WHO'S WHO 1996

AN ANNUAL
BIOGRAPHICAL DICTIONARY

ONE HUNDRED AND FORTY EIGHTH
YEAR OF ISSUE

A & C BLACK
LONDON

PUBLISHED BY A&C BLACK (PUBLISHERS) LIMITED, 35 BEDFORD ROW LONDON WC1R 4JH

ISBN 0 7136 4255 6

The United States
ST MARTIN'S PRESS, NEW YORK

Australia
HODDER HEADLINE (AUSTRALIA) PTY LTD, RYDALMERE, NEW SOUTH WALES

New Zealand
RANDOM CENTURY (NZ) LTD, AUCKLAND

Canada
FITZHENRY & WHITESIDE, MARKHAM, ONTARIO

Southern Africa
BOOK PROMOTIONS (PTY) LTD, CLAREMONT, CAPE TOWN

Middle East
EURAB LTD, ROTTINGDEAN, ENGLAND

India
TR PUBLICATIONS PRIVATE LTD, MADRAS

Hong Kong
PUBLISHERS ASSOCIATES LTD

Singapore
STP DISTRIBUTORS (PTE) LTD

Malaysia
STP DISTRIBUTORS (M) SDN BHD, SHAH ALAM, SELANGOR

TYPESET BY CLOWES COMPUTER COMPOSITION, PRINTED AND BOUND IN GREAT BRITAIN BY WILLIAM CLOWES LIMITED, BECCLES AND LONDON

PAPER MANUFACTURED IN GREAT BRITAIN BY ROBERT FLETCHER (STONECLOUGH), SUPPLIED BY PRECISION PUBLISHING PAPERS (YEOVIL)

WHO WAS WHO

Eight volumes containing the biographies removed from WHO'S WHO each year on account of death, with final details and date of death added. Also a Cumulated Index to the eight volumes giving name, years of birth and death, and the volume in which each entry is to be found.

Volume I	1897-1915
Volume II	1916-1928
Volume III	1929-1940
Volume IV	1941-1950
Volume V	1951-1960
Volume VI	1961-1970
Volume VII	1971-1980
Volume VIII	1981-1990

A CUMULATED INDEX 1897-1990

Volume IX 1991-1995 *in preparation*

WHO'S WHO 1996

CONTENTS

PREFACE *7*

HISTORICAL NOTE *9*

EDITORS' NOTE *11*

OBITUARY *13*

INDEX TO ADVERTISERS *18*

ABBREVIATIONS USED IN THIS BOOK *19*

THE ROYAL FAMILY *62*

BIOGRAPHIES 1

PREFACE

Who's Who is the recognised source book of information on people of influence and interest in all fields.

This, the 1996 edition, contains more than 30,000 biographies, approximately one thousand of these making their first appearance in *Who's Who*. They are of all kinds of people from all parts of the world and from all walks of life: the arts, business and finance, the church, the civil service, education, entertainment and sport, government, the law, local government, the media, medicine, professional institutions, science and the trade unions.

Each entry is in a standard form, full name and present post being followed by date of birth and family details, education, career in date order, publications, recreations and address.

The entries are carefully updated both from information supplied by biographees on their annual proofs and from many independent sources of reference. As a result, tens of thousands of amendments are made, more than half the entries requiring change. The book includes an obituary and a comprehensive list of abbreviations used in the entries.

HISTORICAL NOTE

The first edition of *Who's Who* was published in 1849. It consisted of an almanac followed by thirty-nine lists of ranks and appointments and the names of those holding them. As might be expected, there were lists of peers, members of the House of Commons, judges, archbishops and bishops. Additionally, however, there were the names of the Governor and board of directors of the Bank of England, of British envoys abroad, of the directors of the East India Company and of the officers (including the actuaries) of the life and fire assurance companies in London.

The range of lists was expanded over the next half century to more than two hundred and fifty, to include, amongst others, the Police Commissioners, the officers of the principal railways, the members of the London School Board and the Crown Agents – together with the editors of significant newspapers and magazines whose names, the editor noted, were "given here, not for contributors, but that the public may know who lead public opinion".

In 1897 substantial changes were made to the nature and content of the book. The major change was the addition of a section of biographies in which details were given of the lives of some five and a half thousand leading figures of the day.

Now as then the book aims to list people who, through their careers, affect the political, economic, scientific and artistic life of the country. *Who's Who* places its emphasis on careers whilst giving opportunity for the inclusion of family and other individual details, such as the recreations which have become a distinctive feature of the book.

An invitation to appear in *Who's Who* has, on occasion, been thought of as conferring distinction; that is the last thing it can do. It recognises distinction and influence. The attitude of the present editorial board remains that of the editor of the 1897 edition, who stated in his preface that the book seeks to recognise people whose "prominence is inherited, or depending upon office, or the result of ability which singles them out from their fellows in occupations open to every educated man or woman".

EDITORS' NOTE

A proof of each entry is posted to its subject every year for personal revision, but this cannot be sent unless an address is recorded. Addresses printed in *Who's Who* are those which the subjects of the entries have submitted for publication. It should be noted that the numbers given of the children of a marriage are, unless otherwise indicated, those of the sons and daughters now living; also, that it is the practice to print the names of London clubs unaccompanied by the word London.

It cannot be stated too emphatically that inclusion in *Who's Who* has never at any time been a matter for payment or of obligation to purchase the volume.

Administrator, Musée des Arts Décoratifs, Paris; Special Advr, Internat. Fund for Promotion of Culture, UNESCO, 1991–. Chevalier des Arts et des Lettres (France). *Heir: s* Robert Etienne Eric Abdy, *b* 22 Feb. 1978. *Address:* Hadsley House, Lefebvre Street, St Peter Port, Guernsey, Channel Islands; 13 villa Molitor, 75016 Paris, France; 19 Belgrave Place, SW1X 8BS. *Clubs:* Travellers', Jockey (Paris).

ABEL, Prof. Edward William, PhD, DSc; FRSC; Professor of Inorganic Chemistry, University of Exeter, since 1972 (Head of Department of Chemistry, 1977–88; Deputy Vice-Chancellor, 1991–94); *b* 3 Dec. 1931; *s* of Sydney and Donna Abel; *m* 1960, Margaret R. Edwards; one *s* one *d*. *Educ:* Bridgend Grammar Sch.; University Coll., Cardiff (BSc 1952); Northern Polytechnic, London (PhD 1957). Served Army, 1953–55. Research Fellow, Imperial Coll., 1957–59; Lectr, later Reader, Univ. of Bristol, 1957–71. Vis. Professor: Univ. of British Columbia, 1970; Japanese Soc. for Promotion of Science, 1971; Tech. Univ. of Braunschweig, 1973; ANU, Canberra, 1990; Robert E.Welch Lectures, Texas, 1994. Royal Society of Chemistry: Mem. Council, 1977–82, 1983–87 and 1989–; Pres., 1996–; Chm., Local Affairs Bd, 1983–87; Chm., Divl Affairs Bd, 1989–92; Chm., Scientific Affairs Bd, 1992–95. Main Group Chem. Medal, 1976; Tilden Medal and Lectr, 1981; Mem., Dalton Div. Council, 1977–83, 1987–91 (Sec./Treasurer, 1977–82; Vice-Pres., 1983, 1989–91; Pres., 1987–89). Perm. Sec., Internat. Confs on Organometallic Chem., 1972–89; Mem., UGC, 1986–89 (Chm., Phys. Scis Sub-Cttee, 1986–89); Nat. Advr for Chem., UFC, 1989–92; CNAA: Mem., 1991–93; Chm., Phys. Scis Cttee, 1987–91; Mem., Cttee for Academic Affairs, 1989–91. *Publications:* (ed jtly) Organometallic Chemistry, vols 1–21, 1970–; (exec. editor) Comprehensive Organometallic Chemistry, 9 vols, 1984; papers to learned jls. *Address:* 1A Rosebarn Avenue, Exeter EX4 6DY. *T:* Exeter (01392) 70272; Department of Chemistry, University of Exeter, Exeter EX4 4QD. *T:* Exeter (01392) 263489, *Fax:* (01392) 263434.

ABEL, Kenneth Arthur, CBE 1984; DL; Clerk and Chief Executive, Dorset County Council, 1967–91 (Clerk of the Peace, 1967–73); *b* 4 April 1926; *s* of late Arthur Abel, CBE and Frances Ethel Abel; *m* 1955, Sarah Matilda, *d* of late Capt. M. P. Poynor, TD and Norah Elizabeth Poynor; three *s*. *Educ:* Durham Sch.; Glasgow Univ.; Durham Univ. (LLB). Served RA, 1944–48. Admitted Solicitor, 1953; Assistant Solicitor: Warwicks CC, 1953–54; Leics CC, 1954–59; Sen. Asst Solicitor, Northants CC, 1959–63. Chm., Assoc. of County Chief Execs, 1982–83. Past Pres., Dorset County Golf Union. DL Dorset, 1977. *Recreations:* golf, gardening. *Address:* Herne's Oak, Bradford Road, Sherborne, Dorset DT9 6BP. *T:* Sherborne (01935) 813200. *Club:* Sherborne Golf (Sherborne).

ABEL, Roger Lee; Vice President, Exploration Production, Europe, Conoco Inc., and Chairman, Conoco (UK) Ltd, since 1993; *b* Nebraska, 12 Aug. 1943. *Educ:* Colorado Sch. of Mines (BSc Petroleum Engrg 1965); MIT (MSc 1979). FInstPet. Served US Army, 1966–68 (Capt.). Joined Conoco Inc., 1968: prodn engr, 1968–72; Supervising Reservoir Engr, Lake Charles, Louisiana, 1972–73; Staff Engr, N America, 1973–74; Co-ordinator for W Hemisphere Planning Dept, 1974–75; Exec. Asst, Production, 1975–76; Manager, Planning and Budgets, 1976–77; Exec. Asst to Conoco's Dep. Chm., 1977–78; Sloan Fellow, MIT, 1978–79; Asst Div. Manager, Offshore Div., 1979–80; Vice Pres. and Gen. Manager of Ops for Dubai Petroleum Co., 1980–82; Manager: of Ops, UK and Europe, 1982–84; of Planning, Admin and Engrg, N American Prodn, 1984–86; General Manager: Offshore and Frontier, N American Prodn, 1986–88; Prodn Engrg and Res. Dept, 1988–90; Vice-Pres. and Gen. Manager, Prodn Engrg and Res., 1990–91; Vice Pres., Exploration Prodn–Russia, 1991–93. Pres., Soc. of Petroleum Engrs, 1992. Distinguished Mem., Soc. of Petroleum Engrs. *Address:* Park House, 116 Park Street, W1Y 4NN.

ABEL-SMITH, Prof. Brian; Professor of Social Administration, University of London, at the London School of Economics, 1965–91; *b* 6 Nov. 1926; *s* of late Brig.-Gen. Lionel Abel-Smith. *Educ:* Haileybury Coll.; Clare Coll., Cambridge. MA, PhD, 1955. Served Army: Private 1945; commissioned Oxford and Bucks Light Inf., 1946; Mil. Asst to Dep. Comr, Allied Commn for Austria (Capt.), 1947–48. Res. Fellow, Nat. Inst. of Economic and Social Res., collecting economic evidence for Guillebaud Cttee (cost of NHS), 1953–55. LSE: Asst Lectr in Social Science, 1955; Lectr, 1957; Reader in Social Administration, University of London, 1961. Assoc. Prof., Yale Law Sch., Yale Univ., 1961. Consultant and Expert Adv. to WHO on costs of med. care, 1957–; Consultant: to Social Affairs Div. of UN, 1959, 1961; to ILO, 1967 and 1981–83; Special Adviser: to Sec. of State for Social Services, 1968–70, 1974–78; to Sec. of State for the Environment, 1978–79; Adviser to Comr for Social Affairs, EEC, 1977–80. Member: SW Metrop. Reg. Hosp. Bd, 1956–63; Cent. Health Services Coun. Sub-Cttee on Prescribing Statistics, 1960–64; Sainsbury Cttee (Relationship of Pharmaceut. Industry with NHS), 1965–67; Long-term Study Group (to advise on long-term develt of NHS), 1965–68; Hunter Cttee (Functions of Medical Administrators,) 1970–72; Fisher Cttee (Abuse of Social Security Benefits), 1971–73. Chm., Chelsea and Kensington HMC, 1961–62; Governor: St Thomas' Hosp., 1957–68; Maudsley Hosp. and Inst. of Psychiatry, 1963–67. Hon. MD Limburg, 1981. *Publications:* (with R. M. Titmuss) The Cost of the National Health Service in England and Wales, 1956; A History of the Nursing Profession, 1960; (with R. M. Titmuss) Social Policy and Population Growth in Mauritius, 1961; Paying for Health Services (for WHO), 1963; The Hospitals, 1800–1948, 1964; (with R. M. Titmuss *et al.*) The Health Services of Tanganyika, 1964; (with K. Gales) British Doctors at Home and Abroad, 1964; (with P. Townsend) The Poor and the Poorest, 1965; (with R. Stevens) Lawyers and the Courts, 1967; An International Study of Health Expenditure (for WHO), 1967; (with R. Stevens) In Search of Justice, 1968; (with M. Zander and R. Brooke) Legal Problems and the Citizen, 1973; People Without Choice, 1974; Value for Money in Health Services, 1976; Poverty Development and Health Policy, 1978; National Health Service: the first thirty years, 1978; (with P. Grandjeat) Pharmaceutical Consumption, 1978; (with A. Maynard) The Organisation, Financing and Cost of Health Care in the European Community, 1979; Sharing Health Care Costs, 1980; (with E. Mach) Planning the Finances of the Health Sector, 1984; Cost Containment in Health Care, 1984; (with Marios Raphael) Future Directions for Social Protection, 1986; (ed with Kay Titmuss) The Philosophy of Welfare: selected writings of Richard M. Titmuss, 1987; (with Andrew Creese) Recurrent Costs in the Health Sector, 1989; (jtly) Health Insurance for Developing Countries, 1990; An Introduction to Health: policy, planning and financing, 1994; pamphlets for Fabian Soc., 1953–; articles. *Recreations:* skiing, swimming. *Address:* London School of Economics, Houghton Street, WC2A 2AE. *T:* 0171–405 7686.

ABEL SMITH, Henriette Alice, (Lady Abel Smith), DCVO 1977 (CVO 1964); JP; an Extra Lady-in-Waiting to the Queen (formerly as HRH Princess Elizabeth), since 1987 (a Lady-in-Waiting, 1949–87); *b* 6 June 1914; *d* of late Comdr Francis Charles Cadogan, RN, and late Ruth Evelyn (*née* Howard, *widow* of Captain Gardner Sebastian Bazley); *m* 1st, 1939, Sir Anthony Frederick Mark Palmer, 4th Bt (killed in action, 1941); one *s* one *d*; 2nd, 1953, Sir Alexander Abel Smith, KCVO, TD (*d* 1980); one *s* one *d*. JP Tunbridge Wells 1955, Gloucestershire 1971. *Address:* The Garden House, Quenington, Cirencester, Glos GL7 5BN. *T:* Coln St Aldwyns (0128575) 231.

See also Sir T. S. Bazley, Bt, Sir C. M. Palmer, Bt.

ABEL SMITH, Col Richard Francis; Vice Lord-Lieutenant of Nottinghamshire, since 1991; *b* 11 Oct. 1933; *s* of Col Sir Henry Abel Smith, KCMG, KCVO, DSO and late Lady May Cambridge, *o d* of Earl of Athlone, KG, GCB, GCMG, GCVO, DSO, PC, FRS and Princess Alice, Countess of Athlone, VA, GCVO, GBE; *m* 1960, Marcia Kendrew, DL; one *d*. *Educ:* Eton; RMA Sandhurst; Royal Agric. Coll., Cirencester. Commissioned, 1954, Royal Horse Guards (The Blues); Escort Comdr and ADC to Gov. of Cyprus, 1957–60; Adjutant, 1960–63; Instr, Sandhurst, 1961–63. Comdr, Sherwood Rangers Sqn, Royal Yeomanry Regt, 1967–69, Hon. Col, 1979–89. Chm., Sports Aid Foundn (E Midlands), 1979–90. County Comr, Scouts (Notts), 1966–75. DL 1970, High Sheriff, 1978, Notts. *Recreations:* fishing, shooting, riding. *Address:* Blidworth Dale, Ravenshead, Notts NG15 9AL. *Clubs:* White's, Farmers', Army and Navy.

ABELES, Sir (Emil Herbert) Peter, AC 1991; Kt 1972; Deputy Chairman, TNT (formerly Thomas Nationwide Transport Ltd), Australia, and associated companies, 1967–93 (Managing Director and Chief Executive, 1967–92); Joint Managing Director, 1980–92 and Joint Chairman, 1981, Ansett Transport Industries Ltd; *b* 25 April 1924; *s* of late Alexander Abel and Mrs Anna Deakin; *m* 1969, Katalin Ottilia (*née* Fischer); two *d*. *Educ:* Budapest. Scrap metal industry, Hungary; emigrated to Australia, Sept. 1949; formed Alltrans Pty Ltd, 1950. Director: Ansett Transport Industries Ltd Group; Bliss Corp.; Morael Pty Ltd Gp; Reserve Bank of Australia; Union Shipping Gp. Trustee, Australian Cancer Foundn for Medical Res. *Recreations:* swimming, bridge. *Clubs:* Carlton; American National, Royal Automobile of Australia, Royal Motor Yacht, Tattersalls, Australian Jockey (Sydney).

ABELL, (John) David; Chairman and Chief Executive, Suter plc (formerly Suter Electrical), since 1981; *b* 15 Dec. 1942; *s* of Leonard Abell and Irene (*née* Anderson); *m* 1st, 1967, Anne Janette Priestley (marr. diss. 1977); three *s*; 2nd, 1981, Sandra Dawn Atkinson (marr. diss. 1986); one *s* one *d*; 3rd, 1988, Juliana, *d* of late Prof. J. L. I. Fennell, PhD, FRSL and of Marina Lopukhin. *Educ:* Univ. of Leeds (BAEcon); London School of Economics (Dip. Business Admin). Assistant to Cash and Investment Manager, Ford Motor Co., 1962–65; Asst, Treasurer's Office, AEI, 1965–67; British Leyland: Central Staffs, 1968–69; Manager, Investments and Banking, 1969–70; Chm. and Chief Exec., Prestcold Div., 1970–72; Corporate Treasurer, 1972; First Nat. Finance Corp., Nov. 1972–Aug. 1973; re-joined British Leyland as Man. Dir, Leyland Australia, 1974–75; Group Man. Dir, Leyland Special Products, 1975; Man. Dir, BL Commercial Vehicles, Chm. and Chief Exec., Leyland Vehicles Ltd, 1978–81. *Recreations:* horse racing and breeding, wine, tennis, music. *Address:* Suter plc, St Vincent's, Grantham, Lincs NG31 9EJ.

ABELL, John Norman; Chairman, Europe, CIBC Wood Gundy Inc., 1990–91; Vice-Chairman, Wood Gundy Inc., London, 1988–91; *b* 18 Sept. 1931; *s* of Sir George Edmond Brackenbury Abell; *m* 1957, Mora Delia (*née* Clifton-Brown); two *s* one *d*. *Educ:* Marlborough Coll.; Worcester Coll., Oxford (MA). Wood Gundy Ltd: joined in Vancouver, Canada, 1955; Internat. Man. Dir, Toronto, 1962; Director and Vice-Pres., 1966; Pres., Wood Gundy Inc., New York, 1966; Vice-Chm., Wood Gundy Ltd, Toronto, 1977; Dep. Chm. and Chief Exec., Orion Royal Bank Ltd, 1982, Chm. and Chief Exec. Officer, 1983–85; Vice-Chm., Wood Gundy Inc., Toronto, 1986–88; Director: Echo Bay Mines, Edmonton, Canada, 1980–; First Australia Prime Income Investment Co. Ltd, 1986–92; Minerals & Resources Corp. Ltd, 1985–89; Scotia Synfuels Ltd, Toronto, 1987–; Euro-clear Clearance System, 1989–92; Stelco Inc., Hamilton, Ont, 1993–; A. T. Plastics Inc., Brampton, Ont, 1993–; Longwall Internat., 1993–; Allied Trust Bank, 1993–. Mem., Securities and Investments Bd, 1985–86; Gov., Toronto Stock Exchange, 1987–88. Chairman: Arthritis Soc. of Canada, 1981–82; Canada Meml Foundn, 1992–. Mem.Council, GAP Activity Projects, 1983–. Dir, London House for Overseas Graduates, 1984; Mem. Council, Reading Univ., 1984. *Address:* Whittonditch House, Ramsbury, Marlborough, Wilts SN8 2PZ. *T:* Marlborough (01672) 20449. *Clubs:* Boodle's, MCC; Toronto, York (Toronto).

ABER, Prof. Geoffrey Michael, FRCP; Professor of Renal Medicine, University of Keele, 1982–93; *b* 19 Feb. 1928; *s* of David and Hilda Aber; *m* 1964, Eleanor Maureen; one *s* one *d*. *Educ:* Leeds Grammar School; University of Leeds (MB, ChB, MD with distinction); PhD Birmingham. Leeds Gen. Infirmary, 1952–54; RAMC, 1954–56; Queen Elizabeth Hosp., Birmingham (Univ. of Birmingham), 1956–57, 1958–65; Brompton Hosp., London, 1957–58; Research Fellow: Univ. of Birmingham (Depts of Expt Path. and Medicine), 1958–59 and 1960–64; McGill Univ., 1959–60; Wellcome Sen. Res. Fellow in Clinical Sci., 1964–65; Keele University: Prof. and Adviser in Clinical Res., 1979–82; Head of Dept. of Postgrad. Medicine, 1982–89; Dean of Postgrad. Medicine, 1989–91. *Publications:* contribs to: Recent Advances in Renal Medicine, 1983; Postgraduate Nephrology, 1985; Textbook of Genitourinary Surgery, 1985; scientific papers in learned jls. *Recreations:* music, sport, motor cars. *Address:* Greenleaves, Seabridge Lane, Newcastle-under-Lyme, Staffs ST5 3LS. *T:* Stoke-on-Trent (01782) 613692.

ABERCONWAY, 3rd Baron, *cr* 1911, of Bodnant; **Charles Melville McLaren,** Bt 1902; JP; President: John Brown & Co. Ltd, 1978–85 (Director, 1939–85; Chairman, 1953–78); English China Clays Ltd, since 1984 (Director, 1935–87; Chairman, 1963–84); President, Royal Horticultural Society, 1961–84, now President Emeritus; Commissioner-General, International Garden Festival of Liverpool 1984; Director, National Garden Festival (Stoke on Trent) 1986 Ltd; *b* 16 April 1913; *e s* of 2nd Baron Aberconway, CBE, LLD and Christabel (*d* 1974), *y d* of Sir Melville Macnaghten, CB; *S* father, 1953; *m* 1st, 1941, Deirdre Knewstub (marr. diss. 1949); one *s* two *d*; 2nd, 1949, Ann Lindsay Bullard, *o d* of Mrs A. L. Aymer, New York City; one *s*. *Educ:* Eton; New Coll., Oxford. Barrister, Middle Temple, 1937. Served War of 1939–45, 2nd Lieut RA. Deputy Chairman: Sun Alliance & London Insurance, 1976–85 (Dir, London Assurance, 1953); Westland Aircraft, 1979–84 (Dir, 1947–85); Dir, National Westminster Bank (formerly National Provincial Bank), 1953–83. JP Denbighshire 1946; High Sheriff of Denbighshire 1950. *Recreations:* gardening, travel. *Heir: s* Hon. Henry Charles McLaren [*b* 26 May 1948; *m* 1981, Sally, *yr d* of Captain C. N. Lentaigne; one *s* two *d*]. *Address:* 25 Egerton Terrace, SW3 2DP; Bodnant, Tal-y-cafn, Colwyn Bay, Clwyd.

ABERCORN, 5th Duke of, *cr* 1868; **James Hamilton;** Lord of Paisley, 1587; Lord of Abercorn, 1603; Earl of Abercorn and Lord of Hamilton, Mountcastle and Kilpatrick, 1606; Baron of Strabane, 1617; Viscount of Strabane, 1701; Viscount Hamilton, 1786; Marquess of Abercorn, 1790; Marquess of Hamilton, 1868; Bt 1660; Lord Lieutenant of Co. Tyrone, since 1987; company director; *b* 4 July 1934; *er s* of 4th Duke of Abercorn, and Lady Mary Kathleen Crichton (Dowager Duchess of Abercorn, GCVO) (*d* 1990); *S* father, 1979; *m* 1966, Anastasia Alexandra, *e d* of late Lt-Col Harold Phillips, Checkendon Court, Reading; two *s* one *d*. *Educ:* Eton Coll.; Royal Agricultural Coll., Cirencester, Glos. Joined HM Army, Oct. 1952; Lieut, Grenadier Guards. MP (UU) Fermanagh and South Tyrone, 1964–70. Dir, Northern Bank Ltd, 1970–. Chm., Laganside Develt Corp., 1989– (Laganside Ltd, 1986–89); Dir, NI Industrial Develt Bd, 1982–87. Member: Council of Europe, 1968–70; European Economic and Social Cttee, 1973–78. President: Royal UK Beneficent Assoc., 1979–; Building Socs Assoc., 1986–92; Patron, Royal Ulster Agricl Soc., 1990–. Trustee, Winston Churchill Meml Trust, 1991–. High Sheriff of Co. Tyrone, 1970. *Recreations:* shooting, ski-ing. *Heir: s* Marquess of Hamilton, *qv*. *Address:* Barons Court, Omagh, Northern Ireland BT78 4EZ. *T:* Newtownstewart (016626)

A

AARONSON, Graham Raphael; QC 1982; *b* 31 Dec. 1944; *s* of late John Aaronson and of Dora Aaronson (*née* Franks); *m* 1st, 1967, Linda Esther Smith (marr. diss. 1992); two *s* one *d*; 2nd, 1993, Pearl Isobel Buchler. *Educ:* City of London Sch.; Trinity Hall, Cambridge (Thomas Waraker Law Schol.; MA). Called to the Bar, Middle Temple, 1966 (Bencher 1991); practised Revenue law, 1968–73 and 1978–. Chm., Tax Law Review Cttee, 1994–. Advr on tax reform to Treasury, Israel, 1986–90. Chm., Dietary Res. Foundn, 1989–. Founder, Standford Grange residential rehabilitation centre for ex-offenders, 1974; Man. Dir, Worldwide Plastics Development, 1973–77; Dir, Bridgend Group PLC, 1973–92. *Address:* 1 Essex Court, Temple, EC4Y 9AR. *T:* 0171–583 2000.

ABBADO, Claudio; Artistic Director, Berlin Philharmonic Orchestra, since 1989; Generalmusikdirektor of Vienna, since 1987; *b* Milan, 26 June 1933; *m*; two *s* one *d*. *Educ:* Conservatorio G. Verdi, Milan; Musical Academy, Vienna. Guest Conductor of principal orchestras in Europe and America: conductor at principal festivals and opera houses, 1961–. Music Dir, La Scala, Milan, 1968–86; Principal Conductor, LSO, 1979–88; Music Director, Vienna State Opera, 1986–91. Founder and conductor: European Community Youth Orch., 1977–94; Chamber Orchestra of Europe, 1981–; Gustav Mahler Jugend Orchester, 1986–. Founder and Artistic Dir of Festival, Wien Modern, 1988; Artistic Dir, Saltzburg Easter Fest., 1994; Artistic Advr, Chamber Orch. of Europe. Dr *hc*: Aberdeen, 1986; Ferrara, 1990; Cambridge, 1994. Sergei Koussewitzky Prize, Tanglewood, 1958; Dimitri Mitropoulos Prize, 1963; Mozart-Medaille, Mozart-Gemeinde, Vienna, 1973; Goldmedaille der Internat. Gustav Mahler Gesellschaft, Vienna, 1985; winner of major international prizes for recordings (Diapason, Deutscher Schallplatten-Preis, Grand Prix du Disque, Grammy, USA, etc), 1965–. Gran Croce d'Italia, 1984; Cross, Légion d'Honneur; Bundesverdienstkreuz (Germany), 1992. *Address:* Berliner Philharmonisches Orchester, Matthäikirchstasse 1, D-10785 Berlin, Germany.

ABBOTT, Sir Albert (Francis), Kt 1981; CBE 1974; Mayor, City of Mackay, Queensland, 1970–88; *b* Marvel Loch, WA, 10 Dec. 1913; *s* of late Albert Victor and Diana Abbott; *m* 1941, Gwendoline Joyce Maclean; two *s* four *d*. *Educ:* Mount Martin and Mackay State Schs, Qld. Served RAAF, 1941–45. Sugar cane farmer, 1950–; has given twenty years service to sugar industry organisations. Member: Picture, Theatre and Films Commn, 1975–90; Qld Local Govt Grants Commn, 1977–85. Returned Services League of Australia: Mem., 1946–; Pres., Mackay Sub-Br., 1960–65; Dist Pres., Mackay, 1965–74; Pres., Qld State, 1974–90; Hon. Life Pres., Qld State, 1991–. President: N Qld Local Govt Assoc., 1975–84; Qld Local Govt Assoc., 1983–88; Aust. Local Govt Assoc., 1986–87; Lifeline Mackay, 1990–. Mem., Mackay Rotary Club. Governor, Utah Foundn, 1975–88. *Recreations:* golf, tennis, racing. *Address:* 2 Tudor Court, Mackay, Qld 4740, Australia. *Clubs:* United Services (Brisbane); RSL Ex-Services, Bowls, Golf, Trotting, Turf, Amateur Race, Diggers Race, Legacy (all in Mackay).

ABBOTT, Diane Julie; MP (Lab) Hackney North and Stoke Newington, since 1987; *b* 27 Sept. 1953; *d* of late Reginald and Julia Abbott; *m* 1991, David Thompson (marr. diss.); one *s*. *Educ:* Harrow County Girls' Grammar Sch.; Newnham Coll., Cambridge. Formerly: Admin. Trainee, Home Office; Race Relations Officer, NCCL; Researcher, Thames Television; Reporter, TV-am; Equality Officer, ACTT; Press and PR Officer, GLC; Principal Press Officer, Lambeth Borough Council. Joined Labour Party, 1971; Mem., NEC, 1994–. Mem., Westminster City Council, 1982–86. *Address:* House of Commons, SW1A 0AA.

ABBOTT, James Alan, PhD; Manager and Director of Research, Koninklijk/Shell Laboratorium, Amsterdam, Shell Research BV, 1981–88, retired; *b* 2 Dec. 1928; *s* of George Oswald and Eva Abbott; *m* 1954, Rita Marjorie Galloway; one *s* one *d*. *Educ:* Ilkeston Grammar School; University of Nottingham (BSc, PhD). Post-doctoral research, Univ. of Durham, 1952–53; served Royal Air Force, 1953–56 (Flt Lt RAF Technical Coll., Henlow). Shell companies, UK and Holland, 1956–; Dir, Shell Research Ltd, Sittingbourne Research Centre, 1980–81. Officer, Order of Oranje-Nassau (The Netherlands), 1988. *Publications:* papers in Trans Faraday Soc., Proc. Royal Society. *Recreation:* golf.

ABBOTT, Morris Percy; Chief Executive, 1974–83, Chairman, 1977–83, Hogg Robinson Group Ltd; *b* 3 May 1922; *s* of Harry Abbott and Agnes Maud Breeze; *m* 1944, Marjorie Leven; one *s* one *d*. *Educ:* Rothesay Academy. MIB(Scot) Bank of Scotland, 1939–49. Served War as Pilot, 1941–46; Flight Lieut, RAF; seconded to US Navy at Pensacola Naval Air Station, Florida. Senior Executive with National Bank of India (now Grindlays Bank) in India and East Africa, 1949–59. Managing Director: Credit Insurance Assoc. Ltd, 1969; Hogg Robinson & Gardner Mountain Ltd, 1971; Group Man. Dir, Hogg Robinson Group Ltd, 1973. *Recreations:* music, golf, tennis, sailing. *Address:* Broadwater, 39 Hartfield Road, Bexhill-on-Sea, East Sussex TN39 3EA. *Clubs:* City of London, Caledonian; Royal and Ancient Golf, Rye Golf, Royal Calcutta Golf.

ABBOTT, Adm. Sir Peter (Charles), KCB 1994; Commander-in-Chief Fleet, Commander-in-Chief Eastern Atlantic Area and Commander Naval Forces North Western Europe, since 1995; *b* 12 Feb. 1942; *s* of late Lieut-Col Dennis Abbott, Royal Garwhal Rifles and Delphine McConaghey; *m* 1965, Susan Phillippa Grey; three *d*. *Educ:* St Edward's Sch., Oxford. Queens' College, Cambridge (MA 1966). Articled Clerk, Blackburn, Robson Coates, 1963; 2nd Lieut, RMFVR 1963; Sub Lieut, RN 1964; Commanding Officer, HM Ships Chawton, 1972, Ambuscade, 1976, Ajax, 1983 (and First Frigate Sqdn); RCDS 1985; Flag Officer, Flotilla Two, 1989; ACNS, 1991–93; Dep. SACLANT, 1993–95.

ABBOTT, Roderick Evelyn; Director, Directorate-General of External Economic Relations (formerly External Relations), European Commission, Brussels, since 1982; *b* 16 April 1938; *e s* of late Stuart Abbott, OBE; *m* 1963, Elizabeth Isobel McLean; three *d*. *Educ:* Rugby Sch.; Merton Coll., Oxford. Board of Trade, 1962–68 (Private Sec. to Pres. of BoT, 1965–66; seconded to DEA, 1966–68); UK Mission to UN, Geneva, 1968–71; Foreign Office, London, 1971–73; EEC, 1973–75; EEC Delegation, Geneva, 1975–79; EC (formerly EEC), 1980–. *Recreation:* travel. *Address:* c/o European Commission, 200 rue de la Loi, 1049 Brussels, Belgium. *Club:* Commonwealth Trust.

ABBOTT, Ronald William, CVO 1989; CBE 1979; FIA, ASA, FPMI; Consultant Partner, Bacon & Woodrow, Consulting Actuaries, 1982–94 (Senior Partner, 1972–81); *b* 18 Jan. 1917; *s* of late Edgar Abbott and Susan Mary Ann Abbott; *m* 1st, 1948, Hilda Mary Hampson (*d* 1972), *d* of late William George Clarke and Emily Jane Clarke; two *d*; 2nd, 1973, Barbara Constance, *d* of late Gilbert Hugh Clough and Harriet Clough. *Educ:* St Olave's Grammar Sch. FIA 1946; FPMI 1976. Actuarial Assistant: Atlas Assce Co., 1934–38; Friends Provident & Century Life Office, 1938–46; Sen. Actuary, Bacon & Woodrow, 1946, Partner 1948. Mem., Deptl Cttee on Property Bonds and Equity Linked Life Assce, 1971–73. Dep. Chm., 1973–82, Chm., 1982–87, Occupational Pensions Bd. Mem. Council: Inst. of Actuaries, 1966–74 (Hon. Treasurer, 1971–73); Indust. Soc., 1964–84 (Life Mem., 1984); Pensions Management Inst., 1977–81 (Vice-Pres., 1978–80). Master, Worshipful Co. of Ironmongers, 1986–87. FRSA. Finlaison Medal, Inst. of Actuaries, 1988. *Publications:* A Short History of the Association of Consulting Actuaries, 1991; contrib. to Jl of Inst. of Actuaries. *Recreation:* music. *Address:* 43 Rottingdean Place, Falmer Road, Rottingdean, E Sussex BN2 7FS. *T:* Brighton (01273) 303302. *Club:* Royal Automobile.

ABDALLAH, Abdelwaheb; Comdr, Order of November 7th, Tunisia, 1992; Kt, Order of Independence, Tunisia, 1975; Grand Officier, Order of the Republic, Tunisia, 1991; Minister, Counsellor of the President and Spokesman for the Presidency, Tunis, since 1990; *b* 14 Feb. 1940; *s* of (Militant) Ameur Abdallah; *m* Alia Abdallah; four *s*. *Educ:* Univ. of Caen, France. Master Public Law and Pol Sci.; Dipl. Inst. of Admin of Enterprises; Dr Pol Sci. (Paris). Teacher: Higher Inst. of Management, Tunis, 1971; Law Faculty, Tunis, 1972–74; Press Inst., 1974–86. Attaché, Cabinet, Min. of Nat. Educn, 1971; Legal Adviser to Min. of Nat. Educn, 1971–74; Attaché, Cabinet, President of the Republic, 1974; Head of Office: of Minister Dir, Pres. Office, 1974; of Minister, Cultural Affairs, 1976; of Minister, Information, 1978; Man. Dir, Nat. Printing Co., 1978; Editor, La Presse, Tunisia, 1979–86; Man. Dir, Nat. News Agency Tunis-Afrique-Presse, 1986; Minister of Information, 1987; MP Monastir, until 1988; Mem., Central Cttee, RCD Party, 1988; Ambassador to UK, 1988–90. Several foreign decorations. *Publications:* The Maghrebian Policy of Tunisia (thesis of Public Law), 1970; The Role of Governor in the Political and Administrative Life of Tunisia (Pol Sci. thesis), 1973; Gaullism and Jacobinism (Univ. Study), 1972; The Re-Election of the President of the Republic of Tunisia, 1974; articles on political analysis. *Address:* Présidence de la République, Palais de Carthage, Tunis.

ABDUL AZIZ, Mahmood; High Commissioner for Singapore in London, since 1988; *b* 21 May 1935; *s* of Ghulam Mahmood and Fatimah Mohamad; *m* 1961, Fauziah Aziz; two *d*. *Educ:* Univ. of Malaya, Singapore (BA Hons Econ). Joined Singapore Civil Service, 1966; First Sec., Singapore High Commn, Canberra, 1966–68; Min. of Foreign Affairs (MFA), 1968–69; Chargé d'Affaires, Phnom Penh, 1969–70; MFA, 1970–73; Chargé d'Affaires, Paris, 1973–78; MFA, 1979–82; Ambassador to the Philippines, 1982–86; MFA as Dir-Gen., ASEAN Nat. Secretariat, Singapore, 1986–88. Public Admin. Medal (Silver), Singapore, 1986; Order of Sikatuna, Philippines, 1986. *Recreation:* golf. *Address:* Singapore High Commission, 9 Wilton Crescent, SW1X 8SA. *T:* 0171–235 8315. *Clubs:* Highgate Golf; Wentworth; Tanah Merah Country (Singapore).

ABDULAH, Frank Owen; Deputy Secretary-General, Caribbean Community Secretariat, Guyana, 1989–93; *b* 8 Nov. 1928; *m*; four *d*. *Educ:* Queen's Royal Coll., Trinidad; Oxford (MA, DipEd Oxon). Held several govt posts, 1953–62, before entering Diplomatic Service at Trinidad and Tobago's Independence, 1962; Dep. Perm. Rep. (Minister Counsellor), 1970–73, Perm. Rep. (Ambassador), 1975–83, Trinidad and Tobago Perm. Mission to UN, NY; Perm. Sec. (Acting), Ministry of External Affairs, Port of Spain, 1973–75; High Comr for Trinidad and Tobago in London with concurrent accreditations as Ambassador to Denmark, Finland, France, FRG, Norway and Sweden, 1983–85; Permanent Sec., Min. of External Affairs and Internat. Trade, Trinidad and Tobago, 1985–88. *Recreations:* music, sports. *Address:* 8 Nock Road, Maraval, Trinidad.

ABDULLAH bin Ali, Datuk; Chairman: The KAB Group, since 1985; Chicago Bridge (CBI) Malaysia; Waste Management International (Malaysia); Director, Guthrie Ropel Berhad, since 1979; *b* Johore State, 31 Aug. 1922; *m* Datin Badariah binti Haji Abdul Aziz; three *s* two *d*. *Educ:* Raffles Coll., Singapore; ANU, Canberra. Entered Johore Civil Service, 1949, later Malayan Civil Service; with Independence of Malaysia joined Malaysian Foreign Service; served in India, Australia, Indonesia, Thailand, and as Head of Mission in Ethiopia, 1955–57, Rabat, Morocco, 1957–59; Chief of Protocol and Dep. Sec.-Gen., Min. of Foreign Affairs, Kuala Lumpur, 1969–71; High Comr to Singapore, 1971–74; Ambassador to Fed. Rep. of Germany (concurrently to Switzerland and Greece), 1975; High Comr in London and Ambassador to Ireland, 1975–79. Has attended many internat. confs, incl. UNO in Geneva and NY. Holds Orders: Panglima Setia DiRaja (Order of the Sovereign of Malaysia); Dato Paduka Mahkota Johore (Order of Crown of Johore, Malaysia); Kesatria Mangku Negara (Order of Defender of Realm, Malaysia); Order of Djaksa (Indonesia); Order of Sacred Heart (Japan). *Address:* 21st Floor Menara Promet, Jalan Sultan Ismail, 50250 Kuala Lumpur, Malaysia.

ABDY, Sir Valentine (Robert Duff), 6th Bt *cr* 1850; National Board, Smithsonian Institution, Washington DC, 1983–95; *b* 11 Sept. 1937; *s* of Sir Robert Henry Edward Abdy, 5th Bt, and Lady Diana Bridgeman (*d* 1967), *e d* of 5th Earl of Bradford; *S* father, 1976; *m* 1971, Mathilde Coche de la Ferté (marr. diss. 1982); one *s*. *Educ:* Eton.

OBITUARY

Deaths notified from September 1994 to September 1995.

Abell, Sir Anthony Foster, KCMG, 8 Oct. 1994.
Ackroyd, Sir John Robert Whyte, 2nd Bt, 30 Aug. 1995.
Adebo, Simeon Olaosebikan, Chief; The Okanlomo of Itoko and Egbaland, CFR, CMG, 30 Sept. 1994.
Adrian, 2nd Baron; Richard Hume Adrian, FRS, 4 April 1995 (*ext*).
Adshead, Mary, 3 Sept. 1995.
Albu, Austen Harry, 23 Nov. 1994.
Alford, Ven. John Richard, 27 Feb. 1995.
Alfvén, Prof. Hannes Olof Gösta, 2 April 1995.
Allard, Sir Gordon Laidlaw, Oct. 1994.
Allen, Rear-Adm. Sir David, KCVO, CBE, 13 Jan. 1995.
Allen, Walter Ernest, 28 Feb. 1995.
Allenby, Rt Rev. (David Howard) Nicholas, 28 Feb. 1995.
Amritanand, Rt Rev. Joseph, 27 Nov. 1994.
Anderson, Prof. Sir (James) Norman (Dalrymple), OBE, QC, FBA, 2 Dec. 1994.
Anderson, Walter Charles, CBE, 1 March 1995.
Anfinsen, Prof. Christian Boehmer, 14 May 1995.
Antrobus, Sir Philip Coutts, 7th Bt, 1 Aug. 1995.
Archer, Frank Joseph, 31 March 1995.
Ashley, Maurice Percy, CBE, 26 Sept. 1994.
Askwith, Hon. Betty Ellen, 10 April 1995.
Atkinson, Prof. Richard John Copland, CBE, 10 Oct. 1994.
Austin, Prof. Lloyd James, FBA, 30 Dec. 1994.
Austin, Sir Michael Trescawen, 5th Bt, 3 Aug. 1995.
Ayling, Air Vice-Marshal Richard Cecil, CB, CBE, 27 June 1995.

Badham, Leonard, 11 June 1992.
Baerlein, Richard Edgar, 10 March 1995.
Bailey, Harold, CMG, 28 May 1995.
Balfour, Hon. Mark Robin, 30 Sept. 1995.
Barber, Col Sir William Francis, 2nd Bt, TD, 1 April 1995.
Barker, Sir Harry Heaton, KBE, 18 May 1994.
Barnard, Sir (Arthur) Thomas, CB, OBE, 6 July 1995.
Barnard, Captain Sir George Edward, 14 April 1995.
Barneby, Lt-Col Henry Habington, TD, 27 April 1995.
Barnett, Sir Oliver Charles, CBE, QC, 3 Feb. 1995.
Barr, Ian, 3 April 1995.
Barr, Prof. Murray Llewellyn, OC, FRS, 4 May 1995.
Barratt, Herbert George Harold, OBE, July 1995.
Bateson, Andrew James, QC, 22 June 1995.
Baverstock, Donald Leighton, 16 March 1995.
Begg, Admiral of the Fleet Sir Varyl Cargill, GCB, DSO, DSC, 13 July 1995.
Bell, Sir Gawain Westray, KCMG, CBE, 26 July 1995.
Benjamin, Prof. (Thomas) Brooke, FRS, 16 Aug. 1995.
Benson, Baron (Life Peer); Henry Alexander Benson, GBE, 5 March 1995.
Benson, Sir (William) Jeffrey, 13 Nov. 1994.
Berkeley, Humphry John, 15 Nov. 1994.
Bestor, Prof. Arthur Eugene, 13 Dec. 1994.
Beverton, Prof. Raymond John Heaphy, CBE, FRS, 23 July 1995.
Birch, Alexander Hope, CMG, OBE, 6 March 1995.
Birkinshaw, Prof. John Howard, 20 Sept. 1995.
Black, Rev. Prof. Matthew, FBA, 2 Oct. 1994.
Blackburn, John Graham, MP, 12 Oct. 1994.
Blackett, Major Sir Francis Hugh, 11th Bt, 9 Feb. 1995.
Block, Maj.-Gen. Adam Johnstone Cheyne, CB, CBE, DSO, 14 Oct. 1994.
Bloy, Rt Rev. Francis Eric Irving, 23 May 1993.
Boardman, Harold, 1 Aug. 1994.
Boden, Thomas Bennion, OBE, 18 May 1995.
Bolt, Robert Oxton, CBE, 20 Feb. 1995.
Bonham Carter, Richard Erskine, 18 Dec. 1994.
Bony, Prof. Jean V., 7 July 1995.
Boon, William Robert, FRS, 28 Oct. 1994.
Booth, John Wells, 15 Dec. 1994.
Botvinnik, Mikhail Moisseyevich, 5 May 1995.
Bourne, James Gerald, 5 July 1995.
Bourton, Cyril Leonard, CB, 26 Feb. 1995.
Bowen, Rear-Adm. Frank, 21 May 1995.
Bowen, Very Rev. Lawrence, 26 Sept. 1994.
Bowen, Hon. Sir Nigel Hubert, AC, KBE, 27 Sept. 1994.
Bowick, David Marshall, CBE, 9 March 1995.
Braddon, Russell Reading, 20 March 1995.
Braham, Harold, CBE, 16 Jan. 1995.
Brassey, Lt-Col Hon. Peter Esmé, 14 March 1995.
Bray, Hon. John Jefferson, AC, 26 June 1995.
Brett, Jeremy, (Peter Jeremy William Huggins), 12 Sept. 1995.
Brimelow, Baron (Life Peer); Thomas Brimelow, GCMG, OBE, 2 Aug. 1995.
Britten, Maj.-Gen. Robert Wallace Tudor, CB, MC, 11 July 1995.
Broadhurst, Air Chief Marshal Sir Harry, GCB, KBE, DSO, DFC, AFC, 29 Aug. 1995.
Brogan, Lt-Gen. Sir Mervyn Francis, KBE, CB, 8 March 1994.
Broomhall, Maj.-Gen. William Maurice, CB, DSO, OBE, 13 Jan. 1995.
Brophy, Brigid Antonia, (Lady Levey), 7 Aug. 1995.
Broughshane, 2nd Baron; Patrick Owen Alexander Davison, 22 Sept. 1995.
Brown, Sir (Ernest) Henry Phelps, MBE, FBA, 15 Dec. 1994.
Brown, Thomas Walter Falconer, CBE, 18 May 1995.
Brown, William Glanville, TD, 10 July 1995.
Bruce Lockhart, John Macgregor, CB, CMG, OBE, 7 May 1995.
Bryant, Rear-Adm. Benjamin, CB, DSO, DSC, 23 Nov. 1994.
Buckle, Maj.-Gen. Denys Herbert Vintcent, CB, CBE, 18 Dec. 1994.
Buckmaster, Rev. Cuthbert Harold Septimus, 20 Dec. 1994.
Buckton, Raymond William, 7 May 1995.
Bugotu, Francis, CBE, 9 July 1992.
Bull, Megan Patricia, (Lady Bull), OBE, 8 Aug. 1995.
Bull, Sir Walter Edward Avenon, KCVO, 9 Jan. 1995.
Bullard, Denys Gradwell, 2 Nov. 1994.
Bunting, Sir (Edward) John, AC, KBE, 2 May 1995.
Burchmore, Air Cdre Eric, CBE, 11 Oct. 1994.
Burden, 2nd Baron; Philip William Burden, 25 June 1995.
Burger, Warren Earl, 25 June 1995.
Burt-Andrews, Air Cdre Charles Beresford Eaton, CB, CBE, 7 Jan. 1995.
Butenandt, Prof. Adolf Friedrich Johann, 18 Jan. 1995.
Butterworth, Sir (George) Neville, 25 July 1995.

Cadbury, George Woodall, OC, 24 Feb. 1995.
Callinan, Sir Bernard James, AC, CBE, DSO, MC, 20 July 1995.
Calovski, Mitko, 25 Dec. 1994.
Campbell of Eskan, Baron (Life Peer); John Middleton Campbell, (Jock), 26 Dec. 1994.
Campbell, Ian Macdonald, CVO, 1 April 1994.
Camrose, 2nd Viscount; John Seymour Berry, TD, 15 Feb. 1995.
Carlisle, 12th Earl of; Charles James Ruthven Howard, MC, 28 Nov. 1994.
Carter, Dorothy Ethel Fleming, (Jane), 14 May 1995.
Carter, Frank Ernest Lovell, CBE, 29 Jan. 1995.
Cassels, Prof. James Macdonald, FRS, 19 Oct. 1994.
Caulfield, Sir Bernard, 17 Oct. 1994.
Chalmers, Thomas Wightman, CBE, 30 Aug. 1995.
Chandrasekhar, Prof. Subrahmanyan, FRS, 21 Aug. 1995.
Charleston, Robert Jesse, 4 Dec. 1994.
Chesters, John Hugh, OBE, FRS, 14 Dec. 1994.
Chisholm, Prof. Geoffrey Duncan, CBE, 10 Nov. 1994.
Chisholm, Roderick Æneas, CBE, DSO, DFC, AE, 7 Dec. 1994.
Christie, Hon. Sir Vernon Howard Colville, 4 Nov. 1994.
Churchill, Diana Josephine, 8 Oct. 1994.
Clancarty, 8th Earl of; William Francis Brinsley Le Poer Trench, 18 May 1995.
Clark, Sir Colin Douglas, 4th Bt, MC, 26 April 1995.
Clark, Sir (John) Grahame (Douglas), CBE, FBA, 12 Sept. 1995.
Clayton, Jack, 25 Feb. 1995.
Clayton, Michael Thomas Emilius, CB, OBE, 27 May 1995.
Clegg, Ronald Anthony, (Tony), OBE, 1 June 1995.
Clifford-Turner, Raymond, 18 April 1995.
Clutton-Brock, Arthur Guy, 29 Jan. 1995.
Coates, Sir Ernest William, CMG, 10 Feb. 1994.
Cobbold, Patrick Mark, 16 Dec. 1994.
Cohen, His Honour (Nathaniel) Arthur (Jim), 11 June 1995.
Colchester, Rev. Halsey Sparrowe, CMG, OBE, 27 Jan. 1995.
Coleman, Prof. Donald Cuthbert, FBA, 3 Sept. 1995.
Coles, Dame Mabel Irene, DBE, 17 June 1993.
Comfort, Charles Fraser, OC, CD, 5 July 1994.
Cook, Norman Edgar, CBE, 6 May 1995.
Cook, Peter Edward, 9 Jan. 1995.
Cooke, Peter Maurice, 14 July 1995.
Cooke, Thomas Fitzpatrick, TD, 20 Feb. 1994.
Cooper, Susie, (Mrs Susan Vera Barker), OBE, RDI, 28 July 1995.
Cork and Orrery, 13th Earl of; Patrick Reginald Boyle, 8 Aug. 1995.
Cormack, Sir Magnus Cameron, KBE, 26 Nov. 1994.
Cornish, William Herbert, CB, 7 Jan. 1995.
Cornwall, Ian Wolfran, 18 Nov. 1994.
Costar, Sir Norman Edgar, KCMG, 5 July 1995.
Cotts, Sir (Robert) Crichton Mitchell, 3rd Bt, 17 Jan. 1995.
Cowdray, 3rd Viscount; Weetman John Churchill Pearson, TD, 19 Jan. 1995.
Cozens, Brig. Dame (Florence) Barbara, DBE, RRC, 18 July 1995.
Cozens, Air Cdre Henry Iliffe, CB, AFC, 21 June 1995.
Craig, Very Rev. Prof. Robert, CBE, 30 Jan. 1995.
Crawford, Maj.-Gen. George Oswald, CB, CBE, 26 Dec. 1994.
Creeggan, Rt Rev. Jack Burnett, 18 July 1994.
Crooks, Rev. John Robert Megaw, 17 March 1995.
Cruickshank, Herbert James, CBE, 5 Aug. 1995.
Cruickshank, Prof. John, 11 July 1995.
Culhane, Rosalind, (Lady Padmore), LVO, OBE, 4 March 1995.
Cullen, James Reynolds, 8 April 1995.

Cunliffe, His Honour Christopher Joseph, 23 Sept. 1995.
Cunningham, David, CB, 21 March 1995.
Currie, Rear-Adm. Robert Alexander, CB, DSC, 7 Feb. 1995.
Cuthbertson, Sir Harold Alexander, 14 March 1994.

Dalais, Sir (Adrien) Pierre, 7 Nov. 1991.
Daniels, Laurence John, CB, OBE, 16 Sept. 1994.
Darling, Henry Shillington, CBE, 4 Aug. 1995.
Davidson, Howard William, CMG, MBE, 24 June 1995.
Davidson-Houston, Major Aubrey Claud, 10 June 1995.
Davie, Prof. Donald Alfred, FBA, 18 Sept. 1995.
Davies, David Ronald, 8 Sept. 1994.
Davies, Col Lucy Myfanwy, CBE, 2 Aug. 1995.
Davies, Sir Richard Harries, KCVO, CBE, 29 Jan. 1995.
Davies, Stuart Duncan, CBE, 22 Jan. 1995.
Dean, David Edis, 30 Nov. 1994.
Dean, (Frederick) Harold, CB, QC, 29 Oct. 1994.
Dean, Sir Patrick Henry, GCMG, 5 Nov. 1994.
Deans, Rodger William, CB, 7 June 1995.
de Chair, Somerset, 5 Jan. 1995.
Deer, Sir (Arthur) Frederick, CMG, 29 March 1995.
de Grey, Sir Roger, KCVO, RA, 14 Feb. 1995.
de la Mare, Sir Arthur James, KCMG, KCVO, 15 Dec. 1994.
de Mayo, Prof. Paul, FRS, 26 July 1994.
Denbigh, 11th Earl of, **and Desmond,** 10th Earl of; William Rudolph Michael Feilding, 23 March 1995.
Denny, Sir Alistair Maurice Archibald, 3rd Bt, 29 Aug. 1995.
Dent, Harold Collett, 23 Jan. 1995.
Derby, 18th Earl of; Edward John Stanley, MC, 28 Nov. 1994.
Desai, Shri Morarji Ranchhodji, 10 April 1995.
De Vito, Gioconda, 14 Oct. 1994.
Dickens, Geoffrey Kenneth, MP, 17 May 1995.
Dillon, Sir John Vincent, CMG, 20 Nov. 1992.
Dix, Bernard Hubert, 20 April 1995.
Dodds, George Christopher Buchanan, CMG, 29 June 1995.
Domett, Rear-Adm. Douglas Brian, CB, CBE, 6 Dec. 1994.
Douglas, Arthur John Alexander, CMG, OBE, 13 Feb. 1995.
Dowdalls, Edward Joseph, 16 June 1994.
Drew, John Alexander, CB, 26 Jan. 1995.
Dreyfus, Pierre, 25 Dec. 1994.
Duckmanton, Sir Talbot Sydney, CBE, 12 June 1995.
Dugdale, Sir John Robert Stratford, KCVO, 13 Dec. 1994.
Dundas, Sir Hugh Spencer Lisle, CBE, DSO, DFC, 10 July 1995.
Dunlop, (Norman) Gordon (Edward), CBE, 31 Aug. 1995.
Dunn, Lt-Col Sir (Francis) Vivian, KCVO, OBE, 3 April 1995.
Dunnet, Prof. George Mackenzie, CBE, 11 Sept. 1995.
Durack, Dame Mary, (Mrs Horrie Miller), AC, DBE, 16 Dec. 1994.
Durand, Victor Albert Charles, QC, 1 Oct. 1994.
Durrant, Sir William Henry Estridge, 7th Bt, 13 July 1994.
Durrell, Gerald Malcolm, OBE, 30 Jan. 1995.
du Sautoy, Peter Francis, CBE, 17 July 1995.
Dykes Bower, Stephen Ernest, 11 Nov. 1994.

Eastwood, Sir John Bealby, 6 Aug. 1995.
Eburne, Sir Sidney Alfred William, MC, 19 Dec. 1994.
Eden, Conrad W., TD, 16 Oct. 1994.
Edwards, William Philip Neville, CBE, 24 Jan. 1995.
Edwards-Jones, Ian, QC, 3 March 1995.
Ellman-Brown, Hon. Geoffrey, CMG, OBE, 1 July 1994.
Elphinstone, 18th Lord; James Alexander Elphinstone, 19 Dec. 1994.
Elton, Prof. Sir Geoffrey Rudolph, FBA, 4 Dec. 1994.
Emson, Air Marshal Sir Reginald Herbert Embleton, KBE, CB, AFC, 27 March 1995.
England, Frank Raymond Wilton, 30 May 1995.
Ennals, Baron (Life Peer); David Hedley Ennals, PC, 17 June 1995.
Errington, Richard Percy, CMG, 25 Jan. 1995.
Erskine of Rerrick, 2nd Baron; Iain Maxwell Erskine, 7 June 1995 (*ext*).
Ervine-Andrews, Lt-Col Harold Marcus, VC, 30 March 1995.
Essex, Francis William, CMG, 10 July 1995.
Eversley, David Edward Charles, 3 July 1995.

Fairbairn, Douglas Foakes, CBE, 30 Nov. 1994.
Fairbairn of Fordell, Sir Nicholas Hardwick, QC (Scot.), MP, 19 Feb. 1995.
Farrell, James [*Deceased.*
Fedrick, Geoffrey Courtis, 25 July 1994.
Feeny, Max Howard, 24 March 1995.
Ferrie, Maj.-Gen. Alexander Martin, CBE, 29 June 1995.
Finley, Sir Peter Hamilton, OBE, DFC, 27 April 1994.
Fischer, Annie, 10 April 1995.
Fisher, Patricia, (Lady Fisher), 23 May 1995.
Fistoulari, Anatole, 21 Aug. 1995.
FitzGeorge-Balfour, Gen. Sir (Robert George) Victor, KCB, CBE, DSO, MC, 28 Dec. 1994.
Flavell, Geoffrey, 28 Nov. 1994.
Fleetwood, Susan Maureen, 29 Sept. 1995.
Fleming, Rear-Adm. Sir John, KBE, DSC, 3 Nov. 1994.
Fletcher, Col Archibald Ian, OBE, 27 April 1995.
Fletcher, Geoffrey Bernard Abbott, 8 Feb. 1995.
Ford, Raymond Eustace, CBE, 21 Dec. 1994.
Foster, Maj.-Gen. Norman Leslie, CB, DSO, 3 Jan. 1995.
Fowler, Prof. William Alfred, 14 March 1995.
Fraser, Prof. (Thomas) Russell (Cumming), 26 June 1994.
Fraser-Tytler, Christian Helen, CBE, TD, 30 June 1995.
Freedman, Hon. Samuel, 6 March 1993.
Frere, James Arnold, 26 Nov. 1994.
Fulbright, James William, Hon. KBE, 9 Feb. 1995.
Fürer-Haimendorf, Prof. Christoph von, 11 June 1995.
Furness, 2nd Viscount; William Anthony Furness, 1 May 1995 (*ext*).

Gabb, (William) Harry, CVO, 16 March 1995.
Gadd, John, CBE, 6 Dec. 1994.
Gaon, Solomon, 21 Dec. 1994.
Gardner, James, CBE, RDI, 25 March 1995.
Gardner, Kenneth Burslam, 19 April 1995.
Gardner-Medwin, Prof. Robert Joseph, 29 June 1995.
Garnham, Prof. Percy Cyril Claude, CMG, FRS, 25 Dec. 1994.
Garrett, Hon. Sir Raymond William, AFC, AEA, 12 Oct. 1994.
Gauvain, Timothy John Lund, 15 Nov. 1994.
George, Griffith Owen, TD, 6 Dec. 1994.
Gere, John Arthur Giles, FBA, 11 Jan. 1995.
Gernsheim, Helmut Erich Robert, 20 July 1995.
Gibson, Sir Alexander Drummond, CBE, 14 Jan. 1995.
Gilchrist, (Andrew) Rae, CBE, 1 March 1995.
Giles, Carl Ronald, OBE, 27 Aug. 1995.
Gill, Cyril James, CB, 17 Nov. 1994.
Glass, Ven. Edward Brown, 2 June 1995.
Glentoran, 2nd Baron; Daniel Stewart Thomas Bingham Dixon, KBE, PC (NI), 22 July 1995.
Glyn, Hilary B., 20 June 1995.
Gohel, Sir Jayvantsinhji Kayaji, CBE, 19 May 1995.
Goldsmith, Maj.-Gen. Robert Frederick Kinglake, CB, CBE, 7 April 1995.
Golombek, Harry, OBE, 7 Jan. 1995.
Golt, Sidney, CB, 4 June 1995.
Goodman, Baron (Life Peer); Arnold Abraham Goodman, CH, 12 May 1995.
Goodwin, Prof. Albert, 22 Sept. 1995.
Goodwin, Prof. Geoffrey Lawrence, 26 April 1995.
Goold-Adams, Richard John Moreton, CBE, 23 March 1995.
Gort, 8th Viscount; Colin Leopold Prendergast Vereker, 6 April 1995.
Gowans, Hon. Sir (Urban) Gregory, 1 April 1994.
Graham, Walter Gerald Cloete, CBE, 8 March 1995.
Grant, Douglas Marr Kelso, 19 April 1995.
Grant, James Pineo, 28 Jan. 1995.
Grantchester, 2nd Baron; Kenneth Bent Suenson-Taylor, CBE, QC, 12 Aug. 1995.
Grantley, 7th Baron; John Richard Brinsley Norton, MC, 24 June 1995.
Gray, Maj.-Gen. (Reginald) John, CB, 28 Oct. 1994.
Green, Major George Hugh, MBE, MC, TD, 5 Feb. 1993.
Greenaway, Sir Derek Burdick, 2nd Bt, CBE, TD, 19 Nov. 1994.
Greenewalt, Crawford Hallock, 21 Sept. 1993.
Greensmith, Edward William, OBE, 1 Feb. 1995.
Greenwood, Peter Humphry, FRS, 3 March 1995.

Haferkamp, Wilhelm, 18 Jan. 1995.
Halas, John, OBE, 20 Jan. 1995.
Hallett, Cecil Walter, 5 Dec. 1994.
Hallowes, Odette Marie Celine, GC, MBE, 13 March 1995.
Ham, Rear-Adm. John Dudley Nelson, CB, 20 Nov. 1994.
Hambly, Edmund Cadbury, 28 March 1995.
Hamilton, Adm. Sir John Graham, GBE, CB, 27 Oct. 1994.
Hamilton, Robert William, FBA, 25 Sept. 1995.
Hanbury, Sir John Capel, CBE, 1 March 1995.
Harding, Prof. Anita Elizabeth, 11 Sept. 1995.
Hare, Hon. Alan Victor, MC, 10 April 1995.
Harman, John Bishop, 13 Nov. 1994.
Harmer, Sir Frederic Evelyn, CMG, 24 Feb. 1995.
Harmsworth, St John Bernard Vyvyan, 13 June 1995.
Harris, 6th Baron; George Robert John Harris, 17 Sept. 1995.
Harris, Robert, 18 May 1995.
Harris, Sir Ronald Montague Joseph, KCVO, CB, 22 Jan. 1995.
Harrod, Maj.-Gen. Lionel Alexander Digby, OBE, 18 Jan. 1995.
Havard-Williams, Peter, 16 Aug. 1995.
Haynes, Denys Eyre Lankester, 27 Sept. 1994.
Hayter, Sir William Goodenough, KCMG, 28 March 1995.
Heal, Anthony Standerwick, 25 March 1995.
Hebblethwaite, Peter, 18 Dec. 1994.
Heeps, William, CBE, 1 Feb. 1995.
Helmsing, Most Rev. Charles H., 20 Dec. 1993.
Henderson, Edward Firth, CMG, 13 April 1995.
Henson, Ronald Alfred, 1 Dec. 1994.
Heren, Louis Philip, 26 Jan. 1995.

Heriot, Alexander John, 14 March 1995.
Herries, Sir Michael Alexander Robert Young-, OBE, MC, 6 May 1995.
Herron, Prof. Ronald James, 1 Oct. 1994.
Hewitt, Harold, 23 April 1994.
Hewitt, Richard Thornton, OBE, 1 Oct. 1994.
Highsmith, Patricia, 4 Feb. 1995.
Hilary, David Henry Jephson, CB, 21 Oct. 1994.
Hillier, Jack Ronald, 5 Jan. 1995.
Hilton, Col Sir Peter, KCVO, MC, 30 May 1995.
Hobden, Dennis Harry, 20 April 1995.
Hodge, Sir John Rowland, 2nd Bt, MBE, 1 Jan. 1995.
Holden, Maj.-Gen. John Reid, CB, CBE, DSO, 18 April 1995.
Holloway, David Richard, 31 Aug. 1995.
Holmes, Brig. Kenneth Soar, CB, CBE, 16 Dec. 1994.
Holt, Arthur Frederick, 23 Aug. 1995.
Holt, Rear-Adm. John Bayley, CB, 28 April 1995.
Homans, Prof. George Caspar, 29 May 1989.
Hooper, Ven. Charles German, 22 March 1995.
Hopkins, Prof. Harold Horace, FRS, 22 Oct. 1994.
Hordern, Sir Michael Murray, CBE, 2 May 1995.
Horlick, Sir John James Macdonald, 5th Bt, 20 Feb. 1995.
Hort, Sir James Fenton, 8th Bt, 19 July 1995.
Housden, Rt Rev. James Alan George, 22 April 1994.
Howard, Rev. Canon Ronald Claude, 15 June 1995.
Howell, Rt Rev. Kenneth Walter, 15 Sept. 1995.
Howie, Sir James William, 17 March 1995.
Huckle, Sir (Henry) George, OBE, 29 May 1995.
Hudleston, Air Chief Marshal Sir Edmund C., GCB, CBE, 14 Dec. 1994.
Hudson, William Meredith Fisher, QC, 8 May 1995.
Huijsman, Nicolaas Basil Jacques, CMG, 9 March 1995.
Hulme, Maj.-Gen. Jerrie Anthony, CB, 20 Sept. 1995.
Humphrey, William Gerald, 4 July 1995.
Humphreys, Kenneth William, 4 Nov. 1994.
Hunt, Gilbert Adams, CBE, 17 Aug. 1995.
Hunt, Rt Rev. (William) Warren, 29 Sept. 1994.

Ibiam, Sir (Francis) Akanu, GCON, 1 July 1995.
Ievers, Rear-Adm. John Augustine, CB, OBE, 7 Aug. 1995.
Imms, George, CB, 5 July 1995.
Insch, James Ferguson, CBE, 14 Dec. 1994.
Irving, Sir Charles Graham, 30 March 1995.

Jackson, Frederick Hume, CMG, OBE, 13 Oct. 1994.
Jackson, Hon. Sir Lawrence Walter, KCMG, 5 June 1993.
Jackson-Stops, Gervase Frank Ashworth, OBE, 2 July 1995.
Jacques, Robin, 18 March 1995.
James, (Ernest) Gethin, 7 Sept. 1995.
Jarrett, Sir Clifford George, KBE, CB, 9 July 1995.
Jenkins, Garth John, CB, QC, 11 March 1995.
Jennings, Arnold Harry, CBE, 7 Nov. 1994.
Jennings, Sir Raymond Winter, QC, 6 March 1995.
Jerne, Prof. Niels Kaj, FRS, 7 Oct. 1994.
Johnson, James, 31 Jan. 1995.
Johnson, Rex, 1 March 1995.
Johnson, Robert White, CBE, 10 June 1995.
Johnston, Betty Joan, (Lady Johnston), CBE, 28 Nov. 1994.
Johnstone, Sir Frederic Allan George, 10th Bt, 19 July 1994.
Johnstone, Robert Edgeworth, 3 Dec. 1994.
Jones, Eifion, CMG, OBE, 6 March 1995.
Jones, Sir James Duncan, KCB, 6 Sept. 1995.
Jones, Air Marshal Sir Laurence Alfred, KCB, AFC, 23 Sept. 1995.
Jones, Leslie, 18 July 1994.
Jordan, Henry, 4 Oct. 1994.
Joseph, Baron (Life Peer); Keith Sinjohn Joseph, CH, PC, 10 Dec. 1994.
Josset, Lawrence, 7 May 1995.

Kadoorie, Sir Horace, CBE, 22 April 1995.
Kagan, Baron (Life Peer); Joseph Kagan, 18 Jan. 1995.
Kappel, Frederick R., 10 Nov. 1994.
Katz, Prof. Milton, 9 Aug. 1995.
Kay, Ernest, 25 Nov. 1994.
Keating, Donald Norman, QC, 1 Aug. 1995.
Keeble, Thomas Whitfield, 20 Dec. 1994.
Keighly-Peach, Captain Charles Lindsey, DSO, OBE, 4 Feb. 1995.
Kelsey, Julian George, CB, 25 March 1995.
Kemp, Athole Stephen Horsford, LVO, OBE, 23 March 1995.
Kendall, (William) Denis, 29 July 1995.
Kerr, Andrew Stevenson, CBE, 17 Nov. 1994.
Kettlewell, Richard Wildman, CMG, 17 Nov. 1994.
Key, Maj.-Gen. Clement Denis, MBE, 29 Sept. 1994.
Keys, Prof. Ivor Christopher Banfield, CBE, 7 July 1995.
Kilfedder, Sir James Alexander, MP, 20 March 1995.
Kinahan, Charles Henry Grierson, CBE, 11 Aug. 1995.
Kindersley, David Guy, MBE, 2 Feb. 1995.
King, Alexander Hyatt, 10 March 1995.
King, Prof. Jeffrey William Hitchen, 14 Feb. 1995.
Kingham, His Honour James Frederick, 8 Feb. 1995.
Kirsop, Arthur Michael Benjamin, 6 July 1995.
Kisch, (Alastair) Royalton, 21 March 1995.
Kitchen, Frederick Bruford, CBE, 23 June 1995.
Kneipp, Hon. Sir (Joseph Patrick) George, 15 Feb. 1993.
Kohoban-Wickreme, Alfred Silva, CVO, 7 Aug. 1989.

Lagesen, Air Marshal Sir Philip Jacobus, KCB, DFC, AFC, 9 Oct. 1994.
Lajtha, Prof. Laszlo George, CBE, 14 March 1995.
Lakeman, Enid, OBE, 7 Jan. 1995.
Lamb, Hon. Kenneth Henry Lowry, CBE, 21 June 1995.
Lambert, Hon. Margaret Barbara, CMG, 22 Jan. 1995.
Lane, Prof. Ronald Epey, CBE, 14 March 1995.
Latham, Robert Clifford, CBE, FBA, 4 Jan. 1995.
Laucke, Hon. Sir Condor Louis, KCMG, 30 July 1993.
Lawton, Ven. John Arthur, 29 April 1995.
Ledger, Sir Frank, (Joseph Francis), 8 April 1993.
Leonard-Williams, Air Vice-Marshal Harold Guy, CB, CBE, 21 Nov. 1994.
Leslie, His Honour Gilbert Frank, 24 March 1995.
Lever of Manchester, Baron (Life Peer); Harold Lever, PC, 6 Aug. 1995.
Lewis, Michael Samuel, 6 Aug. 1994.
Ley, Sir Francis Douglas, 4th Bt, MBE, TD, 10 May 1995.
Lindley, Sir Arnold Lewis George, 14 May 1995.
Ling, Maj.-Gen. Fergus Alan Humphrey, CB, CBE, DSO, 7 May 1995.
Lintott, Sir Henry, KCMG, 5 Jan. 1995.
Lissmann, Hans Werner, FRS, 21 April 1995.
Llewellyn, Rev. John Francis Morgan, LVO, 28 June 1995.
Lloyd, Prof. Antony Charles, FBA, 17 Dec. 1994.
Lo, Kenneth Hsiao Chien, 11 Aug. 1995.
Lord, His Honour John Herent, 20 Dec. 1994.
Louis, John Jeffry, Jr, 15 Feb. 1995.
Lovat, 17th Baron; Simon Christopher Joseph Fraser, DSO, MC, TD, 16 March 1995.
Loveridge, Sir John Henry, CBE, 7 Nov. 1994.
Luke, Peter Ambrose Cyprian, MC, 23 Jan. 1995.
Lwoff, Prof. André Michel, 30 Sept. 1994.
Lynn, Wilfred, 13 Oct. 1994.
Lyttleton, Prof. Raymond Arthur, FRS, 16 May 1995.

McCallum, John, (Ian), 12 Feb. 1995.
McCluskie, Samuel Joseph, 15 Sept. 1995.
McDonald, Alistair Ian, CBE, 15 Jan. 1995.
MacDonald, Gen. Sir Arthur Leslie, KBE, CB, 28 Jan. 1995.
Macdonald, Rev. Donald Farquhar Macleod, CBE, 26 April 1995.
McDonald, Thomas Muirhead, 20 June 1995.
MacDougall, Laura Margaret, (Lady MacDougall), 8 March 1995.
McElroy, Roy Granville, CMG, 16 May 1994.
McGilligan, Denis Brian, 8 July 1995.
McGrath, Dr Patrick Gerard, CB, CBE, 18 Oct. 1994.
Macintyre, Angus Donald, 21 Dec. 1994.
Mackenzie, Kenneth Edward, CMG, 24 April 1995.
Macnab, Brig. Sir Geoffrey Alex Colin, KCMG, CB, 17 Jan. 1995.
Maconchy, Dame Elizabeth, (Dame Elizabeth LeFanu), DBE, 11 Nov. 1994.
MacPherson, Stewart Myles, 16 April 1995.
Macqueen, Angus, CMG, 15 July 1995.
McWhirter, Prof. Robert, CBE, 24 Oct. 1994.
Magniac, Rear-Adm. Vernon St Clair Lane, CB, 28 Nov. 1994.
Magor, Major (Edward) Walter (Moyle), CMG, OBE, 1 May 1995.
Mair, Prof. Alexander, OBE, 6 Aug. 1995.
Malcolmson, Kenneth Forbes, 19 Aug. 1995.
Mansel, Rev. Canon James Seymour Denis, KCVO, 22 Sept. 1995.
Marsh, Rt Rev. Henry Hooper, 27 Jan. 1995.
Martin, Thomas Ballantyne, 28 Jan. 1995.
Mason, Sydney, CBE, 24 Jan. 1995.
Matthews, Horatio Keith, CMG, MBE, 31 Dec. 1994.
Matthews, Prof. Richard Ellis Ford, ONZ, FRS, 19 Feb. 1995.
Matthews, Ronald Sydney, CB, 25 May 1995.
May, Peter Barker Howard, CBE, 27 Dec. 1994.
Medley, (Charles) Robert (Owen), CBE, RA, 20 Oct. 1994.
Meldrum, Andrew, CBE, KPM, 10 Jan. 1995.
Menzies, Dame Pattie Maie, GBE, 30 Aug. 1995.
Messervy, Sir (Roney) Godfrey (Collumbell), 22 July 1995.
Middleton, Kenneth William Bruce, 19 Feb. 1995.
Miller, Lt-Comdr John Bryan Peter Duppa-, GC, 15 Dec. 1994.
Milne, Andrew McNicoll, 14 May 1995.
Milner-Barry, Sir (Philip) Stuart, KCVO, CB, OBE, 25 March 1995.
Molyneux, Wilfrid, 7 Feb. 1994.
Montagu, (Alexander) Victor (Edward Paulet), 25 Feb. 1995.
Monteith, Charles Montgomery, 9 May 1995.
Moon, Prof. Philip Burton, FRS, 9 Oct. 1994.
Mootham, Sir Orby Howell, 19 July 1995.
Morgan, (William) Geraint (Oliver), QC, 2 July 1995.
Morley, Very Rev. William Fenton, CBE, 9 July 1995.

Morrison, Rt Hon. Sir Peter Hugh, PC, 13 July 1995.
Mortlock, Herbert Norman, 5 June 1995.
Morton of Shuna, Baron (Life Peer); Hugh Drennan Baird Morton, 26 April 1995.
Moss, Edward Herbert St George, 1 April 1995.
Mote, Harold Trevor, 10 Jan. 1995.
Moynihan, Sir Noël Henry, 5 Oct. 1994.
Mtekateka, Rt Rev. Josiah, 17 June 1995.
Muir, Jean Elizabeth, (Mrs Harry Leuckert), CBE, RDI, 28 May 1995.
Mulley, Baron (Life Peer); Frederick William Mulley, PC, 15 March 1995.
Munro of Foulis, Captain Patrick, TD, 24 Feb. 1995.
Munro, Sir Robert Lindsay, CBE, 12 July 1995.
Murray, Dr Ronald Ormiston, MBE, 5 March 1995.
Musson, Maj.-Gen. Alfred Henry, CB, CBE, 6 Aug. 1995.

Nalder, Hon. Sir Crawford David, 8 Dec. 1994.
Nance, His Honour Francis James, 4 June 1995.
Napier, Barbara Langmuir, OBE, 7 Nov. 1991.
Neale, Sir Alan Derrett, KCB, MBE, 21 March 1995.
Needham, Joseph, CH, FRS, FBA, 24 March 1995.
Nelson of Stafford, 2nd Baron; Henry George Nelson, 19 Jan. 1995.
Newman, Philip Harker, CBE, DSO, MC, 31 Dec. 1994.
Niall, Sir Horace Lionel Richard, CBE, 30 April 1994.
Nickerson, Albert Lindsay, 7 Aug. 1994.
Norman, Mark Richard, CBE, 6 Dec. 1994.

Orr, Sir John Henry, OBE, QPM, 26 Sept. 1995.
Osborne, John James, 24 Dec. 1994.
Owen, Alun Davies, 6 Dec. 1994.
Owen, John Simpson, OBE, 23 Feb. 1995.
Owen, Rowland Hubert, CMG, 25 Jan. 1995.
Owens, Frank Arthur Robert, CBE, 26 June 1995.

Page, Brig. (Edwin) Kenneth, CBE, DSO, MC, 26 Jan. 1995.
Park, Trevor, 6 April 1995.
Parker, Kenneth Alfred Lamport, CB, 11 Sept. 1995.
Parkhurst, Raymond Thurston, 23 Aug. 1993.
Parkinson, Desmond Frederick, CMG, 22 Aug. 1995.
Parnis, Alexander Edward Libor, CBE, 11 Oct. 1994.
Parsons, Geoffrey Penwill, AO, OBE, 26 Jan. 1995.
Parsons-Smith, (Basil) Gerald, OBE, 21 April 1995.
Pasquill, Frank, FRS, 15 Oct. 1994.
Paterson, (James Edmund) Neil, 19 April 1995.
Paterson, Robert Lancelot, OBE, MC, ERD, 8 Feb. 1995.
Pearman, Sir James Eugene, CBE, 13 April 1994.
Peck, Sir John Howard, KCMG, 13 Jan. 1995.
Pedder, Vice-Adm. Sir Arthur Reid, KBE, CB, 22 June 1995.
Peierls, Sir Rudolf Ernst, CBE, FRS, 19 Sept. 1995.
Pembroke, Mary Countess of; Mary Dorothea Herbert, CVO, 16 Jan. 1995.
Pereira, Helio Gelli, FRS, 16 Aug. 1994.
Perry, Frederick John, 2 Feb. 1995.
Philipps, Lady Marion Violet, 18 June 1995.
Pickering, His Honour John Robertson, 25 April 1995.
Pickthorn, Sir Charles William Richards, 2nd Bt, 20 June 1995.
Pilditch, James George Christopher, CBE, 23 Aug. 1995.
Pilkington, Sir Lionel Alexander Bethune, (Sir Alastair), FRS, 5 May 1995.
Pinay, Antoine, 13 Dec. 1994.
Pineau, Christian Paul Francis, 5 April 1995.
Pipkin, (Charles Harry) Broughton, CBE, 31 Jan. 1995.
Pirie, Psyche, 2 June 1995.
Pitchford, John Hereward, CBE, 24 Feb. 1995.
Pitt of Hampstead, Baron (Life Peer); David Thomas Pitt, TC, 18 Dec. 1994.
Place, Rear-Adm. (Basil Charles) Godfrey, VC, CB, CVO, DSC, 27 Dec. 1994.
Pleasence, Donald, OBE, 2 Feb. 1995.
Pope-Hennessy, Sir John Wyndham, CBE, FBA, 31 Oct. 1994.
Porter, Eric Richard, 15 May 1995.
Potter, Sir (William) Ian, 24 Oct. 1994.
Powell, David, 28 June 1995.
Powell, (Elizabeth) Dilys, CBE, 3 June 1995.
Powles, Sir Guy Richardson, ONZ, KBE, CMG, ED, 24 Oct. 1994.
Pratt, Prof. Peter Lynn, 2 March 1995.
Preston, Sir Kenneth Huson, 6 June 1995.
Prestt, Ian, CBE, 24 Jan. 1995.
Price, John Lister Willis, CVO, 1 March 1995.
Price, John Maurice, QC, 15 April 1995.
Price, Brig. Rollo Edward Crwys, CBE, DSO, 24 Feb. 1995.
Pringle, Derek Hair, CBE, 7 July 1995.
Proud, Air Cdre Harold John Granville Ellis, CBE, 19 March 1995.
Putt, Samuel Gorley, OBE, 24 April 1995.
Pyle, Cyril Alfred, 11 May 1994.
Pyrah, Prof. Leslie Norman, CBE, 30 April 1995.

Radford, Sir Ronald Walter, KCB, MBE, 3 Sept. 1995.
Ramsay, Sir Thomas Meek, CMG, 27 Jan. 1995.
Raphael, Chaim, CBE, 10 Oct. 1994.
Rathbone, John Francis Warre, CBE, TD, 22 April 1995.
Rathbone, Very Rev. Norman Stanley, 13 July 1995.
Rathcavan, 2nd Baron; Phelim Robert Hugh O'Neill, PC, 20 Dec. 1994.
Redshaw, Prof. Seymour Cunningham, 25 Jan. 1995.
Rees, Prof. (Florence) Gwendolen, FRS, 4 Oct. 1994.
Reid, Archibald Cameron, CMG, CVO, 24 Nov. 1994.
Reid, Col (Percy Fergus) Ivo, OBE, 9 Dec. 1994.
Reigate, Baron (Life Peer); John Kenyon Vaughan-Morgan, PC, 26 Jan. 1995 (Btcy *ext*).
Rendell, Sir William, 20 Jan. 1995.
Renwick, Prof. James Harrison, 29 Sept. 1994.
Reynolds, Frank Arrowsmith, OBE, 24 Oct. 1994.
Rich, John Rowland, CMG, 13 May 1995.
Richards, Prof. Elfyn John, OBE, 7 Sept. 1995.
Richardson, Kenneth Albert, QC; His Honour Judge Richardson, 6 Dec. 1994.
Rie, Dame Lucy, DBE, 1 April 1995.
Ritchie, Charles Stewart Almon, CC, 8 June 1995.
Roberts, Air Cdre Sir Geoffrey Newland, CBE, AFC, 27 Aug. 1995.
Robinson, Harold George Robert, OBE, 4 Jan. 1995.
Rothman, Sydney, 19 June 1995.
Rouse, Sir Anthony Gerald Roderick, KCMG, OBE, 8 Oct. 1994.
Rowe, Norbert Edward, CBE, 5 Feb. 1995.
Rusk, Dean, Hon. KBE, 20 Dec. 1994.
Russell, Sir Archibald Edward, CBE, FRS, 29 May 1995.
Russell, Prof. Edward Walter, CMG, 22 Oct. 1994.
Ruttle, His Honour Henry Samuel, 11 Sept. 1995.
Ryden, Kenneth, MC, 7 Oct. 1994.

Salaman, Myer Head, 31 Dec. 1994.
Salk, Prof. Jonas Edward, 23 June 1995.
Sandilands, Sir Francis Edwin Prescott, CBE, 29 May 1995.
Saunders, Maj.-Gen. Kenneth, CB, OBE, 23 Dec. 1994.
Scarlett, Hon. John Leopold Campbell, CBE, 19 Aug. 1994.
Schiller, Prof. Karl, 26 Dec. 1994.
Schofield, Alfred, 16 Dec. 1994.
Schon, Baron (Life Peer); Frank Schon, 7 Jan. 1995.
Scott, Prof. Alexander Whiteford, CBE, 6 April 1993.
Scott, Maj.-Gen. Michael Frederick, 13 May 1995.
Scott-Hopkins, Major Sir James Sidney Rawdon, 11 March 1995.
Selkirk, 10th Earl of; George Nigel Douglas-Hamilton, KT, GCMG, GBE, AFC, AE, PC, QC (Scot.), 24 Nov. 1994.
Sempill, Lady (20th in line); Ann Moira Sempill, 6 July 1995.
Senior, Sir Edward Walters, CMG, 18 June 1995.
Series, Prof. George William, FRS, 2 Jan. 1995.
Seton, Lady, (Alice Ida), CBE, 28 July 1995.
Sexton, Maj.-Gen. (Francis) Michael, CB, OBE, 19 June 1995.
Sharpe, William James, CBE, 14 Nov. 1994.
Shearer, Thomas Hamilton, CB, 3 July 1995.
Shindler, His Honour George John, QC, 10 Dec. 1994.
Shoppee, Prof. Charles William, FRS, 20 Oct. 1994.
Shuckburgh, Sir (Charles Arthur) Evelyn, GCMG, CB, 12 Dec. 1994.
Sich, Sir Rupert Leigh, CB, 14 Sept. 1995.
Simmonds, Prof. Kenneth Royston, 29 April 1995.
Simpson, John Ferguson, 12 Sept. 1995.
Sinclair, Ernest Keith, CMG, OBE, DFC, 27 March 1995.
Singh, Giani Zail, 25 Dec. 1994.
Sinnamon, Sir Hercules Vincent, OBE, Feb. 1994.
Skelton, Rear-Adm. Peter, CB, 29 Nov. 1994.
Skinner, Prof. Andrew Forrester, 13 Feb. 1995.
Slater, Gordon James Augustus, 2 March 1995.
Slimmings, Sir William Kenneth MacLeod, CBE, 27 Jan. 1995.
Smijth-Windham, Brig. William Russell, CBE, DSO, 12 Nov. 1994.
Smith, Sir (Frank) Ewart, FRS, 14 June 1995.
Smith, Prof. George, MBE, 12 Sept. 1994.
Smith, George, 25 May 1994.
Smith, Sir John Wilson, CBE, 1 Feb. 1995.
Smith, Sir William Reardon Reardon-, 3rd Bt, 13 June 1995.
Smithers, Prof. Sir David Waldron, 20 July 1995.
Solomons, Prof. David, 12 Feb. 1995.
Somerfield, Stafford William, 13 Jan. 1995.
Somers, 8th Baron; John Patrick Somers Cocks, 15 Feb. 1995.
Somes, Michael George, CBE, 19 Nov. 1994.
Soukop, Wilhelm Josef, RA, 8 Feb. 1995.
Spender, Sir Stephen Harold, CBE, CLit, 16 July 1995.
Spooner, Edward Tenney Casswell, CMG, 30 Aug. 1995.
Spreckley, Sir (John) Nicholas (Teague), KCVO, CMG, 3 Dec. 1994.
Stacey, Prof. Maurice, CBE, FRS, 9 Oct. 1994.
Stallibrass, Geoffrey Ward, CB, OBE, 20 Oct. 1994.
Stamler, Samuel Aaron, QC, 12 Nov. 1994.
Stanier, Brig. Sir Alexander Beville Gibbons, 2nd Bt, DSO, MC, 10 Jan. 1995.
Stapleton, Sir (Henry) Alfred, 10th Bt, 5 Jan. 1995 (*ext*).
Steegmuller, Francis, 20 Oct. 1994.
Steel, Sir James, CBE, 17 Nov. 1994.
Steele-Perkins, Surg. Vice-Adm. Sir Derek Duncombe, KCB, KCVO, 9 Dec. 1994.
Stephens, Cedric John, 14 Oct. 1994.
Stephens, Maj.-Gen. Keith Fielding, CB, OBE, 17 June 1995.

Stevens, (Arthur) Edwin, CBE, 29 Jan. 1995.
Stevenson, Dr Alan Carruth, 18 Sept. 1995.
Stewart, John Anthony Benedict, CMG, OBE, 12 Sept. 1995.
Stewart, John Innes Mackintosh, 12 Nov. 1994.
Stewart, Stephen Malcolm, CBE, QC, 17 April 1995.
Stockwood, Rt Rev. (Arthur) Mervyn, 13 Jan. 1995.
Stoodley, Peter Ernest William, 2 March 1995.
Storey, Christopher, 27 Dec. 1994.
Strachan, Graham Robert, CBE, 1 Jan. 1995.
Stratton, Andrew, 13 Oct. 1994.
Straub, Marianne, OBE, RDI, 8 Nov. 1994.
Strickland-Constable, Sir Robert Frederick, 11th Bt, 11 Dec. 1994.
Sumsion, Herbert Whitton, CBE, 11 Aug. 1995.
Sutcliffe, His Honour Edward Davis, QC, 6 Jan. 1995.
Sutton, Thomas Francis, 9 Dec. 1994.
Swallow, John Crossley, FRS, 3 Dec. 1994.
Sweeting, William Hart, CMG, CBE, 19 Dec. 1994.
Swinburne, Hon. Ivan Archie, CMG, 12 Aug. 1994.
Swindlehurst, Rt Rev. Owen Francis, 28 Aug. 1995.
Swyer, Dr Gerald Isaac Macdonald, 19 Sept. 1995.
Sylvester, George Harold, CBE, 18 Sept. 1994.
Symons, Julian Gustave, 19 Nov. 1994.
Synge, Prof. John Lighton, FRS, 30 March 1995.

Taukalo, Sir (David) Dawea, MBE, 5 Jan. 1993.
Tayler, Alan Breach, CBE, 29 Jan. 1995.
Taylor of Hadfield, Baron (Life Peer); Francis Taylor, 15 Feb. 1995.
Taylor, Eric Scollick, 4 June 1995.
Taylor, Prof. Gerard William, 3 Jan. 1995.
Taylor, Sir James, MBE, 4 Oct. 1994.
Taylor, Kenneth John; His Honour Judge Kenneth Taylor, 20 June 1995.
Taylor, Most Rev. Robert Selby, CBE, OGS, 23 April 1995.
Temple, Sir John Meredith, 10 Dec. 1994.
Terry, Sir George Walter Roberts, CBE, QPM, 18 Aug. 1995.
Terry, Sir John Elliott, 29 March 1995.
Thomas, Rt Rev. John James Absalom, 27 Feb. 1995.
Thompson, Sir John, 11 July 1995.
Thomson, Sir Evan Rees Whitaker, 14 Jan. 1993.
Throckmorton, Sir Anthony John Benedict, 12th Bt, 17 Oct. 1994 (*ext*).
Thurso, 2nd Viscount; Robin Macdonald Sinclair, 29 April 1995.
Tiarks, Henry Frederic, 2 July 1995.
Tinsley, Charles Henry, 6 March 1995.
Todd, John Arthur, FRS, 22 Dec. 1994.
Tolley, Leslie John, CBE, 11 July 1995.
Tonge, Rev. David Theophilus, 16 Jan. 1995.
Torlesse, Rear-Adm. Arthur David, CB, DSO, 19 July 1995.
Touch, Arthur Gerald, CMG, 26 Nov. 1994.
Townsend, Group Captain Peter Wooldridge, CVO, DSO, DFC, 19 June 1995.
Tracy, Walter Valentine, RDI, 28 April 1995.
Traherne, Sir Cennydd George, KG, TD, 26 Jan. 1995.
Trevor, Elleston, 21 July 1995.
Tucker, Edward William, CB, 12 Sept. 1995.
Tudor, Sir James Cameron, KCMG, 9 July 1995.
Tuke, Comdr Seymour Charles, DSO, RN, 11 Oct. 1994.
Turnbull, Reginald Marsh, 17 April 1995.
Turner, Prof. Paul, CBE, 25 Dec. 1994.
Tyrrell, Gerald Fraser, 27 July 1993.

Upham, Captain Charles Hazlitt, VC, 22 Nov. 1994.
Urquhart, Donald John, CBE, 2 Dec. 1994.
Utiger, Ronald Ernest, CBE, 27 July 1995.

Vassar-Smith, Major Sir Richard Rathborne, 3rd Bt, TD, 12 Aug. 1995.

Waddington, Very Rev. John Albert Henry, MBE, TD, 23 Nov. 1994.
Wagner, Sir Anthony Richard, KCB, KCVO, 5 May 1995.
Wakely, Leonard John Dean, CMG, OBE, 24 June 1994.
Waldegrave, 12th Earl; Geoffrey Noel Waldegrave, KG, GCVO, TD, 23 May 1995.
Waley, (Andrew) Felix, VRD, QC; His Honour Judge Waley, 16 April 1995.
Walker, Prof. James, CBE, 27 June 1995.
Walker, Robert Scott, 12 April 1995.
Wallace, Robert, CBE, 16 Aug. 1995.
Waller, Sir (John) Keith, CBE, 14 Nov. 1992.
Waller, Sir John Stanier, 7th Bt, 22 Jan. 1995 (*ext*).
Walton, Ernest Thomas Sinton, 25 June 1995.
Warmington, Lt-Comdr Sir Marshall George Clitheroe, 3rd Bt, RN, 5 Feb. 1995.
Warner, Sir Frederick Archibald, GCVO, KCMG, 30 Sept. 1995.
Warner, Michael Henry Charles, 6 Nov. 1994.
Warsop, Rear-Adm. John Charles, CB, 13 July 1995.
Wasserstein, Prof. Abraham, 20 July 1995.
Waters, Garth Rodney, 17 Feb. 1995.
Waud, Christopher Denis George Pierre, 25 June 1995.
Webster, Prof. John Roger, OBE, 30 March 1995.
Weir, Rev. Cecil James Mullo, 4 March 1995.
Wessel, Robert Leslie, OBE, 21 Feb. 1995.
West, Christopher Robin, 28 Dec. 1994.
Westoll, Prof. Thomas Stanley, FRS, 19 Sept. 1995.
Whewell, Prof. Charles Smalley, 31 May 1995.
Whitbread, William Henry, TD, 23 Nov. 1994.
White of Hull, Baron (Life Peer); Vincent Gordon Lindsay White, KBE, 23 Aug. 1995.
White, Sir Frederick William George, KBE, FRS, 17 Aug. 1994.
White, Captain Richard Taylor, DSO, RN, 3 March 1995.
Whitfield, Prof. John Humphreys, 20 Feb. 1995.
Whitteridge, Sir Gordon Coligny, KCMG, OBE, 11 Jan. 1995.
Whittington, Joseph Basil, OBE, 22 Feb. 1995.
Whitton, Cuthbert Henry, 27 Aug. 1995.
Whitworth, Group Captain Frank, QC, 2 March 1995.
Wickham, Rt Rev. Edward Ralph, 29 Sept. 1994.
Wiesner, Prof. Jerome Bert, 21 Oct. 1994.
Wight, James Alfred, OBE, 23 Feb. 1995.
Wigner, Prof. Eugene Paul, 1 Jan. 1995.
Wilkinson, Prof. Andrew Wood, CBE, 18 Aug. 1995.
Williams, Rear-Adm. David Apthorp, CB, DSC, 20 March 1995.
Williams, David Barry, TD, QC; His Honour Judge Williams, 15 July 1995.
Williams, Dr David Iorwerth, 6 Nov. 1994.
Williams, Sir Edgar Trevor, CB, CBE, DSO, 26 June 1995.
Williams, Maj.-Gen. Edward Alexander Wilmot, CB, CBE, MC, 9 Nov. 1994.
Williams, Sir Francis John Watkin, 8th Bt, QC, 3 Jan. 1995.
Williams, Peter Lancelot, OBE, 10 Aug. 1995.
Wilson of Rievaulx, Baron (Life Peer); James Harold Wilson, KG, OBE, PC, FRS, 24 May 1995.
Wilson, Sir Alan Herries, FRS, 30 Sept. 1995.
Wilson, Prof. Arthur James Cochran, FRS, 1 July 1995.
Wilson, Gilbert, 29 March 1994.
Wilson, Sir John Gardiner, CBE, 22 Aug. 1994.
Wilson, Prof. Raymond, 21 March 1995.
Windeyer, Sir Brian Wellingham, 26 Oct. 1994.
Wood, Robert Eric, CBE, 31 Aug. 1995.
Woodcock, George, 28 Jan. 1995.
Worth, George Arthur, MBE, 25 Aug. 1994.
Wright, Adm. Jerauld, DSM, 27 April 1995.
Wright, John Keith, 24 Dec. 1994.
Wright, Roy William, CBE, 23 Nov. 1994.
Wrigley, Michael Harold, OBE, 13 Jan. 1995.
Wykeham, Air Marshal Sir Peter, KCB, DSO, OBE, DFC, AFC, 23 Feb. 1995.
Wyllie, Robert Lyon, CBE, 26 July 1995.

Yeend, Sir Geoffrey John, AC, CBE, 6 Oct. 1994.
Yonge, Dame (Ida) Felicity (Ann), DBE, 1 April 1995.
Youell, Rev. Canon George, 21 Jan. 1995.
Younger, Charles Frank Johnston, DSO, TD, 6 June 1995.
Yudkin, Prof. John, 12 July 1995.

INDEX TO ADVERTISERS

Action for the Blind, *22*
Amnesty International, *24*

Brighton Society for the Blind, *20*
British Wireless for the Blind Fund, *26*

Cancer & Leukaemia in Childhood, *22*
Children's Society, *20*
Church Army, *30*

Institute of Cancer Research, *40*

Police Dependants' Trust, *50*

Royal Anthropological Institute, *52*
Royal United Kingdom Beneficent Association, *56*

Special Olympics United Kingdom, *50*
Sue Ryder Foundation, *54*

Youth Trust, *60*

ABBREVIATIONS USED IN THIS BOOK

Some of the designatory letters in this list are used merely for economy of space and do not necessarily imply any professional or other qualification.

A

AA	Anti-aircraft; Automobile Association; Architectural Association; Augustinians of the Assumption
AAA	Amateur Athletic Association; American Accounting Association
AAAL	American Academy of Arts and Letters
AA&QMG	Assistant Adjutant and Quartermaster-General
AAAS	American Association for the Advancement of Science
AAC	Army Air Corps
AACCA	Associate, Association of Certified and Corporate Accountants (*now see* ACCA)
AACE	Association for Adult and Continuing Education
AAF	Auxiliary Air Force (*now see* RAux AF)
AAFCE	Allied Air Forces in Central Europe
AAG	Assistant Adjutant-General
AAI	Associate, Chartered Auctioneers' and Estate Agents' Institute (*now* (after amalgamation) *see* ARICS)
AAIL	American Academy and Institute of Arts and Letters (*now see* AAAL)
AAM	Association of Assistant Mistresses in Secondary Schools
AAMC	Australian Army Medical Corps (*now see* RAAMC)
A&AEE	Aeroplane and Armament Experimental Establishment
A and SH	Argyll and Sutherland Highlanders
AAPS	Aquatic and Atmospheric Physical Sciences
AAS	American Astronomical Society
AASA	Associate, Australian Society of Accountants (*now see* FCPA)
AASC	Australian Army Service Corps
AATSE	Australian Academy of Technological Sciences and Engineering
AAUQ	Associate in Accountancy, University of Queensland
AB	Bachelor of Arts (US); able-bodied seaman; airborne
ABA	Amateur Boxing Association; Antiquarian Booksellers' Association; American Bar Association
ABC	Australian Broadcasting Commission; American Broadcasting Companies; Amateur Boxing Club
ABCA	Army Bureau of Current Affairs
ABCC	Association of British Chambers of Commerce
ABCFM	American Board of Commissioners for Foreign Missions
ABI	Association of British Insurers
ABIA	Associate, Bankers' Institute of Australasia
ABINZ	Associate, Bankers' Institute of New Zealand
ABIS	Association of Burglary Insurance Surveyors
ABM	Advisory Board of Ministry
ABNM	American Board of Nuclear Medicine
ABP	Associated British Ports
Abp	Archbishop
ABPsS	Associate, British Psychological Society (*now see* AFBPsS)
ABRC	Advisory Board for the Research Councils
ABS	Associate, Building Societies' Institute (*now see* ACBSI)
ABSA	Association for Business Sponsorship of the Arts
ABSI	Associate, Boot and Shoe Institution
ABSM	Associate, Birmingham and Midland Institute School of Music
ABTA	Association of British Travel Agents
ABTAPL	Association of British Theological and Philosophical Libraries
AC	Companion, Order of Australia; *Ante Christum* (before Christ)
ACA	Associate, Institute of Chartered Accountants
Acad.	Academy
ACARD	Advisory Council for Applied Research and Development
ACAS	Advisory, Conciliation and Arbitration Service; Assistant Chief of the Air Staff
ACBSI	Associate, Chartered Building Societies Institute
ACC	Association of County Councils; Anglican Consultative Council
ACCA	Associate, Chartered Association of Certified Accountants
ACCEL	American College of Cardiology Extended Learning
ACCM	Advisory Council for the Church's Ministry (*now see* ABM)
ACCS	Associate, Corporation of Secretaries (*formerly* of Certified Secretaries)
ACDP	Australian Committee of Directors and Principals
ACDS	Assistant Chief of Defence Staff
ACE	Association of Consulting Engineers; Member, Association of Conference Executives
ACF	Army Cadet Force
ACFA	Army Cadet Force Association
ACFAS	Association Canadienne-Française pour l'avancement des sciences
ACFHE	Association of Colleges for Further and Higher Education
ACG	Assistant Chaplain-General
ACGI	Associate, City and Guilds of London Institute
ACGS	Assistant Chief of the General Staff
ACIArb	Associate, Chartered Institute of Arbitrators
ACIB	Associate, Chartered Institute of Bankers
ACII	Associate, Chartered Insurance Institute
ACIS	Associate, Institute of Chartered Secretaries and Administrators (*formerly* Chartered Institute of Secretaries)
ACIT	Associate, Chartered Institute of Transport
ACLS	American Council of Learned Societies
ACM	Association of Computing Machinery
ACMA	Associate, Chartered Institute of Management Accountants (*formerly* Institute of Cost and Management Accountants)
ACNS	Assistant Chief of Naval Staff
ACommA	Associate, Society of Commercial Accountants (*now see* ASCA)
ACORD	Advisory Committee on Research and Development
ACOS	Assistant Chief of Staff
ACOST	Advisory Council on Science and Technology
ACP	Association of Clinical Pathologists; Associate, College of Preceptors; African/Caribbean/Pacific
ACPO	Association of Chief Police Officers
ACRE	Action with Rural Communities in England
ACS	American Chemical Society; Additional Curates Society
ACSEA	Allied Command South East Asia
ACSM	Associate, Camborne School of Mines
ACT	Australian Capital Territory; Australian College of Theology; Associate, College of Technology; Association of Corporate Treasurers
ACTT	Association of Cinematograph, Television and Allied Technicians
ACTU	Australian Council of Trade Unions
ACU	Association of Commonwealth Universities
ACWA	Associate, Institute of Cost and Works Accountants (*now see* ACMA)
AD	Dame of the Order of Australia; *Anno Domini* (in the year of the Lord); Air Defence
aD	ausser Dienst
ADAS	Agricultural Development and Advisory Service
ADB	Asian Development Bank; Associate of the Drama Board (Education)
ADB/F	African Development Bank/Fund
ADC	Aide-de-camp
ADCM	Archbishop of Canterbury's Diploma in Church Music
AD Corps	Army Dental Corps (*now* RADC)
ADC(P)	Personal Aide-de-camp to HM The Queen
ADEME	Assistant Director Electrical and Mechanical Engineering
Ad eund	*Ad eundem gradum*; and *see under* aeg
ADFManc	Art and Design Fellow, Manchester
ADFW	Assistant Director of Fortifications and Works
ADGB	Air Defence of Great Britain
ADGMS	Assistant Director-General of Medical Services
ADH	Assistant Director of Hygiene
Adjt	Adjutant
ADJAG	Assistant Deputy Judge Advocate General
ADK	Order of Ahli Darjah Kinabalu
Adm.	Admiral
ADMS	Assistant Director of Medical Services
ADOS	Assistant Director of Ordnance Services
ADP	Automatic Data Processing
ADPA	Associate Diploma of Public Administration
ADS&T	Assistant Director of Supplies and Transport
Adv.	Advisory; Advocate
ADVS	Assistant Director of Veterinary Services
ADWE&M	Assistant Director of Works, Electrical and Mechanical
AE	Air Efficiency Award
AEA	Atomic Energy Authority; Air Efficiency Award (*now see* AE)
AEAF	Allied Expeditionary Air Force
AEC	Agriculture Executive Council; Army Educational Corps (*now see* RAEC); Atomic Energy Commission
AECMA	Association Européenne des Constructeurs de Matériel Aérospatial

AEE Atomic Energy Establishment
AEEU Amalgamated Engineering and Electrical Union
AEF Amalgamated Union of Engineering and Foundry Workers (later AEU, *now see* AEEU); American Expeditionary Forces
aeg *ad eundem gradum* (to the same degree—of the admission of a graduate of one university to the same degree at another without examination)
AEGIS Aid for the Elderly in Government Institutions
AEI Associated Electrical Industries
AEM Air Efficiency Medal
AER Army Emergency Reserve
AERE Atomic Energy Research Establishment (Harwell)
Æt., Ætat. *Ætatis* (aged)
AEU Amalgamated Engineering Union (*now see* AEEU)
AF Admiral of the Fleet
AFA Amateur Football Alliance
AFAIAA Associate Fellow, American Institute of Aeronautics and Astronautics
AFASIC Association for All Speech Impaired Children
AFB Air Force Base
AFBPsS Associate Fellow, British Psychological Society
AFC Air Force Cross; Association Football Club
AfC Association for Colleges
AFCAI Associate Fellow, Canadian Aeronautical Institute
AFCEA Armed Forces Communications and Electronics Association
AFCENT Allied Forces in Central Europe
AFD Doctor of Fine Arts (US)
AFDS Air Fighting Development Squadron
AFHQ Allied Force Headquarters
AFI American Film Institute
AFIA Associate, Federal Institute of Accountants (Australia)
AFIAP Artiste, Fédération Internationale de l'Art Photographique
AFIAS Associate Fellow, Institute of Aeronautical Sciences (US) (*now see* AFAIAA)
AFICD Associate Fellow, Institute of Civil Defence
AFIMA Associate Fellow, Institute of Mathematics and its Applications
AFM Air Force Medal
AFNORTH Allied Forces in Northern Europe
AFOM Associate, Faculty of Occupational Medicine
AFRAeS Associate Fellow, Royal Aeronautical Society (*now see* MRAeS)
AFRC Agricultural and Food Research Council (*now see* BBSRC)
AFV Armoured Fighting Vehicles
AG Attorney-General
AGAC American Guild of Authors and Composers
AGARD Advisory Group for Aerospace Research and Development
AGC Adjutant General's Corps
AGH Australian General Hospital
AGI Artistes Graphiques Internationaux; Associate, Institute of Certificated Grocers
AGR Advanced Gas-cooled Reactor
AGRA Army Group Royal Artillery; Association of Genealogists and Record Agents
AGSM Associate, Guildhall School of Music and Drama; Australian Graduate School of Management
AHA Area Health Authority; American Hospitals Association; Associate, Institute of Health Service Administrators (*now see* AHSM)
AHA(T) Area Health Authority (Teaching)
AHQ Army Headquarters
AHSM Associate, Institute of Health Services Management
AH-WC Associate, Heriot-Watt College, Edinburgh
ai *ad interim*
AIA Associate, Institute of Actuaries; American Institute of Architects; Association of International Artists
AIAA American Institute of Aeronautics and Astronautics
AIAgrE Associate, Institution of Agricultural Engineers
AIAL Associate Member, International Institute of Arts and Letters
AIArb Associate, Institute of Arbitrators (*now see* ACIArb)
AIAS Associate Surveyor Member, Incorporated Association of Architects and Surveyors
AIB Associate, Institute of Bankers (*now see* ACIB)
AIBD Associate, Institute of British Decorators
AIBP Associate, Institute of British Photographers
AIBScot Associate, Institute of Bankers in Scotland
AIC Agricultural Improvement Council; Associate of the Institute of Chemistry (later ARIC, MRIC; *now see* MRSC)
AICA Associate Member, Commonwealth Institute of Accountants; Association Internationale des Critiques d'Art
AICC All-India Congress Committee
AICE Associate, Institution of Civil Engineers
AIChE American Institute of Chemical Engineers
AICPA American Institute of Certified Public Accountants
AICS Associate, Institute of Chartered Shipbrokers
AICTA Associate, Imperial College of Tropical Agriculture
AIDS Acquired Immunity Deficiency Syndrome
AIE Associate, Institute of Education
AIEE Associate, Institution of Electrical Engineers
AIF Australian Imperial Forces
AIG Adjutant-Inspector-General
AIH Associate, Institute of Housing
AIHort Associate, Institute of Horticulture
AIIA Associate, Insurance Institute of America; Associate, Indian Institute of Architects
AIIMR Associate, Institute of Investment Management and Research
AIInfSc Associate, Institute of Information Scientists
AIIRA Associate, International Industrial Relations Association
AIL Associate, Institute of Linguists
AILA Associate, Institute of Landscape Architects (*now see* ALI)
AILocoE Associate, Institute of Locomotive Engineers
AIM Associate, Institution of Metallurgists (*now see* MIM); Australian Institute of Management
AIMarE Associate, Institute of Marine Engineers
AIMC Associate, Institute of Management Consultants
AIME American Institute of Mechanical Engineers
AIMgt Associate, Institute of Management
AIMSW Associate, Institute of Medical Social Workers
AInstM Associate Member, Institute of Marketing
AInstP Associate, Institute of Physics
AInstPI Associate, Institute of Patentees and Inventors
AIP Association of Independent Producers
AIPR Associate, Institute of Public Relations
AIProdE Associate, Institution of Production Engineers
AIQS Associate Member, Institute of Quantity Surveyors
AIRTE Associate, Institute of Road Transport Engineers
AIRTO Association of Independent Research and Technology Organizations
AIS Associate, Institute of Statisticians (*later* MIS)
AISA Associate, Incorporated Secretaries' Association
AIStructE Associate, Institution of Structural Engineers
AITI Associate, Institute of Translators and Interpreters
AITP Associate, Institute of Town Planners, India
AJAG Assistant Judge Advocate General
AJEX Association of Jewish Ex-Service Men and Women
AK Knight, Order of Australia; Alaska
AKC Associate, King's College London
AL Alabama
ALA Associate, Library Association; Association of London Authorities
Ala Alabama (US)
ALAA Associate, Library Association of Australia
ALAI Associate, Library Association of Ireland
ALAM Associate, London Academy of Music and Dramatic Art
ALCD Associate, London College of Divinity
ALCM Associate, London College of Music
ALCS Authors Lending and Copyright Society
ALFSEA Allied Land Forces South-East Asia
ALI Argyll Light Infantry; Associate, Landscape Institute
ALICE Autistic and Language Impaired Children's Education
ALLC Association for Literary and Linguistic Computing
ALP Australian Labor Party
ALPSP Association of Learned and Professional Society Publishers
ALS Associate, Linnean Society
Alta Alberta
ALVA Association of Leading Visitor Attractions
AM Albert Medal; Member, Order of Australia; Master of Arts (US); Alpes Maritimes
AMA Association of Metropolitan Authorities; Assistant Masters Association (later AMMA, *now see* ATL); Associate, Museums Association; Australian Medical Association
AMARC Associated Marine and Related Charities
Amb. Ambulance; Ambassador
AMBDA Associate Member, British Dyslexia Association
AMBIM Associate Member, British Institute of Management (*now see* AIMgt)
AMBritIRE Associate Member, British Institution of Radio Engineers (*now see* AMIERE)
AMC Association of Municipal Corporations
AMCST Associate, Manchester College of Science and Technology
AMCT Associate, Manchester College of Technology
AME Association of Municipal Engineers
AMEME Association of Mining Electrical and Mechanical Engineers
AMet Associate of Metallurgy
AMF Australian Military Forces
AMGOT Allied Military Government of Occupied Territory
AMIAE Associate Member, Institution of Automobile Engineers
AMIAgrE Associate Member, Institution of Agricultural Engineers
AMIBF Associate Member, Institute of British Foundrymen
AMICE Associate Member, Institution of Civil Engineers (*now see* MICE)
AMIChemE Associate Member, Institution of Chemical Engineers
AMIE(Aust) Associate Member, Institution of Engineers, Australia

AMIED Associate Member, Institution of Engineering Designers
AMIEE Associate Member, Institution of Electrical Engineers (*now see* MIEE)
AMIE(Ind) Associate Member, Institution of Engineers, India
AMIERE Associate Member, Institution of Electronic and Radio Engineers
AMIH Associate Member, Institute of Housing
AMIMechE Associate Member, Institution of Mechanical Engineers (*now see* MIMechE)
AMIMinE Associate Member, Institution of Mining Engineers
AMIMM Associate Member, Institution of Mining and Metallurgy
AMInstBE Associate Member, Institution of British Engineers
AMInstCE Associate Member, Institution of Civil Engineers (*now see* MICE)
AmInstEE American Institute of Electrical Engineers
AMInstR Associate Member, Institute of Refrigeration
AMInstT Associate Member, Institute of Transport (*now see* ACIT)
AMInstTA Associate Member, Institute of Traffic Administration
AMINucE Associate Member, Institution of Nuclear Engineers
AMIRSE Associate Member, Institute of Railway Signalling Engineers
AMIStructE Associate Member, Institution of Structural Engineers
AMMA Assistant Masters & Mistresses Association (*now see* ATL)
AMN Ahli Mangku Negara (Malaysia)
AMP Advanced Management Program; Air Member for Personnel
AMRINA Associate Member, Royal Institution of Naval Architects
AMS Assistant Military Secretary; Army Medical Services
AMSO Air Member for Supply and Organisation
AMTE Admiralty Marine Technology Establishment
AMTRI Advanced Manufacturing Technology Research Institute
ANA Associate National Academician (America)
ANAF Arab Non-Arab Friendship
Anat. Anatomy; Anatomical
ANC African National Congress
ANECInst Associate, NE Coast Institution of Engineers and Shipbuilders
ANGAU Australian New Guinea Administrative Unit
Anon. Anonymously
ANU Australian National University
ANZAAS Australian and New Zealand Association for the Advancement of Science
Anzac Australian and New Zealand Army Corps
AO Officer, Order of Australia; Air Officer
AOA Air Officer in charge of Administration
AOC Air Officer Commanding
AOC-in-C Air Officer Commanding-in-Chief
AOD Army Ordnance Department
AOER Army Officers Emergency Reserve
APA American Psychiatric Association
APACS Association of Payment and Clearing Systems
APCK Association for Promoting Christian Knowledge, Church of Ireland
APD Army Pay Department
APEX Association of Professional, Executive, Clerical and Computer Staff
APHA American Public Health Association
APIS Army Photographic Intelligence Service
APM Assistant Provost Marshal
APMI Associate, Pensions Management Institute
APR Accredited Public Relations Practitioner
APS Aborigines Protection Society; American Physical Society
APsSI Associate, Psychological Society of Ireland
APSW Association of Psychiatric Social Workers
APT&C Administrative, Professional, Technical and Clerical
APTC Army Physical Training Corps
AQ Administration and Quartering
AQMG Assistant Quartermaster-General
AR Associated Rediffusion (Television); Arkansas
ARA Associate, Royal Academy
ARACI Associate, Royal Australian Chemical Institute
ARAD Associate, Royal Academy of Dancing
ARAeS Associate, Royal Aeronautical Society
ARAgS Associate, Royal Agricultural Societies (*ie* of England, Scotland and Wales)
ARAIA Associate, Royal Australian Institute of Architects
ARAM Associate, Royal Academy of Music
ARAS Associate, Royal Astronomical Society
ARBA Associate, Royal Society of British Artists
ARBC Associate, Royal British Colonial Society of Artists
ARBS Associate, Royal Society of British Sculptors
ARC Architects' Registration Council; Agricultural Research Council (later AFRC); Aeronautical Research Council
ARCA Associate, Royal College of Art; Associate, Royal Canadian Academy
ARCamA Associate, Royal Cambrian Academy of Art
ARCE Academical Rank of Civil Engineer
ARCIC Anglican-Roman Catholic International Commission
ARCM Associate, Royal College of Music
ARCO Associate, Royal College of Organists
ARCO(CHM) Associate, Royal College of Organists with Diploma in Choir Training
ARCPsych Associate Member, Royal College of Psychiatrists
ARCS Associate, Royal College of Science
ARCST Associate, Royal College of Science and Technology (Glasgow)
ARCUK Architects' Registration Council of the United Kingdom
ARCVS Associate, Royal College of Veterinary Surgeons
ARE Associate, Royal Society of Painter-Printmakers (*formerly* of Painter-Etchers and Engravers); Arab Republic of Egypt; Admiralty Research Establishment
AREINZ Associate, Real Estate Institute, New Zealand
ARELS Association of Recognised English Language Schools
ARIAS Associate, Royal Incorporation of Architects in Scotland
ARIBA Associate, Royal Institute of British Architects (*now see* RIBA)
ARIC Associate, Royal Institute of Chemistry (later MRIC; *now see* MRSC)
ARICS Professional Associate, Royal Institution of Chartered Surveyors
ARINA Associate, Royal Institution of Naval Architects
Ark Arkansas (US)
ARLT Association for the Reform of Latin Teaching
ARMS Associate, Royal Society of Miniature Painters
ARP Air Raid Precautions
ARPS Associate, Royal Photographic Society
ARR Association of Radiation Research
ARRC Associate, Royal Red Cross
ARSA Associate, Royal Scottish Academy
ARSC Association of Recorded Sound Collections
ARSCM Associate, Royal School of Church Music
ARSM Associate, Royal School of Mines
ARTC Associate, Royal Technical College (Glasgow) (*now see* ARCST)
ARVIA Associate, Royal Victoria Institute of Architects
ARWA Associate, Royal West of England Academy
ARWS Associate, Royal Society of Painters in Water-Colours
AS Anglo-Saxon
ASA Associate Member, Society of Actuaries; Associate of Society of Actuaries (US); Australian Society of Accountants; Army Sailing Association; Advertising Standards Authority
ASAA Associate, Society of Incorporated Accountants and Auditors
ASAI Associate, Society of Architectural Illustrators
ASAM Associate, Society of Art Masters
AS&TS of SA Associated Scientific and Technical Societies of South Africa
ASBAH Association for Spina Bifida and Hydrocephalus
ASC Administrative Staff College, Henley
ASCA Associate, Society of Company and Commercial Accountants
ASCAB Armed Services Consultant Approval Board
ASCAP American Society of Composers, Authors and Publishers
ASCE American Society of Civil Engineers
ASCHB Association for Study of Conservation of Historic Buildings
AScW Association of Scientific Workers (*now see* ASTMS)
ASD Armament Supply Department
ASE Amalgamated Society of Engineers (later AUEW, then AEU; *now see* AEEU); Association for Science Education
ASEAN Association of South East Asian Nations
ASH Action on Smoking and Health
ASIAD Associate, Society of Industrial Artists and Designers
ASIA(Ed) Associate, Society of Industrial Artists (Education)
ASLE American Society of Lubrication Engineers
ASLEF Associated Society of Locomotive Engineers and Firemen
ASLIB or Aslib Association for Information Management (*formerly* Association of Special Libraries and Information Bureaux)
ASM Association of Senior Members
ASME American Society of Mechanical Engineers; Association for the Study of Medical Education
ASO Air Staff Officer
ASSC Accounting Standards Steering Committee
ASSET Association of Supervisory Staffs, Executives and Technicians (*now see* ASTMS)
AssocISI Associate, Iron and Steel Institute
AssocMCT Associateship of Manchester College of Technology
AssocMIAeE Associate Member, Institution of Aeronautical Engineers
AssocRINA Associate, Royal Institution of Naval Architects
AssocSc Associate in Science
Asst Assistant
ASTA Association of Short Circuit Testing Authorities
ASTC Administrative Service Training Course
ASTMS Association of Scientific, Technical and Managerial Staffs (now part of MSF)
ASVU Army Security Vetting Unit
ASWDU Air Sea Warfare Development Unit
ASWE Admiralty Surface Weapons Establishment
ATA Air Transport Auxiliary
ATAE Association of Tutors in Adult Education
ATAF Allied Tactical Air Force

ATC	Air Training Corps; Art Teacher's Certificate
ATCDE	Association of Teachers in Colleges and Departments of Education (*now see* NATFHE)
ATCL	Associate, Trinity College of Music, London
ATD	Art Teacher's Diploma
ATI	Associate, Textile Institute
ATII	Associate Member, Chartered Institute (*formerly* Incorporated Institute, then Institute) of Taxation
ATL	Association of Teachers and Lecturers
ato	Ammunition Technical Officer
ATPL (A) or **(H)**	Airline Transport Pilot's Licence (Aeroplanes), or (Helicopters)
ATS	Auxiliary Territorial Service (*now see* WRAC)
ATTI	Association of Teachers in Technical Institutions (*now see* NATFHE)
ATV	Association TeleVision
AUA	American Urological Association
AUCAS	Association of University Clinical Academic Staff
AUEW	Amalgamated Union of Engineering Workers (later AEU, *now see* AEEU)
AUS	Army of the United States
AUT	Association of University Teachers
AVCC	Australian Vice-Chancellors' Committee
AVCM	Associate, Victoria College of Music
AVD	Army Veterinary Department
AVLA	Audio Visual Language Association
AVR	Army Volunteer Reserve
AWA	Anglian Water Authority
AWO	Association of Water Officers (*now see* IWO)
AWRE	Atomic Weapons Research Establishment
aws	Graduate of Air Warfare Course
AZ	Arizona

B

b	born; brother
BA	Bachelor of Arts
BAA	British Airports Authority
BAAB	British Amateur Athletic Board
BAAL	British Association for Applied Linguistics
BAAS	British Association for the Advancement of Science
BAB	British Airways Board
BAC	British Aircraft Corporation
BACM	British Association of Colliery Management
BACUP	British Association of Cancer United Patients
BAe	British Aerospace
BAED	Bachelor of Arts in Environmental Design
B&FBS	British and Foreign Bible Society
BAFO	British Air Forces of Occupation
BAFPA	British Association of Fitness Promotion Agencies
BAFTA	British Academy of Film and Television Arts
BAG	Business Art Galleries
BAgrSc	Bachelor of Agricultural Science
BAI	*Baccalarius in Arte Ingeniaria* (Bachelor of Engineering)
BAIE	British Association of Industrial Editors
BALPA	British Air Line Pilots' Association
BAO	Bachelor of Art of Obstetrics
BAOMS	British Association of Oral and Maxillo-Facial Surgeons
BAOR	British Army of the Rhine (formerly *on* the Rhine)
BAOS	British Association of Oral Surgeons (*now see* BAOMS)
BAppSc(MT)	Bachelor of Applied Science (Medical Technology)
BARB	Broadcasters' Audience Research Board
BARC	British Automobile Racing Club
BArch	Bachelor of Architecture
Bart	Baronet
BAS	Bachelor in Agricultural Science
BASc	Bachelor of Applied Science
BASCA	British Academy of Songwriters, Composers and Authors
BASEEFA	British Approvals Service for Electrical Equipment in Flammable Atmospheres
BASW	British Association of Social Workers
Batt.	Battery
BBA	British Bankers' Association; Bachelor of Business Administration
BB&CIRly	Bombay, Baroda and Central India Railway
BBB of C	British Boxing Board of Control
BBC	British Broadcasting Corporation
BBFC	British Board of Film Classification
BBM	Bintang Bakti Masharakat (Public Service Star) (Singapore)
BBS	Bachelor of Business Studies
BBSRC	Biotechnology and Biosciences Research Council
BC	Before Christ; British Columbia; Borough Council
BCAR	British Civil Airworthiness Requirements
BCC	British Council of Churches (*now see* CCBI)
BCE	Bachelor of Civil Engineering; Before the Christian Era
BCh or **BChir**	Bachelor of Surgery
BChD	Bachelor of Dental Surgery
BCIA	British Clothing Industries Association
BCL	Bachelor of Civil Law
BCMF	British Ceramic Manufacturers' Federation
BCMS	Bible Churchmen's Missionary Society
BCOF	British Commonwealth Occupation Force
BCom or **BComm**	Bachelor of Commerce
BComSc	Bachelor of Commercial Science
BCPC	British Crop Protection Council
BCS	Bengal Civil Service; British Computer Society
BCSA	British Constructional Steelwork Association
BCURA	British Coal Utilization Research Association
BCYC	British Corinthian Yacht Club
BD	Bachelor of Divinity
Bd	Board
BDA	British Dental Association; British Deaf Association; British Dyslexia Association
Bde	Brigade
BDQ	Bachelor of Divinity Qualifying
BDS	Bachelor of Dental Surgery
BDSc	Bachelor of Dental Science
BE	Bachelor of Engineering; British Element
BEA	British East Africa; British European Airways; British Epilepsy Association
BEAMA	Federation of British Electrotechnical and Allied Manufacturers' Associations (formerly British Electrical and Allied Manufacturers' Association)
BE&A	Bachelor of Engineering and Architecture (Malta)
BEAS	British Educational Administration Society
BEC	Business Education Council (*now see* BTEC)
BEc	Bachelor of Economics
BECTU	Broadcasting, Entertainment, Cinematograph and Theatre Union
BEd	Bachelor of Education
Beds	Bedfordshire
BEE	Bachelor of Electrical Engineering
BEF	British Expeditionary Force; British Equestrian Federation
BEM	British Empire Medal
BEMAS	British Education Management and Administration Society
BEME	Brigade Electrical and Mechanical Engineer
BEng	Bachelor of Engineering
BEO	Base Engineer Officer
Berks	Berkshire
BESO	British Executive Service Overseas
BEVA	British Equine Veterinary Association
BFI	British Film Institute
BFMIRA	British Food Manufacturing Industries Research Association
BFPO	British Forces Post Office
BFSS	British Field Sports Society
BFWG	British Federation of Women Graduates
BGS	Brigadier General Staff
BHA	British Hospitality Association
Bhd	Berhad
BHF	British Heart Foundation
BHRA	British Hydromechanics Research Association
BHRCA	British Hotels, Restaurants and Caterers' Association (*now see* BHA)
BHS	British Horse Society
BI	British Invisibles
BIBA	British Insurance Brokers' Association (*now see* BIIBA)
BIBRA	British Industrial Biological Research Association
BICC	British Insulated Callender's Cables
BICERA	British Internal Combustion Engine Research Association (*now see* BICERI)
BICERI	British Internal Combustion Engine Research Institute
BICSc	British Institute of Cleaning Science
BIEC	British Invisible Exports Council (*now see* BI)
BIEE	British Institute of Energy Economics
BIF	British Industries Fair
BIFU	Banking Insurance and Finance Union
BIIBA	British Insurance & Investment Brokers' Association
BIM	British Institute of Management
BIR	British Institute of Radiology
BIS	Bank for International Settlements
BISF	British Iron and Steel Federation
BISFA	British Industrial and Scientific Film Association
BISPA	British Independent Steel Producers Association
BISRA	British Iron and Steel Research Association
BITC	Business in the Community
BJ	Bachelor of Journalism
BJSM	British Joint Services Mission
BKSTS	British Kinematograph, Sound and Television Society

BL Bachelor of Law; British Library
BLA British Liberation Army
BLDSA British Long Distance Swimming Association
BLE Brotherhood of Locomotive Engineers; Bachelor of Land Economy
BLegS Bachelor of Legal Studies
BLESMA British Limbless Ex-Servicemen's Association
BLitt Bachelor of Letters
BM British Museum; Bachelor of Medicine; Brigade Major; British Monomark
BMA British Medical Association
BMedSci Bachelor of Medical Science
BMEO British Middle East Office
BMet Bachelor of Metallurgy
BMEWS Ballistic Missile Early Warning System
BMG British Military Government
BMH British Military Hospital
BMilSc Bachelor of Military Science
BMJ British Medical Journal
BMM British Military Mission
BMR Bureau of Mineral Resources
BMRA Brigade Major Royal Artillery
Bn Battalion
BNAF British North Africa Force
BNC Brasenose College
BNEC British National Export Council
BNF British National Formulary
BNFL British Nuclear Fuels Ltd
BNOC British National Oil Corporation; British National Opera Company
BNP Banque Nationale de Paris
BNSC British National Space Centre
BNSc Bachelor of Nursing Science
BOAC British Overseas Airways Corporation
BomCS Bombay Civil Service
BomSC Bombay Staff Corps
BoT Board of Trade
Bot. Botany; Botanical
BOTB British Overseas Trade Board
BOU British Ornithologists' Union
Bp Bishop
BPA British Paediatric Association
BPG Broadcasting Press Guild
BPharm Bachelor of Pharmacy
BPIF British Printing Industries Federation
BPMF British Postgraduate Medical Federation
BPsS British Psychological Society
BR British Rail
Br. Branch
BRA Brigadier Royal Artillery; British Rheumatism & Arthritis Association
BRB British Railways Board
BRCS British Red Cross Society
BRE Building Research Establishment
Brig. Brigadier
BritIRE British Institution of Radio Engineers (*now see* IERE)
BRNC Britannia Royal Naval College
BRS British Road Services
BRurSc Bachelor of Rural Science
BS Bachelor of Surgery; Bachelor of Science; British Standard
BSA Bachelor of Scientific Agriculture; Birmingham Small Arms; Building Societies' Association
BSAA British South American Airways
BSAP British South Africa Police
BSC British Steel Corporation; Bengal Staff Corps
BSc Bachelor of Science
BScA, BScAgr Bachelor of Science in Agriculture
BSc(Dent) Bachelor of Science in Dentistry
BSc (Est. Man.) Bachelor of Science in Estate Management
BScN Bachelor of Science in Nursing
BScSoc Bachelor of Social Sciences
BSE Bachelor of Science in Engineering (US)
BSES British Schools Exploring Society
BSF British Salonica Force
BSFA British Science Fiction Association
BSI British Standards Institution
BSIA British Security Industry Association
BSJA British Show Jumping Association
BSME Bachelor of Science in Mechanical Engineering; British Society of Magazine Editors
BSN Bachelor of Science in Nursing
BSNS Bachelor of Naval Science
BSocSc Bachelor of Social Science
BSRA British Ship Research Association
BSS Bachelor of Science (Social Science)
BST Bachelor of Sacred Theology
BSurv Bachelor of Surveying
BT Bachelor of Teaching; British Telecommunications
Bt Baronet; Brevet
BTA British Tourist Authority (*formerly* British Travel Association)
BTC British Transport Commission
BTCV British Trust for Conservation Volunteers
BTDB British Transport Docks Board (*now see* ABP)
BTEC Business and Technology (*formerly* Technician) Education Council
BTh Bachelor of Theology
BTP Bachelor of Town Planning
Btss Baronetess
BUAS British Universities Association of Slavists
Bucks Buckinghamshire
BUGB Baptist Union of Great Britain
BUPA British United Provident Association
BURA British Urban Regeneration Association
BV Besloten Vennootschap
BVA British Veterinary Association
BVetMed Bachelor of Veterinary Medicine
BVI British Virgin Islands
BVM Blessed Virgin Mary
BVMS Bachelor of Veterinary Medicine and Surgery
BVSc Bachelor of Veterinary Science
BWI British West Indies
BWM British War Medal

C

C Conservative: 100
c child; cousin; *circa* (about)
CA Central America; County Alderman; Chartered Accountant (Scotland and Canada); California
CAA Civil Aviation Authority
CAABU Council for the Advancement of Arab and British Understanding
CAAV (Member of) Central Association of Agricultural Valuers
CAB Citizens' Advice Bureau; Centre for Agricultural and Biosciences (*formerly* Commonwealth Agricultural Bureau)
CACTM Central Advisory Council of Training for the Ministry (later ACCM; *now see* ABM)
CAER Conservative Action for Electoral Reform
CAFOD Catholic Fund for Overseas Development
CALE Canadian Army Liaison Executive
Calif California (US)
CAM Communications, Advertising and Marketing
Cambs Cambridgeshire
CAMC Canadian Army Medical Corps
CAMRA Campaign for Real Ale
CAMS Certificate of Advanced Musical Study
CAMW Central Association for Mental Welfare
C&G City and Guilds of London Institute
Cantab *Cantabrigiensis* (of Cambridge)
Cantuar *Cantuariensis* (of Canterbury)
CARD Campaign against Racial Discrimination
CARE Cottage and Rural Enterprises
CARICOM Caribbean Community
CARIFTA Caribbean Free Trade Area (*now see* CARICOM)
CAS Chief of the Air Staff
CASI Canadian Aeronautics and Space Institute
CAT College of Advanced Technology; Countryside Around Towns
CATE Council for the Accreditation of Teacher Education
Cav. Cavalry
CAWU Clerical and Administrative Workers' Union (later APEX)
CB Companion, Order of the Bath; County Borough
CBC County Borough Council
CBCO Central Board for Conscientious Objectors
CBE Commander, Order of the British Empire
CBI Confederation of British Industry
CBIM Companion, British Institute of Management (*now see* CIMgt)
CBiol Chartered Biologist
CBNS Commander British Navy Staff
CBS Columbia Broadcasting System; Confraternity of the Blessed Sacrament
CBSA Clay Bird Shooting Association
CBSI Chartered Building Societies Institute (*now see* CIB)
CBSO City of Birmingham Symphony Orchestra
CC Companion, Order of Canada; City Council; County Council; Cricket Club; Cycling Club; County Court
CCAB Consultative Committee of Accountancy Bodies
CCAHC Central Council for Agricultural and Horticultural Co-operation

CCBE Commission Consultative des Barreaux de la Communauté Européenne

CCBI Council of Churches for Britain and Ireland

CCC Corpus Christi College; Central Criminal Court; County Cricket Club

CCE Chartered Civil Engineer

CCF Combined Cadet Force

CCFM Combined Cadet Forces Medal

CCG Control Commission Germany

CCH Cacique's Crown of Honour, Order of Service of Guyana

CChem Chartered Chemist

CCHMS Central Committee for Hospital Medical Services

CCIA Commission of Churches on International Affairs

CCIS Command Control Information System

CCJ Council of Christians and Jews

CCPR Central Council of Physical Recreation

CCRA Commander Corps of Royal Artillery

CCRE Commander Corps of Royal Engineers

CCREME Commander Corps of Royal Electrical and Mechanical Engineers

CCRSigs Commander Corps of Royal Signals

CCS Casualty Clearing Station; Ceylon Civil Service; Countryside Commission for Scotland

CCSU Council of Civil Service Unions

CCTA Commission de Coopération Technique pour l'Afrique

CCTS Combat Crew Training Squadron

CD Canadian Forces Decoration; Commander, Order of Distinction (Jamaica); Civil Defence; Compact Disc

CDA Co-operative Development Agency

CDEE Chemical Defence Experimental Establishment

CDipAF Certified Diploma in Accounting and Finance

Cdo Commando

CDRA Committee of Directors of Research Associations

Cdre Commodore

CDS Chief of the Defence Staff

CDU Christlich-Demokratische Union

CE Civil Engineer

CEA Central Electricity Authority

CEC Commission of the European Communities

CECD Confédération Européenne du Commerce de Détail

CECG Consumers in European Community Group

CEDEP Centre Européen d'Education Permanente

CEE Communauté Economique Européenne

CEED Centre for Economic and Environmental Development

CEF Canadian Expeditionary Force

CEFIC Conseil Européen des Fédérations de l'Industrie Chimique

CEGB Central Electricity Generating Board

CEI Council of Engineering Institutions

CEIR Corporation for Economic and Industrial Research

CEM Council of European Municipalities (*now see* CEMR)

CEMA Council for the Encouragement of Music and Arts

CEMR Council of European Municipalities and Regions

CEMS Church of England Men's Society

CEN Comité Européen de Normalisation

CENELEC European Committee for Electrotechnical Standardization

CEng Chartered Engineer

Cento Central Treaty Organisation

CEPT Conférence Européenne des Postes et des Télécommunications

CERL Central Electricity Research Laboratories

CERN Organisation (*formerly* Centre) Européenne pour la Recherche Nucléaire

CERT Charities Effectiveness Review Trust

Cert Ed Certificate of Education

CertITP Certificate of International Teachers' Program (Harvard)

CEST Centre for Exploitation of Science and Technology

CET Council for Educational Technology

CETS Church of England Temperance Society

CF Chaplain to the Forces

CFA Canadian Field Artillery

CFE Central Fighter Establishment

CFM Cadet Forces Medal

CFR Commander, Order of the Federal Republic of Nigeria

CFS Central Flying School

CGA Community of the Glorious Ascension; Country Gentlemen's Association

CGeol Chartered Geologist

CGH Order of the Golden Heart of Kenya (1st class)

CGIA Insignia Award of City and Guilds of London Institute (*now see* FCGI)

CGLI City and Guilds of London Institute (*now see* C&G)

CGM Conspicuous Gallantry Medal

CGRM Commandant-General Royal Marines

CGS Chief of the General Staff

CH Companion of Honour

Chanc. Chancellor; Chancery

Chap. Chaplain

ChapStJ Chaplain, Order of St John of Jerusalem (*now see* ChStJ)

CHAR Campaign for the Homeless and Rootless

CHB Companion of Honour of Barbados

ChB Bachelor of Surgery

CHC Community Health Council

Ch.Ch. Christ Church

Ch.Coll. Christ's College

CHE Campaign for Homosexual Equality

ChLJ Chaplain, Order of St Lazarus of Jerusalem

CHM Chevalier of Honour and Merit (Haiti)

(CHM) *See under* ARCO(CHM), FRCO(CHM)

ChM Master of Surgery

Chm. Chairman or Chairwoman

CHN Community of the Holy Name

CHSC Central Health Services Council

ChStJ Chaplain, Most Venerable Order of the Hospital of St John of Jerusalem

CI Imperial Order of the Crown of India; Channel Islands

CIA Chemical Industries Association; Central Intelligence Agency

CIAD Central Institute of Art and Design

CIAgrE Companion, Institution of Agricultural Engineers

CIAL Corresponding Member of the International Institute of Arts and Letters

CIArb Chartered Institute of Arbitrators

CIB Chartered Institute of Bankers

CIBS Chartered Institution of Building Services (*now see* CIBSE)

CIBSE Chartered Institution of Building Services Engineers

CIC Chemical Institute of Canada

CICB Criminal Injuries Compensation Board

CICHE Committee for International Co-operation in Higher Education

CICI Confederation of Information Communication Industries

CID Criminal Investigation Department

CIDEC Conseil International pour le Développement du Cuivre

CIE Companion, Order of the Indian Empire; Confédération Internationale des Etudiants

CIEx Companion, Institute of Export

CIFRS Comité International de la Rayonne et des Fibres Synthétiques

CIGasE Companion, Institution of Gas Engineers

CIGRE Conférence Internationale des Grands Réseaux Electriques

CIGS Chief of the Imperial General Staff (*now see* CGS)

CIIA Canadian Institute of International Affairs

CIL *Corpus inscriptionum latinarum*

CIM China Inland Mission

CIMA Chartered Institute of Management Accountants

CIMarE Companion, Institute of Marine Engineers

CIMEMME Companion, Institution of Mining Electrical and Mining Mechanical Engineers

CIMgt Companion, Institute of Management

CIMGTechE Companion, Institution of Mechanical and General Technician Engineers

C-in-C Commander-in-Chief

CINCHAN Allied Commander-in-Chief Channel

CIOB Chartered Institute of Building

CIPD Companion, Institute of Personnel and Development

CIPFA Chartered Institute of Public Finance and Accountancy

CIPL Comité International Permanent des Linguistes

CIPM Companion, Institute of Personnel Management (*now see* CIPD)

CIR Commission on Industrial Relations

CIRES Co-operative Institute for Research in Environmental Sciences

CIRIA Construction Industry Research and Information Association

CIRP Collège Internationale pour Recherche et Production

CIS Institute of Chartered Secretaries and Administrators (*formerly* Chartered Institute of Secretaries); Command Control Communications and Information Systems; Commonwealth of Independent States

CISAC Confédération Internationale des Sociétés d'Auteurs et Compositeurs; Centre for International Security and Arms Control

CIT Chartered Institute of Transport; California Institute of Technology

CITB Construction Industry Training Board

CIU Club and Institute Union

CIV City Imperial Volunteers

CJ Chief Justice

CJC Companions of Jesus Christ

CJM Congregation of Jesus and Mary (Eudist Fathers)

CL Commander, Order of Leopold

cl *cum laude*

Cl. Class

CLA Country Landowners' Association

CLIC Cancer and Leukemia in Children

CLIP Common Law Institute of Intellectual Property

CLit Companion of Literature (Royal Society of Literature Award)

CLJ Commander, Order of St Lazarus of Jerusalem

CLP Constituency Labour Party

break, 1940–45, for service in World War II, Nigeria Regt, RWAFF (despatches). Service with the British Council in Peru, E Africa, Colombia, Argentina, Malta, London and Mexico, 1946–77. OBE 1976; Insignia of Aztec Eagle, 1975. *Recreations:* rowing, swimming, pre-Columbian America, the Hispanic world. *Club:* Leander (Henley-on-Thames).

ALLOTT, Prof. Antony Nicolas; Professor of African Law, University of London, 1964–86, now Professor Emeritus; *b* 30 June 1924; *s* of late Reginald William Allott and Dorothy Allott (*née* Dobson); *m* 1952, Anna Joan Sargant, *d* of late Tom Sargant, OBE, and Marie Černy; two *s* two *d*. *Educ:* Downside Sch.; New Coll., Oxford. Lieut Royal Northumberland Fusiliers and King's African Rifles, 1944–46. BA Oxon (1st class Hons Jurisprudence), 1948; PhD London 1954. Lecturer in African Law, School of Oriental and African Studies, London, 1948–60; Reader in African Law, Univ. of London, 1960–64; Prof. of African and Comparative Law, Buckingham Univ., 1987–91. Vis. Prof., Université de Paris I, 1984. Hon. Director, Africa Centre, 1963–66; Pres., African Studies Assoc. of UK, 1969–70 (past Hon. Treas.); Vice-Pres., Internat. African Law Assoc., 1967. Académicien associé, Académie Internat. de Droit Comparé, 1982–; Hon. Corresponding Mem., Académie Royale des Sciences d'Outre-Mer, Belgium, 1980. Chm., Governing Body, Plater Coll., Oxford; Gov., St Bartholomew's Hosp. Med. Sch. Member: Senate, Univ. of London, 1978–86; Council, Commonwealth Magistrates' and Judges' Assoc. (formerly Commonwealth Magistrates' Assoc.), 1972–94; Chm., Mddx Magistrates' Cts Cttee, 1982–86. Chm., Barnet Petty Sessional Area, 1986; Dep. Chm., N Oxfordshire Magistrates' Court, 1993. JP: Middlesex 1969–86 (Chm., Gore Div., 1985–86); Oxfordshire 1987–94. KSG 1990. *Publications:* Essays in African Law, with special reference to the Law of Ghana, 1960; (ed) Judicial and Legal Systems in Africa, 1962, 2nd edn 1970; New Essays in African Law, 1970; The Limits of Law, 1980; (ed with G. Woodman) People's Law and State Law, 1985; articles in legal and other jls. *Recreations:* music, gardening, silviculture. *Address:* Sorbrook Mill, Bodicote, Banbury, Oxon OX15 4AU.
See also R. M. Allott.

ALLOTT, Air Cdre Molly Greenwood, CB 1975; *b* 28 Dec. 1918; *d* of late Gerald William Allott. *Educ:* Sheffield High Sch. for Girls. Served War of 1939–45: joined WAAF, 1941; served in: Egypt, Singapore, Germany. Staff of AOC-in-C: RAF Germany, 1960–63; Fighter Command, 1963–66; Training Command, 1971–73; Dir, WRAF, 1973–76; ADC 1973–76. Nat. Chm., Girls' Venture Corps, 1977–82; Member: Council, Union Jack Club, 1977–91; Main Grants Cttee, RAF Benevolent Fund, 1977–82. FIMgt. *Recreations:* travel, fine and decorative arts. *Address:* 15 Camden Hurst, Milford-on-Sea, Lymington, Hants SO41 0WL. *Clubs:* Royal Air Force, Royal Lymington Yacht.

ALLOTT, Robin Michael; Under-Secretary, Departments of Industry and Trade, 1978–80; *b* 9 May 1926; *s* of Reginald William Allott and Dorothy (*née* Dobson). *Educ:* The Oratory Sch., Caversham; New Coll., Oxford; Sheffield Univ. Asst Principal, BoT, 1948; UK Delegn to OECD, Paris, 1952; Private Sec. to Sec. for Overseas Trade, 1953; Principal, Office for Scotland, Glasgow, 1954; UK Delegn to UN Conf. on Trade and Develt, Geneva, 1964; Asst Sec., BoT, 1965; Counsellor, UK Delegn to EEC, Brussels, 1971; sabbatical year, New Coll., Oxford, 1974–75; Dept of Industry (motor industry), 1975; Under-Sec., Dept of Trade, 1976. *Publications:* The Physical Foundation of Language, 1973; The Motor Theory of Language Origin, 1989; (ed) Studies in Language Origins 3, 1994; contrib. Jl of Social and Evolutionary Systems; contrib. collections on lang. and origin of semiosis, sound symbolism, syntax, etc. *Recreations:* studying the evolutionary relation of language, perception and action; computer programming. *Address:* 5 Fitzgerald Park, Seaford, East Sussex BN25 1AX. *T:* Seaford (01323) 896022.
See also A. N. Allott.

ALLPORT, Denis Ivor; Chairman, 1979–85 and Chief Executive, 1977–85, Metal Box Ltd (Director, 1973–85, Managing Director, 1977–79, Deputy Chairman, 1979); *b* 20 Nov. 1922; *s* of late A. R. Allport and late E. M. Allport (*née* Mashman); *m* 1949, Diana (*née* Marler); two *s* one *d*. *Educ:* Highgate School. Served War, Indian Army, 1941–46; joined Metal Box Ltd, 1946; various appts in UK, Singapore and Pakistan; Man. Dir, Metal Box Co. of India, 1969–70; Dir, Metal Box Overseas Ltd, 1970–74. Chairman: Castle Underwriting Agents Ltd, 1989–94 (Dir, 1988–94); Devonshire Underwriting Agents Ltd, 1991–93; Director: Beecham Gp plc, 1981–88; Marley plc, 1985–91. Member: Nat. Enterprise Bd, 1980–83; NRDC, 1981–83; Neill Cttee of Enquiry into Regulatory Arrangements at Lloyd's, 1986. Gov., Highgate Sch., 1981–94. CIMgt (FBIM 1977). *Recreation:* golf. *Address:* The Barn, Highmoor, Henley-on-Thames, Oxon RG9 5DH. *T:* Nettlebed (01491) 641283. *Clubs:* MCC, Oriental.

ALLSOP, Peter Henry Bruce, CBE 1984; FRSA; FIMgt; Publishing Consultant, Publishers' Management Advisers, since 1983; *b* 22 Aug. 1924; *s* of late Herbert Henry Allsop and Elsie Hilpern (*née* Whittaker); *m* 1950, Patricia Elizabeth Kingwell Bown; two *s* one *d*. *Educ:* Haileybury; Caius Coll., Cambridge (MA). Called to Bar, Lincoln's Inn, 1948, Bencher, 1989. Temp. Asst Principal, Air Min., 1944–48; Barrister in practice, 1948–50; Sweet & Maxwell: Editor, 1950–59; Dir, 1960–64; Man. Dir, 1965–73; Chm., 1974–80; Dir, Associated Book Publishers, 1963, Asst Man. Dir, 1965–67, Man. Dir, 1968–76, Chm., 1976–88. Chm., Teleordering Ltd, 1978–91; Trustee and Vice-Chm., Yale University Press, 1984– (Dir, 1981–84); Director: J. Whitaker & Sons, 1987–; Lloyd's of London Press, 1991–. Mem. Council, Publishers Assoc., 1969–81 (Treasurer, 1973–75, 1979–81; Pres., 1975–77; Vice-Pres., 1977–78; Trustee, 1982–); Member: Printing and Publishing Industry Trng Bd, 1977–79; Publishers' Adv. Cttee, British Council, 1980–85; Chm., Management Cttee, Book House Training Centre, 1980–86. Chm., Social Security Appeal Tribunal, 1982–87 (Mem., 1979–82). Chm., Book Trade Benevolent Soc., 1986–92 (Trustee, 1976–85, 1994–; Dir, 1985). Mem., St Albans City Council, 1955–58. Chm., DAC, Bath and Wells, 1985–94; Trustee, St Andrews Conservation Trust, Wells, 1987–; Mem., Wells Cathedral Fabric Adv. Cttee, 1991–. Chm. Council, King's Coll., Taunton, 1986–94 (Mem., 1983–86). Dir, Woodard Schools (Western Div.) Ltd, 1985–. Editor, later Editor Emeritus: Current Law, 1952–90; Criminal Law Review, 1954–90. *Publications:* (ed) Bowstead's Law of Agency, 11th edn, 1951. *Recreations:* gardening, sculling, theatre. *Address:* Manor Farm, Charlton Mackrell, Somerton, Somerset TA11 7BQ. *Clubs:* Garrick, Farmers'; Leander (Henley-on-Thames); Avon County Rowing.

ALLSOPP, family name of **Baron Hindlip.**

ALLSOPP, Bruce; *see* Allsopp, H. B.

ALLSOPP, (Harold) Bruce, BArch, DipCD, FSA, MRTPI; author and artist; *b* Oxford, 4 July 1912; *s* of Henry Allsopp and Elizabeth May Allsopp (*née* Robertson); *m* 1935, Florence Cyrilla Woodroffe, ARCA (*d* 1991); two *s*. *Educ:* Manchester Grammar Sch.; Liverpool School of Architecture. BArch (1st Cl. Hons), Liverpool, 1933; Rome Finalist, 1934; Diploma in Civic Design 1935; ARIBA 1935; AMTPI 1936; FRIBA 1955; FSA 1968. Asst Architect in Chichester and London, 1934–35; Lecturer, Leeds Coll. of Art, 1935–40. War Service 1940–46, N Africa, Italy, Captain RE. Lecturer in Architecture, Univ. of Durham, 1946; Sen. Lecturer, 1955; Sen. Lecturer, Univ. of Newcastle upon Tyne, 1963, Dir of Architectural Studies, 1965–69; Sen. Lecturer in History of Architecture, 1969–73; Reader, 1973–77. Chm., Oriel Press Ltd, 1962–87; Dir, Routledge & Kegan Paul Books Ltd, 1974–85. Chairman: Soc. of Architectural Historians of GB, 1959–65; Independent Publishers Guild, 1971–73; Master, Art Workers Guild, 1970; Pres., Fedn of Northern Art Socs, 1980–83. Presenter, TV films, including Fancy Gothic, 1974; The Bowes Museum, 1977; Country Houses and Landscape of Northumberland, 1979. *Publications:* Art and the Nature of Architecture, 1952; Decoration and Furniture, Vol. 1 1952, Vol. 2 1953; A General History of Architecture, 1955; Style in the Visual Arts, 1957; Possessed, 1959; The Future of the Arts, 1959; A History of Renaissance Architecture, 1959; The Naked Flame, 1962; Architecture, 1964; To Kill a King, 1965; A History of Classical Architecture, 1965; Historic Architecture of Newcastle upon Tyne, 1967; Civilization, the Next Stage, 1969; The Study of Architectural History, 1970; Modern Architecture of Northern England, 1970; Inigo Jones on Palladio, 1970; Romanesque Architecture, 1971; Ecological Morality, 1972; The Garden Earth, 1973; Towards a Humane Architecture, 1974; Return of the Pagan, 1974; Cecilia, 1975; Inigo Jones and the Lords A'Leaping, 1975; A Modern Theory of Architecture, 1977; Appeal to the Gods, 1980; Should Man Survive?, 1982; The Country Life Companion to British and European Architecture, 1985; Social Responsibility and the Responsible Society, 1985; Guide de l'Architecture, 1985; Larousse Guide to European Architecture, 1985; Patronage and Professionalism, 1993; (with Ursula Clark): Architecture of France, 1963; Architecture of Italy, 1964; Architecture of England, 1964; Photography for Tourists, 1966; Historic Architecture of Northumberland, 1969; Historic Architecture of Northumberland and Newcastle, 1977; English Architecture, 1979; (with U. Clark and H. W. Booton) The Great Tradition of Western Architecture, 1966; *as Simon Grindle:* The Loving Limpet, 1964; *as Rielo:* Blow up the Ark, 1964; What to do with Beetles, 1964; articles in Encyclopedia Americana, Encyclopaedia Britannica, Jl of RSA, Didaskalos, etc. *Recreations:* piano and organ, gardening. *Address:* Woodburn, 3 Batt House Road, Stocksfield, Northumberland NE43 7QZ. *T:* Stocksfield (01661) 842323. *Club:* Athenæum.

ALLTHORPE-GUYTON, Marjorie; Director of Visual Arts, Arts Council of England, since 1993; *b* 29 July 1948; *d* of Maurice Jack Allthorpe-Guyton and Edith Florence (*née* Clark); *m* 1st, 1970, Brian Collison (marr. diss.); 2nd, 1989, John Mullis; one *s* one *d*. *Educ:* Univ. of East Anglia (BA Hons Fine Art); Courtauld Inst. AMA 1974. Asst Keeper, Norwich Castle Mus., 1969–79; Researcher, Norwich Sch. of Art, 1980–82; Selector, British Art Show, Arts Council, 1982–84; Associate Ed., 1988–91, Ed., 1990–92, Artscribe. External Assessor, Fine Art degrees, Goldsmiths' Coll., London Univ., 1988–. FRSA 1994. *Publications:* A Happy Eye: history of Norwich Sch. of Art 1845–1982, 1982; catalogues: Henry Bright, 1973; John Sell Cotman, 1975; John Thirtle, 1977; Norwich Castle Museum, 1979; many essays and articles on contemporary art. *Recreations:* travel, especially Europe, walking, film, theatre, family, cooking. *Address:* 1 Thornhill Road, N1 1HX. *T:* 0171–607 7903. *Clubs:* Chelsea Arts, Blacks.

ALLUM, Sarah Elizabeth Royle, (Mrs R. G. Allum); *see* Walker, S. E. R.

ALLWEIS, Martin Peter; His Honour Judge Allweis; a Circuit Judge, since 1994; *b* 22 Dec. 1947; *s* of late Jack Allweis and of Iris Allweis (*née* Mosco); *m* 1984, Tracy Ruth, *d* of late Hyam Barr and of Bernice Barr; one *s* one *d*. *Educ:* Manchester Grammar Sch.; Sidney Sussex Coll., Cambridge (BA Hons 1969). Called to the Bar, Inner Temple, 1970; in practice on Northern Circuit, 1971–94; a Recorder, 1990–94. *Recreations:* family interests, football (Manchester City FC), squash. *Address:* c/o Bolton Combined Court Centre, Blackhorse Street, Bolton BL1 1SU.

ALMENT, Sir (Edward) Anthony (John), Kt 1980; FRCOG; Consultant Obstetrician and Gynaecologist, Northampton, 1960–85, retired; *b* 3 Feb. 1922; *s* of Edward and Alice Alment; *m* 1946, Elizabeth Innes Bacon. *Educ:* Marlborough Coll.; St Bartholomew's Hosp. Med. Coll. MRCS, LRCP 1945; FRCOG 1967 (MRCOG 1951). Served RAFVR, 1947–48. Trng appointments: St Bartholomew's Hosp., 1945–46 and 1954–60; Norfolk and Norwich Hosp., 1948; Queen Charlotte's Hosp. and Chelsea Hosp. for Women, 1949–50; London Hosp., 1951–52. Royal Coll. of Obstetricians and Gynaecologists: Mem. Council, 1961–67; Hon. Sec., 1968–73; Pres., 1978–81. Chm., Cttee of Enquiry into Competence to Practise, 1973–76; Member: Oxford Reg. Hosp. Bd, 1968–74 (Chm., Med. Adv. Cttee, 1972–74); Oxford RHA, 1973–75; Central Midwives Bd, 1967–68; UK Central Council for Nursing, Midwifery and Health Visiting, 1980–83. Examiner: RCOG; Univs of Cambridge, Leeds and Dar-es-Salaam. Hon. Fellow, Amer. Assoc. of Obstetricians and Gynaecologists, 1973 (Joseph Price Oration, 1972); Hon. FRCPI 1979; Hon. FRCPE 1981; Hon. FRCGP 1982; Hon. FRACOG 1984. Hon. DSc Leicester, 1982. *Publications:* Competence to Practise, 1976; contrib. to med. jls; articles on wine-related subjects. *Recreations:* wine, fishing, engineering, church architecture. *Address:* Winston House, Boughton, Northampton NN2 8RR.

ALMOND, Thomas Clive, OBE 1989; HM Diplomatic Service; Consul-General, Bordeaux, since 1992; *b* 30 Nov. 1939; *s* of late Thomas and Eveline Almond; *m* 1965, Auriol Gala Elizabeth Annette Hendry. *Educ:* Bristol Grammar Sch. Entered HM Diplomatic Service, 1967; Accra, 1968; Paris, 1971; FCO, 1975; Brussels, 1978; Jakarta, 1980; Brazzaville, 1983; Ambassador to People's Republic of the Congo, 1987–88; Asst Marshal of the Diplomatic Corps and Asst Head of Protocol Dept, 1988–92. *Recreations:* travelling, golf. *Address:* c/o Foreign and Commonwealth Office, King Charles Street, SW1A 2AH.

ALPHANDERY, Edmond Gérard; Member, Council General for Maine-et-Loire, since 1976; Mayor of Longué-Jumelles, since 1977; Minister of the Economy, France, 1993–95; *b* 2 Sept. 1943; *m* 1972, Laurence Rivain; one *s*. *Educ:* Frédéric Mistral Lycée, Avignon; Inst. of Political Studies, Paris; Univs of Chicago and California at Berkeley. Asst Lectr, Univ. of Paris, IX, 1968–69; Lectr, Univ. of Aix-en-Provence, 1970–71; Sen. Lectr, and Dean, Faculty of Econ. Sci., Univ. of Nantes, 1971–74; Prof., Univ. of Angers, 1973; Associate Prof., Univ. of Pittsburgh, 1975; Prof. of Political Economy, Univ. of Paris II, 1974–92. Deputy (UDF-CDS) for Maine-et-Loire, French Nat. Assembly, 1978–93 (Mem., Finance Cttee, 1979–93); Vice-Pres., 1991–94, Pres., 1994–, Maine-et-Loire Council General. Vice-Pres., Centre des Démocrates Sociaux; numerous positions with economic and monetary bodies, incl. Mem., Supervisory Bd, Caisse des Dépôts et Consignations, 1988–93; Chm., Supervisory Council, CNP Insurance SA, 1992–93. *Publications:* Les Politiques de stabilisation (with G. Delsupehe), 1974; Cours d'analyse macroéconomique, 1976; Analyse monétaire approfondie, 1978; 1986: le piège, 1986; La Rupture: le liberalisme à l'épreuve des faits (with A. Fourçans), 1987. *Address:* Hôtel du département, Mail de la Préfecture, BP 4104, 49041 Angers Cedex, France.

ALPORT, family name of **Baron Alport.**

ALPORT, Baron, *cr* 1961, of Colchester (Life Peer); **Cuthbert James McCall Alport,** PC 1960; TD 1949; DL; *b* 22 March 1912; *o s* of late Prof. Arthur Cecil Alport, MD, FRCP, and of Janet, *y d* of James McCall, Dumfriesshire; *m* 1945, Rachel Cecilia (*d* 1983), *o d* of late Col R. C. Bingham, CVO, DSO, and late Dorothy Louisa Pratt; one *s* one *d* (and one *d* decd). *Educ:* Haileybury; Pembroke Coll., Cambridge. MA History and Law; Pres., Cambridge Union Society, 1935. Tutor Ashridge Coll., 1935–37. Barrister-at-Law, Middle Temple. Joined Artists Rifles, 1934. Served War of 1939–45: Hon. Lieut-Col;

Director Conservative Political Centre, 1945–50. MP (C) Colchester division of Essex, 1950–61; Chairman Joint East and Central African Board, 1953–55; Governor, Charing Cross Hospital, 1954–55. Asst Postmaster-General, Dec. 1955–Jan. 1957; Parliamentary Under-Secretary of State, Commonwealth Relations Office, 1957–59; Minister of State, Commonwealth Relations Office, Oct. 1959–March 1961; British High Commissioner in the Federation of Rhodesia and Nyasaland, 1961–63; Mem. of Council of Europe, 1964–65; British Govt Representative to Rhodesia, June-July 1967. A Dep. Speaker, House of Lords, 1971–82, 1983–94. Adviser to the Home Secretary, 1974–82. Chm., New Theatre Trust, 1970–83; Pres., Minories Art Gall., Colchester, 1978–91. Life Governor, Haileybury Coll. Master, Skinners' Co., 1969–70, 1982–83. Pro-Chancellor, City Univ., 1972–79. Chm., Acad. Adv. Cttee, Gresham Coll., 1984–86. High Steward of Colchester, 1967–; DL Essex 1974. Hon. Freeman, Colchester, 1992. Hon. DCL City Univ., 1979. *Publications:* Kingdoms in Partnership, 1937; Hope in Africa, 1952; The Sudden Assignment, 1965. *Address:* The Cross House, Layer de la Haye, Colchester, Essex CO2 0JG. *T:* Layer de la Haye (01206) 734217. *Club:* Farmers'.

See also I. C. Taylor.

AL-SABAH, Shaikh Saud Nasir; Minister of Information, Kuwait; *b* 3 Oct. 1944; *m* 1962, Shaikha Awatif Al-Sabah; three *s* two *d*. Barrister-at-law, Gray's Inn. Entered Legal Dept, Min. of Foreign Affairs, Kuwait. Representative of Kuwait: to 6th Cttee of UN Gen. Assembly, 1969–74; to Seabed Cttee of UN, 1969–73; Vice-Chm., Delegn of Kuwait to Conf. of Law of the Sea, 1974–75; Rep. of Delegn to Conf. of Law of Treaties, 1969; Ambassador to: UK, to Norway, Sweden and Denmark, 1975–80; USA, 1981; Canada and Venezuela, 1981–92. *Address:* Ministry of Information, PO Box 193, Safat 13002, Kuwait.

AL SHAKAR, Karim Ebrahim; Ministry of Foreign Affairs, Bahrain, since 1995; *b* 23 Dec. 1945; *m* 1979, Fatima Al Mansouri; three *d*. *Educ:* primary and secondary educn, Bahrain; Delhi Univ. (BA political science 1970). Attaché, Min. of Foreign Affairs, 1970; Mem., Perm. Mission to UN, later Min. of Foreign Affairs, 1972–76; First Sec., 1978; Counsellor, 1981; Perm. Rep. to UN, Geneva and Consul-Gen., 1982–87 (non-resident Ambassador to Germany and Austria and to UN, Vienna, 1984); Ambassador and Perm. Rep to UN, New York, 1987–90; Ambassador to UK, also to Republic of Ireland, the Netherlands and Denmark, 1992–95. *Recreation:* travelling. *Address:* Ministry of Foreign Affairs, POB 547, Government House, Government Road, Manama, Bahrain.

AL-SHAWI, Hisham Ibrahim; Ambassador of the Republic of Iraq to Canada, 1985 (non-resident Ambassador to Jamaica, 1986, to Grenada, 1987); *b* Baghdad, 16 March 1931; *s* of Maj.-Gen. Ibrahim Al-Shawi and Najia Al-Shawi; *m* 1966, Hadia Al-Atia; one *s* one *d*. *Educ:* Baghdad (High Sch. Certif., Lit. Section, 1948); Amer. Univ. of Beirut (BA with Distinction Pol. Science, 1952); Univ. of Oxford (MLitt Internat. Relations, 1956). Asst Instructor, Instructor, then Asst Prof. and Head of Dept of Politics, Univs of Baghdad and Al-Mustansyria, 1958–70; Dean, Coll. of Law and Politics, Mustansyria Univ., 1970–72; Ambassador, Min. of Foreign Affairs, 1972; Perm. Rep. at UN, Geneva, 1972; Minister of Higher Educn and Scientific Res., 1972–74; Minister of State, 1974–75; Minister of State for For. Affairs, 1975–76; Ambassador, Min. of For. Affairs, 1976–77; Perm. Rep. at UN, New York, 1977; Head, Diwan of Presidency of Republic, 1977–78; Ambassador, Min. of For. Affairs, 1978; Ambassador to UK, 1978–82, to Austria, 1982–85. First President: Iraqi Political Science Assoc.; Iraqi UN Assoc.; Chm., Iraqi Atomic Energy Commn, 1972–74; Mem., UN Sub-Commn on Prevention of Racial Discrimination and Protection of Minorities, 1972–74; Rep. on Commn on Human Rights, 26th–30th Sessions. Gov. for Iraq, IAEA, 1974–76. Statue of Victory Personality of the Year, Centro Studi e Ricerche delle Nazioni, Parma, Italy, 1984. *Publications:* From the Essence of the Matter: a collection of articles, 1966; The Art of Negotiation, 1967; An Introduction in Political Science, 1967 (new edn 1978). *Recreations:* horse riding, hunting. *Club:* Iraqi Hunting (Iraq).

ALSOP, William Allen; Principal, Alsop & Störmer, Architects, since 1981; *b* 12 Dec. 1947; *s* of Francis John Alsop and Brenda Hight; *m* 1972, Sheila E. Bean; two *s* one *d*. *Educ:* Architectural Association (DipAA). RIBA. Maxwell Fry, 1971; Cedric Price, 1973–77; Rodrick Ham, 1977–79; Alsop & Störmer, 1981–. Prof. of Architecture, Bremen Acad., 1991. SADG 1973; FRSA. *Publications:* City of Objects, 1992; William Alsop Buildings and Projects, 1992; William Alsop Architect, Four Projects, 1993; Will Alsop and Jan Störmer, Architects, 1993; Le Grand Bleu–Marseille, 1994. *Recreation:* fishing. *Address:* Albert Bridge House, 127 Albert Bridge Road, SW11 4PL. *T:* 0171–978 7878. *Club:* Reform.

ALSTON, John Alistair, CBE 1988; DL; Leader, Norfolk County Council, 1981–87 and since 1989; *b* 24 May 1937; *s* of late David Alston and Bathia Mary (*née* Davidson). *Educ:* Orwell Park, Sherborne; RAC, Cirencester. Norfolk County Council: Mem., 1973–; Vice-Chm., 1987–88; Chm., 1988–89. Chairman: Norfolk Health Commn, 1994–; E Norfolk (formerly Norwich) HA, 1994–. Chm., Broads Bill Steering Cttee, 1984–87; Member: Broads Authority, 1988–; Council, Morley Res. Station, 1981–; Council, UEA, 1986–. DL Norfolk, 1991. *Recreations:* gardening, shooting, fishing. *Address:* Besthorpe Hall, Attleborough, Norfolk NR17 2LJ. *T:* Attleborough (01953) 452138.

ALSTON, Rt. Rev. Mgr. J(oseph) Leo; Parish Priest, Sacred Heart Church, Ainsdale, Southport, since 1972; *b* 17 Dec. 1917; *s* of Benjamin Alston and Mary Elizabeth (*née* Moss). *Educ:* St Mary's School, Chorley; Upholland College, Wigan; English Coll., Rome; Christ's College, Cambridge. Priest, 1942; Licentiate in Theology, Gregorian Univ., Rome, 1942; BA (1st Cl. Hons Classics) Cantab 1945. Classics Master, Upholland Coll., Wigan, 1945–52, Headmaster, 1952–64; Rector, Venerable English Coll., Rome, 1964–71. Protonotary Apostolic, 1988. *Recreation:* music. *Address:* 483 Liverpool Road, Ainsdale, Southport, Merseyside PR8 3BP. *T:* Southport (01704) 77527.

ALSTON, Richard John William; choreographer; Artistic Director, Contemporary Dance Trust and Richard Alston Dance Company, since 1994; *b* 30 Oct. 1948; *s* of Gordon Walter Alston and Margot Alston (*née* Whitworth). *Educ:* Eton; Croydon Coll. of Art. Choreographed for London Contemporary Dance Theatre, 1970–72; founded Strider, 1972; worked in USA, 1975–77; Resident Choreographer, 1980–86, Artistic Dir, 1986–92, Ballet Rambert, subseq. Rambert Dance Co. Principal Ballets: Nowhere Slowly; Tiger Balm; Blue Schubert Fragments; Soft Verges; Rainbow Bandit; Doublework; Soda Lake; for Ballet Rambert: Rainbow Ripples, 1980; The Rite of Spring, 1981; Apollo Distraught, 1982; Dangerous Liaisons, 1985; Zansa, 1986; Dutiful Ducks, 1986; Pulcinella, 1987; Strong Language, 1987; Hymnos, 1988; Roughcut, 1990; Cat's Eye, 1992. Created: The Kingdom of Pagodas, for Royal Danish Ballet, 1982; Midsummer, for Royal Ballet, 1983; Le Marteau Sans Maitre, for Compagnie Chopinot, 1992; Delicious Arbour, for Shobana Jeyasingh Dance Co., 1993; Movements from Petrushka, Lachrymae, Rumours Visions, for Aldeburgh Festival, 1994; Shadow Realm, Something in the City, for Richard Alston Dance Co., 1994. DUniv Surrey, 1993. *Recreations:* music, reading. *Address:* The Place, 17 Dukes Road, WC1H 9AB.

ALSTON, Robert John, CMG 1987; HM Diplomatic Service; High Commissioner to New Zealand, Governor (non-resident) of Pitcairn, Henderson, Ducie and Oeno Islands, and High Commissioner (non-resident) to Western Samoa, since 1994; *b* 10 Feb. 1938; *s* of late Arthur William Alston and of Rita Alston; *m* 1969, Patricia Claire Essex; one *s* one *d*. *Educ:* Ardingly Coll.; New Coll., Oxford (BA Mod. Hist.). Third Sec., Kabul, 1963; Eastern Dept, FO, 1966; Head of Computer Study Team, FCO, 1969; First Sec. (Econ.), Paris, 1971; First Sec. and Head of Chancery, Tehran, 1974; Asst Head, Energy Science and Space Dept, FCO, 1977; Head, Joint Nuclear Unit, FCO, 1978; Political Counsellor, UK Delegn to NATO, 1981; Head, Defence Dept, FCO, 1984; Ambassador to Oman, 1986–90; seconded to Home Civil Service, 1990–92; Asst Under-Sec. of State (Public Depts), FCO, 1992–94. *Recreations:* gardening, travel, music. *Address:* c/o Foreign and Commonwealth Office, King Charles Street, SW1A 2AH.

ALSTON, Prof. Robin Carfrae, OBE 1992; FSA; Professor of Library Studies, London University, and Director, School of Library, Archive and Information Studies, University College London, since 1990; *b* 29 Jan. 1933; *s* of late Wilfred Louis Alston; *m* 1957, Joanna Dorothy Ormiston; two *s* one *d*. *Educ:* Rugby Sch.; Univs of British Columbia (BA), Oxford (MA), Toronto (MA) and London (PhD). Teaching Fellow, University Coll., Toronto, 1956–58; Lectr, New Brunswick Univ., 1958–60; Lectr in English Lit., Leeds Univ., 1964–76; Consultant to British Library, 1977–; Editor-in-Chief, 18th Century Short Title Catalogue, 1978–89; Advr to Develt and Systems Office, Humanities and Social Scis (formerly Ref. Div.), British Library, 1984–; Editl Dir, The Nineteenth Century, series of microfiche texts 1801–1900, 1985–. Hon. Res. Fellow, UCL, 1987–. Klein Vis. Prof., Univ of Texas, 1990; Vis. Prof., Univ. of Malta, 1994. David Murray Lectr, Univ. of Glasgow, 1983; Guest Lectr, Univ. of London, 1983, Sorbonne, 1984, Tokyo Symposium on micro-reproduction, 1984; Cecil Oldman Lectr, Leeds Univ., 1988, 1989; Morris Meml Lectr, Royal Instn, 1991. Jt Editor, Leeds Studies in English and Leeds Texts and Monographs, 1965–72; Editor, Studies in Early Modern English, 1965–72; Jt Editor, The Direction Line, 1976–; Editor: Special Pubns, Bibliographical Soc., 1983–; Libraries and Archives (series), 1991–. Founder, Chm. and principal Editor, Scolar Press Ltd, 1966–72, Man. Dir, 1984–; Founder, Janus Press, devoted to original art prints, 1973. Member: Adv. Cttee, British Library, 1975–; Adv. Cttee, MLA of America for the Wing Project, 1980–; Adv. Panel, Aust. Research Grants Cttee, 1983–; Adv. Bd, Cambridge Hist. of the Book in Britain, 1989–. Member: Organising Cttee, 18th Century Short Title Catalogue, 1976–; Cttee, British Book Trade Index, 1984–. Mem. Council, Bibliographical Soc., 1967– (Vice-Pres., 1978–88, Pres., 1988–90); Founding Mem. Council, Ilkley Literature Festival, 1973–; Jt Founder, Frederic Madden Soc., 1989–. Consultant, Consortium of Univ. Research Libraries, 1985–86; Advr to Govt of Pakistan on estabt of Nat. Liby of Pakistan, 1988. FSA 1987; Hon. FLA, 1986. Samuel Pepys Gold Medal, Ephemera Soc., 1984; Smithsonian Instn award, 1985; Walford Medal, Library Assoc., 1993. *Publications:* An Introduction to Old English, 1961 (rev. edn 1966); A Catalogue of Books relating to the English Language (1500–1800) in Swedish Libraries, 1965; English Language and Medieval English Literature: a Select Reading-List for Students, 1966; A Bibliography of the English Language from the Invention of Printing to the Year 1800: Vol. I, 1965; Vols V and VIII, 1966; Vols VII and IV, 1967; Vol. II, 1968; Vol. VI, 1969; Vol. III, 1970; Vol. IX, 1971; Vol. X, 1972; Vol. XI, 1978; Vol. XII part 1, 1987; Vol. XII part 2, 1988; Alexander Gil's Logonomia Anglica (1619): a translation into Modern English, 1973; (jtly) The Works of William Bullokar, Vol. I, 1966; English Studies (rev. edn of Vol. III, Cambridge Bibl. Eng. Lit.), 1968; English Linguistics 1500–1800: a Collection of Texts in Facsimile (365 vols), 1967–72; European Linguistics 1500–1700: a Collection of Texts in Facsimile (12 vols), 1968–72; A Checklist of the works of Joseph Addison, 1976; Bibliography MARC and ESTC, 1978; Eighteenth-Century Subscription Lists, 1983; ESTC: the British Library Collections, 1983; The arrangement of books in the British Museum Library 1843–1973, and the British Library 1973–1985, 1987; The Nineteenth Century: subject scope and principles of selection, 1987; Index to Pressmarks in use in the British Museum Library and the British Library, 1987; Index to the Classification Schedules of the Map Collections in the British Library, 1987; Computers and Libraries, 1987; The British Library: past, present, future, 1989; Women Writers of Fiction, Verse and Drama: a checklist of works published between 1801 and 1900 in the collections of the British Library, 1990; Handlist of unpublished finding aids to the London Collections of the British Library, 1991; Handlist of catalogues and book lists in the Department of Manuscripts, British Library, 1991; Books with Manuscript: a catalogue, 1994; numerous articles, printed lectures, reviews, etc. *Recreations:* music, photography. *Address:* 16 Medburn Street, NW1 1RJ.

ALSTON-ROBERTS-WEST, Lt-Col George Arthur; *see* West.

ALTHAUS, Sir Nigel (Frederick), Kt 1989; Senior Broker to the Commissioners for the Reduction of the National Debt (Government Broker), 1982–89; *b* 28 Sept. 1929; *er s* of late Frederick Rudolph Althaus, CBE and Margaret Frances (*née* Twist); *m* 1958, Anne, *d* of P. G. Cardew; three *s* one *d*. *Educ:* Eton; Magdalen Coll., Oxford (Roberts Gawen Scholar; 2nd Cl. Lit. Hum. 1954). National Service, 60th Rifles, 1948–50. Joined Pember and Boyle (Stockbrokers), 1954; Partner, 1955–75, Sen. Partner, 1975–82; Sen. Partner, Mullens and Co., 1982–86. Mem., Stock Exchange, 1955–89; Chm., Stock Exchange Benevolent Fund, 1975–82. Treas., ICRF, 1991–. Master, Skinners' Co., 1977–78; Chm. Governors, Skinners' Co. Sch. for Boys, Tunbridge Wells, 1982–89. Chm., British Library of Tape Recordings for Hosp. Patients, 1975–. Comr, Royal Hosp., Chelsea, 1988–94. Queen Victoria's Rifles (TA), 1950–60; Hon. Col, 39 Signal Regt (TA), 1982–88. *Publication:* (ed) British Government Securities in the Twentieth Century, 1976. *Recreations:* golf, shooting, music. *Address:* c/o Bank of England, Threadneedle Street, EC2R 8AH. *Clubs:* Boodle's, Beefsteak; Swinley Forest Golf (Ascot).

ALTHORP, Viscount; Louis Frederick John Spencer; *b* 14 March 1994; *o s* and *heir* of Earl Spencer, *qv*.

ALTMAN, John; His Honour Judge Altman; a Circuit Judge since 1991; *b* 21 June 1944; *s* of Lionel and Vita Altman; *m* 1968, Elizabeth Brown; two *d*. *Educ:* Bootham Sch., York; Univ. of Bristol (LLB); Council of Legal Education. Called to the Bar, Middle Temple, 1967; part-time Chm., Industrial Tribunals, 1983; Asst Recorder, 1985; Chm., Industrial Tribunals, 1986; a Recorder, 1989. *Publications:* contribs to Law Guardian. *Recreations:* reading, photography, music, theatre. *Address:* 14 Dunstarn Drive, Leeds, W Yorks LS16 8EH.

ALTMAN, Lionel Phillips, CBE 1979; special adviser to public bodies and private sector; Chairman: European Cleaning Services Group, since 1991; Hydro-Lock Europe (formerly Hydro-Lock UK), since 1992; Director, Equity & General plc, since 1978 (Chairman, 1978–91); *s* of late Arnold Altman and Catherine Phillips; *m* Diana; one *s* two *d* by previous marriages. *Educ:* University Coll. and Business Sch., also in Paris. FIMI; FCIM; MIPR. Director: Carmo Holdings Ltd, 1947–63; Sears Holdings Motor Gp, 1963–72; Sears Finance, 1965–71; C. & W. Walker Holdings Ltd, 1974–77; H. P. Information plc, 1985–91; Motor Agents Assoc. Ltd, 1986–89 (Mem., Nat. Council, 1965–; Pres., 1975–77); Chm., Pre-Divisional Investments Ltd, 1972– (Chief Exec., 1972–94). Chairman: Motor Industry Educnl Consultative Council Industry Working Party, producing Altman Report on recruitment and training, 1968; Retail Motor Industry Working Party on Single European Market, 1988–92. Vice-Pres., and Mem. Council,

CLRAE Congress (*formerly* Conference) of Local and Regional Authorities of Europe
CLY City of London Yeomanry
CM Member, Order of Canada; Congregation of the Mission (Vincentians); Master in Surgery; Certificated Master; Canadian Militia
CMA Canadian Medical Association; Cost and Management Accountant (NZ)
CMAC Catholic Marriage Advisory Council
CMath Chartered Mathematician
CMB Central Midwives' Board
CMet Chartered Meteorologist
CMF Commonwealth Military Forces; Central Mediterranean Force
CMG Companion, Order of St Michael and St George
CMLJ Commander of Merit, Order of St Lazarus of Jerusalem
CMM Commander, Order of Military Merit (Canada)
CMO Chief Medical Officer
CMP Corps of Military Police (*now see* CRMP)
CMS Church Mission (*formerly* Church Missionary) Society; Certificate in Management Studies
CMT Chaconia Medal of Trinidad
CNAA Council for National Academic Awards
CND Campaign for Nuclear Disarmament
CNI Companion, Nautical Institute
CNO Chief of Naval Operations
CNR Canadian National Railways
CNRS Centre National de la Recherche Scientifique
CO Commanding Officer; Commonwealth Office (after Aug. 1966) (*now see* FCO); Colonial Office (before Aug. 1966); Conscientious Objector; Colorado
Co. County; Company
C of E Church of England
C of S Chief of Staff; Church of Scotland
Coal.L or **Co.L** Coalition Liberal
Coal.U or **Co.U** Coalition Unionist
CODEST Committee for the Development of European Science and Technology
COHSE Confederation of Health Service Employees
COI Central Office of Information
CoID Council of Industrial Design (*now* Design Council)
Col Colonel
Coll. College; Collegiate
Colo Colorado (US)
Col.-Sergt Colour-Sergeant
Com Communist
Comd Command
Comdg Commanding
Comdr Commander
Comdt Commandant
COMEC Council of the Military Education Committees of the Universities of the UK
COMET Committee for Middle East Trade
Commn Commission
Commnd Commissioned
CompAMEME Companion, Association of Mining Electrical and Mechanical Engineers
CompICE Companion, Institution of Civil Engineers
CompIEE Companion, Institution of Electrical Engineers
CompIERE Companion, Institution of Electronic and Radio Engineers
CompIGasE Companion, Institution of Gas Engineers
CompIMechE Companion, Institution of Mechanical Engineers
CompIWES Companion, Institution of Water Engineers and Scientists
CompOR Companion, Operational Research Society
CompTI Companion of the Textile Institute
Comr Commissioner
Comy-Gen. Commissary-General
CON Commander, Order of the Niger
Conn Connecticut (US)
Const. Constitutional
Co-op. Co-operative
COPA Comité des Organisations Professionels Agricoles de la CEE
COPEC Conference of Politics, Economics and Christianity
COPUS Committee on the Public Understanding of Science
Corp. Corporation; Corporal
Corresp. Mem. Corresponding Member
COS Chief of Staff; Charity Organization Society
COSA Colliery Officials and Staffs Association
CoSIRA Council for Small Industries in Rural Areas
COSLA Convention of Scottish Local Authorities
COSPAR Committee on Space Research
COSSAC Chief of Staff to Supreme Allied Commander
COTC Canadian Officers' Training Corps
CP Central Provinces; Cape Province; Congregation of the Passion
CPA Commonwealth Parliamentary Association; Chartered Patent Agent; Certified Public Accountant (Canada) (*now see* CA)
CPAG Child Poverty Action Group
CPAS Church Pastoral Aid Society
CPC Conservative Political Centre
CPEng Chartered Professional Engineer (of Institution of Engineers of Australia)
CPhys Chartered Physicist
CPL Chief Personnel and Logistics
CPM Colonial Police Medal
CPR Canadian Pacific Railway
CPRE Council for the Protection of Rural England
CPRW Campaign for the Protection of Rural Wales
CPS Crown Prosecution Service
CPSA Civil and Public Services Association
CPSU Communist Party of the Soviet Union
CPsychol Chartered Psychologist
CPU Commonwealth Press Union
CQSW Certificate of Qualification in Social Work
CR Community of the Resurrection
cr created or creation
CRA Commandor, Royal Artillery
CRAC Careers Research and Advisory Centre
CRAeS Companion, Royal Aeronautical Society
CRAG Clinical Resources and Audit Group
CRASC Commander, Royal Army Service Corps
CRC Cancer Research Campaign; Community Relations Council
CRCP(C) Certificant, Royal College of Physicians of Canada
CRE Commander, Royal Engineers; Commission for Racial Equality; Commercial Relations and Exports
Cres. Crescent
CRMP Corps of Royal Military Police
CRNCM Companion, Royal Northern College of Music
CRO Commonwealth Relations Office (*now see* FCO)
CS Civil Service; Clerk to the Signet
CSA Confederate States of America
CSAB Civil Service Appeal Board
CSB Bachelor of Christian Science
CSC Conspicuous Service Cross; Congregation of the Holy Cross
CSCA Civil Service Clerical Association (*now see* CPSA)
CSCE Conference on Security and Co-operation in Europe
CSD Civil Service Department; Co-operative Secretaries Diploma; Chartered Society of Designers
CSDE Central Servicing Development Establishment
CSEU Confederation of Shipbuilding and Engineering Unions
CSG Companion, Order of the Star of Ghana; Company of the Servants of God
CSI Companion, Order of the Star of India
CSIR Commonwealth Council for Scientific and Industrial Research (*now see* CSIRO)
CSIRO Commonwealth Scientific and Industrial Research Organization (Australia)
CSO Chief Scientific Officer; Chief Signal Officer; Chief Staff Officer; Central Statistical Office
CSP Chartered Society of Physiotherapists; Civil Service of Pakistan
CSS Companion, Star of Sarawak; Council for Science and Society
CSSB Civil Service Selection Board
CSSp Holy Ghost Father
CSSR Congregation of the Most Holy Redeemer (Redemptorist Order)
CStat Chartered Statistician
CSTI Council of Science and Technology Institutes
CStJ Commander, Most Venerable Order of the Hospital of St John of Jerusalem
CSU Christlich-Soziale Union in Bayern
CSV Community Service Volunteers
CSW Certificate in Social Work
CT Connecticut
CTA Chaplain Territorial Army
CTB College of Teachers of the Blind
CTC Cyclists' Touring Club; Commando Training Centre; City Training College
CText Chartered Textile Technologist
CTR(Harwell) Controlled Thermonuclear Research
CU Cambridge University
CUAC Cambridge University Athletic Club
CUAFC Cambridge University Association Football Club
CUBC Cambridge University Boat Club
CUCC Cambridge University Cricket Club
CUF Common University Fund
CUHC Cambridge University Hockey Club
CUMS Cambridge University Musical Society
CUNY City University of New York
CUP Cambridge University Press
CURUFC Cambridge University Rugby Union Football Club
CV Cross of Valour (Canada)
CVCP Committee of Vice-Chancellors and Principals of the Universities of the United Kingdom
CVO Commander, Royal Victorian Order
CVS Council for Voluntary Service

CVSNA	Council of Voluntary Service National Association
CWA	Crime Writers Association
CWGC	Commonwealth War Graves Commission
CWS	Co-operative Wholesale Society
CWU	Communication Workers Union

D

D	Duke
d	died; daughter
DA	Dame of St Andrew, Order of Barbados; Diploma in Anaesthesia; Diploma in Art
DAA&QMG	Deputy Assistant Adjutant and Quartermaster-General
DAAG	Deputy Assistant Adjutant-General
DA&QMG	Deputy Adjutant and Quartermaster-General
DAC	Development Assistance Committee; Diocesan Advisory Committee
DACG	Deputy Assistant Chaplain-General
DAD	Deputy Assistant Director
DAdmin	Doctor of Administration
DADMS	Deputy Assistant Director of Medical Services
DADOS	Deputy Assistant Director of Ordnance Services
DADQ	Deputy Assistant Director of Quartering
DADST	Deputy Assistant Director of Supplies and Transport
DAG	Deputy Adjutant-General
DAgr	Doctor of Agriculture
DAgrFor	Doctor of Agriculture and Forestry
DAMS	Deputy Assistant Military Secretary
D&AD	Designers and Art Directors Association
DAppSc	Doctor of Applied Science
DAQMG	Deputy Assistant Quartermaster-General
DArch	Doctor of Architecture
DArt	Doctor of Art
DArts	Doctor of Arts
DASc	Doctor in Agricultural Sciences
DATA	Draughtsmen's and Allied Technicians' Association (later AUEW(TASS))
DATEC	Art and Design Committee, Technician Education Council
DBA	Doctor of Business Administration
DBE	Dame Commander, Order of the British Empire
DC	District Council; District of Columbia (US)
DCAe	Diploma of College of Aeronautics
DCAS	Deputy Chief of the Air Staff
DCB	Dame Commander, Order of the Bath
DCC	Diploma of Chelsea College
DCCH	Diploma in Community Child Health
DCDS	Deputy Chief of Defence Staff
DCE	Diploma of a College of Education
DCG	Deputy Chaplain-General
DCGRM	Department of the Commandant General Royal Marines
DCGS	Deputy Chief of the General Staff
DCh	Doctor of Surgery
DCH	Diploma in Child Health
DCIGS	Deputy Chief of the Imperial General Staff (*now see* DCGS)
DCL	Doctor of Civil Law
DCLI	Duke of Cornwall's Light Infantry
DCLJ	Dame Commander, Order of St Lazarus of Jerusalem
DCM	Distinguished Conduct Medal
DCMG	Dame Commander, Order of St Michael and St George
DCMHE	Diploma of Contents and Methods in Health Education
DCnL	Doctor of Canon Law
DCO	Duke of Cambridge's Own
DComm	Doctor of Commerce
DCP	Diploma in Clinical Pathology; Diploma in Conservation of Paintings
DCS	Deputy Chief of Staff; Doctor of Commercial Sciences
DCSO	Deputy Chief Scientific Officer
DCT	Doctor of Christian Theology
DCVO	Dame Commander, Royal Victorian Order
DD	Doctor of Divinity
DDes	Doctor of Design
DDGAMS	Deputy Director General, Army Medical Services
DDH	Diploma in Dental Health
DDL	Deputy Director of Labour
DDME	Deputy Director of Mechanical Engineering
DDMI	Deputy Director of Military Intelligence
DDMO	Deputy Director of Military Operations
DDMS	Deputy Director of Medical Services
DDMT	Deputy Director of Military Training
DDNI	Deputy Director of Naval Intelligence
DDO	Diploma in Dental Orthopaedics
DDPH	Diploma in Dental Public Health
DDPR	Deputy Director of Public Relations
DDPS	Deputy Director of Personal Services
DDR	Deutsche Demokratische Republik
DDRA	Deputy Director Royal Artillery
DDS	Doctor of Dental Surgery; Director of Dental Services
DDSc	Doctor of Dental Science
DDSD	Deputy Director Staff Duties
DDSM	Defense Distinguished Service Medal
DDST	Deputy Director of Supplies and Transport
DDWE&M	Deputy Director of Works, Electrical and Mechanical
DE	Doctor of Engineering; Delaware
DEA	Department of Economic Affairs
decd	deceased
DEconSc	Doctor of Economic Science
DEd	Doctor of Education
Del	Delaware (US)
Deleg.	Delegate
DEME	Directorate of Electrical and Mechanical Engineering
DEMS	Defensively Equipped Merchant Ships
(DemU)	Democratic Unionist
DenD	Docteur en Droit
DEng	Doctor of Engineering
DenM	Docteur en Médicine
DEOVR	Duke of Edinburgh's Own Volunteer Rifles
DEP	Department of Employment and Productivity; European Progressive Democrats
Dep.	Deputy
DERA	Defence Evaluation and Research Agency
DES	Department of Education and Science (*now see* DFE)
DèsL	Docteur ès lettres
DèS or **DèsSc**	Docteur ès sciences
DesRCA	Designer of the Royal College of Art
DFA	Doctor of Fine Arts
DFAS	Decorative and Fine Art Society
DFC	Distinguished Flying Cross
DFE	Department for Education
DFH	Diploma of Faraday House
DFLS	Day Fighter Leaders' School
DFM	Distinguished Flying Medal
DG	Director General; Dragoon Guards
DGAA	Distressed Gentlefolks Aid Association
DGAMS	Director-General Army Medical Services
DGEME	Director General Electrical and Mechanical Engineering
DGLP(A)	Director General Logistic Policy (Army)
DGMS	Director-General of Medical Services
DGMT	Director-General of Military Training
DGMW	Director-General of Military Works
DGNPS	Director-General of Naval Personal Services
DGP	Director-General of Personnel
DGPS	Director-General of Personal Services
DGS	Diploma in Graduate Studies
DGStJ	Dame of Grace, Order of St John of Jerusalem (*now see* DStJ)
DGU	Doctor of Griffith University
DH	Doctor of Humanities
DHA	District Health Authority
Dhc	Doctor *honoris causa*
DHEW	Department of Health Education and Welfare (US)
DHL	Doctor of Humane Letters; Doctor of Hebrew Literature
DHM	Dean Hole Medal
DHMSA	Diploma in the History of Medicine (Society of Apothecaries)
DHQ	District Headquarters
DHSS	Department of Health and Social Security (*now see* DoH *and* DSS)
DHum	Doctor of Humanities
DHumLit	Doctor of Humane Letters
DIAS	Dublin Institute of Advanced Sciences
DIC	Diploma of the Imperial College
DICTA	Diploma of Imperial College of Tropical Agriculture
DIG	Deputy Inspector-General
DIH	Diploma in Industrial Health
DIMP	Darjah Indera Mahkota Pahang
DIntLaw	Diploma in International Law
Dio.	Diocese
DipAA	Diploma in Applied Art
DipAD	Diploma in Art and Design
DipAe	Diploma in Aeronautics
DipArch	Diploma in Architecture
DipASE	Diploma in Advanced Study of Education, College of Preceptors
DipAvMed	Diploma of Aviation Medicine, Royal College of Physicians
DipBA	Diploma in Business Administration
DipBS	Diploma in Fine Art, Byam Shaw School
DipCAM	Diploma in Communications, Advertising and Marketing of CAM Foundation
DipCC	Diploma of the Central College
DipCD	Diploma in Civic Design
DipCE	Diploma in Civil Engineering

DipEcon	Diploma in Economics
DipEd	Diploma in Education
DipEE	Diploma in Electrical Engineering
DipEl	Diploma in Electronics
DipESL	Diploma in English as a Second Language
DipEth	Diploma in Ethnology
DipFD	Diploma in Funeral Directing
DipFE	Diploma in Further Education
DipGSM	Diploma in Music, Guildhall School of Music and Drama
DipHA	Diploma in Hospital Administration
DipHSM	Diploma in Health Services Management
DipHum	Diploma in Humanities
DipLA	Diploma in Landscape Architecture
DipLib	Diploma of Librarianship
DipM	Diploma in Marketing
DipN	Diploma in Nursing
DipNEC	Diploma of Northampton Engineering College (*now* City University)
DipPA	Diploma of Practitioners in Advertising (*now see* DipCAM)
DipPSA	Diploma in Public Service Administration
DipREM	Diploma in Rural Estate Management
DipSMS	Diploma in School Management Studies
DipSoc	Diploma in Sociology
DipTA	Diploma in Tropical Agriculture
DipT&CP	Diploma in Town and Country Planning
DipTh	Diploma in Theology
DipTMHA	Diploma in Training and Further Education of Mentally Handicapped Adults
DipTP	Diploma in Town Planning
DipTPT	Diploma in Theory and Practice of Teaching
DIS	Diploma in Industrial Studies
DistTP	Distinction in Town Planning
DIur	Doctor of Law
Div.	Division; Divorced
Div.Test	Divinity Testimonium (of Trinity College, Dublin)
DJAG	Deputy Judge Advocate General
DJPD	Dato Jasa Purba Di-Raja Negeri Sembilan (Malaysia)
DJStJ	Dame of Justice, Order of St John of Jerusalem (*now see* DStJ)
DJur	*Doctor Juris* (Doctor of Law)
DK	Most Esteemed Family Order (Brunei)
DL	Deputy Lieutenant
DLC	Diploma of Loughborough College
DLES	Doctor of Letters in Economic Studies
DLI	Durham Light Infantry
DLit or **DLitt**	Doctor of Literature; Doctor of Letters
DLittS	Doctor of Sacred Letters
DLJ	Dame of Grace, Order of St Lazarus of Jerusalem
DLO	Diploma in Laryngology and Otology
DM	Doctor of Medicine
DMA	Diploma in Municipal Administration
DMD	Doctor of Medical Dentistry (Australia)
DME	Director of Mechanical Engineering
DMet	Doctor of Metallurgy
DMI	Director of Military Intelligence
DMin	Doctor of Ministry
DMiss	Doctor of Missiology
DMJ	Diploma in Medical Jurisprudence
DMJ(Path)	Diploma in Medical Jurisprudence (Pathology)
DMLJ	Dame of Merit, Order of St Lazarus of Jerusalem
DMO	Director of Military Operations
DMR	Diploma in Medical Radiology
DMRD	Diploma in Medical Radiological Diagnosis
DMRE	Diploma in Medical Radiology and Electrology
DMRT	Diploma in Medical Radio-Therapy
DMS	Director of Medical Services; Decoration for Meritorious Service (South Africa); Diploma in Management Studies
DMSc	Doctor of Medical Science
DMSSB	Direct Mail Services Standards Board
DMT	Director of Military Training
DMus	Doctor of Music
DN	Diploma in Nursing
DNB	Dictionary of National Biography
DNE	Director of Naval Equipment
DNI	Director of Naval Intelligence
DO	Diploma in Ophthalmology
DOAE	Defence Operational Analysis Establishment
DObstRCOG	Diploma of Royal College of Obstetricians and Gynaecologists (*now see* DRCOG)
DOC	District Officer Commanding
DocEng	Doctor of Engineering
DoE	Department of the Environment
DoH	Department of Health
DoI	Department of Industry
DOL	Doctor of Oriental Learning
Dom.	*Dominus* (Lord)
DOMS	Diploma in Ophthalmic Medicine and Surgery
DOR	Director of Operational Requirements
DOrthRCS	Diploma in Orthodontics, Royal College of Surgeons
DOS	Director of Ordnance Services; Doctor of Ocular Science
Dow.	Dowager
DP	Data Processing
DPA	Diploma in Public Administration; Discharged Prisoners' Aid
DPD	Diploma in Public Dentistry
DPEc	Doctor of Political Economy
DPed	Doctor of Pedagogy
DPH	Diploma in Public Health
DPh or **DPhil**	Doctor of Philosophy
DPharm	Doctor of Pharmacy
DPhilMed	Diploma in Philosophy of Medicine
DPhysMed	Diploma in Physical Medicine
DPLG	Diplômé par le Gouvernement
DPM	Diploma in Psychological Medicine
DPMS	Dato Paduka Mahkota Selangor (Malaysia)
DPP	Director of Public Prosecutions
DPR	Director of Public Relations
DPS	Director of Postal Services; Director of Personal Services; Doctor of Public Service
DPSA	Diploma in Public and Social Administration
DPSE	Diploma in Professional Studies in Education
DPsych	Doctor of Psychology
DQMG	Deputy Quartermaster-General
Dr	Doctor
DRA	Defence Research Agency (*now see* DERA)
DRAC	Director Royal Armoured Corps
DRC	Diploma of Royal College of Science and Technology, Glasgow
DRCOG	Diploma of Royal College of Obstetricians and Gynaecologists
DRD	Diploma in Restorative Dentistry
Dr ing	Doctor of Engineering
Dr jur	Doctor of Laws
DrŒcPol	*Doctor Œconomiæ Politicæ* (Doctor of Political Economy)
Dr rer. nat.	Doctor of Natural Science
Dr rer. pol.	Doctor of Political Science
DRS	Diploma in Religious Studies
DRSAMD	Diploma of the Royal Scottish Academy of Music and Drama
DS	Directing Staff; Doctor of Science
DSA	Diploma in Social Administration
DSAC	Defence Scientific Advisory Council
DSAO	Diplomatic Service Administration Office
DSC	Distinguished Service Cross
DSc	Doctor of Science
DScA	Docteur en sciences agricoles
DSCHE	Diploma of the Scottish Council for Health Education
DScMil	Doctor of Military Science
DSc (SocSci)	Doctor of Science in Social Science
DSD	Director Staff Duties
DSF	Director Special Forces
DSIR	Department of Scientific and Industrial Research (later SRC; then SERC)
DSL	Doctor of Sacred Letters
DSLJ	Dato Seri Laila Jasa (Brunei)
DSM	Distinguished Service Medal
DSNB	Dato Setia Negara Brunei
DSNS	Dato Setia Negeri Sembilan (Malaysia)
DSO	Companion of the Distinguished Service Order
DSocSc	Doctor of Social Science
DSP	Director of Selection of Personnel; Docteur en sciences politiques (Montreal)
dsp	*decessit sine prole* (died without issue)
DSS	Department of Social Security; Doctor of Sacred Scripture
Dss	Deaconess
DSSc	Doctor of Social Science
DST	Director of Supplies and Transport
DStJ	Dame of Grace, Most Venerable Order of the Hospital of St John of Jerusalem; Dame of Justice, Most Venerable Order of the Hospital of St John of Jerusalem
DTA	Diploma in Tropical Agriculture
DTD	Dekoratie voor Trouwe Dienst (Decoration for Devoted Service)
DTech	Doctor of Technology
DTH	Diploma in Tropical Hygiene
DTh or **DTheol**	Doctor of Theology
DThPT	Diploma in Theory and Practice of Teaching
DTI	Department of Trade and Industry
DTM&H	Diploma in Tropical Medicine and Hygiene
DU	Honorary Doctor of the University
Dunelm	*Dunelmensis* (of Durham)
DUniv	Honorary Doctor of the University
DUP	Democratic Unionist Party; Docteur de l'Université de Paris
DVA	Diploma of Veterinary Anaesthesia

DVH	Diploma in Veterinary Hygiene
DVLA	Driver and Vehicle Licensing Authority
DVLC	Driver and Vehicle Licensing Centre
DVM	Doctor of Veterinary Medicine
DVMS or **DVM&S**	Doctor of Veterinary Medicine and Surgery
DVR	Diploma in Veterinary Radiology
DVSc	Doctor of Veterinary Science
DVSM	Diploma in Veterinary State Medicine

E

E	East; Earl; England
e	eldest
EAA	Edinburgh Architectural Association
EACR	European Association for Cancer Research
EAGA	Energy Action Grants Agency
EAHY	European Architectural Heritage Year
EAP	East Africa Protectorate
EAW	Electrical Association for Women
EBC	English Benedictine Congregation
Ebor	*Eboracensis* (of York)
EBRD	European Bank for Reconstruction and Development
EBU	European Broadcasting Union
EC	Etoile du Courage (Canada); European Community; European Commission; Emergency Commission
ECA	Economic Co-operation Administration; Economic Commission for Africa
ECAFE	Economic Commission for Asia and the Far East (*now see* ESCAP)
ECCTIS	Education Courses and Credit Transfer Information Systems
ECE	Economic Commission for Europe
ECGD	Export Credits Guarantee Department
ECLA	Economic Commission for Latin America
ECLAC	United Nations Economic Commission for Latin America and the Caribbean
ECOVAST	European Council for the Village and Small Town
ECSC	European Coal and Steel Community
ECU	English Church Union
ED	Efficiency Decoration; Doctor of Engineering (US); European Democrat
ed	edited
EdB	Bachelor of Education
EDC	Economic Development Committee
EdD	Doctor of Education
EDF	European Development Fund
EDG	European Democratic Group; Employment Department Group
Edin.	Edinburgh
Edn	Edition
EDP	Executive Development Programme
Educ	Educated
Educn	Education
EEC	European Economic Community (*now see* EC); Commission of the European Communities
EEF	Engineering Employers' Federation; Egyptian Expeditionary Force
EEIBA	Electrical and Electronic Industries Benevolent Association
EETPU	Electrical Electronic Telecommunication & Plumbing Union (*now see* AEEU)
EETS	Early English Text Society
EFCE	European Federation of Chemical Engineering
EFTA	European Free Trade Association
eh	ehrenhalber (honorary)
EI	East Indian; East Indies
EIA	Engineering Industries Association
EIB	European Investment Bank
EICS	East India Company's Service
E-in-C	Engineer-in-Chief
EIS	Educational Institute of Scotland
EISCAT	European Incoherent Scatter Association
EIU	Economist Intelligence Unit
ELBS	English Language Book Society
ELSE	European Life Science Editors
ELT	English Language Teaching
EM	Edward Medal; Earl Marshal
EMBL	European Molecular Biology Laboratory
EMBO	European Molecular Biology Organisation
EMP	Electro Magnetic Pulse; Executive Management Program Diploma
EMS	Emergency Medical Service
Enc.Brit.	Encylopaedia Britannica
Eng.	England
Engr	Engineer
ENO	English National Opera
ENSA	Entertainments National Service Association
ENT	Ear Nose and Throat
EO	Executive Officer
EOC	Equal Opportunities Commission
EOPH	Examined Officer of Public Health
EORTC	European Organisation for Research on Treatment of Cancer
EP	European Parliament
EPP	European People's Party
EPSRC	Engineering and Physical Sciences Research Council
er	elder
ER	Eastern Region (BR)
ERA	Electrical Research Association
ERC	Electronics Research Council
ERD	Emergency Reserve Decoration (Army)
ESA	European Space Agency
ESCAP	Economic and Social Commission for Asia and the Pacific
ESF	European Science Foundn
ESL	English as a Second Language
ESNS	Educational Sub-Normal Serious
ESRC	Economic and Social Research Council; Electricity Supply Research Council
ESRO	European Space Research Organization (*now see* ESA)
ESTA	European Sciences and Technology Assembly
ESU	English-Speaking Union
ETA	Engineering Training Authority
ETH	Eidgenössische Technische Hochschule
ETUC	European Trade Union Confederation
ETUCE	European Trade Union Committee for Education
EU	European Union
EUDISED	European Documentation and Information Service for Education
Euratom	European Atomic Energy Community
EurChem	European Chemist
Eur Ing	European Engineer
EUROM	European Federation for Optics and Precision Mechanics
EUW	European Union of Women
eV	eingetragener Verein
Ext	Extinct

F

FA	Football Association
FAA	Fellow, Australian Academy of Science; Fleet Air Arm
FAAAI	Fellow, American Association for Artificial Intelligence
FAAAS	Fellow, American Association for the Advancement of Science
FAAO	Fellow, American Academy of Optometry
FAAP	Fellow, American Academy of Pediatrics
FAARM	Fellow, American Academy of Reproductive Medicine
FAAV	Fellow, Central Association of Agricultural Valuers
FAAVCT	Fellow, American Academy of Veterinary and Comparative Toxicology
FABE	Fellow, Association of Building Engineers
FACC	Fellow, American College of Cardiology
FACCA	Fellow, Association of Certified and Corporate Accountants (*now see* FCCA)
FACCP	Fellow, American College of Chest Physicians
FACD	Fellow, American College of Dentistry
FACDS	Fellow, Australian College of Dental Surgeons (*now see* FRACDS)
FACE	Fellow, Australian College of Education
FACerS	Fellow, American Ceramic Society
FACI	Fellow, Australian Chemical Institute (*now see* FRACI)
FACMA	Fellow, Australian College of Medical Administrators (*now see* FRACMA)
FACMG	Fellow, American College of Medicinal Genetics
FACOG	Fellow, American College of Obstetricians and Gynæcologists
FACOM	Fellow, Australian College of Occupational Medicine
FACP	Fellow, American College of Physicians
FACR	Fellow, American College of Radiology
FACRM	Fellow, Australian College of Rehabilitation Medicine
FACS	Fellow, American College of Surgeons
FACVT	Fellow, American College of Veterinary Toxicology (*now see* FAAVCT)
FADM	Fellow, Academy of Dental Materials
FAeSI	Fellow, Aeronautical Society of India
FAFPHM	Fellow, Australian Faculty of Public Health Medicine
FAGO	Fellowship in Australia in Obstetrics and Gynaecology
FAGS	Fellow, American Geographical Society
FAHA	Fellow, Australian Academy of the Humanities
FAI	Fellow, Chartered Auctioneers' and Estate Agents' Institute (*now* (after amalgamation) *see* FRICS); Fédération Aéronautique Internationale
FAIA	Fellow, American Institute of Architects
FAIAA	Fellow, American Institute of Aeronautics and Astronautics

FAIAS Fellow, Australian Institute of Agricultural Science
FAIB Fellow, Australian Institute of Bankers
FAIBiol Fellow, Australian Institute of Biology
FAICD Fellow, Australian Institute of Company Directors
FAIE Fellow, Australian Institute of Energy
FAIEx Fellow, Australian Institute of Export
FAIFST Fellow, Australian Institute of Food Science and Technology
FAII Fellow, Australian Insurance Institute
FAIM Fellow, Australian Institute of Management
FAIP Fellow, Australian Institute of Physics
FAMA Fellow, Australian Medical Association
FAMI Fellow, Australian Marketing Institute
FAmNucSoc Fellow, American Nuclear Society
FAMS Fellow, Ancient Monuments Society
F and GP Finance and General Purposes
FANY First Aid Nursing Yeomanry
FANZCA Fellow, Australian and New Zealand College of Anaesthetists
FANZCP Fellow, Australian and New Zealand College of Psychiatrists (*now see* FRANZCP)
FAO Food and Agriculture Organization of the United Nations
FAOrthA Fellow, Australian Orthopaedic Association
FAPA Fellow, American Psychiatric Association
FAPHA Fellow, American Public Health Association
FAPI Fellow, Australian Planning Institute (*now see* FRAPI)
FAPM Fellow, Association of Project Managers
FAPS Fellow, American Phytopathological Society
FArborA Fellow, Aboricultural Association
FARE Federation of Alcoholic Rehabilitation Establishments
FARELF Far East Land Forces
FAS Fellow, Antiquarian Society; Fellow, Nigerian Academy of Science; Funding Agency for Schools
FASA Fellow, Australian Society of Accountants (*now see* FCPA)
FASc Fellow, Indian Academy of Sciences
fasc. fascicule
FASCE Fellow, American Society of Civil Engineers
FASI Fellow, Architects' and Surveyors' Institute
FASME Fellow, American Society of Mechanical Engineers
FASPOG Fellow, Australian Society for Psychosomatic Obstetrics and Gynaecology
FASSA Fellow, Academy of the Social Sciences in Australia
FAusIMM Fellow, Australasian Institute of Mining and Metallurgy
FAustCOG Fellow, Australian College of Obstetricians and Gynæcologists (*now see* FRACOG)
FBA Fellow, British Academy; Federation of British Artists
FBCO Fellow, British College of Optometrists (*formerly* of Ophthalmic Opticians (Optometrists)) (*now see* FCOptom)
FBCS Fellow, British Computer Society
FBEC(S) Fellow, Business Education Council (Scotland)
FBES Fellow, Biological Engineering Society
FBHA Fellow, British Hospitality Association
FBHI Fellow, British Horological Institute
FBHS Fellow, British Horse Society
FBI Federation of British Industries (*now see* CBI); Federal Bureau of Investigation
FBIA Fellow, Bankers' Institute of Australasia (*now see* FAIB)
FBIAT Fellow, British Institute of Architectural Technicians
FBIBA Fellow, British Insurance Brokers' Association (*now see* FBIIBA)
FBID Fellow, British Institute of Interior Design
FBIIBA Fellow, British Insurance and Investment Brokers' Association
FBIM Fellow, British Institute of Management (*now see* FIMgt)
FBINZ Fellow, Bankers' Institute of New Zealand
FBIPP Fellow, British Institute of Professional Photography
FBIRA Fellow, British Institute of Regulatory Affairs
FBIS Fellow, British Interplanetary Society
FBKS Fellow, British Kinematograph Society (*now see* FBKSTS)
FBKSTS Fellow, British Kinematograph, Sound and Television Society
FBOA Fellow, British Optical Association
FBOU Fellow, British Ornithologists' Union
FBPICS Fellow, British Production and Inventory Control Society
FBPsS Fellow, British Psychological Society
FBritIRE Fellow, British Institution of Radio Engineers (later FIERE)
FBS Fellow, Building Societies Institute (later FCBSI; *now see* FCIB)
FBSI Fellow, Boot and Shoe Institution (*now see* FCFI)
FBSM Fellow, Birmingham School of Music
FC Football Club
FCA Fellow, Institute of Chartered Accountants; Fellow, Institute of Chartered Accountants in Australia; Fellow, New Zealand Society of Accountants; Federation of Canadian Artists
FCAI Fellow, New Zealand Institute of Cost Accountants; Fellow, Canadian Aeronautical Institute (*now see* FCASI)
FCAM Fellow, CAM Foundation
FCAnaes Fellow, College of Anaesthetists (*now see* FRCA)
FCASI Fellow, Canadian Aeronautics and Space Institute
FCBSI Fellow, Chartered Building Societies Institute (*now see* FCIB)
FCCA Fellow, Chartered Association of Certified Accountants
FCCEA Fellow, Commonwealth Council for Educational Administration
FCCS Fellow, Corporation of Secretaries (*formerly* of Certified Secretaries)
FCCT Fellow, Canadian College of Teachers
FCEC Federation of Civil Engineering Contractors
FCFI Fellow, Clothing and Footwear Institute
FCGI Fellow, City and Guilds of London Institute
FCGP Fellow, College of General Practitioners (*now see* FRCGP)
FCH Fellow, Coopers Hill College
FChS Fellow, Society of Chiropodists
FCI Fellow, Institute of Commerce
FCIA Fellow, Corporation of Insurance Agents
FCIArb Fellow, Chartered Institute of Arbitrators
FCIB Fellow, Corporation of Insurance Brokers; Fellow, Chartered Institute of Bankers
FCIBS Fellow, Chartered Institution of Building Services (*now see* FCIBSE); Fellow, Chartered Institute of Bankers in Scotland
FCIBSE Fellow, Chartered Institution of Building Services Engineers
FCIC Fellow, Chemical Institute of Canada (*formerly* Canadian Institute of Chemistry)
FCIH Fellow, Chartered Institute of Housing
FCII Fellow, Chartered Insurance Institute
FCIJ Fellow, Chartered Institute of Journalists
FCILA Fellow, Chartered Institute of Loss Adjusters
FCIM Fellow, Chartered Institute of Marketing; Fellow, Institute of Corporate Managers (Australia)
FCIOB Fellow, Chartered Institute of Building
FCIPA Fellow, Chartered Institute of Patent Agents (*now see* CPA)
FCIPS Fellow, Chartered Institute of Purchasing and Supply
FCIS Fellow, Institute of Chartered Secretaries and Administrators (*formerly* Chartered Institute of Secretaries)
FCISA Fellow, Chartered Institute of Secretaries and Administrators (Australia)
FCIT Fellow, Chartered Institute of Transport
FCIWEM Fellow, Chartered Institution of Water and Environmental Management
FCM Faculty of Community Medicine
FCMA Fellow, Chartered Institute of Management Accountants (*formerly* Institute of Cost and Management Accountants)
FCMSA Fellow, College of Medicine of South Africa
FCNA Fellow, College of Nursing, Australia
FCO Foreign and Commonwealth Office
FCOG(SA) Fellow, South African College of Obstetrics and Gynæcology
FCollH Fellow, College of Handicraft
FCollP Fellow, College of Preceptors
FCommA Fellow, Society of Commercial Accountants (*now see* FSCA)
FCOphth Fellow, College of Ophthalmologists (*now see* FRCOphth)
FCOptom Fellow, College of Optometrists
FCP Fellow, College of Preceptors
FCPA Fellow, Australian Society of Certified Practising Accountants
FCPath Fellow, College of Pathologists (*now see* FRCPath)
FCPS Fellow, College of Physicians and Surgeons
FCP(SoAf) Fellow, College of Physicians, South Africa
FCPSO(SoAf) Fellow, College of Physicians and Surgeons and Obstetricians, South Africa
FCPS (Pak) Fellow, College of Physicians and Surgeons of Pakistan
FCRA Fellow, College of Radiologists of Australia (*now see* FRACR)
FCS Federation of Conservative Students
FCS or **FChemSoc** Fellow, Chemical Society (now absorbed into Royal Society of Chemistry)
FCSD Fellow, Chartered Society of Designers
FCSHK Fellow, College of Surgeons of Hong Kong
FCSLT Fellow, College of Speech and Language Therapists
FCSP Fellow, Chartered Society of Physiotherapy
FCSSA or **FCS(SoAf)** Fellow, College of Surgeons, South Africa
FCSSL Fellow, College of Surgeons of Sri Lanka
FCST Fellow, College of Speech Therapists (*now see* FCSLT)
FCT Federal Capital Territory (*now see* ACT); Fellow, Association of Corporate Treasurers
FCTB Fellow, College of Teachers of the Blind
FCU Fighter Control Unit
FCWA Fellow, Institute of Costs and Works Accountants (*now see* FCMA)
FDA Association of First Division Civil Servants
FDF Food and Drink Federation
FDI Fédération Dentaire Internationale
FDP Freie Demokratische Partei
FDS Fellow in Dental Surgery
FDSRCPSGlas Fellow in Dental Surgery, Royal College of Physicians and Surgeons of Glasgow
FDSRCS or **FDS RCS** Fellow in Dental Surgery, Royal College of Surgeons of England
FDSRCSE Fellow in Dental Surgery, Royal College of Surgeons of Edinburgh
FE Far East

FEAF Far East Air Force
FEANI Fédération Européenne d'Associations Nationales d'Ingénieurs
FEBS Federation of European Biochemical Societies
FECI Fellow, Institute of Employment Consultants
FEE Fédération des Expertes Comptables Européens
FEF Far East Fleet
FEFC or **FEFCE** Further Education Funding Council for England
FEI Fédération Equestre Internationale
FEIDCT Fellow, Educational Institute of Design Craft and Technology
FEIS Fellow, Educational Institute of Scotland
FELCO Federation of English Language Course Opportunities
FEng Fellow, Royal Academy (*formerly* Fellowship) of Engineering
FES Fellow, Entomological Society; Fellow, Ethnological Society
FESC Fellow, European Society of Cardiology
FF Fianna Fáil; Field Force
FFA Fellow, Faculty of Actuaries (in Scotland); Fellow, Institute of Financial Accountants
FFAEM Fellow, Faculty of Accident and Emergency Medicine
FFARACS Fellow, Faculty of Anaesthetists, Royal Australasian College of Surgeons (*now see* FANZCA)
FFARCS Fellow, Faculty of Anaesthetists, Royal College of Surgeons of England (*now see* FRCA)
FFARCSI Fellow, Faculty of Anaesthetists, Royal College of Surgeons in Ireland
FFAS Fellow, Faculty of Architects and Surveyors, London (*now see* FASI)
FFA(SA) Fellow, Faculty of Anaesthetists (South Africa)
FFB Fellow, Faculty of Building
FFCM Fellow, Faculty of Community Medicine (*now see* FFPHM)
FFCMI Fellow, Faculty of Community Medicine of Ireland
FFDRCSI Fellow, Faculty of Dentistry, Royal College of Surgeons in Ireland
FFF Free French Forces
FFFP Fellow, Faculty of Family Planning of the Royal College of Obstetricians and Gynaecologists
FFHC Freedom from Hunger Campaign
FFHom Fellow, Faculty of Homœopathy
FFI French Forces of the Interior; Finance for Industry
FFOM Fellow, Faculty of Occupational Medicine
FFOMI Fellow, Faculty of Occupational Medicine of Ireland
FFPath, RCPI Fellow, Faculty of Pathologists of the Royal College of Physicians of Ireland
FFPHM Fellow, Faculty of Public Health Medicine
FFPHMI Fellow, Faculty of Public Health Medicine of Ireland
FFPM Fellow, Faculty of Pharmaceutical Medicine
FFPS Fauna and Flora Preservation Society
FFR Fellow, Faculty of Radiologists (*now see* FRCR)
FG Fine Gael
FGA Fellow, Gemmological Association
FGCL Fellow, Goldsmiths' College, London
FGCM Fellow, Guild of Church Musicians
FGDS Fédération de la Gauche Démocratique et Socialiste
FGGE Fellow, Guild of Glass Engineers
FGI Fellow, Institute of Certificated Grocers
FGS Fellow, Geological Society
FGSM Fellow, Guildhall School of Music and Drama
FGSM(MT) Fellow, Guildhall School of Music and Drama (Music Therapy)
FHA Fellow, Institute of Health Service Administrators (*formerly* Hospital Administrators; *now see* FHSM)
FHAS Fellow, Highland and Agricultural Society of Scotland
FHCIMA Fellow, Hotel Catering and Institutional Management Association
FHFS Fellow, Human Factors Society
FHKIE Fellow, Hong Kong Institution of Engineers
FHMAAAS Foreign Honorary Member, American Academy of Arts and Sciences
FHS Fellow, Heraldry Society; Forces Help Society and Lord Roberts Workshops
FHSA Family Health Services Authority
FHSM Fellow, Institute of Health Services Management
FH-WC Fellow, Heriot-Watt College (*now* University), Edinburgh
FIA Fellow, Institute of Actuaries
FIAA Fellow, Institute of Actuaries of Australia
FIAAS Fellow, Institute of Australian Agricultural Science
FIAA&S Fellow, Incorporated Association of Architects and Surveyors
FIAgrE Fellow, Institution of Agricultural Engineers
FIAgrM Fellow, Institute of Agricultural Management
FIAI Fellow, Institute of Industrial and Commercial Accountants
FIAL Fellow, International Institute of Arts and Letters
FIAM Fellow, International Academy of Management
FIAP Fellow, Institution of Analysts and Programmers
FIArb Fellow, Institute of Arbitrators (*now see* FCIArb)
FIArbA Fellow, Institute of Arbitrators of Australia
FIAS Fellow, Institute of Aeronautical Sciences (US) (*now see* FAIAA)
FIASc Fellow, Indian Academy of Sciences
FIAWS Fellow, International Academy of Wood Sciences
FIB Fellow, Institute of Bankers (*now see* FCIB)
FIBA Fellow, Institute of Business Administration, Australia (*now see* FCIM)
FIBD Fellow, Institute of British Decorators
FIBiol Fellow, Institute of Biology
FIBiotech Fellow, Institute for Biotechnical Studies
FIBMS Fellow, Institute of Biomedical Sciences
FIBP Fellow, Institute of British Photographers
FIBScot Fellow, Institute of Bankers in Scotland (*now see* FCIBS)
FIC Fellow, Institute of Chemistry (*now see* FRIC, FRSC); Fellow, Imperial College, London
FICA Fellow, Commonwealth Institute of Accountants; Fellow, Institute of Chartered Accountants in England and Wales (*now see* FCA)
FICAI Fellow, Institute of Chartered Accountants in Ireland
FICD Fellow, Institute of Civil Defence (*now see* FICDDS); Fellow, Indian College of Dentists; Fellow, International College of Dentists
FICDDS Fellow, Institute of Civil Defence and Disaster Studies
FICE Fellow, Institution of Civil Engineers
FICeram Fellow, Institute of Ceramics (*now see* FIM)
FICFM Fellow, Institute of Charity Fundraising Managers
FICFor Fellow, Institute of Chartered Foresters
FIChemE Fellow, Institution of Chemical Engineers
FICI Fellow, Institute of Chemistry of Ireland; Fellow, International Colonial Institute
FICM Fellow, Institute of Credit Management
FICMA Fellow, Institute of Cost and Management Accountants
FICorrST Fellow, Institution of Corrosion Science and Technology
FICS Fellow, Institute of Chartered Shipbrokers; Fellow, International College of Surgeons
FICT Fellow, Institute of Concrete Technologists
FICW Fellow, Institute of Clerks of Works of Great Britain
FIDA Fellow, Institute of Directors, Australia
FIDCA Fellow, Industrial Design Council of Australia
FIDE Fédération Internationale des Echecs; Fellow, Institute of Design Engineers; Fédération Internationale pour le Droit Européen
FIDEM Fédération Internationale de la Médaille
FIEAust Fellow, Institution of Engineers, Australia
FIEC Fellow, Institute of Employment Consultants
FIED Fellow, Institution of Engineering Designers
FIEE Fellow, Institution of Electrical Engineers
FIEEE Fellow, Institute of Electrical and Electronics Engineers (NY)
FIEHK Fellow, Institution of Engineering, Hong Kong
FIElecIE Fellow, Institution of Electronic Incorporated Engineers (*now see* FIEIE)
FIEI Fellow, Institution of Engineering Inspection (*now see* FIQA); Fellow, Institution of Engineers of Ireland
FIEIE Fellow, Institution of Electronics and Electrical Incorporated Engineers
FIEJ Fédération Internationale des Editeurs de Journaux et Publications
FIERE Fellow, Institution of Electronic and Radio Engineers (*now see* FIEE)
FIES Fellow, Illuminating Engineering Society (later FIllumES; *now see* FCIBSE); Fellow, Institution of Engineers and Shipbuilders, Scotland
FIET Fédération Internationale des Employés, Techniciens et Cadres
FIEx Fellow, Institute of Export
FIExpE Fellow, Institute of Explosives Engineers
FIFA Fédération Internationale de Football Association
FIFF Fellow, Institute of Freight Forwarders
FIFireE Fellow, Institution of Fire Engineers
FIFM Fellow, Institute of Fisheries Management
FIFor Fellow, Institute of Foresters (*now see* FICFor)
FIFST Fellow, Institute of Food Science and Technology
FIGasE Fellow, Institution of Gas Engineers
FIGCM Fellow, Incorporated Guild of Church Musicians
FIGD Fellow, Institute of Grocery Distribution
FIGO International Federation of Gynaecology and Obstetrics
FIH Fellow, Institute of Housing (*now see* FCIH); Fellow, Institute of the Horse
FIHE Fellow, Institute of Health Education
FIHM Fellow, Institute of Housing Managers (later FIH; *now see* FCIH)
FIHort Fellow, Institute of Horticulture
FIHospE Fellow, Institute of Hospital Engineering
FIHT Fellow, Institution of Highways and Transportation
FIHVE Fellow, Institution of Heating & Ventilating Engineers (later FCIBS and MCIBS; *now see* FCIBSE)
FIIA Fellow, Institute of Industrial Administration (later CBIM and FBIM); Fellow, Institute of Internal Auditors
FIIB Fellow, International Institute of Biotechnology

FIIC Fellow, International Institute for Conservation of Historic and Artistic Works
FIIDA Fellow, International Interior Design Association
FIIM Fellow, Institution of Industrial Managers
FIInfSc Fellow, Institute of Information Scientists
FIInst Fellow, Imperial Institute
FIIP Fellow, Institute of Incorporated Photographers (*now see* FBIPP)
FIIPC Fellow, India International Photographic Council
FIIPE Fellow, Indian Institution of Production Engineers
FIL Fellow, Institute of Linguists
FILA Fellow, Institute of Landscape Architects (*now see* FLI)
FILDM Fellow, Institute of Logistics and Distribution Management (*now see* FILog)
FilDr Doctor of Philosophy
Fil.Hed. Filosofie Hedersdoktor
FILLM Fédération Internationale des Langues et Littératures Modernes
FIllumES Fellow, Illuminating Engineering Society (*now see* FCIBSE)
FILog Fellow, Institute of Logistics
FIM Fellow, Institute of Materials (*formerly* Institution of Metallurgists, then Institute of Metals)
FIMA Fellow, Institute of Mathematics and its Applications
FIMarE Fellow, Institute of Marine Engineers
FIMatM Fellow, Institute of Materials Management (*now see* FILog)
FIMBRA Financial Intermediaries, Managers and Brokers Regulatory Association
FIMC Fellow, Institute of Management Consultants
FIMCB Fellow, International Management Centre from Buckingham
FIMechE Fellow, Institution of Mechanical Engineers
FIMfgE Fellow, Institution of Manufacturing Engineers (*now see* FIEE)
FIMFT Fellow, Institute of Maxillo-facial Technology
FIMgt Fellow, Institute of Management
FIMGTechE Fellow, Institution of Mechanical and General Technician Engineers
FIMH Fellow, Institute of Materials Handling (later FIMatM); Fellow, Institute of Military History
FIMI Fellow, Institute of the Motor Industry
FIMinE Fellow, Institution of Mining Engineers
FIMIT Fellow, Institute of Musical Instrument Technology
FIMLS Fellow, Institute of Medical Laboratory Sciences (*now see* FIBMS)
FIMLT Fellow, Institute of Medical Laboratory Technology (later FIMLS)
FIMM Fellow, Institution of Mining and Metallurgy
FIMMA Fellow, Institute of Metals and Materials Australasia
FIMS Fellow, Institute of Mathematical Statistics
FIMT Fellow, Institute of the Motor Trade (*now see* FIMI)
FIMTA Fellow, Institute of Municipal Treasurers and Accountants (*now see* IPFA)
FIMunE Fellow, Institution of Municipal Engineers (now amalgamated with Institution of Civil Engineers)
FIN Fellow, Institute of Navigation (*now see* FRIN)
FINA Fédération Internationale de Natation Amateur
FInstAM Fellow, Institute of Administrative Management
FInstArb(NZ) Fellow, Institute of Arbitrators of New Zealand
FInstB Fellow, Institution of Buyers
FInstBiol Fellow, Institute of Biology (*now see* FIBiol)
FInstD Fellow, Institute of Directors
FInstE Fellow, Institute of Energy
FInstEnvSci Fellow, Institute of Environmental Sciences
FInstF Fellow, Institute of Fuel (*now see* FInstE)
FInstFF Fellow, Institute of Freight Forwarders Ltd (*now see* FIFF)
FInstHE Fellow, Institution of Highways Engineers (*now see* FIHT)
FInstLEx Fellow, Institute of Legal Executives
FInstM Fellow, Institute of Meat; Fellow, Institute of Marketing (*now see* FCIM)
FInstMC Fellow, Institute of Measurement and Control
FInstMSM Fellow, Institute of Marketing and Sales Management (later FInstM; *now see* FCIM)
FInstMet Fellow, Institute of Metals (later part of Metals Society; *now see* FIM)
FInstNDT Fellow, Institute of Non-Destructive Testing
FInstP Fellow, Institute of Physics
FInstPet Fellow, Institute of Petroleum
FInstPI Fellow, Institute of Patentees and Inventors
FInstPS Fellow, Institute of Purchasing and Supply (*now see* FCIPS)
FInstSM Fellow, Institute of Sales Management (*now see* FInstSMM)
FInstSMM Fellow, Institute of Sales and Marketing Management
FInstW Fellow, Institute of Welding (*now see* FWeldI)
FINucE Fellow, Institution of Nuclear Engineers
FIOA Fellow, Institute of Acoustics
FIOB Fellow, Institute of Building (*now see* FCIOB)
FIOH Fellow, Institute of Occupational Hygiene
FIOM Fellow, Institute of Office Management (*now see* FIAM)
FIOP Fellow, Institute of Printing
FIOSH Fellow, Institute of Occupational Safety and Health
FIP Fellow, Australian Institute of Petroleum
FIPA Fellow, Institute of Practitioners in Advertising
FIPD Fellow, Institute of Personnel and Development
FIPDM Fellow, Institute of Physical Distribution Management (later FILDM)
FIPENZ Fellow, Institution of Professional Engineers, New Zealand
FIPG Fellow, Institute of Professional Goldsmiths
FIPHE Fellow, Institution of Public Health Engineers (*now see* FIWEM)
FIPlantE Fellow, Institute of Plant Engineers (*now see* FIIM)
FIPM Fellow, Institute of Personnel Management (*now see* FIPD)
FIPR Fellow, Institute of Public Relations
FIProdE Fellow, Institution of Production Engineers (later FIMfgE; *now see* FIEE)
FIQ Fellow, Institute of Quarrying
FIQA Fellow, Institute of Quality Assurance
FIQS Fellow, Institute of Quantity Surveyors
FIRA Furniture Industry Research Association
FIRA(Ind) Fellow, Institute of Railway Auditors and Accountants (India)
FIRE(Aust) Fellow, Institution of Radio Engineers (Australia) (*now see* FIREE(Aust))
FIREE(Aust) Fellow, Institution of Radio and Electronics Engineers (Australia)
FIRI Fellow, Institution of the Rubber Industry (later FPRI)
FIRM Fellow, Institute of Risk Management
FIRSE Fellow, Institute of Railway Signalling Engineers
FIRTE Fellow, Institute of Road Transport Engineers
FIS Fellow, Institute of Statisticians
FISA Fellow, Incorporated Secretaries' Association; Fédération Internationale des Sociétés d'Aviron
FISE Fellow, Institution of Sales Engineers; Fellow, Institution of Sanitary Engineers
FISITA Fédération Internationale des Sociétés d'Ingénieurs des Techniques de l'Automobile
FISM Fellow, Institute of Supervisory Managers
FISOB Fellow, Incorporated Society of Organ Builders
FISP Fédération Internationale des Sociétés de Philosophie
FIST Fellow, Institute of Science Technology
FISTC Fellow, Institute of Scientific and Technical Communicators
FISTD Fellow, Imperial Society of Teachers of Dancing
FIStructE Fellow, Institution of Structural Engineers
FISW Fellow, Institute of Social Work
FITD Fellow, Institute of Training and Development (*now see* FIPD)
FITE Fellow, Institution of Electrical and Electronics Technician Engineers
FIW Fellow, Welding Institute (*now see* FWeldI)
FIWE Fellow, Institution of Water Engineers (later FIWES; then FIWEM; *now see* FCIWEM)
FIWEM Fellow, Institution of Water and Environmental Management (*now see* FCIWEM)
FIWES Fellow, Institution of Water Engineers and Scientists (later FIWEM; *now see* FCIWEM)
FIWM Fellow, Institution of Works Managers (*now see* FIIM)
FIWPC Fellow, Institute of Water Pollution Control (later FIWEM; *now see* FCIWEM)
FIWSc Fellow, Institute of Wood Science
FIWSP Fellow, Institute of Work Study Practitioners (*now see* FMS)
FJI Fellow, Institute of Journalists (*now see* FCIJ)
FJIE Fellow, Junior Institution of Engineers (*now see* CIMGTechE)
FKC Fellow, King's College London
FKCHMS Fellow, King's College Hospital Medical School
FL Florida
FLA Fellow, Library Association
Fla Florida (US)
FLAI Fellow, Library Association of Ireland
FLAS Fellow, Chartered Land Agents' Society (*now* (after amalgamation) *see* FRICS)
FLCM Fellow, London College of Music
FLHS Fellow, London Historical Society
FLI Fellow, Landscape Institute
FLIA Fellow, Life Insurance Association
FLS Fellow, Linnean Society
Flt Flight
FM Field-Marshal
FMA Fellow, Museums Association
FMAAT Fellow Member, Association of Accounting Technicians
FMANZ Fellow, Medical Association of New Zealand
FMES Fellow, Minerals Engineering Society
FMF Fiji Military Forces
FMI Foundation for Manufacturing and Industry
FMS Federated Malay States; Fellow, Medical Society; Fellow, Institute of Management Services
FMSA Fellow, Mineralogical Society of America
FNA Fellow, Indian National Science Academy
FNAEA Fellow, National Association of Estate Agents
FNCO Fleet Naval Constructor Officer

FNECInst Fellow, North East Coast Institution of Engineers and Shipbuilders
FNI Fellow, Nautical Institute; Fellow, National Institute of Sciences in India (*now see* FNA)
FNIA Fellow, Nigerian Institute of Architects
FNM Free National Movement
FNZEI Fellow, New Zealand Educational Institute
FNZIA Fellow, New Zealand Institute of Architects
FNZIAS Fellow, New Zealand Institute of Agricultural Science
FNZIC Fellow, New Zealand Institute of Chemistry
FNZIE Fellow, New Zealand Institution of Engineers (*now see* FIPENZ)
FNZIM Fellow, New Zealand Institute of Management
FNZPsS Fellow, New Zealand Psychological Society
FO Foreign Office (*now see* FCO); Field Officer; Flying Officer
FODA Fellow, Overseas Doctors' Association
FODC Franciscan Order of the Divine Compassion
FOIC Flag Officer in charge
FOMI Faculty of Occupational Medicine of Ireland
FONA Flag Officer, Naval Aviation
FONAC Flag Officer Naval Air Command
FOR Fellowship of Operational Research
For. Foreign
FOREST Freedom Organisation for the Right to Enjoy Smoking Tobacco
FOX Futures and Options Exchange
FPA Family Planning Association
FPC Family Practitioner Committee (*now see* FHSA)
FPEA Fellow, Physical Education Association
FPHM Faculty of Public Health Medicine
FPhS Fellow, Philosophical Society of England
FPI Fellow, Plastics Institute (later FPRI)
FPIA Fellow, Plastics Institute of Australia
FPMI Fellow, Pensions Management Institute
FPRI Fellow, Plastics and Rubber Institute (*now see* FIM)
FPS Fellow, Pharmaceutical Society (*now see* FRPharmS); Fauna Preservation Society (*now see* FFPS)
FPhysS Fellow, Physical Society
f r fuori ruole
FRA Fellow, Royal Academy
FRACDS Fellow, Royal Australian College of Dental Surgeons
FRACGP Fellow, Royal Australian College of General Practitioners
FRACI Fellow, Royal Australian Chemical Institute
FRACMA Fellow, Royal Australian College of Medical Administrators
FRACO Fellow, Royal Australian College of Ophthalmologists
FRACOG Fellow, Royal Australian College of Obstetricians and Gynaecologists
FRACP Fellow, Royal Australasian College of Physicians
FRACR Fellow, Royal Australasian College of Radiologists
FRACS Fellow, Royal Australasian College of Surgeons
FRAD Fellow, Royal Academy of Dancing
FRAeS Fellow, Royal Aeronautical Society
FRAgS Fellow, Royal Agricultural Societies (*ie* of England, Scotland and Wales)
FRAHS Fellow, Royal Australian Historical Society
FRAI Fellow, Royal Anthropological Institute of Great Britain & Ireland
FRAIA Fellow, Royal Australian Institute of Architects
FRAIB Fellow, Royal Australian Institute of Building
FRAIC Fellow, Royal Architectural Institute of Canada
FRAIPA Fellow, Royal Australian Institute of Public Administration
FRAM Fellow, Royal Academy of Music
FRAME Fund for the Replacement of Animals in Medical Experiments
FRANZCP Fellow, Royal Australian and New Zealand College of Psychiatrists
FRAPI Fellow, Royal Australian Planning Institute
FRAS Fellow, Royal Astronomical Society; Fellow, Royal Asiatic Society
FRASB Fellow, Royal Asiatic Society of Bengal
FRASE Fellow, Royal Agricultural Society of England
FRBS Fellow, Royal Society of British Sculptors; Fellow, Royal Botanic Society
FRCA Fellow, Royal College of Art; Fellow, Royal College of Anaesthetists
FRCCO Fellow, Royal Canadian College of Organists
FRCD(Can.) Fellow, Royal College of Dentists of Canada
FRCGP Fellow, Royal College of General Practitioners
FRCM Fellow, Royal College of Music
FRCN Fellow, Royal College of Nursing
FRCO Fellow, Royal College of Organists
FRCO(CHM) Fellow, Royal College of Organists with Diploma in Choir Training
FRCOG Fellow, Royal College of Obstetricians and Gynaecologists
FRCOphth Fellow, Royal College of Ophthalmologists
FRCP Fellow, Royal College of Physicians, London
FRCPA Fellow, Royal College of Pathologists of Australasia
FRCP&S (Canada) Fellow, Royal College of Physicians and Surgeons of Canada
FRCPath Fellow, Royal College of Pathologists
FRCP(C) Fellow, Royal College of Physicians of Canada
FRCPE or **FRCPEd** Fellow, Royal College of Physicians, Edinburgh
FRCPGlas Fellow, Royal College of Physicians and Surgeons of Glasgow
FRCPI Fellow, Royal College of Physicians of Ireland
FRCPSGlas Hon. Fellow, Royal College of Physicians and Surgeons of Glasgow
FRCPsych Fellow, Royal College of Psychiatrists
FRCR Fellow, Royal College of Radiologists
FRCS Fellow, Royal College of Surgeons of England
FRCSCan Fellow, Royal College of Surgeons of Canada
FRCSE or **FRCSEd** Fellow, Royal College of Surgeons of Edinburgh
FRCSGlas Fellow, Royal College of Physicians and Surgeons of Glasgow
FRCSI Fellow, Royal College of Surgeons in Ireland
FRCSoc Fellow, Royal Commonwealth Society
FRCUS Fellow, Royal College of University Surgeons (Denmark)
FRCVS Fellow, Royal College of Veterinary Surgeons
FREconS Fellow, Royal Economic Society
FREI Fellow, Real Estate Institute (Australia)
FRES Fellow, Royal Entomological Society of London
FRFPSG Fellow, Royal Faculty of Physicians and Surgeons, Glasgow (*now see* FRCPGlas)
FRG Federal Republic of Germany
FRGS Fellow, Royal Geographical Society
FRGSA Fellow, Royal Geographical Society of Australasia
FRHistS Fellow, Royal Historical Society
FRHS Fellow, Royal Horticultural Society (*now see* MRHS)
FRHSV Fellow, Royal Historical Society of Victoria
FRIAS Fellow, Royal Incorporation of Architects of Scotland; Royal Institute for the Advancement of Science
FRIBA Fellow, Royal Institute of British Architects (*and see* RIBA)
FRIC Fellow, Royal Institute of Chemistry (*now see* FRSC)
FRICS Fellow, Royal Institution of Chartered Surveyors
FRIH Fellow, Royal Institute of Horticulture (NZ)
FRIN Fellow, Royal Institute of Navigation
FRINA Fellow, Royal Institution of Naval Architects
FRIPA Fellow, Royal Institute of Public Administration (the Institute no longer has Fellows)
FRIPHH Fellow, Royal Institute of Public Health and Hygiene
FRMCM Fellow, Royal Manchester College of Music
FRMedSoc Fellow, Royal Medical Society
FRMetS Fellow, Royal Meteorological Society
FRMIA Fellow, Retail Management Institute of Australia
FRMS Fellow, Royal Microscopical Society
FRNCM Fellow, Royal Northern College of Music
FRNS Fellow, Royal Numismatic Society
FRPharmS Fellow, Royal Pharmaceutical Society
FRPS Fellow, Royal Photographic Society
FRPSL Fellow, Royal Philatelic Society, London
FRS Fellow, Royal Society
FRSA Fellow, Royal Society of Arts
FRSAI Fellow, Royal Society of Antiquaries of Ireland
FRSAMD Fellow, Royal Scottish Academy of Music and Drama
FRSanI Fellow, Royal Sanitary Institute (*now see* FRSH)
FRSC Fellow, Royal Society of Canada; Fellow, Royal Society of Chemistry
FRS(Can) Fellow, Royal Society of Canada (used when a person is also a Fellow of the Royal Society of Chemistry)
FRSCM Hon. Fellow, Royal School of Church Music
FRSC (UK) Fellow, Royal Society of Chemistry (used when a person is also a Fellow of the Royal Society of Canada)
FRSE Fellow, Royal Society of Edinburgh
FRSGS Fellow, Royal Scottish Geographical Society
FRSH Fellow, Royal Society for the Promotion of Health
FRSL Fellow, Royal Society of Literature
FRSM or **FRSocMed** Fellow, Royal Society of Medicine
FRSNZ Fellow, Royal Society of New Zealand
FRSSAf Fellow, Royal Society of South Africa
FRST Fellow, Royal Society of Teachers
FRSTM&H Fellow, Royal Society of Tropical Medicine and Hygiene
FRTPI Fellow, Royal Town Planning Institute
FRTS Fellow, Royal Television Society
FRVA Fellow, Rating and Valuation Association (*now see* IRRV)
FRVC Fellow, Royal Veterinary College
FRVIA Fellow, Royal Victorian Institute of Architects
FRZSScot Fellow, Royal Zoological Society of Scotland
FS Field Security
fs Graduate, Royal Air Force Staff College
FSA Fellow, Society of Antiquaries
FSAA Fellow, Society of Incorporated Accountants and Auditors

FSAE Fellow, Society of Automotive Engineers; Fellow, Society of Art Education
FSAI Fellow, Society of Architectural Illustrators
FSAIEE Fellow, South African Institute of Electrical Engineers
FSAM Fellow, Society of Art Masters
FSArc Fellow, Society of Architects (merged with the RIBA 1952)
FSaRS Fellow, Safety and Reliability Society
FSAScot Fellow, Society of Antiquaries of Scotland
FSASM Fellow, South Australian School of Mines
FSBI Fellow, Savings Banks Institute
fsc Foreign Staff College
FSCA Fellow, Society of Company and Commercial Accountants
FScotvec Fellow, Scottish Vocational Education Council
FSCRE Fellow, Scottish Council for Research in Education
FSDC Fellow, Society of Dyers and Colourists
FSE Fellow, Society of Engineers
FSG Fellow, Society of Genealogists
FSGT Fellow, Society of Glass Technology
FSI Fellow, Chartered Surveyors' Institution (*now see* FRICS); Fellow, Securities Institute
FSIAD Fellow, Society of Industrial Artists and Designers (*now see* FCSD)
FSLAET Fellow, Society of Licensed Aircraft Engineers and Technologists
FSLCOG Fellow, Sri Lankan College of Obstetrics and Gynaecology
FSLTC Fellow, Society of Leather Technologists and Chemists
FSMA Fellow, Incorporated Sales Managers' Association (later FInstMSM, then FInstM)
FSMC Freeman of the Spectacle-Makers' Company
FSME Fellow, Society of Manufacturing Engineers
FSMPTE Fellow, Society of Motion Picture and Television Engineers (USA)
FSNAD Fellow, Society of Numismatic Artists and Designers
FSNAME Fellow, American Society of Naval Architects and Marine Engineers
FSRHE Fellow, Society for Research into Higher Education
FSRP Fellow, Society for Radiological Protection
FSS Fellow, Royal Statistical Society
FSTD Fellow, Society of Typographic Designers
FSVA Fellow, Incorporated Society of Valuers and Auctioneers
FT Financial Times
FTAT Furniture, Timber and Allied Trades Union
FTC Flying Training Command; Full Technological Certificate, City and Guilds of London Institute
FTCD Fellow, Trinity College, Dublin
FTCL Fellow, Trinity College of Music, London
FTI Fellow, Textile Institute
FTII Fellow, Chartered Institute (*formerly* Incorporated Institute, then Institute) of Taxation
FTMA Fellow, Telecommunications Managers Association
FTP Fellow, Thames Polytechnic
FTS Fellow, Australian Academy of Technological Sciences and Engineering; Flying Training School; Fellow, Tourism Society
FTSC Fellow, Tonic Sol-fa College
FUCUA Federation of University Conservative and Unionist Associations (*now see* FCS)
FUMIST Fellow, University of Manchester Institute of Science and Technology
FVRDE Fighting Vehicles Research and Development Establishment
FWAAS Fellow, World Academy of Arts and Sciences
FWACP Fellow, West African College of Physicians
FWCMD Fellow, Welsh College of Music and Drama
FWeldI Fellow, Welding Institute
FWSOM Fellow, Institute of Practitioners in Work Study, Organisation and Method (*now see* FMS)
FZS Fellow, Zoological Society
FZSScot Fellow, Zoological Society of Scotland (*now see* FRZSScot)

G

GA Geologists' Association; Gaelic Athletic (Club); Georgia
Ga Georgia (US)
GAI Guild of Architectural Ironmongers
GAP Gap Activity Projects
GAPAN Guild of Air Pilots and Air Navigators
GATT General Agreement on Tariffs and Trade (*now* World Trade Organisation)
GB Great Britain
GBA Governing Bodies Association
GBE Knight or Dame Grand Cross, Order of the British Empire
GBGSA Governing Bodies of Girls' Schools Association (*formerly* Association of Governing Bodies of Girls' Public Schools)
GBSM Graduate of Birmingham and Midland Institute School of Music
GC George Cross
GCB Knight or Dame Grand Cross, Order of the Bath
GCBS General Council of British Shipping
GCCC Gonville and Caius College, Cambridge
GCFR Grand Commander, Order of the Federal Republic of Nigeria
GCH Knight Grand Cross, Hanoverian Order
GCHQ Government Communications Headquarters
GCIE Knight Grand Commander, Order of the Indian Empire
GCLJ Grand Cross, St Lazarus of Jerusalem
GCLM Grand Commander, Order of the Legion of Merit of Rhodesia
GCM Gold Crown of Merit (Barbados)
GCMG Knight or Dame Grand Cross, Order of St Michael and St George
GCON Grand Cross, Order of the Niger
GCSE General Certificate of Secondary Education
GCSG Knight Grand Cross, Order of St Gregory the Great
GCSI Knight Grand Commander, Order of the Star of India
GCSJ Knight Grand Cross of Justice, Order of St John of Jerusalem (Knights Hospitaller)
GCSL Grand Cross, Order of St Lucia
GCStJ Bailiff or Dame Grand Cross, Most Venerable Order of the Hospital of St John of Jerusalem
GCVO Knight or Dame Grand Cross, Royal Victorian Order
gd grand-daughter
GDBA Guide Dogs for the Blind Association
GDC General Dental Council
Gdns Gardens
GDR German Democratic Republic
Gen. General
Ges. Gesellschaft
GFD Geophysical Fluid Dynamics
GFS Girls' Friendly Society
ggd great-grand-daughter
ggs great-grandson
GGSM Graduate in Music, Guildhall School of Music and Drama
GHQ General Headquarters
Gib. Gibraltar
GIMechE Graduate, Institution of Mechanical Engineers
GL Grand Lodge
GLAA Greater London Arts Association (*now see* GLAB)
GLAB Greater London Arts Board
GLC Greater London Council
Glos Gloucestershire
GM George Medal; Grand Medal (Ghana)
GMB (Union for) General, Municipal, Boilermakers
GMBATU General, Municipal, Boilermakers and Allied Trades Union (*now see* GMB)
GmbH Gesellschaft mit beschränkter Haftung
GMC General Medical Council; Guild of Memorial Craftsmen; General Management Course (Henley)
GMIE Grand Master, Order of the Indian Empire
GMSI Grand Master, Order of the Star of India
GMWU General and Municipal Workers' Union (later GMBATU; *now see* GMB)
GNC General Nursing Council
GOC General Officer Commanding
GOC-in-C General Officer Commanding-in-Chief
GOE General Ordination Examination
Gov. Governor
Govt Government
GP General Practitioner; Grand Prix
GPDST Girls' Public Day School Trust
GPMU Graphical, Paper and Media Union
GPO General Post Office
GQG Grand Quartier Général
GR General Reconaissance
Gr. Greek
GRSM Graduate of the Royal Schools of Music
GS General Staff; Grammar School
gs grandson
GSA Girls' Schools Association
GSM General Service Medal; (Member of) Guildhall School of Music and Drama
GSMD Guildhall School of Music and Drama
GSO General Staff Officer
GTCL Graduate, Trinity College of Music
GTS General Theological Seminary (New York)
GUI Golfing Union of Ireland
GWR Great Western Railway

H

HA Historical Association; Health Authority
HAA Heavy Anti-Aircraft
HAC Honourable Artillery Company

HACAS	Housing Association Consultancy and Advisory Service
Hants	Hampshire
HARCVS	Honorary Associate, Royal College of Veterinary Surgeons
Harv.	Harvard
HAT	Housing Action Trust
HBM	His (or Her) Britannic Majesty (Majesty's); Humming Bird Gold Medal (Trinidad)
hc	*honoris causa* (honorary)
HCEG	Honourable Company of Edinburgh Golfers
HCF	Honorary Chaplain to the Forces
HCIMA	Hotel, Catering and Institutional Management Association
HCO	Higher Clerical Officer
HCSC	Higher Command and Staff Course
HDA	Hawkesbury Diploma in Agriculture (Australia)
HDD	Higher Dental Diploma
HDFA	Higher Diploma in Fine Art
HDipEd	Higher Diploma in Education
HE	His (or Her) Excellency; His Eminence
HEA	Health Education Authority
HEC	Ecole des Hautes Etudes Commerciales; Higher Education Corporation
HEFCE	Higher Education Funding Council for England
HEFCW	Higher Education Funding Council for Wales
HEH	His (or Her) Exalted Highness
HEIC	Honourable East India Company
HEICS	Honourable East India Company's Service
Heir-pres.	Heir-presumptive
HEO	Higher Executive Officer
HEQC	Higher Education Quality Council
Herts	Hertfordshire
HFARA	Honorary Foreign Associate of the Royal Academy
HFEA	Human Fertilisation and Embryology Authority
HFRA	Honorary Foreign Member of the Royal Academy
HG	Home Guard
HGTAC	Home Grown Timber Advisory Committee
HH	His (or Her) Highness; His Holiness; Member, Hesketh Hubbard Art Society
HHA	Historic Houses Association
HHD	Doctor of Humanities (US)
HI	Hawaii
HIH	His (or Her) Imperial Highness
HIM	His (or Her) Imperial Majesty
HJ	Hilal-e-Jurat (Pakistan)
HKIA	Hong Kong Institute of Architects
HKIPM	Hong Kong Institute of Personnel Management
HLD	Doctor of Humane Letters
HLI	Highland Light Infantry
HM	His (or Her) Majesty, or Majesty's
HMA	Head Masters' Association
HMAS	His (or Her) Majesty's Australian Ship
HMC	Headmasters' Conference; Hospital Management Committee
HMCIC	His (or Her) Majesty's Chief Inspector of Constabulary
HMCS	His (or Her) Majesty's Canadian Ship
HMHS	His (or Her) Majesty's Hospital Ship
HMI	His (or Her) Majesty's Inspector
HMIED	Honorary Member, Institute of Engineering Designers
HMMTB	His (or Her) Majesty's Motor Torpedo Boat
HMOCS	His (or Her) Majesty's Overseas Civil Service
HMS	His (or Her) Majesty's Ship
HMSO	His (or Her) Majesty's Stationery Office
HNC	Higher National Certificate
HND	Higher National Diploma
H of C	House of Commons
H of L	House of Lords
Hon.	Honourable; Honorary
HPk	Hilal-e-Pakistan
HQ	Headquarters
HQA	Hilali-Quaid-i-Azam (Pakistan)
HRCA	Honorary Royal Cambrian Academician
HRGI	Honorary Member, The Royal Glasgow Institute of the Fine Arts
HRH	His (or Her) Royal Highness
HRHA	Honorary Member, Royal Hibernian Academy
HRI	Honorary Member, Royal Institute of Painters in Water Colours
HROI	Honorary Member, Royal Institute of Oil Painters
HRSA	Honorary Member, Royal Scottish Academy
HRSW	Honorary Member, Royal Scottish Water Colour Society
HSC	Health and Safety Commission
HSE	Health and Safety Executive
HSH	His (or Her) Serene Highness
Hum.	Humanity, Humanities (Classics)
Hunts	Huntingdonshire
HVCert	Health Visitor's Certificate
Hy	Heavy

I

I	Island; Ireland
IA	Indian Army; Iowa
Ia	Iowa (US)
IAAF	International Amateur Athletic Federation
IAC	Indian Armoured Corps; Institute of Amateur Cinematographers
IACP	International Association of Chiefs of Police
IADB	Inter American Development Bank
IADR	International Association for Dental Research
IAEA	International Atomic Energy Agency
IAF	Indian Air Force; Indian Auxiliary Force
IAHM	Incorporated Association of Headmasters
IAM	Institute of Advanced Motorists; Institute of Aviation Medicine
IAMAS	International Association of Meteorology and Atmospheric Sciences
IAMC	Indian Army Medical Corps
IAMTACT	Institute of Advanced Machine Tool and Control Technology
IAO	Incorporated Association of Organists
IAOC	Indian Army Ordnance Corps
IAPS	Incorporated Association of Preparatory Schools
IAPSO	International Association for the Physical Sciences of the Oceans
IARO	Indian Army Reserve of Officers
IAS	Indian Administrative Service; Institute for Advanced Studies; International Academy of Science
IASC	International Arctic Science Committee
IASS	International Association for Scandinavian Studies
IATA	International Air Transport Association
IATUL	International Association of Technological University Libraries
IAU	International Astronomical Union
IAWPRC	International Association on Water Pollution Research and Control
ib. or **ibid.**	*ibidem* (in the same place)
IBA	Independent Broadcasting Authority; International Bar Association
IBCA	International Braille Chess Association
IBG	Institute of British Geographers (*now see* RGS)
IBRD	International Bank for Reconstruction and Development (World Bank)
IBRO	International Bank Research Organisation; International Brain Research Organisation
IBTE	Institution of British Telecommunications Engineers
i/c	in charge; in command
ICA	Institute of Contemporary Arts; Institute of Chartered Accountants in England and Wales (*now see* ICAEW)
ICAA	Invalid Children's Aid Association
ICAEW	Institute of Chartered Accountants in England and Wales
ICAI	Institute of Chartered Accountants in Ireland
ICAO	International Civil Aviation Organization
ICBP	International Council for Bird Preservation
ICBS	Irish Christian Brothers' School
ICC	International Chamber of Commerce
ICCROM	International Centre for Conservation at Rome
ICD	*Iuris Canonici Doctor* (Doctor of Canon Law); Independence Commemorative Decoration (Rhodesia)
ICE	Institution of Civil Engineers
ICED	International Council for Educational Development
ICEF	International Federation of Chemical, Energy and General Workers' Unions
Icel.	Icelandic
ICES	International Council for the Exploration of the Sea
ICF	International Federation of Chemical and General Workers' Unions (*now see* ICEF)
ICFC	Industrial and Commercial Finance Corporation (later part of Investors in Industry)
ICFTU	International Confederation of Free Trade Unions
ICHCA	International Cargo Handling Co-ordination Association
IChemE	Institution of Chemical Engineers
ICI	Imperial Chemical Industries
ICJ	International Commission of Jurists
ICL	International Computers Ltd
ICM	International Confederation of Midwives
ICMA	Institute of Cost and Management Accountants (*now see* CIMA)
ICME	International Commission for Mathematical Education
ICOM	International Council of Museums
ICOMOS	International Council of Monuments and Sites
ICorrST	Institution of Corrosion Science and Technology
ICPO	International Criminal Police Organization (Interpol)
ICRC	International Committee of the Red Cross
ICRF	Imperial Cancer Research Fund
ICS	Indian Civil Service
ICSA	Institute of Chartered Secretaries and Administrators
ICSD	International Council for Scientific Development
ICSID	International Council of Societies of Industrial Design; International Centre for Settlement of Investment Disputes

ICSS International Committee for the Sociology of Sport
ICSTIS Independent Committee for Supervision of Telephone Information Services
ICSTM Imperial College of Science, Technology and Medicine, London
ICSU International Council of Scientific Unions
ICT International Computers and Tabulators Ltd (*now see* ICL)
ID Independence Decoration (Rhodesia); Idaho
Id Idaho (US)
IDA International Development Association
IDB Internal Drainage Board; Industrial Development Board
IDC Imperial Defence College (*now see* RCDS); Inter-Diocesan Certificate
idc completed a course at, or served for a year on the Staff of, the Imperial Defence College (*now see* rcds)
IDRC International Development Research Centre
IDS Institute of Development Studies; Industry Department for Scotland
IEA Institute of Economic Affairs
IEC International Electrotechnical Commission
IEE Institution of Electrical Engineers
IEEE Institute of Electrical and Electronics Engineers (NY)
IEEIE Institution of Electrical and Electronics Incorporated Engineers (*now see* IEIE)
IEETE Institution of Electrical and Electronics Technician Engineers (later IEEIE; *now see* IEIE)
IEI Institution of Engineers of Ireland
IEIE Institution of Electronics and Electrical Incorporated Engineers
IEME Inspectorate of Electrical and Mechanical Engineering
IEng Incorporated Engineer
IERE Institution of Electronic and Radio Engineers
IES Indian Educational Service; Institution of Engineers and Shipbuilders in Scotland; International Electron Paramagnetic Resonance Society
IExpE Institute of Explosives Engineers
IFAC International Federation of Automatic Control
IFAD International Fund for Agricultural Development (UNO)
IFAW International Fund for Animal Welfare
IFBWW International Federation of Building Woodworkers
IFC International Finance Corporation
IFIAS International Federation of Institutes of Advanced Study
IFIP International Federation for Information Processing
IFL International Friendship League
IFLA International Federation of Library Associations
IFORS International Federation of Operational Research Societies
IFPI International Federation of the Phonographic Industry
IFRA World Press Research Association
IFS Irish Free State; Indian Forest Service
IG Instructor in Gunnery
IGasE Institution of Gas Engineers
IGPP Institute of Geophysics and Planetary Physics
IGS Independent Grammar School
IGU International Geographical Union; International Gas Union
IHA Institute of Health Service Administrators
IHospE Institute of Hospital Engineering
IHSM Institute of Health Services Management
IHVE Institution of Heating and Ventilating Engineers (later CIBS)
IIExE Institution of Incorporated Executive Engineers
IILS International Institute for Labour Studies
IIM Institution of Industrial Managers
IIMR Institute of Investment Management and Research
IIMT International Institute for the Management of Technology
IInfSc Institute of Information Scientists
IIS International Institute of Sociology
IISI International Iron and Steel Institute
IISS International Institute of Strategic Studies
IIT Indian Institute of Technology
IL Illinois
ILA International Law Association
ILEA Inner London Education Authority
ILEC Inner London Education Committee
Ill Illinois (US)
ILO International Labour Office; International Labour Organisation
ILP Independent Labour Party
ILR Independent Local Radio; International Labour Review
IM Individual Merit
IMA International Music Association; Institute of Mathematics and its Applications
IMCB International Management Centre from Buckingham
IMCO Inter-Governmental Maritime Consultative Organization (*now see* IMO)
IME Institute of Medical Ethics
IMEA Incorporated Municipal Electrical Association
IMechE Institution of Mechanical Engineers
IMechIE Institution of Mechanical Incorporated Engineers
IMEDE Institut pour l'Etude des Méthodes de Direction de l'Entreprise
IMF International Monetary Fund
IMGTechE Institution of Mechanical and General Technician Engineers
IMinE Institution of Mining Engineers
IMM Institution of Mining and Metallurgy
IMMLEP Immunology of Leprosy
IMMTS Indian Mercantile Marine Training Ship
IMO International Maritime Organization
Imp. Imperial
IMRO Investment Management Regulatory Organisation
IMS Indian Medical Service; Institute of Management Services; International Military Staff
IMTA Institute of Municipal Treasurers and Accountants (*now see* CIPFA)
IMU International Mathematical Union
IMunE Institution of Municipal Engineers (now amalgamated with Institution of Civil Engineers)
IN Indian Navy; Indiana
INASFMH International Sports Association for People with Mental Handicap
Inc. Incorporated
INCA International Newspaper Colour Association
Incog. Incognito
Ind. Independent; Indiana (US)
Inf. Infantry
INFORM Information Network Focus on New Religious Movements
INSA Indian National Science Academy
INSEA International Society for Education through Art
INSEAD or **Insead** Institut Européen d'Administration des Affaires
Insp. Inspector
Inst. Institute
InstBE Institution of British Engineers
Instn Institution
InstSMM Institute of Sales and Marketing Management
InstT Institute of Transport (*now see* CIT)
INTELSAT International Telecommunications Satellite Organisation
IOB Institute of Banking (*now see* CIOB)
IOC International Olympic Committee; Intergovernmental Oceanographic Commission
IOCD International Organisation for Chemical Science in Development
IODE Imperial Order of the Daughters of the Empire
I of M Isle of Man
IOGT International Order of Good Templars
IOM Isle of Man; Indian Order of Merit
IOOF Independent Order of Odd-fellows
IOP Institute of Painters in Oil Colours
IOTA (Fellow of) Institute of Transport Administration
IoW Isle of Wight
IPA International Publishers' Association
IPCS Institution of Professional Civil Servants
IPFA Member or Associate, Chartered Institute of Public Finance and Accountancy
IPHE Institution of Public Health Engineers (*now see* IWEM)
IPI International Press Institute; Institute of Patentees and Inventors
IPlantE Institution of Plant Engineers (*now see* IIM)
IPM Institute of Personnel Management
IPPA Independent Programme Producers' Association
IPPF International Planned Parenthood Federation
IPPR Institute for Public Policy Research
IPPS Institute of Physics and The Physical Society
IProdE Institution of Production Engineers (later Institution of Manufacturing Engineering; *now see* IEE)
IPS Indian Police Service; Indian Political Service; Institute of Purchasing and Supply
IPU Inter-Parliamentary Union
IRA Irish Republican Army
IRAD Institute for Research on Animal Diseases
IRC Industrial Reorganization Corporation; Interdisciplinary Research Centre
IRCAM Institute for Research and Co-ordination in Acoustics and Music
IRCert Industrial Relations Certificate
IREE(Aust) Institution of Radio and Electronics Engineers (Australia)
IRI Institution of the Rubber Industry (*now see* PRI)
IRO International Refugee Organization
IRPA International Radiation Protection Association
IRRV (Fellow/Member of) Institute of Revenues, Rating and Valuation
IRTE Institute of Road Transport Engineers
IS International Society of Sculptors, Painters and Gravers
Is Island(s)
ISBA Incorporated Society of British Advertisers
ISC Imperial Service College, Haileybury; Indian Staff Corps
ISCM International Society for Contemporary Music
ISCO Independent Schools Careers Organisation
ISE Indian Service of Engineers
ISI International Statistical Institute

ISIS Independent Schools Information Service
ISJC Independent Schools Joint Council
ISM Incorporated Society of Musicians
ISMAR International Society of Magnetic Resonance
ISME International Society for Musical Education
ISMRC Inter-Services Metallurgical Research Council
ISO Imperial Service Order; International Organization for Standardization
ISSA International Social Security Association
ISSTIP International Society for Study of Tension in Performance
ISTC Iron and Steel Trades Confederation; Institute of Scientific and Technical Communicators
ISTD Imperial Society of Teachers of Dancing
IStructE Institution of Structural Engineers
IT Information Technology; Indian Territory (US)
It. or **Ital.** Italian
ITA Independent Television Authority (later IBA)
ITAB Information Technology Advisory Board
ITB Industry Training Board
ITC International Trade Centre; Independent Television Commission
ITCA Independent Television Association (*formerly* Independent Television Companies Association Ltd)
ITDG Intermediate Technology Development Group
ITEME Institution of Technician Engineers in Mechanical Engineering
ITF International Transport Workers' Federation
ITN Independent Television News
ITO International Trade Organization
ITU International Telecommunication Union
ITV Independent Television
ITVA International Television Association
IUA International Union of Architects
IUB International Union of Biochemistry (*now see* IUBMB)
IUBMB International Union of Biochemistry and Molecular Biology
IUC Inter-University Council for Higher Education Overseas (*now see* IUPC)
IUCN World Conservation Union (*formerly* International Union for the Conservation of Nature and Natural Resources)
IUCW International Union for Child Welfare
IUGS International Union of Geological Sciences
IUHPS International Union of the History and Philosophy of Science
IULA International Union of Local Authorities
IUP Association of Independent Unionist Peers
IUPAC International Union of Pure and Applied Chemistry
IUPAP International Union of Pure and Applied Physics
IUPC Inter-University and Polytechnic Council for Higher Education Overseas
IUPS International Union of Physiological Sciences
IUTAM International Union of Theoretical and Applied Mechanics
IVF In-vitro Fertilisation
IVS International Voluntary Service
IWA Inland Waterways Association
IWEM Institution of Water and Environmental Management
IWES Institution of Water Engineers and Scientists (*now see* IWEM)
IWGC Imperial War Graves Commission (*now see* CWGC)
IWM Institution of Works Managers (*now see* IIM)
IWO Institution of Water Officers
IWPC Institute of Water Pollution Control (*now see* IWEM)
IWS International Wool Secretariat
IWSA International Water Supply Association
IWSOM Institute of Practitioners in Work Study Organisation and Methods (*now see* IMS)
IWSP Institute of Work Study Practitioners (*now see* IMS)
IY Imperial Yeomanry
IYRU International Yacht Racing Union
IZ I Zingari

J

JA Judge Advocate
JACT Joint Association of Classical Teachers
JAG Judge Advocate General
Jas James
JCB *Juris Canonici* (or *Civilis*) *Baccalaureus* (Bachelor of Canon (or Civil) Law)
JCR Junior Common Room
JCS Journal of the Chemical Society
JCD *Juris Canonici* (or *Civilis*) *Doctor* (Doctor of Canon (or Civil) Law)
JCI Junior Chamber International
JCL *Juris Canonici* (or *Civilis*) *Licentiatus* (Licentiate in Canon (or Civil) Law)
JCO Joint Consultative Organisation (of AFRC, MAFF, and Department of Agriculture and Fisheries for Scotland)
JD Doctor of Jurisprudence
jd *jure dignitatis* (by virtue of status)
JDipMA Joint Diploma in Management Accounting Services
JG Junior Grade
JInstE Junior Institution of Engineers (*now see* IMGTechE)
jl(s) journal(s)
JMB Joint Matriculation Board
JMN Johan Mangku Negara (Malaysia)
JMOTS Joint Maritime Operational Training Staff
Jno. or **Joh.** John
JP Justice of the Peace
Jr Junior
jsc qualified at a Junior Staff Course, or the equivalent, 1942–46
JSD Doctor of Juristic Science
JSDC Joint Service Defence College
jsdc completed a course at Joint Service Defence College
JSLS Joint Services Liaison Staff
JSM Johan Setia Mahkota (Malaysia)
JSPS Japan Society for the Promotion of Science
JSSC Joint Services Staff College
jssc completed a course at Joint Services Staff College
jt, jtly joint, jointly
JUD *Juris Utriusque Doctor* (Doctor of Both Laws (Canon and Civil))
Jun. Junior
Jun.Opt. Junior Optime
JWS or **jws** Joint Warfare Staff

K

KA Knight of St Andrew, Order of Barbados
Kans Kansas (US)
KAR King's African Rifles
KBE Knight Commander, Order of the British Empire
KC King's Counsel
KCB Knight Commander, Order of the Bath
KCC Commander, Order of the Crown, Belgium and Congo Free State
KCH King's College Hospital; Knight Commander, Hanoverian Order
KCHS Knight Commander, Order of the Holy Sepulchre
KCIE Knight Commander, Order of the Indian Empire
KCL King's College London
KCLJ Knight Commander, Order of St Lazarus of Jerusalem
KCMG Knight Commander, Order of St Michael and St George
KCSA Knight Commander, Military Order of the Collar of St Agatha of Paternò
KCSG Knight Commander, Order of St Gregory the Great
KCSHS Knight Commander with Star, Order of the Holy Sepulchre
KCSI Knight Commander, Order of the Star of India
KCSJ Knight Commander, Order of St John of Jerusalem (Knights Hospitaller)
KCSS Knight Commander, Order of St Silvester
KCVO Knight Commander, Royal Victorian Order
KCVSA King's Commendation for Valuable Services in the Air
KDG King's Dragoon Guards
KEH King Edward's Horse
KEO King Edward's Own
KG Knight, Order of the Garter
KGCSS Knight Grand Cross, Order of St Silvester
KGStJ Knight of Grace, Order of St John of Jerusalem (*now see* KStJ)
KH Knight, Hanoverian Order
KHC Hon. Chaplain to the King
KHDS Hon. Dental Surgeon to the King
KHNS Hon. Nursing Sister to the King
KHP Hon. Physician to the King
KHS Hon. Surgeon to the King; Knight, Order of the Holy Sepulchre
K-i-H Kaisar-i-Hind
KJStJ Knight of Justice, Order of St John of Jerusalem (*now see* KStJ)
KLJ Knight, Order of St Lazarus of Jerusalem
KM Knight of Malta
KORR King's Own Royal Regiment
KOSB King's Own Scottish Borderers
KOYLI King's Own Yorkshire Light Infantry
KP Knight, Order of St Patrick
KPM King's Police Medal
KRRC King's Royal Rifle Corps
KS King's Scholar; Kansas
KSC Knight of St Columba
KSG Knight, Order of St Gregory the Great
KSJ Knight, Order of St John of Jerusalem (Knights Hospitaller)
KSLI King's Shropshire Light Infantry
KSS Knight, Order of St Silvester
KStJ Knight, Most Venerable Order of the Hospital of St John of Jerusalem

KStJ(A)	Associate Knight of Justice, Most Venerable Order of the Hospital of St John of Jerusalem
KT	Knight, Order of the Thistle
Kt	Knight
KY	Kentucky
Ky	Kentucky (US)

L

L	Liberal
LA	Los Angeles; Library Association; Literate in Arts; Liverpool Academy; Louisiana
La	Louisiana (US)
LAA	Light Anti-Aircraft
Lab	Labour
LAC	London Athletic Club
LACSAB	Local Authorities Conditions of Service Advisory Board
LAE	London Association of Engineers
LAMDA	London Academy of Music and Dramatic Art
LAMSAC	Local Authorities' Management Services and Computer Committee
LAMTPI	Legal Associate Member, Town Planning Institute (*now see* LMRTPI)
L-Corp. or **Lance-Corp.**	Lance-Corporal
Lancs	Lancashire
LAPADA	London & Provincial Antique Dealers' Association
LARSP	Language Assessment, Remediation and Screening Procedure
Lautro	Life Assurance and Unit Trust Regulatory Organisation
LBC	London Broadcasting Company
LBHI	Licentiate, British Horological Institute
LC	Cross of Leo
LCAD	London Certificate in Art and Design (University of London)
LCC	London County Council (later GLC)
LCh	Licentiate in Surgery
LCJ	Lord Chief Justice
LCL	Licentiate of Canon Law
LCP	Licentiate, College of Preceptors
LCSP	London and Counties Society of Physiologists
LCST	Licentiate, College of Speech Therapists
LD	Liberal and Democratic; Licentiate in Divinity
LDDC	London Docklands Development Corporation
LDiv	Licentiate in Divinity
LDS	Licentiate in Dental Surgery
LDV	Local Defence Volunteers
LEA	Local Education Authority
LEDU	Local Enterprise Development Unit
LEP	Local Ecumenical Project
LEPRA	British Leprosy Relief Association
LèsL	Licencié ès lettres
LG	Lady Companion, Order of the Garter
LGSM	Licentiate, Guildhall School of Music and Drama
LGTB	Local Government Training Board
LH	Light Horse
LHD	*Literarum Humaniorum Doctor* (Doctor of Literature)
LHSM	Licentiate, Institute of Health Services Management
LI	Light Infantry; Long Island
LIBA	Lloyd's Insurance Brokers' Association
Lib Dem	Liberal Democrat
LIBER	Ligue des Bibliothèques Européennes de Recherche
LicMed	Licentiate in Medicine
Lieut	Lieutenant
LIFFE	London International Financial Futures and Options Exchange
Lincs	Lincolnshire
LIOB	Licentiate, Institute of Building
Lit.	Literature; Literary
LitD	Doctor of Literature; Doctor of Letters
Lit.Hum.	*Literae Humaniores* (Classics)
LittD	Doctor of Literature; Doctor of Letters
LJ	Lord Justice
LLA	Lady Literate in Arts
LLB	Bachelor of Laws
LLCM	Licentiate, London College of Music
LLD	Doctor of Laws
LLL	Licentiate in Laws
LLM	Master of Laws
LM	Licentiate in Midwifery
LMBC	Lady Margaret Boat Club
LMC	Local Medical Committee
LMCC	Licentiate, Medical Council of Canada
LMed	Licentiate in Medicine
LMH	Lady Margaret Hall, Oxford
LMR	London Midland Region (BR)
LMS	London, Midland and Scottish Railway; London Missionary Society
LMSSA	Licentiate in Medicine and Surgery, Society of Apothecaries
LMRTPI	Legal Member, Royal Town Planning Institute
LNat	Liberal National
LNER	London and North Eastern Railway
LOB	Location of Offices Bureau
L of C	Library of Congress; Lines of Communication
LP	Limited Partnership
LPH	Licentiate in Philosophy
LPO	London Philharmonic Orchestra
LPTB	London Passenger Transport Board (later LTE; *now see* LRT)
LRAD	Licentiate, Royal Academy of Dancing
LRAM	Licentiate, Royal Academy of Music
LRCP	Licentiate, Royal College of Physicians, London
LRCPE	Licentiate, Royal College of Physicians, Edinburgh
LRCPI	Licentiate, Royal College of Physicians of Ireland
LRCPSGlas	Licentiate, Royal College of Physicians and Surgeons of Glasgow
LRCS	Licentiate, Royal College of Surgeons of England
LRCSE	Licentiate, Royal College of Surgeons, Edinburgh
LRCSI	Licentiate, Royal College of Surgeons in Ireland
LRFPS(G)	Licentiate, Royal Faculty of Physicians and Surgeons, Glasgow (*now see* LRCPSGlas)
LRIBA	Licentiate, Royal Institute of British Architects (*now see* RIBA)
LRPS	Licentiate, Royal Photographic Society
LRT	London Regional Transport
LSA	Licentiate, Society of Apothecaries; Licence in Agricultural Sciences
LSE	London School of Economics and Political Science
LSHTM	London School of Hygiene and Tropical Medicine
LSO	London Symphony Orchestra
Lt	Lieutenant; Light
LT	London Transport (*now see* LRT); Licentiate in Teaching
LTA	Lawn Tennis Association
LTB	London Transport Board (later LTE; *now see* LRT)
LTCL	Licentiate of Trinity College of Music, London
Lt Col	Lieutenant Colonel
LTE	London Transport Executive (*now see* LRT)
Lt Gen.	Lieutenant General
LTh	Licentiate in Theology
LU	Liberal Unionist
LUOTC	London University Officers' Training Corps
LVO	Lieutenant, Royal Victorian Order (*formerly* MVO (Fourth Class))
LWT	London Weekend Television
LXX	Septuagint

M

M	Marquess; Member; Monsieur
m	married
MA	Master of Arts; Military Assistant; Massachusetts
MAA	Manufacturers' Agents Association of Great Britain
MAAF	Mediterranean Allied Air Forces
MAAT	Member, Association of Accounting Technicians
MACE	Member, Australian College of Education; Member, Association of Conference Executives
MACI	Member, American Concrete Institute
MACM	Member, Association of Computing Machines
MACS	Member, American Chemical Society
MADO	Member, Association of Dispensing Opticians
MAE	Member, Academia Europaea
MAEE	Marine Aircraft Experimental Establishment
MAF	Ministry of Agriculture and Fisheries
MAFF	Ministry of Agriculture, Fisheries and Food
MAI	*Magister in Arte Ingeniaria* (Master of Engineering)
MAIAA	Member, American Institute of Aeronautics and Astronautics
MAICE	Member, American Institute of Consulting Engineers
MAIChE	Member, American Institute of Chemical Engineers
Maj. Gen.	Major General
MALD	Master of Arts in Law and Diplomacy
Man	Manitoba (Canada)
M&A	Mergers and Acquisitions
MAO	Master of Obstetric Art
MAOT	Member, Association of Occupational Therapists
MAOU	Member, American Ornithologists' Union
MAP	Ministry of Aircraft Production
MAPsS	Member, Australian Psychological Society
MARAC	Member, Australasian Register of Agricultural Consultants
MArch	Master of Architecture
Marq.	Marquess
MASAE	Member, American Society of Agricultural Engineers
MASC	Member, Australian Society of Calligraphers

MASc Master of Applied Science
MASCE Member, American Society of Civil Engineers
MASME Member, American Society of Mechanical Engineers
Mass Massachusetts (US)
MATh Master of Arts in Theology
Math. Mathematics; Mathematical
MATSA Managerial Administrative Technical Staff Association
MAusIMM Member, Australasian Institute of Mining and Metallurgy
MB Medal of Bravery (Canada); Bachelor of Medicine
MBA Master of Business Administration
MBASW Member, British Association of Social Workers
MBC Metropolitan/Municipal Borough Council
MBCS Member, British Computer Society
MBE Member, Order of the British Empire
MBES Member, Biological Engineering Society
MBFR Mutual and Balanced Force Reductions (negotiations)
MBHI Member, British Horological Institute
MBIFD Member, British Institute of Funeral Directors
MBIM Member, British Institute of Management (*now see* MIMgt)
MBKS Member, British Kinematograph Society (*now see* MBKSTS)
MBKSTS Member, British Kinematograph, Sound and Television Society
MBOU Member, British Ornithologists' Union
MBPICS Member, British Production and Inventory Control Society
MBritIRE Member, British Institution of Radio Engineers (later MIERE; *now see* MIEE)
MBS Member, Building Societies Institute (*now see* MCBSI)
MBSc Master of Business Science
MC Military Cross; Missionaries of Charity
MCAM Member, CAM Foundation
MCB Master in Clinical Biochemistry
MCBSI Member, Chartered Building Societies Institute
MCC Marylebone Cricket Club; Metropolitan County Council
MCCDRCS Member in Clinical Community Dentistry, Royal College of Surgeons
MCD Master of Civic Design
MCE Master of Civil Engineering
MCFP Member, College of Family Physicians (Canada)
MCh or **MChir** Master in Surgery
MChE Master of Chemical Engineering
MChemA Master in Chemical Analysis
MChOrth Master of Orthopaedic Surgery
MCIBS Member, Chartered Institution of Building Services (*now see* MCIBSE)
MCIBSE Member, Chartered Institution of Building Services Engineers
MCIH Member, Chartered Institute of Housing
MCIM Member, Chartered Institute of Marketing
MCIOB Member, Chartered Institute of Building
M.CIRP Member, International Institution for Production Engineering Research
MCIS Member, Institute of Chartered Secretaries and Administrators
MCIT Member, Chartered Institute of Transport
MCIWEM Member, Chartered Institution of Water and Environmental Management
MCL Master in Civil Law
MCMES Member, Civil and Mechanical Engineers' Society
MCom Master of Commerce
MConsE Member, Association of Consulting Engineers
MConsEI Member, Association of Consulting Engineers of Ireland
MCOphth Member, College of Ophthalmologists (*now see* MRCOphth)
MCP Member of Colonial Parliament; Master of City Planning (US)
MCPA Member, College of Pathologists of Australia (*now see* MRCPA)
MCPath Member, College of Pathologists (*now see* MRCPath)
MCPP Member, College of Pharmacy Practice
MCPS Member, College of Physicians and Surgeons
MCS Madras Civil Service; Malayan Civil Service
MCSD Member, Chartered Society of Designers
MCSEE Member, Canadian Society of Electrical Engineers
MCSP Member, Chartered Society of Physiotherapy
MCST Member, College of Speech Therapists
MCT Member, Association of Corporate Treasurers
MD Doctor of Medicine; Military District; Maryland
Md Maryland (US)
MDC Metropolitan District Council
MDes Master of Design
MDS Master of Dental Surgery
MDSc Master of Dental Science
Me Maine (US)
ME Mining Engineer; Middle East; Master of Engineering; Maine
MEAF Middle East Air Force
MEC Member of Executive Council; Middle East Command
MEc Master of Economics
MECAS Middle East Centre for Arab Studies
Mech. Mechanics; Mechanical
MECI Member, Institute of Employment Consultants
Med. Medical
MEd Master of Education
MEF Middle East Force
MEIC Member, Engineering Institute of Canada
MELF Middle East Land Forces
Mencap Royal Society for Mentally Handicapped Children and Adults
MEng Master of Engineering
MEO Marine Engineering Officer
MEP Member of the European Parliament
MESc Master of Engineering Science
MetR Metropolitan Railway
MetSoc Metals Society (formed by amalgamation of Institute of Metals and Iron and Steel Institute; now merged with Institution of Metallurgists to form Institute of Metals)
MEXE Military Engineering Experimental Establishment
MF Master of Forestry
MFA Master of Fine Arts
MFC Mastership in Food Control
MFCM Member, Faculty of Community Medicine (*now see* MFPHM)
MFGB Miners' Federation of Great Britain (*now see* NUM)
MFH Master of Foxhounds
MFHom Member, Faculty of Homœopathy
MFOM Member, Faculty of Occupational Medicine
MFPaed Member, Faculty of Paediatrics, Royal College of Physicians of Ireland
MFPHM Member, Faculty of Public Health Medicine
MGA Major General in charge of Administration
MGC Machine Gun Corps
MGDSRCS Member in General Dental Surgery, Royal College of Surgeons
MGGS Major General, General Staff
MGI Member, Institute of Certificated Grocers
MGO Master General of the Ordnance; Master of Gynaecology and Obstetrics
Mgr Monsignor
MHA Member of House of Assembly
MHCIMA Member, Hotel Catering and Institutional Management Association
MHK Member of the House of Keys
MHort (RHS) Master of Horticulture, Royal Horticultural Society
MHR Member of the House of Representatives
MHRA Modern Humanities Research Association
MHRF Mental Health Research Fund
MHSM Member, Institute of Health Services Management
MI Military Intelligence; Michigan
MIAeE Member, Institute of Aeronautical Engineers
MIAgrE Member, Institution of Agricultural Engineers
MIAM Member, Institute of Administrative Management
MIAS Member, Institute of Aeronautical Science (US) (*now see* MAIAA)
MIBC Member, Institute of Business Counsellors
MIBF Member, Institute of British Foundrymen
MIBiol Member, Institute of Biology
MIBritE Member, Institution of British Engineers
MIB(Scot) Member, Institute of Bankers in Scotland
MICE Member, Institution of Civil Engineers
MICEI Member, Institution of Civil Engineers of Ireland
MICFor Member, Institute of Chartered Foresters
Mich Michigan (US)
MIChemE Member, Institution of Chemical Engineers
MICM Member, Institute of Credit Management
MICorrST Member, Institution of Corrosion Science and Technology
MICS Member, Institute of Chartered Shipbrokers
MIDPM Member, Institute of Data Processing Management
MIE(Aust) Member, Institution of Engineers, Australia
MIED Member, Institution of Engineering Designers
MIEE Member, Institution of Electrical Engineers
MIEEE Member, Institute of Electrical and Electronics Engineers (NY)
MIEEM Member, Institute of Ecology and Environmental Management
MIEI Member, Institution of Engineering Inspection
MIEIE Member, Institution of Electronics and Electrical Incorporated Engineers
MIE(Ind) Member, Institution of Engineers, India
MIEnvSc Member, Institute of Environmental Science
MIERE Member, Institution of Electronic and Radio Engineers (*now see* MIEE)
MIES Member, Institution of Engineers and Shipbuilders, Scotland
MIET Member, Institute of Engineers and Technicians
MIEx Member, Institute of Export
MIExpE Member, Institute of Explosives Engineers
MIFA Member, Institute of Field Archaeologists
MIFF Member, Institute of Freight Forwarders
MIFireE Member, Institution of Fire Engineers
MIFM Member, Institute of Fisheries Management
MIFor Member, Institute of Foresters (*now see* MICFor)
MIGasE Member, Institution of Gas Engineers

MIGeol Member, Institution of Geologists
MIH Member, Institute of Housing (*now see* MCIH)
MIHM Member, Institute of Housing Managers (later MIH)
MIHort Member, Institute of Horticulture
MIHT Member, Institution of Highways and Transportation
MIHVE Member, Institution of Heating and Ventilating Engineers (later MCIBS)
MIIA Member, Institute of Industrial Administration (later FBIM)
MIIM Member, Institution of Industrial Managers
MIInfSc Member, Institute of Information Sciences
MIL Member, Institute of Linguists
Mil. Military
MILGA Member, Institute of Local Government Administrators
MILocoE Member, Institution of Locomotive Engineers
MIM Member, Institute of Metals (*formerly* Institution of Metallurgists)
MIMarE Member, Institute of Marine Engineers
MIMC Member, Institute of Management Consultants
MIMechE Member, Institution of Mechanical Engineers
MIMEMME Member, Institution of Mining Electrical & Mining Mechanical Engineers
MIMgt Member, Institute of Management
MIMGTechE Member, Institution of Mechanical and General Technician Engineers
MIMI Member, Institute of the Motor Industry
MIMinE Member, Institution of Mining Engineers
MIMM Member, Institution of Mining and Metallurgy
MIMunE Member, Institution of Municipal Engineers (now amalgamated with Institution of Civil Engineers)
MIN Member, Institute of Navigation (*now see* MRIN)
Min. Ministry
Minn Minnesota (US)
MInstAM Member, Institute of Administrative Management
MInstBE Member, Institution of British Engineers
MInstCE Member, Institution of Civil Engineers (*now see* FICE)
MInstD Member, Institute of Directors
MInstE Member, Institute of Energy
MInstEnvSci Member, Institute of Environmental Sciences
MInstF Member, Institute of Fuel (*now see* MInstE)
MInstHE Member, Institution of Highway Engineers (*now see* MIHT)
MInstM Member, Institute of Marketing (*now see* MCIM)
MInstMC Member, Institute of Measurement and Control
MInstME Member, Institution of Mining Engineers
MInstMet Member, Institute of Metals (later part of Metals Society, *now see* MIM)
MInstP Member, Institute of Physics
MInstPet Member, Institute of Petroleum
MInstPI Member, Institute of Patentees and Inventors
MInstPkg Member, Institute of Packaging
MInstPS Member, Institute of Purchasing and Supply
MInstR Member, Institute of Refrigeration
MInstRA Member, Institute of Registered Architects
MInstT Member, Institute of Transport (*now see* MCIT)
MInstTM Member, Institute of Travel Managers in Industry and Commerce
MInstW Member, Institute of Welding (*now see* MWeldI)
MInstWM Member, Institute of Wastes Management
MINucE Member, Institution of Nuclear Engineers
MIOA Member, Institute of Acoustics
MIOB Member, Institute of Building (*now see* MCIOB)
MIOM Member, Institute of Office Management (*now see* MIAM)
MIOSH Member, Institution of Occupational Safety and Health
MIPA Member, Institute of Practitioners in Advertising
MIPD Member, Institute of Personnel and Development
MIPlantE Member, Institution of Plant Engineers (*now see* MIIM)
MIPM Member, Institute of Personnel Management (*now see* MIPD)
MIPR Member, Institute of Public Relations
MIProdE Member, Institution of Production Engineers (*now see* MIEE)
MIQ Member, Institute of Quarrying
MIQA Member, Institute of Quality Assurance
MIRE Member, Institution of Radio Engineers (later MIERE)
MIREE(Aust) Member, Institution of Radio and Electronics Engineers (Australia)
MIRO Mineral Industry Research Organisation
MIRT Member, Institute of Reprographic Technicians
MIRTE Member, Institute of Road Transport Engineers
MIS Member, Institute of Statisticians
MISI Member, Iron and Steel Institute (later part of Metals Society)
MIS(India) Member, Institution of Surveyors of India
Miss Mississippi (US)
MIStructE Member, Institution of Structural Engineers
MIT Massachusetts Institute of Technology
MITA Member, Industrial Transport Association
MITD Member, Institute of Training and Development (*now see* MIPD)
MITE Member, Institution of Electrical and Electronics Technician Engineers
MITI Member, Institute of Translation & Interpreting
MITT Member, Institute of Travel and Tourism
MIWE Member, Institution of Water Engineers (later MIWES; then MIWEM; *now see* MCIWEM)
MIWEM Member, Institution of Water and Environmental Management (*now see* MCIWEM)
MIWES Member, Institution of Water Engineers and Scientists (later MIWEM; *now see* MCIWEM)
MIWM Member, Institution of Works Managers (*now see* MIIM)
MIWPC Member, Institute of Water Pollution Control (later MIWEM; *now see* MCIWEM)
MIWSP Member, Institute of Work Study Practitioners (*now see* MMS)
MJA Medical Journalists Association
MJI Member, Institute of Journalists
MJIE Member, Junior Institution of Engineers (*now see* MIGTechE)
MJS Member, Japan Society
MJur *Magister Juris* (Master of Law)
ML Licentiate in Medicine; Master of Laws
MLA Member of Legislative Assembly; Modern Language Association; Master in Landscape Architecture
MLC Member of Legislative Council
MLCOM Member, London College of Osteopathic Medicine
MLitt Master of Letters
Mlle Mademoiselle
MLM Member, Order of the Legion of Merit (Rhodesia)
MLO Military Liaison Officer
MLR Modern Language Review
MM Military Medal; Merchant Marine
MMA Metropolitan Museum of Art
MMB Milk Marketing Board
MMD Movement for Multi-Party Democracy
MME Master of Mining Engineering
Mme Madame
MMechE Master of Mechanical Engineering
MMet Master of Metallurgy
MMGI Member, Mining, Geological and Metallurgical Institute of India
MMin Master of Ministry
MMM Member, Order of Military Merit (Canada)
MMS Member, Institute of Management Services
MMSA Master of Midwifery, Society of Apothecaries
MN Merchant Navy; Minnesota
MNAS Member, National Academy of Sciences (US)
MNECInst Member, North East Coast Institution of Engineers and Shipbuilders
MNI Member, Nautical Institute
MNSE Member, Nigerian Society of Engineers
MNZIS Member, New Zealand Institute of Surveyors
MNZPI Member, New Zealand Planning Institute
MO Medical Officer; Military Operations; Missouri
Mo Missouri (US)
MoD Ministry of Defence
Mods Moderations (Oxford)
MOF Ministry of Food
MOH Medical Officer(s) of Health
MOI Ministry of Information
MOMI Museum of the Moving Image
Mon Monmouthshire
Mont Montana (US); Montgomeryshire
MOP Ministry of Power
MOrthRCS Member in Orthodontics, Royal College of Surgeons
MoS Ministry of Supply
Most Rev. Most Reverend
MoT Ministry of Transport
MOV Member, Order of Volta (Ghana)
MP Member of Parliament
MPA Master of Public Administration; Member, Parliamentary Assembly, Northern Ireland
MPBW Ministry of Public Building and Works
MPH Master of Public Health
MPIA Master of Public and International Affairs
MPMI Member, Property Management Institute
MPO Management and Personnel Office
MPP Member, Provincial Parliament
MPRISA Member, Public Relations Institute of South Africa
MPS Member, Pharmaceutical Society (*now see* MRPharmS)
MR Master of the Rolls; Municipal Reform
MRAC Member, Royal Agricultural College
MRACP Member, Royal Australasian College of Physicians
MRACS Member, Royal Australasian College of Surgeons
MRAeS Member, Royal Aeronautical Society
MRAIC Member, Royal Architectural Institute of Canada
MRAS Member, Royal Asiatic Society
MRC Medical Research Council

MRCA Multi-Role Combat Aircraft
MRCGP Member, Royal College of General Practitioners
MRC-LMB Medical Research Council Laboratory of Molecular Biology
MRCOG Member, Royal College of Obstetricians and Gynaecologists
MRCOphth Member, Royal College of Ophthalmologists
MRCP Member, Royal College of Physicians, London
MRCPA Member, Royal College of Pathologists of Australia
MRCPath Member, Royal College of Pathologists
MRCPE Member, Royal College of Physicians, Edinburgh
MRCPGlas Member, Royal College of Physicians and Surgeons of Glasgow
MRCPI Member, Royal College of Physicians of Ireland
MRCPsych Member, Royal College of Psychiatrists
MRCS Member, Royal College of Surgeons of England
MRCSE Member, Royal College of Surgeons of Edinburgh
MRCSI Member, Royal College of Surgeons in Ireland
MRCVS Member, Royal College of Veterinary Surgeons
MRE Master of Religious Education
MRES or **MREmpS** Member, Royal Empire Society
MRHS Member, Royal Horticultural Society
MRI Member, Royal Institution
MRIA Member, Royal Irish Academy
MRIAI Member, Royal Institute of the Architects of Ireland
MRIC Member, Royal Institute of Chemistry (*now see* MRSC)
MRIN Member, Royal Institute of Navigation
MRINA Member, Royal Institution of Naval Architects
MRPharmS Member, Royal Pharmaceutical Society
MRSanI Member, Royal Sanitary Institute (*now see* MRSH)
MRSC Member, Royal Society of Chemistry
MRSH Member, Royal Society for the Promotion of Health
MRSL Member, Order of the Republic of Sierra Leone
MRSM or **MRSocMed** Member, Royal Society of Medicine
MRST Member, Royal Society of Teachers
MRTPI Member, Royal Town Planning Institute
MRurSc Master of Rural Science
MRUSI Member, Royal United Service Institution
MRVA Member, Rating and Valuation Association
MS Master of Surgery; Master of Science (US); Mississippi
MS, MSS Manuscript, Manuscripts
MSA Master of Science, Agriculture (US); Mineralogical Society of America
MSAAIE Member, Southern African Association of Industrial Editors
MSAE Member, Society of Automotive Engineeers (US)
MSAICE Member, South African Institution of Civil Engineers
MSAInstMM Member, South African Institute of Mining and Metallurgy
MS&R Merchant Shipbuilding and Repairs
MSAutE Member, Society of Automobile Engineers
MSC Manpower Services Commission; Missionaries of the Sacred Heart; Madras Staff Corps
MSc Master of Science
MScD Master of Dental Science
MSD Meritorious Service Decoration (Fiji)
MSE Master of Science in Engineering (US)
MSF (Union for) Manufacturing, Science, Finance
MSH Master of Stag Hounds
MSI Member, Securities Institute
MSIAD Member, Society of Industrial Artists and Designers (*now see* MCSD)
MSINZ Member, Surveyors' Institute of New Zealand
MSIT Member, Society of Instrument Technology (*now see* MInstMC)
MSM Meritorious Service Medal; Madras Sappers and Miners
MSN Master of Science in Nursing
MSocIS Member, Société des Ingénieurs et Scientifiques de France
MSocSc Master of Social Sciences
MSocWork Master of Social Work
MSR Member, Society of Radiographers
MSt Master of Studies
MSTD Member, Society of Typographic Designers
MT Mechanical Transport; Montana
Mt Mount, Mountain
MTA Music Trades Association
MTAI Member, Institute of Travel Agents
MTB Motor Torpedo Boat
MTCA Ministry of Transport and Civil Aviation
MTD Midwife Teachers' Diploma
MTech Master of Technology
MTEFL Master in the Teaching of English as a Foreign or Second Language
MTh Master of Theology
MTIRA Machine Tool Industry Research Association (*now see* AMTRI)
MTPI Member, Town Planning Institute (*now see* MRTPI)
MTS Master of Theological Studies
MUniv Honorary Master of the University
MusB Bachelor of Music
MusD Doctor of Music
MusM Master of Music
MV Merchant Vessel, Motor Vessel (naval)
MVEE Military Vehicles and Engineering Establishment
MVO Member, Royal Victorian Order
MVSc Master of Veterinary Science
MW Master of Wine
MWA Mystery Writers of America
MWeldI Member, Welding Institute
MWSOM Member, Institute of Practitioners in Work Study Organisation and Methods (*now see* MMS)

N

N Nationalist; Navigating Duties; North
n nephew
NA National Academician (America)
NAACP National Association for the Advancement of Colored People
NAAFI Navy, Army and Air Force Institutes
NAAS National Agricultural Advisory Service
NAB National Advisory Body for Public Sector Higher Education
NABC National Association of Boys' Clubs
NAC National Agriculture Centre
NACAB National Association of Citizens' Advice Bureaux
NACCB National Accreditation Council for Certification Bodies
NACETT National Advisory Council for Education and Training
NACF National Art-Collections Fund
NACRO National Association for the Care and Resettlement of Offenders
NADFAS National Association of Decorative and Fine Arts Societies
NAE National Academy of Engineering
NAEW Nato Airborn Early Warning
NAHA National Association of Health Authorities (*now see* NAHAT)
NAHAT National Association of Health Authorities and Trusts
NALGO or **Nalgo** National and Local Government Officers' Association
NAMAS National Measurement and Accreditation Service
NAMCW National Association for Maternal and Child Welfare
NAMH MIND (National Association for Mental Health)
NAMMA NATO MRCA Management Agency
NAPT National Association for the Prevention of Tuberculosis
NARM National Association of Recording Merchandisers (US)
NAS National Academy of Sciences
NASA National Aeronautics and Space Administration (US)
NASDIM National Association of Security Dealers and Investment Managers (later FIMBRA)
NAS/UWT National Association of Schoolmasters/Union of Women Teachers
NATCS National Air Traffic Control Services (*now see* NATS)
NATFHE National Association of Teachers in Further and Higher Education (combining ATCDE and ATTI)
NATLAS National Testing Laboratory Accreditation Scheme
NATO North Atlantic Treaty Organisation
NATS National Air Traffic Services
Nat. Sci. Natural Sciences
NATSOPA National Society of Operative Printers, Graphical and Media Personnel (*formerly* of Operative Printers and Assistants)
NAYC Youth Clubs UK (*formerly* National Association of Youth Clubs)
NB New Brunswick; Nebraska
NBA North British Academy
NBC National Book Council (later NBL); National Broadcasting Company (US)
NBL National Book League
NBPI National Board for Prices and Incomes
NC National Certificate; North Carolina (US)
NCA National Certificate of Agriculture
NCARB National Council of Architectural Registration Boards
NCB National Coal Board
NCC National Computing Centre; Nature Conservancy Council (*now see* NCCE); National Consumer Council
NCCE Nature Conservancy Council for England (English Nature)
NCCI National Committee for Commonwealth Immigrants
NCCL National Council for Civil Liberties
NCD National Capital District, Papua New Guinea
NCDAD National Council for Diplomas in Art and Design
NCET National Council for Educational Technology
NCH National Children's Homes
NCLC National Council of Labour Colleges
NCOPF National Council for One Parent Families
NCSE National Council for Special Education
NCSS National Council of Social Service
NCTA National Community Television Association (US)

NCTJ National Council for the Training of Journalists
NCU National Cyclists' Union
NCVCCO National Council of Voluntary Child Care Organisations
NCVO National Council for Voluntary Organisations
NCVQ National Council for Vocational Qualifications
ND North Dakota
NDA National Diploma in Agriculture
NDak North Dakota (US)
ndc National Defence College
NDD National Diploma in Dairying; National Diploma in Design
NDH National Diploma in Horticulture
NDIC National Defence Industries Council
NDP New Democratic Party
NDTA National Defense Transportation Association (US)
NE North-east
NEAB Northern Examinations and Assessment Board
NEAC New English Art Club
NEAF Near East Air Force
NEARELF Near East Land Forces
NEB National Enterprise Board
Neb Nebraska (US)
NEBSS National Examinations Board for Supervisory Studies
NEC National Executive Committee
NECCTA National Education Closed Circuit Television Association
NECInst North East Coast Institution of Engineers and Shipbuilders
NEDC National Economic Development Council; North East Development Council
NEDO National Economic Development Office
NEH National Endowment for the Humanities
NEL National Engineering Laboratory
NERC Natural Environment Research Council
Nev Nevada (US)
New M New Mexico (US)
NFC National Freight Consortium (*formerly* Corporation, then Company)
NFCG National Federation of Consumer Groups
NFER National Foundation for Educational Research
NFHA National Federation of Housing Associations
NFMS National Federation of Music Societies
NFS National Fire Service
NFSH National Federation of Spiritual Healers
NFT National Film Theatre
NFU National Farmers' Union
NFWI National Federation of Women's Institutes
NGO Non-Governmental Organisation(s)
NGTE National Gas Turbine Establishment
NH New Hampshire (US)
NHBC National House-Building Council
NHS National Health Service
NI Northern Ireland; Native Infantry
NIAB National Institute of Agricultural Botany
NIACRO Northern Ireland Association for the Care and Resettlement of Offenders
NIAE National Institute of Agricultural Engineering
NIAID National Institute of Allergy and Infectious Diseases
NICEC National Institute for Careers Education and Counselling
NICG Nationalised Industries Chairmen's Group
NICS Northern Ireland Civil Service
NID Naval Intelligence Division; National Institute for the Deaf; Northern Ireland District; National Institute of Design (India)
NIESR National Institute of Economic and Social Research
NIH National Institutes of Health (US)
NIHCA Northern Ireland Hotels and Caterers Association
NII Nuclear Installations Inspectorate
NILP Northern Ireland Labour Party
NIMR National Institute for Medical Research
NISTRO Northern Ireland Science and Technology Regional Organisation
NJ New Jersey (US)
NL National Liberal; No Liability
NLCS North London Collegiate School
NLF National Liberal Federation
NLYL National League of Young Liberals
NM New Mexico
NMR Nuclear Magnetic Resonance
NNMA Nigerian National Merit Award
NNOM Nigerian National Order of Merit
Northants Northamptonshire
NOTB National Ophthalmic Treatment Board
Notts Nottinghamshire
NP Notary Public
NPA Newspaper Publishers' Association
NPFA National Playing Fields Association
NPk Nishan-e-Pakistan
NPL National Physical Laboratory
NRA National Rifle Association; National Recovery Administration (US); National Rivers Authority
NRAO National Radio Astronomy Observatory
NRCC National Research Council of Canada
NRD National Registered Designer
NRDC National Research Development Corporation
NRPB National Radiological Protection Board
NRR Northern Rhodesia Regiment
NS Nova Scotia; New Style in the Calendar (in Great Britain since 1752); National Society; National Service
ns Graduate of Royal Naval Staff College, Greenwich
NSA National Skating Association
NSAIV Distinguished Order of Shaheed Ali (Maldives)
NSF National Science Foundation (US)
NSM Non-Stipendiary Minister
NSMHC National Society for Mentally Handicapped Children (*now see* Mencap)
NSPCC National Society for Prevention of Cruelty to Children
NSQT National Society for Quality through Teamwork
NSRA National Small-bore Rifle Association
N/SSF Novice, Society of St Francis
NSTC Nova Scotia Technical College
NSW New South Wales
NT New Testament; Northern Territory (Australia); National Theatre (*now see* RNT); National Trust
NT&SA National Trust & Savings Association
NTDA National Trade Development Association
NTUC National Trades Union Congress
NUAAW National Union of Agricultural and Allied Workers
NUBE National Union of Bank Employees (*now see* BIFU)
NUFLAT National Union of Footwear Leather and Allied Trades (*now see* NUKFAT)
NUGMW National Union of General and Municipal Workers (later GMBATU)
NUHKW National Union of Hosiery and Knitwear Workers (*now see* NUKFAT)
NUI National University of Ireland
NUJ National Union of Journalists
NUJMB Northern Universities Joint Matriculation Board
NUKFAT National Union of Knitwear, Footwear and Apparel Trades
NUM National Union of Mineworkers
NUMAST National Union of Marine, Aviation and Shipping Transport Officers
NUPE National Union of Public Employees
NUR National Union of Railwaymen (*now see* RMT)
NUS National Union of Students
NUT National Union of Teachers
NUTG National Union of Townswomen's Guilds
NUTN National Union of Trained Nurses
NUU New University of Ulster
NV Nevada
NVQ National Vocational Qualification
NW North-west
NWC National Water Council
NWFP North-West Frontier Province
NWP North-Western Province
NWT North-Western Territories
NY New York
NYC New York City
NYO National Youth Orchestra
NZ New Zealand
NZEF New Zealand Expeditionary Force
NZIA New Zealand Institute of Architects
NZRSA New Zealand Retired Services Association

O

O Ohio (US)
o only
OA Officier d'Académie
OAM Medal of the Order of Australia
O & E Operations and Engineers (US)
O & M organisation and method
O & O Oriental and Occidental Steamship Co.
OAS Organisation of American States; On Active Service
OASC Officer Aircrew Selection Centre
OAU Organisation for African Unity
OB Order of Barbados
ob *obiit* (died)
OBE Officer, Order of the British Empire
OBI Order of British India
OC Officer, Order of Canada (equivalent to former award SM)
OC or **o/c** Officer Commanding

o c	only child
OCA	Old Comrades Association
OCC	Order of the Caribbean Community
OCDS or **ocds Can**	Overseas College of Defence Studies (Canada)
OCF	Officiating Chaplain to the Forces
OCS	Officer Candidates School
OCSS	Oxford and Cambridge Shakespeare Society
OCTU	Officer Cadet Training Unit
OCU	Operational Conversion Unit
OD	Officer, Order of Distinction (Jamaica)
ODA	Overseas Development Administration
ODI	Overseas Development Institute
ODM	Ministry of Overseas Development
ODSM	Order of Diplomatic Service Merit (Lesotho)
OE	Order of Excellence (Guyana)
OEA	Overseas Education Association
OECD	Organization for Economic Co-operation and Development
OED	Oxford English Dictionary
OEEC	Organization for European Economic Co-operation (*now see* OECD)
OF	Order of the Founder, Salvation Army
OFEMA	Office Française d'Exportation de Matériel Aéronautique
OFFER	Office of Electricity Regulation
OFM	Order of Friars Minor (Franciscans)
OFMCap	Order of Friars Minor Capuchin (Franciscans)
OFMConv	Order of Friars Minor Conventual (Franciscans)
OFR	Order of the Federal Republic of Nigeria
OFS	Orange Free State
OFSTED	Office for Standards in Education
OFT	Office of Fair Trading
Oftel	Office of Telecommunications
OGS	Oratory of the Good Shepherd
OH	Ohio
OHMS	On His (or Her) Majesty's Service
O i/c	Officer in charge
OJ	Order of Jamaica
OK	Oklahoma
OL	Officer, Order of Leopold; Order of the Leopard (Lesotho)
OLJ	Officer, Order of St Lazarus of Jerusalem
OLM	Officer, Legion of Merit (Rhodesia)
OM	Order of Merit
OMCS	Office of the Minister for the Civil Service
OMI	Oblate of Mary Immaculate
OMM	Officer, Order of Military Merit (Canada)
ON	Order of the Nation (Jamaica)
OND	Ordinary National Diploma
Ont	Ontario
ONZ	Order of New Zealand
OO	Order of Ontario
OON	Officer, Order of the Niger
OP	*Ordinis Praedicatorum* (of the Order of Preachers (Dominican)); Observation Post
OPCON	Operational Control
OPCS	Office of Population Censuses and Surveys
OPSS	Office of Public Service and Science
OQ	Officer, National Order of Quebec
OR	Order of Rorima (Guyana); Operational Research; Oregon
ORC	Orange River Colony
Ore	Oregon (US)
ORGALIME	Organisme de Liaison des Industries Métalliques Européennes
ORL	Otorhinolaryngology
ORS	Operational Research Society
ORSA	Operations Research Society of America
ORSL	Order of the Republic of Sierra Leone
ORT	Organization for Rehabilitation through Training
ORTF	Office de la Radiodiffusion et Télévision Française
o s	only son
OSA	Order of St Augustine (Augustinian); Ontario Society of Artists
OSB	Order of St Benedict (Benedictine)
osc	Graduate of Overseas Staff College
OSFC	Franciscan (Capuchin) Order
O/Sig	Ordinary Signalman
OSNC	Orient Steam Navigation Co.
osp	*obiit sine prole* (died without issue)
OSRD	Office of Scientific Research and Development
OSS	Office of Strategic Services
OST	Office of Science and Technology
OStJ	Officer, Most Venerable Order of the Hospital of St John of Jerusalem
OSUK	Ophthalmological Society of the United Kingdom
OT	Old Testament
OTC	Officers' Training Corps
OTL	Officer, Order of Toussaint L'Ouverture (Haiti)
OTU	Operational Training Unit
OTWSA	Ou-Testamentiese Werkgemeenskap in Suider-Afrika
OU	Oxford University; Open University
OUAC	Oxford University Athletic Club
OUAFC	Oxford University Association Football Club
OUBC	Oxford University Boat Club
OUCC	Oxford University Cricket Club
OUDS	Oxford University Dramatic Society
OUP	Oxford University Press; Official Unionist Party
OURC	Oxford University Rifle Club
OURFC	Oxford University Rugby Football Club
OURT	Order of the United Republic of Tanzania
Oxon	Oxfordshire; *Oxoniensis* (of Oxford)

P

PA	Pakistan Army; Personal Assistant; Pennsylvania
Pa	Pennsylvania (US)
PAA	President, Australian Academy of Science
pac	passed the final examination of the Advanced Class, The Military College of Science
PACE	Protestant and Catholic Encounter
PAg	Professional Agronomist
P&O	Peninsular and Oriental Steamship Co.
P&OSNCo.	Peninsular and Oriental Steam Navigation Co.
PAO	Prince Albert's Own
PASI	Professional Associate, Chartered Surveyors' Institution (*now see* ARICS)
PBS	Public Broadcasting Service
PC	Privy Counsellor; Police Constable; Perpetual Curate; Peace Commissioner (Ireland); Progressive Conservative (Canada)
pc	*per centum* (in the hundred)
PCC	Parochial Church Council
PCE	Postgraduate Certificate of Education
PCEF	Polytechnic and Colleges Employers' Forum
PCFC	Polytechnics and Colleges Funding Council
PCL	Polytechnic of Central London
PCMO	Principal Colonial Medical Officer
PdD	Doctor of Pedagogy (US)
PDG	Président Directeur Général
PDR	People's Democratic Republic
PDRA	post doctoral research assistant
PDSA	People's Dispensary for Sick Animals
PDTC	Professional Dancer's Training Course Diploma
PE	Procurement Executive
PEI	Prince Edward Island
PEN	Poets, Playwrights, Editors, Essayists, Novelists (Club)
PEng	Registered Professional Engineer (Canada); Member, Society of Professional Engineers
Penn	Pennsylvania
PEP	Political and Economic Planning (*now see* PSI)
PER	Professional and Executive Recruitment
PEST	Pressure for Economic and Social Toryism
PETRAS	Polytechnic Educational Technology Resources Advisory Service
PF	Procurator-Fiscal
PFA	Professional Footballers' Association
pfc	Graduate of RAF Flying College
PFE	Program for Executives
PGA	Professional Golfers' Association
PGCE	Post Graduate Certificate of Education
PH	Presidential Order of Honour (Botswana)
PHAB	Physically Handicapped & Able-bodied
PhB	Bachelor of Philosophy
PhC	Pharmaceutical Chemist
PhD	Doctor of Philosophy
Phil.	Philology, Philological; Philosophy, Philosophical
PhL	Licentiate of Philosophy
PHLS	Public Health Laboratory Service
PhM	Master of Philosophy (USA)
PhmB	Bachelor of Pharmacy
Phys.	Physical
PIA	Personal Investment Authority
PIARC	Permanent International Association of Road Congresses
PIB	Prices and Incomes Board (later NBPI)
PICAO	Provisional International Civil Aviation Organization (*now* ICAO)
pinx.	*pinxit* (he painted it)
PIRA	Paper Industries Research Association
PITCOM	Parliamentary Information Technology Committee
PJG	Pingat Jasa Gemilang (Singapore)
PJK	Pingkat Jasa Kebaktian (Malaysia)
Pl.	Place; Plural
PLA	Port of London Authority
PLC or **plc**	public limited company

Plen.	Plenipotentiary
PLI	President, Landscape Institute
PLP	Parliamentary Labour Party; Progressive Liberal Party (Bahamas)
PMA	Personal Military Assistant
PMC	Personnel Management Centre
PMD	Program for Management Development
PMG	Postmaster-General
PMN	Panglima Mangku Negara (Malaysia)
PMO	Principal Medical Officer
PMRAFNS	Princess Mary's Royal Air Force Nursing Service
PMS	Presidential Order of Meritorious Service (Botswana); President, Miniature Society
PNBS	Panglima Negara Bintang Sarawak
PNEU	Parents' National Educational Union
PNG	Papua New Guinea
PNP	People's National Party
PO	Post Office
POB	Presidential Order of Botswana
POMEF	Political Office Middle East Force
Pop.	Population
POUNC	Post Office Users' National Council
POW	Prisoner of War; Prince of Wales's
PP	Parish Priest; Past President
pp	pages
PPA	Periodical Publishers Association
PPARC	Particle Physics and Astronomy Research Council
PPCLI	Princess Patricia's Canadian Light Infantry
PPE	Philosophy, Politics and Economics
PPInstHE	Past President, Institution of Highway Engineers
PPIStructE	Past President, Institution of Structural Engineers
PPITB	Printing and Publishing Industry Training Board
PPP	Private Patients Plan
PPRA	Past President, Royal Academy
PPRBA	Past President, Royal Society of British Artists
PPRBS	Past President, Royal Society of British Sculptors
PPRE	Past President, Royal Society of Painter-Printmakers (*formerly* of Painter-Etchers and Engravers)
PPRIBA	Past President, Royal Institute of British Architects
PPROI	Past President, Royal Institute of Oil Painters
PPRP	Past President, Royal Society of Portrait Painters
PPRTPI	Past President, Royal Town Planning Institute
PPRWA	Past President, Royal Watercolour Association
PPS	Parliamentary Private Secretary
PPSIAD	Past President, Society of Industrial Artists and Designers
PQ	Province of Quebec
PR	Public Relations; Parti républicain
PRA	President, Royal Academy
PRBS	President, Royal Society of British Sculptors
PRCS	President, Royal College of Surgeons
PRE	President, Royal Society of Painter-Printmakers (*formerly* of Painter-Etchers and Engravers)
Preb.	Prebendary
PrEng.	Professional Engineer
Pres.	President
PRHA	President, Royal Hibernian Academy
PRI	President, Royal Institute of Painters in Water Colours; Plastics and Rubber Institute
PRIA	President, Royal Irish Academy
PRIAS	President, Royal Incorporation of Architects in Scotland
Prin.	Principal
PRISA	Public Relations Institute of South Africa
PRO	Public Relations Officer; Public Records Office
Proc.	Proctor; Proceedings
Prof.	Professor; Professional
PROI	President, Royal Institute of Oil Painters
PRO NED	Promotion of Non-Executive Directors
PRORM	Pay and Records Office, Royal Marines
Pro tem.	*Pro tempore* (for the time being)
Prov.	Provost; Provincial
Prox.	*Proximo* (next)
Prox.acc.	*Proxime accessit* (next in order of merit to the winner)
PRS	President, Royal Society; Performing Right Society Ltd
PRSA	President, Royal Scottish Academy
PRSE	President, Royal Society of Edinburgh
PRSH	President, Royal Society for the Promotion of Health
PRSW	President, Royal Scottish Water Colour Society
PRUAA	President, Royal Ulster Academy of Arts
PRWA	President, Royal West of England Academy
PRWS	President, Royal Society of Painters in Water Colours
PS	Pastel Society; Paddle Steamer
ps	passed School of Instruction (of Officers)
PSA	Property Services Agency; Petty Sessions Area
psa	Graduate of RAF Staff College
psc	Graduate of Staff College († indicates Graduate of Senior Wing Staff College)
PSD	Petty Sessional Division; Social Democratic Party (Portugal)
PSGB	Pharmaceutical Society of Great Britain (*now see* RPSGB)
PSI	Policy Studies Institute
PSIAD	President, Society of Industrial Artists and Designers
PSM	Panglima Setia Mahkota (Malaysia)
psm	Certificate of Royal Military School of Music
PSMA	President, Society of Marine Artists
PSNC	Pacific Steam Navigation Co.
PSO	Principal Scientific Officer; Personal Staff Officer
PSOE	Partido Socialista Obrero Español
PSSC	Personal Social Services Council
PTA	Passenger Transport Authority; Parent-Teacher Association
PTE	Passenger Transport Executive
Pte	Private
ptsc	passed Technical Staff College
Pty	Proprietary
PUP	People's United Party
PVSM	Param Vishishc Seva Medal (India)
PWD	Public Works Department
PWE	Political Welfare Executive
PWO	Prince of Wales's Own
PWR	Pressurized Water Reactor

Q

Q	Queen
QAIMNS	Queen Alexandra's Imperial Military Nursing Service
QALAS	Qualified Associate, Chartered Land Agents' Society (*now* (after amalgamation) *see* ARICS)
QARANC	Queen Alexandra's Royal Army Nursing Corps
QARNNS	Queen Alexandra's Royal Naval Nursing Service
QBD	Queen's Bench Division
QC	Queen's Counsel
QCVSA	Queen's Commendation for Valuable Service in the Air
QEH	Queen Elizabeth Hall
QEO	Queen Elizabeth's Own
QFSM	Queen's Fire Service Medal for Distinguished Service
QGM	Queen's Gallantry Medal
QHC	Honorary Chaplain to the Queen
QHDS	Honorary Dental Surgeon to the Queen
QHNS	Honorary Nursing Sister to the Queen
QHP	Honorary Physician to the Queen
QHS	Honorary Surgeon to the Queen
Qld	Queensland
Qly	Quarterly
QMAAC	Queen Mary's Army Auxiliary Corps
QMC	Queen Mary College, London (*now see* QMW)
QMG	Quartermaster-General
QMW	Queen Mary and Westfield College, London
QO	Qualified Officer
QOOH	Queen's Own Oxfordshire Hussars
Q(ops)	Quartering (operations)
QOY	Queen's Own Yeomanry
QPM	Queen's Police Medal
Qr	Quarter
QRIH	Queen's Royal Irish Hussars
QRV	Qualified Valuer, Real Estate Institute of New South Wales
QS	Quarter Sessions; Quantity Surveying
qs	RAF graduates of the Military or Naval Staff College
QSM	Queen's Service Medal (NZ)
QSO	Queen's Service Order (NZ)
QUB	Queen's University, Belfast
qv	*quod vide* (which see)
qwi	Qualified Weapons Instructor

R

(R)	Reserve
RA	Royal Academician; Royal (Regiment of) Artillery
RAA	Regional Arts Association
RAAF	Royal Australian Air Force
RAAMC	Royal Australian Army Medical Corps
RABI	Royal Agricultural Benevolent Institution
RAC	Royal Automobile Club; Royal Agricultural College; Royal Armoured Corps
RACDS	Royal Australian College of Dental Surgeons
RACGP	Royal Australian College of General Practitioners
RAChD	Royal Army Chaplains' Department
RACI	Royal Australian Chemical Institute
RACO	Royal Australian College of Ophthalmologists

RACOG Royal Australian College of Obstetricians and Gynaecologists
RACP Royal Australasian College of Physicians
RACS Royal Australasian College of Surgeons; Royal Arsenal Co-operative Society
RADA Royal Academy of Dramatic Art
RADAR Royal Association for Disability and Rehabilitation
RADC Royal Army Dental Corps
RADIUS Religious Drama Society of Great Britain
RAE Royal Australian Engineers; Royal Aerospace Establishment (*formerly* Royal Aircraft Establishment)
RAEC Royal Army Educational Corps
RAeS Royal Aeronautical Society
RAF Royal Air Force
RAFA Royal Air Force Association
RAFO Reserve of Air Force Officers (*now see* RAFRO)
RAFRO Royal Air Force Reserve of Officers
RAFVR Royal Air Force Volunteer Reserve
RAI Royal Anthropological Institute of Great Britain & Ireland; Radio Audizioni Italiane
RAIA Royal Australian Institute of Architects
RAIC Royal Architectural Institute of Canada
RAM (Member of) Royal Academy of Music
RAMC Royal Army Medical Corps
RAN Royal Australian Navy
R&D Research and Development
RANR Royal Australian Naval Reserve
RANVR Royal Australian Naval Volunteer Reserve
RAOC Royal Army Ordnance Corps
RAPC Royal Army Pay Corps
RARDE Royal Armament Research and Development Establishment
RARO Regular Army Reserve of Officers
RAS Royal Astronomical Society; Royal Asiatic Society; Recruitment and Assessment Services
RASC Royal Army Service Corps (*now see* RCT)
RASE Royal Agricultural Society of England
RAuxAF Royal Auxiliary Air Force
RAVC Royal Army Veterinary Corps
RB Rifle Brigade
RBA Member, Royal Society of British Artists
RBC Royal British Colonial Society of Artists
RBK&C Royal Borough of Kensington and Chelsea
RBL Royal British Legion
RBS Royal Society of British Sculptors
RBSA (Member of) Royal Birmingham Society of Artists
RBY Royal Bucks Yeomanry
RC Roman Catholic
RCA Member, Royal Canadian Academy of Arts; Royal College of Art; (Member of) Royal Cambrian Academy
RCAC Royal Canadian Armoured Corps
RCAF Royal Canadian Air Force
RCamA Member, Royal Cambrian Academy
RCAS Royal Central Asian Society (*now see* RSAA)
RCDS Royal College of Defence Studies
rcds completed a course at, or served for a year on the Staff of, the Royal College of Defence Studies
RCGP Royal College of General Practitioners
RCHA Royal Canadian Horse Artillery
RCHM Royal Commission on Historical Monuments
RCM (Member of) Royal College of Music
RCN Royal Canadian Navy; Royal College of Nursing
RCNC Royal Corps of Naval Constructors
RCNR Royal Canadian Naval Reserve
RCNVR Royal Canadian Naval Volunteer Reserve
RCO Royal College of Organists
RCOG Royal College of Obstetricians and Gynaecologists
RCP Royal College of Physicians, London
RCPath Royal College of Pathologists
RCPE or **RCPEd** Royal College of Physicians, Edinburgh
RCPI Royal College of Physicians of Ireland
RCPSG Royal College of Physicians and Surgeons of Glasgow
RCPsych Royal College of Psychiatrists
RCR Royal College of Radiologists
RCS Royal College of Surgeons of England; Royal Corps of Signals; Royal College of Science
RCSE or **RCSEd** Royal College of Surgeons of Edinburgh
RCSI Royal College of Surgeons in Ireland
RCT Royal Corps of Transport
RCVS Royal College of Veterinary Surgeons
RD Rural Dean; Royal Naval and Royal Marine Forces Reserve Decoration
Rd Road
RDA Royal Defence Academy
RDC Rural District Council
RDF Royal Dublin Fusiliers
RDI Royal Designer for Industry (Royal Society of Arts)
RDS Royal Dublin Society
RE Royal Engineers; Fellow, Royal Society of Painter-Printmakers (*formerly* of Painter-Etchers and Engravers); Religious Education
REACH Retired Executives Action Clearing House
react Research Education and Aid for Children with potentially Terminal illness
Rear Adm. Rear Admiral
REconS Royal Economic Society
Regt Regiment
REME Royal Electrical and Mechanical Engineers
REngDes Registered Engineering Designer
REOWS Royal Engineers Officers' Widows' Society
REPC Regional Economic Planning Council
RERO Royal Engineers Reserve of Officers
RES Royal Empire Society (*now* Royal Commonwealth Society)
Res. Resigned; Reserve; Resident; Research
RETI Association of Traditional Industrial Regions
Rev. Reverend; Review
RFA Royal Field Artillery
RFC Royal Flying Corps (*now* RAF); Rugby Football Club
RFD Reserve Force Decoration
RFH Royal Festival Hall
RFN Registered Fever Nurse
RFPS(G) Royal Faculty of Physicians and Surgeons, Glasgow (*now see* RCPSG)
RFR Rassemblement des Français pour la République
RFU Rugby Football Union
RGA Royal Garrison Artillery
RGI Royal Glasgow Institute of the Fine Arts
RGJ Royal Green Jackets
RGN Registered General Nurse
RGS Royal Geographical Society
RGSA Royal Geographical Society of Australasia
RHA Royal Hibernian Academy; Royal Horse Artillery; Regional Health Authority
RHAS Royal Highland and Agricultural Society of Scotland
RHB Regional Hospital Board
RHBNC Royal Holloway and Bedford New College, London
RHC Royal Holloway College, London (*now see* RHBNC)
RHF Royal Highland Fusiliers
RHG Royal Horse Guards
RHistS Royal Historical Society
RHQ Regional Headquarters
RHR Royal Highland Regiment
RHS Royal Horticultural Society; Royal Humane Society
RHV Royal Health Visitor
RI (Member of) Royal Institute of Painters in Water Colours; Rhode Island
RIA Royal Irish Academy
RIAI Royal Institute of the Architects of Ireland
RIAM Royal Irish Academy of Music
RIAS Royal Incorporation of Architects in Scotland
RIASC Royal Indian Army Service Corps
RIBA (Member of) Royal Institute of British Architects
RIBI Rotary International in Great Britain and Ireland
RIC Royal Irish Constabulary; Royal Institute of Chemistry (*now see* RSC)
RICS Royal Institution of Chartered Surveyors
RIE Royal Indian Engineering (College)
RIF Royal Inniskilling Fusiliers
RIIA Royal Institute of International Affairs
RILEM Réunion internationale des laboratoires d'essais et de recherches sur les matériaux et les constructions
RIM Royal Indian Marines
RIN Royal Indian Navy
RINA Royal Institution of Naval Architects
RINVR Royal Indian Naval Volunteer Reserve
RIPA Royal Institute of Public Administration
RIPH&H Royal Institute of Public Health and Hygiene
RIrF Royal Irish Fusiliers
RLC Royal Logistic Corps
RLSS Royal Life Saving Society
RM Royal Marines; Resident Magistrate; Registered Midwife
RMA Royal Marine Artillery; Royal Military Academy Sandhurst (*now* incorporating Royal Military Academy, Woolwich)
RMB Rural Mail Base
RMC Royal Military College Sandhurst (*now see* RMA)
RMCM (Member of) Royal Manchester College of Music
RMCS Royal Military College of Science
RMedSoc Royal Medical Society, Edinburgh
RMetS Royal Meteorological Society
RMFVR Royal Marine Forces Volunteer Reserve
RMIT Royal Melbourne Institute of Technology
RMLI Royal Marine Light Infantry

RMN Registered Mental Nurse
RMO Resident Medical Officer(s)
RMP Royal Military Police
RMPA Royal Medico-Psychological Association
RMS Royal Microscopical Society; Royal Mail Steamer; Royal Society of Miniature Painters
RMT Rail, Maritime and Transport Union
RN Royal Navy; Royal Naval; Registered Nurse
RNAS Royal Naval Air Service
RNAY Royal Naval Aircraft Yard
RNC Royal Naval College
RNCM (Member of) Royal Northern College of Music
RNEC Royal Naval Engineering College
RNIB Royal National Institute for the Blind
RNID Royal National Institute for Deaf People (*formerly* Royal National Institute for the Deaf)
RNLI Royal National Life-boat Institution
RNLO Royal Naval Liaison Officer
RNR Royal Naval Reserve
RNS Royal Numismatic Society
RNSA Royal Naval Sailing Association
RNSC Royal Naval Staff College
RNT Registered Nurse Tutor; Royal National Theatre
RNTNEH Royal National Throat, Nose and Ear Hospital
RNUR Régie Nationale des Usines Renault
RNVR Royal Naval Volunteer Reserve
RNVSR Royal Naval Volunteer Supplementary Reserve
RNXS Royal Naval Auxiliary Service
RNZAC Royal New Zealand Armoured Corps
RNZAF Royal New Zealand Air Force
RNZIR Royal New Zealand Infantry Regiment
RNZN Royal New Zealand Navy
RNZNVR Royal New Zealand Naval Volunteer Reserve
ROC Royal Observer Corps
ROF Royal Ordnance Factories
R of O Reserve of Officers
ROI Member, Royal Institute of Oil Painters
RoSPA Royal Society for the Prevention of Accidents
(Rot.) Rotunda Hospital, Dublin (after degree)
RP Member, Royal Society of Portrait Painters
RPC Royal Pioneer Corps
RPE Rocket Propulsion Establishment
RPMS Royal Postgraduate Medical School
RPO Royal Philharmonic Orchestra
RPR Rassemblement pour la République
RPS Royal Photographic Society
RPSGB Royal Pharmaceutical Society of Great Britain
RRC Royal Red Cross
RRE Royal Radar Establishment (*now see* RSRE)
RRF Royal Regiment of Fusiliers
RRS Royal Research Ship
RSA Royal Scottish Academician; Royal Society of Arts; Republic of South Africa
RSAA Royal Society for Asian Affairs
RSAF Royal Small Arms Factory
RSAI Royal Society of Antiquaries of Ireland
RSAMD Royal Scottish Academy of Music and Drama
RSanI Royal Sanitary Institute (*now see* RSH)
RSAS Royal Surgical Aid Society
RSC Royal Society of Canada; Royal Society of Chemistry; Royal Shakespeare Company
RSCM Royal School of Church Music
RSCN Registered Sick Children's Nurse
RSE Royal Society of Edinburgh
RSF Royal Scots Fusiliers
RSFSR Russian Soviet Federated Socialist Republic
RSGS Royal Scottish Geographical Society
RSH Royal Society for the Promotion of Health
RSL Royal Society of Literature; Returned Services League of Australia
RSM Royal School of Mines
RSM or **RSocMed** Royal Society of Medicine
RSMA Royal Society of Marine Artists
RSME Royal School of Military Engineering
RSMHCA Royal Society for Mentally Handicapped Children and Adults (*see* Mencap)
RSNC Royal Society for Nature Conservation
RSO Rural Sub-Office; Railway Sub-Office; Resident Surgical Officer
RSPB Royal Society for Protection of Birds
RSPCA Royal Society for Prevention of Cruelty to Animals
RSRE Royal Signals and Radar Establishment
RSSAf Royal Society of South Africa
RSSAILA Returned Sailors, Soldiers and Airmen's Imperial League of Australia (*now see* RSL)
RSSPCC Royal Scottish Society for Prevention of Cruelty to Children
RSTM&H Royal Society of Tropical Medicine and Hygiene
RSUA Royal Society of Ulster Architects
RSV Revised Standard Version
RSW Member, Royal Scottish Society of Painters in Water Colours
RTE Radio Telefis Eireann
Rt Hon. Right Honourable
RTL Radio-Télévision Luxembourg
RTO Railway Transport Officer
RTPI Royal Town Planning Institute
RTR Royal Tank Regiment
Rt Rev. Right Reverend
RTS Religious Tract Society; Royal Toxophilite Society; Royal Television Society
RTYC Royal Thames Yacht Club
RU Rugby Union
RUC Royal Ulster Constabulary
RUI Royal University of Ireland
RUKBA Royal United Kingdom Beneficent Association
RUR Royal Ulster Regiment
RURAL Society for the Responsible Use of Resources in Agriculture & on the Land
RUSI Royal United Services Institute for Defence Studies (*formerly* Royal United Service Institution)
RVC Royal Veterinary College
RWA or **RWEA** (Member of) Royal West of England Academy
RWAFF Royal West African Frontier Force
RWF Royal Welch Fusiliers
RWS (Member of) Royal Society of Painters in Water Colours
RYA Royal Yachting Association
RYS Royal Yacht Squadron
RZSScot Royal Zoological Society of Scotland

S

(S) (in Navy) Paymaster; Scotland
S Succeeded; South; Saint
s son
SA South Australia; South Africa; Société Anonyme
SAAF South African Air Force
SABC South African Broadcasting Corporation
SAC Scientific Advisory Committee
sac qualified at small arms technical long course
SACEUR Supreme Allied Commander Europe
SACIF sociedad anónima commercial industrial financiera
SACLANT Supreme Allied Commander Atlantic
SACRO Scottish Association for the Care and Resettlement of Offenders
SACSEA Supreme Allied Command, SE Asia
SA de CV sociedad anónima de capital variable
SADF Sudanese Auxiliary Defence Force
SADG Société des Architectes Diplômés par le Gouvernement
SAE Society of Automobile Engineers (US)
SAMC South African Medical Corps
SARL Société à Responsabilité Limitée
Sarum Salisbury
SAS Special Air Service
Sask Saskatchewan
SASO Senior Air Staff Officer
SAT Senior Member, Association of Accounting Technicians
SATB Soprano, Alto, Tenor, Bass
SATRO Science and Technology Regional Organisation
SB Bachelor of Science (US)
SBAA Sovereign Base Areas Administration
SBAC Society of British Aerospace Companies (*formerly* Society of British Aircraft Constructors)
SBS Special Boat Service
SBStJ Serving Brother, Most Venerable Order of the Hospital of St John of Jerusalem
SC Star of Courage (Canada); Senior Counsel; South Carolina (US)
sc student at the Staff College
SCA Society of Catholic Apostolate (Pallottine Fathers); Société en Commandité par Actions
SCAA School Curriculum and Assessment Authority
SCAO Senior Civil Affairs Officer
SCAPA Society for Checking the Abuses of Public Advertising
SCAR Scientific Committee for Antarctic Research
ScD Doctor of Science
SCDC Schools Curriculum Development Committee
SCF Senior Chaplain to the Forces; Save the Children Fund
Sch. School
SCI Society of Chemical Industry
SCIS Scottish Council of Independent Schools
SCL Student in Civil Law

SCM State Certified Midwife; Student Christian Movement
SCONUL Standing Conference of National and University Libraries
Scot. Scotland
ScotBIC Scottish Business in the Community
SCOTMEG Scottish Management Efficiency Group
SCOTVEC Scottish Vocational Education Council
SD Staff Duties; South Dakota
SDA Social Democratic Alliance; Scottish Diploma in Agriculture; Scottish Development Agency
SDak South Dakota (US)
SDB Salesian of Don Bosco
SDF Sudan Defence Force; Social Democratic Federation
SDI Strategic Defence Initiative
SDLP Social Democratic and Labour Party
SDP Social Democratic Party
SE South-east
SEAC South-East Asia Command
SEALF South-East Asia Land Forces
SEATO South-East Asia Treaty Organization
SEC Security Exchange Commission
Sec. Secretary
SED Scottish Education Department
SEE Society of Environmental Engineers
SEFI European Society for Engineering Education
SEN State Enrolled Nurse
SEPM Society of Economic Palaeontologists and Mineralogists
SERC Science and Engineering Research Council (*now see* EPSRC and PPARC)
SERT Society of Electronic and Radio Technicians (*now see* IEIE)
SESO Senior Equipment Staff Officer
SFA Securities and Futures Authority
SFInstE Senior Fellow, Institute of Energy
SFInstF Senior Fellow, Institute of Fuel (*now see* SFInstE)
SFTA Society of Film and Television Arts (*now see* BAFTA)
SFTCD Senior Fellow, Trinity College Dublin
SG Solicitor-General
SGA Member, Society of Graphic Art
SGBI Schoolmistresses' and Governesses' Benevolent Institution
Sgt Sergeant
SHA Secondary Heads Association; Special Health Authority
SHAC London Housing Aid Centre
SHAEF Supreme Headquarters, Allied Expeditionary Force
SH&MA Scottish Horse and Motormen's Association
SHAPE Supreme Headquarters, Allied Powers, Europe
SHEFC Scottish Higher Education Funding Council
SHHD Scottish Home and Health Department
SIAD Society of Industrial Artists and Designers (*now see* CSD)
SIAM Society of Industrial and Applied Mathematics (US)
SIB Shipbuilding Industry Board; Securities and Investments Board
SICOT Société Internationale de Chirurgie Orthopédique et de Traumatologie
SID Society for International Development
SIESO Society of Industrial and Emergency Services Officers
SIMA Scientific Instrument Manufacturers' Association of Great Britain
SIME Security Intelligence Middle East
SIMG *Societas Internationalis Medicinae Generalis*
SinDrs Doctor of Chinese
SIROT Société Internationale pour Recherche en Orthopédie et Traumatologie
SIS Secret Intelligence Service
SITA Société Internationale de Télécommunications Aéronautiques
SITPRO Simpler Trade Procedures Board (*formerly* Simplification of International Trade Procedures)
SJ Society of Jesus (Jesuits)
SJAB St John Ambulance Brigade
SJD Doctor of Juristic Science
SJJ Setia Jubli Perak Tuanku Ja'afar
SL Serjeant-at-Law; Sociedad Limitada
SLA Special Libraries Association
SLAC Stanford Linear Accelerator Centre
SLAET Society of Licensed Aircraft Engineers and Technologists
SLAS Society for Latin-American Studies
SLD Social and Liberal Democrats
SLP Scottish Labour Party
SM Medal of Service (Canada) (*now see* OC); Master of Science; Officer qualified for Submarine Duties
SMA Society of Marine Artists (*now see* RSMA)
SMB Setia Mahkota Brunei
SME School of Military Engineering (*now see* RSME)
SMHO Sovereign Military Hospitaller Order (Malta)
SMIEE Senior Member, Institute of Electrical and Electronics Engineers (New York)
SMIRE Senior Member, Institute of Radio Engineers (New York)
SMMT Society of Motor Manufacturers and Traders Ltd
SMN Seri Maharaja Mangku Negara (Malaysia)
SMO Senior Medical Officer; Sovereign Military Order
SMP Senior Managers' Program
SMPTE Society of Motion Picture and Television Engineers (US)
SMRTB Ship and Marine Requirements Technology Board
SNAME Society of Naval Architects and Marine Engineers (US)
SNCF Société Nationale des Chemins de Fer Français
SND Sisters of Notre Dame
SNH Scottish Natural Heritage
SNP Scottish National Party
SNTS Society for New Testament Studies
SO Staff Officer; Scientific Officer; Symphony Orchestra
SOAS School of Oriental and African Studies
Soc. Society
Soc & Lib Dem Social and Liberal Democrats (*now see* Lib Dem)
SocCE(France) Société des Ingénieurs Civils de France
SODEPAX Committee on Society, Development and Peace
SOE Special Operations Executive
SOGAT Society of Graphical and Allied Trades (*now see* GPMU)
SOLACE or **Solace** Society of Local Authority Chief Executives
SOLT Society of London Theatre
SOM Society of Occupational Medicine
SOSc Society of Ordained Scientists
SOTS Society for Old Testament Study
sowc Senior Officers' War Course
SP Self-Propelled (Anti-Tank Regiment)
sp *sine prole* (without issue)
SpA Società per Azioni
SPAB Society for the Protection of Ancient Buildings
SPARKS Sport Aiding Medical Research for Children
SPCA Society for the Prevention of Cruelty to Animals
SPCK Society for Promoting Christian Knowledge
SPCM Darjah Seri Paduka Cura Si Manja Kini (Malaysia)
SPD Salisbury Plain District; Sozialdemokratische Partei Deutschlands
SPDK Seri Panglima Darjal Kinabalu
SPG Society for the Propagation of the Gospel (*now see* USPG)
SPk Sitara-e-Pakistan
SPMB Seri Paduka Makhota Brunei
SPMK Darjah Kebasaran Seri Paduka Mahkota Kelantan (Malaysia)
SPMO Senior Principal Medical Officer
SPNC Society for the Promotion of Nature Conservation (*now see* RSNC)
SPNM Society for the Promotion of New Music
SPR Society for Psychical Research
SPRC Society for Prevention and Relief of Cancer
sprl société de personnes à responsabilité limitée
SPSO Senior Principal Scientific Officer
SPTL Society of Public Teachers of Law
SPUC Society for the Protection of the Unborn Child
Sq. Square
sq staff qualified
SQA Sitara-i-Quaid-i-Azam (Pakistan)
Sqdn or **Sqn** Squadron
SR Special Reserve; Southern Railway; Southern Region (BR)
SRC Science Research Council (later SERC); Students' Representative Council
SRCh State Registered Chiropodist
SRHE Society for Research into Higher Education
SRIS Science Reference Information Service
SRN State Registered Nurse
SRNA Shipbuilders and Repairers National Association
SRO Supplementary Reserve of Officers; Self-Regulatory Organisation
SRP State Registered Physiotherapist
SRY Sherwood Rangers Yeomanry
SS Saints; Straits Settlements; Steamship
SSA Society of Scottish Artists
SSAC Social Security Advisory Committee
SSAFA or **SS&AFA** Soldiers', Sailors', and Airmen's Families Association
SSBN Nuclear Submarine, Ballistic
SSC Solicitor before Supreme Court (Scotland); Sculptors Society of Canada; *Societas Sanctae Crucis* (Society of the Holy Cross); Short Service Commission
SSEB South of Scotland Electricity Board
SSEES School of Slavonic and East European Studies
SSF Society of St Francis
SSJE Society of St John the Evangelist
SSM Society of the Sacred Mission; Seri Setia Mahkota (Malaysia)
SSO Senior Supply Officer; Senior Scientific Officer
SSRC Social Science Research Council (*now see* ESRC)
SSSI Sites of Special Scientific Interest
SSStJ Serving Sister, Most Venerable Order of the Hospital of St John of Jerusalem

St Street; Saint
STA Sail Training Association
STB *Sacrae Theologiae Baccalaureus* (Bachelor of Sacred Theology)
STC Senior Training Corps
STD *Sacrae Theologiae Doctor* (Doctor of Sacred Theology)
STh Scholar in Theology
Stip. Stipend; Stipendiary
STL *Sacrae Theologiae Lector* (Reader or a Professor of Sacred Theology)
STM *Sacrae Theologiae Magister* (Master of Sacred Theology)
STP *Sacrae Theologiae Professor* (Professor of Divinity, old form of DD)
STRIVE Society for Preservation of Rural Industries and Village Enterprises
STSO Senior Technical Staff Officer
STV Scottish Television
SUNY State University of New York
Supp. Res. Supplementary Reserve (of Officers)
Supt Superintendent
Surg. Surgeon
Surv. Surviving
SW South-west
SWET Society of West End Theatre (*now see* SOLT)
SWIA Society of Wildlife Artists
SWPA South West Pacific Area
SWRB Sadler's Wells Royal Ballet
Syd. Sydney

T

T Telephone; Territorial
TA Telegraphic Address; Territorial Army
TAA Territorial Army Association
TAF Tactical Air Force
T&AFA Territorial and Auxiliary Forces Association
T&AVR Territorial and Army Volunteer Reserve
TANS Territorial Army Nursing Service
TANU Tanganyika African National Union
TARO Territorial Army Reserve of Officers
TAS Torpedo and Anti Submarine Course
TASS Technical, Administrative and Supervisory Section of AUEW (now part of MSF)
TAVRA or **TA&VRA** Territorial Auxiliary and Volunteer Reserve Association
TC Order of the Trinity Cross (Trinidad and Tobago)
TCCB Test and County Cricket Board
TCD Trinity College, Dublin (University of Dublin, Trinity College)
TCF Temporary Chaplain to the Forces
TCPA Town and Country Planning Association
TD Territorial Efficiency Decoration; Efficiency Decoration (T&AVR) (since April 1967); Teachta Dala (Member of the Dáil, Eire)
TDD Tubercular Diseases Diploma
TE Technical Engineer
TEAC Technical Educational Advisory Council
TEC Technician Education Council (*now see* BTEC); Training and Enterprise Council
Tech(CEI) Technician
TEFL Teaching English as a Foreign Language
TEFLA Teaching English as a Foreign Language to Adults
TEM Territorial Efficiency Medal
TEMA Telecommunication Engineering and Manufacturing Association
Temp. Temperature; Temporary
TEng(CEI) Technician Engineer (*now see* IEng)
Tenn Tennessee (US)
TeolD Doctor of Theology
TES Times Educational Supplement
TESL Teaching English as a Second Language
TESOL Teaching English to Speakers of other Languages
TET Teacher of Electrotherapy
Tex Texas (US)
TF Territorial Force
TFR Territorial Force Reserve
TFTS Tactical Fighter Training Squadron
TGEW Timber Growers England and Wales Ltd
TGO Timber Growers' Organisation (*now see* TGEW)
TGWU Transport and General Workers' Union
ThD Doctor of Theology
THED Transvaal Higher Education Diploma
THELEP Therapy of Leprosy
THES Times Higher Education Supplement
ThL Theological Licentiate
ThSchol Scholar in Theology
TIMS The Institute of Management Sciences
TLS Times Literary Supplement
TMMG Teacher of Massage and Medical Gymnastics
TN Tennessee
TNC Theatres National Committee
TOSD Tertiary Order of St Dominic
TP Transvaal Province
TPI Town Planning Institute (*now see* RTPI)
Trans. Translation; Translated
Transf. Transferred
TRC Thames Rowing Club
TRE Telecommunications Research Establishment (later RRE)
TRH Their Royal Highnesses
TRIC Television and Radio Industries Club
Trin. Trinity
TRRL Transport and Road Research Laboratory
TS Training Ship
TSB Trustee Savings Bank
tsc passed a Territorial Army Course in Staff Duties
TSD Tertiary of St Dominic
TSSA Transport Salaried Staffs' Association
TUC Trades Union Congress
TULV Trade Unions for a Labour Victory
TUS Trade Union Side
TV Television
TVEI Technical and Vocational Education Initiative
TWA Thames Water Authority
TX Texas
TYC Thames Yacht Club (*now see* RTYC)

U

U Unionist
u uncle
UAE United Arab Emirates
UAR United Arab Republic
UAU Universities Athletic Union
UBC University of British Columbia
UBI Understanding British Industry
UC University College
UCAS Universities and Colleges Admissions Service
UCCA Universities Central Council on Admissions
UCCF Universities and Colleges Christian Fellowship of Evangelical Unions
UCET Universities Council for Education of Teachers
UCH University College Hospital (London)
UCL University College London
UCLA University of California at Los Angeles
UCLES University of Cambridge Local Examinations Syndicate
UCMSM University College and Middlesex School of Medicine
UCNS Universities' Council for Non-academic Staff
UCNW University College of North Wales
UCRN University College of Rhodesia and Nyasaland
UCS University College School
UCSD University of California at San Diego
UCW University College of Wales; Union of Communication Workers (*now see* CWU)
UDC Urban District Council; Urban Development Corporation
UDF Union Defence Force; Union démocratique française
UDR Ulster Defence Regiment; Union des Démocrates pour la Vème République (*now see* RPR)
UDSR Union Démocratique et Socialiste de la Résistance
UE United Empire Loyalist (Canada)
UEA University of East Anglia
UED University Education Diploma
UEFA Union of European Football Associations
UF United Free Church
UFAW Universities Federation for Animal Welfare
UFC Universities' Funding Council
UGC University Grants Committee (later UFC)
UIAA Union Internationale des Associations d'Alpinisme
UICC Union Internationale contre le Cancer
UIE Union Internationale des Etudiants
UISPP Union Internationale des Sciences Préhistoriques et Protohistoriques
UITP International Union of Public Transport
UJD *Utriusque Juris Doctor* (Doctor of both Laws, Doctor of Canon and Civil Law)
UK United Kingdom
UKAC United Kingdom Automation Council
UKAEA United Kingdom Atomic Energy Authority
UKCC United Kingdom Central Council for Nursing, Midwifery and Health Visiting

UKCIS United Kingdom Chemical Information Service
UKERNA United Kingdom Education and Research Networking Association
UKIAS United Kingdom Immigrants' Advisory Service
UKISC United Kingdom Industrial Space Committee
UKLF United Kingdom Land Forces
UKMF(L) United Kingdom Military Forces (Land)
UKMIS United Kingdom Mission
UKOOA United Kingdom Offshore Operators Association
UKPIA United Kingdom Petroleum Industry Association Ltd
UKSLS United Kingdom Services Liaison Staff
ULCI Union of Lancashire and Cheshire Institutes
ULPS Union of Liberal and Progressive Synagogues
UMDS United Medical and Dental Schools
UMIST University of Manchester Institute of Science and Technology
UN United Nations
UNA United Nations Association
UNCAST United Nations Conference on the Applications of Science and Technology
UNCIO United Nations Conference on International Organisation
UNCITRAL United Nations Commission on International Trade Law
UNCSTD United Nations Conference on Science and Technology for Development
UNCTAD or **Unctad** United Nations Commission for Trade and Development
UNDP United Nations Development Programme
UNDRO United Nations Disaster Relief Organisation
UNECA United Nations Economic Commission for Asia
UNEP United Nations Environment Programme
UNESCO or **Unesco** United Nations Educational, Scientific and Cultural Organisation
UNFAO United Nations Food and Agriculture Organisation
UNFICYP United Nations Force in Cyprus
UNHCR United Nations High Commissioner for Refugees
UNICE Union des Industries de la Communauté Européenne
UNICEF or **Unicef** United Nations Children's Fund (*formerly* United Nations International Children's Emergency Fund)
UNIDO United Nations Industrial Development Organisation
UNIDROIT Institut International pour l'Unification du Droit Privé
UNIFEM United Nations Development Fund for Women
UNIFIL United Nations Interim Force in Lebanon
UNIPEDE Union Internationale des Producteurs et Distributeurs d'Energie Electrique
UNISIST Universal System for Information in Science and Technology
UNITAR United Nations Institute of Training and Research
Univ. University
UNO United Nations Organization
UNRRA United Nations Relief and Rehabilitation Administration
UNRWA United Nations Relief and Works Agency
UNSCOB United Nations Special Commission on the Balkans
UP United Provinces; Uttar Pradesh; United Presbyterian
UPGC University and Polytechnic Grants Committee
UPNI Unionist Party of Northern Ireland
UPU Universal Postal Union
UPUP Ulster Popular Unionist Party
URC United Reformed Church
URSI Union Radio-Scientifique Internationale
US United States
USA United States of America
USAAF United States Army Air Force
USAF United States Air Force
USAID United States Agency for International Development
USAR United States Army Reserve
USC University of Southern California
USDAW Union of Shop Distributive and Allied Workers
USM Unlisted Securities Market
USMA United States Military Academy
USN United States Navy
USNR United States Naval Reserve
USPG United Society for the Propagation of the Gospel
USPHS United States Public Health Service
USPS United States Postal Service
USR Universities' Statistical Record
USS United States Ship
USSR Union of Soviet Socialist Republics
USVI United States Virgin Islands
UT Utah
UTC University Training Corps
UU Ulster Unionist
UUUC United Ulster Unionist Coalition
UUUP United Ulster Unionist Party
UWCC University of Wales College of Cardiff
UWE University of the West of England
UWIST University of Wales Institute of Science and Technology
UWT Union of Women Teachers

V

V Five (Roman numerals); Version; Vicar; Viscount; Vice
v *versus* (against)
v or **vid.** *vide* (see)
VA Virginia
Va Virginia (US)
VAD Voluntary Aid Detachment
V&A Victoria and Albert
VAT Value Added Tax
VC Victoria Cross; Voluntary Controlled
VCAS Vice Chief of the Air Staff
VCDS Vice Chief of the Defence Staff
VCGS Vice Chief of the General Staff
VCNS Vice Chief of the Naval Staff
VD Royal Naval Volunteer Reserve Officers' Decoration (*now* VRD); Volunteer Officers' Decoration; Victorian Decoration
VDC Volunteer Defence Corps
Ven. Venerable
Vet. Veterinary
VG Vicar-General
VHS Hon. Surgeon to Viceroy of India
VIC Victoria Institute of Colleges
Vice Adm. Vice Admiral
Visc. Viscount
VM Victory Medal
VMH Victoria Medal of Honour (Royal Horticultural Society)
Vol. Volume; Volunteers
VP Vice-President
VPP Volunteer Political Party
VPRP Vice-President, Royal Society of Portrait Painters
VQMG Vice-Quartermaster-General
VR *Victoria Regina* (Queen Victoria); Volunteer Reserve
VRD Royal Naval Volunteer Reserve Officers' Decoration
VSO Voluntary Service Overseas
VT Vermont
Vt Vermont (US)
VUP Vanguard Unionist Party

W

W West
WA Western Australia; Washington
WAAF Women's Auxiliary Air Force (later WRAF)
WAOS Welsh Agricultural Organisations Society
Wash Washington State (US)
WCC World Council of Churches
W/Cdr Wing Commander
WCMD Welsh College of Music and Drama
WDA Welsh Development Agency
WEA Workers' Educational Association; Royal West of England Academy
WES/PNEU Worldwide Education Service of Parents' National Educational Union
WEU Western European Union
WFSW World Federation of Scientific Workers
WFTU World Federation of Trade Unions
WhF Whitworth Fellow
WHO World Health Organization
WhSch Whitworth Scholar
WI West Indies; Women's Institute; Wisconsin
Wilts Wiltshire
WIPO World Intellectual Property Organization
Wis Wisconsin (US)
Wits Witwatersrand
WJEC Welsh Joint Education Committee
WLA Women's Land Army
WLD Women Liberal Democrats
WLF Women's Liberal Federation
Wm William
WMO World Meteorological Organization
WNO Welsh National Opera
WO War Office; Warrant Officer
Worcs Worcestershire
WOSB War Office Selection Board
WR West Riding; Western Region (BR)
WRAC Women's Royal Army Corps
WRAF Women's Royal Air Force
WRNS Women's Royal Naval Service

WRVS Women's Royal Voluntary Service
WS Writer to the Signet
WSAVA World Small Animal Veterinary Association
WSPA World Society for the Protection of Animals
WSPU Women's Social and Political Union
WUS World University Service
WV West Virginia
WVa West Virginia (US)
WVS Women's Voluntary Services (*now see* WRVS)
WWF World Wide Fund for Nature (*formerly* World Wildlife Fund)
WY Wyoming
Wyo Wyoming (US)

X

X Ten (Roman numerals)
XO Executive Officer

Y

y youngest
YC Young Conservative
YCNAC Young Conservatives National Advisory Committee
Yeo. Yeomanry
YES Youth Enterprise Scheme
YHA Youth Hostels Association
YMCA Young Men's Christian Association
YOI Young Offenders Institute
Yorks Yorkshire
YPTES Young People's Trust for Endangered Species
yr younger
yrs years
YTS Youth Training Scheme
YVFF Young Volunteer Force Foundation
YWCA Young Women's Christian Association

Z

ZANU Zimbabwe African National Union
ZAPU Zimbabwe African People's Union

THE ROYAL FAMILY

THE SOVEREIGN

	Born
Her Majesty Queen Elizabeth II, (Elizabeth Alexandra Mary).	21 April 1926

Succeeded her father, King George VI, 6 February 1952

Married 20 Nov. 1947, HRH The Duke of Edinburgh, *now* HRH The Prince Philip, Duke of Edinburgh, KG, KT, OM, GBE (*b* 10 June 1921; *s* of HRH Prince Andrew of Greece (*d* 1944) and of HRH Princess Andrew of Greece (*d* 1969), *gg-d* of Queen Victoria; *cr* 1947, Baron Greenwich, Earl of Merioneth and Duke of Edinburgh)

Residences: Buckingham Palace, SW1A 1AA; Windsor Castle, Berkshire SL4 1NJ; Sandringham House, Norfolk PE35 6EN; Balmoral Castle, Aberdeenshire AB35 5TB.

SONS AND DAUGHTER OF HER MAJESTY

HRH The Prince of Wales, (Prince Charles Philip Arthur George), KG, KT, GCB; . . . 14 Nov. 1948
cr 1958, Prince of Wales and Earl of Chester; Duke of Cornwall; Duke of Rothesay, Earl of Carrick and Baron of Renfrew; Lord of the Isles and Great Steward of Scotland

Married 29 July 1981, Lady Diana Frances Spencer, *now* HRH The Princess of Wales (*b* 1 July 1961; *y d* of 8th Earl Spencer, LVO), and has issue –

HRH PRINCE WILLIAM OF WALES, (PRINCE WILLIAM ARTHUR PHILIP LOUIS) . . . . 21 June 1982

HRH PRINCE HENRY OF WALES, (PRINCE HENRY CHARLES ALBERT DAVID) . . . . 15 Sept. 1984

Office: St James's Palace, SW1A 1BS; *residence:* Highgrove, Doughton, Tetbury, Gloucestershire GL8 8TN.

HRH The Duke of York, (Prince Andrew Albert Christian Edward), CVO; . . . . . 19 Feb. 1960
cr 1986, Baron Killyleagh, Earl of Inverness and Duke of York

Married 23 July 1986, Sarah Margaret Ferguson (*b* 15 Oct. 1959; 2nd *d* of Major Ronald Ivor Ferguson, Life Guards (retired)), and has issue –

HRH PRINCESS BEATRICE OF YORK, (PRINCESS BEATRICE ELIZABETH MARY). . . . 8 Aug. 1988

HRH PRINCESS EUGENIE OF YORK, (PRINCESS EUGENIE VICTORIA HELENA) . . . . 23 March 1990

Residences: Buckingham Palace, SW1A 1AA; Sunninghill Park, Ascot, Berkshire SL5 7TH.

HRH The Prince Edward (Antony Richard Louis), CVO . . . . 10 March 1964

Residence: Buckingham Palace, SW1A 1AA.

HRH The Princess Royal, (Princess Anne Elizabeth Alice Louise), ... 15 Aug. 1950
Lady of the Order of the Garter, GCVO

Married 1st, 14 Nov. 1973, Captain Mark Anthony Peter Phillips, *qv* (marriage dissolved, 1992), and has issue –

PETER MARK ANDREW PHILLIPS . . . . 15 Nov. 1977

ZARA ANNE ELIZABETH PHILLIPS . . . . 15 May 1981

Married 2nd, 12 Dec. 1992, Captain Timothy James Hamilton Laurence, *qv*

Office: Buckingham Palace, SW1A 1AA; *residence:* Gatcombe Park, Minchinhampton, Stroud, Gloucestershire GL6 9AT.

SISTER OF HER MAJESTY

HRH The Princess Margaret (Rose), Countess of Snowdon, CI, GCVO . . . . 21 Aug. 1930

Married 6 May 1960, Antony Charles Robert Armstrong-Jones, *now* 1st Earl of Snowdon, *qv* (marriage dissolved, 1978), and has issue –

DAVID ALBERT CHARLES ARMSTRONG-JONES, (VISCOUNT LINLEY, *qv*) . . . . . 3 Nov. 1961

SARAH FRANCES ELIZABETH ARMSTRONG-JONES, (LADY SARAH CHATTO) . . . . 1 May 1964

Married 14 July 1994, Daniel Chatto, *s* of late Tim Chatto and of Rosalind Chatto

Residence: Kensington Palace, W8 4PU.

MOTHER OF HER MAJESTY

Her Majesty Queen Elizabeth The Queen Mother, (Elizabeth Angela Marguerite), . . . 4 Aug. 1900
Lady of the Order of the Garter, Lady of the Order of the Thistle, CI, GCVO, GBE

Married 26 April 1923 (as Lady Elizabeth Bowes-Lyon, *d* of 14th Earl of Strathmore and Kinghorne), HRH The Duke of York (Prince Albert), who succeeded as King George VI, 11 Dec. 1936 and *d* 6 Feb. 1952

Residences: Clarence House, St James's, SW1A 1BA; Royal Lodge, The Great Park, Windsor, Berkshire; Birkhall, Ballater, Aberdeenshire; Castle of Mey, Caithness-shire.

WIDOW OF UNCLE OF HER MAJESTY

HRH Princess Alice (Christabel), Duchess of Gloucester, GCB, CI, GCVO, GBE, ... 25 Dec. 1901
3rd *d* of 7th Duke of Buccleuch

Married 6 Nov. 1935, HRH The Duke of Gloucester (Prince Henry William Frederick Albert, *b* 31 March 1900, *d* 10 June 1974), and has issue –

HRH PRINCE WILLIAM OF GLOUCESTER, (PRINCE WILLIAM HENRY ANDREW FREDERICK), *b* 18 Dec. 1941; *d* 28 Aug. 1972

HRH THE DUKE OF GLOUCESTER, (PRINCE RICHARD ALEXANDER WALTER GEORGE) (*see below*)

Residence: Kensington Palace, W8 4PU.

COUSINS OF HER MAJESTY

Child of HRH The Duke of Gloucester and of HRH Princess Alice Duchess of Gloucester (*see above*)

HRH The Duke of Gloucester, (Prince Richard Alexander Walter George), GCVO . . . 26 Aug. 1944

Married 8 July 1972, Brigitte Eva van Deurs, GCVO, *d* of Asger Preben Wissing Henriksen, and has issue –

ALEXANDER PATRICK GREGERS RICHARD, (EARL OF ULSTER, *qv*) . . . . 24 Oct. 1974

DAVINA ELIZABETH ALICE BENEDIKTE, (LADY DAVINA WINDSOR) . . . . . . 19 Nov. 1977

ROSE VICTORIA BIRGITTE LOUISE, (LADY ROSE WINDSOR) . . . . 1 March 1980

Residence: Kensington Palace, W8 4PU.

Children of HRH The Duke of Kent (Prince George Edward Alexander Edmund, *b* 20 Dec. 1902, *d* 25 Aug. 1942) and HRH Princess Marina, Duchess of Kent (*b* 13 Dec. 1906, *d* 27 Aug. 1968), *y d* of late Prince Nicholas of Greece

HRH The Duke of Kent, (Prince Edward George Nicholas Paul Patrick), KG, GCMG, GCVO 9 Oct. 1935

Married 8 June 1961, Katharine Lucy Mary Worsley, GCVO (*b* 22 Feb. 1933, *o d* of Sir William Worsley, 4th Bt) and has issue –

GEORGE PHILIP NICHOLAS, (EARL OF ST ANDREWS, *qv*) . . . . 26 June 1962

NICHOLAS CHARLES EDWARD JONATHAN, (LORD NICHOLAS WINDSOR) . . . . . 25 July 1970

HELEN MARINA LUCY, (LADY HELEN TAYLOR) . . . . 28 April 1964

Married 18 July 1992, Timothy Verner Taylor, *e s* of Commander Michael Taylor, RN and Mrs Colin Walkinshaw, and has issue –

COLUMBUS GEORGE DONALD TAYLOR . . . . 6 Aug. 1994

Residences: York House, St James's Palace, SW1A 1BQ; Crocker End House, Nettlebed, Henley-on-Thames, Oxon RG9 5BJ.

HRH Prince Michael of Kent, (Prince Michael George Charles Franklin), KCVO . . . 4 July 1942

Married 30 June 1978, Baroness Marie-Christine Agnes Hedwig Ida von Reibnitz, *d* of Baron Günther Hubertus von Reibnitz, and has issue –

FREDERICK MICHAEL GEORGE DAVID LOUIS, (LORD FREDERICK WINDSOR) . . . . 6 April 1979

GABRIELLA MARINA ALEXANDRA OPHELIA, (LADY GABRIELLA WINDSOR) . . . . 23 April 1981

Residences: Kensington Palace, W8 4PU; Nether Lypiatt Manor, Stroud, Gloucestershire GL6 7LS.

HRH Princess Alexandra (Helen Elizabeth Olga Christabel), The Hon. Lady Ogilvy, GCVO 25 Dec. 1936

Married 24 April 1963, Hon. Sir Angus (James Bruce) Ogilvy, *qv*, and has issue –

JAMES ROBERT BRUCE OGILVY . . . . 29 Feb. 1964

Married 30 July 1988, Julia, *d* of Charles Frederick Melville Rawlinson, *qv*

MARINA VICTORIA ALEXANDRA, (MRS PAUL MOWATT) . . . . 31 July 1966

Married 2 Feb. 1990, Paul Julian Mowatt, and has issue –

CHRISTIAN ALEXANDER MOWATT . . . . 4 June 1993

ZENOUSKA MAY MOWATT . . . . 26 May 1990

Office: Buckingham Palace, SW1A 1AA; *residence:* Thatched House Lodge, Richmond, Surrey TW10 5HP.

61470, *Fax:* Newtownstewart (016626) 62059; 10 Little Chester Street, SW1X 7AL. *T:* 0171-235 5518. *Clubs:* Royal Automobile, Brooks's.

ABERCROMBY, Sir Ian George, 10th Bt *cr* 1636, of Birkenbog; *b* 30 June 1925; *s* of Robert Ogilvie Abercromby (*g s* of 5th Bt); *S* kinsman, 1972; *m* 1st, 1950, Joyce Beryl, *d* of Leonard Griffiths; 2nd, 1959, Fanny Mary, *d* of late Dr Graham Udale-Smith; one *d*; 3rd, 1976, Diana Marjorie, *d* of H. G. Cockell, and *widow* of Captain Ian Charles Palliser Galloway. *Educ:* Lancing Coll.; Bloxham Sch. *Heir:* none. *Address:* c/o National Westminster Bank, 14 Sloane Square, SW1W 8EQ. *Clubs:* Ski Club of Great Britain; Kandahar; Kildare Street (Dublin).

ABERDARE, 4th Baron, *cr* 1873, of Duffryn; **Morys George Lyndhurst Bruce,** KBE 1984; PC 1974; DL; a Deputy Speaker, House of Lords; *b* 16 June 1919; *s* of 3rd Baron Aberdare, GBE, and Margaret Bethune (*née* Black); *S* father 1957; *m* 1946, Maud Helen Sarah, *o d* of Sir John Dashwood, 10th Bt, CVO; four *s*. *Educ:* Winchester; New College, Oxford (MA). Welsh Guards, 1939–46. Minister of State, DHSS, 1970–74; Minister Without Portfolio, 1974; Chm. of Cttees, H of L, 1976–92. Chairman: Albany Life Assurance Co. Ltd, 1975–92; Metlife (UK) Ltd, 1986–92. Chm., The Football Trust, 1979–; President: Welsh Nat. Council of YMCAs; Kidney Res. Unit for Wales Foundn; Tennis and Rackets Assoc. Hon. LLD Wales, 1985. DL Dyfed, 1985. Bailiff Grand Cross, 1974, Prior for Wales, 1958–88, OStJ. *Publications:* The Story of Tennis, 1959; Willis Faber Book of Tennis and Rackets, 1980. *Recreations:* Real tennis and rackets. *Heir:* *s* Hon. Alastair John Lyndhurst Bruce [*b* 2 May 1947; *m* 1971, Elizabeth Mary Culbert, *d* of John Foulkes; one *s* one *d*]. *Address:* 32 Elthiron Road, SW6 4BW. *T:* 0171–736 0825. *Clubs:* Lansdowne, MCC, Queen's (Pres., 1993–).

ABERDEEN, Bishop of, (RC), since 1977; **Rt. Rev. Mario Joseph Conti;** *b* Elgin, Moray, 20 March 1934; *s* of Louis Joseph Conti and Josephine Quintilia Panicali. *Educ:* St Marie's Convent School and Springfield, Elgin; Blairs Coll., Aberdeen; Pontifical Gregorian Univ. (Scots College), Rome. PhL 1955, STL 1959. FRSE 1995. Ordained, Rome, 1958; Curate, St Mary's Cathedral, Aberdeen, 1959–62; Parish Priest, St Joachim's, Wick and St Anne's, Thurso (joint charge), 1962–77. Chairman: Scottish Catholic Heritage Commn, 1980–; Commn for the Pastoral Care of Migrant Workers and Tourists (incl. Apostleship of the Sea, Scotland), 1978–85; Pres.-Treasurer, Scottish Catholic Internat. Aid Fund, 1978–85; Pres., National Liturgy Commn, 1981–85; Scottish Mem., Episcopal Bd, Internat. Commn for English in the Liturgy, 1978–87; Mem., Bishops' Jt Cttee for Bio-ethical Issues, 1982–; Pres., Nat. Christian Doctrine and Unity Commn, 1985–; Consultor-Mem., Secretariat, later Council, for Promotion of Christian Unity (Rome), 1984–; Convener, Action of Churches Together in Scotland, 1990–93; Mem., Pontifical Commn for Cultural Heritage of the Church, Rome, 1994–. Conventual Chaplain *ad honorem*, 1991, Principal Chaplain, British Assoc., 1995–, SMO Malta. Hon. DD Aberdeen, 1989. KCHS 1989. Commendatore, Order of Merit of the Italian Republic, 1981. *Recreations:* music, art, book browsing, TV, travel, swimming. *Address:* Bishop's House, 3 Queen's Cross, Aberdeen AB9 2NL.

ABERDEEN, (St Andrew's Cathedral), Provost of; *see* Wightman, Very Rev. W. D.

ABERDEEN AND ORKNEY, Bishop of, since 1992; **Rt. Rev. Andrew Bruce Cameron;** *b* 2 May 1941; *s* of Andrew and Helen Cameron; *m* 1974, Elaine Gingles; two *s*. *Educ:* Eastwood Secondary Sch., Glasgow; Edinburgh Theol Coll.; Edinburgh Univ. (Cert. in Past. Studies); Urban Theology Unit, Sheffield (Dip. in Theology and Mission). Ordained deacon 1964, priest 1965; Assistant Curate: St Michael and All Angels, Helensburgh, 1964–67; Holy Cross, Edinburgh, 1967–70; Diocesan and Provincial Youth Chaplain and Chaplain, St Mary's Cathedral, Edinburgh, 1970–75; Rector, St Mary's, Dalmahoy and Anglican Chaplain, Heriot-Watt Univ., 1975–82; Churches Devlt Officer in Livingston Ecumenical Parish, 1982–88; Rector, St John's, Perth and Convenor of Provincial Mission Bd, 1988–92. *Recreations:* golf, swimming, walking, singing, listening to music, theatre, reading 'whodunnits'. *Address:* Ashley House, 16 Ashley Gardens, Aberdeen AB1 6RQ. *T:* Aberdeen (01224) 208142, (office) (01224) 636653, *Fax:* (01224) 636186.

See also Bishop of Argyll and the Isles.

ABERDEEN AND ORKNEY, Dean of; *see* Stranraer-Mull, Very Rev. G.

ABERDEEN AND TEMAIR, 6th Marquess of, *cr* 1916; **Alastair Ninian John Gordon;** Bt (NS) 1642; Earl of Aberdeen, Viscount Formartine, Lord Haddo, Methlic, Tarves and Kellie, 1682 (Scot.); Viscount Gordon 1814, Earl of Haddo 1916 (UK); painter; exhibitions of botanical painting in London, New York, Chicago, Sydney; *b* 20 July 1920; *s* of 3rd Marquess of Aberdeen and Temair, DSO, and Cécile Elizabeth (*d* 1948), *d* of George Drummond, Swaylands, Penshurst, Kent; *S* brother, 1984; *m* 1950, Anne, *d* of late Lt-Col Gerald Barry, MC; one *s* two *d*. *Educ:* Harrow; Camberwell Sch. of Art. Served War of 1939–45, Captain Scots Guards. Member: Internat. Assoc. of Art Critics; Bach Choir, 1939–82. *Recreations:* wine, women and song. *Heir:* *s* Earl of Haddo, *qv*. *Address:* Quick's Green, near Pangbourne, Berks RG8 8SN. *Clubs:* Arts (Chm., 1966–76), MCC; Puffins (Edinburgh).

ABERDEEN AND TEMAIR, June Marchioness of; (Beatrice Mary) June Gordon, CBE 1989 (MBE 1971); DL; Musical Director and Conductor, Haddo House Choral and Operatic Society (formerly Haddo House Choral Society), since 1945; *d* of Arthur Paul Boissier, MA, and Dorothy Christina Leslie Smith; *m* 1939, David George Ian Alexander Gordon (later 4th Marquess of Aberdeen and Temair, CBE, TD) (*d* 1974); two adopted *s* two adopted *d*. *Educ:* Southlands School, Harrow; Royal Coll. of Music. GRSM, ARCM. Teacher of Music, Bromley High School for Girls, 1936–39. Director of Haddo House Choral and Operatic Soc. and Arts Centre, 1945–. Chairman: Scottish Children's League, 1969–94; NE Scotland Music School, 1975–; Adv. Council, Scottish Opera, 1979–92; Chm. (local), Adv. Cttee, Aberdeen Internat. Festival of Music and the Performing Arts, 1980–94. Governor: Gordonstoun Sch., 1971–86; Royal Scottish Acad. of Music and Drama, 1979–82. FRCM 1967; FRSE 1983; FRSAMD 1985. DStJ 1977. DL Aberdeenshire, 1971. Hon. LLD Aberdeen, 1968; Hon. DMus CNAA, 1991. *Publications:* contribs to Aberdeen Univ. Jl, RCM magazine. *Address:* Haddo House, Aberdeen AB4 0ER. *T:* Tarves (01651) 851216. *Club:* Naval & Military.

ABERDOUR, Lord; John Stewart Sholto Douglas; *b* 17 Jan. 1952; *s* and *heir* of 22nd Earl of Morton, *qv*; *m* 1985, Amanda, *yr d* of David Mitchell, Kirkcudbright; one *s* two *d*. *Educ:* Dunrobin Castle School. Studied Agriculture, Aberdeen Univ. *Heir:* *s* Master of Aberdour, *qv*. *Address:* Haggs Farm, Kirknewton, Midlothian.

ABERDOUR, Master of; Hon. John David Sholto Douglas; *b* 28 May 1986; *s* and *heir* of Lord Aberdour, *qv*.

ABERGAVENNY, 5th Marquess of, *cr* 1876; **John Henry Guy Nevill,** KG 1974; OBE 1945; JP; Baron Abergavenny, 1450; Earl of Abergavenny and Viscount Nevill, 1784; Earl of Lewes, 1876; Lt-Col late Life Guards; Lord-Lieutenant of East Sussex, 1974–89 (Vice-Lieutenant of Sussex, 1970–74); Chancellor, Order of the Garter, 1977–94; *b* 8 Nov. 1914; *er s* of 4th Marquess and Isabel Nellie (*d* 1953), *d* of James Walker Larnach; *S* father, 1954; *m* 1938, Patricia (*see* Marchioness of Abergavenny); three *d* (and one *s* one *d* decd). *Educ:* Eton; Trinity Coll., Cambridge. Joined Life Guards, 1936; served War of 1939–45 (despatches, OBE); Lt-Col, retired 1946; Hon. Col, Kent & Co. of London Yeomanry, 1948–62. Director: Massey-Ferguson Holdings Ltd, 1955–85; Lloyds Bank Ltd, 1962–85; Lloyds Bank UK Management, 1962–85; Lloyds Bank SE Regional Bd (Chm.), 1962–85; Whitbread Investment Co. Trustee, Ascot Authority, 1953–; HM Representative at Ascot, 1972–82; President: Royal Assoc. of British Dairy Farmers, 1955 and 1963; Assoc. of Agriculture, 1961–63; Royal Agric. Soc. of England, 1967 (Dep. Pres. 1968, 1972); Hunters' Improvement Soc., 1959; British Horse Soc., 1970–71; Vice-Chm., Turf Bd, 1967–68; Mem. Nat. Hunt Cttee, 1942 (Senior Steward, 1953 and 1963); Mem. Jockey Club, 1952. Member: E Sussex CC, 1947–54 (Alderman 1954–62); E Sussex Agric. Cttee, 1948–54. JP Sussex, 1948; DL Sussex, 1955. KStJ 1976 (Pres. Council, Order of St John, Sussex, 1975). *Heir:* *nephew* Christopher George Charles Nevill [*b* 23 April 1955; *m* 1985, Venetia, *er d* of Frederick Maynard; one *s* decd]. *Address:* (seat) Eridge Park, Tunbridge Wells, East Sussex TN3 9JT. *T:* Tunbridge Wells (01892) 527378; Flat 2, 46 Pont Street, SW1X 0AD. *T:* 0171–581 3967. *Club:* White's.

See also Earl of Cottenham.

ABERGAVENNY, Marchioness of; Mary Patricia Nevill, DCVO 1981 (CVO 1970); an Extra Lady of the Bedchamber to the Queen, 1960–66 and since 1987 (a Lady of the Bedchamber, 1966–87); *b* 20 Oct. 1915; *d* of late Lt-Col John Fenwick Harrison, Royal Horse Guards, and Hon. Margery Olive Edith, *d* of 3rd Baron Burnham, DSO; *m* 1938, Marquess of Abergavenny, *qv*; three *d* (and one *s* one *d* decd). *Address:* Eridge Park, Tunbridge Wells, East Sussex; Flat 2, 46 Pont Street, SW1.

ABERNETHY, Hon. Lord; John Alastair Cameron; a Senator of the College of Justice in Scotland, since 1992; *b* 1 Feb. 1938; *s* of William Philip Legerwood Cameron and Kathleen Milthorpe (*née* Parker); *m* 1968, Elspeth Mary Dunlop Miller; three *s*. *Educ:* St Mary's, Melrose; Trinity Coll., Glenalmond; Pembroke Coll., Oxford (MA; Hon. Fellow, 1993). Nat. Service, 1956–58 (2nd Lieut, RASC). Called to the Bar, Inner Temple, 1963; admitted Mem., Faculty of Advocates, 1966, Vice-Dean, 1983–92; QC (Scotland) 1979. Advocate-Depute, 1972–75; Standing Jun. Counsel; to Dept of Energy, 1976–79; to Scottish Develt Dept, 1978–79. Legal Chm., Pensions Appeal Tribunals for Scotland, 1979–92 (Pres., 1985–92). *Publications:* Medical Negligence: an introduction, 1983; (contrib.) Reproductive Medicine and the Law, 1990. *Recreations:* travel, sport, Africana. *Address:* Court of Session, Parliament House, Edinburgh EH1 1RQ.

ABERNETHY, William Leslie, CBE 1972; FCA, IPFA; Managing Trustee, Municipal Mutual Insurance Ltd, and Director of associated companies, 1973–87; Comptroller of Financial Services, Greater London Council, 1972–73 (Treasurer, 1964–72) and Chief Financial Officer, Inner London Education Authority, 1967–73; *b* 10 June 1910; *s* of Robert and Margaret Abernethy; *m* 1937, Irene Holden; one *s*. *Educ:* Darwen Grammar Sch., Lancs. Hindle & Jepson, Chartered Accts, Darwen, 1925–31; Borough Treasurer's Dept, Darwen, 1931–37; Derbyshire CC, Treasurer's Dept, 1937–48 (Dep. Co. Treas., 1944–48); 1st Treas., Newcastle upon Tyne Regional Hosp. Bd, 1948–50. LCC: Asst Comptroller, 1950–56; Dep. Comptroller, 1956–64; Comptroller, Sept. 1964–Mar. 1965. Chm. Exec. Coun., RIPA, 1959–60. Mem. Council, IMTA, 1966–73. *Publications:* Housing Finance and Accounts (with A. R. Holmes), 1953; Internal Audit in Local Authorities and Hospitals, 1957; Internal Audit in the Public Boards, 1957; contribs professional jls. *Address:* 6 Thornhill Close, Port Erin, Isle of Man IM9 6NF. *T:* Port Erin (01624) 835316.

ABINGDON, Earl of; *see* Lindsey and Abingdon, Earl of.

ABINGER, 8th Baron, *cr* 1835; **James Richard Scarlett,** DL; Lt-Col, late Royal Artillery; farmer and company director; *b* 28 Sept. 1914; *e s* of 7th Baron and Marjorie (*d* 1965), 2nd *d* of John McPhillamy, Blair Athol, Bathurst, NSW; *S* father, 1943; *m* 1957, Isla Carolyn, *o d* of late Vice-Adm. J. W. Rivett-Carnac, CB, CBE, DSC; two *s*. *Educ:* Eton; Magdalene College, Cambridge (MA 1952). India, France, Airborne Corps, and attached RAF; RNXS, 1968. DL Essex, 1968. KStJ. *Heir:* *s* Hon. James Harry Scarlett [*b* 28 May 1959; *m* 1995, Tracy, *d* of N. Cloutier]. *Address:* Sheepcote House, Queen Street, Castle Hedingham, Halstead, Essex CO9 3HA. *T:* Halstead (01787) 460388; 7 Cumberland Street, SW1V 4LS. *T:* 0171–828 4708. *Clubs:* Carlton, Royal Automobile.

ABNEY-HASTINGS, family name of **Countess of Loudoun.**

ABOYNE, Earl of; Alistair Granville Gordon; *b* 26 July 1973; *s* and *heir* of Marquess of Huntly, *qv*. *Educ:* Harrow. *Address:* c/o Aboyne Castle, Aberdeenshire.

ABRAHAM, Ann; Chief Executive, National Association of Citizens Advice Bureaux, since 1991; *b* 25 Aug. 1952; *d* of John Kenneth and Kathleen Mary Marsden. *Educ:* Bedford Coll., Univ. of London (BA Hons German); Postgrad. DMS. MIH. Housing Manager, Local Govt, 1975–80; Ops Manager, Regional Dir and Ops Dir, Housing Corp., 1980–90. *Recreations:* walking, family, friends, football. *Address:* National Association of Citizens Advice Bureaux, Myddelton House, 115–123 Pentonville Road, N1 9LZ. *T:* 0171–833 2181.

ABRAHAM, Sir Edward (Penley), Kt 1980; CBE 1973; FRS 1958; MA, DPhil (Oxon); Fellow of Lincoln College, Oxford, 1948–80, Honorary Fellow, since 1980; Professor of Chemical Pathology, Oxford, 1964–80, now Emeritus Professor; *b* 10 June 1913; *s* of Albert Penley Abraham and Mary Abraham (*née* Hearn); *m* 1939, Asbjörg Harung, Bergen, Norway; one *s*. *Educ:* King Edward VI School, Southampton; The Queen's College, Oxford (1st cl. Hons Sch. of Natural Science), Hon. Fellow 1973. Rockefeller Foundation Travelling Fellow at Universities of Stockholm (1939) and California (1948). Ciba lecturer at Rutgers University, NJ, 1957; Guest lecturer, Univ. of Sydney, 1960; Reader in Chemical Pathology, Oxford, 1960–64. Founder: Edward Penley Abraham Res. Fund; Edward Penley Abraham Cephalosporin Fund. Lectures: Rennebohm, Univ. of Wisconsin, 1966–67; Squibb, Rutgers Univ., 72; Perlman, Univ. of Wisconsin, 1985; A. L. P. Garrod, RCP, 1986; Sarton, Univ. of Gent, 1989. Hon. Fellow: Linacre Coll., Oxford, 1976; Lady Margaret Hall, Oxford, 1978; Wolfson Coll., Oxford, 1982; St Peter's Coll., Oxford, 1983. For. Hon. Mem., Amer. Acad. of Arts and Scis, 1983. Hon. DSc: Exeter, 1980; Oxon, 1984; Strathclyde, 1989. Royal Medal, Royal Soc., 1973; Mullard Prize and Medal, Royal Soc., 1980; Scheele Medal, Swedish Academy of Pharmaceut. Sciences, 1975; Chemical Soc. Award in Medicinal Chemistry, 1975; Internat. Soc. Chemotherapy Award, 1983; Sarton Medal, Gent, 1989. *Publications:* Biochemistry of Some Peptide and Steroid Antibiotics, 1957; Biosynthesis and Enzymic Hydrolysis of Penicillins and Cephalosporins, 1974; contribs to: Antibiotics, 1949; The Chemistry of Penicillin, 1949; General Pathology, 1957, 4th edn 1970; Cephalosporins and Penicillins, Chemistry and Biology, 1972; scientific papers on the biochemistry of natural products, incl. penicillins and cephalosporins; contrib. Biographical Memoirs of Fellows of Royal Society (Lord Florey, 1971; Sir Ernst Chain, 1983). *Recreations:* walking, ski-ing. *Address:* Badger's Wood, Bedwells Heath, Boars Hill, Oxford OX1 5JE. *T:* Oxford (01865) 735395; Sir William Dunn School of Pathology, South Parks Road, Oxford OX1 3RE. *T:* Oxford (01865) 275571. *Club:* Athenæum.

ABRAHAM, Maj.-Gen. (Sutton) Martin (O'Heguerty), CB 1973; MC 1942 and Bar, 1943; Secretary, Bedford College, University of London, 1976–82, retired; *b* 26 Jan. 1919; *s* of Capt. E. G. F. Abraham, CB, late Indian Civil Service, and Ruth Eostre Abraham; *m* 1950, Iona Margaret, *d* of Sir John Stirling, KT, MBE; two *s* one *d*. *Educ:* Durnford; Eton; Trinity Coll., Cambridge (BA Modern Languages). Commissioned in RA, 1939; transf. to 12th Royal Lancers, 1941; Egypt, 1941; Armoured Car Troop Leader, desert campaigns; Armoured Car Sqdn 2nd-in-Comd, Italian campaign; accepted surrender of Trieste (Sqdn Ldr); Mil. Asst to C-in-C Austria, and BAOR, 1946; psc 1948; Mem. Chiefs of Staff Secretariat, 1949–52; Sqdn Ldr 12th Lancers, Malaya, 1953–54; Mem. Staff Coll. Directing Staff, 1955–57; 2nd-in-Comd 12th Lancers, 1957–58; CO 12th Lancers, 1958–62 (Cyprus, 1959–60); Asst Mil. Sec., Southern Comd, 1960–62; GSO1, Staff Coll. (Minley Div.), 1960–62; Comdr RAC (Brig.), 1st Brit. Corps, Germany, 1964–66; idc 1967; Dir, Combat Develt (Army), MoD, 1968–71; Chief of Jt Services Liaison Orgn, BAOR, 1971–73; Mil. Adviser to Arms Control and Disarmament Res. Unit and Western Organisations Dept, FCO, 1973–76, retd. Col, 9/12 Royal Lancers, 1977–81. Governor, Bedford Coll., 1982–85. *Recreations:* painting, reading, sundry country pursuits. *Address:* c/o C. Hoare & Co., 37 Fleet Street, EC4P 4DQ. *Club:* Cavalry and Guards.

ABRAHAMS, Anthony Claud Walter; advocate and solicitor, Brunei Darussalam, since 1987; *b* 16 June 1923; *s* of late Rt Hon. Sir Sidney Abrahams, QC, and of Ruth Bowman; *m* 1st, 1950, Laila Myking; two *s* one *d;* 2nd, 1982, Elizabeth, *d* of late Comdr A. E. Bryant, RN. *Educ:* Bedford Sch.; Emmanuel Coll., Cambridge (MA). Barrister-at-law. Served War: Wavell Cadet, Bangalore, 1942–43; commnd 3/12 Royal Bn, Frontier Force Regt, 1943–45; India, N Africa, Italy, Greece (despatches). Called to the Bar, Middle Temple, 1951; practised Midland Circuit, 1951–64. Gov., 1966–88, Chm., 1978–88, Harpur Trust (the Bedford Charity). Centre for British Teachers: Founder, 1964; Dir, 1973–82; Life Pres., 1982. Mem., Educn Cttee, British-Malaysian Soc., 1986–. Liveryman, Worshipful Co. of Glaziers. *Recreations:* golf, watching cricket and Rugby, wine, travel. *Address:* Goldsmith Building, Temple, EC4Y 7BL. *T:* 0171–353 7913. *Clubs:* Garrick, MCC, Jesters.

ABRAHAMS, Gerald Milton, CBE 1967; President, Aquascutum Group plc, since 1991 (Chairman and Managing Director, 1947–91); *b* 20 June 1917; *s* of late Isidor Abrahams; *m* 1st, 1946, Doris, *d* of Mark Cole, Brookline, Mass, USA; two *d;* 2nd, 1972, Marianne Wilson, *d* of David Kay, London. *Educ:* Westminster Sch. Served War of 1939–45, Major HAC, RHA, in Greece, W Desert and Ceylon. Member: Council, FBI, 1962–65, CBI, 1965–87; British Menswear Guild (Chm., 1959–61, 1964–66); Clothing Export Council (Chm., 1966–70; Vice-Pres., 1970–); Clothing Manufacturers Fedn of GB, 1960–82 (Chm., 1965–66); EDC for Clothing Industry, 1966–69; British Clothing Industry Assoc., 1982–87; BNEC Cttee for Exports to Canada, 1965–70; North American Adv. Gp, BOTB, 1978–87 (Vice Chm., 1983–87). FRSA 1972; CIMgt (CBIM 1973). *Recreations:* golf, tennis. *Address:* 100 Regent Street, W1A 2AQ. *T:* 0171–734 6090. *Club:* Buck's.

ABRAHAMS, Ivor, RA 1991 (ARA 1989); sculptor; *b* 10 Jan. 1935; *s* of Harry Abrahams and Rachel Kalisky; *m* 1st, 1966, Victoria Taylor; one *s*; 2nd, 1974, Evelyne Horvais; one *s*. *Educ:* Wigan Grammar Sch.; St Martin's and Camberwell Schools of Art. NDD(ScSp). Visiting Lecturer: Birmingham College of Art, 1960–63; Coventry College of Art, 1963–66; RCA, Slade Sch., 1980–82. *Major Exhibitions:* Kölnischer Kunstverein, Cologne, 1973; Ikon Gall., Birmingham, 1976; Yorkshire Sculpture Park, Wakefield, 1984. *Public Collections:* Arts Council of GB; Bibliotheque Nat., Paris; Brit. Council; Denver Mus., Colorado; Metropolitan Mus., NY; Nat. Gall. of Australia, Canberra; Tate Gall.; Mus. of Modern Art, NY; V&A Mus.; Wilhelm Lembruck Mus., Duisburg, W Germany; Boymans Mus., Rotterdam, etc. Winston Churchill Fellow, 1990. *Publications:* E. A. Poe: poems and tales (foreword Norbert Lynton), 1976; Oxford Garden Sketchbook (foreword Robert Melville), 1977. *Recreations:* golf, photography. *Address:* 67 Bathurst Gardens, NW10 5JH. *T:* 0181–969 2505. *Clubs:* Chelsea Arts, Colony Rooms.

ABRAHAMSEN, Egil; Comdr, Order of St Olav, 1987 (Kt Comdr 1979); Chairman, Norwegian Telecommunications, since 1980; *b* 7 Feb. 1923; *s* of Anker Christian Abrahamsen and Aagot (*née* Kjølberg); *m* 1950, Randi Wiborg; two *s* one *d*. *Educ:* Technical Univ. of Norway (Naval Architect, 1949); Durham Univ., King's Coll., Newcastle upon Tyne (post-grad. studies and res.); Univ. of Calif, Berkeley (post-grad. studies). Sales Engr, Maschienen-Fabrik Augsburg-Nürnberg, and Karlstads Mekaniska Verkstad AB, Sweden, 1949–50; projects and planning, A/S Rosenberg Mekanisk Verksted, Stavanger, 1951–52; Det Norske Veritas, 1952–85: Surveyor, 1952; Sen. Surveyor, 1954 (resp. for building up Res. Dept); Principal Surveyor, 1957; Dep. Pres., 1966; Vice Pres., 1967; Pres., 1967. Chairman: Norsk Hydro, 1985–92; OPAK, 1985–; Royal Caribbean Cruise-Line, 1987–88; Kosmos, 1988–; IKO Group, 1988–; Eikland, 1990–; Vice-Chm., IM Skaugen A/S, 1990–. Editor, European Shipbuilding, 1952–60. Fellow, Nat. Acad. of Engrg, USA, 1978; Member: Norwegian Acad. of Technical Scis, 1968; Royal Swedish Acad. of Engrg Scis, 1979; Hon. Mem., Soc. of Naval Architects and Marine Engrs, Norway, 1987. DTech *hc* Royal Inst. of Technol., Sweden, 1977. Owes Hon. Prize, for contribn to res. and educn, 1971. Grand Officer, Order of Infante Dom Henrique (Portugal), 1977; Comdr, Order of the Lion (Finland), 1982; Kt, Nat. Order of Merit (France), 1982. *Address:* Norwegian Telecom, PO Box 6701, St Olavs Plass, 0130 Oslo, Norway.

ABRAMS, Dr Michael Ellis, CB 1992; FRCP, FFPHM; public health consultant, since 1992; Deputy Chief Medical Officer, Department of Health (formerly of Health and Social Security), 1985–92; *b* 17 Sept. 1932; *s* of late Sam Philip and Ruhamah Emmie Abrams; *m* 1962, Rosalind J. Beckman; four *c*. *Educ:* King Edward's Sch., Birmingham; Univ. of Birmingham (BSc 1st Cl. Anat. and Physiol. 1953; MB ChB Distinction in Medicine 1956). FRCP 1972; MFCM (Founder Mem.) 1972, FFCM 1983. Ho. Officer posts in United Birmingham Hosps, 1957–58; Univ. Research Fellow, Dept of Exp. Pathology, Univ. of Birmingham, and Medical Registrar, Queen Elizabeth Hosp., Birmingham, 1959; Medical Registrar and MRC Clinical Res. Fellow, Queen Elizabeth Hosp., Birmingham, 1959–62; MRC Clin. Res. Fellow, Dept of Medicine, Guy's Hosp., London, 1962–63; Rockefeller Travelling Fellow, Cardiovascular Res. Inst., Univ. of California Med. Centre, San Francisco, 1963–64; Lectr/Sen. Lectr and Hon. Cons. Phys., Guy's Hosp., 1964–75; Chief Med. Adviser, Guy's Hosp./Essex Gen. Practice Computing Unit, 1968–73; Dir, Inter-Deptl Laboratory, Guy's Hosp., 1971–75; DHSS: SMO, 1975–78; PMO, 1978–79; SPMO, 1979–85. Vice-Chm., Haringey Healthcare NHS Trust, 1993–. Mem., WHO Council on Earth Summit Action Prog. for Health and Envmt, 1993–. Hon. Cons. Phys. Emeritus, Guy's Hosp. and Hon. Lectr in Medicine, Guy's Hosp. Med. Sch.; Examr in Human Communication, London Univ., 1972–84. President, Section of Measurement in Medicine, RSM, 1981–83; Chm., Computer Cttee, RCP, 1981–89. *Publications:* (ed) Medical Computing Progress and Problems, 1970; (ed) Spectrum 71, 1971; (ed) The Computer in the Doctor's Office, 1980; articles on biomedical computing, pulmonary surfactant and glucose tolerance in diabetes. *Recreations:* reading, gardening, beachcombing. *Address:* 97 Wood Vale, N10 3DL. *Club:* Athenæum.

ABRAMSKY, Jennifer, (Mrs Alasdair Liddell); Controller, BBC Radio Five Live and of Ceefax, since 1993; *b* 7 Oct. 1946; *d* of Chimen Abramsky and Miriam (*née* Nirenstein); *m* 1976, Alasdair D. MacDuff Liddell, *qv*; one *s* one *d*. *Educ:* Holland Park Sch.; Univ. of East Anglia (BA Hons English) (Dep. Chm., New Univs Fest., 1968). BBC: joined as Prog. Operations Asst, 1969; Producer, World at One, 1973; Jt Producer and Compiler of Special Prog. on 'Nixon', 1974; Editor: PM Prog., 1978–81; Radio Four Budget Prog., 1979–86; World at One, 1981–86; Today, 1986–87; News and Current Affairs, BBC Radio, 1987–93; set up Radio 4 News FM for duration of Gulf War, 1991. Member: ESRC, 1992–; Editl Bd, British Journalism Rev., 1993–. Hon. Prof., Univ. of Thames Valley, 1994. Woman of Distinction, Jewish Care, 1990. *Recreations:* theatre, music. *Address:* BBC, Broadcasting House, Portland Place, W1A 1AA. *T:* 0171–580 4468.

ABSE, Dr Dannie, FRSL; Specialist in charge of chest clinic, Central Medical Establishment, London, 1954–89; writer; *b* 22 Sept. 1923; *s* of Rudolph Abse and Kate (*née* Shepherd); *m* 1951, Joan (*née* Mercer); one *s* two *d*. *Educ:* St Illtyd's Coll., Cardiff; University Coll., Cardiff; King's Coll., London; Westminster Hosp., London. MRCS, LRCP. First book of poems accepted for publication, 1946. Qualified at Westminster Hosp., 1950; RAF, 1951–54, Sqdn Ldr; Sen. Fellow of the Humanities, Princeton Univ., 1973–74. Pres., Poetry Soc., 1978–92. FRSL 1983; Fellow, Welsh Acad., 1985. Hon. DLitt Wales, 1989. *Publications: poetry:* After Every Green Thing, 1948; Walking Under Water, 1952; Tenants of the House, 1957; Poems, Golders Green, 1962; A Small Desperation, 1968; Funland and other Poems, 1973; Collected Poems, 1977; Way Out in the Centre, 1981; Ask the Bloody Horse, 1986; White Coat, Purple Coat, 1989; Remembrance of Crimes Past, 1990; Selected Poems, 1994; On the Evening Road, 1994; *prose:* Ash on a Young Man's Sleeve, 1954; Journals from the Ant Heap, 1986; Intermittent Journals, 1994; *novels:* Some Corner of an English Field, 1957; O. Jones, O. Jones, 1970; There Was a Young Man from Cardiff, 1991; *autobiography:* A Poet in the Family, 1974; A Strong Dose of Myself, 1983; *plays:* House of Cowards, (first prod.) Questors Theatre, Ealing, 1960; The Dogs of Pavlov, (first prod.) Questors, 1969; Pythagoras, (first prod.) Birmingham Rep. Th., 1976; Gone in January, (first prod.) Young Vic, 1978; *anthologies edited:* (with Howard Sergeant) Mavericks, 1957; Modern European Verse, 1964; (with Joan Abse) Voices in the Gallery, 1986; (with Joan Abse) The Music Lover's Literary Companion, 1988; The Hutchinson Book of Post-War British Poets, 1989. *Recreations:* chess, watching Cardiff City FC. *Address:* 85 Hodford Road, NW11 8NH; Green Hollows, Craig-yr-Eos Road, Ogmore-by-Sea, Glamorgan, South Wales.
See also Leo Abse.

ABSE, Leo; *b* 22 April 1917; *s* of Rudolph and Kate Abse; *m* 1955, Marjorie Davies; one *s* one *d*. *Educ:* Howard Gardens High Sch.; LSE. Served RAF, 1940–45 (arrest for political activities in ME, 1944, precipitated parly debate). Solicitor; sen. partner, subseq. consultant in Cardiff law firm; first solicitor to be granted audience in High Court, 1986. Chm., Cardiff City Lab Party, 1951–53; Mem., Cardiff CC, 1953–58. Contested (Lab) Cardiff N, 1955. Fought a record 17 UK parly and local elections. MP (Lab): Pontypool, Nov. 1958–1983; Torfaen, 1983–87. Chm., Welsh Parly Party, 1976–87. Mem., Home Office Adv. Cttees on the Penal System, 1968, on adoption, 1972; first Chm., Select Cttee on Welsh Affairs, 1980; Mem., Select Cttee on Abortion, 1975–76; Sec., British-Taiwan Parly Gp, 1983–87. Led final parly campaign for abolition of capital punishment, 1969; sponsor or co-sponsor of Private Mem.'s Acts relating to divorce, homosexuality, family planning, legitimacy, widows' damages, industrial injuries, congenital disabilities and relief from forfeiture; sponsored Children's Bill, 1973, later taken over by Govt to become Children's Act, 1975; sponsored Divorce Bill, 1983, later taken over by Govt to become Matrimonial and Family Proceedings Act, 1985; initiated first Commons debates on genetic engineering, Windscale, *in vitro* pregnancies. Led Labour anti-devolution campaign in Wales, 1979. Mem. Council, Inst. for Study and Treatment of Delinquency, 1964–94, Vice-Pres., 1995–; Chm., Winnicott Clinic of Psychotherapy, 1988–91 (Trustee, 1980–); Pres., National Council for the Divorced and Separated, 1974–92; Vice-Pres., British Assoc. for Counselling, 1985–90; Chm., Parly Friends of WNO, 1985–87. Gov., Nat. Mus. of Wales, 1981–87; Member of Court: Univ. of Wales, 1981–87; UWIST. Regents' Lectr, Univ. of Calif, 1984. Received best dressed man award of Clothing Fedn, 1962. Wingate literary prize for non-fiction, Jewish Quarterly, 1994. Order of Brilliant Star (China), 1988. *Publications:* Private Member: a psychoanalytically orientated study of contemporary politics, 1973; (contrib.) In Vitro Fertilisation: past, present and future, 1986; Margaret, daughter of Beatrice: a psychobiography of Margaret Thatcher, 1989; Wotan, my enemy: can Britain live with the Germans?, 1994. *Recreations:* Italian wines, psycho-biography. *Address:* 54 Strand-on-the-Green, W4 3PD. *T:* 0181–994 1166; Via Poggio di Mezzo, Nugola Vecchia, Livorno, Italy. *T:* (586) 977022. *Club:* Savile.
See also D. Abse.

ABUBAKAR, Prof. Iya; Wali of Mubi; Director, National Mathematical Centre, Abuja; Pro-Chancellor and Chairman of Council, University of Ibadan, since 1993; *b* 14 Dec. 1934; *s* of Buba Abubakar, Wali of Mubi, and Fatima Abubakar; *m* 1963, Ummu; one *s* three *d*. *Educ:* Univ. of Ibadan (BSc London (External)); Cambridge Univ. (PhD). FRAS, FIMA. Ahmadu Bello Univ., Zaria, Nigeria: Prof. of Maths, 1967–75, 1978; Dean, Faculty of Science, 1968–69, 1973–75; Vice-Chancellor, 1975–78. Minister of Defence, Nigeria, 1979–82. Visiting Professor: Univ. of Michigan, 1965–66; City Univ. of New York, 1971–72. Chairman: Natural Sciences Reg. Council of Nigeria, 1972–75; Nat. Manpower Commn of Nigeria, 1992–. Mem., Nigerian Univs Commn, 1968–73. Dir, Central Bank of Nigeria, 1972–75. Hon. DSc Ife, 1977: Ahmadu Bello, 1980. *Publications:* Entebbe Modern Mathematics, 1970; several research papers on mathematics in internat. jls. *Recreations:* chess, golf, horse riding. *Address:* National Mathematical Centre, PMB 118, Abuja, Nigeria.

ACHEBE, Prof. Chinua, FRSL 1983; author; Professor Emeritus, University of Nigeria, since 1984; Pro-Chancellor and Chairman of Council, Anambra State University of Technology, Enugu, 1986–88; *b* 16 Nov. 1930; *s* of Isaiah and Janet Achebe; *m* 1961, Christiana Okoli; two *s* two *d*. *Educ:* Univ. of Ibadan. Nigerian Broadcasting Corp.: Talks Producer, 1954; Controller, 1959; Dir, 1961–66. Rockefeller Fellowship, 1960; Unesco Fellowship, 1963; Professor of English: Univ. of Massachusetts, 1972–75; Univ. of Connecticut, Storrs, 1975–76; Univ. of Nigeria, Nsukka, 1973–81. Fulbright Prof., Univ. of Massachusetts, 1987–88; Vis. Distinguished Prof. of English, City Coll., City Univ. of NY, 1989; Vis. Prof., Stanford Univ., 1990. Chairman: Soc. of Nigerian Authors, 1966; Assoc. of Nigerian Authors, 1982–86. Member: Council, Univ. of Lagos, 1966; Exec. Cttee, Commonwealth Arts Orgn, London, 1981–. Neil Gunn Internat. Fellowship, Scottish Arts Council, 1975; Hon. Fellow: Modern Language Assoc. of America, 1975; Amer. Acad. and Inst. of Arts and Letters, 1982. Editor, Okike, 1971–. Patron, Writers and Scholars Educnl Trust, London, and Writers and Scholars Internat., 1972–; Governor, Newsconcern Internat. Foundn, London, 1983–. Hon. DLitt: Dartmouth Coll., 1972; Southampton, 1975; Ife, 1978; Nigeria, 1981; Kent, 1982; Guelph and Mount Allison, 1984; Franklin Pierce Coll., 1985; Ibadan, 1989; Skidmore Coll., 1990; DUniv: Open, 1989; Stirling, 1975; Hon. LLD Prince Edward Island, 1976; Hon. DHL: Massachusetts, 1977; Westfield Coll., 1989; Georgetown Univ., 1990. Jock Campbell New Statesman Award, 1965; Commonwealth Poetry Prize, 1972; Commonwealth Foundn Sen. Vis. Practitioner Award, 1983. Nigerian Nat. Merit Award, 1979; Order of the Fed. Repub. (Nigeria), 1979. Chm. and Publisher, African Commentary Magazine. *Publications:* Things

Fall Apart, 1958; No Longer at Ease, 1960; Arrow of God, 1964; A Man of the People, 1966; Beware Soul-brother (poems), 1971; Girls at War, 1972; Morning Yet on Creation Day (essays), 1975; The Trouble with Nigeria (essays), 1983; Anthills of the Savannah, 1987; Hopes and Impediments (essays), 1987; *for children:* Chike and the River, 1966; (jt) How the Leopard Got its Claws, 1971; The Flute, 1978; The Drum, 1978. *Recreation:* music. *Address:* PO Box 53, Nsukka, Nigeria.

ACHESON, family name of **Earl of Gosford.**

ACHESON, Sir (Ernest) Donald, KBE 1986; Chief Medical Officer, Departments of Health and of Social Security (formerly Department of Health and Social Security), Department of Education and Science and Home Office, 1983–91; *b* 17 Sept. 1926; *s* of Malcolm King Acheson, MC, MD, and Dorothy Josephine Rennoldson; *m* Barbara Mary Castle; one *s* four *d* (and one *d* decd). *Educ:* Merchiston Castle Sch., Edinburgh; Brasenose Coll., Oxford (Theodore Williams Schol. in pathology, 1946; MA, DM; Hon. Fellow, 1989); Middlesex Hospital (Sen. Broderip Schol. in Med., Surg. and Pathol., 1950). FRCP; FRCS; FFPHM; FFOM. Sqdn Leader, RAF Med. Br., 1953–55. Medical Practitioner, 1951; various clinical posts at Middlesex Hosp.; Radcliffe Trav. Fellow of University Coll., Oxford, 1957–59; Medical Tutor, Nuffield Dept of Medicine, Radcliffe Infirmary, Oxford, 1960; Dir, Oxford Record Linkage Study and Unit of Clin. Epidemiology, 1962; May Reader in Medicine, 1965; Fellow, Brasenose Coll., Oxford, 1968; Prof. of Clinical Epidemiology, Univ. of Southampton, and Hon. Consultant Physician, Royal South Hants Hosp., 1968–83; Foundation Dean, Faculty of Med., Southampton Univ., 1968–78; Dir, MRC Unit in Environmental Epidemiology, 1979–83. Member: Wessex Regional Hosp. Bd, 1968–74; Hampshire AHA (Teaching) 1974–78; Chm., SW Hants and Southampton DHA, 1981–83; Member: Adv. Cttee on Asbestos, Health and Safety Exec., 1978; Royal Commn on Environmental Pollution, 1979–83; UGC, 1982–83; GMC, 1984–91; MRC, 1984–91; Chairman: Slow Virus Group, DHSS, 1979–80; Primary Health Care Inner London Gp, DHSS, 1980–81; Enquiry into Public Health in England, 1988; Home Office Adv. Cttee on Health of Prisoners, 1992–. UK Rep., Exec. Bd, WHO, 1988–90; Special Rep. of WHO in former Yugoslavia, 1992–93. Trustee, SCF, 1991–93. R. Samuel McLaughlin Vis. Prof., McMaster Univ., 1977; King's Fund Travelling Fellow, NZ Postgrad. Med. Fedn, 1979; Vis. Prof. of Internat. Health, Dept of Public Health and Policy, LSHTM, 1991–. Lectures: inaugural Adolf Streicher Meml, Stoke-on-Trent, 1978; Walter Hubert, British Assoc. for Cancer Res., 1981; Christie Gordon, Univ. of Birmingham, 1982; Edwin Chadwick Centennial, LSHTM, 1990, etc. Examiner in Community Medicine: Univ. of Aberdeen, 1971–74; Univ. of Leicester, 1981–82; Examiner in Medicine, Univ. of Newcastle upon Tyne, 1975. Mem., Assoc. of Physicians of GB and Ire, 1965– (Pres. 1979). Hon. Fellow: LSHTM; UCL. Hon. FRSocMed 1994. Hon. DM Southampton, 1984; Hon. DSc: Newcastle, 1984; Salford, 1991; Hon. MD: QUB, 1987; Nottingham, 1989; Birmingham, 1991; Hon. LLD Aberdeen, 1988. Leon Bernard Foundn Prize, WHO, 1994. *Publications:* Medical Record Linkage, 1967; Multiple Sclerosis, a reappraisal, 1966; Medicine, an outline for the intending student, 1970; scientific papers on epidemiology of cancer and chronic disease, medical education and organisation of medical care. *Recreations:* family, gardening, music. *Address:* London School of Hygiene and Tropical Medicine, Keppel Street, WC1E 7HT. *Club:* Athenæum.

See also R. M. Acheson.

ACHESON, Prof. Roy Malcolm, ScD, DM; FRCP, FFCM, FFOM; Professor of Community Medicine, University of Cambridge, 1976–88, now Emeritus; Fellow, Churchill College, Cambridge, since 1976; *b* 18 Aug. 1921; *s* of Malcolm King Acheson, MC, MD and Dorothy Rennoldson; *m* 1950, Fiona Marigo O'Brien (marr. diss. 1990); two *s* one *d*. *Educ:* Merchiston Castle Sch., Edinburgh; TCD (MA, ScD); Brasenose Coll., Oxford (MA, DM); Radcliffe Infirmary, Oxford. FRCP 1973; FFCM 1972; FFOM (by distinction) 1984. Clin. and res. posts, Radcliffe Infirmary and Univ. of Oxford; Rockefeller Trav. Fellow, Western Reserve and Harvard Univs, 1955–56; Radcliffe Trav. Fellow, Univ. of Oxford, 1955–57; Lectr in Social Med., Univ. of Dublin, 1955–59; FTCD, 1957–59; Sen. Lectr, then Reader in Social and Preventive Med., Guy's Hosp. Med. Sch. and London Sch. of Hygiene and Trop. Med., 1959–62, Yale University: Associate Prof. of Epidemiology, 1962; Prof. of Epidemiology, 1964–72; Fellow, Jonathan Edwards Coll., 1966–75; London Sch. of Hygiene and Tropical Medicine: Commonwealth Fund Sen. Trav. Fellow in Med., 1968–69; Dir, Centre for Extension Trng in Community Med., 1972–76. Hon. Cons. in Community Med., NE Thames RHA (formerly NE Metrop. RHB), 1972–76, E Anglian RHA, 1976–88; Prof. of Health Service Studies, Univ. of London, 1974–76. Samuel R. McLaughlin Vis. Prof. in Med., McMaster Univ., Hamilton, Ont, 1976. Member: Exec. Cttee and Council, Internat. Epidemiol Soc., 1964–75; Expert Cttee, Methods in Chronic Disease Epidemiol., WHO, 1966; GMC, 1979–88 (Mem. Exec. Cttee, 1979–88; Mem. Educn Cttee, 1979–86); GDC, 1985–88 (Mem. Educn Cttee, 1985–88); Cambridge HA, 1986–88. Cons., Argentina, Colombia, Guatemala, India, Venezuela, WHO, 1965–76; Rapporteur, Adv. Cttee on Med. Res., WHO, 1976–79. Faculty of Community Medicine: Mem. Bd, 1974–84; Sec. to Examrs, 1974–77; Vice Pres., 1986–88; and Mem., numerous cttees. Gov., Action in Internat. Medicine, 1989–92; Councillor, Oral and Dental Res. Trust, 1989–91. Hon. Fellow: Buenos Aires Acad. of Medicine, 1980; Singapore Acad. of Medicine, 1988. Hon. MA Yale, 1964. *Publications:* (ed) Comparability in International Epidemiology, 1965; Seminars in Community Medicine: (ed with L. Aird) I: Sociology, 1976; (ed with L. Aird and D. J. Hall) II: Health Information, Planning and Monitoring, 1971; (with S. Hagard) Health, Society and Medicine: an introduction to community medicine, 1985; (jtly) Costs and Benefits of the Heart Transplantation Programmes at Harefield and Papworth Hospitals, 1985; (jtly) History of Education in Public Health, 1991. *Recreations:* golf (when time permits); country matters; meditating in the bath. *Address:* Churchill College, Cambridge CB3 0DS. *T:* Cambridge (01223) 336000. *Clubs:* United Oxford & Cambridge University; Gog Magog Golf.

See also Sir E. D. Acheson.

ACHONRY, Bishop of, (RC), since 1977; **Most Rev. Thomas Flynn,** DD; *b* 8 July 1931; *s* of Robert and Margaret Flynn. *Educ:* St Nathy's, Ballaghaderreen; Maynooth College. BD, LPh, MA. Diocesan Religious Inspector of Schools, 1957–64; teaching in St Nathy's College, Ballaghaderreen, 1964–73; President and Headmaster of St Nathy's Coll., 1973–77. DD 1977. *Recreations:* gardening, fishing, golf. *Address:* St Nathy's, Ballaghaderreen, Co. Roscommon, Eire. *T:* Ballaghaderreen (0907) 60021.

ACKERMANN, Georg K.; *see* Kahn-Ackermann.

ACKERS, Sir James George, Kt 1987; Chairman, West Midlands Regional Health Authority, 1982–93; *b* 20 Oct. 1935; *s* of James Ackers and Vera Harriet Ackers (*née* Edwards). *Educ:* Oundle Sch., Northants; LSE. Bsc(Econ). Man. Dir, 1963, Chm., 1974–91, Ackers Jarrett Ltd; Chm., Ackers Jarrett Leasing Ltd, 1982–91; Vice Pres., Michael Doud Gill & Associates, Washington, DC, 1968–71. Pres., Walsall Chamber of Industry and Commerce, 1978; Association of British Chambers of Commerce, 1982–: Dep. Chm., 1982–84; Chm., 1984–86; Pres., 1986–90. Member: Cttee of Inquiry into Civil Service Pay, 1981–; Monopolies and Mergers Commn, 1981–90; Nat. Trng Task Force, 1989–91; NEDC, 1989–92. Chm., Fedn of Univ. Conservative Assocs, 1958; Vice-Chm., Bow Group, 1962–63. Pres., Jerome K. Jerome Soc., 1985–93. *Address:* 39 Newstead, The Alders, Tamworth, Staffordshire B79 7UU.

ACKLAND, Joss, (Sidney Edmond Jocelyn); actor; *b* 29 Feb. 1928; *s* of Major Norman Ackland, Journalist, Daily Telegraph and Morning Post, and Ruth Izod; *m* 1951, Rosemary Jean Kirkcaldy, actress; one *s* five *d* (and one *s* decd). *Educ:* Cork Grammar Sch.; Dame Alice Owens Sch.; Central Sch. of Speech Training and Dramatic Art. *Plays:* The Hasty Heart, Aldwych, 1945; The Rising Sun, Arts, 1946; Dir, Winterset, 20th Century, 1946; Shakespeare Fest., Stratford-on-Avon, 1947; various try-out plays at Irving, Q, and Watergate Theatres, and toured, with Easy Money, in Germany, 1948; acted for Anthony Hawtrey, Embassy, Buxton and Croydon; then Arts Council tour, first Pitlochry Fest.; tours, and Repertory at Windsor, Chesterfield and Coventry. Went, with family, to Malawi, Central Africa, to work as a tea planter, 1954. S Africa: acting, directing, script writing and disc-jockeying, 1955–57; returned to England and joined Oxford Playhouse Co., 1957. Old Vic Co.: (incl. tours of America, Canada, USSR, Yugoslavia and Poland) Falstaff, Toby Belch, Caliban, Pistol, etc, 1958–61; Associate Dir, Mermaid Theatre: casting, choosing plays, Dir, Plough and the Stars, and playing numerous leading rôles, 1961–63. In 1963 his house burnt down so concentrated on television and did not return to theatre until 1965. Leading rôles on London stage: The Professor, in The Professor, 1966; Jorrocks, in Jorrocks, 1967; Hotel in Amsterdam, 1968–69; Come As You Are, 1969–70; Brassbound, in Captain Brassbound's Conversion, 1971; The Collaborators, 1973; Mitch, in A Streetcar Named Desire, 1974; Frederick, in A Little Night Music, 1975–76; The Madras House, 1977; Juan Perón, in Evita, 1978; Falstaff, in Henry IV pts 1 and 2, RSC, opening of Barbican Theatre, 1982; Captain Hook and Mr Darling, in Peter Pan, Barbican, 1982; Romain Gary, in Jean Seberg, NT, 1983; Stewart, in Pack of Lies, 1984; Captain Hook in Peter Pan, 1985; Clarence Darrow, in Never the Sinner, Playhouse, 1990; tours: Petruchio, in The Taming of the Shrew, 1977; Sir, in The Dresser; Gaev in The Cherry Orchard, Chichester, 1981. *Films:* Seven Days to Noon, 1949; Crescendo, 1969; The House that Dripped Blood, Villain, 1970; The Happiness Cage, England Made Me, 1971; Penny Gold, The Little Prince, The Black Windmill, S-P-Y-S, The Three Musketeers, 1973; Great Expectations, One of our Dinosaurs is Missing, 1974; Operation Daybreak, Royal Flash, 1975; The Silver Bears, 1976; The End of Civilisation as we know it, The Greek Tycoon, Someone is killing the Great Chefs of Europe, 1977; Saint Jack, The Apple, Rough Cut, 1978; Lady Jane, 1984; A Zed and Two Noughts, 1985; Don Masino, in The Sicilian, 1987; Sir Jock Broughton, in White Mischief, The Colonel, in To Kill a Priest, 1988; Lethal Weapon II, The Hunt for Red October, To Forget Palermo, 1989; The Object of Beauty, The Sheltering Desert, 1991; The Bridge, Bill and Ted's Bogus Adventure, Voices in the Garden, The Mighty Ducks, Nowhere to Run, Pin for the Butterfly, 1992; Occhio Pinocchio (Italy), 1995; Giorgino (France), 1995; Miracle on 34th Street, Mad Dogs and Englishmen, 1995. Numerous appearances on TV, incl. Alan Holly in First and Last, C. S. Lewis in Shadowlands, Barrett in The Barretts of Wimpole Street, Goering in The Man Who Lived at the Ritz, Queenie, the photographer in When We Are Married, They Do It With Mirrors, Onassis in A Woman Named Jackie (US), A Murder of Quality; also TV series: Kipling; The Crezz; Tinker, Tailor, Soldier, Spy; Shroud for a Nightingale; Killing on the Exchange; The Colonel's Lady; Codename Kyril; A Quiet Conspiracy; The Justice Game; Ashenden; The Bible (US). *Publication:* I Must Be in There Somewhere, 1989. *Recreations:* his children, writing, painting. *Club:* Garrick.

ACKNER, family name of **Baron Ackner.**

ACKNER, Baron *cr* 1986 (Life Peer), of Sutton in the county of West Sussex; **Desmond James Conrad Ackner;** Kt 1971; PC 1980; a Lord of Appeal in Ordinary, 1986–92; *b* 18 Sept. 1920; *s* of Dr Conrad and Rhoda Ackner; *m* 1946, Joan, *d* of late John Evans, JP, and widow of K. B. Spence; one *s* two *d*. *Educ:* Highgate Sch.; Clare Coll., Cambridge (MA; Hon. Fellow, 1983). Served in RA, 1941–42; Admty Naval Law Br., 1942–45. Called to Bar, Middle Temple, 1945; QC 1961; Recorder of Swindon, 1962–71; Judge of Courts of Appeal of Jersey and Guernsey, 1967–71; a Judge of the High Court of Justice, Queen's Bench Div., 1971–80; Judge of the Commercial Court, 1973–80; Presiding Judge, Western Circuit, 1976–79; a Lord Justice of Appeal, 1980–86. Mem. Gen. Council of Bar, 1957–61, 1963–70 (Hon. Treas., 1964–66; Vice-Chm., 1966–68; Chm., 1968–70); Bencher Middle Temple, 1965, Dep. Treasurer, 1983, Treasurer, 1984; Mem. Senate of the Four Inns of Court, 1966–70 (Vice-Pres., 1968–70); Pres., Senate of the Inns of Court and the Bar, 1980–82. Chm., Law Adv. Cttee, British Council, 1980–90 (Mem., 1991–); Mem., Lloyd's Arbitration Panel, 1992–. Pres., Arb. Appeal Tribunal, SFA, 1994–. Appeal Comr, PIA, 1994–; Dir, City Disputes Panel, 1994–. Hon. Mem., Canadian Bar Assoc., 1973–. Pres., Soc. of Sussex Downsmen, 1993–. *Recreations:* swimming, gardening, theatre. *Address:* Law Lords' Office, House of Lords, SW1A 0PW. *T:* 0171–219 3243; 4 Pump Court, Temple, EC4Y 7AN. *T:* 0171–353 2656; Browns House, Sutton, near Pulborough, West Sussex RH20 1PU. *T:* Sutton (Sussex) (01798) 869206.

ACKRILL, Prof. John Lloyd, FBA 1981; Professor of the History of Philosophy, Oxford University, 1966–89, now Emeritus; Fellow of Brasenose College, Oxford, 1953–89, now Emeritus; *b* 30 Dec. 1921; *s* of late Frederick William Ackrill and Jessie Anne Ackrill; *m* 1953, Margaret Walker Kerr; one *s* three *d*. *Educ:* Reading School; St John's Coll., Oxford (Scholar) (1940–41 and 1945–48). War service (Royal Berks Regt and GS, Capt.), 1941–45. Assistant Lecturer in Logic, Glasgow Univ., 1948–49; Univ. Lectr in Ancient Philosophy, Oxford, 1951–52; Tutorial Fellow, Brasenose Coll., 1953–66. Mem., Inst. for Adv. Study, Princeton, 1950–51, 1961–62; Fellow Coun. of Humanities, and Vis. Prof., Princeton Univ., 1955, 1964. *Publications:* Aristotle's *Categories* and *De Interpretatione* (trans. with notes), 1963; Aristotle's Ethics, 1973; Aristotle the Philosopher, 1981; New Aristotle Reader, 1987; articles in philos. and class. jls. *Address:* 22 Charlbury Road, Oxford OX2 6UU. *T:* Oxford (01865) 56098.

ACKROYD, Keith, CBE 1994; FRPharmS; Chairman: Trent Regional Health Authority, since 1994; Silentnight Holdings plc, since 1995 (Director, since 1993); *b* 6 July 1934; *s* of Edward Ackroyd and Ethel (*née* Bate); *m* 1958, Ellen Gwenda Thomas; two *s* one *d*. *Educ:* Heath Grammar Sch.; Bradford Sch. of Pharmacy; London Business Sch. FRPharmS 1981. Boots The Chemists Ltd: Apprentice Pharmacist, 1952; Dir, 1975–94; Midlands Area Dir, 1976–77; Man. Dir, 1983–89; Pres., Boots Drug Stores (Canada) Ltd, 1977–79; Boots Company plc: Dir, 1979–94; Man. Dir, Retail Div., 1984–94; Chairman: Halfords Ltd, 1989–94; A. G. Stanley, 1989–94; Do It All Ltd, 1992–94; Director: Takare plc, 1994–; Nottingham Gp plc, 1994–; Cowie plc, 1994–. Chairman: Company Chemists Assoc., 1983–89; British Retailers Assoc., 1988–92; British Retail Consortium, 1992–94. Member: Passport Agency Bd, 1991–; Nat. Bd for Crime Prevention, 1993–95. CIMgt 1981; FInstD 1979. Liveryman, Soc. of Apothecaries, 1990–. *Recreations:* drinking wine, country sport. *Address:* Millfield, Bradmore, Nottingham NG11 6PF. *T:* Nottingham (0115) 921 6052. *Club:* Royal Automobile.

ACKROYD, Norman, RA 1991 (ARA 1988); RE 1985; artist (painter and etcher); *b* 26 March 1938; *s* of late Albert Ackroyd, master butcher, and Clara Briggs, weaver; *m* 1st,

1963, Sylvia Buckland (marr. diss. 1975); two *d*; 2nd, 1978, Penelope Hughes-Stanton; one *s* one *d*. *Educ:* Cockburn High Sch., Leeds; Leeds Coll. of Art; Royal Coll. of Art (ARCA 1964). Teaches occasionally at RA, Slade, RCA and in N. America; Tutor in Etching, Central Sch. of Arts, London, 1965–93. Over 50 one-man exhibns, 1970–, mainly in UK and USA; work in public collections includes: Tate Gall.; BM; V&A; Arts Council; British Council; Mus. of Modern Art, NY; Nat. Galls of Scotland, Norway, Canada, S Africa; Albertina, Vienna; Rijksmus. and Stedelyk, Amsterdam; Musée d'Art Histoire, Geneva; Nat. Gall. of Art, Washington. Mural commissions include: Albany, Glasgow, 1975; Haringey Cultural Centre, 1985; Lloyds Bank Technol. Centre, London, 1990; British Airways, 1991; Freshfields, London, 1992; Tetrapak, London, 1993. TV work includes: Artists in Print (etching), BBC 2, 1981; A Prospect of Rivers, Channel 4, 1988. Awards: Bradford Internat. Biennale, 1972, 1982; Royal Soc. of Etchers and Engravers, 1984, 1985; Bronze Medal, Frechen, Germany, 1986. *Publications:* A Cumberland Journey, 1981; Travels with Copper and Zinc, 1983; (with Douglas Dunn) The Pictish Coast, 1988; St Kilda: the furthest land, 1989; Windrush, 1990; numerous collections of etchings from travels in the British Isles, occasionally with poets. *Recreations:* cricket, archæology. *Address:* Royal Academy of Arts, Piccadilly, W1V 0DS. *T:* 0171–378 6001. *Clubs:* Chelsea Arts, Arts.

ACKROYD, Peter; writer; Chief Book Reviewer, The Times, since 1986; *b* 5 Oct. 1949; *s* of Graham Ackroyd and Audrey Whiteside. *Educ:* St Benedict's Sch., Ealing; Clare Coll., Cambridge (MA); Yale Univ. (Mellon Fellow). Literary Editor, 1973–77, Jt Managing Editor, 1978–82, The Spectator. FRSL 1984. Hon. DLitt Exeter, 1992. *Publications: poetry:* London Lickpenny, 1973; Country Life, 1978; The Diversions of Purley, 1987; *novels:* The Great Fire of London, 1982; The Last Testament of Oscar Wilde, 1983 (Somerset Maugham Prize, 1984); Hawksmoor, 1985 (Whitbread Award; Guardian Fiction Prize); Chatterton, 1987; First Light, 1989; English Music, 1992; The House of Doctor Dee, 1993; Dan Leno and the Limehouse Golem, 1994; *non-fiction:* Notes for a New Culture, 1976; Dressing Up, 1979; Ezra Pound and his World, 1980; T. S. Eliot, 1984 (Whitbread Award; Heinemann Award); Dickens, 1990; Introduction to Dickens, 1991; Blake, 1995. *Address:* c/o Anthony Sheil Associates Ltd, 43 Doughty Street, WC1N 2LF. *T:* 0171–405 9351.

ACKROYD, Rev. Prof. Peter Runham, MA, PhD Cantab, BD, MTh, DD London; Samuel Davidson Professor of Old Testament Studies, University of London, 1961–82, now Emeritus Professor; *b* 15 Sept. 1917; *s* of Jabez Robert Ackroyd and Winifred (*née* Brown); *m* 1st, 1940, Evelyn Alice Nutt (*d* 1990), BSc (Manch.), *d* of William Young Nutt; two *s* three *d*; 2nd, 1991, Ann, MA (Oxon), *d* of James Golden. *Educ:* Harrow County School for Boys; Downing and Trinity Colleges, Cambridge. Open Exhibition in Modern Languages, Downing Coll., Cambridge, 1935; Mod. and Med. Langs Tripos, Pt I, 1936, Pt II, 1938; BDHons London, 1940; Stanton Student, Trin. Coll., Cambridge, 1941–43; Dr Williams's Trust Exhibnr, 1941; MTh London, 1942; PhD Cambridge, 1945; DD London, 1970. Minister of: Roydon Congregational Church, Essex, 1943–47; Balham Congregational Church, London, 1947–48; Lectr in Old Testament and Biblical Hebrew, Leeds Univ., 1948–52; Cambridge University: Univ. Lectr in Divinity, 1952–61; Select Preacher, 1955; Mem. Council of Senate, 1957–61; Hulsean Lectr, 1960–62; Select Preacher, Oxford, 1962, 1981 (McBride Sermon); Dean of Faculty of Theology, King's Coll., London, 1968–69; FKC 1969; Mem. Senate, London Univ., 1971–79; Dean, Univ. Faculty of Theology, 1976–80. Vis. Professor: Lutheran Sch. of Theology, Chicago, 1967 and 1976; Univ. of Toronto, 1972; Univ. of Notre Dame, Indiana, 1982; Emory Univ., Atlanta, 1984. Lectures: Selwyn, NZ, 1970; Ethel M. Wood, Univ. of London, 1982; (first) Walter S. Williams, Denver, 1982; Tübingen, 1983; Haskell, Oberlin, Ohio, 1984; series of lectures, Japan, 1983. External Examiner, Belfast, Bristol, Durham, Cambridge, Edinburgh, Leeds, Nottingham, Exeter, West Indies. Ordained Deacon, 1957; Priest, 1958; Hon. Curate, Holy Trinity, Cambridge, 1957–61. Proctor in Convocation, Cambridge Univ., 1960–64. Pres., Soc. for Old Testament Study, 1972 (Foreign Sec., 1986–89); Hon. Mem., Soc. of Biblical Literature, 1982–; Chairman: Council, British Sch. of Archaeology in Jerusalem, 1979–83; Palestine Exploration Fund, 1986–90 (Hon. Sec., 1962–70). Hon. DD St Andrews, 1970. *Publications:* Freedom in Action, 1951; The People of the Old Testament, 1959, new edn 1981; Continuity, 1962; The Old Testament Tradition, 1963; Exile and Restoration, 1968; Israel under Babylon and Persia, 1970; 1 & 2 Chronicles, Ezra, Nehemiah, Ruth, Jonah, Maccabees, 1970; 1 Samuel (Cambridge Bible Commentary), 1971; I & II Chronicles, Ezra, Nehemiah (Torch Bible Commentary), 1973; 2 Samuel, 1977; Doors of Perception, 1978, new edn 1983; Studies in the Religious Tradition of the Old Testament, 1987; The Chronicler in His Age, 1991; articles and reviews in various learned jls, dictionaries, etc; *translations:* E. Würthein's The Text of the Old Testament, 1957; L. Köhler's Hebrew Man, 1957, repr. 1973; O. Eissfeldt's The Old Testament: An Introduction, 1965; *editor:* Bible Key Words, 1961–64; Society for Old Testament Study Book List, 1967–73; Palestine Exploration Quarterly, 1971–86; *joint editor:* SCM Press OT Library, 1960–80; Cambridge Bible Commentary, 1961–79; SCM Studies in Biblical Theol., 1962–77; Words and Meanings: Essays presented to D. W. Thomas, 1968; Cambridge History of the Bible; vol. I, 1970; Oxford Bible Series, 1979–92; Cambridge Commentaries: Jewish and Christian Writings of the period 200 BC to AD 200, 1979–. *Recreations:* reading, music. *Address:* 155 Northumberland Road North, Harrow, Middlesex HA2 7RB. *T:* 0181–429 0396.

ACKROYD, Sir Timothy Robert Whyte, 3rd Bt *cr* 1956, of Dewsbury, West Riding of Yorkshire; actor; *b* 7 Oct. 1958; *er s* of Sir John Robert Whyte Ackroyd, 2nd Bt and of Jennifer Eileen McLeod, *d* of H. G. S. Bishop; *S* father, 1995. *Educ:* Bradfield; LAMDA. *Heir: b* Andrew John Armitage Ackroyd, *b* 17 Sept. 1961.

ACLAND, Sir Antony (Arthur), GCMG 1986 (KCMG 1982; CMG 1976); GCVO 1991 (KCVO 1976); HM Diplomatic Service, retired; Provost of Eton, since 1991; *b* 12 March 1930; *s* of late Brig. P. B. E. Acland, OBE, MC, TD and of Bridget Susan Acland; *m* 1956, Clare Anne Verdon (*d* 1984); two *s* one *d*; *m* 1987, Jennifer McGougan (*née* Dyke). *Educ:* Eton; Christ Church, Oxford (MA 1956). Joined Diplomatic Service, 1953; ME Centre for Arab Studies, 1954; Dubai, 1955; Kuwait, 1956; FO, 1958–62; Asst Private Sec. to Sec. of State, 1959–62; UK Mission to UN, 1962–66; Head of Chancery, UK Mission, Geneva, 1966–68; FCO, 1968, Hd of Arabian Dept, 1970–72; Principal Private Sec. to Foreign and Commonwealth Sec., 1972–75; Ambassador to Luxembourg, 1975–77, to Spain, 1977–79; Deputy Under-Sec. of State, FCO, 1980–82, Perm. Under-Sec. of State, FCO, and Head of Diplomatic Service, 1982–86; Ambassador to Washington, 1986–91. Director: Shell Transport and Trading, 1991–; Booker plc, 1992–. Chairman: Council, Ditchley Foundn, 1991–; Tidy Britain Gp, 1992–. Trustee, Nat. Portrait Gall., 1991–. Chancellor, Order of St Michael and St George, 1994. Hon. DCL: Exeter, 1988; William and Mary Coll., USA, 1990; Reading, 1992. *Address:* Provost's Lodge, Eton College, Windsor, Berks SL4 6DH. *Club:* Brooks's.

See also Maj.-Gen. Sir J. H. B. Acland.

ACLAND, Lt-Col Sir (Christopher) Guy (Dyke), 6th Bt *cr* 1890; MVO 1990; Deputy Master of the Household and Equerry to Her Majesty, since 1994; *b* 24 March 1946; *s* of Major Sir Antony Guy Acland, 5th Bt, and of Margaret Joan, *e d* of late Major Nelson Rooke; *S* father, 1983; *m* 1971, Christine Mary Carden, *y d* of Dr John Waring, Totland Bay, Isle of Wight; two *s*. *Educ:* Allhallows School; RMA Sandhurst. Commissioned RA, 1966; served BAOR (26 Field Regt), 1967–70; UK and Hong Kong, (3 RHA), 1970–73; BAOR and UK (22 AD Regt), 1974–77; Staff Coll., Camberley, 1978 (psc); served on Staff of HQ Eastern District, 1979–80; commanded Q (Sanna's Post) Bty in BAOR (5 Regt), 1981–83; SO2, Army Staff Duties Directorate, MoD, 1983–85; 2 i/c 1 RHA BAOR, 1986–88; Equerry to HRH The Duke of Edinburgh, 1988–90; SO1, Management Services Orgn 3, MoD, 1990–92; retired 1994. CO, Southampton Univ. OTC, 1992–94. *Recreations:* sailing, shooting, gardening. *Heir: s* Alexander John Dyke Acland, *b* 29 May 1973. *Clubs:* Royal Yacht Squadron, Royal Artillery Yacht.

ACLAND, Sir John (Dyke), 16th Bt *cr* 1644, of Columb John, Devon; *b* 13 May 1939; *s* of Sir Richard Thomas Dyke Acland, 15th Bt and Anne Stella (*née* Alford) (*d* 1992); *S* father, 1990; *m* 1961, Virginia, *yr d* of Roland Forge; two *s* one *d*. *Educ:* Clifton; Magdalene Coll., Cambridge; Univ. of West Indies (MSc). *Heir: s* Dominic Dyke Acland [*b* 19 Nov. 1962; *m* 1990, Sarah Anne, 3rd *d* of Ven. Kenneth Unwin, *qv*; one *s* one *d* (twins)]. *Address:* Sprydon, Broadclyst, Exeter, Devon EX5 3JN.

ACLAND, Maj.-Gen. Sir John (Hugh Bevil), KCB 1980; CBE 1978; Vice Lord-Lieutenant of Devon, since 1995; farmer; *b* 26 Nov. 1928; *s* of late Brig. Peter Acland, OBE, MC, TD and of Bridget Susan Acland; *m* 1953, Myrtle Christian Euing, *d* of Brig. and Mrs Alastair Crawford, Auchentroig, Stirlingshire; one *s* one *d*. *Educ:* Eton. Enlisted Scots Guards, 1946; commnd, 1948; served with 1st or 2nd Bn in Malaya, Cyprus, Egypt, Germany, Kenya, Zanzibar and NI, 1949–70; Equerry to HRH the Duke of Gloucester, 1957–59; Staff Coll., 1959; Bde Major, 4th Guards Armoured Bde, 1964–66; CO 2nd Bn Scots Guards, 1968–71; Col GS ASD, MoD, 1971–74; BGS, MoD, 1975; Comd Land Forces and Dep. Comd British Forces Cyprus, 1976–78; GOC South West Dist, 1978–81; Comd Monitoring Force, Southern Rhodesia, and Military Advr to the Governor, 1979–80. Dir of Liaison Res., Allied Vintners, 1982–93. Hon. Colonel: Exeter Univ. OTC, 1980–90; Royal Devon Yeomanry, 1983–92; Royal Wessex Yeomanry, 1989–92. Pres., Royal British Legion, Devon, 1982–90; Mem., Dartmoor National Park Authority, 1986. Chm., SW Regl Working Party on Alcohol, 1987–93. Mem. Steering Gp, Schools Health Educn Unit, Exeter Univ., 1986–92. Trustee, Exeter Cathedral Preservation Trust, 1994–. Governor: Allhallows Sch., 1982–94; King's Sch., Ottery St Mary, 1994–. DL Devon, 1984. *Publications:* articles in British Army Review and other jls. *Recreations:* fishing, arboriculture, destroying vermin. *Address:* Feniton Court, Honiton, Devon EX14 0BE. *Clubs:* MCC, Blue Seal.

See also Sir Antony Acland.

ACRES, Dr Douglas Ian, CBE 1987 (OBE 1981); JP; DL; Chairman of Council, Magistrates' Association, 1984–87; *b* Brockley, 21 Nov. 1924; *y s* of Sydney Herbert and Hilda Emily Acres; *m* Joan Marjorie, *o d* of William Charles and Alice Emily Bloxham, Benfleet. *Educ:* Westcliff High Sch.; Borland's, Victoria; London Hosp. Med. Coll. MRCS, LRCP 1949; DMJ (Clin.); MRCGP 1968. House Surgeon and Casualty Registrar, King George Hosp., Ilford, 1949–51; RAF Med. Branch, 1951–53 (Dep. Pres., Air Crew Med. Bd, Hornchurch; AOC's Commendation and Vote of Thanks, OStJ, East Coast Flood Disaster, 1953); gen. med. practice, Benfleet, 1953–84; MO, Remploy Ltd, 1965–. Med. Adviser, Congregational Fedn, 1985–; Member: Cttee on Mentally Abnormal Offenders, 1972–75; Barclay Cttee on Role and Task of Social Worker, 1979; Parole Bd, 1984–87; Sec., Fedn of Alcohol Rehab. Estabts, 1980–82; Mem., Exec. Cttee, Alcohol Concern, 1983–87; Chairman: Essex Council on Alcoholism, 1981–86; Out of Court (Alt. for Drunkenness Offenders), 1982–89; Churches' Council on Alcohol and Drugs, 1986–89; Mem., Interdeptl Cttee on Alcoholism, 1975–78; Chm., Educn Cttee, Inst. for Study and Treatment and Deliquency, 1985–89. Cropwood Fellow, Inst. of Criminology, 1973; Mem., BMA (Chm., SE Essex Div., 1979). Magistrates' Association: Dep. Chm., 1983; Chm., Sentencing of Offenders Cttee, 1978–83; Chm., Essex and NE London Br., 1975–78; Chm., Trng Sub-Cttee, 1978–91. JP Essex, 1958; Chm., Rochford Bench, 1974–84; Member: Lord Chancellor's Essex Adv. Cttee, 1973–87; Essex Magistrates' Courts Cttee, 1973–92 (Chm., Trng Sub-Cttee, 1978–92); Essex Probation Cttee, 1972–92 (Chm., R&D Sub-Cttee, 1980–90); Pres., Essex Br., Nat. Assoc. of Probation Officers, 1983–89. Indep. Mem., Benfleet UDC, 1960–65 (Chm., Public Health Cttee). Mem., Board of Visitors, HM Borstal, Bullwood Hall, 1970–83 (Vice-Chm., 1976–82); Member, Governing Body: King John Sch., Thundersley, 1967–89 (Chm., 1971–89); SE Essex Sixth Form Coll., 1982–88. Lay Pastor, Battlesbridge Free Church, 1984–, and Woodham Ferrers Congregational Church, 1984–92. DL Essex 1978. CStJ. Med. corresp., SE Essex Evening Echo, 1968–. *Publications:* articles and chapters on medico-legal matters. *Address:* Thundersley Lodge, Runnymede Chase, Thundersley, Benfleet, Essex SS7 3DB. *T:* South Benfleet (01268) 793241. *Club:* Royal Society of Medicine.

ACTON, 4th Baron *cr* 1869, of Aldenham, Salop; **Richard Gerald Lyon-Dalberg-Acton;** Bt 1644; Hereditary Duke of Dalberg; Patrician of Naples; writer; *b* 30 July 1941; *s* of 3rd Baron Acton, CMG, MBE, TD and of Daphne, *o d* of 4th Baron Rayleigh, FRS and late Mary Hilda, 2nd *d* of 4th Earl of Leitrim; *S* father, 1989; *m* 1st, 1965, Hilary Juliet Sarah (*d* 1973), *d* of Dr Osmond Laurence Charles Cookson, Perth, WA; one *s*; 2nd, 1974, Judith (writer) (marr. diss. 1987), *d* of Hon. Sir Garfield Todd, *qv*; 3rd, 1988, Patricia (Law Professor and writer), *o d* of late M. Morey Nassif and of Mrs Nassif, Iowa, USA. *Educ:* St George's Coll., Salisbury, Rhodesia; Trinity Coll., Oxford (BA History 1963, MA 1988). Mgt trainee, Amalgamated Packaging Industries Ltd, Britain, Rhodesia, USA and S Africa, 1963–66; Trainee Dir, 1967–70, Dir, 1970–74, Coutts & Co.; law student, Council of Legal Educn Inns of Court Sch. of Law, 1974–76; called to the Bar, Inner Temple, 1976; barrister, 1977–81; a Senior Law Officer, Min. of Justice, Legal and Parly Affairs, Zimbabwe, 1981–85. A cross-bencher, H of L, 1989–. Commentaries and personal essays for The Weekend Edition, Monitor Radio. *Publications:* (with Prof. P. Acton) To Go Free: a treasury of Iowa's legal heritage, 1995; contribs to newspapers, historical and literary jls, anthologies. *Heir: s* Hon. John Charles Ferdinand Harold Lyon-Dalberg-Acton, *b* 19 Aug. 1966. *Address:* 152 Whitehall Court, SW1A 2EL. *T:* 0171-839 3077; 100 Red Oak Lane SE, Cedar Rapids, IA 52403, USA. *T:* (319) 3626181.

ACWORTH, Ven. Richard Foote; Archdeacon of Wells, since 1993; *b* 19 Oct. 1936; *s* of Oswald Roney Acworth and Jean Margaret Acworth; *m* 1966, Margaret Caroline Marie Jennings; two *s* one *d*. *Educ:* St John's Sch., Leatherhead; Sidney Sussex Coll., Cambridge (BA Hist. and Theol. 1962; MA 1965); Cuddesdon Theol Coll. Nat. service, RNVR, 1956–58. Ordained deacon, 1963, priest, 1964; Assistant Curate: St Etheldreda's, Fulham, 1963; All Saints and Martyrs, Langley, Mancs, 1964–66; St Mary's, Bridgwater, 1966–69; Vicar, Yatton, 1969–81; Priest-in-charge, St John's and St Mary's, Taunton, 1981–85; Vicar of St Mary Magdalene, Taunton, 1985–93. *Recreations:* walking, gardening, DIY, ornithology. *Address:* The Old Rectory, Croscombe, Wells, Som BA5 3QN. *T:* Wells (01749) 342242, *Fax:* (01749) 330060.

See also Brig. R. W. Acworth.

ACWORTH, Brig. Robert William, CBE 1986; Registrar of St Paul's Cathedral, since 1991; *b* 11 Dec. 1938; *s* of Rev. Oswald Roney Acworth and Jean Margaret (*née* Coupland); *m* 1967, Elizabeth Mary, *e d* of J. N. S. Ridgers, *qv*; two *s* one *d*. *Educ:* St

John's Sch., Leatherhead; RMA, Sandhurst. Commnd, Queen's Royal Regt, 1958; served in Germany, Holland, Norway, Gibraltar, Aden, Oman, Hong Kong, UK and NI; sc 1970; GS01, Oman, 1979–81; Comdr, 10 UDR, 1981–83; Asst COS, HQ NI, 1983–85; Coll. Comdr, RMA, Sandhurst, 1985–87; Asst COS (Intelligence), HQ AFCENT, 1987–90; Dep. Comdr and COS, SE Dist, 1990–91, retd. Deputy Colonel: Queen's Regt, 1986–92; Princess of Wales's Royal Regt, 1992–94. Pres., Queen's Royal Surrey Regt Assoc., 1995–. *Recreations:* gardening, shooting, fishing, tennis. *Address:* St Paul's Cathedral, EC4M 8AD. *T:* 0171–489 1997. *Club:* Army and Navy.

See also Ven. R. F. Acworth.

ADAIR, Brian Campbell, TD 1979; NP 1975; Senior Partner, Adairs, Solicitors, Dumbarton, since 1973; President, Law Society of Scotland, 1992–93; *b* 28 Aug. 1945; *s* of Alan William Adair and Helen Mary Scott or Adair; *m* 1969, Elaine Jean Morrison; one *s* two *d*. *Educ:* Milngavie Primary Sch.; High Sch., Glasgow; Glasgow Univ. (LLB). Apprentice Solicitor, McGrigor Donald, Glasgow, 1967–70; Solicitor, Dumbarton CC, 1970–73; constituted own firm, 1973. Mem. Council, Law Soc. of Scotland, 1980–94 (Vice Pres., 1991–92). Elder, St Paul's Church, Milngavie. *Recreations:* holidaying in Arran, golf at Milngavie Golf Club (Captain, Centenary Year, 1995). *Address:* (office) 3/13 Castle Street, Dumbarton G82 1QS. *T:* Dumbarton (01389) 67625; 21 James Watt Road, Milngavie, Glasgow G62 7JX. *T:* 0141–956 3070.

ADAM, Sir Christopher Eric Forbes, 3rd Bt *cr* 1917; *b* 12 Feb. 1920; *s* of Eric Graham Forbes Adam, CMG (*d* 1925) (2nd *s* of 1st Bt) and of Agatha Perrin, *d* of Reginald Walter Macan; *S* uncle, 1982; *m* 1957, Patricia Ann Wreford, *y d* of late John Neville Wreford Brown; one adopted *d*. *Heir: cousin* Rev. (Stephen) Timothy Beilby Forbes Adam [*b* 19 Nov. 1923; *m* 1954, Penelope, *d* of George Campbell Munday, MC; four *d*]. *Address:* 46 Rawlings Street, SW3 2LS.

ADAM, (David Stuart) Gordon; Director, Barclays Bank UK, 1977–87; Chairman, International Trust Group Ltd, 1983–89 (Director, 1982–93); *b* 21 Dec. 1927; *o s* of late James Adam, RCNC and Florence (*née* Kilpatrick); *m* 1965, Rosanne, *er d* of late William Watson of Ardlamont; two *s* one *d*. *Educ:* Upper Canada College; Queen's Univ., Belfast (LLB); Trinity Hall, Cambridge (MA, LLM); AMP, Harvard Business Sch. Called to the Bar, Gray's Inn, 1951 (scholar and exhibnr). War Office, 1952–53; joined Barclays Bank, 1954; Southern and Central Africa, 1956–57; Local Dir, 1959, Gen. Man., 1968; Dep. Chm., Barclays Bank Trust Co., 1977–82; Chm., Barclays Internat. Devlt Fund, 1985–87; Dir, various cos in Barclays' Group. Indep. Dir, Henry Ansbacher Ltd, 1989–. Mem. Council, CBI, 1972–77. Chairman: Council, Wycombe Abbey Sch., 1981–91; Girls Education Co., 1981–91 (Dir, 1977–). Trustee, Combined Trusts Scholarship Trust, 1987–. *Address:* Mulberry Hill, Wendover, Bucks HP22 6NQ. *T:* Wendover (01296) 623200. *Clubs:* Boodle's, Kandahar.

ADAM, Gordon; *see* Adam, D. S. G.

ADAM, Gordon Johnston, PhD; Member (Lab) Northumbria, European Parliament, since 1979; *b* 28 March 1934; *s* of John Craig Adam and Deborah Armstrong Johnston; *m* 1973, Sarah Jane Seely; one *s*. *Educ:* Leeds Univ. (BSc Hons, PhD). CEng, MIMinE. Mining Engr, NCB, 1959–79. Mem., Whitley Bay Bor. Council, 1971–74; Mem. 1973–80, and Dep. Leader 1975–80, North Tyneside Metrop. Bor. Council (Chm., 1973–74; Mayor, 1974–75). Mem., Whitley Bay Playhouse Theatre Trust, 1975– (Chm., 1975–80); Vice-Chm., Energy, Res. and Technol. Cttee, Eur. Parlt, 1984–; Member: Northern Econ. Planning Council, 1974–79; Northern Arts Gen. Council, 1975–78; Northern Sinfonia Management Cttee, 1978–80; Board Member: Newcastle Free Fest. 1989–; Northern Stage Co., 1989–. Contested (Lab): Tynemouth, 1966; Berwick-upon-Tweed, Nov. 1973 (by-election), Feb. 1974 and 1992. *Recreation:* gardening. *Address:* The Old Farm House, East House Farm, Killingworth Village, Newcastle upon Tyne NE12 0BQ. *T:* 0191–216 0154; (office) 10 Coach Road, Wallsend, Tyne and Wear NE28 6JA. *T:* 0191-263 5838.

ADAM, Madge Gertrude, MA, DPhil; FRAS; University Lecturer (Astronomy), Department of Astrophysics, University Observatory, Oxford, 1947–79; Research Fellow of St Hugh's College, 1957–79, now Emeritus Fellow, *b* 6 March 1912, 2nd *d* of late John Gill Simpson and late Gertrude Adam; unmarried. *Educ:* Municipal High School, Doncaster; St Hugh's College, Oxford (Scholar). Research Scholar, Lady Margaret Hall, 1935–37; Junior British Scholarship, 1936–37; Assistant Tutor of St Hugh's College and Research Assistant at Oxford University Observatory, 1937; lately Fellow and Tutor, St Hugh's College. *Publications:* papers in Monthly Notices of Royal Astronomical Society from 1937. *Address:* 17 Dove House Close, Upper Wolvercote, Oxford OX2 8BG.

ADAM SMITH, Janet (Buchanan), (Mrs John Carleton), OBE 1982; author and journalist; *b* 9 Dec. 1905; *d* of late Very Rev. Sir George Adam Smith, Principal of Aberdeen Univ. and late Lady Adam Smith; *m* 1st, 1935, Michael Roberts (*d* 1948); three *s* one *d*; 2nd, 1965, John Carleton (*d* 1974). *Educ:* Cheltenham Ladies' College (scholar); Somerville College, Oxford (exhibitioner). BBC, 1928–35; Asst Editor, The Listener, 1930–35; Asst Literary Editor, New Statesman and Nation, 1949–52, Literary Editor, 1952–60. Virginia Gildersleeve Vis. Prof., Barnard Coll., New York, 1961 and 1964. Trustee, National Library of Scotland, 1950–85; Pres., Royal Literary Fund, 1976–84. Hon. LLD Aberdeen, 1962. *Publications:* Poems of Tomorrow (ed), 1935; R. L. Stevenson, 1937; Mountain Holidays, 1946; Life Among the Scots, 1946; Henry James and Robert Louis Stevenson (ed) 1948; Collected Poems of R. L. Stevenson (ed), 1950; Faber Book of Children's Verse (ed), 1953; Collected Poems of Michael Roberts (ed), 1958; John Buchan: a Biography, 1965; John Buchan and his World, 1979. *Recreation:* mountain walking. *Address:* 57 Lansdowne Road, W11 2LG. *T:* 0171–727 9324. *Club:* Alpine (Vice-Pres., 1978–80; Hon. Mem., 1993).

See also E. A. Roberts.

ADAMI, Edward F.; *see* Fenech-Adami, E.

ADAMS, Dr Aileen Kirkpatrick, CBE 1988; FRCS; FFARCS; Emeritus Consultant Anaesthetist, Addenbrooke's Hospital, Cambridge, since 1983; *b* 5 Sept. 1923; *d* of F. Joseph Adams and M. Agnes Adams (*née* Munro). *Educ:* Farringtons School, Chislehurst; Sheffield Univ. MB ChB Sheffield, 1946; MA Cantab 1977; FFARCS 1954; FFA(SA) 1987; FRCS 1988; FDSRCS 1989. Fellow in anaesthesia, Harvard Univ. and Mass. Gen. Hosp., Boston, 1955–57; Consultant Anaesthetist, Addenbrooke's Hosp., Cambridge, 1960–83; Associate Lectr, Univ. of Cambridge, 1977–85; Dean, Faculty of Anaesthetists, RCS, 1985–88. Sen. Lectr, Lagos Univ. Med. Sch., Nigeria, 1963–64. Mem., Cambridge Health Authy, 1978–82. Council Mem., RCS, 1982–88; Royal Society of Medicine: formerly Pres., Anaesthetic Section; Pres., History of Medicine Section, 1994–95 (Hon. Sec., 1992); Pres., History of Anaesthesia Soc., 1990–92. Hon. Archivist, Royal Coll. of Anaesthetists, 1989–. Former Examr, Cambridge Univ. and FFARCS. Hunterian Prof., RCS, 1993. Hon. Mem., Assoc. of Anaesthetists, GB and Ire. Mem., Editl Bd, Anaesthesia, 1972–85. Silver Jubilee Medal, 1977. *Publications:* book chapters and papers in med. jls on anaesthetic and related topics. *Recreations:* choral singing, outdoor activities, including walking, ski-ing, history. *Address:* 12 Redwood Lodge, Grange Road, Cambridge CB3 9AR. *T:* Cambridge (01223) 356460.

ADAMS, Rt. Rev. (Albert) James; Acting Vicar, Ridgeway Team Ministry, Diocese of Salisbury, 1984–87; *b* 9 Nov. 1915; *s* of James and Evelyn Adams, Rayleigh, Essex; *m* 1943, Malvena Jones; three *s*. *Educ:* Brentwood Sch.; King's Coll., London; Community of St Andrew, Whittlesford, Cambridge. Ordained Deacon, 1942; Priest, 1943; Curate of Walkley, Sheffield, 1942–44; Succentor, 1944, Precentor, 1945–47, Sheffield Cathedral. Rector of Bermondsey, 1947–55; Rural Dean of Bermondsey, 1954–55; Rector of: Stoke Damerel, Devonport, 1955–63; Wanstead, 1963–71. Sub-Dean, Wanstead and Woodford, 1968–69; Asst Rural Dean, Redbridge, 1970–71; Archdeacon of West Ham, 1970–75; Bishop Suffragan of Barking, 1975–83. *Address:* 89 Hardens Mead, Chippenham, Wilts SN15 3AQ. *T:* Chippenham (01249) 660728.

ADAMS, Alec Cecil Stanley, CMG 1960; CBE 1952; HM Diplomatic Service, retired; *b* 25 July 1909; *e s* of late Stanley A. Adams. *Educ:* King's School, Canterbury; Corpus Christi Coll., Cambridge. One of HM Vice-Consuls in Siam, 1933; served in Portuguese East Africa (acting Consul at Beira, June 1936–Feb. 1937); local rank 2nd Secretary, Bangkok Legation, 1937; Acting Consul, Sourabaya, 1938; Bangkok Legation, 1939–40; Foreign Office, Ministry of Information, 1940; Consul, in Foreign Office, 1945; Bangkok, 1946, Acting Consul-General and Chargé d'Affaires, 1948; Consul, Cincinnati, 1949; HM Chargé d'Affaires in Korea, 1950; HM Consul-General at Houston, Texas, 1953–55; Counsellor and Consul-General at HM Embassy, Bangkok, 1956–62; Deputy Commissioner-General for South East Asia, 1962–63; Political Advisor to C-in-C (Far East) at Singapore, 1963–67; retired 1967. *Address:* Flat 513, 97 Southampton Row, WC1B 4HH. *Club:* Travellers'.

ADAMS, Prof. Anthony Peter, FRCA, FANZCA, Professor of Anaesthetics in the University of London, at the United Medical and Dental Schools of Guy's and St Thomas's Hospitals (formerly at Guy's Hospital Medical School), since 1979; Vice Chairman, Division of Anaesthetics, United Medical and Dental Schools, since 1989 (Chairman, 1984–89); *b* 17 Oct. 1936; *s* of late H. W. J. Adams and W. L. Adams; *m* 1973, Veronica Rosemary John; three *s* one *d*. *Educ:* Epsom College; London Univ. MB BS 1960, PhD 1970; DA 1962; MRCS 1960, LRCP 1960, FRCA (FFARCS 1964); FANZCA (FFARACS 1987). Wellcome Res. Fellow, RPMS, 1964–66; Consultant Anaesthetist and Clinical Lectr, Nuffield Dept of Anaesthetics, Univ. of Oxford, 1968–79. Member: Standing Cttee, Bd of Studies in Surgery, London Univ., 1979–92; Academic Bd of Medicine, London Univ., 1980–83; Jt Cttee for Higher Trng of Anaesthetists, 1985–90; Specialist Adv. Cttee on Accident and Emergency Medicine, Jt Cttee for Higher Trng in Medicine, 1986–90; Exec. Cttee, Fedn of Assocs of Clin. Profs, 1979–87; Exec. Cttee, Anaesthetic Res. Soc., 1983– (Chm., 1991–94); Council, Assoc. of Anaesthetists of GB and Ireland, 1984–89 (Chm., Safety Cttee, 1987–89); Council, Coll. of Anaesthetists, 1989–; Chm., Assoc. of Profs of Anaesthesia, 1984–88; Senator, Eur. Acad. of Anaesthesiology, 1985–. Regional Educnl Adviser (SE Thames RHA) to Faculty of Anaesthetists of RCS, 1980–87; Examiner: FFARCS, 1974–86; DVA, 1986–93; DA and DM, Univ. of WI, 1986–88; MSc, Univ. of Wales Coll. of Medicine, 1988–93; PhD: Univ. of London, 1989; Univ. of Manchester, 1993; Univ. of Liverpool, 1995; MB ChB Chinese Univ. of Hong Kong, 1990. Asst Editor, Anaesthesia, 1976–82; Associate Editor: Survey of Anesthesiology, 1984–94; European Jl of Anaesthesiology, 1987–94; Mem. Editl Bd, British Jl of Anaesthesia, 1984–. Mem., Bd of Govs, Sutton High Sch. for Girls, 1988– (Chm., 1991–). *Publications:* Principles and Practice of Blood Gas Analysis, 1979, 2nd edn 1982; Intensive Care, 1984; (ed jtly) Recent Advances in Anaesthesia and Analgesia, 1984, 1989, 1993 and 1995; Emergency Anaesthesia, 1986; (ed jtly) Anaesthesia, Analgesia and Intensive Care, 1991; contribs to medical jls. *Recreations:* badger watching, English castles, history, tennis, croquet, cinema, theatre, ballet. *Address:* Department of Anaesthetics, Guy's Hospital, London Bridge, SE1 9RT. *T:* 0171–955 4047. *Clubs:* Royal Society of Medicine; Halifax House (Oxford).

ADAMS, Bernard Charles; architect; *b* 29 Oct. 1915; *s* of late Charles Willoughby Adams and Emily Alice (*née* Ambrose); *m* 1st, 1942, Marjorie Barrett Weller (*d* 1986); one *d* (and two *d* decd); 2nd, 1989, Betty Isabel Tucker (*née* Feist) (*d* 1992); *m* 1995, Ruth Atkinson (*née* Johnson). *Educ:* King James I Sch., Newport, IoW. ARIBA 1948, FRIBA 1968. TA, 1938–39; served 1939–41 (Battle of Britain), 219 Battery, 57 (Wessex) HAA Regt, RA; commissioned 1941; served 1941–46, 107 HAA Regt RA, France (Normandy), Belgium, Holland, Germany; Captain RA (despatches). Sen. Architect, Derbs CC, 1951–54; Asst County Architect, Kent CC, 1954–59; Dep. County Architect, Herts CC, 1959–60; County Architect, Somerset CC, 1960–80. Mem. Council, RIBA, 1963–69 and 1970–76 (Vice-Pres., 1970–72; Chm., S-W Regional Council, 1972–74); Chm., Structure of the Profession Study, RIBA, 1976–79; Mem., Nat. Consultative Council for Building and Civil Engrg Industries, 1974–80; Pres., County Architects' Soc., 1973–74 (Vice-Pres., 1971–73); Hon. Mem., Soc. of Ch. Architects of Local Authorities (founded 1974), 1983 (Sen. Vice-Pres., 1974–75; Pres. 1975–76); Architect Adviser to ACC, 1971–80; Mem., Bd of Architectural Studies, Bristol Univ., 1964–74; Founder Chm., Architects' Cttee, Consortium for Method Building, 1961–68. Chm., Taunton Theatre Trust, 1986–89 (Founder Mem., 1972). RIBA Architecture Award, 1970, and Commendation, 1974; Heritage Year Award (EAHY), 1975; Civic Trust Awards, 1962, 1968, 1971, and Commendation, 1965. FRSA 1972. *Publications:* contrib. Jl of RIBA and other jls. *Recreations:* arts, music, theatre, travel, languages. *Address:* Meadowside, Wild Oak Lane, Trull, Taunton, Somerset TA3 7JT. *T:* Taunton (01823) 272485.

ADAMS, (Charles) Christian (Wilfred), CMG 1992; HM Diplomatic Service; Ambassador to Thailand and (non-resident) to Laos, since 1992; *b* 2 June 1939; *s* of Flying Officer Wilfred Sydney Charles Adams, RAF (killed in action 1940) and of Katherine (*née* Hampton); *m* 1965, (Elinor) Pauline Lepper; three *s* one *d*. *Educ:* King's Sch., Canterbury; New Coll., Oxford (BA 2nd cl. Hons Mod. Hist.). Joined CRO, 1962; Asst Private Sec. to Commonwealth Sec., 1965–66; Rio de Janeiro, 1966–70; ODA, 1970–72; CSCE, Helsinki, 1972–74; Dep. Pol Advr, British Mil. Govt, Berlin, 1974–78; Head, Mech. and Electrical Engrg Br. I (Robotics, Machine Tools and Flexible Manufacturing Systems), DoI, 1979–82; Sen. British Trade Comr, Hong Kong, 1982–85; Head: SE Asia Dept, FCO, 1986–88; Project Exports Policy Div., DTI, 1988–91. *Recreations:* history, music, tennis, mountain walking, dogs, Scottish dancing. *Address:* c/o Foreign and Commonwealth Office, SW1A 2AH. *Clubs:* Athenæum; Hong Kong; Royal Varuna Yacht (Pattaya).

ADAMS, Rev. David; *see* Adams, Rev. J. D. A.

ADAMS, Douglas Noël; author; *b* 11 March 1952; *s* of Christopher Douglas Adams and Janet Dora Adams (*née* Donovan, now Thrift); *m* 1991, Jane Belson; one *d*. *Educ:* Brentwood Sch., Essex; St John's Coll., Cambridge (BA, MA). Radio and TV writer, 1974–78; BBC Radio Producer, 1978; BBV TV Script Editor, 1978–80; novelist, 1979–. *Publications:* The Hitch Hiker's Guide to the Galaxy, 1979; The Restaurant at the End of the Universe, 1980; Life, the Universe and Everything, 1982; So Long, and Thanks for all the Fish, 1984; (with John Lloyd) The Meaning of Liff, 1984; The Original Hitch Hiker Radio Scripts, 1985; Dirk Gently's Holistic Detective Agency, 1987; The Long Dark Tea

Time of the Soul, 1988; (with Mark Carwardine) Last Chance to See . . ., 1990; (with John Lloyd) The Deeper Meaning of Liff, 1990; Mostly Harmless, 1992. *Recreations:* buying equipment for recreations he thinks he would like to take up one day. *Address:* c/o Ed Victor Ltd, 6 Bayley Street, Bedford Square, WC1B 3HB. *T:* 0171–304 4100. *Club:* Groucho.

ADAMS, Ernest Victor, CB 1978; Deputy Secretary and Commissioner, Inland Revenue, 1975–81; *b* 17 Jan. 1920; *s* of Ernest and Amelia Adams; *m* 1st, 1943, Joan Bastin, Halesworth, Suffolk (*d* 1985); one *s* one *d*; 2nd, 1987, Mavisse Evelyn Surtees, Henley-on-Thames. *Educ:* Manchester Grammar Sch.; Keble Coll., Oxford (MA). HM Forces, RA, 1940–45. Inland Revenue Dept, 1947; Sen. Inspector of Taxes, 1956; Principal Inspector of Taxes, 1961; Sen. Principal Inspector of Taxes, 1966; Dep. Chief Inspector of Taxes, 1969. *Address:* 5 Northfield Court, Henley-on-Thames RG9 2LH. *T:* Henley-on-Thames (01491) 572586. *Club:* Phyllis Court (Henley).

ADAMS, Frank Alexander, CB 1964; Member, Public Health Laboratory Service Board, 1968–79; *b* 9 July 1907; *m* 1928, Esther Metcalfe (*d* 1988); two *d*. *Educ:* Selhurst Grammar Sch.; London School of Economics, Univ. of London. HM Inspector of Taxes, 1928; Assistant Secretary, Board of Inland Revenue, 1945; Counsellor (Economic and Financial), UK Delegation to OEEC, Paris, 1957–59; Director, Civil Service Pay Research Unit, 1960–63; Under-Sec. (Finance) and Accountant-General, Min. of Health, 1963–67. Mem. Council, Hosp. Saving Assoc., 1968–89. *Address:* 6 Magpie Way, Winslow, Buckingham MK18 3JT. *T:* Winslow (0129671) 3848. *Clubs:* Climbers'; Swiss Alpine (Geneva).

ADAMS, Frederick Baldwin, Jr; Director, Pierpont Morgan Library, 1948–69, now Emeritus; *b* 28 March 1910; *s* of Frederick B. Adams and Ellen Walters Delano; *m* 1st, 1933, Ruth Potter; 2nd, 1941, Betty Abbott; four *d*; 3rd, 1969, Marie-Louise de Croy. *Educ:* St Paul's Sch.; Yale Univ. (BA). Empl. Air Reduction Co. Inc., 1933–48. President: New-York Historical Soc., 1963–71; Bd Governors, Yale University Press, 1959–71; Hon. Pres., Assoc. Internationale de Bibliophilie (Pres., 1974–83); Trustee, Yale Univ., 1964–71; Fellow: Amer. Acad. Arts and Sciences; Amer. Philosophical Soc.; Amer. Antiquarian Soc.; Mass. Historical Soc.; Mem., Phi Beta Kappa. Hon. degrees: LittD: Hofstra Coll., 1959; Williams Coll., 1966; DFA, Union Coll., 1959; MA, Yale Univ., 1965; LHD, New York Univ., 1966. Chevalier, Légion d'Honneur, 1950; Comdr, Order of the Crown of Belgium, 1979. *Publications:* Radical Literature in America, 1939; One Hundred Influential American Books (with Streeter and Wilson), 1947; To Russia with Frost, 1963; contrib. to books and jls in bibliography, printing, collecting. *Address:* 208 rue de Rivoli, 75001 Paris, France. *Clubs:* Athenæum, Roxburghe; Century, Grolier (NY); Cercle Interallié (Paris).
See also S. H. Nowell-Smith.

ADAMS, Gerald Edward, PhD, DSc; Director, Medical Research Council Radiobiology Unit, Chilton, Oxon, since 1982; *b* 8 March 1930; *m* 1955, Margaret Ray; three *s*. *Educ:* Royal Technical Coll., Salford (BSc London, 1955); Univ. of Manchester (PhD 1958, DSc 1970). Post-doctoral Fellow, Argonne National Lab., USA, 1958–60; Vis. Scientist, Centre d'Etude Nucléaire, Saclay, France, 1961–62; Lectr, 1962–66, Sen. Lectr, 1966–70, Cancer Campaign Res. Unit in Radiobiol., Mount Vernon Hosp. (later CRC Gray Lab.); Dir of Molecular Radiobiol., 1970–72, Dep. Dir of Lab., 1972–76, CRC Gray Lab.; Prof. of Physics as Applied to Medicine, Inst. of Cancer Res. (Univ. of London), Sutton, 1976–82. Hon. Vis. Prof., Dept of Pharmacy, Univ. of Manchester, 1984–; Vis. Prof. of Radiobiol., Shanghai Med. Univ., 1986–87. Adrian Fellow, Univ. of Leicester, 1986–. Lectures: 2nd Milford Schulz Annual, Harvard Med. Sch., 1979; Maurice Lenz Annual, Columbia Univ., NY, 1981. Pres., British Inst. of Radiology, 1995–96. Chm., Gray Lab. Cancer Res. Trust, 1995–. Hon. FACR 1981. Hon. doctorate, Univ. of Bologna, 1982. Radiation Res. Award, 1969, Failla Gold Medal, 1990, Radiation Res. Soc., USA; David Anderson-Berry Prize, RSE, 1969; Silvanus Thompson Medal, British Inst. of Radiol., 1979; Röntgen Medal, Soc. of Friends of German Röntgen Mus., 1989; Henry Kaplan Medal, Internat. Assoc. of Radiation Res., 1995. Specialist Editor, Encyc. of Pharmacology and Therapeutics, 1975–; Member Editorial Board: Internat. Jl of Radiation Oncology, Biology and Physics, 1978–; British Jl of Cancer, 1981–; Internat. Jl of Radiation Biology, 1983–91; Radiation Research, 1987–90. *Recreations:* music, golf, walking. *Address:* MRC Radiobiology Unit, Chilton, Didcot, Oxon OX11 0RD. *T:* Abingdon (01235) 834393.

ADAMS, Gerard, (Gerry); President, Sinn Féin, since 1983 (Vice-President, 1978–83); *b* 6 Oct. 1948; *s* of Gerard Adams and Annie (*née* Hannaway); *m* 1971, Colette McArdle; one *s*. *Educ:* St Mary's Christian Brothers' Sch., Belfast. Interned for suspected terrorist activity, 1971, 1973; subseq. imprisoned; released, 1976. Mem., NI Assembly, 1982; MP (Provisional Sinn Féin) Belfast W, 1983–92. Thorr Award, Switzerland, 1995. *Publications:* Falls Memories (autobiog.), 1982; Politics of Irish Freedom; Pathway to Peace, 1988; Cage Eleven (autobiog.), 1990; The Street and Other Stories, 1992; Selected Writings, 1994. *Address:* Sinn Féin, 55 Falls Road, Belfast, N Ireland BT12 4PD.

ADAMS, Hervey Cadwallader, RBA 1932; FRSA 1951; landscape painter; lecturer on art; *b* Kensington, 15 Feb. 1903; *o s* of late Cadwallader Edmund Adams and Dorothy Jane, *y d* of Rev. J. W. Knight; *m* 1928, Iris Gabrielle, (*d* 1984), *y d* of late F. V. Bruce, St Fagans, Glamorgan; two *s*. *Educ:* Charterhouse. Studied languages and singing in France and Spain, 1922–26; studied painting under Bernard Adams, 1929. Art Master, Tonbridge Sch., 1940–63. *Publications:* The Student's Approach to Landscape Painting, 1938; Art and Everyman, 1945; Eighteenth Century Painting, 1949; Nineteenth Century Painting, 1949; The Adventure of Looking, 1949. *Address:* Priory Nursing Home, Horsley, near Stroud, Glos GL6 0PT.

ADAMS, Irene; *see* Adams, Katherine.

ADAMS, Rt. Rev. James; *see* Adams, Rt Rev. A. J.

ADAMS, Sir James; *see* Adams, Sir W. J.

ADAMS, Prof. James Noel, FBA 1992; Professor of Latin, University of Manchester, since 1993; *b* 24 Sept. 1943; *m* 1971, Geneviève Lucienne Baudon; one *s*. *Educ:* North Sydney Boys' High Sch.; Univ. of Sydney (BA); Brasenose Coll., Oxford (DPhil). MA Cantab. Teaching Fellow, Dept of Latin, Univ. of Sydney, 1965–66; Commonwealth Schol., Brasenose Coll., Oxford, 1967–70; Rouse Res. Fellow in Classics, Christ's Coll., Cambridge, 1970–72; University of Manchester: Lectr and Sen. Lectr in Greek and Latin, 1972–82; Reader in Latin, 1982–93. Vis. Sen. Res. Fellow, St John's Coll., Oxford, 1994–95. *Publications:* The Text and Language of a Vulgar Latin Chronicle (Anonymus Valesianus), 1976; The Vulgar Latin of the Letters of Claudius Terentianus, 1977; The Latin Sexual Vocabulary, 1982; Wackernagel's Law and the Placement of the Copula *Esse* in Classical Latin, 1994; articles in learned jls. *Recreation:* cricket. *Address:* Department of Greek and Latin, The University, Manchester M13 9PL. *T:* 0161–275 3024.

ADAMS, Jennifer, LVO 1993; Superintendent, Central Royal Parks, since 1983; *b* 1 Feb. 1948; *d* of Arthur Roy Thomas Crisp and Joyce Muriel Crisp (*née* Davey); *m* 1968, Terence William Adams. *Educ:* City of London School for Girls. Final Diploma, Inst. of Leisure and Amenity (FILAM DipPRA); FIHort. Various positions in Parks Dept, London Borough of Wandsworth, 1971–83. Pres.-elect, 1994–Oct. 1996, Pres., Oct. 1996–, Inst. of Horticulture. Liveryman, Gardeners' Co., 1985. *Recreations:* walking, gardening, nature conservation.

ADAMS, John Crawford, OBE 1977; MD, MS, FRCS; in consulting orthopaedic practice; Hon. Consulting Orthopaedic Surgeon, St Mary's Hospital, London; Hon. Civil Consultant in Orthopædic Surgery, Royal Air Force, since 1984 (Civil Consultant, 1964–84); *b* 25 Sept. 1913; *s* of Archibald Crawford Adams, W Hallam, Derbys; *m* 1940, Joan Bower Elphinstone (*d* 1981); *m* 1990, Marguerite Kyle. MB, BS 1937; MRCS 1937; LRCP 1937; FRCS 1941; MD (London) 1943; MS (London) 1965. Formerly: Chief Asst, Orthopædic and Accident Dept, London Hosp.; Orthopædic Specialist, RAFVR; Resident Surgical Officer, Wingfield-Morris Orthopædic Hosp., Oxford; Consultant Orthopaedic Surgeon: St Mary's Hosp., London and Paddington Green Children's Hosp., 1948–79; Brighton Gen. Hosp., 1948–58; St Vincent's Orthopaedic Hosp., Pinner, 1952–65. FRSM; Fellow, British Orthopædic Assoc. (Hon. Sec., 1959–62; Vice-Pres., 1974–75; Robert Jones Gold Medal and Prize, 1961). Mem, Council, Jl of Bone and Joint Surgery, 1974–84 (formerly Production Editor). *Publications:* Outline of Orthopædics, 1956, 11th edn 1990; Outline of Fractures, 1957, 10th edn 1992; Ischio-femoral Arthrodesis, 1966; Arthritis and Back Pain, 1972; Standard Orthopaedic Operations, 1976, 4th edn 1992; Recurrent Dislocation of Shoulder (chapter in Techniques in British Surgery, ed Maingot), 1950; Shakespeare's Physic, Lore and Love, 1989; Francis, Forgiven Fraud, 1991; Associate Editor and Contributor Operative Surgery (ed Rob and Smith); contributions to the Journal of Bone and Joint Surgery, etc. *Recreations:* history, writing, silversmithing. *Address:* 126 Harley Street, W1N 1AH; 33 Denman's Lane, Lindfield, Sussex RH16 2JN.

ADAMS, Rev. (John) David (Andrew); Headmaster, Weydon School, since 1982; Chaplain to the Queen, since 1994; *b* 27 Nov. 1937; *s* of John McCullough McConnell Adams and Sylvia Pansy (*née* Pinner); *m* 1970, Maria Carmen de Azpiazu-Cruz; one *s* one *d*. *Educ:* Trinity Coll., Dublin (BA 1960; Div. Test. 1961; MA 1964; BD 1965); Univ. of Reading (MEd 1974). Curate, St Stephen's, Belfast, 1962–65; part-time teaching and vol. chaplaincy in Europe, 1965–67; Hd, Religious Educn, Tower Ramparts, Ipswich, 1967–70; Counsellor, later Sen. Teacher, Robert Haining Sch., Surrey, 1970–74; Headmaster, St Paul's, Addlestone, 1974–82. Non-stipendiary Curate, St Thomas-on-the-Bourne, Farnham, 1976–. *Recreations:* gardening, household chores; the life of George Morley, Bishop of Winchester, 1597–1684. *Address:* Brookside Farm, Oast House Crescent, Farnham, Surrey GU9 0NP. *T:* Farnham (01252) 726888.

ADAMS, John Douglas Richard; Registrar of Civil Appeals, since 1982; a Recorder, since 1992; *b* 19 March 1940; *o s* of late Gordon Arthur Richard Adams and Marjorie Ethel Adams (*née* Ongley); *m* 1966, Anne Easton Todd, *o d* of late Robert Easton Todd and Mary Ann Margaret Todd (*née* Isaac); two *d*. *Educ:* Watford Grammar School; Durham Univ. (LLB 1963). Called to Bar, Lincoln's Inn, 1967. Lecturer: Newcastle Univ., 1963–71; University College London, 1971–78; also practised at Revenue Bar until 1978; Special Comr of Income Tax, 1978–82. Hon. Lecturer, St Edmund Hall, Oxford, 1978–; Vis. Lectr, Oxford Univ., 1995–. *Publications:* (with J. Whalley) The International Taxation of Multinational Enterprises, 1977; (contrib.) Atkin's Court Forms, 1984, 1992; (ed jtly) Supreme Court Practice, 1985, 1991, 1993, 1995; (ed jtly) Chitty and Jacob's Queen's Bench Forms, 21st edn, 1986. *Recreations:* music, walking, dining. *Address:* Royal Courts of Justice, Strand, WC2A 2LL.

ADAMS, Rear-Adm. John Harold, CB 1967; LVO 1957; Senior Partner, John Adams Interviews, since 1993; *b* Newcastle-on-Tyne, 19 Dec. 1918; *m* 1st, 1943, Mary Parker (marr. diss. 1961); one *s* decd; 2nd, 1961, Ione Eadie, MVO, JP; two *s* two *d*. *Educ:* Glenalmond. Joined Navy, 1936; Home Fleet, 1937–39; Western Approaches, Channel and N Africa, 1939–42 (despatches); Staff Capt. (D), Liverpool, 1943–45; Staff Course, Greenwich, 1945; jssc 1949; Comdr, HM Yacht Britannia, 1954–57; Asst Dir, Underwater Weapons Matériel Dept, 1957–58; Capt. (SM) 3rd Submarine Sqdn, HMS Adamant, 1958–60; Captain Supt, Underwater Detection Estab., Portland, subseq. Admty Underwater Weapons Estab., 1960–62; idc 1963; comd HMS Albion, 1964–66; Asst Chief of Naval Staff (Policy), 1966–68; retd 1968. Lieut 1941; Lieut-Comdr 1949; Comdr 1951; Capt. 1957; Rear-Adm. 1966. Dir, Paper and Paper Products Industry Training Bd, 1968–71; Dir, Employers' Federation of Papermakers and Boardmakers, 1972–73; Dir Gen., British Paper and Board Industry Fedn, 1974–83. Dir, DUO (UK) Ltd, 1983–93. Chm. Governors, Cheam Sch, 1975–87. *Recreations:* fishing, photography. *Address:* The Oxdrove House, Burghclere, Newbury, Berks RG15 9HJ. *T:* Burghclere (01635) 278385. *Club:* Army and Navy.

ADAMS, John Kenneth; Editor of Country Life, 1958–73; Editorial Director, Country Life Ltd, 1959–73; *b* 3 June 1915; *o c* of late Thomas John Adams and late Mabel Adams (*née* Jarvis), Oxford; *m* 1944, Margaret, *o c* of late Edward Claude Fortescue, Banbury, Oxon. *Educ:* City of Oxford Sch.; Balliol Coll., Oxford. Asst Master, Stonyhurst Coll., 1939–40; served with RAFVR, 1940–41 (invalided); Asst Master, Wellington Coll., 1941–44; attached to Manchester Guardian as Leader-writer, 1942–44; Leader-writer, The Scotsman, 1944–46; joined editorial staff of Country Life, 1946; Asst Editor, 1952; Deputy Editor, 1956; Editor, 1958; Editorial Director, 1959. *Recreations:* gardening, ornithology, travel. *Address:* 95 Alleyn Park, West Dulwich, SE21 8AA. *T:* 0181–693 1736. *Club:* Athenæum.

ADAMS, John Nicholas William B.; *see* Bridges-Adams.

ADAMS, John Roderick Seton; His Honour Judge Adams; a Circuit Judge, since 1990; *b* 29 Feb. 1936; *s* of George Adams and Winifred (*née* Wilson); *m* 1965, Pamela Bridget, *e d* of Rev. D. E. Rice, MC; three *s*. *Educ:* Whitgift Sch.; Trinity Coll., Cambridge. BA, 1959, MA 1963. Commnd, Seaforth Highlanders, 1955–56; Parachute Regt, TA, 1959–66. Legal Adviser in industry, 1960–66. Called to the Bar, Inner Temple, 1962; began practice at the Bar, 1967; Dep. Circuit Judge, 1978–80; a Recorder, 1980–90. *Recreations:* music, fishing, growing old roses. *Address:* 6 Pump Court, Temple, EC4Y 7AR. *T:* 0171–583 6013; Melness House, Sutherland IV27 4YR. *T:* Talmine (01847) 601255.

ADAMS, Katherine, (Irene Adams); JP; MP (Lab) Paisley North, since Nov. 1990; *b* 1948; *m* 1968, Allen S. Adams (*d* 1990), MP Paisley North; one *s* two *d*. Councillor, Paisley Town, 1970. *Address:* c/o House of Commons, SW1A 0AA.

ADAMS, Major Kenneth Galt, CVO 1979; CBE 1989; Industry Fellow, Comino Foundation, since 1987; *b* 6 Jan. 1920; *s* of late William Adams, OBE, and Christina Elisabeth (*née* Hall); *m* 1988, Sally, *d* of late Col John Middleton and *widow* of Douglas Long. *Educ:* Doncaster Grammar Sch.; Staff Coll., Camberley (psc 1953). Served RASC, 1940–59: War Service, ME and N Africa; DADST WO, 1946–48; DAA&QMG, Aldershot, 1952; DAQMG HQ Northern Comd, 1954–56; Sen. Instr, RASC Officers Sch., 1956–59. Sec., S London Indust. Mission, 1959–61; Proprietors of Hay's Wharf Ltd, 1960–70, Exec. Dir, 1966–70; non-exec. dir and consultant, other cos, until 1985. St

George's House, Windsor Castle: Dir of Studies, 1969–76; Fellow, 1976–82; Hon. Fellow, 1990. Comino Fellow, RSA, 1979–89. Chairman: S London Indust. Mission, 1971–74; Indust. Christian Fellowship, 1977–86; Vice Chairman: Archbishops' Council on Evangelism, 1965–77; Southwark Cathedral Council, 1967–70; Member: Indust. Cttee, Bd for Social Responsibility of C of E, 1973–81; Bldg EDC, NEDC, 1977–81; Prof. Standards Cttee, BIM, 1976–81; Dept of Employment's Services Resettlement Cttee for SE England, 1967–77; Adv. Cttee, Christian Assoc. of Business Execs, 1975–; Adv. Cttee, Inst. of Business Ethics, 1986–; Hon. Mem., Foundn for Manufg and Industry (Chm., 1993); Trustee, Industrial Trng Foundn, 1980–91. Lay Steward, St George's Chapel, Windsor, 1969–. Freeman, City of London, 1967; Liveryman, Pattenmakers' Co., 1976–. CIMgt (CBIM 1972); FRSA 1979; FCIT 1981. MA Lambeth, 1979; Hon. DPhil Internat. Management Centres, 1991. *Publications:* lectures and papers on developing an affirmative cultural attitude to industry in Britain. *Recreations:* 19th century novels, Border terriers. *Address:* 8 Datchet Road, Windsor, Berks SL4 1QE. *T:* Windsor (01753) 869708. *Club:* Army and Navy.

ADAMS, Lewis Drummond; General Secretary, Associated Society of Locomotive Engineers and Firemen, since 1994; *b* London, 16 Aug. 1939; *s* of Lewis John Adams and Margaret (*née* Drummond); *m* 1958, Jean Marion Bass; one *s* one *d*. *Educ:* Impington Coll., Cambridge; NCLC; Tavistock Inst., London. British Railways: engine cleaner, 1954–55; engine fireman and driver asst, 1955–67; engine driver, 1967–80. Associated Society of Locomotive Engineers and Firemen: Sec., London Dist Council No 1, 1970–80; Executive Committee: Mem., 1981–90; Vice-Pres., 1985–90; Asst Gen. Sec., 1990–93. British Railways: Mem., later Chm., Pension Fund, 1982–93; Member: Wages Grade Pension Fund, 1982–93; Superannuation Fund, 1982–93. Member: TUC Pension Cttee, 1987–90; Railway Industries Adv. Cttee, 1985–90. *Recreations:* travel, gardening. *Address:* (office) 9 Arkwright Road, Hampstead, NW3 6AB. *T:* 0171–431 0275. *Clubs:* Working Mens' (CIU), Railway (Chelmsford).

ADAMS, Air Vice-Marshal Michael Keith, CB 1986; AFC 1970; FRAeS; Director, International Aerospace Ltd; *b* 23 Jan. 1934; *s* of late William Frederick Adams and Jean Mary Adams; *m* 1966, Susan (*née* Trudgian); two *s* one *d*. *Educ:* Bedford Sch.; City of London Sch. FRAeS 1978. Joined RAF, 1952; qualified Pilot, 1954; Flying Instr, 1960; Test Pilot, 1963 (QCVSA 1967); Staff Coll., Toronto, 1969; CO Empire Test Pilots' Sch., 1975; Dir of Operational Requirements, 1978–81; RCDS, 1982; AOC Training Units, 1983; ACAS (Op. Requirements), MoD, 1984; ACDS (Op. Requirements) Air, MoD, 1985–86; Sen. Directing Staff (Air), RCDS, 1987–88; retd. Dir, Thomson-CSF (UK) Ltd, 1988–94. Vice-Pres., RAeS, 1992–. *Recreations:* walking, silversmithing. *Club:* Royal Air Force.

ADAMS, Norman (Edward Albert), RA 1972 (ARA 1967); ARCA 1951; artist (painter); Keeper of the Royal Academy, since 1986; *b* 9 Feb. 1927; *s* of Albert Henry Adams and Winifred Elizabeth Rose Adams; *m* 1947, Anna Theresa; two *s*. *Educ:* Royal Coll. of Art. Head of Sch. of Painting, Manchester Coll. of Art and Design, 1962–70; Lectr, Leeds Univ., 1975–78; Prof. of Fine Art, and Dir of King Edward VII Coll. (formerly Sch.), Univ. of Newcastle upon Tyne, 1981–86. Exhibitions in most European capitals, also in America (New York, Pittsburgh); Retrospective exhibns, Royal College of Art, 1969, Whitechapel Gall., RA, 1988. Paintings in collections of: most British Provincial Art Galleries; Tate Gall., London; Nat. Galls, New Zealand; work purchased by: Arts Coun. of Gt Brit.; Contemp. Art Soc.; Chantrey Bequest; various Educn Authorities. Murals at: Broad Lane Comprehensive Sch., Coventry; St Anselm's Church, S London; Our Lady of Lourdes, Milton Keynes; Stations of the Cross, St Mary's RC Church, Mulberry Street, Manchester, 1994–95. Decor for ballets, Covent Garden and Sadler's Wells. *Publications:* Alibis and Convictions, 1978; A Decade of Painting, 1971–81, 1981; (with A. Adams): Angels of Soho, 1988; Island Chapters, 1991; Life on Limestone, 1994. *Address:* Butts, Horton-in-Ribblesdale, Settle, North Yorks BD24 0HD. *T:* Horton-in-Ribblesdale (017296) 201, Royal Academy of Arts, W1V 0DS.

ADAMS, Sir Philip (George Doyne), KCMG 1969 (CMG 1959); HM Diplomatic Service, retired; *b* 17 Dec. 1915; *s* of late George Basil Doyne Adams, MD, and Arline Maud Adams (*née* Dodgson); *m* 1954, Hon. (Mary) Elizabeth Lawrence, *e d* of Baron Trevethin and Oaksey (3rd and 1st Baron respectively); two *s* two *d*. *Educ:* Lancing Coll.; Christ Church, Oxford. Entered Consular Service, 1939; served at: Beirut, 1939; Cairo, 1941; Jedda, 1945; FO, 1947; First Sec., 1948; Vienna, 1951; Counsellor, Khartoum, 1954; Beirut, 1956; FO, 1959; Chicago, 1963; Ambassador to Jordan, 1966–70; Asst Under-Sec., FCO, 1970; Dep. Sec., Cabinet Office, 1971–72; Ambassador to Egypt, 1973–75. Dir, Ditchley Foundn, 1977–82. Member: Board, British Council, 1977–82; Marshall Aid Commem. Commn, 1979–88. *Address:* 54 Sussex Square, W2 2SR. *Club:* Brooks's.

ADAMS, Richard Borlase, CBE 1983; Managing Director, Peninsular & Oriental Steam Navigation Co., 1979–84 (Director, 1970, Deputy Managing Director, 1974); *b* 9 Sept. 1921; *s* of James Elwin Cokayne Adams and Susan Mercer Porter; *m* 1951, Susan Elizabeth Lambert; two *s* one *d*. *Educ:* Winchester Coll.; Trinity Coll., Oxford, 1940. War service, Rifle Bde, 1940–46 (Major). Mackinnon Mackenzie Gp of Cos, Calcutta, New Delhi and Hongkong, 1947–63; Chm., Islay Kerr & Co. Ltd, Singapore, 1963–66; British India Steam Navigation Co. Ltd: Dir, 1966; Man. Dir, 1969; Chm., 1970. Dir, Clerical, Medical & General Life Assurance Soc., 1975–88. *Recreations:* gardening, tennis, golf. *Address:* 6 Leicester Close, Henley-on-Thames, Oxon RG9 2LD. *T:* Henley-on-Thames (01491) 574184. *Club:* Oriental.

ADAMS, Richard George; author; *b* 9 May 1920; *s* of Evelyn George Beadon Adams, FRCS, and Lilian Rosa Adams (*née* Button); *m* 1949, Barbara Elizabeth Acland; two *d*. *Educ:* Bradfield Coll., Berks; Worcester Coll., Oxford (MA, Mod. Hist.). Entered Home Civil Service, 1948; retd as Asst Sec., DoE, 1974. Writer-in-residence: Univ. of Florida, 1975; Hollins Univ., Virginia, 1976. Pres., RSPCA, 1980–82. Carnegie Medal, 1972; Guardian Award for Children's Literature, 1972. FRSL 1975; FRSA. *Publications:* Watership Down, 1972 (numerous subseq. edns in various languages; filmed 1978); Shardik, 1974; Nature through the Seasons, 1975; The Tyger Voyage, 1976; The Ship's Cat, 1977; The Plague Dogs, 1977 (filmed 1982); Nature Day and Night, 1978; The Girl in a Swing, 1980 (filmed 1988); The Iron Wolf, 1980; (with Ronald Lockley) Voyage through the Antarctic, 1982; Maia, 1984; The Bureaucats, 1985; A Nature Diary, 1985; (ed and contrib.) Occasional Poets (anthology), 1986; The Legend of Te Tuna, 1986; Traveller, 1989; The Day Gone By (autobiog.), 1990. *Recreations:* folk-song, chess, country pursuits, fly-fishing, travel. *Address:* 26 Church Street, Whitchurch, Hants RG28 7AR.

ADAMS, Sir (William) James, KCMG 1991 (CMG 1976); HM Diplomatic Service, retired; Consultant, Control Risks Group, since 1992; *b* 30 April 1932; *s* of late William Adams and late Norah (*née* Walker); *m* 1961, Donatella, *d* of late Andrea Pais-Tarsilia; two *s* one *d*. *Educ:* Wolverhampton Grammar Sch.; Shrewsbury Sch.; Queen's Coll., Oxford. 2nd Lieut RA, MELF, 1950–51. Foreign Office, 1954; MECAS, 1955; 3rd Sec., Bahrain, 1956; Asst Political Agent, Trucial States, 1957; FO, 1958; 2nd Sec., 1959; Manila, 1960; 1st Sec. and Private Sec. to Minister of State, FO, 1963; 1st Sec. (Information), Paris, 1965–69; FCO, 1969; Counsellor, 1971; Head of European Integration Dept (2), FCO, 1971–72; seconded to Economic Commn for Africa, Addis Ababa, 1972–73; Counsellor (Developing Countries), UK Permanent Representation to EEC, 1973–77; Head of Chancery and Counsellor (Economic), Rome, 1977–80; Asst Under-Sec. of State (Public Depts, then Energy), FCO, 1980–84; Ambassador to Tunisia, 1984–87, to Egypt, 1987–92. Chm., Egyptian-British Chamber of Commerce, 1992–. Order of the Star of Honour (Hon.), Ethiopia, 1965; Order of the Two Niles (Hon.), Sudan, 1965. *Address:* 13 Kensington Court Place, W8 5BJ. *Club:* Reform.

ADAMS-SCHNEIDER, Rt. Hon. Sir Lancelot (Raymond), KCMG 1984; PC 1980; Ambassador of New Zealand to the United States, 1982–84; *b* Wellington, NZ, 11 Nov. 1919; *s* of A. A. Adams; *m* 1945, Shirley Lois, *d* of L. A. Brunton; two *s* one *d*. *Educ:* Mt Albert Grammar School. Served War of 1939–45, NZ Medical Corps. Formerly Gen. Manager of department store, Taumarunui; Mem. Borough Council and Pres., Chamber of Commerce, Taumarunui; Exec. Member, NZ Retailers' Fedn. Vice-Chm. of Nat. Party in Waitomo electorate; Mem. S Auckland Div. Exec.; MP for Hamilton, 1959–69, for Waikato, 1969–81; Minister of Broadcasting, and Assistant to Minister of Customs, 1969; Minister of Customs, Asst Minister of Industries and Commerce, 1969–72; Minister of Health, Social Security and Social Welfare, Feb.–Nov. 1972; Opposition Spokesman on Health and Social Welfare, 1972–75, and on Industry, Commerce and Customs, 1974–75; Minister of Trade and Industry, 1975–81. *Address:* 6 Kimberley Way, Khandallah, Wellington 4, New Zealand.

ADAMSON, Sir Campbell; *see* Adamson, Sir W. O. C.

ADAMSON, Hamish Christopher; Director (International), The Law Society, since 1987; *b* 17 Sept. 1935; *s* of John Adamson, Perth, Scotland, and Denise Adamson (*née* Colman-Sadd). *Educ:* Stonyhurst Coll.; Lincoln Coll., Oxford (Schol.; MA Hons Jurisprudence). Solicitor (Hons). Law Society: Asst Sec., then Sen. Asst Sec. (Law Reform), 1966–81; Sec., Law Reform and Internat. Relations, 1981–87. Sec., UK Delegn, Council of the Bars and Law Socs of EC, 1981–; Exec. Sec., Commonwealth Lawyers' Assoc., 1983–. Chm., Trustee Cttee, Commonwealth Human Rights Initiative, 1993–. *Publications:* The Solicitors Act 1974, 1975; Free Movement of Lawyers, 1992. *Recreations:* plants, books, travel. *Address:* 133 Hartington Road, SW8 2EY.

ADAMSON, Norman Joseph, CB 1981; QC (Scot.) 1979; Legal Secretary to the Lord Advocate and First Parliamentary Draftsman for Scotland, 1979–89, retired; Assistant Counsel to the Lord Chairman of Committees, House of Lords, since 1989; *b* 29 Sept. 1930; *o s* of Joseph Adamson, wine and spirit merchant, and Lily Thorrat, Glasgow; *m* 1961, Patricia Mary, *er d* of Walter Scott Murray Guthrie and Christine Gillies Greenfield, Edinburgh; four *d*. *Educ:* Hillhead High Sch., Glasgow; Glasgow Univ. MA (Hons Philosophy and Economics) 1952; LLB 1955; Faculty of Advocates, Scotland, 1957; called to English Bar, Gray's Inn, 1959. Army Legal Aid (Civil) (UK), 1956–57; practice at Scottish Bar, 1957–65; Standing Jun. Counsel, Bible Board, 1962; Standing Jun. Counsel, MoD (Army), 1963–65; Hon. Sheriff Substitute, 1963–65; Parly Draftsman and Legal Sec., Lord Advocate's Dept, London, 1965–89. Elder of the Church of Scotland. *Recreations:* music, theatre. *Address:* Prospect House, 53 Lodge Hill Road, Lower Bourne, Farnham, Surrey GU10 3RD. *T:* Farnham (01252) 721988. *Club:* Royal Over-Seas League (London and Edinburgh).

ADAMSON, Sir (William Owen) Campbell, Kt 1976; Chairman, Abbey National plc (formerly Abbey National Building Society), 1978–91; *b* 26 June 1922; *o s* of late John Adamson, CA; *m* 1st, 1945, Gilvray (*née* Allan) (marr. diss. 1984); two *s* two *d*; 2nd, 1984, Mrs J. (Mimi) Lloyd-Chandler. *Educ:* Rugby Sch.; Corpus Christi Coll., Cambridge. Royal Inst. of Internat. Affairs, 1944–45; Baldwins Ltd as Management Trainee, 1945; successive managerial appts with Richard Thomas & Baldwins Ltd and Steel Co. of Wales Ltd, 1947–69; Gen. Man. i/c of construction and future operation of Spencer Steelworks, Llanwern; Dir, Richard Thomas & Baldwins Ltd, 1959–69, seconded as Dep. Under-Sec. of State, and Co-ordinator of Industrial Advisers, DEA, 1967–69; Dir-Gen., CBI, 1969–76. Director: Imperial Group, 1976–86; Renold, 1976–86 (Dep. Chm., 1981–82; Chm., 1982–86), Revertex Chemicals, 1977–82 (Chm., 1979–82); Lazard Bros & Co., 1977–87; Tarmac, 1980–90, Yule Catto, 1983–84. Member: BBC Adv. Cttee, 1964–67 and 1967–75; SSRC (on formation), 1965–69; NEDC, 1969–76; Council, Industrial Soc.; Design Council, 1971–73; Council, Iron and Steel Inst., 1960–72; Iron and Steel Industry Delegn to Russia, 1956, and to India, 1968; Vice-Chm., National Savings Cttee for England and Wales, 1975–77. Chairman: Independent Broadcasting Telethon Trust, 1988–; Pres., NCVO, 1992–. Re-Action Trust, 1991–; Vis. Fellow: Lancaster Univ., 1970–90; Nuffield Coll., Oxford, 1971–79. Governor: Rugby Sch., 1979–93; Bedford Coll., London Univ., 1983–85. Hon. DSocSc Birmingham, 1993. *Publications:* various technical articles. *Recreations:* walking, music, arguing. *Address:* 32 Grosvenor Square, W1X 9LL. *T:* 0171–491 4616.

ADAMSON-MACEDO, Prof. Emeritus Colin, DSc; FIEE; engineering and higher education consultant; *b* 23 Nov. 1922; British; *m* 1983, Dr Elvidina Nabuco Macedo; one *s* (one *d*, and one *s* decd, of former marriage). *Educ:* Pocklington Sch., Yorks. BSc 1947, MSc(Eng.) 1952, London; DSc Manchester, 1961. REME (Capt.), 1942–46. Asst Lectr, then with A. Reyrolle & Co. (power systems analysis), 1946–52; Sen. Lectr, then Reader, in Electrical Power Systems Engrg, UMIST, 1952–61; Chm., Dept of Electrical Engineering and Electronics, Univ. of Manchester Institute of Science and Technology, 1961–70; Rector, The Polytechnic of Central London, 1970–83; Overseas Adviser to Univ. of Salford, 1983–86. Mem., Conference Internationale des Grands Réseaux Electriques; Chm. of Consultants, Educational Overseas Services, 1975–; Chm. of Panel 1 (and Mem. Council), British Calibration Service, 1969–83. Mem., Exec. Cttee, Inter-Univ. Council for Service Overseas, 1972–82. Mem., Bd of Trustees, Ecole Supérieure Interafricaine d'Electricité, Abidjan, 1979–90; UN Team leader for Yarmouk Univ. of Technology, Jordan, 1978–80. Vis. Professor: Univ. of Roorkee, India, 1954–55; Univs of Washington and Wisconsin, 1959; Middle East Techn. Univ., Ankara, 1967–68; Univ. of Technology, Baghdad, 1975–83; Fed. Univ. of Rio de Janeiro, 1983– (UNESCO Energy Conslt to Coordenação dos Programas de Pós-graduação de Engenharia, 1986); Advisor to Rector, Mahidol Univ., Thailand, 1984–92; NATO Fellow, Electrical/Electronics Res. Inst., ME Technical Univ., Ankara, 1987; Vis. Prof. and Energy Conslt, Inst. de Pesquisas Tecnológicas, Univ. of São Paulo, 1987–88; Consultant, Trng Policy Div., ILO, 1991–. Mem. Governing Council, Polytechnic of Huddersfield HEC, 1989–92. *Publications:* (jtly) High Voltage Direct Current Power Transmission, 1960; High Voltage DC Power Convertors and Systems, 1963; University Perspectives, 1970; UNESCO reports: Higher Technical Education (Egypt), 1972; Alternative University Structures (UK), 1973, 3rd edn 1977; Technical Higher Education (Iraq), 1974; Post-secondary Education for Persons Gainfully-employed, 1976 and 1977; contribs to Proc. IEE and other learned jls. *Recreations:* yachting, oriental science and technology. *Address:* Yetts o' Huaxu, Glendevon by Dollar, Clackmannanshire FK14 7JY. *T:* Muckhart (01259) 781241; Rua Barata Ribeira 664/503, Copacabana, 22.051-000 Rio de Janeiro-RJ, Brazil. *Clubs:* Athenæum; Royal Mersey Yacht.

ADCOCK, Robert Wadsworth, CBE 1992; DL; Chief Executive and Clerk, Essex County Council, 1976–95; *b* 29 Dec. 1932; *s* of Sir Robert Adcock, CBE; *m* 1957, Valerie Colston Robins; one *s* one *d*. *Educ:* Rugby Sch. Solicitor. Asst Solicitor, Lancs CC, 1955–56; Asst Solicitor, Manchester City Council, 1956–59; Sen. Solicitor, Berks CC, 1959–63; Asst Clerk, later Dep. Clerk, Northumberland CC, 1963–70; Dep. Chief Exec., Essex CC, 1970–76; Clerk of Essex Lieutenancy, 1976–95. Assoc. of County Councils: Advisor, Police Cttee, 1976–83; Advisor, Policy Cttee, 1983–95; Chm., Officers Adv. Gp, 1987–95. Hon. Sec., Assoc. of County Chief Executives, 1983–90 (Chm., 1991–92); Chm., Officers Adv. Panel, SE Regional Planning Conference, 1984–88. DL Essex, 1978. *Recreations:* gardening, ornithology. *Address:* The Christmas Cottage, Great Sampford, Saffron Walden, Essex CB10 2RQ. *T:* Great Sampford (0179986) 363. *Club:* Law Society.

ADDERLEY, family name of **Baron Norton.**

ADDINGTON, family name of **Viscount Sidmouth.**

ADDINGTON, 6th Baron *cr* 1887; **Dominic Bryce Hubbard;** *b* 24 Aug. 1963; *s* of 5th Baron Addington and of Alexandra Patricia, *yr d* of late Norman Ford Millar; *S* father, 1982. *Educ:* Aberdeen Univ. (MA Hons). *Heir: b* Hon. Michael Walter Leslie Hubbard, *b* 6 July 1965. *Address:* 9/11 Chalk Hill Road, Norwich NR1 1SL.

ADDISON, family name of **Viscount Addison.**

ADDISON, 4th Viscount *cr* 1945, of Stallingborough; **William Matthew Wand Addison;** Baron Addison 1937; *b* 13 June 1945; *s* of 3rd Viscount and of Kathleen Amy, *d* of Rt Rev. and Rt Hon. J. W. C. Wand, PC, KCVO; *S* father, 1992; *m* 1st, 1970, Joanna Mary (marr. diss. 1990), *e d* of late J. I. C. Dickinson; one *s* two *d*; 2nd, 1991, Lesley Ann, *d* of George Colin Mawer. *Educ:* King's Sch., Bruton; Essex Inst. of Agriculture. *Heir: s* Hon. Paul Wand Addison, *b* 18 March 1973. *Address:* Church Barn, Oundle, Peterborough PE8 4AX.

ADDISON, Kenneth George, OBE 1978; company director; Director, 1971–89, and Deputy Chief General Manager, 1976–84, Sun Alliance & London Insurance Group; *b* 1 Jan. 1923; *s* of Herbert George Addison and Ruby (*née* Leathers); *m* 1945, Maureen Newman; one *s* one *d*. *Educ:* Felixstowe Grammar Sch. LLB Hons London. Served RAF, 1942–46. Joined Alliance Assurance Co. Ltd, 1939; various subsequent appts; Asst Sec., Law Fire Insurance Office, 1960–64; Gen. Manager, Sun Alliance & London Insurance Group, 1971. Chm., Bourne Home Develts Ltd, 1989–93; Dir, Sabre Insurance Co. Ltd, 1990–. Chairman: Fire Insurers' Res. & Testing Orgn, 1977–84; Management Cttee, Associated Insurers (British Electricity), 1977–84; Internat. Oil Insurers, 1979–82; Dir, Insurance Technical Bureau, 1977–84; Advr, Med. Defence Union, 1986–94 (Dir, 1991–94). Chm., Hearing Aid Council, 1971–78. Dir, Croydon Community Trust, 1990–94. FCIS; FCII (Pres., 1980); FCIArb (Pres., 1968–69). *Publications:* papers on insurance and allied subjects. *Recreations:* swimming, carpentry, gardening. *Address:* Ockley, 13 Hillcroft Avenue, Purley, Surrey CR8 3DJ. *T:* 0181–660 2793.

ADDISON, Mark Eric; Director, Safety Policy Division, Health and Safety Executive, since 1994; *b* 22 Jan. 1951; *s* of Sydney Robert James Addison and Prudence Margaret Addison (*née* Russell); *m* 1987, Lucinda Clare Booth. *Educ:* Marlborough Coll.; St John's Coll., Cambridge (BA, MA); City Univ. (MSc); Imperial Coll. (DIC, PhD). Department of Employment, 1978–: Private Sec. to Parly Under-Sec. of State, 1982; Private Sec. to Prime Minister (Home Affairs, then Parly Affairs), 1985–88; Regl Dir for London, Training Agency, 1988–91; Dir, Finance and Resource Management, 1991–94. *Recreations:* British motorcycles, windsurfing, photography. *Address:* Health and Safety Executive, Rose Court, 2 Southwark Bridge, SE1 9HS.

ADDISON, Michael Francis; His Honour Judge Addison; a Circuit Judge, since 1987; *b* 14 Sept. 1942; *s* of late Joseph Addison and of Wendy Blyth Addison; *m* 1979, Rosemary Hardy (*d* 1994); one *s*. *Educ:* Eton; Trinity College, Cambridge (BA). Called to the Bar, Inner Temple, 1965. *Recreation:* gardening. *Address:* 2 Harcourt Buildings, Temple, EC4Y 9DB. *T:* 0171–353 2112.

ADDISON, Dr Philip Harold, MRCS, LRCP; Hon. Consulting Secretary, The Medical Defence Union, since 1974 (Secretary, 1959–74); *b* 28 June 1909; 2nd *s* of late Dr Joseph Bartlett Addison and Mauricia Renée Addison; *m* 1934, Mary Norah Ryan; one *s* one *d*. *Educ:* Clifton Coll., Bristol; St Mary's Hosp. Medical Sch. MRCS, LRCP 1933; Gold Medallist, Military Medicine and Bronze Medallist Pathology, Army Medical Sch., Millbank, SW1, 1935. Permanent Commission, IMS, 1935; served Burma Campaign, 1943–45 (despatches). Chm., Ethical Cttee of Family Planning Assoc., 1956–60; Vice-Pres., Medico-Legal Soc., 1965–74. *Publications:* Professional Negligence, in Compendium of Emergencies, 1971; The Medico-Legal Aspects of General Anaesthesia, in, Clinical Practice of General Anaesthesia, 1971; contrib. Brit. Med. Jl, Irish Med. Jl, Proc. R.Soc.Med, Medico-Legal Jl, Lancet. *Recreations:* fishing, golf, bridge. *Address:* Red-Wyn-Byn, Monkmead Lane, West Chiltington, Pulborough, West Sussex RH20 2PF. *T:* West Chiltington (017983) 3047. *Clubs:* East India, Devonshire, Sports and Public Schools; Shark Angling Club of Gt Britain; West Sussex Golf; BMA Bridge (Founder Mem.).

ADDYMAN, Peter Vincent, FSA; Director, York Archaeological Trust, since 1972; *b* 12 July 1939; *y s* of Erik Thomas Waterhouse Addyman and Evelyn Mary (*née* Fisher); *m* 1965, Shelton (*née* Oliver), Atlanta, Ga; one *s* one *d*. *Educ:* Sedbergh Sch.; Peterhouse, Cambridge (MA). MIFA 1982; FSA 1967. Asst Lectr in Archaeology, 1962–64, Lectr, 1964–67, QUB; Lectr in Archaeol., Univ. of Southampton, 1967–72. Hon. Fellow, Univ. of York, 1972–; Hon. Reader, Univ. of Bradford, 1974–81. Directed excavations: Maxey, 1960; Lydford, 1964–67; Ludgershall Castle, 1964–72; Chalton, 1970–72. Vice-President: Council for British Archaeol., 1981–85 (Pres., 1992–95); Royal Archaeol. Inst., 1979–83; Chairman: Standing Conf. of Archaeol Unit Managers, 1975–78; Inst. of Field Archaeologists, 1983–85. Chm., Cultural Resource Management Ltd, 1989– (Dir, 1979–); Academic Dir, Heritage Projects Ltd, 1984–; Jt Instigator, Jorvik Viking Centre, York. Hon. DSc Bradford, 1984; DUniv York, 1985. *Publications:* (gen. editor) The Archaeology of York, vols 1–20, 1976–91; (ed with V. E. Black) Archaeological Papers from York, 1984; papers in archaeol jls. *Recreations:* gardening, watercolours, travel. *Address:* 50 Bootham, York YO3 7BZ. *T:* York (01904) 624311; York Archaeological Trust, Piccadilly House, 55 Piccadilly, York YO1 1PL. *T:* York (01904) 663003. *Clubs:* Athenæum; Yorkshire (York).

ADEANE, Hon. (George) Edward, CVO 1985; an Extra Equerry to HRH the Prince of Wales, since 1985; Director: Hambros plc, since 1992; Hambros Bank Ltd, since 1986 (Executive Director, since 1991); Guardian Royal Exchange plc, since 1985; English and Scottish Investors plc, since 1986; *b* 4 Oct. 1939; *s* of Baron Adeane, GCB, GCVO, PC and Lady Adeane. *Educ:* Eton; Magdalene College, Cambridge (MA). Called to Bar, Middle Temple, July 1962. Page of Honour to HM the Queen, 1954–55; Private Sec. and Treas. to HRH the Prince of Wales, 1979–85; Treas. to TRH the Prince and Princess of Wales, 1981–85; Private Sec. to HRH the Princess of Wales, 1984–85. Mem., British Library Bd, 1993–. Trustee, Leeds Castle Foundn, 1991–. *Address:* B4 Albany, Piccadilly, W1V 9RE. *T:* 0171–734 9410.

ADELAIDE, Archbishop of, and Metropolitan of South Australia, since 1991; **Most Rev. Ian Gordon Combe George,** AM 1989; *b* 12 Aug. 1934; *s* of late Gordon Frank George and Kathleen Mary George (*née* Combe); *m* 1964, Barbara Dorothy (*née* Peterson); one *d* (one *s* decd). *Educ:* St Peter's Coll., Adelaide; Univ. of Adelaide (LLB 1957); Gen. Theol Seminary, NY (MDiv 1964). Judges' Associate, Supreme Court of S Australia, 1955–57; barrister and solicitor, Australia, 1957–61. Ordained deacon and priest, New York, 1964; Assistant Curate: St Thomas', Mamaroneck, NY, USA, 1964–65; St David's, Burnside, SA, 1966–67; Priest-in-charge, St Barbara's, Woomera, SA and Chaplain and Welfare Officer, Australian Regular Army, 1967–69; Sub-Warden and Chaplain, St George's Coll., 1969–73, Lectr in History, 1969–73, Univ. of W Australia; Dean of Brisbane, Qld, 1973–81; Senior Chaplain (Army), Qld, 1975–81; Archdeacon of Canberra, 1981–89; Rector, St John's Church, Canberra, 1981–89; Asst Bp, Dio. of Canberra and Goulburn, 1989–91. Art Critic, The News, Adelaide, 1965–67. Trustee, Qld Art Gall., 1974–81. Founding Pres., Alcohol and Drug Problems Assoc. of Qld, 1975–81. Hon. DD Gen. Theol Seminary, NY, 1990. ChStJ 1992. *Publications:* Meditations on the Life of Jesus, 1991; Making Worship Work, 1992; many articles in theol, church and aesthetics jls on art and religion. *Recreations:* gardening, reading, the Arts, wine, ski-ing. *Address:* Bishop's Court, 45 Palmer Place, North Adelaide, SA 5006, Australia. *T:* (8) 2672364; Church Office, 45 Currie Street, Adelaide, SA 5000, Australia. *T:* (8) 2312402, *Fax:* (8) 2118748.

ADELAIDE, Archbishop of, (RC), since 1985; **Most Rev. Leonard Anthony Faulkner;** *b* Booleroo Centre, South Australia, 5 Dec. 1926. *Educ:* Sacred Heart Coll., Glenelg; Corpus Christi Coll., Werribee; Pontifical Urban University, Rome. Ordained Propaganda Fide Coll., Rome, 1 Jan. 1950. Asst Priest, Woodville, SA, 1950–57; Administrator, St Francis Xavier Cathedral, Adelaide, 1957–67; Diocesan Chaplain, Young Christian Workers, 1955–67; Mem., Nat. Fitness Council of SA, 1958–67; Bishop of Townsville, 1967–83; Coadjutor Archbishop of Adelaide, 1983–85. Chm., Aust. Catholic Bishops' Conf. Cttee for the Family and for Life, 1993–. *Address:* Catholic Diocesan Centre, Box 1364 GPO, Adelaide, SA 5001, Australia.

ADELAIDE, Assistant Bishop of; *see* Smith, Rt Rev. S. M.

ADELAIDE, Dean of; *see* Renfrey, Rt Rev. L. E. W.

ADETILOYE, Most Rev. Joseph Abiodun; *see* Nigeria, Metropolitan Archbishop and Primate of.

ADIE, Kathryn, (Kate), OBE 1993; Chief News Correspondent, BBC TV, since 1989; *b* 19 Sept. 1945; *d* of Babe Dunnet (*née* Issitt), and adopted *d* of late John Wilfrid Adie and Maud Adie (*née* Fambely). *Educ:* Sunderland Church High Sch.; Newcastle Univ. (BA Hons Scandinavian Studies). FJI 1990. Technician and Producer, BBC Radio, 1969–76; Reporter, BBC TV South, 1977–78; Reporter, TV News, 1979–81, Correspondent, 1982. Hon. Prof., Broadcasting and Journalism, Univ. of Sunderland, 1995. Hon. MA: Bath, 1987; Newcastle upon Tyne, 1990; Hon. DLitt: City, 1989; Loughborough, 1991; Univ. of Sunderland, 1993. RTS News Award, 1981 and 1987, Judges' Award, 1989; Monte Carlo Internat. TV News Award, 1981 and 1990; BAFTA Richard Dimbleby Award, 1989. Hon. Freeman, Borough of Sunderland, 1989. *Address:* c/o BBC TV, Wood Lane, W12 7RJ. *T:* 0181–576 8830.

ADIE, Rt. Rev. Michael Edgar, CBE 1994; Bishop of Guildford, 1983–94; *b* 22 Nov. 1929; *s* of Walter Granville Adie and Kate Emily Adie (*née* Parish); *m* 1957, Anne Devonald Roynon; one *s* three *d*. *Educ:* Westminster School; St John's Coll., Oxford (MA). Assistant Curate, St Luke, Pallion, Sunderland, 1954–57; Resident Chaplain to the Archbishop of Canterbury, 1957–60; Vicar of St Mark, Sheffield, 1960–69; Rural Dean of Hallam, 1966–69; Rector of Louth, 1969–76; Vicar of Morton with Hacconby, 1976–83; Archdeacon of Lincoln, 1977–83. Chm., Gen. Synod Bd of Education and of National Soc., 1989–94. *Recreations:* gardening, walking, sneezing. *Address:* Greenslade, Froxfield, Petersfield, Hants GU32 1EB.

ADKINS, Richard David; QC 1995; *b* 21 Oct. 1954; *s* of Walter David Adkins and Patricia (*née* Chimes); *m* 1977, Jane Margaret, *d* of Derek and Ella Sparrow; one *s* one *d*. *Educ:* Leamington Coll. for Boys; Hertford Coll., Oxford (MA). Articled Clerk, Lovell, White & King, 1976–78; admitted as solicitor, 1978; Solicitor: Lovell, White & King, 1978–79; Freshfields, 1978–82; called to the Bar, Middle Temple, 1982. Cttee Mem., Chancery Bar Assoc., 1991–93. *Publications:* Encyclopaedia of Forms and Precedents, Vol. 3: Arrangements with Creditors, 1985; Company Receivers: a new status?, 1988; contrib. Gore Browne on Companies, 44th edn, 1992. *Recreations:* opera, tennis. *Address:* 3–4 South Square, Gray's Inn, WC1R 5HP. *T:* 0171–696 9900. *Club:* Bromley Cricket.

ADLER, George Fritz Werner, OBE 1982; FEng, FIMechE; FICE; Director of Research, British Hydromechanics Research Association, 1971–86; *b* 12 Jan. 1926; *s* of Fritz Jacob Sigismund Adler and Hildegard Julie Adler (*née* Lippmann); *m* 1949, June Moonaheim Margaret Nash; three *d*. *Educ:* Penarth County School; Cardiff Technical Coll.; University Coll., Cardiff; Imperial Coll., London. BSc (Eng), DIC. Design Engineer, 1948, Chief, Mechanical Develt, 1953, English Electric, Rugby; Chief Mechanical Engineer, 1958, Gen. Manager Mech. Products, Marconi, 1962; Manager, Mech. Products Div., English Electric, 1966. Dir, Fluid Engineering Products Ltd, 1982–84. Vice-Pres., 1979, Pres., 1983, IMechE; Chm., CDRA (Fedn of Technology Centres), 1981–83; Mem., Engineering Council, 1986–89; Treasurer, Fellowship of Engrg, 1988–91. FIMgt (FBIM 1979); FInstD 1985. Eur Ing, FEANI, 1987. *Publications:* chapter, Water Turbines (jtly), in Kempe's Engineers' Year Book, 1956; articles in technical jls. *Recreations:* gardening, swimming, music. *Address:* The Haining, Orchard Close, Longburton, Sherborne, Dorset DT9 5PP. *T:* Holnest (01963) 210641. *Club:* Carlton.

ADLER, Larry, (Lawrence Cecil Adler); mouth organist; *b* 10 Feb. 1914; *s* of Louis Adler and Sadie Hack; *m* 1st, 1938, Eileen Walser (marr. diss. 1961); one *s* two *d*; 2nd, 1969, Sally Cline (marr. diss. 1977); one *d*. *Educ:* Baltimore City Coll. Won Maryland Harmonica Championship, 1927; first stage appearance, 1928 (NY); first British appearance, 1934 (in C. B. Cochran's Streamline revue); first appearance as soloist with Symphony Orchestra, Sydney, Australia, 1939; jt recital tours with dancer Paul Draper, US, 1941–49; soloist with NY Philharmonic and other major US Orchestras, also orchestras in England, Japan and Europe; war tours for Allied Troops, 1943, 1944, 1945; Germany, 1947, 1949; Korea (Brit. Commonwealth Div.), 1951; Israel (Six Day War), 1967; (Yom Kippur War), 1973; articles and book reviews in Sunday Times, New Statesman, Spectator, New Society, Observer, Punch; restaurant critic: Harpers & Queen, London Portrait; Boardroom; Chamber Life; columnist: What's On in London, Jazz Express, Jewish Gazette; numerous TV One Man Shows; soloist, Edinburgh Festival, playing first performance of unpublished Gershwin quartet (MS gift to Adler from I. Gershwin, 1963); works composed for Adler by: Dr Ralph Vaughan Williams, Malcolm Arnold, Darius Milhaud, Arthur Benjamin, Gordon Jacob, Cyril Scott, Francis Chagrin, Joaquin Rodrigo and others. Hon. Diploma: Peabody Conservatory of Music, Baltimore, 1986; City Coll., Baltimore, 1986. *Compositions:* film scores: Genevieve; King and Country; High Wind in Jamaica; The Great Chase, etc; TV scores: Midnight Men (BBC serial); various TV plays and documentaries; music for TV commercials, children's records, stage plays, etc; concert music: Theme and Variations; Camera III; One Man Show, From Hand to Mouth, Edinburgh Festival, 1965 (other festivals, 1965–). *Publications:* How I Play, 1937; Larry Adler's Own Arrangements, 1960; Jokes and How to Tell Them, 1963; It Ain't Necessarily So (autobiog.), 1985. *Recreations:* tennis, journalism, cycling, conversation; obsession: writing letters to Private Eye. *Address:* c/o MBA Literary Agents Ltd, 45 Fitzroy Street, W1P 5HR. *T:* 0171–387 2076. *Clubs:* Groucho, Scribes; Paddington Tennis.

ADLER, Prof. Michael William, MD; FRCP, FFPHM; Professor of Genito Urinary Medicine, and Consultant Physician, University College London (formerly Middlesex Hospital) Medical School, since 1979; *b* 12 June 1939; *s* of late Gerhard and of Hella Adler; *m* 1st, 1966, Susan Jean (marr. diss. 1978); 2nd, 1979, Karen Hope Dunnell (marr. diss. 1994); two *d;* 3rd, 1994, Margaret Jay (*see* Baroness Jay of Paddington). *Educ:* Bryanston Sch.; Middlesex Hosp. Med. Sch. MB BS 1965, MD 1977; MRCP 1970, FRCP 1984; FFPHM (MFCM 1977, FFCM 1983). House Officer and Registrar in Medicine, Middlesex, Central Middlesex and Whittington Hosps, 1965–69; Lectr, St Thomas' Hosp. Med. Sch., 1970–75; Sen. Lectr, Middlesex Hosp. Med. Sch., 1975–79. Advr in Venereology, WHO, 1983–; Department of Health (formerly DHSS): Mem., Expert Adv. Gp on AIDS, 1984–92; Mem., Sub-Gps on Monitoring and Surveillance, 1987–88 and Health Care Workers, 1987–92; Chief Scientist's Advr, Res. Liaison Gp (Child Health), 1985–. Non-exec. Dir, Camden and Islington Community Health Services NHS Trust, 1992–94. Medical Research Council: Member: Res. Adv. Gp on Epidemiol Studies of Sexually Transmitted Diseases, 1975–80; Working Party to co-ordinate Lab. Studies on the Gonococcus, 1979–83; Working Party on AIDS, 1981–87; Sub-Cttee on Therapeutic Studies, 1985–87; Cttee on Epidemiol Studies on AIDS, 1985–94; Cttee on Clinical Studies of Prototype Vaccines against AIDS, 1987–; RCS Cttee on HIV infection/AIDS, 1991–. Member: Med. Adv. Cttee, Brook Adv. Centres, 1984–94; Working Gp on AIDS, European Commn, 1985–; AIDS Working Party, BMA, 1986–; Exec. Cttee, Internat. Union Against the Venereal Diseases and Treponematoses, 1986–94; ODA Health and Population Adv. Cttee on R&D, 1995–. Mem., Specialist Adv. Cttee on Genito Urinary Medicine, Jt Cttee of Higher Med. Trng, 1981–86 (Sec., 1981–82; Chm., 1983–86). Royal College of Physicians: Member: Cttee on Genito Urinary Medicine, 1984– (Sec., 1984–87; Chm., 1987–91); AIDS Action Gp, 1991–92; Working Gp on AIDS, FCM (now FPHM), 1985–; Member Council: Med. Soc. for the Study of Venereal Diseases; RIPH&H, 1993–94. Dir, Terrence Higgins Trust, 1982–88; Mem. Adv. Bd, Internat. AIDS Soc., 1993–; Trustee, 1987–, Chm., 1991–, Nat. AIDS Trust (Chm., Grants and Gen. Purposes Cttee, 1988–); Adviser: AIDS Crisis Trust, 1986–; Parly All Party Cttee on AIDS, 1987–. Patron, Albany Soc., 1987–91. Evian Health Award, 1990. Member, Editorial Panel: Genito Urinary Medicine; Current Opinion on Infections Diseases; Enfermedades de Transmission Sexual; Venereology; also Ed., AIDS, 1986–94; Consultant Editor, AIDS Letter, RSM, 1987–89. *Publications:* ABC of Sexually Transmitted Diseases, 1984, 3rd edn 1995; (ed) ABC of AIDS, 1987, 3rd edn 1993; (ed) Diseases in the Homosexual Male, 1988; articles on sexually transmitted diseases and AIDS in med. jls. *Recreations:* yoga, jogging. *Address:* Academic Department of Genito Urinary Medicine, Mortimer Market Centre, Capper Street, WC1E 6AU. *T:* 0171–380 9660.

ADMANI, Dr (Abdul) Karim, OBE 1987; JP; consultant physician, with special interest in strokes and the elderly; *b* 19 Sept. 1937; *s* of late Haji Razzak Admani, Palitana, India, and of Hajiani Rahima Admani; *m* Seema, *d* of late Charles Robson, South Shields; one *s* one *d. Educ:* Gujarat Univ., India (BSc 1st cl. Hons); Karachi Univ., Pakistan (MB, BS); Univ. of London. DTM&H 1963; FRCP; FRCPE 1979; FRCPGlas 1988; FRSM 1988; FRIPHH. Teacher, Trent RHA (formerly Sheffield AHA), 1970–; Clin. Lectr, Sheffield Med. Sch., 1972–; Clin. Dir of Medicine, Northern Gen. Hosp. Trust, 1990–92. Vis. Prof. of Medicine and Neurol., Quaide-Azam Med. Coll., Bahawalpur, Pakistan, 1990–. WHO External Examr, Coll. of Physicians and Surgeons of Bangladesh, 1990–93. Director: Ranmoor Grange Nursing Home Ltd, 1975–80; Sunningdale Yorks Ltd, 1983–. Overseas Doctors' Association in UK: Dir, 1976–; Chm., 1981–87; Pres., 1987–94; Chm., ODTS, 1979– (Chm., Educn and Post-grad. Trng Cttee, 1982–). General Medical Council: Mem., 1979–; Chm., L Cttee, 1990–92; Member: Prof. Conduct Cttee, 1979–91; Preliminary Proc. Council, 1991–; Educn Cttee, 1990–92 and 1994; Racial Equality Cttee, 1994–. Member: Exec. Cttee, BMA, Sheffield, 1974–; Central Cttee of Consultants and Specialists, 1979–93; Sheffield HA, 1977–82; Council, British Geriatric Soc., 1989–93 (Chm., Trent Region, 1989–93); Council, BRCS, 1991–94 (Chm., Region III, 1991–94; Pres., S Yorks 1982–); Exec. Cttee for Racial Equality in Sheffield, 1972–90 (Chm., 1978–); Exec. Cttee, Age Concern, Sheffield, 1982–90; Management Bd, Pakistan Muslim Centre, 1987–; NHS Nursing Home Tribunal, 1989–; Medico-Chirurgical Soc. of Sheffield. Chm., Inst. of Transcultural Health Care, 1991–. President: Muslim Council of Sheffield, Rotherham and Dists, 1978–; Union of Pakistani Orgns in UK and Europe, 1979–94. Chm., Pakistan Enterprise Center, 1993–. JP City of Sheffield, 1974. Member, Editorial Board: Pakistan Medical Bull., 1974–; Medi-Scene, 1981–; ODA News Rev., 1985–. *Publication:* (ed) Guidance for Overseas Doctors in National Health Service in UK, 1982, 1991. *Recreations:* tennis, table tennis, snooker, chess. *Address:* 1 Derriman Glen, Silverdale Road, Sheffield S11 9LQ. *T:* Sheffield (0114) 236 0465; Northern General Hospital, Barnsley Road, Sheffield. *Clubs:* Abbeydale Rotary (Pres., 1995), Conservative (Sheffield).

ADRIEN, Sir J. F. M. L.; *see* Latour-Adrien.

ADYE, Sir John (Anthony), KCMG 1993; Director, Government Communications Headquarters, since 1989; *b* 24 Oct. 1939; *s* of Arthur Francis Capel Adye and Hilda Marjorie Adye (*née* Elkes); *m* 1961, Anne Barbara, *d* of Dr John Aeschlimann, Montclair, NJ; two *s* one *d. Educ:* Leighton Park Sch.; Lincoln Coll., Oxford (MA). Joined GCHQ, 1962; Principal, 1968; British Embassy, Washington, 1973–75; Nat. Defence Coll., Latimer, 1975–76; Asst Sec., 1977–83; Under Sec., 1983–89; Dep. Sec., 1989–92; 2nd Perm. Sec., 1992–. Gov., Dean Close Sch., Cheltenham. *Address:* Government Communications Headquarters, Priors Road, Cheltenham, Glos GL52 5AJ. *Club:* Naval and Military.

AGA KHAN (IV), His Highness Prince Karim, granted title His Highness by the Queen, 1957, granted title His Royal Highness by the Shah of Iran, 1959; *b* Genthod, Geneva, 13 Dec. 1936; *s* of late Prince Aly Salomon Khan and of Princess Joan Aly Khan, now Viscountess Camrose (*née* Joan Barbara Yarde-Buller, *e d* of 3rd Baron Churston, MVO, OBE); became Aga Khan, spiritual leader and Imam of Ismaili Muslims all over the world on the death of his grandfather, Sir Sultan Mahomed Shah, Aga Khan III, GCSI, GCIE, GCVO, 11 July 1957; *m* 1969, Sarah Frances Croker-Poole; two *s* one *d. Educ:* Le Rosey, Switzerland; Harvard University (BA Hons 1959). Leading owner and breeder of race horses in France and Ireland; won Derby, 1981 (Shergar), 1986 (Shahrastani), 1988 (Kahyasi) and Prix de L'Arc de Triomphe, 1982 (Akiyda); Prix de Jockey Club: Charlottesville, 1980; Top Ville, 1979; Darshaan, 1984; Mouktar, 1985; Natroun, 1987. President: Aga Khan Foundn, Geneva, 1967 (also branches in Bangladesh, Canada, Egypt, India, Kenya, Tanzania, Pakistan, Portugal, UK and US); Aga Khan Award for Architecture, 1976–; Inst. of Ismaili Studies, 1977–; Aga Khan Trust for Culture, Geneva, 1988. Founder and Chancellor, Aga Khan Univ., Pakistan, 1983. Hon. FRIBA 1991; Hon. Mem., AIA, 1992. Doctor of Laws (*hc*): Peshawar Univ., Pakistan, 1967; Sind Univ., Pakistan, 1970; McGill, 1983; McMaster, 1987; Wales, 1993; Hon. DLitt London, 1989. Thomas Jefferson Meml Foundn Medal in Architecture, 1984; Amer. Inst. of Architects' Inst. Honor, 1984; Medalla de Oro, Consejo Superior de Colegios de Arquitectos, Spain, 1987; Médaille d'argent, Académie d'Architecture, Paris 1991; Huesped de Honor de Granada, Spain, 1991. Commandeur, Ordre du Mérite Mauritanien, 1960; Grand Croix: Order of Prince Henry the Navigator, Portugal, 1960; l'Ordre National de la Côte d'Ivoire, 1965; l'Ordre National de la Haute-Volta, 1965; l'Ordre Malgache, 1966; l'Ordre du Croissant Vert des Comores, 1966; Grand Cordon, Order of the Taj, Iran, 1967; Nishan-i-Imtiaz, Pakistan, 1970; Cavaliere di Gran Croce della Republica Italiana, 1977; Grand Officier, l'Ordre National du Lion, Sénégal, 1982; Nishan-e-Pakistan, Pakistan, 1983; Grand Cordon, Ouissam-al Arch, Morocco, 1986; Cavaliere del Lavoro, Italy, 1988; Commandeur, Légion d'Honneur, France, 1990; Gran Cruz, Merito Civil, Spain, 1991. *Recreations:* ski-ing, yachting. *Address:* Aiglemont, 60270 Gouvieux, France. *Clubs:* Royal Yacht Squadron; Yacht Club Costa Smeralda (Founder Pres.) (Sardinia).

AGA KHAN, Prince Sadruddin; Consultant and Chargé de Mission to the Secretary-General of the UN, since 1978; Founding Member and President, Groupe de Bellerive; Founding Member and Chairman, Independent Commission on Internal Humanitarian Issues, 1983; *b* 17 Jan. 1933; *s* of His late Highness Sir Sultan Mohamed Shah, Aga Khan III, GCSI, GCIE, GCVO and of Andrée Joséphine Caron; *m* 1957, Nina Sheila Dyer (marr. diss., 1962); *m* 1972, Catherine Aleya Sursock. *Educ:* Harvard Univ. (BA); Harvard Grad. Sch. Arts and Sciences; Centre of Middle Eastern Studies. Unesco Consultant for Afro-Asian Projects, 1958; Head of Mission and Adviser to UN High Comr for Refugees, 1959–60; Unesco Special Consultant to Dir-Gen., 1961; Exec. Sec., Internat. Action Cttee for Preservation of Nubian Monuments, 1961; UN Dep. High Comr for Refugees, 1962–65; UN High Comr for Refugees, 1965–77; Co-ordinator, UN Humanitarian and Econ. Assistance Progs relating to Afghanistan, 1988–90; Personal Rep. of UN Sec.-Gen. for Humanitarian Assistance relating to Iraq-Kuwait crisis, 1990–91. Vice Pres., WWF, 1986–. Hon. Fellow, Amer. Acad. of Arts and Scis. Dr *hc:* Fletcher Sch. of Law and Diplomacy, 1986; Univ. of Nice, 1988; Hon. LLD Leeds, 1992. Hon. Citizen Geneva, 1978. UN Human Rights Award, 1978; Hammarsköld Medal, German UN Assoc., 1979; Olympia Prize, Alexander S. Onassis Foundn, 1982; Man of Peace Award, Together for Peace Foundn, 1989; Freedom Award, Internat. Rescue Cttee, USA. Grand Cross: Order of St Silvestro (Papal), 1963; Order of Homayoun (Iran), 1967; Order of the Royal Star of Great Comoro (Comoro Is), 1970; Order of the Two Niles (First Class) Sudan, 1973; Commander's Cross with Star, Order of Merit of Polish People's Republic, 1977; Commandeur de la Légion d'Honneur (France), 1979; Hilal-e-Pakistan, 1991; Commander of Golden Ark (Netherlands). *Publications:* Lectures on refugee problems delivered to RSA and Acad. Internat. Law, The Hague; Violations of Human Rights and Mass Exodus, study for UN Commn on Human Rights, 1981. *Recreations:* Islamic art, sailing, ski-ing, hiking, kite-flying. *Address:* Château de Bellerive, 1245 Collonge-Bellerive, Canton of Geneva, Switzerland. *Clubs:* Travellers' (Paris); Knickerbocker (New York).

AGAR, family name of **Earl of Normanton.**

AGER, Rear-Adm. Kenneth Gordon, CB 1977; retired Royal Navy 1977; *b* 22 May 1920; *s* of Harold Stoddart Ager and Nellie Maud (*née* Tate); *m* 1944, Muriel Lydia Lanham; one *s* one *d. Educ:* Dulwich Central Sch. and Royal Navy. Called up for War Service, RN, 1940; Sub Lt (Special Br.) RNVR, 1943; Lieut (Electrical) RN, 1944; Weapons and Elect. Engr; Comdr (WE) 1958; Captain (E) 1966; Fleet Weapons and Elect. Engr Officer, 1969–71; Sen. Officers' War Course, 1971–72; CSO (Eng) to Flag Off. Scotland and NI, and Captain Fleet Maintenance, Rosyth, 1972–75; Rear-Adm. (E) 1975; Flag Off., Admiralty Interview Bd, 1975–77. *Recreations:* bowls, reading.

AGIUS, Marcus Ambrose Paul; Vice-Chairman, Lazard Brothers & Co. Ltd, since 1990; *b* 22 July 1946; *s* of Lt-Col Alfred Victor Louis Benedict Agius, MC, TD and Ena Eleanora Alberta Agius (*née* Hueffer); *m* 1971, Kate Juliette de Rothschild; two *d. Educ.* Trinity Hall, Cambridge (MA Mech. Scis and Econs); Grad. Sch. of Business Admin, Harvard Univ. (MBA). With Vickers plc, 1968–70; Lazard Brothers & Co. Ltd, 1972–: Dir, 1981–83, Man. Dir, 1984–89; Lazard Frères & Co., 1987–: Limited Partner, 1987–88; Gen. Partner, 1989–. *Recreations:* gardening, shooting, ski ing, tennis, sailing. *Address:* 7 South Terrace, SW7 2TB. *T:* 0171–589 9440; Marise Cottage, Exbury, Hants SO45 1AH. *T:* Southampton (01703) 891195. *Clubs:* White's; Swinley Forest Golf; Beaulieu River Sailing.

AGLIONBY, Francis John; His Honour Judge Aglionby; a Circuit Judge, since 1980; *b* 17 May 1932; *s* of Francis Basil and Marjorie Wycliffe Aglionby; *m* 1967, Susan Victoria Mary Vaughan; one *s* one *d. Educ:* Charterhouse; Corpus Christi Coll., Oxford (MA). Nat. Service, 1950–52, commnd Nigeria Regt. Barrister, Inner Temple, 1956, Bencher, 1976; a Recorder of the Crown Court, 1975–80. Chancellor of Diocese: of Birmingham, 1971–; of Portsmouth, 1978–; of Carlisle, 1991–. Held Home Office enquiry into Horserace Totalisator Bd's bets transmissions procedures, 1979. *Recreations:* variable. *Address:* The Croft, Houghton, Carlisle, Cumbria CA3 0LD. *T:* Carlisle (01228) 23747; 8 King's Bench Walk, Temple EC4Y 7DU. *T:* 0171–583 4306. *Club:* Brooks's.

AGNELLI, Dr Giovanni; industrialist; Chairman: Fiat, since 1966; Istituto Finanziario Industriale, since 1959; EXOR, SA, Luxembourg, since 1974; Giovanni Agnelli Foundation, since 1968; Chairman, Editrice La Stampa, since 1982; *b* Turin, Italy, 12 March 1921; *s* of Edoardo Agnelli, and *g s* of Giovanni Agnelli, founder of Fabbrica Italiana Automobili Torino (FIAT); *m* 1953, Princess Marella Caracciolo di Castagneto; one *s* one *d. Educ:* Turin. DrJur, Univ. of Turin, 1943. Member Board: Eurafrance, Paris; Italian Stock Cos Assoc.; Turin Industrial Assoc.; Member: Exec. Bd, Confedn of Italian Industry; Internat. Adv. Cttee, Chase Manhattan Bank, NY; Adv. Bd, Petrofina; Adv. Bd, Bilderberg Meetings; Business Adv. Council, EBRD; European Round Table of Industrialists. Vice-Chm., Assoc. for Monetary Union of Europe. Hon. Chm., Council for US and Italy. Romanes Lectr, Univ. of Oxford, 1991. Hon. Fellow, Magdalen Coll., Oxford, 1991. Corresp. Mem., Moral and Political Scis Acad., Institut de France. *Address:* 10 Corso Marconi, Turin 10125, Italy. *T:* (11) 6861111.

AGNEW OF LOCHNAW, Sir Crispin Hamlyn, 11th Bt *cr* 1629; Chief of the Name and Arms of Agnew; Advocate; Rothesay Herald of Arms, since 1986; *b* 13 May 1944; *s* of (Sir) Fulque Melville Gerald Noel Agnew of Lochnaw, 10th Bt and of Swanzie, *d* of late Major Esmé Nourse Erskine, CMG, MC; *S* father, 1975; *m* 1980, Susan (journalist, broadcaster; formerly Advertising Exec.), *yr d* of late J. W. Strang Steel, Kirriemuir, Angus; one *s* three *d. Educ:* Uppingham; RMA, Sandhurst. Major RARO (retd 1981), late RHF. Slains Pursuivant of Arms to Lord High Constable of Scotland, 1978–81; Unicorn Pursuivant of Arms, 1981–86. Leader: Army Expedn to E Greenland, 1968; Jt Services Expedn to Chilean Patagonia, 1972–73; Army Expedn to Api, NW Nepal, 1980; Member: RN Expedn to E Greenland, 1966; Jt Services to Elephant Island (Antaŕctica), 1970–71; Army Nuptse Expedn, 1975; Jt British and Royal Nepalese Army Everest Expedn, 1976 (reached the South Col). *Publications:* (jtly) Allan and Chapman, Licensing (Scotland) Act 1976, 2nd edn 1989, 3rd edn 1992; articles in newspapers and magazines, and in legal and heraldic jls. *Recreations:* mountaineering, sailing (Yacht Pippa's Song), heraldry. *Heir:* s Mark Douglas Noel Agnew of Lochnaw, yr, b 24 April 1991. *Address:* 6 Palmerston Road, Edinburgh EH9 1TN. *Club:* Army and Navy.

AGNEW, Sir Godfrey; *see* Agnew, Sir W. G.

AGNEW, Sir John (Keith), 6th Bt *cr* 1895, of Great Stanhope Street, London; *b* 19 Dec. 1950; *er s* of Major Sir (George) Keith Agnew, 5th Bt, TD, and of Anne Merete Louise, *yr d* of Baron Johann Schaffalitzky de Muckadell, Fyn, Denmark; *S* father, 1994. *Educ:* Gresham's Sch., Holt. *Heir: b* George Anthony Agnew, *b* 18 Aug. 1953. *Address:* Rougham Estate, Rougham, Bury St Edmunds, Suffolk IP30 9LZ.

AGNEW, Jonathan Geoffrey William; Chairman: J. G. W. Agnew & Co. Ltd, since 1993; London Insurance Market Investments Trust plc, since 1993; non-executive Director: Greenfriar Investment Co. Ltd, since 1993; Thos Agnew & Sons Ltd, since 1969; *b* 30 July 1941; *er s* of Sir Geoffrey Agnew and Hon. Doreen Maud, *y d* of 1st Baron Jessel, CB, CMG; *m* 1st, 1966, Hon. Joanna Campbell (marr. diss. 1985); one *s* two *d;* 2nd, 1990, Marie-Claire Dreesmann; one *d. Educ:* Eton College; Trinity College, Cambridge (MA). The Economist, 1964–65; World Bank, 1965–67; Hill Samuel & Co., 1967–73, Dir, 1971; Morgan Stanley & Co., 1973–82, a Managing Dir, 1977; financial consultant, 1983–86; Chief Exec., ISRO, 1986; Kleinwort Benson Gp, 1987–93 (Head of Securities Div., 1987–89; Gp Chief Exec., 1989–93); Chm., Kleinwort Benson Ltd, 1989–93. Mem. Council, Lloyd's, 1995–. *Address:* Flat E, 51 Eaton Square, SW1W 9BE. *T:* 0171-235 7589. *Clubs:* White's; Automobile (Paris).

AGNEW, Peter Graeme, MBE 1946; BA; retired; Deputy Chairman, Bradbury Agnew & Co. Ltd (Proprietors of Punch), 1969–84; *b* 7 April 1914; *s* of late Alan Graeme Agnew; *m* 1937, Mary Diana (*née* Hervey); two *s* two *d. Educ:* Kingsmead, Seaford; Stowe School; Trinity College, Cambridge. Student Printer, 1935–37. Joined Bradbury Agnew & Co. Ltd, 1937. RAFVR 1937. Served War of 1939–45; Demobilised, 1945, as Wing Commander. *Recreations:* sailing, gardening. *Address:* The Old House, Manaccan, Helston, Cornwall TR12 6HR.

See also Col N. T. Davies.

AGNEW, Rudolph Ion Joseph; Chairman: Stena Sealink Ltd (formerly Sealink Stena Line), since 1990; Bona Shipholding Ltd, Bermuda, since 1993; LASMO PLC, since 1994; Redland plc, since 1995; Star Mining Corporation, since 1995; *b* 12 March 1934; *s* of Rudolph John Agnew and Pamela Geraldine (*née* Campbell); *m* 1980, Whitney Warren. *Educ:* Downside School. Commissioned officer, 8th King's Royal Irish Hussars, 1953–57. Joined Consolidated Gold Fields, 1957; Dep. Chm., 1978–82; Gp Chief Exec., 1978–89; Chm., 1983–89; Mem., Cttee of Man. Dirs, 1986–89. Chm. and Chief Exec., TVS Entertainment, 1990–93; Chm., Federated Aggregates PLC, 1991–; Jt Chm., Global Stone Corp. (Canada), 1993–94; Non-executive Director: New London PLC, 1985–; Standard Chartered PLC, 1988–; Newmont Mining Corp., USA, 1989–; Newmont Gold Co., USA, 1989–; Director: Gold Fields of South Africa Ltd, 1978–89; Renison Goldfields Consolidated, 1978–90; Anglo American Corp. of South Africa, 1980–88; Hanson PLC, 1989–91. Vice President: Nat. Assoc. of Boys' Clubs; Game Conservancy (Fellow); Hawk Trust; Chm., World Conservation Monitoring Centre, 1989–; Mem. Council, WWF (UK), 1989– (Trustee, 1983–89). CIMgt (FBIM 1980); FRSA. *Recreation:* shooting. *Address:* 7 Eccleston Street, SW1W 9LX. *Clubs:* Cavalry and Guards, White's.

AGNEW, Spiro Theodore, (Ted); *b* Baltimore, Md, 9 Nov. 1918; *s* of Theodore S. Agnew and Margaret Akers; *m* 1942, Elinor Isabel Judefind; one *s* three *d. Educ:* Forest Park High Sch., Baltimore; Johns Hopkins Univ.; Law Sch., Univ. Baltimore (LLB). Served War of 1939–45 with 8th and 10th Armd Divs, 1941–46, company combat comdr in France and Germany (Bronze Star). Apptd to Zoning Bd of Appeals of Baltimore County, 1957 (Chm., 1958–61); County Executive, Baltimore County, 1962–66; Governor of Maryland, 1967–68; Vice-President of the United States, 1969–73. Republican. With Pathlite Inc., Crofton, Md, 1974. *Publication:* The Canfield Decision, 1976. *Recreations:* golf, tennis.

AGNEW, Stanley Clarke, CB 1985; FEng 1985; FICE; Chief Engineer, Scottish Development Department, 1976–87, retired; *b* 18 May 1926; *s* of Christopher Gerald Agnew and Margaret Eleanor Agnew (*née* Clarke); *m* 1950, Isbell Evelyn Parker (*née* Davidson); two *d. Educ:* Royal Belfast Academical Instn; Queen's Univ., Belfast (BSc Civil Eng., 1947). FIWEM. Service with contractors, consulting engineers and local authorities, 1947–62; Eng. Inspector, Scottish Develt Dept, 1962–68, Dep. Chief Engr, 1968–75. *Recreations:* golf, photography, motoring, gardening. *Address:* Duncraig, 52 Blinkbonny Road, Edinburgh EH4 3HX. *T:* 0131–332 4072. *Club:* Murrayfield Golf (Edinburgh).

AGNEW, Sir (William) Godfrey, KCVO 1965 (CVO 1953); CB 1975; Chairman, Lady Clare Ltd, 1970–87 (Director, 1948–87); Vice-Chairman, Sun Life Assurance Society plc, 1983–84 (Director, 1974–84); Director, Sun Life Properties Ltd, 1980–84; *b* 11 Oct. 1913; *o s* of late Lennox Edelsten Agnew and Elsie Blyth (*née* Nott), Tunbridge Wells; *m* 1st, 1939, Ruth Mary (*d* 1962), *e d* of late Charles J. H. O'H. Moore, CVO, MC, and late Lady Dorothie Moore; three *s* three *d;* 2nd, 1965, Lady (Nancy Veronica) Tyrwhitt, *widow* of Adm. Sir St John Reginald Joseph Tyrwhitt, 2nd Bt, KCB, DSO, DSC; two step *s* one step *d. Educ:* Tonbridge. Solicitor, 1935; entered Public Trustee Office, 1936. Served RA and Surrey and Sussex Yeomanry, 1939–46; Major, 1945. Senior Clerk, Privy Council Office, 1946–51; Clerk of the Privy Council, 1953–74 (Deputy Clerk, 1951–53); Dep. Sec., Cabinet Office, 1972–74. Director: Seaway Shipping Agencies Ltd, 1971–80; Seaway Holdings Ltd, 1971–80; Artagen Properties Ltd, 1976–80. Chairman, Sembal Trust, 1967–73. Mem., Bd of Hon. Tutors, Council of Legal Educn, Univ. of WI, 1973–; Consultant: CEI, 1974–79; University Coll., Cardiff, 1982–84; Univ. of Wales Inst. of Science and Technol., 1982–84. Hon. FIMechE, 1968; Hon. FIMunE, 1974; Hon. FCIBSE (formerly Hon. FCIBS), 1975; Hon. FICE, 1984. *Clubs:* Army and Navy; Swinley Forest Golf; Rye Golf.

See also Sir J. M. H. Pollen, Bt, Sir Reginald Tyrwhitt, Bt.

AGNEW-SOMERVILLE, Sir Quentin (Charles Somerville), 2nd Bt *cr* 1957, of Clendry, Co. Wigtown; insurance consultant; *b* 8 March 1929; *s* of Comdr Sir Peter Agnew, 1st Bt and Enid Frances (*d* 1982), *d* of late Henry Boan; assumed additional name of Somerville by Royal licence, 1950; *S* father, 1990; *m* 1963, Hon. April, *y d* and a *co-heiress* of 15th Baron Strange; one *s* two *d. Educ:* RNC Dartmouth. *Heir: s* James Lockett Charles Agnew-Somerville, *b* 26 May 1970. *Address:* Mount Auldyn House, Ramsey, Isle of Man IM8 3PF. *T:* Ramsey (01624) 813724, *Fax:* (01624) 816498.

AGUIRRE, Marcelino O.; *see* Oreja Aguirre.

ÁGÚSTSSON, Helgi, Hon. GCVO 1990; Icelandic Grand Order of the Falcon, 1990 (Order of the Falcon, 1979); Ministry of Foreign Affairs, Iceland, since 1995; *b* 16 Oct. 1941; *s* of Ágúst Pétursson and Helga Jóhannesdóttir; *m* 1963, Hervör Jónasdóttir; three *s* one *d. Educ:* Univ. of Iceland (Law degree 1970). Joined Foreign Ministry, 1970; served London, 1973–77; Counsellor, 1977; Dir, Defence Div., Foreign Min., 1979 and Chm., US-Icelandic Defence Council; Minister-Counsellor, 1980; served Washington, 1983–87; Dep. Permt Under-Sec., Foreign Min., 1987, in rank of Ambassador; Ambassador to UK, 1989–94, and to Ireland, Holland and Nigeria, 1990–94. Former Pres., Icelandic Basketball Fedn. Mem., Rotary Club of London. Decorations from Finland, Denmark, Sweden, Italy, Spain. *Recreations:* theatre, music, reading. *Address:* Ministry of Foreign Affairs, Hverfisgötu 115, 150 Reykjavik, Iceland.

AGUTTER, Jennifer Ann; actress; *b* 20 Dec. 1952; *d* of Derek and Catherine Agutter; *m* 1990, Johan Tham; one *s. Educ:* Elmhurst Ballet School, Camberley. *Films:* East of Sudan, 1964; Ballerina, 1964; Gates of Paradise, 1967; Star, 1968; Walkabout, I Start Counting, The Railway Children, 1969 (Royal Variety Club Most Promising Artist, 1971); Logan's Run, 1975; The Eagle Has Landed, Equus (BAFTA Best Supporting Actress, 1977), The Man In The Iron Mask, 1976; Dominique, Clayton and Catherine, 1977; The Riddle of the Sands, Sweet William, 1978; The Survivor, 1980; An American Werewolf in London, 1981; Secret Places, 1983; Dark Tower, 1987; King of the Wind, 1989; Child's Play 2, 1991; Freddie as Fro7, 1992; Blue Juice, 1995; *stage:* School for Scandal, 1972; Rooted, Arms and the Man, The Ride Across Lake Constance, 1973; National Theatre: The Tempest, Spring Awakening, 1974; Hedda, Betrayal, 1980; Royal Shakespeare Co.: Arden of Faversham, Lear, King Lear, The Body, 1982–83; Breaking the Silence, 1985; Shrew, The Unified Field, LA, 1987; Breaking the Code, NY, 1987; Love's Labour's Lost, Barbican, 1995; *television includes:* Long After Summer, 1967; The Wild Duck, The Cherry Orchard, The Snow Goose (Emmy Best Supporting Actress), 1971; A War of Children, 1972; School Play, 1979; Amy, 1980; Love's Labour's Lost, This Office Life, 1984; Silas Marner, 1985; Murder She Wrote, 1986; The Equaliser, Magnum, 1988; Dear John, 1989; Not a Penny More, Not a Penny Less, Tecx, 1990; The Good Guys, Puss in Boots, 1991; The Buccaneers, 1995. *Publication:* Snap, 1983. *Address:* c/o JY Publicity, 100 Ebury Street, SW1W 9QD. *T:* 0171–730 9009.

AHEARNE, Stephen James, FCA; Chief Financial Officer, since 1990 and Managing Director, since 1992, British Petroleum Company PLC; *b* 7 Sept. 1939; *s* of James Joseph Ahearne and Phyllis Eva (*née* Grigsby); *m* 1965, Janet Elizabeth Edwards; two *s.* Qualified as Chartered Accountant, 1962; joined British Petroleum, 1964: Man. Dir, BP Denmark, 1978–81; Exec. Dir, BP Chems, 1981–86; Gp Controller, 1986–88; Gp Planner, 1988–90. Mem., Restrictive Practices Court, 1993–. *Recreations:* tennis, gardening, sailing, walking, reading. *Address:* c/o British Petroleum Co. PLC, Britannic House, 1 Finsbury Circus, EC2M 7BA. *T:* 0171–496 4157.

AHERN, Bertie; Member of the Dáil (TD) (FF), since 1977; Leader of the Opposition, since 1994; President, Fianna Fáil, since 1994; *b* 12 Sept. 1951; *s* of Cornelius and Julia Ahern; *m* 1975; two *d. Educ:* Rathmines Coll. of Commerce; University Coll., Dublin. Accountant. Asst Chief Whip, 1980–81; spokesman on youth affairs, 1981; Govt Chief Whip and Minister of State at Depts of Taoiseach and Defence, 1982; Minister for Labour, 1987–91; Minister for Finance, 1991–94. Lord Mayor of Dublin, 1986–87. Former Member, Board of Governors: IMF; World Bank; EIB (Chm., 1991–92). Grand Cross, Order of Merit with Star and Sash (Germany), 1991. *Recreations:* sports, reading. *Address:* St Luke's, 161 Lower Drumcondra Road, Dublin 9.

AHERN, Most Rev. John J.; *b* 31 Aug 1911; *s* of James Ahern and Ellen Mulcahy. *Educ:* St Colman's Coll., Fermoy; St Patrick's Coll., Maynooth; Irish Coll., Rome. Ordained, 1936. Prof. at St Colman's Coll., Fermoy, 1940–44; St Patrick's Coll., Maynooth, 1946–57; Bishop of Cloyne, 1957–87. *Address:* Nazareth House, Mallow, Co. Cork, Ireland.

AHMAD, Khurshid; Chairman: Institute of Policy Studies, Islamabad, Pakistan, since 1979; Board of Trustees, Islamic Foundation, Leicester, since 1985; Member, Senate of Pakistan, since 1978; *b* 23 March 1934; three *s* three *d. Educ:* Karachi Univ. (LLB; MA Economics; MA Islamic Studies). Dir-Gen., Islamic Foundn, Leicester, 1973–78; Federal Minister for Planning and Develt and Dep. Chm., Planning Commn, Govt of Pakistan, 1978–79. Chm., Internat. Inst. of Islamic Econs, Islamic Univ., Islamabad, 1983–87. Hon. PhD Educn, Nat. Univ. of Malaya. Islamic Develt Bank Laureate for dist. contribn to Islamic econs, 1988; King Faisal, Internat. Prize for service to Islam, 1990. *Publications:* Essays on Pakistan Economy (Karachi), 1958; An Analysis of Munir Report (Lahore), 1958; (ed) Studies in the Family Law of Islam (Karachi), 1960; (ed) The Quran: an Introduction (Karachi), 1966; The Prophet of Islam (Karachi), 1967; Principles of Islamic Education (Lahore), 1970; Fanaticism, Intolerance and Islam (Lahore), 1970; Islam and the West (Lahore), 1972; The Religion of Islam (Lahore), 1973; (ed) Islam: its meaning and message (London, Islamic Council of Europe), 1976; Development Strategy for the Sixth Plan (Islamabad), 1983; *for Islamic Foundation, Leicester:* Islam: Basic Principles and Characteristics, 1974; Family Life in Islam, 1974; Islamic Perspectives: Studies in honour of Maulana Mawdudi, 1979; The Quran: Basic Teachings, 1979; Studies in Islamic Economics, 1980; contrib. The Third World's Dilemma of Development, Non-Aligned Third World Annual, (USA) 1970. *Recreations:* travelling, reading. *Address:* Markfield Dawah Centre, Ratby Lane, Markfield, Leics LE67 9RN. *T:* Markfield (01530) 244944; Institute of Policy Studies, Block 19, Markaz F-7, Islamabad, Pakistan. *T:* (51) 818230.

AHMED, Prof. Haroon, PhD; FEng 1990; Professor of Microelectronics, University of Cambridge, since 1992; Fellow of Corpus Christi College, Cambridge, since 1967 (Warden of Leckhampton, since 1993); *b* 2 March 1936; *s* of Mohammad Nizam Ahmed and Bilquis Jehan Ahmed; *m* 1969, Evelyn Anne Travers; one *s* two *d. Educ:* St Patrick's Sch., Karachi; Imperial College London; King's College, Cambridge (PhD 1963). GEC and Hirst Research Centre, 1958–59; Turner and Newall Res. Fellow, 1962–63; University of Cambridge: Univ. Demonstrator, Engineering Dept, 1963–66; Lectr, Engineering Dept, 1966–84; Reader in Microelectronics, 1984–92. *Publications:* (with A. H. W. Beck) Introduction to Physical Electronics, 1968; (with P. J. Spreadbury) Electronics for Engineers, 1973, 2nd edn 1984. *Recreations:* golf, tennis, ski-ing. *Address:* Microelectronics Research Centre, Cavendish Laboratory, Madingley Road, Cambridge CB3 0HE. *T:* Cambridge (01223) 337557.

AHO, Esko Tapani; MP (Centre Party), since 1983; Prime Minister of Finalnd, since 1991; *b* Veteli, 20 May 1954; *s* of Kauko Kaleva Aho and Laura Kyllikki Aho (*née* Harjupatana); *m* 1980, Kirsti Hannele Söderkultalahti; two *s* one *d. Educ:* Master of Pol Scis. Political Sec. to Minister for Foreign Affairs, Finland, 1979–80; Chm., Finnish Parlt, April 1991; Member: Traffic Commn, 1983–86; Finances Commn, 1987–90. Member: CSCE Cttee, 1984–90; Finnish Delegn, Nordic Council, 1983–89; Finnish Delegn, Council of Europe, 1989–91. Chairman: League, Centre Party Youth, 1974–80; Finnish Centre Party, 1990–. Member, Advisory Board: Outokumpu Oy (Metal Ind.), 1985–91; OKO (Bank), 1991; SOK (Diversified Co-op.), 1990–91. Grand Cross, Order of White Rose (Finland), 1992; Cavaliere di Gran Croce, Order of Merit (Italy), 1993. *Recreations:* tennis, literature. *Address:* Prime Minister's Office, Aleksanterinkatu 3 D, 00170 Helsinki, Finland. *T:* (0) 1601.

AHRENDS, Peter; Founding Partner and Director, Ahrends Burton & Koralek, Architects, since 1961; *b* 30 April 1933; *s* of Steffen Bruno Ahrends and Margarete Marie Sophie Visino; *m* 1954, Elizabeth Robertson; two *d. Educ:* King Edward VII Sch., Johannesburg; Architectural Assoc. Sch. of Architecture (Dipl., Hons). RIBA 1959. Steffen Ahrends &

Partners, Johannesburg, 1957–58; Denys Lasdun & Partners, 1959–60; Julian Keable & Partners; major-projects, 1961–, include: *public buildings:* Hampton Site, Nat. Gall. Extn, 1982–85 (comp. winning entry); St Mary's Hosp., Newport, IoW (nucleus low energy hosp.), 1990; White Cliffs Heritage Centre, Dover, 1991; Quest Science Centre, 1992–; *educational buildings:* New Liby, TCD, 1961 (internat. comp.); Templeton Coll., Oxford, 1969–; residential bldg, Keble Coll., Oxford, 1976 (RIBA Arch. Award, 1978); Arts Faculty Bldg, TCD, 1979; *residential buildings:* Nebenzahl House, Jerusalem, 1972; Whitmore Court Housing, 1975 (RIBA Good Design in Housing Award, 1977); *commercial/industrial buildings:* warehouse, showroom and offices, Habitat, 1974 (Structural Steel Design Award, FT Industrial Arch. Award, 1976); factory, Cummins Engines (Struct. Steel Design Award, 1980); John Lewis dept store, Kingston-upon-Thames, 1990; Sainsbury supermarket, Canterbury, 1984– (Struct. Steel Design Award, 1985); W. H. Smith offices, Swindon, 1985; British Embassy, Moscow, 1988–; office develt for Stanhope Trafalgar, 1990–; *transport:* Docklands Light Railway Beckton Extension stations, 1987–93; *development plans:* won internat. competition for Campus Develt Plan, Univ. of Grenoble, 1990–93; MBA Sch., Templeton Coll., Univ. of Oxford, 1992; Falmer Develt Plan, Univ. of Brighton, 1992; Cardiff Inner Harbour, 1993. Chair, UK Architects Against Apartheid, 1988–; Member: Design Council, 1988–; Council, AA, 1965–67. Vis. Prof. of Architecture, Kingston Poly., 1983–84; Bartlett Prof. of Arch., Bartlett Sch. of Arch. and Planning, UCL, 1986–89; part-time teaching posts and workshops at AA Sch. of Arch., Canterbury Sch. of Art, Edinburgh Univ., Winter Sch. Edinburgh, Plymouth Poly., Kingston Poly., and Plymouth Sch. of Art; vis. critic and/or ext. examr at Kumasi Univ., AA Sch. of Arch., Nova Scotia Tech. Univ., Strathclyde Univ. Exhibitions of drawings and works: RIBA Heinz Gall., 1980; RIAI, 1981; Douglas Hyde Gall., Dublin, 1981; Braunschweig Tech. Univ., Tech. Univ. of Hanover, Museum of Finnish Arch., 1982; Univ. of Oulu, Alvar Aalto Museum, Finland, 1982; AA HQ, Oslo, 1983. *Publications:* (contrib.) Ahrends Burton & Koralek, Architects (monograph), 1991; papers and articles in RIBA Jl and other prof. jls. *Recreations:* architecture, France. *Address:* (home) 16 Rochester Road, NW1 9JH; (office) 7 Chalcot Road, NW1 8LH. *T:* 0171–586 3311.

AHTISAARI, Martti; President, Republic of Finland, since 1994; *b* 23 June 1937; *s* of Oiva and Tyyne Ahtisaari; *m* Eeva Irmeli. Finnish diplomat; UN envoy; head, operation monitoring Namibia's transition to independence, 1989–90; senior envoy in Yugoslavia, 1992–93. *Address:* Presidential Palace, Helsinki, Finland.

AIKEN, Joan Delano, (Mrs Julius Goldstein); writer of historical, mystery and children's novels, plays and poetry; *b* 4 Sept. 1924; *d* of Conrad Potter Aiken and Jessie McDonald; *m* 1st, 1945, Ronald George Brown (*d* 1955); one *s* one *d*; 2nd, 1976, Julius Goldstein. *Educ:* Wychwood Sch., Oxford. Inf. Officer, subseq. Librarian, UN London Inf. Centre, 1943–49; Features Editor, Argosy magazine, 1955–60; Copy-writer, J. Walter Thompson London office, 1960–61; time thereafter devoted to writing. Mem., Soc. of Authors. Guardian Award for Children's Literature, 1969; Lewis Carroll Award, 1970. *Publications:* (most also published in USA and as paperbacks): The Silence of Herondale, 1964; The Fortune Hunters, 1965; Trouble with Product X, 1966 (Beware of the Bouquet, USA 1966); Hate Begins at Home, 1967 (Dark Interval, USA 1967); The Ribs of Death, 1967 (The Crystal Crow, USA 1968); The Windscreen Weepers (stories), 1969; The Embroidered Sunset, 1970; The Butterfly Picnic, 1970 (A Cluster of Separate Sparks, USA 1972); Died on a Rainy Sunday, 1972; Voices in an Empty House, 1975; Castle Barebane, 1976; Last Movement, 1977; The Five-Minute Marriage, 1977; The Smile of the Stranger, 1978; A Touch of Chill (horror stories), 1979; The Lightning Tree, 1980 (The Weeping Ash, USA); The Girl from Paris, 1982; The Way to Write for Children, 1982; A Whisper in the Night, 1982; Foul Matter, 1983; Mansfield Revisited, 1984; Deception, 1987; Jane Fairfax, 1990; *for children:* (many also published in USA): All You've Ever Wanted (stories), 1953; More Than You Bargained For (stories), 1955; The Kingdom and the Cave, 1960; The Wolves of Willoughby Chase, 1962; Black Hearts in Battersea, 1964; Night Birds on Nantucket, 1966; The Whispering Mountain, 1968; A Necklace of Raindrops (stories), 1968; A Small Pinch of Weather (stories), 1969; Night Fall, 1969; Armitage, Armitage, Fly Away Home (stories), USA 1970; Smoke From Cromwell's Time, USA 1970; The Cuckoo Tree, 1971; The Kingdom Under the Sea (folktales), 1971; The Green Flash (fantasy and horror stories), USA 1971; A Harp of Fishbones (stories), 1972; Winterthing (play), USA 1972; The Mooncusser's Daughter (play), USA 1973; Winterthing & The Mooncusser's Daughter, 1973; Midnight is a Place, 1974; Arabel's Raven, USA 1974; Tales of Arabel's Raven, 1974; Not What You Expected (stories), USA 1974; Tale of a One-Way Street (stories), 1976; The Skin Spinners (poems), USA 1976; A Bundle of Nerves (horror stories), 1976; The Angel Inn (trans. from French), 1976; The Faithless Lollybird (stories), 1977; Mice and Mendelson, 1978; Go Saddle the Sea, 1978; Street (play), USA 1978; Arabel and Mortimer, 1979; The Shadow Guests, 1980; The Stolen Lake, 1981; Mortimer's Cross, 1983; Bridle the Wind, 1983; Up the Chimney Down and Other Stories, 1984; Fog Hounds, Wind Cat, Sea Mice, 1984; The Kitchen Warriors, 1984; The Last Slice of Rainbow, 1985; Mortimer Says Nothing, 1985; Dido and Pa, 1986; Past Eight O'Clock, 1986; A Goose on Your Grave, 1987; Beware of the Moon, 1987; The Teeth of the Gale, 1988; The Erl King's Daughter, 1988; Blackground, 1989; Give Yourself a Fright, 1989; Voices, 1989; A Foot in the Grave, 1990; A Fit of Shivers (horror stories), 1990; Morningquest, 1992; (with Lizza Aiken) Mortimer and Arabel, 1992; A Creepy Company, 1993; The Midnight Moropus, 1993; The Shoemaker's Boy, 1993; Is, 1993; Eliza's Daughter, 1994; The Winter Sleepwalker, 1994; Cold Shoulder Road, 1995; A Handful of Gold, 1995. *Recreations:* listening to music, looking at art, travel, reading, gardening, walking, talking to friends. *Address:* The Hermitage, East Street, Petworth, West Sussex GU28 0AB. *T:* Petworth (01798) 42279. *Clubs:* Society of Authors, Writers' Guild, Crime Writers' Association, PEN; Mystery Writers of America.

AIKEN, Air Chief Marshal Sir John (Alexander Carlisle), KCB 1973 (CB 1967); Director General of Intelligence, Ministry of Defence, 1978–81; *b* 22 Dec. 1921; *s* of Thomas Leonard and Margaret Aiken; *m* 1948, Pamela Jane (*née* Bartlett); one *s* one *d*. *Educ:* Birkenhead School. Joined RAF, 1941; Fighter Sqdns, Europe and Far East, 1942–45; Fighter Comd, 1946–47; CFS, 1948; Staff of RAF Coll., Cranwell, 1948–50; OC Univ. of Birmingham Air Sqdn, 1950–52; Staff Coll., 1953; HQ Fighter Comd, 1954–55; OC 29 Fighter Sqdn, 1956–57; jssc 1958; Headquarters AF North, 1958–60; Air Min., 1960–63; Station Comdr, RAF Finningley, 1963–64; Air Cdre Intelligence, Min. of Defence, 1965–67; idc 1968; Dep. Comdr, RAF, Germany, 1969–71; Dir-Gen. Training, RAF, 1971–72; Head of Economy Project Team (RAF), 1972–73; AOC-in-C, NEAF, Comdr British Forces Near East, and Administrator, Sovereign Base Areas, Cyprus, 1973–76; Air Member for Personnel, 1976–78. Pres., RAFA, 1984–85 and 1987–88 (Chm., Central Council, 1981–84); Council, RAF Benevolent Fund, 1988–. Mem. Council, Chatham House, 1984–90. *Recreations:* walking, ski-ing, music. *Club:* Royal Air Force.

AIKENS, Richard John Pearson; QC 1986; a Recorder, since 1993; *b* 28 Aug. 1948; *s* of late Basil Aikens and of Jean Eleanor Aikens; *m* 1979, Penelope Anne Hartley Rockley (*née* Baker); two *s* two step *d*. *Educ:* Norwich Sch.; St John's Coll., Cambridge (MA). Called to Bar, Middle Temple, 1973; Harmsworth scholar, 1974; Bencher, 1994; in practice, 1974–; a Junior Counsel to the Crown, Common Law, 1981–86. Mem., Supreme Court Rules Cttee, 1984–88. Dir, Bar Mutual Indemnity Fund Ltd, 1988–. Governor, Sedbergh Sch., 1988–. *Publication:* (contributing editor) Bullen and Leake and Jacob, Precedents of Pleading, 13th edn 1990. *Recreations:* music, gardening, wine. *Address:* Brick Court Chambers, 15/19 Devereux Court, WC2R 3JJ. *T:* 0171–583 0777. *Clubs:* Groucho; Leander.

AIKIN, Olga Lindholm, (Mrs J. M. Driver); Partner, Aikin Driver Partnership, since 1988; Visiting Lecturer, London Business School, since 1985; Council Member, Advisory Conciliation and Arbitration Service, since 1982; *b* 10 Sept. 1934; *d* of Sidney Richard Daly and Lilian May Daly (*née* Lindholm); *m* 1st, 1959, Ronald Sidney Aikin (marr. diss. 1979); one *d*; 2nd, 1982, John Michael Driver; one step *d*. *Educ:* London School of Economics (LLB); King's Coll., London. Called to Bar, Gray's Inn, 1956. Assistant Lecturer, King's Coll., London, 1956–59; Lecturer, London School of Economics, 1959–70; London Business School: Sloan Fellowship Programme, 1970–71; Vis. Lectr, 1971–79; Lectr in Law, 1979–85. Dir, Gen. Law Div., Lion Internat. (Keiser Enterprises Inc.), 1985–90; Chm. Bd of Mgt, Nat. Conciliation Service of Qualitas Furnishing Standards Ltd, 1992–. *Publications:* (with Judith Reid) Employment, Welfare and Safety at Work, 1971; (with Sonia Pearson) Legal Problems of Employment Contracts, 1990; (ed) IPM Law and Employment series (Discipline; Industrial Tribunals; Redundancy), 1992; articles in Personnel Management. *Recreation:* collecting cookery books and pressed glass. *Address:* 22 St Luke's Road, W11 1DP. *T:* 0171–727 9791.

See also Hon. Francis Daly.

AIKMAN, Colin Campbell, CBE 1990; PhD; consultant; *b* 24 Feb. 1919; *s* of Colin Campbell Aikman and Bertha Egmont Aikman (*née* Harwood); *m* 1952, Betty Alicia, *d* of R. Y. James; three *d* (one *s* decd). *Educ:* Palmerston North Boys' High Sch.; Victoria University Coll., Wellington, NZ (LLM); London Sch. of Economics (PhD). Law Clerk in Legal Offices, 1935–41; Barrister and Solicitor of Supreme Court of New Zealand, 1940–41; Prime Minister's Dept and Dept of External Affairs (Legal Adviser, 1949–55), 1943–55; Mem. NZ Delgn to San Francisco Conf., 1945; Prof. of Jurisprudence and Constitutional Law, Victoria Univ. of Wellington (Dean of Law Faculty, 1957–59, 1962–67), 1955–68; Mem. Council, NZ Inst. of Internat. Affairs (Nat. Pres., 1960–63, Dir. 1979–84), 1955–; Advr to NZ Govt on Constitutional Develt of Cook Is, Western Samoa and Niue, 1956–68, 1975; Vice-Chancellor, The Univ. of the South Pacific, Suva, Fiji, 1968–74; NZ High Comr to India, accredited also to Bangladesh and Nepal, 1975–78. Member: Council of Volunteer Service Abroad (Inc.) (Chm. 1962–65), 1962–68; Adv. Cttee on External Aid and Develt, 1980–88. Consultant, NZ Law Commn, 1988–91. Trustee, Norman Kirk Meml Trust, 1979– (Chm., 1994–). Mem. Council, Nat. Univ. of Samoa, 1985–. Hon. LLD Victoria Univ. of Wellington, 1992; DU Univ. of South Pacific, 1992. Silver Jubilee Medal, 1977; Western Samoa Order of Tiafau, 1993. *Publications:* (co-author): A Report to Members of the Legislative Assembly of the Cook Islands on Constitutional Development, 1963; New Zealand, The Development of its Laws and Constitution (ed Robson), 1967 (2nd edn); New Zealand's Record in the Pacific Islands in the Twentieth Century (ed Angus Ross), 1969; contribs to NZ Internat. Review, Victoria Univ. of Wellington Law Review. *Recreations:* golf, cricket, carpentry. *Address:* 28 Korokoro Road, Petone, New Zealand. *T:* (4) 5891518. *Clubs:* Wellington; Wellington Golf (Heretaunga).

AILESBURY, 8th Marquess of, *cr* 1821; **Michael Sydney Cedric Brudenell-Bruce;** Bt 1611; Baron Brudenell 1628; Earl of Cardigan 1661; Baron Bruce 1746; Earl of Ailesbury 1776; Earl Bruce 1821; Viscount Savernake 1821; 30th Hereditary Warden of Savernake Forest; *b* 31 March 1926; *e s* of 7th Marquess of Ailesbury and Joan (*d* 1937), *d* of Stephen Salter, Ryde, Isle of Wight; *S* father, 1974; *m* 1st, 1952, Edwina Sylvia de Winton (from whom he obtained a divorce, 1961), *yr d* of Lt-Col Sir (Ernest) Edward de Winton Wills, 4th Bt; one *s* two *d*; 2nd, 1963, Juliet Adrienne (marr. diss. 1974), *d* of late Hilary Lethbridge Kingsford and of Mrs Latham Hobrow, Marlborough; two *d*; 3rd, 1974, Mrs Caroline Elizabeth Romilly (marr. diss. 1990), *d* of late Commander O. F. M. Wethered, RN, DL, JP. *Educ:* Eton. Lt RHG, 1946. Mem., London Stock Exchange, 1954. *Heir: s* Earl of Cardigan, *qv*. *Address:* Luton Lye, Savernake Forest, near Marlborough, Wilts SN8 3HP.

AILSA, 8th Marquess of *cr* 1831; **Archibald Angus Charles Kennedy;** Baron Kennedy 1452; Earl of Cassillis 1509; Baron Ailsa (UK) 1806; *b* 13 Sept. 1956; *er s* of 7th Marquess of Ailsa, OBE and of Mary, 7th *c* of John Burn; *S* father, 1994; *m* 1979, Dawn Leslie Anne Keen (marr. diss. 1989); two *d*. *Recreations:* shooting, ski-ing, cadets and youth-work. *Heir: b* Lord David Thomas Kennedy [*b* 3 July 1958; *m* 1991, Anne Kelly; one *d*]. *Address:* Cassillis House, Maybole, Ayrshire KA19 7JN. *T:* Dalrymple (01292560) 310. *Club:* New (Edinburgh).

AINGER, Nicholas Richard, (Nick); MP (Lab) Pembroke, since 1992; *b* Sheffield, 24 Oct. 1949; *m* 1976, Sally Robinson; one *d*. *Educ:* Netherthorpe Grammar Sch., Staveley. Rigger, Marine and Port Services Ltd, Pembroke Dock, 1977–92. Mem. (Lab) Dyfed CC, 1981–93. Branch Sec., TGWU, 1978–92. *Address:* House of Commons, SW1A 0AA.

AINLEY, David Geoffrey, CEng, FIMechE, FRAeS; Deputy Director (Projects and Research), Military Vehicles and Engineering Establishment, Chertsey, 1978–84; *b* 5 July 1924; *s* of Cyril Edward and Constance Ainley; *m* 1st, 1948, Dorothy Emily (*née* Roberts); one *s* one *d*; 2nd, 1959, Diana Margery Hill (*née* Sayles); one *d*; 3rd, 1988, Joyce Dinah (*née* Jessett). *Educ:* Brentwood Sch., Essex; Queen Mary Coll., London Univ. (BSc, 1st Cl. Hons). Engine Dept, RAE, Farnborough, 1943–44; Power Jets (R&D) Ltd, 1944–46; National Gas Turbine Estabt, Pyestock, 1946–66; idc 1967; Dir of Engine Develt, MoD (Procurement Exec.), 1968–78. George Stephenson Research Prize, IMechE, 1953. *Publications:* contrib. books and learned jls on gas turbine technology. *Recreations:* painting, sketching, golf. *Address:* 20 Hampton Close, Church Crookham, Fleet, Hants GU13 0LB. *T:* Fleet (01252) 622577.

AINSCOW, Robert Morrison, CB 1989; Deputy Secretary, Overseas Development Administration, Foreign and Commonwealth Office, since 1986; *b* 3 June 1936; *s* of Robert M. Ainscow and Hilda Ainscow (*née* Cleminson); *m* 1965, Faye Bider; one *s* one *d*. *Educ:* Salford Grammar School; Liverpool Univ. (BA Econ Hons). Statistician: Govt of Rhodesia and Nyasaland, 1957–61; UN Secretariat, New York, 1961–65 and 1966–68; Dept of Economic Affairs, London, 1965–66. Ministry of Overseas Development: Economic Adviser, 1968–70; Senior Economic Adviser, 1971–76; Head, South Asia Dept, 1976–79; Under Secretary, FCO (ODA), 1979–86. Chm., OECD (DAC) Working Party on Financial Aspects of Develt Assistance, 1982–86. *Address:* Overseas Development Administration, 94 Victoria Street, SW1E 5JL.

AINSWORTH, Sir David; *see* Ainsworth, Sir T. D.

AINSWORTH, (Mervyn) John, FCIS, FInstAM; Chief Executive and Secretary, Institute of Chartered Secretaries and Administrators, since 1990; *b* 28 Jan. 1947; *s* of late Gordon John Ainsworth and Eileen Ainsworth; *m* 1973, Marta Christina Marmolak; two *s* one *d*. *Educ:* Stanfields Technical High Sch., Stoke-on-Trent; Goldsmiths' Coll., Univ. of

London (DipEd). Asst Clerk to Govs and Bursar, Dulwich Coll., 1969–74; Principal Assistant, Sec. and Solicitors' Dept, CEGB, 1974–77; Secretarial Asst, BTDB, 1977–78; Sec., 1978–83, Sec. and Dir of Finance, 1983–84, BPIF; Sec. General, Inst. of Administrative Management, 1984–90. Director: ICSA Publishing, 1990–; ICSA Consultants, 1992–; ICSA Software, 1993–; Inst. of Business Administration, 1992–. Member: Bd, Nat. Examining Bd for Supervisory Management, 1984–; Academic Bd, Greenwich Coll., 1984–; Court, Cranfield Univ. (formerly Inst. of Technology), 1990–; Administration Lead Body, 1991–; Council for Certification of Correspondence Colls, 1994–. FIMgt. Hon. Fellow, Canadian Inst. of Certified Administrative Managers, 1987. Liveryman, Worshipful Co. of Chartered Secs and Administrators. *Publications:* articles on management education and administrative systems. *Recreations:* sailing, gardening, family life. *Address:* 3 Silverdale Drive, SE9 4DH. *T:* 0181–857 2630; (office) 16 Park Crescent, W1N 4AH. *T:* 0171–580 4741.

AINSWORTH, Peter Michael; MP (C) Surrey East, since 1992; *b* 16 Nov. 1956; *s* of late Lt-Comdr Michael Lionel Yeoward Ainsworth, RN and of Patricia Mary Ainsworth (*née* Bedford); *m* 1981, Claire Alison Burnett; one *s* two *d.* *Educ:* Ludgrove, Wokingham; Bradfield Coll.; Lincoln Coll., Oxford (MA Eng. Lit and Lang.). Res. Asst to Sir J. Stewart-Clark, MEP, 1979–81; Investment Analyst, Laing & Cruickshank, 1981–85; Sen. Investment Analyst, S. G. Warburg Securities, 1985–87; Asst Dir, 1987–89, Dir, 1989–92, S. G. Warburg Securities Corporate Finance. Mem., Wandsworth Borough Council, 1986– (Chm., Cons. Group, 1990–92). Mem. Council, Bow Group, 1984–86; Chm., Bow Educnl Trust, 1985–86. Mem., Editl Bd, Crossbow, 1985–86. *Recreations:* family, music, gardening. *Address:* House of Commons, SW1A 0AA.

AINSWORTH, Robert William; MP (Lab) Coventry North East, since 1992; *b* 19 June 1952; *s* of late Stanley Ewart Ainsworth and Monica Pearl Ainsworth (later Mrs D. J. Scullion); *m* 1974, Gloria Jean Sandall; two *d.* *Educ:* Foxford Comprehensive School. Sheet metal worker and fitter, Jaguar, 1971–91 (Shop Steward, MSF, 1974–91; Sec., Joint Stewards, 1980–91). City Councillor, Coventry, 1984–93 (Dep. Leader, 1988–91; Chm., Finance, 1989–92). Mem., Select Cttee on environmental affairs, 1993–. Vice-Chm., W Midlands Gp of Labour MPs, 1995–. *Recreations:* walking, reading, chess. *Address:* House of Commons, SW1A 0AA. *T:* 0171–219 4047. *Clubs:* Bell Green Working Men's (Coventry); Broad Street Old Boy's RFC (Coventry).

AINSWORTH, Sir (Thomas) David, 4th Bt *cr* 1916; *b* 22 Aug. 1926; *s* of Sir Thomas Ainsworth, 2nd Bt, and Marie Eleanor (May) (*d* 1969), *d* of Compton Charles Domvile; *S* half-brother, 1981; *m* 1957, Sarah Mary, *d* of late Lt-Col H. C. Walford; two *s* two *d.* *Educ:* Eton. Formerly Lt 11th Hussars. *Recreations:* shooting, fishing. *Heir:* *s* Anthony Thomas Hugh Ainsworth, *b* 30 March 1962. *Address:* 80 Elm Park Gardens, SW10 9PD; Ashley House, Wootton, Woodstock, Oxon OX20 1DX. *Club:* Cavalry and Guards.

AIRD, Captain Sir Alastair (Sturgis), KCVO 1984 (CVO 1977; LVO 1969); Comptroller, since 1974 and Private Secretary and Equerry, since 1993, to Queen Elizabeth the Queen Mother; *b* 14 Jan. 1931; *s* of Col Malcolm Aird; *m* 1963, Fiona Violet, LVO 1980, *d* of late Lt-Col Ririd Myddelton, MVO; two *d.* *Educ:* Eton; RMA Sandhurst. Commnd 9th Queen's Royal Lancers, 1951; served in BAOR; Adjt 9th Lancers, 1956–59; retd from Army, 1964. Equerry to Queen Elizabeth the Queen Mother, 1960; Asst Private Sec. to the Queen Mother, 1964. Mem. Council, Feathers Assoc. of Youth Clubs, 1973–93; Trustee, RSAS Develt Trust, 1986–. Hon. Bencher, Middle Temple, 1991. *Recreations:* shooting, fishing, tennis. *Address:* 31B St James's Palace, SW1A 1BA. *T:* 0171–839 6700. *Clubs:* Cavalry and Guards; Eton Ramblers; I Zingari.

AIRD, Sir (George) John, 4th Bt *cr* 1901; Chairman and Managing Director, Sir John Aird & Co Ltd, since 1969; *b* 30 Jan. 1940; *e s* of Sir John Renton Aird, 3rd Bt, MVO, MC, and of Lady Priscilla Aird, *yr d* of 2nd Earl of Ancaster; *S* father, 1973; *m* 1968, Margaret, *yr d* of Sir John Muir, 3rd Bt; one *s* two *d.* *Educ:* Eton; Oxford Univ.; Harvard Business Sch. MICE. Trainee, Sir Alexander Gibb & Partners, 1961–65; Manager, John Laing & Son Ltd, 1967–69. Chm., MATCON plc, 1981–; Dir, Chance China Ltd, 1992–. *Recreations:* skiing, tennis, hunting. *Heir:* *s* James John Aird, *b* 12 June 1978. *Address:* Grange Farm, Evenlode, Moreton-in-Marsh, Glos GL56 0NT. *T:* Moreton-in-Marsh (01608) 650607. *Club:* White's.

AIREDALE, 4th Baron, *cr* 1907; **Oliver James Vandeleur Kitson;** Bt, *cr* 1886; Deputy Chairman of Committees, House of Lords, since 1961; Deputy Speaker, House of Lords, since 1962; *b* 22 April 1915; *o s* of 3rd Baron Airedale, DSO, MC, and Sheila Grace (*d* 1935), *d* of late Frank E. Vandeleur, London; *S* father, 1958; unmarried. *Educ:* Eton; Trinity College, Cambridge. Major, The Green Howards. Called to the Bar, Inner Temple, 1941. *Heir:* none. *Address:* (seat) Ufford Hall, Stamford, Lincs PE9 3BH.

AIREY, David Lawrence; Managing Director, Bunge & Co. Ltd, 1987–90, retired; *b* 28 April 1935; *s* of Samuel Airey and Helena Florence Lever; *m* 1961, Joan Mary Stewart; three *d.* *Educ:* Oldershaw Grammar Sch., Wallasey. J. Bibby & Sons Ltd: Management trainee, various sales/commercial management positions, 1952–74; Chief Exec., Edible Oils Div., 1974–78; Man. Dir, J. Bibby Edible Oils Ltd, 1979–86; Dep. Man. Dir, Bunge & Co. Ltd, 1986. Chm., Seed Crushers & Oil Processors Assoc., 1980–82. JP Liverpool, 1980–86. *Recreations:* Rugby Union football (Birkenhead Park FC, 1955–66, Cheshire, 1958–65, North West Counties, 1964, Barbarians, 1965), fishing, cooking, gardening. *Address:* Darnley, Church Road, Woodborough, Pewsey, Wilts SN9 5PH. *T:* Marlborough (01672) 851647. *Clubs:* Birkenhead Park FC; Wasps FC.

AIREY, Dawn Elizabeth; Controller of Arts and Entertainment, Channel 4, since 1994; *b* Preston, Lancs, 15 Nov. 1960; partner, 1979, Martin Pearce. *Educ:* Kelly College; Girton College, Cambridge (MA Hons). Central TV: management trainee, 1985–86; Channel 4 Liaison Officer, 1987; Associate Producer, 1988; Controller, later Dir, Programme Planning, Central Broadcasting, 1988–93; Controller of Network Children's and Daytime Progs, ITV Network Centre, 1993–94. Dir, Birmingham Film and TV Festival, 1993. *Recreations:* tennis, fine wines, cinema, TV, collecting antique maps. *Address:* Channel 4, 124–126 Horseferry Road, SW1P 2TX.

AIREY, Sir Lawrence, KCB 1978 (CB 1976); Chairman of the Board of Inland Revenue, 1980–86, retired; Director (non-executive), 1987–94, and Deputy Chairman, 1988–94, Standard Life Assurance Co.; *b* 10 March 1926; *s* of late Lawrence Clark Airey and Isabella Marshall Pearson; *m* 1953, Patricia Anne, *d* of late Edward George Williams and Mary Selway; two *s* one *d.* *Educ:* Newcastle Royal Grammar Sch.; Peterhouse, Cambridge. Served RM, 1945–47. Entered Civil Service, 1949; General Register Office, 1949–56; Cabinet Office, 1956–58; HM Treasury, 1958–79: Under-Sec., 1969–73; Dep. Sec., 1973–77; Second Perm. Sec., 1977–79. Research Fellow, Nuffield Coll., Oxford, 1961–62. Member: Bd of British Nat. Oil Corp., 1976–77; Govt Contracts Rev. Bd, 1986–. *Recreations:* collecting books; music. *Address:* Lions House, Berwick-on-Tweed, Northumberland TD15 1JG. *T:* Berwick-on-Tweed (01289) 304384.

AIRLIE, 13th Earl of, *cr* 1639 (*de facto* 10th Earl, 13th but for the Attainder); **David George Coke Patrick Ogilvy,** KT 1985; GCVO 1984; PC 1984; JP; Baron Ogilvy of Airlie, 1491; Captain late Scots Guards; Lord Chamberlain of HM Household, since 1984; Chancellor, Royal Victorian Order, since 1984; Lord-Lieutenant of Angus, since 1989; *b* 17 May 1926; *e s* of 12th (*de facto* 9th) Earl of Airlie, KT, GCVO, MC, and Lady Alexandra Marie Bridget Coke (*d* 1984), *d* of 3rd Earl of Leicester, GCVO; *S* father, 1968; *m* 1952, Virginia Fortune Ryan (*see* Countess of Airlie); three *s* three *d.* *Educ:* Eton. Lieutenant Scots Guards, 1944; serving 2nd Battalion Germany, 1945; Captain, ADC to High Comr and C-in-C Austria, 1947–48; Malaya, 1948–49; resigned commission, 1950. Ensign, 1975–85, Lieutenant, 1985–, Queen's Body Guard for Scotland, Royal Company of Archers. Chairman: Schroders plc, 1977–84; Gen. Accident Fire & Life Assurance Corp., 1987– (Dir, 1962–; Dep. Chm., 1975–87); Ashdown Investment Trust Ltd, 1968–82; Director: J. Henry Schroder Wagg & Co. Ltd, 1961–84 (Chm., 1973–77); Scottish & Newcastle Breweries plc, 1969–83; The Royal Bank of Scotland Gp, 1983–93; Baring Stratton Investment Trust (formerly Stratton Investment Trust), 1986–. Treasurer, Scout Assoc., 1962–86; Hon. Pres., Scottish Council of Scout Assoc., 1988–. DL Angus, 1964; JP Angus, 1990. Governor, Nuffield Nursing Homes Trust, 1985–89; Chancellor, Univ. of Abertay Dundee, 1994–. Hon. LLD Dundee, 1990. *Heir:* *s* Lord Ogilvy, *qv.* *Address:* Cortachy Castle, Kirriemuir, Angus DD8 4LX. *T:* Cortachy (01575) 540231; 5 Swan Walk, Chelsea SW3 4JJ.

See also Hon. Sir Angus Ogilvy, Sir Hereward Wake.

AIRLIE, Countess of; Virginia Fortune Ogilvy, DCVO 1995 (CVO 1983); Lady of the Bedchamber to the Queen since 1973; *b* 9 Feb. 1933; *d* of John Barry Ryan, Newport, RI, USA; *m* 1952, Lord Ogilvy (now Earl of Airlie, *qv*); three *s* three *d.* *Educ:* Brearley School, New York City. Founder Governor, Cobham School, Kent, 1958. Mem., Industrial Design Panel, British Rail, 1974–.Trustee: Tate Gallery, 1983– (Chm. Friends of Tate Gallery, 1978–83); Amer. Mus. in Britain, 1985–89; Nat. Gallery, 1989–. Pres., Angus Br., BRCS, 1988. *Address:* Cortachy Castle, Kirriemuir, Angus DD8 4LX; 5 Swan Walk, SW3 4JJ.

AIRY, Maj.-Gen. Sir Christopher (John), KCVO 1989; CBE 1984; Private Secretary and Treasurer to TRH The Prince and Princess of Wales, 1990–91, an Extra Equerry, since 1991; *b* 8 March 1934; *m*; one *s* two *d.* 2nd Lieut, Grenadier Guards, 1954; Scots Guards, 1974. PMA to Sec. of State for War, 1960; sc 1966; DAAG, Regtl Adjt, 1967; Bde Major, 4th Guards Armoured Bde, 1971; ndc 1973; CO, 1st Bn Scots Guards, 1974; Mil. Asst (GSO1) to Master Gen. of the Ordnance, 1976; Comdr 5th Field Force, 1979; rcds 1981; ACOS, HQ UKLF, 1982–83; Sen. Army Mem., RCDS, 1984–85; GOC London District and Maj.-Gen. Comdg Household Div., 1986; retd 1989. Chm., Not Forgotten Assoc., 1993–; Comr, Royal Hosp., Chelsea, 1990–; Mem., Prince of Wales's Council, 1990–91. Dir, Hedley Foundn, 1994–. *Recreations:* gardens, architecture, travel. *Clubs:* Pratt's, Buck's.

AITCHISON, Sir Charles (Walter de Lancey), 4th Bt, *cr* 1938; Director, De Lancey Lands Ltd; *b* 27 May 1951; *er s* of Sir Stephen Charles de Lancey Aitchison, 3rd Bt, and (Elizabeth) Anne (Milburn), *er d* of late Lt-Col Edward Reed, Ghyllheugh, Longhorsley, Northumberland; *S* father 1958; *m* 1984, Susan, *yr d* of late Edward Ellis; one *s* one *d.* Lieut, 15/19th The King's Royal Hussars, 1974; RARO 1974–78. ARICS. *Recreation:* field sports. *Heir:* *s* Rory Edward de Lancey Aitchison, *b* 7 March 1986. *Address:* Middle Bank House, Barbon, Carnforth, Lancs LA6 5SG.

AITCHISON, Craigie (Ronald John), RA 1988 (ARA 1978); painter; *b* 13 Jan. 1926; *yr s* of late Rt Hon. Lord Aitchison, PC, KC, LLD. *Educ:* Scotland; Slade Sch. of Fine Art. British Council Italian Govt Scholarship for painting, 1955; Edwin Austin Abbey Premier Scholarship, 1965; Lorne Scholarship, 1974–75. One-man Exhibitions: Beaux Arts Gall., 1959, 1960, 1964; Marlborough Fine Art (London) Ltd, 1968; Compass Gall., Glasgow, 1970; Basil Jacobs Gall., 1971; Rutland Gall., 1975; Knoedler Gall., 1977; Kettle's Yard Gall., Cambridge, 1979; Serpentine Gall. (major retrospective, 1953–81), 1981–82; Artis, Monte Carlo, Monaco, 1986; Albemarle Gall., 1987, 1989; Castlefield Gall., Manchester, 1990; Thomas Gibson Fine Art, London, 1993; Harewood House, Leeds (retrospective, 1954–94). Exhibited: Calouste Gulbenkian Internat. Exhibn, 1964; Il Tempo del imagine, 2nd Internat. Biennale, Bologna, 1967; Modern British Painters, Tokyo, Japan, 1969; 23rd Salon Actualité de l'Esprit, Paris, 1975; The Proper Study, British Council Lalit Kala Akademi, Delhi, 1984; Hard Won Image, Tate Gall., 1985; British Council Exhibn, Picturing People, Hong Kong and Zimbabwe, 1990; The Journey, Lincoln Cathedral, 1990; Nine Contemporary Painters, City of Bristol Mus. and Art Gall., 1990; British Council Exhibn, British Figurative Painting of 20th Century, Israel Mus., Jerusalem, 1992. Pictures in public collections: Tate Gall., Arts Council, Contemp. Art Soc., Scottish National Gall. of Modern Art, Glasgow Mus. and Art Gall., and Nat. Gall. of Melbourne, Australia. 1st Johnson Wax Prize, Royal Acad., 1982; Korn Ferry Internat. Award, Royal Acad., 1989 and 1991; 1st Jerwood Foundn Award, 1994. *Address:* c/o Royal Academy of Arts, Burlington House, Piccadilly, W1V 0DS.

AITCHISON, Prof. Jean Margaret; Rupert Murdoch Professor of Language and Communication, University of Oxford, since 1993; Fellow, Worcester College, Oxford, since 1993; *b* 3 July 1938; *d* of John Frederick and Joan Eileen Aitchison. *Educ:* Wimbledon High Sch.; Girton Coll., Cambridge (BA 1st Cl. Hons Classics, MA); Radcliffe Coll., Harvard (AM Linguistics 1961). University of London: Asst Lectr in Ancient Greek, Bedford Coll., 1960–65; Lectr, 1965–82, Sen. Lectr, 1982–92, Reader, 1992, in Linguistics, LSE, 1965–92. Reith Lectr, 1996. *Publications:* Linguistics, 1972, 4th edn 1992; The Articulate Mammal: an introduction to psycholinguistics, 1976, 3rd edn 1989; Language Change: progress or decay?, 1981, 2nd edn 1991; Words in the Mind: an introduction to the mental lexicon, 1987, 2nd edn 1994; Introducing Language and Mind, 1992. *Recreation:* windsurfing. *Address:* Worcester College, Oxford OX1 2HB. *T:* Oxford (01865) 278392.

AITCHISON, June Rosemary, (Mrs T. J. Aitchison); *see* Whitfield, J. R.

AITCHISON, Thomas Nisbet; Chief Executive, City of Edinburgh Council, since 1995; *b* 24 Feb. 1951; *s* of Thomas Aitchison and Mary (*née* Millar); *m* 1973, Kathleen Sadler; one *s* two *d.* *Educ:* Univ. of Glasgow (MA 1st Class Hons Geography); Heriot-Watt Univ. (MSc). Lothian Regional Council: Policy Planning, 1975–78; PA to Chief Exec., 1978–81; seconded to Chief Exec's Co-ordination Team, 1981–82; Co-ordination Unit, Dept of Manpower Services, 1982–85; Dept of Management and Inf. Services, 1985–87; Corporate Planning Manager and Depute Dir, 1987–91; Depute Chief Exec., 1991–94; Chief Exec., 1994–95. *Recreations:* hill-walking, football, music. *Address:* City of Edinburgh Council, PO Box 3232, Edinburgh EH1 1YX. *Fax:* 0131–469 3010.

AITKEN, family name of **Baron Beaverbrook.**

AITKEN, Gillon Reid; literary agent; Chairman, Aitken, Stone & Wylie Ltd, since 1985; Vice-President, Wylie, Aitken & Stone, Inc. (New York), since 1986; *b* 29 March 1938; *s* of James Aitken and Margaret Joane Aitken (*née* Simpson); *m* 1982, Cari Margareta Bengtsson; one *d.* *Educ:* Charterhouse Sch.; privately. Private schoolmaster, Surbiton, 1955–56; National Service, 1956–58: Somerset LI; Intelligence Corps; Jt Services Sch. for Linguists (Russian course); Royal Signal Corps, Berlin. Stuart's Advertising Agency Ltd, 1958–59; Editor: Chapman & Hall Ltd, 1959–66; Hodder & Stoughton Ltd, 1966–67;

Dir, Anthony Sheil Associates Ltd, 1967–71; Man. Dir, Hamish Hamilton Ltd, 1971–74; Vice-Pres., Wallace, Aitken & Sheil, Inc. (NY), 1974–77; Chairman: Gillon Aitken Ltd, 1977–85; Christy & Moore Ltd, 1977–; Dir, Hughes Massie Ltd, 1985–. *Publications:* translations from Russian: The Captain's Daughter & Other Stories by Alexander Sergeyevitch Pushkin, 1962; The Complete Prose Tales of Pushkin, 1966; One Day in the Life of Ivan Denisovich by Alexander Solzhenitsyn, 1970. *Recreations:* crossword puzzles, ping-pong. *Address:* c/o Aitken, Stone & Wylie Ltd, 29 Fernshaw Road, SW10 0TG. *T:* 0171–351 7561; 55 Addison Road, W14 8JJ. *T:* 0171–603 7917. *Clubs:* Beefsteak, Brooks's.

AITKEN, Ian Levack; columnist, The Guardian, since 1992; contributing editor, New Statesman, since 1994; *b* 19 Sept. 1927; *s* of George Aitken and Agnes Levack Aitken; *m* 1956, Dr Catherine Hay Mackie, *y d* of late Maitland Mackie, OBE; two *d. Educ:* King Alfred Sch., Hampstead; Regent Street Polytechnic; Lincoln Coll., Oxford (BA PPE; MA); LSE. Served Fleet Air Arm, 1945–48. HM Inspector of Factories, 1951; Res. Officer, CSEU, 1952; Industrial Reporter, Tribune, 1953–54; Industrial Reporter, subseq. Foreign Correspondent and Political Correspondent, Daily Express, 1954–64; political staff, The Guardian, 1964–92 (Political Editor, 1975–90; political columnist, 1990–92). Gerald Barry Award for journalism, 1984. *Recreation:* music. *Address:* 52A North Hill, N6 4RH. *T:* 0181–340 5914. *Clubs:* Garrick, Wig and Pen.

See also Baron Mackie of Benshie, Sir M. Mackie.

AITKEN, Rt. Hon. Jonathan (William Patrick), PC 1994; MP (C) Thanet South, since 1983 (Thanet East, Feb. 1974–1983); *b* 30 Aug. 1942; *s* of late Sir William Aitken, KBE and of Hon. Lady Aitken, MBE, JP; *m* 1979, Lolicia Olivera, *d* of Mr and Mrs O. Azucki, Zürich; one *s* twin *d. Educ:* Eton Coll.; Christ Church, Oxford. MA Hons Law. Private Sec. to Selwyn Lloyd, 1964–66; Foreign Corresp., London Evening Standard, 1966–71; Man. Dir, Slater Walker (Middle East) Ltd, 1973–75; Dep. Chm., Aitken Hume Internat. PLC, 1990–92 (Co-founder, 1981; Chm., 1981–90); Dir, TV-am PLC, 1981–88. Minister of State for Defence Procurement, MoD, 1992–94; Chief Sec. to HM Treasury, 1994–95. Mem., Select Cttee on Employment, 1979–82. *Publications:* A Short Walk on the Campus, 1966; The Young Meteors, 1967; Land of Fortune: A Study of Australia, 1969; Officially Secret, 1970; Richard Nixon: a life, 1993; articles in Spectator, Sunday Telegraph, Sydney Morning Herald, Washington Post, The Independent, etc. *Recreations:* squash, cross-country ski-ing, running. *Address:* House of Commons, SW1A 0AA. *Clubs:* Pratt's, Turf, Beefsteak.

See also M. P. K. Aitken.

AITKEN, Maria Penelope Katharine; actress; Director, Dramatis Personae Co.; *b* 12 Sept. 1945; *d* of Sir William Traven Aitken, and Hon. Penelope Loader Maffey, MBE, JP; *m* 1st, 1968, Mark Durden-Smith (marr. diss.); 2nd, 1972, Arthur Nigel Davenport, *qv* (marr. diss.); one *s*; 3rd, 1992, Patrick McGrath. *Educ:* Riddlesworth Hall, Norfolk; Sherborne Girls' Sch.; St Anne's Coll., Oxford. *Stage includes:* first professional appearance, Belgrade Th., Coventry, 1967; rep., Th. Royal, Northampton, 1970–71; Travesties, RSC, 1974; A Little Night Music, Adelphi, 1975; Blithe Spirit, NT, 1976; Bedroom Farce, NT, 1977; Private Lives, Duchess, 1980; Design for Living, Greenwich, 1982; Sister Mary Ignatius (also dir.), Ambassadors, 1983; Happy Family (dir.), Duke of York's, 1983; Private Lives (also dir.), 1984; After the Ball (dir.), Old Vic, 1985; The Rivals (dir.), Court, Chicago, 1985; Waste, RSC, 1985; The Women, Old Vic, 1986; The Vortex, Garrick, 1989; Other People's Money, Lyric, 1990; The Mystery of Irma Vep (dir.), Ambassadors, 1990; As You Like It (dir.), Regent's Park Open Air Th., 1992; Hay Fever, Albery, 1992; The Picture of Dorian Gray, Lyric, Hammersmith, 1994; *films:* Some Girls Do, 1968; A Fish Called Wanda, 1988; producer, director and actor for TV. *Publication:* A Girdle Round the Earth, 1986. *Address:* c/o Michael Whitehall, 125 Gloucester Road, SW7 4TE.

See also Rt Hon. J. W. P. Aitken.

AITKEN, Prof. Martin Jim, FRS 1983; FSA; FRAS; Professor of Archaeometry, 1985–89, and Deputy Director, Research Laboratory for Archaeology, 1957–89, Oxford University; Fellow of Linacre College, Oxford, 1965–89; *b* 11 March 1922; *s* of Percy Aitken and Ethel Brittain; *m* Joan Killick; one *s* four *d. Educ:* Stamford Sch., Lincs; Wadham Coll. and Clarendon Lab., Oxford Univ. (MA, DPhil). Served War, RAF Radar Officer, 1942–46 (Burma Star, 1945). Mem., Former Physical Soc., 1951–; MRI, 1972–89. Editor, Archaeometry, 1958–89. *Publications:* Physics and Archaeology, 1961, 2nd edn 1974; Thermoluminescence Dating, 1985; Science-based dating in Archaeology, 1990. *Recreations:* sailing, dinghy-racing. *Address:* Ofslang House, Islip, Oxford OX5 2SZ. *T:* Kidlington (01865) 373377; Le Garret, 63930 Augerolles, France. *T:* 73726120.

AITKEN, Sir Robert (Stevenson), Kt 1960; MD (New Zealand), DPhil (Oxford); FRCP, FRACP; retired; *b* NZ; *s* of late Rev. James Aitken; *m* 1929, Margaret G. Kane (*d* 1991); one *s* two *d. Educ:* Gisborne High School, Gisborne, NZ; University of Otago, Dunedin, NZ; Oxford. Medical Qualification in New Zealand, 1922; Rhodes Scholar, Balliol College, Oxford, 1924–26; attached to Medical Unit, The London Hospital, 1926–34; Reader in Medicine, British Post-Graduate Medical School, Univ. of London, 1935–38; Regius Prof. of Medicine, Univ. of Aberdeen, 1939–48; Vice-Chancellor, Univ. of Otago, Dunedin, NZ, 1948–53; Vice-Chancellor, Univ. of Birmingham, 1953–68. Vice-Chm. Association of Univs of the British Commonwealth, 1955–58; Dep. Chm., UGC, 1968–73; Chairman: Committee of Vice-Chancellors and Principals, 1958–61; Birmingham Repertory Theatre, 1962–74. DL Co. Warwick, 1967, West Midlands, 1974–93. Hon. FRCPE; Hon. FDSRCS; Hon. DCL Oxford; Hon. LLD: Dalhousie, Melbourne, Panjab, McGill, Pennsylvania, Aberdeen, Newfoundland, Leicester, Birmingham, Otago; Hon. DSc: Sydney, Liverpool. *Publications:* papers in medical and scientific journals. *Address:* 6 Hintlesham Avenue, Birmingham B15 2PH.

See also T. H. D. Arie.

AITKIN, Prof. Donald Alexander, PhD; Vice-Chancellor, University of Canberra, since 1991; *b* 4 Aug. 1937; *e s* of late Alexander George Aitkin and Edna Irene (*née* Taylor); *m* 1st, 1958, Janice Wood (marr. diss. 1977); one *s* three *d*; 2nd, 1977, Susan Elderton (marr. diss. 1991); one *s*; 3rd, 1991, Beverley Benger. *Educ:* Univ. of New England (MA 1961); ANU (PhD 1964). Postdoctoral Travelling Fellow, Nuffield Coll., Oxford, 1964; Australian National University: Res. Fellow in Pol Sci., 1965–68; Sen. Res. Fellow, 1968–71; Prof. of Politics (Foundn Prof.), Macquarie Univ., 1971–80; Institute of Advanced Studies, Australian National University: Prof. of Pol Sci., 1980–88; Chm. Bd, 1986–88. Chm., Aust. Res. Council, 1988–90. Vice-Pres., Australian Vice-Chancellors' Cttee, 1994–. FASSA 1975. *Publications:* The Colonel, 1969; The Country Party in New South Wales, 1972; Stability and Change in Australian Politics, 1977, 2nd edn 1982; The Second Chair (novel), 1977; (with B. Jinks) Australian Political Institutions, 1980 (trans. Japanese, 1985), 4th edn 1989; (ed) The Life of Politics, 1984; (ed) Surveys of Australian Political Science, 1985. *Recreations:* bushwalking, ski-ing, music, cooking. *Address:* 26 Borrowdale Street, Red Hill, ACT 2603, Australia. *T:* (6) 2015000. *Club:* Commonwealth (Canberra).

AJAYI, Prof. Jacob Festus Ade; Professor of History, University of Ibadan, 1963–89, now Emeritus; ; *b* 26 May 1929; *s* of late Chief E. Ade Ajayi and Mrs C. Bolajoko Ajayi; *m* 1956, Christie Aduke Martins; one *s* four *d. Educ:* University College, Ibadan; University College, Leicester; Univ. of London; BA, PhD (London). Research Fellow, Inst. of Historical Research, London, 1957–58; Lectr, Univ. of Ibadan, 1958–62, Sen. Lectr, 1962–63; Dean, Faculty of Arts, 1964–66; Asst to Vice-Chancellor, 1966–68. Fellow, Centre for Advanced Study in the Behavioural Sciences, Stanford, Calif, 1970–71; Vice-Chancellor, Univ. of Lagos, 1972–78; Pro-Chancellor, Ondo State Univ., Ado-Ekiti, 1984–88. Member: UN University Council, 1974–80 (Chm., 1975–77); Nat. Archives Cttee, Nigeria, 1961–72; Nat. Antiquities Commn, Nigeria, 1970–74; Exec. Council, Internat. African Inst. London, 1971– (Chm., 1975–87); Exec. Bd, Assoc. of African Univs, 1974–80; Admin. Bd., Internat. Assoc. of Univs, 1980–90; Pres., Historical Soc. of Nigeria, 1972–81; Pres., Internat. Congress of African Studies, 1978–85. Dir, BCN plc, 1988–92. Chm., Jadeas Trust, 1989–. Hon. LLD Leicester, 1975; Hon. DLitt: Birmingham, 1984; Ondo State Univ., Ado-Ekiti, 1992. Hon. Fellow, SOAS, Univ. of London, 1994. Fellow, Hist. Soc. of Nigeria, 1980; Overseas FRHistS, 1982. National Merit Award, Nigeria, 1986. Traditional titles, Bobapitan of Ikole-Ekiti and Onikoyi of Ife, 1983. *Publications:* Milestones in Nigerian History, 1962; (ed, with Ian Espie) A Thousand Years of West African History, 1964; (with R. S. Smith) Yoruba Warfare in the Nineteenth Century, 1964; Christian Missions in Nigeria: the making of a new elite, 1965; (ed, with Michael Crowder) A History of West Africa, vol. I, 1972; vol. II, 1974; (ed jtly) The University of Ibadan, 1948–73, 1973; (ed with Bashir Ikara) Evolution of Political Culture in Nigeria, 1985; (ed with M. Crowder) A Historical Atlas of Africa, 1985; (ed) Africa in the Nineteenth Century until the 1880s, vol. VI of Unesco General History of Africa, 1989; History and the Nation, and other Addresses, 1990; (with Peter Pugh) Cementing a Partnership: the story of WAPCO 1960–1990, 1990; A Patriot to the Core: Samuel Ajayi Crowther, 1992; contribs to Jl Historical Soc. of Nigeria, Jl of African History, etc. *Recreations:* dancing, tennis. *Address:* 1 Ojobadan Avenue, Bodija, Ibadan, Nigeria; PO Box 14617 UI, Ibadan, Nigeria.

AKEHURST, Gen. Sir John (Bryan), KCB 1984; CBE 1976; Deputy Supreme Allied Commander, Europe, 1987–90; *b* 12 Feb. 1930; *s* of late Geoffrey and Doris Akehurst; *m* 1955, Shirley Ann, *er d* of late Major W. G. Webb, MBE, and of Ethel Webb; one *s* one *d* decd. *Educ:* Cranbrook Sch.; RMA, Sandhurst. Commnd Northamptonshire Regt, 1949; Malay Regt (despatches), 1952–55; Adjt, 5th Northamptonshire Regt (TA), 1959–60; Staff Coll., Camberley, 1961; Brigade Major, 12 Infantry Bde Gp, 1962–64; Instructor, Staff Coll., Camberley, 1966–68; commanded 2nd Royal Anglian Regt, 1968–70; Directing Staff, IDC/RCDS, 1970–72; Comdt, Jun. Div., Staff Coll., 1972–74; Comdr, Dhofar Bde, Sultan of Oman's Armed Forces, 1974–76; Dep. Mil. Sec. (A), MoD (Army), 1976–79; GOC 4th Armoured Div., BAOR, 1979–81; Comdt, The Staff Coll., Camberley, 1982–83; Comdr, UK Field Army, and Inspector Gen., TA, 1984–87. Sen. Mil. Visitor to Saudi Arabia, 1985–87; Dep. Col, 1981–86, Col, 1986–91, Royal Anglian Regt. Mem., Commonwealth War Graves Commn, 1993–. Chm., Council, TA&VRA, 1990–95; Mem. Council, RUSI, 1985–88; Pres., Reserve Forces Assoc., 1991–. Chm., 1982–84, Pres., 1984–90, Army Golf Assoc.; Vice Patron, Army Officers' Golf Soc., 1986– (Pres., 1983–86). Gov., Royal Star and Garter Home, 1990–91. Governor: Harrow Sch., 1982– (Chm. of Govs, 1991–); John Lyon Sch., 1989–91; Princecroft Primary Sch., Warminster, 1990–. Order of Oman, 3rd Class (mil.), 1976. *Publication:* We Won a War, 1982. *Recreations:* golf, trout fishing, travel. *Address:* c/o Midland Bank, Minehead, Somerset TA24 5LH. *Clubs:* Army and Navy; Bath Golf.

AKENHEAD, Robert; QC 1989; a Recorder, since 1994; *b* 15 Sept. 1949; *s* of late Edmund and of Angela Akenhead; *m* 1972, Elizabeth Anne Jackson; one *s* three *d. Educ:* Rugby School; Exeter Univ. (LLB). Called to the Bar, Inner Temple, 1972; in practice as barrister, 1973–; an Asst Recorder, 1991–94. Examiner, Dio. of Canterbury, 1991–. *Publication:* Site Investigation and the Law, 1984. *Recreations:* theatre, cricket, ski-ing. *Address:* 1 Atkin Building, Gray's Inn, WC1R 5BQ. *T:* 0171–404 0102.

AKERLOF, Prof. George Arthur, PhD; teaching in Economics Department, University of California at Berkeley, since 1980; Cassel Professor of Economics, London School of Economics and Political Science, 1978–81; *b* 17 June 1940; *s* of Gosta C. Akerlof and Rosalie C. Akerlof; *m* 1978, Janet Yellen. *Educ:* Yale Univ. (BA 1962); MIT (PhD 1966). Fellowships: Woodrow Wilson, 1962–63, National Science Co-op., 1963–66; Fulbright, 1967–68; Guggenheim, 1973–74. Univ. of Calif, Berkeley: Asst Prof. of Econs, 1966–70; Associate Prof., 1970–77; Prof., 1977–78. Vis. Prof., Indian Statistical Inst., New Delhi, 1967–68. Sen. Economist, Council of Econ. Advisors, USA, 1973–74; Vis. Economist, Bd of Governors of Fed. Reserve System, USA, 1977–78. *Publications:* contrib. American Econ. Rev., Econ. Jl, Qly Jl Econs, Jl Polit. Econ., Rev. of Econ. Studies, Internat. Econ. Rev., Jl Econ. Theory, Indian Econ. Rev., and Rev. of Econs and Stats. *Address:* Economics Department, University of California, Berkeley, Calif 94720, USA. *Club:* Piggy (Center Harbor, NH, USA).

AKERS, John Fellows; Chairman, International Business Machines Corp., 1986–93; *b* 1934; *m* 1960, Susan Davis; one *s* two *d. Educ:* Yale Univ. (BS). International Business Machines Corp., 1960–93: Pres., Data Processing Div., 1974–76; Vice Pres., Asst Gp Exec., plans and controls, Data Processing Product Gp, 1976–78; Vice Pres., Gp Exec., Data Processing Marketing Gp, 1978–81, Inf. Systems and Communications Gp, 1981–82, Sen. Vice Pres., 1982–83; Dir, 1983–93; Pres., 1983–89; Chief Exec. Officer, 1985–93. Dir, New York Times Co., 1985–; formerly Dir, PepsiCo. Inc. Formerly Mem., President's Educn Policy Adv. Cttee. Trustee: MMA; CIT; Mem. Bd of Governors, United Way of America. *Address:* c/o IBM Corp., Old Orchard Road, Armonk, NY 10504, USA.

AKERS-DOUGLAS, family name of **Viscount Chilston.**

AKERS-JONES, Sir David, KBE 1985; CMG 1978; Chief Secretary, Hong Kong, 1985–86; Acting Governor, Hong Kong, Dec. 1986–April 1987; *b* 14 April 1927; *s* of Walter George and Dorothy Jones; *m* 1951, Jane Spickernell (MBE 1988); one *d* (one *s* decd). *Educ:* Worthing High Sch.; Brasenose Coll., Oxford (MA). British India Steam Navigation Co., 1945–49. Malayan Civil Service (studied Hokkien and Malay), 1954–57; Hong Kong Civil Service, 1957–86; Government Secretary: for New Territories, 1973–81; for City and New Territories, 1981–83; for Dist Admin, 1983–85; Advr to Gov., April–Sept. 1987. Chm., Hong Kong Housing Authy, 1988–93; Advr to China on Hong Kong Affairs, 1993–. Vice-Pres., WWF Hong Kong, 1995–; Chm., Hong Kong Artists' Guild, 1987–. Pres., Outward Bound Trust, Hong Kong, 1986–; Vice-Patron, Hong Kong Football Assoc. Hon. Mem., RICS, 1991. Hon. DCL Kent, 1987; Hon. LLD Chinese Univ. of Hong Kong, 1988. *Recreations:* painting, gardening, walking, music. *Address:* Dragon View, 128 Castle Peak Road, Tsing Lung Tau, New Territories, Hong Kong. *Clubs:* Athenæum, Royal Over-Seas League; Hong Kong, Kowloon, Dynasty, China, Gold Coast Country and Yacht (Hong Kong).

AKHTAR, Prof. Muhammad, FRS 1980; Professor of Biochemistry, University of Southampton, since 1978; *b* 23 Feb. 1933; *m* 1963, Monika E. Schurmann; two *s. Educ:* Punjab Univ., Pakistan (MSc 1st class 1954); Imperial College, London (PhD, DIC 1959). Research Scientist, Inst. for Medicine and Chemistry, Cambridge, Mass, USA, 1959–63;

University of Southampton: Lecturer in Biochemistry, 1963–66; Senior Lectr, 1966–68; Reader, 1968–73; Hd of Dept of Biochemistry, 1978–93; Chm., Sch. of Biochem. and Physiol. Scis, 1983–87; Dir, SERC Centre for Molecular Recognition, 1990–. Chm., Inst. of Biomolecular Scis, 1989–90. Member: Chemical Soc. of GB; American Chemical Soc.; Biochemical Soc. of GB; Council, Royal Soc., 1983–85; Founding Fellow, Third World Acad. of Sciences, 1983. Flintoff Medal, RSC, 1993. Sitara-I-Imtiaz (Pakistan), 1981. *Publications:* numerous works on: enzyme mechanisms; synthesis and biosynthesis of steroids and porphyrins; biochemistry of vision; synthesis of anti-microbial compounds. *Address:* Department of Biochemistry, University of Southampton, Southampton SO9 3TU. *T:* Southampton (01703) 594338.

AKIHITO, HM the Emperor of Japan; Collar, Supreme Order of Chrysanthemum, 1989; *b* Tokyo, 23 Dec. 1933; *e s* of His late Majesty Emperor Hirohito (Showa) and of HM Empress Dowager Nagako; *S* father, 1989; *m* 1959, Michiko Shoda; two *s* one *d*. *Educ:* Gakushuin Primary, Jun. and Sen. High Schs; Dept of Politics, Faculty of Politics and Econs, Gakushuin Univ. Official Investiture as Crown Prince of Japan, 1952. Res. Associate, Australian Mus.; Mem., Ichthyological Soc. of Japan; Hon. Mem., Linnean Soc. of London. *Heir: er s* Crown Prince Naruhito [*b* Tokyo, 23 Feb. 1960; *m* 1993, Masako Owada]. *Publications:* (contrib. jtly) Fishes of the Japanese Archipelago, 1984; (jtly) The Fresh Water Fishes of Japan, 1987; 27 papers on gobies. *Recreation:* tennis. *Address:* Imperial Palace, 1-1 Chiyoda, Chiyoda-ku, Tokyo 100, Japan. *T:* (3) 32131111.

AKINKUGBE, Prof. Oladipo Olujimi, CON 1979; Officier de l'Ordre National de la République de Côte d'Ivoire, 1981; MD, DPhil; FRCP, FWACP, FAS; Professor of Medicine, University of Ibadan, Nigeria, since 1968; *b* 17 July 1933; *s* of late Chief David Akinbobola and of Chief (Mrs) Grace Akinkugbe; *m* 1965, Dr Folasade Modupeore Dina, *d* of late Chief I. O. Dina, CFR, OBE; two *s*. *Educ:* Univs of Ibadan, London (MD), Liverpool (DTM&H) and Oxford (DPhil). FRCP 1968; FWACP 1975; FAS 1980. House Surg., London Hosp., 1958; House Phys., King's Coll. Hosp., London, 1959; Commonwealth Res. Fellow, Balliol Coll. and Regius Dept of Medicine, Oxford, 1962–64; Head of Dept of Medicine, 1972, Dean of Medicine, 1970–74, and Chm., Cttee of Deans, 1972–74, Univ. of Ibadan; Vice-Chancellor: Univ. of Ilorin, 1977–78 (Principal, 1975–77); Ahmadu Bello Univ., Zaria, 1978–79. Rockefeller Vis. Fellow, US Renal Centres, 1966; Vis. Fellow in Medicine, Univs of Manchester, Cambridge and London, 1969; Vis. Prof. of Medicine, Harvard Univ., 1974–75; Vis. Prof. of Medicine, Univ. of Oxford and Vis. Fellow, Balliol Coll., Oxford, 1981–82. Adviser on Postgrad. Med. Educn to Fed. Govt of Nigeria, 1972–75; Chm., Nat. Implementation Commn on Rev. of Higher Educn in Nigeria, 1992; Member: Univ. Grants Commn, Uganda Govt; OAU Scientific Panels on Health Manpower Develt; Council, Internat. Soc. of Hypertension, 1982–90; Bd of Trustees, African Assoc. of Nephrology, 1986–; internat. socs of hypertension, cardiology, and nephrology; Med. Res. Soc. of GB; Scientific Adv. Panel, Ciba Foundn; WHO Expert Adv. Panels on Cardiovascular Diseases, 1973–78, on Health Manpower 1979–; WHO Adv. Council on Health Res., 1990–; Sec. to WHO 1984 Technical Discussions. Pro-Chancellor, and Chm. of Council, Univ. of Port-Harcourt, Nigeria, 1986–90; Member: Governing Council and Bd of Trustees, Obafemi Awolowo Foundn, 1992; Governing Council, Nigeria Heartcare Foundn, 1994. Pres., Nigerian Assoc. of Nephrology, 1987–90. Member, Editorial Bd: Jl of Hypertension, 1984–90; Jl of Human Hypertension, 1988–; Kidney International, 1990–; Blood Pressure, 1991–; News in Physiological Scis, 1992–. Hon. DSc: Ilorin, 1982; Fed. Univ. of Technol., Akure, 1992. Searle Dist. Res. Award, 1989. Traditional title, Atobase of Ife, 1991; Babalofin of Ijebu-Igbo, 1994. *Publications:* High Blood Pressure in the African, 1972; (ed) Priorities in National Health Planning, 1974; (ed) Cardiovascular Disease in Africa, 1976; (ed) Nigeria and Education: the challenges ahead; (ed jtly) Clinical Medicine in the Tropics Series, 1987–; papers on hypertension and renal disease in African, Eur. and Amer. med. jls, and papers on med. and higher educn. *Recreations:* music, gardening, birdwatching. *Address:* Department of Medicine, University of Ibadan, Ibadan, Nigeria. *T:* 22317717. *Clubs:* Dining (Ibadan); Oxford and Cambridge (Nigeria).

AKKER, John Richard; General Secretary, National Association of Teachers in Further and Higher Education, since 1994; *b* 6 May 1943; *s* of Alec Louis Morris Akker and Ruby (*née* Bryant); *m* 1967, Jean-Anne Roxburgh (marr. diss. 1990); two *d*. *Educ:* SW Essex Tech. Coll.; Ruskin Coll., Oxford (L. C. White Schol.; Dip. Econ./Pol.); Univ. of York (BA Hons 1969); Cranfield Inst. of Technol. Mgt Sch. Clerical Officer, Ministry of Works, 1959–64; Asst Nat. Officer, 1969–71, Dep. Nat. Local Govt Officer, 1972–73, NALGO; Association of University Teachers: Asst Gen. Sec., 1973–77; Dep. Gen. Sec., 1978–94. Advr to EC, 1985–88. Visiting Lecturer: CIT, 1970–74; Univ. of Wisconsin, 1977–78. Winston Churchill Fellowship, USA, 1976. *Recreations:* growing vegetables, motor sport, sailing, football. *Address:* (office) 27 Britannia Street, WC1X 9JP. *T:* 0171–837 3636.

ALANBROOKE, 3rd Viscount *cr* 1946; **Alan Victor Harold Brooke;** Baron Alanbrooke, 1945; *b* 24 Nov. 1932; *s* of 1st Viscount Alanbrooke, KG, GCB, OM, GCVO, DSO, and Benita Blanche (*d* 1968), *d* of Sir Harold Pelly, 4th Bt; *S* half-brother, 1972. *Educ:* Harrow; Bristol Univ. (BEd Hons 1976). Qualified teacher, 1975. Served Army, 1952–72; Captain RA, retired. *Heir:* none.

ALBEE, Edward; American dramatist; *b* 12 March 1928. *Publications: plays:* The Zoo Story, 1958; The Death of Bessie Smith, 1959; The Sandbox, 1959; The American Dream, 1960; Who's Afraid of Virginia Woolf?, 1962; (adapted from Carson McCullers' novella) The Ballad of the Sad Café, 1963; Tiny Alice, 1964; (adapted from the novel by James Purdy) Malcolm, 1965; A Delicate Balance, 1966 (Pulitzer Prize, 1967); (adapted from the play by Giles Cooper) Everything in the Garden, 1967; Box and Quotations from Chairman Mao Tse-Tung, 1968; All Over, 1971; Seascape, 1974 (Pulitzer Prize, 1975); Listening, 1975; Counting the Ways, 1976; The Lady from Dubuque, 1978; Lolita (adapted from V. Nabakov), 1979; The Man Who Had Three Arms, 1981; Finding the Sun, 1982; Marriage Play, 1986; Three Tall Women, 1991 (Pulitzer Prize, 1994); The Lorca Play, 1992; Fragments, 1993. *Address:* (office) 14 Harrison Street, New York, NY 10013, USA.

ALBEMARLE, 10th Earl of, *cr* 1696; **Rufus Arnold Alexis Keppel;** Baron Ashford, 1696; Viscount Bury, 1696; *b* 16 July 1965; *s* of Derek William Charles Keppel, Viscount Bury (*d* 1968), and Marina, *yr d* of late Count Serge Orloff-Davidoff; *S* grandfather, 1979. *Educ:* Central Sch. of Art (BA (Hons) Industrial Design, 1990). *Heir: cousin* Crispian Walter John Keppel [*b* 29 Oct. 1948; *m* 1990, Tina Ammann; one *d*]. *Address:* 20A Pembroke Square, W8 6PA.

ALBEMARLE, Countess of, (Diana Cicely), DBE 1956; Chairman: Development Commission, 1948–74; The Drama Board, 1964–78; *b* 6 Aug. 1909; *o c* of John Archibald Grove; *m* 1931, 9th Earl of Albemarle, MC (*d* 1979); one *d*. *Educ:* Sherborne Sch. for Girls. Norfolk County Organiser, WVS, 1939–44. Chairman: Exec. Cttee, Nat. Fedn of Women's Institutes, 1946–51; Departmental Cttee on Youth Service, 1958–60; Nat. Youth Employment Council, 1962–68. Vice-Chm., British Council, 1959–74. Member: Arts Council, 1951; Royal Commn on Civil Service, 1954; Harkness Fellowship Cttee of Award, 1963–69; UGC, 1956–70; Standing Commn on Museums and Galleries, 1958–71; English Local Govt Boundary Commn, 1971–77; Youth Develt Council, 1960–68; Council, Univ. of E Anglia, 1964–72. Life Trustee, Carnegie UK Trust (Chm., 1977–82); Trustee of: The Observer until 1977; Glyndebourne Arts Trust, 1968–80. RD Councillor, Wayland, Norfolk, 1935–46. Hon. DLitt Reading, 1959; Hon. DCL Oxon, 1960; Hon. LLD London, 1960. *Recreations:* gardening, reading. *Address:* Seymours, Melton, Woodbridge, Suffolk IP12 1LW. *T:* Woodbridge (01394) 382151.

See also Sir Hew Hamilton-Dalrymple.

ALBERT, Sir Alexis (François), Kt 1972; CMG 1967; VRD 1942; Chairman: Albert Investments Pty Ltd, since 1962; J. Albert & Son Pty Ltd, Sydney, since 1962; The Australian Broadcasting Company Pty Ltd, Sydney, since 1962; *b* 15 Oct. 1904; *s* of late M. F. and M. E. Albert, Sydney; *m* 1934, Elsa K. R. (decd), *d* of late Capt. A. E. Lundgren, Sydney; three *s*. *Educ:* Knox College, Sydney; St Paul's College, University of Sydney. BEc 1930. Director: Amalgamated Television Services Pty Ltd, 1955–87; Australasian Performing Right Association Ltd, 1946–76. Underwriting Member of Lloyd's, 1944–74; President, Royal Blind Soc. of NSW, 1962–78; Fellow of Council, St Paul's Coll., Univ. of Sydney, 1965–; Council, Nat. Heart Foundn of Aust., NSW Div. 1959–. RANR, 1918–49; Lt-Comdr, retd. Hon. ADC to Governors of NSW, 1937–57. KStJ 1985. *Recreations:* swimming, yachting. *Address:* 25 Coolong Road, Vaucluse, NSW 2030, Australia; (office) 175 Macquarie Street, Sydney, NSW 2000. *T:* (2) 2322144. *Clubs:* Naval and Military; Australian (Sydney); Royal Sydney Golf, Royal Sydney Yacht Squadron (Commodore 1971–75); New York Yacht.

ALBERT, Carl (Bert); Speaker, US House of Representatives, 1971–77; Member, Third Oklahoma District, 1947–77 (Democratic Whip, 1955–62; Majority Leader, 1962–71); *b* McAlester, Oklahoma, 10 May 1908; *s* of Ernest Homer and Leona Ann (Scott) Albert; *m* 1942, Mary Sue Greene Harmon; one *s* one *d*. *Educ:* Univ. of Oklahoma (AB 1931); Oxford Univ. (Rhodes Scholar, BA 1933, BCL 1934). Served US Army, 1941–46. Admitted Oklahoma Bar, 1935; Legal Clerk, Fed. Housing Admin, 1935–37; attorney and accountant, Sayre Oil Co., 1937–38; legal dept, Ohio Oil Co., 1939–40. Practised law: Oklahoma City, 1938; Mattoon, Ill, 1938–39; McAlester, Oklahoma, 1946–47. Bronze Star, 1945. *Recreation:* reading. *Address:* 1831 Wood Road, McAlester, Oklahoma 74501, USA.

ALBERTI, Prof. Kurt George Matthew Mayer, DPhil; FRCP, FRCPE, FRCPath; Professor of Medicine, since 1985, and Dean of Medicine, since 1995, University of Newcastle upon Tyne; *b* 27 Sept. 1937; *s* of William Peter Matthew Alberti and Edith Elizabeth Alberti; *m* 1964; three *s*. *Educ:* Balliol Coll., Oxford (MA; DPhil 1964; BM, BCh 1965). FRCP 1978; FRCPath 1985; FRCPE 1988. Res. Fellow, Harvard Univ., Boston, USA, 1966–69; Res. Officer, Dept of Medicine, Oxford Univ., 1969–73; Prof. of Chemical Pathology and Human Metabolism, 1973–78, Prof. of Clinical Biochemistry and Metabolic Medicine, 1978–85, Univ. of Southampton. Vice-Pres., Internat. Diabetes Fedn, 1988–94. Fellow, All India Inst. of Diabetes, 1976; Hon. Member: Hungarian Diabetes Assoc., 1986; Argentinian Diabetes Assoc., 1991. *Publications:* edited more than 30 medical books, including: Diabetes Annual, Vols 1–6; Recent Advances in Clinical Biochemistry, Vols 1–3; Internat. Textbook of Diabetes Mellitus, 1992; author of more than 800 pubns in learned jls. *Recreations:* hill walking, jogging, crime fiction, Mozart.

ALBERTYN, Rt. Rev. Charles Henry; a Bishop Suffragan, Diocese of Cape Town, 1983–93; *b* 24 Dec. 1928; *s* of Adam and Annie Albertyn; *m* 1965, Berenice Lategan; one *s* two *d*. *Educ:* Hewat Training College (Teacher's Diploma 1948); Diocesan Clergy School, Cape Town (LTh 1956). Teaching, 1948–52. Deacon 1955, priest 1956; Assistant, St Nicholas, Matroosfontein, 1955–60; Priest-in-charge, St Helena Bay, 1960–64; Assistant, St George's, Silvertown, 1965–70; Rector: Church of Holy Spirit, Heideveld, 1970–75; St Mary's, Kraaifontein, 1975–78; Church of Resurrection, Bonteheuwel, 1978–83; Canon of St George Cathedral, Cape Town, 1972–83; Archdeacon of Bellville, 1981–83. *Recreation:* watching soccer. *Address:* 7 Myn Road, Vanguard Estate, Athlone, Cape 7764, S Africa.

ALBERY, Ian Bronson; Chief Executive, Sadler's Wells and Lilian Baylis Theatres; *b* 21 Sept. 1936; *s* of Sir Donald Albery and Rubina Albery (*née* McGilchrist); one *d*; *m* Barbara Yuling Lee (marr. diss.); two *s*. *Educ:* Stowe; Lycée de Briançon, France. Stage, Production or Technical Manager for over 100 West End productions, 1958–70; Technical Dir, London Festival Ballet, 1964–68; Theatre Consultant, UK and overseas, 1968–; Managing Director: Wyndham Theatres, Piccadilly Theatre, Donmar Productions, Omega Stage, 1978–87; Ticketmaster (UK) Ltd, 1985–92; Theatre of Comedy, 1987–90. Consultant, Japan Satellite Broadcasting, 1991–92. Theatres Trust, 1977–; Chief Exec., Sadler's Wells Trust, 1994–. Pres., 1977–79, Vice-Pres., 1979–80, SWET. *Address:* Sadler's Wells Theatre, Rosebery Avenue, EC1R 4TN. *T:* 0171–278 6563. *Club:* Garrick.

ALBERY, John; *see* Albery, W. J.

ALBERY, Tim; theatre and opera director; *b* 20 May 1952. *Theatre* productions include: War Crimes, ICA, 1981; Secret Gardens, Amsterdam and ICA, 1983; Venice Preserv'd, Almeida, 1983; Hedda Gabler, Almeida, 1984; The Princess of Cleves, ICA, 1985; Mary Stuart, Greenwich, 1988; As You Like It, Old Vic, 1989; Berenice, NT, 1990; Wallenstein, RSC, 1993; *opera* productions include: for English National Opera: Billy Budd, 1988; Beatrice and Benedict, 1990; Peter Grimes, 1991; Lohengrin, 1993; for Opera North: The Midsummer Marriage, 1985; The Trojans, 1986; La finta giardiniera, 1989; Don Giovanni, 1991; Don Carlos, 1992; Luisa Miller, 1995; for Royal Opera: Chérubin, 1994; for Welsh National Opera: The Trojans, 1987; La finta giardiniera, 1994; Nabucco, 1995; for Scottish Opera: The Midsummer Marriage, 1988; The Trojans, 1990; Fidelio, 1994; for Australian Opera: The Marriage of Figaro, 1992; for Netherlands Opera: Benvenuto Cellini, 1991; La Wally, 1993; for Batignano Fest., Italy, The Turn of the Screw, 1983; for Bregenz Fest., Austria, La Wally, 1990; for Bayerische Staatsoper, Munich: Peter Grimes, 1991; Simon Boccanegra, 1995. *Address:* c/o Harriet Cruickshank, Cruickshank Cazenove, 97 Old South Lambeth Road, SW8 1XU.

ALBERY, Prof. Wyndham John, FRS 1985; FRSC; Master, University College, Oxford, since 1989; *b* 5 April 1936; *s* of late Michael James Albery, QC, and Mary Lawton Albery. *Educ:* Winchester Coll.; Balliol Coll., Oxford (MA, DPhil). Weir Jun. Research Fellow, 1962, Fellow, 1963–78, University Coll., Oxford; Lectr, Phys. Chem., Univ. of Oxford, 1964–78; Imperial College, London: Prof., Phys. Chemistry, 1978–89; Staff Orator, 1980–83; Dean, RCS, 1986–89. Vis. Fellow, Univ. of Minnesota, 1965; Vis. Prof., Harvard Univ., 1976. Tilden Lectr, RSC, 1979; Sherman Fairchild Schol., Calif. Inst. of Tech., 1985. Chairman: SERC Chemistry Cttee, 1982–85; Electrochem. Gp, RSC, 1985–89. Mem. Council, Royal Instn, 1985–88; Pres., Chemistry Section, British Assoc., 1992. Writer for television series That Was The Week That Was, 1963–64; also (with John Gould) two musicals, Who Was That Lady?, and On The Boil. Curator, Oxford Playhouse, 1974–78; Governor, Old Vic, 1979–89; Chm., Burton Taylor Theatre Management Cttee, 1990–93. Gov., Rugby Sch., 1987–. Fellow, Winchester Coll., 1989–. Hon. DSc Kent, 1990. *Publications:* Ring-Disc Electrodes, 1971; Electrode Kinetics, 1975; papers in jls: Faraday I, Nature, and Jls of Electrochemical Soc., Electroanalytical

Chemistry, etc. *Recreations:* theatre, skiing. *Address:* Master's Lodgings, University College, Oxford OX1 4BH. *T:* Oxford (01865) 276600. *Club:* Garrick.

ALBRIGHT, Madeleine Korbel, PhD; United States Permanent Representative to the United Nations, since 1993; Member, National Security Council, USA, since 1993; *b* 15 May 1937; *m* Joseph Albright (marr. diss.); three *d. Educ:* Wellesley Coll. (BA Hons Pol Sci. 1959); Sch. of Advanced Internat. Studies, Johns Hopkins Univ.; Columbia Univ (BA 1968; PhD 1976). Chief Legislative Asst to Senator Edmund Muskie, 1976–78; Staff Mem., Nat. Security Council and Mem., White House Staff, 1978–81; Sen. Fellow in Soviet and E European Affairs, Center for Strategic and Internat. Studies; Fellow, Woodrow Wilson Internat. Center for Scholars, 1981–82; Res. Prof. of Internat. Affairs and Dir, Women in Foreign Service Program, Georgetown Univ. Sch. of Foreign Service, 1982–92; Pres., Center for Nat. Policy, 1989–92 (Mem., Bd of Dirs). Member: Bd of Dirs, Atlantic Council of US; US Nat. Commn, UNESCO. Vice-Chm., Nat. Democratic Inst. for Internat. Affairs. *Publications:* Poland: the role of the press in political change, 1983; articles in professional jls and chapters in books. *Address:* US Mission to the United Nations, 799 United Nations Plaza, New York, NY 10017, USA; Suite 6333, Department of State, 2201 C Street NW, Washington, DC 20520-6319, USA.

ALBROW, Desmond; an Assistant Editor, Sunday Telegraph, 1976–87; *b* 22 Jan. 1925; *er s* of Frederick and Agnes Albrow; *m* 1950, Aileen Mary Jennings; one *s* three *d. Educ:* St Bede's Grammar Sch., Bradford; Keble Coll., Oxford (MA). RN, 1944–47. On the Editorial Staff of the Yorkshire Observer, 1950–51, Manchester Guardian, 1951–56, Daily Telegraph, 1956–60; Sunday Telegraph, 1960–66: Chief Sub-Editor, News Editor, and Night Editor; Editor, Catholic Herald, 1966–71; Features Editor, Sunday Telegraph, 1971–76. *Recreations:* drinking in moderation and talking to excess; watching other people cultivate their gardens. *Address:* Totyngton Cottage, 18 Victoria Road, Teddington, Mddx TW11 0BG. *T:* 0181–977 4220. *Clubs:* Garrick, Presscala.

ALBU, Sir George, 3rd Bt, *cr* (UK) 1912, of Grosvenor Place, City of Westminster, and Johannesburg, Province of Transvaal, South Africa; farmer; *b* 5 June 1944; *o s* of Major Sir George Werner Albu, 2nd Bt, and Kathleen Betty (*d* 1956), *d* of Edward Charles Dicey, Parktown, Johannesburg; *S* father, 1963; *m* 1969, Joan Valerie Millar, London; two *d. Recreations:* horse racing, tennis, golf. *Heir:* none. *Address:* Glen Hamish Farm, PO Box 62, Richmond, Natal, 3780, South Africa. *T:* Richmond (Natal) 2587. *Clubs:* Victoria (Pietermaritzburg, Natal); Richmond Country (Richmond, Natal).

ALBU, Marie, (Mrs A. H. Albu); *see* Jahoda, Prof. Marie.

ALCOCK, Prof. Leslie, OBE 1991; Hon. Professorial Research Fellow, University of Glasgow, since 1990; *b* 24 April 1925; *o s* of Philip John Alcock and Mary Ethel (*née* Bagley); *m* 1950, Elizabeth A. Blair; one *s* one *d. Educ:* Manchester Grammar Sch.; Brasenose Coll., Oxford. BA 1949, MA 1950. Supt of Exploration, Dept of Archaeology, Govt of Pakistan, 1950; Curator, Abbey House Museum, Leeds, 1952; Asst Lectr, etc, UC Cardiff, 1953; Professor of Archaeology: UC Cardiff, 1973; Univ. of Glasgow, 1973–90. Member: Bd of Trustees, Nat. Mus. of Antiquities, Scotland, 1973–85; Ancient Monuments Bd, Scotland, 1974–90; Royal Commn on Ancient and Historical Monuments of Scotland, 1977–92; Royal Commn on Ancient and Historical Monuments in Wales, 1986–90. President: Cambrian Archaeological Assoc., 1982; Glasgow Archaeological Soc., 1984–85; Soc. of Antiquaries, Scotland, 1984–87. Lectures: Jarrow, 1988; Rhind, Soc. of Antiquaries, Scotland, 1988–89. FSA 1957; FRHistS 1969; FRSE 1976–87. Hon. FSAScot, 1994. *Publications:* Dinas Powys, 1963; Arthur's Britain, 1971; Cadbury/Camelot, 1972; Economy, Society and Warfare, 1987; (co-ed) From the Baltic to the Black Sea, 1988; Cadbury Castle, Somerset, 1995; articles and reviews in British and Amer. jls. *Recreations:* mountain and coastal scenery, music. *Address:* 29 Hamilton Drive, Hillhead, Glasgow G12 8DN.

ALCOCK, Air Chief Marshal Sir (Robert James) Michael, KBE 1992; CB 1989; Air Member for Logistics and Air Officer Commanding-in-Chief Logistics Command, since 1994; *b* 11 July 1936; *s* of late William George and Doris Alcock; *m* 1965, Pauline Mary Oades; two *d. Educ:* Victoria College, Jersey; Royal Aircraft Establishment. CEng, FIMechE; FRAeS. Commissioned, Engineer Branch, RAF, 1959; RAF Tech. Coll., Henlow, 1961; Goose Bay, Labrador, 1961; Units in Bomber Comd, 1959–69; RAF Staff Coll., Bracknell, 1970; PSO to DGEng (RAF), 1971–73; OC Eng. Wing, RAF Coningsby, 1973–75; OC No 23 Maintenance Unit, RAF Aldergrove, 1975–77; Group Captain (Plans), HQ RAF Support Command, 1977–79; MoD, 1979–81; Dep. Comdt, RAF Staff Coll., Bracknell, 1981–84; RCDS, 1984; Dir Gen. of Communications, Inf. Systems and Orgn (RAF), 1985–88; AO Engrg, HQ Strike Comd, 1988–91; Chief Engr and Chief of Logistic Support, RAF, 1991–93; Air Mem. for Supply and Orgn, MoD, 1993–94. Hon. DSc Cranfield, 1994. *Recreations:* golf, model aircraft, sailing. *Address:* c/o National Westminster Bank, Farnborough, Hants. *Clubs:* Royal Air Force; Berkshire Golf, Trevose Golf.

ALDENHAM, 6th Baron *cr* 1896, of Aldenham, Co. Hertford, **AND HUNSDON OF HUNSDON,** 4th Baron *cr* 1923, of Briggens, Co. Hertford; **Vicary Tyser Gibbs;** *b* 9 June 1948; *s* of 5th Baron Aldenham and of Mary Elizabeth, *o d* of late Walter Parkyns Tyser; *S* father, 1986; *m* 1980, Josephine Nicola, *er d* of John Richmond Fell, Lower Bourne, Farnham, Surrey; two *s* one *d. Educ:* Eton; Oriel College, Oxford; RAC, Cirencester. Capel-Cure Myers Ltd, 1975–79; Dir, Montclare Shipping Co., 1986–. Freeman, City of London, 1979. *Heir: s* Hon. Humphrey William Fell Gibbs, *b* 31 Jan. 1989. *Address:* House of Lords, SW1A 0PW.

ALDER, Lucette, (Mrs Alan Alder); *see* Aldous, Lucette.

ALDER, Michael; Controller, English Regional Television, British Broadcasting Corporation, 1977–86, retired; *b* 3 Nov. 1928; *s* of late Thomas Alder and Winifred Miller; *m* 1955, Freda, *d* of late John and Doris Hall; two *d. Educ:* Ranelagh Sch., Bracknell, Berks; Rutherford Coll., Newcastle-upon-Tyne. Newcastle Evening Chronicle, 1947–59; BBC North-East: Chief News Asst, Newcastle; Area News Editor, Newcastle; Representative, NE England, 1959–69; Head of Regional Television Development, BBC, 1969–77. Mem., Exec. Cttee, Relate (formerly Nat. Marriage Guidance Council), 1987–94 (Chm., S Warwicks, 1987–89; Chm., Appeals Cttee, 1988–94). Vice Chm., Tanworth Educnl Foundn, 1994–. Mem., Incorporated Co. of Butchers, 1948. Freeman, City of Newcastle upon Tyne. *Recreations:* gardening, fishing, walking, country pursuits. *Address:* Red Roofs, Bates Lane, Tanworth-in-Arden, Warwicks B94 5AR. *T:* Tanworth-in-Arden (01564) 742403.

ALDERSLADE, Prof. Richard, FRCP, FFPHM; Professor of Community Care, University of Sheffield, since 1994; Special Professor of Health Policy, Nottingham University, since 1993; *b* 11 Aug. 1947; *s* of Herbert Raymond Alderslade and Edna F. Alderslade; *m* 1974, Elizabeth Rose; two *s* one *d* (and one *d* decd). *Educ:* Chichester High Sch. for Boys; Christ Church, Oxford (BM BCh; MA); St George's Hosp. FFPHM 1987; FRCP 1993. GP, 1974–76; Registrar in Community Medicine, 1976–78, Lectr, 1978–79; MO and SMO, DHSS, 1979–85; Specialist in Community Medicine, 1985–88 and Community Unit Gen. Manager, 1986–88, Hull HA; Regl Dir of Public Health and Regl MO, Trent RHA, 1988–94. *Publications:* articles on public health, BMJ and other jls. *Recreations:* walking, railways, photography. *Address:* 85 Market Place, South Cave, Brough, N Humberside HU15 2AS. *T:* Howden (01430) 421362.

ALDERSON, Brian Wouldhave; freelance editor and writer; Children's Books Consultant, The Times, since 1967; *b* 19 Sept. 1930; *s* of John William Alderson and Helen Marjory (*née* Hogg), *m* 1953, Valerie Christine (*née* Wells); three *s* (and two *s* decd). *Educ:* Ackworth Sch.; University College of the South-West, Exeter (BA Hons). Work in the book trade, 1952–63; Tutor-librarian, East Herts Coll. of Further Educn, 1963–65; Sen. Lectr, (on Children's Literature and on the Book Trade), Polytechnic of N London, 1965–83. Visiting Professor: Univ. of Southern Mississippi, 1985; UCLA, 1986. Founder and first Chmn., Children's Books Hist. Soc., 1969–78 and 1995–. Pres., Beatrix Potter Soc., 1995–. Exhibition organiser: (with descriptive notes): Looking at Picture Books, NBL, 1973; Grimm Tales in England, British Library, 1985–86; Be Merry and Wise: the early development of English children's books, Pierpont Morgan Library, NY, 1990–91; Randolph Caldecott and the Art of the English Picture Book, British Library, 1986–87; Childhood Re-Collected, Christ Church, Oxford, 1994. Eleanor Farjeon Award, 1968. *Publications:* Sing a Song for Sixpence, 1986; (with Iona and Robert Opie) Treasures of Childhood, 1989; The Arabian Nights, 1992; Ezra Jack Keats: artist and picture book maker, 1994; *translations:* Hürlimann: Three Centuries of Children's Books in Europe, 1967; Picture-book World, 1968; Grimm, Popular Folk Tales, 1978; *edited:* The Juvenile Library, 1966–74; The Colour Fairy Books, by Andrew Lang, 1975–82; Lear, a Book of Bosh, 1975; Children's Books in England, by F. J. Harvey Darton, 1982; Hans Christian Andersen and his Eventyr in England, 1982. *Recreations:* bibliography, dale-walking. *Address:* 28–30 Victoria Road, Richmond, North Yorks DL10 4AS. *T:* Richmond (01748) 823648.

ALDERSON, Daphne Elizabeth, (Mrs J. K. A. Alderson); *see* Wickham, D. E.

ALDERSON, John Cottingham, CBE 1981; QPM 1974; writer and commentator on police and penal affairs; Chief Constable of Devon and Cornwall, 1973–82; *b* 28 May 1922; *e s* of late Ernest Cottingham Alderson and Elsie Lavinia Rose; *m* 1948, Irené Macmillan Stirling; one *s. Educ:* Barnsley Elem. Schs and Techn. College. Called to Bar, Middle Temple. British Meml Foundn Fellow, Australia, 1956; Extension Certif. in Criminology, Univ. of Leeds. Highland LI, 1938–41 (Corp.); Army Phys. Trng Corps, N Africa and Italy, 1941–46 (Warrant Officer). West Riding Constabulary as Constable, 1946; Police Coll., 1954; Inspector, 1955; Sub-Divisional Comd, 1960; Sen. Comd Course, Police Coll., 1963–64; Dep. Chief Constable, Dorset, 1964–66; Metropolitan Police, Dep. Comdr (Admin and Ops), 1966; 2nd-in-comd No 3 Police District, 1967; Dep. Asst Comr (Trng), 1968; Comdt, Police Coll., 1970; Asst Comr (Personnel and Trng), 1973. Consultant on Human Rights to Council of Europe, 1981–. Member: BBC Gen. Adv. Council, 1971–78; Royal Humane Soc. Cttee, 1973–81; Pres., Royal Life-Saving Soc., 1974–78. Vis. Prof. of Police Studies, Strathclyde Univ., 1983–89. External Examiner, Leadership Studies, Univ. of Exeter, 1994–. Fellow Commoner, Corpus Christi Coll., Cambridge, 1982; Fellow, Inst. of Criminology, Cambridge, 1982; Gwilym Gibbon Res. Fellow, Nuffield Coll., Oxford, 1982–83; Australian Commonwealth Fellow, Australian Govt, 1987; Hon. Res. Fellow, Centre for Police Studies, Univ. of Exeter, 1987–95. Contested (L) Teignbridge, Devon, 1983. Hon. LLD Exeter, 1979; Hon. DLitt Bradford, 1982. *Publications:* (contrib.) Encyclopedia of Crime and Criminals, 1960; (ed jtly) The Police We Deserve, 1973; Policing Freedom, 1979; Law and Disorder, 1984; Human Rights and the Police, 1984; articles in professional jls and newspapers. *Recreations:* reading, writing, keeping fit.

ALDERSON, Margaret Hanne, (Maggie); journalist; Editor, Mode, since 1994; *b* 31 July 1959; *d* of Douglas Arthur Alderson and Margaret Dura Alderson (*née* Mackay); *m* 1991, Geoffrey Francis Laurence. *Educ:* Alleyne's Sch., Stone, Staffs; Univ. of St Andrews (MA Hons History of Art). Features Editor: Look Now, 1983; Honey, 1984; Commng Editor, You, 1985; Metropolitan Features Editor, Evening Standard, 1986; Editor: ES Magazine, 1988; Elle, 1989–92; Dep. Editor, Cleo magazine, 1993–94. Editor of the Year, Colour Supplements, British Soc. of Magazine Eds, 1989. *Recreations:* reading, gardening, painting, travelling. *Address:* 45/2A Ithaca Road, Elizabeth Bay, Sydney, NSW 2011, Australia. *Club:* Groucho.

ALDERTON, John; actor (stage, films, television); *b* Gainsborough, Lincs, 27 Nov. 1940; *s* of Gordon John Alderton and Ivy Handley; *m* 1st, 1964, Jill Browne (marr. diss. 1970; she *d* 1991); 2nd, Pauline Collins, *qv*; two *s* one *d. Educ:* Kingston High Sch., Hull. *Stage:* 1st appearance (Rep.) Theatre Royal, York, in Badger's Green, 1961; cont. Rep.; 1st London appearance, Spring and Port Wine, Mermaid (later Apollo), 1965; Dutch Uncle, RSC, Aldwych, 1969; The Night I chased the Women with an Eel, Comedy, 1969; Punch and Judy Stories, Howff, 1973; Judies, Comedy, 1974; The Birthday Party, Shaw, 1975; Confusions (4 parts), Apollo, 1976; Rattle of a Simple Man, Savoy, 1980; Special Occasions, Ambassadors, 1983; The Maintenance Man, Comedy, 1986; Waiting for Godot, NT, 1987; What the Butler Saw, RNT, 1995; *films:* (1962–): incl. Duffy, Hannibal Brooks, Zardoz, It Shouldn't Happen to a Vet, Please Sir, Clockwork Mice; *television:* series: Please Sir, No Honestly, My Wife Next Door, P. G. Wodehouse, The Upchat Line, Thomas and Sarah, Father's Day, Forever Green and various plays. *Address:* c/o James Sharkey Associates Ltd, 21 Golden Square, W1R 3PA.

ALDINGTON, 1st Baron, *cr* 1962; **Toby (Austin Richard William) Low,** PC 1954; KCMG 1957; CBE 1945 (MBE 1944); DSO 1941; TD and clasp, 1950; DL; Chairman, Leeds Castle Foundation, 1984–94; Barrister-at-Law; *b* 25 May 1914; *s* of Col Stuart Low, DSO (killed at sea by enemy action, Dec. 1942), and of late Hon. Mrs Spear; *m* 1947, Araminta Bowman, *e d* of late Sir Harold MacMichael, GCMG, DSO; one *s* two *d. Educ:* Winchester; New Coll., Oxford (Hon. Fellow 1976). Called to the Bar, 1939. TA; 2nd Lieut 1934; Brig. BGS 5 Corps Italy, Aug. 1944–June 1945; served Greece, Crete, Egypt, Libya, Tunisia, Sicily, Italy, Austria (DSO, MBE, CBE, Croix de guerre avec palmes, Commander of Legion of Merit, USA); Hon. Col 288 LAA Regt RA (TA), 1947–59. MP (C) Blackpool North, 1945–62; Parliamentary Secretary, Ministry of Supply, 1951–54; Minister of State, Board of Trade, 1954–57; Dep. Chm., Cons. Party Organisation, Oct. 1959–63; Chairman: H of L Select Cttee on Overseas Trade, 1984–85; Sub-Cttee A, H of L European Communities Select Cttee, 1989–92. Chm., GEC, 1964–68, Dep. Chm. 1968–84; Chairman: Grindlays Bank Ltd, 1964–76; Sun Alliance and London Insurance Co., 1971–85; Westland Aircraft, 1977–85 (Pres., 1985). Director: Lloyds Bank, 1967–85; Citicorp, 1969–84. Chairman: Port of London Authority, 1971–77; Jt Special Cttee on Ports Industry, 1972. Chairman: Cttee of Management, Inst. of Neurology, 1962–80; BBC Gen. Adv. Council, 1971–78; ISJC, 1986–89; Kent Foundn, 1986–94; President: BSI, 1986–89; Brain Res. Trust, 1987– (Chm., 1974–87). Fellow, Winchester Coll., 1972–87 (Warden, 1979–87). DL Kent, 1973. *Recreation:* golf. *Heir: s* Hon. Charles Harold Stuart Low [*b* 22 June 1948; *m* 1989, Regine, *d* of late Erwin von Csongrady-Schopf; one *s* two *d* (twins)]. *Address:* Knoll Farm, Aldington, Ashford, Kent TN25 7BY. *T:* Aldington (01233720) 292. *Club:* Carlton.

See also Hon. P. J. S. Roberts.

ALDISS, Brian Wilson; writer; critic; *b* 18 Aug. 1925; *s* of Stanley and Elizabeth May Aldiss; *m* 1965, Margaret Manson; one *s* one *d*, and one *s* one *d* by previous *m*. *Educ:* Framlingham Coll.; West Buckland School. FRSL 1990. Royal Signals, 1943–47; book-selling, 1947–56; writer, 1956–; Literary Editor, Oxford Mail, 1958–69. Pres., British Science Fiction Assoc., 1960–64. Editor, SF Horizons, 1964–. Chairman, Oxford Branch Conservation Soc., 1968–69; Vice Pres., The Stapledon Soc., 1975–; Jt Pres., European SF Cttees, 1976–79; Society of Authors: Mem., Cttee of Management, 1976–78, Chm., 1978; Chm., Cultural Exchanges Cttee, 1979–; Member: Arts Council Literature Panel, 1978–80; Internat. PEN, 1983–; Pres., World SF, 1982–84; Vice-President: H. G. Wells Soc., 1983–; Soc. for Anglo-Chinese Understanding, 1987–91. Mem. Council, Council for Posterity, 1990–. Observer Book Award for Science Fiction, 1956; Ditmar Award for Best Contemporary Writer of Science Fiction, 1969; first James Blish Award, for SF criticism, 1977; Pilgrim Award, 1978; first Award for Distinguished Scholarship, Internat. Assoc. for the Fantastic in the Arts, Houston, 1986. *Publications:* The Brightfount Diaries, 1955; Space, Time and Nathaniel, 1957; Non-Stop, 1958 (Prix Jules Verne, 1977); Canopy of Time, 1959; The Male Response, 1961; Hothouse, 1962 (Hugo Award, 1961); Best Fantasy Stories, 1962; The Airs of Earth, 1963; The Dark Light Years, 1964; Introducing SF, 1964; Greybeard, 1964; Best SF Stories of Brian W. Aldiss, 1965; Earthworks, 1965; The Saliva Tree, 1966 (Nebula Award, 1965); Cities and Stones: A Traveller's Jugoslavia, 1966; An Age, 1967; Report on Probability A, 1968; Farewell, Fantastic Venus!, 1968; Intangibles Inc. and other Stories, 1969; A Brian Aldiss Omnibus, 1969; Barefoot in the Head, 1969; The Hand-Reared Boy, 1970; The Shape of Further Things, 1970; The Moment of Eclipse, 1971 (BSFA Award, 1972); A Soldier Erect, 1971; Brian Aldiss Omnibus II, 1971; Billion Year Spree: a history of science fiction, 1973 (Special BSFA Award, 1974; Eurocon Merit Award, 1976); Frankenstein Unbound, 1973 (filmed, 1990); The Eighty-Minute Hour, 1974; (ed) Space Opera, 1974; (ed) Space Odysseys: an Anthology of Way-Back-When Futures, 1975; (ed) Hell's Cartographers, 1975; (ed) Evil Earths, 1975; Science Fiction Art: the fantasies of SF, 1975 (Ferrara Silver Comet, 1977); (ed with H. Harrison) Decade: the 1940s, 1976; (ed with H. Harrison) Decade: the 1950s, 1976; The Malacia Tapestry, 1976; (ed) Galactic Empires, vols 1 and 2, 1976; (ed with H. Harrison) The Year's Best Science Fiction No 9, 1976; Brothers of the Head, 1977; Last Orders, 1977; (ed with H. Harrison) Decade: the 1960's, 1977; A Rude Awakening, 1978; Enemies of the System, 1978; (ed) Perilous Planets, 1978; This World and Nearer Ones, 1979; New Arrivals, Old Encounters, 1979; Life in the West, 1980; Moreau's Other Island, 1980; Foreign Bodies, 1981; Helliconia Spring, 1982 (BSFA Award, John W. Campbell Meml Award); Helliconia Summer, 1983; Seasons in Flight, 1984; Helliconia Winter, 1985; Helliconia Trilogy (boxed set of Helliconia Spring, Helliconia Summer, and Helliconia Winter), 1985; The Horatio Stubbs Saga, 1985; The Pale Shadow of Science, 1985; . . . And the Lurid Glare of the Comet, 1986; (with David Wingrove) Trillion Year Spree, 1986 (Hugo Award, 1987); Cracken at Critical, 1987; Ruins, 1987; Forgotten Life, 1988; Best SF Stories of Brian W. Aldiss, 1988; Science Fiction Blues, 1988; A Romance of the Equator, 1989; Bury My Heart at W. H. Smith's, 1990; Dracula Unbound, 1991; Home Life with Cats, 1992; Remembrance Day, 1993; A Tupolev Too Far, 1993; Somewhere East of Life, 1994; The Detached Retina, 1995; At the Caligula Hotel, 1995. *Recreations:* fame, obscurity, trances. *Address:* Woodlands, Foxcombe Road, Boars Hill, Oxford OX1 5DL. *Clubs:* Groucho; Writers in Oxford.

ALDOUS, Charles; QC 1985; *b* 3 June 1943; *s* of Guy Travers Aldous and Elizabeth Angela Aldous (*née* Paul); *m* 1969, Hermione Sara de Courcy-Ireland; one *s* two *d* (and one *d* decd). *Educ:* Harrow; University College London (LLB). Called to the Bar, Inner Temple, 1967, Bencher, 1994. *Address:* Ravensfield Farm, Bures Hamlet, Suffolk CO8 5DP.

See also Rt Hon. Sir W. Aldous.

ALDOUS, Prof. David John, PhD; FRS 1994; Professor of Statistics, University of California, Berkeley, since 1986; *b* 13 July 1952; *s* of Kenneth George Aldous and Joyce Minnie Aldous (*née* Finch); *m* 1986, Katy Edwards; one *s*. *Educ:* St John's Coll., Cambridge (BA 1973; PhD 1977). Res. Fellow, St John's Coll., Cambridge, 1977–79; University of California, Berkeley: Asst Prof., 1979–82; Associate Prof., 1982–86. *Publication:* Probability Approximations via the Poisson Clumping Heuristic, 1989. *Recreations:* volley-ball, science fiction. *Address:* Department of Statistics, University of California, Berkeley, Calif 94720, USA. *T:* (510) 6422781.

ALDOUS, Lucette; Head of Classical Dance, Dance Department, Western Australian Academy of Performing Arts; Senior Adjudicator, National Eisteddfods, since 1979; *b* 26 Sept. 1938; *d* of Charles Fellows Aldous and Marie (*née* Rutherford); *m* 1972, Alan Alder; one *d*. *Educ:* Toronto Public Sch., NSW; Brisbane Public Sch., Qld; Randwick Girls' High Sch., NSW. Awarded Frances Scully Meml Schol. (Aust.) to study at Royal Ballet Sch., London, 1955; joined Ballet Rambert, 1957, Ballerina, 1958–63; Ballerina with: London Fest. Ballet, 1963–66; Royal Ballet, 1966–71; Prima Ballerina, The Australian Ballet, 1971; Master Teacher, Australian Ballet Sch., 1979; Guest Teacher: Australian Ballet, 1988–; Royal NZ Ballet Co., 1988–; West Australian Ballet Co., 1988–. Rep. Australia, 1st Internat. Ballet Competition, Jackson, Miss, USA, 1979; Guest, Kirov Ballet and Ballet School, Leningrad, 1975–76. Guest appearances: Giselle, with John Gilpin, NY, 1968; Lisbon, 1969; with Rudolf Nureyev, in Don Quixote: Aust., 1970, NY, Hamburg and Marseilles, 1971; Carmen, Johannesburg, 1970; The Sleeping Beauty: E Berlin, 1970, Teheran, 1970, 1975; partnered Edward Villela at Expo '74, Spokane, USA. *Television:* title rôle, La Sylphide, with Fleming Flindt, BBC, 1960. *Films:* as Kitri, in Don Quixote, with Rudolf Nureyev and Robert Helpmann, Aust., 1972; The Turning Point, 1977. Patron, Australian Cecchetti Soc., 1991–. *Recreations:* music, reading, gardening, breeding Burmese cats. *Address:* c/o Dance Department, Western Australian Academy of Performing Arts, 2 Bradford Street, Mount Lawley, Perth, WA 6050, Australia.

ALDOUS, Rt Hon. Sir William, Kt 1988; PC 1995; **Rt Hon. Lord Justice Aldous;** a Lord Justice of Appeal, since 1995; *b* 17 March 1936; *s* of Guy Travers Aldous, QC; *m* 1960, Gillian Frances Henson; one *s* two *d*. *Educ:* Harrow; Trinity Coll., Cambridge (MA). Barrister, Inner Temple, 1960, Bencher, 1985; Jun. Counsel, DTI, 1972–76; QC 1976; appointed to exercise appellate jurisdiction of BoT under Trade Marks Act, 1981–88; a Judge of the High Court, Chancery Div., 1988–95. Chm., Performing Rights Tribunal, 1986–88. *Address:* Royal Courts of Justice, Strand, WC2A 2LL.

See also C. Aldous.

ALDRED, Brian Gordon; County Treasurer, Lancashire County Council, since 1992; *b* 27 April 1951; *s* of late James Bernard Aldred and of Jean Margaret Layton Aldred; *m* 1973, Miriam Constance Shaw; one *s* one *d*. *Educ:* Queen Elizabeth's Grammar Sch., Blackburn; Jesus Coll., Oxford (BA Modern Hist.; MA); Liverpool Poly. (IPFA). Cheshire CC, 1972–82; Dep. Dir of Finance, Bolton MBC, 1982–85; Dep. County Treas., Lancs CC, 1985–92. *Recreations:* cycling, walking, gardening. *Address:* (office) PO Box 100, County Hall, Preston PR1 0LD. *T:* Preston (01772) 264701.

ALDRIDGE, Frederick Jesse; Member, Public Health Laboratory Service Board, 1977–83; Under-Secretary and Controller of Supply, Department of Health and Social Security, 1968–75; *b* 13 Oct. 1915; *s* of late Jesse and Clara Amelia Aldridge; *m* 1940, Grace Hetty Palser; two *d*. *Educ:* Westminster City Sch. Clerical Off., Air Min., 1933; Exec. Off., Min. of Health, 1935; RAF, 1940–46; Acct-General's Div., Min. of Health: Asst Acct-Gen., 1956; Dep. Acct-Gen., 1958; Asst Sec. for Finance and Dep. Acct-Gen., 1964; Asst Sec., Food, Health and Nutrition, also Civil Defence, 1966. *Recreation:* music. *Address:* High Trees, 17 Tanglewood Close, Croydon CR0 5HX. *T:* 0181–656 3623.

ALDRIDGE, (Harold Edward) James; author; *b* 10 July 1918; *s* of William Thomas Aldridge and Edith Quayle Aldridge; *m* 1942, Dina Mitchnik; two *s*. With Herald and Sun, Melbourne, 1937–38; Daily Sketch, and Sunday Dispatch, London, 1939; subsequently Australian Newspaper Service and North American Newspaper Alliance (war correspondent), Finland, Norway, Middle East, Greece, USSR, until 1945; also correspondent for Time and Life, Teheran, 1944. Rhys Meml Award, 1945; Lenin Peace Prize, 1972. *Plays:* The 49th State, Lyric, Hammersmith, 1947; One Last Colinysse, Prague Vinohrady Th., 1981. *Publications:* Signed With Their Honour, 1942; The Sea Eagle, 1944; Of Many Men, 1946; The Diplomat, 1950; The Hunter, 1951; Heroes of the Empty View, 1954; Underwater Hunting for Inexperienced Englishmen, 1955; I Wish He Would Not Die, 1958; Gold and Sand (short stories), 1960; The Last Exile, 1961; A Captive in the Land, 1962; The Statesman's Game, 1966; My Brother Tom, 1966; The Flying 19, 1966; (with Paul Strand) Living Egypt, 1969; Cairo: Biography of a City, 1970; A Sporting Proposition, 1973; The Marvellous Mongolian, 1974; Mockery in Arms, 1974; The Untouchable Juli, 1975; One Last Glimpse, 1977; Goodbye Un-America, 1979; The Broken Saddle, 1983; The True Story of Lilli Stubek, 1984 (Australian Children's Book of the Year, 1985); The True Story of Spit MacPhee, 1986 (Guardian Children's Fiction Prize; NSW Premier's Literary Award, 1986); The True Story of Lola MacKellar, 1993. *Recreations:* trout fishing, etc. *Address:* c/o Curtis Brown, 28/29 Haymarket, SW1Y 4SP.

ALDRIDGE, Dr John Frederick Lewis, OBE 1990, FRCP, FRCPEd, FFOM; consultant in occupational medicine, since 1987; Civil Consultant in Occupational Medicine to the Royal Navy, 1983–92, Emeritus Consultant since 1992; *b* 28 Dec. 1926; *s* of Dr Frederick James Aldridge and Kathleen Marietta Micaela (*née* White); *m* 1955, Barbara Sheila Bolland; three *s* one *d*. *Educ:* Gresham's Sch.; St Thomas's Hosp. Med. Sch. (MB, BS 1951). DIH 1963; FRCPEd 1980; FFOM 1981; FRCP 1984. Served RAMC, 1953–60 (retd, Major). Indust. MO, Reed Paper Gp, 1960–63; CMO, IBM United Kingdom Ltd, 1963–87; part-time Hon. Clin. Asst, Dept of Psychol Medicine, UCH, 1970–76. Faculty of Occupational Medicine, Royal Coll. of Physicians: Vice-Dean, 1984–86; Dean, 1986–88; Chm., Ethics Cttee, 1991–95; Royal Soc. of Medicine: Fellow, 1964; Hon. Sec., 1970–72 and Vice-Pres., 1974–77, Occupl Medicine Section; Soc. of Occupational Medicine: Mem., 1960–; Hon. Meetings Sec., 1969–71. Member: Specialist Adv. Cttee on Occupl Medicine, Jt Cttee of Higher Med. Trng, 1970–74; Nat. Occupl Health and Safety Cttee, RoSPA, 1979–81; Standing Med. Adv. Cttee, DHSS, 1986–88; Defence Med. Emergency Steering Cttee, 1986–88; Indust. Soc. Med. Adv. Cttee, 1986–89 (Chm., 1987–89); CEGB Med. Adv. Cttee, 1988–89. Mem., Council and Cttee of Management, Shipwrecked Mariners' Royal Benevolent Soc., 1987–; Mem. Standing Cttee, 1991–, Chm., 1995–, W Sussex Assoc. for the Disabled; Trustee, Southampton and Wessex Med. Sch. Trust, 1978–82. Liveryman, Worshipful Soc. of Apothecaries, 1984–. *Publications:* papers on occupl med. topics and occupl mental health. *Recreations:* 18th century English porcelain, watercolours, walking, shooting. *Address:* East House, Charlton, Chichester, W Sussex PO18 0HU. *T:* Singleton (0124363) 392. *Clubs:* Lansdowne; Itchenor Sailing.

ALDRIDGE, Trevor Martin; solicitor; President, Special Educational Needs Tribunal, since 1994; Law Commissioner, 1984–93; *b* 22 Dec. 1933; *s* of Dr Sidney and Isabel Aldridge; *m* 1966, Joanna, *d* of C. J. v. D. Edwards; one *s* one *d*. *Educ:* Frensham Heights School; Sorbonne; St John's College, Cambridge (MA). Partner in Bower Cotton & Bower, 1962–84. Chairman: Conveyancing Standing Cttee, 1989 (Mem., 1985–89); Commonhold Working Gp, reported 1987. Hon. Vis. Prof., City Univ., 1994–95. Chm. of Governors, Frensham Heights School, 1977–. Hon. QC 1992. General editor, Property Law Bulletin, 1980–84. *Publications:* Boundaries, Walls and Fences, 1962, 7th edn 1992; Finding Your Facts, 1963; Directory of Registers and Records, 1963, (consulting ed.) 5th edn 1993; Service Agreements, 1964, 4th edn 1982; Rent Control and Leasehold Enfranchisement, 1965, 10th edn as Aldridge's Residential Lettings, 1993; Betterment Levy, 1967; Letting Business Premises, 1971, 6th edn 1989; Your Home and the Law, 1975, 2nd edn 1979; (jtly) Managing Business Property, 1978; Criminal Law Act 1977, 1978; Guide to Enquiries of Local Authorities, 1978, 2nd edn 1982; Guide to Enquiries Before Contract, 1978; Guide to National Conditions of Sale, 1979, 2nd edn 1981; Leasehold Law, 1980; Housing Act, 1980, and as amended 1984, 2nd edn 1984; (ed) Powers of Attorney, 6th edn 1986 to 8th edn 1991; Guide to Law Society's Conditions of Sale, 1981, 2nd edn 1984; Questions of Law: Homes, 1982; Law of Flats, 1982, 3rd edn 1994; Practical Conveyancing Precedents, 1984; Practical Lease Precedents, 1987; Companion to Standard Conditions of Sale, 1990, 2nd edn 1992; Companion to Property Information Forms, 1990; First Registration, 1991; Companion to Enquiries of Local Authorities, 1991; Companion to the Law Society Business Lease, 1991; Implied Covenants for Title, 1995. *Address:* Birkitt Hill House, Offley, Hitchin, Herts SG5 3DB. *T:* Offley (01462) 768261, *Fax:* (01462) 768680. *Club:* United Oxford & Cambridge University.

ALDRIN, Dr Buzz; President, Starcraft Enterprises International (research and development of space technology, manned flight to Mars), since 1988; *b* Montclair, NJ, USA, 20 Jan. 1930; *s* of late Col Edwin E. Aldrin, USAF retd, Brielle, NJ, and Marion Aldrin (*née* Moon); *m* 1988, Lois Driggs-Cannon; two *s* one *d* of former marriage. *Educ:* Montclair High Sch., Montclair, NJ (grad.); US Mil. Academy, West Point, NY (BSc); Mass Inst. of Technology (DSc in Astronautics). Received wings (USAF), 1952. Served in Korea (66 combat missions) with 51st Fighter Interceptor Wing. Aerial Gunnery Instr, Nellis Air Force Base, Nevada; attended Sqdn Officers Sch., Air Univ., Maxwell Air Force Base, Alabama; Aide to Dean of Faculty, USAF Academy; Flt Comdr with 36th Tactical Fighter Wing, Bitburg, Germany. Subseq. assigned to Gemini Target Office of Air Force Space Systems Div., Los Angeles, Calif; later transf. to USAF Field Office, Manned Spacecraft Center. One of 3rd group of astronauts named by NASA, Oct. 1963; served as back up pilot, Gemini 9 Mission and prime pilot, Gemini 12 Mission (launched into space, with James Lovell, 11 Nov. 1966), 4 day 59 revolution flight which brought Gemini Program to successful close; he established a new record for extravehicular activity and obtained first pictures taken from space of an eclipse of the sun; also made a rendezvous with the previously launched Agena; later assigned to 2nd manned Apollo flight, as back-up command module pilot; Lunar Module Pilot, Apollo 11 rocket flight to the Moon; first lunar landing with Neil Armstrong, July 1969; left NASA to return to USAF as Commandant, Aerospace Res. Pilots Sch., Edwards Air Force Base, Calif, 1971; retired USAF 1972. Mem., Soc. of Experimental Test Pilots; FAIAA; Tau Beta Pi, Sigma Xi. Further honours include Presidential Medal of Freedom, 1969; Air Force DSM with Oak Leaf Cluster; Legion of Merit; Air Force DFC with Oak Leaf Cluster; Air Medal with 2 Oak Leaf Clusters; and NASA DSM, Exceptional Service Medal, and Group Achievement Award. Various hon. memberships and hon. doctorates. *Publications:* Return to Earth (autobiography), 1973; Men From Earth: the Apollo Project, 1989. *Recreations:* athletics, scuba diving, skiing, etc. *Address:* 233 Emerald Bay, Laguna Beach, Calif 92651, USA.

ALDRIN, Dr Edwin E(ugene), Jr; *see* Aldrin, Dr Buzz.

ALEKSANDER, Prof. Igor, PhD; FEng 1989; Professor of Neural Systems Engineering, and Head of Department of Electrical Engineering, Imperial College of Science, Technology and Medicine, University of London, since 1988; *b* 26 Jan. 1937. *Educ:* Marist Brothers' Coll., S Africa; Univ. of the Witwatersrand (BSc Eng); Univ. of London (PhD). Section Head of STC, Footscray, 1958–61; Lectr, Queen Mary Coll., Univ. of London, 1961–65; Reader in Electronics, Univ. of Kent, 1965–74; Prof. of Electronics and Head of Electrical Engrg Dept, Brunel Univ., 1974–84; Prof. of Information Technology Management, Computing Dept, Imperial Coll., 1984–88. FCGI 1994. *Publications:* An Introduction to Logic Circuit Theory, 1971; Automata Theory: an engineering approach, 1976; The Human Machine, 1978; Reinventing Man, 1983 (USA 1984); Designing Intelligent Systems, 1984; Thinking Machines, 1987; An Introduction to Neural Computing, 1990; Neurons and Symbols: the stuff that mind is made of, 1993; *c* 120 papers on computing and human modelling. *Recreations:* tennis, skiing, music, architecture. *Address:* c/o Department of Electrical Engineering, Imperial College of Science, Technology and Medicine, Exhibition Road, SW7 2BT. *T:* 0171–225 8501.

ALEPOUDELIS, Odysseus; *see* Elytis, Odysseus.

ALEXANDER, family name of **Baron Alexander of Weedon,** of **Earl Alexander of Tunis,** and of **Earl of Caledon.**

ALEXANDER, Viscount; Frederick James Alexander; *b* 15 Oct. 1990; *s* and *heir* of Earl of Caledon, *qv*.

ALEXANDER OF TUNIS, 2nd Earl *cr* 1952; **Shane William Desmond Alexander;** Viscount, 1946; Baron Rideau, 1952; Lieutenant Irish Guards, retired, 1958; Director: International Hospitals Group and associated companies, since 1981; Pathfinder Financial Corporation, Toronto, since 1980; *b* 30 June 1935; *er s* of 1st Earl Alexander of Tunis, KG, PC, GCB, OM, GCMG, CSI, DSO, MC, and Lady Margaret Diana Bingham (Countess Alexander of Tunis), GBE, DStJ, DL (*d* 1977), *yr d* of 5th Earl of Lucan, PC, GCVO, KBE, CB; *S* father, 1969; *m* 1981, Hon. Davina Woodhouse (LVO 1991; Lady-in-Waiting to Princess Margaret, 1975–), *y d* of 4th Baron Terrington, *qv*; two *d*. *Educ:* Ashbury Coll., Ottawa, Canada; Harrow. A Lord in Waiting (Govt Whip), 1974. Chm., Canada Meml Foundn, 1989–; Pres., British-American-Canadian Associates, 1989–94. Patron, British-Tunisian Soc., 1979–. Liveryman, Mercers Company. *Heir: b* Hon. Brian James Alexander, *b* 31 July 1939. *Address:* c/o House of Lords, SW1A 0PW. *Club:* MCC.

ALEXANDER OF WEEDON, Baron *cr* 1988 (Life Peer), of Newcastle-under-Lyme in the County of Staffordshire; **Robert Scott Alexander,** QC 1973; QC (NSW) 1983; Chairman, National Westminster Bank, since 1989 (Deputy Chairman, 1989); *b* 5 Sept. 1936; *s* of late Samuel James and of Hannah May Alexander; *m* Marie Anderson; two *s* one *d* (and one *s* decd) from previous marriages. *Educ:* Brighton Coll.; King's Coll., Cambridge. BA 1959, MA 1963. Called to Bar, Middle Temple, 1961; Bencher, 1979; Vice Chm., 1984–85, Chm., 1985–86, of the Bar Council. Chm., Panel on Takeovers and Mergers, 1987–89; Dep. Chm., SIB, 1994–; Mem., Govt Panel on Sustainable Develt, 1994–. Non-executive Director: RTZ Corp., 1991–; Internat. Stock Exchange of UK and Republic of Ireland, 1991–93. Chairman: Council, Justice, 1990–; Trustees, Crisis, 1990–. Trustee: National Gall., 1987–93; The Economist, 1990–. President: King's Coll. Assoc., 1980–81; Council, Brighton Coll., 1993–; Mem., Council of Governors, Wycombe Abbey Sch., 1986–92. FRSA 1991. Hon. LLD: Sheffield, 1991; Buckingham, 1992; Keele, 1993; Exeter, 1994. *Recreations:* tennis, gardening. *Address:* National Westminster Bank, 41 Lothbury, EC2P 2BP. *Club:* Garrick.

ALEXANDER, Prof. Alan; Head, Department of Human Resource Management, and Professor of Local and Public Management, since 1993, University of Strathclyde; *b* 13 Dec. 1943; *s* of Alexander Alexander and Rose (*née* Rein); *m* 1964, Morag MacInnes; one *s* one *d*. *Educ:* Possil Secondary Sch., Glasgow; Albert Secondary Sch., Glasgow; Univ. of Glasgow (MA 1965). Lectr/Asst Prof. of Political Sci., Lakehead Univ., Ontario, 1966–71; Lectr in Politics, Univ. of Reading, 1971–87; Prof. of (Management in) Local Govt and Dir, Scottish Local Authorities Management Centre, Strathclyde Univ., 1987–93. Scholar-in-Residence, Rockefeller Foundn, Villa Serbelloni, Bellagio, Italy, Feb.–March 1984; Fulbright Vis. Prof. of Politics, Randolph-Macon Woman's Coll., Virginia, 1986. Mem. Board, Housing Corp., 1977–80. Member: Reading BC, 1972–74; Berks CC, 1973–77. Mem., Standing Res. Cttee on Local and Central Govt Relns, Joseph Rowntree Foundn, 1988–92. Conducted independent inquiry into relations between Western Isles Islands Council and Bank of Credit and Commerce Internat., 1991. Contested (Lab) Henley, Feb. 1974. Pres., Raglan Housing Assoc., 1987– (Chm., 1975–87). *Publications:* Local Government in Britain since Reorganisation, 1982 (Italian edn, revised, 1984); The Politics of Local Government in the United Kingdom, 1982; Borough Government and Politics: Reading 1835–1985, 1985; Managing the Fragmented Authority, 1994; articles in Local Govt Studies, Public Admin, Brit. Jl Pol. Sci. and others. *Recreations:* hill walking, theatre, opera, cinema, avoiding gardening. *Address:* Department of Human Resource Management, University of Strathclyde, Sir Graham Hills Building, 50 Richmond Street, Glasgow G1 1XT. *T:* 0141–553 4167, *Fax:* 0141–552 3581.

ALEXANDER, Prof. Albert Geoffrey, FDSRCS; Professor of Conservative Dentistry, University of London, 1972–92, now Emeritus; *b* 22 Sept. 1932; *s* of William Francis Alexander and Muriel Katherine (*née* Boreham); *m* 1956, Dorothy Constance (*née* Johnson); one *d*. *Educ:* Bridlington Sch.; UCH Dental Sch., Univ. of London (BDS 1956; MDS 1968). LDSRCS 1955, FDSRCS 1961. Dental House Surgeon, Nat. Dental Hosp., 1955–56; Nat. Service, RADC, 1956–58; Clinical Asst, UCH Dental Dept, 1958; private dental practice, 1958–59; Lectr in Cons. Dentistry, 1959–62, Sen. Lectr in Cons. Dentistry and Periodontics, 1962–69, UCH Dental Sch.; Hon. Consultant, UCH Dental Hosp., 1967–92; Vice-Dean of Dental Studies, 1974–77, Dean, 1977–92, UCL Dental Sch., later UC and Middlesex Sch. of Dentistry; Vice-Dean, Faculty of Clinical Sciences, UCMSM, 1977–91; Prof. of Conservative Dentistry, Univ. of Hong Kong, 1992–94. Fellow, UCL, 1986; Member: Council, UCL, 1984–91; Senate, Univ. of London, 1987–91. Chm., Dental Educn Adv. Council, 1986–90; Member: GDC, 1986–92 (Treasurer, 1989–92); Bloomsbury HA, 1981–90. Fellow: Internat. Coll. of Dentists, 1975; Hong Kong Acad. of Medicine, 1993. *Publications:* (co-ed) The Prevention of Periodontal Disease, 1971; (jtly) Self-Assessment Manual, No 3, Clinical Dentistry, 1978; (co-ed) Companion to Dental Studies, Vol. 3, 1986, Vol. 2, 1988; scientific, technical and clinical articles on dentistry and dental research. *Recreations:* photography, blue and white Chinese ceramics. *Address:* 18 Masefield View, Orpington, Kent BR6 8PH. *T:* Orpington (01689) 858852.

ALEXANDER, Andrew Clive; City Editor, Daily Mail, since 1984; Director, Associated Newspapers plc, since 1992; *b* 12 May 1935; *s* of Ronald and Doreen Alexander. *Educ:* Lancing College. Leader Writer, Yorkshire Post, 1960–65; Parly Sketch-Writer, Daily Telegraph, 1966–72; Parly Sketch-Writer and Columnist, Daily Mail, 1972–84. Contested (C) Colne Valley, March 1963, 1964. *Publication:* (with Alan Watkins) The Making of the Prime Minister, 1970. *Recreations:* music, gardening, history, weight training. *Address:* c/o Associated Newspapers plc, 141–143 Drury Lane, WC2B 5TS. *T:* 0171–938 6000. *Clubs:* Reform, Espree.

ALEXANDER, Anthony George Laurence; Director, Hanson PLC, since 1976, and UK Chief Operating Officer, since 1986; *b* 4 April 1938; *s* of George and Margaret Alexander; *m* 1962, Frances, *d* of Cyril Burdett; one *s* two *d*. *Educ:* St Edward's School, Oxford. FCA. Chm., subsids of Hanson plc; Director: Shanks & McEwan Group PLC, 1986–; Inchcape Plc, 1993–. *Recreations:* tennis, golf. *Address:* Crafnant, Gregories Farm Lane, Beaconsfield, Bucks HP9 1HJ. *T:* Beaconsfield (01494) 672882.

ALEXANDER, Anthony Victor, CBE 1987; Director, Sedgwick Group, 1978–89; *b* 17 Sept. 1928; *s* of Aaron and Victoria Alexander; *m* 1958, Hélène Esther; one *d*. *Educ:* Harrow School; St John's Coll., Cambridge (BA, LLB, Mod. Langs and Law). FINucE. Sedgwick Collins & Co: joined 1954; Exec., UK Co., 1954–64; Dir, 1964–68; Sedgwick Collins Holdings Ltd: Dir, 1968–73, and Chm., SCUK; Sedgwick Forbes Holdings: Dir and Chm., SFUK, 1973–77; Dep. Chm., Sedgwick Forbes, 1977–78; Sedgwick Group: Chm., Underwriting Services and Special Services, 1978–84; Director: Securicor Group and Security Services, 1976–; ARV Aviation, 1985–88. Member: Overseas Projects Bd, 1978–79; British Invisible Exports Council, 1983–90; Marketing of Investments Bd, 1985–86; Dir, Securities and Investments Bd, 1986–89. Chm., Trustees, Victor Adda Foundn and Fan Museum Trust; Chm., British Insurance Brokers Assoc., 1982–87 (Dep. Chm., 1981–82). *Recreations:* gardening, sailing, fishing, forestry, antique collecting. *Address:* 1 St Germans Place, Blackheath, SE3 0NH. *T:* 0181–858 5509. *Clubs:* Lloyd's Yacht, Bar Yacht, Medway Yacht.

ALEXANDER, Bill, (William Alexander Paterson); Artistic Director, Birmingham Repertory Theatre, since 1993; Hon. Associate Director, Royal Shakespeare Company, since 1991 (Associate Director, 1984–91); *b* 23 Feb. 1948; *s* of Bill and Rosemary Paterson; *m* 1977, Juliet Harmer; two *d*. *Educ:* St Lawrence Coll., Ramsgate; Keele Univ. (BA Hons English/Politics). Seasons with The Other Company, Bristol Old Vic, Royal Court, 1972–78; Asst Dir, 1978–80, Resident Dir, 1980–84, RSC. Laurence Olivier award, Best Director, 1986. *Productions directed:* 1972–78: *Bristol Old Vic:* The Ride Across Lake Constance; Twelfth Night; Old Times; Butley; How the Other Half Loves; *Royal Court:* Sex and Kinship in a Savage Society, 1976; Amy and the Price of Cotton, 1977; Class Enemy, 1978; Sugar and Spice, 1979; Entertaining Mr Sloane, Nottingham Playhouse, 1977; The Gingerbread Lady, Ipswich, 1977; The Last of the Knuckle Men, Edin. Fest. Fringe, 1977; Julius Caesar, Newcastle upon Tyne, 1979; One White Day, Soho Poly, 1976; Mates, Leicester Square, 1976; Betrayal, 1980; Anna Christie, 1981, Cameri Th., Tel Aviv; Talk of the Devil, Watford Palace, 1986; *Royal Shakespeare Company:* Factory Birds, 1977; Shout Across the River, The Hang of the Gaol, Captain Swing, 1978; Men's Beano, 1979; Bastard Angel, Henry IV tour, 1980; Accrington Pals, 1981; Money, Clay, Molière, 1982; Tartuffe, Volpone, 1983; Richard III, Today, The Merry Wives of Windsor, 1984; Crimes in Hot Countries, Downchild (co-dir), 1985; Country Dancing, A Midsummer Night's Dream, 1986; Cymbeline, Twelfth Night, The Merchant of Venice, 1987; The Duchess of Malfi, Cymbeline, 1989; Much Ado About Nothing, 1990; The Taming of the Shrew (dir, regional tour), 1990; The Bright and Bold Design, 1991; The Taming of the Shrew, 1992; The School of Night, 1992; *Birmingham:* Othello, 1993; Volpone, 1993; Old Times, 1993; The Snowman, 1993; Awake and Sing, 1994; The Tempest, 1994; The Servant, 1995; *other productions* include: Romeo and Juliet, Victory Theatre, NY, 1990; Troilus and Cressida, Shakespeare Theatre, Washington, 1992. *Recreation:* tennis. *Address:* Rose Cottage, Tunley, Glos GL7 6LP; Birmingham Repertory Theatre, Broad Street, Birmingham B1 2EP. *T:* 0121–236 6771.

ALEXANDER, Sir Charles G(undry), 2nd Bt *cr* 1945; MA, AIMarE; Chairman, Alexander Shipping Co. Ltd, 1959–87; *b* 5 May 1923; *s* of Sir Frank Alexander, 1st Bt, and Elsa Mary (*d* 1959), *d* of Sir Charles Collett, 1st Bt; *S* father 1959; *m* 1st, 1944, Mary Neale, *o d* of S. R. Richardson; one *s* one *d*; 2nd, 1979, Eileen Ann Stewart. *Educ:* Bishop's Stortford College; St John's College, Cambridge. Served War as Lieut (E), RN, 1943–46. Chm., Governors Care Ltd, 1975–86; formerly Dep. Chm., Houlder Bros and Co. Ltd; Director: Furness-Houlder Insurance Ltd, until 1988; Furness-Houlder (Reinsurance Services) Ltd, until 1988; Inner London Region, National Westminster Bank Ltd, until 1987; Chm., Hull, Blyth & Co. Ltd, 1972–75. Chm., Bd of Governors, Bishop's Stortford College, until 1986. Mem. Court of Common Council, 1969; Alderman (Bridge Ward), 1970–76. Master, Merchant Taylors' Co., 1981–82; Prime Warden, Shipwrights' Co., 1983–84. *Heir: s* Richard Alexander [*b* 1 Sept. 1947; *m* 1971, Lesley Jane, *d* of Frederick William Jordan, Bishop's Stortford; two *s*]. *Address:* Hollytree Farmhouse, North Cadbury, Yeovil, Somerset BA22 7DD. *T:* North Cadbury (01963) 40159. *Club:* Royal Automobile.

ALEXANDER of Ballochmyle, Sir Claud Hagart-, 3rd Bt, *cr* 1886 of Ballochmyle; JP; Vice Lord-Lieutenant, Ayr and Arran, since 1983; *b* 6 Jan. 1927; *s* of late Wilfred Archibald Alexander (2nd *s* of 2nd Bt) and Mary Prudence, *d* of Guy Acheson; *S* grandfather, 1945; assumed additional surname of Hagart, 1949; *m* 1959, Hilda Etain, 2nd *d* of Miles Malcolm Acheson, Ganges, BC, Canada; two *s* two *d*. *Educ:* Sherborne; Corpus Christi Coll., Cambridge (BA 1948). MInstMC 1980. DL Ayrshire, 1973; JP Cumnock and Doon Valley, 1983. *Heir: s* Claud Hagart-Alexander [*b* 5 Nov. 1963; *m* 1994, Elaine Susan, *d* of Vincent Park, Winnipeg]. *Address:* Kingencleugh House, Mauchline, Ayrshire KA5 5JL. *T:* Mauchline (01290) 550217. *Club:* New (Edinburgh).

ALEXANDER, David; *see* Alexander, J. D.

ALEXANDER, Maj.-Gen. David Crichton, CB 1976; Commandant, Scottish Police College, 1979–87, retired; *b* 28 Nov. 1926; *s* of James Alexander and Margaret (*née* Craig); *m* 1957, Diana Joyce (Jane) (*née* Fisher) (*d* 1995); one *s* two *d* and one step *s*. *Educ:* Edinburgh Academy. Joined RM, 1944; East Indies Fleet; 45 Commando, Malaya, Malta, Canal Zone, 1951–54; Parade Adjt, Lympstone, 1954–57; Equerry and Acting Treasurer to Duke of Edinburgh, 1957–60; psc 1960; Directing Staff, Staff Coll., Camberley, 1962–65; 45 Commando (2IC), Aden, 1965–66; Staff of Chief of Defence Staff, incl. service with Sec. of State, 1966–69; CO 40 Commando, Singapore, 1969–70; Col GS to CGRM, 1970–73; ADC to the Queen, 1973–75; RCDS 1974; Comdr, Training Gp RM, 1975–77. Dir-Gen., English-Speaking Union, 1977–79. Governor, Corps of Commissionaires, 1978– (Pres., 1994–); Member: Civil Service Final Selection Bd, 1978–88; MoD Police Review Cttee, 1985; Transport Users' Consultative Cttee for Scotland, 1989–93. Dir, Edinburgh Acad., 1980–89 (Chm., 1985–89). Pres., SSAFA, Fife, 1990–94. Freeman, City of London; Liveryman, Painter Stainers' Co., 1978. *Recreations:* fishing, gardening, golf. *Address:* Baldinnie, Park Place, Elie, Fife KY9 1DH. *T:* Elie (01333) 330882. *Club:* Army and Navy.

ALEXANDER, Sir Douglas, 3rd Bt *cr* 1921; with Cowen & Co.; *b* 9 Sept. 1936; *s* of Lt-Comdr Archibald Gillespie Alexander (*d* 1978) (2nd *s* of 1st Bt), and of Margery Isabel, *d* of Arthur Brown Griffith; *S* uncle, 1983; *m* 1958, Marylon, *d* of Leonidas Collins Scatterday; two *s*. *Educ:* Rice Univ., Houston, Texas (MA 1961). PhD 1967 (Univ. of N Carolina). Formerly Assoc. Prof. and Chairman, French, State Univ. of New York at Albany. *Heir: s* Douglas Gillespie Alexander, *b* 24 July 1962. *Address:* 2499 Windsor Way Court, Wellington, Fla 33414, USA.

ALEXANDER, Ian Douglas Gavin; QC 1989; a Recorder of the Crown Court, since 1982; *b* 10 April 1941; *s* of late Dr A. D. P. Alexander, MB ChB, and of Mrs D. Alexander; *m* 1969, Rosemary Kirkbride Richards; one *s* one *d*. *Educ:* Tonbridge; University College London (LLB). Called to Bar, Lincoln's Inn, 1964; Recorder, Midland and Oxford Circuit, 1982–. *Recreations:* horses, sailing, gardening, ski-ing. *Address:* 11 Bolt Court, Fleet Street, EC4A 3DQ. *T:* 0171–353 2300, *Fax:* 0171–353 1878. *Club:* Naval and Military.

ALEXANDER, Prof. (John) David, DPhil; Trustees' Professor, Pomona College, since 1991 (President, 1969–91); American Secretary, Rhodes Scholarship Trust, since 1981; *b* 18 Oct. 1932; *s* of John David Alexander, Sr and Mary Agnes McKinnon; *m* 1956, Catharine Coleman; one *s* two *d*. *Educ:* Southwestern at Memphis (BA); Louisville Presbyterian Theological Seminary; Oxford University (DPhil). Instructor to Associate Prof., San Francisco Theol Seminary, 1957–64; Pres., Southwestern at Memphis, 1965–69. Trustee, Teachers Insurance and Annuity Assoc., NY, 1970–; Director: Great Western Financial Corp., Beverly Hills, 1973–; KCET (Community Supported TV of S Calif.), 1979–89; Amer. Council on Educn, Washington DC, 1981–84; National Assoc. of Indep. Colls and Univs, 1984–88; British Inst., 1979–87 (Mem., Bd of Advrs, 1987–); Member: Nat. Panel on Academic Tenure, 1971–72; Assoc. of Amer. Med. Colls Panel on Gen. Professional Preparation of Physicians, 1981–84; Bd of Overseers, Huntington Library, Art Collections and Botanical Gardens, 1991–. Dir, Children's Hosp. of Los Angeles, 1993–. Trustee: Woodrow Wilson Nat. Fellowship Foundn, 1978–; Seaver Inst., 1992–; Wenner-Gren Foundn for Anthropological Res., NY, 1995–. Hon. LLD: Univ. of S California, 1970; Occidental Coll., 1970; Centre Coll. of Kentucky, 1971; Pepperdine Univ., Calif, 1991; Albertson Coll. of Idaho, 1992; Hon. LHD Loyola Marymount Univ., 1983; Hon. LittD Rhodes Coll., Memphis, 1986. *Publications:* articles in Biblical studies; articles and chapters on higher educn in USA. *Recreations:* music, book collecting. *Address:* 807 North College Avenue, Claremont, CA 91711, USA. *T:* (714) 6247848. *Clubs:* Century Association (NY); California (Los Angeles); Bohemian (San Francisco).

ALEXANDER, Sir (John) Lindsay, Kt 1975; MA; Deputy Chairman, Lloyds Bank PLC, 1980–88 (Director, 1970–91); Director: British Petroleum Co. PLC, 1975–91; Hawker Siddeley plc, 1981–91; *b* 12 Sept. 1920; *e s* of Ernest Daniel Alexander and Florence Mary Mainsmith; *m* 1944, Maud Lilian, 2nd *d* of Oliver Ernest and Bridget Collard; two *s* one *d*. *Educ:* Alleyn's Sch.; Brasenose Coll., Oxford (Thomas Wall Schol.; Hon. Fellow 1977). Royal Engineers, 1940–45 (Capt.); served Middle East and Italy. Chairman: The Ocean Steam Ship Co. Ltd, later Ocean Transport and Trading Ltd, 1971–80 (Man. Dir, 1955–71; Dir, 1955–86); Lloyds Bank Internat., 1980–85 (Dir, 1975–85; Dep. Chm., 1979–80); Lloyds Merchant Bank Hldgs, 1988 (Dep. Chm. and Dir, 1985–88). Director: Overseas Containers Holdings Ltd, 1971–82 (Chm., 1976–82); Jebsens Drilling PLC, 1980–86; Wellington Underwriting Holdings Ltd, 1986–; Wellington Underwriting Agencies Ltd, 1986–; Britoil, 1988–90; Abbey Life Gp, later Lloyds Abbey Life, 1988–91. Chairman: Liverpool Port Employers' Assoc., 1964–67; Cttee, European Nat. Shipowners' Assocs, 1971–73; Vice-Chm., Nat. Assoc. of Port Employers, 1965–69; President: Chamber of Shipping of UK, 1974–75 (Vice-Pres., 1973–74); Gen. Council, British Shipping Ltd, 1974–75. Hon. Mem., Master Mariners' Co., 1974–. FCIT (MInstT 1968); CBIM 1980 (FBIM 1972). JP Cheshire, 1965–75. Comdr, Royal Order of St Olav, Norway. *Recreations:* gardening, music, photography. *Address:* Lloyds Bank Plc, 71 Lombard Street, EC3P 3BS. *T:* 0171–626 1500.

ALEXANDER, Prof. John Malcolm; Emeritus Professor, University of Wales; *b* 14 Oct. 1921; *s* of Robert Henry Alexander and Gladys Irene Lightfoot Alexander (*née* Domville); *m* 1946, Margaret, *d* of F. A. Ingram; two *s*. *Educ:* Ipswich Sch.; City and Guilds Coll. DSc (Eng) London; PhD; FCGI; FICE; FIMechE; FIEE; FIM; FEng; FRSA. REME commn, 1942–47; Aluminium Labs Ltd, 1953–55; English Electric, 1955–57; London University: Reader in Plasticity, 1957–63; Prof. of Engrg Plasticity, 1963–69; Chm. Board of Studies in Civil and Mech. Engrg, 1966–68; Prof. of Applied Mechanics, Imp. Coll., 1969–78; Prof. and Head of Dept of Mech. Engrg, University Coll. of Swansea, 1978–83. Stocker Vis. Prof. in Engrg and Technol., 1985–87, Adjunct Prof., 1987–, Univ. of Ohio. Chm., Applied Mechanics Gp, IMechE, 1963–65; Mem., CIRP, 1965–; Vice-President: Inst. of Metals, 1968–71; Inst. of Sheet Metal Engrg, 1979–. Gov., Ipswich Sch., 1977–86. Chm., British Cold Forging Gp, 1973–79. Assessor, Sizewell 'B' Public Inquiry, 1983–85; Mem., Adv. Cttee on Safe Transport of Radioactive Materials, 1985–89. Liveryman, Blacksmiths' Co., 1976. Series Editor, Ellis Horwood Ltd, 1970–; Mem. Editorial Board: Internat. Jl Mech. Sciences, 1968–91; Internat. Jl Machine Tool Design and Research, 1973–. Joseph Bramah Medal, IMechE, 1970. *Publications:* Advanced Mechanics of Materials, Manufacturing Properties of Materials, 1963; Hydrostatic Extrusion, 1971; Strength of Materials, 1980; Manufacturing Technology, 1987; papers to Royal Soc., IMechE, Iron and Steel Inst., Inst. Metals, Metals Soc. *Recreations:* music, gardening, golf. *Address:* Rowan Cottage, Furze Hill Road, Headley Down, Hants GU35 8NP. *Club:* Army and Navy.

ALEXANDER, Jonathan James Graham, DPhil; FBA 1985; FSA 1981; Professor of Fine Arts, Institute of Fine Arts, New York, since 1988; *b* 20 Aug. 1935; *s* of Arthur Ronald Brown and Frederica Emma Graham (who *m* 2nd, Boyd Alexander); *m* 1974, Mary Davey (marr. diss. 1995); one *s*. *Educ:* Magdalen Coll., Oxford (BA, MA, DPhil). Assistant, Dept of Western MSS, Bodleian Library, Oxford, 1963–71; Lecturer, 1971–73, Reader, 1973–87, History of Art Dept, Manchester Univ. Lyell Reader in Bibliography, Univ. of Oxford, 1982–83; Sen. Kress Fellow, Center for Adv. Study in Visual Arts, Nat. Gall. of Art, Washington DC, 1984–85; Sandars Reader in Bibliography, Cambridge Univ., 1984–85. Vis. Prof., UCL, 1991–93. *Publications:* (with Otto Pächt) Illuminated Manuscripts in the Bodleian Library, Oxford, 3 vols, 1966, 1970, 1973; (with A. C. de la Mare) Italian Illuminated Manuscripts in the Library of Major J. R. Abbey, 1969; Norman Illumination at Mont St Michel *c* 966–1100, 1970; The Master of Mary of Burgundy, A Book of Hours, 1970; Italian Renaissance Illuminations, 1977; Insular Manuscripts 6th–9th Century, 1978; The Decorated Letter, 1978; (with E. Temple) Illuminated Manuscripts in Oxford College Libraries, 1986; (ed with Paul Binski) Age of Chivalry: Art in Plantagenet England 1200–1400, 1987; Medieval Illuminators and Their Methods of Work, 1993; (ed) The Painted Page: Italian Renaissance book illumination 1450–1550, 1994; articles in Burlington Magazine, Arte Veneta, Pantheon, etc. *Recreations:* music, gardening. *Address:* Institute of Fine Arts, 1 East 78th Street, New York, NY 10021, USA.

ALEXANDER, Sir Kenneth (John Wilson), Kt 1978; DL; BSc (Econ.); FRSE 1978; Chancellor, University of Aberdeen, since 1986; *b* Edinburgh, 14 March 1922; *o s* of late William Wilson Alexander; *m* 1949, Angela-May, *d* of late Capt. G. H. Lane, RN; one *s* four *d*. *Educ:* George Heriot's Sch., Edinburgh; Sch. of Economics, Dundee. Research Asst, Univ. of Leeds, 1949–51; Lectr, Univ. of Sheffield, 1951–56; Lectr, Univ. of Aberdeen, 1957–62; Dean of Scottish Business Sch., 1973–75 (Chm., Acad. Exec. Cttee, 1972–73); Prof. of Econs, Strathclyde Univ., 1963–80, on leave of absence, 1976–80; Chm., Highlands and Islands Develt Bd, 1976–80; Principal and Vice-Chancellor, Stirling Univ., 1981–86. Mem. Adv. Cttee on University of the Air, 1965; Director: Fairfields (Glasgow) Ltd, 1966–68; Upper Clyde Shipbuilders Ltd, 1968–71; Scottish Television, 1982–92; Stakis plc, 1987–93; Aberdeen Univ. Press, 1989–92 (Chm., 1990–92); Scottish Daily Record and Sunday Mail (1986) Ltd, 1990–92; Chairman: Govan Shipbuilders, 1974–76; Michael Kelly Associates, 1986–94; Scottish Industrial Exhibitions Ltd, 1991–. Dir, Glasgow Chamber of Commerce, 1969–73; Economic Consultant to Sec. of State for Scotland, 1968–91; Chm., Cttee on Adult Educn in Scotland, 1970–73; Mem. Exec. Cttee, 1968–91, Dep. Chm. 1982–91, Scottish Council (Develt and Industry); Member: (part-time) Scottish Transport Gp, 1969–76; SSRC, 1975–76; Scottish Develt Agency, 1975–86; Bd, UK CEED, 1985–. Governor: Technical Change Centre, 1981–87; Newbattle Abbey Coll., 1967–73; President: Section F, British Assoc., 1974; Saltire Soc., 1975–81; Scottish Section, Town and Country Planning, 1982–; Hon. Pres., The Highland Fund, 1983–; Chairman: John Muir Trust, 1985–88; Edinburgh Book Fest., 1987–91; Paxton Trust, 1989–94; Trustee, Nat. Museums of Scotland, 1985–87. CIMgt (CBIM 1980); FEIS 1983; FBEC(S) 1984; FRIAS 1988. DL Fife, 1992. Hon. LLD: CNAA, 1976; Aberdeen, 1986; Dundee, 1986; DUniv: Stirling, 1977; Open 1985. *Publications:* The Economist in Business, 1967; Productivity Bargaining and the Reform of Industrial Relations, 1969; (with C. L. Jenkins) Fairfields, a study of industrial change, 1971; (ed) The Political Economy of Change, 1976; articles in Oxford Econ. Papers, Quarterly Jl of Econ., Scottish Jl of Pol. Econ., Economica, Yorkshire Bulletin Economics, and other jls. *Recreation:* Scottish antiquarianism. *Address:* 9 West Shore, Pittenweem, Fife KY10 2NV.

ALEXANDER, Sir Lindsay; *see* Alexander, Sir J. L.

ALEXANDER, Rt. Rev. Mervyn Alban Newman; *see* Clifton, Bishop of, (RC).

ALEXANDER, Michael Charles; writer; *b* 20 Nov. 1920; *s* of late Rear-Adm. Charles Otway Alexander and Antonia Geermans; *m* 1963, Sarah Wignall (marr. diss.); one *d*. *Educ:* Stowe; RMC, Sandhurst; Oflag IVC, Colditz. Served War: DCLI; 5 (Ski) Bn Scots Gds; 8 Commando (Layforce); HQ 13 Corps (GSO 3); Special Boat Section; (POW, 1942–44); 2nd SAS Regt; War Office (Civil Affairs). Intergovtl Cttee on Refugees, 1946; Editorial Dir, Common Ground Ltd, 1946–50. Located Firuzkoh, Central Afghanistan, 1952; Himalayan Hovercraft Expedn, 1972; Yucatan Straits Hovercraft Expedn, 1975; Upper Ganges Hovercraft Expedn, 1980; Promoter, Scottish Highlands & Is Inflatable Boat Race, 1990, 1991, 1992. Founder and Hon. Pres., British Inflatable Boat Owners' Assoc., 1994. Director: Acorn Productions Ltd; Adastra Productions Co. Ltd. Founded: Woburn Safari Service, 1977; Chelsea Wharf Restaurant, 1983. Holder, Barony of Skelbo, Skelbo Castle, Sutherland. FZS, FRGS; Fellow, Royal Soc. for Asian Affairs. Co-publisher, Wildlife magazine, 1982–86. *Publications:* The Privileged Nightmare (with Giles Romilly), 1952 (republ., as Hostages at Colditz, 1975); Offbeat in Asia, 1953; The Reluctant Legionnaire, 1955; The True Blue, 1957; Mrs Fraser on the Fatal Shore, 1972; Discovering the New World, 1976; Omai: Noble Savage, 1977; Queen Victoria's Maharajah, 1980; Delhi-Agra: a traveller's companion, 1987; *filmscript:* Ada. *Address:* 48 Eaton Place, SW1X 8AL. *T:* 0171–235 2724. *Clubs:* Beefsteak, Chelsea Arts.

ALEXANDER, Sir Michael (O'Donel Bjarne), GCMG 1992 (KCMG 1988; CMG 1982); HM Diplomatic Service, retired; Deputy Chairman, Wasserstein Perella Eastern Europe, since 1992; *b* 19 June 1936; *s* of late Conel Hugh O'Donel Alexander, CMG, CBE, and Enid Constance Crichton Neate; *m* 1960, Traute Krohn; two *s* one *d*. *Educ:* Foyle Coll., Londonderry; Hall Sch., Hampstead; St Paul's Sch. (Schol.); King's Coll., Cambridge (Schol.); Harkness Fellow (Yale and Berkeley) 1960–62. MA (Cantab), AM (Yale). Royal Navy, 1955–57. Entered HM Foreign (later Diplomatic) Service, 1962; Moscow, 1963–65; Office of Political Adviser, Singapore, 1965–68; FCO, 1968–72; Asst Private Sec. to Secretary of State (Rt Hon. Sir Alec Douglas-Home, MP, and Rt Hon. James Callaghan, MP) 1972–74; Counsellor (Conf. on Security and Co-operation in Europe) and later Head of Chancery, UK Mission, Geneva, 1974–77; Dep. Head, 1977–78, Head, 1978–79, Personnel Operations Dept, FCO; Private Sec. (Overseas Affairs) to the Prime Minister (Rt Hon. Margaret Thatcher, MP), 1979–81; Ambassador, Vienna, 1982–86; concurrently Hd of UK Delegn to the Negotiations on Mutual and Balanced Reduction of Forces and Armaments in Central Europe, 1985–86; Ambassador and UK Permanent Rep. on North Atlantic Council, Brussels, 1986–92 (Dean of Council, 1991–92). Chm., KINTO Securities, Kiev, 1994–; Dep. Chm. (and co-founder), Capital SA, Bucharest, 1993–; Dir (and co-founder) Sector Capital, Moscow, 1995–. Sen. Advr, Bain & Co., 1994–. Organised: Britain in Vienna Fest., 1986; Grosses Goldenes Ehrenzeichen (Wien), 1986. Vice-Pres., Atlantic Council of UK, 1993–; Member: Council, RUSI, 1992– (Chm., 1993–); Exec. Cttee, Anglo-Austrian Soc., 1992–. Former Public Schools', British Universities' and National Junior Foil Champion; fenced for Cambridge Univ., 1957–60 (Captain, 1959–60); English Internat., 1958; Silver Medallist (Epée Team) Olympic Games, 1960; Gold Medallist, US Championships, 1961; Captained England, 1963. Represented Cambridge in Field Events Match with Oxford, 1959, 1960. *Publications:* articles on East/West relations and international security. *Recreations:* reading history; watching or participating in sport of any kind. *Address:* (office) 3 Burlington Gardens, W1X 1LE. *Clubs:* Athenæum, Garrick, Epée, All England Fencing; Hawks (Cambridge).

ALEXANDER, Sir Norman (Stanley), Kt 1966; CBE 1959. Professor of Physics: Raffles Coll., Singapore, 1936–49; Univ. of Malaya, Singapore, 1949–52; University Coll., Ibadan, Nigeria, 1952–60; Vice-Chancellor, Ahmadu Bello Univ., Nigeria, 1961–66.

ALEXANDER, Lt-Col Sir Patrick Desmond William C.; *see* Cable-Alexander.

ALEXANDER, Maj.-Gen. Paul Donald, CB 1989; MBE 1968; freelance consultant; Policy Director (Army), Ministry of Defence, 1989–94; *b* 30 Nov. 1934; *s* of Donald Alexander and Alice Louisa Alexander (*née* Dunn); *m* 1958, Christine Winifred Marjorie Coakley; three *s*. *Educ:* Dudley Grammar Sch.; RMA Sandhurst; Staff Coll., Camberley; NDC; RCDS. Enlisted 1953; commissioned Royal Signals, 1955; served Hong Kong, E Africa, Germany; Comd 1st Div. Signal Regt, 1974–76; MoD, 1977–79; Comdr, Corps Royal Signals, 1st (Br) Corps, 1979–81; Dep. Mil. Sec. (B), 1982–85; Signal Officer in Chief (Army), 1985–89, retired. Col Comdt, RCS, 1989–95; Hon. Col, 35th Signal Regt, 1991–. Chm., Royal Signals Assoc., 1990–95; Mem., E Anglian TA&VRA, 1991–. *Publications:* occasional contribs to professional jls. *Recreations:* gardening, fly-fishing, unstructured hedonism. *Clubs:* Army and Navy; Royal Signals Yacht (Adm., 1989–93).

ALEXANDER, Richard Thain; MP (C) Newark, since 1979; *b* 29 June 1934; *s* of Richard Rennie Alexander and Gladys Alexander; *m* 1st, 1966, Valerie Ann Winn (marr. diss. 1985); one *s* one *d*; 2nd, 1987, Pat Hanson. *Educ:* Dewsbury Grammar Sch., Yorks; University Coll. London (LLB Hons). Articled with Sir Francis Hill, Messrs Andrew & Co., Lincoln, 1957–60; Asst Solicitor, Messrs McKinnell, Ervin & Holmes, Scunthorpe, 1960–64; Sen. Partner, Messrs Jones, Alexander & Co., Retford, 1964–85, Consultant, 1986–90. *Recreation:* occasional golf. *Address:* 51 London Road, Newark, Notts NG24 1RZ. *Club:* Newark Conservative.

ALEXANDER, Prof. (Robert) McNeill, FRS 1987; FIBiol; Professor of Zoology, University of Leeds, since 1969; *b* 7 July 1934; *s* of Robert Priestley Alexander and Janet McNeill; *m* 1961, Ann Elizabeth Coulton; one *s* one *d*. *Educ:* Tonbridge School; Trinity Hall, Cambridge (MA, PhD); DSc Wales. Asst Lectr in Zoology, University Coll. of

North Wales, 1958, Lectr 1961, Sen. Lectr 1968; Head, Dept of Pure and Applied Zoology, Univ. of Leeds, 1969–78 and 1983–87. Visiting Professor: Harvard, 1973; Duke, 1975; Nairobi, 1976, 1977, 1978; Basle, 1986; St Francis Xavier Univ. (NS), 1990; Univ. of Calif, Davis, 1992. Mem., Biological Scis Cttee, SRC, 1974–77. Sec., Zool Soc. of London, 1992– (Mem. Council, 1988–91; Vice Pres., 1990–91); Pres., Soc. for Experimental Biology, 1995– (Vice Pres., 1993–95). Hon. Mem., Amer. Soc. of Zoologists, 1986. Scientific Medal, Zoological Soc., 1969; Linnean Medal, Linnean Soc., 1979; Muybridge Medal, Internat. Soc. for Biomechanics, 1991. *Publications:* Functional Design in Fishes, 1967, 3rd edn 1974; Animal Mechanics, 1968, 2nd edn 1983; Size and Shape, 1971; The Chordates, 1975, 2nd edn 1981; Biomechanics, 1975; The Invertebrates, 1979; Locomotion of Animals, 1982; Optima for Animals, 1982; Elastic Mechanisms in Animal Movement, 1988; Dynamics of Dinosaurs and other Extinct Giants, 1989; Animals, 1990; The Human Machine, 1992; Exploring Biomechanics, 1992; Bones, 1994; papers on mechanics of human and animal movement. *Recreations:* history of natural history, local history. *Address:* 14 Moor Park Mount, Leeds LS6 4BU. *T:* Leeds (0113) 275 9218.

ALEXANDER, Thomas John; Director for Education, Employment, Labour and Social Affairs (formerly Social Affairs, Manpower and Education), OECD, Paris, since 1989; *b* 11 March 1940; *s* of late John Alexander and of Agnes Douglas Stewart (*née* Creedican); *m* 1961, Pamela Mason; two *s* one *d. Educ:* Royal High Sch., Edinburgh. Entered FO, 1958; MECAS, 1961; Third Sec. (Commercial), Kuwait, 1963; Asst Private Sec. to the Minister of State, FO, 1965; Second Sec. (Commercial), Tripoli, 1967; seconded to industry (ICI), 1970; Vice Consul (Commercial), Seattle, 1970; First Sec., FCO, 1974; special unpaid leave to act as Private Sec. to Sec.-Gen. of OECD, Paris, 1977–82; Counsellor and Head of Chancery, Khartoum, 1982–83; Dep. Head of Planning, 1984, Head of Private Office of Sec.-Gen., 1984–89, OECD. *Recreations:* squash, tennis. *Address:* c/o OECD, 2 rue André Pascal, 75016 Paris, France.

ALEXANDER, Walter Ronald, CBE 1984; Chairman, Walter Alexander plc, 1979–90 (Managing Director, 1973–79); company director; *b* 6 April 1931; *s* of Walter Alexander and Katherine Mary Turnbull; *m* 1st, 1956, Rosemary Anne Sleigh (marr. diss. 1975); two *s* two *d*; 2nd, 1979, Mrs Lorna Elwes, *d* of Lydia Duchess of Bedford. *Educ:* Loretto Sch.; Cambridge Univ. (MA Hons). Chm. and Man. Dir, Tayforth Ltd, 1961–71; Chm., Scottish Automobile Co. Ltd, 1971–73. Director: Scotcros plc, 1965–82 (Chm., 1972–82); Investors Capital Trust plc, 1967–; Clydesdale Bank plc, 1971–; RIT and Northern plc (formerly Great Northern Investment Trust plc), 1973–84; Dawson Internat. plc, 1979–. Chm., Scottish Appeals Cttee, Police Dependants' Trust, 1974–81; Pres., Public Schs Golfing Soc., 1973–79; Chairman: PGA, 1982–85; Royal and Ancient Golf Club of St Andrews Trust, 1987–. Governor, Loretto Sch., 1961–89; Comr, Queen Victoria Sch., 1987–92. Scottish Free Enterprise Award, 1977. *Recreation:* golf. *Address:* Moonzie Mill, Balmullo, St Andrews, Fife KY16 0AH. *T:* St Andrews (01334) 870864. *Clubs:* Royal and Ancient Golf (Captain, 1980–81); Hon. Company of Edinburgh Golfers; Prestwick Golf; Royal St George's Golf; Royal County Down Golf; Pine Valley Golf, Augusta National Golf (USA).

ALEXANDER, William Gemmell, MBE 1945; *b* 19 Aug. 1918; *s* of Harold Gemmell Alexander and Winifred Ada Alexander (*née* Stott); *m* 1945, Janet Rona Page Alexander (*née* Elias); four *s* one *d. Educ:* Tre Arddur Bay Sch.; Sedbergh Sch.; Oxford Univ. (MA). Served War of 1939–45 (despatches, war stars and clasps): Driver Mechanic, 2nd Lieut, Lieut, Capt., Maj.; served in France, S Africa, Eritrea, Egypt, Middle East, Sicily, Italy, Algeria, NW Europe. HM Overseas Civil Service, 1946–59: Gilbert and Ellice Is, 1946–51; Mauritius, 1951–55; Cyprus, 1955–59; Man., Cooperative Wholesale Soc., Agricultural Dept, 1960–63; Dir, Internat. Cooperative Alliance, 1963–68; Dir-Gen., RoSPA, 1968–74; County Road Safety Officer, W Yorks MCC, 1974–78; Chm., W. H. Stott & Co. Ltd, 1979–83 (Dir, 1968–83). Mem., BSI Quality Assurance Council, 1975–83. Member: Bradford Dio. Bd of Finance, 1985–91; Ewecross Deanery Synod, 1985–; Dent PCC, 1978–. Clerk, Dent Parish Council, 1980–86. Chm., Bd of Govs, Dent GS. AMBIM 1963. *Recreations:* all sports and long distance walking. *Address:* Cross House, Dent, Cumbria LA10 5TF. *T.* Dent (015396) 25228. *Club:* Commonwealth Trust.

ALEXANDER-SINCLAIR of Freswick, Maj.-Gen. David Boyd, CB 1981, retired 1982; *b* 2 May 1927; *s* of late Comdr M. B. Alexander-Sinclair of Freswick, RN and late Avril N. Fergusson-Buchanan; *m* 1958, Ann Ruth, *d* of late Lt-Col Graeme Daglish; two *s* one *d. Educ:* Eton. Commnd into Rifle Bde, 1946, served in Germany, Kenya, Cyprus; ADC to GOC South Malaya District and Maj.-Gen. Bde of Gurkhas, 1950–51; psc 1958; Bde Major, 6th Inf. Bde Gp, 1959–61; GSO2 (Dirg Staff) Staff Coll., 1963–65; comdg 3rd Bn Royal Green Jackets, 1967–69; MoD, 1965–67 and 1969–71; Comdr, 6th Armd Bde, 1971–73; Student, RCDS, 1974; GOC 1st Division, 1975–77; COS, UKLF, 1978–80; Comdt, Staff Coll., 1980–82.

AL FAYED, Mohamed; Chairman: Harrods Holdings plc, since 1994; Harrods Ltd, since 1985; Chairman and Owner, Ritz Hotel, Paris, since 1979; *b* Egypt, Jan. 1933; *m*; five *c. Educ:* Alexandria Univ. Officier, Légion d'Honneur, 1993; La Grande Médaille de la Ville de Paris, 1985; Plaque de Paris, 1989; Commendatore, Order of Merit (Italy), 1990. *Address:* Harrods Ltd, Brompton Road, SW1 7XL.

ALFÖLDY, Tádé; Ambassador of the Republic of Hungary to the Court of St James's, since 1994; *b* 6 Aug. 1946; *s* of László Alföldy and Erzsébet (*née* Újvári); *m* 1968, Orsolya Baraczka; two *d. Educ:* Karl Marx Univ. of Economics, Budapest. Hungarian Shipping Agency, 1968–70; Hungarian Youth Union, 1970–74; Sec.-Gen., Internat. Cttee, Children's and Adolescents' Movements, 1974–79; Ministry of Foreign Affairs, Hungary, 1979–: Arab Desk Officer, 1979–80; 2nd, later 1st, Sec., Kuwait, 1980–85; British Desk Officer, 1985–89; Dir, N Atlantic Dept, 1989–90; Dep. State Sec., 1990–91; Ambassador to Greece, 1991–94. Mem., Foreign Policy Assoc., Budapest. *Recreations:* family, tennis, gardening. *Address:* Embassy of the Republic of Hungary, 35 Eaton Place, SW1X 8BY. *T:* 0171–235 4048/7191. *Clubs:* Athenæum, Queen's.

ALFONSÍN, Dr Raúl Ricardo; President of Argentina, 1983–89; *b* 12 March 1927; *s* of Serafín Raúl Alfonsín and Ana María Foulkes; *m* 1949, María Lorenza Barreneche; three *s* three *d. Educ:* Regional Normal School, Chascomus; Gen. San Martín Mil. Acad.; Law Sch., Nat. Univ. of La Plata. Mem., Radical Civic Union, 1945, Pres., 1983–91. Journalist, founder El Imparcial, Chascomus; Mem., Chascomus City Cttee, 1951, Councilman, 1954–55 (Pres., 1955 and 1959–61); Mem., Buenos Aires Provincial Legislature, 1952; Provincial Deputy, 1958–62; Deputy, Nat. Congress, 1963–66, 1973–76. Founder, Renovation and Change movement. Dr *hc* Univ. of New Mexico, 1985. Human Rights Prize (jtly), Council of Europe, 1986; numerous awards. *Publications:* La Cuestión Argentina, 1980; Ahora, mi Propuesta Política, 1983; Que es el Radicalismo?, 1983. *Address:* c/o President's Office, Buenos Aires, Argentina.

ALFORD, Richard Harding, OBE 1988; Regional Director, Central Europe, British Council, since 1993; *b* 28 Dec. 1943; *s* of Jack Harding Alford and Sylvia Alford; *m* 1968, Penelope Jane Wort; one *s* two *d. Educ:* Dulwich Coll.; Keble Coll., Oxford (BA; Diploma in History and Philosophy of Science). Asst Cultural Attaché, British Embassy, Prague, 1969–72; posts in ME Dept, Policy Res. Dept, and Educnl Contracts Dept, British Council, 1972–77; Project Planning Centre, Bradford Univ., 1977; Inst. of Educn, London Univ., 1978; British Council: Asst Rep., New Delhi, 1978–81; Dir, E Europe and N Asia Dept, 1982–85; Rep., Poland, 1985–89; Dir of Personnel, 1989–93. Gov., Centre for Internat. Briefing, Farnham Castle, 1992–. *Recreations:* squash, theatre, walking the dog. *Address:* c/o The British Council, 10 Spring Gardens, SW1A 2BN. *T:* 0171–930 8466. *Club:* Friends of Dulwich College Sports.

ALFRED, (Arnold) Montague; Deputy Chairman: Ward Lock Educational Co. Ltd, 1985–88; BLA Publishing Ltd, 1985–88; Ling Kee (UK) Ltd, 1985–88; retired; *b* 21 March 1925; *s* of Reuben Alfred and Bessie Alfred (*née* Arbesfield); *m* 1947, Sheila Jacqueline Gold; three *s. Educ:* Central Foundation Boys' Sch.; Imperial Coll., London; London Sch. of Economics. Head of Economics Dept, Courtaulds Ltd, 1953–69; Director, Nylon Div., Courtaulds Ltd, 1964–69; Dir, BPC Ltd, 1969–81; Chairman: BPC Publishing Ltd, 1971–81; Caxton Publishing Holdings Ltd, 1971–81; Second Permanent Sec., and Chief Exec., PSA, DoE, 1982–84. *Publications:* Discounted Cash Flow (jointly), 1965; Business Economics (jointly), 1968. Numerous articles in: Accountant, Textile Jl, Investment Analyst, etc. *Recreation:* active in Jewish community affairs. *Address:* c/o Institute of Directors, 168 Pall Mall, SW1Y 5ED.

ALGOMA, Bishop of, since 1995; **Rt Rev. Ronald Curry Ferris;** *b* 2 July 1945; *s* of Herald Bland Ferris and Marjorie May Ferris; *m* 1965, Janet Agnes (*née* Waller); two *s* four *d. Educ:* Toronto Teachers' Coll. (diploma); Univ. of W Ontario (BA); Huron Coll., London, Ont. (MDiv). Teacher, Pape Avenue Elem. School, Toronto, 1965; Principal Teacher, Carcross Elem. School, Yukon, 1966–68. Incumbent, St Luke's Church, Old Crow, Yukon, 1970–72; Rector, St Stephen's Memorial Church, London, Ont., 1973–81; Bishop of Yukon, 1981–95. Hon. DD Huron Coll., London, Ont., 1982; Hon. DMin Pacific Sch. of Religion, 1995. *Address:* PO Box 1168, 619 Wellington Street E, Sault Ste Marie, ON P6A 5N7, Canada.

ALGOSAIBI, Dr Ghazi; Saudi Arabian Ambassador to the Court of St James's and to Ireland, since 1992; *b* 2 March 1940; *s* of Abdul Rahman and Fatma; *m* 1968, Sigrid Presser; three *s* one *d. Educ:* primary and secondary schs, Bahrain; Cairo Univ. (LLB); Univ. of Southern California (MA Internat. Relations); Univ. of London (PhD). Asst Prof., King Saud Univ., Riyadh, 1965, later Prof. and Head of Political Science and Dean, Faculty of Commerce; Dir, Saudi Railways, 1974; Minister: Industry and Electricity, 1975; Health, 1982; Ambassador to Bahrain, 1984. Numerous foreign awards. *Publications:* 10 collections of essays; 11 collections of poems in Arabic (5 trans. English); The Gulf Crisis: an attempt to understand, 1993; Apartment Freedom, 1994. *Recreations:* swimming, fishing, table tennis. *Address:* Royal Embassy of Saudi Arabia, 30 Charles Street, W1X 7PM. *T:* 0171–917 3000. *Clubs:* Brooks's, Travellers', Army and Navy (Hon. Mem.).

ALHAJI, Alhaji Abubakar, Hon. KBE 1989; High Commissioner for Nigeria in the United Kingdom, since 1992; *b* 22 Nov. 1938; *m* Hajiya Amina Abubakar; three *s* three *d. Educ:* Univ. of Reading (BA Hons Political Economy); IMF Inst. course in public finance, 1974; Hague Inst. for Social Scis (course on industrialisation, 1970). Permanent Secretary, Ministries of: Trade, 1975–78; Industries, 1978–79; Finance, 1979–84; Nat. Planning, 1984–88; Hon. Minister, Ministries of: Budget and Planning, 1988–90; Finance and Economic Develt, 1990–92. Chm., Group 24 Cttee, 1991–92. Vice-Pres., Commonwealth Soc. for the Deaf. Sardauna of Sokoto, 1991. Hon. DSc Sokoto Univ., 1991. *Recreations:* horse riding, walking, reading. *Address:* Nigeria High Commission, 9 Northumberland Avenue, WC2 5BX. *T:* 0171–839 2037.

ALHEGELAN, Sheikh Faisal Al Abdul Aziz, Hon. GBE 1987; Grand Cross and Cordon, Order of King Abdul Aziz, Saudi Arabia; Saudi Arabian diplomat; Minister of Health, Saudi Arabia, since 1984; *b* Jeddah, 7 Oct. 1929; *s* of Sheikh Abdulaziz Alhegelan and Fatima Al-Eissa; *m* 1961, Nouha Tarazi; three *s. Educ:* Faculty of Law, Fouad Univ., Cairo. Min. of Foreign Affairs, 1952–54; Saudi Arabian Embassy, Washington, USA, 1954–58; Chief of Protocol, Min. of Foreign Affairs, 1958–60; Polit. Adviser to King Sa'ud, 1960–61; Ambassador to: Spain, 1961–68; Venezuela and Argentina (concurrently), 1968–75; Denmark, 1975–76; Court of St James's, 1976–79; USA, 1979–83. Chm. Bd of Dirs, Saudi Red Crescent Soc., 1984– . Order of Isabel la Católica, Spain; Gran Cordon, Orden del Libertador, Venezuela; Grande Official, Orden Rio Branco, Brazil; May Grand Decoration, Argentina. *Recreations:* golf, bridge, collecting selective books and objets d'art. *Address:* c/o Ministry of Health, Riyadh, Saudi Arabia. *T:* 4011443, 4033567.

ALI, Rt. Rev. Dr Michael N.; *see* Nazir-Ali.

ALISON, Rt. Hon. Michael James Hugh; PC 1981; MP (C) Selby, since 1983 (Barkston Ash, 1964–83); Second Church Estates Commissioner, since 1987; *b* 27 June 1926; *m* 1958, Sylvia Mary Haigh; two *s* one *d. Educ:* Eton; Wadham Coll., Oxford. Coldstream Guards, 1944–48; Wadham Coll., Oxford, 1948–51; Lazard Bros & Co. Ltd, 1951–53; London Municipal Soc., 1954–58; Conservative Research Dept, 1958–64. Parly Under-Sec. of State, DHSS, 1970–74; Minister of State: Northern Ireland Office, 1979–81; Dept of Employment, 1981–83; PPS to Prime Minister, 1983–87. *Publication:* (ed jtly) Christianity and Conservatism, 1990. *Address:* House of Commons, SW1A 0AA.

ALISON, William Andrew Greig, FLA; Director of Libraries, City of Glasgow, 1975–81; *b* 23 Oct. 1916; *m* 1942, Jessie Youngson Henderson; two *d. Educ:* Daniel Stewart's Coll., Edinburgh. Served War, Royal Air Force, 1940–46. Edinburgh Public Libraries, 1935–62: Assistant, 1935–46; Librarian, Fine Art Dept, 1946–55; Branch Librarian, 1955–61; Librarian, Scottish and Local History Depts, 1961–62; Glasgow City Libraries, 1962–81: Supt of District Libraries, 1962–64; Depute City Librarian, 1964–74; City Librarian, 1974–75. President: Scottish Library Assoc., 1975; Library Assoc., 1979 (also Mem. Council, 1979–82; Chm., Library Assoc. Publishing, 1981–82); Member: British Library Adv. Council, 1979–82; Nat. Library of Scotland Library Co-operation Cttee, 1974–81. British Council visits to: Zimbabwe, 1981; Bahrain, 1982; Syria, 1983. Church of Scotland elder. Silver Jubilee Medal, 1977. *Publication:* (assoc. ed.) New Library Buildings 1984–1989, 1990. *Recreations:* travel, philately. *Address:* St Mawgan, 103 Mossgiel Road, Glasgow G43 2BY. *T:* 0141–632 6036.

ALKER, Doug; Chief Executive, Royal National Institute for Deaf People, since 1995; *b* 23 Nov. 1940. *Educ:* London Univ. (BSc 1967); Birmingham Univ. (MBA 1993). Analytical Chemist, Pilkington Bros, 1959–64; Exptl Officer, ICI, 1964–85; Researcher, BBC, 1985–87; Royal National Institute for Deaf People: Principal Regl Officer, 1987; Dir, Community Services, 1987–90; Dir, Quality and Res., 1990–94. *Address:* c/o Royal National Institute for Deaf People, 105 Gower Street, WC1E 6AH. *T:* 0171–387 8033.

ALLAIN, Prof. Jean-Pierre Charles, MD, PhD; FRCPath; Professor of Transfusion Medicine, University of Cambridge, since 1991; *b* 26 Jan. 1942; *s* of Jacques Louis Allain and Marthe Charlotte (*née* Petitjean); *m* 1st, 1962, DucDung Nguyen (marr. diss.); two *s* two *d*; 2nd, 1978, Helen Lee. *Educ:* Univ. of Paris (MD 1967; PhD 1986). FRCPath 1992. Asst Prof. of Haematol., Univ. of Paris, 1967–70; Dir, French Red Cross Haemophilia Centre, 1970–77; Head, Coagulation Res. Lab., Nat. Blood Transfusion Centre, Paris, 1977–81; Head, Dept of R&D Plasma Protein Derivatives, Nat. Blood Transfusion Centre, Paris, 1981–86; Dir of Med. Res., Diagnostic Div., Abbott Labs,

Chicago, 1986–91; Dir, E Anglian Blood Transfusion Centre, 1991–94. *Publications:* 140 papers in learned jls incl. N Engl. Jl Med., Lancet, Jl of Clin. Invest., Jl Lab. Clin. Med., BMJ, Blood, Transfusion. *Recreations:* tennis, ceramics.

ALLAIRE, Paul Arthur; Chief Executive Officer, since 1990, and Chairman, since 1991, Xerox Corporation, PO Box 1600, Stamford, Connecticut; *b* 21 July 1938; *s* of late Arthur E. Allaire and of Mrs G. P. Murphy; *m* 1963, Kathleen Buckley; one *s* one *d. Educ:* Worcester Polytechnic Inst., USA (BS Elect. Eng., 1960); Carnegie-Mellon Univ., USA (MS Industrial Admin, 1966). Engineer, Univac, 1960–62; Project Manager, General Electric, 1962–64; Manager Financial Planning and Pricing, Xerox Corp., 1966–70; Financial Controller, Rank Xerox Ltd, 1970–73; Xerox Corporation: Dir, Internat. Finance, 1973–74; Dir, Internat. Ops, 1974–75; Rank Xerox Ltd: Chief Staff Officer, 1975–79; Dep. Man. Dir, 1979–80; Man. Dir, 1980–83; Mem., Bd of Dirs; Sen. Vice-Pres., Xerox Corp., 1983–86, Pres., 1986–91; Member, Board of Directors: Fuji Xerox Co.; Sara Lee Corp.; SmithKline Beecham; NY Stock Exchange. Chm., Council on Competitiveness. Mem., Council on For. Relations. Member: Bd of Dirs, NY City Ballet; Bd, Catalyst. Trustee, Nat. Planning Assoc.; Member, Board of Trustees: Carnegie Mellon Univ. (Mem., Business Adv. Council, Grad. Sch. of Indust. Admin); Worcester Polytechnic Inst., Mass. *Recreations:* horse riding, tennis.

ALLAIS, Prof. Maurice; Commandeur de la Légion d'honneur, 1989; Officier des Palmes académiques, 1949; Chevalier de l'économie nationale, 1962; French economist and engineer; *b* 31 May 1911; *s* of Maurice Allais and Louise (*née* Caubet); *m* 1960, Jacqueline Bouteloup; one *d. Educ:* Lycée Lakanal à Sceaux; Lycée Louis-le-Grand; Ecole Polytechnique; Ecole Nationale Supérieure des Mines de Paris. Engineer, Dept of Mines and Quarries, Nantes, 1937–43; Dir, Bureau de Documentation Minière, 1943–48; Prof. of Economic Analysis, Ecole Nationale Supérieure des Mines de Paris, 1944–88; Dir, Centre for Economic Analysis, 1946–; Prof. of Economic Theory, Inst. of Statistics, Univ. of Paris, 1947–68; research in economics, 1948–; Dir of Res., Centre National de la Recherche Scientifique, 1954–80; Prof., Graduate Inst. of Internat. Studies, Geneva, 1967–70; Dir, Clément Juglar Centre of Monetary Analysis, Univ of Paris, 1970–85. Fellow: Operations Res. Soc., 1958; Internat. Soc. of Econometrics, 1949. Mem. de l'Académie des Sciences Morales et Politiques, 1990; Hon. Mem., Amer. Econ. Assoc., 1976; Associate Foreign Member: US Nat. Acad. of Scis, 1989; Accademia Nazionale dei Lincei, Rome, 1991. Dr *hc* Univ. of Groningen, 1964; Univ. of Mons, 1992; Amer. Univ. of Paris, 1992. Prizes from: L'Académie des Sciences, 1933; L'Académie des Sciences Morales et Politiques, 1954, 1959, 1983, 1984. Gravity Res. Foundn, 1959; also Lanchester Prize, Amer. Economic Assoc., 1958; Prix Galabert, 1959; Grand Prix André Arnoux, 1968; Gold Medal, Centre National de la Recherche Scientifique, 1978; Nobel Prize for Economics, 1988. *Publications* include: A la recherche d'une discipline économique, 1943, 3rd edn 1992; Abondance ou misère, 1946; Economie et Intérêt, 1947, 2nd edn 1992; Les fondements comptables de la macroéconomique, 1954; Manifeste pour une société libre, 1959; L'Europe unie, route de la prosperité, 1960; The Role of Capital in Economic Development, 1963; Growth without Inflation, 1968; Les théories de l'équilibre économique général et de l'efficacité maximale, 1971; Inequality and Civilization, 1973; L'impôt sur le capital et la réforme monétaire, 1977, 2nd edn 1988; La théorie générale des surplus, 1980, 2nd edn 1989; Frequency, Probability and Chance, 1982; Determination of Cardinal Utility, 1985; Les conditions monétaires d'une économie de marché, 1987; Autoportraits, 1989; Pour l'indexation, 1990; Pour la réforme de la fiscalité, 1990; L'Europe face à son avenir, que faire, 1991; Erreurs et impasses de la construction européenne, 1992. *Address:* (office) 60 boulevard Saint Michel, 75006 Paris, France.

ALLAM, Peter John; Architect Principal in private practice of Peter Allam, Chartered Architect, Dollar, 1964–68, 1971–78 and since 1981; *b* 17 June 1927; *er s* of late Leslie Francis Allam and Annette Farquharson (*née* Lawson); *m* 1961, Pamela Mackie Haynes; two *d. Educ:* Royal High Sch., Edinburgh; Glasgow Sch. of Architecture. War service, 1944–48, Far East; commnd in Seaforth Highlanders, 1946. Architectural trng, 1948–53. Bahrain Petroleum Co., Engrg Div., 1954–55; Asst in private architectural practices, 1956–64; Partner in private practice of Haswell-Smith & Partners, Edinburgh, 1978–79; Director, Saltire Soc., 1968–70; Dir of Sales, Smith & Wellstood Ltd, Manfg Ironfounders, 1979–81. ARIBA 1964; FRIAS 1985 (Associate, 1964). Red Cross Speaker on Internat. Humanitarian Law. Advanced Driving Observer. *Recreations:* study and practice of conservation, both architectural and natural; music, painting. *Address:* Seberham Flat, 1 Bridge Street, Dollar, Clackmannanshire FK14 7DF. *T:* Dollar (01259) 742973.

ALLAN; *see* Havelock-Allan.

ALLAN, Alexander Claud Stuart; Principal Private Secretary to the Prime Minister, since 1992; *b* 9 Feb. 1951; *s* of Lord Allan of Kilmahew, DSO, OBE and of Maureen (*née* Stuart Clark); *m* 1978, Katie Christine Clemson. *Educ:* Harrow Sch.; Clare College, Cambridge; University College London (MSc). HM Customs and Excise, 1973–76; HM Treasury, 1976–; secondments in Australia, 1983–84; Principal Private Sec. to Chancellor of the Exchequer, 1986–89; Under Sec. (Internat. Finance), 1989–90; Under Sec. (Gen. Expenditure Policy Gp), 1990–92. *Recreations:* Grateful Dead music, sailing, computers. *Address:* c/o 10 Downing Street, SW1A 2AA. *Club:* Royal Ocean Racing.

ALLAN, Andrew Norman; Chief Executive, Carlton UK Television, since 1994; *b* 26 Sept. 1943; *s* of Andrew Allan and Elizabeth (*née* Davison); *m* 1978, Joanna Forrest; two *s* one *d*, and two *d* of a former marriage. *Educ:* Birmingham Univ. (BA). Presenter, ABC Television, 1965–66; Producer: Thames Television, 1966–69; ITN, 1970; Thames TV, 1971–75; Head of News, Thames TV, 1976–78; Tyne Tees Television: Dir of Progs, 1978–83; Dep. Man. Dir, 1982–83; Man. Dir, 1983–84; Dir of Progs, Central Indep. TV, 1984–90; Managing Director: Central Broadcasting, 1990–93; Central Indep. TV, 1993–94. *Recreations:* reading, dining. *Address:* Carlton UK Television, 101 St Martin's Lane, WC2N 4AZ. *T:* 0171–240 4000, *Fax:* 0171–240 4174.

ALLAN, (Charles) Lewis (Cuthbert), MA, CEng, FICE, FIEE, FIMgt; Chairman, South of Scotland Electricity Board, 1967–73 (Deputy Chairman, 1964–67); Member, North of Scotland Hydro-Electric Board, 1967–73; *b* 22 July 1911; *s* of Charles W. Allan, Edinburgh, and Isabella H. Young; *m* 1938, Kathleen Mary Robinson, Chesterfield, Derbyshire; one *s* three *d. Educ:* Merchiston Castle School, Edinburgh; Pembroke College, Cambridge (Mechanical Sciences Tripos). Bruce Peebles & Co. Ltd, Edinburgh, 1933–35; Balfour Beatty & Co. Ltd, 1935–38; Central Electricity Board, 1938–41; Ipswich Corp. Electric Supply and Transport Dept, 1941–44; North of Scotland Hydro-Electric Board, 1944–63 (Chief Electrical and Mechanical Engineer, 1954–63). *Publications:* articles in the electrical technical press and for World Power Conference. *Recreations:* gardening, walking, fishing, piping, Church work. *Address:* 19 Bonaly Avenue, Colinton, Edinburgh EH13 0ET.

ALLAN, Christopher David; QC 1995; a Recorder, since 1993; *b* 5 April 1952; *s* of Herbert Roy Allan and Joan (*née* Womersly); *m* 1977, Lynne Margaret Hosking; one *s* three *d. Educ:* Teignmouth Grammar Sch.; Manchester Univ. (LLB). Called to the Bar, Gray's Inn, 1974; Mem., Northern Circuit, 1975–. *Recreations:* tennis, theatre, walking. *Address:* 25 Byrom Street, Manchester M3 4PF. *T:* 0161–834 5238; 61 Fleet Street, EC4Y 1JU.

ALLAN, Colin Faulds, CB 1976; Chief Planning Inspector (Director of Planning Inspectorate), Department of the Environment, 1971–78, retired; *b* Newcastle upon Tyne, 1917; *s* of late Jack Stanley and Ruth Allan; *m* 1941, Aurea, 2nd *d* of Algernon Noble, Hexham; one *s* one *d. Educ:* Royal Grammar Sch., Newcastle upon Tyne; King's Coll. (Newcastle), Durham Univ. DipArch, ARIBA, DipTP (Distinction), FRTPI. Capt., RA, 1940–45; served in Iraq, India, Burma (despatches). Chief Asst to Dr Thomas Sharp, CBE, PPTPI, Planning Consultant, 1945–47; Area Planning Officer, Cumberland and Staffs CC, 1947–57; joined Housing and Planning Inspectorate, 1957; Chief Housing and Planning Inspector, DoE (formerly Min. of Housing and Local Govt), 1967–71. *Recreations:* painting, bird-watching, eighteenth-century wineglasses. *Address:* Fieldfares, Chinthurst Lane, Shalford, Guildford, Surrey GU4 8JR. *T:* Guildford (01483) 61528.

ALLAN, Diana Rosemary, (Mrs R. B. Allan); *see* Cotton, D. R.

ALLAN, Douglas; *see* Allan, J. D.

ALLAN, George Alexander, MA; Headmaster, Robert Gordon's College, Aberdeen, since 1978; *b* 3 Feb. 1936; *s* of William Allan and Janet Peters (*née* Watt); *m* 1962, Anne Violet Veevers; two *s. Educ:* Daniel Stewart's Coll., Edinburgh; Edinburgh Univ. (MA 1st Cl. Hons Classics; Bruce of Grangehill Scholar, 1957). Classics Master, Glasgow Acad., 1958–60; Daniel Stewart's College: Classics Master, 1960–63; Head of Classics, 1963–73; Housemaster, 1966–73; Schoolmaster Fellow, Corpus Christi Coll., Cambridge, 1972; Dep. Headmaster, Robert Gordon's Coll., 1973–77. Headmasters' Conference: Sec., 1980–86, Chm., 1988, 1989, Scottish Div.; Mem. Cttee, 1982, 1983; Mem., ISIS Scotland Cttee, 1984–93; Council Mem., Scottish Council of Indep. Schs, 1988–. Governor, Welbeck Coll., 1980–89. *Recreations:* golf, gardening, music. *Address:* 24 Woodend Road, Aberdeen AB2 6YH. *T:* Aberdeen (01224) 321733. *Clubs:* East India, Devonshire Sports and Public Schools; Royal Northern & University (Aberdeen).

ALLAN, Rt. Rev. Hugh James Pearson, DD; Assistant Bishop of Nova Scotia, 1991–94; *b* 7 Aug. 1928; *s* of Hugh Blomfield Allan and Agnes Dorothy (*née* Pearson); *m* 1955, Beverley Edith Baker; one *s* three *d. Educ:* St John's Coll., Univ. of Manitoba (LTh 1955, BA 1957). Deacon 1954, priest 1955; Assistant: St Aidan's, Winnipeg, 1954; All Saints, Winnipeg, 1955; Missionary, Peguis Indian Reserve, 1956–60; Rector, St Mark's, Winnipeg, 1960–68; Hon. Canon, Diocese of Rupert's Land, 1967; Rector, St Stephen's Swift Current, Sask., 1968–70; Rural Dean of Cypress, 1968–70; Dean of Qu'Appelle and Rector of St Paul's Cathedral, Regina, Sask., 1970–74; Bishop of Keewatin, 1974–91. Hon. DD, St John's Coll., Univ. of Manitoba, 1974. *Recreations:* ornithology, boating. *Address:* #16–120 Ulster Street, Winnipeg, MB R3T 3A2, Canada.

ALLAN, Ian, OBE 1995; Chairman, Ian Allan Group Ltd, since 1962; *b* 29 June 1922; *s* of George A. T. Allan, OBE, and Mary Louise (*née* Barnes); *m* 1947, Mollie Eileen (*née* Franklin); two *s. Educ:* St Paul's Sch. Joined Southern Railway Co., 1939. Founded Ian Allan Ltd, Publishers, 1945; other cos co-ordinated into Ian Allan Group Ltd, 1962. Chm., Dart Valley Light Railway PLC, 1976–87. Governor, Christ's Hosp., 1944–, Almoner, 1980–89; Chm., King Edward's Sch., Witley, 1983– (Governor, 1975–); Treas., Bridewell Royal Hosp. 1983–. Vice Pres., Transport Trust, 1979–; Mem., Transport Users Consultative Cttee for London, 1982–84; Chm., Assoc. of Indep. Rlys, 1987–. Freeman, City of London, 1986. FCIT 1992. *Publications:* compiled and edited many books on railways and transport subjects, 1939–. *Recreations:* swimming, touring, miniature railways. *Address:* Terminal House, Shepperton TW17 8AS. *T:* Walton-on-Thames (01932) 228950; The Jetty, Middleton-on-Sea, Bognor Regis, W Sussex PO22 7TS. *T:* Middleton-on-Sea (01243) 693378.

ALLAN, James Nicholas, CMG 1989; CBE 1976; HM Diplomatic Service, retired; *b* 22 May 1932; *s* of late Morris Edward Allan and Joan Bach; *m* 1961, Helena Susara Crouse; one *s* one *d. Educ:* Gresham's Sch.; London Sch. of Economics. HM Forces, 1950–53. Asst Principal, CRO, 1956–58; Third, later Second Sec., Cape Town/Pretoria, 1958–59; Private Sec. to Parly Under-Sec., 1959–61; First Secretary: Freetown, 1961–64; Nicosia, 1964; CRO, later FCO, 1964–68; Head of Chancery, Peking, 1969–71; Luxembourg, 1971–73; Counsellor, seconded to Northern Ireland Office, Belfast, 1973–75; Counsellor, FCO, 1976; Head of Overseas Inf. Dept., FCO, 1978–81 (Governor's Staff, Salisbury, Dec. 1979–March 1980); High Comr in Mauritius, 1981–85, concurrently Ambassador (non-resident) to the Comoros, 1984–85; Ambassador to Mozambique, 1986–89; Sen. Directing Staff, RCDS, 1989–92. Mem., Commonwealth Observer Gp, S African elecns, 1994. *Address:* c/o Foreign and Commonwealth Office, SW1A 2AH. *Club:* Athenæum.

ALLAN, Dr James Wilson; Keeper of Eastern Art, Ashmolean Museum, Oxford, since 1991; Fellow of St Cross College, Oxford, since 1990; *b* 5 May 1945; *s* of John Bellerby Allan and Evelyn Mary Allan; *m* 1970, Jennifer Robin Hawksworth; two *s* two *d. Educ:* Marlborough Coll.; St Edmund Hall, Oxford (MA 1966; DPhil 1976). Eastern Art Department, Ashmolean Museum: Asst Keeper, 1966–88; Sen. Asst Keeper, 1988–91. *Publications:* Medieval Middle Eastern Pottery, 1971; Persian Metal Technology 700–1300 AD, 1978; Islamic Metalwork: the Nuhad Es-Said Collection, 1982; Nishapur: metalwork of the early Islamic period, 1982; Metalwork of the Islamic World: the Aron Collection, 1986; (ed) Creswell: A Short Account of Early Muslim Architecture, 1989. *Recreations:* music, ornithology, walking, travel. *Address:* Ashmolean Museum, Oxford OX1 2PH. *T:* Oxford (01865) 278068.

ALLAN, John Clifford, RCNC; Director, Manpower, Dockyards, 1975–79; *b* 3 Feb. 1920; *s* of James Arthur and Mary Alice Allan; *m* 1947, Dorothy Mary (*née* Dossett); two *d. Educ:* Royal Naval Coll., Greenwich. Entered Royal Corps of Naval Constructors, 1945; service at HM Dockyards: Portsmouth, Chatham, Devonport, Gibraltar, Singapore, 1950–75; Chief Constructor, Chief Executive Dockyard HQ, 1967–69, Asst Dir, 1969, Dir, 1975. *Recreations:* painting, tennis, squash (Past Pres., Lansdown Lawn Tennis & Squash Racquets Club). *Address:* 21 Henrietta Street, Bath, Avon BA2 6LP. *T:* Bath (01225) 446570.

ALLAN, (John) Douglas; Sheriff of South Strathclyde, Dumfries and Galloway at Lanark, since 1988; *b* 2 Oct. 1941; *s* of Robert Taylor Allan and late Christina Helen Blythe Reid or Allan; *m* 1966, Helen Elizabeth Jean Aiton or Allan; one *s* one *d. Educ:* George Watson's Coll.; Edinburgh Univ. (BL); Napier Coll., Edinburgh (DMS); FBIM. Solicitor and Notary Public. Solicitor, 1963–67; Depute Procurator Fiscal, 1967–71; Sen. Legal Asst, Crown Office, 1971–76; Asst Procurator Fiscal, Glasgow, 1976–77; Sen. Asst Procurator Fiscal, Glasgow, 1978–79; Asst Solicitor, Crown Office, 1979–83; Regl Procurator Fiscal for Lothian and Borders and Procurator Fiscal for Edinburgh, 1983–88. *Recreations:* youth work, church work, walking. *Address:* Sheriff Court, Hope Street, Lanark ML11 7NE; Minard, 80 Greenbank Crescent, Edinburgh EH10 5SW. *T:* 0131–447 2593.

ALLAN, John Murray; Chief Executive, Ocean Group plc, since 1994; *b* 20 Aug. 1948; *s* of Archibald John and Anna Allan; *m* 1970, Ewa Anna Gaczol; two *d. Educ:* Edinburgh Univ. (BSc Hons Mathematical Sci.). Brand Manager, Lever Bros, 1970–73; Mkting

Manager, Bristol Myers, 1973–77; Fine Fare: Mkting Dir, 1977–83; Dir, 1980; Mkting and Buying Dir, 1983–84; Dir and Gen. Manager, 1984–85; BET: Divl Chm., 1985–87; Dir, 1987–94. FInstD. Recreations: reading, conversation, history. *Address:* Ocean Group plc, Ocean House, The Ring, Bracknell, Berks RG12 1AN. *T:* Bracknell (01344) 30200. *Club:* Caledonian.

ALLAN, Lewis; *see* Allan, C. L. C.

ALLAN, Richard Andrew; Head of Local and Urban Transport Directorate, Department of Transport, since 1994; *b* 28 Feb. 1948; *s* of Kenneth and Mary Allan; *m* 1975, Katharine Mary Tait; one *s* one *d*. *Educ:* Bolton Sch.; Balliol Coll., Oxford (MA Mod. Hist.). VSO, Nigeria, 1970. Asst Principal, DTI, 1970; Asst British Trade Comr, Hong Kong, 1973; Department of Industry: Private Sec. to Perm. Sec., 1974–75; Principal, 1975–79; First Sec. (Civil Aviation and Shipping), Washington, 1980–84; Department of Transport: Asst Sec., 1984; Principal Private Sec. to Sec. of State for Transport, 1985–87; Under Sec., 1988; seconded to BRB, 1988–90; Dir of Personnel, 1990–94. *Recreations:* choral singing, theatre, walking. *Address:* Department of Transport, 2 Marsham Street, SW1P 3EB.

ALLAN, William Roderick Buchanan; formerly Arts Consultant to United Technologies Corporation, working with Tate Gallery, National Portrait Gallery and National Maritime Museum; *b* 11 Sept. 1945; *s* of James Buchanan Allan and Mildred Pattenden; *m* 1973, Gillian Gail Colgan; two *s*. *Educ:* Stowe; Trinity Coll., Cambridge (MA Hons History, 1970). Joined staff of The Connoisseur, 1972, Editor 1976–80; Editorial Consultant to Ommific, 1980–83. Author of seven radio plays with nineteenth century historical themes. *Publications:* contrib. to several books dealing with British history; contrib. to History Today, The Connoisseur, and Antique Collector. *Recreations:* military history, cooking. *Address:* 52 Jamieson House, Edgar Road, Hounslow, Middlesex TW3 8NB.

ALLANBRIDGE, Hon. Lord; William Ian Stewart; a Senator of the College of Justice in Scotland, since 1977; *b* 8 Nov. 1925; *s* of late John Stewart, FRIBA, and Mrs Maysie Shepherd Service or Stewart, Drimfearn, Bridge of Allan; *m* 1955, Naomi Joan Douglas, *d* of late Sir James Boyd Douglas, CBE, and of Lady Douglas, Barstibly, Castle Douglas; one *s* one *d*. *Educ:* Loretto; Glasgow and Edinburgh Univs. Sub-Lt, RNVR, 1944–46. Called to the Bar, 1951; QC (Scot.) 1965; Advocate-Depute, 1959–64; Mem., Criminal Injuries Compensation Bd, 1969–70; Home Advocate-Depute, 1970–72; Solicitor-General for Scotland, 1972–74; Temp. Sheriff-Principal of Dumfries and Galloway, Apr.-Dec. 1974. Mem., Criminal Injuries Compensation Bd, 1976–77. *Address:* 60 Northumberland Street, Edinburgh EH3 6JE. *T:* 0131–556 2823. *Club:* New (Edinburgh).

ALLARD, General Jean Victor, CC (Canada) 1968; CBE 1946; DSO 1943 (Bars 1944, 1945); ED 1946; CD 1958; Chief of Canadian Defence Staff, 1966–69; Representative of the Province of Quebec in New York, Sept. 1969–June 1970; *b* Nicolet, PQ, 12 June 1913; *s* of late Ernest Allard and Victorine Trudel; *m* 1939, Simone, *d* of Gustave Piche, OBE; two *d*. *Educ:* St Laurent Coll., Montreal; St Jerome Coll., Kitchener, Ont. Joined Three Rivers Regt, 1933; Capt., 1938; Major, 1939; War of 1939–45: Co. of London Yeomanry, 1940–41; Canadian Army Staff Coll., Kingston, 1941–42 (Instructor, 1942); 5th Canadian Armoured Div.; second in command: Régt de la Chaudière; Royal 22e Regt, 1943 (Italy); Lt-Col 1944; CO Royal 22e Regt; Brig. 1945; Comd 6th Canadian Infantry Brigade, 1945 (Holland); Military Attaché Canadian Embassy, Moscow, 1945–48; Comd Eastern Quebec Area, 1948–50; idc 1951; Vice Quarter-Master Gen., Canada, 1952; Comdr, 25th Canadian Infantry Brigade Group, in Korea, 1953; Comdr 3rd Canadian Infantry Brigade, 1954; Comd Eastern Quebec Area, 1956; Maj.-Gen. 1958; Vice Chief of the General Staff, Canada, 1958; Comdr 4th Division, BAOR, 1961–63 (first Canadian to command a British Div.); Maj. Gen. Survival, Ottawa, 1963; Lt-Gen. 1964; Chief of Operational Readiness, Canada, 1964–65; Comdr, Mobile Command, Canada, Oct. 1965–June 1966; General, 1966; Col Comdt, 12 Regt Blindé du Canada; Col, Royal 22e Regt, 1985. Member: Royal 22e Regt Assoc.; La Régie du 22e; Royal Canadian Air Force Assoc.; Royal Canadian Naval Service Assoc.; Cercle Universitaire d'Ottawa; Chm. Bd of Governors, Ottawa Univ., 1966–69, Member Bd, 1969–. Hon. DSS Laval, 1958; Hon. LLD: Ottawa, 1959; St Thomas, 1966; St Mary's, Halifax, 1969, Hon. DScMil RMC Canada, 1970. FRSA. Bronze Lion (Netherlands), 1945; Légion d'Honneur and Croix de Guerre (France), 1945; Legion of Merit (US), 1954. Kt of Magistral Grace, Sovereign and Military Order of Malta, 1967. *Publication:* Mémoires, 1985. *Recreation:* music. *Address:* 3265 Boulevard du Carmel, Trois-Rivieres, Quebec, Canada.

ALLARDICE, William Arthur Llewellyn; His Honour Judge Allardice; DL; a Circuit Judge since 1972 (Midland and Oxford Circuit); *b* 18 Dec. 1924; *s* of late W. C. Allardice, MD, FRCSEd, JP, and late Constance Winifred Allardice; *m* 1956, Jennifer Ann, *d* of late G. H. Jackson; one *s* one *d*. *Educ:* Stonyhurst Coll.; University Coll., Oxford (MA). Open Schol., Classics, 1942; joined Rifle Bde, 1943, commnd 1944; served with 52nd LI, Europe and Palestine, 1945; Oxford, 1946–48; called to Bar, Lincoln's Inn, 1950; practised Oxford Circuit, 1950–71. Chm., Trustees, William Salt Liby, 1990–. DL Staffs, 1980. *Recreations:* local history, matters equestrian. *Address:* Stafford Crown and County Courts, Stafford ST18 2QQ. *T:* Stafford (01785) 55217.

ALLASON, Lt-Col James Harry, OBE 1953; *b* 6 Sept. 1912; *s* of late Brigadier-General Walter Allason, DSO; *m* 1946, Nuala Elveen (marr. diss. 1974), *d* of late J. A. McArevey, Foxrock, Co. Dublin; two *s*. *Educ:* Haileybury; RMA, Woolwich. Commissioned RA, 1932; transferred 3rd DG, 1937; War Service India and Burma, 1939–44; retired 1953. Member Kensington Borough Council, 1956–65. Contested (C) Hackney Central, General Election, 1955; MP (C) Hemel Hempstead, 1959–Sept. 1974; PPS to Sec. of State for War, 1960–64. *Address:* 82 Ebury Mews, SW1W 9NX. *T:* 0171–730 1576. *Clubs:* White's; Royal Yacht Squadron.

See also R. W. S. Allason.

ALLASON, Rupert William Simon; MP (C) Torbay, since 1987; European Editor, Intelligence Quarterly, since 1985; *b* 8 Nov. 1951; *s* of Lt-Col J. H. Allason, *qv*; *m* 1979, Nicole Jane, *y d* of late M. L. Van Moppes; one *s* one *d*. *Educ:* Downside; Grenoble Univ.; London Univ. (external). Special Constable, 1975–82. BBC TV, 1978–82. Contested (C): Kettering, 1979; Battersea, 1983. *Publications:* The Branch: A History of the Metropolitan Police Special Branch 1883–1983, 1983; *as Nigel West:* non-fiction: Spy! (with Richard Deacon), 1980; MI5: British Security Service Operations 1909–45, 1981; A Matter of Trust: MI5 1945–72, 1982; MI6: British Secret Intelligence Service Operations 1909–45, 1983; Unreliable Witnesses: espionage myths of World War II, 1984; Garbo (with Juan Pujol), 1985; GCHQ: The Secret Wireless War, 1986; Molehunt, 1987; The Friends: Britain's post-war secret intelligence operations, 1988; Games of Intelligence, 1989; Seven Spies Who Changed the World, 1991; Secret War, 1992; The Illegals, 1993; (ed) Faber Book of Espionage, 1993; fiction: The Blue List, 1989; Cuban Bluff, 1990; Murder in the Commons, 1992; Murder in the Lords, 1994. *Recreation:* sailing close to the wind. *Address:* c/o House of Commons, SW1A 0AA. *Clubs:* White's, Special Forces; Royal Yacht Squadron (Cowes); Royal Torbay Yacht Club (Torquay).

ALLAUN, Frank; *b* 27 Feb. 1913; *s* of Harry and Hannah Allaun; *m* 1st, 1941, Lilian Ball (*d* 1986); one *s* one *d*; 2nd, 1989, Millie Bobker. *Educ:* Manchester Grammar Sch. BA (Com); ACA. Town Hall Correspondent, and later Industrial Correspondent, Manchester Evening News; Northern Industrial Correspondent, Daily Herald; Editor, Labour's Northern Voice, 1951–67. Mem., NUJ; formerly Mem. AEU and Shop Assistants' Union; Pres., Labour Action for Peace, 1965–; Vice-Pres., Campaign for Nuclear Disarmament, 1983–; helped organise first Aldermaston march. MP (Lab) East Salford, 1955–83; PPS to the Secretary of State for the Colonies, Oct. 1964–March 1965, resigned. Mem., Labour Party National Executive, 1967–83, Dep. Chm., 1977–78, Chm., 1978–79. *Publications:* Stop the H Bomb Race, 1959; Heartbreak Housing, 1966; Your Trade Union and You, 1950; No Place Like Home, 1972; The Wasted '30 Billions, 1975; Questions and Answers on Nuclear Weapons, 1981; Spreading the News: a guide to media reform, 1989; The Struggle for Peace, 1992; numerous broadcasts. *Recreations:* walking, swimming. *Address:* 11 Eastleigh Road, Prestwich, Manchester M25 0BQ. *T:* 0161–740 5085.

ALLAWAY, Percy Albert, CBE 1973; FEng; Director, EMI Ltd, 1965–81; Chairman, EMI Electronics Ltd, 1968–81; Member, Executive Management Board, THORN EMI Ltd, 1980–81, Consultant, 1981–82; *b* 22 Aug. 1915; *s* of Albert Edward Allaway and Frances Beatrice (*née* Rogers); *m* 1959, Margaret Lilian Petyt. *Educ:* Southall Technical College. FEng 1980, FIProdE, FIEE, FIQA. Trained EMI Ltd, 1930–35, returned 1940; Man. Dir, 1961–81, Chm., 1969–81, EMI Electronics Ltd; Chairman: EMI-Varian Ltd, 1969–81; EMI-MEC Ltd, 1968–81; Director: Nuclear Enterprises Ltd, 1961–81; SE Labs (EMI) Ltd, 1967–81. Pres., EEA, 1969–70 (former Mem. Council). Chm., Defence Industries Quality Assurance Panel, 1971–78; Past Chm. and Hon. Mem., NCQR; Member: Nat. Electronics Council, 1965–80; Raby Cttee, 1968–69; Parly and Scientific Cttee, 1976–82; Pres., IERE, 1975; a Vice-Pres., and Mem. Council, IQA; Member: Bd and Exec. Cttee, CEI, 1974–78 (Vice-Chm., 1979–80, Chm., 1980–81); Design Council, 1978–80; PO Engrg Adv. Cttee, 1977–81, British Telecom Engrg Adv. Cttee, 1981–82. Mem., Court and Council, Brunel Univ., 1976–82. Liveryman, 1978, and Mem. Court, 1981–86, Worshipful Co. of Scientific Instrument Makers. FRSA. DTech (hc) Brunel, 1973. *Address:* Kroller, 54 Howards Wood Drive, Gerrards Cross, Bucks SL9 7HW. *T:* Gerrards Cross (01753) 885028.

ALLCHIN, Rev. Canon Arthur Macdonald; Director, St Theosevia Centre for Christian Spirituality, Oxford, since 1987; *b* 20 April 1930; *s* of late Dr Frank Macdonald Allchin and Louise Maude Allchin. *Educ:* Westminster Sch.; Christ Church, Oxford (BLitt, MA); Cuddesdon Coll., Oxford. Curate, St Mary Abbots, Kensington, 1956–60; Librarian, Pusey House, Oxford, 1960–69; Warden, Community of Sisters of Love of God, Oxford, 1967–; Res. Canon of Canterbury, 1973–87, Hon. Canon, 1988–. Visiting Lecturer: General Theological Seminary, NY, 1967 and 1968; Catholic Theological Faculty, Lyons, 1980; Trinity Inst., NY, 1983; Vis. Prof., Nashotah House, Wisconsin, 1984. Hon. Prof., UCNW, Bangor, 1992. Editor, Sobornost, 1960–77; Jt Editor, Christian, 1975–80. Hon. DD: Bucharest Theol Inst., 1977; Nashotah House, 1985; Aarhus, 1992; Wales, 1993. *Publications:* The Silent Rebellion, 1958; The Spirit and the Word, 1963; (with J. Coulson) The Rediscovery of Newman, 1967; Ann Griffiths, 1976; The World is a Wedding, 1978; The Kingdom of Love and Knowledge, 1979; The Dynamic of Tradition, 1981; A Taste of Liberty, 1982; The Joy of All Creation, 1984, 2nd edn 1993; (with E. de Waal) Threshold of Light, 1986; Participation in God, 1988; The Heart of Compassion, 1989; Landscapes of Glory, 1989; Praise Above All, 1991; (ed with D. Jasper and contrib.) Heritage and Prophecy, 1993; contrib. Studia Liturgica, Irenikon, Theology, Eastern Churches Review, Worship, One in Christ, Planet, Logos. *Recreations:* music, poetry, walking in hill country. *Address:* 1 Trem yr Wyddfa, Bangor LL57 2ER. *T:* Bangor (01248) 353744.

See also F. R. Allchin.

ALLCHIN, Frank Raymond, PhD; FBA 1981; Fellow of Churchill College, since 1963, and Reader in Indian Studies, 1972–90, University of Cambridge; Reader Emeritus, since 1990; *b* 9 July 1923; *s* of late Frank MacDonald Allchin and Louise Maude Wright; *m* 1951, Bridget Gordon; one *s* one *d*. *Educ:* Westminster Sch.; Regent Street Polytechnic; Sch. of Oriental and African Studies, London Univ. (BA, PhD 1954), MA Cantab. Lectr in Indian Archaeology, SOAS, 1954–59; Univ. Lectr in Indian Studies, Cambridge, 1959–72. Jt Dir, Cambridge Univ. (British) Archaeol Mission to Pakistan, 1975–92. Treas., Ancient India and Iran Trust, 1978–; Vice Chm., British Assoc. for Conservation of Cultural Heritage of Sri Lanka, 1982–91; Dir, British Anuradhapura Project, Sri Lanka, 1989–. Consultant: UNESCO, 1969, 1972, 1975; UNDP, 1971. *Publications:* Piklihal Excavations, 1960; Utnur Excavations, 1961; Neolithic Cattle Keepers of South India, 1963; Kavitāvalī, 1964; The Petition to Rām, 1966; (with B. Allchin) Birth of Indian Civilization, 1968; (with N. Hammond) The Archaeology of Afghanistan, 1978; (with D. K. Chakrabarti) Sourcebook of Indian Archaeology, vol. 1, 1979; (with B. Allchin) The Rise of Civilization in India and Pakistan, 1982; contribs to learned journals. *Recreations:* gardening, walking. *Address:* 2 Shepreth Road, Barrington, Cambridge CB2 5SB. *T:* Cambridge (01223) 870494. *Clubs:* Royal Over-Seas League; Indian International Centre (New Delhi).

See also Rev. Canon A. M. Allchin.

ALLCOCK, Stephen James; QC 1993; *b* 29 Jan. 1952; *s* of James Allcock and Pamela Eve Allcock. *Educ:* Bristol Grammar Sch.; Jesus Coll., Cambridge (BA). Called to the Bar, Gray's Inn, 1975; private practice, 1977–. *Recreations:* motor cars, business, stock market, godfatherhood. *Club:* Groucho.

ALLDAY, Coningsby, CBE 1971; BSc (Hons); Chairman and Chief Executive, British Nuclear Fuels plc, 1983–86 (Managing Director, 1971–83); Director, Allday Nuclear Consultants Ltd, since 1986; *b* 21 Nov. 1920; *s* of late Esca and Margaret Allday; *m* 1st, 1945, Iris Helena (Bobbin) Adams (*d* 1990); one *s* one *d*; 2nd, 1993, Rosalind Roberts. *Educ:* Solihull Sch.; BSc (Hons) Chemistry, London. CEng, FIChemE 1979; CIMgt (CBIM 1984). ICI, 1939–59; UKAEA, 1959–71: Chief Chemist, Technical Dir, Commercial Dir, Dep. Man. Dir; Mem. UKAEA, 1976–86. Chairman, NIMTECH NW, 1986–90; Director: North Region, National Westminster Bank, 1985–92; Sonomatic Ltd, 1988–90. FRSA. Hon. DSc Salford, 1985. Chevalier, Légion d'Honneur, 1983. *Address:* 54 Goughs Lane, Knutsford, Cheshire WA16 8QN.

ALLDIS, Air Cdre Cecil Anderson, CBE 1962; DFC 1941; AFC 1956; RAF (retd); *b* 28 Sept. 1918; 2nd *s* of John Henry and Margaret Wright Alldis, Birkenhead; *m* 1942, Jeanette Claire Tarrant, *d* of Albert Edward Collingwood and Aida Mary Tarrant, Johannesburg; no *c*. *Educ:* Birkenhead Institute; Emmanuel Coll., Cambridge (MA). Served War, 1939–45 (despatches, DFC): Pilot, Wing Comdr, RAF, Bomber Command. Asst Air Attaché, Moscow, 1947–49; Flying and Staff appts, RAF, 1949–59; Dir of Administrative Plans, Air Ministry, 1959–62; Air Attaché, Bonn, 1963–66. Retd from RAF and entered Home Civil Service, 1966; MoD, 1966–69; seconded to HM Diplomatic Service, 1969; Counsellor (Defence Supply), HM Embassy, Bonn, 1969–80; retired from Home Civil Service, 1980. Sec. Gen., The Air League, 1982–90. *Recreations:* golf, fishing, beagling. *Address:* Tudor Cottage, Oxshott Way, Cobham, Surrey KT11 2RU. *T:* Cobham (01932) 866092. *Club:* Naval and Military.

ALLDIS, John; conductor; Chorus Master, Hallé Choir, since 1992; *b* 10 Aug. 1929; *s* of W. J. and N. Alldis; *m* 1960, Ursula Margaret Mason; two *s*. *Educ:* Felsted School; King's Coll., Cambridge (MA). ARCO. Formed John Alldis Choir, 1962; Founder and Conductor, London Symphony Chorus, 1966–69; Conductor, London Philharmonic Choir, 1969–82; Joint Chief Conductor, Radio Denmark, 1971–77; Conductor, Groupe Vocal de France, 1979–83. Choral Prof., Guildhall Sch. of Music, 1966–79 (FGSM 1976); Music Consultant, Israel Chamber Choir (Cameran Singers), 1989–91. Mem., Vaughan Williams Trust, 1976–. Fellow, Westminster Choir Coll., Princeton, NJ, 1978. Chevalier des Arts et des Lettres (France), 1984. *Address:* 3 Wool Road, Wimbledon, SW20 0HN. *T:* 0181–946 4168.

ALLEN, family name of **Baron Allen of Abbeydale** and **Baron Croham.**

ALLEN OF ABBEYDALE, Baron *cr* 1976 (Life Peer), of the City of Sheffield; **Philip Allen,** GCB 1970 (KCB 1964; CB 1954); *b* 8 July 1912; *yr s* of late Arthur Allen and Louie Tipper, Sheffield; *m* 1938, Marjorie Brenda Coe. *Educ:* King Edward VII Sch., Sheffield; Queens' Coll., Cambridge (Whewell Schol. in Internat. Law, 1934; Hon. Fellow 1974). Entered Home Office, 1934; Offices of War Cabinet, 1943–44; Commonwealth Fellowship in USA, 1948–49; Deputy Chm. of Prison Commn for England and Wales, 1950–52; Asst Under Sec. of State, Home Office, 1952–55; Deputy Sec., Min. of Housing and Local Govt, 1955–60; Deputy Under-Sec. of State, Home Office, 1960–62; Second Sec., HM Treasury, 1963–66; Permanent Under-Sec. of State, Home Office, 1966–72. Chairman: Occupational Pensions Bd, 1973–78; Nat. Council of Social Service, 1973–77; Gaming Bd for GB, 1977–85 (Mem., 1975); Mencap, 1982–88. Member Royal Commissions: on Standards of Conduct in Public Life, 1974–76; on Civil Liability and Compensation for Personal Injury, 1973–78; Member: Security Commn, 1973–91; tribunal of inquiry into Crown Agents, 1978–82. Chief Counting Officer, EEC Referendum, 1975. Chm. Council, RHBNC, London Univ., 1985–92 (Visitor, 1992–). *Address:* Holly Lodge, Middle Hill, Englefield Green, Surrey TW20 0JP. *T:* Egham (01784) 432291.

ALLEN, Anthony John, CBE 1994; Chief Executive, National House Building Council, since 1994; *b* 7 Oct. 1939; *s* of late Raymond Houghton Allen and Elsie Zillah Allen; *m* 1st, 1964, Suzanne Myfanwy Davies; two *s*; 2nd, 1987, Helen Leah Graney; one *s*. *Educ:* Battersea Grammar Sch.; Univ. of Exeter (LLB 1961). Admitted Solicitor, 1964. Asst Solicitor: Hendon Bor. Council, 1964–65; Barnet Bor. Council, 1965; Watford Bor. Council, 1966–68; Asst Town Clerk, Coventry CBC, 1968–71; Asst. Chief Exec., Lewisham Bor. Council, 1971–72; Solicitor to the Council and Dep. Town Clerk, Southwark Bor. Council, 1972–76; Chief Exec., Hammersmith and Fulham Bor. Council, 1976–86; Chief Exec., and Clerk to Lieutenancy, Royal Co. of Berks, 1986–93. Non-exec. Dir, BSI, 1992–. Promoter and Dir, London Youth Games Ltd, 1979–. CIMgt 1992. *Publications:* (contrib.) Practical Corporate Planning, ed John Skitt, 1975. *Recreations:* golf, travel. *Address:* The Fifteenth, 7 Broadlands Close, Calcot Park, Reading, Berks RG3 5RP. *T:* Reading (01734) 427310.

ALLEN, His Honour Anthony Kenway, OBE 1946; a Circuit Judge, 1978–90; *b* 31 Oct. 1917; *s* of Charles Valentine Allen and Edith Kenway Allen; *m* 1975, Maureen Murtough. *Educ:* St George's Coll., Weybridge, Surrey; St John's Coll., Cambridge (BA Hons); Freiburg and Grenoble Univs. Served War, RAF Special Intelligence, 1939–45 (Wing Comdr). Called to the Bar, Inner Temple, 1947. *Recreations:* gardening, walking, music. *Address:* 73 Downswood, Epsom Downs, Surrey KT18 5UJ.

ALLEN, Arnold Millman, CBE 1977; Chairman, UKAEA, 1984–86; *b* 30 Dec. 1924; *s* of Wilfrid Millman and Edith Muriel Allen; *m* 1947, Beatrice Mary Whitaker; three *s* one *d*. *Educ:* Hackney Downs Sec. Sch.; Peterhouse, Cambridge (Scholar). Entered HM Treasury, 1945; Private Sec. to Financial Secretary, 1951–52; Principal, HM Treasury, 1953–55; Private Sec. to Chm. of UKAEA (Lord Plowden), 1956–57; HM Treasury, 1958; Dir of Personnel and Admin., Development and Engineering Group (subseq. Reactor Group), UKAEA, 1959–63; Gen. Manager, British Waterways Bd, 1963–68, and Mem. of Bd 1965–68; UKAEA: Personnel Officer, 1968–69; Personnel and Programmes Officer, 1970; Secretary and Mem. for Administration, 1971; Mem. for Finance and Admin, 1976–84; Dep. Chm., 1981–84; Chief Exec., 1982–84. *Address:* Duntish Cottage, Duntish, Dorchester, Dorset DT2 7DR. *T:* Buckland Newton (01300) 345258.

ALLEN, Charles Lamb, FCMA; Chief Executive: Granada Television, since 1992; London Weekend Television, since 1994; Deputy Chairman, GMTV, since 1994; *b* 4 Jan. 1957. *Educ:* Bell Coll., Hamilton. FCMA 1989. Accountant, British Steel, 1974–79; Dep. Audit Manager, Galaghers plc, 1979–82; Dir, Management Services, Grandmet Internat. Services Ltd, 1982–85; Gp Man. Dir, Compass Vending, Grandmet Innovations Ltd, 1986–87; Man. Dir, Grandmet Internat. Services Ltd, 1987–88; Man. Dir, Compass Gp Ltd, 1988–91; Chief Exec., Leisure Div., Granada Gp, 1991–92. Chairman: Granada Leisure, 1993–; Granada Services to Business, 1993–. Gov., RNCM, 1993–. *Recreations:* boating, ski-ing, swimming. *Address:* (office) London Television Centre, Upper Ground, SE1 9LT. *T:* 0171–261 3059; 44 Addison Road, W14 8JH. *T:* 0171–371 3695.

ALLEN, Colin Mervyn Gordon, CBE 1978; General Manager, Covent Garden Market Authority, 1967–89; *b* 17 April 1929; *s* of late Cecil G. Allen and late Gwendoline L. Allen (*née* Hutchinson); *m* 1953, Patricia, *d* of late William and late Doris Seddon; two *s* one *d*. *Educ:* King Edward's Sch., Bath. BA Open, 1985; MA London, 1986; MA London (Dist.), 1991. FCIPS. Naval Store Dept, Admiralty, 1948–56; National Coal Board: London HQ, 1956–59; Area Stores Officer, NE Div., 1959–64; Covent Garden Market Authority: Planning Officer, 1964–66; Asst Gen. Man., 1967. President: Assoc. of Wholesale Markets within Internat. Union of Local Authorities, 1972–78; IPS, 1982–83. Chm., Vauxhall Cross Amenity Trust, 1982–83. *Publications:* various papers on horticultural marketing and allied topics, and on supply and logistics matters. *Recreation:* archaeology. *Address:* 33 Butts Road, Horspath, Oxford OX33 1RJ. *T:* Oxford (01865) 872388.

ALLEN, Prof. Deryck Norman de Garrs; Professor of Applied Mathematics in the University of Sheffield, 1955–80, now Emeritus; Warden of Ranmoor House, 1968–82; *b* 22 April 1918; *s* of Leonard Lincoln Allen and Dorothy Allen (*née* Asplin). *Educ:* King Edward VII School, Sheffield; Christ Church, Oxford. Messrs Rolls Royce, 1940; Research Asst to Sir Richard Southwell, FRS, 1941; Lectr in Applied Mathematics at Imperial Coll., London, 1945; Visiting Prof. in Dept of Mechanical Engineering, Massachusetts Inst. of Technology, 1949; Reader in Applied Mathematics at Imperial Coll. in Univ. of London, 1950. Pro-Vice-Chancellor, Sheffield Univ., 1966–70; Chm., Jt Matriculation Bd, 1973–76. *Publications:* Relaxation Methods, 1954 (US); papers on Applied Maths and Engineering Maths in: Proc. Royal Soc.; Philosophical Trans. of Royal Soc.; Quarterly Jl of Mechanics and Applied Maths; Jl of Instn of Civil Engineers. *Recreation:* travel. *Address:* 18 Storth Park, Fulwood Road, Sheffield S10 3QH. *T:* Sheffield (0114) 230 8751.

ALLEN, Donald George, CMG 1981; Deputy Parliamentary Commissioner for Administration (Ombudsman), 1982–90; Member, Broadcasting Complaints Commission, since 1990; *b* 26 June 1930; *s* of Sidney George Allen and Doris Elsie (*née* Abercombie); *m* 1955, Sheila Isobel Bebbington; three *s*. *Educ:* Southall Grammar School. Foreign Office, 1948; HM Forces, 1949–51; FO, 1951–54; The Hague, 1954–57; 2nd Sec. (Commercial), La Paz, 1957–60; FO, 1961–65: 1st Sec. 1962; Asst Private Sec. to Lord Privy Seal, 1961–63 and to Minister without Portfolio, 1963–64; 1st Sec., Head of Chancery and Consul, Panama, 1966–69; FCO, 1969–72; Counsellor on secondment to NI Office, Belfast, 1972–74; Counsellor and Head of Chancery, UK Permanent Delegn to OECD, Paris, 1974–78; Inspector, 1978–80; Dir, Office of Parly Comr (Ombudsman), 1980–82, on secondment. *Recreations:* squash, tennis, golf. *Address:* 99 Parkland Grove, Ashford, Mddx TW15 2JF. *T:* Ashford (01784) 255617. *Club:* Royal Automobile.

ALLEN, Fergus Hamilton, CB 1969; ScD, MA, MAI; First Civil Service Commissioner, Civil Service Department, 1974–81; *b* 3 Sept. 1921; *s* of late Charles Winckworth Allen and Marjorie Helen, *d* of F. J. S. Budge; *m* 1947, Margaret Joan, *d* of Prof. M. J. Gorman; two *d*. *Educ:* Newtown Sch., Waterford; Trinity Coll., Dublin. ScD 1966. Asst Engineer, Sir Cyril Kirkpatrick and Partners, 1943–48; Port of London Authority, 1949–52; Asst Director, Hydraulics Research Station, DSIR, 1952–58; Dir of Hydraulics Research, DSIR, 1958–65; Chief Scientific Officer, Cabinet Office, 1965–69; Civil Service Comr, 1969–74; Scientific and Technological Advr, CSD, 1969–72. Consultant, Boyden Internat. Ltd, 1982–86. Instn Civil Engrs: Mem., 1947–57; Fellow, 1957–86; Telford Gold Medal, 1958; Mem. Council, 1962–67, 1968–71. *Publications:* The Brown Parrots of Providencia (poems), 1993; papers in technical journals. *Address:* Dundrum, Wantage Road, Streatley, Berks RG8 9LB. *T:* Goring-on-Thames (01491) 873234. *Club:* Athenæum.
See also M. Allen.

ALLEN, Francis Andrew; His Honour Judge Francis Allen; a Circuit Judge, since 1979; *b* 7 Dec. 1933; *s* of Andrew Eric Allen and Joan Elizabeth Allen; *m* 1961, Marjorie Pearce; one *s* three *d*; *m* 1994, Sheila Baggaley. *Educ:* Solihull School; Merton College, Oxford. MA. 2nd Lieut, Highland Light Infantry, 1957; called to the Bar, Gray's Inn, 1958. A Recorder of the Crown Court, 1978–79. Chm., Magisterial Cttee, Judicial Studies Bd, 1990–. *Recreation:* walking. *Club:* Mountain Bothies Association (Scottish Highlands).

ALLEN, Frank Graham, CB 1984; Clerk of the Journals, House of Commons, 1975–84; *b* 13 June 1920; *s* of Percy and Gertrude Allen; *m* 1947, Barbara Caulton; one *d* (one *s* decd). Educ: Shrewsbury Sch. (Schol.); Keble Coll., Oxford (Exhibr, BA). 7th Bn Worcs Regt, 1940–46, India, 1942–44. Asst Clerk, House of Commons, 1946; Principal Clerk, 1973. Mem., House of Laity, Gen. Synod, 1970–80. Silver Jubilee Medal, 1977. *Recreation:* involvement in Chorleywood CARE and in St Andrew's old people's day centre. *Address:* March Mount, Haddon Road, Chorleywood, Herts WD3 5AN. *T:* Chorleywood (01923) 282709. *Club:* Rhinefield Owners (Brockenhurst).

ALLEN, Gary James, CBE 1991; DL; Managing Director, IMI plc, since 1986; *b* 30 Sept. 1944; *s* of Alfred and Alice Allen; *m* 1966, Judith Anne Nattrass; three *s*. *Educ:* King Edward VI Grammar School, Aston, Birmingham; Liverpool University (BCom). FCMA. Managing Dir, IMI Range, 1973–77; Dir, IMI, 1978–; Chm., IMI Components, 1981–85; Asst Man. Dir, IMI, 1985–86; Chairman: Optilon, 1979–84; Eley, 1981–85; Dep. Chm., Marley, 1993– (Dir, 1989–); Director: (non-exec.) NV Bekaert SA, Belgium, 1987–; Birmingham European Airways, 1989–91; London Stock Exchange, 1994–. Mem. Council, CBI, 1986– (Mem., W Midlands Regional Council, 1983–89); Mem. Council, Birmingham Chamber of Industry & Commerce, 1983– (Pres., 1991–92; Mem. Bd, 1994–). Mem. Council, Univ. of Birmingham, 1985–90 (Hon. Life Mem., Court, 1984). Mem. Adv. Bd, Birmingham Royal Ballet, 1993–. DL West Midlands, 1993. CIMgt; FRSA. Midland Businessman of the Year, 1989. *Recreations:* sport, reading. *Address:* IMI plc, PO Box 216, Birmingham B6 7BA. *T:* 0121–356 4848. *Club:* Lord's Taverners'.

ALLEN, Prof. Sir Geoffrey, Kt 1979; PhD; FRS 1976; FEng; FRSC; FInstP; FIM; Executive Adviser, Kobe Steel Ltd, since 1990; Head of Research, Unilever PLC, 1981–90 (Director, Unilever PLC and NV, 1982–90); *b* 29 Oct. 1928; *s* of John James and Marjorie Allen; *m* 1973, Valerie Frances Duckworth; one *d*. *Educ:* Clay Cross Tupton Hall Grammar Sch.; Univ. of Leeds (BSc, PhD). FInstP 1972; FPRI 1974; FIM 1991; FEng 1993. Postdoctoral Fellow, Nat. Res. Council, Canada, 1952–54; Lectr, Univ. of Manchester, 1955–65, Prof. of Chemical Physics, 1965–75; Prof. of Polymer Science, 1975–76, Prof. of Chemical Technology, 1976–81, Imperial Coll. of Science and Technology (Fellow, 1986); Vis. Fellow, Robinson Coll., Cambridge, 1980–. Non-exec. Dir, Courtaulds, 1987–93. Member: Science Research Council, 1976, Chm., 1977–81; Royal Commn on Envmtl Pollution, 1991–; Nat. Consumer Council, 1993–; Council, Foundn for Sci. and Technol., 1995–; President: PRI, 1990–92; Inst. of Materials. A Vice-Pres., Royal Soc., 1991–93. Chancellor, UEA, 1994–. Fellow, St Catherine's Coll., Oxford, 1992. Hon. FCGI 1990. Hon. FUMIST 1993. Hon. MSc Manchester; DUniv Open, 1981; Hon. DSc: Durham, East Anglia, 1984; Bath, Bradford, Loughborough, 1985; Essex, Keele, Leeds, 1986; Cranfield, 1988; Surrey, 1989; Sheffield, 1993. *Publications:* papers on chemical physics of polymers in Trans Faraday Soc., Polymer. *Recreations:* opera, walking, talking. *Address:* Kobe Steel Ltd, Alton House, 174 High Holborn, WC1V 7AA. *T:* 0171–836 1225.

ALLEN, Graham William; MP (Lab) Nottingham North, since 1987; *b* 11 Jan. 1953; *s* of William and Edna Allen. *Educ:* Robert Shaw Primary Sch.; Forest Fields Grammar Sch.; City of London Polytechnic; Leeds Univ. Warehouseman, Nottingham, 1971–72; Labour Party Res. Officer, 1978–83; Local Govt Officer, GLC, 1983–84; Trades Union National Co-ordinator, Political Fund Ballots Campaign, 1984–86; Regional Res. and Educn Officer, GMBATU, 1986–87. Opposition front bench spokesman on social security, 1991–92, on democracy and the constitution, 1992–94, on the media, 1994. Member: Public Accounts Cttee, 1988–91; Procedure Cttee, 1989–91; 1990 Financial Bill Cttee. Chm., PLP Treasury Cttee, 1990–91. *Recreations:* cricket, football, golf, walking. *Address:* House of Commons, SW1A 0AA. *T:* 0171–219 4343. *Clubs:* Long Eaton Labour, Strelley Social, Beechdale Community Centre, Bulwell Community Centre, Dunkirk Cricket (Nottingham).

ALLEN, Hamish McEwan, CB 1984; Head of Administration Department, House of Commons, 1981–85; *b* 7 Sept. 1920; *s* of late Ernest Frank Allen and Ada Florence Allen (*née* Weeks); *m* 1951, Peggy Joan Fifoot; one *s*. *Educ:* City of Bath Sch.; Portsmouth Southern Secondary Sch. Served RAF, 1941–46. Air Ministry: Clerical Officer, 1938; Exec. Officer, 1948; House of Commons: Asst Accountant, 1959; Dep. Accountant, 1962; Head of Estabs Office, 1968. *Address:* 124 Ridge Langley, South Croydon, Surrey CR2 0AS.

ALLEN, (Harold) Norman (Gwynne), CBE 1965; FEng; retired 1977; *b* 30 April 1912; *yr s* of Harold Gwynne Allen and Hilda Margaret Allen (*née* Langley), Bedford; *m* 1938, Marjorie Ellen (*née* Brown); one *s* three *d*. *Educ:* Westminster Sch.; Trinity Coll., Cambridge, BA 1933, MA 1936, Cantab; FEng 1979, FICE, FIMechE, FRINA, FIMarE, FIEE. Engrg trng, John Samuel White & Co. Ltd, Cowes, John Brown & Co. Ltd, Clydebank, and in Merchant Navy, 1933–37; W. H. Allen Sons & Co. Ltd, Bedford: progressive staff appts, 1937–43; Dir 1943–77; Techn. Dir 1945–52; Jt Man. Dir 1952–; Dep. Chm. 1962–70; Chm. 1970–77; Amalgamated Power Engrg Ltd, Bedford: Techn.

Dir 1968–70; Dep. Chm. 1970–77. Belliss & Morcom Ltd, Birmingham, 1968–77. Mem. Bedfordshire CC, 1947–50. Mem. Council: British Internal Combustion Engrg Res. Assoc., 1952–60 (Chm. 1953–54); British Hydromechanics Res. Assoc., 1947–59; IMechE, 1952–70 (Vice-Pres. 1959–65, Pres. 1965); Mem. Adv. Cttee, Nat. Engrg Lab., 1971–73 (Mem. Steering Cttee 1962–68); Mem. British Transport Commn Res. Adv. Council, 1958–60; Vice-Chm. of Council, Mander Coll., Bedford, 1958–74; Governor, Coll. of Aeronautics, Cranfield, 1955–69 (Vice-Chm. 1962–69); Charter Pro-Chancellor, Cranfield Inst. of Technology, 1969–75; Mem. Bd, Council of Engrg Instns, 1964–66; Mem. Exec. Bd, BSI, 1970–76. Provost, Buffalo Hunt of Manitoba, 1960. Dir, Son et Lumière, Woburn Abbey, 1957. Hon. DSc Bath, 1967; Hon. DSc Cranfield, 1977. *Publications:* papers in jls of IMarE, S African IMechE, Engrg Inst. Canada, IMechE. *Recreations:* gardening (MRHS), countryside (Mem. Nat. Trust), magic (Mem. Magic Circle). *Address:* 15 Mullings Court, Dollar Street, Cirencester, Glos GL7 2AW.

ALLEN, Prof. Harry Cranbrook, MC 1944; Professor of American Studies, 1971–80, now Emeritus, and Dean of the School of English and American Studies, 1974–76, University of East Anglia; *b* 23 March 1917; *s* of Christopher Albert Allen and Margaret Enid (*née* Hebb); *m* 1947, Mary Kathleen Andrews (*d* 1992); one *s* two *d*. *Educ:* Bedford School; Pembroke College, Oxford (Open Scholar; 1st cl. hons Modern History; MA). Elected Fellow, Commonwealth Fund of New York, 1939 (held Fellowship, Harvard Univ., Jan–Sept. 1946). Served War of 1939–45, with Hertfordshire and Dorsetshire Regts, in France and Germany (Major); comdt 43rd Division Educational Coll., June–Nov. 1945. Fellow and Tutor in Modern History, Lincoln College, Oxford, 1946–55; Commonwealth Fund Prof. of American History, University Coll., 1955–71, and Dir, Inst. of United States Studies, 1966–71, Univ. of London; Senior Research Fellow, Austr. Nat. Univ., Canberra, and Visiting Scholar, Univ. of California, Berkeley, 1953–54; Schouler Lecturer, The Johns Hopkins University, April 1956; American Studies Fellow, Commonwealth Fund of New York, 1957, at the University of Virginia; Vis. Mem., Inst. for Advanced Study, Princeton, NJ, 1959; Vis. Professor: Univ. of Rochester, New York, 1963; Univ. of Michigan, Ann Arbor, 1966. Member: Dartmouth Royal Naval College Review Cttee, 1958, Naval Education Adv. Cttee, 1960–66; Academic Planning Board, Univ. of Essex, 1962; Chm., British Assoc. for American Studies, 1974–77; Pres., European Assoc. for American Studies, 1976–80. *Publications:* Great Britain and the United States, 1955; Bush and Backwoods, 1959; The Anglo-American Relationship since 1783, 1960; The Anglo-American Predicament, 1960; The United States of America, 1964; Joint Editor: British Essays in American History, 1957; Contrast and Connection, 1976. *Recreation:* retirement. *Address:* B#121 1400 Waverly Road, Gladwyne, PA 19035, USA.

ALLEN, Prof. Ingrid Victoria, (Mrs Alan Barnes), CBE 1993; MD, DSc, FRCPath, FRCPI, FRCPSG, FRCPE; Professor of Neuropathology, Queen's University of Belfast, since 1979; *b* 30 July 1932; *d* of Rev. Robert Allen, MA, PhD, DD and Doris V. Allen; *m* 1972, Alan Watson Barnes, MA, ARIBA, Past Pres., RSUA. *Educ:* Cheltenham Ladies College; QUB. House Officer, Royal Victoria Hosp., Belfast, 1957–58; Musgrave Res. Fellow, Tutor in Path., Calvert Res. Fellow, QUB, 1958–64; Sen. Registrar, RVH, 1964–65; Sen. Lectr and Consultant in Neuropath., QUB/RVH, 1966–78; Reader and Consultant, 1978–79; Head, NI Regional Neuropath. Service, RVH, Belfast, 1979–. Mem., MRC, 1989–93 (Chm., Neuroscis Bd, 1989–92); President: British Neuropathological Soc., 1993–95; Irish Neurological Assoc., 1993–; Vice-President: Internat. Soc. of Neuropath., 1988–92; RCPath, 1994–. MRIA (Fellow, 1993). DL Belfast 1989. Mem. editl bds of various scientific jls. *Publications:* (contrib.) Greenfield's Neuropathology, 1984; (contrib.) McAlpine's Multiple Sclerosis, 1990; contribs to jls on neuropathology, demyelinating diseases, neurovirology and neuro-oncology. *Recreations:* tennis, sailing, reading, history, architecture. *Address:* Department of Neuropathology, Royal Victoria Hospital, Grosvenor Road, Belfast BT12 6BA. *T:* Belfast (01232) 240503. *Clubs:* Royal Society of Medicine; Royal Ulster Yacht.

ALLEN, James Hendricuss; QC 1995; a Recorder, since 1995; *b* 19 Sept. 1949; *s* of James Ede Allen and Anna Catarina Allen; *m* 1974, Heather Boocock (marr. diss. 1994); one *s* two *d*. *Educ:* Morley Grammar Sch.; Newcastle upon Tyne Poly (BA Hons Law). Called to the Bar, Gray's Inn, 1973. *Recreations:* theatre, opera, foreign travel, shooting, tennis, bridge. *Address:* 39 Park Square, Leeds LS1 2NU. *T:* Leeds (0113) 245 6633.

ALLEN, Janet Rosemary; Headmistress of Benenden School, Kent, 1976–85; *b* 11 April 1936; *d* of John Algernon Allen and Edna Mary Allen (*née* Orton). *Educ:* Cheltenham Ladies' Coll.; University Coll., Leicester; Hughes Hall, Cambridge. BA London 1958; CertEd Cambridge 1959. Asst Mistress, Howell's Sch., Denbigh, North Wales, 1959: Head of History Dept, 1961; in charge of First Year Sixth Form, 1968; Housemistress, 1968 and 1973–75. Acting Headmistress: Sch. of St Mary and St Anne, Abbots Bromley, Sept.–Dec. 1988; Selwyn Sch., Gloucester, 1989–90. Member: E-SU Scholarship Selection Panel, 1977–85; South East ISIS Cttee, 1978–84; Boarding Schs Assoc. Cttee, 1980–83; GSA Educnl sub-cttee, 1983–85; Gloucester Diocesan Bd of Educn, 1992–. Vice-Pres., Women's Career Foundn (formerly Girls of the Realm Guild), 1981–. Gov., St Catherine's Sch., Bramley, 1986–. *Recreations:* music, theatre, swimming, helping to preserve national heritage. *Address:* Bourne Rise, Queen's Square, Winchcombe, Cheltenham, Glos GL54 5LR. *Club:* Royal Over-Seas League.

ALLEN, Prof. John Anthony, PhD, DSc; FIBiol; FRSE; Professor of Marine Biology, University of London, and Director, University Marine Biological Station, Millport, Isle of Cumbrae, 1976–91, now Professor Emeritus; Hon. Research Fellow, University Marine Biological Station, since 1991; *b* 27 May 1926; *s* of George Leonard John Allen and Dorothy Mary Allen; *m* 1st, 1952, Marion Ferguson Crow (marr. diss. 1983); one *s* one *d*; 2nd, 1983, Margaret Porteous Aitken. *Educ:* High Pavement Sch., Nottingham; London Univ. (PhD, DSc). FIBiol 1969; FRSE 1968 (Mem. Council, 1970–73). Served in Sherwood Foresters, 1945–46, and RAMC, 1946–48. Asst Lectr, Univ. of Glasgow, 1951–54; John Murray Student, Royal Soc., 1952–54; Lectr/Sen. Lectr in Zool., then Reader in Marine Biol., Univ. of Newcastle upon Tyne, 1954–76. Post Doctoral Fellow and Guest Investigator, Woods Hole Oceanographic Instn, USA, 1965–; Vis. Prof., Univ. of Washington, 1968, 1970, 1971; Royal Soc. Vis. Prof., Univ. of West Indies, 1976. Member: NERC, 1977–83 (Chm., Univ. Affairs Cttee, 1978–83); Council, Scottish Marine Biol Assoc., 1977–83; Council, Marine Biol Assoc. UK, 1981–83, 1990–93; Life Sciences Bd, CNAA, 1981–84; Nature Conservancy Council, 1982–90 (Chm., Adv. Cttee Sci., 1984–90); British Nat. Cttee for Oceanic Res., 1988–90. Pres., Malacological Soc. of London, 1982–84. *Publications:* many papers on decapod crustacea and molluscs, and deep sea benthos, in learned jls. *Recreations:* travel, appreciation of gardens, publunching. *Address:* Drialstone, Millport, Isle of Cumbrae, Scotland KA28 0EP. *T:* Millport (01475) 530479.

ALLEN, Sir John (Derek), Kt 1994; CBE 1987; FCIOB; Chairman, Housing for Wales, since 1988; Deputy Chairman, Land Authority for Wales, since 1988 (Member, since 1976); *b* 6 Nov. 1928; *s* of late William Henry Allen and Lalla Dorothy Allen (*née* Bowen); *m* 1951, (Thelma) Jean Hooper; one *s*. *Educ:* Cardiff High Sch.; Cardiff Coll. of Technology (BA). FCIOB 1979. Civil Engr, then Chm. and Man. Dir, John Morgan Gp, Cardiff, 1947–79; Mgt Consultancy Practice, 1979–86. Dep. Chm., then Chm., Cwmbran Develt Corp., 1979–88. Pres., Nat. Fedn of Building Trade Employers, 1979 (Treas., 1980–83). FIMgt 1980. Freeman, City of London, 1980. *Recreations:* fly-fishing, golf, gardening. *Address:* 6 Egremont Road, Penylan, Cardiff, S Glam CF2 5LN. *T:* Cardiff (01222) 499461. *Clubs:* Cardiff and County; Cardiff Golf.

ALLEN, Very Rev. John Edward; Provost of Wakefield, since 1982; *b* 9 June 1932; *s* of Rev. Canon Ronald and Mrs Isabel Allen; *m* 1957, Eleanor (*née* Prynne); one *s* three *d*. *Educ:* Rugby; University Coll., Oxford (MA); Fitzwilliam Coll., Cambridge (MA); Westcott House. Colonial Service, Kenya, 1957–63; Sales and Marketing, Kimberly-Clark Ltd, 1963–66; Theological College, 1966–68; Curate, Deal, Kent, 1968–71; Senior Chaplain to Univ. of Bristol and Vicar of St Paul's, Clifton, 1971–78; Vicar of Chippenham, Wilts, 1978–82. Mem., Gen. Synod of C of E, 1985–. *Recreations:* walking, fishing and people. *Address:* 1 Cathedral Close, Margaret Street, Wakefield, West Yorkshire WF1 2DQ. *T:* Wakefield (01924) 372402.

ALLEN, Prof. John Frank, FRS 1949; Professor of Natural Philosophy in the School of Physical Sciences, University of St Andrews, 1947–78, now Emeritus; *b* 6 May 1908; *s* of late Prof. Frank Allen, FRSC; *m* 1933, Elfriede Hiebert (marr. diss. 1951); one adopted *s*. *Educ:* Public schools of Winnipeg, Canada. BA (University of Manitoba, 1928), MA (University of Toronto, 1930), PhD (University of Toronto, 1933). Bursar, Student and Fellow of National Research Council of Canada, 1930–33; Fellow of National Research Council of USA, 1933–35; Research Assistant, Royal Society Mond Laboratory, Cambridge, 1935–44; MA Cantab, 1936; Lecturer in Physics, Univ. of Cambridge and Fellow and Lecturer of St John's College, Cambridge, 1944–47. Hon. DSc: Manitoba, 1979; Heriot-Watt, 1984. *Publications:* numerous scientific papers and articles, mainly on experimental low temperature physics. *Recreations:* scientific cinefilms, golf. *Address:* 2 Shorehead, St Andrews, Fife KY16 9RG. *T:* St Andrews (01334) 72717.

See also W. A. Allen.

ALLEN, Maj.-Gen. John Geoffrey Robyn, CB 1976; Lay Observer attached to Lord Chancellor's Department, 1979–85; *b* 19 Aug. 1923; *s* of R. A. Allen and Mrs Allen (*née* Youngman); *m* 1959, Ann Monica (*née* Morford); one *s* one *d*. *Educ:* Haileybury. Commissioned KRRC, 1942; trans. RTR, 1947; Bt Lt-Col, 1961; Lt-Col, CO 2 RTR, 1963; Mil. Asst (GSO1) to CGS, MoD, 1965; Brig., Comd 20 Armd Bde, 1967; IDC, 1970; Dir of Operational Requirements 3 (Army), MoD, 1971; Maj.-Gen., Dir-Gen., Fighting Vehicles and Engineer Equipment, MoD, 1973–74; Dir, RAC, 1974–76; Sen. Army Directing Staff, RCDS, 1976–78; retired 1979. Col Comdt, RTR, 1976–80; Hon. Colonel: Westminster Dragoons, 1982–87; Royal Yeomanry, 1982–87. Member: Adv. Cttee on Legal Aid, 1979–86; Booth Cttee on Procedure in Matrimonial Causes, 1982–85. *Address:* Meadowleys, Charlton, Chichester, W Sussex PO18 0HU. *T:* Singleton (01243) 811638. *Club:* Army and Navy.

ALLEN, John Hunter, OBE 1978; company director; District Councillor, Antrim, since 1963 (Mayor, 1973–90); *s* of John Allen and Jane Kerr Hunter; *m* 1952, Elizabeth Irwin Graham; three *d*. *Educ:* Larne Grammar Sch., NI; Orange's Acad., NI. Served RAF, pilot, 1942–47. Civil Service Excise, 1947–59; Proprietor: Ulster Farm Feeds Ltd, 1959–76; Antrim Feeds Ltd, 1959–76; Roadway Transport Ltd, 1959–; Aldergrove Farms Ltd, 1965–; A.B. Fuels, 1969–; Downtown Developments Ltd, 1975–; Allen Service Stns, 1977–; Century Supplies, 1984–. Chm., NI Sports Council, 1977–84. Chm., Antrim Royal British Legion. Member: Ulster Games Foundn, 1983–; NI Gen. Consumers Council, 1984–. Life Mem., Royal Ulster Agricl Soc, 1972. *Recreations:* Rugby, sailing, boxing, tennis. *Clubs:* Royal Air Force; Antrim Rugby (Pres.); Antrim Hockey (Pres.); Antrim Boxing (Pres.); Antrim Boat (Trustee); Muckamore Cricket (Life Member).

ALLEN, John Piers, OBE 1979; *b* 30 March 1912; *s* of Percy Allen and Marjorie Nash; *m* 1937; two *s*; *m* 1945; two *s* two *d*; *m* 1982. *Educ:* Aldenham Sch. Old Vic Theatre, 1933–35; Victor Gollancz Ltd, 1936–37; London Theatre Studio, 1937–39; RNVR, 1940–45; Dir, Glyndebourne Children's Theatre, 1945–51; writer-producer, BBC, 1951–61; Adjudicator, Dominion Drama Festival, Canada, 1956; UNESCO Drama Specialist, Australia, 1959, 1961; HM Inspector of Schs, 1961–72. Principal, Central School of Speech and Drama, 1972–78. Vis. Prof. of Drama, Westfield Coll., Univ. of London, 1979–83; Vis. Lectr, Centre for Arts, City Univ., 1979–83. Vice-Chm., British Theatre Assoc., 1978–83; Chairman: Accreditation Bd, Nat. Council of Drama Trng, 1979–83; Council of Dance Educn and Trng, 1982– (Chm., Accreditation Bd, 1979–82); Mem., CNAA Dance and Drama Panels, 1979–82; Vice-Pres., British Centre, Internat. Amateur Theatre Assoc., 1982–. Chm., Old Meeting House Trust, Helmsley, 1993–. *Publications:* Going to the Theatre, 1949; Great Moments in the Theatre, 1949; Masters of British Drama, 1957; Masters of European Drama, 1962; Drama in Schools, 1978; Theatre in Europe, 1981; A History of the Theatre in Europe, 1983; (ed) Three Medieval Plays, 1956. *Address:* The Old Orchard, Lastingham, York YO6 6TQ. *T:* Lastingham (017515) 334.

ALLEN, Prof. John Robert Lawrence, DSc; FRS 1979; Research Professor, Postgraduate Research Institute for Sedimentology, University of Reading, since 1993 (Director, 1988–93); *b* 25 Oct. 1932; *s* of George Eustace Allen and Alice Josephine (*née* Formby); *m* 1960, Jean Mary (*née* Wood); four *s* one *d*. *Educ:* St Philip's Grammar Sch., Birmingham; Univ. of Sheffield (BSc; DSc 1972; LLD 1994). Academic career in University of Reading, 1959–, Prof. of Geology, then of Sedimentology, 1972. Mem., NERC, 1992–. FGS 1955; FSA 1991. Assoc. Mem., Royal Belgian Acad. of Scis, 1991. Lyell Medal, Geolog. Soc., 1980; David Linton Award, British Geomorphological Research Group, 1983; Twenhofel Medal, Soc. of Economic Paleontologists and Mineralogists, 1987; G. K. Warren Prize, Nat. Acad. of Scis, USA, 1990; Sorby Medal, Internat. Assoc. of Sedimentologists, 1994. *Publications:* Current Ripples, 1968; Physical Processes of Sedimentation, 1970; Sedimentary Structures, 1982; Principles of Physical Sedimentology, 1985; numerous contribs to professional jls. *Recreations:* cooking, music, opera. *Address:* 17c Whiteknights Road, Reading RG6 2BY. *T:* Reading (01734) 264621.

ALLEN, Prof. Joseph Stanley; (first) Professor and Head of Department of Town and Country Planning, University of Newcastle upon Tyne (formerly King's College, Durham University), 1946–63 (developing first University Degree Course in Town and Country Planning); now Professor Emeritus; *b* 15 March 1898; *s* of late Harry Charles Allen and of Elizabeth S. Allen; *m* 1931, Guinevere Mary Aubrey Pugh (*d* 1974); one *s* one *d*; *m* 1977, Meryl (*d* 1992), *d* of late Charles and Eveline Watts. *Educ:* Liverpool Collegiate School; Liverpool University; post-graduate study in USA. RIBA Athens Bursar. Lectr, Liverpool Univ., 1929–33; Head, Leeds School of Architecture, 1933–45; founded Leeds Sch. of Town and Country Planning, 1934. Vice-Chm. RIBA Bd of Architectural Education and Chm. Recognised Schools Cttee, 1943–45; Member of Council RIBA, 1943–50; Pres. Royal Town Planning Institute, 1959–60 (Vice-Pres. 1957–59). Architect and Town Planning Consultant; undertakings include: Develt Plan for Durham Univ.; Quadrangle, King's College, Newcastle; Courthouse, Chesterfield; Nat. Park Residential Study Centre, Maentwrog; Science Wing, Durham Univ. Consultant, Snowdonia National Park, 1957–74; Member, North of England Regional Advisory Committee, Forestry Commission, 1951–74; Member Diocesan Committees for Care of Churches: Ripon,

Newcastle and York Dioceses. Hon. DLitt Heriot-Watt, 1978. *Publications:* (with R. H. Mattocks): Report and Plan for West Cumberland; Report and Plan for Accrington (Industry and Prudence), 1950. Founder-Editor, Planning Outlook (founded 1948); contrib. to professional journals on architecture and town and country planning. *Recreations:* motoring and walking in the countryside, music, farming and breeding Welsh ponies. *Address:* Bleach Green Farm, Ovingham, Northumberland NE42 6BL. *T:* Prudhoe (01661) 32340.

ALLEN, Sir Kenneth; *see* Allen, Sir William Kenneth G.

ALLEN, Prof. Kenneth William; Professor of Nuclear Structure, 1963–91, Professor Emeritus, since 1991, and Head of Department of Nuclear Physics, 1976–79 and 1982–85, University of Oxford; Fellow, 1963–92, Emeritus Fellow, since 1992, Balliol College, Oxford (Estates Bursar, 1980–83 and 1991–93); *b* 17 Nov. 1923; *m* 1947, Josephine E. Boreham; two *s*. *Educ:* Ilford County High School; London University (Drapers' Scholar); St Catharine's College, Cambridge University. PhD (Cantab) 1947. Physics Division, Atomic Energy of Canada, Chalk River, 1947–51; Leverhulme Research Fellow and Lecturer, Liverpool University, 1951–54; Deputy Chief Scientist, UKAEA, 1954–63. Sen. Vis. Scientist, Lawrence Berkeley Lab., Univ. of California, 1988–89. Mem., Nuclear Physics Bd, SRC, 1970–73. *Publications:* contribs to Nuclear Physics, Physical Review, Review of Scientific Instruments, Nature, etc. *Recreations:* music, chess. *Address:* Ridgeway, Lincombe Lane, Boars Hill, Oxford OX1 5DZ. *T:* Oxford (01865) 739327.

ALLEN, Mark Echalaz, CMG 1966; CVO 1961; HM Diplomatic Service, retired; *b* 19 March 1917; *s* of late Lancelot John Allen and Eleanor Mary (*née* Carlisle); *m* 1948, Elizabeth Joan, *d* of late Richard Hope Bowdler and Elsie (*née* Bryning); two *s* one *d* (and one *d* decd). *Educ:* Charterhouse; Christ Church, Oxford (MA). Appointed Asst Principal, Dominions Office, 1939. Served War of 1939–45 in Western Desert, Sicily and Italy. Dublin, 1945; Bombay, 1948; United Nations, New York, 1953; Madras, 1960; New Delhi, 1961; Diplomatic Service Inspector, 1964; Dep. Chief of Administration, DSAO, 1966; Minister (Econ. and Social Affairs), UK Mission to UN, New York, 1968; Ambassador to Zaïre and Burundi, 1971, and to Congo Republic, 1973; Permanent UK Rep. to Disarmament Conf., Geneva, 1974–77, retired from Diplomatic Service, 1977. Mem., Jt Inspection Unit, UN, 1978–84. *Address:* The Gate House, 65 Albion Street, Stratton, Cirencester, Glos GL7 2HT. *T:* Cirencester (01285) 653510.

ALLEN, Mary; Secretary-General, Arts Council of England, since 1994 (Deputy Secretary-General, Arts Council of GB, 1992–94); *b* 22 Aug. 1951; *d* of Dr Fergus Hamilton Allen, *qv* and Joan Allen; *m* 1st, 1980, Robin Woodhead (marr. diss.); 2nd, 1991, Nigel Pantling. *Educ:* School of St Helen and St Katherine; New Hall, Cambridge. Actress, West End and repertory, 1973–76; Agent, London Management, 1977–78; Arts, Sponsorship Manager, Mobil Oil Co., 1978–81; Assoc. for Business Sponsorship of the Arts, 1982–83; arts management consultant, 1983–90; Dir, Waterman's Arts Centre, 1990–92; Dir, Cheek by Jowl Theatre Co., 1989–92. Public Art Develt Trust: Trustee, 1983–92; Chm., 1987–92. *Publication:* Sponsoring the Arts: new business strategies for the 1990s, 1990. *Recreations:* opera, theatre, collecting contemporary art, gardening. *Address:* Arts Council of England, 14 Great Peter Street, SW1P 3NQ.

ALLEN, Norman; *see* Allen, H. N. G.

ALLEN, Prof. Percival, FRS 1973; Professor of Geology, and Head of Geology Department, University of Reading, 1952–82, now Emeritus Professor; Director, Sedimentology Research Laboratory, 1965–82; *b* 15 March 1917; *s* of late Norman Williams Allen and Mildred Kathleen Hoad; British; *m* 1941, Frances Margaret Hepworth, BSc; three *s* one *d*. *Educ:* Brede Council Sch.; Rye Grammar School; University of Reading. BSc 1939, PhD 1943, Hon. DSc, 1992, Reading; MA Cantab 1947. Univ. Demonstrator, 1942–45, Univ. Asst Lectr, 1945–46, Reading; University Demonstrator, 1946–47, Univ. Lectr, 1947–52, Cambridge; Dean of Science Faculty, Reading, 1963–66. Vis. Prof., Univ. of Kuwait, 1970. Served War of 1939–45. In Royal Air Force, 1941–42. Sedgwick Prize, Univ. of Cambridge, 1952; Daniel Pidgeon Fund, Geological Soc. of London, 1944; Leverhulme Fellowships Research Grant, 1948, 1949. Geological Soc. of London: Mem. Council, 1964–67; Lyell Medal, 1971; Pres., 1978–80; Royal Society: Mem. Council, 1977–79; a Vice-Pres., 1977–79; Chairman: Expeditions Cttee, 1974–; British Nat. Cttee for Geology, 1982–90; Sectional Cttee 5, 1983–88; Actg Chm., Earth Sciences Res. Priorities, 1987–89. Chm., Scottish Regional Cttee and Mem., Nat. and Eastern Reg. Cttees, UGC Earth Sciences Rev., 1987–90; Council Mem., NERC, 1971–74 and Royal Soc. Assessor, 1977–80; Chm., vis. group to Palaeont. Dept in British Mus. (Nat. Hist.), 1975, and Univ. of Strathclyde, 1982; External Appraiser (Geol. Depts): Meml Univ., Newfoundland, 1968; Jadavpur Univ., India, 1977; Univ. of Western Ontario, 1982; Univ. of London, 1982; Univ. of Malaya, 1983; Adv. Panel, UNDP Project on Nile Delta, 1972–; UNESCO/UNDP Geology Consultant, India, 1976–77. UK Editor, Sedimentology, 1961–67; Jt Editor, OUP Monographs in Geology and Geophysics series, 1980–87. Chm., Org. Cttees: VII Internat. Sedimentological Congress, 1967; first European Earth and Planetary Physics Colloquium, 1971; first Meeting European Geological Socs, 1975; UK Delegate to Internat. Union of Geol Sciences, Moscow, 1984; UK Corresp., IGCP Project 245, 1986–91. Sec.-Gen., Internat. Assoc. Sedimentologists, 1967–71; Pres., Reading Geol. Soc., 1976–78, 1987–88; Chm., British Inst. for Geological Conservation, 1987–91. Algerian Sahara Glacials Expedn, 1970; Sec., Philpots Quarry Ltd. Hon. Member: American Soc. of Economic Paleontologists and Mineralogists; Bulgarian Geological Soc.; Geologists' Assoc.; Internat. Assoc. of Sedimentologists; For. Fellow, Indian Nat. Sci. Acad., 1979. *Publications:* papers on Wealden (Lower Cretaceous) and Torridonian (Proterozoic) in various scientific journals. *Recreations:* chess, natural history, gardening, bicycling. *Address:* Orchard End, Hazeley Bottom, Hartley Wintney, Hants RG27 8LU. *T:* Hartley Wintney (01252) 842229; Postgraduate Research Institute for Sedimentology, University of Reading, Reading RG6 2AB. *T:* Reading (01734) 316713.

ALLEN, Hon. Sir Peter (Austin Philip Jermyn), Kt 1987; High Court Judge, Lesotho, 1987–89; *b* 20 Oct. 1929; *yr s* of late Donovan Jermyn Allen and Edith Jane Bates. *Educ:* Headlands School, Swindon. LLB London. Army service, 1947–55, Lieut RA, 1952–55. HM Overseas Police Service, Asst Supt Uganda Police, 1955–62; ADC to Governor of Uganda, 1957; called to the Bar, Gray's Inn, 1964; Lectr, 1962–64, Principal, 1964–70, Uganda Law School; Judicial Adviser, Buganda Kingdom, 1964; Advocate, High Court of Uganda, 1965; Chief Magistrate, Uganda, 1970–73; Judge, Uganda High Court, 1973–85; Chief Justice (Head of Uganda Judiciary, Chm., Judicial Service Commn), 1985–86. Member: Uganda Law Reform Commn, 1964–68; Foundn Cttee, Uganda YMCA, 1959; Dir, Mbarara Branch, YMCA, 1970–73; Chairman: Presidential Commn of Inquiry into Kampala City Council, 1971; Judicial Review of Caribbean Dependent Territories (Allen Report for FCO), 1990; Commn of Inquiry into Grand Cayman New Hospital Contracts, 1993; Mem., Uganda Law Soc., 1964–70. Uganda Independence Medal, 1962. *Publications:* An Introduction to the Law of Uganda (co-author), 1968; Days of Judgment, 1987. *Address:* PO Box 38, Savannah, Grand Cayman, Cayman Islands, British West Indies. *Club:* Commonwealth Trust.

ALLEN, Peter William, FCA; Deputy Chairman, Coopers & Lybrand, 1990–94; *b* 22 July 1938; *s* of late Alfred William Allen, Sittingbourne, Kent, and Myra Nora (*née* Rogers); *m* 1965, Patricia Mary, *d* of late Joseph Frederick Dunk, FCA, Sheffield; three *d*. *Educ:* Cambridge Univ. (MA). Served RAF, 1957–59. Joined Coopers & Lybrand, 1963; qualified CA, 1966; Partner, 1973; Chm., Internat. Personnel Cttee, 1975–78; Partner in Charge, London Office, 1983; Man. Partner, 1984–90; Member: UK Bd, 1984–94; Internat. Exec. Cttee, 1988–90, 1992–94. Non-executive Director: Charter, 1994–; Schroder Ventures, 1994–. CIMgt 1993. Freeman, City of London, 1988; Liveryman, Co. of Glaziers and Painters of Glass, 1989. *Recreations:* golf, bridge. *Address:* John O'Gaddesden's House, Little Gaddesden, Berkhamsted, Herts HP4 1PF. *Club:* Reform.

ALLEN, (Philip) Richard (Hernaman); Under Secretary, Division A, Social Security Policy Group, Department of Social Security, since 1994; *b* 26 Jan. 1949; *s* of late Philip Hernaman Allen and of Dorothy Allen (*née* Modral); *m* 1970, Vanessa (*née* Lampard); two *d*. *Educ:* Loughborough Grammar Sch.; Merton Coll., Oxford (BA (Hons) Mod. History). Asst Principal, HM Customs and Excise, 1970; Assistant Private Secretary: to Paymaster Gen., 1973; to Chancellor of the Duchy of Lancaster, 1974; HM Customs and Excise: Principal, 1975; Asst Sec., 1984; Comr of Customs and Excise, 1990; Director: Internal Taxes, 1990; Orgn, 1991. *Recreations:* music, badminton, keeping fit. *Address:* Department of Social Security, The Adelphi, John Adam Street, WC2N 6HT. *T:* 0171–962 8010.

ALLEN, Sir Richard (Hugh Sedley), KCMG 1960 (CMG 1953); retired; *b* 3 Feb. 1903; *s* of late Sir Hugh Allen, GCVO; *m* 1945, Juliet Home Thomson (*d* 1983); one step *s* (and one *s* decd). *Educ:* Royal Naval Colleges, Osborne and Dartmouth; New College, Oxford. Junior Asst Sec., Govt of Palestine, 1925–27. Entered Foreign Office and Diplomatic Service, 1927; Second Sec., 1932; First Sec., 1939; Counsellor, 1946; Minister, British Embassy, Buenos Aires, 1950–54; Minister to Guatemala, 1954–56; British Ambassador to Burma, 1956–62. *Publications:* Malaysia: Prospect and Retrospect, 1968; A Short Introduction to the History and Politics of Southeast Asia, 1970; Imperialism and Nationalism in the Fertile Crescent, 1974. *Recreation:* sailing. *Address:* 42 Somerstown, Chichester, Sussex PO19 4AL. *T:* Chichester (01243) 781182. *Club:* Bosham and Itchenor Sailing.

ALLEN, Richard Ian Gordon; Financial Adviser, Government of Bahrain, since 1995; *b* 13 Dec. 1944; *s* of Reginald Arthur Hill Allen and Edith Alice Allen (*née* Manger); *m* 1988, Lynn Conroy. *Educ:* Edinburgh Academy; Edinburgh Univ. (MA); York Univ. (BPhil). Consultant, UN Economic Commn for Europe, Geneva, 1970; Research Officer, NIESR, 1971–75; Economic Adviser: Dept of Energy, 1975–78; HM Treasury, 1978–81; Senior Economic Adviser, later Asst Sec., HM Treasury, 1981–85; Counsellor (Economic), Washington, 1985–87; Press Sec. to Chancellor of the Exchequer, 1987–88; Under Sec., HM Treasury, 1988–95. Mem., Bd of Dirs, European Investment Bank, 1988–90. *Recreations:* the ways and whims of my American wife, learning to cope with life on the golf course. *Club:* Royal Wimbledon Golf.

ALLEN, Robert Geoffrey Bruère, (Robin); QC 1995; *b* 13 Feb. 1951; of Rev. Canon R. E. T. Allen and Isabel (*née* Otter-Barry); *m* 1979, Elizabeth Gay Moon; two *s*. *Educ:* Rugby; University Coll., Oxford (BA PPE 1972). Called to the Bar, Middle Temple, 1974; in practice, specialising in discrimination, employment and public law, and human rights, 1976–. Co-organiser and first Treas., Free Representation Unit, 1973. Employment Law Advr to Legal Action Gp, 1978–80; Legal Advr to Local Govt Gp, Inst. Public Relns, 1988–90; expert advr to EC on law affecting most disadvantaged, 1993. Founder Mem. Cttee, Employment Law Bar Assoc., 1994–. Sec., Lambeth Central CLP, 1977. Chm., London Youth Adv. Centre, 1984–90. Chairman: Bd of Govs, Eleanor Palmer Primary Sch., 1988–91; Brandon Centre for Psychotherapy, 1991–93. *Publication:* How to Prepare a Case for an Industrial Tribunal, 1987. *Recreations:* family life, fishing. *Address:* Cloisters, 1 Pump Court, Temple, EC4Y 7AA. *T:* 0171–583 0303. *Club:* Vincent's (Oxford).
See also Very Rev. J. E. Allen.

ALLEN, Thomas, CBE 1989; singer; *b* 10 Sept. 1944; *s* of Thomas Boaz Allen and Florence Allen; *m* 1st, 1968, Margaret Holley (marr. diss. 1986); one *s*; 2nd, 1988, Jeannie Gordon Lascelles. *Educ:* Robert Richardson Grammar Sch., Ryhope; Royal College of Music. ARCM; FRCM 1988. Welsh Nat. Opera, 1969–72; Principal Baritone, Royal Opera, Covent Garden, 1972–78; appearances include: Glyndebourne Fest. Opera; English Opera Group; Paris Opera; Florence; Teatro Colon, Buenos Aires; Met. Opera, NY; Hamburg; La Scala, Milan; BBC TV (The Gondoliers, The Marriage of Figaro); all major orchestras and various concert engagements abroad. Major rôles include: Figaro in Barber of Seville; Figaro and the Count in Marriage of Figaro; Papageno in The Magic Flute; Billy Budd; Marcello in La Bohême; Belcore in l'Elisir d'Amore; Sid in Albert Herring; Tarquinius in Rape of Lucretia; Guglielmo in Così fan Tutte; Demetrius in A Midsummer Night's Dream; Valentin in Faust; Dr Falke in Die Fledermaus; King Arthur; The Count in Voice of Ariadne; Silvio in Pagliacci; Pelléas in Pelléas and Mélisande; Germont in La Traviata; Don Giovanni; Mandryka in Arabella; Malatesta in Don Pasquale; title rôle in Il ritorno d'Ulisse; Beckmesser in Die Meistersinger, and many others. Hon. RAM, 1988. Hon. MA Newcastle, 1984; Hon. DMus Durham, 1988. *Publication:* Foreign Parts: a singer's journal, 1993. *Recreations:* gardening, golf, sailing, reading, ornithology. *Address:* c/o Lies Askonas Ltd, 6 Henrietta Street, WC2E 8LA.

ALLEN, Walter John Gardener; Controller, Capital Taxes Office (formerly Estate Duty Office), Inland Revenue, 1974–78; *b* 8 Dec. 1916; *s* of late John Gardiner Allen and late Hester Lucy Allen, Deal, Kent; *m* 1944, Irene (*d* 1983), *d* of late John Joseph and Sarah Henderson, Lisburn, N Ireland; one *s* one *d*. *Educ:* Manwoods, Sandwich; London Univ. (LLB). Entered Inland Revenue, 1934. Served RAF, 1940–46 (Flying Officer). FGS 1982. *Recreations:* amateur geologist; gardening. *Address:* 43 The Chase, Eastcote, Pinner, Mddx HA5 1SH. *T:* 0181–868 7101.

ALLEN, William Alexander, CBE 1980; RIBA; Founder Chairman, Bickerdike Allen Partners, architects, 1962–89, retired; *b* 29 June 1914; *s* of late Professor Frank Allen, FRSC; *m* 1938; Beatrice Mary Teresa Pearson; two *s* one *d*. *Educ:* public schools in Winnipeg; University of Manitoba. Royal Architectural Inst. of Canada Silver Medal, 1935. Univ. Gold Medal in Architecture, 1936. Appointed to Building Research Station, Watford, 1937; Chief Architect, Bldg Res. Stn, 1953–61; Principal of the Architectural Assoc. School of Architecture, 1961–66. Mem. Council, RIBA, 1953–72, 1982–89 (Chm. various cttees); ARIBA 1937; FRIBA 1965; Chm., Fire Research Adv. Cttee, 1973–83, Visitor, 1983–88; President: Institute of Acoustics, 1975–76; Ecclesiastic Arch. Assoc., 1980. Hon. Associate NZIA, 1965; Hon. Fellow, American Inst. Of Architects, 1984. Hon. LLD Manitoba, 1977. Commander, Ordem do Mérito, Portugal, 1972. *Publications:* (with R. Fitzmaurice) Sound Transmission in Buildings, 1939. Papers, etc, on scientific and technical aspects of architecture and urban design, professionalism, and modern architectural history and education. *Recreations:* writing, drawing, music. *Address:* 4 Ashley Close, Welwyn Garden City, Herts AL8 7LH. *T:* Welwyn Garden (01707) 324178. *Club:* Athenæum.
See also Prof. J. F. Allen.

ALLEN, William Anthony; Deputy Director, Bank of England, since 1994 (Head of Foreign Exchange Division, 1990–94); *b* 13 May 1949; *s* of Derek William Allen and Margaret Winifred Allen (*née* Jones); *m* 1972, Rosemary Margaret Eminson; one *s* two *d*. *Educ:* King's College Sch., Wimbledon; Balliol College, Oxford (BA); LSE (MScEcon). Joined Bank of England, 1972; Economic Intell. Dept, 1972–77; Gold and Foreign Exchange Office, 1977–78; seconded to Bank for Internat. Settlements, Basle, 1978–80; Asst Adviser, Economics Div., Bank of England (working on monetary policy), 1980–82; Manager, Gilt-Edged Div., 1982–86; Hd of Money Market Operations Div., 1986–90. Pt-time Advr, Nat. Bank of Poland, 1990–. *Publications:* articles in economics jls. *Recreations:* gardening, jazz. *Address:* Bank of England, Threadneedle Street, EC2R 8AH. *T:* 0171–601 4444.

ALLEN, Sir William (Guilford), Kt 1981; Chairman, family group of companies; *b* 22 April 1932; *s* of Sir William Guilford Allen, CBE, and Mona Maree Allen; *m* 1959, Elaine Therese Doyle; two *s* one *d*. *Educ:* Downlands Coll., Toowoomba, Qld. In grazing industry, Merino sheep; Principal, Historic Malvern Hills Registered Merino Stud; stud Santa Gertrudis cattle breeder. Commercial broadcasting industry. Treasurer and Trustee, Nat. Party, Qld. Councillor, Longreach Shire. Chm., Qld Transport and Technology Centre, 1984–; Director: Qantas, 1981–; Suncorp Building Soc., 1985–89; Power Brewing Co., 1989–. Trustee, National Party, Qld, 1989–. Fellow, GAPAN. *Recreation:* aviation. *Address:* Toorak House, Hipwood Road, Hamilton, Brisbane, Qld 4007, Australia. *T:* (7) 2624111. *Clubs:* Brisbane, Tattersalls, Australian, Longreach, Queensland Turf, Brisbane Amateur Turf (Brisbane); Australian, Royal Sydney Golf (Sydney).

ALLEN, Sir (William) Kenneth (Gwynne), Kt 1961; *b* 23 May 1907; *er s* of Harold Gwynne Allen and Hilda Allen, Bedford; *m* 1931, Eleanor Mary (*née* Eeles) (*d* 1990); one *s* one *d*. *Educ:* Westminster Sch.; Univ. of Neuchâtel, Switzerland. Started as engineering pupil, Harland & Wolff Ltd, Glasgow and Belfast; subsequently at W. H. Allen, Sons & Co. Ltd, Bedford; Dir, 1937–70, Man. Dir, 1946–70, Chm., 1955–70, W. H. Allen, Sons & Co. Ltd; Chm., Amalgamated Power Engineering, 1968–70; Director: Whessoe Ltd, 1954–65; Electrolux, 1970–78. Chm., Brit. Internal Combustion Engine Manufacturers' Assoc., 1955–57; Pres., British Engineers' Assoc., 1957–59 (now British Mechanical Engineering Fedn); Chm., BEAMA, 1959–61; Pres., Engineering Employers' Fedn, 1962–64; Chm., Labour and Social Affairs Cttee of CBI, 1965–67. FIMarE; MRINA. Freeman of City of London. Liveryman, Worshipful Company of Shipwrights. Mem. Beds CC, 1945–55; High Sheriff Beds, 1958–59; DL Beds, 1978–91. *Address:* 12 The Mews, Amesbury Abbey, Amesbury, Wilts SP4 7EX. *T:* Amesbury (01980) 624048.

ALLEN, Maj.-Gen. William Maurice, CB 1983; FCIT, FIMI, FILDM, FIMgt; MInstPet; Managing Director, Fortis International Ltd, 1991–92; *b* 29 May 1931; *s* of William James Allen and Elizabeth Jane Henrietta Allen; *m* 1955, Patricia Mary (*née* Fletcher); one *d* decd. *Educ:* Dunstable Sch. FCIT 1972; FIMI 1982; FILDM (FIPDM 1982); FIMgt (FBIM 1983); MInstPet 1982. Commnd RASC, 1950; RCT, 1965; regtl and staff appts, Korea, Cyprus, Germany and UK; Student, Staff Coll., Camberley, 1961; Instructor, Staff Coll., Camberley and RMCS Shrivenham, 1968–70; Student, RCDS, 1976; Asst Comdt, RMA Sandhurst, 1979–81; Dir Gen. of Transport and Movements (Army), 1981–83. Dir of Educn and Trng, Burroughs Machines Ltd, 1983–85. Jt Man. Dir, Marina Moraira Yacht Brokers, 1989–92; Sen. Mil. Consultant to Mondial Defence Systems (formerly Mondial & Co.), 1985–; Director: Govt Projects, Unisys Corp. (formerly Systems Develt Corp.), Heidelberg, 1985–86; Fortis Aviation Gp, Spain, 1988–89; European Management Information, 1989–. Member, Council: IAM, 1982–85; NDTA, 1983–. Chm., Milton Keynes Information Technol. Trng Centre, 1983–85. Associate, St George's House. Freeman, City of London, 1981; Hon. Liveryman, Worshipful Co. of Carmen, 1981. *Recreations:* economics, trout fishing, squash, gardening, rough shooting, ocean cruising. *Address:* c/o Royal Bank of Scotland, Holts Farnborough Branch, Lawrie House, 31–37 Victoria Road, Farnborough, Hants GU14 7NR. *Club:* Bristol Channel Yacht (Swansea).

ALLEN, Prof. William Sidney, MA, PhD (Cantab); FBA 1971; Professor of Comparative Philology in the University of Cambridge, 1955–82; Fellow of Trinity College, since 1955; *b* 18 March 1918; *er s* of late W. P. Allen and Ethel (*née* Pearce); *m* 1955, Aenea, *yr d* of late Rev. D. McCallum and Mrs McCallum, Invergordon. *Educ:* Christ's Hosp.; Trinity Coll., Cambridge (Classical Scholar); Porson Scholarship, 1939. War of 1939–45: RTR and General Staff (Int) (despatches). Lecturer in Phonetics, 1948–51, and in Comparative Linguistics, 1951–55, School of Oriental and African Studies, Univ. of London. Dialect research in India, 1952; Fellow of Rockefeller Foundation, USA, 1953; Brit. Council visitor, Univ. of W Indies, 1959. Linguistic Soc. of America's Professor, 1961; Collitz Professor, Linguistic Institute, USA, 1962; Ida Beam Lectr, Univ. of Iowa, 1983. Pres., Philological Soc., 1965–67. Hon. Fellow, Soc. for Cycladic Studies (Athens), 1977. Chm. Editorial Bd, CUP linguistic series, 1969–82; Editor, Lingua, 1963–85. *Publications:* Phonetics in Ancient India, 1953; On the Linguistic Study of Languages (inaugural lecture), 1957; Sandhi, 1962; Vox Latina, 1965; Vox Graeca, 1968, 3rd edn 1987; Accent and Rhythm, 1973; articles on general and comparative linguistics, phonetics, metrics, classical, Indian and Caucasian languages, Icelandic, Aegean cartography. *Address:* 24 Sherlock Road, Cambridge CB3 0HR. *T:* Cambridge (01223) 356739.

ALLEN, Woody; writer, actor, director; *b* Brooklyn, 1 Dec. 1935; *s* of Martin and Nettie Konigsberg; *m* 1966, Louise Lasser (marr. diss.); one *s* by Mia Farrow, *qv*. TV script writer, 1953–64, and appeared as a comedian in nightclubs and on TV shows. Sylvania Award, 1957. *Plays:* (writer) Don't Drink the Water, 1966; (writer and actor) Play It Again Sam, 1969 (filmed 1972); The Floating Light Bulb, 1990. *Films:* (writer and actor) What's New Pussycat?, 1965; (actor): Casino Royale, 1967; Scenes from a Mall, 1991; (writer, actor and director): What's Up Tiger Lily?, 1966; Take the Money and Run, 1969; Bananas, 1971; Everything You Always Wanted to Know About Sex But Were Afraid to Ask, 1972; Sleeper, 1973; Love and Death, 1975; The Front, 1976; Annie Hall (Academy Award), 1977; Manhattan, 1979; Stardust Memories, 1980; A Midsummer Night's Sex Comedy, 1982; Zelig, 1983; Broadway Danny Rose, 1984; Hannah and her Sisters (Academy Award), 1986; New York Stories, 1989; Shadows and Fog, 1992; Husbands and Wives, 1992; Manhattan Murder Mystery, 1994; (writer and director): Interiors, 1978; The Purple Rose of Cairo, 1985; Radio Days, 1987; September, 1988; Another Woman, 1989; Crimes and Misdemeanours, 1989; Alice, 1990; Bullets over Broadway, 1995. *Publications:* Getting Even, 1971; Without Feathers, 1975; Side Effects, 1981; contribs to New Yorker, etc.

ALLEN-JONES, Air Vice-Marshal John Ernest, CBE 1966; Director of RAF Legal Services, 1961–70, retired; *b* 13 Oct. 1909; *s* of Rev. John Allen-Jones, Llanyblodwel Vicarage, Oswestry; *m* 1st, 1937, Margaret Rix (*d* 1973), Sawbridgeworth; one *s* two *d*; 2nd, 1973, Diana Gibbons. *Educ:* Rugby; Worcester Coll., Oxford (MA). Solicitor (Honours), 1934; Partner with Vaudrey, Osborne & Mellor, Manchester. Joined RAF, 1939. Air Vice-Marshal, 1967. Gordon-Shepherd Memorial Prizeman, 1963. *Recreations:* tennis, bridge. *Address:* Hartfield, Duton Hill, Dunmow, Essex CM6 2DX. *T:* Great Easton (0137184) 554.

ALLENBY, family name of **Viscount Allenby.**

ALLENBY, 3rd Viscount *cr* 1919, of Megiddo and of Felixstowe; **Michael Jaffray Hynman Allenby;** Lieutenant-Colonel, The Royal Hussars, retired 1986; Chairman, Quickrest Ltd, 1987–90; a Deputy Speaker, House of Lords, since 1993; *b* 20 April 1931; *s* of 2nd Viscount Allenby and of Mary Lethbridge Allenby (*d* 1988), *d* of Edward Champneys; *S* father, 1984; *m* 1965, Sara Margaret, *d* of Lt-Col Peter Milner Wiggin; one *s*. *Educ:* Eton; RMA Sandhurst. Commnd 2/Lieut 11th Hussars (PAO), 1951; served Malaya, 1953–56; ADC to Governor, Cyprus, 1957–58; Bde Major, 51 Brigade, Hong Kong, 1967–70; comd Royal Yeomanry (TA), 1974–77; GS01 Instructor, Nigerian Staff Coll., Kaduna, 1977–79. *Recreations:* horses, sailing. *Heir:* *s* Hon. Henry Jaffray Hynman Allenby, *b* 29 July 1968. *Club:* Cavalry and Guards.

ALLENDALE, 3rd Viscount, *cr* 1911; **Wentworth Hubert Charles Beaumont,** DL; Baron, 1906; *b* 12 Sept. 1922; *e s* of 2nd Viscount Allendale, KG, CB, CBE, MC, and Violet (*d* 1979), *d* of Sir Charles Seely, 2nd Bt; *S* father 1956; *m* 1948, Hon. Sarah Ismay (marr. diss.), 2nd *d* of 1st Baron Ismay, KG, PC, GCB, CH, DSO; three *s*. *Educ:* Eton. RAFVR, 1940; Flight-Lieutenant 1943; ADC to Viceroy of India, 1946–47. DL Northumberland, 1961. *Heir:* *s* Hon. Wentworth Peter Ismay Beaumont [*b* 13 Nov. 1948; *m* 1975, Theresa Mary, *d* of F. A. More O'Ferrall; one *s* three *d*]. *Address:* Bywell Hall, Stocksfield on Tyne, Northumberland NE43 7AQ. *T:* Stocksfield (01661) 3169; Allenheads, Hexham, Northumberland. *T:* Allenheads (0143485) 205. *Clubs:* Turf, White's; Northern Counties (Newcastle upon Tyne).

See also Earl of Carlisle, Hon. Sir E. N. C. Beaumont.

ALLERTON, Air Vice-Marshal Richard Christopher, CB 1989; DL; Director General of Supply, Royal Air Force, 1987–90, retired; *b* 7 Dec. 1935; *er s* of late Air Cdre Ord Denny Allerton, CB, CBE, and Kathleen Allerton; *m* 1964, Marie Isobel Campbell Mackenzie, *er d* of Captain Sir Roderick Mackenzie, 11th Bt, CBE, DSC, RN, and of Marie, Lady Mackenzie; two *s*. *Educ:* Stone House, Broadstairs; Stowe Sch. Commissioned RAF, 1954; served, 1955–78: RAF Hullavington, Oakington, Feltwell, Kinloss, RAF Unit HQ Coastal Command, Hereford, Little Rissington; Instructor, RAF Coll., Cranwell; Student, RAF Staff Coll., Bracknell; Staff, HQ RAF Germany; Chief Instructor, Supply and Secretarial Trng, RAF Coll., Cranwell; Student, Nat. Defence Coll., Latimer; MoD Harrogate; Dep. Dir, RAF Supply Policy, MoD, 1978–80; Station Comdr, RAF Stafford, 1980–82; RCDS 1983; Air Cdre, Supply and Movements, HQ Strike Comd, 1983–86. ADC to the Queen, 1980–82. Pres., RAF Cricket Assoc., 1987–89. DL Cornwall, 1995. *Recreations:* shooting, fishing, cricket. *Address:* c/o Lloyds Bank, 13 Broad Street, Launceston, Cornwall PL15 8AG. *Club:* Royal Air Force.

ALLEY, Ronald Edgar; artist; Keeper of the Modern Collection, Tate Gallery, London, 1965–86; *b* 12 March 1926; *s* of late Edgar Thomas Alley; *m* 1955, Anthea Oswell (marr. diss.) (now painter and sculptor, as Anthea Alley); two *d*. *Educ:* Bristol Grammar School; Courtauld Institute of Art, London University. Tate Gallery staff as Asst Keeper II, 1951–54; Deputy Keeper, 1954–65. Member: Museum Board, Cecil Higgins Art Gallery, Bedford, 1957; Art Cttee, Ulster Museum, Belfast, 1962; Art Panel of Arts Council, 1963–70. *Publications:* Tate Gallery: Foreign Paintings, Drawings and Sculpture, 1959; Gauguin, 1962; William Scott, 1963; Ben Nicholson, 1963; Francis Bacon (with Sir John Rothenstein), 1964; British Painting since 1945, 1966; Picasso's "Three Dancers" 1967; Barbara Hepworth, 1968; Recent American Art, 1969; [illegible] Catalogue of the Tate Gallery's Collection of Modern [illegible] Artists, 1981. *Recreation:* ornithology. *Address:* 61 Deodar Road, SW15 2NU. *T:* [illegible] 2016. *Club:* Institute of Contemporary Arts.

ALLEYNE, Sir George (Allanmore Ogarren), Kt 1990; MD, FRCP; Director, Pan American Health Organization, since 1995 (Assistant Director, 1990–95); *b* 7 Oct. 1932; *s* of Clinton O. Alleyne and Eileen A. Alleyne (*née* Gaskin); *m* 1958, Sylvan Ionie (*née* Chen); two *s* one *d*. *Educ:* Harrison College, Barbados; University College of the West Indies (MB BS London 1977, MD). Completed training as physician in Barbados and UCH, London, 1958–62; Sen. Med. Registrar, UCH, Jamaica, 1962–63; Res. Fellow, Sen. Res. Fellow, MRC Tropical Metabolism Res. Unit, 1963–72; Prof. of Medicine, Univ. of W Indies, 1972–81 (Chm., Dept of Medicine, 1976–81); Pan American Health Organization: Head of Res. Unit, 1981–83; Dir of Health Programs Develt, 1983–90. Sir Arthur Sims Travelling Prof., 1977. Hon. FACP. Hon. DSc Univ. of W Indies, 1989. Jamaica Assoc. of Scientists Award, 1979. Jamaica Centenary Medal, 1980. *Publications:* contribs to learned jls on medicine, renal physiology and biochemistry, health and develt issues. *Recreations:* reading, gardening. *Address:* Pan American Health Organization, 525 23rd Street NW, Washington, DC 20037, USA. *T:* (202) 8613408.

ALLEYNE, Rev. Sir John (Olpherts Campbell), 5th Bt *cr* 1769; Rector of Weeke, Diocese of Winchester, 1975–93; *b* 18 Jan. 1928; *s* of Captain Sir John Meynell Alleyne, 4th Bt, DSO, DSC, RN, and Alice Violet (*d* 1985), *d* of late James Campbell; *S* father, 1983; *m* 1968, Honor, *d* of late William Albert Irwin, Belfast; one *s* one *d*. *Educ:* Eton; Jesus Coll., Cambridge (BA 1950, MA 1955). Deacon 1955, priest 1956; Curate, Southampton, 1955–58; Chaplain: Coventry Cathedral, 1958–62; Clare Coll., Cambridge, 1962–66; to Bishop of Bristol, 1966–68; Toc H Area Sec., SW England, 1968–71; Vicar of Speke, 1971–73, Rector, 1973–75. *Heir:* *s* Richard Meynell Alleyne, *b* 23 June 1972. *Address:* 2 Ash Grove, Guildford, Surrey GU2 5UT.

ALLEYNE, Selwyn Eugene, CBE 1986; Hong Kong Commissioner in London, 1987–89, retired; *b* 4 Dec. 1930; *s* of Gilbert Sydney Alleyne and Dorothy Alleyne; *m* 1956, Ellie Lynn Wong, MBE. *Educ:* Queen's Royal Coll., Trinidad; Jesus Coll., Oxford (MA). Joined Hong Kong Govt, 1956; Dep. Dir of Urban Services, 1974; Dep. Sec. for Civil Service, 1979; Dir of Social Welfare, and MLC, 1980; Dep. Financial Sec., 1983–87. *Recreations:* tennis, chess, collecting Chinese ceramics. *Address:* 118 Whitehall Court, SW1A 2EL. *Club:* Commonwealth Trust.

ALLFORD, David, CBE 1984; FRIBA; architect, retired; Senior Partner, YRM Partnership, 1975–87 (Partner since 1958); Chairman, YRM plc, 1987–89; Visiting Professor, Bartlett School of Architecture, University College London, since 1989; *b* 12 July 1927; *s* of Frank Allford and Martha Blanche Allford; *m* 1953, Margaret Beryl Roebuck; one *s* three *d*. *Educ:* High Storrs Grammar Sch., Sheffield; Univ. of Sheffield (BA Hons Architecture, 1952). FRIBA 1969. Served RAF, 1945–48. Joined Yorke Rosenberg Mardall, Architects (now YRM plc), 1952; Partner i/c architectural projects: schools, univs (principally Univ. of Warwick), Newcastle Airport, hosps and commercial projs in UK and overseas. Mem. Council, Architectural Assoc., 1970–71 and 1977–78. Hon DLitt Sheffield, 1994. *Publications:* articles in architectural press and related jls. *Recreations:* drawing, painting, following Sheffield Wednesday Football Club. *Address:* 39 Belsize Road, NW6 4RX. *T:* 0171–722 6724. *Clubs:* Garrick, Arts, MCC.

ALLHUSEN, Major Derek Swithin, CVO 1984; DL; farmer; Standard Bearer, HM's Body Guard of Honourable Corps of Gentlemen at Arms, 1981–84; *b* 9 Jan. 1914; 2nd *s* of late Lt-Col F. H. Allhusen, CMG, DSO, Fulmer House, Fulmer, Bucks; *m* 1937, Hon. Claudia Violet Betterton, *yr d* of 1st and last Baron Rushcliffe, PC, GBE (*d* 1949); one *s* one *d* (and one *s* decd). *Educ:* Eton; Chillon Coll., Montreux, Switzerland; Trinity Coll., Cambridge (MA). Lieut, 9th Queen's Royal Lancers, 1935. Served War of 1939–45:

France, 1940, North Africa, Italy (wounded twice) (Silver Star Medal of USA, 1944); Major 1942; 2 i/c 1945–47; retired, 1949. One of HM's Body Guard of Hon. Corps of Gentlemen at Arms, 1963–84. Chm., Riding for the Disabled, Norwich and Dist. Gp, 1968– (Vice-Pres., Eastern Region); President: Royal Norfolk Agric. Assoc., 1974; Nat. Pony Soc., 1982; Cambridge Univ. Equestrian Club; Norfolk Schs Athletic Assoc.; Pres., British Horse Soc., 1986–88 (Mem. Council, 1962–). Freeman, City of London; Hon. Yeoman, Worshipful Co. of Saddlers, 1969; Hon. Freeman, Worshipful Co. of Farriers, 1969. High Sheriff, 1958, DL 1969, Norfolk. *Recreations:* riding, shooting, skiing. Represented GB: Winter Pentathlon Olympic Games, 1948; Equestrianism European Championships Three-Day Event, 1957, 1959, 1965, 1967, 1969 (Winners of Team Championship, 1957, 1967, 1969); Olympic Games, Mexico, 1968 (Gold Medal, Team; Silver Medal, Individual); lent his horse Laurieston to British Olympic Equestrian Team, Munich, 1972 (individual and team Gold Medals). *Address:* Manor House, Claxton, Norwich, Norfolk NR14 7AS. *T:* Thurton (0150843) 228. *Clubs:* Cavalry and Guards, Army and Navy.

ALLIANCE, Sir David, Kt 1989; CBE 1984; Chairman: Coats Viyella, since 1989 (Group Chief Executive, 1975–90); N. Brown Group, since 1968; Tootal Group, since 1991; *b* June 1932. *Educ:* Iran. First acquisition, Thomas Hoghton (Oswaldtwistle), 1956; acquired Spirella, 1968, then Vantona Ltd, 1975, to form Vantona Group, 1975; acquired Carrington Viyella to form Vantona Viyella, 1983, Nottingham Manufacturing, 1985, Coats Patons to form Coats Viyella, 1986. Mem., British Coal Corp., 1993–. CIMgt (CBIM 1985); CompTI 1984. FRSA 1988. Hon. Fellow UMIST 1988; Hon. Fellow, Shenkar Coll. of Textile Tech. and Fashion, Israel, 1990. Hon. FCGI 1991. Hon. LLD Manchester, 1989; Hon. DSc Heriot-Watt, 1991. *Address:* Coats Viyella plc, 28 Savile Row, W1X 2DD. *T:* 0171–734 4030.

ALLIBONE, Thomas Edward, CBE 1960; DSc Sheffield; FRS 1948; FEng; External Professor of Electrical Engineering, University of Leeds, 1967–79, now Emeritus; Visiting Professor of Physics, City University, since 1971; also Robert Kitchin (Saddlers) Research Professor, since 1983, and first Frank Poynton Professor, Physics Department, since 1984, City University; *b* 11 Nov. 1903; *s* of Henry J. Allibone; *m* 1931, Dorothy Margery, LRAM, ARCM, *d* of Frederick Boulden, BSc, MEng, MIMechE; two *d*. *Educ:* Central Sch., Sheffield (Birley Scholar); Sheffield Univ. (Linley Scholar); Gonville and Caius Coll., Cambridge (Wollaston Scholar). PhD Sheffield; PhD Cantab. 1851 Exhibition Sen. Student, Cavendish Laboratory, Cambridge, 1926–30; i/c High-Voltage Laboratory, Metropolitan-Vickers Electrical Co., Manchester, 1930–46; Director: Res. Laboratory, AEI, Aldermaston, 1946–63; AEI (Woolwich) Ltd, 1948–63; Scientific Adviser, AEI, 1963; Chief Scientist, Central Electricity Generating Bd, 1963–70. Mem., British Mission on Atomic Energy, Berkeley, Calif, and Oakridge, Tenn, 1944–45; Visitor: BISRA, 1949–55; ASLIB, 1955–62. Lectures: Faraday, 1946, 1956; Royal Instn Christmas, 1959; Wm Menelaus, 1959; Bernard Price, 1959; Trotter Patterson, 1963; Fison Memorial, 1963; Royal Soc. Rutherford Memorial, 1964 and 1972; Baird Memorial, 1967; Melchett, 1970. President: Section A, British Assoc., 1958; EIBA, 1958–59; Inst. of Information Scientists, 1964–67. Vice-President: Inst. of Physics, 1948–52; Royal Instn, 1955–57, 1970–72. Chm., Res. Cttee, British Electrical and Allied Industries Res. Assoc., 1955–62. [illegible] Inst. of Radiology, 1935–38; Council, IEE, 1937–40, 1946–49, [illegible] Laboratory, 1950–60; Govt Cttee on Copyright, 1951; [illegible] (Mem., Industrial Grants Cttee, 1950–58); Council, Physical Soc., 1953–56; Council, Southern Electricity Bd, 1953–62; Adv. Council, Science Museum; Adv. Council, RMC; Adv. Court, AEA; Nuclear Safety Adv. Council, Min. of Power, 1959–88. Trustee, British Museum, 1968–74. Governor, Downe House, 1959–69; Chm. Governors, Reading Technical Coll., 1959–68. Lord of the Manor, Aldermaston, 1953–87. Mem. Court, Worshipful Co. of Broderers, 1985– (Liveryman, 1967). FInstP; Founder FEng; Hon. FIEE; Fellow, Amer. Inst. of Electrical Engineers. Hon. DSc: Reading, 1960; City, 1970; Hon. DEng Sheffield, 1969. Röntgen Medal, British Inst. of Radiology; Thornton and Cooper Hill Medals, IEE; Melchett Medal, Inst. of Fuel. *Publications:* The Release and Use of Nuclear Energy, 1961; Rutherford: Father of Nuclear Energy (Rutherford Lecture 1972), 1973; The Royal Society and its Dining Clubs, 1975; Lightning: the long spark, 1977; Cockcroft and the Atom, 1983; Metropolitan-Vickers Electrical Co. and the Cavendish Laboratory, 1984; The Making of Physicists, 1987; Philately and the Royal Society, 1990; papers on high voltage and transient electrical phenomena, fission and fusion. *Recreations:* photography, travel, gardening, philately. *Address:* York Cottage, Lovel Road, Winkfield, Windsor, Berks SL4 2ES. *T:* Winkfield Row (01344) 884501.

ALLIN, George, RCNC; Director General Ship Refitting, Ministry of Defence, 1989–93, retired; *b* 21 June 1933; *s* of late Henry Richard Allin and Mary Elizabeth Allin (*née* Wyatt); *m* 1st, 1956, Barbara May Short (marr. diss.); two *s*; 2nd, 1977, Janice Annette Richardson-Sandell. *Educ:* Devonport High Sch.; Devonport Dockyard Tech. Coll.; RNEC Manadon; RNC Greenwich. WhSch, BSc, CEng, MIEE, FIIM; FBIM. Asst Elect. Engineer, 1957–59; HMS Belfast, 1959; Admiralty, Bath, 1959–62; Elect. Engineer, MoD (Navy), Bath, 1963–68; HM Dockyard, Devonport: Line Manager, 1968–70; Project Manager Frigates, 1970–71; Supt Elect. Engineer, Dep. Personnel Manager, 1971–74; Industrial Relations Manager, 1975; Org. and Develt. Div., Dockyard HQ, Bath, 1975–79; HM Dockyard, Rosyth: Project Manager, SSBN Refit, 1980–81; Production Dir, 1981–83; Dockyard HQ, Bath: Management Systems and Audit Div., 1984–85; Principal Dir, Policy and Plans, 1985–86; Principal Dir, Ship Refitting, MoD (Navy), Bath, 1986–87; Dir, Aldermaston Projects, Brown & Root (on secondment), 1987–89. *Recreations:* chess, music, squash, snooker. *Club:* Bath and County (Bath).

ALLINSON, Sir Leonard; *see* Allinson, Sir W. L.

ALLINSON, Sir (Walter) Leonard, KCVO 1979 (MVO 1961); CMG 1976; HM Diplomatic Service, retired; *b* 1 May 1926; *o s* of Walter Allinson and Alice Frances Cassidy; *m* 1951, Margaret Patricia Watts; three *d* (of whom two are twins). *Educ:* Friern Barnet Grammar Sch.; Merton Coll., Oxford. First class in History, 1947; MA. Asst Principal, Ministry of Fuel and Power (Petroleum Div.), 1947–48; Asst Principal, later Principal, Min. of Education, 1948–58 (Asst Private Sec. to Minister, 1953–54); transf. CRO, 1958; First Sec. in Lahore and Karachi, 1960–62, Madras and New Delhi, 1963–66; Counsellor and Head of Political Affairs Dept, March 1968; Dep. Head, later Head, of Permanent Under Secretary's Dept, FCO, 1968–70; Counsellor and Head of Chancery, subsequently Deputy High Comr, Nairobi, 1970–73; RCDS, 1974; Diplomatic Service Inspectorate, 1975; Dep. High Comr and Minister, New Delhi, 1975–77; High Comr, Lusaka, 1978–80; Asst Under-Sec. of State (Africa), 1980–82; High Comr in Kenya and Ambassador to UN Environment Programme, 1982–86. Vice Pres., Royal African Soc., 1982–; Mem. Council, East Africa Inst., 1986–92; Hon. Vice Chm., Kenya Soc., 1989–. Gov., Wendron Voluntary Primary Sch., 1990–. *Address:* Tregarthen, Wendron, Helston, Cornwall TR13 0NA. *Club:* Oriental.

ALLIOTT, Hon. Sir John (Downes), Kt 1986; **Hon. Mr Justice Alliott;** Judge of the High Court of Justice, Queen's Bench Division, since 1986; *b* 9 Jan. 1932; *er s* of late Alexander Clifford Alliott and Ena Kathleen Alliott (*née* Downes); *m* 1957, Patsy Jennifer, *d* of late Gordon Beckles Willson; two *s* one *d*. *Educ:* Charterhouse; Peterhouse, Cambridge (Schol., BA). Coldstream Guards, 1950–51; Peterhouse, 1951–54; called to Bar, Inner Temple, 1955, Bencher 1980; QC 1973. Dep. Chm., E Sussex QS, 1970–71; Recorder, 1972–86; Leader, 1983–86, Presiding Judge, 1989–92, SE Circuit. Member: Home Office Adv. Bd on Restricted Patients, 1983–86; Parole Bd, 1994–. *Recreations:* rural pursuits, France and Italy, military history. *Address:* Royal Courts of Justice, Strand, WC2A 2LL.

ALLISON, Brian George; Chairman, Holt Lloyd International Ltd, since 1995; *b* 4 April 1933; *s* of late Donald Brian Allison and Edith Maud Allison (*née* Humphries); *m* 1958, Glennis Mary Taylor (*d* 1993); one *s* one *d*. *Educ:* Hele's Sch., Exeter; University Coll. London (BSc Econ). FCIM 1981. Flying Officer, RAF, 1955–58. Economist Statistician, Shell-Mex & BP, 1958; Marketing Res. Manager, Spicers, 1958–64; Business Intelligence Services, subseq. The BIS Group: Dir, 1964–91; Gen. Manager, 1964–69; Man. Dir and Dep. Chm., 1969–74; Chm. and Man. Dir, 1974–81; Chm. and Chief Exec., 1981–85; Exec. Chm., 1985–87. Director: English China Clays, subseq. ECC Gp, 1984–92; NYNEX Inf. Solutions Gp, 1987–90; Brammer, 1988–; Electra Corporate Ventures, 1989–; NYNEX Network Systems Co. (Brussels) SA, 1991–93; Microgen Holdings, 1992–; Unitech, 1993–; Mem, London Bd, Halifax Building Soc., 1991–. Vis. Prof., Univ. of Surrey, 1976–92, 1994–. Mem., ESRC, 1986–90. Distinguished Scholar, QUB, 1989. *Recreations:* tennis, travel, motoring, restoring historic properties. *Club:* Reform.

ALLISON, Air Vice-Marshal Dennis, CB 1987; Chief Executive, North Western Regional Health Authority, 1990–94 (General Manager, 1986–90); *b* 15 Oct. 1932; *m* 1964, Rachel Anne, *d* of Air Vice-Marshal J. G. Franks, *qv*; one *s* four *d*. *Educ:* RAF Halton; RAF Coll., Cranwell; Manchester Univ. (MA 1994). Commnd, 1954; No 87 Sqdn, 1955–58; cfs 1958; Flying Instructor and Coll. Adjt, RAF Coll., 1958–61; CO, RAF Sharjah, 1961–62; Indian Jt Services Staff Coll., 1965; MoD Central Staffs, 1968–70; ndc, 1973; MoD Central Staffs, 1973–74; CO, RAF Coningsby, 1974–76; Canadian Nat. Defence Coll., 1977; MoD Central Staffs, 1978–79; Comdt, Central Flying Sch., 1979–83; Dir of Training (Flying), MoD, 1983–84; Dir of Management and Support of Intelligence, MoD, 1985–86; retired 1987. Chm., Family Health Service Computer Unit, 1992–94; Member: NHS Trng Authority, 1988–91; Standing Cttee on Postgrad. Medical Educn, 1988–93; Steering Cttee on Pharmacist Postgrad. Educn, 1991–94; Adv. Bd, NHS Estates, 1991–; Nat. Blood Authority, 1993– (Vice Chm., 1994–). Gov., Salford Coll. of Technology, 1987–89. QCVSA 1959. *Recreations:* bridge, golf, keeping geese. *Address:* The Old Forge, Castle Bytham, Grantham, Lincs NG33 4RU. *T:* Castle Bytham (0178081) 372. *Club:* Royal Air Force.

ALLISON, John, CBE 1975; JP, DL; company director; *b* 4 Oct. 1919; *m* 1948, Elvira Gwendoline Lewis; one *s* two *d*. *Educ:* Morriston Elementary Sch.; Glanmor Secondary Sch.; Swansea Tech. Coll. In family business of quarrying to 1968, and musical instrument retailing, 1957–. Mem. (Lab) Swansea City Council, 1957–74, Leader, 1967–74 (Dep. Mayor, 1966–67 and 1972–73); Mem. (Lab) W Glamorgan County Council, 1974–89, Leader, 1977–89 (Chm., 1975–76); Chm., ACC, 1986–88. Contested (Lab) Barry, 1970. Chm., S Wales Police Authority, 1987–89. DL W Glam 1975; JP Swansea 1966. *Recreations:* fishing, gardening. *Address:* Penbryn, 155 Vicarage Road, Morriston, Swansea SA6 6DT. *T:* Swansea (01792) 71331. *Club:* Morriston Golf.

ALLISON, Air Marshal Sir John Shakespeare, KCB 1995; CBE 1986 (MBE 1971); Chief of Staff and Deputy Commander-in-Chief, Strike Command, since 1994; *b* 24 March 1943; *o s* of Walter Allison and Mollie Emmie Allison (*née* Poole); *m* 1966, Gillian Patricia Middleton; two *s* three *d*. *Educ:* Royal Grammar Sch., Guildford; RAF College, Cranwell; psc, rcds. Commissioned 1964; flying and staff appts include: 5 Sqn; 226 OCU; 310 TFTS (USAF), Arizona; OC 228 OCU; Station Comdr, RAF Wildenrath; Sec., Chiefs of Staff Cttee; Dir, Air Force Plans and Programmes, 1987–89; ACDS Operational Requirements (Air), MoD, 1989–91; AOC No 11 Gp, 1991–94. *Recreations:* air display flying, gliding, preservation of old cars and aircraft. *Address:* c/o National Westminster Bank, 24 Broadgate, Coventry CV1 1NB. *Club:* Royal Air Force.

ALLISON, Roderick Stuart; Chief Executive, Offshore Safety Division, Health and Safety Executive, since 1994; *b* 28 Nov. 1936; *s* of Stuart Frew Allison and Poppy (*née* Hodges); *m* 1968, Anne Sergeant; one *s* one *d*. *Educ:* Manchester Grammar Sch.; Balliol Coll., Oxford. Entered Ministry of Labour, 1959; Private Sec. to Perm. Sec., 1963–64; Principal, 1964; Civil Service Dept, 1969–71; Asst Sec., 1971, Under Sec., 1977, Dept of Employment; HSE, 1989–, Dir, Safety Policy Div., 1992–94. Chm., Adv. Cttee on Dangerous Substances, HSC, 1989–94; Mem., Channel Tunnel Safety Authority, 1992–94. *Recreations:* reading, music, sailing. *Address:* c/o Health and Safety Executive, Rose Court, 2 Southwark Bridge, SE1 9HS.

ALLISON, Ronald William Paul, CVO 1978; journalist, broadcaster; television consultant; Chairman: Television Barter International, since 1990; Grand Slam Sports, since 1991; *b* 26 Jan. 1932; *o s* of Percy Allison and Dorothy (*née* Doyle); *m* 1st, 1956, Maureen Angela Macdonald (*d* 1992); two *d*; 2nd, 1993, Jennifer Loy Weider. *Educ:* Weymouth Grammar Sch.; Taunton's Sch., Southampton. Reporter, Hampshire Chronicle, 1952–57; Reporter, BBC, 1957–67; freelance broadcaster, 1968–69; special correspondent, BBC, 1969–73; Press Sec. to Queen, 1973–78; regular presenter and commentator, Thames TV, 1978–; Controller of Sport and Outside Broadcasts, 1980–85, Dir of Corporate Affairs, 1986–89, Thames TV. *Publications:* Look Back in Wonder, 1968; The Queen, 1973; Charles, Prince of our Time, 1978; The Country Life Book of Britain in the Seventies, 1980; (ed with Sarah Riddell) The Royal Encyclopedia, 1991. *Recreations:* photography, watching football. *Address:* 14 Storey Court, 39 St John's Wood Road, NW8 8QX. *Clubs:* Royal Automobile; Stage Golf Soc.; Old Tauntonians (Southampton).

ALLISS, Peter; golfer; television commentator; *b* 28 Feb. 1931; *s* of Percy Alliss and Dorothy Alliss (*née* Rust); *m* 1st, 1953, Joan; one *s* one *d*; 2nd, 1969, Jacqueline Anne; two *s* one *d*. *Educ:* Queen Elizabeth's Grammar Sch., Wimborne; Crosby House, Bournemouth. Nat. Service, RAF Regt, 1949–51. Professional golfer, 1946; played in 8 Ryder Cup matches and 10 Canada Cup (now World Cup) matches; winner of 21 major events; open championships of Spain, Portugal, Italy, Brazil. Past Pres., Ladies' PGA and British Green Keepers' Assoc.; twice Captain, British PGA; golf course architect. *Publications:* Easier Golf (with Paul Trevillion), 1969; Bedside Golf, 1980; Shell Book of Golf, 1981; The Duke, 1983; Play Golf with Peter Alliss, 1983; The Who's Who of Golf, 1983; (with Michael Hobbs) The Open, 1984; Golfer's Logbook, 1984; Lasting the Course, 1984; More Bedside Golf, 1984; Peter Alliss' Most Memorable Golf, 1986; Peter Alliss' Supreme Champions of Golf, 1986; (ed) Winning Golf, 1986; Yet More Bedside Golf, 1986; Play Better Golf with Peter Alliss, 1989; (with Michael Hobbs) Peter Alliss' Best 100 Golfers, 1989; (with Bob Ferrier) The Best of Golf, 1989; *autobiography:* Alliss in Wonderland, 1964; Peter Alliss: an autobiography, 1981. *Recreation:* talking and taking wine with chums. *Address:* Bucklands, Hindhead, Surrey GU26 6HY. *Clubs:* Lansdowne, Crockfords, Ritz Casino.

ALLNUTT, Ian Peter, OBE; MA; *b* 26 April 1917; *s* of Col E. B. Allnutt, CBE, MC, and Joan C. Gainsford; *m* 1946, Doreen Louise Lenagan; four *d*. *Educ:* Imperial Service Coll., Windsor; Sidney Sussex Coll., Cambridge. HM Colonial Service, 1939–46, Nigeria, with

Inst. of Motor Industry, 1970–78. Chairman: Publicity Club of London, 1961–62; Industry Taxation Panel, 1977–86; United Technologists Estabt, 1980–; Dep. Chm., Technology Transfer Assoc., 1984–90; Member: Council, CBI, 1977–88; CBI Industrial Policy Cttee, 1979–85; Dun & Bradstreet Industry Panel, 1982–86. Chm., Automotive VIP Club, 1988–92. Various TV and radio broadcasts. Freeman: City of London, 1973; City of Glasgow, 1974; Liveryman and former Hon. Treas., Coachmakers' and Coach Harness Makers' Co.; Burgess Guild Brother, Cordwainers' Co. *Publications:* articles. *Address:* (office) 405 Gilbert House, Barbican, EC2Y 8BD. *T:* and *Fax:* 0171–638 3023.

ALTMAN, Robert; film director; *b* Kansas City, 20 Feb. 1925; *m* 3rd, Kathryn Altman; one *s* and one adopted *s* (and two *s* one *d* by previous marriages). *Educ:* Univ. of Missouri. Served US Army, 1943–47. Industrial film maker, Calvin Co., Kansas City, 1950–57. Television writer, producer and director, 1957–65. Films directed: That Cold Day in the Park, 1969; M*A*S*H*, 1970 (Grand Prix, Cannes, 1970); Brewster McCloud, 1971; McCabe and Mrs Miller, 1971; Images, 1972; The Long Goodbye, 1973; Thieves Like Us, 1974; California Split, 1974; Nashville, 1975; Buffalo Bill and the Indians, 1976; 3 Women, 1977; A Wedding, 1978; Quintet, 1979; A Perfect Couple, 1979; Health, 1979; Popeye, 1980; Come Back to the 5 & Dime Jimmy Dean, Jimmy Dean, 1982; Streamers, 1983; Fool for Love, 1986; Beyond Therapy, 1987; (jtly) Aria, 1987; Vincent & Theo, 1990; The Player, 1992 (Best Dir, Cannes Film Fest. 1992); Short Cuts, 1993; directed and produced: Secret Honor, 1984; Tanner '88, 1988 (series); produced: Welcome to LA, 1977; The Late Show, 1977; Remember My Name, 1978; Rich Kids, 1979; Mrs Parker and the Vicious Circle, 1995. *Address:* c/o Sandcastle 5 Productions, Inc., 502 Park Avenue #15-G, New York City, NY 10022, USA.

ALTON, David Patrick; MP Mossley Hill Division of Liverpool, since 1983 (Edge Hill Division, March 1979–1983) (L 1979–88, Lib Dem since 1988); *b* 15 March 1951; *s* of Frederick and Bridget Alton; *m* 1988, Dilys Elizabeth, *yr d* of Rev. Philip Bell; two *s* one *d*. *Educ:* Edmund Campion Sch., Hornchurch; Christ's College of Education, Liverpool. Elected to Liverpool City Council as Britain's youngest City Councillor, 1972; CC, 1972–80; Deputy Leader of the Council and Housing Chairman, 1978; Vice-Pres., AMA, 1979–. MP (L) Liverpool, Edge Hill (by-election), with a 32 per cent swing, March 1979 (youngest member of that parliament); Liberal Party spokesman on: the environment and race relations, 1979–81; home affairs, 1981–82; NI, 1987–88 (Alliance spokesman on NI, 1987); Chief Whip, Liberal Party, 1985–87; Member: Select Cttee on the Environment, 1981–85; H of C Privileges Cttee, 1994–. All Party Groups: Vice Chairman: Drugs Misuse; Mental Health; Treas., Pro-Life; Chm., Street Children, 1992–; Sec., Ukraine. Chm., Liberal Candidates Cttee, 1985. Nat. Pres., Nat. League of Young Liberals, 1979. Co-founder, Movement for Christian Democracy in Britain, 1990. Former Chm., Council for Educn in Commonwealth. Nat. Vice-Pres., Life; Pres., Liverpool Old People's Hostels Assoc.; Vice-Pres., Liverpool YMCA; Chm., Forget-me-not Appeal (Royal Liverpool Hosp.). Vice-Pres., Assoc. of Councillors. Trustee: Crisis at Christmas; Liverpool Hostels for Victims of Violent Crime; Western Care Assoc. Patron: Jubilee Campaign for the release of prisoners of conscience, 1986–; Belfast Trust for Integrated Educn. Mem., Inst. of Journalists. Columnist: Catholic Pictorial, 1982–; Merseymart, 1983–; Liverpool Star, 1987–; The Universe, 1989–. *Publications:* What Kind of Country?, 1987; Whose Choice Anyway?, 1988; Faith in Britain, 1991. *Recreations:* gardening, reading, walking. *Address:* 25 North Mossley Hill Road, Liverpool L18 8BL. *T:* 0151–724 6106.

ALTON, Euan Beresford Seaton, MBE 1945; MC 1943; Under Secretary, Department of Health and Social Security, 1968–76; *b* 22 April 1919; *y s* of late William Lester St John Alton and Ellen Seaton Alton; *m* 1953, Diana Margaret Ede; one *s* one *d*. *Educ:* St Paul's Sch.; Magdalen Coll., Oxford (Exhibnr; MA). Served with Army, 1939–45; Major RA. Admin. Officer, Colonial Service and HM OCS, Gold Coast and Ghana, 1946–58; Admin. Officer, Class 1, 1957. Entered Civil Service as Asst Principal, Min. of Health, 1958; Principal, 1958; Asst Sec., 1961; Under Sec., 1968. *Recreations:* sailing, walking. *Address:* Spindlehurst, School Lane, Brantham, Manningtree, Essex CO11 1QE. *T:* Colchester (01206) 393419. *Clubs:* Cruising Association; Stour Sailing (Manningtree).

ALTRINCHAM, Barony of, *cr* 1945, of Tormarton; title disclaimed by 2nd Baron. *Heir to barony:* Hon. Anthony Ulick David Dundas Grigg [*b* 12 Jan. 1934; *m* 1965, Eliane de Miramon; two *s* one *d*].

ALUN-JONES, Sir (John) Derek, Kt 1987; Chairman: Spectrum Energy & Information Technology Ltd, since 1990; Straker Holdings Ltd, since 1991; Boulton and Paul Ltd, since 1993, and several other private companies; *b* 6 June 1933; *s* of Thomas Alun-Jones, LLB and Madge Beatrice Edwards; *m* 1960, Gillian Palmer; two *s* three *d*. *Educ:* Lancing College; St Edmund Hall, Oxford (MA Hons Jurisp.). Philips Electrical, 1957–59; H. C. Stephens, 1959–60; Expandite, 1960–71 (Man. Dir, 1966–71); Man. Dir, Burmah Industrial Products, 1971–74; Man. Dir and Chief Exec., 1975–87, Chm., 1987–90, Ferranti, subseq. Ferranti Internat. Signal, then Ferranti Internat.; Director: Burmah Oil Trading, 1974–75; Royal Insurance Holdings plc (formerly Royal Insurance), 1981–; Throgmorton Trust, 1978–84; SBAC, 1982–90; Reed International PLC, 1984–90; GKN plc, 1986–88; Consolidated Gold Fields PLC, 1988–89. *Recreations:* shooting, fishing, golf. *Address:* The Willows, Effingham Common, Surrey KT24 5JE. *T:* Bookham (01372) 458158.

ALVAREZ, Alfred; poet and author; *b* London, 1929; *s* of late Bertie Alvarez and Katie Alvarez (*née* Levy); *m* 1st, 1956, Ursula Barr (marr. diss. 1961); one *s*; 2nd, 1966, Anne Adams; one *s* one *d*. *Educ:* Oundle Sch.; Corpus Christi Coll., Oxford. BA (Oxon) 1952, MA 1956. Research Schol., CCC, Oxon, and Research Schol. of Goldsmiths' Company, 1952–53, 1954–55. Procter Visiting Fellowship, Princeton, 1953–54; Vis. Fellow of Rockefeller Foundn, USA, 1955–56, 1958; gave Christian Gauss Seminars in Criticism, Princeton, and was Lectr in Creative Writing, 1957–58; D. H. Lawrence Fellowship, New Mexico Univ., 1958; Poetry Critic, The Observer, 1956–66. Visiting Professor: Brandeis Univ., 1960; New York State Univ., Buffalo, 1966. Vachel Lindsay Prize for Poetry (from Poetry, Chicago), 1961. *Publications:* The Shaping Spirit (US title, Stewards of Excellence), 1958; The School of Donne, 1961; The New Poetry (ed and introd), 1962; Under Pressure, 1965; Beyond All This Fiddle, 1968; Lost (poems), 1968; Penguin Modern Poets, No 18, 1970; Apparition (poems, with paintings by Charles Blackman), 1971; The Savage God, 1971; Beckett, 1973; Hers (novel), 1974; Hunt (novel), 1978; Autumn to Autumn and Selected Poems 1953–76, 1978; Life After Marriage, 1982; The Biggest Game in Town, 1983; Offshore, 1986; Feeding the Rat, 1988; Rain Forest (with paintings by Charles Blackman), 1988; Day of Atonement (novel), 1991; The Faber Book of Modern European Poetry (ed and introd.), 1992; Night, 1995. *Recreations:* poker, music. *Address:* c/o Aitken & Stone, 29 Fernshaw Road, SW10 0TG. *Clubs:* Beefsteak, Climbers', Alpine.

ALVES, Colin, OBE 1990; General Secretary: General Synod Board of Education, 1984–90; National Society for Promoting Religious Education, 1984–90; *b* 19 April 1930; *s* of Donald Alexander Alves and Marjorie Alice (*née* Marsh); *m* 1953, Peggy (*née* Kember); two *s* one *d*. *Educ:* Christ's Hospital, Horsham; Worcester Coll., Oxford (MA). School teaching, 1952–59; Lectr, King Alfred's Coll., Winchester, 1959–68; Head of Dept, Brighton Coll. of Educn, 1968–74; Dir, RE Centre, St Gabriel's Coll., 1974–77; Colleges Officer, General Synod Bd of Educn, 1977–84. Mem., Durham Commn on RE, 1967–70; Chm., Schs Council RE Cttee, 1971–77; Sec., Assoc. of Voluntary Colls, 1978–84; Member: Adv. Cttee on Supply and Educn of Teachers, 1980–85; Nat. Adv. Body for Public Sector Higher Educn, 1983–88; Voluntary Sector Consultative Council, 1984–88. Review Officer, Churches Together in England, 1993–94. Governor: Christ Church Coll., Canterbury, 1981–95; Haywards Heath Coll., 1982–; Digby Stuart Coll., 1990–; Trustee: Shoei Coll., Winchester, 1982–94; St Gabriel's Trust, 1984–; St Pierre Internat. Youth Trust, 1990–; St Gregory's Trust, 1991–95. MLitt Lambeth, 1989. *Publications:* Religion and the Secondary School, 1968; The Christian in Education, 1972; The Question of Jesus, 1987; Free to Choose, 1991; contrib. various symposia on RE. *Recreations:* music, walking, gardening. *Address:* 9 Park Road, Haywards Heath, Sussex RH16 4HY. *T:* Haywards Heath (01444) 454496.

ALVEY, John, CB 1980; FEng 1984; Chairman, SIRA Ltd, 1987–94; *b* 19 June 1925; *s* of George C. V. Alvey and Hilda E. Alvey (*née* Pellatt); *m* 1955, Celia Edmed Marson; three *s*. *Educ:* Reeds Sch.; London Univ.; BSc (Eng), DipNEC. FIEE; MBCS. London Stock Exchange, to 1943. Royal Navy, 1943–46; Royal Naval Scientific Service, 1950; Head of Weapons Projects, Admiralty Surface Weapons Estabt, 1968–72; Dir-Gen. Electronics Radar, PE, MoD, 1972–73; Dir-Gen., Airborne Electronic Systems, PE, MoD, 1974–75; Dir, Admiralty Surface Weapons Estabt, 1976–77; Dep. Controller, R&D Estabts and Res. C, and Chief Scientist (RAF), MoD, 1977–80; Senior Dir, Technology, 1980–83, Man. Dir, Develt and Procurement, and Engr-in-Chief, 1983–86, British Telecom. Dir (non-exec.), LSI Logic Ltd, 1986–91. Member Council: Fellowship of Engrg, 1985–92 (Vice-Pres., 1989–92); Foundn for Sci. and Technology, 1986–90; City Univ., 1985–93. Fellow, Queen Mary and Westfield Coll. (formerly QMC), London, 1988. FRSA 1983. Hon. DSc City, 1984; Hon. DTech CNAA, 1991. *Recreations:* reading, Rugby, skiing, theatre going. *Address:* c/o SIRA Ltd, South Hill, Chislehurst, Kent BR7 5EH.

ALVINGHAM, 2nd Baron, *cr* 1929, of Woodfold; **Maj.-Gen. Robert Guy Eardley Yerburgh,** CBE 1978 (OBE 1972); *b* 16 Dec. 1926; *s* of 1st Baron and Dorothea Gertrude (*d* 1927), *d* of late J. Eardley Yerburgh; *S* father 1955; *m* 1952, Beryl Elliott, *d* of late W. D. Williams; one *s* one *d*. *Educ:* Eton. Commissioned 1946, Coldstream Guards; served UK, Palestine, Tripolitania, BAOR, Farelf, British Guiana; Head of Staff, CDS, 1972–75; Dep. Dir, Army Staff Duties, 1975–78; Dir of Army Quartering, 1978–81, retired. *Heir: s* Captain Hon. Robert Richard Guy Yerburgh, 17th/21st Lancers, retired [*b* 10 Dec. 1956; *m* 1st, 1981, Vanessa, *yr d* of Captain Duncan Kirk (marr. diss. 1993); two *s*; 2nd, 1994, Karen, *er d* of Antony Baldwin].

AMANN, Prof. Ronald, PhD; Chief Executive and Deputy Chairman, Economic and Social Research Council, since 1994; Professor of Comparative Politics (formerly of Soviet Politics), University of Birmingham, since 1986 (on leave of absence); *b* 21 Aug. 1943; *s* of George James Amann and Elizabeth Clementson Amann (*née* Towell); *m* 1965, Susan Frances Peters; two *s* one *d*. *Educ:* Heaton Grammar Sch., Newcastle upon Tyne; Univ. of Birmingham (MSocSc, PhD). Consultant, OECD, and Res. Associate, 1965–68; University of Birmingham: Asst Lectr, then Lectr and Sen. Lectr, 1968–83; Dir, Centre for Russian and E European Studies, 1983–89; Dean, Faculty of Commerce and Soc. Sci., 1989–91; Pro-Vice-Chancellor, 1991–94. Vis. Fellow, Osteuropa Inst., Munich, 1975. Special Advr, H of C Select Cttee on Sci. and Technol., 1976. Mem. Council, SSEES, London Univ., 1986–89. *Publications:* jointly: Science Policy in the USSR, 1969; The Technological Level of Soviet Industry, 1977; Industrial Innovation in the Soviet Union, 1982; Technical Progress and Soviet Economic Development, 1986. *Recreations:* modern jazz, walking. *Address:* 26 Spring Road, Edgbaston, Birmingham B15 2HA. *T:* 0121–440 6186. *Club:* Athenæum.

AMBARTSUMIAN, Victor; Hero of Socialist Labour (twice); Order of Lenin (five times); Order of Labour Red Banner (twice); Hon. President, Academy of Sciences of Armenia, since 1993 (President, 1947–93); *b* 18 Sept. 1908; *m* 1931, Vera Ambartsumian; two *s* two *d*. *Educ:* Univ. of Leningrad. Lecturer in Astronomy, 1931–34, Prof. of Astrophysics, 1934–44, Univ. of Leningrad; Prof. of Astrophysics, Univ. of Erevan, 1944–. Full Mem., Russian Academy of Sciences, 1953–. Pres., Internat. Council of Scientific Unions, 1968–72. Hon. Dr of Science: Univs of Canberra, 1963; Paris, 1965; Liege, 1967; Prague, 1967; Torun, 1973; La Plata, 1974; Foreign Member of Academies of Science: Washington, Paris, Rome, Vienna, Berlin, Amsterdam, Copenhagen, Sofia, Stockholm, Boston, New York, New Delhi, Cordoba, Prague, Budapest; Foreign Member of Royal Society, London. *Publications:* Theoretical Astrophysics, 1953 (in Russian; trans. into German, English, Spanish, Chinese); about 100 papers in learned jls. *Address:* Academy of Sciences of Armenia, Marshal Bagramian Avenue 24, Erevan, Armenia.

AMBERLEY, Viscount; Nicholas Lyulph Russell; *b* 12 Sept. 1968; *s* and *heir* of Earl Russell, *qv*.

AMBLER, Eric, OBE 1981; novelist and screenwriter; *b* 28 June 1909; *s* of Alfred Percy and Amy Madeleine Ambler; *m* 1st, 1939, Louise Crombie; 2nd, 1958, Joan Harrison (*d* 1994). *Educ:* Colfe's Grammar Sch.; London Univ. Apprenticeship in engineering, 1927–28; advertisement copywriter, 1929–35; professional writer, 1936–. Served War of 1939–45: RA, 1940; commissioned, 1941; served in Italy, 1943; Lt-Col, 1944; Asst Dir of Army Kinematography, War Office, 1944–46. US Bronze Star, 1946. Wrote and produced film, The October Man, 1947 and resumed writing career. Diamond Dagger Award, CWA, 1986. Hon. DLitt City, 1992. *Screenplays* include: The Way Ahead, 1944; The October Man, 1947; The Passionate Friends, 1948; Highly Dangerous, 1950; The Magic Box, 1951; Gigolo and Gigolette, in Encore, 1952; The Card, 1952; Rough Shoot, 1953; The Cruel Sea, 1953; Lease of Life, 1954; The Purple Plain, 1954; Yangtse Incident, 1957; A Night to Remember, 1958; Wreck of the Mary Deare, 1959; Love Hate Love, 1970. *Publications:* The Dark Frontier, 1936; Uncommon Danger, 1937; Epitaph for a Spy, 1938; Cause for Alarm, 1938; The Mask of Dimitrios, 1939; Journey into Fear, 1940; Judgment on Deltchev, 1951; The Schirmer Inheritance, 1953; The Night-comers, 1956; Passage of Arms, 1959; The Light of Day, 1962; The Ability to Kill (essays), 1963; (ed and introd) To Catch a Spy, 1964; A Kind of Anger, 1964 (Edgar Allan Poe award, 1964); Dirty Story, 1967; The Intercom Conspiracy, 1969; The Levanter, 1972 (Golden Dagger award, 1973); Doctor Frigo, 1974 (MWA Grand Master award, 1975); Send No More Roses, 1977; The Care of Time, 1981; Here Lies (autobiog.), 1985; The Story So Far, 1993. *Address:* 14 Bryanston Square, W1H 7FF. *Club:* Garrick.

AMBLER, John Doss; Vice-President, since 1980, Vice-President, Human Resources, since 1989, Texaco Inc.; *b* 24 July 1934; *m*; one *s* one *d*. *Educ:* Virginia Polytechnic Inst. (BSc Business Admin). Texaco Inc., USA: various assignments, Marketing Dept, Alexandra, Va, 1956–65; Dist Sales Manager, Harrisburg, Pa, 1965–67; Asst Divl Manager, Norfolk, Va, 1967–68; Staff Asst to Gen. Man. Marketing US, New York, 1968; various assignments, Chicago and New York, 1969–72; Gen. Man., Texaco Olie Maatschappij BV, Rotterdam, 1972–75; Man. Dir, Texaco Oil AB, Stockholm, 1975–77; Asst to Pres., 1977, Asst to Chm. of the Bd, 1980, Texaco Inc., USA; Pres., Texaco Europe, New York, 1981–82; Chm. and Chief Exec. Officer, Texaco Ltd, 1982–89. *Recreations:* hunting, fishing, tennis, photography. *Address:* Texaco Inc., 2000 Westchester Avenue, White Plains, New York, NY 10650, USA.

AMBO, Rt. Rev. George Somboba, KBE 1988 (OBE 1978); Archbishop of Papua New Guinea, 1983–89; Bishop of Popondota, 1977–89; Chairman, South Pacific Anglican Council, 1986–89; *b* Gona, Nov. 1925; *s* of late J. O. Ambo, Gona; *m* 1946, Marcella O., *d* of Karau; two *s* two *d. Educ:* St Aidan's College, Dogura; Newton Theological Coll., Dogura. Deacon, 1955; Priest, 1958. Curate of: Menapi, 1955–57; Dogura, 1957–58; Priest in charge of Boianai, Diocese of New Guinea, 1958–63; Missionary at Wamira, 1963–69; an Asst Bishop of Papua New Guinea, 1960 (first Papuan-born Anglican Bishop). *Publication:* St John's Gospel in Ewage. *Recreations:* reading, carpentry. *Address:* c/o Anglican Diocesan Office, PO Box 26, Popondetta, Papua New Guinea.

AMBRASEYS, Prof. Nicholas, FEng 1985, FICE; Professor of Engineering Seismology, University of London, at Imperial College, since 1973; Head of Engineering Seismology Section, since 1969; *b* 19 Jan. 1929; *s* of Neocles Ambraseys, Athens, and Cleopatra Jambany; *m* 1955, Xeni, *d* of A. Stavrou. *Educ:* National Technical Univ. of Athens (DipEng); Univ. of London (DIC; PhD; DSc 1980). Lectr in Civil Engineering, Imperial Coll., 1958–62; Associate Prof. of Civil Engrg, Univ. of Illinois, 1963; Prof. of Hydrodynamics, Nat. Tech. Univ., Athens, 1964; Imperial College: Lectr, 1965–68; Univ. Reader in Engrg Seismology, 1969–72. Chm., British Nat. Cttee for Earthquake Eng., 1961–71; Dir, Internat. Assoc. for Earthquake Engrg, 1961–77; Vice-Pres., European Assoc. for Earthquake Engrg, 1964–75; Mem., 1969–78, Vice-Chm., 1979–81, Unesco Internat. Adv. Cttee of Earthquake Risk; leader, UN/Unesco earthquake reconnaisance missions to Pakistan, Iran, Turkey, Romania, Jugoslavia, Italy, Greece, Algeria, Nicaragua, East and Central Africa; Chm., Internat. Commn for earthquake protection of historical monuments, 1977–81; Royal Soc. rep., British Nat. Cttee for Geodesy and Geophysics, 1975–85; consultant to Binnie & Partners, UN/Unesco. Hon. Fellow, Internat. Assoc. for Earthquake Engrg, 1992. Dr Eng *hc* Nat. Tech. Univ. of Athens, 1993. Decennial Award, European Assoc. for Earthquake Engrg, 1975; Busk Medal, RGS, 1975. *Publications:* A History of Persian Earthquakes (with C. Melville), 1982; papers on engrg seismology, soil mechanics, tectonics, historical seismicity. *Recreations:* history, philately. *Address:* Imperial College, SW7 2BU. *T:* 0171–589 5111; 19 Bede House, Manor Fields, SW15 3LT. *T:* 0181–788 4219.

AMBROSE, Prof. Edmund Jack, MA (Cantab), DSc (London); Professor of Cell Biology, University of London, Institute of Cancer Research, 1967–76, now Emeritus Professor; Staff of Chester Beatty Research Institute, Institute of Cancer Research: Royal Cancer Hospital, 1952–75; *b* 2 March 1914; *s* of Alderman Harry Edmund Ambrose and Kate (*née* Stanley); *m* 1943, Andrée (*née* Huck), Seine, France; one *s* one *d. Educ:* Perse Sch., Cambridge; Emmanuel Coll., Cambridge. Wartime research for Admiralty on infra-red detectors, 1940–45; subseq. research on structure of proteins using infra-red radiation at Courtauld Fundamental Research Laboratory. Formerly Convener of Brit. Soc. for Cell Biology. Formerly Special Adviser in Cancer to Govt of India at Tata Meml Centre, Bombay. Special Adviser in Leprosy, Foundn for Med. Res., Bombay, 1978– (awarded St Elizabeth Meml Medal, Order of St John, Paris, 1981 for leprosy work); Adviser, Regional Cancer Centre, Kerala, India, 1984–. Pres., Internat. Cell Tissue and Organ Culture Group. Research on structure of proteins, on structure of normal and cancer cells, and on characteristics of surface of cancer cells, cell biology and microbiology of leprosy, using labelled metabolites. *Publications:* Cell Electrophoresis, 1965; The Biology of Cancer, 1966, 2nd edn 1975; The Cancer Cell *in vitro.* 1967; (jtly) Cell Biology, 1970, rev. edn 1976; Nature of the Biological World, 1982; The Mirror of Creation, 1990; publications on Protein Structure and Cell Biology, in Proc. Royal Soc., biological jls. *Recreation:* sailing. *Address:* The Mill House, Westfield, Hastings, E Sussex TN35 4SU. *Clubs:* Chelsea Arts; Royal Bombay Yacht.

AMBROZIC, Most Rev. Aloysius Matthew; *see* Toronto, Archbishop of, (RC).

AMERY, family name of **Baron Amery of Lustleigh.**

AMERY OF LUSTLEIGH, Baron *cr* 1992 (Life Peer), of Preston, in the County of Lancashire and of Brighton in the County of East Sussex; **Julian Amery,** PC 1960; *b* 27 March 1919; *s* of late Rt Hon. Leopold Amery, PC, CH; *m* 1950, Lady Catherine (*d* 1991), *d* of 1st Earl of Stockton, OM, PC, FRS; one *s* three *d. Educ:* Summer Fields; Eton; Balliol Coll., Oxford. War Corresp. in Spanish Civil War, 1938–39; Attaché HM Legation, Belgrade, and on special missions in Bulgaria, Turkey, Roumania and Middle East, 1939–40; Sergeant in RAF, 1940–41; commissioned and transferred to army, 1941; on active service, Egypt, Palestine and Adriatic, 1941–42; liaison officer to Albanian resistance movement, 1944; served on staff of Gen. Carton de Wiart, VC, Mr Churchill's personal representative with Generalissimo Chiang Kai-Shek, 1945. Contested Preston in Conservative interest, July 1945; MP (C): Preston North, 1950–66; Brighton Pavilion, 1969–92. Delegate to Consultative Assembly of Council of Europe, 1950–53 and 1956. Member Round Table Conference on Malta, 1955. Parly Under-Sec. of State and Financial Sec., War Office, 1957–58; Parly Under-Sec. of State, Colonial Office, 1958–60; Sec. of State for Air, Oct. 1960–July 1962; Minister of Aviation, 1962–64; Minister of Public Building and Works, June–Oct. 1970; Minister for Housing and Construction, DoE, 1970–72; Minister of State, FCO, 1972–74. Hon. LLD Westminster Coll., Fulton, Miss. Kt Comdr, Order of Phœnix, Greece; Grand Cordon, Order of Skanderbeg, Albania; Order of Oman, first class. *Publications:* Sons of the Eagle, 1948; The Life of Joseph Chamberlain: vol. IV, 1901–3: At the Height of his Power, 1951; vols V and VI, 1901–14: Joseph Chamberlain and the Tariff Reform Campaign, 1969; Approach March (autobiog.), 1973; articles in National Review, Nineteenth Century and Daily Telegraph. *Recreations:* ski-ing, mountaineering, travel. *Address:* 112 Eaton Square, SW1W 9AE. *T:* 0171–235 1543; Forest Farm House, Chelwood Gate, East Sussex RH17 7DA. *Clubs:* White's, Beefsteak, Carlton, Buck's.

AMERY, Colin Robert; architectural writer, critic and historian; *b* 29 May 1944; *yr s* of Kenneth George Amery and late Florence Ellen Amery (*née* Young). *Educ:* King's College London; Univ. of Sussex (BA Hons). Editor and Inf. Officer, TCPA, 1968–70; Asst Editor and Features Editor, Architectural Review, 1970–79; Architecture Corresp., Financial Times, 1979–. Advr for Sainsbury Wing, Nat. Gall., 1985–91; Arch. consultant to J. Sainsbury plc, 1985–. Vis. Fellow, Jesus Coll., Cambridge, 1989. Member: Arts Panel, Arts Council, 1984–86; Exec. Cttee, Georgian Gp, 1985–93; Adv. Cttee, Geffrye Mus., 1985–87; Architecture Panel, NT, 1986–; London Adv. Cttee, English Heritage, 1987–90; Building Cttee, Nat. Gallery, 1988–92; British Council, Visual Art Adv. Cttee, 1989–93; Dir, Sir John Soane Soc., 1987–; Dir of Develt, Prince of Wales's Inst. of Architecture, 1993–; Chairman: Organising Cttee, Lutyens Exhibn, 1981–82; Lutyens Trust, 1984–93 (Patron, 1993–); Duchy of Cornwall Commercial Property Develt Cttee, 1990; Perspectives on Architecture Ltd, 1994–. Trustee: Spitalfields Trust, 1977–85; Brooking Collection, 1985–94; Nat. Museums and Galls on Merseyside, 1988–; World Monuments Fund in Britain, 1992–; Gov., Museum of London, 1992–. *Publications:* Period Houses and Their Details, 1974; (jtly) The Rape of Britain, 1975; Three Centuries of Architectural Craftsmanship, 1977; (jtly) The Victorian Buildings of London 1837–1887, 1980; (compiled jtly) Lutyens 1869–1944, 1981; (contrib.) Architecture of the British Empire, 1986; Wren's London, 1988; A Celebration of Art and Architecture: the National Gallery Sainsbury Wing, 1991; Bracken House, 1992; articles in professional jls. *Address:* c/o Financial Times, 1 Southwark Bridge, SE1 9HL.

AMES, Rachel, (Sarah), (Mrs Kenneth Ames); *see* Gainham, R.

AMESS, David Anthony Andrew; MP (C) Basildon, since 1983; Chairman, Accountancy Aims, since 1990; *b* Plaistow, 26 March 1952; *s* of late James Henry Valentine Amess and of Maud Ethel Martin; *m* 1983, Julia Monica Margaret Arnold; one *s* four *d. Educ:* St Bonaventure's Grammar Sch.; Bournemouth Coll. of Technol. (BScEcon Hons 2.2., special subject Govt). Teacher, St John the Baptist Jun. Mixed Sch., Bethnal Green, 1970–71; Jun. Underwriter, Leslie & Godwin Agencies, 1974–77; Sen. Manager of Temporary Div., Accountancy Personnel, 1977–80. Mem., Redbridge Council, 1982–86 (Vice Chm., Housing Cttee, 1982–85). Contested (C) Newham NW, 1979. Parliamentary Private Secretary: to Parly Under-Secs of State (Health), DHSS, 1987–88; to Minister of State and Parly Under-Sec. of State, Dept of Transport, 1988–90; to Minister of State, DoE, 1990–92; to Chief Sec. to the Treasury, 1992–94; to Sec. of State for Employment, 1994–95; to Sec. of State for Defence, 1995–. *Publications:* The Road to Basildon, 1993; Basildon Experience: Conservatives fight back, 1994; contrib. magazines and pamphlets. *Recreations:* gardening, music, sport, animals, theatre, antiques. *Address:* c/o House of Commons, SW1A 0AA. *Clubs:* Carlton; Kingswood Squash and Racketball (Basildon).

AMET, Hon. Sir Arnold (Karibone), Kt 1993; CBE 1987; **Hon. Mr Justice Amet;** Chief Justice, Papua New Guinea, since 1993; *b* 30 Oct. 1952; *m* 1972, Miaru; three *s* two *d. Educ:* Univ. of PNG (LLB 1975); Legal Trng Inst., PNG. Joined Public Solicitor's Office, PNG, 1976; qualified as barrister and solicitor, 1977; Legal Officer and Sec., Nat. Airline Commn, 1979–80; Dep. Public Solicitor, 1980–81; Public Solicitor, 1981–83; Judge of National Trial Court and Supreme Court of Appeal, 1983–93. Hon. LLD PNG, 1993. *Recreations:* Christian Ministry, watching Rugby and cricket. *Address:* Supreme Court, PO Box 7018, Boroko, Papua New Guinea.

AMHERST OF HACKNEY, 4th Baron *cr* 1892; **William Hugh Amherst Cecil;** Director: E. A. Gibson Shipbrokers Ltd, 1975–90; Seascope Sale and Purchase Ltd; *b* 28 Dec. 1940; *s* of 3rd Baron Amherst of Hackney, CBE, and of Margaret Eirene Clifton Brown, *d* of late Brig.-Gen. Howard Clifton Brown; *S* father, 1980; *m* 1965, Elisabeth, *d* of Hugh Humphrey Merriman, DSO, MC, TD, DL; one *s* one *d. Educ:* Eton. *Heir: s* Hon. Hugh William Amherst Cecil, *b* 17 July 1968. *Address:* Hillside House, Hyde, near Fordingbridge, Hants SP6 2HD. *Clubs:* Royal Yacht Squadron (Vice-Cdre), Royal Ocean Racing.

AMIES, Sir (Edwin) Hardy, KCVO 1989 (CVO 1977); RDI 1964; FRSA 1965; Dressmaker by Appointment to HM The Queen, since 1955; Director Hardy Amies Ltd, since 1946; Design Consultant to manufacturers in the UK, EEC, USA, Canada, Australia, New Zealand, Japan, and Korea; *b* 17 July 1909; *s* of late Herbert William Amies and Mary (*née* Hardy). *Educ:* Brentwood. Studied languages in France and Germany, 1927–30; trainee at W. & T. Avery Ltd, Birmingham, 1930–34; managing designer at Lachasse, Farm Street, W1, 1934–39. War Service, 1939–45: joined Intelligence Corps, 1939, becoming Lt-Col and head of Special Forces Mission to Belgium, 1944; founded dressmaking business, 1946. Chairman, Incorporated Society of London Fashion Designers, 1959–60 (Vice-Chm., 1954–56). Awards: Harper's Bazaar, 1962; Caswell-Massey, 1962, 1964, 1968; Ambassador Magazine, 1964; Sunday Times Special Award, 1965; Personnalité de l'Année (Haute Couture), Paris, 1986; Hall of Fame Award, British Fashion Council, 1989. Officier de l'Ordre de la Couronne (Belgium), 1946. *Publications:* Just So Far, 1954; ABC of Men's Fashion, 1964; Still Here, 1984; The Englishman's Suit, 1994. *Recreations:* lawn tennis, gardening, opera, needlepoint. *Address:* The Old School, Langford, near Lechlade, Glos GL7 3LF; Hardy Amies Ltd, 14 Savile Row, W1X 2JN. *T:* 0171–734 2436. *Clubs:* Queen's, Buck's.

AMIS, Sir Kingsley, Kt 1990; CBE 1981; author; *b* 16 April 1922; *o c* of William Robert and Rosa Amis; *m* 1st, 1948, Hilary Ann (marr. diss. 1965), *d* of Leonard Sidney and Margery Bardwell; two *s* one *d;* 2nd, 1965, Elizabeth Jane Howard, *qv* (marr. diss. 1983). *Educ:* City of London School; St John's, Oxford (Hon. Fellow, 1976). Served in Army, 1942–45. Lectr in English, University Coll. of Swansea, 1949–61 (Hon. Fellow, 1985); Fellow of Peterhouse, Cambridge, 1961–63. Cholmondeley Award, 1990. *Publications: novels:* Lucky Jim, 1954 (Somerset Maugham Prize, 1955; filmed, 1957); That Uncertain Feeling, 1955 (filmed as Only Two Can Play, 1962); I Like it Here, 1958; Take a Girl Like You, 1960; One Fat Englishman, 1963; (with Robert Conquest) The Egyptologists, 1965; The Anti-Death League, 1966; (as Robert Markham) Colonel Sun, 1968; I Want it Now, 1968; The Green Man, 1969; Girl, 20, 1971; The Riverside Villas Murder, 1973; Ending Up, 1974; The Alteration, 1976; Jake's Thing, 1978; Russian Hide-and-Seek, 1980; Stanley and the Women, 1984; The Old Devils (Booker Prize), 1986 (adapted for stage, 1989); The Crime of the Century, 1987; Difficulties with Girls, 1988; The Folks that Live on the Hill, 1990; We Are All Guilty, 1991; The Russian Girl, 1992; You Can't Do Both, 1994; The Biographer's Moustache, 1995; *short stories:* My Enemy's Enemy, 1962; Collected Short Stories, 1980, enlarged edn, 1987; Mr Barrett's Secret and Other Stories, 1993; *verse:* A Frame of Mind, 1953; A Case of Samples, 1956; A Look Round the Estate, 1967; Collected Poems 1944–1979, 1979; *belles-lettres:* New Maps of Hell, 1960; The James Bond Dossier, 1965; (as William Tanner) The Book of Bond, or Every Man His Own 007, 1966; What Became of Jane Austen?, 1970; *non-fiction:* On Drink, 1972; Rudyard Kipling and his World, 1975; Every Day Drinking, 1983; How's Your Glass?, 1984; (with J. Cochrane) Great British Songbook, 1986; Memoirs, 1991; *edited:* G. K. Chesterton selected stories, 1972; Tennyson, 1972; Harold's Years, 1977; The New Oxford Book of Light Verse, 1978; The Faber Popular Reciter, 1978; The Golden Age of Science Fiction, 1981; The Amis Anthology, 1988; The Crime of the Century, 1989; The Amis Collection, 1990; The Amis Story Anthology, 1992. *Recreations:* music, thrillers, television. *Address:* c/o Jonathan Clowes, Iron Bridge House, Bridge Approach, NW1 8BD. *Club:* Garrick.

See also M. L. Amis.

AMIS, Martin Louis; author; special writer for The Observer, since 1980; *b* 25 Aug. 1949; *s* of Sir Kingsley Amis, *qv* and Hilary Bardwell; *m* 1984, Antonia Phillips; two *s. Educ:* various schools; Exeter Coll., Oxford (BA Hons 1st cl. in English). Fiction and Poetry Editor, TLS, 1974; Literary Editor, New Statesman, 1977–79. *Publications:* The Rachel Papers, 1973 (Somerset Maugham Award, 1974); Dead Babies, 1975; Success, 1978; Other People: a mystery story, 1981; Money, 1984; The Moronic Inferno and Other Visits to America, 1986; Einstein's Monsters (short stories), 1987; London Fields, 1989; Time's Arrow, 1991; Visiting Mrs Nabakov and Other Excursions, 1993; The Information, 1995. *Recreations:* tennis, chess, snooker. *Address:* c/o Peters Fraser & Dunlop, 5th Floor, The Chambers, Chelsea Harbour, Lots Road, SW10 0XF. *Club:* United Oxford & Cambridge University.

AMLOT, Roy Douglas; QC 1989; barrister; *b* 22 Sept. 1942; *s* of Douglas Lloyd Amlot and Ruby Luise Amlot; *m* 1969, Susan Margaret (*née* McDowell); two *s. Educ:* Dulwich

Coll. Called to the Bar, Lincoln's Inn, 1963, Bencher, 1986. Second Prosecuting Counsel to the Inland Revenue, Central Criminal Court and London Crown Courts, 1974; First Prosecuting Counsel to the Crown, Inner London Crown Court, 1975; Jun. Prosecuting Counsel to the Crown, Central Criminal Court, 1977, Sen. Prosecuting Counsel, 1981; First Sen. Prosecuting Counsel, 1987. *Publication:* (ed) 11th edn, Phipson on Evidence. *Recreations:* skiing, squash, music. *Address:* 6 King's Bench Walk, Temple, EC4Y 7DR. *T:* 0171–583 0410.

AMOORE, Rt. Rev. Frederick Andrew; Provincial Executive Officer, Church of the Province of South Africa, 1982–87, retired; *b* 6 June 1913; *s* of Harold Frederick Newnham Amoore and Emily Clara Amoore, Worthing; *m* 1948, Mary Dobson; three *s*. *Educ:* Worthing Boys' High Sch.; University of Leeds. BA (Hons Hist) Leeds, 1934. Curate of: Clapham, London, 1936; St Mary's, Port Elizabeth, S Africa, 1939; Rector of St Saviour's, E London, S Africa, 1945; Dean of St Albans Cathedral, Pretoria, 1950; Exec. Officer for Church of Province of S Africa, 1962–67; Bishop of Bloemfontein, 1967–82. *Recreations:* music, italic script. *Address:* 503 Salwood Court, Main Road, Rondebosch, CP, 7700, South Africa.

AMORY; *see* Heathcoat Amory and Heathcoat-Amory.

AMOS, Alan Thomas; *b* 10 Nov. 1952; *s* of William Edmond Amos and Cynthia Florence Kathleen Amos. *Educ:* St Albans Sch.; St John's Coll., Oxford (MA(PPE) Hons); London Univ. Inst. of Educn (PGCE 1976). Pres., Oxford Univ. Cons. Assoc., 1974–75. Dir of Studies, Hd of Sixth Form, Hd of Econs and Politics Dept, Dame Alice Owen's Sch., Potters Bar, 1976–84; Hd of Agric. and Environment Sect., Cons. Res. Dept, 1984–86; Asst Prin., College of Further Educn, 1986–87. Councillor, 1978–90, Dep. Leader, and Chm. Educn Cttee, 1983–87, Enfield Bor. Council; Chm., London Boroughs Assoc. Educn Cttee, 1986–87. Contested (C): Tottenham, GLC, 1981; Walthamstow, 1983; MP (C) Hexham, 1987–92. Mem., Agriculture Select Cttee, 1989–92; Chairman: Cons. backbench Forestry Cttee, 1987–92; Parly ASH Gp, 1991–92; Secretary: Cons. backbench Transport Cttee, 1988–92 (Vice Chm., 1991–92); Cons. backbench Educn Cttee, 1989–92; British-Bulgarian All Party Gp, 1991–92; Chm., Northern Gp of Cons. MPs, 1991–92. Sec., Nat. Agricl and Countryside Forum, 1984–86. A Vice-Pres., Gtr London YCs, 1981–. Member: ESU, 1982–; ASH, 1987–; SPUC, 1987–. Hon. US Citizen, 1991. *Recreations:* travel, badminton, USA politics, bibliophilia.

AMOS, Air Comdt Barbara Mary D.; *see* Ducat-Amos.

AMOS, Francis John Clarke, CBE 1973; BSc(Soc); DipArch, SPDip, ARIBA, PPRTPI; international consultant on institutional development; Chief Executive, Birmingham City Council, 1973–77; Senior Fellow, University of Birmingham, since 1977; *b* 10 Sept. 1924; *s* of late Frank Amos, FALPA (Director, H. J. Furlong & Sons, Ltd, London), and Alice Mary Amos; *m* 1956, Geraldine Mercy Sutton, MBE, JP, BSc (Econ), MRTPI; one *s* one *d* (and one *d* decd). *Educ:* Alleyns Sch., and Dulwich Coll., London; Sch. of Architecture, The Polytechnic, London (DipArch); Sch. of Planning and Regional Research, London (SPDip); LSE and Birkbeck Coll., Univ. of London (BSc(Soc)). Served War: Royal Corps of Signals, 1942–44; RIASC, 1944–47. Harlow Develt Corp, 1951; LCC, Planning Div., 1953–58; Min. of Housing and Local Govt, 1958–59 and 1962–63; Adviser to Imperial Ethiopian Govt, 1959–62; Liverpool Corp. City Planning Dept, 1962–74, Chief Planning Officer 1966–74; Chairman: Planning Sub-Cttee, Merseyside Area Land Use/Transportation Study, 1967–73; Working Gp, Educnl Objectives in Urban and Regional Planning, Centre for Environmental Studies, 1970–72; Examination in Public Buckinghamshire Structure Plan, 1981–82. Consultant, Halcrow Fox and Associates , 1984–. Member: Exec. Cttee, Internat. Centre for Regional Planning and Develt, 1954–59; various Cttees, Liverpool Council of Social Service, 1965–72; Exec. Cttee, Town and Country Planning Summer Sch., 1969–70; Planning, Architecture and Bldg Studies Sub-Cttee, UGC, 1968–74; Community Work Gp of Calouste Gulbenkian Foundn, 1970–82; Constitution Cttee, Liverpool Community Relations Council, 1970–73; Planning and Transport Res. Adv. Council, DoE, 1971–77; Town and Country Planning Council and Exec. Cttee, 1972–74; Adv. Cttee, Bldg Res. Estabt, 1972–77 (Chm., Planning Cttee, 1972–80); SSRC Planning and Human Geography and Planning Cttees, 1972–76; Social Studies Sub-Cttee, UGC, 1974–76; W Midlands Economic Planning Council, 1974–77; Environmental Bd, DoE, 1975–78; Trustee, Community Projects Foundn, 1978–88; Council of Management, Action Resource Centre, 1978–86; Study Commn on Family, 1978–83; Arts Council Regional Cttee, 1979–; Exec. Cttee, Watt Cttee on Energy, 1980–82; Planning Cttee, CNAA, 1980–83. Comr, London and Metropolitan Govt Staff Commn, 1984–87; Asst Comr, Local Govt Boundary Commn, 1986–. Chm., Birmingham Gp, Internat. Year for Shelter for the Homeless 1987. Special Prof. of Planning Practice and Management, Univ. of Nottingham, 1979–; Vis. Prof., QUB, 1991–. External Examiner in Planning: Univs of: Liverpool, 1967–70; Newcastle, 1968–71; Aston (Birmingham), 1970–71; Queen's (Belfast), 1972–74; Heriot-Watt, 1972–74; Nottingham, 1973–76; UCL 1975–77; Sheffield, 1979–82; Glasgow, 1979–82; Hong Kong, 1982–85; Polytechnics of: Leeds, 1967–68; Central London, 1967–70; Birmingham, 1975–79; Liverpool, 1977–82. Since 1977, has acted as adviser to govts in aid programmes: Bangladesh (UN); Belize (World Bank); Dubai; Ghana (UN); Hong Kong (UK); Hungary; India (ODA); Iraq; Jordan; Laos; Poland; Tanzania (ODA); Trinidad and Tobago (UN); Turkey (OECD); Venezuela (IBRD); Kenya, Pakistan, Romania and Zimbabwe (UN); Uganda (ODA); Zambia (British Council). Mem., County Exec. Cttee, Scout Assoc., 1977–85. Mem., Court, Univ. of Nottingham, 1975–. Chm., Sir Herbert Manzoni Scholarship Trust, 1975–. Adviser to AMA Social Services Cttee, 1974–77; Chm., W Midlands Area, 1978–82, Mem. Nat. Exec., 1982–86, Nat. Assoc. of CAB. Member: Jt Land Requirements Cttee, 1983–; Nuffield Inquiry into Town and Country Planning, 1984–86. Pres., Royal Town Planning Inst., 1971–72 (AMTPI, 1955; Fellow 1967; Hon. Sec., 1979–90); Architect RIBA, 1951. FRSA 1977. Freeman of City of London, 1968. *Publications:* Education for Planning (CES Report), 1973; various reports on Liverpool incl.: Annual Reviews of Plans, Study of Social Malaise; RTPI Report on Future of Planning, 1971, 1977; (part) City Centre Redevelopment; (part) Low Income Housing in the Developing World; articles on Planning and Management in Local Govt in various professional jls. *Recreations:* travel; unsystematic philately and unskilled building. *Address:* Grindstones, 20 Westfield Road, Edgbaston, Birmingham B15 3QG. *T:* 0121–454 5661, *Fax:* 0121–454 8331; The Coach House, Ashton Gifford Lane, Codford St Peter, Warminster, Wilts BA12 0NJ. *T:* Warminster (01985) 50610.

AMOS, Valerie; Managing Director, Quality and Equality, since 1994; *b* 13 March 1954; *d* of E. Michael Amos and Eunice Amos. *Educ:* Univ. of Warwick (BA Sociol.); Univ. of Birmingham (MA Cultural Studies); Univ. of E Anglia (doctoral research). With London Boroughs: Lambeth, 1981–82; Camden, 1983–85; Hackney, 1985–89 (Head of Trng; Head of Management Services); Management Consultant, 1984–89; Chief Exec., Equal Opportunities Commn, 1989–94. Member: Adv. Cttee, Centre for Educnl Develt Appraisal and Res., Univ. of Warwick, 1991–; Gen. Adv. Council, BBC Cttee, King's Fund Coll., 1992–; Council, Inst. of Employment Studies, 1993–. External Examiner: (MA Equal Opportunities), Univ. of Northumbria, at Newcastle (formerly Newcastle Poly.), 1989–93; Liverpool Univ., 1992–. Dir, Hampstead Theatre, 1992–; Dep. Chm., Runnymede Trust, 1990–; Trustee, Women's Therapy Centre, 1989–. *Publications:* various articles on race and gender issues. *Address:* Summerton Business Centre, 18–24 Middle Way, Oxford OX2 7LG. *T:* Oxford (01865) 310651, *Fax:* (01865) 311381.

AMPLEFORTH, Abbot of; *see* Barry, Rt. Rev. N. P.

AMPTHILL, 4th Baron *cr* 1881; **Geoffrey Denis Erskine Russell,** CBE 1986; PC 1995; Deputy Speaker, House of Lords, since 1983; Deputy Chairman: Express Newspapers, since 1989 (Director, since 1985); United Newspapers, since 1991 (Director, since 1981); *b* 15 Oct. 1921; *s* of 3rd Baron Ampthill, CBE, and Christabel, Lady Ampthill (*d* 1976); *S* father, 1973; *m* 1st, 1946, Susan Mary (marr. diss. 1971), *d* of late Hon. Charles John Frederic Winn; two *s* one *d* (and one *s* decd); 2nd, 1972, Elisabeth Anne Marie (marr. diss. 1987), *d* of late Claude Henri Gustave Mallon. *Educ:* Stowe. Irish Guards, 1941–46; 2nd Lt 1941, Captain 1944. Gen. Manager, Fortnum and Mason, 1947–51; Chairman, New Providence Hotel Co. Ltd, 1951–64; Dir, Dualvest plc, 1981–87. Managing Director of theatre owning and producing companies, 1953–81. Dep. Chm., 1980–92, Chm., 1992–94, of Cttees, H of L. Dir, Leeds Castle Foundn, 1980–82. Chm., Select Cttee on Channel Tunnel Bill, 1987. *Heir: s* Hon. David Whitney Erskine Russell [*b* 27 May 1947; *m* 1980, April McKenzie Arbon, *y d* of Paul Arbon, New York; two *d*]. *Address:* 51 Sutherland Street, SW1V 4JX.

AMWELL, 3rd Baron *cr* 1947, of Islington; **Keith Norman Montague;** Director: Thorburn Holdings plc, since 1994; Thorburn Colquhoun Ltd, Consulting Engineers, since 1994; *b* 1 April 1943; *o s* of 2nd Baron Amwell and of Kathleen Elizabeth Montague (*née* Fountain); *S* father, 1990; *m* 1970, Mary, *d* of Frank Palfreyman; two *s*. *Educ:* Ealing Grammar Sch. for Boys; Nottingham Univ. BSc (Civil Engineering); CEng; FICE; CGeol, FGS; MIHT. Consulting civil engineer, 1965–. *Publications:* papers to international construction confs. *Recreations:* gardening, walking, photography, badminton. *Heir: s* Hon. Ian Keith Montague, *b* 20 Sept. 1973.

AMY, Dennis Oldrieve, CMG 1992; OBE 1984; HM Diplomatic Service, retired; Ambassador to the Democratic Republic of Madagascar, 1990–92, and Ambassador (non-resident) to Federal Islamic Republic of the Comoros, 1991–92; *b* 21 Oct. 1932; *s* of late George Arthur Amy and Isabella Thompson (*née* Crosby); *m* 1956, Helen Rosamunde, *d* of late Wilfred Leslie Clemens; one *s* one *d*. *Educ:* Southall Grammar Sch. Served RM, 1951–53. Entered HM Foreign, later HM Diplomatic Service, 1949; FO, 1949–51 and 1953–58; Athens, 1958–61; Second Sec. and Vice Consul, Moscow, 1961–63; FO, 1963–65; DSAO, 1965; Second Sec. and Passport Officer, Canberra, 1966–70; First Sec., Ibadan, 1971–74; seconded to Dept of Trade, 1974–75; FCO, 1976–78; First Sec. (Commercial), Santiago, 1978–83 (Chargé d'Affaires, 1979); FCO, 1983–86 (Counsellor, 1985–86); Consul Gen., Bordeaux, 1986–89. *Recreations:* Scottish country dancing, golf, gardening. *Address:* Timbers, Hambledon Road, Godalming, Surrey GU7 1PJ.

AMYOT, Léopold Henri, CVO 1990; Secretary to Governor General of Canada and Secretary General of Order of Canada and of Order of Military Merit, 1985–90; Herald Chancellor of Canada, 1988–90; *b* 25 Aug. 1930; *s* of S. Eugène Amyot and Juliette Gagnon; *m* 1958, (Marie Jeanne) Andrée Jobin; one *s* two *d*. *Educ:* Laval Univ., Québec (BLSc, BScSoc); Ottawa Univ. (BA); Geneva Univ. (course on Internat. Instns). Joined External Affairs, 1957; Second Secretary: Canberra, 1960; New Delhi, 1961; Counsellor, Paris, 1968; Amb. to Lebanon (with accredn to Syria, Jordan, Iraq), 1974; Dep. Sec. Gen., Agence de Co-opération culturelle et technique, Paris, 1976; Chief of Protocol, Ext. Affairs, Ottawa, 1980; Exec. Dir, Task Force, on Pope's Visit to Canada, 1983; Amb. to Morocco, 1983. Chm., Official Residences Collections (formerly Official Residences Arts) Adv. Cttee, 1985–. Member: Professional Assoc. of For. Service Officers, Ottawa, 1957–; l'Inst. canadien des Affaires internat., Québec, 1985–. Prix d'honneur (Sect. de Québec) l'Inst. canadien des Affaires internat., 1985. *Recreations:* tennis, golf, swimming, contemporary art collector. *Address:* 140 Rideau Terrace #15, Ottawa, Ontario K1M 0Z2, Canada. *T:* (613) 7479077.

AMYOT, René, QC; barrister; Counsel, Jolin, Fournier, Morisset; *b* Quebec City, 1 Nov. 1926; *s* of Omer Amyot and Caroline L'Espérance (*née* Barry); *m* 1954, Monique, *d* of Fernand Boutin; two *s* two *d*. *Educ:* Collège des Jésuites de Québec (BA 1946); Laval Univ. Law Sch. (LLL 1949); Harvard Univ. Grad. Sch. of Business Admin (MBA 1951). Called to Bar of Québec, 1949; QC Canada 1965. Joined Procter & Gamble, Montreal, 1951; Bouffard & Associates, Quebec, 1952; Asst Prof., Faculty of Admin. Scis, Laval Univ., 1954–69; Asst Prof., Fiscal Law, Laval Univ. Law Sch., 1960–70; Consul for Belgium, 1966–82. Dir, and Mem. Exec. Cttee, Centre de Recherche Industrielle de Québec, 1971–76; Pres., Quebec Dist Chamber of Commerce, 1972; Founding Pres., Centre Internat. Recherches et Etudes en Management, 1972; Chairman, Air Canada, 1981–83; Director: Bank of Nova Scotia, 1972–81; Logistec Corp.; Rothmans Inc.; Palmar Inc.; Fidusco Ltd; Ferme Charlevoix Inc.; Expand Images Canada Inc.; Cedar Gp Inc.; Dominion Bridge Inc. Dir, Council for Business and the Arts in Canada. Member: Canadian Bar Assoc.; Québec Bar Assoc.; Canadian Tax Foundn; Cttee, Internat. Chamber; Assoc. des MBA du Québec. Gov., Faculty of Administrative Scis, Laval Univ. Chevalier de l'Ordre de Léopold (Belgium), 1985. *Recreations:* skiing, swimming, tennis, farming. *Address:* Jolin, Fournier, Morisset, Edifice Iberville 3, Suite 500, 2960 Boulevard Laurier, Sainte-Foy, Québec G1V 4S1, Canada. *Clubs:* Québec Garrison, Toronto.

ANCRAM, Earl of; Michael Andrew Foster Jude Kerr; DL; advocate; MP (C) Devizes, since 1992; Minister of State, Northern Ireland Office, since 1994; *b* 7 July 1945; *s* and *heir* of 12th Marquess of Lothian, *qv*; *m* 1975, Lady Jane Fitzalan-Howard, *y d* of 16th Duke of Norfolk, KG, PC, GCVO, GBE, TD, and of Lavinia Duchess of Norfolk, *qv*; two *d*. *Educ:* Ampleforth; Christ Church, Oxford (BA); Edinburgh Univ. (LLB). Advocate, Scottish Bar, 1970. Contested (C) Edinburgh S, 1987. MP (C): Berwickshire and East Lothian, Feb.–Sept. 1974; Edinburgh S, 1979–87. Parly Under-Sec. of State, Scottish Office, 1983–87, NI Office, 1993–94. Mem., Select Cttee on Energy, 1979–83. Chm., Cons. Party in Scotland, 1980–83 (Vice-Chm., 1975–80). Chm., Northern Corporate Communications, 1989–91; Dir, CSM Parly Consultants, 1988–92; Mem. Bd, Scottish Homes, 1988–90. DL Roxburgh, Ettrick and Lauderdale, 1990. *Recreations:* ski-ing, photography, folksinging. *Address:* House of Commons, SW1A 0AA.

ANDERSEN, Valdemar Jens, CMG 1965; OBE 1960 (MBE 1955); VRD 1962; Resident Commissioner, Gilbert and Ellice Islands Colony, 1962–70, retired; *b* 21 March 1919; 2nd *s* of Max Andersen, Maraenui, NZ; *m* 1946, Alison Leone, 2nd *d* of G. A. Edmonds, Remuera, Auckland, NZ; one *s* one *d*. *Educ:* Napier Boys High Sch. NZ; Auckland University Coll. (BSc). Lieut, RNZNVR, 1940–46; Lieut, RANVR, 1947–62. British Solomon Islands Protectorate: Administrative Officer, 1947; Class A, Administrative Officer, 1954; Secretary Protectorate Affairs, 1958. *Recreations:* drama, gardening.

ANDERSON, family name of **Viscount Waverley.**

ANDERSON, Maj.-Gen. Alistair Andrew Gibson, CB 1980; *b* 26 Feb. 1927; *s* of Lt-Col John Gibson Anderson and Margaret Alice (*née* Scott); *m* 1953, Dr Margaret Grace Smith; one *s* two *d*. *Educ:* George Watson's Boys Coll., Edinburgh; University Coll. of

SW of England, Exeter (Short Univ. Course, 1944); Staff Coll., Camberley; Jt Services Staff Coll., Latimer. Enlisted 1944; commnd Royal Corps of Signals, 1946; comd 18 Signal Regt, 1967–69; Defence Ops Centre, 1969–72; staff of Signal Officer-in-Chief, 1972–74; Comdt, Sch. of Signals, 1974–76; Signal Officer-in-Chief (Army), 1977–80, retired; Dir, Communications and Electronics Security Gp, GCHQ, 1980–85. Col Comdt, Royal Corps of Signals, 1980–86; Chm., Royal Signals Assoc., 1982–87. *Recreations:* hill walking, sailing, gardening. *Club:* Army and Navy.

See also Sir J. E. Anderson.

ANDERSON, Dr Alun Mark; Editor, New Scientist, since 1992; *b* 27 May 1948; *s* of Peter Marchmont Anderson and Jane Watkin Anderson (*née* James). *Educ:* Univ. of Sussex (BSc 1968); Univ. of Edinburgh (PhD 1972). IBM Res. Fellow, 1972–74, Jun. Res. Fellow, Wolfson Coll., 1972–76, Oxford; Royal Soc. Res. Fellow, Kyoto Univ., 1977–79; Nature: News and Views Ed., 1980–83; Tokyo Bureau Chief, 1984–86; Washington Ed., 1986–90; Internat. Ed., Science, 1991–92. *Publications:* Science and Technology in Japan, 1984, 2nd edn 1991. *Recreations:* mountain walking, travel. *Address:* New Scientist, IPC, King's Reach Tower, Stamford Street, SE1 9LS. *T:* 0171–261 7301.

ANDERSON, Anthony John; QC 1982; a Recorder, since 1995; *b* 12 Sept. 1938; *s* of late A. Fraser Anderson and Margaret Anderson; *m* 1970, Fenja Ragnhild Gunn. *Educ:* Harrow; Magdalen Coll., Oxford. MA. 2nd Lieut, The Gordon Highlanders, 1957–59. Called to the Bar, Inner Temple, 1964, Bencher, 1992. Chm. of Tribunals, SFA (formerly The Securities Assoc.), 1988–. *Recreations:* golf, fishing. *Address:* 2 Mitre Court Buildings, Temple, EC4Y 7BX. *T:* 0171–583 1380. *Clubs:* Garrick, MCC.

ANDERSON, Dr Arthur John Ritchie, (Iain), CBE 1984; MA; MRCGP; General Medical and Hospital Practitioner, Trainer, 1961–94; final year tutor, Royal Free Hospital, 1985–94; *b* 19 July 1933; *s* of Dr John Anderson and Dorothy Mary Anderson; *m* 1959, Janet Edith Norrish; two *s* one *d*. *Educ:* Bromsgrove Sch.; Downing Coll., Cambridge; St Mary's Hospital Medical Sch. MA, MB BChir (Cantab). MRCS; LRCP; DCH; DObstRCOG. Various hospital posts, 1958–61. Hemel Hempstead RDC, 1967–74, Vice-Chm., 1970–74; Councillor (C), Hertfordshire CC, 1973–, Vice-Chm., 1985–87 (Leader, 1977–83), Chief Whip, Cons. Gp, 1989–. Member: Herts Police Authority, 1973–87 and 1993– (Chm., 1985–87); NW Thames Regional Health Authority, 1978–84; Regional Planning Council for South East, 1977–79; Police Cttee, ACC, 1977–87. President, Hertfordshire Branch, BMA, 1973–74. Member, various governing bodies of primary, secondary, further and higher educn instns. Chm., Crouchfield Trust, 1989–. FRSM 1985. *Publications:* numerous articles, mainly in periodicals. *Recreations:* writing, hockey, walking. *Address:* Leaside, Rucklers Lane, King's Langley, Herts WD4 9NQ. *T:* King's Langley (01923) 262884. *Club:* Herts 100.

ANDERSON, Mrs Beverly Jean; educational consultant and broadcaster; a Director, Railtrack, since 1993; *b* 9 Dec. 1940; *d* of Arthur Benjamin Phillpotts and Sylvia Tomlinson Phillpotts; *m* 1st, 1968, Angus Walker, *qv* (marr. diss. 1976); 2nd, 1976, Andrew Anderson (marr. diss. 1986); one *s*. *Educ:* Wellesley Coll., Mass (BA History, and Politics 1962); London Univ. (PGCE 1967). Jamaican Foreign Service, Kingston and Washington, 1963–66; primary sch. teacher, London, 1968–71, Oxfordshire primary schs, 1971–81; Headteacher, Berwood First Sch., Oxford, 1981–83; Sen. Lectr in Educn, Oxford Poly., 1985–89; Lectr in Educn, Warwick Univ., and educn consultant, 1989–93; Chief Exec., Book Trust, 1993–94. Chairman: Equal Opportunities Wkg Gp, NAB, 1987–88; CNAA Steering Cttee on Accesss Courses to HE Framework, 1988–89; Member: Nat. Curriculum Council, 1989–91; Council, ABSA, 1989–; Arts Council, 1990–94; Governor: BFI, 1985–93; Oxford Stage Co. Bd, 1986–; S Bank Bd, 1989–. Mem., Nuffield Council on Bioethics, 1991–94; Chm. Council, Charter '88, 1989–93. Columnist, TES, 1989–93. Television includes: Presenter: Black on Black, 1982–83; Nothing but the Best; Sixty Minutes; After Dark, 1989–90; Behind the Headlines, 1990–91. FRSA 1991. *Publications:* Learning with Logo: a teacher's guide, 1985; numerous articles on education, social issues and media education. *Recreations:* plays, paintings, poems, movies, dancing. *Address:* c/o Railtrack, 40 Bernard Street, WC1N 1BY.

ANDERSON, Brian David Outram, AO 1993; PhD; FRS 1989; Professor of Systems Engineering, since 1981, and Director, Research School of Information Sciences and Engineering, since 1994, Australian National University; *b* 15 Jan. 1941; *s* of David Outram Anderson and late Nancy Anderson; *m* 1968, Dianne, *d* of M. Allen; three *d*. *Educ:* Sydney Univ.; Stanford Univ. (PhD 1966); California Univ. Res. Asst, Stanford Electronics Labs, 1964; Lectr in Electrical Engrg, Stanford Univ., 1965; Asst Prof. and Staff Consultant, Vidar Corp., Mount View, Calif., 1966; Hd of Dept, 1967–75, Prof., 1967–81, Dept of Electrical Engrg, Univ. of Newcastle. Mem., Scientific Adv. Bd, CRA Ltd, 1982–; Dir, Telectronics Hldgs Ltd, 1986–. Member: Aust. Res. Grants Cttee, 1972–77; Aust. Science and Technology Council, 1977–82; UNESCO Nat. Commn, 1982–83; Aust. Industrial Res. and Develt Incentives Bd, 1984–86; Prime Minister's Sci. and Engrg Council, 1989–93. FAA; FTS; FIEEE; Hon. FIE(Aust). Dr *hc* Louvain, 1991; Swiss Federal Inst. of Technol., 1993. *Publications* include: Linear Optimal Control, 1971; Network Analysis and Synthesis, 1975; Optimal Filtering, 1980; Optimal Control, 1990. *Address:* Research School of Information Sciences and Engineering, Australian National University, Canberra, ACT 0200, Australia.

ANDERSON, Campbell McCheyne; Managing Director, North Limited, since 1994; *b* 17 Sept. 1941; *s* of Allen Taylor Anderson and Ethel Catherine Rundle; *m* 1965, Sandra Maclean Harper; two *s* one *d*. *Educ:* The Armidale Sch., NSW, Aust.; Univ. of Sydney (BEcon). AASA. Trainee and General Administration, Boral Ltd, Australia, 1962–69; Gen. Manager/Man. Dir, Reef Oil NL, Australia, 1969–71; Asst Chief Representative, Burmah Oil Australia Ltd, 1972; Corporate Development, Burmah Oil Incorporated, New York, 1973; Corporate Development, 1974; Finance Director and Group Planning, Burmah Oil Trading Ltd, UK, 1975; Special Projects Dir, 1976, Shipping Dir, 1978, Industrial Dir, 1979, Man. Dir, 1982–84, Burmah Oil Co.; Man. Dir, 1985–93, Chief Exec. Officer, 1986–93, Renison Goldfields Consolidated. Dir, Consolidated Gold Fields, 1985–89. Chm., Ampolex Ltd, 1991–. Dir, Aust. Mines and Metals Assoc., 1985–93; Councillor: Aust. Mining Industry Council, 1985– (Pres., 1991–93); Business Council of Aust., 1986–; Chm., Energy Resources Aust. Ltd, 1994–. *Recreations:* golf, swimming, horse-racing, shooting. *Address:* Apt 5.3 Domain Park, 193 Domain Road, South Yarra, Melbourne, Vic 3141, Australia. *Clubs:* Oil Industries; Frilford Heath Golf; Australian (Sydney); Australian (Melbourne); Royal Sydney Golf, Royal Melbourne Golf; Australian Jockey; Elanora Country (NSW).

ANDERSON, Rear-Adm. (Charles) Courtney, CB 1971; Flag Officer, Admiralty Interview Board, 1969–71, retired; *b* 8 Nov. 1916; *s* of late Lt-Col Charles Anderson, Australian Light Horse, and Mrs Constance Powell-Anderson, OBE, JP; *m* 1940, Pamela Ruth Miles; three *s*. *Educ:* RNC, Dartmouth. Joined RN, 1930. Served War of 1939–45: in command of Motor Torpedo Boats, Destroyers and Frigates. Naval Intelligence, 1946–49 and 1955–57; Commanded HMS Contest, 1949–51; Comdr, 1952; BJSM, Washington, 1953–55; Capt., 1959; Naval Attaché, Bonn, 1962–65; Director, Naval Recruiting, 1966–68; ADC to Queen, 1968; Rear-Adm., 1969. Editor, The Board Bulletin, 1971–78. *Publications:* The Drum Beats Still, 1951. Numerous articles and short stories. *Recreations:* gardening, do-it-yourself. *Address:* Bybrook Cottage, Bustlers Hill, Sherston, Malmesbury, Wilts SN16 0ND.

ANDERSON, (Clarence) Eugene; Chairman and Chief Executive, Ferranti International plc, 1990–94; *b* 31 Aug. 1938; *s* of Clarence Leslie Anderson and Wilda Faye Anderson; *m* 1977, Daniela Leopolda Proche; one *d*, and one *s* two *d* from a previous marriage. *Educ:* Univ. of Texas (BSc Chem. Engrg, 1961); Harvard Univ. (MBA 1963). Process Engr, New Orleans, 1961, Ops Analyst, Houston, 1963–66, Tenneco Oil Co.; Man. Dir, Globe Petroleum Sales Ltd, Lincs, 1966–69; Dir, Supply and Transportation, Houston, 1969–72, Dir, Operational Planning, Houston, 1972, Tenneco Oil Co.; Vice Pres., Tenneco International Co., Houston, 1973; Exec. Dir, Albright & Wilson Ltd, London, 1973–75; Vice Pres., Corporate Develt, Tenneco Inc., Houston, 1975–78; Dep. Man. Dir, Ops, Albright & Wilson Ltd, London, 1979–81; Pres., Celanese International Co., and Vice Pres., Celanese Corp., New York, 1981–85; Chief Exec., Johnson Matthey PLC, London, 1985–89. *Publication:* (jtly) report on microencapsulation. *Recreations:* music, literature, theatre, various sports.

ANDERSON, Clive Stuart; barrister; television presenter and writer; *b* 10 Dec. 1952; *s* of Gordon Menzies Randall Anderson and Doris Elizabeth Anderson; *m* 1981, Dr Jane Hughes; one *s* two *d*. *Educ:* Harrow County Sch. for Boys; Selwyn Coll., Cambridge (MA). Called to the Bar, Middle Temple, 1976. *Radio:* Host, Cabaret Upstairs, 1986–88; Chm., Whose Line is it Anyway?, 1988; Presenter, Devil's Advocate, 1991–92; *television:* Whose Line is it Anyway?, 1988–; Clive Anderson Talks Back, 1989–; Notes & Queries, 1993; Our Man In . . ., 1995; various other progs. *Publications:* (jtly) Great Railway Journeys, 1994; (with Ian Brown) Patent Nonsense, 1994; Our Man In . . ., 1995. *Recreations:* history, comedy, football. *Address:* London Management, 2–4 Noel Street, W1V 3RB. *T:* 0171–287 9000; 4 King's Bench Walk, Temple, EC4Y 7DL. *T:* 0171–353 0478.

ANDERSON, Courtney; *see* Anderson, (Charles) Courtney.

ANDERSON, Rev. David; Principal Lecturer in Religious Studies, Hertfordshire College of Higher Education (formerly Wall Hall College), Aldenham, Herts, 1974–84 (Senior Lecturer, 1970–74); *b* 30 Oct. 1919; *s* of William and Nancy Anderson, Newcastle upon Tyne; *m* 1953, Helen Finlay Robinson, 3rd *d* of Johnson and Eleanor Robinson, Whitley Bay, Northumberland; one *s* two *d*. *Educ:* Royal Grammar Sch. Newcastle upon Tyne; Selwyn Coll., Cambridge. Served in RA, 1940–42, Intelligence Corps, 1942–46, Lieut. Deacon, 1949, Priest, 1950; Curate of parish of St Gabriel, Sunderland, 1949–52; Tutor of St Aidan's Coll., Birkenhead, 1952–56; Warden of Melville Hall, Ibadan, Nigeria, 1956–58; Principal of: Immanuel Coll., Ibadan, Nigeria, 1958–62; Wycliffe Hall, Oxford, 1962–69. Examining Chaplain: to Bishop of Liverpool, 1969–75; to Bishop of St Albans, 1972–80. *Publications:* The Tragic Protest, 1969; Simone Weil, 1971; contrib: Religion and Modern Literature, 1975; William Golding: some critical considerations, 1978; The Passion of Man, 1980. *Recreations:* listening to music, hi-fi gramophones. *Address:* 6 Flassburn Road, Durham DH1 4LX. *T:* Durham (0191) 3843063.

ANDERSON, David Colville, VRD 1947, and Clasp, 1958; QC (Scotland) 1957; *b* 8 Sept. 1916; *yr s* of late J. L. Anderson of Pittormie, Fife, solicitor and farmer, and late Etta Colville; *m* 1948, Juliet, *yr d* of late Hon. Lord Hill Watson, MC, LLD; two *s* one *d*. *Educ:* Trinity Coll., Glenalmond; Pembroke Coll., Oxford; Edinburgh Univ. BA (Hons) Oxford 1938; LLB (Distinction) 1946. Thow Scholar, Maclagan Prizeman, Dalgety Prizeman, Edinburgh Univ. Lecturer in Scots Law, Edinburgh Univ., 1947–60; Advocate, 1946; Standing Junior Counsel to Ministry of Works, 1954–55, and to War Office, 1955–57. Contested (C) Coatbridge and Airdrie, 1955, and East Dunbartonshire, 1959; MP (C) Dumfries, Dec. 1963–Sept. 1964. Solicitor-General for Scotland, 1960–64; Vice-Chairman, Commissioners of Northern Lighthouses, 1963–64; Hon. Sheriff-Substitute, Lothians and Peebles, 1965–; Chm., Industrial Tribunals (Scotland), 1971–72; Chief Reporter for Public Inquiries and Under Sec., Scottish Office, 1972–74. Joined RNVR, 1935. In VIII awarded Ashburton Shield, Bisley, 1933 (Trinity Coll., Glenalmond; schools event); Inter-Services XX at Bisley, 1936–38. Served War of 1939–45 in destroyers (despatches); Lieut 1940; Egerton Prizeman in Naval Gunnery, 1943; Flotilla Gunnery Officer, Rosyth Escort Force, 1943–45; led special operation N Norway, 1945; Lt-Comdr 1948. King Haakon VII Liberty Medal, 1946. *Relevant Play:* The Case of David Anderson QC by John Hale (Manchester, and Traverse Theatre, Edinburgh, 1980; Lyric Studio Hammersmith, 1981). *Address:* 8 Arboretum Road, Edinburgh EH3 5PD. *T:* 0131–552 3003. *Club:* New (Edinburgh).

ANDERSON, David Heywood, CMG 1982; HM Diplomatic Service; Second Legal Adviser, Foreign and Commonwealth Office, since 1989; Barrister-at-Law; *b* 14 Sept. 1937; *s* of late Harry Anderson; *m* 1961, Jennifer Ratcliffe; one *s* one *d*. *Educ:* King James' Grammar Sch., Almondbury. LLB (Leeds); LLM (London). Called to Bar, Gray's Inn, 1963. Asst Legal Adviser, FCO, 1960–69; Legal Adviser, British Embassy, Bonn, 1969–72; Legal Counsellor, FCO, 1972–79; Legal Adviser, UK Mission to UN, NY, 1979–82; Legal Counsellor, FCO, 1982–87; Dep. Legal Advr, FCO, 1987–89. *Publications:* (contrib.) International Maritime Boundaries, 1993; contrib. British Yearbook of Internat. Law and learned jls. *Recreation:* gardening. *Address:* c/o Foreign and Commonwealth Office, King Charles Street, SW1A 2AH.

ANDERSON, David Munro; Chairman, Allingham Anderson Roll Ross Ltd, since 1990; *b* 15 Dec. 1937; *s* of Alexander Anderson and Jessica Anderson (*née* Vincent-Innes); *m* 1st, 1965, Veronica Jane (*née* Stevens) (marr. diss.); two *s* one *d*; 2nd, 1989, Ruth Lewis-Bowen. *Educ:* Morrison's Academy, Perthshire; Strathallan, Perthshire. Commissioned Black Watch; served W Africa; tea production with James Finlay & Co., India, 1959–62; London Chamber of Commerce and Industry, 1962–63; joined E. D. & F. Man Ltd, 1963; formed Anderson Man Ltd, 1981; formed E. D. & F. Man International Ltd, 1985, Chm., 1986–90; Man. Dir, Commodity Analysis Ltd, 1968; numerous directorships. Chairman, formation cttees: Internat. Petroleum Exchange; Baltic Internat. Freight Futures Exchange (jtly); former Vice-Chm., London Commodity Exchange; Member: Securities and Investments Bd, 1986–87; Futures and Commodity Exchanges. *Recreations:* ski-ing, shooting. *Address:* Clees Hall, Bures, Suffolk CO8 5DZ. *T:* Bures (01787) 227271. *Club:* Caledonian.

ANDERSON, Brig. David William, CBE 1976 (OBE 1972); Chief Executive, Cumbernauld Development Corporation, 1985–88; *b* 4 Jan. 1929; *s* of David Anderson and Frances Anderson; *m* 1954, Eileen Dorothy Scott; one *s* two *d*. *Educ:* St Cuthbert's Grammar Sch., Newcastle on Tyne. Black Watch, 1946; RMA, Sandhurst, 1947; commnd HLI, 1948; served ME and Malaya; RHF, Staff Coll., Trucial Oman Scouts, Sch. of Inf., I RHF, Germany, and HQ NORTHAG, 1959–66; Instr, Staff Coll., 1967–69; CO I RHF, Scotland, N Ireland, Singapore, 1969–72; Colonel GS: MoD, 1972–73; HQ Dir of Inf., 1974; Comdr, 3 Inf. Bde, N Ireland, 1975–76; Comdt, Sch. of Infantry, 1976–79; Comdr, Highlands, 1979–81, Comdr 51 Highland Bde, 1982; ADC to the Queen, 1981–82. Chief Exec., NE Fife DC, 1982–85. Hon. Colonel: Aberdeen Univ. OTC, 1982–87; 1/52 Lowland Vol., 1987–88; Member: RHF Council, 1970–88; Highland

TA&VRA, 1984–88; Lowland TA & VRA, 1987–88. Chm., Fife Area Scout Council, 1985–86. Mem., St John Assoc., 1984–85. Hon. Vice-Pres., Cumbernauld Br., Royal British Legion (Scotland), 1985–88. *Recreations:* moving house, Scottish history.

ANDERSON, Prof. Declan John; Professor of Oral Biology, University of Bristol, 1966–85, now Professor Emeritus; Founder, The Oral and Dental Research Trust, 1989 (Director, 1989–92); *b* 20 June 1920; *s* of Arthur John Anderson and Katherine Mary Coffey; *m* 1947, Vivian Joy Dunkerton; four *s* three *d*. *Educ:* Christ's Hospital; Guy's Hospital Medical School, Univ. of London. BDS (London) 1942; LDSRCS 1943, BSc 1946, MSc 1947, PhD 1955. Prof. of Physiology, Univ. of Oregon, USA, 1957–58; Prof. of Physiology in Relation to Dentistry, Univ. of London, 1963–66. *Publications:* Physiology for Dental Students, 1952; How to Dissect and Understand Medical Terms, 1992; scientific papers in professional jls. *Recreations:* silversmithing, forging, music. *Address:* Little Dene, Stonequarry Road, Chelwood Gate, East Sussex RH17 7LS.

ANDERSON, Dr Digby Carter; Director, Social Affairs Unit, since 1980; *b* 25 May 1944; *s* of late Donald Anderson and Elizabeth Nance Ethel Anderson; *m* 1965, Judith Harris. *Educ:* St Lawrence Coll.; Univ. of Reading (BA Hons); Brunel Univ. (MPhil, PhD). Lectr, then Sen. Lectr, Luton Coll. of Higher Educn, 1965–77; Tutor, Brunel Univ. Youth Work Trng Unit, 1974–78; Res. Fellow, Univ. of Nottingham, 1977–80; Associate Lectr, Brunel Univ., 1977–78. Mem., ESRC, 1989–93. Mem., Health Studies Cttee, CNAA, 1987–92. Columnist: The Times, 1984–88; Sunday Telegraph, 1988–89; Sunday Times, 1989–90; Spectator, 1984–; National Review, 1991–. Ordained deacon 1985, priest 1986. Mem., Mont Pelerin Soc. *Publications:* (ed) Health Education in Practice, 1979; Evaluation by Classroom Experience, 1979; Evaluating Curriculum Proposals, 1980; (ed) The Ignorance of Social Intervention, 1980; Breaking the Spell of the Welfare State, 1981; (ed) The Kindness that Kills, 1984; (ed) A Diet of Reason, 1986; The Spectator Book of Imperative Cooking, 1987; (ed) Full Circle, 1988; (ed) Health, Lifestyle and Environment, 1992; (ed) The Loss of Virtue: moral confusion and social disorder in Britain and America, 1993; (ed) This Will Hurt: the restoration of civic order in America and Britain, 1995; contrib. Sociology, Jl Curriculum Studies, Econ. Affairs, Social Policy Rev. *Recreations:* non-Germanic music, the seaside, dinner. *Address:* 17 Hardwick Place, Woburn Sands, Bucks MK17 8QQ. *T:* Milton Keynes (01908) 584526.

ANDERSON, Donald; MP (Lab) Swansea East, since Oct. 1974; barrister-at-law; *b* 17 June 1939; *s* of David Robert Anderson and Eva (*née* Mathias); *m* 1963, Dr Dorothy Trotman, BSc, PhD; three *s*. *Educ:* Swansea Grammar Sch.; University Coll. of Swansea (Hon. Fellow, 1985). 1st cl. hons Modern History and Politics, Swansea, 1960. Barrister; called to Bar, Inner Temple, 1969. Member of HM Foreign Service, 1960–64: Foreign Office, 1960–63; 3rd Sec., British Embassy, Budapest, 1963–64; lectured in Dept of Political Theory and Govt, University Coll., Swansea, 1964–66. Councillor, Kensington and Chelsea, 1971–75. MP (Lab) Monmouth, 1966–70; Mem. Estimates Cttee, 1966–69; Vice-Chm., Welsh Labour Group, 1969–70, Chm., 1977–78; PPS to Min. of Defence (Administration), 1969–70; PPS to Attorney General, 1974–79; opposition front-bench spokesman on foreign affairs, 1983–92, on defence, 1993–94; Shadow Solicitor General, 1994–. Member: Select Cttee on Welsh Affairs, 1980–83 (Chm., 1981–83); Select Cttee on Home Affairs, 1992–93; Chairman: Parly Lab. Party Environment Gp, 1974–79; Welsh Lab. Gp, 1977–78; British-Zimbabwe Parly Gp, 1989–; Vice-Chairman: British-French Parly Gp, 1984–; British-Norwegian Parly Gp, 1988–; Jt Hon. Sec., British-German Parly Gp, 1975– (Jt Chm., 1994); Treas., Anglo-Austrian Soc., 1988–92; Vice-Chairman: Exec., IPU, 1985–88 (Treas., 1988–90, 1992–); CPA, 1986– (Treas., 1990–93). Sen. Vice-Pres., Assoc. of European Parliamentarians for Africa (Southern), 1984–; Mem., North Atlantic Assembly, 1992–. Pres., Gower Soc., 1976–78. Chairman: Parly Christian Fellowship, 1990–93, Nat. Prayer Breakfast, 1989, President: Boys' Brigade of Wales, 1992–94; Swansea Male Choir. Local preacher. Commander's Cross, Order of Merit (FRG), 1986. *Recreations:* church work, walking and talking. *Address:* House of Commons, SW1A 0AA.

ANDERSON, Prof. Donald Thomas, AO 1986; PhD, DSc; FRS 1977; Challis Professor of Biology, University of Sydney, 1984–91, Professor Emeritus, since 1992 (Professor of Biology, 1972–84); *b* 29 Dec. 1931; *s* of Thomas and Flora Anderson; *m* 1960, Joanne Trevathan (*née* Claridge). *Educ:* King's Coll., London Univ. DSc London, 1966; DSc Sydney, 1983. Lectr in Zoology, Sydney Univ., 1958–61; Sen. Lectr, 1962–66; Reader in Biology, 1967–71. Clarke Medal, Royal Soc. of NSW, 1979. *Publication:* Embryology and Phylogeny, of Annelids and Arthropods, 1973; Barnacles: structure, function, development and evolution, 1993; papers in zool. jls. *Recreations:* gardening, photography. *Address:* 5 Angophora Close, Wamberal, NSW 2260, Australia. *T:* (043) 846670.

ANDERSON, Dr Ephraim Saul, CBE 1976; FRCP; FRS 1968; Director, Enteric Reference Laboratory, Public Health Laboratory Service, 1954–78; *b* 1911; *e s* of Benjamin and Ada Anderson, Newcastle upon Tyne; *m* 1959, Carol Jean (*née* Thompson) (marr. diss.); three *s*. *Educ:* Rutherford Coll., and King's Coll. Med. Sch. (Univ. of Durham), Newcastle upon Tyne. MB, BS 1934; MD Durham, 1953; Dip.Bact. London, 1948; Founder Fellow, Royal Coll. of Pathologists, 1963. GP, 1935–39; RAMC, 1940–46; Pathologist, 1943–46; Registrar in Bacteriology, Postgrad. Med. Sch., 1946–47; Staff, Enteric Reference Lab., 1947–52, Dep. Dir, 1952–54. WHO Fellow, 1953; FIBiol 1973; FRCP 1975. Hon. Chm., Internat. Fedn for Enteric Phage Typing of Internat. Union of Microbiol. Socs, 1986– (Jt Chm., 1958–66; Chm., 1966–86); Dir, Internat. Ref. Lab. for Enteric Phage Typing of Internat. Fedn for Enteric Phage Typing, 1954–; Dir, Collab. Centre for Phage Typing and Resistance of Enterobacteria of WHO, 1960–; Mem., WHO Expert Adv. Panel for Enteric Diseases. Vis. Prof., Sch. of Biol Sciences, Brunel Univ., 1973–77; Royal Soc.–Israel Acad. Vis. Res. Prof., 1978–79. Lectures: Scientific Basis of Medicine, British Postgrad. Med. Fedn, 1966; Almroth Wright, Wright-Fleming Inst. of Microbiol., 1967; Holme, UCH, 1970; Cutter, Sch. of Public Health, Harvard, 1972; Marjory Stephenson Meml, Soc. for Gen. Microbiol., 1975. Hon. DSc Newcastle, 1975. *Publications:* contrib. to: The Bacteriophages (Mark Adams), 1959; The World Problem of Salmonellosis (Van Oye), 1964; Ciba Symposium: Bacterial Episomes and Plasmids, 1969; articles on bacteriophage typing and its genetic basis, microbial ecology, transferable drug resistance in bacteria, its evolution, and epidemiology, with special ref. to significance of bacterial plasmids. *Recreations:* music, photography. *Address:* 10 Rosecroft Avenue, NW3 7QB.

ANDERSON, Eric; *see* Anderson, W. E. K.

ANDERSON, Eugene; *see* Anderson, C. E.

ANDERSON, Sir Ferguson; *see* Anderson, Sir W. F.

ANDERSON, Rev. Prof. George Wishart, FRSE 1977; FBA 1972; Professor of Old Testament Literature and Theology, 1962–68, of Hebrew and Old Testament Studies, 1968–82, University of Edinburgh; *b* 25 Jan. 1913; *s* of George Anderson and Margaret Gordon Wishart; *m* 1st, 1941, Edith Joyce Marjorie Walter (decd); one *s* one *d*; 2nd, 1959, Anne Phyllis Walter. *Educ:* Arbroath High Sch.; Univs of St Andrews, Cambridge, Lund. United Coll., St Andrews: Harkness Scholar; MA 1st Cl. Hons Classics, 1935. Fitzwilliam House and Wesley House, Cambridge: 1st Cl. Theol Tripos Part I, 1937; 2nd Cl. Theol Tripos Part II, 1938; BA 1937; MA 1946. Asst Tutor, Richmond Coll., 1939–41. Chaplain, RAF, 1941–46; Tutor in OT Lang. and Lit., Handsworth Coll., 1946–56; Lecturer in OT Lit. and Theol., Univ. of St Andrews, 1956–58; Prof. of OT Studies, Univ. of Durham, 1958–62. Hon. Sec., Internat. Organization of Old Testament Scholars, 1953–71 (Pres., 1971–74); Mem. Editorial Bd of Vetus Testamentum, 1950–75; Editor, Book List of Soc. for OT Study, 1957–66; President, Soc. for OT Study, 1963; Hon. Sec. (Foreign Correspondence), Soc. for OT Study, 1964–74; Charles Ryder Smith Meml Lectr, 1964; Fernley-Hartley Lectr, 1969; Speaker's Lectr in Biblical Studies, Univ. of Oxford, 1976–80; Henton Davies Lectr, 1977; A. S. Peake Meml Lectr, 1984. Hon. DD St Andrews, 1959; Hon. TeolD Lund, 1971. Burkitt Medal for Biblical Studies, British Acad., 1982. *Publications:* He That Cometh (trans. from Norwegian of S. Mowinckel), 1956; A Critical Introduction to the Old Testament, 1959, 2nd edn 1994; The Ras Shamra Discoveries and the Old Testament (trans. from Norwegian of A. S. Kapelrud, US 1963, UK 1965); The History and Religion of Israel, 1966 (trans. Chinese 1990); (ed) A Decade of Bible Bibliography, 1967; (ed) Tradition and Interpretation, 1979; articles in: The Old Testament and Modern Study (ed H. H. Rowley), 1951; The New Peake Commentary (ed M. Black and H. H. Rowley), 1962; The Cambridge History of the Bible, Vol. I (ed P. R. Ackroyd and C. F. Evans), 1970, and in various learned jls. *Recreations:* reading, music, walking. *Address:* 51 Fountainhall Road, Edinburgh EH9 2LH.

ANDERSON, Gordon Alexander, CA, FCMA; Chartered Accountant; *b* 9 Aug. 1931; *s* of Cecil Brown Anderson and Janet Davidson Bell; *m* 1958, Eirené Cochrane Howie Douglas; two *s* one *d*. *Educ:* High School of Glasgow. Qualified as Chartered Accountant, 1955; FCMA 1984. National Service, RN, 1955–57. Partner: Moores Carson & Watson, 1958 (subseq. McClelland Moores & Co., Arthur Young McClelland Moores & Co., Arthur Young (Chm., 1987–89), and Ernst & Young (Dep. Sen. Partner, 1989–90)); McLintock Moores & Murray, 1963–69. Chairman: Bitmac Ltd, 1990– (Dir, 1984–); TSB Bank Scotland, 1994– (Dir, 1991–); Director: Douglas Firebrick Co. Ltd, 1961–70; TSB Group, 1993–. Mem., Scottish Milk Marketing Bd, 1979–85. Mem., Council on Tribunals, 1990– (Mem., Scottish Cttee, 1990–). Institute of Chartered Accountants of Scotland: Mem. Council, 1980–84; Vice-Pres., 1984–86; Pres., 1986–87. Chm. of Govs, High Sch. of Glasgow, 1992–. *Recreations:* golf, gardening, Rugby football. *Address:* Ardwell, 41 Manse Road, Bearsden, Glasgow G61 3PN. *T:* 0141–942 2803. *Clubs:* Caledonian; Western (Glasgow); Glasgow Golf; Buchanan Castle Golf (Captain 1979–80).

ANDERSON, H(ector) John, FRCP; Physician: St Thomas' Hospital, since 1948 (Special Trustee, 1972–81); Lambeth Hospital, since 1960; South Western Hospital, since 1948; French Hospital, since 1950; *b* Central Provinces, India, 5 Jan. 1915; *s* of H. J. Anderson; *m* 1st, 1940, Frances Pearce (marr. diss.), *er d* of Rev. W. P. Putt; one *s* one *d*; 2nd, 1956, Pauline Mary, *d* of A. Hammond; one *d*. *Educ:* Exeter Sch.; St Catharine's Coll., Cambridge; St Thomas' Hospital. MA, MB (Cantab), FRCP 1950. Medical Registrar and Res. Asst Physician, St Thomas' Hospital, 1941 and 1942. Hon. Lt-Col RAMC; served MEF, 1944–47. Kitchener Scholar; Mead Prizeman, St Thomas' Hospital; Murchison Scholar, RCP, 1942; Goulstonian Lectr, RCP, 1951; Examiner: MB London; Medicine, Conjoint Bd, London and England; RCP. Mem. AHA, Lambeth, Southwark, Lewisham Area (T). Member: Assoc. of Physicians of Gt Britain; Thoracic Soc.; FRSoc.Med. *Publications:* Brim of Day, 1944; contrib. to medical literature. *Address:* Churchill Clinic, 80 Lambeth Road, SE1 7PW. *T:* 0171–928 5633; 102 Lambeth Road, SE1 7PT. *T:* 0171–928 1533.

ANDERSON, Rev. Prof. Hugh, MA, BD, PhD, DD, FRSE; Professor of New Testament Language, Literature and Theology, University of Edinburgh, 1966–85, now Professor Emeritus; *b* 18 May 1920; *s* of Hugh Anderson and Jeannie Muir; *m* 1945, Jean Goldie Torbit; one *s* one *d* (and one *s* decd). *Educ:* Galston Sch.; Kilmarnock Acad.; Univ. of Glasgow (MA (Hons Classics and Semitic Langs I), BD (Dist. New Testament); PhD); post-doctoral Fellow, Univs of Oxford and Heidelberg. FRSE 1987. Chaplain, Egypt and Palestine, 1945–46; Lectr in Old Testament, Univ. of Glasgow, 1946–51; Minister, Trinity Presb. Church, Glasgow, 1951–57; A. B. Bruce Lectr, Univ. of Glasgow, 1954–57; Prof. of Biblical Criticism, Duke Univ., N Carolina, 1957–66. Dir, Postgrad. Studies in Theology, Univ. of Edinburgh, 1968–72; Select Preacher, Oxford Univ., 1970; Haskell Lectr, Oberlin Coll., Ohio, 1971; McBride Vis. Prof. of Religion, Bryn Mawr Coll., Pa, 1974–75; Vis. Prof. of Religion, Meredith Coll., N Carolina, 1982; James A. Gray Lectr, 1982, Kenneth Willis Clark Meml Lectr, 1985, Duke Univ., N Carolina; Scholar-in-res., Florida Southern Coll., Lakeland, Fla, 1983; Warner Hall Lectr, St Andrews Presbyterian Coll., N Carolina, 1985; Bishop E. J. Pendergrass Prof. of Religion, Florida Southern Coll., 1986; J. Wallace Hamilton Lectr, Fla, 1988. Convener of Ch. of Scotland's Special Commn on Priorities of Mission in 70s and 80s, 1969–71; Chm., Internat. Selection Council for Albert Schweitzer Internat. Prizes, 1972–91. Hon. DD Glasgow, 1970. *Publications:* Psalms I-XLV, 1951; Historians of Israel, 1957; Jesus and Christian Origins, 1964; The Inter-Testamental Period in The Bible and History (ed W. Barclay), 1965; (ed with W. Barclay) The New Testament in Historical and Contemporary Perspective, 1965; Jesus, 1967; The Gospel of Mark, 1976; Commentary on 3 and 4 Maccabees, Doubleday Pseudepigrapha Vol. 2, 1982; (with Walter Weaver) Perspectives on Christology, 1989; contribs to Religion in Life, Interpretation, Scottish Jl of Theology, Expos. Times, Anchor Bible Dictionary, Theologische Realenzyklopaedia. *Recreations:* golf, gardening, music. *Address:* 5 Comiston Springs Avenue, Edinburgh EH10 6NT. *T:* 0131–447 1401. *Clubs:* Greek (Edinburgh); Luffness Golf (E Lothian).

ANDERSON, Iain; *see* Anderson, A. J. R.

ANDERSON, James Frazer Gillan, CBE 1979; JP; DL; Member, Scottish Development Agency, 1986–89; *b* 25 March 1929; *m* 1956, May Harley; one *s* one *d*. *Educ:* Maddiston Primary Sch.; Graeme High Sch., Falkirk. Member: Stirling CC, 1958–75 (Convener, 1971–75); Central Regional Council, Scotland, 1974– (Convener, 1974–86). Mem., Health and Safety Commission, 1974–80. OStJ. DUniv Stirling, 1987. *Recreations:* gardening, walking.

ANDERSON, Janet; MP (Lab) Rossendale and Darwen, since 1992; *b* 6 Dec. 1949; *d* of late Thomas Anderson and Ethel Pearson; *m* 1972, Vincent William Humphreys; two *s* one *d*. *Educ:* Kingsfield Comprehensive Sch.; Polytechnic of Central London; Univ. of Nantes (Dip. Bi-lingual Business Studies). Asst to Rt Hon. Barbara Castle, 1974–81, to Jack Straw, MP, 1981–87; Campaign Officer, PLP, 1988–89; Regl Organiser, Shopping Hours Reform Council, 1991–92. Contested (Lab) Rossendale and Darwen, 1987. PPS to Dep. Leader of Labour Party, 1992–93. Secretary: All Party Footwear Gp; Tribune Gp of Lab MPs, 1993–. Member: H of C Commn, 1993–94; Select Cttee on Home Affairs, 1994– (Home Affairs Campaigns Co-ordinator, 1994–). *Recreations:* playing the piano, listening to opera. *Address:* House of Commons, SW1A 0AA. *T:* 0171–219 6629. *Club:* Rosemount Working Men's (Stacksteads, Rossendale).

ANDERSON, Prof. John, MD, FRCP; Professor of Medicine, King's College Hospital Medical School, 1964–86, now Emeritus; *b* 11 Sept. 1921; *s* of James and Margaret Anderson; *m* 1952, Beatrice May Venner; three *s*. *Educ:* Durham Univ. BA Hons, Dunelm (Mod. Hist.) 1942; MB, BS Hons, 1950; BSc Hons, 1952 (Physiology); MA (Mod. Hist.),

MD. Served War, Lt, RA (Field) (Ayrshire Yeomanry), 1940–45. MRC Fellow in Clin. Med., Univ. Coll. Hosp., London, 1952–55; Rockefeller Travelling Fellowship, 1956–57; Reader in Medicine, King's Coll. Hosp. Med. Sch., Med. Unit, 1962–64. Mem., Med. Research Soc. FRCP 1962; FBCS 1969; FIBiol 1977. *Publications:* A New Look at Medical Education, 1965; Information Processing of Medical Records, 1970; articles in Lancet and BMJ, on: nutron activation, medical computing, cancer, endocrinology, med. educn. *Recreation:* computing. *Address:* 14 Styles Way, Park Langley, Beckenham, Kent BR3 3AJ. *T:* (office) 0171–274 6222. *Club:* University (Durham).

ANDERSON, Prof. John, FRCP; FRCPGlas; FRCOG; Postgraduate Dean and Director, Postgraduate Institute for Medicine and Dentistry, and Professor of Medical Education, University of Newcastle upon Tyne, since 1985; *b* 2 Feb. 1936; *s* of John and Norah Anderson, Newcastle upon Tyne; *m* Mary Bynon, Whitley Bay; one *s* one *d. Educ:* Royal Grammar Sch., Newcastle upon Tyne; Med. Sch., King's Coll., Univ. of Durham (MB, BS 2nd Cl. Hons). FRCP 1973 (MRCP 1961); FRCOG (*ad eundem*) 1983; FRCPGlas 1992. Med. Registrar, Royal Victoria Inf., Newcastle upon Tyne, 1962–64; Res. Fellow, Univ. of Virginia, Charlottesville, 1965–66; University of Newcastle upon Tyne: First Asst in Medicine 1967–68; Sen. Lectr in Medicine 1968–85; Academic Sub-Dean, Med. Sch., 1975–85. Hon. Cons. Phys., Newcastle HA, 1968–. Mem. Council, RCP, 1974–77; Member: Assoc. of Phys of GB and Ire., 1976–; Exec. Cttee, ASME, 1979– (Hon. Treas., 1980–88; Gen. Sec., 1990–92; Chm. Council, 1992–); GMC, 1980–. *Publications:* The Multiple Choice Question in Medicine, 1976, 2nd edn 1982; numerous chapters in books, and papers in sci. jls on medicine, diabetes and med. educn. *Recreations:* listening to music, watching cricket, reading, thinking. *Address:* 6 Wilson Gardens, Newcastle upon Tyne NE3 4JA. *T:* 0191–285 4745. *Club:* Yorkshire CC.

ANDERSON, Prof. John Allan Dalrymple, TD 1967; DL; FRCP; FRCGP; FFPHM; FFOM; Professor of Community Medicine, University of London, at United Medical and Dental Schools (Guy's Campus), 1975–90, now Professor Emeritus; Professor and Chairman, Department of Public Health and Occupational Medicine, University of the United Arab Emirates, since 1990; *b* 16 June 1926; *s* of John Allan Anderson and Mary Winifred (*née* Lawson); *m* 1965, Mairead Mary MacLaren; three *d. Educ:* Loretto Sch.; Worcester Coll., Oxford (MA); Edinburgh Univ. (MD); London Univ. (DPH); DObstRCOG. Lectr in gen. practice, 1954–59, Dir, Industrial Survey Unit, 1960–63, Univ. of Edinburgh; Sen. Lectr, Social Medicine, LSHTM, 1963–69; Dir, Dept of Community Medicine, Guy's Hosp. Med. Sch., 1970–90; Hon. Consultant Guy's Hosp., 1970–90. Dir, Occupational Health Service, Lewisham and N Southwark HA, 1984–90. Acad. Registrar, FCM, RCP, 1983–89. OC London Scot. Co. 1/51 Highland Vols, TA, 1967–70; CO 221 Fd Amb. (TA), 1978–81; TA Col HQ Lond. Dist, 1981–84; Regtl Col Lond. Scot. Regt, 1983–89. Hon. Civilian Consultant to the Army in Public Health Medicine, 1990–. Elder, Ch. of Scotland, 1977–; Area Surg., SJAB, SW Lond., 1984–90. DL Greater London, 1985; Rep. DL, Borough of Richmond, 1986–90. *Publications:* A New Look at Community Medicine, 1965; Self Medication, 1982; (with Dr R. Grahame) Bibliography of Low Back Pain, 1982; Epidemiological, Sociological and Environmental Aspects of Rheumatic Diseases, 1987; sci. papers on public health and occupational med. and rheumatology. *Recreations:* hill walking, golf, bridge. *Address:* 24 Lytton Grove, Putney, SW15 2HB. *T:* 0181–788 9420. *Clubs:* Hurlingham; New (Edinburgh).

ANDERSON, Sir John (Anthony), KBE 1994; FCA; Chief Executive and Director: South Pacific Merchant Finance Ltd, since 1979; National Bank of New Zealand Ltd, since 1990; Rural Bank of New Zealand Ltd, since 1992; *b* 2 Aug. 1945; *s* of Donald Ian Mogine Anderson and Elizabeth Grace Anderson (*née* Plummer); *m* 1970, Carol Margaret Tuck; two *s* one *d. Educ:* Christ's Coll.; Victoria Univ. of Wellington. ACA 1967, FCA 1991. With Deloitte Ross Tohmatsu, Wellington, 1962–69; Guest & Bell, Melbourne, 1969–72. Director: NZ Steel, 1986–87; Lloyds Merchant Bank (London), 1986–92; Lloyds Bank NZA, 1989–; Chm., Petroleum Corp. of NZ, 1986–88. Chairman: Adv. Bd, NZ Debt Mgt Office, 1989–; Prime Minister's NZ Employment Taskforce, 1994. Chairman: NZ Merchant Banks Assoc., 1982–89; NZ Bankers' Assoc., 1991–92; Pres., NZ Bankers' Inst., 1990. NZ Commemoration Medal, 1990. *Recreations:* cricket, tennis, golf, bridge. *Address:* 5 Fancourt Street, Karori, Wellington, New Zealand. *T:* (4) 4944000. *Clubs:* Wellington, Wellesley (NZ).

ANDERSON, Maj.-Gen. Sir John (Evelyn), KBE 1971 (CBE 1963); CEng, FIEE; CIMgt; Associate and Director, Space and Maritime Applications Inc., 1988–93; *b* 28 June 1916; *e s* of Lt-Col John Gibson Anderson, Christchurch, NZ, and Margaret (*née* Scott), Edinburgh; *m* 1944, Jean Isobel, *d* of Charles Tait, farmer, Aberdeenshire; one *s* one *d. Educ:* King's Sch., Rochester; RMA, Woolwich. Commissioned in Royal Signals, 1936; Lt-Col 1956; Col 1960; Brig. 1964; Maj.-Gen. 1967; Signal Officer in Chief (Army), MoD, 1967–69; ACDS (signals), 1969–72. Col Comdt, Royal Corps of Signals, 1969–74. Hon. Col 71st (Yeomanry) Signal Regt TAVR, 1969–76; Hon. Col Women's Transport Corps (FANY), 1970–76. Dir Gen., NATO Integrated Communications System Management Agency, 1977–81; Exec. Dir, Europe Gp, AFCEA, 1981–88. Pres., Piscatorial Soc., 1981–87. *Recreation:* fishing. *Address:* The Beeches, Amport, Andover, Hampshire SP11 8BW. *Clubs:* Army and Navy, Flyfishers'.

See also Maj.-Gen. A. A. G. Anderson.

ANDERSON, John Graeme, CBE 1989, CEng, FInstE; Deputy Chairman, Northern Engineering Industries plc, 1986–89; Director, Team General Partner, since 1993; *b* 3 June 1927; *s* of John Anderson and Ella (*née* Pusey); *m* 1953, Nancy Clarice Taylor Johnson; one *s* twin *d. Educ:* Merchant Taylors' Sch., Sandy Lodge; London Univ. (BScEng Hons). MIMechE. Served RN, Fleet Air Arm, 1945–48. International Combustion Ltd: graduate apprentice, 1952; Dir, 1968; Dep. Chief Exec., 1969; Man. Dir, 1974; Northern Engineering Industries: Man. Dir, NEI-Internat. Combustion Ltd, 1977; Managing Director: Mechanical Gp, 1980; Power Gp, 1982; Internat. and Projects Gp, 1984; Chm., NEI Pacific, 1984–88. Chm., Internat. Combustion-HUD Hong Kong, 1978–82; Dir, British Nuclear Associates, 1985–88; Alternate Dir, Nat. Nuclear Corp., 1986–88; Director: Tyne and Wear Develt Corp., 1987–93; The Newcastle Initiative, 1988–90. Mem., Duke of Kent's BOTB mission to Turkey, 1984. Chairman: Solid Waste Assoc., 1972–74; Watertube Boilermakers' Assoc., 1976–80; Member: Process Plant Assoc., 1968–87; Process Plant, EDC, 1972–76; Heavy Electrical, EDC, 1976–80. Gov., Derby Coll. of Technology, 1969–74. Chm., Upstage, 1977–79. *Recreations:* shooting, painting, music, fell walking. *Address:* Trinity Barns, Corbridge, Northumberland NE45 5HP. *T:* Hexham (01434) 633228.

ANDERSON, John Huxley Fordyce, FCIOB; Managing Director, Bovis Construction Ltd, since 1993; Director: Bovis Construction Group, since 1988 (non-executive, 1988–92); P&O Property Holdings, since 1985; *b* 13 Jan. 1945; *s* of Alexander Robert Fordyce Anderson and Agnes Joan (*née* Huxley); *m* 1973, Tucker Lee Etherington; one *s* one *d. Educ:* Fan Court Sch.; Milton Abbey Sch.; Brixton Sch. of Building; Harvard Bus. Sch. (post-grad. PMD 1983). FCIOB 1988. Joined Higgs & Hill as indentured student, 1962; Project Planner on projects such as BBC TV Centre, RMA Sandhurst, 1966–69; Contract Manager, Sales and Marketing Manager then Dep. Man. Dir, Costains, Vale do Lobo, Portugal, 1969–74; with Town & City Properties in Holland, 1975–76; Develt Project Manager, Town & City Develts in London, 1976–83; Man. Dir, Town & City, then P&O, Develts, 1984–92; Dir, Chelsea Harbour, 1984–92. Man. Dir, PSA Building Management (on secondment to Govt), 1991–93. *Recreations:* parish council, local amenity society, golf, ski-ing, gardening, watching sport, theatre, ballet, eating and drinking with friends. *Address:* Bovis Construction Ltd, Liscartan House, 127 Sloane Street, SW1X 9BA. *Club:* Royal Automobile.

ANDERSON, Prof. John Kinloch, FSA; Professor of Classical Archaeology, University of California, Berkeley, 1958–93, now Emeritus; *b* 3 Jan. 1924; *s* of late Sir James Anderson, KCIE, and of Lady Anderson; *m* 1954, Esperance, *d* of Guy Batham, Dunedin, NZ; one *s* two *d. Educ:* Trinity Coll., Glenalmond; Christ Church, Oxford (MA). Served War, in Black Watch (RHR) and Intelligence Corps, 1942–46 (final rank, Lieut). Student, British Sch. at Athens, 1949–52; Lecturer in Classics, Univ. of Otago, NZ, 1953–58. FSA 1976. Award for Distinction in Teaching, Phi Beta Kappa (N Calif. Chapter), 1988. *Publications:* Greek Vases in the Otago Museum, 1955; Ancient Greek Horsemanship, 1961; Military Theory and Practice in the Age of Xenophon, 1970; Xenophon, 1974; Hunting in the Ancient World, 1985; articles and reviews in Annual of British Sch. at Athens; Jl of Hellenic Studies, etc. *Recreations:* gardening, riding (Qualified Riding Mem., Calif Dressage Soc.). *Address:* 1020 Middlefield Road, Berkeley, CA 94708, USA. *T:* (510) 8415335.

ANDERSON, John M., PhD; FBA 1991; Professor of English Language, University of Edinburgh, since 1988. *Educ:* Edinburgh Univ. (MA, PhD). Lectr until 1975, Reader, 1975–88, Edinburgh Univ. *Publications:* Grammar of Case: towards a localistic theory, 1971; (ed with C. Jones) Historical Linguistics, 2 vols, 1974; (with R. Lass) Old English Phonology, 1975; (with C. Jones) Phonological Structure and the History of English, 1977; (with C. J. Ewen) Principles of Dependency Phonology, 1987. *Address:* Department of English Language, David Hume Tower, George Square, Edinburgh EH8 9JX.

ANDERSON, Sir John (Muir), Kt 1969; CMG 1957; Commissioner of State Savings Bank of Victoria, 1962–83, Chairman of Commissioners, 1967; *b* 14 Sept. 1914; *s* of John Weir Anderson; *m* 1949, Audrey Drayton Jamieson; one *s* one *d. Educ:* Brighton Grammar Sch.; Melbourne Univ. 2/6th Commando Co., 1941; Lieut, 1st Australian Parachute Bn, 1944; served SE Asia, 1941–45. Established John M. Anderson & Co. Pty Ltd, Manufacturers, Agents and Importers, 1951; Managing Director, King Oscar Fine Foods Pty Ltd. Pres. of Liberal and Country Party of Victoria, 1952–56 (Treasurer, 1957–61, 1978–80). Comr, Melbourne Harbour Trust, 1972–83. Trustee, Melbourne Exhibn, 1960, Chm. of Trustees, 1968. *Recreations:* swimming, fishing. *Address:* 25 Cosham Street, Brighton, Vic 3186, Australia. *T:* 5924790.

ANDERSON, Professor John Neil; (first) Professor of Dental Prosthetics, 1964–82 (now Emeritus), (first) Dean of Dentistry, 1972–76, 1980–82, University of Dundee; *b* 11 Feb. 1922; *m* 1945, Mary G. Croll; one *s* one *d. Educ:* High Storrs Gram. Sch., Sheffield; Sheffield Univ. Asst Lectr, Sheffield Univ., 1945–46; Lectr, Durham Univ., 1946–48; Lectr, Birmingham Univ., 1948–52; Sen. Lectr, St Andrews Univ., 1952–64. External Examiner, Univs of Malaya, Baghdad, Newcastle upon Tyne, Bristol, Birmingham, Liverpool, RCSI. *Publications:* Applied Dental Materials, 1956; (with R. Storer) Immediate and Replacement Dentures, 1966, 3rd edn, 1981; contribs to leading dental jls. *Recreations:* music, gardening, carpentry. *Address:* Wyndham, Derwent Drive, Baslow, Bakewell, Derbyshire DE4 1RS.

ANDERSON, Prof. John Russell, CBE 1980; Professor of Pathology at the Western Infirmary, Glasgow University, 1967–83, retired; *b* 31 May 1918; *s* of William Gregg Anderson and Mary Gordon Adam; *m* 1956, Audrey Margaret Shaw Wilson; two *s* one *d* (and one *d* decd). *Educ:* Worksop Coll.; St Andrews Univ. BSc (St Andrews) 1939, MB, ChB (St Andrews) 1942, MD (St Andrews) 1955; MRCP 1961; FRCPGlas 1965; FRCPath 1966; FRSE 1968. RAMC, 1944–47 (Emergency Commn). Lecturer and Senior Lecturer in Pathology, Glasgow Univ., 1947–65; George Holt Prof. of Pathology, Liverpool Univ., 1965–67. Rockefeller travelling fellowship in Medicine, at Rochester, NY, 1953–54. Pres., RCPath, 1978–81 (Vice-Pres., 1975). Hon. FRCPI, 1981. Hon. LLD Dundee, 1981. *Publications:* Autoimmunity, Clinical and Experimental (jtly), 1967; (ed) Muir's Textbook of Pathology, 9th edn 1972 to 12th edn 1985; various papers on immunopathology in scientific jls. *Recreations:* golf, ski-ing, gardening. *Address:* 3 Connell Crescent, Milngavie, Glasgow G62 6AR.

ANDERSON, Dame Josephine; *see* Barstow, Dame J.

ANDERSON, Julian Anthony; Director General, Country Landowners' Association, since 1990; *b* 12 June 1938; *s* of Sir Kenneth Anderson, KBE, CB. *Educ:* King Alfred Sch.; Wadham Coll., Oxford (MA). Entered MAFF as Asst Principal, 1961; Asst Private Sec. to Minister of Agriculture, 1964–66; Principal, 1966; seconded to FCO, 1970–73; Asst Sec., 1973, Under Sec., 1982–90, MAFF; seconded as Minister (Food and Agriculture), UK Perm. Rep. to EEC, 1982–85. *Recreations:* music, sport, travel, photography, gardening, DIY. *Address:* c/o Country Landowners' Association, 16 Belgrave Square, SW1X 8PQ. *Clubs:* United Oxford & Cambridge University, Civil Service.

ANDERSON, Hon. Sir Kevin (Victor), Kt 1980; Judge of the Supreme Court of Victoria, 1969–84; *b* 4 Sept. 1912; *s* of Robert Victor Anderson and Margaret Anderson (*née* Collins); *m* 1942, Claire Margaret Murphy; six *d. Educ:* Xavier Coll., Kew; Melbourne Univ. (LLB). Victorian Crown Law Dept, 1929–42: Courts Branch, 1929–35; Professional Asst, Crown Solicitor's Office, 1935–42; Lt, RAN, 1942–46; Victorian Bar, 1946–69; QC (Victoria) 1962. Chm., Bd of Inquiry into Scientology, 1963–65. Chm., Victorian Bar Council, 1966–67; Treasurer, Australian Law Council, 1966–68. Kt, Australian Assoc. of SMO of Malta, 1979. *Publications:* Stamp Duties in Victoria, 1949, 2nd edn 1968; joint author: Price Control, 1947; Landlord and Tenant Law, 1948, 3rd edn 1958; Victorian Licensing Law, 1952; Victoria Police Manual, 1956, 2nd edn 1969; Workers' Compensation, 1958, 2nd edn 1966; Fossil in the Sandstone: the Recollecting Judge, 1986; (ed) Victorian Law Reports, 1956–69. *Recreations:* yachting, woodworking. *Address:* 12 Power Avenue, Toorak, Victoria 3142, Australia. *T:* (3) 8222901. *Clubs:* Victoria Racing, Royal Automobile of Victoria, Celtic, Essoign (Melbourne).

ANDERSON, Prof. Malcolm Grove; Professor, since 1989, and Head of Department of Geography, since 1990, University of Bristol; *b* 27 June 1949; *s* of Wilfred Roy Anderson and Frances Betty Anderson; *m* 1972, Elizabeth Ann Roger; one *d. Educ:* Univ. of Nottingham (BSc); Univ. of Cambridge (PhD); Univ. of Bristol (DSc). Research Fellow, Sidney Sussex Coll., Cambridge, 1972; Lectr, 1973, Reader, 1985, Univ. of Bristol. Res. Hydrologist, US Corps of Engrs, 1981–82; Sen. Res. Geotechnical Engr, Hong Kong Govt, 1982–83. Editor-in-Chief, Hydrological Processes. Gill Meml Award, RGS, 1986. *Publications:* (ed with T. P. Burt) Hydrological Forecasting, 1985; (ed with K. S. Richards) Slope Stability: geotechnical engineering and geomorphology, 1987; (ed) Modelling Geomorphological Systems, 1988; (ed with T. P. Burt) Process Studies in Hillslope Hydrology, 1990. *Recreations:* France, sailing, piano. *Address:* Department of Geography, University of Bristol, University Road, Bristol BS8 1SS. *T:* Bristol (0117) 928 7871.

ANDERSON, Brig. Hon. Dame Mary Mackenzie; *see* Pihl, Brig. Hon. Dame M. M.

ANDERSON, Mary Margaret, FRCOG; Consultant Obstetrician and Gynaecologist, Lewisham Hospital, since 1967; *b* 12 Feb. 1932; *d* of William Anderson and Lily Adams. *Educ:* Forres Acad.; Edinburgh Univ. (MB, ChB 1956). FRCOG 1974. Jun. hosp. posts in Scotland and England, including Hammersmith Hosp., and St Mary's Hosp., London (Sen. Registrar); Chm., Div. of Obst. and Gynaecol., Lewisham Hosp., 1984–87. Consultant Advr, CMO, 1990–. Royal College of Obstetricians and Gynaecologists: Chm., Hosp. Recognition Cttee, 1987–89; Jun. Vice Pres., 1989–92. Chm., SE Thames RHA Specialist Sub Cttee, 1986–88; Member: Scientific Cttee, National Birthday Trust, 1990–; Council, Med. Defence Union, 1987–. *Publications:* Anatomy and Physiology of Obstetrics, 1979; Handbook of Obstetrics and Gynaecology, 1981; The Menopause, 1983; Pregnancy after Thirty, 1984; An A–Z of Gynaecology, 1986; Infertility, 1987; (contrib.) Ten Teachers in Obstetrics and Gynaecology, 1990. *Recreations:* reading, music, gardening. *Address:* Green Roof Cottage, 1 Heathway, Blackheath, SE3 7AN; 96 Harley Street, W1N 1AF. *T:* 0171–487 4146.

ANDERSON, Prof. Michael, FRSE; FBA 1989; Professor of Economic History, University of Edinburgh, since 1979; *b* 21 Feb. 1942; *s* of Douglas Henry and Rose Lillian Anderson; *m* 1966, Rosemary Elizabeth Kitching; one *s* one *d*. *Educ:* Kingston Grammar Sch.; Queens' Coll., Cambridge (BA 1964; MA 1968; PhD 1969). FRSE 1990. University of Edinburgh: Department of Sociology: Asst Lectr, 1967; Lectr, 1969; Reader, 1975; Department of Economic and Social History, 1979; Dean, Faculty of Social Scis, 1985–89; Vice-Principal, 1989–93; Acting Principal, April–Aug. 1994. Member: Economic and Social History Cttee, SSRC, 1974–78; Computing Cttee, SSRC, 1980–82; Scot. Records Adv. Council, 1984–93; ESRC, 1990–94 (Member: Res. Resources and Methods Cttee, 1982–84; Society and Politics Res. Develt Gp, 1989–92; Res. Resources Bd, 1992–94); History of Medicine Cttee, Wellcome Trust, 1988–92; BL Bd, 1994–. *Publications:* Family Structure in Nineteenth Century Lancashire, 1971; (ed) Sociology of the Family, 1972; Approaches to the History of the Western Family 1500–1914, 1981; The 1851 Census: a national sample of the enumerators returns, 1987; Population Change in Northwestern Europe 1750–1850, 1988. *Recreations:* natural history, gardening, study of ancient civilizations. *Address:* 30 Kings Park, Longniddry, East Lothian EH32 0QL.

ANDERSON, Vice Adm. Sir Neil (Dudley), KBE 1982 (CBE 1976); CB 1979; Chief of Defence Staff (NZ), 1980–83; *b* 5 April 1927; *s* of Eric Dudley Anderson and Margaret Evelyn (*née* Craig); *m* 1951, Barbara Lillias Romaine Wright; two *s*. *Educ:* Hastings High Sch.; BRNC. Joined RNZN, 1944; trng and sea service with RN, 1944–49; Korean War Service, 1950–51; qual. as navigation specialist; Navigator: HMS Vanguard, 1952–53; HMNZS Lachlan, 1954; HMS Saintes, 1958–59; Commanding Officer, HMNZS: Taranaki, 1961–62; Waikato, 1968–69; Philomel, 1969–70; Dep. Chief of Def. Staff, 1976–77; Chief of Naval Staff, 1977–80. Lieut 1949, Lt-Comdr 1957, Comdr 1960, Captain 1968, Cdre 1972, Rear Adm. 1977, Vice Adm. 1980. *Recreations:* golf, fishing. *Address:* 36 Beauchamp Street, Karori, Wellington, New Zealand. *T:* (4) 4766257. *Club:* Wellington (Wellington, NZ).

ANDERSON, Paul James; journalist; Deputy Editor, New Statesman, since 1993; *b* 3 Oct. 1959; *s* of James George Anderson and Marjorie Rosemary Anderson (*née* Thorpe). *Educ:* Ipswich Sch.; Balliol Coll., Oxford (BA Hons PPE 1981); London College of Printing. Dep. Ed., European Nuclear Disarmament Jl, 1984–87; Reviews Ed., 1986–91, Editor, 1991–93, Tribune. *Publications:* (ed jtly) Mad Dogs: The US Raid on Libya, 1986. *Address:* 75 Devonshire Road, Forest Hill, SE23 3LX.

ANDERSON, Prof. Philip Warren; Joseph Henry Professor of Physics, Princeton University, New Jersey, since 1975; *b* 13 Dec. 1923; *s* of Prof. H. W. Anderson and Mrs Elsie O. Anderson; *m* 1947, Joyce Gothwaite; one *d*. *Educ:* Harvard Univ. BS 1943; MA 1947; PhD 1949, Harvard. Naval Res. Lab., Washington, DC, 1943–45 (Chief Petty Officer, USN). Mem., Technical Staff, 1949–76, Dir, 1976–84, Bell Telephone Labs. Fulbright Lectr, Tokyo Univ., 1952–53; Overseas Fellow, Churchill Coll., Cambridge, 1961–62; Vis. Prof. of Theoretical Physics, Univ. of Cambridge, 1967–75, and Fellow of Jesus College, Cambridge, 1969–75, Hon. Fellow, 1978–; Cherwell-Simon Meml Lectureship, 1979–80, George Eastman Prof., 1993–94, Oxford Univ. Member: Amer. Acad. of Arts and Sciences, 1966; Nat. Acad. of Sciences, US, 1967; Amer. Philosophical Soc., 1991; Foreign Member: Royal Society, London, 1980; Japan Acad., 1988; Indian Nat. Acad. of Scis, 1990; Russian Nat. Acad. of Sci., 1994; Foreign Associate, Accademia Lincei, Rome, 1985. Hon. FInstP, 1986. Hon. DSc: Illinois, 1978; Rutgers, 1991; Ecole Normale Supérieure, Paris, 1995. O. E. Buckley Prize, Amer. Phys. Soc., 1964; Dannie Heinemann Prize, Akad. Wiss. Göttingen, 1975; (jtly) Nobel Prize for Physics, 1977; Guthrie Medal, Inst. of Physics, 1978; Nat. Medal of Science, US, 1984. *Publications:* Concepts in Solids, 1963; Basic Notions of Condensed Matter Physics, 1984; numerous articles in scholarly jls. *Recreations:* go (Japanese game), rank sho-dan, walking. *Address:* 74 Aunt Molly Road, Hopewell, NJ 08525, USA.

ANDERSON, Ray Thomas; Agent-General for Queensland, since 1991; *b* 23 Nov. 1936; *s* of late Thomas James Anderson and Daisy Eva D'Arcy-Irvine (*née* Woodhouse); *m* 1962, Margaret, *d* of Ronald George Geach; one *s* three *d*. *Educ:* State Commercial High Sch., Brisbane; Univ. of Queensland (BCom Hons); Macquarie Univ. (BLegS). Public servant, Brisbane, 1956–60; RAAF Psychologist, Brisbane, 1961–62; Trainee Trade Comr, Canberra, 1963; First Sec. and Asst Trade Comr, Australian High Commn, Singapore, 1964–67; Trade Commissioner: Johannesburg, 1968; Cape Town, 1969–70; Counsellor (Commercial) and Sen. Trade Comr, Aust. High Commn, New Delhi, 1971–73; Regl Dir, DTI, Brisbane, 1974–76; Counsellor (Commercial) and Trade Comr (Mktg), Aust. Embassy, Tokyo, 1977–80; Asst Sec., Dept. of Trade, 1980–82; First Asst Sec., Depts of Foreign Affairs and Trade, Trade, Immigration and Ethnic Affairs, 1982–87; Manager, Nat. Ops, AUSTRADE, 1987–89; Minister (Marketing) and Sen. Trade Comr, London and Minister (Commercial), The Hague, 1990–91. Admitted Barrister, Supreme Court, NSW and High Court of Australia, and Barrister and Solicitor, Supreme Court, ACT, 1989. Freeman, City of London, 1991. Flying Officer, RAAF Reserve. Hon. FAIEx. *Recreations:* tennis, reading, travel, theatre. *Address:* Queensland House, 392 Strand, WC2R 0LZ. *T:* 0171–836 1333. *Clubs:* Royal Automobile (Hon.), East India (Hon.), Royal Over-Seas League (Hon.); Singapore Town; Commonwealth (Canberra); United Services, Queensland (Brisbane).

ANDERSON, Reginald, CMG 1974; Chairman, International Explosives Disposal Ltd, since 1991; *b* 3 Nov. 1921; *s* of late Herbert Anderson and late Anne Mary (*née* Hicks); *m* 1945, Audrey Gabrielle Williams; two *d*. *Educ:* Palmers, Grays, Essex. Cabinet Office, 1938–40. Served War, RAF, Flt Lt, 1941–46. Ministry of: Supply, 1947–57; Supply Staff, Australia, 1957–59; Aviation, 1960–67; Counsellor, British Embassy, Washington, 1967–70; Asst Under-Sec. of State, 1970–76, Dep. Under-Sec. of State, 1976–81, MoD. *Address:* Reynosa, Heronway, Shenfield, Essex CM13 2LX. *T:* Brentwood (01277) 213077. *Club:* Royal Air Force.

ANDERSON, Robert Geoffrey William; Director, British Museum, since 1992; *b* 2 May 1944; *er s* of Herbert Patrick Anderson and Kathleen Diana Anderson (*née* Burns); *m* 1973, Margaret Elizabeth Callis Lea; two *s*. *Educ:* Woodhouse Sch., London; St John's Coll., Oxford (Casberd exhibitioner) (BSc, MA, DPhil). FRSC 1984; FSA 1986; FRSE 1990. Assistant Keeper: Royal Scottish Museum, 1970–75; Science Museum, 1975–78; Dep. Keeper, Wellcome Museum of History of Medicine, and Sec., Adv. Council, Science Museum, 1978–80; Keeper, Dept of Chemistry, Science Mus., 1980–84; Director: Royal Scottish Mus., 1984–85; Nat. Museums of Scotland, 1985–92. Sec., Royal Scottish Soc. of Arts, 1973–75; Member Council: Soc. for History of Alchemy and Chemistry, 1978–; Gp for Scientific, Technological and Medical Collections, 1979–83; British Soc. History of Science, 1981–84 (Pres., 1988–90); Scottish Museums, 1984–91; Museums Assoc., 1988–92; Mem., British Nat. Cttee for Hist. of Science, 1985–89; Pres., Scientific Instrument Commn, IUHPS, 1982–. Member Editorial Board: Annals of Science, 1981–; Annali di Storia della Scienza, 1986–. Trustee, Boerhaave Mus., Leiden, 1994–. Hon. FSAScot 1991. Hon. DSc Edinburgh, 1995. Dexter Prize, Amer. Chemical Soc., 1986. *Publications:* The Mariner's Astrolabe, 1972; Edinburgh and Medicine, 1976; (ed) The Early Years of the Edinburgh Medical School, 1976; The Playfair Collection and the Teaching of Chemistry at the University of Edinburgh, 1978; (contrib.) The History of Technology, Vol. VI, ed T. I. Williams, 1978; Science in India, 1982; (ed) Science, Medicine and Dissent: Joseph Priestley (1733–1804), 1987; Scientific Instrument Makers Trade Catalogues, 1990; (ed) A New Museum for Scotland, 1990; (with G. Fyffe) Joseph Black: a Bibliography, 1992; (ed) Making Instruments Count, 1993. *Recreation:* books. *Address:* British Museum, WC1B 3DG. *T:* 0171-636 1555. *Club:* Athenæum.

ANDERSON, Prof. Robert Henry; Joseph Levy Professor of Paediatric Cardiac Morphology, National Heart and Lung Institute (formerly Cardiothoracic Institute), University of London, since 1979; *b* 4 April 1942; *s* of Henry Anderson and Doris Amy Anderson (*née* Callear); *m* 1966, Christine (*née* Ibbotson); one *s* one *d*. *Educ:* Wellington Grammar Sch., Shropshire; Manchester Univ. BSc (Hons); MD; FRCPath. House Officer, Professorial Surgical Unit, 1966, Medical Unit, 1967, Manchester Royal Infirmary; Asst Lectr in Anatomy, 1967–69, Lectr, 1969–73, Manchester Univ.; MRC Travelling Fellow, Dept of Cardiology, Univ. of Amsterdam, 1973–74; Cardiothoracic Institute, University of London: British Heart Foundn Sen. Res. Fellow and Sen. Lectr in Paediatrics, 1974–77; Joseph Levy Reader in Paediatric Cardiac Morphology, 1977–79. Hon. Prof. of Surgery, Univ. of N Carolina, USA, 1984–; Visiting Professor: Univ. of Pittsburgh, Pa, 1985–; Liverpool Univ., 1989–. Excerpta Medica Travel Award, 1977; British Heart Foundn Prize for Cardiovascular Research, 1984. Associate Editor, Internat. Jl of Cardiology, 1985–91; Exec. Ed., Cardiology in the Young, 1992–. *Publications:* (ed jtly) Paediatric Cardiology, 1977, vol. 3, 1981, vol. 5, 1983, vol. 6, 1986; (with A. E. Becker) Cardiac Anatomy, 1980; (with E. A. Shinebourne) Current Paediatric Cardiology, 1980; (with A. E. Becker) Pathology of Congenital Heart Disease, 1981; (with M. J. Davies and A. E. Becker) Pathology of the Conduction Tissues, 1983; (jtly) Morphology of Congenital Heart Disease, 1983; (with A. E. Becker) Cardiac Pathology, 1984; (with G. A. H. Miller and M. L. Rigby) The Diagnosis of Congenital Heart Disease, 1985; (with B. R. Wilcox) Surgical Anatomy of the Heart, 1985, 2nd edn 1992; (jtly) Paediatric Cardiology, 2 vols, 1987; (with P. J. Oldershaw and J. R. Dawson) Clinician's Illustrated Dictionary of Cardiology, 1988; (jtly) Atlas of the Heart, 1988; (jtly) Transesogophagal Echocardiography in Clinical Practice, 1991; (with A. E. Becker) The Heart Structure in Health and Disease, 1992; over 200 invited chapters in published books and over 370 papers in jls. *Recreations:* golf, tennis, music, wine. *Address:* 60 Earlsfield Road, SW18 3DN. *T:* 0181-870 4368. *Clubs:* Saintsbury, Roehampton.

ANDERSON, Robert (Woodruff); playwright; *b* NYC, 28 April 1917; *s* of James Hewston Anderson and Myra Esther (*née* Grigg); *m* 1st, 1940, Phyllis Stohl (*d* 1956); 2nd, 1959, Teresa Wright (marr. diss. 1978). *Educ:* Phillips Exeter Acad.; Harvard Univ. AB (*magna cum laude*) 1939, MA 1940. Served USNR, 1942–46 (Lt); won prize (sponsored by War Dept) for best play written by a serviceman overseas, Come Marching Home, 1945, subseq. prod, Univ. of Iowa and Blackfriars Guild, NY. Rockefeller Fellowship, 1946; taught playwrighting, American Theatre Wing Professional Trng Prog., 1946–50; organized and taught Playwright's Unit, Actors Studio, 1955; Writer in Residence, Univ. of N Carolina, 1969; Faculty: Salzburg Seminar in Amer. Studies, 1968; Univ. of Iowa Writers' Workshop, 1976. Member: Playwrights Co., 1953–60; Bd of Governors, American Playwrights Theatre, 1963–; Council, Dramatists Guild, 1954– (Pres., 1971–73); New Dramatists Cttee, 1949– (Pres., 1955–57); Vice-Pres., Authors' League of America; Chm., Harvard Bd of Overseers' Cttee to visit the Performing Arts, 1970–76. Wrote and adapted plays for TV and Radio, 1948–53. Elected to Theater Hall of Fame, 1980. Connecticut Commn on the Arts Award, 1992. *Plays:* Eden Rose, 1948; Love Revisited, 1952; Tea and Sympathy, 1953; All Summer Long, 1954; Silent Night, Lonely Night, 1959; The Days Between, 1965; You Know I Can't Hear You When the Water's Running (four short plays), 1967; I Never Sang For My Father, 1968; Solitaire/Double Solitaire, 1971; Free and Clear, 1983; The Kissing was Always the Best, 1987; The Last Act is a Solo, 1989; *screenplays:* Tea and Sympathy, 1956; Until They Sail, 1957; The Nun's Story, 1959; The Sand Pebbles, 1965; I Never Sang For My Father, 1970 (Writers Guild Award for Best Screenplay, 1971); The Patricia Neal Story, TV, 1981; Absolute Strangers, TV, 1991; The Last Act is a Solo, TV, 1991 (ACE Award). *Publications: novels:* After, 1973; Getting Up and Going Home, 1978; *anthology:* (jtly) Elements of Literature, 6 vols, 1988. *Recreations:* photography, tennis. *Address:* Roxbury, CT 06783, USA. *Club:* Harvard (New York City).

ANDERSON, Roy Arnold; Chairman Emeritus, Lockheed Corporation, since 1989; *b* Ripon, Calif, 15 Dec. 1920; *s* of Carl Gustav Anderson and Esther Marie Johnson; *m* 1948, Betty Leona Boehme; two *s* two *d*. *Educ:* Ripon Union High Sch.; Humphreys Sch. of Business; Stanford Univ. AB 1947; MBA 1949; Phi Beta Kappa; CPA. Served War, USNR, 1942–46 and 1950–52. Westinghouse Electric Corporation: Manager, Factory Accounting, 1952–56; Lockheed Missiles and Space Co.: Manager, Accounting and Finance, and Dir, Management Controls, 1956–65; Lockheed Georgia Co.: Dir of Finance, 1965–68; Lockheed Corporation: Asst Treas., 1968–69; Vice-Pres. and Controller, 1969–71; Sen. Vice-Pres., Finance, 1971–75; Vice-Chm. of Board, also Chief Financial and Admin. Officer, 1975–77; Chm. and Chief Exec. Officer, 1977–85; Chm., Exec. Cttee, Dir and Consultant, 1985–88. Director of cos in California. Chm. and Chief Exec., Weingart Foundn, 1994–. *Recreation:* tennis. *Address:* c/o Lockheed Corporation, 606 South Olive Street, Los Angeles, CA 90014, USA. *T:* (213) 6898701.

ANDERSON, Prof. Roy Malcolm, FRS 1986; Linacre Professor of Zoology, University of Oxford, since 1993; Fellow, Merton College, Oxford, since 1993; *b* 12 April 1947; *s* of James Anderson and Betty Watson-Weatherburn; *m* 1st, 1975, Dr Mary Joan Anderson (marr. diss. 1989); 2nd, 1990, Dr Claire Baron. *Educ:* Duncombe Sch., Bengeo; Richard Hale Sch., Hertford; Imperial Coll., London (BSc, ARCS, PhD, DIC). CBiol, FIBiol; FSS. IBM Research Fellow, Univ. of Oxford, 1971–73; Lectr, King's Coll., London, 1973–77; Lectr, 1977–80, Reader, 1980–82, Prof., 1982–93, Head of Dept of Biology, 1984–93, Imperial Coll., London Univ. Vis. Prof., McGill Univ., 1982–; Alexander Langmuir Vis. Prof., Harvard, 1990–. Member: NERC, 1988–91 (Chm., Services and Facilities Cttee, 1989–90); ACOST, 1989–93 (Chm., Standing Cttee on Envmt, 1990–93); Council: Zoological Soc., 1988–90; Royal Soc., 1989–91; RSTM&H, 1989–; RPMS. Gov., Wellcome Trust Ltd, 1992– (Trustee, Wellcome Trust, 1991–92; Chm., Infection and Immunity Grant Panel, 1990–92). Hon. Fellow, Linacre Coll., Oxford, 1993. Zoological Soc. Scientific Medal, 1982; Huxley Meml Medal, Imperial Coll., London, 1983; Wright Meml Medal, British Soc. of Parasitology, 1986; David Starr Jordan Medal, Univs of Stanford, Connell and Indiana, 1986; Chalmers Medal, RSTM&H, 1988; Weldon Medal, Oxford Univ., 1989; John Hill Grundy Medal, Royal Army Med. Coll., 1990; Frink Medal, Zoological Soc. of London, 1993; Joseph Smadel Medal, Infectious Diseases Soc. of Amer. *Publications:* (ed) Population Dynamics of Infectious Disease Agents: theory and applications, 1982; (ed jtly) Population Biology of Infectious Diseases, 1982; (with R. M. May) Infectious Diseases of Humans: dynamics and control, 1991. *Recreations:* hill walking, croquet, natural history, photography. *Address:* Merton College, Oxford OX1 4JD. *Club:* Athenæum.

ANDERSON, (William) Eric (Kinloch), MA, BLitt, DLitt, FRSE; Rector, Lincoln College, Oxford, since 1994; *b* 27 May 1936; *er s* of W. J. Kinloch Anderson, Edinburgh; *m* 1960, Poppy, *d* of W. M. Mason, Skipton; one *s* one *d*. *Educ:* George Watson's Coll.; Univ. of St Andrews (MA); Balliol Coll., Oxford (BLitt; Hon. Fellow, 1989). Asst Master: Fettes Coll., 1960–64; Gordonstoun, 1964–66; Asst Master, Fettes Coll., and Housemaster, Arniston House, 1967–70; Headmaster: Abingdon Sch., 1970–75; Shrewsbury Sch., 1975–80; Eton Coll., 1980–94. Council Mem., Royal Holloway, London Univ. (formerly RHBNC), 1990–95. President: Edinburgh Sir Walter Scott Club, 1981; Johnson Soc., 1992; Mem., Royal Shakespeare Theatre Trust, 1991–94 (Mem. Foundn Bd, 1994–). Gov., Shrewsbury Sch., 1994–. FRSE 1985. Hon. DLitt: St Andrews, 1981; Hull, 1994. *Publications:* The Written Word, 1964; (ed) The Journal of Sir Walter Scott, 1972; (ed) The Percy Letters, vol IX, 1988; articles and reviews. *Recreations:* theatre, golf, fishing. *Address:* Lincoln College, Oxford OX1 3DR. *T:* Oxford (01865) 279800. *Club:* Leander (Henley).

ANDERSON, Professor Sir (William) Ferguson, Kt 1974; OBE 1961; David Cargill Professor of Geriatric Medicine, University of Glasgow, 1965–79; *b* 8 April 1914; *s* of James Kirkwood Anderson, Capt. 7th Scottish Rifles (killed on active service Gaza 1917) and late Sarah Barr Anderson; *m* 1940, Margaret Battison Gebbie; one *s* two *d*. *Educ:* Merchiston Castle Sch.; Glasgow Academy; Glasgow Univ. (MB Hons 1936; MD Hons 1942, with Bellahouston Gold Medal). FRFPSG 1939 (now FRCPG); FRCPE 1961; FRCP 1964; FRCPI 1975; FRCP (C) 1976. Med. Registrar, Univ. Med. Clinic, 1939–41; Army Service, 1941–46, Major (Med. Specialist). Sen. Lectr, Dept of Materia Medica and Therapeutics, Univ. of Glasgow, and Asst Phys., Univ. Med. Clinic, Stobhill Hosp., Glasgow, 1946–49; Sen. Univ. Lectr, Medical Unit, also Hon. Cons. Phys., Cardiff Royal Infirmary, 1949–52; Physician in Geriatric Medicine, Stobhill Gen. Hosp., Adviser in Diseases of Old Age and Chronic Sickness, Western Reg. Hosp. Bd, Scotland, 1952–74. Mem., adv. panel on organization of medical care, WHO, 1973–83. Fogarty Internat. Scholar, Nat. Inst. on Aging, Bethesda, 1979. President: RCPGlas, 1974–76; British Geriatric Soc., 1975–78; BMA, 1977–78. Vice-President: Age Concern (Scotland); Marie Curie Meml Foundn. Hon. Vice-Pres., Scottish Retirement Council; Hon. Pres., Crossroads (Scotland) Care Attendant Schemes. Hon. Chairman: St Mungo's Old Folks' Club, Glasgow; European Clin. Sect., Internat. Assoc. Gerontology. Patron, Abbeyfield Soc. for Scotland. Fellow, Australasian Coll. of Biomedical Scientists (formerly Australasian Coll. of Technologists), 1971; Hon. Fellow, Amer. Coll. of Physicians, 1980. St Mungo Prize, Glasgow, 1968; Brookdale Award, Gerontological Soc. of America, 1984. KStJ 1974. *Publications:* Practical Management of the Elderly, 1967, 5th edn (with Dr B. Williams) 1989; Current Achievements in Geriatrics (ed with Dr B. Isaacs), 1964; articles on Geriatric Medicine and Preventive aspects of Geriatrics in med. jls. *Recreation:* walking. *Address:* Rodel, Moor Road, Strathblane, Glasgow G63 9EX. *T:* Blanefield (01360) 770862. *Clubs:* University Staff, Royal Scottish Automobile (Glasgow).

ANDERTON, Prof. Brian Henry; PhD; Professor of Neuroscience, Institute of Psychiatry, since 1989; *b* 25 Dec. 1945; *s* of Henry Anderton and Mary Anderton (*née* Ashcroft); *m* 1969, Thérèse L. F. Loviny; one *s*. *Educ:* Allsop High Sch. for Boys, Liverpool; University College London (BSc 1967; PhD 1970). MRC Biophysics Unit, KCL, 1970–72; Lectr in Biochem., Poly. of Central London, 1972–77; Lectr in Biochem. and Immunology, Chelsea Coll., Univ. of London, 1977–79; St George's Hospital Medical School, University of London: Lectr in Immunology, 1979–81; Sen. Lectr in Immunology, 1981–86; Reader in Molecular Pathology, 1986–88. *Publications:* contribs to sci. jls on nervous system and molecular pathology of Alzheimer's disease and other neurodegenerative diseases. *Recreations:* hill walking, cycling, general reading, theatre, cinema, listening to music. *Address:* Department of Neuroscience, Institute of Psychiatry, De Crespigny Park, SE5 8AF. *T:* 0171–703 5411.

ANDERTON, Sir (Cyril) James, Kt 1991; CBE 1982; QPM 1977; DL; Chief Constable, Greater Manchester Police Force, 1976–91 (Deputy Chief Constable, 1975); *b* 24 May 1932; *o s* of late James Anderton and late Lucy Anderton (*née* Occleshaw); *m* 1955, Joan Baron; one *d*. *Educ:* St Matthew's Church Sch., Highfield; Wigan Grammar Sch. Certif. Criminology, Manchester Univ., 1960; Sen. Comd Course, Police Coll., 1967. Corps of Royal Mil. Police, 1950–53; Constable to Chief Inspector, Manchester City Police, 1953–67; Chief Supt, Cheshire Constab., 1967–68; Asst Chief Constable, Leicester and Rutland Constab., 1968–72; Asst to HM Chief Inspector of Constab. for England and Wales, Home Office, London, 1972–75; Dep. Chief Constable, Leics Constabulary, 1975. Mem., ACPO, 1968–91 (Pres., 1986–87). British Institute of Management: Pres., Manchester Br., 1984–93; Chm., 1986–90, Mem., 1985–90, NW Regl Bd. President: Manchester NSPCC Jun. League, 1979–93; Christian Police Assoc., 1979–81; Manchester and Dist RSPCA, 1984– (Vice-Pres., 1981–84); Wythenshawe Hosp. League of Friends, 1991–; Greater Manchester Youth Field Gun Assoc., 1992–; Altrincham Town Centre Partnership, 1994–; Member: Manchester Adv. Bd, Salvation Army, 1977– (Chm., 1993–); Exec. Cttee, Manchester NSPCC, 1979–93; Bd, Henshaws Soc. for the Blind, 1991–; Royal Soc. of St George, 1992–; Comdr, St John Amb. Assoc., Greater Manchester, 1989– (County Dir, 1976–89); Vice-President: Manchester YMCA, 1976–; Manchester and District RLSS, 1976–; Adelphi Lads' Club, Salford, 1979–; Sharp Street Ragged Sch., Manchester, 1982–; Manchester Schools Football Assoc., 1976–91; Greater Manchester East Scout Council, 1977–91; Greater Manchester Fedn of Boys' Clubs, 1984–; 318 (Sale) Sqn, ATC, 1985–; Wigan Hospice, 1990–; Bolton Outward Bound Assoc., 1991–; Greater Manchester West Scout Council, 1992–; Manchester and Dist NSPCC, 1994–. Boys' Brigade: Pres., Leics Bn, 1972–76; Hon. Nat. Vice-Pres., 1983–. Patron: NW Counties Schs ABA, 1980–91; NW Campaign for Kidney Donors, 1983–; NW Eye Res. Trust, 1982–91; N Manchester Hosp. Broadcasting Service, 1983–; Internat. Spinal Res. Trust (Greater Manchester Cttee), 1983–91; Sale RNLI, 1986–; Wigan and Dist RSPCA, 1987–; Stockport Canal Trust, 1989–; Disabled Living Services, Manchester, 1991–; The British Trust, 1991–; St Ann's Hospice, Little Hulton, 1991–; Stockport ACROSS, 1993–; Trafford Multiple Sclerosis Soc., 1994–; Mottram and Hattersley ABC, 1994–; RLSS; Catholic Union of GB. British College of Accordionists: Chm., Governing Council, 1972–77; Vice-Pres., 1977–84; Pres., 1984–91; Patron, 1991–. Trustee, Manchester Olympic Bid Cttee, 1985–93. CIMgt (CBIM 1980); Hon. FBCA 1976; Hon. RNCM 1984. Member: RSCM; RSPB; NT; Wigan Little Theatre; Corps of Royal Mil. Police Assoc.; Manchester Lit. and Phil. Soc. Mancunian of The Year, 1980. DL Greater Manchester, 1989. Freeman, City of London, 1990. KStJ 1989 (OStJ 1978; CStJ 1982). Cross Pro Ecclesia et Pontifice, 1982. Chevalier de la Confrérie des Chevaliers du Tastevin, 1985. *Recreations:* opera, fell-walking; Rugby League supporter. *Address:* 9 The Avenue, Sale, Cheshire M33 4PB. *Club:* St John House.

ANDERTON, James, CBE 1966 (OBE 1956); CEng, MIMinE; *b* 3 Nov. 1904; *s* of Richard and Rebecca Anderton; *m* 1st, 1931, Margaret Asbridge (*d* 1945); no *c*; 2nd, 1949, Lucy Mackie; no *c*. *Educ:* Wigan and District Mining and Technical Coll. Manager of various collieries. On nationalisation of mining industry in 1947 became Asst Agent for a group of collieries in St Helens, Lancs; later made Prod. Man., St Helens Area, N Western Div.; Area Gen. Man., St Helens Area, 1949; Dep. Chm., Scottish Div., NCB, 1958. Chm., North Western Div., NCB, 1961–67. Gullick Ltd, Wigan: Dir, 1967–70; Mining Consultant, 1970–81. Hon. MIMinE, 1968. Medal, Instn of Mining Engineers, 1965. Alfried Krupp von Bohlen und Halbach Prize for Energy Research, 1979. *Recreation:* golf. *Address:* The Knoll, Mere Road, Newton-le-Willows, Merseyside WA12 0BJ. *T:* Newton-le-Willows (019252) 5901.

ANDERTON, Sir James; *see* Anderton, Sir C. J.

ANDOVER, Viscount; Alexander Charles Michael Winston Robsahm Howard; student, University of Bristol, since 1994; *b* 17 Sept. 1974; *s* and *heir* of 21st Earl of Suffolk and Berkshire, *qv*. *Educ:* Eton Coll.

ANDREAE-JONES, William Pearce; QC 1984; a Recorder of the Crown Court, since 1982; *b* 21 July 1942. *Educ:* Canford Sch.; Corpus Christi Coll., Cambridge (MA Hons). Called to the Bar, Inner Temple, 1965. *Address:* 1 Sergeants' Inn, Fleet Street, EC4 1LL; Coleridge Chambers, The Citadel, Corporation Street, Birmingham B4 6QD.

ANDREOTTI, Giulio; Life Senator, Chamber of Deputies, since 1992; Prime Minister (President of the Council of Ministers) of Italy, 1972–73, 1976–79 and 1989–92; *b* 14 Jan. 1919; *s* of Filippo and Rosa Andreotti; *m* 1945, Livia Danese; two *s* two *d*. *Educ:* Univ. of Rome. Mem. for Rome Latina Viterbo Frosinone, Chamber of Deputies, 1946–92. Under Sec. of State, Council of Ministers, 1947–54; Minister of Interior, 1954; Minister of Finance, 1955–58; Minister of the Treasury, 1958–59; Minister of Defence, 1959–65; Minister of Industry and Commerce, 1966–68; Chm., Christian Democrats, 1968–72; Minister of Defence, March–Oct. 1974; Minister for Budget and Economic Planning, 1974–76; Minister of Foreign Affairs, 1983–89. Founder, and Editor, Concretezza (political weekly), 1955–76. Hon. Dr: Sorbonne; Loyola Univ., Chicago; Copernican Univ. of Torun, Poland; La Plata; Salamanca; St John's, NY; Warsaw; Univ. of Sci. and Technol., Beijing; New York; Jewish Theol Seminary, NY. Bancarella Prize, 1985. *Publications* include: Pranzo di magro per il cardinale, 1954; De Gasperi e il suo tempo, 1965; La Sciarada di Papa Mastai, 1967; Ore 13: il Ministro deve morire, 1975; Ad Ogni morte di Papa, 1980; Il diario 1976–79, 1981; De Gasperi visto da vicino, 1986; Visti da vicino (4 vols of profiles): Onorevole, stia zitto, 1987, vol II, 1992; L'URSS vista da vicino, 1988, Gli USA visti da vicino, 1989; Il potere logora . . . ma è meglio non perderlo, 1990; Governare con la crisi, 1991; The USA Up Close, 1992; many articles. *Address:* Senato della Repubblica, Palazzo Giustiniani, Via della Dogana Vecchia 29, 00816 Rome, Italy.

ANDRESKI, Prof. Stanislav Leonard; Professor of Sociology, University of Reading, 1964–84, now Emeritus; Professor of Comparative Sociology, Polish University in London, since 1982; *b* 18 May 1919; two *s* two *d*. *Educ:* Secondary sch. in Poznan, 1928–37; Univ. of Poznan (Faculty of Economics and Jurisprudence), 1938–39; London Sch. of Economics, 1942–43. Military service in Polish Army (with exception of academic year 1942–43), 1937–38 and 1939–47 (commissioned, 1944). Lectr in Sociology, Rhodes Univ., SA, 1947–53; Sen. Research Fellow in Anthropology, Manchester Univ., 1954–56; Lectr in Economics, Acton Technical Coll., London, 1956–57; Lectr in Management Studies, Brunel Coll. of Technology, London, 1957–60; Prof. of Sociology, Sch. of Social Sciences, Santiago, Chile, 1960–61; Sen. Res. Fellow, Nigerian Inst. of Social and Economic Research, Ibadan, Nigeria, 1962–64; Hd, Dept of Sociology, Univ. of Reading, 1964–82. Vis. Prof. of Sociology and Anthropology, City Coll., City Univ. of New York, 1968–69; Vis. Prof. of Sociology, Simon Frazer Univ., Vancouver, 1976–77. *Publications:* Military Organization and Society (Internat. Library of Sociology and Social Reconstruction), 1954 (2nd aug. edn, 1968, USA, 1968, paperback, 1969); Class Structure and Social Development (with Jan Ostaszewski and others), (London), 1964 (in Polish); Elements of Comparative Sociology (The Nature of Human Society Series), 1964, Spanish edn 1972; The Uses of Comparative Sociology (American edn of the foregoing), 1965, paperback 1969; Parasitism and Subversion: the case of Latin America, 1966 (NY, 1967, rev. edn 1968, etc; Buenos Aires (in Spanish with a postscript), 1968; paperback edn, London, 1970); The African Predicament: a study in pathology of modernisation, 1968 (USA, 1969); Social Sciences as Sorcery, 1972, Spanish edn 1973, German edn 1974, French edn 1975, Italian edn 1977, Japanese edn 1982; Prospects of a Revolution in the USA, 1973; The Essential Comte, 1974; Reflections on Inequality, 1975; Max Weber's Insights and Errors, 1984, Polish edn 1992; Syphilis, Puritanism and Witch-Hunts, 1989; Wars, Revolutions, Dictatorships, 1992; Editor: Herbert Spencer, Principles of Sociology, 1968; Herbert Spencer, Structure, Function and Evolution, 1970; Max Weber on Capitalism, Bureaucracy and Religion, 1983; contribs to: A Dictionary of the Social Sciences (UNESCO); A Dictionary of Sociology (ed D. Mitchell); Brit. Jl of Sociology; Japanese Jl of Sociology; The Nature of Fascism (ed S. Woolf); Science Jl, Man, European Jl of Sociology, Encounter, etc. *Recreations:* sailing, horse-riding. *Address:* Farriers, Village Green, Upper Basildon, Berkshire RG8 8LS. *T:* Upper Basildon (01491) 671318.

ANDREW, Prof. Christopher Maurice, PhD; FRHistS; Professor of Modern and Contemporary History, University of Cambridge, since 1993; Fellow, Corpus Christi College, Cambridge, since 1967; *b* 23 July 1941; *s* of Maurice Viccars Andrew and Freda Mary (*née* Sandall); *m* 1962, Jennifer Ann Alicia Garratt; one *s* two *d*. *Educ:* Norwich Sch.; Corpus Christi Coll., Cambridge (MA, PhD). FRHistS 1976. Res. Fellow, Gonville and Caius Coll., Cambridge, 1965–67; Dir of Studies in History, 1967–81 and 1988–, Sen. Tutor, 1981–87, Corpus Christi Coll., Cambridge; Univ. Lectr in History, 1972–89, Reader in Mod. and Contemp. Hist., 1989–93, Univ. of Cambridge. Ext. Examr in History, NUI, 1977–84. Specialist Adviser, H of C Select Cttee on Educn, Science and the Arts, 1982–83. Visiting Professor: Univ. of Toronto, 1991; Harvard Univ., 1992. Visiting Fellow: ANU, 1987; Wilson Center, Washington, 1987. TV Presenter: The Fatal Attraction of Adolf Hitler, 1989; Hess: an edge of conspiracy, 1990; The Cambridge Moles, 1990; All the King's Jews, 1990; A Cold War, 1991; BBC Radio Presenter (series): Tampering with the Past, 1990; What if?, 1990–94; Hindsight, 1993–95. Editor: The Historical Journal, 1976–85; Intelligence and National Security, 1986–. *Publications:* Théophile Delcasse and the making of the Entente Cordiale, 1968; The First World War: causes and consequences, 1970 (vol. 19 of Hamlyn History of the World); (with A. S. Kanya-Forstner) France Overseas: the First World War and the climax of French imperial expansion, 1981; (ed with Prof. D. Dilks) The Missing Dimension: governments and intelligence communities in the Twentieth Century, 1984; Secret Service: the making of the British Intelligence Community, 1985; Codebreaking and Signals Intelligence, 1986;

(ed with Jeremy Noakes) Intelligence and International Relations 1900–1945, 1987; (with Oleg Gordievsky) KGB: the inside story of its foreign operations from Lenin to Gorbachev, 1990; (with Oleg Gordievsky) Instructions from The Centre: top secret files on KGB foreign operations, 1991; (with Oleg Gordievsky) More Instructions from The Centre, 1992; For The President's Eyes Only: secret intelligence and the American presidency from Washington to Bush, 1995; broadcasts and articles on mod. history, Association football, secret intelligence, internat. relations. *Address:* 67 Grantchester Meadows, Cambridge CB3 9JL. *T:* Cambridge (01223) 353773.

ANDREW, Prof. Colin, FIMechE; Professor of Manufacturing Engineering, Cambridge University, 1986–94; Fellow, Christ's College, Cambridge, 1986–94; *b* 22 May 1934; *s* of Arnold Roy and Kathleen Andrew; *m* 1952, Ruth E. Probert; two *s* two *d*. *Educ:* Bristol Grammar Sch.; Christ's Coll., Cambridge Univ. MA; PhD. Res. Engr, Rolls-Royce, 1955–58; research, Cambridge, 1958–60; Develt Engr, James Archdale & Co., 1960–61; Bristol University: Lectr, 1961–68; Reader, 1968–71; Prof. of Applied Mechanics, 1971–82; Hon. Prof., 1982–86; Chm. Council, Sch. of Technology, Cambridge Univ., 1993–. Managing Director: Flamgard Ltd, 1982–85; Bristol Technical Develts Ltd, 1985–94. Chairman: Engrg Processes Cttee, SERC, 1981–83; Production Cttee, SERC, 1983–84; Member: Technology Sub-Cttee, UGC, 1986–89; Engrg Council, 1990–94 (Chm., Bd of Engrs Registration, 1992–94). *Publications:* (jtly) Creep Feed Grinding, 1985; papers in scientific jls. *Address:* 17 High Street, Orwell, Cambs SG8 5QN. *T:* Cambridge (01223) 207662.

ANDREW, Prof. Edward Raymond, MA, PhD, ScD (Cambridge); FRS 1984; CPhys; FInstP; FRSE; Graduate Research Professor, University of Florida, since 1983; *b* Boston, Lincs, 27 June 1921; *o s* of late Edward Richard Andrew and Anne (*née* Henderson); *m* 1948, Mary Farnham (*decd* 1965); two *d*; *m* 1972, Eunice Tinning. *Educ:* Wellingborough Sch.; Christ's (Open Scholarship) and Pembroke Colls, Univ. of Cambridge. Scientific Officer, Royal Radar Establishment, Malvern, 1942–45; Cavendish Laboratory, Cambridge, 1945–48; Stokes Student, Pembroke Coll., Cambridge, 1947–49; Commonwealth Fund Fellow, Harvard Univ., 1948–49; Lectr in Natural Philosophy, Univ. of St Andrews, 1949–54; Prof. of Physics, University of Wales, Bangor, 1954–64; Lancashire-Spencer Prof. of Physics, 1964–83, and Dean of Faculty of Science, 1975–78, Univ. of Nottingham; Fellow, Christ's Coll., Cambridge, 1989. Vis. Prof. of Physics, Univ. of Florida, 1969–70. President: Groupement Ampère, 1974–80 (Hon. Pres., 1980–); Internat. Soc. of Magnetic Resonance, 1984–87; Chm., Standing Conf. of Profs of Physics, 1976–79; Mem. Council, European Physical Soc., 1976–79; Chm., British Radio Spectroscopy Gp, 1981–83 (Founder-Chm., 1956–59); Mem., Bd of Trustees, Soc. of Magnetic Resonance in Medicine, 1983–91; Mem., Planning Cttee, US Nat. High Magnetic Field Lab., Fla, 1990–. Selby Fellow, Aust. Academy of Sci., 1989; Fellow, Amer. Physical Soc., 1989. Hon. Mem., British Biophysical Soc., 1992. Hon. DSc: Univ. of Turku, Finland, 1980; Leipzig Univ., 1990; Dr *hc* Adam Mickiewicz Univ., Poznan, Poland, 1989. Wellcome Medal and Prize, Royal Soc., 1984; Distinguished Service Medal, Soc. of Magnetic Resonance in Med., 1991. Editor, Physics Reports, 1974–90; Editor-in-Chief, Magnetic Resonance in Medicine, 1983–91; Member, Editorial Board: Chemical Physics Letters, 1984–87; Solid State Nuclear Magnetic Resonance, 1991–. *Publications:* Nuclear Magnetic Resonance, 1955; (jtly) Clinical Magnetic Resonance, 1990; (jtly) Nuclear Magnetic Resonance at High Magnetic Fields, 1992; scientific papers in learned jls. *Recreation:* travel. *Address:* Department of Physics, University of Florida, 215 Williamson Hall, Gainesville, FL 32611, USA. *T:* (904) 3926691.

ANDREW, Herbert Henry; QC 1982; **His Honour Judge Andrew;** a Circuit Judge, since 1984; *b* 26 July 1928; *s* of Herbert Henry Andrew and Nora Andrew (*née* Gough); *m* 1966, Annette Josephine Colbert; two *s* two *d*. *Educ:* Preston Grammar Sch.; Queens' Coll., Cambridge (BA). Called to the Bar, Gray's Inn, 1952; practised on Northern Circuit, 1953–84; a Recorder, 1978–84. *Recreation:* fell walking. *Address:* Peel House, 5/7 Harrington Street, Liverpool L2 9QA. *T:* 0151–236 4321. *Club:* Liverpool Racquet.

ANDREW, Sir Robert (John), KCB 1986 (CB 1979); civil servant, retired; *b* 25 Oct. 1928; *s* of late Robert Young Andrew and Elsie (*née* Heritage); *m* 1963, Elizabeth Bayley; two *s*. *Educ:* King's College Sch., Wimbledon; Merton Coll., Oxford (MA). Intelligence Corps, 1947–49. Joined Civil Service, 1952: Asst Principal, War Office, Principal, 1957; Min. of Defence, 1963; Asst Sec., 1965; Defence Counsellor, UK Delegn to NATO, 1967–70. Private Sec. to Sec. of State for Defence, 1971–73; Under-Sec., CSD, 1973–75; Asst Under-Sec. of State, MoD, 1975–76; Dep. Under-Sec. of State, Home Office, 1976–83; Perm. Under-Sec. of State, NI Office, 1984–88; Cabinet Office, Review of Govt Legal Services, 1988. Dir, Esmée Fairbairn Trust, 1989–94. Conservator of Wimbledon and Putney Commons, 1973–. Governor, King's College Sch., 1975– (Chm., 1990–). Mem. Council, RHBNC, 1989– (Chm., 1992–). FRSA 1992. *Recreations:* walking, carpentry. *Club:* United Oxford & Cambridge University.

ANDREW, Sydney Percy Smith, FRS 1976; FEng, FIChemE, MIMechE; consultant chemical engineer; ICI Senior Research Associate, 1976–88; *b* 16 May 1926; *s* of Harold C. Andrew and Kathleen M. (*née* Smith); *m* 1986, Ruth Harrison Kenyon (*née* Treanor). *Educ:* Barnard Castl Sch.; King's Coll., Durham Univ. (Open Schol.; BSc); Trinity Hall, Cambridge (Schol. and Prizeman; MA). Joined ICI Billingham Div., 1950; Chemical Engrg Res., 1951; Plant Engr, 1953; Section Manager: Reactor Res., 1955; Process Design, 1959; Gp Man., Catalysts and Chemicals Res., 1963–76. Vis. Prof., Univ. of Bath, 1988–. Chm., Res. Cttee, IChemE. Hon. DSc Leeds, 1979. Soc. of Chemical Industry Medal, 1989. *Publications:* Catalyst Handbook, 1970; various papers in chemical engrg, applied chemistry and plant physiology. *Recreations:* archaeology, ancient and medieval history. *Address:* 1 The Wynd, Stainton in Cleveland, Middlesbrough TS8 9BP. *T:* Middlesbrough (01642) 596348.

ANDREWS, Air Cdre Charles Beresford Eaton B.; *see* Burt-Andrews.

ANDREWS, David; Member of the Dáil (TD) (FF) for Dún Laoghaire, since 1965; *b* 15 March 1935; *s* of Christopher Andrews and Mary Coyle; *m* Annette Cusack; two *s* three *d*. *Educ:* Colaiste Mhuire, CBS; Cistercian College, Roscrea; University College Dublin (BCL). Called to the Bar, King's Inns, 1962; Senior Counsel. Parly Sec. to Taoiseach, and Govt Chief Whip, 1970–73; opposition frontbench spokesman on justice and social welfare, 1973–77; Minister of State: Dept of Foreign Affairs, 1977–79; Dept of Justice, 1978–79; Minister: for Foreign Affairs, 1992–93; for Defence and the Marine, 1993–94; opposition spokesman on tourism and trade, 1995–. Member: Cttee on the Constitution, 1967; New Ireland Forum, 1983–84. Mem., British–Irish Interparly Body, 1990–92. *Recreations:* fly fishing, walking, theatre. *Address:* Dáil Eireann, Leinster House, Dublin 2, Ireland. *T:* Dublin 6789911.

ANDREWS, David Roger Griffith, CBE 1981; Chairman, Gwion Ltd, since 1986; *b* 27 March 1933; *s* of C. H. R. Andrews and G. M. Andrews; *m* 1963, Dorothy Ann Campbell; two *s* one *d*. *Educ:* Abingdon Sch.; Pembroke Coll., Oxford (MA). FCMA, CIMgt. Pirelli-General, 1956–59; Ford Motor Company, 1960–69: Controller: Product Engrg, 1965–66; Transmission and Chassis Div., 1967; European Sales Ops, 1967–69; Asst Controller, Ford of Europe, 1969; BLMC: Controller, 1970; Finance Dir, Austin Morris, 1971–72; Man. Dir, Power and Transmission Div., 1973–75; British Leyland Ltd: Man. Dir, Leyland International, 1975–77; Exec. Vice Chm., BL Ltd, 1977–82; Chm., Leyland Gp and Land Rover Gp, 1981–82; Chm. and Chief Exec., Land Rover-Leyland, 1982–86. Director: Clarges Pharmaceutical Trustees Ltd, 1983–91; Glaxo Trustees Ltd, 1983–91; Ex-Cell-O Ltd, 1987–88; Foundn for Sci. and Technology, 1990– (Mem. Council and Hon. Treas., 1990–). Member: CBI Council, 1981–86; Exec. Cttee, SMMT, 1981–86; Open Univ. Visiting Cttee, 1982–85. FRSA. *Recreations:* reading, sailing. *Address:* Gainford, Mill Lane, Gerrards Cross, Bucks SL9 8BA. *T:* Gerrards Cross (01753) 884310.

ANDREWS, Sir Derek (Henry), KCB 1991 (CB 1984); CBE 1970; Permanent Secretary, Ministry of Agriculture, Fisheries and Food, 1987–93, retired; *b* 17 Feb. 1933; *s* of late Henry Andrews and Emma Jane Andrews; *m* 1st, 1956, Catharine May (*née* Childe) (*d* 1982); two *s* one *d*; 2nd, 1991, Alison Margaret Blackburn, *d* of Sir William Nield, GCMG, KCB. *Educ:* LSE. BA (Hons) 1955. Ministry of Agriculture, Fisheries and Food: Asst Principal, 1957; Asst Private Sec. to Minister of Agriculture, Fisheries and Food, 1960–61; Principal, 1961; Asst Sec., 1968; Private Sec. to Prime Minister, 1966–70; Harvard Univ., USA, 1970–71; Under-Sec., 1973; Dep. Sec., 1981. Mem., RGS. *Clubs:* Reform; Aldeburgh Yacht.

ANDREWS, Hon. Sir Dormer (George), Kt 1987; Chief Justice of Queensland, 1985–89; *b* 8 April 1919; *s* of Miles Dormer Andrews and Margaret Mary Andrews (*née* Robertson); *m* 1943, Joan Merle Tear; three *s*. *Educ:* University of Queensland (BA, LLB). Flying Officer, RAAF, served UK and ME, 1940–44. Admitted Queensland Bar, 1947; District Court Judge, Queensland, 1959; Chm., District Courts, 1965; Judge, 1971, Senior Puisne Judge, 1982, Supreme Court of Queensland. Chm., Law Reform Commn, Queensland, 1973–82. *Recreations:* walking, reading. *Address:* 2 Gleneagle Street, Kenmore, Brisbane, Queensland, Australia. *T:* (7) 3784298. *Clubs:* Queensland, Tattersalls, United Service (Brisbane).

ANDREWS, Brig. George Lewis Williams, CBE 1960; DSO 1944; *b* 1 July 1910; *o s* of Captain C. G. W. Andrews, The Border Regt (killed in action, 1914) and of late Mrs Diana Gambier-Parry (*née* Norrington); *m* 1938, Marianne, *d* of late Carl Strindberg, Stockholm and late Fru Greta Winbergh (*née* Skjöldebrand); one *s*. *Educ:* Haileybury; Sandhurst. Commissioned 2nd Lieut, The Seaforth Highlanders, 1930; active service, Palestine, 1936. Served War of 1939–45; BEF, 1939, MEF, 1941–43, BLA, 1944–45; Comd 2nd Bn The Seaforth Highlanders, 1943–45. Comd 1st Bn Seaforth Highlanders, 1953–54; Comd 152nd Highland Infantry Brigade (TA), 1954–57; Assistant Commandant, RMA Sandhurst, 1957–60. Hon. Col, 2nd Bn 51st Highland Volunteers, 1975–79. Lieut-Col, 1953; Colonel, 1955; Hon. Brig., 1960; psc 1940; jssc 1948. Chevalier, Order of Leopold, Belgium, 1945; Croix de Guerre with palm, Belgium, 1945. *Address:* West Kingsteps, Nairn, Scotland IV12 5LF. *T:* Nairn (01667) 453231.

ANDREWS, His Honour James Roland Blake F.; *see* Fox-Andrews.

ANDREWS, Prof. John Albert; Chief Executive, Further and High Education Funding Councils for Wales, since 1992; *b* 29 Jan. 1935; *s* of late Arthur George Andrews and Hilda May Andrews (*née* Banwell); *m* 1960, Elizabeth Ann Mary Wilkes; two *d*. *Educ:* Newport High Sch.; Wadham Coll., Oxford (MA, BCL). Called to the Bar, Gray's Inn, 1960, Bencher, 1991. Asst Lectr, Univ. of Manchester, 1957–58; Lectr in English Law, Univ. of Birmingham, 1958–67; University College of Wales, Aberystwyth: Prof. of Law, 1967–92; Hon. Prof., 1992–; Head of Dept of Law, 1970–92; Vice-Principal, 1985–88. Visiting Professor: Thessaloniki, 1974, 1990; Cracow, 1978; Maryland, 1983. Former chm. or mem., numerous educnl, police and adv. bodies; Member: Welsh Econ. Council, 1994–; Police Trng Council, 1987–; Chm., Police Promotion Exams Bd, 1987–. Pres., SPTL, 1988–89. Trustee, Hamlyn Trust, 1969–. FRSA 1992. JP N Ceredigion, 1975–91. Editor, Legal Studies, 1981–93. *Publications:* (ed) Welsh Studies in Public Law, 1970; (ed) Human Rights in Criminal Procedure, 1982; (with L. G. Henshaw) The Welsh Language in the Courts, 1984; (with W. D. Hines) Keyguide to the International Protection of Human Rights, 1987; (with D. M. Hirst) Criminal Evidence, 1987, 2nd edn 1992; Criminal Evidence: statutes and materials, 1990; contribs to legal jls. *Recreations:* walking, theatre, food. *Address:* Welsh Funding Councils, Lambourne House, Cardiff CF4 5GL. *T:* Cardiff (01222) 761861; 7 Maeshendre, Aberystwyth, Dyfed SY23 3PR. *T:* Aberystwyth (01970) 623921. *Club:* Brynamlwg.

ANDREWS, John Hayward, CMG 1988; Director, Logan Motorway Group (formerly Logan Toll Motorway Group), 1987–95; *b* 9 Nov. 1919; *s* of James Andrews and Florence Elizabeth Andrews; *m* 1947; one *s* one *d* (and one *s* decd). *Educ:* Univ. of Queensland (BEc). FIE(Aust); FAIM; DipT&CP; DipCE. Served Royal Aust. Engineers, 1940–45. Local Govt City Engineer, Wagga Wagga and Tamworth, NSW, 1946–60; Deputy Commissioner, Main Roads Dept, Queensland, 1961–78; Administrator, Gold Coast City, 1978–79; private practice, 1979–81; Agent-Gen. for Qld, 1981–84; Chairman: Electoral Redistribution Commn for Qld, 1985–86; Sugar Bd (Qld), subseq. Qld Sugar Corp., 1986–92. Dir, White Industries Ltd, 1986–88. *Recreations:* golf, painting, walking. *Address:* 7/34 Sandford Street, St Lucia, Brisbane, Qld 4067, Australia. *Club:* Toowong RSL.

ANDREWS, John Robert; General Secretary, Professional Association of Teachers, since 1992; *b* 15 June 1942; *s* of John Henry Andrews, ERD, MA, FCCA, and Marjorie Andrews (*née* Kirkman); *m* 1966, Minna D. L. Stevenson; two *d*. *Educ:* Nottingham High Sch.; Nottingham Coll. of Educn (CertEd 1963). ACP 1973; FCollP 1982; DipSMS 1982. Teacher in primary and secondary schs, 1963–72; Headteacher, Birmingham LEA, 1972–81; Professional Association of Teachers: Asst Gen. Sec., 1982–91; Mem. Council, 1972–81; Chairman: Educn Cttee, 1975–77; Pay and Conditions Cttee, 1977–81. Council of Managerial and Professional Staffs: Mem., Exec. Cttee, 1988–; Sec., Industrial Relns Cttee, 1990–92; Pres., 1992–. Mem., Econ. and Social Cttee, EU, 1994–. Chm., Indep. Unions Trng Council, 1989–; Vice-Pres., European Confedn of Indep. Trade Unions, 1992–94; Mem. Bd, Confédération Européene des Cadres, 1994–. Director: GTC (England & Wales) Trust, 1992–. Member: Lichfield Deanery Synod, 1970–; Lichfield Diocesan Synod, 1979–; Exec. Cttee, Lichfield Diocesan Bd of Finance, 1987–; Reader, Lichfield Diocese (Gentleshaw and Farewell), 1967–. Mem., Parish Council, Longdon, Staffs, 1973– (Chm., 1991–93). Governor, Gentleshaw Sch., 1993–. FIMgt 1992 (MBIM 1982); FRSA 1992. *Publications:* contribs to various jls on multi-cultural educn, general educnl issues and educn law. *Recreations:* hill walking, horse riding, listening to music. *Address:* (office) 2 St James' Court, Friar Gate, Derby DE1 1BT. *T:* Derby (01332) 372337; 1 Chaseley Gardens, Burntwood, Staffs WS7 9DJ. *T:* Burntwood (01543) 674354. *Club:* Royal Over-Seas League.

ANDREWS, Julie (Elizabeth); actress; *b* 1 Oct. 1935; *m* 1st, Anthony J. Walton (marr. diss. 1968); one *d*; 2nd, 1969, Blake Edwards; one step *s* one step *d*, and two adopted *d*. *Educ:* Woodbrook Girls' Sch., Beckenham and private governess. Appeared in The Boy Friend, Broadway, New York, 1954; My Fair Lady: New York, 1956, London, 1958; Camelot, New York, 1960. *Films:* (Walt Disney) Mary Poppins, 1963 (Academy Award, 1964); Americanisation of Emily, 1964; Sound of Music, 1964; Hawaii, 1965; Torn Curtain, 1966; Thoroughly Modern Millie, 1966; Star, 1967; Darling Lili, 1970; The

Tamarind Seed, 1973; "10", 1980; Little Miss Marker, 1980; S.O.B., 1981; Victor/Victoria, 1982; The Man Who Loved Women, 1983; Duet for One, 1987; That's Life, 1987. *TV:* Julie & Carol at Carnegie Hall, 1961; An Evening with Julie Andrews and Harry Belafonte, 1969; Julie & Carol at Lincoln Center, 1971; The Julie Andrews Hour, 1972–73; Julie & Dick at Covent Garden, 1973–74; Julie & Jackie—How Sweet it is, 1973–74; Julie & Perry & The Muppets, 1973–74; My Favourite Things, 1975; The Puzzle Children, 1976; ABC's Silver Anniversary Celebration, 1978; Julie Andrews . . . One Step into Spring, 1978; The Sound of Christmas (Emmy Award), 1987; Julie & Carol Together Again, 1989; Great Performances Live in Concert, 1990; Our Sons, 1991; The Julie Show, 1992. *Publications:* (as Julie Andrews Edwards) Mandy, 1972; Last of the Really Great Whangdoodles, 1973. *Recreations:* boating, ski-ing, riding.

ANDREWS, Prof. Kenneth Raymond, FBA 1986; Professor of History, University of Hull, 1979–88 (part-time, 1986–88), now Emeritus; *b* 26 Aug. 1921; *s* of Arthur Walter and Marion Gertrude Andrews; *m* 1969, Ottilie Kalman, Olomouc, Czechoslovakia; two step *s*. *Educ:* Henry Thornton Sch., Clapham; King's College London (BA 1948, PhD 1951). Lectr, Univ. of Liverpool, 1963–64; Lectr and Sen. Lectr, Univ. of Hull, 1964–79; active research in English maritime history. *Publications:* English Privateering Voyages to the West Indies, 1959; Elizabethan Privateering, 1964; Drake's Voyages, 1967; The Last Voyage of Drake and Hawkins, 1972; The Spanish Caribbean, 1978; Trade, Plunder and Settlement, 1984; Ships, Money and Politics, 1991; articles in learned jls.

ANDREWS, Peter John; QC 1991; a Recorder of the Crown Court, since 1990; *b* 14 Nov. 1946; *s* of Reginald and Dora Andrews; *m* 1976, Ann Chavasse; two *d*. *Educ:* Bishop Vesey Grammar Sch.; Bristol Univ. (Undergraduate Scholar; LLB); Christ's Coll., Cambridge (Dip. Criminology). Called to the Bar, Lincoln's Inn (Hardwicke Scholar), 1970; Junior, Midland and Oxford Circuit, 1973–74; Asst Recorder, 1986–90. *Address:* 199 Strand, WC2R 1DR. *T:* 0171–379 9779.

ANDREWS, Raymond Denzil Anthony, MBE 1953; VRD 1960; Consultant, Andrews, Downie & Partners, Architects, since 1990 (Senior Partner, 1960–90); *b* 5 June 1925; *s* of Michael Joseph Andrews, BA, and Phylis Marie Andrews (*née* Crowley); *m* 1958, Gillian Whitlaw Small, BA; one *s* one *d*. *Educ:* Highgate Sch.; Christ's Coll., Cambridge; University Coll. London (DipArch, DipTP); Univ. of Michigan (MArch). RIBA. Lieut, Royal Marines, 1943–46; RM Reserve, 1948–68 (Major). King George VI Meml Fellow of English-Speaking Union of US, 1954–55; Chm., London Region, RIBA, 1968–72; Vice-Pres., RIBA, 1972–74, 1978–81; Chm., Festival of Architecture, 1984; Pres., Architectural Assoc., 1975–77. Civic Trust Award, 1971 and 1978; 1st Prize, Royal Mint Square Housing Competition, GLC, 1974. Order of Al Rafadain (Iraq), 1956. *Recreation:* sailing. *Address:* 6 Addison Avenue, W11 4QR. *T:* 0171–602 7701. *Clubs:* Bosham Sailing; RIBA Sailing (Cdre, 1983–87).

ANDREWS, Robert Graham M.; *see* Marshall-Andrews.

ANDREWS, Stuart Morrison; Head Master of Clifton College, 1975–90; *b* 23 June 1932; *s* of William Hannaford Andrews and Eileen Elizabeth Andrews; *m* 1962, Marie Elizabeth van Wyk; two *s*. *Educ:* Newton Abbot Grammar Sch.; St Dunstan's Coll.; Sidney Sussex Coll., Cambridge (MA). Nat. service with Parachute Bde, 1952–53. Sen. History Master and Librarian, St Dunstan's Coll., 1956–60; Chief History Master and Librarian, Repton Sch., 1961–67; Head Master, Norwich Sch., 1967–75. Chm., Direct-grant Sub-cttee of Headmasters' Conf., 1974–75; Dep. Chm., Assisted Places Cttee, 1982–91; Nat. Rep., HMC, 1986–87. Trustee, Glastonbury Abbey Develt Trust, 1992–. Editor, Conference, 1972–82. *Publications:* Eighteenth-century Europe, 1965; Enlightened Despotism, 1967; Methodism and Society, 1970; articles in various historical jls. *Recreations:* walking, writing. *Address:* 34 St Thomas Street, Wells, Somerset BA5 2UX.

ANDREWS, William Denys Cathcart, CBE 1980; WS; Partner, Shepherd & Wedderburn, WS, Edinburgh, 1962–91; *b* 3 June 1931; *s* of Eugene Andrews and Agnes Armstrong; *m* 1955, May O'Beirne; two *s* two *d*. *Educ:* Girvan High Sch.; Worksop Coll.; Edinburgh Univ. (BL). Served RASC, 1950–52. Law Society of Scotland: Mem. Council, 1972–81; Vice Pres., 1977–78; Pres., 1978–79. Examr in Conveyancing, Edinburgh Univ., 1974–77. Pt-time Mem., Lands Tribunal for Scotland, 1980–91. Fiscal to Soc. of Writers to HM Signet, 1987–91. *Recreation:* gardening. *Address:* Auchairne, Ballantrae, South Ayrshire KA26 0NX. *T:* Ballantrae (0146583) 344.

ANDRIESSEN, Prof. Frans, (Franciscus H. J. J.), Kt, Order of Dutch Lion; Grand Cross, Order of Orange-Nassau; Grand Cross, Order of Leopold II; LLD; Member, 1981–92, Vice-President, 1985–92, the European Commission (responsible for external relations); *b* Utrecht, 2 April 1929; *m*; four *c*. *Educ:* Univ. of Utrecht (LLD). Served at Catholic Housing Institute, latterly as Director, 1954–72. Member: Provincial Estates of Utrecht, 1958–67; Lower House of the States-General, initially as specialist in housing matters, 1967–77; Chairman, KVP party in Lower House, 1971–77; Minister of Finance, 1977–80; Member, Upper House of States-General (Senate), 1980. Prof. of European Integration, Rijksuniversiteit, Utrecht, 1989–. *Address:* Gouvernementsweg 200, 1950 Kraainem, Belgium.

ANDRUS, Francis Sedley, LVO 1982; Beaumont Herald of Arms Extraordinary, since 1982; *b* 26 Feb. 1915; *o s* of late Brig.-Gen. Thomas Alchin Andrus, CMG, JP, and Alice Loveday (*née* Parr); unmarried. *Educ:* Wellington Coll.; St Peter's Hall (now Coll.), Oxford (MA). Entered College of Arms as Member of Staff, 1938; Bluemantle Pursuivant of Arms, 1970–72; Lancaster Herald of Arms, 1972–82. Freeman, City of London, 1988. Lord of the Manor of Southfleet, Kent, 1952–. *Address:* 8 Oakwood Rise, Longfield, Dartford, Kent DA3 7PA. *T:* Longfield (01474) 705424.

ANELAY, Dame Joyce (Anne), DBE 1995 (OBE 1990); JP; Chairman, Conservative Women's National Committee, since 1993; *b* 17 July 1947; *d* of late Stanley Charles Clarke and of Annette Marjorie Clarke; *m* 1970, Richard Alfred Anelay, *qv*. *Educ:* Merryhills Primary Sch., Enfield; Enfield Co. Sch.; Bristol Univ. (BA Hons Hist.); London Univ. Inst. of Educn (Cert Ed); Brunel Univ. (MA Public and Social Admin). Teacher, St David's Sch., Ashford, Middx, 1969–74; Voluntary Advr, Woking CAB, 1976–85 (Chm., 1988–93). Member: Social Security Appeal Tribunal, 1983–; Social Security Adv. Cttee for GB and NI, 1989–. Conservative Women's Committee: Chm., SE Area, 1987–90; Vice-Chm., SE Area Exec. Cttee, 1990–93; Member: Nat. Union of Cons. Party, 1987–; Women's Nat. Commission, 1990–93. JP NW Surrey, 1985–. Chm. Govs, Hermitage First and Middle Schs, 1981–88. FRSA 1991. *Recreations:* golf, reading. *Address:* Conservative Central Office, 32 Smith Square, SW1P 3HH. *Clubs:* Carlton; Woking Golf.

ANELAY, Richard Alfred; QC 1993; *b* 26 March 1946; *s* of late Maurice Alfred Anelay and of Bertha Anelay; *m* 1970, Joyce Anne Clarke (*see* Dame Joyce Anelay). *Educ:* Dodmire Primary Sch., Darlington; Queen Elizabeth Grammar Sch., Darlington; Bristol Univ. (BA Classics and Philosophy); Council of Legal Educn. Called to the Bar, Middle Temple, 1970; Asst Recorder, 1987; Recorder, 1992. *Recreation:* golf. *Address:* 1 King's Bench Walk, Temple, EC4Y 7DB. *T:* 0171–583 6266. *Club:* Woking Golf.

ANFOM, Emmanuel E.; *see* Evans-Anfom.

ANGEL, Gerald Bernard Nathaniel Aylmer; Senior District Judge, Family Division of the High Court, since 1991 (Registrar, 1980–90; District Judge, 1991); *b* 4 Nov. 1937; *s* of late Bernard Francis and Ethel Angel; *m* 1968, Lesley Susan Kemp; three *s* one *d* (and one *s* decd). *Educ:* St Mary's Sch., Nairobi. Served Kenya Regt, 1956–57. Called to Bar, Inner Temple, 1959, Bencher 1992; Advocate, Kenya, 1960–62; practice at Bar, 1962–80. Member: Judicial Studies Bd, 1989–90 (Mem., Civil and Family Cttee, 1985–90); Supreme Ct Procedure Cttee, 1990–; Matrimonial Causes Rule Cttee, 1991; Family Proceedings Rule Cttee, 1991–. *Publications:* (ed) Industrial Tribunals Reports, 1966–78; (contrib.) Atkin's Court Forms (Adv. Editor), 1988. *Recreations:* reading, walking. *Address:* c/o Principal Registry of the Family Division, Somerset House, WC2R 1LP. *T:* 0181–670 7184. *Club:* Athenæum.

ANGEL, Heather, FRPS, FBIPP; professional wildlife photographer, author and lecturer; *b* 21 July 1941; *d* of Stanley Paul Le Rougetel and Hazel Marie Le Rougetel (*née* Sherwood); *m* 1964, Martin Vivian Angel; one *s*. *Educ:* 14 schools in England and NZ; Bristol Univ. (BSc Hons (Zoology) 1962; MSc 1965). FRPS 1972; FBIPP 1974. One-man Exhibitions: The Natural History of Britain and Ireland, Sci. Mus., 1981; Nature in Focus, Natural Hist. Mus., 1987; The Art of Wildlife Photography, Gloucester, 1989. Television: demonstrating photographic techniques, Me and My Camera I, 1981; Me and My Camera II, 1983; Gardener's World, 1983; Nature, 1984; Nocon on Photography, 1988. Led British Photographic Delegn to China, 1985. Photos used worldwide in books, magazines, on TV, advertising, etc, 1972–. Special Prof., Dept of Life Sci., Nottingham Univ., 1994–. Hon. FRPS 1986 (Pres., 1984–86). Hon. DSc Bath, 1986. Hood Medal, RPS, 1975; Médaille de Salverte, Soc. Française de Photographie, 1984. *Publications:* Nature Photography: its art and techniques, 1972; All Colour Book of Ocean Life, 1975; Photographing Nature: Trees, 1975, Insects, 1975, Seashore, 1975, Flowers, 1975, Fungi, 1975; Seashore Life on Rocky Shores, 1975; Seashore Life on Sandy Beaches, 1975; Seashells of the Seashore, 1976; Wild Animals in the Garden, 1976; Life in the Oceans, 1977; Life in our Estuaries, 1977; Life in our Rivers, 1977; British Wild Orchids, 1977; The Countryside of the New Forest, 1977; The Countryside of South Wales, 1977; Seaweeds of the Seashore, 1977; Seashells of the Seashore, Book 1, 1978, Book 2, 1978; The Countryside of Devon, 1980; The Guinness Book of Seashore Life, 1981; The Natural History of Britain and Ireland, 1981; The Family Water Naturalist, 1982; The Book of Nature Photography, 1982; The Book of Close-up Photography, 1983; Heather Angel's Countryside, 1983; A Camera in the Garden, 1984; Close-up Photography, 1986; Kodak Calendar, The Thames, 1987; A View from a Window, 1988; Nature in Focus, 1988; Landscape Photography, 1989; Animal Photography, 1991; Kew: a world of plants, 1993; Photographing the Natural World, 1994; *for children:* Your Book of Fishes, 1972; The World of an Estuary, 1975; Fact Finder—Seashore, 1976; The World of a Stream, 1976; Fungi, 1979; Lichens, 1980; Mosses and Ferns, 1980. *Recreation:* travelling to remote parts of the world to photograph wilderness areas and unusual aspects of animal behaviour. *Address:* Highways, 6 Vicarage Hill, Farnham, Surrey GU9 8HJ. *T:* Farnham (01252) 716700, *Fax:* Farnham (01252) 727464.

ANGEL, Prof. James Roger Prior, FRS 1990; Regents Professor of Astronomy, since 1990, and Director, Steward Observatory Mirror Laboratory, since 1985, University of Arizona; *b* 7 Feb. 1941; *s* of James Lee Angel and Joan Angel; *m* 1965, Ellinor M. Goonan; one *s* one *d*. *Educ:* St Peter's Coll., Oxford (Hon. Schol.; BA 1963; Hon. Fellow, 1993); Calif. Inst. of Technology (MS 1966); DPhil Oxon 1967. Post Doctoral Assistant, then Asst Prof., later Associate Prof. of Physics, Columbia Univ., 1967–72; Alfred P. Sloan Res. Fellow, 1970–74; Associate Prof. and Prof. of Astronomy, Arizona Univ., 1973–90. Vice-Pres., Amer. Astronomical Soc., 1987–90 (Pierce Prize, 1976); Fellow, Amer. Acad. of Arts and Scis, 1990. *Publications:* numerous papers on white dwarfs, quasars, astronomical instruments, and telescopes. *Recreation:* piano. *Address:* Steward Observatory, University of Arizona, Tucson, AZ 85721, USA. *T:* (602) 6216541.

ANGELES, Victoria de los; *see* de los Angeles.

ANGELL-JAMES, John, CBE 1967; MD, FRCP, FRCS; Hon. Consulting Surgeon in Otolaryngology, United Bristol Hospitals, 1966–87; *b* 23 Aug. 1901; *s* of Dr John Angell James, MRCS, LRCP and Emily Cormell (*née* Ashwin), Bristol; *m* 1930, Evelyn Miriam Everard, *d* of Francis Over and Ada Miriam Everard, Birmingham; one *s* two *d*. *Educ:* Bristol Grammar Sch.; Univ. of Bristol; London Hosp.; Guy's Hosp. MB ChB 1st Cl. Hons 1924, Bristol; MBBS London (Hons) 1924; MD 1927; FRCS 1928; FRCP 1965. Res. appts, 1924–28, Bristol and London; Hon. ENT Registrar, Bristol Royal Infirmary, 1928–29; Hon. ENT Surg., Bristol Children's Hosp., 1928–48; Cons. ENT Surg., 1948–66; Hon. Asst ENT Surg., later Hon. ENT Surg., Bristol Royal Infirmary, 1929–48; Clin. Tutor, Univ. of Bristol, 1928–55, Lectr and Head of Dept of Otolaryngology, 1955–66; Cons. ENT Surg., United Bristol Hosps, 1948–66. Lt-Col RAMC, 1942–46; Adviser in Otorhinolaryngol., MEF, 1945. Hunterian Prof., RCS, 1962; Semon Lectr in Laryngol., Univ. of London, 1965; James Yearsley Lectr, 1966; Sir William Wilde Meml Lectr, Irish Otolaryngol. Soc., 1966; Vis. Lectr, Univs of Toronto, Vermont, Cornell, Baylor, Chicago and Johns Hopkins Hosp. Royal Soc. of Medicine: Former Fellow, Hon. FRSM 1976; Hon. Mem., Sections of Laryngol. (Pres., 1955) and otology. Member: SW Laryngolog. Assoc. (Chm. 1956); Brit. Medical Assoc. (Pres. Sect. of Otolaryngol., 1959; Chm. Bristol Div., 1966–67; Pres., Bath, Bristol and Som Br., 1968–69); Bristol Med.-Chirurg. Soc. (Pres. 1961); Visiting Assoc. of ENT Surgs of GB, 1948 (Pres. 1965–66); Brit. Assoc. of Otolaryngologists, 1942 (Pres. 1966–69); Collegium Oto-Rhino-Laryngologicum Amicitiae Sacrum, 1948 (Councillor, 1966–74; Pres., 1974); Barany Soc.; Pres., Otolaryngological Res. Soc., 1978. Extern. Examr, Univ. of Manchester, 1964. Hon. Member: Irish Otolaryngol. Soc.; S Africa Soc. of Otolaryngol.; Corresp. Mem., Deutsche Gesellschaft für Hals-Nasen-Ohren-Heilkunde Kopf-und Hals-Chirurgie. Hon. FRCSE 1971; Jobson Horne Prize, BMA, 1962; Colles Medal, RCSI, 1963; Dalby Prize, RSM, 1963; W. J. Harrison Prize in Laryngology, RSM, 1968. President: Gloucester Soc., 1977; Colston Soc., 1983–84. Chm. Editorial Cttee, Clinical Otolaryngology. *Publications:* Chapters in: British Surgical Practice, 1951; Diseases of the Ear, Nose and Throat, 1952 (2nd edn 1966); Ultrasound as a diagnostic and surgical tool, 1964; Clinical Surgery, 1966; Ménière's Disease, 1969; Family Medical Guide, 1980; articles in learned jls in Eng., USA, Canada, Germany and Sweden. *Recreations:* farming; shooting. *Address:* The Leaze, Sundayshill Lane, Falfield, Wotton-under-Edge, Glos GL12 8DQ.

ANGELOU, Marguerite Annie, (Maya); writer, singer and actress; *b* St Louis, 4 April 1928; *d* of Bailey Johnson and Vivian Baxter Johnson; one *s*. *Educ:* George Washington High Sch., San Francisco; California Labor Sch. Yale Univ. Fellowship, 1970; Rockefeller Foundn Scholar, 1975; Reynolds Prof. of Amer. Studies, Wake Forest Univ., 1981–. Writer, director, or actor: *stage:* Medea, 1966; The Least of These, 1966; Ajax, 1974; Look Away, 1975; Moon and Rainbow Shawl, 1988; *films:* Georgia, Georgia, 1972; All Day Long, 1974; Poetic Justice, 1993; *television:* Black, Blue, Black, 1968; Roots, 1977; Sister, Sister, 1982. Awards include: Amer. Revolution Bicentennial, 1975; Woman of the Year in Communications, 1976; Horatio Alger, 1992. *Publications:* autobiography: I Know Why the Caged Bird Sings, 1970 (televised, 1979); Gather Together in My Name, 1974; Singin' and Swingin' and Gettin' Merry Like Christmas, 1976; The Heart of a Woman, 1981; All God's Children Need Travelling Shoes, 1986; *essays:* Lessons in Life, 1993; Wouldn't Take Nothing for my Journey Now, 1994; *poetry:* Just Give Me a Cool Drink of Water 'Fore I Die, 1971; Oh Pray My Wings are Gonna Fit Me Well, 1975; And Still I Rise, 1978; Shaker, Why Don't You Sing?, 1983; Now Sheba Sings the Song, 1987; I shall not be Moved, 1990; On the Pulse of Morning, 1993 (delivered personally at Presidential Inauguration). *Address:* c/o Dave Le Camera Lordly and Dame Inc., 51 Church Street, Boston, Mass 02116, USA.

ANGLESEY, 7th Marquess of, *cr* 1815; **George Charles Henry Victor Paget;** Baron Paget, of Beau Desert, 1549; Earl of Uxbridge, 1784; Bt 1730; Lord-Lieutenant of Gwynedd, 1983–89; *b* 8 Oct. 1922; *o s* of 6th Marquess of Anglesey, GCVO, and Lady Victoria Marjorie Harriet Manners (*d* 1946), *d* of 8th Duke of Rutland; *S* father, 1947; *m* 1948, Elizabeth Shirley Vaughan Morgan (*see* Marchioness of Anglesey); two *s* three *d*. *Educ:* Wixenford, Wokingham; Eton Coll. Major, RHG, 1946. Div. Dir, Wales, Nationwide Building Soc., 1973–89. President: Anglesey Conservative Assoc., 1948–83; Nat. Museum of Wales, 1962–68; Friends of Friendless Churches, 1966–84; Ancient Monuments Soc., 1979–84. Treasurer, Danilo Dolci Trust (Britain), 1964–86. Vice-Chm., Welsh Cttee, Nat. Trust, 1975–85; Member: Historic Buildings Council for Wales, 1953–92 (Chm., 1977–92); Royal Fine Art Commn, 1965–71; Redundant Churches Fund, 1969–78; Royal Commn on Historical Manuscripts, 1984–92; Council, Soc. of Army Historical Research; Trustee: Nat. Portrait Gall., 1979–91; Nat. Heritage Memorial Fund, 1980–92. Hon. Prof., UCW, 1986. FSA 1952; FRSL 1969; Hon. FRIBA, 1971; FRHistS, 1975. Anglesey: CC, 1951–67; JP, 1959–68, 1983–89; DL, 1960, Vice-Lieut, 1960. Hon. Fellow, Royal Cambrian Acad. Freeman of the City of London. Hon. DLitt Wales, 1984. CStJ 1984. *Publications:* (ed) The Capel Letters, 1814–1817, 1955; One-Leg: the Life and Letters of 1st Marquess of Anglesey, 1961; (ed) Sergeant Pearman's Memoirs, 1968; (ed) Little Hodge, 1971; A History of the British Cavalry, 1816–1919, vol I, 1973, vol. II, 1975, vol. III, 1982, vol. IV, 1986, vol. V, 1995. *Recreations:* gardening, music. *Heir: s* Earl of Uxbridge, *qv*. *Address:* Plâs-Newydd, Llanfairpwll, Anglesey LL61 6DZ. *T:* Llanfairpwll (01248) 714330.

ANGLESEY, Marchioness of; (Elizabeth) Shirley Vaughan Paget, DBE 1983 (CBE 1977); LVO 1993; Member of Board, British Council, since 1985 (Chairman, Drama and Dance Advisory Committee, 1981–91); Vice-Chairman, Museums and Galleries Commission, since 1989 (Member, since 1981); *b* 4 Dec. 1924; *d* of late Charles Morgan and Hilda Vaughan (both novelists); *m* 1948, Marquess of Anglesey, *qv*; two *s* three *d*. *Educ:* Francis Holland Sch., London; St James', West Malvern; Kent Place Sch., USA. Personal Secretary to Gladwyn Jebb, FO, until marriage. Chm., Broadcasting Complaints Commn, 1987–91. Dep. Chm., Prince of Wales Cttee, 1970–80. Member: Civic Trust for Wales, 1967–76; Arts Council, 1972–81 (Chm., Welsh Arts Council, 1975–81); Royal Commn on Environmental Pollution, 1973–79; IBA, 1976–82; Radioactive Waste Management Adv. Cttee, 1981–92; Vice-Chm., Govt Working Party on Methods of Sewage Disposal, 1969–70. Chm., NFWI, 1966–69. Mem., Theatres Trust, 1992–. Trustee, Pilgrim Trust, 1982–. Hon. Fellow, UCNW, Bangor, 1990. Hon. LLD Wales, 1977. *Address:* Plâs-Newydd, Llanfairpwll, Gwynedd LL61 6DZ. *T:* Llanfairpwll (01248) 714330.

See also R. H. V. C. Morgan.

ANGLIN, Prof. Douglas (George); Professor of Political Science, Carleton University, Ottawa, Canada, 1958–89, Adjunct Professor, 1989–93, now Professor Emeritus; *b* Toronto, Canada, 16 Dec. 1923; *s* of George Chambers Anglin, MD, and Ruth Cecilia Cale, MD; *m* 1948, Mary Elizabeth Watson; two *d*. *Educ:* Toronto Univ.; Corpus Christi and Nuffield Colls, Oxford Univ. BA Toronto; MA, DPhil Oxon. Lieut, RCNVR, 1943–45. Asst (later Associate) Prof. of Polit. Sci. and Internat. Relations, Univ. of Manitoba, Winnipeg, 1951–58; Associate Prof. (later Prof.), Carleton Univ., 1958–89. Vice-Chancellor, Univ. of Zambia, Lusaka, Zambia, 1965–69; Associate Research Fellow, Nigerian Inst. of Social and Economic Research, Univ. of Ibadan, Ibadan, Nigeria, 1962–63; Research Associate, Center of Internat. Studies, Princeton Univ., 1969–70. Pres., Canadian Assoc. of African Studies, 1973–74. Consultant, Educn for Democracy Prog., South African Council of Churches, Johannesburg, 1992–94. *Publications:* The St Pierre and Miquelon Affairs of 1941: a study in diplomacy in the North Atlantic quadrangle, 1966; Zambia's Foreign Policy: studies in diplomacy and dependence, 1979; Zambian Crisis Behaviour: confronting Rhodesia's unilateral declaration of independence 1965–1966, 1994; edited jointly: Africa: Problems and Prospects 1961; Conflict and Change in Southern Africa, 1978; Canada, Scandinavia and Southern Africa, 1978; articles on Internat. and African affairs in a variety of learned jls. *Address:* Carleton University, Colonel By Drive, Ottawa, Ontario K1S 5B6, Canada.

ANGLIN, Eric Jack; HM Diplomatic Service, retired; Consul-General, Melbourne, 1979–83; *b* 9 Aug. 1923; *m* 1954, Patricia Farr; three *s*. Joined Foreign Service (subseq. Diplomatic Service), 1948; FO, 1948–52; HM Missions in: Damascus, 1952–56; Rangoon, 1956–59; Madrid, 1960–64; FO, 1964–67; La Paz, 1967–70; Khartoum, 1970–72; Inspector, Diplomatic Service, FCO, 1973–76; Buenos Aires, 1976–78; Chargé d'Affaires and Consul-Gen., Santiago, 1978–79. Dir, Aberdeen Sea Products Ltd, 1989–. *Recreations:* auctions, food. *Address:* Treetops, The Glade, Kingswood, Tadworth, Surrey KT20 6LH. *T:* Mogador (01737) 832858.

ANGLO, Margaret Mary, (Mrs Sydney Anglo); *see* McGowan, M. M.

ANGUS, Rev. (James Alexander) Keith, LVO 1990; TD; Minister of Braemar and Crathie Parish Churches, since 1979; Domestic Chaplain to the Queen, since 1979; *b* 16 April 1929; *s* of late Rev. Walter C. S. Angus and late Margaret I. Stephen; *m* 1956, Alison Jane Daly; one *s* one *d*. *Educ:* High School of Dundee; Univ. of St Andrews (MA). National Service, Army, 1947–49; served with TA, 1950–76; Captain RA (TA), 1955; Chaplain to 5, KOSB (TA), 1957–67, to 154 Regt, RCT (V), 1967–76. Assistant Minister, The Cathedral, Glasgow, 1955–56; Minister: Hoddam Parish Church, 1956–67; Gourock Old Parish Church, 1967–79. Convener, Gen. Assembly's Cttee on Chaplains to HM Forces, 1981–85. *Recreations:* fishing, hill walking, golf. *Address:* The Manse of Crathie, Crathie, near Ballater, Aberdeenshire AB35 5UL. *T:* Crathie (013397) 42208. *Club:* New (Edinburgh).

ANGUS, Sir Michael (Richardson), Kt 1990; Chairman: Whitbread PLC, since 1992 (Director, since 1986; Deputy Chairman, 1992); The Boots Company PLC, since 1994; *b* 5 May 1930; *s* of William Richardson Angus and Doris Margaret Breach; *m* 1952, Eileen Isabel May Elliott; two *s* one *d*. *Educ:* Marling Sch., Stroud, Glos; Bristol Univ. (BSc Hons). CIMgt (CBIM 1979). Served RAF, 1951–54. Unilever, 1954–92: Marketing Dir, Thibaud Gibbs, Paris, 1962–65; Man. Dir, Res. Bureau, 1965–67; Sales Dir, Lever Brothers UK, 1967–70; Toilet Preparations Co-ordinator, 1970–76; Chemicals Co-ordinator, 1976–80; Regional Dir, N America, 1979–84; Chairman and Chief Exec. Officer: Unilever United States, Inc., New York, 1980–84; Lever Brothers Co., New York, 1980–84; Chm., Unilever PLC, 1986–92 (Dir, 1970–92); Vice Chm., Unilever NV, 1986–92 (Dir, 1970–92). Jt Dep. Chm., British Airways, 1989– (Dir, 1988–); Dir, Nat. Westminster Bank, 1991– (a Dep. Chm., 1991–94); non-exec. Dir, Thorn EMI plc, 1988–93. Jt Chm., Netherlands-British Chamber of Commerce, 1984–89; Internat. Counsellor, The Conference Board, 1984–. Pres., CBI, 1992–94 (Dep. Pres., 1991–92, 1994–95). Vis. Fellow, Nuffield Coll., Oxford, 1986–92. Dir, Ditchley Foundn, 1994–. Trustee, Leverhulme Trust, 1984–. Chairman of Governors: Ashridge Management Coll., 1991– (Governor, 1974–); RAC, Cirencester, 1992–; Mem. Court of Govs, LSE, 1985–. Hon. DSc: Bristol, 1990; Buckingham, 1994. Holland Trade Award, 1990. Comdr, Order of Oranje-Nassau (Netherlands), 1992. *Recreations:* countryside, wine, mathematical puzzles. *Address:* Whitbread PLC, Chiswell Street, EC1Y 4SD. *T:* 0171–606 4455. *Clubs:* Athenæum; University, Knickerbocker (New York).

ANNALY, 6th Baron *cr* 1863; **Luke Richard White;** a Lord in Waiting (Government Whip), 1994; *b* 29 June 1954; *o s* of 5th Baron Annaly and Lady Marye Isabel Pepys (*d* 1958), *d* of 7th Earl of Cottenham; *S* father, 1990; *m* 1983, Caroline Nina, *yr d* of Col Robert Garnett, MBE: one *s* two *d*. *Educ:* Eton; RMA Sandhurst. Commnd Royal Hussars, 1974–78, RARO. *Heir: s* Hon. Luke Henry White, *b* 20 Sept. 1990. *Address:* House of Lords, SW1A 0PW.

ANNAN, family name of **Baron Annan.**

ANNAN, Baron, *cr* 1965 (Life Peer); **Noël Gilroy Annan,** OBE 1946; Chairman, Board of Trustees, National Gallery, 1980–85 (Trustee, 1978–85); *b* 25 Dec. 1916; *s* of late James Gilroy Annan; *m* 1950, Gabriele, *d* of Louis Ferdinand Ullstein, Berlin; two *d*. *Educ:* Stowe Sch.; King's Coll., Cambridge (Exhibitioner and Scholar). Served War of 1939–45: WO, War Cabinet Offices, and Military Intelligence, 1940–44; France and Germany, 1944–46; GSO1, Political Div. of British Control Commn, 1945–46. University of Cambridge: Fellow of King's Coll., 1944–56, 1966; Asst Tutor, 1947; Lectr in Politics, 1948–66; Provost of King's Coll., 1956–66; Provost of University Coll., London, 1966–78; Vice-Chancellor, Univ. of London, 1978–81. Romanes Lectr, Oxford, 1965. Chairman: Departmental Cttee on Teaching of Russian in Schools, 1960; Academic Planning Bd, Univ. of Essex, 1965–70; Cttee on Future of Broadcasting, 1974–77, report published 1977. Member: Academic Adv. Cttee, Brunel Coll., 1966–73; Academic Planning Bd, Univ. of East Anglia, 1964–71; Public Schools Commn, 1966–70. Chm., Enquiry on the disturbances in Essex Univ. (report published 1974). Sen. Fellow Eton Coll., 1956–66. Governor: Stowe Sch., 1945–66; Queen Mary Coll., London, 1956–60. Trustee: Churchill Coll., Cambridge, 1958–76; British Museum, 1963–80; Pres., London Library, 1980–. Dir, Royal Opera House, Covent Garden, 1967–78; Gulbenkian Foundation: Mem., Arts Cttee, 1957–64; Chm., Educn Cttee, 1971–76. FRHistS; Fellow, Berkeley Coll., Yale, 1963; Hon. Fellow: UCL, 1968; Churchill Coll., Cambridge, 1988; Emer. Fellow, Leverhulme Trust, 1984. For. Hon. Mem., Amer. Acad. of Arts and Sciences, 1973. Hon. DLitt: York, Ontario, 1966; New York, 1981; DUniv Essex, 1967; Hon. LLD Pennsylvania, 1980, Le Bas Prize, 1948; Diamond Jubilee Medal, Inst. of Linguists, 1971; Clerk Kerr Medal, Univ. of Calif, Berkeley, 1985. Comdr, Royal Order of King George I of the Hellenes (Greece), 1962. *Publications:* Leslie Stephen: his thought and character in relation to his time, 1951 (awarded James Tait Black Memorial Prize, 1951), rev. edn 1984; The Intellectual Aristocracy (in Studies in Social History, a tribute to G. M. Trevelyan, 1956); Kipling's Place in the History of Ideas (in Kipling's Mind and Art, 1964); The Curious Strength of Positivism in English Political Thought, 1959; Roxburgh of Stowe, 1965; Our Age: portrait of a generation, 1990; articles in NY Rev. of Books and other periodicals. *Recreation:* writing English prose. *Address:* 16 St John's Wood Road, NW8 8RE. *Club:* Brooks's.

ANNAND, John Angus; Under Secretary, Welsh Office, 1975–85; *b* 13 May 1926; *s* of James Annand and Lilias Annand (*née* Smith); *m* 1971, Julia Dawn Hardman (marr. diss. 1986). *Educ:* Hillhead High Sch., Glasgow; Glasgow Univ. (MA, 1st Cl. Hons); Brasenose Coll., Oxford (MLitt). Lecturer: Univ. of Ceylon; Univ. of South Australia, 1951–53; Asst Dir, Civil Service Commn, 1953–57; Principal, 1957, Asst Sec., 1967, HM Treasury; Civil Service Dept, 1968; Welsh Office, 1971; Under Sec., Health and Social Work Dept, Welsh Office, 1975; Economic Policy Gp, 1978. Mem., GMC, 1986–90. *Address:* 21 Fairwater Road, Llandaff, Cardiff CF5 2LD.

ANNAND, Richard Wallace, VC 1940; DL; Personnel Officer at Finchale Abbey Training Centre for the Disabled, near Durham, 1948–79; late Captain Durham Light Infantry (RARO); *b* 5 Nov. 1914; *s* of Lt-Comdr Wallace Moir Annand, Royal Naval Division (killed Gallipoli 1915), and late Dora Elizabeth Chapman, South Shields; *m* 1940, Shirley Osborne, MBE 1978; JP 1957. *Educ:* Pocklington Sch., East Yorks. Staff of National Provincial Bank, 1933–37; commissioned in RNVR 1933 (Tyne and London Divisions), Midshipman, 1933, Sub-Lieut, 1936; transferred to Durham Light Infantry, Jan. 1938; served in France and Belgium, 1939–40 (wounded, VC (first Army VC of 2nd World War)). Invalided, Dec. 1948. Col in Chief, Europ. Legion of Frontiersmen. President: Durham and Cleveland Cos Br., Royal British Legion; Durham Co. Assoc. for Disabled; N Eastern League of Hard of Hearing; S Shields Br., Normandy Veterans; Durham City Br., DLI Assoc.; St James's Art Sch. for Deafened, 1948–; Past Pres., Newcastle and Gateshead Br., Dunkirk Veterans' Assoc.; Founder Mem., British Assoc. of Hard of Hearing, 1946. Hon. Freeman Co. Borough of South Shields, 1940. DL Co. of Durham, 1956. *Recreation:* golf. *Address:* Springwell House, Whitesmocks, Durham DH1 4LL. *Clubs:* Royal Over-Seas League; County (Durham).

ANNANDALE AND HARTFELL, 11th Earl of, *cr* 1662 (S) with precedence to 1643; **Patrick Andrew Wentworth Hope Johnstone of Annandale and of that Ilk;** Earl of the territorial earldom of Annandale and Hartfell, and of the Lordship of Johnstone; Hereditary Steward of the Stewartry of Annandale; Hereditary Keeper of the Castle of Lochmaben; Chief of the Name and Arms of Johnstone; landowner; Vice-Lord Lieutenant, Dumfries and Galloway Region, districts of Nithsdale, Annandale and Eskdale, since 1992; *b* 19 April 1941; *s* of Major Percy Wentworth Hope Johnstone of Annandale and of that Ilk, TD (*d* 1983) (*de jure* 10th Earl) and of Margaret Jane (now Margaret Countess of Annandale and Hartfell), *d* of Herbert William Francis Hunter-Arundell; claim to earldom admitted by Committee for Privileges, House of Lords, 1985; *m* 1969, Susan Josephine, *d* of late Col Walter John Macdonald Ross, CB, OBE, MC, TD, Netherhall, Castle Douglas; one *s* one *d*. *Educ:* Stowe School; RAC, Cirencester. Member: Dumfries CC, 1970–75; Dumfries and Galloway Regional Council, 1974–86; Scottish Valuation Advisory Council, 1983–85. Director: Bowring Members Agency, 1985–88; Murray Lawrence Members Agency, 1988–92; Solway River Purification Bd, 1970–86; Chm., Royal Jubilee and Prince's Trusts for Dumfries and Galloway, 1984–88. Underwriting Member of Lloyds, 1976–. DL Nithsdale and Annandale and Eskdale, 1987. *Recreations:* golf, shooting. *Heir: s* Lord Johnstone, *qv*. *Address:* House of Lords, SW1A 0PW. *Clubs:* Brooks's; Puffin's (Edinburgh).

ANNENBERG, Walter H., KBE (Hon.) 1976; US Ambassador to the Court of St James's, 1969–74; *b* 13 March 1908; *s* of M. L. Annenberg; *m* 1951, Leonore Cohn; one *d*. *Educ:* Peddie Sch.; Univ. of Pennsylvania. President, Triangle Publications Inc., Philadelphia, Pa; Publisher: Seventeen Magazine; TV Guide; Daily Racing Form. Hon. Bencher, Middle Temple, 1969; Hon. Old Etonian, 1990; Trustee, Winston Churchill Traveling

Fellowships. Medal of Freedom, 1986; holds foreign decorations. *Address:* Llanfair Road, Wynnewood, PA 19096, USA; Suite A200, St David's Center, 150 Radnor-Chester Road, St Davids, PA 19087, USA. *Clubs:* White's; Racquet, Rittenhouse (Philadelphia); Lyford Cay (Bahamas); National Press (Washington, DC); Swinley Forest Golf.

ANNESLEY, family name of **Earl Annesley** and **Viscount Valentia.**

ANNESLEY, 10th Earl *cr* 1789; **Patrick Annesley;** Baron Annesley, 1758; Viscount Glerawly, 1766; *b* 12 August 1924; *e s* of 9th Earl Annesley, and of Nora, *y d* of late Walter Harrison; *S* father, 1979; *m* 1947, Catherine, *d* of John Burgess, Edinburgh; four *d*. *Heir: b* Hon. Philip Harrison Annesley [*b* 29 March 1927; *m* 1951, Florence Eileen (*d* 1995), *o d* of late John Arthur Johnston].

ANNESLEY, Sir Hugh (Norman), Kt 1992; QPM 1986; Chief Constable, Royal Ulster Constabulary, since 1989; *b* 22 June 1939; *s* of late William Henry Annesley and of Agnes Annesley (*née* Redmond); *m* 1970, Elizabeth Ann (*née* MacPherson); one *s* one *d*. *Educ:* St Andrew's Prep. Sch., Dublin; Avoca Sch. for Boys, Blackrock. Joined Metropolitan Police, 1958; Chief Supt, 1974; Police Staff College: Special Course, 1963; Intermed. Comd Course, 1971; Sen. Comd Course, 1975; Asst Chief Constable, Personnel and Ops, Sussex Police, 1976; RCDS 1980; Metropolitan Police, Deputy Assistant Commissioner: Central and NW London, 1981; Personnel, 1983; Dir, Force Re-organisation Team, 1984; Assistant Commissioner: Personnel and Training, 1985; Specialist Ops, 1987. Member: Nat. Exec. Inst., FBI, 1986–; Exec. Cttee, Interpol (British Rep.), 1987–90, and 1993–94. *Recreations:* hockey, sailing. *Address:* Brooklyn, Knock Road, Belfast BT5 6LE.

ANNETT, David Maurice, MA; Headmaster of King's School, Worcester, 1959–79; *b* 27 April 1917; *s* of late M. W. Annett and Marguerite, *d* of Rev. W. M. Hobson; *m* 1953, Evelyn Rosemary, *d* of late W. M. Gordon, Headmaster of Wrekin Coll., and *widow* of R. E. Upcott; one *d* (one step-*s* two step-*d*). *Educ:* Haileybury Coll.; Queens' Coll., Cambridge. Head of Classical Dept at Oundle Sch., 1939–53, and Housemaster, 1948–53; Headmaster of Marling Sch., Stroud, 1953–59. Served with 27th Field Regt, RA, in India and Burma (Capt.), 1941–45. *Address:* The Old Shop, Whitbourne, Worcester WR6 5SR. *T:* Knightwick (01886) 821727.

ANNING, Raymon Harry, CBE 1982; QPM 1975; Commissioner of Police, The Royal Hong Kong Police Force, 1985–90; Chairman, Securicor Consultancy Ltd, since 1991; *b* 22 July 1930; *s* of Frederick Charles Anning and Doris Mabel Anning (*née* Wakefield); *m* 1949, Beryl Joan Boxall; one *s* one *d*. *Educ:* Richmond and East Sheen Grammar School. Army (East Surrey Regt and Royal Military Police), 1948–50. Metropolitan Police, 1952–79: Constable to Chief Supt, Divisions and Headquarters, 1952–69; Officer i/c Anguilla Police Unit, W Indies, 1969; Chief Supt i/c Discipline Office, New Scotland Yard, 1970–72; Commander i/c A 10 (Complaints Investigation) Branch, NSY, 1972–75; seconded to Hong Kong Govt, 1974; Dep. Asst Commissioner C (CID) Dept, 1975–78; Inspector of Metropolitan Police (Dep. Asst Comr), 1979; HM Inspector of Constabulary for England and Wales, 1979–83; Dep. Comr of Police, Hong Kong, 1983–85. Graduate of Nat. Exec. Inst., FBI Academy, Quantico, Virginia, USA, 1979. *Recreation:* walking. *Address:* Sutton Park House, 15 Carshalton Road, Sutton, Surrey SM1 4LE. *Clubs:* Royal Automobile; Royal Hong Kong Golf Club.

ANNIS, David, MD; FRCS; Senior Research Fellow, University of Liverpool, since 1981 (Science and Engineering Research Council Senior Research Fellow, Institute of Medical and Dental Engineering, 1981–86); *b* 28 Feb. 1921; *s* of Harold and Gertrude Annis; *m* 1948, Nesta Roberts; three *s* one *d*. *Educ:* Manchester Grammar Sch.; Univ. of Liverpool. ChM 1953, MD 1959; FRCS 1946. Res. Fellow in Exptl Surgery, Mayo Clinic, Minn., 1949–51. Liverpool University: Sen. Lectr in Surgery, 1951–54; Dir of Studies, Surg. Sci., 1964–69; Dir, Bioengineering Unit, Dept of Surgery, 1969–85; Consultant Gen. Surgeon, Royal Liverpool Hosp., 1954–81. Member: Biomaterials Sub-Cttee, SRC, 1978–80; Physiolog. Systems and Disorders Bd, MRC, 1980–. Mem. Ct of Examrs, RCS, 1963–69; Examiner in Surgery, Univs of Leeds, Glasgow, Cardiff, Dundee, Liverpool and Lagos. Member, Editorial Committee: Bioengineering Jl, 1980–; British Jl of Surgery, 1965–80. *Publications:* contribs to: Wells and Kyle, Scientific Foundations of Surgery, 1967, 3rd edn 1982; Cuschieri, Moosa and Giles, Companion to Surgical Practice, 1982; papers on surgical and med. bioengrg subjects in learned jls. *Recreation:* countryside. *Address:* Little Hey, Dibbinsdale Road, Bromborough, Merseyside L63 0HQ. *T:* 0151–334 3422.

ANNIS, Francesca; actress; *b* 1945. *Theatre:* Royal Shakespeare Company: Romeo and Juliet, 1976; Troilus and Cressida, 1976; Luciana in Comedy of Errors, 1976; Natalya in A Month in the Country, Nat. Theatre, 1981; Masha in Three Sisters, Albery, 1987; Melitta in Mrs Klein, NT, 1988; Rosmersholm, Young Vic, 1992; Lady Windermere's Fan, Albery, 1994. *Films* include: Penny Gold, 1972; Macbeth, 1973; Krull, 1983; Dune, 1984; The Golden River; Under the Cherry Moon. *Television:* A Pin to see the Peepshow, 1973; Madame Bovary, 1975; Stronger than the Sun, 1977; The Ragazza, 1978; Lillie (series), 1978; Partners in Crime (series), 1983; Inside Story (series), 1986; Parnell and the Englishwoman, Absolute Hell, 1991; The Gravy Train Goes East (series), 1991; Between the Lines (series), 1993. *Address:* c/o Dennis Selinger, ICM, 76 Oxford Street, W1R 1RB.

ANNIS, Philip Geoffrey Walter; Manager, Regimental History Project, Royal Regiment of Artillery, since 1986; *b* 7 Feb. 1936; *s* of Walter and Lilian Annis; *m* 1967, Olive, *d* of Mr & Mrs E. W. A. Scarlett; one *s*. *Educ:* Sale Grammar Sch.; Kelsick Grammar Sch., Ambleside; Manchester Univ. FSA 1973; FRHistS 1975. Served RA, 1957–59, and RA (TA), 1961–66. Board of Inland Revenue, 1959–62. Joined National Maritime Museum, 1962; Head of Museum Services, 1971; Dep. Dir, 1979–86. Mem., British Commn, Internat. Commn for Maritime History, 1980–88. Comdr, Order of Lion of Finland, 1986. *Publications:* Naval Swords, 1970; (with Comdr W. E. May) Swords For Sea Service, 1970; articles on the history of naval uniform. *Recreation:* gardening. *Address:* The Royal Artillery Institution, Old Royal Military Academy, Woolwich, SE18 4DN. *T:* 0181–781 5613.

ANSBRO, David Anthony; Managing Partner, Eversheds (formerly Hepworth & Chadwick), solicitors, Leeds, since 1994 (Partner, since 1991); *b* 3 April 1945; *s* of late David T. Ansbro and of Kathleen Mary Ansbro (*née* Mallett); *m* 1967, Veronica Mary (*née* Auton); two *d*. *Educ:* Xaverian Coll., Manchester; Leeds Univ. (LLB Hons). Articled to Town Clerk, Leeds, 1966–69; admitted Solicitor, 1969; Solicitor, Leeds City Council, 1969–73; Asst Dir of Admin, 1973–77, Dep. Dir of Admin, 1977–81, W Yorks County Council; Town Clerk and Chief Exec., York City Council, 1981–85; Chief Exec., Kirklees Council, 1985–87; Rees & Co., Solicitors, Huddersfield, 1987–88; Chief Exec., Leeds City Council, 1988–91. Mem., Local Govt Commn for England, 1992–. Dir, Leeds TEC, 1990–. Papal Medal Pro Ecclesia et Pontifice, 1982. *Recreations:* family, friends, golf, watching Manchester City. *Address:* Cloth Hall Court, Infirmary Street, Leeds LS1 2JB. *T:* Leeds (0113) 2430391. *Club:* Honley Cricket.

ANSCOMBE, Gertrude Elizabeth Margaret, FBA 1967; Professor of Philosophy, University of Cambridge, 1970–86; Fellow, New Hall, Cambridge, 1970–86, Hon. Fellow, since 1986; *b* 1919; *d* of Allen Wells Anscombe and Gertrude Elizabeth Anscombe (*née* Thomas); *m* 1941, Prof. Peter Thomas Geach, *qv;* three *s* four *d*. *Educ:* Sydenham High Sch.; St Hugh's Coll., Oxford (Schol.); Newnham Coll., Cambridge. 2nd cl. Hon. Mods 1939, 1st cl. Greats 1941, Oxford. Research studentships, Oxford and Cambridge, 1941–44; research fellowships, Somerville Coll., Oxford, 1946–64; Fellow, Somerville Coll., 1964–70, Hon. Fellow, 1970–; Hon. Fellow, St Hugh's Coll., Oxford, 1972. Hon. Dr Laws Notre Dame Univ., 1986; Hon. DPhil and Letters Navarra Univ., 1989; Hon. DPhil Univ. of Louvain-la-Neuve, 1990. For. Hon. Mem., Amer. Acad. of Arts and Sciences, 1979. Ehrenkreuz Pro Litteris et Artibus (Austria), 1978; Forschungspreis, Alexander von Humboldt Stiftung, 1983. *Publications:* Intention, 1957; An Introduction to Wittgenstein's Tractatus, 1959; (with Peter Geach) Three Philosophers, 1961; Collected Papers: 1, Parmenides to Wittgenstein, 2, Metaphysics and the Philosophy of Mind, 3, Ethics, Religion and Politics, 1981; translator and co-editor of posthumous works of Ludwig Wittgenstein. *Address:* 3 Richmond Road, Cambridge CB4 3PP.

ANSELL, Dr Barbara Mary, CBE 1982; Consultant Physician (Rheumatology), Wexham Park Hospital, Slough, 1985–88; Head of Division of Rheumatology, Clinical Research Centre, Northwick Park Hospital, Harrow, 1976–88; *b* 30 Aug. 1923; *m* A. H. Weston, MB, FRCGP. *Educ:* Kings High Sch. for Girls, Warwick; Birmingham Univ. (MD 1969). MRCP 1951, FRCP 1967. Consultant Physician (Rheumatol.), Canadian Red Cross Hosp., Taplow, 1962–85. Mem., Cttee for the Review of Medicines, 1979–82. Member: British Assoc. for Rheumatism and Rehabilitation (Mem. Council, 1978–81); Arthritis and Rheumatism Council (Member: Educn Cttee, 1961–77 (Chm., 1966–68); Scientific Co-ordinating Cttee, 1981–; Exec. Cttee, 1987–); RCP Cttee on Rheumatology, 1972–82; Warnock Cttee of Enquiry into Educn of Handicapped Children, 1975; Exec. Cttee, British League Against Rheumatism, 1976–; Standing Cttee, European League Against Rheumatism, 1979– (Chm., Cttee on Paedriatic Rheumatology, 1979–); Heberden Soc. (Pres., 1976); Council, RCP, 1986–87 (2nd Vice-Pres., 1987–88); Rheumatology Chm., RCP Cttee on Higher Med. Trng, 1977–79. Hon. FRCS, 1984; Hon. FRSM, 1989. Hon. Member: Amer. Coll. of Physicians; American, Australian, Finnish, French, German and South African Rheumatism Associations; Spanish Soc. of Rheumatology. Editor, Medicine, 1974, 1976, 1978–79. *Publications:* (ed) Clinics in Rheumatic Diseases, 1976; Chronic Ailments in Childhood, 1976; (ed jtly) Surgical Management of Juvenile Chronic Polyarthritis, 1978; Rheumatic Disorders in Childhood, 1980; Inflammatory Disorders of Muscle, 1984; (ed jtly) Paediatric Rheumatology Update, 1990; (jtly) A Colour Atlas of Paediatric Rheumatology, 1991. *Recreations:* travelling, cooking. *Address:* Dumgoyne, Templewood Lane, Stoke Poges, Bucks SL2 4BG. *T:* Fulmer (01753) 662321; (consulting rooms) 9 Beaumont Road, Windsor, Berks SL4 1HY. *Club:* Royal Society of Medicine.

ANSELL, Maj.-Gen. Nicholas George Picton, CB 1992; OBE 1980; JP; Clerk of the Course, Exeter Racecourse, since 1995; *b* 17 Aug. 1937; *s* of Col Sir Michael Ansell, CBE, DSO and late Victoria Jacintha Fleetwood Fuller; *m* 1961, Vivien, *e d* of Col Anthony Taylor, DSO, MC; two *s* one *d*. *Educ:* Wellington Coll.; Magdalene Coll., Cambridge (MA). Commnd into 5th Royal Inniskilling Dragoon Guards, 1956; served BAOR, Libya, Cyprus; sc Camberley, 1970; Bde Major RAC HQ 1 (BR) Corps, 1971–72; Instructor Staff Coll., 1976–77; CO 5th Royal Inniskilling Dragoon Guards, 1977–80; Col GS Staff Coll., 1980–81; comd 20 Armd Bde, 1982–83; RCDS, 1984; Dep. Chief of Staff HQ BAOR, 1985–86; Dir, RAC, 1987–89; Sen. DS, Army, RCDS, 1990–92. JP Bideford and Gt Torrington, 1994. *Recreations:* country pursuits—horses, fishing, shooting, birdwatching. *Address:* Exeter Racecourse, Kennford, Exeter EX6 7XS. *Club:* Cavalry and Guards.

ANSON, family name of **Earl of Lichfield.**

ANSON, Viscount; Thomas William Robert Hugh Anson; *b* 19 July 1978; *s* and *heir* of Earl of Lichfield, *qv*.

ANSON, Charles Vernon, LVO 1983; Press Secretary to the Queen, since 1990; *b* 11 March 1944; *s* of Philip Vernon Anson and Stella Anson (*née* Parish); *m* 1976, Clarissa Rosamund Denton; one *s* one *d*. *Educ:* Lancing College; Jesus College, Cambridge (BA History). Joined Diplomatic Service, 1966; Third, later Second Sec. (Commercial), Washington, 1968–71; FCO, 1971–74; Asst Private Sec. to Minister of State, 1974–76; Second Sec. (Commercial), Tehran, 1976–79; seconded to Press Office, 10 Downing St., 1979–81; First Sec. (Inf.), Washington, 1981–85; FCO, 1985–87; Dir of Public Relations, Kleinwort Benson, 1987–90. *Address:* c/o Buckingham Palace, SW1A 1AA. *Club:* Hurlingham.

ANSON, Vice-Adm. Sir Edward (Rosebery), KCB 1984; FRAeS 1982; Senior Naval Adviser, British Aerospace plc, 1989–91, retired; Aerospace Consultant (part-time), I.A.D. Aerospace Ltd, Worthing, 1991–93; *b* 11 May 1929; *s* of Ross Rosebery Anson and Ethel Jane (*née* Green); *m* 1960, Rosemary Anne Radcliffe; one *s* one *d*. *Educ:* Prince of Wales Sch., Nairobi, Kenya; BRNC, Dartmouth; Empire Test Pilots Sch., Farnborough (grad. 1957). Served, 1952–64: Naval Air Sqdns, and 700X and 700Z Flts (Blackburn Aircraft Ltd, 1959–61); comd HMS Eskimo, 1964–66; Commander (Air): RNAS Lossiemouth, 1967–68; HMS Eagle, 1969–70; comd Inter Service Hovercraft Trials Unit, 1971; Naval and Air Attaché, Tokyo and Seoul, 1972–74; comd HMS Juno and Captain F4, 1974–76; comd HMS Ark Royal, 1976–78; Flag Officer, Naval Air Command, 1979–82 C of S to C-in-C Fleet, 1982–84, retired. Exec. Dir, Sales, BAe Bristol Div., 1985–86; Pres. and Chief Exec. Officer, BAe, Washington, 1986–89. *Recreations:* walking, golf, tennis, photography. *Address:* c/o Lloyds Bank, High Street, Yeovil, Somerset.

ANSON, Dame Elizabeth (Audrey), (Lady Anson), DBE 1995; JP, DL; Deputy Chairman, and Chairman of Executive Committee, Association of District Councils of England and Wales, since 1993; *b* 9 Jan. 1931; *d* of late Rear-Adm. Sir Philip Clarke, KBE, CB, DSO, and Audrey (*née* White); *m* 1955, Rear-Adm. Sir Peter Anson, Bt, *qv;* two *s* two *d*. *Educ:* Weirfield Sch., Taunton; Royal Naval Sch., Haslemere; King's Coll., London (LLB). Called to Bar, Inner Temple, 1953; joined Western Circuit, 1953; practice at Bar, 1952–56; part-time Adjudicator, 1977–87, an Adjudicator, 1987–91, Immigration Appeals; Ind. Monitor, Entry Clearance Refusals, 1994–. Chm., Ind. Appeals Authority for Sch. Examinations, 1990–. Councillor, Waverley Bor. Council, 1974–, Mayor, 1987–88. Association of District Councils of England and Wales: Mem., 1983–; Vice-Chm., 1989–91; Chm., 1991–93; Chm., Housing and Environmental Health Cttee, 1987–89. Dep. Chm., Local Govt Management Bd, 1991–93; Member: Local Govt Audit Commn, 1987–90; Cons. Nat. Local Govt Adv. Cttee, 1991–; Nat. Union Exec. Cttee, 1992–; Local and Central Govt Relations Res. Cttee, Joseph Rowntree Meml Trust, 1992–; EU Cttee of the Regions, 1993–; Packaging Standards Council, 1992–. Chm., Surrey and NE Hampshire Radio Ltd, 1993–. Chm., Nat. Mobility Scheme, 1987–88. Vice Pres., Inst. of Envmtl Health Officers, 1989–. FRSA 1992. JP 1977, DL 1984, Surrey. *Recreations:* travel, needlecraft. *Address:* Rosefield, Rowledge, Farnham, Surrey GU10 4AT. *T:* Farnham (01252) 792724.

ANSON, Sir John, KCB 1990 (CB 1981); Second Permanent Secretary (Public Expenditure), HM Treasury, 1987–90; *b* 3 Aug. 1930; *yr s* of Sir Edward Anson, 6th Bt, and of Dowager Lady Anson; *m* 1957, Myrica Fergie-Woods; two *s* two *d*. *Educ:* Winchester, Magdalene Coll., Cambridge (MA; Smith's Prize). Served in HM Treasury,

1954–68; Financial Counsellor, British Embassy, Paris, 1968–71; Asst Sec., 1971–72, Under-Sec., 1972–74, Cabinet Office; Under-Sec., 1974–77, Dep. Sec., 1977–87, HM Treasury; Economic Minister, British Embassy, Washington, and UK Exec. Dir, IMF and World Bank, 1980–83. Chairman: Public Finance Foundn, 1991–94; Retirement Income Inquiry, 1994–95. Hon. Treas., Council of Churches for Britain and Ireland, 1990–92. *Address:* 18 Church Road, Barnes, SW13 9HN. *T:* 0181–748 6557.

See also Sir Peter Anson, Bt.

ANSON, Rear-Adm. Sir Peter, 7th Bt, *cr* 1831; CB 1974; DL; CEng, FIEE; Chairman, IGG Component Technology Ltd, since 1992; *b* 31 July 1924; *er s* of Sir Edward R. Anson, 6th Bt, and Alison, *o d* of late Hugh Pollock; *S* father 1951; *m* 1955, Elizabeth Audrey Clarke (*see* Dame Elizabeth Anson); two *s* two *d*. *Educ:* RNC, Dartmouth. Joined RN 1938; Lieut 1944. Served War of 1939–45, HMS Prince of Wales, HMS Exeter. Lieut-Comdr, 1952; Comdr 1956. Commanding Officer, HMS Alert, 1957–58; Staff of RN Tactical Sch., Woolwich, 1959–61; Commanding Officer, HMS Broadsword, 1961–62; Captain, 1963; Director Weapons, Radio (Naval), 1965–66 (Dep. Director, 1963–65); CO HMS Naiad and Captain (D) Londonderry Squadron, 1966–68; Captain, HM Signal School, 1968–70; Commodore, Commander Naval Forces Gulf, 1970–72; ACDS (Signals), 1972–74, retired 1975. Marconi Space and Defence Systems, later Marconi Space Systems: Divl Manager, Satellites, 1977–84; Man. Dir, 1984–85; Chm., 1985–91. Chm., UK Industrial Space Cttee, 1980–82. FIERE 1972. High Sheriff, Surrey, 1993. DL Surrey, 1993. *Heir: s* Philip Roland Anson, *b* 4 Oct. 1957. *Address:* Rosefield, Rowledge, Farnham, Surrey GU10 4AT. *T:* and *Fax:* Farnham (01252) 792724.

See also Sir John Anson.

ANSTEE, Dame Margaret (Joan), DCMG 1994; lecturer, writer and consultant; Adviser to the President and Government of Bolivia; Under-Secretary-General of the United Nations, 1987–93; *b* 25 June 1926; *d* of Edward Curtis Anstee and Anne Adaliza (*née* Mills). *Educ:* Chelmsford County High Sch. for Girls; Newnham Coll., Cambridge (MA; 1st cl. Hons, Mod. and Med. Langs Tripos; Hon. Fellow, 1991); BSc(Econ) London. Lectr in Spanish, QUB, 1947–48; Third Sec., FO, 1948–52; Admin. Officer, UN Technical Assistance Bd, Manila, Philippines, 1952–54; Spanish Supervisor, Cambridge Univ., 1955–56; UN Technical Assistance Board: O i/c Bogotá, Colombia, 1956–57; Resident Rep., Uruguay, 1957–59; Resident Rep., UN Tech. Assistance Bd, Dir of Special Fund Progs, and Dir of UN Inf. Centre, Bolivia, 1960–65; Resident Rep., UNDP, Ethiopia, and UNDP Liaison Officer with UN Econ. Commn for Africa, 1965–67; Sen. Econ. Adviser, Prime Minister's Office, UK, 1967–68; Sen. Asst to Comr i/c Study of Capacity of UN Develt System, 1968–69; Resident Rep., UNDP, Morocco, 1969–72; Resident Rep., UNDP, Chile, and UNDP Liaison Officer with UN Econ. Commn for Latin America, 1972–74; Dep. to UN Under Sec.-Gen. i/c UN Relief Operation to Bangladesh, and Dep. Co-ordinator of UN Emergency Assistance to Zambia, June–Dec. 1973; United Nations Development Programme, New York: Dep. Asst Adminr, and Dep. Reg Dir for Latin America, 1974–76; Dir, Adminr's Unit for Special Assignments, Feb.–July 1976; Asst Dep. Adminr, July–Dec. 1976; Asst Adminr and Dir, Bureau for Prog. Policy and Evaluation, 1977–78; Asst Sec.-Gen. of UN (Dept of Technical Co-operation for Develt), NY, 1978–87; Dir-Gen., UN Office, Vienna, and Head, Centre for Social Develt and Humanitarian Affairs, 1987–92. Special Representative of Secretary-General: for Bolivia, 1982–92; for co-ordination of internat. assistance to Mexico following the earthquake, 1985–87; for UN Conf. for adoption of convention against illicit traffic in narcotic drugs and psychotropic substances, 1988; for Peru, 1991–92; Special Rep. of Sec.-Gen. for Angola, and Head, UN Angola Verification Mission UNAVEM II), 1992–93; Sec.-Gen.'s Personal rep., to co-ordinate UN efforts, Kuwait (burning oil wells and envmtl impact of Gulf war in whole reg.), 1991–92. Chm., Adv. Gp on review of World Food Council, UN, 1985–86; Special Co-ordinator of UN Sec. Gen. to ensure implementation of Gen. Assembly resolution on financial and admin. reform of UN, 1986–87; Co-ordinator for all UN Drug-Control-Related Activities, 1987–90; UN Co-ordinator of Internat. Co-operation for Chernobyl, 1991–92. Sec.-Gen., 8th UN Congress on Prevention of Crime and Treatment of Offenders, 1990. DU Essex, 1994. Reves Peace Prize, Coll. of William and Mary, Williamsburg, USA, 1993. Comdr, Order of Ouissam Alaouite, Morocco, 1972; Gran Cruz de Dama, Condor of the Andes, Bolivia, 1986; Grosse Goldene Ehrenzeichen am Bande, Austria, 1992. *Publications:* The Administration of International Development Aid, USA 1969; Gate of the Sun: a prospect of Bolivia, 1970 (USA 1971); (ed with R. K. A. Gardiner and C. Patterson) Africa and the World (Haile Selassie Prize Trust Symposium), 1970. *Recreations:* writing, gardening, hill-walking (preferably in the Andes), bird-watching, swimming. *Address:* c/o PNUD, Casilla 9072, La Paz, Bolivia. *Club:* United Oxford & Cambridge University (Lady Associate Member).

ANSTEY, Edgar, MA, PhD; Deputy Chief Scientific Officer, Civil Service Department, and Head of Behavioural Sciences Research Division, 1969–77; *b* 5 March 1917; British; *s* of late Percy Lewis Anstey and Dr Vera Anstey; *m* 1939, Zoë Lilian Robertson; one *s*. *Educ:* Winchester Coll.; King's Coll, Cambridge. Assistant Principal, Dominions Office, 1938; Private Sec. to Duke of Devonshire, 1939. 2nd Lieut Dorset Regt, 1940; Major, War Office (DSP), 1941. Founder-Head of Civil Service Commission Research Unit, 1945; Principal, Home Office, 1951; Senior Principal Psychologist, Min. of Defence, 1958; Chief Psychologist, Civil Service Commn, 1964–69. Pres., N Cornwall Liberal Democrat Assoc., 1988–90 (N Cornwall Liberal Assoc., 1985–88). *Publications:* Interviewing for the Selection of Staff (with Dr E. O. Mercer), 1956; Staff Reporting and Staff Development, 1961; Committees-How they work and how to work them, 1962; Psychological Tests, 1966; The Techniques of Interviewing, 1968; (with Dr C. A. Fletcher and Dr. J. Walker) Staff Appraisal and Development, 1976; An Introduction to Selection Interviewing, 1978; articles in Brit. Jl of Psychology, Occupational Psychology, etc. *Recreations:* fell-walking, surfing, bridge. *Address:* Sandrock, 3 Higher Tristram, Polzeath, Wadebridge, Cornwall PL27 6TF. *T:* Trebetherick (01208) 863324. *Club:* Commonwealth Trust.

ANSTEY, Brig. Sir John, Kt 1975; CBE 1946; TD; DL; President and Chairman, National Savings Committee, 1975–78 (a Vice-Chairman, 1968–75); retired as Chairman and Managing Director, John Player & Sons; Director, Imperial Tobacco Co., Ltd, 1949–67; *b* 3 Jan. 1907; *s* of late Major Alfred Anstey, Matford House, Exeter, Devon; *m* 1935, Elizabeth Mary (*d* 1990), *d* of late William Garnett, Backwell, Somerset; one *s* one *d*. *Educ:* Clifton; Trinity Coll., Oxford; Harvard Univ. (MBA 1952). Served War of 1939–45: N Africa, France, SEAC (despatches); Lt-Col 1944; Brig. 1944. Mem. Council, Nottingham Univ., 1948–93 (Treasurer, 1979–81; Pro-Chancellor, 1982–93); Member: (part-time) East Midlands Gas Board, 1968–72; Univ. Authorities Panel, 1979–82. Governor, Clifton Coll. Mem. Council, The Queen's Silver Jubilee Appeal, 1976. High Sheriff of Nottinghamshire, 1967; DL Notts 1970. Hon. LLD Nottingham, 1975. Legion of Honour; Croix de Guerre (France); Legion of Merit (USA). *Address:* Southwell, Notts.

ANSTRUTHER of that Ilk, Sir Ralph (Hugo), 7th Bt, *cr* 1694 (S), of Balcaskie, and 12th Bt *cr* 1700 (S), of Anstruther; GCVO 1992 (KCVO 1976; CVO 1967); MC 1943; DL; Hereditary Carver to the Queen; Equerry to the Queen Mother since 1959, also Treasurer, since 1961; *b* 13 June 1921; *o s* of Capt. Robert Edward Anstruther (*d* 1921), MC, The Black Watch, *o s* of 6th Bt, and Marguerite Blanche Lily (*d* 1992), *d* of Hugo de Burgh; *S* grandfather, 1934, and cousin, Sir Windham Eric Francis Carmichael-Anstruther, 11th Bt, 1980. *Educ:* Eton; Magdalene Coll., Cambridge (BA). Major (retd), Coldstream Gds. Served Malaya, 1950 (despatches). Mem. Queen's Body Guard for Scotland (Royal Co. of Archers). DL Fife, 1960, Caithness-shire, 1965. *Heir: cousin,* Ian Fife Campbell Anstruther, Capt. late Royal Corps of Signals [*b* 11 May 1922; *m* 1st, 1951, Honor (marr. diss. 1963), *er d* of late Capt. Gerald Blake, MC; one *d*; 2nd, 1963, Susan Margaret Walker, *e d* of H. St J. B. Paten; two *s* three *d*]. *Address:* Balcaskie, Pittenweem, Fife KY10 2RD; Watten Mains, Caithness KW1 5UH.

See also Sir T. D. Erskine.

ANSTRUTHER-GOUGH-CALTHORPE, Sir Euan (Hamilton), 3rd Bt *cr* 1929; property manager; *b* 22 June 1966; *s* of Niall Hamilton Anstruther-Gough-Calthorpe (*d* 1970) and of Martha Rodman (who *m* 2nd, 1975, Sir Charles C. Nicholson, Bt, *qv*), *d* of Stuart Warren Don; *S* grandfather, 1985. *Educ:* Hawtreys, Savernake Forest; Harrow School; Royal Agricultural Coll., Cirencester. *Clubs:* Brooks's, Lansdowne.

ANTALPÉTER, Tibor; Order of Merit of Hungarian Republic, Middle Cross, 1995; Director, Hungarian Investment Company Ltd, since 1995; *b* 4 Feb. 1930; *s* of late István Antalpéter and Viktória Dobai; *m* 1956, Adél Máthé; two *d*. *Educ:* Univ. of Economics, Budapest; graduated 1954. Importtex, foreign trade co., 1954; Commercial Sec. in London, 1956–60; Department of International Commercial Relations, Ministry of Foreign Trade: Head of Section, 1960; Dir of Dept, 1964; Dep. Dir-Gen., 1968–73; Dir-Gen. of Dept, 1977–88; Commercial Counsellor, London, 1973–77, 1988–90; Ambassador to UK, 1990–94. Vice-Chm., CAB Internat., 1992–94. Internat. volley-ball player, 1947–56; Chm., Hungarian Volley-ball Assoc. and Mem., Hungarian Olympic Cttee, 1980–86. Hon. FRSA 1992. Order of Merit for Labour, Bronze 1966, Gold 1979. Order of the Finnish Lion, 1st Cl., 1969; Comdr, Order of Prince Henry the Navigator (Portugal), 1979; Order of Merit, Grand Silver Grade (Austria), 1983. *Recreations:* sport, music. *Address:* Kavics u. 11, 1025 Budapest, Hungary. *Clubs:* Athenæum, Army and Navy, Queen's.

ANTHONY, Metropolitan, of Sourozh; Head of the Russian Orthodox Patriarchal Church in Great Britain and Ireland (Diocese of Sourozh); *né* André Borisovich Bloom; *b* Lausanne, Switzerland, 19 June 1914; *o c* of Boris Edwardovich Bloom (Russian Imperial Diplomatic Service) and Xenia Nikolaevna Scriabin (sister of the composer Alexander Scriabin). *Educ:* Lycée Condorcet and Sorbonne, Paris. Dr of Med., Sorbonne, 1943. Army service, med. corps French Army and Resistance, 1939–45. Gen. Practitioner, 1945–49. Took monastic vows, 1943; Priest, Russian Orthodox Church in Paris, 1948; Chaplain to Fellowship of St Alban and St Sergius, London, 1949–50; Vicar, Russian Orthodox Church of St Philip, London, 1950; apptd Hegumen, 1953, Archimandrite, 1956; consecrated Bishop of Sergievo, Suffragan Bishop, Exarchate of Western Europe, 1957; Archbishop of Sourozh, 1960, acting Exarch, 1962–65; Metropolitan of Sourozh and Exarch of the Patriarch of Moscow and All Russia in Western Europe, 1965–74. Member: Ecumenical Commn of Russian Orthodox Church; Central Cttee and Christian Medical Commn of World Council of Churches, 1968. Hulsean Preacher, Cambridge, 1972–73; Preacher, Lambeth Conf., 1978; Firth Lectures, Nottingham Univ., 1982; Eliot Lectures, Kent Univ., 1982; Constantinople Lecture, 1982. Médaille de Bronze de la Société d'encouragement au bien (France), 1945; Browning Award (for spreading of the Christian gospel), USA, 1974. Orders of: St Vladimir 1st Cl. (Russia), 1962; St Andrew (Ecumenical Patriarchate), 1963; St Sergius (Russia), 1977. Lambeth Cross, 1975. Hon. DD (Aberdeen), 1973. *Publications:* Living Prayer, 1965; School for Prayer, 1970; God and Man, 1971; Meditations on a Theme, 1972; Courage to Pray, 1973. *Address:* Russian Orthodox Cathedral, Ennismore Gardens, SW7 1NH. *T:* 0171–584 0096.

ANTHONY, Rt. Hon. Douglas; *see* Anthony, Rt Hon. J. D.

ANTHONY, Evelyn Bridget Patricia, (Mrs Michael Ward-Thomas); author; *b* 3 July 1928; *d* of Henry Christian Stephens, inventor of the Dome Trainer in World War II, and Elizabeth (*née* Sharkey); *g g d* of Henry Stephens of Cholderton, Wilts, inventor of Stephens Ink; *m* 1955, Michael Ward-Thomas; four *s* one *d* (and one *d* decd). *Educ:* Convent of Sacred Heart, Roehampton. Freeman, City of London, 1987; Liveryman, Needlemakers' Co., 1987. High Sheriff, Essex, 1994–95. *Publications:* Imperial Highness, 1953; Curse Not the King, 1954; Far Fly the Eagles, 1955; Anne Boleyn, 1956 (US Literary Guild Award); Victoria, 1957 (US Literary Guild Award); Elizabeth, 1959; Charles the King, 1961; Clandara, 1963; The Heiress, 1964; Valentina, 1965; The Rendezvous, 1967; Anne of Austria, 1968; The Legend, 1969; The Assassin, 1970; The Tamarind Seed, 1971; The Poellenberg Inheritance, 1972; The Occupying Power, 1973 (Yorkshire Post Fiction Prize); The Malaspiga Exit, 1974; The Persian Ransom, 1975; The Silver Falcon, 1977; The Return, 1978; The Grave of Truth, 1979; The Defector, 1980; The Avenue of the Dead, 1981; Albatross, 1982; The Company of Saints, 1983; Voices on the Wind, 1985; No Enemy But Time, 1987; The House of Vandekar, 1988; The Scarlet Thread, 1989; The Relic, 1991; The Dolls' House, 1992; Exposure, 1993. *Recreations:* racing (National Hunt), gardening, going to sale rooms, preferably Christie's. *Address:* Horham Hall, Thaxted, Essex CM6 2NN.

ANTHONY, Graham George, CEng; Director, Industry and Regions, Engineering Council, 1983–90; *b* 25 Oct. 1931; *s* of George Alfred and Dorothy Anthony; *m* 1957, Thelma Jane Firmstone; two *s* one *d*. *Educ:* Fletton Grammar Sch.; King's College London (BSc Eng). Projects Manager, ICI Fibres, 1956; Works Engineer, ICI India, 1964; Chief Engineer, Ilford Ltd, 1968; Gen. Manager, Bonded Structures, 1975; Commercial Dir, Ciba-Geigy (UK) Ltd, 1979. FRSA. *Recreations:* offshore sailing, woodworking. *Address:* 45 Tower Bridge Wharf, St Katharine's Way, E1 9UR. *T:* 0171–709 0977.

ANTHONY, Rt. Hon. (John) Douglas, CH 1982; PC 1971; company director and farmer; Chairman: Resource Finance Corporation, since 1987; Baskin Robbins 31 Flavours Pty Ltd, since 1987; Director: John Swires & Sons Pty Ltd (Australia), since 1987; Clyde Agriculture Ltd, since 1988; Poseidon Gold Ltd, since 1992; *b* 31 Dec. 1929; *s* of late H. L. Anthony; *m* 1957, Margot Macdonald Budd; two *s* one *d*. *Educ:* Murwillumbah Primary and High Schs, The King's Sch., Parramatta; Queensland Agricultural Coll. (QDA). MP, Country Party, later National Party, Richmond, NSW, 1957–84, (Mem., Exec. Council, 1963–72, 1975–83). Minister for Interior, 1964–67; Minister for Primary Industry, 1967–71; Dep. Prime Minister and Minister for Trade and Industry, 1971–72; Minister for Overseas Trade, Minerals and Energy, Nov.–Dec. 1975; Dep. Prime Minister and Minister for Trade and Resources, 1975–83. Dep. Leader, Aust. Country Party, 1966–71; Leader, Nat. Country Party, later Nat. Party, 1971–84. Chm., Pan Australian Mining Ltd, then Mt Leyshon Gold Mines, 1986–92. Hon. Fellow, AATSE, 1990. Hon. LLD Victoria Univ. of Wellington, NZ, 1983. Council Gold Medal, Qld Agricl Coll., 1985. NZ Commemorative Medal, 1990. *Recreations:* golf, tennis, fishing, swimming. *Address:* Sunnymeadows, Murwillumbah, NSW 2484, Australia. *Clubs:* Union, Royal Sydney Golf (Sydney); Queensland (Brisbane).

ANTHONY, Ronald Desmond; consultant in safety and engineering, since 1986; Chief Inspector of Nuclear Installations, Health and Safety Executive, 1981–85; *b* 21 Nov. 1925;

s of William Arthur Anthony and Olive Frances Anthony (*née* Buck); *m* 1948, Betty Margaret Croft; four *d*. *Educ:* Chislehurst and Sidcup Grammar School; City and Guilds Coll., Imperial Coll. of Science and Technology (BSc, ACGI). CEng, FIMechE, MRAeS. Vickers Armstrongs (Supermarine), 1950; Nuclear Power Plant Co., 1957; Inspectorate of Nuclear Installations, 1960; Deputy Chief Inspector, 1973; Dir, Safety Policy Div., 1977, Hazardous Installations Gp, 1981–82, Health and Safety Exec. *Publications:* papers in technical journals. *Recreation:* golf. *Address:* 2 Perry House, Chislehurst Road, Sidcup, Kent DA14 6BE. *T:* 0181-302 6090.

ANTHONY, Vivian Stanley; Secretary, Headmasters' Conference, since 1990; *b* 5 May 1938; *s* of Captain and Mrs A. S. Anthony; *m* 1969, Rosamund Anne MacDermot Byrn; one *s* one *d*. *Educ:* Cardiff High Sch.; LSE (1st Div. 2nd Cl. Hons BSc Econ); Fitzwilliam Coll., Cambridge (DipEd); Merton Coll., Oxford (schoolmaster student). Asst Master, Leeds Grammar Sch., 1960–64; Asst Master and Housemaster, Tonbridge Sch., 1964–69; Lectr in Educn, Univ. of Leeds, 1969–71; Dep. Headmaster, The King's Sch., Macclesfield, 1971–76; Headmaster, Colfe's Sch., London, 1976–90. Asst Examr, Econ. Hist., London Univ., 1964–71; Asst Examr, Econs, Oxford and Cambridge Bd, 1970–76, Chief Examr (Awarder), Econs, 1976–92; Ext. Examr, Educn, Univs of Manchester, 1972–75, Birmingham, 1975–78, and Lancaster, 1977–79. Chm., Econs Assoc., 1974–77; Member: Schools Council Social Science Cttee, 1976–83; London Univ. Schs Examinations Cttee, 1981–85; Secondary Examinations Council Economics Panel, 1984–89; CBI/Schools Panel, 1984–88; Court, Univ. Kent, 1985–90. Sabbatical tour, US indep. schools, 1983. Chm., London Area, 1988–89, Mem. Council, 1989–, SHA; elected Headmasters' Conf., 1980, Chm., Academic Policy Cttee, 1988–90 (Mem., 1983–), Member, Professional Develt Cttee, 1985–89, Teacher Shortage Wkg Party, 1987–88, Assisted Places Cttee, 1987–89, Chm., Records of Achievement Wkg Party, 1987–90. Comr, Inland Revenue, 1989–90. Governor: Stamford Sch., 1992–; King's Sch., Macclesfield, 1993–. Hon. Freeman, Leathersellers' Co., 1990. Hon. FCP 1991. *Publications:* Monopoly, 1968, 3rd edn 1976; Overseas Trade, 1969, 4th edn 1981; Banks and Markets, 1970, 3rd edn 1979; Objective Tests in A Level Economics, 1971, 2nd edn 1974; Objective Tests in Introductory Economics, 1975, 3rd edn 1983; History of Rugby Football at Colfe's, 1980; US Independent Schools, 1984; 150 Years of Cricket at Colfe's, 1986; (ed) Head to Head, 1993; (ed) Manual of Guidance, 1995; *contributor:* The Teaching of Economics in Secondary Schools, 1970; Curriculum Development in Secondary Schools, 1973; Control of the Economy, 1974; Comparative Economics in Teaching Economics, 1984; The Search for Standards, 1992; Access and Affordability, 1994; articles in Economics. *Recreations:* choral singing, Rugby football, squash, tennis. *Address:* 130 Regent Road, Leicester LE1 7PG. *T:* Leicester (0116) 285 4810, *Fax:* Leicester (0116) 247 1152. *Clubs:* East India, Devonshire, Sports and Public Schools, English-Speaking Union, Old Colfeians Association.

ANTICO, Sir Tristan, AC 1983; Kt 1973; President, Pioneer International Ltd (formerly Pioneer Concrete Services), since 1993 (Founding Chairman, 1949; Managing Director, 1949–88); *b* 25 March 1923; *s* of Terribile Giovanni Antico and Erminia Bertin; *m* 1950, Dorothy Bridget Shields; three *s* four *d*. *Educ:* Sydney High Sch. Began career as Accountant; subseq. became Company Secretary, Melocco Bros; Founder of Pioneer Concrete Services Ltd. Chm., Tregoyd Holdings Pty Ltd; formerly Chairman: Ampol Ltd; Papuan Oil Search; Société Générale Australia Hldgs; Quantas Ltd. AC and Knighthood awarded for services to industry and the community. Comdr, Order of Star of Solidarity (Italy), 1967. *Recreations:* horse breeding and horse racing, swimming, yachting. *Address:* 161 Raglan Street, Mosman, NSW 2088, Australia. *T:* (2) 99694070. *Clubs:* Tattersall's, Australian Jockey, Sydney Turf, American National, Royal Sydney Yacht Squadron (Sydney); Manly Golf.

ANTIGUA (diocese)**;** *see* North-Eastern Caribbean and Aruba.

ANTON, Alexander Elder, CBE 1973; FBA 1972; *b* 1922; *m* 1949, Doris May Lawrence; one *s*. *Educ:* Aberdeen Univ. (MA, LLB with dist.; Hon. LLD 1993). Solicitor, 1949; Lectr, Aberdeen, 1953–59; Prof. of Jurisprudence, Univ. of Glasgow, 1959–73. Hon. Vis. Prof., 1982–84, Hon. Prof., 1984, Aberdeen Univ. Mem., Scottish Law Commission, 1966–82. Literary Dir, Stair Soc., 1960–66; Chm., Scottish Rights of Way Soc., 1988–92. *Publications:* Private International Law, 1967, 2nd edn (with P. R. Beaumont), 1990; Civil Jurisdiction in Scotland, 1984; contribs to legal and historical jls. *Recreation:* hill walking. *Address:* 5 Seafield Drive West, Aberdeen AB1 7XA.

ANTONIO; *see* Ruiz Soler, Antonio.

ANTONIONI, Michelangelo; Film Director; *b* Ferrara, Italy, 29 Sept. 1912; *s* of Ismaele and Elisabetta Roncagli; *m* (marr. diss.). *Educ:* degree in Economics and Commerce, Univ. of Bologna. Formerly an Asst Dir, Film Critic to newspapers, and Script Writer. Films directed include: 8 documentaries, etc, 1943–50; subseq. long films: Cronaca di un Amore, 1950; one episode in Amore in Città, 1951; I Vinti, 1952; La Signora Senza Camelie, 1953; Le Amiche, 1955; Il Grido, 1957; L'Avventura, 1959–60; La Notte, 1961; L'Eclisse, 1962; Il Deserto Rosso, 1964; one episode in I Tre Volti, 1965; Blow-Up, 1967; Zabriskie Point, 1969; Chung Kuo-China, 1972; The Passenger, 1974; Il Mistero di Oberwald, 1979; Identificazione di una Donna, 1981; documentaries: Fumbha Mela, 1989; Roma, 1989. *Recreations:* collecting blown glass, tennis, ping-pong. *Address:* Via Vincenzo Tiberio 18, Rome, Italy.

ANTRIM, 14th Earl of, *cr* 1620; **Alexander Randal Mark McDonnell;** Viscount Dunluce; Keeper of Conservation, 1975–95, and Director (formerly Head) of Collection Services, 1990–95, Tate Gallery; *b* 3 Feb. 1935; *er s* of 13th Earl of Antrim, KBE, and Angela Christina (*d* 1984), *d* of Sir Mark Sykes, 6th Bt; *S* father, 1977 (but continued to be known as Viscount Dunluce until 1995); *m* 1963, Sarah Elizabeth Anne (marr. diss. 1974), 2nd *d* of St John Harmsworth; one *s* two *d*; *m* 1977, Elizabeth, *d* of late Michael Moses Sacher; one *d*. *Educ:* Downside; Christ Church, Oxford; Ruskin Sch. of Art. Restorer: the Ulster Museum, 1969–71; Tate Gall., 1965–75. Dir, Ulster Television, 1982–. Mem., Exec. Cttee, City and Guilds Art School, 1983–. FRSA 1984. *Recreations:* painting, vintage cars. *Heir:* *s* Viscount Dunluce, *qv*. *Address:* Deerpark Cottage, Castle Lane, Glenarm, Ballymena, Co. Antrim BT44 6BQ. *Club:* Beefsteak.

ANTROBUS, Sir Edward Philip, 8th Bt *cr* 1815, of Antrobus, Cheshire; *b* 28 Sept. 1938; *er s* of Sir Philip Coutts Antrobus, 7th Bt and his 1st wife, Dorothy Margaret Mary (*d* 1973), *d* of Rev. W. G. Davis; *S* father, 1995; *m* 1966, Janet Sarah Elizabeth (*d* 1990), *d* of Philip Sceales, Johannesburg; one *s* two *d*. *Educ:* Witwatersrand Univ. (BSc Mining Engrg); Magdalene Coll., Cambridge (MA). *Heir:* *s* Francis Edward Sceales Antrobus, *b* 1972. *Address:* 70 Harry Street, Robertsham, Johannesburg, South Africa.

ANWYL, Shirley Anne, QC 1979; **Her Honour Judge Anwyl;** a Circuit Judge, since 1995; *b* 10 Dec. 1940; *d* of James Ritchie and Helen Sutherland Ritchie; *m* 1969, Robin Hamilton Corson Anwyl; two *s*. *Educ:* St Mary's Diocesan Sch. for Girls, Pretoria; Rhodes Univ., S Africa (BA, LLB). Called to the South African Bar, 1963; called to the Bar, Inner Temple, 1966, Bencher, 1985. A Recorder, 1981–95. Member: Senate of Inns of Court and Bar, 1978–81; Gen. Council of the Bar, 1987; Criminal Injuries Compensation Bd, 1980–95; Mental Health Review Tribunal, 1983–. Chm., Barristers' Benevolent Assoc., 1989–95. FRSA 1989. Freeman, City of London, 1994. *Recreations:* theatre, sailing. *Club:* Guild of Freemen of City of London.

ANWYL-DAVIES, His Honour Marcus John, MA; QC 1967; a Circuit Judge, 1972–93; *b* 11 July 1923; *s* of late Thomas Anwyl-Davies and Kathleen Beryl Anwyl-Davies (*née* Oakshott); *m* 1st, 1954, Eva Hilda Elisabeth Paulson (marr. diss. 1974); one *s* one *d*; 2nd, 1983, Myrna Dashoff. *Educ:* Harrow Sch.; Christ Church, Oxford. Royal Artillery, including service with Hong Kong and Singapore RA, 1942–47 (despatches 1945). Called to Bar, Inner Temple, 1949. Legal Assessor, GMC and GDC, 1969–72; Liaison Judge to Herts Magistrates, 1972–82; Resident Judge, St Albans Crown Court, 1972–82. Vice-Pres., Herts Magistrates' Assoc., 1975; Pres., Council of HM's Circuit Judges, 1989. Member: Panel, Amer. Arbitration Assoc., 1993–; London Court of Internat. Arbitration, 1994–; Bd of Dirs, Center for Internat. Commercial Arbitration; Nat. Assoc. of Securities Dealers Bd of Arbitrators. FCIArb 1992 (Mem. Cttee, N Amer. Br., 1993). *Recreation:* photography. *Address:* 39 Essex Street, WC2R 3AT. *T:* 0171–353 4741; 16624 Calle Arbolada, Pacific Palisades, CA 90272–1934, USA. *T:* (310) 4599234, *Fax:* (310) 4598220. *Club:* Reform.

ANYAOKU, Eleazar Chukwuemeka, (Emeka), CON 1982; Ndichie Chief Adazie of Obosi; Ugwumba of Idemili; Secretary-General of the Commonwealth, since 1990; *b* 18 Jan. 1933; *e s* of late Emmanuel Chukwuemeka Anyaoku, Ononukpo of Okpuno Ire, Obosi, Nigeria, and Cecilia Adiba (*née* Ogbogu); *m* 1962, Ebunola Olubunmi, *yr d* of late barrister Olusola Akanbi Solanke, of Abeokuta, Nigeria; three *s* one *d*. *Educ:* Merchants of Light Sch., Oba; Univ. of Ibadan (Schol.), Nigeria; courses in England and France.Exec. Asst, Commonwealth Develt Corp., in London and Lagos, 1959–62. Joined Nigerian Diplomatic Service, 1962; Mem. Nigerian Permanent Mission to the UN, New York, 1963–66; seconded to Commonwealth Secretariat as Asst Dir, 1966–71, and Dir, 1971–75, Internat. Affairs Div.; Asst Sec.-Gen., 1975–77, Dep. Sec.-Gen. (Political), 1977–83 and 1984–90, of the Commonwealth. Minister of External Affairs, Nigeria, Nov.-Dec. 1983. Served as Secretary: Review Cttee on Commonwealth inter-governmental organisations, June-Aug., 1966; Commonwealth Observer Team for Gibraltar Referendum, Aug.-Sept., 1967; Anguilla Commn, WI, Jan.-Sept. 1970; Leader, Commonwealth Mission for Mozambique, 1975; Commonwealth Observer, Zimbabwe Talks, Geneva, 1976; accompanied Commonwealth Eminent Persons Gp, SA, 1986. Vice-Pres., Royal Commonwealth Society, London, 1975–; Mem. Council, Overseas Develt Inst., 1979–90. Mem., Governing Council: SCF, 1984–90; IISS, London, 1987–; Hon. Mem., Club of Rome, 1992–. FRSA 1984. Hon. DLitt: Ibadan, 1990; Buckingham, 1994; Hon. DPhil Ahmadu Bello, 1991; Hon. LLD: Nigeria, 1991; Aberdeen, 1992; Reading, 1992; Bristol, 1993. *Publications:* essays in various pubns. *Recreations:* tennis, swimming, reading. *Address:* Commonwealth Secretariat, Marlborough House, Pall Mall, SW1Y 5HX. *T:* 0171–839 3411; Orimili, Okpuno Ire, Obosi, Anambra State, Nigeria. *Clubs:* Commonwealth Trust, Africa Centre, Travellers'; Metropolitan (Lagos).

AOTEAROA, Bishop of, since 1981; **Rt. Rev. Whakahuihui Vercoe,** MBE 1970; *b* 4 June 1928; *s* of Joseph and Wyness Vercoe; *m* 1951, Dorothy Eivers; three *s*. *Educ:* Torere Primary; Feilding Agricultural High School; College House Theological Coll.; Canterbury Univ. LTh 1985. Curate, St John's Church, Feilding, 1951–53; Priest-in-Charge, Wellington Pastorate, 1953–54; Pastor: Wairarapa, 1954–57; Rangitikei, 1957–61; Chaplain: Armed Forces, Malaya, 1961–64; Papakura Military Camp, 1964–65; ANZAC Brigade, Vietnam, 1968–69; Burnham Mil. Camp, 1965–71; Principal, Te Waipounamu Girls' School, 1971–76; Vicar: Ohinemutu Pastorate, 1976–78; Te Rohe o Whakaari, 1978–81; Archdeacon of Tairawhiti and Vicar-General to Bishopric of Aotearoa, 1978–81. *Recreations:* Rugby, golf, reading, tennis, cricket, fishing. *Address:* PO Box 146, Rotorua, New Zealand. *T:* (home) (7) 3479241, (office) (7) 3486093.

APEL, Dr Hans Eberhard; Social-democratic Member of Bundestag, 1965–90 (Deputy-Chairman of Group, 1969–72); *b* Hamburg, 25 Feb. 1932; *m* 1956, Ingrid Schwingel; two *d*. *Educ:* Hamburg Univ. Diplom-Volkswirt, 1957, Dr.rer.pol, 1960. Apprentice in Hamburg export and import business, 1951–54; Sec., Socialist Group in European Parlt, 1958–61; Head of Economics, Finance and Transportation Dept of European Parlt, 1962–65. Chm., Bundestag Cttee on Transportation, 1969–72. Mem. Nat. Bd, Social-democratic Party (SPD), 1970–88; Parly Sec. of State, Min. for Foreign Affairs, 1972–74; Federal Minister of Finance, 1974–78, of Defence, 1978–82. Prof. in Econ. Dept, Rostock Univ. *Publications:* Edwin Cannan und seine Schüler (Doct. Thesis), 1961; Raumordnung der Bundesrepublik, in: Deutschland 1975, 1964; Europas neue Grenzen, 1964; Der deutsche Parlamentarismus, 1968; Bonn, den . . ., Tagebuch eines Bundestagsabgeordneten, 1972; Der Abstieg, 1990; Die deformierte Demokratie, 1991; Der kranke Koloss, 1994. *Recreations:* sailing, soccer. *Address:* Rögenfeld 42c, 22359 Hamburg, Germany.

APLEY, Alan Graham, FRCS; Consulting Editor, Journal of Bone and Joint Surgery, since 1989 (Editor, 1983–89); *b* 10 Nov. 1914; *s* of Samuel Apley and Mary Tanis; *m* 1st, 1939, Janie Kandler (decd); one *s* one *d*; 2nd, 1988, Violet Chambers. *Educ:* Regent Street Polytechnic; University Coll. London; University College Hosp., London (MB BS); MRCS, LRCP 1938, FRCS 1941; Hon. FRCSE 1987. Served RAMC, 1944–47. Cons. Surg., Rowley Bristow Orthopaedic Hosp., Pyrford, 1947; Dir of Accident and Emergency Centre, St Peter's Hosp., Chertsey, 1964; Hon. Dir, Dept of Orthopaedics, St Thomas' Hosp., London, 1972; Mem. Council, 1973–85, Vice-Pres. 1984–85, RCS; Pres., Orthopaedic Sect., RSM, 1979. *Publications:* System of Orthopaedics and Fractures, 1959, 7th edn 1993; (jtly) Replacement of the Knee, 1984; (jtly) Atlas of Skeletal Dysplasias, 1985; (ed) Recent Advances in Orthopaedics, 1969; (ed) Modern Trends in Orthopaedics, 1972; (jtly) A Concise System of Orthopaedics and Fractures, 1988, 2nd edn 1994; various articles in surg. jls. *Recreations:* music, ski-ing, travelling. *Address:* Singleton Lodge, West Byfleet, Surrey KT14 6PW. *T:* Byfleet (019323) 43353.

APPEL, Karel Christian; Dutch artist (painter); *b* 25 April 1921; *s* of Jan Appel and Johanna Chevallier. *Educ:* Royal Academy of Art, Amsterdam. Began career as artist in 1938. Has had one-man exhibitions in Europe, America and Asia, including: Palais des Beaux-Arts, Brussels, 1953; Stedelijk Mus., Amsterdam, 1955, 1956, 1965; ICA, London, 1957; Palazzo dei Medici, Florence, 1985; travelling exhibitions: museums in Calif, 1961; museums in Canada and USA, 1972, 1973; museums in Brazil, Colombia, Mexico, 1978, 1981; 5 museums in Japan, 1989; Europe, 1990–92. UNESCO Prize, Venice Biennale, 1953; Lissone Prize, Italy, 1958; Acquisition Prize, São Paulo Biennale, Brazil, 1959; Graphique Internat. Prize, Ljubljana, Jugoslavia, 1959; Guggenheim National Prize, Holland, 1961; Guggenheim International Prize, 1961. *Publications:* Works on Paper, 1980; Street Art, 1985; Dupe of Being, 1989; Complete Sculptures 1936–1990, 1990; Karel Appel Sculpture: catalogue raisonné, 1994; *relevant publications:* Karel Appel, 1980; Karel Appel: the early years 1937–1957, 1988.

APPLEBY, Brian John, QC 1971; **His Honour Judge Appleby;** a Circuit Judge, since 1988; *b* 25 Feb. 1930; *s* of Ernest Joel and Gertrude Appleby; *m* 1958, Rosa Helena (*née* Flitterman); one *s* one *d*. *Educ:* Uppingham; St John's Coll., Cambridge (BA). Called to

Bar, Middle Temple, 1953; Bencher, 1980. Dep. Chm., Notts QS, 1970–71; a Recorder, 1972–88. Mem., Nottingham City Council, 1955–58 and 1960–63. District Referee, Nottinghamshire Wages Conciliation Board, NCB, 1980–. *Recreations:* watching good football (preferably Nottingham Forest: Mem. Club Cttee, 1965–82, Life Mem., 1982; Vice-Chm., 1972–75, Chm., 1975–78); swimming, reading and enjoying, when possible, company of wife and children. *Address:* The Poplars, Edwalton Village, Notts NG12 4AB. *T:* Nottingham (0115) 923 2814.

APPLEBY, Douglas Edward Surtees; farmer; retired as Managing Director, The Boots Co. Ltd; *b* 17 May 1929; *s* of Robert Appleby, MSc and Muriel (*née* Surtees); *m* 1952; one *s* one *d*. *Educ:* Durham Johnston Sch.; Univ. of London (BSc); Univ. of Nottingham (BSc). Chartered Accountant, 1957. Commissioned, RAF, Cranwell, 1950–54. Moore, Stephens & Co., Chartered Accountants, London, 1954–57; Distillers Co. Ltd, 1957–58; Corn Products Co., New York, 1959–63; Wilkinson Sword Ltd, 1964–68; The Boots Co Ltd, 1968–81 (Finance Dir, 1968–72, Man. Dir, 1973–81). Regional Dir, Nat. Westminster Bank, 1979–88; Chairman: John H. Mason Ltd, 1982–87; Meadow Farm Produce plc, 1984–86; Sims Food Gp plc, 1987–89. Member Council: Inst. Chartered Accountants, 1971–75; Loughborough Univ., 1973–75; CBI, 1977–81. *Address:* Gorse Farm, Fulletby, Horncastle, Lincs LN9 6LA.

APPLEBY, (Lesley) Elizabeth, (Mrs Michael Kenneth Collins), QC 1979; barrister-at-law; a Recorder, since 1989; *b* 12 Aug. 1942; *o d* of Arthur Leslie Appleby and late Dorothy Evelyn Appleby (*née* Edwards); *m* 1978, Michael Kenneth Collins, OBE, BSc, MICE; one *s* one *d*. *Educ:* Dominican Convent, Brewood, Staffs; Wolverhampton Girls' High Sch.; Manchester Univ. (LLB Hons). Called to Bar, Gray's Inn, 1965 (Richardson Schol.); *ad eundem* Lincoln's Inn, 1975, Bencher, 1986; in practice at Chancery Bar, 1966–; Member, Senate of Inns of Court and Bar, 1977–80, 1981–82. *Recreations:* sailing, swimming, music, golf, gardening. *Address:* 4/5 Gray's Inn Square, Gray's Inn, WC1R 5AY. *T:* 0171–404 5252; Glebe House, West Grinstead, Horsham, West Sussex RH13 8LR. *T:* Partridge Green (01403) 711228.

APPLEBY, Malcolm Arthur; engraver designer; *b* 6 Jan. 1946; *s* of James William and Marjory Appleby. *Educ:* Haws Down County Secondary Modern School for Boys; Beckenham Sch. of Art; Ravensbourne Coll. of Art and Design; Central Sch. of Arts and Crafts; Sir John Cass Sch. of Art; Royal Coll. of Art. Set up trade, 1968; bought Crathes station, 1970; developed fresh approaches to engraving on silver, forging after engraving; works designed and executed include: engraving on Prince of Wales coronet; model of moon (subseq. gift to first moon astronauts); steel and gold cylinder box for Goldsmiths' Co.; steel, gold, ivory and silver chess set, 1977; 500th anniv. silver for London Assay Office; King George VI Diamond Stakes trophy, 1978; seal for the Board of Trustees, V & A; silver condiment set for 10 Downing Street, commnd by Silver Trust; major silver commn for Royal Mus. of Scotland; sporting guns, silver bowls, jewels, prints. Work in collections: Aberdeen Art Gallery; Royal Scottish Museum; Scottish Craft Collection; East Midlands Arts; British Museum; Goldsmiths' Co., V&A; Crafts Council; Contemporary Arts Soc.; Tower of London Royal Armouries; Nat. Mus. of Finland; Åland Maritime Mus.; S Australia Maritime Mus.; one-man show, Liberty, 1994. Founder, British Art Postage Stamp Soc., 1986; Mem., British Art Medal Soc., 1987–. Chm., Crathes Drumoak Community Council, 1981. Life Member: NT for Scotland, 1971; SPAB, 1989. Liveryman, Goldsmiths' Co. *Recreations:* work, walking, looking at garden, drinking herbal tea with friends, acting in pantomime, cat (Fluffeena Purbright), conservation matters, supporter of NE Mountain Trust, breeding silver spangled Hamburg bantam hens. *Address:* Crathes Station, Banchory, Kincardineshire AB31 3JN. *T:* Crathes (0133044) 642. *Club:* Banchory Golf (non-playing mem.).

APPLEBY, Dom Raphael; National Chaplain to Catholic Students' Council, 1974–94; *b* 18 July 1931; *s* of Harold Thompson Appleby and Margaret Morgan. *Educ:* Downside; Christ's Coll., Cambridge (MA). Downside novitiate, 1951. Housemaster at Downside, 1962–75, Head Master, 1975–80; Nat. Co-ordinator for RC Chaplains in Higher Educn, 1980–87. Diocesan Youth Chaplain, Clifton Dio., 1983–89. *Publications:* Dear Church, What's the Point?, 1984; Glimpses of God, 1993. *Recreations:* books, music. *Address:* Downside Abbey, Bath BA3 4RH.

APPLEBY, Rt. Rev. Richard Franklin; *see* Northern Territory (Australia), Bishop of the.

APPLEBY, Robert, CBE 1969; Chairman, Black & Decker Ltd, 1956–75 (Managing Director, 1956–72); *b* 1913; *s* of Robert James Appleby; *m* 1957, Elisabeth Friederike (*d* 1975), *d* of Prof. Eidmann. *Educ:* Graham Sea Training and Engineering Sch., Scarborough. Dep. Chm., Black & Decker Manufacturing Co., Maryland, 1968–72. Mem., Post Office Bd, 1972–73. CEng, FIEE; CIMgt.

APPLETON, John Fortnam; His Honour Judge Appleton; a Circuit Judge, since 1992; *b* 8 April 1946; *s* of George Fortnam Appleton, OBE, TD, JP, DL and Patricia Margaret Appleton; *m* 1983, Maureen Sellers; one *s*. *Educ:* Harrow; Bristol Univ. (LLB Hons). Called to the Bar, Middle Temple, 1969; a Recorder of the Crown Court, 1985. *Recreations:* salmon fishing, shooting, gardening. *Address:* The Old Vicarage, Abbeystead, Lancaster LA2 9BG. *T:* Lancaster (01524) 791727.

APPLETON, Brig. John Roper; Executive Secretary, Royal Academy of Engineering, since 1993; *b* 29 April 1938; *s* of John Jackson Appleton and Ada Mary Appleton (*née* Roper); *m* 1st, 1959, Jenifer Jane Worman; one *s* one *d*; 2nd, 1978, Elizabeth Ann Cullen; two *d*. *Educ:* Liverpool Collegiate Sch.; Alun Grammar Sch., Mold; RMA Sandhurst; RMC Shrivenham. BScEng, CEng, FIMechE. Commnd REME, 1958; regtl and staff appts in UK, BAOR, Cyprus, Canada, 1961–78; MoD, 1978–79; Comdr REME, 1st Armd Div., BAOR, 1979–82; British Liaison Officer, HQ US Army, Pentagon, 1982–83; MoD, 1983–84; Asst Dir, Defence Commitments Staff, MoD, 1984–87, retired 1987. Fellowship of Engineering: Head of Engineering Affairs, 1987; Head of Corporate Affairs, 1991. *Recreations:* gardening, garden construction. *Address:* Royal Academy of Engineering, 29 Great Peter Street, SW1P 3LW. *T:* 0171–222 2688. *Club:* Army and Navy.

APPLEYARD, Joan Ena, (Lady Appleyard); Headmistress, St Swithun's School, Winchester, 1986–94; *b* 15 Aug. 1946; *d* of William Jefferson and Ruth Ena Leake; *m* 1994, Sir Leonard Appleyard, *qv*. *Educ:* Univ. of Newcastle (BA Hons History); Westminster Coll., Oxford (Dip Ed). Asst Mistress, 1968–70, Head of History, 1970–73, Scarborough Girls' High Sch.; Head of Humanities, Graham Sch., Scarborough, 1973–75; Dep. Head, 1975–79, Headmistress, 1979–86, Hunmanby Hall Sch., Filey. Pres., GSA, 1992–93. *Recreations:* drama, theatre, reading, cooking, photography. *Address:* Vine Cottage, Old Vicarage Lane, King's Somborne, Hants SO20 6PZ. *T:* Romsey (01794) 388224.

APPLEYARD, Sir Leonard (Vincent), KCMG 1994 (CMG 1986); HM Diplomatic Service; Ambassador to People's Republic of China, since 1994; *b* 2 Sept. 1938; *s* of Thomas William Appleyard; *m* 1964, Elizabeth Margaret West (marr. diss. 1994); two *d*; *m* 1994, Joan Ena Jefferson (*see* J. E. Appleyard). *Educ:* Read School, Drax, W Yorks; Queens' Coll., Cambridge (MA). Foreign Office, 1962; Third Secretary, Hong Kong, 1964; Second Secretary, Peking, 1966; Second, later First, Secretary, Foreign Office, 1969; First Secretary, Delhi, 1971, Moscow, 1975; HM Treasury, 1978; Financial Counsellor, Paris, 1979–82; Head of Economic Relations Dept, FCO, 1982–84; Principal Private Sec. to Sec. of State for Foreign and Commonwealth Affairs, 1984–86; Ambassador to Hungary, 1986–89; Dep. Sec., Cabinet Office, 1989–91 (on secondment); Political Dir and Dep. Under-Sec. of State, FCO, 1991–94. *Recreations:* music, reading, tennis. *Address:* c/o Foreign and Commonwealth Office, SW1A 2AH. *Club:* Brooks's.

APPLEYARD, Sir Raymond (Kenelm), KBE 1986; PhD; Director-General for Information Market and Innovation, Commission of the European Communities, 1981–86; *b* 5 Oct. 1922; *s* of late Maj.-Gen. K. C. Appleyard, CBE, TD, DL, and Monica Mary Louis; *m* 1947, Joan Greenwood; one *s* two *d*. *Educ:* Rugby; Cambridge. BA 1943, MA 1948, PhD 1950. Instructor, Yale Univ., 1949–51; Fellow, Rockefeller Foundn, California Inst. of Technology, 1951–53; Research Officer, Atomic Energy of Canada Ltd, 1953–56; Sec., UN Scientific Cttee on effects of atomic radiation, 1956–61; Dir, Biology Services, Commn of European Atomic Energy Community, 1961–73; Dir-Gen. for Scientific and Tech. Information and Information Management, EEC Commn, 1973–80. Exec. Sec., European Molecular Biology Organisation, 1965–73; Sec., European Molecular Biology Conf., 1969–73; President: Inst. of Information Scientists, 1981–82; Inst. of Translation and Interpreting, 1989–. Hon. Dr.med Ulm, 1977. *Publications:* contribs to: Nature, Jl Gen. Microbiol., Genetics. *Recreations:* bridge, tennis. *Clubs:* Athenæum; Fondation Universitaire (Brussels).

APPLEYARD, Dr William James, FRCP; Consultant Paediatrician, since 1971, and Clinical Director, Paediatric Directorate, since 1992, Kent and Canterbury Hospitals NHS Trust (formerly Canterbury and Thanet Health District); *b* 25 Oct. 1935; *s* of late E. R. Appleyard and Maud Oliver Collingwood (*née* Marshall); *m* 1964, Elizabeth Anne Ward; one *s* two *d*. *Educ:* Canford Sch.; Exeter College, Oxford (BM BCh, MA); Guy 's Hosp. Med. Sch., Univ. of London. DObstRCOG; FRCP 1978. Junior paediat. posts, Guy's and Gt Ormond St; Resident in Pediat., Univ. of Louisville, 1964–65; Dyers' Co. Res. Registrar, St Thomas' Hosp., 1968–69. Treasurer, BPA, 1983–88; Mem., GMC, 1984– (Mem., Educn Cttee, 1993–); Member Council: RCP, 1988–91 (Member: Standing Cttee, 1970–72; Res. Cttee, 1971–74; Paed. Cttee, 1987–91; Examng Bd, 1992–); BMA, 1973– (Mem., Jt Consultants Cttee, 1976–95; Dep. Chm., Consultants Cttee, 1979–83; Dep. Chm., 1989–91, Chm., 1992–95, Repr. Body); World Med. Assoc., 1995–; Member: Health Service Inf. Steering Gp, Korner Cttee, 1985; DoH Inf. Adv. Gp, 1986–90; London Univ. Nominee, Kent AHA, 1974–78. Hon. Tutor in Paed., Guy's Hosp.; Hon. Lectr in Paed., St Thomas' Hosp.; Dean of Clin. Studies, (UK), St George's Univ. Sch. of Medicine, Grenada, 1995– (Associate Prof., 1985–90; Prof. of Paediatrics, 1991–95; Chm., Senate, 1991–93). Patron, Dyspraxia Trust, 1988–. Liveryman, Apothecaries' Soc., 1983. Alumnus Award for Paed. Res., Univ. of Louisville, 1965. *Publications:* contribs to med. jls. *Recreations:* lawn tennis, photography, erstwhile allotment digger. *Address:* 20 St Stephen's Road, Canterbury, Kent CT2 7HT. *T:* Canterbury (01227) 781771. *Clubs:* Athenæum, Penn.

ap REES, Prof. Thomas; Professor of Botany and Head of Department of Plant Sciences, since 1991 and Fellow of Gonville and Caius College, Cambridge; *b* 19 Oct. 1930; *s* of Elfan Rees and Frances Rees (*née* Boston); *m* 1955, Wendy Ruth, *d* of late Reginald Holroyde and Marjorie Holroyde; three *s*. *Educ:* Llandovery Coll., Dyfed; Lincoln Coll., Oxford (BA 1955; MA, DPhil 1958); ScD Cantab 1983. Nat. service, commnd Royal Signals, 1949–51. Lectr in Mycology, Univ. of Sydney, 1959–61; res. officer and sen. res. officer, CSIRO, 1961–64; University of Cambridge: Lectr in Botany, 1964–91; Reader in Plant Biochem., 1991; Gonville and Caius College: Fellow, 1965–91, Professorial Fellow, 1991–; College Lectr, 1965–91; Dir of Studies in Biol Scis, 1986–91. Science and Engineering Research Council: Mem., Plant Sci. and Microbiol. Cttee, 1982–87 (Chm., 1985–87); Mem., Biol Scis Cttee, 1984–87. Trustee, Llandovery Coll., 1966–. *Publications:* (jtly) Plant Biochemistry, 1964; sci. papers in learned jls. *Recreations:* mountaineering, gardening. *Address:* Department of Plant Sciences, Downing Site, Downing Street, Cambridge CB2 3EA. *T:* Cambridge (01223) 333900; The Elms, High Street, Little Eversden, Cambridge CB3 7HE.

ap ROBERT, His Honour Hywel Wyn Jones; a Circuit Judge, 1975–94 (Judge of Cardiff County Court, 1993–94); *b* 19 Nov. 1923; *s* of Rev. Robert John Jones, BA, BD and Mrs Jones (*née* Evans); *m* 1956, Elizabeth Davies; two *d*. *Educ:* Cardiff High Sch.; Corpus Christi Coll., Oxford (MA). War Service, FO and Intell. Corps. 1942–46, in Britain and India. Called to Bar, Middle Temple, 1950. A Recorder of the Crown Court, 1972–75; Stipendiary Magistrate, Cardiff, later S Glamorgan, 1972–75. Contested (Plaid Cymru) Cardiganshire, 1970. Hon. Mem., Gorsedd of Bards, 1973. *Recreations:* Welsh literature, classical and modern languages. *Address:* Cefn Bryn, 56 Plymouth Road, Penarth, S Glam CF6 2DJ. *Club:* Cardiff and County (Cardiff).

APSLEY, Lord; Allen Christopher Bertram Bathurst; *b* 11 March 1961; *s* and *heir* of 8th Earl Bathurst, *qv*; *m* 1986, Hilary, *d* of John F. George, Weston Lodge Albury, Guildford; one *s* one *d*. *Heir:* *s* Hon. Benjamin George Henry Bathurst, *b* 6 March 1990. *Address:* Cirencester Park, Cirencester, Glos GL7 2BT.

APTHORP, John Dorrington; Chairman: Wizard Wine, Borehamwood, since 1989; Majestic Wine Warehouses, since 1992; *b* 25 April 1935; *s* of late Eric and Mildred Apthorp; *m* 1959, Jane Frances Arnold; three *s* one *d*. *Educ:* Aldenham School. FBIM 1977; FInstD 1978; FIGD 1981. Sub-Lieut RNVR, 1953–55. Family business, Appypak, 1956–68; started Bejam Group, 1968, Exec. Chm., 1968–87, non-exec. Chm., 1987–88. Guardian Young Business Man of Year, 1974. Councillor, London Bor. of Barnet, 1968–74. Liveryman, Butchers' Company, 1974–. Commandeur d'Honneur pour Commanderie du Bontemps de Medoc et des Graves, 1977. *Recreations:* shooting, wine. *Address:* The Field House, Newlands Avenue, Radlett, Herts WD7 8EL. *T:* Radlett (01923) 855201. *Clubs:* St Hubert's, Radlett Tennis and Squash (Pres., 1982–).

AQUILECCHIA, Prof. Giovanni; Professor of Italian, University of London, 1970–89, now Emeritus (Bedford College, 1970–85; Royal Holloway and Bedford New College, 1985–89); Hon. Research Fellow, University College London, since 1984; *b* Nettuno, Rome, 28 Nov. 1923; *s* of late Gen. Vincenzo Aquilecchia and Maria L. Filibeck; *m* 1st, 1951, Costantina M. Bacchetta (marr. diss. 1973); two *s* one *d*; 2nd, 1992, Catherine M. Posford. *Educ:* Liceo T. Tasso, Rome; Univ. of Rome. Dott. Lett., 1946, Diploma of Perfezionamento in Filologia Moderna, 1948, Univ. of Rome. Asst in Italian, Univ. of Rome, 1946–49; Boursier du Gouvernement Français at Collège de France, Univ. of Paris, 1949–50; British Council Scholar, Warburg Inst., Univ. of London, 1950–51; Asst, Dept of Italian Studies, Univ. of Manchester, 1951–53; Asst Lectr in Italian, University Coll., London, 1953–55, Lectr, 1955–59; Libero Docente di Letteratura Italiana, Univ. of Rome, 1958–; Reader in Italian, Univ. of London, at University Coll., 1959–61; Prof. of Italian Lang. and Lit., Univ. of Manchester, 1961–70. Corr. Fellow, Arcadia, 1961. Visiting Professor: Univ. of Melbourne, 1983; Univ. of Naples, 1990. MA (Manchester) 1965. *Publications:* Giordano Bruno, 1971; Schede di italianistica, 1976; Le opere italiane di Giordano Bruno: critica testuale e oltre, 1991; Il dilemma matematico di Bruno tra atomismo e infinitismo, 1992; Schede bruniane, 1993; Nuove schede di italianistica, 1994; critical editions of: Giordano Bruno: La Cena de le Ceneri, 1955, 2nd edn (trans. French) 1994; Due Dialoghi sconosciuti, 1957; Dialoghi Italiani, 1958, repr. 1972, 1985; Praelectiones geometricæ e Ars deformationum, 1964; De la causa, principio et uno, 1973; Candelaio, 1993; Cabala del cavallo pegaseo, 1994; De l'infinito, universo e mondi, 1995; Pietro Aretino: Sei Giornate, 1969, 2nd edn with Introduction, 1975, reprint 1980; Sonetti sopra i xvi modi, 1992; (co-editor) Poesie varie, 1992; Giovanni Villani: Cronica con le continuazioni di Matteo e Filippo, 1979; G. B. Della Porta: Metoposcopia, 1990; (co-editor) Collected essays on Italian Language and Literature, 1971; contrib.: Atti dell'Accad. Nazionale Lincei, Atti e Memorie dell'Arcadia, Bull. dell'Accad. della Crusca, Bull. John Rylands Library, Cultura Neolatina, Dizionario Biografico degli Italiani, Enciclopedia Dantesca, Encyclopædia Britannica, English Miscellany, Filologia e critica, Giornale critico della filosofia italiana, Giornale storico della letteratura italiana, Italian Studies, Letteratura italiana (Opere), Lingua Nostra, Quaderni veneti, Renaissance Studies, Storia della cultura veneta, Studi Secenteschi, Studi Tassiani, etc. *Address:* Department of Italian, University College, Gower Street, WC1E 6BT.

AQUINO, Maria Corazón Cojuangco, (Cory Aquino); President of the Philippines, 1986–92; *b* 25 Jan. 1933; *d* of late José and Demetria Cojuangco; *m* 1954, Benigno S. Aquino (*d* 1983); one *s* four *d*. *Educ:* St Scholastica's Coll. and Assumption Convent, Manila; Ravenhill Acad., Philadelphia; Notre Dame Sch., NY; Mount St Vincent Coll., NY (BA); Far Eastern Univ., Manila. Numerous honours, awards and hon. degrees from Philippine and overseas bodies. *Address:* 25 Times Street, Quezon City, Philippines.

ARAFAT, Yasser; President, Palestine National Authority; *b* 24 Aug. 1929; *m* 1991, Sulia Tawil; one *d*. *Educ:* Cairo Univ. Joined League of Palestinian Students, 1944, Mem. Exec. Cttee, 1950, Pres., 1952–56; formed jointly, Al Fatah, 1956; engineer in Egypt, 1956, in Kuwait, 1957–65; Pres., Exec. Cttee, Palestine Nat. Liberation Movt, and Chm., Exec. Cttee, Palestine Liberation Orgn, 1968–; Pres., Central Cttee and Head, Political Dept, PLO, 1973–; Comdr Palestinian Revolutionary Forces; signed Declaration of Principles on Interim Self-Government, 1993, with Yitzhak Rabin. Joliot-Curie Gold Medal, 1975; Nobel Peace Prize, 1994. *Address:* c/o Palestine National Authority, Jericho Area, West Bank.

ARAI, Ikuo; Managing Director, Sumitomo Corporation, Japan, since 1990; *b* 27 Jan. 1934; *s* of Gentaro Arai and Iku Arai; *m* Keiko Hayashi; two *d*. *Educ:* Kyoto Univ. Joined Sumitomo Corp., 1957; Chief Rep., Cairo Office, 1965; Asst Manager, Import & Export Section, Oil Country Tubular Goods, Iron & Steel Div. (to Manager), 1969; Asst Gen. Manager, Crude Oil Dept, Petroleum & Carbon Div. (to Gen. Manager), 1972; Dir and Gen. Manager, Petroleum & Carbon Div., 1986; Dir Gen. Manager for Europe and Man. Dir UK, 1989. *Recreations:* music, reading, golf. *Address:* Sumitomo Corporation, 2–2 Hitotsubashi 1–chome, Chiyoda–ku, Tokyo 100, Japan.

ARAIN, Shafiq; Ugandan politician and diplomat; *b* 20 Nov. 1933; *s* of late Din Mohd Arain; *m* 1966, Maria Leana Godinho; one *s* two *d*. *Educ:* Government Sch., Kampala; Regent's Polytechnic, London; Nottingham Univ. MP (UPC), 1962–71; Member, E African Legislative Assembly, 1963–71; E African Minister for Common Market and Economic Affairs, later E African Minister for Communications, Research and Social Services; Chairman: Minimum Wages Commission, 1964; Statutory Commn on Cooperative Movement, 1967. Uganda's Delegate to UN General Assembly, 1965–66; Leader, Uganda Delegn to Canada and CPA Conf., Trinidad and Tobago, 1969. Member, Governing Council, Univ. of Dar es Salaam, 1967–68; Chm., Commonwealth Parly Assoc., Uganda Br., 1969–70. Pres., Uganda Cricket Assoc., 1968–69. Left for exile in London following coup in 1971; returned to Uganda, 1979; elections were held in Dec. 1980; Minister without Portfolio, President's Office, and High Comr for Uganda to London, 1980–85. Dir, Equatorial Bank, 1989–94. *Recreations:* golf, walking, reading. *Address:* 30 Roland Way, SW7 3RE. *T:* 0171–835 1277. *Clubs:* Uganda, Commonwealth Trust, Mark's.

ARBER, Prof. Werner; Professor of Molecular Microbiology, Basle University, since 1971. Discovered restriction enzymes at Geneva in 1960's; Nobel Prize in Physiology or Medicine (jointly), 1978. *Address:* Department of Microbiology, Biozentrum der Universität Basel, 70 Klingelbergstrasse, 4056 Basel, Switzerland.

ARBUTHNOT, Andrew Robert Coghill; Missioner, London Healing Mission, since 1983; Director, Sun Alliance and London Insurance Ltd, 1970–91; *b* 14 Jan. 1926; *s* of Robert Wemyss Muir Arbuthnot and Mary Arbuthnot (*née* Coghill); *m* 1952, Audrey Dutton-Barker; one *s* one *d*. *Educ:* Eton. Served 1944–47, Captain, Scots Guards, wounded. Dir, Arbuthnot Latham & Co. Ltd, 1953–82; Chm. and Chief Exec., Arbuthnot Latham Holdings, 1974–81; Chm., Arbuthnot Insurance Services, 1968–83. Contested (C) Houghton-le-Spring, 1959. Ordained Deacon, 1974; Priest, 1975. *Publications:* (with Audrey Arbuthnot) Love that Heals, 1986; Christian Prayer and Healing, 1989; All You Need is More and More of Jesus, 1993. *Recreations:* water colour painting, walking. *Address:* Monksfield House, Tilford, Farnham, Surrey GU10 2AL. *T:* Farnham (01252) 782233.

ARBUTHNOT, James Norwich; MP (C) Wanstead and Woodford, since 1987; Minister of State for Defence Procurement, Ministry of Defence, since 1995; *b* 4 Aug. 1952; 2nd *s* of Sir John Arbuthnot, 1st Bt, MBE, TD and of Margaret Jean, *yr d* of late Alexander G. Duff; *heir pres.* of Sir William Arbuthnot, Bt, *qv*; *m* 1984, Emma Louise Broadbent; one *s* two *d*. *Educ:* Wellesley House, Broadstairs; Eton Coll. (Captain of School); Trinity Coll., Cambridge. MA. Called to the Bar, 1975. Practising barrister, 1977–92. Councillor, Royal Bor. of Kensington and Chelsea, 1978–87. Contested (C) Cynon Valley, 1983, May 1984. PPS to Minister of State for Armed Forces, 1988–90, to Sec. of State, DTI, 1990–92; an Asst Govt Whip, 1992–94; Parly Under-Sec. of State, DSS, 1994–95. Pres., Cynon Valley Cons. Assoc., 1983–92. *Recreations:* playing guitar, ski-ing, computers. *Address:* House of Commons, SW1A 0AA. *T:* 0171–219 3000.

ARBUTHNOT, Sir Keith Robert Charles, 8th Bt *cr* 1823, of Edinburgh; *b* 23 Sept. 1951; *s* of Sir Hugh Fitz-Gerald Arbuthnot, 7th Bt and Elizabeth Kathleen (*d* 1972), *d* of late Sqdn-Ldr G. G. A. Williams; *S* father, 1983; *m* 1982, Anne, *yr d* of late Brig. Peter Moore; two *s* one *d*. *Educ:* Wellington; Univ. of Edinburgh. BSc (Soc. Sci.). *Heir:* *s* Robert Hugh Peter Arbuthnot, *b* 2 March 1986. *Address:* Whitebridge, Peebles, Peeblesshire EH45 9HS.

ARBUTHNOT, Sir William (Reierson), 2nd Bt *cr* 1964, of Kittybrewster, Aberdeen; *b* 2 Sept. 1950; *s* of Sir John Sinclair-Wemyss Arbuthnot, 1st Bt, MBE, TD, sometime MP (C) Dover Div. of Kent, and of (Margaret) Jean, *yr d* of late Alexander Gordon Duff; *S* father, 1992. *Educ:* Eton; Coll. of Law, London. Arbuthnot Latham Holdings, 1970–76; Joynson-Hicks & Co., solicitors, 1978–81. Member of Lloyd's. Vice Chm., High Premium Gp. Liveryman, Grocers' Co., 1981. *Recreation:* genealogy. *Heir:* *b* James Norwich Arbuthnot, *qv*. *Address:* 14 Ashburn Gardens, SW7 4DG. *T:* 0171–370 4907.

ARBUTHNOTT, family name of **Viscount of Arbuthnott.**

ARBUTHNOTT, 16th Viscount of, *cr* 1641; **John Campbell Arbuthnott,** CBE 1986; DSC 1945; FRSE 1984; Lord-Lieutenant Grampian Region (Kincardineshire), since 1977; Lord High Commissioner to General Assembly, Church of Scotland, 1986, 1987; Director, British Petroleum Scottish Advisory Board, since 1990; *b* 26 Oct. 1924; *e s* of 15th Viscount of Arbuthnott, CB, CBE, DSO, MC, and Ursula Collingwood (*d* 1989); *S* father, 1966; *m* 1949, Mary Elizabeth Darley (*née* Oxley); one *s* one *d*. *Educ:* Fettes Coll.; Gonville and Caius Coll., Cambridge. Served RNVR (Fleet Air Arm), 1942–46; Near and Far East, British Pacific Fleet, 1945. Cambridge University, 1946–49 (Estate Management), MA 1967. Chartered Surveyor and Land Agent; Agricultural Land Service, 1949–55; Land Agent (Scotland), The Nature Conservancy, 1955–67. Chm., Aberdeen and Northern Marts, 1986–91 (Dir, 1973–91); Director: Scottish Widows' Fund and Life Assurance Soc., 1978–94 (Dep. Chm., 1982–84, 1987–88; Chm., 1984–87); Clydesdale Bank, 1985–92 (Northern Area, 1975–85); Britoil, 1988–90. Member: Countryside Commn for Scotland, 1967–71; Aberdeen Univ. Court, 1978–84; Royal Commn on Historical MSS, 1987–94; Chm., Red Deer Commn, 1969–75; President: British Assoc. for Shooting and Conservation (formerly Wildfowlers Assoc. of GB and Ireland), 1973–92; The Scottish Landowners' Fedn, 1974–79 (Convener, 1971–74); Royal Zool Soc. of Scotland, 1976–; Scottish Agricl Orgn Soc., 1980–83; RSGS, 1983–87; Fedn of Agricl Co-operatives (UK) Ltd, 1983–87; Dep. Chm., Nature Conservancy Council, 1980–85, Chm., Adv. Cttee for Scotland, 1980–85. FRSA. GCStJ 1994; Prior of Scotland, OStJ, 1983. *Recreations:* countryside activities, historical research. *Heir:* *s* Master of Arbuthnott, *qv*. *Address:* Arbuthnott House, by Laurencekirk, Kincardineshire, Scotland AB30 1PA. *T:* Inverbervie (01561) 361226. *Clubs:* Army and Navy; New (Edinburgh).

ARBUTHNOTT, Master of; Hon. John Keith Oxley Arbuthnott; *b* 18 July 1950; *s* and *heir* of 16th Viscount of Arbuthnott, *qv*; *m* 1974, Jill Mary, *er d* of Captain Colin Farquharson, *qv*; one *s* two *d*. *Educ:* Fettes College; Aberdeen Univ. *Address:* Kilternan, Arbuthnott, Laurencekirk, Kincardineshire AB30 1NA. *T:* Inverbervie (01561) 61203.

ARBUTHNOTT, Hugh James, CMG 1984; HM Diplomatic Service; Ambassador to Denmark, since 1993; *b* 27 Dec. 1936; *m*; two *s* (and one *s* decd). *Educ:* Ampleforth Coll., Yorks; New Coll., Oxford. Nat. Service, Black Watch, 1955–57. Joined Foreign (subseq. Diplomatic) Service, 1960; 3rd Sec., Tehran, 1962–64; 2nd, later 1st Sec., FO, 1964–66; Private Sec., Minister of State for Foreign Affairs, 1966–68; Lagos, 1968–71; 1st Sec. (Head of Chancery), Tehran, 1971–74; Asst, later Head of European Integration Dept (External), FCO, 1974–77; Counsellor (Agric. and Econ.), Paris, 1978–80; Head of Chancery, Paris, 1980–83; Under Sec., Internat. Div., ODA, 1983–85; Ambassador to Romania, 1986–89, to Portugal, 1989–93. *Publication:* Common Man's Guide to the Common Market (ed with G. Edwards), 1979, 2nd edn (co-author with G. Edwards), 1989. *Address:* c/o Foreign and Commonwealth Office, SW1A 2AH.

ARBUTHNOTT, Prof. John Peebles, PhD, ScD; FIBiol; FRSE; Principal and Vice Chancellor, University of Strathclyde, since 1991; *b* 8 April 1939; *s* of James Anderson Arbuthnott and Jean (*née* Kelly); *m* 1962, Elinor Rutherford Smillie; one *s* two *d*. *Educ:* Univ. of Glasgow (BSc 1960; PhD 1964); Trinity Coll., Dublin (ScD 1984). FIBiol 1988; FRSE 1993; FIIB 1993. University of Glasgow: Lectr, Dept of Bacteriology, 1963–67; Alan Johnston, Lawrence and Moseley Res. Fellow of Royal Soc., 1968–72; Sen. Lectr, Dept of Microbiol., 1972–73; Sen. Lectr, Dept of Bacteriol., 1973–75; Professor of Microbiology: TCD, 1976–88 (Bursar, 1983–86); Univ. of Nottingham, 1988–91. Vis. Lectr, Dept of Microbiol., New York Univ. Med. Centre, 1966–67. Mem. Bd, PHLS, 1991–. Chm., Jt Inf. Systems Cttee, HEFC, 1994–; Convenor, Cttee of Scottish Higher Educn Principals, 1994–. Treasurer, Soc. for Gen. Microbiol., 1987–92. MRIA 1985; FRSA 1989. *Publications:* edited: (jtly) Isoelectric Focusing, 1975; (jtly) The Determinants of Bacterial and Viral Pathogencity, 1983; (jtly) Foodborne Illness: a Lancet review, 1991; more than 100 in prestigious scientific learned jls and books. *Recreations:* Scottish country dancing, golf, attending soccer matches. *Address:* University of Strathclyde, Glasgow G1 1XQ. *T:* 0141–552 4400.

ARBUTHNOTT, Robert, CBE 1991; Minister (Cultural Affairs), India, British Council, 1988–93; *b* 28 Sept. 1936; *s* of late Archibald Arbuthnott, MBE, ED, and Barbara Joan (*née* Worters); *m* 1962, Sophie Robina (*née* Axford); one *s* two *d*. *Educ:* Sedbergh Sch. (scholar); Emmanuel Coll., Cambridge (exhibnr; BA Mod Langs, MA). Nat. service, 1955–57 (2nd Lieut The Black Watch RHR). British Council, 1960–94: Karachi, 1960–62; Lahore, 1962–64; London, 1964–67; Representative, Nepal, 1967–72; London Inst. of Education, 1972–73; Representative, Malaysia, 1973–76; Director, Educational Contracts Dept, 1976–77; Controller, Personnel and Staff Recruitment Div., 1978–81; Representative, Germany, 1981–85; RCDS, 1986; Controller, America, Pacific and S Asia Div., 1987. *Recreations:* music-making, the arts, historic buildings, sport. *Club:* United Oxford & Cambridge University.

ARCAYA, Ignacio; Ambassador of Venezuela to the Court of St James's, since 1992; non-resident Ambassador to Ireland, since 1994; *b* 3 June 1939; *s* of Ignacio Luis Arcaya and Antonieta Smith; *m* 1966, Lydia Vincenti; one *s* one *d*. *Educ:* Central Univ. of Venezuela (Internat. Affairs, 1964; Law, 1968). Officer, Dept of Trade, Min. for Foreign Affairs, Venezuela, 1964–66; Third Sec., Perm. Mission of Venezuela in Geneva, 1966–68; Second Sec., Min. for Foreign Affairs, 1968–69; First Sec., Mission to OAS, Washington, 1969–72; Counsellor, Inst. of Foreign Trade, Min. for Foreign Affairs, 1972–75; Minister Counsellor of Econ. Affairs, Paris, 1975–78; Ambassador to Australia and non-resident Ambassador to NZ, Fiji and Philippines, 1978–84; Sec. Gen., Assoc. of Iron Ore Exporting Countries, 1984–88; Ambassador-at-large, Min. of Foreign Affairs, 1988; Ambassador to Chile, 1989–92. Order of Liberator (Venezuela), 1992; numerous foreign orders. *Recreations:* computers, cigars, polo, golf, tennis, ski-ing. *Address:* Venezuelan Embassy, 1 Cromwell Road, SW7 2HW. *T:* 0171–584 5375; 25 Melbury Road, W14 8AB. *T:* 0171–602 3234. *Clubs:* Garrick, Travellers'; Caracas Country; Cowdray Park Polo, Ham Polo; Royal & Ancient Golf; Sunningdale, Coombe Hill.

ARCHDALE, Sir Edward (Folmer), 3rd Bt, *cr* 1928; DSC 1943; Captain, RN, retired; *b* 8 Sept. 1921; *s* of Vice-Adm. Sir Nicholas Edward Archdale, 2nd Bt, CBE, and Gerda (*d* 1969), 2nd *d* of late F. C. Sievers, Copenhagen; *S* father 1955; *m* 1954, Elizabeth Ann Stewart (marr. diss. 1978), *d* of late Maj.-Gen. Wilfrid Boyd Fellowes Lukis, CBE; one *s* two *d*. *Educ:* Royal Naval Coll., Dartmouth. Joined Royal Navy, 1935; served War of 1939–45 (despatches, DSC). *Recreation:* civilization. *Heir:* *s* Nicholas Edward Archdale, *b* 2 Dec. 1965. *Address:* 46 Coleshill Park, Enniskillen, Co. Fermanagh BT74 7LD.

ARCHER, family name of **Barons Archer of Sandwell** and **Archer of Weston-super-Mare.**

ARCHER OF SANDWELL, Baron *cr* 1992 (Life Peer), of Sandwell in the County of West Midlands; **Peter Kingsley Archer,** PC 1977; QC 1971; a Recorder of the Crown Court, since 1982; *b* 20 Nov. 1926; *s* of Cyril Kingsley Archer and May (*née* Baker); *m* 1954, Margaret Irene (*née* Smith); one *s*. *Educ:* Wednesday Boys' High Sch.; LSE; University Coll., London (Fellow 1978). Called to Bar, Gray's Inn, 1952; Bencher, 1974; commenced practice, 1953. MP (Lab) Rowley Regis and Tipton, 1966–74, Warley West, 1974–92. PPS to Attorney-Gen., 1967–70; Solicitor General, 1974–79; chief Opposition spokesman on legal affairs, 1979–82, on trade, 1982–83, on N Ireland, 1983–87. UK Deleg. to UN Gen. Assembly (Third Cttee), 1969. Chm., Council on Tribunals, 1992–. Chm., Amnesty International (British Section), 1971–74; Chm., Parly gp for World Govt, 1970–74; Chm., Soc. of Labour Lawyers, 1971–74, 1979–93; Vice-Chm., Anti-Slavery Soc., 1970–74; Mem., Exec. Cttee, Fabian Soc., 1974–86 (Chm., 1980–81; Pres., 1993–). Ombudsman for Mirror Group Newspapers, 1989–90. Pres., World Disarmament Assoc., 1993–. Pres., Methodist Homes for the Aged, 1992–. *Publications:* the Queen's Courts, 1956; ed Social Welfare and the Citizen, 1957; Communism and the Law, 1963; (with Lord Reay) Freedom at Stake, 1966; Human Rights, 1969; (jtly) Purpose in Socialism, 1973; The Role of the Law Officers, 1978; contributions to: Trends in Social Welfare, 1965; Atkin's, Court Forms, 1965; The International Protection of Human Rights, 1967; Renewal, 1983; Fabian Centenary Essays, 1984; (ed) More Law Reform Now, 1984. *Recreations:* music, writing, talking. *Address:* House of Lords, SW1A 0PW.

ARCHER OF WESTON-SUPER-MARE, Baron *cr* 1992 (Life Peer), of Mark in the County of Somerset; **Jeffrey Howard Archer;** politician and author; *b* 15 April 1940; *s* of William Archer and Lola Archer (*née* Cook); *m* 1966, Mary Weeden (*see* M. D. Archer); two *s*. *Educ:* by my wife since leaving Wellington Sch., Somerset; Brasenose Coll., Oxford. Athletics Blues, 1963–65, Gymnastics Blue, 1963, Pres. OUAC 1965; ran for Great Britain (never fast enough); Oxford 100 yards record (9.6 sec.), 1966. Mem. GLC for Havering, 1966–70; MP (C) Louth, Dec. 1969–Sept. 1974. Dep. Chm., Cons. Party, 1985–86. Trustee, RWS, 1989–. Pres., Somerset AAA, 1973; Hon. Pres., Glasgow Univ. Dialectic Soc., 1984–. Chm., Simple Truth Campaign (raised fifty-seven million pounds for Kurdish Relief), 1991. FRSA 1973. *Plays:* Beyond Reasonable Doubt, Queen's, 1987; Exclusive, Queen's, 1990. *Publications:* Not a Penny More, Not a Penny Less, 1975 (televised, 1990); Shall We Tell the President?, 1977; Kane and Abel, 1979 (televised, 1986); A Quiver Full of Arrows (short stories), 1980; The Prodigal Daughter, 1982; First Among Equals, 1984 (televised, 1986); A Matter of Honour, 1986; A Twist in the Tale (short stories), 1988; As the Crow Flies, 1991; Honour Among Thieves, 1993; Twelve Red Herrings (short stories), 1994; The Proprietors, 1996. *Recreations:* theatre, watching Somerset play cricket (represented Somerset CCC in benefit match, 1981; Pres., Somerset Wyverns, 1983), amateur auctioneer. *Address:* Alembic House, 93 Albert Embankment, SE1 7TY; The Old Vicarage, Grantchester CB3 9ND. *Clubs:* MCC; Louth Working Men's.

ARCHER OF WESTON-SUPER-MARE, Lady; *see* Archer, M. D.

ARCHER, Albert, MBE 1980; Member, Royal Commission on Environmental Pollution, 1981–85; *b* 7 March 1915; *s* of Arthur Archer and Margaret Alice Norris; *m* 1st, 1939; two *s*; 2nd, 1975, Peggy, *widow* of John F. Marsh; two step *s*. *Educ:* Manchester Grammar Sch.; Manchester Coll. of Technology. Fellow, Instn of Environmental Health Officers, 1961. Chief Public Health Inspector, Bor. of Halesowen, 1943–73; City of Birmingham: Environmtl Protection Officer, 1973–75; Dep. City Environmtl Officer, 1975–76; City Environmtl Officer, 1976–80. Mem., govt working parties on air pollution. Pres., Inst. of Environmental Health Officers, 1979–83. *Publications:* articles on air pollution in technical jls. *Recreation:* watching cricket. *Address:* 8 Portland Drive, Stourbridge, West Midlands DY9 0SD. *T:* Hagley (01562) 883366.

ARCHER, Gen. Sir (Arthur) John, KCB 1976; OBE 1964 (MBE 1959); Chief Executive, Royal Hong Kong Jockey Club, 1980–86, retired; *b* 12 Feb. 1924; *s* of Alfred and Mildred Archer, Fakenham; *m* 1950, Cynthia Marie, *d* of Col Alexander and Eileen Allan, Swallowcliffe, Wilts; two *s*. *Educ:* King's Sch., Peterborough; St Catharine's Coll., Cambridge. Entered Army, 1943; commnd 1944; regular commn Dorset Regt, 1946; psc 1956; jssc 1959; GSO1 3rd Div., 1963–65; CO 1 Devon and Dorset Regt, 1965–67; Comdr Land Forces Gulf, 1968–69; idc 1970; Dir of Public Relations (Army), 1970–72; Comdr 2nd Div., 1972–74; Dir of Army Staff Duties, 1974–76; Comdr British Forces Hong Kong, 1976–78 and Lt-Gen. Brigade of Gurkhas, 1977–78, C-in-C, UKLF, 1978–79. Col, Devonshire and Dorset Regt, 1977–79. Pres., Officers' Pension Soc., 1994–. *Recreations:* light aviation, gliding, sailing. *Address:* c/o Lloyds Bank, 38 Blue Boar Row, Salisbury, Wilts SP1 1DB. *Clubs:* Army and Navy; Royal Motor Yacht (Sandbanks, Dorset); Hong Kong, Royal Hong Kong Jockey (Hong Kong).

ARCHER, Bruce; *see* Archer, L. B.

ARCHER, Graham Robertson; HM Diplomatic Service; High Commissioner to Malta, since 1995; *b* 4 July 1939; *s* of late Henry Robertson Archer and Winifred Archer; *m* 1963, Pauline Cowan; two *d*. *Educ:* Judd School, Tonbridge. Joined Commonwealth Relations Office, 1962; British High Commission, New Delhi, 1964; Vice Consul, Kuwait, 1966; CRO (later FCO), 1967; Second Secretary (Commercial), Washington, 1970; First Secretary: FCO, 1972; Wellington, NZ, 1975; FCO, 1979; Counsellor: Pretoria, 1982; The Hague, 1986; FCO, 1990. *Recreations:* listening to music, gardening, hill walking. *Address:* c/o Foreign and Commonwealth Office, Whitehall, SW1A 2AH.

ARCHER, Mrs Jean Mary; Under-Secretary, Ministry of Agriculture, Fisheries and Food, 1973–86; *b* 24 Aug. 1932; *e d* of late Reginald R. and D. Jane Harvey, Braiseworth Hall, Tannington, Suffolk; *m* 1954, G. Michéal D. Archer, MB, BChir, FFARCS, *er s* of Maj.-Gen. G. T. L. Archer, CB; two *d*. *Educ:* Fleet House, Felixstowe; St Felix Sch., Southwold; Newnham Coll., Cambridge. MA Econs 1954. Asst Principal, Min. of Agriculture, 1954; Private Sec. to successive Perm. Secs, MAFF, 1956–59; Principal 1960; Sec., Reorganisation Commn for Eggs, 1967; Asst Sec. 1968; Under-Sec. i/c Food Policy Gp, MAFF, 1973; Under-Sec., Dept of Prices and Consumer Protection, 1974–76; returned to MAFF, as Under-Sec., Milk and Marketing Group, 1976; Under-Sec., Meat, Poultry and Eggs Div., 1980. *Recreations:* travel, music, tennis, watching sport, swimming administration (Team Man., Chelsea/Kensington Swimming Club; Hon. Sec., Swimmers' Parents' and Supporters' Assoc.). *Address:* Friary Cottage, Mendlesham, Suffolk. *T:* Stowmarket (01449) 766395. *Club:* Hurlingham.

See also Rt Hon. Sir A. J. D. McCowan.

ARCHER, Sir John; *see* Archer, Sir A. J.

ARCHER, John Francis Ashweek, QC 1975; a Recorder of the Crown Court since 1974; *b* 9 July 1925; *s* of late George Eric Archer, FRCSE, and late Frances Archer (*née* Ashweek); *m* 1960, Doris Mary Hennessey (*d* 1988). *Educ:* Winchester Coll., 1938–43; New Coll., Oxford, 1947–49 (BA 1949). Served War of 1939–45, 1944–47; Lieut RA, 1948. Called to Bar, Inner Temple, 1950, Bencher, 1984. Mem., Criminal Injuries Compensation Bd, 1987–. *Recreations:* motoring, bridge. *Address:* 7 King's Bench Walk, Temple, EC4.

ARCHER, John Norman; Managing Director, International Tanker Owners Pollution Federation Ltd, 1979–86; *b* 27 Feb. 1921; *s* of late Clifford Banks Archer and Grace Archer; *m* 1st, 1952, Gladys Joy (*née* Barnes) (*d* 1985); one step *d*; 2nd, 1986, Mrs Anne L. M. Appleby (*née* Padwick). *Educ:* Wandsworth School. Served with RA, 1939–46 (Major). Entered Civil Service, Board of Educn, 1937; Asst Principal 1947, Principal 1949, Min. of Educn; attended Admin. Staff Coll., Henley, 1960; Asst Sec. (Joint Head, Architects and Buildings Br.), 1962; technical assistance assignments etc educn, Nigeria, Yugoslavia, Tunisia, 1961–63; Asst Sec., Treasury, O&M Div., 1964; Civil Service Department: Asst Sec., Management Services Development Div., 1968; Under-Sec., Management Services, 1970; Under-Sec., Marine Div., DTI, later Dept of Trade, 1972–79. Member: Cttee of Management, RNLI; Council, Marine Soc.; Internat. Lawn Tennis Club of GB. Freeman, City of London, 1985; Liveryman, Shipwrights' Co., 1986–. *Recreations:* lawn tennis, bridge, watching cricket. *Address:* 17 Sovereign House, Draxmont, Wimbledon Hill Road, SW19 7PG. *T:* 0181–946 6429. *Clubs:* All England Lawn Tennis, Hurlingham, MCC; Kent CC; International Lawn Tennis of Great Britain.

ARCHER, Prof. John Stuart, PhD; FEng 1992; FIMM, FInstE, FInstPet; Deputy (formerly Pro) Rector, since 1991 and Professor of Petroleum Engineering, since 1986, Imperial College of Science, Technology and Medicine, University of London; *b* 15 June 1943; *s* of Stuart Leonard Archer and Joan (*née* Watkinson); *m* 1967, Lesley Oaksford; one *s* one *d*. *Educ:* County Grammar Sch., Chiswick; City Univ. (BSc Hons Ind. Chem.); Imperial Coll., London (DIC Advanced Chem. Engrg, PhD Combustion Engrg). FIMM; FInstE; FInstPet. Sen. Res. Engr, Imperial Oil (Exxon), Canada, 1969–73; Sen. Petroleum Engr, British Gas Corp., 1973–74; Manager, Reservoir Engrg, D&S Petroleum Consultants, 1974–77; Energy Resource Consultants Ltd: Founder Dir, 1977; Dir of Reservoir Studies, 1977–81; Non-exec. Dir, 1982–90; Imperial College, London: Reader in Petroleum Engrg, 1980–86; Hd, Petroleum Engrg, 1984–; Hd, Dept of Mineral Resources Engrg, 1986–; Dean, RSM, 1989–91. Vis. Prof., Univ. of Delft, 1990–93. Director: IMPEL Ltd, 1989–; MTD Ltd, 1993–. Associate Editor: Jl Petroleum Sci. and Engrg, 1990–; Jls of Soc. Petroleum Engrs; Adv. Editor, Petroleum Engineering and Development Studies series, 1987–. Mem., Soc. Petroleum Engrs, 1973–. FRSA 1990. Distinguished Achievement Award, Soc. Petroleum Engrs, 1992. *Publications:* Petroleum Engineering: principles and practice, 1986; numerous papers in learned jls on petroleum reservoir engrg. *Recreations:* golf, gardening, theatre, music. *Address:* Deputy Rector's Office, Sherfield Building, Imperial College of Science, Technology and Medicine, SW7 2AZ. *T:* 0171–589 5111. *Clubs:* Athenæum; Aspect Park Golf (Henley-on-Thames).

ARCHER, Prof. (Leonard) Bruce, CBE 1976; DrRCA; CEng, MIMechE; Director of Research, Royal College of Art, 1985–88, now Emeritus Professor; Director and Secretary, Southwood House Estate Residents Co. Ltd, since 1986; *b* 22 Nov. 1922; *s* of Leonard Castella Archer and Ivy Hilda Archer; *m* 1950, Joan Henrietta Allen; one *d*. *Educ:* Henry Thornton Sch., London; City Univ., London. MIED. Served, Scots Guards, 1941–44. City Univ., 1946–50. Various posts in manufacturing industry, 1950–57; Lectr, Central Sch. of Art and Design, London, 1957–60; Guest Prof., Hochschule für Gestaltung, Ulm, 1960–61; Research Fellow, later Prof., Royal Coll. of Art, 1961–88; Hd of Dept of Design Research, RCA, 1968–85. Examiner res. degrees, various univs, 1985–. Various public appointments in design, educn and industrial and scientific policy, 1968–; Member: Design Council, 1972–80; Internat. Science Policy Foundn, 1979–; Council, Assoc. of Art Instns, 1980–90; Chm., Confedn of Art and Design Assocs, 1981–88. Director: Gore Projects Ltd, 1982–90; Design Research Innovation Centre Ltd, 1982–86. Hon. FRCA, 1988. Hon. DSc City, 1986. *Publications:* varied, on the theory and practice of research, design, develt and educn. *Recreations:* music, the theatre. *Address:* 15 Church Vale, N2 9PB. *T:* 0181–444 4363, *Fax:* 0181–883 0351.

ARCHER, Dr Mary Doreen; scientist; *b* 22 Dec. 1944; *d* of late Harold Norman Weeden and of Doreen Weeden (*née* Cox); *m* 1966, Jeffrey Howard Archer (*see* Baron Archer of Weston-super-Mare); two *s*. *Educ:* Cheltenham Ladies' College; St Anne's Coll., Oxford (Nuffield Schol.; MA 1972); Imperial Coll., London Univ. (PhD 1968); MA Cantab 1976. FRSC 1987. Junior Res. Fellow, St Hilda's Coll., Oxford, 1968–71; temp. Lectr in Chemistry, Somerville Coll., Oxford, 1971–72; Res. Fellow, Royal Instn of GB, 1972–76 (Dewar Fellow, 1975–76); Lector in Chemistry, Trinity Coll., Cambridge, 1976–86; Fellow and Coll. Lectr in Chem., Newnham Coll., Cambridge, 1976–86 (Bye-Fellow, 1987–). Sen. Academic Fellow, De Montfort Univ. (formerly Leicester Polytechnic), 1990–; Vis. Prof., Dept of Biochem., Imperial Coll., London, 1991–; Visitor, Univ. of Hertfordshire, 1993–. Member: Renewable Energy Adv. Gp, Dept of Energy/DTI, 1991–92; Energy Adv. Panel, DTI, 1992–; COPUS, 1995–. Trustee, Science Mus., 1990–. Mem. Council, Cheltenham Ladies' Coll., 1991–. Mem. Bd of Dirs, Internat. Solar Energy Soc., 1975–81 (Sec., UK Section, 1973–76); Manager, 1982–84, Mem. Council, 1984–85, Royal Instn; Chm., Nat. Energy Foundn, 1990–. Director: Anglia Television Gp, 1987–95; Mid Anglia Radio, 1988–94; Q103 (formerly Cambridge & Newmarket FM Radio), 1988–; Addenbrooke's Hosp. NHS Trust, 1992–. Mem. Council of Lloyd's, 1989–92. Pres., Guild of Church Musicians, 1989–. *Publications:* Rupert Brooke and the Old Vicarage, Grantchester, 1989; contribs to chem. jls. *Recreations:* village choirmistress, cats, squash, picking up litter. *Address:* The Old Vicarage, Grantchester, Cambridge CB3 9ND. *T:* Cambridge (01223) 840213.

ARCHER, Dr Mildred Agnes, (Mrs W. G. Archer), OBE 1979; in charge of Prints and Drawings Section, India Office Library, London, 1954–80; *b* 28 Dec. 1911; *d* of V. A. Bell, MBE; *m* 1934, William George Archer (*d* 1979); one *s* one *d*. *Educ:* St Hilda's College, Oxford (MA, DLitt 1978; Hon. Fellow 1978). Art historian (British period, India); resided India, 1934–47; revisited India (study tours), 1966, 1972, 1976, 1981–82, 1984, 1989. *Publications:* Patna Painting, 1947; (with W. G. Archer) Indian Painting for the British, 1955; Tippoo's Tiger, 1959; Natural History Drawings in the India Office Library, 1962; Indian Miniatures and Folk Paintings, 1967; Indian Architecture and the British, 1968; British Drawings in the India Office Library (2 vols), 1969; Indian Paintings from Court, Town and Village, 1970; Company Drawings in the India Office Library, 1972; Artist Adventurers in Eighteenth Century India, 1974; Indian Popular Painting, 1977; India and British Portraiture, 1770–1825, 1979; (with John Bastin) The Raffles Drawings in the India Office Library, 1979; Early Views of India, 1980; (with T. Falk) Indian Miniatures in the India Office Library, 1981; (with R. Lightbown) India Observed, 1982; Oil Paintings and Sculpture in the India Office Collection, 1986; Visions of India: the sketchbooks of William Simpson 1859–62, 1986; (with T. Falk) India Revealed: the art and adventures of James and William Fraser 1801–35, 1989; Company Drawings in the Victoria and Albert Museum, 1992; (with William Archer) India Served and Observed, 1994; articles in Country Life, Apollo, Connoisseur, History Today, Geographical Mag. *Recreations:* grandchildren, gardening, travel. *Address:* 5 Frog Meadow, Dedham, Colchester, Essex CO7 6AD. *T:* Colchester (01206) 323099.

ARCHIBALD, Barony of, *cr* 1949, of Woodside, Glasgow; title disclaimed by 2nd Baron; *see under* Archibald, George Christopher.

ARCHIBALD, George Christopher, FRSC 1979; Professor of Economics, University of British Columbia, 1970–91, now Emeritus; *b* 30 Dec. 1926; *s* of 1st Baron Archibald, CBE, and Dorothy Holroyd Edwards (*d* 1960); *S* father, 1975, as 2nd Baron Archibald, but disclaimed his peerage for life; *m* 1st, 1951, Liliana Barou (marr. diss. 1965); 2nd, 1971, Daphne May Vincent. *Educ:* Phillips Exeter Academy, USA; King's Coll., Cambridge (MA); London Sch. of Economics (BSc Econ.). Served in Army, 1945–48, Captain RAEC. Formerly: Prof. of Economics, Univ. of Essex; Lectr in Economics, Otago Univ. and LSE; Leon Fellow, London Univ. Fellow, Econometric Soc., 1976. *Publications:* (ed) Theory of the Firm, 1971; (with R. G. Lipsey) Introduction to a Mathematical Treatment of Economics, 1973; Information, Incentives and the Economics of Control, 1992. *Address:* Cumbria.

ARCHIBALD, Dr (Harry) Munro, CB 1976; MBE 1945; Deputy Chief Medical Officer (Deputy Secretary), Department of Health and Social Security, 1973–77; *b* 17 June 1915; *s* of James and Isabella Archibald; unmarried. *Educ:* Hillhead High Sch.; Univ. of Glasgow. MB, ChB 1938; DPH 1956. War Service: RAMC, 1940–43; IMS/IAMC, 1943–46; Lt-Col; Italian Campaign (despatches). Colonial Medical Service, Nigeria, 1946–62: Senior Specialist (Malariologist), 1958; Principal Med. Officer, Prevent. Services, N Nigeria, 1960; Med. Officer, Min. of Health, 1962; Sen. Med. Off., 1964; Principal Med. Off., DHSS, 1970; Sen. Principal Med. Off., 1972. Mem. Bd, Public Health Laboratory Service, 1975–77. Fellow, Faculty of Community Medicine, 1973. *Recreation:* travel. *Address:* 1 Camborne House, Camborne Road, Sutton, Surrey SM2 6RL. *T:* 0181–643 1076. *Club:* Caledonian.

ARCHIBALD, Liliana; Chairman: Adam Brothers Contingency Ltd, 1991–92 (Director, 1957–73 and 1977–85); Wilton Park Academic Council, since 1992; *b* 25 May 1928; *d* of late Noah and Sophie Barou; *m* 1951, George Christopher Archibald (marr. diss. 1965). *Educ:* Kingsley Sch.; Geneva University. Univ. Lectr, Otago Univ., 1952–55; Director: Const & Co. Ltd, 1955–73, 1977–83; Credit Consultants Ltd, 1957–73, 1977–85; Fenchurch Gp Internat., 1985–88; Holman Wade, 1989–92; CLM Insurance Fund, 1993–. Head of Division (Credit Insurance and Export Credit), EEC, 1973–77; EEC Advr to Lloyd's and the British Insurance Brokers Assoc., 1978–85; Internat. Affairs Advr to Lloyd's, 1981–85; Advr to Internat. Gp of Protection & Indemnity Clubs, 1980–85. Frequent lecturer on insurance-related problems. Member: Liberalisation of Trade in Services Cttee, British Invisible Exports Council, 1981–; British Export Finance Adv. Council, 1982–91; Action Resource Centre, 1986–91; Govt Inquiry into Shops Act—Sunday and Late-Night Trading, 1984–85; Review Cttee, Banking Law Services, 1987–88; Lord Chancellor's Adv. Cttee on Legal Educn and Conduct, 1991–94; Vice-Chm., ICC Insurance Commn, 1982–87; Chm., Insurance Cttee, British Nat. Cttee, ICC, 1983–87. Member of Lloyd's, 1973–94. *Publications:* (trans. and ed) Peter the Great, 1958; (trans. and ed) Rise of the Romanovs, 1970; contrib. Bankers Magazine. *Recreations:* driving fast cars, ski-ing, gardening. *Address:* 21 Langland Gardens, NW3 6QE.
See also A. Kennaway.

ARCHIBALD, Munro; *see* Archibald, H. M.

ARCTIC, Bishop of The, since 1991; **Rt. Rev. (John) Christopher (Richard) Williams;** *b* 22 May 1936; *s* of Frank Harold and Ceridwen Roberts Williams; *m* 1964, Rona Macrae (*née* Aitken); one *s* one *d. Educ:* Manchester Grammar Sch.; Univ. of Manchester (BA Comm); Univ. of Durham, Cranmer Hall (DipTh). Ordained: deacon, Stretford, England, 1960; priest, Sugluk, PQ, 1962; Missionary, diocese of The Arctic: Sugluk, PQ, 1961–72; Cape Dorset, NWT, 1972–75; Baker Lake, NWT, 1975–78; Archdeacon of The Keewatin, 1975–87; Rector, Yellowknife, NWT, 1978–87; Bp Suffragan, 1987–90, Coadjutor Bp, 1990, dio. of The Arctic. *Recreations:* walking, cross country ski-ing. *Address:* PO Box 164, Iqaluit, NWT X0A 0H0, Canada. *T:* (819) 9794745, *Fax:* (819) 9792481.

ARCULUS, Sir Ronald, KCMG 1979 (CMG 1968); KCVO 1980; HM Diplomatic Service, retired; *b* 11 Feb. 1923; *s* of late Cecil Arculus, MC and Ethel L. Arculus; *m* 1953, Sheila Mary Faux; one *s* one *d. Educ:* Solihull; Exeter Coll., Oxford (MA; Hon. Fellow, 1989). 4th Queen's Own Hussars (now Queen's Royal Hussars), 1942–45 (Captain). Joined HM Diplomatic Service, 1947; FO, 1947; San Francisco, 1948; La Paz, 1950; FO, 1951; Ankara, 1953; FO, 1957; Washington, 1961; Counsellor, 1965; New York, 1965–68; IDC, 1969; Head of Science and Technology Dept, FCO, 1970–72; Minister (Economic), Paris, 1973–77; Ambassador and Permt Leader, UK Delegn to UN Conf. on Law of the Sea, 1977–79; Ambassador to Italy, 1979–83. Dir, 1983–91, Trustee, 1986–93, Consultant, 1992–95, Glaxo Hldgs. Special Advr to Govt on Channel Tunnel trains, 1987–88. Consultant: Trusthouse Forte, 1983–86; London and Continental Bankers Ltd, 1985–90. Dir of Appeals, King's Med. Res. Trust, 1984–88. Governor, British Institute, Florence, 1983–94. FIMgt (FBIM 1984). Freeman, City of London, 1981. Kt Grand Cross, Order of Merit, Italy, 1980. *Recreations:* travel, music, fine arts, antiques. *Address:* 20 Kensington Court Gardens, W8 5QF. *Clubs:* Army and Navy, Hurlingham; Cowdray Park Polo.

ARDAGH AND CLONMACNOISE, Bishop of, (RC), since 1983; **Most Rev. Colm O'Reilly;** *b* 11 Jan. 1935; *s* of John and Alicia O'Reilly. Ordained priest, 1960. *Address:* St Michael's, Longford, Ireland. *T:* Longford (43) 46432.

ARDEE, Lord; John Anthony Brabazon; *b* 11 May 1941; *e s* of 14th Earl of Meath, *qv*; *m* 1973, Xenia Goudime; one *s* two *d. Educ:* Harrow. Page of Honour to the Queen, 1956–57. Served Grenadier Guards, 1959–62. *Heir: s* Hon. Anthony Jaques Brabazon, *b* 30 Jan. 1977. *Address:* Ballinacor, Rathdrum, Co. Wicklow, Ireland.

ARDEN, Andrew Paul Russel; QC 1991; *b* 20 April 1948; *m* 1991, Joanne Leahy; one *d. Educ:* Stowe; University College Sch.; University Coll. London (LLB). Called to the Bar, Gray's Inn, 1974; Dir, Small Heath Community Law Centre, Birmingham, 1976–78. Local government inquiries/reviews: for GLC, 1982–83; for Bristol CC, 1985; for Hackney BC, 1985–87, 1993–98; for Camden BC, 1992. General Editor: Encyclopaedia of Housing Law, 1978–; Housing Law Reports, 1981–. *Publications:* Manual of Housing Law, 1978, 6th edn (with Caroline Hunter), 1996; Housing Act 1980 (annotations), 1980; (with Prof. M. Partington) Quiet Enjoyment, 1980, 2nd edn 1985; (with Prof. M. Partington) Housing Law, 1983, 2nd edn (also with C. Hunter), 1994; (with Prof. J. T. Farrand) Rent Acts & Regulations, amended and annotated, 1981; (with C. Cross) Housing & Building Control Act 1984 (annotations), 1984; Private Tenants Handbook, 1985, 2nd edn 1989; Public Tenants Handbook, 1985, 2nd edn 1989; (with S. McGrath) Landlord & Tenant Act 1985 (annotations), 1986; Housing Act 1985 (annotations), 1986; (with J. Ramage) Housing Associations Act 1985 (annotations), 1986; Homeless Persons Handbook, 1986, 2nd edn 1988; Homeless Persons: Part III, Housing Act 1985, 3rd edn 1988; (with C. Hunter) Housing Act 1988 (annotations), 1989; (with Sir Robert Megarry) Assured Tenancies, Vol. 3, The Rent Acts, 11th edn 1989; (with C. Hunter) Local Government & Housing Act 1989 (annotations), 1990; (with C. Hunter) Local Government Finance Law, 1994; *fiction:* The Motive Not The Deed, 1974; No Certain Roof, 1985; The Object Man, 1986; four thrillers under pseudonym, 1990–91. *Recreations:* Southern Comfort, Hill Street Blues, Camel cigarettes. *Address:* Arden Chambers, 59 Fleet Street, EC4Y 1JU. *T:* 071–353 3132, *Fax:* 071–353 2774.

ARDEN, Rt. Rev. Donald Seymour, CBE 1981; Assistant Bishop of London, since 1981, and voluntary assistant priest, St Alban's, North Harrow, since 1986; *b* 12 April 1916; *s* of Stanley and Winifred Arden; *m* 1962, Jane Grace Riddle; two *s. Educ:* St Peter's Coll., Adelaide; University of Leeds (BA); College of the Resurrection, Mirfield. Deacon, 1939; Priest, 1940. Curate of: St Catherine's, Hatcham, 1939–40; Nettleden with Potten End, 1941–43; Asst Priest, Pretoria African Mission, 1944–51; Director of Usuthu Mission, Swaziland, 1951–61; Bishop of Nyasaland, 1961 (name of diocese changed, when Nyasaland was granted independence, July 1964); Bishop of Malaŵi, 1964–71, of Southern Malaŵi, 1971–81; Archbishop of Central Africa, 1971–80; Priest-in-charge of St Margaret's, Uxbridge, 1981–86. Commissary, dioceses of Southern Malaŵi and Lake Malaŵi, 1981, of Niassa, Mozambique, 1989–. *Publication:* Out of Africa Something New, 1976. *Recreation:* photography. *Address:* 6 Frobisher Close, Pinner, Mddx HA5 1NN. *T:* and *Fax:* 0181–866 6009.

ARDEN, John; playwright; *b* 26 Oct. 1930; *s* of C. A. Arden and A. E. Layland; *m* 1957, Margaretta Ruth D'Arcy; four *s* (and one *s* decd). *Educ:* Sedbergh Sch.; King's Coll., Cambridge; Edinburgh Coll. of Art. *Plays produced include:* All Fall Down, 1955; The Life of Man, 1956; The Waters of Babylon, 1957; Live Like Pigs, 1958; Serjeant Musgrave's Dance, 1959; Soldier, Soldier, 1960; Wet Fish, 1962; The Workhouse Donkey, 1963; Ironhand, 1963; Armstrong's Last Goodnight, 1964; Left-Handed Liberty, 1965; The True History of Squire Jonathan and his Unfortunate Treasure, 1968; The Bagman, 1970; Pearl, 1978; To Put It Frankly, 1979; Don Quixote, 1980; Garland for a Hoar Head, 1982; The Old Man Sleeps Alone, 1982; *with Margaretta D'Arcy:* The Business of Good Government, 1960; The Happy Haven, 1960; Ars Longa Vita Brevis, 1964; Friday's Hiding, 1966; The Royal Pardon, 1966; The Hero Rises Up, 1968; Island of the Mighty, 1972; The Ballygombeen Bequest, 1972; The Non-Stop Connolly Cycle, 1975; Vandaleur's Folly, 1978; The Little Gray Home in the West, 1978; The Manchester Enthusiasts, 1984; Whose is the Kingdom?, 1988; A Suburban Suicide, 1994. *Publications:* To Present the Pretence (essays), 1977; Silence Among the Weapons (novella), 1982; Books of Bale (novel), 1988; (with Margaretta D'Arcy) Awkward Corners, 1988; Cogs Tyrannic (novellas), 1991. *Recreations:* antiquarianism, mythology. *Address:* c/o Casarotto Ramsay Ltd, National House, 60–66 Wardour Street, W1V 3HP.

ARDEN, Hon. Dame Mary (Howarth), (Dame Mary Mance), DBE 1993; **Hon. Mrs Justice Arden;** a Judge of the High Court of Justice, Chancery Division, since 1993; *b* 23 Jan. 1947; *d* of late Lt-Col E. C. Arden, LLB, TD and of M. M. Arden (*née* Smith); *m* 1973, Hon. Sir Jonathan Hugh Mance, *qv*; one *s* two *d. Educ:* Huyton College; Girton College, Cambridge (MA, LLM); Harvard Law School (LLM). Called to the Bar, Gray's Inn, 1971 (Arden and Birkenhead Scholarships, 1971); admitted *ad eundem* to Lincoln's Inn, 1973 (Bencher, 1993); QC 1986; Attorney Gen., Duchy of Lancaster, 1991–93. Bar Mem., Law Society's Standing Cttee on Company Law, 1976–. DTI Inspector, Rotaprint PLC, 1988–91. *Publications:* Negligence and the Public Accountant (contrib.), 1972; Legal Editor, Current Accounting Law and Practice, by Robert Willott, 1976; (with George Eccles) Tolley's Companies Act 1980, 1980; Legal Consultant Editor: Tolley's Companies Act 1981, 1981; Tolley's Accounting Problems of the Companies Acts, 1984; Accounting Provisions of the Companies Act 1985, 1985; Coopers & Lybrand Deloitte Manual of Accounting, vols 1 and 2, 1990; Jt Gen. Editor and Contributor, Buckley on the Companies Acts, 14th edn: Special Bulletin, 1990. *Recreations:* family activities, reading, swimming. *Address:* Royal Courts of Justice, Strand, WC2A 2LL.

ARFIELD, John Alan; University Librarian, Loughborough University of Technology, since 1992; *b* 15 March 1949; *s* of Donald Sidney Arfield and Barbara Winifred Arfield (*née* Alderton); *m* 1970, Paula May Perrin; one *s* two *d. Educ:* Kingston Grammar Sch.; Jesus Coll., Cambridge (BA 1971; MA 1975); Univ. of Sheffield (MA 1973). Cambridge University Library: Asst Liby Officer, 1973–78; Asst Under-Librarian, 1978–79; Under-Librarian, 1979–81; Sub-Librarian (Tech. Services), UC, Cardiff, 1981–88; Dep. Librarian, Reading Univ., 1988–92. *Publications:* articles in librarianship. *Recreations:* squash, cricket, theatre, music. *Address:* Pilkington Library, Loughborough University of Technology, Loughborough, Leics LE11 3TU.

ARGENT, Eric William, FCA; FCIB; Director, Nationwide Anglia Building Society, 1987–88, retired (Joint General Manager, 1978–81, Director, 1978–87, Anglia Building Society); *b* 5 Sept. 1923; *s* of Eric George Argent and Florence Mary Argent; *m* 1949, Pauline Grant; two *d. Educ:* Chiswick Grammar Sch. FCA 1951. War Service, 1942–47. With City Chartered Accountants, 1940–42 and 1947–51; with London Banking House, Antony Gibbs & Sons Ltd, 1951–59; Hastings & Thanet Building Society, 1959–78: Sec. and Chief Accountant, 1962; Dep. Gen. Man., 1964; Gen. Man. and Sec., 1966; Dir and Gen. Man., 1976. *Recreations:* reading, gardening, travel. *Address:* Fairmount, 104 Longcliffe Road, Grantham, Lincs NG31 8DY. *T:* Grantham (01476) 591433.

ARGENT, Malcolm, CBE 1985; Director, British Telecommunications plc, since 1989 (Secretary, 1984–94); Deputy Chairman, Civil Aviation Authority, since 1995; *b* 14 Aug. 1935; *s* of Leonard James and Winifred Hilda Argent; *m* 1st, 1961, Mary Patricia Addis Stimson (marr. diss. 1983); one *s* one *d*; 2nd, 1986, Thelma Hazel Eddleston. *Educ:* Palmer's Sch., Grays, Essex. General Post Office, London Telecommunications Region: Exec. Officer, 1953–62; Higher Exec. Officer, 1962–66; Principal, PO Headquarters, 1966–70; Private Sec., Man. Dir, Telecommunications, 1970–74; Personnel Controller, External Telecommun. Exec., 1974–75; Dir, Chairman's Office, PO Central Headquarters, 1975–77; Dir, Eastern Telecommun. Region, 1977; Secretary: of the Post Office, 1978–81; of British Telecommunications Corp., 1981–94; Trustee, British Telecommunications Staff Superannuation Fund, 1981–94. Director: McCaw Cellular Communications Inc., 1989–94; Westminster Health Care plc, 1992–; Clerical, Medical & Gen. Assce Soc., 1994–. Mem. Council, CBI, 1994–. Freeman, City of London, 1987. CIMgt 1992 (CBIM 1991; FBIM 1980). *Recreation:* tennis. *Address:* Chestnuts, Fryerning Lane, Ingatestone, Essex CM4 0DF.

ARGENTINA, Bishop of, since 1990; **Rt. Rev. David Leake;** Presiding Bishop, Province of the Anglican Church of the Southern Cone of America, 1982–89; *b* 26 June 1935; *s* of Rev. Canon William Alfred Leake and Dorothy Violet Leake; *m* 1961, Rachel Yarham; two *s* one *d. Educ:* St Alban's Coll., Buenos Aires; London Coll. of Divinity. ALCD 1959 (LTh). Deacon 1959, priest 1960; Assistant Bishop: Paraguay and N Argentina, 1969–73; N Argentina, 1973–79; Bishop of Northern Argentina, 1979–89. *Recreations:* observing people's behaviour at airports, railway stations and bus terminals. *Address:* Casilla Correo 4293, 1000 Correo Central, Buenos Aires, Argentina.

ARGOV, Shlomo; Ambassador of Israel to the Court of St James's, 1979–82; *b* 1929; *m* Hava Argov; one *s* two *d. Educ:* Georgetown Univ., USA (BSc Pol. Science); London School of Economics (Internat. Relns) (MSc Econ; Hon. Fellow, 1983). Israel Defence Force, 1947–50; Prime Minister's Office, Jerusalem, 1955–59; Consul General of Israel, Lagos, 1959–60; Counsellor, Accra, 1960–61; Consul, Consulate General of Israel, New York, 1961–64; Dep. Director, United States Div., Min. of Foreign Affairs, Jerusalem, 1965–68; Minister, Embassy of Israel, Washington, 1968–71; Ambassador of Israel, Mexico, 1971–74; Asst Dir Gen. (Dir of Israel Information Services), Min. of Foreign Affairs, Jerusalem, 1974–77; Ambassador of Israel, Netherlands, 1977–79. *Address:* c/o Ministry of Foreign Affairs, Jerusalem, Israel.

ARGYLE, His Honour Major Michael Victor, MC 1945; QC 1961; a Circuit Judge (formerly an Additional Judge of the Central Criminal Court), 1970–88; *b* 31 Aug. 1915; *e s* of late Harold Victor Argyle and Elsie Marion, Repton, Derbyshire; *m* 1951, Ann Norah (*d* 1994), *d* of late Charles Newton and M. Newton, later Mrs Jobson; three *d. Educ:* Shardlow Hall, Derbyshire; Westminster Sch.; Trinity Coll., Cambridge (MA).

Served War of 1939–45: with 7th QO Hussars in India, ME and Italy (immediate MC), 1939–47. Called to Bar, Lincoln's Inn, 1938, Bencher, 1967, Treasurer, 1984; resumed practice at Bar, 1947 (Midland Circuit); Recorder of Northampton, 1962–65, of Birmingham, 1965–70; Dep. Chm., Holland QS, 1965–71; Lay Judge, Arches Court, Province of Canterbury, 1968–92. General Elections, contested (C) Belper, 1950, and Loughborough, 1955. Master, Worshipful Co. of Makers of Playing Cards, 1984–85. *Publications:* (ed) Phipson on Evidence, 10th edn. *Recreations:* chess, boxing. *Address:* The Red House, Fiskerton, near Southwell, Notts NG25 0UL. *T:* Newark (01636) 830530. *Club:* Kennel.

ARGYLL, 12th Duke of, *cr* 1701 (Scotland), 1892 (UK); **Ian Campbell;** Marquess of Lorne and Kintyre; Earl of Campbell and Cowal; Viscount Lochow and Glenyla; Baron Inveraray, Mull, Morvern, and Tiry, 1701; Baron Campbell, 1445; Earl of Argyll, 1457; Baron Lorne, 1470; Baron Kintyre, 1633 (Scotland); Baron Sundridge, 1766; Baron Hamilton of Hameldon, 1776; Bt 1627; 36th Baron and 46th Knight of Lochow; Celtic title, Mac Cailein Mhor, Chief of Clan Campbell (from Sir Colin Campbell, knighted 1280); Hereditary Master of the Royal Household, Scotland; Hereditary High Sheriff of the County of Argyll; Admiral of the Western Coast and Isles; Keeper of the Great Seal of Scotland and of the Castles of Dunstaffnage, Dunoon, and Carrick and Tarbert; Vice Lord-Lieutenant of Argyll and Bute, since 1994; *b* 28 Aug. 1937; *e s* of 11th Duke of Argyll, TD, and Louise (*d* 1970), *o d* of Henry Clews; *S* father, 1973; *m* 1964, Iona Mary, *d* of Captain Sir Ivar Colquhoun, *qv*; one *s* one *d*. *Educ:* Le Rosey, Switzerland; Glenalmond; McGill Univ., Montreal. Captain (retd) Argyll and Sutherland Highlanders. Member, Queen's Body Guard for Scotland, the Royal Company of Archers, retd. Chm., Beinn Bhuidhe Holdings, 1977–; Director: S. Campbell & Son, 1982–; Aberlour Glenlivet Distillery Co.; White Heather Distillers; Muir, MacKenzie & Co., 1973–; Visual Sound Programmes, 1970–. President: Royal Caledonian Schs; Argyll Scouts Assoc.; Highland Soc. of London, 1985–90. Hon. Col, Argyll and Sutherland Highlanders Bn (ACF), 1981–91. DL Argyll and Bute, 1987. KStJ 1975. *Heir: s* Marquess of Lorne, *qv*. *Address:* Inveraray Castle, Inveraray, Argyll PA32 8XF. *T:* Inveraray (01499) 302275, *Fax:* (01499) 302421. *Clubs:* White's; New (Edinburgh).

ARGYLL AND THE ISLES, Bishop of, since 1993; **Rt. Rev. Douglas Maclean Cameron;** *b* 23 March 1935; *s* of Andrew McIntyre Cameron and Helen Adam McKechnie; *m* 1969, Anne Patricia Purnell; two *d*. *Educ:* Eastwood Grammar Sch., Clarkston, Glasgow; Theol Coll., Edinburgh; Univ. of the South, Sewanee, Tennessee, USA. Bank of Scotland, 1951–59; RAF, 1953–55. Ordained: deacon, 1962; priest, 1963; curate, Christ Church, Falkirk, 1962–65; Anglican Church in Papua New Guinea: Mission Priest, 1966–67; priest in charge, Movi, 1967–72; Rector, St Francis, Goroka, 1972–74; Archdeacon of New Guinea Mainland, 1972–74; Priest in charge, St Fillan's, Edinburgh, 1974, Rector, 1978–88; Rector: St Hilda's, Edinburgh, 1977–88; St Mary's, Dalkeith and St Leonard's, Lasswade, 1988–93; Canon, St Mary's Cathedral, Edinburgh and Synod Clerk, 1990–91; Dean of Edinburgh, 1991–92. *Recreations:* hill-walking, listening to music, gardening, cooking. *Address:* The Pines, Ardconnel Road, Oban PA34 5DR. *T:* Oban (01631) 66912.

See also Bishop of Aberdeen and Orkney.

ARGYLL AND THE ISLES, Bishop of, (RC), since 1991; **Rt. Rev. Roderick Wright;** *b* 28 June 1940. *Educ:* St Mary's Coll., Blairs, Grampian; St Peter's Coll., Cardross, Strathclyde. Ordained 1964; Assistant Priest: St Laurence's, Drumchapel, 1964–66; St Jude's, Barlanark, 1966–69; Procurator, Blairs Coll., Grampian, 1969–74; Assistant Priest: Dunoon, Argyll, 1974–76; Fort William, 1976–80; Parish priest: Ardkenneth, South Uist, 1980–87; St Anne's Corpach and St John the Evangelist, Caol, 1987–91. Mem., Cttee on local and regl ecumenism of Action of Churches Together in Scotland. *Address:* Bishop's House, Esplanade, Oban, Argyll PA34 5AB.

ARGYLL AND THE ISLES, Dean of; *see* Macleay, Very Rev. J. H. J.

ARGYLL AND THE ISLES, Provosts in; *see* McCubbin, Very Rev. D.; Maclean, Very Rev. A. M.

ARGYRIS, Prof. John, DScEng, DE Munich; FRS 1986; FEng 1990; FRAeS 1955; Professor of Aeronautical Structures in the University of London, at Imperial College of Science and Technology, 1955–75, Visiting Professor 1975–78, now Emeritus Professor; Director, Institute for Computer Applications, Stuttgart, since 1984; *b* 19 Aug. 1916; *s* of Nicolas and Lucie Argyris; *m* 1953, Inga-Lisa (*née* Johansson); one *s*. *Educ:* 3rd Gymnasium, Athens; Technical Universities, Athens, Munich and Zurich. With J. Gollnow u. Son, Stettin, Research in Structures, 1937–39; Royal Aeronautical Soc., Research and Technical Officer, 1943–49; Univ. of London, Imperial Coll. of Science and Technology, Dept of Aeronautics: Senior Lecturer, 1949; Reader in Theory of Aeronautical Structures, 1950; Hon. FIC 1985. Dir, Inst. for Statics and Dynamics, Stuttgart, 1959–84. Principal Editor, Jl of Computer Methods in Applied Mechanics and Engineering, 1972–. Hon. Professor: Northwestern Polytech. Univ., Xian, China, 1980; Tech. Univ. of Beijing, 1983; Qinghua Univ., Beijing, 1984. Corresp. Mem., Acad. of Scis, Athens, 1973; Life Mem., ASME, 1981; Hon. Life Mem., NY Acad. of Scis, 1983; Foreign Associate, US Nat. Acad. of Engrg, 1986. FAIAA 1983; FAAAS 1985; FASCE 1991; Hon. Fellow, Groupe pour l'Avancement des Méthodes Numériques de l'Ingénieur, Paris, 1974; Hon. FCGI 1976; Hon. Fellow, Aeronautical Soc. of India, 1985; Hon. FRAeS 1986; Hon. Fellow, Romanian Acad., 1992; Hon. Mem., Greek Assoc. of Computational Mechs, 1994. Hon. Dott Ing Genoa, 1970; Hon. dr.tech Trondheim, 1972; Hon. Dr Ing Tech. Hanover, 1983; Hon. Tek. Dr Linköping, 1986; Hon. DSc (Maths) Athens, 1989; Hon. DSc (Mechs) Vilnius, 1991; Hon. DSc (Computer Mechs): Iasi, 1992; Tallinn, Estonia, 1993; Technical Univ., St Petersburg, 1993; Hon. DSc (phys, comput. and mechs) Tech. Univ. and Univ. of Timisoara, Romania, 1993; Hon. DSc (sci of mechs), Technical Univ. of Athens, 1995. Silver Medal, RAeS, 1971; Von Kármán Medal, ASCE, 1975; Copernicus Medal, Polish Acad. of Scis, 1979; Timoshenko Medal, ASME, 1981; I. B. Laskowitz Award with Gold Medal in Aerospace Engrg, NY Acad. of Scis, 1982; World Prize in Culture, and election as Personality of the Year 1984, Centro Studi e Ricerce delle Nazione, Acad. Italia, 1983; Royal Medal, Royal Soc., 1985; Daidalus Gold Medal, Sir George Cayley Inst., 1988; Gold Medal, Bulgarian Acad. of Scis, 1991; Henri Coenda Medal in Gold, 1992. Gold Medal, Land Baden-Württemberg, 1980; Grand Cross of Merit, FRG, 1985; Grand Cross of Merit with Star, FRG, 1989. *Publications:* Handbook of Aeronautics, Vol. I, 1952: Energy Theorems and Structural Analysis, 1960; Modern Fuselage Analysis and the Elastic Aircraft, 1963; Recent Advances in Matrix Methods of Structural Analysis, 1964; Introduction into the Finite Element Method, vols I, II and III, 1986–88; Dynamics of Structures, 1991; An overview of aerolasticity, 1992; The Dynamics of Chaos, 1992; articles and publications in Ingenieur Archiv, Reports and Memoranda of Aeronautical Research Council, Journal of Royal Aeronautical Society and Aircraft Engineering, CMAME, Jl of AIAA, etc; over 400 scientific publications. *Recreations:* reading, music, hiking, archæology. *Address:* Institute for Computer Applications, 27 Pfaffenwaldring, D-70569 Stuttgart, Germany. *T:* (711) 6853594; c/o Department of Aeronautics, Imperial College, Prince Consort Road, SW7. *T:* 071–589 5111. *Club:* English-Speaking Union.

ARGYRIS, Nicholas John; Director, Telecommunications and Postal Services, European Commission, since 1993; *b* 22 March 1943; *s* of Costas Argyris and Eileen Argyris (*née* Pollard); *m* 1st, 1966, Carol Bartlett (marr. diss.); one *s* two *d*; 2nd, 1992, Danielle Canneel. *Educ:* St Paul's Sch.; Clare Coll., Cambridge (BA Econs 1965; Cert. Ed. 1966). Schoolmaster, 1966–68; with Govt Econ. Service, in Depts of Econ. Affairs, Technol. and Trade and Ind., 1968–73; joined European Commission, 1973: worked in Directorate General for: Competition, 1973–84; Develt, 1985–86; Competition, 1987–91; Dir for internal market, DG for Energy, 1991–93. *Publications:* articles on air transport, energy and telecommunications policy. *Recreations:* reading, walking, the arts, dancing. . . *Address:* Commission of the European Communities, 200 rue de la Loi, 1049 Brussels, Belgium. *T:* (2) 2955899.

ARIAS-SALGADO Y MONTALVO, Fernando; Ambassador of Spain to Tunisia, since 1993; Barrister-at-Law; *b* 3 May 1938; *s* of Gabriel Arias-Salgado y Cubas and Maria Montalvo Gutierrez; *m* 1969, Maria Isabel Garrigues Lopez-Chicheri; one *s* one *d*. *Educ:* Univ. of Madrid. Mem., Illustrious Coll. of Lawyers of Madrid. Entered Diplomatic Sch., 1963; Sec., Permanent Rep. of Spain to UN, 1966; Advr, UN Security Council, 1968–69; Asst Dir Gen., Promotion of Research, 1971, Asst Dir Gen., Internat. Co-operation, 1972, Min. of Educn and Science; Legal Advr (internat. matters), Legal Dept, Min. of Foreign Affairs, 1973; Counsellor, Spanish Delegn to Internat. Court of Justice, 1975; Tech. Sec. Gen., Min. of Foreign Affairs, 1976; Dir Gen., Radiotelevisión Española, 1977; Ambassador to the Court of St James's, 1981–83; Dir, Internat. Legal Dept, Min. of Foreign Affairs, 1983–85; Consul-Gen. for Spain in Zürich, 1985–90; Ambassador and Perm. Rep. of Spain to Internat. Orgns in Vienna, 1990–93. Comendador: Orden de Isabel la Católica; Orden del Merito Civil; Orden de San Raimundo de Peñafort; Caballero, Orden de Carlos III. *Address:* 24 Docteur Conseil, Cité Jardin, 1002 Tunis, Tunisia.

ARIAS SÁNCHEZ, Oscar, PhD; President of Costa Rica, 1986–90; President, Arias Foundation for Peace, since 1990; *b* 13 Sept. 1940; *m* Margarita; one *s* one *d*. *Educ:* Univ. of Costa Rica; Univ. of Essex. Prof., Sch. of Political Sciences, Univ. of Costa Rica, 1969–72; Minister of Nat. Planning and Economic Policy, 1972–77; Gen. Sec., 1979–86, Liberación Nacional Party; Congressman, 1978–82. Formulated Central American Peace Agreement, 1986–87. Member: Stockholm Internat. Peace Res. Inst.; Carter Center; Inst. for Internat. Studies, Stanford Univ.; ILD Rockefeller Foundn; Internat. Centre for Human Rights and Democratic Develt; Inter Press Service; Bd of Dirs, WWF. Hon. PhD: Harvard, 1988; Essex, 1988; Dartmouth, 1992. Nobel Peace Prize, 1987; Martin Luther King Peace Prize, Martin Luther King Foundn, 1987; Prince of Asturias Prize, 1988; Nat. Audubon Soc. Prize, 1988; Liberty Medal, Univ. of Pennsylvania, 1991. *Publications:* Pressure Groups in Costa Rica, 1970; Who Governs in Costa Rica?, 1976; Latin American Democracy, Independence and Society, 1977; Roads for Costa Rica's Development, 1977; New Ways for Costa Rican Development, 1980. *Address:* c/o Arias Foundation/Center for Peace, PO Box 8–6410–1000, San José, Costa Rica.

ARIE, Prof. Thomas Harry David, CBE 1995; FRCPsych, FRCP, FFPHM; Foundation Professor of Health Care of the Elderly, University of Nottingham, since 1977, and Hon. Consultant Psychiatrist, Nottingham Health Authority; *b* 9 Aug. 1933; *s* of late Dr O. M. Arie and Hedy (*née* Glaser); *m* 1963, Eleanor, FRCP, *yr d* of Sir Robert Aitken, *qv*; two *d* one *s*. *Educ:* Reading Sch.; Balliol Coll., Oxford (Open Exhibnr in Classics; 1st cl. Hons, Classical Mods); MA, BM 1960; DPM. Training, Radcliffe Infirmary, Oxford, and Maudsley and London Hosps; Consultant Psychiatrist, Goodmayes Hosp., 1969–77; Sen. Lectr in Social Medicine, London Hosp. Med. Coll.; Hon. Sen. Lectr in Psychiatry, UCH Med. Sch. Royal College of Psychiatrists: Mem. Council, 1975–79, 1981–86, 1991–; Vice-Pres., 1984–86; Chm., Specialist Section on Psychiatry of Old Age, 1981–86; Jt Cttee on Higher Psychiatric Training, 1978–84; Royal College of Physicians: Geriatrics Cttee, 1984–90; Examining Bd for Dipl. in Geriatric Medicine, 1983–92. Member: Central Council for Educn and Trng in Social Work, 1975–81; Standing Med. Adv. Cttee, DHSS, 1980–84; Cttee on Review of Medicines, 1981–90; Res. Adv. Council, Nat. Inst. for Social Work, 1982–90; Med. Adv. Cttee to Registrar General, 1990–93. Fotheringham Lectr, Univ. of Toronto, 1979; Vis. Prof., NZ Geriatrics Soc., 1980; Dozor Vis. Prof., Univ. of the Negev, Israel, 1988; Fröhlich Vis. Prof., UCLA, 1991. Chm., Geriatric Psych. Section, World Psych. Assoc., 1989–93. Governor, Centre for Policy on Ageing, 1992–. *Publications:* (ed) Health Care of the Elderly, 1981; (ed) Recent Advances in Psychogeriatrics, Vol. 1 1985, Vol. 2 1992; articles in med. jls and chapters in other people's books. *Address:* Department of Health Care of the Elderly, Queen's Medical Centre, Nottingham NG7 2UH. *T:* Nottingham (0115) 970 9408.

ARIS, Aung San Suu Kyi, (Mrs M. V. Aris); *see* Aung San Suu Kyi.

ARIS, John Bernard Benedict, TD 1967; Director, IMPACT Programme, since 1990; *b* 6 June 1934; *s* of John (Jack) Woodbridge Aris and Joyce Mary (*née* Williams). *Educ:* Eton (King's Schol.); Magdalen Coll., Oxford (MA). FBCS; FInstD; FRSA. LEO Computers, 1958–63; English Electric Computers, 1963–69; ICL, 1969–75; Imperial Group, 1975–85 (Man., Gp Management Services, 1982–85); Dir, NCC, 1985–90. Non-exec. Dir, NCC, 1981–85; Chairman: FOCUS Private Sector Users Cttee (DTI), 1984–85; Alvey IT User Panel, 1985–88; Mem., IT 86 Cttee, 1986. Founder Freeman, Co. of Information Technologists, 1987. *Recreations:* travel, music, art, scuba diving, gastronomy.

ARKELL, John Hardy, MA; Headmaster, Gresham's School, Holt, since 1991; *b* 10 July 1939; *s* of Hardy Arkell and Vivienne (*née* Le Sueur); *m* 1963, Jean Harding, JP; two *s* one *d*. *Educ:* Stowe Sch.; Selwyn Coll., Cambridge (BA Hons English Tripos; MA). National Service, HM Submarines, 1958–60 (Sub Lieut). Asst Master, Abingdon Sch., 1963–64; Head of VI form English, Framlingham Coll., 1964–70; Fettes College, 1970–83: Head of English Dept, 1971–73, 1976–78; Founder Headmaster, Fettes Jun. Sch., 1973–79; Housemaster, Glencorse House, 1979–83; Headmaster, Wrekin Coll., 1983–91. Chm., ISIS, Central England, 1989–91; Sec., HMC Midland Div., 1990–91; HMC Rep., ISJC Special Needs Cttee, 1991–. *Recreations:* tennis, sailing, motor cars, drama. *Address:* Lockhart House, Gresham's School, Holt, Norfolk NR25 6DZ. *T:* Holt (01263) 713739.

ARKELL, John Heward, CBE 1961; TD; MA; CIMgt, FIPM; Director of Administration, BBC, 1960–70; *b* 20 May 1909; *s* of Rev. H. H. Arkell, MA, and Gertrude Mary Arkell; *m* 1st, 1940, Helen Birgit, *d* of Emil Huitfeldt, formerly Norwegian Ambassador to Denmark, and Dorothy Huitfeldt; two *s* one *d*; 2nd, 1956, Meta Bachke Grundtvig (marr. diss.); one *s*. *Educ:* Dragon Sch.; Radley Coll.; Christ Church, Oxford (MA). Sir Max Michaelis (Investment) Trust, 1931–37. Asst Sec., CPRE, 1937–39, Mem. of Exec. Cttee, 1945–75, Vice-Chm., 1967–74, Vice-Pres., 1975–. Commissioned Territorial Officer, 1st Bn Queen's Westminsters, KRRC, 1939; Instructor, then Chief Instructor, Army Infantry Signalling Sch., 1940; served in BLA as special infantry signalling liaison officer, 1944; demobilised 1945, Major. Personnel Manager, J. Lyons, 1945–49; BBC: Controller, Staff Admin, 1949–58; Dir, Staff Admin, 1958–60. Director: The Boots Co. Ltd, 1970–79; UK Provident Instn, 1971–80; Sen. Associate, Kramer Internat. Ltd, 1980–86. Chm., Air Transport and Travel ITB, 1970–80. Lay Mem., Nat. Industrial Relations Ct, 1971–74. Lectr on indust. subjects; occasional indep. management consultancies include P&O and

Coates Group of Cos (Dir, 1970–76). Founder, Exec. Pres. then Jt Pres., and former Gen. Hon. Sec., then Chm., Christ Church (Oxford) United Clubs (Community Centre, SE London), 1932–. Chm. Council, British Institute of Management, 1972–74 (Fellow, 1964–, now Companion; Vice-Chm., 1966–72; Chm. Exec. Cttee, 1966–69; Vice Pres., 1974–); Chm. BIM/CBI Educl Panel, 1971–72; Dir, BIM Foundn, 1976–81; Member Council: CBI, 1973–75; Industry for Management Educn, 1971–; Foundn for Management Educn, 1971–75; National Trust, 1971–84 (Chm., NT Council's Adv. Cttee on the Trust, its members and public, which produced the Arkell Report, 1982–83); Adv. Council, Business Graduates Assoc., 1973–85; Action Resources Centre, 1975–86 (special advr, 1986–90). Mem., later Dir, Christian Frontier Council, 1955–65; Chm., Cttee of British Council of Churches responsible for report on further educn of young people, 1960–61; Member: Finance Cttee, C of E Bd of Finance, 1960–68; CS Deptl Cttee to consider application of Fulton Report to Civil Service, 1968–70; Final Selection Bd, CS Commn, 1978–81. Trustee, Visnews, 1960–69; Vis. Fellow, Henley Management Coll. (formerly Administrative Staff Coll.), 1971–; Governor, Radley Coll., 1965–70; Chm., Radley Coll. War Meml Cttee, 1963–88. Chm., Ringstead Bay Protection Soc., 1983–. Inherited Lordship of the Manor, Fawley, 1992. FRSA. Olaf Medal, Norway. *Publications:* composer of light music (The Leander Waltz, Bless Them Lord, Seringa, Candlelight and others); contrib. to jls on management and indust. subjects. *Recreations:* walking, swimming, music. *Address:* Pinnocks, Fawley, near Henley-on-Thames, Oxon RG9 6JH. *T:* Henley (01491) 573017; Glen Cottage, Ringstead Bay, Dorchester, Dorset DT2 8NG. *T:* Warmwell (01305) 852686. *Clubs:* Savile, Lansdowne; Leander.

ARKFELD, Most Rev. Leo, CBE (Hon.) 1976; Archbishop of Madang, (RC), 1976–87; *b* 4 Feb. 1912; *s* of George Arkfeld and Mary Siemer. *Educ:* St Mary's Seminary, Techny, Ill., USA (BA). Bishop of Wewak, Papua New Guinea, 1948–76; Administrator Apostolic of Wewak, 1976. *Address:* PO Box 107, Wewak, Papua New Guinea.

ARMAGH, Archbishop of, and Primate of All Ireland, since 1986; **Most Rev. Dr Robert Henry Alexander Eames;** Baron Eames *cr* 1995 (Life Peer), of Armagh, in the County of Armagh; *b* 27 April 1937; *s* of William Edward and Mary Eleanor Thompson Eames; *m* 1966 Ann Christine Daly (*see* Lady Eames); two *s*. *Educ:* Belfast Royal Acad.; Methodist Coll., Belfast; Queen's Univ., Belfast (LLB (hons), PhD); Trinity Coll., Dublin. Research Scholar and Tutor, Faculty of Laws, QUB, 1960–63; Curate Assistant, Bangor Parish Church, 1963–66; Rector of St Dorothea's, Belfast, 1966–74; Examining Chaplain to Bishop of Down, 1973; Rector of St Mark's, Dundela, 1974–75; Bishop of Derry and Raphoe, 1975–80; Bishop of Down and Dromore, 1980–86. Select Preacher, Oxford Univ., 1987. Irish Rep., 1984, Mem. Standing Cttee, 1985, ACC; Chairman: Commn on Communion and Women in the Episcopate, 1988–; Commn on Inter-Anglican Relations, 1988–. Governor, Church Army, 1985–. Hon. LLD: QUB, 1989; TCD, 1992; Lancaster, 1994; Hon. DD Cambridge, 1994. *Publications:* A Form of Worship for Teenagers, 1965; The Quiet Revolution—Irish Disestablishment, 1970; Through Suffering, 1973; Thinking through Lent, 1978; Through Lent, 1984; Chains to be Broken, 1992; contribs to New Divinity, Irish Legal Quarterly, Criminal Law Review. The Furrow. *Address:* The See House, Cathedral Close, Armagh, Co. Armagh BT61 7EE.

ARMAGH, Archbishop of, (RC), and Primate of All Ireland, since 1990; **His Eminence Cardinal Cahal Brendan Daly;** *b* Oct. 1917. *Educ:* St Malachy's, Belfast; Queen's Univ., Belfast (BA Hons, Classics, MA); St Patrick's, Maynooth (DD); Institut Catholique, Paris (LPh). Ordained, 1941. Lecturer in Scholastic Philosophy, Queen's Univ., Belfast, 1946–62; Reader, 1962–67; consecrated Bishop, 1967; Bishop of Ardagh and Clonmacnois, 1967–82; Bishop of Down and Connor, 1982–90. Cardinal, 1991. *Publications:* Morals, Law and Life, 1962; Natural Law Morality Today, 1965; Violence in Ireland and Christian Conscience, 1973; Theologians and the Magisterium, 1977; Peace the Work of Justice, 1979; The Price of Peace, 1991; chapters in: Prospect for Metaphysics, 1961; Intellect and Hope, 1968; New Essays in Religious Language, 1969; Understanding the Eucharist, 1969. *Address:* Ara Coeli, Armagh, Ireland.

ARMAGH, Coadjutor Archbishop of, (RC); *see* Brady, Most Rev. Sean.

ARMAGH, Dean of; *see* Cassidy, Very Rev. H.

ARME, Prof. Christopher, PhD, DSc; CBiol, FIBiol; Professor of Zoology, University of Keele, since 1979; *b* 10 Aug. 1939; *s* of Cyril Boddington and Monica Henrietta Arme; *m* 1962; three *s*. *Educ:* Heanor Grammar Sch.; Univ. of Leeds (BSc 1961; PhD 1964); Univ. of Keele (DSc 1985). FIBiol 1980; CBiol 1980. SRC/NATO Res. Fellow, Univ. of Leeds, 1964–66; Res. Associate, Rice Univ., Texas, 1966–68; Lectr, later Reader, QUB, 1968–76; Head of Biology Gp, N Staffs Polytechnic, 1976–79; Head, Dept of Biol Scis, Univ. of Keele, 1981–88; Dir of Terrestrial and Freshwater Scis, NERC, 1993–95 (on leave of absence from Keele Univ.). British Society for Parasitology: Hon. Gen. Sec., 1980–83; Silver Jubilee Lectr, 1987; Vice Pres., 1988–90; Pres., 1990–92. Chm., Heads of Zool. Depts of Univs Gp, 1981–82; Institute of Biology: Hon. Treas. and Chm., Finance Cttee, 1986–93; Chm., Staffing Cttee, 1993–; Treas., Europ. Fedn of Parasitologists, 1992–; Mem., Biol Scis Cttee, and Chm., Animal Scis and Psychol. Sub-Cttee, SERC, 1989–92; Chm., Steering Cttee, NERC special topic prog. on wildlife diseases, 1992–93. Hon. Member: Czechoslovakian Parasitological Soc., 1989; All-Russia Soc. of Helminthologists, 1992; British Soc. for Parasitology, 1992; Bulgarian Soc. for Parasitology, 1995. Jt Editor, Parasitology, 1987–. K. I. Skryabin Medal, All-Russian Soc. of Helminthologists, 1994. *Publications:* (ed jtly) Biology of the Eucestoda, Vols I and II, 1983; (ed) Molecular Transfer across Parasite Membranes, 1988; (ed jtly) Toxic Reactions of the Liver, 1992; contribs to parasitological jls. *Address:* Department of Biological Sciences, University of Keele, Keele, Staffs ST5 5BG. *T:* Newcastle (Staffs) (01782) 583025.

ARMFIELD, Diana Maxwell, (Mrs Bernard Dunstan), RA 1991 (ARA 1989); RWS 1983 (ARWS 1977); RWA; RCA 1991; NEAC; painter, since 1965; *b* 11 June 1920; *d* of Joseph Harold Armfield and Gertrude Mary Uttley; *m* 1949, Bernard Dunstan, *qv*; three *s*. *Educ:* Bedales; Bournemouth Art Sch.; Slade Sch.; Central School of Arts and Crafts. MCSD. Textile/wallpaper designer, 1949–65; work in Fest. of Britain, 1951, and Permanent Collection, V&A Mus. Regular one woman exhibns, Browse & Darby (London), 1979–; exhibn, Friends' Room, RA, also Cardiff and Llanbedrog, 1995; Artist in Residence: Perth, WA, 1985; Jackson, Wyoming, 1989. Work in Permanent Collections: Govt picture collection, RWA; Yale Center for British Art; Nat. Trust; Contemporary Art Soc. for Wales; Lancaster City Mus.; RWS collection, BM; Faringdon Trust; Commissions: Reuters, Nat. Trust, 1989; Prince of Wales, 1989; Royal Acad. diploma collection. Hon. Mem., Pastel Soc., 1988. *Relevant publication:* The Art of Diana Armfield, by Julian Halsby, 1995. *Recreations:* music, gardening, travel. *Address:* 10 High Park Road, Kew, Richmond, Surrey TW9 4BH; Llwynhir, Parc, Bala, Gwynedd, North Wales LL23 7YU. *Club:* Arts.

ARMIDALE, Bishop of, since 1976; **Rt. Rev. Peter Chiswell;** *b* 18 Feb. 1934; *s* of Ernest and Florence Ruth Chiswell; *m* 1960, Betty Marie Craik; two *s* one *d*. *Educ:* Univ. of New South Wales (BE); Moore Theological College (BD London, Th. Schol.). Vicar of Bingara, 1961–68; Vicar of Gunnedah, 1968–76; Archdeacon of Tamworth, 1971–76. *Address:* Bishopscourt, Armidale, NSW 2350, Australia. *T:* (67) 724555.

ARMITAGE, Edward, CB 1974; Comptroller-General, Patent Office and Industrial Property and Copyright Department, Department of Trade (formerly Trade and Industry), 1969–77; *b* 16 July 1917; *s* of Harry and Florence Armitage; *m* 1940, Marjorie Pope; one *s* two *d*. *Educ:* Huddersfield Coll.; St Catharine's Coll., Cambridge. Patent Office, BoT: Asst Examr 1939; Examr 1944; Sen. Examr 1949; Principal Examr 1960; Suptg Examr 1962; Asst Comptroller 1966. Governor, Centre d'Etudes Internationales de la Propriété Industrielle, Strasbourg, 1975–85; Mem. Council, Common Law Inst. of Intellectual Property, 1981–. *Recreations:* bowls, bridge, gardening. *Address:* Lynwood, Lascot Hill, Wedmore, Somerset BS28 4AE. *T:* Wedmore (01934) 712079.

See also Peter Armitage.

ARMITAGE, Maj.-Gen. Geoffrey Thomas Alexander, CBE 1968 (MBE 1945); *b* 5 July 1917; *s* of late Lt-Col H. G. P. Armitage and late Mary Madeline (*née* Drought); *m* 1949, Monica Wall Kent (*widow, née* Poat); one *s* one step *d*. *Educ:* Haileybury Coll.; RMA, Woolwich (Sword of Honour). Commissioned Royal Artillery, 1937. Served War of 1939–45 (despatches, MBE), BEF, Middle East, Italy, NW Europe. Transferred to Royal Dragoons (1st Dragoons), 1951, comd 1956–59; Instructor (GSO1), IDC, 1959–60; Col GS, War Office, 1960–62; Comdt RAC Centre, 1962–65; Chief of Staff, HQ1 (BR) Corps, 1966–68; Dir, Royal Armoured Corps, 1968–70; GOC Northumbrian Dist, 1970–72; retd 1973. Dir, CLA Game Fair, 1974–80. *Recreations:* writing, some field sports. *Address:* Clyffe Cottage, Tincleton, near Dorchester, Dorset DT2 8QR. *Clubs:* Army and Navy, Kennel.

ARMITAGE, Henry St John Basil, CBE 1978 (OBE 1968); HM Diplomatic Service, retired; Middle East consultant; Honorary Secretary to British/Saudi Arabian Parliamentary Group; *b* 5 May 1924; *s* of Henry John Armitage and late Amelia Eleanor Armitage; *m* 1956, Jennifer Gerda Bruford, *d* of Prof. W. H. Bruford, FBA; one *s* one *d*. *Educ:* St Bede's and Bradford Grammar Schs; Lincoln Christ's Hosp.; Trinity Coll., Cambridge. Served Army, 1943–49; Arab Legion, 1946; British Mil. Mission to Saudi Arabia, 1946–49. Mil. Adviser to Saudi Arabian Minister of Defence, 1949–51; Desert Locust Control, Kenya and Aden Protectorates, 1952; in mil. service of Sultan of Muscat and Oman in Oman and Dhofar, 1952–59; Resident Manager, Gen. Geophysical Co. (Houston), Libya, 1959–60; Oil Conslt, Astor Associates, Libya, 1960–61; Business consIt, Beirut, 1962; joined HM Diplomatic Service, 1962; First Secretary (Commercial): Baghdad, 1963–67; Beirut, 1967–68; First Sec., Jedda, 1968 and 1969–74; Chargé d'Affaires: Jedda, 1969 and 1973; Abu Dhabi, 1975, 1976 and 1977; Counsellor and Consul Gen. in charge British Embassy, Dubai, 1974–78. *Recreations:* reading, travel. *Address:* The Old Vicarage, East Horrington, Wells, Somerset BA5 3EA. *Club:* Travellers'.

ARMITAGE, John Vernon, PhD; Principal, College of St Hild and St Bede, Durham, since 1975; *b* 21 May 1932; *s* of Horace Armitage and Evelyn (*née* Hauton); *m* 1963, Sarah Catherine Clay; two *s*. *Educ:* Rothwell Grammar Sch., Yorks; UCL (BSc, PhD); Cuddesdon Coll., Oxford. Asst Master: Pontefract High Sch., 1956–58; Shrewsbury Sch., 1958–59; Lectr in Maths, Univ. of Durham, 1959–67; Sen. Lectr in Maths, King's Coll., London, 1967–70; Prof. of Mathematical Educn, Univ. of Nottingham, 1970–75; Special Prof., Nottingham Univ., 1976–79. Chm., Math. Instruction Sub-Cttee, Brit. Nat. Cttee for Maths, Royal Soc., 1975–78. *Publications:* A Companion to Advanced Mathematics (with H. B. Griffiths), 1969; papers on theory of numbers in various jls. *Recreations:* railways, cricket and most games inexpertly. *Address:* The Principal's House, Leazes Lane, Durham DH1 1TB. *T:* Durham (0191) 3743050. *Club:* Athenæum.

ARMITAGE, Kenneth, CBE 1969; RA 1994; sculptor; *b* 18 July 1916; *m* 1940. Studied at Slade Sch., London, 1937–39. Served War of 1939–45 in the Army. Teacher of Sculpture, Bath Academy of Art, 1946–56. *One-man exhibitions:* Gimpel Fils, London, regularly 1952–; New York, 1954–58, the last at Paul Rosenberg & Co.; Marlborough Fine Art London, 1962, 1965; Arts Council Exhibn touring 10 English cities, 1972–73; Gall. Kasahara, Osaka, 1974, 1978 and Fuji Telecasting Gall., Tokyo, and Gal. Humanite, Nagoya; Stoke-on-Trent City Mus. and Art Gall., 1981; Sala Mendoza, Caracas, Venezuela, 1982; Taranman Gall., London, 1982; Retrospective Exhibn, Artcurial, Paris, 1985. Gregory Fellowship in sculpture, Leeds Univ., 1953–55; *Guest Artist:* Caracas, Venezuela, 1963; City of Berlin, 1967–69. *Work shown in:* Exhibn of Recent Sculpture in British Pavilion at 26th Venice Biennale, 1952; Internat. Open-Air Exhibns of sculpture in Antwerp, London, Sonsbeek, Varese, and Sydney; British Council Exhibns of sculpture since 1952, which have toured Denmark, Germany, Holland, Norway, Sweden, Switzerland, Canada, USA, and S America; New Decade Exhibn, Museum of Modern Art, New York, 1955; British Section of 4th Internat. São Paulo Biennial, Brazil, 1957; 5th Internat. Exhibn of Drawings and Engravings, Lugano, 1958 (prize-winner); British Pavilion at 29th Venice Biennale, 1958; Art since 1945, Kassel Exhibition, 1959; work in British Sculpture in the 'Sixties' exhibition, Tate Gallery, 1965; Internat. Open-air Exhibn, Hakone, Japan, 1969, 1971; 24 English Sculptors, Burlington House, 1971; Jubilee sculpture exhibn, Battersea Park, 1977; World Expo 88, Brisbane; Seoul Olympic sculpture exhibn, 1988; Twelve Stars, Europ. Parlt Art Collection, 1992; Chelsea Harbour Sculpture, 1993. Work represented in: Victoria and Albert Museum, Tate Gallery; Museum of Modern Art, New York; Musée D'Art Moderne, Paris; Galleria Nazionale d' Arti Moderne, Rome; Hakone Open-Air Sculpture Museum, Japan, and other galleries throughout the world. *Address:* 22a Avonmore Road, W14 8RR.

ARMITAGE, Air Chief Marshal Sir Michael (John), KCB 1983; CBE 1975; Commandant, Royal College of Defence Studies, 1988–89; *b* 25 Aug. 1930; *m* 1st, 1955 (marr. diss. 1969); three *s*; 2nd, 1970, Gretl Renate Steinig. *Educ:* Newport Grammar Sch., IW; Halton Apprentice; RAF Coll., Cranwell. psc 1965, jssc 1970, rcds 1975. Commnd 1953; flying and staff appts, incl. 28 Sqn, Hong Kong, and No 4 and No 1 Flying Trng Schools; Personal Staff Officer to Comdr 2ATAF, 1966; OC 17 Sqdn, 1967–70; Stn Comdr, RAF Luqa, Malta, 1972–74; Dir Forward Policy, Ministry of Defence (Air Force Dept), 1976–78; Dep. Comdr, RAF Germany, 1978–80; Senior RAF Mem., RCDS, 1980–81; Dir of Service Intelligence, 1982; Dep. Chief of Defence Staff (Intelligence), 1983–84; Chief of Defence Intelligence, 1985–86; Air Mem. for Supply and Orgn, Air Force Dept, MoD, 1986–87. Mem. Council, RUSI, 1986. Lectures on air power, defence and internat. affairs. *Publications:* (jtly) Air Power in the Nuclear Age, 1982; Unmanned Aircraft, 1988; The Royal Air Force: an illustrated history, 1993, 2nd edn 1995; contrib. prof. jls. *Recreations:* military history, shooting, reading, writing. *Address:* c/o Lloyds Bank, Cox & King's Branch, 7 Pall Mall, SW1Y 5NA. *Club:* Royal Air Force.

ARMITAGE, Prof. Peter, CBE 1984; Professor of Applied Statistics (formerly of Biomathematics), 1976–90, now Emeritus, and Fellow, St Peter's College, University of Oxford, 1976–90, now Emeritus Fellow; *b* 15 June 1924; *s* of Harry and Florence Armitage, Huddersfield; *m* 1947, Phyllis Enid Perry, London: one *s* two *d*. *Educ:* Huddersfield Coll.; Trinity Coll., Cambridge. Wrangler, 1947; MA Cambridge, 1952; PhD London, 1951; Ministry of Supply, 1943–45; National Physical Laboratory, 1945–46; Mem. Statistical Research Unit of Med. Research Council, London Sch. of Hygiene and

Trop. Med., 1947–61; Prof. of Medical Statistics, Univ. of London, 1961–76. President: Biometric Soc., 1972–73; Royal Statistical Soc., 1982–84 (Hon. Sec., 1958–64); Internat. Soc. for Clinical Biostatistics, 1990–91; Mem., International Statistical Institute, 1961. Hon. FFPM 1991. (Jtly) J. Allyn Taylor Prize, John P. Roberts Res. Inst., London, Ont, 1987; Guy Medals in bronze, silver and gold, Royal Statistical Soc., 1962, 1978, 1990. Editor, Biometrics, 1980–84. *Publications:* Sequential Medical Trials, 1960, 2nd edn 1975; Statistical Methods in Medical Research, 1971, 3rd edn 1994; papers in statistical and medical journals. *Recreation:* music. *Address:* 2 Reading Road, Wallingford, Oxon OX10 9DP. *T:* Wallingford (01491) 835840.

See also Edward Armitage.

ARMITAGE, (William) Kenneth; *see* Armitage, Kenneth.

ARMITT, John Alexander, FEng, FICE; Chief Executive, Union Railways, since 1993; *b* 2 Feb. 1946; *s* of Alexander Walter Armitt and Lily Irene (*née* Dunce); *m* 1969, Mavis Dorothy Sage; one *s* one *d*. *Educ:* Portsmouth Northern Grammar Sch.; Portsmouth Coll. of Technology. FEng 1993; FICE 1989. John Laing Construction, 1966–93; Jt Man. Dir, 1988–93; Chairman: J. Laing Internat., 1988–93; Laing Civil Engrg, 1988–93. Council Member: ICE, 1989–92 (Chm., Mgt Bd, 1989–92); FCEC, 1986–93 (Chm., European Affairs Cttee, 1989–92). Pres., Export Gp for Constructional Inds, 1992–93; Mem., Overseas Project Bd, DTI, 1992–93. Mem. Bd, Major Projects Assoc., 1994–. *Recreations:* sailing, golf, theatre, music. *Address:* c/o Union Railways Network Technical Centre, Wellesley Grove, Croydon CR9 1DY.

ARMOUR, Prof. Sir James, Kt 1995; CBE 1989; FRSE; FRCVS; Vice-Principal, 1990–95, and Professor Emeritus, since 1995, University of Glasgow; Chairman, Glasgow Dental Hospital and School NHS Trust, since 1995; *b* 17 Sept. 1929; *s* of James Angus Armour and Margaret Brown Roy; *m* 1st, 1953, Irene Morris (*d* 1988); two *s* two *d*; 2nd, 1992, Christine Strickland. *Educ:* Marr Coll., Troon; Univ. of Glasgow (PhD 1967). MRCVS 1952, FRCVS 1995; FRSE 1991. Colonial Service, Nigeria: Vet. Officer, 1953–57; Vet. Parasitologist, 1957–60; Parasitologist, Cooper Technical Bureau, Berkhamsted, 1960–63; University of Glasgow: Research Fellow, 1963–67; Lectr, 1967–70; Sen. Lectr, 1970–73; Reader, 1973–76; Professor of Veterinary Parasitology, 1976–90; Dean, Vet. Faculty, 1986–91. Dr *hc* Utrecht 1981; DVM&S Edinburgh, 1995. *Publications:* (with Urquhart and Duncan) Veterinary Parasitology, 1988; numerous contribs to vet. and parasitology jls. *Recreations:* golf, watching soccer and Rugby. *Address:* Mokoia, 11 Crosbie Road, Troon KA10 6HE. *Club:* Royal Troon Golf (Captain, 1990–92).

ARMOUR, Mary Nicol Neill, RSA 1958 (ARSA 1940); RSW 1956; RGI 1977 (Vice-President, 1982; Hon. President, 1983); Teacher of Still Life, Glasgow School of Art, 1952–62 (Hon. Life President, 1982); *b* 27 March 1902; *d* of William Steel; *m* 1927, William Armour, RSA, RSW, RGI (*d* 1979). *Educ:* Glasgow Sch. of Art (Hon. Fellow 1993). Has exhibited at Royal Academy, Royal Scottish Academy, Soc. of Scottish Artists, and Royal Glasgow Institute. Work in permanent collections: Glasgow Municipal Gallery; Edinburgh Corporation; Art Galleries of Aberdeen, Perth, Dundee, Newport, Paisley, Greenock and Victoria (Australia). Fellow, Paisley Coll. of Technol., 1989; Hon. Life Vice Pres., Paisley Inst., 1983. Hon. LLD Glasgow, 1980. *Recreations:* weaving, gardening. *Address:* 2 Gateside, Kilbarchan, Renfrewshire PA10 2LY. *T:* Kilbarchan (01505) 702873.

ARMOUR, Nicholas Hilary Stuart; HM Diplomatic Service; Head of Branch 1, Projects Export Promotion Division, Department of Trade and Industry, since 1994; *b* 12 June 1951; *s* of late Brig. William Stanley Gibson Armour and of Penelope Jean Armour; *m* 1982, Georgina Elizabeth Fortescue; two *d*. *Educ:* Ampleforth Coll.; Exeter Univ. (BA). FCO, 1974; MECAS, Lebanon, Beaconsfield, Jordan, 1975; Beirut, 1977; FCO, 1980; Head of Chancery, Athens, 1984; Asst Head of Dept, FCO, 1989; Counsellor, Muscat, 1991. *Recreations:* music, singing, sailing. *Address:* c/o Foreign and Commonwealth Office, King Charles Street, SW1A 2AH.

ARMSON, (Frederick) Simon (Arden); Chief Executive, The Samaritans, since 1990; *b* 11 Sept. 1948; *s* of late Frank Gerald Arden Armson and of Margaret Fenella Armson (*née* Newton); *m* 1975, Marion Albinia (*née* Hamilton-Russell); one *s* two *d*. *Educ:* Denstone Coll. Various administrative and managerial posts, NHS, 1970–84; Asst Gen. Sec. 1984–89, Gen. Sec. 1989, The Samaritans. FRSA 1993. *Recreations:* music, photography, cycling (cross country), walking, sailing. *Address:* Broad Oak, Hurley, Maidenhead, Berkshire SL6 5LW. *T:* Littlewick Green (01628) 824322.

ARMSON, Rev. Canon John Moss; Canon Residentiary, Rochester Cathedral, since 1989; *b* 21 Dec. 1939; *s* of Arthur Eric Armson and Edith Isobel Moss. *Educ:* Wyggeston Sch.; Selwyn Coll., Cambridge (MA); St Andrews Univ. (PhD); College of the Resurrection, Mirfield. Curate, St John, Notting Hill, 1966; Chaplain and Fellow, Downing Coll., Cambridge, 1969; Chaplain, 1973–77, Vice-Principal, 1977–82, Westcott House, Cambridge; Principal, Edinburgh Theol Coll., 1982–89. *Recreation:* landscaping. *Address:* Easter Garth, King's Orchard, Rochester, Kent ME1 1SX.

ARMSON, Simon; *see* Armson, F. S. A.

ARMSTRONG, family name of **Baron Armstrong of Ilminster.**

ARMSTRONG OF ILMINSTER, Baron *cr* 1988 (Life Peer), of Ashill in the county of Somerset; **Robert Temple Armstrong,** GCB 1983 (KCB 1978; CB 1974); CVO 1975; Secretary of the Cabinet, 1979–87, and Head of the Home Civil Service, 1983–87 (Joint Head, 1981–83), retired; Chairman: Biotechnology Investments Ltd, since 1989; Bristol and West Building Society, since 1993 (Director, since 1988); director of companies; *b* 30 March 1927; *o s* of Sir Thomas (Henry Wait) Armstrong, FRCM; *m* 1st, 1953, Serena Mary Benedicta (marr. diss. 1985), *er d* of Sir Roger Chance, 3rd Bt, MC; two *d*; 2nd, 1985, (Mary) Patricia, *d* of late C. C. Carlow. *Educ:* Dragon Sch., Oxford; Eton; Christ Church, Oxford (Hon. Student 1985). Asst Principal, Treasury, 1950–55; Private Secretary to: Rt Hon. Reginald Maudling, MP (when Economic Sec. to Treasury), 1953–54; Rt Hon. R. A. Butler, CH, MP (when Chancellor of the Exchequer), 1954–55; Principal, Treasury, 1955–57; Sec., Radcliffe Cttee on Working of Monetary System, 1957–59; returned to Treasury as Principal, 1959–64; Sec., Armitage Cttee on Pay of Postmen, 1964; Asst Sec., Cabinet Office, 1964–66; Sec. of Kindersley Review Body on Doctors' and Dentists' Remuneration and of Franks Cttee on Pay of Higher Civil Service, 1964–66; Asst Sec., Treasury, 1967–68; Jt Prin. Private Sec. to Rt Hon. Roy Jenkins, MP (Chancellor of the Exchequer), 1968; Under Secretary (Home Finance), Treasury, 1968–70; Principal Private Sec. to Prime Minister, 1970–75; Dep. Sec., 1973; Dep. Under-Sec. of State, Home Office, 1975–77, Permt Under Sec. of State, 1977–79. Director: BAT Industries, 1988–; Inchcape, 1988–95; Lucas Industries, 1989–92; N. M. Rothschild & Sons, 1988–; RTZ Corporation, 1988–; Shell Transport & Trading Co., 1988–; Carlton Television, 1991–; Mem., Supervisory Bd, Robeco Gp, 1988–. Chancellor, Univ. of Hull, 1994–. Chairman: Bd of Trustees, V & A Museum, 1988–; Royal Acad. of Music Foundn, 1988–; Trustee, Leeds Castle Foundn, 1988–; Dir, RAM (Hon. Fellow 1985); Member: Council of Management, Royal Philharmonic Soc., 1975–; Rhodes Trust, 1975–; Bd of Dirs, Royal Opera House, Covent Garden, 1988–93 (Sec., 1968–88). Fellow of Eton Coll., 1979–94. Hon. Bencher, Inner Temple, 1986. *Recreation:* music. *Address:* House of Lords, SW1A 0PW.

ARMSTRONG, Alan Gordon; Senior Lecturer in Economics, University of Bristol, since 1977; *b* 11 Feb. 1937; *s* of late Joseph Gordon Armstrong and of Evelyn Armstrong (*née* Aird); *m* 1963, Margaret Louise Harwood; one *s* one *d*. *Educ:* Bede Grammar Sch., Sunderland; Queens' Coll., Cambridge (MA). Economist, Reed Paper Gp, 1960–62; Res. Officer, Dept of Applied Econs, Univ. of Cambridge, 1962–69; Fellow, Selwyn Coll., Cambridge, 1967–69; Lectr in Econs, Univ. of Bristol, 1970–77. Part-time Mem., Monopolies and Mergers Commn, 1989–; Consultant on Economic Statistics to: UN Statistical Office, OECD, EEC, UK Central Statistical Office, DTI, NEDO, various times, 1970–; Member: EC Adv. Cttee on Econ. and Social Statistics, 1992–; UK Central Statistical Office (formerly Central Statistical Office Users') Adv. Cttee, 1992–. *Publications:* Input–Output Tables and Analysis, 1973; Structural Change in UK, 1974; Review of DTI Statistics, 1989; res. papers and jl articles on input–output, nat. accounts and the motor industry. *Recreations:* gardening (by necessity), badminton, cricket, church affairs. *Address:* Rock House, King's Hill, Nailsea, Bristol BS19 2AU. *T:* Bristol (01275) 853197.

ARMSTRONG, Sir Andrew (Clarence Francis), 6th Bt *cr* 1841, of Gallen Priory, King's County; CMG 1959; Permanent Secretary, Ministry of Mines and Power, Federation of Nigeria, retired; *b* 1 May 1907; *s* of E. C. R. Armstrong (*d* 1923) (*g s* of 1st Bt), FSA, MRIA, Keeper of Irish Antiquities and later Bluemantle Pursuivant, Herald's Coll., and Mary Frances (*d* 1953), *d* of Sir Francis Cruise; *S* cousin, 1987; *m* 1st, 1930, Phyllis Marguerite (*d* 1930), *e d* of Lt-Col H. Waithman, DSO; 2nd, 1932, Laurel May (*d* 1988), *d* of late A. W. Stuart; one *s* (and one *s* decd). *Educ:* St Edmund's Coll., Old Hall, Ware; Christ's Coll., Cambridge; BA. Colonial Administrative Service : Western Pacific, 1929; Nigeria, 1940. *Recreation:* croquet. *Heir:* *s* Christopher John Edmund Stuart Armstrong, MBE, Lt-Col RCT [*b* 15 Jan. 1940; *m* 1972, Georgina Elizabeth Carey, *d* of Lt-Col W. G. Lewis; three *s* one *d*]. *Address:* No 5 Thamesfield Court, Wargrave Road, Henley-on-Thames, Oxon RG9 2LX. *T:* Henley-on-Thames (01491) 577635. *Club:* Phyllis Court.

ARMSTRONG, Anne Legendre, (Mrs Tobin Armstrong); Member, Board of Directors: General Motors, and Halliburton Company, since 1977; Boise Cascade Corporation, since 1978; American Express, 1975–76 and since 1981; Glaxo Holding plc, since 1991; *b* New Orleans, Louisiana, 27 Dec. 1927; *d* of Armant Legendre and Olive Martindale; *m* 1950, Tobin Armstrong; three *s* two *d*. *Educ:* Foxcroft Sch., Middleburg, Va; Vassar Coll., NY (BA). Deleg. Nat. Conventions, 1964, 1968, 1972, 1980, 1984; Mem. Republican Nat. Cttee, 1968–73 (Co-Chm., 1971–73); Counselor to the President, with Cabinet rank, 1973–74; Ambassador to the Court of St James's, 1976–77. Co-Chm., Reagan/Bush Campaign, 1980; Chm., President's Foreign Intelligence Adv. Bd, 1981–90. Chm., Bd of Trustees, Center for Strategic and Internat. Studies, Georgetown Univ., 1987–. Member: Council on Foreign Relations, 1977–; Chm. E-SU of the US, 1977–80. Trustee: Southern Methodist Univ., 1977–86; Economic Club of NY, 1978–81 (Mem., 1982–); Amer. Associates of the Royal Acad. Citizen Regent, Smithsonian Instn, 1978–. Hon. Mem., City of London Br., Royal Soc. of St George, 1978; Mem. and Governor, Ditchley Foundn, 1977–87. Pres., Blair House Restoration Fund, 1985–. Hon. LLD: Bristol, 1976; Washington and Lee, 1976; Williams Coll., 1977; St Mary's Univ., 1978; Tulane, 1978; Hon. LHD: Mt Vernon Coll., 1978; Ripon Coll., 1986; Hamilton Coll., 1990. Gold Medal, Nat. Inst. Social Scis, 1977. Josephine Meredith Langstaff Award, Nat. Soc. Daughters of British Empire in US, 1978; Republican Woman of the Year Award, 1979; Texan of the Year Award, 1981; Texas Women's Hall of Fame, 1986; Presidential Medal of Freedom, 1987; Golden Plate Award, Amer. Acad. of Achievement, 1989. Phi Beta Kappa. *Address:* Armstrong Ranch, Armstrong, TX 78338, USA. *Club:* Pilgrims (New York).

ARMSTRONG, Prof. Arthur Hilary, MA Cantab; FBA 1970; Emeritus Professor: University of Liverpool, since 1972; Dalhousie University, Halifax, Nova Scotia, since 1983; *b* 13 Aug. 1909; *s* of the Rev. W. A. Armstrong and Mrs E. M. Armstrong (*née* Cripps); *m* 1933, Deborah, *d* of Alfred Wilson and Agnes Claudia Fox Pease; two *s* two *d* (and one *d* decd). *Educ:* Lancing Coll.; Jesus Coll., Cambridge. Asst Lectr in Classics, University Coll., Swansea, 1936–39; Professor of Classics, Royal University of Malta, Valletta, 1939–43; Classical VIth Form Master, Beaumont Coll., Old Windsor, Berks, 1943–46; Lectr in Latin, University Coll., Cardiff, 1946–50; Gladstone Professor of Greek, Univ. of Liverpool, 1950–72; Vis. Prof. of Classics and Phil., Dalhousie Univ., Halifax, NS, 1972–83. Killam Sen. Fellow, Dalhousie Univ., 1970–71. *Publications:* The Architecture of the Intelligible Universe in the Philosophy of Plotinus, 1940, repr. 1967 (French trans. with new preface, 1984); An Introduction to Ancient Philosophy, 1947 (American edn, 1949, 4th edn, 1965, last repr. 1981); Plotinus, 1953 (American edn, 1963); Christian Faith and Greek Philosophy (with R. A. Markus), 1960 (American edn, 1964); Plotinus I–VII (Loeb Classical Library), 1966–88; Cambridge History of Later Greek and Early Mediæval Philosophy (Editor and part author), 1967, repr. 1970; St Augustine and Christian Platonism, 1968; Plotinian and Christian Studies, 1979; Classical Mediterranean Spirituality (Vol. 15 of World Spirituality) (Editor and part author), 1986; Hellenic and Christian Studies, 1990; contribs to Classical Qly, Jl Hellenic Studies, Jl Theological Studies, etc. *Recreations:* travel, gardening. *Address:* Minia, Livesey Road, Ludlow, Shropshire SY8 1EX. *T:* Ludlow (01584) 872854.

ARMSTRONG, Rt. Hon. Ernest, PC 1979; *b* 12 Jan. 1915; *s* of John and Elizabeth Armstrong; *m* 1941, Hannah P. Lamb; one *s* one *d*. *Educ:* Wolsingham Grammar Sch. Schoolmaster, 1937–52; Headmaster, 1952–64. Chm., Sunderland Educn Cttee, 1960–65. MP (Lab) NW Durham, 1964–87. Asst Govt Whip, 1967–69; Lord Comr, HM Treasury, 1969–70; an Opposition Whip, 1970–73; Parly Under-Sec. of State, DES, 1974–75, DoE, 1975–79; Dep. Chm., Ways and Means and Dep. Speaker, 1981–87. Vice-Pres., Methodist Conf., 1974–75. Pres., Northern Football League, 1982–. *Recreation:* walking. *Address:* Penny Well, Witton-le-Wear, Bishop Auckland, Co. Durham DL14 0AR. *T:* Witton-le-Wear (01388) 488397.

See also H. J. Armstrong.

ARMSTRONG, Dr Ernest McAlpine, FRCPGlas, FRCGP; Secretary, British Medical Association, since 1993; *b* 3 June 1945; *s* of Ernest Armstrong and Mary Brownlie McLean Armstrong (*née* McAlpine); *m* 1970, Dr Katherine Mary Dickson Young; two *s*. *Educ:* Hamilton Acad.; Glasgow Univ. (BSc (Hons) 1968; MB ChB (Hons) 1970). MRCP 1975; FRCGP 1987; FRCPGlas 1988. Lectr in Pathology, Glasgow Univ., 1971–74; Trainee Assistant, Douglas, 1974–75; Principal in gen. practice, Argyll, 1975–93. Chairman: Argyll and Clyde Area Med. Cttee, 1981–84; Scottish Gen. Med. Services Cttee, 1989–92; British Medical Association: Negotiator, Gen. Med. Services Cttee, 1990–93 (Dep. Chm., 1992–93); Chm., Scottish Council, 1992–93. *Publications:* articles on ultrastructure, clinical immunology and med. politics. *Recreations:* church music, opera, sailing, travelling. *Address:* British Medical Association, Tavistock House, Tavistock Square, WC1H 9JP. *T:* 0171–387 4499; Craiglora, Connel, Argyll PA37 1PH. *T:* Connel (01631) 71232. *Club:* Caledonian.

ARMSTRONG, Frank William, FEng 1991; FIMechE; FRAeS; independent technical consultant, since 1991; *b* 26 March 1931; *s* of Frank Armstrong and Millicent L. Armstrong;

m 1957, Diane T. Varley; three *d*. *Educ:* Stretford Grammar Sch.; Royal Technical Coll., Salford; Queen Mary Coll., Univ. of London (BSc Eng; MSc Eng 1956). FIMechE 1981; FRAeS 1981. Massey-Harris Ltd, 1947–51; De Havilland Engine Co., 1956–58; Admiralty Engineering Lab., 1958–59; NGTE, 1959–78; Engine Div., MoD (PE), 1978–81; Dep. Dir, R&D, NGTE, 1981–83; Royal Aircraft, later Royal Aerospace, Establishment: Head of Propulsion Dept, 1983–87; Dep. Dir (Aircraft), 1987–88; Dep. Dir (Aerospace Vehicles), 1988–90; Dir (Aerospace Vehicles), 1990–91. *Publications:* contribs on aeronautics research, gas turbines and aircraft propulsion to learned jls. *Recreations:* mountaineering, music, aviation history. *Address:* 6 Corringway, Crookham, Fleet, Hants GU13 0AN. *T:* Fleet (01252) 616526.

ARMSTRONG, Hilary Jane; MP (Lab) Durham North West, since 1987; *b* 30 Nov. 1945; *d* of Rt Hon. Ernest Armstrong, *qv*. *Educ:* Monkwearmouth Comp. Sch., Sunderland; West Ham Coll. of Technology (BSc Sociology); Univ. of Birmingham (Dip in Social Work). VSO, Murray Girls' High Sch., Kenya, 1967–69; Social Worker, Newcastle City Social Services Dept, 1970–73; Community Worker, Southwick Neighbourhood Action Project, Sunderland, 1973–75; Lectr, Community and Youth Work, Sunderland Polytechnic, 1975–86. Frontbench spokesperson on education, 1988–92 (under-fives, primary, and special educn), on Treasury affairs, 1994–; PPS to Leader of the Opposition, 1992–94. *Recreations:* reading, knitting. *Address:* House of Commons, Westminster, SW1A 0AA. *T:* 0171–219 5076; (constituency) Bishop Auckland (01388) 767065.

ARMSTRONG, Jack; *see* Armstrong, J. A.

ARMSTRONG, John Archibald, (Jack), OC 1983; retired; Chief Executive Officer, 1973–82, and Chairman, 1974–82, Imperial Oil Ltd; *b* Dauphin, Manitoba, 24 March 1917. *Educ:* Univ. of Manitoba (BSc Geol.); Queen's Univ. at Kingston (BSc Chem. Engrg). Worked for short time with Geol Survey of Canada and in mining industry; joined Imperial Oil Ltd as geologist, Regina, 1940; appts as: exploration geophysicist, western Canada, and with affiliated cos in USA and S America; Asst Reg. Manager, Producing Dept, 1949; Asst Co-ordinator, Producing Dept of Standard Oil Co. (NJ), New York; Gen. Man., Imperial's Producing Dept, Toronto, 1960; Dir, 1961; Dir resp. for Marketing Ops, 1963–65; Exec. Vice-Pres., 1966, Pres. 1970, Chief Exec. Officer, 1973, Chm., 1974. Chm., Commonwealth Study Conf. Assoc. Life Mem., Fraser Inst. Hon. LLD: Winnipeg, 1978; Calgary, 1980.

ARMSTRONG, Neil A.; Chairman, CTA Inc., since 1982; formerly NASA Astronaut (Commander, Apollo 11 Rocket Flight to the Moon, 1969); *b* Wapakoneta, Ohio, USA, 5 Aug. 1930; *s* of Stephen and Viola Armstrong, Wapakoneta; *m* 1956, Janet Shearon, Evanston, Ill; two *s*. *Educ:* High Sch., Wapakoneta, Ohio; Univ. of Southern California (MS); Purdue Univ. (BSc). Pilot's licence obtained at age of 16. Served in Korea (78 combat missions) being a naval aviator, 1949–52. He joined NASA's Lewis Research Center, 1955 (then NACA Lewis Flight Propulsion Lab.) and later transf. to NASA High Speed Flight Station at Edwards Air Force Base, Calif, as an aeronautical research pilot for NACA and NASA; in this capacity, he performed as an X-15 project pilot, flying that aircraft to over 200,000 feet and approximately 4,000 miles per hour; other flight test work included piloting the X-1 rocket airplane, the F-100, F-101, F-102, F-104, F5D, B-47, the paraglider, and others; as pilot of the B-29 "drop" aircraft, he participated in the launches of over 100 rocket airplane flights. Selected as an astronaut by NASA, Sept. 1962; served as backup Command Pilot for Gemini 5 flight; as Command Pilot for Gemini 8 mission, launched 16 March 1966; he performed the first successful docking of 2 vehicles in space; served as backup Command Pilot for Gemini 11 mission; assigned as backup Comdr for Apollo VIII Flight, 1969; Dep. Associate Administrator of Aeronautics, NASA HQ, Washington, 1970–71; University Prof. of Aerospace Engrg, Univ. of Cincinnati, 1971–79; Chm., Cardwell International Ltd, 1980–82. Director: Cincinnati Gas and Electric Co.; Eaton Corp.; Cincinnati Milacron; UAL Inc. Mem., Nat. Acad. of Engrg. Fellow, Soc. of Experimental Test Pilots; FRAeS. Honours include NASA Exceptional Service Medal, and AIAA Astronautics Award for 1966; RGS Gold Medal, 1970. Presidential Medal for Freedom, 1969.

ARMSTRONG, Richard, CBE 1993; conductor; Music Director, Scottish Opera, since 1993; *b* 7 Jan. 1943. *Educ:* Wyggeston School, Leicester; Corpus Christi College, Cambridge (Hon. Fellow, 1994). Music staff, Royal Opera House, Covent Garden, 1966–68; Welsh National Opera: head of music staff, 1968–73; Musical Director, 1973–86; Principal Guest Conductor, 1987–; Principal Guest Conductor, Frankfurt Opera, 1987–90. Hon. DMus De Montfort, 1992. Janáček Medal, 1978. *Recreations:* walking, food. *Address:* c/o Ingpen & Williams, 14 Kensington Court, W8 5DN.

ARMSTRONG, Robert George, CBE 1972; MC 1946; TD 1958; Deputy Director and Controller, Savings Bank, Department for National Savings, 1969–74, retired (Deputy Director and Controller, Post Office Savings Bank, 1964); *b* 26 Oct. 1913; *s* of late George William Armstrong; *m* 1947, Clara Christine Hyde; one *s* one *d*. *Educ:* Marylebone Grammar Sch.; University Coll., London. Post Office Engineering Dept, 1936–50. Served War of 1939–45, Royal Signals. Principal, PO Headquarters, 1950; Asst Sec., 1962; Dep. Dir of Savings, 1963; Under-Sec., 1972. *Address:* Barryleigh, Wheelers Lane, Brockham, Betchworth, Surrey RH3 7HJ. *T:* Betchworth (01737) 843217.

ARMSTRONG, Sheila Ann; soprano; *b* 13 Aug. 1942; *m* 1980, Prof. D. E. Cooper, *qv*. *Educ:* Hirst Park Girls' Sch., Ashington, Northumberland; Royal Academy of Music, London. Debut Sadler's Wells, 1965 Glyndebourne, 1966, Covent Garden, 1973. Sings all over Europe, Far East, N and S America; has made many recordings. K. Ferrier and Mozart Prize, 1965; Hon. RAM 1970, FRAM 1973. Hon. MA Newcastle, 1979; Hon. DMus Durham, 1991. *Recreations:* interior decoration, collecting antique keys, gardening.

ARMSTRONG, Dr Terence Edward; Founder Fellow, Clare Hall, since 1964, Vice-President, 1985–87, and Reader in Arctic Studies, 1977–83, now Emeritus, Cambridge University; *b* 7 April 1920; *s* of Thomas Mandeville Emerson Armstrong and Jane Crawford (*née* Young); *m* 1943, Iris Decima Forbes; two *s* two *d*. *Educ:* Winchester; Magdalene Coll., Cambridge (BA 1941; MA 1947; PhD 1951). Served Army, 1940–46 (Intelligence Corps, parachutist, wounded at Arnhem). Scott Polar Research Institute: Res. Fellow in Russian, 1947–56; Asst Dir of Res. (Polar), 1956–77; Actg Dir, 1982–83; Tutor, Clare Hall, Cambridge, 1967–74. Extensive travel in Arctic and sub-Arctic, incl. voyage through NW Passage, 1954. US Nat. Sci. Foundn Sen. For. Scientist Fellowship, Univ. of Alaska, 1970; Vis. Prof. of Northern Studies, Trent Univ., Ontario, 1988. Chm., Wkg Gp on Arctic Science Policy, NERC, 1987–88. Jt Hon. Sec., Hakluyt Soc., 1965–90. Hon. LLD McGill, 1963; Hon. DSc Alaska, 1980. Cuthbert Peek Award, RGS, 1954; Victoria Medal, RGS, 1978. *Publications:* The Northern Sea Route, 1952; Sea Ice North of the USSR, 1958; The Russians in the Arctic, 1958; Russian Settlement in the North, 1965; (ed) Yermak's Campaign in Siberia, 1975; (jtly) The Circumpolar North, 1978; contribs to jls on socio-economic problems of Arctic and sub-Arctic regions. *Recreations:* making music, walking, foreign travel. *Address:* Harston House, Harston, Cambridge CB2 5NH. *T:* Cambridge (01223) 870262.

ARMSTRONG-JONES, family name of **Earl of Snowdon.**

ARMYTAGE, Captain David George, CBE 1981; Royal Navy, retired; Secretary General, British Diabetic Association, 1981–91; *b* 4 Sept. 1929; *e s* of late Rear-Adm. Reginald William Armytage, GC, CBE and of Mrs Sylvia Beatrice Armytage; *heir* to Sir (John) Martin Armytage, Bt, *qv*; *m* 1954, Countess Cosima Antonia de Bosdari; two *s* one *d*. *Educ:* RNC, Dartmouth. Comd Motor Torpedo Boats, 1952–53; Direction Officer: 809 Sqn, 1956–58; HMS Chichester, 1958–59; Action Data Automation Project Team, 1959–64; Direction Officer, HMS Eagle, 1964–66; Directorate, Navigation and Tactical Control, 1966–68; comd HMS Minerva, 1968–70; Defence Policy Staff, 1970–72; Naval Asst to First Sea Lord, 1972–74; Internat. Mil. Staff, Brussels, 1975–76; comd, HMS Scylla, 1976 and HMS Jupiter, 1977–78. Capt., 7th Frigate Sqn, 1976–78; Dep. Dir, Naval Warfare, 1978–80; comd, NATO Standing Naval Force Atlantic, 1980–81. ADC to the Queen, 1981. *Recreations:* sailing, gardening, shooting. *Address:* Sharcott Manor, Pewsey, Wilts SN9 5PA. *T:* Marlborough (01672) 63485. *Clubs:* Oriental, Royal Naval Sailing Association; Royal Channel Islands Yacht.

ARMYTAGE, Sir (John) Martin, 9th Bt *cr* 1738, of Kirklees, Yorkshire; *b* 26 Feb. 1933; *s* of Sir John Lionel Armytage, 8th Bt, and of Evelyn Mary Jessamine, *d* of Edward Herbert Fox, Adbury Park, Newbury; *S* father, 1983. *Heir: cousin* Captain David George Armytage, *qv*. *Address:* 5 St James's Place, Cheltenham, Glos GL50 2EG. *T:* Cheltenham (01242) 525869.

ARMYTAGE, Prof. Walter Harry Green; Professor of Education, University of Sheffield, 1954–82, now Emeritus Professor; Gerald Read Professor of Education, Kent State University, Ohio, 1982–85; *b* 22 Nov. 1915; *e s* of Walter Green Armytage and Harriet Jane May Armytage; *m* 1948, Lucy Frances Horsfall; one *s*. *Educ:* Redruth County School; Downing Coll., Cambridge. 1st Cl. Hist. Trip. 1937, Cert. in Educ., 1938. History Master, Dronfield Grammar Sch., 1938–39; served War of 1939–45 (despatches); Captain, London Irish Rifles. Univ. of Sheffield: Lectr, 1946; Sen. Lectr, 1952; Pro-Vice-Chancellor, 1964–68. Visiting Lecturer: Univ. of Michigan, USA, 1955, 1959, 1961, 1963, 1975; Newcastle, NSW, 1977; Lectures: Ballard-Matthews, University Coll. of North Wales, 1973; Cantor, RSA, 1969; Hawkesley, IMechE, 1969; S. P. Thompson, IEE, 1972; Galton, Eugenics Soc., 1974; Clapton, Leeds Univ., 1979. Hon. DLitt: NUU, 1977; Hull, 1980; Hon. LLD Sheffield, 1991. *Publications:* A. J. Mundella 1825–1897: the Liberal background of the Labour Movement, 1951; Thomas Hughes: the life of the author of Tom Brown's Schooldays, 1953 (with E. C. Mack); Civic Universities: aspects of a British tradition, 1955; Sir Richard Gregory: his life and work, 1957; A Social History of Engineering, 1961; Heavens Below: Utopian experiments in England 1560–1960, 1962; Four Hundred Years of English Education, 1964; The Rise of the Technocrats, 1965; The American Influence on English Education, 1967; Yesterday's Tomorrows: a historical survey of future societies, 1968; The French Influence on English Education, 1968; The German Influence on English Education, 1969; The Russian Influence on English Education, 1969; (ed jtly) Perimeters of Social Repair, 1978. *Recreations:* walking, gardening. *Address:* 3 The Green, Totley, Sheffield, South Yorks S17 4AT. *T:* Sheffield (0114) 236 2515. *Club:* University Staff (Sheffield).

ARNAULT, Bernard Jean Etienne; President, since 1989, and Chairman, Louis Vuitton Moët Hennessy; *b* Roubaix, 5 March 1949; *s* of Jean Arnault and Marie-Jo (*née* Savinel); *m* 1991, Hélène Mercier; two *s*; one *s* one *d* by former marriage. *Educ:* Ecole Polytechnique, Paris. Qualified as engineer, 1971. Director General: Ferret Savinel, 1978–84; Financière Agache SA, 1984–89; Boussac Saint-Frères SA, 1984–; Pres., Christian Dior, 1994–. Man of the Year, NY, 1991. Légion d'Honneur; Ordre des Arts et des Lettres, 1995. *Recreations:* music, piano, tennis. *Address:* (office) 30 avenue Hoche, 75008 Paris, France. *T:* 44132222.

ARNDT, Ulrich Wolfgang, MA, PhD; FRS 1982; Member, Scientific Staff of Medical Research Council Laboratory of Molecular Biology, Cambridge, since 1962; *b* 23 April 1924; *o s* of E. J. and C. M. Arndt; *m* 1958, Valerie Howard, *e d* of late Maj.-Gen. F. C. Hilton-Sergeant, CB, CBE, QHP; three *d*. *Educ:* Dulwich Coll.; King Edward VI High Sch., Birmingham; Emmanuel Coll., Cambridge (MA, PhD). Metallurgy Dept, Birmingham Univ., 1948–49; Davy-Faraday Laboratory of Royal Instn, 1950–63; Dewar Fellow of Royal Instn, 1957–61; Univ. of Wisconsin, Madison, 1956; Institut Laue-Langevin, Grenoble, 1972–73. *Publications:* (with B. T. M. Willis) Single Crystal Diffractometry, 1966; (with A. J. Wonacott) The Rotation Method in Crystallography, 1977; papers in scientific jls. *Recreations:* walking, reading. *Address:* 28 Barrow Road, Cambridge CB2 2AS. *T:* Cambridge (01223) 350660.

ARNELL, Richard Anthony Sayer; Hon. FTCL; composer; conductor; poet; Principal Lecturer, Trinity College of Music, 1981–87 (Teacher of Composition, 1949–81); *b* 15 Sept. 1917; *s* of late Richard Sayer Arnell and of Hélène Marie Scherf; *m* 1992, Joan Heycock. *Educ:* The Hall, Hampstead; University Coll. Sch., NW3; Royal Coll. of Music. Music Consultant, BBC North American Service, 1943–46; Lectr, Royal Ballet Sch., 1958–59. Editor, The Composer, 1961–64; Chairman: Composers' Guild of GB, 1965, 1974–75 (Vice-Pres., 1992–); Young Musicians' Symph. Orch. Soc., 1973–75. Vis. Lectr (Fulbright Exchange), Bowdoin Coll., Maine, 1967–68; Vis. Prof. Hofstra Univ., New York, 1968–70. Music Dir and Board Mem., London Internat. Film Sch., 1975–89 (Chm., Film Sch. Trust, 1981–87; Chm., Friends of LIFS, 1982–87, Vice-Pres., 1988–); Music Dir, Ram Filming Ltd, 1980–91; Director: Organic Sounds Ltd, 1982–87; A plus A Ltd, 1984–89. Chm., Friends of TCM Junior Dept, 1986–87 (Vice-Pres., 1987–). Chairman: Tadcaster Civic Soc. Music and Arts Cttee, 1988–91; Saxmundham Music and Arts, 1992–. Composer of the Year 1966 (Music Teachers Assoc. Award); Tadcaster Town Council Merit Award, 1990. Compositions include: 6 symphonies; 2 concertos for violin; concerto for harpsichord; 2 concertos for piano; 6 string quartets; 2 quintets; piano trio; piano works; songs; cantatas; organ works; music for string orchestra, wind ensembles, brass ensembles, song cycles; electronic music. *Opera:* Love in Transit; Moonflowers. *Ballet scores:* Punch and the Child, for Ballet Soc., NY, 1947; Harlequin in April, for Arts Council, 1951; The Great Detective, for Sadler's Wells Theatre Ballet, 1953; The Angels, for SWRB, 1957; Giselle (Adam) re-orchestrated, for Ballet Rambert, 1965. *Film scores:* The Land, 1941; The Third Secret, 1963; The Visit, 1964; The Man Outside, 1966; Topsail Schooner, 1966; Bequest for a Village, 1969; Second Best, 1972; Stained Glass, 1973; Wires Over the Border, 1974; Black Panther, 1977; Antagonist, 1980; Dilemma, 1981; Doctor in the Sky, 1983; Toulouse Lautrec, 1984; Light of the World, 1990; The Europeans, 1992. *Other works:* Symphonic Portrait, Lord Byron, for Sir Thomas Beecham, 1953; Landscapes and Figures, for Sir Thomas Beecham, 1956; Petrified Princess, puppet operetta (libretto by Bryan Guinness), for BBC, 1959; Robert Flaherty, Impression for Radio Eireann, 1960; Musica Pacifica for Edward Benjamin, 1963; Festival Flourish, for Salvation Army, 1965; 2nd piano concerto, for RPO, 1967; Overture, Food of Love, for Portland Symph. Orch., 1968; My Ladye Greene Sleeves, for Hofstra Univ., 1968; Life Boat Voluntary, for RNLI, 1974; Call, for LPO, 1980; Ode to Beecham, for RPO, 1986; War God II, 1987. *Mixed media:* Nocturne: Prague, 1968; I Think of all Soft Limbs, for Canadian Broadcasting Corp., 1971; Astronaut One, 1973; Not Wanted on Voyage, 1990; Con Amore, 1990; Xanadu, 1993. *Address:* Benhall Lodge, Benhall, Saxmundham, Suffolk IP17 1DJ. *Club:* Savage.

ARNOLD, Rev. Duane Wade-Hampton, PhD; Principal, St Chad's College, University of Durham, since 1994; *b* 5 Aug. 1953; *s* of Wade Hampton Arnold and Louise Elizabeth (*née* Hensley); *m* 1980, Janet Lee Drew. *Educ:* Univ. of New York (BA 1979); Concordia Univ. (MA 1981); Philadelphia Univ. (MDiv 1982); Cambridge Univ. (DipTheol 1983); St Chad's Coll., Durham (PhD 1989). STh (Lambeth Dip. in Theol.), 1989. Minister, First Church, Detroit, Michigan, 1985–87; Precentor, St Paul's Cathedral, Detroit, 1987; Chaplain, Wayne State Univ., Detroit, 1988–91; Curate, St Thomas Church, Fifth Ave, NY, 1991–93. Tutor, St Chad's Coll., Durham, 1983–85; Lecturer: in Religious Studies, Univ. of Detroit, 1985–88; in Church History, Ashland Seminary, Ohio, 1987–91. ChStJ 1990. Governor's Award for Distinguished Service, Michigan, 1988. Officer, Order of Polonia Restituta (Poland), 1987; Legion of Merit (USA), 1994. *Publications:* A Lutheran Reader, 1982; The Way, the Truth and the Life, 1982; Francis, A Call to Conversion, 1990; Prayers of the Martyrs, 1991; The Early Episcopal Career of Athanasius of Alexandria, 1991; Praying with John Donne and George Herbert, 1992; *De Doctrina Christiana,* a Classic of Western Civilization, 1995; contribs to numerous learned jls. *Recreations:* shooting, restoring college halls and churches. *Address:* The Principal's Lodge, St Chad's College, Durham DH1 3RH. *T:* 0191–374 3367. *Clubs:* Caledonian, St John's House; New York Athletic (New York).

ARNOLD, Rt. Rev. George Feversham, DD; *b* 30 Dec. 1914; *s* of Arnold Feversham and Elsie Mildred Arnold; *m* 1940, Mary Eleanor Sherman Holmes; one *s* one *d. Educ:* Univ. of King's Coll., Halifax, NS (LTh 1937, BD 1944); Dalhousie Univ. (BA 1935, MA 1938). Rector: Louisbourg, 1938–41; Mahone Bay, 1941–50; St John's, Fairview, 1950–53; Windsor, 1953–58; Clerical Sec. and Diocesan Registrar, 1958–67; Exam. Chaplain to Bishop of Nova Scotia, 1947–70; Hon. Canon of All Saints Cathedral, 1959–63, Canon, 1963–67; Bishop Suffragan of Nova Scotia, 1967–75, Bishop Coadjutor, May–Sept. 1975; Bishop of Nova Scotia, 1975–79. Hon. DD, King's Coll., Halifax, 1968. *Recreation:* yachting. *Address:* 56 Holmes Hill Road, Hantsport, NS B0P 1P0, Canada.

ARNOLD, Glynis, (Mrs Elliott Arnold); *see* Johns, Glynis.

ARNOLD, Jacques Arnold; MP (C) Gravesham, since 1987; *b* London, 27 Aug. 1947; *s* of late Samuel Arnold and Eugenie (*née* Patentine); *m* 1976, Patricia Anne, *er d* of Dennis Maunder, of Windsor; one *s* two *d. Educ:* schools in Brazil and by correspondence; London School of Economics (BSc (Econ) 1972). Asst Gp Rep., Midland Bank, São Paulo, 1976–78; Regl Dir, Thomas Cook Gp, 1978–84; Asst Trade Finance Dir, Midland Bank, 1984–85; Dir, American Express Europe Ltd, 1985–87; has travelled to over 70 countries on business. County Councillor for Oundle, Northants, 1981–85. Contested (C) Coventry SE, 1983. PPS to Minister of State: for Envmt and Countryside, 1992–93; Home Office, 1993–. Mem., Educn, Arts and Sci. Select Cttee, 1989–92; Sec., Cons. Backbench Cttee on Foreign and Commonwealth Affairs, 1990–92. Secetary: British-Latin-American Parly Gp, 1987–; Scout Assoc. Parly Gp, 1987–; Chm., British Brazilian Parly Gp, 1992–. Chm., LSE Cons. Soc., 1971–72; Treasurer, Nat. Assoc. of Cons. Graduates, 1974–76; Chm., Hyde Park Tories, 1975–76; Vice-Chairman: Croydon NE Cons. Assoc., 1974–76; Corby Cons. Assoc., 1983–85. Trustee, Environment Foundn, 1989–. Grand Official, Order of Southern Cross (Brazil), 1993. *Publications:* various political articles and pamphlets. *Recreations:* family life, gardening, philately. *Address:* House of Commons, SW1A 0AA. *T:* 0171–219 4150. *Club:* Carlton.

ARNOLD, Rt. Hon. Sir John Lewis, Kt 1972; PC 1979; President of Family Division, 1979–88; a Judge in the Division, 1972–88; *b* 6 May 1915; *s* of late A. L. Arnold and E. K. Arnold; *m* 1940, Alice Margaret Dorothea (*née* Cookson) (marr. diss., 1963); one *s* one *d; m* 1963, Florence Elizabeth, *d* of H. M. Hague, Montreal; one *s* two *d. Educ:* Wellington Coll.; abroad. Called to Bar, Middle Temple, 1937; served War of 1939–45 in Army (despatches, 1945); resumed practice at Bar, 1946; QC 1958; Chm. Bar Council, 1970–72, Chm., Plant Variety Rights Tribunal for proceedings in England and Wales, 1969–72. Hon. DLitt Reading, 1982. *Recreations:* cricket, travel. *Address:* Villa La Pergola, Via B. Bonci 14, Vagliagli 53010, Siena, Italy.

ARNOLD, Very Rev. John Robert; Dean of Durham, since 1989; *b* 1 Nov. 1933; *s* of John Stanley and Ivy Arnold; *m* 1963, Livia Anneliese Franke; one *s* two *d. Educ:* Christ's Hospital; Sidney Sussex Coll., Cambridge (MA); Westcott House Theol College. Curate of Holy Trinity, Millhouses, Sheffield, 1960–63; Sir Henry Stephenson Fellow, Univ. of Sheffield, 1962–63; Chaplain and Lectr, Univ. of Southampton, 1963–72; Secretary, Board for Mission and Unity, General Synod of the Church of England, 1972–78; Dean of Rochester, 1978–89. Hon. Canon of Winchester Cathedral, 1974–78; Mem., General Synod, 1980–. Mem., European Ecumenical Commn for Church and Society, 1986–; Pres., 1986–, Chm., 1993–, Conference of European Churches (Vice-Chm., 1986–92). Order of Saint Vladimir (Russian Orthodox Church), 1977. Officers' Cross, Order of Merit (Germany), 1991. *Publications:* (trans.) Eucharistic Liturgy of Taizé, 1962; (contrib.) Hewitt, Strategist for the Spirit, 1985; Rochester Cathedral, 1987; contribs to Theology, Crucible, St Luke's Journal of Theology. *Recreations:* music; European languages and literature. *Address:* The Deanery, Durham DH1 3EQ. *T:* Durham (0191) 3847500. *Clubs:* Commonwealth Trust, Christ's Hospital.

ARNOLD, Rt. Rev. Keith Appleby; Hon. Assistant Bishop, Diocese of Newcastle, since 1991; *b* 1 Oct. 1926; *s* of Dr Frederick Arnold, Hale, Cheshire, and Alice Mary Appleby Arnold (*née* Holt); *m* 1955, Deborah Noreen Glenwright; one *s* one *d. Educ:* Winchester; Trinity Coll., Cambridge (MA); Westcott House, Cambridge. Served as Lieut, Coldstream Guards, 1944–48. Curate: Haltwhistle, Northumberland, 1952–55; St John's, Princes St, Edinburgh, 1955–61; Chaplain, TA, 1956–61; Rector of St John's, Edinburgh, 1961–69; Vicar of Kirkby Lonsdale, Cumbria, 1969–73; Team Rector of Hemel Hempstead, 1973–80; Bishop Suffragan of Warwick, 1980–90. Vice-Pres., Abbeyfield Soc., 1981–91; Chairman: Housing Assocs Charitable Trust, 1980–86; English Villages Housing Assoc., 1987–. Pres., Warwicks Marriage Guidance Council, subseq. Relate, 1980–90. *Recreations:* skiing, gardening. *Address:* White Lodge, Dunstan, Alnwick, Northumberland NE66 3TB. *T:* Alnwick (01665) 576485.

ARNOLD, Hon. Lynn Maurice Ferguson; *b* 27 Feb. 1949; *s* of Maurice and Jean Arnold; *m* 1978, Elaine Palmer; two *s* three *d. Educ:* Adelaide Boys' High Sch.; Univ. of Adelaide (BA, BEd). Teacher, Salisbury N High Sch., 1971–74; Adv. Teacher, Health Educn Project Team, 1975–76; Personal Assistant to MHR, 1977–79; MHA (ALP) Salisbury, 1979–87; MP (ALP) Ramsay, 1987–93, Taylor, 1993–94; Minister of: Education, 1982–85; Technology, 1982–87; Children's Services, 1985; Employment and Further Educn, and State Develt, 1985–89; Industry, Trade & Technol., also Agriculture, Fisheries, and Ethnic Affairs, 1989–92; Economic Develt, and Multicultural and Ethnic Affairs, 1992–93; Premier of S Australia, 1992–93; Leader of the Opposition and Shadow Minister of Econ. Develt and of Multicultural and Ethnic Affairs, 1993–94. Sec. and Pres., Campaign for Peace in Vietnam, 1970–73. Mem. Council, Univ. of Adelaide, 1979–. *Publications:* Nigeria-Biafra Conflict, 1968; (jtly) Hoa Binh Third Force in Vietnam, 1970; (jtly) You and Me, 1975; (jtly) All Together, 1976. *Recreations:* sociolinguistics, history. *Address:* PO Box 858, Salisbury, SA 5108, Australia.

ARNOLD, Sir Malcolm (Henry), Kt 1993; CBE 1970; FRCM; composer; *b* 21 Oct. 1921; *s* of William and Annie Arnold, Northampton; *m;* two *s* one *d. Educ:* Royal Coll. of Music, London (Schol., 1938). FRCM 1983; FTCL 1992. Principal Trumpet, London Philharmonic Orchestra, 1941–44; served in the Army, 1944–45; Principal Trumpet, London Philharmonic Orchestra, 1945–48; Mendelssohn Schol. (study in Italy), 1948; Coronation Ballet, Homage to the Queen, performed Royal Opera House, 1953. Awarded Oscar for music for film Bridge on the River Kwai, 1957; Ivor Novello Award for outstanding services to British Music, 1985; Wavendon Allmusic Composer of the Year, 1987; Ivor Novello Award for Inn of Sixth Happiness, 1958. Bard of the Cornish Gorsedd, 1969. Hon. RAM; Hon. Mem., Schubert Soc., 1988. Hon. DMus: Exeter, 1970; Durham, 1982; Leicester, 1984; Hon. Dr Arts and Humane Letters, Miami Univ., Ohio, 1990. Hon. Freeman, Borough of Northampton, 1989. *Publications: symphonies:* No 1, 1949; No 2, 1953; No 3, 1957; No 4, 1960; No 5, 1961; No 6, 1967; No 7, 1973; No 8, 1978; No 9, 1986; Symphony for Brass Instruments, 1979; *other works:* Beckus the Dandipratt, overture, 1943; Tam O'Shanter, overture, 1955; Peterloo, overture, 1967; eighteen concertos; six ballets: Homage to the Queen, Electra, Rinaldo Armida, Flowers of the Forest, Solitaire, Sweeney Todd; two one-act operas; two string quartets; two brass quintets; vocal, choral and chamber music. *Recreations:* reading and foreign travel. *Club:* Savile.

ARNOLD, Dr Richard Bentham; Executive Vice-President, International Federation of Pharmaceutical Manufacturers' Associations, since 1984; *b* 29 Aug. 1932; *s* of George Benjamin and Alice Arnold; *m* 1956, Margaret Evelyn Racey; one *s* one *d. Educ:* Stamford Sch.; King Edward VII Sch., King's Lynn; Nottingham Univ. BSc, PhD. Joined May & Baker Ltd, 1959; Commercial Manager, Pharmaceuticals Div., 1974–76; Dir Designate, 1976, Dir, 1977–83, Assoc. of British Pharmaceutical Industry. *Recreations:* golf, fishing, bird watching. *Address:* IFPMA, 30 rue de St Jean, PO Box 9, 1211 Geneva 18, Switzerland.

ARNOLD, Simon Rory; Chairman and Chief Executive, Bain Clarkson Ltd, since 1986; Main Board Director, Inchcape plc, since 1988; *b* 10 Sept. 1933; *s* of R. W. Arnold and R. A. Arnold; *m* 1960, (Janet) Linda May; one *s* one *d. Educ:* Diocesan Coll., Cape Town. J. H. Minet & Co. Ltd: S. Africa, 1952; London, 1955; Chm. and Chief Exec., 1979; Gp Man. Dir, Minet Holdings, 1983; Chief Exec., Bain Dawes Ltd, 1984. Member: Lloyd's Brokers Cttee, 1979– (Chm., 1986–91); Council, Lloyd's, 1991–. *Recreations:* ski-ing, walking, golf, tennis. *Address:* Meadows, Ditchling Common, Ditchling, Sussex BN6 8TN. *T:* Hassocks (01273) 844246.

ARNOLD, Sir Thomas (Richard), Kt 1990; MP (C) Hazel Grove, since Oct. 1974; *b* 25 Jan. 1947; *s* of late Thomas Charles Arnold, OBE and Helen Breen; *m* 1984, Elizabeth Jane (marr. diss. 1993), *widow* of Robin Smithers; one *d. Educ:* Bedales Sch.; Le Rosey, Geneva; Pembroke Coll., Oxford (MA). Theatre producer; publisher. Contested (C): Manchester Cheetham, 1970; Hazel Grove, Feb. 1974; PPS to Sec. of State for NI, 1979–81, to Lord Privy Seal, FCO, 1981–82; Chm., Treasury and CS Select Cttee, 1994– (Mem., 1992–94). Vice-Chm., Conservative Party, 1983–92. *Address:* House of Commons, SW1A 0AA. *T:* 0171–219 4096. *Clubs:* Carlton, Royal Automobile.

ARNOLD, Wallace; *see* Brown, C. E. M.

ARNOLD, William; Head of Family Law Division, Lord Chancellor's Department, since 1994; *b* 13 May 1953; *s* of Rev. William and Mrs Ruth Arnold; *m* 1992, Elizabeth Anne McLellan. *Educ:* Bury Grammar Sch.; King's Coll., Cambridge (MA Classics). Joined Lord Chancellor's Department, 1974: Asst Private Sec. to Lord Chancellor, 1977–79; Principal, 1979; Head of Legal Services Div., 1987; Head of Remuneration and Competition Div., 1988; Head, Courts and Legal Services Bill Div., 1989; Dir of Corporate Services and Principal Estabt and Finance Officer, PRO, 1991–92; on loan to Dept of PM and Cabinet, Canberra, Australia, 1993–94. Reader, St Margaret's Church, Putney, 1989–. *Recreations:* ski-ing, swimming, long-distance trekking, opera, ballet. *Address:* Lord Chancellor's Department, Southside, 105 Victoria Street, SW1E 6QT. *T:* 0171–210 1697.

ARNOLD-BAKER, Charles, OBE 1966; Consultant Lecturer, since 1978, and Visiting Professor, since 1985, City University; Editor, Road Law, since 1992; occasional broadcaster; *b* 25 June 1918; *s* of Baron Albrecht v. Blumenthal and Alice Wilhelmine (*née* Hainsworth); adopted surname of mother's second husband, Percival Richard Arnold Baker, 1938; *m* 1943, Edith (*née* Woods); one *s* one *d. Educ:* Winchester Coll.; Magdalen Coll., Oxford. BA 1940. Called to Bar, Inner Temple, 1948. Army (Private to Captain), 1940–46. Admty Bar, 1948–52; Sec., Nat. Assoc. of Local Councils, 1953–78; Dep. Eastern Traffic Comr, 1978–90. Mem., Royal Commn on Common Lands, 1955–58; Mem. European Cttee, Internat. Union of Local Authorities, 1960–78; a Deleg. to European Local Govt Assembly, Strasbourg, 1960–78. Gwylim Gibbons Award, Nuffield Coll., Oxford, 1959. King Haakon's Medal of Freedom (Norway), 1945. *Publications:* Norway (pamphlet), 1946; Everyman's Dictionary of Dates, 1954; Parish Administration, 1958; New Law and Practice of Parish Administration, 1966; The 5000 and the Power Tangle, 1967; The Local Government Act 1972, 1973; Local Council Administration, 1975, 3rd rev. edn 1989; The Local Government, Planning and Land Act 1980, 1981; Practical Law for Arts Administrators, 1983, 3rd edn 1992; The Five Thousand and the Living Constitution, 1986; many contribs to British and European local govt and legal jls. *Recreations:* travel, history, writing, music, cooking, journalism, wine and doing nothing. *Address:* Top Floor, 2 Paper Buildings, Inner Temple, EC4Y 7ET. *T:* 0171–353 3490. *Club:* Union (Oxford).

ARNOTT, Sir Alexander John Maxwell, 6th Bt *cr* 1896, of Woodlands, Shandon, Co. Cork; *b* 18 Sept. 1975; *s* of Sir John Robert Alexander Arnott, 5th Bt, and of Ann Margaret, *d* of late T. A. Farrelly, Kilcar, Co. Cavan; *S* father, 1981. *Heir: b* Andrew John Eric Arnott, *b* 20 June 1978. *Address:* 11 Palmerston Road, Dublin 6, Ireland.

ARNOTT, Edward Ian W.; *see* Walker-Arnott.

ARNOTT, Sir Melville; *see* Arnott, Sir W. M.

ARNOTT, Prof. Struther, FRS 1985; Principal and Vice-Chancellor, University of St Andrews, since 1986; *b* 25 Sept. 1934; *s* of Charles McCann and Christina Struthers Arnott; *m* 1970, Greta Edwards (BA); two *s. Educ:* Hamilton Academy, Lanarkshire; Glasgow Univ. (BSc, PhD). FRSC 1970; FIBiol 1987; FRSE 1988. King's College London: scientist, MRC Biophysics Research Unit, 1960–70; demonstrator in Physics, 1960–67; dir of postgraduate studies in Biophysics, 1967–70; Purdue University: Prof. of Molecular Biology, 1970–; Head, Dept of Biol Scis, 1975–80; Vice-Pres. for Research and Dean, Graduate Sch., 1980–86. Oxford University: Sen. Vis. Fellow, Jesus Coll., 1980–81; Nuffield Res. Fellow, Green Coll., 1985–86. Guggenheim Meml Foundn Fellow, 1985. Hon. LLD St Andrews, 1995; Hon. ScD St Andrews, Laurinburg, USA, 1994. *Publications:* papers in learned jls on structures of fibrous biopolymers, especially nucleic acids and polysaccharides, and techniques for visualizing them. *Recreations:* bird watching, botanizing. *Address:* College Gate, St Andrews, Fife KY16 9AJ. *T:* St Andrews (01334) 462545; The Principal's House, 9 The Scores, St Andrews, Fife KY16 9AR. *T:*

St Andrews (01334) 472492. *Clubs:* Athenæum, Caledonian; Royal and Ancient (St Andrews).

ARNOTT, Sir (William) Melville, Kt 1971; TD (and clasps) 1944; MD; FRCP; FRCPE, FRCPath; FRSE; British Heart Foundation Professor of Cardiology, University of Birmingham, 1971–74, now Emeritus Professor of Medicine; Consultant Physician, United Birmingham Hospitals, 1946–74; Hon. Consultant Physician, Queen Elizabeth Hospital, Birmingham, since 1974; *b* 14 Jan. 1909; *s* of Rev. Henry and Jeanette Main Arnott; *m* 1938, Dorothy Eleanor, *er d* of G. F. S. Hill, Edinburgh; one *s*. *Educ:* George Watson's Coll., Edinburgh; Univ. of Edinburgh. MB, ChB (Hons), 1931, BSc (1st Cl. Hons Path.), 1934, MD (Gold Medal and Gunning Prize in Path.), 1937, Edinburgh; Murchison Scholar, 1931, McCunn Res. Schol. in Path., 1933–35, Crichton Res. Schol. in Path., 1935, Shaw Macfie Lang Res. Fellow, 1936–38, Edinburgh. MD Birmingham, 1947. 2nd Lieut RA, 1929; TA 1929–39; War of 1939–45, served as specialist physician; five years foreign service (Siege of Tobruk; despatches, NW Europe); Lt-Col 1942. Asst Physician, Edinburgh Municipal Hosps, 1934–36; Hon. Asst Physician: Church of Scotland Deaconess Hosp., Edinburgh, 1938–46; Edinburgh Royal Infirmary, 1946. Dir, Post-grad. studies in Medicine, Edinburgh Univ., 1945–46; William Withering Prof. of Medicine, Univ. of Birmingham, 1946–71. Consultant Adviser in Research to W Midlands RHA, 1974–79. Associate Examr in Medicine, London Univ., 1948–49; Examr in Medicine, to Univs of Cambridge, 1950–56, London, 1951–54, Wales, 1954–57, Queen's, Belfast, 1956–59, Edinburgh, 1959–62, Leeds, 1959–62, St Andrews, 1961–63, Oxford, 1961–68, Newcastle, 1964–67, Manchester, 1964–67, Singapore, 1965, East Africa, 1965, Malaysia, 1973, NUI, 1975–77. Member: UGC, 1954–63; MRC, 1965–69; Council, University Coll. of Rhodesia, 1964–70; UGC Hong Kong, 1966–75; Home Office Cttee (Brodrick) on Death Registration and Coroners, 1965–71; Tropical Medicine Res. Bd, 1967–71. Dep. Pres., First Internat. Conf. on Med. Educn, 1953. Editor, Clinical Science, 1953–58, Member, Editorial Board: Brit. Jl of Social Medicine; Brit. Jl of Industrial Medicine and Cardiovascular Research. RCPE: Mem., 1933; Fellow, 1937; John Matheson Shaw Lectr, 1958; Cullen Prize, 1958. RCP: Mem., 1947; Fellow, 1951; Mem. Council, 1954–56; Oliver-Sharpey Lectr, 1955; Examr for Membership, 1957–66; Croonian Lectr, 1963; Censor, 1969–71; Sen. Vice-Pres., and Sen. Censor, 1973. Foundation Fellow, Royal Coll. of Pathologists. FRMedSoc 1929 (late Senior Pres.); Hon. FRCP(C), 1957; Hon. FACP, 1968 (Lilly Lectr, 1968); FRSE 1971. Member: Assoc. of Physicians; Physiological Soc.; Pathological Soc.; Med. Res. Soc.; Cardiac Soc.; Thoracic Soc.; Internat. Soc. of Internal Medicine. Sir Arthur Sims Commonwealth Trav. Prof. of Medicine, 1957. Lectures: Frederick Price, Trinity Coll., Dublin, 1959; Hall, Cardiac Soc. of Aust. and NZ, 1962; Henry Cohen, Hebrew Univ. of Jerusalem, 1964; Alexander Brown Meml, Univ. of Ibadan, 1972; John Snow, Soc. of Anaesthetists, 1973. President: Edinburgh Harveian Soc., 1955; British Lung Foundation, 1984–87. Research: Originally into experimental path. of renal hypertension and peripheral vascular disease; at present, into physiology and path. of cardio-respiratory function. Hon. DSc: Edinburgh, 1975; Chinese Univ. of Hong Kong, 1983; Hon. LLD: Rhodesia, 1976; Dundee, 1976. *Publications:* some 50 scientific papers, principally in Lancet, Jl of Physiol., Jl of Path., Brit. Jl of Social Medicine, Edinburgh Med. Jl, etc. *Recreation:* travel. *Address:* Flat 20, Bushwood, 32 St James Road, Edgbaston, Birmingham B15 2NX. *T:* 0121–440 2195. *Club:* Naval and Military.

ARONSOHN, Lotte Therese; *see* Newman, L. T.

ARONSON, Geoffrey Fraser, CB 1977; retired solicitor; Legal Adviser and Solicitor to Ministry of Agriculture, Fisheries and Food, to Forestry Commission, and to (EEC) Intervention Board for Agricultural Produce, 1974–79; *b* 17 April 1914; *er s* of late Victor Rees Aronson, CBE, KC, and Annie Elizabeth Aronson (*née* Fraser); *m* 1940, Marie Louise, *e d* of late George Stewart Rose-Innes; one *s* two *d*. *Educ:* Haileybury. Solicitor (Honours) 1936. Legal Dept, Min. of Agriculture and Fisheries, 1938; served War of 1939–45, Flying Control Officer, RAFVR; promoted Asst Solicitor, MAFF, 1960; Under-Sec. (Principal Asst Solicitor), 1971, when chiefly concerned with UK accession to EEC. Part-time consultant to Law Commn, 1979–84. Co-Founder, 1959, and Chm., 1959–74, Epsom Protection Soc. *Recreations:* environmental, travel, gardening. *Address:* 4 The Oaks, Downs Avenue, Epsom, Surrey KT18 5HH. *T:* Epsom (01372) 722431; 30 Eastergate Green, Rustington, W Sussex. *T:* Rustington (01903) 775736. *Club:* Royal Automobile.

ARONSON, Hazel Josephine, (Mrs John A. Cosgrove); QC (Scot.) 1991; Sheriff of Lothian and Borders at Edinburgh, since 1983; Chairman, Mental Welfare Commission for Scotland, since 1991; *b* 12 Jan. 1946; *d* of late Moses Aron Aronson and Julia Tobias; *m* 1967, John Allan Cosgrove, dental surgeon; one *s* one *d*. *Educ:* Glasgow High Sch. for Girls; Univ. of Glasgow (LLB). Advocate at the Scottish Bar. Admitted to Fac. of Advocates, 1968; Standing Junior Counsel to Dept of Trade, 1977–79; Sheriff of Glasgow and Strathkelvin, 1979–83. Temporary Judge, High Court and Court of Session, Scotland, 1992–. Mem., Parole Bd for Scotland, 1988–91. Vice Chm., Edinburgh Friends of Israel, 1980–. *Recreations:* foreign travel, opera, swimming, walking, reading, langlauf. *Address:* 14 Gordon Terrace, Edinburgh EH16 5QR.

ARRAN, 9th Earl of, *cr* 1762, of the Arran Islands, Co. Galway; **Arthur Desmond Colquhoun Gore;** Bt 1662; Viscount Sudley, Baron Saunders, 1758; Baron Sudley (UK), 1884; Captain of the Yeomen of the Guard (Deputy Government Chief Whip), 1994–95; *b* 14 July 1938; *er s* of 8th Earl of Arran and of Fiona Bryde, *er d* of Sir Iain Colquhoun of Luss, 7th Bt, KT, DSO; *S* father, 1983; *m* 1974, Eleanor, *er d* of Bernard van Cutsem and Lady Margaret Fortescue; two *d*. *Educ:* Eton; Balliol College, Oxford. 2nd Lieutenant, 1st Bn Grenadier Guards (National Service). Asst Manager, Daily Mail, 1972–73; Man. Dir, Clark Nelson, 1973–74; Asst Gen. Manager Daily and Sunday Express, June-Nov. 1974. Dir, Waterstone & Co. Ltd, 1984–87. A Lord in Waiting (Govt Whip), 1987–89; Parliamentary Under-Secretary of State: for the Armed Forces, MoD, 1989–92; NI Office, 1992–94; Parly Under-Sec. of State, DoE, 1994. Co-Chm., Children's Country Holidays Fund. *Recreations:* tennis, shooting, gardening, croquet. *Address:* c/o House of Lords, SW1A 0PW. *Clubs:* White's, Pratt's, Turf, Beefsteak.

ARRAND, Ven. Geoffrey William; Archdeacon of Suffolk, since 1994; *b* 24 July 1944; *s* of Thomas Staniforth Arrand and Alice Ada Arrand; *m* 1968, Mary Marshall (marr. diss.); one *s* two *d*. *Educ:* King's Coll., London (BD 1966, AKC). Ordained deacon, 1967, priest, 1968; Assistant Curate: Washington, dio. of Durham, 1967–70; S Ormsby Gp, 1970–73; Team Vicar, Great Grimsby, 1973–79; Team Rector, Halesworth, 1979–85; Dean of Bocking and Rector of Hadleigh with Layham and Shelley, 1985–94; RD of Hadleigh, 1986–94. Hon. Canon, St Edmundsbury Cathedral, 1991–. OStJ 1994. *Recreation:* golf. *Address:* 38 Saxmundham Road, Aldeburgh, Suffolk IP15 5JE. *T:* Aldeburgh (01728) 454034. *Club:* Stoke by Nayland Golf.

ARRINDELL, Sir Clement Athelston, GCMG 1984; GCVO 1985; Kt 1982; QC; Governor-General, St Christopher and Nevis, since 1983 (Governor, St Kitts-Nevis, 1981–83); *b* Basseterre, 19 April 1931. *Educ:* private school; Basseterre Boys' Elementary Sch.; St Kitts-Nevis Grammar Sch. (Island Scholar). Called to the Bar, Lincoln's Inn, 1958. Post-grad. studies; in practice as barrister and solicitor, 1959–66; Acting Magistrate, 1964–66; Magistrate, 1966–71; Chief Magistrate, 1972–78; Judge, WI Associated States Supreme Court, 1978–81. *Recreations:* piano-playing, classical music, gardening. *Address:* Government House, Basseterre, St Christopher, West Indies. *T:* 2315.

ARROW, Kenneth Joseph; Professor of Economics and Operations Research, Stanford University, 1979–91, Professor Emeritus, 1991; *b* 23 Aug. 1921; *s* of Harry I. and Lillian Arrow; *m* 1947, Selma Schweitzer; two *s*. *Educ:* City College (BS in Social Science 1940); Columbia Univ. (MA 1941, PhD 1951). Captain, US AAF, 1942–46. Research Associate, Cowles Commn for Research in Economics, Univ. of Chicago, 1947–49; Actg Asst Prof., Associate Prof. and Prof. of Economics, Statistics and Operations Research, Stanford Univ., 1949–68; Prof. of Econs, later University Prof., Harvard Univ., 1968–79. Staff Mem., US Council of Economic Advisers, 1962. Consultant, The Rand Corp., 1948–. Fellow, Churchill Coll., Cambridge, 1963–64, 1970, 1973, 1986. President: Internat. Economic Assoc., 1983–86; Internat. Soc. for Inventory Res., 1984–90; Member: Inst. of Management Sciences (Pres., 1963); Nat. Acad. of Sciences; Amer. Inst. of Medicine; Amer. Philosoph. Soc.; Pontifical Acad. of Social Scis; Fellow: Econometric Soc. (Pres., 1956); Amer. Acad. of Arts and Sciences; Amer. Assoc. for Advancement of Science (Chm., Section K, 1982); Amer. Statistical Assoc.; Dist. Fellow: Amer. Econ. Assoc. (Pres., 1972); Western Econ. Assoc. (Pres., 1980–81); Corresp. Fellow, British Acad., 1976; Foreign Hon. Mem., Finnish Acad. of Sciences. John Bates Clark Medal, American Economic Assoc., 1957; Nobel Meml Prize in Economic Science, 1972; von Neumann Prize, Inst. of Management Scis and Ops Res. Soc. of America, 1986. Hon. LLD: Chicago, 1967; City Univ. of NY, 1972; Univ. of Pennsylvania, 1976; Washington Univ., St Louis, Missouri, 1989; Hon. Dr Soc. and Econ. Sciences, Vienna, 1971; Hon. ScD Columbia, 1973; Hon. DSocSci, Yale, 1974; Hon. Dr: Paris, 1974; Hebrew Univ. of Jerusalem, 1975; Helsinki, 1976; Aix-Marseille III, 1985; Sacro Cuore, 1994; Hon. LittD Cambridge, 1985. Order of the Rising Sun (2nd class), Japan, 1984. *Publications:* Social Choice and Individual Values, 1951, 2nd edn 1963; (with S. Karlin and H. Scarf) Studies in the Mathematical Theory of Inventory and Production, 1958; (with M. Hoffenberg) A Time Series Analysis of Interindustry Demands, 1959; (with L. Hurwicz and H. Uzawa) Studies in Linear and Nonlinear Programming, 1959; Aspects of the Theory of Risk Bearing, 1965; (with M. Kurz) Public Investment, the Rate of Return, and Optimal Fiscal Policy, 1971; Essays in the Theory of Risk-Bearing, 1971; (with F. Hahn) General Competitive Analysis, 1972; The Limits of Organization, 1974; (with L. Hurwicz) Studies in Resource Allocation Processes, 1977; Collected Papers, Vols 1–6, 1984–86; (with H. Raynaud) Social Choice and Multicriterion Decision-Making, 1986; 170 articles in jls and collective vols. *Address:* Department of Economics, Stanford University, Stanford, CA 94305–6072, USA.

ARROWSMITH, Pat; pacifist and socialist; on staff of Amnesty International, 1971–94, retired; *b* 2 March 1930; *d* of late George Ernest Arrowsmith and late Margaret Vera (*née* Kingham); *m* Mr Gardner, 11 Aug. 1979, separated 11 Aug. 1979; lesbian partnership with Wendy Butlin, 1962–76. *Educ:* Farringtons; Stover Sch.; Cheltenham Ladies' Coll.; Newnham Coll., Cambridge (BA history); Univ. of Ohio; Liverpool Univ. (Cert. in Social Science). Has held many jobs, incl.: Community Organizer in Chicago, 1952–53; Cinema Usher, 1953–54; Social Caseworker, Liverpool Family Service Unit, 1954; Child Care Officer, 1955 and 1964; Nursing Asst, Deva Psychiatric Hosp., 1956–57; Reporter for Peace News, 1965; Gardener for Camden BC, 1966–68; Researcher for Soc. of Friends Race Relations Cttee, 1969–71; Case Worker for NCCL, 1971; and on farms, as waiter in cafes, in factories, as a toy demonstrator, as a 'temp' in numerous offices, as asst in children's home, as newspaper deliverer and sales agent, as cleaner, as bartender, and in a holiday camp. Organizer for Direct Action Cttee against Nuclear War, Cttee of 100 and Campaign for Nuclear Disarmament, 1958–68; gaoled 11 times as political prisoner, 1958–85 (adopted twice as Prisoner of Conscience by Amnesty International); awarded: Holloway Prison Green Band, 1964; Girl Crusaders knighthood, 1940; Americans Removing Injustice, Suppression and Exploitation peace prize, 1991. Contested: Fulham, 1966 (Radical Alliance) and 1970 (Hammersmith Stop the SE Asia War Cttee), on peace issues; Cardiff South East (Independent Socialist), 1979. Member: War Resisters' Internat.; Campaign for Nuclear Disarmament; Ver Poets. *Publications:* Jericho (novel), 1965; Somewhere Like This (novel), 1970; To Asia in Peace, 1972; The Colour of Six Schools, 1972; Breakout (poems and drawings from prison), 1975; On the Brink (anti-war poems with pictures), 1981; The Prisoner (novel), 1982; Thin Ice (anti-nuclear poems), 1984; Nine Lives (poems and pictures), 1990; I Should Have Been a Hornby Train (fiction-cum-memoirs), 1993. *Recreations:* water colour painting (has held and contrib. exhibns), swimming, writing poetry. *Address:* 132c Middle Lane, N8 7JP. *T:* 0181–340 2661.

ARTHUR, family name of **Baron Glenarthur.**

ARTHUR, Adrian; Editor, The Courier, Dundee, since 1993; *b* 28 Sept. 1937; *s* of Alastair and Jean Arthur, Kirkcaldy; *m* 1962, Patricia Mill; one *s* two *d*. *Educ:* Harris Academy, Dundee; Univ. of St Andrews (BL). Sub-Editor, People's Journal, 1954–56; Nat. Service, RAF, 1956–58; The Courier: editorial staff, 1958–; Dep. Editor, 1978–93. *Recreations:* golf, reading, travel, Rotary. *Address:* The Courier, 80 Kingsway East, Dundee DD4 8SL. *T:* Dundee (01382) 223131. *Clubs:* Carnoustie; Dalhousie Golf.

ARTHUR, Allan James Vincent, MBE 1948; DL; Vice Lord-Lieutenant of Essex, 1978–85; *b* 16 Sept. 1915; *s* of late Col Sir Charles Arthur, MC, VD, and late Lady (Dorothy Grace) Arthur; *m* 1940, Joan Deirdre Heape (marr. diss. 1948); *m* 1949, Dawn Rosemary Everil, *d* of Col F. C. Drake, OBE, MC, DL; two *s* two *d*. *Educ:* Rugby Sch.; Magdalene Coll., Cambridge (MA). CU swimming team, 1935–38 (Capt. 1937); CU water polo team, 1937–38. Indian Civil Service (Punjab), 1938–47; Sub Divl Officer, Murree, 1941, Kasur, 1942–43; Dep. Comr, Attock, 1944–46, Multan, 1946–47; Sudan Political Service, 1948–54; District Comr, Khartoum, 1949–51, Shendi, 1951–54; Dep. Governor, Northern Province, 1954; J. V. Drake and Co. Ltd, Sugar Brokers, 1954–60; Woodhouse, Drake, and Carey Ltd, Commodity Merchants, 1960–75 (Chm., 1972–75). Member, Chelmsford Borough Council, 1973–79, Mayor, 1977–78; Governor: London Hosp. Med. Coll., 1956–74; Chigwell Sch., 1972–82; Brentwood Sch., 1973–85. Pres., Chelmsford Medical Educn and Res. Trust, 1981–88. Trustee, Friends of Essex Youth Orchestras, 1985–94. Member: Bd of Visitors, HM Prison, Chelmsford, 1973–79; Council, Univ. of Essex, 1980–87. Pres., Old Rugbeian Soc., 1982–84. High Sheriff of Essex, 1971–72; DL Essex, 1974. *Publications:* contrib. to: The District Officer in India, 1930–47, 1980; Set under Authority, by K. D. D. Henderson, 1987. *Recreations:* swimming, shooting, gardening. *Address:* Mount Maskall, Boreham, Chelmsford CM3 3HW. *T:* Chelmsford (01245) 467776. *Clubs:* Oriental; Hawks (Cambridge).

ARTHUR, Prof. Geoffrey Herbert; Emeritus Professor of Veterinary Surgery, University of Bristol, since 1980; *b* 6 March 1916; *s* of William Gwyn Arthur and Ethel Jessie Arthur; *m* 1948, Lorna Isabel Simpson; four *s* one *d*. *Educ:* Abersychan Secondary Sch.; Liverpool Univ. BVSc 1939; MRCVS 1939; MVSc 1945; DVSc 1957; FRCVS 1957. Lectr in Veterinary Medicine, Liverpool Univ., 1941–48; Reader in Veterinary Surgery, Royal Veterinary Coll., 1949–51; Reader in Veterinary Surgery and Obstetrics, Univ. of London, 1952–65; Prof. of Veterinary Obstetrics and Diseases of Reproduction, Univ. of London, 1965–73; Prof. and Head of Dept of Vet. Surgery, Bristol Univ., 1974–79. Regl Postgrad.

Vet. Dean, W and SW England and S Wales, 1985–94. Examiner to Univs of Cambridge, Dublin, Edinburgh, Glasgow, Liverpool, London, Reading, Bristol and Ceylon. Visiting Professor: Univ. of Khartoum, 1964; Pahlavi Univ., 1976; Nairobi Univ., 1979; Clinical Prof., King Faisal Univ., Saudi Arabia, 1980–84. Chm., Soc. for Protection of Animals Abroad, 1992–94. *Publications:* Wright's Veterinary Obstetrics (including Diseases of Reproduction, 3rd edn), 1964, 5th edn, as Veterinary Reproduction and Obstetrics, 1982, 6th edn 1989; papers on medicine and reproduction in Veterinary Record, Veterinary Jl, Jl of Comparative Pathology, Jl Reprod. Fert., Equine Vet. Jl and Jl Small Animal Pract. (Editor). *Recreations:* observing natural phenomena and experimenting, North African and Middle Eastern travel. *Address:* Fallodene, Stone Allerton, Axbridge, Som BS26 2NH.

ARTHUR, Prof. James Greig, FRS 1992; FRSC 1981; University Professor since 1987 and Professor of Mathematics since 1979, University of Toronto; *b* 18 May 1944; *s* of John Greig Arthur and Katherine Mary Patricia Scott; *m* 1972, Dorothy Pendleton Helm; two *s*. *Educ:* Upper Canada Coll.; Univ. of Toronto (BSc, MSc); Yale Univ. (PhD). Instructor, Princeton Univ., 1970–72; Asst Prof., Yale Univ., 1972–76; Prof., Duke Univ., 1976–79. Sloan Fellowship, 1976; E. W. R. Steacie Meml Fellowship, 1982. Synge Award, RSC, 1987. *Publication:* Simple Algebras, Base Change and the Advanced Theory of the Trace Formula (with Laurent Clozel), 1989. *Recreations:* tennis, golf. *Address:* 23 Woodlawn Avenue W, Toronto, Ontario M4V 1G6, Canada. *T:* (416) 9640975.

ARTHUR, James Stanley, CMG 1977; HM Diplomatic Service, retired; British High Commissioner in Bridgetown, 1978–82, also British High Commissioner (non-resident) to Dominica, 1978–82, to St Lucia and St Vincent, 1979–82, to Grenada, 1980–82, to Antigua and Barbuda, 1981–82, and concurrently British Government Representative to West Indies Associated State of St Kitts-Nevis; retired 1983; *b* 3 Feb. 1923; *s* of Laurence and Catherine Arthur, Lerwick, Shetland; *m* 1950, Marion North; two *s* two *d*. *Educ:* Trinity Academy, Edinburgh; Liverpool Univ. (BSc). Scientific Civil Service, 1944–46; Asst Principal, Scottish Educn Dept, 1946; Min. of Educn/Dept of Educn and Science, 1947–66: Private Sec. to Parly Sec., 1948–50; Principal Private Sec. to Minister, 1960–62; Counsellor, FO, 1966; Nairobi, 1967–70; Dep. High Comr, Malta, 1970–73; High Comr, Suva, 1974–78, and first High Comr (non-resident), Republic of Nauru, 1977–78. Mem. Court, Liverpool Univ., 1987–. *Recreations:* golf, music. *Address:* Moreton House, Longborough, Moreton-in-Marsh, Glos GL56 0QQ. *T:* Cotswold (01451) 30774. *Club:* Commonwealth Trust.

ARTHUR, Lt-Gen. Sir (John) Norman (Stewart), KCB 1985; DL; General Officer Commanding Scotland and Governor of Edinburgh Castle, 1985–88, retired; *b* 6 March 1931; *s* of Col Evelyn Stewart Arthur and Mrs E. S. Arthur (*née* Burnett-Stuart); *m* 1960, Theresa Mary Hopkinson; one *s* one *d* (and one *s* decd). *Educ:* Eton Coll.; RMA, Sandhurst. rcds, jssc, psc. Commnd Royal Scots Greys, 1951; commanded: Royal Scots Dragoon Guards, 1972–74 (despatches, 1974); 7th Armoured Bde, 1976–77; GOC 3rd Armoured Div., 1980–82; Dir of Personal Services (Army), MoD, 1983–85. Col Comdt, Military Provost Staff Corps, 1985–88; Col, The Royal Scots Dragoon Gds (Carabiniers and Greys), 1984–92; Hon. Col, 205 (Scottish) Gen. Hosp., RAMC(V), 1988–93, The Scottish Yeomanry, 1993–. Chm., Cavalry Colonels, 1987–92. Officer, Royal Co. of Archers, Queen's Body Guard for Scotland. Chairman: Scotland, Army Benevolent Fund, 1988–; Carnsalloch Cheshire Home, Dumfries, 1994–; Vice Pres., Edinburgh and Borders, Riding for the Disabled Assoc., 1988–94; Dir, Edinburgh Mil. Tattoo Co., 1988–91; Pres., Scottish Conservation Projects, 1989–94; Mem., Automobile Assoc. Cttee, 1990–. Mem., British Olympic Team, Equestrian Three-Day Event, 1960. DL Stewartry, 1989. *Recreations:* field and country sports and pursuits, horsemanship, military history. *Address:* Newbarns, Dalbeattie, Kirkcudbrightshire DG5 4PY. *T:* Rockcliffe (01556) 630227. *Clubs:* Cavalry and Guards; Caledonian Hunt.

ARTHUR, His Honour John Rhys, DFC 1944; JP; a Circuit Judge, 1975–93; *b* 29 April 1923; *s* of late John Morgan Arthur and Eleanor Arthur; *m* 1951, Joan Tremearne Pickering; two *s* one *d*. *Educ:* Mill Hill; Christ's Coll., Cambridge (MA). Commnd RAF, 1943, demobilised 1946. Cambridge, 1946–48; called to Bar, Inner Temple, 1949. Asst Recorder, Blackburn QS, 1970; Dep. Chm., Lancs County QS, 1970–71; a Recorder, 1972–75. JP Lancs 1970. *Address:* Orovales, Caldy, Wirral L48 1LP. *T:* 0151-625 8624. *Clubs:* MCC, Old Millhillians; Athenæum (Liverpool); Cardiff Athletic.

ARTHUR, Michael Anthony, CMG 1992; HM Diplomatic Service; Counsellor and Head of Chancery, Paris, since 1993; *b* 28 Aug. 1950; *s* of late John Richard Arthur and of Mary Deirdre (*née* Chaundy); *m* 1974, Plaxy Gillian Beatrice (*née* Corke); two *s* two *d*. *Educ:* Rugby; Balliol Coll., Oxford. Entered HM Diplomatic Service, 1972; UK Mission to UN, NY, 1972; FCO, 1973; 3rd, later 2nd Sec., UK Perm. Representation to Eur. Communities, 1974–76; 2nd Sec., Kinshasa, 1976–78; FCO, 1978–83; Private Secretary: to Lord Privy Seal, 1981; to Minister of State, FCO, 1982; 1st Sec., Bonn, 1984–88; Hd, EC Dept (Internal), FCO, 1988–93; Sen. Associate Mem., St Antony's Coll., Oxford, 1993. *Recreations:* music, travel, books. *Address:* c/o Foreign and Commonwealth Office, King Charles Street, SW1A 2AH.

ARTHUR, Lt-Gen. Sir Norman; *see* Arthur, Lt-Gen. Sir J. N. S.

ARTHUR, Hon. Owen Seymour; MP (Lab) Barbados, since 1984; Prime Minister of Barbados, since 1994; *b* 17 Oct. 1949; *m* 1978, Beverley Jaeane Batchelor. *Educ:* Coleridge and Parry Schs; Harrison Coll., Barbados; Univ. of West Indies at Cave Hill (BA) and at Mona (MSc). Research Asst, UWI, Jamaica, 1973; Asst Economic Planner, then Chief Econ. Planner, Nat. Planning Agency, Jamaica, 1974–79; Dir of Econs, Jamaica Bauxite Inst., 1979–81; Chief Project Analyst, Min. of Finance, Barbados, 1981–83; Lectr, Dept of Management, UWI, Cave Hill, 1986, Res. Fellow, 1993. Mem., Barbados Senate, 1983; Parly Sec., Min. of Finance, 1985–86; Chm., Barbados Labour Party, 1993–; Leader of Opposition, 1993–94. *Publications:* The Commercialisation of Technology in Jamaica, 1979; Energy and Mineral Resource Development in the Jamaican Bauxite Industry, 1981; The IMF and Economic Stabilisation Policies in Barbados, 1984. *Recreations:* cooking, gardening. *Address:* Prime Minister's Office, Government Headquarters, Bay Street, St Michael, Barbados. *T:* 4263179, *Fax:* 4369280; Ilard Court, Two Mill Hill, St Michael, Barbados. *T:* 4295171. *Club:* Barbados External Communications Sports.

ARTHUR, Peter Bernard; Deputy Chairman and Chairman of the Sub-Committees of Classification, Lloyd's Register of Shipping, 1976–84; *b* 29 Aug. 1923; *s* of Charles Frederick Bernard Arthur and Joan (*née* Dyer); *m* 1954, Irène Susy (*née* Schüpbach); one *s* two *d*. *Educ:* Oundle Sch. Commnd 1943; Mahratta LI, 1943–47 (mentioned in despatches, Italy, 1945); RA, 1947–53. Mem. Cttee, Lloyd's Register of Shipping, and Vice-Chm., Sub-Cttees of Classification, 1967. Dir, Bolton Steam Shipping Co. Ltd, 1958–84; Chairman: London Deep Sea Tramp Shipowners' Assoc., 1970–71; Deep Sea Tramp Sect., Chamber of Shipping of UK, 1972–73; Bolton Maritime Management Ltd, 1982–83. *Recreations:* music, water colour painting, gardening. *Address:* Lower Terrace, 37A Peter Avenue, Oxted, Surrey RH8 9LG. *T:* Oxted (01883) 712962.

ARTHUR, Sir Stephen (John), 6th Bt *cr* 1841, of Upper Canada; *b* 1 July 1953; *s* of Hon. Sir Basil Malcolm Arthur, 5th Bt, MP, and of Elizabeth Rita, *d* of late Alan Mervyn Wells; *S* father, 1985; *m* 1978, Carolyn Margaret (marr. diss.), *d* of Burney Lawrence Daimond, Cairns, Queensland; one *s* two *d*. *Educ:* Timaru Boys' High School. *Heir: s* Benjamin Nathan Arthur, *b* 27 March 1979.

ARTHURE, Humphrey George Edgar, CBE 1969; MD, FRCS, FRCOG; Consulting Obstetric and Gynæcological Surgeon: Charing Cross Hospital; Queen Charlotte's Hospital; Mount Vernon Hospital; *b* 22 Jan. 1906; *s* of Rev. H. E. E. Arthure, Vicar of Mickleton, Glos; *m* 1936, Dickie Arthure (*d* 1993). MRCS, LRCP 1931; MB, BS 1933; FRCS 1935; MD London 1938; FRCOG 1950 (Hon. Sec. 1949–56; Vice-Pres. 1964–67); FRSM (Pres., Section of Obstetrics and Gynaecology, 1969); co-opted Mem. Council, RCS 1960; Pres., West London Medico-Chirurgical Soc., 1964; Formerly: Chm., Central Midwives Board, and Adviser, Obstetrics and Gynæcology, DHSS; Mem., Standing Maternity and Midwifery Advisory Cttee; Resident Obstetric Officer and Obstetrical Registrar, Charing Cross Hospital; Resident Medical Officer, Chelsea Hospital for Women. Served War of 1939–45, temp. Lt-Col, RAMC. *Publications:* Simpson Oration, 1972; (jtly) Sterilisation, 1976; contribs med. jls. *Address:* 12 Eyot Green, Chiswick Mall, W4 2PT. *T:* 0181-994 7698.

ARTHURS, Prof. Harry William, OC 1989; FRSC 1982; Professor of Law, Osgoode Hall Law School, York University, Canada, since 1968; *b* 9 May 1935; *s* of Leon and Ellen Arthurs; *m* 1974, Penelope Geraldine Ann Milnes; two *s*. *Educ:* Univ. of Toronto (BA, LLB); Harvard Univ. (LLM). Barrister and Solicitor, 1961. York University: Asst Prof. 1961, Associate Prof. 1964, Associate Dean 1967, Dean 1972–77, Osgoode Hall Law Sch.; Pres., 1985–92, Pres. Emeritus, 1992–. Mem., Economic Council of Can., 1978–82; Bencher, Law Soc. of Upper Can., 1979–84; Chm., Consultative Gp on Res. and Educn in Law, 1981–84; Arbitrator, Mediator in Labour Disputes, 1962–84; Chair, Council of Ontario Univs, 1987–89. Visitor: Univs of Toronto, 1965, and McGill, 1967; Clare Hall, Cambridge, 1971; Inst. for Socio-Legal Res., Oxford, 1977–78; UCL, 1984. Hon. LLD: Sherbrooke, 1986; Brock, 1986; Law Soc. of Upper Can., 1987; Hon. DLitt Lethbridge, 1991. *Publications:* Law and Learning, 1983; (jtly) Industrial Relations and Labour Law in Canada, 1979, 3rd edn 1988; Without the Law, 1985. *Address:* Osgoode Hall Law School, York University, 4700 Keele Street, North York, Ontario M3J 1P3, Canada. *T:* (416) 7365407.

ARTIS, Prof. Michael John, FBA 1988; Professor of Economic Policy, European University Institute, Florence, since 1995; Professor of Economics, Manchester University, since 1975 (on leave of absence); *b* 29 June 1938; *s* of Cyril John and Violet Emily Artis; *m* 1st, 1961, Lilian Gregson (marr. diss. 1982); two *d*; 2nd, 1983, Shirley Knight. *Educ:* Baines Grammar Sch., Poulton-le-Fylde, Lancs; Magdalen Coll., Oxford. BA Hons (PPE) Oxon. Assistant Research Officer, Oxford Univ., 1959; Lectr in Economics, Adelaide Univ., 1964; Lectr and Sen. Lectr in Economics, Flinders Univ., 1966; Research Officer and Review Editor, Nat. Inst. of Economic and Social Research, London, 1967; Prof. of Applied Economics, Swansea Univ. Coll., 1972. *Publications:* Foundations of British Monetary Policy, 1964; (with M. K. Lewis) Monetary Control in the United Kingdom, 1981; Macroeconomics, 1984; (with S. Ostry) International Economic Policy Co-ordination, 1986; (with M. K. Lewis) Money in Britain, 1991; contribs on economics, economic policy to books and learned jls. *Recreation:* eating out. *Address:* Via San Jacopo 19, Pratolino (FI) 50036, Italy. *Club:* Reform.

ARTON; *see* Bourne-Arton.

ARTRO MORRIS, John Evan; District Judge, Principal Registry of the Family Division (formerly a Registrar of the Supreme Court, Family Division), 1977–95; *b* 17 Feb. 1925; *s* of Tudor and Mabel Artro Morris, *m* 1961, Karin Ilsa Alida Russell; two *s*. *Educ:* Liverpool Coll.; The Queen's Coll., Oxford. MA Oxon. Served RN, 1943–47. Called to the Bar, Middle Temple, 1952. *Recreations:* D-I-Y, Alvis TA 21, fishing. *Address:* 69 Gowan Avenue, SW6 6RH. *T:* 0171-736 6492. *Club:* London Welsh RFC.

ARTUS, Ronald Edward, CBE 1991; non-executive Director: Imperial Cancer Research Technology Ltd, since 1988; Electrocomponents plc, since 1990; GEC, since 1990; The Solicitors Indemnity Fund Ltd, since 1990; CLM Insurance Fund plc, since 1993; (independent) Member of Board, Securities and Futures Authority (formerly Securities Association Ltd), since 1990; *b* 8 Oct 1931; *s* of late Ernest and of Doris Artus; *m* 1st, 1956, Brenda M. Touche (marr. diss.); three *s* one *d*; 2nd, 1987, Dr Joan M. Mullaney, MD. *Educ:* Sir Thomas Rich's Sch., Gloucester; Magdalen Coll., Oxford (MA). Joined Prudential, 1954; Head of Economic Intelligence Dept, 1958–71; Sen. Asst Investment Manager, 1971–73; Dep. Investment Manager, 1973–75; Jt Sec. and Chief Investment Manager, 1975–79; Dep. Chm., 1985–90; Prudential Corp. PLC: Gp Chief Investment Manager, 1979–90; an Exec. Dir, 1984–90, non-exec. Dir, 1990–93; Chairman: Prudential Portfolio Managers, 1981–90; Prudential Property Services, 1986–90; a Dir of various cos, Prudential Gp, until 1990. Director: Keyser Ullmann Holdings Ltd, 1972–80; Charterhouse Gp Ltd, 1980–82; Celltech Ltd, 1980–91. Member: City Capital Markets Cttee, 1982–90 (Chm., 1988–90); Accounting Standards Cttee, 1982–86; Financial Law Panel, 1993–; Council, Inst. for Fiscal Studies, 1988–94; CBI City Industry Task Force, 1987; Lloyd's Task Force, 1991. Mem. Finance Cttee, 1975–, Mem. Council, 1994–, ICRF. Hon. Fellow, Soc. of Investment Analysts, 1980 (Mem. Council, 1964–76; Chm., 1973–75). *Publications:* contrib. various jls on economic and investment matters. *Recreations:* music (esp. opera), learning about art (esp. British Sch. and English watercolours). *Address:* GEC, 1 Stanhope Gate, W1A 1EH. *Club:* MCC.

ARUNDEL AND BRIGHTON, Bishop of, (RC), since 1977; **Rt. Rev. Cormac Murphy-O'Connor;** *b* 24 Aug. 1932; *s* of late Dr P. G. Murphy-O'Connor and Ellen (*née* Cuddigan). *Educ:* Prior Park Coll., Bath; English Coll., Rome; Gregorian Univ. PhL, STL. Ordained Priest, 1956. Asst Priest, Portsmouth and Fareham, 1957–66; Sec. to Bp of Portsmouth, 1966–70; Parish Priest, Parish of the Immaculate Conception, Southampton, 1970–71; Rector, English College, Rome, 1971–77. Chairman: Bishops' Cttee for Europe, 1978–83; Cttee for Christian Unity, 1983–; Dept for Mission and Unity, 1994–; Jt Chm., ARCIC-II, 1983–. *Recreations:* music, sport. *Address:* St Joseph's Hall, Greyfriars Lane, Storrington, Pulborough, Sussex RH20 4HE.

ARUNDEL AND SURREY, Earl of; Edward William Fitzalan-Howard; *b* 2 Dec. 1956; *s* and *heir* of 17th Duke of Norfolk, *qv*; *m* 1987, Georgina, *y d* of Jack and Serena Gore; two *s* one *d*. *Educ:* Ampleforth Coll., Yorks; Lincoln Coll., Oxford. *Recreations:* skiing, motor-racing, shooting. *Heir: s* Lord Maltravers, *qv*. *Address:* Arundel Castle, West Sussex BN18 9AB. *T:* Arundel (01903) 883979; Scar House, Arkengarthdale, Reeth, N Yorks DL11 6RD. *T:* Richmond (01748) 884726. *Club:* British Racing Drivers (Silverstone).

ARUNDELL; *see* Monckton-Arundell, family name of Viscount Galway.

ARUNDELL, family name of **Baron Talbot of Malahide**.

ARVILL, Robert; *see* Boote, R. E.

ASAAD, Prof. Fikry Naguib M.; *see* Morcos-Asaad.

ASANTE, Kwaku Baprui, GM 1976; MOV 1978; High Commissioner for Ghana in London, 1991–93; *b* 26 March 1924; *s* of Kweku Asante and Odorso Amoo; *m* 1958, Matilda Dzagbele Anteson; two *s* two *d*. *Educ:* Achimota Coll.; Durham Univ. (BSc); Final Exam., Inst. Statisticians (AIS), London. Sen. Maths Master, Achimota, 1954–56; joined Ghana Foreign Service, 1956; 2nd Sec., London, 1957–58; Chargé d'Affaires, Tel Aviv, 1958–60; Principal Sec., African Affairs Secretariat, Office of Pres., 1960–66; Head of Admin., OAU, 1966–67; Ambassador to Switzerland and Austria and Permanent Delegate to UN Office, Geneva, 1967–72; Principal Sec., Min. of Foreign Affairs, 1972; Sen. Principal Sec., Ministries of Trade and Tourism, and Economic Planning, 1973–76; Ambassador to Belgium, Luxembourg and EEC, 1976–79; Sec.-Gen., Social Democratic Front, 1979–81; Sec. (Minister) for Trade and Tourism, 1982; Private Consultant, 1982–88; Sec. (Minister) for Educn, 1988–91. Dir, 1988–, and Chm., Exec. Cttee, 1993–, La Community Bank. Nat. Pres., Old Achtimotan Assoc., 1993–; Chm., Achimota Sch. Bd, 1993–. *Publications:* articles in Ghanaian and foreign newspapers and jls. *Recreations:* music, cricket. *Address:* Asanteson, Palm Wine Junction, La, PO Box 6616, Accra-North, Ghana. *T:* (21) 774344.

ASBIL, Rt. Rev. Walter Gordon; *see* Niagara, Bishop of.

ASCHERSON, (Charles) Neal; journalist and author; *b* 5 Oct. 1932; *s* of Stephen Romer Ascherson and Evelyn Mabel Ascherson; *m* 1st, 1958, Corinna Adam (marr. diss. 1982); two *d*; 2nd, 1984, Isabel Hilton; one *s* one *d*. *Educ:* Eton College; King's College, Cambridge (MA; Hon. Fellow, 1993). Served RM, 1950–52. Reporter and leader writer, Manchester Guardian, 1956–58; Commonwealth corresp., Scotsman, 1959–60; The Observer: reporter, 1960–63; Central Europe corresp., 1963–68; Eastern Europe corresp., 1968–75; foreign writer, 1979–85; columnist, 1985–90; Associate Editor, 1985–89; columnist, The Independent on Sunday, 1990–. Scottish politics corresp., Scotsman, 1975–79. Hon. DLitt Strathclyde, 1988; Hon. DSc(SocSci) Edinburgh, 1990; DUniv Open, 1991. Reporter of the Year 1982, Journalist of the Year 1987, Granada Awards; James Cameron Award, 1989; David Watt Meml Prize, 1991; (jtly) George Orwell Award, 1993. Golden Insignia, Order of Merit (Poland), 1992. *Publications:* The King Incorporated, 1963; The Polish August, 1981; The Struggles for Poland, 1987; Games with Shadows, 1988; Black Sea, 1995. *Address:* 27 Corsica Street, N5 1JT. *Club:* Ognisko Polskie (Polish Hearth Club).

ASFA WOSSEN HAILE SELLASSIE, HIH Merd Azmatch; GCMG (Hon.) 1965; GCVO (Hon.) 1930; GBE (Hon.) 1932; Crown Prince of Ethiopia, since 1930; *b* 27 July 1916; *e s* and *heir* of late Emperor Haile Sellassie, KG, and Empress Menen; *m* 1st, Princess Wallatta Israel; one *d* decd; 2nd, Princess Madfariash Wark Abebe; one *s* three *d*. *Educ:* privately; Liverpool Univ. Governor of Wollo province; Mem., Crown Council. Fought in Italo-Ethiopian War, 1935–36. Grand Cross: Légion d'Honneur; Belgian Order of Leopold; Order of the Netherlands; Order of Rising Sun, Japan; Order of White Elephant, Siam. *Heir: s* Prince Zara Yacob, *b* 18 Aug. 1953.

ASH, Brian Maxwell; QC 1990; *b* 31 Jan. 1941; *s* of late Carl Ash and of Irene Ash (*née* Atkinson); *m* 1971, Barbara Anne Maxwell, creator and founding editor of BBC TV Question Time; two *s* one *d*. *Educ:* Mercers' Sch.; City of London Sch.; New Coll., Oxford (Open Exhibnr; BA). BBC TV Current Affairs Producer, Reporter and Programme Presenter, 1967–73; called to the Bar, Gray's Inn, 1975. Chm. of Panel, Examination in Public of First Alteration to Devon Structure Plan, 1986; Sec., Local Govt, Planning and Envmtl Bar Assoc., 1990–92. *Recreations:* golf, sailing, ski-ing, music. *Address:* 4/5 Gray's Inn Square, WC1R 5AY. *T:* 0171–404 5252. *Clubs:* Royal Mid-Surrey Golf; Royal Norwich Golf.

ASH, Prof. Sir Eric (Albert), Kt 1990; CBE 1983; FRS 1977; FEng 1978; Professor, Department of Physics, University College London, since 1993; *b* 31 Jan. 1928; *s* of Walter and Dorothea Ash; *m* 1954, Clare (*née* Babb); five *d*. *Educ:* University College Sch.; Imperial Coll. of Science and Technology. BSc(Eng), PhD, DSc; FCGI, DIC. FIEE; FIEEE; FInstP. Research Fellow: Stanford Univ., Calif, 1952–54; QMC, 1954–55; Res. Engr, Standard Telecommunication Laboratories Ltd, 1955–63; Sen. Lectr, 1963–65, Reader, 1965–67, Prof., 1967–85, Pender Prof. and Head of Dept, 1980–85, Dept of Electronic and Electrical Engrg, UCL (Hon. Fellow, 1985); Rector, Imperial Coll., London Univ., 1985–93. Dir (non-exec.), BT (formerly British Telecom), 1987–93. Pres., IEE, 1987–88 (Vice-Pres., 1980–83; Dep. Pres., 1984–86); Member: Royal Soc. Cttees; Exec. Bd, Fellowship of Engrg, 1981–84; ABRC, 1989–; Chm., BBC Science Advisory Cttee, 1987–. Trustee: Science Mus., 1987–; Wolfson Foundn, 1988–. Sec., Royal Instn, 1984–88 (Vice Pres., 1980–82, Manager, 1980–84). Marconi International Fellowship, 1984. Dr *hc*: Aston, 1987; Leicester, 1987; Institut National Polytechnique de Grenoble, 1987; Edinburgh, 1988; Polytechnic Univ., NY, 1988; Westminster, 1992; Sussex, 1993; Glasgow, 1994; Chinese Univ. of Hong Kong, 1994. Faraday Medal, IEE, 1980; Royal Medal, Royal Soc., 1986. National Order of Merit (France), 1990. *Publications:* patents; papers on topics in physical electronics in various engrg and physics jls. *Recreations:* music, skiing, swimming. *Address:* c/o Department of Physics, University College London, Gower Street, WC1E 6BT.

ASH, Maurice Anthony, BSc (Econ); Vice President, Town and Country Planning Association, since 1987 (Chairman of Executive, 1969–83; Chairman of Council, 1983–87); *b* 31 Oct. 1917; *s* of Wilfred Cracroft and Beatrice Ash; *m* 1947, Ruth Whitney Elmhirst (*d* 1986); three *d* (one *s* decd). *Educ:* Gresham's Sch., Holt; LSE; Yale. Served War of 1939–45, armoured forces in Western Desert, Italy, Greece (despatches 1944). Mem., SW Regl Economic Planning Council, 1965–68; Chm., Green Alliance, 1978–83. Trustee, Dartington Hall, 1964– (Chm., 1972–84); Mem., Henry Moore Foundn, 1980–89. *Publications:* The Human Cloud, 1962; Who are the Progressives Now?, 1969; Regions of Tomorrow, 1969; A Guide to the Structure of London, 1972; Green Politics, 1980; New Renaissance, 1987; Journey into the Eye of a Needle, 1989; Fabric of the World, 1992; articles on land use, education and environment. *Recreation:* applying Wittgenstein. *Address:* Sharpham House, Ashprington, Totnes, Devon TQ9 7UT. *T:* Totnes (01803) 732216. *Club:* Reform.

ASH, Raymond; former Director, Business Statistics Office, retired from Civil Service, 1986; Director, Business and Trade Statistics Ltd, since 1986; *b* 2 Jan. 1928; *s* of late Horace Ash and Gladys Ash; *m* 1947, Mavis (*née* Wootton); two *s* one *d*. *Educ:* Wolverhampton Grammar Sch. Civil Service, 1949–86: professional statistician and senior manager working on health, labour, overseas trade, and business statistics. *Publications:* contrib. learned jls. *Recreations:* country walks, tourism, historical studies. *Address:* 20 Taliesin Close, Rogerstone, Newport, Gwent NP1 0DD. *T:* Newport (01633) 895470.

ASH, Rear-Admiral Walter William Hector, CB 1962; WhSch; CEng; FIEE; *b* Portsmouth, Hants, 2 May 1906; *s* of Hector Sidney and Mabel Jessy Ash; *m* 1932, Louisa Adelaide Salt, Jarrow-on-Tyne; three *d*. *Educ:* City & Guilds Coll., Kensington; Royal Naval Coll., Greenwich. Whitworth Scholar, 1926; John Samuel Scholar, 1927. Asst Elect. Engr, Admiralty (submarine design), 1932–37; Elect. Engr, Admiralty (battleship design), 1937–39; Fleet Elect. Engr, Staff C-in-C Med., 1939–40; Supt Elect. Engr, Admiralty (supply and prod.), 1940–45; Supt Elect. Engr, HM Dockyard, Hong Kong, 1945–48; Supt Elect. Engr, Admiralty Engineering Lab., 1948–49; Comdr RN, HMS Montclare, 1950–51; Capt. RN, Admiralty (weapon control design), 1951–54; Capt. RN, Elect. Engr Manager, HM Dockyard, Devonport, 1954–58; Capt. RN, Ship Design Dept, Admiralty, 1959–60; Rear-Adm. 1960; subseq. Ship Dept Directorate, Admty, retd Aug. 1963. Vis. Lectr in electrical machinery design, RN Coll., Greenwich, 1934–37. Chairman IEE, SW Sub Centre, 1957–58. ADC to the Queen, 1958–60. *Recreation:* music (piano and organ). *Address:* 4 Vavasour House, North Embankment, Dartmouth, Devon TQ6 9PW. *T:* Dartmouth (01803) 834630.

ASH, Rear-Adm. William Noel, CB 1977; LVO 1959; *b* 6 March 1921; *s* of late H. Arnold Ash, MRCS, LRCP; *m* 1951, Pamela, *d* of late Harry C. Davies, Hawkes Bay, NZ; one *s* one *d*. *Educ:* Merchant Taylors' School. Joined RN, 1938; HM Yacht Britannia, 1955–58; Captain 1965; Canadian NDC, 1965–66; Staff of SACLANT (NATO), 1966–69; Cabinet Office, 1969–71; comd HMS Ganges, 1971–73; Rear-Adm. 1974; Dir of Service Intelligence, 1974–77. Sec, Defence Press and Broadcasting Cttee, 1980–84. *Address:* c/o National Bank of New Zealand, PO Box 25051, St Heliers, Auckland, New Zealand. *Club:* Commonwealth Trust.

ASHBEE, Paul; Archaeologist, University of East Anglia, 1969–83; *b* 23 June 1918; *s* of Lewis Ashbee and Hannah Mary Elizabeth Ashbee (*née* Brett); *m* 1952, Richmal Crompton Lamburn Disher; one *s* one *d*. *Educ:* sch. in Maidstone, Kent; Univ. of London; Univ. of Leicester (MA; DLitt 1984). Post-grad. Dip. Prehistoric Archaeology, London. Royal W Kent Regt and REME, 1939–46; Control Commn for Germany, 1946–49; Univ. of London, Univ. of Bristol (Redland Coll.), 1949–54; Asst Master and Head of History, Forest Hill Sch., 1954–68. Excavation of prehistoric sites, mostly barrows both long and round for then Min. of Works, 1949–76; Co-dir with R. L. S. Bruce-Mitford of BM excavations at Sutton-Hoo, 1964–69; Mem., Sutton Hoo Research Cttee, 1982–. Mem. Council and Meetings Sec., Prehistoric Soc., 1960–74; Sec. (Wareham Earthwork), British Assoc. Sub-Cttee for Archaeological Field Experiment, 1961–; one-time Sec., Neolithic and Bronze Age Cttee, Council for British Archaeology; Mem. Royal Commn on Historical Monuments (England), 1975–85; Mem., Area Archaeological Adv. Cttee (DoE) for Norfolk and Suffolk, 1975–79. Pres., Cornwall Archæol Soc., 1976–80, Vice-Pres., 1980–84; Chm., Scole Cttee for E Anglian Archaeology, 1979–84. FSA 1958; FRSAI 1987. *Publications:* The Bronze Age Round Barrow in Britain, 1960; The Earthen Long Barrow in Britain, 1970, 2nd edn 1984; Ancient Scilly, 1974; The Ancient British, 1978; chapter in Sutton Hoo, Vol. I, 1976; Wilsford Shaft, 1989; numerous papers, articles and reviews in Archaeologia, Antiquaries Jl, Archaeological Jl, Proc. Prehistoric Soc., Antiquity, Cornish Archaeology, Arch. Cantiana, Proc. Dorset Arch. and Nat. Hist. Soc., Proc. Hants FC, Wilts Archaeol Magazine, Yorks Arch. Jl, etc. *Recreations:* East Anglia, historical architecture, bibliophilia, dog ownership. *Address:* The Old Rectory, Chedgrave, Norfolk NR14 6ND. *T:* Loddon (01508) 520595. *Club:* Norfolk (Norwich).

ASHBOURNE, 4th Baron *cr* 1885; **Edward Barry Greynville Gibson;** Lieut-Comdr RN, retired; *b* 28 Jan. 1933; *s* of 3rd Baron Ashbourne, CB, DSO, and of Reta Frances Manning, *e d* of E. M. Hazeland, Hong Kong; *S* father, 1983; *m* 1967, Yvonne Georgina, *d* of Mrs Flora Ham, of Malin, County Donegal; three *s*. *Educ:* Rugby. RN, 1951–72; Kitcat and Aitken, stockbrokers, 1972–73, 1976–79; Vickers, da Costa & Co., stockbrokers, 1973–76; Save & Prosper Gp, 1979–81; GT Management, 1981–88; Directorate of Naval Staff Duties, 1989–92, of Naval Ops and Trade, 1992–93, MoD. Pres., Petersfield Br., East Hants Cons. Assoc.; Vice-Pres., Hampshire Autistic Soc.; Chm., Joshua Christian Trust. *Heir: s* Hon. Edward Charles d'Olier Gibson, *b* 31 Dec. 1967. *Address:* 107 Sussex Road, Petersfield, Hants GU31 4LB.

ASHBROOK, 10th Viscount, *cr* 1751 (Ire.); **Desmond Llowarch Edward Flower,** KCVO 1977; MBE 1945; DL; Baron Castle Durrow, 1733; Member of Council of Duchy of Lancaster, 1957–77; *b* 9 July 1905; *o s* of 9th Viscount and Gladys, *d* of Gen. Sir George Wentworth A. Higginson, GCB, GCVO; *S* father, 1936; *m* 1934, Elizabeth, *er d* of Capt. John Egerton-Warburton and Hon. Mrs Waters; two *s* one *d*. *Educ:* Eton; Balliol Coll., Oxford (BA 1927). Served War of 1939–45, RA. Formerly a Chartered Accountant. JP, 1946–67, DL 1949–, Vice-Lieutenant, 1961–67, Cheshire. *Heir: s* Hon. Michael Llowarch Warburton Flower, *qv*. *Address:* Woodlands, Arley, Northwich, Cheshire CW9 6LZ.

ASHBROOK, Kate Jessie; General Secretary, Open Spaces Society, since 1984; *b* 1 Feb. 1955; *d* of John Ashbrook and Margaret Balfour. *Educ:* Benenden Sch., Kent; Exeter Univ. (BSc). Member, Executive Committee: Open Spaces Soc., 1978–84; Ramblers' Assoc., 1982– (Vice-Chm., 1993–95; Chm., 1995–; Footpath Sec., Bucks and W Middx, 1986–); Council for National Parks, 1983–; Mem., Common Land Forum, 1984–86; Chm., Central Rights of Way Cttee, 1991–; Sec., Countryside Link, 1989–92; Pres., Dartmoor Preservation Assoc., 1995– (Hon. Sec., 1981–84). Chm., Turville Sch. Trust, 1994–95. Editor, Open Space, 1984–. *Publications:* (contrib.) The Walks of South-East England, 1975; (contrib.) Severnside: a guide to family walks, 1976; pamphlets; contribs to The Countryman and various jls. *Recreations:* pedantry, finding illegally blocked footpaths. *Address:* Telfer's Cottage, Turville, Henley-on-Thames RG9 6QL. *T:* Henley-on-Thames (01491) 638396.

ASHBURNER, Prof. Michael, PhD, ScD; FRS 1990; Professor of Biology, University of Cambridge, since 1991; Fellow, Churchill College, Cambridge, since 1980; *b* 23 May 1942; *s* of Geoffrey Staton Ashburner and Diane Ashburner (*née* Leff); *m* 1963, Francesca Ryan, *d* of Desmond Francis Ryan and Isabel Ryan; one *s* two *d*. *Educ:* Royal Grammar Sch., High Wycombe; Churchill Coll., Cambridge (BA 1964, PhD 1968, ScD 1978). FRES 1975. University of Cambridge: Asst in Research, 1966–68; Univ. Demonstrator, 1968–73; Univ. Lectr, 1973–80; Reader in Developmental Genetics, 1980–91. Gordon Ross Res. Fellow, Calif Inst. of Technology, 1968–69; Visiting Professor: Univ. of California Sch. of Medicine, San Francisco, 1977–78; Univ. of Crete, 1985; Univ. of Pavia, Italy, 1990–; Miller Vis. Prof., Univ. of California at Berkeley, 1986. Lectures: Goldschmidt, Hebrew Univ., Jerusalem, 1985; Osborne, Edinburgh Univ., 1991; Dacre, Peterhouse, Cambridge, 1992. Res. Co-ordinator, EMBL, 1994–. Member: EMBO, 1977, Council, 1988–91; Governing Council, Internat. Centre for Insect Physiology and Ecology, Nairobi, 1991–. Mem., Academia Europaea, 1989; Fellow, Japan Soc. for Promotion of Sci., 1992. Hon. Foreign Mem., Amer. Acad. of Arts and Scis, 1993. *Publications:* (ed) The Genetics and Biology of Drosophila, 1976–86, 12 vols; (ed) Insect Cytogenetics, 1980; (ed) Heat Shock: from bacteria to man, 1982; Drosophila: a laboratory handbook and manual, 2 vols, 1989; contribs to scientific jls. *Recreations:* walking, watching birds. *Address:* 5 Bateman Street, Cambridge CB2 1NB. *T:* Cambridge (01223) 64706; Department of Genetics, Downing Street, Cambridge CB2 3EH. *T:* Cambridge (01223) 333969.

ASHBURNHAM, Captain Sir Denny Reginald, 12th Bt *cr* 1661; Captain South Staffordshire Regiment; *b* 24 March 1916; *o* surv. *s* of Sir Fleetwood Ashburnham, 11th Bt, and Elfrida, *d* of late James Kirkley, JP, Cleadon Park, Co. Durham; *S* father 1953; *m* 1946, Mary Frances, *d* of Major Robert Pascoe Mair, Wick, Udimore, Sussex; two *d* (one *s* decd). *Heir: g s* James Fleetwood Ashburnham, *b* 17 Dec. 1979. *Address:* Little Broomham, Guestling, Hastings, East Sussex TN35 4HS.

ASHBURTON, 7th Baron *cr* 1835; **John Francis Harcourt Baring,** KG 1994; KCVO 1990 (CVO 1980); Kt 1983; DL; Chairman: British Petroleum Co. plc, 1992–95 (Director, 1982–95); Barings plc, 1985–89 (non-executive Director, 1989–94); Baring Brothers & Co. Ltd, 1974–89 (a Managing Director, 1955–74); Lord Warden of the Stannaries, Duchy of Cornwall, 1990–94 (Receiver-General, 1974–90); *b* 2 Nov. 1928; *er s* of 6th Baron Ashburton, KG, KCVO and Hon. Doris Mary Thérèse Harcourt (*d* 1981), *e d* of 1st Viscount Harcourt; *S* father, 1991; *m* 1st, 1955, Susan Mary Renwick (marr. diss. 1984), *e d* of 1st Baron Renwick, KBE, and Mrs John Ormiston; two *s* two *d*; 2nd, 1987, Mrs Sarah Crewe, *d* of late J. G. Spencer Churchill. *Educ:* Eton (Fellow, 1982); Trinity Coll., Oxford (MA; Hon. Fellow 1989). Dep. Chm., Royal Insurance Co. Ltd, 1975–82 (Dir, 1964–82); Chairman: Outwich Investment Trust Ltd, 1968–86; Baring Stratton Investment Trust, 1986–; Director: Dunlop Holdings Ltd, 1981–84; Bank of England, 1983–91; Jaguar, 1989–91. Vice-Pres., British Bankers' Assoc., 1977–81; Pres., Overseas Bankers' Club, 1977–78. Chm., Accepting Houses Cttee, 1977–81; Chm., Cttee on Finance for Industry, NEDC, 1980–86. Member: British Transport Docks Bd, 1966–71; President's Cttee, CBI, 1976–79; Trustee and Hon. Treas., Police Foundn, 1989–; Member: Council, Baring Foundn, 1971– (Chm., 1987–); Exec. Cttee, NACF, 1989–. Trustee: Rhodes Trust, 1970– (Chm., 1987–); Southampton Univ. Develt Trust, 1986– (Chm., 1989); Nat. Gall., 1981–87. High Steward, Winchester Cathedral, 1991–. DL Hants, 1994. Hon. Fellow, Hertford Coll., Oxford, 1976. *Heir: s* Hon. Mark Francis Robert Baring [*b* 17 Aug. 1958; *m* 1983, Miranda Caroline, *d* of Captain Charles St John Graham Moncrief; one *s* one *d*]. *Address:* Lake House, Northington, Alresford, Hants SO24 9TG; 3 Stanley House, 13 Stanley Crescent, W11 2NA. *Clubs:* Pratt's, Flyfishers'.

ASHBY, David Glynn; MP (C) North-West Leicestershire, since 1983; barrister; *b* 14 May 1940; *s* of Robert M. Ashby and Isobel A. Davidson; *m* 1965, Silvana Morena; one *d*. *Educ:* Royal Grammar Sch., High Wycombe; Bristol Univ. (LLB Hons). Called to the Bar, Gray's Inn, 1963; in practice on SE Circuit. Member: Hammersmith Bor. Council, 1968–71; for W Woolwich, GLC, 1977–81; ILEA, 1977–81. *Recreations:* gardening, skiing, music. *Address:* House of Commons, SW1A 0AA.

ASHBY, Francis Dalton, OBE 1975; Director, National Counties Building Society, 1980–90; retired; *b* 20 Jan. 1920; *s* of late John Frederick Ashby and late Jessie Ashby; *m* 1948, Mollie Isabel Mitchell; one *s* one *d* (and one *d* decd). *Educ:* Watford Grammar Sch. Diploma in Govt Admin. War Service, Royal Signals, 1940–46: POW, Far East, 1942–45. National Debt Office: Exec. Officer, 1938; Asst Comptroller and Estabt Officer, 1966–76; Comptroller-General, 1976–80. *Recreation:* local voluntary work. *Address:* Moorfield, Carpenters Wood Drive, Chorleywood, Herts WD3 5RP.

ASHBY, Rt Rev. Godfrey William Ernest Candler; Assistant Bishop of Leicester, 1988–95; Priest-in-charge, Newtown Linford, 1992–95; *b* 6 Nov. 1930; *s* of late William Candler Ashby and Vera Fane Ashby (*née* Hickey); *m* 1957, Sally Hawtree; four *s* two *d*. *Educ:* King's School, Chester; King's Coll., London (BD, AKC, PhD). Deacon 1955, priest 1956; Assistant Curate: St Peter, St Helier, Morden, 1955–57; Clydesdale Mission, 1958; Priest-in-charge, St Mark's Mission, 1958–60; Subwarden, St Paul's Coll., Grahamstown, 1960–65; Rector of Alice and Lectr, Federal Theological Seminary, 1966–68; Sen. Lecturer, Old Testament and Hebrew, Rhodes Univ., Grahamstown, 1969–75; Assoc. Professor, 1974–75; Overseas Visiting Scholar, St John's Coll., Cambridge, 1975; Dean and Archdeacon, Cathedral of St Michael and St George, Grahamstown, 1976–80; Bishop of St John's (Transkei and S Africa), 1980–84; Prof. of Divinity, Univ. of Witwatersrand, Johannesburg, 1985–88. Hon. Canon, Leicester Cathedral, 1994–. *Publications:* Theodoret of Cyrrhus as Exegete of the Old Testament, 1970; Sacrifice, 1988; Exodus (commentary), 1995; articles in theological jls. *Recreation:* ornithology. *Address:* 7 Graham Street, Kynsna, 6570, S Africa.

ASHBY, Prof. Michael Farries, FRS 1979; FEng 1993; Royal Society Research Professor, Department of Engineering, University of Cambridge, since 1989 (Professor of Engineering Materials, 1973–89); *b* 20 Nov. 1935; *s* of Lord Ashby, FRS; *m* 1962, Maureen Stewart; two *s* one *d*. *Educ:* Campbell Coll., Belfast; Queens' Coll., Cambridge (BA, MA, PhD). Post-doctoral work, Cambridge, 1960–62; Asst, Univ. of Göttingen, 1962–65; Asst Prof., Harvard Univ., 1965–69; Prof. of Metallurgy, Harvard Univ., 1969–73. Mem., Akad. der Wissenschaften zu Göttingen, 1980–. Hon. MA Harvard, 1969. Editor, Acta Metallurgica, 1974–. *Recreations:* music, design. *Address:* 51 Maids Causeway, Cambridge CB5 8DE. *T:* Cambridge (01223) 303015.

ASHCOMBE, 4th Baron, *cr* 1892; **Henry Edward Cubitt;** late RAF; Chairman, Cubitt Estates Ltd; *b* 31 March 1924; *er s* of 3rd Baron Ashcombe; *S* father, 1962; *m* 1955, Ghislaine (marr. diss. 1968), *o d* of Cornelius Willem Dresselhuys, Long Island, New York; *m* 1973, Hon. Virginia Carington, *yr d* of Baron Carrington, *qv*; *m* 1979, Mrs Elizabeth Dent-Brocklehurst. *Educ:* Eton. Served War of 1939–45, RAF. Consul-General in London for the Principality of Monaco, 1961–68. *Heir: cousin* Mark Edward Cubitt [*b* 29 Feb. 1964; *m* 1992, Melissa Mary, *o d* of Maj. Charles Hay; one *s*]. *Address:* Sudeley Castle, Winchcombe, Cheltenham, Glos GL54 5JD. *Club:* White's.

See also Earl of Harrington.

ASHCROFT, David, TD 1957; MA Cantab; Headmaster, Cheltenham College, 1959–78; *b* 20 May 1920; *s* of late A. H. Ashcroft, DSO; *m* 1949, Joan Elizabeth Young; two *s* three *d*. *Educ:* Rugby Sch.; Gonville and Caius Coll., Cambridge. War Service, 1940–46 (despatches). Asst Master, Rossall Sch., 1946–50; Asst Master, Rugby Sch., 1950–59. *Address:* London House, Ashton Keynes, Swindon, Wilts SN6 6NL. *T:* Cirencester (01285) 861319.

ASHCROFT, James Geoffrey, CB 1988; Deputy Under Secretary of State, Finance, Ministry of Defence, 1985–88; *b* 19 May 1928; *s* of James Ashcroft and Elizabeth (*née* Fillingham); *m* 1953, Margery (*née* Barratt); one *s*. *Educ:* Cowley Sch., St Helens; Peterhouse, Cambridge. BA (Hons Hist.). Min. of Supply, 1950–59; Min. of Aviation, 1959–61, 1964–65; Min. of Defence, 1961–64, 1965–68, 1970–73; Inst. of Strategic Studies, 1968–70; Under-Sec., Pay Board, 1973–74; Asst Under Sec. of State, Management Services, PE, 1974–76; Asst Under Sec. of State, Gen. Finance, MoD, 1976–84. *Publications:* papers on international collaboration in military logistics. *Recreation:* golf. *Address:* 39 Hill Rise, Hinchley Wood, Esher, Surrey KT10 0AL. *T:* 0181–398 5637.

ASHCROFT, John Kevin, CBE 1990; Crabtree Consultancy Group Ltd, since 1990; *b* 24 Dec. 1948; *s* of Cumania Manion and late John Ashcroft; *m* 1972, Jennifer Ann (*née* King); two *s* one *d*. *Educ:* Upholland Grammar School; LSE (BSc Econ Hons). Marketing Trainee, Tube Investments, 1970; Brand Manager, Crown Wallcoverings Internat. Div., 1974; Marketing Dir, Crown Wallcoverings French Subsidiary, 1976; Man. Dir, Coloroll, 1978–82, Dep. Chm. and Chief Exec., 1982–86, Chm., 1986–90. Young Business Man of the Year, The Guardian, 1987. *Recreations:* fine arts, opera, sports, shooting, wine.

ASHCROFT, Ven. Lawrence; retired as Archdeacon of Stow and Vicar of Burton-on-Stather (1954–62); *b* 1901; *s* of Lawrence Ashcroft; *m* 1927, Barbara Louise Casson; two *s* three *d*. *Educ:* University Coll., Durham; Lichfield Theological Coll. Deacon, 1926; Priest, 1927; Curate of Ulverston, 1926–29, of Egremont, 1929–30; District Sec., Brit. and Foreign Bible Society, 1930–33; hon. mem. of staff, Southwell Minster, 1930–33; Vicar of St Saviour's, Retford, 1934–40; Chaplain to the Forces (Emergency Commission), 1940–43, now Hon. Chaplain; Rector of St Michael Stoke, Coventry, 1943; Rural Dean of Coventry, 1949–53; Hon. Canon of Coventry, 1952–53; Hon. Canon of Lincoln, 1954–62; Proctor in Convocation, Canterbury, 1955–62; Chaplain to High Sheriff of Lincolnshire, 1958, to British Embassy, Oslo, 1967, Luxembourg, 1968; Rector, St Philip's, Antigua, 1969, Manvers St Crispin, Toronto, 1970–79. Mem., Church Assembly, 1955–62. Governor, De Aston Grammar Sch., 1955–62; Founder and Chm., Brigg Church Sch., 1956–62.

ASHCROFT, Philip Giles; Legal Consultant, Registry of Friendly Societies and Building Societies Commission, since 1988; *b* 15 Nov. 1926; *s* of Edmund Samuel Ashcroft and Constance Ruth Ashcroft (*née* Giles); *m* 1st, 1968, Kathleen Margaret Senior (marr. diss. 1983); one *s*; 2nd, 1985, Valerie May Smith, *d* of late E. T. G. Smith. *Educ:* Royal Grammar Sch., Newcastle upon Tyne; Durham Univ. Admitted solicitor, 1951. Joined Treasury Solicitor's Dept, 1955; Asst Legal Adviser, Land Commn, 1967; Asst Treasury Solicitor, 1971; Under-Sec. (Legal), DTI, 1973; Legal Adviser, Dept of Energy, 1974–80; Dep. Solicitor to the Post Office, 1980–81; Solicitor, British Telecommunications, 1981–87, retired. *Recreations:* reading, listening to music, walking. *Address:* 24A Rudd's Lane, Haddenham, Aylesbury, Bucks HP17 8JP. *T:* Haddenham (01844) 291921.

ASHDOWN, Rt. Hon. Jeremy John Durham, (Paddy); PC 1989; MP Yeovil (L 1983–88, Lib Dem since 1988); Leader of the Liberal Democrats, since 1988; *b* 27 Feb. 1941; *s* of late John W. R. D. Ashdown and Lois A. Ashdown; *m* 1961, Jane (*née* Courtenay); one *s* one *d*. *Educ:* Bedford Sch. Served RM, 1959–71: 41 and 42 Commando; commanded 2 Special Boat Section; Captain RM; HM Diplomatic Service, 1st Sec., UK Mission to UN, Geneva, 1971–76; Commercial Manager's Dept, Westlands Gp, 1976–78; Sen. Manager, Morlands Ltd, 1978–81; employed by Dorset CC, 1982–83. L spokesman for Trade and Industry, 1983–86; Lib/SDP Alliance spokesman on education and science, 1987; Lib Dem spokesman on NI, 1988–. *Publications:* Citizen's Britain, 1989; Beyond Westminster, 1994; Making Change our Ally, 1994. *Recreations:* walking, gardening, wine making. *Address:* Vane Cottage, Norton sub Hamdon, Som TA14 6SG. *T:* Chiselborough (0193588) 491. *Club:* National Liberal.

ASHE, Sir Derick (Rosslyn), KCMG 1978 (CMG 1966); HM Diplomatic Service, retired 1979; Ambassador and Permanent UK Representative to Disarmament Conference, Geneva, 1977–79 and Permanent Head of UK Delegation to UN Special Session on Disarmament, New York, 1977–78; *b* 20 Jan. 1919; *s* of late Frederick Allen Ashe and late Rosalind Ashe (*née* Mitchell); *m* 1957, Rissa Guinness, *d* of late Capt. Hon. Trevor Tempest Parker, DSC, Royal Navy and Mrs Parker; one *s* one *d*. *Educ:* Bradfield Coll.; Trinity Coll., Oxford. HM Forces, 1940–46 (despatches 1945). Second Sec., Berlin and Frankfurt-am-Main, 1947–49; Private Sec. to Permanent Under-Sec. of State for German Section of FO, 1950–53; First Sec., La Paz, 1953–55; FO, 1955–57; First Sec. (Information), Madrid, 1957–61; FO, 1961–62; Counsellor and Head of Chancery: Addis Ababa, 1962–64; Havana, 1964–66; Head of Security Dept, FCO (formerly FO), 1966–69; Minister, Tokyo, 1969–71; Ambassador to: Romania, 1972–75; Argentina, 1975–77. Knight of the Order of Orange-Nassau (with swords), 1945. *Recreations:* gardening, antiques. *Address:* Dalton House, Hurstbourne Tarrant, Andover, Hants SP11 0AX. *T:* Hurstbourne Tarrant (01264) 736276. *Clubs:* White's, Travellers', Beefsteak.

ASHE, Thomas Michael; QC 1994; *b* 10 March 1949; *s* of John Ashe and Nancy (*née* O'Connor); *m* 1977, Helen Morag Nicholson. *Educ:* Finchley Catholic Grammar Sch. Called to the Bar, Middle Temple, 1971; called to Irish Bar, 1975, Northern Irish Bar, 1993. Estate Duty Office, CS, 1967–70; merchant banking, 1971–76; practice at the Bar, 1978– Dep. Public Prosecutor, Min. of Finance, Singapore, 1988–90. Editor, Company Lawyer, 1983–. Hon. General Counsel to Brit. Inst. of Securities Laws, 1980–; Hon. Consultant to Commercial Crime Unit, Commonwealth Secretariat, 1980–84. Mem. Bd, Centre for Internat. Documentation on Organised and Economic Crime, Cambridge, 1990–; Guest Lectr, Fac. of Laws, Univ. of Cambridge, 1990–. *Publications:* (jtly) Insider Trading, 1990, 2nd edn 1994; (jtly) Insider Dealing (Ireland), 1992; (jtly) Insider Crime, 1994; contrib. Money, 1980, and (jtly) Injunctions, 1991, in Halsbury's Laws of England, 4th edn; articles in legal periodicals. *Recreations:* walking, railways, Gregorian Chant, classical music, Irish traditional music. *Address:* 11 Stone Buildings, Lincoln's Inn, WC2A 3TG. *T:* 0171–404 5055.

ASHE LINCOLN, Fredman; *see* Lincoln, F. A.

ASHENHURST, Maj.-Gen. Francis Ernest; Director, Defence Dental Services, 1990–92, retired; *b* 1 April 1933; *s* of Charles Ashenhurst and Margaret Jane (*née* MacLaine); *m* 1959, Hilary Chapman; two *d*. *Educ:* Methodist Coll., Belfast; Queen's Univ., Belfast (BDS); London Univ. (MSc). Commnd RADC, 1963; OC Rhine Area Dental Unit, 1964–66; Instr and Chief Instr, Depot and Trng Estabt, RADC, 1967–71; Commanding Officer: Army Dental Centres, Hong Kong, 1971–73; 6 Dental Gp, UKLF, 1973–76; postgrad. studies, 1976–77; Asst Dir, Army Dental Service, 1977–78; 1 Dental Gp, BAOR, 1978–81; Dep. Dir, Army Dental Service, 1981–84; Comdt, HQ and Central Gp, RADC, 1984; Dep. Comdr, Med. (Dentistry), BAOR, 1984–86; Comdr, HQ and Tech. Services, RADC, BAOR, 1986–88; Dir, Army Dental Service, 1989–90. QHDS, 1989–92. OStJ 1974. *Recreations:* gardening, listening to music, cooking, discovering Great Britain.

ASHER, Bernard Harry; Chairman: HSBC Investment Bank Ltd, since 1993; James Capel & Co., since 1991; Samuel Montagu, since 1993; *b* 9 March 1936; *s* of Samuel Asher and Rebecca (*née* Fisher); *m* 1961, Batia Sislin; one *s* two *d*. *Educ:* LSE (BSc). S. Japhet & Co., 1957–59; English Electric Co., 1960–67; ITT Inc., 1967–74 and 1978–80; on secondment to NEDO, 1974–78; Hong Kong Bank, 1980–92; Director: HSBC Hldgs, 1991–; Midland Bank, 1991–. *Recreations:* opera, touring airports. *Address:* Thames Exchange, 10 Queen Street Place, EC4R 1BL. *T:* 0171–621 0011. *Clubs:* Reform; Hong Kong, Royal Hong Kong Jockey.

ASHER, Jane; actress and writer; *b* 5 April 1946; *d* of Richard A. J. Asher, MD, FRCP and Margaret Asher (*née* Eliot); *m* Gerald Scarfe, *qv*; two *s* one *d*. *Educ:* North Bridge House; Miss Lambert's PNEU. *Stage:* Will You Walk a Little Faster, Duke of York's, 1960; Wendy in Peter Pan, Scala, 1961; Bristol Old Vic, 1965; Romeo and Juliet and Measure for Measure, NY, 1967; Look Back in Anger, Royal Court, 1969; The Philanthropist, Mayfair and NY, 1970; Treats, Royal Court, 1975; National Theatre, 1976; Whose Life is it Anyway?, Mermaid and Savoy, 1978; Before the Party, Queen's, 1978; Blithe Spirit, Vaudeville, 1986; Henceforward, Vaudeville, 1988; The School for Scandal, NT, 1990; Making it Better, Criterion, 1992; *films include:* Mandy, 1951; Greengage Summer, 1961; Alfie, 1966; Deep End, 1970; Henry VIII and his Six Wives, 1970; Runners, 1984; Dream Child, 1985; Paris by Night, 1988; *television includes:* Brideshead Revisited, 1981; The Mistress, 1986; Wish Me Luck, 1987–89; Eats for Treats, 1990; Tonight at 8.30, Murder Most Horrid, 1991; Closing Numbers, 1993; The Choir, 1995; numerous plays for radio; Radio Actress of the Year Award, 1986. Member: BBC Gen. Adv. Council, 1991–; BAFTA, 1985; Forum, 1993–. Vice Pres., Nat. Autistic Soc., 1990–; Trustee: WWF;

Child Accident Prevention Trust; Ford Martin Trust for Cancer in Children; Children in Need. Governor, Molecule Theatre. Started business, Jane Asher Party Cakes, London, 1990; designer and consultant for Sainsbury's cakes, 1992–. Columnist, Today newspaper, 1994–. FRSA 1989. *Publications:* Jane Asher's Party Cakes, 1982; Jane Asher's Fancy Dress, 1983; Silent Nights for You and Your Baby, 1984; Jane Asher's Quick Party Cakes, 1986; The Moppy Stories, 1987; Easy Entertaining, 1987; Keep Your Baby Safe, 1988; Children's Parties, 1988; Calendar of Cakes, 1989; Eats for Treats, 1990; Jane Asher's Book of Cake Decorating Ideas, 1993; Round the World Cookbook, 1994; Time to Play, 1995; Bearing Down, 1996; 101 Things I wish I'd known before . . ., 1996; journalism for newspapers and magazines. *Recreations:* reading, ski-ing. *Address:* c/o ICM, Oxford House, 76 Oxford Street, W1R 1RB.

ASHFORD, (Albert) Reginald, CMG 1962; Assistant Secretary, Board of Customs and Excise, 1952–73; *b* 30 June 1914; *s* of Ernest and Ethel Ashford; *m* 1946, Mary Anne Ross Davidson (*d* 1990); one *s*. *Educ:* Ealing Grammar Sch.; London Sch. of Economics (BSc Econ). Entered Civil Service, 1931 as Clerical Officer, MoT; Exec. Officer, Customs and Excise, 1934; Private Sec. to Chm. of Bd, 1943–46; Principal, 1946; UK Delegate: to internat. confs on reduction of barriers to trade, incl. GATT, Geneva, 1947, Havana, 1947–48, Annecy, 1949, Torquay, 1950, and intermediate meetings (sometime Chm., wkg parties); to Econ. Commn for Europe, 1948–56 (TIR Convention, 1949); to UNESCO, Florence, 1950 (Chm., Drafting Cttee of Internat. Convention on Importation of Educnl, Scientific and Cultural Materials); to Customs Co-operation Council, Brussels, 1953–60 (Chm., Perm. Tech. Cttee, 1954, and Finance Cttee, 1958–59). European Tariff discussions and European Free Trade Area Agreement, Brussels, Paris, Stockholm, 1953–60; transferred by choice to home div., 1960. Vice Chm., Bucks Assoc. for Blind, 1979–81. *Address:* 4 Tithe Green, Rustington, West Sussex BN16 3QX. *T:* Rustington (01903) 776545.

ASHFORD, George Francis, OBE 1945; retired; *b* 5 July 1911; *s* of G. W. Ashford and L. M. Redfern; *m* 1950, Eleanor Vera Alexander; two *s*. *Educ:* Malvern Coll.; Trinity Hall, Cambridge; Birmingham Univ. Served War of 1939–45, Army, N Africa and Italy (despatches 1944). Distillers Co. Ltd, 1937–67: Solicitor, 1937; Legal Adviser, 1945; Dir, 1956; Management Cttee, 1963–67; Dir, BP Co. Ltd, 1967–73, Man. Dir, 1969–73; Dir, Albright & Wilson Ltd, 1973–79. Mem., Monopolies and Mergers Commn, 1973–80. Pres., British Plastics Fedn, 1966–67; Vice-President: Soc. of Chemical Industry, 1966–69; Chem. Ind. Assoc., 1967–70. Mem. Economic Policy Cttee for Chemical Industry, 1967–74; Chm., Working Party on Industrial Review, 1973. Organiser, Meals on Wheels, Woodley and Sonning, 1983–86. *Recreation:* gardening. *Address:* The Old House, Sonning, Berks RG4 0UR. *T:* Reading (01734) 692122.

ASHFORD, Ven. Percival Leonard; Chaplain to the Queen, since 1982; *b* 5 June 1927; *s* of late Edwin and Gwendoline Emily Ashford; *m* 1955, Dorothy Helen Harwood; two *s*. *Educ:* Kemp Welch Sch., Poole; Bristol Univ.; Tyndale Hall Theol Coll., Bristol. Asst Curate, St Philip and St James, Ilfracombe, 1954; Curate-in-Charge, Church of Good Shepherd, Aylesbury, 1956; Vicar, St Olaf's, Poughill, Bude, 1959; HM Prison Service: Asst Chaplain, Wormwood Scrubs, 1965; Chaplain: Risley Remand Centre, 1966; Durham, 1969; Wandsworth, 1971; Winchester, 1975; SW Reg. Chaplain of Prisons, 1977; Chaplain General of Prisons, 1981–85; Archdeacon to the Prison Service, 1982–85; Vicar of Hambledon, 1985–87; Permission to officiate, dio. Sarum, 1991–. Mem. Gen. Synod, C of E, 1985. Exam. Chaplain to Bishop of Portsmouth, 1986. Selector Chm., ACCM, 1988–89. *Recreations:* choral and classical music, reading. *Address:* 45 Windsor Way, Alderholt, near Fordingbridge, Hants SP6 3BN. *T:* Fordingbridge (01425) 655493.

ASHFORD, Reginald; *see* Ashford, A. R.

ASHFORD, Ronald, CBE 1992; CEng, FIMechE, FRAeS; aviation and safety consultant; *b* 24 Aug. 1932; *s* of Russell Sutcliffe Ashford and Dorothy Ashford (*née* Shorland); *m* 1955, Françoise Louisa Gabrielle Génestal du Chaumeil; two *s*. *Educ:* St Edward's Sch., Oxford; De Havilland Aeronautical Tech. Sch. Flight Develt Engr, De Havilland Aircraft Co., 1953–56; Pilot Officer, RAF, 1956–58; Flight Develt Engr and Sen. Aerodynamicist, De Havilland/Hawker Siddeley Aviation, 1958–68; Design Surveyor, Air Registration Bd, 1968–72; Civil Aviation Authority: Surveyor and Head, Flight Dept, 1972–83; Dir-Gen., Airworthiness, 1983–88; Group Dir, Safety Regulation, and Board Mem., 1988–92; Sec. Gen., Eur. Jt Aviation Authorities, 1992–94. Wakefield Gold Medal, 1989, Hodgson Prize, 1991, RAeS; Dist. Service Award, Flight Safety Foundn, 1992; Award for Dist. Service, US Fed. Aviation Admin, 1992; Cumberbatch Trophy, GAPAN, 1992. *Publications:* papers in Jl RAeS. *Recreations:* walking, gardening, light aircraft flying. *Address:* Chartcote, Goodley Stock Road, Crockham Hill, Edenbridge, Kent TN8 6TA. *T:* Edenbridge (01732) 866252.

ASHFORD, Air Vice-Marshal Ronald Gordon, CBE 1978; Senior Traffic Commissioner, Western Traffic Area and Licensing Authority, since 1991; *b* 2 May 1931; *s* of Richard Ashford and Phyllis Lancaster; *m* 1966, Patricia Ann Turner; two *d*. *Educ:* Ilfracombe Grammar Sch.; Bristol Univ. (LLB). Joined RAF, 1952; qualified as Navigator, 1953; OC No 115 Squadron, 1971–72; OC RAF Finningley, 1976–77; RCDS, 1978; Air Cdre Intelligence, 1979–83; Comdr, Southern Maritime Air Region, 1983–84; Dir Gen., Personal Services (RAF), MoD, 1984–85; retired. Chm., Metropolitan Traffic Comrs, 1985–91. *Recreation:* golf. *Address:* Old Courthay, Church Lane, Brent Knoll, Som TA9 4DG. *Club:* Royal Air Force.

ASHFORD, William Stanton, OBE 1971; HM Diplomatic Service, retired; *b* 4 July 1924; *s* of Thomas and May Ashford; *m* 1957, Rosalind Anne Collett; two *s*. *Educ:* Winchester Coll.; Balliol Coll., Oxford. Served RAF, 1943–47; Air Ministry, 1948; Commonwealth Relations Office, 1961; Director of British Information Services, Sierra Leone, 1961, Ghana, 1962; Acting Consul-General, Tangier, 1965; Regional Information Officer, Bombay, 1966; Head of Chancery, British Government Office, Montreal, 1967; seconded to Northern Ireland Office, 1972; FCO, 1974; Consul-General, Adelaide, 1977; High Comr, Vanuatu, 1980–82. *Recreations:* 18th Century music, smallholder farming. *Address:* c/o Lloyds Bank, PO Box 770, St Helier, Jersey JE4 8ZZ. *T:* Jersey (01534) 59655.

ASHIOTIS, Costas; High Commissioner of Cyprus in London, 1966–79; Cyprus Ambassador to Denmark, Sweden, Norway and Malta, 1966–79; *b* 1908; *m*. *Educ:* Pancyprian Gymnasium, Nicosia; London Sch. of Economics. Journalist and editor; joined Govt Service, 1942; Asst Comr of Labour, 1948; Dir-Gen., Min. of Foreign Affairs, 1960. Mem. Cyprus delegns to UN and to internat. confs. Retired from Foreign Service, 1979. MBE 1952. *Publications:* Labour Conditions in Cyprus during the War Years, 1939–45; literary articles. *Address:* 10 Ev. Pallikarides Street, Nicosia, Cyprus.

ASHKEN, Kenneth Richard; Director (Policy), Crown Prosecution Service, since 1993; *b* 13 June 1945; *s* of Karol and Dulcinea Ashken; *m* 1969, Linda Salemink (separated); two *s* one *d*; partner, Patricia Almond; one *d*. *Educ:* Whitgift Sch., Croydon; London Univ. (LLB Hons); Cambridge Inst. of Criminology (DipCrim). Office of Director of Public Prosecutions, 1972; Asst Dir of Public Prosecutions, 1984; Hd of Policy and Inf. Div., 1986, Dir, Policy and Communications Gp (Grade 3), 1990, Crown Prosecution Service. *Recreation:* mountain-biking. *Address:* Crown Prosecution Service, 50 Ludgate Hill, EC4M 7JJ. *Club:* Royal Automobile.

ASHKENAZY, Vladimir; concert pianist; conductor; Chief Conductor, Deutsches Symphonie-Orchester Berlin (formerly Berlin Radio Symphony Orchestra), since 1989; *b* Gorky, Russia, 6 July 1937; *m* 1961, Thorunn Johannsdottir, *d* of Johann Tryggvason, Iceland; two *s* three *d*. *Educ:* Central Musical Sch., Moscow; Conservatoire, Moscow. Studied under Sumbatyan; Lev Oborin class, 1955: grad 1960. Internat. Chopin Comp., Warsaw, at age of 17 (gained 2nd prize); won Queen Elizabeth Internat. Piano Comp., Brussels, at age of 18 (gold medal). Joint winner (with John Ogdon) of Tchaikovsky Piano Comp., Moscow, 1962. London debut with London Symph. Orch. under George Hurst, and subseq, solo recital, Festival Hall, 1963. Music Dir, RPO, 1987–94. Has played in many countries. Makes recordings. Hon. RAM 1972. Icelandic Order of the Falcon, 1971. *Publication:* (with Jasper Parrott) Beyond Frontiers, 1985. *Address:* Käppelistrasse 15, 6045 Meggen, Switzerland.

ASHLEY, family name of **Baron Ashley of Stoke.**

ASHLEY OF STOKE, Baron *cr* 1992 (Life Peer), of Widnes in the County of Cheshire; **Jack Ashley,** CH 1975; PC 1979; *b* 6 Dec. 1922; *s* of John Ashley and Isabella Bridge; *m* 1951, Pauline Kay Crispin; three *d*. *Educ:* St Patrick's Elem. Sch., Widnes, Lancs; Ruskin Coll., Oxford; Gonville and Caius Coll., Cambridge. Labourer and cranedriver, 1936–46; Shop Steward Convenor and Nat. Exec. Mem., Chemical Workers' Union, 1946; Scholarship, Ruskin Coll., 1946–48 and Caius Coll., 1948–51 (Chm. Cambridge Labour Club, 1950; Pres. Cambridge Union, 1951); BBC Radio Producer, 1951–57; Commonwealth Fund Fellow, 1955; BBC Senior Television Producer, 1957–66; Mem., General Advisory Council, BBC, 1967–69, 1970–74. MP (Lab) Stoke-on-Trent, South, 1966–92. Parliamentary Private Secretary to: Sec. of State for Econ. Affairs, 1967–68; Sec. of State, DHSS, 1974–76. Mem., Lab. Party Nat. Exec. Cttee, 1976–78. Pres., Hearing and Speech Trust, 1985–. Councillor, Borough of Widnes, 1945. *Publications:* Journey into Silence (autobiog.), 1973; Acts of Defiance (autobiog.), 1992. *Address:* House of Lords, SW1A 0PW.

ASHLEY, Lord; Anthony Nils Christian Ashley-Cooper; *b* 24 June 1977; *s* and *heir* of Earl of Shaftesbury, *qv*.

ASHLEY, Sir Bernard (Albert), Kt 1987; FCSD; Hon. Life President, Laura Ashley Holdings plc, 1993 (Chairman, 1985–93; non-executive Director, since 1991); *b* 11 Aug. 1926; *s* of Albert Ashley and Hilda Maud Ashley; *m* 1st, 1949, Laura Mountney (*d* 1985); two *s* two *d*; 2nd, 1990, Mme Regine Burnell. *Educ:* Whitgift Middle Sch., Croydon, Surrey. Army commission, 1944; Royal Fusiliers, 1944–46, seconded 1 Gurkha Rifles, 1944–45. Incorporated Ashley, Mountney Ltd, 1954; Chm., Ashley, Mountney Ltd, later Laura Ashley Ltd, 1954–93. Hon. DScEcon Wales, 1986. *Recreations:* sailing, flying. *Address:* 128 rue Defaqz, 1050 Bruxelles, Belgium. *Clubs:* Garrick; Royal Thames Yacht (Southampton), Army Sailing Association; Lyford Cay (Bahamas).

ASHLEY, Cedric, CBE 1984; PhD; CEng, FIMechE; automotive engineering consultant; Chairman, Cedric Ashley and Associates, since 1989; Director, Euromotor, University of Birmingham, since 1992; Managing Director, Steyr Power Technology, since 1992; *b* 11 Nov. 1936; *s* of Ronald Ashley and Gladys Fincher; *m* 1st, 1960, Pamela Jane Turner (decd); one *s*; 2nd, 1965, (Marjorie) Vivien Gooch (marr. diss. 1991); one *s* one *d*; 3rd, 1991, Auriol Mary Keogh. *Educ:* King Edward's Sch., Birmingham; Mech. Engrg Dept, Univ. of Birmingham (BSc 1958, PhD 1964). CEng 1972; FIMechE 1978. Rolls-Royce Ltd, Derby, 1955–60; Univ. of Birmingham, 1960–73: ICI Res. Fellow, 1963; Lectr, 1966; Internat. Technical Dir, Bostrom Div., Universal Oil Products Ltd, 1973–77; Dir, Motor Industry Res. Assoc., 1977–87; Man. Dir, Lotus Engineering, 1987; Chief Exec., BICERI, 1989–91. Chairman: SEE, 1970–72; RAC Tech. Cttee, 1980–87; Member: SMMT Technical Bds, 1977–87; Board, Assoc. Ind. Contract Res. Orgns, 1977–86 (Pres., 1982–84); Coventry and District Engineering Employers Assoc., 1978–85; Board, Automobile Div., IMechE, 1978–93 (Chm., 1990–91); Court, Cranfield Inst. of Technol., 1977–87; Engine and Vehicles Cttee, DTI, 1980–88; Three-Dimensional Design Bd, CNAA, 1981–87. FRSA 1983. Cementation Muffelite Award, SEE, 1968; Design Council Award, 1974. TA, 1959–68. *Publications:* (contrib.) Infrasound and Low Frequency Vibration, ed Tempest, 1976; papers on electro-hydraulics, vehicle ride, and effect of vibration and shock on man and buildings, in learned jls. *Recreations:* travel, reading. *Address:* (office) 29 High Street, Burnham, Bucks SL1 7JD. *T:* Maidenhead (01628) 662399. *Club:* Royal Automobile.

ASHLEY, Prof. Francis Paul, PhD; FDSRCS; Professor of Periodontology and Preventive Dentistry, since 1984 and Dean, Dental School, since 1991, United Medical and Dental Schools of Guy's and St Thomas' Hospitals; *b* 21 July 1942; *s* of late George Francis Ashley and Mary (*née* McIntyre); *m* 1967, Carolyn Patricia Whittenbury; one *s* one *d*. *Educ:* De La Salle Coll., Pendleton; Turner Dental Sch., Univ. of Manchester (BDS 1964); Guy's Hosp. Dental Sch. (PhD 1974). FDSRCS 1969. House Surgeon, Manchester Dental Hosp., 1965; Gen. Dental Practitioner, 1965–68; Guy's Hospital Dental School: Res Asst in Preventive Dentistry, 1968–71; Lectr in Periodontology and Preventive Dentistry, 1971–73; Sen. Lectr, 1973–79; Hon. Consultant, 1975; Reader in Periodontology and Preventive Dentistry, Univ. of London, 1979–84. Mem., Health Educn Council, 1984–87; Chairman: Dental Health Adv. Panel, 1984–90; Dentifrice Accreditation Panel, BDA, 1990–; Mem., GDC, 1994–. Chairman: Teachers' Section, Brit. Soc. Periodontology, 1980–83; Periodontal Res. Gp, Brit. Soc. for Dental Res., 1984–86. Hon. Sec., Assoc. of Profs of Dentistry, 1990–93. Scientific Advr, British Dental Jl, 1980– (Scientific Asst Ed, 1980–85). *Publications:* various contribs to scientific literature. *Recreations:* gardening, walking, reading, opera. *Address:* 62 Fitzjames Avenue, Croydon, Surrey CR0 5DD. *T:* 0181–654 2456.

ASHLEY-COOPER, family name of **Earl of Shaftesbury.**

ASHLEY-MILLER, Dr Michael, CBE 1995; DPH; FFPHM; FRCPE; FRCP; Secretary, Nuffield Provincial Hospitals Trust, London, since 1986; *b* 1 Dec. 1930; *s* of Cyril and Marjorie Ashley-Miller; *m* 1958, Yvonne Townend; three *d*. *Educ:* Charterhouse; Oxford Univ.; King's Coll. Hosp.; London Sch. of Hygiene and Tropical Med. MA Oxon; BM BCh; DObstRCOG. FFPHM (FFCM 1977); FRCPE 1985; FRCP 1990. Ho. Surg., Ho. Phys., King's Coll. Hosp., 1956–57; SMO, Dulwich Hosp., 1957; MO/SMO, RAF, 1958–61; SMO, IoW CC, 1961–64; MO/SMO, MRC (HQ Staff), 1964–74; PMO, SPMO, Scottish Home and Health Dept, 1974–86. Pres., Gen. Practice Sec., RSocMed, 1994–95. Hon. MRCP 1986; Hon. FRCGP. *Publications:* (invited contributor to) Vol. III, Textbook of Public Health, 1985; (jt ed) Screening for Risk of Coronary Heart Disease, 1987; contrib. to The Practitioner, Public Health, The Medical Officer, Health Bull., BMJ. *Recreations:* tennis, golf, reading, visiting cathedrals. *Address:* 28 Fitzwarren Gardens, N19 3TP. *T:* 0171–272 7017. *Clubs:* Royal Society of Medicine, Royal Over-Seas League.

ASHLEY-SMITH, Jonathan, PhD; FMA; Head of Conservation, Victoria and Albert Museum, since 1977; *b* 25 Aug. 1946; *s* of Ewart Trist and Marian Tanfield Ashley-Smith; *m* 1967, Diane Louise (*née* Wagland); one *s* one *d*. *Educ:* Sutton Valence Public Sch.; Bristol Univ. (BSc (Hons), PhD). FMA 1988. Post-doctoral research, Cambridge Univ., 1970–72; Victoria and Albert Museum, 1973–. Leverhulme Fellow, 1994–95. Member: UK Inst. for Conservation, 1974– (Mem., Exec Cttee, 1978–; Vice-Chm., 1980–); Crafts Council, 1980–83; Conservation Cttee, Crafts Council, 1978–83; Council for Care of Churches Conservation Cttee, 1978–85; Board of Governors, London Coll. of Furniture, 1983–85; Chm., UK Inst. for Conservation, 1983–84. FRSC 1987; FIIC 1985; Hon. FRCA 1992. Scientific Editor, Science for Conservators (Crafts Council series), 1983–84. *Publications:* articles in learned jls on organometallic chemistry, spectroscopy and scientific examination of art objects. *Recreations:* loud music, good beer. *Address:* Victoria and Albert Museum, Exhibition Road, SW7 2RL. *T:* 0171–938 8568.

ASHMOLE, (Harold) David; Senior Principal Dancer, 1984–93, Guest Artist, since 1994, Australian Ballet; *b* 31 Oct. 1949; *s* of Richard Thomas Ashmole and Edith Ashmole. *Educ:* Sandye Place, Beds; Royal Ballet Sch. Solo Seal, Royal Acad. of Dancing; ARAD. Joined Royal Ballet Co., 1968; Soloist, 1972; Principal, 1975; transf. to Sadler's Wells Royal Ballet, 1976, Sen. Principal, 1978–84. Appeared in: Dame Alicia Markova's Master Classes, BBC Television, 1980; Maina Gielgud's Steps, Notes and Squeaks, Aberdeen Internat. Festival, 1981. Guest appearances with Scottish Ballet, 1981, with Bolshoi (for UNESCO Gala), 1986, with Sadlers Wells Royal Ballet at Royal Opera House, 1986 (season) and in Japan, Germany, S Africa and France. *Classical ballets include:* La Bayadère, Coppélia, Daphnis and Chloe, Giselle, Nutcracker, Raymonda, The Seasons, Sleeping Beauty, Swan Lake, La Sylphide; *other ballets include:* (choreography by Ashton): Cinderella, The Two Pigeons, La Fille Mal Gardée, Les Rendezvous, The Dream, Lament of the Waves, Symphonic Variations, Birthday Offering; (Balanchine): Apollo, Prodigal Son, Serenade, The Four Temperaments, Agon, Tchaikovsky Pas de Deux; (Béjart): Gaîté Parisienne, Webern Opus 5, Songs of a Wayfarer, Le Concours; (Bintley): Night Moves, Homage to Chopin, The Swan of Tuonela; (Cranko): Brouillards, Pineapple Poll, The Taming of the Shrew, Onegin; (Darrell): The Tales of Hoffmann; (de Valois): Checkmate, The Rake's Progress; (Fokine): Les Sylphides, Petrushka; (Hynd): Papillon; (Lander): Etudes; (Lifar): Suite en Blanc; (MacMillan): Concerto, Elite Syncopations, Romeo and Juliet, Quartet, Song of the Earth, Symphony; (Massine): La Boutique Fantasque; (Miller-Ashmole): Snugglepot-and-Cuddlepie; (Nijinska): Les Biches; (Nureyev): Don Quixote; (Robbins): Dances at a Gathering, Requiem Canticles, In the Night, Concert; (Seymour): Intimate Letters, Rashamond; (Samsova): Paquita; (Tetley): Gemini, Laborintus, Orpheus; (van Manen): Grosse Fugue, 5 Tangos; (Wright): Summertide; (Prokovsky): The Three Musketeers; (Seregei): Spartacus. *Recreations:* Moorcroft pottery collection, gardening, shooting, fishing. *Address:* c/o Australian Ballet, 2 Kavanagh Street, South Melbourne, Vic 3205, Australia.

ASHMORE, Dr Alick, CBE 1979; Director, Daresbury Laboratory, Science Research Council, 1970–81; *b* 7 Nov. 1920; *s* of Frank Owen Ashmore and Beatrice Maud Swindells; *m* 1947, Eileen Elsie Fuller; two *s* three *d*. *Educ:* King Edward VII Sch., Lytham; King's Coll., London. Experimental Officer, RRDE, Malvern, 1941–47; Lecturer in physics, University of Liverpool, 1947–59; Queen Mary Coll., London: Reader in experimental physics, 1960–64; Prof. of Nuclear Physics, 1964–70, also Head of Physics Dept, 1968–70. *Publications:* research publications on nuclear and elementary-particle physics in Proc. Phys. Soc., Nuclear Physics, Physical Review. *Recreations:* walking, travel. *Address:* Farnham House, Hesket Newmarket, Wigton, Cumbria CA7 8JG. *T:* Caldbeck (016974) 78414.

ASHMORE, Admiral of the Fleet Sir Edward (Beckwith), GCB 1974 (KCB 1971; CB 1966); DSC 1942; *b* 11 Dec. 1919; *er s* of late Vice-Admiral L. H. Ashmore, CB, DSO and late Tamara Vasilevna Schutt, St Petersburg; *m* 1942, Elizabeth Mary Doveton Sturdee, *d* of late Rear-Admiral Sir Lionel Sturdee, 2nd Bt, CBE; one *s* one *d* (and one *d* decd). *Educ:* RNC, Dartmouth. Served HMS Birmingham, Jupiter, Middleton, 1938–42; qualified in Signals, 1943; Staff of C-in-C Home Fleet, Flag Lieut, 4th Cruiser Sqdn, 1944–45; qualified Interpreter in Russian, 1946; Asst Naval Attaché, Moscow, 1946–47; Squadron Communications Officer, 3rd Aircraft Carrier Squadron, 1950; Commander 1950; comd HMS Alert, 1952–53; Captain 1955; Captain (F) 6th Frigate Sqdn, and CO HMS Blackpool, 1958; Director of Plans, Admiralty and Min. of Defence, 1960–62; Commander British Forces Caribbean Area, 1963–64; Rear-Adm., 1965; Asst Chief of the Defence Staff, Signals, 1965–67; Flag Officer, Second-in-Command, Far East Fleet, 1967–68; Vice-Adm. 1968; Vice-Chief, Naval Staff, 1969–71; Adm. 1970; C-in-C Western Fleet, Sept.-Oct. 1971; C-in-C, Fleet, 1971–74; Chief of Naval Staff and First Sea Lord, 1974–77; First and Principal Naval Aide-de-Camp to the Queen, 1974–77; CDS, Feb.-Aug. 1977. Gov., Suttons Hosp. in Charterhouse, 1976–. *Recreations:* usual. *Club:* Naval and Military.

See also Vice-Adm. Sir P. W. B. Ashmore, Sir John Sykes, Bt.

ASHMORE, Gillian Margaret; Regional Director, Government Office for the South East, since 1994; *b* 14 Oct. 1949; *d* of John Oxenham and Joan Oxenham; *m* 1971, Frederick Scott Ashmore; two *s* two *d*. *Educ:* Walthamstow Hall, Sevenoaks; Winchester Co. High Sch. for Girls; Newnham Coll., Cambridge (BA Hons Hist.). Depts of the Envmt and Tspt, 1971–86; seconded to Housing Corp., 1974; Dep. Dir, Enterprise and Regulation Unit, Dept of Employment, 1986–87, then DTI, 1987–89; Head, Central Finance Div., Dept of Transport, 1990–92; Dir, Privatisation Studies, BRB, 1992–94. Trustee, Kingston Friends Workshop Gp, 1993–. FRSA 1995. *Recreations:* children and all their doings, dancing, novels, eating and talking. *Address:* Charles House, 375 Kensington High Street, W14 8QH. *T:* 0171–605 9095.

ASHMORE, Vice-Adm. Sir Peter (William Beckwith), KCB 1972 (CB 1968); KCVO 1980 (MVO (4th Class) 1948); DSC 1942; Extra Equerry to the Queen, since 1952; *b* 4 Feb. 1921; *yr s* of late Vice-Adm. L. H. Ashmore, CB, DSO and late Tamara Vasilevna Schutt, St Petersburg; *m* 1952, Patricia Moray Buller, *o d* of late Admiral Sir Henry Buller, GCVO, CB and of Lady Hermione Stuart; one *s* three *d*. *Educ:* Yardley Court; RN Coll., Dartmouth. Midshipman, 1939. Served War of 1939–45, principally in destroyers (despatches); Lieut, 1941; Equerry (temp.) to King George VI, 1946–48; Extra Equerry, 1948; Comdr, 1951; Captain, 1957; Deputy Director, RN Staff Coll., Greenwich, 1957; Captain (F) Dartmouth Training Squadron, 1960–61; Imperial Defence Coll., 1962; Admiralty, Plans Division, 1963; Rear-Adm. 1966; Flag Officer, Admiralty Interview Board, 1966–67; Chief of Staff to C-in-C Western Fleet and to NATO C-in-C Eastern Atlantic, 1967–69; Vice-Adm. 1969; Chief of Allied Staff, NATO Naval HQ, S Europe, 1970–72, retired 1972. Master of HM's Household, 1973–86. *Recreations:* fishing, golf. *Address:* Netherdowns, Sundridge, near Sevenoaks, Kent TN14 6AR.

See also Adm. of the Fleet Sir E. B. Ashmore.

ASHMORE, Prof. Philip George; Professor of Physical Chemistry, The University of Manchester Institute of Science and Technology, 1963–81, now Professor Emeritus; *b* 5 May 1916; *m* 1943, Ann Elizabeth Scott; three *s* one *d*. *Educ:* Emmanuel Coll., Cambridge. Fellow, Asst Tutor and Dir of Studies of Natural Sciences, Emmanuel Coll., Cambridge, 1949–59; Lecturer in Physical Chem., Univ. of Cambridge, 1953–63; Fellow and Tutor to Advanced Students, Churchill Coll., Cambridge, 1959–63. Vice-Principal Acad. Affairs, UMIST, 1973, 1974. Course Consultant, Open Univ., 1981–85. *Publications:* The Catalysis and Inhibition of Chemical Reactions, 1963; (ed) Reaction Kinetics, 1975; RIC Monographs for Teachers: No 5 and No 9; many papers in: TFS, International Symposium on Combustion, Jl of Catalysis. *Address:* 30 Queen Edith's Way, Cambridge CB1 4PN. *T:* Cambridge (01223) 248225.

ASHTON, family name of **Baron Ashton of Hyde.**

ASHTON OF HYDE, 3rd Baron *cr* 1911; **Thomas John Ashton,** TD; Director, Barclays Bank PLC and subsidiary companies, 1969–87; *b* 19 Nov. 1926; *s* of 2nd Baron Ashton of Hyde and Marjorie Nell (*d* 1993), *d* of late Hon. Marshall Jones Brooks; *S* father, 1983; *m* 1957, Pauline Trewlove, *er d* of late Lt-Col R. H. L. Brackenbury, OBE; two *s* two *d*. *Educ:* Eton; New Coll., Oxford (BA 1950, MA 1955). Sen. Exec. Local Dir, Barclays Bank, Manchester, 1968–81. Major retd, Royal Glos Hussars (TA). JP Oxon, 1965–68. *Heir: s* Hon. Thomas Henry Ashton [*b* 18 July 1958; *m* 1987, Emma, *d* of Colin Allinson; three *d*]. *Address:* Fir Farm, Upper Slaughter, Bourton-on-the-Water GL54 2JR. *Club:* Boodle's.

ASHTON, Anthony Southcliffe; *b* 5 July 1916; *s* of late Prof. Thomas Southcliffe Ashton, FBA, and of Mrs Marion Hague Ashton; *m* 1939, Katharine Marion Louise Vivian; two *d*. *Educ:* Manchester Grammar Sch.; Hertford Coll., Oxford (MA). Economist, Export Credits Guarantee Dept, 1937. Served War of 1939–45, as driver and Lt-Col, RASC. Asst Financial Editor, Manchester Guardian, 1945; Dep. Asst Dir of Marketing, NCB, 1947; Manager, various depts of Vacuum Oil Co. (later Mobil Oil Co.), 1949; attended Advanced Management Programme, Harvard Business Sch., 1961; Treasurer, 1961, Finance Director, 1967–69, Esso Petroleum Co.; Mem. Bd (Finance and Corporate Planning), Post Office Corp., 1970–73. Director: Tyzack and Partners Ltd, 1974–79; Provincial Insce Co., 1974–86. Member: Shipbuilding Industry Bd, 1967–71; Council of Manchester Business Sch., 1968–81; Dir, Oxford Univ. Business Summer Sch., 1974 (Mem., Steering Cttee, 1978–81). Trustee: PO Pension Fund, 1975–83; Tyzack Employee Trust, 1979–84; Dir, Exeter Trust, 1980–86 (Chm., 1982–86). Vice-Pres., Hertford Coll. Soc., 1977–. *Address:* Quarry Field, Stonewall Hill, Presteigne, Powys LD8 2HB. *T:* Presteigne (01544) 267447. *Club:* Army and Navy.

ASHTON, George Arthur, CEng; FIMechE; engineering and management consultant, retired; *b* 27 Nov. 1921; *s* of Lewis and Mary Ashton; *m* 1st, 1948, Joan Rutter (decd); one *s*; 2nd, 1978, Pauline Jennifer Margett. *Educ:* Llanidloes Grammar Sch.; Birmingham Central Tech. Coll. Student Engrg Apprentice, Austin Motor Co., 1939–42. HM Forces, 1943–47 (Major, REME). Works Dir, Tubes Ltd, 1958; Tech. Dir, 1962, Dep. Man. Dir, 1966, TI Steel Tube Div.; Dir, Tube Investments, 1969; Man. Dir, Machine Div., 1974, Technical Dir and Business Area Chm., 1978–84, TI Group plc; Chm., Seamless Tubes Ltd, 1983–86. Dir, A. Lee & Sons plc, 1981–91. Dep. Chm., Steering Cttee, WINTECH, Welsh Develt Agency, 1984–87. Pres., BISPA, 1974–75; Vice-Pres., AMTRI, 1986– (Chm. Council, 1982–86). FRSA 1981; CIMgt. *Recreations:* gardening, walking, cycling, theatre-going. *Address:* Barn Cottage, Longford, Ashbourne, Derbys DE6 3DT. *T:* Great Cubley (01335) 330561. *Club:* Naval and Military.

ASHTON, John Russell, CB 1988; retired engineer; *b* 28 Feb. 1925; *s* of Jessie Florence and John William Ashton; *m* 1951, Isobel Burbury; two *d*. *Educ:* Canberra Grammar School; Sydney University. BE (Civil Engineering). Hydro-Electric Commission, Tasmania: Engineer, 1947–54; System Development Engineer, 1954–71; Dep. Engineer for Civil Investigation, 1971–72; Asst to Comr, 1972–77; Commissioner, 1977–87. In-service training Fellowship with US Bureau of Reclamation, 1960. *Recreations:* golf, photography, carpentry, gardening. *Address:* 3 Lanrick Court, Lindisfarne, Tasmania 7015, Australia. *T:* (02) 438758. *Club:* Royal Hobart Golf.

ASHTON, Joseph William; MP (Lab) Bassetlaw Division of Notts since Nov. 1968; journalist; *b* 9 Oct. 1933; *s* of Arthur and Nellie Ashton, Sheffield; *m* 1957, Margaret Patricia Lee; one *d*. *Educ:* High Storrs Grammar Sch.; Rotherham Technical Coll. Engineering Apprentice, 1949–54; RAF National Service, 1954–56; Cost Control Design Engineer, 1956–68; Sheffield City Councillor, 1962–69. PPS to Sec. of State for Energy, formerly Sec. of State for Industry, 1975–76; an Asst Govt Whip, 1976–77; Opposition Spokesman on Energy, 1979–81. Member, Select Committee: on Trade and Industry, 1987–92; on Home Affairs, 1989–92; on Nat. Heritage, 1992–; Chm., Parly All-Party Football Cttee, 1992–. Columnist for: Sheffield Star, 1970–75, 1979–80; Labour Weekly, 1971–82; Daily Star, 1979–87; Sunday People, 1987–88; Plus magazine, 1988–89. Columnist of the Year, What the Papers Say, Granada TV, 1984. *Publications:* Grass Roots, 1977; A Majority of One (stage play), 1981. *Recreations:* being a Director of Sheffield Wednesday and Vice-Pres. of supporters' club, reading, do-it-yourself, motoring, travel, films, theatre. *Address:* 16 Ranmoor Park Road, Sheffield S10 3GX. *T:* Sheffield (0114) 230 1763. *Clubs:* Foundry Working Men's (Sheffield); Doncaster Road Working Men's (Langold); various Miners' Institutes, etc.

ASHTON, Kenneth Bruce; General Secretary, National Union of Journalists, 1977–85; *b* 9 Nov. 1925; *m* 1955, Amy Anne Sidebotham; four *s*. *Educ:* Latymer Upper School. Served Army, 1942–46. Reporter: Hampstead and Highgate Express, 1947–50; Devon and Somerset News, Mansfield Reporter, Sheffield Star, 1950–58; Sub-Editor, Sheffield Telegraph, Daily Express, London and Daily Mail, Manchester, 1958–75. Nat. Exec. Cttee Mem., NUJ, 1968–75, Pres., 1975, Regional Organiser, 1975–77. Member: TUC Printing Industries' Cttee, 1975—86; Printing and Publishers' Industry Training Bd, 1977–83; British Cttee, Journalists in Europe, 1980–86; Communications Adv. Cttee, UK Nat. Commn for Unesco, 1981–86; consultative Mem., Press Council, 1977–80; Pres., Internat. Fedn of Journalists, 1982–86. *Address:* High Blean, Raydaleside, Askrigg, Leyburn, N Yorks DL8 3DJ.

ASHTON, Rt. Rev. Leonard (James), CB 1970; Bishop in Cyprus and The Gulf, 1976–83; Hon. Assistant Bishop, Diocese of Oxford, since 1984; *b* 27 June 1915; *s* of late Henry Ashton and Sarah Ashton (*née* Ing). *Educ:* Tyndale Hall, Bristol. Ordained, Chester, 1942; Curate, Cheadle, 1942–45; Chap. RAF, 1945–74; N Wales, 1945; AHQ Malaya and Singapore, 1946; BC Air Forces, Japan, 1947–48; Halton, 1948–49; Feltwell, 1949–50; Chap. and Lectr, RAF Chap. Sch., Cheltenham, 1950–53; Sen. Chap., AHQ Iraq, 1954–55; RAF Coll., Cranwell, 1956–60; Br. Forces Arabian Peninsular and Mid. East Command, 1960–61; Asst Chap. Chief, Trng Commands, 1962–65; Res. Chap., St Clement Danes, Strand, 1965–69; Chaplain-in-Chief, (with relative rank of Air Vice-Marshal) RAF, and Archdeacon of RAF, 1969–73; QHC, 1967–73; Hon. Canon and Prebendary of St Botolph, Lincoln Cathedral, 1969–73, Canon Emeritus, 1973–; Asst Bishop in Jerusalem, 1974–76; Episcopal Canon: St George's Cathedral, Jerusalem, 1976–83; St Paul's Cath., Nicosia, Cyprus, 1989–; Commissary for Bishop in Iran and Bishop in Jerusalem, 1984–. ChStJ 1976. *Publication:* Winged Words, 1990. *Recreations:* gardening, photography. *Address:* 60 Lowndes Avenue, Chesham, Bucks HP5 2HJ. *T:* Chesham (01494) 782952. *Club:* Royal Air Force.

ASHTON, Prof. Norman (Henry), CBE 1976; DSc (London); FRS 1971; FRCP, FRCS, FRCPath, FRCOphth; Professor of Pathology, University of London, 1957–78, now Emeritus; Director, Department of Pathology, Institute of Ophthalmology, University of London, 1948–78; Consultant Pathologist, Moorfields Eye Hospital, 1948–78; *b* 11 Sept. 1913; 2nd *s* of Henry James and Margaret Ann Ashton. *Educ:* West Kensington Central Sch.; King's Coll. and Westminster Hosp. Med. Sch., Univ. of London. Westminster Hospital: Prize in Bacteriology, 1938; Editor Hosp. Gazette, 1939–40; House Surg., House Phys., Sen. Casualty Officer and RMO, 1939–41. Asst Pathologist, Princess Beatrice Hosp., 1939; Dir of Pathology, Kent and Canterbury Hosp., and Blood Transfusion Officer of East Kent, 1941. Lieut-Col RAMC, Asst Dir of Pathology and Officer i/c Central Pathological Lab., Middle East, 1946. Pathologist to the Gordon Hosp., 1947; Reader in Pathology, Univ. of London, 1953; Fellow in Residence, Johns Hopkins Hosp., Baltimore, 1953, and Visiting Prof. there, 1959. Emeritus Fellow, Leverhulme Trust. Vis. Research Fellow, Merton Coll., Oxford, 1980. Lectures: Walter Wright, 1959; Banting, 1960; Clapp (USA), 1964; Proctor (USA), 1965; Bradshaw (RCP), 1971; Montgomery, 1973; Foundation, RCPath, 1974; Jackson (USA), 1978; Foundn, Assoc. of Clinical Pathologists, 1985. Chm., Fight for Sight Appeal, 1980–91; Trustee, Sir John Soane's Museum, 1977–82. Member, Board of Governors: Moorfields Eye Hosp., 1963–66 and 1975–78; Hosp. for Sick Children, Gt Ormond St, 1977–80; Royal Nat. Coll. for the Blind, 1977–92; Member: Brit. Nat. Cttee for Prevention of Blindness, 1973–78; Royal Postgrad. Med. Sch. Council, 1977–80; Council, RCPath, 1963–66 and 1976–78 (Founder Fellow); Governing Body, Brit. Postgrad. Med. Fedn, 1967–82, and Cent. Acad. Council, 1957–78 (Chm., 1967–70); Council, RSM, 1971–79, and Exec. Cttee, 1976–81; Med. Adv. Bd, British Retinitis Pigmentosa Soc.; Pathological Soc. of Great Britain and Ireland; European Assoc. for Study of Diabetes; Chapter Gen. and Hosp. Cttee of St John; Oxford Ophthalmological Congress; Medical Art Soc.; Member, Cttee of Management: Inst. of Ophthalmology, 1953–78, 1984–92; Inst. of Child Health, 1960–65; Cardio-Thoracic Inst., 1972–78; Inst. of Rheumatology, 1973–77; Mem. Bd of Governors, Brendoncare Foundn, 1984–. President: Ophth. Sect., RSM, 1972–74; Assoc. of Clinical Pathologists, 1978–79; Ophth. Soc. of UK, 1979–81; Chm., Brit. Diab. Assoc. Cttee on Blindness in Diabetes, 1967–70. Fellow, Inst. of Ophthalmology; FRSocMed. Hon. Life Mem., British Diabetic Association; Life Pres. European Ophth. Pathology Soc.; Pres. Brit. Div. Internat. Acad. of Pathology, 1962. Hon. Member: Assoc. for Eye Research; Hellenic Ophth. Soc.; British Div., Internat. Acad. of Pathology; Amer. Ophth. Soc.; Amer. Assoc. of Ophthalmic Pathologists; Gonin Club. Hon. Fellow: RSocMed; Royal Coll. of Ophthalmologists; Royal Coll. of Pathologists; Coll. of Physicians, Philadelphia; Amer. Acad. Ophthal. and Otolaryng. Mem. Ed. Bd, Brit. Jl Ophthalmology, 1963–78, and Jl Histopathology. Master, Soc. of Apothecaries of London, 1984–85; Freeman, City of London. Hon. Steward, Westminster Abbey, 1969–84. Hon. DSc Chicago. KStJ. Edward Nettleship Prize for Research in Ophthalmology, 1953; BMA Middlemore Prize, 1955; Proctor Medal for Research in Ophthalmology (USA), 1957; Doyne Medal (Oxford), 1960; William Julius Mickle Fellow, Univ. London, 1961; Bowman Medal, 1965; Donder's Medal, 1967; Wm Mackenzie Memorial Medal, 1967; Gonin Medal, 1978; 1st Jules Stein Award, USA, 1981; Francis Richardson Cross Medal, 1982; Lord Crook Gold Medal, Spectacle Makers' Co., 1989; Internat. Pizart Vision Award, USA, 1991. *Publications:* contrib. to books and numerous scientific articles in Jl of Pathology and Bacteriology, Brit. Jl of Ophthalmology, and Amer. Jl of Ophthalmology. *Recreations:* painting, gardening. *Address:* 4 Blomfield Road, Little Venice, W9 1AH. *T:* 0171–286 5536. *Clubs:* Athenæum, Garrick.

ASHTON, Prof. Robert, PhD; Professor of English History, University of East Anglia, 1963–89, now Emeritus; *b* 21 July 1924; *s* of late Joseph and late Edith F. Ashton; *m* 1946, Margaret Alice Sedgwick; two *d. Educ:* Magdalen Coll. Sch., Oxford; University Coll., Southampton (1942–43, 1946–49); London Sch. of Economics (1949–52). BA 1st Cl. hons (London) 1949; PhD (London) 1953; Asst Lecturer in Economic History, Univ. of Nottingham, 1952; Lecturer, 1954; Senior Lecturer, 1961; Vis. Associate Prof. in History, Univ. of California, Berkeley, 1962–63; Prof. of English History, 1963, and Dean of Sch. of English Studies, 1964–67, Univ. of East Anglia. Vis. Fellow, All Souls Coll., Oxford, 1973–74 and 1987; James Ford Special Lectr in History, Oxford, 1982; Leverhulme Emeritus Fellow, 1989–91. FRHistS 1960 (Vice-Pres., 1983–86). *Publications:* The Crown and the Money Market, 1603–1640, 1960; Charles I and the City, in Essays in the Economic and Social History of Tudor and Stuart England in honour of R. H. Tawney (ed F. J. Fisher), 1961; James I by his Contemporaries, 1969; The Civil War and the Class Struggle, in The English Civil War and After 1642–1658 (ed R. H. Parry), 1970; The English Civil War: Conservatism and Revolution 1603–49, 1978, 2nd edn 1989; The City and the Court 1603–1643, 1979; Reformation and Revolution 1558–1660, 1984; Counter-Revolution: the second Civil War and its origins, 1646–8, 1994; articles in learned periodicals. *Recreations:* music, looking at old buildings, wine. *Address:* The Manor House, Brundall, Norwich NR13 5JY. *T:* Norwich (01603) 713368.

ASHTON, Roy; a Recorder of the Crown Court, since 1979; barrister-at-law; *b* 20 Oct. 1928; *s* of Charles and Lilian Ashton; *m* 1954, Brenda Alice Dales; one *s* one *d. Educ:* Boston Grammar Sch.; Nottingham Univ. (LLB Hons). National Service, Directorate of Legal Services, RAF, 1951–53. Called to the Bar, Lincoln's Inn, 1954. Dep. Chairman, Agricultural Land Tribunal, 1978–. *Recreations:* reading, horse racing, film collecting. *Address:* (chambers) 22 Albion Place, Northampton NN1 1UD. *Club:* Northampton and County.

ASHTON, Ruth Mary, (Mrs E. F. Henschel), OBE 1991; RN, RM, MTD; Non-executive Director, Optimum Health Services NHS Trust, since 1994; General Secretary, Royal College of Midwives, 1980–94; *b* 27 March 1939; *d* of Leigh Perry Ashton and Marion Lucy Ashton (*née* Tryon); *m* 1984, E. Fred Henschel. *Educ:* Kenya High Sch. for Girls; Clarendon Sch. (lately Abergele). London Hosp. and Queen Mother's Hosp., Glasgow; High Coombe Midwife Teachers' Training College (RN 1964; RM 1967; MTD 1970). Staff Midwife and Midwifery Sister, Queen Mother's Hosp., Glasgow, 1967–69; Nursing Officer and Midwifery Tutor, King's College Hosp., 1971–75; Tutor, 1975–79 and Professional Officer, 1979, Royal College of Midwives. Temp. Prof., March of Dimes, Los Angeles, 1982. ACIArb. OStJ 1988. *Publications:* midwifery related articles. *Recreations:* gardening, sailing, travel. *Address:* c/o National Westminster Bank, 1 Mincing Lane, EC3M 3JH. *T:* (home) 0181–851 7403. *Club:* Queenborough Yacht.

ASHTON, William Michael Allingham, MBE 1978; Musical Director, National Youth Jazz Orchestra of Great Britain, since 1968; *b* Blackpool, 6 Dec. 1936; *s* of Eric Sandiford Ashton and Zilla Dorothea (*née* Miles); *m* 1966, Kay Carol Watkins; two *s* one *d. Educ:* Rossall Sch., Fleetwood; St Peter's Coll., Oxford (BA Hons Mod. Langs 1961; DipEd 1962). Nat. Service, RAF, 1955–57. Professional musician, 1962–63; teacher of French in London schs, 1963–73. Founded London Schs Jazz Orch., 1965; became Nat. Youth Jazz Orch., 1968. Editor, News from NYJO, 1988–. Appeared in Royal Variety Perf., 1978; visits to America, Russia, Australasia, France, Poland, Portugal, Germany, Bulgaria, Turkey, Malta, Spain, Italy, etc; appearances at festivals, film premières, etc. Numerous recordings. Member: Arts Sub-cttee, Internat. Year of the Child, 1979; Cttee, Assoc. British Jazz Musicians, 1988–. BP ABSA Award, 1991; Music Retailers Assoc. Annual Awards for Excellence, 1984, 1990; NYJO voted Best British Big Band, British Jazz Awards, 1993. *Recreations:* song writing, swimming, reading. *Address:* 11 Victor Road, Harrow, Middx HA2 6PT. *T:* 0181–863 2717, *Fax:* 0181–863 8685.

ASHTOWN, 7th Baron *cr* 1800; **Nigel Clive Cosby Trench,** KCMG 1976 (CMG 1966); HM Diplomatic Service, retired; *b* 27 Oct. 1916; *s* of Clive Newcome Trench (*d* 1964), *g s* of 2nd Baron, and Kathleen (*d* 1979), 2nd *d* of Major Ivar MacIvor, CIE; *S* cousin, 1990; *m* 1939, Marcelle Catherine Clotterbooke Patyn (*d* 1994); one *s. Educ:* Eton; Univ. of Cambridge. Served in KRRC, 1940–46 (despatches). Appointed a Member of the Foreign (subseq. Diplomatic) Service, 1946; Lisbon, 1946; First Secretary, 1948; returned Foreign Office, 1949; First Secretary (Commercial) Lima, 1952; transf. Foreign Office, 1955; Counsellor, Tokyo, 1961; Counsellor, Washington, 1963; Cabinet Office, 1967; HM Ambassador to Korea, 1969–71; CS Selection Board, 1971–73; Ambassador to Portugal, 1974–76. Mem., Police, Prison and Fire Service Selection Bds, 1977–86. Sungrye Medal, Order of Diplomatic Service Merit (Korea), 1984. *Heir: s* Hon. Roderick Nigel Godolphin Trench [*b* 17 Nov. 1944; *m* 1st, 1967, Janet (*d* 1971), *d* of Harold Hamilton-Faulkner; one *s*; 2nd, 1973, Susan Barbara, *d* of L. F. Day, FRCS, DLO; one *d*]. *Address:* 4 Kensington Court Gardens, Kensington Court Place, W8 5QE. *Club:* Naval and Military.

ASHURST, Kenneth William Stewart; Chief Executive and Clerk, Essex County Council, since 1995; *b* 19 May 1945; *s* of Kenneth Latham Ashurst, OBE and Helen Ferguson Ashurst (*née* Rae); *m* 1984, Catherine Mary Sample; two *s* one *d. Educ:* Royal Grammar Sch., Newcastle upon Tyne; King Edward VI Grammar Sch., Lichfield; Exeter Coll., Oxford Univ. (MA); Guildford Coll. of Law; Birmingham Univ. (MSocSc). Trainee solicitor, Leicester and Newcastle upon Tyne CBCs, 1967–68; Assistant Solicitor: Newcastle upon Tyne, 1968–71; Cumberland CC, 1972–73; Asst Co. Clerk, Cumbria CC, 1973–79; Dep. Co. Sec., 1979–81, Co. Solicitor and Dep. Co. Clerk, 1981–85, Suffolk CC; Dep. Chief Exec. and Clerk, Essex CC, 1985–94. Clerk to: Essex Police Authy, 1995–; Essex Lieutenancy, 1995–; River Crouch Harbour Authy, 1995–; Secretary: Lord Chancellor's Adv. Cttee in Essex, 1995–; Stansted Airport Consultative Cttee, 1995–; Mem., Essex TEC Bd, 1995–. Law Society: Council Mem., 1989–; Chm., Local Govt Gp, 1986–87. FIMgt 1982. *Recreations:* family, wine tasting, day dreaming. *Address:* Essex County Council, PO Box 11, County Hall, Chelmsford CM1 1LX. *T:* Chelmsford (01245) 492211.

ASHWORTH, Prof. Andrew John, PhD, DCL; FBA 1993; Edmund-Davies Professor of Criminal Law and Criminal Justice, King's College, London University, since 1988; *b* 11 Oct. 1947; *s* of late Clifford Ashworth and of Amy (*née* Ogden); *m* 1971, Gillian Frisby; two *d. Educ:* London Sch. of Economics (LLB 1968); New Coll., Oxford (BCL 1970; DCL 1993); Manchester Univ. (PhD 1973). Lectr, then Sen. Lectr, in Law, Manchester Univ., 1970–78; Fellow and Tutor in Law, Worcester Coll., Oxford, 1978–88. Editor, Criminal Law Rev., 1975–. *Publications:* Sentencing and Penal Policy, 1983; Principles of Criminal Law, 1991; Sentencing and Criminal Justice, 1992; The Criminal Process, 1994. *Recreations:* bridge, golf, travel.

ASHWORTH, Prof. Graham William, CBE 1980; DL; Professor of Urban Environmental Studies, University of Salford, 1973–87, part-time Research Professor, since 1987; Director General, Tidy Britain (formerly Keep Britain Tidy) Group, since 1987; *b* 14 July 1935; *s* of Frederick William Ashworth and Ivy Alice Ashworth; *m* 1960, Gwyneth Mai Morgan-Jones; three *d. Educ:* Devonport High Sch., Plymouth; Univ. of Liverpool (Master of Civic Design, BArch). RIBA, PPRTPI, FRSA, FInstEnvSci, FBIM. LCC (Hook New Town Project), 1959–61; consultancy with Graeme Shankland, 1961–64; architect to Civic Trust, 1964–65; Dir, Civic Trust for North-West, 1965–73 (Chm., Exec. Cttee, 1973–87); Director: Univ. of Salford Environmental Inst., 1978–87; CAMPUS (Campaign to Promote Univ. of Salford), 1981–87. Member: Skeffington Cttee on Public Participation in Planning, 1969; North-West Adv. Council of BBC, 1970–75 (Chm.); NW Economic Planning Council (and Sub-gp Chm.), 1968–79; Countryside Commn, 1974–77; Merseyside Urban Develt Corp., 1981–92; (non-exec.) North Western Electricity Bd, 1985–88; Chairman: Ravenhead Renaissance, 1988–; Going for Green, 1994–. Governor, Northern Baptist Coll., 1966–82; Pres., Royal Town Planning Inst., 1973–74; Chm., Instn of Environmental Sciences, 1980–82. Member: Council, St George's House, Windsor, 1982–88; Council, Baptist Union, 1983–. Trustee, Manchester Mus. of Science and Industry, 1988–90. Editor, Internat. Jl of Environmental Educn, 1981–. DL Lancs 1991. *Publications:* An Encyclopædia of Planning, 1973; Britain in Bloom, 1991; The Role of Local Government in Environmental Protection, 1992. *Recreations:* gardening, painting, church and social work. *Address:* Manor Court Farm, Preston New Road, Samlesbury, Preston PR5 0UP. *Clubs:* Athenæum, National Liberal.

ASHWORTH, Sir Herbert, Kt 1972; Chairman: Nationwide Building Society, 1970–82 (Deputy-Chairman, 1968–70); Nationwide Housing Trust, 1983–87; *b* 30 Jan. 1910; *s* of Joseph Hartley Ashworth; *m* 1936, Barbara Helen Mary, *d* of late Douglas D. Henderson; two *s* one *d. Educ:* Burnley Grammar Sch.; London Univ. (grad. econ. and law). General Manager, Portman Building Soc., 1938–50; General Manager, Co-operative Permanent Building Soc., 1950–61; Director and General Manager, Hallmark Securities Ltd, 1961–66. Dep. Chm., 1964–68, Chm., 1968–73, Housing Corp. Dir, The Builder Ltd, 1975–80. Chm., Surrey and W Sussex Agricl Wages Cttee, 1974–87. Vice-Pres., Building Socs Assoc., 1975–. *Publications:* Housing in Great Britain, 1951; Building Society Work Explained, 1942, 18th edn 1987; The Building Society Story, 1980. *Address:* 8 Tracery, Park Road, Banstead, Surrey SM7 3DD. *T:* Burgh Heath (01737) 352608.

ASHWORTH, Ian Edward; *b* 3 March 1930; *s* of late William Holt and Cicely Ashworth, Rochdale; *m* Pauline, *er d* of late Maurice James Heddle, MBE, JP, and Gladys Heddle, Westliff-on-Sea; two *s* one *d. Educ:* Manchester Grammar Sch.; The Queen's Coll., Oxford (BCL, MA). Admitted Solicitor, 1956; FGA 1983. Asst Solicitor, Rochdale, 1956–58; Dep. Town Clerk, Dep. Clerk of Peace, Canterbury, 1958–63; Town Clerk, Clerk of Peace, Deal, 1963–66; Town Clerk, Rugby, 1966–70; Circuit Administrator, Western Circuit, Lord Chancellor's Office (Under Sec.), 1970–87; Planning Inspector, 1987–95. *Recreations:* music, gemmology, gardening. *Address:* Westdale Edge, Beer Road, Seaton, Devon EX12 2PT. *T:* Seaton (01297) 21212. *Club:* United Oxford & Cambridge University.

ASHWORTH, James Louis, FIMechE, FIEE, ARTC (Salford); Full-Time Member for Operations, Central Electricity Generating Board, 1966–70, retired; *b* 7 March 1906; *s* of late James and late Janet Ashworth; *m* 1931 Clara Evelyn Arnold (*d* 1992); one *s* two *d. Educ:* Stockport Grammar Sch.; Salford Royal Coll. of Technology. Apprenticeship with Mirrlees, Bickerton & Day Ltd, Stockport (Diesel Oil Engine Manufrs), 1924–29; Metro-Vickers Electrical Co. Ltd, 1929; Manchester Corp. Elec. Dept, Stuart Street Gen. Stn, 1930–32; Hull Corp. Elec. Dept, 1932–35; Halifax Corp. Elec. Dept, 1935–40; Mersey Power Co. Ltd, Runcorn, 1940–48; British Elec. Authority, N West: Chief Generation Engr (O), 1948–57; Dep. Divisional Controller, 1957–58; Central Elec. Gen. Bd, N West, Merseyside and N Wales Region: Dep. Regional Dir, 1958–62; Regional Dir,

1962–66. *Recreations:* gardening, photography, travel, reading. *Address:* Chase Cottage, 23 The Chase, Reigate, Surrey RH2 7DJ. *T:* Redhill (01737) 61279.

ASHWORTH, Dr John Michael, FIBiol; Director, London School of Economics and Political Science, 1990–Sept. 1996; *b* 27 Nov. 1938; *s* of late Jack Ashworth and late Constance Mary Ousman; *m* 1st, 1963, Ann Knight (*d* 1985); one *s* three *d*; 2nd, 1988, Auriol Stevens. *Educ:* West Buckland Sch., N Devon; Exeter Coll., Oxford (MA, DSc; Hon. Fellow, 1983); Leicester Univ. (PhD). FIBiol 1974. Dept of Biochemistry, Univ. of Leicester: Res. Demonstr, 1961–63; Lectr, 1963–71; Reader, 1971–73; Prof. of Biology, Univ. of Essex, 1974–79 (on secondment to Cabinet Office, 1976–79); Under-Sec., Cabinet Office, 1979–81 and Chief Scientist, Central Policy Review Staff, 1976–81; Vice-Chancellor, Univ. of Salford, 1981–90. Harkness Fellow of Commonwealth Fund, NY, at Brandeis Univ. and Univ. of Calif, 1965–67. NEDO: Chm., Information Technology EDC, 1983–86; Mem., Electronics EDC, 1983–86. Chairman: Nat. Accreditation Council for Certification Bodies, BSI, 1984–88; NCC, 1983–92. Director: Granada TV, 1987–89; Granada Group, 1990–; J. Sainsbury, 1993–; London First, 1993–. Colworth Medal, Biochem. Soc., 1972. *Publications:* Cell Differentiation, 1972; (with J. Dee) The Slime Moulds, 1976; over 100 pubns in prof. jls on biochem., genet., cell biolog. and educnl topics. *Recreation:* fell walking. *Address:* London School of Economics and Political Science, Houghton Street, Aldwych, WC2A 2AE; (from Sept. 1996) Garden House, Wivenhoe, Essex CO7 9DB.

ASHWORTH, Peter Anthony Frank; Director, Leeds Permanent Building Society, 1971–92 (President, 1978); *b* 24 Aug. 1935; *s* of Peter Ormerod and Dorothy Christine Ashworth; *m* 1964, Elisabeth Crompton; one *s* one *d*. *Educ:* Leeds Grammar School. Articled to Hollis & Webb, Chartered Surveyors, Leeds (now Weatherall, Green & Smith), 1953–56; Partner, 1961–80. *Recreations:* golf, gardening. *Address:* 4 Bridge Paddock, Collingham, Wetherby LS22 5BN. *T:* Collingham Bridge (01937) 572953. *Club:* Alwoodley Golf (Leeds).

ASHWORTH, Piers, QC 1973; a Recorder of the Crown Court, since 1974; *b* 27 May 1931; *s* of Tom and Mollie Ashworth; *m* 1st, 1959, Iolene Jennifer (marr. diss. 1978), *yr d* of W. G. Foxley; three *s* one *d*; 2nd, 1980, Elizabeth, *er d* of A. J. S. Aston. *Educ:* Christ's Hospital; Pembroke Coll., Cambridge (scholar). Commnd Royal Signals, 1951. BA (Cantab) 1955; Harmsworth Law Scholar, 1956; called to Bar, Middle Temple, 1956, Bencher, 1984; Midland and Oxford circuit. Chm., Bar Mutual Indemnity Fund Ltd, 1987–. Gov. and Almoner, Christ's Hosp, 1986–. *Recreations:* sailing, squash, tennis, bridge. *Address:* 2 Harcourt Buildings, Temple, EC4Y 9DB. *T:* 0171–583 9020.

ASIROGLU, Vahap; Member: Board of Co-ordination, and Counsel for Foreign Relations, Kavala Group of companies, since 1983; Board, Association for the Co-ordination of Foreign Investment, since 1988; *b* Karamürsel, 1916; *m*; one *c*. *Educ:* Galatasaray High Sch.; Istanbul Univ. (Faculty of Law). Third Sec., Second Political Dept, Min. of Foreign Affairs, 1943–46; successively, Third, Second, First Sec., Turkish Embassy, Prague, 1946–51; First Sec., Dept of Internat. Economic Affairs, MFA, 1951–53; First Sec. and Counsellor, Turkish Perm. Mission to UN, 1953–59; Asst Dir Gen., Dept of Internat. Econ. Affairs, MFA, 1959–60; Asst Dir Gen. and Dir Gen., Personnel and Admin. Dept, MFA, 1960; Dir Gen., UN and Internat. Instns Dept, MFA, 1960–62; Asst Perm. Rep., Turkish Perm. Mission to UN, 1962–65; Turkish Ambassador: to Copenhagen, 1965–68; to Jakarta, 1968–71; Sec. Gen., Reg. Cooperation for Develt (a reg. org. between Turkey, Iran and Pakistan), 1971–74; Sen. Counsellor, MFA, 1974; Director General: Dept of Consular Affairs, MFA, 1974–75; Dept of Cultural Affairs, MFA, 1975–76; Asst Sec. Gen. for Inf. and Cultural Affairs, MFA, 1976; Ambassador to UK, 1978–81; retd from Min. of Foreign Affairs, 1981. Mem., UN Human Rights Commn, 1953–56; Turkish Rep., ICAO Conf., Montreal, 1956–57; Head of Turkish Delegn, GATT Conf., Tokyo, 1959; Asst Chm., Conf. on Immunities and Diplomatic Relns, Vienna, 1961; Chm., Fifth Commn, UN Gen. Assembly, 1967. Vice-Pres., Turkish Higher Educn Council, 1981–83.

ASKE, Rev. Sir Conan, 2nd Bt *cr* 1922; Assistant Curate of St John-in-Bedwardine, Worcester, 1972–80; *b* 22 April 1912; *s* of Sir Robert William Aske, 1st Bt, TD, QC, LLD, and Edith (*d* 1918), *d* of Sir Walter Herbert Cockerline; *S* father 1954; *m* 1st, 1948, Vera Faulkner (*d* 1960); 2nd, 1965, Rebecca, *d* of Hugh Grant, Wick, Caithness. *Educ:* Rugby; Balliol Coll., Oxford. TA, London Irish Rifles, 1939; served, 1939–49, with East York Regt, Sudan Defence Force, Somalia Gendarmerie. Major, Civil Affairs Officer, Reserved Area of Ethiopia and The Ogaden, 1949–51; Schoolmaster, Hillstone, Malvern, 1952–69; Asst Curate, Hagley, Stourbridge, 1970–72. Hon. Padre, Worcs Br., 1940 Dunkirk Veterans' Assoc., 1988–. *Heir: b* Robert Edward Aske [*b* 21 March 1915; *m* 1940, Joan Bingham, *o d* of Captain Bingham Ackerley, Cobham; one *s*]. *Address:* 167 Malvern Road, Worcester WR2 4NN. *T:* Worcester (01905) 422817.

ASKEW, Barry Reginald William; journalist, broadcaster and public relations consultant; *b* 13 Dec. 1936; *s* of late Reginald Ewart Askew and Jane Elizabeth Askew; *m* 1st, 1958, June Roberts (marr. diss. 1978), *d* of Vernon and late Betty Roberts; one *s* one *d*; 2nd, 1980, Deborah Parker, *d* of Harold and Enid Parker. *Educ:* Lady Manners Grammar Sch., Bakewell, Derbys. Trainee reporter upwards, Derbyshire Times, 1952–57; Reporter and sub-ed., Sheffield Telegraph, 1957–59; reporter, feature writer and broadcaster, Raymonds News Agency, Derby, 1959–61; Editor, Matlock Mercury, 1961–63; Industrial Correspondent, Asst Ed., Dep. Ed., Sheffield Telegraph, later Morning Telegraph, Sheffield, 1964–68; Associate Ed., The Star, Sheffield, 1968; Editor, 1968–81, Dir, 1978–81, Lancashire Evening Post; Editor, News of the World, 1981. Presenter and anchor man: ITV, 1970–81; BBC Radio 4, 1971–72; BBC 1, 1972; BBC 2, 1972–76. Consultant in TV, radio, PR and commerce, 1982–95. Mem., Davies Cttee to reform hosp. complaints procedures in UK, 1971–73. Campaigning Journalist of 1971, IPC Nat. Press Awards; Journalist of 1977, British Press Awards; Crime Reporter of 1977, Witness Box Awards. *Recreations:* Rugby, chess, reading military history, golf. *Address:* School House Cottage, Rosemary Lane, Bartle, Preston, Lancs PR4 0HB. *T:* Preston (01772) 731817, (office) Preston (01772) 690459. *Club:* Preston Grasshoppers RF.

ASKEW, Sir Bryan, Kt 1989; Personnel Director, Samuel Smith Old Brewery (Tadcaster), 1982–95; Chairman, Yorkshire Regional Health Authority, 1983–94; *b* 18 Aug. 1930; *s* of John Pinkney Askew and Matilda Askew; *m* 1955, Millicent Rose Holder; two *d*. *Educ:* Wellfield Grammar Sch., Wingate, Co. Durham; Fitzwilliam Coll., Cambridge (MA Hons History). ICI Ltd, 1952–59; Consett Iron Co. Ltd (later part of British Steel Corporation), 1959–71; own consultancy, 1971–74; Samuel Smith Old Brewery (Tadcaster), 1974–95. Member, Consett UDC, 1967–71; contested (C) General Elections: Penistone, 1964 and 1966; York, 1970. Mem., Duke of Edinburgh's Third Commonwealth Study Conf., Australia, 1968. Mem., Working Gp on Young People and Alcohol, Home Office Standing Conf. on Crime Prevention, 1987. Mem. Court, 1985–, Mem. Council, 1988–, Univ. of Leeds. FRSA 1986; FRSM 1988. Hon. LLD Hull, 1992. *Recreations:* listening to music, reading. *Address:* 27 Golf Links Avenue, Tadcaster LS24 9HF. *T:* Tadcaster (01937) 833216.

ASKEW, John Marjoribanks Eskdale, CBE 1974; *b* 22 Sept. 1908; *o s* of late William Haggerston Askew, JP, Ladykirk, Berwicks, and Castle Hills, Berwick-on-Tweed; *m* 1st, 1933, Lady Susan Egerton (marr. diss., 1966), 4th *d* of 4th Earl of Ellesmere, MVO; one *s* one *d*; *m* 1976, Priscilla Anne, *e d* of late Algernon Ross-Farrow. *Educ:* Eton; Magdalene Coll., Cambridge (BA). Lieut 2 Bn Grenadier Guards, 1932; Capt. 1940; Major 1943; served NW Europe 1939–40 and 1944–45. Brigadier, Royal Company of Archers, Queen's Body Guard for Scotland. Convener: Berwicks CC, 1961; Border Regional Council, 1974–82. *Address:* Ladykirk, Berwicks TD15 1SU. *T:* Berwick (01289) 82229; Castle Hills, Berwick-on-Tweed TD15 1PB. *Clubs:* Boodle's; New (Edinburgh).

See also Baron Faringdon, Duke of Sutherland.

ASKEW, Rev. Canon Reginald James Albert; Dean of King's College, London, 1988–93; Canon Emeritus, Salisbury Cathedral, since 1988; *b* 16 May 1928; *s* of late Paul Askew and Amy Wainwright; *m* 1953, Kate, *yr d* of late Rev. Henry Townsend Wigley; one *s* two *d*. *Educ:* Harrow; Corpus Christi Coll., Cambridge (MA); Lincoln Theological College. Curate of Highgate, 1957–61; Tutor and Chaplain of Wells Theol Coll., 1961–65, Vice-Principal 1966–69; Priest Vicar of Wells Cath., 1961–69; Vicar of Christ Church, Lancaster Gate, London, 1969–73; Principal, Salisbury and Wells Theol Coll., 1973–87; Canon of Salisbury Cathedral and Prebendary of Grantham Borealis, 1975–87. Proctor in Convocation for London Univ., Gen. Synod of C of E, 1990–93. Mem., Corrymeela Community, 1990–. *Publication:* The Tree of Noah, 1971. *Recreations:* music, gardening, making wood-cuts and lino-cuts. *Address:* Carters Cottage, North Wootton, Shepton Mallet, Somerset BA4 4AF. *T:* Pilton (01749) 890728. *Club:* Athenæum.

ASKONAS, Brigitte Alice, PhD; FRS 1973; with Institute of Molecular Medicine (Molecular Immunology), John Radcliffe Hospital, Oxford, since 1989 (part-time); attached to Department of Biology, Imperial College of Science, Technology and Medicine (part-time); *b* 1 April 1923; *d* of late Charles F. Askonas and Rose Askonas. *Educ:* McGill Univ., Montreal (BSc, MSc); Cambridge Univ. (PhD; Hon. Fellow, New Hall and Girton Coll.). Research student, Sch. of Biochemistry, Univ. of Cambridge, 1949–52; Immunology Div., NIMR, 1953–89 (Head of Div., 1977–88); Dept of Bacteriology and Immunology, Harvard Med. Sch., Boston, 1961–62; Basel Inst. for Immunology, Basel, Switzerland, 1971–72. Visiting Professor: Dept of Medicine, St Mary's Hosp. Med. Sch., London, 1988–94; Dept of Biol., ICSTM, 1995–. Hon. Member: Amer. Soc. of Immunology; Soc. française d'Immunologie; German Ges. für Immunologie. Hon. DSc McGill, 1987. *Publications:* contrib. scientific papers to various biochemical and immunological jls and books. *Recreations:* art, travel. *Address:* 23 Hillside Gardens, N6 5SU. *T:* 0181–348 6792; Department of Biology, Imperial College of Science, Technology and Medicine, Prince Consort Road, SW7 2BB. *T:* 0171–594 5404, *Fax:* 0171–584 9075.

ASLET, Clive William; Editor, Country Life, since 1993 (Deputy Editor, 1989–92); Editor in Chief, Country Life Books, since 1994; *b* 15 Feb. 1955; *s* of Kenneth and Monica Aslet; *m* 1980, Naomi Roth; one *s*. *Educ:* King's College Sch., Wimbledon; Peterhouse, Cambridge. Joined Country Life, 1977, Architectural Editor, 1984–88. Founding Hon. Sec., Thirties Soc., 1979–87. FRSA. *Publications:* The Last Country Houses, 1982; (with Alan Powers) The National Trust Book of the English House, 1985; Quinlan Terry, the Revival of Architecture, 1986; The American Country House, 1990; Countryblast, 1991; (introd.) The American Houses of Robert A. M. Stern, 1991. *Recreations:* the arts, books, hunting. *Address:* c/o Country Life, King's Reach Tower, Stamford Street, SE1 9LS. *T:* 0171–261 6969. *Club:* Garrick.

ASPEL, Michael Terence, OBE 1993; broadcaster and writer; *b* 12 Jan. 1933; *s* of late Edward and of Violet Aspel; *m* 1st, 1957, Dian; one *s* (and one *s* decd); 2nd, 1962, Ann; twin *s* and *d*; 3rd 1977, Elizabeth; two *s*. *Educ:* Emanuel School. Tea boy, publishers, 1949–51. Nat. Service, KRRC and Para Regt, TA, 1951–53. Radio actor, 1954–57; television announcer, 1957–60, newsreader, 1960–68; freelance broadcaster, radio and TV, 1968–; presenter: Aspel and Company, 1984–93; This is Your Life, 1988–; occasional stage appearances. Pres., Stackpole Trust, 1985–; Vice-President: BLISS (Baby Life Support Systems), 1981–; ASBAH (Assoc. for Spina Bifida and Hydrocephalus), 1985–; Patron, Plan International, 1986–. Member: Equity, 1955–; Lord's Taverners; RYA. FZS. *Publications:* Polly Wants a Zebra (autobiog.), 1974; Hang On! (for children), 1982; (with Richard Hearsey) Child's Play, 1985; regular contribs to magazines. *Recreations:* water sports, theatre, cinema, eating, travel. *Address:* c/o Bagenal Harvey Organisation, 141–143 Drury Lane, WC2B 5TB.

ASPELL, Col Gerald Laycock, TD (2 clasps); DL, FCA; Vice Lord-Lieutenant of Leicestershire, 1984–90; *b* 10 April 1915; *s* of Samuel Frederick Aspell and Agnes Maude (*née* Laycock); *m* 1939, Mary Leeson Carroll, *d* of Rev. Ion Carroll, Cork; one *s* two *d*. *Educ:* Uppingham Sch. FCA 1938. Commnd 2nd Lieut, 4th Bn Leicestershire Regt, TA, 1933; served War of 1939–45 in UK and Burma, RE, RA, RAF; commanded 579 Light Anti-Aircraft Regt, RA (TA), 1946–51. Partner, Coopers & Lybrand, 1952–78; mem. of various nat. and local cttees of Inst. of Chartered Accountants during that time. Dir, 1964–85, Chm., 1978–85, Leicester Building Soc.; Dep. Chm., Alliance and Leicester Building Soc., 1985; Local Dir, Eagle Star Insce Gp, 1949–84 (Chm., Midlands Bd, 1970–84). Chairman: Leicester and Dist Local Employment Cttee, then Leics Dist Manpower Cttee, 1971–79. Mem., Leicester Diocesan Bd of Finance, 1952–77. Civil Defence Controller, then Sub-Regl Dir CD, Leics, Rutland and Northants, 1956–65. Member: Leics and Rutland TAA, then E Midlands TAVRA, 1947–80 (Chm., Leics Cttee, 1969–80). Hon. Colonel: Royal Anglian Regt (Leics), 1972–79; Leics and Northants ACF, 1979–84. Grand Treasurer, United Grand Lodge of England, 1974–75. Trustee, Uppingham Sch., 1964–87 (Chm., 1977–87). DL Leics, 1952. *Recreations:* cricket, tennis, squash, fishing, charitable involvements. *Address:* Laburnum House, Great Dalby, Melton Mowbray, Leics LE14 2HA. *T:* Melton Mowbray (01664) 63604.

ASPIN, Norman, CMG 1968; HM Diplomatic Service, retired; Adviser and Secretary, East Africa Association, 1981–84; *b* 9 Nov. 1922; *s* of Thomas and Eleanor Aspin; *m* 1948, Elizabeth Irving; three *s*. *Educ:* Darwen Grammar Sch.; Durham Univ. (MA). War Service, 1942–45, Lieut RNVR. Demonstrator in Geography, Durham Univ., 1947–48; Asst Principal, Commonwealth Relations Office, 1948; served in India, 1948–51; Principal, Commonwealth Relations Office, 1952; served in Federation of Rhodesia and Nyasaland, 1954–57; British Deputy High Commissioner in Sierra Leone, 1961–63; Commonwealth Relations Office, 1963–65; British Embassy, Tel Aviv, 1966–69; IDC 1970; Head of Personnel Policy Dept, FCO, 1971–73; Under-Sec., FCO, 1973–76; Comr, British Indian Ocean Territory, 1976; British High Comr in Malta, 1976–79; Asst Under-Sec. of State, FCO, 1979–80. *Recreations:* sailing, tennis. *Address:* Mounsey Bank, Dacre, Cumbria CA11 0HL.

ASPINALL, John Michael; QC 1995; a Recorder, since 1990; *b* 19 Feb. 1948; *s* of Kenneth James Aspinall and Joan Mary Aspinall; *m* 1980, Frances Helen Parks. *Educ:* Kampala Kindergarten; Wigan and Dist Mining and Tech. Coll.; Liverpool Univ. (LLB Hons). Called to the Bar, Inner Temple, 1971; Asst Recorder, 1985–90. RAC Motor Sports Council: Mem., 1990–, Chm., 1994–, Judicial Cttee; Mem., 1994–. Winner,

Observer Mace Nat. Debating Comp., 1971. *Recreations:* motor sports, being with my wife and friends at the Drax Arms. *Address:* 3 Pump Court, Temple, EC4Y 7AJ. *T:* 0171–353 0711. *Club:* Savile.

ASPINALL, John Victor; Chairman of the Trustees, Howletts and Port Lympne Foundation, since 1984; *b* 11 June 1926; *s* of late Col Robert Aspinall and Mary (*née* Horn, later Lady Osborne); *m* 1st, 1956, Jane Gordon Hastings (marr. diss. 1966); one *s* one *d*; 2nd, 1966, Belinda Musker (marr. diss. 1972); 3rd, 1972, Lady Sarah Courage (*née* Curzon); one *s*. *Educ:* Rugby Sch.; Jesus Coll., Oxford. Founded: Howletts Zoo Park, 1958; Clermont Club, 1962; Port Lympne Zoo Park, 1973; Aspinall's Club, 1978; Aspinall Curzon Club, 1984; Aspinalls, 1992–. Won gaming case Crown *v* Aspinall, 1958. *Publications:* The Best of Friends, 1976, Amer. edn 1977, German edn 1978; contributor to numerous publications. *Recreations:* wild animals, gambling. *Address:* 64 Sloane Street, SW1X 9SH. *T:* 0171–235 2768, *Fax:* 0171–235 4701.

ASPINALL, Wilfred; Member, European Economic and Social Consultative Assembly, since 1986; European Union adviser/consultant; *b* 14 Sept. 1942; *s* of late Charles Aspinall and Elizabeth Aspinall; *m* 1973, Judith Mary, *d* of late Leonard James Pimlott and Kathleen Mary Pimlott; one *d*. *Educ:* Poynton Secondary Modern; Stockport Coll. for Further Educn. Staff, National Provincial Bank Ltd, 1960–69; Asst Gen. Sec., National Westminster Staff Assoc., 1969–75; Dep. Sec. (part-time), Council of Bank Staff Assocs, 1969–75; Mem., Banking Staff Council, 1970–77; Gen. Sec., Confedn of Bank Staff Assocs, 1975–79; Exec. Dir, Fedn of Managerial, Professional and Gen. Assocs, 1978–94. Vice-Pres., Confédération Internat. des Cadres, 1979–94. Member: N Herts DHA, 1981–86; NW Thames RHA, 1986–88; Hammersmith and Queen Charlotte's SHA, 1981–90; Professions Allied to Medicine, Whitley Management Negotiating Cttee, 1983–87. *Recreations:* motoring, travel—particularly to places of historical interest, social affairs and political history. *Address:* The Croft, Shillington Road, Pirton, Hitchin, Herts SG5 3QJ. *T:* Hitchin (01462) 712316, *Fax:* (01462) 712293; Economic and Social Consultative Assembly, rue Ravenstein 2, Brussels 1000, Belgium. *T:* (2) 5199011; (Brussels private office) Rue de la Tourelle 23, 1040 Brussels. *T:* (2) 2308510, *Fax:* (2) 2307818.

ASPINWALL, Jack Heywood; MP (C) Wansdyke, since 1983 (Kingswood, 1979–83); company director; *b* 5 Feb. 1933; *m* 1954, Brenda Jean Aspinwall; one *s* two *d*. *Educ:* Prescot Grammar School, Lancs; Marconi College, Chelmsford. Served RAF, 1949–56. Director: family retail business, 1956–66; food distbn co., 1966–71; investment co., 1971–. Mem., Avon County Council. Contested (L) Kingswood, Feb. and Oct. 1974. *Publication:* (comp.) Kindly Sit Down!: best after-dinner stories from both Houses of Parliament, 1983. *Address:* House of Commons, SW1A 0AA; 154 Bath Road, Willsbridge, Bristol BS15 6EF.

ASPRAY, Rodney George, FCA; Managing Director, Worthbase Ltd, since 1990; *b* 1934. Secretary, Manchester and Salford Cooperative Society, 1965–69; Chief Exec. Officer, Norwest Co-op Soc., 1969–91. Director: Co-operative Bank, 1980–89 (Chm., 1986–89); Co-operative Wholesale Soc. Ltd, 1980–89; Mersey Docks & Harbour Co., 1987–; Piccadilly Radio Plc, 1989–90. Mem., Monopolies and Mergers Commn, 1975–81. FCA 1960. *Address:* Kambara, 4 Green Lane, Higher Poynton, Cheshire SK12 1TJ.

ASQUITH, family name of **Earl of Oxford and Asquith.**

ASQUITH, Viscount; Raymond Benedict Bartholomew Michael Asquith, OBE 1992; HM Diplomatic Service; Counsellor, Kiev, since 1992; *b* 24 Aug. 1952; *er s* and *heir* of 2nd Earl of Oxford and Asquith, *qv*; *m* 1978, Mary Clare, *e d* of Francis Pollen; one *s* four *d*. *Educ:* Ampleforth; Balliol College, Oxford. FCO, 1980–83; First Sec., Moscow, 1983–85; Cabinet Office and FCO, 1985–92. *Heir: s* Hon. Mark Julian Asquith, *b* 13 May 1979.

ASSCHER, Sir (Adolf) William, Kt 1992; MD, FRCP; Principal (formerly Dean), St George's Hospital Medical School, London University, since 1988; Hon. Consultant Physician, St George's Hospital, since 1988; *b* 20 March 1931; *s* of William Benjamin Asscher and Roosje van der Molen; *m* 1st, 1959, Corrie van Welt (*d* 1961); 2nd, 1962, Dr Jennifer Lloyd, *d* of Wynne Llewelyn Lloyd, CB; two *d*. *Educ:* Maerlant Lyceum, The Hague; London Hosp. Med. Coll. BSc 1954; MB 1957; MD 1963; MRCP 1959, FRCP 1971. Nat. service, Lieut RE, 1949–51. Jun. appts, London Hosp., 1957–59; Lectr in Medicine, London Hosp. Med. Coll., 1959–64; Welsh National School of Medicine, later University of Wales College of Medicine: Sen. Lectr, 1964–70, and Hon. Cons. Physician, Royal Inf., Cardiff; Reader, 1970–76; Prof. of Medicine, 1976–80; Head of Dept of Renal Medicine, 1980–88. Chairman: Cttee on Review of Medicines, DHSS, 1985–87; Cttee on Safety of Medicines, Dept of Health (formerly DHSS), 1987–92 (Mem., 1984–87); Member: Medicines Commn, DHSS, 1981–84; SW Thames RHA, 1987–90; Jt Consultants Cttee, 1992–; Welsh Arts Council, 1985–88. Non-executive Director: Wandsworth DHA, 1991–93; St George's Health Care Trust, 1993–. Chairman: Med. Benefit Risk Foundn UK, 1993–; Welsh Med. Technology Forum, 1993–. Regl Advr, 1976–79, Mem. Council, 1977–80, RCP. Examnr, Final MB, Wales, London, Bristol and Edinburgh. Pres., Renal Assoc., 1986–89. *Publications:* Urinary Tract Infection, 1973 (with W. Brumfitt); The Challenge of Urinary Tract Infections, 1980; (with D. B. Moffat and E. Sanders) Nephrology Illustrated, 1982; (with D. B. Moffat) Nephro-Urology, 1983; (with W. Brumfitt) Microbial Diseases in Nephrology, 1986; (with S. R. Walker) Medicines and Risk-Benefit Decisions, 1986; (with J. D. Williams) Clinical Atlas of the Kidney, 1991; papers on nephrology and drug regulation in learned jls. *Recreations:* visual arts, golf, tennis. *Address:* Principal's Office, St George's Hospital Medical School, Cranmer Terrace, Tooting, SW17 0RE. *T:* 0181–672 3122. *Club:* Reform.

ASSHETON, family name of **Baron Clitheroe.**

ASTAIRE, Jarvis Joseph; Deputy Chairman, Wembley Stadium, since 1984; Chairman, Viewsport Ltd, since 1964; *b* 6 Oct. 1923; *s* of late Max and of Esther Astaire; *m* 1st, 1948, Phyllis Oppenheim (*d* 1974); one *s* one *d*; 2nd, 1981, Nadine Hyman (*d* 1986). *Educ:* Kilburn Grammar Sch., London. Dir, Lewis & Burrows Ltd, 1957–60; Managing Director: Mappin & Webb Ltd, 1958–60; Hurst Park Syndicate, 1962–71; Director: Perthpoint Investments Ltd, 1959–70; Associated Suburban Properties Ltd, 1963–81; Anglo-Continental Investment & Finance Co. Ltd, 1964–75; William Hill Org., 1971–82; First Artists Prodns Inc. (USA), 1976–79; Wembley PLC (formerly GRA Gp), 1987–; Revlon Group Ltd, 1991–; Greyhound Racing Assoc., 1991–. Mem. Bd, British Greyhound Racing, 1991–. Introduced into UK showing of sporting events on large screen in cinemas, 1964. Pres., Royal Free Hosp. and Med. Sch. Appeal Trust, 1991– (Chm., 1974); Hon. Treas., London Fedn of Boys' Clubs, 1976–; Trustee, Bowles Outdoor Centre, 1985–; Patron, Nightingale House Home for Aged Jews, 1984–. Chm., Associated City Properties, 1981–. Chief Barker (Pres.), Variety Club of GB, 1983; Pres., Variety Clubs Internat. (Worldwide), 1991–93. Freeman, City of London, 1983. *Recreations:* playing tennis, watching cricket and football. *Address:* Broughton House, 6–8 Sackville Street, W1X 1DD. *T:* 0171–287 4601. *Clubs:* East India, MCC, Queen's; Friars (USA).

ASTBURY, Prof. Alan, PhD; FRS 1993; FRS(Can) 1988; R. M. Pearce Professor of Physics, University of Victoria, British Columbia, since 1983; Director, TRIUMF, since 1994; *b* 27 Nov. 1934; *s* of Harold Astbury and Jane Astbury (*née* Horton); *m* 1964, Kathleen Ann Stratmeyer; two *d*. *Educ:* Nantwich and Acton Grammar Sch.; Univ. of Liverpool (BSc, PhD). Leverhulme Research Fellow, Univ. of Liverpool, 1959–61; Res. Associate, Lawrence Radiation Lab., Berkeley, Calif., 1961–63; Res. Physicist, Rutherford Appleton Lab., UK, 1963–83. Vis. Scientist, CERN, Geneva, 1970–74 and 1980–83. Rutherford Medal, Inst. Physics, 1986. *Publications:* numerous in learned jls. *Recreations:* ski-ing, jazz, playing piano. *Address:* TRIUMF, 4004 Wesbrook, Vancouver, BC V6T 2A3, Canada. *T:* (604) 2227353; 1383 St Patrick Street, Victoria, BC V8S 4Y5, Canada. *T:* (604) 5955315.

ASTILL, Michael John; His Honour Judge Astill; a Circuit Judge, since 1984; *b* 31 Jan. 1938; *s* of Cyril Norman Astill and Winifred Astill; *m* 1968, Jean Elizabeth, *d* of Dr J. C. H. Mackenzie; three *s* one *d*. *Educ:* Blackfriars School, Laxton, Northants. Admitted solicitor, 1962; called to the Bar, Middle Temple, 1972; a Recorder, 1980–84. A Pres., Mental Health Tribunals, 1986–. *Recreations:* music, reading, sport.

ASTLEY, family name of **Baron Hastings.**

ASTLEY, Philip Sinton, LVO 1979; HM Diplomatic Service; Counsellor, Foreign and Commonwealth Office, since 1994; *b* 18 Aug. 1943; *s* of Bernard Astley and Barbara Astley (*née* Sinton); *m* 1966, Susanne Poulsen; two *d*. *Educ:* St Albans Sch.; Magdalene Coll., Cambridge (BA 1965). Asst Representative, British Council, Madras, 1966–70; British Council, London, 1970–73; First Sec., FCO, 1973–76, Copenhagen, 1976–79; First Sec. and Head of Chancery, East Berlin, 1980–82; First Sec., FCO, 1982–84; Counsellor and Head of Management Review Staff, FCO, 1984–86; Econ. Counsellor and Consul Gen., Islamabad, 1986–90; Dep. Head of Mission, Copenhagen, 1990–94. Kt, Order of Dannebrog (Denmark), 1979. *Recreations:* oriental textiles, gardening. *Address:* c/o Foreign and Commonwealth Office, SW1A 2AH.

ASTLING, Alistair Vivian; Chief Executive, Dudley Metropolitan Borough Council, since 1988; *b* 6 Sept. 1943; *s* of Alec William and Barbara Grace Astling; *m* 1967, Hazel Ruth Clarke. *Educ:* Glyn Grammar Sch., Epsom; Sheffield Univ. (LLB 1965; LLM 1967); Birmingham Univ. (MSocSci 1973). West Bromwich County Borough Council: articled clerk, 1967; Asst Solicitor, 1971; Asst Town Clerk, 1973; Walsall Metropolitan Borough Council: Corporate Planner, 1974; Chief Exec. and Town Clerk, 1982; Clerk to W Midlands Police Authy, 1988–; Sec. to Birmingham Internat. Airport Shareholders' Forum, 1988–. *Recreations:* squash, theatre, music. *Address:* Dudley Metropolitan Borough Council, Council House, Dudley DY1 1HF. *T:* Dudley (01384) 453201; 16 Knighton Drive, Sutton Coldfield, W Midlands B74 4QP.

ASTON, Bishop Suffragan of, since 1992; **Rt. Rev. John Michael Austin;** *b* 4 March 1939; *s* of John Fenner Austin and Margaret Austin; *m* 1971, Rosemary Joan Elizabeth King; two *s* one *d*. *Educ:* Worksop Coll.; St Edmund Hall, Oxford (BA 1963); St Stephen's House, Oxford. Ordained deacon, 1964, priest, 1965; Assistant Curate: St John the Evangelist, E Dulwich, 1964–68; St James Cathedral, Chicago, 1968–69; St Christopher's, Pembroke Coll. Mission, 1969–76; Social Responsibility Advr, St Alban's Dio., 1976–84; Dir, London Diocesan Bd for Social Responsibility, 1984–92. Prebendary, St Paul's Cathedral, 1982–87. Founding Chm., Church Action on Poverty, 1980–85; Mem., Follow-up Cttee for the Archbishop's Report, Faith in the City, 1986–92. *Recreations:* walking, cycling, playing the violin very badly! *Address:* Strensham House, 8 Strensham Hill, Birmingham B13 8AG. *T:* 0121–449 0675.

ASTON, Archdeacon of; *see* Barton, Ven. C. J. G.

ASTON, Sir Harold (George), Kt 1983; CBE 1976; Chairman and Chief Executive, Bonds Coats Patons Ltd, 1981–87 (Deputy Chairman, 1970–80); Director, Central Sydney Area Health Service, 1988–92; *b* Sydney, 13 March 1923; *s* of Harold John Aston and Annie Dorothea McKeown; *m* 1947, Joyce Thelma Smith (decd); one *s* one *d*. *Educ:* Crown Street Boys' Sch., Sydney, Australia. Manager, Buckinghams Ltd, Sydney, 1948–55; Bonds Industries Ltd: Merchandising Manager, 1955–63; Gen. Man., 1963–67; Man. Dir, 1967–70; Director: Bonds Coats Patons Ltd (formerly Bonds Industries Ltd); Manufacturers Mutual Insurance, 1982– (Vice Chm., 1987–); Downard-Pickfords Pty Ltd, 1983–89 (Chm.); Australian Guarantee Corp. Ltd, 1983–88; Australian Manufacturing Life Assce Ltd, 1984–88; Rothmans Hldgs Ltd, 1986– (Dep. Chm., 1989–); Westpac Banking Corp., 1988–92; Chm., Television and Telecasters Ltd, 1991–92; Consultant, Pacific Dunlop Ltd, 1987–. President: Textile Council of Australia, 1973–80 (Life Mem., 1984); Confedn of Aust. Industry, 1980–82; Hon. Trustee, Cttee for Econ. Develt of Australia, 1988–; Governor: Aesop Foundn, 1988–; (Founding), Heart Inst. of Australia, 1986–93. CompTI 1984; FCFI 1986; KStJ 1993 (Dep. Receiver-Gen., Finance Cttee, 1985–). *Recreations:* walking, gardening, travelling. *Address:* 44 Greenway Drive, Pymble, NSW 2073, Australia. *Clubs:* American, Australian, Royal Sydney Yacht Squadron (Sydney); Concord Golf.

See also Hon. Sir William Aston.

ASTON, Dr Margaret Evelyn, (Hon. Mrs Buxton), FSA, FRHistS; FBA 1994; historian; *b* 9 Oct. 1932; *d* of 1st Baron Bridges, KG, GCB, GCVO, MC, PC, FRS and of late Katharine Dianthe, *d* of 2nd Baron Farrer; *m* 1st, 1954, Trevor Henry Aston (marr. diss. 1969; he *d* 1985); 2nd, 1971, Paul William Jex Buxton, *qv*; two *d*. *Educ:* Downe House; Lady Margaret Hall, Oxford (BA, MA; DPhil 1962). FRHistS 1962; FSA 1987. Lectr, St Anne's Coll., Oxford, 1956–59; Theodor Heuss Schol., W Germany, 1960–61; Res. Fellow, Newnham Coll., Cambridge, 1961–66; Res. Fellow, Folger Shakespeare Liby, and teaching post, Catholic Univ. of America, Washington, 1966–69; Hon. Sen. Res. Fellow, QUB, 1984–85. *Publications:* Thomas Arundel: a study of church life in the reign of Richard II, 1967; The Fifteenth Century: the prospect of Europe, 1968, repr. 1994; Lollards and Reformers: images and literacy in late medieval religion, 1984; England's Iconoclasts: laws against images, 1988; Faith and Fire: popular and unpopular religion 1350–1600, 1993; The King's Bedpost: reformation and iconography in a Tudor group portrait, 1994; contrib. learned jls, TLS etc. *Recreation:* visiting art galleries and exhibitions. *Address:* Castle House, Chipping Ongar, Essex CM5 9JT. *T:* Ongar (01277) 362642.

ASTON, Prof. Peter George, DPhil; Professor of Music, University of East Anglia, since 1974; *b* 5 Oct. 1938; *s* of late George William Aston and Elizabeth Oliver Smith; *m* 1960, Elaine Veronica Neale; one *s*. *Educ:* Tettenhall Coll.; Birmingham Sch. of Music (GBSM); Univ of York (DPhil); FTCL, ARCM. Lectr in Music, 1964–72, Sen. Lectr, 1972–74, Univ. of York; Dean, Sch. of Fine Arts and Music, UEA, 1981–84. Dir, Tudor Consort, 1958–65; Conductor: English Baroque Ensemble, 1968–70; Aldeburgh Festival Singers, 1975–88; Principal Guest Conductor, Sacramento Bach Fest., USA, 1993–; Jt Artistic Dir, Norwich Fest. of Contemporary Church Music, 1981–; Chorus Master, Norfolk and Norwich Triennial Fest., 1982–88. Chairman: Eastern Arts Assoc. Music Panel, 1976–81; Norfolk Assoc. for the Advancement of Music, 1990–93 (Pres., 1993–); Pres., Trianon Music Gp, 1984–. Patron, Lowestoft Choral Soc., 1986–. Gen. Editor, UEA Recording Series, 1979–. FRSA 1980. Hon. Fellow, Curwen Inst., 1987; Hon. RCM 1991. *Compositions:* song cycles, chamber music, choral and orchestral works, church music, opera. *Publications:* George Jeffreys and the English Baroque, 1970; The Music of York Minster, 1972; Sound and Silence (jtly), 1970, German edn 1972, Italian edn 1979, Japanese edn 1982; (ed) The Collected Works of George Jeffreys, 3 vols, 1977; (jtly) Music Theory in Practice, vol. 1, 1992, vols 2 and 3, 1993; contrib. to internat. music jls. *Recreations:* Association football, cricket, bridge, chess. *Address:* University of East Anglia, Music Centre, School of Music, Norwich NR4 7TJ. *T:* Norwich (01603) 56161. *Clubs:* Athenæum; Norfolk (Norwich).

ASTON, Hon. Sir William (John), KCMG 1970; JP; Speaker, House of Representatives, Australia, 1967–73; MP for Phillip, 1955–61, 1963–72; *b* 19 Sept. 1916; *s* of Harold John Aston and Dorothea (*née* McKeown); *m* 1941, Beatrice Delaney Burrett; one *s* two *d.* *Educ:* Randwick Boys' High School. Served War, 1939–45, AIF in New Guinea, Lieut. Mayor of Waverley, 1952–53. Dep. Govt Whip, 1959–61 and 1963–64; Chief Govt Whip, 1964–67; Trustee, Parlt Retiring Allowances, 1964–67; Mem. and Dep. Chm., Joint Select Cttee on New and Perm. Parlt House, 1965–72; Chairman: House of Reps Standing Orders Cttee, 1967–72; Joint House Cttee, 1967–72; Library Cttee, 1967–72; Joint Cttee on Broadcasting of Parly Proceedings, 1967–72; Jt Chm., Inter-Parliamentary Union (Commonwealth of Aust. Br.) and Commonwealth Parly Assoc. (Aust. Br.), 1967–72; Leader, Aust. Delegn to IPU Conf., Ottawa, 1964; Convenor and Chm., First Conf. of Aust. Presiding Officers, 1968; rep. Australia at: opening of Zambian Parlt Bldg; Funeral of Israeli Prime Minister Eshkol and IPU Symposium, Geneva, 1968; Conf. of Commonwealth Presiding Officers, Ottawa, 1969, New Delhi, 1971; opened Aust. House, Mt Scopus, Univ. of Israel, 1971; led Parly delegn to Turkey, Yugoslavia, UK and to Council of Europe, 1971. JP NSW 1954. Korean Order of Distinguished Service Merit (1st Class), 1969. *Recreations:* cricket, golf, football, fishing, bowls. *Address:* 55 Olola Avenue, Vaucluse, NSW 2030, Australia. *T:* (2) 3375992. *Clubs:* Royal Automobile of Australia (Sydney); Waverley Bowling, Royal Sydney Golf.
See also Sir H. G. Aston.

ASTOR, family name of **Viscount Astor** and **Baron Astor of Hever.**

ASTOR, 4th Viscount, *cr* 1917, of Hever Castle; Baron *cr* 1916; **William Waldorf Astor;** *b* 27 Dec. 1951; *s* of 3rd Viscount Astor; *S* father 1966; *m* 1976, Annabel Sheffield, *d* of T. Jones; two *s* one *d.* *Educ:* Eton Coll. A Lord in Waiting (Govt Whip), 1990–93; Parliamentary Under-Secretary of State: DSS, 1993–94; Dept of Nat. Heritage, 1994–95. *Heir:* *s* Hon. William Waldorf Astor, *b* 18 Jan. 1979. *Address:* Ginge Manor, Wantage, Oxon OX12 8QT. *Clubs:* White's, Turf.

ASTOR OF HEVER, 3rd Baron *cr* 1956, of Hever Castle; **John Jacob Astor;** *b* 16 June 1946; *s* of 2nd Baron Astor of Hever and of Lady Irene Haig, *d* of Field Marshal 1st Earl Haig, KT, GCB, OM, GCVO, KCIE; *S* father, 1984; *m* 1st, 1970, Fiona Diana Lennox Harvey (marr. diss. 1990), *d* of Captain Roger Harvey; three *d*; 2nd, 1990, Hon. Elizabeth, *d* of 2nd Viscount Mackintosh of Halifax, OBE, BEM; one *s* one *d.* *Educ:* Eton College. Lieut Life Guards, 1966–70, Malaysia, Hong Kong, Ulster. Director: Terres Blanches Services Sarl, 1975–77; Valberg Plaza Sarl, 1977–82; Managing Director: Honon et Cie, 1982–; Astor France Sarl, 1989–; Pres., Astor Enterprises Inc., 1983–. Sec., Anglo-Swiss Parly Assoc., 1992–; Jt Treas., British–S African Parly Assoc. Trustee: Rochester Cathedral Trust; Canterbury Cathedral Trust; Astor Foundn; Astor of Hever Trust; Patron: Edenbridge Music and Arts Trust; Kent Assoc. of Youth Clubs, 1994–; President: Sevenoaks Westminster Patrons Club; Earl Haig Br., Royal British Legion; Vice-President: Royal British Legion Village; Tree Council. Gov., Cobham Hall Sch., 1993–. Chm., Council of St John, Kent, 1987–; OStJ 1991. *Heir:* *s* Hon. Charles Gavin John Astor, *b* 10 Nov. 1990. *Address:* Frenchstreet House, Westerham, Kent TN16 1PW. *Clubs:* White's; House of Lords Yacht; Riviera Golf.
See also Hon. H. W. Astor.

ASTOR, David Waldorf, CBE 1994; farmer, since 1973; Director, Priory Investments Ltd (formerly Priory Investments Holdings), since 1990; *b* 9 Aug. 1943; *s* of late Michael Langhorne Astor and Barbara Mary (*née* McNeil); *m* 1968, Clare Pamela St John; two *s* two *d.* *Educ:* Eton Coll. Short service commn in Royal Scots Greys, 1962–65. United Newspapers, 1970–72; Housing Corp., 1972–75; Head of Develt, National Th., 1976–77; Chm., CPRE, 1983–93. Dir, Jupiter Tarbutt Merlin, 1985–91. Contested (SDP/Alliance) Plymouth Drake, 1987. FRSA. *Recreations:* books, sport. *Address:* Bruern Grange, Milton under Wychwood, Oxford OX7 6HA. *T:* Shipton-under-Wychwood (01993) 830413. *Clubs:* Brook's, MCC.

ASTOR, Hon. (Francis) David (Langhorne), CH 1994; Editor of The Observer, 1948–75; Director, The Observer, 1976–81; *b* 5 March 1912; *s* of 2nd Viscount Astor and Nancy, Viscountess Astor, CH, MP (*d* 1964); *m* 1st, 1945, Melanie Hauser; one *d*; 2nd, 1952, Bridget Aphra Wreford; two *s* three *d.* *Educ:* Eton; Balliol, Oxford. Yorkshire Post, 1936. Served War of 1939–45, with Royal Marines, 1940–45. Foreign Editor of the Observer, 1946–48. Croix de Guerre, 1944. *Publication:* (with V. Yorke) Peace in the Middle East: super powers and security guarantees, 1978. *Address:* 24 St Ann's Terrace, NW8 6PJ. *T:* 0171–586 8689; Manor House, Sutton Courtenay, Oxon OX14 4AD. *T:* Abingdon (01235) 848221. *Clubs:* Athenæum, Reform.

ASTOR, Hon. Hugh Waldorf, JP; Director, Hambro's plc, 1960–91, retired; *b* 20 Nov. 1920; 2nd *s* of 1st Baron Astor of Hever; *m* 1950, Emily Lucy, *d* of Sir Alexander Kinloch, 12th Bt; two *s* three *d.* *Educ:* Eton; New Coll., Oxford. Served War of 1939–45; Intelligence Corps, Europe and SE Asia (Lieut-Col). Joined The Times as Asst Middle East Correspondent, 1947; elected to Board of The Times, 1956; Dep. Chm., 1959, resigned 1967 on merger with Sunday Times; Chm., The Times Book Co. Ltd, 1960, resigned 1967 on merger with Sunday Times. Chairman: Times Trust, 1967–82; Trust Houses Forte Council, 1971– (Mem. Council, 1962–); Exec. Vice Chm., Olympia Ltd, 1971–73; Director: Winterbottom Energy Trust plc, 1961–86; Phoenix Assurance plc, 1962–85. Dep. Chm., Middlesex Hosp., 1965–74; Chm., King Edward's Hospital Fund for London, 1983–88. Governor, Peabody Donation Fund, 1973–92 (Chm., 1981–92); Hon. Treasurer: Franco-British Soc., 1969–76; Marine Biol Assoc. UK, 1968–78; has served on Council or governing body of: RNLI; RYA; RORC; Air League. Mem. Ct of Assts, Fishmongers' Co. (Prime Warden, 1976–77). In partnership with Sir William Dugdale participated in air races, London-Sydney 1969, London-Victoria 1971. JP Berks, 1953; High Sheriff of Berks, 1963. *Recreations:* sailing, flying, shooting, diving. *Address:* Folly Farm, Sulhamstead, Berks RG7 4DF. *T:* Reading (01734) 302326; 79 Ashley Gardens, Thirleby Road, SW1P 1HG. *T:* 0171–976 6818. *Clubs:* Brooks's, Buck's, Pratt's; Royal Yacht Squadron, Royal Ocean Racing.
See also Baron Astor of Hever.

ASTOR, Major Hon. Sir John (Jacob), Kt 1978; MBE 1945; ERD 1989; DL; Major, Life Guards; *b* 29 Aug. 1918; 4th *s* of 2nd Viscount Astor; *m* 1st, 1944, Ana Inez (marr. diss. 1972; she *d* 1992), *yr d* of late Señor Dr Don Miguel Carcano, KCMG, KBE; one *s* one *d*; 2nd, 1976, Susan Sheppard (marr. diss. 1985), *d* of late Major M. Eveleigh; 3rd, 1988, Marcia de Savary. *Educ:* Eton; New Coll., Oxford. Served War of 1939–45 (MBE, Legion of Honour, French Croix de Guerre). Contested (C) Sutton Div. of Plymouth, 1950; MP (C) Sutton Div. of Plymouth, 1951–Sept. 1959. PPS to Financial Sec. of Treasury, 1951–52. Chairman: Governing Body of Nat. Inst. of Agricultural Engineering, 1963–68; Agric. Res. Council, 1968–78; NEDC for Agricultural Industry, 1978–83. Member: Horserace Totalisator Bd, 1962–68; Horserace Betting Levy Bd, 1976–80. Steward of Jockey Club, 1968–71 and 1983–85. DL 1962, JP, Cambs, 1960–74. *Address:* The Dower House, Hatley Park, Hatley St George, Sandy, Beds SG19 3HL. *T:* Gamlingay (01767) 650266. *Club:* White's.

ASTWOOD, Hon. Sir James (Rufus), KBE 1994; Kt 1982; JP; President, Court of Appeal, Bermuda, since 1994; *b* 4 Oct. 1923; *s* of late James Rufus Astwood, Sr, and Mabel Winifred Astwood; *m* 1952, Gloria Preston Norton; one *s* two *d.* *Educ:* Berkeley Inst., Bermuda; Univ. of Toronto, Canada. Called to the Bar, Gray's Inn, London, Feb. 1956, Hon. Bencher, 1985; admitted to practice at Jamaican Bar, Oct. 1956; joined Jamaican Legal Service, 1957; Dep. Clerk of Courts, 1957–58; Clerk of Courts, Jamaica, 1958–63; Stipendiary Magistrate and Judge of Grand Court, Cayman Islands (on secondment from Jamaica), 1958–59; Resident Magistrate, Jamaica, 1963–74; Puisne Judge, Jamaica, during 1971 and 1973; retd from Jamaican Legal Service, 1974; Sen. Magistrate, Bermuda, 1974–76; Solicitor General, 1976–77; Acting Attorney General, during 1976 and 1977; Acting Dep. Governor for a period in 1977; Chief Justice, 1977–93, Justice of Appeal, 1993–94, Bermuda. Has served on several cttees, tribunals and bds of enquiry, both in Bermuda and Jamaica. *Recreations:* golf, cricket, photography, reading, bridge, travel, cycling. *Address:* Clifton, 8 Middle Road, Devonshire DVO3, Bermuda; PO Box HM 1674, Hamilton HMGX, Bermuda. *Clubs:* Kingston Cricket (Kingston, Jamaica); Castle Harbour Golf, Bermuda Senior Golfers Society, Royal Hamilton Amateur Dinghy, Coral Beach and Tennis, Mid Ocean (Bermuda).

ASTWOOD, Lt-Col Sir Jeffrey (Carlton), Kt 1972; CBE 1966; OBE (mil.) 1946; ED 1942; Speaker of House of Assembly, Bermuda, 1968–72, retired; *b* 5 Oct. 1907; *s* of late Jeffrey Burgess Astwood, Neston, Bermuda, and Lilian Maude (*née* Searles); *m* 1928, Hilda Elizabeth Kay (*née* Onions); one *s* one *d.* *Educ:* Saltus Grammar School, Bermuda. Served local TA, 1922–60; retired as Lt-Col, having commanded since 1943. House of Assembly, Bermuda, 1948–72; Minister of Agriculture, of Immigration and Labour, of Health; Member of Exec. Council; Dep. Speaker, 1957–68. President: Exec. Cttee, Sandys Grammar Sch., 1950–57 (Chm. Trustees, 1950–); Bermuda Sea Cadet Assoc., 1974–78; Chm., St James' Church Vestry. President: Atlantic Investment and Development Co. Ltd; J. B. Astwood & Son Ltd; Belfield-in-Somerset Ltd; Aberfeldy Nurseries Ltd. FInstD. *Recreations:* theatre, horticulture. *Address:* Greenfield, Somerset MA03, Bermuda. *T:* (business) Hamilton 2922245; (home) 2341729. *Clubs:* Royal Bermuda Yacht, Sandys Boat, Somerset Lawn Tennis (Bermuda).

ATCHERLEY, Sir Harold Winter, Kt 1977; Chairman: Aldeburgh Foundation, 1989–94 (Deputy Chairman, 1988–89); Toynbee Hall, 1985–90 (Member, Management Committee, 1979–90); *b* 30 Aug. 1918; *s* of L. W. Atcherley and Maude Lester (*née* Nash); *m* 1st, 1946, Anita Helen (*née* Leslie) (marr. diss. 1990); one *s* two *d*; 2nd, 1990, Mrs Elke Jessett, *d* of late Dr Carl Langbehn. *Educ:* Gresham's Sch.; Heidelberg and Geneva Univs. Joined Royal Dutch Shell Gp, 1937. Served War: Queen's Westminster Rifles, 1939; commissioned Intelligence Corps, 1940; served 18th Infty Div., Singapore; PoW, 1942–45. Rejoined Royal Dutch Shell Gp, 1946: served Egypt, Lebanon, Syria, Argentina, Brazil, 1946–59. Personnel Co-ordinator, Royal Dutch Shell Group, 1964–70, retd. Recruitment Advisor to Ministry of Defence, 1970–71. Chm., Tyzack & Partners, 1979–85; Dir, British Home Stores Ltd, 1973–87. Chairman: Armed Forces Pay Review Body, 1971–82; Police Negotiating Bd, 1983–86 (Dep. Chm., 1982); Member: Top Salaries Review Body, 1971–87; Nat. Staff Cttee for Nurses and Midwives, 1973–77; Cttee of Inquiry into Pay and Related Conditions of Service of Nurses, 1974; Cttee of Inquiry into Remuneration of Members of Local Authorities, 1977. Vice-Chm., Suffolk Wildlife Trust, 1987–90; Mem. Management Cttee, Suffolk Rural Housing Assoc., 1984–. Empress Leopoldina Medal (Brazil), 1958. *Recreations:* music, skiing, good food. *Address:* Conduit House, The Green, Long Melford, Suffolk CO10 9DU. *T:* Sudbury (01787) 310897.

ATHA, Bernard Peter, OBE 1991; Principal Lecturer in Business Studies, Huddersfield Technical College, 1973–90; *b* 27 Aug. 1928; *s* of Horace Michael Atha and Mary Quinlan; unmarried. *Educ:* Leeds Modern Sch.; Leeds Univ. (LLB Hons). Barrister-at-law, Gray's Inn. Commn, RAF, 1950–52. Variety artist on stage; Mem. Equity; films and TV plays. Elected Leeds City Council, 1957; Chm., Leeds Leisure Services Cttee, 1988–; former Chairman: Watch Cttee; Social Services Cttee; Educn Cttee. Vice-Chm., W Leeds HA, 1988–90. Contested (Lab): Penrith and the Border, 1959; Pudsey, 1964. Pres., Leeds Co-op. Soc.; Chm., Leeds Playhouse and Leeds Grand Theatre; Dir, Opera North. Member: Arts Council, 1979–82; Ministerial Working Party on Sport and Recreation, 1974, on Sport for the Disabled, 1989; EU (formerly EC) Sport for Disabled Cttee, 1992–; Internat. Paralympic Cttee, 1993–; Vice-Chm., Sports Council, 1976–80; Chairman: Yorks and Humberside Reg. Sports Council, 1966–76; Nat. Water Sports Centre, 1978–84; UK Sports Assoc. for People with Mental Handicap, 1980– (Pres., INASFMH, 1993–); British Paralympics Assoc., 1989. Vice-Chm., St James' Univ. Hosp. NHS Trust, 1993– (Dir, 1990–). Chairman: Yorks Dance Centre Trust; Red Ladder Theatre Co. Governor, Sports Aid Foundn. FRSA. *Recreations:* sport, the arts, travel. *Address:* 25 Moseley Wood Croft, Leeds, West Yorks LS16 7JJ. *T:* Leeds (0113) 267 2485.

ATHABASCA, Bishop of, since 1992; **Rt. Rev. John Robert Clarke;** *b* 27 July 1938; *s* of Rt Rev. Neville and Alice Clarke; *m* 1964, Nadia Juliann Slusar; one *s* two *d.* *Educ:* Univ. of W Ontario (BA); Huron Coll., London, Ontario (LTh; DD *jure dignitatis,* 1992). Ordained: deacon, 1963; priest, 1964; Curate, St Michael and All Angels, Toronto, 1964–66; Priest-in-charge, Church of the Apostles, Moosonee, 1966–84; Exec. Archdeacon and Treas., Dio. of Athabasca, 1984–91. *Recreations:* woodworking, travelling, canoeing, gardening. *Address:* PO Box 6868, Peace River, Alberta T8S 1S6, Canada. *T:* (home) (403) 6241008; (office) (403) 6242767.

ATHERTON, Alan Royle, CB 1990; Chairman, The Argyll Consultancies PLC, since 1994 (Deputy Chairman, 1992–94); *b* 25 April 1931; *s* of Harold Atherton and Hilda (*née* Royle); *m* 1959, Valerie Kemp (separated 1991); three *s* one *d.* *Educ:* Cowley Sch., St Helens; Sheffield Univ. (BSc (Hons Chem.)). ICI Ltd, 1955–58; Department of Scientific and Industrial Research: SSO, 1959–64; Private Sec. to Permanent Sec., 1960–64; PSO, Road Res. Lab., 1964–65; Principal, Min. of Housing and Local Govt, 1965–70; Asst Sec., Ordnance Survey, 1970–74; Under-Sec., 1975–87, Dep. Sec., 1987–91, DoE. Consultant, Nabarro Nathanson, 1991–. Chm., Local Govt Staff Commn (Eng.), 1993–. Vice Chm., CS Med. Assoc., 1987–. Chm., Queen Elizabeth II Conf. Centre Bd, 1990–93; Dir, Internat. Centre for Facilities, Canada, 1993–; Member: Letchworth Garden City Corp., 1991–94; Historic Royal Palaces Agency Adv. Gp, 1991–. *Recreations:* walking, gardening, opera, Rugby. *Clubs:* Arts, Civil Service.

ATHERTON, David; Music Director: Hong Kong Philharmonic Orchestra, since 1989; Mainly Mozart Festival, Southern California and Northern Mexico, since 1989; Principal Guest Conductor, BBC National Orchestra of Wales, since 1994; *b* 3 Jan. 1944; *s* of Robert and Lavinia Atherton; *m* 1970, Ann Gianetta Drake; one *s* two *d.* *Educ:* Cambridge Univ. (MA). LRAM, LTCL. Music Dir, London Sinfonietta, 1967–73 and 1989–91

(Founder, 1967); Repetiteur, Royal Opera House, Covent Garden, 1967–68; Resident Conductor, Royal Opera House, 1968–79; Principal Conductor and Artistic Advr, 1980–83, Principal Guest Conductor, 1983–86, Royal Liverpool Philharmonic Orch.; Music Dir and Principal Conductor, San Diego Symphony Orch., 1980–87; Artistic Dir and Conductor: London Stravinsky Fest., 1979–82; Ravel/Varèse Fest., 1983–84; Principal Guest Conductor, BBC Symphony Orch., 1985–89. Became youngest conductor in history of Henry Wood Promenade Concerts at Royal Albert Hall, and also at Royal Opera House, 1968; Royal Festival Hall debut, 1969; from 1970 performances in Europe, Middle East, Far East, Australasia, N America. Adapted and arranged Pandora by Roberto Gerhard for Royal Ballet, 1975. Conductor of the year award (Composers' Guild of GB), 1971; Edison award, 1973; Grand Prix du Disque award, 1977; Koussevitzky Award, 1981; Internat. Record Critics Award, 1982; Prix Caecilia, 1982. *Publications:* (ed) The Complete Instrumental and Chamber Music of Arnold Schoenberg and Roberto Gerhard, 1973; (ed) Pandora and Don Quixote Suites by Roberto Gerhard, 1973; contrib., The Musical Companion, 1978, The New Grove Dictionary, 1981. *Recreations:* travel, computers, theatre. *Address:* c/o Harold Holt Ltd, 31 Sinclair Road, W14 0NS.

ATHERTON, James Bernard; Secretary-General, British Bankers' Association, 1982–85; *b* 3 Dec. 1927; *s* of late James Atherton and Edith (*née* Atkinson); *m* 1953, Eileen Margaret Birch; two *s*. *Educ:* Alsop High Sch., Liverpool. Served RAF, 1946–48; Martins Bank, 1943–46 and 1948–69 (Asst Chief Accountant, 1966–69); Barclays Bank, 1969–82 (Chief Clearing Manager, 1969–73, Asst Gen. Manager, 1973–78, Divl Gen. Manager, 1978–82). *Recreations:* opera, gardening. *Address:* Spring House, Empshott, Liss, Hants GU33 6HR. *T:* Blackmoor (01420) 538185.

ATHERTON, Michael; Captain, England cricket team, since 1993; *b* 23 March 1968; *s* of Alan and Wendy Atherton. *Educ:* Manchester Grammar Sch.; Downing Coll., Cambridge (BA Hons History; MA). 1st class début, Cambridge *v* Essex, 1987; joined Lancashire, 1987; Captain: Young England, Sri Lanka 1987, Australia 1988; Cambridge Univ., 1988–89; Combined Universities, 1989; first played for England 1989, *v* Australia. Mem., Editl Board, Wisden Cricket Monthly, 1993–95. *Recreations:* golf, reading; is cricket still a recreation?! *Address:* c/o Lancashire County Cricket Club, Old Trafford, Manchester M16 0PX. *Club:* Groucho.

ATHERTON, Rt. Rev. Mgr. Richard, OBE 1989; President of Ushaw College, since 1991; *b* 15 Feb. 1928; *s* of Richard Atherton and Winifred Mary Atherton (*née* Hurst). *Educ:* St Francis Xavier's Coll., Liverpool; Upholland Coll., Wigan. Ordained priest, 1954; Curate: St Cecilia's, Tuebrook, Liverpool, 1954–60; St Philip Neri's, Liverpool, 1960–65; Prison Chaplain: Walton, Liverpool, 1965–75; Appleton Thorne, Warrington, 1975–77; Principal RC Prison Chaplain, 1977–87; Parish Priest, St Joseph's Leigh, Lancs, 1987–89. *Publications:* Summons to Serve, 1987; New Light on the Psalms, 1993. *Recreations:* walking, reading. *Address:* Ushaw College, Durham DH7 9RH. *T:* 0191–373 1366.

ATHOLL, 10th Duke of, *cr* 1703; **George Iain Murray;** DL; Lord Murray of Tullibardine, 1604; Earl of Tullibardine, Lord Gask and Balquhidder, 1606; Earl of Atholl, 1629; Marquess of Atholl, Viscount Balquhidder, Lord Balvenie, 1676; Marquess of Tullibardine, Earl of Strathtay, Earl of Strathardle, Viscount Glenalmond, Viscount Glenlyon, 1703—all in the peerage of Scotland; Representative Peer for Scotland in the House of Lords, 1958–63; *b* 19 June 1931; *s* of Lieut-Col George Anthony Murray, OBE, Scottish Horse (killed in action, Italy, 1945), and Hon. Mrs Angela Campbell-Preston, (*d* 1981), *d* of 2nd Viscount Cowdray (she *m* 2nd, 1950, Robert Campbell-Preston of Ardchattan, *qv*); *S* kinsman 1957. *Educ:* Eton; Christ Church, Oxford. Director: Westminster Press (Chm., 1974–93); BPM Holdings, 1972–83; Pearson Longman Ltd, 1975–83. Pres., Scottish Landowners Fedn, 1986–91 (Vice-Convener, 1971–76, Convener, 1976–79); Chm., RNLI, 1979–89 (Dep. Chm., 1972–79); Member: Cttee on the Preparation of Legislation, 1973–75; Exec. Cttee, Nat. Trust for Scotland (Vice-Pres., 1977–); Red Deer Commn, 1969–83. DL Perth and Kinross, 1980. *Heir: cousin* John Murray [*b* 19 Jan. 1929; *m* 1956, Margaret Yvonne, *o d* of late Ronald Leonard Leach; two *s* one *d*]. *Address:* Blair Castle, Blair Atholl, Perthshire PH18 5TJ. *T:* Blair Atholl (01796) 481212; 31 Marlborough Hill, NW8 0NG. *Clubs:* Turf, White's; New (Edinburgh).

ATIYAH, Sir Michael (Francis), OM 1992; Kt 1983; MA, PhD Cantab; FRS 1962; FRSE 1985; Master of Trinity College, Cambridge, since 1990; Director, Isaac Newton Institute for Mathematical Sciences, Cambridge, since 1990; *b* 22 April 1929; *e s* of late Edward Atiyah and Jean Levens; *m* 1955, Lily Brown; three *s*. *Educ:* Victoria Coll., Egypt; Manchester Grammar Sch.; Trinity Coll., Cambridge. Research Fellow, Trinity Coll., Camb., 1954–58, Hon. Fellow, 1976; First Smith's Prize, 1954; Commonwealth Fund Fellow, 1955–56; Mem. Inst. for Advanced Study, Princeton, 1955–56, 1959–60, 1967–68, 1987; Asst Lectr in Mathematics, 1957–58, Lectr 1958–61, Univ. of Cambridge; Fellow Pembroke Coll., Cambridge, 1958–61 (Hon. Fellow, 1983); Reader in Mathematics, Univ. of Oxford, and Professorial Fellow of St Catherine's Coll., Oxford, 1961–63 (Hon. Fellow, 1992); Savilian Prof. of Geometry, and Fellow of New College, Oxford, 1963–69; Prof. of Mathematics, Inst. for Advanced Study, Princeton, NJ, 1969–72; Royal Soc. Res. Prof., Mathematical Inst., Oxford, and Professorial Fellow, St Catherine's Coll., Oxford, 1973–90. Visiting Lecturer, Harvard, 1962–63 and 1964–65. Member: Exec. Cttee, Internat. Mathematical Union, 1966–74; SERC, 1984–89; ACOST, 1991–93; President: London Mathematical Soc., 1975–77; Mathematical Assoc., 1981–82; Royal Soc., 1990–95; Chm., European Mathematical Council, 1978–90. Chancellor, Univ. of Leicester, 1995–. Hon. FEng, 1993. Foreign Member: Amer. Acad. of Arts and Scis; Swedish Royal Acad.; Leopoldina Acad.; Nat. Acad. of Scis, USA; Acad. des Sciences, France; Royal Irish Acad.; Czechoslovak Union of Mathematicians and Physicists; Amer. Philos. Soc.; Indian Nat. Science Acad.; Australian Acad. of Scis; Ukrainian Acad. of Scis; Russian Acad. of Scis. Hon. Prof., Chinese Acad. of Scis; Hon. Fellow, Darwin Coll., Cambridge, 1992. Hon. DSc: Bonn, 1968; Warwick, 1969; Durham, 1979; St Andrew's, 1981; Dublin, Chicago, 1983; Edinburgh, 1984; Essex, London, 1985; Sussex, 1986; Ghent, 1987; Reading, Helsinki, 1990; Leicester, 1991; Salamanca, Rutgers, 1992; Wales, Montreal, Waterloo, 1993; Lebanese Univ., Birmingham, Keele, Queen's (Ontario), 1994; Hon. ScD Cantab, 1984; DUniv Open, 1995. Fields Medal, Internat. Congress of Mathematicians, Moscow, 1966; Royal Medal, Royal Soc., 1968; De Morgan Medal, London Mathematical Soc., 1980; Antonio Feltrinelli Prize for mathematical sciences, Accademia Nazionale dei Lincei, Rome, 1981; King Faisal Foundn Internat. Prize for Science, Saudi Arabia, 1987; Copley Medal, Royal Soc., 1988; Gunning Victoria Jubilee Prize, RSE, 1990; Nehru Meml Medal, INSA, 1993; Franklin Medal, Amer. Phil. Soc., 1993. Commander, Order of Cedar (Lebanon), 1994. *Publications:* Collected Works, 5 vols, 1988; The Geometry and Physics of Knots, 1990; papers in mathematical journals. *Recreation:* gardening. *Address:* Master's Lodge, Trinity College, Cambridge CB2 1TQ. *Clubs:* Athenæum, United Oxford & Cambridge University.

See also P. S. Atiyah.

ATIYAH, Prof. Patrick Selim, DCL; FBA 1978; QC 1989; Professor of English Law, and Fellow of St John's College, Oxford University, 1977–88, Hon. Fellow, 1988; *b* 5 March 1931; *s* of Edward Atiyah and D. J. C. Levens; *m* 1951, Christine Best; four *s*. *Educ:* Woking County Grammar Sch. for Boys; Magdalen Coll., Oxford (MA 1957, DCL 1974). Called to the Bar, Inner Temple, 1956. Asst Lectr, LSE, 1954–55; Lectr, Univ. of Khartoum, 1955–59; Legal Asst, BoT, 1961–64; Fellow, New Coll., Oxford, 1964–69; Professor of Law: ANU, 1970–73; Warwick Univ., 1973–77; Visiting Professor: Univ of Texas, 1979; Harvard Law Sch., 1982–83; Duke Univ., 1985. Lectures: Lionel Cohen, Hebrew Univ., Jerusalem, 1980; Oliver Wendell Holmes, Harvard Law Sch., 1981; Cecil Wright Meml, Univ. of Toronto, 1983; Viscount Bennett, Univ. of New Brunswick, 1984; Chorley, LSE, 1985; Hamlyn, Leeds Univ., 1987. Hon. LLD Warwick, 1989. General Editor, Oxford Jl of Legal Studies, 1981–86. *Publications:* The Sale of Goods, 1957, 8th edn 1990; Introduction to the Law of Contract, 1961, 5th edn 1995; Vicarious Liability, 1967; Accidents, Compensation and the Law, 1970, 5th edn (ed Peter Cane), 1993; The Rise and Fall of Freedom of Contract, 1979; Promises, Morals and Law, 1981 (Swiney Prize, RSA/RSP, 1984); Law and Modern Society, 1983, 2nd edn 1995; Essays on Contract, 1987; Pragmatism and Theory in English Law, 1987; (with R. S. Summers) Form and Substance in Anglo-American Law, 1987; articles in legal jls. *Recreations:* gardening, cooking. *Address:* 75 Main Road, Long Hanborough, Witney, Oxon OX8 8JX. *T:* Freeland (01993) 882938.

See also Sir M. F. Atiyah.

ATKIN, Alec Field, CBE 1978; FEng 1979; FIMechE, FRAeS; Managing Director, Marketing, Aircraft Group, British Aerospace, 1981–82, retired; Director, AWA (Consultancy) Ltd, since 1983; *b* 26 April 1925; *s* of Alec and Grace Atkin; *m* 1948, Nora Helen Darby (marr. diss. 1982); two *s* one *d*; *m* 1982, Wendy Atkin. *Educ:* Riley High Sch.; Hull Technical Coll. (DipAe); Hull Univ. (BSc Hons). FIMechE 1955; FRAeS 1952. English Electric Co., Preston: Aerodynamicist, 1950; Dep. Chief Aerodyn., 1954; Head of Exper. Aerodyns, 1957; Asst Chief Engr, then Proj. Manager, 1959; Warton Div., British Aircraft Corporation Ltd: Special Dir, 1964; Dir, 1970; Asst Man. Dir, 1973–75; Dep. Man. Dir, 1975–76; Man. Dir, 1976–77; Man. Dir (Mil.), Aircraft Gp of British Aerospace, and Chm., Warton, Kingston-Brough and Manchester Divs, 1978–81. FRSA. *Recreation:* sailing. *Address:* Les Fougères d'Icart, Icart Road, St Martin, Guernsey GY4 6JG.

ATKINS, family name of **Baron Colnbrook.**

ATKINS, Eileen, CBE 1990; actress; *b* 16 June 1934; *d* of Arthur Thomas Atkins and late Annie Ellen (*née* Elkins); *m* Bill Shepherd. *Educ:* Latymers Grammar Sch., Edmonton; Guildhall Sch. of Music and Drama. *Stage appearances include:* Twelfth Night, Richard III, The Tempest, Old Vic, 1962; The Killing of Sister George, Bristol Old Vic, transf. Duke of York's, 1965 (Best Actress, Standard Awards); The Cocktail Party, Wyndham's, transf. Haymarket, 1968; Vivat! Vivat Regina!, Piccadilly, 1970; Suzanne Andler, Aldwych, 1973; As You Like It, Stratford, 1973; St Joan, Old Vic, 1977; Passion Play, Aldwych, 1981; Medea, Young Vic, 1986; The Winter's Tale, Cymbeline, Mountain Language, NT, 1988; A Room of One's Own, Hampstead, 1989; Exclusive, Strand, 1989; Prin, NY, 1990; The Night of the Iguana, NT, 1992; Vita and Virginia, Ambassadors, 1993; *films include:* Equus, 1974; The Dresser, 1984; Let Him Have It, 1990; Wolf, 1994; *TV appearances include:* The Duchess of Malfi; Sons and Lovers; Smiley's People; Nelly's Version; The Burston Rebellion; Breaking Up; The Vision; Mrs Pankhurst in In My Defence (series), 1990; A Room of One's Own, 1990; The Lost Language of Cranes, 1993; The Maitlands, 1993; Cold Comfort Farm, 1995. Co-created television series: Upstairs Downstairs; The House of Eliott. BAFTA Award, 1985. *Address:* c/o Jonathan Altaras Associates, 2 Goodwins Court, WC2N 4LL.

ATKINS, Leonard B. W.; *see* Walsh-Atkins.

ATKINS, Rt. Rev. Peter Geoffrey; Dean, Theological College of St John the Evangelist, Auckland, since 1991; Lecturer in Liturgy and Evangelism, University of Auckland and Melbourne College of Divinity, since 1991; *b* 29 April 1936; *s* of late Lt-Col Owen Ivan Atkins and Mrs Mary Atkins; *m* 1968, Rosemary Elizabeth (*née* Allen); one *d*. *Educ:* Merchant Taylors' School, Crosby, Liverpool; Sidney Sussex Coll., Cambridge; St John's Coll., Auckland, NZ. MA (Cantab), BD (Otago), LTh (NZ). Deacon 1962, priest 1963; Curate, Karori Parish, Wellington, 1962–66; Priest-Tutor, St Peter's Theological Coll., Siota, Solomon Is, 1966–67; Curate, Dannevirke Parish, dio. Waiapu, 1968–70; Vicar of Waipukurau Parish, 1970–73; Diocesan Sec. and Registrar, Diocese of Waiapu, 1973–79; Canon of St John's Cathedral, Napier, 1974–79; Vicar of Havelock North, 1979–83; Archdeacon of Hawkes Bay, 1979–83; Vicar-Gen., Diocese of Waiapu, 1980–83; Commissary to Archbishop of NZ, 1983; Bishop of Waiapu, 1983–90. *Publications:* Good News in Evangelism, 1992; (contrib.) Pastoral Care in the South Pacific, 1995. *Recreations:* gardening, tennis, music. *Address:* Dean's Lodge, St John's College, 200 St John's Road, Meadowbank, Auckland 5, New Zealand. *T:* (home) (9) 5287086; (office) (9) 5212725, *Fax:* (9) 5212420.

ATKINS, Rt Hon. Robert James; PC 1995; MP (C) South Ribble, since 1983 (Preston North, 1979–83); *b* 5 Feb. 1946; *s* of late Reginald Alfred and of Winifred Margaret Atkins; *m* 1969, Dulcie Mary (*née* Chaplin); one *s* one *d*. *Educ:* Highgate School. Councillor, London Borough of Haringey, 1968–77; Vice-Chm., Greater London Young Conservatives, 1969–70, 1971–72. Contested (C) Luton West, Feb. 1974 and Oct. 1974 general elections. PPS to Minister of State, DoI, then DTI, 1982–84, to Minister without Portfolio, 1984–85, to Sec. of State for Employment, 1985–87; Parly Under Sec. of State, DTI, 1987–89, Dept of Transport, 1989–90, DoE (Minister for Sport), 1990, DES (Minister for Sport), 1990–92; Minister of State, NI Office, 1992–94; Minister of State for the Environment and the Countryside, DoE, 1994–95. Vice-Chm., Cons. Aviation Cttee, 1979–82; Jt Sec., Cons. Defence Cttee, 1979–82. President: Cons. Trade Unionists, 1984–87; Lancs Young Conservatives, 1984–86. Member: Victorian Soc.; Sherlock Holmes Soc. of London; English Heritage; Historic Churches Preservation Trust. Freeman, City of London, 1989. *Publication:* (contrib.) Changing Gear, 1981. *Recreations:* cricket, ecclesiology, wine, Holmesiaria. *Address:* c/o House of Commons, SW1A 0AA. *T:* 0171–219 5080. *Clubs:* MCC, Lord's Taverners', Middlesex County Cricket, Lords and Commons Cricket, Lancashire County Cricket.

ATKINS, Ronald Henry; *b* Barry, Glam, 13 June 1916; *s* of Frank and Elizabeth Atkins; *m*; three *s* two *d*. *Educ:* Barry County Sch.; London Univ. (BA Hons). Teacher, 1949–66 (latterly Head, Eng. Dept, Halstead Sec. Sch.); Lectr, Accrington Coll. of Further Educn, 1970–74. Member: Braintree RDC, 1952–61; Preston Dist Council, 1974–76, 1980–. Contested (Lab) Lowestoft, 1964; MP (Lab) Preston North, 1966–70 and Feb. 1974–1979. *Recreations:* jazz, dancing, walking. *Address:* 38 James Street, Preston, Lancs PR1 4JU *T:* Preston (01772) 251910.

ATKINSON, Sir Alec; *see* Atkinson, Sir J. A.

ATKINSON, Anthony Barnes, FBA 1984; Warden of Nuffield College, Oxford, since 1994; *b* 4 Sept. 1944; *s* of Norman Joseph Atkinson and Esther Muriel Atkinson; *m* 1965, Judith Mary (*née* Mandeville); two *s* one *d*. *Educ:* Cranbrook Sch.; Churchill Coll., Cambridge (MA). Fellow, St John's Coll., Cambridge, 1967–71; Prof. of Econs, Univ. of

Essex, 1971–76; Prof. and Hd of Dept of Political Economy, UCL, 1976–79; Prof. of Econs, LSE, 1980–92; Prof. of Political Economy, and Fellow, Churchill Coll., Cambridge, 1992–94. Vis. Prof. MIT, 1973. Member: Royal Commn on Distribution of Income and Wealth, 1978–79; Retail Prices Index Adv. Cttee, 1984–90; Pension Law Review Cttee, 1992–93; Social Justice Commn, 1992–94. President: European Econ. Assoc., 1989 (Vice-Pres., 1986–88); Internat. Econ. Assoc., 1989–92; Vice-Pres., British Acad., 1988–90. Fellow, Econometric Soc., 1975 (Vice-Pres., 1986–87, Pres., 1988). Hon. Mem., Amer. Econ. Assoc., 1985. Hon. Dr Rer. Pol. Univ. of Frankfurt, 1987; Hon. Dr en Sci. Econ., Univ. of Lausanne, 1988; Hon. Dr: Univ. of Liège, 1989; Athens Univ. of Econs, 1991; Stirling, 1992; Edinburgh, 1994. Scientific Prize, Union des Assurances de Paris, 1986. Editor, Jl of Public Economics, 1972–. *Publications:* Poverty in Britain and the Reform of Social Security, 1969; Unequal Shares, 1972; The Tax Credit Scheme, 1973; Economics of Inequality, 1975; (with A. J. Harrison) Distribution of Personal Wealth in Britain, 1978; (with J. E. Stiglitz) Lectures on Public Economics, 1980; Social Justice and Public Policy, 1982; (jtly) Parents and Children, 1983; (with J. Micklewright) Unemployment Benefits and Unemployment Duration, 1985; Poverty and Social Security, 1989; (with J. Micklewright) Economic Transformation in Eastern Europe and the Distribution of Income, 1992; Public Economics in Action, 1995; articles in Rev. of Econ. Studies, Econ. Jl, Jl of Public Econs, Jl of Econ. Theory. *Address:* 39 Park Town, Oxford OX2 6SL. *T:* Oxford (01865) 56064; Nuffield College, Oxford OX1 1NF.

ATKINSON, Arthur Kingsley Hall, CB 1985; Chief Executive, Intervention Board for Agricultural Produce, 1980–86; *b* 24 Dec. 1926; *er s* of Arthur Hall Atkinson and Florence (*née* Gerrans). *Educ:* Priory Sch., Shrewsbury; Emmanuel Coll., Cambridge (MA). RAF, 1948; MAFF: Asst Principal 1950; Private Sec. 1953; Principal 1956; Asst Sec. 1965; Under Sec., 1973; Cabinet Office, 1976–78; MAFF, 1978–80. *Recreations:* travel, music, gardening. *Address:* Fortfield Lawn, Manor Road, Sidmouth, Devon EX10 8RP.

ATKINSON, Prof. Bernard, FEng, FIChemE; Director-General, BRF International (formerly Director, Brewing Research Foundation), since 1981; *b* 17 March 1936; *s* of late Thomas Atkinson and of Elizabeth Ann (*née* Wilcox); *m* 1957, Kathleen Mary Richardson; two *s*. *Educ:* Farnworth Grammar Sch.; Univ. of Birmingham (BSc); Univ. of Manchester Inst. of Science and Technology; PhD Univ. of Manchester. FEng 1980. Post-Doctoral Fellow and Asst Prof., Rice Univ., Houston, Texas, 1960–63; Lectr, Sen. Lectr in Chem. Engrg, and latterly Reader in Biochem. Engrg, University Coll. of Swansea, 1963–74 (Hon. Fellow, 1991); Prof. and Head of Dept of Chem. Engrg, UMIST, 1974–81; Visiting Professor: UMIST, 1981–86; Swansea, 1986–; Heriot-Watt, 1991–. European Brewery Convention: Mem., Management Cttee and Council, 1990–; Vice Pres., 1991–. Editor, Biochemical Engineering Journal, 1983–93. Senior Moulton Medal, IChemE, 1976; Gairn EEC Medal, Soc. of Engrs, 1985; Presidential Award, Master Brewers' Assoc. of the Americas, 1988. *Publications:* Biochemical Reactors, 1974, trans. Japanese, Russian, Spanish; (with P. F. Cooper) Biological Fluidised Bed Treatment of Water and Waste Water, 1981; (with F. Mavituna) Biochemical Engineering and Biotechnology Handbook, 1982, 2nd edn 1991; (ed) Research and Innovation in the 1990s: the chemical engineering challenge, 1986; (with C. Webb and G. M. Black) Process Engineering Aspects of Immobilised Cell Systems, 1986; numerous contribs to chemical engrg and biochemical engrg jls. *Recreations:* cycling, sailing, walking. *Address:* BRF International, Lyttel Hall, Nutfield, Surrey RH1 4HX. *T:* Nutfield Ridge (01737) 822272; Little Mieders, Borers Arms Road, Copthorne, Crawley, West Sussex RH10 3LJ. *T:* Copthorne (01342) 713181.

ATKINSON, Prof. Bruce Wilson, PhD; Professor of Geography, Queen Mary and Westfield College (formerly at Queen Mary College), University of London, since 1983; *b* 28 Sept. 1941; *s* of J. and S. A. Atkinson. *Educ:* University Coll., London (BSc, PhD). Queen Mary, subseq. Queen Mary and Westfield College, University of London: Lectr, 1964–78; Reader, 1978–83; Hd, Dept of Geog., 1985–89; Dean of Social Scis, 1991–94; Mem., Senate and Acad. Council, Univ. of London, 1991–94. Natural Environment Research Council: Mem., 1982–85, Chm., 1988–91, Aquatic & Atmospheric Phys. Sci. Cttee; Mem., Atmos. Sci., Marine Sci., Terrestrial and Freshwater Sci. and Higher Educn Affairs Cttees, 1988–91. Mem., Meteorol and Atmos. Phys. Sub-cttee, Nat. Cttee on Geodesy and Geophysics, 1988–90. Mem. Council and cttees, and Editor, Weather, RMetS, 1972–79; Chm., Pubns Cttee, 1992–, Mem. Council, 1993–, RGS; Mem., Assoc. Brit. Climatologists, 1970– (Chm., 1976–78). Ed., Progress in Physical Geography, 1977–. Hugh Robert Mill Medal, RMetS, 1974; Back Award, RGS, 1981. *Publications:* Weather Business, 1968; (ed) Dynamical Meteorology, 1981; Meso-scale Atmospheric Circulations, 1981; Weather: Review of UK Statistical Sources, 1985; (ed jtly) Encyclopædic Dictionary of Physical Geography, 1986; (with A. Gadd) Weather: a modern guide to forecasting, 1986; articles in Qly Jl RMetS, Jl Applied Met., Boundary Layer Meteorol., Monthly Weather Rev., Trans IBG, Geog., Weather, Canadian Geog. *Recreations:* walking, music. *Address:* Department of Geography, Queen Mary and Westfield College, Mile End Road, E1 4NS. *T:* 0171–975 5402. *Clubs:* Athenæum, Geographical.

ATKINSON, David Anthony; MP (C) Bournemouth East, since Nov. 1977; *b* 24 March 1940; *s* of late Arthur Joseph Atkinson and of Joan Margaret Atkinson (*née* Zink); *m* 1968, Susan Nicola Pilsworth; one *s* one *d*. *Educ:* St George's Coll., Weybridge; Coll. of Automobile and Aeronautical Engrg, Chelsea. Diplomas in Auto. Engrg and Motor Industry Management. Member: Southend County Borough Council, 1969–72; Essex CC, 1973–78. Mem., Council of Europe, 1979–86, 1987–. PPS, 1979–87, to Rt Hon. Paul Channon, MP (Minister of State, Civil Service Dept, 1979–81, Minister for the Arts, 1981–83, Minister of State, DTI, 1983–86, Sec. of State for Trade and Industry, 1986–87). Nat. Chm., Young Conservative Orgn, 1970–71; President: Christian Solidarity Internat. (UK), 1983– (Chm., 1979–83); Internat. Soc. for Human Rights (UK), 1985–. *Recreations:* mountaineering, art and architecture, travel. *Address:* House of Commons, SW1A 0AA.

ATKINSON, David Rowland; Regional Chairman, British Gas East Midlands, 1987–92; *b* 18 June 1930; *s* of late Rowland Hodgson Atkinson and Nora Marian (*née* Coleman); *m* 1956, Marian Eileen Sales; one *d*. *Educ:* Wrekin College. FCA, CIMgt, CompIGasE. National Coal Board: NW Div., 1955; E Midlands Div., 1961; Chief Accountant, W Midlands Gas, 1969; Dir of Finance, E Midlands Gas, 1977; Dep. Chm., SE Gas, 1983; Dir of Finance, British Gas, 1985. *Recreations:* Rugby, gardening, ciné photography. *Address:* Russetts, 124 The Ridings, Rothley, Leics LE7 7SL.

ATKINSON, Air Marshal Sir David (William), KBE 1982; FFOM; FRCPE; FFPHM; Director-General, Stroke (formerly Chest, Heart and Stroke) Association, 1985–93; Director-General, RAF Medical Services, 1981–84; *b* 29 Sept. 1924; *s* of late David William Atkinson and of Margaret Atkinson; *m* 1948, Mary (*née* Sowerby); one *s*. *Educ:* Edinburgh Univ. (MB, ChB 1948). DPH and DIH, London; FFPHM (FFCM 1976); MFOM 1978, FFOM 1983; FRCPE 1983. Joined RAF, 1949; med. officer appts, UK, Jordan and Egypt, 1949–63; Student, RAF Staff Coll., 1963–64; SMO, RAF Brüggen, Germany, 1964–67; Dep. PMO, HQ Air Support Comd, 1967–70; PMO, HQ Brit. Forces Gulf, Bahrain, 1970–71; OC RAF Hosp., Wegberg, Germany, 1971–73; Dir of Health and Research (RAF), 1974–78; QHP 1977–84; PMO, RAF Strike Command, 1978–81. Freeman, City of London, 1984; Liveryman, Soc. of Apothecaries. CStJ 1981. *Publication:* (jtly) Double Crew Continuous Flying Operations: a study of aircrew sleep patterns, 1970. *Recreations:* walking, gardening, reading, looking at pictures. *Address:* Rosedene, Woodside Lane, Lymington, Hants SO41 8FJ. *Club:* Royal Air Force.

ATKINSON, Frank, CBE 1995 (OBE 1980); FSA; FMA; Director, Beamish North of England Open Air Museum, 1970–87; *b* 13 April 1924; *s* of Ernest Atkinson and Elfrida (*née* Bedford); *m* 1953, Joan Peirson; three *s*. *Educ:* Holgate Grammar Sch., Barnsley; Sheffield Univ. (BSc). Director: Wakefield City Art Gall. and Mus., 1949; Halifax Museums, 1951; Bowes Mus. and Durham Co. Mus. Service, 1958. Member: Working Party on Preservation of Technolog. Material, 1970–71; Wright Cttee on Provincial Museums and Galls, 1971–73; Working Party of Standing Commn on Museums and Galls (Drew Report), 1975–78; Museums and Galleries Commn, 1987–94 (Chm., Registration Cttee, 1988–94). Chairman: Thomas Bewick Birthplace Trust, 1985–91; Northumbrian Tourism Co-ordination Gp, 1989–93. Pres., Museums Assoc., 1974–75. Hon. MA Newcastle upon Tyne, 1971; Hon. DCL Durham, 1987. *Publications:* Aspects of the 18th century Woollen and Worsted Trade, 1956; The Great Northern Coalfield, 1966, 3rd edn 1979; Industrial Archaeology of North East England, 1974; Life and Traditions in Northumberland and Durham, 1977, 2nd edn 1986; North East England: people at work 1860–1950, 1980; Victorian Britain: North East England, 1989; Northern Life, 1991; contribs to Trans Newcomen Soc., Procs of British Spel. Soc., Antiquaries Jl, Museums Jl, etc. *Recreations:* pot-holing (now only in retrospect), computer programming. *Address:* The Old Vicarage, Ovingham, Prudhoe, Northumberland NE42 6BW. *T:* Prudhoe (01661) 835445.

ATKINSON, Sir Frederick John, (Sir Fred Atkinson), KCB 1979 (CB 1971); Hon. Fellow of Jesus College, Oxford, since 1979; *b* 7 Dec. 1919; *s* of George Edward Atkinson and of late Elizabeth Sabina Cooper; *m* 1947, Margaret Grace Gibson; two *d*. *Educ:* Dulwich Coll.; Jesus Coll., Oxford; Hon. Fellow, Jesus Coll., 1979. Lectr, Jesus and Trinity Colls, Oxford, 1947–49; Economic Section, Cabinet Office, 1949–51; British Embassy, Washington, 1952–54; HM Treasury, 1955–62; Economic Adviser, Foreign Office, 1962–63; HM Treasury, 1963–69 (Dep. Dir, Economic Section, Treasury, 1965–69); Controller, Economics and Statistics, Min. of Technology, 1970; Chief Econ. Adviser, DTI, 1970–73; an Asst Sec.-Gen., OECD, Paris, 1973–75; Dep. Sec. and Chief Econ. Advr, Dept of Energy, 1975–77; Chief Economic Adviser, HM Treasury, and Head of Govt Econ. Service, 1977–79. *Publication:* (with S. Hall) Oil and the British Economy, 1983. *Recreation:* reading. *Address:* 26 Lee Terrace, Blackheath, SE3 9TZ. *T:* 0181–852 1040; Tickner Cottage, Aldington, Kent TN25 7EG. *T:* Aldington (01233) 720514.

ATKINSON, Brig. Geoffrey Arthur; Executive Secretary, Royal Academy of Engineering (formerly Fellowship of Engineering), 1990–93; *b* 17 March 1931; *s* of Arthur Vivian Atkinson and Flora Muriel Atkinson (*née* Lucas); *m* 1952, Joyce Eileen Pavey; one *s* one *d*. *Educ:* Berkhamsted Sch.; Royal Military College of Science (BScEng); Manchester Business Sch. CEng, FIMechE. Commnd REME, 1950; Regtl and technical employment, UK, Malaya, BAOR, 1950–60; EME, Queen's Own Hussars, 1960; Instr, RMA Sandhurst, 1962; Technical Staff trng, RMCS, 1963; BEME 20 Armd Bde, 1965; Weapons Staff, Army Sch. of Transport, 1967; CO 7 Armd Workshop, 1970; GSO1(W) DGFVE, 1972; ADEME 1/3 HQ DEME, 1975; Mil. Dir of Studies, Weapons and Vehicles, RMCS, 1977; CCREME HQ 1 BR Corps, BAOR, 1978; Dir of Equipment Engrg, HQ DGEME, 1981; Comdr HQ REME TA, 1983, retired 1984. Hon. Col REME Specialist Units TA, 1986–89. Dep. Sec., Fellowship of Engineering, 1984. Member: Council, Parly and Scientific Cttee, 1991–93; Cttee, Parly Gp for Engrg Develt, 1991–93. Freeman, City of London, 1990; Liveryman, Co. of Engineers, 1991. *Recreations:* sailing, antique furniture restoration.

ATKINSON, Harry Hindmarsh, PhD; consultant; Under Secretary, Director (Special Responsibilities), Science and Engineering Research Council, 1988–92; *b* 5 Aug. 1929; *s* of late Harry Temple Atkinson and Constance Hindmarsh Atkinson (*née* Shields); *m* 1958, Anne Judith Barrett; two *s* one *d*. *Educ:* Nelson Coll., Nelson, NZ; Canterbury University Coll., NZ (BSc, sen. schol.; MSc (1st cl. Hons)), 1948–52. Asst Lectr, Physics, CUC, 1952–53; Research Asst, Cornell Univ., USA, 1954–55; Corpus Christi Coll. and Cavendish Laboratory, Cambridge Univ., 1955–58 (PhD); Sen. Research Fellow, AERE, Harwell, 1958–61; Head, General Physics Group, Rutherford Laboratory, 1961–69; Staff Chief Scientific Adviser, Cabinet Office, 1969–72; Dep. Chief Scientific Officer and Head of Astronomy, Space and Radio Division, SRC, 1972–78; Dir (Astronomy, Space and Radio, and Nuclear Physics), SRC later SERC, 1979–83; Dir Science, SERC, 1983–88. Chm. Council, ESA, 1984–87 (Vice-Chm., 1981–84, UK Deleg., 1974–87); UK Member: EISCAT Council, 1976–86; Bd, Anglo-Aust. Telescope, 1979–88; Council, European Synchrotron Radiation Facility, 1986–88; Chairman: Cttee on Netherlands/UK Astronomy Collaboration, 1981–88; Steering Cttee, Inst. Laue-Langevin, Grenoble, 1984 and 1987 (UK deleg., 1983–88); Assessor, UGC, 1987–89; Member: NI Cttee, UFC, 1989–93; Working Gp on Internat. Collaboration (Cabinet Office), ACOST, 1989; Co-ordinator, UK, Australia, NZ sci. collaboration, 1989–94. Chief Scientist, Loss Prevention Council, 1990–. *Publications:* papers on various branches of physics, science and higher education policy, international comparisons. *Address:* Bampton, Oxon. *Club:* Athenæum.

ATKINSON, Prof. James; Founder Director, Centre for Reformation Studies, Sheffield, since 1983; Professor of Biblical Studies, University of Sheffield, 1967–79, now Emeritus; *b* 27 April 1914; *s* of Nicholas Ridley Atkinson and Margaret (*née* Hindhaugh); *m* 1939, Laura Jean Nutley (decd); one *s* one *d*. *Educ:* Tynemouth High Sch.; Univ. of Durham. MA 1939, MLitt 1950 Durham; DrTheol, Münster, Germany, 1955. Curate, Newcastle upon Tyne, 1937; Precentor, Sheffield Cath., 1941; Vicar, Sheffield, 1944; Fellow, Univ. of Sheffield, 1951; Canon Theologian: Leicester, 1954–70; Sheffield, 1971–93; Reader in Theology, Univ. of Hull, 1956; Vis. Prof., Chicago, 1966; Public Orator, Univ. of Sheffield, 1972–79; Consultant Prof. with Evangelical Anglican Res. Centre, Latimer House, Oxford, 1981–84; Special Prof. in Reformation Theol., Univ. of Nottingham, 1993–. Examining Chaplain to: Bp of Leicester, 1968–79; Bp of Derby, 1978–88. Member: Anglican-Roman Catholic Preparatory Commission, 1967–; Gen. Synod of Church of England, 1975–80; Marriage Commn, 1976–78. Pres., Soc. for Study of Theology, 1978–80; Mem., Acad. Internat. des Sciences Religieuses, 1980–. *Publications:* Library of Christian Classics, Vol. XVI, 1962; Rome and Reformation, 1965; Luther's Works, Vol. 44, 1966; Luther and the Birth of Protestantism, 1968; (trans. Spanish 1971, Italian 1983); The Reformation, Paternoster Church History, Vol. 4, 1968; The Trial of Luther, 1971; Martin Luther: Prophet to the Church Catholic, 1983; The Darkness of Faith, 1987; contribs to learned jls, also essays and parts of books. *Recreations:* gardening, music. *Address:* Leach House, Hathersage, Derbyshire S30 1BA. *T:* Hope Valley (01433) 650570; Centre for Reformation Studies, St George's Hall, Portobello, Sheffield S1 4DP. *T:* Sheffield (0114) 276 8555, ext. 5015.

See also Sir Robert Atkinson.

ATKINSON, Sir John Alexander, (Sir Alec Atkinson), KCB 1978 (CB 1976); DFC 1943; Second Permanent Secretary, Department of Health and Social Security, 1977–79; *b* 9 June 1919; *yr s* of late Rev. R. F. Atkinson and late Harriet Harrold Atkinson, BSc (*née* Lowdon); *m* 1945, Marguerite Louise Pearson, MA; one *d*. *Educ:* Kingswood Sch.;

Queen's Coll., Oxford. Served in RAF, 1939–45. Asst Prin., 1946, Prin., 1949, Min. of Nat. Insce; Cabinet Office, 1950–52; Prin. Private Sec. to Minister of Pensions and Nat. Insce, 1957–58; Asst Sec., 1958; Under-Sec., Min. of Social Security, later DHSS, 1966–73; Dep. Sec., DHSS, 1973–76. Member: Panel of Chairmen, CSSB, 1979–88; Occupational Pensions Bd, 1981–88. Chm., Working Gp on Pensions and Divorce, Pensions Management Inst. with Law Soc., 1992–93. Pres., Kingswood Assoc., 1983. *Address:* Bleak House, The Drive, Belmont, Sutton, Surrey SM2 7DH. *T:* 0181–642 6479. *Club:* United Oxford & Cambridge University.

ATKINSON, Kenneth Neil, FIPD; Managing Director, Tavel Training Co. Ltd, since 1995; *b* 4 April 1931; *s* of William Atkinson and Alice Reid. *Educ:* Kingussie High Sch., Inverness-shire. ARCM 1961; FIPD (FIPM 1986). Various appts, Min. of Labour and Dept of Employment, 1948–67; Dep. Chief Conciliation Officer, Dept of Employment, 1968–72; Dir, Industry Trng Bd Relations, MSC, 1973–78; Manpower Services Dir, Scotland, 1979–82; Dir of Youth Training, Training Agency (formerly Manpower Services/Training Commn), 1983–89; Dir, then Chief Exec., ABTA Nat. Trng Bd, 1989–94. Chm., Prince's Trust Community Venture, 1989–92; Mem. Bd, Prince's Trust Volunteers, 1993–94. Mem., Council, CGLI, 1991–. *Recreations:* tennis, choral and solo singing, conducting. *Address:* 57 St Andrews Wharf, 12 Shad Thames, SE1 2YN. *T:* 0171–407 7491. *Club:* Royal Scottish Automobile (Glasgow).

ATKINSON, Leonard Allan, CMG 1963; *b* 6 Dec. 1906; *s* of L. Atkinson; *m* 1933, Annie R., *d* of A. E. Wells; one *s* two *d*. *Educ:* Wellington Coll. and Victoria Univ. of Wellington, New Zealand. Joined Customs Dept, 1924; Inspector, Public Service Commission, 1941–44; Sec., 1944–47; Asst Comr, 1947–54; Commission Member, 1954–58; Chm., 1958–62; Chm., State Services Commission, NZ, 1963–66. *Recreation:* bowls. *Address:* 181 The Parade, Island Bay, Wellington, NZ. *Club:* Wellington (NZ).

ATKINSON, Mary; *see under* Hardwick, Mollie.

ATKINSON, Michael William, CMG 1985; MBE 1970; HM Diplomatic Service, retired; *b* 11 April 1932; *m* 1963, Veronica Bobrovsky; two *s* one *d*. *Educ:* Purley County Grammar School; Queen's College, Oxford (BA Hons). Served FO, Vientiane, Buenos Aires, British Honduras, Madrid; FCO 1975; NATO Defence Coll., 1976; Counsellor, Budapest, 1977–80, Peking, 1980–82; Hd of Consular Dept, FCO, 1982–85; Ambassador: to Ecuador, 1985–89; to Romania, 1989–92.

ATKINSON, Norman; *b* 25 March 1923; *s* of George Atkinson, Manchester; *m* 1948, Irene Parry. *Educ:* elementary and technical schs. Served apprenticeship, Metropolitan Vickers Ltd, Trafford Park. Member of Manchester City Council, 1945–49. Chief Design Engineer, Manchester University, 1957–64. Contested (Lab) Wythenshawe, 1955, Altrincham and Sale, 1959. MP (Lab) Tottenham, 1964–87. Treasurer, Labour Party, 1976–81. Mem., Governing Body, Imperial Coll., London, 1975–. *Recreations:* walking, cricket, football, oil painting. *Address:* 4 Willow Court, 31 Willow Place, SW1P 1JJ. *Club:* Arts.

ATKINSON, Rev. Canon Peter Gordon; Rector, Lavant, since 1994; *b* 26 Aug. 1952; *m* 1983, Lynne Wilcock; two *s* one *d*. *Educ:* St John's Coll., Oxford (BA 1974; MA 1978); Westcott House, Cambridge. Ordained: deacon, 1979; priest, 1980; Asst Curate, Clapham Old Town Team Ministry, 1979–83; Priest-in-charge, St Mary, Tatsfield, 1983–90; Rector, Holy Trinity, Bath, 1990–91; Principal, Chichester Theol Coll., 1991–94; Bursalis Preb., Chichester Cathedral, 1991–. *Publication:* (contrib.) Stepping Stones: joint essays on Anglican Catholic and Evangelical Unity, ed C. Baxter, 1987. *Recreations:* reading, walking, painting. *Address:* The Rectory, Pook Lane, East Lavant, Chichester, West Sussex PO18 0AH. *T:* Chichester (01243) 527313.

ATKINSON, Peter Landreth; MP (C) Hexham, since 1992; *b* 19 Jan. 1943; *s* of Major Douglas Wilson Atkinson, 19th King George's Own Lancers (*d* Burma, 1945) and of Amy Landreth; *m* 1976, Brione, *d* of late Comdr Arthur Darley, RN and Elspeth Darley; two *d*. *Educ:* Cheltenham Coll. Journalist, 1961–87 (formerly News Editor, Evening Standard); Dep. Dir, British Field Sports Soc., 1987–92. Councillor: London Borough of Wandsworth, 1978–82; Suffolk County Council, 1989–92. Member: Select Cttee on Scottish Affairs, 1992–; European Legislation Cttee, 1992–. *Recreations:* shooting, racing, gardening. *Address:* House of Commons, SW1A 0AA. *Clubs:* Turf; Albert Edward (Hexham).

ATKINSON, Reay; *see* Atkinson, W. R.

ATKINSON, Sir Robert, Kt 1983; DSC 1941; RD 1947; FEng; Chairman, British Shipbuilders, 1980–84; *b* 7 March 1916; *s* of Nicholas and Margaret Atkinson; *m* 1st, 1941, Joyce Forster (*d* 1973); one *s* one *d*; 2nd, 1977, Margaret Hazel Walker. *Educ:* London Univ. (BSc(Eng) Hons). MIMechE, CEng, FEng 1983. Served War 1939–45 (DSC 1941 and two Bars, 1st, 1943, 2nd, 1944, mentioned in Despatches, 1943). Managing Director: Wm Doxford, 1957–61; Tube Investments (Eng), 1961–67; Unicorn Industries, 1967–72; Chm., Aurora Holdings, Sheffield, 1972–84; Dir, Stag Furniture Hldgs, 1973–92. *Publications:* The Design and Operating Experience of an Ore Carrier Built Abroad, 1957; The Manufacture of Steel Crankshafts, 1960; Some Crankshaft Failures: Investigation into Causes and Remedies, 1960; technical papers. *Recreations:* salmon fishing, walking, gardening. *Address:* Southwood House, Itchen Abbas, Winchester, Hants SO21 1AT. *Club:* Royal Thames Yacht.

See also Prof. James Atkinson.

ATKINSON, Rowan Sebastian; actor and writer; *b* 6 Jan. 1955; *s* of late Eric Atkinson and of Ella May Atkinson; *m* 1990, Sunetra Sastry; one *s*. *Educ:* Durham Cathedral Choristers' Sch.; St Bees Sch.; Newcastle Univ.; Oxford Univ. (BSc, MSc). *Stage:* Beyond a Joke, Hampstead, 1978; Oxford Univ. Revues at Edinburgh Festival Fringe; youngest person to have a one-man show in the West End of London, 1981; The Nerd, 1984; The New Revue, 1986; The Sneeze, 1988; *television:* Not the Nine O'clock News, 1979–82; The Black Adder, 1983; Blackadder II, 1985; Blackadder the Third, 1987; Blackadder goes Forth, 1989; Mr Bean, The Return of Mr Bean, The Curse of Mr Bean, 1990–94; *films:* The Tall Guy, 1989; The Appointment of Dennis Jennings, 1989; The Witches, 1990; Hot Shots—Part Deux, 1993; Four Weddings and a Funeral, 1994; The Lion King, 1994. *Recreations:* motor cars, motor sport. *Address:* c/o PBJ Management Ltd, 5 Soho Square, W1V 5DE. *T:* 0171–287 1112.

ATKINSON, Prof. Thomas, PhD, DSc, DEng; FEng 1987; Professor and Head of Department of Mining Engineering, Nottingham University, 1977–88, now Emeritus; Chairman, Consolidated Coalfields Ltd, 1986–91; *b* 23 Jan. 1924; *s* of Thomas Bell and Elizabeth Atkinson; *m* 1948, Dorothy; one *d*. *Educ:* Imperial Coll., London. DIC; PhD London, 1973; DSc Nottingham, 1988; DEng Witwatersrand, 1989. FIMM, FIMinE, FIEE, FIMechE. FRSA. Served RN, 1942–46. Charlaw and Sacriston Collieries Ltd, Durham, 1938–42; NCB, 1946–49; Andrew Yule, India, 1949–53; KWPR, Australia, 1953–56; Mining Engr, Powell Duffryn Technical Services Ltd, 1956–68; Sen. Lectr, Imperial Coll., 1968–73; Head of Coal Mining Div., Shell Internat. Petroleum Maatschappij BV, Holland, 1973–77. Dir, British Mining Consultants Ltd, 1969–88. Chm., Nat. Awards Tribunal, British Coal (formerly NCB), 1984–. *Publications:* contribs to Mining Engrg, Mineral Econs, Mine Electrics, etc. *Recreation:* painting. *Address:* 27 Kirk Lane, Ruddington, Nottingham NG11 6NN. *T:* Nottingham (0115) 984 2400. *Club:* Chaps.

ATKINSON, (William) Reay, CB 1985; FBCS; Under Secretary, 1978–86, and Regional Director, North Eastern Region, 1981–86, Department of Industry; *b* 15 March 1926; *s* of William Edwin Atkinson and Lena Marion (*née* Haselhurst); *m*; one *s* two *d*; *m* 1983, Rita Katherine (*née* Bunn). *Educ:* Gosforth Grammar Sch., Newcastle upon Tyne; King's Coll., Durham Univ.; Worcester Coll., Oxford. Served RNVR, 1943–46. Entered Civil Service as Inspector of Taxes, 1950; Principal, 1958, Asst. Sec., 1965; Secretaries Office, Inland Revenue, 1958–61 and 1962–69; Asst Sec., Royal Commn on the Press, 1961–62; Civil Service Dept, 1969; Under Sec., and Dir, Central Computer Agency, CSD, 1973–78. Chm., Northern Development Co. Ltd, 1986–90; Director: English Estates Corp., 1986–94; Northern Rock Building Soc., 1987–; Belasis Hall Technol. Park, 1989–; Maryport Develt Co. Ltd, 1989–. Chm of Governors, Univ. of Northumbria at Newcastle (formerly Newcastle-upon-Tyne Polytechnic), 1989– (Hon. Fellow, 1987). *Recreations:* fell walking, music. *Address:* High Dryburn, Garrigill, near Alston, Cumbria CA9 3EJ.

ATTALI, Jacques; Member, Conseil d'Etat, France, 1981–90 and since 1993; Président, Attali et Associés, since 1994; *b* 1 Nov. 1943. *Educ:* Ecole Polytechnique; Inst. d'Etudes Politiques de Paris; Ecole des Mines; Ecole Nat. d'Admin. Dr d'Etat en Sci. Econ. Conseil d'Etat: Auditeur, 1970; Maître des Requêtes, 1977; Conseiller, 1989; Special Advr to President of French Republic, 1981–91; Pres., EBRD, 1991–93. *Publications:* Analyse économique de la vie politique, 1972; Modèles Politiques, 1973; (with Marc Guillaume) L'Anti-Economique, 1974; La Parole et l'outil, 1975; Bruits, 1976; La nouvelle Economie Française, 1977; L'Ordre Cannibale, 1979; Les Trois Mondes, 1981; Histoire du Temps, 1982; La figure de Fraser, 1984; Un homme d'influence, 1985; Au propre et au figuré, 1988; Lignes d'Horizon, 1990; 1492, 1991; Verbatim, 1993; Europe(s), 1994; L'Economie de l'Apocalypse, 1995; Verbatim II, 1995; *fiction:* La vie eternelle, roman, 1989; Le premier Jour après moi, 1990; Il viendra, 1994; Manuel, l'Enfant Rêve, 1994. *Address:* 28 rue Bayard, 75008 Paris, France.

ATTALLAH, Naim Ibrahim; Book Publisher and Proprietor: Quartet Books, since 1976; The Women's Press, since 1977; Robin Clark, since 1980; Group Chief Executive, Asprey PLC; Managing Director: Mappin & Webb, since 1990; Watches of Switzerland; Executive Director, Garrard, since 1990; *b* 1 May 1931; *s* of Ibrahim and Genevieve Attallah; *m* 1957, Maria Attallah (*née* Nykolyn); one *s*. *Educ:* Battersea Polytechnic. Foreign Exchange Dealer, 1957; Financial Consultant, 1966; Dir of cos, 1969–; Financial Dir and Jt Man. Dir, Asprey of Bond Street, 1979–92; Magazine Proprietor: The Literary Review, 1981–; The Wire, 1984–; The Oldie, 1991–94. Proprietor, Academy Club, 1989–. Launched Parfums Namara, Avant l'Amour and Après l'Amour, 1985, Naïdor, 1987, l'Amour de Namara, 1990. *Theatre:* co-presenter, Happy End, Lyric, 1975; presented and produced, The Beastly Beatitudes of Balthazar B, Duke of York's, 1981; co-prod, Trafford Tanzi, Mermaid, 1982; *films:* co-prod (with David Frost), The Slipper and the Rose, 1974–75; exec. producer, Brimstone and Treacle, 1982; also prod and presented TV docs. *Publications:* Women, 1987; Singular Encounters, 1990; Of a Certain Age, 1992; More of a Certain Age, 1993; Speaking for the Oldie, 1995; A Timeless Passion (novel), 1995; contrib. Literary Review, Oldie, and most nat. newspapers. *Recreations:* classical music, opera, theatre, cinema, photography. *Address:* 106 Regent Street, W1R 6JH. *T:* 0171–734 5842.

ATTENBOROUGH, family name of **Baron Attenborough**.

ATTENBOROUGH, Baron *cr* 1993 (Life Peer), of Richmond upon Thames, in the London Borough of Richmond upon Thames; **Richard Samuel Attenborough,** Kt 1976; CBE 1967; actor, producer and director; Goodwill Ambassador for UNICEF, since 1987; *b* 29 Aug. 1923; *s* of late Frederick L. Attenborough; *m* 1945, Sheila Beryl Grant Sim; one *s* two *d*. *Educ:* Wyggeston Grammar Sch., Leicester. Leverhulme Schol. to Royal Acad. of Dramatic Art, 1941 (Bancroft Medal). First stage appearance as Richard Miller in Ah Wilderness, Intimate Theatre, Palmers Green, 1941; Ralph Berger in Awake and Sing, Arts Theatre (West End début), 1942; The Little Foxes, Piccadilly Theatre, 1942; Brighton Rock, Garrick, 1943. Joined RAF 1943; seconded to RAF Film Unit for Journey Together, 1944; demobilised, 1946. Returned to stage in The Way Back (Home of the Brave), Westminster, 1949; To Dorothy, a Son, Savoy, 1950, Garrick, 1951; Sweet Madness, Vaudeville, 1952; The Mousetrap, Ambassadors, 1952–54; Double Image, Savoy, 1956–57, St James's, 1957; The Rape of the Belt, Piccadilly, 1957–58. *Film: appearances:* In Which We Serve (screen début), 1942; School for Secrets, The Man Within, Dancing With Crime, Brighton Rock, London Belongs to Me, The Guinea Pig, The Lost People, Boys in Brown, Morning Departure, Hell is Sold Out, The Magic Box, Gift Horse, Father's Doing Fine, Eight O'Clock Walk, The Ship That Died of Shame, Private's Progress, The Baby and the Battleship, Brothers in Law, The Scamp, Dunkirk, The Man Upstairs, Sea of Sand, Danger Within, I'm All Right Jack, Jet Storm, SOS Pacific; The Angry Silence (also co-prod), 1959; The League of Gentlemen, 1960; Only Two Can Play, All Night Long, 1961; The Dock Brief, The Great Escape, 1962; Séance On a Wet Afternoon (also prod; Best actor, San Sebastian Film Fest. and British Film Acad.), The Third Secret, 1963; Guns at Batasi (Best actor, British Film Acad.), 1964; The Flight of the Phœnix, 1965; The Sand Pebbles (Hollywood Golden Globe), 1966; Dr Dolittle (Hollywood Golden Globe), The Bliss of Mrs Blossom, 1967; Only When I Larf, 1968; The Last Grenade, A Severed Head, David Copperfield, Loot, 1969; 10 Rillington Place, 1970; And Then There Were None, Rosebud, Brannigan, Conduct Unbecoming, 1974; The Chess Players, 1977; The Human Factor, 1979; Jurassic Park, 1993; Miracle on 34th Street, 1994; *produced:* Whistle Down the Wind, 1961; The L-Shaped Room, 1962; *directed:* Young Winston (Hollywood Golden Globe), 1972; A Bridge Too Far (Evening News Best Drama Award), 1976; Magic, 1978; A Chorus Line, 1985; *produced and directed:* Oh! What a Lovely War (16 Internat. Awards incl. Hollywood Golden Globe and SFTA UN Award), 1968; Gandhi (8 Oscars, 5 BAFTA Awards, 5 Hollywood Golden Globes, Dirs' Guild of America Award for Outstanding Directorial Achievement), 1980–81; Cry Freedom (Berlinale Kamera; BFI Award for Technical Achievement), 1987; Chaplin, 1992; Shadowlands, 1993 (Alexander Korda Award for Outstanding British Film of the Year, BAFTA). Formed: Beaver Films with Bryan Forbes, 1959; Allied Film Makers, 1960. Chairman: Goldcrest Films & Television Ltd, 1982–87; Channel Four Television, 1987–92 (Dep. Chm., 1980–86); Capital Radio, 1972–92 (Life Pres., 1992–); Duke of York's Theatre, 1979–92. Dir, Chelsea Football Club, 1969–82 (Life Vice Pres., 1993). Chairman: Actor's Charitable Trust, 1956–88 (Pres., 1988–); Combined Theatrical Charities Appeals Council, 1964–88 (Pres., 1988–); BAFTA (formerly SFTA), 1969–70 (Vice-Pres., 1971–94); RADA, 1972– (Mem. Council, 1963–); UK Trustees, Waterford-Kamhlaba Sch., Swaziland, 1976– (Gov., 1987–); BFI, 1981–92; Cttee of Inquiry into the Arts and Disabled People, 1983–85; British Screen Adv. Council, 1987–; European Script Fund, 1988–; Member: British Actors' Equity Assoc. Council, 1949–73; Cinematograph Films Council, 1967–73; Arts Council of GB, 1970–73. Trustee: Tate Gall., 1976–82 and 1994– (Tate Foundn, 1986–); Foundn for Sport and the Arts, 1991–. Gov., Nat. Film Sch., 1970–81; Dir, Young Vic, 1974–84. Pres., Muscular Dystrophy Gp of GB, 1971– (Vice-Pres., 1962–71); Chm., Help a London Child; Gov., Motability, 1977–. Patron:

Kingsley Hall Community Centre, 1982–; RA Centre for Disability and the Arts, Leicester, 1990–. President: The Gandhi Foundn, 1983–; Brighton Festival, 1984–; British Film Year, 1984–86; Arts for Health, 1989–; Gardner Centre for the Arts, Sussex Univ., 1990– (Patron, 1969–90). Pro-Chancellor, Sussex Univ., 1970–. Fleming Meml Lect., RTS, 1989. Fellow: BAFTA, 1983; BFI, 1992; FKC 1993. Freeman, City of Leicester, 1990. Hon. DLitt: Leicester, 1970; Kent, 1981; Sussex, 1987; Hon. DCL Newcastle, 1974; Hon. LLD Dickinson, Penn., 1983. Evening Standard Film Award, 40 years service to British Cinema, 1983; Award of Merit for Humanitarianism in Film Making, European Film Awards, 1988; Shakespeare Prize, FVS Foundn, Hamburg, 1992. Martin Luther King, Jr Peace Prize, 1983. Padma Bhushan (India), 1983; Commandeur, Ordre des Arts et des Lettres (France), 1985; Chevalier, Légion d'Honneur (France), 1988. *Publications:* In Search of Gandhi, 1982; (with Diana Carter) Richard Attenborough's Chorus Line, 1986; Cry Freedom, A Pictorial Record, 1987. *Recreations:* collecting paintings and sculpture, listening to music, watching football. *Address:* Old Friars, Richmond Green, Surrey TW9 1NQ. *Clubs:* Garrick, Beefsteak.

See also Sir D. F. Attenborough.

ATTENBOROUGH, Sir David (Frederick), Kt 1985; CVO 1991; CBE 1974; FRS 1983; broadcaster and naturalist; *b* 8 May 1926; *s* of late Frederick Levi Attenborough; *m* 1950, Jane Elizabeth Ebsworth Oriel; one *s* one *d*. *Educ:* Wyggeston Grammar Sch. for Boys, Leicester; Clare Coll., Cambridge (Hon. Fellow, 1980). Served in Royal Navy, 1947–49. Editorial Asst in an educational publishing house, 1949–52; joined BBC Television Service as trainee producer, 1952; undertook zoological and ethnographic filming expeditions to: Sierra Leone, 1954; British Guiana, 1955; Indonesia, 1956; New Guinea, 1957; Paraguay and Argentina, 1958; South West Pacific, 1959; Madagascar, 1960; Northern Territory of Australia, 1962; the Zambesi, 1964; Bali, 1969; Central New Guinea, 1971; Celebes, Borneo, Peru and Colombia, 1973; Mali, British Columbia, Iran, Solomon Islands, 1974; Nigeria, 1975; Controller, BBC-2, BBC Television Service, 1965–68; Dir of Programmes, Television, and Mem., Bd of Management, BBC, 1969–72. Writer and presenter, BBC series: Tribal Eye, 1976; Wildlife on One, annually 1977–; Life on Earth, 1979; The Living Planet, 1984; The First Eden, 1987; Lost Worlds, Vanished Lives, 1989; The Trials of Life, 1990; Life in the Freezer, 1993; The Private Life of Plants, 1995. Huw Wheldon Meml Lecture, RTS, 1987. President: BAAS, 1990–91; RSNC, 1991–; Mem., Nature Conservancy Council, 1973–82. Trustee: WWF UK, 1965–69, 1972–82, 1984–90; WWF Internat., 1979–86; British Museum, 1980–; Science Museum, 1984–87; Royal Botanic Gardens, Kew, 1986–92. Corresp. Mem., Amer. Mus. Nat. Hist., 1985. Fellow, BAFTA 1980. Hon. Fellow: Manchester Polytechnic, 1976; UMIST, 1980; Hon. FRCP 1991. Special Award, SFTA, 1961; Silver Medal, Zool Soc. of London, 1966; Silver Medal, RTS, 1966; Desmond Davis Award, SFTA, 1970; Cherry Kearton Medal, RGS, 1972; Kalinga Prize, UNESCO, 1981; Washburn Award, Boston Mus. of Sci., 1983; Hopper Day Medal, Acad. of Natural Scis, Philadelphia, 1983; Founder's Gold Medal, RGS, 1985; Internat. Emmy Award, 1985; Encyclopaedia Britannica Award, 1987; Livingstone Medal, RSGS, 1990; Franklin Medal, RSA, 1990; Golden Kamera Award, Berlin, 1993. Hon. DLitt: Leicester, 1970; City, 1972; London, 1980; Birmingham, 1982; Hon. DSc: Liverpool, 1974; Heriot-Watt, 1978; Sussex, 1979; Bath, 1981; Ulster, Durham, 1982; Keele, 1986; Oxford, 1988; Plymouth, 1992; Hon. LLD: Bristol, 1977; Glasgow, 1980; DUniv: Open Univ., 1980; Essex, 1987; Antwerp, 1993; Hon. ScD Cambridge, 1984; Hon. DVetMed Edinburgh, 1994. Hon. Freeman, City of Leicester, 1990. Comdr of Golden Ark (Netherlands), 1983. *Publications:* Zoo Quest to Guiana, 1956; Zoo Quest for a Dragon, 1957; Zoo Quest in Paraguay, 1959; Quest in Paradise, 1960; Zoo Quest to Madagascar, 1961; Quest under Capricorn, 1963; The Tribal Eye, 1976; Life on Earth, 1979; The Living Planet, 1984, rev. edn 1985; The First Eden, 1987; The Trials of Life, 1990; The Private Life of Plants, 1994. *Recreations:* music, tribal art, natural history. *Address:* 5 Park Road, Richmond, Surrey TW10 6NS.

See also Baron Attenborough.

ATTENBOROUGH, John Philip, CMG 1958; CBE 1953 (OBE 1946); retired; *b* 6 Nov. 1901; *s* of late Frederick Samuel and Edith Attenborough; *m* 1947, Lucie Blanche Woods, *y d* of late Rev. J. R. and Mrs Prenter and *widow* of late Dr P. P. Murphy; one step *s*. *Educ:* Manchester Grammar Sch.; Corpus Christi Coll., Oxford (MA). Superintendent of Education, Northern Nigeria, 1924–30; Lecturer and Senior Inspector, Education Dept, Palestine, 1930–37; Dir of Education, Aden, 1937–46; Deputy Dir of Education, Palestine, 1946–48; Asst Educational Adviser, Colonial Office, 1948; Dir of Education, Tanganyika, 1948–55; Mem. for Social Services, Tanganyika, 1955–57; Min. for Social Services, Tanganyika, 1957–58; Consultant: UNICEF, 1963–65; UNESCO, 1967; Devon, CC, 1961–68; Mem. SW Regional Hosp. Bd, 1965–71. Pres. Torbay Conservative Assoc., 1967–79. *Address:* 21 Thorncliff Close, Torquay, Devon TQ1 2QW. *T:* Torquay (01803) 297291.

ATTENBOROUGH, Peter John; Director of Educational and Community Care Projects, The Rank Foundation, since 1994; Headmaster of Charterhouse, 1982–93; *b* 4 April 1938; *m* 1967, Alexandra Deidre Campbell Page; one *s* one *d*. *Educ:* Christ's Hospital; Peterhouse, Cambridge. BA Classics 1960, MA 1964. Asst Master, Uppingham Sch., 1960–75 (Housemaster, Senior Classics Master); Asst Master, Starehe Boys' Centre, Nairobi, 1966–67; Headmaster, Sedbergh Sch., 1975–81. Chairman: Common Entrance Cttee of Independent Schs, 1983–88; Schools Arabic Project, 1986–87; Mem., HMC Cttee, 1986–90. Almoner, Christ's Hosp., 1987–; Governor: Ashdown House, 1983–93; Haslemere Prep. Sch., 1986–93; St Edmund's Sch., 1986–94; Brambletye Sch., 1989–; Caldicott Sch., 1990–93; Trustee, Uppingham Sch., 1993–. Freeman, City of London, 1965; Liveryman, Skinners' Co., 1978. *Address:* Rawmarsh Cottage, Linton, near Ross-on-Wye, Herefords HR9 7RX.

ATTENBOROUGH, Philip John, CBE 1994; publisher; Deputy Chairman, Hodder Headline plc, since 1993 (Chairman, Hodder & Stoughton Ltd and Hodder & Stoughton Holdings Ltd, 1975–93); *b* 3 June 1936; *er s* of late John Attenborough, CBE, and Barbara (*née* Sandle); *m* 1963, Rosemary, *y d* of Dr W. B. Littler, *qv*; one *s* one *d*. *Educ:* Rugby; Trinity Coll., Oxford. Christmas postman (parcels), 1952–54; Nat. Service, Sergeant 68th Regt RA, Oswestry, 1956; lumberjack, Blind River, Ont, 1957; joined Hodder & Stoughton, 1957: Export Manager, 1960; Dir, 1963; Sales Dir, 1969. Chm., The Lancet Ltd, 1977–91; Dir, Book Tokens Ltd, 1985–. Publishers Association: Mem. Council, 1976–92 (Treasurer, 1981–82; Vice-Pres., 1982–83, 1985–86; Pres., 1983–85); Leader, delegns of Brit. publishers to China, 1978, to Bangladesh, India and Pakistan, 1986, to India, 1990; Mem., Exec. Cttee, IPA, 1988– (Vice-Pres., 1992–); Chairman: Book Develt Council, 1977–79; PA Freedom to Publish Cttee, 1987–92; Member: British Council Publishers Adv. Cttee, 1977–93 (Chm., 1989–93); British Library Adv. Council, 1986–89; UK Rep., Fédération des Editeurs Européens, 1986–93; Advr, UNESCO Publishing, 1992–. Gov., Judd Sch., Tonbridge, 1987–. Liveryman, Skinners' Co., 1970 (extra Mem. Court, 1985–88). *Publication:* The Rebirth of European Publishing: an Anglo-European perspective of 1992, 1991. *Recreations:* trout fishing, playing golf and tennis, watching cricket. *Address:* Coldhanger, Seal Chart, near Sevenoaks, Kent TN15 0EJ. *T:* Sevenoaks (01732) 761516. *Clubs:* Garrick, MCC; Kent CC; Rye Golf, Senior Golfers' Society; Piscatorial Society.

ATTERTON, David Valentine, CBE 1981; PhD; FEng; FIM; Chairman, Guinness Mahon Holdings, since 1993; *b* 13 Feb. 1927; *s* of Frank Arthur Shepherd Atterton and Ella Constance (*née* Collins); *m* 1948, Sheila Ann McMahon; two *s* one *d*. *Educ:* Bishop Wordsworth's Sch., Salisbury; Peterhouse, Cambridge. MA, PhD Cantab. Post-doctorate research, Cambridge, 1950–52; joined Foundry Services Ltd, 1952; Managing Director: Foseco Ltd, 1966; Foseco Minsep Ltd, 1969; Chm., Foseco Minsep plc, 1979–86. Dep. Chm., Associated Engineering plc, 1979–86 (Dir 1972–); Director: Investors in Industry plc (formerly Finance Corp. for Industry and FFI), 1974–92; IMI plc, 1976–89; Barclays Bank UK Ltd, 1982–84; Bank of England, 1984–92; Barclays Bank, 1984–92; (part-time) British Coal, 1986–; Marks and Spencer plc, 1987–92; Rank Organisation, 1987–; Dimex Ltd, 1988–89; Chm., Peripheral Vision Ltd, 1992–. Chm., NEDO Iron and Steel Sector Working Party, 1977–82; Member: ACARD, 1982–85; British N Amer. Assoc., 1982–92; Bd of Governors, United World Coll. of the Atlantic, 1968–85 (Chm., 1973–79). Pres., Birmingham Chamber of Commerce and Industry, 1974–75. Pres., Inst. of Metals, 1987–88. Master, Founders' Co., 1994–95. *Publications:* numerous scientific papers in learned jls. *Recreations:* cartography, notaphilia, Japanese language, photography. *Address:* Cathedral Green House, Wells, Somerset BA5 2UB. *T:* Wells (01749) 74907.

ATTEWELL, Brian; HM Diplomatic Service; High Commissioner to the Bahamas, since 1992; *b* 29 May 1937; *s* of late William John Geldard Attewell and of Marie Evelyn Attewell; *m* 1963, Mary Gillian Tandy; two *s* one *d*. *Educ:* Dulwich Coll.; London School of Economics and Political Science (BScEcon 1961). BoT, 1956–58, 1961–66; Private Sec. to Parly Sec., 1964–66; transf. to Diplomatic Service, 1966: Washington, 1967–70; Buenos Aires, 1970–73; FCO, 1974–78; Canberra, 1978–80; FCO, 1980–83; Dubai, 1984–87; Brussels, 1988–92. *Recreations:* golf, tennis, walking, listening to music (classical and jazz), following fortunes of Charlton Athletic. *Address:* c/o Foreign and Commonwealth Office, King Charles Street, SW1A 2AH. *Club:* Lyford Cay (Nassau).

ATTLEE, family name of **Earl Attlee.**

ATTLEE, 3rd Earl *cr* 1955; **John Richard Attlee;** Viscount Prestwood, 1955; *b* 3 Oct. 1956; *s* of 2nd Earl Attlee and Anne Barbara, *er d* of late James Henderson, CBE; *S* father, 1991; *m* 1993, Celia Jane, *y d* of Dexter Plummer. *Educ:* Stowe.

ATTLEE, Air Vice-Marshal Donald Laurence, CB 1978; LVO 1964; DL; fruit farmer, since 1977; *b* 2 Sept. 1922; *s* of Major Laurence Attlee; *m* 1952, Jane Hamilton Young; one *s* two *d*. *Educ:* Haileybury. Pilot trng in Canada, 1942–44; Flying Instructor, 1944–48; Staff, Trng Comd, 1949–52; 12 Sqdn, 1952–54; Air Ministry, Air Staff, 1954–55; RAF Staff Coll., 1956; 59 Sqdn, 1957–59; CO, The Queen's Flight (W/Cdr), 1960–63; HQ, RAF Germany, 1964–67; CO, RAF Brize Norton, 1968–69; IDC, 1970; MoD Policy Staff, 1971–72; Dir of RAF Recruiting, 1973–74; Air Cdre, Intell., 1974–75; AOA Trng Comd, 1975–77, retired. Chm., Mid-Devon Business Club, 1985–87; Mem. Bd, Mid-Devon Enterprise Agency, 1983–93. Mem., Mid-Devon DC, 1982– (Vice-Chm., 1987–89; Chm., 1989–91). DL Devon, 1991. *Recreations:* genealogy, Do-it-Yourself, gardening. *Address:* Jerwoods, Culmstock, Cullompton, Devon EX15 3JU. *T:* Hemyock (01823) 680317. *Club:* Royal Air Force.

ATTRIDGE, Elizabeth Ann Johnston, (Mrs John Attridge); Senior Clerk/Adviser, European Legislation Committee, House of Commons; *b* 26 Jan. 1934; *d* of late Rev. John Worthington Johnston, MA, CF, and Mary Isabel Giraud (*née* McFadden); *m* 1956, John Attridge; one *s*. *Educ:* Richmond Lodge Sch., Belfast; St Andrews Univ., Fife. Assistant Principal, Min. of Education, NI, 1955, reappointed on marriage (marriage bar), MAFF, London, 1956; assisted on Agriculture Acts, 1957 and 1958; Head Plant Health Br., 1963–66, Finance, 1966–69, External Relations (GATT) Br., 1969–72; Assistant Secretary: Animal Health I, 1972–75; Marketing Policy and Potatoes, 1975–78; Tropical Foods Div., 1978–83; Under Secretary: European Community Group, 1983–85; Emergencies, Food Quality and Pest Control, 1985–89; Animal Health Gp, 1989–91; Agricl Inputs, Plant Protection and Emergencies Gp, 1991–94. Chairman, International Coffee Council, 1982–83. *Recreations:* collecting fabric, opera. *Address:* Croxley East, The Heath, Weybridge, Surrey KT13 0UA.

ATTWOOD, Thomas Jaymril; Chairman, Cargill, Attwood and Thomas Ltd, Management Consultancy Group, since 1965; *b* 30 March 1931; *s* of George Frederick Attwood and Avril Sandys (*née* Cargill, NZ); *m* 1963, Lynette O. E. Lewis; one *s* one *d*. *Educ:* Haileybury and Imperial Service Coll.; RMA Sandhurst; Harvard Grad. Sch. of Business Admin; INSEAD, Fontainebleau. Pres., Internat. Consultants' Foundn, 1978–81. Conducted seminars for UN Secretariat, European Commn and World Council of Churches, 1970–80; presented papers to Eur. Top Management Symposium, Davos, Internat. Training Conf. and to World Public Relations Conf. Mem. Exec. Cttee, Brit. Management Training Export Council, 1978–85; Chm., Post Office Users National Council, 1982–83. Mem. Court, Worshipful Company of Marketors, 1985–93 (Liveryman, 1980). FCIM; FIMC; FIMgt; Fellow, Inst. of Dirs. Mem., Richmond upon Thames Borough Council, 1969–71. *Publications:* (jtly) Bow Group pubn on United Nations, 1961; contrib. to reference books, incl. Systems Thinking, Innovation in Global Consultation, Handbook of Management Development, and Helping Across Cultures; articles on marketing, management and business topics. *Recreations:* travel, music, chess, City of London, cricket. *Address:* 8 Teddington Park, Teddington, Mddx TW11 8DA. *T:* 0181–977 8091. *Clubs:* City Livery, MCC, Lord's Taverners.

ATTYGALLE, Gen. Don Sepala, Hon. LVO 1954; Chairman and Managing Director, Air Lanka Ltd, since 1993; High Commissioner for Democratic Socialist Republic of Sri Lanka in London, 1990–93; *b* 14 Oct. 1921; *m* 1958, Ithali Mercia Attygalle; one *s*. *Educ:* Royal College, Colombo; psc 1953, idc 1966. Commissioned into Army, 1940; Ceylon Light Infantry; Extra ADC to Governor-General of Ceylon, 1952–65; CO, Ceylon Armoured Corps, 1955; Comdr, Sri Lanka Army, 1967–77; Chief Co-Ordinating Authority, 1977, Sec., 1983–90, Min. of Defence. Deshamanya, 1990. *Recreations:* sports. *Address:* Air Lanka Ltd, 37 York Street, Colombo 1, Sri Lanka.

ATWELL, Very Rev. James Edgar; Provost of St Edmundsbury, since 1995; *b* 3 June 1946; *s* of Joseph Norman Edgar Atwell and Sybil Marion Atwell (*née* Burnett); *m* 1976, Lorna Goodwin; one *s* two *d*. *Educ:* Dauntsey's Sch.; Exeter Coll., Oxford (MA, BD); Harvard Univ. (ThM). Ordained deacon, 1970, priest, 1971; Assistant Curate: St John the Evangelist, E Dulwich, 1970–74; Great St Mary's, Cambridge, 1974–77; Chaplain, Jesus Coll., Cambridge, 1977–81; Vicar of Towcester, 1981–95; RD, Towcester, 1983–91. *Recreations:* countryside, walking, driving a Land Rover, travel, fairground organs, theology. *Address:* The Provost's House, Bury St Edmunds, Suffolk IP33 1RS. *T:* (home) Bury St Edmunds (01284) 754852, (Cathedral office) (01284) 754933, *Fax:* (01284) 768655.

ATWELL, Sir John (William), Kt 1976; CBE 1970; FEng; FIMechE, FRSE; Chairman, Omega Software Ltd, 1982–84; *b* 24 Nov. 1911; *s* of William Atwell and Sarah Workman; *m* 1945, Dorothy Hendry Baxter, *d* of J. H. Baxter and Janet Muir; no *c*. *Educ:* Hyndland Secondary Sch., Glasgow; Royal Technical Coll., Glasgow (ARTC); Cambridge Univ. (MSc). General Management, Stewarts and Lloyds Ltd, 1939–54; Dir 1955–61, Man. Dir

1961–68, G. & J. Weir Ltd; Dir, The Weir Group Ltd, 1961–74, and Chm., Engineering Div., 1968–74; Mem., BRB (Scottish), 1975–81. Chm., Scottish Offshore Partnership, 1975–81; Director: Anderson Strathclyde Ltd, 1975–78; Govan Shipbuilders Ltd, 1975–79. Mem., Bd of Royal Ordnance Factories, 1974–79. Chm., Requirements Bd for Mechanical Engineering and Machine Tools, DTI, 1972–76. Member: University Grants Cttee, 1965–69; NEDC Mech. Eng Cttee, 1969–74; Court, Strathclyde Univ., 1967–83 (Chm., 1975–80); Council, RSE, 1974–85 (Treas., 1977–82; Pres., 1982–85); Exec. Cttee, Scottish Council of Develt and Industry, 1972–77; Adv. Council for Applied R&D, 1976–80; Scottish Hosps Res. Trust, 1972–84; Council, Scottish Business Sch., 1972–80. Vice-Pres., IMechE, 1966–73, Pres., 1973–74; Vice-Chm., 1977–78, Chm., 1978–79, CEI. Hon. Fellow, Strathclyde Univ., 1990. Hon. LLD Strathclyde, 1973. *Recreation:* golf. *Address:* Elmfield, Buchanan Drive, Rutherglen, Glasgow G73 3PE. *T:* 0141–647 1824. *Clubs:* New (Edinburgh); Western (Glasgow).

ATWILL, Sir (Milton) John (Napier), Kt 1979; Director, MEPC Australia Ltd, since 1980; *b* 16 Jan. 1926; *s* of Milton Spencer Atwill and Isabella Caroline Atwill; *m* 1955, Susan Playfair; two *d*. *Educ:* Cranbrook Sch., Sydney; Geelong Church of England Grammar Sch.; Jesus Coll., Cambridge (MA). Called to the Bar, Gray's Inn, 1953, NSW Bar, 1953. President, NSW Division, Liberal Party of Australia, 1970–75; Hon. Treas., 1968–69; Federal Pres., Liberal Party, 1975–82; Chm., Pacific Democrat Union, 1982; Vice-Chm., Internat. Democrat Union, 1983. *Recreations:* cricket, tennis. *Address:* 5 Fullerton Street, Woollahra, NSW 2025, Australia. *T:* (2) 3631522. *Clubs:* Australian, Union, Royal Sydney Golf, Melbourne.

ATWOOD, Barry Thomas; Principal Assistant Solicitor (Under Secretary), Legal Group A (legislation and advisory work), Ministry of Agriculture, Fisheries and Food, since 1992; *b* 25 Feb. 1940; *s* of Percival Atwood and Vera Fanny Atwood (*née* Stoneham); *m* 1965, Jennifer Ann Burgess; two *s*. *Educ:* Bristol Grammar Sch.; Bristol Univ. (LLB); University College London. Solicitor. Articled John Robinson and Jarvis, Isle of Wight, 1961; Solicitor with Robert Smith & Co., Bristol, 1965; Legal Dept, Ministry of Agriculture, Fisheries and Food: conveyancing, 1966; food legislation, 1970; Common Agricultural Policy, 1977; i/c European Court litigation, 1982; Agricultural Commodities and Food Safety Bill, 1986; Legal Gp B (domestic and EC litigation and commercial work), 1989. *Recreations:* family, music, swimming, walking, France. *Address:* Ministry of Agriculture, Fisheries and Food, 55 Whitehall, SW1A 2EY. *T:* 0171–270 8339, *Fax:* 0171–270 8166.

ATWOOD, Margaret, CC (Can.) 1981; FRSC 1987; writer; *b* Ottawa, 18 Nov. 1939; *m* Graeme Gibson; one *d*. *Educ:* Univ. of Toronto (BA 1961); Radcliffe Coll., Cambridge, Mass (AM 1962); Harvard Univ., Cambridge, Mass. Lectr in English, Univ. of BC, Vancouver, 1964–65; Instructor in English: Sir George Williams Univ., Montreal, 1967–68; Univ. of Alberta, 1969–70; Asst Prof. of English, York Univ., Toronto, 1971–72; Writer-in-Residence: Univ. of Toronto, 1972–73; Tuscaloosa, Alabama, 1985; Berg Prof., New York Univ., 1986; Macquarie Univ., Australia, 1987. Holds hon. degrees from univs and colls; recipient of awards, medals and prizes for writing. TV scripts: The Servant Girl, 1974; Snowbird, 1981; (with Peter Pearson) Heaven on Earth, 1986; radio script, The Trumpets of Summer, 1964. *Publications: poetry:* Double Persephone, 1961; Kaleidoscopes Baroque: a poem, 1965; Talismans for Children, 1965; Speeches for Doctor Frankenstein, 1966; The Circle Game, 1966; The Animals in That Country, 1969; The Journals of Susanna Moodie, 1970; Procedures for Underground, 1970; Power Politics, 1971; You Are Happy, 1974; Selected Poems, 1976; Marsh, Hawk, 1977; Two-Headed Poems, 1978; True Stories, 1981; Notes Towards a Poem that Can Never be Written, 1981; Snake Poems, 1983; Interlunar, 1984; Selected Poems II, 1986; Selected Poems 1966–84, 1990; Margaret Atwood Poems, 1991; Poems 1976–1986, 1992; Morning in the Burned House, 1995; *fiction:* The Edible Woman, 1969; Surfacing, 1972; Lady Oracle, 1976; Dancing Girls (short stories), 1977; Up in the Tree (for children), 1978; Anna's Pet (for children), 1980; Life Before Man, 1979; Bodily Harm, 1981; Encounters with the Element Man, 1982; Murder in the Dark, 1983; Bluebeard's Egg, 1983; Unearthing Suite, 1983; The Handmaid's Tale, 1986 (Governor General's Award, 1986; filmed 1990); Cat's Eye, 1989; (ed with Shannon Ravenel) The Best American Short Stories, 1989; Wilderness Tips (short stories), 1991; Good Bones (short stories), 1992; The Robber Bride, 1993; *non-fiction:* Survival: a thematic guide to Canadian literature, 1972; Days of the Rebels 1815–1840, 1977; Second Words: selected critical prose, 1982; For the Birds (for children), 1990. *Address:* c/o Jonathan Cape, 32 Bedford Square, WC1B 3EL.

AUBREY, John Melbourn, CBE 1979; *b* 5 March 1921; *s* of Melbourn Evans Aubrey and Edith Maria Aubrey; *m* 1949, Judith Christine Fairbairn; two *s* two *d* (and one *s* decd). *Educ:* St Paul's Sch.; Corpus Christi Coll., Cambridge (Mech. Sciences Tripos). FCIPA 1952. Armstrong Siddeley Motors Ltd, 1942–43; RE, 1943–47; Tootal Broadhurst Lee Co., 1947–49; Gill Jennings and Every, Chartered Patent Agents, 1949–55; Courtaulds Ltd, 1955–81, Consultant 1982–86. Chm., Baptist Insurance Co. Ltd, 1980– (Dir, 1971–); Mem. Council, Baptist Union of GB and Ireland, 1970–89. *Recreations:* gardening, sailing, swimming, skiing. *Address:* Clarence Cottage, 45 Clarence Hill, Dartmouth TQ6 9NY. *T:* Dartmouth (01803) 833194. *Clubs:* United Oxford & Cambridge University, Ski of GB; Dartmouth Yacht.

AUBREY-FLETCHER, family name of **Baroness Braye.**

AUBREY-FLETCHER, Sir Henry (Egerton), 8th Bt *cr* 1782, of Clea Hall, Cumberland; farmer and company director; *b* 27 Nov. 1945; *s* of Sir John Henry Lancelot Aubrey-Fletcher, 7th Bt and of Diana Mary Fynvola, *o c* of Lt-Col Arthur Egerton; *S* father, 1992; *m* 1976, Sara Roberta, *d* of late Major Robert Gilliam Buchanan and Mrs Margaret Ogden-White; three *s*. *Educ:* Eton. Chm., Chilton House Nursing Home, 1987–; Director: Fox FM ILR, 1987–; Mix 96 ILR, 1994–. Member: Council, CLA, 1987–; Landscape Adv. Cttee, Dept of Transport, 1990–94; Council, Berks, Bucks, Oxon Wildlife Trust, 1992–; Council, NT, 1995–. High Sheriff Bucks, 1995–96. *Recreations:* computers, media and rural affairs. *Heir: s* John Robert Aubrey-Fletcher, *b* 20 June 1977. *Address:* Estate Office, Chilton, Aylesbury, Bucks HP18 9LR. *T:* Long Crendon (01844) 208196.

AUCHINCLOSS, Louis Stanton; author; Partner, Hawkins Delafield and Wood, NYC, since 1957 (Associate, 1954–57); *b* NY, 27 Sept. 1917; *s* of J. H. Auchincloss and P. Stanton; *m* 1957, Adèle Lawrence; three *s*. *Educ:* Groton Sch.; Yale Univ.; Univ. of Virginia (LLB). Lieut USNR; served, 1941–45. Admitted to NY Bar, 1941; Associate Sullivan and Cromwell, 1941–51. Mem. Exec. Cttee, Assoc. of Bar of NY City. Pres., Museum of City of NY, 1967; Trustee, Josiah Macy Jr Foundn. Mem., Nat. Inst. of Arts and Letters. *Publications:* The Indifferent Children, 1947; The Injustice Collectors, 1950; Sybil, 1952; A Law for the Lion, 1953; The Romantic Egoists, 1954; The Great World and Timothy Colt, 1956; Venus in Sparta, 1958; Pursuit of the Prodigal, 1959; The House of Five Talents, 1960; Reflections of a Jacobite, 1961; Portrait in Brownstone, 1962; Powers of Attorney, 1963; The Rector of Justin, 1964; Pioneers and Caretakers, 1966; The Embezzler, 1966; Tales of Manhattan, 1967; A World of Profit, 1969; Second Chance: tales to two generations, 1970; Edith Wharton, 1972; I Come as a Thief, 1972; Richelieu, 1972; The Partners, 1974; A Writer's Capital, 1974; Reading Henry James, 1975; The Winthrop Covenant, 1976; The Dark Lady, 1977; The Country Cousin, 1978; The House of the Prophet, 1980; The Cat and the King, 1981; Watch Fires, 1982; Honourable Men, 1986; Diary of a Yuppie, 1987; The Golden Calves, 1989; (ed) Hone and Strong Diaries of Old Manhattan, 1989; Fellow Passengers, 1990; J. P. Morgan, 1990; House of the Prophet, 1991; Lady of Situations, 1991; pamphlets on American writers. *Address:* 1111 Park Avenue, New York, NY 10028, USA; (office) 67 Wall Street, New York, NY 10005. *Club:* Century Association (NY).

AUCKLAND, 9th Baron (*cr* Irish Barony, 1789; British 1793); **Ian George Eden;** Non-executive Director: C. J. Sims & Co. Ltd; George S. Hall & Co. Ltd; *b* 23 June 1926; *s* of 8th Baron Auckland; *S* father 1957; *m* 1954, Dorothy Margaret, *d* of H. J. Manser, Eastbourne; one *s* two *d*. *Educ:* Blundell's Sch. Royal Signals, 1945–48; 3/4 County of London Yeomanry (Sharpshooters) (TA), 1948–53. Underwriting Mem. of Lloyd's, 1956–64. Pres., Inst. of Insurance Consultants, 1977–89. Chm., Anglo-S Pacific Group, CPA, 1985–. Member: New Zealand Soc.; Anglo-Finnish Parly Gp, 1965–. Pres., Surrey Co., Royal British Legion, 1983–; Council, RoSPA. Master, Broderers' Co., 1967–68; Hon. Mem., Court of Assistants, Blacksmiths' Co. Knight, 1st cl., White Rose (Finland), 1984. *Recreations:* music, theatre, tennis and walking. *Heir: s* Hon. Robert Ian Burnard Eden, *b* 25 July 1962; *m* 1986, Geraldine. *Address:* Tudor Rose House, 30 Links Road, Ashtead, Surrey KT21 2HF. *T:* Ashtead (01372) 274393. *Clubs:* City Livery, World Traders.

AUCKLAND (Dio. Durham), **Archdeacon of;** *see* Gibson, Ven. G. G.

AUCKLAND (NZ), Bishop of, since 1995; **Rt Rev. John Campbell Paterson;** *b* 4 Jan. 1945; *s* of Thomas Paterson and Lucy Mary Paterson; *m* 1968, Marion Reid Anderson; two *d*. *Educ:* King's Coll., Auckland; Auckland Univ. (BA); St John's Coll., Auckland (LTh (Hons)); Dip. Public Speaking (NZ Speech Bd), 1969. Ordained, deacon, 1969, priest, 1970; Assistant Curate, Whangarei, 1969–71; Vicar, Waimate North Maori Pastorate, 1971–76; Co-Missioner, Auckland Maori Mission, 1976; Chaplain, Queen Victoria Sch., 1976–82; TF Chaplain, 1976–84; Sec., Te Pihopatanga o Aotearoa, 1978–86; Provincial Sec., Church of the Province of NZ, 1986–92; Gen. Sec., Anglican Church in Aotearoa, NZ and Polynesia, 1992–95. Mem., ACC, 1990–96. *Publication:* (ed) He Toenga Whatiwhatinga, 1983. *Recreations:* music, sport, literature. *Address:* PO Box 37–242, Parnell, Auckland, New Zealand. *T:* (9) 3771989.

AUDLAND, Sir Christopher (John), KCMG 1987 (CMG 1973); HM Diplomatic Service and Commission of the European Communities, retired; *b* 7 July 1926; *s* of late Brig. Edward Gordon Audland, CB, CBE, MC, and Violet Mary, *d* of late Herbert Shepherd-Cross, MP; *m* 1955, Maura Daphne Sullivan; two *s* one *d*. *Educ:* Winchester Coll. RA, 1944–48 (Temp. Capt.). Entered Foreign (subseq. Diplomatic) Service, 1948; served in: Bonn; British Representation to Council of Europe, Strasbourg; Washington; UK Delegn to negotiations for British Membership of European Communities, Brussels, 1961–63; Buenos Aires; Head of Science and Technology Dept, FCO, 1968–70; Counsellor (Head of Chancery), Bonn, 1970–72; seconded to Commn of Eur. Communities, 1973: Dep. Sec.-Gen., 1973–81; Dir-Gen. for Energy, 1981–86. Head, UK Delegn to 1st UN Conf. on Seabed and Ocean Floor, 1968; Dep. Head, UK Delegn to Four-Power Negotiations on Berlin, 1970–72. Hon. Fellow, Faculty of Law, and Vis. Lectr on European Instns, Edinburgh Univ., 1986–. Vice President: Europa Nostra, 1988–91; Internat. Castles Inst., 1988–90 (Pres., 1990–91); Europa Nostra united with Internat. Castles Inst., 1991– (Exec. Pres., 1992). Member: NW Regl Cttee, National Trust, 1987–; European Strategy Bd, ICL, 1988–; Lake District Nat. Park Authority, 1989–; Pro-Chancellor, Lancaster Univ., 1990– (Mem., Council, 1988–). Trustee: Peter Kirk Meml Fund, 1989–; Ruskin Foundn, 1994–. *Address:* The Old House, Ackenthwaite, Milnthorpe, Cumbria LA7 7DH. *T:* Milnthorpe (015395) 62202, *Fax:* (015395) 64041. *Club:* United Oxford & Cambridge University.

AUDLEY, 25th Baron *cr* 1312–13; **Richard Michael Thomas Souter;** Director, Graham Miller & Co. Ltd, retired 1983; *b* 31 May 1914; *s* of Sir Charles Alexander Souter, KCIE, CSI (*d* 1958) and Lady Charlotte Dorothy Souter (*née* Jesson) (*d* 1958); *S* kinswoman, Baroness Audley (24th in line), 1973; *m* 1941, Pauline, *d* of D. L. Eskell; three *d*. *Educ:* Uppingham. Fellow, CILA. Military Service, 1939–46; Control Commission, Germany, 1946–50. Insurance Broker until 1955; Loss Adjuster, 1955–84. *Recreations:* shooting, gardening. *Heir:* three co-heiresses. *Address:* Friendly Green, Cowden, near Edenbridge, Kent TN8 7DU. *T:* Cowden (01342) 850682.

AUDLEY, Sir (George) Bernard, Kt 1985; Chairman: Caverswall Holdings, since 1990; Pergamon AGB plc, 1988–90; Founder, and Chairman, AGB Research PLC, 1973–88; *b* Stockton Brook, N Staffs, 24 April 1924; *s* of late Charles Bernard Audley and Millicent Claudia Audley; *m* 1950, Barbara, *d* of late Richard Arthur Heath; two *s* one *d*. *Educ:* Wolstanton Grammar Sch.; Corpus Christi Coll., Oxford (MA). Lieut, Kings Dragoon Guards, 1943–46. Asst Gen. Man., Hulton Press Ltd, 1949–57; Man. Dir, Television Audience Measurement Ltd, 1957–61; founded AGB Research, 1962. Chairman: Netherhall Trust, 1962–; Industry and Commerce Adv. Cttee, William and Mary Tercentenary Trust, 1985–89; Arts Access, 1986–; Pres., EUROPANEL, 1966–70; Vice-Pres., Periodical Publishers Assoc., 1989– (Pres., 1985–89); Mem. Cttee, St Bride's World Wide Trust, 1991–. Vis. Prof. in Business and Management, Middlesex Univ. (formerly Poly.), 1989–. Governor, Hong Kong Coll., 1984–94. FRSA 1986. Freeman of City of London, 1978; Liveryman, Gold and Silver Wyre Drawers' Company, 1975–. *Recreations:* golf, reading, travel. *Address:* 56 River Court, SE1 9DE. *T:* 0171–928 6576; Le Collet du Puits, Montauroux, 83440 Fayence, France. *T:* (94) 765287. *Clubs:* Cavalry and Guards, MCC; Rye Golf, Hadley Wood Golf.

AUDLEY, Prof. Robert John, PhD; FBPsS; Professor of Psychology, since 1965, Head of Psychology Department, since 1979, and Vice-Provost, since 1988, University College London; *b* 15 Dec. 1928; *s* of Walter Audley and Agnes Lilian (*née* Baker); *m* 1st, 1952, Patricia Mary Bannister (marr. diss. 1977); two *s*; 2nd, 1990, Vera Elyashiv Bickerdike. *Educ:* Battersea Grammar Sch.; University Coll. London (BSc 1st Cl. Hons Psychology, 1952; PhD 1955). Fullbright Scholar and Res. Asst, Washington State Univ., 1952; University College London: Res. Worker, MRC Gp for Exptl Investigation of Behaviour, 1955–57; Lectr in Psychology, 1957–64; Reader in Psychology, 1964; Dean, Faculty of Science, 1985–88; Fellow, 1989. Vis. Prof., Columbia Univ., NY, 1962; Vis. Miller Prof., Univ. of Calif, Berkeley, 1971; Vis Fellow, Inst. for Advanced Study, Princeton, 1970. Member: UGC Social Studies Sub-Cttee, 1975–82; UGC Equipment Sub-Cttee, 1982–89; Computer Bd for Univs and Res. Councils, 1986–90; MRC/RN Personnel Res. Cttee, 1984– (Chm., Psychology Sub-Cttee, 1984–); Chm., Jt Wkg Gp, ESRC/HEFC Jt. Inf. Systems Cttee, 1990– (Mem., New Technology Sub-Cttee, Jt Inf. Systems Cttee, 1993–). President: British Psychological Soc., 1969–70; Exptl Psychology Soc., 1975–76. Editor, British Jl of Math. and Stat. Psychology, 1965–70. *Publications:* papers on choice, judgement, medical mishaps. *Recreations:* crosswords, cooking, the arts. *Address:* Psychology Department, University College London, Gower Street, WC1E 6BT. *T:* 0171–380 7558.

AUDLEY-CHARLES, Prof. Michael Geoffrey, PhD; Yates-Goldsmid Professor of Geology, 1982–93, now Emeritus Professor, and Head of the Department of Geological Sciences, 1982–92, University College London; *b* 10 Jan. 1935; *s* of Lawrence Geoffrey and Elsie Ada Audley-Charles; *m* 1965, Brenda Amy Cordeiro; one *s* one *d*. *Educ:* Royal Wanstead Sch.; Chelsea Polytechnic (BSc); Imperial Coll., London (PhD). Geologist with mining and petroleum cos, Canada and Australia, 1957–62; Imperial Coll. of Science and Technology, London: research in geology, 1962–67; Lectr in Geol., 1967–73; Reader in Geol., 1973–77; Prof. of Geol. and Head of Dept of Geol Sciences, Queen Mary Coll., London, 1977–82. *Publications:* geological papers dealing with stratigraphy of British Triassic, regional geol. of Indonesia and Crete and evolution of Gondwanaland, in learned jls. *Recreation:* gardening. *Address:* La Serre, St Pantaléon, 46800 Montcuq, France. *T:* 65318067.

AUDU, Rev. Ishaya Shu'aibu, FRCPE; Medical Director, Savannah Polyclinic, Zaria, since 1984; *b* 1 March 1927; *s* of Malam Bulus Audu and Malama Rakiya Audu; *m* 1958, Victoria Abosede Ohiorhenuan; two *s* five *d*. *Educ:* Ibadan and London Univs. House Officer, Sen. House Officer, Registrar in Surgery, Medicine, Obstetrics and Gynæcology and Pædiatrics, King's Coll. Hosp., London and Univ. Coll. Hosp., Ibadan, 1954–58; postgrad. studies, UK, 1959–60; Specialist Physician, Pædiatrician to Govt of Northern Nigeria and Personal Physician to Premier of North Region Govt, 1960–62; Lectr to Associate Professorship in Pæds, Univ. of Lagos Med. Sch., 1962–66; Vis. Res. Associate Prof., Univ. of Rochester Med. Sch., NY, 1964–65; Dep. Chm., Lagos Univ. Teaching Hosp. Man. Bd and Mem. Council, Univ. Lagos Med. Coll., 1962–66; Mem. Senate, Lagos Univ., 1963–66; Vice-Chancellor, Ahmadu Bello Univ., 1966–1975; Prof. of Medicine, 1967–77; Sen. Medical Officer, Ashaka Cement Co. Ltd, 1977–79; Minister of External Affairs, Fed. Republic of Nigeria, 1979–83; Ambassador and Perm. Rep. of Nigeria to UN, 1983–84. Pres., Christian Health Assoc. of Nigeria, 1986–93 (Trustee, 1993–); Chm., Nat. Primary Health Care Develt Agency of Nigeria, 1992–. Pro-Chancellor and Chm. of Council, Univ. of Nigeria, Nsukka, 1993–. Ordained Minister, United Church of Christ in Nigeria, 1986. Hon. LHD Ohio, 1968; Hon DSc Nigeria, 1971; Hon. LLD Ibadan, 1973; FMC (Pæd) Nigerian Med. Council; FRSocMed. *Publications:* contribs to learned jls. *Recreations:* walking, table tennis. *Address:* (office) Sarki Road, Samaru, Zaria, Nigeria; (home) 23a Ibrahim Babangida Road, GRA, Zaria.

AUDUS, Prof. Leslie John, MA, PhD, ScD Cantab; FIBiol; Hildred Carlile Professor of Botany, Bedford College, University of London, 1948–79; *b* 9 Dec. 1911; English; *m* 1938, Rowena Mabel Ferguson (*d* 1987); two *d*. *Educ:* Downing Coll., Cambridge Univ. Downing Coll. Exhibitioner, 1929–31; Frank Smart Research Student (Cambridge Univ.), 1934–35; Lecturer in Botany, University Coll., Cardiff, 1935–40. Served War of 1939–45: RAFVR (Technical, Radar, Officer), 1940–46; PoW South Pacific, 1942–45. Scientific Officer, Agricultural Research Council, Unit of Soil Metabolism, Cardiff, 1946–47; Monsanto Lecturer in Plant Physiology, University Coll., Cardiff, 1948. Recorder, 1961–65, Pres., 1967–68, Section K, British Assoc. for the Advancement of Science. Vis. Prof. of Botany: Univ. of California, Berkeley, 1958; Univ. of Minnesota, Minneapolis, 1965. Vice-Pres. Linnean Soc. of London, 1959–60 (Hon. FLS); Life Mem. New York Academy of Sciences, 1961. Editor, Journal Exp. Botany, 1965–74. *Publications:* Plant Growth Substances, 1953, 3rd edn 1972; (ed) The Physiology and Biochemistry of Herbicides, 1964; (ed) Herbicides: physiology, biochemistry and ecology, 1976; original research on plant respiration, hormones, responses to gravity, soil micro-biology in relation to pesticides, etc in Annals of Botany, New Phytologist, Nature, Journal of Experimental Botany, Weed Research, etc. *Recreations:* furniture construction and restoration, electronics, amateur radio. *Address:* 38 Belmont Lane, Stanmore, Middlesex HA7 2PT.

AUERBACH, Frank Helmuth; painter; *b* 29 April 1931; *s* of Max Auerbach, lawyer, and Charlotte Norah Auerbach; *m* 1958, Julia Wolstenholme; one *s*. *Educ:* privately; St Martin's Sch. of Art; Royal Coll. of Art. *One-man exhibitions:* Beaux Arts Gallery, 1956, 1959, 1961, 1962, 1963; Marlborough Fine Art, 1965, 1967, 1971, 1974, 1983, 1987, 1990; Marlborough-Gerson, New York, 1969; Villiers, Sydney, Australia, 1972; Bergamini, Milan, 1973; Univ. of Essex, 1973; Mun. Gall. of Modern Art, Dublin, 1975; Marlborough, Zurich, 1976; Anthony D'Offay, London; Arts Council Retrospective, Hayward Gall., 1978; Edinburgh, 1978; Jacobson, NY, 1979; Marlborough, NY, 1982, 1994; Anne Berthoud, London, 1983; Venice Biennale, British Pavilion, 1986 (Golden Lion Prize); Kunstverein, Hamburg; Museum Folkwang, Essen; Centro de Arte Reina Sofia, Madrid, 1986–87; Rijksmuseum Vincent van Gogh, Amsterdam, 1989; Paul Mellon Centre of British Art, New Haven, 1991; Nat. Gall., 1995. *Mixed exhibitions:* Carnegie International, Pittsburgh, 1958, 1962; Dunn International, Fredericton, 1963; Gulbenkian International, Tate Gallery, 1964; European Painting in the Seventies, USA, 1976; Annual Exhbn, part I, Hayward Gall., 1977; Westkunst, Cologne, 1981; Internat. Survey, Moma, NY, 1984; The Hard Won Image, Tate Gall., 1984; The British Show, Australia, 1985; British Art in the Twentieth Century, RA, 1987; Current Affairs, Mus. of Modern Art, Oxford, and tour, 1987; A School of London, Kunstnernes Hus. Oslo, and tour, 1987–88; British Figurative Painting of the Twentieth Century, Israel Mus., Jerusalem, 1992–93; *public collections:* Arts Council; Brit. Council; Brit. Museum; Tate Gallery, London; Metropolitan Museum, NY; Mus. of Modern Art, NY; National Gallery of Victoria, Melbourne; Nat. Galls of Australia, W Australia and NSW; County Museum of LA, Calif; Cleveland Mus., Ohio; Art Inst., Chicago; Univ. of Cincinnati; St Louis Art Mus.; Tamayo Mus., Mexico; Aberdeen, Bedford, Bolton, Cambridge, Edinburgh, Hartlepool, Huddersfield, Hull, Leeds, Leicester, Manchester, Nottingham, Oldham, Rochdale, Sheffield, Southampton Galls; Arts Council, Contemporary Art Soc., etc. *Address:* c/o Marlborough Fine Art, 6 Albemarle Street, W1X 4BY.

AUKIN, David; Head of Drama, Channel 4 Television, since 1990; *b* 12 Feb. 1942; *s* of Charles and Regina Aukin; *m* 1969, Nancy Meckler, theatre director; two *s*. *Educ:* St Paul's Sch., London; St Edmund Hall, Oxford (BA). Admitted Solicitor, 1965. Literary Advr, Traverse Theatre Club, 1970–73; Administrator, Oxford Playhouse Co., 1974–75; Administrator, 1975–79, Dir, 1979–84, Hampstead Theatre; Dir, Leicester Haymarket Theatre, 1984–86; Exec. Dir, NT, 1986–90. FRSA 1989. *Recreation:* golf. *Address:* c/o Channel 4 Television, 124 Horseferry Road, SW1P 2TX. *T:* 0171–396 4444. *Club:* Groucho.

AULD, Alasdair Alpin, FMA; Director, Glasgow Museums and Art Galleries, 1979–88, retired; *b* 16 Nov. 1930; *s* of Herbert Bruce Auld and Janetta Isabel MacAlpine; *m* 1959, Mary Hendry Paul; one *s* one *d*. *Educ:* Shawlands Acad., Glasgow; Glasgow Sch. of Art (DA). FMA 1971. Glasgow Museums and Art Galleries: Asst Curator, 1956–72; Keeper of Fine Art, 1972–76; Depute Dir, 1976–79. Pres., Scottish Fedn of Museums and Art Galls, 1981–84. *Publications:* catalogues; articles on museum subjects. *Recreations:* golf, travel. *Address:* 3 Dalziel Drive, Pollokshields, Glasgow G41 4JA. *T:* 0141–427 1720.

AULD, Margaret Gibson, RGN, RM; FRCN; MPhil; Chief Nursing Officer, Scottish Home and Health Department, 1977–88, retired; *b* 11 July 1932; *d* of late Alexander John Sutton Auld and Eleanor Margaret Ingram. *Educ:* Glasgow; Cardiff High Sch. for Girls; Radcliffe Infirm., Oxford (SRN 1953); St David's Hosp., Cardiff; Queen's Park Hosp., Blackburn (SCM 1954). Midwife Teacher's Dipl., 1962; Certif. of Nursing Admin, 1966, MPhil 1974, Edinburgh. Queen's Park Hosp., Blackburn, 1953–54; Staff Midwife, Cardiff Maternity Hosp., 1955, Sister, 1957; Sister, Queen Mary Hosp., Dunedin, NZ, 1959–60; Deptl Sister, Cardiff Maternity Hosp., 1960–66; Asst Matron, Simpson Meml Maternity Pavilion, Edinburgh, 1966–68, Matron, 1968–73; Actg Chief Reg. Nursing Officer, S-Eastern Reg. Hosp. Bd, Edinburgh, 1973; Chief Area Nursing Off., Borders Health Bd, 1973–76. Life Vice Pres., Royal Coll. of Midwives of UK, 1988. Chm., CRAG/SCOTMEG Review of Maternity Services in Scotland, 1992–95; Member: GNC (Scotland), 1973–76; Central Midwives Bd (Scotland), 1972–76; Cttee on Nursing (Briggs), 1970–72; Maternity Services Cttee, Integration of Maternity Work (Tennent Report), 1972–73; Human Fertilization and Embryol. Authy, 1990–92; Cttee on Ethics of Gene Therapy, 1990–93; Nuffield Council on Bioethics, 1991–94. Gov., Queen Margaret Coll., Edinburgh, 1989–. FRCN 1981; CIMgt (CBIM 1983). Hon. DSc CNAA, 1987. *Recreations:* reading, music, entertaining. *Address:* Staddlestones, Neidpath Road, Peebles EH45 8NN. *T:* Peebles (01721) 729594.

AULD, Rt Hon. Sir Robin Ernest, Kt 1988; PC 1995; **Rt Hon. Lord Justice Auld;** a Lord Justice of Appeal, since 1995; *b* 19 July 1937; *s* of late Ernest Auld; *m* 1963, Catherine Eleanor Mary, *er d* of late David Henry Pritchard; one *s* one *d*. *Educ:* Brooklands Coll.; King's Coll., London (LLB 1st cl. Hons 1958; PhD 1963; FKC 1987). Called to Bar, Gray's Inn, 1959 (Macaskie Schol., Lord Justice Holker Sen. Schol.), Bencher, 1984; SE Circuit; in practice at English Bar, 1959–87; admitted to Bar, State of NY, USA, 1984. Prosecuting Counsel to Dept of Trade, 1969–75; QC 1975; a Recorder, 1977–87; a Judge of the High Court of Justice, QBD, 1987–95; Presiding Judge, Western Circuit, 1991–94. Mem., Judicial Studies Bd, 1989–91 (Chm., Criminal Cttee, 1989–91). Mem., Commn of Inquiry into Casino Gambling in the Bahamas, 1967; Chm., William Tyndale Schools' Inquiry, 1975–76; Counsel to Inquiry into Brixton Disorders, 1981; Chm., Home Office Cttee of Inquiry into Sunday Trading, 1983–84. Dept of Trade Inspector, Ashbourne Investments Ltd, 1975–79; Legal Assessor, GMC and GDC, 1982–87. Master, Woolmen's Co., 1984–85. *Address:* Royal Courts of Justice, Strand, WC2A 2LL. *Club:* Athenæum.

AUNG SAN SUU KYI; Co-Founder and General Secretary, National League for Democracy, Burma, since 1988; Burmese prisoner of conscience, 1989–95; *b* Rangoon, 19 June 1945; *d* of Bogyoke Aung San (assassinated, 19 July 1947) and late Daw Khin Kyi; *m* 1972, Michael Vaillancourt Aris; two *s*. *Educ:* St Francis Convent, Rangoon; Methodist English High Sch., Rangoon; Lady Shri Ram Coll., Delhi Univ.; St Hugh's Coll., Oxford (BA PPE 1967; MA; Hon. Fellow, 1990). Asst Sec., Adv. Cttee on Admin. and Budgetary Questions, UN Secretariat, NY, 1969–71; Res. Officer, Min. of Foreign Affairs, Bhutan, 1972. Vis. Schol., Centre for SE Asian Studies, Kyoto Univ., Japan, 1985–86. Fellow, Indian Inst. of Advanced Studies, Simla, 1987. Hon. Mem., World Commn on Culture and Develt, Unesco, 1992; Mem., Acad. Universelle des Cultures, Paris, 1993. Hon. Pres., LSE Students' Union, 1992; Hon. Life Mem., Univ. of London Union, 1992. Hon. doctorates: Thammasat Univ., Bangkok, 1992; Toronto Univ., 1993; Vrije Univ., Brussels, 1994. Thorolf Rafto Award for Human Rights, Norway, 1990; Nobel Peace Prize, 1991; Sakharov Prize for Freedom of Thought, European Parlt, 1991; Annual Award, Internat. Human Rights Law Group, USA, 1992; Simón Bolívar Prize, Unesco, 1992; Prix Littéraire des Droits de l'Homme, Paris, 1992; Rose Prize, Internat. Forum of Danish Lab. Movement, 1993; Victor Jara Internat. Human Rights Award Center for Human Rights and Constitutional Law, LA, 1993; Bremen Solidarity Prize, 1993. *Publications:* (ed with Michael Aris) Tibetan Studies in Honour of Hugh Richardson, 1980; Aung San, 1984, 2nd edn as Aung San of Burma: a biographical portrait by his daughter, 1990; (contrib.) Burma and Japan: basic studies on their cultural and social structure, 1987; Burma and India: some aspects of intellectual life under colonialism, 1990; Freedom from Fear and Other Writings, 1991; Towards a True Refuge (Joyce Pearce Meml Lect.), 1993; numerous speeches. *Address:* 56 University Avenue, Rangoon, Burma.

AUST, Anthony Ivall, CMG 1995; Legal Counsellor, Foreign and Commonwealth Office, 1984–88 and since 1991; *b* 9 March 1942; *s* of Ivall George Aust and Jessie Anne Salmon; *m* 1st, 1969, Jacqueline Antoinette Thérèse Paris (marr. diss. 1987); two *d*; 2nd, 1988, Dr Kirsten Kaarre Jensen. *Educ:* Wilson Central Sch., Reading; Stoneham Grammar Sch., Reading; London Sch. of Econs and Pol Science (LLB 1963, LLM 1967). Admitted Solicitor, 1967. Asst Legal Adviser, FCO (formerly CO), 1967–76; Legal Adviser, British Mil. Govt, Berlin, 1976–79; Asst Legal Adviser, FCO, 1979–84; Counsellor (Legal Advr) UK Mission to UN, NY, 1988–91. *Recreations:* architecture, cinema, theatre, gardening, parlour games. *Address:* c/o Foreign and Commonwealth Office, SW1A 2AH.

AUSTEN, Patrick George; Chief Executive, Liberty plc, since 1993; *b* 22 Sept. 1943; *m* 1968, Margaret; three *s* one *d*. *Educ:* Bristol Coll. of Commerce; Leicester Sch. of Textiles; Leicester Poly.; Centre d'Etudes Industrielles, Geneva. ICI Fibres, 1961–83: commercial apprentice, British Nylon Spinners (later ICI Fibres), 1961–65; mgt trainee, 1965–67; Trade Sales Manager, 1967–70; Fibres Manager, Republic of Ireland, 1970–73; Business Area Manager, 1974–79; Commercial Manager, Textile Fibres, 1979–83; BTR, 1983–; Managing Director: Pretty Polly, 1983–85; Pretty Polly and Dunlopillo, 1985–87; BTR plc, 1983–; Gp Chief Exec., Consumer Products Gp, 1987–. *Recreations:* golf, motor-racing. *Address:* Chanticleer, 14 Chantry View Road, Guildford, Surrey GU1 3XR. *T:* Guildford (01483) 301667.

AUSTEN-SMITH, Air Marshal Sir Roy (David), KBE 1979; CB 1975; CVO 1994; DFC 1953; retired; a Gentleman Usher to HM the Queen, 1982–94, an Extra Gentleman Usher, since 1994; *b* 28 June 1924; *m* 1951, Ann (*née* Alderson); two *s*. *Educ:* Hurstpierpoint College. Pilot trng, Canada, 1943–44; 41 Sqn (2 TAF), 1945; 33 Sqdn, Malaya, 1950–53; Cranwell, 1953–56; 73 Sqdn, Cyprus, 1956–59; Air Min., 1960–63; 57 Sqdn, 1964–66; HQ 2 ATAF, 1966–68; CO, RAF Wattisham; MoD, 1970–72; AOC and Comdt, RAF Coll., Cranwell, 1972–75; SASO Near East Air Force, 1975–76; Comdr British Forces, Cyprus, AOC Air HQ Cyprus and Administrator, Sovereign Base Areas, Cyprus, 1976–78; Hd of British Defence Staff, Washington, and Defence Attaché, 1978–81. *Recreation:* golf. *Address:* c/o National Westminster Bank, Swanley, Kent. *Club:* Royal Air Force.

AUSTERBERRY, Ven. Sidney Denham; Archdeacon of Salop, 1959–79, now Archdeacon Emeritus; *b* 28 Oct. 1908; *s* of late Mr and Mrs H. Austerberry; *m* 1934, Eleanor Jane Naylor; two *s* two *d*. *Educ:* Hanley High Sch.; Egerton Hall, Manchester. Curate, Newcastle-under-Lyme Parish Church, 1931–38; Vicar of S Alkmund, Shrewsbury, 1938–52; Vicar of Brewood, 1952–59; Hon. Clerical Sec., Lichfield Diocesan Conf., 1954–70; Rural Dean of Penkridge, 1958–59; Vicar of Great Ness, 1959–77. Hon. Canon, Lichfield Cathedral, 1968–79. *Address:* 6 Honeysuckle Row, Sutton Park, Shrewsbury SY3 7TW. *T:* Shrewsbury (01743) 368080.

AUSTICK, David; Chairman, Austicks Bookshops Ltd, since 1991 (Senior Partner, 1964–91); *b* 8 March 1920; *m* 1944, Florence Elizabeth Lomath. Member: Leeds City Council (for W Hunslet), 1969–74, Hon. Alderman, 1988; Leeds Metropolitan District Council (for Hunslet), 1969–75; W Yorkshire County Council (for Otley and Lower Wharfedale), 1974–79. MP (L) Ripon, July 1973–Feb. 1974; Contested (L) Ripon, 1974, (L) Cheadle, 1979, (L) Leeds, European Parlt, 1979. Vice Pres., Electoral Reform Soc. (Exec. Chm., 1984–86; Co-Sec., 1985–92); Member: European Movement; Fellowship of Reconciliation. Co. and Financial Sec., E. R. Ballot Services Ltd, 1989–91. *Address:* Austicks Bookshops, 16 Oxford Street, Harrogate HG1 1SN; Clarence House, Clarence Place, Burley in Wharfedale, Ilkley LS29 7DW. *Club:* National Liberal.

AUSTIN, Sir Anthony Leonard, 6th Bt *cr* 1894, of Red Hill, Castleford, West Riding; *b* 30 Sept. 1930; *yr s* of Sir William Ronald Austin, 4th Bt (*d* 1989) and his 1st wife, Dorothy Mary (*d* 1957), *d* of L. A. Bidwell, FRCS; *S* brother, 1995; *m* 1st, 1956, Mary Annette (marr. diss. 1966), *d* of Richard Kelly; two *s* one *d*; 2nd, 1967, Aileen Morrison Hall, *d* of William Hall Stewart; one *d*. *Educ:* Downside. *Heir: s* Peter John Austin, *b* 29 July 1958. *Address:* Stanbury Manor, Morwenstow, Bude, Cornwall EX23 9JQ.

AUSTIN, Brian Patrick; HM Diplomatic Service; Consul-General, Vancouver, since 1993; *b* 18 March 1938; *s* of Edward William Austin and Winifred Alice Austin; *m* 1968, Augusta Francisca Maria Lina; one *s* one *d*. *Educ:* St Olave's Grammar Sch.; Clare Coll., Cambridge. National Service, 1956–58. Joined CRO, 1961; Central African Office, 1962; Lagos, 1963; The Hague, 1966; First Sec., FCO, 1969; Montreal, 1973; FCO, 1978; Dep. High Comr, Kaduna, 1981–84; Counsellor: FCO, 1984–88; Stockholm, 1989–93. *Recreation:* birdwatching. *Address:* c/o Foreign and Commonwealth Office, SW1A 2AH.

AUSTIN, Dr Colin François Lloyd, FBA 1983; Director of Studies in Classics and Fellow, Trinity Hall, Cambridge, since 1965; Reader in Greek Language and Literature, University of Cambridge, since 1988; *b* Melbourne, Australia, 26 July 1941; *s* of Prof. Lloyd James Austin, FBA; *m* 1967, Mishtu Mazumdar, Calcutta, India; one *s* one *d*. *Educ:* Lycée Lakanal, Paris; Manchester Grammar Sch.; Jesus Coll., Cambridge (Scholar; MA 1965); Christ Church, Oxford (Sen. Scholar; MA, DPhil 1965); Freie Universität, West Berlin (Post-grad. Student). Univ. of Cambridge: John Stewart of Rannoch Scholar in Greek and Latin, 1960; Battie Scholar, Henry Arthur Thomas Scholar and Hallam Prize, 1961; Sir William Browne Medal for a Latin Epigram, 1961; Porson Prize, 1962; Prendergast Greek Student, 1962; Res. Fellow, Trinity Hall, 1965–69; Asst Univ. Lectr in Classics, 1969–73, Lectr, 1973–88; Leverhulme Res. Fellow, 1979 and 1981. Treasurer: Jt Cttee, Greek and Roman Socs, London, 1983–; Cambridge Philological Soc., 1971–. *Publications:* De nouveaux fragments de l'Erechthée d'Euripide, 1967; Nova Fragmenta Euripidea, 1968; (with Prof. R. Kasser) Papyrus Bodmer XXV et XXVI, 2 vols, 1969; Menandri Aspis et Samia, 2 vols, 1969–70; Comicorum Graecorum Fragmenta in papyris reperta, 1973; (with Prof. R. Kassel) Poetae Comici Graeci: vol. IV, Aristophon—Crobylus, 1983, vol. III 2, Aristophanes, Testimonia et Fragmenta, 1984, vol. V, Damoxenus—Magnes, 1986, vol. VII, Menecrates-Xenophon, 1989, vol. II, Agathenor—Aristonymus, 1991, vol. VIII, Adespota, 1995; notes and reviews in classical periodicals. *Recreations:* cycling, philately, wine tasting. *Address:* 7 Park Terrace, Cambridge CB1 1JH. *T:* Cambridge (01223) 62732; Trinity Hall, Cambridge CB2 1TJ.

AUSTIN, Prof. Colin Russell, FAA; Charles Darwin Professor of Animal Embryology, and Fellow of Fitzwilliam College, University of Cambridge, 1967–81, now Professor Emeritus; *b* 12 Sept. 1914; *s* of Ernest Russell Austin and Linda Mabel King; *m* 1941, Patricia Constance Jack; two *s*. *Educ:* Univ. of Sydney, Australia (BVSc 1936; DSc 1954); MA Cantab 1967. FAA 1987; FAIBiol 1987. Mem. Research Staff, CSIRO, Australia, 1938–54; Mem. Scientific Staff of MRC, UK, 1954–64; Editor, Jl of Reproduction and Fertility, 1959–64; Head of Genetic and Developmental Disorders Research Program, Delta Regional Primate Research Center, and Prof. of Embryology, Tulane Univ., New Orleans, 1964–67. F. R. Lillie Meml Fellow, Marine Biol Lab, Woods Hole, Mass, 1961. Visiting Professor: Florida State Univ., 1962; Univ. of Palermo, 1969; Univ. of NSW, 1974; Murdoch Univ., 1979; Univ. of Auckland, 1980; Chulalongkorn Univ., Bangkok, 1985; Goding Lectr, Australian Soc. for Reproductive Biol., 1991. Editor: Reproduction in Mammals, 1972–86; Biological Reviews, 1981–84. Hon. Mem., Amer. Assoc. Anatomists, 1984; Hon. Member: Soc. Chilena Reprod. y Desarrollo, 1989; Eur. Soc. of Human Reproduction and Embryol., 1990. Medal and Citation, Istituto Sperimentale Italiano Lazzaro Spallanzani, 1972; Marshall Medal, Soc. for Study of Fertility, 1981; Pioneer Award, Internat. Embryo Transfer Soc., 1995. *Publications:* The Mammalian Egg, 1961; Fertilization, 1965; Ultrastructure of Fertilization, 1968; Human Embryos: the debate on assisted reproduction, 1989; numerous research papers. *Recreations:* gardening, swimming, tennis. *Address:* 47 Dixon Road, Buderim, Qld 4556, Australia.

AUSTIN, Ven. George Bernard; Archdeacon of York, since 1988; broadcaster, writer; *b* 16 July 1931; *s* of Oswald Hulton Austin and Evelyn Austin; *m* 1962, Roberta Anise Thompson; one *s*. *Educ:* St David's Coll., Lampeter (BA); Chichester Theological Coll. Deacon 1955, priest 1956; Assistant Curate: St Peter's, Chorley, 1955–57; St Clement's, Notting Dale, 1957–59; Asst Chaplain, Univ. of London, 1960; Asst Curate, Dunstable Priory, 1961–64; Vicar: St Mary the Virgin, Eaton Bray, 1964–70; St Peter, Bushey Heath, 1970–88. Hon. Canon: St Albans, 1978–88; York, 1988–. Proctor in Convocation, 1970–; a Church Commr, 1978–. *Publications:* Life of our Lord, 1960; WCC Programme to Combat Racism, 1979; (contrib.) When will ye be Wise?, 1983; (contrib.) Building in Love, 1990; Journey to Faith, 1992; Affairs of State, 1995; contrib. to national press. *Recreations:* cooking, theatre. *Address:* 7 Lang Road, Bishopthorpe, York YO2 1QJ. *T:* York (01904) 709541.

AUSTIN, Hon. Jacob, (Jack), PC (Canada) 1981; QC (British Columbia) 1970; Member of the Senate, Canadian Parliament, since 1975; *b* 2 March 1932; *s* of Morris Austin and Clara Edith (*née* Chetner); *m* (marr. diss.); three *d*; *m* 1978, Natalie Veiner Freeman. *Educ:* Univ. of British Columbia (BA, LLB); Harvard Univ. (LLM). Barrister and Solicitor, BC and Yukon Territory. Asst Prof. of Law, Univ. of Brit. Columbia, 1955–58; practising lawyer, Vancouver, BC, 1958–63; Exec. Asst to Minister of Northern Affairs and Nat. Resources, 1963–65; contested (Liberal) Vancouver-Kingsway, Can. Federal Election, 1965; practising lawyer, Vancouver, BC, 1966–70; Dep. Minister, Dept of Energy, Mines and Resources, Ottawa, 1970–74; Principal Sec. to Prime Minister, Ottawa, May 1974–Aug. 1975; Minister of State, 1981–82; Minister of State for Social Develt, responsible for Canada Develt Investment Corp., 1982–84; Chm., Ministerial Sub-Cttee on Broadcasting and Cultural Affairs, 1982–84. Pres., Internat. Div., Bank of British Columbia, 1985–86; Associate Counsel: Swinton & Co., 1986–92; Boughton Peterson & Co., 1992–; Chairman of Board and Director: Elite Insurance Management Ltd, 1986–90. Hon. DSocSc Univ. East Asia, 1987. *Publications:* articles on law and public affairs in Canadian Bar Rev., Amer. Soc. of Internat. Law and other publns. *Recreations:* sailing, tennis, reading, theatre. *Address:* Suite 304, 140 Wellington Street, The Senate, Ottawa, Ontario K1A 0A4, Canada. *T:* (613) 9921437. *Clubs:* Rideau (Ottawa); Cercle Universitaire d'Ottawa; Vancouver (Vancouver, BC); Metropolitan (NY).

AUSTIN, Rt. Rev. John Michael; *see* Aston, Bishop Suffragan of.

AUSTIN, Vice-Adm. Sir Peter (Murray), KCB 1976; Director, Mastiff Electronic Systems, since 1987 (Managing Director, 1990–91); *b* 16 April 1921; *er s* of late Vice-Adm. Sir Francis Austin, KBE, CB, and late Lady (Marjorie) Austin (*née* Barker); *m* 1959, Josephine Rhoda Ann Shutte-Smith; three *s* one *d*. *Educ:* RNC, Dartmouth. Cadet, Dartmouth, 1935. Served War of 1939–45: at sea in HMS Cornwall, 1939–40; destroyers, 1941–45. Qualif. as pilot in FAA, 1946; served in 807 Sqdn, 1947–49; CO 736 Sqdn, 1950–52; grad. from RAF Flying Coll., Manby, 1953; comd 850 Sqdn in HMAS Sydney, incl. Korea, 1953–54; Lt-Cmdr (Flying), HMS Bulwark, 1954–56; Comdr (Air), RNAS Brawdy, 1956–58; Comdr (Air), HMS Eagle, 1958–59; Captain, 1961; Captain F7 in HMS Lynx, 1963–65; CO, RNAS Brawdy, 1965–67; Staff of SACLANT, 1967–69; comd aircraft carrier, HMS Hermes, 1969–70; Rear-Adm., 1971; Asst Chief of Naval Staff (Ops and Air), 1971–73; Flag Officer, Naval Air Comd, 1973–76, retired; Vice-Adm., 1974. Operations Dir, Mersey Docks and Harbour Co., 1976–80; Dir, Avanova Internat. Consultants, 1980–89; Chm., Special Training Services, 1984–90. Vice-Chm. Council, Air League, 1987–. Liveryman, GAPAN, 1987–. CIMgt. *Recreations:* golf, skiing, sailing, walking, swimming. *Clubs:* Army and Navy; Royal Yacht Squadron.

AUSTIN, Air Marshal Sir Roger (Mark), KCB 1992; AFC 1973; FRAeS; Controller, Aircraft, since 1994, and Deputy Chief of Defence Procurement (Operations), since 1995, Ministry of Defence; *b* 9 March 1940; *s* of Mark and Sylvia Joan Austin; *m* 1st, 1963, Carolyn de Recourt Martyn (marr. diss. 1981); two *s* one *d*; 2nd, 1986, Glenys Amy Beckley (*née* Roberts); two step *d*. *Educ:* King Alfred's Grammar Sch., Wantage. Commissioned in RAF, 1957; flying appts as Qualified Flying Instructor and with Nos 20 and 54 Sqns, 1960–68; commanded No 54 Sqn, 1969; flying appt with No 4 Sqn, 1970–72; Staff Coll., Camberley, 1973; commanded 233 OCU, 1974–77; PSO to AOC-in-C Strike Command, 1977–80; commanded RAF Chivenor, 1980–82; ADC to the Queen, 1980–82; Staff of HQ Strike Command, 1982–84; Dir of Op. Requirements, 1984–85; RCDS, 1986; AO i/c Central Tactics and Trials Orgn, 1987; DG Aircraft 1, MoD (PE), 1987–89; AOC and Comdt, RAF Coll., Cranwell, 1989–92; DCDS (Systems), MoD, 1992–94. *Recreations:* walking, transport systems. *Club:* Royal Air Force.

AUSTIN-SMITH, Michael Gerard; QC 1990; a Recorder, since 1986; *b* 4 Sept. 1944; *s* of late Cyril John Austin-Smith and of Joyce Austin-Smith; *m* 1971, Stephanie Maddocks; one *s* one *d*. *Educ:* Hampton Grammar Sch.; Exeter Univ. (LLB Hons). Called to the Bar, Inner Temple, 1969. DTI Inspector, 1988–89 and 1989–90. *Address:* 36 Essex Street, Strand, WC2 3AS.

AUSTIN-WALKER, John Eric; MP (Lab) Woolwich, since 1992; *b* 21 Aug. 1944; *s* of late Stanley George Austin and Ellen Elizabeth (*née* Day); *m* 1965, Linda Margaret Walker (separated 1988); two *s* one *d*. *Educ:* Glyn Grammar Sch., Epsom; Goldsmiths' Coll., Univ. of London (Cert. Community and Youth Work 1972); Sch. for Advanced Urban Studies, Univ. of Bristol (MSc Policy Studies 1990). Hosp. lab. technician, 1961–63; Labour Party organiser, 1963–70; social worker/community worker, Bexley, 1972–74; Race Equality Officer (Dir, Bexley Council for Racial Equality), 1974–92. London Borough of Greenwich Council: Mem., 1970–94; Vice-Chm., 1971–74, Chm., 1974–78, Social Services; Dep. Leader, 1981–82; Leader, 1982–87; Mayor of Greenwich, 1987–88 and 1988–89. Vice-Chairman: ALA, 1983–87 (Envmt Spokesperson, 1989–92); London Strategic Policy Unit, 1986–88; Chaiman: London Ecology Unit, 1990–92; London Emergency Planning Inf. Centre, 1990–92. Chairman: British Youth Council, 1969–71; Assoc. CHCs for England and Wales, 1986–88. Contested (Lab) Woolwich, 1987. Mem., Select Ctte on Health, 1994–. Vice Chm., London Gp of Labour MPs, 1992–; Chm., Socialist Campaign Gp of Labour MPs, 1994–. *Recreations:* cooking, gardening, marathon running, travel. *Address:* House of Commons, SW1A 0AA. *T:* 0171–219 5195, *Fax:* 0171–219 2706; (constituency office) *T:* 0181–317 9001, *Fax:* 0181–317 3005. *Club:* St Patrick's Social (Plumstead).

AUSTRALIA, Primate of; *see* Melbourne, Archbishop of.

AUSTRALIA, North-West, Bishop of, since 1992; **Rt. Rev. Anthony Howard Nichols;** *b* 29 March 1938; *m* 1968, Judith Margaret Ross; two *s* two *d*. *Educ:* Univ. of Sydney (BA; MEd); Univ. of London (BD Hons); Macquarrie Univ. (MA Hons); Moore Coll., ACT (Theol. scholar). Latin and history teacher, 1960–63. Assistant Curate: St Paul's Chatswood, 1966; St Bede's, Drummoyne, 1967; Lectr, Biblical Studies, Moore Coll., Sydney, 1968–72; Lectr, Biblical Studies and Educn, 1972–81, Dean of Faculty of Theology, 1977–81, Satya Wacana Christian Univ., Salatiga, Indonesia; Principal: Nungalinya Coll., Darwin (Training Coll. for Aboriginal theol students), 1982–87; St Andrew's Hall, Melbourne (CMS Training Coll.), 1988–91. Stephen Bayne Scholar, Univ. of Sheffield, 1985–86. *Publications:* jl articles on Bible translation, missiology, Indonesian religions, Aboriginal culture, and philosophy of educn. *Address:* Bishop's House, PO Box 140, Geraldton, WA 6530, Australia. *T:* (99) 217277, *Fax:* (99) 642220.

AUSTWICK, Prof. Kenneth, JP; Professor of Education, Bath University, 1966–91, now Emeritus; *b* 26 May 1927; *s* of Harry and Beatrice Austwick; *m* 1956, Gillian Griffin; one *s* one *d*. *Educ:* Morecambe Grammar Sch.; Sheffield Univ. BSc Maths, DipEd, MSc, PhD Sheffield. Fellow, Royal Statistical Soc.; FRSA. Schoolmaster, Bromsgrove, Frome and Nottingham, 1950–59; Lectr/Sen. Lectr, Sheffield Univ., 1959–65; Dep. Dir, Inst. of Educn, Reading Univ., 1965–66; Pro-Vice-Chancellor, Bath Univ., 1972–75. Vis. Lecturer: Univ. of BC, 1963; Univ. of Michigan, 1963; Univ. of Wits., 1967. Consultant, OECD, 1965; Adviser, Home Office, 1967–81; Chm., Nat. Savings SW Regional Educn, 1975–78. JP Bath 1970. *Publications:* Logarithms, 1962; Equations and Graphs, 1963; (ed) Teaching Machines and Programming, 1964; (ed) Aspects of Educational Technology, 1972; Maths at Work, 1985; Mathematics Connections, 1985; Level by Level Mathematics, 1991; (ed) Working Science, 1991; (ed) Working English, 1991; (ed) Working Technology, 1992; (ed) Working Geography, 1992; (ed) Working Mathematics, 1993; articles and contribs on maths teaching and educnl technology. *Recreations:* gardening, wine making. *Address:* Brook House, Combe Hay, Bath BA2 7EG. *T:* Bath (01225) 832541. *Club:* Commonwealth Trust.

AUTY, Richard Mossop, CBE 1978 (OBE 1968); retired British Council officer; *b* 29 Jan. 1920; *s* of Rev. Thomas Richard Auty and Mrs Edith Blanche Auty (*née* Mossop); *m* 1st, 1944, Noreen Collins (marr. diss. 1949); one *d*; 2nd, 1956, (Anne) Marguerite Marie Poncet; one *s* one *d*. *Educ:* Hanley High Sch.; LSE, Univ. of London. Planning Br., Min. of Agriculture and Fisheries, 1942–46; Bureau of Current Affairs, 1946–49; Lectr, Goldsmiths' Coll. and Morley Coll., 1947–49; British Council, 1949–80: Lectr, Milan, 1949–57; Head, Overseas Students Centre, London, 1957–61; Reg. Rep., S India, 1961–65; Cultural Attaché, Brit. Embassy, Budapest, 1965–68; Director: S Asia Dept, 1968–70; Personnel Dept, 1970–72; Controller, European Div., 1972–76; Rep., France, and Cultural Counsellor, British Embassy, Paris, 1976–80. *Recreations:* literature, theatre, cinema. *Address:* 4 Thurlow Road, NW3 5PJ. *T:* 0171–435 8982.

AVEBURY, 4th Baron *cr* 1900; **Eric Reginald Lubbock;** Bt 1806; *b* 29 Sept. 1928; *s* of Hon. Maurice Fox Pitt Lubbock (6th *s* of 1st Baron) (*d* 1957), and Hon. Mary Katherine Adelaide Stanley (*d* 1981), *d* of 5th Baron Stanley of Alderley; *S* cousin, 1971; *m* 1953, Kina Maria (marr. diss. 1983) (*see* Lady Avebury); two *s* one *d*; 2nd, 1985, Lindsay Stewart; one *s*. *Educ:* Upper Canada Coll.; Harrow Sch.; Balliol Coll., Oxford (BA Engineering; boxing blue). Welsh Guards (Gdsman, 2nd Lieut), 1949–51; Rolls Royce Ltd, 1951–56; Grad. Apprentice; Export Sales Dept; Tech. Assistant to Foundry Manager. Management Consultant: Production Engineering Ltd, 1953–60; Charterhouse Group Ltd, 1960. MP (L) Orpington, 1962–70; Liberal Whip in House of Commons, 1963–70. Dir, C. L. Projects Ltd, 1966–; Consultant, Morgan-Grampian Ltd, 1970–. President: Data Processing Management Assoc., 1972–75; Fluoridation Soc., 1972–84; Conservation Soc., 1973–83.

Member: Council, Inst. of Race Relations, 1972–74; Royal Commn on Standards of Conduct in Public Life, 1974–76; Chm., British Parly Human Rights Gp, 1976–. Pres., London Bach Soc. and Steinitz Bach Players, 1984–. MIMechE. *Recreations:* listening to music, reading. *Heir: s* Hon. Lyulph Ambrose Jonathan Lubbock [*b* 15 June 1954; *m* 1977, Susan (*née* MacDonald); one *s* one *d*]. *Address:* House of Lords, SW1A 0PW.

AVEBURY, Lady; Kina-Maria Lubbock, (Kina Lady Avebury); consultant on mental health; *b* 2 Sept. 1934; *d* of late Count Joseph O'Kelly de Gallagh and of Mrs M. Bruce; *m* 1953, 4th Baron Avebury, *qv* (marr. diss. 1983); two *s* one *d*. *Educ:* Convent of the Sacred Heart, Tunbridge Wells; Goldsmiths' College (BScSoc Hons) and LSE, Univ. of London. Lectr, Royal Coll. of Nursing, 1970–74; campaign organizer, European Movement, 1975; Asst Dir, Nat. Assoc. for Mental Health, 1976–82; Sociologist, Dept of Psychiatry, London Hosp. Med. Coll., 1983–85; Mental Health Planner, Tower Hamlets Social Services, 1986–94. Chairman: Nat. Marriage Guidance Council, 1975–82; Family Service Units, 1984–87; Avebury Working Party, 1982–84 (produced Code of Practice for Residential Care for DHSS); Mem., Central Council for Educn and Trng in Social Work, 1986–90. JP Kent, 1974–79. *Publications:* Volunteers in Mental Health, 1985; articles on mental health and related social policy. *Recreations:* painting, opera, cooking.

AVELING, Alan John, CB 1986; Consultant, Mott Macdonald Group, since 1988; Under Secretary, Director of Home Regional Services, Property Services Agency, Department of the Environment, 1980–88; *b* 4 Jan. 1928; *s* of late Herbert Ashley Aveling and Ethel Aveling; *m* 1960, Stella May Reed; one *s* one *d*. *Educ:* Fletton Grammar Sch.; Rugby Technical Coll. CEng; FIEE, FIMechE, FCIBSE. Air Min. Works Dir, Newmarket, 1951–52; RAF Airfield Construction, 2nd Allied Tactical Air Force, 1952–55; Air Min. HQ, 1955–61; Sen. Engr, War Office Works Dept, 1961–63; BAOR Services, Germany, MPBW, 1963–66; Directorate Personnel, MPBW, 1966–67; Superintending Engr, Overseas Defence and FCO Services, 1967–72; Reg. Works Officer, later Regional Dir, British Forces, Germany, PSA/DoE, 1972–76; Dir of Estate Management Overseas, 1976–78; Dir Eastern Region, PSA/DoE, 1978–80. *Recreations:* aviculture, ski-ing. *Club:* Royal Air Force.

AVERY, Gillian Elise, (Mrs A. O. J. Cockshut); writer; *b* 1926; *d* of late Norman and Grace Avery; *m* 1952, A. O. J. Cockshut; one *d*. *Educ:* Dunottar Sch., Reigate. Chm., Children's Books History Soc., 1987–90; Mem., American Antiquarian Soc., 1988. *Publications: children's fiction:* The Warden's Niece, 1957; Trespassers at Charlcote, 1958; James without Thomas, 1959; The Elephant War, 1960; To Tame a Sister, 1961; The Greatest Gresham, 1962; The Peacock House, 1963; The Italian Spring, 1964; The Call of the Valley, 1966; A Likely Lad, 1971 (Guardian Award, 1972); Huck and her Time Machine, 1977; *adult fiction:* The Lost Railway, 1980; Onlookers, 1983; *non-fiction:* 19th Century Children: heroes and heroines in English children's stories (with Angela Bull), 1965; Victorian People in Life and Literature, 1970; The Echoing Green: memories of Regency and Victorian youth, 1974; Childhood's Pattern, 1975; Children and Their Books: a celebration of the work of Iona and Peter Opie (ed with Julia Briggs), 1989; The Best Type of Girl: a history of girls' independent schools, 1991; Behold the Child: a history of American children and their books 1622–1921, 1994. Ed, Gollancz revivals of early children's books, 1967–70, and anthologies of stories and extracts from early children's books. *Recreations:* music, laughing. *Address:* 32 Charlbury Road, Oxford OX2 6UU.

AVERY, Graham John Lloyd; a Director, European Commission (formerly Commission of the European Communities), Brussels, since 1987; *b* 29 Oct. 1943; *s* of Rev. Edward Avery and Alice Avery; *m* 1967, Susan Steele (separated 1982); two *s*; partner, 1989, Annalisa Cecchi; one *s*. *Educ:* Kingswood Sch., Bath; Balliol Coll., Oxford (MA). Fellow, Center for Internat. Affairs, Harvard Univ. Joined MAFF, 1965; Principal responsible for negotiations for British entry to European Communities, 1969–72; PPS to Ministers, Frederick Peart, John Silkin, 1976; Commission of the European Communities, Brussels: Member of Cabinets: of President, Roy Jenkins, 1977–80; of Vice-Pres. for External Relns, Christopher Soames, 1973–76; of Comrs for Agric., Finn Gundelach 1981, Poul Dalsager 1981, Frans Andriessen 1985–86; served in Directorate Gen. for Agric. as Hd of Div. for Econ. Affairs and Gen. Problems, 1981–84, as Dir for Agricl Structures, 1987–89, as Dir for Rural Develt, 1989–90; served: in Directorate Gen. for External Relations as Dir for relns with USA, Canada, Australia, NZ and S Africa, 1990–92; as Dir for relns with Austria, Switzerland, Iceland, Norway, Sweden and Finland, 1992–93; in Task Force for Enlargement as Dir, 1993–94. *Publications:* articles in Internat. Affairs, World Today, Europ. Affairs, Oxford Internat. Rev., Jl of Agricl Econs, Europ. Environment Rev., etc. *Address:* European Commission, 1049 Brussels, Belgium. *T:* (2) 2992202.

AVERY, James Royle, (Roy Avery); Headmaster, Bristol Grammar School, 1975–86; *b* 7 Dec. 1925; *s* of Charles James Avery and Dorothy May Avery; *m* 1954, Marjorie Louise (*née* Smith); one *s* one *d*. *Educ:* Queen Elizabeth's Hosp., Bristol; Magdalen Coll., Oxford; Bristol Univ. MA Oxon, CertifEd Bristol; FRSA. Asst History Master, Bristol Grammar Sch., 1951–59; Sen. History Master, Haberdashers' Aske's Sch. at Hampstead, then Elstree, 1960–65; Head Master, Harrow County Boys' Sch., 1965–75. *Publications:* The Story of Aldenham House, 1961; The Elstree Murder, 1962; The History of Queen Elizabeth's Hospital 1590–1990, 1990; contrib. Dictionary of World History, 1973; articles, reviews in educnl jls. *Recreations:* reading, walking, sport, music, the Ecumenical Movement, international studies. *Address:* First Floor Flat, 4 Rockleaze, Sneyd Park, Bristol BS9 1ND. *T:* Bristol (0117) 968 6805.

AVERY, John Ernest; Deputy Parliamentary Commissioner for Administration, since 1990; *b* 18 April 1940; *s* of Ernest Charles Avery and Pauline Margaret Avery; *m* 1966, Anna Meddings; two *d*. *Educ:* Plymouth Coll.; Leeds Univ. (BSc). Called to the Bar, Gray's Inn, 1972. Patent Examiner, Bd of Trade, 1964–72; Office of Fair Trading, 1972–76; Dept of Industry, later DTI, 1976–89; Dir of Investigations, Office of Parly Comr for Admin (Ombudsman), 1989–90. *Recreations:* squash, theatre. *Address:* Office of Parliamentary Commissioner for Administration, Church House, Great Smith Street, SW1P 3BW. *T:* 0171–276 2119.

AVERY, Percy Leonard; Chairman, staff side, Civil Service National Whitley Council, 1977–80; General Secretary, Association of Government Supervisors and Radio Officers, 1951–79; *b* 10 March 1915; *s* of Percy James Avery and Frances Elisabeth Avery; *m* 1940, Joan Mahala Breakspear; one *s* one *d* (and one *d* decd). *Educ:* Woolwich Polytechnic. Served War: Navigator, RAF Bomber Comd, 1941–45; Flt Lieut. Exec. Sec., Internat. Fedn of Air Traffic Electronics Assoc., 1972–79. Member: Kent Area Health Authority, 1973–79; MoD Management Review Body, 1975–76; Civil Service Pay Rev. Board, 1978–79; CS Deptl Whitley Councils (various), 1949–77. Dir of Admin, British Karate Bd, 1979–82; Dir, Internat. Amateur Karate Fedn, 1983–; Treasurer: English Karate Council, 1981–82; European Amateur Karate Fedn, 1982–. Governor, Ruskin Coll; Mem., Kent Age Concern, 1980–83. *Recreations:* athletics, Rugby, music, gardening. *Address:* Edificio Oromar no 136, Piso 9, Avenida Columbretes, Oropesa del Mar, Castellon, Spain. *T:* (64) 311017.

AVERY, Roy; *see* Avery, J. R.

AVERY JONES, Sir Francis, Kt 1970; CBE 1966; FRCP; retired; Consulting Physician, Gastroenterological Department, Central Middlesex Hospital (Physician, 1940–74); Consulting Gastroenterologist: St Mark's Hospital (Consultant, 1948–78); Royal Navy (Consultant, 1950–78); Hon. Consulting Physician, St Bartholomew's Hospital, 1978; *b* 31 May 1910; *s* of Francis Samuel and Marion Rosa Jones; *m* 1st, 1934, Dorothea Pfirter (*d* 1983); one *s*; 2nd, 1983, K. Joan Edmunds. *Educ:* Sir John Leman Sch., Beccles; St Bartholomew's Hosp. Baly Research Scholarship, St Bart's, 1936; Julius Mickle Fellowship, University of London, 1952. Goulstonian Lecturer, Royal College of Physicians, 1947; Lumleian Lectr, RCP; Nuffield Lectr in Australia, 1952; First Memorial Lectr, Amer. Gastroenterological Assoc., 1954; Croonian Lectr, RCP, 1969; Harveian Orator, RCP, 1980; Caroline Walker Meml Lectr, Caroline Walker Trust, 1992. Formerly Examiner: RCP; Univ. of London; Univ. of Leeds. Chairman: Emergency Bed Service, 1967–72; Med. Records Cttee, Dept of Health and Social Security; Medical Adv. Cttee, British Council, 1973–79; Member: Med. Sub-cttee, UGC, 1966–71; Brent and Harrow AHA, 1975–78; Dep. Chm., Management Cttee, King Edward VII Hosp. Fund, 1976–79; Mem. Council, Surrey Univ., 1975–82. Pres., United Services Section, RSM, 1974–75 (formerly Pres., section of Proctology); 2nd Vice-Pres., RCP, 1972–73; President: Medical Soc. of London, 1977–78; Medical Artists Assoc., 1980–91; British Digestive Foundn, 1981–92. Editor of Gut, 1965–70. Hon. FRCS 1981; Hon. FACP 1985; Hon. Mem., Amer., Canadian, French, Scandinavian and Australian Gastroenterological Assocs. Master, Worshipful Co. of Barbers, 1977–78. Hon. MD Melbourne, 1952; DUniv Surrey, 1980. Ambuj Nath Bose Prize, RCP, 1971; Moxon Medal, RCP, 1978; Fothergillian Gold Medal, Med. Soc., London, 1980; Henry L. Bockus Medal, World Orgn of Gastroenterology, 1982. *Publications:* Clinical Gastroenterology (jt author), 2nd edn 1967; Editor of Modern Trends in Gastroenterology First and Second Series, 1952 and 1958; many articles on Gastroenterology in the Medical Press. *Recreation:* water-side and herb gardening. *Address:* Mill House, Nutbourne, Pulborough, West Sussex RH20 2HE. *T:* West Chiltington (01798) 813314. *Club:* Athenæum.

See also J. F. Avery Jones.

AVERY JONES, Dr John Francis, CBE 1987; FTII; Senior Partner, Speechly Bircham, since 1985; *b* 5 April 1940; *s* of Sir Francis Avery Jones, *qv*; *m* 1994, Catherine Susan Bobbett. *Educ:* Rugby Sch.; Trinity Coll., Cambridge (MA, LLM, PhD 1993). Solicitor, 1966; Partner in Bircham & Co., 1970. Member: Meade Cttee, 1975–77; Keith Cttee, 1980–84. Pres., Inst. of Taxation, 1980–82; Chm., Law Soc.'s Revenue Law Cttee, 1983–87; Member Council: Law Soc., 1986–90; Inst. for Fiscal Studies, 1988–; Exec. Cttee, Internat. Fiscal Assoc., 1988–94 (1st Vice-Pres., 1993–94; Chm., British Br., 1989–91); Mem., Bd of Trustees, Internat. Bureau of Fiscal Documentation, 1989– (Chm., 1991–). Vis. Prof. of Taxation, LSE, 1988–. Dep. Special Comr of Income Tax, 1991–; Chm., VAT Tribunals, 1991–. Mem. Bd of Governors, Voluntary Hosp. of St Bartholomew, 1984–; Chm., Addington Soc., 1985–87. Master, Co. of Barbers, 1985–86. Consulting Ed., Encyclopedia of VAT, 1989–93 (Gen. Ed., 1972–89); Jt Editor, British Tax Review, 1974–; Mem. Editl Bd, Simon's Taxes, 1977–. *Publications:* (ed) Tax Havens and Measures Against Tax Avoidance and Evasion in the EEC, 1974; numerous articles on tax. *Recreations:* music, particularly opera. *Address:* 65 Castlebar Road, W5 2DA. *T:* 0181–998 2143. *Club:* Athenæum.

AVNER, Yehuda; Ambassador of Israel to Australia, since 1992; *b* 30 Dec. 1928; *m* Miriam Avner; one *s* three *d*. *Educ:* High School, Manchester. Editor of publications, Jewish Agency, Jerusalem, 1956–64; Editor of Political Publications, Min. of Foreign Affairs, and Asst to Prime Minister Levi Eshkol, 1964–67; Consul, New York, 1967–68; First Sec. then Counsellor, Washington, 1968–72; Dir of Foreign Press Bureau, Foreign Ministry, and Asst to PM Golda Meir, 1972–74; seconded to PM's Bureau, and Adviser to PM Yitzhak Rabin, 1974–77; Adviser to PM Menachem Begin, 1977–83; Ambassador to UK, 1983–88; Dir Gen., Clore Foundn, Israel, 1989–90; Inspector General of Foreign Service, Israel, 1990–92. *Publication:* The Young Inheritors: a portrait of Israeli youth, 1982. *Address:* Embassy of Israel, 6 Turrana Street, Yarralumla, ACT 2600, Australia.

AVONSIDE, Rt. Hon. Lord; Ian Hamilton Shearer, PC 1962; a Senator of the College of Justice in Scotland, 1964–84; *b* 6 Nov. 1914; *s* of Andrew Shearer, OBE, and Jessie Macdonald; *m* 1st, 1942; one *s* one *d*; 2nd, 1954, Janet Sutherland Murray (*see* Lady Avonside). *Educ:* Dunfermline High Sch.; Glasgow Univ.; Edinburgh Univ. MA Glasgow, 1934; LLB Edinburgh, 1937. Admitted to Faculty of Advocates, 1938; QC (Scotland) 1952. Served War of 1939–45, RA; Major. Standing Counsel: to Customs and Excise, Bd of Trade and Min. of Labour, 1947–49; to Inland Revenue, 1949–51; to City of Edinburgh Assessor, 1949–51; Junior Legal Assessor to City of Edinburgh, 1951; Sheriff of Renfrew and Argyll, 1960–62; Lord Advocate, 1962–64. Mem., Lands Valuation Court, 1964 (Chm., 1975–84). Chm. Nat. Health Service Tribunal, Scotland, 1954–62; Mem. Scottish Cttee of Coun. on Tribunals, 1958–62; Chm. Scottish Valuation Advisory Coun., 1965–68; Mem., Scottish Univs Cttee of the Privy Council, 1971–. Pres., Stair Soc., 1975–87. *Publications:* Purves on Licensing Laws, 1947; Acta Dominorum Concilii et Sessionis, 1951. *Recreations:* golf, gardening. *Address:* The Mill House, Samuelston, East Lothian EH41 4HG. *T:* Haddington (01620) 822396. *Club:* New (Edinburgh).

AVONSIDE, Lady; Janet Sutherland Shearer, OBE 1958; Scottish Governor, BBC, 1971–76; *b* 31 May 1917; *d* of William Murray, MB, ChB, and Janet Harley Watson; *m* 1954, Ian Hamilton Shearer, Rt Hon. Lord Avonside, *qv*. *Educ:* St Columba's Sch., Kilmacolm; Erlenhaus, Baden Baden; Univ. of Edinburgh. LLB, Dip. of Social Science. Asst Labour Officer (Scot.), Min. of Supply, 1941–45; Sec. (Scot.), King George's Fund for Sailors, 1945–53; Hon. Sec. (Scot.), Federal Union and United Europe, 1945–64; Scottish Delegate: Congress of Europe, 1947; Council of Europe, Strasburg, 1949. Contested (C), elections: Maryhill, Glasgow, 1950; Dundee East, 1951; Leith, 1955. Lectr in Social Studies, Dept of Educational Studies, Univ. of Edinburgh, 1962–70. Governor, Queen Margaret Coll., Edinburgh, 1986–89. *Recreation:* gardening. *Address:* The Mill House, Samuelston, East Lothian EH41 4HG. *T:* Haddington (01620) 822396. *Clubs:* Caledonian (Associate Mem.); New (Edinburgh).

AWAD, Muhammad Hadi; Director, Western Europe Department, Ministry of Foreign Affairs, Yemen, since 1990; *b* 5 May 1934; Yemeni; *m* 1956, Adla; one *s* three *d*. *Educ:* Murray House Coll. of Educn. DipEd, Certif. Social Anthrop. Edinburgh. Teacher, 1953–59; Educn Officer, 1960–62; Chief Inspector of Schs, 1963–65; Vice-Principal, As-Shaab Coll., 1965–67; Perm. Rep. to Arab League, Ambassador to UAR and non-resident Ambassador to Sudan, Lebanon, Libya and Iraq, 1968–70; Perm. Sec., Min. of For. Affairs, 1970–73; Ambassador to London, 1973–80, to Sweden and Spain, 1974–80, to Denmark, Portugal and the Netherlands, 1975–80, to Tunisia, 1980–86; Perm. Rep. to Arab League, 1980–86. *Recreation:* photography. *Address:* c/o Ministry of Foreign Affairs, PO Box 19262, Sana'a, Yemen.

AWDRY, Daniel (Edmund), TD; DL; *b* 10 Sept. 1924; *s* of late Col Edmund Portman Awdry, MC, TD, DL, Coters, Chippenham, Wilts, and Mrs Evelyn Daphne Alexandra Awdry, JP (formerly French); *m* 1950, Elizabeth Cattley; three *d*. *Educ:* Winchester Coll. RAC, OCTU, Sandhurst, 1943–44 (Belt of Honour). Served with 10th Hussars as Lieut, Italy, 1944–45; ADC to GOC 56th London Div., Italy, 1945; Royal Wilts Yeo., 1947–62;

Major and Sqdn Comdr, 1955–62. Qualified Solicitor, 1950. Mayor of Chippenham, 1958–59; Pres., Southern Boroughs Assoc., 1959–60. MP (C) Chippenham, Wilts, Nov. 1962–1979; PPS to Minister of State, Board of Trade, Jan.-Oct. 1964; PPS to Solicitor-Gen., 1973–74. Director: BET Omnibus Services, 1966–80; Sheepbridge Engineering, 1968–79; Rediffusion Ltd, 1973–85; Colonial Mutual Life Assurance Ltd, 1974–89. DL Wilts, 1979. *Recreation:* chess. *Address:* Old Manor, Beanacre, near Melksham, Wilts SN12 7PT. *T:* Melksham (01225) 702315.

AWDRY, Rev. Wilbert Vere; Church of England clergyman, and author; *b* 15 June 1911; *s* of Rev. Vere Awdry and Lucy Louisa (*née* Bury); *m* 1938, Margaret Emily (*née*Wale) (*d* 1989); one *s* two *d*. *Educ:* Dauntsey's, W Lavington, Wilts; St Peter's Hall. Oxford (MA); Wycliffe Hall, Oxford (DipTh). Asst Master, St George's Sch., Jerusalem, 1933–36; Curate: Odiham, Hants, 1936–38; W Lavington, 1938–40; King's Norton, Birmingham, 1940–46; Rector, Elsworth with Knapwell, Cambs, 1946–53; Rural Dean, Bourn, Cambs, 1950–53; Vicar, Emneth, Wisbech, 1953–65; authorised to officiate in Dio. of Gloucester, 1965–. *Publications: for children:* The Three Railway Engines, 1945; Thomas the Tank-engine, 1946; James the Red Engine, 1948; Tank-engine Thomas again, 1949; Troublesome Engines, 1950; Henry the Green Engine, 1951; Toby the Tram Engine, 1952; Gordon the Big Engine, 1953; Edward the Blue Engine, 1954; Four Little Engines,, 1955; Percy the Small Engine, 1956; The Eight Famous Engines, 1957; Duck & the Diesel Engine, 1958; Belinda the Beetle, 1958; The Little Old Engine, 1959; The Twin Engines, 1960; Branch Line Engines, 1961; Belinda beats the Band, 1961; Gallant Old Engine, 1962; Stepney the Bluebell Engine, 1963; Mountain Engines, 1964; Very Old Engines, 1965; Main Line Engines, 1966; Small Railway Engines, 1967; Enterprising Engines, 1968; Oliver the Western Engine, 1969; Duke the Lost Engine, 1970; Tramway Engines, 1972; Thomas' Christmas Party, 1984; Map of the Island of Sodor, 1958, 4th edn 1988; (jtly) The Island of Sodor: its people, history and railways, 1987; *non fiction:* (ed) Industrial Archaeology in Gloucestershire, 1973, 3rd edn 1983; (jt ed) A Guide to Steam Railways of Great Britain, 1979, 3rd edn 1984; (jtly) The Birmingham and Gloucester Railway, 1987. *Recreations:* reading, railway modelling, photography, family history. *Address:* Sodor, 30 Rodborough Avenue, Stroud, Glos GL5 3RS. *T:* Stroud (01453) 762321.

AXELROD, Julius, PhD; Guest Researcher, Laboratory of Cell Biology, since 1984, Chief, Section on Pharmacology, Laboratory of Clinical Science, 1955–84 (Acting Chief, Jan.-Oct. 1955), National Institute of Mental Health, USA; Laboratory of Cell Biology, since 1984; *b* NYC, 30 May 1912; *s* of Isadore Axelrod, Michaliev, Poland, and Molly Liechtling, Striej, Poland (formerly Austria); *m* 1938, Sally (*née* Taub); two *s*. *Educ:* George Washington Univ., Wash., DC (PhD); New York Univ. (MA); New York City Coll. (BS). Lab. Asst. Dept Bacteriology, NY Univ. Med. Sch., 1933–35; Chemist, Lab. Industrial Hygiene, 1935–46; Res. Associate, Third NY Univ.; Research Div., Goldwater Memorial Hosp., 1946–49; Nat. Heart Inst., NIH: Associate Chemist, Section on Chem. Pharmacology, 1949–50; Chemist, 1950–53; Sen. Chemist, 1953–55. Jt Nobel Prize for Physiology-Medicine, 1970; Mem., Nat. Academy of Sciences, 1971; Fellow, Amer. Acad. of Arts and Sciences; Senior Mem., Amer. Inst. of Medicine, 1979. Thudicum Medal and Lecture, British Biochem Soc., 1989. Foreign Member: Royal Society, 1979; Deutsche Akademie der Naturforscher, 1984. Hon. LLD: George Washington, 1971; College City, NY, 1972; Hon. DSc: Chicago, 1966; Med. Coll., Wisconsin, 1971; New York, 1971; Pennsylvania Coll. of Med., 1973; Hahnemann Univ., 1987; McGill Univ., 1988; Doctor *hc* Panama, 1972; DPhil *hc*: Ripon Coll., 1984; Tel Aviv Univ., 1984. Winner of 15 awards; holds 23 hon. lectureships; Member: 13 editorial boards; 5 Sci. Adv. Cttees. *Publications:* (with Richard J. Wurtman and Douglas E. Kelly) The Pineal, 1968; numerous original papers and contribs to jls in Biochem., Pharmacol. and Physiology. *Recreations:* reading and listening to music. *Address:* 10401 Grosvenor Place, Rockville, MD 20852, USA. *T:* (301) 4936376.

AXFORD, David Norman, PhD, CMet, CEng, FIEE; international consultant meteorologist; Special Executive Adviser to the Secretary-General, World Meteorological Organisation, since 1995; *b* 14 June 1934; *s* of Norman Axford and Joy Alicia Axford (*née* Williams); *m* 1st, 1962, Elizabeth Anne (*née* Stiles) (marr. diss. 1980); one *s* two *d*; 2nd, 1980, Diana Rosemary Joan (*née* Bufton); three step *s* one step *d*. *Educ:* Merchant Taylors' School, Sandy Lodge; Plymouth Coll.; St John's Coll., Cambridge (Baylis Open Scholarship in Maths; BA 1956, MA 1960, PhD (Met.) 1972); MSc (Electronics) Southampton 1963; FIEE 1982. Entered Met. Office, 1958; Flying Officer, RAF, 1958–60; Meteorological Office: Forecasting and Research, 1960–68; Met. Research Flight, and Radiosondes, 1968–76; Operational Instrumentation, 1976–80; Telecommunications, 1980–82; Dep. Dir, Observational Services, 1982–84; Dir of Services, 1984–89; Dep. Sec.-Gen., WMO, 1989–95. Chm., Cttee on Operational World Weather Watch Systems Evaluation, N Atlantic (CONA), 1985–89. Pres., N Atlantic Observing Stations (NAOS) Bd, 1983–86; Vice Pres., RMetS, 1989–91 (Mem. Council and Hon. Gen. Sec., 1983–88). L. G. Groves 2nd Meml Prize for Met., 1970. *Publications:* papers in learned jls on met. and aspects of met. instrumentation in GB and USA. *Recreations:* home and garden, music, travel, good food. *Address:* Rudgewick Cottage, Binfield Heath, Henley-on-Thames, Oxon RG9 4JY. *T:* Henley-on-Thames (01491) 574423; c/o World Meteorological Organisation, Case Postale No 2300, 1211 Genève 2, Switzerland. *Club:* Phyllis Court (Henley-on-Thames).

AXFORD, Dr William Ian, FRS 1986; Director, Max Planck Institut für Aeronomie, Katlenburg-Lindau, West Germany, 1974–82 and since 1985; *b* 2 Jan. 1933; *s* of John Edgar Axford and May Victoria Axford; *m* 1955, Catherine Joy; two *s* two *d*. *Educ:* Univ. of Canterbury, NZ (MSc Hons, ME Dist.); Univ. of Manchester (PhD); Univ. of Cambridge. NZ Defence Science Corps, 1957–63; seconded to Defence Res. Bd, Ottawa, 1960–62; Associate Prof. of Astronomy, 1963–66, Prof. of Astronomy, 1966–67, Cornell Univ., Ithaca, NY; Prof. of Physics and Applied Physics, Univ. of Calif at San Diego, 1967–74; Vice-Chancellor, Victoria Univ. of Wellington, NZ, 1982–85. Pres., COSPAR, 1986–94; Vice-Pres., Scientific Cttee on Solar-Terrestrial Physics, 1986–90. Hon. Prof., Göttingen Univ., 1978; Appleton Meml Lectr, URSI, 1969. Chm. Bd, NZ Foundn for Res., Sci. and Technol., 1992–95. Pres., European Geophysical Soc., 1990–92. Fellow, Amer. Geophysical Union, 1971; ARAS 1981; For. Associate, US Nat. Acad. of Scis, 1983; Member: Internat. Acad. of Astronautics, 1985; Academia Europaea, 1989. Hon. FRSNZ 1993. Space Science Award, AIAA, 1970; John Adam Fleming Medal, Amer. Geophysical Union, 1972; Tsiolkovsky Medal, Kosmonautical Fedn, USSR, 1987; Chapman Medal, RAS, 1994; NZ Sci. and Technol. Gold Medal, 1994. *Publications:* about 250 articles in scientific jls on aspects of space physics and astrophysics. *Address:* Max Planck Institut für Aeronomie, Postfach 20, 37189 Katlenburg-Lindau, Germany. *T:* (5556) 979439, *Fax:* (5556) 979240; 2 Gladstone Road, Napier, New Zealand. *T* and *Fax:* (68) 352188.

AXISA, John Francis, MBE 1950; *b* 20 Nov. 1906; *s* of late Emmanuel Axisa and Vincenzina (*née* Micallef); *m* 1939, Ariadne Cachia; three *s* one *d*. *Educ:* St Paul's Sch., Malta and privately. Joined Malta Civil Service, 1927; Dir of Emigration, 1947–56; Dir of Technical Education, 1956–59; Dir of Emigration, Labour and Social Welfare, 1959–60; Under-Sec., 1960–61; Commissioner-Gen. for Malta in London, 1961–64; Malta's first High Commissioner on Malta's Independence, 1964–69; Ambassador of Malta to: France, 1966–69; Fed. Republic of Germany, 1967–69; Libya, 1966–68; Belgium, 1967–68; Netherlands, 1968–69. Chm., Bd of Govs, St Edward's Coll., Malta, 1988–90 (Trustee, 1988–93). *Recreations:* carpentry, fishing, reading. *Address:* 5/8 Tower Road, Sliema, Malta, GC. *Club:* Union (Malta).

AXTON, Henry Stuart, (Harry), FCA; Chairman, Brixton Estate plc, 1983–93; *b* 6 May 1923; *s* of Wilfrid George Axton and Mary Louise Laver; *m* 1947, Constance Mary Godefroy; one *d*. *Educ:* Rock Ferry. RMC, Sandhurst, commissioned 1942; served: N Africa, Royal Tank Regt, NW Europe, Fife and Forfar Yeo.; wounded three times, invalided out, 1945. Articles, G. E. Holt & Son; Chartered Accountant 1948. Treas., United Sheffield Hosps and other hosp. appts, 1948–55; Company Sec., Midland Assurance, 1955–61; Brixton Estate, 1961–93: Man. Dir, 1964–83; Dep. Chm., 1971–83; Chm., Investment Cos in Australia and Switzerland. Pres., British Property Fedn, 1984–86 (Mem. Council, 1974–93; Vice-Pres., 1983–84; Hon. Life Mem., 1993). Dep. Chm., Audit Commn, 1987–91 (Mem., 1986–91). Chairman: Council, St George's Hosp. Med. Sch., 1977–92 (Mem., 1969–92; Dep. Chm. 1974–77; first Hon. Fellow 1992); St George's New Hosp. Bldg Cttee, 1972–92 (Mem., 1969–92); Nuffield Hosps, 1976–93 (Governor, 1968–93; Dep. Chm. 1975–76); BUPA Medical Centre, 1973–82 (Governor, 1970–82); Mem., Chichester HA, 1985–87; Governor: BUPA, 1969–80; St George's Hosp., 1970–74, Special Trustee, 1974–77. Chm., Chichester Festivities, 1989–. Dir, Cathedral Works Organisation (Chichester), 1985–91. Mem., Archbp's Council for Church Urban Fund, 1990–94. Freeman, City of London, 1987. Lord of the Manor of Aldingbourne, 1993. *Recreations:* sailing, music. *Address:* Hook Place, Aldingbourne, near Chichester, Sussex PO20 6TS. *T:* Eastergate (01243) 542291. *Clubs:* Royal Thames Yacht, Royal Ocean Racing.

AYALA, Jaime Z. de; *see* Zobel de Ayala.

AYALA-LASSO, José; United Nations Commissioner for Human Rights, since 1994; *b* 29 Jan. 1932; *m* Monique Wiets de Ayala Lasso; one *s* three *d*. *Educ:* Catholic Univ. of Leuven, Belgium; Catholic Univ. of Ecuador; Central Univ. of Ecuador. Ministry of Foreign Affairs, Ecuador, 1955; served Tokyo, Lima, Rome and Min. of Foreign Affairs, to 1974; Ambassador of the Foreign Service, 1975; Under-Sec.-Gen., Min. of Foreign Affairs, 1975; Minister of Foreign Affairs, 1977; Ambassador to Belgium, Luxembourg and EC, 1979, to Peru, 1983; Ambassador and Perm. Rep. of Ecuador to UN, 1989–94. Order of Al Mérito, Ecuador; numerous orders from foreign counties. *Recreation:* classical music. *Address:* High Commisioner for Human Rights, Palais des Nations, United Nations, Geneva, Switzerland.

AYCKBOURN, Alan, CBE 1987; playwright; Artistic Director, Stephen Joseph Theatre-in-the-Round, Scarborough; *b* 12 April 1939; *s* of Horace Ayckbourn and Irene Maude (*née* Worley); *m* 1959, Christine Helen (*née* Roland); two *s*. *Educ:* Haileybury. Worked in repertory as Stage Manager/Actor at Edinburgh, Worthing, Leatherhead, Oxford, and with late Stephen Joseph's Theatre-in-the-Round Co., at Scarborough. Founder Mem., Victoria Theatre, Stoke-on-Trent, 1962. BBC Radio Drama Producer, Leeds, 1964–70; Co. Dir, NT, 1986–87. Vis. Prof. of Contemporary Theatre, and Fellow, St Catherine's Coll., Oxford, 1991–92. Has written numerous full-length plays. London productions: Mr Whatnot, Arts, 1964; Relatively Speaking, Duke of York's, 1967, Greenwich, 1986 (televised, 1969, 1989); How the Other Half Loves, Lyric, 1970, Duke of York's, 1988; Time and Time Again, Comedy, 1972 (televised, 1976); Absurd Person Singular, Criterion, 1973 (Evening Standard Drama Award, Best Comedy, 1973) (televised, 1985); The Norman Conquests (Trilogy), Globe, 1974 (Evening Standard Drama Award, Best Play; Variety Club of GB Award; Plays and Players Award) (televised, 1977); Jeeves (musical, with Andrew Lloyd Webber), Her Majesty's, 1975; Absent Friends, Garrick, 1975 (televised, 1985); Confusions, Apollo, 1976; Bedroom Farce, Nat. Theatre, 1977 (televised, 1980); Just Between Ourselves, Queen's, 1977 (Evening Standard Drama Award, Best Play) (televised, 1978); Ten Times Table, Globe (dir), 1978; Joking Apart, Globe, 1979 (Plays and Players Award); Sisterly Feelings, Nat. Theatre, 1980; Taking Steps, Lyric, 1980; Suburban Strains (musical with Paul Todd), Round House, 1981; Season's Greetings, Apollo, 1982; Way Upstream, Nat. Theatre (dir), 1982 (televised, 1988); Making Tracks (musical with Paul Todd), Greenwich, 1983; Intimate Exchanges, Ambassadors, 1984; A Chorus of Disapproval, Nat. Theatre (dir), 1985 (Standard Drama Award, Best Comedy; Olivier Award, Best Comedy; Drama Award, Best Comedy, 1985), transf. Lyric, 1986 (filmed, 1989); Woman in Mind, Vaudeville (dir), 1986; A Small Family Business, Nat. Theatre (dir), 1987 (Evening Standard Drama Award, Best Play); Henceforward . . ., Vaudeville (dir), 1988 (Evening Standard Drama Award, Best Comedy, 1989); Man of the Moment, Globe (dir), 1990 (Evening Standard Drama Award, Best Comedy, 1990); The Revengers' Comedies, Strand, 1991; Time of My Life, Vaudeville (dir), 1993; Wildest Dreams, Barbican (dir), 1993; Scarborough: Body Language, 1990; Dreams from a Summer House (play with music by John Pattison), 1992; Communicating Doors, 1994; Haunting Julia, 1994; A Word from our Sponsor (musical with John Pattison), 1995; other plays directed: Tons of Money, Nat. Theatre, 1986; A View from the Bridge, Nat. Theatre, transf. Aldwych, 1987; 'Tis Pity she's a Whore, Nat. Theatre, 1988; Two Weeks with the Queen, Nat.Theatre, 1994; Conversations with my Father, Old Vic, 1995. *Plays for children:* Callisto 5, 1990; My Very Own Story, 1991; This Is Where We Came In, 1991; Invisible Friends, Nat. Theatre (dir), 1991; Mr A's Amazing Maze Plays, Nat. Theatre, 1993; The Musical Jigsaw Play, 1994. Hon. DLitt: Hull, 1981; Keele, 1987; Leeds, 1987; York, 1992; Bradford, 1994. *Publications:* The Norman Conquests, 1975; Three Plays (Absurd Person Singular, Absent Friends, Bedroom Farce), 1977; Joking Apart and Other Plays (Just Between Ourselves, Ten Times Table), 1979; Sisterly Feelings, and Taking Steps, 1981; A Chorus of Disapproval, 1986; Woman in Mind, 1986; A Small Family Business, 1987; Henceforward . . ., 1988; Mr A's Amazing Maze Plays, 1989; Man of the Moment, 1990; Invisible Friends (play for children), 1991; The Revengers' Comedies, 1991; Time of My Life, 1993; Wildest Dreams, 1993; Callisto 5, This is Where We Came In, My Very Own Story, 1995. *Recreations:* music, reading, cricket, films. *Address:* c/o Casarotto Ramsay Ltd, National House, 60–66 Wardour Street, W1V 3HP. *T:* 0171–287 4450. *Club:* Garrick.

AYERS, John Gilbert; Keeper, Far Eastern Department, Victoria and Albert Museum, 1970–82; *b* 27 July 1922; *s* of H. W. Ayers, CB, CBE; *m* 1957, Bridget Elspeth Jacqualine Fanshawe; one *s* two *d*. *Educ:* St Paul's Sch.; St Edmund Hall, Oxford. Served in RAF, 1941–46 (Sgt). Asst Keeper, Dept of Ceramics, Victoria and Albert Museum, 1950, Dep. Keeper 1963. Pres., Oriental Ceramic Soc., 1984–87. *Publications:* The Seligman Collection of Oriental Art, II, 1964; The Baur Collection: Chinese Ceramics, I-IV, 1968–74, Japanese Ceramics, 1982; (with R. J. Charleston) The James A. de Rothschild Collection: Meissen and Oriental Porcelain, 1971; Oriental Ceramics, The World's Great Collections: Victoria and Albert Museum, 1975; (with J. Rawson) Chinese Jade throughout the Ages, exhbn catalogue, 1975; (with D. Howard) China for the West, 2 vols, 1978; (with D. Howard) Masterpieces of Chinese Export Porcelain, 1980; Oriental Art in the Victoria and Albert Museum, 1983; (ed) Chinese Ceramics in the Topkapi Saray Museum, Istanbul, 3 vols, 1986; (with O. Impey and J. V. G. Mallet) Porcelain for Palaces: the fashion for Japan in

Europe 1650–1750, 1990; Chinese Ceramic Tea Vessels: the K. S. Lo Collection, Hong Kong, 1991; A Jade Menagerie: creatures real and imaginary from the Worrell Collection, 1993. *Address:* 3 Bedford Gardens, W8 7ED. *T:* 0171–229 5168.

AYERST, Rev. Edward Richard; Chaplain to the Queen, 1987–95; *m* 1959, Pauline Clarke; one *s* two *d*. *Educ:* Coopers' Company's School; Leeds Univ. (BA Hons 1951); College of the Resurrection, Mirfield. Vicar of St Mary with St John, Edmonton, N18, 1960–66; Rector of East Cowes with Whippingham, IoW, 1966–77; Vicar of Bridgwater, 1977–90. Mem., Philosophical Soc., 1981. *Recreations:* sailing; helping the Sea Cadet Corps. *Address:* 56 Maple Drive, Burnham-on-Sea, Somerset TA8 1DH. *T:* Burnham-on-Sea (01278) 780701.

AYKROYD, Sir James (Alexander Frederic), 3rd Bt *cr* 1929, of Birstwith Hall, Hampsthwaite, co. York; Chairman, Alexander Muir & Son Ltd, since 1993; *b* 6 Sept. 1943; *s* of Bertram Aykroyd (*d* 1983), *y s* of Sir Frederic Alfred Aykroyd, 1st Bt, and his 1st wife, Margot Aykroyd (*née* Graham Brown) (*see* Dame Margot Smith); *S* uncle, 1993; *m* 1973, Jennifer Marshall; two *d*. *Educ:* Eton Coll.; Univ. of Aix en Provence; Univ. of Madrid. Sen. Export Dir, James Buchanan & Co. Ltd, 1965–83; Export Man. Dir, Martini & Rossi SpA, 1983–87; Sen. Partner, Aykroyd Marketing Consultants, 1987–. *Recreations:* active sports esp. tennis and golf. *Heir: half b* Toby Nigel Bertram Aykroyd, *b* 13 Nov. 1955. *Address:* 5 Highbury Terrace, N5 1UP. *T:* 0171–226 9750. *Club:* Alwoodley Golf.

AYKROYD, Sir William Miles, 3rd Bt *cr* 1920; MC 1944; *b* 24 Aug. 1923; *s* of Sir Alfred Hammond Aykroyd, 2nd Bt, and Sylvia Ambler Aykroyd (*née* Walker) (*d* 1992), *widow* of Lieut-Col Foster Newton Thorne; *S* father, 1965. *Educ:* Charterhouse. Served in 5th Royal Inniskilling Dragoon Guards, Lieut, 1943–47. Dir, Hardy Amies Ltd, 1950–69. *Heir: cousin* Michael David Aykroyd [*b* 14 June 1928; *m* 1952, Oenone Gillian Diana, *o d* of Donald George Cowling, MBE; one *s* three *d*]. *Address:* Buckland Newton Place, Dorchester, Dorset DT2 7BX. *T:* Buckland Newton (01300) 345259. *Club:* Boodle's.

AYLARD, Comdr Richard John, CVO 1994; RN, retired; Private Secretary and Treasurer to the Prince of Wales, since 1991; *b* 10 April 1952; *s* of John and Joy Aylard; *m* 1st, 1977, Sally Williams (marr. diss. 1984); 2nd, 1984, Suzanne Walker; two *d*. *Educ:* Queen Elizabeth's Grammar Sch., Barnet; Reading Univ. (BSc Hons Applied Zoology with Maths). Joined RN as university cadet, 1972; served HM Ships Shavington, Ark Royal, Fox, 1974–77; Staff of Flag Officer Submarines, 1977–79; Flag Lieut to Dep. SACLANT, Norfolk, USA, 1979–81; Capt's Sec., HMS Invincible, 1981–83; Supply Officer, HMS Brazen, 1984–85; Equerry to the Princess of Wales, 1985–88; Asst Private Sec. and Comptroller to the Prince and Princess of Wales, 1988–91; Comdr RN, 1987; RN retd, 1989. *Recreations:* sailing, fishing, gardening, ski-ing. *Address:* Wren House, Kensington Palace, W8 4PU.

AYLEN, Rear-Adm. Ian Gerald, CB 1962; OBE 1946; DSC 1942; CEng; FIMechE; *b* 12 Oct. 1910; *s* of late Commander A. E. Aylen, RN and Mrs S. C. M. Aylen; *m* 1937, Alice Brough Maltby; one *s* two *d*. *Educ:* Blundell's, Tiverton. RNE Coll., Keyham, 1929–33; served in HMS Rodney; Curacoa; Galatea, 1939–40; Kelvin, 1940–42; 30 Assault Unit, 1945; Cossack; Fleet Engineer Officer, Home Fleet, 1957–58; CO HMS Thunderer, RNE Coll., 1958–60; Rear-Admiral, 1960; Admiral Superintendent, HM Dockyard, Rosyth, 1960–63; Dep. Sec., Instn Mechanical Engineers, 1963–65; Asst Sec., Council of Engineering Instns, 1966–71, retired 1971. *Address:* Tracey Mill Barn, Honiton, Devon EX14 8SL.

AYLEN, Walter Stafford; QC 1983; a Recorder, since 1985; *b* St Helena, 21 May 1937; *s* of late Rt Rev. Charles Arthur William Aylen and Elisabeth Margaret Anna (*née* Hills); *m* 1967, Peggy Elizabeth Lainé Woodford, three *d*. *Educ*. Summer Fields Sch.; Winchester Coll. (schol.); New Coll., Oxford (schol., sen. schol.; BCL; MA). Commnd 2nd Lieut KRRC, 1956–57. Called to the Bar, Middle Temple, 1962 (Bencher 1991); Asst Recorder, 1982; Bar Council, 1994–. Chm., BSITC, 1994. Vice-Chm., Finance Cttee, 1995. FRSA 1989. *Recreations:* reading novels (especially his wife's), theatre, music. *Address:* 27 Gauden Road, SW4 6LR. *T:* 0171–622 7871; Hardwicke Building, New Square, Lincoln's Inn, WC2A 3SB. *T:* 0171–242 2523.

AYLESFORD, 11th Earl of; **Charles Ian Finch-Knightley,** JP; Baron Guernsey, 1703; Lord-Lieutenant of West Midlands, 1974–93; *b* 2 Nov. 1918; *er s* of 10th Earl of Aylesford; *S* father, 1958; *m* 1946, Margaret Rosemary Tyer (*d* 1989); one *s* two *d*. *Educ:* Oundle. Lieut RSF, 1939; Captain Black Watch, 1947. Regional Dir, Birmingham and W Midlands Bd, Lloyds Bank, 1982–88. Mem., Water Space Amenity Commn, 1973–83. County Comr for Scouts, 1949–74, Patron 1974–. JP 1948, DL 1954, Vice-Lieutenant 1964–74, Warwicks. KStJ 1974. Hon. LLD Birmingham, 1989. *Recreations:* wild life and nature conservation. *Heir: s* Lord Guernsey, *qv*. *Address:* Packington Old Hall, Coventry, West Midlands CV7 7HG. *T:* (home) Meriden (01676) 23273; (office) Meriden (01676) 23467. *Club:* Warwickshire CC (President, 1980–).

AYLING, Peter William, OBE 1989; BSc, CEng, FRINA; Secretary, Royal Institution of Naval Architects, 1967–89; *b* 25 Sept. 1925; *s* of late William Frank and Edith Louise Ayling; *m* 1949, Sheila Bargery; two *s* two *d*. *Educ:* Royal Dockyard Sch., Portsmouth; King's Coll., Univ. of Durham (BSc). Shipwright apprentice, HM Dockyard, Portsmouth, 1942–47; King's Coll., Univ. of Durham, 1947–50; Research and Principal Research Officer, British Ship Research Assoc., London, 1950–65; Principal Scientific Officer, Ship Div., Nat. Physical Laboratory, Feltham (now British Maritime Technology Ltd), 1965–67. *Publications:* papers on ship strength and vibration, Trans RINA, NECInst and IESS. *Recreations:* music, gardening, walking, motoring. *Address:* Oakmead, School Road, Camelsdale, Haslemere, Surrey GU27 3RN. *T:* Haslemere (01428) 644474.

AYLMER, family name of **Baron Aylmer.**

AYLMER, 13th Baron *cr* 1718; **Michael Anthony Aylmer;** Bt 1662; *b* 27 March 1923; *s* of Christopher Aylmer (*d* 1955) and Marjorie (*d* 1981), *d* of Percival Ellison Barber, surgeon, Sheffield; *S* cousin, 1982; *m* 1950, Countess Maddalena Sofia, *d* of late Count Arbeno Attems, Aiello del Friuli, Italy; one *s* one *d*. *Educ:* privately and Trinity Hall, Cambridge (Exhibnr, MA, LLM). Admitted a solicitor, 1948. Employed in Legal Dept of Equity & Law Life Assurance Society plc, 1951 until retirement, 1983. *Recreations:* reading and music. *Heir: s* Hon. (Anthony) Julian Aylmer [*b* 10 Dec. 1951; *m* 1990, Belinda Rosemary, *d* of Maj. Peter Parker; one *s* one *d*]. *Address:* 42 Brampton Grove, NW4 4AQ. *T:* 0181–202 8300.

AYLMER, Dr Gerald Edward, FBA 1976; Master of St Peter's College, Oxford, 1978–91, Hon. Fellow, 1991; *b* 30 April 1926; *s* of late Captain E. A. Aylmer, RN, and Mrs G. P. Aylmer (*née* Evans); *m* 1955, Ursula Nixon; one *s* one *d*. *Educ:* Winchester; Balliol Coll., Oxford (MA, DPhil). Served RN, 1944–47. Jane Eliza Proctor Vis. Fellow, Princeton Univ., NJ, USA, 1950–51; Jun. Res. Fellow, Balliol Coll., Oxford, 1951–54; Asst Lectr in History, Univ. of Manchester, 1954–57, Lectr, 1957–62; Prof. of History and Head of Dept of History, Univ. of York, 1963–78; Mem., Oxford History Faculty, 1978–. Vis. Mem., Inst. for Advanced Study, Princeton, 1975. Mem., Royal Commn on Historical Manuscripts, 1978– (Chm., 1989–94). Pres., RHistS, 1984–88 (Hon. Vice Pres., 1988–); Hon. Vice-President: Cromwell Assoc., 1991–; Historical Assoc., 1992–. Mem., Editorial Bd, History of Parliament, 1969– (Chm., 1989–). Hon. DLitt Exeter, 1991; Hon. LittD Manchester, 1991. *Publications:* The King's Servants, 1961 (2nd edn 1974); (ed) The Diary of William Lawrence, 1962; The Struggle for the Constitution, 1963 (5th edn 1975); (ed) The Interregnum, 1972 (2nd edn 1974); The State's Servants, 1973; (ed) The Levellers in the English Revolution, 1975; (ed with Reginald Cant) A History of York Minster, 1978; Rebellion or Revolution?: England 1640–1660, 1986; articles and revs in learned jls. *Address:* The Old Captains, Hereford Road, Ledbury, Herefordshire HR8 2PX. *T:* Ledbury (01531) 670817; 18 Albert Street, Jericho, Oxford OX2 6AZ. *T:* Oxford (01865) 512383.

AYLMER, Sir Richard John, 16th Bt *cr* 1622, of Donadea, Co. Kildare; writer; *b* 23 April 1937; *s* of Sir Fenton Gerald Aylmer, 15th Bt and Rosalind Boultbee (*d* 1991), *d* of J. Percival Bell; *S* father, 1987; *m* 1962, Lise, *d* of Paul Demers; one *s* one *d*. *Educ:* Lower Canada Coll., Montreal; Western Ontario, London, Canada; Harvard Univ., Cambridge, Mass, USA. *Heir: s* Fenton Paul Aylmer, *b* 31 Oct. 1965. *Address:* 3573 Lorne Avenue, Montreal, Quebec H2X 2A4, Canada.

AYNSLEY-GREEN, Prof. Albert, DPhil; FRCP, FRCPE; Nuffield Professor of Child Health, since 1993, and Head, Division of Clinical Sciences, Institute of Child Health, since 1993, University of London; Director, Clinical Research and Development, Great Ormond Street Hospital for Children, since 1993; Hon. Consultant Paediatrician, Great Ormond Street Hospital and University College Hospital, since 1993; *b* 30 May 1943; *m* 1967, Rosemary Anne Boucher; two *d*. *Educ:* Glyn Grammar Sch., Epsom; Guy's Hosp. Med. Sch., Univ. of London (MB BS); Oriel Coll., Oxford (MA, DPhil). MRCS 1967; FRCP 1982; FRCPE 1987. House Officer posts at Guy's Hosp., London, St Luke's Hosp., Guildford, Radcliffe Infirmary, Oxford and RPMS, Hammersmith Hosp., London, 1967–70; Radcliffe Infirmary, Oxford: Wellcome Res. Fellow, 1970–72; Clinical Lectr in Internal Medicine, 1972–73; Sen. House Officer and Registrar posts in Paediatrics, Radcliffe Infirmary and John Radcliffe Hosp., Oxford, 1973–74; European Sci. Exchange Fellow, Royal Soc. and Swiss Nat. Res. Council, Univ. Children's Hosp., Zurich, 1974–75; University of Oxford: Clinical Lectr in Paediatrics, 1975–78; Univ. Lectr, 1978–83; Fellow, Green Coll., 1980–83; Hon. Consultant Paediatrician, Oxford AHA, 1978–83; University of Newcastle upon Tyne: James Spence Prof. of Child Health and Hd of Dept, 1984–93; Hd, Sch. of Clinical Med. Scis, 1991–93; Hon. Consultant Paediatrician, Royal Victoria Infirmary, Newcastle upon Tyne, 1984–93. Non-Exec. Mem., Bd of Govs, Hosp. for Sick Children, Gt Ormond St, 1990–93; Exec. Mem., Trust Bd, Gt Ormond St Hosp. for Children NHS Trust, 1993–. Chm., Adv. Gp on NHS Priorities for R&D in Mother and Child Health, DoH, 1994–95. Visiting Professor: Univ. of Ulm, FRG, 1986; Harvard Univ., 1987; Columbus Children's Hosp., Ohio State Univ., 1991; Vis. Paediatrician in Residence, Royal Children's Hosp., Univ. of Qld, 1989; Vis. Lectr, Children's Hosp., Camperdown, Sydney, 1992. Numerous lectures in Europe, USA and Australia including: Lockyer, RCP, 1988; Assoc. of Paediatric Anaesthetists of GB and Ire. (and Medal), 1990; Niilo Hallman, Univs of Helsinki and Tampere, Finland (and Medal), 1991. External Examiner in Paediatrics: Univ. of Malaya, 1990; Chinese Univ. of Hong Kong, 1994; Univ. of Kuwait, 1996. European Society for Paediatric Endocrinology: Sec., 1982–87; Pres., 1994–95. Hon. Mem., Hungarian Paediatric Assoc., 1988. Andrea Prader Prize and Medal, European Soc. for Paediatric Endocrinology, 1991. *Publications:* papers and articles on child health in general, and specifically on endocrinology and metabolism in infancy and childhood. *Recreations:* family, walking, music, photography. *Address:* Institute of Child Health, 30 Guilford Street, WC1N 1EH. *T:* 0171–242 9789. *Club:* Royal Society of Medicine.

AYOUB, Fouad; Order of Istiqlal I, 1991; Ambassador of the Hashemite Kingdom of Jordan to the Court of St James's, since 1991, and non-resident Ambassador to Iceland and to Ireland, since 1992; *b* 15 Aug. 1944; *m* 1974, Marie Vernazza; two *s* one *d*. *Educ:* California State Univ., San Francisco (BA; MA philosophy 1974). Press Secretary to King Hussein, 1977–91; Mem., Jordanian Delegn to Madrid Peace Conf., 1991. Fellow, Centre for Internat. Affairs, Harvard, 1983–84. Numerous foreign orders. *Recreation:* reading. *Address:* Embassy of the Hashemite Kingdom of Jordan, 6 Upper Phillimore Gardens, W8 7HB. *T:* 0171–937 3685.

AYOUB, John Edward Moussa, FRCS; Consulting Surgeon, Moorfields Eye Hospital, since 1973 (Surgeon, 1950–73); Consulting Ophthalmic Surgeon, London Hospital (now Royal London Hospital), since 1973 (Surgeon, 1947–73); Consulting Ophthalmic Surgeon, Royal Masonic Hospital, since 1973 (Consultant, 1967–73); Consulting Ophthalmic Surgeon, Royal Navy; *b* 7 Sept. 1908; British; *m* 1939, Madeleine Marion Coniston Martin; one *s* one *d*. *Educ:* St Paul's Sch.; Lincoln Coll., Oxford; St Thomas' Hospital. BM, BCh Oxon 1933; FRCS 1935. Fellow, and past Vice-Pres. Section of Ophthalmology, RSM; Past Mem. Council, Faculty of Ophthalmologists (Vice-Pres., 1959–). Served War of 1939–45, Surg. Lieut-Comdr RNVR, specialist in ophthalmology. Visiting consultant ophthalmologist to Western Memorial Hosp., Newfoundland, 1974–. *Publications:* contributions to medical journals. *Recreation:* gardening. *Address:* 2 Clarendon Road, Boston Spa, near Wetherby, West Yorks LS23 6NG. *Clubs:* Leander; Royal Cruising.

AYRES, Gillian, OBE 1986; RA 1991 (ARA 1982); painter, artist; *b* 3 Feb. 1930; *d* of Stephen and Florence Ayres; *m* Henry Mundy (marr. diss.); two *s*. *Educ:* St Paul's Girls' Sch.; Camberwell Sch. of Art. Student, 1946–50; taught, 1959–81 (incl. Sen. Lectr, St Martin's Sch. of Art, and Head of Painting, Winchester Sch. of Art, 1978–81). One-woman Exhibitions include: Gallery One, 1956; Redfern Gall., 1958; Moulton Gall., 1960 and 1962; Kasmin Gall., 1965, 1966 and 1969; William Darby Gall., 1976; Women's Internat. Centre, New York, 1976; Knoedler Gall., 1979, 1982, 1987; Mus. of Mod. Art, Oxford, 1981; retrospective exhibn, Serpentine Gall., 1983; also exhibited: Redfern Gall., 1957; 1st Paris Biennale, 1959; Hayward Gall., 1971; Silver Jubilee Exhibn, RA, 1977; Knoedler Gall., NY, 1985; Tate Gall., 1995. Works in public collections: Tate Gall.; Mus. of Mod. Art, NY; Olinda Mus., Brazil; Gulbenkian Foundn, Lisbon; V&A Mus.; British Council. Hon. DLit London, 1994. Prize winner: Tokyo Biennale, 1963; John Moores Prize, 1982; Indian Trienale, Gold Medal, 1991. *Address:* Tall Trees, Gooseham, near Bude, Cornwall EX23 9PQ. *T:* Morwenstow (01288) 331206.

AYRTON, Norman Walter; international theatre and opera director; Dean, British American Drama Academy, London, since 1986; *b* London, 25 Sept. 1924. Served War of 1939–45, RNVR. Trained as an actor at Old Vic Theatre School under Michael Saint Denis, 1947–48; joined Old Vic Company, 1948; repertory experience at Farnham and Oxford, 1949–50; on staff of Old Vic Sch., 1949–52; rejoined Old Vic Company for 1951 Festival Season; opened own teaching studio, 1952; began dramatic coaching for Royal Opera House, Covent Garden, 1953; apptd Asst Principal of London Academy of Music and Dramatic Art, 1954; taught at Shakespeare Festival, Stratford, Ont, and Royal Shakespeare Theatre, Stratford-upon-Avon, 1959–62; apptd GHQ Drama Adviser to Girl Guide Movement, 1960–74; Principal, LAMDA, 1966–72; Dean, World Shakespeare Study Centre, Bankside, 1972; Dir of Opera, Royal Acad. of Music, 1986–90. *Director:* Artaxerxes, for Handel Opera Soc., Camden Festival, 1963; La Traviata, Covent Garden,

1963; Manon, Covent Garden, 1964; Sutherland-Williamson Grand Opera Season, in Australia, 1965; Twelfth Night at Dallas Theatre Center, Texas, 1967; The Way of the World, NY, 1976; Lakmé, Sydney Opera House, 1976; Der Rosenkavalier, Sydney Opera House, 1983; *Guest Director:* Australian Council for Arts, Sydney and Brisbane, 1973; Loeb Drama Center, Harvard (and teacher), 1974, 1976, 1978; Faculty, Juillard Sch., NY, 1974–85; Melbourne Theatre Co., 1974–; Nat. Inst. of Dramatic Art, Sydney, 1974; Vancouver Opera Assoc., 1975–; Sydney Opera House, 1976–81, 1983; Williamstown Festival, USA, 1977; Hartford Stage Co. and Amer. Stage Fest., 1978–; Missouri Rep. Theatre, 1980–81; Nat. Opera Studio, London, 1980–81; Spoleto Fest., USA, 1984; Sarah Lawrence Coll., NY, 1993–94; Utah Shakespeare Fest., 1994; Resident Stage Director: Amer. Opera Center, NY, 1981–85; Vassar Coll., NY, 1990–94; Cornell Univ., 1995. Hon. RAM 1989. *Recreations:* reading, music, gardens, travel. *Address:* 40A Birchington Road, NW6 4LJ.

AZA, Alberto; Spanish Ambassador to the Court of St James's, since 1992; *b* 22 May 1937; *s* of Alberto Aza and Marcela Arias; *m* 1963, María Eulalia Custodio Martí; two *s* four *d*. *Educ:* Univ. de Oviedo; Law Faculty of Madrid (Law Degree); BA, BSc. Joined Diplomatic Service, 1965; served Libreville, Algiers, Rome, Madrid; Dir, Cabinet of the Spanish Prime Minister, 1977–83; Chief Dir, OAS, Latin-America Dept, Min. of Foreign Affairs, 1983; Minister Counsellor, Lisbon, 1983–85; Ambassador: to OAS, Washington, 1985–89; to Belize (resident in Washington), 1985–89; to Mexico, 1990–92. Gran Cruz del Mérito Civil (Spain), 1979. *Recreations:* fishing, golf, walking. *Address:* 24 Belgrave Square, SW1X 8QA. *T:* 0171–235 8363. *Clubs:* Athenæum, White's, Travellers'.

AZIKIWE, Rt. Hon. Nnamdi, GCFR 1980; PC 1960; LLD, DLitt, MA, MSc; Ndichie Chief Owelle of Onitsha, 1973; Leader, Nigeria People's Party, since 1979; (First) President of the Federal Republic of Nigeria, 1963–66; Governor-General and Commander-in-Chief of Nigeria, 1960–63; *b* Zungeru, Northern Nigeria, 16 Nov. 1904; *s* of Obededom Chukwuemeka and Rachel Chinwe Azikiwe; *m* 1936, Flora Ogbenyeanu Ogoegbunam, *d* of Chief Ogoegbunam, the Adazia of Onitsha (Ndichie Chief); three *s* one *d*. *Educ:* CMS Central Sch., Onitsha; Methodist Boys' High Sch., Lagos; Storer Coll., Harpers Ferry, W Va, USA; Howard Univ., Washington, DC; Lincoln Univ., Pa; Univ. of Pennsylvania. Overseas Fellow, Inst. Journalists, London, 1962 (Mem., 1933–). Editor-in-Chief, African Morning Post, Accra, 1934–37; Editor-in-Chief, West African Pilot, 1937–45; Correspondent for Associated Negro Press, 1944–47; Gen. Sec., Nat. Council of Nigeria and the Cameroons, 1944–46 (Pres., 1946–60); Correspondent for Reuter's, 1944–46; Chm. African Continental Bank Ltd, 1944–53. MLC Nigeria, 1947–51; Mem. Foot Commission for Nigerianisation of Civil Service, 1948. Leader of Opposition in the Western House of Assembly, 1952–53; Mem. Eastern House of Assembly, 1954–59; MHR 1954; Minister, Eastern Nigeria, 1954–57; Leader, Educational Missions to UK and USA, for establishment of Univ. of Nigeria, 1955 and 1959; Premier of Eastern Nigeria, 1954–59; Pres., Exec. Council of Govt of E Nigeria, 1957–59; President of Senate of Federation, Jan–Nov. 1960. NPP Candidate, Presidential Election, 1979. Mem., Council of State, 1979–83. Ndichie Chief Ozizani Obi of Onitsha, 1963–72. Chm., Provisional Council of Univ. of Nigeria, 1960–61; Chancellor of Univ. of Nigeria, 1961–66, of Univ. of Lagos, 1970–76. Jt Pres., Anti-Slavery Soc. for Human Rights, London, 1970– (Vice-Pres., 1966–69). (Life) FREconS; (Life) FRAI; (Life) Mem. British Association for Advancement of Science; Member: American Soc. of International Law; American Anthropological Assoc. Pres. numerous sporting assocs and boards, 1940–60; Mem., Nigerian Olympic Cttee, 1950–60. Hon. DCL Liberia, 1969; Hon. DSc Lagos, 1972. KStJ 1960–66. *Publications:* Liberia in World Politics, 1934; Renascent Africa, 1937; The African in Ancient and Mediaeval History, 1938; Land Tenure in Northern Nigeria, 1942; Political Blueprint of Nigeria, 1943; Economic Reconstruction of Nigeria, 1943; Economic Rehabilitation of Eastern Nigeria, 1955; Zik: a selection of speeches, 1961; Meditations: a collection of poems, 1965; My Odyssey, 1971; Military Revolution in Nigeria, 1972; Dialogue on a New Capital for Nigeria, 1974; Treasury of West African Poetry; Democracy with Military Vigilance, 1974; Onitsha Market Crisis, 1975; Civil War Soliloquies: further collection of poems, 1976; Ideology for Nigeria, 1978. *Recreations:* athletics, boxing, cricket, soccer, swimming, tennis, reading. *Address:* Onuiyi Haven, PO Box 7, Nsukka, Nigeria.

AZIZ, Suhail Ibne; international management consultant, since 1981; Chairman and Managing Director, Brettonwood Partnership Ltd, since 1990; *b* Bangladesh (then India), 3 Oct. 1937; permanently resident in England, since 1966; *s* of Azizur Rahman and Lutfunnessa Khatoon; *m* 1960, Elizabeth Ann Pyne, Dartmouth, Devon; two *d*. *Educ:* Govt High Sec. Sch., Sylhet; Murarichand Coll., Dacca Univ., Sylhet (Intermed. in Science, 1954); Jt Services Pre-Cadet Trng Sch., Quetta; Cadet Trng Sch., PNS Himalaya, Karachi; BRNC, Dartmouth (Actg Sub-Lieut 1958); (mature student) Kingston upon Thames Polytechnic and Trent Polytech., Nottingham (Dipl. in Man. Studies, 1970); (ext. student) London Univ. (BScEcon Hons 1972); (internal student) Birkbeck Coll., London Univ., (MScEcon 1976). FIMgt; MIMC 1986. Sub-Lieut and Lieut, Pakistan Navy Destroyers/Mine Sweeper (Exec. Br.), 1954–61. Personnel and indust. relations: Unilever (Pakistan); Royal Air Force; Commn on Indust. Relations, London; Ford Motor Co. (GB); Mars Ltd, 1963–78; Dir of Gen. Services Div., CRE, 1978–81; Dep. Dir of Econ. Develt, London Borough of Lewisham, 1984–88; Management Consultant, Fullemploy Consultancy Ltd, 1989–90; Dir and Mem. Exec. Sub-Cttee, Education Business Partnership. Mem., London Electricity Consumer Cttee, 1991–. Leading Mem., Bangladesh Movement in UK, 1971. Member: Exec., Standing Conf. of Asian Orgs in UK, 1972–; N Metropol. Conciliation Cttee, Race Relations Bd, 1971–74; Exec., Post Conf. Constituent Cttee, Black People in Britain—the Way Forward, 1975–76; Adv. Cttee to Gulbenkian Foundn on Area Resource Centre and Community Support Forum, 1976–81; Exec., Nottingham and Dist Community Relations Council, 1975–78; Dept of Employment Race Relations Employment Adv. Gp, 1977–78; BBC Asian programme Adv. Cttee, 1977–81; Industrial Tribunals, 1977–; Exec., Nat. Org. of African, Asian and Caribbean Peoples, 1976–77; Home Sec.'s Standing Adv. Council on Race Relations, 1976–78; Steering Cttee, Asian Support Forum, 1984–86; Jt Consultative Cttee with Ethnic Minorities, Merton BC, 1985–; Plunkett Foundn for Co-operative Studies, 1985–; "One World", 1986–; Adv. Gp, City of London Polytechnic Ethnic Minority Business Develt Unit, 1987–; Res. Adv. Bd, QMC, London Univ., 1988–; (co-opted), Exec. Cttee, Tower Hamlets Assoc. for Racial Equality, 1988– (Mem., Action Tower Hamlets, 1987); Exec. Cttee, Docklands Forum; Bangladeshis in Britain—a Response Forum, 1987–; Chairman: Jalalabad Overseas Orgn in UK, 1983–; London Boroughs Bangladesh Assoc., 1984–; Founder Chm., East London Bangladeshi Enterprise Agency, 1985–. CRE Bursary to study Minority Business Develt initiatives in USA, 1986. Mem., Labour Econ. Finance Taxation Assoc., 1973–80; Institute of Management Consultants: Chm., Third World Specialist Gp, 1984–; Treasurer, London Reg., 1985–87. Jt Trustee, United Action-Bangladesh Relief Fund, 1971–; Trustee: Trust for Educn and Develt; Greater Sylhet Develt and Welfare Council; Brixton Neighbourhood Assoc., 1979–82; East End Tourism Trust. Deeply interested in community and race relations and believes profoundly that future health of Brit. society depends on achieving good race relations. *Recreations:* travelling, seeing places of historical interest, meeting people, reading (*eg* political economy). *Address:* 126 St Julian's Farm Road, West Norwood, SE27 0RR. *Clubs:* Royal Air Force; Sudan (Khartoum).

B

BABCOCK, Horace Welcome; astronomer; Director, Mount Wilson and Palomar Observatories, 1964–78; *b* 13 Sept. 1912; *s* of Harold D. Babcock and Mary G. (*née* Henderson); *m* 1st, 1940; one *s* one *d*; 2nd, 1958; one *s*. *Educ:* California Institute of Technology (BS); Univ. of California (PhD). Instructor, Yerkes and McDonald Observatories, 1939–41; Radiation Laboratory, Mass Inst. of Tech., 1941–42; Calif Inst. of Tech., 1942–45; Staff Mem., Mount Wilson Observatory, 1946–51; Astronomer, Mount Wilson and Palomar Observatories, 1951–80; Founding Dir, Las Campanas Observatory, Chile, of Carnegie Instn, Washington, 1968–78. Elected to: National Acad. of Sciences, 1954 (Councillor, 1973–76); American Acad. of Arts and Sciences, 1959; American Philosophical Soc., 1966; Corres. Mem., Société Royale des Sciences de Liège, 1968; Associate, Royal Astronomical Soc., 1969; Member: American Astronomical Soc.; Astronomical Soc. of the Pacific; Internat. Astronomical Union. Hon. DSc Univ. of Newcastle upon Tyne, 1965. US Navy Bureau of Ordnance Development Award, 1945; Eddington Gold Medal, RAS, 1958; Henry Draper Medal of the National Acad. of Sciences, 1957; Bruce Medal, Astronomical Soc. of the Pacific, 1969; Gold Medal, RAS, 1970; Hale Prize, Amer. Astronomical Soc., 1992; Rank Prize in Opto-electronics, 1993. *Publications:* scientific papers in Astrophysical Jl, Publications of the Astronomical Soc. of the Pacific, Jl of Optical Soc. of America, etc, primarily on magnetic fields of the stars and sun, astrophysics, diffraction gratings, adaptive optics, and astronomical instruments. *Address:* The Observatories, Carnegie Institution of Washington, 813 Santa Barbara Street, Pasadena, CA 91101–1292, USA. *T:* (818) 5771122.

BABINGTON, His Honour Anthony Patrick; a Circuit Judge, 1972–87; *b* 4 April 1920; 2nd *s* of late Oscar John Gilmore Babington, MAI, AMICE, Monkstown, Co. Cork. *Educ:* Reading Sch. Served with Royal Ulster Rifles and Dorset Regt, 1939–45 (wounded twice); Croix de Guerre with Gold Star (France), 1944. Called to the Bar, Middle Temple, 1948; Bencher, 1977, Autumn Reader, 1994; South Eastern Circuit; Prosecuting Counsel to Post Office, SE Circuit (South), 1959–64; Metropolitan Stipendiary Magistrate, 1964–72. Mem., Home Office Working Party on Bail, 1971–73. Mem., Nat. Exec. Cttee, Internat. PEN English Centre, 1979–82. Trustee: New Bridge, 1985–; PEN Literary Foundn, 1990–. *Publications:* No Memorial, 1954; The Power to Silence, 1968; A House in Bow Street, 1969; The English Bastille, 1971; The Only Liberty, 1975; For the Sake of Example, 1983; Military Intervention in Britain, 1990; The Devil to Pay, 1991. *Recreations:* music, theatre, reading. *Address:* 3 Gledhow Gardens, South Kensington, SW5 0BL. *T:* 0171–373 4014; Thydon Cottage, Chilham, near Canterbury, Kent CT4 8BX. *T:* Canterbury (01227) 730300. *Clubs:* Garrick, Special Forces.

BABINGTON, His Honour Robert John, DSC 1943; QC (NI) 1965; appointed County Court Judge for Fermanagh and Tyrone, 1978; *b* 9 April 1920; *s* of David Louis James Babington and Alice Marie (*née* McClintock); *m* 1952, Elizabeth Bryanna Marguerite Alton, *d* of Dr E. H. Alton, Provost of Trinity College, Dublin; two *s* one *d*. *Educ:* St Columba's Coll., Rathfarnham, Dublin; Trinity Coll., Dublin (BA). Called to the Bar, Inn of Court of NI, 1947. MP North Down, Stormont, 1968–72. *Recreations:* golf, bird-watching. *Address:* c/o Royal Courts of Justice, Chichester Street, Belfast BT1 3JF. *Clubs:* Special Forces; Tyrone County (Omagh); Fermanagh County (Enniskillen); Royal Belfast Golf.

BABINGTON, Roger Vincent, FRINA; Director General Ships, Ministry of Defence, since 1995; *b* 6 April 1943; *s* of George Cyril Babington and late Rita Mary Babington (*née* Simpkins); *m* 1967, Susan Wendy Eaton; two *s* two *d*. *Educ:* King Edward's Sch., Bath; Univ. of Birmingham (BSc); University Coll. London (MSc). CEng; RCNC. MoD, 1967–76; Constructor, Principal Naval Overseer, Barrow-in-Furness, 1976–81; HM Dockyard, Rosyth: Constructor, 1981–82; Chief Constructor, 1982–86; Dir of Progs and Planning, 1986–87; Ministry of Defence, Bath: Dir, Surface Ships/D, 1987–89; Dir, SSN20, 1989–91; Dir, Submarines, 1991–93; Dir-Gen., Ship Refitting, 1993; Dir-Gen., Fleet Support (Ships), 1993–95. FIMgt. *Recreations:* Badminton, house, garden and vehicle maintenance, watching sport, listening. *Address:* Director General Ships, Ministry of Defence, Carpenter House, Broad Quay, Bath BA1 5AB. *T:* Bath (01225) 472285. *Club:* Bath and County (Bath).

BABINGTON, William, CBE 1972; QFSM 1969; Chief Officer, Kent County Fire Brigade, 1966–76, retired; *b* 23 Dec. 1916; *s* of William and Annie Babington; *m* 1940, Marjorie Perdue Le Seelleur; one *d*. *Educ:* King Edward's Grammar Sch., Birmingham. Addtl Supt of Police, Assam, India, 1942–44; Instructor, Fire Service Coll., 1951–53; Divl Officer, Hampshire Fire Service, 1954–59; Asst Chief Officer, Suffolk and Ipswich Fire Service, 1959–62; Dep. Chief Officer, Lancashire Fire Brigade, 1962–66. *Recreations:* sailing, travel. *Address:* Alpine Cottage, Grouville, Jersey, CI. *T:* Jersey (01534) 52737.

BABINGTON-BROWNE, Gillian Brenda, (Mrs K. J. Wilson); a Metropolitan Stipendiary Magistrate, since 1991; *b* 20 May 1949; *d* of Derek Keith Babington-Browne and Olive Maude (*née* Seymour); *m* 1983, Kenneth John Wilson. *Educ:* Rochester Girls' Grammar Sch.; Coll. of Law, London. Admitted Solicitor, 1973; Asst Solicitor with Arnold, Tuff & Grimwade, Rochester, 1973–74; Assistant with Ronald A. Prior, 1974, with Edward Lewis Possart, London, 1974–78; own practice, 1978–89; freelance advocate and consultant, 1989–91. Associate Mem., London Criminal Courts Solicitors' Assoc. (former Pres.). *Publications:* contribs to legal jls. *Recreations:* gardening, interior design/decorating, reading. *Address:* c/o Old Street Magistrates' Court, EC1V 9LJ. *T:* 0171–739 2373.

BACHE, Andrew Philip Foley, CMG 1992; HM Diplomatic Service; Ambassador to Romania, since 1992; *b* 29 Dec. 1939; *s* of late Robert Philip Sidney Bache, OBE and Jessie Bache; *m* 1963, Shân Headley; two *s* one *d*. *Educ:* Shrewsbury Sch.; Emmanuel Coll., Cambridge (MA). Joined HM Diplomatic Service, 1963; 3rd Sec., Nicosia, 1964–66; Treasury Centre for Admin. Studies, 1966; 2nd Sec., Sofia, 1966–68; FCO, 1968–71; 1st Sec., Lagos, 1971–74; FCO, 1974–78; 1st Sec. (Commercial), Vienna, 1978–81; Counsellor and Head of Chancery, Tokyo, 1981–85; Counsellor, Ankara, 1985–87; Hd of Personnel Services Dept, FCO, 1988–90; on secondment as Diplomatic Service Chm. to CSSB, 1990–91. *Recreations:* diverse, including travel, history, ornithology, fine arts, squash, tennis, cricket. *Address:* c/o Foreign and Commonwealth Office, King Charles Street, SW1A 2AH. *Club:* MCC.

BACHER, Dr Aron, (Ali Bacher); Managing Director, United Cricket Board of South Africa, since 1991; *b* 24 May 1942; *s* of Rose and Koppel Bacher; *m* 1965, Shira Ruth Teeger; one *s* two *d*. *Educ:* Yeoville Boys' Primary Sch.; King Edward VII High Sch.; Witwatersrand Univ. (MB BCh). Junior appts, Baragwanath and Natalspruit Hosps, 1968–69; private practice, Rosebank, Johannesburg, 1970–79. Managing Director: Delta Distributors, 1979–81; Transvaal Cricket Council, 1981–86; South African Cricket Union, 1986–91. Cricket début for Transvaal, 1959–60; captained S Africa, 1970; played 12 Test matches, made 120 1st cl. appearances, 7,894 runs, 18 centuries, 110 catches, one stumping; retired, 1974; Transvaal and Nat. Selectors' Panels, 1976–83; Dir S African Cricket Develt Club, 1986. Numerous awards include Jack Cheetham Meml, 1990, for doing the most to normalise sport in S Africa. *Recreation:* jogging. *Address:* PO Box 55041, Northlands 2116, South Africa. *T:* (11)8802810, (11)7831263.

BACK, Kathleen, (Mrs J. H. Back); *see* Harrison, Kathleen.

BACK, Kenneth John Campbell, AO 1984; MSc, PhD; higher education consultant; *b* 13 Aug. 1925; *s* of J. L. Back; *m* 1950, Patricia, *d* of R. O. Cummings; two *d*. *Educ:* Sydney High Sch.; Sydney Univ. (MSc); Univ. of Queensland (PhD). Res. Bacteriologist, Davis Gelatine (Aust.) Pty Ltd, 1947–49; Queensland University: Lectr in Bacteriology, 1950–56; Sen. Lectr in Microbiology, 1957–61; Actg Prof. of Microbiology, 1962; Warden, University Coll. of Townsville, Queensland, 1963–70; Vice-Chancellor, James Cook Univ. of N Queensland, 1970–85, Prof. Emeritus, 1986–; Exec. Dir, Internat. Develt Program of Australian Univs and Colls Ltd, 1986–90. Chm., Standing Cttee, Australian Univs Internat. Develt Prog. (formerly Australian-Asian Univs Co-operation Scheme), 1977–85. Hon. DSc: Queensland, 1982; James Cook, 1995; DUniv South Pacific, 1992. *Publications:* papers on microbiological metabolism, international education. *Recreations:* golf, bridge. *Address:* 13 Steinwedel Street, Farrer, ACT 2607, Australia. *T:* (6) 2865014. *Club:* Royal Canberra Golf (Canberra).

BACK, Patrick, QC 1970; a Recorder of the Crown Court, since 1972; *b* 23 Aug. 1917; *s* of late Ivor Back, FRCS, and Barbara Back (*née* Nash). *Educ:* Marlborough; Trinity Hall, Cambridge. Captain, 14th Punjab Regt, 1941–46. Called to Bar, 1940; Bencher, Gray's Inn, 1978. Commenced practice, Western Circuit, 1948, Leader, 1984–89, Dep. Chm., Devon Q3, 1968. *Recreation:* fly-fishing. *Address:* Paddock Edge, Broadwindsor, Dorset. *T:* Broadwindsor (01308) 644; 3 Temple Gardens, EC4Y 9AU; Flat 71, 8 New Crane Place, Garnet Street, Wapping, E1 9TT. *T:* 0171–488 4371.

BACKETT, Prof. Edward Maurice; Foundation Professor of Community Health, University of Nottingham, 1969–81, now Professor Emeritus; *b* 12 Jan. 1916; *o s* of late Frederick and Louisa Backett; *m* 1940, Shirley Paul-Thompson; one *s* two *d*. *Educ:* University Coll., London; Westminster Hospital. Operational Research with RAF; Nuffield Fellow in Social Medicine; Research Worker, Medical Research Council; Lecturer, Queen's Univ., Belfast; Senior Lecturer, Guy's Hospital and London Sch. of Hygiene and Tropical Medicine; Prof. and Head of Dept of Public Health and Social Medicine, Univ. of Aberdeen, 1958–69. Hon. Member: Internat. Epidemiol Assoc., 1984; Soc. for Social Medicine, 1986. *Publications:* The Risk Approach to Health Care, 1984; papers in scientific journals. *Recreations:* swimming, walking, sailing. *Address:* Lidstones, South Town, Dartmouth, Devon TQ6 9BU. *T:* Dartmouth (01803) 833788.

BACKHOUSE, David Miles; Chairman, Henderson Administration Group PLC, 1990–92; *b* 30 Jan. 1939; *s* of late Jonathan Backhouse and Alice Joan (*née* Woodroffe); *m* 1969, Sophia Ann (*née* Townsend); one *s* one *d*. *Educ:* Summerfields, Oxford; Bradfield Coll. Commenced career in banking with Schroders PLC, 1966. Non-executive Director: TSB Group, 1985–92; Witan Investment Company, 1985–92; RAC, Cirencester, 1987–; Bradstock Group, 1990–; IFG Group, 1993–; Clayhithe plc, 1994–. Trustee, Mental Health Foundn, 1991–. *Recreations:* tennis, riding. *Address:* South Farm, Fairford, Glos GL7 3PN. *T:* Cirencester (01285) 712225. *Clubs:* Boodle's; Vanderbilt Racquet.

BACKHOUSE, Sir Jonathan Roger, 4th Bt, *cr* 1901; formerly Managing Director, W. H. Freeman & Co. Ltd, Publishers; *b* 30 Dec. 1939; *s* of Major Sir John Edmund Backhouse, 3rd Bt, MC, and Jean Marie Frances, *d* of Lieut-Col G. R. V. Hume-Gore, MC, The Gordon Highlanders; *S* father, 1944. *Educ:* Oxford. *Heir: b* Oliver Richard Backhouse [*b* 18 July 1941; *m* 1970, Gillian Irene, *o d* of L. W. Lincoln, Northwood, Middx].

BACKHOUSE, Roger Bainbridge; QC 1984; *b* 8 March 1938; *s* of Leslie Bainbridge Backhouse and Jean Backhouse; *m* 1962, Elizabeth Constance, *d* of Comdr J. A. Lowe, DSO, DSC; two *s* one *d*. *Educ:* Liverpool Coll.; Trinity Hall, Cambridge (History Tripos parts I & II). Nat. Service, RAF, 1956–58 (Pilot Officer). Worked in family business, 1961–62; Schoolmaster, 1962–64; called to the Bar, Middle Temple, 1965. *Recreations:* shooting, golf, opera. *Address:* Preston House, Colebrook Street, Winchester, Hants SO23 9LH. *T:* Winchester (01962) 863053; (chambers) 1 Middle Temple Lane, WC2 9AA. *Clubs:* Royal Air Force; Hockley Golf.

BACON, Prof. George Edward, MA, ScD Cantab, PhD London; Professor of Physics, University of Sheffield, 1963–81, now Emeritus; *b* 5 Dec. 1917; *s* of late George H. Bacon and Lilian A. Bacon, Derby; *m* 1945, Enid Trigg; one *s* one *d*. *Educ:* Derby Sch.; Emmanuel Coll., Cambridge (Open and Sen. Schol.); CPhys. Air Ministry, Telecommunications Research Estabt, 1939–46. Dep. Chief Scientific Officer, AERE, Harwell, 1946–63; Dean, Faculty of Pure Science, Sheffield Univ., 1969–71. Leverhulme Emeritus Fellow, 1988. FInstP. *Publications:* Neutron Diffraction, 1955; Applications of Neutron Diffraction in Chemistry, 1963; X-ray and Neutron Diffraction, 1966; Neutron Physics, 1969; Neutron Scattering in Chemistry, 1977; The Architecture of Solids, 1981; Fifty Years of Neutron Diffraction, 1987; many scientific pubns on X-ray and neutron crystallographic studies in Proc. Royal Society, Acta Cryst., etc. *Recreations:* gardening, photography, genealogy. *Address:* Windrush Way, Guiting Power, Cheltenham GL54 5US. *T:* Cotswold (01451) 850631.

BACON, Jennifer Helen, CB 1995; Director General, Health and Safety Executive, since 1995 (Deputy Director General (Policy), 1992–95); *b* 16 April 1945; *d* of Dr Lionel James Bacon and Joyce Bacon (*née* Chapman). *Educ:* Bedales Sch., Petersfield; New Hall, Cambridge (BA Hons 1st cl.). Joined Civil Service as Asst Principal, Min. of Labour, 1967; Private Sec. to Minister of State for Employment, 1971–72; Principal, 1972–78, worked on health and safety and industrial relations legislation; Principal Private Sec. to Sec. of State for Employment, 1977–78; Asst Sec., Controller of Trng Services, MSC, 1978–80; sabbatical, travelling in Latin America, 1980–81; Asst Sec., Machinery of Govt Div., CSD, later MPO, 1981–82; Under Sec., Dir of Adult (formerly Occupational) Trng, MSC, 1982–86; Under Sec., School Curriculum and Exams, DES, 1986–89; Department of Employment: Prin. Finance Officer (Grade 3), 1989–91; Dir of Resources and Strategy (Grade 2), 1991–92. Mem. Bd, Sheffield Develt Corp., 1992–. Vis. Fellow, Nuffield Coll., Oxford, 1989–. *Recreations:* classical music especially opera, travelling, walking.

BACON, Sir Nicholas (Hickman Ponsonby), 14th Bt of Redgrave, *cr* 1611, and 15th Bt of Mildenhall, *cr* 1627; Premier Baronet of England; *b* 17 May 1953; *s* of Sir Edmund Castell Bacon, 13th and 14th Bt, KG, KBE, TD and of Priscilla Dora, *d* of Col Sir Charles Edward Ponsonby, 1st Bt, TD; *S* father, 1982; *m* 1981, Susan, *d* of Raymond Dinnis, Edenbridge, Kent; four *s*. *Educ:* Eton; Dundee Univ. (MA). Barrister-at-law, Gray's Inn. A Page of Honour to the Queen, 1966–69. *Heir: s* Henry Hickman Bacon, *b* 23 April 1984. *Address:* Raveningham Hall, Norfolk NR14 6NS. *Club:* Pratt's.

BACON, Peter James; HM Diplomatic Service; Counsellor (Commercial and Development), Jakarta, since 1992; *b* 17 Sept. 1941; *s* of Alfred J. Bacon and Mildred (*née* Randall); *m* 1963, Valerie Ann Colby; one *s* one *d*. *Educ:* Richard Huish Grammar Sch., Taunton. GPO, 1958–63; joined HM Diplomatic Service, 1963; CRO, 1963–64; Nicosia, 1964–66; Kota Kinabalu, 1967–70; Brussels, 1970–71; Beirut, 1971–75; Asst Private Sec. to Minister of State, FCO, 1975–78; Suva, 1978–80; First Sec. (Energy), Washington, 1980–84; Hd, Parly Relns Unit, FCO, 1984–88; Consul (Commercial), Johannesburg, 1988–92. *Recreations:* golf, travel. *Address:* c/o Foreign and Commonwealth Office, King Charles Street, SW1A 2AH.

BACON, Sir Sidney (Charles), Kt 1977; CB 1971; BSc(Eng); FEng, FIMechE, FIEE, FTP; Managing Director, Royal Ordnance Factories, 1972–79; Deputy Chairman, Royal Ordnance Factories Board, 1972–79; *b* 11 Feb. 1919; *s* of Charles and Alice Bacon. *Educ:* Woolwich Polytechnic; London Univ. Military Service, 1943–48, Capt. REME. Royal Arsenal, Woolwich, 1933–58; Regional Supt of Inspection, N Midland Region, 1958–60; Asst Dir, ROF, Nottingham, 1960–61; Director, ROF: Leeds, 1961–62; Woolwich, 1962–63; Birtley, 1965; idc, 1964; Dir of Ordnance Factories, Weapons and Fighting Vehicles, 1965–66; Dep. Controller, ROFs, 1966–69; Controller, ROFs, 1969–72. Dir, Short Brothers, 1980–89. Pres., IProdE, 1979; Mem. Council, CGLI, 1979–91. Hon. FCGI 1991. *Recreations:* golf, listening to music. *Address:* 228 Erith Road, Bexleyheath, Kent DA7 6HP. *Club:* Shooters Hill Golf.

BADCOCK, Maj.-Gen. John Michael Watson, CB 1976; MBE 1959; DL; Chairman, S. W. Mount & Sons, 1982–86; *b* 10 Nov. 1922; *s* of late R. D. Badcock, MC, JP and Mrs J. D. Badcock; *m* 1948, Gillian Pauline (*née* Attfield); one *s* two *d*. *Educ:* Sherborne Sch.; Worcester Coll., Oxford. Enlisted in ranks (Army), 1941; commnd Royal Corps of Signals, 1942; war service UK and BAOR; Ceylon, 1945–47; served in UK, Persian Gulf, BAOR and Cyprus; Comdr 2 Inf. Bde and Dep. Constable of Dover Castle, 1968–71; Dep. Mil. Sec., 1971–72; Dir of Manning (Army), 1972–74; Defence Advr and Head of British Defence Liaison Staff, Canberra, 1974–77; retired. psc, jssc, idc. Col Comdt, Royal Signals, 1974–80 and 1982–90; Master of Signals, 1982–90; Hon. Col, 31 (London) Signal Regt (Volunteers), 1978–83. Chm., SE TA&VRA, 1979–85. Chief Appeals Officer, CRC, 1978–82. DL Kent, 1980. *Recreations:* Rugby football, cricket, hockey, most field sports less horsemanship. *Address:* c/o RHQ Royal Signals, 56 Regency Street, SW1P 4AD. *T:* 071–414 8243. *Club:* Army and Navy.

BADDELEY, Prof. Alan David, PhD; FRS 1993; Director, Applied Psychology Unit, Medical Research Council, Cambridge, since 1974; Senior Research Fellow, Churchill College, Cambridge, since 1988; *b* 23 March 1934; *s* of Donald and Nellie Baddeley; *m* 1964, Hilary Ann White; three *s*. *Educ:* University Coll., London (BA); Princeton Univ. (MA). PhD Cantab, 1962. Walker Fellow, Princeton Univ., 1956–57; Scientist, MRC Applied Psychology Unit, Cambridge, 1958–67; Lectr then Reader, Sussex Univ., 1969–72; Prof. of Psychology, Stirling Univ., 1972–74. Hon. Prof. of Cognitive Psychology, Cambridge Univ., 1991–. Vis. Fellow, Univ. of California, San Diego, 1970–71; Visiting Professor: Harvard Univ., 1984; Univ. of Queensland, 1990; Univ. of Texas, Austin, 1991. President: Experimental Psychology Soc., 1984–86; European Soc. for Cognitive Psychology, 1986–90. Mem., Academia Europaea, 1989. *Publications:* The Psychology of Memory, 1976; Your Memory: a user's guide, 1982; Working Memory, 1986; Human Memory: theory and practice, 1990. *Recreations:* walking, reading, travel. *Address:* MRC Applied Psychology Unit, 15 Chaucer Road, Cambridge CB2 2EF. *T:* Cambridge (01223) 355294.

BADDELEY, Sir John (Wolsey Beresford), 4th Bt *cr* 1922; *b* 27 Jan. 1938; *s* of Sir John Beresford Baddeley, 3rd Bt, and Nancy Winifred (*d* 1994), *d* of late Thomas Wolsey; *S* father, 1979; *m* 1962, Sara Rosalind Crofts (marr. diss. 1992); three *d*. *Educ:* Bradfield College, Berks. FCA. Qualified as Chartered Accountant, 1961. *Recreations:* inland waterways, tennis, squash, destructive gardening. *Heir: cousin* Mark David Baddeley, *b* 10 May 1921. *Address:* Springwood, Sandgate Lane, Storrington, Sussex RH20 3HJ. *T:* Storrington (01903) 743054.

BADDELEY, Very Rev. William Pye, BA; Dean Emeritus of Brisbane, 1981; *b* 20 March 1914; *s* of W. H. Clinton-Baddeley and Louise Bourdin, Shropshire; *m* 1947, Mary Frances Shirley, *d* of Col E. R. C. Wyatt, CBE, DSO; one *d*. *Educ:* Durham Univ.; St Chad's Coll., Durham; Cuddesdon Coll., Oxford. Deacon, 1941; Priest, 1942; Curate of St Luke, Camberwell, 1941–44; St Anne, Wandsworth, 1944–46; St Stephen, Bournemouth, 1946–49; Vicar of St Pancras (with St James and Christ Church from 1954), 1949–58; Dean of Brisbane, 1958–67; Rector of St James's, Piccadilly, 1967–80; RD of Westminster (St Margaret's), 1974–79; Commissary to: Archbishop of Brisbane, 1967–; Bishop of Wangaratta, 1970–; Archbishop of Papua New Guinea, 1972–80; Bishop of Newcastle, NSW, 1976–. Member: London Diocesan Synod, 1970–80; Bishop of London's Council, 1975–80. Chaplain: Elizabeth Garrett Anderson Hospital, London, 1949–59; St Luke's Hostel, 1952–54; Qld Univ. Anglican Soc., 1960–64; St Martin's Hosp., Brisbane, 1960–67; London Companions of St Francis, 1968–80; Lord Mayor of Westminster, 1968–69 and 1974–75; Actors' Church Union, 1968–70; Royal Acad. of Arts, 1968–80; Vis. Chaplain, Westminster Abbey, 1980–. Hon. Chaplain to: Archbishop of Brisbane (Diocesan Chaplain, 1963–67); Union Soc. of Westminster, 1972–80. President: Brisbane Repertory Theatre, 1961–64; Qld Univ. Dramatic Soc., 1961–67; Qld Ballet Co., 1962–67; Dir, Australian Elizabethan Theatre Trust, 1963–67; Mem. Council of Management, Friends of Royal Academy, 1978–; Chairman: Diocesan Radio and Television Council, 1961–67; weekly television Panel "Round Table", 1962–66; monthly television Panel "What Do YOU Think", 1960–67; Pres., Connard and Seckford Players, 1984–. Governor: Burlington Sch., 1967–76; Archbishop Tenison's Sch., 1967–80; Chairman: Assoc. for Promoting Retreats, 1967–80; Malcolm Sargent Cancer Fund for Children, 1968–92 (Hon. Consultant, 1992–); Cttee for Commonwealth Citizens in China, 1970–73; Mem. Council, Metropolitan Hosp. Sunday Fund, 1968–78; Vice-Pres., Cancer Relief Appeal, 1977–. Life Governor of Thomas Coram Foundation, 1955–. Mem. Chapter-Gen., OStJ, 1974–. ChStJ 1971 (SBStJ 1959). *Recreations:* theatre, music, photography. *Address:* Cumberland House, Woodbridge, Suffolk IP12 4AH. *T:* Woodbridge (01394) 384104. *Clubs:* East India, Carlton, Arts.

BADDILEY, Prof. Sir James, Kt 1977; PhD, DSc, ScD; FRS 1961; FRSE 1962; Professor of Chemical Microbiology, 1977–83, now Emeritus, and Director, Microbiological Chemistry Research Laboratory, 1975–83, University of Newcastle upon Tyne; SERC Senior Research Fellow, and Fellow of Pembroke College, University of Cambridge, 1981–85, now Emeritus; *b* 15 May 1918; *s* of late James Baddiley and Ivy Logan Cato; *m* 1944, Hazel Mary, *yr d* of Wesley Wilfrid Townsend and Ann Rayner Townsend (*née* Kilner); one *s*. *Educ:* Manchester Grammar Sch.; Manchester University (BSc 1941, PhD 1944, DSc 1953; Sir Clement Royds Meml Schol., 1942, Beyer Fellow, 1943–44); MA 1981, ScD 1986, Cantab. Imperial Chemical Industries Fellow, University of Cambridge, 1945–49; Swedish Medical Research Council Fellow, Wenner-Grens Institute for Cell Biology, Stockholm, 1947–49; Mem. of Staff, Dept of Biochemistry, Lister Institute of Preventive Medicine, London, 1949–55; Rockefeller Fellowship, Mass. Gen. Hosp., Harvard Med. Sch., 1954; Prof. of Organic Chem., King's Coll., Univ. of Durham, 1955–77 (later Univ. of Newcastle upon Tyne); Head of Sch. of Chemistry, Newcastle upon Tyne Univ., 1968–78. Member: Council, Chemical Soc., 1962–65; Cttee, Biochemical Soc., 1964–67; Council, Soc. of Gen. Microbiol., 1973–75; Council, SERC (formerly SRC), 1979–81 (Mem., Enzyme Chem. and Technol Cttee, 1972–75, Biol Scis Cttee, 1976–79; Mem., Science Bd, 1979–81); Council, Royal Soc., 1977–79; Editorial Boards, Biochemical Preparations, 1960–70, Biochimica et Biophysica Acta, 1970–77, Cambridge Studies in Biotechnology, 1985–. Karl Folkers Vis. Prof. in Biochem., Illinois Univ., 1962; Tilden Lectr, Chem. Soc., 1959; Special Vis. Lectr, Dept of Microbiology, Temple Univ., Pa, 1966; Leeuwenhoek Lectr, Royal Society, 1967; Pedler Lectr, Chem. Soc., 1978; Endowment Lectr, Bose Inst., Calcutta, 1980. Hon. Mem., Amer. Soc. Biochem. and Molecular Biol. Hon. DSc Heriot Watt, 1979; Bath, 1986. Meldola Medal, RIC, 1947; Corday-Morgan Medal, Chem. Soc., 1952; Davy Medal, Royal Soc., 1974. *Publications:* numerous contribs on chemistry and biochemistry of co-enzymes, bacterial cell walls and membranes in Journal of the Chemical Society, Nature, Biochemical Journal, etc; articles in various microbiological and biochemical reviews. *Recreations:* photography, music, fine arts. *Address:* Hill Top Cottage, Hildersham, Cambridge CB1 6DA. *T:* Cambridge (01223) 893055; Department of Biochemistry, University of Cambridge, Tennis Court Road, Cambridge CB2 1QW. *T:* Cambridge (01223) 333600.

BADEN, (Edwin) John, CA; Director, since 1987, Chairman, since 1995, Girobank plc; *b* 18 Aug. 1928; *s* of Percy Baden and Jacoba (*née* de Blank); *m* 1952, Christine Irene (*née* Grose); two *s* three *d*. *Educ:* Winchester Coll.; Corpus Christi Coll., Cambridge (MA Econ and Law). Mem. Inst. of Taxation. Audit Clerk, Deloitte Haskins & Sells, CA, 1951–54; Financial Dir/Co. Sec., H. Parrot & Co., Wine Importer, 1954–61; Dir of various subsids, C & A Modes, 1961–63; a Man. Dir, Samuel Montagu & Co. Ltd, 1963–78; Man. Dir/Chief Exec., Italian International Bank Plc, 1978–89; Girobank: Chief Exec., 1989–91; Dep Chm., 1989–90; Man. Dir, 1990–91. Dir, Alliance & Leicester Building Soc., 1990–. Member, Management Committee: Pan European Property Unit Trust, 1973–; N American Property Unit Trust, 1975–93 (Chm., 1980–93). Sec. Gen., Eurogiro (formerly European Post/Giro Dirs Gp), 1993– (Chm., 1990–92); Mem., EU Payment Systems Technical Develt Gp, 1990–. Institute of Chartered Accountants of Scotland: Mem., Council, 1984–90; Mem., Res. Cttee, 1966–74, 1985–88, 1991–. Trustee, Internat. Centre for Res. in Accounting, Univ. of Lancaster, 1975–. Mem., Review Panel, Financial Reporting Council, 1990–. Liveryman, Co. of Information Technologists, 1992–. FRSA; CIMgt; FCIB. Cavaliere Ufficiale, Order of Merit, Italian Republic, 1986. *Publications:* (contrib.): Making Corporate Reports Valuable, 1988; Auditing into the 21st Century, 1993; Post Giro Banking in Europe, 1993; International Control and Financial Reporting; articles in professional magazines. *Recreations:* reading, sailing, shooting. *Address:* Lanaways Barn, Two Mile Ash Road, Horsham, Sussex RH13 7LA. *T:* Southwater (01403) 733834.

BADEN-POWELL, family name of **Baron Baden-Powell.**

BADEN-POWELL, 3rd Baron, *cr* 1929, of Gilwell; **Robert Crause Baden-Powell;** Bt, *cr* 1922; Vice-President, Scout Association, since 1982; Chairman, Quarter Horse Racing UK, since 1985; *b* 15 Oct. 1936; *s* of 2nd Baron and Carine Crause Baden-Powell (*née* Boardman) (*d* 1993); *S* father, 1962; *m* 1963, Patience Hélène Mary Batty (*see* Lady Baden-Powell). *Educ:* Bryanston (Blandford). Chief Scouts Comr, 1965–82; Pres., West Yorks Scout Council, 1972–88; Mem., 1965–, Mem. Cttee, 1972–78, Council, Scout Assoc. Mem. Council, British Quarter Horse Assoc., 1984–90 (Chm., 1990); Chm., Quarter Horse Racing UK, 1985–88. Pres., Camping and Caravanning Club, 1992–. *Recreation:* breeding racing Quarter Horses. *Heir: b* Hon. David Michael Baden-Powell [*b* 11 Dec. 1940; *m* 1966, Joan Phillips, *d* of H. W. Berryman, Melbourne, Australia; three *s*]. *Address:* Clandon Manor Farm, Back Lane, East Clandon, Guildford, Surrey GU4 7SA. *T:* Guildford (01483) 224262.

BADEN-POWELL, Lady; Patience Hélène Mary Baden-Powell, CBE 1986; Vice President, The Girl Guides Association, since 1990; President, Commonwealth Youth Exchange Council, 1982–86; *b* 27 Oct. 1936; *d* of Mr and Mrs D. M. Batty, Zimbabwe; *m* 1963, Baron Baden-Powell, *qv*. *Educ:* St Peter's Diocesan Sch., Bulawayo. Internat. Comr, 1975–79, Chief Comr, 1980–85, Girl Guides Assoc. Director: Laurentian Financial Gp, 1981–; Fieldguard Ltd, 1986–. President: Surrey Council for Voluntary Youth Services, 1986–; National Playbus Assoc., 1979–; Trustee, Painshill Park Trust, 1992–; Patron: Woodlarks Camp Site for the Disabled, 1978–; Surrey Antiques Fair, 1969–. *Address:* Clandon Manor Farm, Back Lane, East Clandon, Guildford, Surrey GU4 7SA. *T:* Guildford (01483) 224262, *Fax:* (01483) 222087.

BADENOCH, (Ian) James (Forster); QC 1989; a Recorder, since 1987; *b* 24 July 1945; *s* of Sir John Badenoch, *qv*; *m* 1979, Marie-Thérèse Victoria Cabourn-Smith; two *s* one *d*. *Educ:* Dragon Sch., Oxford; Rugby Sch.; Magdalen Coll., Oxford (MA). Called to the

Bar, Lincoln's Inn, 1968; Mem., Inner Temple. Member: Medico-Legal Soc.; Harveian Soc.; London Common Law Bar Assoc.; Professional Negligence Bar Assoc. *Publication:* (contrib.) Medical Negligence, 1990, 2nd edn 1994. *Recreations:* family, tennis, travel. *Address:* 1 Crown Office Row, Temple, EC4Y 7HH. *T:* 0171–797 7500.

BADENOCH, Sir John, Kt 1984; DM; FRCP, FRCPE; Hans Sloane Fellow, Royal College of Physicians, 1985–91; Emeritus Fellow, Merton College, Oxford University, 1987; *b* 8 March 1920; *s* of William Minty Badenoch, MB, and Ann Dyer Badenoch (*née* Coutts); *m* 1944, Anne Newnham, *d* of Prof. Lancelot Forster; two *s* two *d*. *Educ:* Rugby Sch.; Oriel College, Oxford. MA; DM 1952; FRCP 1959; FRCPE 1982. Rockefeller Med. Studentship, Cornell Univ. Med. Coll., 1941. Res. Asst, Nuffield Dept of Clin. Medicine, Oxford, 1949–56; Dir, Clin. Studies, Univ. of Oxford, 1954–65; Consultant Phys., Oxfordshire HA, 1956–85; Univ. Lectr in Medicine, Univ. of Oxford, 1956–85. Former Mem., Board of Governors of United Oxford Hosps; Mem. Board, Oxford AHA(T), 1974–83; Mem., GMC, 1984–89. Royal College of Physicians: Pro-Censor and Censor, 1972–73; Sen. Censor and Sen. Vice-Pres., 1975–76; Goulstonian Lectr, 1960; Lumleian Lectr, 1977. Examiner in Medicine at various times for the Universities of: Oxford, Cambridge, Manchester, QUB and NUI. Member: Assoc. of Physicians of GB and Ireland; Med. Res. Soc.; British Soc. of Haematology; British Soc. of Gastroenterology. Liveryman, Soc. of Apothecaries. *Publications:* (ed jtly) Recent Advances in Gastroenterology, 1965, 2nd edn 1972; various papers in the field of gastroenterology and medicine. *Recreations:* reading, walking, natural history. *Address:* 21 Hartley Court, 84 Woodstock Road, Oxford OX2 7PF. *T:* Oxford (01865) 511311.

See also I. J. F. Badenoch.

BADGE, Peter Gilmour Noto; Chief Metropolitan Stipendiary Magistrate, since 1992; a Chairman, Inner London Juvenile Panel, since 1979; a Recorder of the Crown Court, since 1980; *b* 20 Nov. 1931; *s* of late Ernest Desmond Badge, LDS and Marie Benson Badge (*née* Clough); *m* 1956, Mary Rose Noble; four *d*. *Educ:* Univ. of Liverpool (LLB). National Service, 1956–58: RNVR, lower deck and commnd; UK, ME and FE; RNR, 1958–62. Solicitor, 1956; Mem., Solicitor's Dept, New Scotland Yard, 1958–61; Asst Solicitor and later Partner, 1961–75, Kidd, Rapinet, Badge & Co.; Notary Public; Metropolitan Stipendiary Magistrate, 1975–. Member: Lord Chancellor's Adv. Cttee for Inner London, 1983–; Magisterial Cttee, Judicial Studies Bd, 1985–90; Chm., Legal Cttee, Magistrates' Assoc., 1990–93. Mem., Basket Makers' Assoc., 1987–; Chairman: Coracle Soc., 1985–; Binney Meml Awards Cttee, 1992–. Mem. Bd of Green Cloth, Verge of the Palaces of St James's, Whitehall etc, 1992–. Liveryman, Co. of Basket Makers, 1995–. Contested (L) Windsor and Maidenhead, 1964. *Publications:* articles on coracles. *Address:* Bow Street Magistrates' Court, Bow Street, WC2E 7AS. *Club:* Garrick.

BADGER, Prof. Anthony John, PhD; Paul Mellon Professor of American History, Cambridge University, since 1992; Fellow, Sidney Sussex College, Cambridge, since 1992; *b* 6 March 1947; *s* of Kenneth Badger and Iris G. (*née* Summerill); *m* 1981, Ruth Catherine Davis; two *s*. *Educ:* Cotham Grammar Sch.; Sidney Sussex Coll., Cambridge (BA, MA); Hull Univ. (PhD). Department of History, Newcastle University: Lectr, 1971–81; Sen. Lectr, 1981–91; Prof., 1991. *Publications:* Prosperity Road: the New Deal, North Carolina and tobacco, 1980; North Carolina and the New Deal, 1981; The New Deal: the Depression years, 1989. *Recreations:* walking, supporting Bristol Rovers. *Address:* Sidney Sussex College, Cambridge CB2 3HU. *T:* Cambridge (01223) 338876.

BADGER, Sir Geoffrey Malcolm, Kt 1979; AO 1975; PhD, DSc; FRSC, FRACI, FACE, FTS, FAA; Chairman, Australian Science and Technology Council, 1977–82; *b* 10 Oct. 1916; *s* of J. McD. Badger; *m* 1941, Edith Maud, *d* of Henry Chevis. *Educ:* Geelong Coll.; Gordon Inst. of Technology; Univs of Melbourne, London (PhD), Glasgow (DSc). Instructor Lieut, RN, 1943–46. Finney-Howell Research Fellow, London, 1940–41; Research Chemist, ICI, 1941–43; Research Fellow, Glasgow, 1946–49. Univ. of Adelaide: Sen. Lectr, 1949–51; Reader, 1951–54; Prof. of Organic Chemistry, 1955–64, now Emeritus Professor; Dep. Vice Chancellor, 1966–67; Vice-Chancellor, 1967–77; Res. Professor, 1977–79. Dir, Western Mining Corp., 1979–88. Mem. Executive, CSIRO, 1964–65. President: Aust. Acad. of Science, 1974–78; Aust. and NZ Assoc. for Advancement of Science, 1979–80; Chm., Order of Australia Assoc., 1989–92. DUniv Adelaide. H. G. Smith Medal, 1951, A. E. Leighton Medal, 1971, RACI; W. D. Chapman Medal, Instn of Engrs, Australia, 1974; ANZAAS Medal, 1981. *Publications:* Structures and Reactions of Aromatic Compounds, 1954; Chemistry of Heterocyclic Compounds, 1961; The Chemical Basis of Carcinogenic Activity, 1962; Aromatic Character and Aromaticity, 1969; (ed) Captain Cook, 1970; The Explorers of the Pacific, 1988; numerous papers in Jl Chem. Soc., etc. *Address:* 1 Anna Court, West Lakes, SA 5021, Australia. *T:* (8) 494594. *Club:* Adelaide (Adelaide).

BADHAM, Douglas George, CBE 1975; JP; HM Lord-Lieutenant for Mid Glamorgan, 1985–89; company director; Chairman, Hamell (West) Ltd, since 1968; *b* 1 Dec. 1914; *s* of late David Badham, JP; *m* 1939, Doreen Spencer Phillips; two *d*. *Educ:* Leys Sch., Cambridge. CA. Exec. Director: Powell Duffryn Gp, 1938–69; Pascoe Hldgs, 1983–88; Alignrite, 1984–87; T. H. Couch, 1984–88; World Trade Centre Wales, 1984–; Chairman: Powell Duffryn Wagon Co., 1965–85; T. T. Pascoe, 1983–89; Economic Forestry Gp PLC, 1981–88 (Dir, 1978–88). Chm., Nat. Health Service Staff Commn, 1972–75; Mem., 1978–84, Dep. Chm., 1980–84, Welsh Develt Agency. Member: Wales and the Marches Telecommunications Bd, 1973–80; British Gas Corp., 1974–83; Forestry Commn, S Wales Reg. Adv. Cttee, 1946–76 (Chm., 1973–76); Western Region Adv. Bd, BR, 1977–82; Welsh Council (Chm., Industry and Planning Panel), 1971–80; Nature Conservancy Council Adv. Cttee for Wales; Council, UWIST, 1975–80; Develt Corp. for Wales, 1965–83 (Chm., 1971–80). JP Glamorgan, 1962; DL, 1975–82, High Sheriff, 1976, Lieut, 1982, Mid Glamorgan. KStJ 1991. *Recreations:* forestry, trout breeding. *Address:* Swyn-y-Coed, Watford Road, Caerphilly, Mid Glamorgan CF8 1NE. *T:* Caerphilly (01222) 882094. *Club:* Cardiff and County (Cardiff).

BADIAN, Ernst, FBA 1965; Professor of History, since 1971, John Moors Cabot Professor, since 1982, Harvard University; *b* 8 Aug. 1925; *s* of Joseph Badian and Sally (*née* Horinger), Vienna (later Christchurch, NZ); *m* 1950, Nathlie Anne (*née* Wimsett); one *s* one *d*. *Educ:* Christchurch Boys' High Sch.; Canterbury Univ. Coll., Christchurch, NZ; University Coll., Oxford (Hon. Fellow 1987). MA (1st cl. hons), NZ, 1946; LitD, Victoria, NZ, 1962. University of Oxford: Chancellor's Prize for Latin Prose, 1950; Craven Fellow, 1950; Conington Prize, 1959; BA (1st cl. hons Lit. Hum.) 1950; MA 1954; DPhil 1956. Asst Lectr in Classics, Victoria University Coll., Wellington, 1947–48; Rome Scholar in Classics, British Sch. at Rome, 1950–52; Asst Lectr in Classics and Ancient History, Univ. of Sheffield, 1952–54; Lectr in Classics, Univ. of Durham, 1954–65; Prof. of Ancient History, Univ. of Leeds, 1965–69; Prof. of Classics and History, State Univ. of NY at Buffalo, 1969–71. John Simon Guggenheim Fellow, 1985; Fellow, Nat. Humanities Center, 1988. Vis. Professor: Univs of Oregon, Washington and California (Los Angeles), 1961; Univ. of S Africa, 1965, 1973; Harvard, 1967; State Univ. of NY (Buffalo), 1967–68; Heidelberg, 1973; Univ. of California (Sather Prof.), 1976; Univ. of Colorado, 1978; Univ. of Tel-Aviv, 1981; Martin Classical Lectr, Oberlin Coll., 1978; lecturing visits to Australia, Canada, France, Germany, Holland, Israel, Italy, NZ, Rhodesia, Switzerland, and S Africa. Fellow: Amer. Acad. of Arts and Sciences, 1974; Amer. Numismatic Soc., 1987; Corresponding Member: Austrian Acad. of Scis, 1975; German Archaeol Inst., 1981; Foreign Mem., Finnish Acad. of Sci. and Letters, 1985. Hon. Mem., Soc. for Promotion of Roman Studies, 1983. Hon. DLitt Macquarie, 1993. Editor, Amer. Jl of Ancient History. *Publications:* Foreign Clientelae (264–70 BC), 1958; Studies in Greek and Roman History, 1964; (ed) Ancient Society and Institutions, 1966; Polybius (The Great Histories Series), 1966; Roman Imperialism in the Late Republic, 1967 (2nd edn 1968); Publicans and Sinners, 1972; (ed) Sir Ronald Syme, Roman Papers, Vols 1–2, 1979; From Plataea to Potidaea, 1993; contribs to collections, dictionaries and encyclopaedias and to classical and historical journals. *Recreations:* travelling, reading. *Address:* Department of History, Harvard University, Cambridge, MA 02138, USA.

BAELZ, Very Rev. Peter Richard; Dean of Durham, 1980–88, Dean Emeritus since 1988; *b* 27 July 1923; 3rd *s* of Eberhard and Dora Baelz; *m* 1950, Anne Thelma Cleall-Harding; three *s*. *Educ:* Dulwich Coll.; Cambridge Univ. BA 1944, MA 1948, BD 1971; DD Oxon 1979. Asst Curate: Bournville, 1947–50; Sherborne, 1950–52; Asst Chap. Ripon Hall, Oxford, 1952–53; Rector of Wishaw, Birmingham, 1953–56; Vicar of Bournville, 1956–60; Fellow and Dean, Jesus Coll., Cambridge, 1960–72; University Lectr in Divinity, Cambridge, 1966–72; Canon of Christ Church and Regius Prof. of Moral and Pastoral Theology, Univ. of Oxford, 1972–79. Hon. Prof., Univ. of Wales, 1993. Hulsean Lectr, 1965–66; Bampton Lectr, 1974. Hon. DD Durham, 1993. *Publications:* Prayer and Providence, 1968; Christian Theology and Metaphysics, 1968; The Forgotten Dream, 1975; Ethics and Belief, 1977; Does God Answer Prayer?, 1982; contributor to: Traditional Virtues Reassessed, 1964; Faith, Fact and Fantasy, 1964; The Phenomenon of Christian Belief, 1970; Christianity and Change, 1971; Christ, Faith and History, 1972; Is Christianity Credible?, 1981; God Incarnate: story and belief, 1981; Ministers of the Kingdom, 1985; By What Authority?, 1987; Embracing the Chaos, 1990; The Weight of Glory, 1991; Tradition and Unity, 1991; Using the Bible Today, 1991; Companion to Contemporary Architectural Thought, 1993; This Sumptuous Church, 1993; Veritatis Splendor: a response, 1994. *Recreations:* walking, motoring. *Address:* 36 Brynteg, Llandrindod Wells, Powys LD1 5HB. *T:* Llandrindod Wells (01597) 825404.

BAER, Jack Mervyn Frank; Chairman, Hazlitt, Gooden & Fox, 1992–94, Consultant, since 1994; *b* 29 Aug. 1924; *yr s* of late Frank and Alix Baer; *m* 1st, 1952, Jean St Clair (marr. diss. 1969; she *d* 1973), *o c* of late L. F. St Clair and Evelyn Synnott; one *d*; 2nd, 1970, Diana Downes Baillieu, *yr d* of Aubrey Clare Robinson and Mollie Panter-Downes, *qv*; two step *d*. *Educ:* Bryanston; Slade Sch. of Fine Art, University Coll., London. Served RAF (Combined Ops), 1942–46. Proprietor, Hazlitt Gallery, 1948 until merger with Gooden & Fox, 1973; Man. Dir, Hazlitt, Gooden & Fox, 1973–92. Chm., Fine Arts and Antiques Export Adv. Cttee to Dept of Trade, 1971–73 (Vice-Chm., 1969–71). Member: Reviewing Cttee on Export of Works of Art, 1992–; Museums and Galls Commn, 1993–. Pres., Fine Art Provident Institution, 1972–75. Chm., Soc. of London Art Dealers, 1977–80 (Vice Chm. 1974–77). Trustee, Burlington Magazine Foundn, 1991–. *Publications:* numerous exhibition catalogues; articles in various jls. *Recreation:* drawing. *Address:* 9 Phillimore Terrace, W8 6BJ. *T:* 0171–937 6899. *Clubs:* Brooks's, Beefsteak.

BAGGE, Sir (John) Jeremy (Picton), 7th Bt *cr* 1867, of Stradsett Hall, Norfolk; *b* 21 June 1945; *s* of Sir John Bagge, 6th Bt, ED, DL and of Elizabeth Helena, *d* of late Daniel James Davies, CBE; *S* father, 1990; *m* 1979, Sarah Margaret Phipps, *d* of late Maj. James Shelley Phipps Armstrong; two *s* one *d*. *Educ:* Eton. FCA 1968. *Heir: s* Alfred James John Bagge, *b* 1 July 1980. *Address:* Stradsett Hall, King's Lynn, Norfolk PE33 9HA.

BAGGLEY, Charles David Aubrey, CBE 1980; MA; Headmaster of Bolton School, 1966–83; *b* 1 Feb. 1923; *s* of A. C. and M. Baggley, Bradford, Yorks; *m* 1st, 1949, Marjorie Asquith Wood (marr. diss. 1983), *d* of M. H. Wood, Harrogate; one *s* one *d*; 2nd, 1983, Julia Hazel Yorke, *d* of S. Morris, Sonning-on-Thames. *Educ:* Bradford Grammar Sch.; King's Coll., Cambridge (1942 and 1945–47) (Exhibitioner in Classics, Scholar in History; Class I, Part II of Historical Tripos, 1947; BA 1947, MA 1952). Temp. Sub. Lieut, RNVR, 1942–45. History Master, Clifton Coll., 1947–50; Head of History Side, Dulwich Coll., 1950–57; Headmaster, King Edward VII Sch., Lytham, 1957–66. Chm., HMC, 1978. Schools Liaison Advr, Salford Univ., 1983–91. Mem., Bolton Civic Trust, 1968–94. Gov., Giggleswick School, 1985–94. *Recreations:* walking, gardening, reading. *Address:* Masters, Thames Street, Sonning-on-Thames, Reading RG4 0UR.

BAGIER, Gordon Alexander Thomas; DL; *b* 7 July 1924; *m* 1949, Violet Sinclair; two *s* two *d*. *Educ:* Pendower Secondary Technical Sch., Newcastle upon Tyne. Signals Inspector, British Railways; Pres., Yorks District Council, NUR, 1962–64. Mem. of Keighley Borough Council, 1956–60; Mem. of Sowerby Bridge Urban Council, 1962–65. MP (Lab) Sunderland South, 1964–87. PPS to Home Secretary, 1968–69. Chm., Select Cttee on Transport, 1985–87. DL Tyne and Wear, 1988. *Recreation:* golf. *Address:* Rahana, Whickham Highway, Dunston, Gateshead, Tyne and Wear NE11 9QH. *Club:* Westerhope Golf (Newcastle upon Tyne).

BAGLIN, Richard John; Chairman: Wigwam Information plc, since 1993; Greenwich Healthcare NHS Trust, since 1995 (Director, since 1993); *b* 30 Oct. 1942; *s* of F. W. and C. C. Baglin; *m* 1964, Anne Christine; one *d*. *Educ:* Preston Manor County Grammar Sch.; St John's Coll., Cambridge (MA). Various posts with Abbey National BS, later Abbey National plc, 1964–93: Gen. Man., 1981–88; Dir, various subsidiaries, 1987–93; Man. Dir, New Businesses, 1988–92. Mem., SE London Probation Service Cttee, 1993–. *Recreations:* theatre, the arts. *Address:* 2 Feathers Place, Greenwich, SE10 9NE. *T:* 0181–858 9895.

BAGNALL, Air Vice-Marshal Anthony John Crowther, CB 1994; OBE 1982; Air Officer Commanding No 11 Group, since 1994; *b* 8 June 1945; *s* of Maurice Arthur Bagnall and Marjorie (*née* Crowther); *m* 1970, Pamela Diane Wilson; one *s* two *d*. *Educ:* Stretford Grammar Sch. RAF Coll., Cranwell, 1964; Flight Comdr, 5 Sqn, 1975; Advanced Staff College, 1978; Sqn Comdr, 43 Sqn, 1983, 23 Sqn, 1985; Dir, Air Staff Briefing and Co-ordination, 1985; Station Comdr, RAF Leuchars, 1987; RCDS 1990; Dir, Air Force Staff Duties, 1991; ACAS, 1992. *Recreations:* golf, bridge, fell walking. *Address:* c/o Lloyds Bank, 53 King Street, Manchester M60 2ES. *Club:* Royal Air Force.

BAGNALL, Kenneth Reginald, QC 1973; QC (Hong Kong) 1983; Chairman, The New Law Publishing Co. plc, since 1993; Editor-in-Chief, New Property Cases, since 1986; *b* 26 Nov. 1927; *s* of Reginald and Elizabeth Bagnall; *m* 1st, 1955, Margaret Edith Wall; one *s* one *d*; 2nd, 1963, Rosemary Hearn; one *s* one *d*. *Educ:* King Edward VI Sch., Birmingham; Univ. of Birmingham. LLB (Hons). Yardley Scholar. Served Royal Air Force; Pilot Officer, 1947, Flt Lt, 1948. Called to the Bar, Gray's Inn, 1950; a Dep. Judge of Crown Court, 1975–83. Co-founder, 1980, Chm., 1980–82, and Life Govr, 1983, Anglo-American Real Property Inst. Mem., Crafts Council, 1982–85; Co-founder, Bagnall Gall., Crafts Council, 1982. Founder, The New Law Fax Reporting Service, 1992. Mem., Inst. of Dirs. Freeman, City and Corp. of London, 1972; Freeman and Liveryman, Barber-Surgeons' Co, 1972. *Publications:* Guide to Business Tenancies, 1956; Atkins Court Forms and Precedents (Town Planning), 1973; (with K. Lewison) Development Land Tax, 1978; Judicial Review, 1985. *Recreations:* yachting, motoring, travel. *Address:* Brookfield House, Wentworth, Surrey GU25 4JZ. *Clubs:* Carlton, 1900, United and Cecil.

BAGNALL, Field Marshal Sir Nigel (Thomas), GCB 1985 (KCB 1981); CVO 1978; MC 1950 and Bar 1953; Chief of the General Staff, 1985–88; *b* 10 Feb. 1927; *s* of Lt-Col Harry Stephen Bagnall and Marjory May Bagnall; *m* 1959, Anna Caroline Church; two *d.* *Educ:* Wellington Coll. Joined Army, 1945; commnd Green Howards, 1946; Palestine, 1946–48, 6th Airborne Div.; Malaya, 1949–53, Canal Zone and Cyprus, 1954–56, Green Howards; GSO1 (Intell.), Dir of Borneo Ops, 1966–67; comd 4/7 Royal Dragoon Guards, NI and BAOR, 1967–69; Sen. Directing Staff (Army), Jt Services Staff Coll., 1970; comd Royal Armoured Corps HQ 1 (Br.) Corps, 1970–72; Defence Fellow, Balliol Coll., Oxford, 1972–73; Sec., Chief of Staff Cttee, 1973–75; GOC 4th Div., 1975–77; ACDS (Policy), MoD, 1978–80; Comdr, 1 (Br.) Corps, 1980–83; C-in-C BAOR and Comdr, Northern Army Gp, 1983–85. Col Comdt, APTC, 1981–88, RAC, 1985–88; ADC Gen. to the Queen, 1985–88. Hon. Fellow, Balliol Coll., Oxford, 1986. Pres., Anglo-German Officers' Assoc., 1992. Comdr's Cross, Order of Merit (Germany), 1993. *Publication:* The Punic Wars, 1991. *Recreations:* writing, reading, gardening. *Address:* c/o Royal Bank of Scotland, 49 Charing Cross Road, SW1A 2DX.

BAGNALL, Peter Hill; Chairman, Oxford Radcliffe NHS Trust Hospital, since 1993; *b* 8 Oct. 1931; *s* of Reginald Stuart Bagnall and Mary Adelaide (*née* Hill); *m* 1st, 1955, Edith Ann Wood (marr. diss. 1979); one *s* one *d* (and one *s* decd); 2nd, 1979, Diana Elizabeth Rayner. *Educ:* Newcastle-under-Lyme Sch.; St Catharine's Coll., Cambridge (MA). Nat. Service and TA Commns, N Staffs Regt. Dir, W. H. Smith & Son Ltd, 1968–88; Dir and Man. Dir, W. H. Smith PLC, 1974–88, retd; Chm., Book Club Associates, 1972–88; Director: Book Tokens Ltd, 1975–; W. H. Smith Pension Trustees Ltd, 1979–; TSB/Trustcard, 1986–89; The Book Trust, 1986–93 (Chm., 1989–91); Longman/Ladybird Books, 1987–90; British Museum Pubns, 1988–; Blackwell Ltd, Oxford, 1989–. Dir, Oxon HA, 1990–93. Mem., Vis. Cttee, Open Univ., 1988–92; Chm. Govs, Oxford Brooke's Univ., 1993–. Churchwarden, St Peter's, Alvescot. *Recreations:* fell-walking, book collecting, theatre, travel, local affairs. *Address:* Oxford Radcliffe NHS Trust, The John Radcliffe, Headley Way, Headington, Oxford OX3 9DX. *T:* Oxford (01865) 741741; The Old Rectory, Alvescot, Bampton, Oxford OX18 2PS. *Clubs:* Garrick, Sloane.

BAGNALL, Richard Maurice, MBE 1945; Deputy Chairman, Tube Investments Ltd, 1976–81, Managing Director, 1974–81, Director, 1969–81; *b* 20 Nov. 1917; *s* of late Francis Edward Bagnall, OBE and Edith Bagnall; *m* 1946, Irene Pickford; one *s* one *d.* *Educ:* Repton. Served War, 1939–45: RA, Shropshire Yeomanry, 1939–43 (despatches); Bde Major, 6 AGRA Italy, 1943–45. Joined Tube Investments Ltd, 1937. Chm., Round Oak Steel Works Ltd, 1976–81 (Dir, 1974–81). Governor, King's Sch., Worcester, 1977–81. Bronze Star, USA, 1945. *Recreations:* golf, gardening, photography. *Address:* Apartment 29A, Alto Club, Alvor, 8500 Portimao, Algarve, Portugal. *Club:* MCC.

BAGOT, family name of **Baron Bagot.**

BAGOT, 9th Baron *cr* 1780; **Heneage Charles Bagot;** Bt 1627; *b* 11 June 1914; *s* of Charles Frederick Heneage Bagot (*d* 1939) (4th *s* of *g s* of 1st Baron) and of Alice Lorina, *d* of Thomas Farr; *S* half-brother, 1979; *m* 1939, Muriel Patricia Moore, *y d* of late Maxwell James Moore Boyle; one *s* one *d.* *Educ:* Harrow. Formerly Major, QEO 6th Gurkha Rifles. *Recreations:* shooting, skiing, sailing. *Heir: s* Hon. Charles Hugh Shaun Bagot [*b* 23 Feb. 1944; *m* 1986, Mrs Sally A. Stone, *d* of D. G. Blunden]. *Address:* Llithfaen, near Pwllheli, Gwynedd LL53 6PD; 16 Barclay Road, SW6 1EH. *Clubs:* Alpine Ski; Himalayan.

BAGSHAWE, Prof. Kenneth Dawson, CBE 1990; MD; FRCP; FRCR; FRS 1989; Professor of Medical Oncology in the University of London at Charing Cross and Westminster Medical School (formerly Charing Cross Hospital Medical School), 1974–90, now Emeritus; Hon. Consultant Physician, Charing Cross Hospital, since 1990 (Consultant Physician, 1961–90); *b* 17 Aug. 1925; *s* of Harry Bagshawe and Gladys (*née* Dawson); *m* 1st, 1946, Ann Kelly; one *s* one *d*; 2nd, 1977, Sylvia Dorothy Lawler (*née* Corben). *Educ:* Harrow County Sch.; London Sch. of Econs and Pol Science; St Mary's Hosp. Med. Sch. (MB, BS 1952; MD 1964). FRCP 1969; FRCR 1983; FRCOG *ad eundem* 1978. Served RN, 1942–46. Fellow, Johns Hopkins Univ., Baltimore, USA, 1955–56; Sen. Registrar, St Mary's Hosp., 1956–60. Visiting Professor: Down State Univ., NY, 1977; Univ. of Hong Kong, 1982, 1994. Chm., DHSS Wkg Gp on Acute Cancer Services, 1980–84. Cancer Research Campaign: Chm., Scientific Cttee, 1983–88; Chm., Exec. Cttee, 1988–90; Vice Chm. Bd, 1988–. Hon. FRSM 1993. Hon. DSc Bradford, 1990. Galen Medal, London Soc. of Apothecaries, 1993. *Publications:* Choriocarcinoma, 1969; Medical Oncology, 1975; 300 papers on cancer chemotherapy, tumour markers, drug targeting, etc. *Recreations:* (passive) music, art; (active) demolition, conservation. *Address:* 115 George Street, W1H 5TA. *T:* 0171–262 6033, (office) 0181–846 7517. *Club:* Athenæum.

BAHL, Kamlesh, (Mrs N. Lakhani); Chairwoman, Equal Opportunities Commission, since 1993; *b* 28 May 1956; *d* of Swinder Nath Bahl and Leela Wati Bahl; *m* 1986, Dr Nitin Lakhani. *Educ:* Univ. of Birmingham (LLB 1977). Admitted Solicitor, 1980. GLC, 1978–81; BSC, 1981–84; Texaco Ltd, 1984–87; Data Logic Ltd: Legal and Commercial Manager, 1987–89; Company Sec. and Manager, Legal Services, 1989–93; Legal Consultant, 1993–. Mem., Barnet HA, 1989–90; Non-Exec. Dir, Parkside HA, 1990–93. Law Society: Chm., Commerce and Industry Gp, 1988–89; Mem. Council, 1990–. Member: Justice Sub-Cttee on Judiciary, 1991–92; Ethnic Minorities Adv. Cttee and Tribunals Cttee (Cttees of Lord Chancellor's Judicial Studies Bd), 1991–; Council and Standing Cttee on HAs, NAHAT, 1993–; Council, Justice, 1993–94. Indep. Mem., Diplomatic Service Appeal Bd, FCO, 1993–. EC Rep., EC Consultative Commn on Racism and Xenophobia, 1994–. FRSA 1993. *Publication:* (ed) Managing Legal Practice in Business, 1989. *Recreations:* swimming, dancing, travelling, theatre. *Address:* Overseas House, Quay Street, Manchester M3 3HN. *T:* 0161–833 9244, 0161–838 8201.

BAILES, Alyson Judith Kirtley; HM Diplomatic Service; Head of Security Policy Department, Foreign and Commonwealth Office, since 1994; *b* 6 April 1949; *d* of John-Lloyd Bailes and Barbara (*née* Martin). *Educ:* Belvedere Sch., Liverpool; Somerville Coll., Oxford (MA Modern Hist.). Entered Diplomatic Service, 1969; Budapest, 1970–74; UK Delgn to NATO, 1974–76; FCO, 1976–78; Asst to EC 'Cttee of Wise Men' (which reported on ways of improving functioning of EC instns), 1979; on loan to MoD, 1979–81; Bonn, 1981–84; Dep. Head of Planning Staff, FCO, 1984–86; Counsellor, Peking, 1987–89; on attachment to RIIA, 1990; Consul-Gen. and Dep. Head of Mission, Oslo, 1990–93. *Recreations:* music, nature, travel. *Address:* c/o Foreign and Commonwealth Office, SW1A 2AF. *T:* (home) 0171–373 1259.

BAILEY, family name of **Baron Glanusk.**

BAILEY, Sir Alan (Marshall), KCB 1986 (CB 1982); Permanent Secretary, Department of Transport, 1986–91; *b* 26 June 1931; *s* of John Marshall Bailey and Muriel May Bailey; *m* 1st, 1959, Stella Mary Scott (marr. diss. 1981); three *s*; 2nd, 1981, Shirley Jane Barrett. *Educ:* Bedford Sch.; St John's and Merton Colls, Oxford (MA, BPhil; Hon. Fellow, St John's Coll., 1991). Harmsworth Senior Scholarship, 1954; Harkness Commonwealth Fellowship, USA, 1963–64. Principal Private Sec. to Chancellor of the Exchequer, 1971–73; Under-Sec., HM Treasury, 1973–78, Dep. Sec., 1978–83 (Central Policy Review Staff, Cabinet Office, 1981–82), 2nd Perm. Sec., 1983–85. Board Mem., London Transport, 1991–; Chm., London Buses Ltd, 1994–. Trustee, Orchestra of the Age of Enlightenment, 1990–. *Address:* 11 Park Row, SE10 9NG. *T:* 0181–858 3015.

BAILEY, Prof. Allen Jackson, FRSC; Professor of Biochemistry, University of Bristol, since 1980; *b* 31 Jan. 1931; *s* of late Horace Jackson Bailey and Mabel Bailey (*née* Young); *m* 1956, Beryl Lee; twin *s* two *d.* *Educ:* Eccles Grammar Sch. BSc London (Chem.) 1954; MSc (Physics) 1958, PhD (Chem.) 1960, Birmingham; MA 1967, ScD 1973, Cambridge. FIFST. Shell Chemicals, 1954–57; Low Temp. Res. Station, Univ. of Cambridge, 1960–67; Harkness Fellow, Commonwealth Fund, Biol. Dept, CIT, 1963–65; joined AFRC Meat Res. Inst., Bristol, 1967: SPSO (Special Merit), 1972; Head of Biochem. Dept, 1977–79; Director (DCSO), 1979–85; Hd of Lab., AFRC Inst. of Food Res., Bristol, 1985–90. Vis. Prof., São Paulo Univ., 1991. Scott Robertson Meml Lectr, QUB, 1986; Proctor Meml Lectr, Leeds, 1991. Hon. Fellow, British Connective Tissue Soc. Senior Medal Food Science, RSC, 1987; Internat. Lectureship Award, Amer. Meat Sci. Assoc., 1989. Mem. Editl Bds, sci. jls. *Publications:* Recent Advances in Meat Science, 1985; Collagen as a Food, 1987; Connective Tissue in Meat and Meat Products, 1989; sci. papers in learned jls. *Recreations:* travel, photography. *Address:* Seasons, Bridgwater Road, Winscombe, Avon BS25 1NA. *T:* Winscombe (0193484) 3447. *Club:* Farmers'.

BAILEY, Sir Brian (Harry), Kt 1983; OBE 1976; JP; DL; Chairman, Television South West Ltd, 1980–93; Director: Channel Four Television, 1985–91 (Deputy Chairman, 1989–91); Oracle Teletext Ltd, 1983–93; *b* 25 March 1923; *s* of Harry Bailey and Lilian (*née* Pulfer); *m* 1948, Nina Olive Sylvia (*née* Saunders); two *d.* *Educ:* Lowestoft Grammar Sch. RAF, 1941–45. SW Dist Organisation Officer, NALGO, 1951–82; South Western Reg. Sec., TUC, 1968–81. Chairman: South Western RHA, 1975–82; Health Educn Council, 1983–87; Health Educn Authority, 1987–89; Member: Somerset CC, 1966–84; SW Econ. Planning Council, 1969–79; Central Health Services Council, 1978–80; MRC, 1978–86; Adv. Cttee on Severn Barrage, Dept of Energy, 1978–81; Business Educn Council, 1980–84; NHS Management Inquiry Team, 1983–84. Chm. Council, Indep. Television Assoc., 1991; Vice-Chm., BBC Radio Bristol Adv. Council, 1971–78; Member: BBC West Reg. Adv. Council, 1973–78; Council, ITCA, 1982–86; South and West Adv. Bd, Legal and General Assurance Soc. Ltd, 1985–87. Director: Independent Television Publications Ltd, 1985–90; Bournemouth Orchs (formerly Western Orchestral Soc. Ltd), 1982–. SW Regl Pres., MENCAP, 1984–90; Nat. Pres., Hosp. Caterers Assoc., 1987–. Trustee, EEC Chamber Orchestra, 1987–. Gen. Governor, British Nutrition Foundn, 1987–91. Chm. of Govs, Dartington Coll. of Arts, 1992–. JP Somerset, 1964 (Chm., Taunton Deane Magistrates Bench, 1987–92); DL Somerset, 1988. *Recreations:* football, cricket and tennis (watching), music, golf (playing). *Address:* Runnerstones, 32 Stonegallows, Taunton, Somerset TA1 5JP. *T:* Taunton (01823) 461265. *Club:* Enmore Park Golf.

BAILEY, David, FRPS, FCSD; photographer, film director; *b* 2 Jan. 1938; *s* of William Bailey and Agnes (*née* Green); *m* 1st, 1960, Rosemary Bramble; 2nd, 1967, Catherine Deneuve, *qv*; 3rd, 1975, Marie Helvin (marr. diss. 1985); 4th, 1986, Catherine Dyer; two *s* one *d.* *Educ:* self taught. FRPS 1972; FSIAD 1975. Photographer for Vogue, 1959–; dir of television commercials, 1966–, of documentaries, 1968–; dir. and prod., Who Dealt? (TV film), 1993. Exhibitions: Nat. Portrait Gall., 1971; one-man retrospective, V&A, 1983; Internat. Centre of Photograph, NY, 1984; Photographs from the Sudan, ICA and tour, 1985; Bailey Now!, Nat. Centre of Photography, Bath, 1989; Hamilton's Gall., 1995. FRSA. Hon. FCGI. *Publications:* Box of Pinups, 1964; Goodbye Baby and Amen, 1969; Warhol, 1974; Beady Minces, 1974; Papua New Guinea, 1975; Mixed Moments, 1976; Trouble and Strife, 1980; David Bailey's London NW1, 1982; Black and White Memories, 1983; Nudes 1981–84, 1984; Imagine, 1985; If We Shadows, 1992; The Lady is a Tramp, 1995 (filmed, 1995). *Recreations:* aviculture, photography, travelling, painting. *Address:* 24–26 Brownlow Mews, WC1N 2LA.

BAILEY, D(avid) R(oy) Shackleton, LittD; FBA 1958; Pope Professor of the Latin Language and Literature, Harvard University, 1982–88, now Emeritus; Adjunct Professor, University of Michigan, since 1989; *b* 10 Dec. 1917; *y s* of late Rev. J. H. Shackleton Bailey, DD, and Rosamund Maud (*née* Giles); *m* 1967, Hilary Ann (marr. diss. 1974), *d* of Leonard Sidney and Margery Bardwell; *m* 1994, Kristine Zvirbulis. *Educ:* Lancaster Royal Grammar Sch.; Gonville and Caius Coll., Cambridge. Fellow of Gonville and Caius Coll., 1944–55, Praelector, 1954–55; Fellow and Dir of Studies in Classics, Jesus Coll., Cambridge, 1955–64; Visiting Lecturer in Classics, Harvard Coll., 1963; Fellow and Dep. Bursar, Gonville and Caius Coll., 1964; Senior Bursar 1965–68; Univ. Lectr in Tibetan, 1948–68; Prof. of Latin, Univ. of Michigan, 1968–74; Prof. of Greek and Latin, Harvard Univ., 1975–82. Andrew V. V. Raymond Vis. Prof., State Univ. of NY at Buffalo, 1973–74; Vis. Fellow of Peterhouse, Cambridge, 1980–81; Nat. Endowment of Humanities Fellowship, 1980–81. Mem., Amer. Philosophical Soc., 1977. Fellow, Amer. Acad. of Arts and Sciences, 1979. Editor, Harvard Studies in Classical Philology, 1978–84. Hon. LittD Dublin, 1984. Charles J. Goodwin Award of Merit, Amer. Philol Assoc., 1978; Kenyon Medal, British Acad., 1985. *Publications:* The Śatapañcāśatka of Mātrceta, 1951; Propertiana, 1956; Towards a Text of Cicero, *ad Atticum*, 1960; Ciceronis Epistulae ad Atticum IX-XVI, 1961; Cicero's Letters to Atticus, Vols I and II, 1965; Vol. V, 1966, Vol. VI, 1967, Vols III and IV, 1968, Vol. VII, 1970; Cicero, 1971; Two Studies in Roman Nomenclature, 1976; Cicero: *Epistulae ad Familiares*, 2 vols, 1977; (trans.) Cicero's Letters to Atticus, 1978; (trans.) Cicero's Letters to his Friends, 2 Vols, 1978; Towards a Text of *Anthologia Latina*, 1979; Selected Letters of Cicero, 1980; Cicero: *Epistulae ad Q. Fratrem et M. Brutum*, 1981; Profile of Horace, 1982; Anthologia Latina, I.1, 1982; Horatius, 1985; Cicero: Philippics, 1986; (trans.) Cicero, Selected Letters, 1986; Ciceronis Epistulae, 4 vols, 1987–88; Lucanus, 1988; Onomasticon to Cicero's speeches, 1988; Quintilianus: *Declamationes minores*, 1989; Martialis, 1990; Back from Exile, 1991; Martial, 3 vols, 1993; Homoeoteleuton in Latin dactylic verse, 1994; articles in Classical and Orientalist periodicals. *Recreation:* cats. *Address:* 303 North Division, Ann Arbor, MI 48104, USA.

BAILEY, Dennis, RDI 1980; ARCA; graphic designer and illustrator; Partner, Bailey and Kenny, since 1988; *b* 20 Jan. 1931; *s* of Leonard Charles Bailey and Ethel Louise Funnell; *m* 1985, Nicola Anne Roberts; one *s* one *d.* *Educ:* West Sussex Sch. of Art, Worthing; Royal College of Art. Asst Editor, Graphis magazine, Zürich, 1956; free-lance design practice, London, 1957–87; Paris, 1961–64; Art Dir, Town magazine, London, 1964–66; Lectr in graphic design, Chelsea Sch. of Art, 1970–81, Middlesex Polytechnic, 1985–89. *Clients and work include:* Economist Newspaper: covers and typographic advisor; Economist Publications: The World in 1987–1995; Architectural Assoc.: art dir of magazine AA Files; Arts Council of GB: design of exhibn catalogues and posters for Dada and Surrealism Reviewed, 1978, Picasso's Picassos, 1981, Renoir, 1985, Torres-Garcia, 1985, Le Corbusier, 1987, Art in Latin America, 1989, Dali: the early years, 1994; Royal Academy: catalogue and graphics for Pompeii AD 79, 1977, graphics and publicity for The Genius of Venice, 1984, Inigo Jones, 1989, Frans Hals, 1990, Egon Schiele, 1990; Mantegna, 1992; Imperial War Museum: graphics for Cabinet War Rooms, Whitehall, 1984; RSA: housestyle, 1989; A. d'Offay Gallery: catalogues and housestyle, 1990–91; design of business print for Cons. Gold Fields, Ultramar, London Merchant Securities and N. M. Rothschild & Sons. Illustrations for The Economist, Esquire, Harpers Bazaar (USA), Harpers and Queen, Illustrated London News, Listener, Nova, Observer, Olympia (Paris), Town; book jackets for Jonathan Cape, Penguin Books and Anglo-German Foundn. *Address:* Cunningham Place, NW8 8JU. *T:* (studio) 0171–377 5483.

BAILEY, Sir Derrick Thomas Louis, 3rd Bt, *cr* 1919; DFC; *b* 15 Aug. 1918; 2nd *s* of Sir Abe Bailey, 1st Bt, KCMG; *S* half-brother, 1946; *m* 1st, 1946, Katharine Nancy Stormonth Darling; four *s* one *d*; 2nd, 1980, Mrs Jean Roscoe (marr. diss. 1990). *Educ:* Winchester. Engaged in farming. *Recreations:* all sports, all games. *Heir: s* John Richard Bailey [*b* 11 June 1947; *m* 1977, Jane, *o d* of John Pearson Gregory; two *s* one *d*]. *Address:* Bluestones, Alderney, CI. *Club:* Rand (Johannesburg).

BAILEY, His Honour Desmond Patrick; a Circuit Judge (formerly Judge of County Courts), 1965–79; *b* 6 May 1907; 3rd *s* of Alfred John Bailey, Bowdon, Cheshire, and of Ethel Ellis Johnson; unmarried. *Educ:* Brighton Coll.; Queens' Coll., Cambridge (BA, LLB). Called to Bar, Inner Temple, 1931. Northern Circuit. Served War of 1939–45: Rifle Brigade, Lancashire Fusiliers, Special Operations Executive, North Africa, Italy (Major). Recorder of Carlisle, 1963–65. *Address:* c/o Davies Wallis Foyster, 37 Peter Street, Manchester M2 5GB.

BAILEY, Air Vice-Marshal Dudley Graham, CB 1979; CBE 1970; Deputy Managing Director, The Services Sound and Vision Corporation (formerly Services Kinema Corporation), 1980–93; *b* 12 Sept. 1924; *s* of P. J. Bailey and D. M. Bailey (*née* Taylor); *m* 1948, Dorothy Barbara Lovelace-Hunt; two *d*. Pilot trng, Canada, 1943–45; Intell. Officer, Air HQ Italy, 1946–47 and HQ 23 Gp, 1948–49; Berlin Airlift, 1949; Flt Comdr No 50 and 61 Sqdns, Lincolns, 1950–52; exchange duties, USAF, B-36 aircraft, 1952–54; Canberra Sqdn: Flt Comdr, 1955; Sqdn Comdr, 1956; Air Min., 1956–58; Army Staff Coll., Camberley, 1959; OC No 57 (Victor) Sqdn, 1960–62; Air Warfare course, Manby, 1962; Wing Comdr Ops, HQ Air Forces Middle East, 1963–65; MoD Central Staffs, 1965–66; MoD (Air) Directorate of Air Staff Plans, 1966–68; OC RAF Wildenrath, 1968–70; Sen. Personnel Staff Officer, HQ Strike Comd, 1970–71; Royal Coll. of Defence Studies, 1972; Dir of Personnel (Air), RAF, 1972–74; SASO, RAF Germany, 1974–75; Dep. Comdr, RAF Germany, 1975–76; Dir Gen., Personal Services (RAF), MoD, 1976–80, retired. Chm., Central Council, RAFA, 1990–. Gov., Piper's Corner Sch., Gt Kingshill, Bucks, 1991–. *Address:* Firs Corner, Abbotswood, Speen, Bucks HP27 0SR. *T:* High Wycombe (01494) 488462. *Club:* Royal Air Force.

BAILEY, Eric; Director, Plymouth Polytechnic, 1970–74, retired; *b* 2 Nov. 1913; *s* of Enoch Whittaker Bailey, Overton Hall, Sandbach, Cheshire; *m* 1942, Dorothy Margaret Laing, Stockport; one *s* one *d*. *Educ:* King's Sch., Macclesfield; Manchester Univ. BSc Hons; CEng, FRIC, MIChemE; DipEd. Lectr, Stockport Coll. of Technology, 1936–41; Industrial Chemist, 1941–45; Lectr, Enfield Coll. of Technology, 1945–46; Vice-Principal, Technical Coll., Worksop, 1946–51; Principal: Walker Technical Coll., Oakengates, Salop, 1951–59; Plymouth Coll. of Technology, 1959–69. *Recreations:* putting colour into gardens, photography, pursuing leisure and voluntary activities. *Address:* 3 St Bridget Avenue, Crownhill, Plymouth, Devon PL6 5BB. *T:* Plymouth (01752) 771426. *Club:* Rotary (Plymouth).

BAILEY, Glenda Adrianne; Editor, Marie Claire, since 1988; *b* 16 Nov. 1958; *d* of John Ernest Bailey and Constance Groome. *Educ:* Noel Baker Sch., Derby; Kingston Poly. (BA Fashion Design; Hon. MA). Editor: Honey Magazine, 1986; Folio Magazine, 1987. Women's Magazine Editor of the Year, BSME, 1989, 1992; Editor's Editor of the Year, BSME, 1992. *Address:* 2 Hatfields, SE1 9PG. *T:* 0171–261 5240.

BAILEY, Sir Harold (Walter), Kt 1960; FBA 1944; MA, W Aust.; MA, DPhil Oxon; Professor of Sanskrit, Cambridge University, 1936–67, Professor Emeritus, 1967; Life Fellow, Queens' College, Cambridge, 1956 (Fellow, 1936–56; Hon. Fellow, 1967); *b* Devizes, Wilts, 16 Dec. 1899. Was Lecturer in Iranian Studies at Sch. of Oriental Studies. Member of: Danish Academy, 1946; Norwegian Academy, 1947; Kungl. Vitterhets Historie och Antikvitets Akademien, Stockholm, 1948; Governing Body, SOAS, Univ. of London, 1946–70; L'Institut de France, Associé étranger, Académie des Inscriptions et Belles-Lettres, 1968. President: Philological Soc., 1948–52; Royal Asiatic Society, 1964–67 (Gold Medal, 1972; Denis Sinor Medal for Inner Asian Studies, 1993); Soc. for Afghan Studies, 1972–79; Soc. of Mithraic Studies (1971), 1975–; Corpus Inscriptionum Iranicarum, 1987– (Mem., 1954; Chm., 1967–87); Chm., Anglo-Mongolian Soc., 1979–81. Chm., Ancient India and Iran Trust, 1978–. FAHA 1971; Hon. Fellow: SOAS, London Univ., 1963–; Queens' Coll., Cambridge, 1967; St Catherine's Coll., Oxford, 1976. Hon. Mem., Bhandarkar Oriental Res. Inst., Poona, 1968. Hon. DLitt: W Aust., 1963; ANU, 1970; Oxon, 1976; Hon. DD Manchester, 1979. *Publications:* Zoroastrian Problems in the Ninth Century Books, 1938; Indo-Scythian Studies, Khotanese Texts, I–VIII, 1945–85; Khotanese Buddhist Texts, 1951, 2nd edn 1981; Saka Documents I–IV (portfolios) 1960–67; Saka Documents V (text vol.), 1968; Dictionary of Khotan Saka, 1979; The Culture of the Sakas in Ancient Iranian Khotan, 1981; numerous articles, 1930–. *Address:* Queens' College, Cambridge CB3 9ET.

BAILEY, Jack Arthur; Secretary, MCC, 1974–87; Secretary, International Cricket Conference, 1974–87; *b* 22 June 1930; *s* of Horace Arthur and Elsie Winifred Bailey; *m* 1st, 1957, Julianne Mary Squier (marr. diss.); one *s* two *d*; 2nd, 1991, Vivian Mary Robins. *Educ:* Christ's Hospital; University Coll., Oxford (BA). Asst Master, Bedford Sch., 1958–60; Reed Paper Group, 1960–67; Rugby Football Correspondent, Sunday Telegraph, 1962–74; Asst Sec., MCC, 1967–74. Regular contributor to The Times, 1987–. Mem., Cricket Writers' Club. *Publications:* Conflicts in Cricket, 1989; Trevor Bailey: a life in cricket, 1993. *Recreations:* cricket (played for Essex and for Oxford Univ.), golf. *Address:* 132 Cranbrook Road, W4 2LJ. *T:* 0181–994 6622. *Clubs:* MCC; Vincent's (Oxford).

BAILEY, John; *see* Bailey, W. J. J.

BAILEY, Sir John Bilsland, KCB 1987 (CB 1982); Director, Personal Investment Authority and Chairman, Disciplinary Tribunal, since 1994; HM Procurator General and Treasury Solicitor, 1984–88; *b* 5 Nov. 1928; *o s* of late Walter Bailey and Ethel Edith Bailey, FRAM (who *m* 2nd, Sir Thomas George Spencer); *m* 1952, Marion Rosemary (*née* Carroll); two *s* one *d*. *Educ:* Eltham Coll.; University Coll., London (LLB). Solicitor of Supreme Court. Legal Asst, Office of HM Treasury Solicitor, 1957; Sen. Legal Asst, 1962; Asst Treasury Solicitor, 1971; Principal Asst Treasury Solicitor, 1973; Under-Sec. (Legal), Dept of HM Procurator General and Treasury Solicitor, 1973–77; Legal Dir, Office of Fair Trading, 1977–79; Dep. Treasury Solicitor, 1979–84. Chief Adjudicator, Cttee for Supervision of Standards of Telephone Inf. Services, 1989–. Pres., Disciplinary Cttee, 1994, Public Interest Dir, 1993–, LAUTRO. Gov., Anglo-European Coll. of Chiropractic, 1990–94. Chm., Westminster Soc., 1994–. *Recreations:* walking, reading, listening to music. *Club:* Reform.

BAILEY, John Everett Creighton, CBE 1947; Executive Chairman, Difco Laboratories (UK) Ltd, 1970–75; Chairman and Managing Director, Baird & Tatlock Group of Cos, 1941–69; *b* 2 Nov. 1905; *s* of late John Edred Bailey and late Violet Constance Masters; *m* 1928, Hilda Anne Jones (*d* 1982); one *s* four *d*. *Educ:* Brentwood Sch. Peat Marwick Mitchell & Co., 1925–31; Director: Derbyshire Stone Ltd, 1959–69; Tarmac Derby Ltd, 1969–70; G. D. Searle & Co., 1969–70, and other companies. Mem., Admlty Chemical Adv. Panel, 1940–50; Pres. Scientific Instrument Manufacturers Assoc., 1945–50; Chm. Brit. Laboratory Ware Assoc., 1950–52, Pres., 1974–83; Chm. Brit. Sci. Instr. Research Assoc., 1952–64 (Pres. 1964–71), first Companion, SIRA Inst.; Mem., Grand Council FBI, 1945–58; Mem. BoT Exhibns Adv. Cttee, 1957–65, and Census of Production Adv. Cttee, 1960–68. Formerly Special Member, Prices and Incomes Board. Master, 1957–58 and 1974–75, Worshipful Co. of Scientific Instrument Makers; Master, Worshipful Co. of Needlemakers, 1981–83; Freeman of City of London, 1955. Fellow, Inst. of Export, 1955; MRI; CIMgt (CBIM 1961). *Recreation:* golf. *Address:* Wayford Manor, Wayford, Crewkerne, Somerset TA18 8QG. *Club:* Athenæum.

BAILEY, Rt Rev. Jonathan Sansbury; *see* Derby, Bishop of.

BAILEY, Norman Stanley, CBE 1977; operatic and concert baritone; *b* Birmingham, 23 March 1933; *s* of late Stanley and Agnes Bailey; *m* 1st, 1957, Doreen Simpson (marr. diss. 1983); two *s* one *d*; 2nd, 1985, Kristine Ciesinski. *Educ:* Rhodes Univ., S Africa; Vienna State Academy. BMus; Performer's and Teacher's Licentiate in Singing; Diplomas, opera, lieder, oratorio. Principal baritone, Sadler's Wells Opera, 1967–71; regular engagements at world's major opera houses and festivals, including: La Scala, Milan; Royal Opera House, Covent Garden; Bayreuth Wagner Festival (first British Hans Sachs in Meistersinger, 1969); Vienna State Opera (first British Wanderer in Siegfried, 1976); Metropolitan Opera, NY; Paris Opera; Edinburgh Festival; Hamburg State Opera; Munich State Opera. BBC Television performances in Falstaff, La Traviata, The Flying Dutchman, Macbeth. Recordings include The Ring (Goodall); Meistersinger and Der Fliegende Holländer (Solti); Walküre (Klemperer), among others. Hon. RAM, 1981; Hon. DMus, Rhodes, 1986. *Recreations:* Mem., Baha'i world community; chess, notaphily, golf, microcomputing. *Address:* 84 Warham Road, South Croydon, Surrey CR2 6LB.

BAILEY, Patrick Edward Robert; Director, Dan-Air Associated Services, 1985–92; *b* 16 Feb. 1925; *s* of late Edward Bailey and Mary Elizabeth Bailey; *m* 1947, Rowena Evelyn Nichols; two *s* three *d*. *Educ:* Clapham Coll.; St Joseph's Coll., Mark Cross; LSE. BSc(Econ). MIPM; FCIT 1971 (Mem. Council, 1982–85 and 1987–89). RAPC and RAEC (Captain), 1943–48; Labour Management, Min. of Supply and Army Department: ROF Glascoed, 1951–54; RAE Farnborough, 1954–58; RSAF Enfield, 1958–59; ROF Radway Green, 1959–61; ROFs Woolwich, 1961–66. British Airports Authority: Dep. Personnel Dir, 1966; Personnel Dir, 1970; Airport Services Dir, 1974; Dir, Gatwick and Stansted Airports, 1977–85. Chm. Trustees, British Airports Authority Superannuation Scheme, 1975–86. Mem., Air Transport and Travel Industry Trng Bd, 1971–76; Mem. Bd, Internat. Civil Airports Assoc., 1974–77. Mem., Mid-Sussex DC, 1986– (Chm., 1991–93). *Address:* 17 Lucastes Lane, Haywards Heath, W Sussex RH16 1LE.

BAILEY, Paul, (christened **Peter Harry**); freelance writer, since 1967; radio broadcaster; *b* 16 Feb. 1937; *s* of Arthur Oswald Bailey and Helen Maud Burgess. *Educ:* Sir Walter St John's Sch., London; Central School of Speech and Drama. Actor, 1956–64: appeared in first productions of Ann Jellicoe's The Sport of My Mad Mother, 1958, and John Osborne's and Anthony Creighton's Epitaph for George Dillon, 1958. Literary Fellow at Univ. of Newcastle and Univ. of Durham, 1972–74; Bicentennial Fellowship, 1976; Visiting Lectr in English Literature, North Dakota State Univ., 1977–79. Frequent radio broadcaster, mainly on Radio 3; has written and presented programmes on Karen Blixen, Henry Green, I. B. Singer and Primo Levi, among others. FRSL, 1982–84. E. M. Forster Award, 1974; George Orwell Meml Prize, 1978, for broadcast essay The Limitations of Despair. *Publications:* At the Jerusalem, 1967 (Somerset Maugham Award, 1968; Arts Council Prize, 1968); Trespasses, 1970; A Distant Likeness, 1973; Peter Smart's Confessions, 1977; Old Soldiers, 1980; An English Madam, 1982; Gabriel's Lament, 1986; An Immaculate Mistake: scenes from childhood and beyond (autobiog.), 1990; Sugar Cane, 1993; (ed) The Oxford Book of London, 1995; contribs to Observer, TLS, Daily Telegraph, Guardian. *Recreations:* visiting churches, travel, watching tennis. *Address:* 79 Davisville Road, W12 9SH. *T:* 0181–749 2279.

BAILEY, Reginald Bertram, CBE 1976; Member, Employers' Panel, Industrial Tribunals in England and Wales, 1977–85; *b* 15 July 1916; *s* of late George Bertram Bailey and Elizabeth Bailey, Ilford; *m* 1942, Phyllis Joan Firman; one *s* one *d*. *Educ:* Owen's School. Served War of 1939–45: RAPC, 1940–42; RE, 1942–46 (Captain). Entered Post Office as Exec. Officer, 1935; Higher Exec. Officer, 1947; Sen. Exec. Officer, 1948; Principal, 1950; Instructor, Management Trng Centre, 1957; Staff Controller, SW Region, 1958; Comdt, Management Trng Centre, 1962; Asst Sec., 1965; Dir, Wales and the Marches Postal Region, 1967; Dir, South-Eastern Postal Region, 1970–76. *Recreations:* walking, gardening, philately, old railway timetables. *Address:* 21 Preston Paddock, Rustington, Littlehampton, West Sussex BN16 2AA. *T:* Rustington (01903) 772451.

BAILEY, Sir Richard (John), Kt 1984; CBE 1977; Deputy Chairman, British Ceramic Research Limited, 1990–94 (Chairman, 1982–83 and 1987–90); Director, Central Independent Television plc, 1986–94; *b* 8 July 1923; *s* of Philip Bailey and Doris Margaret (*née* Freebody); *m* 1945, Marcia Rachel Cureton Webb; one *s* three *d*. *Educ:* Newcastle; Shrewsbury. FICeram 1955 (Founder Fellow). Served RNVR 1942–46 (Lieut). Doulton Fine China Ltd: Technical Dir, 1955–63; Man. Dir, 1963–72; Dir, Doulton & Co. Ltd, 1967–82; Man. Dir, Royal Doulton Tableware Ltd, 1972–80, Chm., 1980–83; Chairman: Royal Crown Derby Porcelain Co. Ltd, 1983–87; Royal Doulton Ltd, 1983–87. Member: Ceramics Industry Nat. Jt Council, 1961–84 (Jt Chm., 1969–84); Ceramic Industry Training Bd, 1967–70; Dir, W Midlands Industrial Develt Assoc., 1983–87; President: BCMF, 1973–74; British Ceramic Soc., 1980–81; Chm., North Staffs Business Initiative, 1981–91. Pres., North Staffs Med. Inst., 1987–. Hon. Freeman, City of Stoke-on-Trent, 1987. Hon. Fellow, Staffordshire Univ. (formerly Poly.), 1988. MUniv Keele, 1983. FRSA 1977. *Recreations:* golf, walking, gardening. *Address:* Lea Cottage, School Lane, Aston, near Market Drayton, Shropshire TF9 4JD.

BAILEY, Ronald William, CMG 1961; HM Diplomatic Service, retired; *b* 14 June 1917; *o s* of William Staveley Bailey and May Eveline (*née* Cudlipp), Southampton; *m* 1946, Joan Hassall, *d* of late A. E. Gray, JP, Stoke-on-Trent; one *s* one *d*. *Educ:* King Edward VI Sch., Southampton; Trinity Hall, Cambridge (Wootton Isaacson Scholar in Spanish). Probationer Vice-Consul, Beirut, 1939–41; HM Vice-Consul, Alexandria, 1941–45; Asst Oriental Sec., British Embassy, Cairo, 1945–48; 1st Sec., Foreign Office, 1948–49; British Legation, Beirut, 1949–52 (acted as Chargé d'Affaires, 1949, 1950 and 1951); British Embassy, Washington, 1952–55; Counsellor, Washington, 1955–57; Khartoum, 1957–60 (acted as Chargé d'Affaires in each of these years); Chargé d'Affaires, Taiz, 1960–62; Consul-Gen., Gothenburg, 1963–65; Minister, British Embassy, Baghdad, 1965–67; Ambassador to

Bolivia, 1967–71; Ambassador to Morocco, 1971–75. Mem. Council, Anglo-Arab Assoc., 1978–85. Vice-Pres., 1975–87, Pres., 1987–89, Hon. Life Vice-Pres., 1989, Soc. for Protection of Animals in N Africa; Chm., Black Down Cttee, Nat. Trust, 1982–87; Hon. Life Pres., British-Moroccan Soc., 1989. *Publication:* (ed) Records of Oman 1867–1960 (12 vols), 1989–92. *Recreations:* walking, photography, gardening. *Address:* Redwood, Tennyson's Lane, Haslemere, Surrey GU27 3AF. *T:* Haslemere (01428) 642800. *Club:* Oriental.

BAILEY, Sir Stanley (Ernest), Kt 1986; CBE 1980; QPM 1975; DL; security consultant; *b* 30 Sept. 1926; *m* 1954, Marguerita Dorothea Whitbread. Joined Metropolitan Police, 1947; Asst Chief Constable, Staffs, 1966; Dir, Police Res., Home Office, 1970–72; Dep. Chief Constable, Staffs, 1973–75; Chief Constable, Northumbria, 1975–91; Regl Police Comdr, No 1 Home Defence Reg., 1981–91. Mem., IACP, 1970– (Chairman: Adv. Cttee on Internat. Policy, 1984–89; Europ. Sub-Cttee, 1984–89; Mem. Exec. Cttee, 1986–91); Rep., ICPO, 1986–88. Pres., ACPO, England, Wales & NI, 1985–86 (Vice-Pres., 1984–85; Immediate Past Pres., 1986–87; Chm., Crime Prevention Sub-cttee, 1986–91); Vice Pres., Police Mutual Assce Soc., 1986–94. Chairman: Cttee on Burglar Alarms, BSI, 1975–93; Cttee on Security Standards, BSI, 1976–93; Founder and Chm., 1st Internat. Police Exhibn and Conf., London, 1987; Founder and Jt Chm., Centre for Res. into Crime, Community and Policing, Univ. of Newcastle upon Tyne, 1989–92; Vice Chm., Crime Concern, 1989–93 (Mem., Adv. Bd, 1988–94); Member: Home Office Standing Conf. on Crime Prevention, 1977–91; Bd, Northumbria Coalition Against Crime, 1989–92; Chm. of cttees and working parties on crime prevention, intruder alarms, criminal intelligence, computer privacy, and physical stress in police work. Observer, VIII UN Congress on Crime Prevention, Havana, 1990 (Organiser and Chm., First UN Meeting of Sen. Police Officials). Police Advr, AMA, 1987–91. Pres., Security Services Assoc., 1991–; Vice Pres., Ex Police in Commerce, 1992–. Has presented papers etc in USA, Denmark, France, Hong Kong, NZ, Japan, Germany, Spain, Thailand, China, Holland, Portugal, Italy, Belgium and USSR on community crime prevention, measurement of effectiveness, and Private Security industry. Trustee, Suzy Lamplugh Trust, 1991–93. Patron, Assoc. of Security Consultants, 1992–. Mem., Bd of Govs, Internat. Inst. of Security, 1990–. Grad., Nat. Exec. Inst., FBI Washington, 1984. Freeman, City of London, 1988. CIMgt (CBIM 1987). DL Tyne and Wear, 1986. ABIS—Ken Bolton Award for outstanding contribution to crime prevention, 1990. OStJ 1981. *Publications:* articles in learned jls on policy issues. *Recreations:* gardening, travel. *Address:* 2 Hadrian Court, Darras Hall, Ponteland, Newcastle upon Tyne NE20 9JU.

BAILEY, Thomas Aubrey, MBE 1959; Director, Peter Cox Ltd, Building Restoration Specialists (Member of SGB Group of Cos), 1970–76; *b* 20 Jan. 1912; *o s* of late Thomas Edward Bailey and Emma Bailey; *m* 1944, Joan Woodman, *d* of late John Woodman Hooper; one *s*. *Educ:* Adams' Grammar Sch., Newport, Shropshire; Regent Street Polytechnic Sch. of Architecture. Entered HM Office of Works, Ancient Monuments Br., 1935; Asst Architect, 1945–49; Architect, London and E Anglia, 1949–54; Sen. Architect in charge Ancient Monuments Br., Eng., Wales and Overseas, Min. of Public Building and Works, 1954–69; Architectural Adv. to Oxford Historic Bldgs Fund, 1963–69. Served on various cttees on stone decay and preservation; seconded to Sir Giles G. Scott, OM, RA, for Rebuilding of House of Commons, 1944–49. *Principal works:* Direction of MPBW Survey for Oxford Historic Bldg Appeal, 1957–62 and Cambridge Appeal, 1963; re-erection of fallen Trilithons at Stonehenge, 1958–64; Conservation of Claudian Aqueduct and Aurelian Wall, Brit. Embassy at Rome, 1957–69; etc. Resigned professional membership of RIBA and ARCUK, to enter specialised Bldg Industry, 1969. Mem. Conservation Cttee, for Council for Places of Worship, 1968; Mem. Council, Ancient Monuments Soc., 1970–. FSA 1957; FRSA 1969; Fellow of Faculty of Bldg, 1970. Freeman of City of London, 1967; Freeman and Liveryman, Worshipful Company of Masons, 1973. Hon. MA Oxon, 1963. *Publications:* (jointly) The Claudian Aqueduct in the Grounds of the British Embassy, Rome, 1966; many technical reports on conservation of Historic Monuments. *Recreations:* music, photography, travel, motoring. *Address:* 32 Anne Boleyn's Walk, Cheam, Sutton, Surrey SM3 8DF. *T:* 0181–642 3185. *Club:* City Livery.

BAILEY, (William) John (Joseph); journalist; *b* 11 June 1940; *s* of Ernest Robert Bailey and Josephine Smith; *m* 1963, Maureen Anne, *d* of James Gibbs Neenan and Marjorie Dorema Wrigglesworth; five *s* three *d*. *Educ:* St Joseph's, Stanford-le-Hope, Essex; Campion Hall, Jamaica; St George's Coll., Kingston, Jamaica; St Chad's Coll., Wolverhampton. Reporter: Southend Standard, Essex, and Essex and Thurrock Gazette, 1960–63; Northern Daily Mail, 1963–64; Chief Reporter, Billingham and Stockton Express, 1964–72; Sub-Editor, Mail, Hartlepool, 1972–75; Features Editor, Echo, Sunderland, 1975–. Member: Press Council, 1974–80; Complaints Cttee, 1974–76, 1977–; Cttee for Evidence to Royal Commission on Press, 1975–76; Gen. Purposes Cttee, 1976–77; Secretariat Cttee, 1976–. Nat. Union of Journalists: Mem., Nat. Exec. Council, 1966–82; Vice-Pres., 1972–73; Pres., 1973–74; Gen. Treasurer, 1975–83. Sec., Hartlepool People Ltd, 1983–. Provincial Journalist of the Year (jtly with Carol Roberton), British Press Awards, 1977 (commended, 1979); Special award Northern Cross, Tom Cordner North East Press Awards, 1984–85, 1989. *Address:* 225 Park Road, Hartlepool, Cleveland TS26 9NG. *T:* Hartlepool (01429) 264577. *Club:* Press (Glasgow).

BAILHACHE, Philip Martin; Bailiff of Jersey, since 1995 (Deputy Bailiff, 1994–95); *b* 28 Feb. 1946; *s* of Jurat Lester Vivian Bailhache (Lieut-Bailiff of Jersey, 1980–82) and Nanette Ross (*née* Ferguson); *m* 1st, 1967 (marr. diss. 1982); two *s* two *d*; 2nd, 1984, Linda (*née* Le Vavasseur dit Durell); one *s* one *d*. *Educ:* Charterhouse; Pembroke Coll., Oxford. Called to the Bar, Middle Temple, 1968; called to the Jersey Bar, 1969; QC (Jersey) 1989. In private practice as Advocate, Jersey, 1969–74; States of Jersey Dep. for Grouville, 1972–74; Solicitor-Gen., Jersey, 1975–85; Attorney Gen. for Jersey, 1986–93. Chm., Jersey Arts Council, 1987–89. *Recreations:* books, wine, gardening, the arts. *Address:* L'Anquetinerie, Grouville, Jersey, Channel Islands JE3 9UX. *T:* Jersey (01534) 852533. *Clubs:* Reform; United (Jersey).

BAILIE, Rt. Hon. Robin John, PC (N Ire) 1971; Solicitor of the Supreme Court of Judicature, Northern Ireland, since 1961; *b* 6 March 1937; *m* 1961, Margaret F. (*née* Boggs); one *s* three *d*. *Educ:* Rainey Endowed Sch. Magherafelt, Co. Londonderry; The Queen's Univ. of Belfast (LLB). MP (N Ire) for Newtonabbey, 1969–72; Minister of Commerce, Govt of NI, 1971–72. Chm., Fine Wine Wholesalers, 1985–; Director: Goodyear Tyre & Rubber Co. (GB), 1984–91; Lummus Mackie Ltd, 1990–. *Recreations:* wine drinking, ski-ing, squash, golf, tennis. *Address:* 5 Thurloe Close, SW7 2SE. *T:* 0171–581 4898.

BAILLIE, family name of **Baron Burton.**

BAILLIE, Alastair Turner; HM Diplomatic Service, retired; Deputy High Commissioner in Calcutta, 1987–91; *b* 24 Dec. 1932; *s* of late Archibald Turner Baillie and Margaret Pinkerton Baillie; *m* 1st, 1965, Wilma Noreen Armstrong (marr. diss. 1974); one *s*; 2nd, 1977, Irena Maria Gregor; one step *s* one step *d*. *Educ:* Dame Allan's Sch., Newcastle upon Tyne; Christ's Coll., Cambridge (BA). National Service, commissioned Queen's Own Cameron Highlanders, 1951–53. HMOCS: North Borneo, subseq. Sabah, Malaysia, 1957–67; joined HM Diplomatic Service, 1967; FCO, 1967–73; Consul (Commercial), Karachi, 1973–77; First Sec. and Head of Chancery, Manila, 1977–80; Counsellor, Addis Ababa, 1980–81; Counsellor (Commercial), Caracas, 1981–83; Governor of Anguilla, 1983–87. *Recreations:* sport, reading, travelling.

BAILLIE, Sir Gawaine George Hope, 7th Bt, of Polkemmet, *cr* 1823; *b* 8 March 1934; *s* of Sir Adrian Baillie, 6th Bt, and Hon. Olive Cecilia (*d* 1974), *d* of 1st Baron Queenborough, GBE; *S* father, 1947; *m* 1966, Margot, *d* of Senator Louis Beaubien, Montreal; one *s* one *d*. *Heir: s* Adrian Louis Baillie, *b* 26 March 1973. *Address:* Freechase, Warninglid, Sussex RH17 5SZ.

BAILLIE, Ian Fowler, CMG 1966; OBE 1962; Director, The Thistle Foundation, Edinburgh, 1970–81; *b* 16 Feb. 1921; *s* of late Very Rev. Principal John Baillie, CH, DLitt, DD, LLD and Florence Jewel (*née* Fowler); *m* 1951, Sheila Barbour (*née* Mathewson); two *s* one *d*. *Educ:* Edinburgh Acad,; Corpus Christi Coll., Oxford (MA). War service, British and Indian Armies, 1941–46. HM Overseas Civil Service (formerly Colonial Service), 1946–66: Admin. Officer (District Comr), Gold Coast, 1946–54; Registrar of Co-operative Socs and Chief Marketing Officer, Aden, 1955; Protectorate Financial Sec., Aden, 1959; Dep. British Agent, Aden, 1962; Brit. Agent and Asst High Comr, Aden, 1963; Dir, Aden Airways 1959–66; Sen. Research Associate and Administrative Officer, Agricultural Adjustment Unit, Dept of Agricultural Economics, Univ. of Newcastle upon Tyne, 1966–69. *Publication:* (ed with S. J. Sheehy) Irish Agriculture in a Changing World, 1971. *Recreation:* angling. *Address:* 4 Grange Loan Gardens, Edinburgh EH9 2EB. *T:* 0131–667 2647.

BAILLIE, Prof. John, CA; Visiting Professor of Accountancy, Heriot-Watt University, since 1989; Partner, Scott-Moncrieff, since 1993; *b* 7 Oct. 1944; *s* of Arthur and Agnes Baillie; *m* 1972, Annette Alexander; one *s* one *d*. *Educ:* Whitehill Sch. CA 1967 (Gold Medal and Distinction in final exams). Partner, Thomson McLintock & Co., later KPMG Peat Marwick, 1978–93. Johnstone-Smith Prof. of Accountancy, Univ. of Glasgow, 1983–88. Mem. various technical and professional affairs cttees, Inst. of Chartered Accountants of Scotland. Hon. MA Glasgow, 1983. *Publications:* Systems of Profit Measurement, 1985; Consolidated Accounts and the Seventh Directive, 1985; technical and professional papers; contribs to Accountants' Magazine and other professional jls. *Recreations:* keeping fit, reading, music, golf. *Address:* The Glen, Glencairn Road, Kilmacolm, Renfrewshire PA13 4PB. *T:* Kilmacolm (01505) 873254. *Club:* Western (Glasgow).

BAILLIE, William James Laidlaw, RSA 1979 (ARSA 1968); PPRSW (PRSW 1974; RSW 1963); painter; President, Royal Scottish Academy, since 1990 (Treasurer, 1980–90); *b* 19 April 1923; *s* of James and Helen Baillie; *m* 1961, Helen Gillon; one *s* two *d*. *Educ:* Dunfermline High Sch.; Edinburgh College of Art (Andrew Grant Schol., 1941–50; Dip. Drawing and Painting 1950). Studies interrupted by war service with Royal Corps of Signals, mainly in Far East, 1942–47. Taught in Edinburgh schools, 1951–60; Mem., Teaching Staff, Edin. College of Art, 1960–88, Sen. Lectr, 1968–88; Visiting Tutor, National Gallery of Canada Summer Sch., near Ottawa, 1955. Exhibits at Thackeray Gall., London, but mostly in Scotland, mainly at Scottish Gall., Edinburgh; first retrospective exhibn in Kirkcaldy Art Gallery, 1977. *Recreations:* music, travel. *Address:* 6A Esslemont Road, Edinburgh EH16 5PX. *T:* 0131–667 1538.

BAILLIE-HAMILTON, family name of **Earl of Haddington.**

BAILLIEU, family name of **Baron Baillieu.**

BAILLIEU, 3rd Baron *cr* 1953, of Sefton, Australia and Parkwood, Surrey; **James William Latham Baillieu;** Assistant Director, Standard Chartered Asia Ltd; *b* 16 Nov. 1950; *s* of 2nd Baron Baillieu and Anne Bayliss, *d* of Leslie William Page, Southport, Queensland; *S* father, 1973; *m* 1st, 1974, Cornelia Masters Ladd (marr. diss.), *d* of W. Ladd; one *s*; 2nd, 1987, Clare Stephenson, *d* of Peter Stephenson of Benalla, Victoria. *Educ:* Radley College; Monash Univ., Melbourne (BEc 1977). Short Service Commission, Coldstream Guards, 1970–73. Manager Asst, Banque Nationale de Paris, Melbourne, 1980; Rothschild Australia Ltd, 1980–88 (Manager, 1983; Sen. Manager, 1984; Associate Dir, 1985); Rothschild Australia Asset Management Ltd, 1980–88 (Associate Dir, 1985); Dir, Manufacturers Hanover Australia Ltd, 1988–90. *Heir: s* Hon. Robert Latham Baillieu, *b* 2 Feb. 1979. *Address:* c/o Mutual Trust Pty Ltd, 360 Collins Street, Melbourne, Victoria 3000, Australia. *Clubs:* Boodle's; Australian (Melbourne).

BAILLIEU, Colin Clive; Chairman, Gresham Underwriting Agencies, 1990–92; *b* 2 July 1930; *s* of Ian Baillieu and Joanna Baillieu (*née* Brinton); *m* 1st, 1955, Diana Robinson (marr. diss. 1968); two *d*; 2nd, 1968, Renata Richter; two *s*. *Educ:* Dragon Sch.; Eton. Commissioned Coldstream Guards, 1949. Local newspaper, Evening Standard, 1951–52; British Metal Corp., 1952–58; British Aluminium, 1958–60; Monsanto Fibres, 1960–66; Arthur Sanderson, 1966–68; Ultrasonic Machines, 1968–76. Member: Council of Lloyd's, 1983–88; Monopolies and Mergers Commn, 1984–93. Contested (C) Rossendale, Lancs, 1964 and 1966. Chm., Nat. Assoc. of Lay Inspectors in Schools, 1993. *Recreations:* skiing, teaching boys to play polo, 17th Century history. *Address:* Hoyle Farm, Heyshott, Midhurst, West Sussex GU29 0DY. *T:* Graffham (01798) 867230. *Clubs:* Travellers', Beefsteak, Shikar, MCC.

BAIN, Andrew David, FRSE 1980; Visiting Professor of Political Economy, University of Glasgow, since 1991; Board Member, Scottish Enterprise, since 1991; *b* 21 March 1936; *s* of Hugh Bain and Kathleen (*née* Eadie); *m* 1st, 1960, Anneliese Minna Frieda Kroggel (marr. diss. 1988); three *s*; 2nd, 1989, Eleanor Riches. *Educ:* Glasgow Academy; Christ's Coll., Cambridge. PhD Cantab 1963. Junior Res. Officer, Dept of Applied Econs, Cambridge Univ., 1958–60; Res. Fellow, Christ's Coll., Cambridge, 1960; Instructor, Cowles Foundn, Yale Univ., 1960–61; Lectr, Cambridge, 1961–66; Fellow, Corpus Christi Coll., Cambridge, 1962; on secondment to Bank of England, 1965–67; Prof. of Econs, 1967–70, Esmee Fairbairn Prof. of Econs of Finance and Investment, 1970–77, Univ. of Stirling; Walton Prof. of Monetary and Financial Econs, Univ. of Strathclyde, 1977–84; Gp Econ. Advr, Midland Bank, 1984–90. Member: Cttee to Review the Functioning of Financial Institutions, 1977–80; (part-time) Monopolies and Mergers Commn, 1981–82; TEC Nat. Council, 1994–. *Publications:* The Growth of Television Ownership in the United Kingdom (monograph), 1964; The Control of the Money Supply, 1970; Company Financing in the UK, 1975; The Economics of the Financial System, 1981, 2nd edn 1992; articles on demand analysis, monetary policy and other subjects. *Address:* 1 Stafford Street, Helensburgh, Glasgow G84 9HU. *Club:* Reform.

BAIN, Douglas John; Industrial Adviser to the Secretary of State for Scotland, 1983–85; *b* 9 July 1924; *s* of Alexander Gillan Bain and Fanny Heaford; *m* 1946, Jean Wallace Fairbairn; three *d*. *Educ:* Pollokshields Secondary School; Royal Technical Coll. (now Strathclyde Univ.), Glasgow (DRTC). ATI. Royal Tech. Coll., 1941–43 and 1948–51. RAF, 1943–48. J. & P. Coats Ltd, 1951–83: graduate trainee, 1951–55; overseas management, 1955–60; central management, 1960–68; Director, 1968–83; seconded to Scottish Office (Scottish Econ. Planning Dept) as Under Sec., 1979–82. *Recreations:* golf, walking, geology, flying. *Address:* 49 Bimbadeen Crescent, Yallambie, Melbourne, Vic 3085, Australia.

BAIN, Prof. George Sayers, DPhil; Principal, London Business School, since 1989; *b* 24 Feb. 1939; *s* of George Alexander Bain and Margaret Ioleen Bamford; *m* 1st, 1962, Carol Lynn Ogden White (marr. diss. 1987); one *s* one *d*; 2nd, 1988, Frances Gwynneth Rigby (*née* Vickers). *Educ:* Univ. of Manitoba (BA Hons 1961, MA 1964); Oxford Univ. (DPhil 1968). Lectr in Econs, Univ. of Manitoba, 1962–63; Res. Fellow, Nuffield Coll., Oxford, 1966–69; Frank Thomas Prof. of Indust. Relations, UMIST, 1969–70; University of Warwick: Dep. Dir, 1970–74, Dir, 1974–81, SSRC Industrial Relations Res. Unit; Pressed Steel Fisher Prof. of Industrial Relations, 1979–89; Chm., Sch. of Industrial and Business Studies, 1983–89. Member: Mech. Engrg Econ. Develt Cttee, NEDO, 1974–76; Cttee of Inquiry on Indust. Democracy, Dept of Trade (Chm., Lord Bullock), 1975–76; Council: ESRC, 1986–91; Nat. Forum for Management Educn and Develt, 1987–90; Chm. Council, Univ. Management Schs, 1987–90. Member: Bd of Trustees, 1990–, and Exec. Vice-Pres., 1991–, European Foundn for Management Develt; Internat. Affairs Cttee, 1990–92, Bd of Dirs, 1992–94, Amer. Assembly of Collegiate Schs of Business; Council, Foundn for Management Educn, 1991–; Council, IMgt (formerly BIM), 1991–93; Senior Salaries Review Body, 1993–; Internat. Council, Amer. Management Assoc., 1993–; Foundn for Canadian Studies in UK, 1993–. Chairman: Food Sector Wkg Gp, NEDO, 1991–92; Commn on Public Policy and British Business, 1995–. Director: Blackwell Publishers (formerly Basil Blackwell Ltd), 1990–; The Economist, 1993–; Canada Life Assurance Co. of GB, 1993–. Consultant: Royal Commn on Trade Unions and Employers' Assocs (Donovan Commn), 1966–67; NBPI, 1967–69; Canadian Task Force on Labour Relns, 1968; acted as Consultant to Dept of Employment, and to the Manitoba and Canada Depts of Labour; frequently acts as arbitrator and mediator in indust. disputes. FRSA 1987. *Publications:* Trade Union Growth and Recognition, 1967; The Growth of White-Collar Unionism, 1970; (jtly) The Reform of Collective Bargaining at Plant and Company Level, 1971; (jtly) Social Stratification and Trade Unionism, 1973; (jtly) Union Growth and the Business Cycle, 1976; (jtly) A Bibliography of British Industrial Relations, 1979; (jtly) Profiles of Union Growth, 1980; (ed) Industrial Relations in Britain, 1983; (jtly) A Bibliography of British Industrial Relations 1971–1979, 1985; contrib. prof. and learned jls. *Recreations:* reading, genealogy, family history. *Address:* London Business School, Sussex Place, Regent's Park, NW1 4SA. *T:* 0171–262 5050. *Club:* Reform.

BAIN, Iain Andrew; Editor, Nairnshire Telegraph, since 1987; *b* 25 Feb. 1949; *s* of Alistair I. R. Bain and late Jean R. Forrest; *m* 1974, Maureen Beattie; three *d*. *Educ:* Nairn Acad.; Univ. of Aberdeen (MA). Research, Univ. of Durham, 1971–74; Sub-editor, 1974, Asst Editor, 1980, Editor, 1981–87, The Geographical Magazine. *Publications:* Mountains and People, 1982; Water on the Land, 1983; Mountains and Earth Movements, 1984; various articles. *Recreations:* reading, walking, photography, gardening. *Address:* Rosebank, Leopold Street, Nairn IV12 4BE. *Club:* Nairn Golf.

BAIN, John; *see* Bain, K. J.

BAIN, John Taylor, CBE 1975; Director of Education, Glasgow, 1968–75; Lay Observer (Solicitors Act) in Scotland, 1977–83; *b* 9 May 1912; *m*; one *s* two *d*. *Educ:* St Andrews Univ. (BSc, MA); Edinburgh Univ. (BEd). War Service, RAF (Technical Br.). Entered educational administration in 1947. JP Glasgow, 1971.

BAIN, (Kenneth) John, MA; Headmaster, The Purcell School, since 1983; *b* 8 July 1939; *s* of Allan John and Hetty Bain; *m* 1962, Cynthia Mary Spain; one *s* one *d*. *Educ:* Bancroft's School; St Peter's College, Oxford (MA). Assistant Master, Stanbridge Earls School, 1962–70; Assistant Master and Housemaster, Cranleigh School, 1970–83. FRSA 1992. *Publications:* occasional articles in educational jls. *Recreations:* music, golf, walking, rough gardening. *Address:* The Purcell School, Mount Park Road, Harrow on the Hill, Middx HA1 3JS; Candida House, Whitechurch Canonicorum, Bridport, Dorset DT6 6RQ. *T:* Chideock (01297) 89629.

BAIN, Margaret Anne; *see* Ewing, M. A.

BAIN, Neville Clifford, FCA, FCIS; Group Chief Executive, Coats Viyella PLC, since 1989; *b* 14 July 1940; *s* of Charles Alexander Bain and Gertrude Mae Bain; *m* 1987, Anne Patricia (*née* Kemp); one step *d*, and one *s* one *d* by previous marriage. *Educ:* King's High Sch., Dunedin, NZ; Otago Univ., Dunedin (BCom Acctcy 1964; BCom Econ 1966; MCom Hons 1968). CMA; ACA 1959, FCA 1989; FCIS 1962. Trainee Inspector, Inland Revenue, NZ, 1957–59; Manager, Anderson & Co., Chartered Accountants, NZ, 1960–62; Cadbury Schweppes Hudson: Cost Accountant, subseq. Financial Controller, and Co. Sec., NZ, 1963–68; Finance Dir, NZ, 1968–75; Cadbury Schweppes: Group Chief Exec., S Africa, 1975–80; Group Strategic Planning Dir, 1980–83 (apptd to Main Bd, 1981); Managing Director: Cadbury Ltd, 1983–86; Cadbury World Wide, 1986–89; Dep. Group Chief Exec. and Finance Dir, Cadbury Schweppes Plc, 1989–90. Director: London Internat. Gp, 1988–93; Gartmore Scotland Investment Trust, 1992–; Argyll Group, 1993–. CIMgt (CBIM 1988). Hon. LLD Otago, NZ, 1993. *Recreations:* sport, walking, music. *Address:* 28 Savile Row, W1X 2DD. *T:* 0171–734 4030, *Fax:* 0171–437 2016.

BAINBRIDGE, Beryl, FRSL; actress, writer; *b* 21 Nov. 1934; *d* of Richard Bainbridge and Winifred Baines; *m* 1954, Austin Davies (marr. diss.); one *s* two *d*. *Educ:* Merchant Taylors' Sch., Liverpool; Arts Educational Schools, Ltd, Tring. Weekly columnist, Evening Standard, 1987–. FRSL 1978. Hon. LittD Liverpool, 1986. *Plays:* Tiptoe Through the Tulips, 1976; The Warrior's Return, 1977; Its a Lovely Day Tomorrow, 1977; Journal of Bridget Hitler, 1981; Somewhere More Central (TV), 1981; Evensong (TV), 1986. *Publications:* A Weekend with Claud, 1967, rev. edn 1981; Another Part of the Wood, 1968, rev. edn 1979; Harriet Said. . . ., 1972; The Dressmaker, 1973 (film, 1989); The Bottle Factory Outing, 1974 (Guardian Fiction Award); Sweet William, 1975 (film, 1980); A Quiet Life, 1976; Injury Time, 1977 (Whitbread Award); Young Adolf, 1978; Winter Garden, 1980; English Journey, 1984 (TV series, 1984); Watson's Apology, 1984; Mum and Mr Armitage, 1985; Forever England, 1986 (TV series, 1986); Filthy Lucre, 1986; An Awfully Big Adventure, 1989 (staged, 1992); The Birthday Boys, 1991; Something Happened Yesterday (essays), 1993; Kiss Me Hardy, 1996. *Recreations:* painting, sleeping. *Address:* 42 Albert Street, NW1 7NU. *T:* 0171–387 3113.

BAINBRIDGE, Cyril, FCIJ; author and journalist; *b* 15 Nov. 1928; *o s* of late Arthur Herman and Edith Bainbridge; *m* 1953, Barbara Hannah (*née* Crook); one *s* two *d*. *Educ:* privately (Negus Coll., Bradford). Served Army, staff of CGS, WO, 1947–49. Entered journalism as Reporter, Bingley Guardian, 1944–45; Telegraph and Argus, and Yorkshire Observer, Bradford, 1945–54; Press Assoc., 1954–63; joined The Times, 1963: Asst News Editor, 1967; Dep. News Editor, 1967–69; Regional News Editor, 1969–77; Managing News Editor, 1977–82; Asst Managing Editor, 1982–86; Editorial Data Manager, Times Newspapers, 1986–88. Vice-Pres., 1977–78, Pres., 1978–79, Fellow, 1986, Chartered Inst. of Journalists; Member: Press Council, 1980–90; Nat. Council for Trng of Journalists, 1983–86. *Publications:* Taught With Care: a Century of Church Schooling, 1974; The Brontës and their Country, 1978, 3rd edn 1993; Brass Triumphant, 1980; North Yorkshire and North Humberside, 1984, 2nd edn 1989; (ed) One Hundred Years of Journalism, 1984; Pavilions on the Sea, 1986; (jtly) The News of the World Story, 1993. *Recreations:* reading, brass bands, collecting old bookmarks. *Address:* 6 Lea Road, Hemingford Grey, Huntingdon, Cambs PE18 9ED.

BAINES, Anthony Cuthbert, DLitt; FBA 1980; *b* 6 Oct. 1912; *s* of Cuthbert Edward Baines and Margaret Clemency Lane Poole; *m* 1960, Patricia Margaret Stammers. *Educ:* Westminster Sch. (KS); Christ Church Oxford; Royal College of Music. BA 1933, MA 1970, DLitt 1977, Oxon. Member, London Philharmonic Orchestra, 1935–39, 1946–49. Commissioned Royal Tank Regt, 1940–45. Associate Conductor, International Ballet Co., 1950–53; Member, Music Staff: Uppingham Sch., 1954–65; Dean Close Sch., 1965–70; Curator, Bate Collection of Historical Wind Instruments, Oxford Univ., 1970–80, retired. Fellow, University Coll., Oxford, 1974–80, retired. Editor, Galpin Society Jl, 1956–63 and 1970–84. Hon. DMus Edinburgh, 1994. *Publications:* Woodwind Instruments and their History, 1957, 5th edn 1977; Bagpipes, 1960, 4th edn 1979; ed and contrib. Musical Instruments through the Ages, 1961, 6th edn 1978; Victoria and Albert Museum, Catalogue of Musical Instruments, vol. II, Non-Keyboard, 1968; European and American Musical Instruments, 1966, 2nd edn 1981; Brass Instruments, their History and Development, 1976, 3rd edn 1980; The Oxford Companion to Musical Instruments, 1992. *Recreations:* painting, wild life. *Address:* 18 Bridge Square, Farnham, Surrey GU9 7QR.

BAINES, Sir George G.; *see* Grenfell-Baines.

BAINES, Prof. John Robert, MA, DPhil; Professor of Egyptology, Oxford University and Fellow of Queen's College, Oxford, since 1976; *b* 17 March 1946; *o s* of late Edward Russell Baines and of Dora Margaret Jean (*née* O'Brien); *m* 1971, Jennifer Christine Ann, *e d* of S. T. Smith; one *s* one *d*. *Educ:* Winchester Coll.; New Coll., Linacre Coll., Worcester Coll., Oxford (BA 1967, MA, DPhil 1976). Lectr in Egyptology, Univ. of Durham, 1970–75; Laycock Student, Worcester Coll., Oxford, 1973–75. Visiting Professor: Univ. of Arizona, 1982, 1988; Univ. of Michigan, 1989; Ecole Pratique des Hautes Etudes, Paris, 1994; Harvard Univ., 1995–96; Fellow, Humboldt-Stiftung, 1982, 1989. *Publications:* (trans. and ed) H. Schäfer, Principles of Egyptian Art, 1974, rev. edn 1986; (with J. Málek) Atlas of Ancient Egypt, 1980; (trans. and ed) E. Hornung, Conceptions of God in Ancient Egypt, 1982; Fecundity Figures, 1985; (ed jtly) Pyramid Studies and Other Essays presented to I. E. S. Edwards, 1988; (jtly) Religion in Ancient Egypt (ed B. Shafer), 1991; (ed jtly) Civilizations of the Ancient Near East, 4 vols, 1995; (jtly) Ancient Egyptian Kingship, 1995; articles in collections and in Acta Orientalia, American Anthropologist, Art History, Encyclopaedia Britannica, Jl Egypt. Archaeol., Man, Orientalia, Studien altägypt. Kultur, etc. *Address:* Oriental Institute, Pusey Lane, Oxford OX1 2LE.

BAINS, Lawrence Arthur, CBE 1983; DL; Director: Bains Brothers Ltd; Crowland Leasings Ltd; Bains Finance Management Ltd, and associated companies; Chairman, Haringey District Health Authority, 1982–93; *b* 11 May 1920; *s* of late Arthur Bains and Mabel (*née* Payn); *m* 1954, Margaret, *d* of late Sir William and Lady Grimshaw; two *s* one *d*. *Educ:* Stationers' Company's School. Served War, 1939–46: Middlesex Yeomanry, 1939; N Africa, 1940; POW, 1942, escaped, 1943. Member of Lloyd's. Hornsey Borough Council: Mem., 1949–65; Dep. Leader, 1958–64; Mayor, 1964–65; Council, London Borough of Haringey: Mem., 1964–74; Finance Chm., 1968–71; Greater London Council: Chm., 1977–78; Mem. for Hornsey/Haringey, 1967–81; Chm., South Area Planning Bd, 1970–73; Dep. Leader, Housing Policy Cttee, 1979–81; Chm., GLC/Tower Hamlets Jt Housing Management Cttee, 1979–81; Mem., Lee Valley Regional Park Authority, 1968–81 (Chm., 1980–81). Chm., N London Coll. of Health Studies, 1991–95. Trustee, Help the Homeless, 1979–. Liveryman, Worshipful Co. of Basketmakers. DL Greater London, 1978 (Rep. DL for Borough of Barnet, 1983). Officer, Order of St Lazarus of Jerusalem. *Recreation:* being a grandfather. *Address:* Crowland Lodge, 100 Galley Lane, Arkley, Barnet EN5 4AL. *T:* 0181–440 3499. *Club:* City Livery.

BAINS, Malcolm Arnold; JP, DL; Clerk of the Kent County Council and Clerk to the Lieutenancy of Kent, 1970–74; *b* 12 Sept. 1921; *s* of Herbert Bains, Newcastle-upon-Tyne; *m* 1st, 1942, Winifred Agnes Davies (marr. diss. 1961); three *s*; 2nd, 1968, Margaret Hunter. *Educ:* Hymers Coll.; Durham Univ. (LLB (Hons)); Solicitor. Commnd as Pilot in RAF, 1942–46. Solicitor with Taunton and Sunderland and with Notts and Hants County Councils, 1946–55; Dep. Clerk of Hants County Council and Dep. Clerk of the Peace, 1955–60; Dep. Clerk of Kent County Council, 1960–70; Chm., Working Group which advised Secretary of State for Environment on future management of Local Authorities, 1971–73. Chm., Local Govt Review Bd of Victoria, 1978–79. Fellow, ANU and Advr to NSW Govt, 1977–78. Head of Norfolk Island Public Service, 1979–82. FRSA 1976. DL Kent 1976; JP Norfolk Is, 1980. *Publications:* The Bains Report, 1972; Management Reform in English Local Government, 1978; Local Government in NSW, 1980. *Recreations:* swimming, tennis. *Address:* c/o 51 Priest Hill, Caversham, Reading RG4 7RY; PO Box 244, Norfolk Island, 2899, via Australia.

BAIRD, Anthony; *see* Baird, E. A. B.

BAIRD, Charles Fitz; Chairman and Chief Executive Officer, Inco Ltd, 1980–87, retired; *b* 4 Sept. 1922; *s* of George White and Julia (Fitz) Baird; *m* 1947, Norma Adele White; two *s* two *d*. *Educ:* Middlebury Coll. (BA); New York Univ. (Grad. Sch. of Bus. Admin); Harvard Univ. (Advanced Management Program). US Marine Corps, 1943–46, 1951–52 (Capt.). Standard Oil Co. (NJ), now Exxon, 1948–65: Dep. European Financial Rep., London, 1955–58; Asst Treas., 1958–62; Dir, Esso Standard SA Française, 1962–65; Asst Sec., Financial Man., US Navy, 1965–67, Under Secretary, 1967–69; Internat. Nickel Co. of Canada Ltd (Inco Ltd): Vice Pres. Finance, 1969–72, Sen. Vice Pres., 1972–76; Dir, 1974–93; Vice Chm., 1976–77; Pres., 1977–80. Director: Bank of Montreal, 1975–93; Aetna Life and Casualty Co., 1982–93. Nat. Advr, Council on Oceans and Atmosphere, 1972–74; Member: Presidential Commn on Marine Sci. Engrg and Resources, 1967–69; Council on Foreign Relations. Mem., Bd of Trustees, Bucknell Univ., 1969– (Chm., 1976–82); Trustee: Logistic Management Inst., 1987–; Center for Naval Analyses, 1989– (Chm., 1993–). Hon. LLD Bucknell Univ. 1976. US Navy Distinguished Civilian Service Award, 1969. *Recreations:* tennis, platform tennis, golf. *Clubs:* Chevy Chase (Washington, DC); Maidstone (E Hampton, NY); Bridgehampton (NY).

BAIRD, Sir David Charles, 5th Bt of Newbyth, *cr* 1809; *b* 6 July 1912; *s* of late William Arthur Baird, of Lennoxlove, and Lady Hersey Baird; *S* uncle, 1941. *Educ:* Eton; Cambridge. *Heir: nephew* Charles William Stuart Baird [*b* 8 June 1939; *m* 1965, Jane Joanna, *d* of late Brig. A. Darley Bridge; three *d*]. *Address:* 52 Old High Street, Kirkcudbright DG6 4JX.

BAIRD, Prof. David Tennent, FRCPE; FRCOG: Medical Research Council Clinical Research Professor of Reproductive Endocrinology, Edinburgh University, since 1985; *b* 13 March 1935; *s* of Sir Dugald Baird, MD, FRCOG and Lady (May) Baird (*née* Tennent),

CBE; *m* 1965, Frances Diana Lichtveld (separated); two *s*. *Educ:* Aberdeen Grammar Sch., Aberdeen Univ.; Trinity Coll., Cambridge (BA); Edinburgh Univ. (MB, ChB; DSc). Junior med. posts, Royal Infirmary, Edinburgh, 1959–65; MRC Travelling Research Fellow, Worcester Foundn of Experimental Biology, USA, 1965–68; Lectr, later Sen. Lectr, Dept of Obstetrics, Univ. of Edinburgh, 1968–72; Dep. Dir, MRC Unit of Reproductive Biology, Edinburgh, 1972–77; Prof. of Obst. and Gyn., Univ. of Edinburgh, 1977–85. Consultant Gynaecologist, Royal Infirmary, Edinburgh, 1970–. FRSE 1990. *Publications:* Mechanism of Menstrual Bleeding, 1985; contribs in med. and sci. jls on reproductive endocrinology. *Recreations:* ski mountaineering, golf. *Address:* 22 India Street, Edinburgh EH3 6HB. *T:* 0131–225 3962. *Club:* Royal Society of Medicine.

BAIRD, (Eric) Anthony (Bamber); Director, Institute for Complementary Medicine, since 1980; *b* 11 Dec. 1920; *s* of Oswald Baird and Marion Bamber; *m* 1st, 1952, Margareta Toss (marr. diss. 1957); 2nd, 1959, Inger Bohman (marr. diss. 1977); two *d*. *Educ:* LSE (BScEcon). Served RA, 1941–46. Swedish Broadcasting Corp., 1950–65; Public Relations Ltd, 1965–72; Civil Service, 1973–78; Inst. for Complementary Medicine, 1979–. FRSA 1992. *Publications:* Notes on Canada, 1962; (jtly) The Charm of Sweden, 1962. *Recreations:* writing children's stories, gardening. *Address:* 24 Backwoods Lane, Lindfield, Haywards Heath, West Sussex RH16 2ED. *T:* Lindfield (01444) 482018.

BAIRD, James Hewson; Chief Executive and Company Secretary, British Veterinary Association, since 1987; *b* 28 March 1944; *s* of James Baird, MBE, MRCVS and Ann Sarah Baird (*née* Hewson); *m* 1969, Clare Rosalind (*née* Langstaff); three *d*. *Educ:* Austin Friars; Creighton, Carlisle; Newcastle upon Tyne Univ. (BSc Hons Agric). Hydrologist, Essex River Authy, 1968–75; Policy Officer, Nat. Water Council, 1975–80 (Mem., DoE/NWC Waste of Water Gp, 1978–80). Inst. of Civil Engineers: Asst Dir, 1980–81; Dir of Admin., 1981–86; Mem., Infrastructure Planning Gp, 1982–86; Dir, Assoc. of Municipal Engineers, 1984–86; Dir, External Affairs, Fedn of Civil Engineering Contractors, 1986–87; Sec., London and SE Section, FCEC, 1986–87. FRSA. *Recreations:* Rugby, gardening, farming, countryside. *Address:* British Veterinary Association, 7 Mansfield Street, W1M 0AT. *T:* 0171–636 6541. *Clubs:* Farmers', Royal Society of Medicine, Rugby of London.

BAIRD, Lt-Gen. Sir James (Parlane), KBE 1973; MD, FRCP, FRCPEd; Medical Adviser, National Advice Centre for Postgraduate Education, 1977–84; *b* 12 May 1915; *s* of Rev. David Baird and Sara Kathleen Black; *m* 1948, Anne Patricia Anderson; one *s* one *d*. *Educ:* Bathgate Academy; Univ. of Edinburgh. FRCPEd 1952, MD 1958, FRCP 1959. Commissioned, RAMC, 1939; Lt-Col 1956; Prof. of Military Medicine, Royal Army Medical Coll., 1965; Cons. Physician, BAOR, 1967; Dir of Medicine and Consulting Physician to the Army, 1969–71; Comdt and Dir of Studies, Royal Army Med. Coll., 1971–73; Dir Gen., Army Medical Services, 1973–77. QHP 1969. QHA (Pakistan), 1982. *Publications:* Tropical Diseases Supplement to Principles and Practice of Medicine, 1968; (contrib.) The Oxford Companion to Medicine, 1986. *Recreation:* golf. *Club:* West Sussex Golf.

BAIRD, Sir James Richard Gardiner, 10th Bt *cr* 1695; MC 1945; *b* 12 July 1913; *er s* of Captain William Frank Gardiner Baird (killed in action 1914) (2nd *s* of 8th Bt) and Violet Mary (*d* 1947), *d* of late Richard Benyon Croft; *S* uncle, Sir James Hozier Gardiner Baird, 9th Bt, 1966; *m* 1941, Mabel Ann (Gay), *d* of A. Algernon Gill; two *s* one *d*. *Educ:* Eton. Served War of 1939–45. Lieut, Royal Artillery, 1940; Captain, Kent Yeomanry, 1944. *Recreation:* shooting. *Heir:* *s* James Andrew Gardiner Baird [*b* 2 May 1946; *m* 1984, Jean Margaret (marr. diss. 1988), *yr d* of Brig. Sir Ian Jardine, 4th Bt; one *s*. *Educ:* Eton]. *Address:* Church Farm House, Guist, Norfolk NR20 5AJ. *T:* Foulsham (0136284) 808. *Club:* Naval and Military.

BAIRD, Air Vice-Marshal John Alexander, QHP 1991; Director General, Royal Air Force Medical Services, since 1994; *b* 25 July 1937; *s* of Dr David A. Baird and Isobel T. Baird; *m* 1963, Mary Clews. *Educ:* Merchiston Castle Sch.; Edinburgh Univ. (MB ChB). FFOM; DipAvMed; MRAeS. Western Gen. Hosp., Edinburgh, 1961–62; MO Sarawak, 1962–63; commnd RAF, 1963; RAF Stations, UK and Singapore, 1963–80; exchange post, USA, 1970–73; HQ Strike Comd, 1980–83; MoD, 1983–86; OC Princess of Wales RAF Hosp., Ely, 1987–88; PMO, RAF Germany, 1988–91; PMO, HQ RAF Strike Comd, 1991–94. Mem., Internat. Acad. of Aviation and Space Medicine, 1983. FRSocMed 1983; Fellow, Aerospace Med. Assoc., 1992. *Publications:* contribs to med. jls on aviation medicine subjects. *Recreations:* ornithology, wild-life conservation, cricket, music. *Address:* HQ Personnel and Training Command, RAF Innsworth, Gloucester GL3 1EZ. *Club:* Royal Air Force.

BAIRD, Joyce Elizabeth Leslie, OBE 1991; Joint General Secretary, Assistant Masters and Mistresses Association, 1978–90; *b* 8 Dec. 1929; *d* of Dr J. C. H. Baird and Mrs J. E. Baird. *Educ:* The Abbey School, Reading; Newnham College, Cambridge (MA); secretarial training. FEIS 1987. Secretary to Sir Austin Robinson and editorial assistant, Royal Economic Soc., 1952–60; Senior Geography Mistress, Hertfordshire and Essex High School, Bishop's Stortford, 1961–77 (Dep. Head, 1973–75). President: Assoc. of Assistant Mistresses, 1976–77; Internat. Fedn of Secondary Teachers, 1981–85; Vice Pres., NFER, 1991–. Mem., Cambridge City Council, 1992–. *Recreations:* walking, thinking about gardening, travel. *Address:* 26 Fulbrooke Road, Cambridge CB3 9EE. *T:* Cambridge (01223) 354909. *Club:* Commonwealth Trust.

BAIRD, Kenneth William; Music Director, Arts Council, 1988–94; *b* 14 July 1950; *s* of William and Christine Baird. *Educ:* Uppingham School; St Andrews Univ. (MA); Royal College of Music. LRAM, ARCM. English National Opera, 1974–82; Gen. Manager, Aldeburgh Foundn, 1982–88. Chm., Snape Historical Trust, 1986–. *Address:* 59 High Street, Wickham Market, Suffolk IP13 0HE. *Club:* Chelsea Arts.

BAIRD, Ronald; Vice-Chairman, Saatchi & Saatchi Advertising, since 1992 (Director, since 1974); *b* 9 Dec. 1930; *s* of Richard Baird and Emma Baird (*née* Martin); *m* 1957, Helen Lilian, *d* of His Honour Judge John and Lilian Charlesworth. *Educ:* Grammar School, Blyth, Northumberland; King's College, Univ. of Durham. 13th/18th Royal Hussars (QMO), 1949–51. Saward Baker & Co., 1954–63; Chief Exec. Officer, Stuart Advtg, 1963–68; Man. Dir, Holmwood Advtg, 1968–74; Dir, Notley Advtg, 1970–74. Member: Derwent Howe Steering Group (Cumbria), 1982–90; Council, Think British, 1980–; Board, Nat. Theatre, 1984–91 (Vice-Chm., Nat. Theatre Develt Council, 1985); Royal Life Saving Soc. (Vice-Pres.); London Fedn of Boys' Clubs. *Recreations:* Irish wolfhounds, music, painting, fell walking, field sports. *Address:* Berry Corner, Berry Lane, Chorleywood, Herts WD3 5EY. *T:* Chorleywood (01923) 283251; Spout House, Gosforth, Cumbria CA20 1AZ.

BAIRD, Susan, CBE 1991; JP; DL; Lord Provost and Lord-Lieutenant of Glasgow, 1988–92; *b* 26 May 1940; *d* of Archie and Susan Reilly; *m* 1957, George Baird; three *s* one *d*. *Educ:* St Mark's Secondary School, Glasgow. Mem. Labour Party, 1969; City of Glasgow Council (formerly Glasgow District Council, then Glasgow City Council): Mem. (Lab), 1974–; Bailie of the City, 1980–84; Convener, Manpower Cttee, 1980–84; Vice-Convener, Parks and Recreation Cttee, 1984–88. JP 1977, DL 1992, Glasgow. DUniv Glasgow, 1990. St Mungo Prize, St Mungo Trust, 1991. OStJ. *Recreations:* reading, walking. *Address:* 138 Downfield Street, Parkhead, Glasgow G32 8RZ. *T:* 0141–778 7641.

BAIRD, Vice-Adm. Sir Thomas (Henry Eustace), KCB 1980; DL; *b* Canterbury, Kent, 17 May 1924; *s* of Geoffrey Henry and Helen Jane Baird; *m* 1953, Angela Florence Ann Paul, Symington, Ayrshire; one *s* one *d*. *Educ:* RNC, Dartmouth. Served HM Ships: Trinidad, in support of convoys to Russia, 1941, Midshipman; Bermuda, Russian convoys and landings in N Africa, and Orwell, Russian convoys and Atlantic escort force, 1942; Howe, E Indies, 1943, Sub-Lt; Rapid, E Indies, 1944 until VJ Day, Lieut; St James, Home Fleet, 1946; Ganges, Ratings' New Entry Trng, 1948; Plucky, Exec. Officer, mine clearance in Mediterranean, 1950; Lt Comdr 1952; Veryan Bay, Exec. Officer, W Indies and Falkland Is., 1953; O-in-C, Petty Officers' Leadership Sch., Malta, 1954; Exec. Officer, HMS Whirlwind, Home Fleet and Med., for Suez Op., 1956; Comd, HMS Acute, Dartmouth Trng Sqdn, 1958; Comdr 1959; Comd, HMS Ulysses, Home Fleet, 1960; Staff, C-in-C, Home Fleet, Northwood, 1961; Exec. Officer, Jt Anti-Sub. Sch., Londonderry, 1963; EO, HMS Bulwark, Far East, 1965; Ch. Staff Officer to Cdre, Naval Drafting, 1966; Captain 1967; Dep. Dir, Naval Equipment, Adm., Bath, 1967; Captain: Mine Countermeasures; Fishery Protection and HMS Lochinvar (comd), 1969; Comd, HMS Glamorgan, Far East, W Indies, S Amer., Med., and UK Waters, 1971; Captain of the Fleet, 1973; Rear Adm. 1976; Chief of Staff to C-in-C Naval Home Comd, 1976–77; Dir Gen., Naval Personal Services, 1978–79; Vice-Adm. 1979; Flag Officer Scotland and NI, 1979–82. Chm. Exec. Cttee, Erskine Hosp., 1986–95. DL Ayr and Arran, 1982. *Recreations:* cricket, golf, shooting, fishing. *Address:* Craigrethill, Symington, Ayrshire KA1 5QN. *Club:* Prestwick Golf (Prestwick).

BAIRD, Dr Thomas Terence, CB 1977; Chief Medical Officer, Department of Health and Social Services, Northern Ireland, 1972–78, retired; *b* 31 May 1916; *s* of Thomas Baird, Archdeacon of Derry, and Hildegarde Nolan; *m* 1st, 1940, Joan Crosbie; two *d*; 2nd, 1982, Mary Wilson Powell. *Educ:* Haileybury Coll.; Queen's Univ. of Belfast. MB, BCh, BAO, 1939; DPH, 1947; FFPHM (FFCM (RCP), 1972); MRCPI 1973, FRCPI 1975; MRCPEd 1975, FRCPEd 1994. FFCM Ireland (Founder Fellow), 1977; Fellow, Royal Acad. of Medicine in Ire., 1991. Ho. Surg./Ho. Phys., North Lonsdale Hosp., Barrow-in-Furness, 1939–40. Served War, RNVR, 1940–46. Queen's Univ. of Belfast, DPH course, 1946–47. Berks CC: Asst MO, 1947–49; Dep. County MO and Dep. Principal Sch. MO, 1949–54. Welsh Bd of Health: MO, 1954–57; Sen. MO, 1957–62; Min. of Health and Local Govt, Northern Ireland: PMO, 1962–64; Dep. Chief MO, 1964–68; Min. of Health and Social Services, NI, Sen. Dep. Chief MO, 1968–72. Chairman: NI Med. Manpower Adv. Cttee; NI Adv. Cttee on infant mortality and handicaps. Member: GMC, 1973–79; Faculty of Medicine, QUB; NI Council for Postgrad. Med. Educn; Bd, Faculty of Community Medicine, RCPI. Chief Surgeon for Wales, St John Ambulance Bde, 1959–62. QUB Boat Club: Capt. of Boats, 1937–38; Vice-Pres., 1989–90. QHP 1974–77. CStJ 1959. *Publications:* (jtly) Infection in Hospital—a code of practice, 1971; papers in various learned jls. *Recreations:* fishing, forestry. *Address:* Port-a-Chapel, Greencastle, Co. Donegal. *T:* Greencastle (077) 81038. *Club:* Carlton.

BAIRD, William; Under Secretary, Scottish Home and Health Department, 1978–87; *b* 13 Oct. 1927; *s* of Peter and Christina Baird, Airdrie; *m* 1954, Anne Templeton Macfarlane; two *d*. *Educ:* Airdrie Academy; Glasgow Univ. Entered Scottish Home Dept, 1952; Private Sec. to Perm. Under-Sec. of State, Scottish Office, 1957; Principal, Scottish Educn Dept, 1958–63; Private Sec. to Minister of State and successive Secs of State for Scotland, 1963–65; Asst Sec., Scottish Educn Dept, 1965–66; Dept of Agriculture and Fisheries for Scotland, 1966–71; Scottish Office Finance Div., 1971–73; Registrar General for Scotland, 1973–78. *Address:* 8 Strathearn Road, North Berwick EH39 5BZ. *T:* North Berwick (01620) 893190.

BAIRSTO, Air Marshal Sir Peter (Edward), KBE 1981 (CBE 1973); CB 1980; AFC 1957; DL; *b* 3 Aug. 1926; *s* of late Arthur Bairsto and Beatrice (*née* Lewis); *m* 1947, Kathleen (*née* Clarbour); two *s* one *d*. *Educ:* Rhyl Grammar Sch. Pilot, FAA, 1944–46; 1946–62: FO RAF Regt, Palestine, Aden Protectorate; Flying Instr; Fighter Pilot, Fighter Comd and Near East; Flight Comdr, 43 Sqdn, and Leader, RAF Aerobatic Team; Sqdn Comdr, 66 Sqdn; RAF Staff Coll.; Wing Comdr, Flying, Nicosia, 1963–64; Op. Requirements, MoD, 1965–67; JSSC Latimer, 1967; Instr, RAF Staff Coll., 1968–70; Stn Comdr, RAF Honington, 1971–73; Dir, Op. Requirements, MoD, 1974–77; AOC Training Units, Support Command, 1977–79; Comdr, Northern Maritime Air Region, 1979–81; Dep. C-in-C, Strike Command, 1981–84. Vice-Chm. (Air), Highland TAVRA, 1984–90. Hon. Col, Northern Gp Field Sqns RE (Airfield Damage Repair) (Vol.), 1989–92. Mem., Scottish Sports Council, 1985–90. HM Comr, Queen Victoria Sch., Dunblane, 1984–93; Chm. Management Bd, RAF Benevolent Fund Home, Alastrean House, Tarland, 1984–94. Mem., St Andrews Links Trust, 1989– (Chm., 1993–). Queen's Commendation for Valuable Services in the Air, 1955 and 1960. CIMgt. DL Fife, 1992. *Recreations:* golf, fishing, shooting, gardening. *Address:* Bearwood, Hepburn Gardens, St Andrews, Fife KY16 9LT. *T:* St Andrews (01334) 475505. *Clubs:* Royal Air Force; Royal and Ancient Golf.

BAIRSTOW, John; Founder, 1968, Chairman, 1972–93, Queens Moat Houses PLC (formerly Queens Modern Hotels Ltd); *b* 25 Aug. 1930; *m*; four *d*. *Educ:* City of London Sch. FSVA. Founded Bairstow, Eves and Son, Valuers and Estate Agents, 1953. *Recreation:* salmon fishing.

BAKER, Prof. Alan, FRS 1973; Professor of Pure Mathematics, University of Cambridge, since 1974; Fellow of Trinity College, Cambridge, since 1964; *b* 19 Aug. 1939; *o c* of Barnet and Bessie Baker. *Educ:* Stratford Grammar Sch.; University Coll. London; Trinity Coll., Cambridge. BSc (London); MA, PhD (Cantab). Mem., Dept of Mathematics, UCL, 1964–65 and Fellow, UCL, 1979; Research Fellow, 1964–68, and Dir of Studies in Mathematics, 1968–74, Trinity Coll., Cambridge; Mem., Dept of Pure Maths and Math. Statistics, Univ. of Cambridge, 1966–; Reader in Theory of Numbers, 1972–74. Visiting Professor: Univs of Michigan and Colorado, 1969; Stanford Univ., 1974; Royal Soc. Kan Tong Po Prof., Univ. of Hong Kong, 1988; ETH, Zürich, 1989; Mem., Inst. for Advanced Study, Princeton, 1970; Mathematical Scis Res. Inst., Berkeley, 1993; First Turán Lectr, J. Bolyai Math. Soc. Hungary, 1978. For. Fellow, Indian Nat. Sci. Acad., 1980. Fields Medal, Internat. Congress of Mathematicians, Nice, 1970; Adams Prize of Univ. of Cambridge, 1971–72. *Publications:* Transcendental Number Theory, 1975; (ed jtly) Transcendence Theory: advances and applications, 1977; A Concise Introduction to the Theory of Numbers, 1984; (ed) New Advances in Transcendence Theory, 1988; papers in various mathematical jls. *Recreation:* travel. *Address:* Trinity College, Cambridge CB2 1TQ. *T:* Cambridge (01223) 338400.

BAKER, Alex Anthony, CBE 1973; MD, MRCP, DPM; FRCPsych; Consultant Psychiatrist with special interest in the elderly to Gloucestershire Clinical Area, 1973–77, retired; *b* 22 March 1922; *m* 1944; two *s* two *d*. *Educ:* St Mary's Hosp. Med. Sch. Consultant Psychiatrist: Banstead Hosp., 1955; Mother and Baby Unit, Downview Hosp., 1958; St Mary Abbotts Hosp., 1967; Medical Administrator, Banstead Hosp., 1964;

sometime Consultant to WHO; Sen. Principal Medical Officer, Dept of Health, 1968; Dir, NHS Hospital Adv. Service, 1969–73. *Publications:* (jtly) Psychiatric Services and Architecture, 1958; (jtly) Social Psychiatry; Psychiatric Disorders in Obstetrics, 1967; Comprehensive Psychiatric Care, 1976; chapters in sundry books; papers in numerous jls on research, psychiatric treatment, organisation of psychiatric services, etc. *Address:* Pineholm, High Close, Bovey Tracey, Devon TQ13 9EX.

BAKER, Ann Maureen, (Mrs D. R. Baker); *see* Jenner, A. M.

BAKER, Anthony Baxter, CBE 1983; JP; Regional Administrator, Northern Regional Health Authority, 1973–83; *b* 12 June 1923; *s* of late Anthony Thurlbeck Baker and Robina Frances Jane (*née* Baxter); *m* 1st, 1946, Mary Margherita Patterson (*d* 1978); one *s* three *d*; 2nd, 1981, Judith Margaret Ayers, JP. *Educ:* Tynemouth High Sch.; Durham Univ. DPA; FHA. RAFVR, UK, Canada and Iceland, 1942–46. Admin. Asst, later Dep. Sec., SE Northumberland HMC, 1949–60; Asst Sec., later Principal Asst Sec., Newcastle Regional Hosp. Bd, 1960–73. JP Tynemouth 1965; former Chm., North Tyneside PSD. *Recreations:* Rugby football (PP Percy Park RFC; PP Northumberland RFU), golf. *Address:* 59 Broadway, Tynemouth, North Shields NE30 2LJ. *T:* Tyneside 0191–257 4660.

BAKER, Anthony Castelli, LVO 1980; MBE 1975; HM Diplomatic Service, retired; *b* 27 Dec. 1921; *s* of late Alfred Guy Baker and of Luciana (*née* Castelli). *Educ:* Merchant Taylors' Sch., Northwood, Mddx. Served War: munitions worker, 1940–41; volunteered for RAFVR and served in UK, ME and Italy, 1941–46 (Flt Lieut). Joined HM Diplomatic Service, 1946; served in Rome and Paris, 1946–50; Third Sec., Prague, 1951; Hamburg, 1953; Vice-Consul, Milan, 1954; Third, later Second Sec., Athens, 1959; Second Sec., Beirut, 1963; First Sec., Cairo, 1965; Naples, 1968; Turin, 1970; First Sec. Commercial, Calcutta, 1972; Consul, Montreal, 1975; First Sec. Commercial, Port of Spain, 1976; Consul, Genoa, 1979–81. Officer, Order of Merit (Italy), 1980. *Recreations:* tennis, watching cricket, travelling, jazz music. *Address:* Flat 16, Mourne House, 11 Maresfield Gardens, NW3 3BU. *Clubs:* Royal Air Force, MCC; Gloucestershire CC.

BAKER, Arthur John, CBE 1981; Principal, Brockenhurst Tertiary College (formerly Brockenhurst Grammar School, then Brockenhurst Sixth Form College), 1969–88, retired; *b* 29 Nov. 1928; *s* of Arthur Reginald and Ruth Baker; *m* 1953, June Henrietta Dunham; one *s* two *d*. *Educ:* Southampton Univ. (BSc; DipEd). Mathematics Master, Hampton Grammar Sch., 1952–55; Dep. Head, Sunbury Grammar Sch., 1955–61; Headmaster, Christchurch Grammar Sch., 1961–69. *Recreations:* walking, gardening, travel. *Address:* 93 New Forest Drive, Brockenhurst, Hampshire SO42 7QT. *T:* Lymington (01590) 23138.

BAKER, Cecil John; Director, Alliance & Leicester Building Society (formerly Alliance Building Society), 1970–92 (Chairman, 1981–91); *b* 2 Sept. 1915; *s* of late Frederick William Baker and Mildred Beatrice Palmer; *m* 1st, 1942, Kathleen Cecilia Henning (marr. diss. 1965); one *s*; 2nd, 1971, Joan Beatrice Barnes; one *d*. *Educ:* Whitgift Sch.; LSE (LLB 1939; BSc(Econ) 1949); Inst. of Actuaries. FIA 1948; ACII 1937. Sec., Insurance Inst. of London, 1945–49; Investment Manager, London Assurance, 1950–64; Investment Consultant, Hambros Bank Ltd, 1964–74; Chairman: Pension Fund Property Unit Trust, 1966–87; Charities Property Unit Trust, 1967–87; Agricl Property Unit Trust for Pension Funds and Charities, 1976–87; Victory Insurance Holdings Ltd, 1979–85; British American Property Unit Trust, 1982–87; United Real Property Trust plc, 1983–86 (Dir, 1982–86); Hunting Gate Group, 1980–90; Dir, Abbey Life Group plc, 1985–88. *Recreations:* golf, travel. *Address:* 3 Tennyson Court, 12 Dorset Square, NW1 6QB. *T:* 0171–724 9716. *Club:* Savile.

BAKER, Charles A.; *see* Arnold-Baker.

BAKER, Air Vice-Marshal Christopher Paul, CB 1991; FCIPS; FIMgt; Chairman, Taylor Curnow Ltd, since 1994; *b* 14 June 1938; *er s* of late Paul Hocking Baker, FCA and Kathleen Minnie Florence Baker; *m* 1st, 1961, Heather Ann Laity (decd), *d* of late Cecil Henry Laity and of Eleanor Hocking Laity; three *s*, 2nd, 1981, Francesca R. Aghabi, *er d* of George Khalil Aghabi and Elizabeth Maria Regina Aghabi; two *s*. *Educ:* Bickley Hall, Kent; Tonbridge School. FCIPS (FInstPS 1989). Commnd RAF, 1958; served 1958–61: RAF Khormaksar (Air Movements), Aden; Supply Sqdn, RAF Coll., Cranwell; RAF Labuan, N Borneo; No 389 Maintenance Unit, RAF Seletar, Singapore; MoD Harrogate; student, RAF Staff Coll., Bracknell; OC Supply Sqdn, RAF Linton-on-Ouse; SHAPE, Two ATAF; ndc; Directing Staff, RAF Staff Coll., Bracknell; HQ RAF Support Comd; Dep. Dir, RAF Supply Systems, MoD; Comd Supply Movements Officer, HQ Strike Comd, RAF High Wycombe, 1982–84; RCDS, 1985; Dir, Supply Systems, MoD, 1986–87; Dir, Supply Policy and Logistics Plans, MoD, 1988–89; Dir Gen. of Support Management, RAF, 1989–93. Gen. Manager, Defence Sector Business Gp, TNT Express (UK) Ltd, 1993–94. FIMgt (FBIM 1979); MInstD 1993. Freeman, City of London; Liveryman, Bakers' Co. *Publications:* papers on the crisis of authority, oil potential of the Arctic Basin, and German reunification. *Recreations:* Rugby, rowing, ski-ing, modern history. *Address:* Lloyds Bank, Cox's & King's Branch, PO Box 1190, 7 Pall Mall, SW1Y 5NA. *T:* 0171–839 1333. *Club:* Royal Air Force.

BAKER, Derek; *see* Baker, L. G.

BAKER, Douglas Robert Pelham, FCA; Chairman: Portman Building Society, since 1990; Hardy Oil and Gas plc, since 1989; Deputy Chairman, London International Group, since 1989; *b* 21 May 1929. With Touche Ross & Co., Chartered Accountants, 1945–47 and 1949–89 (Chm., 1984–88). Dep. Chm., 1987–88, Chm., 1988–90, Regency and W of England Building Soc. (merged with Portman Wessex Building Soc., 1990); Dir, Merrett Hldgs, 1988–94. Royal Naval Service, 1947–49. Chm., Brighton HA, 1988–91. *Address:* Hamsey Manor, Hamsey, E Sussex BN8 5TD.

BAKER, Elizabeth Margaret; Headmistress, Wimbledon High School, 1992–95, retired; *b* 13 Sept. 1945; *d* of Walter and Betty Gale; *m* 1965, Stuart Baker; one *d*. *Educ:* University College of Wales, Swansea (BA, DipEd). Lectr, Derby Coll. of Further Educn, 1968–71; Classics Teacher: West Monmouth Sch., 1971–74; Cheltenham Bournside, 1974–81; Cheltenham Ladies' Coll., 1981–88; Headmistress, Ellerslie, Malvern, 1988–92. *Recreations:* wine, letter-writing, keeping the classics alive. *Address:* 33 Ashen Grove, SW19 8BW. *T:* 0181–946 5023.

BAKER, Hon. Francis Edward N.; *see* Noel-Baker.

BAKER, Francis Eustace, CBE 1984 (OBE 1979); business interests in property, farming and the automotive industry; Partner, Crossroads Motors, since 1988; *b* 19 April 1933; *s* of Stephen and Jessica Wilhelmina Baker; *m* 1957, Constance Anne Shilling; two *s* two *d*. *Educ:* Borden Grammar Sch.; New Coll., Oxford (MA). Nat. Service, RN, 1955–57 (Sub Lieut). Admin. Officer, HMOCS, 1957; Solomon Is, 1958–63; farming, 1963–67; Admin. Officer, Condominium of New Hebrides, 1967–79; Chief Sec. to Falkland Is Govt, 1979–83; Gov. and C-in-C, St Helena and Dependencies, 1984–88. Silver Jubilee Medal, 1977. *Recreations:* swimming, reading, farming, interesting motor cars. *Address:* Dark Orchard, Primrose Lane, Bredgar, near Sittingbourne, Kent ME9 8EH. *T:* Wormshill (01622) 884295.

BAKER, His Honour Geoffrey; QC 1970; a Circuit Judge, 1978–95; *b* 5 April 1925; *er s* of late Sidney and Cecilia Baker, Bradford; *m* 1948, Sheila (*née* Hill); two *s* one *d*. *Educ:* Bradford Grammar Sch.; Leeds Univ.; LLB (Hons). Called to Bar, Inner Temple, 1947. Recorder: of Pontefract, 1967–71; of Sunderland, 1971; a Recorder of the Crown Court, 1972–78. Pres., Leeds and WR Medico-Legal Soc., 1984–85 (Mem. Cttee, 1980–94). Chm., Standing Council, Convocation of Leeds Univ., 1986–90 (Mem. 1980–); Member: Adv. Cttee on Law, Leeds Univ., 1983–; Court, Leeds Univ., 1984–88; Pres., Leeds Univ. Law Graduates' Assoc., 1981–. *Recreations:* gardening, painting, photography. *Address:* c/o Courts Administrator, Bank House, Park Place, Leeds LS1 5QS.

BAKER, Geoffrey Hunter, CMG 1962; HM Diplomatic Service, retired; *b* 4 Aug. 1916; *s* of late Thomas Evelyn Baker and Gladys Beatrice Baker (*née* Marsh); *m* 1963, Anita Wägeler; one *d*. *Educ:* Haberdashers' Aske's Hampstead Sch.; Royal Masonic Sch., Bushey, Herts; Gonville and Caius Coll., Cambridge (Scholar). Joined Consular Service, 1938; Vice-Consul at Hamburg, 1938, Danzig, 1939, Bergen, 1939; captured by German forces there, April 1940; Vice-Consul, Basra, 1942, Jedda, 1942; Foreign Office, 1945–47; First Sec., Rangoon, 1947–51, Tehran, 1951–52; FO, 1953–54; NATO Def. Coll., Paris, 1954; Consul-Gen., Hanoi, 1954–56; UK Delegation, UN, Nov. 1956–March 1957; Cabinet Office, 1957–60; UK Delegation to the European Free Trade Association, Geneva, 1960–66; Consul-General, Munich, 1966–71, Zagreb, 1971–74. Order of Merit (Bavaria), 1971. *Recreation:* listening to music. *Address:* 10 Leigh Road, Highfield, Southampton SO17 1EF. *Clubs:* United Oxford & Cambridge University; Cambridge University Cruising (Cambridge).

BAKER, George William, CBE 1977 (OBE 1971); VRD 1952 (Clasp 1979); HM Diplomatic Service, retired; *b* 7 July 1917; *e s* of late George William Baker and of Lilian Turnbull Baker; *m* 1942, Audrey Martha Elizabeth, *e d* of Harry and Martha Day; two *d*. *Educ:* Chigwell Sch.; Hertford Coll., Oxford (Colonial Service Second Devonshire Course). London Div., RNVR, 1937–62; served War, RN, 1939–45. Colonial Admin. Service, Tanganyika, 1946–62: Asst Colonial Attaché, Washington (incl. service in UK Delegn to Trusteeship Council at UN), 1957; Defence Sec., Tanganyika, 1959; Head of Tanganyika Govt Information Dept, 1959–62; retd after Tanganyika Independence, 1962. Joined CRO, 1962; Head of Chancery, First Sec. (Information) and Dir of British Inf. Services, British High Commn, Freetown, 1962–65; served in FCO (Consular and Defence Depts), 1965–69; First Sec. and Head of Chancery, Kinshasa, 1969–72; Dep. British Govt Rep., St Vincent and Grenada, Windward Is, 1972–74; British Commissioner, Port Moresby, Papua New Guinea, 1974–75, High Comr to Papua New Guinea, 1975–77. Mem., E Sussex Cttee, VSO, 1984– (Chm., 1980–84). A Vice-Pres., Royal African Soc., 1973–92 (Hon. Vice-Pres., 1992–); Hon. Mem. and Foreign Affairs Advr, Scientific Exploration Soc., 1965–; Consultant to Operation Raleigh, 1987–. Chm., Heathfield Cttee, Sussex Housing Assoc. for Aged, 1979–84; Chm., Waldron Br., Wealden Cons. Assoc. and Vice-Chm., Constituency Political Cttee, 1983–84. Mem. Guild of Freemen of City of London, 1980–94; Freeman, City of London, 1980; Liveryman, Clockmakers' Co., 1984– (Mem., 1981–; Steward, 1987–; Ed., Clockmaker's Times, 1987–93). Mem., Queenhithe Ward Club, City of London, 1970–93. Member: Exeter Flotilla (Chm., 1987–90); Hertford Soc.; Cttee, Devon Br., Oxford Soc.; E Devon Luncheon Club (Chm., 1989–); sundry E Devon clubs and socs. *Publications:* official booklets and contribs to learned jls. *Recreations:* photography, fishing, sailing, climbing, tennis, Rugby Union, cricket, flying, clock and cabinet-making. *Address:* Crosswinds, Coreway, Sidford, Sidmouth, Devon EX10 9SD. *T:* Sidmouth (01395) 578845. *Club:* MCC.

See also Baron Coleridge.

BAKER, Gordon Meldrum; HM Diplomatic Service; High Commissioner, Belize, since 1995; *b* 4 July 1941; *o s* of Walter John Ralph Gordon Baker and Kathleen Margaret Henrietta Dawe Baker (*née* Meldrum); *m* 1978, Sheila Mary Megson. *Educ:* St Andrew's Sch., Bawdrip, near Bridgwater. MSc Bradford 1976. Lord Chancellor's Dept, 1959–66; transf. to HM Diplomatic Service, 1966; Commonwealth Office, 1966–68; FO (later FCO), 1968–69; Lagos, 1969–72; First Sec., FCO, 1973–75 (Resident Clerk, 1974–75); sabbatical at Postgrad. Sch. of Studies in Industrial Technol., Univ. of Bradford, 1975–76; FCO, 1976–78 (Res. Clerk, 1976–78); First Sec. (Chancery/Information), subseq. First Sec., Head of Chancery and Consul, Brasilia, 1978–81; Asst Head, Mexico and Central America Dept, FCO, 1982–84; Counsellor, 1984; on secondment to British Aerospace, 1984–86; Counsellor, Head of Chancery then Dep. Hd of Mission, and Consul-General, Santiago, 1986–89, Chargé d'Affaires, 1986, 1987 and 1989; RCDS, 1990–91; Head of W Indian and Atlantic Dept, FCO, 1991–94. *Recreations:* walking, watching birds, amateur dramatics, browsing. *Address:* c/o Foreign and Commonwealth Office, King Charles Street, SW1A 2AH.

BAKER, Howard Henry, Jr; Chief of Staff at the White House, 1987–88; Senior Partner, Baker, Worthington, Crossley, Stansberry & Woolf, law firm; *b* 15 Nov. 1925; *s* of Howard H. Baker and Dora Ladd; *m* 1951, Joy Dirksen; one *s* one *d*. *Educ:* McCallie Sch.; Tulane Univ.; Univ. of Tennessee (LLB 1949). Served USN, 1943–46. Director: Federal Express; Waste Management; United Technologies; Pennzoil. Chm. of Bd, Newstar Inc. US Senate: Senator from Tennessee 1967–85; Minority Leader, 1977–81; Majority Leader, 1981–85; former Co-Chm., Senate Select Cttee on Presidential Campaign Activities, and mem. other Senate cttees. Mem., Trustees Bd, Mayo Clinic. Mem., Amer. Bar Assoc. Presidential Medal of Freedom, 1984. *Address:* (office) Courthouse Square, Huntsville, TN 37756, USA.

BAKER, Maj.-Gen. Ian Helstrip, CBE 1977 (MBE 1965); rcds, psc; General Officer Commanding, North East District, 1980–82; Secretary, University College London, 1982–91; *b* 26 Nov. 1927; *s* of late Henry Hubert Baker and Mary Clare Baker (*née* Coles); *m* 1956, Susan Anne, *d* of late Major and Mrs Henry Osmond Lock, York House, Dorchester, Dorset; one *s* one *d* (and one *s* decd). *Educ:* St Peter's Sch., York; St Edmund Hall, Oxford; RMA, Sandhurst; Open Univ. (BA 1994). Commnd, 1948; 10th Fd Regt RA, 1949–51; 2nd Regt RHA, 1951–53; RAC Centre, 1953–55; transf. RTR, 1955; 4th Royal Tank Regt, 1955–57; HQ 10th Inf. Bde, 1957–58; Staff Coll., Camberley, 1959; Major 1960; DAAG HQ 17 Gurkha Div., Overseas Commonwealth Land Forces, Malaya and Singapore, 1960–62; OC Parachute Sqdn RAC (C Sqdn 2nd Royal Tank Regt), 1962–65; Instr Staff Coll., Camberley, and Bt Lt-Col, 1965; GSO1 and Asst Sec., Chiefs of Staff Cttee, MoD, 1966–67; Lt-Col 1966; CO, 1st Royal Tank Regt, UK and BAOR, 1967–69; Col 1970; Col, RTR, 1970–71; Brig. 1972; Comdr, 7th Armoured Bde, BAOR, 1972–74; RCDS, 1974; Brig. Gen. Staff, HQ UKLF, 1975–77; Services Fellow, St Catharine's Coll., Cambridge, 1977; Maj.-Gen., 1978; Asst Chief of the Gen. Staff, 1978–80. Col Comdt, Royal Tank Regt, 1981–86. Member: UK Conf. of Univ. Registrars and Secs, 1982–91; Organising Cttee for 4th Internat. Conf. of Univ. Administrators, Delhi, 1985, for 5th Internat. Conf., Sydney, 1987, for 6th Internat. Conf., Maryland, USA, 1989, for 7th Internat. Conf., Twente, The Netherlands, 1991; Univ. of London Mil. Educn Cttee, 1987–91. Pres., Crabtree Foundn, UCL, 1995; Hon. President: Medical Students Soc., UCL, 1983–88; UCL Boat Club, 1986–93. Mem., RAC Benevolent Fund Cttee, 1985–89. Governor, Welbeck Coll., 1980–82. *Publications:*

contribs to service and university papers and journals. *Recreations:* sailing, golf, outdoor pursuits, history, reading. *Address:* Owen's Farm, Hook, Hampshire RG27 9NG. *Club:* Sandford Springs Golf.

BAKER, Ian Michael; Metropolitan Stipendiary Magistrate, since 1990; *b* 8 May 1947; *s* of late David Ernest Baker and of Phyllis Hinds; *m* 1st, 1976, Sue Joel (marr. diss. 1985); one *s*; 2nd, 1991, Jill Sack. *Educ:* Cynffig Grammar Sch., Mid Glam; St Catharine's Coll., Cambridge (MA). Articled, then Asst Solicitor to John Clitheroe, Kingsley Napley, 1972–76; Partner, Heninghem, Ambler & Gildener, York, 1976–79; Assistant Solicitor: Claude, Hornby & Cox, 1979; Seifert Sedley, 1980–83; Clinton Davis, 1984–87; Partner, T. V. Edwards, 1987–90. Trustee, Nat. Council for Welfare of Prisoners Abroad, 1986– (Chm., 1993–). *Recreations:* jazz, travel, kitchen gardening, theatre, photography, cooking, bird-watching. *Address:* Wells Street Magistrates' Court, 59–65 Wells Street, W1A 3AE. *Club:* Ronnie Scott's.

BAKER, James Addison, III; Senior Partner, Baker & Botts, since 1993; Secretary of State, United States of America, 1989–92; Chief of Staff and Senior Counsellor to the President of the United States of America, 1992–93; *b* 28 April 1930; *s* of James A. Baker, Jr and late Bonner Means Baker; *m* 1973, Susan Garrett; eight *c*. *Educ:* Princeton Univ. (BA); Univ. of Texas at Austin (law degree). Served US Marine Corps, 1952–54. Practised law, firm of Andrews, Kurth, Campbell and Jones, Houston, Texas, 1957–75, 1977–81. Under Sec. of Commerce, US Govt, 1975; National Chairman: President Ford's re-elecn campaign, 1976; George Bush for President Cttee, 1979–80; Dep. Dir, Reagan–Bush Transition and Sen. Advr to 1980 Reagan–Bush Cttee, 1980–Jan. 1981; Chief of Staff to US President, 1981–85; Sec. of US Treasury, 1985–88. Numerous hon. degrees. *Recreations:* hunting, fishing, tennis, golf. *Address:* Baker & Botts, 555 13th Street NW, Suite 500 East, Washington, DC 20004, USA. *Clubs:* numerous social, civic and paternal.

BAKER, Dame Janet (Abbott), CH 1994; DBE 1976 (CBE 1970); professional singer; Member, Opera Board, Royal Opera House, Covent Garden, since 1994; *b* 21 Aug. 1933; *d* of Robert Abbott Baker and May (*née* Pollard); *m* 1957, James Keith Shelley. *Educ:* The College for Girls, York; Wintringham, Grimsby. Mem., Munster Trust. Chancellor, Univ. of York, 1991–. Trustee: Foundn for Sport and the Arts, 1991–; Tillett Trust, 1987–94; Kathleen Ferrier Meml Scholarship, 1976. Daily Mail Kathleen Ferrier Award, 1956; Queen's Prize, Royal College of Music, 1959; Shakespeare Prize, Hamburg, 1971; Copenhagen Sonning Prize, 1979. Hon. DMus: Birmingham, 1968; Leicester, 1974; London, 1974; Hull, 1975; Oxon, 1975; Leeds, 1980; Lancaster, 1983; York, 1984; Hon. MusD Cantab, 1984; Hon. LLD Aberdeen, 1980; Hon. DLitt Bradford, 1983. Hon. Fellow: St Anne's Coll., Oxford, 1975; Downing Coll., Cambridge, 1985. FRSA 1979. Gold Medal, Royal Philharmonic Soc., 1990. *Publication:* Full Circle (autobiog.), 1982. *Recreations:* reading, walking.

BAKER, John Arnold, DL; **His Honour Judge Baker;** a Circuit Judge, since 1973; *b* Calcutta, 5 Nov. 1925; *s* of late William Sydney Baker, MC and Hilda Dora Baker (*née* Swiss); *m* 1954, Edith Muriel Joy Heward; two *d*. *Educ:* Plymouth Coll.; Wellington Sch., Somerset; Wadham Coll., Oxford (MA, BCL). Treas., Oxford Union, 1948. Admitted Solicitor, 1951; called to Bar, Gray's Inn, 1960. A Recorder, 1972–73. Chm., Nat. League of Young Liberals, 1952–53; contested (L): Richmond, 1959 and 1964; Dorking, 1970; Vice-Pres., Liberal Party, 1968–69; Chm., Liberal Party Exec., 1969–70. Pres., Medico-Legal Soc., 1986–88. Lay FRSocMed. DL Surrey, 1986. *Recreation:* music. *Address:* c/o The Crown Court, Canbury Park Road, Kingston upon Thames, Surrey KT2 6JV. *T:* 0181–549 5241.

BAKER, Rt Rev. John Austin; Bishop of Salisbury, 1982–93; *b* 11 Jan. 1928; *s* of George Austin Baker and Grace Edna Baker; *m* 1974, Gillian Mary Leach. *Educ:* Marlborough; Oriel Coll., Oxford (MA, MLitt). Asst Curate, All Saints', Cuddesdon, and Lectr in Old Testament, Cuddesdon Theol Coll., 1954–57; Priest 1955; Asst Curate, St Anselm's, Hatch End, and Asst Lectr in NT Greek, King's Coll., London, 1957–59; Official Fellow, Chaplain and Lectr in Divinity, Corpus Christi Coll., Oxford, 1959–73, Emeritus Fellow, 1977; Lectr in Theology, Brasenose and Lincoln Colls, Oxford, 1959–73; Hebrew Lectr, Exeter Coll., Oxford, 1969–73; Canon of Westminster, 1973–82; Treas., 1974–78; Sub-Dean and Lector Theologiae, 1978–82; Rector of St Margaret's, Westminster, and Speaker's Chaplain, 1978–82. Hon. Asst Bp, dio. Winchester, 1994–. Governor of Pusey House, Oxford, 1970–78; Exam. Chaplain to Bp of Oxford, 1960–78, to Bp of Southwark, 1973–78. Governor: Westminster Sch., 1974–81; Ripon Coll., Cuddesdon, 1974–80; Westminster City Sch., 1978–82; Dorset Inst. of Higher Educn, 1982–86; Bishop Wordsworth's Sch., 1982–93; Sherborne Sch., 1982–93; Salisbury & Wells Theological Coll., 1982–93; Pres. of Council, Marlborough Coll., 1982–93; Trustee, Harold Buxton Trust, 1973–79. Dorrance Vis. Prof., Trinity Coll., Hartford, Conn, USA, 1967; Vis. Prof., King's Coll., London, 1974–77; Hulsean Preacher, Univ. of Cambridge, 1979; Select Preacher, Univ. of Oxford, 1983; Stephenson Lectr, Univ. of Sheffield, 1994; Warburton Lectr, Inns of Court, 1994. Chairman: Defence Theol Working Party, C of E Bd for Social Responsibility, 1980–82; C of E Doctrine Commn, 1985–87 (Mem. 1967–76, 1977–81, 1984–87); House of Bps Working Party on Nature of Christian Belief on Issues in Human Sexuality, 1990–91; Member: Faith and Order Advisory Gp, C of E Bd for Mission and Unity, 1976–81; Council of Christians and Jews, 1979– (Exec. Cttee, 1995–); Cttee for Theological Education, 1982–85; Standing Cttee, WCC Faith and Order Commn, 1983–87; Vice-Pres., Nat. Family Mediation, 1993–. Chaplain, Playing Card Makers' Co., 1977. DD Lambeth, 1991. *Publications:* The Foolishness of God, 1970; Travels in Oudamovia, 1976; The Living Splendour of Westminster Abbey, 1977; The Whole Family of God, 1981; Evidence for the Resurrection, 1986; The Faith of a Christian, 1996; contrib. to: Man: Fallen and Free (ed Kemp), 1969; Thinking about the Eucharist (ed Ramsey), 1972; Church Membership and Intercommunion (ed Kent and Murray), 1973; What about the New Testament? (ed Hooker and Hickling), 1975; Man and Nature (ed Montefiore), 1975; Studia Biblica I, 1978; Religious Studies and Public Examinations (ed Hulmes and Watson), 1980; Believing in the Church, 1981; Hospice: the living Idea (ed Saunders, Summers and Teller), 1981; Darwin: a Commemoration (ed R. J. Berry), 1982; Unholy Warfare (ed D. Martin and P. Mullen), 1983; The Challenge of Northern Ireland, 1984; Lessons before Midnight (ed J. White), 1984; Feminine in the Church (ed M. Furlong), 1984; Dropping the Bomb (ed J. Gladwin), 1985; Theology and Racism, I (ed K. Leech), 1985; Peace Together (ed C. Barrett), 1986; Working for the Kingdom (ed J. Fuller), 1986; Faith and Renewal (ed T. F. Best), 1986; Women Priests? (ed A. Peberdy), 1988; For the Love of Animals (ed B. and M. Annett), 1989; Liberating Life (ed S. McFague *et al*), 1990; The Extended Circle (ed J. Wynne Tyson), 1990; Praying for Peace (ed M. Hare Duke), 1991; Animals on the Agenda (ed. A. Linzey), 1995; *translations:* W. Eichrodt, Theology of the Old Testament, vol. 1 1961, vol. 2 1967; T. Bovet, That They May Have Life, 1964; J. Daniélou, Theology of Jewish Christianity, 1964; H. von Campenhausen, Ecclesiastical Authority and Spiritual Power, 1969; H. von Campenhausen, The Formation of the Christian Bible, 1972; J. Daniélou, Gospel Message and Hellenistic Culture, 1973; (with David Smith) J. Daniélou, The Origins of Latin Christianity, 1977. *Recreations:* music, walking. *Address:* 4 Mede Villas, Kingsgate Road, Winchester, Hants SO23 9QQ. *T:* Winchester (01962) 861388. *Club:* United Oxford & Cambridge University.

BAKER, John B.; *see* Brayne-Baker.

BAKER, John Burkett, QC 1975; **His Honour Judge J. Burkett Baker;** a Circuit Judge, since 1978; *b* 17 Sept. 1931; *s* of Philip and Grace Baker; *m* 1955, Margaret Mary Smeaton; two *s* seven *d* (and one *s* decd). *Educ:* Finchley Catholic Grammar Sch.; White Fathers, Bishops Waltham; UC Exeter. LLB London. RAF, 1955–58. Called to Bar, Gray's Inn, 1957; practised from 1958. Prosecuting Counsel to Dept of Health and Social Security, 1969–75; Dep. Chm., Shropshire QS, 1970–71; a Recorder of the Crown Court, 1972–78. Mem. Cttee, Council of Circuit Judges, 1991–. Marriage Counsellor, Catholic Marriage Adv. Council, 1970–87 (Chm., 1981–83); Pres., Barnet, Haringey and Hertsmere Marriage Guidance Council, 1982–92. Governor: Bedford Coll., London, 1983–85; Holy Family Convent, Enfield, 1984–89. Papal Cross Pro Ecclesia et Pontifice, 1986. *Recreation:* theatre. *Address:* 43 The Ridgeway, Enfield, Mddx EN2 8PD.

BAKER, Prof. John Hamilton, LLD; FBA 1984; Professor of English Legal History, Cambridge University, since 1988; Fellow of St Catharine's College, since 1971; *b* 10 April 1944; *s* of Kenneth Lee Vincent Baker, QPM and Marjorie (*née* Bagshaw); *m* 1968, Veronica Margaret, *d* of Rev. W. S. Lloyd; two *d*. *Educ:* King Edward VI Grammar School, Chelmsford; UCL (LLB 1965 (Andrews Medal), PhD 1968; Fellow 1990); MA Cantab 1971, LLD 1984, Yorke Prize, 1975. FRHistS 1980. Called to the Bar, Inner Temple, 1966 (Hon. Bencher 1988), *aeg* Gray's Inn, 1978. Asst Lectr, Faculty of Laws, UCL, 1965–67, Lectr, 1967–71; Cambridge University: Librarian, Squire Law Library, 1971–73; Univ. Lectr in Law, 1973–83; Reader in English Legal History, 1983–88; Junior Proctor, 1980–81; Chm., Faculty of Law, 1990–92. Visiting Professor: European Univ. Inst., Florence, 1979; Yale Law Sch., 1987; NY Univ. Sch. of Law, 1988–; Vis. Lectr, Harvard Law Sch., 1982; Mellon Senior Res. Fellow, H. E. Huntington Lib., San Marino, Calif., 1983; Ford Special Lectr, Oxford Univ., 1984; Vis. Fellow, All Souls Coll., Oxford, 1995. Corresp. Fellow, Amer. Soc. Legal History, 1993. Literary Dir, Selden Soc., 1981– (Jt Dir, 1981–90). Hon. LLD Chicago, 1992. Ames Prize, Harvard, 1985. *Publications:* An Introduction to English Legal History, 1971, 3rd edn 1990; English Legal Manuscripts, vol. I, 1975, vol. II, 1978; The Reports of Sir John Spelman, 1977–78; (ed) Legal Records and the Historian, 1978; Manual of Law French, 1979, 2nd edn 1990; The Order of Serjeants at Law, 1984; English Legal Manuscripts in the USA, vol. I 1985, vol. II 1991; The Legal Profession and the Common Law, 1986; (with S. F. C. Milsom) Sources of English Legal History, 1986; The Notebook of Sir John Port, 1986; (ed) Judicial Records, Law Reports and the Growth of Case Law, 1989; Readings and Moots in the Inns of Court, vol. II, 1990; Cases from the lost notebooks of Sir James Dyer, 1994; articles in legal and hist. jls. *Address:* 75 Hurst Park Avenue, Cambridge CB4 2AB. *T:* Cambridge (01223) 565054; St Catharine's College, Cambridge CB2 1RL. *T:* Cambridge (01223) 338317.

BAKER, John William; Chairman, National Power plc, since 1995 (Chief Executive, 1990–95); *b* 5 Dec. 1937; *s* of Reginald and Wilhelmina Baker; *m* 1st, 1962, Pauline (*née* Moore); one *s*; 2nd, 1975, Gillian (*née* Bullen). *Educ:* Harrow Weald County Grammar Sch.; Oriel Coll., Oxford. Served Army, 1959–61. MoT, 1961–70; DoE, 1970–74; Dep. Chief Exec., Housing Corp., 1974–78; Sec., 1979–80, Bd Mem., 1980–89, Corporate Man. Dir, 1986–89, CEGB. *Recreations:* tennis, bridge, music, theatre. *Address:* National Power plc, Senator House, 85 Queen Victoria Street, EC4V 4DP. *T:* 0171–454 9494.

BAKER, Rt. Hon. Kenneth (Wilfred), CH 1992; PC 1984; MP (C) Mole Valley, since 1983 (St Marylebone, Oct. 1970–1983; Acton, March 1968–1970); *b* 3 Nov. 1934; *s* of late W. M. Baker, OBE and of Mrs Baker (*née* Harries); *m* 1963, Mary Elizabeth Gray-Muir; one *s* two *d*. *Educ:* St Paul's Sch.; Magdalen Coll., Oxford. Nat. Service, 1953–55: Lieut in Gunners, N Africa; Artillery Instructor to Libyan Army. Oxford, 1955–58 (Sec. of Union). Served Twickenham Borough Council, 1960–62. Contested (C): Poplar, 1964; Acton, 1966. Parly Sec., CSD, 1972–74; PPS to Leader of Opposition, 1974–75; Minister of State and Minister for Information Technology, DTI, 1981–84; a Minister for Local Govt, DoE, 1984–85; Sec. of State for the Environment, 1985–86; Sec. of State for Educn and Sci., 1986–89; Chancellor of the Duchy of Lancaster, 1989–90; Chm., Conservative Party, 1989–90; Sec. of State for Home Dept, 1990–92. Mem., Public Accounts Cttee, 1969–70. Mem. Exec., 1922 Cttee. Chm., Hansard Soc., 1978–81. Sec. Gen., UN Conf. of Parliamentarians on World Population and Development, 1978. *Publications:* (ed) I Have No Gun But I Can Spit, 1980; (ed) London Lines, 1982; (ed) The Faber Book of English History in Verse, 1988; (ed) Unauthorized Versions: poems and their parodies, 1990; (ed) The Faber Book of Conservatism, 1993; The Turbulent Years: my life in politics, 1993. *Recreation:* collecting books. *Address:* House of Commons, SW1A 0AA. *Clubs:* Athenæum, Carlton, Garrick.

BAKER, Prof. (Leonard Graham) Derek, MA, BLitt; Professor of History, since 1986, Director, Institute for Medieval Renaissance and Hispanic Studies, since 1989, Director, Centre for Undergraduate Study and Research, since 1990, University of Texas; *b* 21 April 1931; *s* of Leonard and late Phoebe Caroline Baker; *m* 1970, Jean Dorothy Johnston; one *s* one *d*. *Educ:* Christ's Hospital; Oriel Coll., Oxford (1st Class Hons Modern History 1955, MA, BLitt). Captain, Royal Signals, 1950–52. Senior History Master, The Leys School, 1956–66; Lecturer in Medieval History, Univ. of Edinburgh, 1966–79; Headmaster, Christ's Hosp., 1979–85. Editor, Ecclesiastical History Soc., 1969; Pres., British Sub-Commission, Commission Internationale d'Histoire Ecclésiastique Comparée, 1971. Dir, Exec. Cttee, Haskins Soc., 1990–. FRHistS 1969. *Publications:* Portraits and Documents, Vol. 1 1967, Vol. 2 1969; Partnership in Excellence, 1974; (ed) Studies in Church History, 7–17, 1970–80 (subsidia 1–2, 1978–79); numerous articles in historical jls. *Recreations:* singing; climbing, mountaineering, pot-holing, camping; good company; food and wine; travel. *Address:* 5 Allendale, Southwater, Horsham, Sussex RH13 7UE. *T:* Southwater (01403) 731459; 30 Dick Place, Edinburgh EH9 2JB. *T:* 0131–667 5920; 1300 Dallas Drive, #1023, Denton, TX 76201, USA. *T:* (817) 3873282. *Clubs:* National Liberal; Leander (Henley-on-Thames).

BAKER, Mark Alexander Wyndham; Executive Director, Corporate Affairs and Personnel, Nuclear Electric plc, 1989–96; Chairman, Magnox Electric, from April 1996; *b* 19 June 1940; *s* of late Lt-Comdr Alexander Arthur Wyndham Baker, RN and Renée Gavrelle Stenson (*née* Macnaghten); *m* 1964, Meriel, *yr d* of Capt. Hugh Chetwynd-Talbot, MBE and Cynthia Chetwynd-Talbot; one *s* one *d*. *Educ:* Prince Edward Sch., Salisbury, S Rhodesia; University Coll. of Rhodesia & Nyasaland (Beit Schol.; BA London); Christ Church, Oxford (Rhodes Schol.; MA). United Kingdom Atomic Energy Authority, 1964–89: Sec., 1976–78, Gen. Sec., 1978–81, AERE, Harwell; Dir of Personnel and Admin, Northern Div., 1981–84; Authority Personnel Officer, 1984–86; Authority Sec., 1986–89. FRSA 1992. *Recreations:* bridge, gardening, golf, walking, words. *Address:* (office) Berkeley Technology Centre, Berkeley, Glos GL13 9PB. *Clubs:* Reform; Antrobus Dining (Cheshire).

BAKER, Martyn Murray; Head of Exports to Asia, Africa and Australasia Division, Department of Trade and Industry, since 1993; *b* 10 March 1944; *s* of late Norman and Constance Baker; *m* 1970, Rosemary Caroline Holdich. *Educ:* Dulwich Coll.; Pembroke Coll., Oxford (MA). Asst Principal, Min. of Aviation, 1965–67; Asst Private Sec. to

Minister of State, Min. of Technology, 1968–69; Private Sec. to Parly Under Secs of State, Min. of Technology, Min. of Aviation Supply, DTI, 1969–71; Principal, 1971; Principal Private Sec. to Sec. of State for Trade, 1977–78; Asst Sec., Dept of Trade, 1978; Counsellor, Civil Aviation and Shipping, Washington, 1978–82; Department of Trade and Industry: Asst Sec., Air Div., 1982–85; Projects and Export Policy Div., 1985–86; Under Sec., 1986; Regl Dir, NW, 1986–88; Dir, Enterprise and Deregulation Unit, 1988–90; Head of Overseas Trade Div., 1990–93. Mem., Export Guarantees Advisory Council, 1985–86. Leader, Manchester-Salford City Action Team, 1986–88. Hon. Vis. Sen. Fellow, Manchester Business Sch., 1988–. FRSA 1988. *Address:* Department of Trade and Industry, 66–74 Victoria Street, SW1E 6SW.

BAKER, Mary Geraldine, MBE 1995; National Welfare Director, Parkinson's Disease Society, 1984–91 and since 1992 (Acting Chief Executive, 1991–92); *b* 27 Oct. 1936; *d* of George and Emily Wheeler; *m* 1960, Robert William John Baker; three *s*. *Educ:* Bromley High Sch.; Leeds Univ. (BA); Inst. of Almoners. AIMSW. Almoner, St Thomas' Hosp., 1959–61; housewife and mother, 1961–75; Social Worker, 1975–82; Principal Med. Social Worker, Frimley Park Hosp., 1983. Mem., Adv. Gp on Rehabilitation, DoH, 1992–94. Pres., European Parkinson's Disease Assoc., 1992–96. Mem., Nat. Hosp. for Neurology and Neurosurgery SHA, 1994–. Member, Council: CSP, 1994–; Queen's Nursing Inst. Hon. FCSLT 1991. *Publications:* Speech Therapy in Practice, 1988; (with B. McCall) Care of the Elderly, 1990; (with P. Smith) The Role of the Social Worker in the Management of Parkinson's Disease, 1991; contribs to learned jls. *Recreations:* music, theatre, reading, bridge, caravanning. *Address:* Parkinson's Disease Society, 22 Upper Woburn Place, WC1H 0RA; Kailua, Maybourne Rise, Mayford, Woking, Surrey GU22 0SM. *T:* Woking (01483) 763626. *Club:* Soroptimists'.

BAKER, Maurice S.; Managing Director, F. W. Woolworth & Co. Ltd, 1967–71, retired; *b* 27 Jan. 1911; *s* of Sidney B. Baker and Ellen Elizabeth (*née* Airey); *m* 1st, 1935, Helen Johnstone (*née* Tweedie) (*d* 1977); one *s*; 2nd, 1978, Kirsten Randine (*née* Haugen). *Educ:* Lowestoft Grammar School. Trainee Manager, F. W. Woolworth & Co. Ltd, 1928; RAOC, 1940–46 (Major); rejoined company, 1946; Dir 1962. Officer, Legion of Merit (US), 1945. *Recreation:* bowls (Pres., 1975, Hon. Life Mem., 1983, Surrey County Bowling Assoc.).

BAKER, Michael Findlay; QC 1990; **His Honour Judge Findlay Baker;** a Circuit Judge, since 1995; *b* 26 May 1943; *s* of Rt Hon. Sir George Baker, PC, OBE; *m* 1973, Sarah Hartley Overton; two *d*. *Educ:* Haileybury; Brasenose Coll., Oxford. Called to the Bar, Inner Temple, 1966; a Recorder, 1991–95. Sec., National Reference Tribunals for the Coal-mining Industry, 1973–95. *Recreations:* mountain climbing and walking, cross country running. *Address:* The Crown Court, Bricket Road, St Albans, Herts. *Clubs:* Alpine; Thames Hare and Hounds.

See also Hon. Sir T. S. G. Baker.

BAKER, Prof. Michael John, TD 1971; Professor of Marketing, since 1971, and Senior Adviser to the Principal, since 1991, Strathclyde University; Chairman, Westburn Publishers Ltd, since 1984; *b* 5 Nov. 1935; *s* of John Overend Baker and Constance Dorothy (*née* Smith); *m* 1959, Sheila (*née* Bell); one *s* two *d*. *Educ:* Worksop Coll.; Gosforth and Harvey Grammar Schs; Durham Univ. (BA); London Univ. (BScEcon); Harvard Univ. (CertITP, DBA); DipM. FCIM; FCAM; FRSA; FScotvec. 2nd Lieut, RA, 1956–57. Salesman, Richard Thomas & Baldwins (Sales) Ltd, 1958–64; Asst Lectr, Medway Coll. of Technology, 1964–66; Lectr, Hull Coll. of Technology, 1966–68; Foundn for Management Educn Fellow, 1968–71, Res. Associate, 1969–71, Harvard Business Sch.; Dean, Strathclyde Bus. Sch., 1978–84; Dep. Principal, Strathclyde Univ., 1984–91. Mem., Vice Chm. and Chm., Scottish Bus. Educn Council, 1973–85; Pres., Marketing Educn Gp, 1986– (Chm., 1973–86); Member: Food and Drink, EDC, 1976–78; SSRC Management and Industrial Relns Cttee, 1976–80; Nat. Councillor, Inst. of Marketing, 1977, Vice Chm. 1984–86, Chm. 1987. Member: Scottish Hosps Endowment Res. Trust, 1983–; Chief Scientist's Cttee, SHHD, 1985–; Bus. and Management Sub-Cttee, UGC, 1985–89. Chairman: Scottish Marketing Projects Ltd, 1986–; IBEX Ltd, 1991–; Director: Stoddard Sekers International (formerly Stoddard Hldgs) PLC, 1983–; Scottish Transport Gp, 1986–90; ARIS plc, 1990–94; Reid Gp, 1989–91; SGBS Ltd, 1990–; STAMP Ltd, 1992–. Dir, Scottish Med. Res. Fund, 1992–. Lomond Sch., 1984–. Founding Editor, Jl of Marketing Management, 1985. *Publications:* Marketing, 1971, 5th edn 1991; Marketing New Industrial Products, 1975; (with R. McTavish) Product Policy, 1976; (ed) Marketing in Adversity, 1976; (ed) Marketing Theory and Practice, 1976, 2nd edn 1983; (ed) Industrial Innovation, 1979; Market Development, 1983; (ed) Dictionary of Marketing, 1984, 2nd edn 1990; Marketing Strategy and Management, 1985, 2nd edn 1992; (with S. T. Parkinson) Organisational Buying Behaviour, 1986; (ed) The Marketing Book, 1987, 3rd edn 1994; (with D. Ughanwa) The Role of Design in International Competitiveness, 1989; (with S. Hart) Marketing and Competitive Success, 1989; Research for Marketing, 1991; (ed) Perspectives on Marketing Management, vol. 1, 1991, vol. 2, 1992, vol. 3, 1993, vol. 4, 1994. *Recreations:* hill walking, sailing, foreign travel. *Address:* Westburn, Helensburgh G84 9NH. *T:* Helensburgh (01436) 674686. *Club:* Royal Over-Seas League.

BAKER, Michael John David; His Honour Judge Michael Baker; a Circuit Judge, since 1988; *b* 17 April 1934; *s* of late Ernest Bowden Baker and of Dulcie Baker; *m* 1958, Edna Harriet Lane; one *s* one *d*. *Educ:* Trinity Sch. of John Whitgift; Bristol Univ. (LLB Hons). Admitted solicitor, 1957. Flying Officer, RAF, 1957–60. Joined firm of Glanvilles, Solicitors, Portsmouth, 1960; Partner, 1963–88; a Recorder, 1980–88. Coroner, S Hampshire, 1973–88 (Asst Dep. Coroner, 1971; Dep. Coroner, 1972). Pres., Southern Coroners Soc., 1975–76; Mem. Council, Coroners Soc. of England and Wales, 1979–88 (Jun. Vice-Pres., 1987–88). *Recreations:* walking, tennis, the theatre, music (particularly choral singing), photography. *Address:* c/o 131 London Road, Waterlooville, Hants PO7 7SS. *T:* Waterlooville (01705) 251414. *Clubs:* Royal Air Force, Law Society; Emsworth Sailing.

BAKER, Nicholas Brian; MP (C) North Dorset, since 1979; Parliamentary Under-Secretary of State, Home Office, since 1994; *b* 23 Nov. 1938; *m* 1970, Penelope Carol d'Abo; one *s* one *d*. *Educ:* Clifton Coll.; Exeter Coll., Oxford (MA). Partner in Frere Cholmeley, subseq. Frere Cholmeley Bischoff, solicitors, EC4, 1973–94. Parliamentary Private Secretary to: Minister of State for the Armed Forces, 1981–83, for Defence Procurement, MoD, 1983–84; Sec. of State for Defence, MoD, 1984–86; Sec. of State for Trade and Industry, 1987–88; an Asst Govt Whip, 1989–90; a Lord Comr of HM Treasury (Govt Whip), 1990–94. *Publications:* pamphlets. *Recreations:* exercise, music, English countryside. *Address:* House of Commons, SW1A 0AA. *Clubs:* Wimborne Conservative, Blandford Constitutional.

BAKER, Nigel Robert James; QC 1988; a Recorder, since 1985; *b* 21 Dec. 1942; *s* of late Herbert James Baker and of Amy Beatrice Baker; *m* 1973, Stephanie Joy Stephenson; one *s*. *Educ:* Norwich Sch.; Univ. of Southampton (BA Law); Queens' Coll., Cambridge (LLM). Lectr in Law, Univ. of Leicester, 1968–70; called to the Bar, Middle Temple, 1969; practice on Midland and Oxford Circuit. Mem., Bar Council, 1985. *Recreations:* football, fell walking, gardening. *Address:* 9 Bedford Row, WC1R 4AZ. *T:* 0171–242 3555.

BAKER, Paul Vivian; His Honour Judge Paul Baker; a Circuit Judge, since 1983; *b* 27 March 1923; *er s* of Vivian Cyril Baker and Maud Lydia Baker; *m* 1957, Stella Paterson Eadie, *d* of William Eadie, MD; one *s* one *d*. *Educ:* City of London Sch.; University Coll., Oxford (BCL, MA). Called to Bar, Lincoln's Inn, 1950, Bencher, 1979; QC 1972. Editor, Law Quarterly Review, 1971–87. Chm., Incorporated Council of Law Reporting for England and Wales, 1992–. *Recreations:* music, walking. *Address:* 9 Old Square, Lincoln's Inn, WC2A 3SR. *T:* 0171–242 2633. *Clubs:* Athenæum, Authors'.

BAKER, Peter Maxwell; QC 1974; **His Honour Judge Peter Baker;** a Circuit Judge, since 1983; *b* 26 March 1930; *s* of late Harold Baker and of Rose Baker; *m* 1954, Jacqueline Mary Marshall; three *d*; *m* 1988, Sandra Elizabeth Hughes. *Educ:* King Edward VII Sch., Sheffield; Exeter Coll., Oxford. MA Oxon. Called to Bar, Gray's Inn, 1956 (Holker Senior Exhibitioner); Junior, NE Circuit, 1960; a Recorder of the Crown Court, 1972–83. *Recreations:* yachting, music, watching others garden. *Address:* c/o Circuit Administrator, 17th Floor, West Riding House, Albion Street, Leeds LS1 5AA. *Club:* Sheffield (Sheffield).

BAKER, Prof. Raymond, PhD; FRS 1994; Executive Director of Medicinal Chemistry, Merck Sharp & Dohme Research Laboratories, since 1989; *b* 1 Nov. 1936; *s* of Alfred Baker and May (*née* Golds); *m* 1960, Marian Slater; one *s* two *d*. *Educ:* Ilkeston Grammar Sch.; Leicester Univ. (BSc, PhD). Postdoctoral Fellow, UCLA, 1962–64; University of Southampton: Lectr in Organic Chem., 1964–72; Sen. Lectr, 1972–74; Reader, 1974–77; Prof., 1977–84; Dir, Wolfson Unit of Chemical Entomology, 1976–84; Dir of Medicinal Chem., Merck Sharpe Dohme Res. Labs. 1984–89. Vis. Prof., Univ. of Edinburgh, 1988. Hon. DSc Nottingham Trent, 1990. *Publications:* Mechanism in Organic Chemistry, 1971; contrib. numerous articles to Jl Chemical Soc., Jl Medicinal Chem., and other scientific jls. *Recreations:* golf, gardening. *Address:* (office) Terlings Park, Harlow, Essex CM20 2QR. *T:* Harlow (01279) 440152.

BAKER, Richard Douglas James, OBE 1976; RD 1979; broadcaster and author; Member, Broadcasting Standards Council, 1988–93; *b* Willesden, London, 15 June 1925; *s* of Albert and Jane Isobel Baker; *m* 1961, Margaret Celia Martin; two *s*. *Educ:* Kilburn Grammar Sch.; Peterhouse, Cambridge (MA). Served War, Royal Navy, 1943–46. Actor, 1948; Teacher, 1949; Third Programme Announcer, 1950–53; BBC TV Newsreader, 1954–82; Commentator for State Occasion Outside Broadcasts, 1967–70; TV Introductions to Promenade Concerts, 1960–95; Panellist on BBC2's Face the Music, 1966–79; Presenter, Omnibus, BBC TV, 1983; on Radio 4: Presenter of Start the Week with Richard Baker, 1970–87; These You Have Loved, 1972–77; Baker's Dozen, 1978–87; Rollercoaster, 1984; Music in Mind, 1987–88; Richard Baker Compares Notes, 1987–95; on Radio 3: Mainly for Pleasure, 1986–92; In Tune, 1992–95; Rush Hour concerts, 1994–95; on Radio 2: Presenter of Melodies for You, 1986–95; presenter, Classic Countdown, Classic FM, 1995–. Columnist, Now! Magazine, 1979–80. Dir, Youth and Music; Mem., Exec. Cttee, Friends of Covent Garden; Trustee, D'Oyly Carte Opera Co., 1985–; Governor, NYO of GB, 1985–. TV Newscaster of the Year (Radio Industries Club), 1972, 1974, 1979; BBC Radio Personality of the Year (Variety Club of GB), 1984. Hon. FLCM 1974; Hon. RCM 1988. Hon. LLD: Strathclyde, 1979; Aberdeen, 1983. *Publications:* Here is the News (broadcasts), 1966; The Terror of Tobermory, 1972; The Magic of Music, 1975; Dry Ginger, 1977; Richard Baker's Music Guide, 1979; Mozart, 1982, rev. edn 1991; London, a theme with variations, 1989; Richard Baker's Companion to Music, 1993. *Recreations:* gardening, the gramophone. *Address:* c/o Bagenal Harvey Organisation, 141–143 Drury Lane, WC2B 5TB. *T:* 0171–379 4625. *Club:* Garrick.

BAKER, Richard Hugh; HM Diplomatic Service, retired; *b* 22 Oct. 1935; *s* of Hugh Cuthbert Baker and Muriel Lovenda Baker (*née* Owens); *m* 1963, Patricia Marianne Haigh Thomas; one *s* three *d*. *Educ:* Marlborough Coll.; New Coll., Oxford. Army (2nd Lieut RA), 1954–56. Plebiscite Officer, UN Plebiscite, S Cameroons, 1960–61; joined Diplomatic Service, 1962; 3rd, later 2nd, then 1st Sec., Addis Ababa, 1963–66; Foreign Office, 1967; Private Sec. to Permanent Under-Sec. of State, Foreign Office (later FCO), 1967–70; 1st Sec. and Head of Chancery, Warsaw, 1970–72; FCO, 1973–76; RCDS 1977; Econ. and Financial Counsellor, and Dep. Head, UK Perm. Delegn to OECD, Paris, 1978–82; Dep. High Comr, Ottawa, 1982–86; Asst Under-Sec. of State, and Civilian Mem., Sen. Directing Staff, RCDS, 1986–89. *Recreations:* music, painting, literature, pottery, printmaking, writing.

BAKER, Sir Robert George Humphrey S.; *see* Sherston-Baker.

BAKER, Scott; *see* Baker, T. S. G.

BAKER, Stephen, OBE 1987; consultant; Managing Director, British Electricity International Ltd, 1978–86; *b* 27 March 1926; *s* of late Arthur and Nancy Baker; *m* 1950, Margaret Julia Wright; one *s* two *d*. *Educ:* Epsom Coll.; Clare Coll., Cambridge (MA). FIMechE. Engr Officer, RN, 1944–47; Apprentice, Davy United Engineering Co. Ltd, 1947–49; Works Engr, John Baker & Bessemer Ltd, 1949–51; Davy United Engrg Co. Ltd, 1951: Dir of Prodn, 1960; Gen. Man., 1961; Dir, Davy Ashmore Ltd, 1963; Dir of Ops, Davy-Ashmore Engrg Ltd, 1964; Chm. and Chief Exec. of Davy United Engrg Co. Ltd, Ashmore Benson Pease Ltd and Loewy Robertson Engrg Co. Ltd, 1968; Man. Dir, Kearney & Trecker Ltd, 1970; Co-ordinator of Industrial Advrs, Depts of Trade and Industry, 1974–78. *Recreations:* fishing, gardening. *Address:* 75 Slayleigh Lane, Sheffield S10 3RG.

BAKER, Very Rev. Thomas George Adames, MA; DD Lambeth, 1987; Dean of Worcester, 1975–86, Dean Emeritus since 1986; *b* 22 Dec. 1920; *s* of late Walter and Marion Baker, Southampton; unmarried. *Educ:* King Edward VI Sch., Southampton; Exeter Coll., Oxford; Lincoln Theological Coll. Curate of All Saints, King's Heath, Birmingham, 1944–47; Vicar of St James, Edgbaston, 1947–54; Sub-Warden of Lincoln Theological Coll., 1954–60; Principal of Wells Theological College and Prebendary of Combe II in Wells Cathedral, 1960–71; Archdeacon of Bath, 1971–75. Canon Theologian of Leicester Cathedral, 1959–66. Select Preacher, Univ. of Cambridge, 1963, Univ. of Oxford, 1973. Recognised Teacher, Bristol Univ., 1969–74. *Publications:* What is the New Testament?, 1969; Questioning Worship, 1977. *Recreation:* music. *Address:* Charterhouse, EC1M 6AN.

BAKER, Hon. Sir (Thomas) Scott (Gillespie), Kt 1988; **Hon. Mr Justice Scott Baker;** a Judge of the High Court of Justice, Queen's Bench Division, since 1993 (Family Division, 1988–92); Presiding Judge, Wales and Chester Circuit, 1991–95; *b* 10 Dec. 1937; *s* of late Rt Hon. Sir George Baker, PC, OBE and Jessie McCall Baker; *m* 1973, (Margaret) Joy Strange; two *s* one *d*. *Educ:* Haileybury; Brasenose Coll., Oxford. Called to the Bar, Middle Temple, 1961 (Astbury Schol.), Bencher 1985; a Recorder, 1976–88; QC 1978; Family Div. Liaison Judge (Wales and Chester Circuit), 1990–92. Member: Senate, Inns of Court, 1977–84; Bar Council, 1988. Mem., Govt Cttee of Inquiry into Human Fertilisation (Warnock Cttee), 1982–84. Mem., Chorleywood UDC, 1965–68. Dep. Chm., Cricket Council Appeals Cttee, 1986–88. Gov., Caldecott Sch., 1991–. *Recreations:* golf, fishing, shooting. *Address:* Royal Courts of Justice, Strand, WC2A 2LL.

Clubs: MCC; Denham Golf (Captain, 1992).
See also M. F. Baker.

BAKER, Wallis James, CB 1989; Chairman, Land Administration Commission, Queensland, 1983–89, retired; *b* 19 March 1931; *s* of James Campbell Baker and Doris Isabel (*née* Nowland); *m* 1960, Eileen Merle Seeney; one *s* one *d*. *Educ:* Downlands Coll., Toowoomba, Qld. Admitted Solicitor, Supreme Court of Qld, 1954, re-admitted, 1990; called to the Bar, Qld, 1969. Practised as Solicitor, Monto, Qld, 1955–68; entered Qld Public Service as career public servant, 1968. *Recreations:* tennis, ancient history, rock collecting. *Address:* 61 Montrose Street, Gordon Park, Brisbane, Qld 4031, Australia. *T:* (7) 33576618.

BAKER, Willfred Harold Kerton, TD; *b* 6 Jan. 1920; *o s* of late W. H. Baker; *m* 1st, 1945, Kathleen Helen Sloan (*née* Murray Bisset) (*d* 1987); one *s* two *d*; 2nd, Jean Gordon Scott (*née* Skinner). *Educ:* Hardye's Sch.; Edinburgh Univ.; Cornell Univ., USA. Joined TA, and served War of 1939–45 (Major). Edinburgh Univ. (BSc Agriculture), 1946–49. MP (C) Banffshire, 1964–Feb. 1974. *Recreations:* golf, philately. *Address:* Ashdown, 42 Southfield Avenue, Paignton, South Devon TQ3 1LH. *T:* Paignton (01803) 550861.

BAKER, Wilson, FRS 1946; FRSC; BSc, MSc, PhD, DSc (Manchester); MA (Oxon.); retired; Alfred Capper Pass Professor of Organic Chemistry, University of Bristol, 1945–65 (Dean of the Faculty of Science, 1948–51; Emeritus Professor, University of Bristol, 1965); *b* 24 Jan. 1900; *yr s* of Harry and Mary Baker, Runcorn, Cheshire; *m* 1927, Juliet Elizabeth, *d* of Henry and Julia R. Glaisyer, Birmingham; one *s* two *d*. *Educ:* Liverpool Coll. Upper Sch.; Victoria Univ. of Manchester (Mercer Schol., Baeyer Fellow and Dalton Scholar). Asst Lecturer in Chemistry, Univ. of Manchester, 1924–27; Tutor in Chemistry, Dalton Hall, Manchester, 1926–27; Univ. Lecturer and Demonstrator in Chemistry, Univ. of Oxford, 1927–44; Fellow and Praelector in Chemistry, The Queen's Coll., Oxford, 1937–44. Vice-Pres. of the Chemical Society, 1957–60. *Publications:* numerous original papers on organic chemistry, dealing chiefly with the synthesis of natural products, the development of synthetical processes, compounds of abnormal aromatic type, organic inclusion compounds, and the preparation of large-ring compounds, and the chemistry of penicillin, published mainly in Journal of the Chemical Society; (with T. W. J. Taylor) 2nd Edition of Professor N. V. Sidgwick's The Organic Chemistry of Nitrogen, 1937. *Recreations:* walking, gardening, music, mineralogy. *Address:* Lane's End, 54 Church Road, Winscombe, Avon BS25 1BJ. *T:* Winscombe (01934) 843112.

BAKER-BATES, Merrick Stuart; HM Diplomatic Service; Consul-General, Los Angeles, since 1992; *b* 22 July 1939; *s* of late E. T. Baker-Bates, MD, FRCP, and of Norah Stuart (*née* Kirkham); *m* 1963, Chrystal Jacqueline Goodacre; one *s* one *d*. *Educ:* Shrewsbury Sch.; Hertford Coll., Oxford (MA); College of Europe, Bruges. Journalist, Brussels, 1962–63; entered HM Diplomatic Service, 1963; 3rd, later 2nd Sec., Tokyo, 1963–68; 1st Secretary: FCO, 1968–73; (Inf.), Washington, 1973–76; (Commercial), Tokyo, 1976–79; Counsellor (Commercial), Tokyo, 1979–82. Dir, Cornes & Co., Tokyo, 1982–85; Representative Dir, Gestetner Ltd (Japan), 1982–85; Dep. High Comr and Counsellor (Commercial/Econ.), Kuala Lumpur, 1986–89; Hd of S Atlantic and Antarctic Dept, FCO, and Comr, British Antarctic Territory, 1989–92. *Recreations:* photography, golf, cycling. *Address:* c/o Foreign and Commonwealth Office, SW1A 2AH. *Clubs:* Brooks's; Tokyo (Tokyo).
See also R. P. Baker-Bates.

BAKER-BATES, Rodney Pennington; Director of Finance and Information Technology, British Broadcasting Corporation, since 1993; *b* 25 April 1944; *s* of Eric Tom Baker-Bates and Norah Stuart Baker-Bates; *m* 1972, Gail Elizabeth Roberts; one *s*. *Educ:* Shrewsbury Sch.; Hertford Coll., Oxford (MA History). FICA 1971; AIMC 1975; FCIB 1991. Glyn Mills & Co., 1966–68; Arthur Andersen & Co., 1968–77; Chase Manhattan Bank, 1977–84; Midland Bank, 1984–92. Governor, Bedales Sch., 1993–. *Recreations:* gardening, performing arts, country pursuits. *Address:* c/o British Broadcasting Corporation, 201 Wood Lane, W12 7TS. *T:* 0181–752 4311. *Club:* City of London.
See also M. S. Baker-Bates.

BAKER-CARR, Air Marshal Sir John (Darcy), KBE 1962 (CBE 1951); CB 1957; AFC 1944; Controller of Engineering and Equipment, Air Ministry, 1962–64, retired; *b* 13 January 1906; *s* of late Brigadier-General C. D. Baker-Carr, CMG, DSO and Sarah Quinan; *m* 1934, Margery Dallas; no *c*. *Educ:* England and USA. Entered RAF as Pilot Officer, 1929; No 32 Fighter Sqdn 1930, Flying Officer; Flying Boats at home and overseas, 1931; Armament Specialist Course, 1934; Flight-Lieut; Armament and Air Staff appts, 1935–38; Sqdn Ldr, 1938; Armament Research and Development, 1939–45 (AFC); Wing Comdr, 1940; Gp Captain, 1942; Central Fighter Estab., 1946–47; Dep. Dir Postings, Air Min., 1947–48; Air Cdre, 1948; Dir of Armament Research and Development, Min. of Supply, 1948–51 (CBE); idc 1952; Comdt RAF, St Athan, 1953–56; Senior Technical Staff Officer, HQ Fighter Command, RAF, 1956–59; Air Vice-Marshal, 1957; Air Officer Commanding, No 41 Group, Maintenance Command, 1959–61; Air Marshal, 1962. *Recreations:* sailing and carpentry. *Address:* Thatchwell Cottage, King's Somborne, Hants SO20 6PH. *Club:* Royal Air Force Yacht (Hamble, Hants).

BAKER WILBRAHAM, Sir Richard, 8th Bt *cr* 1776; DL; Director, J. Henry Schroder Wagg & Co. Ltd, 1969–89; Chairman, Bibby Line Group, since 1992 (Deputy Chairman, 1989–92); *b* 5 Feb. 1934; *s* of Sir Randle Baker Wilbraham, 7th Bt, and Betty Ann, CBE (*d* 1975), *d* of W. Matt Torrens; *S* father, 1980; *m* 1962, Anne Christine Peto, *d* of late Charles Peto Bennett, OBE; one *s* three *d*. *Educ:* Harrow. Welsh Guards, 1952–54. J. Henry Schroder Wagg & Co. Ltd, 1954–89. Director: Westpool Investment Trust, 1974–92; Brixton Estate, 1985– (Dep. Chm., 1994–); The Really Useful Group plc, 1985–90; Charles Barker Group, 1986–89; Grosvenor Estates Hldgs, 1989– (Dep. Chm., 1989–); Severn Trent, 1989–94; Majedie Investments, 1989–; Christie Hosp. NHS Trust, 1990–. Mem., Gen. Council, King Edward's Hosp. Fund for London, 1986–. Gov., Nuffield Hosps, 1990–. A Church Comr, 1994–. Trustee, Grosvenor Estate, 1981–. Governor: Harrow Sch., 1982–92; The King's Sch., Macclesfield, 1986–. High Sheriff, Cheshire, 1991–92; DL Cheshire, 1992. *Recreations:* field sports. *Heir:* *s* Randle Baker Wilbraham, *b* 28 May 1963. *Address:* Rode Hall, Scholar Green, Cheshire ST7 3QP. *T:* Alsager (01270) 882961. *Clubs:* Brooks's, Pratt's.

BAKEWELL, Joan Dawson; broadcaster and writer; *b* 16 April; *d* of John Rowlands and Rose Bland; *m* 1st, 1955, Michael Bakewell (marr. diss. 1972); one *s* one *d*; 2nd, 1975, Jack Emery. *Educ:* Stockport High Sch. for Girls; Newnham Coll., Cambridge (BA History and Econs). Associate, 1980–91, Associate Fellow, 1984–87, Newnham Coll., Cambridge. Gov., BFI, 1994–. Pres., Soc. of Arts Publicists, 1984–90. *BBC Television incl:* Meeting Point, 1964; The Second Sex, 1964; Late Night Line Up, 1965–72; The Youthful Eye, 1968; Moviemakers at the National Film Theatre, 1971; Film 72, and Film 73, 1972–73; For the Sake of Appearance, Where is Your God?, Who Cares?, and The Affirmative Way (series), 1973; Holiday '74, '75, '76, '77 and '78 (series); What's it all About? (2 series) and Time Running Out (series), 1974; The Shakespeare Business, The Brontë Business, and Generation to Generation (series), 1976; My Day with the Children, 1977; The Moving Line, 1979; Arts UK: OK?, 1980; Arts Correspondent, 1981–87; The Heart of the Matter, 1988–. *ITV incl.* Sunday Break, 1962; Home at 4.30, 1964; (writer and producer) Thank You, Ron (documentary), 1974; Fairest Fortune and Edinburgh Festival Report, 1974; Reports Action (4 series), 1976–78. *Radio:* Away from it All, 1978–79; PM, 1979–81; plays: There and Back; Parish Magazine. *Theatre:* Brontës: The Private Faces, Edinburgh Fest., 1979. *Publications:* (with Nicholas Garnham) The New Priesthood: British television today, 1970; (with John Drummond) A Fine and Private Place, 1977; The Complete Traveller, 1977; journalism for Punch, Radio Times; Television Critic of The Times, 1978–81; columnist, Sunday Times, 1988–90. *Recreations:* theatre, travel, talk. *Address:* Knight Ayton Management, 70A Berwick Street, W1V 3PE.

BALCHIN, John Alfred; General Manager, Stevenage Development Corporation, 1969–76, retired; *b* 8 Aug. 1914; *er s* of Alfred and Florence Balchin; *m* 1st, 1940, Elsie Dormer (*d* 1982); one *s* two *d*; 2nd, 1986, Edna Bilton (*née* Morgan). *Educ:* Sir Walter St John's Sch., Battersea; Sir John Cass Coll., City of London. DPA (London), DMA, FCIS, FCIH. LCC Clerk's Dept, 1932–38; civil defence co-ordination work, 1938–45; to Housing Dept, 1946–65; Principal Clerk, 1952; Asst Dir (Finance), 1960; Asst Dir (Housing Management), 1963; Sen. Asst Dir of Housing, GLC, 1965–69. Assoc. Sen. Lectr, for Housing Management and Administration, Brunel Univ., 1969–71. Member: Housing Services Adv. Gp, DoE, 1976–80; North British Housing Assoc., 1976–89; Auriol Housing Foundn, 1986–88. *Publications:* Housing: programming and development of estates, 1971, revd edn 1978; Housing Management: history, principles and practice, 1972; Housing Studies, 1st series, 1979, 2nd series, 1980, revd edn 1981; First New Town: an autobiography of the Stevenage Development Corporation, 1980. *Address:* Rhoswiel Lodge, Weston Rhyn, Oswestry, Shropshire SY10 7TG. *T:* Chirk (01691) 773139.

BALCHIN, Sir Robert (George Alexander), Kt 1993; Chairman, The Grant-Maintained Schools Foundation (formerly Trust), since 1989; *b* 31 July 1942; *s* of late Leonard George and Elizabeth Balchin; *m* 1970, Jennifer, SSStJ, BA (Mus), ACP, *d* of late Bernard Kevin Kinlay, Cape Town; twin *s*. *Educ:* Bec Sch.; Univs of London (Teaching Cert.) and Hull. (MEd, Adv. DipEd). Asst Master, Chinthurst Sch., 1964–68; Hd of English Dept, Ewell Sch., 1968–69; Res., Univ. of Hull Inst. of Educn, 1969–71; Headmaster, Hill Sch., Westerham, 1972–80; Company Director, 1980–; Chairman: Pardoe-Blacker (Publishing) Ltd, 1989–; Grant-Maintained Schs Mutual Insce Ltd, 1992–. St John Ambulance: Nat. Schs Advr, 1978–82; Asst Dir-Gen., 1982–84; Dir-Gen., 1984–90; Mem. Chapter-Gen., Order of St John, 1984–. Mem. Council, Imperial Soc. of Kts Bachelor, 1995–. Member: Standing Conf. on Sch. Sci. and Technol., 1976–79; FAS, 1994– (Chm., New Schs Cttee, 1994–); Jt Founder/Treas., Catch 'em Young Project Trust, 1984–; Chm./Founder, Campaign for a Gen. Teaching Council, 1981–85; Chm., St John Nat. Schs Project, 1990–. Mem. Editorial Bd, Education Today, 1981–87. Mem., Centre for Policy Studies, 1982–; Lecture Sec., Heraldry Soc., 1982–88; Chm., Balchin Family Soc., 1993–. Trustee, Adeline Genée Th., 1982–87. Mem., Surrey CC, 1981–85 (Mem., Educn and Social Services Cttees); Vice-Pres., Lambeth Cons. Assoc., 1976–81; Treas., E Surrey Cons. Assoc., 1982–85; Cons. Party Dep. Area Treas., 1983–86; Cons. Vice-Chm. (SE Area), 1986–89; Cons. Bd of Finance, 1990–93; Cons. Party Chm. for SE England, 1993–96 (Treas., 1990–93); Consultant-Dir, Cons. Central Office, 1988–93. Hon. Mem. CGLI, 1983. FCP 1971 (Hon. FCP 1987); Hon. FHS 1987. Hon. DPhil Northland Open Univ., Canada, 1985. Freeman, 1980, Liveryman, 1987, Goldsmiths' Co. KStJ 1984. Cross of Merit (Comdr), SMO Malta, 1987; Comdr, Order of Polonia Restituta, 1990. *Publications:* Emergency Aid in Schools, 1984; New Money, 1985, 2nd edn 1989; (jtly) Choosing a State School, 1989; (jtly) Emergency Aid at Work, 1990; numerous articles on educn/politics. *Address:* New Place, Lingfield, Surrey RH7 6EF. *T:* Lingfield (Surrey) (01342) 834543; 88 Marsham Court, Westminster, SW1P 4LA. *Clubs:* Athenæum, St Stephen's Constitutional.

BALCHIN, Prof. William George Victor, MA, PhD; FKC; FRGS, FRMetS; Emeritus Professor of Geography in the University of Wales (Swansea), 1978 (Professor of Geography, 1954–78); *b* 20 June 1916; *s* of Victor Balchin and Ellen Winifred Gertrude Chapple; *m* 1939, Lily Kettlewood; one *s* one *d* (and one *d* decd). *Educ:* Aldershot County High Sch. (State Scholar and County Major Scholar, 1934); St Catharine's Coll., Cambridge (1st Cl. Pt I Geographical Tripos, 1936; College Prize for Geography, 1936; BA 1937; MA 1941). PhD KCL 1951; FKC 1984. FRGS 1937; FRMetS 1945. Jun. Demonstrator in Geog., Univ. of Cambridge, 1937–39 (Geomorphologist on Spitsbergen Expedn, 1938); Hydrographic Officer, Hydrographic Dept, Admiralty, 1939–45 (also part-time Lectr for Univ. of Bristol Regional Cttee on Educn and WEA Tutor and Lectr); Lectr in Geog., KCL, 1945–54 (Geomorphologist on US Sonora-Mohave Desert Expedn, 1952); University Coll. of Swansea, Univ. of Wales: Head, Dept of Geog., 1954–78; Dean, Faculty of Pure and Applied Science, 1959–61; Vice-Principal, 1964–66 and 1970–73. Leverhulme Emeritus Fellow, 1982. Royal Geographical Society: Open Essay Prize, 1936; Gill Meml Award, 1954; Mem. Council, 1962–65, 1975–82, 1984–88; Chm., Educn Cttee, 1975–88; Vice-Pres., 1978–82; Chm., Ordnance Survey Cons. Cttee for Educn, 1983–92. Geographical Association: Hon. Annual Conf. Organiser, 1950–54; Mem. Council, 1950–81; Trustee, 1954–77; Pres., 1971; Hon. Mem., 1980. Pres., Section E (Geog.), BAAS, 1972. Member: Met. Res. Cttee, MoD, 1963–69; British Nat. Cttee for Cartography, 1961–71 and 1976–79, for Geography, 1964–70 and 1976–78; Council, British Geography, 1988–92. Treasurer, Second Land Utilisation Survey of Britain, 1961–; Chm., Land Decade Educnl Council, 1978–83. Mem., Nature Conservancy Cttee for Wales, 1959–68; Vice-Pres., Glam Co. Naturalists' Trust, 1961–80. Pres., Balchin Family Hist. Soc., 1993–. Member: Hydrology Cttee, ICE, 1962–76; Bradford Univ. Disaster Prevention and Limitation Unit, 1989–. Member, Court of Governors: Nat. Mus. of Wales, 1966–74; UCW, Swansea, 1980–; Mem. Council, St David's UC, 1968–80. *Publications:* (ed) Geography and Man (3 vols), 1947; (with A. W. Richards) Practical and Experimental Geography, 1952; Cornwall (The Making of the English Landscape Series), 1954; (ed and contrib.) Geography: an outline for the intending student, 1970; (ed and contrib.) Swansea and its Region, 1971; (ed and contrib.) Living History of Britain, 1981; Concern for Geography, 1981; The Cornish Landscape, 1983; The Geographical Association: the first hundred years, 1993; over 150 res. papers, articles and contribs on geomorphology, climatology, hydrology, econ. geography and cartography in learned jls. *Recreations:* travel, writing. *Address:* 10 Low Wood Rise, Ben Rhydding, Ilkley, West Yorks LS29 8AZ. *T:* Ilkley (01943) 600768. *Clubs:* Commonwealth Trust, Geographical.

BALCOMBE, Rt. Hon. Sir (Alfred) John, Kt 1977; PC 1985; a Lord Justice of Appeal, 1985–95; *b* 29 Sept. 1925; *er s* of late Edwin Kesteven Balcombe; *m* 1950, Jacqueline Rosemary, *yr d* of late Julian Cowan; two *s* one *d*. *Educ:* Winchester (schol.); New Coll., Oxford (exhibnr). Served, 1943–47: Royal Signals; commnd 1945. BA 1949 (1st class Hons Jurisprudence), MA 1950. Called to Bar, Lincoln's Inn, 1950, Bencher 1977; QC 1969; practised at Chancery Bar, 1951–77; Judge of the High Court of Justice, Family Div., 1977–85; Judge of the Employment Appeal Tribunal, 1983–85. Mem., Gen. Council of the Bar, 1967–71. Lectures: Maccabæan, British Acad., 1993; Stevens, RSocMed, 1995. Chm., London Marriage Guidance Council, 1982–88. Master, Worshipful Company of Tin Plate Workers, 1971–72. *Publications:* Exempt Private Companies, 1953; (ed) Estoppel, in Halsbury's Laws of England, 4th edn. *Address:* Alban Place, 1A Lingfield Road, Wimbledon, SW19 4QA. *T:* 0181–947 0980. *Club:* Garrick.

BALCOMBE, Frederick James; Lord Mayor of Manchester, 1974–75, Deputy Lord Mayor, 1975–76; *b* 17 Dec. 1911; *s* of late Sidney and late Agnes Balcombe; *m* 1st, 1936, Clarice (*née* Cassel) (*d* 1949); two *s* (and two *c* decd); 2nd, 1956, Rhoda (*née* Jaffe) (*d* 1989); one *d*. *Educ:* St Anthony's RC Sch., Forest Gate; West Ham Secondary Central Sch., Stratford, London. Served War of 1939–45, RAF (commnd). Chm., family co. of insurance loss assessors. President: Manchester and District Fedn of Community Assocs, 1962–78; Manchester and District Allotments Council, 1963–78; Higher Blackley Community Assoc., 1963–; Vice-President: Blackley Prize Band, 1964–; Mem., League of Friends, and Cttee, and Hon. Treas., Crumpsall Hosp., 1964–72; connected with 199th Manchester Scout Gp. Mem. Manchester City Council, Crumpsall Ward, subseq. St Peter's Ward, Collegiate Church Ward, 1958–82; served as Chm. Central Purchasing Cttee, 1964–67, Gen. and Parly (now Policy), Markets, 1958–82, Airports, 1971–82 (Chm.), Parks, 1958–67, and Finance, 1964–73, Cttees (Dep. Chm.). Chm., Manchester Internat. Airport, 1975–79. Mem., Airport Owners' Assoc., 1979–82. Founder, Hillel House, Manchester Univ, 1958 (Hon. Sec., 1958–68, now Sen. Life Vice-Pres.); Chm. of Governors, Coll. of Building, Manchester, 1964–67; Mem. Council, BBC Radio Manchester, 1970–76; Mem. Council, Manchester and Salford Police Authority, 1968–74; Mem., AMC Rating Cttee, 1973–74. Mem., Bd of Deputies of British Jews, 1956–64; Mem., Council, Manchester and Salford Jews, 1958– (Exec. Mem., 1963–68); Founder Mem., Manchester Jewish Blind Soc., 1956– (Hon. Sec. 13 years, now Vice-Pres.); Adjutant, Jewish Lads' Brigade and Club, Manchester, 1946–49, Chm. 1972–78. Trustee/Mem., NW Liver Research, 1986–. Governor, King David Schs, Manchester, 1954–84; Vice-Pres., Fedn of Boys' Clubs, 1969–; President: Manchester Cttee, Central British Fund, 1969–; RAFA Manchester South, 1981–84; Manchester City Swimming Club, 1981–90. Founder Mem., Variety Club of Israel, 1972; Barker of Variety Club, 1970– (Chm. Manchester Cttee, 1976). JP Manchester, 1967–. Mem. Jewish Faith. Life long blood donor. *Recreations:* family, communal endeavour, swimming, walking. *Address:* Flat 3, Filleigh Park Road, Bowdon, Cheshire WA14 3JG. *T:* 0161–929 0847; (office) 0161–941 6231.

BALCOMBE, Rt. Hon. Sir John; *see* Balcombe, Rt. Hon. Sir A. J.

BALCON, Dr Raphael, MD; FRCP, FACC; Consultant Cardiologist, Royal Brompton & National Heart and Lung Hospitals NHS Trust; *b* 26 Aug. 1936; *s* of Henry and Rhoda Balcon; *m* 1959, Elizabeth Ann Henry; one *d*. *Educ:* King's Coll., London; King's Coll. Hosp. Med. Sch. (MB, BS 1960, MD 1969). LRCP, MRCS 1960, MRCP 1965, FRCP 1977; FACC 1973. House Phys., Med. Unit, KCH, 1960; House Surg., KCH, Dulwich, 1960; House Phys., London Chest Hosp., 1961; Sen. House Officer, St Stephen's Hosp., 1962; Public Health Fellow in Cardiology, Wayne State Univ. Med. Sch., USA, 1963; British Heart Foundn Fellow, Dept of Cardiol., KCH, 1964, Med. Registrar 1965; Registrar, then Sen. Registrar, National Heart Hosp., 1966–70; Consultant Cardiologist, Nat. Heart and Chest Hosps, London Chest Hosp., subseq. Royal Brompton and Nat. Heart and Lung Hosps, Victoria Park, now Royal Brompton & Nat. Heart and Lung Hosps NHS Trust, 1970–. Dean, Cardiothoracic Inst., 1976–80. Hon. Treasurer, 1981–86, Pres., 1995–, British Cardiac Soc. *Publications:* contrib. books on cardiological subjects; papers in BMJ, Lancet, Brit. Heart Jl, Amer. Jl of Cardiol., Circulation, Eur. Jl of Cardiol., Acta Medica Scandinavica. *Recreations:* ski-ing, tennis, mountain walking.

BALDERSTONE, Sir James (Schofield), AC 1992; Kt 1983; company director, now retired, and grazier; Chairman: Australian Mutual Provident Society, 1990–93 (Director, 1979–93); Chase AMP Bank, 1990–91 (Director, 1985–91); Broken Hill Proprietary Co. Ltd, 1984–89 (Director, 1971–89); Stanbroke Pastoral Co., 1982–93 (Managing Director, 1964–81); *b* 2 May 1921; *s* of late James Schofield and Mary Essendon Balderstone; *m* 1946, Mary Henrietta Tyree; two *s* two *d*. *Educ:* Scotch College, Melbourne. Service with RANR, WWII, 1940–45. General Manager for Aust., Thos Borthwick & Sons, 1953–67; Dep. Chm., Westpac Banking Corp., 1992–93 (Dir, 1981–84); Director: NW Shelf Develt Pty, 1976–83; Woodside Petroleum, 1976–83; ICI (Australia), 1981–84. Founding Chm., Australian Meat Exporters' Fed. Council, 1963–64; Mem., Australian Meat Bd, 1964–67. Chairman: Commonwealth Govt Policy Discussion Gp on Agriculture, 1981–82; Scotch Coll. Council, 1991–. Mem., Council, Aust. War Meml, 1994–. Patron, Australian British Chamber of Commerce. Pres., Inst. of Public Affairs (Vic.), 1981–84. DUniv Newcastle, NSW, 1985. Commander's Cross, Order of Merit (Germany), 1991. *Recreations:* farming, reading, sport. *Address:* 115 Mont Albert Road, Canterbury, Victoria 3126, Australia. *T:* (3) 8363137. *Clubs:* Australian, Melbourne (Melbourne); Union (Sydney), Queensland (Brisbane).

BALDOCK, Brian Ford; Director, since 1986, Group Managing Director, since 1989, and Deputy Chairman, since 1992, Guinness PLC; *b* 10 June 1934; *s* of Ernest A. and Florence F. Baldock; *m* 1st, 1956, Mary Lillian Bartolo (marr. diss. 1966); two *s*; 2nd, 1968, Carole Anthea Mason; one *s*. *Educ:* Clapham Coll., London. Army Officer, 1952–55. Procter & Gamble, 1956–61; Ted Bates Inc., 1961–63; Rank Orgn, 1963–66; Smith & Nephew, 1966–75; Revlon Inc., 1975–78; Imperial Group, 1978–86. Chm., Portman Group, 1989–; Dir, Dalgety. Freeman, City of London, 1989. CInstM 1991 (FInstM 1976); Fellow, Marketing Soc., 1988. FRSA 1987. *Recreations:* theatre (opera), cricket. *Address:* The White House, Donnington, Newbury, Berks RG13 2JT. *T:* Newbury (01635) 41200. *Clubs:* Mark's, Lord's Taverners (Mem. Council; Chm., 1992–).

BALDOCK, John Markham, VRD 1949; Lieutenant Commander RNVR 1948; Chairman Lenscrete Ltd, 1949; Director CIBA-GEIGY (UK) Ltd; *b* 19 Nov. 1915; *s* of late Captain W. P. Baldock, and Mrs H. Chalcraft; *m* 1949, Pauline Ruth Gauntlett; two *s*. *Educ:* Rugby Sch.; Balliol Coll., Oxford. Agric. degree, 1937. Served War of 1939–45, with Royal Navy, Atlantic, Mediterranean, Indian Ocean; Russian convoys, 1942–43. Lloyds, EC3, 1945. Joined Board of Lenscrete, 1946. MP (C) Harborough Div. of Leics, 1950–Sept. 1959, retd, also as Parl. Private Sec. to Rt Hon. D. Ormsby Gore (Minister of State, Foreign Office). Founder, Hollycombe steam collection and steam fair. *Recreations:* country life, sailing, steam engines, industrial archæology, theatre. *Address:* Duffryn, Wheatsheaf Enclosure, Liphook, Hants GU30 7EJ. *T:* Liphook (01428) 723233. *Club:* Farmers'.

BALDOCK, Lionel Trevor; Agent-General for Victoria, 1990–93; *b* 26 Nov. 1936; *s* of late Lionel Vernon Baldock and of Alice Thelma Baldock; *m* 1967, Carolynne Cutting (marr. diss.); one *s* one *d*. *Educ:* Melbourne Univ. (BCom). Man. Dir, Evasoft Leather Co., 1958–73; General Manager: Tecnicast Pty Ltd, 1974–80; (also Dir) Centrifugal Castings Australia Pty Ltd, 1974–80; J. C. & Howard Wright Pty Ltd, 1983–84; Pacific Dunlop Ltd (NSW), 1984–85; Sen. Trade Comr, Australian Trade Commn, Paris, 1985–90. *Recreations:* swimming, ski-ing, sailing, walking. *Clubs:* Royal Automobile, Royal Overseas League; Royal Automobile, Royal South Yarra Lawn Tennis (Melbourne).

BALDOCK, (Richard) Stephen; High Master, St Paul's School, since 1992; *b* 19 Nov. 1944; *s* of John Allan Baldock and Marjorie Procter Baldock; *m* 1969, Dr Janet Elizabeth Cottrell; one *s* three *d*. *Educ:* St Paul's Sch.; King's Coll., Cambridge (John Stewart of Rannoch schol. in Greek and Latin 1964; BA 1967 Part I Classics, Part II Theology, MA 1970). St Paul's School: Asst Master, 1970–77; Housemaster, School House, 1977–84; Surmaster, 1984–92. Council Mem. and Educnl Advr, Overseas Missionary Fellowship, 1989–. Governor: Newland House Prep. Sch., Twickenham, 1987–; Durston House Prep. Sch., Ealing, 1992–; Hall Sch., Hampstead, 1993–. *Recreations:* family, computers, sport. *Address:* St Paul's School, Lonsdale Road, Barnes, SW13 9JT. *T:* 0181–748 8135. *Clubs:* East India, Devonshire, Sports and Public Schools, MCC.

BALDRY, Antony Brian, (Tony); MP (C) Banbury, since 1983; Minister of State, Ministry of Agriculture, Fisheries and Food, since 1995; *b* 10 July 1950; *e s* of Peter Edward Baldry and Oina (*née* Paterson); *m* 1979, Catherine Elizabeth, 2nd *d* of Captain James Weir, RN and Elizabeth Weir; one *s* one *d*. *Educ:* Leighton Park Sch., Reading; Univ. of Sussex (BA, LLB). Called to the Bar, Lincoln's Inn, 1975; barrister. Director: New Opportunity Press, 1975–90; Newpoint Publishing Gp, 1983–90. Contested (C) Thurrock, 1979. PPS to Minister of State for Foreign and Commonwealth Affairs, 1986–87, to Lord Privy Seal and Leader of the House, 1987–89, to Sec. of State for Energy, 1989–90; Parliamentary Under-Secretary of State: Dept of Energy, 1990; DoE, 1990–94; FCO, 1994–95. Mem., Parly Select Cttee on Employment, 1983–86. Joined Sussex Yeomanry, 1971; TA Officer, resigned 1990. Robert Schuman Silver Medal, Stiftung FVS Hamburg, 1978. *Recreations:* walking in the country, reading historical biography, gardening, cricket, beagling. *Address:* House of Commons, SW1A 0AA. *Clubs:* Carlton; Brass Monkey; Banbury Conservative.

BALDRY, Jack Thomas; Director, Purchasing and Supplies, Post Office, 1969–72; *b* 5 Oct. 1911; *s* of late John and Ellen Baldry; *m* 1936, Ruby Berenice (*née* Frost); three *d*. *Educ:* Framlingham Coll. Post Office: Asst Traffic Supt, 1930; Asst Surveyor, 1935; Asst Princ., 1940; Princ., 1947 (Private Sec. to PMG, 1950–53); Asst Sec., 1953; Dep. Dir, External Telecommunications, 1960; Dir of Personnel, 1967. *Recreations:* farming, foreign travel. *Address:* Village End, Bruisyard Road, Badingham, Woodbridge IP13 8NA. *T:* Badingham (01728) 638331.

BALDRY, Tony; *see* Baldry, A. B.

BALDWIN, family name of **Earl Baldwin of Bewdley.**

BALDWIN OF BEWDLEY, 4th Earl *cr* 1937; **Edward Alfred Alexander Baldwin;** Viscount Corvedale, 1937; *b* 3 Jan. 1938; *o s* of 3rd Earl Baldwin of Bewdley and Joan Elspeth, *y d* of late C. Alexander Tomes, New York, USA; *S* father, 1976; *m* 1970, Sarah MacMurray, *er d* of Evan James, *qv;* three *s*. *Educ:* Eton; Trinity Coll., Cambridge (MA, PGCE). Chm., British Acupuncture Accreditation Bd, 1990–. Jt Chm., Parly Gp for Alternative and Complementary Medicine, 1992–. *Heir: s* Viscount Corvedale, *qv*. *Address:* Manor Farm House, Godstow Road, Upper Wolvercote, Oxford OX2 8AJ. *T:* Oxford (01865) 52683. *Club:* MCC.

BALDWIN, Alan Charles; Metropolitan Stipendiary Magistrate, since 1990; *b* 14 April 1948; *s* of Frederick Baldwin and Millicent Baldwin (*née* McCarthy); *m* 1974, Denise Maureen Jagger; two *s*. Admitted Solicitor, 1976. *Address:* Marylebone Magistrates' Court, 181 Marylebone Road, NW1 5QJ.

BALDWIN, David Arthur, CBE 1990; Chairman, Hewlett-Packard Ltd, since 1988; *b* 1 Sept. 1936; *s* of late Isaac Arthur Baldwin and Edith Mary Baldwin (*née* Collins); *m* 1961, (Jacqueline) Anne Westcott; one *s* one *d*. *Educ:* Twickenham Technical Coll.; Wimbledon Technical Coll. (qualified electronic engineer). CEng, FIEE; FCIM. R&D Engineer, EMI, 1954–63; Sales Engineer, Solartron, 1963–65; Hewlett-Packard: Sales Engineer and Sales Manager, 1965–73; European Marketing Manager, 1973–78; Man. Dir, Hewlett-Packard Ltd, 1978–88. Man. Dir, Hewlett-Packard Europ. Multi-Country Region, 1990–; Pres., Hewlett-Packard Belgium, 1991–; Chm., Hewlett-Packard Spain, 1991–; Director, Hewlett-Packard Finland, Sweden, Denmark, Netherlands and Austria. Mem. Court, Cranfield Inst. of Technol., 1987–. DUniv Strathclyde, 1990. *Recreations:* golf, ski-ing, photography, painting, sailing. *Address:* Hewlett-Packard Ltd, Cain Road, Bracknell, Berks RG12 1HN. *T:* Bracknell (01344) 360000. *Club:* Royal Automobile.

BALDWIN, Captain George Clifton, CBE 1968; DSC 1941 and Bar 1944; RN (retd); Member: Press Council, 1973–78; Press Council Appointments Commission, 1978–90; *b* 17 Jan. 1921; *s* of late George and late Louisa Baldwin; *m* 1947, Hasle Mary McMahon; three *s*. *Educ:* Sleaford Grammar Sch., Lincs; Hitchin Grammar Sch., Herts. Served War: joined RN, 1939, Pilot in Fleet Air Arm; in comd: 807 Sqdn, 1943; No 4 Naval Fighter Wing, 1944–45. Qual. at Empire Test Pilots' Sch., 1946; in comd, 800 Sqdn, 1952; in comd, RN Air Station, Lossiemouth, 1961–62; IDC course, 1963; Dir, Naval Air Warfare, MoD, 1964–66; in comd, RN Air Station, Yeovilton, 1966–68; ADC, 1967; retd, 1968. Chm., Fleet Air Arm Officers' Assoc., 1973–78 (Vice Pres., 1978–). *Address:* Applegarth, Church Lane, Lodsworth, Petworth, West Sussex GU28 9DD. *T:* Lodsworth (01798) 861236.

BALDWIN, Prof. Jack Edward, PhD; FRS 1978; Waynflete Professor of Chemistry and Fellow of Magdalen College, University of Oxford, since 1978; *b* 8 Aug. 1938; *s* of Frederick Charles Baldwin and Olive Frances Headland; *m* 1977, Christine Louise, *d* of William B. Franchi. *Educ:* Lewes County Grammar Sch.; Imperial Coll., London Univ. (BSc, DIC, PhD). ARCS. Asst Lectr in Chem., Imperial Coll., 1963, Lectr, 1966; Asst Prof. of Chem., Pa State Univ., 1967, Associate Prof., 1969; Alfred P. Sloan Fellow, 1969–70, Associate Prof. of Chem., 1970, Prof., 1972, MIT; Daniell Prof. of Chem., King's Coll., London, 1972; Prof. of Chem., MIT, 1972–78. Mem., BBSRC, 1994–. Lectures: Tilden, RSC, 1979; Simonsen, RSC, 1982. Corresp. Mem., Academia Scientiarum Gottingensis, Göttingen, 1988. Hon. DSc: Warwick, 1988, Strathclyde, 1989. Corday Morgan Medal and Prize, Chem. Soc., 1975; Medal and Prize for Synthetic Organic Chemistry, RSC, 1980; Paul Karrer Medal and Prize, Zürich Univ., 1984; Medal and Prize for Natural Product Chemistry, RSC, 1984; Hugo Müller Medal, RSC, 1987; Max Tischler Award, Harvard Univ., 1987; Dr Paul Jansen Prize for Creativity in Organic Synthesis, Belgium, 1988; Davy Medal, Royal Soc., 1994. *Publications:* res. pubns in Jl of Amer. Chem. Soc., Jl of Chem. Soc., Tetrahedron. *Address:* Dyson Perrins Laboratory, South Parks Road, Oxford OX1 3QY.

BALDWIN, John, OBE 1978; National Secretary, Amalgamated Engineering Union (formerly Amalgamated Union of Engineering Workers) Workers/Construction Section, 1976–88; *b* 16 Aug. 1923; *s* of Stephen John Baldwin and Elizabeth (*née* Hutchinson); *m* 1945, Grace May Florence (*née* Wilson); two *d*. *Educ:* Laindon High Road Sen. Sch., Essex. Boy service, RN, HMS Ganges, 1938; returned to civilian life, 1948; Steel Erector, CEU, 1950; played active part as Shop Steward and Site Convenor; elected full-time official, 1957; Asst Gen. Sec., AUEW/Construction Sect., 1969–76. Chm., Mechanical Handling Sector Working Party of NEDO; Member: Engrg Construction EDC, 1975–; Construction Equipment and Mobile Cranes Sector Working Party of NEDO; National Jt Council for the Engrg Construction Industry. Mem., Labour Party, 1962–. *Recreations:* most sports. *Address:* 7 Ridge Langley, Sanderstead, South Croydon, Surrey CR2 0AP. *T:* 0181–651 1643.

BALDWIN, Prof. John Evan, PhD; FRS 1991; Professor of Radioastronomy, and Fellow of Queens' College, University of Cambridge, since 1989; Head of Mullard Radio Astronomy Observatory, Cavendish Laboratory, since 1987; *b* 6 Dec. 1931; *s* of Evan Baldwin and Mary Wild; *m* 1969, Joyce Cox. *Educ:* Merchant Taylors', Crosby; Queens' Coll., Cambridge (MA; Clerk Maxwell Student, 1955–57; PhD 1956). Cambridge University: Research Fellow, later Fellow, Queens' Coll., 1956–74; Univ. Demonstrator in Physics, 1957–62; Asst Dir of Research, 1962–81; Reader, 1981–89. *Publications:* contribs to scientific jls. *Recreations:* gardening, mountain walking. *Address:* Cavendish Laboratory, Madingley Road, Cambridge CB3 0HE. *T:* Cambridge (01223) 337299.

BALDWIN, Dr John Paul; QC 1991; *b* 15 Aug. 1947; *s* of Frank Baldwin and of late Marjorie Baldwin (*née* Jay); *m* 1981, Julie Campbell; two *d*. *Educ:* Nelson Grammar Sch.; Univ. of Leeds (BSc 1st Cl. Hons 1968); St John's Coll., Oxford (DPhil 1972). Res. Fellow, Univ. of Oxford, 1972–75; called to the Bar, Gray's Inn, 1977. *Publications:* numerous scientific pubns, 1969–75. *Recreations:* tennis, gardening. *Address:* 8 New Square, Lincoln's Inn, WC2A 3QP. *T:* 0171–405 4321. *Clubs:* Harbour, Campden Hill Lawn Tennis; Portcullis (Wallingford).

BALDWIN, Air Vice-Marshal Nigel Bruce, CBE 1992; Assistant Chief of Defence Staff (Overseas), since 1993; *b* 20 Sept. 1941; *s* of Peter William Baldwin and Doris Baldwin; *m* 1963, Jennifer; one *d* (and one *d* decd). *Educ:* Peter Symonds' Sch., Winchester; RAF Coll., Cranwell. Pilot, Vulcans, 9/35 Sqns, 1963–68; ADC to AOC 11 Gp, 1968–70; Sqn Ldr, Vulcans, 35 Sqn, Cyprus, 1970–73; Staff Coll., Bracknell, 1974; HQ Strike Command, 1975–76; OC 50 Sqn, Vulcans, 1977–79; US Air War Coll. and Faculty, US Air Command and Staff Coll., 1979–82; Gp Captain and Station Comdr, Wyton, 1983–85; Internat. Fellow, Nat. Defense Univ., Washington, 1986; Asst Dir of Defence Policy, MoD, 1986–88; Air Cdre Plans, HQ Strike Command, 1989–92. *Recreations:* hill walking, Schubert, Nelson. *Address:* Ministry of Defence, Main Building, Whitehall, SW1A 2HB. *T:* 0171–218 7170. *Club:* Royal Air Force.

BALDWIN, Maj.-Gen. Peter Alan Charles, CBE 1994; Consultant, Thomson Foundation, since 1995; *b* 19 Feb. 1927; *s* of Alec Baldwin and Anne Dance; *m* 1st, 1953, Judith Elizabeth Mace; 2nd, 1982, Gail J. Roberts. *Educ:* King Edward VI Grammar Sch., Chelmsford. Enlisted 1942; commnd R Signals 1947; early service included Berlin, 1948–49 (during airlift), and Korean War, 1950; Staff Coll., 1960; JSSC, 1964; Borneo operations (despatches, 1967); Directing Staff, Staff Coll., 1967–69; Comdr, 13 Signal Regt, BAOR, 1969–71; Sec. for Studies, NATO Defence Coll., 1971–74; Comdr, 2 Signal Group, 1974–76; ACOS Jt Exercises Div., Allied Forces Central Europe, 1976–77; Maj.-Gen. and Chief Signal Officer, BAOR, 1977–79. Dep. Dir of Radio, 1979–87, Dir of Radio, 1987–90, IBA; Chief Exec., Radio Authy, 1991–95. Fellow, Radio Acad., 1992; FRSA 1993. *Recreations:* cricket, music, theatre. *Address:* c/o Lloyds Bank, 7 Pall Mall, SW1Y 5NA. *Clubs:* Army and Navy, MCC.

BALDWIN, Sir Peter (Robert), KCB 1977 (CB 1973); MA; Chairman, SE Thames Regional Health Authority, 1983–91; *b* 10 Nov. 1922; *s* of Charles Baldwin and Katie Baldwin (*née* Field); *m* 1951, Margaret Helen Moar; two *s*. *Educ:* City of London Sch.; Corpus Christi Coll., Oxford (Hon. Fellow, 1980). Foreign Office, 1942–45; Gen. Register Office, 1948–54; HM Treasury, 1954–62; Cabinet Office, 1962–64; HM Treasury, 1964–76; Principal Private Sec. to Chancellor of Exchequer, July 1966–Jan. 1968; Under-Sec., HM Treasury, 1968–72; Dep. Sec., HM Treasury, 1972–76; Second Permanent Sec., DoE, 1976; Permanent Sec., Dept of Transport, 1976–82. Dir, Mitchell Cotts, 1983–87; Chairman: Rural Village Develt Foundn, 1983–85 (Vice-Chm., 1985–90); Brent Dial-a-Ride, 1983–85; Westminster Dial-a-Ride, 1984–87; Community Transport, 1985–87; Tripscope, 1986–; Disabled Persons Transport Adv. Cttee, 1986–; Exec. Cttee, RADAR, 1992– (Mem., 1983–); Kent Air Ambulance Appeal, 1992–94; President: Readibus, 1981–84; Disability Action Westminster, 1986– (Chm., 1983–86); Hearing Dogs for the Deaf, 1987– (Chm., 1983–86); Vice-President: RNID, 1983–91; Disabled Drivers Motoring Club, 1985–; PHAB, 1988– (Vice-Chm., 1981, Chm., 1982–88; Vice-Pres., N Ireland, 1990–); Mem. Bd, 1988–, Chm., 1994–, Charities Aid Foundn (Vice Chm., 1993). Member: Cttee, AA, 1983–93 (Vice-Chm., 1990–; Chm., AA Road Safety Res. Foundn, 1990–); Nat. Railway Mus. Cttee, 1983–87; Bd, Public Finance Foundn, 1984–; Bd, RSA Exams, 1989–; Bd, City Lit. Inst., 1990–; Council, KCL, 1992–; Chairman: Council, Royal Soc. of Arts, 1985–87 (Vice-Pres., 1987–; FRSA); Delegacy, KCH Med. and Dental Sch., 1991–; Bd of Govs, UMDS of Guy's and St Thomas's Hosp., 1993–. Life Vice-Pres., Civil Service Sports Council, 1982– (Chm., 1978–82; Vice-Chm., 1974–78). Chm., St Catherine's Home and Sch., Ventnor, 1961–78; Governor, Eltham Coll., 1984–85. Trustee, Pets as Therapy, 1990–. FKC; FCIT; Hon. FIHT; CIMgt. Freeman, City of London, 1992. *Recreations:* painting, watching cricket. *Address:* 123 Alderney Street, SW1V 4HE. *T:* 0171–821 7157. *Club:* Reform.

BALES, Kenneth Frederick, CBE 1990; Regional Managing Director, West Midlands Regional Health Authority, 1984–92; *b* 2 March 1931; *s* of Frederick Charles Bales and Deborah Alice Bales; *m* 1958, Margaret Hazel Austin; two *s* one *d*. *Educ:* Buckhurst Hill Grammar Sch.; LSE; Univ. of Manchester. BScSoc; DipSocAdmin. Hosp. Sec., Newhall & Hesketh Park Hosps, 1958–62; Regional Trng Officer, Birmingham Regional Hosp. Bd, 1962–65; Regional Staff Officer, Birmingham Regional Staff Cttee, 1965–68; Group Sec., W Birmingham HMC, 1968–73; Regional Administrator, W Midlands RHA, 1973–84. Associate, Inst. Health Service Management. *Recreations:* painting, sport. *Address:* Stronefield, 4 St Catherine's Close, Blackwell, near Bromsgrove, Worcestershire B60 1BP. *T:* 0121–445 1424.

BALFE, Richard Andrew; Member (Lab) London South Inner, European Parliament, since 1979; Chair, Political Committee, Co-operative Wholesale Society, since 1984; *b* 14 May 1944; *s* of Dr Richard J. Balfe and Mrs Dorothy L. Balfe (*née* de Cann); *m* 1986, Susan Jane Honeyford; one *s* one *d*, and one *s* by a previous marriage. *Educ:* Brook Secondary Sch., Sheffield; LSE (BSc Hons 1971). Fellow Royal Statistical Soc., 1972. HM Diplomatic Service, 1965–70; Res. Officer, Finer Cttee on One Parent Families, 1970–73; Political Sec., RACS, 1973–79; Dir, RACS and associated cos, 1978–85. European Parliament: Quaestor, 1994–; Member: Foreign and Security Cttee, 1981–; Civil Liberties Cttee, 1994–; spokesman on defence; Mem. for relns between EP and Near East. Parly Candidate (Labour), Paddington South, 1970; contested (Lab) Southwark and Bermondsey, 1992. Mem., GLC for Southwark/Dulwich, 1973–77; Chairman: Thamesmead New Town Cttee, 1973–75; GLC Housing Cttee, 1975–77. Member: Exec. Cttee, Fabian Soc., 1981–82; London Labour Party Exec., 1973– (Chair Policy Cttee, 1983–85). Member: Ct of Governors, LSE, 1973–91; RIIA, 1982–. *Publications:* Housing: a new Socialist perspective, 1976; Role and Problems of the Co-operative Movement in the 1980s (with Tony Banks), 1977. *Recreations:* collecting books and pamphlets on political and social history topics, music. *Address:* 132 Powis Street, SE18 6NL. *T:* (office) 0181–855 2128; (home) 081–761 2510. *Clubs:* Reform; Lewisham Labour.

BALFOUR, family name of **Earl of Balfour** and **Barons Balfour of Inchrye, Kinross** and **Riverdale.**

BALFOUR, 4th Earl of, *cr* 1922; **Gerald Arthur James Balfour;** Viscount Traprain 1922; JP; *b* 23 Dec. 1925; *er s* of 3rd Earl of Balfour and Jean (*d* 1981), 4th *d* of late Rev. Canon J. J. Cooke-Yarborough; *S* father, 1968; *m* 1956, Natasha Georgina (*d* 1994), *d* of late Captain George Anton. *Educ:* Eton; HMS Conway. Holds Master Mariner's certificate. Mem., E Lothian CC, 1960–75. JP East Lothian, 1970. *Heir: cousin* Eustace Arthur Goschen Balfour [*b* 26 May 1921; *m* 1st, 1946, Anne, *d* of late Major Victor Yule; two *s*; 2nd, 1971, Mrs Paula Cuene-Grandidier]. *Address:* The Tower, Whittingehame, Haddington, Scotland EH41 4QA. *Clubs:* English-Speaking Union; International Association of Cape Horners.

BALFOUR OF BURLEIGH, Lord *cr* 1607 (*de facto* 8th Lord, 12th but for the Attainder); **Robert Bruce,** CEng, FIEE; FRSE; Director: Scottish Investment Trust plc, since 1971; William Lawson Distillers Ltd, since 1984; Television Educational Network Ltd, since 1990; Edinburgh Book Festival, since 1981 (Chairman, 1981–87); Chairman, United Artists Communications (Scotland) Ltd, since 1983; Chancellor, Stirling University, since 1988; *b* 6 Jan. 1927; *e s* of 11th Lord Balfour of Burleigh and Dorothy (*d* 1977), *d* of late R. H. Done; *S* father, 1967; *m* 1st, 1971, Mrs Jennifer Brittain-Catlin (marr. diss. 1993), *d* of late E. S. Manasseh; two *d*; 2nd, 1993, Janet Morgan (*see* Lady Balfour of Burleigh). *Educ:* Westminster Sch. Served RN, 1945–48, as Ldg Radio Electrician's Mate. Joined English Electric Co. Ltd, 1951; graduate apprentice, 1951–52; Asst Foreman, Heavy Electrical Plant Dept, Stafford Works, 1952–54; Asst Superintendent, Heavy Electrical Plant Dept, Netherton Works, Liverpool, 1954–57; Manager, English Electric Co. of India (Pvt) Ltd, Madras, 1957–60; Dir and Gen. Manager, English Electric Co. India Ltd, 1960–64; Dep. Gen. Manager, English Electric Co. Ltd, Netherton, Liverpool, 1964–65, Gen. Manager 1965–66; Dir and Gen. Manager, D. Napier & Son Ltd, 1966–68; Dep. Gov., Bank of Scotland, 1977–91 (Dir, 1968–91). Chairman: Viking Oil, 1971–80; NWS Bank (formerly North West Securities), 1978–91; Capella Nova, 1988–; Canongate Press, 1991–93; Director: Tarmac, 1981–90; UAPT Infolink, 1991–94; Member: British Railways (Scottish) Board, 1982–93; Forestry Commn, 1971–74. Chm., Fedn of Scottish Bank Employers, 1977–86. Chairman: Scottish Arts Council, 1971–80; NBL Scotland, 1981–85; Turing Inst., 1983–91; Scottish Cttee, ABSA, 1990–94 (Mem. Council, 1976–94). Pres., Friends of Vellore, 1973–. Vice-Pres., RNID, 1987–; Treasurer: Royal Scottish Corp., 1967–; RSE, 1989–94. Hon. FRIAS, 1982. DUniv Stirling, 1988; Hon. DLitt Robert Gordon, 1995. *Recreations:* music, climbing, woodwork. *Heir: d* Hon. Victoria Bruce, *b* 7 May 1973. *Address:* House of Lords, Westminster, SW1A 0PW.
See also G. J. D. Bruce.

BALFOUR OF BURLEIGH, Lady; Janet Bruce; writer and consultant; *b* 5 Dec. 1945; *e d* of Frank Morgan and Shiela Sadler; *m* 1993, Lord Balfour of Burleigh, *qv*. *Educ:* Newbury Co. Girls Grammar Sch.; St Hugh's Coll., Oxford. MA, DPhil Oxon, MA Sussex. FSAScot 1992. Kennedy Meml Scholar, Harvard Univ., 1968–69; Student, Nuffield Coll., Oxford, 1969–71; Res. Fellow, Wolfson Coll., Oxford and Res. Officer, Univ. of Essex, 1971–72; Res. Fellow, Nuffield Coll., Oxford, 1972–74; Lectr in Politics, Exeter Coll., Oxford, 1974–76; Dir of Studies, St Hugh's Coll., Oxford, 1975–76 and Lectr in Politics, 1976–78; Mem., Central Policy Rev. Staff, Cabinet Office, 1978–81. Mem. Bd, British Council, 1989–. Vis. Fellow, All Souls Coll., Oxford, 1983. Dir, Satellite Television PLC, 1981–83; Special Advr to Dir-Gen., BBC, 1983–86; Advr to Bd, Granada Gp, 1986–89; Mem., London Adv. Bd, Nat. and Provincial Bldg Soc., 1988–89; Chm., Cable & Wireless Resource Ltd, 1993–; non-executive Director: Cable & Wireless, 1988–; W. H. Smith, 1989–95; Midlands Electricity, 1990–; Pitney Bowes, 1991–93; Scottish American Investment Co., 1991–; Scottish Med. Res. Fund, 1993–; Scottish Life, 1995–. Vice-Pres., Videotext Industries Assoc., 1985–91; Dir, Hulton Deutsch Collection, 1988–90. Member: Lord Chancellor's Adv. Council on Public Records, 1982–86; Scottish Museums Council Develt Resource, 1988–; Adv. Council, Inst. for Advanced Studies in the Humanities, Univ. of Edinburgh, 1988–; Ancient Monuments Bd for Scotland, 1990–; Book Trust (Scotland), 1992–; Scottish Econ. Council, 1993–; Chm., Scotland's Book Campaign, 1994–. Trustee: Amer. Sch. in London, 1985–88; Fairground Heritage Trust, 1987–90; Cyclotron Trust, 1988–90; Scottish Hosp. Endowments Res. Trust, 1992–; Carnegie Endowment for Univs of Scotland, 1994–; Chm., Dorothy Burns Charitable Trust, 1992–. Mem., Editorial Bd, Political Quarterly, 1980–90. *Publications*(as Janet Morgan): The House of Lords and the Labour Government 1964–70, 1975; Reinforcing Parliament, 1976; (ed) The Diaries of a Cabinet Minister 1964–70 by Richard Crossman, 3 vols 1975, 1976, 1977; (ed) Backbench Diaries 1951–63 by Richard Crossman, 1980; (ed with Richard Hoggart) The Future of Broadcasting, 1982; Agatha Christie: a biography, 1984; Edwina Mountbatten: a life of her own, 1991. *Recreations:* music of Handel, sea-bathing, gardens. *Address:* c/o David Higham Associates Ltd, 5–8 Lower John Street, Golden Square, W1R 4HA. *T:* 0171–437 7888.

BALFOUR OF INCHRYE, 2nd Baron *cr* 1945, of Shefford; **Ian Balfour;** *b* 21 Dec. 1924; *s* of 1st Baron Balfour of Inchrye, PC, MC and Diana Blanche (*d* 1982), *d* of Sir Robert Grenville Harvey, 2nd Bt; *S* father, 1988; *m* 1953, Josephine Maria Jane, *d* of late Morogh Percy Wyndham Bernard and of the Hon. Mrs Bernard; one *d*. *Educ:* Eton, spasmodically, and Magdalen College, Oxford (MA). Business consultant, author and composer. *Publication:* Famous Diamonds, 1987, 2nd edn 1992. *Recreations:* watching cricket and Association football, walking, writing, thinking, drinking, dreaming. *Address:* 10 Limerston Street, SW10 0HH. *T:* 0171–351 0343.

BALFOUR, David Mathers, CBE 1970; MA; CEng, MICE; Director, R. M. Douglas Construction Ltd, 1975–83; Chairman, Balfour, Beatty & Co. Ltd, 1971–74 (Managing Director, 1966–72); *b* 11 Jan. 1910; *s* of late George Balfour, MP and Margaret (*née* Mathers); *m* 1938, Elisabeth, *d* of John Murdoch Beddall; two *s* one *d*. *Educ:* Shrewsbury Sch.; Pembroke Coll., Cambridge (MA). Served War of 1939–45, Lt-Col RE. Joined Balfour, Beatty & Co. Ltd, as Civil Engineer, 1930 (Dir, 1942); Chairman: Power Securities Corporation Ltd, 1971–74; Balfour Kilpatrick Ltd, 1971–72 (Dir, 1971–75); Exec. Dir, British Insulated Callender's Cables Ltd, 1970–72. Chairman: Export Gp for the Constructional Industries, 1963–65; Fedn of Civil Engineering Contractors, 1966–67. *Recreations:* golf, shooting. *Address:* Little Garnstone Manor, Seal, Sevenoaks, Kent TN15 0HY. *T:* Sevenoaks (01732) 761221. *Clubs:* East India, Devonshire, Sports and Public Schools; Rye Golf (Rye); Wildernesse Golf (Sevenoaks).

BALFOUR, (Elizabeth) Jean, CBE 1981; FRSE 1980; FRSA; FICFor; FIBiol; JP; Chairman, Countryside Commission for Scotland, 1972–82; *b* 4 Nov. 1927; 2nd *d* of late Maj.-Gen. Sir James Syme Drew, KBE, CB, DSO, MC, and late Victoria Maxwell of Munches; *m* 1950, John Charles Balfour, *qv*; three *s*. *Educ:* Edinburgh Univ. (BSc). Partner/Owner, Balbirnie Home Farms; Dir, A. & J. Bowen & Co. Ltd. Pres., Royal Scottish Forestry Soc., 1969–71; Mem., Fife CC, 1958–70; Chm., Fife County and City and Royal Burgh of Dunfermline Joint Probation Cttee, 1967–69; Governor, East of Scotland Coll. of Agriculture, 1958–88, Vice Pres. 1982–88; Dir, Scottish Agricl Colls, 1987–88, Dir, Council, 1974–87; Member: Scottish Agric. Develt Council, 1972–77; Verney Working Party on Natural Resources, 1971–72; Nature Conservancy Council, 1973–80; Oil Develt Council, 1973–78; Scottish Economic Council, 1978–83; Forth River Purification Bd, 1992–; Vice-Chm., Scottish Wildlife Trust, 1968–72 (Founder

Council Mem.); Chairman: Regional Adv. Cttee, East (Scotland) Forestry Commn, 1976–85; Regional Adv. Cttee, Mid (Scotland) Forestry Commn, 1988–; Food and Farming Adv. Cttee, Scottish Cons. and Unionist Assoc., 1985–88; Crarae Gardens Charitable Trust, 1986–93. Deputy Chairman: Seafish Industry Authority, 1987–90; Cttee on Women in Science, Engrg and Technol., OST, Cabinet Office, 1993–94. Mem., Cttee of Enquiry on handling of geographical information, 1985–87. Trustee: Buckland Foundn, 1989–94; Royal Botanic Gdns, Edinburgh, 1992–. Mem. Council, RSE, 1983–86; Mem. Council and Chm., Policy and Legislation Cttee, Inst. of Chartered Foresters, 1986–88. Hon. Vice-Pres., Scottish YHA, 1983–. Mem. Court, St Andrews Univ., 1983–87 (Chm. Ct Cttee, Estates and Buildings, 1983–87); Gov., Duncan of Jordanstone Coll. of Art, 1992–. JP Fife, 1963. FRSA 1981; FRZSScot 1983; FIBiol 1988. Hon. DSc St Andrews, 1977; DUniv Stirling, 1991. Report to Government, A New Look at the Northern Ireland Countryside, 1984–85. *Recreations:* hill walking, fishing, painting, exploring arctic vegetation, shooting. *Address:* Kirkforthar House, Markinch, Fife KY7 6LS. *T:* Glenrothes (01592) 752233; Scourie, by Lairg, Sutherland IV27 4TH. *Clubs:* Farmers', Commonwealth Trust; (Assoc. Mem.) New (Edinburgh).

BALFOUR, Rear-Adm. George Ian Mackintosh, CB 1962; DSC 1943; *b* 14 Jan. 1912; *yr s* of late Dr T. Stevenson Balfour, Chard, Som, and Mrs Balfour; *m* 1939, Pamela Carlyle Forrester, *y d* of late Major Hugh C. C. Forrester, DL, JP, Tullibody House, Cambus, and late Mrs Forrester; two *s* one *d*. *Educ:* Royal Naval Coll., Dartmouth. Served in China, 1930–32; South Africa, 1935–37. Commanded Destroyers for most of War of 1939–45, on various stations. Mediterranean, 1948, Far East, 1949–50, USA 1951–53, Captain (D) 2nd Destroyer Flotilla, 1956–58; Dir of Officer Appointments, 1958–59; Senior Naval Mem., Imperial Defence Coll., 1960–63; retired list, 1963. Chief Appeals Officer, Cancer Res. Campaign, 1963–77. *Address:* Westover, Farnham Lane, Haslemere, Surrey GU27 1HD. *T:* Haslemere (01428) 643876.

BALFOUR, Rear-Adm. Hugh Maxwell, CB 1990; LVO 1974; consultant; *b* 29 April 1933; *s* of Ronald Hugh Balfour and Ann Smith; *m* 1958, Sheila Ann Weldon; one *s* two *d*. *Educ:* Ardvreck; Crieff; Kelly College, Tavistock. Joined RN 1951; qualified as Signal Officer, 1959; Commanded HM Ships Sheraton, Phoebe, Whitby and Fifth Destroyer Squadron in HMS Exeter, to 1985 (Exec. Officer, HM Yacht Britannia, 1972–74); Comdr, Sultan of Oman's Navy, 1985–90. Order of Oman, 1990. *Recreations:* sailing, shooting, gardening. *Club:* Naval and Military.

BALFOUR, Jean; *see* Balfour, E. J.

BALFOUR, John Charles, OBE 1978; MC 1943; JP; Vice Lord-Lieutenant for Fife, since 1988; Chairman, Fife Area Health Board, 1983–87 (Member, 1981–87); *b* 28 July 1919; *s* of late Brig. E. W. S. Balfour, CVO, DSO, OBE, MC, and Lady Ruth Balfour, CBE; *m* 1950, (Elizabeth) Jean Drew (*see* (Elizabeth) Jean Balfour); three *s*. *Educ:* Eton Coll.; Trinity Coll., Cambridge (BA). Served war, Royal Artillery, 1939–45 (Major), N Africa and Europe. Member, Royal Company of Archers, Queen's Body Guard for Scotland, 1949–. Member: Inter-departmental Cttee on Children and Young Persons, Scotland (Chm., Lord Kilbrandon), 1961–64; Scottish Council on Crime, 1972–75; Chairman: Children's Panel, Fife County, 1970–75, Fife Region 1975–77; Scottish Assoc. of Youth Clubs, 1968–79. JP 1957, DL 1958, Fife. *Recreations:* shooting, fishing. *Address:* Kirkforthar House, Markinch, Glenrothes, Fife KY7 6LS. *T:* Glenrothes (01592) 752233, *Fax:* (01592) 610314. *Club:* New (Edinburgh).
See also P. E. G. Balfour.

BALFOUR, Hon. Mark Robin; Chairman: Finglands Services Ltd, since 1981; Light Trades House Ltd, since 1973; *b* 16 July 1927; *s* and *heir* of 2nd Baron Riverdale, *qv*; *m* 1959, Susan Ann Phillips; one *s* two *d*. *Educ:* Aysgarth Sch., Yorks; Lisgar Collegiate, Ottawa, Canada; Trinity Coll. Sch., Port Hope, Ont; Millfield Sch.; Rotherham Technical Coll. (Intermediate Cert. in Metallurgy). Served RN, 1944–47. Arthur Balfour & Co. Ltd: Dir, 1955; Manager, London Office, Home and Export, 1957; Asst Man. Dir, 1959; negotiated merger with Darwins Group Ltd, 1960; Man. Dir, Balfour Darwins Ltd, 1961, Chm. 1971–75; following formation of Sheffield Rolling Mills Ltd (consortium of BSC, James Neill subsid., Balfour Darwins Ltd subsid.), 1969, Chm. 1970–74; non-exec. Dir, Special Steels Div., BSC, 1971–73; negotiated sale of Sheffield Rolling Mills Ltd to BSC, 1973; Dir, Overseas Ops, Edgar Allen Balfour Ltd (formed by merger of Balfour Darwins Ltd and Edgar Allen Ltd), 1975–79. British Independent Steel Producers' Association: Mem., Exec. Cttee, 1969–75; Mem., Product Group (Special Steels), 1962–75 (Chm., 1970–71); Mem., Steelmakers' Cttee, 1970–75. Pres., National Fedn of Engineers' Tool Manufrs, 1974–76; Member: EDC for Machine Tools, 1976–78; Council, Fedn of British Hand Tool Manufrs, 1972–77; Econs and Management Cttee, Iron and Steel Inst., 1970–75; Iron and Steel Industry Regional Trng Bd, 1964–68; Sheffield and Dist Br. Cttee, Inst. of Dirs, 1969–77; Council, Sheffield Chamber of Commerce, 1959–93 (Pres., 1978); Australian British Trade Assoc. Council, BOTB, 1975–85; ANZ Trade Adv. Cttee, BOTB, 1975–85. Mem. Council, Yorkshire Cancer Res. Campaign, 1991–. Chm., Ashdell Schs Trust, 1985–. Master, Cutlers' Co. of Hallamshire, 1969–70; Mem., Worshipful Co. of Blacksmiths, 1972–; Freeman, City of London, 1972. High Sheriff, S Yorks, 1986–87. Vice-Consul for Finland in Sheffield, 1962–, Consul, 1994. Order of the Lion, Finland, 1975. Silver Jubilee Medal, 1977. *Recreations:* fishing, shooting. *Address:* Fairways, Saltergate, Bamford, near Sheffield S30 2BE. *T:* Hope Valley (01433) 651314. *Club:* The Club (Sheffield).

BALFOUR, Michael John; JP; Director: SIGECO (UK) Ltd (formerly IMI Capital Markets (UK) Ltd), since 1987 (Chairman, 1987–92); IMI Bank (International), since 1987 (Deputy Chairman, 1987–92); *b* 17 Oct. 1925; *s* of Duncan and Jeanne Germaine Balfour; *m* 1951, Mary Campbell Penney, *d* of Maj.-Gen. Sir (William) Ronald Campbell Penney, KBE, CB, DSO, MC; two *s* one *d* (and *e s* decd). *Educ:* Eton Coll.; Christ Church, Oxford (MA Hons Modern Languages 1949). War service, RAF, 1944–47. Entered Bank of England, 1950: Senior Adviser, European affairs, 1973, Chief Adviser, 1976; Asst Dir, 1980–85. Alternate Director, Bank for International Settlements, 1972–85; Member, EEC Monetary Cttee, 1974–85. Director, Balgonie Estates Ltd, 1955–; Chm., IMI Securities Ltd, 1988–94. JP Roxburgh, 1988. *Recreations:* music, fishing, boating, etc. *Address:* Harrietfield, Kelso, Roxburghshire TD5 7SY. *T:* Kelso (01573) 224825; 17 Shrewsbury Mews, W2 5PN. *T:* 0171-229 8013.

BALFOUR, Nancy, OBE 1965; President, Contemporary Art Society, since 1984 (Chairman, 1976–82); *b* 1911; *d* of Alexander Balfour and Ruth Macfarland Balfour. *Educ:* Wycombe Abbey Sch.; Lady Margaret Hall, Oxford (MA). Foreign Office Research Dept, 1941–45; BBC N American Service, 1945–48; Economist Newspaper, 1948–72: Asst Editor with responsibility for American Survey, 1954–72; Fellow, Inst. of Politics, Kennedy Sch. of Govt, Harvard Univ., 1973–74. Member: Council, RIIA, 1963–84; Bd, British–American Arts Assoc., 1980–; Hon. Treasurer, Contemporary Art Soc., 1971–76; Chm., Art Services Grants, 1982–89; Vice-Chm., Crafts Council, 1983–85 (Mem., 1980–85); Chairperson, Southern Arts Craft Panel, 1986–90; Chm., Arts Research Ltd, 1990–. Trustee, Public Art Develt Trust, 1983–91. FRSA 1985. *Recreations:* sightseeing, ancient and modern; viewing work by living artists. *Address:* 36E Eaton Square, SW1W 9DH. *T:* 0171-235 7874. *Club:* Arts.

BALFOUR, Neil Roxburgh; Chairman: York Trust Ltd, since 1983; Yorkshire General Unit Trust, since 1985; *b* 12 Aug. 1944; *s* of Archibald Roxburgh Balfour and Lilian Helen Cooper; *m* 1st, 1969, HRH Princess Elizabeth of Yugoslavia; one *s*; 2nd, 1978, Serena Mary Churchill Russell; one *s* one *d*. *Educ:* Ampleforth Coll., Yorks; University Coll., Oxford Univ. (BA History); called to the Bar, Middle Temple, 1969. Baring Brothers & Co., 1968–74; European Banking Co. Ltd, 1974–83 (Exec. Dir, 1980–83). Chm., York Trust Group plc, 1986–91. Mem. (C) N Yorks, European Parlt, 1979–84. *Publication:* Paul of Yugoslavia (biography), 1980. *Recreations:* bridge, golf, tennis, shooting, fishing. *Address:* York Trust Ltd, 12th Floor, Moor House, 119 London Wall, EC2Y 5ET. *T:* 0171-374 2344; 55 Warwick Square, SW1V 2AJ. *Clubs:* Turf, Pratt's; Harbour Tennis; Royal St George's (Sandwich); Mentmore Golf; Arcangues Golf (Biarritz).

BALFOUR, Peter Edward Gerald, CBE 1984; Chairman, Charterhouse plc, 1985–90; a Vice-Chairman, Royal Bank of Scotland, 1985–90 (Director, 1971–90); Director, 1978–91, Vice-Chairman, 1981–91, Royal Bank of Scotland Group; *b* 9 July 1921; *y s* of late Brig. Edward William Sturgis Balfour, CVO, DSO, OBE, MC and Lady Ruth Balfour, CBE, MB; *m* 1st, 1948, Grizelda Davina Roberta Ogilvy (marr. diss. 1967); two *s* one *d*; 2nd, 1968, Diana Rosemary Wainman; one *s* one *d*. *Educ:* Eton College. Scots Guards, 1940–54. Joined Wm McEwan & Co. Ltd, 1954; Chm. and Chief Exec., Scottish & Newcastle Breweries, 1970–83. Director: British Assets Trust Ltd, 1962–91; Selective Assets Trust (formerly Edinburgh American Assets Trust), 1962–92 (Chm., 1978–92); First Charlotte Assets Trust, 1980–92 (Chm., 1981–92). Chm., Scottish Council for Develt and Industry, 1978–85. Mem., Hansard Soc. Commn on Electoral Reform, 1975–76. *Address:* Scadlaw House, Humbie, East Lothian EH36 5PH. *T:* Humbie (01875) 833252. *Clubs:* Cavalry and Guards; New (Edinburgh).
See also J. C. Balfour.

BALFOUR, Raymond Lewis, MVO 1965; HM Diplomatic Service, retired; Counsellor, Kuwait, 1979–83; *b* 23 April 1923; *s* of Henry James Balfour and Vera Alice (*née* Dunford); *m* 1975, Vanda Gaye Crompton. RMA Sandhurst, 1942; commnd RAC; served with IV Queen's Own Hussars, 1942–47. Diplomatic Service, 1947–87; served at Munich, Beirut, Gdansk (Poland), Baghdad, Khartoum, Geneva, Damascus; Counsellor, Tripoli, 1976–79. Order of the Blue Nile, Sudan, 1965. *Recreations:* travel, gardening. *Address:* 25 Chenery Drive, Sprowston, Norwich, Norfolk NR7 8RR.

BALFOUR, Richard Creighton, MBE 1945; retired; *b* 3 Feb. 1916; *s* of Donald Creighton Balfour and Muriel Fonçeca; *m* 1943, Adela Rosemary Welch; two *s*. *Educ:* St Edward's Sch., Oxford (Pres., Sch. Soc., 1985–86). FIB. Joined Bank of England, 1935; Agent, Leeds, 1961–65; Deputy Chief Cashier, 1965–70; Chief Accountant, 1970–75. Dir, Datasaab Ltd, 1975–81. Naval Service, Lt-Comdr RNVR, 1939–46. President: Royal National Rose Soc., 1973 and 1974; World Fedn of Rose Socs, 1983–85 (Vice-Pres. for Europe, 1981–83; Chm., Classification Cttee, 1981–88); Chairman: 1976—The Year of the Rose; Internat. Rose Conf., Oxford, 1976; organiser and designer of the British Garden at Montreal Floralies, 1980. Master, Worshipful Co. of Gardeners, 1991–92; Freeman, City of London. DHM 1974. Gold Medal, World Fedn of Rose Socs, 1985; Australian Rose Award, 1989. *Publications:* articles in many horticultural magazines and photographs in many publications. *Recreations:* roses, gardening, photography, dancing, sea floating, collecting rocks and hat pins, travel, watching sport. *Address:* Albion House, Little Waltham, Chelmsford, Essex CM3 3LA. *T:* Chelmsford (01245) 360410.

BALFOUR-PAUL, (Hugh) Glencairn, CMG 1968; HM Diplomatic Service, retired; Director General, Middle East Association, 1978–79; Research Fellow, University of Exeter, since 1979, *b* 23 Sept. 1917; *s* of late Lt-Col J. W. Balfour Paul, DSO; *m* 1st, 1950, Margaret Clare Ogilvy (*d* 1971); one *s* three *d*; 2nd, 1974, Janet Alison Scott; one *s* one *d*. *Educ:* Sedbergh; Magdalen Coll., Oxford. Served War of 1939–45, Sudan Defence Force. Sudan Political Service, Blue Nile and Darfur, 1946–54; joined Foreign Office, 1955; Santiago, 1957; Beirut, 1960; Counsellor, Dubai, 1964; Dep. Political Resident, Persian Gulf, 1966; Counsellor, FO, attached St Antony's Coll., Oxford, 1968; Ambassador to Iraq, 1969–71; Ambassador to Jordan, 1972–75; Ambassador to Tunisia, 1975–77. *Publication:* The End of Empire in the Middle East, 1990. *Recreations:* archaeology, poetry, pew ends. *Address:* Uppincott Barton, Shobrooke, Crediton, Devon EX17 1BE. *T:* Crediton (01363) 772104.

BALGONIE, Lord; David Alexander Leslie Melville; Director: Wood Conversion Ltd, since 1984; The Treske Shop Ltd, since 1988; *b* 26 Jan. 1954; *s* and *heir* of Earl of Leven and Melville, *qv*; *m* 1981, Julia Clare, *yr d* of Col I. R. Critchley, Lindores, Muthill, Perthshire; one *s* one *d*. *Educ:* Eton. Lieut (acting Captain), Queen's Own Highlanders (GSM for N Ireland); RARO 1979–89. *Heir: s* Hon. Alexander Ian Leslie Melville, *b* 29 Nov. 1984. *Address:* Old Farmhouse, West Street, Burghclere, Newbury, Berkshire RG15 9LB.

BALKWILL, Bryan Havell; conductor; Professor of Conducting, Indiana University, Bloomington, 1977–92; *b* 2 July 1922; *s* of Arthur William Balkwill and Dorothy Silver Balkwill (*née* Wright); *m* 1949, Susan Elizabeth Roberts; one *s* one *d*. *Educ:* Merchant Taylors' Sch.; Royal Academy of Music. Asst Conductor, New London Opera Co., 1947–48; Associate Conductor, Internat. Ballet, 1948–49; Musical Director and Principal Conductor, London Festival Ballet, 1950–52; Music staff and subseq. Associate Conductor, Glyndebourne Opera, 1950–58; Musical Dir, Arts Council 'Opera For All', 1953–63; Resident Conductor, Royal Opera House, Covent Garden, 1959–65; Musical Director: Welsh Nat. Opera Company, 1963–67; Sadler's Wells Opera, 1966–69; free-lance opera and concert conducting in N America, Europe and GB, 1970–. Guest Conductor: Royal Opera House, Covent Garden, English Nat. Opera, Glyndebourne, Wexford Festival, Aldeburgh, RPO, LPO, BBC. Life Mem. Royal Philharmonic Society; FRAM. *Address:* 8 The Green, Wimbledon Common, SW19 5AZ. *T:* 0181-947 4250.

BALL, Air Marshal Sir Alfred (Henry Wynne), KCB 1976 (CB 1967); DSO 1943; DFC 1942; Vice-Chairman (Air), Council of Territorial, Auxiliary and Volunteer Reserve Associations, 1979–84; *b* 18 Jan. 1921; *s* of Captain J. A. E. Ball, MC, BA, BE, sometime Actg Chief Engineer, Bengal Nagpur Railway; *m* 1942, Nan McDonald; three *s* one *d*. *Educ:* Campbell Coll., Belfast; RAF Coll., Cranwell; idc, jssc, psc, pfc. Served War of 1939–45 (Despatches twice; US Air Medal 1943); Sqdn Ldr 1942; Wing Comdr 1944; air operations, Lysanders, Spitfires, Mosquitoes; commanded: 4 Photo. Reconn. Unit; 682, 542, 540 and 13 Photo. Reconn. Sqdns in N Africa, UK, France and Middle East; E Africa, 1947; RAF Staff Coll., 1952; Canberras, RAF Wyton, 1953; Bomber Comd, 1952; BJSM, Washington, 1959; Comdr, Honington V Bomber Base, 1963–64; Air Officer, Administration, Aden, 1965; IDC, 1967; Dir of Operations, (RAF), MoD, 1967–68; Air Vice-Marshal, 1968; ACOS, Automatic Data Processing Div., SHAPE, 1968–71; Dir-Gen. Organisation (RAF), 1971–75; Air Marshal, 1975; UK Rep., Perm. Mil. Deputies Gp, Cento, 1975–77; Dep. C-in-C, RAF Strike Command, 1977–79, retired 1979. Mil. Affairs Advr, Internat. Computers Ltd, 1979–83. Hon. Air Cdre, No

2624 (Co. of Oxford) RAuxAF Regt Sqdn, 1984–90. Hon. FBCS 1974. *Recreations:* golf, bridge. *Clubs:* Royal Air Force; Phyllis Court; Huntercombe.

BALL, Alison; QC 1995; *b* 12 Jan. 1948; *d* of Winifred Alice Ball and Hilary Noble Ball; *m* 1980, Richard; two *d. Educ:* Bedales Sch.; King's Coll., London (LLB Hons). Called to the Bar, Middle Temple, 1972; founded Specialist Family Law Chambers, 1989, Joint Head, 1990–; Asst Recorder and Dep. District Judge, 1992–. *Recreations:* my family and other animals. *Address:* 1 Garden Court, Temple, EC4Y 9BJ. *T:* 0171–797 7900.

BALL, Anthony George, (Tony Ball), MBE 1986; FCIM; FIMI; ACIArb; Chairman: Tony Ball Associates plc, since 1983; TBA plc, since 1993; *b* 14 Nov. 1934; *s* of Harry Ball and Mary Irene Ball, Bridgwater; *m* 1957, Ruth Parry Davies; two *s* one *d. Educ:* Grammar Sch., Bridgwater. Indentured engineering apprentice, Austin Motor Co., 1951–55; responsible for launch of Mini, 1959; UK Car Sales Manager, 1962–66, Austin Motor Co.; Sales and Marketing Exec., British Motor Corp., 1966–67; Chm. and Man. Dir, Barlow Rand UK Motor Gp, 1967–78; Managing Director: Barlow Rand Ford, S Africa, 1971–73; Barlow Rand European Operations, 1973–78; returned to British Leyland as Man. Dir, Overseas Trading Operations, 1978; Director: Leyland Australia, Leyland S Africa, Leyland Kenya and all BL African subsids; Dep. Man. Dir, Austin Morris Ltd, 1979; Chm. and Man. Dir, BL Europe & Overseas, 1979–82; Director, 1979–82: BL Cars Ltd (World Sales Chief, 1979–82; responsible for conducting BL's Buy British campaign and launch of the Austin Metro in 1980); Austin Morris Ltd; Rover Triumph Ltd; Jaguar Rover Triumph Inc. (USA); Dir, Jaguar Cars Ltd, 1980–82; Chief Exec. and Gp Man. Dir, Henlys plc, 1982–83. Dep. Chm., Lumley Insce Gp, 1983–95; Director: Jetmaster UK, 1989–; Theatre Agents Billy Marsh Associates, 1993–. Dir, producer and stager of 'Industrial Theatre' Motivational confs, sponsorship, marketing, promotions and new product launches, 1983–. Responsible for: staging General Motors' UK launch of Vauxhall Astra, 1984, Lada Samara/Proton Cars launches, annually 1989–, Mercedes-Benz and Fiat Uno launches, 1990, 1991, promotion and opening ceremony of Rugby World Cup, Twickenham, 1991, Leyland DAF (LDV) Focus on Vans, 1992; DoH European drug abuse prevention campaign, 1992. Apptd special Marketing Adviser: to Sec. of State for Agric. on launch of Food from Britain campaign, 1982; to Sec. of State for Energy, 1984–87 (responsible for staging Nat. Energy Management Confs and Exhibns, 1985 and 86); to Sec. of State for Wales, 1988–91 (with responsibility for review of Welsh craft and giftware industry); to SMMT for producing and promoting British Internat. Motor Show, Nat. Exhibn Centre, Birmingham, 1992, 1994; created and devised "Wales—Land of Quality" corporate marketing theme; responsible for: marketing and promoting London Zoo, 1993; creating and producing Lloyds Bank's Playwright of the Year Award, 1994. Lectr, public and after dinner speaker; TV and radio broadcasts on motoring, marketing and industrial subjects; producer, The Birth of Rugby; panellist, Any Questions. Mason Meml Lecture, Birmingham Univ., 1983. Governor, N Worcs Coll., 1984–91. Freeman of City of London, 1980; Liveryman: Worshipful Co. of Coach Makers and Coach Harness Makers, 1980; Worshipful Co. of Carmen, 1982. Fellowship of Inst. of Marketing awarded 1981, for launch of the Metro and services to Brit. Motor Industry; Hon. Mem. CGLI, 1982, for services to technical and vocational educn; Prince Philip Medal, CGLI, 1984, for outstanding contribution to marketing and the motor industry; Benedictine Business After-Dinner Speaker of the Year Award, 1991, 1992. *Publications:* (contrib.) Metro: the vital launch, 1981; (contrib.) Tales out of School, 1983; A Marketing Study of the Welsh Craft Industry (Welsh Office report, 1988); (contrib.) Making Better Business Presentations, 1988; contribs to numerous industrial, management and marketing books and jls. *Recreations:* theatre, British military history, sharing good humour. *Address:* Tony Ball Associates plc, 174–178 North Gower Street, NW1 2NB. *T:* 0171–380 0953; Blythe House, Bidford-on-Avon, Warwickshire B50 4BY. *T:* Bidford-on-Avon (01789) 778015; 249 Grove End Gardens, St John's Wood, NW8 9LU. *T:* 0171–286 0899. *Clubs:* Oriental, Royal Automobile.

BALL, Arthur Beresford, OBE 1973; HM Diplomatic Service, retired; history teacher, Gresham's School, 1989–91, language teacher, since 1991; *b* 15 Aug. 1923; *s* of Charles Henry and Lilian Ball; *m* 1961, June Stella Luckett; one *s* two *d. Educ:* Bede Collegiate Boys' Sch., Sunderland; Univ. of E Anglia (BA Hons 1987; MA 1989). Joined HM Diplomatic Service, 1949: Bahrain, 1949; Tripoli, 1950; Middle East Centre for Arab Studies, 1952; Ramullah, 1953; Damascus, 1954; Foreign Office, 1957; Kuwait, 1959; HM Consul, New Orleans, 1963; Jedda, 1965; FO, 1967; São Paulo, 1969; Lisbon, 1972; Ankara, 1975; Consul-Gen., Perth, WA, 1978–80. *Recreations:* sailing, ice skating, historical studies. *Address:* 15 Eccles Road, Holt, Norfolk NR25 6HJ.

BALL, Sir Charles (Irwin), 4th Bt *cr* 1911; Deputy Chairman, Associated British Ports Holdings, since 1982; *b* 12 Jan. 1924; *s* of Sir Nigel Gresley Ball, 3rd Bt, and Florine Isabel (*d* 1992), *d* of late Col Herbert Edwardes Irwin; *S* father, 1978; *m* 1st, 1950, Alison Mary Bentley (marr. diss. 1983); one *s* one *d*; 2nd, 1994, Christine Trilby Knowles. *Educ:* Sherborne Sch. FCA 1960. Served RA, 1942–47. Chartered Accountant, 1950; Peat, Marwick, Mitchell & Co., 1950–54; joined Robert, Benson, Lonsdale & Co. Ltd (now Kleinwort, Benson Ltd), 1954; Director: Kleinwort, Benson Ltd, 1964–76 (Vice-Chm., 1974–76); Kleinwort, Benson, Lonsdale Ltd, 1974–76; Cadbury Schweppes Ltd, 1971–76; Chubb & Son Ltd, 1971–76; Sun Alliance and London Insurance Ltd, 1971–83; Telephone Rentals plc, 1971–89 (Vice-Chm., 1978–81, Chm., 1981–89); Tunnel Holdings Ltd, 1976–82; Barclays Bank Ltd, 1976–77 (Chm., Barclays Merchant Bank Ltd, 1976–77); Rockware Group plc, 1978–84; Peachey Property Corporation plc, 1978–88 (Chm., 1981–88); British Transport Docks Bd, 1971–82; Chm., Silkolene plc, 1989–94; Dep. Chm., Century Oils Group plc, 1991–94. Liveryman, 1960, Mem. Ct of Assts, 1979–87, Master, 1985, Clockmakers' Co. *Heir: s* Richard Bentley Ball, *b* 29 Jan. 1953. *Address:* Killybegs, Eddystone Road, Thurlestone, Kingsbridge, Devon TQ7 3NU. *T:* Kingsbridge (01548) 560062.

BALL, Sir Christopher (John Elinger), Kt 1988; MA; Director of Learning, Royal Society of Arts, since 1992; *b* 22 April 1935; *er s* of late Laurence Elinger Ball, OBE, and Christine Florence Mary Ball (*née* Howe); *m* 1958, Wendy Ruth Colyer, *d* of late Cecil Frederick Colyer and Ruth Colyer (*née* Reddaway); three *s* three *d. Educ:* St George's School, Harpenden; Merton College, Oxford (Harmsworth Scholar 1959; Hon. Fellow, 1987); 1st Cl. English Language and Literature, 1959; Dipl. in Comparative Philology, 1962; MA Oxon, 1963. 2nd Lieut, Parachute Regt, 1955–56. Lectr in English Language, Merton Coll., Oxford, 1960–61; Lectr in Comparative Linguistics, Sch. of Oriental and African Studies (Univ. of London), 1961–64; Fellow and Tutor in English Language, Lincoln Coll., Oxford, 1964–79 (Sen. Tutor and Tutor for Admissions, 1971–72; Bursar, 1972–79; Hon. Fellow, 1981); Warden, Keble College, Oxford, 1980–88 (Hon. Fellow, 1989). Founding Fellow, Kellogg Forum for Continuing Educn, Univ. of Oxford, 1988–89; Fellow in Continuing Educn, RSA, 1989–92; Vis. Prof. in Higher Educn, Leeds Poly., 1989–91. Sec., Linguistics Assoc. of GB, 1964–67; Pres., Oxford Assoc. of University Teachers, 1968–71; Publications Sec., Philological Soc., 1969–75; Chairman: Oxford Univ. English Bd, 1977–79; Bd of NAB, 1982–88; Higher Educn Inf. Services Trust, 1987–90; Education—Industry Forum (Industry Matters), RSA, 1988–90; Member: General Bd of the Faculties, 1979–82; Hebdomadal Council, 1985–89; CNAA, 1982–88 (Chm., English Studies Bd, 1973–80, Linguistics Bd, 1977–82); BTEC, 1984–89 (Chm., Quality Assurance & Control Cttee, 1989–90); IT Skills Shortages Cttee (Butcher Cttee), 1984–85; CBI IT Skills Agency, 1985–88; CBI Task Force, 1988–89. Chairman: NICEC, 1989–93; Pegasus, 1989–92; Strategic Educn Fora for Kent, Oxfordshire and Gtr Peterborough, 1992–95; Educn Policy Cttee, RSA Exams Bd, 1993–. Member: Council and Exec., Templeton Coll., Oxford, 1981–92; Centre for Medieval and Renaissance Studies, Oxford, 1987–90; Brathay Hall Trust, 1988–91 (Chm, 1990–91); Manchester Polytechnic, 1989–91 (Hon. Fellow, 1988). Pres., ACFHE, 1990–92. Gov., St George's Sch., Harpenden, 1985–89. Jt Founding Editor (with late Angus Cameron), Toronto Dictionary of Old English, 1970; Member Editorial Board: Oxford Rev. of Education, 1984–95; Science and Public Affairs, 1989–94. FRSA 1987. Hon. Fellow: Univ. of Westminster (formerly Poly. of Central London), 1991; Auckland Inst. of Technol., NZ, 1992. Hon. DLitt CNAA, 1989; DUniv N London, 1993; Hon. DEd Greenwich, 1994. *Publications:* Fitness for Purpose, 1985; Aim Higher, 1989; (ed jtly) Higher Education in the 1990s, 1989; More Means Different, 1990; Learning Pays, 1991; Sharks and Splashes, 1991; Profitable Learning, 1992; Start Right, 1994; pamphlets and various contributions to philological, linguistic and educational jls. *Address:* 45 Richmond Road, Oxford OX1 2JJ. *T* and *Fax:* Oxford (0865) 310800.

BALL, Christopher John Watkins; Chairman, SA Housing, since 1994; Chief Executive Officer, Cape Town 2004 Olympic Bid, since 1995; *b* 2 Nov. 1939; *s* of Clifford George and Cynthia Lindsay Watkins-Ball; *m* 1968, Susan Anne Nellist; one *s* two *d. Educ:* St John's Coll., Johannesburg; Univ. of the Witwatersrand (Dipl. Iuris 1963); Jesus Coll., Cambridge (MA Econs 1967). Outwich South Africa Ltd, 1968–72, Dir 1970; Barclays Group, 1972–89: Barclays Nat. Merchant Bank, S Africa, 1972–78; Manager, Corporate Finance, 1972–75; Gen. Manager, 1975–78; Man. Dir, Barclays Nat. Western Bank, S Africa, 1978–80; Regional Gen. Manager, London, Barclays Bank, 1980–83; Barclays Nat. Bank Ltd (now First Nat. Bank of Southern Africa), S Africa, 1983, Man. Dir, 1984–89; Chief Exec., Pvte Bank & Trust Co., 1989–93. Pres., Clearing Bankers' Assoc. of S Africa, 1985. *Recreations:* golf, tennis. *Address:* Cape Town Olympic Bid Co., Dock House, V & A Waterfront, Cape Town, 8001, S Africa. *Club:* Leander.

BALL, Denis William, MBE 1971; industrial and financial consultant; Director: Perkins Foods PLC, since 1987; Redbridge Properties Ltd, since 1990; *b* 20 Oct. 1928; *er s* of William Charles Thomas and late Dora Adelaide Ball, Eastbourne; *m* 1972, Marja Tellervo Lumijärvi (*d* 1987), *er d* of Osmo Kullervo and Leila Tellervo Lumijärvi, Toijala, Finland; two *s* one *d. Educ:* Brunswick Sch.; Tonbridge Sch. (Scholar); Brasenose Coll., Oxford (MA). Sub-Lt, RNR, 1953; Lieut 1954; Lt-Comdr 1958. Asst Master, 1953–72, Housemaster, 1954–72, The King's Sch., Canterbury; Headmaster, Kelly Coll., 1972–85. Director: James Wilkes, 1977–78; Western Bloodstock, 1987–92; Cons., Throgmorton Investment Management, 1977–78. Trustee, Tavistock Sch., 1972–85; Vice-Chm. of Governors, St Michael's Sch., Tawstock Court, 1974–93 (Hon. Gov., 1993–; Headmaster during interregnum, 1986); Mem., Political and PR Sub-Cttee, HMC, 1979–84. Treas., Ickham PCC, 1990–. Mem., Johnson Club, 1987–. *Recreations:* Elizabethan history, cryptography, literary and mathematical puzzles, cricket, real tennis, squash (played for Oxford Univ. and Kent), golf. *Address:* Ickham Hall, Ickham, Canterbury, Kent CT3 1QT. *Clubs:* East India, Devonshire, Sports and Public Schools, MCC.

BALL, Dr Harold William; Keeper of Palæontology, British Museum (Natural History), 1966–86; *b* 11 July 1926; *s* of Harold Ball and Florence (*née* Harris); *m* 1955, Patricia Mary (*née* Silvester); two *s* two *d. Educ:* Yardley Gram. Sch.; Birmingham Univ. BSc 1947, PhD 1949, Birmingham. Geologist, Nyasaland Geological Survey, 1949–51; Asst Lectr in Geology, King's Coll., London, 1951–54; Dept of Palæontology, British Museum (Nat. Hist.), 1954–86: Dep. Keeper, 1965; Keeper, 1966. Adrian Vis. Fellow, Univ. of Leicester, 1972–77. Sec., 1968–72, Vice-Pres., 1972–73, 1984–86, Geological Soc. of London; Pres., 1981–84, Vice-Pres., 1984–86, Soc. for the History of Natural History. Wollaston Fund, Geological Soc. of London, 1965. *Publications:* papers on the stratigraphy of the Old Red Sandstone and on the palæontology of the Antarctic in several scientific jls. *Recreations:* music, wine, gardening. *Address:* Wilderbrook, Dormans Park, East Grinstead, West Sussex RH19 2LT. *T:* Dormans Park (0134287) 426.

BALL, Sir James; *see* Ball, Sir R. J.

BALL, Prof. John Geoffrey, CEng; consultant metallurgist; Professor of Physical Metallurgy, Imperial College, University of London, 1956–80, now Emeritus (Head of Metallurgy Department, 1957–79; Senior Research Fellow, 1980–86); *b* 27 Sept. 1916; *s* of late I. H. Ball and late Mrs E. M. Ball; *m* 1941, Joan C. M., *d* of late Arthur Wiltshire, JP, Bournemouth. *Educ:* Wellington (Salop) High Sch.; Univ. of Birmingham. British Welding Res. Assoc., 1941–49; Sen. Metallurgist, 1945–49; AERE, Harwell, 1949–56; Head of Reactor Metallurgy, 1953–56. Min. of Tech. Visitor to British Non-Ferrous Metals Res. Assoc., 1962–72. Dean, Royal Sch. of Mines, Imperial Coll., 1962–65 and 1971–74; Dean, Faculty of Engineering, Univ. of London, 1970–74. Chairman: Res. Bd, 1964–74, and Mem. of Council Br. Welding Res. Assoc., 1964–81; Engrg Physics Sub-Cttee, Aeronautical Res. Council, 1964–68; Metallurgy Bd, CNAA, 1965–71; Metallurgy and Materials Cttee and Univ. Science and Technology Bd, SRC, 1967–70; Engrg Bd, SRC, 1969–71; Manpower Utilisation Working Party, 1967–69; Mem., Light Water Reactor Pressure Vessel Study Gp, Dept of Energy, 1974–77. Consultant on Materials, SERC, 1983–84. President: Inst. of Welding, 1965–66; Instn of Metallurgists, 1966–67 (Mem. Council 1951–56, 1958–70); Member: Council, Br. Nuclear Forum, 1964–71; Manpower Resources Cttee, 1965–68; Council, Inst. of Metals, 1965; Council, Iron and Steel Inst., 1965; Council, City Univ., 1966–90; Brain Drain Cttee, 1966–67; Public Enquiry into loss of "Sea Gem", 1967; Materials and Structures Cttee, 1967–70; Technology Sub-Cttee of UGC, 1968–73; Chartered Engineer Section Bd, CEI, 1978–83; Mem., Group IV Exec. Cttee, Engineering Council, 1983–94. Governor, Sir John Cass Coll., 1958–67. Hon. ARSM 1961. Brooker Medal, Welding Inst., 1979; Freedom of Inst. and Distinguished Service Award, Indian Inst. of Technology, Delhi, 1985. *Recreations:* gardening, painting, travel. *Address:* 3 Sylvan Close, Limpsfield, Surrey RH8 0DX. *T:* Oxted (01883) 713511.

BALL, Prof. John Macleod, DPhil; FRS 1989; FRSE; Professor of Applied Analysis, Department of Mathematics, Heriot-Watt University, since 1982; *b* 19 May 1948; *s* of Ernest Frederick Ball and Dorothy Forbes Ball; *m* 1st, 1973, Mary Judith Hodges (marr. diss. 1977); 2nd, 1992, Sedhar Chozam. *Educ:* Mill Hill Sch.; St John's Coll., Cambridge (BA Maths, 1969); Univ. of Sussex (DPhil 1972). FRSE 1980. SRC Postdoctoral Res. Fellow, Dept of Maths, Heriot-Watt Univ., and Lefschetz Center for Dynamical Systems, Brown Univ., USA, 1972–74; Lectr in Maths, 1974–78, Reader in Maths, 1978–82, SERC Sen. Fellow, 1980–85, Heriot-Watt Univ. Visiting Professor: Dept of Maths, Univ. of Calif, Berkeley, 1979–80; Laboratoire d'Analyse Numérique, Université Pierre et Marie Curie, Paris, 1987–88, 1994; Inst. for Advanced Study, Princeton, 1993–94. Member: EPSRC, 1994–; Edinburgh Mathematical Soc., 1972– (Pres., 1989–90); London Math. Soc., 1982–; Amer. Math. Soc., 1987–; Soc. for Nat. Phil., 1978–. Mem. Exec. Cttee, Internat. Centre for Mathematical Scis, Edinburgh, 1991– (Chm., 1991–93). Hon. DSc Ecole Polytechnique Fédérale, Lausanne, 1992. Whittaker Prize, Edinburgh Math. Soc.,

1981; Jun. Whitehead Prize, 1982, Naylor Prize, 1994, London Math. Soc.; Keith Prize, RSE, 1990. Mem. Editorial Boards of various math. and scientific jls. *Publications:* articles in math. and scientific jls. *Recreations:* travel, music, chess. *Address:* 11 Gloucester Place, Edinburgh EH3 6EE. *T:* 0131–226 4384.

BALL, Rt. Rev. Michael Thomas; *see* Truro, Bishop of.

BALL, Rt. Rev. Peter John, CGA; Bishop of Gloucester, 1992–93; *b* 14 Feb. 1932; *s* of Thomas James and Kathleen Obena Bradley Ball. *Educ:* Lancing; Queens' Coll., Cambridge; Wells Theological College. MA (Nat. Sci.). Ordained, 1956; Curate of Rottingdean, 1956–58; Co-founder and Brother of Monastic Community of the Glorious Ascension, 1960 (Prior, 1960–77); Suffragan Bishop of Lewes, 1977–92; Prebendary, Chichester Cathedral, 1978–. Fellow of Woodard Corporation, 1962–71; Member: Archbishops' Council of Evangelism, 1965–68; Midlands Religious Broadcasting Council of the BBC, 1967–69; Admin. Council, Royal Jubilee Trusts, 1986–88. Archbishop of Canterbury's Adviser to HMC, 1985–90. Governor: Wellington Coll., 1985–93; Radley Coll., 1986–93; Lancing Coll., 1972–82, 1990–. Freeman, Bor. of Eastbourne, 1992. DUniv Sussex, 1992. *Recreations:* squash (Cambridge Blue, 1953) and music. *Address:* South Downs, King Harry Road, Feock, Truro, Cornwall TR3 6QN.
See also Bishop of Truro.

BALL, Rev. Canon Peter William; Canon Emeritus, St Paul's Cathedral, since 1990 (Residentiary Canon, 1984–90); Public Preacher, diocese of Salisbury, since 1990; *b* 17 Jan. 1930; *s* of Leonard Wevell Ball and Dorothy Mary Ball; *m* 1956, Angela Jane Dunlop; one *s* two *d*. *Educ:* Aldenham School; Worcester Coll., Oxford (MA); Cuddesdon Coll., Oxford. Asst Curate, All Saints, Poplar, 1955; Vicar, The Ascension, Wembley, 1961; Rector, St Nicholas, Shepperton, 1968; Area Dean of Spelthorne, 1972–83; Prebendary of St Paul's Cathedral, 1976. Dir, Post Ordination Trng and Continuing Ministerial Educn, Kensington Episcopal Area, 1984–87. Chaplain: Rediffusion Television, 1961–68; Thames Television, 1970–93. First Dir, Brent Samaritans, 1965–68; Dep. Dir, NW Surrey Samaritans, 1973–79. Mem., European Conf. on the Catechumenate, 1975– (Chm., 1983). *Publications:* Journey into Faith, 1984; Adult Believing, 1988; Adult Way to Faith, 1992. *Recreations:* gardening, walking, music. *Address:* Whittonedge, Whittonditch Road, Ramsbury, Marlborough, Wilts SN8 2PX.

BALL, Prof. Sir (Robert) James, Kt 1984; MA, PhD; Professor of Economics, London Business School, since 1965; Director: IBM UK Holdings Ltd, since 1979; IBM United Kingdom Pensions Trust Ltd, since 1994; Royal Bank of Canada, since 1990; Economic Adviser, Touche Ross & Co., since 1984; *b* 15 July 1933; *s* of Arnold James Hector Ball; *m* 1st, 1954, Patricia Mary Hart Davies (marr. diss. 1970); one *s* three *d* (and one *d* decd); 2nd, 1970, Lindsay Jackson (*née* Wonnacott); one step *s*. *Educ:* St Marylebone Grammar Sch.; The Queen's College, Oxford; Styring Schol.; George Webb Medley Junior Schol. (Univ. Prizeman), 1956. BA 1957 (First cl. Hons PPE), MA 1960; PhD Univ. of Pennsylvania, 1973. RAF 1952–54 (Pilot-Officer, Navigator). Research Officer, Oxford University Inst. of Statistics, 1957–58; IBM Fellow, Univ. of Pennsylvania, 1958–60; Lectr, Manchester Univ., 1960, Sen. Lectr, 1963–65; London Business School: Governor, 1969–84; Dep. Principal, 1971–72; Principal, 1972–84. Director: Ogilvy and Mather Ltd, 1969–71; Economic Models Ltd, 1971–72; Barclays Bank Trust Co., 1973–86; Tube Investments, 1974–84; Legal & General Gp, 1978–94 (Chm., 1980–94); LASMO plc, 1988–94. Member: Cttee to Review National Savings (Page Cttee), 1971–73; Economics Cttee of SSRC, 1971–74; Cttee on Social Forecasting, SSRC, 1971–72; Cttee of Enquiry into Electricity Supply Industry (Plowden Cttee), 1974–75; Chm., Treasury Cttee on Policy Optimisation, 1976–78. Marshall Aid Commemoration Comr, 1987–. Governor, NIESR, 1973–. Vice-Pres., Chartered Inst. of Marketing, 1991–94; Member Council: REconS, 1973–79; BIM, 1974–82 (Chm., Economic and Social Affairs Cttee, 1979–82); British–N American Cttee, 1985–. Pres., Sect. F, BAAS, 1990–91. Vice-Pres., CAM Foundn, 1983–92; Trustee: Foulkes Foundn, 1984–; Civic Trust, 1986–91; The Economist, 1987–; Re Action Trust, 1991–93. Fellow, Econometric Soc., 1973; CIMgt (CBIM 1974); FIAM 1985. Freeman, City of London, 1987. Hon. DSc Aston, 1987; Hon. DSocSc Manchester, 1988. *Publications:* An Econometric Model of the United Kingdom, 1961; Inflation and the Theory of Money, 1964; (ed) Inflation, 1969; (ed) The International Linkage of National Economic Models, 1972; Money and Employment, 1982; (with M. Albert) Toward European Economic Recovery in the 1980s (report to European Parliament), 1984; (ed) The Economics of Wealth Creation, 1992; articles in professional jls. *Recreations:* gardening, bridge, chess. *Address:* London Business School, Sussex Place, Regent's Park, NW1 4SA. *T:* 0171–262 5050. *Club:* Royal Automobile.

BALL, Tessa; *see* Hilton, T.

BALLADUR, Edouard; Chevalier, Légion d'Honneur; Deputy (RPR) for Paris, French National Assembly, since 1988; Prime Minister of France, 1993–95; *b* 2 May 1929; *s* of Pierre Balladur and Emilie Latour; *m* 1957, Marie-Josèphe Delacour; four *s*. *Educ:* Lycée Thiers, Marseilles; Faculté de Droit, Aix-en-Provence; Inst. d'etudes Politiques; Ecole Nat. d'Admin. Jun. Auditeur, 1957, Maître des Requêtes, 1963, Conseil d'Etat; Adviser to Dir-Gen., ORTF, 1962–63 (Mem. Admin Council, 1967–68); Tech. Adviser, Office of Prime Minister Pompidou, 1966–68; Pres., French Co. for routier tunnel under Mont Blanc, 1968–81; Mem., Admin Council, Nat. Forestry Office, 1968–73; Asst Sec. Gen., later Sec. Gen., French President's Office, 1969–74; Chm. and Chief Exec., Générale de Service Informatique, 1977–86; Chm. and Chief Exec., Co. européene d'accumulateurs, 1980–86; Mem., Conseil d'Etat, 1984–; Minister for Economy, Finance and Privatization, 1986–88; Mem., Paris City Council, 1989–. Numerous medals and awards, incl. Louise Michel Prize, 1993. *Publications:* l'Arbre de mai, 1979; Je crois en l'homme plus qu'en l'Etat, 1987; (jtly) Passion et longueur de temps, 1989; Douze lettres aux Français trop tranquilles, 1990; Des modes et des convictions, 1992; Le dictionnaire de la réforme, 1992. *Address:* Assemblée nationale, 126 rue de l'Université, 75355 Paris, France.

BALLANTINE, (David) Grant, FFA; Directing Actuary, Government Actuary's Department, since 1991; *b* 24 March 1941; *s* of James Williamson Ballantine and Robertha (*née* Fairley); *m* 1969, Marjorie Campbell Brown; one *s* one *d*. *Educ:* Daniel Stewart's Coll.; Edinburgh Univ. (BSc 1st Cl.). Scottish Widows' Fund, 1963–68; Asst Vice-Pres., Amer. Insce Gp (Far East), 1968–73; Government Actuary's Department, 1973–: Actuary, 1973–82; Chief Actuary, 1983–90. Mem. Council, Faculty of Actuaries, 1991–94. *Publications:* articles in trade and professional jls. *Address:* Government Actuary's Department, 22 Kingsway, WC2B 6LE. *T:* 0171–242 6828.

BALLARAT, Bishop of, since 1994; **Rt. Rev. (Robert) David Silk;** *b* 23 Aug. 1936; *s* of Robert Reeve Silk and Winifred Patience Silk; *m* 1957, Joyce Irene Bracey; one *s* one *d*. *Educ:* Gillingham Grammar School; Univ. of Exeter (BA Hons Theology 1958); St Stephen's House, Oxford. Deacon 1959, priest 1960, Rochester; Curate: St Barnabas, Gillingham, 1959–63; Holy Redeemer, Lamorbey, 1963–69; Priest-in-Charge of the Good Shepherd, Blackfen, 1967–69; Rector of Swanscombe, 1969–75; Rector of Beckenham, St George, 1975–80; Team Rector, Holy Spirit, Leicester, 1982–88; Archdeacon of Leicester, 1980–94. Proctor in Convocation, 1970–94; Prolocutor of Lower House of Convocation of Canterbury, 1980–94; Member of Liturgical Commn, 1976–91; Chm., Leicester Council of Faiths, 1986–93; Moderator, Churches Commn for Inter-Faith Relations (formerly Cttee for Relations with Peoples of Other Faiths), 1990–93. *Publications:* Prayers for Use at the Alternative Services, 1980; Compline—an Alternative Order, 1980; In Penitence and Faith, 1988. *Recreations:* Richard III Society, Leicester FC, theatre. *Address:* Bishopscourt, 454 Wendouree Parade, Ballarat, Vic 3350, Australia. *Club:* Athenæum.

BALLARAT, Bishop of, (RC), since 1971; **Most Rev. Ronald Austin Mulkearns,** DD, DCL; *b* 11 Nov. 1930. *Educ:* De La Salle Coll., Malvern; Corpus Christi Coll., Werribee; Pontifical Lateran Univ., Rome. Ordained, 1956; Coadjutor Bishop, 1968–71. *Address:* 1444 Sturt Street, Ballarat, Victoria 3350, Australia.

BALLARD, Prof. Clifford Frederick; Professor Emeritus in Orthodontics, University of London; Hon. Consultant, Eastman Dental Hospital, London; *b* 26 June 1910; *s* of Frederick John Ballard and Eliza Susannah (*née* Wilkinson); *m* 1937, Muriel Mabel Burling; one *s* one *d*. *Educ:* Kilburn Grammar Sch.; Charing Cross Hosp. and Royal Dental Hospital. LDS 1934; MRCS, LRCP 1940. Hd of Dept of Orthodontics, Inst. of Dental Surgery, British Post-Grad. Med. Fedn, Univ. of London, 1948–72; Prof. of Orthodontics, London Univ., 1956–72; Dental Surgeon, Victoria Hosp. for Children, SW3, 1948–64, Tooting, 1964–71. Pres. of Brit. Soc. for the Study of Orthodontics, 1957, Senior Vice-Pres., 1963, 1964; Mem. Council of Odontological Section of Royal Society Med., 1954–56, 1959–62 (Sec., 1957, Vice-Pres., 1969–72); Mem. Board, Faculty of Dental Surgery. RCS, 1966–74. FDS 1949; Diploma in Orthodontics, 1954 (RCS); FFDRCS Ire., 1964. Charles Tomes Lectr, RCS, 1966; Northcroft Memorial Lectr, Brit. Soc. for Study of Orthocorties, 1967. Hon. Life Mem., British Dental Assoc., 1982; Hon. Member: British Soc. for Study of Orthodontics; Israel Orthodontic Soc.; NZ Orthodontic Soc.; European Orthodontic Soc.; Membre d'Honneur, Société Française d'Orthopédie Dento-faciale. Colyer Gold Medal, RCS, 1975; (first recipient) C. F. Ballard Award, Consultant Orthodontists' Gp, 1990. *Publications:* numerous contributions to learned journals, 1948–. *Recreation:* indoor bowls. *Address:* Flat 20, The Maltings, Salisbury, Wilts SP1 1BD. *T:* Salisbury (01722) 335099.

BALLARD, James Graham; novelist and short story writer; *b* 15 Nov. 1930; *s* of James Ballard and Edna Ballard (*née* Johnstone); *m* 1954, Helen Mary Matthews (*d* 1964); one *s* two *d*. *Educ:* Leys School, Cambridge; King's College, Cambridge. *Publications:* The Drowned World, 1963; The 4–Dimensional Nightmare, 1963 (re-issued as The Voices of Time, 1985); The Terminal Beach, 1964; The Drought, 1965; The Crystal World, 1966; The Disaster Area, 1967; The Atrocity Exhibition, 1970; Crash, 1973; Vermilion Sands, 1973; Concrete Island, 1974; High Rise, 1975; Low-Flying Aircraft, 1976; The Unlimited Dream Company, 1979; Myths of the Near Future, 1982; Empire of the Sun, 1984 (filmed, 1988); The Venus Hunters, 1986; The Day of Creation, 1987; Running Wild, 1988; War Fever, 1990; The Kindness of Women, 1991; Rushing to Paradise, 1994. *Address:* 36 Old Charlton Road, Shepperton, Middlesex TW17 8AT. *T:* Walton-on-Thames (01932) 225692.

BALLARD, John Frederick; Director, Planning Directorate, Department of the Environment, since 1993; *b* 8 Aug. 1943; *s* of Frederick and Margaret Ballard; *m* 1976 (separated 1986); one *s* two *d*. *Educ:* Roundhay Grammar Sch., Leeds; Ifield Grammar Sch., W Sussex; Southampton Univ. (BA); Exeter Univ. (CertEd). Academic Registrar's Dept, Univ. of Surrey, 1965–69; Asst Principal, MoT, 1969; Principal, DoE, 1972; Treasury, 1976; Asst Sec. 1978, Sec., Top Salaries Review Body and Police Negotiating Bd; DoE, 1979; Prin. Private Sec. to Sec. of State for the Environment, 1983–85; Under Sec., DoE and Dept of Transport, and Regl Dir, Yorks and Humberside Region, 1986; Dir, Housing Assocs and the Private Sector, DoE, 1990–92; Dir, Maxwell Pensions Unit, DSS, 1992–93 (on secondment); Trustee, Maxwell Pensioners Trust, 1993–. Special Trustee, Gt Ormond St Hosp. for Sick Children, 1992–. *Recreations:* squash, singing, reading. *Address:* Department of the Environment, 2 Marsham Street, SW1P 3EB. *T:* 0171–276 3854.

BALLARD, Ronald Alfred; Head of Technical Services of the Central Computers and Telecommunications Agency, HM Treasury (formerly Civil Service Department), 1980–85; consultant, 1985–95; voluntary work, Help the Aged, since 1989; *b* 17 Feb. 1925; *s* of Joseph William and Ivy Amy Ballard; *m* 1948, Eileen Margaret Edwards; one *d*. *Educ:* Univ. of Birmingham (BSc (Hons) Physics). National Service, RN, 1945–47. Admiralty Surface Weapons Establishment, Portsmouth: Scientific Officer, then Sen. Scientific Officer, Research and Development Seaborne Radar Systems, 1948–55; Application of Computers to Naval Comd and Control Systems, 1955–69; PSO, 1960, responsibilities for Action Data Automation (ADA), on HMS Eagle and destroyers; SPSO, to Head Computer Systems and Techniques in Civil Service Dept (Central Computers Agency in 1972), 1969; Head of Central Computers Facility, 1972–76; DCSO, to Head Technical Services Div. of Central Computers Agency, 1977; CSO(B), 1980–85. Treas., Sutton Assoc. for the Blind, 1985–; Asst Treas., League of Friends, Queen Mary's Hosp., Carshalton, 1986–.

BALLENTYNE, Donald Francis, CMG 1985; HM Diplomatic Service, retired; Consul-General, Los Angeles, 1985–89; *b* 5 May 1929; *s* of late Henry Q. Ballentyne and Frances R. MacLaren; *m* 1950, Elizabeth Heywood, *d* of Leslie A. Heywood; one *s* one *d*. *Educ:* Haberdashers' Aske's Hatcham Sch. FO, 1950–53; Berne and Ankara, 1953–56; Consul: Munich, 1957; Stanleyville, 1961; Cape Town, 1962; First Secretary: Luxembourg, 1965–69, Havana, 1969–72; FCO, 1972–74; Counsellor (Commercial), The Hague, 1974–78, Bonn, 1978–81; Counsellor, E Berlin, 1982–84. *Recreations:* sailing, riding. *Address:* Orford, Suffolk.

BALLESTEROS, Severiano; golfer; *b* Santander, Spain, 9 April 1957; *m* 1988, Carmen Botin; two *s* one *d*. Professional golfer, 1974–; won Spanish Young Professional title, 1975, 1978; French Open, 1977, 1982, 1985, 1986; Japan Open, 1977, 1978; Swiss Open, 1977, 1978, 1989; German Open, 1978, 1988; Open Champion, Lytham St Anne's, 1979 and 1988, St Andrews, 1984; won US Masters, 1980, 1983; World Matchplay Champion, Wentworth, 1981, 1982, 1984, 1985; Australian PGA Championship, 1981; Spanish Open, 1985, 1995; Dutch Open, 1986; British Masters, 1991; PGA Championship, 1991; Internat. Open, 1994; numerous other titles in Europe, USA, Australasia; Mem. Ryder Cup team, 1979, 1983, 1985, 1987, 1989. Prince of Asturias prize for sport, 1989. *Address:* Houston Palace, 7 Avenue Princess Grace, Monte Carlo, Monaco.

BALLIN, Dame (Reubina) Ann, DBE 1993 (CBE 1981); Chairman (New Zealand), Australia New Zealand Council for the Care of Animals in Research and Teaching, since 1993; *b* 20 Feb. 1932; *d* of late Jack Ballin and of Thelma Joyce (*née* Penberthy). *Educ:* St Hilda's Collegiate Sch.; Waikato Diocesan Sch.; Univ. of Auckland; Univ. of Canterbury (MA 1964). Vis. Psychologist, Princess Margaret Hosp., 1964–69; private Psychologist, Calvary Psychiatric Clinic, 1964–73; Student Counsellor, Univ. of Canterbury, 1974–86. Mem., Royal Commn on Social Policy, 1987–88; Nat. Chm., Internat. Year of Disabled People, 1979–82; Chm., NZ Council of Recreation and Sport, 1985–86; Mem., Hillary Commn for Sport and Recreation, 1986–88; Chm., Victims' Task Force, 1988–93. Pres., NZ Psychological Soc., 1978–79. Mem., Cambodia Trust, 1993–. Patron, Family Help

Trust, 1993–. Sesquicentennial Medal, NZ, 1990. *Recreations:* sport, literature, food, embroidery, all broadcast media, gardens. *Address:* 2/91 Mays Road, Christchurch 8005, New Zealand. *T:* and *Fax:* (3) 3557955.

BALLS, Alastair Gordon, CB 1995; Chief Executive, Tyne and Wear Development Corporation, since 1987; *b* 18 March 1944; *s* of Dr Ernest George Balls and Mrs Elspeth Russell Balls; *m* 1978, Beryl May Nichol; one *s* one *d. Educ:* Hamilton Acad.; Univ. of St Andrews (MA); Univ. of Manchester (MA). Economist: Treasury, Govt of Tanzania, 1966–68; Min. of Transport, UK, 1969–74; Sec., Adv. Cttee on Channel Tunnel, 1974–75; Sen. Econ. Adviser, HM Treasury, 1976–79; Asst Sec., Dept of Environment, 1979–83; Regl Dir, Depts of Environment and Transport (Northern Region), 1984–87. Mem. Council, Univ. of Newcastle upon Tyne, 1990–. *Recreations:* sailing, cycling, walking, camping in the company of my family. *Address:* Tyne and Wear Development Corporation, Scotswood House, Newcastle Business Park, Newcastle upon Tyne NE4 7YL. *T:* 0191–226 1234, *Fax:* 0191–226 0905.

BALMER, Colin Victor; Assistant Under-Secretary of State (Financial Management), Ministry of Defence, since 1994; *b* 22 Aug. 1946; *s* of Peter Lionel Balmer and Adelaide Currie Balmer; *m* 1978, Frances Mary Montrésor; two *s* one *d. Educ:* Liverpool Inst. High Sch. War Office, 1963, later Ministry of Defence: Asst Private Sec. to Minister of State, 1972; Private Sec. to Parly Under-Sec. of State (RAF), 1973; Civil Advr to GOC N Ireland, 1973; Cabinet Office, 1977; Private Sec. to Minister of State (Defence Procurement), 1980; UK Delegn to NATO, 1982; MoD 1984; Minister (Defence Materiel), Washington, 1990; Asst Under-Sec. of State, MoD, 1992–. *Recreations:* golf, tennis, gardening, bridge, rock and roll music, playing guitar (badly). *Address:* 36 Pensford Avenue, Richmond, Surrey TW9 4HP. *T:* 0181–878 2224.

BALMFORTH, Ven. Anthony James; Archdeacon of Bristol, 1979–90, now Archdeacon Emeritus; *b* 3 Sept. 1926; *s* of Joseph Henry and Daisy Florence Balmforth; *m* 1952, Eileen Julia, *d* of James Raymond and Kitty Anne Evans; one *s* two *d. Educ:* Sebright School, Wolverley; Brasenose Coll., Oxford (BA 1950, MA 1951); Lincoln Theological Coll. Army service, 1944–48. Deacon 1952, priest 1953, dio. Southwell; Curate of Mansfield, 1952–55; Vicar of Skegby, Notts, 1955–61; Vicar of St John's, Kidderminster, Worcs, 1961–65; Rector of St Nicolas, King's Norton, Birmingham, 1965–79; Hon. Canon of Birmingham Cathedral, 1975–79; RD of King's Norton, 1973–79; Examining Chaplain to: Bishop of Birmingham, 1978–79; Bishop of Bristol, 1981–90. Hon. Canon of Bristol Cathedral, 1979–. Mem., Gen. Synod of C of E, 1982–90. *Recreations:* cricket, gardening. *Address:* Slipper Cottage, Stag Hill, Yorkley, near Lydney, Glos GL15 4TB. *T:* Dean (01594) 564016.

BALNIEL, Lord; Anthony Robert Lindsay; Director, J. O. Hambro Investment Management, since 1987; *b* 24 Nov. 1958; *s* and *heir* of Earl of Crawford and Balcarres, *qv*; *m* 1989, Nicola A., *y d* of Antony Bicket; two *s. Educ:* Eton Coll.; Univ. of Edinburgh. *Heir: s* Master of Lindsay, *qv. Address:* 6 Pembridge Place, W2 4XB. *Clubs:* New (Edinburgh); XII.

BALSTON, Antony Francis; His Honour Judge Balston; a Circuit Judge, since 1985; *b* 18 Jan. 1939; *s* of Comdr E. F. Balston, DSO, RN, and late D. B. L. Balston (*née* Ferrers); *m* 1966, Anne Marie Judith Ball; two *s* one *d. Educ:* Downside; Christ's Coll., Cambridge (MA). Served Royal Navy, 1957–59; Univ. of Cambridge, 1959–62; admitted Solicitor, 1966. Partner, Herington Willings & Penry Davey, Solicitors, Hastings, 1967–85; a Recorder of the Crown Court, 1980–85; Hon. Recorder, Hastings, 1984–. *Recreation:* gardening.

BALTIMORE, Prof. David, PhD; Ivan R. Cottrell Professor of Molecular Biology and Immunology, Massachusetts Institute of Technology, since 1994; *b* New York, 7 March 1938; *s* of Richard and Gertrude Baltimore; *m* 1968, Alice Huang; one *d. Educ:* Swarthmore Coll. (BA 1960); Rockefeller Univ. (PhD 1964). Postdoctoral Fellow, MIT, 1963–64; Albert Einstein Coll. of Med., NY, 1964–65; Research Associate, Salk Inst., La Jolla, Calif, 1965–68; Massachusetts Institute of Technology: Associate Prof., 1968–72; Amer. Cancer Soc. Prof. of Microbiol., 1973–83; Prof. of Biology, 1972–90; Dir, Whitehead Inst., 1982–90; Prof., 1990–94, Pres., 1990–91, Rockefeller Univ. FAAAS 1980. Member: Nat. Acad. of Scis, 1974; Amer. Acad. of Arts and Scis, 1974; Pontifical Acad. of Scis, 1978; Foreign Mem., Royal Soc., 1987. Eli Lilly Award in Microbiology and Immunology, 1971; US Steel Foundn Award in Molecular Biology, 1974; (jtly) Nobel Prize for Physiology or Medicine, 1975. *Address:* Massachusetts Institute of Technology, Building 68, Room 380, 77 Massachusetts Avenue, Cambridge, MA 02139, USA.

BAMBERG, Harold Rolf, CBE 1968; Chairman: Glos Air Cos; Eagle Aircraft Ltd; Via Nova Properties Ltd; Bamberg Organisation; *b* 17 Nov. 1923; *m* 1957, (marr. diss. 1990); one *s* two *d* (and one *s* one *d* of a former marriage). *Educ:* Hampstead. Former Chairman: British Independent Air Transport Assoc.; GAMTA; former Director: Cunard Steamship Co.; BOAC Cunard, etc.; Founder, Lunn Poly Ltd, 1956. FRSA; FRAeS 1993. Mem., Skal Club. Kt, Order of Merit, Italian Republic, 1960. *Recreations:* horses, travel, golf. *Address:* Park House, Pinecote Drive, Sunninghill, Berks SL5 9PS. *T:* Ascot (01344) 22817, *Fax:* (01344) 21375. *Clubs:* Guards' Polo; Wentworth Golf.

BAMBOROUGH, John Bernard; Principal of Linacre College, Oxford, 1962–88; Pro-Vice-Chancellor, Oxford University, 1966–88; *b* 3 Jan. 1921; *s* of John George Bamborough; *m* 1947, Anne, *d* of Olav Indrehus, Indrehus, Norway; one *s* one *d. Educ:* Haberdashers' Aske's Hampstead Sch. (Scholar); New College, Oxford (Scholar). 1st Class, English Language and Literature, 1941; MA 1946. Service in RN, 1941–46 (in Coastal Forces as Lieut RNVR; afterwards as Educ. Officer with rank of Instructor Lieut, RN). Junior Lectr, New Coll., Oxford, 1946; Fellow and Tutor, Wadham Coll., Oxford, 1947–62 (Dean, 1947–54; Domestic Bursar, 1954–56; Sen. Tutor, 1957–61); Univ. Lectr in English, 1951–62; Mem. Hebdomadal Council, Oxford Univ., 1961–79. Hon. Fellow: New Coll., Oxford, 1967; Linacre Coll., Oxford, 1988; Wadham Coll., Oxford, 1988. Editor, Review of English Studies, 1964–78. Cavaliere Ufficiale, Order of Merit (Italy), 1991. *Publications:* The Little World of Man, 1952; Ben Jonson, 1959; (ed) Pope's Life of Ward, 1961; Jonson's Volpone, 1963; The Alchemist, 1967; Ben Jonson, 1970; (ed) Burton's Anatomy of Melancholy, 1989. *Address:* 18 Winchester Road, Oxford OX2 6NA. *T:* Oxford (01865) 59886.

BAMFIELD, Clifford, CB 1981; Civil Service Commission Panel of Selection Board Chairmen, 1982–93; *b* 21 March 1922; *s* of G. H. Bamfield. *Educ:* Wintringham Grammar Sch., Grimsby; Manchester Business Sch., 1966. Served War, RNVR, 1941–46. Customs and Excise: Exec. Officer, 1946; Private Sec. to Chm., 1959–61; Principal, 1961; Asst Sec., 1967; Under Sec., Comr and Dir of Estabs, 1973; Under Sec., CSD, 1974–80; Mem., 1982–91, Dep. Chm., 1989–91, CSAB. *Address:* 15 The Linkway, Sutton, Surrey SM2 5SE. *T:* 0181–642 5377. *Club:* Army and Navy.

BAMFORD, Alan George, CBE 1985; Principal, Homerton College, Cambridge, 1985–91; *b* 12 July 1930; *s* of James Ross and Margaret Emily Bamford; *m* 1954, Joan Margaret, *e d* of Arthur W. Vint; four *s. Educ:* Prescot Grammar School; Borough Road College, London; Liverpool University (DipEd, MEd); MA Cantab; Cert. Ed. London. Teacher and Dep. Headmaster, Lancashire primary schs, 1952–62; Lectr in Primary Educn, Liverpool Univ., 1962–63; Sen. Lectr in Educn, Chester Coll., 1963–66; Principal Lectr and Head of Educn Dept, S Katharine's Coll., Liverpool, 1966–71; Principal, Westhill Coll., Birmingham, 1971–85. Pres., Birmingham Council of Christian Educn, 1972–74, Vice-Pres., 1974–91; Vice-Pres., Colls of Educn Christian Union, 1965–86, Pres., 1966–67, 1972–73; Chm., Birmingham Assoc. of Youth Clubs, 1972–85, Vice-Pres., 1985–; Member: Standing Conf. on Studies in Educn, 1974–91 (Exec. Cttee and Editl Bd, 1978–87, Sec., 1982–84); Council of Nat. Youth Bureau, 1974–80 (Exec. Cttee, 1978–80); Adv. Cttee on religious broadcasts, BBC Radio Birmingham, 1972–80; Educn Cttee, Free Church Fed. Council, 1978–89; BCC Standing Cttee on Theol Educn, 1979–82; Council, British and Foreign School Soc., 1979–85; Exec. Cttee, Assoc. of Voluntary Colls, 1979–86; Standing Cttee on Educn and Training of Teachers, 1985– (Vice-Chm., 1988; Chm. , 1989); Cttee, Standing Conf. of Principals and Dirs of Colls and Insts of Higher Educn, 1986–91; Voluntary Sector Consultative Council, 1987–88; Cambridge HA, 1987–90 (Trustee, 1988–90); Chairman: Colls Cttee, NATFHE, 1981–82; Central Register and Clearing House Cttee, 1981–82 (Mem. Council of Management, 1982–92). Governor: London Bible Coll., 1981–89; Cambridge Inst. of Educn, 1985–91. JP Birmingham 1977–85. FRSA. Hon. MA Birmingham, 1981. *Publications:* articles on educn and church-related subjects. *Recreations:* travel, photography. *Address:* Shiloh, 2 Bayham Road, Tunbridge Wells, Kent TN2 5HP. *Club:* Commonwealth Trust.

BAMFORD, Sir Anthony (Paul), Kt 1990; DL; Chairman and Managing Director, J. C. Bamford Group, since 1975; *b* 23 Oct. 1945; *s* of Joseph Cyril Bamford, *qv*; *m* 1974, Carole Gray Whitt; two *s* one *d. Educ:* Ampleforth Coll.; Grenoble Univ. Joined JCB on shop floor, 1962. Dir, Tarmac, 1987–94. Member: Design Council, 1987–89; President's Cttee, CBI, 1986–88. Pres., Staffs Agricl Soc., 1987–88. Pres., Burton on Trent Cons. Assoc., 1987–90. High Sheriff, Staffs, 1985–86. DL Staffs, 1989. Hon. FCGLI 1993; Hon. FCSD 1994. Hon. MEng Birmingham, 1987; DUniv Keele, 1988; Hon. DSc Cranfield, 1994. Young Exporter of the Year, 1972; Young Businessman of the Year, 1979. Chevalier, l'Ordre National du Mérite (France), 1989. *Recreations:* riding, farming, classic and vintage racing cars. *Address:* c/o J. C. Bamford Excavators Ltd, Rocester, Uttoxeter, Staffs ST14 5JP. *Clubs:* Pratt's, Lighthouse, British Racing Drivers'.

BAMFORD, Prof. Clement Henry, FRS 1964; MA, PhD, ScD Cantab; CChem, FRSC; Honorary Senior Fellow, Department of Clinical Engineering (formerly Institute of Medical and Dental Bioengineering), University of Liverpool, since 1980; Campbell Brown Professor of Industrial Chemistry, University of Liverpool, 1962–80, now Emeritus Professor; *b* 10 Oct. 1912; *s* of Frederic Jesse Bamford and Catherine Mary Bamford (*née* Shelley), Stafford; *m* 1938, Daphne Ailsa Stephan, BSc Sydney, PhD Cantab, of Sydney, Australia; one *s* one *d. Educ:* St Patrick's and King Edward VI Schs, Stafford; Trinity Coll., Cambridge (Senior Scholar, 1931). Fellow, Trinity Coll., Cambridge, 1937; Dir of Studies in Chemistry, Emmanuel Coll., Cambridge, 1937. Joined Special Operations Executive, 1941; joined Fundamental Research Laboratory of Messrs Courtaulds Ltd, at Maidenhead, 1945; head of laboratory, 1947–62; Liverpool University: Dean, Faculty of Science, 1965–68; Pro-Vice-Chancellor, 1972–75; Hd, Dept of Inorganic, Physical and Industrial Chemistry, 1973–78. Member: Council, Chem. Soc., 1972–75; Council, Soc. Chem. Ind., 1974–75. Pres., British Assoc. Section B (Chemistry), 1975–76; Vice-Pres., 1977–81, Pres., 1981–85, Macromolecular Div., Internat. Union of Pure and Applied Chemistry. Vis. Professor: Kyoto Univ., 1977; Univ. of NSW, 1981. Mem. Edit. Bd, Polymer, 1958–; European Ed., Jl of Biomaterials Sci., 1988–. Hon. DSc: Bradford, 1980; Lancaster, 1988. Meldola Medal, Royal Inst. of Chemistry, 1941; Macromolecules and Polymers Award, Chemical Soc., 1977; Award for dist. service in advancement of polymer science, Soc. of Polymer Science, Japan, 1989; George Winter Award, European Soc. for Biomaterials, 1992. *Publications:* Synthetic Polypeptides (with A. Elliott and W. E. Hanby), 1956; The Kinetics of Vinyl Polymerization by Radical Mechanisms (with W. G. Barb, A. D. Jenkins and P. F. Onyon), 1958; (ed with late C. F. H. Tipper and R. G. Compton) Comprehensive Chemical Kinetics, 26 vols, 1969–86; papers on physical chemistry, polymer science and biomaterials science in learned journals. *Recreations:* music, especially violin playing, hill walking, gardening. *Address:* Broom Bank, Tower Road, Prenton, Birkenhead, Merseyside L42 8LH. *T:* 0151–608 3979.

BAMFORD, Joseph Cyril, CBE 1969; formerly Chairman and Managing Director: J. C. Bamford Excavators Ltd; JCB Farms Ltd; JCB Research Ltd; JCB Sales Ltd; JCB Service; JCB Earthmovers Ltd; *b* 21 June 1916; *m* 1941, Marjorie Griffin; two *s. Educ:* St John's, Alton, Staffs; Stonyhurst Coll. Founded J. C. Bamford Excavators Ltd, 1945; more than seventy per cent of total production now goes to export market; initials JCB have entered the language as term for excavator. Hon. DTech Loughborough Univ. of Technol., 1983; Hon. DBA Buckingham, 1991; Hon. DEng Sheffield, 1992. *Recreations:* yacht designing, landscaping, landscape gardening. *Address:* Les Tourelles, Bon Port 15, 1820 Montreux-Territet, Switzerland.

See also Sir A. P. Bamford.

BAMFORD, Louis Neville Jules; Legal Executive with Margetts & Ritchie, Solicitors, Birmingham, since 1960; *b* 2 July 1932; *s* of Neville Barnes Bamford and Elise Marie Bamford; unmarried. *Educ:* local schools in Birmingham. Member (Lab): Birmingham CC, 1971–74; W Midlands CC, 1974–86 (Chm., 1981–82; Chm., Legal and Parly Cttee, 1974–77; Mem. of various cttees); Birmingham CC, 1986– (Mem. various cttees incl. Gen. Purposes, Envmtl Health and Trading Services (Vice-Chm.)). Chm., Birmingham Convention and Visitors Bureau. *Recreations:* football, music. *Address:* 15 Chilton Court, Park Approach, Erdington, Birmingham B23 7XY.

BAMMEL, Caroline Penrose, PhD; FBA 1994; Reader in Early Church History, since 1992, and Fellow of Girton College, since 1968, University of Cambridge; *b* 6 July 1940; *d* of Prof. Nicholas Geoffrey Lemprière Hammond, *qv*; *m* 1979, Prof. Ernst Bammel. *Educ.* Clifton High Sch., Bristol; Girton Coll., Cambridge (MA; PhD 1966). Girton College, Cambridge: Res. Fellow, 1966–68; Lectr in Classics, 1968–; Dir of Studies in Theology, 1976–; Asst Lectr, 1975–80, Lectr, 1980–92, in Early Church History, Cambridge Univ. Faculty of Divinity. *Publications:* Der Römerbrieftext des Rufin und seine Origenesübersetzung, 1985; Origenis in Epistulam Pauli ad Romanos explanationum libri, Vol. I, 1990; contrib. Jl of Theol Studies, Augustinianum, Zeitschrift für Kirchengeschichte, etc. *Address:* Girton College, Cambridge CB3 0JG. *T:* Cambridge (01223) 338999.

BAMPFYLDE, family name of **Baron Poltimore.**

BANANA, Rev. Dr Canaan Sodindo; President of Zimbabwe, 1980–87; *b* Esiphezini, Matabeleland, 5 March 1936; *s* of Aaron and Jese Banana; *m* 1961, Janet Mbuyazwe; three *s* one *d. Educ:* Mzinyati Mission; Tegwani Trng Inst.; Epworth Theol Coll., Salisbury; Kansai Industrial Centre, Japan; Wesley Theol Seminary, Washington, DC; Univ. of S Africa. Dip. in Urban and Industrial Mission, Kansai, 1970; MTS Hons, Wesley Theol Seminary, 1974; BA Hons Univ. of SA, 1980. Methodist Minister and Manager of Schools: Wankie Area, 1963–64; Plumtree Area, 1965–66 (Sch. Chaplain, Tegwani High Sch.); Methodist Minister, Fort Viet Area, 1967–68; Methodist Minister, Bulawayo and Chm.,

Bulaway Council of Churches, 1969–70; with Mambo Press as Promotion Officer for Moto, Catholic newspaper, 1971; Founder Mem. and first Vice Pres., ANC, Zimbabwe, 1971–73; ANC Rep. in N America and UN, 1973–75; Chaplain, American Univ., 1974–75; Publicity Sec., People's Movement Internal Co-ordinating Cttee (ZANU-PF), 1976–77; Reg. Co-ordinator, Matabeleland N and S Provinces, 1979–80. Chm., Southern Africa Contact Gp, 1970–73; Mem., Adv. Cttee, WCC, 1970–80. Hon. LLD: Amer. Univ., 1981; Univ. of Zimbabwe, 1983. *Publications:* The Zimbabwe Exodus, 1974; The Gospel According to the Ghetto, 1974, 3rd edn 1980; The Woman of my Imagination, 1980 (also in Ndebele and Shona versions); Theology of Promise, 1982; The Ethos of Socialism, 1988; various articles. *Recreations:* tennis, table tennis; soccer (player, referee and coach); volley ball (umpire); music. *Address:* c/o State House, Box 368, Harare, Zimbabwe. *T:* Harare (4) 26666.

BANBURY, family name of **Baron Banbury of Southam.**

BANBURY OF SOUTHAM, 3rd Baron *cr* 1924, of Southam; **Charles William Banbury;** Bt 1902; *b* 29 July 1953; *s* of 2nd Baron Banbury of Southam and of Hilda Ruth, *d* of late A. H. R. Carr; *S* father, 1981; *m* 1st, 1984, Lucinda Trehearne (marr. diss. 1986); 2nd, 1989, Inger Marianne Norton; two *d. Educ:* Eton College. *Heir:* none. *Address:* The Mill, Fossebridge, Glos GL54 3JN.

BANBURY, (Frederick Harold) Frith; theatrical director, producer and actor; *b* 4 May 1912; *s* of Rear-Adm. Frederick Arthur Frith Banbury and Winifred (*née* Fink); unmarried. *Educ:* Stowe Sch.; Hertford Coll., Oxford; Royal Academy of Dramatic Art. First stage appearance in "If I Were You", Shaftesbury Theatre, 1933; for next 14 years appeared both in London and Provinces in every branch of theatre from Shakespeare to revue. Appearances included: Hamlet, New Theatre, 1934; Goodness How Sad, Vaudeville, 1938; (revue) New Faces, Comedy, 1939; Uncle Vanya, Westminster, 1943; Jacobowsky and the Colonel, Piccadilly, 1945; Caste, Duke of York's, 1947. During this time he also appeared in numerous films including The Life and Death of Colonel Blimp and The History of Mr Polly, and also on the television screen. Since 1947 he has devoted his time to production and direction, starting with Dark Summer at Lyric, Hammersmith (later transferred St Martin's), 1947; subseq. many, in both London and New York, including The Holly and the Ivy, Duchess, 1950; Waters of the Moon, Haymarket, 1951; The Deep Blue Sea, Duchess, 1951, and Morosco, New York, 1952; A Question of Fact, Piccadilly, 1953; Marching Song, St Martin's, 1954; Love's Labour's Lost, Old Vic, 1954; The Diary of Anne Frank, Phoenix, 1956; A Dead Secret, Piccadilly, 1957; Flowering Cherry, Haymarket, 1957, and Lyceum, New York, 1959; A Touch of the Sun, Saville, 1958; The Ring of Truth, Savoy, 1959; The Tiger and the Horse, Queen's, 1960; The Wings of the Dove, Lyric, 1963; The Right Honourable Gentleman, Billy Rose, New York, 1965; Howards End, New, 1967; Dear Octopus, Haymarket, 1967; Enter A Free Man, St Martin's, 1968; A Day In the Death of Joe Egg, Cameri Theatre, Tel Aviv, 1968; Le Valet, Théâtre de la Renaissance, Paris, 1968; On the Rocks, Dublin Theatre Festival, 1969; My Darling Daisy, Lyric, 1970; The Winslow Boy, New, 1970; Captain Brassbound's Conversion, Cambridge, 1971; Reunion in Vienna, Chichester Festival, 1971, Piccadilly, 1972; The Day After the Fair, Lyric, 1972, Shubert, Los Angeles, 1973; Glasstown, Westminster, 1973; Ardèle, Queen's, 1975; On Approval, Canada and SA, 1976, Vaudeville, 1977; directed in Australia, Kenya, USA, 1978–79; Motherdear, Ambassadors, 1980; Dear Liar, Mermaid, 1982; The Aspern Papers, Haymarket, 1984; The Corn is Green, Old Vic, 1985; The Admirable Crichton, Haymarket, 1988; Screamers, Arts, 1989. *Recreation:* playing the piano.

BANBURY, Frith; *see* Banbury, Frederick Harold F.

BANCROFT, family name of **Baron Bancroft.**

BANCROFT, Baron *cr* 1982 (Life Peer), of Coatham in the county of Cleveland; **Ian Powell Bancroft,** GCB 1979 (KCB 1975; CB 1971); Head of the Home Civil Service and Permanent Secretary to the Civil Service Department, 1978–81; *b* 23 Dec. 1922; *s* of A. E. and L. Bancroft; *m* 1950, Jean Swaine; two *s* one *d. Educ:* Coatham Sch.; Balliol Coll., Oxford (Scholar; Hon. Fellow 1981). Served Rifle Brigade, 1942–45. Entered Treasury, 1947; Private Secretary: to Sir Henry Wilson Smith, 1948–50; to Chancellor of the Exchequer, 1953–55; to Lord Privy Seal, 1955–57; Cabinet Office, 1957–59; Principal Private Sec. to successive Chancellors of the Exchequer, 1964–66; Under-Sec., HM Treasury, 1966–68, Civil Service Dept, 1968–70; Dep. Sec., Dir Gen. of Organization and Establishments, DoE, 1970–72; a Comr of Customs and Excise, and Dep. Chm. of Bd, 1972–73; Second Permanent Sec., CSD, 1973–75; Permanent Sec., DoE, 1975–77. Mem., Adv. Council on Public Records, 1983–88. Dep. Chm., Sun Life Corp. plc, 1987–93 (Dir, 1983–93); a Vice-Chm., 1986–87); Director: Rugby Group (formerly Rugby Portland Cement), 1982–93; Bass Plc, 1982–93; ANZ Grindlays Bank plc, 1983–93; Bass Leisure Ltd, 1984–93. Pres., Building Centre Trust, 1987–93. Vis. Fellow, Nuffield Coll., Oxford, 1973–81; Chm. Trustees, Mansfield Coll., Oxford, 1988– (Chm. Council, 1981–88). Chm., Royal Hosp. and Home, Putney, 1984–88 (Mem., Management Board, 1988–); Governor, Cranleigh Sch., 1983–92; Patron, Friends of Public Record Office, 1993–. *Address:* House of Lords, SW1A 0PW. *T:* 0171–219 3000. *Clubs:* United Oxford & Cambridge University, Civil Service.

BAND, David; Chief Executive, Barclays de Zoete Wedd, since 1988; Director: Barclays PLC, since 1988; Barclays Bank PLC, since 1988; *b* 14 Dec. 1942; *s* of David Band and Elisabeth Aitken Band; *m* 1973, Olivia Rose (*née* Brind); one *s* one *d. Educ:* Rugby; St Edmund Hall, Oxford (MA). Joined J. P. Morgan & Co. in London, 1964; General Manager: Singapore, 1976; Paris, 1978; Sen. Vice Pres., Morgan Guaranty Trust Co., New York, 1981; Man. Dir, Morgan Guaranty Ltd, London, 1986; Exec. Vice Pres., Morgan Guaranty Trust Co., and Chm., J. P. Morgan Securities Ltd, London, 1987. Dep. Chm., Securities Assoc., 1986–88. *Recreation:* tennis. *Address:* c/o BZW, Ebbgate House, 2 Swan Lane, EC4R 3TS. *T:* 0171–956 4007.

BAND, His Honour Robert Murray Niven, MC 1944; QC 1974; a Circuit Judge, 1978–91; *b* 23 Nov. 1919; *s* of Robert Niven Band and Agnes Jane Band; *m* 1948, Nancy Margery Redhead; two *d. Educ:* Trinity Coll., Glenalmond; Hertford Coll., Oxford (MA). Served in Royal Artillery, 1940–46. Called to the Bar, Inner Temple, 1947; Junior Treasury Counsel in Probate Matters, 1972–74; Chm. Family Law Bar Assoc., 1972–74; a Recorder of the Crown Court, 1977–78. Chm., St Teresa's Hosp., Wimbledon, 1969–83. *Recreations:* the countryside, gardens, old buildings, treen.

BAND, Thomas Mollison, FSAScot; FTS; Chairman, Made in Scotland Ltd, since 1994; *b* 28 March 1934; *s* of late Robert Boyce Band and Elizabeth Band; *m* 1959, Jean McKenzie Brien; one *s* two *d. Educ:* Perth Academy. National Service, RAF, 1952–54. Joined Civil Service, 1954; Principal, BoT, 1969; Sen. Principal, Dept of Industry, 1973; Scottish Econ. Planning Dept, 1975, Asst Sec., 1976; Scottish Development Dept, 1978; Scottish Office, Finance, 1981; Dir, Historic Bldgs and Monuments, Scottish Develt Dept, 1984–87; Chief Exec., Scottish Tourist Bd, 1987–94. Chairman: Anderson Enterprises Ltd, 1994–; Edinburgh Europa Ltd, 1994–; Dir, Perth Rep. Theatre Ltd, 1994–. Dir, Edinburgh Telford Coll., 1989–. Chm., Industrial Cttee, Napier Univ. (formerly Napier Poly. of Edinburgh), 1989–. FRSA 1993. *Recreations:* skiing, gardening, beating. *Address:* Heathfield, Pitcairngreen, Perthshire PH1 3LT. *T:* Almondbank (01738) 83403.

BANDA, Hastings Kamuzu, MD, **(Ngwazi Dr H. Kamuzu Banda);** President of Malaŵi 1966–94; Chancellor, University of Malaŵi, 1965–94; Life President, Malaŵi Congress Party; *b* Nyasaland, 1905. *Educ:* Meharry Medical Coll., Nashville, USA (MD); Universities of Glasgow and Edinburgh. Further degrees: BSc, MB, ChB, LRCSE; and several hon. degrees awarded later. Practised medicine in Liverpool and on Tyneside during War of 1939–45 and in London, 1945–53. Returned to Africa, 1953, and practised in Gold Coast. Took over leadership of Nyasaland African Congress in Blantyre, 1958, and became Pres.-Gen.; was imprisoned for political reasons, 1959; unconditionally released, 1960; Minister of Natural Resources and Local Government, Nyasaland, 1961–63; Prime Minister of Malaŵi (formerly Nyasaland), 1963–66. *Address:* Blantyre, Malaŵi.

BANDARANAIKE, Mrs Sirimavo; Prime Minister of Sri Lanka (Ceylon until 1972), 1960–65, 1970–77 and since 1994; President, Sri Lanka Freedom Party, since 1960; *b* 17 April 1916; *d* of Barnes Ratwatte, Ratemahatmaya of Ratnapura Dist, Mem. of Ceylon Senate; *m* 1940, Solomon West Ridgeway Dias Bandaranaike (*d* 1959), Prime Minister of Ceylon, 1956–59; one *s* two *d. Educ:* Ratnapura Ferguson Sch.; St Bridget's Convent, Colombo. Assisted S. W. R. D. Bandaranaike in political career. Campaigned for Sri Lanka Freedom Party in election campaigns, March and July 1960. Formerly Pres. and Treasurer, Lanka Mahila Samiti. MP, 1960–80, and 1989–; Minister of Defence and External Affairs, 1960–65; Minister of Information and Broadcasting, 1964–65; Leader of the Opposition, 1965–70, and 1989–94; Minister of Defence and Foreign Affairs, of Planning and Econ. Affairs, and of Plan Implementation, 1970–77. Chm., Non Aligned Movt, 1976–77. Ceres Medal, FAO, 1977. *Address:* 65 Rosmead Place, Colombo 7, Sri Lanka.

BANFIELD, Ven. David John; Archdeacon of Bristol, since 1990; *b* 25 June 1933; *s* of Norman Charles Banfield and Muriel Gladys Honor Banfield (*née* Pippard); *m* 1967, Rita (*née* Woolhouse); three *d. Educ:* Yeovil Sch.; London Coll. of Divinity, London Univ. (ALCD). RAF, 1951–53. Deacon 1957, priest 1958; Curate, Middleton, Manchester, 1957–62; Chaplain and Asst Warden, Scargill House, Yorks, 1962–67; Vicar of Addiscombe, Croydon, 1967–80; Vicar of Luton, Beds, 1980–90. *Recreations:* travel, walking, music, gardening. *Address:* 10 Great Brockeridge, Westbury-on-Trym, Bristol BS9 3TY. *T:* Bristol (0117) 962 2438.

BANFIELD, John Martin; Chairman, Mobil Oil Co., since 1994; *b* 15 Nov. 1947; *s* of Jack Banfield and Peggy Winifred Banfield (*née* Parker); *m* 1978, Mary Gerrey Morton; one *s* one *d. Educ:* Haberdashers' Aske's; St John's Coll., Cambridge (MA Geography). Mobil Oil Co., 1969; Man. Dir, Mobil Cyprus, 1986; Sales Dir, Mobil Benelux, 1988; Marketing Dir, Mobil Oil Co., 1990; Pres., Mobil Benelux, 1992; Marketing Dir, Mobil Germany, 1993. *Recreations:* music, sailing, travel. *Address:* Mobil Oil Co., Mobil House, 500–600 Witan Gate, Central Milton Keynes MK9 1ES. *T:* Milton Keynes (01908) 853000. *Club:* MCC.

BANGEMANN, Dr Martin; a Member, European Commission (formerly Commission of the European Community), since 1989 (a Vice-President, 1989–93); *b* 15 Nov. 1934; *s* of Martin Bangemann and Lotte Telge; *m* 1962, Renate Bauer; three *s* two *d. Educ:* Univ. of Tübingen; Univ. of Munich (DJur). Lawyer, 1964–. Mem., Bundestag, 1972–80 and 1986–89; Mem., European Parliament, 1973–84; Minister of Econs, FRG, 1984–88. Freie Demokratische Partei: Mem., 1963–; Chm., 1985–88. Fed. Cross of Merit with star (Germany); Bavarian Order of Merit. *Address:* Rue de la Loi 200, 1049 Brussels, Belgium.

BANGHAM, Alec Douglas, MD; FRS 1977; retired; Research Worker, Agricultural Research Council, Institute of Animal Physiology, Babraham, 1952–82 and Head, Biophysics Unit, 1971–82; *b* 10 Nov. 1921; *s* of Dr Donald Hugh and Edith Bangham; *m* 1943, Rosalind Barbara Reiss; three *s* one *d. Educ:* Bryanston Sch.; UCL and UCH Med. Sch. (MD). Captain, RAMC, 1946–48. Lectr, Dept of Exper. Pathology, UCH, 1949–52; Principal Scientific Officer, 1952–63, Senior Principal Scientific Officer (Merit Award), 1963–82, ARC, Babraham. Fellow, UCL, 1981–. *Publications:* contrib. Nature, Biochim. Biophys. Acta, and Methods in Membrane Biol. *Recreations:* horticulture, photographic arts, sailing. *Address:* 17 High Green, Great Shelford, Cambridge CB2 5EG. *T:* Cambridge (01223) 843192, *Fax:* (01223) 844683.

BANGOR, 8th Viscount *cr* 1781 (Ire.); **William Maxwell David Ward;** Baron 1770 (Ire.); antiquarian bookseller; *b* 9 Aug. 1948; *s* of 7th Viscount Bangor and his 3rd wife, Leila Mary Heaton (*d* 1959); *S* father, 1993; *m* 1976, Sarah Mary Malet Bradford (*née* Hayes). *Educ:* University Coll., London. *Recreations:* history, music, antiquity, Bolton Wanderers. *Heir presumptive:* *b* Hon. (Edward) Nicholas Ward [*b* 16 Jan. 1953; *m* 1985, Rachel Mary, *d* of Hon. Hugh Waldorf Astor, *qv*; two *d*]. *Address:* 31 Britannia Road, SW6 2HJ. *Club:* Chelsea Arts.

BANGOR, Bishop of, since 1993; **Rt. Rev. Barry Cennydd Morgan,** PhD; *b* 31 Jan. 1947; *s* of Rees Haydn Morgan and Mary Gwyneth Morgan; *m* 1969, Hilary Patricia Lewis; one *s* one *d. Educ:* Ystalyfera Grammar Sch.; University Coll. London (BA Hons History 1969); Selwyn Coll., Cambridge (BA Hons Theol. 1971); Westcott House, Cambridge. MA Cantab 1974; PhD Wales 1986. Priest, Llandaff, 1973; Curate, St Andrew's Major, Dinas Powis, 1972–75; Chaplain, Bryn-y-Don Community Sch., 1972–75; Chaplain and Lectr, St Michael's Coll., Llandaff, 1975–77; Lectr, University Coll., Cardiff, 1975–77; Warden of Church Hostel, Bangor, Anglican Chap., UCNW and Lectr in Theology, UCNW, 1977–84; Rector of Wrexham, 1984–86; Archdeacon of Merioneth and Rector of Criccieth, 1986–92. Editor, Welsh Churchman, 1975–82. Exam. Chaplain to Abp of Wales, 1978–82, to Bp of Bangor, 1983; Diocese of Bangor: In-Service Trng Officer, 1979–84; Warden of Ordinands, 1982–84; Canon of Bangor Cathedral, 1983–84. Mem., Archbishop's Doctrinal Commn, 1982–93 (Chm. 1989–93); Chm., Div. of Stewardship, Provincial Bd of Mission, 1988–95. *Publications:* O Ddydd i Ddydd, Pwyllgor Darlleniadau Beiblaidd Cygnor Eglwysi Cymru, 1980; History of the Church Hostel and Anglican Chaplaincy at University College of North Wales, Bangor, 1986; Concepts of Mission and Ministry in Anglican University Chaplaincy Work, 1988. *Recreation:* golf. *Address:* Ty'r Esgob, Bangor, Gwynedd LL57 2SS. *T:* Bangor (01248) 362895.

BANGOR, Dean of; *see* Edwards, Very Rev. T. E. P.

BANHAM, Mrs Belinda Joan, CBE 1977; JP; Part time Consultant, Health Division, Business Sciences Ltd; *d* of late Col Charles Unwin and Winifred Unwin; *m* 1939, Terence Middlecott Banham; two *s* two *d. Educ:* privately; West Bank Sch.; Brussels. BSc (Hons) London; Dip. Social Studies London. RGN. Work in health services, 1937–; work in theory and practice on aspects of social deviance and deprivation, Cornwall CC, 1954–67; Mem., SW RHB, 1965–74; Chairman: Cornwall and Isles of Scilly HMC, 1967–74 (Mem., 1964–77); Cornwall and Isles of Scilly AHA, 1974–77; Kensington, Chelsea and Westminster FPC, 1979–85 (Mem. 1977–79); Paddington and N Kensington DHA, 1981–86; Mem., Lambeth, Southwark and Lewisham FPC, 1987–90; Chm., Lambeth,

Southwark and Lewisham FHSA, 1993– (Vice-Chm., 1990–93); Vice-Chm., Lambeth, Southwark and Lewisham Health Commn, 1993–. Mem., MRC, 1980–87 (Chm., Standing Cttee on Use of Medical Inf. in Research, 1980–87). Mem., Industrial Tribunals, 1974–87. Marriage Guidance Councillor, 1960–72. A Vice-Chm., Disabled Living Foundn, 1984–91 (Dir, then Hon. Dir, 1977–83); Pres., Friends of St Mary's Hosp., Paddington, 1983–; Vice-President: KIDS, 1987– (Chm., 1982–87); AFASIC, 1990–. Trustee, Wytham Hall, 1985– (Vice Chm., 1990–). JP Cornwall, 1972. Special interests: social deprivation and deviance, Health Service management and use of resources. *Publications:* Snapshots in Time: some experiences in health care 1936–1991, 1991; (jtly) (paper) Systems Science in Health Care (NATO Conf., Paris, 1977); (jtly) (report) Partnership in Action: a study of healthcare services for elderly and physically handicapped in Newcastle, 1989. *Recreations:* gardening, plant biology, theatre. *Address:* Ponsmaen, St Feock, Truro, Cornwall TR3 6QG. *T:* Truro (01872) 862 275; 81 Vandon Court, Petty France, SW1H 9HG. *T:* 0171–222 1414.

See also Sir J. M. M. Banham.

BANHAM, Sir John (Michael Middlecott), Kt 1992; Chairman: Westcountry Television Ltd, since 1992; Labatt Breweries of Europe (formerly John Labatt (Europe)), since 1992; ECI Ventures Ltd, since 1992; Tarmac, since 1994; *b* 22 Aug. 1940; *s* of Terence Middlecott Banham, FRCS and Belinda Joan Banham, *qv*; *m* 1965, Frances Barbara Molyneux Favell; one *s* two *d*. *Educ:* Charterhouse; Queens' Coll., Cambridge (Foundn Schol.; BA 1st cl. in Natural Scis, 1962; Hon. Fellow, 1989). Asst Principal, HM Foreign Service, 1962–64; Dir of Marketing, Wallcoverings Div., Reed International, 1965–69; McKinsey & Co. Inc.: Associate, 1969–75; Principal, 1975–80; Dir, 1980–83. Controller, Audit Commn, 1983–87; Dir-Gen., CBI, 1987–92; Chm., Local Govt Commn for England, 1992–95. Director: National Westminster Bank, 1992–; National Power, 1992–; John Labatt; Merchants Trust. Mem., BOTB, 1989–92; Dir and Mem. Bd, Business in the Community, 1989–92. Member Council: PSI, 1986–92; Forum for Management Educn and Develt, 1988–93; BESO, 1991–92. Member: Council of Management, PDSA, 1982–93; Governing Body, London Business Sch., 1987–92; Managing Trustee, Nuffield Foundn, 1988–; Hon. Treas., Cancer Res. Campaign, 1991–. Hon. LLD Bath, 1987; Hon. DSc: Loughborough, 1989; Exeter, 1993. *Publications:* Future of the British Car Industry, 1975; Realizing the Promise of a National Health Service, 1977; The Anatomy of Change: blueprint for a new era, 1994; numerous reports for Audit Commn on education, housing, social services and local government finance, 1984–87, and for CBI on UK economy, skills, transport, the infrastructure, urban regeneration and manufacturing. *Recreations:* walking, gardening, music. *Address:* c/o Westcountry Management, Brettenham House, Lancaster Place, WC2E 7EN. *T:* 0171–379 1697, *Fax:* 0171–379 1659. *Clubs:* Travellers', Oriental.

BANISTER, Stephen Michael Alvin; Secretary, British and Foreign School Society, since 1978; Editor, Transport Reviews, since 1981; *b* 7 Oct. 1918; *s* of late Harry Banister and Idwen Banister (*née* Thomas); *m* 1944, Rachel Joan Rawlence; four *s*. *Educ:* Eton; King's Coll., Cambridge (MA). With Foreign Office, 1939–45; Home Guard (Major, 1944). Asst Principal, Min. of Civil Aviation, 1946; Principal, 1947; Private Sec. to six successive Ministers of Transport and Civil Aviation, 1950–56; Asst Sec., Min. of Transport and BoT, 1956–70; Under Sec., DoE, 1970–76, Dept of Transport, 1976–78. UK Shipping Delegate, UNCTAD, 1964; UK Dep., European Conf. of Ministers of Transport, 1976–78. Dir, Taylor and Francis, 1978–91. Mem., Nat. Insurance Tribunal, Kingston upon Thames, 1979–85. MCIT 1994. *Compositions:* (amateur) for singers, including Bluebeard. *Recreations:* countryside, walking, singing (formerly in opera, now in choirs); formerly cricket (Cambridge Crusader); played for CU *v* Australians, 1938. *Address:* Bramshaw, Lower Farm Road, Effingham, Surrey KT24 5JJ. *T:* Bookham (01372) 52778.

BANKS, family name of **Baron Banks.**

BANKS, Baron *cr* 1974 (Life Peer), of Kenton in Greater London; **Desmond Anderson Harvie Banks,** CBE 1972; *b* 23 Oct. 1918; *s* of James Harvie Banks, OBE and Sheena Muriel Watt; *m* 1948, Barbara Wells (OBE 1987); two *s*. *Educ:* Alpha Prep. Sch.; University College Sch. Served with KRRC and RA, 1939–46, Middle East and Italy (Major); Chief Public Relations Officer to Allied Mil. Govt, Trieste, 1946. Joined Canada Life Assce Co., subseq. Life Assoc. of Scotland; life assce broker from 1959; Director: Tweddle French & Co. (Life & Pensions Consultants) Ltd, 1973–82; Lincoln Consultants Ltd, 1982–89. Liberal Party: Pres., 1968–69; Chm. Exec., 1961–63 and 1969–70; Dir of Policy Promotion, 1972–74; Chm. Res. Cttee, 1966; Hon. Sec., Home Counties Liberal Fedn, 1960–61; Chairman: Working Party on Machinery of Govt, 1971–74; Liberal Summer Sch. Cttee, 1979–92; Member: For. Affairs Panel, 1961–88 (sometime Vice-Chm.); Social Security Panel, 1961–88; Hon. Sec., Liberal Candidates Assoc., 1947–52; contested (L): Harrow East, 1950; St Ives, 1955; SW Herts, 1959. Vice-Chm., Liberal Party Standing Cttee, 1973–79; Dep. Liberal Whip, House of Lords, 1977–83; spokesman on: social security, 1975–89; social services, 1977–83. Pres., Liberal European Action Gp, 1971–87; Vice-Pres., European Atlantic Gp, 1985– (Vice Chm., 1979–85); a Pres., British Council, European Movement, 1986– (Vice-Chm., 1979–86). Elder, United Reformed Church. *Publications:* Clyde Steamers, 1947, 2nd edn 1951; numerous political pamphlets. *Recreations:* pursuing interest in Gilbert and Sullivan opera and in Clyde river steamers; reading. *Address:* Lincoln House, The Lincolns, Little Kingshill, Great Missenden, Bucks HP16 0EH. *T:* High Wycombe (01494) 866164. *Club:* National Liberal (President, 1981–93).

BANKS, Alan George; HM Diplomatic Service, retired; *b* 7 April 1911; *s* of George Arthur Banks and Sarah Napthen; *m* 1946, Joyce Frances Telford Yates; two *s*. *Educ:* Preston Gram. Sch. Served in HM Forces, 1939–43; at Consulate-Gen., Dakar, 1943–45; Actg Consul, Warsaw, 1945–48; HM Vice-Consul: Bordeaux, 1948–50; Istanbul, 1950–52; Zagreb, 1952–55; FO, 1955–58; HM Consul, Split, 1958–60; 1st Sec. and Consul, Madrid, 1960–62; 1st Sec., FO, 1962–67; Consul-General, Alexandria, 1967–71. *Recreations:* classical music, gardening, photography. *Address:* Ferney Field, Parkgate Road, Newdigate, Dorking, Surrey RH5 5AH. *T:* Newdigate (0130677) 434.

BANKS, (Arthur) David; Editorial Director, Mirror Group Newspapers, since 1994; *b* 13 Feb. 1948; *s* of Arthur Banks and Helen (*née* Renton); *m* 1975, Gemma Newton; one *s* one *d*. *Educ:* Boteler Grammar Sch., Warrington. Asst Man. Editor, NY Post, 1979–81; Night Editor, then Asst Editor, The Sun, 1981–86; Dep. Man. Editor, NY Daily News, 1986–87; Dep. Editor, The Australian, 1987–89; Editor: Daily Telegraph Mirror (Sydney), 1989–92; Daily Mirror, 1992–94. *Recreations:* dining, dieting. *Address:* Mirror Group Newspapers, 1 Canada Square, Canary Wharf, E14 5AP. *T:* 0171–510 3000.

BANKS, Colin; Founder Partner, Banks and Miles, graphic designers, London, since 1958 (Hamburg, 1990–93, and Brussels, 1991–93); *b* 16 Jan. 1932; *s* of William James Banks and late Ida Jenny (*née* Hood); *m* 1961, Caroline Grigson, PhD; one *s* (one *d* decd). Prodn Editor (with John Miles) of Which? and other Consumers' Assoc. magazines, 1964–93. Design Consultant to: Zool Soc., 1962–82; British Council, 1968–83; E Midlands Arts Assoc., 1974–77; English National Opera, 1975–76; Direct Election Campaign, European Parlt, 1978, 1984; (new visual identity for) Post Office: Royal Mail, Telecommunications, etc, 1972–; British Telecom., 1980; US Govt Social Marketing Project, Family Planning in Indonesia, 1985–; NERC, 1986; City Univ., 1987; CNAA, 1988; IMechE, 1988; Fondation Roi Baudouin, 1988–89; SERC, 1989. Designer/Design Adviser to: City and Guilds; Commn for Racial Equality; UN Univ., Japan, 1991–; BTEC, 1993–; other instns and commercial cos; Graphic Consultant to London Transport, 1964–. Exhibitions: London, Paris, Amsterdam, Glasgow, Brussels, Kyoto, Hamburg. Vice-Pres., SIAD, 1974–76. Pres., Soc. of Typographic Designers, 1988–93; Design and Industries Assoc. Manager, Blackheath Sch. of Art, 1981–89; Treas., Project Mala for children's educn and welfare, India, 1989–92. Lectured in Europe, India, Japan, SE Asia, USA. FRSA. Fifty Best German Printed Books, W Germany, 1989; Internationalen Buchkunst Ausstellung Medal, Leipzig, 1971, 1989; Gold Medal, Brno Biennale, 1986; RSA Green Award, 1989; BBC Envmtl Design Prize, 1990; Technol. and Creation Prize, Paris Cité, 1991. *Publications:* Social Communication, 1979; (with E. Schumacher Gebler) 26 Letters, Vol. I 1989, Vol. II 1992; contrib. jls, London, Budapest, Copenhagen, USA etc. *Recreation:* India. *Address:* 1 Tranquil Vale, Blackheath, SE3 0BU. *T:* 0181–318 1131; Little Town, Wilts. *Clubs:* Arts; Double Crown (Pres., 1989–90), Wynkyn de Worde (Chm., 1984–85).

BANKS, David; *see* Banks, A. D.

BANKS, Frank David, FCA; business consultant; Chairman, H. Berkeley (Holdings) Ltd, 1984–90; *b* 11 April 1933; *s* of Samuel and Elizabeth Banks; *m* 1st, 1955, Catherine Jacob; one *s* two *d*; 2nd, 1967, Sonia Gay Coleman; one *d*. *Educ:* Liverpool Collegiate Sch.; Carnegie Mellon Univ. (PFE); Open Univ. (BA 1988); Univ. of Sussex (MA 1992). British Oxygen Co. Ltd, 1957–58; Imperial Chemical Industries Ltd, 1959–62; English Electric Co. Ltd, 1963–68; Finance Dir, Platt International Ltd, 1969–71; Industrial Advr, DTI, 1972–73; Constructors John Brown Ltd, 1974–80; Man. Dir, Agribusiness Div., Tate & Lyle Ltd, 1981–83. *Recreations:* music, history. *Address:* 8 Church Road, Flitwick, Beds MK45 1AE.

BANKS, Mrs Gillian Theresa, CB 1990; Director of Studies, Retirement Income Inquiry; *b* 7 Feb. 1933; *d* of Percy and Enid Brimblecombe; *m* 1960, John Anthony Gorst Banks; one *s* two *d*. *Educ:* Walthamstow Hall Sch., Sevenoaks; Lady Margaret Hall, Oxford (BA). Asst Principal, Colonial Office, 1955; Principal, Treasury, 1966; Department of Health and Social Security: Asst Sec., 1972; Under Sec. 1981; Dir, Health Authy Finance, 1985; Dir, OPCS and Registrar Gen. for Eng. and Wales, 1986; Dir, Carnegie Inquiry into the Third Age, 1990; Functions and Manpower Review of Wider DoH, 1994. *Recreation:* hill walking. *Address:* 16 Chalcot Square, NW1 8YA. *T:* 0171–722 3962.

BANKS, John, FEng, FIEE; Chairman, Adacom 3270 Communications Ltd, 1986–90; *b* 2 Dec. 1920; *s* of John Banks and Jane Dewhurst; *m* 1943, Nancy Olive Yates; two *s*. *Educ:* Univ. of Liverpool (BEng Hons; MEng). FEng 1983; FIEE 1959. Chief Engr, Power Cables Div., BICC, 1956–67; Divl Dir and Gen Man., Supertension Cables Div., BICC, 1968–74; Exec. Dir, 1975–78, Chm., 1978–84, BICC Research and Engineering Ltd; Exec. Dir, BICC, 1979–84. Vis. Prof., Liverpool Univ., 1987–. Pres., IEE, 1982–83. *Recreations:* golf, swimming, music and the arts. *Address:* Flat B1 Marine Gate, Marine Drive, Brighton BN2 5TQ. *T:* Brighton (01273) 690756. *Club:* Seaford Golf.

BANKS, Lynne Reid; writer; *b* 1929; *d* of Dr James Reid-Banks and Muriel (Pat) (*née* Marsh); *m* Chaim Stephenson, sculptor; three *s*. *Educ:* schooling mainly in Canada; RADA. Actress, 1949–54; reporter for ITN, 1955–62; English teacher in kibbutz in Western Galilee, Israel, 1963–71; full-time writer, 1971–; writing includes plays for stage, television and radio. *Publications: plays:* It Never Rains, 1954; All in a Row, 1956; The Killer Dies Twice, 1956; Already, It's Tomorrow, 1962; (for children) Travels of Yoshi and the Tea-Kettle, 1993; *fiction:* The L-Shaped Room, 1960 (trans. 10 langs; filmed 1962); An End to Running, 1962 (trans. 2 langs); Children at the Gate, 1968; The Backward Shadow, 1970; Two is Lonely, 1974; Defy the Wilderness, 1981; The Warning Bell, 1984; Casualties, 1986; *biographical fiction:* Dark Quartet: the story of the Brontes, 1976 (Yorks Arts Lit. Award, 1977); Path to the Silent Country: Charlotte Bronte's years of fame, 1977; *history:* Letters to my Israeli Sons, 1979; Torn Country, USA 1982; *for young adults:* One More River, 1973; Sarah and After, 1975; My Darling Villain, 1977 (trans. 3 langs); The Writing on the Wall, 1981; Melusine, 1988 (trans 3 langs); *for children:* The Adventures of King Midas, 1976; The Farthest-Away Mountain, 1977; I, Houdini, 1978; The Indian in the Cupboard, 1980 (trans. 11 langs) (Pacific NW Choice Award, 1984; Calif. Young Readers Medal, 1985; Va Children's Choice, 1988; Mass. Children's Choice, 1988; Rebecca Caudill Award, Ill, 1989; Arizona Children's Choice, 1989); Maura's Angel, 1984 (trans. 2 langs); The Fairy Rebel, 1985; Return of the Indian, 1986; The Secret of the Indian, 1989; The Magic Hare, 1992; Mystery of the Cupboard, 1993; Broken Bridge, 1994; short stories; articles in The Times, The Guardian, Sunday Telegraph, Observer, TES, TLS, Independent on Sunday, Sunday Times, Spectator, and in overseas periodicals. *Recreations:* theatre, gardening, teaching EFL abroad. *Address:* c/o Watson, Little Ltd, 12 Egbert Street, NW1 8LJ. *T:* 071–722 9514.

BANKS, Matthew Richard William; MP (C) Southport, since 1992; *b* 21 June 1961; *s* of Harry and Audrey Banks; *m* 1992, Jane, *d* of Michael Miller. *Educ:* Calday Grange Grammar Sch.; Sheffield City Polytechnic (BA Hons History and Econs); RMA Sandhurst. Commnd, The Gordon Highlanders, 1980–83; War Disablement Pension, 1983. Barclays Bank, 1983–87; Private Sec. to Cecil Franks, MP, 1987–89; Dir, LBJ Ltd, management consultancy, 1989–. Mem., Wirral BC, 1984–90 (Chairman: Schs Cttee, 1985–86; Works Cttee, 1986–87). Contested (C) Manchester Central, 1987. Mem., Select Cttee on Transport, 1992–; Vice-Chm., Cons. Back bench Transport Cttee, 1993–; Chm., Anglo-Venezeula Parly Gp, 1993–; Sec., Anglo-UAE Parly Gp, 1993–. FRGS 1983. *Recreations:* golf, walking, travel, reading. *Address:* House of Commons, SW1A 0AA. *T:* 0171–219 6924. *Clubs:* Heswall Golf; West Lancashire Sailing.

BANKS, Richard Alford, CBE 1965; *b* 11 July 1902; *s* of William Hartland Banks, Hergest Croft, Kington, Hereford; *m* 1st, 1937, Lilian Jean (*d* 1974), *d* of Dr R. R. Walker, Presteigne, Radnorshire; two *s* one *d*; 2nd, 1976, Rosamund Gould. *Educ:* Rugby; Trinity Coll., Cambridge (BA). Dir of Imperial Chemical Industries Ltd, 1952–64; Chm. of the Industrial Training Council, 1962–64; Mem., Water Resources Bd, 1964–74. Veitch Meml Medal, RHS, 1983. JP Hereford, 1963–73. *Recreations:* arboriculture, gardening and travel. *Address:* Haywood Cottages, Kington, Herefordshire HR5 3EJ.

BANKS, Robert George; MP (C) Harrogate, since Feb. 1974; *b* 18 Jan. 1937; *s* of late George Walmsley Banks, MBE, and of Olive Beryl Banks (*née* Tyler); *m* 1967, Diana Margaret Payne Crawfurd; four *s* one *d* (of whom one *s* one *d* are twins). *Educ:* Haileybury. Lt-Comdr RNR. Jt Founder Dir, Antocks Lairn Ltd, 1963–67. Member of Lloyd's. Mem., Alcohol Educn and Res. Council, 1982–88. Mem., Paddington BC, 1959–65. PPS to Minister of State and to Under-Sec. of State, FCO, 1979–82. Member: Select Cttee on Foreign Affairs (and its Overseas Develt Sub-Cttee), 1982; Select Cttee on Trade and Industry, 1994–; Jt Sec., Cons. Defence Cttee, 1976–79; Chairman: British-Sudan All Party Parly Gp, 1984–; All-Party Tourism Gp (Sec., 1973–79; Vice-Chm., 1979); Vice-Chm., Yorks Cons. Mems' Cttee, 1983–. Member: Council of Europe, 1977–81; WEU, 1977–81; N Atlantic Assembly, 1981–. Introd Licensing (Alcohol Educn and Res.) Act, 1981; sponsored Licensing (Restaurants Meals) Act, 1987. Reports: for Mil. Cttee of

WEU, Report on Nuclear, Biol. and Chem. Protection, adopted by WEU Assembly April 1980; North Atlantic Assembly document, The Technology of Military Space Systems, 1982; New Jobs from Pleasure, report on tourism, 1985. *Publications:* (jtly) Britain's Home Defence Gamble (pamphlet), 1979; committee reports. *Recreations:* travel, farming, architecture, contemporary art. *Address:* House of Commons, SW1A 0AA.

BANKS, Tony; MP (Lab) Newham North West, since 1983. *Educ:* St John's Primary Sch., Brixton; Archbishop Tenison's Grammar Sch., Kensington; York Univ. (BA); London School of Economics. Former trade union research worker; Head of Research, AUEW, 1969–75; an Asst Gen. Sec., Assoc. of Broadcasting and Allied Staffs, 1976–83. Political Advr to Minister for Overseas Develt, 1975. Joined Labour Party, 1964; Greater London Council: Mem. for Hammersmith, 1970–77, for Tooting, 1981–86; Chairman: Gen. Purposes Cttee, 1975–77; Arts and Recreation Cttee, 1981–83; GLC, 1985–86. Contested (Lab): E Grinstead, 1970; Newcastle upon Tyne N, Oct. 1974; Watford, 1979. Member: Select Cttee, HM Treasury, 1986–87; Select Cttee on Procedure, 1987–; Jt Lords/Commons Cttee on Private Bill Procedure, 1987–88; Council of Europe Parly Assembly and WEU, 1989–. Chm., London Gp, Labour MP's, 1987–91. Member: ENO Bd, 1981–83; London Festival Ballet Bd, 1981–83; Nat. Theatre Bd, 1981–85. *Publication:* (jtly) Out of Order, 1993. *Address:* 306 High Street, Stratford, E15 1AJ. *T:* 0181–555 0036.

BANKS, William Hartley; Member, West Yorkshire County Council, 1977–86 (Chairman, 1982–83); *b* 5 July 1909; *s* of Hartley and Edith Banks; *m* 1935, Elsie Kendrew; four *s* one *d* (and one *s* decd). *Educ:* Holbeck Technical Sch. Entered local politics, 1947; Mem., Divl Educn Exec., 1948; Mem., Rothwell UDC, 1959–74 (Chm., 1972–73); Chairman: Sch. Governors, Rothwell, 1964–68; Rothwell Primary Schs, 1974–; Rothwell Secondary Schs, 1982–. Chairman: Rothwell Accident Prevention Cttee, 1960–72; Rothwell Road Safety Cttee, 1987 (Vice-Chm., 1974–87); Sec., Rothwell and Dist Civic Soc., 1974–77; President: Rothwell Athletic Club, 1974– (Treasurer, 1951–74); Rothwell Cricket Club, 1960–; Rothwell Civic Soc., 1980–; Rothwell Pensioners' Assoc., 1986–; Chairman: Rothwell Gateway Club, 1980–88; Rothwell Theatre Gp, 1986–; Rothwell and Dist Probus Club, 1992–; Rothwell Methodist Church Men's Supper Club, 1992–; Leader, Rothwell Windmill Youth Club, 1950–55. Accompanist and on Preaching Plan, Rothwell Methodist Church, 1984–; talks to local schs and orgns on aspects of life in 1920s. *Publication:* The History of Rothwell Cricket Club 1875–1990, 1991. *Recreations:* classical music, most sports. *Address:* 6 Prospect Place, Rothwell, Leeds LS26 0AL. *T:* Leeds (0113) 282 1502.

BANNENBERG, Jon, RDI 1978; AMRINA; *b* Australia, 8 July 1929; *s* of Henryk and Kay Bannenberg; *m* 1960, Beaupré Robinson; two *s*. *Educ:* Canterbury High Sch., Sydney; Sydney Conservatorium of Music. RDI (Motor Yacht Design) 1978. Designed: 'Siècle d'Elégance' Exhibn, Louvre, Paris, 1959; CINOA Exhibn, V&A Museum, London, 1960; Motor and Sail Boat Designs include: Queen Elizabeth 2, 1967; Tiawana, Tamahine, 1968; Carinthia V, Anemos II, 1969; Benedic, 1970; Carinthia VI, Arjuna, Aetos, 1971; Blue Lady, Yellowbird, Firebird, Heron 21, 1972; Stilvi, Pegasus III, 1973; My Gail, Xiphas, Mediterranean Sky, 1974; Boule Dogue, Southern Breeze, 1975; Solitaire, 1976; Majestic, 1977; Rodis Island, Nabila, Cimba, 1979; My Gail II, Nahema, 1981; Acajou, Azteca, Paraiso, Bobbara, Three Y's, 1983; My Gail III, Cedar Sea, Shirley B, Highlander, Sterling One, Never Say Never, Garuda, 1985; Southern Cross III, Lady Ghislaine, 1987; Acharné, Starlight, 1988; Beaupré, Stefaren, G. Whiz, Mercedes, Mystique, 1989; Gee. Dee, Oceana, Opal C, 1991; Siran, Moecca, 1992. Member, RYA. *Recreations:* running, swimming, sailing, music, Polynesian and Pacific history. *Address:* 35 Carlyle Square, Chelsea, SW3 6HA. *T:* 0171–352 6129; 6 Burnsall Street, SW3 3ST. *T:* 0171–352 4851, *Fax:* 0171–352 8444.

BANNER, Josephina, (Mrs Delmar Banner); *see* Vasconcellos, J. de.

BANNER, Rev. Prof. Michael Charles, DPhil; F. D. Maurice Professor of Moral and Social Theology, King's College, London, since 1994; *b* 19 April 1961; *s* of Maurice Banner and Maureen (*née* Ince); *m* 1983, Elizabeth Jane Wheare; two *d*. *Educ:* Bromsgrove Sch.; Balliol Coll., Oxford (BA 1983; MA 1985; DPhil 1986). Ordained Deacon 1986; Priest 1987. Bampton Res. Fellow, St Peter's Coll., Oxford, 1985–88; Dean, Chaplain, Fellow and Dir of Studies in Philosophy and Theol., 1988–94, Tutor 1989–94, Peterhouse, Cambridge. Vis. Res. Fellow, Merton Coll., Oxford, 1993. Chm., HM Govt Cttee of Enquiry on Ethics of Emerging Technologies in Breeding of Farm Animals, 1993–95. *Publications:* The Justification of Science and the Rationality of Religious Belief, 1990; various articles in learned jls. *Recreations:* walking, gardening, reading. *Address:* Department of Theology and Religious Studies, King's College, Strand, WC2R 1LS. *T:* 0171–873 2073.

BANNERMAN, Sir David (Gordon), 15th Bt, *cr* 1682 (NS), of Elsick, Kincardineshire; OBE 1977; with Ministry of Defence, since 1963; *b* 18 Aug. 1935; *s* of Lt-Col Sir Donald Arthur Gordon Bannerman, 13th Bt and of Barbara Charlotte, *d* of late Lt-Col Alexander Cameron, OBE, IMS; *S* brother, Sir Alexander Patrick Bannerman, 14th Bt, 1989; *m* 1960, Mary Prudence, *d* of Rev. Philip Frank Ardagh-Walter; four *d*. *Educ:* Gordonstoun; New Coll., Oxford (MA). 2nd Lieut Queen's Own Cameron Highlanders, 1954–56. HMOCS (Tanzania), 1960–63. *Recreations:* painting, ornithology, tennis, squash. *Address:* c/o Drummond's Bank, 49 Charing Cross, SW1A 2DX.

BANNISTER, (Richard) Matthew; Controller, BBC Radio 1, since 1993; *b* 16 March 1957; *s* of Richard Neville Bannister and Olga Margaret Bannister; *m* 1st, 1984, Amanda Gerrard Walker (*d* 1988); one *d*; 2nd, 1989, Shelagh Margaret Macleod; one *s*. *Educ:* King Edward VII Sch., Sheffield; Nottingham Univ. (LLB Hons). Presenter, BBC Radio Nottingham, 1978–81; Reporter/Presenter: Capital Radio, 1981–83; Newsbeat, Radio 1, 1983–85; Dep. Head, 1985–87, Head, 1987–88, News and Talks, Capital Radio; BBC 1988–: Man. Ed., Gtr London Radio, 1988–91; Project Co-ordinator: Charter Renewal, 1991–93; Prog. Strategy Review, 1993. *Recreations:* rock music, collecting P. G. Wodehouse first editions. *Address:* BBC Radio 1, Egton House, Langham Street, W1A 1AA. *T:* 0171–580 4468. *Club:* Reform.

BANNISTER, Sir Roger (Gilbert), Kt 1975; CBE 1955; DM (Oxon); FRCP; Master of Pembroke College, Oxford, 1985–93; Chairman, Medical Commission on Accident Prevention, since 1994; Hon. Consultant Physician and non-executive Director, National Hospital for Neurology and Neurosurgery, Queen Square, WC1 (formerly Consultant Physician, National Hospital for Nervous Diseases); Hon. Consultant Neurologist: Oxford Regional and District Health Authorities; St Mary's Hospital, W2 (formerly Consultant Neurologist); *b* 23 March 1929; *s* of late Ralph and of Alice Bannister, Harrow; *m* 1955, Moyra Elver, *d* of late Per Jacobsson, Chairman IMF; two *s* two *d*. *Educ:* City of Bath Boys' Sch.; University Coll. Sch., London; Exeter and Merton Colls, Oxford; St Mary's Hospital Medical Sch., London. Amelia Jackson Studentship, Exeter Coll., Oxford, 1947; BA (hons) Physiology, Junior Demonstrator in Physiology, Harmsworth Senior Scholar, Merton Coll., Oxford, 1950; Open and State Schol., St Mary's Hosp., 1951; MSc Thesis in Physiology, 1952; MRCS, LRCP, 1954; BM, BCh Oxford, 1954; DM Oxford, 1963. William Hyde Award for research relating physical education to medicine; MRCP 1957. Junior Medical Specialist, RAMC, 1958; Radcliffe Travelling Fellowship from Oxford Univ., at Harvard, USA, 1962–63. Correspondent, Sunday Times, 1955–62. Consultant Neurologist, Western Ophthalmic Hosp., 1963–85. Chm., Hon. Consultants, King Edward VII Convalescent Home for Officers, Osborne, 1979–87. Chm., Medical Cttee, St Mary's Hosp., 1983–85; Deleg., Imperial Coll., representing St Mary's Hosp. Med. Sch., 1988–; Trustee, St Mary's Hosp. Med. Sch. Develt Trust, 1994–. President: National Fitness Panel, NABC, 1956–59; Alzheimer's Disease Soc., 1982–84; Sports Medicine Sect., RSM, 1994–; Gen. Sect., BAAS, 1995; Chm., Clinical Autonomic Res. Soc., 1982–84. Mem. Council, King George's Jubilee Trust, 1961–67; Pres., Sussex Assoc. of Youth Clubs, 1972–79; Chm., Res. Cttee, Adv. Sports Council, 1965–71; Mem., Min. of Health Adv. Cttee on Drug Dependence, 1967–70; Chm., Sports Council, 1971–74; Pres., Internat. Council for Sport and Physical Recreation, 1976–83. Mem., Management Cttee, 1979–84, Council, 1984–, King Edward's Hosp. Fund for London; Trustee: King George VI and Queen Elizabeth Foundn of St Catharine's, Cumberland Lodge, Windsor, 1985–; Leeds Castle, 1989–; Henry and Proctor Amer. Fellowships, 1987–; Winston Churchill Fellowships, 1988–; Mem. of Commn, Marshall Fellowships; Governor: Atlantic Coll., 1985–93; Sherborne Sch., 1989–93. Saville Lectr, West End Hosp., London, 1970; Chadwick Trust Lectr, 1972; George Cecil Clarke Lectr, Univ. of Nottingham, 1982; Goodman Lectr, Aitchison Meml Fund, 1987; Tetelman Lectr, Yale Univ., 1990. Winner Oxford *v* Cambridge Mile, 1947–50; Pres. OUAC, 1948; Capt. Oxford & Cambridge Combined American Team, 1949; Finalist, Olympic Games, Helsinki, 1952; British Mile Champion, 1951, 1953, 1954; World Record for One Mile, 1954; British Empire Mile title and record, 1954; European 1500 metres title and record, 1954. FIC 1992. Hon. FUMIST, 1974; Hon. Fellow: Exeter Coll., Oxford, 1979; Merton Coll., Oxford, 1986. Hon. LLD Liverpool, 1972; Hon. DLitt Sheffield, 1978; Hon. Doctorates: Univ. of Jyvaskyla, Finland; Univ. of Bath, Univ. of Grinnell, 1984; Univ. Rochester, NY, 1985; Univ. of Pavia, Italy, 1986; Williams Coll., USA, 1987; Victoria Univ., Canada, 1993. Hans-Heinrich Siegbert Prize, 1977. Chm. Editorial Bd, Clinical Autonomic Res., 1991–; Mem., Editorial Bd, Jl of the Autonomic Nervous System, 1980–95; Associate Editor, Jl Neurol Sci., 1985–95. *Publications:* First Four Minutes, 1955; (ed) Brain's Clinical Neurology, 3rd edn 1969 to 6th edn 1985, 7th edn 1992 (as Brain and Bannister's Clinical Neurology); (ed) Autonomic Failure, 1983 to 3rd edn 1992 (ed with C. J. Mathias); papers on physiology of exercise, heat illness and neurological subjects. *Address:* 21 Bardwell Road, Oxford OX2 6SU. *T:* Oxford (01865) 511413; 7 Pembroke Court, South Edwardes Square, W8 6HN. *T:* 0171–938 1980. *Clubs:* Athenæum, United Oxford & Cambridge University; Vincent's (Oxford).

BANNON, John Kernan, ISO 1969; Director of Services, Meteorological Office, 1973–76; *b* 26 April 1916; *s* of Frederick J. Bannon, Clerk in Holy Orders and Eveline Bannon, Muckamore, NI; *m* 1947, Pauline Mary Roch Thomas, Pembroke; one *s* one *d*. *Educ:* Royal Sch., Armagh; Emmanuel Coll., Cambridge (Braithwaite Batty Scholar). BA (Wrangler) 1938. Technical Officer, Meteorological Office, 1938; commnd RAFVR, 1943–46 (Temp. Sqdn Ldr); Met. Office, 1946–76; idc 1963. *Publications:* some official scientific works; articles in meteorological jls. *Recreations:* walking, gardening. *Address:* 18 Courtenay Drive, Emmer Green, Reading RG4 8XH. *T:* Reading (01734) 473696.

BANTOCK, Prof. Geoffrey Herman; Emeritus Professor of Education, University of Leicester, 1975; *b* 12 Oct. 1914; *s* of Herman S. and Annie Bantock; *m* 1950, Dorothy Jean Pick; no *c*. *Educ:* Wallasey Grammar Sch.; Emmanuel Coll., Cambridge. BA 1936, MA 1942, Cantab. Taught in grammar schs, training coll.; Lectr in Educn, University Coll. of Leicester, 1950–54; Reader in Educn, University Coll., Leicester, later Univ. of Leicester, 1954–64; Prof. of Educn, 1964–75; Leverhulme Emeritus Fellow, 1976–78. Vis. Prof., Monash Univ., Melbourne, 1971. *Publications:* Freedom and Authority in Education, 1952 (2nd edn 1965); L. H. Myers: a critical study, 1956; Education in an Industrial Society, 1963 (2nd edn 1973); Education and Values, 1965; Education, Culture and the Emotions, 1967; Education, Culture and Industrialization, 1968; T. S. Eliot and Education, 1969 (paperback 1970); Studies in the History of Educational Theory: Vol. I, Artifice and Nature 1350–1765, 1980, Vol. II, The Minds and the Masses 1760–1980, 1984 (Book Prize, Standing Conf. on Studies in Educn, 1985); Dilemmas of the Curriculum, 1980; The Parochialism of the Present, 1981. *Recreations:* music, art, foreign travel. *Address:* c/o The University, Leicester.

BANTOCK, John Leonard; Assistant Under Secretary of State, Home Office Police Department, 1980–84; *b* 21 Oct. 1927; *s* of Edward Bantock and Agnes Bantock; *m* 1947, Maureen McKinney; two *s*. *Educ:* Colfe's Sch., SE13; King George V Sch., Southport, Lancs; LSE, London Univ. (LLB 1951). Unilever Ltd, 1943–45; Army, 1945–48 (Staff Captain, UK, India and Cyprus); Colonial Office, 1951–52; Inland Revenue, 1952–69; Secretariat, Royal Commn on Constitution, 1969–73; Cabinet Office, 1973–76; Sec., Cttee of Privy Counsellors on Recruitment of Mercenaries, 1976; Asst Under Sec. of State, Home Office Radio Regulatory Dept, 1976–79 (Head, UK Delegn, World Admin. Radio Conf., 1979). *Club:* MCC.

BANTON, Prof. Michael Parker; JP; PhD, DSc; Professor of Sociology, 1965–92, now Emeritus, and Pro-Vice-Chancellor, 1985–88, University of Bristol; *b* 8 Sept. 1926; *s* of Francis Clive Banton and Kathleen Blanche (*née* Parkes); *m* 1952, Rut Marianne (*née* Jacobson), Luleå; one *s* two *d* (and one *s* decd). *Educ:* King Edward's Sch., Birmingham; London Sch. of Economics. BSc Econ. 1950; PhD 1954; DSc 1964. Midn, then Sub-Lieut RNVR, 1945–47. Asst, then Lecturer, then Reader, in Social Anthropology, University of Edinburgh, 1950–65. Dir, SSRC Res. Unit on Ethnic Relations, 1970–78. Visiting Professor: MIT, 1962–63; Wayne State Univ., Detroit, 1971; Univ. of Delaware, 1976; ANU, 1981; Duke Univ., 1982. Editor, Sociology, 1966–69. President: Section N, 1969–70 and Section H, 1985–86, BAAS; Royal Anthropological Inst., 1987–89; Mem., Vetenskapssocieteten, Lund, Sweden, 1972; Member: Royal Commn on Criminal Procedure, 1978–80; Royal Commn on Bermuda, 1978; UK National Commn for UNESCO, 1963–66 and 1980–85; UN Cttee for the Elimination of Racial Discrimination, 1986–; Ethnic Minorities Adv. Cttee, Judicial Studies Bd, 1993–; SW Regl Hosp. Board, 1966–70. JP Bristol, 1966. FRSA 1981. *Publications:* The Coloured Quarter, 1955; West African City, 1957; White and Coloured, 1959; The Policeman in the Community, 1964; Roles, 1965; Race Relations, 1967; Racial Minorities, 1972; Police-Community Relations, 1973; (with J. Harwood) The Race Concept, 1975; The Idea of Race, 1977; Racial and Ethnic Competition, 1983; Promoting Racial Harmony, 1985; Investigating Robbery, 1985; Racial Theories, 1987; Racial Consciousness, 1988; Discrimination, 1994. *Address:* The Court House, Llanvair Discoed, Gwent NP6 6LX. *T:* Penhow (01633) 400208.

BANWELL, Derick Frank, CBE 1978; Member: Refuge Housing Association Ltd (formerly BCAR (Housing) Ltd) (Chairman, 1979–89); Refuge Housing Society Ltd (formerly BCAR (Homes) Ltd) (Chairman, 1979–86); *b* 19 July 1919; *s* of Frank Edward Banwell; *m* 1945, Rose Kathleen Worby; two *s* one *d*. *Educ:* Kent Coll., Canterbury. RA, 1939–46. Admitted as Solicitor, 1947; Asst Solicitor, Southend-on-Sea Co. Borough Coun., 1947–48; Sen. Asst Solicitor, Rochdale Co. Borough Coun., 1948–51; Chief Common Law Solicitor, City of Sheffield, 1951–56; Sen. Asst Solicitor, 1956–59, Asst

Town Clerk, 1959–60, Southend-on-Sea Co. Borough Coun.; Dep. Town Clerk and Dep. Clerk of the Peace, Swansea Co. Borough Council, 1960–64; Gen. Manager, Runcorn Develt Corp., 1964–78. Sec., Church Bldgs Cttee, United Reformed Church, 1978–85. *Recreations:* history, music, model railways. *Address:* 57 Broad Street, Canterbury, Kent CT1 2LS.

BARBACK, Ronald Henry; Professor of Economics, University of Hull, 1965–76 (Dean, Faculty of Social Sciences and Law, 1966–69); *b* 31 Oct. 1919; *s* of late Harry Barback and Winifred Florence (*née* Norris); *m* 1950, Sylvia Chambers; one *s* one *d*. *Educ:* Woodside Sch., Glasgow; Univ. Coll., Nottingham (BScEcon); Queen's and Nuffield Colls, Oxford (MLitt). Asst Lectr in Econs, Univ. of Nottingham, 1946–48; Lectr in Econs, subseq. Sen. Lectr, Canberra University Coll., Australia, 1949–56; Univ. of Ibadan (formerly University Coll., Ibadan): Prof. of Econs and Social Studies, 1956–63; Dean, Faculty of Arts, 1958–59; Dean, Faculty of Econs and Social Studies, 1959–63; Dir, Nigerian (formerly W African) Inst. of Social and Econ. Res., 1956–63; Sen. Res. Fellow, Econ. Res. Inst., Dublin, 1963–64; Prof. of Econs, TCD, 1964–65; Vis. Prof., Brunel Univ., 1984–86. Dep. Econ. Dir and Head, Econ. Res., CBI, 1977–81, Consultant, 1981–82. Nigeria: Mem., Ibadan Univ. Hosp. Bd of Management, 1958–63; Mem., Jt Econ. Planning Cttee, Fedn of Nigeria, 1959–61; Sole Arbitrator, Trade Disputes in Ports and Railways, 1958; Chm., Fed. Govt Cttee to advise on fostering a share market, 1959. UK Official Delegate, FAO meeting on investment in fisheries, 1970; Mem., FAO mission to Sri Lanka, 1975. Consultant, Div. of Fisheries, Europ. Commn Directorate-Gen. of Agriculture, 1974; Specialist Advr, H of L Select Cttee on Eur. Communities, 1980–83; Commonwealth Scholarships Commn Adviser on Econs, 1971–76. Mem., Schools Council Social Sciences Cttee, 1971–80; Chm., Schs Council Econs and Business Studies Syllabus Steering Gp, 1975–77. Member: Hull and Dist Local Employment Cttee, 1966–73; N Humberside Dist Manpower Cttee, 1973–76; CNAA Business and Management Studies Bd, 1978–81, Economics Bd, 1982–86; Ct, Brunel Univ., 1979–83. Chm., Royal Tunbridge Wells Civic Soc., 1991–93. Member: Editorial Bd, Bull. of Economic Research (formerly Yorks Bull. of Social and Economic Research), 1965–76 (Jt Editor, 1966–67); Editorial Adv. Bd, Applied Economics, 1969–80; Editor, Humberside Statistical Bull., nos 1–3, 1974, 1975, 1977. *Publications:* (contrib.) The Commonwealth in the World Today, ed J. Eppstein, 1956; (ed with Prof. Sir Douglas Copland) The Conflict of Expansion and Stability, 1957; (contrib.) The Commonwealth and Europe (EIU), 1960; The Pricing of Manufactures, 1964; (contrib.) Insurance Markets of the World, ed M. Grossmann 1964; (contrib.) Webster's New World Companion to English and American Literature, 1973; Forms of Co-operation in the British Fishing Industry, 1976; (with M. Breimer and A. F. Haug) Development of the East Coast Fisheries of Sri Lanka, 1976; The Firm and its Environment, 1984; contrib. New Internat. Encyc., FAO Fisheries Reports, and jls. *Recreations:* walking, music. *Address:* 14a Calverley Park Gardens, Tunbridge Wells, Kent TN1 2JN. *T:* Tunbridge Wells (01892) 533290. *Club:* Commonwealth Trust.

BARBARA, Agatha, Companion of Honour, National Order of Merit (Malta), 1990; social/welfare worker; President of the Republic of Malta, 1982–87; Chairperson, The Samaritans – Malta, since 1988; *b* Zabbar, 11 March 1923. *Educ:* Government Grammar School. School teacher, 1945; entered politics, 1946; first woman Member of Parliament, 1947; became first woman Minister, in Labour Govt, 1955, as Minister of Education; also Minister of Educn, 1971–74; Minister of Labour, Culture, and Welfare, 1974–81. Was Acting Prime Minister of Malta on various occasions, and elected President of the Republic, 16 Feb. 1982. Patron: Ad Vitam St Michael's Band Club, Zabbar; Malta-China Friendship and Cultural Soc. Hon. Academician, Accademia Universale A. Magno, Prato, Italy; Hon. PhD Univ. of Beijing, China, 1984. Keys and Freedom of: Lahore, Buenos Aires, Lima, San José, Bogotà and Montevideo, 1986; Aden, 1987. Malta GC 50th anniversary medal for service in civil defence, 1992. Stara Planina, 1st cl. with ribbon (Bulgaria), 1983; Order of National Flag 1st Class (Democratic People's Republic of Korea), 1985; Hishan-e-Pakistan (Islamic Republic of Pakistan), 1986; Sceptre of Authority of the Incas (Peru), 1986. *Recreations:* philately, classical and modern music. *Address:* Kenn Taghna, Wied Il-Ghajn Street, Zabbar, Republic of Malta.

BARBARITO, Most Rev. Luigi, DD, JCD; Titular Archbishop of Fiorentino; Apostolic Nuncio to the Court of St James's, since 1986; *b* Atripalda, Avellino, Italy, 19 April 1922; *s* of Vincenzo Barbarito and Alfonsina Armerini. *Educ:* Pontifical Seminary, Benevento, Italy; Gregorian Univ., Rome (JCD); Papal Diplomatic Academy, Rome (Diploma). Priest, 1944; served Diocese of Avellino, 1944–52; entered Diplomatic Service of Holy See, 1953; Sec., Apostolic Delegn, Australia, 1953–59; Secretariat of State of Vatican (Council for Public Affairs of the Church), 1959–67; Counsellor, Apostolic Nunciature, Paris, 1967–69; Archbishop and Papal Nuncio to Haiti and Delegate to the Antilles, 1969–75; Pro-Nuncio to Senegal, Bourkina Fasso, Niger, Mali, Mauretania, Cape Verde Is and Guinea Bissau, 1975–78; Apostolic Pro-Nuncio to Australia, 1978–86. Mem., Mexican Acad. of Internat. Law. Grand Cross, National Order of Haiti, 1975; Grand Cross, Order of the Lion (Senegal), 1978; Knight Commander, Order of Merit (Italy), 1966, (Portugal), 1967. *Recreations:* music, walking, snooker. *Address:* Apostolic Nunciature, 54 Parkside, Wimbledon, SW19 5NF. *T:* 0181–946 1410.

BARBER, family name of **Baron Barber.**

BARBER, Baron *cr* 1974 (Life Peer), of Wentbridge; **Anthony Perrinott Lysberg Barber,** PC 1963; TD; DL; Chairman, Standard Chartered Bank plc, 1974–87; *b* 4 July 1920; *s* of John Barber, CBE, Doncaster; *m* 1st, 1950, Jean Patricia (*d* 1983), *d* of Milton Asquith, Wentbridge, Yorks; two *d*; 2nd, 1989, Mrs Rosemary Youens, *d* of Rev. Canon Fearnly Youens. *Educ:* Retford Grammar Sch.; Oriel Coll., Oxford Univ. (PPE, MA) (Hon. Fellow 1971). Served War of 1939–45: commnd in Army (Dunkirk); seconded to RAF as pilot, 1940–45 (despatches; prisoner of war, 1942–45, took Law Degree with 1st Class Hons while POW, escaped from Poland, prisoner of the Russians). Barrister-at-law, Inner Temple, 1948 (Inner Temple Scholarship). MP (C): Doncaster, 1951–64; Altrincham and Sale, Feb. 1965–Sept. 1974; PPS to the Under-Sec. of State for Air, 1952–55; Asst Whip, 1955–57; a Lord Comr of the Treasury, 1957–58; PPS to the Prime Minister, 1958–59; Economic Sec. to the Treasury, 1959–62; Financial Sec. to the Treasury, 1962–63; Minister of Health and Mem. of the Cabinet, 1963–64; Chancellor of the Duchy of Lancaster, June-July 1970; Chancellor of the Exchequer, 1970–74. Chm., Conservative Party Organisation, 1967–70; Pres., Nat. Union of Cons. & Unionist Assocs, 1973. Dir, BP, 1979–88. Mem., Falkland Islands Inquiry (Franks Cttee), 1982. British Mem., Eminent Persons Gp on S Africa, 1986. Vice-Chm. Council, Charing Cross and Westminster Med. Sch., 1984– (Chm. Council, Westminster Med. Sch., 1975–84). Chm., RAF Benevolent Fund, 1991–. DL W Yorks, 1987. *Address:* House of Lords, SW1A 0PW. *Clubs:* Carlton, Royal Air Force.

BARBER OF TEWKESBURY, Baron *cr* 1992 (Life Peer), of Gotherington in the County of Gloucestershire; **Derek Coates Barber,** Kt 1984; Chairman: Booker Countryside Advisory Board, 1990–95; Countryside Commission, 1981–91; *s* of Thomas Smith-Barber and Elsie Coates; 1st marr. diss. 1981; *m* 2nd, 1983, Rosemary Jennifer Brougham, *o d* of late Lt-Comdr Randolph Brougham Pearson, RN, and of Hilary Diana Mackinlay Pearson (*née* Bennett). *Educ:* Royal Agricl Coll., Cirencester (MRAC; Gold Medal, Practical Agriculture). Served War: invalided, Armed Forces, 1942. Farmed in Glos Cotswolds; Mem., Cheltenham Rural District Council, 1948–52; Dist Adv. Officer, National Agricl Adv. Service, MAFF, 1946–57; County Agricl Advisor, Glos, 1957–72; Environment Consultant to Humberts, Chartered Surveyors, 1972–93; MAFF Assessor: Pilkington Cttee on Agric. Educ., 1966; Agric. and Hort. Trng Bd, 1968. Member: H of L Sub-Cttee D (Food and Agric.), 1992–; H of L Select Cttee on Sustainable Devel t, 1994–95. Chairman: BBC's Central Agricl Adv. Cttee, 1974–80 (*ex officio* Mem., BBC's Gen. Adv. Council, 1972–80); New National Forest Adv. Bd, 1991–. Royal Soc. for Protection of Birds: Mem., 1970–75, Chm., 1976–81, Council; Chm., Educn Cttee, 1972–75; Vice-Pres., 1982; Pres., 1990–91. President: RASE, 1991–92; Rare Breeds Survival Trust, 1991–95 (Mem. Council, 1987–); Hawk and Owl Trust, 1992–; British Pig Assoc., 1995–96; Glos Naturalists' Soc., 1981–; Vice-Pres., Ornithol Soc. of Mid-East, 1987–; Mem. Council, British Trust for Ornithology, 1987–90; Founder Mem., 1969, Farming and Wildlife Adv. Gp of landowning, farming and wildlife conservation bodies; Member: Ordnance Survey Adv. Bd, 1982–85; Bd, RURAL Council, 1983–94; Bd, CEED, 1984–; Centre for Agricl Strategy, 1985–91; Agricl Res. Insts Assoc., 1991–; Long Ashton Res. Stn Cttee, 1991–. Dep. Chm., Bd, Groundwork Foundn, 1985–91; Patron, Woodland Trust, 1991–. FRAgS 1992; FIAgrM 1992. Hon. FRASE 1986. Hon. DSc Bradford, 1986. First Recipient, Summers Trophy for services to agric. in practice or science, 1955; Bledisloe Gold Medal for distinguished service to UK agriculture, 1967; RSPB Gold Medal for services to bird protection, 1982; Massey-Ferguson Award for services to agric., 1989; RASE Gold Medal, for distinguished service to UK agric., 1991. Silver Jubilee Medal, 1977. Editor, Humberts Commentary, 1973–88; columnist, Power Farming, 1973–91; Spec. Correspondent, Waitaki NZR Times, 1982–88. *Publications:* (with Keith Dexter) Farming for Profits, 1961, 2nd edn 1967; (with J. G. S. and Frances Donaldson) Farming in Britain Today, 1969, 2nd edn 1972; (ed) Farming with Wildlife, 1971; A History of Humberts, 1980; contrib. farming and wildlife conservation jls. *Recreations:* birds, wildlife conservation, farming. *Address:* Chough House, Gotherington, Glos GL52 4QU. *T:* Cheltenham (01242) 673908. *Club:* Farmers'.

BARBER, Chris; *see* Barber, D. C.

BARBER, Sir David; *see* Barber, Sir T. D.

BARBER, (Donald) Chris(topher), OBE 1991; band leader, Chris Barber's Jazz and Blues Band; *b* 17 April 1930; *s* of Henrietta Mary Evelyn Barber, MA Cantab and Donald Barber, CBE, BA Cantab; *m* Renate M. Hilbich; one *s* one *d*. *Educ:* King Alfred School; St Paul's School. Formed first amateur band, 1949; present band commenced on professional basis, 1954; plays trombone, trumpet, baritone horn, contra bass. Hon. Citizen, New Orleans. Numerous recordings, including over 100 LPs, with records in the hit parade of over 40 countries world wide. *Recreations:* motor racing, snooker. *Address:* c/o Cromwell Management, 4 & 5 High Street, Huntingdon, Cambs PE18 6TE. *T:* Huntingdon (01480) 435600, *Fax:* (01480) 435155.

BARBER, Frank; Senior Partner, Morgan, Fentiman & Barber; Deputy Chairman of Lloyd's, 1983, 1984; *b* 5 July 1923; *s* of Sidney Barber and Florence (*née* Seath); *m* 1945, Gertrude Kathleen Carson (decd); one *s* one *d* (and one *s* decd); *m* 1994, Elizabeth Joan Charvet. *Educ:* West Norwood Central School. RAFVR, 1942–46; Underwriter, Lloyd's syndicate, Frank Barber & others, 1962–81; Member: Cttee of Lloyd's, 1977–80, 1982–85 and 1987; Council of Lloyd's, 1983–85 and 1987; Dep. Chm., Lloyd's Underwriters' Non-Marine Assoc., 1971, Chm., 1972; Dep. Chm., British Insurers' European Cttee, 1983. Partner: Morgan, Fentiman & Barber, 1968–; G. S. Christanson & Partners, 1985–; Chm., A. E. Grant (Underwriting Agencies) Ltd, 1991–. *Recreations:* music, walking, sailing. *Address:* Doiley Hill House, Hurstbourne Tarrant, Andover, Hants SP11 0ER. *T:* Hurstbourne Tarrant (01264) 736595, *Fax:* (01264) 736229.

BARBER, Giles Gaudard; Librarian, Taylor Institution, University of Oxford, since 1970; Fellow, Linacre College, Oxford, since 1963 (Vice-Principal, 1988–90); *b* 15 Aug. 1930; *s* of Eric Arthur Barber and Madeleine Barber (*née* Gaudard); *m* 1st, 1958, Monique Fluchère (*d* 1969); one *d*; 2nd, 1970, Gemma Miani; two *s* one *d*. *Educ:* Dragon Sch., Oxford; Leighton Park Sch.; St John's Coll., Oxford (MA, BLitt). Asst, Bodleian Library, 1954–70; Univ. Lectr in Continental Bibliography, Oxford, 1969–. Pres., Oxford Bibliographical Soc., 1992–; Vice-Pres., Bibliographical Soc., 1983–93; Chm., Voltaire Foundn, 1987–89; Mem. Council, Internat. Soc. for 18th Century Studies, 1979–83. Vis. Lectr, Univ. of Paris IV (Sorbonne), 1980; Lectures: 1st Graham Pollard Meml, 1984; Moses Tyson Meml, Manchester Univ., 1985; Panizzi, British Library, 1988. Gordon Duff Prize in Bibliography, 1962. Officier, Ordre des Arts et des Lettres (France), 1992. *Publications:* Fine Bindings 1500–1700, 1968 (ed jtly); A checklist of French printing manuals, 1969; Textile and embroidered bookbindings, 1971; (ed) Book making in Diderot's Encyclopédie, 1973; (ed) Contat, Anecdotes typographiques, 1980; (ed jtly) Buch und Buch-handel in Europa im achtzehnten Jahrhundert, 1981; Daphnis and Chloe, 1989; Studies of the booktrade of the European Enlightenment, 1994; Arks for Learning, 1995; articles in learned jls. *Recreations:* book-collecting, looking at Oxford, drawing. *Address:* 2 Linton Road, Oxford OX2 6UG. *T:* Oxford (01865) 511500.

BARBER, Prof. James, PhD; FIBiol, FRSC; Ernst Chain Professor of Biochemistry and Head of Department of Biochemistry, Imperial College of Science, Technology and Medicine, since 1989; *b* 16 July 1940; *s* of Stanley William George Barber and Sophia Helen Barber; *m* 1965, Marilyn Jane Emily Tyrrell; one *s* one *d*. *Educ:* Portsmouth Southern Grammar Sch.; Univ. of Wales (BSc Hons Chem.); Univ. of East Anglia (MSc, PhD Biophys.). FIBiol 1979; FRSC 1983. Unilever Biochem. Soc. European Fellow, Univ. of Leiden, 1967–68; Imperial College: Lectr, Dept of Botany, 1968–74; Reader in Plant Physiology, 1974–79, Prof., 1979–89; Dean, Royal Coll. of Science, 1989–91. Mem., Academia Europaea, 1989. Hon. Dr Univ. of Stockholm, 1992. *Publications:* The Intact Chloroplast, 1976; Primary Processes in Photosynthesis, 1977; Photosynthesis in Relation to Model Systems, 1979; Electron Transport and Photophosphorylation, 1982; Chloroplast Biogenesis, 1984; Photosynthetic Mechanisms and the Environment, 1986; The Light Reactions, 1987; The Photosystems: structure, function and molecular biology, 1992; articles and reviews. *Recreations:* running, sailing, gardening. *Address:* Wolfson Laboratories, Biochemistry Department, Imperial College of Science, Technology and Medicine, SW7 2AY. *T:* 0171–581 1316.

BARBER, Prof. James Peden, PhD; Master, Hatfield College, Durham, since 1980; Professor of Politics, Durham University, since 1992; *b* 6 Nov. 1931; *s* of John and Carrie Barber; *m* 1955, Margaret June (*née* McCormac); three *s* one *d*. *Educ:* Liverpool Inst. High Sch.; Pembroke Coll., Cambridge (MA, PhD); The Queen's Coll., Oxford. Served RAF, 1950–52 (Pilot Officer). Colonial Service, Uganda: Dist Officer, subseq. Asst Sec. to Prime Minister and Clerk to the Cabinet, 1956–63; Lectr, Univ. of NSW, Australia, 1963–65; Lectr in Govt, Univ. of Exeter, 1965–69 (seconded to University Coll. of Rhodesia, 1965–67); Prof. of Political Science, Open Univ., 1969–80; Pro-Vice-Chancellor, 1987–92 and Sub-Warden, 1990–92, Durham Univ. Res. Fellow, S African Inst. of Internat. Affairs, 1995. Advr, Commons Select Cttee on Foreign Affairs, 1990–91. Mem. RIIA; Part-time Dir, Chatham House study, Southern Africa in Conflict, 1979–81.

Mem., Amnesty International. President: Durham Univ. Soc. of Fellows, 1988; Durham Univ. Hockey Club, 1981–. JP Bedford, 1977–80. *Publications:* Rhodesia: the road to rebellion, 1967; Imperial Frontier, 1968; South Africa's Foreign Policy, 1973; European Community: vision and reality, 1974; The Nature of Foreign Policy, 1975; Who Makes British Foreign Policy?, 1977; The West and South Africa, 1982; The Uneasy Relationship: Britain and South Africa, 1983; South Africa: the search for status and security, 1990; The Prime Minister since 1945, 1991; Forging the New South Africa, 1994. *Recreations:* choral music, all kinds of sport, walking. *Address:* Kingsgate House, Bow Lane, Durham DH1 3ER. *T:* Durham (0191) 3848651. *Club:* Commonwealth Trust.

BARBER, Rear-Adm. John L.; *see* Lee-Barber.

BARBER, John Norman Romney; company director and business consultant; *s* of George Ernest and Gladys Eleanor Barber; *m* 1941, Babette Chalu; one *s*. *Educ:* Westcliff. Served with Army, 1939–46 (Capt.). Min. of Supply, 1946–55 (Princ.). Joined Ford Motor Co. Ltd, 1955, Finance Dir, 1962; Chm., Ford Motor Credit Co. Ltd, 1963; Dir, Henry Ford & Son Ltd, Cork, 1963; Dir Autolite Motor Products Ltd, 1963; Finance Dir, AEI Ltd, 1965; Chm., Telephone Cables Ltd, 1967; Dir of Finance and Planning, 1968–71, Dep. Man. Dir, 1971–73, Dep. Chm. and Man. Dir, 1973–75, British Leyland Motor Corp. Ltd; Chairman, 1973–75: British Leyland International Ltd; Leyland Innocenti, SpA; Leyland Motor Corp. of Australia Ltd; Director: Leyland España SA; Automóviles de Turismo Hispano Ingleses SA; NZ Motor Corp. Ltd; British Leyland Motors Inc.; Metalurgica de Santa Ana SA; Chairman: Pullmaflex International Ltd, 1976–79; Aberhurst Ltd, 1976–88; A. C. Edwards Engineering Ltd, 1976–81; Cox & Kings Financial Services Ltd, 1980–85; C & K Executive Search Ltd, 1980–85; C & K Consulting Group Ltd, 1982–88; Director: Acrow plc, 1977–84; Good Relations Group plc, 1979–86; Amalgamated Metal Corp. Ltd, 1980–81; Spear & Jackson International plc, 1980–85; Economists Advisory Group Ltd, 1981–; UK Investments Ltd, 1985–; The Communications Group Hldgs plc, 1990–; Deputy Chairman: Cox & Kings Ltd, 1980–81; John E. Wiltshier Group plc, 1980–88 (Dir, 1979–88). Mem., Royal Commn on Medical Educn, 1965–68; Chm., Adv. Cttee to BoT on Investment Grants, 1967–68; Mem., Adv. Council for Energy Conservation, 1974–75. Vice Pres., SMMT, 1974–76. CBIM; Mem. Council BIM, 1967–71. *Publications:* papers on management subjects in various jls. *Recreations:* motor sport, forestry, photography. *Address:* 38 Spring Street, W2 1JA. *Club:* British Automobile Racing.

BARBER, Nicholas Charles Faithorn; Deputy Chairman, Royal Insurance Holdings plc, since 1994 (Director, since 1991); *b* 7 Sept. 1940; *s* of Bertram Harold and Nancy Lorraine Barber; *m* 1966, Sheena Macrae Graham; two *s* one *d*. *Educ:* Ludgrove Sch.; Shrewsbury Sch.; Wadham Coll., Oxford (MA); Columbia Univ., New York, 1969–71 (MBA). Lectr, Marlboro Coll., Vermont, USA, 1963–64; joined Ocean Steam Ship, then Ocean Transport and Trading, subseq. Ocean Group, 1964; Dir, 1980–94; Chief Exec., 1986–94. Divl Dir, NEB, 1977–79; Director: Costain Gp, 1990–93; Barings plc, 1994–; Bristol & West Bldg Soc., 1994–; Albright & Wilson, 1995–. Mem., NW Industrial Develt Bd, 1982–85; Gov., NIESR, 1991–. Trustee: Nat. Museums and Galls on Merseyside, 1986–94; British Mus., 1993–; Chm., British Mus. Soc., 1992–. Governor: Shrewsbury Sch., 1983–; London Business Sch., 1993–; Mem. Council, Liverpool Univ., 1985–88; Vice-Pres., Liverpool Sch. of Tropical Medicine, 1988–; Dir, Liverpool Playhouse, 1982–87; Mem., Adv. Cttee, Tate Gall., Liverpool, 1988–92. *Recreations:* hill-walking, cricket, destructive gardening. *Address:* Flat 6, Lytton Court, 14 Barter Street, WC1A 2AH. *Clubs:* United Oxford & Cambridge University, MCC.

BARBER, Rt. Rev. Paul Everard; *see* Brixworth, Bishop Suffragan of.

BARBER, Sir (Thomas) David, 3rd Bt *cr* 1960, of Greasley, Nottingham; self-employed philatelist; *b* 18 Nov. 1937; *o s* of Col Sir William Francis Barber, 2nd Bt and his 1st wife, Diana Constance Barber (*née* Lloyd) (*d* 1984); *S* father, 1995; *m* 1st, 1971, Amanda Mary Healing (*née* Rabone) (marr. diss. 1976); one *s*; 2nd, 1978 Jeannine Mary Boyle (*née* Gurney), one *s* one *d*. *Educ:* Eton; Trinity Coll., Cambridge (MA). 2nd Lieut, RA, 1958–61. *Heir: s* Thomas Edward Barber, *b* 14 March 1973. *Address:* Windrush House, Inkpen, Hungerford, Berks RG17 9QY. *Clubs:* MCC; Free Foresters.

BARBER, Trevor Wing; His Honour Judge Barber; a Circuit Judge, since 1992; *b* 10 June 1943; *s* of Robert and Margaret Barber; *m* 1967, Judith Penelope Downey; one *s* one *d*. *Educ:* Worksop Coll.; Newcastle Univ. (LLB). Called to the Bar, Inner Temple, 1967; practice in Sheffield, 1967–92. *Recreations:* gardening, hockey, reading. *Address:* Juniper Lodge, Hillfoot Road, Totley, Sheffield S17 2AY. *Club:* Sheffield (Sheffield).

BARBER, Prof. William Joseph, Hon. OBE 1981; Professor of Economics, Wesleyan University, Middletown, Conn, USA, 1965–93; *b* 13 Jan. 1925; *s* of Ward Barber; *m* 1955, Sheila Mary Marr; three *s*. *Educ:* Harvard Univ. (AB); Balliol Coll., Oxford. BA, 1st Cl. Hons, 1951, MA 1955; DPhil (Nuffield Coll.) 1958. Served War, US Army, 1943–46. Lectr in Econs, Balliol Coll., Oxford, 1956; Wesleyan University: Dept of Economics, 1957–93; Asst Prof., 1957–61; Associate Prof., 1961–65; Prof., 1965–93; Andrews Prof., 1972–93; Andrews Prof. Emeritus, 1994–; Acting Pres., Aug.–Oct. 1988. Research Associate: Oxford Univ. Inst. of Economics and Statistics, 1962–63; Twentieth Century Fund, South Asian Study, 1961–62. Amer. Sec., Rhodes Scholarship Trust, 1970–80. Pres., Hist. of Econs Soc., 1989–90. *Publications:* The Economy of British Central Africa, 1961; A History of Economic Thought, 1967; contributor to Asian Drama: an inquiry into the poverty of nations (with Gunnar Myrdal and others), 1968; British Economic Thought and India 1600–1858, 1975; (jtly) Exhortation and Controls: the search for a wage-price policy, 1975; Energy Policy in Perspective, 1981; From New Era to New Deal: Herbert Hoover, the economists, and American economic policy 1921–1933, 1985; (ed, and jt author) Breaking the Academic Mould: economists and American higher learning in the nineteenth century, 1988; (ed) Perspectives on the History of Economic Thought, vols V and VI, 1991; contribs to professional jls. *Address:* 306 Pine Street, Middletown, CT 06457, USA. *T:* (203) 3462612.

BARBIERI, Margaret Elizabeth, (Mrs M. E. Barbieri-Webb); freelance ballet teacher and coach, since 1990; guest teacher, Royal Ballet School, since 1990; Artistic Director, Images of Dance, since 1990; *b* 2 March 1947; *d* of Ettore Barbieri and Lea Barbieri; *m* 1983, Iain Webb, soloist SWRB; one *s*. *Educ:* Convent High Sch., Durban, S Africa. Trained with Iris Manning and Brownie Sutton, S Africa; Royal Ballet Sen. Sch., 1963; joined Royal Ballet, 1965; Principal, 1970; Sen. Principal, SWRB, 1974–89. Dir, Classical Graduate Course, London Studio Centre, 1990–. Gypsy Girl, Two Pigeons, 1966; 1st Giselle, Covent Garden, 1968; 1st Sleeping Beauty, Leeds, 1969; 1st Swan Lake, Frankfurt, 1977, Covent Garden, 1983; 1st Romeo and Juliet, Covent Garden, 1979; 1st Sleeping Beauty, Covent Garden, 1985. Other roles with Royal Ballet: La Fille mal Gardée, Two Pigeons, The Dream, Façade, Wedding Bouquet, Rendezvous (Ashton); Lady and the Fool, Card Game, Pineapple Poll (Cranko); The Invitation, Solitaire, (Summer) The Four Seasons (MacMillan); Checkmate, The Rake's Progress (de Valois); Grosse Fugue, Tilt (van Manen); Lilac Garden (Tudor); Fête Etrange (Howard); Grand Tour (Layton); Summer Garden (Hynd); Game Piano (Thorpe), 1978; Cinderella (Killar), 1978; Cinderella (Rodrigues), 1979; Papillon, The Taming of the Shrew, 1980; Coppélia, Les Sylphides, Raymonda Act III, Spectre de la Rose; La Vivandière, 1982; Petrushka, 1984. Roles created: Knight Errant (Tudor), 1968; From Waking Sleep (Drew), 1970; Ante-Room (Cauley), 1971; Oscar Wilde (Layton), 1972; Sacred Circles and The Sword (Drew), 1973; The Entertainers (Killar), 1974; Charlotte Brontë (Hynd), 1974; Summertide (Wright), 1977; Metamorphosis (Bintley), 1984; Flowers of the Forest (Bintley), 1985; The Wand of Youth (Corder), 1985. Recreated: Pavlova's Dragonfly Solo, 1977; The Dying Swan, produced by Dame Alicia Markova after Fokine, 1985. Guest artist, 1990–92, guest teacher, 1991–92, Birmingham Royal Ballet. Staged for Images of Dance: Les Sylphides, Façade, 1991; Rake's Progress, 1992; Pineapple Poll, La Bayadère, 1993. Travelled with Royal Ballet to Australia, Canada, China, Egypt, Far East, France, Germany, Greece, Holland, Israel, Italy, Japan, New Zealand, Portugal, Spain, Switzerland, Yugoslavia, India and North and South America; guest appearances, USA, Germany, S Africa, France, Norway, Czechoslovakia. TV Appearances in: Spectre de la Rose; Grosse Fugue; Giselle; Coppelia; Checkmate; Markova master classes. Gov., Royal Ballet, 1991–. *Recreations:* music (classical), theatre, gardening. *Address:* Chiswick.

BARBOSA, Rubens Antonio, Hon. LVO 1969; Brazilian Ambassador to the Court of St James's, since 1994; *b* 13 June 1938; *s* of José Orlando Barbosa and Lice Farina Barbosa; *m* 1969, Maria Ignez Correa da Costa Barbosa; one *s* one *d*. *Educ:* Univ. of Brazil (Law graduate); LSE (MA); other degrees in economics, finance and politics. Exec. Sec., Brazilian Trade Commn with socialist countries of Eastern Europe, 1976–84; Head of Staff, Min. of External Relations, 1985–86; Under-Sec. Gen., Multilateral and Special Pol Affairs, 1986; Head, Internat. Affairs, Min. of Economy, 1987–88; Ambassador and Perm. Rep. to Latin-Amer. Integration Assoc., 1988–91; Under-Sec. Gen., Regl Integration, Econ. Affairs and Foreign Trade, Min. of External Relations, and Co-ordinator for Mercosur, Brazil, 1991–93. Grand Cross, Order of Rio Branco (Brazil); French Legion of Honour; orders from Argentina and Mexico; honours from Germany, Belgium, Italy, Iran, Portugal. *Publications:* America Latina em Perpectiva: a integração regional da retórica à realidade, 1991; articles in newspapers and learned jls. *Recreations:* tennis, classical music. *Address:* Brazilian Embassy, 32 Green Street, W1Y 4AT. *T:* 0171–629 6044, *Fax:* 0171–493 5105.

BARBOUR, James Jack, OBE 1992; Chief Executive Officer, Central Manchester NHS Trust, since 1994; *b* 16 Jan. 1953; *s* of late Thomas Jack Barbour and of Flora Jean Barbour (*née* Murray); *m* 1985, Rosalind Marjorie Doig; one *s* two *d*. *Educ:* Madras Coll., St Andrews; Univ. of Strathclyde (BA Jt Hons Politics, Sociol., Econs). MHSM 1983. Grad. Mgt Trainee, NHS in Scotland, 1977–79; Administrator, Gtr Glasgow Health Bd, 1979–83; EEC Exchange scholarship in Germany, 1981; Unit Administration, Gt Ormond St Gp of Hosps, 1983–86; General Manager: Royal Manchester Children's Hosp., 1986–87; Aberdeen Royal Infirmary, 1987–92; Chief Exec., Aberdeen Royal Hosps NHS Trust, 1992–94. Alumnus, London Business Sch. Develt Prog., 1989. FRSA 1993. Burgess, City of Aberdeen, 1992. *Recreations:* spoiling my children, trying to stay fit! *Address:* Central Manchester Healthcare NHS Trust, Manchester Royal Infirmary, Cobbett House, Oxford Road, Manchester M13 9WL. *T:* 0161–276 4755. *Club:* Royal Northern (Aberdeen).

BARBOUR, Very Rev. Prof. Robert Alexander Stewart, KCVO 1991; MC 1945; Professor of New Testament Exegesis, University of Aberdeen, 1971–82; Master of Christ's College, Aberdeen, 1977–82; an Extra Chaplain to the Queen in Scotland since 1991 (Chaplain-in-Ordinary to the Queen, 1976–91); Dean of the Chapel Royal in Scotland, 1981–91; Prelate of the Priory of Scotland of the Order of St John, 1977–93; *b* 11 May 1921; *s* of George Freeland Barbour and Helen Victoria (*née* Hepburne-Scott); *m* 1950, Margaret Isobel Pigot; three *s* one *d*. *Educ:* Rugby Sch.; Balliol Coll., Oxford (MA 1946); Univ. of St Andrews (BD 1952); Yale Univ. (STM 1953). Sec., Edinburgh Christian Council for Overseas Students, 1953–55; Lectr and Sen. Lectr in NT Lang., Lit. and Theol., Univ. of Edinburgh, 1955–71. Hensley Henson Lectr, Univ. of Oxford, 1983–84. Moderator, Gen. Assembly of Church of Scotland, 1979–80. Chm., Scottish Churches' Council, 1982–86. Hon. Sec., Studiorum Novi Testamenti Societas, 1970–77. Chm. Governors, Rannoch Sch., 1973–79. Hon. DD St Andrews, 1979. *Publications:* The Scottish Horse 1939–45, 1950; Traditio-Historical Criticism of the Gospels, 1972; What is the Church for?, 1973; articles in various jls. *Recreations:* music, walking, forestry. *Address:* Fincastle, Pitlochry, Perthshire PH16 5RJ. *T:* Pitlochry (01796) 473209. *Club:* New (Edinburgh).

BARBOZA, Mario G.; *see* Gibson-Barboza.

BARCLAY, (Alan) Neil, DPhil, Scientific Staff, Medical Research Council, Cellular Immunology Unit, Oxford, since 1978; *b* 12 March 1950; *s* of Frank Rodney Barclay and late Betty Cowie Barclay (*née* Watson); *m* 1975, Ella Geraldine Quinn; two *s* one *d*. *Educ:* Hardye's Sch., Dorchester; Oriel Coll., Oxford (DPhil Biochem 1976). Res. Fellow, Inst. of Neurobiology, Univ. of Göteborg, Sweden, 1976–78. Hon. Mem., Scandinavian Soc. of Immunology, 1993. *Publications:* (jtly) The Leucocyte Antigen Factsbook, 1993; contribs to scientific jls. *Recreations:* literature, listening to music, writing stories (unpublished). *Address:* MRC Cellular Immunology Unit, Sir William Dunn School of Pathology, Oxford University, Oxford OX1 3RE. *T:* Oxford (01865) 275598.

BARCLAY, Christopher Francis Robert, CMG 1967; Secretary, Government Hospitality Fund, 1976–80; *b* 8 June 1919; *s* of late Captain Robert Barclay, RA (retired) and late Annie Douglas Dowdeswell Barclay (*née* Davidson); *m* 1st, 1950, Clare Justice Troutbeck (marr. diss., 1962); two *s* one *d*; 2nd, 1962, Diana Elizabeth Goodman; one *s* one *d*. *Educ:* Eton Coll.; Magdalen Coll., Oxford (MA). 2nd Lieut The Rifle Bde, 1940; Capt. 1942; Major 1943; served in Middle East; Political Officer, Northern Iraq, 1945; Brit. Embassy, Baghdad, 1946. Foreign Office, 1946; Second Sec., British Embassy, Cairo, 1947; First Sec., Foreign Office, 1950; Brit. Embassy, Bonn, 1953; FO, 1956; Regional Information Officer, Beirut, 1960; FO, 1961; Counsellor and Head of Information Research Dept, 1962–66; Head of Personnel Dept (Training and General), FCO, 1967–69; Asst Sec., CSD, 1969–73, DoE, 1973–76. Chm., Jt Nat. Horse Educn and Trng Council, 1988–90. Mem. Council, City Univ., 1976–84. Master, Saddlers' Co., 1983–84. FRSA 1984. *Recreations:* fishing, gardening. *Address:* Croft Edge, Painswick, Glos GL6 6XH. *T:* Painswick (01452) 812332. *Club:* Army and Navy.

BARCLAY, Sir Colville Herbert Sanford, 14th Bt, *cr* 1668; Painter; *b* 7 May 1913; *s* of late Rt Hon. Sir Colville Adrian de Rune Barclay, 3rd *s* of 11th Bt, and Sarita Enriqueta, *d* of late Herbert Ward; *S* uncle, 1930; *m* 1949, Rosamond Grant Renton Elliott; three *s*. *Educ:* Eton, Trinity Coll., Oxford. Third Sec., Diplomatic Service, 1937–41; enlisted in Navy, Nov. 1941; Sub-Lieut RNVR 1942; Lieut 1943; Lieut Commander 1945; demobilised, 1946. Exhibitor: Royal Academy, RBA, London Group, Bradford City and Brighton Art Galleries. Chm. Royal London Homoeopathic Hospital, 1970–74 (Vice-Chm., 1961–65; Chm., League of Friends, 1974–84). Plant-hunting expedns to Crete, Turkey, Cyprus, Réunion, Mauritius and Nepal, 1966–81. *Publications:* Crete: checklist of the vascular plants, 1986; articles in botanical jls. *Recreation:* gardening. *Heir: s* Robert Colraine Barclay [*b* 12 Feb. 1950; *m* 1980, Lucilia Saboia, *y d* of Carlos Saboia de

Albuquerque, Rio de Janeiro; one *s* one *d*]. *Address:* Pitshill, Petworth, West Sussex GU28 9AZ. *T:* Lodsworth (01798) 861341. *Club:* Naval.

BARCLAY, Hugh Maben, CB 1992; Clerk of Public Bills, House of Commons, 1988–91; *b* 20 Feb. 1927; *s* of late William Barclay, FRCS, and late Mary Barclay; *m* 1956, Hilda Johnston; one *s* one *d*. *Educ:* Fettes Coll., Edinburgh (exhbnr); Gonville and Caius Coll., Cambridge (schol.). Served Royal Artillery, 1948. House of Commons: Asst Clerk, 1950; Sen. Clerk, 1955; Dep. Principal Clerk, 1967; Principal Clerk, 1976; Clerk of Standing Cttees, 1976; Clerk of Private Bills, 1982. *Address:* 37 Stockwell Green, SW9 9HZ. *T:* 0171–274 7375.

BARCLAY, James Christopher; Chairman, Cater Allen Holdings PLC, since 1985 (Deputy Chairman, 1981–85); *b* 7 July 1945; *s* of late Theodore David Barclay and of Anne Barclay; *m* 1974, Rolleen Anne, *d* of late Lt-Col Arthur Forbes and of Joan Forbes; one *s* one *d*. *Educ:* Harrow. Served 15th/19th The King's Royal Hussars, 1964–67. Chm., Cater Ryder & Co. Ltd, 1981. Chm., London Discount Market Assoc., 1988–90. *Recreations:* fresh air pursuits. *Address:* Rivers Hall, Waldringfield, Woodbridge, Suffolk IP12 4QX; (office) 20 Birchin Lane, EC3V 9DJ. *Clubs:* Boodle's, Pratt's.

BARCLAY, John Alistair; Deputy Group Chief Executive, Royal Bank of Scotland, since 1992; *b* 5 Dec. 1933; *m* 1963, Mary Tierney (*née* Brown); three *d*. *Educ:* Banff Academy. FCIBS. Royal Bank of Scotland, 1949–: Chief City Manager, 1982–84; seconded to Williams & Glyn's Bank (Asst Gen. Manager), 1984–85; Exec. Vice-Pres., NY, 1985–88; Sen. Gen. Manager, UK Banking, 1988–89; Exec. Dir, International, 1989–90; Man. Dir, Corporate and Institutional Banking, 1990–92. *Recreations:* travel, golf, reading, gardening, curling, photography, good food and wine. *Address:* Royal Bank of Scotland, 67 Lombard Street, EC3P 3DL. *T:* 0171–615 5026.

BARCLAY, Neil; *see* Barclay, A. N.

BARCLAY, Sir Peter (Maurice), Kt 1992; CBE 1984; Partner, Beachcrofts, Solicitors, 1974–88, retired; *b* 6 March 1926; *s* of George Ronald Barclay and Josephine (*née* Lambert); *m* 1953, Elizabeth Mary Wright; one *s* two *d*. *Educ:* Bryanston Sch.; Magdalene Coll., Cambridge (MA). Served RNVR, 1944–46. Admitted Solicitor, 1952; Senior Partner, Beachcroft & Co., 1964–74. Chairman: Cttee on Roles and Tasks of Social Workers, 1981–82; Social Security Adv. Cttee, 1984–93; Nat. Family Mediation, 1994–. Non-exec. Mem., DSS Deptl Bd, 1994–. Pres., National Inst. for Social Work, 1988 (Chm., 1973–85); Chm., Horticultural Therapy, 1989–94; Vice Pres., St Pancras Housing Assoc., 1994– (Mem., 1971–93, Chm., 1983–91, Management Cttee). Trustee, Joseph Rowntree Foundn (formerly Joseph Rowntree Meml Trust), 1972– (Vice-Chm., 1994–); Governor, Bryanston Sch., 1972–88; Council Mem., PSI, 1989–. DUniv Stirling, 1994. *Recreations:* gardening, painting. *Address:* 4/43 Ladbroke Grove, W11 3AR. *T:* 0171–727 4613.

BARCLAY, Sir Roderick (Edward), GCVO 1966 (KCVO 1957; CVO 1953); KCMG 1955 (CMG 1948); HM Diplomatic Service, retired; *b* 22 Feb. 1909; *s* of late J. Gurney Barclay and Gillian (*née* Birkbeck); *m* 1934, Jean Cecil, *d* of late Sir Hugh Gladstone; one *s* three *d*. *Educ:* Harrow; Trinity Coll., Cambridge. Entered Diplomatic Service, 1932. Served at HM Embassies at Brussels, Paris, Washington and in FO; Counsellor in FO 1946; Principal Private Sec. to Sec. of State for Foreign Affairs, 1949–51; Asst Under-Sec. of State, 1951; Dep. Under-Sec. of State, 1953–56; HM Ambassador to Denmark, 1956–60; Adviser on European Trade Questions, Foreign Office, and Dep. Under-Sec. of State for Foreign Affairs, 1960–63; Ambassador to Belgium, 1963–69. Director: Slough Estates, 1969–84; Barclays Bank SA, 1969–79 (Chm., 1970–74); Barclays Bank Internat., 1971–77; Banque de Bruxelles, 1971–77. Knight Grand Cross of the Dannebrog (Denmark) and of the Couronne (Belgium). *Publication:* Ernest Bevin and the Foreign Office 1932–69, 1975; contrib. Country Life, etc. *Recreations:* shooting, fishing. *Address:* Garden Cottage, Great White End, Latimer, Chesham, Bucks HP5 1UJ. *T:* Little Chalfont (01494) 765919. *Club:* Brooks's.
See also A. E. Palmer.

BARCLAY, Yvonne Fay, (Mrs William Barclay); *see* Minton, Y. F.

BARCROFT, Prof. Henry, FRS 1953; MA; MD; FRCP; Professor of Physiology, St Thomas's Hospital Medical School, London, 1948–71, Emeritus since 1971; a Wellcome Trustee, 1966–75; *b* 18 Oct. 1904; *s* of late Sir Joseph Barcroft, CBE, FRS; *m* 1933, Bridget Mary (*d* 1990), *d* of late A. S. Ramsey; three *s* one *d*. *Educ:* Marlborough Coll.; King's Coll. Cambridge; Exhibitioner, 1923. Natural Science Tripos Class I, Parts I and II; Harold Fry and George Henry Lewes studentships at Cambridge, 1927–29; Gedge Prize, 1930; Harmsworth Scholar, St Mary's Hospital, London, 1929–32; Lectr in Physiology, University Coll., London, 1932–35; Dunville Prof. of Physiology, Queen's Univ., Belfast, 1935–48. Arris and Gale Lectr, RCS, 1945; Bertram Louis Abrahams Lectr, RCP, 1960; Robert Campbell Meml Orator, Ulster Med. Soc., 1975; Bayliss-Starling Meml Lectr, Physiological Soc., 1976; Vis. Prof., Univ. of Adelaide, 1963. Chairman: Editorial Bd, Monographs of Physiological Soc., 1957–65; Research Defence Soc., 1968–71, Sec. 1972–77, Vice-Pres., 1978–. Hon. Member: British Microcirculation Soc.; Société Française d'Angiologie; Japanese Coll. of Angiology; Czechoslovak Med. Soc. J. E. Purkinje. Hon. DSc Univ. Western Australia, 1963; Hon. MD Leopold-Franzens Univ., Innsbruck, 1969; Hon. DSc QUB, 1975. Pro meritis médaille in silver, Karl Franzens Univ., Graz. *Publications:* (with H. J. C. Swan) Sympathetic Control of Human Blood Vessels, 1953; papers in the Journal of Physiology. *Recreations:* sailing, golf. *Address:* 73 Erskine Hill, NW11 6EY. *T:* 0181–458 1066.

BARD, Dr Basil Joseph Asher, CBE 1968; Innovation consultant, retired; Director, Scanning Technology Ltd, since 1984; *b* London, 20 Aug. 1914; *s* of late Abram Isaac Bard and Anita Bard; *m* 1942, Ena Dora Birk; three *s*. *Educ:* Owen's Sch.; RCS (Imperial Coll.). BSc(Chem.), ARCS 1934, DIC (Chem. Engrg and Fuel Technology) 1935, PhD (Chem. Constitution of Coal) 1936, London; Bar Finals (1st cl. hons) and Studentship, Coun. of Legal Educn, 1937; called to Bar, Gray's Inn (Birkenhead and William Shaw Schol.), 1938. Practised at Bar, 1938–39; Legal Dept, Coal Commn, 1939–41; Explosives Prodn Dept, Min. of Supply, 1941–43; Materials Dept, Min. of Aircraft Production, 1943–45; Depts of Industrial Res., Educn, Design, etc, FBI, 1945–49; NRDC, 1950–74; in turn, Commercial Man., Techn. Dir and Exec. Dir, Dept of Applied Science; Mem., NRDC, 1956–73, Man. Dir, 1971–73; Exec. Dir, First National Finance Corp., 1974–76; Chm., Birmingham Mint Ltd, 1977–81. Director: Allied Insulators Ltd, 1975–77; Interflex Group, 1984–89; Chairman: NPM Gp, 1977–83; Xtec Ltd, 1983–86 (Dir, 1981–86); ProMicro Ltd, 1985–91. Founder and Chm., 1968–70, subsequently Vice-Pres., UK Licensing Execs Soc. (awarded Gold Medal 1973; Hon. Life Member, 1989). Consultant to UNIDO, 1972–74; Hon. Mem., Foundn for Sci. and Technol., 1990– (Hon. Treasurer, 1984–90); has served on various Govt Cttees. Pres., Jewish Meml Council, 1982–89; Vice-Pres., Anglo-Jewish Assoc., 1983– (Pres., 1977–83); Chm., Administration Cttee, UK Friends of Hebrew Univ. of Jerusalem, 1991– (Hon. Fellow, 1993). *Publications:* (ed) Industry and Research, 1947; (ed) The Patent System, 1975; various articles on science, technology, patents, industry, commerce and their inter-relationships. *Recreations:* music, bridge, chess, social life. *Address:* 23 Mourne House, Maresfield Gardens, Hampstead, NW3 5SL. *T:* 0171–435 5340. *Club:* Athenæum.

BARDEN, Prof. Laing, CBE 1990; PhD, DSc; Vice-Chancellor, University of Northumbria at Newcastle, since 1992 (Director, Newcastle upon Tyne Polytechnic, 1978–92); *b* 29 Aug. 1931; *s* of Alfred Eversfield Barden and Edna (*née* Laing); *m* 1956, Nancy Carr; two *s* one *d*. *Educ:* Washington Grammar Sch.; Durham Univ. (BSc, MSc). R. T. James & Partners, 1954–59. Liverpool Univ., 1959–62 (PhD); Manchester Univ., 1962–69 (DSc); Strathclyde Univ., 1969–74; Newcastle upon Tyne Polytechnic, subseq. Univ. of Northumbria at Newcastle, 1974–. Director: Microelectronics Applications Res. Inst. Ltd, 1980–90; Tyne and Wear Enterprise Trust Ltd, 1982–; Newcastle Technology Centre Ltd, 1985–90; Newcastle Initiative, 1988–. Mem., Council for Industry and Higher Educn, 1987–. *Publications:* contribs to Geotechnique, Proc. ICE, Jl Amer. Soc. CE, Qly Jl Eng. Geol. *Recreations:* cricket, soccer, snooker. *Address:* 7 Westfarm Road, Cleadon, Tyne and Wear SR6 7UG. *T:* Wearside (091) 5362317. *Clubs:* National Liberal; Mid Boldon (Boldon).

BARDER, Sir Brian (Leon), KCMG 1992; HM Diplomatic Service, retired; High Commissioner to Australia, 1991–94; *b* 20 June 1934; *s* of Harry and Vivien Barder; *m* 1958, Jane Maureen Cornwell; two *d* one *s*. *Educ:* Sherborne; St Catharine's Coll., Cambridge (BA). 2nd Lieut, 7 Royal Tank Regt, 1952–54. Colonial Office, 1957; Private Sec. to Permanent Under-Sec., 1960–61; HM Diplomatic Service, 1965; First Secretary, UK Mission to UN, 1964–68; FCO, 1968–70; First Sec. and Press Attaché, Moscow, 1971–73; Counsellor and Head of Chancery, British High Commn, Canberra, 1973–77; Canadian Nat. Defence Coll., Kingston, Ontario, 1977–78; Head of Central and Southern, later Southern African Dept, FCO, 1978–82; Ambassador to Ethiopia, 1982–86; Ambassador to Poland, 1986–88; High Comr to Nigeria, and concurrently Ambassador to Benin, 1988–91. CON 1989. *Address:* 10 Melrose Road, SW18 1NE. *Club:* United Oxford & Cambridge University.
See also E. L. Wen.

BARDSLEY, Andrew Tromlow; JP; General Manager and Chief Executive, Harlow Development Corporation, 1973–80; *b* 7 Dec. 1927; *o s* of Andrew and Gladys Ada Bardsley; *m* 1954, June Patricia (*née* Ford); one *s* one *d*. *Educ:* Ashton-under-Lyne Grammar Sch.; Manchester Coll. of Art. CEng, FICE. Royal Navy, 1947–49. Entered Local Govt (Municipal Engrg), 1950; various appts leading to Borough Engr and Surveyor, Worksop MB, 1962–69; Director of Technical Services: Corby New Town, 1969–71; Luton CBC, 1971–73; Principal, Westgate Develt Consultancy, 1981–93. Gen. Comr. of Taxes in England and Wales, 1987–92. JP Essex, 1975 (Dep. Chm., Harlow Bench, 1987–92). *Publications:* papers on engrg and associated matters incl. housing and town centre re-development. *Recreations:* golf, music, gardening, most spectator sports. *Address:* 25 Charlotte Close, Talbot Village, Poole, Dorset BH12 5HR. *T:* Poole (01202) 537954. *Club:* Ferndown Golf.

BARENBLATT, Prof. Grigory Isaakovich, PhD, ScD; G. I. Taylor Professor of Fluid Mechanics, University of Cambridge, 1992–94; Fellow, Gonville and Caius College, Cambridge, since 1994; *b* 10 July 1927; *s* of Isaak Grigorievich Barenblatt and Nadezhda Veniaminovna (*née* Kagan); *m* 1952, Iraida Nikolaevna Kochina; two *d*. *Educ:* Moscow Univ. (MSc 1950; PhD 1953; ScD 1957); Univ. of Cambridge (MA 1993). Res. Scientist, Inst. of Petroleum, USSR Acad. of Sci., Moscow, 1953–61; Prof. and Hd, Dept of Mechanics of Solids, Inst. of Mechanics, Moscow Univ., 1961–75; Hd, Theoretical Dept, Inst. of Oceanology, USSR Acad. of Sci., Moscow, 1975–92. Foreign Mem., Amer. Acad. of Arts and Scis, 1975; Foreign Associate, US Nat. Acad. of Engrg, 1992; MAE, 1993. Hon. DTech Royal Inst. of Technol., Stockholm, 1989. *Publications:* Similarity, Self-Similarity, and Intermediate Asymptotics, 1979; Dimensional Analysis, 1987; (jtly) Theory of Fluid Flows in Porous Media, 1990; contrib. Jl Applied Maths and Mechanics, Physics of Atmosphere and Ocean, Jl Fluid Mechanics. *Recreation:* historical reading. *Address:* Gonville and Caius College, Cambridge CB2 1TA.

BARENBOIM, Daniel; pianist and conductor; Musical Director: Chicago Symphony Orchestra, since 1991; Berlin State Opera, since 1992; *b* Buenos Aires, 15 Nov. 1942; *s* of Enrique Barenboim and late Aida Barenboim (*née* Schuster); *m* 1st, 1967, Jacqueline du Pré (*d* 1987); 2nd, 1988, Elena Bashkirova; two *s*. *Educ:* Santa Cecilia Acad., Rome; studied with his father; coached by Edwin Fischer, Nadia Boulanger, and Igor Markevitch. Debut as pianist with: Israel Philharmonic Orchestra, 1953; Royal Philharmonic Orchestra, 1956; Berlin Philharmonic Orchestra, 1963; NY Philharmonic Orchestra, 1964; Musical Dir, Orchestre de Paris, 1975–88; tours include: Australia, North and South America, Far East; regular appearances at Bayreuth, Edinburgh, Lucerne, Prague and Salzburg Festivals. Many recordings as conductor and pianist. Beethoven Medal, 1958; Paderewski Medal, 1963; subsequently other awards. Legion of Honour (France), 1987. *Publication:* A Life in Music, 1991. *Address:* c/o Daniel Barenboim Secretariat, 5 place de la Fusterie, 1204 Génève, Switzerland.

BARFETT, Ven. Thomas; Archdeacon of Hereford and Canon Residentiary of Hereford Cathedral, 1977–82, now Emeritus; Prebendary of Colwall and Treasurer, 1977–82; Chaplain to the Queen, 1975–86; *b* 2 Oct. 1916; *s* of Rev. Thomas Clarence Fairchild Barfett and Dr Mary Deborah Barfett, LRCP, LRCS, MA; *m* 1945, Edna, *d* of Robert Toy; one *s* one *d*. *Educ:* St John's Sch., Leatherhead; Keble Coll., Oxford (BA 1938; MA 1942); Wells Theol Coll. Ordained deacon, Portsmouth, 1939; priest, 1940; Curate: Christ Church, Gosport, 1939–44; St Francis of Assisi, Gladstone Park, London, 1944–47; St Andrew Undershaft with St Mary Axe, City of London, 1947–49; Asst Sec., London Diocesan Council for Youth, 1944–49; Vicar, St Paul, Penzance, dio. of Truro, 1949–55; Rector of Falmouth, 1955–77; Officiating Chaplain, 1102 Marine Craft Unit, RAF, 1957–75; Sec., Truro Diocesan Conf., 1952–67; Proctor in Convocation, dio. of Truro, 1958–76; Hon. Canon, Truro, 1964–77; licensed to officiate, dioceses of Bermuda, 1984, Europe, 1986. Chm., House of Clergy, and Vice-Pres., Truro Diocesan Synod, 1970–76; Mem., Gen. Synod, 1977–82. Chaplain to lay Sheriff, City of London, 1976–77. Church Comr, 1975–82; Mem. C of E Central Bd of Finance, 1969–77, Pensions Board, 1973–86. Chairman: Missions to Seamen, Cornwall, 1957–77; Cornwall Family History Soc., 1985–88 (Pres., 1994–). Mem., St John Council for Cornwall, 1983–93. Freeman, City of London, 1973; Freeman and Liveryman, Scriveners Co., 1976. Sub ChStJ, 1971 (Asst ChStJ, 1963). Silver Jubilee Medal, 1977. *Publications:* Trebarfoote: a Cornish family, 1975, 2nd edn 1989; ed Cornish section, Hatchments in Britain, 1988. *Recreations:* heraldry, genealogy. *Address:* Treberveth, 57 Falmouth Road, Truro, Cornwall TR1 2HL. *T:* Truro (01872) 73726. *Club:* United Oxford & Cambridge University.

BARHAM, Geoffrey Simon; His Honour Judge Barham; a Circuit Judge, since 1993; *b* 23 Dec. 1945; *s* of Denis Patrick Barham and Pleasance (*née* Brooke); *m* 1976, Sarah Seebold; one *s* one *d*. *Educ:* Malvern Coll.; Christ's Coll., Cambridge (MA). Called to the Bar, Lincoln's Inn, 1968; Asst Recorder, 1983; Recorder, 1987. *Recreation:* golf. *Address:* c/o SE Circuit Office, New Cavendish House, 18 Maltravers Street, WC2R 3EU. *Club:* Norfolk (Norwich).

BARING, family name of **Baron Ashburton,** of **Earl of Cromer,** of **Baron Howick of Glendale,** of **Baron Northbrook,** and of **Baron Revelstoke.**

BARING, Sir John (Francis), 3rd Bt *cr* 1911, of Nubia House, Isle of Wight; Chairman: Hackman, Baring & Co., since 1994 (Partner, 1991–94); HB Communications Acquisition Corporation, since 1993; *b* 21 May 1947; *s* of Raymond Alexander Baring (*d* 1967) (2nd *s* of 1st Bt) and of Margaret Fleetwood Baring (who *m* 1991, Earl of Malmesbury, *qv*), *d* of late Col R. W. P. C. Campbell-Preston; *S* uncle, 1990; *m* 1971, Elizabeth Anne, *yr d* of Robert D. H. Pillitz; two *s* one *d*. Citibank NA, 1971–72; Chemical Bank, 1972–84; Kidder, Peabody & Co. Inc., 1984–89; GPA Group Ltd, 1989. *Recreations:* gardening, fishing. *Heir: s* Julian Alexander David Baring, *b* 10 Feb. 1975. *Address:* 89 June Road, North Salem, NY 10560, USA. *T:* (914) 6695750. *Club:* Union (New York).

BARING, Nicholas Hugo; Chairman, Commercial Union plc, since 1990 (Director, since 1968; Deputy Chairman, 1983–90); *b* 2 Jan. 1934; *er s* of late Francis Anthony Baring (killed in action, 1940) and Lady Rose Baring, DCVO; *m* 1972, (Elizabeth) Diana, *d* of late Brig. Charles Crawfurd; three *s*. *Educ:* Eton (King's Schol.); Magdalene Coll., Cambridge (exhibnr, BA). Nat. service, 2nd Lieut Coldstream Guards, 1952–54. ADC to Governor of Kenya, 1957–58; joined Baring Brothers, 1958; Man. Dir, Baring Brothers & Co., 1963–86; Dir, Barings plc, 1985–94 (Dep. Chm., 1986–89). Mem., City Capital Markets Cttee, 1983–89 (Chm., 1983–87). Pres., Liverpool Sch. of Tropical Medicine, 1989–. Chm., Bd of Trustees, Nat. Gall., 1992– (Trustee, 1989–). National Trust: Mem. Exec. Cttee, 1965–69 and 1979–; Mem. Council, 1978–; Chm., Finance Cttee, 1980–91. Member: Council, Baring Foundn, 1969–; Council of Management, Architectl Heritage Fund, 1987–. *Address:* St Helen's, 1 Undershaft, EC3P 3DQ. *Club:* Brooks's.
See also P. Baring.

BARING, Peter; *b* 28 Oct. 1935; *yr s* of Francis Anthony Baring (killed in action, 1940) and Lady Rose Baring, DCVO; *m* 1960, Teresa Anne Bridgeman; three *s*. *Educ:* Magdalene College, Cambridge (MA English). Joined Baring Brothers & Co., 1959, Director, 1967; Chairman: Barings plc, 1989–95; Baring Asset Management, 1993–95. Dir, Inchcape, 1978–. Dep. Chm., Provident Mutual Life Assurance Assoc., 1989–95. Chm., London Investment Banking Assoc., 1991–94. Gov., London Business Sch., 1991–. Chm., Glyndebourne Arts Trust, 1994–. *Address:* 8 Bishopsgate, EC2N 4AE. *T:* 0171–280 1000.
See also N. H. Baring.

BARKER, family name of **Baroness Trumpington.**

BARKER, Sir Alwyn (Bowman), Kt 1969; CMG 1962; BSc, BE; CEng, FIEE, FIEAust; Chairman, Kelvinator Australia Ltd, 1967–80 (Managing Director, 1952–67); *b* 5 Aug. 1900; *s* of late A. J. Barker, Mt Barker, South Australia; *m* 1926, Isabel Barron Lucas, *d* of late Sir Edward Lucas; one *d* (one *s* decd). *Educ:* St Peter's Coll., Adelaide; Geelong C of E Grammar Sch.; Univ. of Adelaide. British Thomson Houston Co. Ltd, England, 1923–24; Hudson Motor Car Co., Detroit, 1924–25; Production Manager, Holden's Motor Body Builders Ltd, Adelaide, 1925–30; Works Manager, Kelvinator Aust. Ltd, Adelaide, 1931–40; Gen. Man., Chrysler Aust. Ltd, Adelaide, 1940–52; Chm., Municipal Tramways Trust SA, 1953–68; Dir, public companies. Mem. Faculty of Engineering, Univ. of Adelaide, 1937–66 (Lectr in Industrial Engineering, 1929–53). Chm., Industrial Develt Adv. Council, 1968–70; Fellow, Internat. Acad. of Management; Member: Manufacturing Industries Adv. Council, 1958–72; Res. and Develt Adv. Cttee, 1967–72. Hon. Life Mem., Australian Mineral Foundn; Hon. Fellow Australian Inst. of Management (Federal Pres., 1952–53, 1959–61; Pres. Adelaide Div., 1952–54); Pres., Australian Council, Inst. of Prodn Engrs, 1970–72. John Storey Meml Medal, 1965; Jack Finlay Nat. Award, 1964. *Publications:* Three Presidential Addresses, 1954; William Queale Memorial Lecture, 1965. *Recreations:* pastoral. *Address:* 51 Hackney Road, Hackney, SA 5069, Australia. *T:* (8) 3622838. *Club:* Adelaide.

BARKER, Anne Judith, (Mrs B. J. Barker); *see* Rafferty, A. J.

BARKER, Anthony; QC 1985; a Recorder, since 1985; *b* 10 Jan. 1944; *s* of Robert Herbert Barker and Ellen Doreen Barker; *m* 1st, 1969, (marr. diss. 1980); two *d*; 2nd, 1983, Mrs Valerie Ann Ellis; one step *s*. *Educ:* Newcastle-under-Lyme High Sch.; Clare Coll., Cambridge (BA Hons). Called to the Bar, Middle Temple, 1966. Asst Recorder, 1981. *Recreations:* gardening, walking, music. *Address:* Hilderstone House, Hilderstone, near Stone, Staffs ST15 8SF. *T:* Hilderstone (01889) 505331.

BARKER, Arthur Vincent, CBE 1974 (OBE 1955); Chartered Accountant; financial planning consultant; *b* 10 Nov. 1911; *e s* of late Arthur and Susannah Mary Barker; *m* 1936, Dorothy Drew; one *d*. *Educ:* Whitley and Monkseaton High Sch.; London Sch. of Economics. Qual. as CA, 1934; with Price Waterhouse & Co., 1934–35; with NAAFI in Middle East and UK, 1935–62 (Jt Gen. Man., 1955); British Railways: Member: Southern Region Bd, 1962–65; LMR Bd, 1965–68; Chm., Shipping and Internat. Services Div., 1968–69; Chairman: British Rail Hovercraft, 1970–71; British Transport Hotels Ltd, 1968–74; Mem., British Railways Bd, 1968–74. *Recreation:* fly-fishing. *Address:* 24 West Mount, The Mount, Guildford, Surrey GU2 5HL. *T:* Guildford (01483) 39524.

BARKER, Audrey Lilian; writer; *b* 13 April 1918; *d* of Harry and Elsie Barker. *Educ:* County secondary schools in Beckenham, Kent and Wallington, Surrey. Editorial office, Amalgamated Press, 1936; Publisher's reader, Cresset Press, 1947; BBC, 1949–78. Atlantic Award in Literature, 1946; Somerset Maugham Award, 1947; Cheltenham Festival of Literature Award, 1963; SE Arts Creative Book Award, 1981. FRSL 1970; Mem. Exec. Cttee, PEN, 1981–85; Member Panel of Judges: Katherine Mansfield Prize, 1984; Macmillan Silver Pen Award for Fiction, 1986 and 1989. *Publications: collected stories:* Innocents, 1947; Novelette, 1951; Lost Upon the Roundabouts, 1964; Femina Real, 1971; Life Stories, 1981; No Word of Love, 1985; Any Excuse for a Party, 1991; Element of Doubt: ghost stories, 1992; *novels:* Apology for a Hero, 1950; The Joy-Ride (three novellas), 1963; A Case Examined, 1965; The Middling, 1967; John Brown's Body, 1969 (shortlisted for Booker Prize, 1969); A Source of Embarrassment, 1974; A Heavy Feather, 1978; Relative Successes, 1984; The Gooseboy, 1987; The Woman Who Talked to Herself, 1989; Zeph, 1992. *Address:* Carshalton, Surrey.

BARKER, Barry, MBE 1960; FCIS; Secretary and Chief Executive, Institute of Chartered Secretaries and Administrators (formerly Chartered Institute of Secretaries), 1976–89; *b* 1929; *s* of late Francis Walter Barker and Amy Barker; *m* 1954, Dr Vira Dubash; two *s*. *Educ:* Ipswich Sch.; Trinity Coll., Oxford (MA Class. Greats). Secretary: Bombay Chamber of Commerce and Industry, 1956–62; The Metal Box Co. of India Ltd, 1962–67. Dir, Shipbuilding Industry Bd, 1967–71; Consultant at Dept of Industry, 1972; Sec., Pye Holdings Ltd, 1972–76. Chairman: Consultative Council of Professional Management Orgns, 1981–90; Nat. Endorsement Bd, Management Charter Initiative, 1990–94. Member: BTEC, 1985–94; RSA Exams Bd, 1987–94; NCVQ, 1989–92; Bd of Management, Young Vic Co., 1984–90. *Recreations:* the theatre and the arts. *Address:* 82 Darwin Court, Gloucester Avenue, NW1 7BQ. *T:* 0171–911 0570. *Club:* Oriental.

BARKER, Brian John; QC 1990; a Recorder of the Crown Court, since 1985; *b* 15 Jan. 1945; *s* of William Barker and Irene Barker (*née* Gillow); *m* 1977, Anne Judith Rafferty, *qv*; three *d* (and one *d* decd). *Educ:* Strode's School, Egham; Univ. of Birmingham (LLB); Univ. of Kansas (MA). Called to the Bar, Gray's Inn, 1969. Mem., Senate and Bar Council, 1976–79. A Pres., Mental Health Review Tribunals, 1993–. Gov., Strode's Coll., Egham. Freeman, City of London; Liveryman, Coopers' Co., 1989. *Recreations:* sheep rearing, golf. *Address:* Queen Elizabeth Building, Temple, EC4Y 9BS. *T:* 0171–583 5766. *Clubs:* City Livery; Royal Mid-Surrey Golf, Rye Golf; Pett Cricket.

BARKER, Rt. Rev. Clifford Conder, TD 1970; Bishop Suffragan of Selby, 1983–91; Hon. Assistant Bishop of York, since 1991; *b* 22 April 1926; *s* of Sidney and Kathleen Alice Barker; *m* 1952, Marie Edwards (*d* 1982); one *s* two *d*; 2nd, 1983, Mrs Audrey Gregson; two step *s* one step *d*. *Educ:* Oriel Coll., Oxford (BA 1950, MA 1955); St Chad's Coll., Durham (Dip. in Theol. 1952). Emergency Commun, The Green Howards, 1944–48; deacon 1952, priest 1953; Curate: All Saints', Scarborough, 1952–55; Redcar, 1955–57; Vicar: All Saints', Sculcoates, Hull, 1957–63; Rudby-in-Cleveland, 1963–70; RD of Stokesley, 1965–70; Vicar, St Olave with St Giles, York, 1970–76; RD of York, 1971–76; Canon of York, 1973–76; Bishop Suffragan of Whitby, 1976–83. CF (TA), 1958–74. *Recreations:* golf, gardening, music. *Address:* Wylde Green, 15 Oak Tree Close, Strensall, York YO3 5TE. *T:* York (01904) 490406.

BARKER, Sir Colin, Kt 1991; Chairman, British Technology Group Ltd, 1983–1993 (Chief Executive, 1983–85); *b* 20 Oct. 1926; *m* 1951, Beryl; three *s* one *d*. *Educ:* Hull Grammar Sch.; London and Edinburgh Univs. Ford UK, 1960–67 (Finance Dir, 1967); Finance Director: Blue Circle, 1968–70; STC, 1970–80; British Steel Corp., 1980–83. Chairman: CIN Management, 1985–93; British Investment Trust, 1985–93; MCD (UK), 1990–; Anglian Windows, 1991–; Director: Reed Internat., 1983–92; British Coal Corp., 1984–91; Edinburgh Fund Managers, 1988–93. *Address:* 12 Clune Court, Hutton Road, Shenfield, Essex CM15 8NQ.

BARKER, David, QC 1976; a Recorder of the Crown Court, since 1974; *b* 13 April 1932; *s* of late Frederick Barker and of Amy Evelyn Barker; *m* 1957, Diana Mary Vinson Barker (*née* Duckworth); one *s* three *d*. *Educ:* Sir John Deane's Grammar Sch., Northwich; University Coll., London; Univ. of Michigan. 1st cl. hons LLB London; LLM Michigan. RAF, 1956–59. Called to Bar, Inner Temple, 1954, Bencher, 1985; practised Midland and Oxford Circuit; Mem., Senate of Inns of Court and the Bar, 1981–84. Mem., Criminal Injuries Compensation Bd, 1990–. Contested (Lab) Runcorn, 1955. *Recreations:* gardening, walking, sailing. *Address:* Nanhill, Woodhouse Eaves, Leics LE12 8TL. *T:* Woodhouse Eaves (01509) 890224; Francis Taylor Building, Temple, EC4Y 7BY. *T:* 0171–353 7768. *Club:* Western (Glasgow).

BARKER, Prof. David (Faubert), MA, DPhil, DSc; Professor of Zoology, University of Durham, 1962–87, now Professor Emeritus; *b* 18 Feb. 1922; *s* of Faubert and Doreen Barker; *m* 1st, 1945, Kathleen Mary Frances Pocock; three *s* two *d*; 2nd, 1978, Patricia Margaret Drake; one *s* one *d*. *Educ:* Bryanston Sch.; Magdalen Coll., Oxford. DSc 1972. Senior Demy of Magdalen Coll., 1946; Leverhulme Research Scholar, Royal Coll. of Surgeons, 1946; Demonstrator in Zoology and Comparative Anatomy, Oxford, 1947; DPhil 1948; Rolleston Prizeman, 1948; Prof. of Zoology, Univ. of Hong Kong, 1950–62; led scientific expeditions to Tunisia, 1950, North Borneo, 1952; Dean of Faculty of Science, Hong Kong, 1959–60; Public Orator, Hong Kong, 1961; Sir Derman Christopherson Fellow, Durham Univ. Research Foundn, 1984–85. Emeritus Fellow, Leverhulme Trust, 1989–92. *Publications:* (Founder) Editor, Hong Kong Univ. Fisheries Journal, 1954–60; Editor, Symposium on Muscle Receptors, 1962; scientific papers, mostly on muscle innervation. *Address:* Department of Biological Sciences, Science Laboratories, South Road, Durham DH1 3LE. *T:* Durham (091) 3743342.

BARKER, Prof. David James Purslove, MD, PhD; FRCP, FFPHM; Professor of Clinical Epidemiology, since 1979 and Director, Medical Research Council Environmental Epidemiology Unit, since 1984, University of Southampton; *b* 29 June 1938; *s* of Hugh Purslove and Joye Frances Barker; *m* 1st, 1960, Angela Beatrice Coddington (*d* 1980); three *s* two *d*; 2nd, 1983, Janet Elizabeth Franklin; one step *s* two step *d*. *Educ:* Oundle Sch.; Guy's Hosp. Med. Sch., London Univ. (BSc 1st Cl. Hons, 1959; MB BS 1962; PhD 1966; MD 1973). FRCP 1979; FFPHM (FFCM 1979). University of Birmingham: Research Fellow in Social Medicine, 1963–66; Lectr in Medicine, 1966–69; Lectr in Preventive Medicine, Makerere Univ., Uganda, 1969–72; Sen. Lectr in Clinical Epidemiology and Consultant Physician, Univ. of Southampton, 1972–79. Hon. FRCOG, 1993. Royal Soc. Wellcome Gold Medal, 1994. *Publications:* Practical Epidemiology, 1973, 4th edn 1992; (with G. Rose) Epidemiology in Medical Practice, 1976, 4th edn 1990; (with G. Rose) Epidemiology for the Uninitiated, 1979, 3rd edn 1993; Fetal and infant origins of adult disease, 1992; Mothers, babies and disease in later life, 1994. *Recreations:* writing, drawing, golf, fishing, craic. *Address:* Manor Farm, East Dean, near Salisbury, Wilts SP5 1HB. *T:* Lockerley (01794) 340016.

BARKER, Edward, OBE 1966; QPM 1961; Chief Constable of Sheffield and Rotherham Constabulary, 1967–72; *b* 1 Nov. 1909; *s* of George and Gertrude Barker; *m* 1935, Clare Garth; one *d*. *Educ:* The Grammar School, Malton. Joined Preston Borough Police, 1931; transf. Lancs Constabulary, 1938; Inspector/Chief Inspector, Comdt of Constabulary Trng Sch., 1946–51; Supt 1954; Vis. Lectr to Bermuda Police, 1955; Chief Supt 1956; Asst Comdt, Police Coll., Bramshill, 1956–57; Chief Constable: Bolton Borough Police, 1957; Sheffield City Police, 1964. Hon. Fellow, Sheffield Poly., 1973. Police Long Service and Good Conduct Medal, 1953. SBStJ. *Recreations:* golf, gardening, watching field sports. *Address:* 21 Woodstock Road, Aberdeen AB2 4ET. *T:* Aberdeen (01224) 318484. *Club:* Deeside Golf.

BARKER, Prof. Graeme William Walter, FSA; Professor and Head of School of Archaeological Studies, Leicester University, since 1988; *b* 23 Oct. 1946; *s* of Reginald Walter Barker and Kathleen (*née* Walton); *m* 1976, Sarah Miranda Buchanan (marr. diss. 1991); one *s* one *d*. *Educ:* Alleyn's Sch., Dulwich; St John's Coll., Cambridge (Henry Arthur Thomas Schol., 1965–67; MA, PhD). FSA 1979. Rome Schol. in Classical Studies, British Sch. at Rome, 1969–71; Lectr, 1972–81, Sen. Lectr, 1981–88, in Prehist. and Archaeol., Sheffield Univ.; Dir., British Sch. at Rome, 1984–88. Dir, Molise survey and excavation project, S Italy, 1974–78; Co-Director: UNESCO Libyan Valleys Survey, 1979–89; Tuscania Project, 1986–91. *Publications:* Landscape and Society: Prehistoric Central Italy, 1981, Italian edn 1984; (with R. Hodges) Archaeology and Italian Society, 1981; Prehistoric Communities in Northern England, 1981; (jtly) La Casatico di Marcaria, 1983; (jtly) Cyrenaica in Classical Antiquity, 1984; Prehistoric Farming in Europe, 1985; (with C. S. Gamble) Beyond Domestication in Prehistoric Europe: Investigations in Subsistence Archaeology and Social Complexity, 1985; (with J. A. Lloyd) Roman Landscapes, 1991; (with R. Maggi and R. Nisbet) Archeologia della Pastorizia nell'Europa Meridionale, 1993; contribs, esp. on archaeol survey, archaeozool. and ancient agric., to learned jls. *Address:* School of Archaeological Studies, University of Leicester, University Road, Leicester LE1 7RH. *T:* Leicester (0116) 252 2611.

BARKER, Harold; retired; Keeper, Department of Conservation and Technical Services, British Museum, 1975–79; Member: Council for Care of Churches, 1976–81; Crafts Council, 1979–80; *b* 15 Feb. 1919; *s* of William Frampton Barker and Lily (*née* Pack); *m*

1942, Everilda Alice Whittle; one *s* one *d*. *Educ:* City Secondary Sch., Sheffield; Sheffield Univ. (BSc). Experimental Asst, 1940, Experimental Officer, 1942, Chemical Inspectorate, Min. of Supply; British Museum: Experimental Officer, Research Lab., 1947; Sen. Experimental Officer, 1953; Chief Experimental Officer, 1960; Principal Scientific Officer, 1966; Acting Keeper, 1975. *Publications:* papers on radiocarbon dating and scientific examination of antiquities in various jls. *Recreations:* music, walking, videography. *Address:* 27 Westbourne Park, Falsgrave, Scarborough, N Yorks YO12 4AS. *T:* Scarborough (01723) 353273.

BARKER, Howard; playwright and poet; *b* 28 June 1946. *Educ:* Univ. of Sussex (MA). Theatre productions, 1970–, include: *Royal Court:* No End of Blame, 1981; Victory, 1983; version of Thomas Middleton's Women Beware Women, 1986; The Last Supper, 1988; Golgo, 1990; *RSC* at The Pit: The Castle, 1985; Downchild: a fantasy, 1985; The Bite of the Night, 1988; other productions: A Passion in Six Days, Crucible, Sheffield, 1983; The Power of the Dog, Hampstead, 1985; Possibilities, Almeida, 1988; The Last Supper, 1989, Seven Lears, 1990, Leicester. TV and radio plays include: Scenes from an Execution, Radio 3, 1984 (Best Drama Script, Sony Radio Awards, 1985; Prix Italia, 1985; perf. Almeida, 1990); Pity in History, BBC 2, 1985; A Hard Heart, Radio 3, 1992 (perf. Almeida, 1992); The Early Hours of a Reviled Man, Radio 3, 1992. Opera (with Nigel Osborne) Terrible Mouth, ENO, Almeida, 1992. Formed The Wrestling School (company to perform own work), 1989. *Publications: plays:* Stripwell, and Claw, 1977; Fair Slaughter, 1978; Love of a Good Man, and All Bleeding, 1981; That Good Between Us, and Credentials of a Sympathiser, 1981; No End of Blame: scenes of overcoming, 1981; Two Plays for the Right: Birth on a Hard Shouder, and The Loud Boy's Life, 1982; Hang of the Gaol, 1982; Victory: choices in reaction, 1983; The Castle, and Scenes from an Execution, 1984; Crimes in Hot Countries, and Fair Slaughter, 1984; Power of the Dog, 1985; A Passion in Six Days, and Downchild, 1985; The Last Supper: a New Testament, 1988; Lullabies for the Impatient, 1988; Possibilities, 1988; Pity in History, 1989; Seven Lears, and Golgo, 1990; Europeans, and Judith, 1990; Collected Plays, vol. I, 1990; A Hard Heart, 1992; The Early Hours of a Reviled Man, 1992; Collected Plays, vol. II, 1993; *poetry:* Don't Exaggerate (Desire and Abuse), 1985; Breath of the Crowd, 1986; Gary the Thief/Gary Upright, 1987; The Ascent of Monte Grappa, 1991; *essays:* Arguments for a Theatre, 1989. *Address:* c/o Judy Daish Associates, 83 Eastbourne Mews, W2 6LQ.

BARKER, Hon. Sir Ian; *see* Barker, Hon. Sir R. I.

BARKER, John Francis Holroyd, CB 1984; Consultant, Cabinet Office, 1985–93; *b* 3 Feb. 1925; *s* of Rev. C.H. Barker and B.A. Barker (*née* Bullivant); *m* 1954, Felicity Ann (*née* Martindale); three *d*. *Educ:* King Edward's School, Stourbridge; Oriel College, Oxford. RNVR, 1943–46. Director of Music, Abingdon School, 1950–54; War Office/Ministry of Defence, 1954–85. *Recreation:* music. *Address:* c/o Coutts & Co., 440 Strand, WC2R 0QS. *Club:* Athenæum.

BARKER, Air Vice-Marshal John Lindsay, CB 1963; CBE 1946; DFC 1945; RAF (retired); *b* 12 Nov. 1910; *s* of Abraham Cockroft Barker and Lilian Alice (*née* Woods); *m* 1948, Eleanor Margaret Hannah; one *s*. *Educ:* Trent Coll., Derbys; Brasenose Coll., Oxford. Called to the Bar, Middle Temple, 1947. RAFO, 1930, RAF, 1933. Served War of 1939–45: France, 1939–40; N Africa, 1942–44; Bomber Command, 1944–45; Far East, 1945–46; Palestine, 1946–48; Egypt, 1950–53; Air Attaché, Rome, 1955–58; Cmdr Royal Ceylon Air Force, 1958–63. Air Vice-Marshal, 1959. Retd, 1963. Order of Merit, Italy, 1958. *Recreations:* golf, photography, sailing. *Address:* The Old Cider Press, Mill Court, Frogmore, Kingsbridge, S Devon TQ7 2PB. *T:* Frogmore (01548) 531746. *Club:* Royal Air Force.

BARKER, John Michael Adrian; His Honour Judge Barker; a Circuit Judge, since 1979; *b* 4 Nov. 1932; *s* of Robert Henry Barker and Annie Robson Barker (*née* Charlton); *m* 1971, Gillian Marsha (*née* Greenstone). *Educ:* Marist Coll., Hull Univs of Sheffield and Hull. BSc, LLB. Called to Bar, Middle Temple, 1959. Schoolmaster, Stonyhurst Coll., 1957–59; Lectr in Law, Univ. of Hull, 1960–63. A Recorder of the Crown Court, 1974–79. Mem., Hull CC, 1965–71. *Publications:* articles in Conveyancer and Property Lawyer, Solicitors' Jl, Criminal Law Review and Solicitor. *Recreations:* walking, gardening. *Address:* Combined Court Centre, Lowgate, Hull HU1 2EZ.

BARKER, Rear-Adm. John Perronet, CB 1985; RN retired, 1986; Administration Secretary, Missions to Seamen, 1987–93; *b* 24 June 1930; *s* of late Gilbert Barker and Dorothy G. Barker (*née* Moore); *m* 1955, Priscilla, *d* of late Sir William Christie, KCIE, CSI, MC; two *s*. *Educ:* Edgbaston Prep. Sch., Birmingham; Nautical Coll., Pangbourne; BRNC, Dartmouth. Entered RN, 1948; served, 1949–72: HMS King George V, Glory, Condor, Ceres, Lagos, Hampshire and Centurion; staff of C-in-C Home Fleet, of C-in-C Nore and of Comdr British Navy Staff, Washington; Sec. to ACNS (OR), MoD (Navy), to Flag Officer 2FEF, and to Flag Officer Plymouth; Sec. to Controller of the Navy, 1972–76; Student, RCDS, 1977; Dir, Fleet Supply Duties, MoD (Navy), 1978–80; Cdre, HMS Centurion, 1980–83; Chief of Staff to C-in-C, Naval Home Command, 1983–85. Chairman: IYRU World Youth Sailing, 1986–; Assoc. of RN Officers, 1987–; Royalist Mgt Cttee, Sea Cadet Assoc., 1986–; Member Council: Shaftesbury Homes and Arethusa, 1986–; Sea Cadet Assoc., 1986–; Life Rear Cdre, RNSA, 1986. Freeman, Co. of Shipwrights, 1983. *Recreations:* sailing, gardening, DIY. *Address:* c/o Lloyds Bank, 125 Colmore Row, Birmingham B3 3AD. *Clubs:* Royal Yacht Squadron (Cowes); Royal Naval Sailing Association (Portsmouth); Midland Sailing (Birmingham).

BARKER, Prof. Kenneth, CBE 1994; Chief Executive and Vice-Chancellor, De Montfort University, since 1992 (Director, Leicester Polytechnic, 1987–92); *b* 26 June 1934; *s* of Thomas William and Lillian Barker; *m* 1958, Jean Ivy Pearl; one *s* one *d*. *Educ:* Royal Coll. of Music (ARCM); King's Coll., London (BMus); Sussex Univ. (MA). GRSM, FTCL, FLCM. Schoolmaster, 1958–62; lectr and university teacher, 1962–75; Principal, Gipsy Hill Coll., 1975; Pro-Dir, Kingston Polytechnic, 1975–86; Dep. Dir/Dir Designate, Leicester Poly., 1986–87. FRSA; CIMgt. Hon. DSc Moscow State Tech. Univ., 1995. *Publications:* contribs to jls. *Recreations:* music, theatre, watching Rugby. *Address:* De Montfort University, The Gateway, Leicester LE1 9BH; Bramshott, Church Road, Surbiton, Surrey KT6 5HH. *T:* 0181–398 4700. *Clubs:* Athenæum, Reform, Institute of Directors.

BARKER, Nicolas John; Editor, Book Collector, since 1965; *b* 6 Dec. 1932; *s* of Sir Ernest Barker, FBA, and Olivia Stuart Horner; *m* 1962, Joanna Mary Sophia Nyda Cotton; two *s* three *d*. *Educ:* Westminster Sch.; New Coll., Oxford (MA). With Bailliere, Tindall & Cox, 1959 and Rupert Hart-Davis, 1959; Asst Keeper, National Portrait Gallery, 1964; with Macmillan & Co. Ltd, 1965; with OUP, 1971; Dep. Keeper, British Library, 1976–92. William Andrews Clark Vis. Prof, UCLA, 1986–87. President: Amici Thomae Mori, 1978–89; Double Crown Club, 1980–81; Bibliographical Soc., 1981–85; Chm., London Liby Cttee, 1994–; Member: Publication Bd of Dirs, RNIB, 1969–92; London Library Cttee, 1971–; BBC and ITV Appeals Adv. Cttee, 1977–86; Nat. Trust Arts Panel, 1979–91 (Libraries Advr, 1991–); Trustee, The Pilgrim Trust, 1977–; Chm., Laurence Sterne Trust, 1984–. DUniv York, 1994. *Publications:* The Publications of the Roxburghe Club, 1962; The Printer and the Poet, 1970; Stanley Morison, 1972; (ed) Essays and Papers of A. N. L. Munby, 1977; (ed) The Early Life of James McBey: an autobiography, 1883–1911, 1977; Bibliotheca Lindesiana, 1977; The Oxford University Press and the Spread of Learning 1478–1978, 1978; (with John Collins) A Sequel to an Enquiry,1983; Aldus Manutius and the Development of Greek Script and Type, 1985; The Butterfly Books, 1987; Two East Anglian Picture Books, 1988; (ed) Treasures of the British Library, 1989; (ed) S. Morison, Early Italian Writing-Books, 1990; (with Sir Anthony Wagner and A. Payne) Medieval Pageant, 1993; Hortus Eystettensis: the Bishop's Garden and Besler's Magnificent Book, 1994. *Address:* 22 Clarendon Road, W11 3AB. *T:* 0171–727 4340. *Clubs:* Garrick, Beefsteak, Roxburghe; Roxburghe (San Francisco); Zamorano (Los Angeles).

BARKER, Paul; writer and broadcaster; *b* 24 Aug. 1935; *s* of Donald and Marion Barker; *m* 1960, Sally, *e d* of James and Marion Huddleston; three *s* one *d*. *Educ:* Hebden Bridge Grammar Sch.; Calder High Sch.; Brasenose Coll., Oxford (Hulme Exhibr), MA. Intell. Corps (commn), 1953–55. Lecteur, Ecole Normale Supérieure, Paris, 1958–59; The Times, 1959–63; New Society, staff writer, 1964; The Economist, 1964–65; New Society: Assistant Editor, 1965–68; Editor, 1968–86; Social Policy Ed., Sunday Telegraph, 1986–88; Associate Ed., The Independent Magazine, 1988–90. Townscape and arts columnist, Evening Standard, 1987–92; social and political columnist, Sunday Times, 1990–91. Leverhulme Res. Fellow, 1993–95. Dir and Adv. Editor, The Fiction Magazine, 1982–87. Dir, Pennine Heritage, 1978–86. Vis. Fellow, Centre for Analysis of Social Policy, Univ. of Bath, 1986–. Trustee, 1991–, Fellow, 1992, Sen. Fellow, 1995, Inst. of Community Studies. FRSA 1990. (Jtly) BPG Award for outstanding radio prog., My Country, Right or Wrong, 1988. *Publications:* (ed) A Sociological Portrait, 1972; (ed and contrib.) One for Sorrow, Two for Joy, 1972; (ed) The Social Sciences Today, 1975; (ed and contrib.) Arts in Society, 1977; (ed and contrib.) The Other Britain, 1982; (ed) Founders of the Welfare State, 1985; (contrib.) Britain in the Eighties, 1989; (contrib.) Towards a New Landscape, 1993. *Recreation:* driving along the motorway to a baroque church, with the radio on. *Address:* 15 Dartmouth Park Avenue, NW5 1JL. *T:* 0171–485 8861. *Club:* Academy.

BARKER, Peter William, CBE 1988; DL; Chairman, Fenner (formerly J. H. Fenner (Holdings)) PLC, 1982–93; *b* 24 Aug. 1928; *s* of William Henry George and Mabel Irene Barker; *m* 1961, Mary Rose Hainsworth, JP; one *s* one *d*. *Educ:* Royal Liberty Sch., Romford; Dorking County High Sch.; South London Polytechnic. CIMgt; FIIM; FInstD; FCIM. J. H. Fenner & Co., 1953–67; Jt Managing Dir, Fenner International, 1967–71; Chief Exec., J. H. Fenner (Holdings), 1971–82. Chm., Neepsend plc, 1993 (Dir, 1984–93). Member: Yorks and Humberside Regional Council, CBI, 1981– (Chm., 1991–93); National Council, CBI, 1985–; Yorks and Humberside Regional Indust. Develt Bd, 1981– (Chm., 1992–). Pro-Chancellor, Univ. of Hull, 1993–. Hon. DSc (Econ) Hull, 1992. FRSA. DL Humberside, 1990, High Sheriff, 1993–94. *Recreations:* sailing, ski-ing, tennis, music. *Address:* Swanland Rise, West Ella, North Humberside HU10 7SF. *T:* Hull (01482) 653050. *Clubs:* Royal Yorkshire Yacht, Royal Thames Yacht.

BARKER, Hon. Sir (Richard) Ian, Kt 1994; **Hon. Justice Barker;** Senior Judge, High Court of New Zealand, since 1991; *b* 17 March 1934; *s* of Archibald Henry Barker and Kate Dorothy Barker (*née* Humphrys); *m* 1965, Mary Christine Allardyce; two *s* three *d*. *Educ:* Auckland Univ. (BA, LLB, 1958). Called to the Bar, NZ, 1958; Partner, Morpeth, Gould & Co., solicitors, Auckland, 1968–80; Barrister, 1968–76; QC (NZ) 1973; Judge, High Court of NZ, 1976–. Chancellor, Univ. of Auckland, 1991–. Pres., Legal Res. Foundn of NZ, 1981–90. *Publications:* contrib. articles to NZ and Australian jls. *Recreations:* walking, reading, music, railways. *Address:* High Court of New Zealand, Box 60, Auckland, New Zealand. *T:* (9) 3098836. *Club:* Northern (Auckland).

BARKER, Richard Philip; Headmaster, Sevenoaks School, 1981–July 1996; *b* 17 July 1939; *s* of late Philip Watson Barker and Helen May Barker; *m* 1966, Imogen Margaret Harris; two *s* one *d*. *Educ:* Repton; Trinity Coll., Cambridge (MA 1962); Bristol Univ. (Cert. Ed. 1963). Head of Geography, Bedales Sch., 1963–65; Dir, A level business studies project, 1966–73; Lectr, Inst. of Education, London Univ., 1973–74; Housemaster, Marlborough Coll., 1973–81. Mem., RSA. *Publications:* (ed) Understanding Business Series, (annually) 1976–. *Recreations:* educational interests, beekeeping, fishing, sailing, travelling. *Address:* (until July 1996) Headmaster's House, Sevenoaks School, Kent TN13 1HU. *T:* Sevenoaks (01732) 455133.

BARKER, Ronald Hugh, PhD, BSc; CEng, FIEE, FIMechE; Deputy Director, Royal Armament Research and Development Establishment, 1965–75, retired; *b* 28 Oct. 1915; *s* of E. W. Barker and L. A. Taylor; *m* 1943, W. E. Hunt; two *s*. *Educ:* University of Hull. Physicist, Standard Telephones and Cables, 1938–41; Ministry of Supply, 1941–59; Dep. Dir, Central Electricity Research Laboratories, 1959–62; Technical Dir, The Pullin Group Ltd, 1962–65. *Publications:* various, on servomechanisms and control systems. *Address:* Cramond, 17 Dewlands Way, Verwood, Dorset BH31 6JN.

BARKER, Ronnie, (Ronald William George Barker), OBE 1978; actor, retired 1987; *b* 25 Sept. 1929; *s* of Leonard and Edith Barker; *m* 1957, Joy Tubb; two *s* one *d*. *Educ:* Oxford High Sch. Started acting career, Aylesbury Rep. Co., 1948. *Plays (West End):* Mourning Becomes Electra, 1955; Summertime, 1955; Listen to the Wind, 1955; Double Image, 1956; Camino Real, 1957; Lysistrata, 1958; Irma la Douce, 1958; Platanov, 1960; On the Brighter Side, 1961; Midsummer Night's Dream, 1962; Real Inspector Hound, 1968; The Two Ronnies, Palladium, 1978. *Films include:* Robin and Marian, 1975; Picnic, 1975; Porridge, 1979. *Television: series:* Seven Faces of Jim, 1965; Frost Report, 1966–67; Hark at Barker, 1968–69; Six Dates with Barker, 1970; The Two Ronnies, 10 series, 1971–86; Twenty Years of the Two Ronnies, 1986; Porridge, 1974, 1975, 1976, 1977; Open All Hours, 1976, 1981, 1982; Going Straight, 1978; Clarence, 1987. Awards: Variety Club, 1969, 1974, 1980; SFTA, 1971; Radio Industries Club, 1973, 1974, 1977, 1981; Water Rats, 1975; British Acad. Award, 1975, 1977, 1978; Royal Television Society's award for outstanding creative achievement, 1975; British Comedy Award for lifetime achievement, 1990. *Publications:* Book of Bathing Beauties, 1974; Book of Boudoir Beauties, 1975; It's Goodnight From Him, 1976; Sauce, 1977; Gentlemen's Relish, 1979; Sugar and Spice, 1981; Ooh-la-la!, 1983; Pebbles on the Beach, 1985; A Pennyworth of Art, 1986; Dancing in the Moonlight (autobiog.), 1993. *Recreations:* writing song lyrics, collecting postcards.

BARKER, Prof. Theodore Cardwell, PhD, FRHistS; Professor of Economic History, University of London, 1976–83, now Emeritus and engaged in research; *b* 19 July 1923; *s* of Norman Humphrey Barker and Louie Nettleton Barker; *m* 1955, Joy Marie (Judith) Pierce. *Educ:* Cowley Sch., St Helens; Jesus Coll., Oxford (MA); Manchester Univ. (PhD). FRHistS 1963. Econ. History staff, LSE, 1953–64; first Prof. of Econ. and Social Hist., Univ. of Kent at Canterbury, 1964–76. President: Internat. Historical Congress, 1990–95 (Chm., British Nat. Cttee, 1978–93); Econ. Hist. Soc., 1986–89 (Hon. Sec., 1960–86); Railway and Canal Hist. Soc., 1986–88; Chairman: Management Cttee, Inst. of Historical Res., London Univ., 1977–88; Hist. Bd, CNAA, 1977–81; Management Cttee, London Univ. Business History Unit, 1979–86; Debrett's Business History Research Ltd, 1984–89; Athlone Press Adv. Cttee, 1988–. Chairman: Oral Hist. Soc., 1973–76; Transport History

Res. Trust, 1991–. Mem. Council, RHistS, 1967–70 and 1974–77. *Publications:* A Merseyside Town in the Industrial Revolution (with J. R. Harris), 1954, repr. 1993; A History of the Girdlers Company, 1957; Pilkington Brothers and the Glass Industry, 1960; (with R. H. Campbell, Peter Mathias and B. S. Yamey) Business History, 1960, 2nd edn 1970; (with R. M. Robbins) A History of London Transport: Vol. I, 1963, Vol. II, 1974; (ed with J. C. McKenzie and John Yudkin) Our Changing Fare: two hundred years of British food habits, 1966; (with B. W. E. Alford) A History of the Worshipful Company of Carpenters, 1968; (ed) The Long March of Everyman, 1974; (with M. J. Hatcher) A History of British Pewter, 1974; (with C. I. Savage) An Economic History of Transport, 1975; The Glassmakers, 1977; The Transport Contractors of Rye, 1982; (ed with Michael Drake) The Population Factor, 1982; (ed) The Economic and Social Effects of the Spread of Motor Vehicles, 1987; Moving Millions, 1990; (with Dorian Gerhold) The Rise and Rise of Road Transport 1700–1990, 1993; (ed with Anthony Sutcliffe) Megalopolis: the giant city in history, 1993; A Short, Illustrated and Updated History of Pilkington, 1994. *Recreations:* walking, motoring, visiting parts of Europe which many others do not reach. *Address:* Minsen Dane, Brogdale Road, Faversham, Kent ME13 8YA. *T:* Faversham (01795) 533523. *Club:* Reform.

BARKER, Thomas Christopher; HM Diplomatic Service, retired; *b* 28 June 1928; *m* 1960, Griselda Helen Cormack; two *s* one *d*. *Educ:* Uppingham (Schol.); New Coll., Oxford (Schol.). MA, Lit Hum, 1952; Gaisford Prize for Greek Verse. 2nd Lt, 1st Bn, The Worcestershire Regt, 1947–48. HM Foreign Service, 1952; Third Sec., Paris, 1953–55; Second Sec., Baghdad, 1955–58; FO, 1958–62; First Sec., Head of Chancery and Consul, Mexico City, 1962–67; FO, 1967–69; Counsellor and Head of Chancery, Caracas, 1969–71; FCO, 1971–75; seconded as Under Sec., NI Office, Belfast, 1976. Curator, 1978–87, Secretary to Trustees, 1987–93, Scottish Nat. War Meml, Edinburgh.

BARKER, Timothy Gwynne; Vice Chairman: Kleinwort Benson Group plc, since 1993 (Director, since 1988; Deputy Chief Executive, 1990–93); Vice Chairman, Kleinwort Benson Ltd, since 1989 (Director, since 1973); *b* 8 April 1940; *s* of Frank Richard Peter Barker and Hon. Olwen Gwynne (*née* Philipps); *m* 1964, Philippa Rachel Mary Thursby-Pelham; one *s* one *d*. *Educ:* Eton Coll.; McGill Univ., Montreal; Jesus Coll., Cambridge (MA). Director-General: City Panel on Take-overs and Mergers, 1984–85; Council for the Securities Industry, 1984–85; Head of Corporate Finance Div., Kleinwort Benson Ltd, 1986–90. *Address:* 20 Fenchurch Street, EC3P 3DB. *T:* 0171-623 8000.

BARKER, Trevor; Chairman: Alpha Consolidated Holdings Ltd, since 1988; Micklegate Group, since 1989; Drew Scientific Group PLC, since 1993; Deputy Chairman, Blanchards PLC, since 1988; *b* 24 March 1935; *s* of Samuel Lawrence Barker and Lilian Barker (*née* Dawson); *m* 1957, Joan Elizabeth Cross; one *s* one *d*. *Educ:* Acklam Hall Grammar School. FCA. Price Waterhouse & Co., 1957–58; Cooper Brothers, 1958–62; sole practitioner, 1962–70; Chm. and Chief Exec., Gold Case Travel, 1964–77; Dir, Ellerman Wilson Lines, 1977–80; Chairman: John Crowther Gp, 1980–88; William Morris Fine Arts plc, 1981–88; Dir, Darlington Bldg Soc., 1994–. FRSA 1989. Liveryman, Co. of Woolmen, 1986. *Recreations:* breeding and racing thoroughbred horses, opera, music, literature, the arts. *Address:* Windways, 323 Coniscliffe Road, Darlington, Co. Durham DL3 8AH. *T:* Darlington (01325) 350436.

BARKING, Area Bishop of, since 1991; **Rt. Rev. Roger Frederick Sainsbury;** *b* 2 Oct. 1936; *s* of Frederick William Sainsbury and Lillian Maude Sainsbury; *m* 1960, Jennifer Marguerite Carey. *Educ:* High Wycombe Royal Grammar School; Jesus Coll., Cambridge (MA); Clifton Theological Coll., Curate, Christ Church, Spitalfields, 1960–63; Missioner, Shrewsbury House, Liverpool, 1963–74; Warden, Mayflower Family Centre, Canning Town, 1974–81; Priest-in-Charge, St Luke, Victoria Dock, 1978–81; Vicar of Walsall, 1981–87; Rector, Walsall Team Ministry, 1987–88; Archdeacon of West Ham, 1988–91. Alderman, London Borough of Newham, 1976–78. Chairman: Frontier Youth Trustees, 1985–; Evangelical Coalition for Urban Mission, 1988–; London Churches Docklands Gp, 1989–; Urban Learning Foundn, 1992. Comr, Churches Commn for Racial Justice, 1992. *Publications:* From a Mersey Wall, 1970; Justice on the Agenda, 1985; Lifestyle, 1986; Rooted and Grounded in Love, 1988; God of New Beginnings, 1990. *Recreations:* cricket, football supporting, stone polishing. *Address:* Barking Lodge, 110 Capel Road, Forest Gate, E7 0JS. *T:* 0181–478 2456. *Club:* Sion College.

BARKLEY, Rev. Prof. John Montieth; retired; Principal, Union Theological College, Belfast, 1978–81; *b* 16 Oct. 1910; *s* of Rev. Robert James Barkley, BD, and Mary Monteith; *m* 1st, 1936, Irene Graham Anderson (*d* 1987); one *d*; 2nd, 1988, Caroline Margaret Barnett. *Educ:* Magee Univ. Coll. Derry; Trinity Coll., Dublin; The Presbyterian Coll., Belfast. BA 1934, MA 1941, BD 1944, PhD 1946, DD 1949, Trinity Coll., Dublin; BA 1952, MA 1953, Queen's Univ., Belfast. Thompson Memorial Prizeman in Philosophy, 1934; Larmour Memorial Exhibitioner in Theology, 1944; Paul Memorial Prizeman in History, 1953; Carey Lecturer, 1954–56; Lecturer in Ecclesiastical History, Queen's Univ., Belfast, 1951–54; Prof. in Ecclesiastical Hist., 1954–79, Vice-Principal, 1964–76, Principal, 1976–78, Presbyterian Coll., Belfast, until amalgamated with Magee Coll. to form Union Theological Coll. FRHistS. Ordained, Drumreagh Presbyterian Church, 1935; installed in II Ballybay and Rockcorry, 1939; installed in Cooke Centenary, Belfast, 1949. *Publications:* Handbook on Evangelical Christianity and Romanism, 1949; Presbyterianism, 1951; Westminster Formularies in Irish Presbyterianism, 1956; History of the Presbyterian Church in Ireland, 1959; Weltkirchenlexikon (arts), 1960; History of the Sabbath School Society for Ireland, 1961; The Eldership in Irish Presbyterianism; The Baptism of Infants, 1963; The Presbyterian Orphan Society, 1966; Worship of the Reformed Church, 1966; St Enoch's 1872–1972, 1972; (ed) Handbook to Church Hymnary, 3rd edn, 1979; Fasti of the Presbyterian Church in Ireland 1840–1910, 1987; Blackmouth and Dissenter (autobiog.), 1991; articles in Scottish Journal of Theology, Verbum Caro, Biblical Theology, Dictionary of Worship. *Recreations:* bowls, golf. *Address:* 14 Clonallon Park, Belfast BT4 2BZ. *T:* Belfast (01232) 650842.

BARKSHIRE, John; *see* Barkshire, R. R. St J.

BARKSHIRE, Robert Hugh, CBE 1968; *b* 24 Oct. 1909; *yr s* of late Lt-Col Charles Robert Barkshire, OBE; *m* 1934, Sally Blunt (*d* 1992); one *s*. *Educ:* King's Sch., Bruton. Bank of England, 1927–55: Private Sec. to the Governor (C. F. Cobbold, later Lord Cobbold), 1949–53; Sec. to Cttee of London Clearing Bankers, British Bankers' Assoc., Bankers' Clearing House, and Mem., various inter-Bank Cttees, 1955–70; Hon. Sec., Meetings of Officers of European Bankers' Assocs, 1959–72; Gen. Comr of Income Tax for City of London, 1969–78; Governor, NIESR, 1970–78. FCIB (FIB 1960). Freeman, City of London. *Address:* The Dower House, Headbourne Worthy, Winchester, Hants SO23 7JG. *Club:* Royal Thames Yacht.

See also R. R. St J. Barkshire.

BARKSHIRE, Robert Renny St John, (John), CBE 1990; TD; JP; DL; banker; Chairman, Eastbourne Hospitals NHS Trust, since 1993; *b* 31 Aug. 1935; *s* of Robert Hugh Barkshire, *qv*; *m* 1st, 1960, Margaret Elizabeth Robinson (marr. diss. 1990); two *s* one *d*; 2nd, 1990, Audrey Mary Anne Witham. *Educ:* Bedford School. ACIB. Served Duke of Wellington's Regt, 2nd Lieut, 1953–55; HAC, 1955–74 (CO, 1970–72; Regtl Col, 1972–74). Joined Cater Ryder & Co., 1955, Jt Man. Dir, 1963–72; Chm., Mercantile House Holdings plc, 1972–87; Non-exec. Dir, Extel Gp PLC, 1979–87 (Dep. Chm., 1986–87); Chairman: CL-Alexanders Laing & Cruickshank Hldgs Ltd, 1984–88; Internat. Commodities Clearing House Ltd, 1986–90. Chm., Financial Futures Wkg Pty, 1980, later LIFFE Steering Cttee, 1981–82; Dir, LIFFE, 1982–91 (Chm., 1982–85); Member: Adv. Bd, Internat. Monetary Market Div., Chicago Mercantile Exchange, 1981–84; London Adv. Bd, Bank Julius Baer, 1988–91. Chairman: Uplink Ltd (EPN Satellite Service), 1988–90; Chaco Investments Ltd, 1994–; non-executive Director: Household Mortgage Corp., 1985–94; Savills, 1988–95; Sun Life Corp. (formerly Assce Soc.), 1988–; TR Property Investment Trust plc, 1993–. Chm., Cttee on Market in Single Properties, 1985–. Gen. Comr for Income Tax, City of London, 1981–. Chairman: Reserve Forces Assoc., 1983–87; Sussex TA Cttee, 1983–85; SE TAVRA, 1985–91; Dep. Chm., TA Sport Bd, 1983– (Mem., 1979–). Financial Advisor: Victory Services Assoc. (formerly Club), 1981–95; RE Central Mgt Investments Policy Cttee, 1988–; Dir, Officers' Pensions Soc. Investment Co. Ltd, 1982–; Mem., Regular Forces Employment Assoc. Council, 1986–95; Man. Trustee, Regtl Assoc., Duke of Wellington's Regt, 1990–. Chairman: E Sussex Br., Magistrates' Assoc., 1986–91; E Sussex Magistrates' Courts Cttee, 1993–. Mem., Chiddingly Parish Council, 1979–86; Chm. and Treas., Chiddingly PCC, 1976–86; Chm., Chiddingly and Dist Royal British Legion, 1982–87; Vice Pres., St James Br., Royal British Legion, 1991–. Governor: Harpur Trust, 1984–89 (Chm., Bedford Sch. Cttee, 1984–89); Eastbourne Coll., 1980–March 1995 (Vice Chm., 1983–92); Roedean Sch., 1984–89; Comr, Duke of York's Royal Military Sch., 1986–. Freeman, City of London, 1973; Liveryman, Worshipful Co. of Farmers, 1981. JP Lewes, 1980; DL E Sussex, 1986. *Recreations:* sailing, shooting. *Address:* Denes House, High Street, Burwash, East Sussex TN19 7EH. *T:* Burwash (01435) 882646. *Clubs:* City of London, Cavalry and Guards, MCC; Royal Fowey Yacht (Cornwall).

BARKWORTH, Peter Wynn; actor, since 1948; director, since 1980; *b* 14 Jan. 1929; *s* of Walter Wynn Barkworth and Irene May Barkworth. *Educ:* Stockport Sch.; Royal Academy of Dramatic Art. Folkestone and Sheffield Repertory Cos, 1948–51. West End plays include: A Woman of No Importance, Savoy, 1953; Roar Like a Dove, Phoenix, 1957–60; The School for Scandal, Haymarket, 1962; Crown Matrimonial, Haymarket, 1972; Donkeys' Years, Globe, 1976; Can You Hear Me at the Back?, Piccadilly, 1979; A Coat of Varnish, Haymarket, 1982; Siegfried Sassoon, Apollo, 1987; Hidden Laughter, Vaudeville, 1990; The Winslow Boy, Globe, 1994. Director: Night and Day, Leatherhead, 1980; Sisterly Feelings, nat. tour, 1982; The Eight O'Clock Muse, Riverside Studios, 1989. Television serials: The Power Game, 1966; Manhunt, 1969; Telford's Change, 1979; Winston Churchill: the wilderness years, 1981; The Price, 1985; Late Starter, 1985; The Gospel According to St Matthew, 1986. Film: Champions, 1984. Awards: Best Actor, BAFTA, 1974 and 1977; Royal TV Soc. and Broadcasting Press Guild, 1977 (both 1977 awards for Professional Foul). *Publications:* About Acting, 1980; First Houses, 1983; More About Acting, 1984; The Complete About Acting, 1991. *Recreations:*walking, gardening, music, looking at paintings. *Address:* 47 Flask Walk, NW3 1HH. *T:* 0171–794 4591. *Club:* British Academy of Film and Television Arts.

BARLING, Gerald Edward; QC 1991; practising in EC Law, London and Brussels, since 1981; a Recorder, since 1993; *b* 18 Sept. 1949; *s* of Banks Hubert Barling and Barbara Margarita (*née* Myerscough); *m* 1983, Myriam Frances (*née* Ponsford); three *d*. *Educ:* St Mary's Coll., Blackburn; New Coll., Oxford (Burnett Open Exhibnr in Classics, 1968; Hons Sch. of Jurisprudence (1st Cl.), 1971; MA). Called to the Bar, Middle Temple, 1972 (Harmsworth Entrance Exhibnr, 1971; Astbury Law Scholar, 1973). Practised at Common Law Bar, Manchester, 1973–81; an Asst Recorder, 1990–93. Lectr in Law, New Coll., Oxford, 1972–77. Chairman: Western European Sub-Cttee, Bar Council, 1991–92; Bar European Gp, 1994– (Vice-Chm., 1992–94). *Publications:* (contrib.) Butterworth's European Court Practice, 1991; papers on different aspects of EC Law. *Recreations:* fishing, forestry, family. *Address:* 15/19 Devereux Court, WC2R 3JJ. *T:* 0171–583 0777; avenue de la Joyeuse Entrée 8, B1040 Brussels, Belgium.

BARLOW, Sir Christopher Hilaro, 7th Bt, *cr* 1803; architect; *b* 1 Dec. 1929; *s* of Sir Richard Barlow, 6th Bt, AFC, and Rosamund Sylvia, *d* of late F. S. Anderton (she *m* 2nd, 1950, Rev. Leonard Haslet Morrison, MA); *S* father, 1946; *m* 1952, J. C. de M. Audley, *e d* of late J. E. Audley, Cheshire; one *s* two *d* (and one *s* decd). *Educ:* Eton; McGill Univ., Montreal. BArch. MRAIC. Past Pres., Newfoundland Architects' Assoc. Lt Governor's Silver Medal, 1953. *Heir: s* Crispian John Edmund Audley Barlow, Inspector, Royal Hong Kong Police, [*b* 20 April 1958; *m* 1981, Anne Waiching Siu]. *Address:* 18 Winter Avenue, St John's, Newfoundland A1A 1T3, Canada.

BARLOW, Prof. David Hearnshaw, MD; Nuffield Professor of Obstetrics and Gynaecology, University of Oxford, since 1990; Fellow, Oriel College, Oxford, since 1990; *b* 26 Dec. 1949; *s* of Archibald and Anne Barlow; *m* 1973, Norma Christie Woodrow; one *s* one *d*. *Educ:* Clydebank High Sch.; Univ. of Glasgow (BSc Hons Biochem. 1971; MB ChB 1975; MD 1982); MA Oxon 1985. MRCOG 1980. MRC Trng Fellowship, 1977–78; Hall Tutorial Fellow, Univ. of Glasgow, 1979–81; Sen. Registrar, Queen Mother's Hosp., Glasgow, 1981–84; Clinical Reader in Obstetrics and Gynaecology, Univ. of Oxford, 1984–90; Fellow, Green Coll., Oxford, 1984–90, Hon. Sen. Associate Mem., 1990; Hon. Consultant Obstetrician and Gynaecologist, John Radcliffe Hosp., Oxford, 1984–. Blair Bell Meml Lectr, RCOG, 1985. *Publications:* scientific publications in field of reproduction, particularly on endometriosis, the menopause and IVF. *Recreations:* wide-ranging interest in music, painting. *Address:* Nuffield Department of Obstetrics and Gynaecology, John Radcliffe Hospital, Headington, Oxford OX3 9DU. *T:* Oxford (01865) 221008.

BARLOW, David John; freelance broadcasting consultant; Adviser on International Relations, BBC, since 1993; househusband and passionate carer for young family; *b* 20 Oct. 1937; *s* of Ralph and Joan Barlow; *m* 1981, Sanchia Béatrice Oppenheimer; two *s* one *d*, and three *s* of previous marr. *Educ:* Leighton Park Sch.; The Queen's Coll., Oxford; Leeds Univ. MA, DipEd (Oxon); DipESL (Leeds). British Council, 1962–63; BBC, 1963–: Producer, African Service; Schools Broadcasting, 1965–67; Programme Organiser, Hindi, Tamil, Nepali and Bengali Service, 1967–70; Further Educn Radio, 1970–71; UNESCO, British Council Consultancies, 1970–73; Head of Liaison Internat. Relations, 1974–76; Chief Asst Regions, 1977–79; Gen. Sec., ITCA, 1980–81; BBC: Sec., 1981–84; Controller: Public Affairs and Internat. Relations, 1984–86; Public Affairs, 1986–87; Regional Broadcasting, 1987–90; seconded to EBU as Co-ordinator for Audio Visual Eureka Project, 1990–91; Controller, Information Services and Internat. Relns, 1991–92. Mem., RTS, 1985–. *Recreations:* bird watching, mountains, books. *Address:* 1 St Joseph Close, Olney, Bucks MK46 5HD. *T:* Bedford (01234) 712960. *Club:* English-Speaking Union.

BARLOW, David Michael Rigby; Under Secretary, Government Legal Service, since 1989; *b* 8 June 1936; *s* of late Samuel Gordon Barlow and Eunice Hodson Barlow; *m* 1973, Valeree Elizabeth Rush-Smith; one *s*; one *d* by previous marr. *Educ:* Shrewsbury Sch.; Christ Church, Oxford (MA Law). National Service: Midshipman RNVR in Submarine Br. of RN, 1954–56; Sub-Lieut and Lieut in permanent RNR, 1956–61.

Solicitor, England and Wales, 1965, NI, 1991. Appointments as a lawyer in the public service, 1965–73; Asst Sec. in Govt Legal Service, 1973–89. *Recreations:* Spanish language and culture, horse riding, cinema. *Address:* Royal Courts of Justice, Chichester Street, Belfast BT1 4NX. *T:* Belfast (01232) 235111.

BARLOW, Prof. Frank, CBE 1989; MA, DPhil; FBA 1970; FRSL 1971; Professor of History and Head of Department, University of Exeter, 1953–76, now Emeritus Professor; *b* 19 April 1911; *e s* of Percy Hawthorn and Margaret Julia Barlow; *m* 1936, Moira Stella Brigid Garvey; two *s*. *Educ:* Newcastle High Sch.; St John's Coll., Oxford. Open Schol., St John's Coll., Oxford, 1929; 1st Cl. Hons Sch. of Modern History, 1933; Bryce Student, 1933; Oxford Senior Student, 1934.; BLitt, 1934; Fereday Fellow, St John's Coll., Oxford, 1935–38; DPhil 1937. Asst Lecturer, University Coll., London, 1936–40; War service in the Army, 1941–46, commissioned into Intelligence Corps, demobilised as Major; Lecturer 1946, Reader 1949, Dep. Vice-Chancellor, 1961–63, Public Orator, 1974–76, University of Exeter. Hon. DLitt Exon, 1981. *Publications:* The Letters of Arnulf of Lisieux, 1939; Durham Annals and Documents of the Thirteenth Century, 1945; Durham Jurisdictional Peculiars, 1950; The Feudal Kingdom of England, 1955; (ed and trans.) The Life of King Edward the Confessor, 1962; The English Church, 1000–1066, 1963; William I and the Norman Conquest, 1965; Edward the Confessor, 1970; (with Martin Biddle, Olof von Feilitzen and D. J. Keene) Winchester in the Early Middle Ages, 1976; The English Church 1066–1154, 1979; The Norman Conquest and Beyond (selected papers), 1983; William Rufus, 1983; Thomas Becket, 1986; Introduction to Devonshire Domesday Book, 1991; English Episcopal Acta, xi–xii (Exeter 1046–1257), 1995. *Recreation:* gardening. *Address:* Middle Court Hall, Kenton, Exeter EX6 8NA. *T:* Starcross (01626) 890438.

BARLOW, Frank, CBE 1993; Managing Director, Pearson plc, since 1990; Chairman: BSkyB, 1991–95; Financial Times Group, since 1993; *b* 25 March 1930; *s* of John and Isabella Barlow; *m* 1950, Constance Patricia Ginns; one *s* two *d*. *Educ:* Barrow Grammar Sch., Cumbria. Nigerian Electricity Supply Corp., 1952–59; Daily Times, Nigeria, 1960–62; Managing Director: Ghana Graphic, 1962–63; Barbados Advocate, 1963; Trinidad Mirror Newspapers, 1963–64; Gen. Manager, Daily Mirror, 1964–67; Man. Dir, King & Hutchings, 1967–75; Dir and Gen. Manager, Westminster Press, 1975–83; Dir, Economist, 1983–; Chief Executive: Financial Times Group, 1983–90; Westminster Press Group, 1985–90. Pres., Les Echos, Paris, 1988–90. Director: Elsevier (UK), 1991–; Logica, 1995–. Dir, Press Assoc., 1985–93. Chm., Printers' Charitable Corp., 1995–. Dir, Royal Philharmonic Orch., 1988–93. *Recreations:* golf, fell walking, angling. *Address:* (office) 3 Burlington Gardens, W1X 1LE. *Clubs:* MCC; Gerrards Cross Golf.

BARLOW, George Francis, FRICS; Chief Executive (formerly Director), Peabody Trust, since 1987; *b* 26 May 1939; *s* of late George and Agnes Barlow; *m* 1969, Judith Alice Newton; one *s* two *d*. *Educ:* Wimbledon Coll.; Hammersmith Sch. of Art and Building; Polytechnic of Central London. Surveyor, Building Design Partnership, 1962–67; Develt Surveyor, GLC Housing Dept, 1967–70; The Housing Develt Officer, London Borough of Camden, 1970–76; Dir/Sec., Metropolitan Housing Trust, 1976–87 (incl. Winding-up Sec. of Omnium (Central) and Strongbridge & SE Regional Housing Assocs). External Examiner, Polytechnic of Central London, 1989–90. Sec., Metropolitan Home Ownership Ltd, 1981–87; Chm., London Housing Assocs Council, 1978–82; Member: Central YMCA Housing Assoc., 1982–85; Council, Nat. Fedn of Housing Assocs, 1985–89; Housing Cttee, RICS, 1986–91; Council, BITC, 1989–; Cttee, Community Self Build Agency, 1989–94; Cttee, Broomleigh Housing Assoc., 1989–95; Trustee, Kent Community Housing Trust, 1989–92; Mem. Bd, East London Partnership, 1991–. Chm., Youth Homelessness Cttee, Prince's Trust/BITC, 1994–. *Publications:* articles in Housing Review and Voluntary Housing. *Recreations:* swimming, music, supporter of Crystal Palace FC. *Address:* (office) 45 Westminster Bridge Road, SE1 7JB. *T:* 0171–928 7811.

BARLOW, Sir (George) William, Kt 1977; BSc Tech, FEng, FIMechE, FIEE; President, Royal Academy of Engineering (formerly Fellowship of Engineering), 1991–July 1996; Chairman, Ericsson Ltd, 1981–94; *b* 8 June 1924; *s* of Albert Edward and Annice Barlow; *m* 1948, Elaine Mary Atherton (*née* Adamson); one *s* one *d*. *Educ:* Manchester Grammar Sch.; Manchester Univ. (Kitchener Schol., Louis Atkinson Schol.; BSc Tech. 1st cl. Hons Elec. Engrg, 1944). Served as Elec. Lt, RNVR, 1944–47. Various appts, The English Electric Co. Ltd (in Spain, 1952–55, Canada, 1958–62); Gen. Manager, Liverpool and Netherton, 1964–67; Managing Director: English Electric Domestic Appliance Co. Ltd, 1965–67; English Electric Computers Ltd, 1967–68. Gp Chief Exec., 1969–77, Chm., 1971–77, Ransome Hoffman Pollard Ltd. Chm., Post Office, 1977–80, organized separation of Post Office and British Telecom, 1980; Chairman: BICC, 1984–91 (Dir, 1980–91); SKF (UK), 1990–92; Barking Power Ltd, 1992–93; Director: Vodafone Group, 1988–; Waste Management International, 1992–; Chemring Gp, 1994–. Chm., NICG, 1980. Member: Industrial Develt Adv. Bd, 1972–79; Electronics EDC, 1981–83; Council, IEE, 1969–72 (Vice-Pres., 1978–80, Dep. Pres., 1983–84; Hon. Fellow, 1990); Council, IMechE, 1971–74; National Electronics Council, 1982–; President: IWM, 1976–77; BEAMA, 1986–87; ORGALIME, 1990–; Chm., Ferrous Foundries Adv. Cttee, 1975–78; Vice Pres., City and Guilds of London Inst., 1982–92. Chairman: Design Council, 1980–86; Engineering Council, 1988–90. Pres., Assoc. of Lancastrians in London, 1981 and 1992. Trustee, Brain Res. Trust, 1987–. Governor, London Business Sch., 1979–92 (Hon. Fellow, 1991). Liveryman, Worshipful Company of Glaziers; Master, Worshipful Company of Engineers, 1986–87. CIMgt (CBIM 1971). Hon. FUMIST 1978; Hon. FICE 1991. Hon. DSc: Cranfield, 1979; Bath, 1986; Aston, 1988; City, 1989; Hon. DTech: CNAA, 1988; Loughborough, 1993. *Recreation:* golf. *Address:* 4 Parkside, Henley-on-Thames, Oxon RG9 1TX. *T:* Henley-on-Thames (01491) 411101. *Clubs:* Army and Navy, Brooks's; Leander (Henley-on-Thames); Huntercombe, Royal Birkdale Golf.

BARLOW, Dr Horace Basil, FRS 1969; Royal Society Research Professor, Physiological Laboratory, Cambridge University, 1973–87; *b* 8 Dec. 1921; *s* of Sir (James) Alan (Noel) Barlow, 2nd Bt, GCB, KBE and Nora Barlow (*née* Darwin); *m* 1st, 1954, Ruthala (marr. diss., 1970), *d* of late Dr M. H. Salaman; four *d*; 2nd, 1980, Miranda, *d* of John Weston Smith; one *s* three *d*. *Educ:* Winchester; Trinity Coll., Cambridge. Research Fellow, Trinity Coll., 1950–54, Lectr, King's Coll., Cambridge, 1954–64. Demonstrator and Asst Dir of Research, Physiological Lab., Cambridge, 1954–64; Prof. of Physiological Optics and Physiology, Univ. of Calif, Berkeley, 1964–73. *Publications:* several, on neurophysiology of vision in Jl of Physiology, and elsewhere. *Address:* Trinity College, Cambridge CB2 1TQ.

See also Sir T. E. Barlow, Bt.

BARLOW, Sir John (Kemp), 3rd Bt *cr* 1907, of Bradwall Hall, Sandbach; merchant banker and farmer; Chairman: Thomas Barlow and Bro. Ltd; Barlow Services Ltd; Majedie Investments plc; Director of other companies; *b* 22 April 1934; *s* of Sir John Denman Barlow, 2nd Bt and Hon. Diana Helen (*d* 1986), *d* of 1st Baron Rochdale, CB and *sister* of 1st Viscount Rochdale, OBE, TD; *S* father, 1986; *m* 1962, Susan, *er d* of Col Sir Andrew Horsbrugh-Porter, *qv*; four *s*. *Educ:* Winchester; Trinity Coll., Cambridge (MA 1958). Chm., Rubber Growers' Assoc., 1974. Steward of the Jockey Club, 1988–90. High Sheriff, Cheshire, 1979. *Recreations:* steeplechasing, hunting, shooting. *Heir: s* John William Marshall Barlow [*b* 12 March 1964; *m* 1991, Sarah Nobes; one *s*]. *Address:* Bulkeley Grange, Malpas, Cheshire SY14 8BT. *Clubs:* Brooks's, City of London, Jockey.

BARLOW, Patrick; actor, writer, director; *b* 18 March 1947; *s* of Edward Morgan and Sheila Maud Barlow; two *s*. *Educ:* Uppingham Sch.; Birmingham Univ. (BA 1968). Founder mem., Inter-Action Community Arts, 1968–72; Dir, Lancaster Young People's Theatre, 1972–74; Founder Dir, Solent People's Theatre, 1974–76; created Henrietta Sluggett and appeared nationwide in clubs, streets, theatres, incl. Crucible, Sheffield, Haymarket, Leicester and NT, 1976–79; created *National Theatre of Brent*, 1980, appeared in and wrote jointly: stage: Charge of the Light Brigade, 1980; Zulu!, 1981; Black Hole of Calcutta, 1982; Götterdämmerung, 1982; Messiah, 1983; Complete Guide to Sex, 1984; Greatest Story Ever Told, 1987; television: Messiah, 1983; Mighty Moments from World History, Lawrence of Arabia, Dawn of Man, Boadicea, Arthur and Guinevere, 1985; Revolution!!, 1989; created Royal Dingle Co. for Oh Dear Purcell!, 1995; *other stage appearances* incl.: Truscott, in Loot, Manchester Royal Exchange, 1987; Humphry, in Common Pursuit, Phoenix, 1988; Pseudolus, in A Funny Thing Happened on the Way to the Forum, Manchester Liby Th., 1988; Sidney, in Silly Cow, Haymarket, 1991; Toad, in Wind in the Willows, RNT, 1994; *television* incl.: Talk to Me, 1983; All Passion Spent, 1986; Thank You Miss Jones, 1987; *radio* incl.: All the World's a Globe, Midsummer Wedding, 1990; Noah, 1991; Looking Forward to the Past, 1991–93; Desmond Dingle's Compleat Life and Works of William Shakespeare, 1995; Writer for television: The Ghost of Faffner Hall (jtly), 1989; adaptation, The Growing Pains of Adrian Mole, 1986; screenplay, Van Gogh (Prix Futura, Berlin Film Fest.), 1990; Scarfe on Sex, 1991; The True Adventures of Christopher Columbus (also actor and dir), 1992; Queen of the East, 1994 (also actor); also libretto, Judgement of Paris, Garden Venture, Royal Opera, 1991. *Publications:* All the World's a Globe, 1987 (adapted for radio) (Sony Radio award), 1990; Premier Ondas award, 1991); Shakespeare: The Truth, 1993. *Address:* Peters Fraser & Dunlop, 503 The Chambers, Chelsea Harbour, SW10 0XS. *T:* 0171–344 1010. *Club:* Groucho.

BARLOW, Roy Oxspring; solicitor; a Recorder of the Crown Court, since 1975; *b* 13 Feb. 1927; *s* of George and Clarice Barlow; *m* 1957, Kathleen Mary Roberts; two *s* one *d*. *Educ:* King Edward VII Sch., Sheffield; Queen's Coll., Oxford; Sheffield Univ. (LLB). Local Government, 1952–62; solicitor in private practice, 1962–. Asst Comr, Parly Boundary Commn, 1992–95. *Recreations:* farming, walking, reading. *Address:* The Cottage, Oxton Rakes, Barlow, Sheffield S18 5TH. *T:* Sheffield (0114) 289 0652.

BARLOW, Sir Thomas (Erasmus), 3rd Bt *cr* 1902; DSC 1945; DL; *b* 23 Jan. 1914; *s* of Sir Alan Barlow, 2nd Bt, GCB, KBE, and Nora (*d* 1989), *d* of late Sir Horace Darwin, KBE; *S* father, 1968; *m* 1955, Isabel, *d* of late Dr T. M. Body, Middlesbrough, Yorks; two *s* two *d*. *Educ:* Winchester College. Entered RN as cadet, 1932; qualified Submarines, 1937; served in Submarines in Atlantic, Mediterranean, Indian Ocean and Far East during War of 1939–45; Naval Staff Course, 1946; Joint Services Staff Course, 1947, Commander, 1950. British Joint Services Mission, Washington, 1950–53; Captain 1954; Imperial Defence Coll., 1957; Chief Staff Officer to Flag Officer Submarines, 1960–62; Commodore, HMS Drake, Devonport, 1962–64; retired, 1964. Actively concerned in Wildlife and Countryside Conservation: Royal Soc. for Nature Conservation; Berks, Bucks and Oxfordshire Naturalists' Trust; Charles Darwin Foundn for Galapogos Is. DL Bucks, 1977. *Recreations:* bird watching, the countryside. *Heir: s* James Alan Barlow, *b* 10 July 1956. *Address:* 45 Shepherds Hill, Highgate, N6 5QJ. *T:* 0181–340 9653. *Clubs:* Athenæum, Savile.

See also H. B Barlow.

BARLOW, Sir William; *see* Barlow, Sir G. W.

BARLTROP, Roger Arnold Rowlandson, CMG 1987; CVO 1982; HM Diplomatic Service, retired; Ambassador to Fiji, 1988–89 (High Commissioner, 1982–88) and High Commissioner (non-resident) to Republic of Nauru and to Tuvalu, 1982–89; *b* 19 Jan. 1930; *s* of late Ernest William Barltrop, CMG, CBE, DSO, and Ethel Alice Lucy Barltrop (*née* Baker); *m* 1962, Penelope Pierrepont Dalton (separated 1992); two *s* two *d*. *Educ:* Solihull Sch.; Leeds Grammar Sch.; Exeter Coll., Oxford. MA. Served RN, 1949–50, RNVR/RNR, 1950–64 (Lt-Comdr 1962). Asst Principal, CRO, 1954–56; Second Sec., New Delhi, 1956–57; Private Sec. to Parly Under-Sec. of State and Minister of State, CRO, 1957–60; First Sec., E Nigeria, 1960–62; Actg Dep. High Comr, W Nigeria, 1962; First Sec., Salisbury, Rhodesia, 1962–65; CO and FO, later FCO, 1965–69; First Sec. and Head of Chancery, Ankara, 1969–70; Dep. British Govt Rep., WI Associated States, 1971–73; Counsellor and Head of Chancery, Addis Ababa, 1973–77; Head of Commonwealth Coordination Dept, FCO, 1978–82. Mem., Commonwealth Observer Gp for elections in Bangladesh, Feb. 1991, and in St Kitts/Nevis, 1995; Foreign Affairs Trng Advr, Solomon Is, 1994. Chm., Pacific Is Soc. of UK and Ireland, 1992–. *Recreations:* sailing, genealogy, opera. *Address:* 35 Highfield Drive, Hurstpierpoint, West Sussex BN6 9AU. *Clubs:* Commonwealth Trust, Royal Over-Seas League; Royal Suva Yacht (Suva).

BARNA, Prof. Tibor, CBE 1974; Professor of Economics, University of Sussex, 1962–82, Professor Emeritus 1984; Member, Monopolies and Mergers Commission, 1963–78; *b* 1919. *Educ:* London School of Economics. Lecturer, London School of Economics, 1944; Official Fellow, Nuffield College, Oxford, 1947; senior posts in UN Economic Commission for Europe, 1949; Assistant Director, National Institute of Economic and Social Research, London, 1955. *Publications:* Redistribution of Income through Public Finance in 1937, 1945; Investment and Growth Policies in British Industrial Firms, 1962; Agriculture towards the Year 2000, 1979; European Process Plant Industry, 1981; papers in Jl Royal Statistical Soc., Economic Jl, European Econ. Review. *Address:* Beanacre, Westmeston, Hassocks, West Sussex BN6 8XE. *T:* Hassocks (01273) 842384.

BARNARD, 11th Baron, *cr* 1698; **Harry John Neville Vane,** TD 1960; landowner; Lord-Lieutenant and Custos Rotulorum of County Durham, 1970–88; a Vice-Chairman, Council, British Red Cross Society, 1987–93 (Member Council 1982–85); *b* 21 Sept. 1923; *er s* of 10th Baron Barnard, CMG, OBE, MC, TD, and Sylvia Mary (*d* 1993), *d* of Herbert Straker; *S* father, 1964; *m* 1952, Lady Davina Mary Cecil, DStJ (marr. diss. 1992), *e d* of 6th Marquess of Exeter, KCMG; one *s* four *d*. *Educ:* Eton. MSc Durham, 1986. Served War of 1939–45, RAFVR, 1942–46 (Flying Officer, 1945). Northumberland Hussars (TA), 1948–66; Lt-Col Commanding, 1964–66. Vice-Pres., N of England TA&VRA, 1970 and 1977–88, Pres., 1974–77. Hon. Col, 7 (Durham) Bn The Light Infantry, 1979–89. County Councillor, Durham, 1952–61. Member: Durham Co. AEC, 1953–72 (Chm., 1970–72); N Regional Panel, MAFF, 1972–76; CLA Council, 1950–80; Dir, NE Housing Assoc., 1964–77. President: Farmway Ltd, 1965–; Durham Co. Br., CLA, 1965–89; Durham Co. St John Council, 1971–88; Durham Co. Scouts Assoc., 1972–88; Durham and Cleveland Co. Br. RBL, 1973–92; Durham Wildlife Trust (formerly Durham Co. Conservation Trust), 1984–; Durham Co. Fedn of Young Farmers Clubs, 1991–92. Patron, Durham Co. Br., BRCS, 1993– (Pres., 1969–87). DL Durham, 1956, Vice-Lieutenant, 1969–70; JP Durham, 1961. Joint Master of Zetland Hounds, 1963–65. KStJ 1971. *Heir: s* Hon. Henry Francis Cecil Vane, *b* 11 March 1959. *Address:*

Raby Castle, PO Box 50, Staindrop, Darlington, Co. Durham DL2 3AY. *T:* Staindrop (01833) 660751. *Clubs:* Brooks's; Durham County (Durham); Northern Counties (Newcastle upon Tyne).

BARNARD, Prof. Christiaan Neethling, MD, MMed, PhD; Professor of Surgical Science, Cape Town University, 1968–83, Professor Emeritus, 1984; Senior Consultant and Scientist in Residence, Oklahoma Heart Centre, Baptist Medical Centre, since 1985; *b* 8 Nov. 1922; *s* of Adam Hendrik Barnard and Maria Elizabeth Barnard (*née* De Swart); *m* 1st, 1948, Aletta Gertruida Louw (marr. diss. 1970); one *d* (one *s* decd); 2nd, 1970, Barbara Maria Zoellner (marr. diss. 1982); two *s*; 3rd, 1988, Karin Setzkorn; one *s*. *Educ:* Beaufort West High Sch.; Univs of Cape Town and Minnesota. MB, ChB 1946, MD 1953, Cape Town; MS, PhD 1958, Minnesota. Private practice, Ceres, CP, 1948–51; Sen. Resident MO, City Hosp., Cape Town, 1951–53; subseq. Registrar, Groote Schuur Hosp.; Registrar, Surgery Dept, Cape Town Univ.; Charles Adams Meml Schol. and Dazian Foundn Bursary for study in USA; US Public Health Grant for further res. in cardiac surgery; Specialist Cardio-Thoracic Surgeon, Lectr and Dir of Surg. Res., Cape Town Univ. and Groote Schuur Hosp., 1958; Head of Cardio-Thoracic Surgery, Cape Town Univ. Teaching Hosps, 1961; Assoc. Prof., Cape Town Univ., 1962. Oppenheimer Meml Trust Bursary for overseas study, 1960. Performed world's first human heart transplant operation, 3 Dec. 1967, and world's first double-heart transplant, 25 Nov. 1974. Holds numerous hon. doctorates, foreign orders and awards, hon. citizenships and freedoms, medallions, etc; Dag Hammarskjöld Internat. Prize and Peace Prize, Kennedy Foundn Award, Milan Internat. Prize for Science, etc; hon. fellow or member various colleges, societies, etc. FACS 1963; Fellow NY Cardiological Soc. 1965; FACC 1967. *Publications:* (with V. Schrire) Surgery of Common Congenital Cardiac Malformations, 1968; One Life, 1969; Heart Attack: You Don't Have to Die, 1971; The Unwanted, 1974; South Africa: Sharp Dissection, 1977; In The Night Season, 1977; Best Medicine, 1979; Good Life—Good Death, 1980; (jtly) The Arthritis Handbook, 1984; numerous contribs to med. jls. *Recreations:* viticulture, ornithology, farming. *Address:* PO Box 6143, Welgemoed, 7538 Cape Town, Republic of South Africa.

BARNARD, Prof. Eric Albert, PhD; FRS 1981; Director, Molecular Neurobiology Unit, and Professor of Neurobiology, Royal Free Hospital School of Medicine, London University, since 1992; *b* 2 July 1927; *m* 1956, Penelope J. Hennessy; two *s* two *d*. *Educ:* Davenant Foundn Sch.; King's Coll., London. BSc, PhD 1956. King's College, London: Nuffield Foundn Fellow, 1956–59; Asst Lectr, 1959–60; Lectr, 1960–64. State University of New York at Buffalo: Associate Prof. of Biochemical Pharmacol., 1964–65; Prof. of Biochemistry, 1965–76; Head of Biochemistry Dept, 1969–76; Imperial College of Science and Technology, London: Rank Prof. of Physiol Biochemistry, 1976–85; Chm., Div. of Life Sciences, 1977–85; Head, Dept of Biochem., 1979–85; Dir, MRC Molecular Neurobiol. Unit, Cambridge, 1985–92. Rockefeller Fellow, Univ. of Calif, Berkeley, 1960–61; Guggenheim Fellow, MRC Lab. of Molecular Biol., Cambridge, 1971. Visiting Professor: Univ. of Marburg, Germany, 1965; Tokyo Univ., 1993; Vis. Scientist, Inst. Pasteur, France, 1973. Member: Amer. Soc. Biol Chemists; Internat. Soc. Neurochem; EMBO; IBRO; Internat. Union of Pharmacology; Cttee Mem., CNRS, France. UK rep., EC Cttee on Decade of the Brain. Josiah Macy Faculty Scholar Award, USA, 1975; Medal of Polish Acad. of Scis, 1980; Ciba Medal and Prize, 1985; Eastman Kodak Award, USA, 1988; Erspamer Internat. Award for Neuroscience, 1991. Editor-in-Chief, Receptors and Channels, 1993–; ed., or mem. editl bd, eight other scientific jls. *Publications:* editor of eight scientific books; several hundred papers in learned jls. *Recreation:* the pursuit of good claret. *Address:* Molecular Neurobiology Unit, Division of Basic Medical Sciences, Royal Free Hospital Medical School, Rowland Hill Street, NW3 2PF.

BARNARD, Surg. Rear Adm. Ernest Edward Peter, DPhil; FFCM; Surgeon Rear Admiral, Operational Medical Services, 1982–84; retired 1984; *b* 22 Feb. 1927; *s* of Lionel Edward Barnard and Ernestine (*née* Lethbridge); *m* 1955, Dr Joan Barnard (*née* Gunn); one *s* one *d*. *Educ:* schools in England and Australia; Univ. of Adelaide; St Mary's Hosp., Univ. of London (MB, BS 1955); St John's Coll., Univ. of Oxford (student, 1966–68; DPhil 1969). MRCS, LRCP 1955; MFOM 1979; FFCM 1980. After house appts, joined RN, 1956; served, 1957–76: HMS Bulwark, Reclaim and Dolphin; RN Physiol Lab.; RN Med. Sch.; Inst. of Naval Medicine; Dept of Med. Dir Gen. (Naval); exchange service with US Navy at Naval Med. Res. Inst., Bethesda, Md, 1976–78; Inst. of Naval Medicine, 1978–80; QHP 1980–84; Dep. Med. Dir Gen. (Naval), 1980–82; Surgeon Rear-Adm., Inst. of Naval Medicine, and Dean of Naval Medicine, 1982. FRSM 1962. *Publications:* papers on underwater medicine and physiology. *Recreations:* gardening, literature, photography. *Address:* c/o Barclays Bank, 12 The Square, Wickham, Hants PO17 5JQ.

BARNARD, Prof. George Alfred, MA, DSc; Emeritus Professor of Mathematics, University of Essex, *b* 23 Sept. 1915; *s* of Frederick C. and Ethel C. Barnard; *m* 1st, 1942, Helen J. B. Davies; three *s*; 2nd, 1949, Mary M. L. Jones; one *s*. *Educ:* Sir George Monoux Grammar Sch., Walthamstow; St John's Coll., Cambridge. Math. Trip., Pt III, 1936, Res. Studentship, St John's Coll., spent at Grad. Sch. Princeton, NJ, USA, 1937–39. Plessey Co., Ilford, as Math. Consultant, 1940–42; Ministry of Supply Adv. Unit, 1942–45; Maths Dept, Imperial Coll., London: Lectr, 1945–47; Reader in Math. Statistics, 1948–54, Professor, 1954–66; Prof. of Mathematics, Univ. of Essex, 1966–75; Prof. of Statistics, Univ. of Waterloo, 1975–81. Visiting Professor: Yale, 1966; Univ. of Waterloo, 1972–73; Univ. of Nottingham, 1975–77. Member: UGC, 1967–72; Computer Bd, 1970–72; SSRC, 1971–74. Royal Statistical Society: Council Mem. and Vice-Pres., 1952, 1962, Pres. 1971–72 (Chm. Res. Sect., 1958; Guy Medal in Silver, 1958, in Gold, 1975); Hon. Fellow, 1993. Mem. Internat. Statistical Inst., 1952; Statistical Adviser, Brit. Standards Instn (with Prof. E. S. Pearson), 1954; Chm. Inst. of Statisticians, 1960–62; President: Operational Res. Soc., 1962–64; Inst. of Mathematics and its Applications, 1970–71 (Gold Medal, 1986); Fellow: Amer. Statistical Assoc.; Inst. of Mathematical Statistics; Amer. Assoc. for Advancement of Science. Hon. Dr Math. Waterloo, 1983; DUniv: Open, 1986; Essex, 1994; Hon. DSc City, 1991. Deming Medal, Amer. Soc. for Quality Control, 1991. *Publications:* (ed) The Foundations of Statistical Inference, 1962; papers in Jl Royal Statistical Society; Technometrics; Biometrika. *Recreation:* viola playing. *Address:* Mill House, Hurst Green, Brightlingsea, Essex CO7 0EH. *T:* Brightlingsea (0120630) 2388.

See also D. E. C. Wedderburn.

BARNARD, Hermione; *see* Lee, H.

BARNARD, Prof. John Michael; Professor of English Literature, School of English, University of Leeds, since 1978; *b* Folkestone, 13 Feb. 1936; *s* of John Claude Southard Barnard and Dora Grace Barnard; *m* 1st, 1961, Katherine Duckham (marr. diss. 1973); one *s* two *d*; partner, 1975, *m* 2nd, 1991, Hermione Lee, *qv*. *Educ:* Wadham Coll., Oxford (BA (Hons) Eng. Lang. and Lit.; BLitt; MA). Res. Asst, English Dept, Yale Univ., 1961–64; Vis. Lectr, English Dept, Univ. of California at Santa Barbara, 1964–65; Post-doctoral Fellow, William Andrews Clark Meml Liby, UCLA, 1965; Leeds University: Lectr and Sen. Lectr, Sch. of English, 1965–78; Actg Dir, Inst. of Bibliography and Textual Criticism, Sch. of English, 1982–. Res. Fellow, William Andrews Clark Meml Liby, UCLA, and Huntingdon Liby, 1994. Member: British Cttee, Eighteenth Century Short Title Catalogue, 1983–89; Council, Bibliographical Soc., 1989–94. British Academy Warton Lecture, 1989. Internat. expert Verkenningscommissie Moderne Letteren, Netherlands, 1992–93. Gen. Editor, Longman Annotated Poets, 1976–; Mem. Editl Bd, English Poetry Full Text Database, 1991–93. *Publications:* (ed) William Congreve, The Way of the World, 1972; (ed) Pope: The Critical Heritage, 1973; (ed) John Keats: the complete poems, 1973, 3rd edn 1988; (ed) Etherege: The Man of Mode, 1979; John Keats, 1987; (ed) John Keats: selected poems, 1988; (jtly) The Early Seventeenth-Century York Book Trade and John Foster's Inventory of 1616, 1994; articles in Brit. and Amer. learned jls, occasional reviews, etc. *Recreations:* travel, walking. *Address:* Lane End, Weeton Lane, Weeton, near Leeds LS17 0AN. *T:* Harrogate (01423) 734814. *Club:* Johnson.

BARNARD, Sir Joseph (Brian), Kt 1986; DL; Chairman, International Business Group, since 1993; *b* 22 Jan. 1928; *s* of Joseph Ernest Barnard and Elizabeth Loudon (*née* Constantine); *m* 1959, Suzanne Hamilton Bray; three *s* (incl. twins). *Educ:* Bramcote School, Scarborough; Sedbergh School. Served Army, 1946–48, commissioned KRRC. Director: Joseph Constantine Steamship Line, 1952–66; Teesside Warehousing Co., 1966–; Indeck Energy Services, 1991–. Farms at East Harlsey. Dir, Northern Electric (formerly NE Electricity Bd), 1986–90; Chm., NE Electricity Cons. Council, 1986–90; Mem., Electricity Consumers' Council, 1986–90. Vice-Chm., 1988–91, Chm., 1991–92, Nat. Union of Cons. and Unionist Assocs (Chm., Yorks Area, 1983–88); Chm., Cons. Assoc. for Cleveland and Yorks N Euro Constituency, 1993–94. Chm. Governors, Ingleby Arncliffe C of E Primary School, 1979–91; Patron, St Oswald's, E Harlsey. JP Northallerton, 1973–94; Chm., Northallerton (formerly Allertonshire PSD), 1981–93; Mem., N Yorks Magistrates' Courts Cttee, 1981–93. DL N Yorks, 1988. *Recreations:* walking, shooting, gardening. *Address:* Harlsey Hall, Northallerton, N Yorks DL6 2BL. *T:* Northallerton (01609) 82203. *Club:* Carlton.

BARNARD, Hon. Lance Herbert, AO 1979; retired; Director, Office of Australian War Graves, Department of Veterans' Affairs, Commonwealth of Australia, 1981–83; *b* 1 May 1919; *s* of Hon. H. C. Barnard and M. M. Barnard (*née* McKenzie); *m* 2nd, 1962, Jill Denise Carstairs, *d* of Senator H. G. J. Cant; one *s* two *d* (and one *d* decd); also one *d* by a former marriage. *Educ:* Launceston Technical Coll. Served War, overseas, AIF 9th Div., 1940. Formerly teacher, Tasmanian Educn Dept. Elected to House of Representatives as Member for Bass, 1954, 1955, 1958, 1961, 1963, 1966, 1969, 1972, 1974. From Dec. 1972: Minister of Defence, Navy, Army, Air, Supply, Postmaster-Gen., Labour and National Service, Immigration, Social Services, Repatriation, Health, Primary Industry, National Development, and of the Interior. Dep. Leader, Federal Parliamentary Labor Party, 1967–72; Deputy Prime Minister, 1972–74; Minister for Defence (Navy, Army, Air and Supply), 1973–75. Australian Ambassador to Sweden, Norway and Finland, 1975–78. Captain, Aust. Cadet Corps, post War of 1939–45. State Pres., Tasmanian Br., Aust. Labor Party; Tasmanian deleg., Federal Exec., Aust. Labor Party. *Publication:* Labor's Defence Policy, 1969. *Recreation:* gardening. *Address:* 6 Bertland Court, Launceston, Tasmania 7250, Australia.

BARNE, Major Nicholas Michael Lancelot; Private Secretary, Comptroller and Equerry to Princess Alice, Duchess of Gloucester, and to the Duke and Duchess of Gloucester, since 1989; *b* 25 Nov. 1943; *m* 1974, Hon. Janet Elizabeth, *d* of Baron Maclean, KT, GCVO, KBE, PC; two *s*. *Educ:* Eton Coll. Regular officer, Scots Guards, 1965–79; fruit farming, 1979–84; Co. Comdt, Norfolk Army Cadet Force, 1985–89. *Recreations:* golf, ski-ing, shooting. *Address:* Blofield House, Blofield, Norwich, Norfolk NR13 4RW; Tower Flat, Kensington Palace, W8 4PU.

BARNES; *see* Oppenheim-Barnes.

BARNES, family name of **Baron Gorell.**

BARNES, Adrian Francis Patrick; Remembrancer of the City of London, since 1986; *b* 25 Jan. 1943; *s* of Francis Walter Ibbetson Barnes, *qv* and Heather Katherine (*née* Tamplin), *m* 1980, Sally Eve Whatley; one *s* one *d*. *Educ:* St Paul's School; MA City of London Polytechnic 1981. Called to the Bar, Gray's Inn, 1973; Solicitor's Dept, DTI, 1975; Dep. Remembrancer, Corp. of London, 1982. Freeman, City of London, 1982. Liveryman, Merchant Taylors' Co., 1989–. *Recreations:* music, chess, cricket, biography, circuit training, City lore. *Address:* Guildhall, EC2P 2EJ. *T:* 0171–332 1200, *Fax:* 0171–332 1895. *Clubs:* Brooks's, Guildhall; Cannons Sports.

BARNES, Alan Robert, CBE 1976; JP; Headmaster, Ruffwood School, Kirkby, Liverpool, 1959–87; Field Officer, Secondary Heads Association, since 1987; *b* 9 Aug. 1927; *s* of Arthur Barnes and Ida Barnes; *m* 1951, Pearl Muriel Boughton; (two *s* decd). *Educ:* Enfield Grammar Sch.; Queens' Coll., Cambridge (MA). National Service, RAEC. Wallington County Grammar Sch., 1951–55; Churchfields Sch., West Bromwich, 1955–59. Pres., Headmasters' Assoc., 1974, Treas., 1975–77; Chm., Jt Four Secondary Assocs, 1978; Treas., Secondary Heads Assoc., 1978–82; Vice-Chm., British Educn Management and Admin Soc., 1980–82, Chm. 1982–84. Schools Liaison Officer, Univ. of Essex, 1988–92. Chm., HMA Benevolent Fund, 1975–. JP Knowsley, Merseyside, 1967. *Publications:* (contrib.) Going Comprehensive (ed Halsall), 1970; (contrib.) Management and Headship in the Secondary School (ed Jennings), 1978; contrib. to: Education, BEMAS Jl, SHA publications. *Recreation:* bridge. *Address:* 2 Lark Valley Drive, Fornham St Martin, Bury St Edmunds, Suffolk IP28 6UF.

BARNES, Dame (Alice) Josephine (Mary Taylor), (Dame Josephine Warren), DBE 1974; FRCP, FRCS, FRCOG; Consulting Obstetrician and Gynaecologist, Charing Cross Hospital and Elizabeth Garrett Anderson Hospital; President, Women's National Cancer Control Campaign, 1974–95 (Chairman 1969–72; Vice-President, 1972–74); *b* 18 Aug. 1912; *er d* of late Rev. Walter W. Barnes, MA(Oxon), and Alice Mary Ibbetson, FRCO, ARCM; *m* 1942, Sir Brian Warren, *qv* (marr. diss. 1964); one *s* two *d*. *Educ:* Oxford High Sch.; Lady Margaret Hall, Oxford (Hon. Fellow, 1980); University College Hosp. Med. Sch. 1st class Hons Physiology, Oxford, BA 1934, MA, BM, BCh 1937, DM 1941. University College Hospital: Goldschmid Scholar; Aitchison Scholar; Tuke Silver Medal; Fellowes Silver Medal; F. T. Roberts Prize; Suckling Prize. Various appointments at UCH, Samaritan Hosp., Queen Charlotte's Hosp., and Radcliffe Infirmary, Oxford; Dep. Academic Head, Obstetric Unit, UCH, 1947–52; Surgeon, Marie Curie Hosp., 1947–67. Medical Women's Federation: Hon. Sec., 1951–57; Pres., London Assoc., 1958–60; Pres., 1966–67. Royal Society of Medicine: Mem. Council, 1949–50; Pres., Sect. of Obstetrics and Gynaecology, 1972–73; Pres., Sect. of History of Medicine, 1995–Oct. 1996; Hon. Editor, Sect. of Obstetrics, 1951–71; Hon. Fellow, 1988. President: W London Medico-Chirurgical Soc., 1969–70; Nat. Assoc. of Family Planning Doctors, 1976–93; Obstetric Physiotherapists Assoc., 1976–94; BMA, 1979–80 (Pres.-elect, 1978–79; Life Mem., 1994); Union Professionnelle Internationale de Gynécologie et d'Obstétrique, 1977–79; Royal Medical Benevolent Fund, 1982–. Examiner in Obstetrics and Gynaecology: Univ. of London; RCOG; Examining Bd in England, Queen's Univ., Belfast; Univ. of Oxford; Univ. of Kampala; Univ. of Ibadan; Univ. of Maiduguri. Member: Council, Med. Defence Union, 1961–82 (Vice-Pres. 1982–87; Hon. Fellow 1988); Royal Commn on Med. Educn, 1965–68; Council, RCOG, 1965–71 (Jun. Vice-Pres., 1972–74, Sen. Vice-Pres., 1974–75); MRC Cttee on Analgesia in Midwifery; Min. of Health Med. Manpower Cttee; Medico-Legal Soc.; Population Investigation Cttee,

Eugenics Soc.; Cttee on the Working of the Abortion Act, 1971–73; Standing Med. Adv. Cttee, DHSS, 1976–80; Council, Advertising Standards Authority, 1980–93; DHSS Inquiry into Human Fertilisation and Embryology, 1982–84; Vice-Pres., Nat. Union of Townswomen's Guilds, 1979–82; President: Nat. Assoc. of Family Planning Nurses, 1980–; Osler Club of London, 1988–89; Friends of GPDST, 1988–. Mem. of Honour, French Gynaecological Soc., 1945; Hon. Member: British Paediatric Assoc., 1974; Italian Soc. of Obstetrics and Gynaecology, 1979; Nigerian Soc. of Gynaecology and Obstetrics, 1981; Corresp. Mem., Royal Belgian Soc. of Obstetricians and Gynaecologists, 1949. Governor: Charing Cross Hosp.; Chelsea Coll. of Science and Technology, 1958–85; Member Council: Benenden Sch., 1966–91; Bedford Coll., 1976–85; King's Coll., London, 1985–93 (FKC 1985); Mem. Court of Patrons, RCOG, 1984. Lectures: Fawcett, Bedford Coll., 1969; Rhys-Williams, Nat. Birthday Trust, 1970; Winston Churchill Meml, Postgrad. Med. Centre, Canterbury, 1971; Bartholomew Mosse, Rotunda Hosp., Dublin, 1975; Simpson Oration, RCOG, 1977; Annual, Liverpool Med. Instn, 1979; Sophia, Univ. of Newcastle upon Tyne, 1980; Ann Horler, Newcastle upon Tyne, 1984; Helena Wright Meml, 1988; Margaret Jackson Meml, 1988. Hunterian Orator, Hunterian Soc., 1994. Hon. FRCPI 1977; Hon. Fellow, Edinburgh Obstetrical Soc., 1980; Hon. FCSP 1991; Hon. FRCOG 1994; Hon. Fellow, RHBNC, London Univ., 1985. Hon. MD: Liverpool, 1979; Southampton, 1981; Hon. DSc: Leicester, 1980; Oxon, 1990. Hon. Bencher, Gray's Inn, 1992. Commandeur du Bontemps de Médoc et des Graves, 1966. *Publications:* Gynaecological Histology, 1948; The Care of the Expectant Mother, 1954; Lecture Notes on Gynaecology, 1966; (ed, jtly) Scientific Foundations of Obstetrics and Gynaecology, 1970; Essentials of Family Planning, 1976; numerous contribs to med. jls, etc. *Recreations:* music, gastronomy, motoring, foreign travel; formerly hockey (Oxford Univ. Women's Hockey XI, 1932, 1933, 1934). *Address:* 8 Aubrey Walk, W8 7JG. *T:* 0171–727 9832.

See also F. W. I. Barnes, A. I. Holden, M. G. J. Neary.

BARNES, Anthony Hugh; Secretary, Norfolk Churches Trust, since 1992; *b* 16 June 1931; *s* of Sir George Barnes and Anne Barnes; *m* 1st, 1956, Susan Dempsey; two *s* one *d*; 2nd, 1984, Jennifer Carey. *Educ:* King's Coll., Cambridge (MA). FIPD. Schweppes Ltd, 1954–66; Royal Opera House, 1966–70; ICI, 1970–82; self-employed, 1982–84; Dir, Redundant Churches Fund, 1984–92. *Address:* 1 Dixon's Court, 52 Bethel Street, Norwich NR2 1NR. *T:* Norwich (01603) 666783.

BARNES, Christopher John Andrew; Director of Establishments, Ministry of Agriculture, Fisheries and Food, since 1995; *b* 11 Oct. 1944; *s* of late Eric Vernon Barnes and of Joan Mary Barnes; *m* 1st, 1978, Carolyn Elizabeth Douglass Johnston (*d* 1990); two *s*; 2nd, 1990, Susan Elizabeth Bird; two *s*. *Educ:* City of London Sch.; London School of Economics (BScEcon). Exec. Officer, MAFF, 1962; Asst Principal, 1967; Private Sec. to Parly Sec., 1969–71; Principal, 1971; Sec. to Northfield Cttee on Agricultural Land Ownership and Occupancy, 1977–79; Asst Sec., 1980; Chief Reg. Officer, Nottingham and Reading, 1980–83; Hd of Personnel and R&D Requirements Divs, 1983–90; 'Barnes Review' of near market R&D, 1988; Under Sec. (Grade 3), 1990–; Arable Crops and Hortic., later Arable Crops and Alcoholic Drinks Gp, 1990–95. Non-exec. Dir, Booker Food Services, 1987–90. Mem. CS Medical Aid Assoc., Management Cttee, 1992–. *Recreations:* off-road vehicles, country living, France. *Address:* Ministry of Agriculture, Fisheries and Food, Whitehall Place, SW1A 2HH. *T:* 0171–270 8139.

BARNES, Clive Alexander, CBE 1975; Associate Editor and Chief Drama and Dance Critic, New York Post, since 1977; *b* London, 13 May 1927; *s* of Arthur Lionel Barnes and Freda Marguerite Garratt; *m* 1958, Patricia Winckley; one *s* one *d*. *Educ:* King's Coll., London; St Catherine's Coll., Oxford. Served RAF, 1946–48. Admin. Officer, Town Planning Dept, LCC, 1952–61; concurrently freelance journalist; Chief Dance Critic, The Times, 1961–65; Exec. Editor, Dance and Dancers, Music and Musicians, and Plays and Players, 1961–65; a London Correspondent, New York Times, 1963–65, Dance Critic, 1965–77, Drama Critic (weekdays only), 1967–77; a NY correspondent, The Times, 1970–. Knight of the Order of Dannebrog (Denmark), 1972. *Publications:* Ballet in Britain since the War, 1953; (ed, with others) Ballet Here and Now, 1961; Frederick Ashton and his Ballets, 1961; Dance Scene, USA (commentary), 1967; (ed with J. Gassner) Best American Plays, 6th series, 1963–67, 1971, and 7th series, 1974; (ed) New York Times Directory of the Theatre, 1973; Nureyev, 1983; contribs to jls, inc. Punch, The New Statesman, The Spectator, The New Republic. *Recreations:* eating, drinking, walking, theatregoing. *Address:* c/o New York Post, 210 South Street, New York, NY 10002, USA. *Club:* Century (NY).

BARNES, Rev. Cyril Arthur; Dean of Moray, Ross and Caithness, 1980–84. *b* 10 Jan. 1926; *s* of Reginald William and Mary Adeline Barnes; *m* 1951, Patricia Patience Allen. *Educ:* Penistone Grammar School; Edinburgh Theological Coll. (GOE 1950). King's Own Scottish Borderers and RAEC, 1944–47. Curate, St John's, Aberdeen, 1950–53; Rector, St John's, Forres, 1953–55; Priest-in-Charge, Wentbridge, Yorks, 1955–58; Vicar, St Bartholomew's, Ripponden with St John's, Rishworth, 1958–67, also St John's, Thorpe, 1966–67; Rector, Christ Church, Huntly with St Marnan's, Aberchirder, 1967–84, also Holy Trinity, Keith, 1974–84; Canon of Inverness Cathedral, 1971–80; Synod Clerk, 1977–80. Editor: Huntly Express, 1985–91; Northern See, 1990–; Newscan, 1991–93. *Recreations:* gardening, do-it-yourself. *Address:* Tillytarmont Cottage, Bridge of Isla, Huntly, Aberdeenshire AB54 4SP.

BARNES, Daniel Sennett, CBE 1977; CEng, FIEE; Chairman, Berkshire and Oxfordshire Manpower Board, 1983–88; *b* 13 Sept. 1924; *s* of Paula Sennett Barnes and John Daniel Barnes; *m* 1955, Jean A. Steadman; one *s*. *Educ:* Dulwich Coll.; Battersea Polytechnic (BScEng, 1st Cl. Hons). Apprenticeship at Philips, 1941–46; served REME, 1946–48; Battersea Polytechnic, 1948–51; Sperry Gyroscope, 1951–82: Dir of Engineering, 1962–68; Manager, Defence Systems, 1968–70; Gen. Manager, 1970–71; Man. Dir, 1971–82; British Aerospace PLC (formerly Sperry Gyroscope): Man. Dir, Electronic Systems and Equipment Div., 1982–85; HQ Dir, 1985–86; Director: Sperry Ltd UK, 1971–82; Sperry AG Switzerland, 1979–83. Pres., Electronic Engrg Assoc., 1981–82. *Recreations:* sailing, joinery, music and ballet, gardening.

BARNES, David; *see* Barnes, J. D. F.

BARNES, David John; Head Master, Pate's Grammar School, Cheltenham, since 1986; *b* 6 Nov. 1939; *s* of David Alan Barnes and Norah Barnes (*née* Fleming); *m* 1961, Jan Crofts; one *s* one *d*. *Educ:* The Grammar Sch., Wolstanton, Staffs; Queen's Coll., Oxford (Open Schol.; MA); DipEd London. Assistant Master: Pocklington Sch., York, 1962–66; Nottingham High Sch., 1966–68; Vice-Principal, Newcastle-under-Lyme Sch., 1968–86. *Publications:* A Parent's Guide to GCSE, 1988; various check-lists and guides to students' reading, 1991. *Recreations:* fly-fishing, Homer, digging holes and other honest labour. *Address:* Pate's Grammar School, Princess Elizabeth Way, Cheltenham, Glos GL51 0HG. *T:* Cheltenham (01242) 523169.

BARNES, (David) Michael (William), QC 1981; a Recorder, since 1985; *b* 16 July 1943; *s* of David Charles Barnes and Florence Maud Barnes; *m* 1970, Susan Dorothy Turner; three *s*. *Educ:* Monmouth Sch.; Wadham Coll., Oxford. Called to Bar, Middle Temple, 1965, Bencher, 1989. Hon. Research Fellow, Lady Margaret Hall, Oxford, 1979. Chm., Hinckley Point 'C' Public Inquiry, 1988. *Publications:* Leasehold Reform Act 1967, 1967; Hill and Redman's Law of Landlord and Tenant, 15th edn 1970– 18th edn 1988. *Recreations:* walking, crime fiction. *Address:* 4 Breams Buildings, EC4A 1AQ. *Club:* Beefsteak.

BARNES, Edward Campbell; independent television producer/director and television consultant, since 1986; Head of Children's Programmes, BBC Television, 1978–86; *b* 8 Oct. 1928; *s* of Hubert Turnbull Barnes and Annie Mabel Barnes; *m* 1950, Dorothy Smith (*d* 1992); one *s* two *d*. *Educ:* Wigan Coll. British Forces Network, Vienna, 1946–49; stage management, provincial and West End theatre, 1949–55; BBC Television: studio management, 1955–62; Producer, Blue Peter, 1962–70; Dep. Head of Children's Progs, 1970–78, incl.: original Editor, John Craven's Newsround; Producer: Blue Peter Royal Safari with Princess Anne; 6 series of Blue Peter Special Assignments; Producer and Director: Treasure Houses, 1986; All Our Children, 1987–90; Boxpops, 1992; The Lowdown, 1992; Exec. Prod., Parallel 9, 1992. Mem. Bd, Children's Film and Television Foundn Ltd, 1983–. Mem., RTS (Mem., Awards Cttee, 1989–91). SFTA Award, 1969; RTS Silver Medal, 1986; Pye Television Award, 1985. *Publications:* 25 Blue Peter Books and 8 Blue Peter Mini Books, 1964–; 6 Blue Peter Special Assignment Books, 1973–75; Blue Peter Royal Safari, 1971; Petra: a dog for everyone, 1977; Blue Peter: the inside story, 1989; numerous articles for nat. press. *Recreations:* cricket, opera, birding, walking, Venice, Bali. *Club:* Tewin Irregulars Cricket.

BARNES, Rt Rev. Edwin Ronald; *see* Richborough, Bishop Suffragan of.

BARNES, Eric Charles, CBE 1992; High Court Judge, Hong Kong, 1981–91; *b* 12 Sept. 1924; *m* 1st, Estelle Fay Barnes (*née* Darnell); four *s* one *d*; 2nd, 1978, Judianna Wai Ling Barnes (*née* Chang); one *s* one *d*. *Educ:* Univ. of Queensland (LLB). *Recreations:* tennis, racing (horse), sports. *Address:* Flat 41 King's Park Flats, 12 King's Park Rise, Yaumatei, Kowloon, Hong Kong. *Clubs:* United Services Recreation, Kowloon Cricket, Royal Hong Kong Jockey (Hong Kong); Tattersall's (Brisbane).

BARNES, Francis Walter Ibbetson; Chairman, Industrial Tribunals, 1976–87 (Resident Chairman, Exeter, 1984–87); *b* 10 May 1914; *e s* of late Rev. Walter W. Barnes, MA (Oxon) and Alice Mary Ibbetson, FRCO, ARCM; *m* 1st, 1941, Heather Katherine (marr. diss. 1953), *d* of Frank Tamplin; two *s*; 2nd, 1955, Sonia Nina (Nina Walker, pianist), *d* of late Harold Higginbottom; two *s* one *d*. *Educ:* Dragon Sch., Oxford; Mill Hill Sch.; Balliol Coll., Oxford. BA Jurisprudence (Hons), Oxford, 1937; MA 1967. Called to Bar, Inner Temple, 1938. Profumo Prize, Inner Temple, 1939. Served War, 1939–46 in Army (Middlesex Regt) and Home Office and Military Fire Services; Sen. Company Officer NFS and Capt. comdg military Fire Fighting Co. on BLA; later Staff Capt. in Amsterdam, and in JAG (War Crimes Section), GHQ Germany. After release from Army, functioned as Judge Advocate or Prosecutor in various trials of war criminals in Germany, 1947–48. Recorder of Smethwick, 1964–66; Dep. Chm., Oxfordshire QS, 1965–71; Recorder of Warley, 1966–71, Hon. Recorder, 1972; a Recorder of the Crown Court, 1972–76. Life Governor, Mill Hill Sch., 1939–; Mem., Dame Henrietta Barnett Bd (Educnl Trust), 1951–. Elected to Bar Council, 1961. Bar Council's rep. (observer) on Cons. cttee of Lawyers of the Common Market countries, 1962–71; contrib. to Common Market Law Review. Union Internat. des Avocats: Mem. Council, 1964–; Rapporteur Général at Vienna Congress, 1967; Rapporteur National at Paris Congress, 1971. Mem., Exec. Cttee, Friends of Farnham Park Rehabilitation Centre, 1988–93; Dir, Farnham Park Ltd, 1989–93. Freeman, City of London, 1991. *Recreations:* music, languages, gardening. *Address:* 83 St George's Drive, Ickenham, Mddx UB10 8HR. *T:* Ruislip (01895) 672532.

See also A. F. P. Barnes, Dame A. J. M. T. Barnes.

BARNES, Geoffrey Thomas, CBE 1989; HM Overseas Civil Service, retired; *b* 18 Aug. 1932; *s* of late Thomas Arthur Barnes and Ethel Maud (*née* Walker); *m* 1962, Agnete Scot Madsen; three *s* one *d*. *Educ:* Dover College; St Catharine's College, Cambridge (MA). Nat. Service, 2nd Lieut QO Royal West Kent Regt; served Malaya, 1951–52; Lieut, Royal Warwickshire Regt, TA, 1952–55. Admin Officer, HMOCS Sarawak, 1956–68; City and Guilds of London, 1968–70; HMOCS Hong Kong: Asst Defence Sec., 1970–72; Police Civil Sec., 1972–76; Asst Dir, Commerce and Industry Dept, 1976–77; Dep. Sec. for Security, 1977–81, for Health and Welfare, 1981–84; Comr, Indep. Commn Against Corruption, 1985–88; Sec. for Security, Hong Kong Govt, and Official Mem., Legislative Council, 1988–90. Consultant to FCO on anti-corruption measures in Jamaica, 1990, Peru, 1991, Venezuela, 1992 and Ecuador, 1993. JP Hong Kong, 1980. *Recreations:* walking, painting, golf, gardening, sailing. *Address:* Alloways, Cranleigh Road, Ewhurst, Surrey GU6 7RJ. *T:* Cranleigh (01483) 276490. *Clubs:* Royal Over-Seas League; Hong Kong (Hong Kong) (Life Mem.).

See also K. J. Barnes.

BARNES, Harold, (Harry); MP (Lab) Derbyshire North East, since 1987; *b* 22 July 1936; *s* of Joseph and Betsy Barnes; *m* 1963, Elizabeth Ann Stephenson; one *s* one *d*. *Educ:* Ruskin Coll., Oxford (Dip. Econs and Political Science); Hull Univ. (BA Philosophy and Political Studies). National Service, 1954–56. Railway clerk, 1952–54 and 1956–60; adult student, 1960–65; further educn lectr, 1965–66; Lectr, Sheffield Univ., 1966–87. Jt Pres., New Consensus (Britain), 1992– (Chm., 1990–92). Mem., National Admin. Council, Ind. Labour Publications, 1977–80 and 1982–85. *Publications:* pamphlets on local govt and on the public face of Militant; articles and reviews in Labour Leader, London Labour Briefing, Tribune, Morning Star, Local Socialism, New Socialist, Derbyshire Miner, Leeds Weekly Citizen, Sheffield Forward, Industrial Tutor, Political Studies. *Address:* House of Commons, SW1A 0AA. *T:* 0171–219 4521. *Clubs:* Dronfield Contact; Chesterfield Labour.

BARNES, Ingrid Victoria, (Mrs Alan Barnes); *see* Allen, I. V.

BARNES, Jack Henry; Under Secretary, Department of Health, since 1991; *b* 11 Dec. 1943; *s* of James Barnes and Joan Ivy (*née* Sears); *m* 1966, Nicola Pearse; two *d*. *Educ:* Hatfield Sch., Herts; Univ. of Sussex (BA); LSE (MSc). Dep. Chief Inspector, Social Services Inspectorate, DHSS, 1983–88; Dep. Chief Scientist and Dir, Res. Management, Dept of Health, 1988–91. *Address:* Quarry House, Leeds LS2 7UE.

BARNES, (James) David (Francis), CBE 1987; Chief Executive Officer, Zeneca Group PLC, since 1993; *b* 4 March 1936; *s* of Eric Cecil Barnes, CMG, and of Jean Margaret Barnes; *m* 1963, Wendy Fiona Mary (*née* Riddell); one *s* one *d*. *Educ:* Shrewsbury Sch.; Liverpool Univ. FInstD; CBIM. National Service, commnd 'N' Battery (Eagle Troop), 2nd Regt RA, 1958–60 (Malaya). Overseas Dir 1971–77, Dep. Chm. 1977–83, ICI Pharmaceuticals Div.; Chm., Paints Div., 1983–86; Exec. Dir, ICI, 1986–93. Non-Executive Director: Thorn-EMI, 1987–; Redland, 1994–. Chairman: Pharmaceuticals EDC, NEDO, 1983–92; Biotechnology Industries Working Party, NEDO, 1989–91. Vice-Pres., Thames Valley Hospice, 1986–. Mem. Bd of Governors, Ashridge (Bonar Law Meml) Trust, 1993–. FRSA 1988. *Recreations:* fishing, shooting, walking. *Address:* c/o Zeneca Group PLC, 15 Stanhope Gate, W1Y 6LN.

BARNES, James Frederick, CB 1982; Stewardship Adviser, Diocese of Monmouth, since 1989; Deputy Chief Scientific Adviser, and Head of Profession for the Science Group, Ministry of Defence, 1987–89; *b* 8 March 1932; *s* of Wilfred and Doris M. Barnes; *m* 1957, Dorothy Jean Drew; one *s* two *d*. *Educ:* Taunton's Sch., Southampton; Queen's Coll., Oxford. BA 1953, MA 1957; CEng, FRAeS. Bristol Aeroplane Co. (Engine Div.), 1953; Min. of Supply, Nat. Gas Turbine Estabt: Sci. Officer 1955; Sen. Sci. Off. 1957; Principal Sci. Off. 1962; Sen. Principal Sci. Off. (Individual Merit) 1965; Min. of Aviation Supply, Asst Dir, Engine R&D, 1970; seconded to HM Diplomatic Service, Counsellor (Science and Technology), British Embassy, Washington, 1972; Under-Sec., MoD, 1974; Dir Gen. Res. (C), MoD (Procurement Exec.), 1974–77; Dep. Dir (Weapons), RAE, 1978–79; Dep. Chief Scientific Adviser (Projs), MoD, 1979–82; Dep. Controller, Establishments Resources and Personnel, MoD, 1982–84; Dep. Controller, Estabts and Res., MoD, 1984–86. Chm., MoD Individual Merit Promotion Panel, 1990–. Sec., Monmouth DAC for Care of Churches, 1994–; Chm., CCBI Stewardship Network, 1993–; Mem., Council on Christian Approaches to Defence and Disarmament, 1980–; Lay Member: Guildford Diocesan Synod, 1978–84; Winchester Diocesan Synod, 1985–89; Chm., Deanery Finance Cttee, 1987–89; Co-opted Mem., Monmouth Diocesan Conf.; Churchwarden, All Saints', Farringdon, 1985–89. Member: Monmouth & Llandaff Housing Assoc., 1991–93; Gwerin (Cymru) Housing Assoc., 1993–94; Trustee, Roger Williams & Queen Victoria Almshouses, Newport, 1990–. Chm. of Govs, Yateley Manor Prep. Sch., 1981–89. James Clayton Fund Prize, IMechE, 1964. *Publications:* contrib. books and learned jls on mech. engrg, esp. gas turbine technology, heat transfer and stress analysis. *Recreation:* making things. *Address:* 64 Caerau Road, Newport, Gwent NP9 4HJ.

BARNES, Sir James George, Kt 1976; MBE (mil.) 1946; JP; Mayor of Dunedin, New Zealand, 1968–77; sharebroker; *b* Dunedin, NZ, 1908; *s* of Richard R. Barnes; *m* 1938, Elsie, *d* of James D. Clark; one *d*. *Educ:* King Edward Technical High Sch. Served War, RNZAF 75 Sqdn, 1940–46 (POW, 1942–45). Mem., Dunedin City Council, 1947–53 and 1959–80 (Dep. Mayor 1951–53 and 1959–68); MP, 1951–57. Exec. Mem.: Otago Peninsula Trust; NZ Fedn for the Blind; Chm., Bd of Ocean Beach Domain. Past Pres., Otago Savings Bank. Chm. or Dir, Sch. Bds and Youth orgs. NZ mile champion, 1932; NZ Cross Country Champion, 1933; Manager NZ Empire Games Team, 1950; Asst Man., NZ Olympic Team, 1956; Past Pres., NZ AAA; Mem. Otago AAA; Mem. NZ Trotting Conf. (Pres., 1979–80); Sen. Vice Pres., Aust. Trotting Council, 1977–80; Exec. Mem., World Trotting Congress, 1980; Past Pres., Forbury Park Trotting Club. CStJ 1979. *Recreations:* golf, trotting. *Address:* 35 Cliffs Road, Dunedin, New Zealand; PO Box 221, Dunedin.

BARNES, John Alfred, CBE 1993; Director-General, City and Guilds of London Institute, 1985–93; *b* 29 April 1930; *s* of John Joseph and Margaret Carr Barnes; *m* 1954, Ivy May (*née* Walker); two *d*. *Educ:* Bede Boys Grammar Sch., Sunderland; Durham Univ. (MA, BSc, MEd). Teacher, Grangefield Grammar Sch., Stockton-on-Tees, 1953–57; Asst Educn Officer, Barnsley, 1957–61; Dep. Dir, then Dir of Educn, City of Wakefield, 1963–68; Chief Educn Officer, City of Salford, 1968–84. Mem. Council, Assoc. of Colls of Further and Higher Educn, 1976–82 (Chm. 1980–81); Chairman: Northern Examining Assoc., 1979–82; Associated Lancs Schs Examg Bd, 1972–84; Member: Associated Examg Bd, Nat. Exams Bd for Supervisory Studies, 1985–93; Further Educn Unit Management Bd, 1986–89; YTS Certification Bd, 1986–89; various ind. trng bds, 1969–78, and MSC cttees, 1978–84; Review of Vocational Qualifications Working Gp, 1985–86; Task Gp on Assessment and Testing, 1987–88; Exec. Mem., Standing Conf. on Sch. Sci. and Technol., 1985–89 (Chm., Exec. Cttee, 1988–89). Mem., Nat. Exec. Cttee, Soc. of Educn Officers, 1979–84; Sec., Assoc. of Educn Officers, 1977–84; Treas., NFER, 1979–84; Pres., Educnl Develt Assoc., 1980–85. Chm., Sir Isaac Pitman Ltd, 1990–93; Sec., UK Skills, 1990–93. Mem. Council, City Technology Colls Trust, 1990–93; Gov., Imperial Coll., 1987–93; Mem. Court, Reading Univ., 1994–. Mem. (C), Bucks CC, 1993– (Chm., Personnel Cttee, 1994–; Vice-Chm., Educn Cttee, 1994–). FRSA 1973; FITD 1986 (Hon. FIID 1993); FCollP 1991; Hon. FCGI 1993; Hon. CIPD 1994. *Publications:* occasional papers in educnl press. *Recreations:* cultural activities, foreign travel. *Address:* 37 Woodfield Park, Amersham, Bucks HP6 5QH. *T:* Amersham (012043) 6120. *Club:* Athenæum.

BARNES, Prof. John Arundel, DSC 1944; FBA 1981; Fellow of Churchill College, Cambridge, since 1969; Program Visitor, Sociology, Research School of Social Sciences, Australian National University, since 1993 (Visiting Fellow, 1978–79, 1985–92); *b* Reading, 9 Sept. 1918; *s* of T. D. and M. G. Barnes, Bath; *m* 1942, Helen Frances, *d* of Charles Bastable; three *s* one *d*. *Educ:* Christ's Hosp.; St John's Coll., Cambridge; Sch. of African Studies, Univ. of Cape Town; Balliol Coll., Oxford. Fellow, St John's Coll., Cambridge, 1950–53; Simon Research Fellow, Manchester Univ., 1951–53; Reader in Anthropology, London Univ., 1954–56; Prof. of Anthropology, Sydney Univ., 1956–58; Prof. of Anthropology, Inst. of Advanced Studies, ANU, Canberra, 1958–69; Overseas Fellow, Churchill Coll., Cambridge, 1965–66; Prof. of Sociology, Univ. of Cambridge, 1969–82, now Emeritus. *Publications:* Marriage in a Changing Society, 1951; Politics in a Changing Society, 1954; Inquest on the Murngin, 1967; Sociology in Cambridge, 1970; Three Styles in the Study of Kinship, 1971; Social Networks, 1972; The Ethics of Inquiry in Social Science, 1977; Who Should Know What?, 1979; Models and interpretations, 1990; A Pack of Lies, 1994. *Address:* Sociology Program, Research School of Social Sciences, Australian National University, Canberra, ACT 0200, Australia.

BARNES, Prof. Jonathan, FBA 1987; Professor of Ancient Philosophy, University of Geneva, since 1994; *b* 26 Dec. 1942; *s* of late A. L. Barnes and of K. M. Barnes; *m* 1965, Jennifer Postgate; two *d*. *Educ:* City of London Sch.; Balliol Coll., Oxford. Fellow, Oriel Coll., Oxford, 1968–78; Fellow of Balliol Coll., 1978–94, Prof. of Ancient Philosophy, 1989–94, Oxford Univ. Visiting posts at: Inst. for Advanced Study, Princeton, 1972; Univ. of Texas, 1981; Wissenschaftskolleg zu Berlin, 1985; Univ. of Alberta, 1986; Univ. of Zurich, 1987; Istituto Italiano per gli studi filosofici, 1988. *Publications:* The Ontological Argument, 1972; Aristotle's Posterior Analytics, 1975; The Presocratic Philosophers, 1979; Aristotle, 1982; Early Greek Philosophy, 1987; The Toils of Scepticism, 1991. *Address:* Les Charmilles, 36200 Ceaulmont, France.

See also J. P. Barnes.

BARNES, Joseph Harry George; Chairman, Baxters of Speyside, since 1994; Director, 1969–93, Joint Managing Director, 1988–90, J. Sainsbury plc; *b* 24 July 1930; *s* of William Henry Joseph Barnes and Dorothy Eleanor Barnes; *m* 1958, Rosemary Gander; two *s*. *Educ:* John Ruskin Grammar Sch., Croydon. FCA 1963. Articled clerk, Lever Honeyman & Co., 1946–52. National Service, 2nd Lieut RAPC, 1953–55. Joined J. Sainsbury plc, 1956. *Recreations:* tennis, fishing. *Address:* Tudor Court, 29 Grimwade Avenue, Croydon, Surrey CR0 5DJ. *T:* 0181–654 5696.

BARNES, Dame Josephine; *see* Barnes, Dame A. J. M. T.

BARNES, Julian Patrick; writer; *b* 19 Jan. 1946; *m* Pat Kavanagh. *Educ:* City of London Sch.; Magdalen Coll., Oxford. Lexicographer, OED Supplement, 1969–72; freelance journalist; Contributing Ed., New Review, 1977; Asst Literary Ed., 1977–79, TV Critic, 1977–81, New Statesman; Dep. Literary Ed., Sunday Times, 1980–82; TV Critic, Observer, 1982–86; Letters from London: 1990–1995, 1995. *Publications:* Metroland, 1980 (Somerset Maugham Award, 1981); Before She Met Me, 1982; Flaubert's Parrot, 1984 (Prix Médicis, 1986); Staring at the Sun, 1986; A History of the World in 10½ Chapters, 1989; Talking it Over, 1991; The Porcupine, 1992; Love, Etc (Prix Femina, 1992); (as Dan Kavanagh): Duffy, 1980; Fiddle City, 1981; Putting the Boot In, 1985; Going to the Dogs, 1987. Officier de l'Ordre des Arts et des Lettres (France), 1995. *Address:* c/o A. D. Peters, The Chambers, Chelsea Harbour, Lots Road, SW10 0XF.

See also Jonathan Barnes.

BARNES, Sir Kenneth, KCB 1977 (CB 1970); Permanent Secretary, Department of Employment, 1976–82; *b* 26 Aug. 1922; *s* of Arthur and Doris Barnes, Accrington, Lancs; *m* 1948, Barbara Ainsworth; one *s* two *d*. *Educ:* Accrington Grammar Sch.; Balliol Coll., Oxford. Lancs Fusiliers, 1942–45. Entered Ministry of Labour, 1948; Under-Sec., Cabinet Office, 1966–68; Dep. Sec., Dept of Employment, 1968–75. *Address:* South Sandhills, Sandy Lane, Betchworth, Surrey RH3 7AA. *T:* Betchworth (01737) 842445.

BARNES, Kenneth James, CBE 1969 (MBE 1964); Advisor (Finance), Directorate General for Development, Commission of the European Communities, 1982–87; *b* 8 May 1930; *s* of late Thomas Arthur Barnes and Ethel Maud Barnes; *m* 1st, 1953, Lesley Dawn Grummett Wright (*d* 1976); two *s* one *d*; 2nd, 1981, Anna Elisabeth Gustaf Maria Vanoorlé (marr. diss. 1988). *Educ:* Guilford and Hale Schs, Perth, WA; Dover Coll.; St Catharine's Coll., Cambridge (Crabtree exhibnr; MA); London Univ. Pilot Officer, RAF, 1949–50; Flying Officer, RAFVR, 1950–53. Administrative Officer, HMOCS Eastern Nigeria, 1954–60; Asst Sec., Min. of Finance, Malaŵi, 1960–64, Sen. Asst Sec., 1965, Dep. Sec., 1966, Permanent Sec., 1967–71; Asst Sec., British Steel Corp., 1971–73; EEC: Principal Administrator, Directorate-Gen. for Develt, 1973–75; Head of Div. for Ind. Co-operation, Trade Promotion and Regional Co-operation, 1976–78; Hd of Div. for Caribbean, Indian and Pacific Oceans, 1979–80; Advr (Political), 1981–82; Advr (Finance), 1983–87. Chm., Newbury Dist Liaison Group on Disablement, 1990–; Jt Treas., Anti-Slavery Internat., 1991–. *Recreations:* reading, esp. history, listening to music, mediaeval fortifications, strengthening European Community links, charities for the disabled. *Address:* 29 Bearwater, Charnham Street, Hungerford, Berks RG17 0NN. *T:* Hungerford (01488) 684329. *Clubs:* Commonwealth Trust, Royal Over-Seas League.

See also G. T. Barnes.

BARNES, Mark Richard Purcell; QC 1992. Called to the Bar, Lincoln's Inn, 1974. *Address:* 1 Essex Court, Temple, EC4Y 9AR. *T:* 0171–583 2000.

BARNES, Melvyn Peter Keith, OBE 1990; ALA; Guildhall Librarian and Director of Libraries and Art Galleries, Corporation of London, since 1984; *b* 26 Sept. 1942; *s* of Harry and Doris Barnes; *m* 1965, Judith Anne Leicester; two *s*. *Educ:* Chatham House Sch., Ramsgate; North-Western Polytechnic, London. ALA 1965; DMA 1972; FBIM 1980; FRSA 1983. Public library posts in Kent, Herts and Manchester, 1958–68; Dep. Bor. Librarian, Newcastle-under-Lyme, 1968–72; Chief Librarian, Ipswich, 1972–74; Bor. Librarian and Arts Officer, Kensington and Chelsea, 1974–80; City Librarian, Westminster, 1980–84. Hon. Librarian to Clockmakers' Co., Gardeners' Co. Member: LA Council, 1974– (Chm. Exec. Cttee, 1987–92; Vice-Pres., 1991–93; Pres., 1995); Liby and Inf. Services Council, 1984–89; Brit. Liby Adv. Council, 1986–91; Brit. Liby SRIS Adv. Cttee, 1986–91. Pres., Internat. Assoc. of Metropolitan City Libraries, 1989–92; Dep. Chm., Liby Services Trust and Liby Services Ltd, 1983–93. Hon. Treas., Victoria County History of Inner Middlesex, 1979–90. Gov., St Bride Inst., 1984–. Liveryman, Clockmakers' Co., 1990–. Editorial Cons., Journal of Librarianship, 1980–94. *Publications:* Youth Library Work, 1968, 2nd edn 1976; Best Detective Fiction, 1975; Murder in Print, 1986; Dick Francis, 1986; Root and Branch: a history of the Worshipful Company of Gardeners of London, 1994; (ed) Deerstalker series of classic crime fiction reprints, 1977–82; contributor to numerous books and jls in fields of librarianship and crime fiction criticism. *Recreations:* reading and writing, going to the theatre, studying the history of the movies and stage musicals, performing amateur operatics. *Address:* Guildhall Library, Aldermanbury, EC2P 2EJ. *T:* 0171–332 1850.

BARNES, Michael; *see* Barnes, D. M. W.

BARNES, Michael Cecil John; Legal Services Ombudsman for England and Wales, since 1991; *b* 22 Sept. 1932; *s* of late Major C. H. R. Barnes, OBE and of Katherine Louise (*née* Kennedy); *m* 1962, Anne Mason; one *s* one *d*. *Educ:* Malvern; Corpus Christi Coll., Oxford. Nat. Service, 2nd Lieut, Wilts Regt, served in Hong Kong, 1952–53. MP (Lab) Brentford and Chiswick, 1966–Feb. 1974, an Opposition Spokesman on food and food prices, 1970–71; Chairman: Parly Labour Party Social Security Group, 1969–70; ASTMS Parly Cttee, 1970–71; Jt Hon. Sec., Labour Cttee for Europe, 1969–71; Mem., Public Accounts Cttee, 1967–74. Contested (Lab): Wycombe, 1964; Brentford and Isleworth, Feb. 1974; Mem. Labour Party, 1957–79; helped form SDP, 1981; rejoined Labour Party, 1983–. Chm., Electricity Consumers' Council, 1977–83; Dir, UKIAS, 1984–90. Member: Council of Management, War on Want, 1972–77; Nat. Consumer Council, 1975–80; Arts Council Trng Cttee, 1977–83; Energy Commn, 1977–79; Internat. Cttee of Nat. Council for Voluntary Organisations, 1977–83; Advertising Standards Authority, 1979–85; Direct Mail Services Standards Bd, 1983–86; Data Protection Tribunal, 1985–90; Investigation Cttee, Solicitors' Complaints Bureau, 1987–90; Chairman: UK Adv. Cttee on EEC Action Against Poverty Programme, 1975–76; Notting Hill Social Council, 1976–79; West London Fair Housing Gp Ltd, 1980–87; Vice Chm., Bangabandhu Soc., 1980–90; Organising Secretary: Gulbenkian Foundn Drama Trng Inquiry, 1974–75; Music Trng Inquiry, 1976–77; Sec., Nat. Council for Drama Trng, 1976–84; Chm., Hounslow Arts Trust, 1974–82; Trustee, Project Hand Trust, 1974–77; Governor, Internat. Musicians Seminar, Prussia Cove, 1978–81. *Recreations:* walking, swimming, dogs. *Address:* 45 Ladbroke Grove, W11 3AR. *T:* 0171–727 2533.

BARNES, Prof. Michael Patrick; Professor of Scandinavian Studies, University College London, since 1995 (Professor of Scandinavian Philology, 1983–94); *b* 28 June 1940; *s* of William Edward Clement Barnes and Gladys Constance Barnes (*née* Hooper); *m* 1970, Kirsten Heiberg (*née* Røer); one *s* three *d*. *Educ:* University College London (BA, MA); Univ. of Oslo. Asst Lectr, Lectr and Reader in Scandinavian Philology, UCL, 1964–83. Visiting Professor: Tórshavn, Faroe Islands, 1979; Uppsala Univ., 1984. Mem., Gustav Adolfs Akademien, Uppsala, 1984 (Corresp. Mem., 1977). Mem., Editl Bd, North-Western European Language Evolution, 1989– (Mem. Adv. Bd, 1981–88); Jt Hon. Sec., Viking Soc. for Northern Research, 1982– (Mem. Editl Bd, 1970–76, Chief Editor, 1977–83, Saga Book of the Viking Soc.). Knight, Order of the Falcon (Iceland), 1992. *Publications:* Draumkvæde: an edition and study, 1974; The Runic Inscriptions of Maeshowe, Orkney, 1994; articles in learned jls. *Recreations:* badminton, being with family, walking disused railways. *Address:* 93 Longland Drive, N20 8HN. *T:* 0181–445 4697.

BARNES, Peter; dramatist; *b* 10 Jan. 1931; *s* of Frederick and Martha Barnes; *m* 1958, Charlotte (*née* Beck). *Educ:* Stroud Grammar Sch. 1st Play, Sclerosis, 1965. Adapted and co-directed: Wedekind's Lulu, 1970; The Bewitched, 1974; adapted and dir., Feydeau's The Purging, 1976; directed: Wedekind's The Singer, 1976; Jonson's Bartholomew Fair,

1978, 1987; Marston's Antonio, 1979; Wedekind's The Devil Himself, 1980; adapted Jonson's The Devil is an Ass, 1977; directed: For All Those Who Get Despondent, 1977; Laughter!, 1978; Somersaults, 1981; Red Noses (Laurence Olivier Award for Best Play), 1985; adapted Feydeau's Scenes from a Marriage, 1986; directed: The Spirit of Man (TV plays), 1989; Nobody Here But Us Chickens (TV plays) (RTS Award for Best TV Play), 1990; Sunsets and Glories, 1990; adapted Ninagawa's Tango at the End of Winter, 1991; dir, Bye Bye Columbus (TV play), 1992; *radio plays include:* My Ben Jonson, 1973; The Two Hangmen, from Wedekind and Brecht, 1979; Barnes' People One, 1981; The Jumping Minuses of Byzantinium, 1981 (Giles Cooper Radio Award); A Mad World My Masters, from Middleton, 1983; Barnes' People Two, 1983; The Primrose Path, from Feydeau, 1984; The Old Law, from Middleton, Rowley and Massinger, 1986; Barnes' People Three, 1986; Don Juan and Faust, from Grabbe, 1987; The Magnetic Lady, from Jonson, 1987; More Barnes' People, 1989. *Publications:* The Ruling Class, 1969 (John Whiting Award; Evening Standard Award); Leonardo's Last Supper, 1970; Noonday Demons, 1970; Lulu, 1971; The Bewitched, 1974; The Frontiers of Farce, 1976; Laughter!, 1978; The Collected Plays, 1981; Barnes' People Two, 1984; Red Noses, 1985; The Real Long John Silver (Barnes' People Three), 1986; The Collected Plays, 1989; The Spirit of Man, 1990; Nobody Here But Us Chickens, 1990; Sunsets and Glories, 1991; Collected Plays, vol. II, 1993. *Address:* 7 Archery Close, Connaught Street, W2 2BE. *T:* 0171–262 9205.

BARNES, Prof. Peter John, DM, DSc; FRCP; Professor of Thoracic Medicine, University of London (National Heart and Lung Institute) and Hon. Consultant Physician, Royal Brompton Hospital, since 1987; *b* 29 Oct. 1946; *s* of late John Barnes and Eileen Gertrude Barnes (*née* Thurman); *m* 1976, Olivia Harvard-Watts; three *s*. *Educ:* Leamington Coll.; St Catharine's Coll., Cambridge (MA); Worcester Coll., Oxford (DM, DSc). FRCP 1985. Hammersmith Hospital, London: Sen. Registrar, 1979–82; Sen. Lectr and Consultant Physician, RPMS, 1982–85; Prof. of Clinical Pharmacol., Cardiothoracic Inst., London, 1985–87. *Publications:* Asthma: basic mechanisms and clinical management, 1989, 2nd edn 1992; New Drugs for Asthma, 1982, 2nd edn 1992; Recent Advances in Respiratory Medicine, 1993; Conquering Asthma, 1994; Molecular Biology of Lung Disease, 1994; numerous pubns on lung pharmacol. and asthma. *Recreations:* travel, ethnic art collecting, gardening, film and theatre going. *Address:* Department of Thoracic Medicine, National Heart and Lung Institute, Dovehouse Street, SW3 6LY. *T:* 0171–351 8174; 44 Woodsome Road, NW5 1RZ.

BARNES, Peter Robert, CB 1982; Deputy Director of Public Prosecutions, 1977–82; President, Video Appeals Committee, since 1985; *b* 1 Feb. 1921; *s* of Robert Stanley Barnes and Marguerite (*née* Dunkels); *m* 1955, Pauline Belinda Hannen; two *s* one *d*. *Educ:* Eton Coll.; Trinity Coll., Cambridge (BA). Called to Bar, Inner Temple, 1947. Dir. of Public Prosecutions: Legal Asst, 1951; Sen. Legal Asst, 1958; Asst Solicitor, 1970; Asst Director, 1974; Principal Asst Dir, 1977. *Recreation:* bridge. *Address:* 28 The Paddock, Godalming, Surrey GU7 1XD.

BARNES, Dr Robert Sandford; Chairman, Robert S. Barnes Consultants, since 1978; Principal, Queen Elizabeth College, Kensington, London University, 1978–85, Fellow, 1985; *b* 8 July 1924; *s* of William Edward and Ada Elsie Barnes (*née* Sutherst); *m* 1952, Julia Frances Marriott Grant; one *s* three *d*. *Educ:* Univ. of Manchester. BSc Hons 1948, MSc 1959, DSc 1962. Radar Research, Admiralty Signals Estab., Witley, Surrey, 1944–47; AERE, Harwell: Metallurgical Research, 1948–62; Head of Irradiation Branch, 1962–65; Vis. Scientist, The Science Center, N Amer. Aviation Co., Calif, 1965; Head of Metallurgy Div., AERE, Harwell, 1966–68; Dep. Dir, BISRA, 1968–69; Dir, BISRA, 1969–70; Dir R&D, British Steel Corp., 1970–75; Chief Scientist, BSC, 1975–78. Technical Adviser: Bd of BOC Ltd, 1978–79; Bd of BOC International Ltd, 1979–81; Bd of New Ventures Secretariat, 1978–80. Chm., Ruthner Continuous Crop Systems Ltd, 1976–78. Member: CBI Res. and Technol. Cttee, 1968–75; Adv. Council on R&D for Iron and Steel, 1970–75; Materials Science and Technol. Cttee, SRC, 1975–79; European Industrial Res. Management Assoc., 1970 (Vice-Pres., 1974–78); Parly and Scientific Cttee, 1970–80, 1983–85; Foundn for Science and Technology, 1984– (Mem., Membership Cttee, 1987–); Chm., Materials Technology Panel, Internat. Tin Res. Inst., 1988–. Member: Council, Welding Inst., 1970–75; Council, Instn of Metallurgists, 1970–75 and 1979–85 (Vice Pres., 1979; Sen. Vice Pres., 1982; Pres., 1983–85); Council, Metals Soc., 1974–80, 1982–85 (Chairman: Coordinating Cttee, 1976–78, Executive Cttee, 1976–80). Institute of Metals: Mem., Steering Gp, 1983–84; Mem. Council, 1985–92; Mem. Exec. Cttee, 1985–92; Past Pres., 1985–; Chm., Professional Bd, 1985–92; Institute of Materials Members Trust: Trustee, 1984–; Mem., 1986–; Chm., 1992–. Chairman: Combined Operations Working Party, 1980–81; European Nuclear Steel-making Club, 1973–76; UK Representative: Commn de la Recherche Technique Sidérurgique, 1972–78; Conseil d'Association Européenne pour la Promotion de la Recherche Technique en Sidérurgie, 1972–78; Adv. Council on Energy Conservation, Industry Group, 1977–78; Council, Nat. Backpain Assoc., 1979–. Hon. Mem. Council, Iron and Steel Inst., 1969–73. Governor, Sheffield Polytechnic, 1968–72; Member: Court of Univ. of Surrey, 1968–80; Collegiate Council, Univ. of London, 1978–85; Jt Finance and Gen. Purposes Cttee, Univ. of London, 1978–85; Senate, Univ. of London, 1980–85; Member Council: King's Coll. London, 1982–85; Chelsea Coll., 1983–85; Bd Mem., CSTI, 1984–88. Lectures: Hatfield Meml, Iron and Steel Inst., 1973; John Player, IMechE, 1976. Freeman, City of London, 1984; Liveryman, Worshipful Co. of Engrs, 1985. Rosenhain Medallist, Inst. of Metals, 1964. FInstP 1961; FIM 1965; FRSA 1976; FKC 1985; Life Mem., Royal Instn, 1986. CEng 1977; CPhys 1984. *Publications:* chapters in specialist books of science; scientific papers in various learned jls. *Recreation:* sailing the Mediterranean (yacht Cassis of St Helier). *Address:* Pigeon Forge, Daneshill, The Hockering, Woking, Surrey GU22 7HQ. *T:* Woking (01483) 761529. *Clubs:* Athenæum, Cruising Association.

BARNES, Roger Anthony; Director, Hambros Bank Ltd, since 1993; Assistant Director, Bank of England and Head of Banking Supervision Division, 1988–93; *b* 29 May 1937; *s* of Kenneth Ernest Barnes and Lilian Agnes (*née* King); *m* 1961, Tessa Margaret Soundy; two *s* two *d*. *Educ:* Malvern College; St John's College, Oxford (BA). Bank of England, 1961–93. Mem. Council of Management, European Sch. of Management, 1994–. *Recreations:* golf, music, English folk dancing. *Address:* 40 Battlefield Road, St Albans, Herts AL1 4DD. *T:* St Albans (01727) 851987. *Club:* Bankers'.

BARNES, Roland, CBE 1970; BSc, MB, ChB, FRCS, FRCSE, FRCSGlas; Professor of Orthopaedic Surgery, University of Glasgow, 1959–72, now Professor Emeritus; *b* 21 May 1907; *y s* of Benjamin Barnes and Mary Ann Bridge, Accrington, Lancs.; *m* 1938, Mary Mills Buckley; one *s* two *d*. *Educ:* University of Manchester. BSc 1927; MB, ChB 1930; Medical and Surgical Clinical prizes. Usual resident appointments; Resident Surgical Officer, Manchester Royal Infirmary, 1934–35; Dickinson Travelling Scholar, Univ. of Manchester, 1935–36; visited orthopaedic clinics in USA; Fellow, Hospital for Ruptured and Crippled, New York. Chief Asst to Sir Harry Platt, Bt, Orthopaedic Department, Royal Infirmary, Manchester, 1937–39; Surgeon in Charge of Orthopædic and Peripheral Nerve Injury Centre, EMS Hospital, Winwick, Lancs, 1940–43. Past Pres., British Orthopædic Assoc.; Hon. Mem. French, Finnish, German and S African Orthopædic Assocs; Corresp. Mem. Amer. Orthopædic Assoc. *Publications:* papers on injuries of the peripheral nerves and spine, fractures of neck of femur, and on tumours of bone. *Recreation:* gardening. *Address:* 12 St Germains, Bearsden, Glasgow G61 2RS. *T:* 0141–942 2699.

BARNES, Rosemary Susan, (Rosie); Director, WellBeing (formerly Birthright), since 1992; *b* 16 May 1946; *d* of Alan Allen and Kathleen (*née* Brown); *m* 1967, Graham Barnes; two *s* one *d*. *Educ:* Bilborough Grammar Sch.; Birmingham Univ. (BSocSci Hons). Management Trainee, Research Bureau Ltd, 1967–69; Product Manager, Yardley of London Ltd, 1969–72; primary teacher (briefly), 1972; freelance market researcher, 1973–87. MP Greenwich, Feb. 1987–1992 (SDP, 1987–90, Social Democrat, 1990–92); contested (Soc. Dem.) Greenwich, 1992. *Recreations:* motherhood and a career leave little time. *Address:* (office) 27 Sussex Place, Regent's Park, NW1 4SP.

BARNES, Timothy Paul; QC 1986; a Recorder, since 1987; *b* 23 April 1944; *s* of Arthur Morley Barnes and Valerie Enid Mary Barnes; *m* 1969, Patricia Margaret Gale; one *s* three *d*. *Educ:* Bradfield Coll., Berkshire; Christ's Coll., Cambridge (MA). Called to Bar, Gray's Inn, 1968, Hilbery Exhibn; practises Midland and Oxford Circuit; Asst Recorder, 1983. *Recreations:* gardening, hockey. *Address:* The White House, Crooms Hill, SE10 8HH. *T:* 0181–858 1185. *Club:* MCC.

BARNETT, family name of **Baron Barnett.**

BARNETT, Baron *cr* 1983 (Life Peer), of Heywood and Royton in Greater Manchester; **Joel Barnett;** PC 1975; JP; chairman and director of a number of companies; Vice-Chairman, Board of Governors, BBC, 1986–93; *b* 14 Oct. 1923; *s* of Louis and Ettie Barnett, both of Manchester; *m* 1949, Lilian Goldstone; one *d*. *Educ:* Derby Street Jewish Sch.; Manchester Central High Sch. Certified accountant. Served RASC and British Military Govt in Germany. Mem. of Prestwich, Lancs, Borough Council, 1956–59; JP Lancs 1960; Hon. Treas. Manchester Fabian Society, 1953–65. Contested (Lab) Runcorn Div. of Cheshire, Oct. 1959; MP (Lab) Heywood and Royton Div., Lancs, 1964–83. Member: Public Accounts Cttee, 1965–71 (Chm., 1979–83); Public Expenditure Cttee, 1971–74; Select Cttee on Tax Credits, 1973–74; Chm. Parly Labour Party Economic and Finance Group, 1967–70 and 1972–74 (Vice-Chm., 1966–67); Opposition Spokesman on Treasury matters, 1970–74; Chief Sec. to the Treasury, 1974–79 (Cabinet Mem., 1977–79); Opposition spokesman on the Treasury in House of Lords, 1983–86. Hon. Visiting Fellow, Univ. of Strathclyde, 1980–. Chm., British Screen Finance Ltd (formerly British Screen Finance Consortium), 1985–. Mem., Internat. Adv. Bd, Unisys, 1989–. Chm., Building Societies' Ombudsman Council, 1987–. Trustee, V&A Museum, 1984–. Mem., Hallé Cttee, 1982–93. Chm., Birkbeck Coll. Appeal Cttee, 1990–; Trustee, Open Univ. Foundn, 1994–. Chm., Hansard Soc. for Parly Govt, 1984–90. Pres., RIPA, 1989–92. Hon. Fellow, Birkbeck Coll., London, 1992. Hon. LLD Strathclyde, 1983. *Publication:* Inside the Treasury, 1982. *Recreations:* walking, conversation and reading; good food. *Address:* Flat 92, 24 John Islip Street, SW1P 4LG; 7 Hillingdon Road, Whitefield, Manchester M25 7QQ.

BARNETT, Charles Henry; Managing Director, Aintree Racecourse Co. Ltd, since 1993; *b* 15 July 1948; *s* of Major B. G. Barnett and D. Barnett; *m* 1978, Georgina Greig; one *s* two *d*. *Educ:* Eton Coll.; Christ Church, Oxford (BA 2nd Cl. Hons Jurisprudence; MA). Chief Exec., Haydock Park Racecourse, 1984–93. *Recreation:* country pursuits. *Address:* Aintree Racecourse, Aintree, Liverpool L9 5AS. *T:* 0151–523 2600.

BARNETT, Dr Christopher Andrew; Headmaster, Whitgift School, Croydon, since 1991; *b* 1 Feb. 1953; *s* of Peter Alan Barnett and Joan Barnett (*née* Cullis); *m* 1976, Hon. Laura Miriam Elizabeth, *o c* of Baron Weidenfeld, *qv*; three *s* one *d*. *Educ:* Cedars Sch., Leighton Buzzard; Oriel Coll., Oxford (Exhibnr; BA Hons History 1974; MA 1978; DPhil 1981). Lectr in Econs, Brunel Univ., 1975–77; Head of History Dept, Bradfield Coll., Berks, 1978–87; Second Master, Dauntsey's Sch., Wilts, 1987–91. Fellow Commoner, Downing Coll., Cambridge, 1987; Evelyn Wrench Scholar, ESU, 1990. Pres., Croydon Music Fest., 1992–. Trustee, Warlingham Park Sch., 1994–. *Recreations:* opera, political Victoriana, hill-walking, travel, horse-racing (steeplechases). *Address:* Whitgift School, Haling Park, South Croydon CR2 6YT. *T:* 0181–688 9222.

BARNETT, Christopher John Anthony; His Honour Judge Barnett; a Circuit Judge, since 1988; QC 1983; *b* 18 May 1936; *s* of Richard Adrian Barnett and Phyllis Barnett (*née* Cartwright); *m* 1959, Sylvia Marieliese (*née* Pritt); two *s* one *d*. *Educ:* Repton Sch., Derbyshire; College of Law, London. Called to the Bar, Gray's Inn, 1965. District Officer (Kikuyu Guard) and Kenya Government Service, 1955–60; a District Officer in HM Overseas Civil Service, serving in Kenya, 1960–62; in practice as barrister, 1965–88; a Recorder, 1982–88. Chm., SE Circuit Area Liaison Cttee, 1985–88. Mem., Court of Essex Univ., 1983–. *Recreations:* cricket, tennis, walking. *Address:* 4 Paper Buildings, Temple, EC4Y 7EX. *T:* 0171–583 7765.

BARNETT, Colin Michael; international business consultant, since 1990; Regional Secretary, North-West Regional Council of the Trades Union Congress, 1976–85; Divisional Officer, North-West Division of the National Union of Public Employees, 1971–84; *b* 27 Aug. 1929; *s* of Arthur Barnett and Kathleen Mary Barnett; *m* 1st, 1953, Margaret Barnett (marr. diss. 1980); one *s* one *d*; 2nd, 1982, Hilary Carolyn Hodge, PhD; one *s* one *d*. *Educ:* St Michael's Elem. Sch., Southfields; Wandsworth Grammar Sch.; London Sch. of Econs and Polit. Science; WEA classes. Area Officer, NUPE, 1959, Asst Divl Officer 1961. Chm. Gp H, Duke of Edinburgh Conf. on Industry and Society, 1974. Secretary: NW Peace Council, 1979–; NW Cttee Against Racism, 1980–. Chm., MSC Area Bd, Gtr Manchester and Lancashire, 1978–83. Member: Merseyside District Manpower Bd, 1983–86; Industrial Tribunal, Manchester, 1974–; Liverpool Social Security Appeal Tribunal, 1986–. Dir, AT4 Community Prog. Agency, 1986–89. Debt and Industrial Advr, St Helens CAB, 1984–92; Marriage Guidance Counsellor, 1984–92. Organised: People's March for Jobs, 1981; (jtly) People's March for Jobs, 1983. British Representative: NW Russia Agency for Internat. Co-operation and Develt; St Petersburg British-Russia Soc.; St Petersburg Independent Humanitarian Foundn; Co-ordinator, UK projects for St Petersburg Health Dept. Employment Advr, This is Your Right, Granada TV, 1970–89. Governor, William Temple Foundn, 1980–87. *Recreations:* walking, reading. *Address:* 14 Elm Grove, Eccleston Park, Prescot, Merseyside L34 2RX. *T:* 0151–426 4045, *Fax:* 0191–426 0100.

BARNETT, Correlli (Douglas); author; Fellow, Churchill College, Cambridge, since 1977; Keeper of the Churchill Archives Centre, 1977–95; *b* 28 June 1927; *s* of D. A. Barnett; *m* 1950, Ruth Murby; two *d*. *Educ:* Trinity Sch., Croydon; Exeter Coll., Oxford. Second class hons, Mod. Hist. with Mil. Hist. and the Theory of War as a special subject; MA 1954. Intell. Corps, 1945–48. North Thames Gas Bd, 1952–57; Public Relations, 1957–63. Vice-Pres., E Arts Assoc., 1978–91 (Chm. Literature Panel, and Mem. Exec. Cttee, 1972–78); Pres., East Anglian Writers, 1969–88; Member: Council, Royal Utd Services Inst. for Defence Studies, 1973–85; Cttee, London Library, 1977–79 and 1982–84. Leverhulme Res. Fellowship, 1976; apptd Lectr in Defence Studies, Univ. of Cambridge, 1980; resigned in order to devote more time to writing, 1983. Winston Churchill Meml Lectr, Switzerland, 1982. FRSL; FRHistS. Hon. DSc Cranfield, 1993.

Chesney Gold Medal, RUSI, 1991. *Publications:* The Hump Organisation, 1957; The Channel Tunnel (with Humphrey Slater), 1958; The Desert Generals, 1960, new enlarged edn, 1983; The Swordbearers, 1963; Britain and Her Army, 1970 (RSL award, 1971); The Collapse of British Power, 1972; Marlborough, 1974; Bonaparte, 1978; The Great War, 1979; The Audit of War, 1986 (US edn as The Pride and the Fall, 1987); Engage the Enemy More Closely: the Royal Navy in the Second World War, 1991 (Yorkshire Post Book of the Year Award, 1991); The Lost Victory: British Dreams, British Realities 1945–1950, 1995; (historical consultant and writer to) BBC Television series: The Great War, 1963–64; The Lost Peace, 1965–66; The Commanders, 1972–73; reviews Mil. Hist. for The Sunday Telegraph; contrib. to: The Promise of Greatness (a symposium on the Great War), 1968; Governing Elites (a symposium), 1969; Decisive Battles of the Twentieth Century, 1976; The War Lords, 1976; The Economic System in the UK, 1985; Education for Capability, 1986; (ed) Hitler's Generals, 1989. *Recreations:* gardening, interior decorating, idling, eating, mole-hunting, travelling through France. *Address:* Catbridge House, East Carleton, Norwich NR14 8JX. *T:* Mulbarton (01508) 410.

BARNETT, Geoffrey Grant Fulton; Director, Baring Brothers & Co. Ltd, since 1979; *b* 9 March 1943; *s* of Air Chief Marshal Sir Denis H. F. Barnett, GCB, CBE, DFC; *m* 1968, Fiona Katharine Milligan; two *s* two *d*. *Educ:* Winchester; Clare Coll., Cambridge (MA). Courtaulds Ltd, 1964–67; The Economist Intelligence Unit, 1967–70; British Printing Corp., 1970–71; Baring Brothers & Co. Ltd, 1971–; Man. Dir, Baring Brothers Asia, Hong Kong, 1979–83; seconded as Dir Gen., Panel on Takeovers and Mergers, 1989–92. Hon. Treas., VSO, 1984–; Mem. Cttee, London and Quadrant Housing Trust, 1985–. FRSA 1992. *Recreations:* Scotland, walking, music, bird watching. *Address:* 2 Mill Hill Road, SW13 0HR. *T:* 0181–878 6975.

BARNETT, Jenifer W.; *see* Wilson-Barnett.

BARNETT, Jeremy John, OBE 1982; *b* 26 Jan. 1941; *s* of late Audrey Wickham Barnett and Lt-Comdr Charles Richard Barnett, RN; *m* 1968, Maureen Janet Cullum; one *s* one *d*. *Educ:* St Edward's Sch., Oxford; St Andrews Univ. (MA); Leeds Univ. (Dip TEFL); SOAS, London Univ. (MA 1994). Joined British Council, 1964; teaching, Victory Coll., Cairo, 1965–67; Lectr, Inst. of Educn, Istanbul, 1967–69; MECAS, Lebanon, 1969–70; Dir of Studies, Turco-British Assoc., Ankara, 1970–72; British Council Rep., Riyadh, 1972–75; Dir, ME Dept, 1975–78; Counsellor for British Council and Cultural Affairs, Ankara, 1978–82; British Council Rep., Warsaw, 1982–85; Dir, E Europe and N Asia Dept, 1985–88; Controller, S and W Asia Div., 1988–89; British Council Rep., later Dir, and Cultural Counsellor, British Embassy, Cairo, 1989–93. *Recreation:* hill walking. *Address:* Oakdene Station Road, Groombridge, Tunbridge Wells, Kent TN3 9NB. *T:* Langton (01892) 864626.

BARNETT, Joseph Anthony, CBE 1983 (OBE 1975); Director (formerly Representative), British Council, Tokyo, 1983–91, retired; *b* 19 Dec. 1931; *s* of Joseph Edward Barnett and Helen Johnson; *m* 1960, Carolina Johnson Rice; one *s* one *d*. *Educ:* St Albans Sch.; Pembroke Coll., Cambridge (BA (Hons) English and Psychology); Edinburgh Univ. (Diploma in Applied Linguistics). Served Army, 1950–51 (2nd Lieut). Teaching, Aylesford House, St Albans, 1954–55; Unilever Ltd, 1955–58; apptd British Council, 1958; Asst Educn Officer, Dacca, Pakistan, 1958; trng at Sch. of Applied Linguistics, Edinburgh Univ., 1960; Educn Officer, Dacca, 1961; seconded to Inst. of Educn, London Univ., 1963; Head, English Language Teaching Inst., London, 1964; Dir of Studies, Regional Inst. of English, Bangalore, India, 1968; Representative, Ethiopia, 1971; Controller, English Language Teaching Div., 1975; Representative, Brazil, 1978–82. *Publications:* (jtly) Getting on in English, 1960; Success with English (language laboratory materials), Books 1–3, 1966–69. *Recreation:* sport (tennis, cricket, riding). *Address:* The Thatch, Stebbing Green, Dunmow, Essex CM6 3TE. *T:* Stebbing (01371) 865014. *Club:* Athenæum.

BARNETT, Kenneth Thomas, CB 1979; Director, Abbey Data Systems Ltd, since 1984; *b* 12 Jan. 1921; *yr s* of late Frederick Charles Barnett and Ethel Barnett (*née* Powell); *m* 1943, Emily May Lovering; one *d*. *Educ:* Howard Gardens High Sch., Cardiff. Entered Civil Service (Min. of Transport), 1937; Sea Transport Office, Port Said, 1951–54; Asst Sec., 1965; Under-Sec., Cabinet Office (on secondment), 1971–73; Under-Sec., DoE, 1970–76, Dep. Sec., 1976–80. *Recreations:* gardening, watching Rugby football. *Address:* The Stone House, Frith End, Bordon, Hants GU35 0RA. *T:* Bordon (01420) 472856.

BARNETT, Nicholas John; Hon. Mr Justice Barnett; Judge of the High Court, Hong Kong, since 1987; *b* 13 May 1940. *Educ:* Bristol Grammar Sch.; King's Coll. London (LLB). Solicitor. *Address:* Supreme Court, Hong Kong.

BARNETT, Rt. Rev. Paul William, PhD; Bishop of North Sydney, and an Assistant Bishop, Diocese of Sydney, since 1990; *b* 23 Sept. 1935; *s* of William and Edna Barnett; *m* 1963, Anita Janet Simpson; two *s* two *d*. *Educ:* Univ. of London (BD Hons 1963, PhD 1978); Univ. of Sydney (MA Hons 1975). Deacon, 1963; priest, 1965; Lectr, Moore Theol Coll., 1964–67; Rector, St Barnabas, Broadway, 1967–73; Rector, Holy Trinity, Adelaide, 1973–79; Master, Robert Menzies Coll., Macquarie Univ., 1980–90. Lecturer, part time: Macquarie Univ., 1980–86; Univ. of Sydney, 1982–. Vis. Prof., Regent Coll., Vancouver, 1987, 1991, 1993. Vis. Fellow in History, Macquarie Univ., 1987–. Highly commended author, Christian Booksellers Conf., 1990. *Publications:* Is the New Testament History?, 1986; The Message of 2 Corinthians, 1988; Bethlehem to Patmos, 1989; Apocalypse Now and Then, 1990; The Two Faces of Jesus, 1990; The Servant King, 1991. *Recreations:* tennis, swimming, fishing, fine music. *Address:* Diocese of Sydney, St Andrew's House, Sydney Square, Sydney, NSW 2001, Australia. *T:* (2) 4196761.

BARNETT, Robert William, OBE 1993; HM Diplomatic Service; Counsellor (Science, Technology and Environment), Bonn (with responsibility also for Switzerland), since 1995; *b* 25 May 1954; *s* of Harry Frederick Barnett, Wells-next-the-Sea, Norfolk and Dorothy Anne Barnett (*née* Williamson); *m* 1979, Caroline Sara Weale; two *s*. *Educ:* Wymondham Coll., Norfolk; St Catharine's Coll., Cambridge (BA Hons Mod. & Med. Langs 1977; MA 1979). Joined FCO, 1977: Japanese lang. trng, 1979; Third Sec., Tokyo, 1980–84; Policy Planning Staff, FCO, 1984; Asst Private Sec. to Minister of State, 1984–86; First Secretary: Western European Dept, FCO, 1986–88; Bonn, 1988–91; seconded to Saxony State Govt as Inward Investment Advr, 1992; Asst Hd, Eastern Adriatic Unit, FCO, 1993–94; Ambassador to Bosnia-Herzegovina, 1994–95. *Recreations:* walking, photography, gardening. *Address:* c/o Foreign and Commonwealth Office, King Charles Street, SW1A 2AH; British Embassy, Friedrich Ebert Allee 77, 53113 Bonn, Germany. *T:* (228) 9167177.

BARNETT, William Evans; QC 1984; **His Honour Judge William Barnett;** a Circuit Judge, since 1994; *b* 10 March 1937; *s* of late Alec Barnett and late Esmé (*née* Leon); *m* 1976, Lucinda Jane Gilbert, JP, MA, ARCM; two *s*. *Educ:* Repton; Keble Coll., Oxford (BA Jurisprudence, 1961; MA 1965). National Service, RCS, 1956–58. Called to the Bar, Inner Temple, 1962; Major Scholarship, Inner Temple, 1962. A Recorder, 1981–94. Mem., Personal Injuries Litigation Procedure Wkg Pty, 1976–78; Judicial Mem., Mental Health Rev. Tribunal, 1993–. *Recreations:* golf, photography, gardening. *Address:* Carleon, 6 Castlemaine Avenue, South Croydon, Surrey CR2 7HQ. *T:* 0181–688 9559. *Club:* Royal Automobile.

BARNEVIK, Percy; President and Chief Executive Officer, ABB Asea Brown Boveri Ltd, Zürich, Switzerland, since 1988; *b* Simrishamn, Sweden, 1941. *Educ:* Sch. of Econs, Gothenburg, Sweden (MBA 1964); Stanford Univ. Johnson Group, 1966–69; Sandvik AB: Group Controller, 1969–75; Pres. of Sandvik, USA, 1975–79; Exec. Vice Pres., Sandvik AB Sweden, 1979–80; Chm., 1983–; Pres. and Chief Exec. Officer, Asea, 1980–87. Chm. Bd, Skanska AB, Sweden, 1992–; Member Board: Investor (formerly Providentia), 1987–; Du Pont, 1991–. Hon. DTech: Linköping, Sweden, 1989; Gothenburg, 1991. *Address:* ABB Asea Brown Boveri Ltd, PO Box 8131, 8050 Zürich, Switzerland.

BARNEWALL, family name of **Baron Trimlestown.**

BARNEWALL, Sir Reginald Robert, 13th Bt, *cr* 1622; cattle breeder and orchardist at Mount Tamborine; *b* 1 Oct 1924; *o s* of Sir Reginald J. Barnewall, 12th Bt and of Jessie Ellen, *d* of John Fry; *S* father 1961; *m* 1st, 1946, Elsie Muriel (*d* 1962), *d* of Thomas Matthews-Frederick, Brisbane; three *d* (one *s* decd); 2nd, 1962, Maureen Ellen, *d* of William Joseph Daly, South Caulfield, Vic; one *s*. *Educ:* Xavier Coll., Melbourne. Served War of 1939–45, overseas with Australian Imperial Forces. Served with Citizen Military Forces Unit, Royal Australian Armoured Corps, 1948–56. Managing Dir, Southern Airlines Ltd of Melbourne, 1953–58; Operation Manager, Polynesian Airlines, Apia, Western Samoa, 1958–62; Managing Dir, Orchid Beach (Fraser Island) Pty Ltd, 1962–71; Dir, Island Airways Pty Ltd, Pialba, Qld, 1964–68; owner and operator, Coastal-Air Co. (Qld), 1971–76; Dir and Vice-Chm., J. Roy Stevens Pty Ltd, to 1975. *Heir:* *s* Peter Joseph Barnewall, *b* 26 Oct. 1963. *Address:* Mount Tamborine, Queensland 4272, Australia. *Clubs:* United Service (Brisbane); RSL (Surfers Paradise).

BARNISH, Alan; Chief Executive, Shropshire County Council, since 1993; *b* 13 Oct. 1949; *s* of Sydney and Dora Barnish; *m* 1972, Elizabeth Sanders; one *s* one *d*. *Educ:* Leeds Univ. (BCom); IPFA. Mid Glam CC, 1975–90; Chief Exec. and Co. Treas., Powys CC, 1990–93. *Address:* Shirehall, Shropshire County Council, Shrewsbury SY2 6ND. *T:* Shrewsbury (01743) 252901.

BARNSTAPLE, Archdeacon of; *see* Lloyd, Ven. B. T.

BARON, Alexander; *see* Baron, J. A.

BARON, Florence Jacqueline; QC 1995; *b* 7 Oct. 1952; *d* of Jose Baron and Ellen Elizabeth Jane Baron (*née* McLennan). *Educ:* Jersey Coll. for Girls; St Hugh's Coll., Oxford (BA Juris.). Called to the Bar, Middle Temple, 1976. *Recreation:* relaxing. *Address:* Queen Elizabeth Building, Temple, EC4Y 9BS.

BARON, Franklin Andrew Merrifield; Permanent Representative of Commonwealth of Dominica to United Nations and to Organisation of American States, since 1982; Dominican High Commissioner to London, 1986–92; *b* 19 Jan. 1923; *m* 1973, Sybil Eva Francisca McIntyre. *Educ:* Portsmouth Govt Sch., St Mary's Acad., Dominica Grammar Sch. A. A. Baron & Co.: entered firm, 1939; Partner, 1945; sole owner, 1978–. Member: Roseau Town Council, 1945–47 and 1956–58; Legislative and Exec. Councils, 1954–61; Founder and Leader, United People's Party, 1954–66; Minister of Trade and Production, 1956–60; Chief Minister and Minister of Finance, 1960–61. Ambassador to USA, 1982–86. Chairman: National Commercial Bank, 1986–90; Fort Young Hotel Co., 1986–; The New Chronicle, 1989– (Dir, 1984–); Proprietor, Paramount Printers Ltd, 1992–. Member: Public Service Commn, 1976–78; Electoral Commn, 1979–90; Dominica Boundaries Commn, 1979–90; Bd, Dominica Electricity Services, 1981–91 (Chm., 1983–91); Bd, Industrial Develt Corp., 1984–89; Chm., Dominica Public Library, 1985–89. *Recreations:* horticulture, reading, travel. *Address:* 11 Cork Street, Roseau, Dominica. *T:* 809 448 2445.

BARON, (Joseph) Alexander; writer; *b* 4 Dec. 1917; *s* of Barnet Baron and Fanny Levinson; *m* 1960, Delores Salzedo; one *s*. *Educ:* Hackney Downs Sch., London. Asst Editor, The Tribune, 1938–39. Served War of 1939–45, Army. Editor, New Theatre, 1946–49. Fellow, QMW, 1992. *Publications: novels:* From the City, From the Plough, 1948; There's No Home, 1950; Rosie Hogarth, 1951; With Hope, Farewell, 1952; The Human Kind, 1953; The Golden Princess, 1954; Queen of the East, 1956; Seeing Life, 1958; The Lowlife, 1963; Strip Jack Naked, 1966; King Dido, 1969; The In-Between Time, 1971; Gentle Folk, 1976; Franco is Dying, 1977; also film scripts and television plays. *Address:* c/o Unna and Durbridge, 24 Pottery Lane, W11 4LZ.

BARON, Dr (Ora) Wendy, OBE 1992; Director (formerly Curator), Government Art Collection, since 1978; *b* 20 March 1937; *d* of late Dr S. B. Dimson and of Gladys Felicia Dimson, *qv*; *m* 1st, 1960, Jeremy Hugh Baron (marr. diss.); one *s* one *d*; 2nd, 1990, David Joseph Wyatt, *qv*. *Educ:* St Paul's Girls' Sch.; Courtauld Institute of Art (BA, PhD). Trustee, Public Art Commns Agency, 1990–. Has selected, researched and catalogued exhibitions, including: Sickert, Fine Art Soc., 1973; Camden Town Recalled, Fine Art Soc., 1976; The Camden Town Group, New Haven, USA, 1980; Late Sickert, Hayward Gall., 1981; Sickert, Royal Acad., 1992, Amsterdam, 1993. FRSA 1993. *Publications:* Sickert, 1973; Miss Ethel Sands and her Circle, 1977; The Camden Town Group, 1979; articles and reviews in professional jls in the field of modern British art. *Address:* Government Art Collection, c/o Department of National Heritage, 2–4 Cockspur Street, SW1Y 5DH.

BARON, Sir Thomas, Kt 1992; CBE 1983; Chairman, Stockbridge Village Trust, Merseyside. FRICS 1948. *Address:* 48 Princess Street, Leigh, Lancs WN7 2RA.

BARÓN CRESPO, Enrique Carlos; lawyer; Member, European Parliament, since 1986 (President, 1989–91); *b* Madrid, 27 March 1944; *m*; one *s*. *Educ:* Univ. of Madrid (LLL); Inst. Católico de Dirección de Empresas (Lic. en Ciencias Empresariales); Ecole Supérieure des Scis Econ. et Commerciales, Paris (Dip.). Lectr in Agricl Econs, Inst. Nacional de Estudios Agrarios, Valladolid, and in Structural Econs, Univ. of Madrid, 1966–70; lawyer in private practice, 1970–77. Mem. (PSOE), Congress of Deputies, Spain, 1977–; spokesman on econ. and budgetary affairs, 1977–82; Minister of Transport, Tourism and Communications, 1982–85. European Parliament: a Vice-Pres., 1987–89; Pres., Spanish Socialist Gp. Pres., Internat. European Movt, 1987–. *Publications:* Población y Hambre en el Mundo; El Final del Campesinado; La Civilización del Automóvil; Europa 92: el rapto del futuro; contribs on economic and social questions to major Spanish periodicals. *Address:* European Parliament, 1040 Brussels, Belgium; Centre Européen, Plateau de Kirchberg, L-2929, Luxembourg.

BARR, A. W. Cleeve, CBE 1972; retired 1977; *b* 1910; *s* of Albert John Barr and Ellen (*née* Cleeve); *m* 1st, 1935, Edith M. Edwards, BA (*d* 1965); one *s* one *d* (and one *s* decd); 2nd, 1966, Mrs Mary W. Harley (*widow*). *Educ:* Borlase, Marlow; Liverpool Univ. Private offices (Charles Holden and Paul Mauger); Herts CC (schools) and LCC (housing). Dep. Housing Architect, LCC, 1956–57; Development Architect, Ministry of Education, 1957–58; Chief Architect, Min. of Housing and Local Govt, 1959–64. Dir, Nat. Building

Agency, 1964–77 (Man. Dir, 1967–77); Dir, Nat. Building Agency Film Unit, 1977–80; Vice-Pres., UK Housing Trust, 1981–89. Hon. Sec. RIBA, 1963–65. *Recreation:* painting. *Address:* 72 Eastwick Road, Walton-on-Thames, Surrey KT12 5AR.

BARR, David; a Metropolitan Stipendiary Magistrate, since 1976; *b* Glasgow, 15 Oct. 1925; *s* of late Walter and Betty Barr; *m* 1960, Ruth Weitzman; one *s* one *d*. *Educ:* Haberdashers' Aske's Hampstead Sch.; Largs Higher Grade Sch.; Brookline High Sch., Boston, USA; Edinburgh Univ.; University Coll., London (LLB). Royal Navy, 1943–47. Solicitor, 1953; private practice, 1953–76 (Partner, Pritchard Englefield & Tobin). JP Inner London Area, 1963–76; Chm., Inner London Juvenile Panel, 1969–76; Dep. Chm., N Westminster PSD, 1968–76. Manager, Finnart House Sch., Weybridge, 1955–73 (Trustee, 1973–, Chm., 1985–). Pres., David Isaacs Fund, 1986–94. *Recreations:* book collecting, bridge. *Address:* Highbury Corner Magistrates' Court, Holloway Road, N7 8JA. *Clubs:* Garrick, MCC.

BARR, Rev. Prof. James, MA, BD, DD; FBA 1969; Professor of Hebrew Bible, Vanderbilt University, Nashville, Tennessee, since 1989; *b* 20 March 1924; *s* of Rev. Prof. Allan Barr, DD; *m* 1950, Jane J. S. Hepburn, MA; two *s* one *d*. *Educ:* Daniel Stewart's Coll., Edinburgh; Edinburgh Univ. (MA 1948, BD 1951); MA 1976, BD DD 1981, Oxon. Served War of 1939–45 as pilot in RNVR (Fleet Air Arm), 1942–45. Minister of Church of Scotland, Tiberias, Israel, 1951–53; Prof. of New Testament Literature and Exegesis, Presbyterian Coll., Montreal, 1953–55; Prof. of Old Testament Literature and Theology, Edinburgh Univ., 1955–61; Prof. of Old Testament Literature and Theology, Princeton Theological Seminary, 1961–65; Prof. of Semitic Languages and Literatures, Manchester Univ., 1965–76; Oriel Prof. of the Interpretation of Holy Scripture, and Fellow of Oriel Coll., Oxford Univ., 1976–78 (Hon. Fellow, 1980); Regius Prof. of Hebrew, Oxford Univ., and Student of Christ Church, 1978–89. Visiting Professor: Hebrew Univ., Jerusalem, 1973; Chicago Univ., 1975, 1981; Strasbourg Univ., 1975–76; Brown Univ., Providence, RI, 1985, 1994; Univ. of Otago, NZ, 1986; Univ. of South Africa, 1986; Vanderbilt Univ., Nashville, Tenn, 1987–88; Heidelberg Univ., 1993; lectured in Princeton Univ., 1962–63; in Union Theol. Seminary, New York, 1963; Lectures: Currie, Austin Theol. Seminary, Texas, 1964; Cadbury, Birmingham Univ., 1969; Croall, Edinburgh Univ., 1970; Grinfield, on the Septuagint, Oxford Univ., 1974–78; Firth, Nottingham Univ., 1978; Sprunt, Richmond, Va, 1982; Sanderson, Ormond Coll., Melbourne, 1982; Faculty, Cardiff, 1986; Schweich, British Acad., 1986; Cole, Vanderbilt, 1988; Sarum, Oxford, 1989; Read-Tuckwell, Bristol, 1990; Gifford, Edinburgh, 1991; Guggenheim Memorial Fellowship for study in biblical semantics, 1965. Mem., Inst. for Advanced Study, Princeton, NJ, 1985. Editor: Jl of Semitic Studies, 1965–76; Oxford Hebrew Dictionary, 1974–80. President: SOTS, 1973; British Assoc. for Jewish Studies, 1978. FRAS 1969; Fellow, Amer. Acad. of Arts and Scis, 1993. Corresp. Mem., Göttingen Acad. of Sciences, 1976; Member: Norwegian Acad. of Science and Letters, 1977; Royal Soc. of Scis, Uppsala, 1991; Amer. Philosophical Soc., 1993; Hon. Mem., Soc. of Biblical Lit. (USA), 1983. Hon. Fellow, SOAS, 1975. Hon. DD: Knox Coll., Toronto, 1964; Dubuque, 1974; St Andrews, 1974; Edinburgh, 1983; Victoria Univ., Toronto, 1988; Hon. DTheol: Univ. of South Africa, 1986; Protestant Theol Faculty, Paris, 1988; Oslo Univ., 1991; Hon. MA Manchester, 1969. *Publications:* The Semantics of Biblical Language, 1961; Biblical Words for Time, 1962; Old and New in Interpretation, 1966; Comparative Philology and the Text of the Old Testament, 1968; The Bible in the Modern World, 1973; Fundamentalism, 1977; The Typology of Literalism, 1979; Explorations in Theology 7: The Scope and Authority of the Bible, 1980; Holy Scripture: Canon, Authority, Criticism, 1983; Escaping from Fundamentalism, 1984; The Variable Spellings of the Hebrew Bible, 1988; The Garden of Eden and the Hope of Immortality, 1992; Biblical Faith and Natural Theology, 1993; articles in Semitic and biblical journals. *Recreation:* bird watching. *Address:* 203 Arden Place, 4400 Belmont Park Terrace, Nashville, TN 37215, USA; 6 Fitzherbert Close, Iffley, Oxford OX4 4EN. *T:* Oxford (01865) 772741; 11 Résidence Galawa, Quai Nord-Est, 34340 Marseillan (Hérault), France; Calle Aspret 21, 03792 Orba (Alicante), Spain.

BARR, Maj.-Gen. John Alexander James Pooler, CB 1993; CBE 1989; Engineer-in-Chief (Army), 1991–93; *b* 29 Jan. 1939. 2nd Lieut, RE, 1960; Lt-Col, 1978; GSO1 (DS) SC, 1978; Brig. 1983; Comdt, Royal Sch. of Mil. Engrg, Chatham, 1983–87; Dir of Army Staff Duties, MoD, 1987–89; DCS (Support), HQ Allied Forces Northern Europe, 1989–91; Maj.-Gen., 1991. Col Comdt, RE, 1993–. CompICE 1992. *Address:* c/o Lloyds Bank, Cox's & King's Branch, PO Box 1190, 7 Pall Mall, SW1Y 5NA.

BARR, Kenneth Glen; Sheriff of South Strathclyde, Dumfries and Galloway at Dumfries, since 1976; *b* 20 Jan. 1941; *o s* of late Rev. Gavin Barr and of Mrs Catherine McLellan Barr (*née* McGhie); *m* 1970, Susanne Crichton Keir. *Educ:* Ardrossan Acad.; Royal High Sch.; Edinburgh Univ. (MA, LLB). Admitted to Faculty of Advocates, 1964. *Address:* Sheriff Court House, Dumfries DG1 2AN.

BARR, His Honour Reginald Alfred; a Circuit Judge (formerly Judge of County Courts), 1970–92; *b* 21 Nov. 1920; *s* of Alfred Charles Barr; *m* 1946, Elaine, 2nd *d* of James William Charles O'Bala Morris, Llanstephan, Carmarthenshire. *Educ:* Christ's Hospital; Trinity Coll., Oxford (MA). Served War, 1941–46, Middle East and Burma. Called to Bar, Middle Temple, 1954; Standing Counsel to Registrar of Restrictive Trading Agreements, 1962–70. Mem. Review Bd for Govt Contracts, 1969–70. *Address:* Gosfield Hall, Halstead, Essex CO9 1SF.

BARR, William Greig, DL; Rector, Exeter College, Oxford, 1972–82; *b* 10 June 1917; *s* of late William S. Barr, Glasgow; *m* 1st, 1954, Helen Georgopoulos (*d* 1988); two *s*; 2nd, 1991, Valerie Bowman (*née* Tatham). *Educ:* Sedbergh Sch.; Magdalen Coll., Oxford. Stanhope Prize, 1938; 1st cl., Hon. Sch. of Modern History, 1939. Served War, 1939–45: Lt-Col, Royal Devon Yeomanry. Exeter College, Oxford: Fellow, 1945–72; Sub-Rector, 1947–54; Sen. Tutor, 1960–66; Hon. Fellow, 1982; Oxford University: Lectr in Modern History, 1949–72; Jun. Proctor, 1951–52; Pro-Vice-Chancellor, 1980–82. Hon. Treas., Oxford Univ. Rugby Football Club, 1948–73. A Rhodes Trustee, 1975–87. Visiting Prof. of Hist., Univ. of South Carolina, 1968. Pres., Brighton Coll. DL Oxon 1974. *Address:* 24 Northmoor Road, Oxford OX2 6UR. *T:* Oxford (01865) 58253.

BARR YOUNG, Gavin Neil; His Honour Judge Barr Young; a Circuit Judge, since 1988; *b* 14 Aug. 1939; *s* of Dr James Barr Young and Elsie Barr Young (*née* Hodgkinson); *m* 1969, Barbara Elizabeth Breckon; two *d*. *Educ:* Loretto Sch., Musselburgh; Leeds Univ. (LLB). Called to the Bar, Gray's Inn, 1963; Member, North Eastern Circuit, 1964–88 (North Eastern Circuit Junior, 1968); a Recorder of the Crown Court, 1979–88. *Recreations:* gardening, music. *Address:* Flaxbourne House, Great Ouseburn, York YO5 9RG. *T:* Boroughbridge (01423) 330629.

BARRACK, William Sample, Jr; Senior Vice-President, Texaco Inc., NY, since 1983; *b* 26 July 1929; *s* of William Sample Barrack and Edna Mae Henderson; *m* 1953, Evelyn Irene Ball; one *s* one *d*. *Educ:* Pittsburgh Univ. BSc (Engr) 1950. FInstPet 1981. Comdr, USN, 1950–53. Joined Texaco Inc., 1953; marketing and management positions in USA, 1953–67; in Europe, 1967–71; Vice-President: in NY, 1971–80; Marketing Dept, Europe, 1971–76; Producing Dept, Eastern Hemisphere, 1976–77; Personnel and Corporate Services Dept, 1977–80; Chm. and Chief Exec., Texaco Ltd, London, 1980–82. Director: Caltex Petroleum Corp.; Texaco Foundn Inc.; Standard Commercial Corp. Governor, Foreign Policy Assoc.; Member: US Naval War College Foundn; Bd of Visitors, Univ. of Pittsburgh. Trustee, Manhattanville College. *Clubs:* Woodway Country; Ox Ridge Hunt; Ida Lewis Yacht; North Sea (Belgium); Clambake (Newport, RI); New York Yacht.

BARRACLOUGH, Air Chief Marshal Sir John, KCB 1970 (CB 1969); CBE 1961; DFC 1942; AFC 1941 (despatches twice); FRAeS; FRSA, FIPD, FIMgt, MIPR; Hon. Inspector General, Royal Auxiliary Air Force, 1984–89; Gentleman Usher to the Sword of State, 1980–88; Vice-Chairman: British Export Finance Advisory Council, 1982–89; Commonwealth War Graves Commission, 1981–86 (Commissioner 1974–86); company director; Chairman, TROIKA Consortium Ltd; *b* 2 May 1918; *s* of late Horatio and Marguerite Maude Barraclough; *m* 1946, Maureen (*née* McCormack), niece of George Noble, Count Plunkett; one *d*. *Educ:* Cranbrook Sch. Service Artists' Rifles, 1935–38. Commissioned RAF, 1938. Air Vice-Marshal, 1964; Air Marshal, 1970; Air Chief Marshal, 1973. Served Near, Middle and Far East; commanded RAF Mogadishu, 1943; first single-engined jet flight to S Africa, 1951. Examining Wing, Central Flying Sch., 1948–51; Staff of IDC, 1952–54; Station Commander, RAF Biggin Hill, 1952–54 and Middleton St George, 1954–56; GC Ops, FEAF, 1958–61; Dir of Public Relations, Air Ministry, 1961–64; AOC No 19 Group, and NATO Air Comdr, Central Sub-Area, Eastern Atlantic Comd, 1964–67; Harvard Business Sch., AMP, 1967; AOA, Bomber Command, 1967–68; AOA, Strike Comd, 1968–70; Vice-Chief of Defence Staff, 1970–72; Air Secretary, 1972–74; Comdt, Royal Coll. of Defence Studies, 1974–76, retired. Hon. Air Cdre, No 3 (County of Devon) Maritime HQ Unit, RAuxAF, 1979–90. Mem., RAF Training and Educn Adv. Bd, 1976–79; Vice Chm., Air League Council, 1977–81; Chm., RUSI Council, 1977–80, Vice-Pres., 1980–90; President: Air Public Relations Assoc., 1976–; West Devon Area, St John Ambulance, 1977–85; Royal Crescent Soc., Bath, 1990–. OStJ 1985. Past President: RAF Modern Pentathlon Assoc.; Combined Services Equitation Assoc. Editl Dir, 1978–81, Vice-Chm. of Editl Bd, 1981–86, NATO's Sixteen Nations. *Publications:* (jtly) The Third World War, 1978; contrib. to The Third World War: The Untold Story, 1982; contribs to professional jls. *Recreations:* country pursuits, sailing (Irish Admiral's Cup Team, 1973). *Address:* c/o Hoare and Co., Fleet Street, EC4P 4DQ. *Clubs:* Boodle's, Royal Air Force, Royal Anglo-Belgian; Royal Western Yacht.

BARRACLOUGH, Sir Kenneth (James Priestley), Kt 1978; CBE 1967 (OBE 1945); TD; JP; Chief Metropolitan Magistrate 1975–78, retired; *b* 1907; *s* of Herbert Barraclough, Leeds; *m* 1931, Gladys Evelyn, *d* of Charles Henderson, Liverpool and Rio de Janeiro; two *s* one *d*. *Educ:* Oundle Sch.; Clare Coll., Cambridge. Barrister, Middle Temple, 1929 (Master of the Bench, 1975), North Eastern Circuit; Inns of Court Regt, TA, 1938; Col 1945. HQ, 21st Army Group (despatches). Metropolitan Magistrate, 1954; Dep. Chm. Appeals Cttee, Hampshire QS, 1957–62; Chm., HO Poisons Board, 1958–76. Member: Adv. Cttee on Drug Dependence, 1966–70; Adv. Council on the Misuse of Drugs, 1972–73; Medicines Commn, 1969–75. JP Hampshire, 1957. *Address:* 18 Fitzroy Road, Fleet, Hants GU13 8JJ.

BARRAN, Sir David Haven, Kt 1971; Chairman, Midland Bank Ltd, 1980–82 (Deputy Chairman, 1975–80); *b* 23 May 1912; *s* of Sir John Barran, 2nd Bt and Alice Margarita (*née* Parks); *m* 1944, Jane Lechmere Macaskie; four *s* three *d*. *Educ:* Winchester; Trinity Coll., Cambridge. BA 1934. Joined Asiatic Petroleum Co., 1934; served in Egypt, Palestine, Sudan, India, 1935–46. Pres., Asiatic Petroleum Corp., New York, 1958; Managing Dir, Royal Dutch/Shell Group, 1961–72; Chm., Shell Oil Co., 1970–72; Director: Shell Transport and Trading Co. Ltd, 1961–83 (Dep. Chm., 1964–67; Chm., 1967–72; Man. Dir, 1964–73); General Accident Insurance; BICC; Glaxo Hldgs. Chairman: CBI Cttee on Inflation Accounting, 1973–74; Adv. Cttee on Appt of Advertising Agents, 1975–78 (Mem., 1973–78); Ct of Governors, Administrative Staff Coll., 1971–76; Governor, Centre for Environmental Studies, 1972–75. Comdr, Order of Oranje Nassau, 1971; Comdr, Order of Merit, Fed. Repub. of Germany, 1980. *Recreations:* gardening, shooting, embroidery (Pres., Embroiderers' Guild, 1982–87). *Address:* 36 Kensington Square, W8 5HP. *T:* 0171–937 5664; Brent Eleigh Hall, Suffolk CO10 9NP. *T:* Lavenham (01787) 247202. *Club:* River (New York).

BARRAN, Sir John (Napoleon Ruthven), 4th Bt *cr* 1895; Head of Information Technology, Central Office of Information, 1985–87, retired; *b* 14 Feb. 1934; *s* of Sir John Leighton Barran, 3rd Bt, and Hon. Alison Mary (*d* 1973), 3rd *d* of 9th Baron Ruthven, CB, CMG, DSO; *S* father, 1974; *m* 1965, Jane Margaret, *d* of Sir Stanley Hooker, CBE, FRS; one *s* one *d*. *Educ:* Heatherdown Sch., Ascot; Winchester Coll.; University Coll., London (BA 1994). National Service, 1952–54, Lieut, 5th Roy. Inniskilling Dragoon Guards; served Canal Zone. Asst Account Executive: Dorland Advertising Ltd, 1956–58; Masius & Fergusson Advertising Ltd, 1958–61; Account Executive, Ogilvy, Benson & Mather (New York) Inc., 1961–63; Overseas TV News Service, COI, 1964; First Sec. (Information), British High Commission, Ottawa, 1965–67; Central Office of Information: Home Documentary Film Section, 1967–72; Overseas TV and Film News Services, 1972–75; TV Commercials and Fillers Unit, 1975–78; Head of Viewdata Unit, 1978–85. Founded Video History to make documentaries, 1986. *Recreations:* entertaining, gardening, shooting. *Heir:* *s* John Ruthven Barran, *b* 10 Nov. 1971. *Address:* 17 St Leonard's Terrace, SW3 4QG. *T:* 0171–730 2801; The Hermitage, East Bergholt, Suffolk; Middle Rigg Farm, Sawley, North Yorks.

BARRASS, Gordon Stephen, CMG 1992; Adviser, International Affairs, Coopers & Lybrand, since 1993; *b* 5 Aug. 1940; *s* of James and Mary Barrass; *m* 1965, Alice Cecile Oberg (*d* 1984). *Educ:* Hertford Grammar Sch.; LSE (BSc (Econs)); SOAS (postgrad.). FCO, 1965–67; Chinese Language student, Hong Kong Univ., 1967–69; in Office of HM Chargé d'Affaires, Peking, 1970–72; Cultural Exchange Dept, FCO, 1972–74; UKMIS Geneva, 1974–78; Planning Staff, FCO, 1979–82; RCDS, 1983; seconded to MoD, 1984, Cabinet Office, 1987; Under Sec., 1991–93. *Recreations:* Chinese and Western art, classical archaeology, opera, travel, books. *Address:* Coopers & Lybrand, 1 Embankment Place, WC2N 6NN.

BARRATT, Francis Russell, CB 1975; Deputy Secretary, HM Treasury, 1973–82; *b* 16 Nov. 1924; *s* of Frederick Russell Barratt; *m* 1st, 1949, Janet Mary Sherborne (marr. diss. 1978); three *s*; 2nd, 1979, Josephine Norah Harrison (*née* McCririck). *Educ:* Durban High Sch., SA; Clifton; University Coll., Oxford. War Service, 1943–46; Captain, Intelligence Corps, 1946. Asst Principal, HM Treasury, 1949; Principal, 1953; First Sec., UK High Commission, Karachi, 1956–58; Asst Sec., 1962, Under Sec., 1968, HM Treasury. Dir, Amdahl (UK), 1983–93; Trustee, Amdahl (UK) Pension Fund, 1984–. Mem., Rev. Bd for Govt Contracts, 1984–93. *Address:* Little Paddocks, Smallhythe Road, Tenterden, Kent TN30 7LY. *T:* Tenterden (01580) 763734. *Club:* Athenæum.

BARRATT, Gilbert Alexander; Master of the Supreme Court, Chancery Division, since 1980; *b* 1930; *s* of Arthur Walter Barratt and Frances Erskine Barratt (*née* Scott); *m* 1964, Fiona MacDermott; one *s* one *d*. *Educ:* Winchester; New Coll., Oxford. BA Modern History. Qualified as Solicitor, 1957; Partner: Stitt & Co., 1960–63; Thicknesse & Hull, 1963–67; Lee Bolton & Lee, 1967–78; Winckworth & Pemberton, 1978–80. *Recreation:*

travel. *Address:* The Old School, Clungunford, Craven Arms, Shropshire SY7 0PN. *Club:* Travellers'.

BARRATT, Sir Lawrence Arthur, (Sir Lawrie Barratt), Kt 1982; FCIS; Chairman, Barratt Developments PLC, and subsidiary companies, 1962–88, and since 1991 (Managing Director, 1962–88; Life President, 1989–91); *b* Newcastle, 14 Nov. 1927; *m* 1st, 1951 (marr. diss. 1984); two *s*; 2nd, 1984, Mary Sheila (*née* Brierley). Founded Barratt Developments, as a private co., 1958. *Recreations:* golf, shooting, sailing. *Address:* Barratt Developments, Wingrove House, Ponteland Road, Newcastle upon Tyne NE5 3DP.

BARRATT, Michael Fieldhouse; communications consultant; broadcaster on radio and television; Chairman: Commercial Video Ltd, since 1981; Michael Barratt Ltd, since 1977; Director, Valley Communications, since 1992; *b* 3 Jan. 1928; *s* of late Wallace Milner Barratt and Doris Barratt; *m* 1st, 1952, Joan Francesca Warner (marr. diss.); three *s* three *d*; 2nd, 1977, Dilys Jane Morgan; two *s* one *d*. *Educ:* Rossall and Paisley Grammar Sch. Entered journalism, Kemsley Newspapers, 1944; Editor, Nigerian Citizen, 1956; *television:* Reporter, Panorama, 1963; Presenter: 24 Hours, 1965–69; Nationwide, 1969–77; Songs of Praise, 1977–82; Reporting London, 1983–88; *radio:* Question-Master, Gardeners' Question Time, 1973–79. Trustee, Temple Holdings, 1992–. Rector, Aberdeen Univ., 1973. Mem., RTS; FRHS; FInstD. Hon. LLD Aberdeen, 1975. *Publications:* Michael Barratt, 1973; Michael Barratt's Down-to-Earth Gardening Book, 1974; Michael Barratt's Complete Gardening Book, 1977; Golf with Tony Jacklin, 1978. *Recreations:* golf, cricket, listening. *Address:* 5/7 Forlease Road, Maidenhead, Berks SL6 1RP. *T:* Maidenhead (01628) 770800. *Club:* Lord's Taverners.

BARRATT, Prof. Michael George; Professor of Mathematics, Northwestern University, Illinois, since 1974; *b* 26 Jan. 1927; *e s* of George Bernard Barratt and Marjorie Holloway Barratt (*née* Oldham); *m* 1952, Jenepher Hudson; one *s* four *d*. *Educ:* Stationers' Company's Sch.; Magdalen Coll., Oxford. Junior Lecturer, Oxford Univ., 1950–52; Fellow, Magdalen Coll., Oxford, 1952–56; Lectr, Brasenose Coll., Oxford, 1955–59; Sen. Lectr and Reader, 1959–63, Prof. of Pure Maths, 1964–74, Manchester Univ. Vis. Prof., Chicago Univ., 1963–64. *Publications:* papers in mathematical jls. *Address:* Department of Mathematics, Northwestern University, Lunt Building, Evanston, Ill 60201, USA.

BARRATT, Sir Richard (Stanley), Kt 1988; CBE 1981; QPM 1974; HM Chief Inspector of Constabulary, 1987–90; *b* 11 Aug. 1928; *s* of Richard Barratt and Mona Barratt; *m* 1952, Sarah Elizabeth Hale; one *s* two *d*. *Educ:* Saltley Grammar Sch., Birmingham. CIMgt. Birmingham City Police (Constable to Chief Inspector), 1949–65; Dir, Home Office Crime Prevention Centre, Stafford, 1963; seconded to Home Office (Res. and Develt), 1964; Sen. Comd Course, Police Coll., 1964; Supt, Cheshire Constab., 1965, Chief Supt, 1966; Asst Chief Constable, Manchester City Police, 1967; Asst Chief Constable, Manchester and Salford Police, 1968, Dep. Chief Constable, 1972; Dep. Chief Constable, Greater Manchester Police, 1974; Chief Constable, S Yorks Police, 1975–78; HM Inspector of Constabulary, 1978–87. Review of the Royal Bahamas Police, 1985. Led Police delegns to China, 1987, Pakistan, 1990. Assessor, Guildford and Woolwich Inquiry, 1990–94. Mem., Gaming Bd for GB, 1991–. OStJ 1978. *Recreations:* reading, gardening, golf. *Address:* c/o Home Office, Room 565, Queen Anne's Gate, SW1H 9AT.

BARRATT, Robin Alexander; QC 1989; a Recorder, since 1993; *b* 24 April 1945; *s* of Harold and Phyllis Barratt; *m* 1972, Gillian Anne Ellis; one *s* three *d*. *Educ:* Charterhouse; Worcester Coll., Oxford (Exhibnr; BA Hons, MA). Harmsworth Entrance Exhibnr, 1965, Schol. 1969; called to the Bar, Middle Temple, 1970. Lectr in Law, Kingston Polytechnic, 1968–71; Western Circuit, 1971; Asst Recorder, 1990. Councillor (C), London Bor. of Merton, 1978–86. *Recreations:* squash, fell walking, music. *Address:* 4/5 Gray's Inn Square, Gray's Inn, WC1R 5AY.

BARRATT-BOYES, Sir Brian (Gerald), KBE 1971 (CBE 1966); Surgeon-in-Charge, Cardio-Thoracic Surgical Unit, Greenlane Hospital, Auckland, 1964–88, now Hon. Consultant; Hon. Senior Cardio-Thoracic Surgeon, Mercy (formerly Mater Misericordiae) Hospital, Auckland, 1966–89; *b* 13 Jan. 1924; *s* of Gerald Cave Boyes and Edna Myrtle Boyes (*née* Barratt); *m* 1st, 1949, Norma Margaret Thompson (marr. diss. 1986); five *s*; 2nd, 1986, Sara Rose Monester. *Educ:* Wellington Coll.; Univ. of Otago. MB, ChB 1946; FRACS 1952; FACS 1960; ChM 1962. Lectr in Anatomy, Otago Univ. Med. Sch., 1947; House Surg. and Registrar, Wellington Hosp., 1948–50; Surgical Registrar and Pathology Registrar, Palmerston North Hosp., 1950–52; Fellow in Cardio-Thoracic Surgery, Mayo Clinic, USA, 1953–55; Nuffield Trav. Fellowship UK (Bristol Univ.), 1956; Sen. Cardio-Thoracic Surg., Greenlane Hosp., 1957. Hon. Prof. of Surgery, Auckland Univ., 1971; Sir Arthur Sims Commonwealth Travelling Prof., 1982. FRSNZ 1970. Hon. FACS 1977; Hon. FRCS 1985; Hon. Fellow, Royal Coll. of Surgeons of Thailand, 1987; Hon. FACC 1988. Hon. DSc, 1985. R. T. Hall Prize for Disting. Cardiac Surgery in Austr. and NZ, 1966; René Leriche Prize, Société Internationale de Chirurgie, 1987. *Publications:* Heart Disease in Infancy: diagnosis and surgical treatment, 1973; (jtly) Cardiac Surgery, 1986, 2nd edn 1993; numerous in med. jls throughout the world. *Recreations:* farming, trout fishing. *Address:* Greenhills, 982 Hibiscus Coast Highway, Waiwera, New Zealand. *Club:* Northern (Auckland).

BARRE, Raymond; Chevalier de la Légion d'Honneur, Chevalier de l'Ordre National du Mérite agricole, Officier des Palmes Académiques; Grand Croix de l'Ordre National du Mérite, 1977; Député, Rhône, French National Assembly; *b* Saint-Denis, Réunion, 12 April 1924; *s* of René Barre and Charlotte Déramond; *m* 1954, Eve Hegedüs; two *s*. *Educ:* Lycée Leconte-de-Lisle, Saint-Denis-de-la-Réunion; Faculté de Droit, Paris; Institut d'Etudes Politiques, Paris. Professor at Faculté de Droit et des Sciences Economiques: Caen, 1950; Paris (Chair of Political Economy), 1963–. Econs Res. Dir Foundation Nat. des Scis Politiques, 1958. Professor at Institut d'Etudes Politiques, Paris, 1961–. Director of Cabinet of Mr J.-M. Jeanneney (Minister of Industry), 1959–62; Member: Cttee of Experts (Comité Lorain) studying financing of investments in France, 1963–64; Gen. Cttee on Economy and Financing of Fifth Plan, 1966; Vice-Chm., Commn of European Communities (responsible for Economic and Financial Affairs), 1967–72; Minister of Foreign Trade, Jan.–Aug. 1976; Minister of Economics and Finance, 1976–78; Prime Minister, 1976–81; elected to National Assembly, from Rhône, 1978. Mem. Gen. Council, Banque de France, 1973; Chm. Cttee for studying Housing Financing Reform, 1975–76. *Publications:* Economie Politique, vol. 1, 1961, vol. 2, 1965; Une Politique pour l'Avenir, 1981; Refléxions pour Demain, 1984; Au Tournant du Siècle, 1987; Questions de Confiaure, 1988. *Address:* 4–6 avenue Emile-Acollas, 75007 Paris, France.

BARRELL, Anthony Charles, CB 1994; FEng; Chief Executive, North Sea Safety, Health and Safety Executive, 1991–94; *b* 4 June 1933; *s* of William Frederick Barrell and Ruth Eleanor Barrell (*née* Painter); *m* 1963, Jean, *d* of Francis Henry Hawkes and Clarice Jean (*née* Silke); one *s* one *d*. *Educ:* Friars Sch., Bangor; Kingston Grammar Sch.; Birmingham Univ.; Imperial Coll. BSc Hons chem. eng. CEng, FEng 1990; FIChemE 1984; EurIng 1988. Chemist, Ministry of Supply, later War Dept, 1959–64; Commissioning Engineer, African Explosives and Chemical Industries, 1964–65; Shift Manager, MoD, 1965–66; Chemical Inspector, then Supt. Specialist Inspector, HM Factory Inspectorate, 1966–78; Head of Major Hazards Assessment Unit, HSE, 1978–85; Dir, Technology, HSE, 1985–90; Chief Exec., N Sea Safety, Dept of Energy, 1990–91. Mem. Council, IChemE, 1989– (Pres., 1993–94). *Publications:* papers on assessment and control of major hazards, on offshore safety and on fire and explosion risks. *Recreations:* off-shore sailing, fell walking. *Address:* Sanderling, Baskervyle Road, Gayton, Wirral L60 8NJ. *T:* 0151–342 8255. *Club:* Royal Northern and University (Aberdeen).

BARRER, Prof. Richard Maling, FRS 1956; PhD Cantab; DSc (NZ); ScD Cantab; FRSC (FRIC 1939); Senior Research Fellow, Imperial College of Science and Technology, since 1977; Professor of Physical Chemistry, Imperial College of Science and Technology, University of London, 1954–77, now Emeritus; Head of Department of Chemistry, 1955–76; *b* 16 June 1910; *s* of T. R. Barrer, 103 Renall Street, Masterton, New Zealand; *m* 1939, Helen Frances Yule, Invercargill, NZ; one *s* three *d*. *Educ:* Canterbury University Coll., NZ (MSc); Clare Coll., Cambridge (1851 Exhibition Scholar). PhD Cantab, 1935; DSc NZ, 1937; ScD Cantab, 1948. Major Research Student, 1935–37, Research Fellow, 1937–39, Clare Coll.; Head of Chemistry Dept, Technical Coll., Bradford, 1939–46; Reader in Chemistry, London Univ., 1946–49; Prof. of Chemistry, Aberdeen Univ., 1949–54. Dean, Royal Coll. of Science, 1964–66. Member Council: Faraday Soc., 1952–55; Chemical Soc., 1956–59, 1974–77; Royal Institute of Chemistry, 1961–64; Soc. of Chemical Industry, 1965–68. Governor, Chelsea Coll. of Sci. and Technol., 1960–81. Hon. Pres., Internat. Zeolite Assoc., 1994. Hon. ARCS 1959; Hon. FRSNZ 1965; Hon. FNZIC 1987; Hon. DSc: Bradford, 1967; Aberdeen, 1983. *Publications:* Diffusion in and through Solids, 1941; Zeolites and Clay Minerals as Sorbents and Molecular Sieves, 1978; Hydrothermal Chemistry of Zeolites, 1982; research papers in British and foreign scientific journals. *Recreations:* tennis, interest in athletics (Full Blue and winner Oxford–Camridge cross-country, 1934; winner UAU cross-country, 1935). *Address:* Flossmoor, Orpington Road, Chislehurst, Kent BR7 6RA. *Clubs:* Hawks (Cambridge); Achilles.

BARRETT, Prof. Ann, MD; FRCP, FRCR; Professor of Radiation Oncology, University of Glasgow, since 1986; *b* 27 Feb. 1943; *d* of Robert Douglas and Elsie Mary Brown; *m* 1989, Adrian Bell; one *s* two *d*. *Educ:* St Bartholomew's Hosp. (MD). Junior posts, St Bartholomew's, UCH, Middlesex, Mount Vernon and Westminster Hosps, 1968–76; Chef de Clinique, Hôpital Tenon, Paris, 1976; Sen. Lectr and Consultant, Royal Marsden Hosp., 1977–86. Dir, Beatson Oncology Centre, Glasgow, 1987–91. Member: COMARE; NRPB; former Mem., Molecular and Cellular Med. Bd, MRC. Chm., Standing Scottish Cttee, RCR, 1992–95; Pres., Scottish Radiological Soc., 1995–. *Publications:* Practical Radiotherapy Planning, 1985, 2nd edn 1992; Cancer in Children, 1986, 2nd edn 1992. *Recreations:* hill walking, the Arts. *Address:* Beatson Oncology Centre, Western Infirmary, Glasgow G12 9XD. *T:* 0141–211 2123.

BARRETT, Rev. Prof. Charles Kingsley, DD; FBA 1961; Professor of Divinity, Durham University, 1958–82; *b* 4 May 1917; *s* of Rev. F. Barrett and Clara (*née* Seed); *m* 1944, Margaret E. Heap, Calverley, Yorks; one *s* one *d*. *Educ:* Shebbear Coll.; Pembroke Coll., Cambridge; Wesley House, Cambridge. DD Cantab, 1956. Asst Tutor, Wesley Coll., Headingley, 1942; Methodist Minister, Darlington, 1943; Lecturer in Theology, Durham Univ., 1945. Lectures: Hewett, USA, 1961; Shaffer, Yale, 1965; Delitzsch, Münster, 1967; Cato, Australia, 1969; Tate-Willson, Dallas, 1975; McMartin, Ottawa, 1976; Sanderson, Melbourne, and West-Watson, Christchurch, NZ, 1983; Alexander Robertson, Univ. of Glasgow, 1984; K. W. Clark, Duke, USA, 1987; Ryan, Asbury Seminary, Kentucky, 1988; Dominion-Chalmers, Ottawa, 1990; Woodruff Vis. Prof., Emory Univ., Atlanta, 1986; Gunning Fellow, Edinburgh Univ., 1994. Vice-Pres., British and Foreign Bible Soc.; Pres., Studiorum Novi Testamenti Societas, 1973; Mem., Royal Norwegian Soc. of Scis and Letters, 1991; Hon. Mem., Soc. of Biblical Literature, USA. Hon. DD: Hull, 1970; Aberdeen, 1972; Hon. DrTheol Hamburg, 1981. Burkitt Medal for Biblical Studies, 1966; von Humboldt Forschungspreis, 1988. *Publications:* The Holy Spirit and the Gospel Tradition, 1947; The Gospel according to St John, 1955, 2nd edn 1978; The New Testament Background: Selected Documents, 1956, 2nd edn 1987; Biblical Preaching and Biblical Scholarship, 1957; The Epistle to the Romans, 1957, 2nd edn 1991; Westcott as Commentator, 1959; Yesterday, Today and Forever: The New Testament Problem, 1959; Luke the Historian in Recent Study, 1961; From First Adam to Last, 1962; The Pastoral Epistles, 1963; Reading Through Romans, 1963; History and Faith: the Story of the Passion, 1967; Jesus and the Gospel Tradition, 1967; The First Epistle to the Corinthians, 1968; The Signs of an Apostle, 1970; Das Johannesevangelium und das Judentum, 1970; The Prologue of St John's Gospel, 1971; New Testament Essays, 1972; The Second Epistle to the Corinthians, 1973; The Fourth Gospel and Judaism, 1975; (ed) Donum Gentilicium, 1978; Essays on Paul, 1982; Essays on John, 1982; Freedom and Obligation, 1985; Church, Ministry and Sacraments in the New Testament, 1985; The Acts of the Apostles, vol. I (Internat. Critical Commentary series), 1994; Paul: an introduction to his thought, 1994; contributions to learned journals and symposia in Britain, the Continent, Australia and USA. *Address:* 22 Rosemount, Plawsworth Road, Pity Me, Durham DH1 5GA. *T:* Durham (0191) 3861340.

BARRETT, David; broadcaster, writer and political commentator on national and provincial media, since 1985; Premier and Minister of Finance, Province of British Columbia, Canada, 1972–75; *b* Vancouver, 2 Oct. 1930; *s* of Samuel Barrett and Rose (*née* Hyatt); father a business man in East Vancouver, after war service; *m* 1953, Shirley Hackman, West Vancouver; two *s* one *d*. *Educ:* Britannia High Sch., Vancouver; Seattle Univ.; St Louis Univ. BA(Phil) Seattle, 1953; Master of Social Work, St Louis, 1956. Personnel and Staff Trng Officer, Haney Correctional Inst., 1957–59; also gained experience in a variety of jobs. Fellow, Inst. of Politics, Harvard Univ., 1987; Vis. Schol., McGill Univ., 1988. Elected: MLA for Dewdney, Sept. 1960 and 1963; to re-distributed riding of Coquitlam 1966, 1969 and 1972; Vancouver East, by-election 1976, 1979; New Democratic Party Leader, June 1970–84 (first Social Democratic Govt in history of Province); Leader, Official Opposition, British Columbia, 1970–72 and 1975–84; MP (NDP) Esquimalt-Juan de Fuca, 1988. Dr of Laws, *hc*, St Louis Univ., 1974; Hon. DPhil Simon Fraser Univ., BC, 1986. *Address:* 1179 Monro Street, Victoria, British Columbia V9A 5P5, Canada.

BARRETT, Lt-Gen. Sir David William S.; *see* Scott-Barrett.

BARRETT, Sir Dennis Charles T.; *see* Titchener-Barrett.

BARRETT, Edmond Fox, OBE 1981; HM Diplomatic Service, retired; First Secretary, Foreign and Commonwealth Office, 1986–88; *b* 24 Aug. 1928; *s* of late Edmond Henry Barrett and Ellen Mary Barrett (*née* Fox); *m* 1959, Catherine Wendy Howard (*née* Slater). *Educ:* St Brendan's Coll., Bristol. Dominions Office, 1946; Royal Navy, 1947–49; CRO, 1949–50; Karachi, 1950–52; New Delhi, 1952–54; CRO, 1954–55; Admiralty, 1955–60; Foreign Office, 1960–63; Bucharest, 1963–65; Rio de Janeiro, 1965–68; Boston, 1968–70; Mexico City, 1971–73; FCO, 1973–76; Santo Domingo, 1976–79; Tehran, 1979–81; Consul Gen., Bilbao, 1981–86. *Recreations:* reading, golf, gardening. *Address:* 10 Greenheys Place, Woking, Surrey GU22 7JD.

BARRETT, Ernest; Chairman: Henry Barrett & Sons Ltd, 1982–87 (Joint Managing Director, 1968–85); Steel Stockholding Division, Henry Barrett & Sons Ltd, 1967–85; Henry Lindsay Ltd, 1974–87; *b* 8 April 1917; *s* of Ernest Barrett and Marian Conyers; *m*

1940, Eileen Maria Peel; one *d*. *Educ:* Charterhouse. Joined Henry Barrett & Sons Ltd, Bradford, 1934. Served War, RA, and commissioned, 1940; served in Mediterranean Theatre, with 1st Army, 1943–46 (despatches, 1944); Major 1945. Apptd Dir, Henry Barrett & Sons Ltd, 1946. Pres., Nat. Assoc. of Steel Stockholders, 1977–79 (Chm., Yorks Assoc., 1964–66; Vice-Pres., 1975–77); Pres., Engineering Industries Assoc., 1971 (Chm. Yorks Region, 1960–65; Vice-Pres. of Assoc., 1965–71). *Recreation:* gardening. *Address:* West Ghyll, Victoria Avenue, Ilkley, W Yorks LS29 9BW. *T:* Ilkley (01943) 609294.

BARRETT, Jack Wheeler, CBE 1971; PhD; FEng; CChem; FIC; Chairman, Cole Group plc, 1979–86 (Director, 1978); *b* 13 June 1912; *s* of John Samuel Barrett, Cheltenham; *m* 1935, Muriel Audley Read; two *s* two *d*. *Educ:* Cheltenham Grammar Sch.; Imperial Coll., Univ. of London. BSc, PhD, CChem, FRSC, FEng, FIChemE. Chief Chemist, London Essence Co. Ltd, 1936–41; joined Monsanto Chemicals Ltd, 1941; Dir of Research, 1955–71; Dir, Monsanto Ltd, 1955–78; Chm., Info-line Ltd, 1976–80. President: IChemE, 1971–72; Chem. Soc., 1974–75; IInfSc, 1976–79; ICSU Abstracting Bd, 1974–77; Chm., Chemical Divl Council, BSI, 1973–79; Mem., British Library Bd, 1973–79. *Publications:* articles in Jl Chem. Soc., Chemistry and Industry, Jl ASLIB, Chemistry in Britain. *Recreation:* gardening. *Address:* West Manor House, Bourton-on-the-Water, Cheltenham, Glos GL54 2AP. *T:* Cotswold (01451) 820296. *Club:* Athenæum.

BARRETT, Rev. John Charles Allanson; Headmaster, The Leys School, Cambridge, since 1990; *b* 8 June 1943; *s* of Leonard Wilfred Allanson Barrett and Marjorie Joyce Barrett; *m* 1967, Sally Elisabeth Hatley; one *s* one *d*. *Educ:* Culford Sch.; Univ. of Newcastle upon Tyne (BA Hons); Fitzwilliam Coll., Cambridge; Wesley House, Cambridge. MA Cantab. Ordained Methodist Minister. Chaplain and Lectr in Divinity, Westminster Coll., Oxford, 1968–69; Asst Tutor, Wesley Coll., Bristol, 1969–71; Circuit Minister, Hanley Trinity Circuit, Stoke on Trent, and actg Hd of Religious Studies, Birches High Sch., Hanley, 1971–73; Chaplain and Hd of Religious and Gen. Studies, Kingswood Sch., Bath, 1973–83; Headmaster, Kent Coll., Pembury, 1983–90. World Methodist Council: Mem. Exec. Cttee, 1981–; Sec., Brit. Cttee, 1986–; Chairman: Educn Cttee, 1991–; Prog. Cttee, 1992–. Mem. Steering Cttee, Bloxham Project, 1986–92. Hon. DD Florida Southern, 1992. *Publications:* What is a Christian School?, 1981; Family Worship in Theory and Practice, 1983; Methodist Education in Britain, 1990; sections on Methodism in Encyc. Britannica Year Books, 1988–94. *Address:* The Leys School, Cambridge CB2 2AD. *T:* Cambridge (01223) 355327. *Club:* East India.

BARRETT, John Edward; Consultant, Dunlop Slazenger International; *b* 17 April 1931; *s* of Alfred Edward Barrett and Margaret Helen Barrett (*née* Walker); *m* 1967, (Florence) Angela (Margaret) Mortimer; one *s* one *d*. *Educ:* University College Sch., Hampstead; St John's Coll., Cambridge (MA History). Joined Slazengers as management trainee, 1957; Tournament Dir, 1975; Dir, 1978; Consultant, 1981– (now Dunlop Slazenger International). Tennis career: RAF champion, 1950, 1951; Captain of Cambridge, 1954; Nat. Indoor Doubles champion (with D. Black), 1953; Davis Cup, 1956–57, non-playing Captain, 1959–62; Dir, LTA Trng Squad (Barrett Boys), 1965–68; qualified LTA coach, 1969; Founded: BP Internat Tennis Fellowship, 1968–80 (and directed); BP Cup (21-and-under), 1973–80; Junior Internat. Series, 1975–79. Financial Times: tennis corresp., 1963–; crossword contribs, 1986–. TV tennis commentator: BBC, 1971–; Australian networks, 1981–; USA. *Publications:* Tennis and Racket Games, 1975; Play Tennis with Rosewall, 1975; 100 Wimbledon Championships, 1986; (with Dan Maskell) From Where I Sit, 1988; (with Dan Maskell) Oh, I Say, 1989; (ed and contrib.) World of Tennis, annually, 1969–. *Recreations:* music, theatre, reading. *Address:* All England Lawn Tennis Club, Church Road, Wimbledon, SW19 5AE. *Clubs:* United Oxford & Cambridge University, All England Lawn Tennis (Mem. Cttee), International Lawn Tennis (Dep. Pres.), Queen's.

BARRETT, Michael Paul, OBE 1987; Director, British Council, Japan, since 1993; *b* 30 July 1941; *s* of William James Barrett and Irene (*née* Beynon); *m* 1966, Marie-Thérèse Françoise Juliette Lombard; two *s*. *Educ:* Westminster City Sch; Univ. of Durham (BA Hons Classics). Asst Tutor in English to Overseas Students, Univ. of Birmingham, 1963–64; British Council: Asst Dir, Port Harcourt, 1964–65; Asst Rep., Addis Ababa, 1966–69; Educnl Television Officer, Tokyo, 1970–72; Dir, Films Dept, 1972–75; Educnl Technologist, Media Dept, 1975–77; Non-Formal Educn Specialist, Nairobi, 1977–80; Dep. Rep., Japan, 1980–84; Cultural Attaché, Washington, 1984–87; Dir, PR, 1987–88; Consultant, Goddard Kay Rogers & Associates Ltd, 1989; Man. Dir, GKR Japan Ltd, 1989–93. Vice-Pres., British Chamber of Commerce in Japan, 1992–. Chm. Bd of Trustees, British Sch. in Tokyo, 1992–. *Recreations:* contemporary art and music, fishing, sailing, Celtic culture. *Address:* 25 Offerton Road, SW4 0DJ; Rosalbert, Roullens 11290, Montréal, France. *Club:* Travellers.

BARRETT, Sir Stephen (Jeremy), KCMG 1991 (CMG 1982); HM Diplomatic Service, retired; Ambassador to Poland, 1988–91; *b* 4 Dec. 1931; *s* of late W. P. Barrett and Dorothy Barrett; *m* 1958, Alison Mary Irvine; three *s*. *Educ:* Westminster Sch.; Christ Church, Oxford (MA). FO, 1955–57; 3rd, later 2nd Sec., Political Office with Middle East Forces, Cyprus, 1957–59; Berlin, 1959–62; 1st Sec., FO, 1962–65; Head of Chancery, Helsinki, 1965–68; 1st Sec., FCO, 1968–72; Counsellor and Head of Chancery, Prague, 1972–74; Head of SW European Dept, FCO, later Principal Private Sec. to Foreign and Commonwealth Sec., 1975; Head of Science and Technology Dept, FCO, 1976–77; Fellow, Center for Internat. Affairs, Harvard, 1977–78; Counsellor, Ankara, 1978–81; Head of British Interests Section, Tehran, 1981; Asst Under-Sec. of State, FCO, 1981–84; Ambassador to Czechoslovakia, 1985–88. *Recreations:* climbing small mountains, reading. *Club:* Ausable (St Huberts, NY).

BARRETT, William Spencer, FBA 1965; Fellow of Keble College, Oxford, 1952–81 and Tutor in Classics, 1939–81, Hon. Fellow, 1981; Reader in Greek Literature, University of Oxford, 1966–81; *b* 29 May 1914; *o s* of William Barrett and Sarah Jessie Barrett (*née* Robbins); *m* 1939, Georgina Margaret Elizabeth (*d* 1989), *e d* of William and Alma Georgina Annie Hill; one *s* one *d*. *Educ:* Derby Sch; Christ Church, Oxford (Scholar). Ireland and Craven Schol. 1933; 1st Class Classical Hon. Mods, 1934; Gaisford Prize for Greek Verse, 1934; de Paravicini Schol., 1934; 1st Class Lit. Hum., 1937; Derby Schol., 1937; Charles Oldham Prize, 1938. Lectr, Christ Church, Oxford, 1938–39; Lectr, Keble Coll. 1939–52; Librarian, 1946–66; Univ. Lectr in Greek Literature, 1947–66; Sub Warden, Keble Coll., 1968–76. Temp. Civilian Officer, Admty (Naval Intelligence Div.), 1942–45. *Publications:* (ed) Euripides, Hippolytos, 1964; Sophocles, Niobe (in Papyrus Fragments of Sophocles, ed R. Carden), 1974; articles in learned jls. *Address:* 8 The Avenue, Clifton, Bristol BS8 3HE. *T:* Bristol (0117) 974 3321.

BARRETT-LENNARD, Rev. Sir Hugh (Dacre), 6th Bt *cr* 1801; Priest, London Oratory; *b* 27 June 1917; *s* of Sir Fiennes Cecil Arthur Barrett-Lennard (*d* 1963) and Winifrede Mignon (*d* 1969), *d* of Alfred Berlyn; *S* cousin, 1977. *Educ:* Radley College, Berks; Pontifical Beda College, Rome. Teaching, 1936. Served War of 1939–45, NW Europe (despatches); enlisted London Scottish, Jan. 1940; commissioned 2nd Lt, Oct. 1940; Captain Essex Regt, 1945. Entered Brompton Oratory, 1946; ordained Priest in Rome, 1950. *Recreations:* on Isle of Eigg, Hebrides. *Heir: cousin* Richard Fynes Barrett-Lennard, *b* 6 April 1941. *Address:* The Oratory, South Kensington, SW7 2RW. *T:* 0171-589 4811.

BARRIE, (Charles) David (Ogilvy); Director, National Art Collections Fund, since 1992; *b* 9 Nov. 1953; *s* of late Alexander Ogilvy Barrie and Patricia Mary Tucker; *m* 1978, Mary Emily, *d* of Rt Hon. Sir Ralph Gibson, *qv*; two *d*. *Educ:* Bryanston Sch.; Brasenose Coll., Oxford (MA Phil and Exp. Psych.). HM Diplomatic Service, 1975; served FCO 1975–76; Dublin, 1976–80; seconded to Cabinet Office, 1980–81; FCO, 1981–87; transf. Cabinet Office, 1988; seconded to Japan Festival 1991, as Exec. Dir, 1989–92; resigned from Cabinet Office, 1992. Companion and Dir, Guild of St George, 1992–. *Publications:* (ed) John Ruskin's Modern Painters, 1987; numerous articles and reviews. *Recreations:* sailing, collecting paintings and drawings. *Address:* National Art Collections Fund, Millais House, 7 Cromwell Place, SW7 2JN. *T:* 0171-225 4800. *Clubs:* Royal Cruising; Emsworth Sailing.

BARRIE, Herbert, MD, FRCP; Consultant Paediatrician: New Victoria Hospital, Kingston, since 1993; Ashtead Hospital, Surrey, since 1986; Hon. Consultant Paediatrician, Charing Cross Hospital, since 1987 (Consultant Paediatrician, 1966–84; Physician in charge, 1984–86); *b* 9 Oct. 1927; *m* 1963, Dinah Barrie, MB, BS, FRCPath; one *s* one *d*. *Educ:* Wallington County Grammar School; University College and Med. Sch., London. MB, BS 1950; MD 1952; MRCP 1957, FRCP 1972. Registrar, Hosp. for Sick Children, Gt Ormond St, 1955–57; Research Fellow, Harvard Univ., Children's Med. Center, 1957; Sen. Registrar and Sen. Lectr, Dept of Paediatrics, St Thomas' Hosp., 1959–65; Consultant Paediatrician, Moor House Sch. for Speech Disorders, 1968–74. Vis. Prof., Downstate Univ. Med. Center, NY, 1976. Member: London Med. Soc.; British Paediatric Assoc.; British Assoc. of Perinatal Paediatrics; Neonatal Soc.; Perinatal Visiting Club; BMA; Vaccine Damage Tribunal Panel. *Publications:* numerous contribs to books and jls on paediatric and neonatal topics, esp. resuscitation of newborn and neonatal special care. *Recreations:* tennis, writing, wishful thinking. *Address:* 3 Burghley Avenue, New Malden, Surrey KT3 4SW. *T:* 0181-942 2836.

BARRIE, Lesley; General Manager, Tayside Health Board, since 1993; *b* 28 Sept. 1944. *Educ:* Glasgow High Sch. for Girls; Univ. of Glasgow (DPA). MHSM; DipHSM. NHS admin. trainee, 1963–66; hosp. mgt, 1966–77; District General Manager: Inverclyde Dist, 1977–81; Glasgow SE, 1981–83; Dir, Admin Services, Glasgow Royal Infirmary, Royal Maternity Hosp. and Glasgow Dental Hosp., 1983–87; Unit Gen. Manager, Stirling Royal Infirmary, 1987–91; Gen. Manager, Forth Valley Health Bd, 1991–93. Chm., Social Security Appeal Tribunals, 1978–90; Mem., Industrial Tribunal, 1992–. MIMgt. *Recreations:* table tennis (Scottish International, 1963–70), badminton, reading. *Address:* Tayside Health Board, Vernonholme, Riverside Drive, Dundee DD1 9NL. *T:* Dundee (01382) 645151.

BARRINGTON, Sir Alexander (Fitzwilliam Croker), 7th Bt *cr* 1831; retired; *b* 19 Nov. 1909; *s* of Sir Charles Burton Barrington, 5th Bt, and Mary Rose (*d* 1943), *d* of Sir Henry Hickman Bacon, 10th and 11th Bt; *S* brother, 1980. *Educ:* Castle Park, Dalkey, Co. Dublin; Shrewsbury School; Christ Church, Oxford. Director of various private companies, 1932–39. Served in Army as Captain, Intelligence Corps, 1939–42; prisoner of war, Singapore and Thailand, 1942–45. Book publishers' executive, editor and production manager, 1946–72. *Recreations:* gardening, travel. *Heir: cousin* John William Barrington, Major retd, Royal Irish Fusiliers [*b* 20 Oct. 1917; *m* 1st, 1949, Annie Wetten (*d* 1985); two *s* one *d*; 2nd, 1986, Evelyn Carol Paterson, *d* of late Oscar Broten]. *Address:* 11 Tedworth Square, SW3 4DU.

BARRINGTON, James Henry; Executive Director, League Against Cruel Sports, since 1988; *b* 18 Nov. 1952; *s* of James Irving Barrington and Bridget Nora (*née* Mullen); *m* 1986, Ursula Barbara Sitko. *Educ:* St Joseph's Acad., London. Admin. Officer, London Electricity Bd, 1969–76; Asst Supervisor, Social Services Dept, London Borough of Greenwich, 1976–79; League Against Cruel Sports: Promotions Manager, 1980–85; Dep. Dir, 1985–88. *Recreations:* music, photography, walking. *Address:* c/o League Against Cruel Sports, Sparling House, 83–87 Union Street, SE1 1SG. *T:* 0171-403 6155.

BARRINGTON, Sir Nicholas (John), KCMG 1990 (CMG 1982); CVO 1975; HM Diplomatic Service, retired; High Commissioner to Pakistan, 1989–94 (Ambassador, 1987–89); non-resident Ambassador to Afghanistan, 1994; *b* 23 July 1934; *s* of late Eric Alan Barrington and Mildred (*née* Bill). *Educ:* Repton; Clare Coll., Cambridge (MA 1957; Hon. Fellow 1992). HM Forces, RA, 1952–54. Joined Diplomatic Service, 1957; Tehran (language student), 1958; Oriental Sec., Kabul, 1959; FO, 1961; 2nd Sec., UK Delegn to European Communities, Brussels, 1963; 1st Sec., Rawalpindi, 1965; FO, 1967; Private Sec. to Permanent Under Sec., Commonwealth Office, April 1968; Asst Private Sec. to Foreign and Commonwealth Sec., Oct. 1968; Head of Chancery, Tokyo, 1972–75 (promoted Counsellor and for a period apptd Chargé d'Affaires, Hanoi, 1973); Head of Guidance and Information Policy (subsequently Information Policy) Dept, FCO, 1976–78; Counsellor, Cairo, 1978–81; Minister and Head of British Interests Section, Tehran, 1981–83; Supernumary Ambassador attached to UK Mission to UN, NY, for Gen. Assembly, autumn 1983; Co-ordinator for London Econ. Summit, 1984; Asst Under-Sec. of State (Public Depts), FCO, 1984–87. Chm., Management Cttee, Southwold Summer Theatre; Member: Support Cttee, Cambridge Univ. Divinity Faculty; Exec. Cttee, Asia House and Pakistan Soc. Trustee, Ancient India and Iran Trust. FRSA 1984. 3rd Cl., Order of the Sacred Treasure, Japan, 1975. *Recreations:* theatre, drawing, prosopography. *Address:* c/o Clare College, Cambridge CB2 1TL. *Clubs:* Athenæum, Commonwealth Trust.

BARRINGTON-WARD, Rt. Rev. Simon; *see* Coventry, Bishop of.

BARRITT, Rev. Dr Gordon Emerson, OBE 1979; Principal, National Children's Home, 1969–86; President of the Methodist Conference, 1984–85; *b* 30 Sept. 1920; *s* of Norman and Doris Barritt; *m* 1st, 1947, Joan Mary Alway (*d* 1984); two *s* one *d*; 2nd, 1993, Karen Lesley Windle. *Educ:* William Hulme's Grammar Sch., Manchester; Manchester Univ.; Cambridge Univ. (Wesley House and Fitzwilliam Coll.). Served War, RAF, 1942–45 (despatches). Methodist Minister: Kempston Methodist Church, Bedford, 1947–52; Westlands Methodist Church, Newcastle-under-Lyme, 1952–57; Chaplain, Univ. of Keele, 1953–57. Dir, Enfield Counselling Service, 1986–89; Treasurer, 1969–86, Chm., 1970–72, Nat. Council of Voluntary Child Care Organisations; Member: Home Office Adv. Council on Child Care, 1968–71; Brit. Assoc. of Social Workers, 1960–; Nat. Children's Bureau, 1963– (Treasurer, 1989–); Internat. Union for Child Welfare, 1969–86; Chm., Kids, 1986–93; Vice Chm. of Council, Selly Oak Colls, Birmingham, 1991– (Fellow, 1987); Governor: Farringtons Sch., 1986– (Chm. of Govs, 1986–93); Queenswood Sch., 1986–93. DUniv Keele, 1985. *Publications:* The Edgworth Story, 1972; (ed) Many Pieces—One Aim, 1975; (ed) Family Life, 1979; Residential Care, 1979; contrib.: Caring for Children, 1969; Giving Our Best, 1982. *Recreations:* music, do-it-yourself. *Address:* 10 Cadogan Gardens, Grange Park, N21 1ER. *T:* 0181-360 8687.

BARRON, Brian Munro; Asia Correspondent, BBC News and Current Affairs, since 1986; *b* 28 April 1940; *s* of Albert and Norah Barron; *m* 1974, Angela Lee, MA; one *d*.

Educ: Bristol Grammar School. Junior Reporter, Western Daily Press, Bristol, 1956–60; Dep. Chief Sub-editor, Evening World, Bristol, 1960–61; Sub-editor, Daily Mirror, 1961–63; Dep. Chief Sub-editor, Evening Post, Bristol, 1963–65; Sub-editor, BBC External Services, London, 1965–67; Correspondent, BBC Radio: Aden, 1967–68; ME, Cairo, 1968–69; SE Asia, Singapore, 1969–71; Reporter, BBC TV News, 1971–73; Correspondent, BBC TV: Far East, Hong Kong, 1973–76; Africa, Nairobi, 1976–81; Ireland, 1981–83; Washington, 1983–86. Royal Television Society: Journalist of the Year, 1979–80; Internat. Reporting Award, 1985. *Recreations:* opera, theatre, tennis. *Address:* British Broadcasting Corporation, Asia Bureau, 1141 Telecom House, 3 Gloucester Road, Hong Kong. *T:* (852) 802 0527, *Fax:* (852) 802 4428. *Clubs:* Nairobi (E Africa): Kenwood Country (Md, USA); Foreign Correspondents (Hong Kong).

BARRON, Derek Donald; Chairman and Chief Executive, Ford Motor Co. Ltd, 1986–91; Chairman, Ford Motor Credit Co., 1986–91; *b* 7 June 1929; *s* of Donald Frederick James Barron and Hettie Barbara Barron; *m* 1963, Rosemary Ingrid Brian; two *s*. *Educ:* Beckenham Grammar School; University College London. Joined Ford Motor Co. Sales, 1951; Tractor Group, 1961; Tractor Manager, Ford Italiana 1963; Marketing Associate, Ford Motor Co. USA, 1970; Gen. Sales Manager, Overseas Markets, 1971; Man. Dir, Ford Italiana, 1973; Group Dir, Southern European Sales, Ford of Europe, 1977; Sales and Marketing Dir, Ford Brazil, 1979; Vice-Pres., Ford Motor de Venezuela, 1982; Dir-Vice-Pres., Operations, Ford Brazil, 1985. DUniv Essex, 1989. *Address:* c/o National Westminster Bank, The Keys, Warley, Essex CM13 3BS.

BARRON, Sir Donald (James), Kt 1972; DL; Chairman, Joseph Rowntree Foundation, since 1981; *b* 17 March 1921; *o s* of Albert Gibson Barron and Elizabeth Macdonald, Edinburgh; *m* 1956, Gillian Mary, *o d* of John Saville, York; three *s* two *d*. *Educ:* George Heriot's Sch., Edinburgh; Edinburgh Univ. (BCom). Member, Inst. Chartered Accountants of Scotland. Joined Rowntree Mackintosh Ltd, 1952; Dir, 1961; Vice-Chm., 1965; Chm., 1966–81. Dir, 1972, Vice-Chm., 1981–82, Chm., 1982–87, Midland Bank plc. Dep. Chm., CLCB, 1983–85; Chm., Cttee of London and Scottish Bankers, 1985–87. Director: Investors in Industry, subseq. 3i, Gp, 1980–91; Canada Life Assurance Co. of GB Ltd, 1980– (Chm., 1991–94; Dep. Chm., 1994–); Canada Life Unit Trust Managers Ltd, 1980– (Chm., 1982–); Canada Life Assurance Co., Toronto, 1980–; Canada Life Assce (Ireland), 1992–; Clydesdale Bank, 1986–87. Mem., Bd of Banking Supervision, 1987–89. Dir, BIM Foundn, 1977–80 and Mem. Council, BIM, 1978–80; Trustee, Joseph Rowntree Foundn (formerly Meml Trust), 1966–73, 1975– (Chm., 1981–); Treasurer, 1966–72, a Pro-Chancellor, 1982–, York Univ.; Member: Council of CBI, 1966–81 (Chm., CBI Educn Foundn, 1981–85); SSRC, 1971–72; UGC, 1972–81; Council, PSI, 1978–85; Council, Inst. of Chartered Accountants of Scotland, 1980–81; NEDC, 1983–85. Governor, London Business Sch., 1982–88. DL N Yorks (formerly WR Yorks and City of York), 1971. Hon. doctorates: Loughborough, 1982; Heriot-Watt, 1983; CNAA, 1983; Edinburgh, 1984; Nottingham, 1985; York, 1986. *Recreations:* travelling, golf, tennis, gardening. *Address:* Greenfield, Sim Balk Lane, Bishopthorpe, York YO2 1QH. *T:* York (01904) 705675. *Clubs:* Athenæum; Yorkshire (York).

BARRON, Iann Marchant, CBE 1994; Chairman, Division Group, since 1990; *b* 16 June 1936; *s* of William Barron; *m* 1961, Jacqueline Almond (marr. diss. 1989); two *s* two *d*. *Educ:* University College School; Christ's College, Cambridge (exhibitioner; MA). Elliott Automation, 1961–65; Managing Director: Computer Technology Ltd, 1965–72; Microcomputer Analysis Ltd, 1973–78; Exec. Dir, 1978–89, Chief Strategic Officer, 1984–89, INMOS International; Man. Dir, INMOS, 1981–88. Vis. Prof., Westfield Coll., London, 1976–78; Vis. Indust. Prof., Bristol Univ., 1985–; Vis. Fellow: QMC, 1976; Science Policy Res. Unit, 1977–78. Exec. Trustee, The Exploratory, 1992–. Mem. Council, UCS, 1983–. Distinguished FBCS, 1986. FIEE 1994. Hon. DSc: Bristol Polytechnic, 1988; Hull, 1989. R. W. Mitchell Medal, 1983; J. J. Thompson Medal, IEE, 1986. *Publications:* The Future with Microelectronics (with Ray Curnow), 1977; technical papers. *Address:* Barrow Court, Barrow Gurney, Avon BS19 3RW.

BARRON, Prof. John Penrose, MA, DPhil, FSA; Master of St Peter's College, Oxford, since 1991; *b* 27 Apr. 1934; *s* of George Barron and Minnie Leslie Marks; *m* 1962, Caroline Mary, *d* of late W. D. Hogarth, OBE; two *d*. *Educ:* Clifton Coll.; Balliol Coll., Oxford (Hon. Exhibnr). 1st Cl., Class. Hon. Mods, 1955; Lit. Hum., 1957; MA 1960, DPhil 1961; Thomas Whitcombe Greene Prizeman, 1955, and Scholar, 1957; Barclay Head Prizeman, 1959; Cromer Prize, British Academy, 1965. London University: Asst Lectr in Latin, Bedford Coll., 1959–61, and Lectr, 1961–64; Lectr in Archaeology, UCL, 1964–67; Reader in Archaeology and Numismatics, 1967–71; Prof. of Greek Lang. and Lit., 1971–91, and Head of Dept of Classics, 1972–84, KCL; Dean, Faculty of Arts, 1976–80; Dir, Inst. of Classical Studies, 1984–91; Dean, Insts for Advanced Study, 1989–91. Mem. Senate, 1977–81, 1987–91, Mem. Academic Council, 1977–81, 1985–89; Public Orator, 1978–81, 1986–88; Pro-Vice-Chancellor, 1987–89. Mem., UFC, 1989–93. FKC 1988. Vis. Mem., Inst. for Advanced Study, Princeton, 1973. Blegen Distinguished Vis. Res. Prof., Vassar Coll., NY, 1981; T. B. L. Webster Vis. Prof., Stanford Univ., 1986; Vis. Prof., Aust. Archaeol Inst., Athens, 1994. Lectures: Eberhard L. Faber, Princeton, 1985; Woodward, Yale, 1985; Sotheby, Edinburgh, 1986; Dill, QUB, 1986; Batchelor, UEA, 1992. Pres., Soc. for Promotion of Hellenic Studies, 1990–93 (Trustee, 1970–; Hon. Sec., 1981–90); Mem., Academia Europaea, 1990. Trustee, Prince of Wales Inst. of Architecture, 1990–. Governor: St Paul's Schools, London, 1991–; SOAS, 1989– (Vice-Chm., 1992–); Almoner, Christ's Hosp., 1975–80. *Publications:* Greek Sculpture, 1965 (new and rev. edn 1981); Silver Coins of Samos, 1966; articles in Classical Quarterly, Jl of Hellenic Studies, Bulletin of Inst. of Classical Studies, etc. *Recreations:* travel, gardens. *Address:* St Peter's College, Oxford OX1 2DL. *Club:* Athenæum.

BARRON, Kevin John; MP (Lab) Rother Valley, since 1983; *b* 26 Oct. 1946; *s* of Richard Barron; *m* 1969; one *s* two *d*. *Educ:* Maltby Hall Secondary Modern Sch.; Ruskin Coll., Oxford. NCB, 1962–83. PPS to Leader of the Opposition, 1985–88; Opposition spokesman on energy, 1988–92, on employment, 1993–. Member: Select Cttee on Energy, 1983–85; Select Cttee on Environmental Affairs, 1992–93. Pres., Rotherham and Dist TUC, 1982–83. *Address:* House of Commons, SW1A 0AA.

BARRON, Maj.-Gen. Richard Edward, CB 1993; *b* 22 Nov. 1940; *s* of John Barron and Lorna Frances Barron; *m* 1968, Margaret Ann Eggar; one *s* one *d*. *Educ:* Oundle; RMA. Commissioned Queen's Royal Irish Hussars, 1962; Staff College, 1973; DAA&QMG 7th Armoured Brigade, 1974–76; Instructor, Staff Coll., 1978–81; CO, QRIH, 1981–84; Comdr, 7th Armoured Brigade, 1984–86; RCDS 1987; QMG's Staff, 1988–89; Dir, RAC, 1989–92. Col, Queen's Royal Hussars, 1993–. *Recreations:* restoration, gardening, fishing. *Address:* Middle Burrow, Timberscombe, Som TA24 7UD. *Clubs:* Cavalry and Guards, MCC.

BARRON, (Thomas) Robert, CBE 1980; Member, British Railways Board, 1978–81; *b* 27 Dec. 1918; *s* of late Robert and Florence May Barron; *m* 1942, Constance Lilian Bolter; one *s* three *d*. *Educ:* Dame Allan's Sch., Newcastle-on-Tyne; King's Coll., Durham Univ. BA 1st class Hons (Econ.). Served RA and 1st Airborne Div., 1940–46. Joined LNER as Traffic Apprentice, 1946; Asst Gen. Manager, London Midland Region, 1966, Western Region, 1967; British Railways Board: Dir Management Staff, 1970; Controller of Corporate Planning, 1972; Dir of Planning and Investment, 1977. Exec. Dir, Channel Tunnel, 1981–82. Mem., NW Economic Planning Council, 1965–67. *Recreations:* music, fishing, watching sport. *Address:* 25 Shotford Road, Harleston, Norfolk IP20 9JN. *T:* Harleston (01379) 853625.

BARRONS, John Lawson; Chief Executive, Century Newspapers Ltd, Belfast, since 1989; *b* 10 Oct. 1932; *s* of late William Cowper Barrons, MBE and Amy Marie Barrons (*née* Lawson); *m* 1st, 1957, Caroline Anne (marr. diss. 1986), *d* of late George Edward Foster; three *s*; 2nd, 1987, Lauren Ruth, *d* of late Robert Z. Friedman. *Educ:* Caterham Sch. Nat. Service, 1st Bn Northamptonshire Regt, 1952–54. Journalist, UK and USA, 1950–57; Gen. Manager, Nuneaton Observer, 1957; Managing Editor, Northampton Chronicle & Echo, 1959; Gen. Manager, Edinburgh Evening News, 1961; Gen. Manager, 1965–76, Man. Dir, 1976–85, Westminster Press. Director: Pearson Longman, 1979–83; Stephen Austin Newspapers, 1986–91; Northern Press, 1986–91; Lincolnshire Standard Gp plc, 1987–88; President: Westminster (Florida) Inc., 1980–85; Westminster (Jacksonville) Inc., 1982–85. Dir, Evening Newspaper Advertising Bureau, 1978–81 (Chm. 1979–80); Dir, The Press Association Ltd, 1985–86; Chm., Printing Industry Res. Assoc., 1983–85 (Mem. Council, 1978, a Vice-Chm., 1979–83); Mem. Bd of Management, Internat. Electronic Publishing Res. Centre, 1981–85. Member, Council: Newspaper Soc., 1975–87 (Pres., 1981–82; Hon. Vice-Pres., 1983–); CPU, 1970–86. *Recreations:* walking, fishing. *Address:* 3 Chesterford Gardens, Hampstead, NW3 7DD. *Clubs:* Flyfishers', MCC.

BARROW, Prof. Geoffrey Wallis Steuart, FBA 1976; Sir William Fraser Professor of Scottish History and Palæography, University of Edinburgh, 1979–92, now Professor Emeritus; *b* Headingley, Leeds, 28 Nov. 1924; *s* of late Charles Embleton Barrow and Marjorie, *d* of Donald Stuart; *m* 1951, Heather Elizabeth, *d* of James McLeish Lownie; one *s* one *d*. *Educ:* St Edward's Sch., Oxford; Inverness Royal Acad.; St Andrews Univ.; Pembroke Coll., Oxford. FRSE 1977. Lecturer in History, University Coll., London, 1950–61; Prof. of Mediaeval Hist., King's Coll., Univ. of Durham, later Univ. of Newcastle upon Tyne, 1961–74; Prof. of Scottish History, Univ. of St Andrews, 1974–79. Mem., Royal Commn on Historical MSS, 1984–90. Ford's Lectr, Univ. of Oxford, 1977; Rhind Lectr, Soc. of Antiquaries of Scotland, 1985. Hon. DLitt: Glasgow, 1988; Newcastle, 1994. *Publications:* Feudal Britain, 1956; Acts of Malcolm IV, King of Scots, 1960; Robert Bruce and the Community of the Realm of Scotland, 1965; Acts of William I, King of Scots, 1971; Kingdom of the Scots, 1973; (ed) The Scottish Tradition, 1974; The Anglo-Norman Era in Scottish History, 1980; Kingship and Unity, 1981; Scotland and its Neighbours, 1992; contrib. Scottish Historical Review, etc. *Recreation:* hill walking. *Address:* 12A Lauder Road, Edinburgh EH9 2EL.

BARROW, Jill Helen; Director of Education, Surrey County Council, since 1993; *b* 26 April 1951; *d* of Philip Eric Horwood and Mavis Mary (*née* Handscombe); *m* (marr. diss.); two *d*. *Educ:* Durham Univ. (Cert Ed 1972; MA Ed 1983); Open Univ. (BA 1980). Teaching in secondary, special and further educn, 1972–86; educn mgt and inspection, 1986–90; Dep. Dir of Educn, Essex CC, 1990–93. *Recreations:* walking, outdoor activities, travelling, reading. *Address:* County Hall, Penrhyn Road, Kingston-upon-Thames, Surrey KT1 2DJ. *T:* 0181–541 9500.

BARROW, Dame Jocelyn (Anita), DBE 1992 (OBE 1972); Deputy Chairman, Broadcasting Standards Council, since 1989; *b* 15 April 1929; *d* of Charles Newton Barrow and Olive Irene Barrow (*née* Pierre); *m* 1970, Henderson Downer. *Educ:* Univ. of London. Mem., Taylor Cttee on School Governors; Gen. Sec., later Vice-Chm., Campaign Against Racial Discrimination, 1964–69; Vice-Chm., Internat. Human Rights Year Cttee, 1968; Member: CRC, 1968–72; Parole Bd, 1983–87. A Governor, BBC, 1981–88. Chairman: Independent Cttee of Management, Optical Consumer Complaints Service, 1992–; Independent Equal Opportunities Inquiry into Ethnicity and Trng and Assessment on Bar Vocational Course, 1993–94; Non-Exec. Dir, Whittington Hosp. NHS Trust, 1993–; Mem., Econ. and Social Cttee, EC, 1990–. Nat. Vice-Pres., Nat. Towns-women's Guilds, 1978–80, 1987–; Pres. and Founder, Community Housing Assoc.; Governor: Farnham Castle, 1977–93; BFI, 1991–. FRSA. Hon. DLitt E London, 1992. *Recreations:* theatre, music, cooking, reading. *Address:* c/o Broadcasting Standards Council, 5–8 The Sanctuary, SW1P 3JS. *T:* 0171–233 0408. *Club:* Reform.

BARROW, John Frederick; HM Diplomatic Service, retired; *b* 28 Dec. 1918; *s* of Frederick William and Caroline Barrow; *m* 1947, Mary Roberta Young; two *d*. *Educ:* King Edward VII Sch., King's Lynn. Home Civil Service, 1936–39; war service in British and Indian Armies, 1939–46 (Major); rejoined Home Civil Service, 1946; Treasury, 1952–62; FCO, 1962; service overseas at Delhi, Kuala Lumpur, Jesselton, Prague, Washington, Hong Kong; retired as Counsellor, 1977. *Address:* 55 Chancellor House, Mount Ephraim, Tunbridge Wells, Kent TN4 8BT.

BARROW, Captain Michael Ernest, DSO 1982; RN; *b* 21 May 1932; *s* of late Captain Guy Runciman Barrow, OBE, RN and late Barbara Barrow (*née* Heinekey); *m* 1962, Judith Ann (*née* Cooper); two *s* one *d*. *Educ:* Wellesley House; RNC, Dartmouth. Served in HM Ships: Devonshire, Liverpool (trng, 1950–52); Agincourt, Euryalus, 1952–53; HM Yacht Britannia, 1954–56; Camperdown, 1958–59; Flag Lt to Cdre Hong Kong, 1956–58; commanded: Caunton, 1960; Laleston, 1961–62; Mohawk, 1963–64; Torquay, 1967–69; Diomede, 1973–75; Glamorgan, 1980–83 (served in Falkland Is conflict); RN Staff Course, 1966; Staff Flag Officer, Malta, 1970–71; Comdr RNC, Dartmouth, 1971–73; Dep. Dir, Recruiting, 1975–77; Asst Chief of Staff (Ops) to Comdr, Allied Naval Forces Southern Europe, Naples, 1978–80; ADC to the Queen, 1982–83; retired RN 1983. Clerk to the Worshipful Co. of Haberdashers, 1983–95. Gentleman Usher to Her Majesty, 1984–. *Recreations:* sailing, skiing, gardening. *Address:* Heathfield, Shear Hill, Petersfield, Hampshire GU31 4BB. *T:* Petersfield (01730) 264198. *Clubs:* Royal Naval Sailing; Royal Naval Ski.

BARROW, Dame Nita; *see* Barrow, Dame R. N.

BARROW, Captain Sir Richard John Uniacke, 6th Bt *cr* 1835; *b* 2 Aug. 1933; *s* of Sir Wilfrid John Wilson Croker Barrow, 5th Bt and (Gwladys) Patricia (*née* Uniacke); *S* father 1960; *m* 1961, Alison Kate (marr. diss. 1974), *yr d* of late Capt. Russell Grenfell, RN, and of Mrs Lindsay-Young; one *s* two *d*. *Educ:* Abbey Sch., Ramsgate; Beaumont Coll., Old Windsor. Commnd 2nd Lieut Irish Guards, 1952; served: Germany, 1952–53; Egypt, 1953–56; Cyprus, 1958; Germany, 1959–60; retired, 1960; joined International Computers and Tabulators Ltd; resigned 1973. *Heir: s* Anthony John Grenfell Barrow, *b* 24 May 1962.

BARROW, Dame (Ruth) Nita, DA 1980; GCMG 1990; FRCN 1980; Governor General of Barbados, since 1990; *b* 15 Nov. 1916. *Educ:* St Michael's Girls' School; Basic Nursing, Barbados (SRN), 1935–41; Midwifery Preparation, Trinidad Registered Midwife, 1941–42; Public Health Diploma, 1943–44, Nursing Educn, 1944–45, Univ. of Toronto; Sister Tutor's Diploma, Edinburgh, 1951–52; BSc Nursing, Columbia Univ., NY, 1962–63. Staff Nurse, Barbados Gen. Hosp., Private Duty Nursing, 1940–41; Nursing Instr, Basic Sch. of Public Health, Jamaica, 1945–51; Sister Tutor, Kingston Sch.

of Nursing, Jamaica, 1952–54; Matron, UCH, Jamaica, 1954–56; Principal Nursing Officer, Jamaica, 1956–63; WHO Nursing Advr, Caribbean Area, Region of the Americas, 1964–71; Associate Dir, 1971–75, Dir, 1975–81, Med. Commn, WCC. Ambassador Extraordinary and Plenipotentiary and Permanent Rep. of Barbados to UN, 1986–90. Mem., Editl Bd, Contact, Christian Med. Commn, Geneva. Gamaliel Lectr, Wisconsin, 1983. Hon. LLD: Univ. of W Indies, 1975; Toronto, 1987; Winnipeg, 1988; Spelman Coll., Atlanta; York Univ., Canada, 1990; Smith Coll., USA, 1991; Queen's Univ., Canada, 1991; LLD (*hc*) Adelphi Univ., NY, 1994; Hon. DSc McMaster, 1983; Hon. DHum: Maurice Brown, Ga, 1987; Mount St Vincent, Canada, 1988; Hon. DHumLit, Morris Brown Univ., Atlanta, 1987; Hon. DLitt, Wilfrid Laurier Univ., Canada, 1994; numerous honours and awards from local and national organizations, including: Presidential Medal, Brooklyn Coll., 1988; Christiane Reiman Award, Internat. Council of Nurses, Geneva, 1989; McManus Medal, Columbia Univ., 1990. Order of the Caribbean Community, 1994. *Publications:* papers on Nursing Educn and Primary Health Care. *Recreations:* travel, reading. *Address:* Government House, Barbados.

BARROW, Simon William; Headmaster, The Oratory School, since 1992; *b* 17 Jan. 1942; *s* of Alfred Francis Lendon Barrow and Ruth Mary Barrow; *m* 1977, Brenda Cora Mary Kelly; one *s* one *d*. *Educ:* Stonyhurst; Reading Univ. (BA Mod Hist). Asst Master, Caldicott Sch., Farnham Royal, 1963–69; The Oratory Sch., Woodcote, 1969– (Housemaster, 1971; Dep. Head, 1982). *Recreations:* Rugby refereeing, walking, gardening, giving others good advice. *Address:* Walled Garden House, The Oratory School, Woodcote, Reading RG8 0PJ. *T:* Checkendon (01491) 680207.

BARROWCLOUGH, Sir Anthony (Richard), Kt 1988; QC 1974; Parliamentary Commissioner for Administration, and Health Service Commissioner for England, Wales and Scotland, 1985–90; *b* 24 June 1924; *m* 1949, Mary Agnes Pery-Knox-Gore; one *s* one *d*. *Educ:* Stowe; New Coll., Oxford. Served RNVR, 1943–46 (Sub-Lieut and later Lieut). Called to the Bar, Inner Temple, 1949, Bencher 1982; Recorder, 1972–84. Part-time Member, Monopolies Commn, 1966–69; Mem., Council on Tribunals (and Mem., Scottish Cttee), 1985–90; Indep. Mem. Council, FIMBRA, 1991–94. Chm., Dartmoor Steering Gp, 1990–. *Recreation:* country pursuits. *Address:* The Old Vicarage, Winsford, near Minehead, Somerset TA24 7JE.

BARRY, Prof. Brian Michael, FBA 1988; Professor of Political Science, London School of Economics and Political Science, since 1987; *b* 7 Aug. 1936; *s* of James Frederick and Doris Rose Barry; *m* 1st, 1960, Joanna Hill Scroggs (marr. diss. 1988); one *s*; 2nd, 1991, Anni Parker. *Educ:* Taunton's Sch., Southampton; Queen's Coll., Oxford (MA; DPhil 1965). Lloyd-Muirhead Res. Fellow, Univ. of Birmingham, 1960–61; Rockefeller Fellow in Legal and Political Philosophy, and Fellow of Harvard College, 1961–62; Asst Lectr, Keele Univ., 1962–63; Lectr, Univ. of Southampton, 1963–65; Tutorial Fellow, University Coll., Oxford, 1965–66; Official Fellow, Nuffield Coll., Oxford, 1966–69 and 1972–75; Prof., Univ. of Essex, 1969–72 (Dean of Social Studies, 1971–72); Prof., Univ. of British Columbia, 1975–76; Fellow, Center for Advanced Study in the Behavioral Scis, 1976–77; Professor: Univ. of Chicago, 1977–82; California Inst. of Technology, 1982–86; European Univ. Inst., Florence, 1986–87. Fellow, Amer. Acad. of Arts and Scis, 1978. Founding Editor, British Jl of Political Science, 1971–72; Editor, Ethics, 1979–82. *Publications:* Political Argument, 1965; Sociologists, Economics and Democracy, 1970; The Liberal Theory of Justice, 1973; (with Russell Hardin) Rational Man and Irrational Society?, 1982; A Treatise on Social Justice: vol. 1, Theories of Justice, 1989, vol. 2, Justice as Impartiality, 1994; Democracy, Power and Justice: collected essays, 1989, rev. edn 1991; articles in learned jls. *Recreations:* music, theatre, cooking. *Address:* London School of Economics, Houghton Street, WC2A 2AE. *T:* 0171–955 7175.

BARRY, Daniel, CB 1988; Permanent Secretary, Department of the Environment for Northern Ireland, 1983–88; *b* 4 March 1928; *s* of William John Graham Barry and Sarah (*née* Wilkinson); *m* 1951, Florence (*née* Matier); two *s* one *d*. *Educ:* Belfast Mercantile Coll. FCIS, FSCA, FIHT. Local Government Officer with various NI Councils, 1944–68; Town Clerk, Carrickfergus Borough Council, 1968–73; Asst Sec. (Roads), Dept of the Environment for NI, 1973–76, Dep. Sec., 1976–80; Dep. Sec., Dept of Educn for NI, 1980–83. *Recreations:* golf, gardening, tobacco producing, wine making.

BARRY, Sir Edward; *see* Barry, Sir L. E. A. T.

BARRY, Edward Norman, CB 1981; Under Secretary, Northern Ireland Office, 1979–81, retired 1981; *b* 22 Feb. 1920; *s* of Samuel and Matilda (*née* Legge); *m* 1952, Inez Anna (*née* Elliott); one *s* two *d*. *Educ:* Bangor Grammar Sch. Northern Ireland Civil Service: Department of Finance: Establishment Div., 1940–51; Works Div., 1951–60; Treasury Div., 1960–67; Establishment Officer, 1967–72; Min. of Home Affairs, 1972–74; Asst Sec., N Ireland Office, 1974–79. *Recreations:* golf, Irish Football Association Ltd (Hon. Treasurer).

BARRY, James Edward; His Honour Judge Barry; a Circuit Judge, since 1994; *b* 27 May 1938; *s* of James Douglas Barry and Margaret (*née* Thornton); *m* 1963, Pauline Pratt; three *s*. *Educ:* Merchant Taylors' Sch., Crosby; Brasenose Coll., Oxford (schol.; MA Jurisp.). Called to the Bar, Inner Temple, 1963; in practice, NE Circuit, 1963–85; Stipendiary Magistrate for S Yorks, 1985–94; a Recorder, 1985–94. *Recreations:* reading, domestic pursuits. *Address:* Leeds Combined Court Centre, 1 Oxford Place, Leeds LS1 3BG.

BARRY, Sir (Lawrence) Edward (Anthony Tress), 5th Bt *cr* 1899; Baron de Barry in Portugal *cr* 1876; *b* 1 Nov. 1939; *s* of Sir Rupert Rodney Francis Tress Barry, 4th Bt, MBE, and Diana Madeline (*d* 1948), *o d* of R. O'Brien Thompson; *S* father, 1977; *m* 1st, 1968, Fenella Hoult (marr. diss. 1991); one *s* one *d*; 2nd, 1992, (Elizabeth) Jill Dawe, *d* of G. Bradley, Fishtoft. *Educ:* Haileybury. Formerly Captain, Grenadier Guards. *Heir:* *s* William Rupert Philip Tress Barry, *b* 13 Dec. 1973. *Address:* 4 The Gables, Argos Hill, Rotherfield, East Sussex TN6 3QJ. *T:* Crowborough (01892) 852322.

BARRY, Michael; *see* Bukht, M. M. J.

BARRY, Rt. Rev. (Noel) Patrick, OSB; Abbot of Ampleforth, since 1984; *b* 6 Dec. 1917; 2nd *s* of Dr T. St J. Barry, Wallasey, Cheshire. *Educ:* Ampleforth Coll.; St Benet's Hall, Oxford. Housemaster, Ampleforth Coll., 1954–64, Headmaster 1964–79. First Asst to Abbot Pres. of English Benedictine Congregation, 1985–. Chairman: Conference of Catholic Colleges, 1973–75; HMC, 1975; Union of Monastic Superiors, 1989–. *Address:* Ampleforth Abbey, York YO6 4EN.

BARRY, Peter; TD (FG) Cork South Central; *b* Cork, 10 Aug. 1928; *s* of Anthony Barry and Rita Costello; *m* 1958, Margaret O'Mullane; four *s* two *d*. *Educ:* Christian Brothers' Coll., Cork. Alderman of Cork Corp., 1967–73; Lord Mayor of Cork, 1970–71. TD: Cork City SE, 1969–82; Cork South Central, 1982–; opposition spokesman on labour and public services, 1972–73; Minister for: Transport and Power, 1973–76; Education, 1976–77; opposition spokesman on finance and economic affairs, 1977–81; Minister for the Environment, 1981–82; opposition spokesman on the environment, 1982; Minister for Foreign Affairs, 1982–87; opposition spokesman on foreign affairs, 1987–91, on industry and commerce, 1991–. Dep. Leader of Fine Gael Party, 1979–87, 1991–; Chm., Nat. Exec., 1982–84. Co-Chm., Anglo-Irish Conf., 1982–87. *Address:* Sherwood, Blackrock, Co. Cork.

BARRY, Maj.-Gen. Richard Hugh, CB 1962; CBE 1953 (OBE 1943); retired; *b* 9 Nov. 1908; *s* of Lieut-Col Alfred Percival Barry and Helen Charlotte (*née* Stephens); *m* 1st, 1940, Rosalind Joyce Evans (*d* 1973); one *s* two *d*; 2nd, 1975, Elizabeth Lucia Middleton (*d* 1994). *Educ:* Winchester; Sandhurst. 2nd Lieut Somerset LI, 1929; Staff Coll., Camberley, Capt., 1938; served War of 1939–45; BEF, SOE, AFHQ, Algiers. Military Attaché, Stockholm, 1947; Deputy Chief of Staff Western Europe Land Forces, 1948; Dir, Standing Group, NATO, 1952; Chief of Staff, HQ British Troops in Egypt, 1954–56; Imperial Defence Coll., 1957; Standing Group Representative, North Atlantic Council, 1959–62; retired, 1962. Maj.-Gen. 1959. Africa Star, 1943; 1939–45 Star; Defence, Victory Medals, 1945. *Recreation:* hunting. *Address:* Little Place, Farringdon, Alton, Hants GU34 3EH. *T:* Tisted (0142058) 8216. *Club:* Army and Navy.

BARSTOW, Dame Josephine (Clare), DBE 1995 (CBE 1985); opera singer, free-lance since 1971; *b* Sheffield, 27 Sept. 1940; *m* 1969, Ande Anderson; no *c*. *Educ:* Birmingham Univ. (BA). Debut with Opera for All, 1964; studied at London Opera Centre, 1965–66; Opera for All, 1966; Glyndebourne Chorus, 1967; Sadler's Wells Contract Principal, 1967–68, sang Cherubino, Euridice, Violetta; *Welsh Nat. Opera:* Contract Principal, 1968–70, sang Violetta, Countess, Fiordiligi, Mimi, Amelia, Simon Boccanegra; Don Carlos, 1973; Jenufa, 1975; Peter Grimes, 1978, 1983; Tatyana in Onegin, 1980; Tosca, 1985; Un Ballo in Maschera, 1986; The Makropoulos Case, 1994; *Covent Garden:* Denise, world première, Tippett's The Knot Garden, 1970 (recorded 1974); Falstaff, 1975; Salome, 1982; Santuzza, 1982; Peter Grimes, 1988 and 1995; Attila, 1990; Fidelio, 1993; *Glyndebourne:* Lady Macbeth (for TV), 1972; Idomeneo, 1974; Fidelio, 1981; *English Nat. Opera:* has sung all parts in Hoffman, Emilia Marty (Makropulos Case), Natasha (War and Peace) and Traviata; Der Rosenkavalier, 1975, 1984; Salome, 1975; Don Carlos, 1976, 1986; Tosca, 1976, 1987; Forza del Destino, 1978, 1992; Aida, 1979; Fidelio, Arabella, 1980; The Flying Dutchman, La Bohème, 1982; The Valkyrie, 1983; Don Giovanni, 1986; Lady Macbeth of Mtsensk, 1987, 1991; Street Scene, 1993; Jenufa, 1994. Other appearances include: Alice in Falstaff, Aix-en-Provence Festival, 1971; Nitocris in Belshazzar, Geneva, 1972; Jeanne, British première, Penderecki's The Devils, 1973; Marguerite, world première, Crosse's The Story of Vasco, 1974; Fidelio, Jenufa, Scottish Opera, 1977; Gayle, world première, Tippett's The Ice Break, 1977; US debut as Lady Macbeth, Miami, 1977; Musetta in La Bohème, NY Met., 1977; Salome, East Berlin, 1979 (Critics Prize), San Francisco, 1982; Abigaille in Nabucco, Miami, 1981; debut in Chicago as Lady Macbeth, 1981; new prod. of Jenufa, Cologne, 1981; La Voix Humaine and Pagliacci, Chicago, 1982; The Makropulos Case (in Italian), Florence, 1983; Gutrune, Göterdämmerung, Bayreuth, 1983; Die Fledermaus, San Francisco, 1984; Peter Grimes, 1984, La Traviata, 1985, Salome, 1987, Der Rosenkavalier, 1990, Houston; Benigna, world première, Penderecki's Die Schwarze Maske, Salzburg, 1986, Vienna Staatsoper, 1986; Manon Lescaut, USA, 1986; Tosca, Bolshoi, Tiblisi, 1986; Tosca, and Macbeth, Bolshoi, Riga, 1986; Macbeth, Zurich, 1986, Munich, 1987; Medea, Boston, 1988; Prokofiev's The Fiery Angel, Adelaide, 1988; Un Ballo in Maschera, Salzburg, 1989, 1990; Fanciulla del West, Toulouse, 1991; Gloriana, Opera North, 1993; Chrysothemis, Houston, 1993; Fidelio, 1992, Salome, 1994, Amsterdam. Sings in other opera houses in USA, Canada and Europe. Recordings include: Un Ballo in Maschera; Verdi arias; scenes from Salome, Medée, Makropulos case and Turandot; Kiss Me Kate; Kurt Weill's Street Scene, Gloriana. Fidelio medal, Assoc. of Internat. Opera Directors, 1985. *Recreation:* farm which she runs with her husband (she breeds pure-bred Arabian horses). *Address:* c/o John Coast, 31 Sinclair Road, W14 0NS.

BARSTOW, Stan; writer; *b* 28 June 1928; *s* of Wilfred Barstow and Elsie Gosnay; *m* 1951, Constance Mary Kershaw; one *s* one *d*. *Educ:* Ossett Grammar Sch. Employed in Engineering Industry, 1944–62, mainly as Draughtsman. Best British Dramatisation, Writers' Guild of GB, 1974; Royal TV Soc. Writers' Award, 1975. Hon. Fellow, Bretton Coll., 1985. Hon. MA Open Univ., 1982. *Radio: dramatisations:* A Kind of Loving, 1964; The Pity of it All, 1967; Bright Day, 1968; The Watchers on the Shore, 1971; We could always fit a sidecar, 1974; The Right True End, 1978; The Apples of Paradise, 1988; Foreign Parts, 1990; My Son, my Son, 1993. *Television: dramatisations:* A Raging Calm, 1974; South Riding, 1974; Joby, 1975; The Cost of Loving, 1977; Travellers, 1978; A Kind of Loving (from A Kind of Loving, The Watchers on the Shore, The Right True End), 1982; A Brother's Tale, 1983; The Man Who Cried, 1993. *Publications:* A Kind of Loving, 1960; The Desperadoes, 1961; Ask Me Tomorrow, 1962; Joby, 1964; The Watchers on the Shore, 1966; A Raging Calm, 1968; A Season with Eros, 1971; The Right True End, 1976; A Brother's Tale, 1980; A Kind of Loving: The Vic Brown Trilogy, 1982; The Glad Eye, 1984; Just You Wait and See, 1986; B-Movie, 1987; Give Us This Day, 1989; Next of Kin, 1991; In My Own Good Time, 1996; *plays:* Listen for the Trains, Love, 1970; Joby (TV script), 1977; An Enemy of the People (ad. Ibsen), 1978; The Human Element, and Albert's Part (TV scripts), 1984; (with Alfred Bradley): Ask Me Tomorrow, 1966; A Kind of Loving, 1970; Stringer's Last Stand, 1972. *Address:* c/o Lemon, Unna & Durbridge Ltd, 24 Pottery Lane, W11 4LZ.

BART, A. S.; *see* Schwarz-Bart.

BART, Lionel; composer, lyricist and playwright; *b* 1 Aug. 1930. Wrote lyrics for Lock Up Your Daughters, 1959; music and lyrics for Fings Ain't Wot They Used T'be, 1959; music, lyrics and book for Oliver!, 1960; music, lyrics and direction of Blitz!, also co-author of book with Joan Maitland, 1962; music and lyrics of Maggie May, 1964; music of Lionel, 1977. Has also written several film scores and many individual hit songs. *Films:* Serious Charge; In the Nick; Heart of a Man; Let's Get Married; Light up the Sky; The Tommy Steele Story; The Duke Wore Jeans; Tommy the Toreador; Sparrers Can't Sing; From Russia with Love; Man in the Middle; Oliver (gold disc for sound track, 1969); The Optimists of Nine Elms. Ivor Novello Awards as a song writer: three in 1957; four in 1959; two in 1960; for best original theme, radio and TV, 1989; Jimmy Kennedy, for life long achievement, 1985; Golden Break Award, 1990. Variety Club Silver Heart as Show Business Personality of the Year, 1960. Broadway, USA; Tony (Antoinette Perry) Award, etc (for Oliver!), best composer and lyricist, 1962. *Address:* c/o 8–10 Bulstrode Street, W1M 6AH.

BARTELL, Anne, (Mrs John Bartell); *see* Gibson, A.

BARTER, Nicholas Arthur Beamish; Principal, Royal Academy of Dramatic Art, since 1993; *b* 12 Sept. 1940; *s* of Paul André Valentine Spencer and Sylvia Theadora Essex Barter; *m* 1961, Brigid Alice Panet (marr. diss. 1977); one *s* one *d*. *Educ:* Cheltenham Coll.; Pembroke Coll., Cambridge (BA Hons, MA). ABC TV Trainee Directors Award, 1963; Asst Dir, Phoenix Th., Leicester, 1963–65; Dir of Prodns, Lincoln Theatre Royal, 1965–68; Dep. Artistic Dir, RSC Theatregoround, 1968; Dir, Ipswich Arts Th., 1968–71; Asst Drama Dir, Arts Council of GB, 1971–75; Artistic Dir, Unicorn Th., 1977–86 (Best Prodn for Young People Award, Drama mag., 1982, for Beowulf); Children's Th. Consultant, Los Angeles, 1986–; Course Dir, and Dep. Principal, RADA, 1988–93. Chm.,

Dharma Trust, 1990–. *Publications:* Playing with Plays, 1979; contrib. Theatre Qly, Theatre Internat. *Recreation:* pottery. *Address:* c/o Royal Academy of Dramatic Art, 62–64 Gower Street, WC1E 6ED. *T:* 0171–636 7076.

BARTHOLOMEW, Prof. David John, PhD; FBA 1987; Professor of Statistics, London School of Economics, since 1973 (Pro-Director, 1988–91); *b* 6 Aug. 1931; *s* of Albert and Joyce Bartholomew; *m* 1955, Marian Elsie Lake; two *d. Educ:* University College London (BSc, PhD). Scientist, NCB, 1955–57; Lectr in Stats, Univ. of Keele, 1957–60; Lectr, then Sen. Lectr, UCW, Aberystwyth, 1960–67; Prof. of Stats, Univ. of Kent, 1967–73. Pres., Royal Statistical Soc., 1993–95 (Hon. Sec., 1976–82; Treas., 1989–93); Vice-Pres., Manpower Soc., 1987–. *Publications:* (jtly) Backbench Opinion in the House of Commons 1955–1959, 1961; Stochastic Models for Social Processes, 1967, 3rd edn 1982; (jtly) Let's Look at the Figures: the quantitative approach to human affairs, 1971; (jtly) Statistical Inference Under Order Restrictions, 1972; (jtly) Statistical Techniques for Manpower Planning, 1979, 2nd edn 1991; Mathematical Methods in Social Science, 1981; God of Chance, 1984; Latent Variable Models and Factor Analysis, 1987; Uncertain Belief, 1995; The Statistical Approach to Social Measurement, 1996; papers in statistical and social science jls. *Recreations:* gardening, steam railways, theology. *Address:* Department of Statistics, London School of Economics, Houghton Street, WC2A 2AE. *T:* 0171–955 7648.

BARTLE, Ronald David; a Metropolitan Stipendiary Magistrate since 1972; *b* 14 April 1929; *s* of late Rev. George Clement Bartle and Winifred Marie Bartle; *m* 1st, 1963; one *s* one *d;* 2nd, 1981, Hisako (*née* Yagi). *Educ:* St John's Sch., Leatherhead; Jesus Coll., Cambridge (MA). Nat. Service, 1947–49 (Army Athletic Colours). Called to Bar, Lincoln's Inn, 1954; practised at Criminal Bar, 1954–72; a Dep. Circuit Judge, 1975–79; a Chm., Inner London Juvenile Courts, 1975–79. Member: Home Office Council on Drug Abuse, 1987–; Home Office Cttee on Magistrates' Court Procedure, 1989–. Lectr on Advocacy, Council of Legal Educn, 1984–89. Contested (C) Islington N, 1958, 1959; Mem., Essex CC, 1963–66. Mem., Lawyers' Christian Fellowship. Freeman, City of London, 1976; Liveryman, Basketmakers' Co., 1976– (Steward, 1990). Patron, Pathway to Recovery Trust. *Publications:* Introduction to Shipping Law, 1958; The Police Officer in Court, 1984; Crime and the New Magistrate, 1985; The Law and the Lawless, 1987; (contrib.) Atkin's Court Forms and Precedents; contrib. to legal jls. *Recreations:* music, reading, swimming. *Address:* Bow Street Magistrates' Court, WC2E 7AS. *Clubs:* Garrick, Lansdowne.

BARTLEET, Rt. Rev. David Henry; Bishop Suffragan of Tonbridge, 1982–93; *b* 11 April 1929; *s* of Edmund Arthur Bartleet and Helen Bartleet (*née* Holford); *m* 1956, Jean Mary (*née* Rees); one *s* two *d. Educ:* St Edward's School, Oxford; AA School of Architecture, London; St Peter's Hall, Oxford; Westcott House, Cambridge. Curate: St Mary-le-Tower, Ipswich, 1957–60; St George's, Doncaster (in charge of St Edmund's), 1960–64; Vicar: Edenbridge, Kent, 1964–73; Bromley, Kent, 1973–82. *Recreations:* music, architecture, icons. *Address:* 21 Lee Road, Aldeburgh, Suffolk IP15 5EY. *T:* Aldeburgh (01728) 452724.

BARTLES-SMITH, Ven. Douglas Leslie; Archdeacon of Southwark, since 1985; *b* 3 June 1937; *s* of late Leslie Charles and Muriel Rose Bartles-Smith; *m* 1967, Patricia Ann Coburn; two *s* one *d. Educ:* Shrewsbury School; St Edmund Hall, Oxford (MA); Wells Theol Coll. Nat. Service (2nd Lieut, RASC), 1956–58. Curate of St Stephen's, Rochester Row, SW1, 1963–68; Curate-in-charge, St Michael and All Angels with Emmanuel and All Souls, Camberwell, 1968–72; Vicar, 1972–75; Vicar of St Luke, Battersea, 1975–85; RD of Battersea, 1981–85. *Publications:* (co-author) Urban Ghetto, 1976; Opportunities for a Strong Church, 1993. *Recreations:* Shrewsbury Town Football Club, reading, walking, travel. *Address:* 1a Dog Kennel Hill, East Dulwich, SE22 8AA. *T:* 0171–274 6767.

BARTLETT, Andrew Vincent Bramwell; QC 1993; *b* 7 Oct. 1952; *s* of John Samuel Bartlett and Doris Jean Bartlett; *m* 1974, Elisabeth Jefferis. *Educ:* Jesus Coll., Oxford (BA). Called to the Bar, Middle Temple, 1974. *Address:* 1 Paper Buildings, Temple, EC4Y 7EP. *T:* 0171–583 7355.

BARTLETT, Charles; *see* Bartlett, Harold Charles.

BARTLETT, George Robert; QC 1986; a Recorder, since 1990; *b* 22 Oct. 1944; *s* of late Commander H. V. Bartlett, RN and of Angela (*née* Webster); *m* 1972, Dr Clare Virginia, *y d* of G. C. Fortin; three *s. Educ:* Tonbridge Sch.; Trinity Coll., Oxford (MA). Called to the Bar, Middle Temple, 1966. An Asst Parly Boundary Comr, 1992–. *Publication:* (ed) Ryde on Rating, 1991–. *Recreations:* cricket and other games. *Address:* 2 Mitre Court Buildings, Temple, EC4Y 7BX. *T:* 0171–583 1380.

BARTLETT, (Harold) Charles, RE 1961 (ARE 1950); RWS 1970 (ARWS 1959); President, Royal Society of Painters in Water Colours, 1987–92; painter and printmaker; *b* Grimsby, 23 Sept. 1921; *s* of Charles Henry and Frances Kate Bartlett; *m;* one *s; m* Olwen Jones, RE, RWS. *Educ:* Eastbourne Grammar Sch.; Eastbourne Sch. of Art; Royal College of Art (ARCA 1949). First one man exhibition in London, 1960. *Recreations:* music, sailing. *Address:* St Andrews, Fingringhoe, near Colchester, Essex CO5 7BG. *T:* Colchester (01206) 729406.

BARTLETT, Henry Francis, CMG 1975; OBE 1964; painter; HM Diplomatic Service, retired; *b* 8 March 1916; *s* of F. V. S. and A. G. Bartlett, London; *m* 1940, A. D. Roy. *Educ:* St Paul's Sch.; Queen's Coll., Oxford; Ruskin Sch. of Drawing; Univ. of California (Commonwealth Fellow). Min. of Inf., 1940–45; Paris, 1944–47; Vice-Consul Lyons, 1948–49; FO, 1949–50; Vice-Consul, Szczecin, 1950; Second, later First, Sec., Warsaw, 1951–53; FO, 1953–55; First Sec. (Commercial), Caracas, 1955–60; First Sec. (Inf.), Mexico City, 1960–63; Consul, Khorramshahr, 1964–67; Dep. High Comr, Brisbane, 1967–69; Counsellor, Manila, 1969–72 (Chargé d'Affaires, 1971); Ambassador to Paraguay, 1972–75. Hon. Prof., Nat. Univ. of Asunción, 1975. Exec. Officer, Utah Foundation, Brisbane, 1976–89. Exhibitions of painting: Paris, 1947; London, 1950; Caracas, 1957, 1959; Mexico City, 1962; Brisbane, 1969, 1978, 1981, 1983, 1985, 1988, 1990, 1992, 1994. Represented: Commonwealth Art Bank; Queensland and S Aust. State Galleries; Queensland Univ. of Technol.; Brisbane Civic Art Gall.; Bendigo Art Gall. Trustee: Queensland Art Gallery, 1977–87; Qld Cultural Centre Trust, 1980–87. *Recreation:* painting. *Address:* 14 Bowen Place, 341 Bowen Terrace, New Farm, Brisbane, Qld 4005, Australia.

BARTLETT, Sir John (Hardington), 4th Bt *cr* 1913, of Hardington Mandeville, Somerset; Chairman and Director of various companies; *b* 11 March 1938; *s* of Sir (Henry) David (Hardington) Bartlett, 3rd Bt, MBE and of Kathleen Rosamund, *d* of late Lt-Col W. H. Stanbury; *S* father, 1989; *m* 1st, 1966, Susan Elizabeth Waldock (*d* 1970); one *d;* 2nd, 1971, Elizabeth Joyce, *d* of George Raine; two *s. Educ:* St Peter's Grammar Sch., Guildford. Career in engineering and construction. *Recreations:* joinery, woodwork, construction, fine wine. *Heir: s* Andrew Alan Bartlett, *b* 26 May 1973. *Address:* Hardington House, Ermyn Way, Leatherhead, Surrey KT22 8TW. *Club:* Naval.

BARTLETT, Maj.-Gen. John Leonard, CB 1985; Paymaster-in-Chief and Inspector of Army Pay Services, 1983–86, retired; *b* 17 Aug. 1926; *s* of late F. Bartlett and E. Bartlett; *m* 1952, Pauline (*née* Waite); two *s. Educ:* Holt Grammar Sch., Liverpool. MBCS, FBIM, jssc, psc, pfc. Commissioned Royal Army Pay Corps, 1946; served Hong Kong, Singapore, BAOR, War Office, Washington, Malta, Libya, HQ MELF, 1966–67 (despatches 1968); Staff Pmr and O i/c FBPO Berlin, 1968–69; GSO1 (Secretary) NATO Mil. Agency for Standardisation, 1969–71; Comd Pmr, Hong Kong, 1972–74; Col GS, MoD (ADP Coord.), 1974–76; Chief Pmr ADP and Station Comdr, Worthy Down, 1976–79; Chief Pmr, BAOR, 1980–82. Col Comdt, RAPC, 1987–90. Freeman, City of London, 1984. *Recreation:* golf. *Address:* c/o Lloyds Bank, The Square, Wickham, Hants PO17 5JQ. *Club:* Lansdowne.

BARTLETT, John Vernon, CBE 1976; MA; FEng, FICE, FASCE, FIE Aust.; Consulting Engineer; Consultant, Mott MacDonald Group (formerly Mott, Hay and Anderson), since 1988; *b* 18 June 1927; *s* of late Vernon F. Bartlett and Olga Bartlett (*née* Testrup); *m* 1951, Gillian, *d* of late Philip Hoffmann, Sturmer Hall, Essex; four *s. Educ:* Stowe; Trinity Coll., Cambridge. Served 9th Airborne Squadron, RE, 1946–48; Engineer and Railway Staff Corps, TA, 1978; Col 1986. Engineer with John Mowlem & Co. Ltd, 1951–57; joined staff of Mott, Hay & Anderson, 1957; Partner, 1966–88; Chm., 1973–88. Pres., ICE, 1983–84 (Vice-Pres., 1979–82; Mem. Council, 1974–77); Chm., British Tunnelling Soc., 1977–79. Gov., Imperial Coll., 1991–. FRSA 1975. Mem. Council, Fellowship of Engrg, 1982–86. Master, Engineers' Co., 1992–93 (Mem., Court of Assts, 1986–). Telford Gold Medal, (jointly) 1971, 1973; S. G. Brown Medal, Royal Soc., 1973. *Publications:* Tunnels: Planning Design and Construction (with T. M. Megaw), vol. 1, 1981, vol. 2, 1982; Ships of North Cornwall, 1995; contrib. various papers to ICE, ASCE, etc. *Recreations:* sailing, maritime history. *Address:* 6 Cottenham Park Road, SW20 0RZ. *T:* 0181–946 9576. *Clubs:* Hawks (Cambridge); Harlequin Football; Royal Engineers Yacht.

BARTLETT, Prof. Maurice Stevenson, FRS 1961; MA Cambridge, DSc London; Professor of Bio-mathematics in the University of Oxford, 1967–75, now Emeritus; *b* 18 June 1910; *s* of W. S. Bartlett, Scrooby; *m* 1957, Sheila, *d* of C. E. Chapman; one *d. Educ:* Latymer Upper Sch.; Queens' Coll., Cambridge. Wrangler, 1932; Rayleigh Prize, 1934. Asst Lectr in Statistics, University Coll., London, 1933–34; Statistician, Imperial Chemical Industries, Ltd, 1934–38; Lectr in Mathematics, Univ. of Cambridge, 1938–47. National Service, Min. of Supply, 1940–45. Visiting Prof. of Mathematical Statistics, Univ. of North Carolina, 1946; Prof. of Mathematical Statistics, Univ. of Manchester, 1947–60; Prof. of Statistics, Univ. of London (University Coll.), 1960–67. Mem. Internat. Statistical Institute, 1949, Hon. Mem., 1980; President: Manchester Statistical Soc., 1959–60; Biometric Soc. (Brit. Reg.), 1964–66; Internat. Assoc. Statistics Phys. Sci., 1965–67; Royal Statistical Society, 1966–67. Foreign Asociate, Nat. Acad. of Scis, USA, 1993. Hon. DSc: Chicago, 1966; Hull, 1976. Gold Medal, Royal Statistical Soc., 1969; Weldon Prize and Medal, Oxford, 1971. *Publications:* An Introduction to Stochastic Processes, 1955; Stochastic Population Models in Ecology and Epidemiology, 1960; Essays in Probability and Statistics, 1962; Probability, Statistics and Time, 1975; Statistical Analysis of Spatial Pattern 1976; Selected Papers, 3 vols, 1988; papers on statistical and biometrical theory and methodology. *Address:* Overcliff, 4 Trefusis Terrace, Exmouth, Devon EX8 2AX.

BARTLETT, Prof. Neil, FRS 1973; Professor of Chemistry, University of California, Berkeley, 1969–94, now Professor Emeritus; Principal Investigator, Chemical Sciences Division, Lawrence Berkeley Laboratory, since 1969; *b* Newcastle upon Tyne, 15 Sept. 1932; *s* of Norman Bartlett and Ann Willins Bartlett (*née* Vock), both of Newcastle upon Tyne; *m* 1957, Christina I., *d* of J. W. F. Cross, Guisborough, Yorks; three *s* one *d. Educ:* Heaton Grammar Sch., Newcastle upon Tyne; King's Coll., Univ. of Durham, Newcastle upon Tyne. BSc 1954, PhD 1958. Senior Chemistry Master, The Duke's Sch., Alnwick, Northumberland, 1957–58; Mem. Faculty (Dept of Chemistry), Univ. of British Columbia, 1958–66; Prof. of Chemistry, Princeton Univ., and Scientist, Bell Telephone Laboratories, Murray Hill, NJ, USA, 1966–69. Visiting Miller Prof., Univ. of Calif, Berkeley, 1967–68; Brotherton Vis. Prof., Univ. of Leeds, 1981; Erskine Fellow, Univ. of Canterbury, NZ, 1983; Vis. Fellow, All Souls, Oxford, 1984, etc. Foreign Associate: Nat. Acad. of Sciences, USA, 1979; Acad. des Scis, France, 1989; Member: Deutsche Akademie der Naturforscher Leopoldina, 1969; Der Akademie der Wissenschaften in Göttingen, 1977; Amer. Chem. Soc., etc; Fellow: Amer. Acad. of Arts and Scis, 1977; Chem. Inst. of Canada; Chem. Soc. (London). Sigma Xi. Hon. DSc: Waterloo, Canada, 1968; Colby Coll., Maine, USA, 1972; Newcastle, 1981; McMaster, 1992; Dr *hc:* Bordeaux, 1976; Ljubljana, 1989; Nantes, 1990; Hon. LLD Simon Fraser, 1993. Corday-Morgan Medal and Prize of Chem. Soc., 1962; Res. Corp. Plaque and Prize, 1965; E. W. R. Steacie Prize, 1965; Robert A. Welch Award, 1976; Medal of Inst. Jožef Stefan, Ljubljana, 1980; W. H. Nichols Medal, NY Section, ACS, 1983; Prix Moissan, 1988; Amer. Chem. Soc. Award for Distinguished Service to Inorganic Chemistry, 1989, for Creative Work in Fluorine Chemistry, 1992; Pauling Medal, 1989; Bonner Chemiepreis, Bonn, 1992. *Publications:* The Chemistry of the Monatomic Gases, 1975; scientific papers to: Jl of Chem. Soc., Inorganic Chem., etc; Mem. various editorial advisory bds in Gt Britain, France and USA. *Recreations:* water colour painting; walking in high country; gardening. *Address:* 6 Oak Drive, Orinda, CA 94563, USA; Chemistry Department, University of California, Berkeley, CA 94720, USA. *T:* (business) (510) 642–7259.

BARTON, Alan Burnell; Under Secretary, Finance Division, Department of Health, since 1993; *b* 2 May 1943; *s* of Charles Henry Barton and Rose Edith Barton; *m* 1969, Jirina Klapstova; one *s* one *d. Educ:* Glyn Grammar Sch., Ewell; Bristol Univ. (BSc Chem.). Operational Research Exec., NCB, 1966–73; Department of Health and Social Security: Principal, 1973–78; Asst Sec., 1979–90; Dir, Medical Devices Directorate, DoH, 1990–93. *Recreations:* jazz, theatre, country houses. *Address:* (office) Richmond House, 79 Whitehall, SW1A 2NS. *T:* 0171–210 4907

BARTON, Anne; *see* Barton, B. A.

BARTON, Prof. (Barbara) Anne, PhD; FBA 1991; Professor of English, Cambridge University, since 1984; Fellow of Trinity College, Cambridge, since 1986; *b* 9 May 1933; *d* of Oscar Charles Roesen and Blanche Godfrey Williams; *m* 1st, 1957, William Harvey Righter; 2nd, 1969, John Bernard Adie Barton, *qv. Educ:* Bryn Mawr College, USA. BA 1954 (*summa cum laude*); PhD Cantab 1960. Lectr in History of Art, Ithaca Coll., NY, 1958–59; Girton College, Cambridge: Rosalind Lady Carlisle Research Fellow, 1960–62; Official Fellow in English, 1962–72; Dir of Studies in English, 1963–72; Univ. Asst Lectr, later Univ. Lectr in English, Cambridge, 1962–72; Hildred Carlile Prof. of English and Head of Dept, Bedford Coll., London, 1972–74; Fellow and Tutor in English, New Coll., Oxford and CUF Lectr, 1974–84. Lectures: British Acad. Chatterton, 1967; Alexander Meml, Univ. Coll., Toronto, 1983; British Acad. Shakespeare, 1991; Northcliffe, UCL, 1994. Hon. Fellow: Shakespeare Inst., Univ. of Birmingham, 1982; New Coll., Oxford, 1989. Member Editorial Advisory Boards: Shakespeare Survey, 1972–; Shakespeare Quarterly, 1981–; Studies in English Literature, 1976–. *Publications:* Shakespeare and the Idea of the Play, 1962, 4th edn 1977, trans. Japanese 1982; Ben Jonson, Dramatist, 1984; The Names of Comedy, 1990; Byron: Don Juan, 1992; Essays, Mainly Shakespearean, 1994; essays and studies in learned jls. *Recreations:* opera, fine arts, travel. *Address:* Trinity

College, Cambridge CB2 1TQ. *T:* Cambridge (01223) 338466; Leverington Hall, Wisbech, Cambs PE13 5DE.

BARTON, Ven. (Charles) John Greenwood; Archdeacon of Aston, since 1990; *b* 5 June 1936; *s* of Charles William Greenwood Barton and Doris Lilian Leach. *Educ:* Battersea Grammar Sch.; London Coll. of Divinity (ALCD). Asst Curate, St Mary Bredin, Canterbury, 1963–66; Vicar, Whitfield with West Langdon, dio. Canterbury, 1966–75; Vicar, St Luke, South Kensington, 1975–83; Area Dean, Chelsea, 1980–83; Chief Broadcasting Officer, Church of England, 1983–90. Chm., BBC W Midlands Regl Adv. Council, 1995–; Mem., English Nat. Forum, 1995–. *Address:* 26 George Road, Edgbaston, Birmingham B15 1PJ. *T:* 0121–454 5525, *Fax:* 0121–455 6085. *Club:* National Liberal.

BARTON, Sir Derek Harold Richard, Kt 1972; FRS 1954; FRSE 1956; Distinguished Professor of Chemistry, Texas A and M University, since 1986; *b* 8 Sept. 1918; *s* of William Thomas and Maude Henrietta Barton; *m* 1st, 1944, Jeanne Kate Wilkins; one *s;* 2nd, 1969, Christiane Cognet (*d* 1992); 3rd, 1993, Judith Von-Leuenberger Cobb. *Educ:* Tonbridge Sch.; Imperial Coll., Univ. of London (Fellow, 1980). BSc Hons (1st Class) 1940; Hofmann Prizeman; PhD (Organic Chemistry) 1942; DSc London 1949. Research Chemist: on Govt project, 1942–44. Albright and Wilson, Birmingham, 1944–45; Asst Lectr, Dept of Chemistry, Imperial Coll., 1945–46, ICI Research Fellow, 1946–49; Visiting Lectr in Chemistry of Natural Products, Harvard Univ., USA, 1949–50; Reader in Organic Chemistry, 1950–53, Prof. of Organic Chemistry, 1953–55, Birkbeck Coll.; Regius Prof. of Chemistry, Glasgow Univ., 1955–57; Prof. of Organic Chem., 1957–70, Hofmann Prof. of Organic Chem., 1970–78, Imperial Coll.; Emeritus Prof. of Organic Chem., Univ. of London, 1978; Dir, Institut de Chimie des Substances Naturelles, CNRS, France, 1977–85. Arthur D. Little Vis. Prof., MIT, 1958; Karl Folkers Vis. Prof., Univs of Illinois and Wisconsin, 1959; Cecil H. and Ida Green Vis. Prof., Univ. of British Columbia, 1977; Firth Vis. Prof. in Chemistry, Univ. of Sheffield, 1978. Lectures: Tilden, Chem. Soc., 1952; Max Tischler, Harvard Univ., 1956; First Simonsen Memorial, Chem. Soc., 1958; Falk-Plaut, Columbia Univ., 1961; Aub, Harvard Med. Sch., 1962; Renaud, Michigan State Univ., 1962; Inaugural 3 M's, Univ. of Western Ontario, 1962; 3 M's, Univ. of Minnesota, 1963; Hugo Müller, Chem. Soc., 1963; Pedler, Chem. Soc., 1967; Sandin, Univ. of Alberta, 1969; Robert Robinson, Chem. Soc., London, 1970; Bakerian, Royal Society, 1970; Bose Endowment, Bose Inst., Calcutta, 1972; Stieglitz, Chicago Univ., 1974; Bachmann, Michigan, 1974; Woodward, Yale, 1974; First Smissman, Kansas, 1976; Benjamin Rush and Priestley, Pennsylvania State Univ., 1977; Romanes, Edinburgh, 1979; (first) Hirst, St Andrews Univ., 1980; Kharasch, Univ. of Chicago, 1987; Nelson Leonard, Illinois Univ., 1988; C. B. Purves, McGill Univ., 1988; Janôt, France, 1989; Rayson Huang, Hong Kong Univ., 1994. President: Section B, British Assoc. for the Advancement of Science, 1969; Organic Chemistry Div., Internat. Union of Pure and Applied Chemistry, 1969; Perkin Div., Chem. Soc., 1971; Pres., Chem. Soc., 1973–74. Mem., Council for Scientific Policy, 1965–68. Hon. Member: Sociedad Quimica de Mexico, 1969; Belgian Chem. Soc., 1970; Chilean Chem. Soc., 1970; Polish Chem. Soc., 1970; Pharmaceutical Soc. of Japan, 1970; Royal Acad. Exact Scis, Madrid, 1971; Acad. of Pharmaceutical Scis, USA, 1971; Danish Acad. Scis, 1972; Argentinian Acad. Scis, 1973; Societa Italiana per il Progresso delle Scienze, 1977; Chem. Soc. of Japan, 1982; Acad. des Scis, France, 1983; Royal Irish Acad. of Sci., 1985; Corresp. Mem., Argentinian Chem. Soc., 1970; Foreign Member: Acad. das Ciencias de Lisboa, 1971; Academia Nazionale dei Lincei, Rome, 1974; Indian Nat. Sci. Acad., 1990; Foreign Hon. Member American Academy of Arts and Sciences, 1960; Kitasato Inst. of Japan, 1990; Foreign Associate: Nat. Acad. of Sciences, USA, 1970; l'Académie des Sciences, Institute de France, 1978. Hon. Fellow: Deutsche Akad. der Naturforscher Leopoldina, 1967; Birkbeck Coll., 1970; ACS Centennial Foreign Fellow, 1976; Hon. FRSC 1985. Hon. DSc: Montpellier Univ., 1962; Dublin, 1963; St Andrews, Columbia NYC, 1970; Coimbra, 1971; Oxon, Manchester, 1972; South Africa, 1973; La Laguna, Western Virginia, 1974; Sydney, 1976; Valencia, Sheffield, Western Ontario, Weizman Inst. of Sci., 1979; London, 1984; Debrechen, 1986; Shanghai Inst. of Organic Chemistry, 1991; Marseille III, Nova de Lisboa, Cordoba (Argentina), Nacionel de Sur (Argentina), 1993; Hong Kong, 1994; Puebla, Salamanca, Conception, Tokushima, Munich, 1995; Hon. Dr: Frankfurt, 1980; Metz, 1981; Lyon, Uruguay, 1983; Paris-Sud, 1988; Hon. DrEng Stevens Inst. of Technol., 1984. Harrison Memorial Prize, Chem. Soc., 1948; First Corday-Morgan Medallist, Chemical Soc., 1951; Fritzsche Medal, Amer. Chem. Soc., 1956; First Roger Adams Medal, Amer. Chem. Soc., 1959; Davy Medal, Royal Society, 1961; Nobel Prize for Chemistry (jointly), 1969; First award in Natural Product Chemistry, Chem. Soc. of London, 1971; Longstaff Medal, Chem. Soc., 1972; B. C. Law Gold Medal, Indian Assoc. for Cultivation of Science, 1972; Medal, Soc. of Cosmetic Chem. of GB, 1972; Royal Medal, Royal Soc., 1972; Second Centennial of Priestley Chemistry Award, Amer. Chem. Soc., 1974; Medal of Union of Sci. Workers, Bulgaria, 1978; Univ. of Sofia Medal, 1978; Acad. of Scis, Bulgaria Medal, 1978; Copley Medal, Royal Soc., 1980; Hanbury Meml Medal, PSGB, 1981; first May & Baker Award, RSC, 1987; Chemical Pioneers award, Amer. Inst. of Chem., 1993; Priestley Medal, Amer. Chem. Soc., 1995. Order of the Rising Sun (2nd class), Japan, 1972; Officier, Légion d'Honneur, 1985 (Chevalier, 1974). *Publications:* numerous, in Journal of Chemical Society and Tetrahedron. *Address:* Department of Chemistry, Texas A and M University, College Station, Texas 77843–3255, USA.

BARTON, Maj.-Gen. Eric Walter, CB 1983; MBE 1966; BSc; FIMgt, FRGS; Director, Caravan Club Ltd, 1984–93; *b* 27 April 1928; *s* of Reginald John Barton and Dorothy (*née* Bradfield); *m* 1963 (marr. diss. 1983); two *s;* *m* 1984, Mrs Pamela Clare Frimann, *d* of late Reginald D. Mason and of Doris Mason, Winchelsea. *Educ:* St Clement Danes Sch., London; Royal Military Coll. of Science (BScEng 1955). Dip. in Photogrammetry, UCL, 1960. FIMgt (FBIM 1979); FRGS 1979. Commnd RE, 1948; served Mid East, 1948–50; Arab Legion, 1951–52; seconded to Dir, Overseas Surveys, E Africa, 1957–59; Sen. Instr, Sch. of Mil. Survey, 1961–63; OC 13 Fd Survey Sqdn, Aden, 1965–67; Dir, Surveys and Prodn, Ordnance Survey, 1977–80; Dir of Mil. Survey, 1980–84. Major 1961, Lt-Col 1967, Col 1972, Brig. 1976, Maj.-Gen. 1980. Col Comdt, RE, 1982–87; Hon. Col, Field Survey Sqn, later 135 Indep. Topographic Sqn RE (V) TA, 1984–89. Pres., Field Survey Assoc., 1991– (Chm., 1984–86); Member: Council, Photogrammetric Soc., 1979–82; Nat. Cttee for Photogrammetry, 1979–84; Council, RGS, 1980–83; Council, British Schs Exploring Soc., 1980–84; Nat. Cttee for Geography, 1981–84. *Recreations:* swimming, water sports, numismatics. *Address:* c/o Barclays Bank, Haywards Heath, W Sussex. *Club:* Geographical.

BARTON, Maj.-Gen. Francis Christopher, CB 1966; CBE 1964; *b* 17 Jan. 1916; *s* of Rev. John Bernard Barton, Elphinstone House, Hastings; *m* 1939, Olivia Mary Darroll-Smith; two *d.* *Educ:* Haileybury Coll. 2nd Lieut, Royal Marines, 1934; Lieut-Col, 1956; Brig., 1961; Maj.-Gen., 1964. Comd 45 Commando, RM, 1958–60; Comd 3 Commando Brigade, RM, 1962–63; Comdt, Joint Warfare Establishment, Old Sarum, 1964–66; retired, 1966. Voluntary Help Organiser, Royal Victoria Hospitals, Bournemouth, 1967–80; Chm., Standing Conf., Voluntary Help Organisers, 1971–72. *Address:* Moorhaven, Frogham, Fordingbridge, Hants SP6 2AJ.

BARTON, Rev. Prof. John, DPhil, DLitt; Oriel and Laing Professor of the Interpretation of Holy Scripture, University of Oxford, since 1991; Fellow of Oriel College, Oxford, since 1991; *b* 17 June 1948; *s* of Bernard Arthur Barton and Gwendolyn Harriet Barton; *m* 1973, Mary Burn; one *d.* *Educ:* Latymer Upper Sch., Hammersmith; Keble Coll., Oxford (MA; DPhil 1974; DLitt 1988). Deacon and priest, 1973. University of Oxford: Jun. Res. Fellow, Merton Coll., 1973–74; Official Fellow, St Cross Coll., 1974–91; University Lectr in Theology (OT), 1974–89; Reader in Biblical Studies, 1989–91; Chaplain, St Cross Coll., 1979–91. Canon Theologian, Winchester Cathedral, 1991–. *Publications:* Amos's Oracles against the Nations, 1980; Reading the Old Testament: method in biblical study, 1984; Oracles of God: perceptions of ancient prophecy in Israel after the Exile, 1986; People of the Book?—the authority of the Bible in Christianity, 1988; Love Unknown: meditations on the Death and Resurrection of Jesus, 1990; What is the Bible?, 1991. *Address:* Oriel College, Oxford OX1 4EW.

BARTON, John Bernard Adie, CBE 1981; Advisory Director, Royal Shakespeare Company, since 1991 (Associate Director, 1964–91); *b* 26 Nov. 1928; *s* of late Sir Harold Montague Barton and Joyce Wale; *m* 1968, Anne Righter (*see* B. A. Barton). *Educ:* Eton Coll.; King's Coll., Cambridge (BA, MA). Fellow, King's Coll., Cambridge, 1954–60 (Lay Dean, 1956–59). Joined Royal Shakespeare Company, 1960; Associate Dir, 1964. Has adapted texts and directed or co-directed many plays for Royal Shakespeare Company, including: The Taming of the Shrew, 1960; The Hollow Crown, 1961; The Art of Seduction, 1962; The Wars of the Roses, 1963–64; Henry IV, Parts I and II, and Henry V, 1964–66; Love's Labour's Lost, 1965; Coriolanus and All's Well That Ends Well, 1967; Julius Caesar and Troilus and Cressida, 1968; Twelfth Night and When Thou Art King, 1969; Measure for Measure and The Tempest, 1970; Richard II, Henry V, and Othello, 1971; Richard II, 1973; King John, Cymbeline, and Dr Faustus, 1974; Perkin Warbeck, 1975; Much Ado About Nothing, The Winter's Tale, and Troilus and Cressida, 1976; A Midsummer Night's Dream, Pillars of the Community, 1977; The Way of the World, The Merchant of Venice, Love's Labour's Lost, 1978; The Greeks, 1979; Hamlet, 1980; The Merchant of Venice, Titus Andronicus and The Two Gentlemen of Verona, 1981; La Ronde, 1982; Life's a Dream, 1983; The Devils, 1984; Waste, Dream Play, 1985; The Rover, 1986; Three Sisters, 1988; Coriolanus, 1989; Peer Gynt, 1994. Directed: The School for Scandal, Haymarket, 1983, Duke of York's, 1983; The Vikings at Helgeland, Den Nationale Scene, Bergen, 1983; Peer Gynt, 1990, Measure for Measure, As You Like It, 1991, Oslo. Wrote and presented Playing Shakespeare, LWT, 1982, Channel 4, 1984; narrated Morte d'Arthur, BBC2, 1984; wrote The War that Never Ends, BBC2, 1990. *Publications:* The Hollow Crown, 1962 (and 1971); The Wars of the Roses, 1970; The Greeks, 1981. *Recreations:* travel, chess, work. *Address:* 14 DeWalden Court, 85 New Cavendish Street, W1M 7RA. *T:* 0171–580 6196.

BARTON, Ven. John Greenwood; *see* Barton, Ven. C. J. G.

BARTON, Roger; Member (Lab) Sheffield, European Parliament, since 1989; *b* 6 Jan. 1945; *s* of late Joseph and Doreen Barton; *m* 1965; two *s.* *Educ:* Burngreave Secondary Modern Sch.; Granville Coll. (Engrg Technician's Cert.). Fitter, 1961–81; Sheffield TUC and Labour Party Sec., 1981–89. Mem., Sheffield CC, 1971–90. *Recreations:* walking, gentle cycling, water sports. *Address:* Labour European Office, 2nd Floor, Barkers Pool House, Burgess Street, Sheffield S1 2HF. *Clubs:* Trades and Labour, Wortley Hall Labour (Sheffield).

BARTON-CHAPPLE, Dorothy, (Mrs Derek Barton-Chapple); *see* Tutin, Dorothy.

BARTOSIK, Rear-Adm. Josef C., CB 1968; DSC 1943; *b* 20 July 1917; *m* 1st, 1943, Cynthia Pamela Bowman; three *s* one *d;* 2nd, 1969, Jeannine Scott (*née* Bridgeman). Joined Polish Navy, 1935; served in Polish destroyers under British operational control, 1939–46; transf. to RN, 1948; commanded: HMS Comus, 1955–56; HMS Scarborough and 5th Frigate Sqn, 1960–61; HMS Seahawk (RN Air Station Culdrose), 1962–63, HMS London, 1964–65; Rear-Adm. 1966; Asst Chief of Naval Staff (Ops), 1966–68; retired 1968. Coordinating Dir, European Jt Org., Australia Europe Container Service and Australia NZ Europe Container Service, 1969–81, retired 1981. *Recreation:* picture framing. *Address:* 33 Cheval Place, SW7 1EW.

BARTTELOT, Col Sir Brian Walter de Stopham, 5th Bt, *cr* 1875; OBE 1983; psc; Vice Lord-Lieutenant for West Sussex, since 1994; Member, HM Body Guard of the Honourable Corps of Gentlemen at Arms, since 1993; *b* 17 July 1941; *s* of Lt-Col Sir Walter de Stopham Barttelot, 4th Bt, and Sara Patricia (who *m* 2nd, 1965, Comdr James Barttelot, RN retd), *d* of late Lieut-Col H. V. Ravenscroft; *S* father, 1944; *m* 1969, Hon. Mary Angela Fiona Weld Forester, OStJ, *y d* of 7th Baron Forester, and of Marie Louise Priscilla, CStJ, *d* of Sir Herbert Perrott, 6th Bt, CH, CB; four *d.* *Educ:* Eton; RMA, Sandhurst. Commnd Coldstream Guards, 1961; Temp. Equerry to HM the Queen, 1970–71. Camberley Staff Coll., 1974; GSO2, Army Staff Duties Directorate, MoD, 1975–76; Second in comd, 2nd Bn, Coldstream Guards, 1977–78; Mil. Sec. to Maj.-Gen. comdg London Dist and Household Div., 1978–81; GSO1, MoD, 1981–82; CO 1st Bn Coldstream Gds, 1982–85; GSO1, HQ BAOR, 1985–86; Regtl Lt-Col Comdg Coldstream Guards, 1986–92. Col, Foot Guards, 1989–92. Pres., W Sussex Scout Council, 1993–. Liveryman, Gunmakers' Co., 1981. DL W Sussex, 1988. *Heir:* *b* Robin Ravenscroft Barttelot [*b* 15 Dec. 1943; *m* 1987, Theresa, *er d* of late Kenneth Greenlees; one *s* one *d*]. *Address:* Stopham Park, Pulborough, W Sussex RH20 1EB. *Clubs:* Cavalry and Guards, Pratt's, Farmers'.

BARWELL, David John Frank; international business consultant; *b* 12 Oct. 1938; *s* of James Howard and Helen Mary Barwell; *m* 1968, Christine Sarah Carter; one *s.* *Educ:* Lancing College; Trinity College, Oxford; Institut des Hautes Etudes Internationales, Geneva. FCO, 1965; served: Aden, 1967; Baghdad, 1968; Bahrain, 1971; Cairo, 1973; FCO, 1976; Nicosia, 1982; Paris, 1985; FCO, 1989–92. *Recreations:* gardening, singing. *Address:* Duckyls Clock House, West Hoathly, Sussex RH19 4LP. *Club:* Athenæum.

BARWICK, David Robert, CBE 1976; QC 1977; Governor of British Virgin Islands, 1982–86; *b* 20 Oct. 1927; *s* of Jack Barwick and Kathleen Barwick (*née* Gould); *m* 1951, Margaret (*née* Funnell); one *s* two *d.* *Educ:* Christchurch Boys' High Sch.; Univ. of New Zealand (LLB). Barrister and Solicitor of the Supreme Court of New Zealand. Private practice, NZ, 1953–56; Asst Attorney-General, Judicial Comr, British Solomon Islands, 1956–62; Judge of the High Court of Western Pacific, Gilbert and Ellice Islands, 1962–67; Parliamentary Draftsman, Solicitor-General, Secretary for Justice, Actg Attorney-General, Malaŵi, 1967–76; Attorney-General: Solomon Islands, 1976; Cayman Islands, 1976–82. *Recreations:* painting, conchology, music, golf. *Address:* PO Box 83, Savannah Post Office, Grand Cayman, Cayman Islands. *T:* 71583. *Club:* Commonwealth Trust.

BARWICK, Rt. Hon. Sir Garfield (Edward John), AK 1981; GCMG 1965; Kt 1953; PC 1964; QC (Australia); Chief Justice of Australia, 1964–81; *b* 22 June 1903; *s* of late Jabez Edward Barwick and Lilian Grace Ellicott; *m* 1929, Norma Mountier Symons; one *s* one *d.* *Educ:* Fort Street Boys' High Sch., Sydney; University of Sydney, BA 1923; LLB (Hons) 1926. New South Wales Bar, 1927; KC 1941; Victorian Bar, 1945; KC (Vic) 1945; Queensland Bar, 1958; QC Queensland, 1958. Practised extensively in all jurisdictions: Supreme Court, High Court of Australia and Privy Council. Pres. NSW Bar Assoc., 1950–52 and 1955–56; Attorney-Gen. Commonwealth of Australia, Dec.

1958–Feb. 1964; Minister for External Affairs, Dec. 1961–April 1964. Judge ad hoc, Internat. Court of Justice, 1973–74. President: Law Council of Australia, 1952–54; Australian Inst. of Internat. Affairs, 1972–83. Hon. Bencher, Lincoln's Inn, 1964. Leader: Australian Delegation, SEATO Council, Bangkok, 1961, Paris, 1963; UN Delegation, 1960, 1962–64; Australian Delegation to ECAFE, Manila, 1963; Australian Delegation, ANZUS, Canberra, 1962, Wellington, 1963. Chancellor, Macquarie Univ., 1967–78. Pres., NSW Inst. for Deaf and Blind Children, 1976–. Hon. LLD: Sydney, 1972; Macquarie, 1987. *Recreations:* fishing, yachting. *Address:* 71 The Cotswolds, Curagul and Bobbin Head Roads, North Turramurra, NSW 2074, Australia. *Clubs:* Australian (Sydney); Royal Sydney Yacht Squadron; Hon. Member: Pioneers' (Australasian); Tattersalls; City Tattersalls; Middle Harbour Yacht.

BARYSHNIKOV, Mikhail; ballet dancer and company director; with Mark Morris formed White Oak Dance Project, 1990; *b* 28 Jan. 1948; *s* of Nicolai Baryshnikov and Alexandra (*née* Kisselov). *Educ:* Ballet Sch. of Riga, Latvia; Kirov Ballet Sch., Leningrad. Soloist, Kirov Ballet Co., 1969–74; Principal Dancer, NY City Ballet, 1978–79; Artistic Dir, 1980–89, Principal Dancer, 1974–78 and 1980–89, American Ballet Theater. Guest Artist, 1974–, with: Royal Ballet; National Ballet of Canada; Hamburg Ballet; Ballet Victoria, Aust.; Stuttgart Ballet; Alvin Ailey Dance Co., and Eliot Feld Ballet, New York; Spoleto Festival. Repertoire includes: Shadowplay (Tudor); Le Jeune Homme et la Morte (Petit); Sacré du Printemps (Tetley); Prodigal Son, Apollo, Theme and Variations (Balanchine); Afternoon of a Faun (Robbins); Romeo and Juliet, Wild Boy (MacMillan); Configurations (Choo San Goh); Les Patineurs, A Month in the Country (Ashton); Spectre de la Rose, Le Pavillon d'Armide, Petrouchka (Fokine); Santa Fe Saga (Feld); La Sylphide, La Bayadère, Coppélia, La Fille mal gardée (Bournonville); Swan Lake (Sergeyev and Bruhn); The Nutcracker, Don Quixote (own choreography). Works created: Medea (Butler), 1975; Push Comes to Shove, and, Once More Frank (Tharp), Connotations on Hamlet (Neumeier), Pas de Duke (Ailey), Other Dances (Robbins), 1976; Variations on America (Feld), 1977; Rubies (Balanchine), Opus Nineteen (Robbins), 1979; Rhapsody (Ashton), 1980. Gold Medal: Varna Competition, Bulgaria, 1966; 1st Internat. Ballet Comp., Moscow, 1968 (also awarded Nijinsky Prize by Paris Acad. of Dance); Dance Magazine Award, NYC, 1978. *Films:* The Turning Point, 1978; White Nights, 1986; Dancers, 1987. *Publication:* (with Charles Engell France, photographs by Martha Swope) Baryshnikov at Work, 1976. *Recreation:* fishing.

BARZEL, Dr Rainer C.; Member of the Bundestag, Federal Republic of Germany, 1957–87; *b* 20 June 1924; *s* of Dr Candidus Barzel, Senior Asst Master, and Maria Barzel. *Educ:* studied Jurisprudence and Political Economy, Univ. of Cologne (Referendar, Dr jur.). With Govt of North Rhine-Westphalia, 1949–56; Federal Minister in the Adenauer Govt, for all-German affairs, Dec. 1962–Oct. 1963; Chairman: Cttee on Economic Affairs, German Fed. Parlt, 1977–79; Cttee on Foreign Affairs, 1980–82; Fed. Minister for Inter-German Affairs, 1982–83; Pres. of Bundestag, 1983–84. Coordinator for German-French cooperation, Feb.-Dec. 1980, 1986–90. Chm., CDU, 1971–73 and Chm., CDU/CSU Group in German Federal Parlt, 1964–73. Pres., German-French Inst., 1980–83. *Publications:* (all publ. in Germany): Die geistigen Grundlagen der politischen Parteien, 1947; Die deutschen Parteien, 1952; Gesichtspunkte eines Deutschen, 1968; Es ist noch nicht zu spät, 1976; Auf dem Drahtseil, 1978; Das Formular, 1979; Unterwegs—Woher und wohin, 1982; Im Streit und umstritten, 1986; Geschichten aus der Politik, 1987; Ermland und Masuren—Zu Besuch, aber nicht als ein Fremder, 1988; Plädoyer für Deutschland, 1989; (ed) Sternstunden des Parlaments, 1989; So Nicht, 1993. *Recreation:* skating. *Address:* Camphausen Allee 8, 53173 Bonn, Germany.

BARZUN, Jacques; University Professor Emeritus, Columbia University; *b* 30 Nov. 1907; *s* of Henri Barzun and Anna-Rose Martin; *m* 1936, Mariana Lowell (*d* 1979); two *s* one *d*; *m* 1980, Marguerite Davenport. *Educ:* Lycée Janson de Sailly; Columbia Univ. Instructor in History, Columbia Univ., 1929; Research Fellow, American Council of Learned Socs, 1933–34; Columbia University: Asst Prof., 1938; Associate Prof., 1942; Prof. of History, 1945–75; University Prof., 1967; Dean of Grad. Faculties, 1955–58, Dean of Faculties and Provost, 1958–67. Dir Emeritus, Council for Basic Educn; Dir, NY Soc. Library; Mem. Adv. Council, Univ. Coll. at Buckingham. Membre Associé de l'Académie Delphinale, Grenoble, 1952; Member: Amer. Acad. of Arts and Letters, USA (President, 1972–75, 1977–79); Amer. Acad. of Arts and Sciences; American Historical Assoc.; Amer. Philos. Soc.; FRSA, USA (Benjamin Franklin Fellow); FRSL. Seth Low Prof. of History, Columbia Univ., 1960; Extraordinary Fellow, Churchill Coll., Cambridge, 1961–. Literary Advisor, Charles Scribner's Sons Ltd, 1975–; Mem. Bd of Editors, Encyclopaedia Britannica, 1962–. Chevalier de la Légion d'Honneur. *Publications:* The French Race: Theories of its Origins, 1932; Race: A Study in Superstition, 1937 (revd, 1965); Of Human Freedom, 1939 (revd, 1964); Darwin, Marx, Wagner, 1941 (revd, 1958); Teacher in America, 1945 (revd, 1981); Berlioz and the Romantic Century, 1950, 4th edn 1982; Pleasures of Music, 1951, rev. edn 1977; Selected Letters of Byron, 1953, 2nd edn 1957; Nouvelles Lettres de Berlioz, 1954, 2nd edn 1974; God's Country and Mine, 1954; Music in American Life, 1956; The Energies of Art, 1956; The Modern Researcher (with Henry F. Graff), 1957, 5th edn 1993; The House of Intellect, 1959, 2nd edn 1961; Classic, Romantic and Modern, 1961; Science: The Glorious Entertainment, 1964; (ed) Follett's Modern American Usage, 1967; The American University, 1968, 3rd edn 1992; (with W. H. Taylor) A Catalogue of Crime, 1971, rev. edn 1989; On Writing, Editing and Publishing, 1971; Berlioz's Evenings with the Orchestra, 1956, 2nd edn 1973; The Use and Abuse of Art, 1974; Clio and the Doctors, 1974; Simple and Direct, 1975; Critical Questions, 1982; A Stroll with William James, 1983; A Word Or Two Before You Go, 1986; The Culture We Deserve, 1989; Begin Here, 1991; An Essay on French Verse for Readers of English Poetry, 1991; contrib. to leading US journals. *Address:* 1170 Fifth Avenue, New York, NY 10029, USA. *Club:* Century (New York).

BASHAM, Brian Arthur; Chairman, Warwick Corporate Ltd, since 1991; *b* 30 July 1943; *s* of Arthur Edgar Basham and Gladys Florence Alice (*née* Turner); *m* 1st, 1968, Charlotte Blackman; two *d*; 2nd, 1988, Eileen Wise. *Educ:* Brownhill Road Primary Sch., Catford; Catford Secondary Sch. GEC Export Clerk, 1961; Daily Mail City Office: Stock Exchange prices collector, 1962; City Press reporter, then chief sub-editor, 1963; Prodn Editor, Daily Mail City Page, 1964; Financial Journalist: Daily Telegraph, 1966; The Times, 1968; Fund Man., Cornhill Consolidated, 1971; Associate Dir, John Addey Associates, 1973; Founder, 1976, subseq. Dep. Chm., Broad Street Gp; Co-Founder and Dep. Chm., Primrose Care; Director: Cyrus Holdings: Cs Csiky Securities. *Recreations:* reading, physical work. *Address:* c/o Warwick Corporate Ltd, 12–13 Clerkenwell Green, EC1R 0DP. *T:* 0171–253 3300.

BASHFORD, Humphrey John Charles, MA; Headmaster, Hessle High School, 1964–81, retired; *b* 5 Oct. 1920; *s* of late Sir Henry Bashford, MD, FRCP, and late Margaret Eveline Sutton; *m* 1942, Alyson Margaret Liddle; one *s* three *d* (and one *s* decd). *Educ:* Sherborne Sch.; Clare Coll., Cambridge. MA Cambridge 1950. Served War of 1939–45: commissioned 2nd Bn Oxford Bucks LI, 1941; GSO3 HQ Airborne Corps 1944–46. Senior History Master, Leys Sch., Cambridge, 1947; Part-time Tutor, WEA, 1950; Headmaster, Wellingborough Sch., 1956–64. *Recreations:* gardening, fly-fishing. *Address:* 11 Cowgate, Welton, Brough, N Humberside HU15 1NB.

BASHMET, Yuri Abramovich; viola player; *b* 24 Jan. 1953; *m* Natalia Timofeevna; one *s* one *d*. *Educ:* Moscow State Conservatory. Winner, Munich International Viola Competititon, 1976; Founder and Dir, Chamber Orchestra Moscow Soloists,1989–. Has performed with many orchestras including: Berlin Philharmonic; Boston Symphony; Concertgebouw; LSO; Los Angeles Philharmonic; Montreal Symphony; first performance of viola concerti by Alfred Schnittke and Aleksander Tchaikovsky. *Address:* c/o Van Walsum Management, 26 Wadham Road, SW15 2LR. *T:* 0181–874 6344; Apartment 16, Nezhdanovoy str. 7, 103009, Moscow, Russia.

BASING, 5th Baron *cr* 1887; **Neil Lutley Sclater-Booth;** *b* 16 Jan. 1939; *s* of 4th Baron Basing and Jeannette (*d* 1957), *d* of late Neil Bruce MacKelvie, New York; *S* father, 1983; *m* 1967, Patricia Ann, *d* of late George Bryan Whitfield, New Haven, Conn; two *s*. *Educ:* Eton; Harvard Univ. (BA). *Heir:* *s* Hon. Stuart Whitfield Sclater-Booth, *b* 18 Dec. 1969.

BASINGSTOKE, Bishop Suffragan of, since 1994; **Rt Rev. Dr (Douglas) Geoffrey Rowell;** *b* 13 Feb. 1943; *s* of Cecil Victor Rowell and late Kate (*née* Hunter). *Educ:* Eggar's Grammar Sch., Alton, Hants; Winchester Coll.; Corpus Christi Coll., Cambridge (MA, PhD); MA, DPhil Oxon; Cuddesdon Theol Coll. Ordained deacon, 1968, priest 1969; Hastings Rashdall Student and Asst Chaplain, New Coll., Oxford, 1968–72; Hon. Asst Curate, St Andrew's, Headington, 1968–71; University of Oxford: Fellow, Chaplain and Tutor in Theology, Keble Coll., 1972–94; Lectr in Theology, 1977–94; Leader, expedn to Ethiopia, 1974; Pro-Proctor, 1980–81. Canon, Chichester Cathedral, 1981–; Vis. Canon-Theologian, St James' Episcopal Cathedral, Chicago, 1988. Member: C of E Liturgical Commn, 1981–91; C of E Doctrine Commn, 1991–; Anglican-Oriental Orthodox Internat. Forum, 1985, 1989, 1993. Examining Chaplain to: Bp of Leicester, 1979–90; Bp of Winchester, 1991–93. Hon. Dir, Archbp's Exam. in Theol., 1985–; Conservator, Mirfield Cert. in Pastoral Theol., 1987–; Mem., Theol Colls Assessment Gp, 1993. Gov., SPCK, 1984–94 (Vice-Pres., 1994–). Member: Council of Almoners, Christ's Hosp., 1979–89; Council of Mgt, St Stephen's Hse, Oxford, 1986–; Governor: Pusey Hse, Oxford, 1979–; Eggar's Sch., Alton, 1994–; Chm. Council, Hse of St Gregory and St Macrina, Oxford, 1987–94. Trustee, Scott Holland Lectureship, 1979– (Chm., 1992–). FRSA 1989. *Publications:* Hell and the Victorians: a study of the 19th century theological controversies concerning eternal punishment and the future life, 1974; (ed with B. E. Juel Jensen) Rock-Hewn Churches of Eastern Tigray, 1976; The Liturgy of Christian Burial: an historical introduction, 1977; The Vision Glorious: themes and personalities of the Catholic Revival in Anglicanism, 1983; (ed) Tradition Renewed: the Oxford Movement Conference Papers, 1986; (ed and contrib.) To the Church of England, by G. Bennett, 1988; (ed with M. Dudley) Confession and Absolution, 1990; The English Religious Tradition and the Genius of Anglicanism, 1992; (ed with M. Dudley) The Oil of Gladness: anointing in the Church, 1993; contributor to various books on theol subjects; articles in Jl Theol Studies, English Hist. Rev., Jl Ecclesiastical Hist., Church Hist., Anglican and Episcopal Hist., Internationale Cardinal-Newman Studien, Studia Urbania, etc. *Recreations:* travel in remote places, reading, music. *Address:* Little Acorns, Boyneswood Road, Medstead, Alton, Hants GU34 5EA. *T:* Alton (01420) 562925, *Fax:* (01420) 561251.

BASINGSTOKE, Archdeacon of; *see* Knight, Ven. A. F.

BASINSKI, Prof. Zbigniew Stanislaw, OC 1985; DPhil, DSc; FRS 1980; FRSC; Research Professor, Department of Materials Science and Engineering, McMaster University, Ont, 1987–92, now Professor Emeritus; *b* Wolkowysk, Poland, 28 April 1928; *s* of Antoni Basinski and Maria Zofia Anna Hilferding Basinska; *m* 1952, Sylvia Joy Pugh; two *s*. *Educ:* Lyceum of Krzemieniec, Poland; Polish Army Cadet Sch., Camp Barbara, Palestine, 1943–47; Univ. of Oxford (BSc, MA, DPhil, DSc). Research Asst, Univ. of Oxford, 1951–54; Staff Member, Dept of Mech. Engrg (Cryogenic Lab.), Massachusetts Inst. of Technol., 1954–56; Nat. Res. Council of Canada, 1956–87, latterly as Principal Res. Officer and Head of Materials Physics (Div. of Physics). Ford Distinguished Vis. Prof., Carnegie Inst. of Technol., Pittsburgh, USA, 1964–65; Commonwealth Vis. Prof., Univ. of Oxford, Fellow of Wolfson Coll., Oxford, 1969–70; Adjunct Prof., Carleton Univ., Ottawa, 1975–77, 1981–; Overseas Fellow, Churchill Coll., Cambridge, 1980–81. Dr *hc* Acad. of Mining and Metallurgy, S Staszic Univ., Krakow, 1991. *Publications:* many original research papers, mainly related to crystal defects and the mechanical properties of metals, in learned jls. *Recreations:* computer design, the stock market, winemaking, general reading. *Address:* Institute for Materials Research, McMaster University, 1280 Main Street West, Hamilton, Ontario L8S 4M1, Canada. *T:* (905) 5259140 (ext. 23498). *Clubs:* Oxford Union, Halifax House (Oxford).

BASKER, Prof. Robin Michael, DDS, Professor of Dental Prosthetics, University of Leeds, since 1978; Consultant in Restorative Dentistry, United Leeds Teaching Hospitals NHS Trust (formerly Leeds Western Health Authority), since 1978; *b* 26 Dec. 1936; *s* of Caryl Ashbourne Basker and Edna Crowden (*née* Russell); *m* 1961, Jacqueline Mary Bowles; two *d*. *Educ:* Wellingborough Sch.; London Hosp. Med. Coll., Univ. of London (BDS 1961); Birmingham Univ. (DDS 1969). LDSRCS 1961, MGDSRCS 1979. General dental practice, 1961–63; Lectr and Sen. Lectr, Univ. of Birmingham, 1963–78; Leeds University: Dean, Sch. of Dentistry, 1985–90; Chm., Bd of Faculty of Medicine and Dentistry, 1990–93. Hon. Scientific Advr, British Dental Jl, 1980–; British Standards Expert Advr, ISO TC/106, 1982–. Mem., Nuffield Foundn Inquiry into trng and educn of personnel auxiliary to dentistry, 1992–93. Member: Dental Cttee, Med. Defence Union, 1985–; GDC, 1986– (Treas., 1992–94; Chm., Registration Sub-Cttee, 1994; Chm., Educn Cttee, 1994–); President: British Soc. for Study of Prosthetic Dentistry, 1988 (Mem. Council and Sec., 1978–81); Yorks Br., BDA, 1991–92. Ext. Examr in Dental Subjects, Univs of Birmingham, Bristol, Dundee, London, Manchester, Newcastle upon Tyne, Sheffield, Wales and UC, Cork; Examr for Membership of Gen. Dental Surgery, RCS, 1979–84 (Chm. Examrs, 1987–92). FRSocMed. *Publications:* Prosthetic Treatment of the Edentulous Patient, 1976, 3rd edn 1992; Overdentures in General Dental Practice, 1983, 3rd edn 1993; A Colour Atlas of Removable Partial Dentures, 1987. *Recreations:* choral singing, walking. *Address:* Leeds Dental Institute, Clarendon Way, Leeds LS2 9LU. *T:* Leeds (0113) 233 6191.

BASKERVYLE-GLEGG, Maj.-Gen. John, MBE 1974; Senior British Loan Service Officer, Oman, 1990–93; *b* 10 Nov. 1940; *s* of late Lt-Col John Baskervyle-Glegg and Ethne Baskervyle-Glegg (*née* Woollan); *m* 1974, Jane Van der Noot. *Educ:* Eton; rcds, psc, osc. Grenadier Guards, 1960; served UK, Germany, Cyprus, Far East, Africa; Staff College, 1974; Comd 1st Bn Grenadier Guards, Berlin and UK, 1980–82; RCDS, 1982–84; Comdr 24 Inf. Bde, Catterick, 1984–86; Comdr British Mil. Adv. Training Team, Zimbabwe, 1987–89. *Recreations:* music, gardening, all sports, travel. *Address:* c/o National Westminster Bank, Colomberie, St Helier, Jersey JE4 8PD. *Clubs:* Cavalry and Guards, MCC; I Zingari, Free Foresters.

BASOV, Prof. Nikolai Gennadievich; Orders of Lenin, 1967, 1969, 1972, 1975, 1982; Hero of Socialist Labour, 1969, 1982; Order of the Patriotic War, II degree, 1985; Physicist, Russia; Member of the Praesidium of the Russian Academy of Sciences, 1967–90, Adviser, since 1990; Director, Quantum Radiophysics Division, P. N. Lebedev Physical Institute, since 1989; Professor, Moscow Institute of Physical Engineers; *b* 14

Dec. 1922; *s* of Prof. Gennady Fedorovich Basov and Zinaida Andreevna Molchanova; *m* 1950, Ksenia Tikhonovna Nazarova Basova; two *s*. *Educ:* secondary; Kiev Military-medical Sch.; Institute of Physical Engineers, Moscow. Joined the P. N. Lebedev Physical Institute, Moscow, 1948: Vice-Dir, 1958–73; Dir, 1973–89; Head, Lab. of Quantum Radiophysics, 1963–. Deputy, USSR Supreme Soviet, 1974–89 (Mem., Praesidium, 1982–89). Mem., Expert Council for President of Russian Fedn, 1991–93, for Prime Minister of Russian Fedn, 1993–. Hon. Chm., All-Union Soc., Znanie, 1990– (Chm. Bd, 1978–90); Vice-Pres., WFSW, 1983–90 (Hon. Mem., 1990–; Vice-Pres., Exec. Council, 1976–83). Editor-in-Chief: Priroda (Nature), Popular Sciences Magazine, 1967–90; Soviet Jl of Quantum Electronics, 1971–; Jl of Soviet Laser Res., 1980. Corresponding Mem., USSR Acad. of Sciences, 1962; Academician, 1966; Mem., Russian Optical Soc., 1991–. Fellow: Optical Soc. of America, 1974 (Mem. 1972); Indian Nat. Sci. Acad., 1987; Member: Acad. of Sciences of GDR, 1967; German Acad. of Natural Scis, Leopoldina, 1971; Bulgarian Acad. of Scis, 1974; Royal Swedish Acad. of Engineering Sciences, 1975; Polish Acad. of Scis, 1977; Czechoslovakian Acad. of Scis, 1977 (Gold Medal, 1975); Hon. Member: Bulgarian Phys. Soc., 1972; Urania Soc., GDR, 1980; Eur. Acad. of Arts, Scis and Humanities, 1980; TIT Soc. (Soc. for Dissemination of Natural Scis), Hungary, 1981; Internat. Acad. of Sciences, 1989; European Acad. of Sci. and Arts, Salzburg, 1991; Russian Acad. of Natural Scis, 1992. Hon. Mem., Mark Twain Soc., USA, 1977. Hon. Dr: Polish Mil.-Tech. Acad., 1972; Jena Univ., 1974; Prague Polytechnic Inst., 1975; Pavia Univ., 1977; Madrid Polytechnic Univ., 1985; Karl-Marx Stadt Technical Univ., 1988. Awarded Lenin Prize, 1959; Nobel Prize for Physics (jointly with Prof. A. M. Prokhorov of the P. N. Lebedev Physical Institute, Moscow, and Prof. C. H. Townes of MIT Cambridge, Mass, USA), 1964; A. Volta Gold Medal, Italian Physical Soc., 1977; E. Henkel Gold Medal, GDR, 1986; Kalinga Prize, UNESCO, 1986; Gold Medal, Slovakian Acad. of Sciences, 1988; M. V. Lomonosov Gold Medal, Acad. of Sciences of USSR, 1989; State Prize, USSR, 1989; Edward Teller Medal for Achievements in Fusion Energy, 1991. Order of Kirill and Mephodii (Bulgaria), 1981; Comdr's Cross, Order of Merit (Poland), 1986. *Address:* P. N. Lebedev Physical Institute, Russian Academy of Sciences, Lenin Prospekt 53, Moscow, Russia.

BASS; *see* Hastings Bass, family name of Earl of Huntingdon.

BASS, Bryan Geoffrey; Headmaster, City of London School, 1990–95; *b* 23 March 1934; *s* of Leslie Horace Bass and Mary Joyce Light; *m* 1956, Cecilia Manning; one *s* two *d*. *Educ:* Wells Cathedral School; Christ Church, Oxford (BA Hons English 1956; MA 1983). Teacher, Manchester Grammar School; Headmaster, Hymers College, Hull, 1983–90. *Recreations:* making music, cooking with friends. *Address:* 10 Gerard Road, Harrow, Middlesex HA1 2ND.

BASS, Harry Godfrey Mitchell, CMG 1972; HM Diplomatic Service, retired; *b* 26 Aug. 1914; *s* of late Rev. Arthur Edward Bass and Mildred Bass; *m* 1948, Monica Mary, *d* of late Rev. H. F. Burroughs (and eponym of the orchid *Oncidium flexuosum* x *Rodriguezia fragrans*); two *s* one *d*. *Educ:* Marlborough Coll.; Gonville and Caius Coll., Cambridge; St John's Coll., Oxford (BA (Oxon) 1937, MA (Cantab) 1940). British Museum, Dept of Egyptian and Assyrian Antiquities, 1939; Admiralty, 1940; Dominions Office, 1946; Asst Sec., Office of UK High Commissioner, Australia, 1948–51; Mem. of Secretariat, Commonwealth Economic Conference, 1952 and Meeting of Commonwealth Prime Ministers, 1953; Counsellor, Office of UK High Commissioner, Calcutta, 1954–57; Dep. UK High Commissioner, Federation of Rhodesia and Nyasaland, 1959–61; British Minister (Pretoria and Cape Town) in the Republic of S Africa, 1961–62; seconded to Central African Office, 1963–64; British Dep. High Commissioner, Ibadan, 1965–67; Head of Consular Dept, FCO, 1967–70; High Comr in Lesotho, 1970–73. Chapter Clerk, St George's Chapel, Windsor, 1974–77. Silver Jubilee Medal, 1977. *Recreation:* birdwatching. *Address:* Tyler's Mead, Reepham, Norfolk NR10 4LA.

See also Baron Crofton.

BASS, Rear-Adm. Paul Eric, CB 1981; CEng, FIMechE, MIMarE; *b* 7 March 1925; *s* of C. H. P. Bass, Ipswich; *m* 1948, Audrey Bruce Tomlinson; one *s*. *Educ:* Northgate School, Ipswich; Royal Naval Engineering Coll., Keyham. Served as Midshipman in HM Ships Cambrian, Mauritius, Premier and Rodney; Lieut in Belfast, Phoebe and Implacable; Lt Comdr in Ulysses; Comdr in Lion and Tiger; Naval Staff Course, 1962; Captain, Weapons Trials, 1969–72; NATO Defense Course, 1972–73; Asst Chief of Staff (Intelligence), SACLANT, 1973–75; Dir, Naval Manning and Training (Engineering), 1975–78; Flag Officer, Portsmouth and Port Admiral, Portsmouth, 1979–81, retired 1981. *Recreation:* sailing. *Clubs:* Royal Yacht Squadron; Royal Naval Sailing Association; Royal Naval and Royal Albert Yacht (Portsmouth).

BASSET, Bryan Ronald; CBE 1988; Chairman, Royal Ordnance plc, 1985–87; *b* 29 Oct. 1932; *s* of late Ronald Lambart Basset and of Lady Elizabeth Basset, *qv*; *m* 1960, Lady Carey Elizabeth Coke, *d* of 5th Earl of Leicester; three *s*. *Educ:* Eton; RMA Sandhurst. Captain, Scots Guards, 1952–57. Stockbroker, Toronto, Canada, 1957–59; Panmure Gordon & Co., Stockbrokers, 1959–72; Managing Director, Philip Hill Investment Trust, 1972–85. *Recreations:* farming, shooting, fishing. *Address:* 67 Cottesmore Court, Kelso Place, Stanford Road, W8 5QW. *T:* 0171–937 1803; Quarles, Wells-next-the-Sea, Norfolk NR23 1RY. *T:* Fakenham (01328) 738105. *Clubs:* White's, Pratt's.

BASSET, Lady Elizabeth, DCVO 1989 (CVO 1976); Extra Woman of the Bedchamber to Queen Elizabeth the Queen Mother, 1959–81 and since 1993 (Woman of the Bedchamber, 1981–93); *b* 5 March 1908; *d* of 7th Earl of Dartmouth, GCVO, TD and Ruperta, Countess of Dartmouth; *m* 1931, Ronald Lambart Basset (*d* 1972); one *s* (and one *s* decd). *Educ:* at home. *Publications: anthologies:* Love is My Meaning, 1973, 2nd edn 1988; Each in His Prison, 1978; The Bridge is Love, 1981. *Recreations:* riding, gardening, reading, writing, needlework. *Address:* 67 Cottesmore Court, Kelso Place, W8 5QW. *T:* 0171–937 1803.

See also B. R. Basset.

BASSETT, Douglas Anthony; Director, National Museum of Wales, 1977–86, now Senior Research Fellow; *b* 11 Aug. 1927; *s* of Hugh Bassett and Annie Jane Bassett; *m* 1955, Elizabeth Menna Roberts; three *d*. *Educ:* Llanelli Boys' Grammar Sch.; University Coll. of Wales, Aberystwyth. Asst Lectr and Lectr, Dept of Geology, Glasgow Univ., 1952–59; Keeper, Dept of Geology, Nat. Museum of Wales, 1959–77. Member: Water Resources Bd, 1965–73; Nature Conservancy Council (and Chm., Adv. Cttee for Wales), 1973–85; Secretary of State for Wales' Celtic Sea Adv. Cttee, 1974–79; Ordnance Survey Rev. Cttee, 1978–79; Adv. Cttee for Wales, British Council, 1983–90; Founder Mem. and first Chm., Assoc. of Teachers of Geology, 1967–68; Chm., Royal Soc. Cttee on History of Geology, 1972–82. Dir, Nat. Welsh-American Foundn, 1980–. Prince of Wales' Cttee, 1977–86. Hon. Professorial Fellow, University Coll., Cardiff, 1977. Editor: Nature in Wales, 1982–87; Manual of Curatorship, Museums Assoc., 1983–. Aberconway Medal, Institn of Geologists, 1985; Silver Medal, Czechoslavakian Soc. for Internat. Relns, 1985. Mem. White Order of Bards of GB, 1979; Officier de l'Ordre des Arts et des Lettres (received from Min. of Culture, Paris), 1983. *Publications:* Bibliography and Index of Geology and Allied Sciences for Wales and the Welsh Borders, 1897–1958, 1961; A Source-book of Geological, Geomorphological and Soil Maps for Wales and the Welsh Borders (1800–1966), 1967; Wales in miniature, 1993; contribs to various geological, museum and historical jls. *Recreations:* bibliography, chronology. *Address:* 4 Romilly Road, Cardiff CF5 1FH.

BASSETT, Nigel F.; *see* Fox Bassett.

BASSETT CROSS, Alistair Robert Sinclair; District Judge, Principal Registry, Family Division, High Court of Justice, since 1991; *b* 25 Aug. 1944; *s* of late Edward Bassett Cross and of Marguerite Sinclair Bassett Cross (*née* Mitchell); *m* 1977, Margaret Victoria Janes; one *s* one *d*. *Educ:* Bishop Challoner Sch., Shortlands; Coll. of Law, Lancaster Gate. FInstLEx 1971. Legal Exec. with Lawrence Graham, 1964–77; solicitor, 1980; Legal Exec. and Solicitor, Payne Hicks Beach, 1977–91 (Partner, 1988–91); Dep. County Court and Dist Registrar, 1990. Mem., Solicitors' Family Law Assoc., 1984; Mem., Family Mediators' Assoc., 1989; Accredited Family Mediator, 1990. HAC, 1965, commnd, 1969. Freeman, City of London, 1993. *Recreations:* family life, gardening, steam and model railway enthusiast. *Address:* Principal Registry (Family Division), Somerset House, Strand, WC2R 1LP.

BASSINGTHWAIGHTE, Keith; His Honour Judge Bassingthwaighte; a Circuit Judge, since 1991; *b* 19 Jan. 1943; *s* of Reginald and Barbara Bassingthwaighte; *m* 1966, Olwyn Burn. *Educ:* Ashford (Middx) County Grammar Sch. Admitted solicitor, 1967. Served RAF Legal Branch as Flt Lt, 1968, Sqdn Ldr 1973, Wing Comdr 1978 and Gp Capt. 1981; retired 1984. Chm., Industrial Tribunals (London Central and S regions), part-time 1984–85, full-time 1985–91; a Recorder of the Crown Court, 1987–91. Pres., Social Security Appeal, Medical Appeal, Disability Appeal, Child Support Appeal and Vaccine Damage Tribunals, 1994–. *Recreations:* golf, tennis, bridge, opera. *Address:* City Gate House, 39–45 Finsbury Square, EC2A 1PX. *Clubs:* Royal Air Force; Worplesdon Golf (Woking).

BASTIN, Prof. John Andrew, MA, PhD; FRAS; Professor, since 1971, and Head of Department of Physics, 1975–80, Queen Mary College, London University; *b* 3 Jan. 1929; *s* of Lucy and Arthur Bastin; *m*; one *s* one *d*; *m* 1985, Aida Baterina Delfino. *Educ:* George Monoux Grammar Sch., London; Corpus Christi Coll., Oxford. MA, PhD. Univ. of Ibadan, Nigeria, 1952–56; Univ. of Reading, 1956–59; Queen Mary Coll., Univ. of London, 1959–. Initiated a group in far infrared astronomy at Queen Mary College, 1960–70. *Publications:* papers on far infrared astronomy and lunar evolution. *Recreations:* English water colours, architecture, Renaissance and Baroque music. *Address:* 27 Endwell Road, SE4 2NE.

BATCHELOR, Prof. George Keith, FRS 1957; Emeritus Professor of Applied Mathematics, University of Cambridge, 1983; *b* Melbourne, 8 March 1920; *s* of George Conybere Batchelor and Ivy Constance Batchelor (*née* Berneye); *m* 1944, Wilma Maud Rätz, MBE; three *d*. *Educ:* Essendon and Melbourne High Schs; Univ. of Melbourne. BSc 1940, MSc 1941, Melbourne; PhD 1948, Adams Prize, 1951, Univ. of Cambridge. Research Officer, Aeronautical Research Laboratory, Melbourne, 1940–44; Fellow of Trinity Coll., Cambridge, 1947–; Lectr, Univ. of Cambridge, 1948–59, Reader in Fluid Dynamics, 1959–64, and Head of Dept of Applied Mathematics and Theoretical Physics, 1959–83; Prof. of Applied Maths, Univ. of Cambridge, 1964–83. Chairman: European Mechanics Cttee, 1964–87; Nat. Cttee for Theoretical and Applied Mechanics, 1967–72. Editor, Cambridge Monographs on Mechanics and Applied Mathematics, 1953–; Editor, Journal of Fluid Mechanics, 1956–. Mem. Council, Royal Soc., 1986–87; Mem., Royal Soc. of Sciences, Uppsala, 1972. Foreign Hon. Member: Amer. Acad. of Arts and Scis, 1959; Polish Acad. of Scis, 1974; French Acad. of Sci., 1984; Aust. Acad. of Sci., 1989; Emeritus MAE, 1990; For. Associate, US Nat. Acad. of Scis, 1994. Dr *hc* Grenoble, 1959; Tech. Univ. of Denmark, 1974; McGill, 1986; Michigan, 1990; Melbourne, 1994. Agostinelli Prize, Accad. Nazionale de Lincei, Rome, 1986; Royal Medal, Royal Soc., 1988; Timoshenko Medal, Amer. Soc. Mech. Engrs, 1988. *Publications:* The Theory of Homogeneous Turbulence, 1953; An Introduction to Fluid Dynamics, 1967; (ed) The Scientific Papers of G. I. Taylor, vol. 1, 1958, vol. 2, 1960, vol. 3, 1963, vol. 4, 1971; papers on fluid mechanics and its applications in scientific jls. *Address:* Cobbers, Conduit Head Road, Cambridge CB3 0EY. *T:* Cambridge (01223) 356387.

BATCHELOR, Sir Ivor (Ralph Campbell), Kt 1981; CBE 1976; FRCPE, DPM, FRCPsych; FRSE; Professor of Psychiatry, University of Dundee, 1967–82, now Emeritus Professor; *b* 29 Nov. 1916; *s* of Ralph C. L. Batchelor, FRCSE, FRCPE, and Muriel (*née* Shaw); *m* 1941, Honor Wallace Williamson; one *s* three *d*. *Educ:* Edinburgh Academy; Edinburgh Univ. MB ChB. FRCPsych 1971 (Hon. 1984). RAFVR, 1941–46; Sqdn Ldr, Comd Neuro-psychiatrist, CMF. Asst Phys. and Dep. Phys. Supt, Royal Edinburgh Hosp., and Sen. Lectr in Psychiatry, Univ. of Edinburgh, 1947–56; Phys. Supt, Dundee Royal Mental Hosp., 1956–62; Prof. of Psychiatry, Univ. of St Andrews, 1962–67. Member: Gen. Nursing Council for Scotland (Chm. Educn Cttee), 1964–71; Standing Med. Adv. Cttee, Scot., 1967–74; Adv. Cttee on Med. Research, Scotland, 1969–73; Scottish Council for Postgraduate Med. Educn, 1970–79; Chief Scientist Cttee, Scotland, 1973–82. Mem., Med. Services Review (Porritt) Cttee, 1958–62; Chm., Cttee on Staffing Mental Deficiency Hosps, 1967–70; Member: Cttee on Nursing (Briggs Cttee), 1970–72; Cttee on the Working of the Abortion Act (Lane Cttee), 1971–74; MRC (Chm. Clinical Research Bd, 1973–74, Chm. Neuro-Sciences Bd, 1974–75), 1972–76; MRC Health Services Res. Panel, 1981–82; Royal Commn on the Nat. Health Service, 1976–79; Indep. Sci. Cttee on Smoking and Health, 1980–86; UK Central Council for Nursing, Midwifery and Health Visiting, 1980–83; Scottish Hosp. Endowments Res. Trust, 1984–90. Chm. Trustees, Orchar Art Gall., Dundee, 1980–87. *Publications:* (with R. N. Ironside) Aviation Neuro-Psychiatry, 1945; Henderson and Gillespie's Textbook of Psychiatry, 8th edn 1956 and subseq. edns to 10th edn 1969; papers on clinical psychiatry and health services. *Recreation:* rural rambles and natural history. *Address:* 55 Hepburn Gardens, St Andrews, Fife KY16 9LS. *T:* St Andrews (01334) 73130. *Clubs:* Athenæum; Royal and Ancient Golf (St Andrews).

BATCHELOR, Prof. (John) Richard; Professor of Immunology, Royal Postgraduate Medical School, Hammersmith Hospital, 1979–94, now Professor Emeritus; *b* 4 Oct. 1931; *s* of B. W. Batchelor, CBE and Mrs C. E. Batchelor; *m* 1955, Moira Ann (*née* McLellan); two *s* two *d*. *Educ:* Marlborough Coll.; Emmanuel Coll., Cambridge; Guy's Hospital, London. MB, BChir Cantab, 1955; MD Cantab 1965. FRCPath 1991; FRCP 1995. Nat. Service, RAMC, 1957–59; Dept of Pathology, Guy's Hospital: Res. Fellow, 1959–61; Lectr and Sen. Lectr, 1961–67; Prof. of Transplantation Research, RCS, 1967; Dir, McIndoe Res. Unit, Queen Victoria Hosp., East Grinstead, 1967–78. Pres., Transplantation Soc., 1988–90 (Hon. Sec., then Vice-Pres. (E Hemisphere), 1976–80); Member Council, Nat. Kidney Res. Fund, 1979–86; Chm., Scientific Co-ord. Cttee, Arthritis and Rheumatism Council, 1988–. MRSocMed. Mem. Court, Skinners' Company. European Editor, Transplantation, 1964–. *Publications:* scientific articles upon tissue transplantation research in various special jls. *Recreations:* sailing; tennis; walking. *Address:* Little Ambrook, Nursery Road, Walton-on-the-Hill, Tadworth, Surrey KT20 7TU. *T:* Tadworth (01737) 2028. *Clubs:* Brooks's, Queen's.

BATE, Prof. (Andrew) Jonathan, PhD; King Alfred Professor of English Literature, University of Liverpool, since 1991; *b* 26 June 1958; *s* of Ronald Montagu Bate and Sylvia Helen Bate; *m* 1984, Hilary Gaskin (marr. diss. 1995). *Educ:* Sevenoaks Sch., Kent; St Catharine's Coll., Cambridge (MA; PhD 1984). Harkness Fellow, Harvard Univ., 1980–81; Research Fellow, St Catharine's Coll., Cambridge, 1983–85; Fellow, Trinity Hall, Cambridge and Lectr, Trinity Hall and Girton Coll., 1985–90; Research Reader, British Acad., 1994–96. Vis. Associate Prof., UCLA, 1989. *Publications:* Shakespeare and the English Romantic Imagination, 1986; (ed) Lamb, Essays of Elia, 1987; Shakespearean Constitutions, 1989; Romantic Ecology, 1991; (ed) The Romantics on Shakespeare, 1992; Shakespeare and Ovid, 1993; The Arden Shakespeare: Titus Andronicus, 1995; (ed) Shakespeare: an illustrated stage history, 1996. *Recreations:* cricket, tennis, opera, walking. *Address:* Department of English, University of Liverpool, PO Box 147, Liverpool L69 3BX. *T:* 0151–794 2704.

BATE, David Christopher; QC 1994; a Recorder, since 1991; *b* 2 May 1945; *s* of late Robert Leslie Bate and Brenda Mabel Bate (*née* Price); *m* 1973, Patricia Joan Bailey; three *s* one *d*. *Educ:* Hendon Co. Grammar Sch.; Manchester Univ. (LLB Hons). Called to the Bar, Gray's Inn, 1969; VSO (UNA) with Melanesian Mission, 1969–70; Crown Counsel, British Solomon Is Protectorate, 1971. *Recreation:* trying to sing in tune. *Address:* Queen Elizabeth Building, Temple, EC4Y 9BS. *T:* 0171–583 5766.

BATE, Sir David (Lindsay), KBE 1978 (CBE 1968); Chief Judge, Benue and Plateau States of Nigeria, 1975–77; Senior Puisne Judge, High Court of Justice, Northern States of Nigeria, 1968–75 (Puisne Judge 1957–68); *b* 3 March 1916; *m* 1948, Thadeen June, *d* of late R. F. O'Donnell Peet; two *s*. *Educ:* Marlborough; Trinity Coll., Cambridge. Called to Bar, Inner Temple, 1938. Commissioned, Royal Artillery, 1939 and served, Royal Artillery, 1939–46. Entered Colonial Legal Service, 1947; Crown Counsel, Nigeria, 1947–52; Senior Crown Counsel, Nigeria, 1952–54; Senior Crown Counsel, Northern Nigeria 1954–56; Solicitor-Gen., Northern Nigeria, 1956. *Recreations:* shooting, fishing. *Address:* 4029 Lanchaster Road, RR2, Duncan, British Columbia V9L 1N9, Canada.

BATE, Jonathan; *see* Bate, A. J.

BATE, Sir (Walter) Edwin, Kt 1969; OBE 1955; Barrister, Solicitor and Notary Public, Hastings, New Zealand, since 1927; *b* 12 March 1901; *s* of Peter and Florence Eleanor Bate; *m* 1925, Louise Jordan; two *s* one *d*. *Educ:* Victoria Univ., Wellington. LLM (first class hons), 1922. Admitted Barrister and Solicitor, 1922; practised: Taumarunui, NZ, 1923; Hastings, NZ, 1927. Mayor, City of Hastings, NZ, 1953–59; Chm., Hawke Bay Hosp. Bd, 1941–74; Pres., Hosp. Bds Assoc. of NZ, 1953–74; Pres., Associated Trustee Savings Banks of NZ, 1968 and 1969. OStJ 1961. Grand Master of Freemasons in NZ, 1972–74. *Recreation:* gardening. *Address:* 38 Busby Hill, Havelock North, New Zealand. *T:* Hastings (6) 8777448.

BATE, Prof. Walter Jackson; Kingsley Porter University Professor, Harvard University, since 1980; *b* 23 May 1918; *s* of William George Bate. *Educ:* Harvard Univ. AB 1939, PhD 1942. Harvard University: Associate Prof. of English, 1949–55; Prof. of English, 1955–62; Chm., Dept of English, 1955–62; Abbott Lawrence Lowell Prof. of the Humanities, 1962–80. Corresp. Fellow, British Acad., 1978. Member: Amer. Acad. of Arts and Sciences; Amer. Philosophical Soc.; Cambridge Scientific Soc. Christian Gauss Award, 1956, 1964, 1970; Pulitzer Prize for Biography, 1964, 1978; Nat. Book Award, 1978; Nat. Book Critics Award, 1978. *Publications:* Stylistic Development of Keats, 1945; From Classic to Romantic, 1946; Criticism: The Major Texts, 1952; The Achievement of Samuel Johnson, 1955; Prefaces to Criticism, 1959; Yale Edition of Samuel Johnson, Vol. II, 1963, Vols III–V, 1969; John Keats, 1963; Coleridge, 1968; The Burden of the Past and The English Poet, 1971; Samuel Johnson, 1977; (ed) Coleridge, *Biographia Literaria,* 1982; (ed) British and American Poets: Chaucer to the present, 1985; Harvard Scholars in English 1890–1990, 1992. *Recreation.* farming. *Address:* 3 Warren House, Cambridge, MA 02138, USA. *Club:* Saturday (Boston, Mass).

BATE, Maj.-Gen. William, CB 1974; OBE 1963; DL; Secretary to the Council of TAVR Associations, 1975–86 (Deputy Secretary, 1973–75); *b* 6 June 1920; *s* of S. Bate, Warrington; *m* 1946, Veronica Mary Josephine (*née* Quinn); two *s* two *d*. Commnd, 1941; war service in Burma, 1941–46 (despatches); Senior Instructor, RASC Officers Sch., 1947–50; Co. Comd 7th and 11th Armoured Divs, 1951–53; psc 1954; DAA&QMG Q (Ops), WO, 1955–57; jssc 1957; Admin. Staff Coll., Henley, 1958; Directing Staff, Staff Coll., Camberley, 1958–60; AA&QMG, Ops and Plans, HQ BAOR, 1961–63; CO, 2 Div. Column, BAOR, 1963–65; Col GS, Staff Coll., Camberley, 1965–67; Brig. Q (Maint.), MoD, 1967–68; ADC to the Queen, 1969; idc 1969; Dir of Admin. Planning (Army), 1970; Dir of Movements (Army), MoD, 1971–73. Col Comdt, 1974–86, Rep. Col Comdt, RCT, 1975, 1977, 1982, 1986. Hon. Col, 163 Movement Control Regt, RCT(V), TAVR, 1974–79. President: RASC/RCT Benevolent Fund; Waggon Club. Chm., Camberley Br., RNLI. FCIT 1967. DL Surrey, 1980. *Recreations:* cricket, tennis. *Address:* Netherbury, 14 Belton Road, Camberley, Surrey GU15 2DE. *T:* Camberley (01276) 63529. *Clubs:* East India, Devonshire, Sports and Public Schools, MCC.

BATELY, Prof. Janet Margaret, (Mrs L. J. Summers), FBA 1990; Sir Israel Gollancz Professor of English Language and Medieval Literature, King's College, University of London, since 1995 (Professor of English Language and Medieval Literature, 1977–95); *b* 3 April 1932; *d* of late Alfred William Bately and Dorothy Maud Bately (*née* Willis); *m* 1964, Leslie John Summers, sculptor; one *s*. *Educ:* Greenhead High Sch., Huddersfield; Westcliff High Sch. for Girls; Somerville Coll., Oxford (Shaw Lefevre Scholar). BA 1st cl. hons English 1954, Dip. in Comparative Philology (with distinction) 1956, MA 1958; FKC 1986. Asst Lectr in English, Birkbeck Coll., Univ. of London, 1955–58, Lectr, 1958–69, Reader, 1970–76. Lectures: Sir Israel Gollancz Meml, British Acad., 1978; Toller Meml, Manchester Univ., 1987. Chm., Scholarships Cttee, Univ. of London, 1988–91. Member: Council, EETS, 1981–; Exec. Cttee, Fontes Anglo-Saxonici, 1985–; Adv. Cttee, Internat. Soc. of Anglo-Saxonists, 1986–91; Adv. Cttee, Sources of Anglo-Saxon Lit. and Culture, 1987–. Governor: Cranleigh Sch., 1982–88; King's Coll. Sch., Wimbledon, 1991–94. Gen. Ed., King's Coll. London Medieval Studies, 1987–. *Publications:* The Old English Orosius, 1980; The Literary Prose of King Alfred's Reign: Translation or Transformation, 1980; (ed) The Anglo-Saxon Chronicle: MS.A, 1986; The Anglo-Saxon Chronicle: texts and textual relationships, 1991; The Tanner Bede, 1992; Anonymous Old English Homilies: a preliminary bibliography, 1993; contribs to: England Before the Conquest, 1971; Saints, Scholars and Heroes (ed M. H. King and W. M. Stevens), 1979; Five Hundred Years of Words and Sounds (ed E. G. Stanley and Douglas Grey), 1983; Learning and Literature in Anglo-Saxon England (ed M. Lapidge and H. Gneuss), 1985; Medieval English Studies (ed D. Kennedy, R. Waldron and J. Wittig), 1988; Words for Robert Burchfield's Sixty-Fifth Birthday (ed E. G. Stanley and T. F. Hoad), 1988; From Anglo-Saxon to Early Middle English (ed M. Godden *et al.*), 1994; Leeds Studies in English, Reading Medieval Studies, Eichstätter Beiträge, Medium Aevum, Rev. of English Studies, Anglia, English Studies, Essays and Studies, Classica et Mediaevalia, Scriptorium, Studies in Philology, Mediev. Arch., Notes and Queries, Archaeologia, Anglo-Saxon England, The Dickensian, Jl Soc. of Archivists, Bull. John Rylands Library, etc. *Recreations:* music, gardening. *Address:* 86 Cawdor Crescent, W7 2DD. *T:* 0181–567 0486.

BATEMAN, Sir Cecil (Joseph), KBE 1967 (MBE 1944); Chairman, G. Heyn & Sons Ltd, 1971–87; Director: Nationwide Building Society, 1970–84; Allied Irish Banks, 1970–80; Allied Irish Investment Bank Ltd, 1971–80; *b* 6 Jan. 1910; *s* of Samuel and Annie Bateman; *m* 1938, Doris M. Simpson; one *s* one *d*. *Educ:* Queen's Univ., Belfast. Served War of 1939–45, Royal Artillery (Major). Entered NI Civil Service, Nov. 1927. Dir of Establishments, Min. of Finance, 1958–63; Sec. to Cabinet and Clerk of Privy Council of N Ireland, 1963–65; Permanent Sec., Min. of Finance, and Head of Northern Ireland Civil Service, 1965–70. *Recreations:* golf, reading. *Address:* 26 Schomberg Park, Belfast BT4 2HH. *T:* Belfast (01232) 763484.

BATEMAN, Sir Geoffrey (Hirst), Kt 1972; FRCS; Surgeon, Ear, Nose and Throat Department, St Thomas' Hospital, London, 1939–71; *b* 24 Oct. 1906; *s* of Dr William Hirst Bateman, JP, Rochdale, Lancs; *m* 1931, Margaret, *d* of Sir Samuel Turner, Rochdale; three *s* one *d*. *Educ:* Epsom Coll.; University Coll., Oxford. Theodore Williams Schol. in Anat., Oxford Univ., 1926; BA Oxon, Hons sch. Physiol., 1927; Epsom schol. to King's Coll. Hosp., 1927; BM, BCh Oxon, 1930; FRCS, 1933; George Herbert Hunt Trav. Schol., Oxford Univ., 1933. RAFVR, Wing Comdr, 1939–45. Mem., Bd Governors, St Thomas' Hosp., 1948; Mem. Collegium Otolaryngologica Amicitiæ Sacrum, 1949; Hon. Corr. Mem. Amer. Laryngological Assoc., 1960; Past Mem. Council, RCS; Editor, Jl of Laryngology and Otology, 1961–77; Formerly Hon. Cons. on Oto-rhino-laryngology to the Army; Cons. Adviser in Otolaryngology, Dept of Health and Social Security. Pres., British Assoc. of Otolaryngologists, 1970–71 (Vice-Pres., 1967–70). Hon. FRSM 1978. *Publications:* Diseases of the Nose and Throat (Asst Editor to V. E. Negus, 6th edn), 1955; contributor various jls, etc. *Recreations:* golf, fishing. *Address:* Thorney, Graffham, Petworth, West Sussex GU28 0QA. *T:* Graffham (01798) 867314.

See also Sir R. M. Bateman.

BATEMAN, Leslie Clifford, CMG 1965; FRS 1968; Secretary-General, International Rubber Study Group, 1976–83; *b* 21 March 1915; *s* of Charles Samuel Bateman; *m* 1st, 1945, Marie Louise Pakes (*d* 1967); two *s*; 2nd, 1973, Mrs Eileen Joyce Jones (*née* Henwood); one step *s* one step *d*. *Educ:* Bishopshalt Sch., Uxbridge; University Coll., London. BSc, 1st cl. Hons Chem., 1935; PhD and Ramsey Memorial Medal, 1938; DSc 1955; Fellow, 1974. Oriel Coll., 1940–41; Chemist, Natural Rubber Producers Research Assoc., 1941–53; Dir of Research, 1953–62; Controller of Rubber Res., Malaysia, 1962–74; Chm., Internat. Rubber R&D Board, 1962–74. Mem., Malaysian Govt Task Force on Rubber Industry, 1983. Hon. DSc: Malaya, 1968; Aston, 1972. Colwyn Medal, 1963, and Jubilee Foundn Lectr, 1971, Inst. of Rubber Industry. Hon. PSM, Malaysia, 1974. *Publications:* (ed and contrib.) The Chemistry and Physics of Rubber-like Substances, 1963; numerous scientific papers in Jl Chem. Soc., etc, and articles on technical-economic status of natural rubber and its developments. *Recreations:* cricket, golf and other outdoor activities. *Address:* 3 Palmerston Close, Welwyn Garden City, Herts AL8 7DL. *T:* Welwyn Garden (01707) 322391.

BATEMAN, Mary-Rose Christine, (Mrs R. D. Farley), MA; Headmistress, Perse School for Girls, Cambridge, 1980–89; *b* 16 March 1935; *d* of Comdr G. A. Bateman, RN, and Mrs G. A. Bateman; *m* 1990, Richard Dashwood Farley. *Educ:* The Abbey, Malvern Wells, Worcs; St Anne's Coll., Oxford (MA); CertEd Cambridge. Assistant English Mistress: Westonbirt Sch., Tetbury, Glos, 1957–60; Ashford Sch., Kent, 1960–61; Lady Eleanor Holles Sch., Mddx, 1961–64; Head of English Department: Westonbirt Sch., Glos, 1964–69; Brighton and Hove High Sch., GPDST, 1969–71; Headmistress, Berkhamsted School for Girls, Herts, 1971–80. Administrator, Women's Nat. Cancer Control Campaign, 1989. *Address:* Yerdley House, Long Compton, Shipston on Stour, Warwickshire CV36 5LH. *T:* Long Compton (0160884) 231.

BATEMAN, Paul Terence; Chief Executive, Save and Prosper Group Ltd, since 1988; *b* 28 April 1946; *s* of Nelson John Bateman and Frances Ellen (*née* Johnston); *m* 1970, Moira (*née* Burdis); two *s*. *Educ:* Westcliff High Sch. for Boys; Univ. of Leicester (BSc). Save and Prosper Gp Ltd, 1967: graduate, secretarial dept, 1967–68; asst to Gp Actuary, 1968–73; Marketing Manager, 1973–75; Gp Marketing Manager, 1975–80; Gp Marketing and Develt Manager, 1980–81; Exec. Dir, Marketing and Develt, 1981–88. *Recreations:* yachting, squash. *Address:* Save and Prosper Group Ltd, 1 Finsbury Avenue, EC2M 2QY. *T:* 0171–588 1717; Bayside, 95 Thorpe Bay Gardens, Thorpe Bay, Essex SS1 3NW. *T:* Southend-on-Sea (01702) 587152. *Club:* Royal Burnham Yacht.

BATEMAN, Sir Ralph (Melton), KBE 1975; MA Oxon; Chairman, Stothert and Pitt, 1977–85; President, Confederation of British Industry, 1974–76 (Deputy President, 1973–74); *b* 15 May 1910; 3rd *s* of William Hirst Bateman, MB, BCh, and of Ethel Jane Bateman, Rochdale, Lancs; *m* 1935, Barbara Yvonne, 2nd *d* of Herbert Percy Litton and Grace Vera Litton, Heywood, Lancs; two *s* two *d*. *Educ:* Epsom Coll.; University Coll., Oxford. Turner & Newall Ltd: joined as management trainee, 1931; held various directorships in Group, 1942–76; Dir, 1957; Dep. Chm., 1959; Chm., 1967–76. Mem., NEDC, 1973–76. Mem. Council, Manchester Business Sch., 1972–76; Vice-Pres., Ashridge Management Coll.; Chm. of Council, University Coll. at Buckingham, 1976–79; Member Court: Manchester Univ.; Salford Univ. FCIS, CBIM; FRSA 1970. Hon. Fellow, UMIST, 1977. Hon. DSc: Salford, 1969; Buckingham, 1983. *Recreations:* family and social affairs. *Address:* 2 Bollin Court, Macclesfield Road, Wilmslow, Cheshire SK9 2AP. *T:* Wilmslow (01625) 530437.

See also Sir G. H. Bateman.

BATEMAN, Richard George Saumarez La T.; *see* La Trobe-Bateman.

BATEMAN, Richard Montague; Executive Secretary, Geological Society, since 1980; *b* 27 Nov. 1943; *s* of Gordon Montague Bateman and Joan Rhoda Bateman (*née* Puddifoot); *m* 1970, Gillian Elizabeth, *er d* of Noel Leslie Costain, *qv*; one *d*. *Educ:* Lyme Regis Grammar Sch. Entered Civil Service, 1964, MoD (Air), 1965–69; Chamber of Shipping of UK, 1969–75, Asst Sec., 1973–75; Gen. Council of British Shipping, 1975–80. Sec., Assoc. of European Geol Socs, 1987–92. Mem., Envmt Council, 1994. Associate Mem., Inst. of Dirs, 1989. *Recreations:* maritime history, classical music. *Address:* Geological Society, Burlington House, Piccadilly, W1V 0JU. *T:* 0171–434 9944. *Club:* Anchorites.

BATES; *see* Baker-Bates.

BATES, Alan (Arthur), CBE 1995; actor; *b* 17 Feb. 1934; *m* 1970, Victoria Ward (*d* 1992); one *s* (one twin *s* decd). *Educ:* Herbert Strutt Grammar Sch., Belper, Derbyshire; RADA. *Theatre:* English Stage Co. (Royal Court Theatre, London): The Mulberry Bush; Cards of Identity; Look Back in Anger; The Country Wife; In Celebration; London (West End): Long Day's Journey into Night; The Caretaker; The Four Seasons; Hamlet; Butley, London and NY (Evening Standard Best Actor award, 1972; Antoinette Perry Best Actor award, 1973); Poor Richard, NY; Richard III and The Merry Wives of Windsor, Stratford, Ont.; Venice Preserved, Bristol Old Vic; Taming of the Shrew, Stratford-on-Avon, 1973; Life Class, 1974; Otherwise Engaged, Queen's, 1975 (Variety Club of GB Best Stage Actor award, 1975); The Seagull, Duke of York's, 1976; Stage Struck,

Vaudeville, 1979; A Patriot for Me, Chichester, Haymarket, 1983, transf. Ahmanson, LA (Variety Club of GB Best Stage Actor award, 1983); Victoria Station, and One for the Road, Lyric Studio, 1984; The Dance of Death, Riverside Studios, Hammersmith, 1985; Yonadab, NT, 1985; Melon, Haymarket, 1987; Ivanov, and Much Ado About Nothing, Strand, 1989; Stages, NT, 1992; The Showman, Almeida, 1993. *Films:* The Entertainer, 1960; Whistle Down the Wind, 1961; A Kind of Loving, 1962; The Running Man, The Caretaker, 1963; Zorba the Greek, Nothing but the Best, 1964; Georgie Girl, 1965; King of Hearts, Far from the Madding Crowd, 1967; The Fixer (Oscar nomination), 1968; Women in Love, 1969; The Three Sisters (National Theatre Co.), 1970; A Day in the Death of Joe Egg, The Go-Between, 1971; Second Best (also prod.), 1972; Impossible Object, 1973; Butley, 1974; In Celebration, Royal Flash, 1975; An Unmarried Woman, 1977; The Shout, 1978; The Rose, 1979; Nijinsky, 1981; Quartet, 1982; The Return of the Soldier, 1983; The Wicked Lady, 1984; Duet for One, 1986; Prayer for the Dying, 1987; We Think the World of You, 1989; Mr Frost, Dr M, 1990; Hamlet, 1991; Losing Track, Secret Friends, 1992; Shuttlecock, 1994; Silent Tongue, 1994; Grotesque, 1995. *Television:* various plays; Plaintiff and Defendant, Two Sundays, The Collection, 1977; The Mayor of Casterbridge, 1978; Very Like a Whale, The Trespasser, 1980; A Voyage Round my Father, Separate Tables, An Englishman Abroad, 1983 (BAFTA Best TV Actor award, 1984); Dr Fisher of Geneva, 1984; One for the Road, 1985; Pack of Lies, 1988; The Dog It Was that Died, 1988; 102 Boulevard Haussmann, 1991; Unnatural Pursuits, 1992; Hard Times, 1994; Oliver's Travels, 1995. *Recreations:* swimming, driving, riding, reading. *Address:* c/o Chatto & Linnit, Prince of Wales Theatre, Coventry Street, W1V 7FE.

BATES, Alfred; Research Assistant, Union of Shop, Distributive and Allied Workers, since 1991; *b* 8 June 1944; *s* of Norman and Alice Bates; single. *Educ:* Stretford Grammar Sch. for Boys; Manchester Univ. (BSc); Corpus Christi Coll., Cambridge. Lectr in Maths, De La Salle Coll. of Educn, Middleton, 1967–74. MP (Lab) Bebington and Ellesmere Port, Feb. 1974–1979; PPS to Minister of State for Social Security, 1974–76; Asst Govt Whip, 1976–79; a Lord Comr, HM Treasury, 1979. Researcher and presenter, 1980–87, and an assistant producer, 1983–87, BBC TV; freelance media consultant, 1987–91. *Recreation:* cricket umpiring. *Address:* 116 Jackson Street, Stretford, Manchester M32 8BB.

BATES, Air Vice-Marshal David Frank, CB 1983; RAF retired; *b* 10 April 1928; *s* of late S. F. Bates, MusB, FRCO, and N. A. Bates (*née* Story); *m* 1954, Margaret Winifred (*née* Biles); one *s* one *d*. *Educ:* Warwick Sch.; RAF Coll., Cranwell. Commnd, 1950; served Egypt, Innsworth, UKSLS Australia, HQ Transport Comd, RAF Technical Coll., Staff Coll., Lyneham, El Adem, Staff Coll., Jt Services Staff Coll., Innsworth, and RCDS, 1950–73; Stn Comdr, Uxbridge, 1974–75; Dir of Personnel Ground, 1975–76; Dir of Personnel Management (ADP), 1976–79; AOA, RAF Support Comd, 1979–82. Bursar, Warwick Sch., 1983–85. Pres., Adastrian Cricket Club, 1977–82. *Recreations:* cricket, most sports, gardening, model railways. *Address:* c/o Lloyds Bank, 73 Parade, Leamington Spa, Warwicks CV32 4BB. *Clubs:* Royal Air Force, MCC.

BATES, Sir Dawson; *see* Bates, Sir J. D.

BATES, Eric; Chairman, Midlands Electricity Board, 1969–72; *b* 1 Nov. 1908; *s* of late John Boon Bates and late Edith Anne Bates; *m* 1933, Beatrice, *d* of late William Henry Herapath and late Beatrice Herapath; one *s* two *d*. Trained Ilford Elec. Dept.; Asst, County of London Elec. Supply Co., 1929–32; Consumers' Engr: West Kent Electric Co., 1933–36; Isle of Thanet Elec. Supply Co., 1937–42; Elec. Engr, Kennedy & Donkin, 1942–44; Consumers' Engr, Luton Elec. Dept, 1944–48; Sect. Head, Eastern Elec. Bd, 1948–49; Dep. Chief Commercial Officer, Eastern Elec. Bd, 1949–57; North Eastern Electricity Board: Chief Commercial Officer, 1957–62; Dep. Chm., 1962–67; Chm., *Recreation: 1967–69. Publications:* contribs to Proc. IEE. *Address:* Broadstairs, Kent.

BATES, Sir Geoffrey Voltelin, 5th Bt, *cr* 1880; MC 1942; *b* 2 Oct. 1921; *s* of Major Cecil Robert Bates, DSO, MC (3rd *s* of 2nd Bt) and Hylda, *d* of Sir James Heath, 1st Bt; *S* uncle, 1946; *m* 1st, 1945, Kitty Kendall Lane (*d* 1956); two *s*; 2nd, 1957, Olivia Gwyneth Zoë (*d* 1969) *d* of Capt. Hon. R. O. FitzRoy (later 2nd Viscount Daventry); one *d* (and one *d* decd); 3rd, 1971, Mrs Juliet Eleanor Hugolyn Whitelocke-Winter, *widow* of Edward Colin Winter and *d* of late Comdr G. C. A. Whitelocke, RN retd, and Mrs S. H. Whitelocke. *Educ:* Radley. High Sheriff, Flintshire, 1969. *Recreations:* hunting, shooting, fishing. *Heir: s* Edward Robert Bates, *b* 4 July 1946. *Address:* Gyrn Castle, Llanasa, near Holywell, Clwyd CH8 9BG. *T:* Prestatyn (017456) 3500.

BATES, Rt. Rev. Gordon; *see* Whitby, Bishop Suffragan of.

BATES, James P. M.; *see* Martin-Bates.

BATES, Sir (John) Dawson, 2nd Bt, *cr* 1937; MC 1943; Regional Director of the National Trust, retired 1981; *b* 21 Sept. 1921; *o s* of Sir (Richard) Dawson Bates, 1st Bt, PC, and Muriel (*d* 1972), *d* of late Sir Charles Cleland, KBE, MVO, LLD; *S* father, 1949; *m* 1953, Mary Murray, *o d* of late Lieut-Col Joseph M. Hoult, Norton Place, Lincoln; two *s* one *d*. *Educ:* Winchester; Balliol. BA 1949. FRICS. Served War of 1939–45, Major, Rifle Brigade (MC). *Heir: s* Richard Dawson Hoult Bates, *b* 12 May 1956. *Address:* Butleigh House, Butleigh, Glastonbury, Somerset.

BATES, John Gerald Higgs; Solicitor, Office of Inland Revenue, 1990–July 1996; *b* 28 July 1936; *o s* of Thomas William Bates and Winifred Alice Higgs; *m* 1971, Antoinette Lotery (*d* 1984); two *s*; *m* 1992, Alba Heather Phyllida Whicher. *Educ:* Kettering Grammar Sch.; St Catharine's Coll., Cambridge (MA); Harvard Law Sch. (LLM). Called to the Bar, Middle Temple, 1959. Practised at the Bar, 1962–66; Office of Solicitor of Inland Revenue, 1966–: Under Sec. (Legal), 1990. *Recreations:* cooking, wine, music. *Address:* Solicitor's Office, Inland Revenue, Somerset House, Strand, WC2R 1LB. *T:* 0171–438 6228.

BATES, Malcolm Rowland, FCIS; FRAeS; Deputy Managing Director, General Electric Co. plc, since 1985; *b* 23 Sept. 1934; *s* of late Rowland Bates and of Ivy Bates (*née* Hope); *m* 1960, Lynda Margaret Price; three *d*. *Educ:* Portsmouth Grammar Sch.; Univ. of Warwick (MSc); Harvard Business Sch. FCIS 1963; FRAeS 1993; CIMgt 1983. Flying Officer, RAF, 1956–58. Delta Group plc, 1959–68 (Man. Dir, Elkington & Co. plc, 1966–68); Adwest Gp plc, 1968–69; Industrial Reorgn Corp., 1969–70; Man. Dir, Spey Investments, 1970–72; Jt Man. Dir, Wm Brandt & Sons Ltd, 1972–75; General Electric Co. plc: Sen. Commercial Dir, 1976–80; Dir, 1980–. Non-exec. Dir, Enterprise Oil, 1991–. Chm., Engrg Deregulation Task Force, 1993–94; Member: Industrial Develt Adv. Bd, 1993–; Private Finance Panel, 1993–. FRSA 1993. Freeman: City of London, 1985; Painter-Stainers' Co., 1985. *Recreations:* classical music, tennis, reading. *Address:* Mulberry Close, Croft Road, Goring-on-Thames, Oxon RG8 9ES. *T:* Goring-on-Thames (01491) 872214. *Club:* Royal Air Force.

BATES, Michael Charles, OBE 1994; HM Diplomatic Service; Deputy Head of News Department, Foreign and Commonwealth Office, since 1995; *b* 9 April 1948; *s* of Stanley Herbert Bates and Winifred (*née* Watkinson); *m* 1971, Janice Kwan Foh Yin; one *s* one *d*. *Educ:* Stratton Grammar Sch. Joined HM Diplomatic Service, 1966: Attaché, New Delhi, 1971–74; Third Sec., Moscow, 1974–77; FCO, 1977–79; Second, later First Sec., Singapore, 1979–83; First Sec., Brussels, 1983–87; Press Officer to Prime Minister, 1987–89; Head, Parly Relns Unit, FCO, 1989–91; Dep. Head of Mission, Riga, 1991–92; Chargé d'Affaires, Bratislava, 1993–94; Ambassador, Slovak Republic, 1994–95. *Recreations:* music, reading, travel. *Address:* c/o Foreign and Commonwealth Office, King Charles Street, SW1A 2AH.

BATES, Michael Walton; MP (C) Langbaugh, since 1992; an Assistant Government Whip, since 1994; *b* 26 May 1961; *s* of John Bates and Ruth Walton; *m* 1983, Carole Whitfield; two *s*. *Educ:* Heathfield Sen. High Sch.; Gateshead Coll. Young Conservatives: Chm., Gateshead, 1982–84; Mem., Nat. Adv. Cttee, 1984–87; Chm., Northern Area, 1984–87; Chm., 1987–90, Pres., 1990, Gateshead Cons. Assoc. Chm., Northern Area Develt Initiative, 1990–92. Contested (C): Tyne Bridge, 1987; Langbaurgh, Nov. 1991. PPS to Minister of State, DSS, 1992–93, NI Office, 1994–95. Member: Select Cttee on Social Security, 1992; Select Cttee on Health, 1994. Secretary: H of C Motor Club, 1992–; Parly Christian Fellowship, 1993–. Vice-President: House Builders' Fedn, 1993–; Fedn of Econ. Develt Authorities, 1993–. Pres., Cleveland Autistic Soc., 1993–. *Recreations:* walking, northern art and artists, watching cricket (Yorkshire) and football (Middlesbrough). *Address:* House of Commons, SW1A 0AA. *T:* 0171–219 4203; (constituency office) 8 Westgate Road, Guisborough, N Yorks. *T:* Guisborough (01287) 636543. *Clubs:* Guisborough, Saltburn and Middlesbrough Conservative.

BATES, Rev. Paul Spencer; consultant, The Alexander Corporation, since 1994; *b* 1 Jan. 1940; *s* of Rev. John Spencer Bates and Margaret Annie Bates (*née* Harwood); *m* 1964, Freda Ann Spillard; two *s*. *Educ:* St Edmund's Sch., Canterbury; Corpus Christi Coll., Cambridge (MA); Lincoln Theol Coll. Deacon 1965, priest 1966; Asst Curate, Hartcliffe, Bristol, 1965–69; Chaplain, Winchester Coll., 1970–80; Dir of Training, dio. of Winchester, 1980–90; Residentiary Canon, Westminster Abbey, 1990–94. *Publications:* contrib. SPCK Taleteller series. *Recreations:* cricket, modern novels, gardening. *Address:* 67 Hillfield Park, Muswell Hill, N10 3QU. *T:* 0181–444 6854.

BATES, Peter Edward Gascoigne, CBE 1987; Deputy Chairman, Plessey Electronic Systems Ltd, 1976–86; *b* 6 Aug. 1924; *s* of James Edward Bates and Esmé Grace Gascoigne Bates (*née* Roy); *m* 1947, Jean Irene Hearn, *d* of late Brig. W. Campbell Grant; two *s* one *d*. *Educ:* Kingston Grammar Sch.; School of Oriental and African Studies, Univ. of London; Lincoln Coll., Oxford. Served War, Intelligence Corps, SEAC and Japan, 1943–46; Captain 1945. Malayan CS, 1947–55; Rolls-Royce, Aero Engine Div., 1955–57; Bristol Aircraft (later British Aircraft Corp.), 1957–64, Special Director, 1963; joined Plessey Co., 1964: Gen. Man., Plessey Radar, 1967–71; Man. Dir, Radar Div., 1971–76. Mem., UK Adv. Cttee, Mitsubishi Electric, 1991–. Member: CBI Overseas Cttee, 1981–86; BOTB, 1984–87. Member: Council, Electronic Engrg Assoc., 1973–86 (Pres. 1976); Council, SBAC, 1978–86 (Pres. 1983–84); Pres., AECMA, 1985–86. *Publication:* Japan and the British Commonwealth Occupation Force 1946–1952, 1993. *Recreations:* golf, theatre, reading history and biography. *Address:* 22 Haygarth Place, Wimbledon, SW19 5BX. *T:* 0181–946 0345. *Clubs:* Army and Navy; Royal Wimbledon Golf.

BATES, Ralph; *b* Swindon, Wilts, 3 Nov. 1899; *s* of Henry Roy and Mabel Stevens Bates; *m* 1940, Eve Salzman; one *s*. *Educ:* Swindon and North Wilts. Secondary Sch. After service in 16th Queen's Royal West Surreys, 1917–19, worked in Great Western Railway Factory at Swindon; in Spain, 1930–37; took active part in Republican politics in Spain; began literary career in 1933 as consequence of unemployment; Capt. in the Spanish Loyalist Army and in the International Brigade, Madrid sector, 1936–37; lecture tour in USA 1937–38; one year resident in Mexico, 1938–39; Adjunct Prof. of Literature, New York Univ. 1948–68, now Professor Emeritus of Literature. *Publications:* Sierra, 1933; Lean Men, 1934, Schubert, 1934, The Olive Field, 1936; Rainbow Fish, 1937; The Miraculous Horde, 1939; The Fields of Paradise, 1941; The Undiscoverables, 1942; The Journey to the Sandalwood Forest, 1947; The Dolphin in the Wood, 1949. *Recreations:* small boating, music. *Address:* 37 Washington Square West, New York, NY 10011–9181, USA. *T:* (212) 2544149.

BATES, His Honour Stewart Taverner, QC 1970; a Circuit Judge, 1989–95; *b* 17 Dec. 1926; *s* of John Bates, Greenock; *m* 1950, Anne Patricia, *d* of David West, Pinner; two *s* four *d*. *Educ:* Univs of Glasgow and St Andrews; Corpus Christi Coll., Oxford. Officers' Trng Sch., Bangalore, 1946, commnd Argyll and Sutherland Highlanders. Called to Bar, Middle Temple, 1954, Bencher, 1975, Lent Reader, 1992; a Recorder, 1981–89. Mem. Bar Council, 1962–66. Chm., Barristers' Benevolent Assoc., 1983–89; Member: Goodman Cttee on Charity Law and Voluntary Organisations, 1976; Cttee of Management, Inst. of Urology, Univ. of London, 1978–89; Chm., St Peter's Hosp. Special Cttee, 1986–89. *Recreations:* theatre, sailing, ski-ing. *Address:* The Grange, Horsington, Templecombe, Somerset BA8 0EF. *T:* Templecombe (01963) 70521. *Club:* Garrick.

BATESON; *see* de Yarburgh-Bateson, family name of Baron Deramore.

BATESON, John Swinburne, FIHT; Group Chief Executive, AMEC plc, 1988–95; *b* 11 Jan. 1942; *s* of William Swinburne Bateson and Katherine Urquart (*née* Lyttle); *m* Jean Vivien Forsyth; one *s* two *d*. *Educ:* Appleby Grammar Sch.; Lancaster Royal Grammar Sch. FIHT 1986. Family business and associated activities, 1959–61; Harbour & General Works Ltd: Trainee Quantity Surveyor, 1961; Quantity Surveyor, 1966; Site Quantity Surveyor, Marples Ridgway Ltd, 1966–68; Leonard Fairclough Ltd: Site Quantity Surveyor, 1969; Contracts Surveyor, 1971; Chief Quantity Surveyor, Scotland, 1974; Fairclough Civil Engineering Ltd: Asst to Chief Exec., 1977; Man. Dir, Southern Div., 1979; Fairclough Construction Group Ltd: Asst to Chief Exec., 1980; Dir, 1981–; AMEC plc: Dir, 1982–86; Dep. Chief Exec., 1986–88. *Recreations:* gardening, aviation, reading, photography, chess, bridge, antiques. *Address:* Clayton Croft, Ribchester Road, Clayton-le-Dale, Blackburn, Lancs BB1 9EE.

BATESON, Prof. (Paul) Patrick (Gordon), FRS 1983; Professor of Ethology, since 1984, and Head of Department of Zoology, since 1994, University of Cambridge; Provost of King's College, Cambridge, since 1988 (Fellow, 1964–84; Professorial Fellow, 1984–88); *b* 31 March 1938; *s* of Richard Gordon Bateson and Sölvi Helene Berg; *m* 1963, Dusha Matthews; two *d*. *Educ:* Westminster Sch.; King's Coll., Cambridge (BA 1960, PhD 1963, MA 1965, ScD 1977). Harkness Fellow, Stanford Univ. Medical Centre, Calif, 1963–65; Sen. Asst in Res., Sub-Dept of Animal Behaviour, Univ. of Cambridge, 1965–69; Lectr in Zoology, Univ. of Cambridge, 1969–78; Dir, Sub-Dept of Animal Behaviour, 1976–88; Reader in Animal Behaviour, 1978–84. Pres., Assoc. for the Study of Animal Behaviour, 1977–80; Member: Council for Sci. and Soc., 1989–92; Council, Zool Soc. of London, 1989–92; Museums and Galls Commn, 1995–. Trustee, Inst. for Public Policy Research, 1988–. Scientific Medal, Zool Soc. of London, 1976. *Publications:* (ed with P. H. Klopfer) Perspectives in Ethology, Vols 1–8, 1973–89; (ed with R. A. Hinde) Growing Points in Ethology, 1976; (ed) Mate Choice, 1983; (contrib.) Defended to Death, 1983; (with Paul Martin) Measuring Behaviour, 1986, 2nd edn 1993; (ed with D. S. Turner) The Domestic Cat: the biology of its behaviour, 1988; (ed) The Development and Integration of Behaviour, 1991. *Address:* Provost's Lodge, King's College, Cambridge CB2 1ST. *T:* Cambridge (01223) 355949.

BATH, 7th Marquess of, *cr* 1789; **Alexander George Thynn,** Bt 1641; Viscount Weymouth and Baron Thynne, 1682; Director: Cheddar Caves, since 1956; Longleat Enterprises, since 1964; *b* 6 May 1932; *s* of 6th Marquess of Bath and of his 1st wife, Hon. Daphne Winifred Louise, *d* of 4th Baron Vivian; *S* father, 1992; *m* 1969, Anna Gael Gyarmathy; one *s* one *d*. *Educ:* Eton College; Christ Church, Oxford (BA, MA). Lieutenant in the Life Guards, 1951–52, and in Royal Wilts Yeomanry, 1953–57. Contested (Wessex Regionalist): Westbury, Feb. 1974; Wells, 1979; contested (Wessex Regionalist and European Federal Party) Wessex, European Election 1979. Permanent exhibn of paintings since 1949 and murals since 1964, first opened to the public in 1962 in private apartments at Longleat House. Record, I Play the Host, singing own compositions, 1974. *Publications:* (as Alexander Thynn) (before 1976 Alexander Thynne) The Carry-cot, 1972; Lord Weymouth's Murals, 1974; A Regionalist Manifesto, 1975; The King is Dead, 1976; Pillars of the Establishment, 1980. *Heir:* *s* Viscount Weymouth, *qv*. *Address:* Longleat, Warminster, Wilts BA12 7NN. *T:* Warminster (01985) 844300.

BATH and WELLS, Bishop of, since 1991; **Rt. Rev. James Lawton Thompson;** *b* 11 Aug. 1936; *s* of Bernard Isaac and Marjorie May Thompson; *m* 1965, Sally Patricia Stallworthy; one *s* one *d*. *Educ:* Dean Close School, Cheltenham; Emmanuel Coll., Cambridge (MA 1964; Hon. Fellow, 1992). FCA 1959. 2nd Lt, 3rd Royal Tank Regt, 1959–61. Deacon, 1966; Curate, East Ham, 1966–68; Chaplain, Cuddesdon Coll., Oxford, 1968–71; Rector of Thamesmead and Ecumenical Team Leader, 1971–78; Suffragan, then Area, Bishop of Stepney, 1978–91. Mem., House of Bishops, Gen. Synod of C of E, 1988–. Chairman: Cttee for Relations with People of Other Faiths, BCC, 1983–89; Urban Studies Centre, then Urban Learning Foundn, 1985–91; Interfaith Network (UK), 1987–92; Church at Work, London, 1989–91; Social Policy Cttee, Bd for Social Responsibility, 1990–; London Churches Broadcasting Gp, 1987–91. Visitor, Wadham Coll., Oxford, 1992. Hon. Fellow, QMC, 1986. Hon. DLitt E London Poly., 1989; Hon. DD Exeter, 1995. (Jointly) Sir Sigmund Sternberg Award for Christian-Jewish Relations, 1987. *Publications:* Halfway: reflections in midlife, 1986; (contrib.) Trevor Huddleston, ed D. D. Honoré, 1989; The Lord's Song, 1990; Stepney Calling, 1991. *Recreations:* riding, painting, a horse, sport. *Address:* The Palace, Wells, Somerset BA5 2PD. *T:* Wells (01749) 672341.

BATH, Archdeacon of; *see* Burgess, Ven. J. E.

BATH, Alan Alfred; Director, Education and Training, Commission of the European Communities, 1973–80; *b* 3 May 1924; *s* of Alfred Edward Bath and Doris Ellen Lawson; *m* 1st, 1946, Joy Roselle Thornton (*d* 1979), *d* of George Jeune, St Saviour, Jersey; one *s* two *d*; 2nd, 1987, Jill Diana Lesley Pearce, *d* of Eric and Nancy Douglas, Blandford Forum, Dorset. Educ: Frays Coll., Uxbridge; Queen's Univ., Belfast (BSc Econ). RAF, 1942–46. Asst Lectr in Econs, QUB, 1950–53; Admin. Officer, Assoc. of Univs of British Commonwealth, 1953–58; Imperial Coll., Univ. of London, 1958–62 (Develt Sec., 1960–62); Sec., Cttee of Vice-Chancellors and Principals of Univs of UK, 1964–73; Sec., UK Nat. Delegn to Council of Europe Cttee for Higher Educn and Research, 1969–73. *Publication:* A Survey of the Work of the Winston Churchill Memorial Trust, 1985. *Recreations:* music, sailing, gardening. *Address:* 6 Sleepers Hill Gardens, Winchester, Hants SO22 4NT. *T:* Winchester (01962) 865848. *Clubs:* Athenæum, Royal Air Force.

BATHERSBY, Most Rev. John Alexius; *see* Brisbane, Archbishop of, (RC).

BATHO, James; *see* Batho, W. J. S.

BATHO, Sir Peter (Ghislain), 3rd Bt *cr* 1928, of Frinton, Essex; *b* 9 Dec. 1939; *s* of Sir Maurice Benjamin Batho, 2nd Bt and Antoinette Marie (*d* 1994), *d* of Baron d'Udekem d'Acoz; *S* father, 1990; *m* 1966, Lucille Mary, *d* of Wilfrid F. Williamson; three *s*. *Educ:* Ampleforth Coll.; Writtle Agricl Coll. Career in agriculture. Mem., Suffolk CC, 1989–93. *Heir:* *s* Rupert Sebastian Ghislain Batho, *b* 26 Oct. 1967. *Address:* Park Farm, Saxmundham, Suffolk IP17 1DQ. *T:* Saxmundham (01728) 602132.

BATHO, (Walter) James (Scott); Chairman, London and Quadrant Housing Trust, since 1989; *b* 13 Nov. 1925; *er s* of Walter Scott Batho and Isabella Laidlaw Batho (*née* Common); *m* 1951, Barbara Kingsford; two *s* two *d*. *Educ:* Epsom County Grammar Sch.; Univ. of Edinburgh (MA Eng. Lit. and Lang.). Served War, RNVR, 1943–46. Air Min., 1950–53; WO, 1953–63 (Private Sec. to Perm. Under Sec. of State, 1956–57); MPBW, 1963–70; DoE, 1970–85, Under Sec., 1979–85 (Regl Dir and Chm., Regl Bd for Eastern Region, DoE and Dept of Transport, 1983–85). Chm., Noise Review Wkg Party, DoE, 1990. Pres., Ashtead Choral Soc., 1990–. *Recreations:* singing, reading, gardening. *Address:* Bushpease, Grays Lane, Ashtead, Surrey KT21 1BU. *T:* Ashtead (01372) 273471. *Club:* Naval.

BATHURST, family name of **Earl Bathurst** and **Viscount Bledisloe.**

BATHURST, 8th Earl, *cr* 1772; **Henry Allen John Bathurst,** DL; Baron Bathurst of Battlesden, Bedfordshire, 1712; Baron Apsley of Apsley, Sussex, 1771; Earl Bathurst of Bathurst, Sussex, 1772; Capt. Royal Gloucestershire Hussars (TA); TARO, 1959; *b* 1 May 1927; *s* of late Lord Apsley, DSO, MC, MP (killed on active service, 1942), and late Lady Apsley, CBE; *g s* of 7th Earl; *S* grandfather, 1943; *m* 1st 1959, Judith Mary (marr. diss. 1977), *d* of Mr and Mrs A. C. Nelson, Springfield House, Foulridge, Lancs; two *s* one *d*; 2nd, 1978, Gloria, *widow* of David Rutherston and *o d* of Harold Edward Clarry, Vancouver, BC. *Educ:* Ridley Coll., Canada; Eton; Christ Church, Oxford, 1948–49. Late Lieut 10th Royal Hussars (PWO). Capt., Royal Glos. Hussars, TA, 1949–57. Hon. Sec. Agricultural Cttee (Conservative), House of Lords, 1957; a Lord-in-Waiting, 1957–61; Joint Parliamentary Under-Sec. of State, Home Office, 1961–July 1962. Governor, Royal Agricultural Coll.; Pres. Glos Branch CPRE. Chancellor, Primrose League, 1959–61. Dir, Forestor Gp, 1986–92. Member: CLA Council, 1965 (Chm., Glos Branch of CLA, 1968–71); Timber Growers' Organisation (TGO) Council, 1966; President: Royal Forestry Soc., 1976–78; InstSMM, 1982–92; Assoc. of Professional Foresters, 1983–87. DL County of Gloucester, 1960. *Heir:* *s* Lord Apsley, *qv*. *Address:* Manor Farm, Sapperton, near Cirencester, Glos GL7 6LE. *Clubs:* White's, Cavalry and Guards.

BATHURST (NSW), Bishop of, since 1989; **Rt. Rev. Bruce Winston Wilson;** *b* 23 Aug. 1942; *s* of Alick Bruce Wilson and Maisie Catherine (*née* Pye); *m* 1966, Zandra Robyn Parkes; one *s* one *d*. *Educ:* Canterbury Boys' High School; Univ. of Sydney (MA); London Univ. (BD); Univ. of NSW (BA); Australian Coll. of Theology (ThL). Curacies, Darling Point and Beverly Hills, Sydney, 1966–69; Anglican Chaplain, Univ. of NSW, 1970–75; Rector of St George's, Paddington, Sydney, 1975–83; Director, St Mark's Theol Coll., Canberra, 1984–89; Asst Bishop, Diocese of Canberra and Goulburn, 1984–89. Exec., Nat. Council of Churches in Australia, 1994–95. *Publications:* The Human Journey: Christianity and Modern Consciousness, 1981; Can God Survive in Australia?, 1983. *Recreations:* jogging, motor car restoration, reading, cooking. *Address:* Bishopscourt, 16 McKell Street, Bathurst, NSW 2795, Australia. *T:* (63) 311175.

BATHURST, Admiral of the Fleet Sir (David) Benjamin, GCB 1991 (KCB 1987); First Sea Lord and Chief of Naval Staff, and First and Principal Naval Aide-de-Camp to the Queen, 1993–95; *b* 27 May 1936; *s* of late Group Captain Peter Bathurst, RAF and Lady Ann Bathurst; *m* 1959, Sarah Peto; one *s* three *d*. *Educ:* Eton College; Britannia RN College, Dartmouth. Joined RN, 1953; qualified as Pilot, 1960, as Helicopter Instructor, 1964; Fleet Air Arm appts incl. 2 years' exchange with RAN, 723 and 725 Sqdns; Senior Pilot, 820 Naval Air Sqdn; CO 819 Naval Air Sqdn; HMS Norfolk, 1971; Naval Staff, 1973; CO, HMS Ariadne, 1975; Naval Asst to First Sea Lord, 1976; Captain, 5th Frigate Sqdn, HMS Minerva, 1978; RCDS 1981; Dir of Naval Air Warfare, 1982; Flag Officer, Second Flotilla, 1983–85; Dir.-Gen., Naval Manpower and Training, 1985–86; Chief of Fleet Support, 1986–89; C-in-C Fleet, Allied C-in-C Channel, and C-in-C Eastern Atlantic Area, 1989–91; Vice Chief of Defence Staff, 1991–93. FRAeS. Younger Brother, Trinity House. Liveryman, GAPAN. *Recreations:* gardening, shooting, fishing. *Address:* c/o Coutts and Co., 440 Strand, WC2. *Clubs:* Army and Navy, MCC.

BATHURST, Sir Frederick Peter Methuen Hervey-, 6th Bt, *cr* 1818; *b* 26 Jan. 1903; *s* of Sir Frederick Edward William Hervey-Bathurst, 5th Bt, DSO and Hon. Moira O'Brien, 2nd *d* of 14th Baron Inchiquin; *S* father 1956; *m* 1st, 1933, Maureen (marr. diss. 1956), *d* of Charles Gordon, Boveridge Park, Salisbury; one *s* one *d*; 2nd, 1958, Mrs Cornelia Shepard Riker, *widow* of Dr John Lawrence Riker, Rumson, NJ, USA. *Educ:* Eton. Served War of 1939–45, Capt. Grenadier Guards. *Recreations:* sailing, riding, ski-ing, flying. *Heir:* *s* Frederick John Charles Gordon Hervey-Bathurst [*b* 23 April 1934; *m* 1957, Caroline Myrtle, *d* of Lieut-Col Sir William Starkey, 2nd Bt, and late Irene Myrtle Francklin; one *s* two *d*]. *Address:* PO Box 236, Rumson, NJ 07760, USA. *T:* (908) 2914194. *Clubs:* Cavalry and Guards, Royal Ocean Racing.

See also Sir J. F. Portal, Bt.

BATHURST, Joan Caroline, (Lady Bathurst); *see* Petrie, J. C.

BATHURST, Sir Maurice (Edward), Kt 1984; CMG 1953; CBE 1947; QC 1964; *b* 2 Dec. 1913; *o s* of late Edward John James Bathurst and Annie Mary Bathurst; *m* 1941, Dorothy (marr. diss. 1963), *d* of late W. S. Stevens, LDS, RCS; one *s*; *m* 1968, Joan Caroline Petrie, *qv*. *Educ:* Haberdashers' Aske's, Hatcham; King's Coll., London; Gonville and Caius Coll., Cambridge; Columbia Univ. LLB, First Class Hons. (London), 1937; University Law Schol. (London), 1937; Post-Grad. Research Studentship (London), 1938; Bartle Frere Exhibitioner (Camb.), 1939; Tutorial Fellow (Chicago), 1939; Special Fellow (Columbia), 1940; LLM (Columbia), 1941; Hon. DCL (Sacred Heart, NB), 1946; PhD (Camb.), 1949; LLD (London), 1966. Solicitor of Supreme Court, 1938–56. Called to Bar, Gray's Inn, 1957; Master of the Bench, 1970; Master of the Library, 1978–81. Legal Adviser, British Information Services, USA, 1941–43; Legal Adviser, British Embassy, Washington, 1943–46 (First Sec., 1944; Counsellor, 1946); Legal Member, UK Delegation to United Nations, 1946–48; UK Representative, Legal Advisory Cttee, Atomic Energy Commission, 1946–48; Legal Adviser to British Chm., Bipartite Control Office, Frankfurt, 1949; Dep. Legal Adviser, CCG, 1949–51; Legal Adviser, UK High Commn, Germany, 1951–55; Judge, Supreme Court, British Zone, Germany, 1953–55; Legal Adviser, British Embassy, Bonn, 1955–57; British Judge, Arbitral Commn, Germany, 1968–69; Mem., Panel of Arbitrators, Internat. Centre for Settlement of Investment Disputes, 1968–87; a Pres., Arbitral Tribunals, Internat. Telecommunication's Satellite Orgn, 1974–78; Judge, Arbitral Tribunal and Mixed Commn for Agreement on German External Debts, 1977–88. Mem. UK Delegations to UNRRA; United Nations San Francisco Conference; Bermuda Civil Aviation Conference; PICAO; Washington Financial Talks; UN Gen. Assembly; FAO; WHO; Internat. Tin Study Group; UK-US Double Taxation Treaty Negotiations; London Nine-Power Conf.; Paris Conf. on W Eur. Union; NATO Status of Forces Conf., Bonn. Internat. Vice-Pres. UN League of Lawyers; Vice President: Brit. Inst. of International and Comparative Law; Brit. Acad. of Experts, 1988–92. Member: UK Cttee, UNICEF, 1959–84; Ct of Assistants, Haberdashers' Co. (Fourth Warden, 1973–74; Second Warden, 1978–79; First Warden, 1979–80, Master, 1980–81); Editorial Cttee, British Yearbook of International Law; *ad eundem*, Inner Temple; Gen. Council of the Bar, 1970–71; Senate of Inns of Court, 1971–73; Council of Legal Educn, 1971–79; Senate of the Inns of Court and the Bar, 1974–77. Hon. Vis. Prof. in Internat. Law, King's Coll., London, 1967–77; Hon. Fellow, King's Coll., London. Chm. Governors, Haberdashers' Aske's Hatcham Schools, 1973–80. Pres., British Insurance Law Assoc., 1971–75. Freeman of the City of London and of the City of Bathurst, NB. *Publications:* Germany and the North Atlantic Community: A Legal Survey (with J. L. Simpson), 1956; (ed, jtly) Legal Problems of an Enlarged European Community, 1972; notes and articles in legal jls, etc., British and American. *Recreation:* theatre. *Address:* Airlie, The Highlands, East Horsley, Surrey KT24 5BG. *T:* East Horsley (01483) 283269. *Club:* Garrick.

BATHURST NORMAN, George Alfred; His Honour Judge Bathurst Norman; a Circuit Judge, since 1986; *b* 15 Jan. 1939; *s* of Charles Phipps Bathurst Norman and Hon. Doreen Albinia de Burgh Norman (*née* Gibbs); *m* 1973, Susan Elizabeth Ball; one *s* one *d*. *Educ:* Harrow Sch.; Magdalen Coll., Oxford (BA). Called to the Bar, Inner Temple, 1961; SE Circuit, 1962; Dep. Circuit Judge, 1975; a Metropolitan Stipendiary Magistrate, 1981–86; a Recorder, 1986. Mem., Home Office Working Party on Coroners Rules, 1976–81. Mem., Gen. Council of the Bar, 1968–70. *Recreations:* wildlife, ornithology, cricket, travel. *Address:* 3 Hare Court, Temple, EC4. *Club:* MCC.

BATISTE, Spencer Lee; MP (C) Elmet, since 1983; solicitor in private practice, since 1970; *b* 5 June 1945; *m* 1969, Susan Elizabeth (*née* Atkin); one *s* one *d*. *Educ:* Carmel Coll.; Sorbonne, Paris; Cambridge Univ. (MA). PPS to Minister of State for Industry and IT, 1985–87, to Minister of State for Defence Procurement, 1987–89; to Sir Leon Brittan, Vice-Pres. of EC Commn, 1989–. Member: Select Cttee on Energy, 1985; Select Cttee on Information, 1991–; Select Cttee on Sci. and Technology, 1992–; Vice-Chairman: Cons. Space Cttee, 1986– (Sec., 1983–85); Cons. Trade and Industry Cttee, 1989–. Pres., Yorks Cons. Trade Unionists, 1984–87 (Nat. Pres., 1990). Vice-Chm., Small Business Bureau, 1983–. Law Clerk to Sheffield Assay Office, 1974–. Mem., British Hallmarking Council, 1988–. *Recreations:* gardening, reading, photography, stamp collecting. *Address:* House of Commons, SW1A 0AA. *Club:* The Club (Sheffield).

BATLEY, John Geoffrey, OBE 1987; CEng; Consultant, Dan-Rail, Copenhagen, since 1988; Transport Consultant, Carl Bro (UK), since 1993; *b* 21 May 1930; *s* of John William and Doris Batley; *m* 1953, Cicely Anne Pindar; one *s* one *d*. *Educ:* Keighley Grammar School. MICE, MCIT. British Rail: trained and qualified as a chartered engineer in NE Region, 1947–53; Asst Divl Engr, Leeds, 1962; Management Services Officer, BR HQ, London, 1965; Dep. Principal, British Transport Staff Coll., Woking, 1970; Divl Manager, Leeds, 1976; Dep. Chief Secretary, BRB, London, 1982; Sec., BRB, 1984–87; Project Co-ordinator, World Bank/Tanzanian Railway Corp., 1988–92. *Recreations:* walking, golf, gardening. *Address:* Wentworth Cottage, Old Lodge Hill, Ilkley, West Yorkshire LS29 0BB. *T:* Ilkley (01943) 601396. *Clubs:* Farmers', Savile.

BATTEN, Sir John (Charles), KCVO 1987; MD, FRCP; Physician to the Queen, 1974–89 (Physician to HM Royal Household, 1970–74), and Head of HM Medical Household, 1982–89; Physician: King Edward VII Hospital for Officers, 1968–89; King Edward VII Hospital, Midhurst, 1969–89; Hon. Physician to: St Dunstan's, since 1960; St George's Hospital, since 1980; Brompton Hospital, since 1986; Chief Medical Officer,

Confederation Life, since 1974 (Deputy Chief Medical Referee, 1958–74); *b* 11 March 1924; *s* of late Raymond Wallis Batten, JP and Gladys (*née* Charles); *m* 1950, Anne Mary Margaret, *d* of late John Oriel, CBE, MC; one *s* two *d* (and one *d* decd). *Educ:* Mill Hill School; St Bartholomew's Medical School. MB, BS 1946 London Univ.; MRCP 1950; MD London 1951; FRCP 1964. Junior appts, St George's Hosp. and Brompton Hosp., 1946–58. Surgeon Captain, Royal Horse Guards, 1947–49. Physician: St George's Hospital, 1958–79; Brompton Hosp., 1959–86. Dorothy Temple Cross Research Fellow, Cornell Univ. Medical Coll., New York, 1954–55. Examiner in Medicine, London Univ., 1968; Marc Daniels Lectr, RCP, 1969; Croonian Lectr, RCP, 1983. Member: Board of Governors, Brompton Hosp., 1966–69; St George's Hosp. Medical School Council, 1969; Council, RSocMed, 1970; Royal College of Physicians: Censor, 1977–78; Senior Censor, 1980–81; Vice-Pres., 1980–81. President: Cystic Fibrosis Trust, 1986–; British Lung Foundn, 1987–94; Medical Protection Soc., 1988–; Chm., Med. and Survival Cttee, RNLI, 1992–94 (Vice Pres., 1994). *Publications:* contributions to medical books and journals. *Recreations:* music and sailing. *Address:* 7 Lion Gate Gardens, Richmond, Surrey TW9 2DF. *T:* 0181–940 3282.

BATTEN, Stephen Duval; QC 1989; barrister; a Recorder, since 1988; *b* 2 April 1945; *s* of Brig. Stephen Alexander Holgate Batten, CBE and of Alice Joan Batten, MBE, *d* of Sir Ernest Royden, 3rd Bt; *m* 1976, Valerie Jean Trim; one *s* one *d*. *Educ:* Uppingham; Pembroke Coll., Oxford (BA). Called to the Bar, Middle Temple, 1968. *Recreations:* golf, sheep farming. *Address:* 3 Raymond Buildings, Gray's Inn, WC1R 5BH. *T:* 0171–831 5833.

BATTERBURY, Paul Tracy Shepherd, TD 1972 (2 bars); DL; **His Honour Judge Batterbury;** a Circuit Judge, since 1983; *b* 25 Jan. 1934; only *s* of late Hugh Basil John Batterbury and of Inez Batterbury; *m* 1962, Sheila Margaret, *d* of John Watson; one *s* one *d*. *Educ:* St Olave's Grammar Sch., Southwark; Univ. of Bristol (LLB). Served RAF, 1952–55, TA, 1959–85 (Major, RA). Called to Bar, Inner Temple, 1959; practising barrister, 1959–83. Councillor: Chislehurst and Sidcup UDC, 1960–62; London Borough of Greenwich, 1968–71 (Chm., Housing Cttee, 1970–71). Founder Trustee, St Olave's Sch., SE9, 1970–; Founder Chm., Gallipoli Meml Lects, 1986–89. Vice-Pres., SE London, SJAB, 1988–91. DL Greater London, 1986; rep. DL, London Borough of Havering, 1989–95. *Recreations:* photography, walking, caravanning. *Address:* 5 Paper Buildings, Temple, EC4Y 9HB. *T:* 0171–583 9275.

BATTERSBY, Sir Alan (Rushton), Kt 1992; MSc, PhD, DSc, ScD; FRS 1966; Professor of Organic Chemistry, and Fellow of St Catharine's College, Cambridge, 1969–92, Professor and Fellow Emeritus, since 1992; Director, Schering Agrochemicals Ltd; *b* Leigh, 4 March 1925; *s* of William and Hilda Battersby; *m* 1949, Margaret Ruth, *d* of Thomas and Annie Hart, Whaley Bridge, Cheshire; two *s*. *Educ:* Grammar Sch., Leigh; Univ. of Manchester (Mercer and Woodiwis Schol.); Univ. of St Andrews. MSc Manchester; PhD St Andrews; DSc Bristol; ScD Cantab. Asst Lectr in Chemistry, Univ. of St Andrews, 1948–53; Commonwealth Fund Fellow at Rockefeller Inst., NY, 1950–51 and at Univ. of Illinois, 1951–52; Lectr in Chemistry, Univ. of Bristol, 1954–62; Prof. of Organic Chemistry, Univ. of Liverpool, 1962–69. Mem. Council, Royal Soc., 1973–75. Mem. Deutsche Akademie der Naturforscher Leopoldina, 1967. Pres., Bürgenstock Conf., 1976. Chm., Exec. Council, 1983–90, Trustee, 1993–, Ciba Foundn. Foreign Fellow: Nat. Acad. of Scis, India, 1990; Indian Nat. Science Acad., 1993. Honorary Member: Soc. Royale de Chimie, Belgium, 1987; Amer. Acad. of Arts and Scis, 1988. Lectures: Treat Johnson, Yale, 1969; Pacific Coast, USA, 1971; Karl Folkers, Wisconsin, 1972; N-E Coast, USA, 1974; Andrews, NSW, 1975; Middle Rhine, 1976; Tishler, Harvard, 1978; August Wilhelm von Hoffmann, Ges. Deutscher Chem., 1979; Pedler, Chem. Soc., 1980–81; Rennebohm, Wisconsin, 1981; Kharasch, Chicago, 1982; Bakerian, Royal Soc., 1984; Baker, Cornell, 1984; Lady Masson Meml, Melbourne, 1987; Atlantic Coast, USA, 1988; Nehru Centenary, Seshadri Meml and Zaheer Meml, India, 1989; Marvel, Illinois, 1989; Gilman, Iowa, 1989; Alder, Cologne, 1991; Dauben, Berkeley, 1994; Alexander Cruickshank, Gordon Confs, 1994; Univ. Lectr, Ottawa, 1993; Visiting Professor: Cornell Univ., 1969; Virginia Univ., 1971; Tohoku Univ., Japan, 1974; ANU, 1975; Technion, Israel, 1977; Univ. of Canterbury, NZ, 1980; Melbourne Univ., 1987; Univ. of Auckland, NZ, 1989, 1993; Univ. of NSW, 1990. Chemical Society: Corday-Morgan Medal, 1959; Tilden Medal and Lectr, 1963; Hügo Müller Medal and Lectr, 1972; Flintoff Medal, 1975; Award in Natural Product Chemistry, 1978; Longstaff Medal, 1984; Robert Robinson Lectr and Medal, 1986. Paul Karrer Medal and Lectr, Univ. Zürich, 1977; Davy Medal, 1977, Royal Medal, 1984, Royal Soc.; Roger Adams Award in Organic Chemistry, ACS, 1983; Havinga Medal, Holland, 1984; Antoni Feltrinelli Internat. Prize for Chemistry, Rome, 1986; Varro Tyler Lect. and Award, Purdue, 1987; Adolf Windaus Medal, Göttingen, 1987; Wolf Prize, Israel, 1989; Arun Guthikonda Meml Award, Columbia, 1991; Hofmann Meml Medal, Ges. Deutscher Chem., 1992. Hon. LLD St Andrews, 1977; Hon. DSc: Rockefeller Univ., USA, 1977; Sheffield, 1986; Heriot-Watt, 1987; Bristol, 1994. *Publications:* papers in chemical jls, particularly Jl Chem. Soc. *Recreations:* music, camping, sailing, fly fishing, gardening. *Address:* University Chemical Laboratory, Lensfield Road, Cambridge CB2 1EW. *T:* Cambridge (01223) 336400.

BATTERSBY, Robert Christopher, CBE 1990 (MBE 1971); *b* 14 Dec. 1924; *s* of late Major Robert Luther Battersby, MM, RFA, late Indian Army, and Dorothea Gladys (*née* Middleton); *m* 1st, 1949, June Scriven (marr. diss.); one *d*; 2nd, 1955, Marjorie Bispham; two *s* one *d*. *Educ:* Firth Park Grammar Sch., Sheffield; Edinburgh Univ. (Gen. Sciences); Fitzwilliam House, Cambridge; Sorbonne; Toulouse Univ. BA Cantab (Hons Russian and Modern Greek) 1950; Cert. of Educn 1952; MA Cantab 1954; Cert. de Langue française, Toulouse, 1953; FIL 1958. Served Royal Artillery (Field) and Intelligence Corps, 1942–47 (Italian Campaign, Greece and Crete 1944, Central and Western Macedonia 1945–47); TA to 1952; Lieut RARO. With Dowsett Gp of shipbuilding and civil engrg cos on major distant water trawler and pre-stressed concrete plant export contracts, 1953–63; Manager, Eastern Trade Dept, Glacier Metal Co. Ltd, 1963–66; Sales Dir, Associated Engrg Export Services Ltd, 1966–71; Sales Dir, GKN Contractors Ltd, 1971–73. Responsible for negotiating and installing USSR, Polish, Czechoslovak and Romanian plain bearing industries, Polish diesel engine component industry, and several other metallurgical and machining plants in E Europe; Export, Financial and Commercial Adviser to various UK and USA cos. Mem. CBI and Soc. of British Engrs delegns to China, Poland, Yugoslavia and Singapore. Mem. Exec. Council, Russo-British Chamber of Commerce, and of London Chamber of Commerce Russian and Polish sections, 1968–73; Adviser to E European Trade Council, 1969–71. Principal Administrator: Credit and Investments Directorate-Gen., EEC Commn, Luxembourg, 1973–75; Agriculture Directorate-Gen., 1975–76; Fisheries Directorate-Gen., Brussels, 1976–79; Mem., first EEC Vice-Presidential delegn to Poland, 1977. MEP (C) Humberside, 1979–89; Mem., Agriculture and Budgetary Control Cttees, 1979; Chm., Fisheries Working Gp, 1979–84; Vice-Chairman: Fisheries Sub-Cttee, 1984–87; Budgetary Control, 1984–89; Vice-Pres., Eur. Parlt Delegn to China, 1981, 1984, and 1987, Eur. Parlt Delegn to USSR, 1987–89; Chief Whip, EDG, 1987–89. Contested (C) Humberside, Eur. Parly Elecn, 1989. Consultant on E Europe, 1990–; Special Advr on E Europe, Cons. Party, 1990–. Vice Pres., Yorkshire and Humberside Develt Assoc., 1980–87. Chm., Friends of Poland Assoc., Eur. Parlt, 1982–93. Occasional lectr at Farnham Castle and at American univs on East/West trade, and in Poland and USSR on automotive component manufg technology; broadcaster. Member: RIIA; Anglo-Hellenic Soc. FIMgt (FBIM 1982). Silver Medal, Order of European Merit, Luxembourg, 1981. KSG 1990. *Publications:* works in English and Russian on distant water trawler operation; articles on fishing technology, shipbuilding and East/West trade; translations from Greek, Russian and other languages. *Recreations:* politics, European and Oriental languages, history, opera, music, travel. *Address:* West Cross, Rockshaw Road, Merstham, Surrey RH1 3BZ. *T:* Merstham (0173764) 3783. *Club:* Carlton.

BATTISCOMBE, Christopher Charles Richard, CMG 1992; HM Diplomatic Service; Assistant Under-Secretary of State (Public Departments), Foreign and Commonwealth Office, since 1994; *b* 27 April 1940; *s* of late Lt-Col Christopher Robert Battiscombe and Karin Sigrid (*née* Timberg); *m* 1972, Brigid Melita Theresa Lunn; one *s* one *d*. *Educ:* Wellington Coll.; New Coll., Oxford (BA Greats). Entered FO, 1963; ME Centre for Arabic Studies, Shemlan, Lebanon, 1963–65; Third/Second Sec., Kuwait, 1965–68; FCO, 1968–71; First Secretary: UK Delegn, OECD, Paris, 1971–74; UK Mission to UN, New York, 1974–78; Asst Head, Eastern European and Soviet Dept, FCO, 1978–80; Commercial Counsellor: Cairo, 1981–84; Paris, 1984–86; Counsellor, FCO, 1986–90; Ambassador to Algeria, 1990–94. *Recreations:* golf, skiing, tennis. *Address:* c/o Foreign and Commonwealth Office, SW1A 2AH. *Club:* Kandahar.

BATTISCOMBE, Mrs (Esther) Georgina, BA; FRSL 1964; author; *b* 21 Nov. 1905; *d* of late George Harwood, MP, Master Cotton Spinner, Bolton, Lancs, and Ellen Hopkinson, *d* of Sir Alfred Hopkinson, KC, MP, First Vice-Chancellor of Manchester Univ.; *m* 1932, Lt-Col Christopher Francis Battiscombe, OBE, FSA (*d* 1964), Grenadier Guards; one *d*. *Educ:* St Michael's Sch., Oxford; Lady Margaret Hall, Oxford. *Publications:* Charlotte Mary Yonge, 1943; Two on Safari, 1946; English Picnics, 1949; Mrs Gladstone, 1956; John Keble (James Tait Black Memorial Prize for best biography of year), 1963; Christina Rossetti (Writers and their Work), 1965; ed, with M. Laski, A Chaplet for Charlotte Yonge, 1965; Queen Alexandra, 1969; Shaftesbury, 1974; Reluctant Pioneer: The Life of Elizabeth Wordsworth, 1978; Christina Rossetti: a divided life, 1981; The Spencers of Althorp, 1984; Winter Song, 1992. *Recreation:* looking at churches. *Address:* 40 Phyllis Court Drive, Henley-on-Thames, Oxfordshire RG9 2HU. *T:* Henley (01491) 574830.

BATTISHILL, Sir Anthony (Michael William), KCB 1989; Chairman, Board of Inland Revenue, since 1986 (Deputy Chairman, 1985); *b* 5 July 1937; *s* of William George Battishill and Kathleen Rose Bishop; *m* 1961, Heather Frances Lawes; one *d*. *Educ:* Taunton Sch.; Hele's Sch., Exeter; London Sch. of Economics. BSc (Econ). 2nd Lieut, RAEC, 1958–60. Inland Revenue, 1960–63; HM Treasury, 1963–65; Inland Revenue, 1965–76, Asst Sec., 1970; Central Policy Review Staff, 1976–77; Principal Private Sec. to Chancellor of the Exchequer, HM Treasury, 1977–80; Under Sec., HM Treasury, 1980–82, 1983–85, Inland Revenue, 1982–83. Mem. Ct of Governors, LSE, 1987–. *Recreations:* gardening, old maps. *Address:* The Board Room, Somerset House, WC2R 1LB. *T:* 071–438 7711.

BATTLE, Dennis Frank Orlando; Commissioner and Director of Personnel and Finance, and Principal Establishments and Finance Officer, HM Customs and Excise, since 1994; *b* 17 Dec. 1942; *s* of Frank William Orlando and Marion Kathleen Battle; *m* 1965, Sandra Moule; one *s* one *d*. *Educ:* Bedford Modern School. Joined Customs and Excise as Exec. Officer, 1962; Higher Exec. Officer, NBPI, 1967; Sen. Exec. Officer, CS Coll., 1972; returned to Customs and Excise, 1975, Grade 7 1978, Asst Sec. 1985; Comr and Dir of Personnel, 1990.

BATTLE, John Dominic; MP (Lab) Leeds West, since 1987; *b* 26 April 1951; *s* of John and Audrey Battle; *m* 1977, Mary Meenan; one *s* two *d*. *Educ:* Leeds Univ. (BA Hons (1st cl.) 1976). Training for RC Priesthood, Upholland Coll., 1969–72; Leeds Univ., 1973–77; Res. Officer to Derek Enright, MEP, 1979–83; Nat. Co-ordinator, Church Action on Poverty, 1983–87. Opposition front-bench spokesman on housing, 1992–94, on science and technology, 1994–. Vice-Chm., All Party Gp on Overseas Develt; Mem., All Party Gp on Homelessness. Main political interests are economic policy, social security, housing, poverty at home and abroad. Columnist, Catholic Herald. *Recreations:* walking, poetry, supporting Leeds United FC. *Address:* House of Commons, SW1A 0AA. *T:* 0171–219 5954.

BATTY, Christina Agnes Lillian, (Mrs Ronald Batty); *see* Foyle, C. A. L.

BATTY, Paul Daniel; QC 1995; a Recorder, since 1994; *b* 13 June 1953; *s* of late Vincent Batty and of Catherine Batty; *m* 1986, Angela Jane Palmer; one *d*. *Educ:* St Aidan's Grammar Sch., Sunderland; Newcastle upon Tyne Univ. (LLB). Called to the Bar, Lincoln's Inn, 1975; Junior, NE Circuit, 1985; Bar Mess Junior, 1982–85; Asst Recorder, 1991. *Recreations:* boating, angling, swimming. *Address:* 33 Broad Chare, Quayside, Newcastle upon Tyne NE1 3DQ. *T:* 0191–232 0541.

BATTY, Peter Wright; television and film producer, director and writer; Chief Executive, Peter Batty Productions, since 1970; *b* 18 June 1931; *s* of late Ernest Faulkner Batty and Gladys Victoria Wright; *m* 1959, Anne Elizabeth Stringer; two *s* one *d*. *Educ:* Bede Grammar Sch., Sunderland; Queen's Coll., Oxford. Feature-writer, Financial Times, 1954–56; freelance journalist, 1956–58; Producer, BBC TV, 1958–64: mem. original Tonight team, other prodns incl. The Quiet Revolution, The Big Freeze, The Katanga Affair, Sons of the Navvy Man; Editor, Tonight, 1963–64; Exec. Producer and Associate Head of Factual Programming, ATV, 1964–68: prodns incl. The Fall and Rise of the House of Krupp (Grand Prix for Documentary, Venice Film Fest., 1965; Silver Dove, Leipzig Film Fest., 1965), The Road to Suez, The Suez Affair, Vietnam Fly-in, Battle for the Desert; freelance work for BBC TV, ITV and Channel 4, 1968–. Progs dir., prod and scripted incl. The Plutocrats, The Aristocrats, Battle for Cassino, Battle for the Bulge, Birth of the Bomb, Farouk: last of the Pharaohs, Operation Barbarossa, Superspy, Sunderland's Pride and Passion, A Rothschild and his Red Gold, Search for the Super, Spy Extraordinary, Story of Wine, World of Television, The Rise and Rise of Laura Ashley, The Gospel According to St Michael, Battle for Warsaw, Battle for Dien Bien Phu, Nuclear Nightmares, A Turn Up in a Million, Il Poverello, Swindle!, The Algerian War, Fonteyn and Nureyev: the perfect partnership, The Divided Union, A Time for Remembrance, Swastika over British Soil; prod and scripted 6 episodes World at War series. *Publications:* The House of Krupp, 1966; (with Peter Parish) The Divided Union, 1987; La Guerre d'Algérie, 1989. *Recreations:* walking, reading, listening to music. *Address:* Claremont House, Renfrew Road, Kingston, Surrey KT2 7NT. *T:* 0181–942 6304. *Club:* White Elephant.

BATTY, Sir William (Bradshaw), Kt 1973; TD 1946; Chairman, Ford Motor Co. Ltd, 1972–75, retired (Managing Director, 1968–73); *b* 15 May 1913; *s* of Rowland and Nellie Batty; *m* 1946, Jean Ella Brice; one *s* one *d* (and one *s* decd). *Educ:* Hulme Grammar Sch., Manchester. Served War of 1939–45, RASC (Lt-Col). Apprentice toolmaker, Ford Motor Co. Ltd, Trafford Park, Manchester, 1930; Co. trainee, 1933; Press liaison, Advertising

Dept, 1936; Service Dept, 1937; Tractor Sales Dept, 1945; Asst Man., Tractor Dept, 1948; Man., Tractor and Implement Product Planning, 1953; Man., Tractor Div., 1955; Gen. Man., Tractor Gp, 1961; Dir, Tractor Gp, 1963; Dir, Car and Truck Gp, 1964; Exec. Dir, 1963–75. Chairman: Ford Motor Credit Co. Ltd, 1968 (Dir, 1963–); Automotive Finance Ltd, 1970–75; Director: Henry Ford & Son Ltd, Cork, 1965–75; Ford Lusitana SARL, Portugal, 1973–75. Mem., Engineering Industries Council, 1975–76. Pres., SMMT, 1975–76. Hon. LLD Manchester, 1976. FBIM. *Recreations:* golf, sailing, gardening. *Address:* Glenhaven Cottage, Riverside Road West, Newton Ferrers, South Devon PL8 1AD. *Club:* Royal Western Yacht.

BAUER, family name of **Baron Bauer.**

BAUER, Baron *cr* 1982 (Life Peer), of Market Ward in the City of Cambridge; **Peter Thomas Bauer,** MA; DSc; FBA; Professor of Economics (with special reference to economic development and under-developed countries) in the University of London, at the London School of Economics, 1960–83, now Emeritus Professor of Economics; Fellow of Gonville and Caius College, Cambridge, 1946–60, and since 1968; unmarried. *Educ:* Scholae Piae, Budapest; Gonville and Caius Coll., Cambridge. Reader in Agricultural Economics, University of London, 1947–48; University Lecturer in Economics, Cambridge Univ., 1948–56; Smuts Reader in Commonwealth Studies, Cambridge Univ., 1956–60. *Publications:* books and articles on applied economics. *Address:* House of Lords, Westminster, SW1A 0PW. *Clubs:* Garrick, Beefsteak.

BAUGH, John Trevor; Director General of Supplies and Transport (Naval), Ministry of Defence, 1986–93; *b* 24 Sept. 1932; *s* of late Thomas Harold Baugh and of Nellie Baugh (*née* Machin); *m* 1st, 1956, Pauline Andrews (decd); three *s*; 2nd, 1981, Noreen Rita Rosemary Sykes; two step *s*. *Educ:* Queen Elizabeth's Hospital, Bristol. MCIT 1956. Asst Naval Store Officer, Devonport, 1953; Dep. Naval Store Officer, Admiralty, 1959; Armament Supply Officer, Alexandria, 1966; Principal, MoD, Bath, 1970; Supt, RN Store Depot, Copenacre, 1974; Asst Sec., MoD (Navy), 1976, Exec. Dir, 1979; MoD (Army), 1983, Asst Under Sec. of State 1985. *Recreations:* bridge, golf. *Address:* Wonham, Lansdown Road, Bath, Avon BA1 5RB. *Clubs:* Athenæum; Bath Golf.

BAUGHAN, Julian James; QC 1990; a Recorder, since 1985; *b* 8 Feb. 1944; *s* of late Prof. E. C. Baughan, CBE, and Mrs E. C. Baughan. *Educ:* Eton Coll. (King's Schol.); Balliol Coll., Oxford (Brassey Italian Schol.; BA History). Called to Bar, Inner Temple, 1967 (Profumo Schol., Philip Teichman Schol., Major Schol.); Prosecuting Counsel to DTI, 1983–90. *Address:* 13 King's Bench Walk, Temple, EC4Y 7EN.

BAUGHEN, Rt. Rev. Michael Alfred; *see* Chester, Bishop of.

BAUM, Prof. (John) David, MD; FRCP; Professor of Child Health, since 1985, and Founding Director, Institute of Child Health, since 1988, University of Bristol; *b* 23 July 1940; *s* of Isidor and Mary Baum; *m* 1967, Angela Rose Goschalk; four *s*. *Educ:* Univ. of Birmingham. MB ChB, MA, MSc, MD, DCH. Royal Postgrad. Med. Sch., 1967; Lectr then Clinical Reader in Paed., Oxford, 1972; Professorial Fellow, St Catherine's Coll., Oxford, 1977. Vis. Prof., Univ. of Colorado Med. Center, 1969. Chm., Adv. Cttee, Winnicot Res. Unit, Cambridge, 1991–; Dir, BPA Res. Unit, 1993–. Founding Chm., Nat. Assoc. for Care of Children with Life Threatening Diseases and their Families, 1990–; Chm., British Assoc. of Community Child Health, 1990–94; Trustee: Cancer & Leukemia in Childhood Trust; MusicSpace; Patron: Bristol Family Conciliation Service; Children's Hospice South West; Guardian, Helen House, Oxford. FRSA. Inventor, Silver Swaddler, 1968; co-inventor, Human Milk Pasteuriser, 1976. Guthrie Medal, BPA, 1976. *Publications:* (ed jtly) Clinical Paediatric Physiology, 1979; (ed jtly) Care of the Child with Diabetes, 1985; (ed jtly) Listen, my child has a lot of living to do: caring for children with life-threatening conditions, 1990; numerous papers on preterm infants, childhood diabetes and internat. child health. *Recreations:* visual arts, politics of child health, the environment. *Address:* 19 Charlotte Street, Bristol BS1 5PZ. *T:* Bristol (0117) 926 0448. *Club:* Oxford University Choolant Society.

See also M. Baum.

BAUM, Prof. Michael, ChM; FRCS; Professor of Surgery, Institute of Cancer Research, Royal Marsden Hospital, London, since 1990; *b* 31 May 1937; *s* of Isidor and Mary Baum; *m* 1965, Judith (*née* Marcus); one *s* two *d*. *Educ:* Univ. of Birmingham (MB, ChB; ChM). FRCS 1965. Lecturer in Surgery, King's College Hosp., 1969–72; Research Fellow, Univ. of Pittsburgh, USA, 1971–72; Reader in Surgery, Welsh National Sch. of Medicine, Cardiff, 1972–78; Hon. Cons. Surgeon, King's College Hosp., 1978–80; Prof. of Surgery, KCH Med. Sch., London, 1980–90. Chairman: SE Thames Regional Cancer Organisation, 1988–90; British Breast Gp, 1989–91; Breast Cancer Trials Cttee, 1989–; UK Co-ordinating Cttee for Cancer Research, 1989–. Mem., Adv. Cttee on Breast Cancer Screening, DHSS, 1987–. Hon. MD Göteborg, 1986. *Publications:* Breast Cancer—The Facts, 1981, 3rd edn 1994; multiple pubns on breast cancer, cancer therapy, cancer biology and the philosophy of science. *Recreations:* painting, sculpting, theatre, reading, philosophizing. *Address:* Garden Flat, 12 Redington Road, NW3 7RG. *T:* 0171–435 0702. *Clubs:* Athenæum, Royal Society of Medicine, Chelsea Arts.

See also J. D. Baum.

BAUMAN, Robert Patten; Chairman, British Aerospace, since 1994; Chief Executive, SmithKline Beecham, 1989–94 (Chairman and Chief Executive, Beecham Group, 1986–89); *b* 27 March 1931; *s* of John Nevan Bauman Jr and Lucille Miller Patten; *m* 1961, Patricia Hughes Jones; one *s* one *d*. *Educ:* Ohio Wesleyan Univ. (BA); Harvard Sch. of Business (MBA). Served USAF, 1955–57. General Foods Corp., 1958–81: Corp. Vice-Pres., 1968; Group Vice-Pres., 1970; Exec. Vice-Pres. and Corp. Dir, 1972–81; Pres., Internat. Ops, 1974–81; Dir, Avco Corp., 1980, Chm. and Chief Exec., 1981–85; Vice-Chm. and Dir, Textron Inc., 1985–86. Director: Cap Cities/ABC Inc., 1986–; Union Pacific Corp., 1987–; CIGNA Corp., 1990–; Reuters Holdings, 1993–; Russell Reynolds Associates Inc., 1994–. Trustee: Ohio Wesleyan Univ., 1982–; Royal Botanic Gardens, Kew, 1990–. *Publication:* Plants as Pets, 1982. *Recreations:* growing orchids, tennis, photography, golf. *Address:* British Aerospace plc, Warwick House, PO Box 87, Farnborough Aerospace Centre, Farnborough GU14 6YU. *Clubs:* Queen's; Blind Brook (New York); Walton Heath Golf.

BAUR, Christopher Frank; writer; Editor, The Scotsman, 1985–87; *b* 28 May 1942; *s* of Mrs Mary Stewart (*née* Sigg) and Frank Baur; *m* 1965, Jaqueline Gilchrist; four *s*. *Educ:* Dalhousie Prep. Sch.; Strathallan Sch., Perthshire. Joined Scotsman as copy boy, 1960; trained as journalist; Scotsman's Industrial Reporter, 1963, additionally Scottish Politics, 1972; Financial Times, Scottish corresp., 1973; Scottish political corresp., BBC, 1976; Asst Editor, Scotsman, 1978, writing on politics and economic affairs; Dep. Editor, Scotsman, 1983–85. *Recreation:* creating. *Address:* 29 Edgehead Village, near Pathhead, Midlothian. *T:* Ford (01875) 320476.

BAVIN, Alfred Robert Walter, CB 1966; Deputy Secretary, Department of Health and Social Security, 1968–73 (Ministry of Health, 1966–68); *b* 4 April 1917; *s* of late Alfred and late Annie Bavin; *m* 1947, Helen Mansfield (*d* 1987); one *s* three *d*. *Educ:* Christ's Hosp.; Balliol Coll., Oxford. 1st cl. Hon. Mods 1937; 1st cl. Lit. Hum. 1939. Min. of Health, Asst Principal, 1939, Principal, 1946; Cabinet Office, 1948–50; Min. of Health, Principal Private Sec. to Minister, 1951; Asst Sec. 1952; Under-Sec. 1960. Nuffield Home Civil Service Travelling Fellowship, 1956. *Address:* 86 Chapel Lane, Sands, High Wycombe, Bucks HP12 4BS. *Clubs:* Athenæum, MCC.

BAVIN, Rt. Rev. Timothy John, FRSCM; OGS; *b* 17 Sept. 1935; *s* of Edward Sydney Durrance and Marjorie Gwendoline Bavin. *Educ:* Brighton Coll.; Worcester Coll., Oxford (2nd Cl. Theol., MA); Cuddesdon Coll. Curate, St Alban's Cathedral Pretoria, 1961–64; Chaplain, St Alban's Coll., Pretoria, 1965–68; Curate of Uckfield, Sussex, 1969–71; Vicar of Good Shepherd, Brighton, 1971–73; Dean and Rector of Cathedral of St Mary the Virgin, Johannesburg, 1973–74; Bishop of Johannesburg, 1974–84; Bishop of Portsmouth, 1985–95; postulant, OSB, 1996. Mem., OGS, 1987–; FRSCM 1991. ChStJ 1975. *Publication:* Deacons in the Ministry of the Church, 1987. *Recreations:* music, theatre, walking, gardening. *Address:* Alton Abbey, Alton, Hants GU34 4AP.

BAWDEN, Prof. Charles Roskelly, FBA; Professor of Mongolian, University of London, 1970–84, now Emeritus Professor; *b* 22 April 1924; *s* of George Charles Bawden and Eleanor Alice Adelaide Bawden (*née* Russell); *m* 1949, Jean Barham Johnson; three *s* one *d*. *Educ:* Weymouth Grammar School; Peterhouse, Cambridge (MA, PhD, Dipl. in Oriental Languages). War Service, RNVR, 1943–46. Asst Principal, German Section, Foreign Office, 1948–49; Lectr in Mongolian, SOAS, 1955; Reader in Mongolian, 1962, and Prof., 1970, Univ. of London; Head of Dept of Far East, SOAS, 1970–84; Pro-Director, SOAS, 1982–84. FBA 1971–80, 1985; Mem. corresp., Soc. Finno-Ougrienne 1975. *Publications:* The Mongol Chronicle Altan Tobči, 1955; The Jebtsundamba Khutukhtus of Urga, 1961; The Modern History of Mongolia, 1968, 2nd edn 1989; The Chester Beatty Library: a catalogue of the Mongolian Collection, 1969; Shamans Lamas and Evangelicals: the English missionaries in Siberia, 1985; articles and reviews in SOAS Bull., Central Asiatic Jl, Zentralasiatische Studien and other periodicals. *Address:* 19 Richings Way, Iver, Bucks SL0 9DA.

BAWDEN, Nina Mary, (Mrs A. S. Kark), CBE 1995; MA; FRSL; JP; novelist; *b* 19 Jan. 1925; *d* of Charles and Ellalaine Ursula May Mabey; *m* 1st, 1946, Henry Walton Bawden; one *s* (and one *s* decd); 2nd, 1954, Austen Steven Kark, *qv*; one *d*. *Educ:* Ilford County High Sch.; Somerville Coll., Oxford (BA). Asst, Town and Country Planning Assoc., 1946–47. JP Surrey, 1968. Mem., ALCS. Pres., Soc. of Women Writers and Journalists. *Publications: novels:* Who Calls the Tune, 1953; The Odd Flamingo, 1954; Change Here for Babylon, 1955; The Solitary Child, 1956; Devil by the Sea, 1958, 2nd edn 1972 (abridged for children, 1976); Just Like a Lady, 1960; In Honour Bound, 1961; Tortoise by Candlelight, 1963; Under the Skin, 1964; A Little Love, a Little Learning, 1965; A Woman of My Age, 1967; The Grain of Truth, 1969; The Birds on the Trees, 1970; Anna Apparent, 1972; George beneath a Paper Moon, 1974; Afternoon of a Good Woman, 1976 (Yorkshire Post Novel of the Year, 1976); Familiar Passions, 1979; Walking Naked, 1981; The Ice House, 1983; Circles of Deceit, 1987 (televised, 1990); Family Money, 1991; *for children:* The Secret Passage, 1963; On the Run, 1964; The White Horse Gang, 1966; Squib, 1966; A Handful of Thieves, 1967; The Witch's Daughter, 1968; The Runaway Summer, 1969; Carrie's War, 1975; The Peppermint Pig, 1975 (Guardian award, 1976); Rebel on a Rock, 1978; The Robbers, 1978; Kept in the Dark, 1982; The Finding, 1985; Princess Alice, 1985; Keeping Henry, 1987; The Outside Child, 1989; Humbug, 1992; The Real Plato Jones, 1993; *autobiography:* In My Own Time, 1994. *Recreations:* travelling, reading, politics, friends. *Address:* 22 Noel Road, N1 8HA. *T:* 0171–226 2839; 19 Kapodistriou, Nauplion, Greece 21100. *Clubs:* Oriental, PEN, Society of Authors.

BAWN, Cecil Edwin Henry, CBE 1956; FRS 1952; BSc, PhD; Brunner Professor of Physical Chemistry in the University of Liverpool, 1969–Dec. 1973, now Emeritus (Grant-Brunner Professor of Inorganic and Physical Chemistry, 1948–69); *b* 6 Nov. 1908; British; *m* 1934, Winifred Mabel Jackson; two *s* one *d*. *Educ:* Cotham Grammar Sch., Bristol. Graduated, Univ. of Bristol, 1929; PhD in Chemistry (Bristol), 1932; Asst Lectr in Chemistry, Univ. of Manchester, 1931–34; Lectr in Chemistry, 1934–38; Lectr in Physical Chemistry, Univ. of Bristol, 1938–45; Reader in Physical Chemistry, 1945–49. During War of 1939–45 was in charge of a Physico-Chemical Section in Armament Research Dept, Min. of Supply. Mem., Univ. Grants Cttee, 1965–74. Swinburne Gold Medal, 1966. Hon. DSc: Bradford, 1966; Birmingham, 1968; Bristol, 1974. *Publications:* The Chemistry of High Polymers, 1948; papers in chemical journals. *Address:* Springfields, Stoodleigh, near Tiverton, Devon EX16 9PT. *T:* Oakford (013985) 220.

BAWTREE, Rear Adm. David Kenneth, CB 1993; EurIng, CEng, FIMechE, FIEE; Civil Emergencies Adviser, Home Office, since 1993; *b* 1 Oct. 1937; *s* of Kenneth Alfred Bawtree and Dorothy Constance Bawtree (*née* Allen); *m* 1962, Ann Cummins; one *s* one *d*. *Educ:* Christ's Hospital; Royal Naval Engineering College. BSc(Eng). Served in HM Ships Maidstone, Jutland, Diamond, Defender, Rothesay, Bristol, and MoD, 1965–76; Staff of C-in-C Fleet, 1979, of DG Weapons, 1981; Dep. Dir, Naval Analysis, 1983; RCDS 1985; Dep. Dir, Op. Requirements (Navy), 1986; Dir, Naval Engrg Training, 1987–90; Flag Officer, and Naval Base Comdr, Portsmouth, 1990–93. Past President: Royal Naval and Royal Albert Yacht Club, Portsmouth; Naval Home Club; RN & RM Children's Home; Royal Naval Squash Rackets Assoc.; Past Member: Victory Technical Adv. Cttee; Mary Rose Trust; Portsmouth Naval Base Heritage Trust; Portsmouth Naval Base Property Trust; Royal Naval Mus.; Trustee: St Mary's Music Foundn, 1990– (Chm.); Portsmouth News Snowball Appeal, 1992–; Director: Hants Foundn for Young Musicians, 1993–; Portsmouth Community Health Care Trust, 1993–; former Patron, Portsmouth MacMillan Appeal. Governor: Portsmouth Grammar Sch., 1993– (Chm.); Penhale First Sch., 1991–. Freeman, City of London; Liveryman, Engineers' Co. *Recreations:* squash, organs and their music, miniature furniture. *Club:* Naval and Military.

BAXANDALL, Prof. Michael David Kighley, FBA 1982; Professor of the History of Art, University of California, Berkeley, since 1987; *b* 18 Aug. 1933; *o s* of late David Baxandall, CBE; *m* 1963, Katharina Simon; one *s* one *d*. *Educ:* Manchester Grammar Sch.; Downing Coll., Cambridge (MA); Univs of Pavia and Munich. Jun. Res. Fellow, Warburg Inst., 1959–61; Asst Keeper, Dept of Architecture and Sculpture, Victoria and Albert Museum, 1961–65; Warburg Institute, University of London: Lectr in Renaissance Studies, 1965–73; Reader, 1973–81; Prof., History of the Classical Tradition, 1981–88. Slade Prof. of Fine Art, Univ. of Oxford, 1974–75; A. D. White Prof.-at-Large, Cornell Univ., 1982–88. *Publications:* Giotto and the Orators, 1971; Painting and Experience in Fifteenth-Century Italy, 1972; South German Sculpture 1480–1530 in the Victoria and Albert Museum, 1974; The Limewood Sculptors of Renaissance Germany, 1980; Patterns of Intention, 1985; (jtly) Tiepolo and the Pictorial Intelligence, 1994; Shadows and Enlightenment, 1995. *Address:* 405 Doe Library, University of California, Berkeley, CA 94720, USA.

BAXENDALE, Presiley Lamorna, (Mrs R. K. FitzGerald); QC 1992; *b* 31 Jan. 1951; *d* of Geoffrey Arthur Baxendale and late Elizabeth (*née* Stevenson); *m* 1978, Richard Kieran FitzGerald; one *s* one *d*. *Educ:* St Mary's Sch., Wantage; St Anne's Coll., Oxford (BA). Called to the Bar, Lincoln's Inn, 1974; Jun. Counsel to Crown, Common Law,

1991. Mem., ICSTIS, 1986–90. Vice Chm., Exec. Cttee, 1994–, and Mem. Council, Justice. Mem., Ct of Govs, LSE, 1988–. *Address:* 2 Hare Court, Temple, EC4Y 7BH. *T:* 0171–583 1770. *Club:* CWIL.

BAXENDELL, Sir Peter (Brian), Kt 1981; CBE 1972; FEng 1978; FIC 1983; Director, Shell Transport and Trading Co., 1973–95 (Chairman, 1979–85); *b* 28 Feb. 1925; *s* of Lesley Wilfred Edward Baxendell and Evelyn Mary Baxendell (*née* Gaskin); *m* 1949, Rosemary (*née* Lacey); two *s* two *d*. *Educ:* St Francis Xavier's, Liverpool; Royal School of Mines, London (ARSM, BSc; FIC 1983). Joined Royal Dutch/Shell Group, 1946; Petroleum Engr in Egypt, 1947, and Venezuela, 1950; Techn. Dir, Shell-BP Nigeria, 1963; Head of SE Asia Div., London, 1966; Man. Dir, Shell-BP Nigeria, 1969; Chm., Shell UK, 1974–79; Man. Dir, 1973, Chm., Cttee of Man. Dirs, 1982–85, Royal Dutch/Shell Gp of Cos; Chm., Shell Canada Ltd, 1980–85; Dir, Shell Oil Co., USA, 1982–85; Chm., Hawker Siddeley Gp, 1986–91 (Dir, 1984–91; Dep. Chm., Jan.–April 1986); Director: Sun Life Assurance Co. of Canada, 1986–; Inchcape, 1986–93. Mem., UGC, 1983–89. Mem., Governing Body, Imperial Coll., London, 1983–. Hon. DSc: Heriot-Watt, 1982; QUB, 1986; London, 1986; Loughborough, 1987. Commander, Order of Orange–Nassau, 1985. *Publications:* articles on petroleum engrg subjects in scientific jls. *Recreations:* tennis, fishing. *Address:* Shell Centre, SE1 7NA. *T:* 0171–934 2772.

BAXTER, Dr Christina Ann; Dean of St John's College, Nottingham, since 1988; Vice-Chairman of House of Laity, General Synod of Church of England, since 1990; *b* 8 March 1947; *d* of Leslie John David and Madge Adeline Baxter. *Educ:* Walthamstow Hall, Sevenoaks, Kent; Durham Univ. (BA, PhD); Bristol Univ. (Cert Ed). Asst Teacher, 1969–73, Head of Religious Educn, 1973–76, John Leggott Sixth Form Coll., Scunthorpe; part-time tutor, St John's Coll., Durham, and Durham research student, 1976–79; Lectr in Christian Doctrine, St John's Coll., Nottingham, 1979–. *Recreation:* swimming. *Address:* St John's College, Chilwell Lane, Bramcote, Nottingham NG9 3DS. *T:* Nottingham (0115) 925 1114; 18 St Michael's Square, Bramcote, Nottingham NG9 3HG. *T:* Nottingham (0115) 922 4087.

BAXTER, Maj.-Gen. Ian Stuart, CBE 1982 (MBE 1973); antiques dealer, since 1990; *b* 20 July 1937; *s* of Charles Baxter and Edith (*née* Trinder); *m* 1961, Meg Bullock; three *d*. *Educ:* Ottershaw Sch. Commissioned RASC, 1958; RCT, 1965; regtl and staff appts UK, NI, Kenya, India, Germany and Falkland Is; sc, Camberley, 1970; ndc, Latimer, 1974; DS, Staff Coll., Camberley, 1975–78; CO, 2nd Armoured Div., Regt RCT, 1978–80; Col AQ Commando Forces, RM, 1980–83 (incl. Falklands Campaign); RCDS, 1984; Dir, Army Recruiting, 1985–87; ACDS (Logistics), 1987–90, retd. Col Comdt, RCT, 1989–93. Dir (non-exec.), Cornwall Community Healthcare NHS Trust, 1990–93; Vice-Chm. (non-exec), Cornwall HealthCare NHS Trust, 1993–. Pres., RCT/RASC Instn, 1993–. *Recreations:* antique restoration, Rugby. *Address:* c/o Barclays Bank, 50 Fore Street, Callington, Cornwall PL17 7AQ.

BAXTER, John Lawson; DL; *b* 25 Nov. 1939; *s* of John Lawson Baxter and Enid Maud Taggart; *m* 1967; three *s*. *Educ:* Trinity Coll., Dublin; Queen's Univ., Belfast; BA, BComm, LLB; LLM Tulane Univ., New Orleans. Solicitor. Mem. (U) N Ireland Assembly, for N Antrim, 1973–75; Minister of Information, N Ireland Executive, 1974. Chm. (part-time), Industrial Tribunals (NI), 1980–83; Mem., Northern Health and Social Services Board, 1982–. DL Co Londonderry, 1988. *Recreations:* golf, fishing. *Address:* Beardiville, Cloyfin, Coleraine, N Ireland. *T:* Bushmills (02657) 31552.

BAXTER, John Stephen; Head Master, Wells Cathedral School, since 1986; *b* 7 Sept. 1939; *s* of George Baxter and Muriel (*née* Firman); *m* 1965, Priscilla Candy; two *s*. *Educ:* Magdalen Coll. Sch., Oxford; Merton Coll., Oxford (BA Modern Hist.); Grey Coll., Durham (DipEd). Assistant Master: Cranleigh Sch., 1964–67; Christ's Coll., NZ, 1967–70; Westminster Sch., 1971–86 (Hd of Hist., 1974–79; Hse Master, 1979–81). Ecclesiastical Insce Gp Scholar, 1993; Korea Foundn Fellow, 1993. Res. Asst, H of C, 1971–79; Reader, Edward Arnold, 1980–83. Mem., Admiralty Interview Bd, 1988–. Chairman: SW Div., HMC, 1991; Choir Schs Assoc., 1995. Gov., St Aubyn's Sch., 1978–; Trustee, Commonwealth Linking Trust, 1972–; Mem., Bd of Mgt, MusicSpace, 1988–. MIMgt 1991; FRSA 1990. Freeman, City of London, 1991; Mem., Musicians' Co., 1991–. *Publications:* (contrib.) History of Lords and Commons Cricket, 1989; papers and articles in educn jls. *Recreations:* music, Cornish history, golf, sport (GB Olympic Hockey Squad, Oxon; Capt., Oxon U19 Rugby; Minor Counties Cricket, Cornwall Veterans Cricket). *Address:* Wells Cathedral School, Wells, Somerset BA5 2ST. *T:* Wells (01749) 672117. *Clubs:* East India, Devonshire, Sports and Public Schools, MCC; Vincent's (Oxford); Cornish Coughs, St Minver Cricket, St Enodoc Golf, (Cornwall).

BAXTER, John Walter, CBE 1974; Consultant, G. Maunsell & Partners (Partner, 1955, Senior Partner, 1959–80); *b* 4 June 1917; *s* of late J. G. Baxter and late D. L. Baxter (*née* Phelps); *m* 1941, Jessie, *d* of late T. Pimblott; one *d*. *Educ:* Westminster City Sch.; City and Guilds Engrg College. BSc(Eng), FCGI, FEng, FICE, FRSA. Civil Engineer: Trussed Concrete Steel Co. Ltd, 1936–41; Shell Refining Co. Ltd, 1941–52; Maunsell Posford & Pavry, 1952–55. President: ICE, 1976–77 (Vice-Pres., 1973–76, Mem. Council, 1963–68 and 1970–79); Smeatonian Soc. of Civil Engrs, 1986; Vice-Chm., ACE, 1979–80, Chm., 1980–81. *Publications:* contrib. Proc. ICE. *Address:* The Down Side, Old Station Road, Itchen Abbas, Hants SO21 1AZ.

BAXTER, Kenneth Peter; Secretary, Department of the Premier and Cabinet, Victoria, since 1992; Chairman, Australian Dairy Corporation, since 1992; *b* 23 Oct. 1943; *s* of P. F. Baxter; *m* 1973, Pamela Annabel Marr; two *s* one *d*. *Educ:* Fort St Boys' High Sch.; Univ. of Sydney (BEc). Farming columnist and press sec., 1972–80; Dir, Corporate Affairs, Philip Morris Ltd and Asst Man. Dir, Philip Morris Aust. Ltd, 1981–82; Cllr, Aust. Rural Adjustment Unit, 1982–87; Mem., Aust. Egg Bd, 1983–85; Man. Dir, NSW Egg Corp., 1983–88; Dir, Grain Handling Authy, NSW, 1986–89; Chairman: Good Food Products Aust. Pty Ltd, 1986–88; Aust. Dairy Res. Council, 1986–; Darling Harbour Authy, 1989–90; Dairy R&D Corp., 1990–92; Aust. Dairy Ltd, 1992–; Dir, Thai Dairy Ind. Co. Ltd, 1992–. Dep. Dir–Gen., Premier's Dept, NSW, 1988–92. FAICD 1980; FAIM 1985. *Publications:* Wool Marketing in New Zealand, 1967, 2nd edn 1972; Statutory Marketing Authorities, 1988. *Recreations:* sailing, surf life-saving, reading. *Address:* (office) 55 Collins Street, Melbourne, Vic 3000, Australia. *T:* (3) 6515072. *Clubs:* Melbourne (Victoria); Royal Sydney Yacht Squadron (Sydney).

BAXTER, Prof. Murdoch Scott, PhD, CChem, FRSC; FRSE; Director, Marine Environment Laboratory of International Atomic Energy Agency (formerly International Laboratory of Marine Radioactivity), Monaco, since 1990, on leave of absence from Glasgow University; *b* 12 March 1944; *s* of John Sawyer Napier Baxter and Margaret Hastie Baxter (*née* Murdoch); *m* 1968, Janice Henderson; one *s*. *Educ:* Univ. of Glasgow. BSc Hons Chem. 1966, PhD Geochem. 1969. Research Fellow, State Univ. of NY (Noble gas history of lunar rocks and meteorites), 1969–70; Lectr, Dept of Chemistry, Univ. of Glasgow (geochem., radiochem. and envtl radioactivity), 1970–85; Vis. Consultant, IAEA (nuclear waste disposal), 1981–82; Dir, Scottish Univs Res. and Reactor Centre, 1985–90; Personal Chair, Univ. of Glasgow, 1985–. Member: Challenger Soc. for Marine Sci.; Scottish Marine Biol Assoc.; NERC Coger Cttee. FRSE 1989. Exec. Editor, JL of Envtl Radioactivity; Mem., Editl Bd, Jl of Radioanalytical and Nuclear Chem. *Publications:* numerous papers to professional jls. *Recreations:* hill walking, golf, sport watching, keeping dogs. *Address:* Marine Environment Laboratory, International Atomic Energy Agency, BP 800, 98012 Monaco.

BAXTER, Raymond Frederic, FRSA; broadcaster and writer; *b* 25 Jan. 1922; *s* of Frederick Garfield Baxter and Rosina Baxter (*née* Rivers); *m* 1945, Sylvia Kathryn (*née* Johnson), Boston, Mass; one *s* one *d*. *Educ:* Ilford County High Sch. Joined RAF, 1940; flew Spitfires with 65, 93 and 602 Sqdns, in UK, Med. and Europe. Entered Forces Broadcasting in Cairo, still as serving officer, 1945; civilian deputy Dir BFN BBC, 1947–49; subseq. short attachment West Region and finally joined Outside Broadcast Dept, London; with BBC until 1966; Dir, Motoring Publicity, BMC, 1967–68. Member Cttee of Management: RNLI, 1979– (Vice Pres., 1987–); Air League, 1980–85. Hon. Freeman, City of London, 1978; Liveryman, GAPAN, 1983. Hon. Admiral, Assoc. of Dunkirk Little Ships, 1982–. CRAeS 1991. *Publications:* (with James Burke and Michael Latham) Tomorrow's World, Vol. 1, 1970, Vol. 2, 1971; Farnborough Commentary, 1980; film commentaries, articles and reports on motoring and aviation subjects, etc. *Recreations:* motoring, boating. *Address:* The Green Cottage, Wargrave Road, Henley-on-Thames, Oxon RG9 3HX. *T:* Henley-on-Thames (01491) 571081. *Clubs:* Royal Air Force, British Racing Drivers, etc.

BAXTER, Prof. Rodney James, FRS 1982; FAA 1977; Professor in the Department of Theoretical Physics, Institute of Advanced Studies, and in the School of Mathematical Sciences, Australian National University, since 1981; *b* 8 Feb. 1940; *s* of Thomas James Baxter and Florence A. Baxter; *m* 1968, Elizabeth Phillips; one *s* one *d*. *Educ:* Bancroft's Sch., Essex; Trinity Coll., Cambridge; Australian National Univ. Reservoir Engineer, Iraq Petroleum Co., 1964–65; Research Fellow, ANU, 1965–68; Asst Prof., Mathematics Dept, Massachusetts Inst. of Technology, 1968–70; Fellow, ANU, 1970–81; Royal Soc. Res. Prof., 1992, Sen. Fellow, 1992–, Isaac Newton Inst. for Mathematical Scis, Cambridge Univ. Pawsey Medal, Aust. Acad. of Science, 1975; Boltzmann Medal, IUPAP, 1980; Heineman Prize, Amer. Inst. of Physics, 1987; Harrie Massey Medal, Inst. of Physics, 1994. *Publications:* Exactly Solved Models in Statistical Mechanics, 1982; contribs to Proc. Royal Soc., Jl of Physics A, Physical Rev., Statistical Physics, Annals of Physics. *Recreation:* theatre. *Address:* Theoretical Physics IAS, Australian National University, Canberra, ACT 2601, Australia. *T:* (62) 492968.

BAXTER, Roger George, PhD; FRAS, FRSA; Headmaster of Sedbergh School, 1982–95; *b* 21 April 1940; *s* of Rev. Benjamin George Baxter and Gweneth Muriel Baxter (*née* Causer); *m* 1967, Dorothy Ann Cook; one *s* one *d*. *Educ:* Handsworth Grammar Sch., Birmingham; Univ. of Sheffield (BSc, PhD). Junior Research Fellow, Univ. of Sheffield, 1965–66, Lectr, Dept of Applied Mathematics, 1966–70; Asst Mathematics Master, Winchester Coll., 1970–81, Under Master, 1976–81. Governor: Bramcote Sch., Scarborough, 1982–; Hurworth Hse Sch., Darlington, 1982–; Cathedral Choir Sch., Ripon, 1984–; Mowden Hall Sch., Northumberland, 1984–; Cundall Manor Sch., York, 1988–. Member: HMC Academic Policy Cttee, 1985–90; Common Entrance Board, 1989–94. Mem. Ct, Univ. of Lancaster, 1994–. Freeman, City of London, 1992; Liveryman, Gunmakers' Co., 1992–. *Publications:* various papers on numerical studies in magnetoplasma diffusion with applications to the F-2 layer of the ionosphere. *Recreations:* opera, music, cooking, wine. *Address:* The Rivelin, The Gill, Lindale, Grange-over-Sands, Cumbria LA11 6LT. *T:* Grange-over-Sands (01539) 535129.

BAXTER, William T., BCom Edinburgh; Professor of Accounting, London School of Economics, 1947–73, Hon. Fellow 1978; *b* 27 July 1906; *s* of W. M. Baxter and Margaret Threipland; *m* 1st, 1940, Marjorie Allanson (*d* 1971); one *s* one *d*; 2nd, 1973, Leena-Kaisa Laitakari-Kaila. *Educ:* George Watson's Coll.; Univ. of Edinburgh (Hon. Fellow, 1994). Chartered Accountant (Edinburgh), 1930; Commonwealth Fund Fellow, 1931, at Harvard Univ.; Lectr in Accounting, Univ. of Edinburgh, 1934; Prof. of Accounting, Univ. of Cape Town, 1937. Hon. DLitt: Kent at Canterbury, 1974; Heriot-Watt, 1976; Hon. DSc Buckingham, 1983; Hon. DSc(Econ) Hull, 1977. *Publications:* Income Tax for Professional Students, 1936; The House of Hancock, 1945; Depreciation, 1971; Accounting Values and Inflation, 1975; Collected Papers on Accounting, 1979; Inflation Accounting, 1984. *Address:* 1 The Ridgeway, NW11 8TD. *T:* 0181–455 6810.

BAYCROFT, Rt Rev. John Arthur; *see* Ottawa, Bishop of.

BAYDA, Hon. Edward Dmytro; Chief Justice of Saskatchewan, since 1981; *b* 9 Sept. 1931; *s* of Dmytro Andrew Bayda and Mary Bilinski; *m* 1953, Marie-Thérèse Yvonne Gagné; one *s* five *d*. *Educ:* Univ. of Saskatchewan (BA 1951, LLB 1953). Called to the Bar, Saskatchewan, 1954; QC (Sask) 1966. Senior Partner, Bayda, Halvorson, Scheibel & Thompson, 1966–72. Judge, Court of Queen's Bench, 1972; Justice, Court of Appeal, 1974. Hon. LLD Saskatchewan, 1989. KM 1975. *Address:* (home) 3000 Albert Street, Regina, Sask S4S 3N7, Canada. *T:* (306) 5862126; (chambers) Court House, 2425 Victoria Avenue, Regina, Sask S4P 3V7. *T:* (306) 7875415.

BAYFIELD, Rabbi Anthony Michael; Chief Executive, Reform Movement and Reform Synagogues of Great Britain, since 1994; *b* 4 July 1946; *s* of Ronald Bayfield and Sheila (*née* Mann); *m* 1969, Linda Gavinia (*née* Rose); one *s* two *d*. *Educ:* Royal Liberty Sch., Gidea Park; Magdalene Coll., Cambridge (MA (Hons) Law); Leo Baeck Coll., London (Rabbinic degree). Rabbi, NW Surrey Synagogue, 1972–82; Dir, Sternberg Centre for Judaism (Manor House Trust), 1983–. Dir, Advancement of Jewish Educn Trust, 1987–93; Co-ordinator of Supervisors, 1987–93, Lectr in Homiletics, Leo Baeck Coll., 1992–. Chairman: Assembly of Rabbis, Reform Synagogues of GB, 1980–82; Council of Reform and Liberal Rabbis, 1984–86. Founder Editor, Manna (Qly Jl of Progressive Judaism), 1983–. *Publications:* Churban: the murder of the Jews of Europe, 1981; (ed) Dialogue with a Difference, 1992; Sinai, Law and Responsible Autonomy: Reform Judaism and the Halakhic tradition, 1993; articles in European Judaism, Brit. Jl of Religious Educn, Church Times. *Recreations:* family life, reading, walking, Essex CCC, suffering with West Ham United FC. *Address:* Reform Synagogues of Great Britain, Sternberg Centre for Judaism, 80 East End Road, Finchley, N3 2SY. *T:* 0181–349 4731, 0181–346 2288.

BAYLEY, Gordon Vernon, CBE 1976; FIA, FIMA, FSS, CIMgt; Director, National Provident Institution, 1970–94; *b* 25 July 1920; *s* of late Capt. Vernon Bayley, King's Regt, and Mrs Gladys Maud Bayley; *m* 1945, Miriam Allenby, *d* of late Frederick Walter Ellis and Miriam Ellis, Eastbourne; one *s* two *d*. *Educ:* Abingdon. Joined HM Forces, 1940; commissioned Royal Artillery, Major 1945. Asst Actuary, Equitable Life Assurance Soc., 1949; Partner, Duncan C. Fraser and Co. (Actuaries), 1954–57; National Provident Institution: Assistant Sec., 1957, Joint Sec. 1959; Gen. Manager and Actuary 1964–85. Chm., Swiss Reinsurance Co., 1985–92; Dir, TR Industrial and Gen. Trust PLC, 1983–88. Mem., Occupational Pensions Bd, 1973–74. Member: Cttee to Review the Functioning of Financial Institutions, 1977–80; Companies House Steering Bd, 1988–90. Institute of Actuaries: Fellow, 1946; Hon. Sec., 1960–62; Vice-Pres., 1964–67; Pres., 1974–76; Chm., Life Offices Assoc., 1969–70 (Dep. Chm., 1967–68); Gold Medal, 1985. Chm., Bd of Governors, Abingdon Sch., 1979–83. *Publications:* contribs to Jl Inst.

Actuaries, Jl Royal Statistical Soc. *Recreation:* sailing. *Address:* The Old Manor, Witley, Surrey GU8 5QW. *T:* Wormley (01428) 682301. *Clubs:* Athenæum, English Speaking Union; Sea View Yacht.

BAYLEY, Hugh; MP (Lab) York, since 1992; *b* 9 Jan. 1952; *s* of Michael and Pauline Bayley; *m* 1984, Fenella Jeffers; one *s* one *d*. *Educ:* Haileybury Sch.; Univ. of Bristol (BSc); Univ. of York (BPhil). Dist Officer, 1975–77, Nat. Officer, 1977–82, NALGO; Gen. Sec., Internat. Broadcasting Trust, 1982–86; Lectr in Social Policy, 1986–87, Res. Fellow in Health Econs, 1987–92, Univ. of York. Councillor, London Bor. of Camden, 1980–86. Mem., York HA, 1988–90. Mem., Select Cttee on Health, 1992–. Chm., Yorks Region, Fabian Soc., 1988–. *Address:* 9 Holly Terrace, York YO1 4DS. *T:* York (01904) 623713.

BAYLEY, Dame Iris; *see* Murdoch, Dame J. I.

BAYLEY, Prof. John Oliver, FBA 1990; Warton Professor of English Literature, and Fellow of St Catherine's College, University of Oxford, 1974–92; *b* 27 March 1925; *s* of F. J. Bayley; *m* 1956, Dame Jean Iris Murdoch, *qv*. *Educ:* Eton; New Coll., Oxford. 1st cl. hons English Oxon 1950. Served in Army, 1943–47. Mem., St Antony's and Magdalen Colls, Oxford, 1951–55; Fellow and Tutor in English, New Coll., Oxford, 1955–74. *Publications:* In Another Country (novel), 1954; The Romantic Survival: A Study in Poetic Evolution, 1956; The Characters of Love, 1961; Tolstoy and the Novel, 1966; Pushkin: A Comparative Commentary, 1971; The Uses of Division: unity and disharmony in literature, 1976; An Essay on Hardy, 1978; Shakespeare and Tragedy, 1981; The Order of Battle at Trafalgar, 1987; The Short Story: Henry James to Elizabeth Bowen, 1988; Housman's Poems, 1992; Alice (novel), 1994; The Queer Captain (novel), 1995.

BAYLEY, Nicola Mary; writer, artist and illustrator; *b* 18 Aug. 1949; *d* of Percy Harold Bayley and Ann Barbara Crowder; *m* 1978, Alan John Howard Hilton, *qv*; one *s*. *Educ:* Farnborough Hill Convent College; St Martin's Sch. of Art (DipAD); Royal College of Art (MA Illus.). *Publications: written and illustrated:* Nicola Bayley's Book of Nursery Rhymes, 1975; One Old Oxford Ox, 1977; Copy Cats (5 books), 1984; As I was Going Up and Down, 1985; Hush-a-bye Baby, 1985; *illustrated:* Tyger Voyage, 1976; Puss in Boots, 1976; La Corona and the Tin Frog, 1979; The Patchwork Cat, 1981; The Mouldy, 1983; Merry Go Rhymes (4 books), 1987; The Mousehole Cat, 1990. *Recreations:* watching the garden, opera, sleeping, cats. *Address:* c/o Walker Books, 87 Vauxhall Walk, SE11 5HJ. *Club:* Art Workers Guild.

BAYLEY, Lt-Comdr Oscar Stewart Morris, RN retd; *b* 15 April 1926; *s* of late Rev. J. H. S. Bayley; *m* Pamela Margaret Harrison (one *s* one *d* by a former marriage). *Educ:* St John's Sch., Leatherhead; King James's Grammar Sch., Knaresborough. Called to Bar, Lincoln's Inn, 1959. Entered RN, 1944: Ceylon, 1956–58; Supply Off., HMS Narvik and Sqdn Supply Off., 5th Submarine Div., 1960–62; Sec. to Comdr British Forces Caribbean Area, 1962–65; retd from RN at own request, 1966. Legal Asst (Unfair Competition), The Distillers Co. Ltd, 1966–68; Clerk, Fishmongers' Co., 1968–73; Accountant, Hawker Siddeley Gp, 1978–81, John Lewis Partnership, 1981–82. Dir, Seed Oysters (UK) Ltd. Clerk to Governors of Gresham's Sch., Holt; Hon. Sec., Salmon and Trout Assoc. and of Shellfish Assoc. of Great Britain; Vice-Chm., National Anglers' Council; Secretary: Atlantic Salmon Research Trust; City and Guilds of London Art Sch. Ltd, 1968–73; Nat. Assoc. of Pension Funds Investment Protection Cttee, 1974–75. Dir and Chief Sec., The Royal Life Saving Soc., 1976–78: Reader: All Saints Church, Footscray, 1989; St Andrew's Church, Orpington, Kent, 1994; Chm., Sidcup Council of Churches, 1990–92. *Address:* 244 Bexley Lane, Sidcup, Kent DA14 4JG.

BAYLEY, Peter Charles; Emeritus Professor, University of St Andrews; Emeritus Fellow, University College, Oxford; *b* 25 Jan. 1921; *y s* of late William Charles Abell Bayley and Irene (*née* Heath); *m* 1951, Patience (marr. diss. 1980), *d* of late Sir George (Norman) Clark and Lady Clark; one *s* two *d*. *Educ:* Crypt Sch., Gloucester; University Coll., Oxford (Sidgwick Exhibnr; MA 1st Cl. Hons English, 1947). Served RA and Intell. Corps (India), 1941–45. Jun. Fellow, University Coll., Oxon, 1947; Fellow and Praelector in English, 1949–72 (at various times Domestic Bursar, Tutor for Admissions, Librarian, Editor of University Coll. Record); Univ. Lectr in English, 1952–72; Proctor, 1957–58; Oxford Univ. Corresp., The Times, 1960–63; Master of Collingwood Coll. and Lectr, Dept of Engish, Univ. of Durham, 1971–78; Berry Prof. and Head of Dept of English, Univ. of St Andrews, 1978–85. Vis. Reader, Birla Inst., Pilani, Rajasthan, India, 1966; Vis. Lectr, Yale Univ., and Robert Bates Vis. Fellow, Jonathan Edwards Coll., 1970; Brown Distinguished Vis. Prof., Univ. of the South, Sewanee, Tenn, 1978; Brown Distinguished Vis. Lectr in British Studies, Vanderbilt Univ., Sewanee, Rhodes, Birmingham-Southern, Millsaps etc., 1985. *Publications:* Edmund Spenser, Prince of Poets, 1971; 'Casebook' on Spenser's The Faerie Queene, 1977; Poems of Milton, 1982; An ABC of Shakespeare, 1985; University College, Oxford: a guide and brief history, 1992; edited: Spenser, The Faerie Queene: Book II, 1965; Book I, 1966; Loves and Deaths: short stories by 19th century novelists, 1972. *Recreations:* nature, art. *Address:* 63 Oxford Street, Woodstock, Oxford OX20 1TJ.

BAYLEY, Prof. Peter James; Drapers Professor of French, since 1985, and Fellow of Gonville and Caius College, since 1971, Cambridge University; *b* 20 Nov. 1944; *s* of John Henry Bayley and Margaret Burness, Portreath, Cornwall. *Educ:* Redruth County Grammar Sch.; Emmanuel Coll., Cambridge (Kitchener Schol., 1963–66; 1st cl. Hons Mod. and Med. Langs Tripos, 1964 and 1966; MA 1970; PhD 1971); Ecole Normale Supérieure, Paris (French Govt Schol., 1967–68). Cambridge University: Fellow of Emmanuel Coll., 1969–71; Coll. Lectr, Gonville and Caius Coll., 1971–85; Tutor, 1973–79; Praelector Rhetoricus, 1980–86; Univ. Asst Lectr in French, 1974–78; Univ. Lectr, 1978–85 (Actg Head, Dept of French, 1983–85). Hon. Sen. Res. Fellow, Inst. of Romance Studies, London Univ., 1990. Vice-Pres., Assoc. of Univ. Profs of French, 1989–95. Pres., Soc. for French Studies, 1990–92; deleg., and Mem. Exec., Univ. Council for Modern Langs, 1994–. Officier des Palmes Académiques, 1988. *Publications:* French Pulpit Oratory 1598–1650, 1980; (ed with D. Coleman) The Equilibrium of Wit: essays for Odette de Mourgues, 1982; (ed) Selected Sermons of the French Baroque, 1983; contributions to: Critique et création littéraires en France (ed Fumaroli), 1977; Bossuet: la Prédication au XVIIe siècle (ed Collinet and Goyet), 1980; Catholicism in Early Modern History: a guide to research (ed O'Malley), 1988; Convergences: rhetoric and poetic in Seventeenth-Century France (ed Rubin and McKinley), 1989; New Oxford Companion to Literature in French (ed France), 1995; Cambridge Rev., Dix-Septième Siècle, French Studies, Mod. Lang. Rev., etc. *Recreations:* Spain, food and wine, gardening, English ecclesiastical history. *Address:* Gonville and Caius College, Cambridge CB2 1TA. *T:* Cambridge (01223) 332439; (vacations) The White House, Hackleton, Northants NN7 2AD. *T:* Northampton (01604) 870059.

BAYLEY, Stephen Paul; Principal, EYE-Q Ltd, since 1990; *b* 13 Oct. 1951; *s* of Donald and Anne Bayley; *m* 1981, Flo Fothergill; one *s* one *d*. *Educ:* Quarry Bank Sch., Liverpool; Manchester Univ.; Liverpool Univ. Sch. of Architecture. Lecturer: Hist. of Art, Open Univ., 1974–76; Hist. and Theory of Art, Univ. of Kent, 1976–80; Dir, Conran Foundn, 1981–89; Dir, Boilerhouse Project, in V&A Mus., 1982–86; Founding Dir, later Chief Exec., Design Mus., 1986–89. A Contributing Editor, GQ, 1991–. Mem., Design Cttee, LRT, 1989–91. Has lectured at: Nat. Inst. of Design, Ahmedabad; India Inst. of Technol., Bombay; Art Gall. of WA, Perth; Nat. Gall. of Victoria, Melbourne; Salon de l'Automobile, Geneva; Sony Design Center, Tokyo; Internat. Expo, Nagoya; Art Coll. Center of Design (Europe), La Tour-de-Peilz, Switzerland; RIBA; RSA; RCA; and at univs, colls and museums throughout Britain and Europe. Gov., History of Advertising Trust, 1985–. Lay Assessor, RIBA Awards, 1991–; Mem. Graphics Jury, D&AD, 1993–. Chevalier de l'Ordre des Arts et des Lettres (France), 1989. *Publications:* In Good Shape, 1979; The Albert Memorial, 1981; Harley Earl and the Dream Machine, 1983; The Conran Directory of Design, 1985; Sex, Drink and Fast Cars, 1986; Twentieth Century Style and Design, 1986; Commerce and Culture, 1989; Taste, 1991; Beefeater 2-Day Guide to London, 1993; General Knowledge: a guide to modern opinions, 1996; numerous Open Univ. books, and Boilerhouse/Design Mus. catalogues inc. Art and Industry, 1982; Sony Design, 1982; Taste, 1983; Robots, 1984; National Characteristics, 1985; Coke, 1986. *Recreations:* indistinguishable from work, but both involve words, pictures, food, drink, sport and travel. *Address:* 74 Fentiman Road, SW8 1LA. *T:* 0171–820 3973. *Clubs:* Savile, Hurlingham, Academy.

BAYLIS, Clifford Henry, CB 1971; Controller, HM Stationery Office, and Queen's Printer of Acts of Parliament, 1969–74; *b* 20 March 1915; *s* of late Arthur Charles and Caroline Jane Baylis, Alcester, Warwicks; *m* 1st, Phyllis Mary Clark; two *s*; 2nd, Margaret A. Hawkins. *Educ:* Alcester Grammar Sch.; Keble Coll., Oxford. Harrods Ltd, 1937–39. Served with HM Forces, 1940–46: Major RASC. Principal, Board of Trade, 1947; Asst Sec., UK Trade Commissioner, Bombay, 1955; Export Credits Guarantee Dept, 1963–66; Under-Sec., Board of Trade, 1966–67; Under-Sec., Min. of Technology, 1967–69. Dir, Shipbuilders' and Repairers' Nat. Assoc., 1974–77; Clerk, Shipwrights' Co., 1977–86. *Address:* 38 Cleaver Street, SE11 4DP. *T:* 0171–587 0817.

BAYLIS, Rear-Adm. Robert Goodwin, CB 1984; OBE 1963; CEng; FIEE; Chief Executive, R. G. Baylis & Associates, since 1984; Director, British Maritime Technology Reliability Consultants Ltd, since 1988; Consultant, GEC-Marconi Avionics; *b* 29 Nov. 1925; *s* of Harold Goodwin Baylis and Evelyn May (*née* Whitworth); *m* 1949, Joyce Rosemary Churchill; two *s* one *d*. *Educ:* Highgate Sch.; Edinburgh Univ.; Loughborough Coll.; RN Engrg Coll.; Trinity Coll., Cambridge. MA Cantab. MRAeS. Joined Royal Navy, 1943; various appts at sea in Far East and Home Fleet and ashore in research and devlt and trng establishments; Staff of C-in-C, S Atlantic and S America, 1958; British Navy Staff, Washington, and Special Projects (Polaris), 1964; Defence Fellow, Southampton Univ., 1969; Naval ADC to HM the Queen, 1978; Staff of Vice Chief of Defence Staff, 1979; President, Ordnance Board, 1981–84. Comdr 1961, Captain 1970, Rear-Adm. 1979. Mem. Steering Gp, Solent Maritime. Mem., Nuffield Theatre Bd, 1988– (Chm., 1989–93). Mem. (Emeritus), Australian Ordnance Council; Mem. Council, IEE, 1984–86; Mem., Euro-Atlantic Gp, 1989–. *Recreations:* tennis, sailing. *Address:* Broadwaters, 4 Cliff Road, Hill Head, Fareham, Hants PO14 3JS. *Clubs:* Lansdowne; Owls (Cape Town).

BAYLISS, David, OBE 1992; FEng 1993; Eur Ing; Director of Planning, London Transport, since 1984; *b* 9 July 1938; *s* of Herbert and Annie Esther Bayliss; *m* 1961, Dorothy Christine Crohill; two *s* one *d*. *Educ:* Arnold Sch., Blackpool; UMIST (BSc Tech 1961); Manchester Univ. (Dip TP 1966). CEng, FICE, 1980, FITE 1984, FIHT 1972, FCIT 1977, FRTPI 1972; Eur Ing 1991. Manchester Corp., 1961–66; GLC, 1966–68; Centre for Environmental Studies, 1968–69; GLC, 1969–84 (Asst Divl Engr; Head, Transport Studies; Chief Transport Planner). Chm., SERC/DoT LINK Transport and Ops Steering Gp, 1991–. Chm., Regional Studies Assoc., 1978–81; Member Council: CIT, 1978–82; IHT, 1992–; President: British Parking Assoc., 1987–89; Transport Studies Soc., 1989–90. FRSA 1994. *Recreations:* writing, travel, wine. *Address:* 37 Ledborough Lane, Beaconsfield, Bucks HP9 2DB. *T:* Beaconsfield (01494) 673313.

BAYLISS, Frederic Joseph; Special Professor, Department of Adult Education, University of Nottingham, since 1988; *b* 15 April 1926; *s* of Gordon and Gertrude Bayliss; *m* 1948, Mary Provost; two *d*. *Educ:* Ashby de la Zouch Grammar Sch.; Hertford Coll., Oxford. PhD Nottingham 1960. RAF, 1944–47. Tutor in Economics, Oxford Univ. Tutorial Classes Cttee, 1950–57; Lectr in Industrial Relations, Dept of Adult Education, Univ. of Nottingham, 1957–65; Industrial Relations Advr, NBPI, 1965–69; Asst Sec., CIR, 1969–71; Sen. Economic Advr, Dept of Employment, 1971–73; Under Sec., Pay Board, 1973–74; Sec., Royal Commn on the Distribution of Income and Wealth, 1974–77; Acct Gen., Dept of Employment, 1977–86. Chairman: Campaign for Work, 1988–92; Employment Policy Inst., 1992–95. Hon. Fellow, City Univ. Business Sch., 1989–. *Publications:* British Wages Councils, 1962; The Standard of Living, 1965; Making a Minimum Wage Work, 1991; (with S. Kessler) Contemporary British Industrial Relations, 1992; Does Britain still have a Pay Problem?, 1993. *Recreations:* gardening, walking. *Address:* 11 Deena Close, Queens Drive, W3 0HR. *T:* 0181–992 1126; Department of Adult Education, University of Nottingham, Nottingham NG7 2RD. *Club:* Reform.

BAYLISS, John; Chairman: Richmount Management Ltd; Broomleigh Housing Association Ltd; *b* 22 Jan. 1934; *s* of Athol Thomas Bayliss and late Elizabeth Rose Bayliss; *m* 1954, Maureen (*née* Smith); one *d*. *Educ:* Haberdashers' Aske's, Hatcham. Westminster Bank, 1950; Abbey National, later Abbey National Building Society, then Abbey National plc, 1957–93: Regional Man., 1969; Personnel Man., 1972; Asst Gen. Man., 1974; General Manager: Field Operations, 1976; Housing, 1981; Marketing, 1983; Man. Dir (Retail Ops), 1988; Dep. Chm., 1991–93. *Recreation:* France. *Address:* The Penthouse, 9 Clevedon House, Holmbury Park, Bromley, Kent BR1 2WG.

BAYLISS, Sir Noel (Stanley), Kt 1979; CBE 1960; PhD, FRACI, FAA; Professor of Chemistry, University of Western Australia, 1938–71, Emeritus Professor, 1972; *b* 19 Dec. 1906; *s* of Henry Bayliss and Nelly Stothers; *m* 1933, Nellie Elise Banks; two *s*. *Educ:* Queen's Coll., Univ. of Melbourne (BSc 1927); Lincoln Coll., Oxford (BA 1930); Univ. of Calif, Berkeley (PhD 1933). FRACI 1942; FAA 1954. Victorian Rhodes Scholar, 1927–30; Commonwealth Fund (Harkness) Fellow, Univ. of Calif, 1930–33; Sen. Lectr in Chem., Univ. of Melbourne, 1933–37. Chm., Murdoch Univ. Planning Bd, 1970–73; Member: Australian Univs Commn, 1959–70; Hong Kong Univ. and Polytech. Grants Cttee, 1966–73. Hon. FACE 1965; Hon. DSc Univ. of WA, 1968; Hon. DUniv Murdoch Univ., 1975. *Publications:* over 70 original papers in scientific jls. *Recreations:* golf, music. *Address:* 62 Dorothy Genders Hostel, 99 McCabe Street, Mosman Park, WA 6012, Australia. *T:* (9) 3852987. *Club:* Royal Perth Yacht (WA).

BAYLISS, Sir Richard (Ian Samuel), KCVO 1978; MD, FRCP; consulting physician; Physician to the Queen, 1970–81, and Head of HM Medical Household, 1973–81; Consultant Physician, King Edward VII's Hospital for Officers, 1964–87; Vice-President, Private Patients Plan, since 1989 (Director, 1979–89); *b* 2 Jan. 1917; *o s* of late Frederick William Bayliss, Tettenhall, and late Muryel Anne Bayliss; *m* 1st, 1941, Margaret Joan Lawson (marr. diss. 1956); one *s* one *d*; 2nd, 1957, Constance Ellen, *d* of Wilbur J. Frey, Connecticut; two *d*; 3rd, 1979, Marina de Borchgrave d'Altena, *widow* of Charles Rankin. *Educ:* Rugby; Clare Coll., Cambridge (Hon. Fellow, 1983); St Thomas' Hosp., London. MB, BChir Cambridge 1941; MRCS, LRCP 1941; MRCP 1942; MD Cambridge 1946; FRCP 1956. Casualty Officer, Ho.-Phys., Registrar, Resident Asst Phys., St Thomas'

Hosp.; Off. i/c Med. Div., RAMC, India; Sen. Med. Registrar and Tutor, Hammersmith Hosp.; Rockefeller Fellow in Medicine, Columbia Univ., New York, 1950–51; Lectr in Medicine and Physician, Postgrad. Med. Sch. of London; Dean, Westminster Med. Sch., 1960–64; Physician to HM Household, 1964–70; Consulting Physician: Westminster Hosp., 1954–81; King Edward VII Hosp., Midhurst, 1973–82; Civilian Consultant in Medicine, RN, 1975–82. Asst Dir, RCP Res. Unit, 1982–88. Hon. Sec., Assoc. of Physicians, 1958–63, Cttee 1965–68, Pres., 1980–81; Pres., Section of Endocrinology, RSM, 1966–68; Examr in Medicine, Cambridge and Oxford Univs; Examr, MRCP. Member: Bd of Governors, Westminster Hosp., 1960–64, 1967–74; Council, Westminster Med. Sch., 1960–75; Soc. for Endocrinology (Council, 1956–60); Brit. Cardiac Soc., 1952; Council, RCP, 1968–71 (Second Vice-Pres., 1983–84); Bd of Advrs, Merck Inst. of Therapeutic Res., 1972–76. Med. Dir, Swiss Reinsurance Co. (UK), 1968–85; Dir, JS Pathology plc, 1984–90; Hon. Med. Adviser, Nuffield Nursing Home Trust, 1981–88. Harveian Orator, RCP, 1983. Hon. FRCPath 1994. *Publications:* Thyroid Disease: the facts, 1982, 2nd edn 1991; Practical Procedures in Clinical Medicine, 3rd edn; various, in med. jls and textbooks, on endocrine, metabolic and cardiac diseases. *Recreations:* ski-ing, music. *Address:* Flat 7, 61 Onslow Square, SW7 3LS. *T:* 0171–589 3087, *Fax:* 0171–581 5937. *Club:* Garrick.

BAYLISS, Valerie June; Under Secretary and Director of Youth and Education Policy (formerly Education Programmes), Department of Education and Employment (formerly Department of Employment), since 1991; *b* 10 June 1944; *d* of George and Ellen Russell; *m* 1971, Derek Andrew Bayliss; one *s*. *Educ:* Wallington County Grammar Sch. for Girls; Univ. of Wales (1st cl. hons History, BA 1965; MA 1967). Research Student, LSE, 1966–68; Dept of Employment, 1968; Manpower Services Commission, subseq. Training Agency: Head of Job Centre Services, 1978–82; Head, YTS Policy, 1982–85; Dir, Field Ops, 1985–87; Dir, Resources and Personnel, 1987–90. Sheffield University: Mem. Council, 1988–; Dir, Management Sch., 1991–. Hon. Mem. Council, Rural Buildings Preservation Trust. FRSA 1990. *Recreations:* walking, reading, listening to music. *Address:* Department of Education and Employment, Moorfoot, Sheffield S1 4PQ. *T:* Sheffield (0114) 259 4573.

BAYLY, Prof. Christopher Alan, DPhil; FRHistS; FBA 1990; Vere Harmsworth Professor of Imperial and Naval History, since 1992 and Fellow of St Catharine's College, since 1970, Cambridge University; *b* 18 May 1945; *s* of Roy Ernest and Elfreda Madeleine Bayly; *m* 1981, Susan Banks Kaufmann. *Educ:* Skinners School, Tunbridge Wells; Balliol College, Oxford (MA); St Antony's, Oxford (DPhil 1970). Stanhope Prize, Oxford, 1965. Cambridge University: Dir of Studies in History, St Catharine's Coll., 1970–92 (Tutor, 1977–80); Smuts Reader in Commonwealth Studies, 1981–87; Reader in Modern Indian History, 1988–91; Prof. of Modern Indian Hist., 1991–92. Directeur d'Etudes associé, CNRS, Ecole des Hautes Etudes, Paris, 1986. Vis. Prof., Univ. of Virginia, Charlottesville, 1975. *Publications:* The Local Roots of Indian Politics: Allahabad 1880–1920, 1975; Rulers, Townsmen and Bazaars: North Indian society in the age of British Expansion 1770–1870, 1983, 2nd edn 1988; Indian Society and the Making of the British Empire, 1988; Imperial Meridian: the British Empire and the world 1780–1830, 1989; (ed) The Raj: India and the British 1600–1947, 1990; contribs to jls. *Recreation:* travelling. *Address:* St Catharine's College, Cambridge CB2 1RL. *T:* Cambridge (01223) 338321.

BAYLY, Vice-Adm. Sir Patrick (Uniacke), KBE 1968; CB 1965; DSC 1944, and 2 bars, 1944, 1951; *b* 4 Aug. 1914; *s* of late Lancelot F. S. Bayly, Nenagh, Eire; *m* 1945, Moy Gourlay Jardine, *d* of Robert Gourlay Jardine, Newtonmearns, Scotland; two *d*. *Educ:* Aravon, Bray, Co. Wicklow; RN Coll., Dartmouth, Midshipman, 1932; Sub-Lieut, 1934; Lieut, 1935; South Africa, 1936; China station, 1938; Combined operations, 1941–44, including Sicily and Salerno; Lieut-Comdr 1944; HMS Mauritius, 1946; Comdr 1948, Naval Staff, 1948; Korean War, 1952–53, in HMS Alacrity and Constance; Captain 1954, Naval Staff; Imperial Defence Coll., 1957; Capt. (D) 6th Destroyer Sqdn, 1958; Staff of SACLANT, Norfolk, Va, 1960; Chief of Staff, Mediterranean, 1962; Rear-Admiral, 1963; Flag Officer, Sea Training, 1963; Adm. Pres., RN Coll., Greenwich, 1965–67; Vice-Adm., 1967; Chief of Staff, COMNAVSOUTH, Malta, 1967–70; retd, 1970. Dir, Maritime Trust, 1971–88. US Legion of Merit, 1951. *Recreation:* golf. *Address:* Dunning House, Liphook, Hants GU30 7EH.

BAYNE, Brian Leicester, PhD; FIBiol; Director, Centre for Coastal and Marine Sciences, Plymouth Marine Laboratory, Natural Environment Research Council, since 1995; *b* 24 July 1938; *s* of John Leonard and Jean Leicester Bayne; *m* 1961, Marianne Middleton; two *d*. *Educ:* Ardingly Coll.; Univ. of Wales (BSc, PhD). Post-doctoral res., Univ. of Copenhagen and Fisheries Laboratory, Conwy, 1963–68; Lectr, Sch. of Biology, Univ. of Leicester, 1968–73; Institute for Marine Environmental Research, Plymouth: Res. Scientist, 1973–83; Dir, 1983–88; Dir, Plymouth Marine Lab., NERC, 1988–95. Hon. Professorial Fellow, Sheffield Univ., 1987; Hon. Prof., Univ. of Wales, 1989. *Publications:* Marine Mussels: ecology and physiology, 1976; res. papers in marine sci. jls, *eg* Jl of Experimental Marine Biol. and Ecol. *Recreation:* sailing. *Address:* Centre for Coastal and Marine Sciences, Plymouth Marine Laboratory, Prospect Place, Plymouth, Devon PL1 3DH. *T:* Plymouth (01752) 222772.

BAYNE, Sir Nicholas (Peter), KCMG 1992 (CMG 1984); HM Diplomatic Service; High Commissioner to Canada, since 1992; *b* 15 Feb. 1937; *s* of late Captain Ronald Bayne, RN and Elisabeth Ashcroft; *m* 1961, Diana Wilde; two *s* (and one *s* decd). *Educ:* Eton Coll.; Christ Church, Oxford (MA, DPhil). Entered Diplomatic Service, 1961; served at British Embassies in Manila, 1963–66, and Bonn, 1969–72; seconded to HM Treasury, 1974–75; Financial Counsellor, Paris, 1975–79; Head of Financial, later Economic Relations, Dept, FCO, 1979–82; attached to RIIA, 1982–83; Ambassador to Zaire, 1983–84, also accredited to the Congo, Rwanda and Burundi, 1984; seconded to CSSB, 1985; Ambassador and UK Perm. Rep. to OECD, Paris, 1985–88; Dep. Under-Sec. of State, FCO, 1988–92. *Publication:* (with R. D. Putnam) Hanging Together: the Seven-Power Summits, 1984, rev. edn 1987 (trans. German, Japanese, Italian). *Recreations:* reading, sightseeing. *Address:* c/o Foreign and Commonwealth Office, King Charles Street, SW1A 2AH. *Club:* Travellers'.

BAYNES, Sir John (Christopher Malcolm), 7th Bt *cr* 1801; Lt-Col retd; *b* 24 April 1928; *s* of Sir Rory Malcolm Stuart Baynes, 6th Bt and Ethel Audrey (*d* 1947), *d* of late Edward Giles, CIE; *S* father, 1979; *m* 1955, Shirley Maxwell, *o d* of late Robert Allan Dodds; four *s*. *Educ:* Sedbergh School; RMA Sandhurst; Edinburgh Univ. (MSc). Commissioned Cameronians (Scottish Rifles), 1949; served Malaya, 1950–53 (despatches); Aden, 1966; Defence Fellow, Edinburgh Univ., 1968–69; comd 52 Lowland Volunteers (TAVR), 1969–72; retired, 1972. Order of the Sword, 1st Class (Sweden), 1965. *Publications:* Morale, 1967, new edn 1987; The Jacobite Rising of 1715, 1970; History of the Cameronians, Vol. IV, 1971; The Soldier in Modern Society, 1971; Soldiers of Scotland, 1988; The Forgotten Victor, 1989; (ed jtly) A Tale of Two Captains, 1990; No Reward but Honour?, 1991; Urquhart of Arnhem, 1993; Far from a Donkey: Gen. Sir Ivor Maxse, 1995; contribs to military and sporting jls. *Recreations:* shooting, fishing, golf. *Heir: s* Christopher Rory Baynes, *b* 11 May 1956. *Address:* Talwrn Bach, Llanfyllin, Powys SY22 5LQ. *T:* Llanfyllin (01691) 648576. *Club:* Army and Navy.

BAYNES, Pauline Diana, (Mrs F. O. Gasch); designer and book illustrator; *b* 9 Sept 1922; *d* of Frederick William Wilberforce Baynes, CIE and Jessie Harriet Maud Cunningham; *m* 1961, Fritz Otto Gasch (*d* 1988). *Educ:* Beaufront Sch., Camberley; Farnham Sch. of Art; Slade Sch. of Art. MSIA 1951. Mem., Women's Internat. Art Club, 1938. Voluntary worker, Camouflage Develt and Trng Centre, RE, 1940–42; Hydrographic Dept, Admty, 1942–45. Designed world's largest crewel embroidery, Plymouth Congregational Church, Minneapolis, 1970. Kate Greenaway Medal, Library Assoc., 1968. *Publications: illustrated:* Farmer Giles of Ham, and subseq. books and posters by J. R. R. Tolkien, 1949; The Lion, the Witch and the Wardrobe, and subseq. Narnia books by C. S. Lewis, 1950; The Arabian Nights, 1957; The Puffin Book of Nursery Rhymes by Iona and Peter Opie, 1963; Recipes from an Old Farmhouse by Alison Uttley, 1966; Dictionary of Chivalry, 1968; Snail and Caterpillar, 1972; A Companion to World Mythology, 1979; The Enchanted Horse, 1981; Frog and Shrew, 1981; All Things Bright and Beautiful, 1986; The Story of Daniel by George MacBeth, 1986; Noah and the Ark, 1988; Bilbo's Last Song, 1990; The Naming by Margaret Greaves, 1992; The Lion, the Witch and the others: a book of Narnians, 1994; numerous other children's books, etc.; *written and illustrated:* Victoria and the Golden Bird, 1948; How Dog Began, 1985; King Wenceslas, 1987; In the beginning, 1990; A book of Narnians, 1994. *Recreation:* going for walks with dogs. *Address:* Rock Barn Cottage, Dockenfield, Farnham, Surrey GU10 4HH. *T:* Headley Down (01428) 713306.

BAYNHAM, Prof. Alexander Christopher; Principal, Cranfield University (formerly Cranfield Institute of Technology) (Shrivenham Campus), since 1989; *b* 22 Dec. 1935; *s* of Alexander Baynham and Dulcie Rowena Rees; *m* 1961, Eileen May Wilson; two *s* one *d*. *Educ:* Marling Sch.; Reading Univ. (BSc); Warwick Univ. (PhD); Royal Coll. of Defence Studies (rcds). Joined Royal Signals and Radar Estab., Malvern, 1955; rejoined, 1961 (univ. studies, 1958–61); Head, Optics and Electronics Gp, 1976; RCDS, 1978; Scientific Adviser to Asst Chief Adviser on Projects, 1979; Dep. Dir, 1980–83, Dir, 1984–86, RSRE; Dir, RARDE, 1986–89. *Publications:* Plasma Effects in Semi-conductors, 1971; assorted papers in Jl of Physics, Jl of Applied Physics and in Proc. Phys. Soc. *Recreations:* church activities, music. *Address:* Cranfield University, Shrivenham Campus, Swindon, Wilts SN6 8LA.

BAYNHAM, Dr John William, CBE 1994; Chairman, Lothian Health Board, since 1990; *b* 20 Jan. 1929; *s* of Rev. Albert J. Baynham and Euphemia Baynham; *m* 1959, Marcella Bridget (Marié) Friel; one *d*. *Educ:* Bathgate Academy; Aberdeen Univ. (BSc, PhD); Imperial College London (DIC). Scottish Agricultural Industries: res. develt chemist, 1955–62; Production Planning/ Techno Commercial, 1962–70; Trade Union negotiating and gen. management, 1970–80; Dir, Sales and Marketing, 1980–84; overall Agribusiness Dir, 1984–87. Founder Dir, Leith Enterprise Trust, 1984 (Chm., 1987–90). Chm., Bd of Govs, Moray House Inst. of Educn, Heriot-Watt Univ., 1991–95. Dr *hc* Edinburgh, 1995. *Publications:* contribs to learned jls and seminars. *Recreations:* golf, good food and wine, grandchildren. *Address:* 2/18 Succoth Court, Succoth Park, Edinburgh EH12 6BZ. *T:* 0131–337 2813. *Club:* Caledonian (Edinburgh).

BAYS, Rt. Rev. Eric; *see* Qu'Appelle, Bishop of.

BAYTON, Rt Rev. John, AM 1983; Episcopal Chaplain, St George's College, Jerusalem, since 1995; *b* 24 March 1930; *s* of Ernest Bayton and Jean Bayton (*née* Edwards); *m* 1959, Elizabeth Anne, *d* of Rt Rev. J. A. G. Housden; one *s* two *d*. *Educ:* Aust. Coll. of Theology, ACT (ThL (Hons)); St Francis Theol Coll., Brisbane. Ordained deacon 1956, priest 1957; Rector, Longreach, Qld, 1958–63; Rector and Sub-dean, Thursday Island (Canon in Residence), 1963–65; Rector, Auchenflower, 1965–68; Dean of St Paul's Cathedral, Rockhampton, 1968–79; Vicar, St Peter's, Eastern Hill, 1980–89; Archdeacon of Malvern, 1986–89; Bishop of Geelong (Asst Bishop, dio. of Melbourne), 1989–95. Chm., Division of Community Care, 1990–93. Founder, 1981, Patron, 1993–, Inst. for Spiritual Studies, Melbourne. Solo Art Exhibitions: Brisbane 1967, 1976, 1978; Rockhampton 1975, 1976; Melbourne 1981, 1984, 1986, 1987. Represented in public and private collections Australia, USA and UK. Prelate, Aust. Priory, Order of St John of Jerusalem and Knights Hospitaler, 1990. GCSJ 1988. *Publications:* Cross over Carpentaria, 1965; Coming of the Light, 1971; The Icon, 1980; (ed) Anglican Spirituality, 1982. *Recreations:* painting, sketching, sculpting, reading, walking. *Address:* St George's College, PO Box 1248, Jerusalem, Israel. *Club:* Melbourne (Melbourne).

BAYÜLKEN, Ümit Halûk; President: Turkish Atlantic Treaty Association, since 1984; Turkish Parliamentarians' Union, since 1992; *b* 7 July 1921; *s* of Staff Officer H. Hüsnü Bayülken and Mrs Melek Bayülken; *m* 1952, Mrs Valihe Salci; one *s* one *d*. *Educ:* Lycée of Haydarpasa, Istanbul; Faculty of Political Science (Diplomatic Sect.), Univ. of Ankara. Joined Min. of For. Affairs, 1944; 3rd Sec., 2nd Political Dept; served in Private Cabinet of Sec.-Gen.; mil. service as reserve Officer, 1945–47; Vice-Consul, Frankfurt-on-Main, 1947–49; 1st Sec., Bonn, 1950–51; Dir of Middle East Sect., Ankara, 1951–53; Mem. Turkish Delegn to UN 7th Gen. Assembly, 1952; Political Adviser, 1953–56, Counsellor, 1956–59, Turkish Perm. Mission to UN; rep. Turkey at London Jt Cttee on Cyprus, 1959–60; Dir-Gen., Policy Planning Gp, Min. of Foreign Affairs, 1960–63; Minister Plenipotentiary, 1963; Dep. Sec.-Gen. for Polit. Affairs, 1963–64; Sec.-Gen. with rank of Ambassador, 1964–66; Ambassador to London, 1966–69, to United Nations, 1969–71; Minister of Foreign Affairs, 1971–74; Secretary-General, Cento, 1975–77; Sec.-Gen., Presidency of Turkish Republic, 1977–80; Senator, 1980; Minister of Defence, 1980–83; MP, Antalya, 1983–87. Mem., Turkish Delegns to 8th-13th, 16th-20th Gen. Assemblies of UN; rep. Turkey at internat. confrs, 1953–66; Leader of Turkish Delegn: at meeting of For. Ministers, 2nd Afro-Asian Conf., Algiers, 1965; to Ministerial Councils of NATO, OECD, Cento and Regl Co-operation for Develt, 1971–74; Turkey and EEC Jt Assoc., 1971–74; to Cttee of Ministers, Council of Europe, 1972; at Conf. on European Security and Co-operation, 1973; Mem., Parly Assembly of European Council, 1984–87. Univ. of Ankara: Mem., Inst. of Internat. Relations; Lectr, Faculty of Polit. Scis, 1963–66. Hon. Gov., Sch. of Oriental and African Studies, London; Hon. Mem., Mexican Acad. of Internat. Law. Isabel la Católica (Spain), 1964; Grand Cross of Merit (Germany), 1965; Hon. GCVO, 1967; Sitara-i-Pakistan (Pakistan), 1970; Star, Order One (Jordan), 1972; Sirdar-i-Ali (Afghanistan), 1972. Tunisia, 1973; UAR, 1973; UN, 1975; Turkish Pres., 1980. *Publications:* lectures, articles, studies and essays on subject of minorities, Cyprus, principles of foreign policy, internat. relations and disputes. *Recreations:* music, painting, reading. *Address:* Nergiz, Sokak no 15/20, Çankaya, Ankara, Turkey.

BAZALGETTE, Rear-Adm. Derek Willoughby, CB 1976; *b* 22 July 1924; *yr s* of late H. L. Bazalgette; *m* 1st, 1947, Angela Hilda Vera (*d* 1991), *d* of late Sir Henry Hinchliffe, JP, DL; four *d*; 2nd, 1994, Ann, *widow* of Adm. Sir Peter Stanford, GCB, LVO. *Educ:* RNC Dartmouth. Served War of 1939–45; specialised in Gunnery, 1949; HMS Centaur, 1952–54; HMS Birmingham, 1956–58; SO 108th Minesweeping Sqdn and in comd HMS Houghton, 1958–59; HMS Centaur, 1963–65; Dep. Dir Naval Ops, 1965–67; comd HMS Aurora, 1967–68; idc 1969; Chief Staff Officer to Comdr British Forces Hong Kong, 1970–72; comd HMS Bulwark, 1972–74; Admiral President, RNC Greenwich, 1974–76; Comdr 1958; Captain 1965; Rear-Adm. 1974. ADC 1974. HQ Comr for Water Activities, Scout Assoc., 1976–87; Principal, Netley Waterside House, 1977–83;

Indep. Inquiry Inspector, 1983–92. Lay Canon, Portsmouth Cathedral, 1984–; Mem., General Synod, 1985–90. Sen. Treas., Corp. of Sons of the Clergy, 1992–94. Chm., Portsmouth Housing Trust, 1989–. Liveryman, Shipwrights' Co., 1986. Freeman, City of London, 1976. FIMgt (FBIM 1976). *Address:* Park House, Hambledon, Waterlooville, Hants PO7 4SB. *Club:* Lansdowne.

BAZLEY, Most Rev. Colin Frederick; *see* Chile, Bishop of.

BAZLEY, Sir Thomas Stafford, 3rd Bt, *cr* 1869; *b* 5 Oct. 1907; *s* of Captain Gardner Sebastian Bazley, DL, *o s* of 2nd Bt (*d* 1911) and Ruth Evelyn (*d* 1962), *d* of late Sir E. S. Howard (she *m* 2nd, Comdr F. C. Cadogan, RN, retd; he *d* 1970); *S* grandfather, 1919; *m* 1945, Carmen, *o d* of late J. Tulla; three *s* two *d*. *Educ:* Harrow; Magdalen Coll., Oxford. *Heir: s* Thomas John Sebastian Bazley, *b* 31 Aug. 1948. *Address:* Eastleach Downs Farm, near Eastleach, Cirencester, Glos GL7 3PX.

See also H. A. Abel Smith.

BEACH; *see* Hicks-Beach, family name of Earl St Aldwyn.

BEACH, Gen. Sir (William Gerald) Hugh, GBE 1980 (OBE 1966); KCB 1976; MC 1944; Chairman, Society for Promoting Christian Knowledge, since 1994; *b* 20 May 1923; *s* of late Maj.-Gen. W. H. Beach, CB, CMG, DSO; *m* 1951, Estelle Mary Henry (*d* 1989); three *s* one *d*. *Educ:* Winchester; Peterhouse, Cambridge (MA; Hon. Fellow 1982). Active service in France, 1944 and Java, 1946; comd: 4 Field Sqn, 1956–57; Cambridge Univ. OTC, 1961–63; 2 Div. RE, 1965–67; 12 Inf. Bde, 1969–70; Defence Fellow, Edinburgh Univ. (MSc), 1971; Dir, Army Staff Duties, MoD, 1971–74; Comdt, Staff Coll., Camberley, 1974–75; Dep. C-in-C, UKLF, 1976–77; Master-Gen. of the Ordnance, 1977–81; Chief Royal Engr, 1982–87; Warden, St George's House, Windsor Castle, 1981–86. Dir, Council for Arms Control, 1986–89. Vice Lord-Lieut for Greater London, 1981–87. Kermit Roosevelt Vis. Lectr to US Armed Forces, 1977; Mountbatten Lectr, Edinburgh Univ., 1981; Gallipoli Meml Lectr, 1985; Wilfred Fish Meml Lectr, GDC, 1986. Colonel Commandant: REME, 1976–81; RPC, 1976–80; RE, 1977–87; Hon. Colonel, Cambridge Univ. OTC, TAVR, 1977–87; Chm., CCF Assoc., 1981–87; Chm., MoD Study Gp on Censorship, 1983. Mem., Security Commn, 1982–91. Chairman: Rochester Cathedral Develt Trust, 1986–; Winchester DAC for Care of Churches, 1988–; Hampshire and the Islands Historic Churches Trust. Member: Winchester Cathedral Fabric Adv. Cttee; Peace Forum, CCBI; Council for Arms Control. Gov., Bedales Sch., 1991–. Patron, Venturers Search and Rescue, 1985–. CIMgt; FRSA. Hon. Fellow CIBSE, 1988. Hon. DCL Kent, 1990. *Publications: chapters on:* nuclear weapons in the defence of North-West Europe, in Unholy Warfare (ed Martin and Mullen), 1983; where does the nuclear-free path lead, in The Cross and the Bomb (ed Francis Bridger), 1983; disarmament and security in Europe, in Armed Peace (ed O'Connor Howe), 1984; military implications of 'No First Use', in Dropping the Bomb (ed John Gladwin), 1985. *Recreations:* sailing, ski-ing. *Address:* The Ropeway, Beaulieu, Hants SO42 7YG. *T:* Beaulieu (01590) 612269. *Clubs:* Farmers'; Royal Lymington Yacht.

BEACH, Surgeon Rear-Adm. William Vincent, CB 1962; OBE 1949; MRCS; LRCP; FRCSE; Retd; *b* 22 Nov. 1903; *yr s* of late William Henry Beach; *m* 1931, Daphne Muriel (*d* 1992), *yr d* of late Eustace Ackworth Joseph, ICS; two *d*. *Educ:* Seaford Coll.; Guy's Hospital, London. Joined RN Medical Service, 1928. Served War of 1939–45 as Surgical specialist in Hospital ships, Atlantic and Pacific Fleets. Surgical Registrar, Royal Victoria Infirmary, Newcastle upon Tyne; Senior Specialist in Surgery, RN Hospitals, Chatham, Haslar, Malta, Portland; Senior Medical Officer, RN Hospital, Malta; Medical Officer i/c RN Hospital, Portland; Sen. Medical Officer, Surgical Division, RN Hospital, Haslar; Medical Officer in charge of Royal Naval Hospital, Chatham, and Command MO on staff of C-in-C the Nore Command, 1960–61; MO i/c RN Hospital, Malta, and on staff of C-in-C, Mediterranean and as Medical Adviser to C-in-C, Allied Forces, Mediterranean, 1961–63. Surg. Rear-Admiral, 1960. QHS 1960. Senior Surgeon i/c Shaw Savill Passenger Liners, 1966–75. Fellow, Assoc. of Surgeons of Great Britain and Ireland, 1947, Senior Fellow, 1963. *Publications:* Urgent Surgery of the Hand, 1940; Inguinal Hernia—a new operation, 1946; The Treatment of Burns, 1950. *Recreations:* shooting, fishing. *Address:* Cherrytree Cottage, Easton, Winchester SO21 1EG. *T:* Itchen Abbas (01962) 779222. *Club:* Naval and Military.

BEACHAM, Prof. Arthur, OBE 1961; MA, PhD; Deputy Vice-Chancellor, Murdoch University, Western Australia, 1976–79 (Acting Vice-Chancellor, 1977–78); *b* 27 July 1913; *s* of William Walter and Maud Elizabeth Beacham; *m* 1938, Margaret Doreen Moseley (*d* 1979); one *s* one *d*. *Educ:* Pontywaun Grammar Sch.; University Coll. of Wales (BA 1935); Univ. of Liverpool (MA 1937); PhD Belfast 1941. Jevons Res. Student, Univ. of Liverpool, 1935–36; Leon Res. Fellow, Univ. of London, 1942–43; Lectr in Economics, Queen's Univ. of Belfast, 1938–45; Sen. Lectr, University Coll. of Wales, 1945–47; Prof. of Indust. Relations, University Coll., Cardiff, 1947–51; Prof. of Economics, University Coll. of Wales, Aberystwyth, 1951–63; Vice-Chancellor, Univ. of Otago, Dunedin, New Zealand, 1964–66; Gonner Prof. of Applied Econs, Liverpool Univ., 1966–75. Chairman: Mid-Wales Industrial Develt Assoc., 1957–63; Post Office Arbitration Tribunal, 1972–73; Member: Advisory Council for Education (Wales), 1949–52; Transp. Consultative Cttee for Wales, 1948–63 (Chm. 1961–63); Central Transp. Consultative Cttee, 1961–63; Economics Cttee of DSIR, 1961–63; North West Economic Planning Council, 1966–74; Merseyside Passenger Transport Authority, 1969–71; Council, Royal Economic Soc., 1970–74. Chm., Cttees on Care of Intellectually Handicapped, Australia, 1982–85; Dir, Superannuation Scheme for Aust. Univs, 1982–83. Hon. LLD Otago, 1969; Hon. DUniv Murdoch, 1982. *Publications:* Economics of Industrial Organisation, 1948 (5th edn 1970); Industries in Welsh Country Towns, 1950. Articles in Econ. Jl, Quarterly Jl of Economics, Oxford Econ. Papers, etc. *Recreations:* golf, gardening. *Address:* 10 Mannersley Street, Carindale, Qld 4152, Australia. *T:* (7) 3986524. *Clubs:* Dunedin (Dunedin, NZ); Cricketers' (Qld).

BEADLES, Anthony Hugh, MA; Headmaster of Epsom College, since 1993; *b* 18 Sept. 1940; *s* of O. H. R. Beadles, OBE and N. K. Beadles; *m* 1970, Heather Iona McFerran; two *s* one *d*. *Educ:* Epsom Coll.; Christ Church, Oxford (MA). Head of History, Ellesmere Coll., 1963–67; Head of History and Asst Housemaster, Harrow Sch., 1967–85; Headmaster, King's Sch., Bruton, 1985–93. *Recreations:* cricket, mountains, golf. *Address:* Headmaster's House, Epsom College, Epsom, Surrey KT17 4JQ. *T:* Epsom (01372) 722118. *Clubs:* MCC; Vincent's (Oxford).

BEAGLEY, Thomas Lorne, CB 1973; Hon. Secretary, Chartered Institute of Transport, since 1983; *b* 2 Jan. 1919; *s* of late Captain T. G. Beagley, Royal Montreal Regt; *m* 1942, Heather Blanche Osmond; two *s* one *d*. *Educ:* Bristol Grammar Sch.; Worcester Coll., Oxford (MA). Served War: 2nd Lieut, Northamptonshire Regt, 1940; Lt-Col, AQMG (Movements), AFHQ, Italy, 1945. Joined Min. of Transport, 1946; Cabinet Office, 1951–52; Min. of Defence, 1952–54; UK Delegn to NATO, 1954–57; UK Shipping Rep., Far East, 1960–63; Asst Under-Sec. of State, Dept of External Affairs, 1966–68; Under-Sec., Min. of Transport, 1968–71; Dep. Sec., Transport Industries, DoE, 1972–76; Dep. Chief Exec., PSA, 1976–79. Member: Nat. Ports Council, 1979–81; Dover Harbour Bd, 1980–89. Chartered Institute of Transport: FCIT, 1972; Pres., 1977; Award of Merit, 1988; Pres., European Soc. of Transport Insts, 1984–90. Hon. FIRTE 1979. Viva Award for Transport Improvement, Carmen's Co, 1985. *Recreation:* galleries. *Address:* 3 Kings Ride House, 289 Sheen Road, Richmond, Surrey TW10 5AW. *T:* 0181–876 1216. *Clubs:* Travellers'; Richmond Golf.

BEAL, Anthony Ridley; publishing consultant; Chairman: Heinemann Educational Books, 1979–84; Heinemann International, 1984–85; Managing Director, Heinemann Educational Books (International), 1979–84; *b* 28 Feb. 1925; *s* of Harold and Nesta Beal; *m* 1st, 1958, Rosemary Jean Howarth (*d* 1989); three *d*; 2nd, 1990, Carmen Dolores Carter (*née* Martinez). *Educ:* Haberdashers' Aske's Hampstead School; Downing College, Cambridge (scholar); 1st class English Tripos 1948. RNVR, 1943–46; Lectr in English, Eastbourne Training Coll., 1949; joined William Heinemann, 1949; Dep. Man. Dir, Heinemann Educational Books, 1962–73, Man. Dir, 1973–79; Dir, Heinemann Group of Publishers, 1973–85; Chairman: Heinemann Publishers (NZ), 1980–85; Heinemann Publishers Australia Pty, 1981–85; Ginn & Co., 1979–84. Chm., Educational Publishers' Council, 1980–83 (Vice-Chm., 1978–80); Mem. Council, Publishers' Assoc., 1982–86. *Publications:* D. H. Lawrence: Selected Literary Criticism, 1956; D. H. Lawrence, 1961; contribs to books on literature, education and publishing. *Recreations:* reading maps, travelling, thinking while gardening. *Address:* 19 Homefield Road, Radlett, Herts WD7 8PX. *T:* Radlett (01923) 854567. *Club:* Garrick.

BEAL, Peter George, PhD; FBA 1993; Manuscript Expert, since 1980, Deputy Director, since 1990, Department of Printed Books and Manuscripts, Sotheby's, London; *b* Coventry, 16 April 1944; *s* of William George Beal and Marjorie Ena (*née* Owen); *m* 1st, 1974, Gwyneth Morgan (marr. diss. 1980); 2nd, 1982, Sally Josephine Taylor (marr. diss. 1994); one step *s*. *Educ:* King Henry VIII Grammar Sch., Coventry; Leeds Univ (BA Hons English, 1966; PhD 1974). Res. editor, Bowker/Mansell Publishing, 1974–79. Lyell Reader in Bibliography, Oxford Univ., 1995–96. *Publications:* Index of English Literary Manuscripts, vol. I, parts 1 and 2, 1450–1625 (2 vols), 1980, vol. II, parts 1 and 2, 1625–1700 (2 vols), 1987, 1993; (gen. ed.) English Verse Miscellanies of the Seventeenth Century (5 vols), 1990; (co-founded and co-ed) English Manuscript Studies 1100–1700, annually, 1989–; contribs, mainly on 16th and 17th century literary MSS, to learned jls. *Recreations:* reading, swimming, films. *Address:* Department of Printed Books and Manuscripts, Sotheby's, 34–35 New Bond Street, W1A 2AA. *T:* 0171–408 5298.

BEAL, Rt. Rev. Robert George; Bishop of Wangaratta, 1985–94; *b* 17 Aug. 1929; *s* of Samuel and Phyllis Beal; *m* 1956, Valerie Francis Illich; two *s* four *d*. *Educ:* Sydney Grammar School; St Francis' College, Brisbane, Qld; Newcastle Univ., NSW (BA, ThL). Ordained, 1953; Priest, Asst Curate, St Francis', Nundah, Brisbane, 1953–55; Rector: South Townsville, 1955–59; Auchenflower, Brisbane, 1959–65; Dean of Wangaratta, 1965–72; Rector of Ipswich, Brisbane, and Residentiary Canon of St John's Cathedral, 1974–75; Dean of Newcastle, NSW, 1975–83; Archdeacon of Albury, 1983–85. *Recreations:* tennis, gardening. *Address:* 1 Pangari Place, New Lambton Gardens, Newcastle, NSW 2299, Australia.

BEALE, Anthony John; Solicitor and Legal Adviser, Welsh Office, 1980–91; Under Secretary (Legal), Welsh Office, 1983–91; *b* 16 March 1932, *o s* of late Edgar Beale and Victoria Beale; *m* 1969, Helen Margaret Owen-Jones; one *s* one *d*. *Educ:* Hitchin Grammar Sch.; King's Coll. London (LLB; AKC). Solicitor of the Supreme Court, 1956. Legal Asst, 1960, Sen. Legal Asst, 1966, Min. of Housing and Local Govt and Min. of Health; Consultant, Council of Europe, 1973; Asst Solicitor, DoE 1974. ARPS. *Recreations:* photography, golf, collecting old cheques.

BEALE, Edward; *see* Beale, T. E.

BEALE, Prof. Geoffrey Herbert, MBE 1947; FRS 19[illegible] Research Professor, Edinburgh University, 1963–78; *b* 11 June 1913; *s* of [illegible] and Elsie Beale; *m* 1949, Betty Brydon McCallum (marr. diss. 1969); three *s*. *Educ:* Sutton County Sch.; Imperial Coll. of Science, London. Scientific Research Worker, John Innes Horticultural Institution, London, 1935–40. Served in HM Forces (1941–46). Research worker, department of Genetics, Carnegie Institute, Cold Spring Harbor, New York, 1947; Rockefeller Fellow, Indiana Univ., 1947–48; Lecturer, Dept of Animal Genetics, 1948–59, Reader in Animal Genetics, 1959–63, Edinburgh Univ. Research Worker (part-time), Chulalongkorn Univ., Bangkok, 1976–. FRSE 1966. *Publications:* The Genetics of Paramecium aurelia, 1954; (with Jonathan Knowles) Extranuclear Genetics, 1978; (with S. Thaithong) Malaria Parasites, 1992. *Address:* 23 Royal Terrace, Edinburgh EH7 5AH. *T:* 0131–557 1329.

BEALE, Josiah Edward Michael; lately Assistant Secretary, Department of Trade and Industry; *b* 29 Sept. 1928; *s* of late Mr and Mrs J. E. Beale, Upminster, Essex; *m* 1958, Jean Margaret McDonald; two *d* (and one *d* decd). *Educ:* Brentwood Sch.; Jesus Coll., Cambridge. UK Shipping Adviser, Singapore, 1968–71. Assistant Secretary, Monopolies and Mergers Commission, 1978–81. Hon. Sec., Friends of Historic Essex, 1987–. *Address:* The Laurels, The Street, Great Waltham, Chelmsford, Essex CM3 1DE.

BEALE, Lt-Gen. Sir Peter (John), KBE 1992; FRCP; Chief Medical Adviser, British Red Cross, since 1994; *b* 18 March 1934; *s* of Basil and Eileen Beale; *m* 1959, Julia Mary Beale; four *s* one *d* (and one *d* decd). *Educ:* St Paul's Cathedral Choir Sch.; Felsted Sch. (Music Schol.); Gonville and Caius Coll., Cambridge (Choral Schol.; BA); Westminster Hosp. MB BChir 1958. DTM&H; FFCM; FFOM. Commissioned RAMC, 1960; medical training, 1964–71; Consultant Physician, Army, 1971; served Far East, Middle East, BAOR; Community Physician, Army, 1981; served BAOR and UK; Comdr Medical, HQ UKLF, 1987–90; DGAMS, 1990–93; Surg. Gen., MoD, 1991–94. QHP 1987–94. OStJ. *Publications:* contribs to professional jls on tropical and military medicine. *Recreations:* music (conductor, tenor, pianist, French Horn player); sport (golf, squash, tennis); bridge. *Address:* The Old Bakery, Avebury, Marlborough, Wilts. *T:* Avebury (01672) 539315.

BEALE, (Thomas) Edward, CBE 1966; JP; Chairman, Beale's Ltd, 1934–90; *b* 5 March 1904; *s* of late Thomas Henderson Beale, London; *m* Beatrice May (*d* 1986), *d* of William Steele McLaughlin, JP, Enniskillen; one *s*. *Educ:* City of London Sch. Mem. Bd, British Travel Assoc., 1950–70, Dep. Chm. 1965–70. Vice-Pres. and Fellow, Hotel and Catering Inst., 1949–71; Chm., Caterers' Assoc. of Gt Britain, 1949–52; Pres., Internat. Ho-Re-Ca (Union of Nat. Hotel, Restaurant & Caterers Assocs), 1954–64. Chm., Treasury Cttee of Enquiry, House of Commons Refreshment Dept, 1951. Master, Worshipful Co. of Bakers, 1955. Mem., Islington Borough Council, 1931–34. Gen. Comr of Income Tax, 1949–60. Creator, Beale Arboretum, West Lodge Park, 1965. JP Inner London, 1950 (Chm. EC Div., Inner London Magistrates, 1970–73). FRSH 1957; FRSA 1968; Hon FHCIMA 1974. Grant of Armorial Bearings and Crest, 1970. Médaille d'Argent de Paris, 1960. *Recreation:* arboriculture. *Address:* West Lodge Park, Hadley Wood, Herts EN4 0PY. *Club:* Carlton.

BEALES, Prof. Derek Edward Dawson, PhD, LittD; FRHistS; FBA 1989; Professor of Modern History, University of Cambridge, since 1980; Fellow of Sidney Sussex College, Cambridge, since 1958; *b* 12 June 1931; *s* of late Edward Beales and Dorothy Kathleen

Beales (*née* Dawson); *m* 1964, Sara Jean (*née* Ledbury); one *s* one *d*. *Educ:* Bishop's Stortford Coll.; Sidney Sussex Coll., Cambridge (MA, PhD, LittD). Sidney Sussex College: Research Fellow, 1955–58; Tutor, 1961–70; Vice-Master, 1973–75; University Asst Lectr, Cambridge, 1962–65; Lectr, 1965–80; Chairman, Faculty Board of History, Cambridge, 1979–81; Member: Cambridge Univ. Liby Syndicate, 1982–88; Gen. Bd of Faculties, Cambridge, 1987–89. Vis. Lectr, Harvard Univ., 1965; Lectures: Founder's Meml, St Deiniol's Liby, Hawarden, 1990; Stenton, Univ. of Reading, 1992; Birkbeck, Trinity Coll., Cambridge, 1993. British rep., Humanities Standing Cttee, ESF, 1994–. Mem. Council, RHistS, 1984–88. Editor, 1971–75, Chm. Editl Bd, 1990–, Historical Jl. *Publications:* England and Italy 1859–60, 1961; From Castlereagh to Gladstone, 1969; The Risorgimento and the Unification of Italy, 1971; History and Biography, 1981; (ed with Geoffrey Best) History, Society and the Churches, 1985; Joseph II: in the shadow of Maria Theresa 1741–80, 1987; Mozart and the Habsburgs, 1993; articles in learned jls. *Recreations:* playing keyboard instruments and bridge, walking, not gardening. *Address:* Sidney Sussex College, Cambridge CB2 3HU. *T:* Cambridge (01223) 338833.

BEALES, Peter Leslie; Chairman and Managing Director, Peter Beales Roses, since 1967; *b* 22 July 1936; *s* of E. M. Howes; *m* 1961, Joan Elizabeth Allington; one *s* one *d*. *Educ:* Aldborough School, Norfolk; Norwich City Tech. Coll. MIHort. Apprenticed E. B. LeGrice Roses (1st apprentice, Horticultural Apprentice Scheme), 1952–57; Nat. Service, RA, 1957–59; Manager, Rose Dept, Hillings Nurseries, Chobham, 1959–66; founded Peter Beales Roses, 1967. Lecturer, UK and overseas, 1985–. Chm., Attleborough Chamber of Commerce, 1988–89. Hon. Life Mem., Bermuda Rose Soc., 1987; Life Mem., N. Ireland Rose Soc., 1985. Freeman, City of London; Liveryman, Gardeners' Co. Lester E. Harrell Award for significant contrib. to heritage roses, USA, 1988. *Publications:* Georgian and Regency Roses, 1981; Early Victorian Roses, 1981; Late Victorian Roses, 1981; Edwardian Roses, 1981; Classic Roses, 1985; Twentieth-Century Roses, 1988; Roses, 1992. *Recreations:* photography, rose breeding, travelling, sport, book collecting. *Address:* Peter Beales Roses, London Road, Attleborough, Norfolk NR17 1AY. *T:* Attleborough (01953) 454707.

BEALEY, Prof. Frank William; Professor of Politics, University of Aberdeen, 1964–90, now Emeritus; *b* Bilston, Staffs, 31 Aug. 1922; *er s* of Ernest Bealey and Nora (*née* Hampton), both of Netherton, Dudley; *m* 1960, Sheila Hurst; one *s* two *d*. *Educ:* Hill Street Elem. Sch.; King Edward VI Grammar Sch., Stourbridge; London Sch. of Economics (BSc Econ 1948). Seaman in RN, 1941–46; Student, LSE, 1946–48 (1st cl. Hons Govt; DSc Econ. 1990); Finnish Govt Scholar, 1948–49; Research Asst for Passfield Trust, 1950–51; Extra-Mural Lectr, University of Manchester (Burnley Area), 1951–52; Lectr, University of Keele, 1952–64. Vis. Fellow, Yale, 1980. Treas., Soc. for Study of Labour Hist., 1960–63. Organiser, Parly All-Party Gp, Social Sci. and Policy, 1984–89. Trustee, Jan Hus Educnl Foundn, 1981–; Co-ordinator of Jt European Project 0276 (Political Sci. in Czechoslovakia), 1991–93. FRHistS 1974. *Publications:* (with Henry Pelling) Labour and Politics, 1958, 2nd edn 1982; (with J. Blondel and W. P. McCann) Constituency Politics, 1965; The Social and Political Thought of the British Labour Party, 1970; The Post Office Engineering Union, 1976; (with John Sewel) The Politics of Independence, 1981; Democracy in the Contemporary State, 1988; articles in academic jls. *Recreations:* reading poetry, eating and drinking, watching football and cricket, darts. *Address:* 2 Morag House, Oyne, Insch, Aberdeenshire AB52 6QT. *T:* Old Rayne (014645) 457. *Club:* Economicals Association Football and Cricket.

BEAMENT, Sir James (William Longman), Kt 1980; ScD; FRS 1964; Drapers Professor [illegible]riculture, University of Cambridge, 1969–89, now Emeritus; Life Fellow, Queens' [illegible]; *b* 17 Nov. 1921; *o c* of late T. Beament, Crewkerne, [illegible]of. Sir Ernest Barker, Cambridge; two *s*. *Educ:* [illegible], Queens' Coll., Cambridge; London Sch. of Tropical Medicine. Exhibitioner, Queens' Coll., 1941; BA 1943; MA 1946; PhD London 1945; ScD Cantab 1960. Research Officer with Agricultural Research Council, Cambridge, 1946; Cambridge University: Univ. Lectr, 1961; Reader in Insect Physiology, 1966; Hd of Dept of Applied Biol., 1969–89; Queens' College, Cambridge: Fellow and Tutor, 1961; Vice-Pres., 1981–86. Member: Adv. Bd for the Res. Councils, 1977; NERC, 1970–83 (Chm., 1977–80). Mem., Composers' Guild of Great Britain, 1967. Scientific Medal of Zoological Soc., 1963. *Publications:* many papers on insect physiology in scientific journals; Editor of several review volumes. *Recreations:* acoustics, playing the double-bass. *Address:* 19 Sedley Taylor Road, Cambridge CB2 2PW. *T:* Cambridge (01223) 562433; Queens' College, Cambridge CB3 9ET. *T:* Cambridge (01223) 335511.

BEAMISH, Adrian John, CMG 1988; HM Diplomatic Service; Ambassador to Mexico, since 1994; *b* 21 Jan. 1939; *s* of Thomas Charles Constantine Beamish and Josephine Mary (*née* Lee); *m* 1965, Caroline Lipscomb (marr. diss. 1991); two *d*; *m* 1994, Antonia Cavanagh; one step *s* one step *d*. *Educ:* Christian Brothers' Coll., Cork; Prior Park Coll., Bath; Christ's Coll., Cambridge (BA); Università per gli Stranieri, Perugia. Third, later Second Secretary, Tehran, 1963–66; Foreign Office, 1966–69; First Sec., UK Delegn, OECD, Paris, 1970–73; New Delhi, 1973–76; FCO, 1976–78; Counsellor, Dep. Head, Personnel Operations Dept, FCO, 1978–80; Counsellor (Economic), Bonn, 1981–85; Hd, Falkland Is Dept, FCO, 1985–87; Ambassador to Peru, 1987–89; Asst Under-Sec. of State (Americas), FCO, 1989–94. *Recreations:* people, books, plants. *Address:* c/o Foreign and Commonwealth Office, SW1A 2AH.

BEAMISH, Air Vice-Marshal Cecil Howard, CB 1970; FDSRCS; Director of Dental Services, Royal Air Force, 1969–73; *b* 31 March 1915; *s* of Frank George Beamish, Coleraine; *m* 1955, Frances Elizabeth Sarah Goucher; two *s*. *Educ:* Coleraine Acad.; Queen's Univ., Belfast. Joined Royal Air Force, 1936; Group Capt., 1958; Air Cdre, 1968; Air Vice-Marshal, 1969. QHDS 1969–73. *Recreations:* Rugby football, golf, squash. *Address:* East Keal Manor, Spilsby, Lincs PE23 4AS.

BEAMONT, Wing Comdr Roland Prosper, CBE 1969 (OBE 1953); DSO 1943, Bar 1944; DFC 1941, Bar 1943; DFC (US) 1946; FRAeS; author, aviation consultant; *b* 10 Aug. 1920; *s* of Lieut-Col E. C. Beamont and Dorothy Mary (*née* Haynes); *m* 1st, 1942, Shirley Adams (*d* 1945); one *d*; 2nd, 1946, Patricia Raworth; two *d*. *Educ:* Eastbourne Coll. Commissioned in RAF, 1939; served War of 1939–45, Fighter Command, RAF, BEF, Battle of Britain (despatches), Battle of France and Germany. Attached as Test Pilot to Hawker Aircraft Ltd during rest periods, in 1941–42 and 1943–44; Experimental Test Pilot, Gloster Aircraft Co. Ltd, 1946; Chief Test Pilot, English Electric Co., 1947–61; Special Dir and Dep. Chief Test Pilot, BAC, 1961–64; Director, Flight Operations, BAC Preston, later British Aerospace, Warton Division, 1965–78; Dir of Flight Operations, Panavia (Tornado testing), 1971–79. Events while Chief Test Pilot, English Electric Co. Ltd: 1st British pilot to fly at speed of sound (in USA), May 1948; 1st Flight of Britain's 1st jet bomber (the Canberra), May 1949; holder of Atlantic Record, Belfast-Gander, 4 hours 18 mins. Aug. 1951 and 1st two-way Atlantic Record, Belfast-Gander-Belfast, 10 hrs 4 mins Aug. 1952 (in a Canberra); first flight of P1, 1954 (Britain's first fully supersonic fighter); first British pilot in British aircraft to fly faster than sound in level flight, 1954, and first to fly at twice the speed of sound, Nov. 1958; first flight of Lightning supersonic all-weather fighter, 1957; first flight of TSR2, Sept. 1964 (Britain's first supersonic bomber). Britannia Trophy for 1953; Derry and Richards Memorial Medal, 1955; R. P. Alston Memorial Medal, RAeS, 1960; British Silver Medal for Aeronautics, 1965. Pres., Popular Flying Assoc., 1979–84. Master Pilot and Liveryman, Guild of Air Pilots. Hon. Fellow, Soc. of Experimental Testpilots, USA, 1985. DL Lancashire 1977–81. *Publications:* Phoenix into Ashes, 1968; Typhoon and Tempest at War, 1975; Testing Years, 1980; English Electric Canberra, 1984; English Electric P1 Lightning, 1985; Fighter Test Pilot, 1986; My Part of the Sky, 1989; Testing Early Jets, 1990; Tempest over Europe, 1994. *Recreation:* fly-fishing. *Address:* Cross Cottage, Pentridge, Salisbury, Wilts SP5 5QX. *Club:* Royal Air Force.

BEAN, Basil, CBE 1985; Vice President, National House Building Council, since 1994 (Director General, then Chief Executive, 1985–94); Deputy Chairman, Admiral Homes Ltd, since 1994; *b* 2 July 1931; *s* of Walter Bean and Alice Louise Bean; *m* 1956, Janet Mary Brown; one *d*. *Educ:* Archbishop Holgate Sch., York. Mem. CIPFA. York City, 1948–53; West Bromwich Borough, 1953–56; Sutton London Bor., 1957–62; Skelmersdale Develt Corp., 1962–66; Havering London Bor., 1967–69; Northampton Develt Corp., 1969–80 (Gen. Manager, 1977–80); Chief Exec., Merseyside Develt Corp., 1980–85; overseas consultancies. Mem., British Waterways Bd, 1985–88. Hon. FIAA&S. *Publications:* financial and technical papers. *Recreations:* reading, walking, travel. *Address:* The Forge, Manor Farm, Church Lane, Princes Risborough, Bucks HP27 9AW. *T:* Princes Risborough (018444) 6133. *Clubs:* Cheyne Walk; Northampton and County (Northampton).

BEAN, Hugh (Cecil), CBE 1970; violinist (freelance); Professor of Violin, Royal College of Music, since 1954; *b* 22 Sept. 1929; *s* of Cecil Walter Claude Bean and Gertrude Alice Chapman; *m* 1963, Mary Dorothy Harrow; one *d*. *Educ:* Beckenham Grammar Sch. Studied privately, and at RCM, London (principal prize for violin) with Albert Sammons, 1938–57; Boise Trav. Schol., 1952; at Brussels Conservatoire with André Gertler (double premier prix for solo and chamber music playing), 1952–53. National Service, Gren. Gds, 1949–51. Formerly Leader of Harvey Phillips String Orch. and Dennis Brain Chamber Orch.; Leader of Philharmonia and New Philharmonia Orch., 1957–67; Associate Leader, BBC Symph. Orch., 1967–69; Co-Leader, Philharmonia Orch., 1990. Member: Bean-Parkhouse Duo; Music Gp of London. Has made solo commercial records, and has performed as soloist with many major orchestras. Hon. ARCM 1961, FRCM 1968. *Recreations:* design and construction of flying model aircraft; steam-driven passenger hauling model railways; gramophone record collection. *Address:* Rosemary Cottage, 30 Stone Park Avenue, Beckenham, Kent BR3 3LX. *T:* 0181–650 8774.

BEAN, Rev. Canon John Victor; Vicar, St Mary, Cowes, Isle of Wight, 1966–91, and Priest-in-charge, All Saints, Gurnard, IoW, 1978–91; Chaplain to the Queen, since 1980; *b* 1 Dec. 1925; *s* of Albert Victor and Eleanor Ethel Bean; *m* 1955, Nancy Evelyn Evans; two *s* one *d* (and one *d* died in infancy). *Educ:* local schools; Grammar Sch., Gt Yarmouth; Downing Coll., Cambridge (MA); Salisbury Theological Coll., 1948. Served War, RNVR, 1944–46; returned to Cambridge, 1946–48. Assistant Curate: St James, Milton, Portsmouth, 1950–55; St Peter and St Paul, Fareham, 1955–59; Vicar, St Helen's, IoW, 1959–66. Rural Dean of West Wight, 1968–73; Clergy Proctor for Diocese of Portsmouth, 1973–80; Hon. Canon, Portsmouth Cathedral, 1970–91, Canon Emeritus, 1991. *Recreations:* photography, boat-watching, tidying up. *Address:* 4 Parkmead Court, Park Road, Ryde, Isle of Wight PO33 2HD. *Club:* Gurnard Sailing (Gurnard).

BEAN, Leonard, CMG 1964; MBE (mil.) 1945; MA; Secretary, Southern Gas Region, 1966–79, retired; *b* 19 Sept. 1914; *s* of late Harry Bean, Bradford, Yorks, and late Agnes Sherwood Beattie, Worcester; *m* 1938, Nancy Winifred (*d* 1990), *d* of Robert John Neilson, Dunedin, NZ; one *d*. *Educ:* Canterbury Coll., NZ; Queens' Coll., Cambridge. Served War of 1939–45: Major, 2nd NZ Div. (despatches, MBE). Entered Colonial Service, N Rhodesia, 1945; Provincial Comr, 1959; Perm. Sec. (Native Affairs), 1961; acted as Minister for Native Affairs and Natural Resources in periods, 1961–64; Permanent Secretary: to Prime Minister, 1964; also to President, 1964. Adviser to President, Zambia, 1964–66. *Recreations:* golf, gardening. *Address:* Squirrels Gate, 20 Ashley Park, Ringwood, Hants BH24 2HA. *T:* Ringwood (01425) 475262. *Clubs:* MCC; Bramshaw Golf.

BEAN, Marisa; *see* Robles, Marisa.

BEAN, Dame Marjorie (Louise), DBE 1995 (OBE 1981; MBE 1968); Education Officer, Department of Education, Bermuda, 1949–74; *b* 25 May 1909; *d* of E. H. Stuart Bean and Josephine Augusta Bean (*née* Wentworth); *Educ:* Berkeley Inst., Bermuda (Cambridge Sch. Cert. 1924); Wilberforce Univ., Ohio (BSc *cum laude* 1932, Hon. DHum 1950); London Univ. (DipEd 1946); Summer Courses, Teachers' Coll., Columbia Univ., NY, 1938 and 1939. Primary Teacher, Berkeley Prep. Sch., Bermuda, 1925–28; Principal, Sandys Secondary Sch., Bermuda, 1932–36 and 1963–65 (seconded); English and Geography Mistress, Berkeley Inst., 1938–49. First female MLA (Senate), Bermuda, 1981. Founder: Bermuda Nat. Trust; Berkeley Educnl Soc.; Cttee of Six; Queen's Birthday Ball and Presentation of Debutantes. Distinguished Service Award, Salvation Army Adv. Bd; many other local honours and awards. *Recreations:* travel, voluntary, civic and community activities: Church, school, clubs and charities. *Address:* 3 Berkeley Mews, Pembroke, Bermuda. *Clubs:* New Cavendish; Royal Commonwealth Society (Hon. Pres., Bermuda Br.), Business and Professional Women's Association (Bermuda).

BEAR, Leslie William, CBE 1972; Editor of Official Report (Hansard), House of Commons, 1954–72; *b* 16 June 1911; *s* of William Herbert Bear, Falkenham, Suffolk; *m* 1st, 1932, Betsy Sobels (*d* 1934), Lisse, Holland; 2nd, 1936, Annelise Gross (*d* 1979), Trier, Germany; two *s*. *Educ:* Gregg Sch., Ipswich. Served War, 1943–44, Royal Air Force. Mem. of Official Reporting Staff, League of Nations, Geneva, 1930–36; joined Official Report (Hansard), House of Commons, 1936; Asst Ed., 1951. *Recreations:* music, gardening, reading. *Address:* Medleys, Ufford, Woodbridge, Suffolk. *T:* Eyke (01394) 460358.

BEARD, Allan Geoffrey, CB 1979; CBE 1994; Under Secretary, Department of Health and Social Security, 1968–79 (Ministry of Social Security 1966–68); *b* 18 Oct. 1919; *s* of late Major Henry Thomas Beard and Florence Mercy Beard; *m* 1945, Helen McDonagh; one *d*. *Educ:* Ormskirk Grammar Sch. Clerical Officer, Air Min., 1936; Exec. Off., Higher Exec. Off., Asst Principal, Assistance Board, 1938–47; Army Service, 1940–46 (Capt., RE); Principal, Nat. Assistance Board, 1950; Asst Sec., 1962. Governor, 1981–, Hon. Treasurer, 1985–, Motability. *Recreations:* gardening, do-it-yourself. *Address:* 51 Rectory Park, Sanderstead, Surrey CR2 9JR. *T:* 0181–657 4197. *Club:* Royal Automobile.

BEARD, (Christopher) Nigel; Senior Manager, ICI-Zeneca Ltd, since 1993; *b* 10 Oct. 1936; *o s* of Albert Leonard Beard, Castleford, Yorks, and Irene (*née* Bowes); *m* 1969, Jennifer Anne, *d* of T. B. Cotton, Guildford, Surrey; one *s* one *d*. *Educ:* Castleford Grammar Sch., Yorks; University Coll. London. BSc Hons, Special Physics. Asst Mathematics Master, Tadcaster Grammar Sch., Yorks, 1958–59; Physicist with English Electric Atomic Power Div., working on design of Hinckley Point Nuclear Power Station, 1959–61; Market Researcher, Esso Petroleum Co., assessing future UK Energy demands and market for oil, 1961; Ministry of Defence: Scientific Officer, later Principal Scientific

Officer, in Defence Operational Analysis Estabt (engaged in analysis of central defence policy and investment issues), 1961–68, and Supt of Studies pertaining to Land Ops; responsible for policy and investment studies related to Defence of Europe and strategic movement of the Army, Dec. 1968–72; Chief Planner, Strategy, GLC, 1973–74; Dir, London Docklands Develt Team, 1974–79; Sen. Consultant, ICI, 1979–93. Mem., SW Thames RHA, 1978–86; Mem. Bd, Royal Marsden Hosp., 1982–90. Contested (Lab): Woking, 1979; Portsmouth N, 1983; Erith and Crayford, 1992. FRSA. *Publication:* The Practical Use of Linear Programming in Planning and Analysis, 1974 (HMSO). *Recreations:* reading, walking, the theatre. *Address:* Lanquhart, The Ridgway, Pyrford, Woking, Surrey GU22 8PW. *T:* Byfleet (019323) 48630. *Club:* Athenæum.

BEARD, Derek, CBE 1979; Director, Westminster Democratic Studies Ltd, since 1988; *b* 16 May 1930; *s* of Walter Beard and Lily Beard (*née* Mellors); *m* 1st, 1953, Ruth Davies (marr. diss. 1966); two *s*; 2nd, 1966, Renate Else, *d* of late W. E. Kautz, Berlin and Mecklenburg; two *s*. *Educ:* Hulme Grammar Sch., Oldham; Brasenose Coll., Oxford (MA, DipEd). Stand Grammar Sch., Whitefield, 1954–56; HMOCS, Nyasaland, 1956–59; Asst Educn Officer, WR Yorks, 1959–61; Sen. Asst, Oxfordshire, 1961–63; British Council, Pakistan, 1963–65; Producer, BBC Overseas Educnl Recordings Unit, 1965–66; British Council: Dir, Appts, Services Dept, 1966–70; Dep. Rep., India, 1970–73; Controller, Educn and Science Div., 1973–77; Rep. in Germany, 1977–81, Belgium, 1981–84; Asst Dir Gen., 1984–87. Adviser, 21st Century Trust, 1987–88; Academic Dir, Oxford Internat. Summer Sch., 1988. MInstD. *Publications:* articles on educn and cultural relns. *Recreations:* sculpture, music, travel. *Address:* 3 College Avenue, Epsom, Surrey KT17 4HN. *Club:* Royal Anglo-Belgian.

BEARD, Nigel; *see* Beard, C. N.

BEARD, Prof. Richard William, MD 1971; FRCOG 1972; Professor and Head of Department of Obstetrics and Gynaecology, St Mary's Hospital Medical School, since 1972; *b* 4 May 1931; *s* of late William and of Irene Beard; *m* 1st, 1957, Jane; two *s*; 2nd, 1979, Irène Victoire Marie de Marotte de Montigny; one *s*. *Educ:* Westminster Sch.; Christ's Coll., Cambridge (MA, MB Chir); St Bartholomew's Hosp. Obstetrician and Gynaecologist, RAF Changi, Singapore, 1957–60; Chelsea Hosp. for Women, 1961–62; UCH, 1962–63; Senior Lecturer/Hon. Consultant: Queen Charlotte's and Chelsea Hosps, 1964–68; King's Coll. Hosp., 1968–72. Advr to Social Services Select Cttee, H of C (2nd Report on Perinatal and Neonatal Mortality), 1978–80; Civil Consultant in Obstetrics and Gynaecology to RAF, 1983–; Consultant Advr in Obst. and Gyn. to DoH (formerly DHSS), 1985–91. Mem., Acad. Royale de Medécine de Belgique, 1983. *Publications:* Fetal Physiology and Medicine, 1976, 2nd edn 1983; contribs to learned jls. *Recreations:* tennis, sailing, Chinese history. *Address:* 64 Elgin Crescent, W11 2JJ. *T:* 0171–221 1930. *Club:* Garrick.

BEARDMORE, Alexander Francis, OBE 1987; FEng, FIMechE, FIEE; Engineer in Chief, Post Office, 1981–91, retired; *b* 20 Feb. 1931; *s* of Alexander Beardmore and Alice Beardmore (*née* Turner); *m* 1959, Pamela Anne Cozens; two *d*. *Educ:* Mitcham County Grammar School; London Univ. (BScEng, MSc). Nat. Service, Royal Signals, 1954–56. Post Office, 1948–91: Research Engineer, 1948–68; Controller Marketing, London Postal Region, 1972–77; Asst Dir, equipment provision, 1977–81. Chm., Unit Load Tech. Cttee, British Materials Handling Board, 1981–91. FIMgt. *Recreations:* Lions International, gardening, DIY, walking. *Address:* Three Gables, Cheltenham Road, Baunton, Cirencester, Glos GL7 7BE. *T:* Cirencester (01285) 654361.

BEARDMORE, Prof. John Alec, CBiol, FIBiol; Professor of Genetics, since 1966 and Head, School of Biological Sciences, since 1988, University College of Swansea; *b* 1 May 1930; *s* of George Edward Beardmore and Anne Jean (*née* Warrington); *m* 1953, Anne Patricia Wallace; three *s* one *d* (and one *s* decd). *Educ:* Burton on Trent Grammar Sch.; Birmingham Central Tech. Coll.; Univ. of Sheffield. BSc (1st Cl. Botany) 1953, PhD (Genetics) 1956. Research Demonstrator, Dept of Botany, Univ. of Sheffield, 1954–56; Commonwealth Fund Fellow, Columbia Univ., 1956–58; Vis. Asst Prof. in Plant Breeding, Cornell Univ., 1958; Lectr in Genetics, Univ. of Sheffield, 1958–61; Prof. of Genetics and Dir, Genetics Inst., Univ. of Groningen, 1961–66; Nat. Science Foundn Senior Foreign Fellow, Pennsylvania State Univ., 1966; Dean of Science, University Coll. of Swansea, 1974–76, Vice-Principal, 1977–80, Dir, Inst. of Marine Studies, 1983–87. Chm., Univ. of Wales Validation Bd, 1994–; Mem., Univ. of Wales Vice Chancellors' Bd, 1993–. Vis. Prof., Univ. of Ghent, 1992–. Member: NERC Aquatic Life Scis Cttee, 1982–87 (Chm., 1984–87); CNAA: Life Scis Cttee, 1979–85; Cttee for Science, 1985–87; Bd, Council of Sci. and Technology Insts, 1983–85 (Chm., 1984–85); Council, Galton Inst. (formerly Eugenics Soc.), 1980– (Chm., Res. Cttee, 1979–87); British Nat. Cttee for Biology, 1983–87; Council, Linnean Soc., 1989–93; Cttee, Heads of Univ. Biol Scis (Treas., 1989–91, Chm., 1991–94); Adv. Bd, Internat. Foundn for Sci., 1992–; Vice-Pres., Inst. of Biol., 1985–87 (Mem. Council, 1976–79; Hon. Sec., 1980–85); UK rep., Council of European Communities Biologists Assoc., 1980–87. FRSA; FLS. Darwin Lectr, Inst. of Biol. and Eugenics Soc, 1984. Univ. of Helsinki Medal, 1980. *Publications:* (ed with B. Battaglia) Marine Organisms: genetics ecology and evolution, 1977; articles on evolutionary genetics, human genetics and biological educn. *Recreations:* bridge, walking. *Address:* 153 Derwen Fawr Road, Swansea SA2 8ED. *T:* Swansea (01792) 206232.

BEARDSWORTH, Maj.-Gen. Simon John, CB 1984; self-employed consultant in defence procurement; Director, OMI International, since 1993; *b* 18 April 1929; *s* of late Paymaster-Captain Stanley Thomas Beardsworth, RN and Pearl Sylvia Emma (Biddy) Beardsworth (*née* Blake); *m* 1954, Barbara Bingham Turner; three *s*. *Educ:* RC Sch. of St Edmund's Coll., Ware; RMA Sandhurst; RMCS. BSc. Commissioned Royal Tank Regt, 1949; Regtl service, staff training and staff appts, 1950–69; CO 1st RTR, 1970–72; Project Manager, Future Main Battle Tank, 1973–77; Student, Royal Naval War College, 1977; Dir of Projects, Armoured Fighting Vehicles, 1977–80; Dep. Comdt, RMCS, 1980–81; Vice Master Gen. of the Ordnance, 1981–84, retired. *Recreations:* game shooting, travel, support to equestrian events, authorship. *Address:* c/o Lloyds Bank, Crewkerne, Somerset TA18 7LR. *Club:* Army and Navy.

BEARE, Robin Lyell Blin, MB, BS; FRCS; Hon. Consultant Plastic Surgeon: Queen Victoria Hospital, East Grinstead, since 1960; Brighton General Hospital and Brighton and Lewes Group of Hospitals, since 1960; Hon. Consulting Plastic Surgeon, St Mary's Hospital, London, since 1976 (Consultant Plastic Surgeon, 1959–76); *b* 31 July 1922; *s* of late Stanley Samuel Beare, OBE, FRCS, and late Cecil Mary Guise Beare (*née* Lyell); *m* 1947, Iris Bick; two *s* two *d*. *Educ:* Radley (scholar). Middlesex Hosp. Medical Sch. MB, BS (Hons) 1952 (dist. Surg.); FRCS (Eng) 1955. Served with RAF Bomber Command (Aircrew) 1940–46. Formerly Ho. Surg., Casualty Officer, Asst Pathologist and Surgical Registrar, The Middlesex Hosp., 1952–56. Surg. Registrar, Plastic Surgery and Jaw Injuries Centre, Queen Victoria Hosp., East Grinstead, 1957–60. Examr in gen. surgery for FRCS, 1972–78. Fellow Assoc. of Surgeons of Gt Britain and Ireland; Fellow Royal Society Med.; Mem. Brit. Assoc. of Plastic Surgeons; Mem. of Bd of Trustees, McIndoe Memorial Research Unit, E Grinstead; Hon. Mem. Société Française de Chirurgie Plastique et Reconstructive. *Publications:* various on surgical problems in BMJ, Amer. Jl of Surgery, etc. *Recreations:* fishing, shooting. *Address:* Scraggs Farm, Cowden, Kent TN8 7EB. *T:* Cowden (01342) 850386.

BEARE, Stuart Newton; Partner, Richards Butler, Solicitors, since 1969 (Senior Partner, 1988–91); *b* 6 Oct. 1936; *s* of Newton Beare and Joyce (*née* Atkinson); *m* 1974, Cheryl Wells. *Educ:* Clifton Coll.; Clare Coll., Cambridge (MA, LLB). Nat. Service, commnd Royal Signals, attached RWAFF, 1956–57. Plebiscite Supervisory Officer, N Cameroons, 1960–61; admitted solicitor, 1964. Pres., City of London Law Soc., 1995–. Clerk, Ward of Portsoken, 1993–. Master, City of London Solicitors' Co., 1995–96. *Recreations:* mountain walking, ski-ing. *Addresses:* 24 Ripplevale Grove, N1 1HU. *T:* 0171–609 0766. *Clubs:* Alpine, City of London, Oriental.

BEARN, Prof. Alexander Gordon, MD; FRCP, FRCPEd, FACP; Professor of Medicine, Cornell University Medical College, 1966–89, now Professor Emeritus (Stanton Griffis Distinguished Medical Professor, 1976–79); Attending Physician, The New York Hospital, since 1966; Adjunct Professor and Visiting Professor, Rockefeller University, 1966–88, Hon. Physician, since 1988; *b* 29 March 1923; *s* of E. G. Bearn, CB, CBE; *m* 1952, Margaret, *d* of Clarence Slocum, Fanwood, NJ, USA; one *s* one *d*. *Educ:* Epsom Coll.; Guy's Hosp., London. Postgraduate Medical Sch. of London, 1949–51. Rockefeller Univ., 1951–66; Hon. Research Asst, University Coll. (Galton Laboratory), 1959–60; Prof. and Sen. Physician, Rockefeller Univ., 1964–66; Chm., Dept of Medicine, Cornell Univ. Med. Coll., 1966–77; Physician-in-Chief, NY Hosp., 1966–77; Sen. Vice Pres., Medical and Scientific Affairs, Merck Sharp and Dohme Internat., 1979–88. Woodrow Wilson Foundn Vis. Fellow, 1979–80. Trustee: Rockefeller Univ., 1970–; Howard Hughes Medical Inst., 1987–; Dir, Josiah Macy Jr Foundn, 1981–. Mem. Editorial Bd, several scientific and med. jls. Lectures: Lowell, Harvard, 1958; Medical Research Soc., 1969; Lilly, RCP, 1973; Harvey, 1975; Lettsomian, Med. Soc., 1976. Macy Faculty Scholar Award, 1974–75. Alfred Benzon Prize, Denmark, 1979. Member: Nat. Acad. Science; Amer. Philosophical Soc.; Foreign Mem., Norwegian Acad. Science and Letters. Hon. MD Catholic Univ., Korea, 1968; Docteur *hc* Paris, 1975. *Publications:* Archibald Garrod and the individuality of man, 1993; articles on human genetics and liver disease, 1950–; (Co-Editor) Progress in Medical Genetics, annually, 1962–85; (Associate Editor) Cecil and Loeb: Textbook of Medicine. *Recreations:* biography, collecting snuff-mulls, aristology. *Address:* 1225 Park Avenue, New York, NY 10128, USA. *T:* (212) 534 2495; 41 Shoregate, Crail, Fife KY10 3SU. *Clubs:* Knickerbocker, Century (NY); Crail Golf.

BEARNE, Air Vice-Marshal Guy, CB 1956; *b* 5 Nov. 1908; *y s* of late Lieut-Col L. C. Bearne, DSO, AM; *m* 1933, Aileen Cartwright, *e d* of late H. J. Randall, Hove; one *s* two *d*. Commissioned RAF, 1929; served in various Bomber Sqdns, 1930–33; specialist armament course, 1933; armament duties, 1934–44; Bomber Command, 1944–45 (despatches twice); Staff Officer i/c Administration, RAF Malaya, 1946; Joint Services Staff Coll., 1947; Dep. Dir Organisation (Projects), 1947–49; Command of Central Gunnery Sch., 1949–51; SASO, Rhodesian Air Training Gp, 1951–52; AOC Rhodesian Air Training Gp, 1953; Dir of Organisation (Establishments), Air Ministry, 1954–56; Air Officer in Charge of Administration, Technical Training Command, 1956–61; retd, 1961. *Address:* 2 Mill Close, Hill Deverill, Warminster, Wilts BA12 7EE. *T:* Warminster (01985) 840533.

BEARSTED, 4th Viscount *cr* 1925, of Maidstone; **Peter Montefiore Samuel**, MC 1942; TD 1951; Bt 1903; Baron 1921; Banker; Director, Hill Samuel Group, 1965–87 (Deputy Chairman, after merger with Philip Hill, Higginson & Co., 1965–82); Chairman: Dylon International Ltd, 1958–84; Hill Samuel & Co. (Ireland) Ltd, 1964–84; *b* 9 Dec. 1911; second *s* of Viscount Bearsted and Dorothea, *e d* of late E. Montefiore Micholls; *S* brother, 1986; *m* 1st, 1939, Deirdre du Barry (marr. diss. 1942); 2nd, 1946, Hon. Elizabeth Adelaide Pearce Serocold (*d* 1983), *d* of late Baron Cohen, PC; two *s* one *d*; 3rd, 1984, Nina Alice Hilary, *widow* of Michael Pocock, CBE. *Educ:* Eton; New College, Oxford (BA). Served Warwickshire Yeo, Middle East and Italy, 1939–45. Director: M. Samuel & Co. Ltd, 1935 (Dep. Chm. 1948); Shell Transport & Trading Co. Ltd, 1938–82; Samuel Properties Ltd, 1961–86 (Chm., 1982–86); Mayborn Group PLC, 1946– (Chm., 1946–88); Trades Union Unit Trust Managers Ltd, 1961–82; General Consolidated Investment Trust Ltd, 1975–83. President, Norwood Home for Jewish Children, 1962–79; Hon. Treas., Nat. Assoc. for Gifted Children, 1968–81; Chairman: Council, Royal Free Hospital of Medicine, 1973–82 (Mem., 1948–); Bd of Governors, Royal Free Hosp., 1956–68 (Governor, 1939–). *Recreation:* shooting. *Heir:* *s* Hon. Nicholas Alan Samuel [*b* 22 Jan. 1950; *m* 1975, Caroline Jane, *d* of Dr David Sacks; one *s* four *d*]. *Address:* 9 Campden Hill Court, W8 7HX; Farley Hall, Farley Hill, near Reading, Berkshire RG7 1UL. *T:* Eversley (01734) 733242. *Club:* White's.

BEASLEY, John T.; *see* Telford Beasley.

BEASLEY, Michael Charles, IPFA, FCA, FCCA; County Treasurer, Royal County of Berkshire, 1970–88; *b* 20 July 1924; *y s* of late William Isaac Beasley and Mary Gladys (*née* Williams), Ipswich, Suffolk; *m* 1955, Jean Anita Mary, *o d* of late Reginald John Shedrick Webber and Margaret Dorothy (*née* Rees), Penarth, S Glamorgan; one *s*. *Educ:* Northgate Grammar Sch., Ipswich. BScEcon London. Treasurer's Dept, East Suffolk County Council, 1940–48; served Royal Navy, 1943–46; Treasurer's Dept, Staffordshire CC, 1948–51; Educn Accountant, Glamorgan CC, 1951–54; Asst County Treasurer, Nottinghamshire CC, 1954–61; Dep. County Treasurer, Royal County of Berkshire, 1961–70, Acting Chief Exec., 1986. Examiner, CIPFA, 1963–66; Financial Adviser, Assoc. of County Councils and former County Councils Assoc., 1971–87; Hon. Treasurer, Soc. of County Treasurers, 1984–88 (Hon. Sec., 1972–80, Vice-Pres., 1980–81, Pres., 1981–82); Mem., Treasury Cttee on Local Authority Borrowing, 1972–87; Member Council: Local Authorities Mutual Investment Trust, 1974–75; RIPA, 1976–82. *Publications:* contribs to jls on local govt finance and computers. *Recreations:* pottering and pondering. *Address:* Greenacre, Hyde End Road, Spencers Wood, Berkshire RG7 1BU. *T:* Reading (01734) 883868.

BEASLEY, Prof. William Gerald, CBE 1980; BA, PhD; FRHistS; FBA 1967; Professor of the History of the Far East, University of London, 1954–83; Head of Japan Research Centre, School of Oriental and African Studies, 1978–83; *b* 1919; *m* 1955, Hazel Polwin; one *s*. *Educ:* Magdalen Coll. Sch., Brackley; University Coll., London. Served War, 1940–46, RNVR. Lecturer, Sch. of Oriental and African Studies, University of London, 1947. Mem., 1961–68, British Chm., 1964–68, Anglo-Japanese Mixed Cultural Commn. Vice-Pres., British Acad., 1974–75, Treasurer, 1975–79. Hon. Mem., Japan Acad., 1984. Hon. DLitt Hong Kong, 1978. Order of the Rising Sun (Third Class), Japan, 1983. *Publications:* Great Britain and the opening of Japan, 1951; Select Documents on Japanese foreign policy, 1853–1868, 1955; The Modern History of Japan, 1963; The Meiji Restoration, 1972; Japanese Imperialism 1894–1945, 1987; The Rise of Modern Japan, 1990; Japan Encounters the Barbarian: Japanese travellers in America and Europe, 1995. *Address:* 172 Hampton Road, Twickenham TW2 5NJ.

BEASLEY-MURRAY, George Raymond, DD, PhD; Senior Professor of New Testament Interpretation, Southern Baptist Theological Seminary, Louisville, Kentucky, since 1980; *b* 10 Oct. 1916; *s* of George Alfred Beasley; *m* 1942, Ruth Weston; three *s* one *d*. *Educ:* City of Leicester Boys' Sch.; Spurgeon's Coll. and King's Coll., London; Jesus Coll., Cambridge (MA). BD 1941, MTh 1945, PhD 1952, DD 1964, London; DD Cambridge, 1989. Baptist Minister, Ilford, Essex, 1941–48; Cambridge, 1948–50; New Testament Lectr, Spurgeon's Coll., 1950–56; New Testament Prof., Baptist Theological Coll., Rüschlikon, Zürich, 1956–58; Principal, Spurgeon's Coll., 1958–73; Buchanan-Harrison Prof. of New Testament Interpretation, Southern Baptist Theol Seminary, Louisville, Ky, 1973–80. Pres., Baptist Union of Great Britain and Ireland, 1968–69. Hon. DD McMaster, 1973; Hon. LLD CNAA, 1989. *Publications:* Christ is Alive, 1947; Jesus and the Future, 1954; Preaching the Gospel from the Gospels, 1956, new edn 1995; A Commentary on Mark Thirteen, 1957; Baptism in the New Testament, 1962; The Resurrection of Jesus Christ, 1964; Baptism Today and Tomorrow, 1966; Commentary on 2 Corinthians (Broadman Commentary), 1971; The Book of Revelation (New Century Bible), 1974; The Coming of God, 1983; Jesus and the Kingdom of God, 1986; Commentary on the Gospel of John (Word Commentary), 1987; Word Biblical Themes: John, 1989; Gospel of Life: theology in the Fourth Gospel, 1991; Jesus and the Last Days: the interpretation of the Olivet Discourse, 1993; (jtly) The Newell Lectureships II, 1993. *Recreation:* music. *Address:* 4 Holland Road, Hove, E Sussex BN3 1JJ.

See also Rev. Dr P. Beasley-Murray.

BEASLEY-MURRAY, Rev. Dr Paul; Senior Minister, Baptist Church, Victoria Road South, Chelmsford, since 1993; *b* 14 March 1944; *s* of Rev. Dr George R. Beasley-Murray, *qv*; *m* 1967, Caroline (*née* Griffiths); three *s* one *d*. *Educ:* Trinity School of John Whitgift; Jesus Coll., Cambridge (MA); Northern Baptist Coll. and Manchester Univ. (PhD); Baptist Theol Seminary, Rüschlikon and Zürich Univ. Baptist Missionary Soc., Zaire (Professor at National Univ., Theol. Faculty), 1970–72; Pastor of Altrincham Baptist Church, Cheshire, 1973–86; Principal, Spurgeon's Coll., 1986–92. Chm., Richard Baxter Inst. for Ministry, 1994–. Editor, Ministry Today, 1994–. *Publications:* (with A. Wilkinson) Turning the Tide, 1981; Pastors Under Pressure, 1989; Dynamic Leadership, 1990; (ed) Mission to the World, 1991; Faith and Festivity, 1991; Radical Believers, 1992; (ed) Anyone for Ordination?, 1993; A Call to Excellence, 1995. *Recreations:* music, walking. *Address:* The Manse, 12 Beach's Drive, Chelmsford, Essex CM1 2NJ. *T:* Chelmsford (01245) 352996.

BEASTALL, John Sale, CB 1995; Head of Local Government Group, HM Treasury, since 1993; *b* 2 July 1941; *s* of Howard and Marjorie Betty Beastall (*née* Sale). *Educ:* St Paul's School; Balliol College, Oxford (BA 1963). Asst Principal, HM Treasury, 1963–67 (Asst Private Sec. to Chancellor of the Exchequer, 1966–67); Principal: HM Treasury, 1967–68 and 1971–75 (Private Sec. to Paymaster General, 1974–75); CSD, 1968–71; Assistant Secretary: HM Treasury, 1975–79 and 1981–85; CSD, 1979–81; DES, 1985–87; Treasury Officer of Accounts, 1987–93. *Recreation:* Christian youth work. *Address:* c/o HM Treasury, Parliament Street, SW1P 3AG. *Club:* United Oxford & Cambridge University.

BEATON, James Wallace, GC 1974; CVO 1992 (LVO 1987); security manager; Chief Superintendent, Metropolitan Police, 1985–92; *b* St Fergus, Aberdeenshire, 16 Feb. 1943; *s* of J. A. Beaton and B. McDonald; *m* 1965, Anne C. Ballantyne; two *d*. *Educ:* Peterhead Acad., Aberdeenshire. Joined Metropolitan Police, 1962: Notting Hill, 1962–66; Sergeant, Harrow Road, 1966–71; Station Sergeant, Wembley, 1971–73; Royalty Protection Officer, 'A' Division, 1973; Police Officer to The Princess Anne, 1973–79; Police Inspector, 1974; Chief Inspector, 1979; Superintendent, 1983. Director's Honor Award, US Secret Service, 1974. *Recreations:* reading, keeping fit, golf, hill walking. *Address:* 1 Kingswells View, Westhill, Skene, Aberdeenshire AB32 6RZ. *T:* Kingswell (01224) 744361.

BEATSON, Jack; Rouse Ball Professor of English Law, since 1993, and Fellow of St John's College, since 1994, University of Cambridge; a Recorder, since 1994; *b* 3 Nov. 1948; *s* of late John James Beatson and Miriam Beatson (*née* White); *m* 1973, Charlotte, *y d* of Lt-Col J. A. Christie-Miller; one *s* one *d*. *Educ:* Whittingehame Coll., Brighton; Brasenose Coll., Oxford (BCL, MA). Called to the Bar, Inner Temple, 1972, Hon. Bencher, 1993; Lectr in Law, Univ. of Bristol, 1972–73; Fellow and Tutor in Law, Merton Coll., Oxford, 1973–94 (Hon. Fellow, 1995). A Law Comr, 1989–94. Visiting Professor: Osgoode Hall Law Sch., Toronto, 1979; Univ. of Virginia Law Sch., 1980, 1983; Vis. Sen. Teaching Fellow, Nat Univ. of Singapore, 1987; Vis. Fellow, Univ. of WA, 1988. *Publications:* (ed jtly) Chitty on Contract, 25th edn 1982 to 27th edn 1994; (with M. H. Matthews) Administrative Law: Cases and Materials, 1983, 2nd edn 1989; The Use and Abuse of Restitution, 1991; articles on administrative law, contract, and restitution in legal jls. *Recreations:* gardening, travelling. *Address:* St John's College, Cambridge CB2 1TP.

BEATTIE, Hon. Sir Alexander (Craig), Kt 1973; President, The Eryldene Trust, 1983–89; *b* 24 Jan. 1912; *e s* of Edmund Douglas and Amie Louisa Beattie; *m* 1st, 1944, Joyce Pearl Alder (*d* 1977); two *s*; 2nd, 1978, Joyce Elizabeth de Groot. *Educ:* Fort Street High Sch., Sydney; Univ. of Sydney (BA, LLB; Hon. LLD). Admitted to NSW Bar, 1936. Served War of 1939–45: Captain, 2nd AIF, Royal Australian Armoured Corps, New Guinea and Borneo. Pres., Industrial Commn of NSW, 1966–81 (Mem., 1955). Trustee, Royal Botanic Gardens and Govt Domain, Sydney, 1976–82, Chm. 1980–82. *Recreations:* gardening, bowls. *Club:* Australian (Sydney).

BEATTIE, Anthony; *see* Beattie, G. A.

BEATTIE, Prof. Arthur James, FRSE 1957; Professor of Greek at Edinburgh University, 1951–81; Dean of the Faculty of Arts, 1963–65; *b* 28 June 1914, *e s* of Arthur John Rait Beattie. *Educ:* Montrose Academy; Aberdeen Univ.; Sidney Sussex Coll., Cambridge. Wilson Travelling Fellowship, Aberdeen, 1938–40. Served War, 1940–45; RA 1940–41; Int. Corps, 1941–45; Major GS02; despatches, 1945. Fellow and Coll. Lectr, Sidney Sussex Coll., 1946–51; Faculty Asst Lectr and Univ. Lectr in Classics, Cambridge, 1946–51. Chm. Governors, Morrison's Acad., Crieff, 1962–75; Governor, Sedbergh Sch., 1967–78. Comdr, Royal Order of the Phœnix (Greece), 1966. *Publications:* articles contributed to classical jls. *Recreations:* walking, bird-watching. *Club:* New (Edinburgh).

BEATTIE, Charles Noel, QC 1962; retired; *b* 4 Nov. 1912; *s* of Michael William Beattie and Edith Beattie (*née* Lickfold); *m*; three *d*. *Educ:* Lewes Grammar Sch. LLB (London). Admitted a solicitor, 1938. Served War of 1939–45 (despatches), Capt. RASC. Called to the Bar, Lincoln's Inn, 1946; Bencher 1971. *Publication:* My Wartime Escapades, 1987. *Address:* Leckhelm Estate, Loch Broom, Ullapool, Ross-shire IV23 2RL.

BEATTIE, David, CMG 1989; HM Diplomatic Service; Ambassador to the Swiss Confederation, and concurrently (non-resident) to the Principality of Liechtenstein, since 1992; *b* 5 March 1938; *s* of George William David Beattie and Norna Alice (*née* Nicolson); *m* 1966, Ulla Marita Alha, *d* of late Allan Alha and of Brita-Maja (*née* Tuominen), Helsinki, Finland; two *d*. *Educ:* Merchant Taylors' Sch., Crosby; Lincoln Coll., Oxford (BA 1964, MA 1967). National Service, Royal Navy, 1957–59; Sub-Lieut RNR, 1959; Lieut RNR 1962–67. Entered HM Foreign (now Diplomatic) Service, 1963; FO, 1963–64; Moscow, 1964–66; FO, 1966–70; Nicosia, 1970–74; FCO, 1974–78; Counsellor, later Dep. Head, UK Delegn to Negotiations on Mutual Reduction of Forces and Armaments and Associated Measures in Central Europe, Vienna, 1978–82; Counsellor (Commercial), Moscow, 1982–85; Head of Energy, Science and Space Dept, FCO, 1985–87; Min. and Dep. UK Perm. Rep. to NATO, Brussels, 1987–92. Freeman, City of London, 1989. FIL 1990. *Recreations:* bridge, walking, history of the House of Stuart. *Address:* c/o Foreign and Commonwealth Office, SW1A 2AH. *Clubs:* Travellers', Kandahar Ski.

BEATTIE, Hon. Sir David (Stuart), GCMG 1980; GCVO 1981; QSO 1985; Governor-General of New Zealand, 1980–85; Chairman, New Zealand International Festival of the Arts, since 1987; *b* Sydney, Australia, 29 Feb. 1924; *s* of Joseph Nesbitt Beattie; *m* 1950, Norma Macdonald, QSO, *d* of John Macdonald; three *s* four *d*. *Educ:* Dilworth Sch.; Univ. of Auckland (LLB). Served War of 1939–45, Naval Officer. Barrister and Solicitor; President Auckland Dist Law Soc., 1964; QC 1965; Judge of Supreme Court, 1969–80; Chairman, Royal Commission on the Courts, 1977–78; Mem., Commn on Courts of Fiji, 1993–94. Chm., NZ Meat Industry Assoc. (Inc.), 1988–; Pres., NZ Olympic and Commonwealth Games Assoc., 1989–. Chm., Sir Winston Churchill Memorial Trust Board, 1975–80; Pres., NZ Sports Foundn, 1977–80, 1986–93 (Chm. of Trustees, 1977–80). Hon. LLD Auckland, 1983. *Publications:* legal articles. *Address:* 18 Golf Road, Heretaunga, Wellington, New Zealand.

BEATTIE, (George) Anthony; Chief Executive, Natural Resources Institute, Overseas Development Administration, since 1990; *b* 17 April 1944; *s* of James Ellison Beattie and Christine Beattie; *m* 1973, Janet Frances Dring; one *s*. *Educ:* Stationers' Company's Sch., London; Trinity Coll., Cambridge (MA). Economic Planning Div., Office of the President, Malawi, 1966–69; Overseas Development Administration: Economic Planning Staff, 1969–78; Admin. Group, 1978; Dir, Tropical Develt and Res. Inst., 1986; Dir, Overseas Develt Natural Resources Inst., 1987–90. *Recreations:* music, pottering in the country, Border terriers. *Address:* Natural Resources Institute, Central Avenue, Chatham Maritime, Chatham, Kent ME4 4TB. *T:* Medway (01634) 880088.

BEATTIE, Hon. Dame Heather; *see* Steel, Hon. Dame A. H.

BEATTIE, Thomas Brunton, CMG 1981; OBE 1968; HM Diplomatic Service, retired 1982; Management Consultant, Control Risks Ltd, since 1982; *b* 17 March 1924; *s* of Joseph William Beattie and Jessie Dewar (*née* Brunton), Rutherglen; *m* 1st, 1956, Paula Rahkola (marr. diss. 1981); one *d*; 2nd, 1982, Josephine Marion Collins. *Educ:* Rutherglen Acad.; Pembroke Coll., Cambridge. MA. Served RAF, 1943–47. Jt Press Reading Service, British Embassy, Moscow, 1947; Finnish Secretariat, British Legation, Helsinki, 1951; FO, 1954; Second Sec., Madrid, 1956; FO, 1960; First Sec., Athens, 1964; First Sec., later Counsellor, FCO, 1969; Counsellor, Rome, 1977, FCO 1981. Mem., Inst. of Translation and Interpreting, 1991. Treas., Scottish Covenanter Memls Assoc., 1991–. Member: Management Cttee, Pembroke Coll. Cambridge Soc., 1995–; Marie Stuart Soc. *Publications:* translated: Viktor Suvorov, Icebreaker, 1990; Vladimir Kuzichkin, Inside the KGB, 1990. *Recreations:* unremarkable. *Address:* Cairnside, Kirkland of Glencairn, Moniaive, Dumfriesshire DG3 4HD. *Clubs:* Carlton; Royal Scottish Automobile (Glasgow).

BEATTY, 3rd Earl *cr* 1919; **David Beatty;** Viscount Borodale of Wexford, Baron Beatty of the North Sea and of Brooksby, 1919; *b* 21 Nov. 1946; *s* of 2nd Earl Beatty, DSC, and Dorothy Rita, *d* of late M. J. Furey, New Orleans, USA; *S* father, 1972; *m* 1971, Anne (marr. diss. 1983), *d* of A. Please, Wokingham; two *s*; *m* 1984, Anoma Corinne Wijewardene. *Educ:* Eton. *Heir: s* Viscount Borodale, *qv*. *Address:* c/o House of Lords, SW1A 0PW.

BEATTY, Hon. (Henry) Perrin; PC(Can) 1979; *b* 1 June 1950; *m* 1974, Julia Kenny; two *s*. *Educ:* Upper Canada College; Univ. of Western Ontario (BA 1971). MP (Progressive C) Wellington–Grey–Dufferin–Simcoe, Canada, 1972–93; Minister of State for Treasury Bd, 1979; Minister of Nat. Revenue and for Canada Post Corp., 1984; Solicitor General, 1985; Minister of Nat. Defence, 1986–89; Minister of Nat. Health and Welfare, 1989–91; Minister of Communications, 1991–93; Minister for External Affairs, 1993. Former Mem., Special Jt Cttee on Constitution of Canada; Chm., Commonwealth Delegated Legislation Cttee. *Address:* PO Box 33, Fergus, Ont N1M 1Z4, Canada.

BEAUCHAMP, Sir Christopher Radstock Proctor-, 9th Bt *cr* 1744; solicitor with Gilbert Stephens, Exeter; *b* 30 Jan. 1935; *s* of Rev. Sir Ivor Cuthbert Proctor-Beauchamp, 8th Bt, and Caroline Muriel (*d* 1987), *d* of late Frank Densham; *S* father, 1971; *m* 1965, Rosalind Emily Margot, 3rd *d* of G. P. Wainwright, St Leonards-on-Sea; two *s* one *d*. *Educ:* Rugby; Trinity College, Cambridge (MA). *Heir: s* Charles Barclay Proctor-Beauchamp, *b* 7 July 1969. *Address:* The White House, Harpford, near Sidmouth, East Devon EX10 0NJ.

BEAUCLERK, family name of **Duke of St Albans.**

BEAUFORT, 11th Duke of, *cr* 1682; **David Robert Somerset;** Earl of Worcester, 1514; Marquess of Worcester, 1642; Chairman, Marlborough Fine Art Ltd, since 1977; *b* 23 Feb. 1928; *s* of late Captain Henry Robert Somers Fitzroy de Vere Somerset, DSO (*d* 1965) (*g g s* of 8th Duke) and late Bettine Violet Somerset (*née* Malcolm) (*d* 1973); *S* cousin, 1984; *m* 1950, Lady Caroline Jane Thynne (*d* 1995), *d* of 6th Marquess of Bath and of Hon. Daphne Vivian; three *s* one *d*. *Educ:* Eton. Formerly Lieutenant, Coldstream Guards. Pres., British Horse Soc., 1988–90. *Heir: s* Marquess of Worcester, *qv*. *Address:* Badminton, Avon GL9 1DB.

BEAUMONT, family name of **Viscount Allendale** and **Baron Beaumont of Whitley.**

BEAUMONT OF WHITLEY, Baron *cr* 1967 (Life Peer), of Child's Hill; **Rev. Timothy Wentworth Beaumont,** MA (Oxon); politician, priest and writer; Liberal Democrat spokesman on conservation and the countryside, House of Lords, since 1993; *b* 22 Nov. 1928; *o s* of Major and Hon. Mrs M. W. Beaumont; *m* 1955, Mary Rose Wauchope; one *s* two *d* (and one *s* decd). *Educ:* Gordonstoun; Christ Church, Oxford; Westcott House, Cambridge. Asst Chaplain, St John's Cathedral, Hong Kong, 1955–57; Vicar, Christ Church Kowloon Tong, Hong Kong, 1957–59; Hon. Curate, St Stephen's Rochester Row, London, 1960–63; resigned orders, 1973; resumed orders, 1984; Vicar, St Philip and All Saints, with St Luke, Kew, 1986–91. Editor: Prism, 1960–63 and 1964; New Outlook, 1964, 1972–74; Chm., Studio Vista Books Ltd, 1963–68; Proprietor of New Christian, 1965–70. Food Columnist, Illustrated London News, 1976–80. Asst Dir (Public Affairs), Make Children Happy, 1977–78; Co-ordinator, The Green Alliance, 1978–80. Liberal Party Organisation: Jt Hon. Treas., 1962–63; Chm., Liberal Publications Dept, 1963–64; Head of Org., 1965–66; Chm., Liberal Party's Org. Cttee, 1966; Chm., Liberal Party, 1967–68; Pres., Liberal Party, 1969–70; Vice-Chm., Liberal Party Exec. and Dir, Policy Promotion, 1980–83; Mem., Lib Dem Policy Cttee, 1992–. Liberal spokesman on education and the arts, H of L, 1968–86; Alternate Mem., Assemblies of Council of Europe and WEU, 1973–77, Leader of Liberal Delegn, 1977–78, Vice-Chm., Liberal Gp, 1977–78. Pres., British Fedn of Film Socs, 1973–79. Chairman: Albany Trust, 1969–71; Inst. of Res. into Mental and Multiple Handicap, 1971–73; Exit, 1980–81. Mem., Exec. Cttee, British Council, 1974–78. Mem. Exec., Church Action on Poverty, 1983–86, 1991–94. *Publications:* (ed) Modern Religious Verse, 1965; ed and contrib., The Liberal

Cookbook, 1972; (ed) New Christian Reader, 1974; (ed) The Selective Ego: the diaries of James Agate, 1976; Where shall I place my cross?, 1987. *Address:* 40 Elms Road, SW4 9EX. *T:* 0171–498 8664.

BEAUMONT, Bill; *see* Beaumont, W. B.

BEAUMONT, Christopher; *see* Beaumont, H. C.

BEAUMONT, Christopher Hubert; a Recorder of the Crown Court, since 1981; *b* 10 Feb. 1926; *s* of Hubert and Beatrix Beaumont; *m* 1st, 1959, Catherine Sanders Clark (*d* 1971); two *s*; 2nd, 1972, Sara Patricia Magee; one *d*. *Educ:* West Monmouth Sch., Pontypool; Balliol Coll., Oxford (MA). Served RN, 1944–47 (Sub-Lieut RNVR). Called to Bar, Middle Temple, 1950. Asst Dep. Coroner, Inner West London, 1963–81. Chm., Agricultural Land Tribunal, Eastern Area, 1985– (Dep. Chm., 1979–85). *Publications:* Law Relating to Sheriffs, 1968; Town and Country Planning Act 1968, 1969; Housing Act 1969, 1969; Town and Country Planning Acts 1971 and 1972, 1973; (with W. G. Nutley) Land Compensation Act 1973, 1973; (with W. G. Nutley) Community Land Act 1975, 1976; (ed with W. G. Nutley) Planning Appeal Decisions, 1986–. *Address:* Rose Cottage, Lower Eashing, Godalming, Surrey GU7 2QG. *T:* Godalming (01483) 416316; 2 Harcourt Buildings, Temple, EC4Y 9DB. *T:* 0171–353 8415.

BEAUMONT, David Colin Baskcomb; HM Diplomatic Service; High Commissioner, Botswana, since 1995; *b* 16 Aug. 1942; *s* of Colin Baskcomb Beaumont and Denise Heather Smith; *m* 1965, Barbara Enid Morris; two *s* one *d*. *Educ:* St Benedict's Sch., Ealing. Joined CRO, 1961; Private Sec. to Special Rep. in Africa, Nairobi, 1965; Third Sec., Bahrain, 1967; Second Sec., FCO, 1970; Second Sec. (Commercial), Accra, 1974; First Sec., FCO, 1977; First Sec. (Develt), Kathmandu, 1981; First Sec. and Dep. Head of Mission, Addis Ababa, 1983; First Sec., later Counsellor, FCO, 1986; Head of Protocol Dept, 1989–94, and First Asst Marshal of the Diplomatic Corps, 1993–94, FCO. *Recreations:* tennis, walking, cooking. *Address:* c/o Foreign and Commonwealth Office, King Charles Street, SW1A 2AH. *Club:* MCC.

BEAUMONT, Captain Hon. Sir (Edward) Nicholas (Canning), KCVO 1994 (CVO 1986; LVO 1976); Vice Lord-Lieutenant of Berkshire, 1989–94; Director, High Gosforth Park, since 1994; *b* 14 Dec. 1929; 3rd *s* of 2nd Viscount Allendale, KG, CB, CBE, MC and Violet (*d* 1979), *d* of Sir Charles Seely, 2nd Bt; *m* 1953, Jane Caroline, *d* of Alexander Lewis Paget Falconer Wallace, of Candacraig, Strathdon, Aberdeenshire; two *s*. *Educ:* Eton. Joined Life Guards, 1948; Captain 1956; retired 1960. Assistant to Clerk of the Course, Ascot, 1964; Clerk of the Course and Sec. to Ascot Authy, 1969–94. Pres., Berks SJAB, 1988–94. DL Berks 1982. *Address:* Low Shield House, Sparty Lea, Allenheads, Northumberland. *T:* Hexham (01434) 685037. *Club:* White's.

BEAUMONT, Sir George Howland Francis, 12th Bt, *cr* 1661; late Lieutenant 60th Rifles; *b* 24 Sept. 1924; *s* of 11th Bt and Renée Muriel (*d* 1987), 2nd *d* of late Maj.-Gen. Sir Edward Northey, GCMG, CB; *S* father 1933; *m* 1949, Barbara Singleton (marr. annulled, 1951); *m* 1963, Henrietta Anne (marr. diss. 1986), *d* of late Dr A. Waymouth and Mrs J. Rodwell, Riverside Cottage, Donnington, Berks; twin *d*. *Educ:* Stowe Sch. *Address:* Stretton House, Manor Court, Stretton-on-Fosse, near Moreton-in-Marsh, Glos GL56 9SB. *T:* Shipston-on-Stour (01608) 662845. *Club:* Lansdowne.

BEAUMONT, His Honour (Herbert) Christopher, MBE 1948; a Circuit Judge, 1972–85; *b* 3 June 1912; *s* of late Gerald Beaumont, MC and bar, and Gwendolene Beaumont (*née* Haworth); *m* 1940, Helen Margaret Gordon Smail, *d* of William Mitchell Smail; one *s* two *d*. *Educ:* Uppingham Sch.; Worcester Coll., Oxford. Indian Civil and Political Services, 1936–47; Private Sec. to Lord Radcliffe, Chm. of Indo-Pakistan Boundary Commn, 1947; Foreign Office, 1948–52. Called to the Bar, Inner Temple, 1951; Metropolitan Magistrate, 1962–72. Chm. of the London Juvenile Courts, 1964; Dep. Chm., North Riding QS, 1966–71; temp. Resident Judge, Cyprus, 1986. Mem., Parole Bd, 1974–76; a Chm., Police (Disciplinary) Appeal Tribunal, 1988–90. *Recreations:* travel in Europe, growing vegetables. *Address:* Minskip Lodge, Boroughbridge, Yorks YO5 9JF. *T:* Boroughbridge (01423) 322365. *Club:* Brooks's.

See also G. M. Waller.

BEAUMONT, (John) Michael; Seigneur of Sark since 1974; *b* 20 Dec. 1927; *s* of late Lionel (Buster) Beaumont and Enid Beaumont (*née* Ripley), and *g s* of Dame Sibyl Hathaway, Dame of Sark; *m* 1956, Diana (*née* La Trobe-Bateman); two *s*. *Educ:* Loughborough Coll. (DLC). Aircraft Design Engr, 1952–70; Chief Techn. Engr, Beagle Aircraft, 1969–70; Design Engr, BAC GW Div., 1970–75. *Recreations:* theatre, music, gardening. *Heir:* *s* Christopher Beaumont, Major RE, *b* 4 Feb. 1957. *Address:* La Seigneurie, Sark, Channel Islands. *T:* Sark (048183) 2017.

BEAUMONT, John Richard; Director of Marketing, Energis Communications Ltd, since 1995; *b* 24 June 1957, *s* of Jim Beaumont and Betty Marie (*née* Jarratt); *m*; two *d*. *Educ:* Univ. of Durham (BA Geog.). Res. Asst, Univ. of Leeds, 1978–80; Lectr, Univ. of Keele, 1980–83; Consultant, Coopers & Lybrand (London and NY), 1983–85; Jt Man. Dir, Pinpoint Analysis Ltd, London, 1985–87; ICL Prof. of Applied Management Information Systems and Dir, European Centre for Inf. Resource Management, Univ. of Stirling, 1987–90; Prof. and Hd of Sch. of Management, Bath Univ., 1990–92. Man. Dir, Stratatech, 1986–93; Strategy Planning Manager, 1993–94, Head of Corporate Strategy and Affairs, 1994–95, Energis Communications. Hon. Professor: QUB, 1990–93; City Univ., 1994–. Mem. Council, ESRC, 1989–93. *Publications:* (with P. Keys) Future Cities, 1982; (with S. Williams) Projects in Geography, 1983; (with E. Sutherland) Information Resources Management, 1992; (jtly) Managing our Environment, 1993. *Recreations:* good wine, travel, running, golf, watching Rugby, reading and writing fiction. *Address:* 92 Lauderdale Tower, EC2Y 8BY. *Club:* Athenæum.

BEAUMONT, Hon. Sir Nicholas; *see* Beaumont, Hon. Sir E. N. C.

BEAUMONT, Peter John Luther; QC 1986; **His Honour Judge Beaumont;** a Circuit Judge, since 1989; *b* 10 Jan. 1944; *s* of S. P. L. Beaumont, OBE, and D. V. Beaumont; *m* 1970, Ann Jarratt; one *s* one *d*. *Educ:* Peterhouse, Zimbabwe; Univ. of Zimbabwe (BScEcon Hons). Called to the Bar, Lincoln's Inn, 1967; practised South Eastern Circuit; a Recorder, 1986. Mem., Parole Bd, 1992–. Governor, Felsted Sch., 1990–. *Recreations:* cricket, tennis, gardening. *Address:* Chelmsford Crown Court. *T:* Chelmsford (0245) 358222.

BEAUMONT, Sir Richard Ashton, KCMG 1965 (CMG 1955); OBE 1949; HM Diplomatic Service, retired; Chairman, Arab-British Chamber of Commerce, since 1980; *b* 29 Dec. 1912; *s* of A. R. Beaumont, FRCS, Uppingham, and Evelyn Frances (*née* Rendle); *m* 1st, 1942, Alou (*d* 1985), *d* of M. Camran, Istanbul; one *d*; 2nd, 1989, Melanie Anns, *d* of H. Brummell. *Educ:* Repton; Oriel Coll., Oxford. Joined HM Consular Service, 1936; posted Lebanon and Syria, 1936–41. Served War, 1941–44. Returned to Foreign Office, 1944; served in London, Iraq, Venezuela; Imperial Defence Coll., 1958; Head of Arabian Department, Foreign Office, 1959; Ambassador: to Morocco, 1961–65; to Iraq, 1965–67; Dep. Under-Sec. of State, FO, 1967–69; Ambassador to the Arab Republic of Egypt, 1969–72. Dir-Gen., Middle East Assoc., 1973–77; Chairman: Arab British Centre, 1976–77; Anglo-Arab Assoc., 1979–. Governor, SOAS, 1973–78. Trustee, Thomson Foundn, 1974–. *Address:* 82 Peterborough Road, SW6 3EB.

BEAUMONT, William Anderson, CB 1986; OBE (mil.) 1961; AE 1953; Speaker's Secretary, House of Commons, 1982–86; *b* 30 Oct. 1924; *s* of late William Lionel Beaumont and Mrs E. Taverner; *m* 1st, 1946, Kythé (*d* 1988), *d* of late Major K. G. Mackenzie, Victoria, BC; one *d*; 2nd, 1989, Rosalie, *widow* of Judge Michael Underhill, QC. *Educ:* Terrington Hall, York; Cranleigh Sch. (Entrance Exhibnr); Christ Church, Oxford (MA, DipEd). Served RAF, Navigator, 1942–47, 355 Sqdn, 232 Sqdn, SEAC (Flt Lt); RAuxAF 3507 (Co. of Somerset) FCU, 1948–54; 3609 (W Riding) FCU, 1954–61 (Wing Comdr CO, 1958–61); Observer Comdr, No 18 (Leeds) Gp, Royal Observer Corps, 1962–75 (ROC Medal 1975). Asst Master, Bristol Grammar Sch., 1951–54; Beaumont and Smith Ltd, Pudsey, 1954–66 (Man. Dir, 1958–66); Henry Mason (Shipley) Ltd (Man. Dir, 1966–76); Principal, Welsh Office, 1976–79; Asst Sec., Welsh Office, 1979–82. A Chm. of Assessors, CSSB, 1988–92. Dir, St David's Forum, 1986–92; Sec., Prince of Wales Award Gp, 1987–90; Mem., Awards Cttee, RAF Benevolent Fund, 1990–; Vice-Chm., Franco-British Soc., 1991–. FRSA 1977. *Recreations:* inland waterways, reluctant gardening, walking. *Address:* 28 Halford Road, Richmond, Surrey TW10 6AP. *T:* 0181–940 2390. *Clubs:* Royal Air Force; Civil Service; United Services Mess (Cardiff).

BEAUMONT, William Blackledge, (Bill), OBE 1982; Rugby Union footballer, retired; sports broadcaster and writer; Director, J. Blackledge & Son Ltd, since 1981; *b* 9 March 1952; *s* of Ronald Walton Beaumont and Joyce Beaumont; *m* 1977, Hilary Jane Seed; two *s*. *Educ:* Ellesmere Coll., Shropshire. Joined family textile business, 1971. First played Rugby Union for England, 1975; 34 caps (20 caps as Captain); Mem., British Lions, NZ tour, 1977; Captain, British Lions, S Africa tour, 1980; played for Lancashire Barbarians, retd 1982. Television includes A Question of Sport (BBC TV), 1982–. *Publications:* Thanks to Rugby 1982; Bill Beaumont's Tackle Rugby, 1983; Bill Beaumont's Sporting Year Book, 1984. *Recreations:* tennis, golf, water-skiing. *Clubs:* East India, MCC; Fylde Rugby Union Football; Royal Lytham St Anne's Golf.

BEAUMONT-DARK, Sir Anthony (Michael), Kt 1992; investment adviser; *b* Birmingham, 11 Oct. 1932; *s* of Leonard Cecil Dark; *m* 1959, Sheelagh Irene, *d* of R. Cassey; one *s* one *d*. *Educ:* Birmingham Coll. of Arts and Crafts; Birmingham Univ. Mem., Birmingham Stock Exchange, 1958–; Consultant, Smith, Keen, Cutler, subseq. Smith Keen Murray, 1985– (Sen. Partner, 1959–85); Dep. Chm., J. Saville Gordon plc, 1994– (Dir, 1989–); Director: Wigham Poland (Midlands) Ltd, 1960–75; Nat. Exhibition Centre Ltd, 1971–73; Cope Allman Internat. Ltd, 1972–83; Birmid Qualcast PLC, 1983–89; TR High Income Trust PLC, 1990– (Chm., 1994–); Birmingham Executive Airways, 1983– (Chm., 1983–86); ADR Net, 1993–94. Mem., Central Housing Adv. Cttee, DoE, 1970–76. Member: Birmingham City Council, 1956–67 (Alderman, 1967–74, Hon. Alderman, 1976); W Midlands CC, 1973–87 (Chm., Finance Cttee, 1977–83). Contested (C): Birmingham, Aston, 1959, 1964; Birmingham, Selly Oak, 1992. MP (C) Birmingham, Selly Oak, 1979–92. Mem., Treasury and Civil Service Select Cttee, 1979–92. Governor: Aston Univ., 1980–; Birmingham Univ., 1984–92. Trustee, Birmingham Copec Housing Trust, 1975–80. FRSA 1993. *Address:* 124 Lady Byron Lane, Copt Heath, Solihull, Birmingham B93 9BA. *Club:* Carlton.

BEAUREPAIRE, Dame Beryl (Edith), AC 1991; DBE 1981 (OBE 1975); *b* 24 Sept. 1923; *d* of late E. L. Bedggood; *m* 1946, Ian Francis Beaurepaire, *qv*; two *s*. *Educ:* Fintona Girls' Sch., Balwyn, Victoria; Univ. of Melbourne. ASO, WAAAF, 1942–45. Mem. Nat. Exec., YWCA Australia, 1969–77. Liberal Party of Australia: Chm., Victorian Women's Sect., 1973–76; Chm., Federal Women's Sect., 1974–76; Vice Pres., Victorian Div., 1976–86. Mem., Federal Women's Adv. Cttee Working Party, 1977. Pres., Victorian Assoc. of Order of British Empire, 1988–91. Vice Pres., Citizen's Welfare Service, Vic, 1970–86; Convenor, Nat. Women's Adv. Council, Australia, 1978–82. Member: Council, Australian War Memorial, 1982– (Chm., 1985–); Australian Children's Television Foundation Bd, 1982–90; Bd, Victoria's 150th Authy, 1982–87; Australian Bi-centennial Multicultural Foundn, 1989–92. Chm., Bd of Management, Fintona Girls' Sch., 1973–87. Silver Jubilee Medal, 1977. *Recreations:* golf, swimming. *Address:* 18 Barton Drive, Mount Eliza, Vic 3930, Australia. *T:* 787 1129. *Clubs:* Alexandra (Melbourne); Peninsula Country Golf (Frankston).

BEAUREPAIRE, Ian Francis, CMG 1967; Director, Pacific Dunlop Ltd (formerly Dunlop Olympic Ltd), 1980–92; Chairman, Olex Ltd, 1973–92; *b* 14 Sept. 1922; *s* of late Sir Frank and Lady Beaurepaire; *m* 1946, Beryl Edith Bedggood (*see* Dame Beryl Beaurepaire); two *s*. *Educ:* Carey Grammar Sch., Scotch Coll., Melbourne; Royal Melbourne Inst. of Technology. Served RAAF (Flying Officer), 1942–45. Man. Dir, Beaurepaire Tyre Service Pty Ltd, 1953–55; Gen. Man., The Olympic Tyre & Rubber Co. Pty Ltd, 1955–61; Chm., 1959–78, Man. Dir, 1959–75, Chief Exec., 1975–78, Exec. Chm., 1978–80, Olympic Consolidated Industries Ltd. Mem., Melbourne Underground Rail Loop Authority, 1971–83, Chm., 1981–83. Member: Melbourne City Council, 1956–75 (Lord Mayor of Melbourne, 1965–67); Management Cttee of Royal Victorian Eye and Ear Hosp., 1966–88 (Pres., 1982–88). *Recreations:* golf, grazing. *Address:* 18 Barton Drive, Mount Eliza, Victoria 3930, Australia. *Clubs:* Athenæum, Naval and Military, Melbourne (Melbourne); Peninsula Country Golf (Frankston).

BEAVEN, John Lewis, CMG 1986; CVO 1983 (MVO 1974); HM Diplomatic Service, retired; Ambassador to Sudan, 1986–90; *b* 30 July 1930; *s* of Charles and Margaret Beaven; *m* 1960, Jane Beeson (marr. diss.); one *s* one *d*; *m* 1975, Jean McComb Campbell. *Educ:* Newport (Gwent) High Sch. BoT, 1946; RAF, 1948–50; Asst Trade Comr, British High Commn, Karachi, 1956–60; Second Secretary (Commercial), British High Commn, Freetown, 1961–64; First Secretary (Commercial): British High Commn, Nicosia, 1964–66; Nairobi, 1966–68; FCO, 1969–72; Head of Chancery, British Embassy, Jakarta, 1972–74; Counsellor (Economic and Commercial), British High Commn, Lagos, 1975–77; Dep. Consul General and Dir, British Trade Develt Office, NY, 1978–82; Consul-General, San Francisco, 1982–86. US Rep., SCF, 1990–. *Recreations:* music, needlepoint, walking, computing. *Address:* Scannell Road, Ghent, NY 12075–0157, USA. *T:* (518) 3922152, *Fax:* (518) 3929418. *Club:* Brook (New York).

BEAVERBROOK, 3rd Baron *cr* 1917, of Beaverbrook, New Brunswick, and of Cherkley, Surrey; **Maxwell William Humphrey Aitken;** Bt 1916; Chairman, Beaverbrook Foundation, 1985–92; Treasurer, European Democratic Union, 1990–92; *b* 29 Dec. 1951; *s* of Sir (John William) Max Aitken, 2nd Bt, DSO, DFC, and of Violet, *d* of Sir Humphrey de Trafford, 4th Bt, MC; *S* to disclaimed barony of father, 1985; *m* 1974, Susan Angela More O'Ferrall; two *s* two *d*. *Educ:* Charterhouse; Pembroke Coll., Cambridge. Beaverbrook Newspapers Ltd, 1973–77; Trustee, Beaverbrook Foundation, 1974–92; Dir, Ventech, 1983–86; Chm., Ventech Healthcare Corp. Inc., 1986, 1988–92. Govt spokesman for Home Office and DTI, H of L, 1986; a Lord in Waiting (Government Whip), 1986–88; Dep. Treas., 1988–90, Treas., 1990–92, Cons. Party. Chm., Nat. Assoc. of Boys' Clubs, 1989–92. Mem. Council, Homeopathic Trust, 1986–92. *Recreations:*

sailing, motor cars. *Heir:* s Hon. Maxwell Francis Aitken, *b* 17 March 1977. *Address:* c/o House of Lords, SW1A 0PW. *Clubs:* White's; Royal Yacht Squadron.

BEAVIS, Air Chief Marshal Sir Michael (Gordon), KCB 1981; CBE 1977 (OBE 1969); AFC 1962; Director, Black & Edgington (formerly Tubular Edgington) Group, since 1989 (Deputy Chairman, 1989–91 and since 1993); *b* 13 Aug. 1929; *s* of Walter Erle Beavis and Mary Ann (*née* Sarjantson); *m* 1950, Joy Marion (*née* Jones); one *s* one *d*. *Educ:* Kilburn Grammar School. Joined RAF 1947; commnd 1949; served Fighter Comd Squadrons 1950–54, RNZAF 1954–56; flew Vulcan aircraft, Bomber Comd, 1958–62; Staff Coll., 1963; MoD, 1964–66; OC No 10 Squadron (VC10s), 1966–68; Group Captain Flying, Akrotiri, Cyprus, 1968–71; Asst Dir, Defence Policy, MoD, 1971–73; RCDS, 1974; RAF Germany, 1975–77 (SASO 1976–77); Dir Gen. RAF Training, 1977–80; Comdt, RAF Staff Coll, 1980–81; AOC-in-C, RAF Support Comd, 1981–84; Dep. Comdr, AFCENT, 1984–86. CIMgt. Freeman, City of London, 1980; Liveryman, GAPAN, 1983. *Recreations:* golf, ski-ing, travel. *Address:* c/o Lloyds Bank, 202 High Street, Lincoln. *Club:* Royal Air Force.

BEAZER, Brian Cyril; Chairman and Chief Executive, Beazer (formerly C. H. Beazer (Holdings)) PLC, 1983–91; *b* 22 Feb. 1935; *s* of late Cyril Henry George Beazer and of Ada Vera Beazer; *m* 1958, Patricia (*née* White); one *d*. *Educ:* Wells Cathedral School. Joined C.H. Beazer, 1958; Man. Dir, 1968; apptd Chm. and Chief Exec. on death of his father in 1983. *Recreations:* walking, reading. *Address:* The Weavers House, Castle Combe, Wiltshire SN14 7HX.

BEAZLEY, Christopher John Pridham; *b* 5 Sept. 1952; *s* of Peter George Beazley, *qv*. *Educ:* Shrewsbury; Bristol Univ. Formerly Nuffield Research Fellow, School of European Studies, Sussex Univ. Vice Chm., Lewes and Eastbourne branch, European Movement, 1980; Wealden DC, 1979–83. MEP (C) Cornwall and Plymouth, 1984–94; contested (C) Cornwall and W Plymouth, Eur. Parly elecns, 1994. *Address:* The Grange, Devoran, near Truro, Cornwall TR3 6PF. *Club:* Oriental.

BEAZLEY, Hon. Kim Christian; MP (ALP) Swan, Perth, Australia, since 1980; Leader of the House of Representatives, Australia, since 1988 (Vice-President, Executive Council, 1988–91); Minister for Finance, since 1993; *b* 14 Dec. 1948; *s* of Hon. Kim Edward Beazley and Betty Beazley; *m* 1st, 1974, Mary Paltridge (marr. diss. 1989); two *d*; 2nd, 1990, Susanna Annus; one *d*. *Educ:* Univ. of Western Australia (MA); Oxford Univ. (Rhodes Scholar; MPhil). Tutor in Social and Political Theory, Murdoch Univ., WA, 1976–79, Lectr 1980. Minister of State for Aviation, and Minister Assisting the Minister for Defence, 1983–84; Special Minister of State, 1983–84; Minister of State for Defence, 1984–90; Minister for Transport and Communications, 1990–91, for Finance, 1991, for Employment, Educn and Training, 1991–93. Mem. Nat. Exec., ALP, 1991–94. *Publication:* (with I. Clark) The Politics of Intrusion: the Super-Powers in the Indian Ocean, 1979. *Recreations:* swimming, reading. *Address:* Parliament House, Canberra, ACT 2600, Australia. *T:* (6) 2733955.

BEAZLEY, Peter George, CBE 1993; *b* 9 June 1922; *s* of Thomas Alfred and Agnes Alice Mary Beazley; *m* 1945, Joyce Marion Sulman; one *s* two *d*. *Educ:* Highgate Sch.; St John Baptist Coll., Oxford. Final Hons PPE, MA Oxon. Captain, Rifle Brigade, served in N Africa, Italy, Austria, 1942–47. Joined ICI, 1947; served in UK, Portugal, Germany, Belgium and S Africa as Manager, Gen. Manager, Divl Bd Dir, Vice Chm. and Man. Dir of associated cos, 1948–77; retd from ICI 1978. MEP (C) Bedfordshire, 1979–84, Bedfordshire South, 1984–94. Member: European Democratic Gp Bureau, 1982–83; Economic and Monetary Affairs and Industrial Policy Cttee, European Parlt, 1984–94 (Vice Chm., 1984–89); European Parlt Portuguese Parlt Jt delegn, 1979–84; European Parlt Japanese delegn, 1985–89; Vice Chm., SE Asia delegn, 1989–94. MRI; Mem., RIIA (Res. Fellow, 1977–78). *Publication:* The Role of Western Technology Transfer in the Development of the Soviet Union's Chemical Industry (with V. Sobeslavsky), 1979. *Recreations:* golf, gardening. *Address:* Rest Harrow, 14 The Combe, Ratton, Eastbourne, East Sussex BN20 9DB; 4 Bridgewater Court, Little Gaddesden, Herts. *Club:* Oriental.

See also C. J. P. Beazley.

BECHER, Major Sir William Fane Wrixon-, 5th Bt, *cr* 1831; MC 1943; Temp. Major, Rifle Brigade (SRO); *b* 7 Sept. 1915; *o s* of Sir Eustace W. W. W. Becher, 4th Bt, and Hon. Constance Gough-Calthorpe, *d* of 6th Baron Calthorpe; *S* father, 1934; *m* 1st, 1946, Vanda (marr. diss. 1960; she *m* 1962, Rear-Adm. Viscount Kelburn, later 9th Earl of Glasgow; she *d* 1984), *d* of 4th Baron Vivian; one *s* one *d*; 2nd, 1960, Hon. Mrs Yvonne Mostyn. *Educ:* Harrow; Magdalene Coll., Cambridge (BA). Served War of 1939–45; Western Desert and Tunisian Campaigns, 1940–43 (MC, wounded twice); Liaison Officer to Comdr, 13th Corps, Lt-Gen. W. H. Gott, 1941 (taken prisoner at battle of Sidi Rezegh, Nov. 1941, and escaped); Italian Campaign, 1944; ADC to FM Lord Wilson, Supreme Allied Comdr Mediterranean. Lloyd's Underwriter, 1950. Member: British Boxing Bd of Control, 1961–82; Nat. Playing Fields Assoc., 1953–65 (Pres., Wiltshire Branch, NPFA, 1950–56). *Recreations:* golf, cricket (played cricket for Sussex, 1939, captained Wiltshire, 1949–53), reading (biographies and autobiographies of famous men and women). *Heir:* *s* John William Michael Wrixon-Becher, *b* 29 Sept. 1950. *Address:* 37 Clabon Mews, SW1X 0EQ. *T:* 0171–589 7780; 13 Montpelier Crescent, Brighton BN1 3JF. *T:* Brighton (01273) 321728. *Clubs:* MCC, Royal Green Jackets; I Zingari (Sec., 1952–93).

BECHTEL, Stephen Davidson, Jr; Chairman Emeritus: Bechtel Group, Inc., since 1990; Fremont Group, since 1995; Sequoia Ventures, Inc., since 1995; *b* 1925; *s* of Stephen Davidson Bechtel and Laura Peart. Joined Bechtel Group, Inc. (Engineers and Constructors), 1941; Pres., 1960; Chm., 1965–90. Mem., Bd of Trustees, CIT, 1967–. Chairman: Business Council, 1987–88; Nat. Acad. of Engrg, 1982–86. Mem., Inst. for Internat. Studies, Stanford Univ. (Vice Chm. and Mem., Bd of Visitors, 1991–). Numerous awards including: Herbert Hoover Medal, 1981; Chairman's Award, Amer. Acad. of Engrg Socs, 1982; President's Award, ASCE, 1985; Nat. Medal of Technology, 1991. Officer, Legion of Honour (France), 1979. *Address:* c/o Bechtel Group, Inc., PO Box 193965, San Francisco, CA 94119–3965, USA.

BECK, Prof. Arnold Hugh William, BSc (Eng), MA; Professor of Engineering, 1966–83, Head of Electrical Division, 1971–81, University of Cambridge, now Emeritus Professor; Life Fellow of Corpus Christi College, Cambridge, since 1983 (Fellow, 1962); Fellow of University College, London, since 1979; *y s* of Major Hugh Beck and Diana L. Beck; *m* 1947, Katharine Monica, *y d* of S. K. Ratcliffe; no *c*. *Educ:* Gresham's Sch., Holt; University Coll., London. Research Engr, Henry Hughes & Sons, 1937–41; seconded to Admty Signal Estab., 1941–45; Standard Telephones & Cables, 1947–58; Lectr, Cambridge Univ., 1958–64; Reader in Electrical Engrg, 1964–66. FIEEE 1959. *Publications:* Velocity Modulated Thermionic Tubes, 1948; Thermionic Valves, 1953; Space-charge Waves, 1958; Words and Waves, 1967; (with H. Ahmed) Introduction to Physical Electronics, 1968; Handbook of Vacuum Physics, Vol. 2, Parts 5 and 6, 1968; Statistical Mechanics, Fluctuations and Noise, 1976; papers in Jl IEE, Inst. Radio Engrs, etc. *Address:* 18 Earl Street, Cambridge. *T:* Cambridge (01223) 62997.

BECK, Rev. Brian Edgar, MA; President of the Methodist Conference, 1993–94; Secretary of the Conference, since 1984; *b* 27 Sept. 1933; *o s* of late A. G. and C. A. Beck; *m* 1958, Margaret Ludlow; three *d*. *Educ:* City of London School; Corpus Christi College, Cambridge (1st Cl. Classical Tripos pts 1 and 2); Wesley House, Cambridge (1st Cl. Theol. Tripos pt 2). BA 1955, MA 1959. Ordained Methodist Minister, 1960; Asst Tutor, Handsworth Coll., 1957–59; E Suffolk Circuit Minister, 1959–62; St Paul's United Theological Coll., Limuru, Kenya, 1962–68; Tutor, Wesley House, Cambridge, 1968–80, Principal 1980–84. Sec., E African Church Union Consultation Worship and Liturgy Cttee, 1963–68; Mem., World Methodist Council, 1966–71, 1981–; Co-Chm., Oxford Inst. of Methodist Theol. Studies, 1976–. Hon. Chaplain, Guild of St Bride, Fleet Street, 1994–. Fernley-Hartley Lectr, 1978. *Publications:* (contrib.) Christian Belief, a Catholic-Methodist statement, 1970; (contrib.) Unity the Next Step? (ed P. Morgan), 1972; Reading the New Testament Today, 1977; (contrib.) Suffering and Martyrdom in the New Testament (ed Horbury and McNeile), 1981; Christian Character in the Gospel of St Luke, 1989; articles in NT Studies, Epworth Review. *Recreations:* walking, DIY. *Address:* 25 Marylebone Road, NW1 5JR. *T:* 0171–486 5502, *Fax:* 0171–935 2104; 76 Beaumont Road, Purley, Croydon, Surrey CR8 2EG. *T* and *Fax:* 0181–645 9162.

BECK, Clive; Proprietor, Octavia Management Services, since 1992; Chairman, United Kingdom Detention Services Ltd, since 1993; *b* 12 April 1937; *s* of Sir Edgar Beck, *qv*, and Mary Agnes Beck; *m* 1960, Philippa Flood, three *s* three *d*. *Educ:* Ampleforth College. 2nd Lieut, The Life Guards, 1956–57; John Mowlem & Co., 1957–67; SGB Group, 1967–86; Dep. Chm., John Mowlem & Co., 1986–92. Director: Builders' Accident Insurance Ltd, 1990–; Pioneer Concrete Holdings plc. *Recreations:* golf, shooting, fishing. *Address:* (office) 30 Nero Court, Brentford Dock, Middx TW8 8QA. *T:* 0181–560 3066. *Clubs:* Buck's; Royal Wimbledon Golf, Swinley Forest Golf.

See also Sir E. P. Beck.

BECK, Sir Edgar (Charles), Kt 1975; CBE 1967; MA; FEng 1977; Chairman, John Mowlem & Company Ltd, 1961–79, President, since 1981; *b* 11 May 1911; *s* of Edgar Bee Beck and Nellie Stollard Beck (*née* Osborne); *m* 1933, Mary Agnes Sorapure (marr. diss. 1972); three *s* two *d*; *m* 1972, Anne Teresa Corbould. *Educ:* Lancing Coll.; Jesus Coll., Cambridge (MA). Joined John Mowlem & Co. Ltd as Engineer, 1933: Dir 1940; Man. Dir 1958. Director: Scaffolding Great Britain Ltd, 1942–85 (Chm., 1958–78); Builders' Accident Insce Ltd, 1959, Dep. Chm., 1969; Mem., ECGD Adv. Council, 1964–69; President, Fedn of Civil Engrg Contractors, 1971–75 (Chm., 1958–59); Chairman: Export Gp for the Constructional Industries, 1959–63; Brit. Hosps Export Council, 1964–75. Under-writing Mem. of Lloyd's, 1955–. FICE. *Recreations:* golf, salmon fishing. *Address:* Mill Cottage, Wilsford-cum-Lake, near Salisbury, Wilts SP4 7BP. *Clubs:* Buck's; Swinley Forest Golf.

See also C. Beck, Sir E. P. Beck.

BECK, Sir (Edgar) Philip, Kt 1988; Chairman, John Mowlem & Co., 1979–95; *b* 9 Aug. 1934; *s* of Sir Edgar Charles Beck, *qv*; *m* 1st, 1957, Thomasina Joanna Jeal (marr. diss.); two *s*; 2nd, 1991, Bridget Cockerell (*née* Heathcoat-Amory). *Educ:* Ampleforth College; Jesus College, Cambridge (MA). Dir, John Mowlem, 1964, Dep. Chm., 1978–79. Chairman: FCEC, 1982–83; Export Group for Constructional Industries, 1986–88. *Address:* 30 Nero Court, Brentford Dock, Middx TW8 8QA. *Club:* Royal Yacht Squadron.

See also C. Beck.

BECK, (James Henry) John; Director of Industries and Farms, Prison Department, Home Office, 1976–80; *b* 5 April 1920; *s* of James Henry and Elizabeth Kate Beck; *m* 1942, Doris Peacock (*d* 1995); one *d* (and one *d* decd). *Educ:* Polytechnic Secondary Sch., Regent Street, W1. Entered Home Office as Clerical Officer, 1937; HM Forces, 1939; returned to Home Office as Executive Officer, 1946; Higher Exec. Officer, 1950; Sen. Exec. Officer, 1958; Principal, 1963; Asst Sec., 1968. *Address:* Scarlet Oaks, Ridgway, Pyrford, Woking, Surrey GU22 8PN. *T:* Byfleet (01932) 346064.

BECK, Prof. (John) Swanson, FRSE 1984; Foundation Dean, International Medical College, Kuala Lumpur, since 1993; Professor of Pathology, University of Dundee, 1971–93, now Professor Emeritus; *b* 22 Aug. 1928; *s* of late Dr John Beck and Mary (*née* Barbour); *m* 1960, Marion Tudhope Paterson; one *s* one *d*. *Educ:* Glasgow Acad.; Univ. of Glasgow. BSc, MB, ChB, MD, FRCPG, FRCPE, FRCPath, FIBiol, CBiol. Lectr in Pathology, Univ. of Glasgow, 1958–63; Sen. Lectr in Pathology, Univ. of Aberdeen, 1963–71. Consultant Pathologist: N Eastern Regional Hosp. Bd, 1963–71; Eastern Regional Hosp. Bd, 1971–74; Tayside Health Bd, 1974–93. Chairman: Breast Tumour Panel, MRC, 1979–90; Biomedical Res. Cttee, SHHD, 1983–93 (Mem. 1975–79). Member: Cell Biology and Disorders Bd, MRC, 1978–82; Health Services Res. Panel, MRC, 1981–82; Chief Scientist's Cttee, SHHD, 1983–93; Tayside Health Bd, 1983–91; Nat. Biol Standards Bd, 1988–93 (Chm., Scientific Policy Adv. Cttee, 1991–93); Med. Adv. Bd, LEPRA, 1988–. Mem. Council, RSE, 1987–90 (Convenor, Grants Cttee, 1991–94). *Publications:* various papers in Jl of Pathology and other medical and scientific jls. *Recreations:* walking, gardening. *Address:* 598 Perth Road, Dundee DD2 1QA. *T:* Dundee (01382) 562298. *Club:* Commonwealth Trust.

BECK, Sir Philip; see Beck, Sir E. P.

BECK, (Richard) Theodore, FRIBA, FSA, FRSA, MRTPI; architect; *b* 11 March 1905; *s* of Alfred Charles Beck and Grace Sophia Beck (*née* Reading); *m* 1950, Margaret Beryl Page; one *s* one *d*. *Educ:* Haileybury; Architectural Association Sch. Past Mem. Council, Royal Archaeological Inst.; Past Master: Broderers Company; Barber-Surgeons Company; Parish Clerks Co.; Mem. Court of Common Council, Corporation of London, 1963–82; Dep., Ward of Farringdon Within, 1978–82; Sheriff, City of London, 1969–70; former Dep. Chm., Central Criminal Court Extension Cttee. Chm., Governors, City of London Sch., 1971–75, Dep. Chm., 1976 (Hon. Mem., John Carpenter Club); Chm., Schools Cttee, Corporation of London, 1977, Dep. Chm., 1978. Former Governor: Bridewell Royal Hosp.; King Edward's Sch., Witley; Christ's Hospital (Aldermanic Almoner); Reeves Foundn. Vicary Lectr, 1969; Prestonian Lectr, 1975. *Publication:* The Cutting Edge: early history of the surgeons of London, 1975. *Recreations:* gardening, archaeology. *Address:* Blundens House, Upper Froyle, Alton, Hants GU34 4LB. *T:* Bentley (01420) 23147. *Clubs:* Guildhall, City Livery.

BECK, Swanson; *see* Beck, J. S.

BECKE, Mrs Shirley Cameron, OBE 1974; QPM 1972; Vice-Chairman, 1976–83 and Regional Administrator, London Region, 1974–79, Women's Royal Voluntary Service, retired; *b* 29 April 1917; *er d* of late George L. Jennings, AMIGasE and Marion Jennings; *m* 1954, Rev. Justice Becke, MBE, TD, FCA (*d* 1990); no *c*. *Educ:* privately; Ealing Co. Gram. Sch. Trained in Gas Engineering, 1935–40. Joined Metropolitan Police as Constable, 1941; served in various ranks; Woman Commander, 1969–74. OStJ 1975. *Recreations:* reading, bridge. *Address:* 4 North Close, St Martin's Square, Chichester PO19 1NU. *T:* Chichester (01243) 784295.

BECKE, Lt-Col William Hugh Adamson, CMG 1964; DSO 1945; *b* 24 Sept. 1916; *er s* of late Brig.-Gen. J. H. W. Becke, CMG, DSO, AFC, and late Mrs A. P. Becke (*née* Adamson); *m* 1945, Mary Catherine, 3rd *d* of late Major G. M. Richmond, Kincairney, Murthly, Perthshire. *Educ:* Charterhouse; RMC Sandhurst. Commissioned in The Sherwood Foresters, 1937. British Military Mission to Greece, 1949–52; Asst Military Adviser to the High Commissioner for the UK in Pakistan, 1957–59; Military Attaché, Djakarta, 1962–64; retd 1966. Private Sec. and Comptroller to Governor of Victoria, 1969–74; Personnel Officer, Gas and Fuel Corp. of Vic, 1974–82. *Address:* 3 Chambers Street, South Yarra, Vic 3141, Australia. *Clubs:* Army and Navy; Melbourne, Victoria Racing (Melbourne).

BECKER, Prof. Gary Stanley, PhD; University Professor, Departments of Economics and Sociology, University of Chicago, since 1983; *b* 2 Dec. 1930; *s* of Louis William Becker and Anna (*née* Siskind); *m* 1st, 1954, Doria Slote (decd); two *d*; 2nd, 1979, Guity Nashat; two *s*. *Educ:* Princeton Univ. (AB *summa cum laude* 1951); Univ. of Chicago (AM 1953; PhD 1955). Asst Prof., Univ. of Chicago, 1954–57; Columbia University: Asst and Associate Prof of Econs, 1957–60; Prof. of Econs, 1960–68; Arthur Lehman Prof. of Econs, 1968–69; University of Chicago: Ford Foundn Vis. Prof. of Econs, 1969–70; Prof., 1970–83, Chm., 1984–85, Dept of Econs. Member: Domestic Adv. Bd, Hoover Instn, 1973–91 (Sen. Fellow, 1990–); Acad. Adv. Bd, Amer. Enterprise Inst. for Public Policy Res., 1987–91; Associate Mem., Inst. Fiscal and Monetary Policy, Min. of Finance, Japan, 1988–; Res. Associate, Econs Res. Center, Nat. Opinion Res. Center, 1980–. Columnist, Business Week, 1985–. Member: American Economic Association: Vice-Pres., 1974; Pres., 1987; Distinguished Fellow, 1988; Mont Pelerin Society, 1971–: Exec. Bd, 1985–; Vice-Pres., 1989–90; Pres., 1990–92; Editl Bd, Amer. Econ. Rev., 1968–71; Amer. Statistical Assoc. (Fellow 1965); Econometric Soc. (Fellow 1965). Member: Nat. Acad. Scis, 1975–; Internat. Union for Scientific Study of Population, 1982–; Amer. Philosophical Soc., 1986–; Founding Mem., Nat. Acad. Educn (Vice-Pres., 1965–67). Fellow: Amer. Acad. Arts and Scis, 1972; Nat. Assoc. of Business Economists, 1993. Hon. degrees: PhD: Hebrew Univ., Jerusalem, 1985; Palermo, 1993; LLD Knox Coll., Ill, 1985; Dr of Arts, Illinois, 1988; DSc SUNY, 1990; DHL: Princeton, 1991; Columbia, 1993. John Bates Clark Medal, Amer. Econ. Assoc., 1967; Frank E. Seidman Dist. Award in Pol Econ., 1985; Merit Award, NIH, 1986; John R. Commons Award, Omicron Delta Epsilon, 1987; Nobel Prize for Economics, 1992. *Publications:* The Economics of Discrimination, 1957, 2nd edn 1971; Human Capital, 1964, 3rd edn 1994 (trans. Japanese 1975, Spanish 1984); Human capital and the Personal Distribution of Income: an analytical approach, 1967; Economic Theory, 1971 (trans. Japanese, 1976); (ed jtly) Essays in the Economics of Crime and Punishment, 1974; (with G. Ghez) The Allocation of Time and Goods Over the Life Cycle, 1975; The Economic Approach to Human Behaviour, 1976 (trans. German 1982, Polish 1990); A Treatise on the Family, 1981, expanded edn 1991 (trans. Spanish 1987, Chinese 1988); contrib. chaps in numerous books and articles in jls incl. Jl Pol Econ., Qly Jl Econs, Amer. Econ. Rev., Jl Law and Econs, Jl Labor Econs, Business Econs, etc. *Address:* Department of Economics, University of Chicago, 1126 East 59th Street, Chicago, IL 60637, USA. *T:* (312) 7028168; 1308 East 58th Street, Chicago, IL 60637, USA.

BECKERLEG, John; Director of Finance, Buckinghamshire County Council, since 1993; *b* 12 Aug. 1956; *s* of Lewis Beckerleg and Doris (*née* Bundy); *m* 1983, April Cornelia Saunders; one *s* one *d*. *Educ:* Emmanuel Coll., Cambridge (MA 1981). CIPFA 1981. Chief Accountant, Cambs CC, 1985–87; Sen. Asst Co. Treas., Herts CC, 1987–91; Dep. Co. Treas., Bucks CC, 1991–93. *Recreations:* theatre, genealogy. *Address:* Jigglers Cross, 57 High Street, Meppershall, Beds SG17 5LX. *T:* Letchworth (01462) 816547.

BECKERMAN, Wilfred, PhD, DPhil; Fellow of Balliol College, Oxford, 1975–92; Reader in Economics, Oxford University, 1978–92; *b* 19 May 1925; *s* of Morris and Mathilda Beckerman; *m* 1st, 1952, Nicole Geneviève Ritter (*d* 1979); one *s* two *d*; 2nd, 1991, Joanna Pasek. *Educ:* Ealing County Sch.; Trinity Coll., Cambridge (MA, PhD); MA, DPhil Oxon. RNVR, 1943–46. Trinity Coll., Cambridge, 1946–50; Lecturer in Economics, Univ. of Nottingham, 1950–52; OEEC and OECD, Paris, 1952–61; National Inst. of Economic and Social Research, 1962–63. Fellow of Balliol Coll., Oxford, 1964–69; Prof. of Political Economy, Univ. of London, and Head of Dept of Political Economy, UCL, 1969–75; The Economic Adviser to the Pres. of the Board of Trade (leave of absence from Balliol), 1967–69. Mem., Royal Commn on Environmental Pollution, 1970–73. Member: Exec. Cttee, NIESR, 1973–; Council, Royal Economic Soc., 1990–93. Elie Halévy Vis. Prof. Institut d'Etudes Politiques, Paris, 1977; Resident Scholar, Woodrow Wilson Internat. Center for Scholars, Washington, DC, 1982. Consultant: World Bank; OECD; ILO. Pres., Section F (Economics), BAAS, 1978. *Publications:* The British Economy in 1975 (with associates), 1965; International Comparisons of Real Incomes, 1966; An Introduction to National Income Analysis, 1968; (ed and contrib.) The Labour Government's Economic Record, 1972; In Defence of Economic Growth, 1974; Measures of Leisure, Equality and Welfare, 1978; (ed and contrib.) Slow Growth in Britain: Causes and Consequences, 1979; Poverty and the Impact of Income Maintenance Programmes, 1979; (with S. Clark) Poverty and the Impact of Social Security in Britain since 1961, 1982; (ed and contrib.) Wage Rigidity and Unemployment, 1986; Small is Stupid, 1995; Growth, the Environment and the Distribution of Incomes, 1995; articles in Economic Jl, Economica, Econometrica, Review of Economic Studies, Review of Economics and Statistics, etc. *Recreations:* various. *Address:* 1c Norham Gardens, Oxford OX2 6PS.

BECKETT, family name of **Baron Grimthorpe.**

BECKETT, Prof. Arnold Heyworth, OBE 1983; Professor of Pharmacy, Chelsea College (University of London), 1959–85, now Emeritus; *b* 12 Feb. 1920; *m* 1st, 1942, Miriam Eunice Webster; one *s* one *d*; 2nd, Susan Yvonne Harris. *Educ:* Baines Grammar Sch., Poulton-le-Fylde; Sch. of Pharmacy and Birkbeck Coll., University of London. FRPharmS (FPS 1942); BSc 1947; PhD 1950; DSc London, 1959. Head, Dept of Pharmacy, Chelsea Coll. of Sci. and Technology, 1959–79. Chm., Med. Commn, Internat. Tennis Fedn, 1985–; Mem., Med. Commn, Internat. Olympic Cttee, 1968–; Mem., British Olympic Assoc. Med. Commn, until 1986; Chm., Bd of Pharmaceutical Sciences, Fédération Internat. Pharmaceutique, 1960–80; Mem. Council, Pharmaceutical, later Royal Pharmaceutical, Soc. of GB, 1965– (Pres., 1981–82). Vis. Prof. to Univs, USA and Canada. Examr in Pharmaceut. Chem., Univs in UK, Nigeria, Ghana, Singapore. Pereira Medal, 1942; STAS Medal, Belg. Chem. Soc., 1962; Hanbury Meml Medal, 1974; Charter Gold Medal, 1977; Mem. of Olympic Order, Silver Medal, 1980. Hon. DSc: Heriot-Watt, 1976; Uppsala, 1977; Leuven, 1982. *Publications:* (co-author) Practical Pharmaceutical Chemistry, 1962; Part 1, 3rd edn, 1975, Part 2, 3rd edn, 1976; founder Co-editor, Jl of Medicinal Chemistry; research contribs to jls. *Recreations:* travel, sport, photography. *Address:* 20 Braybrooke Gardens, Upper Norwood, SE19 2UN.

BECKETT, Bruce Probart, FRIBA, FRIAS, FRTPI, FCIOB; Chartered Architect, Town and Country Planner and Building Consultant in private practice, since 1984; *b* 7 June 1924; *s* of J. D. L. Beckett and Florence Theresa (*née* Probart); *m* 1957, Jean McDonald; two *s* three *d* (incl. twin *s* and *d*). *Educ:* Rondebosch Boys' High Sch., Cape Town; Univ. of Cape Town (BArch with distinction, 1950); University Coll. London (Diploma in Town Planning, 1963). Active Service SA Navy, 1943; Midshipman, 1943; Sub-Lieut, 1944; seconded RN, 1944; Lieut, 1946. ARIBA 1950, FRIBA 1968; FRIAS 1968. Mem. Inst. S African Architects, 1950; FRTPI (AMTPI 1966); FCIOB 1979. Private practice in S Africa, 1952–59, London, 1960. Sen. Architect, War Office, 1961; Superintending Grade Arch., Directorate-Gen. of Res. and Development, 1963–67; Chief Architect, 1967–84 and Dir of Bldg, 1978–84, Scottish Office, retd. Partner, Hutchison Locke & Monk, 1984–87. Dep. Leader, Timber Trade Mission to Canada, 1964. A Vice-Pres., RIBA, 1972–73, 1975–76, 1976–77; Hon. Librarian, 1976–78. Sec. of State for Scotland's nominee on ARCUK, 1970–85, RIBA nominee, 1985–92; Member Council: EAA, 1970–78; RIAS, 1971–78, 1984–87; RIBA, 1972–78; Member: Sec. of State for Environment's Construction and Housing Res. Adv. Council, 1968–79; Building Res. Estabt Adv. Cttees in England and Scotland, 1970–84; York Adv. Cttee for continuing educn for building professions, 1975–80. Assessor, to Scottish Cttee of Design Council, 1974–84; Civic Trust Adjudicator, 1985–87. *Publications:* papers on industrialised building, contract procedure, etc, in various jls; HMSO publications on Scottish housing, educational and health buildings. *Recreations:* sailing, walking. *Address:* Summerfield, Vines Cross Road, Horam, near Heathfield, East Sussex TN21 0HE. *T:* Horam Road (01435) 812042; 4/4 Liddesdale Place, Glenogle Road, Edinburgh EH3 5WJ. *T:* 0131–556 2867. *Clubs:* Arts; New (Edinburgh); Kelvin (Kelvin Grove, Cape Town).

BECKETT, Maj.-Gen. Denis Arthur, CB 1971; DSO 1944; OBE 1960; *b* 19 May 1917; *o s* of late Archibald Beckett, Woodford Green, Essex; *m* 1946, Elizabeth (marr. diss. 1974), *er d* of late Col Guy Edwards, Upper Slaughter, Glos; one *s*; *m* 1978, Nancy Ann Hitt. *Educ:* Forest Sch.; Chard Sch. Joined Hon. Artillery Co., 1939; commnd into Essex Regt, 1940; served in W Africa, Middle East, Italy and Greece, 1940–45; DAA & QMG and Bde Major, Parachute Bdes, 1948–50; Instructor, RMA Sandhurst, 1951–53; Directing Staff, Staff Coll., Camberley, 1953–56; Second in Comd 3rd Bn Para. Regt, 1956–58; comd 2nd Bn Para. Regt, 1958–60; Directing Staff, JSSC, 1960–61; comd 19 Bde, 1961–63; idc 1964; DAG, BAOR, 1965–66; Chief of Staff, Far East Land Forces, 1966–68; Dir of Personal Services (Army), 1968–71, retired 1971. Trustee: Nehru Meml Centre Trust, 1975–; Airborne Forces Mus., 1985–94; Governor, Forest Sch., 1986–95. Liveryman, Coopers' Co., 1962–. *Address:* 12 Wellington House, Eton Road, NW3 4SY. *Clubs:* Army and Navy, Lansdowne.

BECKETT, Maj.-Gen. Edwin Horace Alexander, CB 1988; MBE 1974; Head of British Defence Staff, Washington, 1988–91, retired; *b* 16 May 1937; *s* of William Alexander Beckett and Doris Beckett; *m* 1963, Micaela Elizabeth Benedicta, *d* of Col Sir Edward Malet, Bt, OBE; three *s* one *d*. *Educ:* Henry Fanshawe School; RMA Sandhurst; ndc, psc, sq. Commissioned 1957 West Yorks Regt; regtl service in Aden (despatches 1968), Gibraltar, Germany and N Ireland; DAA&QMG 11 Armd Brigade, 1972–74; CO 1 PWO, 1976–78 (despatches 1977); GSO1 (DS) Staff Coll., 1979; Comdt Junior Div., Staff Coll., 1980; Comdr UKMF and 6 Field Force, 1981; Comdr UKMF, 1 Inf. Brigade and Tidworth Garrison, 1982; Director: Concepts, MoD, 1983–84; Army Plans and Programmes, MoD, 1984–85; C of S, HQ BAOR, 1985–88. Col Comdt, The King's Div., 1988–94. Dir, Corporate Affairs, IDV Ltd, 1991–. *Recreations:* fishing, picture framing, farming for fun. *Club:* Cavalry and Guards.

BECKETT, Prof. James Camlin, MA; Professor of Irish History, Queen's University of Belfast, 1958–75; *b* 8 Feb. 1912; 3rd *s* of Alfred Beckett and Frances Lucy Bushell. *Educ:* Royal Belfast Academical Instn; Queen's Univ., Belfast. History Master, Belfast Royal Academy, 1934; Lectr in Modern History, Queen's Univ., Belfast, 1945, Reader in Modern History, 1952. Fellow Commoner, Peterhouse, Cambridge, 1955–56; Cummings Lectr, McGill Univ., Montreal, 1976; Mellon Prof., Tulane Univ., New Orleans, 1977; Member: Irish Manuscripts Commn, 1959–86; Royal Commission on Historical Manuscripts, 1960–86. Hon. DLitt New Univ. of Ulster, 1979; NUI, 1990; Hon. DLit Queen's Univ. of Belfast, 1980. FRHistS; MRIA. *Publications:* Protestant Dissent in Ireland, 1687–1780, 1948; Short History of Ireland, 1952; (ed with T. W. Moody) Ulster since 1800: a Political and Economic Survey, 1954; (ed with T. W. Moody) Ulster since 1800: a Social Survey, 1957; (with T. W. Moody) Queen's Belfast, 1845–1949, 1959; The Making of Modern Ireland 1603–1923, 1966; (ed with R. E. Glasscock) Belfast: the Origin and Growth of an Industrial City, 1966; (ed) Historical Studies VII, 1969; Confrontations, 1973; The Anglo-Irish Tradition, 1976; The Cavalier Duke, 1990; contrib. The Ulster Debate, 1972; articles, reviews, etc., in English Hist. Rev., History, Irish Hist. Studies and other jls. *Recreations:* chess, walking. *Address:* 19 Wellington Park Terrace, Belfast, N Ireland BT9 6DR. *Club:* Ulster Reform (Belfast).

BECKETT, Rt. Hon. Margaret M., (Mrs L. A. Beckett); PC 1993; MP (Lab) Derby South, since 1983; Campaigns Co-ordinator and Deputy Leader of the Labour Party, 1992–94 (acting Leader, May–July 1994); *b* 15 Jan. 1943; *d* of late Cyril and Winifred Jackson; *m* 1979, Lionel A. Beckett; two step *s*. *Educ:* Notre Dame High Sch., Norwich; Manchester Coll. of Sci. and Technol. Formerly: engrg apprentice (metallurgy), AEI, Manchester; exptl officer, Manchester Univ.; Labour Party res. asst; political adviser, Minister for Overseas Develt, 1974; Principal Researcher, Granada TV, 1979–83. Contested (Lab) Lincoln, Feb. 1974; MP (Lab) Lincoln, Oct. 1974–1979; PPS to Minister for Overseas Develt, 1974–75; Asst Govt Whip, 1975–76; Parly Under-Sec. of State, DES, 1976–79; Opposition front bench spokesman on health and social security, 1984–89; Shadow Chief Sec. to the Treasury, 1989–92; Shadow Leader, H of C, 1992–94. Mem. NEC, Labour Party, 1980–81, 1985–86, 1988–. *Address:* c/o House of Commons, SW1A 0AA.

BECKETT, Sir Martyn Gervase, 2nd Bt, *cr* 1921; MC 1945; RIBA; Architect; *b* 6 Nov. 1918; *s* of Hon. Sir Gervase Beckett, 1st Bt, and Lady Marjorie Beckett (*d* 1964), *e d* of 5th Earl of Warwick; *S* father, 1937; *m* 1941, Hon. Priscilla Brett, *y d* of 3rd Viscount Esher, GBE; two *s* one *d*. *Educ:* Eton; Trinity Coll., Cambridge (BA). Enlisted in Green Howards, 1939; commnd Welsh Guards, 1940; served War of 1939–45 (MC); Lieut (temp. Captain). DipArch 1951, ARIBA 1952. Built or reconstructed several country houses and housing estates, hotels, libraries etc; works to various scheduled buildings and for National Trust. Architect to King's College Chapel, Cambridge, 1960– (internal alterations and renovations to the Chapel, 1968); Cons. Architect to: Gordonstoun, 1954–58; Savoy Hotel Gp, 1981–; Temple Bar Trust, 1983–; Charterhouse, 1983–; Ampleforth Coll., 1984; Eton Coll., 1986–; Rank Labs, 1987; BRCS, 1994. Exhibited: RA, London, provinces; one man exhibitions: Clarges Gall., 1980 and 1983; Soar Gall., 1986, 1988, 1990, 1992 and 1994. Trustee: The Wallace Collection, 1972–92 (Chm. 1976–92); British Museum, 1978–88; CPRE Trust, 1983–90; Chm., Yorkshire Regional Cttee, Nat. Trust, 1980–85; Member: N York Moor Nat. Park Cttee, 1972–78; Council of Management, Chatsworth House Trust, 1981–; President: Ryedale Br., CPRE, 1964–; Friends of York Art Gall., 1970–83. Mem. Council, RSPB, 1985–87. Trustee, D'Oyly Carte Charity Trust, 1988–. FRSA 1982; FAMS 1955. Freeman, City of London, 1986. *Recreations:* painting, photography, piano. *Heir:* *s* Richard Gervase Beckett, *qv*. *Address:* 3 St Albans Grove, W8 5PN. *T:* 0171–937 7834; Kirkdale Farm, Nawton, Yorks. *Clubs:* Brooks's, MCC.

BECKETT, Richard Gervase; QC 1988; barrister; *b* 27 March 1944; *s* and *heir* of Sir Martyn Beckett, Bt, *qv*; *m* 1976, Elizabeth Ann, *d* of Major Hugo Waterhouse; one *s* three *d*. *Educ:* Eton. Diploma in Economics (Oxford). Called to the Bar, Middle Temple, 1965; practice at the Bar, 1966–. *Recreation:* landscape. *Address:* 33 Groveway, SW9 0AH. *T:* 0171–735 3350. *Clubs:* Pratt's, Portland.

BECKETT, Sir Terence (Norman), KBE 1987 (CBE 1974); Kt 1978; DL; Adviser to Joint Committee of Milk Marketing Board and Dairy Trade Federation, 1987–94; *b* 13 Dec. 1923; *s* of late Horace Norman Beckett, MBE and late Clarice Lillian (*née* Allsop); *m* 1950, Sylvia Gladys Asprey; one *d*. *Educ:* Wolverhampton and S Staffs Tech. Coll.; London Sch. of Econs (Hon. Fellow, 1994). BScEcon, FIMechE, CIMgt, FIMI, FEng. Captain REME, British Army (UK, India, Malaya), 1945–48; RARO, 1949–62. Company Trainee, Ford Motor Co. Ltd, 1950; Asst in office of Dep. Chm. and Man. Dir, 1951; Man., Styling, Briggs Motor Bodies Ltd (Ford subsid.), 1954; Admin Man., Engrg, Briggs, 1955; Manager, Product Staff, 1955; Gen. Man., Product Planning Staff, 1961 (responsible for Cortina, Transit Van, 'D' series truck); Manager, Marketing Staff, 1963; Dir, Car Div., 1964; Exec. Dir, Ford Motor Co. Ltd, 1966 and Dir of Sales, 1968; Vice-Pres., European and Overseas Sales Ops, Ford of Europe Inc., 1969; Man. Dir and Chief Exec., 1974–80 and Chm., 1976–80, Ford Motor Co. Ltd; Chm., Ford Motor Credit Co. Ltd, 1976–80; Director: ICI, 1976–80; Automotive Finance Ltd, 1974–77. Dir Gen. CBI, 1980–87 (Mem. Council, 1976–80); Dep. Chm., CEGB, 1990 (Dir, 1987–90). Member: NEDC, 1980–87; Engineering Industries Council, 1975–80; BIM Council, 1976–77; Top Salaries Review Body, 1987–92; Grand Council, Motor and Cycle Trades Benevolent Fund (BEN), 1976–80; SMMT Council and Exec. Cttee, 1974–80; Council, Automobile Div., IMechE, 1979–80; Vice Pres. and Hon. Fellow, Inst. of the Motor Industry, 1974–80; Vice-Pres., Conference on Schs, Sci. and Technol., 1979–80; Chm., Governing Body, London Business Sch., 1979–86; Mem. Court, Cranfield Inst. of Technology, 1977–82; Pro-Chancellor and Chm. Council, Univ. of Essex, 1989– (Mem. Court, 1985–); Governor, Nat. Inst. of Econ. and Social Res., 1978–; Governor and Mem. Court, LSE, 1978–; Mem. Court of Assts, Worshipful Co. of Engineers, 1983–85. DL Essex, 1991. Pres., IVCA, 1987–91. Patron: MSC Award Scheme for Disabled People, 1979–80; AIESEC, 1985. Lectures: Stamp, London Univ., 1982; Pfizer, Kent at Canterbury Univ., 1983. Hon. Fellow: Sidney Sussex Coll., Cambridge, 1981; London Business Sch., 1988; Hon. DSc: Cranfield, 1977; Heriot-Watt, 1981; Hon. DSc (Econ.) London, 1982; Hon. DTech: Brunel, 1991; Wolverhampton, 1995; DU Essex, 1995. FRSA 1984. Hambro Businessman of the Year, 1978; BIM Gold Medal, 1980. *Recreations:* ornithology, music. *Address:* c/o Barclays Bank plc, 74 High Street, Ingatestone, Essex CM4 9BW. *Club:* Athenæum.

BECKETT, William Cartwright, CB 1978; LLM; Solicitor to the Corporation of Lloyd's, 1985–93; *b* 21 Sept. 1929; *s* of late William Beckett and Emily (*née* Cartwright); *m* 1st, 1956, Marjorie Jean Hoskin; two *s*; 2nd, 1974, Lesley Margaret Furlonger. *Educ:* Salford Grammar Sch.; Manchester Univ. (LLB 1950, LLM 1952). Called to Bar, Middle Temple, 1952. Joined Treasury Solicitor's Dept, 1956; Board of Trade, 1965; Asst Solicitor, DEP, 1969; Under-Sec., DTI, 1972; Dep.-Sec. 1977; Legal Secretary, Law Officers' Dept, 1975–80; Solicitor, DTI, 1980–84. *Recreations:* music, golf. *Address:* Park House, Bradwell, near Braintree, Essex CM7 8EP. *T:* Braintree (01376) 561109. *Club:* Reform.

BECKINGHAM, Prof. Charles Fraser, FBA 1983; Professor of Islamic Studies, University of London, 1965–81, now Emeritus; *b* 18 Feb. 1914; *o c* of Arthur Beckingham, ARBA and Alice Beckingham, Houghton, Hunts; *m* 1946, Margery (*d* 1966), *o d* of John Ansell; one *d*. *Educ:* Grammar Sch., Huntingdon; Queens' Coll., Cambridge (scholar, Members' English prizeman, 1934). Dept of Printed Books, British Museum, 1936–46. Seconded to military and naval Intelligence, 1942–46. Foreign Office (GCHQ), 1946–51; Lectr in Islamic History, Manchester Univ., 1951–55; Sen. Lectr, 1955–58; Prof. of Islamic Studies, 1958–65. Pres., Hakluyt Soc., 1969–72; Treas., Royal Asiatic Soc., 1964–67, Pres., 1967–70, 1976–79, Hon. Fellow, Sri Lanka Branch, 1978. Chm., St Marylebone Soc., 1980–84. Jt Editor, 1961–64, Editor, 1965, Jl of Semitic Studies; Editor, Jl of RAS, 1984–87; Internat. Dir, Fontes Historiae Africanae Project, Union Académique Internationale, 1986–95. Sir Percy Sykes Meml Medal, RSAA, 1987. *Publications:* contribs to Admiralty Handbook of Western Arabia, 1946; (with G. W. B. Huntingford) Some Records of Ethiopia, 1954; Introduction to Atlas of the Arab World and Middle East, 1960; (with G. W. B. Huntingford) A True Relation of the Prester John of the Indies, 1961; Bruce's Travels (ed and selected), 1964; The Achievements of Prester John, 1966; (ed) Islam, in, Religion in the Middle East (ed A. J. Arberry), 1969; (with E. Ullendorff) The Hebrew Letters of Prester John, 1982; Between Islam and Christendom, 1983; (ed) The Itinerário of Jerónimo Lobo, 1984; (with H. A. R. Gibb) The Travels of Ibn Battuta, vol. IV, 1994; articles in learned jls. *Address:* 3 Pipe Passage, Lewes, E Sussex BN7 1YG. *Clubs:* Travellers', Beefsteak.

BECKLAKE, (Ernest) John (Stephen), PhD; CEng; Senior Research Fellow, Science Museum, since 1994; *b* 24 June 1943; *s* of Ernest and Evelyn Becklake; *m* 1965, Susan Elizabeth (*née* Buckle), BSc; two *s*. *Educ:* Bideford Grammar Sch.; Exeter Univ. (BSc, PhD). CEng 1988; MIEE 1988. Engr, EMI Electronics, Wells, 1967–69; Post-Doctoral Fellow, Victoria Univ., BC, Canada, 1969–70; Sen. Scientist, Marconi Space and Def. Systems, Frimley, 1970–72; Science Museum: Asst Keeper, Dept of Earth and Space Sciences, 1972–80; Keeper, Dept of Elect. Engrg, Communications and Circulation, 1980–85; Keeper, Dept of Engrg, subseq. Head of Technology Gp, 1985–94. Mem., Internat. Acad. of Astronautics, 1988–. *Publications:* Man and the Moon, 1980; The Climate Crisis, 1989; The Population Explosion, 1990; Pollution, 1990; (ed) History of Rocketry and Astronautics, vol. XVI, 1995; (series editor) Exploration and Discovery, 1980–; technical pubns in Electronics Letters, Jl of Physics D, Jl of British Interplanetary Soc., and Spaceflight. *Recreations:* gardening, golf, rugby. *Address:* Tree Wood, Robin Hood Lane, Sutton Green, Guildford, Surrey GU7 4QY. *T:* Woking (01483) 766931. *Club:* Puttenham Golf.

BECKMAN, Michael David, QC 1976; *b* 6 April 1932; *s* of Nathan and Esther Beckman; *m* 1990, Jennifer (*née* Redmond); two *d* from former marriage. *Educ:* King's Coll., London (LLB (Hons)). Called to the Bar, Lincoln's Inn, 1954. *Recreations:* various. *Address:* Bullards, Widford, Herts SG12 8SG. *T:* Much Hadham (0127984) 2669; (chambers) 11 Stone Buildings, Lincoln's Inn, WC2A 3TG; 3 East Pallants, Chichester PO19 1TR.

BECKWITH, Prof. Athelstan Laurence Johnson, FRS 1988; FAA; FRACI; Professor of Organic Chemistry, Research School of Chemistry, Australian National University, since 1981 (Dean, 1989–91); *b* 20 Feb. 1930; *s* of Laurence Alfred Beckwith and Doris Grace Beckwith; *m* 1953, Phyllis Kaye Marshall, Perth, WA; one *s* two *d*. *Educ:* Perth Modern Sch.; Univ. of WA (BSc Hons); Oxford Univ. (DPhil 1956). FAA 1973; FRACI 1973. Lectr in Chemistry, Adelaide Univ., 1953; CSIRO Overseas Student, 1954; Res. Officer, CSIRO Melbourne, 1957; Adelaide University: Lectr in Organic Chemistry, 1958; Prof., 1965–81; Dean of Science, 1972–73. Temp. Lectr, Imperial Coll., London, 1962–63; Vis. Lectr, Univ. of York, 1968; Carnegie Fellow, 1968. Federal Pres., RACI, 1965 (Rennie Medal, 1960; H. G. Smith Meml Medal, 1981; Organic Chemistry Medal, 1992); Vice-Pres., Aust. Acad. of Sci., 1985–86. *Publications:* numerous articles in Jl of Chem. Soc., Jl of Amer. Chem. Soc., etc. *Recreations:* golf, music, walking. *Address:* 2/14 Currie Crescent, Kingston, ACT 2604, Australia. *T:* (6) 2494012; (6) 2953694.

BECKWITH, John Lionel, FCA; Chairman, Pacific Investments; Founder Chairman, London & Edinburgh Trust PLC, 1971–92; *b* 19 March 1947; *s* of Col Harold Beckwith and Agnes Camilla McMichael (*née* Duncan); *m* 1975, Heather Marie Robbins; two *s* one *d*. *Educ:* Harrow Sch. FCA 1970; ATII 1970. Arthur Andersen & Co., 1969–71; with London & Edinburgh Trust PLC, 1971–92. Founder Chm., Rutland Trust plc, 1986–91. Member: Develt Bd, Cancer Relief Macmillan Fund; NCH Action for Children's 125th Anniversary Appeal Cttee. Vice-President: RNIB; Youth Clubs of UK; Founder, and Chm. Bd of Trustees, Youth Sport Trust; Trustee, Home Farm Develt Trust; Patron, Teenage Cancer Trust. *Recreations:* sport, music, ballet. *Clubs:* Annabel's, Queen's; Old Harrovian Football; Royal Berkshire Golf, Royal Mid-Surrey Golf, St George's Hill Golf; Riverside Racquet Centre.

See also P. M. Beckwith.

BECKWITH, Peter Michael; Chairman: PMB Holdings Ltd, since 1992; Riverside plc, since 1993; Deputy Chairman, German City Estates NV, since 1992; *b* 20 Jan. 1945; *s* of Col Harold Andrew Beckwith and Agnes Camilla McMichael Beckwith; *m* 1968, Paula Gay Bateman; two *d*. *Educ:* Harrow School; Emmanuel College, Cambridge (MA Hons). Qualified Solicitor, 1970; Asst Solicitor, Norton Rose Botterell & Roche; London & Edinburgh Trust: Joint Founder and shareholder, 1972; Managing Director, 1983–86; Dep. Chm., 1987; Chm., 1992. FRSA. *Recreations:* tennis, ski-ing, opera, dogs, gardening. *Address:* PMB Holdings Ltd, Hill Place House, 55A High Street, SW19 5BA. *Clubs:* Riverside Racquets; Down Hill Only (Wengen).

See also J. L. Beckwith.

BECTIVE, Earl of; Thomas Michael Ronald Christopher Taylour; estate agent, with Bective Davidson, London, since 1995; *b* 10 Feb. 1959; *s* and *heir* of 6th Marquis of Headfort, *qv*; *m* 1987, Susan Jane, *er d* of late C. A. Vandervell and of Mrs Vandervell; two *s*. *Educ:* Harrow; RAC Cirencester. Estate agent with Egerton, London, until 1994. *Heir:* *s* Lord Kenlis, *qv*. *Address:* Thoodyn, Bayview, Ramsey, Isle of Man. *Clubs:* Lansdowne; Royal Dublin Society (Dublin).

BEDBROOK, Jack Harry, CEng, FRINA; FIMgt; RCNC; Managing Director, HM Dockyard, Devonport, 1979–84; *b* 8 Aug. 1924; *s* of Harry Bedbrook and Emma Bedbrook; *m* (marr. diss.); three *d*. *Educ:* Technical Coll., Portsmouth; RNC, Greenwich. Dir Gen. Ships Dept, Admiralty, 1946–51; Asst Constructor, Devonport, 1951–54; Dockyard Dept, Bath, 1954–56; Constructor, Gibraltar Dockyard, 1956–58; Admiralty Exptl Works, Haslar, 1958–62; Dir Gen. Ships Dept, 1962–65; Chief Constructor, Portsmouth, 1965–71; Project Manager, Rosyth, 1971–74; Prodn Dir, Devonport, 1974–77; Man. Dir, HM Dockyard, Rosyth, 1977–79. Registered Mem., Assoc. of Natural Medicines. *Recreations:* badminton, sailing, gardening, music, therapeutic massage. *Address:* Laxtons, Cargreen, Saltash, Cornwall PL12 6PA. *T:* Saltash (01752) 844519.

BEDDALL, Hugh Richard Muir; Chairman, Muir Beddall & Co. Ltd, since 1964; Member of Lloyd's, since 1943; *b* 20 May 1922; *s* of Herbert Muir Beddall and Jennie Beddall (*née* Fowler); *m* 1946, Monique Henriette (*née* Haefliger); three *s* one *d*. *Educ:* Stowe; Ecole de Commerce, Neuchatel, Switzerland. Employee of Muir Beddall & Co., 1939–41. Served War of 1939–45; Royal Marines, 2nd Lieut, 1941; subseq. Captain A Troop 45 RM Commando and No 1 Commando Bde HQ; demob., 1946. Employee, Muir Beddall, Mise & Cie, Paris, 1946–47; returned as employee of Muir Beddall & Co. Ltd, 1947; Dir, 1949; Dep. Chm., 1960; Chm., 1964. FCII. Dir, Muir Beddall Mise & Cie, Paris. *Recreations:* shooting, fishing, racing. *Address:* Flat 4, 53 Cadogan Square, SW1X 0HY. *T:* 0171-235 9461. *Clubs:* Buck's, East India, Special Forces.

BEDDARD, Nicholas Elliot; His Honour Judge Beddard; a Circuit Judge, since 1986; *b* 26 April 1934; *s* of Terence Elliot Beddard and Ursula Mary Hamilton Howard; *m* 1964, Gillian Elisabeth Vaughan Bevan, 2nd *d* of Llewellyn and Molly Bevan; two *s* one *d*. *Educ:* Eton. National Service, 1952–54; commissioned, Royal Sussex Regt, 1953; TA (Royal Sussex Regt), 1955–64. United Africa Co., 1955–58; Asst Public Policy Executive, RAC, 1958–68; called to the Bar, Inner Temple, 1967; A Recorder, 1986. *Recreations:* choral singing, squash, golf. *Address:* Farrar's Building, Temple, EC4Y 7BD. *T:* 0171–583 9241. *Clubs:* Lansdowne; Orford Sailing.

BEDDINGTON, Charles Richard; Metropolitan Magistrate, 1963–80; *b* 22 Aug. 1911; *s* of late Charles Beddington, Inner Temple, and Stella (*née* de Goldschmidt); *m* 1939, Debbie, *d* of late Frederick Appleby Holt and Rae Vera Franz, *d* of Sir George Hutchinson; two *s* one *d*. *Educ:* Eton (scholar); Balliol Coll., Oxford. Barrister, Inner Temple, 1934. Joined TA, 1939; served RA, 1939–45, Major. Practised at the Bar in London and on SE Circuit. Mem. Mental Health Review Tribunal (SE Metropolitan Area), 1960–63. *Recreation:* travel. *Address:* 21 Mytten Close, Cuckfield, West Sussex RH17 5LN. *T:* Haywards Heath (01444) 454063.

BEDDOE, David Sydney R.; *see* Rowe-Beddoe.

BEDFORD, 13th Duke of, *cr* 1694; **John Robert Russell;** Marquess of Tavistock, 1694; Earl of Bedford, 1550; Baron Russell of Chenies, 1540; Baron Russell of Thornhaugh, 1603; Baron Howland of Streatham, 1695; *b* 24 May 1917; *er s* of 12th Duke and Louisa Crommelin Roberta (*d* 1960), *y d* of Robert Jowitt Whitwell; *S* father 1953; *m* 1st, 1939, Clare Gwendolen Hollway, *née* Bridgman (*d* 1945); two *s*; 2nd, Lydia (marr. diss., 1960), *widow* of Capt. Ian de Hoghton Lyle, 3rd *d* of 3rd Baron Churston and late Duchess of Leinster; one *s*; 3rd, 1960, Mme Nicole Milinaire, *d* of Paul Schneider. Coldstream Guards, 1939; invalided out, 1940. *Publications:* A Silver-Plated Spoon, 1959; (with G. Mikes) Book of Snobs, 1965; The Flying Duchess, 1968; (with G. Mikes) How to Run a Stately Home, 1971. *Heir:* *s* Marquess of Tavistock, *qv*. *Address:* Château des Ligures, 2 rue Honoré Labande, Monte Carlo, MC 98000, Monaco. *Clubs:* Brooks's, Pratt's.

BEDFORD, Bishop Suffragan of, since 1994; **Rt. Rev. John Henry Richardson;** *b* 11 July 1937; *s* of John Farquhar Richardson and Elizabeth Mary Richardson; *m* 1963, Felicity-Anne Lowes; three *d*. *Educ:* Winchester; Trinity Hall, Cambridge (BA 1961; MA 1965); Cuddesdon Coll., Oxford. Nat. Service, 1956–58 (despatches, Malaya, 1958). Ordained deacon, 1963, priest, 1964; Asst Curate, St George's, Stevenage, 1963–66; Curate, St Mary's, Eastbourne, 1966–68; Vicar: St Paul's, Chipperfield, 1968–75; St Mary's, Rickmansworth, 1975–86; RD, Rickmansworth, 1977–86; Vicar, St Michael's, Bishops Stortford, 1986–93; Hon. Canon, St Albans Cathedral, 1986–. *Recreations:* walking, bird-watching, windsurfing, fishing, energetic gardening. *Address:* 168 Kimbolton Road, Bedford MK41 8DN. *T:* Bedford (01234) 357551. *Club:* Royal Automobile.

BEDFORD, Archdeacon of; *see* Lesiter, Ven. M. L.

BEDFORD, Alfred William, (Bill), OBE 1961; AFC 1945; FRAeS; Aerospace consultant, since 1986; *b* 18 Nov. 1920; *m* 1941, Mary Averill; one *s*. *Educ:* Loughborough College School, Leics. Electrical engineering apprenticeship, Blackburn Starling & Co. Ltd. RAF 1940–51: served Fighter Sqdns, 605 (County of Warwick) Sqdn, 1941; 135 Sqdn,

1979–80. Chief Econ. Adviser, Min. of Transport, 1964–68; Special Adviser, Treasury and CS Cttee, Nationalised Industry Financing, 1981; Mem., Monopolies and Mergers Commn, 1988–94. Chm., Inst. of Public Sector Management, 1983–87 (Dir, 1978–83). Formerly Member: Cttee on Road Pricing (Smeed Cttee); Cttee on Transport in London; Cttee on Transport Planning (Lady Sharp Cttee); Urban Motorways Inter-Deptl Cttee; Standing Adv. Cttee on Trunk Road Assessment (Sir George Leitch Cttee). Managing Editor, Jl of Transport Economics and Policy, 1975–88. *Publications:* Urban Transport: studies in economic policy, 1973; (ed) Productivity and Amenity: achieving a social balance, 1974; (ed) Industrial Relations in a Changing World, 1975; (with T. C. Evans) Corporate Social Responsibility: a reassessment, 1978; Liberalisation of the Use of British Telecommunications Network: an independent economic enquiry, 1981; (with P. B. Kettle) Improving Railway Financial Performance, 1985; (with B. Laidlaw) The Future of Telecommunications, 1989; Privatisation, Regulation and Deregulation, 1992. *Recreations:* music, table tennis, golf. *Address:* 59 Canons Drive, Edgware, Mddx HA8 7RG. *T:* 0181–952 1320. *Club:* Reform.

BEESLEY, Peter Frederick Barton; Registrar: Faculty Office of the Archbishop of Canterbury, since 1981; Diocese of Guildford, since 1981; (Joint) Diocese of Ely, since 1978; (Joint) Diocese of Hereford, since 1983; Partner, Lee Bolton & Lee, since 1969; *b* 30 April 1943; *s* of Ronald Fitzgerald Barton Beesley and Mary Kurczyn (*née* Parker); *m* 1974, Elizabeth Jane Grahame; one *s* two *d*. *Educ:* King's School, Worcester; Exeter Univ. (LLB); Coll. of Law, Guildford. Articled Clerk and Asst Solicitor, Windeatt & Windeatt, 1965–68; Asst Solicitor, Lee Bolton & Lee, 1968–69. Jt Registrar, Dio. St Albans, 1969–78; Registrar, Woodard Corp., 1987–; Legal Advr, Nat. Soc. (C of E) for Promoting Religious Educn, 1975–; Secretary: Ecclesiastical Law Assoc., 1978–; Ecclesiastical Law Soc., 1987–; Pres., City of Westminster Law Soc., 1991–92. Liveryman, Glaziers' and Painters' of Glass Co., 1981. *Publications:* (contrib. jtly) Encyclopaedia of Forms and Precedents, Vol. 13, Ecclesiastical Law, 1987; Anglican Marriage in England and Wales, a Guide to the Law for Clergy, 1992. *Address:* (office) 1 The Sanctuary, Westminster, SW1P 3JT. *T:* 0171–222 5381. *Clubs:* Athenæum, St Stephen's Constitutional.

BEESON, Prof. Paul Bruce, Hon. KBE 1973; FRCP; Professor of Medicine, University of Washington, 1974–82, now Emeritus; *b* 18 Oct. 1908; *s* of John Bradley Beeson, Livingston, Mont; *m* 1942, Barbara Neal, *d* of Ray C. Neal, Buffalo, NY; two *s* one *d*. *Educ:* Univ. of Washington, McGill Univ. Med. Sch. MD, CM, 1933. Intern, Hosp. of Univ. of Pa, 1933–35; Gen. practice of medicine, Wooster, Ohio, 1935–37; Asst Rockefeller Inst., 1937–39; Chief Med. Resident, Peter Bent Brigham Hosp., 1939–40; Instructor in Med., Havard Med. Sch., and Chief Phys., American Red Cross-Harvard Field Hosp. Unit, Salisbury, 1940–42; Asst and Assoc. Prof. of Med., Emory Med. Sch., 1942–46; Prof. of Med. Emory Med. Sch., 1946–52; Prof. of Med. and Chm. Dept of Med., Yale Univ., 1952–65; Nuffield Prof. of Clinical Med., Oxford Univ., and Fellow of Magdalen Coll., 1965–74, Hon. Fellow, 1975; Hon. Fellow RSM, 1976. Vis. Investigator, Wright-Fleming Inst., St Mary's Hosp., 1958–59. Pres., Assoc. Amer. Physicians, 1967; Master, Amer. Coll. of Physicians, 1970. Phillips Award, Amer. Coll. Physicians, 1975; Flexner Award, Assoc. Amer. Med. Colls, 1977. *Alumnus Summa Laude Dignatus,* Univ. of Washington, 1968; Hon. DSc: Emory Univ., 1968; McGill Univ., 1971; Yale Univ., 1975; Albany Med. Coll., 1975; Ohio Med. Coll., 1979. *Publications:* (ed jtly) The Oxford Companion to Medicine, 1986; edited: Cecil-Loeb Textbook of Medicine, 1959–82; Yale Journal Biology and Medicine, 1959–65; Journal Amer. Geriatric Soc., 1981–84; numerous scientific publications relating to infectious disease, pathogenesis of fever, pyelonephritis and mechanism of eosinophilia. *Address:* 21013 NE 122nd Street, Redmond, WA 98053, USA.

BEESON, Very Rev. Trevor Randall; Dean of Winchester, 1987–Feb. 1996; *b* 2 March 1926; *s* of late Arthur William and Matilda Beeson; *m* 1950, Josephine Grace Cope; two *d*. *Educ:* King's Coll., London (AKC 1950; FKC 1987); St Boniface Coll., Warminster. RAF Met Office, 1944–47. Deacon, 1951; Priest, 1952; Curate, Leadgate, Co. Durham, 1951–54; Priest-in-charge and subseq. Vicar of St Chad, Stockton-on-Tees, 1954–65; Curate of St Martin-in-the-Fields, London, 1965–71; Vicar of Ware, Herts, 1971–76; Canon of Westminster, 1976–87; Treasurer, Westminster, 1978–82; Rector of St Margaret's, Westminster, 1982–87; Chaplain to Speaker of House of Commons, 1982–87. Chaplain of St Bride's, Fleet Street, 1967–84. Religious Programmes Advr, LWT, 1970–86. Chm., Christian Action, 1988–. Gen. Sec., Parish and People, 1962–64; Editor, New Christian, and Man. Dir, Prism Publications Ltd, 1965–70; European Corresp. of The Christian Century (Chicago), 1970–83; Chm., SCM Press Ltd, 1978–87. Select Preacher, Oxford, 1980, 1991. Mem. Council, WWF, 1987–. Hon. MA (Lambeth) 1976. *Publications:* New Area Mission, 1963; (jtly) Worship in a United Church, 1964; An Eye for an Ear, 1972; The Church of England in Crisis, 1973; Discretion and Valour: religious conditions in Russia and Eastern Europe, 1974; Britain Today and Tomorrow, 1978; Westminster Abbey, 1981; A Vision of Hope: the churches and change in Latin America, 1984; (contrib.) God's Truth, 1988; contrib. to DNB, Oxford Dictionary of the Church. *Recreations:* cricket, gardening. *Address:* (until Feb. 1996) The Deanery, The Close, Winchester, Hants SO23 9LS; (from March 1996) 69 Greatbridge Road, Romsey, Hants SO51 8FE. *T:* Romsey (01794) 514627.

BEESTON, Prof. Alfred Felix Landon, MA, DPhil; FBA 1965; Laudian Professor of Arabic, Oxford, 1955–78; Emeritus Fellow, St John's College, Oxford, 1978 (Fellow, 1955–78); *b* 1911; *o s* of Herbert Arthur Beeston and Edith Mary Landon. *Educ:* Westminster Sch.; Christ Church, Oxford. James Mew Arabic Scholarship, Oxford, 1934; MA (Oxford), 1936; DPhil (Oxford), 1937. Lieut, Intell. Corps, 1940; Capt., 1943. Asst in Dept of Oriental Books, Bodleian Library, Oxford, 1935–40; Sub-Librarian and Keeper of Oriental Books, Bodleian Library, 1946–55. Mem., Governing Body, SOAS, Univ. of London, 1980–84 (Hon. Fellow 1980). Hon. Mem., Hungarian Oriental Soc., 1993. Lidzbarski Medal for Semitic Epigraphy, Deutsche Morgenländische Ges., 1983. *Publications:* Baidāwī's Commentary on Sūrah 12, 1963; Written Arabic, 1968; The Arabic Language Today, 1970; Selections from the Poetry of Baššār, 1977; Samples of Arabic Prose, 1977; The 'Epistle on Singing Girls' of Jāhiz, 1980; Sabaic Grammar, 1984; many articles. *Address:* St John's College, Oxford OX1 3JP.

BEESTON, James; Chief Executive, Birmingham Heartlands Development Corporation, since 1992; *b* 2 April 1947; *s* of Richard and Mary Beeston; *m* 1971, Christine, *d* of Barry and Enid Thomas; two *s*. *Educ:* King Edward's, Camp Hill; Birmingham Sch. of Planning. DipTP; MRTPI. Birmingham City Council: Public Works Dept, 1965–74; Central Area Planning Officer, 1974–80; Divl Planning Officer, 1980–85; Asst Dir of Devélt, 1985–87; Project Controller, National Indoor Arena; Co-ordinator, first phase, Birmingham Olympics bid; Develt Manager and Dep. Chief Exec., Birmingham Heartlands, 1987–92. Member: Faculty of Building; Urban Villages Group, Midlands; City 2000 Urban Affairs Cttee, Birmingham; RICS Awards Panel, Midlands, 1994–95; Lunar Soc., Birmingham. *Publication:* (jtly) Negotiating with Planning Authorities. *Recreations:* family, cricket, squash, sport, gardening. *Address:* Birmingham Heartlands Development Corporation, Waterlinks House, Richard Street, Heartlands, Birmingham B7 4AA. *T:* 0121–333 3060.

BEETHAM, Geoffrey Howard, CB 1992; Legal Adviser to Department of Transport, 1983–93; Principal Assistant Solicitor, Treasury Solicitor's Department, 1983–93; *b* 9 Jan. 1933; *s* of Reginald Percy Beetham and Hetty Lilian Beetham (*née* Redman); *m* 1st, 1956, Valerie Douglass (marr. diss. 1975); three *d*; 2nd, 1977, Carol Ann Dorrell; two step *s*. *Educ:* City of London Sch.; St John's Coll., Oxford (BA Jurisp.). Nat. Service, RAF, 1951–53. Solicitor, 1960; Assistant Solicitor: Metropolitan Borough of Battersea, 1960–65; London Borough of Wandsworth, 1965–70; Sen. Legal Assistant and Asst Solicitor, DoE, 1970–77; Asst Solicitor, Dept of Transport, 1977–83. Legal Mem., Mental Health Review Tribunal, 1994. *Recreations:* throwing pots, music, countryside.

BEETHAM, Marshal of the Royal Air Force Sir Michael (James), GCB 1978 (KCB 1976); CBE 1967; DFC 1944; AFC 1960; DL; FRAeS; Chief of the Air Staff, 1977–82; Air ADC to the Queen, 1977–82; *b* 17 May 1923; *s* of Major G. C. Beetham, MC; *m* 1956, Patricia Elizabeth Lane; one *s* one *d*. *Educ:* St Marylebone Grammar School. Joined RAF, 1941; pilot trng, 1941–42; commnd 1942; Bomber Comd: 50, 57 and 35 Sqdns, 1943–46; HQ Staff, 1947–49; 82 (Recce) Sqdn, E Africa, 1949–51; psa 1952; Air Min. (Directorate Operational Requirements), 1953–56; CO 214 (Valiant) Sqdn Marham, 1958–60; Gp Captain Ops, HQ Bomber Comd, 1962–64; CO RAF Khormaksar, Aden, 1964–66; idc 1967; Dir Ops (RAF), MoD, 1968–70; Comdt, RAF Staff Coll., 1970–72; ACOS (Plans and Policy), SHAPE, 1972–75; Dep. C-in-C, Strike Command, 1975–76; C-in-C RAF Germany, and Comdr, 2nd Tactical Allied Air Force, 1976–77. Chm., GEC Avionics Ltd, 1986–90 (Dir, 1984–91); Dir, Brixton Estate PLC, 1983–93. Chm., Trustees, RAF Museum, 1983–. FRSA 1979; FRAeS 1982. DL Norfolk, 1989. *Recreations:* golf, tennis. *Clubs:* Royal Air Force; Royal West Norfolk Golf.

BEETHAM, Roger Campbell, CMG 1993; LVO 1976; HM Diplomatic Service; UK Permanent Representative to the Council of Europe (with personal rank of Ambassador), since 1993; *b* 22 Nov. 1937; *s* of Henry Campbell and Mary Beetham; *m* 1st 1965, Judith Rees (marr. diss. 1986); 2nd, 1986, Christine Marguerite Malerme. *Educ:* Peter Symonds Sch., Winchester; Brasenose Coll., Oxford (MA). Entered HM Diplomatic Service, 1960; FO, 1960–62; UK Delegation to Disarmament Conference, Geneva, 1962–65; Washington, 1965–68; News Dept, FCO, 1969–72; Head of Chancery, Helsinki, 1972–76; FCO, 1976; seconded to European Commission, Brussels, as Spokesman of the President, Rt Hon. Roy Jenkins, 1977–80; Counsellor (Econ. and Commercial), New Delhi, 1981–85; Head of Maritime, Aviation and Envmt Dept, FCO, 1985–90; Ambassador to Senegal and (non-resident) to Cape Verde, Guinea, Guinea-Bissau and Mali, 1990–93. Order of the White Rose of Finland, 1976. *Recreations:* oenology, cooking, travel. *Address:* c/o Foreign and Commonwealth Office, SW1A 2AH. *Club:* Travellers'.

BEETON, David Christopher; Chief Executive, Historic Royal Palaces, since 1989; *b* 25 Aug. 1939; *s* of Ernest Beeton and Ethel Beeton; *m* 1968, Brenda Lomax; two *s*. *Educ:* Ipswich Sch.; King's Coll., London Univ. (LLB). Solicitor. Chief Exec., Bath CC, 1973–85; Sec., National Trust, 1985–89. *Recreations:* swimming, historic buildings, cooking, music. *Address:* Hampton Court Palace, Surrey KT8 9AU. *T:* 0181–781 9751, *Fax:* 0181–781 9754.

BEEVOR, Antony Romer; Executive Director, Hambros Bank Ltd, since 1985; *b* 18 May 1940; *s* of late Miles Beevor and Sybil (*née* Gilliat); *m* 1970, Cecilia Hopton; one *s* one *d*. *Educ:* Winchester; New Coll., Oxford (BA). Admitted Solicitor, 1965. Ashurst Morris Crisp & Co., 1962–72 (on secondment as Sec., Panel on Takeovers and Mergers, 1969–71); joined Hambros Bank, 1972; Dir, 1974; on secondment, as Dir-Gen., Panel on Takeovers and Mergers, 1987–89; Director: Hambros plc, 1990–; (non-exec.), Rugby Gp PLC, 1993–. *Recreations:* ski-ing, shooting. *Address:* 20 Radipole Road, SW6 5DL. *T:* 0171-731 8015. *Club:* Hurlingham.

BEEVOR, Sir Thomas Agnew, 7th Bt, *cr* 1784; *b* 6 Jan. 1929; *s* of Comdr Sir Thomas Beevor, 6th Bt, and Edith Margaret Agnew (who *m* 2nd, 1944, Rear-Adm. R. A. Currie, *qv*, and *d* 1985); *S* father 1943; *m* 1st, 1957, Barbara Clare (marr. diss., 1965), *y d* of Capt. R. L. B. Cunliffe, RN (retd); one *s* two *d*; 2nd, 1966, Carola, *d* of His Honour J. B. Herbert, MC; 3rd, 1976, Mrs Sally Bouwens, White Hall, Saham Toney, Norfolk. *Heir: s* Thomas Hugh Cunliffe Beevor [*b* 1 Oct. 1962; *m* 1988, Charlotte Louise, *e d* of Keith E. Harvey]. *Address:* Hargham Hall, Norwich NR16 2JW.

BEEZLEY, His Honour Frederick Ernest; a Circuit Judge, 1976–93; *b* 30 Jan. 1921; *s* of Frederick William Beezley and Lilian Isabel (*née* Markham); *m* 1969, Sylvia Ruth (*née* Locke). *Educ:* Acton County Sch. Served War, Royal Signals, Combined Operations, 1940–46. Called to Bar, Gray's Inn, 1947; Res. Judge, Cambridge Crown Court, 1987–93. *Recreations:* fly-fishing, horse racing, musician with Ely Mil. Band. *Address:* White Lodge, 25 Northwold, Ely, Cambridge CB6 1BG.

BEFFA, Jean-Louis Guy Henri; Chevalier de la Légion d'Honneur; Officier de l'Ordre National du Mérite; Chairman and Chief Executive Officer, Compagnie de Saint-Gobain, since 1987; *b* 11 Aug. 1941; *m* 1967, Marie-Madeleine Brunel; two *s* one *d*. *Educ:* Ecole Polytechnique (Ing. au Corps des Mines); Dip. de l'Inst. d'Etudes Politiques de Paris. Compagnie de Saint-Gobain: Vice-Pres., Corporate Planning, 1974–77; Pres., Pipe Div., 1978–82; Chief Operating Officer, 1982–86. Order of Merit (Germany); Order of Rio Branco (Brazil). *Recreations:* golf, classical music. *Address:* Compagnie de Saint-Gobain, Les Miroirs, 18 avenue d'Alsace Cédex 27, 92096 Paris La Défense, France. *T:* 47623310.

BEGG, Dr Sir Neil (Colquhoun), KBE 1986 (OBE 1973); Director of Medical Services, Royal New Zealand Plunket Society, 1956–76, retired; *b* 13 April 1915; *s* of Charles Mackie Begg, CB, CMG, Croix de Guerre, and Lillian Helen Lawrance Begg; *m* 1942, Margaret Milne MacLean; two *s* two *d*. *Educ:* John McGlashan Coll., Dunedin, NZ; Otago Univ. Med. Sch. (MB ChB 1940); postgrad. paediatrics, London and Edinburgh, 1947–48. DCH, MRCP London, MRCPE. Served 2 NZ Expedn Force, 1942–46, Med. Corps, ME and Italy. Paediatrician, Dunedin Public Hosp., 1949–56. Chm., NZ Historic Places Trust, 1978–86. Hon. FRCPE 1958, Hon. FRCP 1977. *Publications:* Dusky Bay (with A. C. Begg), 1966; (with A. C. Begg) James Cook and New Zealand, 1969; Child and his Family, 1970, 8th edn 1975; (with A. C. Begg) Port Preservation, 1973; (with A. C. Begg) The World of John Boultbee, 1979; The Intervening Years, 1992; contribs to NZ Med. Jl. *Recreation:* trout fishing. *Address:* 86 Newington Avenue, Dunedin 9001, New Zealand. *T:* (3)4672089.

BEGG, Robert William, CBE 1977; MA; CA; FRSA; Consultant, Moores Rowland, Chartered Accountants, since 1987 (Partner, 1951–86, Consultant, 1986–87, Mann Judd Gordon); *b* 19 Feb. 1922; *s* of late David Begg, CA, FFA, and of Elizabeth Young Thomson; *m* 1948, Sheena Margaret Boyd; two *s*. *Educ:* Greenock Acad.; Glasgow Univ. (MA 1942). Served Royal Navy, 1942–46, Lieut RNVR (despatches). Mem., Institute of Chartered Accountants of Scotland, 1948. Member: Glasgow Univ. General Council Business Cttee, 1973–76; Court, Glasgow Univ., 1986–90. Hon. Treasurer: Royal Philosophical Soc. of Glasgow, 1952–62; Royal Glasgow Inst. of Fine Arts, 1975–86 (Pres., 1987–90); Mem. Bd of Governors, Glasgow School of Art, 1955–77, Chm., 1970–76; Trustee: RIAS Hill House Trust, 1977–82; Pollok Trust, 1987–; Member: Council, National Trust for Scotland, 1984–90 (Mem. Exec. Cttee, 1985–90); Museums and Galls Commn, 1988–91. Gov. of Patrons, Nat. Galls of Scotland, 1984– (Mem., 1974–91, Chm., 1980–87, Bd of Trustees). DUniv Glasgow, 1990. *Recreation:* painting.

Address: Allan House, 25 Bothwell Street, Glasgow G2 6NL. *T:* 0141–221 6991; (home) 3 Colquhoun Drive, Bearsden, Glasgow G61 4NQ. *T:* 0141–942 2436. *Clubs:* Art, XIII (Glasgow).

BEGGS, Roy; MP (UU) East Antrim, since 1983 (resigned seat Dec. 1985 in protest against Anglo-Irish Agreement; re-elected Jan. 1986); *b* 20 Feb. 1936; *s* of John Beggs; *m* 1959, Wilma Lorimer; two *s* two *d. Educ:* Ballyclare High Sch.; Stranmillis Trng Coll. (Certificate/Diploma in Educn). Teacher, 1957–78, Vice-Principal, 1978–83, Larne High Sch. Mem., 1973–, Vice-Chm., 1981–, NE Educn and Library Bd; Pres., Assoc. of Educn and Liby Bds, NI, 1984–85 (Vice-Pres., 1983–84). Mem., Larne Borough Council, 1973–; Mayor of Larne, 1978–83; Mem. for N Antrim, NI Assembly, 1982–86. Mem., Public Accounts Commn, 1984–. *Address:* House of Commons, SW1A 0AA; 9 Carnduff Road, Ballyvernstown, Larne, Co. Antrim. *T:* Larne (01574) 273258.

BEHNE, Edmond Rowlands, CMG 1974; Managing Director, Pioneer Sugar Mills Ltd, Queensland, 1952–76; *b* 20 Nov. 1906; *s* of late Edmund Behne; *m* 1932, Grace Elizabeth Ricketts; two *s* one *d. Educ:* Bendigo Sch. of Mines; Brisbane Boys' Coll.; Univ. of Queensland. BSc and MSc (App.); ARACI. Bureau of Sugar Experiment Stations, 1930–48 (Director, 1947); Pioneer Sugar Mills Ltd, 1948–80. *Recreation:* bowls. *Address:* Craigston, 217 Wickham Terrace, Brisbane, Qld 4000, Australia. *T:* (7) 38315657. *Club:* Johnsonian (Brisbane).

BEHR, Norman Isaac, FRICS; Vice President, London Rent Assessment Panel, 1988–93 (Valuer Member, 1983–87); *b* 28 Sept. 1922; *s* of Moses and Sarah Behr; *m* 1950, Anne Laurette Hilton. *Educ:* Haberdashers' Aske's Sch.; College of Estate Management. Chartered Surveyor. Articled, De Groot & Co., 1939–42; served War, RAOC, REME, 1942–46; joined Valuation Office, 1948; District Valuer and Valuation Officer, Westminster, 1965–67, City of London, 1967–70; Superintending Valuer, 1970; Asst Chief Valuer, 1977; Dep. Chief Valuer (Rating), 1981–83. First Prize, Chartered Auctioneers and Estate Agents Inst., 1941; Wainwright Prize, Royal Instn of Chartered Surveyors, 1950. *Recreations:* opera, cooking, computers. *Address:* 43 Netherhall Gardens, NW3 5RL. *T:* 0171–435 9391.

BEIGHTON, Leonard John Hobhouse, CB 1992; Deputy Chairman, Board of Inland Revenue, 1992–94 (Director General, 1988–92); *b* 20 May 1934; *s* of John Durant Kennedy Beighton and Leonora Hobhouse; *m* 1962, Judith Valerie Bridge (decd); one *s* one *d. Educ:* Tonbridge Sch.; Corpus Christi College, Oxford (MA PPE). Inland Revenue, 1957; seconded HM Treasury, 1968–69 (Private Sec. to Chief Sec.), and 1977–79. Chm., Dio. of Guildford Council for Social Responsibility. Dir, Shared Interest Soc. Ltd; Mem. Council, Shaftesbury Soc. *Address:* 160 Tilt Road, Cobham, Surrey KT11 3HR.

BEILL, Air Vice-Marshal Alfred, CB 1986; Appeals Secretary, King Edward VII's Hospital for Officers, since 1987; *b* 14 Feb. 1931; *s* of late Group Captain Robert Beill, CBE, DFC and Sophie Beill; *m* 1953, Vyvian Mary Crowhurst Archer; four *d. Educ:* Rossall Sch.; RAF Coll., Cranwell. FCIT 1980; FBIM 1976; FInstPS 1985. Commnd RAF, 1952; served, 1952–64: RAF Marham, Stafford and Fauld; HQ Air Forces ME, Aden; RAF Supply Control Centre, Hendon; student, RAF Staff Coll., Andover, 1964; HQ FEAF, Singapore, 1965–67; student, JSSC, Latimer, 1968; OC Supply and Movements Sqdn, RAF Scampton, 1968–69; HQ Maintenance Comd, 1969–70; DS JSSC (later NDC), 1970–73; Comd Supply Officer, HQ NEAF, Cyprus, 1973–75; Dir of Engrg and Supply Policy (RAF), 1976–78; student, RCDS, 1978; Dir of Movements (RAF), 1979–82; Dir of Supply Policy and Logistics Plans (RAF), 1982–84; Dir Gen. of Supply (RAF), 1984–87, retired. ADC to the Queen, 1974–75. Life Vice Pres., RAF Swimming Assoc., 1987– (Pres., 1982–87). *Address:* c/o Lloyds Bank, Cox's & King's Branch, 7 Pall Mall, SW1Y 5NA. *Club:* Royal Air Force.

BEISHON, (Ronald) John, DPhil; CPsychol, CEng; Director, Consumers' Association, 1987–94; Chief Executive, Association for Consumer Research, 1987–94; *b* 10 Nov. 1930; *s* of Arthur and Irene Beishon; *m* 1955, Gwenda Jean Solway; two *s* two *d. Educ:* Battersea Polytechnic; Univ. of London (BSc); Univ. of Birmingham; Univ. of Oxford (DPhil). MIM, MWeldI, AFBPsS. National Service, RASC, 1951–53; Technical Officer, ICI Ltd, 1954–58; Section Leader, BICC Ltd, 1958–61; Sen. Res. Asst, Oxford Univ., 1961–64; Lectr, Bristol Univ., 1964–68; Reader, Sussex Univ., 1968–71; Professor of Systems, Open Univ., 1971–80; Dir, Poly. of South Bank, 1980–85 (Hon. Fellow, 1986); seconded as actg Dir, 1985, Permanent Dir, 1986–87, Poly. of North London. Bd Dir, Internat. Consumer Res. and Testing Ltd, 1990–94; Dir, New Statesman and Soc., 1995–; Publisher, European Bookseller, 1995–. Member, Executive Committee: Internat. Organisation Consumer Unions, 1987–94 (Hon. Sec., 1991–94); Rep., FAO and Codex Alimentarius, 1988–); NHBC, 1988–91. Mem., Governing Bd, Brighton Univ. (formerly Brighton Poly.), 1985– (Chm., Audit Cttee, 1990–92); Chm., Bd of Management, Co-operative Coll., 1995–. FRSA. Hon. Fellow, N London Univ. 1993. DUniv Central England, 1993. *Publications:* (ed with G. Peters) Systems Behaviour, 1973, 2nd edn 1976; articles in various jls. *Recreation:* squash. *Address:* 421 Ditchling Road, Brighton, East Sussex BN1 6XB. *Club:* Wig and Pen.

BEITH, Rt. Hon. Alan (James), PC 1992; MP, Berwick-upon-Tweed since Nov. 1973 (L 1973–88, Lib Dem since 1988); Deputy Leader, Liberal Democrats, since 1992; *b* 20 April 1943; *o s* of James and Joan Beith, Poynton, Ches; *m* 1965, Barbara Jean Ward; one *s* one *d. Educ:* King's Sch., Macclesfield; Balliol and Nuffield Colls, Oxford. BLitt, MA Oxon. Lectr, Dept of Politics, Univ. of Newcastle upon Tyne, 1966–73. Vice-Chm., Northumberland Assoc. of Parish Councils, 1970–71 and 1972–73; Jt Chm., Assoc. of Councillors, 1974–79; Member: Gen. Adv. Council of BBC, 1974–84; Hexham RDC, 1969–74; Corbridge Parish Council, 1970–74; Tynedale District Council, 1973–74; BBC NE Regional Adv. Council, 1971–74; NE Transport Users' Consultative Cttee, 1970–74. Mem., House of Commons Commn, 1979–; UK Rep. to Council of Europe and WEU, 1976–84. Liberal Chief Whip, 1976–85; Dep. Leader, Liberal Party, 1985–88; spokesman on Educn, 1977–83; spokesman on parly and constitutional affairs, 1983–87; Lib. spokesman on foreign affairs, 1985–87 (Alliance spokesman on foreign affairs, 1987); Lib Dem spokesman on Treasury affairs, 1987–94, on Home affairs, 1994–. Member: Select Cttee on Treasury affairs, 1987–94; Intelligence and Security Cttee, 1994–. Trustee, Historic Chapels Trust, 1993–. Methodist Local Preacher. *Publications:* The Case for the Liberal Party and the Alliance, 1983; (jtly) Faith and Politics, 1987; chapter in The British General Election of 1964, ed Butler and King, 1965. *Recreations:* walking, music, boating, looking at old buildings. *Address:* 28 Castle Terrace, Berwick-upon-Tweed TD15 1NZ. *T:* Berwick (01289) 330039. *Club:* National Liberal.

BEITH, Sir John, KCMG 1969 (CMG 1959); HM Diplomatic Service, retired; *b* 4 April 1914; *s* of late William Beith and Margaret Stanley, Toowoomba, Qld; *m* 1949, Diana Gregory-Hood (*d* 1987), *d* of Sir John Little Gilmour, 2nd Bt; one *s* one *d* (and one *d* decd), (one step *s* one step *d*). *Educ:* Eton; King's Coll., Cambridge. Entered Diplomatic Service, 1937, and served in FO until 1940; 3rd Sec., Athens, 1940–41; 2nd Sec., Buenos Aires, 1941–45; served Foreign Office, 1945–49; Head of UK Permanent Delegation to the UN at Geneva, 1950–53; Head of Chancery at Prague, 1953–54; Counsellor, 1954; Counsellor and Head of Chancery, British Embassy, Paris, 1954–59; Head of Levant Dept, FO, 1959–61; Head of North and East African Dept, Foreign Office, 1961–63; Ambassador to Israel, 1963–65; an Asst Sec.-Gen., NATO, 1966–67; Asst Under-Sec. of State, FO, 1967–69; Ambassador to Belgium, 1969–74. *Recreations:* music, racing, books. *Address:* Dean Farm House, Winchester SO21 2LP. *T:* Winchester (01962) 776326. *Clubs:* White's, Anglo-Belgian.

BEITH, John William, CBE 1972; Director Special Duties, Massey Ferguson Holdings Ltd, 1971–74, retired; *b* 13 Jan. 1909; *s* of John William Beith and Ana Theresia (*née* Denk); *m* 1931, Dorothy (*née* Causbrook) (*d* 1986); two *s. Educ:* Spain, Chile, Germany; Llandovery Coll., S Wales. Joined Massey Harris (now Massey Ferguson), 1927, London; occupied senior exec. positions in Argentina, Canada, France and UK; Vice-Pres., Canadian parent co., 1963; Chm., Massey Ferguson (UK) Ltd, 1970. Pres., Agricl Engrs Assoc. Ltd, 1970. *Recreations:* ancient and contemporary history; follower of Rugby; swimming. *Address:* Torre Blanca, 22 Calle de S Hortet, 07669 Cala Serena, Mallorca. *T:* Baleares 657830. *Club:* Oriental.

BÉJART, Maurice (Jean); choreographer; Director, Rudra Béjart Ballet Lausanne, since 1992; *b* 1 Jan. 1927; *s* of Gaston and Germaine Berger. *Educ:* Lycée de Marseilles. Début as ballet dancer with Marseilles Opéra, 1945; International Ballet, 1949–50; Royal Opera, Stockholm, 1951–52; co-founded Les Ballets de l'Etoile, later Ballet-Théâtre de Paris, 1954 (Dir, 1954–59); Director: Twentieth Century Ballet Co., 1959–87; Béjart Ballet Lausanne, 1987–92; Mudra Sch., 1972. Grand Prix National de la Musique, 1970; Prix Erasme de la danse, 1974. Chevalier des Arts et des Lettres; Commandeur de l'Ordre de Léopold (Belgium), 1982; Ordre du Soleil Levant (Japan), 1986; Grand Officier de l'Ordre de la Couronne (Belgium), 1988. Principal works include: La Belle au Boa, Symphonie pour un homme seul, 1955; Orphée, 1958; Le sacre du printemps, 1959; Boléro, 1961; The Tales of Hoffman, 1962; The Merry Widow, The Damnation of Faust, l'Oiseau de Feu, 1964; Romeo and Juliet, 1966; Messe pour le temps présent, 1967; Firebird, 1970; Song of a Wayfarer, Nijinsky: clown de Dieu, 1971; Le Marteau sans Maître, La Traviata, 1973; Ce que l'amour me dit, 1974; Notre Faust, 1975; Heliogabale, Pli selon Pli, 1976; Petrouchka, 1977; Gaîté Parisienne, Ce que la Mort me dit, 1978; Mephisto Waltzer, 1979; Casta Diva, Eros Thanatos, 1980; The Magic Flute, Les Chaises, Light, Les Uns et les Autres (film), Adagietto, 1981; Wien Wien nur du Allein, Thalassa Mare Nostrum, 1982; Salome, Messe pour le Temps Futur, Vie et mort d'une marionnette humaine, 1983; Dionysos, 1984; Le Concours, la Chauve Souris, 1985; Arepo, Malraux ou la Métamorphose des Dieux, 1986; Trois Etudes pour Alexandre, Souvenir de Léningrad, Après-midi d'un Faune, Fiche Signalétique, 1987; Patrice Chéreau . . ., Dibouk, Et Valse, Piaf, Paris-Tokyo, A force de partir . . ., 1988; 1789 et nous, Elégie pour elle, L . . ., aile, 1989; Ring um den Ring, Nijinsky Clown de dieu (theatrical version), Pyramides, Mozart Tangos, 1990; Mr C . . . ., Sissi, Opera, Crucifixion, 1993; Journal: 1st Chapter, 1995. *Publications:* Mathilde, ou le temps perdu (novel), 1963; La Reine Verte (play), 1963; L'autre chant de la danse, 1974; Un instant dans la vie d'autrui, 1979; La Mort Subite, 1991. *Address:* Rudra Béjart Lausanne, Case Postale 25, 1000 Lausanne 22, Switzerland.

BEKER, Prof. Henry Joseph, PhD; Chairman and Chief Executive, Zergo Ltd, since 1989 (Managing Director, 1988–89); Visiting Professor of Information Technology, Royal Holloway (formerly Royal Holloway College, then Royal Holloway and Bedford New College), University of London, since 1984; *b* 22 Dec. 1951; *s* of Jozef and Mary Beker; *m* 1976, Mary Louise (*née* Keilthy); two *d. Educ:* Kilburn Grammar Sch.; Univ. of London (BSc Maths 1973, PhD 1976); Open Univ. (BA 1982). CEng, MIEE 1984; FIS (MIS 1977); CStat; CMath, FIMA 1994 (AFIMA 1978). Sen. Res. Asst, Dept of Statistics, University Coll. of Swansea, 1976–77; Principal Mathematician, Racal-Comsec Ltd, 1977–80, Chief Mathematician, 1980–83; Dir of Research, Racal Research Ltd, 1983–85; Dir of Systems, Racal-Chubb Security Systems Ltd, 1985–86; Man. Dir, Racal-Guardata Ltd, 1986–88. Vis. Prof. of IT, Westfield Coll., Univ. of London, 1983–84. Vice Pres., Inst. of Mathematics and its Applications, 1988–89. FRSA. *Publications:* Cipher Systems, 1982; Secure Speech Communications, 1985. *Recreations:* music, mycology, natural history, reading, travel. *Address:* Zergo Ltd, The Square, Basing View, Basingstoke, Hants RG21 4EG.

BEKOE, Dr Daniel Adzei; Regional Director, International Development Research Centre, Nairobi, since 1986; Member, Pontifical Academy of Sciences, since 1983; *b* 7 Dec. 1928; *s* of Aristocles Silvanus Adzete Bekoe and Jessie Nadu (*née* Awuletey); *m* 1958, Theresa Victoria Anyisaa Annan (marr. diss. 1983); three *s* (and one *s* decd); *m* 1988, Bertha Augustina Ashia Randolph. *Educ:* Achimota Sch.; University Coll. of Gold Coast (BSc London); Univ. of Oxford (DPhil). Jun. Res. Asst, Univ. of Calif, LA, 1957–58; Univ. of Ghana (formerly University Coll. of Ghana): Lectr, 1958–63; Sen. Lectr, 1963–65; Associate Prof., 1965–74; Prof. of Chemistry, 1974–83; Vice-Chancellor, 1976–83; Dir, UNESCO Regl Office for Sci. and Technol. for Africa, 1983–85. Sabbatical year, Univ. of Calif, LA, 1962–63; Vis. Associate Prof., Univ. of Ibadan, 1966–67. Member: UN Univ. Council, 1980–83; UN Adv. Cttee on Science and Technology for Develt, 1980–82. Pres., ICSU, 1980–83. *Publications:* articles on molecular structures in crystallographic and chemical jls; gen. articles in Proc. Ghana Acad. of Arts and Sciences. *Recreations:* music, walking. *Address:* International Development Research Centre, PO Box 62084, Nairobi, Kenya. *T:* (2) 330850.

BELCH, Sir (Alexander) Ross, Kt 1992; CBE 1972; FRSE 1977; FRINA; Chairman: Murray Hotels (Crieff) Ltd, since 1974; Kelvin Travel Ltd, since 1984; Altnacraig Shipping plc, since 1988; Ferguson Marine PLC, since 1991; Altnamara Shipping plc, since 1993; *b* 13 Dec. 1920; *s* of Alexander Belch, CBE, and Agnes Wright Ross; *m* 1947, Janette Finnie Murdoch (*d* 1988); four *d*; *m* 1992, Dorothy West. *Educ:* Morrison's Acad., Crieff, Perthshire; Glasgow Univ. (BSc Naval Arch. 1st Cl. Hons). Lithgows Ltd: Dir and Gen. Manager, 1954–59; Asst Man. Dir, 1959–64; Man. Dir, 1964–69; Scott Lithgow Ltd: Man. Dir, 1969–80; Chm., 1978–80. Director: Jebsen Carriers Ltd, 1990–; Ferguson Shipbuilders, 1993–. Chm., Irvine Develt Corp., 1985–90. Pres., Shipbuilders and Repairers Nat. Assoc., 1974–76. Chm., Council of Trustees, Scottish Maritime Museum, 1983–. CIMgt (CBIM 1981). Hon. LLD Strathclyde, 1978. *Address:* Altnacraig House, Lyle Road, Greenock, Renfrewshire PA16 7XT. *T:* Greenock (01475) 721124.

BELCHER, John Rashleigh, MS 1945; FRCS 1942; Consultant Thoracic Surgeon, NE Metropolitan Regional Hospital Board, 1950–82; Surgeon, London Chest Hospital, 1951–82; Thoracic Surgeon, Middlesex Hospital, 1955–82; *b* 11 Jan. 1917; *s* of late Dr Ormonde Rashleigh Belcher, Liverpool; *m* 1940, Jacqueline Mary, *d* of late C. P. Phillips; two *s* one *d. Educ:* Epsom Coll.; St Thomas' Hosp. MB BS 1939; FRCS 1942; MS 1945; Resident appointments at St Thomas' Hospital, 1939–40. RAF, 1940–46: Medical Service; general duties and surgical specialist; Squadron Leader. Resident and Asst posts at St Thomas', Brompton, London Chest, and Middlesex Hosps; followed by consultant appointments; co-editor, Brit. Jl of Diseases of the Chest. Pres., Assoc. of Thoracic Surgeons, 1980; Member: Thoracic Soc.; Cardiac Soc.; Amer. Coll. of Chest Physicians. Mem. Bd of Govs, Hosps for Diseases of Chest and Heart, 1961–82. Toured: for British Council, Far East 1969, Cyprus and Greece 1973, Yugoslavia 1977; for FCO, Indonesia 1971, Bolivia 1975; personal lecture tours, Nepal and India 1969, Jamaica 1973, Mexico 1975. Hunterian Prof., RCS, 1979. *Publications:* Thoracic Surgical Management, 1953;

chapters in standard text-books; papers in British and foreign medical journals. *Recreations:* photography, picture framing, opera. *Address:* 23 Hornton Court, Hornton Street, W8 7RT. *T:* 0171–937 7006.

BELCHER, Ronald Harry, CMG 1958; Under-Secretary, Ministry of Overseas Development, 1965–75; *b* 5 Jan 1916; *s* of Harry Albert Belcher; *m* 1948, Hildegarde (*née* Hellyer-Jones); one *s*. *Educ:* Christ's Hosp., Horsham; Jesus Coll., Cambridge; Brasenose Coll., Oxford. BA (Hons Classics) Cantab 1937; Dipl. Class. Arch. Cantab 1938; BA Oxon 1938. Indian Civil Service, Punjab, 1939–48; Commonwealth Relations Office, 1948–65; seconded to Foreign Office for service in British Embassy, Washington, 1951–53; Private Sec., 1953–54; Asst Sec., 1954; Deputy High Commissioner for the UK in S Africa, 1956–59; Asst Under Sec. of State, CRO, 1960–61; British Dep. High Comr, Delhi, 1961–65. *Address:* Fieldview, Lower Road, Fetcham, Surrey KT22 9EJ. *Club:* Commonwealth Trust.

BELCOURT, Norma Elizabeth, (Mrs Emile Belcourt); *see* Burrowes, N. E.

BELDAM, Rt. Hon. Sir (Alexander) Roy (Asplan), Kt 1981; PC 1989; **Rt. Hon. Lord Justice Beldam;** a Lord Justice of Appeal, since 1989; *b* 29 March 1925; *s* of George William Beldam and Margaret Frew Shettle (formerly Beldam, *née* Underwood); *m* 1953, Elisabeth Bryant Farr; two *s* one *d*. *Educ:* Oundle Sch.; Brasenose Coll., Oxford. Sub-Lt, RNVR Air Branch, 1943–46. Called to Bar, Inner Temple, 1950; Bencher, 1977; QC 1969; a Recorder of the Crown Court, 1972–81; Presiding Judge, Wales and Chester Circuit, Jan.–Oct. 1985; a Judge of the High Court of Justice, QBD, 1981–89. Chm., Law Commn, 1985–89. *Recreations:* sailing, cricket, naval history. *Address:* Royal Courts of Justice, Strand, WC2A 2LL.

BELFALL, David John; Under Secretary, Health Policy and Public Health Directorate, Scottish Office, since 1991; *b* 26 April 1947; *s* of Frederick Belfall and Ada Belfall (*née* Jacobs); *m* 1972, Lorna McLaughlan; one *s* one *d*. *Educ:* Colchester Royal Grammar Sch.; St John's Coll., Cambridge (BA Hons). Home Office, 1969–88; Under-Sec. (Emergency Services), Home and Health Dept, Scottish Office, 1988–91. *Recreations:* squash, badminton. *Address:* St Andrews House, Regent Road, Edinburgh EH1 3DG.

BELFAST, Earl of; Arthur Patrick Chichester; farmer; *b* 9 May 1952; *s* and *heir* of 7th Marquess of Donegall, *qv*; *m* 1989, Caroline, *er d* of Major Christopher Philipson; one *s*. *Educ:* Harrow; Royal Agricl Coll., Cirencester. Coldstream Guards. *Recreations:* hunting, shooting, fishing. *Heir:* *s* Viscount Chichester, *qv*. *Address:* Dunbrody Park, Arthurstown, Co. Wexford, Eire.

BELFAST, Dean of; *see* Shearer, Very Rev. John.

BELHAM, David Ernest, CB 1975; Principal Assistant Solicitor (Under Secretary), Department of Employment, 1970–77, retired; *b* 9 Aug. 1914; *s* of Ernest George Belham and Grace Belham (*née* Firth); *m* 1938, Eunice Monica (*née* Vine); two *s* two *d*. *Educ:* Whitgift Sch.; Law Society's Sch. of Law. Solicitor (Hons), 1937. Private practice, 1937–39. Served War, RAFVR, 1940–46. Entered Solicitor's Department, Min. of Labour, 1946; Asst Solicitor, 1962. *Address:* 26 The Chase, Findon, Worthing, W Sussex BN14 0TT. *T:* Findon (01903) 873771.

BELHAVEN and STENTON, 13th Lord, *cr* 1647; **Robert Anthony Carmichael Hamilton;** farming; *b* 27 Feb. 1927; *o s* of 12th Lord; *S* father, 1961; *m* 1st, 1952, Elizabeth Ann, *d* of late Col A. H. Moseley, Warrawee, NSW; one *s* one *d*; 2nd, 1973, Rosemary Lady Mactaggart (marr. diss. 1986), *o d* of Sir Herbert Williams, 1st Bt, MP; one *d* (adopted); 3rd, 1986, Malgorzata Maria, *d* of Pobog Tadeusz Hruzik-Mazurkiewicz, Krakow, Poland; one *d*. *Educ:* Eton. Commissioned, The Cameronians, 1947. *Recreation:* cooking. *Heir:* *s* Master of Belhaven, *qv*. *Address:* 16 Broadwater Down, Tunbridge Wells, Kent TN2 5NR; 710 Howard House, Dolphin Square, SW1V 3PQ. *Club:* Army and Navy.

BELHAVEN, Master of; Hon. Frederick Carmichael Arthur Hamilton; *b* 27 Sept. 1953; *s* of 13th Lord Belhaven and Stenton, *qv*; *m* 1st, 1981, Elizabeth Anne (marr. diss. 1988), *d* of S. V. Tredinnick, Wisborough Green, Sussex; two *s*; 2nd, 1991, Philippa Martha Gansel Whitehead, *d* of Sir Rowland Whitehead, Bt, *qv*. *Educ:* Eton.

BELICH, Sir James, Kt 1990; Mayor of Wellington, New Zealand, 1986–92, retired; *b* 25 July 1927; *s* of Yakov Belich and Maria (*née* Batistich); *m* 1951, Valerie Frances Anzulovich; one *s* two *d*. *Educ:* Otahuhu Coll.; Auckland Univ.; Victoria Univ. of Wellington (BA Hons Econs); IBM Teaching Fellow, Massey Univ. Consular/Internat. Trade, Auckland, Sydney, Wellington, 1948–56; Economist, Market Res. Manager, Dir, Chief Exec. and Chm., Research, Marketing, Public Relns, Advertising, 1956–86. Member: Wellington Harbour Bd; Wellington Regional Council. Director: Air NZ, 1987–89; Lambton Harbour Overview Ltd (Chm.); Wellington Internat. Airport. Pres. and Exec., various orgns incl.: Pres., UNA, Wellington and NZ; Founder Pres., UNICEF, NZ. FInstD; Fellow, Inst. of Advertising. *Recreations:* reading, walking, bowls. *Address:* 4 Indus Street, Khandallah, Wellington 4, New Zealand. *T:* (4) 4793339. *Clubs:* Wellington, Wellington Central Rotary (Wellington).

BELISLE, Denton; management consultant; Manager, Social Security Board, Belize, since 1993; *b* 18 March 1948; *s* of George Nathaniel and Laura Ianthe Belisle; *m* 1974, Barrette Johnissa (*née* Sanz); three *s*. *Educ:* Univ. of West Indies (BSc Hons); Univ. of Newcastle upon Tyne. Agricl Officer, 1970–78; Projects Officer (Agric.), 1978–81; Investment Promotion Officer, 1981–83; Dep. Perm. Rep. to UN, 1983–84; Hd, Econs Div., Develt Finance Corp., 1984–85; Chargé d'Affaires *ai*, Washington, 1985; Actg High Comr, 1985–86, High Comr, 1986–87, London. *Recreations:* tennis, reading. *Address:* 10 Mango Street, Belmopan, Belize, Central America. *T:* (8) 23568. *Club:* Belmopan Tennis.

BELL, Alan Scott; Librarian, The London Library, since 1993; *b* 8 May 1942; *s* of late Stanley Bell and Iris Bell (*née* Scott), Sunderland; *m* 1966, Olivia Butt; one *s* one *d*. *Educ:* Ashville Coll., Selwyn Coll., Cambridge (BA 1963, MA 1967); MA Oxon 1981. Asst Registrar, Royal Commn on Historical MSS, 1963–66; Asst Keeper, Nat. Library of Scotland, 1966–81; Librarian, Rhodes House Library, Univ. of Oxford, 1981–93. Vis. Fellow, All Souls Coll., Oxford, 1980. Adv. Editor, New DNB, 1993–. *Publications:* (ed) Scott Bicentenary Essays, 1973; (ed) Sir Leslie Stephen's Mausoleum Book, 1978; (ed) Henry Cockburn, 1979; Sydney Smith, 1980; (contrib.) Illustrated History of Oxford University, 1993. *Address:* The London Library, 14 St James's Square, SW1Y 4LG. *T:* 0171–930 7705; 23 Upland Park Road, Oxford OX2 7RU. *Clubs:* Beefsteak, Brooks's.

BELL, Alexander Gilmour, CB 1991; Chief Reporter for Public Inquiries, Scottish Office, 1979–93, Inquiry Reporter (Consultant), since 1993; *b* 11 March 1933; *s* of Edward and Daisy Bell; *m* 1966, Mary Chisholm; four *s*. *Educ:* Hutchesons' Grammar Sch.; Glasgow Univ. (BL). Admitted Solicitor, 1954. After commercial experience in Far East and in private practice, entered Scottish Office, as Legal Officer, 1967; Dep. Chief Reporter, 1973. *Recreations:* casual outdoor pursuits, choral music. *Address:* Woodend, Haddington, East Lothian EH41 4PE. *T:* Haddington (0162082) 3514.

BELL, (Alexander) Scott; Group Managing Director, Standard Life Assurance Co., since 1988; *b* 4 Dec. 1941; *s* of William Scott Bell and Irene Bell; *m* 1965, Veronica Jane (*née* Simpson); two *s* one *d*. *Educ:* Daniel Stewart's College, Edinburgh. FFA, FPMI. Standard Life Assurance Co.: Asst Actuary for Canada, 1967; Dep. Actuary, 1972; South Region Manager, 1974; Asst Gen. Manager (Finance), 1979; Gen. Manager (Finance), 1985–88. Director: Bank of Scotland, 1988–; Hammerson plc, 1988–; Scottish Financial Enterprise, 1989–; Prime Health Ltd; Prosperity SA. Chm., Associated Scottish Life Offices, 1994–. Hon. Canadian Consul in Scotland, 1994–. *Recreations:* travel, golf, reading. *Address:* Standard Life Assurance Co., 3 George Street, Edinburgh EH2 2XZ. *Clubs:* New (Edinburgh); Bruntsfield Links Golfing Society.

BELL, Alistair Watson; His Honour Judge Bell; a Circuit Judge, since 1978; *b* Edinburgh, 31 March 1930; *s* of Albert William Bell and Alice Elizabeth Watson; *m* 1957, Patricia Margaret Seed; one *s* two *d*. *Educ:* Lanark Grammar Sch.; George Watson's Coll.; Univs of Edinburgh (MA) and Oxford (MA, BCL). 2nd Lieut RASC, 1955. Called to Bar, Middle Temple, 1955; Harmsworth Scholar, 1956; entered practice, Northern Circuit, 1957; a Recorder of the Crown Court, 1972–78. Hon. Recorder, Carlisle, 1990. Contested (L) Chorley, 1964 and Westmorland, 1966. *Recreations:* hill walking, with or without golf clubs, Edinburgh life and letters 1760–1840. *Address:* Courts of Justice, Carlisle.

BELL, Andrew Montgomery; Sheriff of Lothian and Borders, since 1990; *b* 21 Feb. 1940; *s* of James Montgomery Bell and Mary Bell (*née* Cavaye), Edinburgh; *m* 1969, Ann Margaret Robinson; one *s* one *d*. *Educ:* Royal High Sch., Edinburgh; Univ. of Edinburgh (BL). Solicitor, 1961–74; called to Bar, 1975; Sheriff of S Strathclyde, Dumfries and Galloway at Hamilton, 1979–84; Sheriff of Glasgow and Strathkelvin, 1984–90. *Publication:* (contrib.) Stair Memorial Encyclopaedia of Scots Law, 1995. *Recreations:* reading, listening to music. *Address:* 5 York Road, Trinity, Edinburgh EH5 3EJ. *T:* 0131–552 3859. *Club:* New (Edinburgh).

BELL, Archibald Angus, QC (Scot.) 1961; Sheriff of Glasgow and Strathkelvin (formerly Lanark) at Glasgow, since 1973; *b* 13 April 1923; *o s* of James Dunlop Bell, Solicitor, Ayrshire, and Katherine Rachel Gordon Miller; *m* 1949, Dorothy, *d* of Dr Pollok Donald, Edinburgh, and Mrs Dorothy Donald; two *s*. *Educ:* The Leys Sch., Cambridge; Univ. of St Andrews; Univ. of Glasgow. Served War, Royal Navy, 1941–45; Sub-Lieut RNVR. MA, St Andrews, 1947; LLB, Glasgow, 1949; admitted to Faculty of Advocates, 1949; Reporter, Court of Session Cases, 1952–55. Contested (C and U) Maryhill Div. of Glasgow, Gen. Elec., 1955. Standing Junior Counsel in Scotland: to Board of Trade, 1955–57; to War Dept, 1957–61. Comr under NI (Emergency Provisions) Act, 1973–75; Advr to Sec. of State, NI, 1975–. Mem. Court, St Andrews Univ., 1966–70. Pres., Scottish Cricket Union, 1975. *Recreations:* watching the sun rise, getting fun out of games. Formerly: hockey and cricket blue, St Andrews, and Pres. UAU and Dramatic Soc. *Clubs:* Royal Scots (Edinburgh); MCC; Royal and Ancient (St Andrews); RNVR (Scotland).

BELL, Arthur; *see* Bell, E. A.

BELL, Sir Brian (Ernest), KBE 1994 (OBE 1977); Chairman and Managing Director, Brian Bell & Co. Pty Ltd, since 1956; *b* 3 July 1928; *s* of Ernest James Bell and Evelyn Ivy Alice Bell (*née* Zeller); *m* 1962, Jean Ann Clough (*d* 1992); one *s* one *d*. *Educ:* Chinchilla State Sch., Qld, Australia; Toowoomba Grammar Sch., Qld; Queensland Univ. (pharmaceutical chemist, 1949). Went to Papua New Guinea, 1954; Bulk Med. Store, Dept of Health, 1954–56; estabd first Appliance and Service Orgn, 1956. Mem., first Port Moresby CC, 1971–88 (Dep. Lord Mayor, 1973). Citizen of PNG, 1976. Hon. Consul for: Sweden, 1974–88 (Consul Gen., 1988–); Norway, 1984–88 (Consul Gen., 1988–). Mem., Salvation Army Adv. Bd, PNG, 1987–. Chm., Univ. of PNG Foundn, 1985–. Independence Medal (PNG), 1975; Silver Jubilee Medal, 1977; Tenth Anniversary Medal (PNG), 1985; Comdr, Royal Order of Polar Star (Sweden), 1990; Kt 1st Cl., Royal Order of Merit (Norway), 1992. *Recreation:* interest in community affairs. *Address:* Brian Bell and Co. Pty Ltd, PO Box 1228, Boroko, Papua New Guinea. *T:* 255411. *Club:* Papua (Port Moresby).

BELL, Catherine Elisabeth Dorcas, (Mrs R. J. Weber), PhD; Head of Central Policy Unit, Department of Trade and Industry, since 1995; *b* 26 April 1951; *d* of late Frank Douglas Howe and of Phyllis (*née* Walsh); *m* 1993, Richard John Weber; one *s*. *Educ:* Balshaw's Grammar Sch., Leyland, Lancs; Girton Coll., Cambridge (MA); Univ. of Kent (PhD). Joined Department of Trade and Industry, 1975; Pvte Sec. to Sec. of State for Trade and Industry, 1980–81; Principal, 1981; Asst Sec., 1986; Under Sec., 1991; Head of Competition Policy Div., 1991–93; maternity leave, 1993–94; on secondment to Cabinet Office, 1994–95. *Recreations:* opera, ski-ing, gardening. *Address:* Department of Trade and Industry, Ashdown House, 123 Victoria Street, SW1E 6RB. *T:* 0171–215 6712.

BELL, (Charles) Trevor; General Secretary, Colliery Officials and Staffs Area of the National Union of Mineworkers, 1979–89; Member, National Executive Committee of the National Union of Mineworkers, 1979–89; *b* 22 Sept. 1927; *s* of Charles and Annie Bell; *m* 1974, Patricia Ann Tappin. *Educ:* state schools; Technical Coll. (City and Guilds Engrg); Coleg Harlech, N Wales (Trades Union scholarship, 1955). Craftsman in coal mining industry, 1941. Mem., Bd of Trustees, Jim Conway Meml Foundn for Res. and Educn, 1989–. Mem., Labour Party, 1946–. *Recreations:* gardening, golf. *Address:* Wakefield, West Yorks WF2 6SH.

BELL, David Charles Maurice; Chief Executive, Financial Times, since 1993; *b* 30 Sept. 1946; *s* of Roderick Martin Bell and Mary Frances Bell (*née* Wade); *m* 1972, Primrose Frances Moran; two *s* one *d*. *Educ:* Worth Sch.; Trinity Hall, Cambridge (BA 2nd Cl. Hons Hist.); Univ. of Pennsylvania (MA Econs and Pol Sci.). Oxford Mail and Times, 1970–72; Financial Times, 1972–: Washington Corresp., 1975–78; News Editor, Internat. Edn, 1978–80; Features Editor, 1980–85; Man. Editor, 1985–89; Advertisement Dir, 1989–93; Marketing Dir, 1992–93. *Recreations:* cycling, theatre, Victorian social history. *Address:* 35 Belitha Villas, N1 1PE. *T:* 0171–609 4000.

BELL, Dr Donald Atkinson, CEng; Technical Director, Marchland Consulting Ltd, since 1991; *b* 28 May 1941; *s* of late Robert Hamilton Bell and Gladys Mildred Bell; *m* 1967, Joyce Louisa Godber; two *s*. *Educ:* Royal Belfast Academical Instn; Queen's Univ., Belfast (BSc); Southampton Univ. (PhD). FIMechE; MIEE; FBCS. National Physical Lab., 1966–77; Dept of Industry, 1978–82; Dir, Nat. Engrg Lab., 1983–90; Hd of R&D, Strathclyde Inst., 1990–91. *Address:* Marchland Consulting Ltd, 108 East Kilbride Road, Glasgow G76 8JF. *T:* 0141–644 2000.

BELL, Donald L.; *see* Lynden-Bell.

BELL, Prof. Donald Munro; international concert and opera artist; freelance; Professor of Music, Calgary University, since 1982; *b* 19 June 1934; one *s*. *Educ:* South Burnaby High Sch., BC, Canada. Made Wigmore Hall Debut, 1958; since then has sung at Bayreuth Wagner Festival, 1958, 1959, 1960; Lucerne and Berlin Festivals, 1959; Philadelphia and New York debuts with Eugene Ormandy, 1959; Israel, 1962; Russia Recital Tour, 1963;

Glyndebourne Festival, 1963, 1973, 1974, 1982; with Deutsche Oper am Rhein, Düsseldorf, 1964–66; Scottish National Opera, 1974; Scottish Opera, 1978; Basler Kammer Orchestre, 1978; Australian Tour (Musica Viva), 1980. Prof. and Head of Vocal Dept, Ottawa Univ., 1979–82. Directed Opera Workshop at Univ. of Calgary. Dir, Alberta Br., Nat. Opera Assoc, 1986–. Member: Nat. Assoc. of the Teachers Singing, 1985–; Nat. Opera Assoc., 1985– (Dir for Canada, 1988–). Has made recordings. Arnold Bax Medal, 1955. *Address:* University of Calgary, Faculty of Fine Arts, Department of Music, 2500 University Drive NW, Calgary, Alberta T2N 1N4, Canada.

BELL, Edith Alice, OBE 1981; Chief Nursing Officer, Welsh Office, 1972–81; *b* 14 Sept. 1919; *d* of George and Alice Bell. *Educ:* Girls' Grammar Sch., Lancaster. SRN University Hosp., Leeds; SCM St Luke's Hosp., Bradford; Cert. Royal Medico Psychological Assoc., Westwood Hosp., Bradford; Registered Nurse, Mentally Subnormal, Aston Hall, Derby. Ward Sister, Aston Hall Hosp., Derby, 1941–43; Asst Matron, Royal Albert Hosp., Lancaster, 1943–46; Dep. Matron, Darenth Park Hosp., Dartford, 1946–48; Gp Matron, Fountain Gp HMC, London, 1948–60; Management Services Officer, SE RHB, Scotland, 1960–63; Chief Regional Nursing Officer, E Anglian RHB, 1963–72. WHO Fellowship, 1951. Past Member: Gen. Nursing Council, England and Wales; Nat. Council of Nurses; Standing Nursing Adv. Cttee; Services Cttee, Internat. Council of Nurses; Jt Bd, Clinical Nursing Studies; Council, Queen's Inst. of Dist Nursing Service; SW Metrop. RHB: Nursing, Research and Trng Cttees. Chairman: Mental Nurses Cttee; Jt Organizations; Reg. Nursing Officers Gp; Royal Coll. of Nursing Br. Mem., NHS Reorganization Steering Cttee. Hon. Sec., Mental Hosp. Matrons Assoc.; Pres., Inst. of Religion and Medicine. Chairman: CS Retirement Fellowship Gp, 1987– (Chm., N Lancs Br., 1989–; Mem., Cttee of Management, 1988–); Old Girls' Assoc., Girls' Grammar Sch., Lancaster, 1987–. *Publications:* contribs to professional jls. *Recreations:* reading, travel, gardening, supporting ecumenical activities, local Abbeyfield Society. *Address:* Tyla Teg, 51 Farmdale Road, Newlands, Lancaster LA1 4JB. *Club:* Civil Service.

BELL, Edward; Chairman, since 1992, and Publisher, since 1990, HarperCollins UK; Chairman, HarperCollins India, since 1994; *b* 2 Aug. 1949; *s* of Eddie and Jean Bell; *m* 1969, Junette Bannatyne; one *s* two *d*. *Educ:* Airdrie High Sch. Cert. of Business Studies. With Hodder & Stoughton, 1970–85; Man. Dir, Collins General Div., 1985–89; launched Harper Paperbacks in USA, 1989; Dep. Chief Exec., 1990–91, Chief Exec., 1991–92, HarperCollins UK. Dir, Night Kitchen Children's Theatre, New York, 1991–. *Recreations:* reading, golf, supporting Arsenal, opera, collecting old books. *Address:* HarperCollins Publishers, 77–85 Fulham Palace Road, W6 8JB. *T:* 0181–307 4399. *Clubs:* Naval and Military; AutoWink (Epsom).

BELL, Prof. (Ernest) Arthur, CB 1988; PhD; FLS, CChem, FRSC; CBiol, FIBiol; Visiting Professor, King's College London, since 1982; Adjunct Professor, University of Texas at Austin, since 1990; *b* 20 June 1926; *s* of Albert Bell and Rachel Enid (*née* Williams), Gosforth, Northumberland; *m* 1952, Jean Swinton Ogilvie; two *s* one *d*. *Educ:* Dame Allan's Sch., Newcastle upon Tyne; Univ. of Durham (King's Coll., Newcastle upon Tyne) BSc; Trinity Coll., Univ. of Dublin (MA, PhD; Hon. Fellow, 1990). CChem, FRIC (now FRSC) 1961; FIBiol 1987. Res. Chemist, ICI, Billingham, 1946; Demonstr and holder of Sarah Purser Med. Res. Award, TCD, 1947; Asst to Prof. of Biochem., TCD, 1949; Lectr in Biochem., KCL, 1953; Reader in Biochem., Univ. of London, 1964–68; Prof. of Botany, Univ. of Texas, 1968–72; Prof. of Biology, London Univ., and Hd of Dept of Plant Scis, KCL, 1972–81; FKC 1982; Dir, Royal Botanic Gardens, Kew, 1981–88. Sen. Foreign Scientist Fellow, Nat. Sci. Foundn, USA, and Vis. Prof. of Biol., Univ. of Kansas, 1966; Visiting Professor: Univ. of Sierra Leone, 1977; Univ. of Reading, 1982–88; Cecil H. and Ida Green Vis. Prof., Univ. of British Columbia, 1987; Vis. Commonwealth Fellow, Australia, 1980; Emeritus Leverhulme Fellow, 1991–93. Scientific Dir, Texas Botanical Gardens Soc., 1988–. Consultant Dir, CAB-Internat. Mycological Inst. (formerly Commonwealth Mycol. Inst.), 1982–88; Member: Working Party on Naturally Occurring Toxicants in Food, 1983–94; Royal Mint Adv. Cttee, 1992–. Hon. Botanical Adviser, Commonwealth War Graves Commn, 1983–89. President: Section K (Plant Biol.), BAAS, 1985–86; KCL Assoc., 1986–88; Vice Pres., Linnean Soc., 1983–85 (Mem. Council, 1980–85); Mem. Council, RHS, 1985–89; Hon. Mem., Phytochemical Soc. of Europe, 1985. *Publications:* contribs on plant biochem., chemotaxonomy, and chem. ecology to Phytochemistry, and Biochem. Jl. *Recreations:* walking, travel. *Address:* 3 Hillview, Wimbledon, SW20 0TA. *Club:* Athenæum.

BELL, Sir Ewart; *see* Bell, Sir W. E.

BELL, Geoffrey Lakin; President, Geoffrey Bell and Co., New York, since 1982; Chairman, Guinness Mahon Holdings, 1987–93; *b* 8 Nov. 1939; *s* of Walter Lakin Bell and Ann (*née* Barnes); *m* 1973, Joan Abel; one *d*. *Educ:* Grimsby Technical Sch.; London School of Economics and Political Science. Economic Asst, HM Treasury, 1961–63; Vis. Scholar, Fed. Reserve System, principally with Federal Reserve Bank of St Louis, 1963–64; HM Treasury, also Special Lectr at LSE, 1964–66; Economic Advr, British Embassy, Washington, 1966–69; 1969–82: Asst to Chm., J. Henry Schroder Wagg; Dir, Schroder Wagg; Exec. Vice Pres., Schroder Internat. and Sen. Advr, Schroder Bank and Trust Co., NY; Special Columnist on Econs and Finance, The Times, 1969–74; Exec. Sec. and Mem., Gp of Thirty, 1978–. Mem., Court of Govs, LSE, 1994–. Cons. Editor, International Reports, 1983–93. *Publications:* The Euro-Dollar Market and the International Financial System, 1973; numerous articles on internat. econs and finance in UK and USA. *Address:* 17 Abbotsbury House, Abbotsbury Road, W14 8EN. *T:* 0171–603 9408; 300 East 56th Street, New York, NY, USA. *T:* (212) 8381193. *Club:* Reform.

BELL, Sir (George) Raymond, KCMG 1973; CB 1967; Vice-President, European Investment Bank, 1973–78, retired; Hon. Vice-President, European Investment Bank, 1978; *b* 13 March 1916; *e s* of late William Bell and Christabel Bell (*née* Appleton); *m* 1944, Joan Elizabeth, *o d* of late W. G. Coltham and Christina Coltham; two *s* two *d*. *Educ:* Bradford Grammar Sch.; St John's Coll., Cambridge (Scholar). Entered Civil Service, Assistant Principal, 1938; Min. of Health, 1938; transf. Treasury, 1939; served War 1941–44, Royal Navy (Lieut RNVR). Principal, Civil Service, 1945; Asst Sec., 1951; Under-Sec., 1960; Dep. Sec., 1966; Dep. Sec. HM Treasury, 1966–72. Sec. (Finance), Office of HM High Commissioner for the UK in Canada, 1945–48; Counsellor, UK Permanent Delegn to OEEC/NATO, Paris, 1953–56; Principal Private Sec. to Chancellor of Exchequer, 1958–60. Mem. UK Delegation to Brussels Conference, 1961–62 and 1970–72. *Recreations:* music, reading, travel. *Address:* Quartier des Bories, Aouste-sur-Sye, 26400 Crest, Drôme, France. *T:* 75 25 26 94. *Club:* Athenæum.

BELL, Griffin B.; Attorney-General, USA, 1977–79; *b* Americus, Georgia, 31 Oct. 1918; *s* of A. C. Bell and Thelma Pilcher; *m* 1943, Mary Foy Powell; one *s*. *Educ:* Southwestern Coll., Ga; Mercer Univ. (LLB *cum laude* 1948, LLD 1967). Served AUS, 1941–46, reaching rank of Major. Admitted to Georgia Bar, 1947; practice in Savannah and Rome, 1947–53. Partner in King and Spalding, Atlanta, 1953–59, 1976–77, 1979–, Managing Partner, 1959–61; United States Judge, 5th Circuit, 1961–76. Chairman: Atlanta Commn on Crime and Delinquency, 1965–66; CSCE, 1980. Mem., Vis. Cttee, Law Sch., Vanderbilt Univ.; Trustee, Mercer Univ.; Member: Amer. Law Inst.; Amer. Coll. of Trial Lawyers (Pres., 1985–86). *Address:* 206 Townsend Place NW, Atlanta, GA 30327, USA.

BELL, Guy Davies; Director, BAA plc, 1988–89; Managing Director, Gatwick Airport Ltd, 1985–89; *b* 19 May 1933; *s* of Percival and Margaret Bell; *m* 1958, Angela Mary Joan Bickersteth; two *s* one *d* (and one *s* decd). *Educ:* Sedbergh Sch. MICE. British Transport Docks Bd, 1963–68; British Airports Authority, 1968–86, Engrg Dir, 1977–85; BAA, 1986–89. *Recreations:* gardening, open air, music. *Club:* Royal Automobile.

BELL, Prof. Ian Frederick Andrew, PhD; Professor of American Literature, University of Keele, since 1992; *b* 31 Oct. 1947; *s* of Frederick George Bell and Cecilia Bell; *m* 1983, Elizabeth Mary Tagart (marr. diss. 1989); two *s*; one *s*. *Educ:* West Bridgford Grammar Sch.; Univ. of Reading (BA 1970; PhD 1978). Lectr, Sen. Lectr and Reader in Amer. Lit., Univ. of Keele, 1973–92. *Publications:* Critic as Scientist: the modernist poetics of Ezra Pound, 1981; (ed) Ezra Pound: tactics for reading, 1982; (ed) Henry James: fiction as history, 1984; (ed jtly) American Literary Landscapes: the fiction and the fact, 1988; Henry James and the Past: readings into time, 1991; (ed) The Best of O. Henry, 1993; Washington Square: styles of money, 1993. *Recreations:* visual arts, cinema, music. *Address:* Department of American Studies, University of Keele, Staffs ST5 5BG. *T:* Newcastle (Staffs) (01782) 583012.

BELL, Ian Wright, CBE 1964; HM Diplomatic Service, retired; *b* Radlett, Herts, 21 Aug. 1913; *s* of late T. H. D. Bell; *m* 1940, Winifred Mary Ruth Waterfield, *y d* of late E. H. Waterfield, ICS; three *s*. *Educ:* Canford Sch.; St Peter's Hall, Oxford. Vice-Consul: Valparaiso, 1938; Montevideo, 1940; Foreign Office, 1946; First Sec., 1947; First Sec., Addis Ababa, 1949, Chargé d'Affaires, 1949, 1950, 1952 and 1953; Consul, Innsbruck, 1953; First Sec., Prague, 1954, Chargé d'Affaires, 1954 and 1956; Counsellor and Consul-Gen., Jedda, 1956; Counsellor and Official Sec., UK High Commission, Canberra, 1957; HM Consul-Gen., Lyons, 1960–65; Ambassador, Santo Domingo, 1965–69; Consul-Gen., Stuttgart, 1969–73. FRGS. *Publications:* The Scarlet Flower (Poems), 1947; The Dominican Republic, 1981; reviews and articles in various periodicals. *Recreations:* painting, drama, music, walking. *Address:* 4A Fisher Lane, Bingham, Nottingham NG13 8BQ.

BELL, James Steven, CMG 1989; CBE 1964; DFC 1946; QPM 1956; CPM 1950; Director General, Ministry of the Interior, Bahrain, retired; *b* 30 Sept. 1914; *s* of Lachlan Steven Bell and Mary (*née* Bertram). *Educ:* Whitehaven School. Grenadier Guards A Cadet, 1933–35; Kent County Constabulary, 1935–41; RAF, 1941–46; Nigeria Police, 1946–64; Bahrain Public Security, Ministry of the Interior, 1966–93. Nigerian Police Medal, 1960; Order of Bahrain 1st Cl., 1983; Bahrain Public Security Medal for Distinguished Service, 1988. *Recreations:* walking, reading, travel. *Address:* c/o Barclays Bank, Strand Street, Whitehaven, Cumbria CA28 7DL.

BELL, Jocelyn; *see* Bell Burnell, S. J.

BELL, Rear-Adm. John Anthony, CB 1977; Research Fellow, Exeter University, 1986–89, retired; Director, Naval Education Service, 1975–78; Chief Naval Instructor Officer, 1978–79; *b* 25 Nov. 1924; *s* of Mathew Bell, Dundee, and Mary Ann Ellen Bell (*née* Goss), London; *m* 1946, Eileen Joan Woodman; three *d*. *Educ:* St Ignatius Coll., Stamford Hill; London Univ. BA, BSc, LLB. Barrister, Gray's Inn, 1970. RM 1943–45; Schoolmaster, RN, Instr Lt, Courses, Reserve Fleet, service with RAN, 1945–52; HMS Implacable, Theseus, Admiralty, HMS Excellent, 1952–59; HMS Centaur, RN Staff Course, Staff of SACLANT, USA, Directing Staff, RN Staff Course, Western Fleet, 1959–69; Naval Educn Service, Dir, Dept of Naval Oceanography and Meteorology, 1969–75; Instr Captain 1969, Rear-Adm. 1975. Educn Sec. of the BBC, 1979–83; Dep. Chairman: Police Complaints Bd, 1983–85; (Discipline), Police Complaints Authority, 1985–86; Vice Chm., Educn Foundn for Visual Aids, 1986–88; Member: BEC Educn Cttee, 1975–79; C&G Policy Cttee, 1975–79; TEC, 1976–79; Cert. of Extended Educn Cttee, DES, 1978–79; FEFCE SW Cttee, 1993–. Pres., Sea Cadet Corps, Gravesend, 1982–84; Vice-Pres., United Services Catholic Assoc., 1979–; Nat. Vice-Pres., RN Assoc., 1983. Chairman: Kent EC Cttee, 1982–84; RNLI, Wellington, 1988–. Vice-Chm., Bd (formerly Court) of Govs, London Guildhall Univ. (formerly City of London Poly.), 1984–; Governor: SOAS, London Univ., 1975–79; Somerset Coll. of Art and Technology, 1987– (Vice-Chm. of Govs, 1989–); London Coll. of Furniture, 1988–90. Editor-in-Chief, Education Media International, 1988–. KSG 1983. *Recreations:* swimming, wines, travelling, France.

BELL, Prof. John Irving, DM; FRCP; Nuffield Professor of Clinical Medicine, University of Oxford, since 1992; Fellow of Magdalen College, Oxford, since 1990; *b* 1 July 1952; *s* of Robert Edward Bell and Mary Agnes (*née* Wholey). *Educ:* Univ. of Alberta, Canada (BSc Medicine); Oxford Univ. (BA Hons Physiol Sci.; BM, BCh; DM 1990). FRCP 1992. Rhodes Scholar, Univ. of Alberta and Magdalen Coll., Oxford, 1975. Postgraduate training in medicine, 1979–82 (John Radcliffe Hosp., Hammersmith Hosp., Guy's Hosp., Nat. Hosp. for Neurol Disease); Clinical Fellow in Immunology, Stanford Univ., USA, 1982–87; Wellcome Sen. Clin. Fellow, 1987–89, University Lectr, 1989–92, Oxford Univ. *Publications:* scientific papers in immunology and genetics. *Recreations:* rowing, swimming, sailing. *Address:* Magdalen College, Oxford OX1 4AU. *T:* Oxford (01865) 221339. *Clubs:* Leander (Henley-on-Thames); Vincent's (Oxford).

BELL, Sir John Lowthian, 5th Bt *cr* 1885; *b* 14 June 1960; *s* of Sir Hugh Francis Bell, 4th Bt and of Lady Bell (Mary Howson, MB, ChB, *d* of late George Howson, The Hyde, Hambledon); *S* father, 1970; *m* 1985, Venetia, *d* of J. A. Perry, Taunton; one *s* one *d*. *Recreations:* shooting, fishing. *Heir:* *s* John Hugh Bell, *b* 29 July 1988. *Address:* Arncliffe Hall, Ingleby Cross, Northallerton, N Yorks DL6 3PA.

BELL, Prof. (John) Nigel (Berridge), PhD; Professor of Environmental Pollution, Imperial College, University of London, since 1989; *b* 26 April 1943; *s* of John Edward Donald Bell and Dorothy Elise Bell (*née* White); *m* 1st, 1970, Jennifer Margaret Pollard (marr. diss. 1977); 2nd, 1978, Carolyn Mary Davies (marr. diss. 1992); three *s*. *Educ:* Univ. of Manchester (BSc Botany 1964; PhD Plant Ecol. 1969); Univ. of Waterloo, Ont. (MSc Biol. 1965). Teaching Fellow, Univ. of Waterloo, 1964–65; Res. Asst, Bedford Coll., Univ. of London, 1968–70; Imperial College, University of London: Res. Asst, 1970–72; Lectr, 1972–83; Sen. Lectr, 1983–87; Reader in Envmtl Pollution, 1987–89; Dir, Centre for Envmtl Technology, 1986–94; Head, Agricl and Envmtl Mgt Sect., Dept of Biology, 1986–. *Publications:* (ed) Ecological Aspects of Radionuclide Releases, 1983; Air Pollution Injury to Vegetation, 1986; (ed) Acid Rain and Britain's Natural Ecosystems, 1988; Air Pollution and Forest Health in the European Community, 1990; numerous papers in jls on air pollution and radioactive pollution. *Recreations:* classical music, travel, walking, railways. *Address:* Imperial College Centre for Environmental Technology, 48 Prince's Gardens, SW7 2PE. *T:* 0171–594 9288; 48 Western Elms Avenue, Reading, Berks RG3 2AN. *T:* Reading (01734) 580653.

BELL, Joseph Denis Milburn; Chairman, North Western Electricity Board, 1976–85; *b* 2 Sept. 1920; *s* of John Bell, BEM, and Ann Bell; *m* 1949, Wilhelmina Maxwell Miller; one *s* one *d*. *Educ:* Bishop Auckland Grammar Sch.; St Edmund Hall, Oxford (MA). Served

War, RAF, 1941–45. Contested (Lab) Canterbury, 1945. Lectr in Modern Econ. History, Univ. of Glasgow, 1946; National Coal Board: Indust. Relations Dept, 1954; Dep. Indust. Relations Dir, Durham Div., 1963; Electricity Council: Statistical Officer, Indust. Relations Dept, 1966; Dep. Indust. Relations Adviser (Negotiating), 1967; Indust. Relations Adviser, 1972. *Publications:* Industrial Unionism: a critical analysis, 1949 (repr. in Trade Unions: selected readings, ed W. E. J. McCarthy, 1972); (contrib.) The Scottish Economy (ed A. K. Cairncross), 1953; (contrib.) The System of Industrial Relations in Great Britain (ed A. Flanders and H. A. Clegg), 1954; (contrib.) The Lessons of Public Enterprise (ed M. Shanks), 1963. *Address:* Rossways, Broad Lane, Hale, Altrincham, Cheshire WA15 0DH. *T:* 0161–980 4451.

BELL, Prof. Kathleen Myra, CBE 1978; Professor of Social Studies in the University of Newcastle upon Tyne, 1971–83, now Professor Emeritus; *b* 6 March 1920; *d* of late Walter Petty and late Myra Petty; *m* 1945, Rev. Jack Martin Bell (*d* 1993); one *s* one *d*. *Educ:* St Joseph's Coll., Bradford; Univ. of Manchester (Prize in Public Admin. 1940). Asst Personnel Officer, later Trng Officer, Min. of Supply ROF, 1942–45; Tutor and Lectr in Univ. Depts of Extra-Mural Studies, 1945–63; University of Newcastle upon Tyne: Lectr in Social Studies, 1963–67; Sen. Tutor, 1967–69; Sen. Lectr, 1969–71. Member: Lord Chancellor's Council on Tribunals, 1963–81 (Ch. person, Cttee on Functions of the Council, 1977–81); Social Admin. Cttee of Jt Univ. Council for Public and Social Admin., 1965–83; BBC Programmes Complaints Commn, 1978–81; Academic Adviser (apptd by Govt Chief Scientist) to DHSS Social Security Res. Policy Cttee, 1976–83; Expert Adviser to OECD Directorate for Social Affairs and Educn, for their project, Role of Women in the Economy, 1976–77; Mem., AHA for N Tyneside, 1974–77; Mem., Davies Cttee on Hosp. Complaints Procedure, 1971–73; Member Editorial Board: Jl of Social Policy, 1971–78; Jl of Social Welfare Law, 1977–. *Publications:* Tribunals in the Social Services, 1969; Disequilibrium in Welfare, 1973; Research Study on Supplementary Benefit Appeal Tribunals—Review of Main Findings, Conclusions and Recommendations, 1975; The Functions of the Council on Tribunals, 1980; various papers in Jl of Social Policy, Econ. and Social Admin, and other jls. *Address:* Silverton, 86 Trinity Road, Edinburgh EH5 3JU. *Club:* Scottish Arts (Edinburgh).

BELL, Leslie Gladstone, CEng, FRINA; RCNC; Director of Naval Ship Production, Ministry of Defence, 1977–79, retired; *b* 20 Oct. 1919; *s* of late John Gladstone Bell and Jessie Gray Bell (*née* Quigley); *m* 1963, Adriana Agatha Jacoba van den Berg; one *s* one *d*. *Educ:* Portsmouth Dockyard Tech. Coll.; Royal Naval Engineering Coll., Keyham; Royal Naval Coll., Greenwich. Staff Constructor Cdr, Home Fleet, 1953–56; Aircraft Carrier Design, 1956–59; Chief Constructor, Weapon Development, 1959–67; IDC, 1968; Asst Dir, Submarine Design, 1969–72; Director, Submarine Project Team, 1972–77. *Recreations:* gardening, golf, music. *Address:* Haytor, Old Midford Road, Bath, Avon BA2 7DH. *T:* Bath (01225) 833357. *Club:* Bath Golf.

BELL, Martin, OBE 1992; Foreign Affairs Correspondent, BBC TV News, since 1994; *b* 31 Aug. 1938; *s* of late Adrian Hanbury Bell and Marjorie H. Bell; *m* 1971, Nelly Lucienne Gourdon; two *d*; *m* 1985, Rebecca D. Sobel. *Educ:* The Leys Sch., Cambridge; King's Coll., Cambridge (MA). BBC TV News: Reporter, 1965–77; Diplomatic Correspondent, 1977–78; Chief Washington Correspondent, 1978–89; Berlin Correspondent, 1989–93; E European Correspondent, 1993–94. Pool TV Reporter, 7th Armoured Bde, Gulf War, 1991. Royal Television Society Reporter of the Year, 1977, TV Journalist of the Year, 1992. *Address:* c/o Foreign Desk, Room 6236, BBC Television Centre, Wood Lane, W12 7RJ.

BELL, Martin George Henry: Senior Partner, Ashurst Morris Crisp, 1986–92; Director, Laird Group, since 1994; *b* 16 Jan. 1935; *s* of Leonard George Bell and Phyllis Bell (*née* Green); *m* 1965, Shirley Wrightson; two *s*. *Educ:* Charterhouse; Coll. of Law. Nat. Service, 1953–55. Articles, 1956–61, admitted Solicitor, 1961, Assistant, 1961, Partner, 1963, Ashurst Morris Crisp. *Recreations:* walking, scuba diving, ski-ing. *Address:* Mulberry, Woodbury Hill, Loughton, Essex IG10 1JB. *T:* 0181–508 1188.

BELL, Michael John Vincent, CB 1992; Deputy Chief of Defence Procurement (Support), Ministry of Defence, since 1995; *b* 9 Sept. 1941; *e s* of C. R. V. Bell, OBE and late Jane Bell, MBE; *m* 1983, Mary Shippen, *o d* of late J. W. Shippen and Mrs Margaret Shippen; one *s* two *d*. *Educ:* Winchester Coll.; Magdalen Coll., Oxford (BA Lit. Hum.). Res. Associate, Inst. for Strategic Studies, 1964; Ministry of Defence: Asst Principal, 1965; Principal, 1969; Asst Sec., 1975; on loan to HM Treasury, 1977–79; Asst Under Sec. of State (Resources and Programmes), 1982–84; Dir Gen. of Management Audit, 1984–86; Asst Sec. Gen. for Defence Plannning and Policy, NATO, 1986–88; Dep. Under-Sec. of State (Finance), 1988–92, (Defence Procurement), 1992–95. *Recreations:* motorcycling, military history. *Address:* Ministry of Defence, Main Building, Whitehall, SW1A 2HB.

BELL, Nigel; *see* Bell, J. N. B.

BELL, Prof. Peter Robert; Emeritus Professor of Botany, University of London; *b* 18 Feb. 1920; *s* of Andrew and Mabel Bell; *m* 1952, Elizabeth Harrison; two *s*. *Educ:* Simon Langton School, Canterbury; Christ's Coll., Cambridge (MA 1949). University College London: Asst Lecturer in Botany, 1946; Lectr in Botany, 1949; Reader in Botany, 1967; Prof. of Botany, 1967; Quain Prof. of Botany and Head of Dept of Botany and Microbiol., 1978–85; Dean of Science, 1979–82; Mem. Council, 1979–85. Visiting Professor: Univ. of California, Berkeley, 1966–67; Univ. of Delhi, India, 1970. British Council Distinguished Visitor, NZ, 1976; many other visits overseas, including exploration of Ecuadorian Andes. Vice-Pres., Linnean Soc., 1962–65; Mem. Biological Sciences Cttee, 1974–79 (Chm. Panel 1, 1977–79), SRC. *Publications:* Darwin's Biological Work, Some Aspects Reconsidered, 1959; (with C. F. Woodcock) The Diversity of Green Plants, 1968, 3rd edn 1983; (trans., with D. E. Coombe) Strasburger's Textbook of Botany, 8th English edn, 1976; Green Plants: their origin and diversity, 1993; scientific papers on botanical topics, particularly reproductive cells of land plants, and on history of botany. *Recreation:* mountains. *Address:* 13 Granville Road, Barnet, Herts EN5 4DU. *T:* 0181–449 9331.

BELL, Prof. Peter Robert Frank, MD; FRCS, FRCSGlas; Professor of Surgery, University of Leicester, since 1974; *b* 12 June 1938; *s* of Frank and Ruby Bell; *m* 1961, Anne Jennings; one *s* two *d*. *Educ:* Univ. of Sheffield (MB, ChB Hons 1961; MD 1969). FRCS 1965; FRCSGlas 1968. Postgrad. surg. career in Sheffield hosps, 1961–65; Lectr in Surgery, Univ. of Glasgow, 1965–68; Sir Henry Wellcome Travelling Fellow, Univ. of Colorado, 1968–69; Consultant Surgeon and Sen. Lectr, Western Infirm., Glasgow, 1969–74. President: Surgical Res. Soc., 1986–88; European Soc. of Vascular Surgery, 1994; Mem. Council, RCS, 1992–. *Publications:* Surgical Aspects of Haemodialysis, 1974, 2nd edn 1983; Operative Arterial Surgery, 1982; Arterial Surgery of the Lower Limb, 1991; Surgical Management of Vascular Disease, 1992; pubns on vascular disease, transplantation and cancer in med. and surg. jls. *Recreations:* horticulture, oil painting, tennis. *Address:* Department of Surgery, Clinical Sciences Building, PO Box 65, Royal Infirmary, Leicester LE2 7LX. *Club:* Leicestershire (Leicester).

BELL, Prof. Quentin (Claudian Stephen), FRSA; FRSL; Emeritus Professor of the History and Theory of Art, Sussex University; painter, sculptor, potter, author, art critic; *b* 19 Aug. 1910; 2nd *s* of late Clive and Vanessa Bell; *m* 1952, Anne Olivier Popham; one *s* two *d*. *Educ:* Leighton Park. Exhibitions, 1935, 1947, 1949, 1972, 1977, 1981, 1982, 1986. Political warfare executive, 1941–43. Lectr in Art Education, King's Coll., Newcastle, 1952; Senior Lecturer, 1956; Prof. of Fine Art, University of Leeds, 1962–67 (Head of Dept of Fine Art, 1959); Slade Professor of Fine Art, Oxford Univ., 1964–65; Ferens Prof. of Fine Art, University of Hull, 1965–66; Prof. of History and Theory of Art, Sussex Univ., 1967–75. Commissioned Sculpture for Univ. of Leeds. MA Dunelm, 1957. Regular contributor to Listener, 1951–60. *Publications:* On Human Finery, 1947, rev. edn 1976; Those Impossible English (with Helmut Gernsheim), 1951; Roger Montané, 1961; The Schools of Design, 1963; Ruskin, 1963; Victorian Artists, 1967; Bloomsbury, 1968; Virginia Woolf, a Biography, 2 vols, 1972 (James Tait Black Meml Prize; Duff Cooper Meml Prize); A New and Noble School, 1982; Techniques of Terracotta, 1983; The Brandon Papers (novel), 1985; Bad Art, 1989. *Address:* 81 Heighton Street, Firle, Sussex BN8 6NZ. *T:* Glynde (01273) 858201.

BELL, Sir Raymond; *see* Bell, Sir G. R.

BELL, Robert Donald Murray, CB 1966; *b* 8 Oct. 1916; *s* of Robert William and Mary Caroline Bell; *m* 1941, Karin Anna Smith; one *s* one *d*. *Educ:* Christ's Hosp.; Clare Coll., Cambridge. First Class Honours, Natural Sciences Tripos (Physics), 1938. Joined Scottish Office, 1938. War of 1939–45: Royal Artillery, 1940–45 (Mil. Coll. of Science, Bury, 1943). Principal, Scottish Home Dept, 1946; Private Sec. to Sec. of State for Scotland, 1947–50; Under-Secretary in Scottish Depts, 1959–76.

BELL, Hon. Sir Rodger, Kt 1993; **Hon. Mr Justice Bell;** a Judge of the High Court of Justice, Queen's Bench Division, since 1993; a Judge of Employment Appeal Tribunal, since 1994; *b* 13 Sept. 1939; *s* of John Thornton Bell and Edith Bell; *m* 1969, (Sylvia) Claire Tatton Brown; one *s* three *d*. *Educ:* Brentwood Sch.; Brasenose Coll., Oxford (BA). Called to the Bar, Middle Temple, 1963, Bencher, 1989; QC 1982; a Recorder, 1980–93; Chm., NHS Tribunal, 1991–93; Legal Mem., Mental Health Review Tribunals, 1983–93; Mem., Parole Board, 1990–93. *Address:* Royal Courts of Justice, Strand, WC2A 2LL.

BELL, Prof. Ronald Leslie, CB 1988; FEng 1991; FIM, FInstP, FIAgrE; Director-General, Agricultural Development and Advisory Service and the Regional Organisation, and Chief Scientific Adviser, Ministry of Agriculture, Fisheries and Food, 1984–89; *b* 12 Sept. 1929; *s* of Thomas William Alexander Bell and Annie (*née* Mapleston); *m* 1954, Eleanor Joy (*née* Lancaster); one *s* two *d*. *Educ:* The City School, Lincoln; Univ. of Birmingham (BSc, PhD). Research Fellow, Royal Radar Estabt, Malvern, 1954–57; Imperial College, Univ. of London: Lectr in Metallurgy, 1957–62; Reader in Metallurgy, 1962–65; University of Southampton: Prof. of Engrg Materials, 1965–77; Head of Dept of Mech. Engrg, 1968; Dean of Faculty of Engrg and Applied Scis, 1970–72; Dep. Vice Chancellor, 1972–76; Dir, NIAE, 1977–84. Vis. Prof., Cranfield Inst. of Technology, 1979–89. Pres., British Crop Protection Council, 1985–89; Member: AFRC, 1984–89; Council, RASE, 1984–89. Sen. Treas., Methodist Church Div. of Ministries, 1992–. Hon. DSc Southampton, 1985. *Publications:* papers in learned jls dealing with twinning and brittle fracture of metals, grain boundary sliding and creep in metals, dislocations in semi-conductors, agricultural engineering. *Recreations:* the bassoon, painting, Association football, gardening. *Address:* 3 Old Garden Court, Mount Pleasant, St Albans AL3 4RQ.

BELL, Ronald Percy, MA; FRS 1944; FRSE 1968; FRSC; Professor of Chemistry, University of Stirling, 1967–75, now Emeritus; Hon. Research Professor of Chemistry, University of Leeds, 1976–82; *b* 1907; *e s* of E. A. Bell, Maidenhead; *m* 1931, Margery Mary West; one *s*. *Educ:* County Boys' Sch., Maidenhead; Balliol Coll., Oxford. Bedford Lecturer in Physical Chemistry, Balliol Coll., 1932; Fellow of Balliol Coll., 1933 (Vice-Master, 1965); Hon. Fellow, 1967, Univ. Lecturer and Demonstrator, Oxford Univ., 1938; Univ. Reader, Oxford Univ., 1955. George Fisher Baker Lectr, Cornell Univ., 1958; Nat. Science Foundn Fellow, Brown Univ., 1964; Visiting Professor: Weizmann Inst. of Sci., Israel, 1973; Tech. Univ. of Denmark, Lyngby, 1976. President: Faraday Soc., 1956; Chemistry Section, British Assoc. Meeting, Durham, 1970; Vice-Pres. Chemical Soc., 1958 (Tilden Lectureship, 1941; Liversidge Lectureship, 1973–74; Spiers Meml Lectureship, 1975). Foreign Mem. Royal Danish Acad. of Arts and Sciences, 1962; Foreign Associate, Nat. Acad. of Sciences, USA, 1972; Foreign Hon. Mem., Amer. Acad. of Arts and Scis, 1974. Hon. LLD Illinois Inst. of Techn., 1965; Hon. DTech, Tech. Univ. of Denmark, 1969; Hon. DSc Kent, 1974; Hon. DUniv. Stirling, 1977. Leverhulme Emeritus Fellow, 1976. Meldola Medal, Inst. of Chemistry, 1936, Chem. Soc. Award in Kinetics and Mechanism, 1974. *Publications:* Acid-Base Catalysis, 1941; Acids and Bases, 1952, 2nd edn 1969; The Proton in Chemistry, 1959, 2nd edn 1973; The Tunnel Effect in Chemistry, 1980; papers in scientific journals. *Address:* Flat 5, Park Villa Court, Roundhay, Leeds LS8 1EB. *T:* Leeds (0113) 266 4236.

BELL, Scott; *see* Bell, Alexander Scott.

BELL, Stuart; MP (Lab) Middlesbrough, since 1983; barrister; *b* High Spen, Co. Durham, 16 May 1938; *s* of Ernest and Margaret Rose Bell; *m* 1st, 1960, Margaret, *d* of Mary Bruce; one *s* one *d*; 2nd, 1980, Margaret, *d* of Edward and Mary Allan; one *s*. *Educ:* Hookergate Grammar Sch. Formerly colliery clerk, newspaper reporter, typist and novelist. Called to the Bar, Gray's Inn, 1970. Conseil Juridique and Internat. Lawyer, Paris, 1970–77. Member: Newcastle City Council, 1980–83 (Mem., Finance, Health and Environment, Arts and Recreation Cttees; Chm., Youth and Community Cttee; Vice-Chm., Educn Cttee); Educn Cttee, AMA; Council of Local Educn Authorities; Newcastle AHA (T), 1980–83. Contested (Lab) Hexham, 1979. PPS to Dep. Leader of Opposition, Rt Hon. Roy Hattersley, 1983–84; Opposition front bench spokesman: on NI, 1984–87; on trade and industry, 1992–. Founder Mem. and Vice Chm., British–Irish Inter Parly Body, 1990–93; Exec. Mem., IPU British Gp, 1990– (Vice Chm., 1991–). Member: Fabian Soc.; Soc. of Lab. Lawyers; GMBATU. *Publications:* Paris 69 (novel), 1973; Days That Used To Be (novel), 1975; How to Abolish the Lords (Fabian Tract), 1981; Valuation for United States Customs Purposes, 1981; When Salem Came to the Boro: the true story of the Cleveland child abuse crisis, 1989; Annotation of The Children Act, 1989. *Recreation:* writing. *Address:* House of Commons, SW1A 0AA.

BELL, Sir Timothy John Leigh, (Sir Tim), Kt 1990; Chairman, Lowe Bell Communications, since 1987; Director, Centre for Policy Studies, since 1989; *b* 18 Oct. 1941; *s* of Arthur Leigh Bell and Greta Mary Bell (*née* Findlay); *m* 1988, Virginia Wallis Hornbrook; one *s* one *d*. *Educ:* Queen Elizabeth's Grammar Sch., Barnet, Herts. FIPA. ABC Television, 1959–61; Colman Prentis & Varley, 1961–63; Hobson Bates, 1963–66; Geers Gross, 1966–70; Man. Dir, Saatchi & Saatchi, 1970–75; Chm. and Man. Dir, Saatchi & Saatchi Compton, 1975–85; Gp Chief Exec., Lowe Howard-Spink Campbell Ewald, 1985–87; Dep. Chm., Lowe Howard-Spink & Bell, 1987–89. Special Adviser to: Chm. NCB, 1984–86; South Bank Bd, 1985–86. Chm., Charity Projects, 1984–. Member: Industry Cttee, SCF; Public Affairs Cttee, WWF, 1985–88; Public Relations Cttee, Greater London Fund for the Blind, 1979–86; Council, Royal Opera House, 1982–85;

Steering Cttee, Percent Club. Governor, BFI, 1983–86. Council Mem., Sch. of Communication Arts, 1985–87. *Address:* (office) 7 Hertford Street, W1Y 7DY.

BELL, Trevor; *see* Bell, C. T.

BELL, Walter (Fancourt), CMG 1967; *b* 7 Nov. 1909; *s* of Canon George Fancourt Bell; *m* 1948, Katharine Spaatz, Washington, DC, USA; no *c. Educ:* Tonbridge Sch. Barrister, Inner Temple. Vice-Consul (Acting): New York, 1935–40; Mexico City, 1940–41; New York, 1941–42; Foreign Office, London, 1942–45; 1st Sec., Brit. Embassy, Washington, DC, 1946–48; attached E Africa High Commn, Nairobi, Kenya, 1949–52; 1st Sec., Brit. High Commn, New Delhi, 1952–55; attached War Office, London, 1956–57; Adviser, Federal Govt, W Indies, 1957–60; attached Govt of Kenya, 1961–63; Counsellor, British High Commn, Nairobi, Kenya, 1963–67. US Medal of Freedom with Bronze Palm, 1946. *Recreation:* walking. *Address:* 6 Onslow Square, SW7 3NP. *Club:* Travellers'.

BELL, William Archibald Ottley Juxon; Chairman, Heritage of London Trust, since 1980; *b* 7 July 1919; *s* of Maj. William Archibald Juxon Bell and Mary Isabel Maude Bell (*née* Ottley); *m* 1947, Belinda Mary (*née* Dawson); three *s* three *d. Educ:* Eton; Trinity College, Oxford (MA(Hist.)). Temp. Captain, Welsh Guards, 1940–45. Entered HM Foreign Service, 1945; Political Private Sec. to Sir Terence Shone, UK High Comr in India, 1946–47; Sec. to Exec. Dirs, British S Africa Co., 1947–50; Partner and Dir, King & Shaxson Ltd (Bill-brokers), 1950–90. Mem. of Lloyd's, 1970. Mem., for Chelsea, GLC and ILEA, 1970–86. Chairman: Diocesan Bd of Finance for Oxon, 1973–76; GLC Historic Bldgs Cttee, 1977–81; Oxfordshire Buildings Trust, 1987–93; English Heritage Commemorative Plaques Working Gp, 1990–95; Member: Cttee, Oxfordshire Historic Churches Trust, 1970–; UK Cttee for European Architectural Heritage Year, 1973–75; London Adv. Cttee, English Heritage, 1986–90. High Sheriff, Oxon, 1978–79. *Recreations:* shooting, golf, music. *Address:* Cottisford House, near Brackley, Northants NN13 5SW. *T:* Finmere (012804) 247; 165 Cranmer Court, SW3 3HF. *T:* 0171–589 1033. *Clubs:* White's, Pratt's.

BELL, William Bradshaw; JP; Chairman, Northern Ireland Gas Employers' Board, 1984–87; *b* 9 Oct. 1935; *s* of Robert Bell and Mary Ann Bell; *m* 1969, Leona Maxwell; one *s* three *d. Educ:* Fane Street Primary School, Belfast; Grosvenor High School, Belfast. Member: for N Belfast, NI Constitutional Convention, 1975–76; Belfast City Council, 1976–85 (Unionist spokesman on housing, 1976–79); for S Antrim, NI Assembly, 1982–86 (Dep. Chm., Finance and Personnel Cttee, 1984–86); Lisburn Bor. Council, 1989– (Chm., Police Liaison Cttee, 1991–). Lord Mayor of Belfast, 1979–80; JP Belfast, 1985. *Recreations:* music, motoring, gardening, writing.

BELL, William Edwin, CBE 1980; Deputy Chairman, Enterprise Oil plc, since 1991 (Chairman, 1984–91); *b* 4 Aug. 1926; *s* of late Cuthbert Edwin Bell and Winifred Mary Bell (*née* Simpson); *m* 1952, Angela Josephine Vaughan; two *s* two *d. Educ:* Birmingham University (BSc Civil Eng.); Royal School of Mines, Imperial College. Joined Royal Dutch Shell Group, 1948; tech. and managerial appts, Venezuela, USA, Kuwait, Indonesia; Shell International Petroleum Co. (Middle East Coordination), 1965–73; Gen. Man., Shell UK Exploration and Production and Dir, Shell UK, 1973; Man. Dir, Shell UK, 1976–79; Middle East Regional Coordinator and Dir, Shell International Petroleum Co., 1980–84, retired; non-exec. Dir, Costain Group, 1982–92. Pres., UK Offshore Operators Assoc., 1975–76. *Publications:* contribs to internat. tech. jls, papers on offshore oil industry develts. *Recreations:* golf, sailing. *Address:* Fordcombe Manor, near Tunbridge Wells, Kent TN3 0SE. *Club:* Nevill Golf.

BELL, Sir (William) Ewart, KCB 1982 (CB 1978); Head of Northern Ireland Civil Service, 1979–84 and Second Permanent Secretary, Northern Ireland Office, 1981–84, retired; *b* 13 Nov. 1924; *s* of late Rev. Dr Frederick G. Bell and late Margaret Jane Ewart; *m* 1957, Kathleen Ross Boucher; two *d. Educ:* Methodist Coll., Belfast; Wadham Coll., Oxford (MA). Asst Master, Cheltenham Coll., 1946–48; Northern Ireland Civil Service, 1948–84; Min. of Health and Local Govt, 1948–52; Min. (later Dept) of Commerce, 1952–76; Asst Sec., 1963–70; Dep. Sec., 1970–73; Sec., 1973–76; Permanent Sec., Dept of Finance, 1976–79. Dir, Ulster Bank Ltd, 1985–95. Hon. Treas., QUB, 1985–93. Pres., Irish RFU, 1986–87; Chm., Rugby World Cup Ltd, 1993–. *Recreations:* gardening, golf, Rugby football (Irish Rugby International, 1953).

BELL, Sir William H. D. M.; *see* Morrison-Bell.

BELL, William Lewis, CMG 1970; MBE 1945; retired; Information Officer, University of Oxford, 1977–84; *b* 31 Dec. 1919; *s* of Frederick Robinson Bell and Kate Harper Bell (*née* Lewis); *m* 1943, Margaret Giles; one *s* one *d. Educ:* Hymers Coll., Hull; Oriel Coll., Oxford. Served The Gloucestershire Regt (Major), 1940–46. Colonial Administrative Service, Uganda, 1946–63: Dep. Sec. to the Treasury, 1956–58; Perm. Sec., Min. of Social Services, 1958–63; Fellow, Economic Develt Inst., World Bank, 1958. Chm., Uganda National Parks, 1962; Pres., Uganda Sports Union, 1961–62. Director, Cox & Danks Ltd (Metal Industries Group), 1963–64. Sec. to the Governors, Westfield Coll., Univ. of London, 1964–65; Founding Head of British Develt Div. in the Caribbean, ODA, 1966–72; UK Dir, Caribbean Develt Bank, 1970–72; Dir-Gen., Technical Educn and Training Org. for Overseas Countries, 1972–77. *Recreations:* cricket, Caribbeana. *Address:* Hungry Hatch, Fletching, E Sussex TN22 3SH. *Clubs:* MCC; Vincent's (Oxford).

BELL, William Rupert Graham, CB 1978; Under Secretary, Department of Industry, 1975–80; *b* 29 May 1920; *m* 1950, Molly Bolton; two *d. Educ:* Bradford Grammar Sch.; St John's Coll., Cambridge (Scholar). Served Royal Artillery, 1940–45 (despatches). Asst Principal, Min. of Fuel and Power, 1948; Principal, 1949; Asst Sec., 1959; Under-Sec., Min. of Power, 1966–70, DTI, 1970–72; Deputy Principal, Civil Service Coll., 1972–75. Imperial Defence Coll., 1965. *Address:* 47 Chiswick Staithe, Hartington Road, W4 3TP. *T:* 0181–994 2545.

BELL BURNELL, Prof. (Susan) Jocelyn, PhD; FRAS, FInstP; astronomer; Professor of Physics, Open University, since 1991; *b* 15 July 1943; *d* of G. Philip and M. Allison Bell; *m* 1968, Martin Burnell (separated 1989); one *s. Educ:* The Mount Sch., York; Glasgow Univ. (BSc); New Hall, Cambridge (PhD). FRAS 1969. Res. Fellowships, Univ. of Southampton, 1968–73; Res. Asst, Mullard Space Science Lab., UCL, 1974–82; Sen. Res. Fellow, 1982–86, SSO, 1986–89, Grade 7, 1989–91, Royal Observatory, Edinburgh. An Editor, The Observatory, 1973–76. Lectures: Marie Curie, 1994; Appleton, 1994. Mem., IAU, 1979–. Hon. DSc: Heriot-Watt, 1993; Newcastle, 1995; Warwick, 1995; DUniv York, 1994. Michelson Medal, Franklin Inst., Philadelphia (jtly with Prof. A. Hewish), 1973; J. Robert Oppenheimer Meml Prize, Univ. of Miami, 1978; Rennie Taylor Award, Amer. Tentative Soc., NY, 1978; (first) Beatrice M. Tinsley Prize, Amer. Astronomical Soc., 1987; Herschel Medal, RAS, 1989. Discovered the first four pulsars (neutron stars), 1967–68. *Publications:* Broken for Life, 1989; (ed jtly) Next Generation Infrared Space Observatory, 1992; papers in Nature, Astronomy and Astrophysics, Jl of Geophys. Res., Monthly Notices of RAS. *Recreations:* Quaker interests, walking. *Address:* Department of Physics, The Open University, Walton Hall, Milton Keynes MK7 6AA.

BELL DAVIES, Vice-Adm. Sir Lancelot (Richard), KBE 1977; *b* 18 Feb. 1926; *s* of late Vice-Adm. R. Bell Davies, VC, CB, DSO, AFC, and Mrs Bell Davies, Lee on Solent, Hants; *m* 1949, Emmeline Joan (*née* Molengraaff), Wassenaar, Holland; one *s* two *d. Educ:* Boxgrove Preparatory Sch., Guildford; RN Coll., Dartmouth. War of 1939–45: Midshipman, HMS Norfolk, 1943 (Scharnhorst sunk); joined Submarines, 1944. First Command, HMS Subtle, 1953; subseq. commands: HMS Explorer, 1955; Comdr, HMS Leander, 1962; Captain: HMS Forth, also SM7, 1967, and HMS Bulwark, 1972; Rear-Adm., 1973. Ministry of Defence Posts: (Comdr) Naval Staff, 1960; (Captain) Naval Asst to Controller, 1964; Director of Naval Warfare, 1969; Comdr, British Naval Staff, Washington, and UK Rep. to Saclant, 1973–75; Supreme Allied Commander Atlantic's Rep. in Europe, 1975–78; Comdt, Nato Defence Coll., Rome, 1978–81. Chm., Sea Cadet Council, 1983–92. CIMgt (FBIM 1977). *Recreations:* sailing, skiing, gardening. *Address:* Holly Hill Lodge, 123 Barnes Lane, Sarisbury Green, Southampton SO3 6BH. *T:* Locks Heath (01489) 573131. *Clubs:* Naval and Military; Royal Yacht Squadron, Royal Naval Sailing Association.

BELLAK, John George; Chairman, Severn Trent plc (formerly Severn-Trent Water Authority), 1983–94; *b* 19 Nov. 1930; *m* 1960, Mary Prudence Marshall; three *s* one *d. Educ:* Uppingham; Clare College, Cambridge. MA (Economics). Sales and Marketing Dir, Royal Doulton, 1968–80, Man. Dir, 1980–83; Chairman: Royal Crown Derby, 1972–83; Lawleys Ltd, 1972–83. President: British Ceramic Manufacturers' Fedn, 1982–83; Fedn of European Porcelain and Earthenware Manufacturers, 1982–83; European Waste Water Group, 1991–93; Dep. Chm., Water Services Assoc., 1992 (Vice-Chm., 1990–91; Chm., 1991). Chm., Abtrust High Income Investment Trust, 1994–; Dir, Ascot Holdings, 1993–. Mem., Grand Council, CBI, 1984–94. Mem. Court, Keele Univ., 1984–. *Recreations:* ornithology, field sports, reading. *Address:* 1 Council House Court, Shrewsbury SY1 2AU. *Clubs:* Carlton, Beefsteak.

BELLAMY, Rear-Adm. Albert John, CB 1968; OBE 1956; CMath, FIMA; first Deputy Director, Polytechnic of the South Bank, 1970–80; *b* Upton-on-Severn, 26 Feb. 1915; *s* of late A. E. Bellamy and late Mrs A. E. Bellamy; *m* 1942, Dorothy Joan Lawson; one *s* one *d. Educ:* Hanley Castle Grammar Sch.; Downing Coll., Cambridge (Buchanan Exhibitioner; 1st cl. hons Pts I and II, Math. tripos, MA). FIMA 1960; CMath 1992. Asst master, Berkhamsted Sch., 1936–39. Joined RN, 1939, as Instructor Lieut; Fleet Instr and Meteorological Officer, America and WI, 1948–50 (HMS Glasgow); Instr Comdr, 1950; Headmaster, RN Schs, Malta, 1951–54; HMS Ark Royal, 1955–56; Dean of the College, RN Engineering Coll., Manadon, Plymouth, 1956–60; Instr Capt., 1958; staff of Dir, Naval Educn Service, 1960–63; Dir of Studies, RN Electrical, Weapons and Radio Engineering Sch., HMS Collingwood, 1963–65; Instr Rear-Adm., 1965; Dir, Naval Educn Service and Hd of Instructor Branch, MoD, 1965–70. Mem., Home Office Extended Interview non-Service Mems Panel, 1980–87. *Recreations:* gardening, show jumping (BSJA representative for Dorset), crosswords, parish council work, finance work with two charities, keeping old age at bay by being involved. *Address:* The Cottage, Kington Magna, Gillingham, Dorset SP8 5EG. *T:* East Stour (01747) 838668.

BELLAMY, Alexander (William); retired; Senior Legal Assistant, Council on Tribunals, 1967–76 (temporary Legal Assistant, 1963–67); *b* Aug. 1909; *m* 1931, Lena Marie Lauga Massy. *Educ:* Mill Hill Sch.; Clare Coll., Cambridge. Called to Bar, Gray's Inn, 1934; practised at Bar, London, 1934–38; Magistrate, Straits Settlements and FMS, 1938; Penang & Province Wellesley Volunteer Force, 1940–42; escaped from Singapore in 1942; seconded as District Magistrate, Gold Coast, 1942; legal staff, Malaya Planning Unit, WO, 1944; SO2 (Legal) SEAC, 1944; SO1 British Mil. Admin (Malaya), 1945; Pres., Superior Court, Penang, 1945; released from mil. service overseas, 1946, with Hon. rank of Lt Col; Crown Counsel, Singapore, 1946; District Judge (Civil), Singapore, 1948; District Judge and 1st Magistrate, Singapore, 1952; actg Puisne Judge, Fed. of Malaya, 1953–54; Puisne Judge, Supreme Court, Nigeria, 1955; Actg Chief Justice, High Court of Lagos and Southern Cameroons, 1959, 1960; Actg Chief Justice, High Court of Lagos, 1961; a Judge of High Court of Lagos and Southern Cameroons, 1955–62.

BELLAMY, Christopher William; Judge of the Court of First Instance of the European Communities, since 1992; *b* 25 April 1946; *s* of late William Albert Bellamy, TD, MRCS, LRCP and of Vyvienne Hilda, *d* of Albert Meyrick, OBE; *m* 1989, Deirdre Patricia (*née* Turner); one *s* two *d. Educ:* Tonbridge Sch.; Brasenose Coll., Oxford (MA). Called to the Bar, Middle Temple, 1968; Bencher, 1994. Taught in Africa, 1968–69; in practice at Bar, 1970–92; QC 1986; Asst Recorder, 1989–92. Gov., Ravensbourne Coll. of Design and Communication, 1988–92. *Publications:* (with G. Child) Common Market Law of Competition, 1973, 4th edn (ed V. Rose), 1993; papers and articles on legal matters. *Recreations:* history, walking, family life. *Address:* European Court of First Instance, 2925 G.D. Luxembourg. *T:* (352) 4303 3494/3562. *Club:* Athenæum.

BELLAMY, David James, OBE 1994; PhD; FLS; FIBiol; botanist; writer and broadcaster; *b* 18 Jan. 1933; *s* of Thomas Bellamy and Winifred (*née* Green); *m* 1959, Rosemary Froy; two *s* three *d. Educ:* London University: Chelsea Coll. of Science and Technology (BSc); Bedford Coll. (PhD). Lectr, then Sen. Lectr, Dept of Botany, Univ. of Durham, 1960–80; Hon. Prof. of Adult and Continuing Educn, 1980–82; Special Prof., Nottingham Univ., 1987–; Vis. Prof. of Natural Heritage Studies, Massey Univ., NZ, 1988–89. Dir, David Bellamy Associates, envmtl consultants, 1988–; Associate Dir, P-E Internat., 1993–. Founder Dir, Conservation Foundn; Trustee: WWF, 1985–89; Living Landscape Trust, 1985–; President: WATCH, 1982; YHA, 1983–; Population Concern, 1988–; Nat. Assoc. Envmtl Educn, 1989–; Assoc. of Master Thatchers, 1991–; Council, Zool Soc. of London, 1991–94. Governor, Repton Sch., 1983–89. Chief I Spy, 1983. Presenter and script writer for television and radio programmes, BBC and ITV; programmes include Longest Running Show on Earth, 1985; main series: Life in our Sea, 1970; Bellamy on Botany, 1973; Bellamy's Britain, 1975; Bellamy's Europe, 1977; Botanic Man, 1979; Up a Gum Tree, 1980; Backyard Safari, 1981; The Great Seasons, 1982; Bellamy's New World, 1983; You Can't See The Wood, 1984; Discovery, 1985; Seaside Safari, 1985; End of the Rainbow Show, 1985; Bellamy's Bugle, 1986; Turning the Tide, 1986; The End of the Rainbow Show, 1986; Bellamy's Bird's Eye View, 1988; Moa's Ark, 1990; Bellamy Rides Again, 1991, 1992; Wetlands, 1991; England's Last Wilderness, 1992; Blooming Bellamy, 1993; Routes of Wisdom, 1993; Bellamy's Border Raids: the Peak District, 1994. DUniv Open, 1984; Hon. DSc: CNAA, 1990; Nottingham, 1993; Dunelm, 1995. Frances Ritchie Meml Prize, Rambler's Assoc., 1989; UNEP Global 500 Award, 1990. Order of the Golden Ark (Netherlands), 1989. *Publications:* Peatlands, 1974; Bellamy on Botany, 1974; Bellamy's Britain, 1975; Bellamy's Europe, 1977; Life Giving Sea, 1977; Botanic Man, 1978; Half of Paradise, 1979; The Great Seasons, 1981; Backyard Safari, 1981; Discovering the Countryside with David Bellamy: vols I and II, 1982, vols III and IV, 1983; The Mouse Book, 1983; Bellamy's New World, 1983; The Queen's Hidden Garden, 1984; Turning the Tide, 1986; The Vanishing Bogs of Ireland, 1986; Bellamy's Changing Countryside, 4 vols, 1989; (with Brendan Quayle) England's Last Wilderness, 1989; England's Lost Wilderness, 1990; (with Jane Gifford) Wilderness in Britain, 1991; How Green Are You?, 1991; Tomorrow's Earth, 1991; (with Andrea Pfister) World Medicine, 1992; Blooming Bellamy, 1993. *Recreations:* children, ballet. *Address:* Mill House, Bedburn, Bishop Auckland, Co. Durham DL13 3NW.

BELLAMY, Prof. Edmund Henry, MA, PhD; Professor of Physics in the University of London, Westfield College, 1960–84, now Emeritus; *b* 8 April 1923; *s* of Herbert Bellamy and Nellie (*née* Ablett); *m* 1946, Joan Roberts; three *s*. *Educ:* Quarry Bank Sch., Liverpool; King's Coll., Cambridge. Lectr in Natural Philosophy, Univ. of Glasgow, 1951–59, Sen. Lectr, 1959–60; Vis. Physicist, Univ. of Pisa, 1960. Mem., Nuclear Physics Board of Science Research Council, 1965–66. Visiting Professor: Univ. of Stanford, 1966–67; Univ. of Pisa, 1985–86; Emeritus Fellow, Leverhulme Trust, 1987–89; Consultant, Univ. of Florida, 1990. *Publications:* numerous scientific papers in Proc. Phys. Soc. and other journals. *Recreations:* skiing, squash, travel, football, golf. *Address:* 134 Main Road, Long Hanborough, Witney, Oxon OX8 8JY. *T:* Freeland (01993) 882227.

BELLAMY, (Kenneth) Rex; Tennis Correspondent, The Times, 1967–89; *b* 15 Sept. 1928; *s* of Sampson Bellamy and Kathleen May Bellamy; *m* 1951, Hilda O'Shea; one step *d*. *Educ:* Yeovil; Woodhouse Grammar Sch., Sheffield. National Service, RA and RASC, 1946–49. Sports and Feature Writer, Sheffield Telegraph, 1944–46 and 1949–53; Sports Writer: Birmingham Gazette, 1953–56; The Times, 1956–89. World Championship Tennis award for service to tennis, 1988; International Tennis-writing Awards: 5 from Assoc. of Tennis Professionals, 1975–79 (award discontinued); 2 from Women's Tennis Assoc., 1977–78. *Publications:* Teach Yourself Squash (jtly), 1968; The Tennis Set, 1972; The Story of Squash, 1978 rev. edn as Squash—A History, 1988; The Peak District Companion, 1981; Walking the Tops, 1984; Game, Set and Deadline, 1986; Love Thirty, 1990; The Four Peaks, 1992. *Recreations:* hill-walking, golf. *Address:* 8 Guillards Oak, Midhurst, W Sussex GU29 9JZ. *Clubs:* Jesters (Hon. Mem.); Cowdray Park Golf.

BELLANY, Prof. Ian; Professor of Politics, University of Lancaster, since 1979; *b* 21 Feb. 1941; *s* of James Bellany and Jemima Bellany (*née* Emlay); *m* 1965, Wendy Ivey, *d* of Glyndwr and Bronwen Thomas; one *s* one *d*. *Educ:* Preston Lodge, Prestonpans; Firth Park Grammar Sch., Sheffield; Balliol Coll., Oxford (State Scholar, MA, DPhil). Foreign and Commonwealth Office, 1965–68; Res. Fellow in Internat. Relations, ANU, 1968–70; University of Lancaster: Lectr. later Sen. Lectr in Politics, 1970–79; Dir, Centre for Study of Arms Control and Internat. Security, 1979–90; Head, Dept of Politics, 1985–86. Leverhulme Res. Fellow, 1982; NATO Instl Fellow, 1989–90. Mem., Govt Adv. Panel on Disarmament, 1981–. Examr in Internat. Relations, LSE, 1985–88, in Internat. Studies, Birmingham Univ., 1990–93. Founding Editor, Arms Control: Journal of Arms Control and Disarmament, 1980–91. *Publications:* Australia in the Nuclear Age, 1972; A Basis for Arms Control, 1991; Reviewing Britain's Defence, 1994; edited jointly: Antiballistic Missile Defences in the 1980s, 1983; The Verification of Arms Control Agreements, 1983; The Nuclear Non-Proliferation Treaty, 1985; New Conventional Weapons and Western Defence, 1987; contribs to jls. *Recreations:* broadcasting, coarse carpentry, computing. *Address:* 42 Barton Road, Lancaster LA1 4ER. *T:* Lancaster (01524) 68157.

BELLANY, John, CBE 1994; RA 1991 (ARA 1986); artist (painter); *b* Scotland, 18 June 1942; *s* of Richard Weatherhead Bellany and Agnes Craig Bellany; *m* 1st, 1964, Helen Margaret Percy (marr. diss. 1974); two *s* one *d*; 2nd, 1980, Juliet Gray (*née* Lister) (*d* 1985); 3rd, 1986 (for 2nd time), Helen Margaret Bellany. *Educ:* Cockenzie Public Sch., Scotland; Preston Lodge Sch., Scotland; Edinburgh Coll. of Art (DA); Royal Coll. of Art (MA Fine Art; ARCA). Lectr in Fine Art in various art colls and univs in Gt Britain, incl. Winchester Coll. of Art, Goldsmiths' Coll., London Univ., RCA; Artist in Residence, Victorian Coll. of the Arts, Melb., 1982. *One man exhibitions:* Nat. Portrait Gall., 1986; Fischer Fine Art, London, 1988–89, 1991; Scottish Nat. Gall. of Modern Art, 1989; Raab Gall., Berlin and Ruth Siegel Gall., NY, 1990; Fitzwilliam Mus., Cambridge, 1991; Kelvingrove Art Gall. and Mus., Glasgow, 1992; many others in Britain, USA, Australia, Europe; *retrospective exhibitions:* Scottish Nat. Gall. of Modern Art, Edin., and Serpentine Gall., London, 1986; Kunsthalle, Hamburg, 1988. Works represented in major museums and private collections throughout the world, incl. Tate Gall., V&A Mus., Mus. of Modern Art, NY; Metropolitan Mus., NY. Hon. Fellow Commoner, Trinity Hall, Cambridge, 1988. Hon. RSA 1987. *Relevant publications:* John Bellany, by Victor Musgrave and Philip Rawson, 1982; John Bellany, a Retrospective, by Douglas Hall, 1986; John Bellany (Portraits) (The Maxi Hudson Collection), by Robin Gibson, 1986; John Bellany, by Richard Cork, 1986; John Bellany, Retrospective, by Prof. D. Werner Hofmann and Keith Hartley, 1988; John Bellany, by John McEwen, 1994. *Recreation:* climbing to and fro across Hadrian's Wall. *Address:* 2 Windmill Drive, SW4 9DE. *T:* 0181–675 7909, *Fax:* (01799) 42062; 19 Great Stuart Street, Edinburgh EH2 7TP. *T:* 0131–226 5183; Angela Flowers Gallery, 199–205 Richmond Road, E8 3NT. *T:* 0181–985 3333, *Fax:* 0181–985 0067; Berkeley Square Gallery, 23A Bruton Street, W1X 7DA. *T:* 0171–493 7939. *Clubs:* Chelsea Arts; Scottish Arts (Edinburgh).

BELLENGER, Rev. Dr Dominic Terence Joseph, (Rev. Dom Aidan Bellenger), FRHistS; Director of Historical Research, Downside Abbey, since 1995; Parish Priest, St Wulstan's, Little Malvern, since 1995; *b* 21 July 1950; *s* of Gerald Bellenger and Kathleen Bellenger (*née* O'Donnell). *Educ:* Finchley Grammar Sch.; Jesus Coll., Cambridge (Scholar, MA, PhD); Angelicum Univ., Rome. Res. Student in History, 1972–78 and Lightfoot Schol. in Eccl. Hist., Cambridge, 1975–78; Assistant Master: St Mary's Sch., Cambridge, 1975–78; Downside Sch., 1978–82; Benedictine Monk, Downside Abbey, 1982; Priest, 1988; Housemaster, 1989–91, Head Master, 1991–95, Downside Sch. Member: Cttee, Eccl. Hist. Soc., 1982–85; Cttee, English Benedictine Hist. Commn, 1987–; Council, Catholic Record Soc., 1990–; Clifton Diocesan Educn Commn, 1995–; Trustee: Catholic Family Hist. Soc., 1990–; Andrew C. Duncan Catholic History Trust, 1993–; Pres., English Catholic Hist. Gp, 1991–. Governor: Moor Park Sch., Ludlow, 1991–; St Antony's, Leweston, Sherborne, 1991–93; St Mary's Sch., Shaftesbury, 1992–; Moreton Hall, Suffolk, 1995–. Leverhulme Res. Award, 1986. FRSA. Editor, South Western Catholic History, 1982–; English correspondent, Rev. d'Hist. de l'Eglise de France, 1982–85. *Publications:* English and Welsh Priests 1558–1800, 1984; The French Exiled Clergy, 1986; (ed) Opening the Scrolls, 1987; (ed jtly) Les Archives du Nord, Calendar of 20 H, 1987; St Cuthbert, 1987; (ed jtly) Letters of Bede Jarrett, 1989; (ed) Fathers in Faith, 1991; (ed) The Great Return, 1994; *contributed to:* Religion and National Identity, 1982; Dictionnaire de Spiritualité, 1985, 1994; Monks, Hermits and the Ascetic Tradition, 1985; The Churches, Ireland and the Irish, 1988; Mélanges Charles Molette, 1989; The Continuity of Tradition, 1990; The Loveable West, 1990; Martyrs and Martyrologies, 1993; Protestors for Paradise, 1993; articles in learned jls and periodicals. *Recreations:* books, church architecture, talk, travel, visual arts, writing. *Address:* Downside School, Stratton-on-the-Fosse, Bath BA3 4RJ. *T:* Stratton-on-the-Fosse (01761) 232206.

BELLEW, family name of **Baron Bellew.**

BELLEW; *see* Grattan-Bellew.

BELLEW, 7th Baron *cr* 1848; **James Bryan Bellew;** Bt 1688; *b* 5 Jan. 1920; *s* of 6th Baron Bellew, MC, and Jeanie Ellen Agnes (*d* 1973), *d* of late James Ormsby Jameson; *S* father, 1981; *m* 1st, 1942, Mary Elizabeth (*d* 1978), *d* of Rev. Edward Eustace Hill; two *s* one *d*; 2nd, 1978, Gwendoline, formerly wife of Major P. Hall and *d* of late Charles Redmond Clayton-Daubeny. Served War of 1939–45, Irish Guards (Captain). *Heir: s* Hon. Bryan Edward Bellew [*b* 19 March 1943; *m* 1968, Rosemary Sarah, *d* of Major Reginald Kilner Brasier Hitchcock; two *s*]. *Address:* c/o Royal Bank of Scotland, 45 The Promenade, Cheltenham, Glos GL50 1PY.

BELLINGER, Sir Robert (Ian), GBE 1967; Kt 1964; Chairman: Kinloch (PM) Ltd, 1946–75; National Savings Committee, 1970–75, and President, 1972–75; Director, Rank Organisation, 1971–83; *b* Tetbury, Glos, 10 March 1910; *s* of David Morgan Bellinger, Cardiganshire, and Jane Ballantine Deans, Edinburgh; *m* 1962, Christiane Marie Louise Janssens, Brussels; one *s* one *d*. *Educ:* Church of England sch. Elected Court of Common Council, 1953; Chm. City of London Freemen's Sch., 1957; Alderman for Ward of Cheap, 1958; Sheriff, City of London, 1962–63; Lord Mayor of London, 1966–67; one of HM Lieutenants, City of London, 1976–. Chairman: Panel for Civil Service Manpower Review, 1968–71; Adv. Cttee on Magistracy, City of London, 1968–76; Licensing Cttee, City of London; Finance Cttee, BBC; Governor, BBC, 1968–71; Trustee, St Paul's Cathedral Trust, 1977–; Dir, Arsenal Football Club. Chairman: Anglo-Danish Soc., 1976–83; Danish Trade Adv. Bd, 1979–82. Past Master, Broderers' Company; Liveryman, Fletchers' Company. Hon. DSc City Univ., 1966. Gentleman Usher of the Purple Rod, Order of the British Empire, 1969–85. KStJ 1966; Commandeur, Ordre de Léopold, cl. III (Belgium), 1963; Comdr, Royal Order of the Phoenix (Greece), 1963; Officier, Ordre de la Valeur Camerounaise (Cameroons), 1963; Knight Comdr of the Order of Dannebrog (Denmark), 1977. *Recreations:* tennis, football, music, motoring. *Address:* Penn Wood, Fulmer, Bucks SL3 6JL. *T:* Fulmer (01753) 662029. *Club:* City Livery.

BELLINGHAM, Prof. Alastair John, FRCP, PRCPath; Professor of Haematology, King's College London, since 1984; President, Royal College of Pathologists, 1993–Nov. 1996; *b* 27 March 1938; *s* of Stanley Herbert Bellingham and Sybil Mary Milne; *m* 1963, Valerie Jill Morford; three *s*. *Educ:* Tiffin Boys' Sch., Kingston upon Thames; University Coll. Hosp. (MB BS). Research Fellow, Univ. of Washington, 1969–71; Sen. Lectr, UCH, 1971–74; Prof. of Haematology, Univ. of Liverpool, 1974–84. Hon. Consultant Haematologist, KCH. Past Pres., British Soc. for Haematology; Vice-President: Eur. Div., Internat Soc. Haematology, 1992–; RCPath, 1990–93. *Publications:* contribs to books and jls on haematol., esp. red cell physiol. and inherited red cell disorders, incl. enzyme deficiencies, sickle cell disorders and thalassaemia. *Recreations:* oenology, viticulture, cricket, photography. *Address:* 13 Barnmead Road, Beckenham, Kent BR3 1JF. *T:* 0181–778 0730. *Club:* Savage.

BELLINGHAM, Henry Campbell; MP (C) Norfolk North West, since 1983; *b* 29 March 1955; *s* of late Henry Bellingham; *m* 1993, Emma Whiteley. *Educ:* Eton; Magdalene Coll., Cambridge (BA 1977). Called to the Bar, Middle Temple, 1978. Partner in family farming and property co.; Underwriting Mem. of Lloyd's. PPS to Sec. of State for Transport, 1990–92, for Defence, 1992–95, for Foreign and Commonwealth Affairs, 1995–. Chm., Cons. Council on Eastern Europe, 1989–94; Mem., Select Cttee on the Environment, 1987–90; Jt Vice Chm., Cons. Parly Smaller Businesses Cttee, 1987–90 (Sec., 1983–87); Founder Mem. and sponsor, W Norfolk Local Enterprise Agency, 1986–94. *Address:* House of Commons, SW1A 0AA. *Clubs:* White's, Pratt's.

BELLINGHAM, Sir Noel (Peter Roger), 7th Bt (2nd creation) *cr* 1796; accountant; *b* 4 Sept. 1943; *s* of Sir Roger Carroll Patrick Stephen Bellingham, 6th Bt, and of Mary, *d* of late William Norman; *S* father, 1973; *m* 1977, Jane, *d* of late Edwin William and of Joan Taylor, Sale, Cheshire. *Heir: b* Anthony Edward Norman Bellingham, *b* 24 March 1947. *Address:* 20 Davenport Park Road, Davenport, Stockport, Cheshire SK2 6JS. *T:* 0161–483 7168. *Club:* 64 Society (Cheshire).

BELLIS, Bertram Thomas; Headmaster, The Leys School, Cambridge, 1975–86; *b* 4 May 1927; *s* of Rev. Thomas J. Bellis and Mary A. Bellis; *m* 1952, Joan Healey; two *s*. *Educ:* Kingswood Sch., Bath; St John's Coll., Cambridge (Exhibr in Maths, MA). Rossall Sch., 1951–55; Highgate Sch., 1955–65; Headmaster, Daniel Stewart's Coll., 1965–72; Principal, Daniel Stewart's and Melville Coll., 1972–75. Chm., Scottish Educn Dept Cttee on Computers and the Schools (reports, 1969 and 1972); Member: Council, Inst. of Math., 1975–79; Educational Research Bd, SSRC, 1975–80. Governor: Queenswood Sch., 1980–92; St John's Coll. Sch., 1981–86. Pres., Mathematical Assoc., 1971–72. Schoolmaster Fellow, Balliol Coll., Oxford, 1963; FIMA 1964; FRSE 1972. *Recreation:* fell walking. *Address:* 2 Eller Raise, Kendal, Cumbria LA9 6AB.

BELLIS, John Herbert; Regional Chairman of Industrial Tribunals, Nottingham Region, since 1992 (Manchester Region, 1984–92); *b* 11 April 1930; *s* of Thomas and Jane Bellis; *m* 1961, Sheila Helen McNeil Ford; two *s* one *d*. *Educ:* Friars Grammar Sch., Bangor; Liverpool Univ. (LLB). Admitted Solicitor, 1953. National Service, 1953–55. In practice as solicitor on own account, Penmaenmawr, N Wales, 1958–84. Parly Cand. (L) Conway, Caernarvonshire, 1959. *Recreations:* golf, walking, gardening, horse racing. *Address:* Green Acre, Church Lane, Muston, Nottingham NG13 0FD. *T:* Bottesford (01949) 42634.

BELLO, Mohammed; CON 1965; **Hon. Mr Justice Bello;** Chief Justice of Nigeria, since 1987; *b* 1930; *s* of Mallam Muhammadu Gidado; *m* 1962; many *c*. *Educ:* Harvard Law School. Called to the Bar, Lincoln's Inn. Northern Nigeria appointments: Crown Counsel, 1956; Magistrate, 1961; Dir of Public Prosecutions, 1964; Judge of the High Court, 1966; Senior Puisne Judge, North-Central and Kwara States, 1968; occasional Acting Chief Justice, Northern State, 1969–75; Justice of Supreme Court of Nigeria, 1975. Fellow, Nigerian Inst. of Advanced Legal Studies, 1984. Hon. LLD: Ibadan, 1987; Ahmadu Bello, 1990; Lagos, 1992. *Recreation:* rambling. *Address:* (home) 15 Ikoyi Crescent, Lagos, Nigeria. *T:* (1) 618847; Supreme Court of Nigeria, Lagos, Nigeria. *T:* (1) 635426.

BELLOTTI, David Frank; Deputy Chairman and Chief Executive, Brighton and Hove Albion Football Club; *b* 13 Aug. 1943; *s* of Patrick Frank Bellotti and Elsie (*née* Venner); *m* 1st, 1965, Sheila (*née* Jones); one *s* one *d*; 2nd, 1973, Jennifer (*née* Compson) (marr. diss.); one *s*. *Educ:* Exeter Sch.; YMCA National Coll. (Diploma in Youth Service); Brighton Polytechnic (Diploma in Counselling); Univ. of Sussex (MA). Civil Service, 1961–64; Young Men's Christian Association: student, Nat. Coll., 1964–65; Sec., St Helens, Llanelli, Norwich and Lewes, 1965–76; Regional Sec., South-East, 1977–81; Dir, Hove, 1981–90. Mem. (Lib Dem), E Sussex CC, 1981–. MP (Lib Dem) Eastbourne, Oct. 1990–1992; contested same seat, 1992. Contested (Lib Dem) E Sussex and Kent S, Eur. Parly elecns, 1994. *Recreations:* Association Football, politics, snooker. *Address:* 29 St David's Close, Eastbourne BN22 0UZ. *T:* Eastbourne (01323) 505218. *Club:* National Liberal.

BELLOW, family name of **Baron Bellwin.**

BELLOW, Saul; American writer; *b* 10 June 1915; *s* of Abraham and Liza Gordon Bellow; three *s*; *m* 1989, Janis Freedman. *Educ:* Univ. of Chicago; Northwestern Univ. Nobel Prize for Literature, 1976; Malaparté Prize for Literature, Italy, 1984. Hon. DLitt, Northwestern Univ., 1962. Commander, Legion of Honour (France), 1983; Commander, Order of Arts and Letters (France), 1985 (Croix de Chevalier, 1968). *Publications:* Dangling Man, 1944 (reissued 1972); The Victim, 1947; The Adventures of Augie March, 1953 (National Book Award, 1954); Seize the Day, 1956; Henderson the Rain King, 1959; Herzog, 1964 (National Book Award, Internat. Literary Prize, 1965); Mosby's Memoirs and Other Stories, 1969; Mr Sammler's Planet, 1970 (National Book Award, 1970);

Humboldt's Gift, 1975 (Pulitzer Prize 1976); To Jerusalem and Back, 1976; The Dean's December, 1982; (short stories) Him with His Foot in His Mouth, 1984; More Die of Heartbreak, 1987; A Theft, 1989; The Bellarosa Connection, 1989; Something to Remember Me By: three tales, 1991; It All Adds Up (essays), 1994. *Address:* University of Chicago, Chicago, IL 60637, USA.

BELLOWS, James Gilbert; TV, newspaper, on-line consultant; *b* 12 Nov. 1922; *s* of Lyman Hubbard Bellows and Dorothy Gilbert Bellows; *m* 1950, Marian Raines (decd); three *d*; *m* 1964, Maggie Savoy (decd); *m* 1971, Keven Ryan; one *d*. *Educ:* Kenyon Coll. (BA, LLB). Columbus (Ga) Ledger, 1947; News Editor Atlanta (Ga) Jl, 1950–57; Asst Editor, Detroit (Mich.) Free Press, 1957–58; Managing Editor Miami (Fla) News, 1958–61; Exec. Editor (News Ops), NY Herald Tribune, 1961–62; Editor, 1962–66; associate Editor, Los Angeles Times, 1966–75; Editor: Washington Star, 1975–78; Los Angeles Herald Examiner, 1979–82; Managing Editor, Entertainment Tonight (TV show), 1982–83; Exec. Producer, ABC-TV News, 1983–86; Dir of Editorial Develt, Prodigy, 1986–88; Managing Editor, USA Today on TV, 1988–89; Vice Pres. Editorial, MediaNews Gp, 1990–91; Los Angeles Bureau Chief, TV Guide, 1992–94. Member: Kenyon Review Adv. Bd; Amer. Soc. of Newspaper Editors. *Address:* 2337 Canyonback Road, Los Angeles, CA 90049, USA. *Club:* Bel-Air Country (Los Angeles).

BELLWIN, Baron *cr* 1979 (Life Peer), of the City of Leeds; **Irwin Norman Bellow;** JP; DL; *b* 7 Feb. 1923; *s* of Abraham and Leah Bellow; *m* 1948, Doreen Barbara Saperia; one *s* two *d*. *Educ:* Lovell Road; Leeds Grammar School; Leeds Univ. LLB. Leader, Leeds City Council, 1975–79; Vice-Chm. Assoc. of Metropolitan Authorities, 1978–79. Parly Under Sec. of State, DoE, 1979–Jan. 1983; Minister of State, 1983–84. Mem., Commn for New Towns, 1985–; Vice-Pres., Internat. New Towns Assoc, 1985–. Non-executive Director: Taylor Woodrow, 1985–92; Sinclair Goldsmith Holding, 1986–93; Lewis Gp, 1993–; Stewart Title (UK), 1993–; Farr Brokers Ltd, 1994–. Chm., N Hull HAT, 1993–. Mem., Nat. Sports Council, 1972–75; Pres., English Basket Ball Assoc., 1972–75. Master, Guild of World Traders in London, 1989. JP Leeds, 1969; DL W Yorks, 1991. *Recreation:* golf. *Address:* Woodside Lodge, Ling Lane, Scarcroft, Leeds LS14 3HX. *T:* Leeds (0113) 289 2908. *Club:* Moor Allerton Golf (Club Pres.).

BELMONT, Abbot of; *see* Jabalé, Rt Rev. J. M.

BELMORE, 8th Earl of, *cr* 1797; **John Armar Lowry-Corry;** Baron Belmore, 1781; Viscount Belmore, 1789; *b* 4 Sept. 1951; *s* of 7th Earl of Belmore and Gloria Anthea, *d* of late Herbert Bryant Harker, Melbourne, Australia; *S* father 1960; *m* 1984, Lady Mary Meade, *d* of 6th Earl of Clanwilliam; two *s* one *d*. *Educ:* Lancing; Royal Agricultural Coll., Cirencester. *Heir: s* Viscount Corry, *qv*. *Recreation:* fishing. *Address:* The Garden House, Castle Coole, Enniskillen, Co. Fermanagh, N Ireland BT74 6JX. *T:* Enniskillen (01365) 322463. *Club:* Kildare Street and University (Dublin).

BELOFF, family name of **Baron Beloff.**

BELOFF, Baron *cr* 1981 (Life Peer), of Wolvercote in the County of Oxfordshire; **Max Beloff;** Kt 1980; MA, DLitt (Oxon); FBA 1973; FRHistS; FRSA; *b* 2 July 1913; *er s* of late Simon and Mary Beloff; *m* 1938, Helen Dobrin; two *s*. *Educ:* St Paul's Sch.; Corpus Christi Coll., Oxford (Scholar; Hon. Fellow, 1993). Gibbs Schol. in Mod. Hist., 1934; 1st Cl. Hons, School of Modern History, 1935; Senior Demy, Magdalen Coll., Oxford, 1935. Junior Research Fellow, Corpus Christi Coll., 1937; Asst Lecturer in History, Manchester Univ., 1939–46; Nuffield Reader in Comparative Study of Institutions, Oxford Univ., 1946–56; Fellow of Nuffield Coll., 1947–57; Gladstone Prof. of Govt and Public Admin, Oxford Univ., 1957–74, now Professor Emeritus, and Fellow, All Souls Coll., 1957–74, Emeritus Fellow, 1980–; Supernumerary Fellow, St Antony's Coll., Oxford, 1975–84; Principal, University Coll. at Buckingham, 1974–79. Hon. Prof., St Andrews Univ., 1993–. War of 1939–45, Royal Corps of Signals, 1940–41. Governor, Haifa Univ.; Ex-Trustee and Ex-Librarian, Oxford Union Soc. Hon. Fellow, Mansfield Coll., Oxford, 1989. Hon. LLD: Pittsburgh, USA, 1962; Manchester Univ., 1989; Hon. DCL, Bishop's Univ. Canada, 1976; Hon. DLitt Bowdoin Coll., USA, 1976; Hon. DrUniv Aix-Marseille III, 1978; Hon. DLitt Buckingham, 1984. *Publications:* Public Order and Popular Disturbances, 1660–1714, 1938; The Foreign Policy of Soviet Russia, Vol. 1, 1947, Vol. 2, 1949; Thomas Jefferson and American Democracy, 1948; Soviet Policy in the Far East, 1944–51, 1953; The Age of Absolutism, 1660–1815, 1954; Foreign Policy and the Democratic Process, 1955; Europe and the Europeans, 1957; The Great Powers, 1959; The American Federal Government, 1959; New Dimensions in Foreign Policy, 1961; The United States and the Unity of Europe, 1963; The Balance of Power, 1967; The Future of British Foreign Policy, 1969; Imperial Sunset, vol. 1, 1969, 2nd edn 1988, vol. 2, Dream of Commonwealth 1921–42, 1989; The Intellectual in Politics, 1970; (with G. R. Peele) The Government of the United Kingdom, 1980, 2nd edn 1985; Wars and Welfare 1914–1945, 1984; An Historian in the Twentieth Century, 1992; edited: The Federalist 1948, 2nd edn 1987; Mankind and his Story, 1948; The Debate on the American Revolution, 1949, 2nd edn 1989; On the Track of Tyranny, 1959; (jtly) L'Europe du XIXe et XXe siècle, 1960–67; (with V. Vale) American Political Institutions in the 1970's, 1975; articles in English, French, Italian and American journals. *Recreation:* watching cricket. *Address:* c/o House of Lords, SW1A 0PW. *T:* 0171–219 6669. *Club:* Reform.
See also Hon. Michael Beloff.

BELOFF, Hon. Michael Jacob, MA; QC 1981; barrister and writer; a Recorder, 1985–Aug. 1996; a Deputy High Court Judge, 1989–Aug. 1996; President, Trinity College, University of Oxford, from Aug. 1996; *b* 18 April 1942; *s* of Baron Beloff, *qv*; *m* 1969, Judith Mary Arkinstall; one *s* one *d*. *Educ:* Dragon Sch., Oxford; Eton Coll. (King's Schol.; Captain of Sch. 1960); Magdalen Coll., Oxford (Demy; H. W. C. Davis Prizeman, 1962; BA Hist. (1st cl.) 1963, Law 1965; MA 1967). Pres., Oxford Union Soc., 1962; Oxford Union tour of USA, 1964. Called to the Bar, Gray's Inn, 1967 (Gerald Moody Schol., 1963; Atkin Schol., 1967), Bencher, 1988; Jt Head of Chambers, 4–5 Gray's Inn Sq., 1993–. Lectr in Law, Trinity Coll., Oxford, 1965–66. Legal Correspondent: New Society, 1969–79; The Observer, 1979–81. Vice-Pres., Administrative Law Bar Assoc., 1990 (first Chm., 1986–90, now Chm. Emeritus); Member: Bingham Law Reform Cttee on Discovery of Documents and Disclosure, 1982–; Adv. Council, Envmtl Law Foundn, 1990–; Chm., Oxford Univ. Tribunal into Alleged Plagiarism, 1990. Consultant Editor, Judicial Review Bulletins: Commercial Law, Environmental Law. Hon. Mem., Internat. Athletes' Club. Women's Legal Defence Award (first winner), 1991. *Publications:* A Short Walk on the Campus (ed with J. Aitken), 1966; The Plateglass Universities, 1968; The Sex Discrimination Act, 1976; Halsbury's Laws of England (contribution on Time), 1983; (contrib.) Judicial Safeguards in Administrative Proceedings, 1989; (contrib.) Judicial Review, 1991; contrib. Encounter, Minerva, Irish Jurist, Political Qly, Current Legal Problems, Public Law, Statute Law Review, Modern Law Review, etc. *Recreation:* running. *Address:* 38 Park Town, Oxford OX2 6SJ; 41 Campden Hill Square, W8 7JR; 4–5 Gray's Inn Square, Gray's Inn, WC1R 5AY. *T:* 0171–404 5252; (from Aug. 1996) President's Lodgings, Trinity College, Oxford OX1 3BH. *Clubs:* Reform; Vincent's (Oxford).

BELOFF, Nora; author and journalist; *b* 24 Jan. 1919; *m* 1977, Clifford Makins (*d* 1990). *Educ:* King Alfred Sch.; Lady Margaret Hall, Oxford. BA Hons History 1940. Polit. Intell. Dept, FO, 1941–44; British Embassy, Paris, 1944–45; reporter, Reuters News Agency, 1945–46; Paris corresp., The Economist, 1946–48; Observer corresp., Paris, Washington, Moscow, Brussels etc, 1948–78; political correspondent, 1964–76, roving correspondent, 1976–78. Currently engaged in research on internat. responsibilities for the conflict in former Yugoslavia. *Publications:* The General Says No, 1963; The Transit of Britain, 1973; Freedom under Foot, 1976; No Travel like Russian Travel, 1979 (US, as Inside the Soviet Empire: myth and reality, 1980); Tito's Flawed Legacy: Yugoslavia and the West 1939–1984, 1985 (US, as Tito's Flawed Legacy: Yugoslavia and the West 1939 till now, 1986; trans. Italian, 1987, Slovene, 1990, Serbo-Croat, 1991). *Address:* 11 Belsize Road, NW6 4RX. *T and Fax:* 0171–586 0378.

BELPER, 4th Baron *cr* 1856; **Alexander Ronald George Strutt;** formerly Major, Coldstream Guards; *b* 23 April 1912; *s* of 3rd Baron and Hon. Eva Isabel Mary Bruce (*d* 1987), 2nd *d* of 2nd Baron Aberdare (she *m* 2nd, 6th Earl of Rosebery); *S* father 1956; *m* 1940, Zara Sophie Kathleen Mary (marr. diss. 1949), *y d* of Sir Harry Mainwaring, 5th Bt; one *s*. *Educ:* Harrow. Served War with Coldstream Guards, 1939–44 (wounded). *Heir: s* Hon. Richard Henry Strutt [*b* 24 Oct. 1941; *m* 1966, Jennifer Vivian, *d* of late Capt. Peter Winser and of Mrs James Whitaker; one *s* one *d*; *m* 1980, Judith Mary de Jonge, *d* of Mr and Mrs James Twynam, Kitemore House, Faringdon, Oxon]. *Address:* Kingston Hall, Nottingham NG11 0DL.

BELSKY, Franta; sculptor; *b* Brno, 6 April 1921; *s* of Joseph Belsky, economist; *m* Margaret Owen (cartoonist Belsky) (*d* 1989). *Educ:* Acad. of Fine Arts, Prague; Royal Coll. of Art, London. ARCA, Hons Dip. 1950. Served War as gunner (France, 1940; Normandy, 1944; various decorations). Taught in art schs, 1950–55. FRBS (Mem. Council, 1958–92); Pres., Soc. of Portrait Sculptors, 1963–68, 1994–; Governor, St Martin's Sch. of Art, 1967–88. Hon. Churchill Fellow, Westminster Coll., Fulton, Mo, 1994–. Work in Nat. Portrait Gall. and collections in Europe and USA, for numerous co. councils, industrial, shipping and private cos and educn authorities: Paratroop Memorial, Prague, 1947; Lt-Col Peniakoff (Popski), Ravenna, 1952; statue of Cecil Rhodes, 8′, Bulawayo, 1953; RAF memorial, Prague, 1995; groups: Constellation, Colchester, 1953; Lesson, LCC housing develt, 1957–58; Triga, Knightsbridge, 1958; Joy-ride, Stevenage New Town Centre, 1958; Astronomer Herschel Memorial, 18′, Slough, 1969; Oracle, 18′, Temple Way House, Bristol, 1975 (RBS Sir Otto Beit Medal, 1976); Totem, 32′, Manchester Arndale Centre, 1975 (RBS Sir Otto Beit Medal, 1978); fountains: European Shell Centre, 30′, South Bank, 1961; Leap, 26′, Blackwall Basin, 1988; reliefs: Epicentre, Doncaster City Centre, 1965; 1978 Jean Masson Davidson Award for Dist. in Portrait Sculpture; portraits include: Queen Mother, Birmingham Univ., 1962; Prince Philip, 1979 and HM the Queen, 1981, Nat. Portrait Gall.; Prince Andrew, 1963 and 1984; Prince William, 1985; statue of Sir Winston Churchill for Churchill Meml and Library in US, Fulton, Missouri and City of Prague, 1992, and bust in Churchill Archives, Cambridge, 1971 and Nat. Gall., Prague, 1990; Harry S. Truman, Presidential Library, Independence, Mo and H. S. T. Dam, Osage River, Mo; Adm. Cunningham, Trafalgar Square, 1969; Lord Cottesloe, Nat. Theatre; Mountbatten Meml, Horse Guards Parade, 1983, and bust, Queen Elizabeth II Conf. Centre, Westminster, 1986; Adm. Lord Lewin, HMS Dryad, 1985. Queen Mother 80th Birthday Crown coin. *Publications:* illus. and contrib. various books, jls and a monograph. *Recreations:* ski-ing, gardening, amateur archaeology. *Address:* 4 The Green, Sutton Courtenay, Abingdon OX14 4AE.

BELSTEAD, 2nd Baron, *cr* 1938; **John Julian Ganzoni;** Bt 1929; PC 1983; JP; Chairman, Parole Board, since 1992; Lord-Lieutenant of Suffolk, since 1994; *b* 30 Sept. 1932; *o s* of 1st Baron Belstead and Gwendolen Gertrude Turner (*d* 1962); *S* father, 1958. *Educ:* Eton; Christ Church, Oxford. MA 1961. Parliamentary Under-Secretary of State: DES, 1970–73; NI Office, 1973–74; Home Office, 1979–82; Minister of State: FCO, 1982–83; MAFF, 1983–87; DoE, 1987–88; Dep. Leader, H of L, 1983–87; Leader, H of L and Lord Privy Seal, 1988–90; HM Paymaster General and Minister, NI Office, 1990–92. Chm., Assoc. of Governing Bodies of Public Schools, 1974–79. JP Borough of Ipswich, 1962; DL Suffolk, 1979. *Heir:* none. *Address:* House of Lords, SW1A 0PW. *T:* 0171–219 3000. *Clubs:* Boodle's; All England Lawn Tennis (Wimbledon); MCC.

BELTON, Prof. Peter Stanley, PhD; Head of Norwich Laboratory, since 1992, and Deputy Director, since 1994, Institute of Food Research, Biotechnology and Biological Sciences (formerly Agricultural and Food Research Council); *b* 19 June 1947; *s* of Stanley Belton and Bertha (*née* Lawrence); *m* 1976, Teresa Stutz; three *s*. *Educ:* Cooper's Sch., Bow; Chelsea Coll., Univ. of London (BSc 1st Cl. Hons Chem. 1968; PhD 1972). University of East Anglia: Open Univ. Fellowship, 1971–72; ICI Fellowship, 1972–74; Res. Leader, Unilever Res., Port Sunlight, 1974–79; AFRC Institute of Food Research Norwich Laboratory: Hd, Molecular Spectroscopy Gp, 1979–87; Hd, Chem. Physics Dept, 1987–90; Hd, Food Structure & Biopolymer Technol. Dept, 1990–91; Hd, Food Colloid & Biopolymer Sci. Dept, 1991–92. Visiting Professor: Univ. of São Paulo, 1976; Centre D'Etudes Nucléaire, 1989; Hon. Prof., UEA, 1992. Member: SERC Instrumentation Panel, 1989–91; AFRC Food Res. Grants Bd, 1991–94; BBSRC Food Directorate, 1994–; Internat. Scientific Cttee, Sciences des Aliments; Scientific Cttee, Ecole Européenne de Chimie Analytique. FIFST. Member, Editorial Board: Jl Sci. Food & Agric., 1991–; Jl of Magnetic Resonance Analysis, 1994–. *Publications:* (jtly) From Arms Race to World Peace, 1991; contrib. books and jls. *Recreations:* coarse fishing, listening to music, making wine. *Address:* Institute of Food Research Norwich Laboratory, Norwich Research Park, Colney, Norwich NR4 7UA; 79 The Avenues, Norwich, Norfolk NR2 3QB. *T:* Norwich (01603) 453348.

BELTRAM, Geoffrey; Under-Secretary, Department of Health and Social Security, 1973–81; *b* 7 April 1921; *s* of George and Beatrice Dorothy Beltram; *m* 1945, Audrey Mary (*née* Harkett); one *s* one *d*. *Educ:* Dame Alice Owen's School. Tax Officer, Inland Revenue, 1938; served in RAF, 1941–46; Exec. Officer and Higher Exec. Officer, Min. of Town and Country Planning, 1947–51; Asst Principal, Nat. Assistance Bd, 1951–55; Principal 1955–63; Asst Sec. 1963–73 (NAB 1963–66, Min. of Social Security 1966–68, DHSS 1968–73). Vis. Res. Associate, LSE, 1981–84. Vis. social worker, Ind. Living Fund, 1988–93. *Publication:* Testing the Safety Net: a study of the Supplementary Benefit scheme, 1984. *Recreations:* literature, listening to music, opera, ballet, walking, tennis, swimming, writing.

BEN-TOVIM, Atarah, (Mrs Douglas Boyd), MBE 1980 (for services to children's music); Founder and Artistic Director, Children's Concert Centre, since 1975; *b* 1 Oct. 1940; *d* of Tsvi Ben-Tovim and Gladys Ben-Tovim; *m* 1976, Douglas Boyd; one *d*. *Educ:* Royal Acad. of Music, London. ARAM 1967. Principal Flautist, Royal Liverpool Philharmonic Orchestra, 1962–75; children's concerts with Atarah's Band, 1973–88. Hon. DMus 1991. *Publications:* Atarah's Book (autobiog.), 1976, 2nd edn 1979; Atarah's Band Kits (14 published), 1978–; Children and Music, 1979; (jtly) The Right Instrument For Your Child, 1985; You Can Make Music!, 1986; The Young Orchestral Flautist, Books 1–3, 1990; Queen Eleanor's Legacy, 1994. *Recreations:* music, writing, France and the

Mediterranean. *Address:* c/o Watson Little Ltd, 12 Egbert Street, NW1 8LJ. *T:* 0171–722 9514.

BENACERRAF, Prof. Baruj; Fabyan Professor of Comparative Pathology, Harvard Medical School, 1970–91, Professor Emeritus, since 1991; President: Dana-Farber, Inc., since 1991; Dana-Farber Cancer Institute, Boston, 1980–91; *b* 29 Oct. 1920; *m* 1943, Annette Dreyfus; one *d. Educ:* Lycée Janson, Paris (BèsL 1940); Columbia Univ. (BS 1942); Medical Coll. of Virginia (MD 1945). Served US Army, 1946–48. Intern, Queens Gen. Hosp., NY, 1945–46; Res. Fellow, Dept of Micro-biol., Coll. of Physicians and Surgeons, Columbia Univ., 1948–49; Chargé de Recherches, CNRS, Hôpital Broussais, Paris, 1950–56; New York University School of Medicine: Asst Prof. of Pathol., 1956–58; Assoc. Prof. of Pathol., 1958–60; Prof. of Pathol., 1960–68; Chief, Lab. of Immunol., Nat. Inst. of Allergy and Infectious Diseases, NIH, Bethesda, 1968–70. Scientific Advr, WHO; Chm., Scientific Adv. Cttee, Centre d'Immunologie de Marseille, CNRS-INSERM; Member: Immunology A Study Sect., NIH, 1965–69; Adv. Council, National Inst. of Allergy and Infectious Disease, 1985–88; Scientific Adv. Cttee, Basel Inst. of Immunology, 1985–89; Member Scientific Advisory Board: Trudeau Foundn, 1970–76; Mass Gen. Hosp., 1971–74. President: Amer. Assoc. of Immunologists, 1973–74; Fedn of Amer. Socs for Exptl Biol., 1974–75; Internat. Union of Immunol Socs, 1980–83. Fellow, Amer. Acad. of Arts and Scis, 1972. Correspondent Emérite, Institut National de la Santé et de la Recherche Scientifique, 1988. Member: Nat. Acad. of Scis, 1973; Nat. Inst. of Med., 1981; Amer. Assoc. of Pathologists and Bacteriologists; Amer. Soc. for Exptl Pathol.; British Assoc. for Immunol.; French Soc. of Biol Chem.; Harvey Soc. Lectures: R. E. Dyer, NIH, 1969; Harvey, 1971, 1972; J. S. Blumenthal, Univ. of Minnesota, 1980. Hon. MD Geneva, 1980; Hon. DSc: Virginia Commonwealth Univ., 1981; NY Univ., 1981; Yeshiva Univ., 1982; Univ. Aix-Marseille, 1982; Columbia Univ., 1985; Adelphi Univ., 1988; Weizmann Inst., 1989; Harvard Univ., 1992; Univ. Bordeaux, 1993. Rabbi Shai Shacknai Lectr and Prize, Hebrew Univ. of Jerusalem, 1974; T. Duckett Jones Meml Award, Helen Hay Whitney Foundn, 1976; Waterford Biomedical Science Award, 1980; (jtly) Nobel Prize for Physiology or Medicine, 1980; Rous-Whipple Award, Amer. Assoc. of Pathologists, 1985; Nat. Medal of Science, US, 1990. *Publications:* (with D. Katz) Immunological Tolerance, 1974; Immunogenetics and Immunodeficiency, 1975; (with D. Katz) The Role of Products of the Histocompatibility Gene Complex in Immune Responses, 1976; Textbook of Immunology, 1979; 650 articles in professional journals. *Recreations:* music, art collecting. *Address:* Dana-Farber Cancer Institute, 44 Binney Street, Boston, Mass 02115, USA.

BÉNARD, André Pierre Jacques, Hon. KBE 1991; French business executive; non-executive Director, Eurotunnel, since 1994 (Co-Chairman, 1986–90, Chairman, 1990–94); *b* 19 Aug. 1922; *s* of Marcel Bénard and Lucie Thalmann; *m*1946, Jacqueline Preiss; one *s. Educ:* Lycée Janson-de-Sailly; Lycée Georges Clémenceau, Nantes; Lycée Thiers, Marseilles; Ecole Polytechnique, Paris. Joined Royal Dutch Shell Group, 1946; with Société Anonyme des Pétroles Jupiter, 1946–49; Société des Pétroles Shell Berre, 1950–59; Shell Française: Pres. Man. Dir, 1967–70; Regional Co-ordinator Europe, 1970; Man. Dir, 1971–83, Mem. Supervisory Bd, 1983–93, Royal Dutch Shell Group. Director: La Radiotechnique SA, Paris, 1980–; Barclays Bank SA, Paris, 1989–; Seaperfect London. Senior Adviser, Lazard Frères, NY, 1983–90. Mem. Bd, INSEAD, Fontainebleau, 1983–. Hon. Pres., French Chamber of Commerce and Industry, Netherlands, 1980–; Vice-Pres., French Chamber of Commerce, GB, 1985–. Médaille des Evadés; Médaille de la Résistance; Chevalier du Mérite Agricole; Chevalier de l'Ordre National du Mérite; Comdr, Légion d'Honneur; Comdr, Order of Orange Nassau. *Recreation:* golf. *Address:* Channel Tunnel Group, The Adelphi, John Adam Street, WC2N 6JT. *T:* 0171–747 6747.

BENARROCH, Heather Mary, (Mrs E. J. Benarroch); *see* Harper, Heather.

BENAUD, Richard, OBE 1961; international sports consultant, journalist and media representative, television commentator: BBC, since 1960; Nine Network, Australia, since 1977; *b* 6 Oct. 1930; *s* of Louis Richard Benaud and Irene Benaud; *m* 1967, Daphne Elizabeth Surfleet; two *s* by previous marr. *Educ:* Parramatta High Sch. Captain, Australian Cricket Team, 28 Tests, played for Australia 63 Tests, Tours to England, 1953, 1956, 1961; first cricketer to achieve Test double, 2000 runs, 200 wickets, 1963. *Publications:* Way of Cricket, 1960; Tale of Two Tests, 1962; Spin Me a Spinner, 1963; The New Champions, 1965; Willow Patterns, 1972; Benaud on Reflection, 1984; The Appeal of Cricket, 1995. *Recreation:* golf. *Address:* (office) 19/178 Beach Street, Coogee, NSW 2034, Australia. *T:* Sydney (2) 6641124.

BENDALL, David Vere, CMG 1967; MBE 1945; HM Diplomatic Service, retired; *b* 27 Feb. 1920; *s* of John Manley Bendall; *m* 1941, Eve Stephanie Merrilees Galpin; one *d. Educ:* Winchester; King's Coll., Cambridge (BA). Served Grenadier Guards, 1940–46. Third Sec., Allied Force HQ, Caserta, 1946; Rome, 1947; FO, 1949; First Sec., Santiago, 1952; FO, 1955; seconded to NATO Secretariat, Paris 1957; FO, 1960; NATO Secretariat, Paris as Dep. Head, Economic and Finance Div. and Special Advisor on Defence Policy, 1962; Counsellor, 1962; Counsellor, Washington, 1965–69; Asst Under-Sec. of State for Western Europe, 1969–71. Chairman: Banque Morgan Grenfell en Suisse (formerly Morgan Grenfell Switzerland), 1974–90; Morgan Grenfell Internat. Ltd, 1979–85; Morgan Grenfell Italia, 1982–93; Banca Nazionale del Lavoro Investment Bank, 1986–94. Director: Morgan Grenfell (Holdings) Ltd, 1971–85; Morgan Grenfell France, 1986–90; Dep. Chm., Avon Cosmetics, 1979–90; Member: Morgan Grenfell Internat. Adv. Council, 1986–87; Internat. and London Adv. Bds, Banque de l'Indochine et de Suez, 1974–87. Chm., BRCS, 1980–85 (Vice-Chm., 1979–80); Vice-Chm., Finance Cttee, League of Red Cross Socs, 1981–85. CStJ 1985. *Recreations:* golf, tennis, shooting, languages. *Address:* 3 Eaton Terrace Mews, SW1W 8EU. *T:* 0171–730 4229; Ashbocking Hall, near Ipswich, Suffolk IP6 9LG. *T:* Helmingham (01473) 890262. *Club:* Boodle's.

BENDALL, Dr Eve Rosemarie Duffield; Chief Executive Officer, English National Board for Nursing, Midwifery and Health Visiting, 1981–86; *b* 7 Aug. 1927; *d* of Col F. W. D. Bendall, CMG, MA, and Mrs M. L. Bendall, LRAM, ARCM. *Educ:* Malvern Girls' Coll.; London Univ. (MA, PhD); Royal Free Hosp. (SRN). Ward Sister, Dorset County Hosp., 1953–55; Night Supt, Manchester Babies' Hosp., 1955–56; Nurse Tutor: United Sheffield Hosps Sch. of Nursing, 1958–61; St George's Hosp., London, 1961–63; Principal, Sch. of Nursing, Hosp. for Sick Children, Gt Ormond Street, 1963–69. Registrar, GNC, 1973–77. *Publications:* (jtly) Basic Nursing, 1963, 3rd edn 1970; (jtly) A Guide to Medical and Surgical Nursing, 1965, 2nd edn 1970; (jtly) A History of the General Nursing Council, 1969; So You Passed, Nurse (research), 1975. *Recreation:* gardening.

BENDALL, Vivian Walter Hough; MP (C) Ilford North, since March 1978; surveyor and valuer; *b* 14 Dec. 1938; *s* of late Cecil Aubrey Bendall and Olive Alvina Bendall (*née* Hough); *m* 1969, Ann Rosalind Jarvis (marr. diss. 1992). *Educ:* Coombe Hill House, Croydon; Broad Green Coll., Croydon. LRVA 1976, MRSH 1965. Mem. Croydon Council, 1964–78; Mem. GLC, 1970–73; Chm., Greater London Young Conservatives, 1967–68. Backbench Committees: Vice-Chm., Transport Cttee, 1982–83; Sec., Foreign and Commonwealth Affairs Cttee, 1981–84; Vice-Chm., Employment Cttee, 1984–87 (Jt Sec. 1981–84); Former Member: Central Council for Care of the Elderly; South Eastern Area Reg. Assoc. for the Blind; Mem., Dr Barnardo's New Mossford Home Fund Raising Cttee. Contested (C) Hertford and Stevenage, Feb. and Oct. 1974. *Recreation:* cricket. *Address:* 25A Brighton Road, South Croydon, Surrey CR2 6EA. *T:* 0181–688 0341. *Clubs:* Carlton; Essex County Cricket.

BENDER, Prof. Arnold Eric; Emeritus Professor, University of London; Professor of Nutrition and Dietetics, University of London and Head of Department of Food Science and Nutrition, Queen Elizabeth College, 1978–83 (Professor of Nutrition, 1971–78); *b* 24 July 1918; *s* of Isadore and Rose Bender; *m* 1941, Deborah Swift; two *s. Educ:* Liverpool Inst. High Sch.; Univ. of Liverpool (BSc Hons); Univ. of Sheffield (PhD). FRSH, FIFST. Research, Pharmaceutical Industry, 1940–45 and 1950–54; Res. Fellow, National Inst. of Radiotherapy, Sheffield, 1945–47; Lectr, Univ. of Sheffield, 1947–49; Research, Food Industry, 1954–64; Teaching and Research, Univ. of London, 1965–83. Department of Health and Social Security: Gp Sec. of Working Party on Protein Requirements, 1963; Mem., Sub-cttee on Protein Requirements, 1967; Mem., Cttee on Toxic Chemicals in Food and the Environment, 1976–83; Mem., Cttee on Med. Aspects of Food Policy, 1978–85; Chm., Panel on Novel Foods, 1980–85. Ministry of Agriculture, Fisheries and Food: Mem., Cttee on Dietetic Foods, 1969–73 and on Composition of Foods, 1975–77; Mem., Adv. Cttee on Irradiated and Novel Foods, 1981–85 and on Naturally Occurring Toxic Substances in Foods, 1983–90. Society of Chemical Industry: Mem. Council, 1982–85; Food Group: Hon. Sec., 1955–60; Chm., 1979–80; Vice-Chm., 1980–82; Chm., Nutrition Panel, 1960–63 and 1976–78. Royal Society of Health: Mem. Council, 1974–89; Chm. Council, 1987–88; Chm., Examinations Cttee, 1983–85; Chm., Conf. and Meetings Cttee, 1985–86; Chm., Food and Nutrition Gp, 1968–70 (Vice Chm., 1967–68). Member: Royal Soc. British Nat. Cttee for Biochem., 1963–69, for Nutritional Scis, 1976–85; Eur. Cttee for Co-operation in Sci. and Technol. (COST 91), 1980–83 (Chm., Nutrition Sub-cttee, 1982–83); Cttee on Protein Quality Evaluation, ARC, 1955–66; Sector D Res. Cttee, CNAA, 1982–91; Pres., Inst. Food Sci. and Technol., 1989–91; Vice-Pres., Internat. Union of Food Sci. and Technol., 1983–87 (Mem. Exec., 1978–83). Hon. Treasurer, UK Nutrition Soc., 1962–67; Hon. Sec., UK Council for Food Sci. and Technol., 1964–77. Hon. DSc Univ. Complutense, Madrid, 1983. Mem. Editorial Board: Jl of Human Nutrition; Jl of Science of Food and Agriculture; Jl of Food Technol.; British Jl of Nutrition; Jl of Envmtl Mgt and Health. *Publications:* Dictionary of Nutrition and Food Technology, 1960, 6th edn 1990, Japanese edn 1965, Arabic edn 1985; Nutrition and Dietetic Foods, 1967, 2nd edn 1973; Value of Food, 1970, 3rd edn 1979, Spanish edn 1972; Facts of Food, 1975, Polish edn 1979; Food Processing and Nutrition, 1978, Japanese edn 1978; The Pocket Guide to Calories and Nutrition, 1979, 2nd edn 1986, Dutch, US, Italian and Spanish edns, 1981; Nutrition for Medical Students, 1982; Health or Hoax?, 1985, Spanish edn 1987; Food Tables, 1986; Food Labelling, 1992; Meat and meat products in developing countries, 1992; Dictionary of Food and Health, 1995; research papers and review articles in Brit. Jl of Nutrition, Biochem. Jl, BMJ, Jl Human Nutrition, Jl Science Food and Agric., and other professional jls, and reports. *Recreations:* writing, gardening, lecturing. *Address:* 2 Willow Vale, Fetcham, Leatherhead, Surrey KT22 9TE. *T:* Bookham (01372) 454702.

See also B. G. Bender.

BENDER, Dr Brian Geoffrey; Deputy Secretary and Head of European Secretariat, Cabinet Office, since 1994; *b* 25 Feb. 1949; *s* of Arnold Eric Bender, *qv*; *m* 1974, Penelope Clark; one *s* one *d. Educ:* Greenford Grammar Sch.; Imperial Coll., London Univ. (BSc, PhD). Joined DTI, 1973; Private Sec. to Sec. of State for Trade, 1976–77; First Sec. (Trade Policy), Office of UK Permanent Rep. to EC, 1977–82; Principal (responsible for internat. steel issues), DTI, 1982–84; Counsellor (Industry), Office of UK Permanent Rep. to EC, 1985–89; Under Sec. and Dep. Head of European Secretariat, Cabinet Office, 1990–93; Hd of Regl Develt Div., DTI, 1993–94. *Recreations:* family, theatre. *Address:* Cabinet Office, 70 Whitehall, SW1A 2AS.

BENDERSKY, Pamela May H.; *see* Hudson-Bendersky.

BENDJAMA, Amar; Ambassador of Algeria to the Court of St James's, since 1994; *b* Constantine, Algeria, 1 Jan. 1951; *m*; two *c. Educ:* Nat. Sch. of Admin., Algiers. Ministry of Foreign Affairs, Algeria: Hd of Official Visits Desk, Protocol Dept, 1975–79; Counsellor, Moscow, 1980–84; Dep. Dir, European Dept, 1984–89; First Counsellor, Perm. Mission to UN in NY, and Dep. Rep. to Security Council, 1989–90; Chargé d'Affaires, Perm. Mission to UN in NY, 1990–91; Ambassador to Ethiopia, Djibouti and Eritrea, 1992–94. Permanent Representative to OAU and UNECA, 1992–94, Chairman: Conf. Cttee, OAU, 1992–93; Adv. Cttee for Admin. and Budgetary Issues, OAU, 1993–94. *Address:* Algerian Embassy, 54 Holland Park, W11 3RJ. *T:* 0171–221 7800.

BENEDICTUS, David Henry; writer and director for stage, television and radio; *b* 16 Sept. 1938; *s* of late Henry Jules Benedictus and Kathleen Constance (*née* Ricardo); *m* 1971, Yvonne Daphne Antrobus; one *s* one *d. Educ:* Stone House, Broadstairs; Eton College; Balliol College, Oxford (BA English); State Univ. of Iowa. News and current affairs, BBC Radio, 1961; Drama Director, BBC TV, 1962; Story Editor, Wednesday Play and Festival Series, BBC, 1965; Thames TV Trainee Director, at Bristol Old Vic, 1968; Asst Dir, RSC, Aldwych, 1970; Judith E. Wilson Vis. Fellow, Cambridge, and Fellow Commoner, Churchill Coll., Cambridge, 1981–82; Commissioning Editor, Drama Series, Channel 4 TV, 1984–86; BBC Radio: Readings Editor, 1989–91; Editor, Readings, 1991; Editor, Radio 3 Drama, 1992; Sen. Producer, Serial Readings, 1993 (incl. The Bible, 1992; Arcadia, 1993; Jack, 1994; Macbeth, 1995). Writer in Residence: Sutton Library, Surrey, 1975; Kibbutz Gezer, Israel, 1978; Bitterne Library, Southampton, 1983–84. Antiques corresp., Standard, 1977–80; reviewer for books, stage, films, records, for major newspapers and magazines. Dir, Kingston Books, 1988–90. Member: Amnesty International; Writers' Guild; Liberal Democratic Party; Trustee, Performing Arts Lab. Plays include: Betjemania, 1976; The Golden Key, 1982; What A Way To Run A Revolution!, 1985; You Say Potato, 1992. *Publications:* The Fourth of June, 1962; You're a Big Boy Now, 1963; This Animal is Mischievous, 1965; Hump, or Bone by Bone Alive, 1967; The Guru and the Golf Club, 1969; A World of Windows, 1971; The Rabbi's Wife, 1976; Junk, how and where to buy beautiful things at next to nothing prices, 1976; A Twentieth Century Man, 1978; The Antique Collector's Guide, 1980; Lloyd George (from Elaine Morgan's screenplay), 1981; Whose Life is it Anyway? (from Brian Clarke's screenplay), 1981; Who Killed the Prince Consort?, 1982; Local Hero (from Bill Forsyth's screenplay), 1983; The Essential London Guide, 1984; Floating Down to Camelot, 1985; The Streets of London, 1986; The Absolutely Essential London Guide, 1986; Little Sir Nicholas, 1990; (with Prof. Hans Kalmus) Odyssey of a Scientist, 1991; Sunny Intervals and Showers, 1992; The Stamp Collector, 1994. *Recreations:* chess, tennis, cricket, auctions, table tennis, piano playing, horse racing, eating. *Address:* 19 Oxford Road, Teddington, Middlesex TW11 0QA. *T:* 0181–977 4715.

BENEDIKTSSON, Einar, MA; Knight Commander, Order of the Falcon, Iceland; Ambassador for Iceland to USA, also accredited to Canada, Mexico, Chile, Argentina and Uruguay, since 1993; *b* Reykjavik, 30 April 1931; *s* of Stefan M. Benediktsson and Sigridur

Oddsdóttir; *m* 1956, Elsa Petursdóttir; three *s* two *d. Educ:* Colgate Univ., NY; Fletcher Sch. of Law and Diplomacy, Mass; London Sch. of Econs and Pol. Science; Inst. des Etudes Européennes, Turin. With OEEC, 1956–60; Head of Section, Mins of Econ. Affairs and Commerce, 1961–64, and Min. of For. Affairs, 1964; Counsellor, Paris, 1964–68; Head of Section, Min. of For. Affairs, 1968–70; Perm. Rep. to Internat. Orgns, Geneva, 1970–76; Chm., EFTA Council, 1975; Ambassador to France (also accredited to Spain and Portugal, and Perm. Rep. to OECD and UNESCO, 1976–82); Ambassador to UK and concurrently to The Netherlands, Nigeria and Ireland, 1982–86; Perm. Rep. to N Atlantic Council, 1986–90, and Ambassador to Belgium and Luxembourg, 1986–91; Ambassador to Norway, also to Poland and Czechoslovakia, 1991–93. Holds foreign decorations. *Address:* Embassy of Iceland, 1156 15th Street NW, Washington, DC 20005, USA. *T:* (202) 2656653; 2443 Kalorama Road NW, Washington, DC 20008. *T:* (202) 3323040.

BENETTON, Luciano; industrialist; *b* 13 May 1935. Established Fratelli Benetton (with brothers), 1965; founder and Pres., Benetton, 1978; Benetton Holdings, 1981; Vice-Pres. and Man. Dir, Benetton Group SpA; Mem. Board, Edizione Holding SpA; Pres., Benetton Foundn. Mem., Italian Senate, 1992–94. Awards: Civiltà Veneta, 1986; Premio Creatività, 1992. *Publications:* contribs to La Biblioteca di Harvard, economic and business strategies, 1988. *Address:* Benetton Group SpA, via Minelli 1, 31050 Ponzano (TV), Italy. *T:* (422) 4491.

BENGOUGH, Sir Piers (Henry George), KCVO 1986; OBE 1973; DL; Her Majesty's Representative, Ascot, since 1982; *b* 24 May 1929; *s* of Nigel and Alice Bengough; *m* 1952, Bridget Shirley Adams; two *s. Educ:* Eton. Commnd 10th Royal Hussars (PWO), 1948; commanded Royal Hussars (PWO), 1971–73, retired. Formerly amateur rider; wins incl. Grand Military Gold Cup (4 times). Member: Jockey Club, 1965– (Steward, 1974–77, 1990–92); Horserace Betting Levy Board, 1978–81; Director: Cheltenham Steeplechase Co., 1977–90; Hereford Racecourse Co., 1974–; Ludlow Race Club, 1979–; Chm., Compensation Fund for Jockeys, 1981–89. Mem., HM Bodyguard, Hon. Corps of Gentlemen-at-Arms, 1981–. Hon. Col The Royal Hussars (PWO), 1983–90. DL Hereford and Worcester, 1987. *Recreations:* shooting, fishing. *Address:* Great House, Canon Pyon, Hereford HR4 8PD. *Clubs:* Cavalry and Guards, Pratt's.

BENINGFIELD, Gordon George; artist, since 1966; *b* 31 Oct. 1936; *s* of George Robert Edward Beningfield and Emily Ellen (*née* McNally); *m* 1958, Elizabeth Boyce; two *d. Educ:* London Colney Secondary Sch. Ecclesiastical artist, 1952–65. President: Brit. Butterfly Conservation Soc., 1989–; Blackmore Vale Br., NT, 1989–. Designed and engraved 8 meml windows for the Guards Chapel, 1972–94; designed stamps for GPO: Butterfly, 1981; Insects, 1985; many philatelic designs worldwide. One-man exhibns, London, 1967–. Freeman, City of London, 1995; Liveryman, Glass Sellers' Co., 1995–. *Publications:* Beningfield's Butterflies, 1978; Beningfield's Countryside, 1980; Hardy Country, 1983; Beningfield's English Landscapes, 1985; Beningfield's English Farm, 1988; Hardy Landscapes, 1990; Beningfield's Woodland, 1993; Gordon Beningfield, the Artist and his Work: a pictorial autobiography, 1994; *illustrator:* Darkling Thrush, 1985; Poems of the Countryside, 1987; Green and Pleasant Land, 1989; Poems of the Seasons, 1992. *Recreations:* enjoying the rural landscape, natural history, general British history. *Address:* 3 The Moor, Water End, near Hemel Hempstead, Herts HP1 3BL. *T:* Hemel Hempstead (01442) 68356.

BENJAMIN, Prof. Bernard; Professor of Actuarial Science, The City University, London, 1973–75, now Emeritus; *b* 8 March 1910; *s* of Joseph and Lucy Benjamin, London; *m* 1937, May Pate, Horham, Suffolk; two *d. Educ:* Colfe Grammar Sch.; Sir John Cass Coll. (London University). BSc (Hons); PhD London. LCC, 1928; statistician Public Health Dept, 1940; served War, 1943–46, RAF; statistician, General Register Office, 1952; Chief Statistician, 1954; Dir of Statistics, Ministry of Health, 1963–65; Dir of Research and Intelligence, GLC, 1965–70; Dir of Statistical Studies, CS College, 1970–73; Hon. Cons. in Med. Stats to Army, 1966. Chm., Statistics Users Council (formerly Standing Cttee of Statistics Users), 1971–90. Fellow: Inst. of Actuaries (a Vice-Pres. 1963; Pres., 1966–68; Gold Medal, 1975); Royal Statistical Soc. (Pres. 1970–71; Guy Medal in Gold, 1986); Galton Inst. (formerly Eugenics Soc.) (Pres., 1982–87; Galton Lectr, 1981). Hon. DSc: City Univ., London, 1981; Kent Univ. 1987. Internat. Insurance Prize of Italy, 1985. *Publications:* Social and Economic Factors in Mortality, 1965; Health and Vital Statistics, 1968; Demographic Analysis, 1969; The Population Census, 1970; (with H. W. Haycocks) The Analysis of Mortality and Other Actuarial Statistics, 1971; Statistics in Urban Administration, 1976; (ed) Medical Records, 1977; General Insurance, 1977; (jtly) The Analysis of Mortality and Other Actuarial Statistics, 1980, 3rd edn 1993; (jtly) Pensions: the problems of today and tomorrow, 1987; Population Statistics, 1989; (with Amal Soliman) Mortality on the Move, 1993; numerous medical and population statistical papers and contribs to Jl of Royal Statistical Society and Jl of Inst. of Actuaries. *Recreations:* gardening, painting (both kinds). *Address:* c/o Centre for Insurance and Investment, City University, Northampton Square, EC1. *Club:* Athenæum.

BENJAMIN, George William John; composer, occasional conductor and pianist; *b* 31 Jan. 1960; *s* of William Benjamin and Susan Benjamin (*née* Bendon). *Educ:* Westminster School (private tuition with Peter Gellhorn); Paris Conservatoire (Olivier Messiaen); King's College, Cambridge (Alexander Goehr). MA, MusB. First London orchestral performance, BBC Proms, 1980; research at Institut de Recherche et Coordination Acoustique/Musique, Paris, 1984–87; Prince Consort Prof. of Composition, RCM; performs, conducts and lectures on own and other contemp. music, GB, Europe, USA, Far East. Artistic Dir, contemp. music festivals, USA (San Francisco Symphony Orch.), France (Opéra Bastille), 1992, and London (South Bank), 1993. Featured composer, Salzburg Fest., 1995. Hon. FRCM 1993. Lili Boulanger Award, USA, 1985; Koussevitzky Internat. Record Award, 1987; Gramophone Contemp. Music Award, 1990. *Publications include: orchestral:* Altitude, 1977; Ringed by the Flat Horizon, 1980; A Mind of Winter, 1981; At First Light, 1982; Jubilation, 1985; Antara, 1987; Sudden Time, 1993; Three Inventions for Chamber Orchestra, 1995; *chamber music:* Piano Sonata, 1978; Octet, 1978; Flight, 1979; Sortilèges, 1981; Three Studies for Solo Piano, 1985; Upon Silence, 1990, 1991. *Address:* c/o Faber Music Ltd, 3 Queen Square, WC1N 3AU.

BENJAMIN, Pauline, (Mrs Joseph Benjamin); *see* Crabbe, Pauline.

BENJAMIN, Dr Ralph, CB 1980; DSc, PhD, BSc, FCGI, FEng, FIEE; Visiting Professor: University College and Imperial College of Science, Technology and Medicine, University of London, since 1988; University of Bristol, since 1993; *b* 17 Nov. 1922; *s* of Charles Benjamin and Claire Benjamin (*née* Stern); *m* 1951, Kathleen Ruth Bull, BA; one *s* (and one *s* decd). *Educ:* in Germany and Switzerland; St Oswald's Coll., Ellesmere; Imperial Coll. of Science and Technology, London. DSc(Eng) London, 1970; FEng 1983; FCGI 1982. Joined Royal Naval Scientific Service, 1944; Senior Scientific Officer, 1949; Principal Scientific Officer, 1952; Senior Principal Scientific Officer (Special Merit), 1955; Deputy Chief Scientific Officer (Special Merit), 1960; Head of Research and Deputy Chief Scientist, Admiralty Surface Weapons Establishment, 1961; Dir and Chief Scientist, Admiralty Underwater Weapons Estab., 1964–71, and Dir, Underwater Weapons R&D (Navy), 1965–71; Chief Scientist, GCHQ, 1971–82; Head of Communications Techniques, SHAPE Technical Centre, The Hague, 1982–87. Hon. consultant: Univ. of Illinois; US Office of Naval Research, 1956.IEE Marconi Premium, 1964; IERE Heinrich Hertz Premium, 1980, 1983. Chm., Bristol Area IEE, 1992–93; Council Mem., Brit. Acoustical Soc., 1971. Vis. Prof., Dept of Electrical and Electronic Engineering, Univ. of Surrey, 1973–80. FRSA 1984. *Publications:* Modulation, Resolution and Signal Processing for Radar Sonar and Related Systems, 1966; contribs to various advisory cttees, working parties, symposia, etc; articles in Jls of Inst. of Electrical and Electronic Engrs, Instn of Electrical Engineers and Inst. of Electronic and Radio Engineers, etc. *Recreations:* work, mountaineering, ski-ing, swimming, sub-aqua, canoeing, windsurfing. *Address:* 13 Bellhouse Walk, Rockwell Park, Bristol BS11 0UE. *Club:* Athenæum.

BENN, Anthony, OBE 1945; *b* 7 Oct. 1912; *s* of late Francis Hamilton Benn and Arta Clara Benn (*née* Boal); *m* 1943, Maureen Lillian Kathleen Benn (*née* Denbigh) (*d* 1992); two *s* four *d. Educ:* Harrow; Christ Church, Oxford (Scholar). Oxford Univ. Cricket XI, 1935. Price & Pierce Ltd, 1935 (Director, 1947, Chm., 1956–72). Joined Surrey and Sussex Yeomanry, 1936. Served War of 1939–45 (OBE): Staff Coll., 1942; Instructor, Middle East Staff Coll., 1943. Comdr, Order of the Lion of Finland, 1958. *Recreation:* travel.

BENN, Edward, CMG 1981; Minister (Defence Equipment), British Embassy, Washington, 1978–82, retired; *b* 8 May 1922; *s* of John Henry Benn and Alice (*née* Taylor); *m* 1947, Joan Taylor; one *d. Educ:* High Storrs Grammar Sch., Sheffield; Sheffield Univ. (BEng; 1st Cl. Hons Civil Engrg; Mappin Medal, 1943). Operational Research with Army, 1943–48; India and Burma, 1944–46 (Major); entered War Office, 1948; tank research, Supt Special Studies, and later Dep. Dir, Army Op. Res. Estabt, 1961; Asst Sci. Adviser to SACEUR, Paris, 1962–65; Dep. Chief Sci. Adviser, Home Office, 1966–68; Dir, Defence Policy, MoD, 1968–75; Under Sec. and Dep. Chief Scientist (RAF), MoD, 1975–78. *Recreation:* golf. *Address:* Pemberley, St Elizabeths, Eastcombe, Stroud, Glos GL6 7DR. *Clubs:* MCC; Minchinhampton Golf.

BENN, Edward Glanvill; Life President, Benn Brothers plc, Publishers, since 1976, Chairman, 1945–75; *b* 1905; 2nd *s* of late Sir Ernest Benn, 2nd Bt, CBE; *m* 1931, Beatrice Catherine, MBE, *d* of Claude Newbald; one *s* one *d. Educ:* Harrow; Clare Coll., Cambridge. Served War of 1939–45, East Surrey Regt, 1940–45; Brigade Major, 138 Infantry Brigade, Italy, 1944 (despatches). Council Member: Nat. Advertising Benevolent Soc., 1937–61 (Trustee, 1951–80, and Pres. 1961–62); Advertising Assoc., 1951–67 (Hon. Treasurer 1960–65); Commonwealth Press Union, 1956– (Hon. Treasurer 1967–77, Hon. Life Mem. 1975; Astor Award, 1982); Vice Pres., Readers' Pension Cttee, 1950–; Life Vice Pres., Newspaper Press Fund, 1965– (Appeals Pres. 1971); Chm., Advertising Advisory Cttee, Independent Television Authority, 1959–64 (Mackintosh medal, 1967); Dir., Exchange Telegraph Co. Ltd, 1960–72 (Chm. 1969–72); Pres., Periodical Publishers Assoc., 1976–78. Master, Stationers' Company, 1977. *Address:* Crescent Cottage, Aldeburgh, Suffolk IP15 5HW. *Clubs:* Reform (Hon. Life Mem.); Tandridge Golf (Hon. Life Mem.).

See also Sir J. J. Benn.

BENN, Sir (James) Jonathan, 4th Bt *cr* 1914; Chairman, SCA Pension Trusts Ltd, since 1988; Director, Broomhill Trust, since 1991; *b* 27 July 1933; *s* of Sir John Andrews Benn, 3rd Bt, and of Hon. Ursula Lady Benn, *o d* of 1st Baron Hankey, PC, GCB, GCMG, GCVO, FRS; *S* father, 1984; *m* 1960, Jennifer Mary, *e d* of late Dr Wilfred Howells, OBE; one *s* one *d. Educ:* Harrow; Clare College, Cambridge (MA). Various positions with Reed International PLC (formerly A. E. Reed & Co.), 1957–88; Director, Reed Paper & Board (UK) Ltd, 1971, Managing Dir 1976; Director, Reed Group Ltd, 1976; Chm. and Chief Exec., Reed Paper & Board (UK) Ltd, 1977–90; Chm., Reedpack Paper Gp, 1988–90; Dir, Reedpack Ltd, 1988–90. Pres., British Paper and Board Industries Fedn, 1985–87. *Recreations:* golf, skiing, music. *Heir: s* Robert Ernest Benn [*b* 17 Oct. 1963; *m* 1985, Sheila Margaret, 2nd *d* of Dr Alastair Blain]. *Address:* Fielden Lodge, Ightham, Kent TN15 9AN.

See also E. G. Benn, T. J. Benn.

BENN, Sir Jonathan; *see* Benn, Sir (James) J.

BENN, Timothy John; Chairman, Timothy Benn Publishing Ltd, since 1983, and other companies; *b* 27 Oct. 1936; *yr s* of Sir John Andrews Benn, 3rd Bt, and of Hon. Ursula Helen Alers Hankey; *m* 1982, Christina Grace Townsend. *Educ:* Harrow; Clare Coll., Cambridge (MA); Princeton Univ., USA; Harvard Business Sch., USA (National Marketing Council Course; Scholarship Award). FInstM. 2nd Lieut Scots Guards, 1956–57. Benn Brothers Ltd: Board Member, 1961–82; Managing Director, 1972–82; Dep. Chm., 1976–81; Chm., Benn Brothers plc, 1981–82; Ernest Benn: Board Member, 1967–82; Managing Director, 1973–82; Chairman and Managing Director, 1974–82. Chairman: Bouverie Publishing Co., 1983–; Buckley Press (Publr, Post Magazine and Insurance Monitor, Re-insurance, Insurance Directory), 1984–; Henry Greenwood and Co., 1987–; Dalesman Publishing Co. (Publr, The Dalesman, Cumbria), 1989–. Pres., Tonbridge Civic Soc., 1982–87. *Publication:* The (Almost) Compleat Angler, 1985. *Recreations:* writing, gardening, toymaking. *Address:* The Priory, Bordyke, Tonbridge, Kent TN9 1NN. *Club:* Flyfishers'.

See also Sir J. J. Benn.

BENN, Rt. Hon. Tony; PC 1964; MP (Lab) Chesterfield, since March 1984; *b* 3 April 1925; *er* surv. *s* of 1st Viscount Stansgate, DSO, DFC, PC, former Labour MP and Cabinet Minister (*d* 1960); having unsuccessfully attempted to renounce his right of succession, 1955 and 1960, won a bye-election in May 1961 only to be prevented from taking seat; instigated Act to make disclaimer possible, and disclaimed title for life, 1963; *m* 1949, Caroline Middleton De Camp, MA; three *s* one *d.* Served: RAFVR, 1943–45; RNVR, 1945–46. Joined Labour Party, 1943; Mem., NEC, 1959–60, 1962–93 (Chm., 1971–72); candidate for leadership of Labour Party, 1976, 1988, and for dep. leadership, 1971, 1981. MP (Lab) Bristol SE, Nov. 1950–1960 and Aug. 1963–1983; Postmaster-Gen., 1964–66, recommended establishment of GPO as public corp. and founded Giro; Minister of Technology, 1966–70, assumed responsibility for Min. of Aviation, 1967 and Min. of Power, 1969; opposition spokesman on Trade and Industry, 1970–74; Sec. of State for Industry and Minister for Posts and Telecommunications, 1974–75; Sec. of State for Energy, 1975–79. Pres., EEC Council of Energy Ministers, 1977. Pres., Campaign Gp, 1987–. Contested (Lab) Bristol East, 1983. *Publications:* The Privy Council as a Second Chamber, 1957; The Regeneration of Britain, 1964; The New Politics, 1970; Speeches, 1974; Arguments for Socialism, 1979; Arguments for Democracy, 1981; (ed) Writings on the Wall: a radical and socialist anthology 1215–1984, 1984; Out of the Wilderness, Diaries 1963–1967, 1987; Fighting Back: speaking out for Socialism in the Eighties, 1988; Office Without Power, Diaries 1968–72, 1988; Against the Tide, Diaries 1973–76, 1989; Conflicts of Interest, Diaries 1977–80, 1990; A Future for Socialism, 1991; The End of an Era, Diaries 1980–1990, 1992; (jtly) Common Sense, 1993; Years of Hope: Diaries, Letters and Papers 1940–1962, 1994; numerous pamphlets. *Address:* House of Commons, SW1A 0AA.

BENNER, Patrick, CB 1975; Deputy Secretary, Department of Health and Social Security, 1976–84; *b* 26 May 1923; *s* of Henry Grey and Gwendolen Benner; *m* 1952, Joan Christabel Draper; two *d*. *Educ:* Ipswich Sch.; University Coll., Oxford. Entered Min. of Health as Asst Princ., 1949; Princ., 1951; Princ. Private Sec. to Minister, 1955; Asst Sec., 1958; Under-Sec., Min. of Health, 1967–68, DHSS 1968–72; Dep. Sec., Cabinet Office, 1972–76. Chm., Rural Dispensing Cttee, 1987–91; Member: Exec. Council, Hosp. Saving Assoc., 1984–; Exec. Cttee, Musicians Benevolent Fund, 1985–. *Address:* 12 Manor Gardens, Hampton, Mddx TW12 2TU. *T:* 0181–783 0848. *Club:* National Liberal.

BENNET, family name of **Earl of Tankerville.**

BENNETT, Alan; dramatist and actor; *b* 9 May 1934; *s* of Walter Bennett and Lilian Mary Peel; unmarried. *Educ:* Leeds Modern Sch.; Exeter Coll., Oxford (BA Modern History, 1957; Hon. Fellow, 1987). Jun. Lectr, Modern History, Magdalen Coll., Oxford, 1960–62. Trustee, National Gall., 1994–. Hon. DLitt Leeds, 1990. Co-author and actor, Beyond the Fringe, Royal Lyceum, Edinburgh, 1960, Fortune, London, 1961 and Golden, NY, 1962; author and actor, On the Margin (TV series), 1966; *stage plays:* Forty Years On, Apollo, 1968; Getting On, Queen's, 1971; Habeas Corpus, Lyric, 1973; The Old Country, Queen's, 1977; Enjoy, Vaudeville, 1980; Kafka's Dick, Royal Court, 1986; Single Spies (double bill: A Question of Attribution; An Englishman Abroad (also dir)), NT, 1988; The Wind in the Willows (adapted), NT, 1990; The Madness of George III, NT, 1991; *BBC TV films:* A Day Out, 1972; Sunset Across the Bay, 1975; *TV Plays for LWT*, 1978–79: Doris and Doreen; The Old Crowd; Me! I'm Afraid of Virginia Woolf; All Day on the Sands; Afternoon Off; One Fine Day; *BBC TV plays:* A Little Outing, A Visit from Miss Prothero, 1977; Intensive Care, Say Something Happened, Our Winnie, Marks, A Woman of No Importance, Rolling Home; An Englishman Abroad, 1983; The Insurance Man, 1986; Talking Heads (series), 1988 (adapted for stage comedy, 1992); 102 Boulevard Haussmann, 1991; A Question of Attribution, 1991; *BBC TV documentary:* Dinner at Noon, 1988; Portrait or Bust, 1994; The Abbey, 1995; *Channel 4:* Poetry in Motion, 1990; Poetry in Motion 2, 1992; *feature films:* A Private Function, 1984; Prick Up Your Ears, 1987; The Madness of King George, 1995. *Publications:* (with Cook, Miller and Moore) Beyond the Fringe, 1962; Forty Years On, 1969; Getting On, 1972; Habeas Corpus, 1973; The Old Country, 1978; Enjoy, 1980; Office Suite, 1981; Objects of Affection, 1982; A Private Function, 1984; The Writer in Disguise, 1985; Prick Up Your Ears (screenplay), 1987; Two Kafka Plays, 1987; Talking Heads, 1988 (Hawthornden Prize, 1989); Single Spies, 1989; The Lady in the Van, 1990; Poetry in Motion, 1990; The Wind in the Willows (adaptation), 1991; The Madness of George III, 1992; (jtly) Poetry in Motion 2, 1992; Writing Home, 1994 (collected articles); The Madness of King George (screenplay), 1995. *Address:* c/o Peters Fraser & Dunlop, The Chambers, Chelsea Harbour, Lots Road, SW10 0XF. *T:* 0171–376 7676.

BENNETT, (Albert) Edward; Director, G24 Nuclear Safety Assistance Co-ordination Centre, 1992–95, and Directorate of Nuclear Safety, Industry and the Environment, and Civil Protection (formerly of Nuclear Safety and Control of Chemical Pollution), 1987–95, European Commission; *b* 11 Sept. 1931; *s* of Albert Edward and Frances Ann Bennett; *m* 1957, Jean Louise Paston-Cooper; two *s*. *Educ:* University Coll. Sch., Hampstead; London Hosp. Med. Coll. MB BS London; FFCM 1972, FFOM 1984. Surgeon Lieut, RN, 1957–60; Senior Lectr, Dept of Clinical Epidemiology and Social Medicine, St. Thomas's Hosp. Med. Sch., 1964–70; Dir, Health Services Evaluation Gp, Univ. of Oxford, 1970–77; Prof. and Head of Dept of Clinical Epidemiology and Social Medicine, St George's Hosp. Med. Sch., Univ. of London, 1974–81; Director: Health and Safety Directorate, EEC, 1981–87. Hon. Editor, Internat. Jl of Epidemiology, 1977–81. *Publications:* Questionnaires in Medicine, 1975; (ed) Communications between Doctors and Patients, 1976; (ed) Recent Advances in Community Medicine, 1978; numerous sci. reports and contribs on epidemiology of chronic disease and evaluation of health services. *Recreations:* opera, gardening, browsing. *Address:* The Walled Garden, Liston, Sudbury, Suffolk CO10 7HT. *T:* Sudbury (01787) 374746. *Club:* Athenæum.

BENNETT, Albert Joseph, CBE 1966; Secretary, National Health Service Staff Commission, 1972–75; Vice-Chairman, Paddington and North Kensington Health Authority, 1982–85; *b* 9 April 1913; *er s* of late Albert James Bennett and late Alice Bennett, Stourbridge, Worcs; unmarried. *Educ:* King Edward VI Sch., Stourbridge; St John's Coll., Cambridge (MA) Mathematical Tripos (Wrangler). Admin. Officer, LCC, 1936–39; Central Midwives Board: Asst Sec., 1939–45; Sec., 1945–47; Instructor Lieut, later Lt-Comdr, RN, 1940–45; Sec., NW Met. Regional Hosp. Bd, 1947–65; Principal Officer, NHS Nat. Staff Cttee, 1965–72; Under-Sec., DHSS, 1972–75, seconded as Sec., NHS Staff Commn. Member: Nat. Selection Cttee for Recruitment of Trainee Hospital Admin. Staff, 1955–64; Cttee of Inquiry into the Recruitment, Training and Promotion of Admin. and Clerical Staff in Hospital Service, 1962–63; Adv. Cttee on Hospital Engineers Training, 1967–72; Admin. Training Cttee, Cttee of Vice-Chancellors and Principals, 1970–72; Kensington and Chelsea and Westminster AHA(T), 1977–82, and Family Practitioner Cttee, 1977–85. *Recreations:* walking, gardening. *Address:* 19 Garson House, Gloucester Terrace, W2 3DG. *T:* 0171–262 8311.

BENNETT, Andrew Francis; MP (Lab) Denton and Reddish, since 1983 (Stockport North, Feb. 1974–1983); teacher; *b* Manchester, 9 March 1939; *m*; two *s* one *d*. *Educ:* Birmingham Univ. (BSocSc). Joined Labour Party, 1957; Member, Oldham Borough Council, 1964–74. Member, National Union of Teachers. Contested (Lab) Knutsford, 1970; an Opposition spokesperson on educn, 1983–88. Interested especially in social services and education. *Recreations:* photography, walking, climbing. *Address:* 28 Brownsville Road, Stockport SK4 4PF; House of Commons, SW1A 0AA.

BENNETT, Andrew John; Chief Natural Resources Adviser, Overseas Development Administration, Foreign and Commonwealth Office, since 1987; *b* 25 April 1942; *s* of Leonard Charles Bennett and Edna Mary Bennett (*née* Harding). *Educ:* St Edward's Sch., Oxford; University Coll. of N Wales (BSc Agr Scis 1965); Univ. of West Indies, Trinidad (DipTropAg 1967); Univ. of Reading (MSc Crop Protection 1970). VSO Kenya, 1965–66; Agricl Officer (Research), Govt of St Vincent, 1967–69; Maize Agronomist, Govt of Malawi, 1971–74; Crop Develt Manager, 1976–78, Chief Research Officer, 1978–79, S Region, Sudan; Asst Agricl Adviser, ODA, 1980–83; Natural Resources Adviser (ODA), SE Asia Develt Div., Bangkok, 1983–85; Head, British Develt Div. in Pacific (ODA), Fiji, 1985–87. *Recreations:* walking, boating. *Address:* Overseas Development Administration, 94 Victoria Street, SW1E 5JL. *T:* 0171–917 0619.

BENNETT, Charles John Michael, CBE 1974; FCA; Partner in Barton, Mayhew & Co., Chartered Accountants, 1937–71; *b* 29 June 1906; *e s* of late Hon. Sir Charles Alan Bennett and Constance Radeglance, *d* of Major John Nathaniel Still; *m* 1931, Audrey (*d* 1990), *o d* of J. C. C. Thompson (killed in action, 1915) and Norah K. Davenport; two *d*. *Educ:* Clifton Coll.; Trinity Coll., Cambridge. Served with HM Forces, 1939–45: Major, RAPC, India, 1942–45. Member: Electricity Supply Companies Commn, 1959, in Hong Kong; Fiji Sugar Inquiry Commn, 1961; Commn of Inquiry (Sugar Industry) 1962, in Mauritius; Commn of Inquiry into Banana Industry of St Lucia, 1963; Commn of Inquiry (Chm.) into Sugar Industry and Agriculture of Antigua, 1965; Commn of Enquiry into Sugar Industry of Guyana, 1967; Cttee of Enquiry into the pricing of certain contracts for the overhaul of aero-engines by Bristol Siddeley Engines Ltd. Mem. of Council, Institute of Chartered Accountants, 1963–69. Part-time Mem., Commonwealth Development Corp., 1965–73, Dep. Chm. 1970–71, 1972–73; Independent Mem., NEDC for Chemical Industry, and Chm., Pharmaceuticals Working Party, 1969. Mem., E Anglian Regional Cttee of Nat. Trust, 1971–81. *Recreations:* golf, fishing. *Address:* 2 The Beeches, Station Road, Holt, Norfolk, NR25 6BS. *T:* Holt (01263) 713479. *Clubs:* Oriental; Royal West Norfolk Golf; Denham Golf.

See also R. H. Cooke.

BENNETT, Sir Charles (Moihi), Kt 1975; DSO 1943; company director, retired; President, New Zealand Labour Party, 1972–76; *b* 27 July 1913; *s* of Rt Rev. Frederick August Bennett, Bishop of Aotearoa, 1928–50, and Rangioue Bennett; *m* 1947, Elizabeth May Stewart. *Educ:* Univ. of New Zealand; Exeter Coll., Oxford. MA, DipSocSci, DipEd. Director of Maori Welfare, 1954–57; High Comr for New Zealand to Fedn of Malaya, 1959–63; Asst Sec., Dept of Maori Affairs, 1963–69. Mem., NZ Prisons Parole Bd, 1974–76. Hon. LLD Canterbury Univ. of NZ, 1973. Hon. Kt PMN (Malaysia), 1963. *Address:* 72 Boucher Avenue, Te Puke 3071, New Zealand.

See also Sir J. M. Bennett, Rt Rev. M. A. Bennett.

BENNETT, Corinne Gillian, MBE 1988; Cathedrals Architect at English Heritage, since 1992; *b* 3 March 1935; *d* of Gilbert Wilson and Lucile (*née* Terroux); *m* 1979, Keith Charles Hugh Bennett. *Educ:* University Coll. London (BA Hons Arch. 1957; Inst. of Archaeology, London Univ. (Dip. Conservation of Historic Monuments 1964). ARIBA 1959. Assistant Architect: Powell & Moya, 1958–61; Manning & Clamp, 1961–62; Architect, Ancient Monuments Br., MPBW, 1963–68; joined Purcell Miller Tritton, Associate, 1968, Partner, 1972–92. Consulting Surveyor, Archdeacons of Rochester Dio., 1969–84; Architect, Dean and Chapter of Winchester, 1974–89; Consultant Architect, Brighton BC (for Royal Pavilion), 1981–91. *Recreations:* walking, gardening. *Address:* c/o English Heritage, 23 Savile Row, W1X 1AB. *Club:* Arts.

BENNETT, Dudley Paul; His Honour Judge Dudley Bennett; a Circuit Judge, since 1993; *b* 4 Aug. 1948; *s* of late Patrick James Bennett and of Mary Bennett (*née* Edmondson); *m* 1986, Patricia Ann Martin; two *d*. *Educ:* Bradfield Coll.; LSE (LLB). Called to the Bar, Inner Temple, 1972; Recorder of the Crown Court, 1988–93. *Recreations:* travel, gardening, Afghan Hounds. *Address:* The Crown Court, Canal Street, Nottingham NG1 7EJ. *Club:* United Services (Nottingham).

BENNETT, Edward; *see* Bennett, A. E.

BENNETT, Air Vice Marshal Sir Erik Peter, KBE 1990; CB 1984; retired from RAF, 1991; Commander, Royal Air Force of Oman (in the rank of Air Marshal), 1974–90; *s* of Robert Francis and Anne Myra Bennett. *Educ:* The King's Hospital, Dublin. Air Adviser to King Hussein, 1961–62; RAF Staff College, 1963; Jt Services Staff Coll., 1968; RAF Coll. of Air Warfare, 1971. Order of Istiqlal (Jordan), 1960; Order of Oman, 1980; Order of Merit (Oman), 1989; Order of Sultan Qaboos (Oman), 1985; Medal of Honour (Oman), 1989. *Recreations:* riding, sailing, big game fishing. *Address:* Al Hail Farm, Seeb-Hail Al Awahir, PO Box 1751, Postal Code 111, Sultanate of Oman. *Clubs:* Royal Air Force, Beefsteak.

BENNETT, Rt. Hon. Sir Frederic (Mackarness), Kt 1964; PC 1985; DL; *b* 2 Dec. 1918; 2nd *s* of late Sir Ernest Bennett and of Lady (Marguerite) Bennett; *m* 1945, Marion Patricia, *e d* of Cecil Burnham, OBE, FRCSE. *Educ:* Westminster. Served War of 1939–45, enlisted Middx Yeo., 1939; commissioned RA, 1940; commended for gallantry, 1941; Military Experimental Officer in Petroleum Warfare Dept, 1943–46, when released with rank of Major. TA&VRA, 1973–83. Called to English Bar, Lincoln's Inn, 1946, Southern Rhodesian Bar, 1947. Observer, Greek Communist War, 1947–49; Diplomatic correspondent, Birmingham Post, 1950–52. Contested (C) Burslem, 1945, Ladywood Div. of Birmingham, 1950. MP (C): Reading N, 1951–55; Torquay, Dec. 1955–1974; Torbay, 1974–87. PPS: to Under-Sec. of State, Home Office, 1953–55, to Minister of Supply, 1956–57, to Paymaster-Gen., 1957–59, and to Pres. of Bd of Trade, 1959–61. Chm. Exec. Cttee, CPA Gen. Council, 1971–73; Leader, UK Delegation and Chm., Council of Europe and WEU Assemblies, 1979–87; Former Chm., Europ. Democratic Political Gp Council of Europe and CD, ED & RPR Federated Gp, WEU. Director: RHB Trust Co. Ltd; Squibb A/S; Commercial Union Assurance Co. Ltd, West End and Exeter Bds; Gibraltar Building Soc.; Lord of the Manor of Mawddwy. Co-Pres., E-SU of Pakistan, 1988–. DL Greater London, 1990. Freeman, City of London, 1984. Hon. Dr of Law Istanbul, 1984. Comdr, Order of Phœnix, Greece, 1963; (Sithari) Star of Pakistan, 1st cl., 1964; Order of Al-Istiqlal, 1st cl., Jordan, 1980; Comdr, Order of Isabel la Católica, Spain, 1982; Order of Hilal-i-Quaid-i-Azam, Pakistan, 1983; Commander's Cross, Order of Merit, FRG, 1989; Order (first class) of Polonia Restituta, Poland, 1990 (Comdr, 1977; Grand Comdr's Cross, 1984); Knight of Vitezi, Hungary, 1990. *Publications:* Speaking Frankly, 1960; Detente and Security in Europe, 1976; China and European Security, 1978; The Near and Middle East and Western European Security, 1979, 2nd edn 1980; Impact of Individual and Corporate Incentives on Productivity and Standard of Living, 1980; Fear is the Key; Reds under the Bed, or the Enemy at the Gate—and Within, 1979, 3rd edn 1982. *Recreations:* shooting, fishing, yachting. *Address:* Cwmllecoediog, Aberangell, near Machynlleth, Powys SY20 9QP. *T:* Cemmaes Road (01650) 511430, *Fax:* (01650) 511469; 4 Hale Court, Lincoln's Inn, WC2A 3UJ. *T:* 0171–242 3900, *Fax:* 0171–831 8455. *Club:* Carlton.

BENNETT, His Honour Harry Graham, QC 1968; a Circuit Judge, 1972–91; Designated Circuit Judge, Leeds, 1988–91; *b* 19 Sept. 1921; *s* of Ernest and Alice Mary Bennett, Cleckheaton, Yorks; *m* 1987, Elizabeth, *widow* of Judge Allister Lonsdale. *Educ:* Whitcliffe Mount Grammar Sch., Cleckheaton; King's Coll., London. Royal Artillery, 1943–47. Called to Bar, Gray's Inn, 1948. Recorder: Doncaster, 1966–68; York, 1968–71 (Hon. Recorder, 1972–93); Crown Court, 1972; Dep. Chm., ER of Yorks QS, 1964–71. Chm., Agricl Land Tribunal (N Area), 1967–72; Chm., Cttee of Inquiry into Police Interrogation Procedures in NI, 1978–79. *Club:* Leeds (Leeds).

BENNETT, Sir Hubert, Kt 1970; FRIBA; Architect in private practice; Architect to UNESCO Headquarters, Paris, since 1980; former Architect to the Greater London Council (formerly London County Council) and Superintending Architect of Metropolitan Buildings, 1956–71; *b* 4 Sept. 1909; *s* of late Arthur Bennett and Eleanor Bennett; *m* 1938, Louise F. C. Aldred; three *d*. *Educ:* Victoria University, Manchester, School of Architecture. Asst Lecturer, Leeds School of Architecture, 1933–35; Asst Lecturer, Regent Street Polytechnic Sch. of Architecture, 1935–40; Superintending Architect (Lands), War Dept, 1940–43; Borough Architect, Southampton, 1943–45; County Architect, W Riding of Yorks, 1945–56. Exec. Dir, English Property Corp. Ltd, 1971–79. Mem. of Council, RIBA, 1952–55, 1957–62, 1965–66, 1967–69; Hon. Treas., RIBA, 1959–62; Pres., W Yorks Soc. of Architects, 1954–66; Chm., Technical Panel, Standing Conf. on London Regional Planning, 1962–64; Member: Building Res. Bd, 1959–66; Timber Res. and Develt Assoc. Adv. Panel, 1965–68; Housing Study Mission from Britain to Canada, 1968. Dir, Help the Aged Housing Assoc. (UK) Ltd. Prof., Univ of NSW, 1973. Architect for the Hyde Park Corner-Marble Arch Improvement Scheme, Crystal Palace Recreational Centre and South Bank Arts Centre; Consulting Architect, Guest Palace for the Sultan of Oman, Muscat, 1982. RIBA Assessor, South Bank Competition, Vauxhall Cross, 1981; Assessor, City Polytechnic of Hong Kong, 1982–83. RIBA: Silver Medallist for Measured Drawings (Hon. Mention), 1932; Arthur Cates Prize, 1933; Sir John Soane Medallist, 1934; Neale Bursar, 1936; Godwin and Wimperis Bursar, 1948; RIBA London Architecture Bronze Medal, 1959; RIBA Bronze Medal, 1968. Royal Society of Arts Medal, 1934; Rome Scholarship Special Award, 1936; Min. of Housing and Local Govt Housing Medal, 1954, 1963, 1964, 1966, 1968; Civic Trust Awards; Sir Patrick Abercrombie Award (for planning project Thamesmead), Internat. Union of Architects, 1969; Fritz Schumacher Prize, 1970. Hon. Member: Architects in Industry Group; Inst. of Architects of Czechoslovakia; Soc. of Architects of Venezuela. *Address:* Broadfields, Liphook, Hants GU30 7JH. *T:* Liphook (01428) 724176.

BENNETT, Hon. Sir Hugh Peter Derwyn, Kt 1995; **Hon. Mr Justice Bennett;** a Judge of the High Court of Justice, Family Division, since 1995; *b* 8 Sept. 1943; *s* of Peter Ward Bennett, *qv* and Priscilla Ann Bennett; *m* 1969, Elizabeth (*née* Landon); one *s* three *d. Educ:* Haileybury and ISC; Churchill College, Cambridge (MA). Called to the Bar, Inner Temple, 1966, Bencher, 1993; an Assistant Recorder, 1987; QC 1988; a Recorder, 1990–95. Mem., Supreme Court Rule Cttee, 1988–92; a Chm. (part-time), Betting Levy Appeal Tribunal, 1989–95. Hon. Legal Adv, Sussex County Playing Fields Assoc., 1988–95. Fellow of Woodard Corp., 1987–; Mem. Council, Lancing Coll., 1981–95. *Recreations:* cricket, tennis, shooting, fishing. *Address:* Royal Courts of Justice, Strand, WC2A 2LL. *Clubs:* Pilgrims; MCC.

See also Sir M. J. Cholmeley, Bt.

BENNETT, Hywel Thomas; actor; director; *b* Wales, 8 April 1944; *s* of Gordon Bennett and Sarah Gwen Bennett (*née* Lewis); *m* 1967, Cathy McGowan (marr. diss. 1988); one *d. Educ:* Henry Thornton Grammar School, Clapham; RADA (scholarship). *Stage:* Nat. Youth Theatre for 5 years; repertory, Salisbury and Leatherhead; first major roles in The Screwtape Letters and A Smashing Day, Arts Th., 1966; Shakespeare at Mermaid, Young Vic, Shaw Theatres; repertory, 1972–77 (roles included Jimmy Porter, in Look Back in Anger, Belgrade, and Hamlet, S Africa); Otherwise Engaged, Comedy, 1977; Night Must Fall, Shaw Th., 1977; Levantine, Her Majesty's, 1979; Terra Nova, Chichester, 1980; Fly Away Home, Lyric, Hammersmith, 1983; She Stoops to Conquer, Nat. Theatre, 1985; Toad of Toad Hall; Three Sisters, Albery, 1987; Edinburgh Festival, 1967 and 1990 (Long John Silver, in Treasure Island); *directed:* plays at provincial theatres incl. Lincoln, Leatherhead, Birmingham, Coventry, Sheffield and Cardiff; *films:* The Family Way, The Twisted Nerve, The Virgin Soldiers, Loot, The Buttercup Chain, Alice in Wonderland, Endless Night, Murder Elite, War Zone, The Twilight Zone, Checkpoint Chiswick, Age Unknown, Deadly Advice; *TV plays and films* include: Romeo and Juliet; The Idiot; A Month in the Country; Trust Me; Artemis 81; Frankie and Johnnie; The Other Side of Paradise; Murder Most Horrid; Frontiers; Karaoke; *TV series:* Malice Aforethought; Pennies from Heaven; Tinker, Tailor, Soldier, Spy; Shelley (10 series); Where the Buffalo Roam; Death of a Teddy Bear; The Consultant; Absent Friends; Myself a Mandarin; The Secret Agent; A Mind to Kill; Casualty; Virtual Murder; many radio plays, commercial voiceovers and film narrations. *Recreations:* fishing, golf, reading, walking. *Address:* c/o James Sharkey, Third Floor Suite, 15 Golden Square, W1R 3AG. *T:* 0171–434 3801. *Clubs:* Savile, Wig and Pen (Hon. Mem.).

BENNETT, John, MBE 1945; HM Senior Chief Inspector of Schools for Scotland, 1969–73; *b* 14 Nov. 1912; *m* 1940, Johanne R. McAlpine, MA; two *s* one *d. Educ:* Edinburgh Univ. MA (first class hons) 1934. Schoolmaster until 1951. Served War of 1939–45: Capt. REME, 79 Armd Div., 1940–46. HM Inspector of Schools, 1951. *Recreations:* mathematics, golf, bridge. *Address:* 35 Cadzow Drive, Cambuslang, Glasgow G72 8NF. *T:* 0141–641 1058.

BENNETT, Sir John (Mokonuiarangi), Kt 1988; QSO 1978; Chairman: Maori Education Trust, since 1975; Te Kohanga Reo National Trust, since 1982; Nature Conservation Council, 1984 (Member, 1970); Takitini School of Performing Arts Trust, since 1990; *b* 4 Sept. 1912; *e s* of Frederick Augustus Bennett and Arihia Rangioue Bennett; *m* 1939, Moana Hineiwaerea (*d* 1975); two *s* two *d* (and two *s* decd). *Educ:* Clive Sch.; Te Aute Coll.; Christchurch Teachers' Coll. Various teaching positions, 1934–74. Vice Pres., New Zealand Maori Council, 1982–. Adv. Council, Dictionary of NZ Biography, 1993. QSO awarded for Public Service, 1978; knighthood for services to education, 1988. *Address:* 70 Simla Avenue, PO Box 8486, Havelock North, Hawkes Bay, New Zealand. *T:* Hawkes Bay (6) 8777994.

See also Sir C. M. Bennett, Rt Rev. M. A. Bennett.

BENNETT, Rt. Rev. Manu Augustus, ONZ 1989; CMG 1981; DD; *b* 10 Feb. 1916; *s* of Rt Rev. F. A. Bennett, Bishop of Aotearoa, 1928–50, and Alice Rangioue Bennett; *m* 1944, Kathleen Clark; one *d. Educ:* Victoria Univ. Coll., Univ. of Hawaii. BSc 1954. Deacon, 1939; Priest, 1940; Vicar of Tauranga, Te Puke Maori District, Dio. Waiapu, 1940–44; Chaplain to 2 NZEF, 1944–46; Pastor of Rangitikei South-Manawatu Pastorate, Dio. Wellington, 1946–52; Asst Vicar of Church of Holy Nativity, Honolulu, 1953–54; Pastor of Wellington Pastorate, 1952–57; Vicar of Ohinemutu Pastorate, Waikato, 1964–68; Bishop of Aotearoa, 1968–81. Nat. Council of Churches Chaplain, Dept of Justice. Mem., Waitangi Tribunal on Treaty Matters. Faculty Mem., Native Ministries Consortium, Vancouver Sch. of Theology, Univ. of BC; Kaumatua, Te Rau Kahikatea Unit, St John's Coll., Auckland. Hon. DD Jackson Coll., 1964. *Address:* 8/2 Gemini Crescent, Rotorua, New Zealand.

See also Sir C. M. Bennett, Sir J. M. Bennett.

BENNETT, Prof. Martin Arthur, FRS 1995; Professor, Research School of Chemistry, Australian National University, since 1991; *b* 11 Aug. 1935; *s* of late Arthur Edward Charles Bennett and Dorothy Ivy Bennett; *m* 1964, Rae Elizabeth Matthews; two *s. Educ:* Haberdashers' Aske's Hampstead Sch.; Imperial Coll. of Science and Technology, London (BSc 1957; PhD 1960; DSc 1974). FAA. Postdoctoral Fellow, Univ. of California, 1960–61; Turner and Newall Fellow, 1961–63, Lectr, 1963–67, UCL; Fellow, 1967–70, Sen. Fellow, 1970–79, Professorial Fellow, 1979–91, Res. Sch. of Chem., ANU. Vis. Prof. and Vis. Fellow, univs in Canada, Germany, USA and Japan. Numerous awards, Aust. learned instns; Nyholm Medal, RSC, 1991; Max Planck Soc. Res. Award, 1994. *Publications:* chapters on Ruthenium in Comprehensive Organometallic Chemistry; contribs to learned jls. *Recreations:* golf, reading, foreign languages, esp. German and Japanese. *Address:* Research School of Chemistry, Australian National University, Canberra, ACT 0200, Australia. *T:* (6) 2493639; 21 Glasgow Place, Hughes, ACT 2605, Australia. *T:* (6) 2824154.

BENNETT, Mrs Mary Letitia Somerville, MA; Principal, St Hilda's College, Oxford, 1965–80, Hon. Fellow 1980; Pro-Vice-Chancellor, Oxford University, 1979–80; *b* 9 Jan. 1913; *o c* of Rt Hon. H. A. L. Fisher, OM, and Lettice Ilbert; *m* 1955, John Sloman Bennett, CMG (*d* 1990). *Educ:* Oxford High Sch.; Somerville Coll. (Schol.); 2nd Cl. Mods, 1st Cl. Lit. Hum.; Hon. Fellow, 1977. Jt Broadcasting Cttee, 1940–41; Transcription Service of BBC, 1941–45; Colonial Office, 1945–56. Mem., Hebdomodal Council, Oxford Univ., 1973–79. Hon. Sec., Society for the Promotion of Roman Studies, 1960–85. *Publication:* The Ilberts in India, 1995. *Address:* Rock Cottage, Thursley, Surrey GU8 6QJ; 25A Alma Place, Oxford OX4 1JW. *Club:* University Women's.

BENNETT, Nicholas Jerome; Adviser to Price Waterhouse on public affairs, since 1993; Managing Partner, Sussex Associates, public affairs and education consultants, since 1993; *b* 7 May 1949; *s* of Peter Ramsden Bennett and late Antonia Mary Flanagan; *m* 1995, Ruth, *er d* of Andrew and Alma Whitelaw, Barnham Broom, Norfolk. *Educ:* Sedgehill Sch.; Polytechnic of North London (BA Hons Philosophy); Univ. of London Inst. of Educn (PGCE Distinction); Univ. of Sussex (MA). Educnl publishing, 1974; schoolmaster, 1976–85; educn officer, 1985–87. Chm., SE London Young Conservatives, 1972–73; Councillor, London Borough of Lewisham, 1974–82 (Leader of the Opposition, 1979–81); co-opted Mem., ILEA Educn Cttee, 1978–81. Mem., FEFCE, 1992–. Advr, Surrey Heartlands Health Unit, 1993–94. Contested (C): St Pancras N, 1973 and Greenwich, by-elec. 1974, GLC elections; Hackney Central, 1979. MP (C) Pembroke, 1987–92; contested (C) Pembroke, 1992. PPS to Minister of State, Department of Transport, 1990; Parly Under-Sec. of State, Welsh Office, 1990–92. Member: Select Cttee on Welsh Affairs, 1987–90; Select Cttee on Procedure, 1988–90; Vice-Chairman: (Wales), Cons. backbench Party Organisation Cttee, 1990; Assoc. of Cons. Clubs, 1990–92. Member, 1987–92: British-Amer. Parly Gp; IPU; CPA. Mem., Catholic Union. Chm., Nat. Council for Civil Protection, 1990. Mem., Western Front Assoc. *Publication:* (contrib.) Primary Headship in the 1990s, 1989. *Recreations:* swimming, history, transport, browsing in second-hand bookshops, cinema, small scale gardening, visiting battlefields of First and Second World War. *Address:* 7 Haredon Close, SE23 3TG. *T:* and *Fax:* 0181–291 2876. *Club:* Lee Green Constitutional.

BENNETT, Patrick, QC 1969; a Recorder of the Crown Court, since 1972; *b* 12 Jan. 1924; *s* of Michael Bennett; *m* 1951, Lyle Reta Pope; two *d. Educ:* Bablake Sch., Coventry; Magdalen Coll., Oxford. State Scholar, 1941, MA, BCL 1949. Served RNVR, 1943–46, Sub Lt. Called to Bar, Gray's Inn, 1949, Bencher 1976, Master of Students, 1980; Asst Recorder, Coventry, 1969–71; Dep. Chm., Lindsey QS, 1970–71. Mem., Mental Health Act Commn, 1984–86. Fellow: Internat. Soc. of Barristers, 1984; Nat. Inst. of Advocacy, 1980. Pres., Thomas More Soc., 1990–93. *Publications:* Assessment of Damages in Personal Injury and Fatal Accidents, 1980; The Common Jury, 1986; Trial Techniques, 1986. *Recreations:* food, flying. *Address:* (home) 22 Wynnstay Gardens, W8 6UR. *T:* 0171–937 2110; 233 rue Nationale, Boulogne sur Mer, France. *T:* 21913339; (professional) 2 Crown Office Row, Temple, EC4Y 7HJ. *T:* 0171–797 8100. *Clubs:* Hurlingham; Spartan Flying (Denham).

BENNETT, Peter Ward, OBE; Chairman, W. H. Smith & Son Holdings Ltd, 1977–82. *Address:* Dene House, Littledene, Glynde, Lewes, Sussex BN8 6LB.

See also H. P. D. Bennett.

BENNETT, Philip Hugh Penberthy, CBE 1972; FRIBA; FCIArb; Consultant, T. P. Bennett Partnership, architects, since 1980 (Partner, 1948–80, Senior Partner, 1967–80); *b* 14 April 1919; *o s* of late Sir Thomas Penberthy Bennett, KBE, FRIBA, and late Mary Langdon Edis; *m* 1943, Jeanne Heal; one *s* one *d. Educ:* Highgate Sch.; Emmanuel Coll., Cambridge (MA). Lieut (G) RNVR, 1940–46. Principal works: town centres at Bootle and Stratford (London); head offices for Norwich Union Insce Socs, Ford Motor Co. and other commercial cos; dept stores for United Africa Co. in Ghana and Nigeria, Bentalls (Kingston) and Fenwicks (Newcastle); extensions to Middlesex Hosp.; hostel for Internat. Students Trust; Cunard Internat. Hotel; flats for local authorities and private developers; buildings for airfield and dock develt. Chm., Building Regulations Adv. Cttee (DoE), 1965–77; former RIBA rep. on Jt Contracts Tribunal (Chm. 1973–78) and Nat. Jt Consultative Cttee (Chm. 1970); Mem. other cttees of RIBA and NEDO; Governor: Sch. of Building, 1952–72; Vauxhall Coll. of Further Educn, 1972–77; Member: Home Office Deptl Cttee enquiring into Fire Service, 1967–70; Adv. Council for Energy Conservation, 1974–76. Dir, BEC Building Trust Ltd, 1984–91. *Publications:* Architectural Practice and Procedure, 1981; chapter on building, in Britain 1984, 1963; articles in Building, Financial Times, etc. *Recreations:* travel, drawing, theatre. *Address:* Grey Walls, Park Lane, Aldeburgh, Suffolk IP15 5PH. *T:* Aldeburgh (01728) 452766.

BENNETT, Gen. Sir Phillip (Harvey), AC 1985 (AO 1981); KBE 1983; DSO 1969; Governor of Tasmania, 1987–95; *b* 27 Dec. 1928; *m* 1955, Margaret Heywood; two *s* one *d. Educ:* Perth Modern Sch.; Royal Mil. Coll.; jssc, rcds, psc (Aust.). Served, 1950–56: 3rd Bn RAR, Korea (despatches), Sch. of Infantry (Instr), 25 Cdn Bde, Korea, Pacific Is Regt, PNG, and 16th Bn Cameron Highlanders of WA; Commando training, Royal Marines, England, Malta and Cyprus, 1957–58; OC 2 Commando Co., Melb., 1958–61; Aust. Staff Coll., 1961–62; Sen. Instr, then Chief Instr, Officer Cadet Sch., Portsea, 1962–65; AAG Directorate of Personal Services, AHQ, 1965–67; Co 1 RAR, 1967–69 (served Vietnam; DSO); Exchange Instr, Jt Services Staff Coll., England, 1969–71; COL Directorate of Co-ordination and Organization, AHQ, 1971–73; COS HQ Fd Force Comd, 1974–75; RCDS, England, 1976; Comdr 1st Div., 1977–79; Asst Chief of Def. Force Staff, 1979–82; Chief of General Staff, 1982–84; Chief of Defence Force, Australia, 1984–87. Hon. Col, Royal Tasmania Regt, 1987–95. KStJ 1988. Hon. LLD: New South Wales, 1987; Tasmania, 1992. *Recreations:* sailing, golf. *Address:* 6/65 Mountbatten Park, Musgrave Street, Yarralumla, ACT 2600, Australia. *Clubs:* Australian (Sydney); University House, Commonwealth (Canberra).

BENNETT, Ralph Featherstone; *b* 3 Dec. 1923; *o s* of late Mr and Mrs Ralph J. P. Bennett, Plymouth, Devon; *m* 1948, Delia Marie, *o d* of late Mr and Mrs J. E. Baxter, Franklyns, Plymouth; two *s* two *d. Educ:* Plympton Grammar Sch.; Plymouth Technical Coll. Articled pupil to City of Plymouth Transport Manager, 1940–43; Techn. Asst, Plymouth City Transp., 1943–54; Michelin Tyre Co., 1954–55; Dep. Gen. Man., City of Plymouth Transp. Dept, 1955–58; Gen. Manager: Gt Yarmouth Transp. Dept, 1958–60; Bolton Transp. Dept, 1960–65; Manchester City Transp., 1965–68; London Transport Executive (formerly London Transport Board): Mem., 1968–71; Dep. Chm., 1971–78; Chief Exec., 1975–78; Chairman: London Transport Executive, 1978–80; London Transport International, 1976–80. Pres., Confedn of Road Passenger Transport, 1977–78; Vice-President: Internat. Union of Public Transport, 1978–81; CIT, 1979–82. CEng; FIMechE; FCIT; FRSA. *Address:* Buffers, Green Lane, Yelverton, South Devon PL20 6BW. *T:* Yelverton (01822) 852153.

BENNETT, Raymond Clayton Watson; His Honour Judge Raymond Bennett; a Circuit Judge, since 1989; *b* 20 June 1939; *s* of Harold Watson and Doris Helena Bennett (previously Watson); *m* 1965, Elaine Margaret Haworth; one *s* one *d. Educ:* Bury Grammar Sch.; Manchester Univ. (LLB). Solicitor, 1964–72; called to the Bar, Middle Temple, 1972; practising barrister, 1972–89; an Asst Recorder, 1984; a Recorder, 1988. *Recreations:* cycling, tennis, badminton, reading, painting, gardening. *Address:* c/o The Crown Court, Sessions House, Lancaster Road, Preston PR1 2PD.

BENNETT, Sir Reginald (Frederick Brittain), Kt 1979; VRD 1944; MA Oxon; BM, BCh, 1942; LMSSA 1937; DPM 1948; Grand Officer, Italian Order of Merit, 1977;

company director and wine consultant; formerly psychiatrist and politician; *b* 22 July 1911; *e s* of late Samuel Robert Bennett and Gertrude (*née* Brittain); *m* 1947, Henrietta, *d* of Capt. H. B. Crane, CBE, RN; one *s* three *d*. *Educ:* Winchester Coll.; New College, Oxford (sailing Blue, 1931–34); St George's Hosp. Med. Sch., SW1. Oxford Univ. Air Squadron, 1931–34; RNVR, 1934–46; Fleet Air Arm, Medical Officer and Pilot; torpedoed twice. Maudsley Hosp., SE5, 1947–49. MP(C) Gosport and Fareham, 1950–74, Fareham, 1974–79; PPS to Rt Hon. Iain Macleod, MP, 1956–63; Chairman: House of Commons Catering Sub-Cttee, 1970–74, 1976–79; Anglo-Italian Parly Gp, 1971–79 (Hon. Sec. 1961–71); Parly and Scientific Cttee, 1959–62. Vice-Pres., Franco-British Parly Relations Cttee, 1973–79; Mem. Council, Internat. Inst. of Human Nutrition, 1975–. Helmsman: Shamrock V, 1934–35; Evaine, 1936–38; Olympic Games (reserve), 1936; in British-American Cup Team, 1949 and 1953 in USA; various trophies since. Chairman: Amateur Yacht Research Soc., 1972–90; World Sailing Speed Record Council, IYRU, 1980–; Portland/West Kirby Speed Sailing Cttee, RYA, 1980–92; RYA Nat. Match-Racing Championship Cttee, 1989–. Hon. Lieut-Col, Georgia Militia, 1960; Hon. Citizen: of Atlanta, Ga, 1960; of Port-St Louis-du-Rhône, France, 1986. Commandeur du Bontemps-Médoc, 1959; Chevalier du Tastevin, 1970; Galant de la Verte Marennes; Chevalier de St Etienne, Alsace, 1971; Chevalier Bretvin (Muscadet), 1973; Legato del Chianti, 1983. *Publications:* articles on wine, medicine, psychiatry, politics and yacht racing; videotapes of yacht racing in Shamrock V. *Recreations:* sailing, painting, foreign travel, basking in the sun, avoiding exercise. *Address:* 30 Strand-on-the-Green, W4 3PH. *Clubs:* White's; Imperial Poona Yacht (Cdre); Wykehamist Sailing (Cdre); Sea View Yacht; Sea View Buffs, etc.

BENNETT, Richard Clement W.; *see* Wheeler-Bennett.

BENNETT, Richard Rodney, CBE 1977; composer; *b* 29 March 1936; *s* of H. Rodney and Joan Esther Bennett. *Educ:* Leighton Park Sch., Reading; Royal Academy of Music. Works performed, 1953–, at many Festivals in Europe, S Africa, USA, Canada, Australia, etc. Has written music for numerous films including: Indiscreet; The Devil's Disciple; Only Two Can Play; The Wrong Arm of the Law; Heavens Above; Billy Liar; One Way Pendulum; The Nanny; Far from the Madding Crowd; Billion Dollar Brain; Secret Ceremony; The Buttercup Chain; Figures in a Landscape; Nicholas and Alexandra; Lady Caroline Lamb; Voices; Murder on the Orient Express (SFTA award; Academy Award Nomination; Ivor Novello award, PRS); Permission to Kill; Equus (BAFTA Nomination); The Brinks Job; Yanks (BAFTA Nomination); Return of the Soldier; also the music for television series: The Christians; L. P. Hartley trilogy; The Ebony Tower; Tender is the Night; The Charmer; Poor Little Rich Girl; The Hiding Place; The Story of Anne Frank. Commissioned to write 2 full-length operas for Sadler's Wells: The Mines of Sulphur, 1965, A Penny for a Song, 1968; commnd to write opera for Covent Garden: Victory, 1970; (children's opera) All the King's Men, 1969; Guitar Concerto, 1970; Spells (choral work), 1975. *Publications include:* chamber music, orchestral music, educational music, song cycles, etc; articles for periodicals, about music. *Recreations:* cinema, modern jazz. *Address:* c/o Nigel Britten, Lemon Unna & Durbridge Ltd, 24 Pottery Lane, W11 4LZ.

BENNETT, Prof. Robert John, PhD; FBA 1991; Professor of Geography, London School of Economics, since 1985; *b* 23 March 1948; *s* of Thomas Edward Bennett and Kathleen Elizabeth Robson; *m* 1971, Elizabeth Anne Allen; two *s*. *Educ:* Taunton's Sch., Southampton; St Catharine's Coll., Cambridge (BA 1970; PhD 1974). Lecturer: University Coll. London, 1973–78; Univ. of Cambridge, 1978–85; Fellow and Dir of Studies, 1978–85, Tutor, 1981–85, Fitzwilliam Coll., Cambridge. Vis. Prof., Univ. California at Berkeley, 1978; Guest Schol., Brookings Instn, Washington DC, 1978, 1979, 1981; Hubert Humphrey Inst. Fellow, Univ. Minnesota, 1985; Univ. Fellow, Macquarie, 1987; Snyder Lectr, Toronto, 1988. Treas., IBG, 1990–93; Vice Pres., RGS, 1993–95 (Mem. Council, 1990–); Chm., Council of British Geography, 1995–. Murchison Award, RGS, 1982. Gen. Editor, Government and Policy, 1982–; European Co-Editor, Geographical Analysis, 1985–88. *Publications:* Environmental Systems (with R. J. Chorley), 1978; Spatial Time Series, 1979; Geography of Public Finance, 1980; (ed) European Progress in Spatial Analysis, 1981; (ed with N. Wrigley) Quantitative Geography, 1981; Central Grants to Local Government, 1982; (with K. C. Tan) Optimal Control of Spatial Systems, 1984; Intergovernmental Financial Relations in Austria, 1985; (with A. G. Wilson) Mathematical Methods in Human Geography and Planning, 1985; (ed with H. Zimmerman) Local Business Taxes in Britain and Germany, 1986; (with G. Krebs) Die Wirkung Kommunaler Steuern auf die Steuerliche Belastung der Kapitalbildung, 1987; (with G. Krebs) Local Business Taxes in Britain and Germany, 1988; (ed) Territory and Administration in Europe, 1989; (ed) Decentralisation, Local Governments and Markets, 1990; (with G. Krebs) Local Economic Development Initiatives in Britain and Germany, 1991; (ed with R. C. Estall) Global Change and Challenge, 1991; (with A. McCoshan) Enterprise and Human Resource Development, 1993; (jtly) Local Empowerment and Business Services, 1994; (with G. Krebs and H. Zimmermann) Chambers of Commerce in Britain and Germany, 1994. *Recreations:* the family, craftwork. *Address:* Department of Geography, London School of Economics, Houghton Street, WC2A 2AE.

BENNETT, Robin; educational consultant, since 1995; Chairman, Wandsworth Education Shop Ltd, since 1995; *b* 6 Nov. 1934; *s* of Arthur James Bennett, Major RA, and Alice Edith Bennett, Kesgrave, Ipswich; *m* 1st, 1962, Patricia Ann Lloyd (marr. diss. 1991); one *s* one *d*; *m* 2nd, 1992, Margaret Jane Allen. *Educ:* Northgate Grammar School, Ipswich; St. John's Coll., Univ. of Durham (BA); Queen's Coll., and Univ. of Birmingham (Dip Th). MEd Birmingham. Assistant Curate: Prittlewell, 1960–63; St Andrew with St Martin, Plaistow, 1963–65; Vicar, St Cedd, Canning Town, 1965–72; Rector of Loughton, 1972–75; Director, Oxford Inst. for Church and Society, 1975–77; Principal, Aston Training Scheme, 1977–82; Adult Education Officer, Gen. Synod Bd of Education, 1982–85, Archdeacon of Dudley and Dir of Lay Ministerial Develt and Training, Diocese of Worcester, 1985–86; Vice-Principal, Clapham Battersea Adult Educn Inst., 1986–89; Dep. Principal, Wandsworth Adult Coll., 1989–95; Exec. Team Mem., S Thames Coll. Further Educn Corp., 1992–95. Mem. Exec., Nat. Inst. of Adult Continuing Educn, 1982–89. Joined Society of Friends, 1988. *Recreations:* golf, travel, opera, League football. *Address:* 97 Caterham Drive, Old Coulsdon, Surrey CR5 1JQ.

BENNETT, Ronald Alistair, CBE 1986; QC (Scotland) 1959; Vice-President for Scotland, Value Added Tax Tribunals, since 1977; *b* 11 Dec. 1922; *s* of Arthur George Bennett, MC and Edythe Sutherland; *m* 1950, Margret Magnusson, *d* of Sigursteinn Magnusson, Icelandic Consul-Gen. for Scotland; three *s* two *d* (and one *d* decd). *Educ:* Edinburgh Academy; Edinburgh Univ.; Balliol Coll., Oxford. MA, LLB Univ. of Edinburgh, 1942; Muirhead and Dalgety Prizes for Civil Law, 1942. Lieut, 79th (Scottish Horse) Medium Regt RA, 1943–45; Capt. attached RAOC, India and Japan, 1945–46. Called to Scottish Bar, 1947; Vans Dunlop Schol. in Scots Law and Conveyancing, 1948; Standing Counsel to Min. of Labour and National Service, 1957–59; Sheriff-Principal: of Roxburgh, Berwick and Selkirk, 1971–74; of S Strathclyde, Dumfries and Galloway, 1981–82; of N Strathclyde, 1982–83; Temp. Addtl Sheriff-Principal of Grampian, Highland and Islands, 1990–91. Lectr in Mercantile Law: Edinburgh Univ., 1956–68; Heriot-Watt Univ., 1968–75. Chairman: Med. Appeal Tribunals (Scotland), 1971–; Agricultural Wages Bd for Scotland, 1973–; Local Govt Boundary Commn for Scotland, 1974–90; Northern Lighthouse Bd, April-Sept. 1974; Industrial Tribunals, (Scotland), 1977–95; War Pension Tribunals, 1984–. Arbiter, Motor Insurers' Bureau appeals, 1975–; Mem., Scottish Medical Practices Cttee, 1976–88. *Publications:* Bennett's Company Law, 2nd edn, 1950; Fraser's Rent Acts in Scotland, 2nd edn 1952; Editor: Scottish Current Law and Scots Law Times Sheriff Court Reports, 1948–74; Court of Session Reports, 1976–88. *Recreations:* crossword puzzles, reading, music, gardening. *Address:* Laxamyri, 46 Cammo Road, Barnton, Edinburgh EH4 8AP. *T:* 0131–339 6111.

BENNETT, Sir Ronald (Wilfred Murdoch), 3rd Bt, *cr* 1929; *b* 25 March 1930; *o s* of Sir Wilfred Bennett, 2nd Bt, and Marion Agnes, OBE (*d* 1985), *d* of late James Somervell, Sorn Castle, Ayrshire, and step *d* of late Edwin Sandys Dawes; *S* father 1952; *m* 1st, 1953, Rose-Marie Audrey Patricia, *o d* of Major A. L. J. H. Aubépin, France and Co. Mayo, Ireland; two *d*; 2nd, 1968, Anne, *d* of late Leslie George Tooker; *m* 3rd. *Educ:* Wellington Coll.; Trinity Coll., Oxford. *Heir: cousin* Mark Edward Francis Bennett, *b* 5 April 1960. *Clubs:* Kampala, Uganda (Kampala).

BENNETT, Roy Grissell, CMG 1971; TD 1947; Chairman, Maclaine Watson & Co. Ltd, London and Singapore, 1970–72 (Director, 1958–72), retired; Chairman, Beder International Singapore and Beder Malaysia, since 1972; *b* 21 Nov. 1917. *Educ:* privately and RMC Sandhurst. Served War of 1939–45, 17th/21st Lancers, seconded 24th Lancers, 1st Lothian and Border Horse, 2nd i/c, 1944–46; Major. Joined J. H. Vavasseur & Co. Ltd, Penang, 1946; Director, 1949; joined Maclaine, Watson & Co. Ltd, Singapore 1952, Dir London Board 1958–72, Man. Dir, Eastern interests, 1960; Chm. and Man. Dir, London and Singapore, 1970–72; Chm., Pilkington (SE Asia) Private Ltd and Fibreglass Pilkington Malaysia, 1972–89. Chairman: Singapore Internat. Chamber of Commerce, 1967–70; Singapore Chamber of Commerce Rubber Assoc., 1960–72; founder Chm., Rubber Assoc. of Singapore (Dep. Chm. 1966–72); Chm. Council, Singapore Anti-Tuberculosis Assoc., 1962–; Founder Chm. and Governor, United World Coll., SE Asia, 1972– (Chm. Governors, 1972–79); Chm., Racehorse Spelling Station, Cameron Highlands, Malaysia, 1976–. Riding for the Disabled Association of Singapore: Founder Chm., 1982–85; Mem. Cttee, 1982–; Life Hon. Mem., 1989; Patron, 1992–. Patron, Nat. Kidney Foundn. FInstD. *Recreations:* economics, polo, racing, shooting, swimming, photography, motoring, safaris, camping, gardening, zoology, boating, reading, travelling, people especially of the East. *Address:* PO Box 49, Bukit Panjang, Singapore 9168; 22 Jalan Perdana, Johore Bharu 80300, Malaysia. *T:* Johore Bharu (7) 2234505, *Fax:* (7) 2249006; Oak Tree House, South Holmwood, Surrey RH5 4NF. *T:* Dorking (01306) 889414, *Fax:* (01306) 877604. *Clubs:* Cavalry and Guards; Tanglin, British, Turf (Dep. Chm.), Polo (Patron; Past Chm.; Pres. 1958–70), AA Sports (Singapore); Turf, Polo, Town, Swimming (Penang); Victoria Racing (Melbourne).

BENNETT, Hon. William Richards, PC (Can.) 1982; Premier of British Columbia, 1975–86; *b* 14 April 1932; *y s* of late Hon. William Andrew Cecil Bennett, PC (Can.) and of Annie Elizabeth May Richards; *m* 1955, Audrey Lyne, *d* of late Jack James; four *s*. Began a business career. Elected MP for Okanagan South (succeeding to a constituency which had been held by his father), 1973; Leader of Social Credit Group in Provincial House, 1973; formed Social Credit Govt after election of Dec. 1975.

BENNETTS, Rt. Rev. Colin James; *see* Buckingham, Area Bishop of.

BENNEY, (Adrian) Gerald (Sallis), CBE 1995; RDI 1971; goldsmith and silversmith; Professor of Silversmithing and Jewellery, Royal College of Art, 1974–83; *b* 21 April 1930; *s* of late Ernest Alfred Benney and Aileen Mary Benney; *m* 1957, Janet Edwards; three *s* one *d*. *Educ:* Brighton Grammar Sch.; Brighton Coll. of Art (Nat. Dip. in Art); RCA (DesRCA). FSIAD 1975. Estabd 1st workshop, Whitfield Place, London, 1955; Consultant Designer, Viners Ltd, 1957–69; began designing and making Reading civic plate, 1963; discovered technique of texturing on silver, 1964; moved workshop to Bankside, London, 1969; began prodn of Beenham Enamels, 1970. Holds Royal Warrants of Appt to the Queen (designer and maker of 40th Anniversary Mace, for use at Commonwealth Ceremonies, 1992), the Duke of Edinburgh, Queen Elizabeth the Queen Mother and the Prince of Wales. Member: Govt's Craft Adv. Cttee, 1972–77; UK Atomic Energy Ceramics Centre Adv. Cttee, 1979–83; British Hallmarking Council, 1983–88. Metalwork Design Advisor to Indian Govt (UP State), 1977–78; Chm., Govt of India Hallmarking Survey, 1981; Export Advisor and Designer to Royal Selangor Pewter Co., Kuala Lumpur, 1986–. Consultant to Silver Trust, 1977– (commission of silver for loaning to No 10 Downing St and other govt estabs). Major Exhibn, Worshipful Co. of Goldsmiths, 1973; Major one man exhibn of oil paintings, Solomon Gall., 1988. Liveryman, Goldsmiths' Co., 1964. Hon. MA Leicester, 1963. Freeman, Borough of Reading, 1984. *Recreations:* walking, oil painting, landscape gardening. *Address:* Beenham House, Beenham, Berks RG7 5LJ. *T:* Reading (01734) 744370; (show rooms) 73 Walton Street, Knightsbridge, SW3 2HT. *T:* 0171–589 7002. *Club:* Arts.

BENNION, Francis Alan Roscoe; writer; *b* 2 Jan. 1923; *o s* of Thomas Roscoe Bennion, Liverpool; *m* 1st, 1951, Barbara Elisabeth Braendle (separated 1971, marr. diss. 1975); three *d*; 2nd, 1977, Mary Field. *Educ:* John Lyon's, Harrow; Balliol Coll., Oxford. Pilot, RAFVR, 1941–46. Gibbs Law Scholar, Oxford, 1948. Called to Bar, Middle Temple, 1951 (Harmsworth Scholar); practised at Bar, 1951–53, 1985–94. Lectr and Tutor in Law, St Edmund Hall, Oxford, 1951–53; Office of Parly Counsel, 1953–65, and 1973–75; Dep. Parly Counsel, 1964; Parly Counsel, 1973–75; seconded to Govt of Pakistan to advise on drafting of new Constitution, 1956; seconded to Govt of Ghana to advise on legislation and drafting Constitution converting the country into a Republic, 1959–61. Sec., RICS, 1965–68; Governor, College of Estate Management, 1965–68. Co-founder and first Chm., Professional Assoc. of Teachers, 1968–72; Founder: Statute Law Soc., 1968 (Chm., 1978–79); Freedom Under Law, 1971; Dicey Trust, 1973; Towards One World, 1979; Statute Law Trust, 1991; founder and first Chm., World of Property Housing Trust (later Sanctuary Housing Assoc.), 1968–72 (Vice-Pres., 1986–); Co-founder, Areopagitica Educnl Trust, 1979. *Publications:* Constitutional Law of Ghana, 1962; Professional Ethics: The Consultant Professions and their Code, 1969; Tangling with the Law, 1970; Consumer Credit Control, 1976–; Consumer Credit Act Manual, 1978, 3rd edn 1986; Statute Law, 1980, 3rd edn 1990; Statutory Interpretation, 1984, 2nd edn 1992; Victorian Railway Days, 1989; The Sex Code: Morals for Moderns, 1991; articles and contribs to books on legal and other subjects. *Recreations:* studying Oxford origins, admiring the British Empire. *Address:* 29 Pegasus Road, Oxford OX4 5DS. *T:* Oxford (01865) 775164. *Club:* MCC.

BENNITT, Mortimer Wilmot; Secretary, Islington Archaeology Society; *b* 28 Aug. 1910; *s* of Rev. F. W. and Honoria Bennitt. *Educ:* Charterhouse; Trinity Coll., Oxford. Entered Office of Works, 1934; Private Sec. to Sir Philip Sassoon, 1937–38. Served War of 1939–45: RAF, 1943–45. Under Sec., 1951; Dep. Dir, Land Commn, 1967–71; retired 1971. Chairman: Little Theatre Guild of Gt Britain, 1959–60; Tavistock Repertory Company, London, 1975–77. Patron of St Mary's, Bletchley. *Publication:* Guide to Canonbury Tower, 1980. *Recreation:* theatre. *Address:* 3/5 Highbury Grove, N5 1HH. *T:* 0171–704 1335. *Clubs:* United Oxford & Cambridge University, Tower Theatre.

BENSON, Sir Christopher (John), Kt 1988; FRICS; Chairman: Sun Alliance Group, since 1993 (Director, since 1988; Deputy Chairman, 1992–93); Costain plc, since 1993; *b* 20 July 1933; *s* of Charles Woodburn Benson and Catherine Clara (*née* Bishton); *m* 1960, Margaret Josephine, OBE, JP, *d* of Ernest Jefferies Bundy; two *s*. *Educ:* Worcester Cathedral King's Sch.; Thames Nautical Trng Coll., HMS Worcester. FRICS. Chartered surveyor and agricl auctioneer, Worcs, Herefords, Wilts, Dorset, Hants, 1953–64; Dir, Arndale Develts Ltd, 1965–69; Chm., Dolphin Develts Ltd, 1969–71; Asst Man. Dir, Law Land Co. Ltd, 1972–74; Man. Dir, 1976–88, Chm., 1988–93, MEPC; Chm., The Boots Company, 1990–94 (Dir, 1989–94); Dep. Chm., Thorn Lighting Gp, 1994–; Chm., Albright & Wilson, 1995–. Dir, House of Fraser plc, 1982–86; Chairman: LDDC, 1984–88; Reedpack Ltd, 1989–90; Housing Corp., 1990–94; Games for Good Causes plc, 1993–; Funding Agency for Schs, 1994–. Underwriting Mem. of Lloyd's, 1979–. Pres., British Property Fedn, 1981–83; Chm., Property Adv. Gp to DoE, 1988–90; Mem. Council, CBI, 1990–. Dir, Royal Opera House, 1984–92. Chm., Civic Trust, 1985–90; Trustee, Metropolitan Police Museum, 1986–; Vice President: Cancer Relief Macmillan Fund, 1991–; RSA, 1992–. Lay-Gov., London Hosp. Med. Coll., 1993–. Mem. Council, Marlborough Coll., 1982–90. Hon. FRCPath 1992; Hon. FCIOB 1992. Hon. Fellow, Wolfson Coll., Cambridge, 1990. Hon. Bencher, Middle Temple, 1984. Freeman: City of London, 1975; Co. of Watermen and Lightermen, 1985; Liveryman: Worshipful Co. of Gold and Silver Wyre Drawers, 1975; Guild of Air Pilots and Air Navigators, 1981. *Recreations:* farming, aviation, opera, ballet. *Address:* 111 Westminster Bridge Road, SE1 7UE. *Clubs:* Garrick, Royal Automobile, MCC.

BENSON, David Holford; Chairman, Kleinwort Charter Investment Trust, since 1992; Non-executive Director, Kleinwort Benson Group Plc, since 1992 (Vice Chairman, 1989–92); *b* 26 Feb. 1938; *s* of Sir Rex Benson, DSO, MVO, MC, and Lady Leslie Foster Benson; *m* 1964, Lady Elizabeth Mary Charteris, *d* of 12th Earl of Wemyss and March, *qv*; one *s* two *d*. *Educ:* Eton Coll.; Madrid. CIGasE 1989. Shell Transport & Trading, 1957–63; Kleinwort Benson Gp, 1963–. Non-Exec. Director: Marshall Cavendish, 1984–; Rouse Co., 1986–; British Gas, 1988–; Vice Chm., Leach Internat. (formerly Leach Relais), 1992–. Trustee, Charities Official Investment Fund, 1984–. *Recreation:* painting. *Address:* (office) 20 Fenchurch Street, EC3P 3DB; 11 Brunswick Gardens, W8 4AS. *T:* 0171–727 4949. *Clubs:* White's, English-Speaking Union.

BENSON, Prof. Frank Atkinson, OBE 1988; DL; BEng, MEng (Liverpool); PhD, DEng (Sheffield); FIEE, FIEEE; Professor and Head of Department of Electronic and Electrical Engineering, University of Sheffield, 1967–87; Pro-Vice Chancellor, 1972–76; *b* 21 Nov. 1921; *s* of late John and Selina Benson; *m* 1950, Kathleen May Paskell; two *s*. *Educ:* Ulverston Grammar Sch.; Univ. of Liverpool. Mem. research staff, Admty Signal Estab., Witley, 1943–46; Asst Lectr in Electrical Engrg, University of Liverpool, 1946–49; Lectr 1949–59, Sen. Lectr 1959–61, in Electrical Engrg, University of Sheffield; Reader in Electronics, University of Sheffield, 1961–67. DL South Yorks, 1979. *Publications:* Voltage Stabilizers, 1950; Electrical Engineering Problems with Solutions, 1954; Voltage Stabilized Supplies, 1957; Problems in Electronics with Solutions, 1958; Electric Circuit Theory, 1959; Voltage Stabilization, 1965; Electric Circuit Problems with Solutions, 1967; Millimetre and Submillimetre Waves, 1969; Fields, Waves and Transmission Lines, 1991; many papers on microwaves, gas discharges and voltage stabilization in learned jls. *Address:* 64 Grove Road, Sheffield S7 2GZ. *T:* Sheffield (0114) 236 3493.

BENSON, (Harry) Peter (Neville), CBE 1982; MC 1945; FCA; Chairman, Davy Corporation PLC, 1982–85; *b* 10 Feb. 1917; *s* of Harry Leedham Benson and Iolanthe Benson; *m* 1948, Margaret Young Brackenridge; two *s* one *d*. *Educ:* Cheltenham Coll. FCA 1946. Served War, S Staffs Regt, 1939–45 (Major; MC). Moore Stephens, 1946–48; John Mowlem, 1948–51; Dir, 1951–54, Man. Dir, 1954–57, Waring & Gillow; Dir, APV Co., 1957–66; Man. Dir, 1966–77, Chm., 1977–82, APV Holdings. Director: Rolls Royce Motors, 1971–80; Vickers Ltd, 1980–82. *Recreation:* golf. *Address:* The Gate House, Little Chesters, Nursery Road, Walton-on-the-Hill, Tadworth, Surrey KT20 7TX. *T:* Tadworth (01737) 813767. *Club:* Walton Heath Golf.

BENSON, Horace Burford; *b* 3 April 1904; *s* of Augustus W. Benson and Lucy M. (*née* Jarrett); *m* 1930, Marthe Lanier; one *s* one *d*. Called to Bar, Gray's Inn, 1936; practised as Barrister, Seychelles Islands, 1936–46; District Magistrate, Ghana, 1946; Puisne Judge, Ghana, 1952–57; retired, 1957. Temp. Magistrate, Basutoland, 1958–60; Puisne Judge, Basutoland, Bechuanaland Protectorate and Swaziland, 1960–61; Chief Justice, Basutoland (now Lesotho), 1965; Puisne Judge, Malawi, 1967–69. *Recreations:* bowls, bridge. *Address:* c/o Barclays Bank, West Norwood, SE27 9DW.

BENSON, James; President, James Benson Associates Inc., since 1987; *b* 17 July 1925; *s* of Henry Herbert Benson and Olive Benson (*née* Hutchinson); *m* 1950, Honoria Margaret Hurley; one *d*. *Educ:* Bromley Grammar Sch., Kent; Emmanuel Coll., Cambridge (MA). Manager, Res. and Promotion, Kemsley Newspapers, 1948–58; Dir, Mather & Crowther, 1959–65; Man. Dir, 1966–69, Chm., 1970–71 and 1975–78, Ogilvy & Mather Ltd; Vice-Chm., The Ogilvy Group (formerly Ogilvy & Mather Internat.) Inc., 1971–87. Chm., American Associates of the Royal Acad. Trust, 1983–. *Publications:* Above Us The Waves, 1953; The Admiralty Regrets, 1956; Will Not We Fear, 1961; The Broken Column, 1966. *Recreations:* swimming, walking, painting, reading. *Address:* 580 Park Avenue, New York, NY 10021, USA.

BENSON, Jeremy Henry, OBE 1984; architect in private practice (Benson & Bryant, Chartered Architects), since 1954; *b* 25 June 1925; 3rd *s* of late Guy Holford Benson and Lady Violet Benson; *m* 1951, Patricia Stewart; two *s* three *d*. *Educ:* Eton; Architectural Assoc. (AADipl.); FRIBA. Royal Engineers, 1944–47. Pres., Georgian Gp, 1985–90 (Mem., Exec. Cttee, 1967–85; Chm., 1980–85); Chm., SPAB, 1989–90 (Vice-Chm., 1971–89; Mem. Exec. Cttee, 1959–90, 1991–); Chm., Joint Cttee of SPAB, GG, Victorian Soc., Civic Trust, Ancient Monuments Soc. and Council for British Archaeology, 1989– (Mem., 1968–; Vice-Chm., 1972–89), and Chm. of its Tax Group; Member: Forestry Commn's Westonbirt Adv. Cttee, 1969–; Historic Buildings Council for England, 1974–84; Adv. Cttee on Trees in the Royal Parks, 1977–80; Council, Garden History Soc., 1994–. Historic Buildings and Monuments Commission for England: Comr, 1983–88; Mem., Historic Buildings and Areas (formerly Historic Buildings) Adv. Cttee, 1984–93; Chm., Gardens Cttee, 1984–92; Mem., Landscape Gardens Panel, 1992–. Chairman: Old Chiswick Protection Soc., 1993–; Chiswick House Friends, 1993–. *Recreation:* gardening. *Address:* (office) Walpole House, Chiswick Mall, W4 2PS. *T:* 0181–994 1611; Field Barn, Taddington, Temple Guiting, Cheltenham, Glos GL54 5RY. *T:* Stanton (0138673) 228. *Club:* Brooks's.

BENSON, Neil Winston, FCA; Senior Partner, Lewis Golden & Co., Chartered Accountants, since 1980; *b* 17 Oct. 1937; *s* of John William Benson and Rebecca (*née* Winston); *m* 1960, Ann Margery Licht; one *s* one *d*. *Educ:* Clifton Coll. FCA 1961. Articled clerk with Hartleys, Wilkins and Flew, 1955–60; qualified as chartered accountant, 1961; Lewis Golden & Co.: Sen. Clerk, 1961–63; Partner, 1963–. Chairman: Davis Service Gp Plc, 1981–; Moss Bros Gp Plc, 1989–; Director: Shaftesbury Plc, 1986–; Talley Industries Inc. (USA), 1988–; Dep. Chm., Business Post Gp Plc, 1993–. Hon. Treasurer and Trustee: Cystic Fibrosis Res. Trust, 1990–; Liver Res. Trust, 1991–. *Recreations:* Real tennis, golf, watching Rugby, theatre, my Alvis. *Address:* 40 Queen Anne Street, W1M 0EL. *T:* 0171–580 7313. *Clubs:* Royal Automobile, MCC, Saints and Sinners; Roehampton Golf, Hampstead Golf, Lake Nona Golf (Orlando, Fla).

BENSON, Peter; *see* Benson, H. P. N.

BENSON, Maj.-Gen. Peter Herbert, CBE 1974 (MBE 1954); Member of Panel of Independent Inspectors, Planning Inspectorate, Departments of Environment and Transport, 1981–88; *b* 27 Oct. 1923; *s* of Herbert Kamerer Benson and Edith Doris Benson; *m* 1949, Diana Betty Ashmore; one *s* one *d*. Joined Army, 1944; commnd into S Wales Borderers, 1945; transf. to RASC, 1948, and Royal Corps of Transport, 1965; served, Palestine, Cyprus, Malaya and Singapore (three times), Borneo, Africa and Australia; Comdr, 15 Air Despatch Regt, 1966–68; GSO1 (DS) Staff Coll., Camberley, and Australian Staff Coll., 1968–70; Col Q (Movements), MoD (Army), 1971–72; Comdr, 2 Transport Gp RCT (Logistic Support Force), 1972–73. Comdr, ANZUK Support Gp Singapore, Sen. British Officer Singapore, and Leader, UK Jt Services Planning Team, 1973–74; Chief Transport and Movements Officer, BAOR, 1974–76; Dir Gen. of Transport and Movements (Army) (formerly Transport Officer in Chief (Army)), MoD, 1976–78. Chm., Grants Cttee, Army Benevolent Fund, 1980–92. Col Comdt, RCT, 1978–90. Chm., Abbeyfield Soc., Beaminster, 1982–92. Pres., Army Officers' Golfing Soc., 1993–. Liveryman, Co. of Carmen, 1977. *Recreations:* golf, fly-fishing, photography. *Club:* Lyme Regis Golf (Captain, 1993).

BENSON, Richard Anthony; QC 1995; a Recorder, since 1995; *b* 20 Feb. 1946; *s* of Douglas Arthur Benson and Muriel Alice Benson (*née* Fairfield); *m* 1967, Katherine Anne Smith; one *s* two *d*. *Educ:* Wrekin Coll.; Coll. of Law; Inns of Court Sch. of Law. Sailing and overland expedition to Africa, 1964–65; articled to Bircham & Co. (Solicitors), 1965–67; joined Inner Temple as student, 1968; adventuring in Sudan, 1969–70; called to the Bar, Inner Temple, 1974; in practice on Midland and Oxford Circuit, specialising in criminal law; Asst Recorder, 1991–95. *Recreations:* flying (flew Atlantic via Greenland 1983), off-shore cruising, drama, writing and performing in reviews, after-dinner speaking, the company of friends! *Address:* 1 King's Bench Walk, Temple, EC4Y 7DB. *T:* 0171–353 8436. *Clubs:* Northampton and County; Bar Yacht.

BENSON, Richard Stuart Alistair; His Honour Judge Benson; a Circuit Judge, since 1993; *b* 23 Nov. 1943; *s* of late Frank Benson and of Jean Benson; *m* 1980, Susan. *Educ:* Clapham Coll.; Univ. of Nottingham (BA Politics). Called to the Bar, Gray's Inn, 1968; in practice at the Bar, firstly Midland Circuit, later Midland and Oxford Circuit, Nottingham, 1968–92; a Recorder, 1991–93. *Recreations:* steeplechasing, horses (Joint Master, Trent Valley Draghounds), books, France. *Address:* 1 High Pavement, Nottingham NG1 1HF. *T:* Nottingham (0115) 941 8218. *Club:* Nottingham and Notts United Services.

BENT, Margaret (Hilda), PhD; FBA 1993; musicologist; Senior Research Fellow, All Souls College, Oxford, since 1992; *b* 23 Dec. 1940; *d* of Horace Bassington and Miriam (*née* Simpson); *m*; one *s* one *d*. *Educ:* Haberdashers' Aske's Acton Sch.; Girton Coll., Cambridge (organ schol.; BA 1962; MusB 1963; MA; PhD 1969). Lectr, then Sen. Lectr, Music Dept, Goldsmiths' Coll., London Univ., 1972–75; Vis. Prof., then full Prof. and Chm., Music Dept, Brandeis Univ., 1975–81; Prof., later Chm., Music Dept, Princeton Univ., 1981–92. Guggenheim Fellow, 1983–84. Pres., Amer. Musicological Soc., 1984–86. For. Hon. Mem., Amer. Acad. of Arts and Scis, 1994. *Publications:* (ed jtly) Old Hall Manuscript, vols I and II 1969, vol III 1973; (ed jtly) John Dunstable, Complete Works, 1970; (ed) Four Anonymous Masses, 1979; Dunstaple, 1981; (ed jtly) Ciconia, 1985; (ed) Rossini, Il Turco in Italia, 1988; (contrib.) New Grove Dictionary of Music and Musicians, 1980; contrib. Musica Disciplina, Jl of Amer. Musicol Soc., Early Music Hist. etc. *Address:* All Souls College, Oxford OX1 4AL. *T:* Oxford (01865) 279379.

BENTALL, Hugh Henry, MB; FRCS; Emeritus Professor of Cardiac Surgery, Royal Postgraduate Medical School, University of London, since 1985; Hon. Consulting Cardiac Surgeon, Hammersmith Hospital, since 1985; *b* 28 April 1920; *s* of late Henry Bentall and Lilian Alice Greeno; *m* 1944, Jean, *d* of late Hugh Cameron Wilson, MD, FRCS; three *s* one *d*. *Educ:* Seaford Coll., Sussex; Medical Sch. of St Bartholomew's Hospital, London. RNVR, Surg Lieut, 1945–47. Consultant Thoracic Surgeon, Hammersmith Hosp., 1955–85; Lecturer in Thoracic Surgery, Postgraduate Medical Sch., London, 1959; Reader, 1962–65; Prof., 1965–85. Order of Yugoslav Flag with Gold Leaves, 1984. *Publications:* books and papers on surgical subjects. *Recreations:* sailing, antique horology. *Address:* Royal Postgraduate Medical School of London, Ducane Road, W12 0NN. *T:* 0181–743 2030. *Clubs:* Royal Naval Sailing Association (Portsmouth); Royal Air Force Yacht (Hamble).

BENTALL, Leonard Edward; Chairman, Bentalls, since 1982; *b* 26 May 1939; *s* of late Leonard Edward Rowan Bentall and Adelia Elizabeth Bentall (*née* Hawes); *m* 1964, Wendy Ann Daniel; three *d*. *Educ:* Stowe School. FCA. Articled Clerk, Dixon Wilson Tubbs & Gillett, 1958–64. Bentalls, 1964–: Management Accountant, Merchandise Controller, Merchandise Dir, Man. Dir, Chm. and Man. Dir, Chm. and Chief Exec. Non-Exec. Dir, Associated Independent Stores, 1979–82. Pres., Textile Benevolent Assoc. Non-exec. Dir, Kingston Hosp. Trust. Governor: Kingston Coll.; Kingston Grammar Sch. Trustee and Chm., Exec. Cttee, Steadfast Sea Cadet Corps, Kingston upon Thames. FInstD. *Address:* Bentalls PLC, Anstee House, Wood Street, Kingston upon Thames, Surrey KT1 1TS. *T:* 0181–546 2002; Runnymede, Sandpit Hall Road, Chobham, Woking, Surrey GU24 8AN. *T:* Chobham (01276) 858256. *Clubs:* MCC, Surrey Cricket, Saints and Sinners.

BENTHALL, Jonathan Charles Mackenzie; Director, Royal Anthropological Institute, since 1974; Editor, Anthropology Today, since 1985; *b* Calcutta, 12 Sept. 1941; *s* of Sir Arthur Paul Benthall, KBE and Mollie Pringle; *m* 1975, Zamira, *d* of Baron Menuhin, *qv*; two *s* and one step *s*. *Educ:* Eton (KS); King's Coll., Cambridge (MA). Sec., Inst. of Contemporary Arts, 1971–73. Member: UK Adv. Cttee, 1981–87, Overseas Adv. Cttee, 1985–86, 1990–, Council, 1987–90, Assembly, 1990–, SCF; Assoc. of Social Anthropologists, 1983; Bd, Internat. Broadcasting Trust, 1991–. Hon. Res. Fellow, Dept of Anthropology, UCL, 1994. Anthropology in Media Award, Amer. Anthropol Assoc., 1993. Chevalier de l'Ordre des Arts et des Lettres (France), 1973. *Publications:* Science and Technology in Art Today, 1972; (ed) Ecology: the Shaping Enquiry, 1972; (ed) The Limits of Human Nature, 1973; (ed jtly) The Body as a Medium of Expression, 1975; The Body Electric: patterns of western industrial culture, 1976; Disasters, Relief and the Media, 1993. *Recreations:* listening to music, swimming, mountain walking. *Address:* 212 Hammersmith Grove, W6 7HG. *Club:* Athenæum.

BENTHAM, Prof. Richard Walker; Professor of Petroleum and Mineral Law, and Director of the Centre for Petroleum and Mineral Law Studies, University of Dundee, 1983–90; Professor Emeritus, since 1991; *b* 26 June 1930; *s* of Richard Hardy Bentham and Ellen Walker (*née* Fisher); *m* 1956, Stella Winifred Matthews; one *d*. *Educ:* Campbell Coll., Belfast; Trinity Coll., Dublin (BA, LLB). Called to the Bar, Middle Temple, 1955.

Lecturer in Law: Univ. of Tasmania, 1955–57; Univ. of Sydney, 1957–61; Legal Dept, The British Petroleum Co. PLC, 1961–83 (Dep. Legal Advisor, 1979–83). Founder Mem., Scottish Council for Internat. Arbitration, 1988–; Mem. Council, Inst. of Internat. Business Law and Practice, ICC, 1988–94; British nominated Mem., Panel of Arbitrators, Dispute Settlement Centre, IEA, 1989–. Mem. and consultant, Russian Petroleum Legislation Project (sponsored by Univ. of Houston, World Bank and ODAS), 1991–. FRSA 1986. *Publications:* articles in learned jls in UK and overseas. *Recreations:* cricket, military history, military modelling. *Address:* West Bryans, 87 Dundee Road, West Ferry, Dundee DD5 1LZ. *T:* Dundee (01382) 477100.

BENTINCK, family name of **Earl of Portland**.

BENTLEY, (Anthony) Philip; QC 1991; Barrister, Stanbrook and Hooper, European Community Lawyers, Brussels, since 1980; *b* 5 Dec. 1948; *s* of late Kenneth Bentley and of Frances Elizabeth (*née* Scott); *m* 1980, Christine Anne-Marie Odile Bausier; two *s* two *d*. *Educ:* St George's Coll., Weybridge; St Catharine's Coll., Cambridge (MA). Called to the Bar, Lincoln's Inn, 1970. With ICI, 1973–77; Dilley & Custer, 1977–80. *Recreation:* oboist in amateur orchestras. *Address:* 42 rue du Taciturne, 1040 Brussels, Belgium. *T:* Brussels (2) 2305059.

BENTLEY, Rt. Rev. David Edward; *see* Gloucester, Bishop of.

BENTLEY, David Jeffrey, CB 1993; Principal Assistant Legal Adviser, Home Office, since 1988; *b* 5 July 1935; *s* of late Harry Jeffrey Bentley and Katherine (*née* Barnett). *Educ:* Watford Grammar School; New College, Oxford (BCL, MA). Called to the Bar, Lincoln's Inn, 1963; University teaching, 1957–79; Asst Parly Counsel, 1965–67; Legal Adviser's Branch, Home Office, 1979–. *Recreations:* reading, listening to music, walking. *Address:* c/o Home Office, Queen Anne's Gate, SW1H 9AT. *Club:* United Oxford & Cambridge University.

BENTLEY, David Ronald; QC 1984; **His Honour Judge Bentley;** a Circuit Judge, since 1988; *b* 24 Feb. 1942; *s* of Edgar Norman and Hilda Bentley; *m* 1978, Christine Elizabeth Stewart; two *s*. *Educ:* King Edward VII Sch., Sheffield; University Coll. London. LLB (Hons) 1963; LLM and Brigid Cotter Prize, London Univ., 1979; PhD Sheffield, 1994. Called to the Bar, Gray's Inn, 1969 (Macaskie Scholar). In practice at the bar, 1969–88; a Recorder, 1985–88. *Recreations:* legal history, wildlife, dogs, soccer, cinema.

BENTLEY, Ven. Frank William Henry; Archdeacon of Worcester and Canon Residentiary of Worcester Cathedral, since 1984; Chaplain to the Queen, since 1994; *b* 4 March 1934; *s* of Nowell and May Bentley; *m* 1st, 1957, Muriel Bland (*d* 1958); one *s*; 2nd, 1960, Yvonne Wilson; two *s* one *d*. *Educ:* Yeovil School; King's College London (AKC). Deacon 1958, priest 1959; Curate at Shepton Mallet, 1958–62; Rector of Kingsdon with Podymore Milton and Curate-in-charge, Yeovilton, 1962–66; Rector of Babcary, 1964–66; Vicar of Wiveliscombe, 1966–76; Rural Dean of Tone, 1973–76; Vicar of St John-in-Bedwardine, Worcester, 1976–84; Rural Dean of Martley and Worcester West, 1979–84. Hon. Canon of Worcester Cathedral, 1981. *Recreations:* gardening, countryside. *Address:* 56 Battenhall Road, Worcester WR5 2BQ. *T:* Worcester (01905) 764446; (office) The Old Palace, Deansway, Worcester WR1 2JE. *T:* Worcester (01905) 20537.

BENTLEY, Rev. Canon Geoffrey Bryan; Hon. Canon of Windsor, since 1982; *b* 16 July 1909; *s* of late Henry Bentley; *m* 1938, Nina Mary, *d* of late George Coombe Williams, priest; two *s* two *d*. *Educ:* Uppingham Sch.; King's Coll., Cambridge (Scholar); Cuddesdon Coll., Oxford. BA and Carus Greek Testament Prize, 1932; MA 1935. Ordained, 1933; Asst Curate, St Cuthbert's, Copnor, 1933–35; Tutor of Scholae Cancellarii, Lincoln, 1935–38; Lecturer, 1938–52; Priest Vicar of Lincoln Cathedral and Chaplain of Lincoln County Hosp., 1938–52; Proctor in Convocation, 1945–55; Rector of Milton Abbot with Dunterton, Dio. Exeter, 1952–57; Examg Chap. to Bp of Exeter, 1952–74; Commissary of Bp of SW Tanganyika, 1952–61; Canon of Windsor, 1957–82, President, 1962, 1971 and 1976. Member: Archbp's Commns on Atomic Power, 1946, and Divine Healing, 1953; Archbp's Group on Reform of Divorce Law, 1964 (author of report, Putting Asunder). William Jones Golden Lectr, 1965; Scott Holland Lectr., 1966. *Publications:* The Resurrection of the Bible, 1940; Catholic Design for Living, 1940; Reform of the Ecclesiastical Law, 1944; God and Venus, 1964; Dominance or Dialogue?, 1965; (contrib.) Sexual Morality: three views, 1965; (contrib.) Abortion and the Sanctity of Human Life, 1985. *Address:* 5 The Cloisters, Windsor Castle, Berks SL4 1NJ. *T:* Windsor (01753) 863001.

BENTLEY, Prof. George, FRCS; Professor of Orthopaedic Surgery, since 1982, and Director, since 1992, Institute of Orthopaedics, University College and Middlesex School of Medicine, University of London; *b* 19 Jan. 1936; *s* of George and Doris Bentley; *m* 1960, Ann Gillian Hutchings; two *s* one *d*. *Educ:* Rotherham Grammar Sch.; Sheffield Univ. (MB, ChB, ChM), FRCS 1964. House Surgeon, Sheffield Royal Infirmary, 1959–61; Lectr in Anatomy, Birmingham Univ., 1961–62; Surg. Registrar, Sheffield Royal Infirm., 1963–65; Sen. Registrar in Orthopaedics, Nuffield Orthopaedic Centre and Radcliffe Infirm., Oxford, 1967–69; Instructor in Orth., Univ. of Pittsburgh, USA, 1969–70; Lectr, 1970–71, Sen. Lectr and Reader in Orth., 1971–76, Univ. of Oxford; Prof. of Orth. and Accident Surgery, Univ. of Liverpool, 1976–82; Hon. Consultant Orthopaedic Surgeon: Royal Nat. Orthopaedic Hosp., Stanmore; Middlesex Hosp. *Publications:* (ed) 3rd edn vols I and II, Rob and Smith Operative Surgery—Orthopaedics, 1979, 4th edn 1991; (ed) Mercer's Orthopaedic Surgery, 8th edn, 1983; papers on arthritis, accident surgery and scoliosis in leading med. and surg. jls. *Recreations:* golf, tennis, music. *Address:* Institute of Orthopaedics, Royal National Orthopaedic Hospital, Stanmore, Middx HA7 4LP. *T:* 0181–954 2300.

BENTLEY, John Ransome; Director, Wordnet International PLC, since 1983; *b* 19 Feb. 1940; *m* 1st, 1960 (marr. diss. 1969); one *s* one *d*; 2nd, 1982, Katherine Susan (marr. diss. 1986), *d* of Gerald Percy and the Marchioness of Bute. *Educ:* Harrow Sch. Chairman: Bardsey PLC, 1980–81; Intervision Video (Holdings) PLC, 1980–82. *Recreation:* living.

BENTLEY, Philip; *see* Bentley, A. P.

BENTLEY, Sir William, KCMG 1985 (CMG 1977); HM Diplomatic Service, retired; Chairman: Society of Pension Consultants, since 1987; Coflexip UK Ltd, since 1988; DUCO Ltd, since 1990; *b* 15 Feb. 1927; *s* of Lawrence and Elsie Jane Bentley; *m* 1950, Karen Ellen Christensen; two *s* three *d*. *Educ:* Bury High Sch.; Manchester Univ.; Wadham Coll., Oxford (1st cl. Mod. Hist.); Coll. of Europe, Bruges. HM Foreign (later Diplomatic) Service, 1952; 3rd (later 2nd) Sec., Tokyo, 1952–57; United Nations Dept, Foreign Office, 1957–60; 1st Sec., UK Mission to United Nations, 1960–63; Far Eastern Dept, FO, 1963–65; Head of Chancery, Kuala Lumpur, 1965–69; Dep. Comr-Gen., British Pavilion, Expo 70, Osaka, 1969–70; Counsellor, Belgrade, 1970–73; Head of Permanent Under-Sec.'s Dept, FCO, 1973–74; Head of Far Eastern Dept, FCO, 1974–76; Ambassador to the Philippines, 1976–81; High Comr in Malaysia, 1981–83; Ambassador to Norway, 1983–87. *Recreations:* golf, skiing, fishing, shooting. *Address:* 48 Bathgate Road, SW19 5PJ; Les Terriers, Landivy, Mayenne, France. *Clubs:* Brooks's; Roehampton.

BENTON, Joseph Edward; JP; MP (Lab) Bootle, since Nov. 1990; *b* 28 Sept. 1933; *s* of Thomas and Agnes Benton; *m* 1959, Doris Wynne; four *d*. *Educ:* St Monica's Primary and Secondary Sch.; Bootle Technical Coll. Nat. Service, RAF, 1955. Apprentice fitter and turner, 1949; former Personnel Manager, Pacific Steam Navigation Co.; Girobank, 1982–90. Councillor, Sefton Borough Council, 1970–90 (Leader, Labour Gp, 1985–90). An Opposition Whip, 1994–. Mem., Speaker's Panel of Chairmen, 1992–94. Mem., Bd Visitors, Liverpool Prison (Walton), 1974–81. Chm. of Govs, Hugh Baird Coll. of Technology, 1972–93. Assoc. Mem., IPM, 1965; MIL 1963. JP South Sefton, 1969. *Address:* c/o House of Commons, SW1A 0AA.

BENTON, Kenneth Carter, CMG 1966; *b* 4 March 1909; *s* of William Alfred Benton and Amy Adeline Benton (*née* Kirton); *m* 1938, Peggie (*d* 1992), *d* of Maj.-Gen. C. E. Pollock, CB, CBE, DSO; one *s* (and two step *s* decd). *Educ:* Wolverhampton Sch.; London Univ. Teaching and studying languages in Florence and Vienna, 1930–37; employed British Legation, Vienna, 1937–38; Vice-Consul, Riga, 1938–40; 2nd Sec., British Embassy, Madrid, 1941–43; 2nd, later 1st Sec., Rome, 1944–48; FO, 1948–50; 1st Sec., Rome, 1950–53; 1st Sec., Madrid, 1953–56; FO, 1956–62; 1st Sec. and Consul, Lima, 1963–64; FO, 1964–66; Counsellor, Rio de Janeiro, 1966–68; retd from Diplomatic Service, 1968. *Publications:* Twenty-fourth Level, 1969; Sole Agent, 1970; Spy in Chancery, 1972; Craig and the Jaguar, 1973; Craig and the Tunisian Tangle, 1974; Death on the Appian Way, 1974; Craig and the Midas Touch, 1975; A Single Monstrous Act, 1976; The Red Hen Conspiracy, 1977; Ward of Caesar, 1986; as James Kirton: Time for Murder, 1985; Greek Fire, 1985; The Plight of the Baltic States, 1986. *Recreations:* writing, painting. *Address:* 2 Jubilee Terrace, Chichester, West Sussex PO19 1XL. *T:* Chichester (01243) 787148. *Club:* Detection.

BENTON, Margaret Carole; Head of Theatre Museum, Victoria and Albert Museum, since 1990; *b* 14 April 1943; *d* of late Lawrence Benton and Mary (*née* Thomason). *Educ:* The Red Maids Sch., Bristol; Univ. of Wales (BA Hons French). British Broadcasting Corporation: Radio, 1966; News, Paris Office, 1967; Schools Television, 1969; Gen. Features Television, 1970; COI (Overseas Documentaries/Co-prodns), 1971; BBC Television, Bristol, 1975; Nat. Museum of Photography, Film and Television, 1985. Member: Theatres Adv. Council; Council of Management (British Centre), Internat. Theatre Inst.; Pres., Société Internationale des Bibliothèques et des Musées des Arts du Spectacle; Member: RTS; Museums Assoc. FRSA. Prod and dir. television documentaries and other progs for BBC, including: Ours to Keep; Gold on Ice (Omnibus); Journey Back; A Vision of Wiltshire; The Factory. *Recreations:* rural "idylling", theatre, cinema, gardens, historic buildings. *Address:* c/o Theatre Museum, National Museum of the Performing Arts, 1E Tavistock Street, WC2E 7PA. *T:* 0171–836 7891.

BENTON, Peter Faulkner, MA, CIMgt; Chairman, Enterprise Support Group Ltd, since 1993; *b* 6 Oct. 1934; *s* of late S. F. Benton and Mrs H. D. Benton; *m* 1959, Ruth, *d* of late R. S. Cobb, MC, and Mrs J. P. Cobb; two *s* three *d*. *Educ:* Oundle; Queens' Coll., Cambridge (MA Nat. Sciences). 2nd Lieut RE, 1953–55. Unilever Ltd, 1958–60; Shell Chemicals Ltd, 1960–63; Berger Jenson and Nicholson Ltd, 1963–64; McKinsey & Co. Inc., London and Chicago, 1964–71; Gallaher Ltd, 1971, Dir, 1973–77; Man. Dir, Post Office Telecommunications, 1978–81; Dep. Chm., British Telecom, 1981–83. Dir-Gen., BIM, 1987–92. Chairman: Saunders Valve Ltd, 1972–77; Mono Pumps Group, 1976–77; European Practice, Nolan, Norton & Co., 1984–87; Identica Ltd, 1992–93; Director: Singer and Friedlander, 1983–89; Woodside Communications, 1995–; Mem., Supervisory Bd, Hiross Holdings AG, Austria, 1992–94. Dir, Turing Inst., 1985–94. Chm., Enfield Dist HA, 1986–92. Chm., Heating, Ventilating, Air Conditioning and Refrigerating Equipment Sector Working Party, NEDO, 1976–79; Member: Electronics Industry EDC, 1980–83; Econ. and Financial Policy Cttee, CBI, 1979–83; Special Adviser to EEC, 1983–84; Nat. Curriculum Science Wkg Gp, 1987–88; Indust. Develt Adv. Bd, DTI, 1988–94; Ind. Mem., British Liby Adv. Council, 1988–93. Vice-President: British Mech. Engrg Confedn, 1974–77; European Council of Management, 1989–93. Chairman: Ditchley Conf. on Inf. Technol., 1982; Financial Times Conf., World Electronics, 1983; World Bank Conf. on Catastrophe Avoidance, Washington, 1988, Karlstad, 1989; Vis. Gp, Inst. for Systems Engrg and Informatics, Italy, 1994. Royal Signals Instn Lectr, London, 1980; ASLIB Lectr, 1988; Adam Smith Lectr, 1991. Pres., Highgate Literary and Scientific Instn, 1981–88. Chm., N London Hospice Gp, 1985–89. Governor, Molecule Club Theatre, 1985–91. *Publications:* Riding the Whirlwind, 1990; articles on management, science and IT. *Recreations:* reading, golf, conversation, looking at buildings. *Address:* Northgate House, Highgate Hill, N6 5HD. *T:* 0181–341 1122. *Clubs:* Athenæum, United Oxford & Cambridge University, The Pilgrims; Blythe Sappers; Highgate Golf.

BENTON JONES, Sir Simon W. F.; *see* Jones.

BENTSEN, Lloyd Millard, Jr; Secretary to the US Treasury, 1993–94; *b* 11 Feb. 1921; *s* of late Lloyd and of Edna Ruth Bentsen; *m* 1943, Beryl Ann Longino; two *s* one *d*. *Educ:* Univ. of Texas (LLB 1942). Served USAAF, 1942–45 (DFC; Air Medal). Admitted to Texas Bar, 1942; in private practice, 1945–48; Judge, Hidalgo County, Texas, 1946–48. Mem. of Congress, 1948–54; Mem. for Texas, US Senate, 1972–93. Pres., Lincoln Consolidated, Houston, 1955–70. Democratic running mate to Michael Dukakis, US Presidential election, 1988. *Address:* 600 Travis Street, Suite 2600, Houston, TX 77002, USA.

BENYON, Thomas Yates; Director of various companies; *b* 13 Aug. 1942; *s* of late Thomas Yates Benyon and Joan Ida Walters; *m* 1968, Olivia Jane (*née* Scott Plummer); two *s* two *d*. *Educ:* Wellington Sch., Somerset; RMA Sandhurst. Lieut, Scots Guards, 1963–67. Insurance Broker, 1967–71; commodity broking, banking, 1971–78. Chm., Milton Keynes HA, 1989–94; Dir, Bucks Purchasing Authy, 1993–; Mem. Council, NAHAT. Councillor, Aylesbury Vale DC, 1976–79. Contested (C): Huyton, Feb. 1974; Haringey (Wood Green), Oct. 1974; MP (C) Abingdon, 1979–83; Vice Chm., Health and Social Services Cttee, 1982–83; Mem., Social Services Select Cttee, 1980–83. Chairman: Assoc. of Lloyd's Members, 1983–85; Soc. of Names, 1991–. Vice-Pres., Guidepost Trust (charity for mentally sick), 1978–. *Recreation:* family. *Address:* Old Rectory, Adstock, Buckingham MK18 2HY. *Clubs:* Pratt's, Royal Automobile.

BENYON, Sir William (Richard), Kt 1994; DL; farmer, since 1964; *b* 17 Jan. 1930; *e s* of late Vice-Adm. R. Benyon, CB, CBE, and of Mrs. Benyon, The Lambdens, Beenham, Berkshire; *m* Elizabeth Ann Hallifax; two *s* three *d*. *Educ:* Royal Naval Coll., Dartmouth. Royal Navy, 1947–56; Courtaulds Ltd, 1956–64. Mem., Berks CC, 1964–74. MP (C) Buckingham, 1970–83, Milton Keynes, 1983–92. PPS to Minister of Housing and Construction, 1972–74; Conservative Whip, 1974–76. Chairman: Peabody Trust, 1993–; Ernest Cook Charitable Trust, 1993–. JP 1962–78, DL 1970, High Sheriff 1995, Berks. *Address:* Englefield House, Englefield, near Reading, Berkshire RG7 5EN. *T:* Reading (01734) 302221. *Clubs:* Boodle's, Pratt's.

BERESFORD, family name of **Baron Decies** and **Marquess of Waterford.**

BERESFORD, Sir (Alexander) Paul, Kt 1990; dental surgeon; MP (C) Croydon Central, since 1992; Parliamentary Under-Secretary of State, Department of the Environment, since 1994; *b* 6 April 1946; *s* of Raymond and Joan Beresford; *m* Julie Haynes; three *s* one *d*. *Educ:* Richmond Primary Sch., Richmond, Nelson, NZ; Waimea Coll., Richmond; Otago Univ., Dunedin. Mem. (C), Wandsworth BC, 1978–94 (Leader of Council, 1983–92). Mem., Audit Commn, 1991–92. *Address:* c/o House of Commons, SW1A 0AA.

BERESFORD, Prof. Maurice Warwick, FBA 1985; Professor of Economic History, University of Leeds, 1959–85, now Emeritus; *b* 6 Feb. 1920; *s* of late H. B. Beresford and Mrs N. E. Beresford. *Educ:* Boldmere and Green Lane Elementary Schs; Bishop Vesey's Grammar Sch., Sutton Coldfield; Jesus Coll., Cambridge (exhibnr and schol.). Goldsmiths' Co. Open Exhibnr; Historical Tripos, Pt I class I, 1940, Pt II class I, 1941; MA 1945. On Staff of Birmingham Univ. Settlement, 1941–42; Sub-warden, Percival Guildhouse, Rugby, 1942–43; Warden, 1943–48; University of Leeds: Lecturer, 1948–55; Reader, 1955–59; Dean, 1958–60; Chm., Sch. of Economic Studies, 1965–68, 1971–72, 1981–83; Chm. of Faculty Bd, 1968–70. Harrison Vis. Prof. of History, Coll. of William and Mary, Virginia, 1975–76; Vis. Prof. of History, Strathclyde Univ., 1987–90. Voluntary teacher, Wakefield Prison, 1975–92. Chairman: Yorks Citizens' Advice Bureaux Cttee, 1963–69; Parole Review Cttee, Leeds Prison, 1970–92; Northern Area Inst. for Study and Treatment of Delinquency, 1973–78; Co-opted Mem., City of Leeds Probation Cttee, 1972–78; SSRC, Economic and Social History Cttee, 1972–75. Minister's nominee, Yorkshire Dales National Park Cttee, 1964–71; Member: Consumer Council, 1966–71; Hearing Aids Council, 1969–71; Royal Commn on Historical Monuments (England), 1979–90. Hon. Vice-Pres., Yorks Archaeolog. Soc., 1986 (Medallist, 1989); Hon. Patron, Thoresby Soc., 1985. Hon. DLitt: Loughborough, 1984; Hull, 1986. *Publications:* The Leeds Chambers of Commerce, 1951; The Lost Villages of England, 1954, rev. edn 1983; History on the Ground, 1957, rev. edn 1984; (with J. K. S. St Joseph) Medieval England: an Aerial Survey, 1958, rev. edn 1979; Time and Place, 1962; New Towns of the Middle Ages, 1967, rev. edn 1988; (Ed, with G. R. J. Jones) Leeds and Its Region, 1967; (with J. G. Hurst) Deserted Medieval Villages, 1971, rev. edn 1989; (with H. P. R. Finberg) English Medieval Boroughs, 1973; (with B. J. Barber) The West Riding County Council 1889–1974, 1979; Walks Round Red Brick, 1980; Time and Place: collected essays, 1985; East End, West End, 1988; (with J. G. Hurst) Wharram Percy — Deserted Medieval Village, 1990; contribs to Economic History Review, Agricultural History Review, Medieval Archaeology, etc. *Recreations:* music, theatre, maps, delinquency. *Address:* 4 Claremont Avenue, Leeds LS3 1AT. *T:* Leeds (0113) 245 4563.

BERESFORD, Meg; Assistant Director, YMCA Centre, Wiston Lodge, since 1994; *b* 5 Sept. 1937; *d* of late John Tristram Beresford and of Anne Stuart-Wortley; *m* 1959, William Tanner; two *s*. *Educ:* Sherborne School for Girls; Seale Hayne Agricultural Coll., Newton Abbot; Univ. of Warwick. Community worker, Leamington Spa; Organising Sec., European Nuclear Disarmament, 1981–83; Gen. Sec., CND, 1985–90; gardener, 1991–92, Staff Co-ordinator, 1992–94, Iona Community. *Publications:* Into the Twenty First Century, 1989; contributor to End Jl, Sanity. *Recreations:* walking, reading, camping, music. *Address:* Wiston Lodge, Wiston, Biggar ML12 6HT.

BERESFORD-PEIRSE, Sir Henry Grant de la Poer, 6th Bt *cr* 1814; *b* 7 Feb. 1933; *s* of Sir Henry Campbell de la Poer Beresford-Peirse, 5th Bt, CB, and Margaret (*d* 1995), *d* of Frank Morison Seafield Grant, Knockie, Inverness-shire; *S* father, 1972; *m* 1966, Jadranka, *d* of Ivan Njerš, Zagreb, Croatia; two *s*. *Heir: s* Henry Njerš de la Poer Beresford-Peirse, *b* 25 March 1969.

BERESFORD-WEST, Michael Charles; QC 1975; a Recorder of the Crown Court, 1975–83; *b* 3 June 1928; *s* of late Arthur Charles, OBE, KPM and Ida Dagmar West; *m* 1st, 1956, Patricia Eileen Beresford (marr. diss.); two *s* one *d*; 2nd, 1986, Sheilagh Elizabeth Davies. *Educ:* St Peter's, Southbourne; Portsmouth Grammar Sch.; Brasenose Coll., Oxford (MA). Nat. Service, Intell. Corps, Middle East, SIME. Called to Bar, Lincoln's Inn, 1952, Inner Temple, 1980; Western Circuit, 1953–65; SE Circuit, 1965; a Chm., Independent Schools Tribunal and Tribunal (Children's Act 1948), 1974–80. *Recreations:* swimming, opera, music, golf, cruising. *Address:* Goldsmith Chambers, Goldsmith Building, Temple, EC4Y 7BL. *T:* 0171–353 6802, *Fax:* 0171–583 5255; Farnham Hall, Farnham, Saxmundham, Suffolk IP17 1LB. *Clubs:* Hampshire Hogs; Nomads; Aldeburgh Yacht, Bar Yacht; Aldeburgh Golf.

BERG, Adrian, RA 1992; *b* 12 March 1929; *s* of Charles Berg, MD, DPM and Sarah (*née* Sorby). *Educ:* Charterhouse; Gonville and Caius Coll., Cambridge (MA); Trinity Coll., Dublin (HDipEd); St Martin's Sch. of Art (Intermediate Arts & Crafts); Chelsea Sch. of Art (NDD); Royal Coll. of Art (ARCA). Nat. Service, 1947–49. Taught at various art schools, esp. Central Sch. of Art and Design and Camberwell Sch. of Arts and Crafts, 1961–78; Sen. Tutor, RCA, 1987–88. One-man exhibitions include: Arthur Tooth & Sons Ltd, London, 1964, 1967, 1969, 1972 and 1975; Galleria Vaccarino, Florence, 1973; Galerie Burg Diesdonk, Düsseldorf, 1976; Waddington and Tooth Galls, London, 1978; Waddington Galls, Montreal and Toronto and Grace Hokin, Inc., Chicago, 1979; London: Waddington Galls, 1981 and 1983; Serpentine Gall., 1973, 1984 and 1986; Piccadilly Gall., 1985, 1988, 1989, 1991 and 1993; Concourse Gall., Barbican Centre, 1993; Walker Art Gall., Liverpool, 1986; Victoria Art Gall., Bath, 1993; Plymouth City Mus. and Art Gall., 1993; Newport Mus. and Art Gall., Gwent, 1993; Mappin Gall., Sheffield, 1993; Hatton Gall., Newcastle, 1994; Royal Botanic Gdn, Edinburgh, 1994. Lorne Scholarship, 1979–80. Gold Medal, Florence Biennale, 1973; minor and major prizes, John Moores Nat. Exhibns, 1980 and 1982; Major Prize, 3rd Tolly Cobbold, Eastern Arts Nat. Exhibn, 1981; Foundn for Art Award, NT, 1987. *Recreations:* imaginative writing, criticism. *Address:* The Piccadilly Gallery, 16 Cork Street, W1X 1PF. *T:* 0171–629 2875.

BERG, Alan; Stipendiary Magistrate for Greater Manchester, since 1994; *b* 17 Feb. 1943; *s* of Simon and Esther Berg; *m* 1967, Lorna Lewis; two *s*. *Educ:* King George V Grammar Sch., Southport; Law Coll., Liverpool. Solicitor in private practice, Liverpool, 1967–94; Sen. Partner, Canter Levin & Berg; Asst Stipendiary Magistrate, 1991–94. *Recreations:* gardening, swimming, worrying. *Address:* Manchester City Magistrates' Court, Crown Square, Manchester M60 1PR. *T:* 0161–832 7272.

BERG, Rev. John J.; *see* Johansen-Berg.

BERG, Prof. Paul, PhD; Cahill Professor of Biochemistry, since 1994, and Director, Beckman Center for Molecular and Genetic Medicine, since 1985, Stanford University School of Medicine; *b* New York, 30 June 1926; *m* Mildred Levy; one *s*. *Educ:* Pennsylvania State Univ. (BS); Western Reserve Univ. (PhD). Pre-doctoral and post-doctoral med. research, 1950–54; scholar in cancer research, American Cancer Soc., Washington Univ., 1954; Asst to Associate Prof. of Microbiology, Washington Univ., 1955–59; Stanford Univ. Sch. of Medicine: Associate Prof. of Biochem., 1959–60; Prof., Dept of Biochem., 1960, Chm. 1969–74; Willson Prof. of Biochem., 1970–93; Non-resident Fellow, Salk Inst., 1973–83. Editor, Biochemical and Biophysical Res. Communications, 1959–68; Member: NIH Study, Sect. on Physiol Chem.; Editorial Bd, Jl of Molecular Biology, 1966–69; Bd of Sci. Advisors, Jane Coffin Childs Foundn for Med. Res.; Adv. Bds to Nat. Insts of Health, Amer. Cancer Soc., Nat. Sci. Foundn, MIT and Harvard, 1970–80; Council, Nat. Acad. of Scis, 1979. Former Pres., Amer. Soc. of Biological Chemists; Foreign Member: Japan Biochem. Soc., 1978–; French Acad. of Scis, 1981–; Royal Soc., 1992. Lectures: Harvey, 1972; Lynen, 1977; Weizmann Inst., 1977; Univ. of Pittsburgh, 1978; Priestly, Pennsylvania State Univ., 1978; Shell, Univ. of California at Davis, 1978; Dreyfus, Northwestern Univ., 1979; Jesup, Columbia Univ., 1980; Karl-August-Förster, Univ. of Mainz, 1980; David Rivett Meml, CSIR, Melb., 1980. Hon. DSc: Rochester and Yale Univs, 1978; Washington Univ., St Louis, 1986; numerous awards include: Eli Lilly Award, 1959; Calif. Scientist of the Year, 1963; Nat. Acad. of Scis, 1966, 1974; Amer. Acad. of Arts and Scis, 1966; Henry J. Kaiser, Stanford Univ. Sch. of Med., 1969, 1972; Dist. Alumnus, Pennsylvania State Univ.; V. D. Mattia Prize of Roche Inst. for Molec. Biol., 1972; Gairdner Foundn Award, Nobel Prize in Chemistry, New York Acad. of Scis and Albert Lasker Med. Res. awards, 1980; National Medal of Science, 1983. *Publications:* (jtly) Genes and Genomes: a changing perspective, 1990; (jtly) Dealing with Genes: the language of heredity, 1992; many scientific articles and reviews. *Address:* Beckman Center–BO62, Stanford University Medical Center, Stanford, CA 94305, USA.

BERGANZA, Teresa; singer (mezzo-soprano); *b* Madrid, Spain; *d* of Guillermo and Maria Ascension Berganza; *m*; three *c*. Début in Aix-en-Provence, 1957; début in England, Glyndebourne, 1958; appeared at Glyndebourne, 1959; Royal Opera House, Covent Garden, 1959, 1960, 1963, 1964, 1976, 1977, 1979, 1981, 1984, 1985; Royal Festival Hall, 1960, 1961, 1962, 1967, 1971; appears regularly in Vienna, Milan, Aix-en-Provence, Holland, Japan, Edinburgh, Paris, Israel, America; Carmen, opening ceremonies, Expo 92, Seville; participated opening ceremonies, Barcelona Olympics, 1992. Mem. (first elected woman), Spanish Royal Acad. of Arts, 1994. Prizes: Lucretia Arana; Nacional Lírica, Spain; Lily Pons, 1976; Acad. Nat. du Disque Lyrique; USA record award; Harriet Cohen Internat. Music Award, 1974; Grand Prix Rossini; Médaille d'or, Ville Aix-en-Provence; International Critic Award, 1988. Charles Cross (6 times); Grand Cross, Isabel la Católica, Spain; Gran Cruz al Mérito en las Bellas Artes, Spain; Commandeur, l'Ordre des Arts et des Lettres, France. *Publication:* Flor de Soledad y Silencio, 1984. *Recreations:* music, books, the arts. *Address:*La Rossiniana, Archanda 5, PO Box 137, 28200 San Lorenzo del Escorial, Madrid, Spain. *T:* (1) 8960941, *Fax:* (1) 8960816.

BERGER, John; author and art critic; *b* London, 5 Nov. 1926; *s* of late S. J. D. Berger, OBE, MC, and Mrs Miriam Berger (*née* Branson). *Educ:* Central Sch. of Art; Chelsea Sch. of Art. Began career as a painter and teacher of drawing; exhibited at Wildenstein, Redfern and Leicester Galls, London. Art Critic: Tribune; New Statesman. Vis. Fellow, BFI, 1990–. Numerous TV appearances, incl.: Monitor; two series for Granada TV. Scenario: (with Alain Tanner) La Salamandre; Le Milieu du Monde; Jonas (New York Critics Prize for Best Scenario of Year, 1976); Play me Something (also principal rôle) (Europa Prize, Barcelona Film Fest., 1989). George Orwell Meml Prize, 1977; Lannan Foundn Lit. Award for Fiction, USA, 1989; State Prize for Artistic Achievement, Austria, 1990; Petrarca Award, Germany, 1991. *Publications: fiction:* A Painter of Our Time, 1958; The Foot of Clive, 1962; Corker's Freedom, 1964; G (Booker Prize, James Tait Black Meml Prize), 1972; Into their Labours (trilogy), 1992: Pig Earth, 1979; Once in Europa, 1989; Lilac and Flag, 1991; *theatre:* with Nella Bielski: Question of Geography, 1986 (staged Marseilles, 1984, Paris, 1986 and by RSC, Stratford, 1987); Francisco Goya's Last Portrait, 1989; *non-fiction:* Marcel Frishman, 1958; Permanent Red, 1960; The Success and Failure of Picasso, 1965; (with J. Mohr) A Fortunate Man: the story of a country doctor, 1967; Art and Revolution, Moments of Cubism and Other Essays, 1969; The Look of Things, Ways of Seeing, 1972; The Seventh Man, 1975 (Prize for Best Reportage, Union of Journalists and Writers, Paris, 1977); About Looking, 1980; (with J. Mohr) Another Way of Telling, 1982 (televised, 1989); And Our Faces, My Heart, Brief as Photos, 1984; The White Bird, 1985 (USA, as The Sense of Sight, 1985); Keeping a Rendezvous (essays and poems), 1992; *translations:* (with A. Bostock): Poems on the Theatre, by B. Brecht, 1960; Return to My Native Land, by Aime Cesaire, 1969; (with Lisa Appignanesi) Oranges for the Son of Alexander Levy, by Nella Bielski, 1982. *Address:* Quincy, Mieussy, 74440 Taninges, France.

BERGER, Vice-Adm. Sir Peter (Egerton Capel), KCB 1979; LVO 1960; DSC 1949; MA; Bursar, 1981–91, and Fellow, Selwyn College, Cambridge, since 1981; *b* 11 Feb. 1925; *s* of late Capel Colquhoun Berger and Winifred Violet Berger (*née* Levett-Scrivener); *m* 1956, June Kathleen Pigou; three *d*. *Educ:* Harrow Sch. MA Cantab 1984. Served War of 1939–45: entered RN as a Cadet, 1943; Normandy and South of France landings in HMS Ajax, 1944; Sub-Lt, 1945; Lieut, 1946; Yangtse Incident, HMS Amethyst, 1949; Lt-Comdr, 1953; Comdr, 1956; Fleet Navigating Officer, Home Fleet, 1956–58; Navigating Officer, HM Yacht Britannia, 1958–60; Commanded HMS Torquay, 1962–64; Captain, 1964; Defence, Naval and Military Attaché, The Hague, 1964–66; commanded HMS Phoebe, 1966–68; Commodore, Clyde, 1971–73; Rear-Adm., 1973; Asst Chief of Naval Staff (Policy), 1973–75; COS to C-in-C Fleet, 1976–78; Flag Officer Plymouth, Port Admiral Devonport, Comdr Central Sub Area Eastern Atlantic and Comdr Plymouth Sub Area Channel, 1979–81, retired 1981. *Recreations:* shooting, fishing, history. *Address:* Linton End House, Linton Road, Balsham, Cambs CB1 6HA. *T:* Cambridge (01223) 892959.

BERGERSEN, Dr Fraser John, FRS 1981; FAA 1985; Visiting Fellow, Division of Biochemistry and Molecular Biology, School of Life Sciences, Australian National University, since 1994; *b* 26 May 1929; *s* of Victor E. and Arabel H. Bergersen; *m* 1952, Gladys Irene Heather; two *s* one *d*. *Educ:* Univ. of Otago, New Zealand (BSc, MSc (Hons)); Univ. of New Zealand (DSc 1962). Bacteriology Dept, Univ. of Otago, 1952–54; Div. of Plant Industry, CSIRO, Canberra, Aust., 1954–94, Chief Res. Scientist, 1972–94; engaged full-time in scientific research in microbiology, with special reference to symbiotic nitrogen fixation in legume root-nodules. Foreign Sec., Aust. Acad. of Science, 1989–93. David Rivett Medal, CSIRO Officers' Assoc. 1968. *Publications:* Methods for Evaluating Biological Nitrogen Fixation, 1980; Root Nodules of Legumes: structure and functions, 1982; one hundred and fifty articles and chapters in scientific journals and books. *Recreations:* music, gardening. *Address:* 13 Ferdinand Street, Campbell, ACT 2601, Australia. *T:* (62) 2477413.

BERGHUSER, Sir Hugo (Erich), Kt 1989; MBE 1981; Member of Parliament, Papua New Guinea, since 1987; Minister for Civil Aviation, Tourism and Culture, since 1987; *b* Germany, 25 Oct. 1935. *Educ:* Volksschule, Stiepel; Trade School, Bochum. Cabinet-maker. Embarked on ship to emigrate to Australia, 1958; ship (Skaubryn) caught fire and sank in the Indian Ocean; arrived in Papua New Guinea in 1959; active in the building industries, meat trade and timber sawmilling trade, employing over 700. Independence Medal, PNG, 1975; Queen's Jubilee Medal, 1977; Service Medal, PNG, 1980; Long Service Medal, PNG, 1985. Distinctive Cross, 1st Cl. (Germany), 1986; Hon. Consulate Gen. (Turkey). *Address:* PO Box 1785, Boroko, NCD, Papua New Guinea. *Club:* Papua.

BERGMAN, (Ernst) Ingmar; Swedish film producer; Director, Royal Dramatic Theatre, Stockholm; director of productions on television; *b* Uppsala, 14 July 1918; *s* of a Chaplain to the Royal Court at Stockholm; *m* 1971, Mrs Ingrid von Rosen (*d* 1995); (eight *c* by previous marriages). *Educ:* Stockholm Univ. Producer, Royal Theatre, Stockholm, 1940–42; Producer and script-writer, Swedish Film Co., 1940–44; Theatre Director:

Helsingborg, 1944–46; Gothenburg, 1946–49; Malmo, 1952–1959. Produced: Hedda Gabler, Cambridge, 1970; Show, 1971; King Lear, 1985; Hamlet, 1986, Nat. Theatre, 1987; Miss Julie, Nat. Th., 1987; Lady from the Sea, Oslo, A Doll's House, Theatre Royal Glasgow, 1990. Films (British titles) produced include: Torment, 1943; Crisis, 1945; Port of Call, 1948; Summer Interlude, 1950; Waiting Women, 1952; Summer with Monika, 1952; Sawdust and Tinsel, 1953; A Lesson in Love, 1953; Journey into Autumn, 1954; Smiles of a Summer Night, 1955; The Seventh Seal, 1956–57; Wild Strawberries, 1957; So Close to Life, 1957; The Face, 1958; The Virgin Spring, 1960 (shown Edinburgh Fest., 1960); The Devil's Eye, 1961 (shown Edinburgh Fest., 1961); Through a Glass Darkly, 1961; Winter Light, 1962; The Silence, 1963; Now About all these Women, 1964 (first film in colour); Persona, 1967; Hour of the Wolf, 1968; Shame, 1968; The Rite, 1969; The Passion, 1970; The Fâro Document, 1970 (first documentary, shown Vienna Fest., 1980); The Touch, 1971; Cries and Whispers, 1972 (NY Film Critics Best Film Award, 1972); Scenes from a Marriage, 1974 (BBC TV Series, 1975; published, 1975; British première as play, Chichester, 1990); Face to Face, 1976 (BBC TV Series, 1979); The Serpent's Egg, 1977; Autumn Sonata, 1978; From the Life of the Marionettes, 1981; Fanny and Alexander, 1983 (published, 1989); screenplay, The Best Intentions, 1991. Has gained several international awards and prizes for films; Goethe Prize, 1976; Great Gold Medal, Swedish Acad. of Letters, 1977. *Publications:* Four Stories, 1977; The Magic Lantern (autobiog.), 1988; Images: my life in film, 1994.

BERGNE, (Alexander) Paul (A'Court), OBE 1985; HM Diplomatic Service; Research and Analysis Department, Foreign and Commonwealth Office, since 1995; *b* 9 Jan. 1937; *s* of Villiers A'Court Bergne and Diana Daphne Cuthbert (*née* Holman-Hunt); *m* 1963, Suzanne Hedwig Judith Wittich; one *s* one *d*. *Educ:* Winchester Coll.; Trinity Coll., Cambridge (BA); SOAS, London Univ. (MA). Krasicki Iran Expedn film cameraman, 1958–59; joined FO, 1959; served Vienna, 1961–63; Tehran, 1965–68; MECAS, 1970–72; Abu Dhabi, 1972–75; Cairo, 1975–77; Athens, 1980–84; Counsellor, Hong Kong, 1985–87; Cabinet Office, 1988–92; Ambassador to Uzbekistan, 1993–95, and to Tajikstan, 1994–95. *Publications:* articles on art, architecture and archaeology of the Middle East. *Recreations:* mountain walking, numismatics, archaeology. *Address:* c/o Foreign and Commonwealth Office, SW1A 2AH.

BERGONZI, Prof. Bernard, FRSL; Professor of English, University of Warwick, 1971–92, now Emeritus; *b* 13 April 1929; *s* of late Carlo and Louisa Bergonzi; *m* 1st, 1960, Gabriel Wall (*d* 1984); one *s* two *d*; 2nd, 1987, Anne Samson. *Educ:* Wadham Coll., Oxford (BLitt, MA). Asst Lectr in English, Manchester Univ., 1959–62, Lectr, 1962–66; Sen. Lectr, Univ. of Warwick, 1966–71, Pro-Vice-Chancellor, 1979–82. Vis. Lectr, Brandeis Univ., 1964–65; Visiting Professor: Stanford Univ., 1982; Univ. of Louisville, 1988; Nene Coll., 1994–April 1996; Vis. Fellow, New Coll., Oxford, 1987. FRSL 1984. *Publications:* Descartes and the Animals (verse), 1954; The Early H. G. Wells, 1961; Heroes' Twilight, 1965; The Situation of the Novel, 1970; Anthony Powell, 1971; T. S. Eliot, 1972; The Turn of a Century, 1973; Gerard Manley Hopkins, 1977; Reading the Thirties, 1978; Years (verse), 1979; The Roman Persuasion (novel), 1981; The Myth of Modernism and Twentieth Century Literature, 1986; Exploding English, 1990; Wartime and Aftermath, 1993; David Lodge, 1995. *Recreations:* conversation, retrospection. *Address:* 19 St Mary's Crescent, Leamington Spa CV31 1JL. *T:* Leamington (01926) 883115.

BERGQUIST, Prof. Dame Patricia (Rose), DBE 1994; DSc; FRSNZ; Professor of Zoology, since 1981, Assistant Vice-Chancellor Academic, since 1989, University of Auckland; *b* 10 March 1933; *d* of William Smyth and Bertha Ellen Smyth (*née* Penny); *m* 1958, Peter Leonard Bergquist; one *d*. *Educ:* Devonport Primary Sch.; Takapuna Grammar; Univ. of Auckland (BSc 1954; MSc Hons 1957; PhD 1961; DSc 1979). University of Auckland: Lectr, then Sen. Lectr in Zool., 1958–69; Associate Prof., 1970–80; Head of Zool., 1986–92; Dep. Vice-Chancellor, 1993. Research Fellow: Yale 1962 and 1968; Marseille, 1973; Natural Hist. Mus., London, 1978; Amer. Mus. of Natural Hist., 1990; Sen. Queen's Fellow in Marine Sci., Australia, 1984. FRSNZ 1981 (Hector Medal and Prize, 1989). *Publications:* Sponges, 1978; numerous papers and monographs in learned jls. *Recreations:* music, stamp collecting, swimming, wind-surfing. *Address:* School of Biological Sciences, University of Auckland, Private Bag 92019, Auckland, New Zealand. *T:* (9) 373599; 3A Pukerangi Crescent, Ellerslie, Auckland 5, New Zealand.

BERGSTRÖM, Prof. Sune, MD; Swedish biochemist; *b* 10 Jan. 1916; *s* of Sverker Bergström and Wera (*née* Wistrand). *Educ:* Karolinska Inst (MD 1944, DMedSci 1944). Squibb Inst., USA, 1941–42; Med. Nobel Inst., Stockholm, 1942–46; Basle Univ., 1946–47; Prof. of Biochemistry, Lund Univ., 1947–58; Prof at Karolinska Inst, 1958–80, Dean of Med. Faculty, 1963–66, Rector, 1969–77. Consultant to WHO. Chm., Board, Nobel Foundn, 1975–87 (and Chm., Adv. Council, Med. Research, 1977–82). Member: Swedish Acad. of Scis; Swedish Acad. of Engineering; Amer. Acad. of Arts and Scis; Nat. Acad. of Scis, USA; Acad. of Sci., USSR; Acad. of Med. Scis, USSR; Papal Acad. of Sci.; Hon. Mem., Amer. Soc. of Biol. Chemists. Albert Lasker Basic Med. Research Award, 1977; (jtly) Nobel Prize for Physiology or Medicine, 1982. *Publications:* papers on heparin, autoxidation, bile acids and chlorestrol, prostaglandins. *Address:* Karolinska Institutet, Nobel Forum, Box 270, 17177 Stockholm, Sweden.

BERINGER, Prof. John Evelyn, CBE 1993; Professor, School of Biological Sciences, University of Bristol, since 1993; *b* 14 Feb. 1944; *s* of Group Captain William Beringer and Evelyn Joan Beringer (*née* Buckley); *m* 1970, Sheila Murray (*née* Gillies); three *s*. *Educ:* Univ. of Edinburgh (Scottish Dip. in Agric. 1965; BSc 1970); Univ. of East Anglia (PhD 1973). FIBiol 1985. Microbial Geneticist, John Innes Inst., 1970–80; Head, Dept of Microbiology, Rothamsted Exptl Station, Harpenden, 1980–84; University of Bristol: Dir, Molecular Genetics Unit, 1984–88; Head, Dept of Microbiology, 1986–90; Head, Dept of Botany, 1990–93. Chairman, advisory committees: Genetic Manipulation Planned Release Sub-Cttee, 1987–90; Releases to Envmt, 1990–. Fleming Lectr, Soc. for Gen. Microbiology, 1979. *Publications:* sci. contribs to biological jls and proceedings. *Recreations:* gardening, golf, travel. *Address:* 92 Church Lane, Backwell, Bristol BS19 3JW. *T:* Flax Bourton (01275) 462880.

BERIO, Luciano; composer; *b* 24 Oct. 1925; *s* of Ernesto Berio and Ada dal Fiume; *m* 1st, 1950, Cathy Berberian (marr. diss. 1964; she *d* 1983); one *d*; 2nd, 1964, Susan Oyama (marr. diss. 1971); one *s* one *d*; 3rd, 1977, Talia Pecker; two *s*. *Educ:* Liceo Classico, Oneglia; Conservatorio G. Verdi, Milan. Hon. degree in Composition, City Univ., London, 1979. Works include: Differences, 1958; Epifanie, 1959–63; Circles, 1960; Passaggio, 1962; Laborintus II, 1965; Sinfonia, 1968; Concerto for 2 pianos, 1972; Opera, 1969–74; Sequenzas I–XI for solo instruments, and for female voice, 1958–88; A-Ronne for five actors, 1974–75; Coro for chorus and orchestra, 1975–76; La Ritirata Notturna di Madrid, 1975; Ritorno degli Snovidenia, 1977; La Vera Storia, 1981; Un Re in Ascolto, 1983; Voci, 1984; Requies, 1985; Formazioni, 1986; Ricorrenze, 1987; Concerto II (Echoing Curves), 1988; Ofanim, 1988; Canticum Novissimi Testamenti, 1989; Rendering (Schubert), 1990; Continuo, 1991. *Address:* Il Colombaio, Radicondoli (Siena), Italy.

BERIOZOVA, Svetlana; ballerina; *b* 24 Sept. 1932; *d* of Nicolas and Maria Beriozoff (Russian); *m* 1959, Mohammed Masud Khan (marr. diss. 1974; he *d* 1989). *Educ:* New York, USA. Joined Grand Ballet de Monte Carlo, 1947; Metropolitan Ballet, 1948–49; Sadler's Wells Theatre Ballet, 1950–52; Sadler's Wells Ballet (now The Royal Ballet), 1952. Has created leading rôles in Designs for Strings (Taras), Fanciulla delle Rose (Staff), Trumpet Concerto (Balanchine), Pastorale (Cranko), The Shadow (Cranko), Rinaldo and Armida (Ashton), The Prince of the Pagodas (Cranko), Antigone (Cranko), Baiser de la Fée (MacMillan), Diversions (MacMillan), Persephone (Ashton), Images of Love (MacMillan). Classical Roles: Le Lac des Cygnes, The Sleeping Beauty, Giselle, Coppélia, Sylvia, Cinderella. Other rôles currently danced: Les Sylphides, The Firebird, The Lady and Fool, Checkmate, Fête Etrange, Ondine, Nutcracker. Has danced with The Royal Ballet in USA, France, Italy, Australia, S Africa, Russia, and as guest ballerina in Belgrade, Granada, Milan (La Scala), Stuttgart, Bombay, Nervi, Helsinki, Paris, Vienna, New Zealand, Zurich. Played the Princess in The Soldier's Tale (film), 1966. Has frequently appeared on television. *Relevant publications:* Svetlana Beriosova (by C. Swinson), 1956, Svetlana Beriosova (by A. H. Franks), 1958. *Recreation:* the arts. *Address:* 10 Palliser Court, Palliser Road, W14 9ED.

BERKELEY, 18th Baron *cr* 1421; **Anthony Fitzhardinge Gueterbock,** OBE 1989; Public Affairs Manager, Eurotunnel, since 1987; *b* 20 Sept. 1939; *o s* of Brig. E. A. L. Gueterbock (*d* 1984) and Hon. Cynthia Ella Gueterbock (*d* 1991), *sister* of Baroness Berkeley, 17th in line; *S* aunt, 1992; *m* 1965, Diane Christine, *e d* of Eric William John Townsend; two *s* one *d*. *Educ:* Trinity Coll., Cambridge (MA). CEng, MICE. Engineering, construction and planning, Sir Alexander Gibb & Partners, 1961–65; multi-disciplinary engineering and construction, planning and business develt, George Wimpey PLC, 1965–81; The Channel Tunnel Group/Eurotunnel, 1981–. *Recreations:* ski-ing, sailing. *Heir:* *s* Hon. Thomas Fitzhardinge Gueterbock [*b* 5 Jan. 1969; *m* 1995, Helen Ruth, *er d* of Lt-Comdr Brian Walsh, RN retd].

BERKELEY, Frederic George; Chief Master of the Supreme Court Taxing Office, 1988–92 (Master, 1971–88); *b* 21 Dec. 1919; *s* of late Dr Augustus Frederic Millard Berkeley and Anna Louisa Berkeley; *m* 1988, Helen Kathleen Lucy; one step *s* one step *d*, and one *s* one *d* (and one *d* decd) of previous marriage. *Educ:* Elstree Sch.; Aldenham Sch.; Pembroke Coll., Cambridge (MA). Admitted Solicitor, 1948. Served War of 1939–45, Leics Regt, Normandy (wounded); Major; DADAWS Allied Land Forces SE Asia, 1945–46. Partner in Lewis & Lewis (from 1964 Penningtons and Lewis & Lewis), 1951–70. Mem. No 1 (London) Legal Aid Area Cttee (later No 14), 1954–70, Vice-Chm. 1964–70, Chm. 1970. General Editor and contributor, Butterworth's Costs Service, 1984–. *Recreations:* reading, travel. *Address:* 10 Dover House, Abbey Park, Beckenham, Kent BR3 1QB. *T:* 0181–650 4634.

BERKELEY, Michael Fitzhardinge; composer and broadcaster; *b* 29 May 1948; *s* of late Sir Lennox Randal Berkeley and of Elizabeth Freda (*née* Bernstein); *m* 1979, Deborah Jane Coltman-Rogers; one *d*. *Educ:* Westminster Cathedral Choir Sch.; The Oratory Sch.; Royal Acad. of Music (ARAM 1984). Studied privately with Richard Rodney Bennett; rock musician; phlebotomist, St Bartholomew's Hosp., 1969–71; Presentation Asst, LWT, 1973; Announcer, BBC Radio 3, 1974–79; Associate Composer to Scottish Chamber Orch., 1979; regular presenter of arts programmes for BBC (Kaleidoscope, Radio 4, Meridian, World Service, Mainly for Pleasure, In Tune, Radio 3); introduces proms, concerts and festivals for BBC2 and Radio 3, and BBC television documentaries. Jt Artistic Dir, Spitalfields Fest., 1994–; Artistic Dir, Cheltenham Fest., 1995–. Member: Exec. Cttee, Assoc. of Professional Composers, 1982–84; Central Music Adv. Cttee, BBC, 1986–90; Gen. Adv. Council, BBC, 1990–; New Music Sub-Cttee, Arts Council of GB, 1984–86; Music Panel Adviser to Arts Council, 1986–90; Opera Bd, Royal Opera House, Covent Gdn, 1994–; acts as expert witness in cases of musical plagiarism. Vis. Prof., Huddersfield Univ. (formerly Poly.), 1991–94. Gov., NYO, 1994–. *Compositions: orchestral music:* Fanfare and National Anthem, 1979; Primavera, 1979; Flames, 1981; Gregorian Variations, 1982; Daybreak and a Candle End, 1985; Gethsemane Fragment, 1990; *for chamber or small orchestra:* Meditations, 1977 (Guinness Prize for Composition); Fantasia Concertante, 1978; Uprising: Symphony in one movement, 1980; Suite; the Vision of Piers the Ploughman, 1981; The Romance of the Rose, 1982; Coronach, 1988; Entertaining Master Punch, 1991; *concertos:* Concerto for Oboe and String Orch., 1977; Concerto for Cello and Small Orch., 1983; Concerto for Horn and String Orch., 1984; Organ Concerto, 1987; Clarinet Concerto, 1991; Violin Concerto, 1994; *chamber music:* String Trio, 1978; American Suite, 1980; Chamber Symphony, 1980; String Quartet No 1, 1981; Nocturne, 1982; Piano Trio, 1982; Music from Chaucer, 1983; Quintet for Clarinet and Strings, 1983; String Quartet No 2, 1984; The Mayfly, 1984; Pas de deux, 1985; For the Savage Messiah, 1985; Quartet Study, 1987; Catch Me if You Can, 1993; *strings:* Etude de Fleurs, 1979; Sonata for Violin and Piano, 1979; Iberian Notebook, 1980; Variations on Greek Folk-Songs, 1981; Funerals and Fandangos, 1984; A Mosaic for Father Popieluszko, 1985; *guitar:* Lament, 1980; Worry Beads, 1981; Sonata in One Movement, 1982; Impromptu, 1985; *keyboard:* Passacaglia, 1978; Strange Meeting, 1978; Organ Sonata, 1979; Dark Sleep, 1994; *woodwind:* Three Moods, 1979; American Suite, 1980; Fierce Tears, 1984; Flighting, 1985; Keening, 1987; *vocal music for solo voice:* The Wild Winds, 1978; Rain, 1979; Wessex Graves, 1981; Songs of Awakening Love, 1986; Speaking Silence, 1986; *choral music:* At the Round Earth's Imagin'd Corners, 1980; The Crocodile and Father William, 1982; Easter, 1982; As the Wind Doth Blow, 1983; Hereford Communion Service, 1985; Pasce Oves Meas, 1985; Verbum Caro Factum Est, 1987; The Red Macula, 1989; Night Song in the Jungle, 1990; *oratorio:* Or Shall We Die?, 1983 (text by Ian McEwan; filmed for Channel 4); *opera:* Baa Baa Black Sheep, 1993 (libretto by David Malouf); *ballet:* Bastet, 1988; *film music:* Captive, 1986; Twenty-one, 1990. *Publications:* musical compositions; articles in The Observer, The Guardian, The Listener, The Sunday Telegraph, and Vogue. *Recreations:* looking at paintings, reading, walking and hill farming in mid-Wales. *Address:* c/o Rogers, Coleridge & White Ltd, 20 Powis Mews W11 1JN. *T:* 0171–221 3717.

BERKELEY MILNE, Alexander; *see* Milne, A. B.

BERKOFF, Steven; actor, director and writer; *b* 3 Aug. 1937; *s* of Polly and Al Berks (formerly Berkovitch); *m* (marr. diss). *Educ:* Raines Foundation Grammar School, Stepney; Grocers' Co. Sch., Hackney. *Plays acted,* 1965–: Zoo Story; Arturo Ui; *plays directed/acted/wrote,* 1969–: Metamorphosis (also directed on Broadway, 1989, Japan, 1992); Macbeth (directed and acted); Agamemnon; The Trial; The Fall of the House of Usher; East; Kvetch (Evening Standard Comedy of the Year Award, 1992); season of 3 plays, NT; Hamlet (directed and acted); Decadence (filmed, 1993); Greek; West; One Man; *wrote and directed:* Sink the Belgrano, Mermaid, 1986, Acapulco, 1992; *directed:* Coriolanus, NY, 1988, Munich, 1991; Salomé, Edinburgh Festival, NT (and acted), 1989, Phoenix (and acted), 1990; The Trial, NT, 1991; *films acted:* The Clockwork Orange; Barry Lyndon; The Passenger; McVicar; Outlands; Octopussy; Beverley Hills Cop; Rambo; Underworld; Revolution; Sins; Under the Cherry Moon; Absolute Beginners; Prisoner of Rio; The Krays. *Publications:* East, 1977; Gross Intrusion (short stories), 1979; Decadence, 1982; Greek, 1982; West, 1985; Lunch, 1985; Harry's Xmas, 1985; Kvetch, 1987; Acapulco, 1987; Sink the Belgrano, 1987; Massage, 1987; America, 1988; I Am Hamlet, 1989; A Prisoner in Rio, 1989; The Theatre of Steven Berkoff (photograhic),

1992; Coriolanus in Deutschland, 1992; *play adaptations:* The Fall of the House of Usher, 1977; Agamemnon, 1977; The Trial, 1981; Metamorphosis, 1981; In the Penal Colony, 1988. *Recreation:* writing, photography, travel. *Address:* c/o Joanna Marston, 1 Clareville Grove Mews, SW7 5AH. *T:* 0171–370 1080.

BERKSHIRE, Archdeacon of; *see* Hill, Ven. M. A.

BERKSON, David Mayer; a Recorder of the Crown Court, since 1978; an Assistant Judge Advocate General, since 1988; Deputy Judge Advocate General, Germany, since 1994; Magistrate of the Standing Civilian Courts, since 1991; *b* 8 Sept. 1934; *s* of Louis Berkson and Regina Berkson (*née* Globe); *m* 1961, Pamela Anne (*née* Thwaite); one *d.* *Educ:* Birkenhead School. Called to the Bar, Gray's Inn, 1957. Dep. Judge Advocate, 1984–87. Legal Mem., Mental Health Review Tribunal for the Mersey Area, 1982–84. *Address:* c/o Office of the Judge Advocate General, 22 Kingsway, WC2B 6LE. *Clubs:* Lansdowne; Athenæum (Liverpool); Border and County (Carlisle).

BERLIN, Sir Isaiah, OM 1971; Kt 1957; CBE 1946; FBA 1957; MA; President of the British Academy, 1974–78; Fellow of All Souls College, Oxford; *b* 6 June 1909; *s* of Mendel and Marie Berlin; *m* 1956, Aline, *d* of Pierre de Gunzbourg. *Educ:* St Paul's Sch.; Corpus Christi Coll., Oxford. Lectr in Philosophy, New Coll., Oxford, 1932; Fellow: All Souls, 1932–38; New Coll., 1938–50; war service with Min. of Information, in New York, 1941–42, at HM Embassy in Washington, 1942–46, HM Embassy, Moscow, Sept. 1945–Jan. 1946; Fellow, All Souls Coll., Oxford, 1950–66, 1975–; Chichele Prof. of Social and Pol Theory, Oxford Univ., 1957–67; Pres., Wolfson Coll., Oxford 1966–Mar. 1975, Hon. Fellow, 1975. Mem. Cttee of Awards: Commonwealth (Harkness) Fellowships, 1960–64; Kennedy Scholarships, 1967–79. Vice-Pres., British Academy, 1959–61; Pres. Aristotelian Soc., 1963–64. Mem., Academic Adv. Cttee., Univ. of Sussex, 1963–66. Visiting Professor: Harvard Univ., 1949, 1951, 1953, 1962; Bryn Mawr Coll., 1952; Chicago Univ., 1955; Princeton Univ., 1965; ANU, Canberra, 1975; Prof. of Humanities, City Univ. of NY, 1966–71. Lectures: Northcliffe, UCL, 1953; Mellon, Nat. Gall. of Art, Washington, DC, 1965; Danz, Washington Univ., 1971. Foreign Member: American Academy of Arts and Sciences; American Academy-Institute of Arts and Letters; American Philosophical Soc. Member, Board of Directors, Royal Opera House, Covent Garden, 1954–65, 1974–87; a Trustee, Nat. Gall., 1975–85. Hon. Pres., British Friends of the Univ. of Jerusalem. Hon. Fellow: Corpus Christi Coll., Oxford; St Anthony's Coll., Oxford; Wolfson Coll., Cambridge. Hon. doctorates of the following universities: Hull, 1965; Glasgow, 1967; E Anglia, 1967; Brandeis (USA), 1967; Columbia, 1968; Cambridge, 1970; London, 1971; Jerusalem, 1971; Liverpool, 1972; Tel Aviv, 1973; Harvard, 1979; Sussex, 1979; Johns Hopkins, 1981; Northwestern, 1981; NY, 1982; Duke, 1983; City, NY, 1983; New Sch. of Social Research, NY, 1987; Oxford, 1987; Ben Gurion, 1988; Yale, 1989; Toronto, 1994; Bologna, 1995. Erasmus Prize (jtly), 1983; Agnelli Internat. Prize for Ethics, 1987. *Publications:* Karl Marx, 1939, 4th edn 1978; Translation of First Love by I. S. Turgenev, 1950; The Hedgehog and the Fox, 1953, 4th edn 1979; Historical Inevitability, 1954; The Age of Enlightenment, 1956; Moses Hess, 1958; Two Concepts of Liberty, 1959; Mr Churchill in 1940, 1964; Four Essays on Liberty, 1969; Fathers and Children, 1972; Vico and Herder, 1976; Russian Thinkers, 1978; Concepts and Categories, 1978; Against the Current, 1979; Personal Impressions, 1980; translation of A Month in the Country by I. S. Turgenev, 1980; The Crooked Timber of Humanity, 1990; The Magus of the North, 1993. *Address:* All Souls College, Oxford OX1 4AL. *Clubs:* Athenæum, Brooks's, Garrick; Century (New York).

BERLINS, Marcel Joseph; journalist and broadcaster; *b* 30 Oct. 1941; *s* of Jacques and Pearl Berlins. *Educ:* schools in France and South Africa; Univ. of Witwatersrand (BComm, LLB); LSE (LLM). Legal Asst, Lord Chancellor's Dept, 1969–71; Legal Corresp. and leader writer, The Times, 1971–82; freelance writer and TV presenter, 1982–86; Editor, Law Magazine, 1987–88; presenter, Radio 4 Law in Action, 1988–; columnist, The Guardian, 1988–. *Publications:* Barrister behind Bars, 1974; (with Geoffrey Wansell) Caught in the Act, 1974; (with Clare Dyer) Living Together, 1982; (with Clare Dyer) The Law Machine, 1982, 3rd edn 1989; (ed) The Law and You, 1986; numerous articles for newspapers, magazines and legal jls. *Recreations:* cinema, jazz. *Address:* 7 Leighton Crescent, NW5 2QY. *T:* 0171–485 3965.

BERMAN, Edward David, (ED Berman), MBE 1979; social entrepreneur, playwright, theatre director and producer; educationalist; Founder, Chief Executive and Artistic Director, Inter-Action, since 1968; *b* 8 March 1941; 2nd *s* of Jack Berman and Ida (*née* Webber); naturalized British citizen, 1976. *Educ:* Harvard (BA Hons); Exeter Coll., Oxford (Rhodes Schol.); Dept of Educnl Studies, Oxford (1978–). *Plays:* 8 produced since 1966; *director: theatre:* (premières) *inter alia* Dirty Linen (London and Broadway), 1976, and The Dogg's Troupe (15 minute) Hamlet, (ed) by Tom Stoppard, 1976 (also filmed, 1976); The Irish Hebrew Lesson, 1976 and Samson and Delilah, 1978, by Wolf Mankowitz; Dogg's Hamlet, Cahoot's Macbeth, 1979, by Tom Stoppard; *producer: theatre:* 125 stage premières for adults and 170 new plays for children, London, 1967–89; *maker of films:* (educational) The Head, 1971; Two Weeler, 1972; Farm in the City, 1977; Marx for Beginners Cartoon (co-prod., voice dir), 1978; *actor:* over 1200 performances as Prof. Dogg, Otto Première Check, Super Santa. Editor: 18 community arts, action and constructive leisure handbooks, 1972–; 2 anthologies of plays, 1976–78. Trustee and Founder, Inter-Action Trust, 1968; Director and Founder: Ambiance Lunch-Hour Th. Club, 1968; Prof. Dogg's Troupe for Children, 1968; Labrys Trust, 1969; Inter-Action Advisory Service, 1970; Infilms, 1970; The Almost Free Th., 1971; Inprint Publishing Unit, 1972; City Farm 1, 1972; Alternative Education Project, 1973–84; Inter-Action Trust Ltd, 1974; Town and Country Inter-Action (Milton Keynes) Ltd, 1975; Ambiance Inter-Action Inc., 1976; Talacre Centre Ltd, 1977; Co-Founder: Inter-Action Housing Trust Ltd, 1970; NUBS, Neighbourhood Use of Bldgs and Space; Community Design Centre, 1974; Beginners Books Ltd, 1978; Inter-Action Housing Co-operative, 1978. Founder, Artistic Dir, BARC, British Amer. Rep. Co., 1978. Devised: Inter-Action Creative Game Method, 1967; Super Santa, Father Xmas Union, 1967–82; Chairman: Save Piccadilly Campaign, 1971–80; Talacre Action Gp, 1972; Nat. Assoc. of Arts Centres, 1975–79; Dir, Islington Bus Co., 1974–76; Treas., Fair Play for Children Campaign, 1975–77; Founder: City Farm Movement, 1976; WAC—Weekend Arts Coll., 1979; co-founder: Sport-Space, 1976; FUSION—London and Commonwealth Youth Ensemble, 1981. Founder and Co-Director: Internat. Inst. for Social Enterprise, 1980; Country Wings, 1981; OPS, Occupation Preparation Systems, 1982; Options Training Ltd, 1983; Social Enterprise Projects Ltd; Founder and Trustee, Inter-Action Social Enterprise Trust Ltd, Social Enterprise Foundn of Inter-Action, 1984; Cdre, Ships-in-the-City, 1988; Founder and Director: Network Inter-Action; Youth-Tech; Star Dome, 1989; Marketing and Business Services International Ltd, 1992. Special Adviser: on inner city matters to Sec. of State for the Environment, 1982–83; Ministry of Labour, Russia, 1992–94, Min. of Economy, 1993–. As community artist: created 17 formats for participatory theatre, 1968–85; Community Media Van, 1983; Community Cameos, 1977–83; MIY—Make It Yourself, 1978; RIY—Raise It Yourself, 1981; Learning Domes, 1993; Public Art Workshop, 1994; IES—Instant Enterprise Systems. *Publications:* Prof. R. L. Dogg's Zoo's Who I and II, 1975; Selecting Business Software, 1984; Make a Real Job of It, Breaks for Young Bands, 1985; How to Set Up a Small Business, 1987; Healthy Learning Songs & Activities, 1989; New Game Songs & Activities, 1989; The Democracy Handbook, 1995. *Recreations:* solitude, conversation, work, music. *Address:* Inter-Action Trust, HMS President (1918), Victoria Embankment, EC4Y 0HJ. *T:* 0171–583 2652.

BERMAN, Sir Franklin (Delow), KCMG 1994 (CMG 1986); Legal Adviser, Foreign and Commonwealth Office, since 1991; *b* 23 Dec. 1939; *s* of Joshua Zelic Berman and Gertrude (*née* Levin); *m* 1964, Christine Mary Lawler; two *s* three *d.* *Educ:* Rondebosch Boys' High Sch., Cape Town; Univ. of Cape Town; Wadham and Nuffield Colls, Oxford. BA, BSc Cape Town; MA Oxford. Rhodes Scholar, 1961; Martin Wronker Prizeman, 1963; called to Bar (Middle Temple), 1966. HM Diplomatic Service, 1965: Asst Legal Adviser, FO, 1965; Legal Adviser: British Military Govt, Berlin, 1971; British Embassy, Bonn, 1972; Legal Counsellor, FCO, 1974; Counsellor and Legal Adviser, UK Mission to UN, NY, 1982; FCO, 1985, Dep. Legal Advr, 1988. Mem., Appeals Bd, WEU, 1994–. Chairman: Diplomatic Service Assoc., 1979–82; Staff Tribunal, Internat. Oil Pollution Compensation Fund, 1986–. Member: Council of Management, British Inst. of Internat. and Comparative Law, 1992–; Council, British Br., Internat. Law Assoc., 1993–; Gov., Inst. of Advanced Legal Studies, Univ. of London, 1992–. Trustee, Edward Fry Meml Liby, 1992–. Hon. QC 1992. Mem. Editl Bd, British Yearbook of Internat. Law, 1994–. *Recreations:* walking, reading, music, choral singing. *Address:* c/o Foreign and Commonwealth Office, SW1A 2AH. *T:* 0171–270 3000. *Club:* United Oxford & Cambridge University.

BERMAN, Lawrence Sam, CB 1975; retired; *b* 15 May 1928; *yr s* of Jack and Violet Berman; *m* 1954, Kathleen D. Lewis; one *s* one *d.* *Educ:* St Clement Danes Grammar Sch.; London Sch. of Economics. BSc (Econ) 1st cl. hons 1947; MSc (Econ) 1950. Res. Asst, LSE, 1947; Nuffield Coll., Oxford, 1948; Econ. Commn for Europe, 1949; Central Statistical Office: Asst Statistician 1952; Statistician 1955; Chief Statistician 1964; Asst Dir 1968; Dir of Statistics, Depts of Industry and Trade, 1972–83. Statistical Advr, Caribbean Tourism R & D Centre, Barbados, 1984–85. Editor, National Income Blue Book, 1954–60; Member: Council, Royal Statistical Soc., 1970–74 (Vice-Pres., 1973–74); Council Internat. Assoc. for Research in Income and Wealth, 1980–85; ISI. *Publications:* Caribbean Tourism Statistical Reports; articles and papers in Jl of Royal Statistical Soc., Economica, Economic Trends, Statistical News, etc. *Recreations:* travel, theatre, collecting sugar tongs and bow ties. *Address:* 10 Carlton Close, Edgware, Mddx HA8 7PY. *T:* 0181–958 6938.

BERMANT, Chaim Icyk; author, since 1966; *b* 26 Feb. 1929; *s* of Azriel Bermant and Feiga (*née* Daets); *m* 1962, Judy Weil; two *s* two *d.* *Educ:* Queen's Park Sch., Glasgow; Glasgow Yeshiva; Glasgow Univ. (MA Hons; MLitt); London School of Economics (MScEcon). School-master, 1955–57; Economist, 1957–58; Television script writer, 1958–61; Journalist, 1961–66. *Publications:* Jericho Sleep Alone, 1964; Berl Make Tea, 1965; Ben Preserve Us, 1965; Diary of an Old Man, 1966; Israel, 1967; Swinging in the Rain, 1967; Troubled Eden, 1969; The Cousinhood, 1971; Here Endeth the Lesson, 1969; Now Dowager, 1971; Roses are Blooming in Picardy, 1972; The Last Supper, 1973; The Walled Garden, 1974; Point of Arrival, 1975; The Second Mrs Whitberg, 1976; Coming Home, 1976 (Wingate-Jewish Chronicle Book Award); The Squire of Bor Shachor, 1977; The Jews, 1978; Now Newman was Old, 1978; Belshazzar, 1979; (with Dr M. Weitzman) Ebla, 1979; The Patriarch, 1981; On the Other Hand, 1982; The House of Women, 1983; Dancing Bear, 1984; What's the Joke, 1986; Titch, 1987; The Companion, 1987; Lord Jacobovits: the authorised biography of the Chief Rabbi, 1990; Murmurings of a Licensed Heretic, 1990. *Recreations:* walking, sermon-tasting.

BERMINGHAM, Gerald Edward; MP (Lab) St Helens South, since 1983; *b* Dublin, 20 Aug. 1940; *s* of late Patrick Xavier Bermingham and Eva Terescena Bermingham; *m* 1st, 1964, Joan (marr. diss.); two *s*; 2nd, 1978, Judith. *Educ:* Cotton College, N Staffs; Wellingborough Grammar School; Sheffield University. LLB Hons. Admitted Solicitor, 1967; called to the Bar, Gray's Inn, 1985. Councillor, Sheffield City Council, 1975–79, 1980–82. Contested (Lab) SE Derbyshire, 1979. *Recreations:* sport, reading, TV. *Address:* 10 Devonshire Drive, Sheffield S17 3PJ. *T:* St Helens (01744) 810083.

BERNARD, Sir Dallas (Edmund), 2nd Bt *cr* 1954; Chairman: National & Foreign Securities Trust Ltd, 1981–86; Thames Trust Ltd, 1983–86; Consultant, Globalmajor Ltd, since 1989; *b* 14 Dec. 1926; *o s* of Sir Dallas Gerald Mercer Bernard, 1st Bt, and Betty (*d* 1980), *e d* of late Sir Charles Addis, KCMG; *S* father, 1975; *m* 1st, 1959 (marr. diss. 1979); three *d*; 2nd, 1979, Mrs Monica Montford, *d* of late James Edward Hudson; one *d.* *Educ:* Eton Coll.; Corpus Christi Coll., Oxford (MA). FCIS. Director: Dreyfus Intercontinental Investment Fund NV, 1970–91; Morgan Grenfell (Holdings) Ltd, 1972–79; Morgan Grenfell & Co. Ltd, 1964–77; Dominion Securities Ltd, Toronto, 1968–79; Italian Internat. Bank Plc, 1978–89; Dreyfus Dollar Internat. Fund Inc., 1982–91. Mem. Monopolies and Mergers Commn, 1973–79. Mem. Council, GPDST, 1988–93 (Finance Cttee, 1975–92). *Heir:* none. *Address:* 106 Cheyne Walk, SW10 0DG. *T:* 0171–235 2318. *Club:* Lansdowne.

BERNARD, Daniel Camille; President of Managing Board, and Chief Executive Officer, Carrefour Group, since 1992; *b* 18 Feb. 1946; *s* of Paul Bernard and Simone (*née* Doise); *m* 1968, Chantal Leduc; one *s* two *d.* *Educ:* Lycée Camille Desmoulins, Cateau; Lycée Faidherbe, Lille; HEC Business Sch.; Univ. of Paris. Divl Manager, Mammouth, 1976–81; Chief Exec. Officer, Metro France, 1981–89; Mem. Bd, Metro Internat., 1990–92. *Recreations:* mountains, ski-ing, opera. *Address:* Carrefour, 5 avenue du Général de Gaulle, Lisses, 91005, France. *T:* 60869652.

BERNARD, Jeffrey Joseph; columnist, The Spectator, since 1976; *b* 27 May 1932; *s* of Oliver P. Bernard and Fedora Roselli Bernard; *m* 1st, 1951, Anna (*d* 1955); 2nd, 1958, Jacki; 3rd, 1966, Jill; one *d*; 4th, 1978, Susan (marr. diss. 1981). *Educ:* Nautical College, Pangbourne. Odd jobs until 1958; film editor, 1958–62; actor, 1963; journalist and columnist, 1964–, for Sunday Times, New Statesman, Sporting Life and Spectator. 'Jeffrey Bernard is Unwell', a play by Keith Waterhouse based on 10 Spectator columns, Low Life, 1989. *Publications:* High Life – Low Life, 1982; Low Life, 1986; Talking Horses, 1987; More Low Life, 1989. *Recreations:* cricket, racing, cooking, Mozart. *Address:* 29 Greek Street, Soho, W1V 5LL. *T:* 0171–437 5920. *Clubs:* Groucho, Chelsea Arts.

BERNARD, Joan Constance, MA, BD; FKC; Principal of Trevelyan College, University of Durham, and Honorary Lecturer in Theology, 1966–79; *b* 6 April 1918; *d* of late Adm. Vivian Henry Gerald Bernard, CB, and Eileen Mary Bernard. *Educ:* Ascham Sch., Sydney, NSW; St Anne's Coll., Oxford Univ. (BA Lit. Hum. 1940, MA 1943); King's Coll., London (BD 1961). War Service, ATS, 1940–46; AA Comd, 1940–44; SO Air Def. Div., SHAEF, 1944–45 (mentioned in despatches 1945); Special Projectile Ops Gp, July-Nov. 1945. Dep. Admin. Officer, NCB, 1946–50; Asst Sec., Educn, Music and Drama, NFWI, 1950–57; full-time student, 1957–61; Warden, Canterbury Hall, Univ. of London, and part-time Lectr, Dept of Theol., KCL, 1962–65; FKC 1976. Mem., Ordination Candidates' Cttee, ACCM, 1972–91; Examining Chaplain to Bishop of Southwark, 1984–94. Mem., Fabric Adv. Cttee, Southwark Cathedral, 1992–. FRSA 1984. *Recreations:*

music (assisted John Tobin in Handel research for many years); mountaineering, photography. *Address:* 89 Rennie Court, Upper Ground, SE1 9NZ.

BERNBAUM, Prof. Gerald; Vice-Chancellor and Chief Executive, South Bank University, since 1993; *b* 25 March 1936; *s* of Benjamin Bernbaum and Betty (*née* Sack); *m* 1959, Pamela Valerie Cohen (marr. diss. 1987); two *s*. *Educ:* Hackney Downs Grammar Sch.; LSE (BSc Econ 1957); London Inst. of Educn (PGCE 1958). Mitcham Grammar School for Boys: Asst Master, 1958–59; Head of Dept, 1959–62; Head of Dept, Rutherford Comprehensive Sch., 1962–64; University of Leicester School of Education: Lectr, 1964–70; Sen. Lectr, 1970–74; Prof. of Educn, 1974–93; Dir, 1976–85; Pro-Vice-Chancellor, 1985–87; Exec. Pro-Vice-Chancellor and Registrar, 1987–93. *Publications:* Social Change and the Schools, 1967; Knowledge and Ideology in the Sociology of Education, 1977; (ed) Schooling in Decline, 1978; (with H. Patrick and M. Galton) Educational Provision in Small Primary Schools, 1990; articles in Sociol Rev., Brit. Jl Educnl Studies. *Recreations:* public affairs, professional sport, music. *Address:* South Bank University, 103 Borough Road, SE1 0AA. *T:* 0171–928 8989.

BERNERD, Elliott; Chairman, Chelsfield plc, since 1987; *b* 23 May 1945; *s* of Geoffrey Bernerd and Trudie Malawer (*née* Melzack); *m* 1st, 1968, Susan Elizabeth Lynton (marr. diss. 1989); two *d*; 2nd, 1992, Sonia Ramsay (*née* Ramalho). Chm. Wentworth Group Holdings Ltd, 1990–. Chm., London Philharmonic Trust, 1987–94. *Recreations:* tennis, ski-ing. *Address:* Chelsfield plc, 67 Brook Street, W1Y 2NJ. *T:* 0171–493 3977. *Clubs:* Savile, Cavalry and Guards, Royal Automobile; Wentworth.

BERNERS, Baroness (16th in line), *cr* 1455; **Pamela Vivien Kirkham;** *b* 30 Sept. 1929; *er d* of Harold Williams and Baroness Berners, 15th in line (*d* 1992); *S* to Barony of mother (called out of abeyance, 1995); *m* 1952, Michael Joseph Sperry Kirkham; two *s* one *d*. *Educ:* Bredenbury Court, Hereford; Stonar Sch., Wilts. Radcliffe Infirmary, Oxford (SRN, 1951). *Recreations:* painting, drawing, gardening, reading. *Heir:* *s* Hon. Rupert William Tyrwhitt Kirkham [*b* 18 Feb. 1953; *m* 1994, Lisa Carol Judy Lipsey; one *s*].

BERNEY, Sir Julian (Reedham Stuart), 11th Bt *cr* 1620; *b* 26 Sept. 1952; *s* of Lieut John Reedham Erskine Berney (killed on active service in Korea, 1952), Royal Norfolk Regt, and of Hon. Jean Davina, *d* of 1st Viscount Stuart of Findhorn, PC, CH, MVO, MC; *S* grandfather, 1975; *m* 1976, Sheena Mary, *yr d* of Ralph Day and Ann Gordon Day; two *s* one *d*. *Educ:* Wellington Coll.; North-East London Polytechnic. FRICS 1992. *Recreation:* sailing. *Heir:* *s* William Reedham John Berney, *b* 29 June 1980. *Address:* Reeds House, 40 London Road, Maldon, Essex CM9 6HE. *T:* Maldon (01621) 853420. *Club:* Royal Ocean Racing.

BERNSTEIN, Alexander; Chairman, Granada Group plc, since 1979 (Director, since 1964); *b* 15 March 1936; *s* of late Cecil Bernstein and of Myra Ella, *d* of Lesser and Rachel Lesser; *m* 1962, Vanessa Anne (marr. diss. 1993), *d* of Alwyn and Winifred Mills; one *s* one *d*. *Educ:* Stowe Sch.; St John's Coll., Cambridge. Man. Dir, 1964–68, Chm., 1977–86, Granada TV Rental Ltd; Jt Man. Dir, Granada Television Ltd, 1971–75; Dir, Waddington Galleries, 1966–. Trustee: Civic Trust for the North-West, 1964–86; Granada Foundn, 1968–. Chm., Royal Exchange Theatre, 1983–94 (Dep. Chm., 1980–83). Member of Court: Univ. of Salford, 1976–87; Univ. of Manchester, 1983–. Hon. DLitt Salford 1981. *Recreations:* modern art, ski-ing, gardening. *Address:* 36 Golden Square, W1R 4AH.

BERNSTEIN, Prof. Basil Bernard; Karl Mannheim Professor of Sociology of Education, 1979–90, now Emeritus, and Head of Sociological Research Unit, 1963–90, University of London; *b* 1 Nov. 1924; *s* of Percival and Julia Bernstein; *m* 1955, Marion Black; two *s*. *Educ:* LSE (BScEcon); UCL (PhD). Teacher, City Day Coll., Shoreditch, 1954–60; Hon. Research Asst, UCL, 1960–62; University of London Institute of Education: Sen. Lectr, Sociology of Educn, 1963; Reader in Sociology of Educn, 1965; Prof., 1967; Senior Pro-Director, 1983–89. Hon. DLitt: Leicester, 1974, Rochester, 1989; Fil H Dr Univ. of Lund, 1980; DUniv Open, 1983. *Publications:* Class Codes and Control, Vol. I, Theoretical Studies Towards a Sociology of Language, 1971, 2nd edn 1974, (ed) Vol. II, Applied Studies Towards a Sociology of Language, 1973, Vol. III, Towards a Theory of Educational Transmissions, 1975, revd edn 1977, Vol. IV, The Structuring of Pedagogic Discourse, 1990; (with W. Brandis) Selection and Control, 1974; (with U. Lundgren) Macht und Control, 1985; Poder, Educatión y Conciencia: sociología de la tranmisión cultural, 1988; Code Theory and Research, 1995. *Recreations:* music, painting, conversation, etc. *Address:* 90 Farquhar Road, Dulwich, SE19 1LT. *T:* 0181–670 6411.

BERNSTEIN, Ingeborg, (Inge); Her Honour Judge Bernstein; a Circuit Judge, since 1991; *b* 24 Feb. 1931; *d* of Sarah and Eli Bernstein; *m* 1967, Eric Geoffrey Goldrein; one *s* one *d*. *Educ:* Peterborough County School; St Edmund's College, Liverpool; Liverpool University. Called to the Bar, Inner Temple, 1952; practice on Northern Circuit; a Recorder, 1978–91. Chm., Mental Health Review Tribunal; Mem., Mental Health Act Commn, 1984–86. *Recreation:* the domestic arts. *Address:* 14 Castle Street, Liverpool L2 0NE. *T:* 0151–236 4421.

BERNSTEIN, Ronald Harold, DFC 1944; QC 1969; FCIArb; a Recorder of the Crown Court, 1974–90; *b* 18 Aug. 1918; *s* of late Mark and Fanny Bernstein; *m* 1955, Judy, *d* of David Levi, MS, and Vera Levi; three *s* one *d*. *Educ:* Swansea Grammar Sch.; Balliol Coll., Oxford. BA (Jurisprudence) 1939; FCIArb 1982. Served in RA, 1939–46, and in 654 Air OP Sqdn, RAF, 1942–46. Commanded 661 Air OP Sqdn, RAuxAF, 1954–56. Called to the Bar, Middle Temple, 1948, Bencher, 1975–. Mem., Gen. Council of the Bar, 1965–69; Vice-Pres., 1988–91, Vice-Pres. Emeritus, 1991–, CIArb. Pres., Highgate Soc., 1983–93. Hon. ARICS 1986; Hon. FSVA 1987. *Publications:* (jointly) The Restrictive Trade Practices Act, 1956; Handbook of Rent Review, 1981, and subseq. edns to 1994; Handbook of Arbitration Practice, 1987, 2nd edn 1992; Joint Ventures in Property, 1993. *Address:* (professional) Falcon Chambers, Falcon Court, EC4Y 1AA. *T:* 0171–353 2484; (home) 0181–340 9933; *Fax:* 0181–348 7676. *Club:* Athenæum.

BERRAGAN, Maj.-Gen. Gerald Brian, CB 1988; Chief Executive, Institute of Packaging, since 1988; *b* 2 May 1933; *s* of William James and Marion Beatrice Berragan; *m* 1956, Anne Helen Kelly; three *s*. Commissioned REME 1954; attached 7th Hussars, Hong Kong, 1954–55; transf. RAOC 1956; served UK, Belgium, Germany and with 44 Para Bde (TA); Staff College, 1966; Nat. Defence Coll., 1972–73; Comdr RAOC 3 Div., 1973–76; AQMG HQ N Ireland, 1976–78; HQ DGOS, 1978–80; Comdt Central Ordnance Depot, Chilwell, 1980–82; Sen. Management Course, Henley, 1982; Comdt COD Bicester, 1982–83; Dir, Supply Ops (Army), 1983–85; Sen. Internat. Defence Management Course, USA, 1985; Dir Gen. of Ordnance Services, 1985–88. Col Comdt, RAOC, 1988–93, RLC 1993–. FInstPS. *Recreations:* offshore sailing, tennis. *Clubs:* Athenæum, Army and Navy.

BERRIDGE, (Donald) Roy, CBE 1981; FEng; Chairman, South of Scotland Electricity Board, 1977–82 (Deputy Chairman, 1974–77); *b* 24 March 1922; *s* of Alfred Leonard Berridge and Pattie Annie Elizabeth (*née* Holloway); *m* 1945, Marie (*née* Kinder); one *d*. *Educ:* King's Sch., Peterborough; Leicester Coll. of Art and Technology. FEng 1979; FIMechE 1962. Taylor, Taylor & Hobson Ltd, Leicester, 1940; James Gordon & Co., 1946; British Electricity Authority, 1948; seconded to AERE, Harwell, 1952; Reactor Design Engr, CEGB, 1962; Chief Generation Design Engr, 1964–70; Dir-Gen., Gen. Develt Constr. Div., CEGB, 1970–72; Dir of Engrg, SSEB, 1972–74. Dir, Howden Gp, 1982–88. Member: N of Scotland Hydro-Electric Bd, 1977–82; Scottish Economic Council, 1977–83; CBI (Scottish Council), 1977–83. *Address:* East Gate, Chapel Square, Deddington, Oxon OX15 0SG.

BERRIDGE, Dr Michael John, FRS 1984; Fellow of Trinity College, Cambridge, since 1972; *b* 22 Oct. 1938; *s* of George Kirton Berridge and Stella Elaine Hards; *m* 1965, Susan Graham Winter; one *s* one *d*. *Educ:* University Coll. of Rhodesia and Nyasaland (BSc); Univ. of Cambridge (PhD). Post-doctoral Fellow: Univ. of Virginia, 1965–66; Case Western Reserve Univ., Cleveland, Ohio, 1966–69. Member: AFRC Lab. of Molecular Signalling (formerly Unit of Insect Neurophysiology and Pharmacology), Dept of Zoology, Univ. of Cambridge, 1969–90; Babraham Inst. Lab. of Molecular Signalling, 1990–. King Faisal Internat. Prize in Sci., 1986; Jeantet Prize in Medicine, 1986; Gairdner Foundn Internat. Award, 1988; Lasker Basic Med. Res. Award, 1989; Dr H. P. Heineken Prize for Biochemistry and Biophysics, 1994; Wolf Foundn Prize in Medicine, 1995. *Publications:* papers in Jl Exptl Biol., Biochem. Jl and Nature. *Recreations:* golf, gardening. *Address:* 13 Home Close, Histon, Cambridge CB4 4JL. *T:* Cambridge (01223) 232416.

BERRIEDALE, Lord; Alexander James Richard Sinclair; *b* 26 March 1981; *s* and *heir* of Earl of Caithness, *qv*.

BERRILL, Sir Kenneth, GBE 1988; KCB 1971; Chairman of Council, Open University, since 1983 (Pro-Chancellor, 1983–95); *b* 28 Aug. 1920; *m* 1st, 1941, Brenda West (marr. diss.); one *s*; 2nd, 1950, June Phillips (marr. diss.); one *s* one *d*; 3rd, 1977, Jane Marris. *Educ:* London Sch. of Economics; Trinity Coll., Cambridge. BSc(Econ) London; MA Cantab, 1949. Served War, 1939–45, REME. Economic Adviser to Turkey, Guyana, Cameroons, OECD, and World Bank. Univ. Lectr in Economics, Cambridge, 1949–69; Rockefeller Fellowship Stanford and Harvard Univs, 1951–52; Fellow and Bursar, St Catharine's Coll., Cambridge, 1949–62, Hon. Fellow, 1974; Prof., MIT, 1962; Fellow and First Bursar, King's Coll., Cambridge, 1962–69, Hon. Fellow, 1973; HM Treasury Special Adviser (Public Expenditure), 1967–69; Chm., UGC, 1969–73; Head of Govt Econ. Service and Chief Economic Advr, HM Treasury, 1973–74; Head of Central Policy Review Staff, Cabinet Office, 1974–80; Chm., Vickers da Costa Ltd and Vickers da Costa & Co. Hong Kong Ltd, 1981–85; Chm., SIB, 1985–88; Dep. Chm., 1982–87, Chm., 1987–90, Robert Horne Gp; Chm., Commonwealth Equities Fund, 1990–95. Mem., Stock Exchange, London, 1981–85. Member: Council for Scientific Policy, 1969–72; Adv. Bd for Research Councils, 1972–77; Adv. Council for Applied R&D, 1977–80; Brit. Nat. Commn for UNESCO, 1967–70; UN Cttee for Develt Planning, 1984–87; Inter-Univ. Council, 1969–73; UGC, Univ. of S Pacific, 1972–85; Council, Royal Economic Soc., 1972– (Vice Pres., 1986–); Adv. Bd, RCDS, 1974–80; Review Bd for Govt Contracts, 1981–85; Chm. Exec. Cttee, NIESR, 1988–; (Nominated), Governing Council, Lloyd's, 1983–88. Dir, UK-Japan 2000 Gp, 1986–90. Advr, Nippon Credit Internat. Ltd, 1989–; Dep. Chm., General Funds Investment Trust, 1982–85; Director: Investing in Success Investment Trust, 1965–67; Ionian Bank, 1969–73; Dep. Chm., Universities' Superannuation Scheme, 1981–85 (Chm., Jt Negotiating Cttee, 1990–). Trustee: London Philharmonic, 1987–; Newnham Coll. Develt Trust, 1989–95; Nat. Extension Coll., 1990–; Res. Inst. for Consumer Affairs, 1990–. Governor: Admin. Staff Coll., Henley, 1969–84; ODI, 1969–73; Mem. Council, Salford Univ., 1981–84. McDonnell Scholar, World Inst. for Develt Economic Res., 1988, 1990. Mem., Cambridge City Council, 1963–67. CIMgt (CBIM 1987). FRSA 1988; Hon. Fellow: LSE, 1970; Chelsea Coll., London, 1973. Hon. LLD: Cambridge, 1974; Bath, 1974; East Anglia, 1975; Leicester, 1975; DUniv Open, 1974; Hon. DTech Loughborough, 1974; Hon DSc Aston, 1974. Jephcott Lectr and Medallist, 1978; Stamp Meml Lectr, 1980. *Recreations:* ski-ing, sailing. *Address:* Salt Hill, Bridle Way, Grantchester, Cambs CB3 9NY. *T:* Cambridge (01223) 840335, *Fax:* Cambridge (01223) 845939. *Clubs:* Climbers (Hon. Mem.); Himalayan; Cambridge Alpine.

BERRILL, Prof. Norman John, PhD, DSc; FRS 1952; FRSC; FAAAS; lately Strathcona Professor of Zoology, McGill University, Montreal; *b* 28 April 1903. *Educ:* Bristol Gram. Sch., Somerset, England; Bristol Univ.; London Univ. BSc Bristol; PhD, DSc London. FRSC 1936; FAAAS 1979. *Publications:* The Tunicata, 1951; The Living Tide, 1951; Journey into Wonder, 1953; Sex and the Nature of Things, 1954; The Origin of Vertebrates, 1955; Man's Emerging Mind, 1955; You and the Universe, 1958; Growth, Development and Pattern, 1962; Biology in Action, 1966; Worlds Apart, 1966; Life of the Oceans, 1967; The Person in the Womb, 1968, Developmental Biology, 1971; Development, 1976. *Address:* 9 Orchard Drive, Durham, NH 03824, USA.

BERRIMAN, Sir David, Kt 1990; FCIB; CIMgt; Chairman, North East Thames Regional Health Authority, 1984–90; Director (non-executive), Cable and Wireless 1975–88; *b* 20 May 1928; *s* of late Algernon Edward Berriman, OBE and late Enid Kathleen Berriman (*née* Sutcliffe); *m* 1st, 1955, Margaret Lloyd (*née* Owen) (marr. diss. 1970); two *s*; 2nd, 1971, Shirley Elizabeth (*née* Wright) (*d* 1993); 3rd, 1995, Mrs Patricia Salter. *Educ:* Winchester; New Coll., Oxford (MA, Dip. Econ. and Pol. Sc.); Harvard Business Sch. PMD course, 1961. First National City Bank of New York, 1952–56; Ford Motor Co. Ltd, 1956–60; AEI Hotpoint, 1960–63; Gen. Manager, United Leasing Corporation Ltd, 1963–64; Morgan Grenfell & Co. Ltd: Manager, 1964; Exec. Dir, 1968–73; Dir, Guinness Mahon & Co. Ltd, 1973–87 (Exec. Dir, 1973–85). Chairman: Bunzl Textile Holdings Ltd, 1981–88 (Dep. Chm., 1980); Alban Communications Ltd, 1988–90 (Dir, 1983–; Dep. Chm., 1987–88); Knightstone Group Ltd, 1992–93; Privatised Public Service Pension Plan Trustees Ltd, 1994–; Director (non-exec.): Sky Television (formerly Satellite Television), 1981–89 (Chm., 1981–85); Bahrein Telecommunications Corp., 1982–88; Britannia Building Soc., 1983–93; Ashenden Enterprises Ltd, 1983–; E European Develt Ltd, 1990–92; KDB Bank (UK) Ltd, 1991–. Chm., Lewisham and N Southwark DHA, 1981–84. Member: Bd of Trade's Interim Action Cttee for the Film Industry, 1977–85; Govt review body on Harland and Wolff diversification, 1980; British Screen Adv. Council, 1985–91. Director: British Screen Finance Ltd, 1985–91; Nat. Film Develt Fund, 1985–91; Videotron Corp., 1989–. Dep. Chm., Nat. Film and Television School, 1988–92 (Gov., 1977–92). Chm., Assoc. of Lloyd's Members, 1994– (Mem. Cttee, 1993–). Chairman: MacIntyre Care, 1978–92 (Gov., 1977–92); MacIntyre Charitable Trust, 1986–92; MacIntyre Foundn, 1993–; Member, Council: Internat. Hosp. Fedn, 1985–86; King Edward's Hosp. Fund for London, 1985–90. Trustee: New Coll., Oxford Development Fund, 1983–; Kent Community Housing Trust, 1990–. *Recreations:* golf, lawn tennis. *Address:* Leigh House, Leigh, Tonbridge TN11 8RH. *Clubs:* Royal Automobile, International Lawn Tennis; Wildernesse Golf (Sevenoaks); Royal St George's Golf; Valderrama Golf (Spain).

BERRY, family name of **Baron Hartwell, Camrose Viscountcy** and **Viscount Kemsley.**

BERRY, Anthony Arthur; Chairman, Berry Bros & Rudd Ltd, 1965–85; *b* 16 March 1915; *s* of Francis L. Berry and Amy Marie (*née* Freeman); *m* 1953, Sonia Alice, *d* of Sir Harold Graham-Hodgson, KCVO; one *s* one *d*. *Educ:* Charterhouse; Trinity Hall,

Cambridge. Served War, RNVR, 1939–45, incl. 2¼ yrs in the Mediterranean. Joined the wine trade on leaving Cambridge, 1936; rejoined family firm of Berry Bros & Rudd on completion of war service; Dir, 1946–. Worshipful Co. of Vintners: Liveryman, 1946; Mem. Court, 1972–; Master, 1980–81. *Recreations:* golf, walking. *Address:* 4 Cavendish Crescent, Bath, Avon BA1 2UG. *T:* Bath (01225) 422669. *Clubs:* Boodle's, MCC; Saintsbury; Bath and County (Bath); Royal Wimbledon Golf; Royal St George's Golf (Sandwich).

BERRY, Anthony Charles; QC 1994; *b* 4 Oct. 1950; *s* of Geoffrey Vernon Berry and Audrey Millicent Berry (*née* Farrar); *m* 1977, Susan Carmen Traversi; three *s* one *d*. *Educ:* Downside Sch.; Lincoln Coll., Oxford (BA Phil. and Psychol.). Called to the Bar, Gray's Inn, 1976. Sec., Criminal Bar Assoc., 1991–93; Mem., Bar Council, 1993–. *Recreations:* tennis, golf. *Address:* 4 Brick Court, Temple, EC4Y 9AD.

BERRY, (Anthony) Scyld (Ivens); cricket correspondent, The Sunday Telegraph, since 1993; *b* 28 April 1954; *s* of Prof. Francis Berry, *qv*; *m* 1984, Sunita Ghosh; one *s* one *d*. *Educ:* Westbourne School, Sheffield; Ampleforth College; Christ's College, Cambridge (MA Oriental Studies). Cricket correspondent: The Observer, 1978–89; The Sunday Correspondent, 1989–90; The Independent on Sunday, 1991–93. *Publications:* Cricket Wallah, 1982; Train to Julia Creek, 1984; (ed) The Observer on Cricket, 1987; Cricket Odyssey, 1988; (with Phil Edmonds) 100 Great Bowlers, 1989. *Recreations:* playing village cricket, being at home. *Address:* c/o The Sunday Telegraph, 1 Canada Square, Canary Wharf, E14 5DT. *Club:* Hinton Charterhouse Cricket.

BERRY, Cicely Frances, (Mrs H. D. Moore), OBE 1985; Voice Director, Royal Shakespeare Co., since 1969; *b* 17 May 1926; *d* of Cecil and Frances Berry; *m* 1951, Harry Dent Moore (*d* 1978); two *s* one *d*. *Educ:* Eothen Sch., Caterham, Surrey; Central Sch. of Speech and Drama, London. Teacher, Central Sch. of Speech and Drama, 1948–68; 4-week Voice Workshops: Nat. Repertory Co. of Delhi, 1980; Directors and Actors in Australia (org. by Aust. Council), 1983; Directors, Actors, Teachers in China, Chinese Min. of Culture, 1984; text-based workshops: Theatre Voice, Stratford, 1992; Actors in Croatia, Poland, Bulgaria and the Netherlands, 1993; workshop: Writers in Stratford, 1993; Eur. League of Insts of Arts, Berlin, 1994. Hon. Prof., de Montfort Univ.; Vis. Fellow, Central Sch. of Speech and Drama, 1994–. Organised Internat. Voice Conf., Stratford, 1995. Plays directed: Hamlet, Educn Dept, NT, 1985; King Lear, The Other Place, Stratford and Almeida Theatre, 1989. Patron of Northumberland and Leicester Youth Theatres. FRSAMD 1987. *Publications:* Voice and the Actor, 1973, 6th edn 1986; Your Voice and How to Use it Successfully, 1975, 2nd edn as Your Voice and How to Use it, 1994; The Actor and the Text, 1987.

BERRY, Sir Colin (Leonard), Kt 1993; FRCPath; Professor of Morbid Anatomy, University of London, at The London Hospital Medical College, since 1976; Warden of Joint Medical and Dental School, St Bartholomew's and Royal London Hospitals, and Vice-Principal for Medicine and Dentistry, Queen Mary and Westfield College, London University, since 1995; *b* 28 Sept. 1937; *s* of Ronald Leonard Berry and Peggy-Caroline (*née* Benson); *m* 1960, Yvonne Waters; two *s*. *Educ:* privately, and Beckenham Grammar Sch.; Charing Cross Hosp. Med. Sch. (MB, BS; Governors' Clinical Gold Medal, Llewellyn Schol., Pierera Prize in Clinical Subjects, Steadman Prize in Path.); trained in Histopath., Charing Cross Hosp., 1962–64. MD 1968, PhD 1970, DSc 1993 (London). FRCPath 1979; FFPM 1991; FRCP 1993. Lectr and Sen. Lectr, Inst. of Child Health, London, 1964–70; Reader in Pathology, Guy's Hosp. Med. Sch., 1970–76; Dean, London Hosp. Med. Coll., 1994–95. Gillson Scholar, Worshipful Soc. of Apothecaries, 1967–68 and 1970–72; Arris and Gail Lectr, RCS, 1973; Lectures: Bawden, BCPC, 1990; John Hull Grundy, Royal Army Med. Coll., 1992; Simonides, European Soc. of Pathology, 1993; Lucas, RCP, 1994. Chairman: Cttee on Dental and Surgical Materials, 1982–92 (Vice-Chm., 1979–82); Scientific Sub-Cttee on Pesticides, MAFF, 1984–87; Adv. Cttee on Pesticides, MAFF/DHSS, 1988– (Mem., 1982–87); Member: Toxicology Review Panel, WHO, 1976–84, 1987–; Scientific Adv. Cttee on Pesticides, EEC, 1981–88; Cttee on Toxicity of Chemicals in Food, Consumer Products and the Environment, 1982–88; Cttee on Safety of Medicines, Dept. of Health, 1990–92; Ownership Bd, Pesticides Safety Directorate, 1994–; MRC, 1990–; Chm., Physiological Systems and Disorders Bd, MRC, 1990–92 (Mem., 1988–). President: Developmental Path. Soc., 1976–79; European Soc. of Pathology, 1989–91 (Pres. elect, 1987–89); Sec. Fedn of Assocs of Clinical Profs, 1987–; Chm. Council, Res. Defence Soc., 1993–; Hon. Sec., ACP, 1982–85 (Meetings Sec., 1979–82). Scientific Advr, BIBRA, 1987–90. Treasurer, RCPath, 1988– (Asst Registrar, 1981–84). Asst to Court, Apothecaries' Soc., 1990–. *Publications:* Teratology: trends and applications, 1975; Paediatric Pathology, 1981, 2nd edn 1989; Diseases of the Arterial Wall, 1988; contrib. to many texts; numerous publns in LJl of Path., Circulation Res. and other path. jls. *Recreations:* fishing, pond building. *Club:* Reform.

BERRY, Prof. Francis; Emeritus Professor of English Language and Literature, Royal Holloway College, University of London, since 1980; *b* 23 March 1915; *s* of James Berry and Mary Augusta Jane Berry (*née* Ivens); *m* 1st, 1947, Nancy Melloney (*d* 1967), *d* of Cecil Newton Graham; one *s* one *d*; 2nd, 1970, Patricia (marr. diss. 1975), *d* of John Gordon Thomson; 3rd, 1979, Eileen, *d* of Eric Charles Lear. *Educ:* Hereford Cathedral Sch.; Dean Close Sch.; University Coll., Exeter. BA London (1st cl. hons); MA Exeter. Solicitor's articled clerk, 1931; University Coll., Exeter, 1937. War Service, 1939–46. University Coll., Exeter, 1946; successively Asst Lectr, Lectr, Sen. Lectr, Reader in English Literature, and Prof. of English Literature, Univ. of Sheffield, 1947–70; Prof. of English Lang. and Lit., Royal Holloway Coll., Univ. of London, 1970–80. Visiting Lecturer: Carleton Coll., Minn, USA, 1951–52; University Coll. of the West Indies, Jamaica, 1957; W.P. Ker Lectr, Glasgow, 1979; Lectr for British Council: in India, 1966–67; tour of univs in Japan, 1983, of univs of New Zealand, 1988; Vis. Fellow, ANU, Canberra, 1979; Vis. Prof. of English, Univ. of Malaŵi, 1980–81. Pres. SW of England Shakespeare Trust, 1985. FRSL 1968. Hon. Fellow, RHBNC, London Univ., 1987. *Publications:* Gospel of Fire, 1933; Snake in the Moon, 1936; The Iron Christ, 1938; Fall of a Tower, 1942; Murdock and Other Poems, 1947; The Galloping Centaur, 1952, 2nd edn 1970; Herbert Read, 1953, 2nd edn 1961; An Anthology of Medieval Poems (ed), 1954; Poets' Grammar: time, tense and mood in poetry, 1958, 2nd edn, 1974; Morant Bay and other poems, 1961; Poetry and the Physical Voice, 1962; The Shakespeare Inset, 1965, 2nd edn 1971; Ghosts of Greenland, 1967; John Masefield: the Narrative Poet, 1968; (ed) Essays and Studies for the English Association, 1969; Thoughts on Poetic Time, 1972; I Tell of Greenland (novel), 1977; From the Red Fort: new and selected poems, 1984; Collected Poems, 1994; contributor: Review of English Studies; Essays in Criticism; Poetry Nat. Review; BBC Radio Three, ABC, etc. *Recreations:* following first-class cricket, chess, travel, gardening. *Address:* 4 Eastgate Street, Winchester, Hants SO23 8EB. *T:* Winchester (01962) 854439. *Club:* Hampshire (Winchester).

See also A. S. I. Berry.

BERRY, Rt. Rev. Fraser; *see* Berry, Rt Rev. R. E. F.

BERRY, Dr James William; Director General (formerly Director) of Scientific and Technical Intelligence, 1982–89; *b* 5 Oct. 1931; *s* of Arthur Harold Berry and Mary Margaret Berry; *m* 1960, Monica Joan Hill; three *d*. *Educ:* St Mary's Coll., Blackburn; Municipal Technical Coll., Blackburn; Manchester Univ. (BSc); Leeds Univ. (PhD); FIEE. Royal Signals and Radar Estab., Malvern, 1956–60; Admiralty Surface Weapons Estab., Portsdown, 1960–76 (Head of Computer Div., 1972–76); Dir of Long Range Surveillance and Comd and Control Projs, MoD (PE), 1976–79; Dir Gen. Strategic Electronic Systems, MoD (PE), 1979–82. Organist, St Michael's RC Church, Leigh Park, Havant; 'cellist mem. of Petersfield Orch., Fareham Phil. Orch., and Bowes Music Gp. *Recreations:* music (organ, 'cello, piano), walking, bird watching. *Club:* Civil Service.

BERRY, John, CBE 1968; MA (Cantab); PhD (St Andrews); FRSE 1936; DL; consultant on water impoundment biology, 1968–90; Conservation and Fisheries Adviser to: North of Scotland Hydro-Electric Board, 1968–89; South of Scotland Electricity Board, 1973–89; *b* Edinburgh, 5 Aug. 1907; *o s* of late William Berry, OBE, DL, Tayfield, Newport, Fife; *m* 1936, Hon. Bride Fremantle, MA (Cantab), 3rd *d* of 3rd Baron Cottesloe, CB; two *s* one *d*. *Educ:* Eton; Trinity Coll., Cambridge. BA 1929 (Zoo. Chem. Phys. Pt I and Law Pt II); MA 1933; PhD 1935; Salmon research, Fishery Bd for Scotland, 1930–31; Biological Research Station, University Coll., Southampton, Research Officer, 1932–36 and Dir, 1937–39. Press Censor for Scotland, 1940–44; Biologist and Information Officer, North of Scotland Hydro-Electric Bd, 1944–49; Dir of Nature Conservation in Scotland, 1949–67. Consultant Ecologist, Scottish Landowners' Fedn, 1984–87. Chm., Interdepartmental Salmon Res. Gp (UK and Ireland), 1971–82; Dir, British Pavilion, Expo '71, Budapest. Mem., Scottish Marine Biology Assoc., 1947–71 (RSE rep., Exec. Cttee, 1947; Mem Council, 1948–54, 1957–66). Pres. 1954–56, Vice-Pres. 1956–60, and Mem., 1966–72, Commn on Ecology, Internat. Union for Conservation of Natural Resources; UK rep., Exec. Bd, Internat. Wildfowl Research Bureau, 1963–72; Vice-President: RZS Scotland, 1959–82 (Hon. Life Fellow and Hon. Vice-Pres., 1982); Scottish Wildlife Trust; Vice-Pres. and Mem. Council, Wildfowl Trust, 1969– (Hon. Life Fellow, 1983). Mem. Court, Dundee Univ., and Delegate to Commonwealth Univs Congress, 1970–78. Hon. LLD Dundee, 1970; Hon. DSc St Andrews, 1991. DL Fife, 1969. *Publications:* The Status and Distribution of Wild Geese and Wild Duck in Scotland, 1939; various papers and articles on fresh-water fisheries, hydro-electric development and ornithology. *Recreations:* natural history (esp. wild geese and insects), music. *Address:* The Garden House, Tayfield, Newport-on-Tay, Fife DD6 8HA. *T:* Newport-on-Tay (01382) 543118. *Club:* New (Edinburgh).

See also P. F. Berry.

BERRY, Prof. Michael Victor, FRS 1982; Royal Society Research Professor, Bristol University, since 1988; *b* 14 March 1941; *s* of Jack and Marie Berry; *m* 1st, 1961, Eveline Ethel Fitt (marr. diss. 1970); two *s*; 2nd, 1971, Lesley Jane Allen (marr. diss. 1984); two *d*; 3rd, 1984, Monica Suzi Saiovici; one *s* one *d*. *Educ:* Univ. of Exeter (BSc; Hon. PhD 1991); Univ. of St Andrews (PhD). Bristol University: Res. Fellow, 1965–67; Lectr, 1967–74; Reader, 1974–78; Prof. of Physics, 1978–88. Bakerian Lectr, Royal Soc., 1987. Mem., Royal Scientific Soc., Uppsala, 1988. Maxwell Medal and Prize, Inst. of Physics, 1978; Dirac Medal and Prize, Inst. of Physics, 1990; Lilienfeld Prize, Amer. Physical Soc., 1990; Royal Medal, Royal Soc., 1990; Naylor Prize and Lectureship in Applied Maths, London Math. Soc., 1992; Science for Art Prize, LVMH, Paris, 1994; Hewleth Packard Europhysics Prize, 1995. *Publications:* Diffraction of Light by Ultrasound, 1966; Principles of Cosmology and Gravitation, 1976; about 250 research papers, book reviews, etc, on physics. *Recreations:* cooking, walking. *Address:* H. H. Wills Physics Laboratory, Tyndall Avenue, Bristol BS8 1TL. *T:* Bristol (0117) 9288735.

BERRY, Nicholas (William); Chairman: Stancroft Trust Ltd, since 1972; Yeoman Investment Trust plc; Barlows plc; Mintel International Ltd; *b* 3 July 1942; *s* of Baron Hartwell, *qv*; *m* 1977, Evelyn Prouvost; two *s*. *Educ:* Eton; Christ Church, Oxford. Publisher and investor; Man. Dir, 1976–91, Chm., 1981–91, Harrap Publishing; Chm., Manchester Ship Canal, 1986–87. Director: Robert Fleming Far Eastern Investment Trust; Arlen; Caledonian Media Communications; Helicon Publishing. *Address:* Stancroft Trust, 20 Bride Lane, EC4Y 8DX. *T:* 0171–583 3808. *Club:* White's.

BERRY, Very Rev. Peter Austin; Provost of Birmingham, since 1986; *b* 27 April 1935; *s* of Austin James Berry and Phyllis Evelyn Berry. *Educ:* Solihull Sch.; Keble Coll., Oxford (MA, English and Theol.); St Stephen's House, Oxford. Intelligence Corps, 1954–56. Ordained deacon, 1962, priest, 1963; Chaplain to Bishop of Coventry, 1963–70; Midlands Regl Officer, Community Relations Commn, 1970–73; Canon Residentiary, Coventry Cathedral, 1973–77; Vice-Provost of Coventry, 1977–85. Mem., Gen. Synod of C of E, 1990–; Church Comr, 1994–. Chairman: Standing Adv. Cttee for Religious Educn, Birmingham; Birmingham Internat. Council, 1987–; Pre-Raphaelite Soc. Fellow, Coventry Univ. (Fellow, Lanchester Coll., Coventry, 1985). *Recreations:* music, theatre, architecture. *Address:* Birmingham Cathedral, Colmore Row, Birmingham B3 2QB. *T:* 0121–236 6323; 16 Pebble Mill Road, Edgbaston, Birmingham B5 7SA; The Round House, Ilmington, Compton Scorpion, Warwicks CV36 4LQ.

BERRY, Peter Fremantle; Managing Director and Crown Agent, Crown Agents for Oversea Governments and Administrations, since 1988; *b* 17 May 1944; *s* of John Berry, *qv*; *m* 1972, Paola Padovani; one *s* two *d*. *Educ:* Eton Coll.; Lincoln Coll., Oxford (MA Hons Mod. History). Harrisons & Crosfield, London, 1966–73: Manager: Kuala Belait, Brunei, 1968; Indonesia, 1970; Anglo Indonesian Corp., London: Gen. Man., 1973; Dir, 1974–82; Crown Agents for Oversea Governments and Administrations, 1982–: Director: Asia and Pacific, based Singapore, 1982–84; ME, Asia and Pacific, based London, 1984–88; Chm. or Dir of many Crown Agents' subsidiaries and associates. Director: Thomas Tapling Ltd, 1987–; Anglo-Eastern Plantations Plc, 1991–93; TR Pacific Investment Trust, 1994–; Member: Management Bd, Resource, 1989–92; Internat. Bd, Transparency Internat., 1993–. Member: Rubber Growers Assoc., 1978–82; UK Task Force on Kuwait, 1991; UK–Japan 2000 Gp, 1992–; Whitehall Export Promotion Cttee, 1992–; Council: Malaysia, Singapore and Brunei Assoc., 1982–87; Indonesia Assoc., 1974–93 (Chm., 1986–89). FRSA. *Recreations:* wildlife and country pursuits in Britain and Italy, travel and international development. *Address:* St Nicholas House, St Nicholas Road, Sutton, Surrey SM1 1EL. *T:* 0181–643 3311. *Club:* Royal Automobile.

BERRY, Rt. Rev. (Robert Edward) Fraser; Bishop of Kootenay, 1971–89; *b* Ottawa, Ont, 21 Jan. 1926; *s* of Samuel Berry and Claire Hartley; *m* 1951, Margaret Joan Trevorrow Baillie; one *s* one *d*. *Educ:* Sir George Williams Coll., Montreal; McGill Univ., Montreal; Montreal Diocesan Theological Coll. Assistant, Christ Church Cathedral, Victoria, BC, 1953–55; Rector: St Margaret's, Hamilton, Ont, 1955–61; St Mark's, Orangeville, Ont, 1961–63; St Luke's, Winnipeg, Manitoba, 1963–67; St Michael and All Angels, Kelowna, BC, 1967–71. Hon. DD, Montreal Diocesan Theol Coll., 1973. *Recreations:* reading, boating, angling, swimming, walking. *Address:* 1857 Maple Street, Kelowna, BC V1Y 1H4, Canada. *T:* (604) 7622923. *Clubs:* Vancouver (Vancouver); Kelowna Yacht.

BERRY, Prof. Robert James, FRSE 1981; FIBiol; Professor of Genetics in the University of London, since 1974; *b* 26 Oct. 1934; *o s* of Albert Edward James Berry and Nellie (*née* Hodgson); *m* 1958, Anne Caroline Elliott, *d* of Charles Elliott and Evelyn Le Cornu; one *s* two *d*. *Educ:* Shrewsbury Sch.; Caius Coll., Cambridge (MA); University Coll. London

(PhD; DSc 1976). Lectr, subseq. Reader, then Prof., in Genetics, at Royal Free Hospital Sch. of Medicine, 1962–78; Prof. of Genetics at University Coll. London, 1978–. Mem., Human Fertilization and Embryology Authy, 1990–. Member: Gen. Synod, 1970–90; Board of Social Responsibility of the General Synod, 1976–91; Natural Environment Research Council, 1981–87; Council, Zoological Soc. of London, 1986–90 (Vice-Pres., 1988–90); President: Linnean Soc., 1982–85; British Ecological Soc., 1987–89; Christians in Science (formerly Research Scientists' Christian Fellowship), 1993– (Chm., 1968–88); Mammal Soc., 1995–; Chm., Environmental Issues Network, 1992–. Trustee, Nat. Museums and Galleries, Merseyside, 1986–94. Governor, Monkton Combe Sch., 1979–91. *Publications:* Teach Yourself Genetics, 1965, 3rd edn 1977; Adam and the Ape, 1975; Inheritance and Natural History, 1977; (jtly) Natural History of Shetland, 1980; (ed) Biology of the House Mouse, 1981; Neo-Darwinism, 1982; (ed) Evolution in the Galapagos, 1984; (jtly) Free to be Different, 1984; Natural History of Orkney, 1985; (ed jtly) The People of Orkney, 1986; (ed jtly) Nature, Natural History and Ecology, 1987; (ed jtly) Changing Attitudes to Nature Conservation, 1987; God and Evolution, 1988; (ed jtly) Evolution, Ecology and Environmental Stress, 1989; (ed) Real Science, Real Faith, 1991; (ed jtly) Genes in Ecology, 1992; (ed) Environmental Dilemmas, 1993. *Recreations:* remembering hill-walking (especially Munros), recovering. *Address:* Department of Biology, University College London, Gower Street, WC1E 6BT. *T:* 0171–380 7170.

BERRY, Dr Robert Langley Page, CBE 1979; Chairman, 1968–78, Deputy Chairman, 1978–79, Alcoa of Great Britain Ltd; *b* 22 Nov. 1918; *s* of Wilfred Arthur and Mabel Grace Berry; *m* 1946, Eleanor Joyce (*née* Cramp); one *s* one *d.* *Educ:* Sir Thomas Rich's Sch., Gloucester; Birmingham Univ. (BSc (Hons), PhD). Served war, Royal Engrs, 1939–45. ICI Metals Div., 1951–66, Director, 1960–66; Man. Dir, Impalco, 1966–68. Non-Exec. Dir, Royal Mint, 1981–86. Dir, Nat. Anti-Waste Prog., 1976–80. President: Inst. of Metals, 1973; Aluminium Fedn, 1974. *Publications:* several, in scientific jls. *Recreations:* fly-fishing, gardening. *Address:* Waterloo Cottage, Waterloo Lane, Fairford, Glos GL7 4BP. *T:* Cirencester (01285) 712038. *Club:* Army and Navy.

BERRY, Prof. Roger Julian, RD 1987; FRCP; FRCR; FFOM; Director, Westlakes Research Institute, Cumbria, 1992–95; Chairman, British Committee on Radiation Units and Measurements, since 1995 (Member, since 1978; Vice-Chairman, 1984–95); *b* 6 April 1935; *s* of Sidney Norton Berry and Beatrice (*née* Mendelson); *m* 1960, Joseline Valerie Joan (*née* Butler). *Educ:* Stuyvesant High Sch., New York; New York Univ. (BA); Duke Univ. (BSc, MD); Magdalen Coll., Oxford (MA, DPhil). MRC External Staff and Hd, Radiobiol. Lab., Churchill Hosp., Oxford, also Hon. Cons. Med. Radiobiologist, Oxford AHA, and Clin. Lectr, Univ. of Oxford, 1969–74; Hd, Neutrons and therapy-related effects gp, MRC Radiobiol. Unit, Harwell, 1974–76; Sir Brian Windeyer Prof. of Oncology, Mddx Hosp. Med. Sch., 1976–87; Dir, Health, Safety and Environmental Protection, British Nuclear Fuels, 1987–92. Member: Internat. Commn on Radiological Protection, 1985–89; Nat. Radiological Protection Bd, 1982–87; MRC Cttee on Effects of Ionizing Radiation, and Chm., Radiobiol. Sub-Cttee, 1983–87; DoE Radioactive Waste Management Cttee, 1984–87; DHSS Cttee on Med. Aspects of Radiation in the Environment, 1985–87, Black Enquiry on Windscale; HSC Adv. Cttee on Safety of Nuclear Installations, 1992–; CBI Health and Safety Policy Cttee, 1988–92; CIA Health, Safety and Envmt Council, 1990–92. President: BIR, 1986–87; Radiology Sect., RSM, 1985–86; Chm., Sci. Adv. Cttee, Thames Cancer Registry, 1985–87. Surg. Captain, RNR, 1986, and PMO (Reserves), 1987–89. QHP 1987–89. Hon. Fellow, Amer. Coll. of Radiology, 1983. OStJ 1990. Editor, Cell and Tissue Kinetics, 1976–80. *Publications:* Manual on Radiation Dosimetry (jtly), 1970; contributor to Oxford Textbook of Medicine, Florey's Textbook of Pathology; over 160 sci. papers in Brit. Jl of Radiology, etc. *Recreations:* sailing, music, naval history. *Address:* Well Cottage, Parkgate Road, Mollington, Chester CH1 6NE. *T:* Chester (01244) 851367. *Clubs:* Naval and Military, Royal Naval Sailing Association.

BERRY, Dr Roger Leslie; MP (Lab) Kingswood, since 1992; *b* 4 July 1948; *s* of Mary Joyce Berry and Sydney Berry. *Educ:* Dalton County Jun. Sch.; Huddersfield New Coll.; Univ. of Bristol (BSc); Univ. of Sussex (DPhil). Lectr in Econs and Associate Fellow, IDS, Univ. of Sussex, 1973–74; Lecturer in Economics: Univ. of Papua New Guinea, 1974–78; Univ. of Bristol, 1978–92. Avon County Council: Mem., 1981–93; Chm., Finance and Admin. Cttee, 1981–84; Dep. Leader of Council, 1985–86; Leader, Labour Group, 1986–92. Contested (Lab): Weston-super-Mare, 1983; Kingswood, 1987. Sec., All-Party Disablement Gp. Chair, Full Employment Forum, 1994–; Vice-Pres., ACC. *Publications:* contribs to learned jls; newspaper articles and pamphlets. *Recreations:* travel, cooking, reading, cinema, theatre. *Address:* 9 Manor Road, Bristol BS16 2JD. *T:* Bristol (0117) 965 4889. *Clubs:* Kingswood Labour, St George Labour.

BERRY, (Roger) Simon; QC 1990; *b* 9 Sept. 1948; *e s* of Kingsland Jutsum Berry and Kathleen Margaret Berry (*née* Parker); *m* 1974, Jennifer Jane, *d* of Jonas Birtwistle Hall and Edith Emilé Hall (*née* Vester); three *s.* *Educ:* St Brendan's Coll., Bristol; Manchester Univ. (LLB). Admitted Solicitor, 1973; Partner, Stanley, Wasbrough & Co., Solicitors, Bristol (later Veale Wasbrough), 1975–77; removed from Roll, 1977, at own request, in order to seek call to the Bar; called to the Bar, Middle Temple, 1977; Mem., Middle Temple and Lincoln's Inn; Harmsworth Benefactor's Law Schol.; Mem., Western Circuit, 1978–; in practice at Chancery Bar, 1978–. Member: Chancery Bar Assoc., 1978– (Mem. Cttee, 1984, 1985); Professional Negligence Bar Assoc., 1991–. *Recreations:* family, the performing arts, cycling, ski-ing, keeping fit. *Address:* 9 Old Square, Lincoln's Inn, WC2A 3SR. *T:* 0171–405 4682. *Clubs:* Ski of Great Britain, Riverside.

BERRY, Air Cdre Ronald, CBE 1965 (OBE 1946); DSO 1943; DFC 1940 and Bar, 1943; RAF retired; Director of Control Operations, Board of Trade, 1965–68; *b* 3 May 1917; *s* of W. Berry, Hull; *m* 1940, Nancy Watson, Hessle, near Hull; one *d.* *Educ:* Hull Technical Coll. VR Pilot, Brough Flying Sch., 1937–39; 603 F Sqdn, Turnhouse/Hornchurch, 1939–41 (Battle of Britain); Sqdn Ldr, and CO 81 F Sqdn, North Africa, 1942; Wing Comdr, and CO 322 F Wing, North Africa, 1942–43; Camberley Army Staff Coll., 1944; CO, RAF Acklington, 1945–46; jssc 1955; various operational appts in Fighter and Bomber Comd; V Sqdn, 1957–59; Group Capt., Air Min. and HQ Bomber Comd, 1959. *Recreations:* motoring, gardening, flying. *Address:* Aldrian, Mereview Avenue, Hornsea, N Humberside HU18 1RR.

BERRY, Scyld; *see* Berry, A. S. I.

BERRY, Simon; *see* Berry, Roger S.

BERRY, Thomas Henry S.; *see* Seager Berry.

BERTHOIN, Georges Paul; Chevalier, Légion d'Honneur, 1990; Médaille militaire, Croix de Guerre, Médaille de la Résistance avec Rosette, France, 1945; Executive Member of the Trilateral Commission (Japan, N America, W Europe), 1973–75, and since 1993 (Chairman, 1975–92, Hon. European Chairman, since 1992); Honorary International Chairman, the European Movement, since 1981 (Chairman, 1978–81); *b* Nérac, France, 17 May 1925; *s* of Jean Berthoin and Germaine Mourgnot; *m* 1st, 1950, Ann White Whittlesey; four *d*; 2nd, 1965, Pamela Jenkins; two *s.* *Educ:* Grenoble Univ.; École Sciences Politiques, Paris; Harvard Univ. Licencié ès Lettres (Philosophie), Licencié en Droit, Laureate for Economics (Grenoble). Lectr, McGill Univ., Montreal, 1948; Private Sec. to French Minister of Finance, 1948–50; Head of Staff of Superprefect of Alsace-Lorraine-Champagne, 1950–52. Joined High Authority of European Coal and Steel Community, and then Principal Private Sec. to its Pres. (Jean Monnet), 1952–53–55. Dep. Chief Rep. of ECSC in UK, 1956–67; Chargé d'Affaires for Commission of the European Communities (ECSC Euratom-Common Market), 1968; Principal Adviser to the Commission, and its Dep. Chief Rep. in London, 1969–70, Chief Representative, 1971–73. Member: Nine Wise Men Gp on Africa, 1988–89; Bd, Aspen Inst., Berlin; Friends of Jean Monnet; Adv. Bd, Johns Hopkins Univ. Bologna Center Sch. of Advanced Studies. Regular Lectr, RCDS, London. *Recreations:* art, theatre, walking, collecting objects. *Address:* 67 Avenue Niel, 75017 Paris, France.

BERTHON, Vice-Adm. Sir Stephen (Ferrier), KCB 1980; *b* 24 Aug. 1922; *s* of late Rear-Adm. C. P. Berthon, CBE and Mrs C. P. Berthon (*née* Ferrier); *m* 1948, Elizabeth Leigh-Bennett; two *s* two *d.* *Educ:* Old Malthouse, Swanage; RNC Dartmouth. Served War of 1939–45 at sea, Mediterranean, Atlantic, Russia; spec. communications, 1945–46; Flag Lieut Singapore, 1946–48; submarines, 1949–51; East Indies Flagship, 1951–52; HMS Mercury, 1952–54; Staff of Flag Officer Aircraft Carriers, 1954–56; Fleet Communications Officer Mediterranean, 1957–59; jssc 1959; Comdr HMS Mercury, 1959–61; Jt Planning Staff, 1961–64; Naval Attaché, Australia, 1964–66; Dir of Defence Policy, MoD, 1968–71; Cdre HMS Drake, 1971–73; Flag Officer Medway and Port Adm. Chatham, 1974–76; Asst Chief of Naval Staff (Op. Req.), 1976–78; Dep. Chief of Defence Staff (Operational Requirements), 1978–81; retired 1981. Jt MFH, Avon Vale Hunt, 1981–84. *Recreations:* hunting, riding, gardening, walking, painting. *Club:* Army and Navy.

BERTHOUD, Prof. Jacques Alexandre; Professor of English and Head, Department of English and Related Literature, University of York, since 1980; *b* 1 March 1935; *s* of Alexandre L. Berthoud and Madeleine (*née* Bourquin); *m* 1958, Astrid Irene (*née* Titlestad); one *s* two *d.* *Educ:* Univ. of the Witwatersrand, Johannesburg (BA and BA Hons). Lectr, English Dept, Univ. of Natal, Pietermaritzburg, 1960–67; Lectr, subseq. Sen. Lectr, English Dept, Univ. of Southampton, 1967–79. British Chm., Amnesty Internat., 1978–80. *Publications:* (with Dr C. van Heyningen) Uys Krige, 1966; Joseph Conrad, the Major Phase, 1978; (ed) books for OUP and Penguin Books. *Recreation:* sleeping. *Address:* 30 New Walk Terrace, Fishergate, York YO1 4BG. *T:* York (01904) 629212.

BERTHOUD, Sir Martin (Seymour), KCVO 1985; CMG 1985; HM Diplomatic Service, retired; Director, The Wates Foundation, since 1993; *b* 20 Aug. 1931; *s* of Sir Eric Berthoud, KCMG and late Ruth Tilston, *d* of Sir Charles Bright, FRSE; *m* 1960, Marguerite Joan Richarda Phayre; three *s* one *d.* *Educ:* Rugby Sch.; Magdalen Coll., Oxford (BA). Served with British Embassies in: Tehran, 1956–58; Manila, 1961–64; Pretoria/Cape Town, 1967–71; Tehran, 1971–73; Counsellor, Helsinki, 1974–77; Inspector, HM Diplomatic Service, 1977–79; Head of N. American Dept, FCO, 1979–81; Consul-General, Sydney, 1982–85; High Comr, Trinidad and Tobago, 1985–91. EC Monitoring Mission Service Medal, 1994. Commander, Order of the Lion, Finland, 1976; Keys of City of San Fernando, Trinidad, 1991. *Recreations:* golf, tennis, bird-watching, acting as under-gardener to wife. *Address:* Gillyflower, Stoke by Nayland, Suffolk CO6 4RD. *T:* Colchester (01206) 263237; The Wates Foundation, 1260 London Road, SW16 4EG. *Clubs:* United Oxford & Cambridge University; Vincent's (Oxford).

BERTIE, family name of **Earl of Lindsey and Abingdon.**

BERTRAM, Dr Brian Colin Ricardo; Director-General, Wildfowl and Wetlands Trust, 1987–92; *b* 14 April 1944; *s* of Dr Colin Bertram and Dr (Cicely) Kate Bertram, *qv*; *m* 1975, Katharine Jean Gillie; one *s* two *d.* *Educ:* Perse School, Cambridge; St John's Coll., Cambridge (BA 1965; MA 1968); PhD Cambridge, 1969. FIBiol 1981. Research Fellow, Serengeti Res. Inst., Tanzania, 1969–73; Sen. Res. Fellow, King's Coll., Cambridge, 1976–79; Curator of Mammals, 1980–87, and Curator of Aquarium and Invertebrates, 1982–87, Zoological Society of London. Vice-Pres., World Pheasant Assoc., 1990–; Mem. Council, Zool Soc. of London, 1993–. *Publications:* Pride of Lions, 1978; The Ostrich Communal Nesting System, 1992. *Recreations:* family, friends, zoology, garden, travel. *Address:* Fieldhead, Amberley, Stroud, Glos GL5 5AG. *T:* Amberley (01453) 872796. *Club:* Zoological.

BERTRAM, Dr Christoph; Diplomatic Correspondent, Die Zeit, since 1986; *b* 3 Sept. 1937; German national; *m* 1st, 1967, Renate Edith Bergemann (marr. diss. 1980); 2nd, 1980, Ragnhild Lindemann; two *s* two *d.* *Educ:* Free Univ. Berlin and Bonn Univ. (law); Institut d'Etudes Politiques, Paris (political science). Dr of Law 1967. Joined Internat. Inst. for Strategic Studies as Research Associate, 1967, Asst Dir, 1969–74, Dir, 1974–82; Mem. Planning Staff, West German Min. of Defence, 1969–70. Political and Foreign Editor, Die Zeit, 1982–85. *Publications:* (with Alastair Buchan *et al.*) Europe's Futures—Europe's Choices, 1969; Mutual Force Reductions in Europe: the political aspects, 1972; (ed, with Johan J. Holst) New Strategic Factors in the North Atlantic, 1977; Arms Control and Technological Change, 1979. *Recreations:* clocks, sailing. *Address:* Die Zeit, Pressehaus, Speersort 1, 20079 Hamburg, Germany. *Club:* Garrick.

BERTRAM, (Cicely) Kate, MA; PhD; President, Lucy Cavendish College, Cambridge, 1970–79 (Tutor, 1965–70; Hon. Fellow, 1982); *b* 8 July 1912; *d* of late Sir Harry Ralph Ricardo, FRS; *m* 1939, Dr George Colin Lawder Bertram (Fellow and formerly Senior Tutor of St John's Coll., Cambridge); four *s.* *Educ:* Hayes Court, Kent; Newnham Coll., Cambridge. MA, PhD (Cantab), 1940. Jarrow Research Studentship, Girton Coll., Cambridge, 1937–40. Mem. Colonial Office Nutrition Survey, in Nyasaland, 1939; Adviser on Freshwater Fisheries to Govt of Palestine, 1940–43. Mem. Council, New Hall, Cambridge, 1954–66; Associate of Newnham Coll. FLS. JP: Co. Cambridge, and Isle of Ely, 1959; W Sussex, 1981. *Publications:* Lucy Cavendish College, Cambridge: a history of the early years, 1989; Letters from the Swamps, 1991; 2 Crown Agents' Reports on African Fisheries, 1939 and 1942; papers on African Fish, in zoological jls; papers and articles on Sirenia (with G.C.L. Bertram). *Recreations:* foreign travel, gardening. *Address:* Ricardo's, Graffham, near Petworth, Sussex GU28 0PU. *T:* Graffham (01798) 867205. *Club:* English-Speaking Union.

See also B. C. R. Bertram.

BERTRAM, Robert David Darney; Partner, Shepherd & Wedderburn, WS, since 1992; *b* 6 Oct. 1941; *s* of late D. N. S. Bertram; *m* 1967, Patricia Joan Laithwaite; two *s.* *Educ:* Edinburgh Academy; Oxford Univ. (MA); Edinburgh Univ. (LLB (Hons), Berriedale Keith Prize). An Assistant Solicitor, Linklaters & Paines, London, 1968–69; Partner, Dundas & Wilson, CS, 1969–92. Associate, Institute of Taxation, 1970 (Mem., Technical Cttee, 1986–); Examiner, Law Society of Scotland, 1972–75; Member: Scottish Law Commn, 1978–86; (part-time), VAT Tribunal, Scotland, 1984–92. Non-exec. Dir, The Weir Group plc, 1983–. *Publications:* contribs to professional jls. *Address:* (office) Saltire Court, 20 Castle Terrace, Edinburgh EH1 2ET. *T:* 0131–228 9900. *Clubs:* Scottish Arts, Edinburgh University Staff.

BESCH, Anthony John Elwyn, FGSM; opera and theatre director, since 1950; Head of Opera Studies, Guildhall School of Music and Drama, 1986–89; *b* 5 Feb. 1924; *s* of Roy Cressy Frederick Besch and late Anne Gwendolen Besch. *Educ:* Rossall Sch., Lancs; Worcester Coll., Oxford (MA). FGSM 1989. Dir, opera and theatre, 1950–: Royal Opera House, Covent Garden; Glyndebourne Opera; English Nat. Opera, London Coliseum; Scottish Opera; Opera North; New Opera Co., London; Handel Opera Soc.; Edinburgh Festival; Wexford Festival; Deutsche Oper, Berlin; Royal Netherlands Opera; Théâtre de la Monnaie, Brussels; Teatro Colon, Buenos Aires; New York City Opera; San Francisco Opera; Canadian Opera Co.; Nat. Arts Centre, Canada; Australian Opera; State Opera, S Australia; Victoria State Opera. FRSA 1990. *Recreation:* gardening. *Address:* 201 Hammersmith Grove, W6 0NP. *Club:* Garrick.

BESLEY, Christopher; a Metropolitan Magistrate, 1964–88; *b* 18 April 1916; *s* of late C. A. Besley, Tiverton; *m* 1947, Pamela, *d* of Dr W. E. David, Sydney, Australia; four *s* two *d*. *Educ:* King's Coll., Wimbledon; King's Coll., London. Barrister, Gray's Inn, 1938; practised Western Circuit. Served War of 1939–45, Devon Regt (wounded, N Africa). *Address:* Queen Elizabeth Building, Temple, EC4; 15 Belvedere Avenue, SW19 7PP. *T:* 0181–946 2184; Nanquidno House, St Just-in-Penwith, Cornwall TR19 7NU. *Club:* Lansdowne.

BESSBOROUGH, 11th Earl of, *cr* 1739 (Ire.); **Arthur Mountifort Longfield Ponsonby;** Baron Bessborough (Ire.) 1721; Viscount Duncannon (Ire.) 1722; Baron Ponsonby (GB) 1749; Baron Duncannon (UK) 1834; *b* 11 Dec. 1912; *s* of Hon. Cyril Myles Ponsonby (*d* 1915), 2nd *s* of 8th Earl, and Rita Narcissa Longfield (*d* 1977); *S* cousin, 1993; *m* 1st, 1939, Patricia (*d* 1952), *d* of Col Fitzhugh Minnigerode, Va, USA; one *s* one *d*; 2nd, 1956, Anne Marie Galitzine (marr. diss. 1963); 3rd, 1963, Madeleine Lola Margaret, *d* of Maj.-Gen. Laurence Grand, CB, CIE, CBE; two *s*. *Educ:* Harrow; Trinity Coll., Cambridge. Captain, Welsh Guards, 1940–46. *Heir: s* Viscount Duncannon, *qv*. *Address:* Roche Court, Winterslow, Wilts SP5 1BG. *T:* Winterslow (01980) 862204.

BESSER, Prof. (Gordon) Michael, MD, DSc; FRCP; Professor of Medicine and Chairman, Department of Medicine, St Bartholomew's Hospital Medical College, since 1992; Consultant and Physician in charge, Department of Endocrinology, St Bartholomew's Hospital, since 1974; *b* 22 Jan. 1936; *s* of Hyman Besser and Leah Besser (*née* Geller); *m* 1972; one *s* one *d*. *Educ:* Hove County Grammar Sch.; Bart's Med. Coll., Univ. of London (BSc, MB BS, MD, DSc). FRCP 1973. St Bartholomew's Hospital: Lectr in Medicine, 1966–70; Sen. Lectr and Hon. Consultant Physician, 1970–74; Prof. of Endocrinology, Med. Coll., 1974–92; Dir of Medicine, 1989–93; Chief Exec., 1992–94. Consultant Endocrinologist to RN, 1989–. Vis. Prof., univs and med. estabts in Canada, China, Hong Kong, Italy, Malta, USA, Yugoslavia. Cttee work for RCP, RSocMed, Soc. for Endocrinology, Jt Cttee on Higher Med. Training; Medical Research Council: former Mem., Physiol. Systems Bd and Grants Cttee (Chm., 1984–86); Chm., Working Party on Hormone Replacement Therapy, 1992–. Royal College of Physicians: Lectr, 1974, 1993; Censor, 1990–92; Sen. Vice-Pres. and Sen. Censor, 1995–. Hon. MD Turin, 1985. Mem., Editl Bd, Clinics in Endocrinology and Metabolism, 1977–; former Mem., Editl Bd, Clinical Endocrinol., Jl of Endocrinol., and Neuroendocrinol. *Publications:* Fundamentals of Clinical Endocrinology (with R. Hall and J. Anderson), 2nd edn 1978, 3rd edn 1980, (ed with R. Hall) 4th edn 1989; Clinical Neuroendocrinology, 1977; Recent Advances in Medicine, 3 edns, 1981–87; (ed jtly) Endocrinology, 2nd edn 1989, 3rd edn 1994; Clinical Endocrinology, 1986, 2nd edn 1994; Clinical Diabetes, 1988; contribs to learned jls. *Recreations:* early Chinese ceramics, opera, ballet, theatre, keeping fit. *Address:* St Bartholomew's Hospital, EC1A 7BE. *T:* 0171–601 8342. *Club:* Garrick.

BESSEY, Gordon Scott, CBE 1968; *b* 20 Oct. 1910; *s* of late Edward Emerson and Mabel Bessey, Great Yarmouth; *m* 1937, Cynthia (JP 1966), *d* of late William and Mary Bird, Oxford; one *s* three *d*. *Educ:* Heath Sch., Halifax; St Edmund Hall, Oxford. BA 1932, Dip Ed 1933, MA 1937. Teaching: Keighley and Cheltenham, 1933–37; Admin. Asst, Surrey, 1937–39; Asst, later Dep. Educn Officer, Norfolk, 1939–45; Dep. Educn Officer, Somerset, 1945–49. Mem., Youth Service Development Council, 1960–67; Chm., Working Party on part-time training of Youth Leaders, 1961–62; Pres., Assoc. of Chief Educn Officers, 1963; Treas., Soc. of Educn Officers, 1971–74; Chairman: Educnl Adv. Council of IBA (formerly ITA), 1970–74; County Educn Officers' Soc., 1969–70; Dir of Educn, Cumberland, 1949–74, Cumbria, 1974–75. Chairman: East Cumbria Community Health Council, 1974–79; Assoc. of Community Health Councils in England and Wales, 1977–79; Voluntary Action, Cumbria, 1975–84. Hon. DCL Newcastle upon Tyne, 1970. *Recreations:* fishing, golf, fell-walking, ornithology. *Address:* The Lawn, Holybourne, near Alton, Hants. *T:* Alton (01420) 544107.

BEST, family name of **Baron Wynford.**

BEST, Prof. Ernest; Professor of Divinity and Biblical Criticism, University of Glasgow, 1974–82, now Professor Emeritus; Dean of the Faculty of Divinity, 1978–80; *b* 23 May 1917; *s* of John and Louisa Elizabeth Best; *m* 1949, Sarah Elizabeth Kingston; two *d*. *Educ:* Methodist Coll., Belfast; Queen's Univ., Belfast (BA, MA, BD, PhD); Presbyterian Coll., Belfast. Asst Minister, First Bangor Presbyterian Church, 1943–49; Minister, Caledon and Minterburn Presbyt. Churches, 1949–63; Lectr (temp.), Presbyt. Coll., Belfast, 1953–54; Guest Prof., Austin Presbyt. Theol Seminary, Texas, 1955–57; Lectr in Biblical Lit. and Theol., St Andrews Univ., 1963–74 (Sen. Lectr 1971–74). Lectures: Nils W. Lund, Chicago, 1978; Manson Meml, Manchester Univ., 1978; Sprunt, Richmond, Virginia, 1985; Ethel M. Wood, London Univ., 1986. Vis. Prof. of New Testament Studies, Knox Coll., Dunedin, NZ, 1983; Vis. Fellow, Univ. of Otago, 1983; Gunning Fellow, New Coll., Edinburgh Univ., 1993. Jt Editor, Biblical Theology, 1962–72; Associate Editor, Irish Biblical Studies, 1978–. *Publications:* One Body in Christ, 1955; The Temptation and the Passion, 1965, 2nd edn 1990; The Letter of Paul to the Romans, 1967; 1 Peter, 1971; 1 and 2 Thessalonians, 1972; From Text to Sermon, 1977, 2nd edn 1988; Text and Interpretation (ed jtly), 1979; Following Jesus, 1981; Mark: the Gospel as story, 1983; Disciples and Discipleship, 1986; 2 Corinthians, 1987; Paul and His Converts, 1988; Interpreting Christ, 1993; Ephesians: a guide, 1993; contrib. Biblica, Ecumenical Review, Expository Times, Interpretation, Jl Theol Studies, New Testament Studies, Novum Testamentum, Scottish Jl Theology, Catholic Biblical Qly, Zeit. neu. test. Wiss. *Recreations:* vegetable growing, golf. *Address:* 13 Newmill Gardens, St Andrews, Fife KY16 8RY.

BEST, Dr Geoffrey Francis Andrew; Senior Associate Member, St Antony's College, Oxford, since 1988; *b* 20 Nov. 1928; *s* of Frederick Ebenezer Best and Catherine Sarah Vanderbrook (*née* Bultz); *m* 1955, Gwenllyan Marigold Davies; two *s* one *d*. *Educ:* St Paul's Sch.; Trinity Coll., Cambridge (MA, PhD). Army (RAEC), 1946–47; Choate Fellow, Harvard Univ., 1954–55; Fellow of Trinity Hall and Asst Lectr, Cambridge Univ., 1955–61; Lectr, Edinburgh Univ., 1961–66; Sir Richard Lodge Prof. of History, Edinburgh Univ., 1966–74; Prof. of History, Sch. of European Studies, 1974–85 (Hon. Prof., 1982–85), Dean, 1980–82, Univ. of Sussex; Academic Visitor, Dept of Internat. Relations, LSE, 1985–88. Vis. Prof., Chicago Univ., 1964; Visiting Fellow: All Souls Coll., Oxford, 1969–70; LSE, 1983–85; ANU, 1984; Fellow, Woodrow Wilson Internat. Center, Washington, DC, 1978–79. Lees Knowles Lectr, Cambridge, 1970; Joanne Goodman Lectr, Univ. of Western Ontario, 1981. Mem. Council, British Red Cross Soc., 1981–84, Hon. Consultant, 1985–91. Jt Editor, Victorian Studies, 1958–68; Editor, War and Society Newsletter, 1973–82. FRHistS 1977–84. *Publications:* Temporal Pillars, 1964; Shaftesbury, 1964; Bishop Westcott and the Miners, 1968; Mid-Victorian Britain, 1971; (ed) Church's Oxford Movement, 1971; (jt ed) War, Economy and the Military Mind, 1976; Humanity in Warfare, 1980; War and Society in Revolutionary Europe, 1982; Honour Among Men and Nations, 1982; Nuremberg and After: the continuing history of war crimes and crimes against humanity, 1984; (ed jtly) History, Society and the Churches, 1985; (ed) The Permanent Revolution, 1988; War and Law since 1945, 1994; contrib. various jls. *Address:* 19 Buckingham Street, Oxford OX1 4LH.

BEST, His Honour Giles Bernard; a Circuit Judge, 1975–91; *b* 19 Oct. 1925; *yr s* of late Hon. James William Best, OBE. *Educ:* Wellington Coll.; Jesus Coll., Oxford. Called to Bar, Inner Temple, 1951; Dep. Chm., Dorset QS, 1967–71; a Recorder, 1972–75. *Address:* Pitcombe, Little Bredy, Dorset DT2 9HG.

BEST, Keith (Lander); Chief Executive, Immigration Advisory Service, since 1993; *b* 10 June 1949; *s* of late Peter Edwin Wilson Best and Margaret Louisa Best; *m* 1990, Elizabeth Margaret Gibson; two *d*. *Educ:* Brighton Coll.; Keble Coll., Oxford (BA (Hons) Jurisprudence; MA). Assistant Master, Summerfields Sch., Oxford, 1967; called to the Bar, Inner Temple, 1971; Lectr in Law, 1973. Served: 289 Parachute Battery, RHA (V), 1970–76; with RM on HMS Bulwark, 1976; Naval Gunfire Liaison Officer with Commando Forces (Major). Councillor, Brighton Borough Council (Chm. Lands Cttee, Housing Cttee), 1976–80. Dir, Prisoners Abroad, 1989–93. MP (C): Anglesey, 1979–83; Ynys Môn, 1983–87. PPS to Sec. of State for Wales, 1981–84. Former Chm., All Party Alcohol Policy and Services Gp; former Mem., Select Cttee on Welsh Affairs. Chairman: Bow Gp Defence Cttee; British Cttee for Vietnamese Refugees; Internat. Council of Parliamentarians' Global Action; World Federalist Movement, 1987–; Conservative Action for Electoral Reform, 1992–; Member: UN Disarmament Cttee; Young Conservative Nat. Adv. Cttee, 1978. Mem. Cttee, Assoc. of Lloyd's Mems. Founder Member: Two Piers Housing Co-operative, 1977; Brighton Housing Trust, 1976; school manager, Downs County First Sch. and Downs Middle Sch., 1976. *Publications:* Write Your Own Will, 1978 (paperback); The Right Way to Prove a Will, 1980 (paperback); contrib. District Councils Rev. *Recreations:* parachuting, walking, photography, travel. *Address:* 15 St Stephen's Terrace, SW8 1DJ. *Clubs:* New Cavendish; Royal Artillery Mess (Woolwich); Holyhead Conservative.

BEST, Sir Richard (Radford), KCVO 1990; CBE 1989 (MBE 1977); HM Diplomatic Service, retired; *b* 28 July 1933; *s* of Charles and Frances Best (*née* Raymond); *m* 1st, 1957, Elizabeth Vera Wait (*d* 1968); two *d*; 2nd, 1969, Mary Hill (*née* Wait); one *s*. *Educ:* Worthing High Sch.; University Coll. London (BA Hons). Home Office, 1957–66; HM Diplomatic Service, 1966–: CO (formerly CRO), 1966–68; served Lusaka, 1969–72; Stockholm, 1972–76; FCO, 1976–79; served New Delhi, 1979–83; FCO, 1983–84; Dep. High Comr, Kaduna, 1984–88; Ambassador to Iceland, 1989–91; FCO, 1991. BBC 'Brain of Britain', 1966. Life Mem., Kaduna Br., Nigeria–Britain Assoc. Grand Cross, Order of Icelandic Falcon, 1990. *Recreations:* cricket watching, gardening, churchwardening. *Address:* Holly Howe, The Street, Patching, near Worthing, West Sussex BN13 3XF. *Club:* Royal Over-Seas League.

BEST, Richard Stuart, OBE 1988; Director, Joseph Rowntree Foundation (formerly Joseph Rowntree Memorial Trust), since 1988; *b* 22 June 1945; *s* of Walter Stuart Best, DL, JP and Frances Mary Chignell; *m* 1st, 1970, Ima Akpan (marr. diss. 1976); one *s* one *d*; 2nd, 1978, Belinda Janie Tremayne Stemp; one *s* one *d*. *Educ:* Shrewsbury School; University of Nottingham (BA). British Churches Housing Trust, 1968–73 (Dir, 1971–73); Dir, Nat. Fedn of Housing Assocs, 1973–88. Trustee: Sutton Housing Trust, 1971–84 (Dep. Chm., 1983–84); Internat. Year of Shelter for the Homeless 1987 Trust; Chm., Omnium Central Housing Assoc., 1978–80; Committee Member: UK Housing Trust, 1976–88; Sutton Hastoe Housing Assoc., 1982–; Member: Social Policy Cttee, C of E Bd for Social Responsibility, 1986–91; BBC/IBA Central Appeals Cttee, 1989–91; Cttee, Assoc. of Charitable Foundns, 1989–92; Comr, Rural Develt Commn, 1989–; Board Member: Anchor Housing Assoc., 1985–88. Sec., Duke of Edinburgh's Inquiry into British Housing, 1984–91. *Publications:* Rural Housing: problems and solutions, 1981; Housing Associations 1890–1990, 1991; Housing After 2000 AD, 1992. *Address:* West Wing, Grimston Park, near Tadcaster, N Yorks LS24 9DB. *Club:* Travellers'.

BEST-SHAW, Sir John (Michael Robert), 10th Bt *cr* 1665; retired; *b* 28 Sept. 1924; *s* of Sir John James Kenward Best-Shaw, 9th Bt, Commander RN, and Elizabeth Mary Theodora (*d* 1986), *e d* of Sir Robert Hughes, 12th Bt; *S* father, 1984; *m* 1960, Jane Gordon, *d* of A. G. Guthrie; two *s* one *d* (and one *s* decd). *Educ:* Lancing; Hertford Coll., Oxford (MA); Avery Hill Coll., London (Teachers' Cert.). Captain Royal West Kent Regt, 1943–47. Royal Fedn of Malaya Police, 1950–58; church work, 1958–71; teaching, 1972–82. *Recreations:* gardening, writing. *Heir: s* Thomas Joshua Best-Shaw [*b* 7 March 1965; *m* 1992, Emily Susan, *d* of Vivian Rubin; one *s*]. *Address:* Belmont, 104 High Street, West Malling, Kent ME19 6NE. *T:* West Malling (01732) 843823. *Club:* Commonwealth Trust.

BESTERMAN, Edwin Melville Mack, MD, MA, Cantab; FRCP; FACC; Honorary Consultant Cardiologist: Department of Medicine, University of the West Indies (Mona Faculty, Jamaica), since 1985; St Mary's Hospital, London, since 1985; Paddington Green Children's Hospital, since 1985; Hon. Consultant Physician, Department of Medicine, Hammersmith Hospital, since 1981; *b* 4 May 1924; *s* of late Theodore Deodatus Nathaniel Besterman and Evelyn, *y d* of Arthur Mack, NY; *m* 1978, Perri Marjorie Burrowes, *d* of R. Burrowes, Kingston, Jamaica, WI; four *s* by previous marriage. *Educ:* Stowe Sch.; Trinity Coll., Cambridge; Guy's Hospital. BA (Cantab) 1943 (1st cl. hons Physiology), MA 1948; MB, BChir 1947; MRCP 1949; MD 1955 (Raymond Horton Smith Prize); FRCP 1967; FACC 1985. Out-patient Officer, Guy's Hosp., 1947; House Physician, Post-graduate Medical Sch., Hammersmith, 1948; Registrar, Special Unit for Juvenile Rheumatism, Canadian Red Cross Memorial Hosp., Taplow, Berks, 1949–52; First Asst (Lectr), Inst of Cardiology and Nat. Heart Hosp., 1953–56; Sen. Registrar, Middlesex Hosp., 1956–62; Consultant Cardiologist: St Mary's Hosp., London, 1962–85; Paddington Green Children's Hosp., 1972–85. Member: Brit. Cardiac Soc.; Faculty of History of Medicine and Pharmacy; British Pacing Group. *Publications:* contribs to Paul Wood, Diseases of the Heart and Circulation, 3rd edn, 1968; articles on phonocardiography, pulmonary hypertension, atherosclerosis, blood platelet function, lipid fractions and drug trials in angina and hypertension in Brit. Heart Jl, Brit. Med. Jl, Lancet, Circulation, Atherosclerosis Research, etc. *Recreations:* photography, gardening, fishing, tennis, dogs. *Address:* PO Box 340, Stony Hill, Kingston 9, Jamaica, West Indies. *Club:* Liguanea.

BETHE, Prof. Hans Albrecht, PhD; Professor of Theoretical Physics, Cornell University, 1937–75, now Professor Emeritus; *b* Strassburg, Germany, 2 July 1906; *m* 1939, Rose Ewald; one *s* one *d*. *Educ:* Goethe Gymnasium, Frankfurt on Main; Univs of Frankfurt and Munich. PhD Munich, 1928. Instructor in Theoretical Physics, Univs of Frankfurt, Stuttgart, Munich and Tübingen, 1928–33; Lectr, Univs of Manchester and Bristol,

England, 1933–35; Asst Prof., Cornell Univ., Ithaca, 1935–37. Dir, Theoretical Physics Div. of Los Alamos Atomic Scientific Laboratory, 1943–46. Sabbatic leave to Cambridge Univ., academic year, 1955–56. Mem., President's Science Adv. Cttee, 1956–59. Member: Nat. Acad. Sciences; Amer. Physical Soc.; Amer. Astron. Soc.; For. Mem., Royal Society. Holds hon. doctorates in Science. US Medal of Merit, 1946; Planck Medal, German Physical Soc., 1955; Eddington Medal, Royal Astronomical Soc., 1961; Enrico Fermi Award, US Atomic Energy Commn, 1961; Nobel Prize for Physics, 1967. *Publications:* (jt author) Elementary Nuclear Theory, 1947; Mesons and Fields, 1955; Quantum Mechanics of One- and Two-Electron Atoms, 1957; Intermediate Quantum Mechanics, 1964; contributions to: Handbuch der Physik, 1933, 1954; Reviews of Mod. Physics, 1936–37, 1990; Physical Review; Astrophysical Jl. *Address:* Laboratory of Nuclear Studies, Cornell University, Ithaca, NY 14853, USA.

BETHEL, David Percival, CBE 1983; Director, Leicester Polytechnic, 1973–87; *b* Bath, 7 Dec. 1923; *s* of William George Bethell and Elsie (*née* Cossins); *m* 1943, Margaret Elizabeth, *d* of late Alexander Wrigglesworth; one *s* one *d*. *Educ:* King Edward VI Sch., Bath; Crypt Grammar Sch., Glos; West of England Coll. of Art; Bristol Univ., 1946–51; NDD, ATD, FRSA, FSAE, FCSD, RWA. Served with RN, Far East, 1943–45. Lectr, Stafford Coll. of Art, 1951–56; Deputy Principal, Coventry Coll. of Art, 1956–65; Principal, Coventry Coll. of Art, 1965–69; Dep. Dir, Leicester Polytechnic, 1969–73. Pres., Nat. Soc. for Art Educn, 1965–66; Member: Nat. Adv. Cttee for Art Educn, 1965–71; Jt Summerson Coldstream Cttee, 1968–70; The Design Council, 1980–88; Nat. Adv. Bd for Local Authority Higher Educn, 1983–87; OECD Directing Gp for Management of Higher Educn, 1984–87; Cttee for Internat. Co-operation in Higher Educn, British Council, 1981–88; Chairman: CNAA Cttee for Art and Design (and Research Degrees Sub-Cttee), 1975–81; Educn and Trng Bd, Chartered Soc. of Designers, 1987–91; Study Team on Delivery of Primary Health Care Services, 1987–88; Cttee of Dirs of Polytechnics, 1978–80; Vice-Chm., Inter-Univs and Polytechnics Council for Higher Educn Overseas. Sometime Design Consultant to Massey Ferguson, Van Heusen, Monotype Corp., etc. British Council Adviser to Hong Kong Govt, 1971–; Chairman: UGC/NAB Town & Country Planning Courses Cttee, 1985–86; Hong Kong Planning Cttee for Academic Accreditation, 1986–89; Hong Kong Council for Acad. Accreditation, 1989–92; Member: Hong Kong UPGC, 1982–92; World Council, INSEA; Council of Europe; Assessor, Partnership Trust, 1991–93; Convenor, W Midlands Br., Conservative Acad. Liaison Forum, 1993–; Chairman: Cyril Wood Meml Trust; Leicester Haymarket Theatre, 1979–85; Frame-Work Knitters Educnl Bursary Awards Cttee, 1992–. Paintings and prints in Glos. Libraries, Stafford Art Gallery, Coventry, RWA, private collections. Mem., Worshipful Co. of Frame-Work Knitters (Steward, 1994). Aust. Commonwealth Travelling Fellowship, 1979. Hon. LLD Leicester, 1982; Hon. DLitt Loughborough, 1987. *Publications:* A Case of Sorts, 1991; An Industrious People, 1991. *Recreations:* travel; study of art, design, architecture; archæology and music. *Address:* 48 Holmfield Road, Stoneygate, Leicester LE2 1SA. *Clubs:* Athenæum, Royal Over-Seas League.

BETHEL, Dr Keva Marie, CMG 1995; Principal, College of the Bahamas, since 1982; *b* 18 Aug. 1935; *d* of late Sidney Alexander Eldon and of Rowena Beatrice Eldon (*née* Hill); *m* 1962, E. Clement Bethel (*d* 1987); one *s* one *d*. *Educ:* Girton Coll., Cambridge (BA, MA); Univ. of Alberta (PhD 1981). Government High School, Nassau, Bahamas: Asst Mistress, Spanish and French, 1959–66; Head, Mod. Langs Dept, 1966–72; Dep. Headmistress, 1972–75; College of the Bahamas: Chm., Div. of Humanities, 1975–77; Dean, Acad. Affairs, 1977–78; Vice Principal, 1979–81; Actg Principal, Jan.–June 1992. *Publication:* chapter on Higher Education in the Bahamas, in Handbook of World Education, ed Walter Wickremasinghe, 1991. *Recreations:* reading, music. *Address:* College of the Bahamas, PO Box N4912, Nassau, New Providence, Bahamas. *T:* 3238550; PO Box N1232, Nassau, New Providence, Bahamas.

BETHEL, Martin; QC 1983; a Recorder of the Crown Court, since 1979; *b* 12 March 1943; *o s* of late Rev. Ralph Bethel and of Enid Bethel; *m* 1974, Kathryn Denby; two *s* one *d*. *Educ:* Kingswood Sch.; Fitzwilliam Coll., Cambridge (MA, LLM). Called to the Bar, Inner Temple, 1965; North-Eastern Circuit (Circuit Junior, 1969). *Recreations:* family, sailing, skiing. *Address:* (chambers) Pearl Chambers, 22 East Parade, Leeds LS1 5BU. *T:* Leeds (0113) 245 2702.

BETHELL, family name of **Barons Bethell** and **Westbury.**

BETHELL, 4th Baron *cr* 1922, of Romford; **Nicholas William Bethell;** Bt 1911; free-lance writer; *b* 19 July 1938; *s* of Hon. William Gladstone Bethell (*d* 1964) (3rd *s* of 1st Baron), and of Ann Margaret Bethell (*née* Barlow, now Don); *S* kinsman, 1967; *m* 1st, 1964, Cecilia Mary (marr. diss. 1971, she *d* 1977), *er d* of Prof. A. M. Honeyman; two *s*; 2nd, 1992, Bryony Lea Morgan, *e d* of Brian Griffiths; one *s*. *Educ:* Harrow; Pembroke Coll., Cambridge (PhD 1987). On editorial staff of Times Literary Supplement, 1962–64; a Script Editor in BBC Radio Drama, 1964–67. A Lord in Waiting (Govt Whip, House of Lords), June 1970–Jan. 1971. MEP (C), 1975–94 (London NW, 1979–94); contested (C) London NW, Eur. Parly elecns, 1994. Chm., Friends of Cyprus, 1981–; Pres., Friends of Gibraltar's Heritage, 1992–. Comdr, Order of Merit (Poland), 1991. *Publications:* Gomulka: his Poland and his Communism, 1969; The War Hitler Won, 1972; The Last Secret, 1974; Russia Besieged, 1977; The Palestine Triangle, 1979; The Great Betrayal, 1984; Spies and Other Secrets, 1994; *translations:* Six Plays, by Slawomir Mrozek, 1967; Elegy to John Donne, by Joseph Brodsky, 1967; Cancer Ward, by A. Solzhenitsyn, 1968; The Love Girl and the Innocent, by A. Solzhenitsyn, 1969; The Ascent of Mount Fuji, by Chingiz Aitmatov, 1975; dramatic works for radio and TV; occasional journalism. *Recreations:* poker, tennis. *Heir:* *s* Hon. James Nicholas Bethell [*b* 1 Oct. 1967. *Educ:* Harrow; Edinburgh Univ.]. *Address:* 73 Sussex Square, W2 2SS. *T:* 0171–402 6877. *Clubs:* Garrick, Pratt's.

BETHELL, Prof. Leslie Michael; Fellow, St Antony's College, Oxford, since 1993; Professor of Latin American History, 1986–92, now Emeritus, and Director, Institute of Latin American Studies, 1987–92, University of London; *b* 12 Feb. 1937; *s* of late Stanley Bethell and of Bessie Bethell (*née* Stoddart); *m* 1961 (marr. diss. 1983); two *s*; partner since 1984, Felicity Guinness, *d* of Sir Andrew Hunter Carnwath, *qv*; one step *s* three step *d*. *Educ:* Cockburn High Sch., Leeds; University Coll. London (BA, PhD). Lectr in History, Univ. of Bristol, 1961–66; Lectr 1966–74, Reader 1974–86, in Hispanic Amer. and Brazilian History, UCL. Visiting Professor: Instituto Universitario de Pesquisas de Rio de Janeiro, 1979; Univ. of California at San Diego, 1985; Wilson Center, Washington, 1986; Univ. of Chicago, 1992–93. Comdr, Order of the Southern Cross (Brazil), 1994. *Publications:* The Abolition of the Brazilian Slave Trade, 1970; (ed) The Cambridge History of Latin America: vols I and II, Colonial Latin America, 1984; vol. III, From Independence to *c* 1870, 1985; vols IV and V, From *c* 1870 to 1930, 1986; vol. VII, Mexico, Central America and the Caribbean since 1930, 1990; vol. VIII, Spanish South America since 1930, 1991; vol. VI, Economy, Society and Politics since 1930, Part 1, Economy and Society, Part 2, Politics and Society, 1994; vol XI, Bibliographical Essays, 1995; vol. X, Ideas, Culture and Society since 1930, 1995; (ed jtly) Latin America between the Second World War and the Cold War 1944–48, 1992; articles and chapters on Latin American history, slave trade and slavery, Brazilian history and politics, Britain and Latin America, and United States and Latin America. *Address:* 2 Keats Grove, Hampstead, NW3 2RT. *T:* and *Fax:* 0171–435 5861; St Antony's College, Oxford OX2 6JF. *T:* Oxford (01865) 274487, *Fax:* (01865) 58680.

BETHELL, Richard Anthony; Lord-Lieutenant of Humberside, since 1983; *b* 22 March 1922; *s* of late William Adrian Bethell and Cicely Bethell (*née* Cotterell); *m* 1945, Lady Jane Pleydell-Bouverie, *d* of 7th Earl of Radnor, KG, KCVO; two *s* two *d*. *Educ:* Eton. JP, ER Yorks, 1950; DL 1975, High Sheriff 1976–77, Vice Lord-Lieutenant 1980–83, Humberside. *Address:* Manor House Farm, Long Riston, Hull HU11 5JR. *T:* Hornsea (01964) 563245.

BETHUNE, Sir Alexander Maitland Sharp, 10th Bt (NS), *cr* 1683; retired; Director: Copytec Services Ltd, 1964–86; Contoura Photocopying Ltd, 1952–86; *b* 28 March 1909; *o s* of Sir Alexander Sharp Bethune, JP, DL, of Blebo, Cupar, Fife, 9th Bt of Scotscraig, and Elisabeth Constance Carnegie (*d* 1935), 3rd *d* of Frederick Lewis Maitland-Heriot of Ramornie, Fife; *S* father, 1917; *m* 1955, Ruth Mary, *d* of J. H. Hayes; one *d*. *Educ:* Eton; Magdalene Coll., Cambridge. *Recreations:* golf, Scottish history, nature. *Address:* 21 Victoria Grove, W8 5RW.

BETHUNE, Hon. Sir (Walter) Angus, Kt 1979; pastoralist; *b* 10 Sept. 1908; *s* of Frank Pogson Bethune and Laura Eileen Bethune; *m* 1936, Alexandra P., *d* of P. A. Pritchard; one *s* one *d*. *Educ:* Hutchin's Sch., Hobart; Launceston Church of England Grammar Sch. Served War, RAAF Air Crew, Middle East, 1940–43. Member, Hamilton Municipal Council, 1936–56, resigned (Dep. Warden, 1955–56). MHA, Wilmot, Tasmania, 1946–75, resigned; Leader of Opposition, 1960–69; Premier and Treasurer, Tasmania, 1969–72. Leader of Liberal Party, 1960–72, resigned. President: Clarendon Children's Homes, 1977–83; St John's Ambulance Brigade (Tasmania), 1979–86. OStJ 1982. *Address:* 553 Churchill Avenue, Sandy Bay, Tas 7005, Australia. *Clubs:* Tasmanian; Naval, Military and Air Force; Royal Autocar of Tasmania.

BETT, Sir Michael, Kt 1995; CBE 1990; MA; First Civil Service Commissioner, since 1995; Chairman, Cellnet, since 1991; non-executive Director, BT, since 1994 (Deputy Chairman, 1991–94); *b* 18 Jan. 1935; *s* of Arthur Bett, OBE and Nina Daniells; *m* 1959, Christine Angela Reid; one *s* two *d*. *Educ:* St Michael's Coll.; Aldenham Sch.; Pembroke Coll., Cambridge. Dir, Industrial Relations, Engrg Employers' Fedn, 1970–72; Personnel Dir, General Electric Co. Ltd, 1972–77; Dir of Personnel, BBC, 1977–81; British Telecom: Bd Mem. for Personnel, 1981–84; Corporate Dir, Personnel and Corporate Services, 1984–85; Man. Dir Local (Inland) Communications Services, 1985–87; Man. Dir, UK Communications, 1987–88; Man. Dir, British Telecom UK, 1988–91; Vice-Chm., 1990–91. Chm., Workhouse Ltd; Dir, Compel Gp plc. Chairman: Nurses Pay Rev. Body, 1990–95; Social Security Adv. Cttee, 1993–95; Armed Forces Indep. Review on Manpower, 1994–95; Member: Pay Bd, 1973–74; Training Levy Exemption Referee, 1975–82; Civil Service Arbitration Tribunal, 1977–83; Cttee of Inquiry into UK Prison Services, 1978–79; Cttee of Inquiry into Water Service Dispute, 1983; NHS Management Inquiry, 1983; Armed Forces Pay Review Body, 1983–87; Civil Service Coll. Adv. Council, 1983–88; Trng Commn (formerly MSC), 1985–89; Nat. Council, TEC, 1994–95. Mem. Council, Cranfield Inst. of Technology, 1982–87; Pro-Chancellor, Aston Univ., 1993–. Chairman: Bromley CABx, 1985–93; SCF, 1993–. Chm. of Govs, Cranbrook Sch. Dir, English Shakespeare Co., 1988–95. CIPD (Pres., 1993–96); CIMgt; FRSA. Hon. Col, 81 Signal Sqn (Vols), RCS, 1990–. DBA (*hc*): IMCB, 1986; CNAA/Liverpool Poly., 1991. *Recreations:* television and radio, theatre, music, cooking, gardening. *Address:* Office of the Civil Service Commissioners, Horse Guards Road, SW1P 3AL.

BETTRIDGE, Brig. John Bryan, CBE 1983; Principal, Emergency Planning College (formerly Civil Defence College), 1984–93; *b* 16 Aug. 1932; *s* of Henry George Bettridge and Dorothy Bettridge; *m* 1959, one *s* one *d*. *Educ:* Eastbourne Grammar School. Commissioned RA, 1951; regimental duty, 3 RHA and 52 Locating Regt, 1952–59; Instructor, RMA Sandhurst, 1959–61; Student, Staff Coll., Camberley, 1962; War Office, 1964–66; Bty Comd, 1 RHA, 1968–70; Comd, 3 RHA, 1973–75, Hong Kong; Chief Instructor, Tactics, RSA, 1976; Comd RA 2 Div., 1977–78; RCDS 1979; Dep. Comdt, Staff Coll., 1980–82; Comdt, RSA Larkhill, 1983–84. *Recreations:* golf, carpentry. *Address:* Cherry Garth, Main Street, Bishopthorpe, York YO2 1RB. *T:* York (01904) 704270.

BETTS, Prof. Alan Osborn, PhD, MA, BSc, MRCVS; education management consultant, since 1989; Principal and Dean, The Royal Veterinary College, University of London, 1970–89, now Emeritus Professor; *b* 11 March 1927; *s* of late A. O. and D. S. A. Betts; *m* 1st, 1952, Joan M. Battersby; one *s* one *d*; 2nd, 1990, Jane M. Jones. *Educ:* Royal Veterinary Coll.; Magdalene Coll., Cambridge. Asst in Gen. Practice, 1949; Animal Health Trust Research Scholar, 1950–52; Demonstrator, Univ. of Cambridge, 1952–56; Commonwealth Fund Fellow, Cornell Univ., USA, 1955–56; University Lectr, Cambridge, 1956–64; Prof. of Veterinary Microbiology and Parasitology, Univ. of London, 1964–70. Leverhulme Vis. Fellow, Graduate Sch. of Admin, Univ. of Calif, Davis, 1982. Vice-Chm., 1976–88, Acting Chm., 1989, Governing Body of Wye Coll.; University of London: Dep. Vice-Chancellor, 1984–88; Chm., Collegiate Council, 1981–84; Member: Jt Planning Cttee, 1981–88; Univ. Court, 1983–88. OFSTED Lay Inspector, 1993–. Treasurer: BVA, 1967–70; RCVS, 1978–81; Pres., Vet. Res. Club, 1984–85. Member: Brit. Pharmacopoeia Commn, 1978–93; EC Adv. Cttee on Veterinary Trng, 1980–90 (Chm., Working Party, 1984–90); Bucks FHSA, 1992–; Bucks Health Bd, 1995–. Mem. Council, Imperial Cancer Research Fund, 1988–; Sec./Treas., Foundn for Internat. Exchange of Scientific and Cultural Information by Telecommunications, 1988–89. Trustee: Hunterian Mus., RCSE, 1990–; Eastman Dental Res. Foundn, 1994–. Dalrymple-Champneys Cup and Medal of BVA, 1978; Faculty Medal, Vet. Faculty, Univ. of Munich, 1985. *Publications:* Viral and Rickettsial Infections of Animals, 1967; papers in microbiological, veterinary and management jls. *Recreations:* travel, gliding. *Address:* Lower Boycott, Stowe, Buckingham MK18 5JZ. *T:* and *Fax:* Buckingham (01280) 813287. *Club:* Athenæum.

BETTS, Air Vice-Marshal (Charles) Stephen, CBE 1963; MA; Head of Control and Inspection Division, Agency for the Control of Armaments, WEU, Paris, 1974–84; *b* 8 April 1919; *s* of H. C. Betts, Nuneaton; *m* 1st, 1943, Pauline Mary (deceased), *d* of Lt-Col P. Heath; two *d*; 2nd, 1964, Margaret Doreen (*d* 1993), *d* of Col W. H. Young, DSO. *Educ:* King Edward's Sch., Nuneaton; Sidney Sussex Coll., Cambridge. Joined RAF 1941; Air Cdre 1966; Asst Comdt (Eng.), RAF Coll., Cranwell, 1971–72; Air Vice-Marshal 1972; AOC No 24 Group, RAF, 1972–73, retired 1974. *Recreations:* travel, music. *Address:* Cranford, Weston Road, Bath BA1 2XX. *T:* Bath (01225) 310995. *Club:* Royal Air Force.

BETTS, Charles Valentine, FEng 1991, FRINA; Director General Submarines, and Deputy Controller of the Navy, since 1994; Head, Royal Corps of Naval Constructors, since 1992; *b* 10 Jan. 1942; *s* of Harold Blair Betts and late Mary Ellis Betts (*née* France); *m* 1965, Patricia Joyce Bennett; two *s*. *Educ:* St Catharine's Coll., Cambridge (BA Hons, MA Mech. Scis); Royal Naval Coll., Greenwich (Prof. Cert., Naval Arch.); Univ. of London (MPhil Naval Arch.). CEng. Asst Constructor, MoD, 1966–71; Lectr in Naval

Arch., UCL, 1971–74; Constructor, HM Dockyard, Portsmouth, 1974–77; Constructor and Chief Constructor, MoD, Bath, 1977–83; Chief Constructor, MoD, London, 1983–85; Prof. of Naval Arch., UCL, 1985–89; Dir, Surface Ships B, MoD, Bath, 1989–92; Dir Gen., Surface Ships, MoD, 1992–94. FRSA. *Publications:* (jtly) The Marine Technology Reference Book, 1990; papers in professional jls. *Recreations:* cruising under sail, listening to music, patiently waiting to be a curate's husband. *Address:* Ministry of Defence, Foxhill, Bath BA1 5AB. *T:* Bath (0225) 882374, *Fax:* (0225) 883599. *Club:* Royal Naval Sailing Association.

BETTS, Clive James Charles; MP (Lab) Sheffield Attercliffe, since 1992; *b* 13 Jan. 1950; *s* of late Harold and Nellie Betts. *Educ:* Longley Sch., Sheffield; King Edward VII Sch., Sheffield; Pembroke Coll., Cambridge (BA Econ). Sheffield City Council: Councillor (Lab), 1976–92; Chm., Housing Cttee, 1980–86; Chm., Finance Cttee, 1986–88; Dep. Leader, 1986–87; Leader, 1987–92. Chm., S Yorks Pension Authority, 1989–92; Dep. Chm., AMA, 1988–91 (Chm., Housing Cttee, 1985–89). Sec., Labour's Treasury Deptl Cttee, 1995–; Labour Ldr's Campaign Team, 1995–. *Recreations:* Sheffield Wednesday FC, cricket, squash, walking, real ale. *Address:* House of Commons, SW1A 0AA.

BETTS, Lily Edna Minerva, (Mrs John Betts); *see* Mackie, L. E. M.

BETTS, Rt. Rev. Stanley Woodley, CBE 1967; *b* 23 March 1912; *yr s* of Hubert Woodley and Lillian Esther Betts. *Educ:* Perse Sch.; Jesus Coll., Cambridge (MA 1937); Ridley Hall, Cambridge. Curate of St Paul's Cheltenham, 1935–38; Chaplain, RAF, 1938–47 (despatches); Sen. Chaplain of BAFO, Germany, 1946–47; Comdt, RAF Chaplains' Sch., Dowdeswell Court, 1947; Chaplain, Clare Coll., Cambridge, 1947–49; Chaplain, Cambridge Pastorate, 1947–56; Proctor in Convocation, 1952–59; Vicar of Holy Trinity Cambridge, 1949–56; Exam. Chaplain to Bishop of Southwell, 1947–56; Select Preacher to University of Cambridge, 1955; Suffragan Bishop of Maidstone, 1956–66; Archbishop of Canterbury's Episcopal Representative with the three Armed Forces, 1956–66; Dean of Rochester, 1966–77. Chm., Bd of the Church Army, 1970–80; Vice-President: Lee Abbey, 1977–; Wadhurst Coll., 1984– (Chm. Council 1976–84). *Address:* 2 King's Houses, Old Pevensey, Sussex BN24 5JR. *T:* Eastbourne (01323) 762421. *Club:* National.

BETTS, Stephen; *see* Betts, C. S.

BEVAN, (Andrew) David Gilroy; Principal, A. Gilroy Bevan, Incorporated Valuers & Surveyors; *b* 10 April 1928; *s* of Rev. Thomas John Bevan and Norah Gilroy Bevan; *m* 1967, Cynthia Ann Villiers Boulstridge; one *s* three *d*. *Educ:* Woodrough's Sch., Moseley; King Edward VI Sch., Birmingham. Served on Birmingham City Council and later W Midlands County Council, 1959–81; past Mem., Finance and Gen. Purposes Cttee, and Policy and Priorities Cttee; past Chm., City Transport Cttee, W Midlands PTA and Transport and Highways Cttee. MP (C) Birmingham, Yardley, 1979–92; contested same seat 1992. Jt Chm., Parly Road Passenger Transport Cttee, 1987–92; former Member, House of Commons Committees: Select Cttee on Transport, 1983–92; All Party Leisure and Recreation Industry (Jt Chm., 1979–92); Urban Affairs and New Towns (Jt Hon. Sec., 1980–87; Vice Chm., 1987–92); Tourism (Chm., 1984–92); Cdre, H of C Yacht Club, 1989. FIAA&S 1962 (Past Chm., W Midlands Br.); FRVA 1971; FSVA 1968 (Past Chm., W Midlands Br.); FFB 1972; FCIA 1954; MRSH 1957. *Recreations:* gardening, walking. *Address:* The Cottage, 12 Wentworth Road, Four Oaks Park, Sutton Coldfield, West Midlands B74 2SG. *T:* (home) 0121–308 3292; (business) 0121–308 6319. *Club:* Carlton.

See also P. G. Bevan.

BEVAN, Rear-Adm. Christopher Martin, CB 1978; Under Treasurer Gray's Inn, 1980–89; *b* London, 22 Jan. 1923; *s* of Humphrey C. Bevan and Mary F. Bevan (*née* Mackenzie); *m* 1948, Patricia C. Bedford; one *s* three *d*. *Educ:* Stowe Sch., Bucks; Victoria Univ., Wellington, NZ. Trooper in Canterbury Yeoman Cavalry (NZ Mounted Rifles), 1941; joined RN as Ord. Seaman, 1942; served remainder of 1939–45 war, Mediterranean and N Atlantic; commissioned 1943; Comdr 1958; Captain 1967; Supt Weapons and Radio, Dockyard Dept, MoD (Navy), 1967–70; Asst Dir, Weapons Equipment (Surface), later, Captain Surface Weapons Acceptance, Weapons Dept, MoD (Navy), 1970–73; Dir, Naval Officer Appts (Engrs), 1973–76; ADC to the Queen, 1976; Rear-Adm. 1976; Flag Officer Medway and Port Adm. Chatham, 1976–78. *Recreations:* photography, theatre, music, travel. *Address:* c/o Messrs C. Hoare and Co., 37 Fleet Street, EC4P 4DQ. *Clubs:* Boodle's, Hurlingham.

BEVAN, David Gilroy; *see* Bevan, A. D. G.

BEVAN, (Edward) Julian; QC 1991; *b* 23 Oct. 1940; *m* 1966, Bronwen Mary Windsor Lewis; two *s* two *d*. *Educ:* Eton. Called to the Bar, Gray's Inn, 1962, Bencher, 1989; Standing Counsel for the Inland Revenue, 1974; Jun. Treasury Counsel, 1977, Sen. Treasury Counsel, 1985, First Sen. Treasury Counsel, 1989–91, Central Criminal Court. *Address:* 30 Halsey Street, SW3 2PT. *T:* 0171–584 1316. *Club:* Garrick.

BEVAN, Prof. Hugh Keith; JP; Professor of Law, University of Hull, 1969–89; *b* 8 Oct. 1922; *s* of Thomas Edward Bevan and Marjorie Avril Bevan (*née* Trick); *m* 1950, Mary Harris; one *d* (one *s* decd). *Educ:* Neath Grammar Sch.; University Coll. of Wales, Aberystwyth. LLB 1949, LLM 1966. Called to the Bar, Middle Temple, 1959. Served RA, 1943–46. University of Hull: Lectr in Law, 1950–61; Sen. Lectr in Law, 1961–69; Pro Vice-Chancellor, 1979–82; Wolfson College, Cambridge: Vis. Fellow, 1986 and 1989–90; Fellow, 1990–92; Hon. Fellow, 1992. Chm., Rent Assessment Cttees, 1982–92. Pres., Soc. of Public Teachers of Law, 1987–88. JP Kingston-upon-Hull, 1972 (Chm. of Bench, 1984–89). *Publications:* Source Book of Family Law (with P. R. H. Webb), 1964; Law Relating to Children, 1973; (with M. L. Parry) The Children Act 1975, 1978; Child Law, 1988; numerous articles. *Recreations:* music, golf. *Address:* Wolfson College, Cambridge CB3 9BB. *T:* (01223) 335900.

BEVAN, John Penry Vaughan; a Recorder, since 1988; Senior Treasury Counsel, Central Criminal Court, since 1989; *b* 7 Sept. 1947; *s* of late Llewellyn Vaughan Bevan and of Hilda Molly Bevan; *m* 1st, 1971, Dinah Nicholson; two *d*; 2nd, 1978, Veronica Aliaga-Kelly; one *s* one *d*. *Educ:* Radley Coll.; Magdalene Coll., Cambridge (BA). Called to the Bar, Middle Temple, 1970. *Recreation:* sailing. *Clubs:* Leander (Henley-on-Thames); Aldeburgh Yacht; Orford Sailing.

BEVAN, John Stuart, OBE 1995; consultant; *b* 19 Nov. 1935; *s* of Frank Oakland and Ruth Mary Bevan; *m* 1960, Patricia Vera Beatrice (*née* Joyce); two *s* two *d*. *Educ:* Eggar's Grammar Sch.; Jesus Coll., Oxford; S Bartholomew's Hosp. Med. Coll. MA, MSc; FInstP. Health Physicist, UK Atomic Energy Authority, 1960–62; Lectr, then Sen. Lectr in Physics, Polytechnic of the South Bank (previously Borough Polytechnic), 1962–73; Inner London Education Authority: Asst Educn Officer, then Sen. Asst Educn Officer, 1973–76; Dep. Educn Officer, 1977–79; Dir of Educn, 1979–82; Sec., NAB, 1982–88; Dir of Educn Services, London Residuary Body, 1989–92; Chief Exec., ACFHE, 1992–93; Sec., Assoc. for Colls, 1993–94. Former Member, National Executive Committees: Nat. Union of Teachers; Assoc. of Teachers in Technical Instns (Pres., 1972–73). Scout Association: Asst, later Dep. Comr, Kent, 1982–; Chm., Nat. Activities Bd, 1988–93; Nat. Comr for Activities, 1994–. Hon. Fellow: S Bank Univ. (formerly Poly of the S Bank), 1987; Westminster Coll., Oxford, 1990. DUniv Surrey, 1990; Hon. LLD CNAA, 1992. *Publications:* occasional papers in the educnl press. *Recreations:* scouting, mountaineering. *Address:* 4 Woodland Way, Bidborough, Tunbridge Wells, Kent TN4 0UX. *T:* Tunbridge Wells (01892) 527461.

BEVAN, Julian; *see* Bevan, E. J.

BEVAN, Sir Martyn Evan E.; *see* Evans-Bevan.

BEVAN, Prof. Michael John, PhD; FRS 1991; Investigator, Howard Hughes Medical Institute, and Professor, Department of Immunology, University of Washington, Seattle, since 1990; *b* 20 Sept. 1945; *s* of Thomas John Bevan and Doris Mary (*née* Prior); *m* 1985, Pamela Jean Fink; two *s*. *Educ:* Pontypridd Boys' Grammar Sch.; University Coll. London (BSc Zool. 1967; MSc Biochem. 1968); Nat. Inst. for Med. Research, London (PhD 1972). Postdoctoral Fellow, Salk Inst. for Biol Studies, La Jolla, Calif., 1973–76, Asst Res. Prof., 1976–77; Asst, then Associate, Prof., Dept. of Biology, MIT, 1977–82; Associate, then Member, Dept of Immunology, Scripps Res. Inst., La Jolla, Calif., 1982–90. *Publications:* numerous original res. pubns in scientific jls incl. Nature, Science, Cell, Jl Exptl Medicine. *Recreation:* hiking. *Address:* Howard Hughes Medical Institute, Department of Immunology, University of Washington, SL–15, Seattle, WA 98195, USA. *T:* (206) 6853610.

BEVAN, Dr Michael Webster; Head, Department of Molecular Genetics, John Innes Centre, Biotechnical and Biological Sciences Research Council; *b* 5 June 1952; *s* of John Vernon Bevan and Sue (*née* Webster); *m* 1982, Jane Foster; two *s*. *Educ:* Univ. of Auckland (BSc 1973; Msc Hons 1974); Univ. of Cambridge (PhD 1979). Res. Fellow, Washington Univ., St Louis, Mo, 1980; Higher Scientific Officer, 1982–84, SSO, 1984–86, PSO, 1986–88, Plant Breeding Inst., Cambridge; Hd, Dept of Molecular Genetics, Inst. of Plant Sci. Res., AFRC, subseq. John Innes Centre, BBSRC, 1988–. Rank Prize, Rank Foundn, 1986. *Publications:* contrib. numerous chapters in books and articles to learned jls. *Recreations:* reading modern literature, riding, ski-ing, walking. *Address:* 329 Unthank Road, Norwich NR4 7QA. *T:* Norwich (01603) 504181.

BEVAN, Nicolas, CB 1991; Speaker's Secretary, House of Commons, since 1993; *b* 8 March 1942; *s* of late Roger Bevan, BM, and Diana Mary Bevan (*née* Freeman); *m* 1982, Helen Christine, *d* of N. A. Berry. *Educ:* Westminster Sch.; Corpus Christi Coll., Oxford (MA LitHum). Ministry of Defence: Asst Principal, 1964; Principal, 1969; Private Sec. to Chief of Air Staff, 1970–73; Cabinet Office, 1973–75; Asst Sec., 1976; RCDS 1981; Asst Under Sec. of State, 1985; Under Sec., Cabinet Office, 1992–93. *Recreation:* gardening. *Address:* House of Commons, SW1A 0AA.

BEVAN, Prof. Peter Gilroy, CBE 1983; MB, ChB; FRCS; Consultant Surgeon, Dudley Road Hospital, Birmingham, 1958–87; Professor of Surgery and Postgraduate Medical Education, University of Birmingham, 1981–87, now Emeritus Professor; *b* 13 Dec. 1922; *s* of Rev. Thomas John Bevan and Norah (*née* Gilroy); *m* 1st, 1949, Patricia Joan (*née* Laurie) (*d* 1985); one *s* one *d*; 2nd, 1990, Beryl Margaret (*née* Perry). *Educ:* King Edward VI High Sch., Birmingham; Univ. of Birmingham Medical Sch. (MB, ChB 1946; ChM 1958). LRCP MRCS 1946, FRSC 1952; Hon. FRCSI 1984. Served RAMC, BAOR, 1947–49 (Captain). Demonstrator in Anatomy, Univ. of Birmingham, 1949–51; Resident Surgical Officer, Birmingham Children's Hosp., 1954–55; Lectr in Surgery and Sen. Surgical Registrar, Queen Elizabeth Hosp., Birmingham, 1954–58; WHO Vis. Prof. of Surgery to Burma, 1969; Director, Board of Graduate Clinical Studies, Univ. of Birmingham, 1978–87; Pres., Birmingham Medical Inst., 1994– (Postgrad. Tutor, 1989–94). Royal College of Surgeons: Mem. Council, 1971–83; Vice-Pres., 1980–82; Dir, Overseas Doctors Training Scheme Cttee, 1986–90. Founder Chm., W Midlands Oncology Assoc., 1974–79; Vice-Pres., Brit. Assoc. of Surgical Oncology, 1975–78; President: Pancreatic Soc. of GB, 1977; British Inst. of Surgical Technologists, 1980–; Assoc. of Surgeons of GB and Ireland, 1984–85 (Fellow, 1960–; Mem. Council, 1975–85); W Midlands Surgical Soc., 1986; Nat. Assoc. of Theatre Nurses, 1992–94. EEC: UK representative: on Monospecialist Section of Surgery, 1975–84; on Adv. Cttee on Medical Trng, 1980–85. Civil Consultant Advr in Gen. Surgery to RN, 1973–84; Med. Adviser, Midlands Div., Ileostomy Assoc., 1976–87. Chm., Adv. Cttee of Deans, 1986–88. Chairman: Steering Gp on Operating Theatres, Dept of Health, 1988–89; Jt Planning Adv. Cttee, Dept of Health, 1990–; Medical Mem., Pensions Appeal Tribunals, 1987–89; Mem., Medical Appeals Tribunal, 1989–. Former Member: Jt Planning Adv. Cttee; Central Manpower Cttee; Jt Consultants Cttee; Council for Postgraduate Med. Educn. *Publications:* Reconstructive Procedures in Surgery, 1982; Handbook of General Surgery, 1992; various surgical papers in BMJ, Brit. Jl Surgery, Lancet, Annals of RCS. *Recreations:* inland waterways, golf, photography, music, gardening. *Address:* 10 Russell Road, Moseley, Birmingham B13 8RD. *T:* 0121–449 3055. *Clubs:* Royal Navy Medical; Edgbaston Golf (Birmingham).

See also A. D. G. Bevan.

BEVAN, Rev. Canon Richard Justin William, PhD, ThD; Chaplain to The Queen, 1986–92; Canon Emeritus, Carlisle Cathedral, since 1989 (Canon Residentiary, Carlisle Cathedral, 1982–89, Treasurer and Librarian, 1982–89, Vice-Dean, 1987–89); *b* 21 April 1922; *s* of Rev. Richard Bevan, Vicar of St Harmon, Radnorshire and Margaret Bevan; *m* 1948, Sheila Rosemary Barrow, of Fazakerley, Liverpool; three *s* one *d* (and one *s* decd). *Educ:* St Edmund's Sch., Canterbury; St Augustine's Coll., Canterbury; Lichfield Theol Coll.; St Chad's Coll., Univ. of Durham (Theol. Prizeman; BA, LTh). ThD: Geneva Theol. Coll., 1972; Greenwich Univ., USA, 1990; PhD Columbia Pacific Univ., 1980. Ordained Deacon, Lichfield Cathedral, 1945, priest, 1946; Asst Curate, Stoke-on-Trent, 1945–49; Chaplain, Aberlour Orphanage and licence to officiate, dio. of Moray, Ross and Caithness, 1949–51; Asst Master, Burnley Tech. High Sch., 1951–60; Asst Curate, Church Kirk, 1951–56, Whalley, 1956–60; Rector, St Mary-le-Bow, Durham and Chaplain to Durham Univ., 1960; Vicar, St Oswald's United Benefice, 1964–74; Convener of Chaplains, Univ of Durham, 1964–74; Rector of Grasmere, 1974–82. Examg Chaplain to Bishop of Carlisle, 1970–; Chaplain, Durham Girls' High Sch., 1966–74; Vice-Pres., Friends of St Chad's Coll., 1990– (Governor, St Chad's Coll., 1969–89). First Pres., and Founder Mem., Grasmere Village Soc., 1976–78; Dove Cottage Local Cttee, 1974–82. *Publications:* (ed) Steps to Christian Understanding, 1959; (ed) The Churches and Christian Unity, 1964; (ed) Durham Sermons, 1964; Unfurl the Flame (poetry), 1980; A Twig of Evidence: does belief in God make sense?, 1986; articles on ethics and culture. *Recreations:* poetry reading, musical appreciation, train spotting. *Address:* Beck Cottage, West End, Burgh-by-Sands, Carlisle CA5 6BT. *T:* Burgh-by-Sands (01228) 576781. *Club:* Victory Services.

BEVAN, Richard Thomas, MD; FRCP; Chief Medical Officer, Welsh Office, 1965–77, retired; *b* 13 Jan. 1914; *s* of T. Bevan, Bridgend; *m* 1940, Dr Beryl Bevan (*née* Badham) (*d* 1986); two *s* one *d*. *Educ:* Welsh Nat. Sch. of Medicine. MB, BCh 1939; DPH 1941; MD 1955; FRCP; FFCM. Resident Medical Officer, St David's Hosp., Cardiff; RAF, 1941–46; Lecturer, Welsh Nat. Sch. of Medicine, 1946–68; Deputy County MO,

Glamorgan CC, 1948–62. QHP 1974–77. *Address:* 47 Chelveston Crescent, Solihull, W Midlands B91 3YH. *T:* 0121–704 9890.

BEVAN, Sir Timothy (Hugh), Kt 1984; Deputy Chairman, Foreign & Colonial Investment Trust plc, since 1993 (Director, since 1988); *b* 24 May 1927; *y s* of late Hugh Bevan and Pleasance (*née* Scrutton); *m* 1952, Pamela, *e d* of late Norman and Margaret Smith; two *s* two *d*. *Educ:* Eton. Lieut Welsh Guards. Called to Bar, 1950. Joined Barclays Bank Ltd, 1950; Dir, 1966–93; Vice-Chm., 1968–73; Dep. Chm., 1973–81; Chm., 1981–87. Dir, BET, 1987–92 (Chm., 1988–91). Chm., Cttee of London Clearing Bankers, 1983–85. Mem., NEDC, 1986–87. *Recreations:* sailing, gardening. *Address:* c/o Barclays Bank, 54 Lombard Street, EC3V 9EX. *Clubs:* Cavalry and Guards, Royal Ocean Racing; Royal Yacht Squadron.

BEVAN, Rear-Adm. Timothy Michael, CB 1986; Assistant Chief of the Defence Staff (Intelligence), 1984–87, retired; Deputy Director, ACRE, The Rural Communities Charity, since 1990; *b* 7 April 1931; *s* of Thomas Richard and Margaret Richmond Bevan; *m* 1970, Sarah Knight; three *s*. *Educ:* Eton College. psc(n), jssc. Entered RN, 1949; commanded: HMS Decoy, 1966; HMS Caprice, 1967–68; HMS Minerva, 1971–72; HMS Ariadne, 1976–78; HMS Ariadne, and Captain of 8th Frigate Sqdn, 1980–82; Britannia Royal Naval Coll., 1982–84.

BEVAN, Walter Harold, CBE 1977; FCIS; Chairman, Gateshead District Health Authority (formerly of Gateshead Area Health Authority), 1977–84; *b* 22 May 1916; *s* of late Walter Bevan and Sarah (*née* Grainger); *m* 1958, Patricia Edna Sadler, *d* of late Sir Sadler Forster, CBE, DCL; twin *s* and *d*. *Educ:* Gateshead Sch. FCIS 1961. 5th Bn Royal Northumberland Fusiliers, TA, 1938–42; served War: commissioned RA; Arakan campaign, Burma, with 81st W African Div., 1942–46; 4/5 Bn Royal Northumberland Fusiliers, TA, 1947–52. Asst to Sec., North Eastern Trading Estates Ltd, 1937, Chief Accountant 1956; English Industrial Estates Corporation: Chief Accountant, 1960; Sec., 1966; Finance Dir and Sec., 1973; Chief Exec. and Chm., Management Bd, 1974–79. Governor, Gateshead Technical Coll., 1971–81. *Publications:* articles on industrial estates and distribution of industry. *Recreations:* public and voluntary services, bowling, reading. *Address:* Cornerways, Lyndhurst Grove, Low Fell, Gateshead NE9 6AX. *T:* 0191–487 6827.

BEVERIDGE, Crawford William, CBE 1995; Chief Executive, Scottish Enterprise, since 1991; *b* 3 Nov. 1945; *s* of William Wilson Beveridge and Catherine Crawford Beveridge; *m* 1977, Marguerite DeVoe; one *s* one *d*. *Educ:* Edinburgh Univ. (BSc); Bradford Univ. (MSc). Appts with Hewlett Packard in Scotland, Switzerland, USA, 1968–77; European Personnel Manager, Digital Equipment Corp., 1977–81; Vice-Pres., Human Resources, Analog Devices, 1982–85; Vice-Pres., Corporate Resources, Sun Microsystems, 1985–90. *Recreations:* music, cooking, paperweights. *Address:* (office) 120 Bothwell Street, Glasgow G2 7JP.

BEVERIDGE, Sir Gordon (Smith Grieve), Kt 1994; FRSE; FEng; FIChemE; FRSA; MRIA; President and Vice-Chancellor, The Queen's University of Belfast, since 1986; *b* 28 Nov. 1933; *s* of late Victor Beattie Beveridge and Elizabeth Fairbairn Beveridge (*née* Grieve); *m* 1963, Geertruida Hillegonda Johanna, (Trudy), Bruyn, *d* of late Gerrit Hendrik Bruijn and Johanna (*née* Breyaen); two *s* one *d*. *Educ:* Inverness Royal Academy; Univ. of Glasgow (BSc, 1st Cl. Hons Chem. Engrg); Royal College of Science and Technology, Glasgow (ARCST 1st Cl. Hons Chem. Engrg); Univ. of Edinburgh (PhD). Asst Lectr, Univ. of Edinburgh, 1956–60; post-doctoral Harkness Fellow of Commonwealth Fund, New York, at Univ. of Minnesota, 1960–62; Vis. Prof., Univ. of Texas, 1962–64; Lectr, Univ. of Edinburgh and Heriot-Watt Univ., 1962–67; Sen. Lectr/Reader, Heriot-Watt Univ., 1967–71; Prof. of Chem. Engrg and Head of Dept of Chem. and Process Engrg, Univ. of Strathclyde, Glasgow, 1971–86. Consultant to industry. Institution of Chemical Engineers: Fellow, 1969–; Vice-Pres., 1979–81, 1983–84, Pres., 1984–85; Exec. Cttee, 1981–86; Hon. Librarian, 1977–84; Mem., Council, 1975–76, 1977–; Scottish Branch: Sec., 1963–71; Vice-Chm., 1972–74; Chm., 1974–76. Society of Chemical Industry, London: Mem. Council, 1978–88; Vice-Pres., 1985–88; Chm. of W of Scotland Section, 1978–86. Council of Engineering Institutions (Scotland): Member, 1977–82; Vice-Chm., 1979–80; Chm., 1980–81; Organiser of 1981 Exhibn, Engineering in the '80s, Edinburgh. Council for National Academic Awards: Chemical, Instrumentation and Systems Engrg Bd, 1976–81: Vice-Chm., 1979–81; Engineering Bd, 1981–84. Science and Engineering Research Council (formerly Science Research Council), various committees: 1973–76, 1980–83; Mem., Engrg Bd; Chm., Process Engrg Cttee (formerly Chemical Engrg Cttee), 1983–86. Engineering Council: Mem., 1981–95; Vice-Chm., 1984–85; Chm., Standing Cttee for Professional Instns, 1982–88; Chm., Standing Cttee for Regions and Assembly, 1989–95; Mem., Regl Orgn in NI, 1987–. NEDO: Mem., Chemicals EDC, 1983–88; Chm., Petrochemicals Sector Wkg Gp, 1983–87. Chairman: Local Organising Cttee, BAAS, Belfast, 1986–87; Organising Cttee of Celebration of Armagh and St Patrick 1994–95, 1992–; Dep. Chm., Armagh Observatory Bicentenary Cttee, 1990–91; Member: Engrg and Technol. Adv. Cttee, 1986–92, CICHE, 1992–, British Council; NI Partnership, 1987–; Educnl Adv. Cttee, Ulster TV, 1986–93; Adv. Council, ESDU Internat. Ltd, 1983–88 (Chm., 1983–86); Council, OU, 1988–93; Newcomen Soc., 1989–; Smeatonian Soc. of Civil Engrs, 1991–; European Sci. and Technol. Assembly, EC, 1994–; Adv. Council, Ireland's Historic Science Centre, 1995–. Royal Academy of Engineering (formerly Fellowship of Engineering): FEng 1984; Mem. Council, 1991–94, Standing Cttee for Engrg, 1991–94; Hon. Sec., Process Engrg, 1991–94. Chm., Navan Fort Initiative Gp, 1987–89; Director: NI Economic Res. Centre, 1987–95; Navan at Armagh, 1989– (Chm., 1989–); Navan at Armagh Management Ltd, 1990– (Chm., 1990–); Queen's University Bookbinding Ltd, 1989– (Chm., 1989–); QUBIS Ltd, 1986– (Chm., 1991–); The University Book Shop Ltd, 1986–; Textflow Services Ltd, 1992– (Chm., 1992–); Opera NI, 1992–; NI Quality Centre, 1993–; Lennoxvale Developments Ltd, 1993–; Cremer and Warner Ltd, 1984–91 (Chm., 1985–90). President: Retirement Assoc., NI, 1986–; Queen's Univ. Assoc., 1989–90; Queen's Univ. Assoc. London, 1994–95; Patron: Abercorn Trust, 1986–; Linenhall Liby Appeal, 1989; John Whyte Trust Fund, 1990–; NI Business Achievement Award Trust, 1993– (Vice Patron, 1990–92); NI Children's Holiday Scheme, 1994–95. CIMgt (CBIM 1990). FRSA 1987; MRIA 1989. Hon. LLD: Dublin, 1992; NUI, 1995; Hon. DSc: Ulster, 1994; Connecticut Coll., 1995; Queen's Univ., Kingston, 1995; Hon. Dr, Lodz Tech. Univ., Poland, 1995. Associate Editor, Computers and Chemical Engineering, 1974–87. *Publications:* Optimization - theory and practice (with R. S. Schechter), 1970; multiple pubns in learned jls. *Recreations:* Irish, Scottish and Dutch history, Marlburian war-games, model railway system design, family golf, walking, the engineering profession. *Address:* The Office of the Vice-Chancellor, The Queen's University of Belfast, Belfast, Northern Ireland BT7 1NN. *T:* Belfast (01232) 245133, *Fax:* (01232) 330808. *Club:* Caledonian.

BEVERIDGE, John Caldwell, QC 1979; Recorder, Western Circuit, since 1975; *b* 26 Sept. 1937; *s* of William Ian Beardmore Beveridge, *qv*; *m* 1st, 1972, Frances Ann Clunes Grant Martineau (marr. diss. 1988); 2nd, 1989, Lilian Moira Weston Adamson. *Educ:* Jesus Coll., Cambridge (MA, LLB). Called to the Bar, Inner Temple, 1963, Bencher, 1985; Western Circuit; called to the Bar, NSW, 1975, QC (NSW), 1980. Partner, Beveridge & Forwood, Zurich. Conservative Mem., Westminster City Council, 1968–72. Freeman, City of London. Jt Master, Westmeath Foxhounds, 1976–79. *Recreations:* hunting, shooting, travelling. *Address:* Bathealton Court, Taunton, Somerset TA4 2AJ. *T:* Wiveliscombe (01984) 624611; 23b Lennox Gardens, SW1X 0DE. *T:* 0171–584 9898. *Clubs:* Brooks's, Pratt's, Turf, Beefsteak.

BEVERIDGE, William Ian Beardmore, MA, ScD Cantab; DVSc Sydney; Professor of Animal Pathology, Cambridge, 1947–75; Emeritus Fellow of Jesus College; *b* 1908; *s* of J. W. C. and Ada Beveridge; *m* 1935, Patricia, *d* of Rev. E. C. Thomson; one *s*. *Educ:* Cranbrook Sch., Sydney; St Paul's Coll., University of Sydney. ScD Cantab 1974. Research bacteriologist, McMaster Animal Health Laboratory, Sydney, 1931–37; Commonwealth Fund Service Fellow at Rockefeller Inst. and at Washington, 1938–39; Walter and Eliza Hall Inst. for Medical Research, Melbourne, 1941–46; Visiting Worker, Pasteur Inst., Paris, 1946–47; Vis. Prof., Ohio State Univ., 1953; Guest Lectr, Norwegian Veterinary Sch., 1955; first Wesley W. Spink Lectr on Comparative Medicine, Minnesota, 1971. Consultant: WHO, Geneva, 1964–79; Bureau of Animal Health, Canberra, 1979–84; Vis. Fellow, John Curtin Sch. of Med. Res., ANU, Canberra, 1979–84, Fellow, University House, 1980–85. Chm. Permanent Cttee of the World Veterinary Assoc., 1957–75. DVM (*hc*) Hanover, 1963; Hon. Associate RCVS, 1963; Life Fellow, Aust. Vet. Assoc., 1963; Hon. Member: British Veterinary Assoc., 1970; Amer. Vet. Med. Assoc., 1973; World Veterinary Congresses, 1975; Univ. House, Canberra, 1986; Hon. Foreign Mem., Académie Royale de Médicine de Belgique, 1970; Foundation Fellow, Aust. Coll. Vet. Scientists, 1971; Mem., German Acad. for Scientific Research, Leopoldina, 1974; Hon. Dip., Hungarian Microbiological Assoc., Budapest, 1976. Karl F. Meyer Goldheaded Cane Award, 1971; Gamgee Gold Medal, World Vet. Assoc., 1975; Medal of Honour, French Nat. Cttee of World Vet. Assoc., 1976. *Publications:* The Art of Scientific Investigation, 1950; Frontiers in Comparative Medicine, 1972; Influenza: the last great plague, 1977; Seeds of Discovery, 1980; Viral Diseases of Farm Livestock, 1981; Bacterial Diseases of Cattle, Sheep and Goats, 1983; articles on infectious diseases of man and domestic animals and comparative medicine, in scientific jls. *Recreations:* bush-walking, skiing. *Address:* 5 Bellevue Road, Wentworth Falls, Blue Mountains, NSW 2782, Australia. *T:* (47) 571606.

See also J. C. Beveridge.

BEVERLEY, Bishop Suffragan of, since 1994; **Rt Rev. John Scott Gaisford;** Episcopal Visitor for the Province of York, since 1994; *b* 7 Oct. 1934; *s* of Joseph and Margaret Thompson Gaisford; *m* 1962, Gillian Maclean; one *s* one *d*. *Educ:* Univ. of Durham (Exhibnr, St Chad's Coll., Durham; BA Hons Theol. 1959, DipTh with Distinction 1960, MA 1976). Deacon 1960, priest 1961, Manchester; Assistant Curate: S Hilda, Audenshaw, 1960–62; S Michael, Bramhall, 1962–65; Vicar, S Andrew, Crewe, 1965–86; RD of Nantwich, 1974–85; Hon. Canon of Chester Cathedral, 1980–86; Archdeacon of Macclesfield, 1986–94. Proctor in Convocation, Mem. Gen. Synod, 1975–; Church Commissioner, 1986–94; Member: Church of England Pensions Bd, 1982–; Churches Conservation Trust (formerly Redundant Churches Fund), 1989–. *Recreations:* fell walking, caravanning. *Address:* 3 North Lane, Roundhay, Leeds LS8 2QJ. *T:* Leeds (0113) 273 2003, *Fax:* (0113) 273 3002.

BEVERLEY, Lt-Gen. Sir Henry (York La Roche), KCB 1991; OBE 1979; Commandant General Royal Marines, 1990–93; Director-General, Winston Churchill Memorial Trust, since 1993; *b* 25 Oct. 1935; *s* of Vice-Adm. Sir York Beverley, KBE, CB, and Lady Beverley; *m* 1963, Sally Anne Maclean; two *d*. *Educ:* Wellington College. DS Staff Coll., 1976–78; CO 42 Cdo RM, 1978–80; Comdt CTC RM, 1980–82; Director RM Personnel, MoD, 1983–84; Comd 3 Cdo Bde RM, 1984–86; Maj.-Gen. Trng and Reserve Forces RM, 1986–88; CoS to CGRM, 1988–90. *Recreations:* golf, skiing. *Club:* Royal Thames Yacht.

BEVINGTON, Eric Raymond, CMG 1961; *b* 23 Jan. 1914; *s* of late R. Bevington and N. E. Bevington (*née* Sutton); *m* 1939, Enid Mary Selina (*née* Homer); one *s* one *d*. *Educ:* Monkton Combe Sch.; Loughborough Coll.; Queens' Coll., Cambridge. CEng, MIMechE. Cadet, HM Overseas Service, Gilbert and Ellice Islands, 1937; District Officer, Fiji, 1942; Sec., Commn of Enquiry into Cost of Living Allowances, Nigeria, 1945–46; Admin. Officer Cl I, Fiji, 1950; Asst Col Sec. (Develt), Fiji, 1951; Develt Comr, Brunei, 1954; Financial Sec., Fiji, 1958–61, Development Commissioner, 1962–63; Mem., Executive Council, Fiji, 1958–63; Senior Project Engineer, Wrigh Rain Ltd, 1964–67; Appeals Inspector, Min. of Housing and Local Govt, 1967–70; Sen. Housing and Planning Inspector, DoE, 1970–78. Mem., New Forest DC, 1979–83. *Publication:* The Things We Do For England, 1990. *Recreations:* golf, sailing, zymurgy. *Address:* Holmans Cottage, Bisterne Close, Burley, Hants BH24 4AZ. *T:* Burley (01425) 403316.

BEVINS, Anthony John; Political Editor, The Observer, since 1993; *b* 16 Aug. 1942; *s* of Rt. Hon. John Reginald Bevins, *qv* and Mary Leonora (*née* Jones); *m* 1965, Ruchira Mishtuni (*née* Roy); one *s* one *d*. *Educ:* Liverpool Collegiate Grammar Sch.; LSE (BSc Econ). VSO, 1964–66; Sub-Editor, Liverpool Daily Post & Echo, 1967–69; Liverpool Daily Post: Dep. Chief Sub-Editor, 1969–70; Political Corresp., 1970–73; Political Staff, Sunday Express, 1973; Political Correspondent: The Sun, 1973–76; Daily Mail, 1976–81; The Times, 1981–86; Political Editor, The Independent, 1986–93. Political Reporter of the Year, Granada TV What the Papers Say, 1990; Jt Winner, British Press Awards, Exclusive of the Year, 1993. *Address:* Press Gallery, House of Commons, SW1A 0AA. *T:* 0171–219 4700.

BEVINS, Rt. Hon. John Reginald, PC 1959; *b* 20 Aug. 1908; *e s* of John Milton and Grace Eveline Bevins, Liverpool; *m* 1933, Mary Leonora Jones; three *s*. *Educ:* Dovedale Road and Liverpool Collegiate Schs. Served War of 1939–45; gunner, 1940; Major, RASC, 1944; MEF and Europe. Mem. Liverpool City Council, 1935–50. Contested West Toxteth Div., 1945, and Edge Hill (bye-election), 1947; MP (C) Toxteth Div. of Liverpool, 1950–64; PPS to the Minister of Housing and Local Government, 1951–53; Parliamentary Sec., Ministry of Works, 1953–57, Ministry of Housing and Local Govt, 1957–59; Postmaster-General, 1959–64. *Publication:* The Greasy Pole, 1965. *Address:* 37 Queen's Drive, Liverpool L18 2DT. *T:* 0151–722 8484.

See also A. J. Bevins, K. M. Bevins.

BEVINS, Kenneth Milton, CBE 1973; TD 1951; Director: Royal Insurance plc, 1970–88; Royal Insurance Holdings, 1988–89; *b* 2 Nov. 1918; *yr s* of late John Milton Bevins and Grace Eveline Bevins, Liverpool; *m* 1st, 1940, Joan Harding (*d* 1969); two *d*; 2nd, 1971, Diana B. Sellers, *y d* of late Godfrey J. Sellers, Keighley. *Educ:* Liverpool Collegiate Sch. Joined Royal Insurance Co. Ltd, 1937. Served War, 1939–46: 136 Field Regt, RA, incl. with 14th Army in Burma, 1943–46 (Major). Sec., Royal Insurance Co. Ltd, 1957; Gen. Manager, 1963; Dep. Chief Gen. Manager, 1966; Chief Gen. Manager, 1970–80; Director: Trade Indemnity Co. Ltd, 1970–80 (Chm., 1975–80); Mutual & Federal Insurance Co. Ltd, 1971–80; British Aerospace plc, 1981–87. Dir, Fire Protection Assoc., 1963–77 (Chm., 1966–68). Member: Jt Fire Research Organisation Steering Cttee, 1966–68; Home Secretary's Standing Cttee on Crime Prevention, 1967–73; Exec. Cttee, City Communications Centre, 1976–80; Bd, British Aerospace, 1980–81; Govt Cttee to review structure, functions and status of ECGD, 1983–84. Chm., British Insurance Assoc., 1971–73 (Dep. Chm., 1967–71). *Recreations:* travel, gardening, reading, painting. *Address:* Linton, The Drive, Sevenoaks, Kent TN13 3AF. *T:* Sevenoaks (01732) 456909. *Clubs:* Oriental, Army and Navy.

See also Rt Hon. J. R. Bevins.

BEWES, Rev. Preb. Richard Thomas; Rector, All Souls Church, Langham Place, since 1983; Prebendary of St Paul's Cathedral, since 1988; *b* 1 Dec. 1934; *s* of late Rev. Canon Cecil and Sylvia Bewes; *m* 1964, Elisabeth Ingrid Jaques; two *s* one *d*. *Educ:* Marlborough Sch.; Emmanuel Coll., Cambridge (MA); Ridley Hall, Cambridge. Deacon, 1959; priest, 1960; Curate of Christ Church, Beckenham, 1959–65; Vicar: St Peter's, Harold Wood, 1965–74; Emmanuel, Northwood, 1974–83. *Publications:* God in Ward 12, 1973; Advantage Mr Christian, 1975; Talking about Prayer, 1979; The Pocket Handbook of Christian Truth, 1981; John Wesley's England, 1981; The Church Reaches Out, 1981; The Church Overcomes, 1983; On The Way, 1984; Quest for Truth, 1985; Quest for Life, 1985; The Church Marches On, 1986; When God Surprises, 1986; The Resurrection, 1989; A New Beginning, 1989. *Recreations:* tennis, photography, audio-visual production. *Address:* 2 All Souls Place, W1N 3DB. *T:* 0171–580 6029.

BEWICK, Herbert; retired barrister; *b* 4 April 1911; *s* of late James Dicker and Elizabeth Jane Bewick. *Educ:* Whitehill Secondary Sch., Glasgow; Royal Grammar Sch., Newcastle upon Tyne; St Catharine's Coll., Cambridge. Called to Bar, Gray's Inn, 1935; Recorder of Pontefract, 1961–67; Chm. of Industrial Tribunal (Newcastle upon Tyne), 1967–72; practised in common law, 1972–84. *Address:* Flat 38, Cranlea, 1 Kingston Park Avenue, Kingston Park, Newcastle upon Tyne NE3 2HB.

BEWICKE-COPLEY, family name of **Baron Cromwell.**

BEWLEY, Edward de Beauvoir; Hon. Mr Justice Bewley; Judge of the High Court of Hong Kong, since 1980; *b* 12 March 1931; *s* of Harold de Beauvoir Bewley and Phyllis Frances Cowdy; *m* 1st, 1956, Sheelagh Alice Brown; one *s*; 2nd, 1968, Mary Gwenefer Jones; three *d*. *Educ:* Shrewsbury School; Trinity College, Dublin. BA, LLB; Barrister at Law. Administrative Officer, Northern Rhodesia, 1956–59; English Bar, 1960–61; Resident Magistrate, Nyasaland, 1961–64; Magistrate, Hong Kong, 1964–76, District Judge, 1976–80. *Recreations:* golf, skiing, reading, music. *Address:* 76E Peak Road, The Peak, Hong Kong. *T:* 8496111. *Clubs:* Hong Kong; Royal Irish Yacht (Dun Laoghaire), Royal Hong Kong Golf.

BEWLEY, Thomas Henry, Hon. CBE 1988; MA; MD; FRCP, FRCPI, FRCPsych; Hon. Senior Lecturer, St George's Hospital Medical School, University of London, since 1968; Consultant Psychiatrist, Tooting Bec and St Thomas' Hospitals, 1961–88; *b* 8 July 1926; *s* of Geoffrey Bewley and Victoria Jane Wilson; *m* 1955, Beulah Knox, MD, FFCM; one *s* four *d*. *Educ:* St Columba's College, Dublin; Trinity College, Dublin University (MA; MD 1958). FRCPsych 1972, Hon. FRCPsych 1989. Hon. MD Dublin, 1987. Qualified TCD, 1950; trained St Patrick's Hosp., Dublin, Maudsley Hosp., Univ. of Cincinnati. Member: Standing Adv. Cttee on Drug Dependence, 1966–71; Adv. Council on Misuse of Drugs, 1972–84; Consultant Adviser on Drug Dependence to DHSS, 1972–81; Consultant, WHO, 1969–78. Pres., RCPsych, 1984–87 (Dean, 1977–82); Jt Co-founder and Mem. Council, Inst. for Study of Drug Dependence, 1967–. *Publications:* Handbook for Inceptors and Trainees in Psychiatry, 1976, 2nd edn 1980; papers on drug dependence, medical manpower and side effects of drugs. *Address:* 11 Garrads Road, SW16 1JU. *T:* 0181–769 1703. *Club:* London Chapter of Irish Georgian Society.

BEXON, Roger, CBE 1985; Chairman, Laporte plc, 1986–95; Managing Director, British Petroleum Co., 1981–86, and Deputy Chairman, 1983–86; *b* 11 April 1926; *s* of late MacAlister Bexon, CBE, and Nora Hope Bexon (*née* Jenner); *m* 1951, Lois Loughran Walling; one *s* one *d*. *Educ:* Denstone Coll. (schol.); St John's Coll., Oxford (MA); Tulsa Univ. (MS). Geologist and petroleum engineer with Trinidad Petroleum Development Co. Ltd, 1946–57; management positions with British Petroleum Co., E Africa, 1958–59; Libya, 1959–60; Trinidad, 1961–64; London, 1964–66; Manager, North Sea Operations, 1966–68; General Manager, Libya, 1968–70; Regional Coordinator, Middle East, London, 1971–73; Gen. Manager, Exploration and Production, London, 1973–76; Managing Director, BP Exploration Co. Ltd, London, 1976–77; Chm., Goal Petroleum plc, 1990–; Director: Standard Oil Co., 1982–86 (Dir and Sen. Vice Pres., 1977–80); BP Canada Inc., 1983–87; BICC, 1985–92; Lazard Bros, 1986–91; Fenner plc, 1986–89; Cameron Iron Works, 1987–89; Astec (BSR) PLC, 1989–. Mem. Council, British–N American Res. Assoc., 1986–. *Publications:* general and technical contribs to internat. jls on oil and energy matters. *Recreations:* reading, golf, Times crossword puzzles. *Address:* c/o 22 Hill Street, W1X 7FB. *T:* 0171–496 4423.

BEYER, John Charles; Director, China-Britain Trade Group, since 1991; *b* 29 April 1950; *s* of William Herbert Beyer and Doris Irene Beyer (*née* Tomline); *m* 1971, Letty Marindin Minns; one *s* one *d*. *Educ:* Abingdon Sch.; Queens' Coll., Cambridge (MA). Vis. Schol., Université de Paris VII, 1973–74; British Council Schol., Beijing Langs Inst., 1974–75; Lectr, Dept of Oriental Langs, Univ. of Calif, Berkeley, 1979–80; Researcher, Dept of Chinese Studies, Leeds Univ., 1980–82; Missions Exec., Sino-British Trade Council, 1983–85; Editor, China-Britain Trade Rev., 1985–90; Dir, Sino-British Trade Council, 1990–91. *Recreation:* family. *Address:* China-Britain Trade Group, 5th Floor, Abford House, 15 Wilton Road, SW1V 1LT. *T:* 0171–828 5176.

BEYFUS, Drusilla Norman; writer, editor, broadcaster; Lecturer, Central St Martin's College of Art, since 1989; *d* of Norman Beyfus and Florence Noel Barker; *m* 1956, Milton Shulman, *qv*; one *s* two *d*. *Educ:* Royal Naval Sch; Channing Sch. Woman's Editor, Sunday Express, 1950; columnist, Daily Express, 1952–55; Associate Editor, Queen magazine, 1956; Home Editor, The Observer, 1963; Associate Editor, Daily Telegraph magazine, 1966; Editor, Brides and Setting Up Home magazine, 1972–79; Associate Editor, 1979–87, Contributing Editor, 1987–88, Vogue magazine; Editor, Harrods Magazine, 1987–88; columnist, Sunday Telegraph, 1990–91; Contributing Editor, Telegraph Magazine, 1991–; columnist, You magazine (Mail on Sunday), 1994–. TV and radio appearances, incl. Call My Bluff and talks programmes. *Publications:* (with Anne Edwards) Lady Behave, 1956 (rev. edn 1969); The English Marriage, 1968; The Brides Book, 1981; The Art of Giving, 1987; Modern Manners, 1992; The Done Thing (series): Courtship, 1992; Parties, 1992; Business, 1993; Sex, 1993; contrib. to Sunday Times, Punch, New Statesman, Daily Telegraph, Daily Mail. *Recreations:* walking, modern art, cooking. *Address:* 51G Eaton Square, SW1W 9BE. *T:* 0171–235 7162.

See also Marquis of Normanby, A. Shulman.

BEYNON, Ernest Geoffrey; Joint General Secretary, Assistant Masters and Mistresses Association, 1979–87; *b* 4 Oct. 1926; *s* of late Frank William George and Frances Alice Pretoria Beynon; *m* 1956, Denise Gwendoline Rees; two *s* one *d*. *Educ:* Borden Grammar Sch., Kent; Univ. of Bristol, 1944–47, 1949–50 (BSc (Hons Maths) 1947, CertEd 1950). National Service, Royal Artillery, 1947–49. Mathematics Master, Thornbury Grammar Sch., Glos, 1950–56; Mathematics Master and Sixth Form Master, St George Grammar Sch., Bristol, 1956–64; Asst Sec., Assistant Masters Assoc., 1964–78. Last Chm., Teachers' Panel, Burnham Primary and Secondary Cttee, 1985–87. Mem., Univ. of Bristol Court, 1986–; Trustee and Manager, Muntham House Sch., 1979–. Treasurer: Welwyn Garden City Soc., 1988–; Welwyn Garden Decorative and Fine Arts Soc., 1992–. Tower Captain, St John's, Lemsford. Hon. FCP, 1985. *Publications:* many reports/pamphlets for AMA, incl. The Middle School System, Mixed Ability Teaching, Selection for Admission to a University. *Recreations:* family, campanology, canal boating, special interest tours abroad, books. *Address:* 3 Templewood, Welwyn Garden City, Herts AL8 7HT. *T:* Welwyn Garden (01707) 321380.

BEYNON, Sir Granville; *see* Beynon, Sir W. J. G.

BEYNON, Dr John David Emrys, FEng 1988; FIEE; Principal, King's College London, 1990–92; *b* 11 March 1939; *s* of John Emrys and Elvira Beynon; *m* 1964, Hazel Janet Hurley; two *s* one *d*. *Educ:* Univ. of Wales (BSc); Univ. of Southampton (MSc, PhD). FIERE 1977; FIEE 1978. Scientific Officer, Radio Res. Station, Slough, 1962–64; Univ. of Southampton: Lectr, Sen. Lectr and Reader, 1964–77; Prof. of Electronics, UWIST, Cardiff, 1977–79; University of Surrey: Prof. of Elec. Engrg, 1979–90; Head of Dept of Electronic and Elec. Engrg, 1979–83; Pro-Vice-Chancellor, 1983–87; Sen. Pro-Vice-Chancellor, 1987–90. Vis. Prof., Carleton Univ., Ottawa, 1975; Cons. to various cos, Govt estabts and Adviser to British Council, 1964–. Member: Accreditation Cttee, IEE, 1983–89; Adv. Cttee on Engrg and Technology, British Council, 1983–92; Technology Sub-Cttee, UGC, 1984–89; Nat. Electronics Council, 1985–91; Cttee 1, 1990–92, Main Cttee, 1991–94, CICHE; Adv. Cttee, Erasmus, 1990–92; Standing Cttee on Educn and Trng, Royal Acad. of Engrg, 1992–; Adv. Council, British Liby, 1994–; ITC, 1995–. Engrg Professors' Conference: Hon. Sec., 1982–84; Vice-Chm., 1984–85 and 1987–88; Chm., 1985–87. FRSA 1982; FKC 1990. Hon. Fellow, UC Swansea, 1990. *Publications:* Charge-Coupled Devices and Their Applications (with D. R. Lamb), 1980; papers on plasma physics, semiconductor devices and integrated circuits, and engrg educn. *Recreations:* music, photography, travel. *Address:* 13 Great Quarry, Guildford, Surrey GU1 3XN.

BEYNON, Prof. John Herbert, DSc; FRS 1971; Professor Emeritus, University of Wales, since 1991; *b* 29 Dec. 1923; British; *m* 1947, Yvonne Lilian (*née* Fryer); no *c*. *Educ:* UC Swansea, Univ. of Wales. BSc (1st cl. hons Physics); DSc; CPhys; FInstP; CChem; FRSC. Experimental Officer, Min. of Supply, Tank Armament Research, 1943–47; ICI Ltd (Organics Div.), 1947–74; Associate Research Man. i/c Physical Chemistry, 1962–70; Sen. Res. Associate, 1965–74. University College of Swansea, University of Wales: Hon. Professorial Fellow, and Lectr in Chemistry, 1967–74; Royal Soc. Res. Prof., 1974–86; Res. Prof., Depts of Physics and Chemistry, 1987–. Prof. of Chemistry, Purdue Univ., Indiana, 1969–75; Associate Prof. of Molecular Sciences, Univ. of Warwick, 1972–74; Vis. Prof., Univ. of Essex, 1973–74, 1982–; Hon. Prof., Univ. of Warwick, 1977–. Chm., Science Curriculum Develt Cttee, Cttee for Wales, 1983–88; Pres., Europ. Mass Spectrometry Soc., 1993–. Editor, Internat. Jl of Mass Spectrom. Ion Processes, 1983–85; Editor-in-Chief, Rapid Communications in Mass Spectrom., 1987–. Gold Medal: Internat. Mass Spectrometry Soc., 1985; British Mass Spectrometry Soc., 1987; Italian Mass Spectrometry Soc., 1992. *Publications:* Mass Spectrometry and its Applications in Organic Chemistry, 1960; Mass and Abundance Tables for use in Mass Spectrometry, 1963; The Mass Spectra of Organic Molecules, 1968; Table of Ion Energies for Metastable Transitions in Mass Spectrometry, 1970; Metastable Ions, 1973; An Introduction to Mass Spectrometry, 1981; Current Topics in Mass Spectrometry and Chemical Kinetics, 1982; Application of Transition State Theory to Unimolecular Reactions, 1983; papers in Proc. Royal Soc., Nature, Jl Sci. Inst., Jl Applied Physics, Chem. Soc., JACS, Trans Faraday Soc., Int. Jl Mass Spectrom. and Ion Physics, Org. Mass Spectrom., Anal. Chem., etc. *Recreations:* photography, golf. *Address:* Chemistry Building, University College Swansea, Singleton Park, Swansea SA2 8PP. *T:* Swansea (01792) 295298, *Fax:* (01792) 295717; 17 Coltshill Drive, Mumbles, Swansea SA3 4SN. *T:* Swansea (01792) 368718. *Clubs:* Swansea Cricket and Football (Bd Mem., 1990–92), Swansea Sports (Chm., 1988–93); Bristol Channel Yacht.

BEYNON, Timothy George, MA; FRGS 1983; Senior Warden, Saltwells Local Nature Reserve, Dudley, since 1992; *b* 13 Jan. 1939; *s* of George Beynon and Fona I. Beynon; *m* 1973, Sally Jane Wilson; two *d*. *Educ:* Swansea Grammar Sch.; King's Coll., Cambridge (MA). City of London Sch., 1962–63; Merchant Taylors' Sch., 1963–78; Headmaster: Denstone Coll., 1978–86; The Leys Sch., Cambridge, 1986–90. *Recreations:* ornithology, fishing, shooting, sport, music, expeditions. *Address:* The Croft, College Road, Denstone, Uttoxeter, Staffs ST14 5HR.

BEYNON, Prof. Sir (William John) Granville, Kt 1976; CBE 1959; PhD, DSc; FRS 1973; Professor and Head of Department of Physics, University College of Wales, Aberystwyth, 1958–81, now Emeritus; *b* 24 May 1914; *s* of William and Mary Beynon; *m* 1942, Megan Medi, *d* of Arthur and Margaret James; two *s* one *d*. *Educ:* Gowerton Grammar Sch.; University Coll., Swansea. Scientific Officer, later Senior Scientific Officer, National Physical Laboratory, 1938–46; Lecturer, later Senior Lecturer in Physics, University Coll. of Swansea, 1946–58. Mem., SRC, 1976–80. Mem., Schools Council, 1965–76; Pres., 1972–75, Hon. Pres., 1981–, URSI; Hon. Professorial Fellow, UC Swansea, 1981–; Hon. DSc Leicester, 1981. *Publications:* (ed) Solar Eclipses and the Ionosphere, 1956; (ed) Proceedings Mixed Commission on the Ionosphere, 1948–58; numerous publications in scientific jls. *Recreations:* music, cricket, tennis, Rugby. *Address:* Caebryn, Caergôg, Aberystwyth, Dyfed SY23 1ET. *T:* Aberystwyth (01970) 623947.

BHASKAR, Prof. Krishan Nath; with Motor Industry Research Unit Ltd, Norwich (Founder, 1983; Director, 1988–94); *b* 9 Oct. 1945; *s* of late Dr Ragu Nath Bhaskar and Mrs Kamla Bhaskar (*née* Dora Skill); *m* 1977, Fenella Mary (*née* McCann); one *s* one *d*. *Educ:* St Paul's Sch., London; London Sch. of Econs and Pol. Science (BSc Econ 1st Cl. Hons, MSc Econ). Lectr, LSE, 1968–70; Lectr in Accounting, Univ. of Bristol, 1970–78; Prof. of Accountancy and Finance, UEA, 1978–88. Founder, Computer Industry Res. Unit, 1985. *Publications:* (with D. Murray) Macroeconomic Systems, 1976; Building Financial Models: a simulation approach, 1978; Manual to Building Financial Models, 1978; The Future of the UK Motor Industry, 1979; The Future of the World Motor Industry, 1980; (with M. J. R. Shave) Computer Science Applied to Business Systems, 1982; The UK and European Motor Industry: analysis and future prospects, 1983; (jtly) Financial Modelling with a Microcomputer, 1984; (with R. J. Housden) Management Information Systems and Data Processing for the Management Accountant, 1985, new edn, as Information Technology Management, 1990; (with B. C. Williams) The Impact of Microprocessors on the Small Practice, 1985; A Fireside Chat on Databases for Accountants, 1985; Computer Security—Threats and Countermeasures, 1993; *reports:* A Research Report on the Future of the UK and European Motor Industry, 1984; Jaguar: an investor's guide, 1984; Car Pricing in Europe, 1984; (with G. R. Kaye) Financial Planning with Personal Computers, Vol. 1, 1985, Vol. 2, 1986; State Aid to the European Motor Industry, 1985, updated edn 1987; Demand Growth: a boost for employment?, 1985; Japanese Automotive Strategies: a European and US perspective, 1986; Quality and the Japanese Motor Industry: lessons for the West?, 1986; The Future of Car Retailing in the UK, 1987; A Single European Market? an automotive perspective, 1988; Rover: profile, progress and prospects, 1988; Automotive Trade Restrictions in Western Europe,

1989; The Greek Vehicle Market: future opportunities, 1989; Into the 1990s: future strategies of the vehicle producers of South Korea and Malaysia, 1990; UK Local Content of UK and European Cars, 1993; 1993 European Production Forecast, 1993. *Recreations:* gardening, vegetarian cooking, travel, wine. *Address:* Grove Orchard, The Street, Shotesham, Norwich NR15 1XH.

BHATTACHARYYA, Prof. Sushantha Kumar, FEng 1991; Professor of Manufacturing Systems Engineering, University of Warwick, since 1980; *b* 6 June 1940; *s* of Sudhir Bhattacharyya and Hemanalini (*née* Chakraborty); *m* 1981, Bridie Rabbite; three *d*. *Educ:* IIT, Kharagpur (BTech); Univ. of Birmingham (MSc, PhD). MIMechE, FIEE. CAV Ltd, 1960–63; Prodn Engr, Joseph Lucas Ltd, 1964–68; University of Birmingham: Lectr, Dept of Engrg Prodn, 1970; Hd of Warwick Manufacturing Gp, 1972. Advr, nat. and multinat. cos, UK and abroad. Non-exec. Dir, Technology Rover Gp. Member: Nat. Consumer Council, 1990–93; Council for Sci. and Technology, 1993–. Hon. Professor: Min. of Machinery, Beijing; Hong Kong Poly. Univ.; Univ. of Technol., Malaysia. FIMgt. *Publications:* numerous, on operational and technological change in manufacturing industry. *Recreations:* family, flying, cricket. *Address:* Engineering Department, University of Warwick, Coventry CV4 7AL. *T:* Coventry (01203) 523155. *Club:* Athenæum.

BHUTTO, Hon. Benazir; Prime Minister of Pakistan, 1988–90, and since 1993; *b* 21 June 1953; *d* of late Zulfikar Ali Bhutto and of Begum Nusrat Bhutto; *m* 1987, Asif Ali Zardari; one *s* two *d*. *Educ:* Harvard Univ.; Lady Margaret Hall, Oxford. Under house arrest, 1977–84; leader in exile, Pakistan People's Party, with Begum Nusrat Bhutto; returned to Pakistan, 1986. *Publications:* Perspective on Pakistan Foreign Policy, 1978; Daughter of the East, 1988. *Address:* Office of the Prime Minister, Islamabad, Pakistan.

BIANCHERI, Boris, Hon. GCVO 1990; Italian Ambassador to the United States of America, since 1991; *b* 3 Nov. 1930; *s* of Augusto and Olga Wolff von Stomersee; *m* 1979, Flavia Arzeni; one *s* one *d*. *Educ:* Univ. of Rome (Law Degree). Joined Min. of Foreign Affairs, 1956; served Athens, 1959; Economic Dept, Min. of Foreign Affairs, 1964–67; Sec.-Gen., Commn for 1970 Osaka Exhibn, 1968; First Counsellor, Cultural Relations, Min. of Foreign Affairs, 1971; Political Counsellor, London, 1972–75; Chef de Cabinet, Sec. of State for Foreign Affairs, 1978; Minister, 1979; Ambassador, Tokyo, 1980–84; Dir. Gen., Political Affairs, Min. of Foreign Affairs, 1985; Ambassador, UK, 1987–91. Gran Croce, Ordine al Merito della Repubblica Italiana; numerous foreign orders. *Recreations:* gardening, boating, swimming, horse-riding. *Address:* Italian Embassy, 1601 Fuller Street NW, Washington, DC 20009, USA. *Club:* Circolo Della Caccia (Rome).

BIBBY, Benjamin; *see* Bibby, J. B.

BIBBY, Sir Derek (James), 2nd Bt *cr* 1959, of Tarporley, Co. Palatine of Chester; MC 1945; DL; President, Bibby Line Group Ltd (formerly Bibby Line Ltd), since 1992 (Chairman, 1969–92); *b* 29 June 1922; *s* of Major Sir (Arthur) Harold Bibby, 1st Bt, DSO, DL, LLD, and of Marjorie, *d* of Charles J. Williamson; *S* father, 1986; *m* 1961, Christine Maud, *d* of late Rt Rev. F. J. Okell, MA, DD, Bishop of Stockport; four *s* one *d*. *Educ:* Rugby; Trinity Coll., Oxford (MA). Served War, Army, 1942–46. DL Cheshire, 1987. *Recreations:* shooting, gardening. *Heir:* *s* Michael James Bibby [*b* 2 Aug. 1963; *m* 1994, Beverley, *o d* of Donald Graham]. *Address:* Willaston Grange, Willaston, South Wirral L64 2UN. *T:* 0151–327 4913.

BIBBY, (John) Benjamin; Director, 1961–94, Chairman, 1970–78, J. Bibby & Sons PLC; *b* 19 April 1929; *s* of late J. P. and D. D. Bibby; *m* 1956, Susan Lindsay Paterson; two *s* one *d*. *Educ:* Oundle Sch.; St Catharine's Coll., Cambridge (MA). Called to the Bar, Gray's Inn, 1981. Held various positions in J. Bibby & Sons PLC, 1953–94. Mem. Council, Univ. of Liverpool, 1978–81; Mem. Exec. Cttee, West Kirby Residential Sch., 1978–87. Mem. Cttee, 1982–, Hon. Treas., 1987–, Nat. Squib Owners' Assoc. (Chm., 1983–87). JP Liverpool 1975–81. *Publications:* (with C. L. Bibby) A Miller's Tale, 1978; A Birthday Ode and Other Verse, 1994; A Letter to a Grandson and Other Verse, 1994. *Recreations:* sailing, gardening. *Address:* Kirby Mount, Warwick Drive, West Kirby, Wirral, Merseyside L48 2HT. *T:* 0151–625 8071. *Clubs:* Royal Thames Yacht; West Kirby Sailing; Royal Mersey Yacht; Royal Anglesey Yacht.

BIĆANIĆ, Prof. Nenad Josip Nikola, PhD; Regius Professor of Civil Engineering, University of Glasgow, since 1994; *b* Zagreb, Croatia, 6 Sept. 1945; *s* of Vladimir Bićanić and Elizabeta (*née* Kostial-Zivanović); *m* 1969, Jasna Babić; one *s* one *d*. *Educ:* Zagreb Univ., Croatia (Dip. Ing 1968); Univ. of Wales, Swansea (PhD 1978). Structural Engr, Zagreb, 1968–69; Consulting Engr, Arnhem, Netherlands, 1969–72; Zagreb University: Lectr and Researcher, 1972–76; Docent, Prof., 1978–83; Prof., 1984–85; Lectr, Sen. Lectr, then Reader, Univ. of Wales, Swansea, 1985–94. Vis. Prof., Univ. of Colo, Boulder, 1983–84. *Publications:* Computer Aided Analysis and Design of Concrete Structures, 1990; Computational Modelling of Concrete Structures, 1994; papers in learned and professional jls. *Recreations:* international folk-dancing, ski-ing, tennis. *Address:* 20 Ledcameroch Road, Bearsden, Glasgow G61 4AE. *T:* 0141–942 0711. *Club:* College (Glasgow).

BICESTER, 3rd Baron *cr* 1938, of Tusmore; **Angus Edward Vivian Smith;** *b* 20 Feb. 1932; *s* of Lt-Col Hon. Stephen Edward Vivian Smith (*d* 1952) (2nd *s* of 1st Baron) and Elenor Anderson, *d* of Edward S. Hewitt, New York City; *S* uncle, 1968. *Educ:* Eton. *Heir:* *b* Hugh Charles Vivian Smith, *b* 8 Nov. 1934.

BICHARD, Michael George; Permanent Secretary, Employment Department Group, since 1995; *b* 31 Jan. 1947. *Educ:* Manchester Univ. (LLB); Birmingham Univ. (MSocSci). Chief Executive: Brent BC, 1980–86; Gloucestershire CC, 1986–90; Social Security Benefits Agency, 1990–95. DUniv Leeds Metropolitan, 1992. *Address:* Employment Department Group, Caxton House, Tothill Street, SW1H 2NF. *T:* 0171–273 3000.

BICK, Sir Martin James M.; *see* Moore-Bick.

BICKERSTETH, Rt. Rev. John Monier, KCVO 1989; Clerk of the Closet to The Queen, 1979–89; *b* 6 Sept. 1921; *yr s* of late Rev. Canon Edward Monier, OBE and Inez Katharine Bickersteth; *m* 1955, Rosemary, *yr d* of late Edward and Muriel Cleveland-Stevens, Gaines, Oxted; three *s* one *d*. *Educ:* Rugby; Christ Church, Oxford; Wells Theol College. MA Oxon 1953. Captain, Buffs and Royal Artillery, 1941–46. Priest, 1951; Curate, St Matthew, Moorfields, Bristol, 1950–54; Vicar, St John's, Hurst Green, Oxted, 1954–62; St Stephen's, Chatham, 1962–70; Hon. Canon of Rochester, 1968–70; Bishop Suffragan of Warrington, 1970–75; Bishop of Bath and Wells, 1975–87. A C of E delegate to 4th Assembly, WCC, 1968. Chaplain and Sub-Prelate, OStJ, 1977–. Chairman: Royal Sch. of Church Music, 1977–88; Bible Reading Fellowship, 1978–90; Vice Chm., Central Bd of Finance of Church of England, 1981–84. Mem., Marlborough Coll. Council, 1980–91. Freeman of the City of London, 1979. *Publications:* (jtly) Clerks of the Closet in the Royal Household, 1991; A Bickersteth Diary 1914–1918, 1995. *Recreations:* country pursuits. *Address:* Beckfords, Newtown, Tisbury, Wilts SP3 6NY. *T:* Tisbury (01747) 870479. *Club:* Commonwealth Trust.

BICKERTON, Frank Donald, CBE 1966; Director General, Central Office of Information, and Head of Government Information Service, 1971–74; *b* 22 June 1917; *s* of F. M. Bickerton and A. A. Hibbert; *m* 1945, Linda Russell; two *s*. *Educ:* Liverpool Collegiate Sch. Min. of Health, in Public Relations Div., 1935–40. Served War, RNVR, 1940–45. Min. of National Insurance (later Min. of Pensions and Nat. Insurance), 1946–61: initially Asst Press Officer and in charge of Information Div., 1952–61; Chief Information Officer, Min. of Transport, 1961–68; Controller (Home), COI, 1968–71. *Recreations:* walking, gardening. *Address:* 6 Diana Close, Granville Rise, Totland, Isle of Wight PO39 0EE.

BICKFORD, James David Prydeaux, CB 1995; Visiting Professor of Law, Cleveland State University, USA; *b* 28 July 1940; *s* of William A. J. P. Bickford and late Muriel Bickford (*née* Smythe); *m* 1965, Carolyn Jane, *d* of late Major W. A. R. Sumner, RHA; three *s*. *Educ:* Downside; Law Society's College of Law, London. Admitted to Roll of Solicitors, 1963; Solicitor of the Supreme Court. In practice, J. J. Newcombe, Solicitors, Okehampton, 1963–69; Crown Counsel and Legal Advr to Govt of Turks and Caicos Islands, BWI, 1969–71; Asst Legal Advr, FCO, 1971–79 and 1982–84; Legal Advr, British Mil. Govt, Berlin, 1979–82; Legal Counsellor, FCO, 1984–87; Under Sec., MoD, and Legal Advr to Security and Intelligence Services, 1987–95. Lectr in Law, Case Western Reserve Univ., USA. Mem., Panel of Legal Experts, Internat. Telecommunications Satellite Orgn, 1985–; Chm., Assembly of Internat. Maritime Satellite Orgn, 1985–87. Mem., Law Soc. *Publication:* Land Dealings Simplified in the Turks and Caicos Islands, 1971. *Recreations:* the family, sailing, fishing. *Address:* c/o National Westminster Bank, Torrington, Devon EX38 8HP.

BICKFORD SMITH, John Roger, CB 1988; TD 1950; *b* 31 Oct. 1915; *er s* of late Leonard W. Bickford Smith, Camborne, Cornwall, For. Man., ICI, and late Anny Grete (*née* Huth); *m* 1st, 1939, Cecilia Judge Heath (marr. diss.) (decd), *er d* of W. W. Heath, Leicester; two *s*; 2nd, 1972, Baronin Joaise Miranda et Omnes Sancti von Kirchberg-Hohenheim. *Educ:* Eton (King's Schol.); Hertford Coll., Oxford (Schol.). BA 1937; MA 1952. Commnd in Duke of Cornwall's LI (TA), 1939; served 1939–46: UK, India, Burma and Germany; AJAG (Major), 1942; Lieut-Col 1944. Called to Bar, Inner Temple, 1942, Bencher, 1985. Practised at Common Law Bar in London and on Midland Circuit, 1946–67; Master of Supreme Court, QBD, 1967–88, Sen. Master and Queen's Remembrancer, 1983–88. Master, Bowyers' Co., 1986–88. *Publications:* The Crown Proceedings Act 1947, 1948; various contribs to legal pubns. *Recreation:* foreign travel. *Address:* 65 Gibson Square, N1 0RA. *Club:* Garrick.

BICKNELL, Mrs Christine Betty, CBE 1986; MA (Oxon); retired; *b* 23 Dec. 1919; *er d* of Walter Edward and Olive Isabelle Reynolds; *m* 1960, Claud Bicknell, *qv*. *Educ:* St Martin-in-the-Fields High Sch. for Girls; Somerville Coll., Oxford (Exhibr). BA 1941. Board of Trade, 1941–60; Northern Regional Officer, Min. of Land and Natural Resources, 1965–67. Chairman: Prudhoe and Monkton HMC, 1966–70; Leavesden HMC, 1971–74; Kensington and Chelsea and Westminster AHA (T), 1973–77; Victoria HA, 1982–85; Member: Newcastle RHB, 1961–70, and NW Metrop. RHB, 1971–74; Nat. Whitley Council for Nurses and Midwives, 1962–70; Northern Econ. Planning Bd, 1965–67; Bd of Governors, Royal Vic. Infirm., Newcastle upon Tyne, 1965–70 and St Bartholomew's Hosp., 1971–74; Chm., CS Selection Bds, 1970–90; Member: Industrial Tribunals, 1977–88; Newspaper Panel, Monopolies Commn, 1973–83; British Library Board, 1979–82; Pres., Hosp. Domestic Administrators' Assoc., 1970–74. *Recreations:* gardening, mountains, travel, sailing. *Address:* Aikrigg End Cottage, Burneside Road, Kendal LA9 6DZ. *Clubs:* Alpine, United Oxford & Cambridge University.

BICKNELL, Claud, OBE 1946; a Law Commissioner, 1970–75; a part-time Chairman of Industrial Tribunals, 1975–83; *b* Rowlands Gill, near Newcastle upon Tyne, 15 June 1910; 2nd *s* of Raymond Bicknell and Phillis Bicknell (*née* Lovibond); *m* 1st, 1934, Esther Irene (*d* 1958), *e d* of Kenneth Bell; one *s* two *d* (one *d* decd); 2nd, 1960, Christine Betty Reynolds (*see* C. B. Bicknell). *Educ:* Oundle Sch.; Queens' Coll., Cambridge. MA 1935. Pres., Cambridge Univ. Mountaineering Club, 1930–31. Admitted as a solicitor, 1934; Asst Solicitor, 1934–39, and partner, 1939–70, in firm of Stanton, Atkinson & Bird, Newcastle upon Tyne. Dir, Northern Corporation Ltd, 1939–53. Auxiliary Fire Service, Newcastle upon Tyne, 1939–41; Nat. Fire Service, 1941–45; Sen. Fire Staff Officer, Home Office, 1943–45. Mem. Planning Bd, Lake District Nat. Park, 1951–70 (Chm., Development Control Cttee, 1957–70). Chm., Newcastle upon Tyne Housing Improvement Trust Ltd, 1966–70. Pres., Newcastle upon Tyne Incorp. Law Soc., 1969. *Recreation:* mountains. *Address:* Aikrigg End Cottage, Burneside Road, Kendal LA9 6DZ. *Clubs:* Garrick, Alpine.

See also Sir J. R. Shelley, Bt.

BIDDLE, Martin, FBA 1985; FSA, FRHistS; Director, Winchester Research Unit, since 1968; Astor Senior Research Fellow in Medieval Archaeology, Hertford College, Oxford, since 1989; *b* 4 June 1937; *s* of Reginald Samuel Biddle and Gwladys Florence Biddle (*née* Baker); *m* 1966, Birthe, *d* of Landsretssagfører Axel Th. and Anni Kjølbye of Sønderborg, Denmark; two *d* (and two *d* by previous marr.). *Educ:* Merchant Taylors' Sch., Northwood; Pembroke Coll., Cambridge (MA 1965); MA Oxon 1967; MA Pennsylvania 1977. FSA 1964; FRHistS 1970; MIFA 1984. Second Lieut, 4 RTR, 1956; 1 Indep. Sqn, RTR, Berlin, 1956–57. Asst Inspector of Ancient Monuments, MPBW, 1961–63; Lectr in Medieval Archaeology, Univ. of Exeter, 1963–67; Vis. Fellow, All Souls Coll., Oxford, 1967–68; Dir, University Museum, and Prof. of Anthropology and of History of Art, Univ. of Pennsylvania, 1977–81; Lectr of The House, Christ Church, Oxford, 1983–86. Directed excavations and investigations: Nonsuch Palace, 1959–60; Winchester, 1961–71; Repton (with wife), 1974–88, 1993; St Alban's Abbey (with wife), 1978, 1982–84, 1991; Holy Sepulchre, Jerusalem (with wife), 1989–90, 1992, 1993; Qasr Ibrim, Egypt (with wife), 1990, 1992. Archaeological Consultant: Canterbury Cathedral; St Alban's Abbey and Cathedral Church; Eurotunnel, etc. Chm., Rescue, Trust for British Archaeology, 1971–75. Mem., Royal Commn on Historical Monuments of England, 1984–. General Editor, Winchester Studies, 1976–. (With Birthe Biddle) Frend Medal, Soc. of Antiquaries, 1986. *Publications:* (with C. Heighway) The Future of London's Past, 1973; (with F. Barlow and others) Winchester in the Early Middle Ages, 1976; (with H.M. Colvin, J. Summerson and others) The History of the King's Works, vol. iv, pt 2, 1982; Object and Economy in Medieval Winchester, 1990; King Arthur's Round Table, 1990; Approaches in Urban Archaeology, 1990; papers on archaeological, historical and art-historical subjects in learned jls. *Recreations:* travel, esp. Hellenic travel, reading. *Address:* 19 Hamilton Road, Oxford OX2 7PY. *T:* Oxford (01865) 513056. *Club:* Athenæum.

BIDDULPH, family name of **Baron Biddulph.**

BIDDULPH, 5th Baron *cr* 1903; **Anthony Nicholas Colin Maitland Biddulph;** interior designer; sporting manager; *b* 8 April 1959; *s* of 4th Baron Biddulph and of Lady Mary, *d* of Viscount Maitland (killed in action, 1943) and *g d* of 15th Earl of Lauderdale; *S* father, 1988; *m* 1993, Hon. Sian Diana, *y d* of Baron Gibson-Watt, *qv*; one *s*. *Educ:* Cheltenham; RAC, Cirencester. *Heir:* *s* Hon. Robert Julian Maitland Biddulph, *b* 8 July 1994.

Recreations: shooting, fishing, painting. *Address:* 8 Orbel Street, SW11 3NZ; The Old Rectory, Bramdean, Alresford, Hants SO24 0LW. *Clubs:* Cavalry and Guards, Raffles.

BIDDULPH, Constance; *see* Holt, C.

BIDDULPH, Sir Ian D'Olier, (Jack), 11th Bt *cr* 1664, of Westcombe, Kent; *b* 28 Feb. 1940; *s* of Sir Stuart Royden Biddulph, 10th Bt and Muriel Margaret (*d* 1995), *d* of Angus Harkness, Hamley Bridge, S Australia; *S* father, 1986; *m* 1967, Margaret Eleanor, *o d* of late John Gablonski, Oxley, Brisbane; one *s* two *d*. *Heir: s* Paul William Biddulph, *b* 30 Oct. 1967. *Address:* Christensens Road, Mount Walker, M/S 23, via Rosewood, Qld 4340, Australia.

BIDE, Sir Austin (Ernest), Kt 1980; Hon. President, Glaxo Holdings plc, since 1985 (Chief Executive, 1973–80; Chairman, 1973–85); non-executive Chairman, BL plc, 1982–86 (Deputy Chairman, 1980–82; Director, 1977–86); *b* 11 Sept. 1915; *o s* of late Ernest Arthur Bide and Eliza Bide (*née* Young); *m* 1941, Irene (*née* Ward); three *d*. *Educ:* County Sch., Acton; Univ. of London. 1st cl. hons BSc Chemistry; FRSC, CChem. Govt Chemist's Dept, 1932–40; Research Chemist, Glaxo, 1940: i/c Chemical Develt and Intellectual Property, 1944–54; Dep. Sec., 1954–59; Sec., 1959–65; Dir, 1963–71; Dep. Chm., 1971–73; Dir, J. Lyons & Co. Ltd, 1977–78. Member: Review Body, UGC, 1985–87; Working Party on Biotechnology (under auspices of ACARD/ABRD and Royal Soc.) (Report 1980); Adv. Cttee on Industry to the Vice-Chancellors and Principals of UK Univs, 1984–87; Chm., Information Technology 1986 Cttee, 1986. Member: Adv. Council, Inst. of Biotechnological Studies, 1985–89; Council, Inst. of Manpower Studies, 1985–91; Chairman: Visiting Cttee, Open Univ., 1982–89; Adam Smith Inst., 1986– (Mem., 1985–). Chairman: QCA Ltd, 1985–89; Micro-test Res. Ltd, 1987–90; United Environmental Systems, 1988–90; CGEA (UK) Ltd, 1991–; Onyx (UK) Ltd, 1991–; Comatech (UK) Ltd, 1992–; Tyseley Waste Disposal, 1994–; Director: Oxford Consultancy Ltd, 1988– (Chm., 1994–); Cie des Transports et Services Publiques, 1992–. Confederation of British Industry: Member: Council, 1974–85; President's Cttee, 1983–86; Chm., Res. and Technol. Cttee, 1977–86; Institute of Management (formerly British Institute of Management): CIMgt (FBIM 1972); Mem. Council, 1976–88; Chm., Finance Cttee, 1976–79; Vice-Pres., 1992–; Dir, BIM Foundn, 1977–79. Medical Research Council: Mem., 1986–90; Chm., Investment Cttee, 1988–90; Chm., Pensions Trust, 1988–90; Mem., AIDS Cttee, 1987–90; Trustee, Nat. AIDS Trust (Chm., until 1991). Member: Editl Adv. Bd, Science in Parlt, 1994–; Foundn for Sci. and Technol., 1994–. Chm. Court, Freight Transport Assoc., 1992–; Mem. Court, British Shippers Council, 1984–92 (Chm., 1989–92); Trustee, British Motor Industry Heritage Trust, 1983–86. Chm., Salisbury Cathedral Spire Appeal Cttee, 1987–92; Trustee, Salisbury Cathedral Spire Trust, 1987–; Mem., Confraternity of Benefactors, Salisbury Cathedral, 1992–. Chm. of Appeal, RCS, 1992–. Mem. Council, Imperial Soc. of Knights Bachelor, 1980–. CIEx 1987; FInstD 1989; Hon. FIChemE 1983; Hon. FIIM 1983 (Vice-Pres., 1983); Hon. Fellow: Inst. Biotechnological Studies 1985; St Catherine's Coll., Oxford, 1987. Hon. DSc: QUB, 1986; CNAA, 1990; DUniv OU, 1991. Gold Medal, BIM, 1983; Duncan Davies Medal, R&D Soc., 1990. *Publications:* papers in learned jls on organic chemical subjects. *Recreation:* fishing. *Club:* Hurlingham.

BIDGOOD, John Claude, MIEx; Chairman: Anglo-Dominion Finance Co. Ltd; Anglo-Dominion Construction Co. Ltd; Anglo-Dominion Trading Co. Ltd; *b* 12 May 1914; *s* of late Edward Charles Bidgood, Leeds; *m* 1945, Sheila Nancy Walker-Wood; one *s* two *d*. *Educ:* London Choir Sch.; Woodhouse Technical Sch. Served early part of War of 1939–45 as Pilot RAF. Mem. Leeds City Council, 1947–55 (late Chm. Works Cttee and City Architects Cttee); contested (C) N E Leeds, 1950, 1951; MP (C) Bury and Radcliffe, 1955–64; PPS to Joint Parly Secs, Min. of Pensions and Nat. Insurance, 1957–58; Mem. Parly Select Cttee on Estimates, 1958–64. Dir, Bidgood Holdings Ltd; Chm., Yorks Assoc. for the Disabled, 1950–58; Member: Inst. of Export; Leeds and Bradford Joint Aerodrome Cttee, 1951–55. Mayor, Chapeltown Corporation, 1987–88. Hon. Citizen, City of Atlanta, Georgia, 1960; Freeman, City of London, 1961; Liveryman and Mem., Worshipful Co. of Horners. *Recreations:* music, travel. *Address:* The Old Joinery, Walton, near Wetherby, W Yorks LS23 7DQ. *T:* Boston Spa (01937) 844028. *Club:* City Livery.

BIDSTRUP, (Patricia) Lesley, MD, FRCP, FRACP; Member, Medical Appeals Tribunal, 1970–88; private consulting concerned mainly with industrial medicine, since 1958; *b* 24 Oct. 1916; *d* of Clarence Leslie Bidstrup, Chemical Works Manager, South Australia, and Kathleen Helena Bidstrup (*née* O'Brien); *m* 1952, Ronald Frank Guymer, TD, MD, FRCP, FRCS, DPH, DIH; one step *s* one step *d*. *Educ:* Kadina High Sch. and Walford House, Adelaide, SA. MB, BS (Adel.) 1939; MD (Adel.) 1958; FRACP 1954; FRCP (Lond.) 1964. Resident Ho. Phys. and Registrar, Royal Adelaide Hosp., SA, 1939–41. Hon. Capt., AAMC, 1942–45. MO, UNRRA, Glyn-Hughes Hosp., Belsen, 1945–46. General practice: Acting Hon. Asst Phys., Royal Adelaide Hosp.; Tutor in Med., St Mark's Coll., Adelaide, and in Univ. of Adelaide Med. Sch.; Lectr in Med., Univ. of Adelaide Dental Faculty, 1942–45; Asst, Dept for Research in Industrial Medicine, MRC, 1947–58; Clinical Asst (Hon.), Chest Dept, St Thomas' Hosp., 1958–78. Member: Scientific Sub-Cttee on Poisonous Substances used in Agriculture and Food Storage, 1956–58; Industrial Injuries Adv. Council, 1970–83. Visiting Lectr, TUC Centenary Inst. of Occupational Health; Examiner for Diploma in Industrial Health: Conjoint Bd, 1965–71, 1980–82; Society of Apothecaries, 1970–76; External Examiner for Diploma in Industrial Health, Dundee, 1980–82. Fellow, Amer. Coll. of Occupational Medicine. William P. Yant Award, Amer. Industrial Hygiene Assoc., 1989. Mayoress, Royal Borough of Kingston-upon-Thames, 1959, 1960. *Publications:* The Toxicity of Mercury and its Compounds, 1964; chapters in: Cancer Progress, 1960; The Prevention of Cancer, 1967; Clinical Aspects of Inhaled Particles, 1972; contribs to Brit. Jl Indust. Med., Lancet, BMJ, Proc. Royal Soc. Med., ILO Encyclopaedia on Industrial Diseases. *Recreations:* people, theatre, music. *Address:* 11 Sloane Terrace Mansions, Sloane Terrace, SW1X 9DG. *T:* 0171–730 8720.

BIDWELL, Sir Hugh (Charles Philip), GBE 1989; Non-executive Director, Rothschild Asset Management Ltd, since 1992; Lord Mayor of London, 1989–90; *b* 1 Nov. 1934; *s* of Edward and late Elisabeth Bidwell; *m* 1962, Jenifer Celia Webb; two *s* one *d*. *Educ:* Stonyhurst College. Nat. Service, 1953–55; commissioned E Surrey Regt, seconded to 1st Bn KAR, based Nyasaland. Viota Foods, 1956–70 (Dir, 1962–70); Dir, Robertson Foods, 1969–70; Chairman: Pearce Duff & Co. Ltd, 1970–84; Gill & Duffus Foods Ltd, 1984–85. Non-executive Chairman: Riggs AP Bank Ltd, 1989–92; Octavian Gp Ltd, 1993–; Applied Distribution (Gp) plc, 1993–; Non-exec. Dep. Chm., London Forum, 1992–; Non-Executive Director: Argyll Group plc, 1990–95; Fleming Geared Income and Assets Investment Trust plc, 1993–; Bridge Farm Dairies Ltd, 1993–; Alpha Airports Gp plc, 1994–. Chm., London Tourist Bd, 1992–93; Member: London Chamber of Commerce and Industry, 1976–85; Food from Britain Council, 1983–89 (Chm., Export Bd, 1983–86); European Trade Cttee, 1989–91; British-Soviet Chamber of Commerce, 1989–92; China-Britain (formerly Sino-British) Trade Gp, 1989–94; E. European Trade Gp, 1991–92; BOTB, 1992–94. Pres., British Food Export Council, 1980–87; Dep. Pres., Food and Drink Fedn, 1985–86. Alderman, Billingsgate Ward, 1979–; Sheriff of the City of London, 1986–87. Master, Grocers' Co., 1984–85. President: Billingsgate Ward Club; Fishmongers' & Poulterers' Instn. *Recreations:* golf, fishing, tennis, cricket, shooting. *Address:* (office) Five Arrows House, St Swithin's Lane, EC4N 8NR. *T:* 0171–235 7762; (office) 0171–280 5000. *Clubs:* Boodle's, City of London, MCC; Royal & Ancient; Denham Golf, Royal St George's.

BIDWELL, Sydney James; *b* Southall, 14 Jan. 1917; *s* of late Herbert Emmett Bidwell; *m* 1941; one *s* one *d*. *Educ:* Elementary sch., evening classes and trade union study. Railway worker (formerly NUR activist); Tutor and Organiser, Nat. Council of Labour Colls. Mem., TGWU (sponsored as MP by union). TUC Reg. Educn Officer, London, 1963–66. Mem., Southall Bor. Council, 1951–55. Contested (Lab): E Herts, 1959; Herts SW, 1964. MP (Lab) Southall, 1966–74, Ealing, Southall, 1974–92; contested (True Lab) Ealing, Southall, 1992. Mem., Parly Select Cttee on Race Relations and Immigration, 1968–79; Mem., Select Cttee on Transport, 1979–92. *Publications:* Red White and Black Book on Race-Relations, 1976; The Turban Victory, 1977; articles on TU and Labour history. *Recreations:* soccer, painting, cartooning.

BIERICH, Marcus; Chairman, Supervisory Board, Robert Bosch GmbH, Stuttgart, since 1993 (Chairman, Board of Management, 1984–93); *b* 29 April 1926. *Educ:* Univs of Münster and Hamburg (PhD 1951; studies in mathematics, science and philosophy). Bankhaus Delbrück Schickler & Co., 1951–61; Director 1961–67, Mem. Bd of Management 1967–80, Mannesmann AG, Düsseldorf; Chief Financial Officer and Mem. Bd of Management, Allianz Versicherungs-AG, München, 1980–84. Hon. Dr.rer.oec Univ. of Bochum, 1977. *Address:* Robert Bosch GmbH, Postfach 10 60 50, 70049 Stuttgart, Germany. *T:* (711) 8110.

BIFFEN, Rt. Hon. (William) John, PC 1979; DL; MP (C) Shropshire North, since 1983 (Oswestry Division of Salop, Nov. 1961–1983); *b* 3 Nov. 1930; *s* of Victor W. Biffen; *m* 1979, Mrs Sarah Wood (*née* Drew); one step *s* one step *d*. *Educ:* Dr Morgan's Sch., Bridgwater; Jesus Coll., Cambridge (BA). Worked in Tube Investments Ltd, 1953–60; Economist Intelligence Unit, 1960–61. Chief Sec. to the Treasury, 1979–81; Sec. of State for Trade, 1981–82; Lord Pres. of the Council, 1982–83; Leader of House of Commons, 1982–87 and Lord Privy Seal, 1983–87. Director: Glynwed International, 1987–; J. Bibby & Sons, 1988–; Rockware Gp, 1988–91. DL Shropshire, 1993. *Publication:* Inside the House of Commons, 1989. *Address:* c/o House of Commons, SW1A 0AA.

BIGG, Sally; *see* Gunnell, S.

BIGGAM, Sir Robin (Adair), Kt 1993; Chairman, BICC plc, since 1992 (Managing Director, 1986–87; Chief Executive, 1987–91); *b* 8 July 1938; *s* of Thomas and Eileen Biggam; *m* 1962, Elizabeth McArthur McDougall; one *s* two *d*. *Educ:* Lanark Grammar Sch. Chartered accountant. Peat Marwick Mitchell, 1960–63; ICI, 1964–81; Director: ICL, 1981–84; Dunlop Holdings plc, 1984–85; Non Executive Director: Chloride Group plc, 1985–87; Lloyds Abbey Life plc (formerly Abbey Life Gp), 1985–90; Redland Gp plc, 1991–; British Aerospace plc, 1994–; Foreign & Colonial German Investment Trust plc, 1995–. *Recreations:* golf, swimming, gardening. *Address:* Devonshire House, Mayfair Place, W1X 5FH. *T:* 0171–629 6622. *Club:* Royal Automobile.

BIGGAR, (Walter) Andrew, CBE 1980 (OBE 1967); MC 1945; FRAgS; farming since 1956; *b* 6 March 1915; *s* of Walter Biggar and Margaret Sproat; *m* 1945, Patricia Mary Irving Elliot; one *s* one *d*. *Educ:* Sedbergh Sch., Cumbria; Edinburgh Univ. (BScAgric). FRAgS 1969. Commnd Royal Signals, 1938; War Service, 51st Highland Div., 1939–46; POW, Germany, 1940–45. Rowett Res. Inst., 1935–54. Director and Trustee: Scottish Soc. for Research in Plant Breeding, 1958–88; Animal Diseases Res. Assoc., 1966–. Member: Farm Animals Welfare Adv. Cttee, 1967–77; ARC, 1969–80; Scottish Agricultural Develt Council, 1971–82; JCO Consultative Bd, 1980–84; Chm., Animals Bd, JCO, 1973–80. Chm., Moredun Animal Health Trust, 1988–. Governor: St Margaret's Sch., Edinburgh, 1960–81; Grassland Res. Inst., 1962–81 (Hon. Fellow, 1981); Scottish Crop Res. Inst., 1980–83. *Recreation:* photography. *Address:* Magdalenehall, St Boswells, Roxburghshire TD6 0EB. *T:* St Boswells (01835) 823741.

BIGGART, (Thomas) Norman, CBE 1984; WS; Partner, Biggart Baillie & Gifford, WS, Solicitors, Glasgow and Edinburgh, 1959–95; *b* 24 Jan. 1930; *o s* of Andrew Stevenson Biggart, JP and Marjorie Scott Biggart; *m* 1956, Eileen Jean Anne Gemmell; one *s* one *d*. *Educ:* Morrisons Acad., Crieff; Glasgow Univ. (MA 1951, LLB 1954). Served RN, 1954–56 (Sub-Lt RNVR). Law Society of Scotland: Mem. Council, 1977–86; Vice-Pres., 1981–82; Pres., 1982–83. Mem., Council on Tribunals, and Chm., Scottish Cttee, 1990–. Pres., Business Archives Council, Scotland, 1977–86. Member: Exec. Cttee, Scottish Council (Development and Industry), 1984–93; Scottish Tertiary Educn Adv. Council, 1984–87; Scottish Records Adv. Council, 1985–91. Director: Clydesdale Bank, 1985–; Independent (formerly New Scotland) Insurance Gp, 1986– (Chm., 1989–93); Beechwood Glasgow, 1989– (Chm., 1989–). Trustee, Scottish Civic Trust, 1989–. Hon. Mem., American Bar Assoc., 1982. OStJ 1968. *Recreations:* golf, hill walking. *Address:* Gailes, Kilmacolm, Renfrewshire PA13 4LZ. *T:* Kilmacolm (0150587) 2645. *Clubs:* Royal Scottish Automobile, The Western (Glasgow).

BIGGS, Vice-Adm. Sir Geoffrey (William Roger), KCB 1993; Military Adviser to ICL and DESC, since 1995; *b* 23 Nov. 1938; *s* of Vice-Adm. Sir Hilary Biggs, KBE, CB, DSO and Lady Biggs; *m* 1st, 1968, Marcia (*née* Leask) (marr. diss. 1978); three *s*; 2nd, 1981, Caroline Ann (*née* Daly); one *d*, and two step *s*. *Educ:* St Andrews, Eastbourne; Charterhouse. Joined RN 1956, Submarine Service, 1960; commanded HM Ships: Otus, 1969–70; Superb, 1978–79; Brilliant, 1984–85; Broadsword, 1985–86; Capt. 2nd Frigate Sqn, 1985–86; Dir of Naval Ops, 1986–89; Flag Officer Gibraltar, 1990; Comdr British Forces Gibraltar, 1990–92; Dep. Comdr and C of S to C-in-C Fleet, 1992–94; retd, 1995. Comdr, 1975; Capt., 1980; Rear-Adm., 1990; Vice-Adm., 1992. *Recreations:* lawnmowing, crosswords, family and friends. *Address:* c/o Naval Secretary, Victory Building, HM Naval Base, Portsmouth PO1 3LS.

BIGGS, Dr John, FRSC; Chairman, Free Church Federal Council, since 1993 (Moderator, 1992–93); *b* 3 Jan. 1933; *s* of Horace James Biggs and Elsie Alice Biggs, Leicester; *m* 1965, Brenda Muriel Hicklenton. *Educ:* Wyggeston Grammar Sch. for Boys, Leicester; Downing Coll., Cambridge (Graystone Scholar). MA, PhD (Cantab). CChem; FRSC (FCS 1958). DSIR Res. Fellow, Cambridge, 1958–60; Lectr in Chemistry, Univ. of Hull, 1960–87. President: Baptist Students' Fedn, 1955–56; Yorkshire Baptist Assoc., 1973–74; Vice-Pres., Baptist Men's Movement, 1995–; Baptist Union of GB: Chm., Home Mission Working Gp, 1981–88; Mem. Council, 1978–, Chm., 1990–94; Pres., 1989–90; Mem., Scholarships and Ministerial Trng Bursary Cttee, 1978– (Chm., 1995–). Governor, Northern Baptist Coll., Manchester, 1989–; Chm., Relocation Steering Cttee, Baptist Theol Seminary (Mem. Bd of Trustees, Rüschlikon, Zürich, 1989–94, Vice-Chm., 1992–94). *Recreations:* fell-walking, opera, photography. *Address:* Fellcroft, Easedale Road, Grasmere, Ambleside, Cumbria LA22 9QR. *Club:* Penn.

BIGGS, Lewis; Curator, Tate Gallery, Liverpool, since 1990; *b* 22 April 1952; *s* of Lewis Ian Biggs and Penelope Torre Biggs (*née* Torr); *m* 1983, Ann Margaret Compton; one *s* one *d*. *Educ:* New Coll., Oxford (MA Mod. Hist. 1974); Courtauld Inst., Univ. of London

(MA Hist. of Art 1979). Gallery Co-ordinator, Arnolfini Gall., Bristol, 1979–84; Exhibns Officer, British Council, 1984–87; Curator of Exhibns, Tate Gall., Liverpool, 1987–90.

BIGGS, Brig. Michael Worthington, CBE 1962 (OBE 1944); MA; CEng, MICE; *b* 16 Sept. 1911; *s* of late Lt-Col Charles William Biggs, OBE, Cheltenham and late Winifred Jesse Bell Biggs (*née* Dickinson); *m* 1940, Katharine Mary, *d* of late Sir Walter Harragin, CMG, QC, Colonial Legal Service, and Lady Harragin; two *d*. *Educ:* Cheltenham Coll.; RMA Woolwich; Pembroke Coll., Cambridge. MA (Cantab) 1966; MICE 1967. 2nd Lieut RE, 1931; served War of 1939–45, E Africa, Abyssinia (Bde Major), and Burma (GSO1 and CRE); Lt-Col 1942; Col 1954; Mil. Adviser to High Comr, Australia, 1954–57; Brig. 1960; Chief of Staff, E Africa Comd, 1960–62; Dir of Quartering (Army), MoD, 1963–66; retd, 1966. Group Building Exec., Forte's (Holdings) Ltd, 1966–67; Manager, Hatfield and Welwyn Garden City, Commn for New Towns, 1967–78. Member: Council, TCPA, 1978–86; Exec. Cttee, Hertfordshire Soc.; Chm., Herts Bldg Preservation Trust, 1978–86. Pres., KAR and EAF Officers' Dinner Club. Freeman, City of London, 1985. *Recreations:* golf, gardening. *Address:* Strawyards, High Street, Kimpton, Herts SG4 8PT. *T:* Kimpton (01438) 823498. *Club:* Army and Navy.

BIGGS, Sir Norman (Parris), Kt 1977; Director, Banco de Bilbao, 1981–87; *b* 23 Dec. 1907; *s* of John Gordon Biggs and Mary Sharpe Dickson; *m* 1936, Peggy Helena Stammwitz (*d* 1990); two *s* one *d*. *Educ:* John Watson's Sch., Edinburgh. Bank of England, 1927–46; Dir, Kleinwort Sons & Co. Ltd, 1946–52; Esso Petroleum Company, Ltd: Dir, 1952–66, Chm., 1968–72; Chairman: Williams & Glyn's Bank Ltd, 1972–76; United International Bank Ltd, 1970–79; Deputy Chairman: National and Commercial Banking Gp Ltd, 1974–76; Privatbanken Ltd, 1980–83; Director: Royal Bank of Scotland, 1974–76; Gillett Bros Discount Co. Ltd, 1963–77. Mem., Bullock Cttee on Industrial Democracy, 1976. *Address:* Northbrooks, Danworth Lane, Hurstpierpoint, Sussex BN6 9LW. *T:* Hurstpierpoint (01273) 832022.

BIGGS, Prof. Peter Martin, CBE 1987; PhD, DSc; FRS 1976; Director of Animal Health (formerly Animal Disease Research), Agricultural and Food Research Council, 1986–88, retired; Visiting Professor of Veterinary Microbiology, Royal Veterinary College, University of London, since 1982; *b* 13 Aug. 1926; *s* of Ronald Biggs and Cécile Biggs (*née* Player); *m* 1950, Alison Janet Molteno; two *s* one *d*. *Educ:* Bedales Sch.; Cambridge Sch., USA; Queen's Univ., Belfast; Royal Veterinary Coll., Univ. of London (BSc 1953, DSc 1975); Univ. of Bristol (PhD 1958). FRCVS, FRCPath, FIBiol, CBiol. Served RAF, 1944–48; Research Asst, Univ. of Bristol, 1953–55, Lectr, 1955–59; Houghton Poultry Research Station: Head of Leukosis Experimental Unit, 1959–74; Dep. Dir, 1971–74; Dir, 1974–86. Sir William Dick Meml Lectr, Univ. of Edinburgh, 1974 and 1987; E.H.W. Wilmott Guest Lectr, Univ. of Bristol, 1977. Andrew D. White Prof.-at-Large, Cornell Univ., 1988–94. Member: Veterinary Products Cttee, 1973–; Management Bd, AFRC, 1986–88. Hon. Life Pres., World Vet. Poultry Assoc., 1985; President: Inst. of Biol., 1990–92; Internat. Assoc. for Comparative Res. on Leukemia and Related Diseases, 1981–83. Hon. FRASE 1986. Hon. DVM Ludwig-Maximilians Univ., 1976; Dr *hc* Liège, 1991. Tom Newman Meml Award, 1964; Poultry Science Award, British Oil and Cake Mills, 1968; J. T. Edwards Meml Medal, 1969; Dalrymple-Champneys Cup and Medal, 1973; Bledisloe Veterinary Award, 1977; Wooldridge Meml Medal, 1978; Joszef Marek Meml Medal, Vet. Univ. of Budapest, 1979; Victory Medal, Central Vet. Soc., 1980; Gordon Meml Medal, Robert Fraser Gordon Meml Trust, 1989; Wolf Foundn Prize in Agric., 1989. *Publications:* scientific papers on viruses and infectious disease. *Recreations:* music making, boating. *Address:* Willows, London Road, St Ives, Huntingdon, Cambridgeshire PE17 4ES. *T:* St Ives (01480) 463471. *Clubs:* Athenæum, Farmers'.

BIGHAM, family name of **Viscount Mersey** and of **Lady Nairne.**

BIGNALL, John Reginald, FRCP; Physician, Brompton Hospital, 1957–79; *b* 14 Oct. 1913; *s* of Walter and Nellie Bignall; *m* 1939, Ruth Thirtle; one *s* three *d*. *Educ:* Nottingham High Sch.; St John's Coll. Cambridge; London Hospital. MA 1938; MD 1947; FRCP 1961. Served in RAMC, 1941–46, Middle East and Mediterranean (Major).

BIGNELL, (Francis) Geoffrey; Assistant Secretary-General (Management), Law Society, since 1987; *b* 7 March 1949; *s* of Ernest Francis John Bignell and Olive Ethel Bignell (*née* Peatson); *m* 1978, Susan Rachel Harrison; two *s* one *d*. *Educ:* Isleworth Grammar Sch.; Trinity Hall, Cambridge (MA); Coll. of Law. Social work in Basildon and Worksop, 1971–74; articled to Notts CC, 1975–78; admitted Solicitor, 1977; Prosecuting Solicitor, Notts Police Authy, 1978–80; Asst and Sen. Asst Solicitor, Leics CC, 1980–83; Prin. Solicitor, Warwicks CC, 1983–87. *Recreations:* photography, shares, railways, entertaining the children. *Address:* (office) 113 Chancery Lane, WC2A 1PL. *T:* 0171–242 1222.

BIJUR, Peter Isaac; Senior Vice President, Texaco Inc., since 1992; *b* 14 Oct. 1942; *m* 1968, Anne Montgomery; two *s* one *d*. *Educ:* Univ. of Pittsburgh (BA Pol. Sci. 1964); Columbia Univ. (MBA 1966). Texaco, 1966–: Manager, Buffalo sales dist, 1971–73; Asst Manager to Vice-Pres. for public affairs, 1973–75; Staff Co-ordinator, dept of strategic planning, 1975–77; Asst to Exec. Vice-Pres., 1977–80; Manager, Rocky Mountain Refining and Marketing, 1980–81; Asst to Chm. of Bd, 1981–83; Pres., Texaco Oil Trading & Supply Co., 1984; Vice-Pres., special projects, 1984–86; Pres. and Chief Exec., Don Mills, Texaco Canada, 1987–89; Chm., Pres. and Chief Exec., Texaco Canada Resources, Calgary, 1988–89; Chm., Texaco Ltd, 1989–91; Pres., Texaco Europe, 1990–92. *Address:* Texaco Inc., 2000 Westchester Avenue, White Plains, NY 10650, USA.

BILBY, Prof. Bruce Alexander, BA, PhD; FRS 1977; Consultant; Professor of the Theory of Materials, University of Sheffield, 1966–84, now Emeritus; *b* 3 Sept. 1922; *e s* of late George Alexander Bilby and Dorothy Jean (*née* Telfer); *m* 1st, 1946, Hazel Joyce (*née* Casken); two *s* one *d*; 2nd, 1966, Lorette Wendela (*née* Thomas); two *s*. *Educ:* Dover Grammar Sch.; Peterhouse, Cambridge (BA); Univ. of Birmingham (PhD). Admiralty, 1943–46. Research, Birmingham, 1946–51; Univ. of Sheffield: Royal Soc. Sorby Res. Fellow, 1951–57; J. H. Andrew Res. Fellow, 1957–58; Reader in Theoretical Metallurgy, 1958–62, Prof., 1962–66. Has made contributions to theory of dislocations and its application to the deformation, transformation and fracture of metallic crystals. Rosenhain Medal, 1963; Griffith Medal, 1994. *Publications:* contribs to learned jls. *Recreation:* sailing. *Address:* 32 Devonshire Road, Totley, Sheffield S17 3NT. *T:* Sheffield (0114) 236 1086; Department of Mechanical and Process Engineering, The University, Mappin Street, Sheffield S1 3JD. *T:* Sheffield (0114) 276 8555.

BILDT, Carl; MP (Moderate Party), Sweden, since 1979; European Union Co-Chairman, International Conference on Former Yugoslavia, since 1995; *b* Halmstad, 15 July 1949; *s* of Daniel B. Bildt and Kerstin Bildt (*née* Andersson); *m* 1984, Mia Bohman; one *s* one *d*. *Educ:* Stockholm Univ. Mem., Stockholm CC, 1974–77; Under-Sec. of State for Co-ordination and Planning, Cabinet Office, 1979–81; Member: Parly Standing Cttee in Foreign Affairs, 1982–86; Adv. Council on Foreign Affairs, 1982–; Submarine Defence Commn, 1982–83; 1984 Defence Cttee, 1984–87; Prime Minister of Sweden, 1991–94. Moderate Party: Mem., Exec. Cttee, 1981–; Mem., Parly Gp Council, 1982–91; Chm., 1986–. Mem., IISS, 1981–. Mem., Nordic Council, 1986– (Chm., Conservative Gp, 1988–91). Chm., Internat. Democratic Union, 1992–. *Publications:* Landet Som Steg ut i Kylan, 1972; Framtid i Frihet, 1976; Hallänning, Svensk, Europé, 1991. *Address:* Sveriges Riksdag, 10012 Stockholm, Sweden. *T:* (8) 7865390.

BILL, (Edward) Geoffrey (Watson), OBE 1991; FSA, FRHistS; Lambeth Librarian, 1958–91; Lecturer and Archivist, Christ Church, Oxford, 1950–91; *b* 19 Feb. 1924; *s* of Edward Richard Bill and Anne (*née* Greenwood); *m* Margaret Nancy Finch; one *s* one *d*. *Educ:* Kingston Grammar Sch.; Balliol Coll., Oxford (MA). FRHistS 1983; FSA 1984. Served Army, 1943–46 (Lieut). Dept of Western MSS, Bodleian Library, Oxford, 1954–58. DLitt Lambeth, 1983. *Publications:* Christ Church Meadow, 1965; (with Dr J. F. A. Mason) Christ Church and Reform 1850–1867, 1970; University Reform in Nineteenth Century Oxford, 1973; Education at Christ Church Oxford 1660–1800, 1988; Catalogue of MSS in Lambeth Palace Library, 1972–83. *Recreation:* avoiding gardening. *Address:* Moss Cottage West, Foxfield, Broughton-in-Furness, Cumbria LA20 6BT. *T:* Broughton-in-Furness (01229) 716315.

BILLETT, Paul Rodney, CB 1981; *b* 19 Feb. 1921; *s* of late Arthur William and Grace Hilda Billett; *m* 1st, 1945, Muriel Gwendoline Marsh (*d* 1977); one *s*; 2nd, 1985, Eileen May Nourse. *Educ:* Commonweal and College Grammar Schools, Swindon. Entered Exchequer and Audit Dept, 1939. Served RASC, 1941–46. Deputy Secretary, Exchequer and Audit Dept, 1975–81 (retired). *Address:* Wynthorpe, Cornsland, Brentwood, Essex CM14 4JL. *T:* Brentwood (01277) 224830.

BILLINGHAM, Angela Theodora, JP; Member (Lab) Northamptonshire and Blaby, European Parliament, since 1994; *b* 31 July 1939; widow; two *d*. *Educ:* Aylesbury GS; London Univ. Former Teacher and Examiner. Mayor of Banbury, 1976; Member (Lab): Banbury BC, 1970–74; Cherwell DC, 1974–84; Oxfordshire CC, 1993–94. Contested (Lab) Banbury, 1992. Chair, Central Region MEPs, 1995–. JP N Oxfordshire and Bicester, 1976. *Recreations:* tennis, gardening, bridge, cinema. *Address:* European Parliament, 97 Rue Belliard, 1040 Brussels, Belgium; The Green, Oxford Road, Adderbury, near Banbury, Oxon OX17 3NG.

BILLINGHAM, Prof. Rupert Everett, MA, DPhil, DSc Oxon; FRS 1961; Professor and Chairman, Department of Cell Biology and Anatomy, Southwestern Medical School, University of Texas Health Science Center at Dallas, 1971–86; Professor Emeritus, 1990; *b* 15 Oct. 1921; *o s* of Albert Everett and Helen Louise Billingham, Oxford; *m* 1951, Jean Mary Morpeth; two *s* one *d*. *Educ:* City of Oxford High Sch.; Oriel Coll., Oxford. Served 1942–46, as Lieut RNVR. Asst Lectr, later Lectr in Zoology, University of Birmingham, 1947; Junior Research Fellow, British Empire Cancer Campaign, 1950; Intermediate Research Fellow, Brit. Emp. Cancer Campaign, 1953; Hon. Res. Asst, later Res. Associate, Dept of Zoology, University Coll., London, 1951; Wistar Prof. of Zoology, Univ. of Pennsylvania, USA, and Mem. of Wistar Institute of Anatomy and Biology, Philadelphia, 1957; Prof. and Chm., Dept of Medical Genetics, Univ. of Pennsylvania Med. Sch., Pa, 1965–71. Member: Allergy and Immunology Study Section, Nat. Insts of Health, US Public Health Service, 1958–62; Transplantation and Immunology Cttee, Nat. Insts of Health, 1968–70, 1971–73; Scientific Adv. Cttee, Massachusetts General Hospital, 1976–79; Nat. Allergy and Infectious Diseases Council, Nat. Insts of Health, 1980–83; Sigma Xi College of Nat. Lecturers, 1981–83; President: Transplantation Soc., 1974; Internat. Soc. for Immunology of Reproduction, 1983–86. Hon. Mem., British Transplantation Soc., 1988. Fellow, New York Acad. of Sciences, 1962; Fellow, Amer. Acad. of Arts and Sciences, 1965. Lectures: Herman Beerman, Soc. for Investigative Dermatology, 1963; I. S. Ravdin, Amer. College of Surgeons, 1964; *Sigma Xi*, Yale, 1965; Nat. Insts of Health, 1965; J. W. Jenkinson Meml, Oxford, 1965–66; Harvey, NY, 1966; Kinyoun, Nat. Inst. of Allergy and Infectious Diseases, 1979; Dist. Guest, Soc. for Gyn. Investigation, 1982. Hon. DSc: Trinity Coll., Hartford, Conn, 1965; Univ. of Pennsylvania, 1992. Alvarenga Prize, Coll. Physicians, Philadelphia, 1963; Hon. Award Medal, Amer. Assoc. of Plastic Surgeons, 1964; Adair Award, Amer. Gynecological Soc., 1971; AOA Honor Med. Soc., 1974. *Publications:* The Immunobiology of Transplantation (with W. K. Silvers), 1971; The Immunobiology of Mammalian Reproduction (with A. E. Beer) 1976; contribs to scien. jls on biology of skin, immunology of tissue transplantation and immunology of manmalian reproduction. *Recreations:* woodwork, gardening. *Address:* RR3, Box 86P, Vineyard Haven, MA 02568, USA. *T:* (508) 6937939.

BILLINGTON, Brian John, (Bill); Director, Network Management and Maintenance, Highways Agency, since 1995; *b* 25 Feb. 1939; *s* of late Kenneth Jack Billington and Doris Violet Billington; *m* 1965, Gillian Elizabeth Annis; two *d*. *Educ:* Slough Grammar Sch.; The Polytechnic, Regent Street (BSc(Econ)); LSE (MSc). Lectr, The Polytechnic, Regent Street, 1966–68; Min. of Power, later Dept of Energy, 1969–74; Dept of Transport, 1974–; Under Sec., 1991–. *Address:* Highways Agency, Saint Christopher House, Southwark Street, SE1 0TE. *T:* 0171–921 4883.

BILLINGTON, Dr James Hadley; Librarian of Congress, USA, since 1987; *b* 1 June 1929; *s* of Nelson Billington and Jane Coolbaugh; *m* 1957, Marjorie Anne Brennan; two *s* two *d*. *Educ:* Princeton Univ.; Balliol College, Oxford (Rhodes Scholar; DPhil 1953). Served US Army, 1953–56. Harvard University: Instructor in History, 1957–58; Asst Prof. of History and Res. Fellow, Russian Res. Center, 1958–59; Asst Prof. of History, 1958–61; Associate Prof. of History, 1962–64, Prof., 1964–73, Princeton; Dir, Woodrow Wilson Internat. Center for Scholars, Washington, 1973–87. Visiting Research Professor: Inst. of History, Acad. of Scis, USSR, 1966–67; Univ. of Helsinki, 1960–61; Ecole des Hautes Etudes en Scis Sociales, Paris, 1985, 1988; Vis. Lectr, USA, Europe, Asia; Guggenheim Fellow, 1960–61. Member: Amer. Acad. of Arts and Scis; Amer. Philosophical Soc.; numerous hon. degrees. Comd, Ordre des Arts et des Lettres. *Publications:* Mikhailovsky and Russian Populism, 1958; The Icon and the Axe: an interpretive history of Russian culture, 1966; The Arts of Russia, 1970; Fire in the Minds of Men: origins of the Revolutionary Faith, 1980; Russia Transformed: breakthrough to hope, 1992; contribs to learned jls. *Address:* Library of Congress, Washington, DC 20540, USA. *T:* (202) 7075205.

BILLINGTON, Kevin; film, theatre and television director; *b* 12 June 1934; *s* of Richard and Margaret Billington; *m* 1967, Lady Rachel Mary Pakenham (*see* Lady Rachel Billington); two *s* two *d*. *Educ:* Bryanston Sch.; Queens' Coll., Cambridge (BA). Film dir, BBC prog., Tonight, 1960–63; documentary film dir, BBC, 1963–67; films include: A Sort of Paradise; Many Mexicos; The Mexican Attitude; Twilight of Empire; Mary McCarthy's Paris; These Humble Shores; Matador; A Few Castles in Spain; The English Cardinal; A Socialist Childhood; Madison Avenue, USA; ATV documentary, All The Queen's Men. *Feature Film Director:* Interlude, 1967; The Rise and Rise of Michael Rimmer, 1969; The Light at the Edge of the World, 1970; Voices, 1974; Reflections, 1984. *Television Director:* And No One Can Save Her, 1973; Once Upon a Time is Now (documentary), 1978; The Music Will Never Stop (documentary), 1979; Henry VIII, 1979; The Jail Diary of Albie Sachs, 1980; The Good Soldier, 1981; Outside Edge, 1982; The Sonnets of William Shakespeare, 1984; Heartland, 1989; Small Doses, 1990; A Time to Dance, 1992. *Theatre Director:* Find Your Way Home, 1970; Me, 1973; The Birthday Party, 1974; The Caretaker, 1975; Bloody Neighbours, 1975; Emigrés, 1976; The

Homecoming, 1978; Quartermaine's Terms, 1982; The Deliberate Death of a Polish Priest, 1985 (Channel Four, 1986); The Philanthropist, 1986; The Lover, and A Slight Ache (double bill), 1987; The Breadwinner, 1989; Veterans Day, 1989; Quartermaine's Terms, 1993; Old Times, 1994. Chm., BAFTA, 1989–90 and 1990–91. Screenwriters' Guild Award, 1966 and 1967; Guild of TV Producers and Directors Award, 1966 and 1967. *Recreation:* swimming. *Address:* The Court House, Poyntington, Sherborne, Dorset DT9 4LF. *Club:* Garrick.

BILLINGTON, Michael; Drama Critic of The Guardian, since 1971; *b* 16 Nov. 1939; *s* of Alfred Billington and Patricia (*née* Bradshaw); *m* 1978, Jeanine Bradlaugh. *Educ:* Warwick Sch.; St Catherine's Coll., Oxford (BA). Trained as journalist with Liverpool Daily Post and Echo, 1961–62; Public Liaison Officer and Director for Lincoln Theatre Co., 1962–64; reviewed plays, films and television for The Times, 1965–71. Film Critic: Birmingham Post, 1968–78; Illustrated London News, 1968–81; London Arts Correspondent, New York Times, 1978–; Drama Critic, Country Life, 1987–. Contributor to numerous radio and television Arts programmes, incl. Kaleidoscope, Critics' Forum, The Book Programme, Arena. Presenter, The Billington Interview and Theatre Call, BBC World Service. Writer and Presenter, television profiles of Peggy Ashcroft, Peter Hall and Alan Ayckbourn. Prof. of Drama, Colorado Coll., 1981. IPC Critic of the Year, 1974. *Publications:* The Modern Actor, 1974; How Tickled I Am, 1977; (ed) The Performing Arts, 1980; The Guinness Book of Theatre Facts and Feats, 1982; Alan Ayckbourn, 1983; Tom Stoppard, 1987; Peggy Ashcroft, 1988; (ed) Twelfth Night, 1990; One Night Stands, 1993. *Recreations:* work, travel, cricket. *Address:* 15 Hearne Road, W4 3NJ. *T:* 0181–995 0455. *Club:* Garrick.

BILLINGTON, Lady Rachel (Mary); writer; *b* 11 May 1942; *d* of 7th Earl of Longford, *qv*, and Countess of Longford, *qv*; *m* 1967, Kevin Billington, *qv*; two *s* two *d*. *Educ:* London Univ. (BA English). Work includes: short stories; four BBC radio plays; two BBC TV plays, Don't be Silly, 1979, Life After Death, 1981. Reviewer; feature writer, Sunday Telegraph. *Publications:* All Things Nice, 1969; The Big Dipper, 1970; Lilacs out of the Dead Land, 1971; Cock Robin, 1973; Beautiful, 1974; A Painted Devil, 1975; A Woman's Age, 1979; Occasion of Sin, 1982; The Garish Day, 1985; Loving Attitudes, 1988; Theo and Matilda, 1990; Bodily Harm, 1992; The Family Year, 1992; The Great Umbilical: mother, daughter, mother, 1994; *for children:* Rosanna and the Wizard-Robot, 1981; The First Christmas, 1983; Star-Time, 1984; The First Easter, 1987; The First Miracles, 1990. *Recreation:* nature. *Address:* The Court House, Poyntington, near Sherborne, Dorset DT9 4LF. *Clubs:* Society of Authors, PEN.

BILLOT, Barbara Kathleen; Deputy Director (Under-Secretary), Department for National Savings, 1974–80; *b* 26 May 1920; *d* of Alfred Billot and Agnes Billot (*née* Hiner). *Educ:* Petersfield County High Sch. for Girls. Post Office Savings Bank: Clerical Officer 1938; Exec. Off. 1939; Higher Exec. Off. 1946; Sen. Exec. Off. 1953; Chief Exec. Off. 1957; Principal, Post Office Headquarters, 1960; Sen. Chief Exec. Off., PO Savings Dept, 1961; Principal Exec. Off. (Estabt Off.), 1969; Asst Sec., Dept for Nat. Savings, 1971. *Recreations:* reading, theatre-going. *Address:* 6 Springbank, Chichester, W Sussex PO19 4BX. *T:* Chichester (01243) 776295.

bin YEOP, Tan Sri Abdul Aziz, Al-Haj; PSM (Malaysia); Hon. GCVO 1972; Member, Malaysian Parliament; Partner in legal firm, Aziz and Mazlan, Advocates and Solicitors, 1966–71, and since 1973; *b* 5 Oct. 1916; *m* 1942, Puan Sri Hamidah Aziz; six *s* three *d*. *Educ:* King Edward VII Sch., Perak, Malaysia. Malay Administrative Service, 1937; called to Bar, Lincoln's Inn, 1950; Malayan Civil Service, 1951; First Asst State Sec., Perak 1954; London Univ. (course in Community Development), 1955. Permanent Sec., Min. of Agriculture, 1958–62; Dep. Sec., Malaysian Affairs Div., Prime Minister's Dept, 1962–64; Permanent Sec., Min. of Education, 1964–66. Chm. and Dir of firms in Malaysia, 1966–71. High Comr for Malaysia in London, 1971–73. First Chm., Bd of Governors of BERNAMA (Malaysia's National News Agency), 1967–71; Chairman: Council, Universiti Teknologi, Malaysia, 1974– (Pro-chancellor, 1977–80); Majlis Amanah Raayat, Malaysia, 1975–. *Recreations:* walking, reading, fishing. *Address:* c/o Aziz and Mazlan, Advocates and Solicitors, Wisma Getah Asli, 1st Floor, 148 Jalan Ampang, Kuala Lumpur 50450, Malaysia. *T:* Kuala Lumpur (3) 2420804, 2427961, 2420105, *Fax:* (3) 2433525, 2483525.

BINCHY, Maeve, (Mrs Gordon Snell); writer; *b* Dublin, 28 May 1940; *d* of William Binchy and Maureen Blackmore; *m* 1977, Gordon Snell, writer and broadcaster. *Educ:* Holy Child Convent, Killiney, Dublin; University College, Dublin. History teacher in girls' schs, 1960–68; columnist, Irish Times, 1968–. *Publications: novels:* Light a Penny Candle, 1982; Echoes, 1985; Firefly Summer, 1987; Circle of Friends, 1990 (filmed, 1995); Copper Beech, 1992; The Glass Lake, 1994; *short stories:* Central Line, 1978; Victoria Line, 1980; Dublin 4, 1982; The Lilac Bus, 1984; Silver Wedding, 1988. *Recreations:* reading, theatre, very bad bridge, gardening. *Address:* Dalkey, Co. Dublin, Ireland.

BING, Inigo Geoffrey; a Metropolitan Stipendiary Magistrate, since 1989; an Assistant Recorder, since 1991; *b* 1 April 1944; *s* of late Geoffrey Henry Cecil Bing, QC and Christian Frances Bing; *m* 1980, Shirley-Anne Holmes (*née* Benka); three step *c*. *Educ:* St Olave's Grammar Sch., Southwark; Birmingham Univ. (LLB). Called to the Bar, Inner Temple, 1967; practised London and SE Circuit. Mem. (Lab) London Borough of Lambeth, 1971–78 (Chm., F and GP Cttee, 1974–78); Co-founder, Lambeth Community Law Centre. Contested Braintree: (SDP) 1983; (SDP/Alliance) 1987. *Publication:* Criminal Procedure and Sentencing in the Magistrates' Court, 1990, 3rd edn 1994. *Recreations:* reading, writing, music, exploring France, the company of friends. *Address:* c/o Thames Magistrates' Court, Bow Road, E3 4DJ. *Club:* Reform.

BING, Sir Rudolf (Franz Joseph), KBE 1971 (CBE 1956); General Manager, Metropolitan Opera, New York, 1950–72; Distinguished Professor, Brooklyn College, City University of New York, 1972–75; Director Columbia Artists Management, since 1973; *b* Vienna, 9 Jan. 1902; *m* 1929, Nina (*née* Schelemskaja) (*d* 1983); *m* 1987, Carroll Lee Douglass (marr. annulled, 1989). *Educ:* Vienna. Hessian State Theatre, Darmstadt, 1928–30; Civic Opera, Berlin-Charlottenburg, 1930–33. Gen. Manager, Glyndebourne Opera, 1935–49; Artistic Director, Edinburgh Festival, 1947–49. Holds hon. doctorates in music and in letters, from the US. Légion d'Honneur, 1958; Comdr's Cross of Order of Merit, Federal Republic of Germany, 1958; Grand Silver Medal of Honour, Republic of Austria, 1959; Comdr, Order of Merit, Republic of Italy, 1959, Grand Officer, 1970. *Publication:* 5000 Nights at the Opera, 1972.

BINGHAM, family name of **Baron Clanmorris** and of **Earl of Lucan.**

BINGHAM, Lord; George Charles Bingham; *b* 21 Sept. 1967; *s* and *heir* of 7th Earl of Lucan, *qv*. *Educ:* Eton; Trinity Hall, Cambridge.

BINGHAM, Caroline Margery Conyers; professional writer; *b* 7 Feb. 1938; *o d* of Cedric and Muriel Worsdell; *m* 1958, Andrew Bingham (marr. diss. 1972); one *d*. *Educ:* Mount Sch., York; Convent de la Sagesse, Newcastle upon Tyne; Cheltenham Ladies' Coll.; Univ. of Bristol (BA Hons History). Res. Fellow, Dept of History, RHBNC, London Univ., 1985–87. *Publications:* The Making of a King: the early years of James VI and I, 1968 (USA 1969); James V, King of Scots, 1971; (contrib.) The Scottish Nation: a history of the Scots from Independence to Union, 1972; The Life and Times of Edward II, 1973; The Stewart Kingdom of Scotland, 1371–1603, 1974 (USA 1974); The Kings and Queens of Scotland, 1976 (USA 1976); The Crowned Lions: the Early Plantagenet Kings, 1978; James VI of Scotland, 1979; The Voice of the Lion (verse anthology), 1980; James I of England, 1981; Land of the Scots: a short history, 1983; History of Royal Holloway College 1886–1986, 1987; Beyond the Highland Line: Highland history and culture, 1991. *Address:* 164 Regent's Park Road, NW1 8XN.

BINGHAM, Hon. Charlotte Mary Thérèse; playwright and novelist; *b* 29 June 1942; *d* of 7th Baron Clanmorris (John Bingham) and of Madeleine Mary, *d* of late Clement Ebel; *m* 1964, Terence Brady, *qv*; one *s* one *d*. *Educ:* The Priory, Haywards Heath; Sorbonne. *TV series* with Terence Brady: Boy Meets Girl; Take Three Girls; Upstairs Downstairs; Away From It All; Play for Today; No—Honestly; Yes—Honestly; Pig in the Middle; Thomas and Sarah; The Complete Lack of Charm of the Bourgeoisie; Nanny; Oh Madeline! (USA TV); Father Matthew's Daughter; Forever Green; The Upper Hand; *TV films:* Love With a Perfect Stranger, 1986; Losing Control, 1987; The Seventh Raven, 1987; This Magic Moment, 1988; Riders, 1990; Polo, 1993; *stage:* (contrib.) The Sloane Ranger Revue, 1985; I Wish, I Wish, 1989. *Publications:* Coronet among the Weeds, 1963; Lucinda, 1965; Coronet among the Grass, 1972; Belgravia, 1983; Country Life, 1984; At Home, 1986; To Hear A Nightingale, 1988; The Business, 1989; In Sunshine or In Shadow, 1991; Stardust, 1992; By Invitation Only, 1993; Nanny, 1993; Change of Heart, 1994; Debutantes, 1995; with Terence Brady: Victoria, 1972; Rose's Story, 1973; Victoria and Company, 1974; Yes—Honestly, 1977. *Recreations:* horses, watching others garden. *Address:* c/o Peters, Frazer & Dunlop, 5th Floor, The Chambers, Chelsea Harbour, SW10 0XF. *Club:* Society of Authors.

BINGHAM, Sir (Eardley) Max, Kt 1988; QC (Tas.) 1974; Chairman, Queensland Criminal Justice Commission, 1989–92; *b* 18 March 1927; *s* of Thomas Eardley and Olive Bingham; *m* 1952, Margaret Garrett Jesson; three *s* one *d*. *Educ:* Univ. of Tasmania (LLB (Hons)); Lincoln Coll., Oxford (BCL; Rhodes Schol., 1950); Univ. of California at Berkley (Harkness Commonwealth Fund Fellow, 1963). RANR, 1945–46. Legal practice, and teaching, Univ. of Tasmania, 1953–69. MHA Tasmania, 1969–84; Attorney-General, 1969–72; Leader of the Opposition, 1972–79, Dep. Leader of the Opposition, 1982; Dep. Premier of Tas., 1982–84. Mem., Nat. Crime Authority, 1984–87. *Publications:* contribs to jls. *Recreations:* farming, reading, sailing. *Address:* 14 Musgrove Road, Geilston Bay, Tas 7015, Australia. *T:* (02) 438331. *Clubs:* Tasmanian, Royal Yacht of Tasmania (Hobart)

BINGHAM, John, CBE 1991; FRS 1977; Plant Breeding International, Cambridge, 1981–91; *b* 19 June 1930; *s* of Thomas Frederick Bingham and Emma Maud Lusher; *m* 1983, Jadwiga Anna Siedlecka; one *s*. Mem. of staff, Plant Breeding Inst. of Cambridge, subseq. Plant Breeding Internat. Cambridge Ltd, 1954–91. Has researched in plant breeding, culminating in production of improved winter wheat varieties for British agriculture. Pres., Royal Norfolk Agricl Assoc., 1991. Hon. FRASE, 1983. Hon. ScD UEA, 1992. Res. Medal, RASE, 1975; Mullard Medal of Royal Society, 1975; Massey Ferguson Nat. Award for Services to UK Agric., 1984. *Recreations:* farming, conservation of wild life. *Address:* Hereward Barn, Church Lane, Mattishall Burgh, Dereham, Norfolk NR20 3QZ. *T:* Dereham (01362) 858354.

BINGHAM, Sir Max; *see* Bingham, Sir E. M.

BINGHAM, Rt. Hon. Sir Thomas (Henry), Kt 1980; PC 1986; Master of the Rolls, since 1992; *b* 13 Oct. 1933; *o s* of late Dr T. H. Bingham and Dr C. Bingham, Reigate; *m* 1963, Elizabeth, *o d* of late Peter Loxley; two *s* one *d*. *Educ:* Sedbergh; Balliol Coll., Oxford (MA; Hon. Fellow, 1989). Royal Ulster Rifles, 1952–54 (2nd Lt); London Irish Rifles (TA) 1954–59. Univ. of Oxford: Gibbs Schol. in Mod. Hist., 1956; 1st cl. Hons, Mod. Hist., 1957. Eldon Law Schol., 1957; Arden Schol., Gray's Inn, 1959; Cert. of Honour, Bar Finals, 1959; called to Bar, Gray's Inn, 1959; Bencher, 1979. Standing Jun. Counsel to Dept of Employment, 1968–72; QC 1972; a Recorder of the Crown Court, 1975–80; Judge of the High Court of Justice, Queen's Bench Div., and Judge of the Commercial Court, 1980–86; a Lord Justice of Appeal, 1986–92. Leader, Investigation into the supply of petroleum and petroleum products to Rhodesia, 1977–78; Chm., King's Fund Working Parties into Statutory Registration of Osteopaths and Chiropractors, 1989–93; Inquiry into the Supervision of BCCI, 1991–92; Comr, Interception of Communications Act 1985, 1992–94. Mem., Lord Chancellor's Law Reform Cttee; Chairman: Council of Legal Educn, 1982–86; Adv. Council, Centre for Commercial Law Studies, Queen Mary and Westfield Coll., London Univ., 1989–92; Adv. Council on Public Records, 1992–; Magna Carta Trust, 1992–; Royal Commn on Historical Manuscripts, 1994–. President: CIArb, 1991–; British Records Assoc., 1992–. Visitor: Balliol Coll., Oxford, 1986–; RPMS, 1989–; UCL, 1992–; Nuffield Coll., Oxford, 1992–; London Business Sch., 1992–. Governor: Sedbergh, 1978–88; Atlantic Coll., 1984–89. Special Trustee, St Mary's Hosp., 1985–92 (Chm., 1988–92); Member: St Mary's Med. Sch. Delegacy, 1988–92; Council, KCL, 1989–93. Trustee, Pilgrim Trust, 1991–. Fellow, Winchester, 1983–93; Presentation Fellow, KCL, 1992; Fellow, QMW, 1993; Hon. Bencher, Inn of Court of NI, 1993. Hon. LLD Birmingham, 1993; Hon. DCL Oxford, 1994. *Publication:* Chitty on Contracts, (Asst Editor) 22nd edn, 1961. *Address:* Royal Courts of Justice, Strand, WC2A 2LL.

BINGLEY, Juliet Martin, (Lady Bingley), MBE 1991; Research Social Worker, City Corporation Social Services, based at St Mark's Hospital, EC1, since 1990 (Senior Social Worker, 1973–90); *b* 18 July 1925; *d* of Mary Kate Vick and Reginald Vick, OBE, MCh, FRCS; *m* 1948, Adm. Sir Alexander Noel Campbell Bingley, GCB, OBE (*d* 1972); one *s* two *d*. *Educ:* King Alfred School, Hampstead; London Sch. of Economics. Associated Mem., Inst. of Medical Social Workers. Social Worker, St Bartholomew's Hosp., 1945–48. Chairman: Nat. Assoc. of Mental Health, 1979–84; Good Practices in Mental Health, 1989–93; Vice-Chm., Nat. Assoc. for Colitis and Crohn's Disease, 1989–. Counsellor, Dr Aubrey and Partners, Welwyn, Herts, 1990–. CStJ 1962. Companion of Honour, Republic of Malta, 1976. *Recreations:* music, gardening, reading, theatre, moving furniture, collecting Staffordshire figures, lawn mowing. *Address:* Hoddesdonbury Farm, Hoddesdon, Herts EN11 8LS. *T:* Hoddesdon (01992) 463238.

BINMORE, Prof. Kenneth George, PhD; FBA 1995; Professor of Economics, University College London, since 1991; *b* 27 Sept. 1940; *s* of Ernest George Binmore and Maud Alice (*née* Holland); *m* 1968, Josephine Ann Lee; two *s* two *d*. *Educ:* Imperial Coll., London (BSc; PhD 1964). Lectr, Reader and Prof. of Maths, LSE, 1969–88; Prof. of Econs, LSE and Univ. of Michigan, 1988–93; Dir, ESRC Centre for Econ. Learning and Social Learning, 1994–. *Publications:* Mathematical Analysis, 1977, 2nd edn 1982; Logic, Sets and Numbers, 1980; Topological Ideas, 1981; Calculus, 1982; Economic Organizations as Games, 1986; Economics of Bargaining, 1986; Essays on the Foundation of Game Theory, 1991; Fun and Games, 1992; Frontiers of Game Theory, 1993; Game Theory and the Social Contract, 1994; papers. *Recreation:* philosophy. *Address:* Newmills, Whitebrook, near Monmouth, Gwent NP5 4TY. *T:* Monmouth (01600) 860691; (office) 0171–380 7864; (home) 0171–700 5133.

BINNEY, H(arry) A(ugustus) Roy, CB 1950; Director-General, 1951–70, Director-General, International, 1971–72, British Standards Institution; retired; *b* 18 May 1907; *s* of Harry Augustus Binney, Churston, Devon; *m* 1944, Barbara Poole (*d* 1975); three *s* one *d* (and one *d* decd). *Educ:* Royal Dockyard Sch., Devonport; London Univ. BSc(Eng). Entered Board of Trade, 1929, Under-Sec. 1947–51. Chairman: Standardization Cttee, European Productivity Agency, 1953–58; Cttee for European Standards (CEN), 1963–65; Mem. Council, 1951–72, Vice-Pres., 1964–69, ISO. UN Advr on Standards to Govt of Cyprus, 1974–77. Hon. Life Fellow, Standards Engrg Soc. of America; Hon. Life Mem., American Soc. for Testing and Materials. FKC; FRSA. *Recreation:* gardening. *Address:* Hambutts Orchard, Edge Lane, Painswick, Glos GL6 6UW. *T:* Painswick (01452) 813718.

BINNEY, Marcus Hugh Crofton, OBE 1983; writer, journalist, conservationist; Founder, 1975, and President, since 1984, Save Britain's Heritage (Chairman, 1975–84); *s* of late Lt-Col Francis Crofton Simms, MC and of Sonia, *d* of Rear-Adm. Sir William Marcus Charles Beresford-Whyte, KCB, CMG (she *m* 2nd, Sir George Binney, DSO); *m* 1st, 1966, Hon. Sara Anne Vanneck (marr. diss. 1976), *e d* of 6th Baron Huntingfield; 2nd, 1981, Anne Carolyn, *d* of Dr T. H. Hills, Merstham, Surrey; two *s*. *Educ:* Magdalene Coll., Cambridge (BA 1966). Architectural writer, 1968–77, Architectural Editor, 1977–84, Editor, 1984–86, Country Life; Ed., Landscape, 1987–88; envmt correspondent, Harpers & Queen, 1989–90; architectural correspondent, The Times, 1991–. Sec., UK Cttee, Internat. Council on Monuments and Sites, 1972–81; Director: Rly Heritage Trust, 1985–; HMS Warrior; Chairman: Friends of City Churches, 1995–; Save Europe's Heritage, 1995–; Pres., Save Jersey's Heritage; Mem. Council, Jersey Wildlife Preservation Trust. London Conservation Medal, 1985. *Publications:* (with Peter Burman): Change and Decay: the future of our churches, 1977; Chapels and Churches: who cares?, 1977; (with Max Hanna) Preservation Pays, 1978; (ed jtly) Railway Architecture, 1979; (ed jtly) Our Past Before Us, 1981; (with Kit Martin) The Country House: to be or not to be, 1982; (with Max Hanna) Preserve and Prosper, 1983; The Architecture of Sir Robert Taylor, 1984; Our Vanishing Heritage, 1984; Country Manors of Portugal, 1987; Palace on the River, 1991; (with M. Watson-Smyth) The Save Action Guide, 1991; Châteaux of the Loire, 1992; (with R. Runciman) Glyndebourne: building a vision, 1994; The Châteaux of France: photographs by Frederick Evans 1906–7, 1994; contributor to: Satanic Mills, 1979; Elysian Gardens, 1979; Lost Houses of Scotland, 1980; Taking the Plunge, 1982; SAVE Gibraltar's Heritage, 1982; Vanishing Houses of England, 1983; Time Gentlemen Please, 1983. *Address:* Domaine des Vaux, St Lawrence, Jersey JE3 1JG. *T:* Jersey (01534) 864424, *Fax:* (01534) 862612.

BINNIE, David Stark, OBE 1979; FCIT; FBIM; railway and rapid transport consultant; *b* 2 June 1922; *s* of Walter Archibald Binnie and Helen (*née* Baxter), Bonkle, Lanarkshire; *m* 1947, Leslie Archibald; one *s* one *d*. *Educ:* Wishaw High School. British Railways: Gen. and Signalling Asst to Gen. Manager Scottish Region, 1955; Asst District Operating Supt 1961, District Operating Supt 1963, Glasgow North; Divisional Movements Manager, Glasgow Div., 1965; Movements Manager, Scottish Region, 1967; Divisional Manager, SE Div., Southern Region, 1969; Asst Gen. Manager, Southern Region, 1970, Gen. Manager, 1972; Exec. Dir, Freight, BR Board, 1974–76; Gen. Manager, BR, London Midland Region, 1977–80. Lt-Col Engineer and Railway Staff Corps, RE (T&AVR). OStJ. *Recreation:* Dartmoor and Highland life. *Address:* Above Ways, Lower Knowle Road, Lustleigh, Devon TQ13 9SE. *T:* Lustleigh (016477) 386.

BINNIG, Prof. Dr Gerd Karl; IBM Fellow, since 1986; Honorary Professor of Physics, University of Munich, since 1987; *b* 20 July 1947; *m* 1969, Lore; one *s* one *d*. *Educ:* J. W. Goethe Univ., Frankfurt/M (DipPhys; PhD). Research staff mem., IBM Zurich Res. Lab., in fields of superconductivity of semiconductors and scanning tunneling microscopy, 1978–, Gp Leader 1984–; IBM Almaden Res. Center, San José, and collab. with Stanford Univ., 1985–86; Vis. Prof., Stanford Univ., 1985–86. Member: Technology Council, IBM Acad., 1989–92; Supervisory Bd, Mercedes Automobil Holding AG, 1989–. For. Associate Mem., Acad. of Scis, Washington, 1987. Hon. FRMS 1988. Scanning Tunneling Microscopy awards: Physics Prize, German Phys. Soc., 1982; Otto Klung Prize, 1983; (jtly) King Faisal Internat. Prize for Science and Hewlett Packard Europhysics Prize, 1984; (jtly) Nobel Prize in Physics, 1986; Elliot Cresson Medal, Franklin Inst., Philadelphia, 1987; Minnie Rosen Award, Ross Univ., NY, 1988. Grosses Verdienstkreuz mit Stern und Schulterband des Verdienstordens (FRG), 1987; Bayenischer Verdienstorden, 1992. *Recreations:* music, tennis, soccer, golf. *Address:* IBM Research Laboratory, Saemerstrasse 4, 8803 Rueschlikon, Switzerland. *T:* (1) 7248415.

BINNING, Lord; George Edmund Baldred Baillie-Hamilton; *b* 27 Dec. 1985; *s* and *heir* of Earl of Haddington, *qv*.

BINNING, Kenneth George Henry, CMG 1976; Director, Public Policy Unit Ltd, since 1993; *b* 5 Jan. 1928; *o s* of late Henry and Hilda Binning; *m* 1953, Pamela Dorothy, *o d* of A. E. and D. G. Pronger; three *s* one *d*. *Educ:* Bristol Grammar Sch.; Balliol Coll., Oxford. Joined Home Civil Service, 1950; Nat. Service, 1950–52; HM Treasury, 1952–58; Private Sec. to Financial Sec., 1956–57; AEA, 1958–65; seconded to Min. of Technology, 1965; rejoined Civil Service, 1968; Dir-Gen. Concorde, 1972–76 and Under-Sec., DTI later Dept of Industry, 1972–83. Mem., BSC, 1980–83; Director of Government Relations: NEI Internat. subseq. NEI plc, 1983–90; Rolls Royce, 1991–93. *Recreations:* music, gardening. *Address:* 12 Kemerton Road, Beckenham, Kent BR3 2NJ. *T:* 0181–650 0273. *Club:* Reform.

BINNS, David John, CBE 1989; Trust Board Secretary, Halton General Hospital NHS Trust, since 1995 (Non-executive Director, 1992–94); *b* 12 April 1929; *s* of Henry Norman Binns, OBE and Ivy Mary Binns; *m* 1957, Jean Margaret Evans; one *s* (one *d* decd). *Educ:* Fleetwood Grammar Sch.; Rossall Sch.; Sheffield Univ. LLB 1951. Solicitor 1954. Articled Clerk, Sheffield City Council, 1949; Asst Solicitor, Warrington County Borough Council, 1954; Dep. Town Clerk, Warrington County Borough Council, 1958; General Manager: Warrington Develt Corp., 1969–81; Warrington and Runcorn Develt Corp., 1981–89. Mem., Warrington DHA, 1990–92. *Recreations:* walking, gardening, music. *Address:* 4 Cedarways, Appleton, Warrington, Cheshire WA4 5EW. *T:* Warrington (01925) 262169. *Club:* Warrington (Warrington).

BINNS, Geoffrey John; His Honour Judge Binns; a Circuit Judge, since 1980; *b* 12 Oct. 1930; *s* of Rev. Robert Arthur Geoffrey Binns and Elizabeth Marguerite Binns; *m* 1964, Elizabeth Anne Poole Askew. *Educ:* Perse Sch.; Jesus Coll., Cambridge (MA). Admitted solicitor, 1956; Partner, Fraser, Woodgate & Beall, Wisbech, 1958–80; a Recorder of the Crown Court, 1977–80. Chm., N Cambs Hosp. Management Cttee, 1970–74; Member: E Anglian Reg. Hosp. Bd, 1972–74; E Anglian RHA, 1974–76; Panel of Chairmen, Cambridge Univ. Ct of Discipline, 1976–80. Registrar, Archdeaconry of Wisbech, 1972–80. *Publication:* Contributing Ed., Butterworths' County Court Precedents and Pleadings, 1985. *Recreations:* golf, gardening. *Address:* c/o Combined Court Centre, Bishopgate, Norwich NR3 1UR. *T:* Norwich (01603) 761776. *Club:* Norfolk (Norwich).

BINNS, Rev. John Richard, PhD; Vicar, St Mary the Great with St Michael, Cambridge, since 1994; *b* 10 Jan. 1951. *Educ:* St John's Coll., Cambridge (MA 1976); King's Coll., London (PhD 1989); Coll. of the Resurrection, Mirfield. Ordained deacon, 1976, priest, 1977; Assistant Curate: Holy Trinity, Clapham, 1976–78; Clapham Old Town, 1978–80; Team Vicar, Mortlake with E Sheen, 1980–87; Vicar, Holy Trinity, Upper Tooting, 1987–94. *Publications:* Cyril of Scythopolis: Lives of the Monks of Palestine, 1991; Ascetics and Ambassadors of Christ, 1994. *Address:* Great St Mary's Vicarage, 39 Madingley Road, Cambridge CB3 0EL. *T:* Cambridge (01223) 355285.

BINNS, Malcolm; concert pianist; *b* 29 Jan. 1936; *s* of Douglas and May Binns. *Educ:* Bradford Grammar Sch.; Royal Coll. of Music (ARCM, Chappell Gold Medal, Medal of Worshipful Co. of Musicians). London début, 1957; Henry Wood Proms début, 1960; Royal Festival Hall début, 1961; Festival Hall appearances in London Philharmonic Orchestra International series, 1969–; toured with Scottish Nat. Orch., 1989; concerts at Aldeburgh, Leeds, Three Choirs (1975), Bath and Canterbury Festivals; regular appearances at Promenade concerts and broadcasts for BBC Radio. First complete recording of Beethoven piano sonatas on original instruments, 1980; première recordings of Sir William Sterndale Bennett's piano concertos with London Philharmonic and Philharmonia Orchs, 1990. *Recreation:* collecting antique gramophone records. *Address:* 233 Court Road, Orpington, Kent BR6 9BY. *T:* Orpington (01689) 31056.

BINNS, Susan May; Director, Internal Market and Financial Services, European Commission, since 1995; *b* 22 April 1948; *d* of Jack and Mollie Binns. *Educ:* Harrogate Coll.; LSE (BSc Econ Internat. Relations). HM Diplomatic Service, 1968; served FCO and Brussels; New Delhi, 1978–80; Cabinet of Ivor Richard, EC Member, Brussels, 1981–84; Counsellor, EC Delegations: Washington, 1985–88; Belgrade, 1988; Dep. Chef de Cabinet of Bruce Millan, EC Mem. resp. for regl policies, 1989–91, Chef de Cabinet, 1991–95. *Recreation:* tennis. *Address:* European Commission, 200 rue de la Loi, 1049 Brussels, Belgium. *T:* (2) 2963285.

BINNY, John Anthony Francis; *b* 13 Dec. 1911. *Educ:* Wellington College. Supplementary Reserve of Officers, 15th/19th The King's Royal Hussars, 1936. Served War of 1939–45, France and Burma (despatches). Chairman: Blue Circle Industries, 1975–78 (Dir, 1952); Law Debenture Corp., 1950–77 (Dir, 1948); Chm., Mercantile Investment Trust, 1971–77; Dep. Chm., Nat. Westminster Bank plc, 1972–81 (Dir, 1950); Dep. Chm., TI Group, 1975–79. *Recreations:* cricket, fishing, shooting, gardening. *Address:* Pollards Moor Farm, Pollards Moor Road, Copythorne, Cadnam, Southampton SO4 2NZ. *Clubs:* Cavalry and Guards, MCC.

BINTLEY, David Julian; freelance choreographer and dancer; Director, Birmingham Royal Ballet from Aug. 1995; *b* 17 Sept. 1957; *s* of David Bintley and Glenys Bintley (*née* Ellinthorpe); *m* 1981, Jennifer Catherine Ursula Mills; one *s*. *Educ:* Holme Valley Grammar School. Royal Ballet School, 1974; Sadler's Wells Royal Ballet, 1976; first professional choreography, The Outsider, 1978; youngest choreographer to work at the Royal Opera House, for production of Adieu, 1980; first three act ballet, The Swan of Tuonela, 1982; Company Choreographer, 1983–85, Resident Choreographer, 1985–86, Sadler's Wells Royal Ballet; Resident Choreographer and Principal Dancer, Royal Ballet, 1986–93. Evening Standard Award for Ballet, for Choros and Consort Lessons, both 1983; Laurence Olivier Award for Petrushka, 1984; Manchester Evening News Award for Dance, for Still Life at the Penguin Café, 1987. *Address:* Birmingham Royal Ballet, Birmingham Hippodrome, Thorp Street, Birmingham B5 4AU.

BIOBAKU, Dr Saburi Oladeni, CMG 1961; MA, PhD; Research historian and management consultant; Research Professor and Director, Institute of African Studies, University of Ibadan, 1976–83; *b* 16 June 1918; *s* of late Chief S. O. Biobaku, Aré of Iddo, Abeokuta; *m* 1949, Muhabat Folasade, *d* of Alhaji L. B. Agusto, barrister-at-law, Lagos; one *s*. *Educ:* Govt Coll., Ibadan; Higher Coll., Yaba; University Coll., Exeter; Trinity Coll., Cambridge. BA London, 1945; BA Cantab, 1947, MA 1951; PhD London, 1951. Education Officer, Nigeria, 1947–53; Registrar, University Coll., Ibadan, 1953–57; Dir, Yoruba Historical Research Scheme, 1956–; Sec. to Premier and Executive Council, Western Nigeria, 1957–61; Pro-Vice-Chancellor, Univ. of Ife, Nigeria, 1961–65; Vice-Chancellor, Univ. of Lagos, 1965–72; Chairman, Management Consultant Services Ltd, Lagos, 1972–76, 1983–. Hon. DLitt. Created: Aré of Iddo, Abeokuta, 1958; Agbakin of Igbore, 1972; Maye of Ife, 1980; Baapitan of Egbaland, 1980. *Publications:* The Origin of the Yoruba, 1955; The Egba and Their Neighbours, 1842–1872, 1957; Living Cultures of Nigeria, 1977; contribs to Africa, jl of Nigerian Historical Soc., Odu (Joint Ed.), etc. *Recreations:* soccer, tennis, badminton, swimming, walking. *Address:* PO Box 7741, Lagos, Nigeria. *T:* (home) 961430. *Clubs:* Metropolitan (Lagos); Dining (Ibadan).

BIRAN, Yoav; Deputy Director General, in charge of Middle East and peace process, Ministry of Foreign Affairs, Jerusalem, since 1993; *b* 17 July 1939; *s* of Michael and Rachel Barsky; *m* (marr. diss.); one *s* two *d*; *m* 1991, Mrs Jane Moonman. *Educ:* Hebrew University of Jerusalem (post grad. studies, history, internat. relns). Joined Min. of For. Affairs, Jerusalem, 1963; ME and Afr. Depts, 1963–65; Second Sec., Ethiopia, 1965–67; First Sec., Uganda, 1967–70; Prin. Asst to Asst Dir-Gen. in charge of World Jewry and Inf., 1970–72, Dep. Dir of Dir-Gen.'s Cabinet, 1972–74, Min. of For. Affairs; Mem., Israel Delegn to Geneva Peace Conf., Dec. 1973; Dir of Dept, Center for Res. and Policy Planning, Min. of For. Affairs, 1975–77; Minister Plenipotentiary, 1977–82, Chargé d'Affaires, 1982–83, London; elected Distinguished Mem., Israel For. Service and of Israel Civil Service, 1983; Asst Dir Gen., Admin, 1984–87, N Amer. and Disarmament Affairs, 1987–88, FO, Jerusalem; Ambassador to UK, 1988–93. *Recreations:* theatre, collecting antiquarian maps and books. *Address:* Ministry of Foreign Affairs, Hakirya, Romema, Jerusalem 91950, Israel.

BIRCH, Prof. Anthony Harold, PhD; FRSC 1988; Professor of Political Science, University of Victoria, British Columbia, 1977–89, now Emeritus; *b* 17 Feb. 1924; *o s* of late Frederick Harold Birch and Rosalind Dorothy Birch; *m* 1953, Dorothy Madeleine Overton, Bayport, New York; one *s* one *d*. *Educ:* The William Ellis Sch.; University Coll., Nottingham; London Sch. of Economics. BSc (Econ) London, with 1st cl. hons, 1945; PhD London, 1951. Asst Principal, Board of Trade, 1945–47; University of Manchester: Asst Lectr in Govt, 1947–51; Lectr, 1951–58; Senior Lectr in Government, 1958–61; Prof. of Political Studies, Univ. of Hull, 1961–70; Prof. of Political Sci., Exeter Univ., 1970–77. Commonwealth Fund Fellow at Harvard Univ. and University of Chicago, 1951–52. Consultant to Government of Western Region of Nigeria, 1956–58. Vis. Prof. Tufts Univ., 1968; Vis. Fellow, ANU, 1987. Vice-Pres., Internat. Political Sci. Assoc., 1976–79; Life Vice-Pres., UK Political Studies Assoc., 1976– (Chm., 1972–75). *Publications:* Federalism, Finance and Social Legislation, 1955; Small-Town Politics, 1959; Representative and Responsible Government, 1964; The British System of Government, 1967, 9th edn 1993; Representation, 1971; Political Integration and Disintegration in the British Isles, 1977; Nationalism and National Integration, 1989; The Concepts and Theories of Modern Democracy, 1993; articles in various journals. *Recreations:* reading, music, bridge, camping. *Address:* 1901 Fairfield Road, Victoria, BC V8S 1H2, Canada.

BIRCH, Prof. Arthur John, AC 1987; CMG 1979; DPhil (Oxon); FRS 1958; FAA, FRACI; Professor of Organic Chemistry, Australian National University, 1967–80, now Emeritus; Professorial Fellow, Lincoln College, Oxford, since 1980; *b* 3 Aug. 1915; *s* of

Arthur Spencer and Lily Birch; *m* 1948, Jessie Williams; three *s* two *d*. *Educ:* Sydney Technical High Sch.; Sydney Univ. MA Oxon 1981; MSc: Sydney, 1939; Manchester, 1957. Scholar of the Royal Commission for the Exhibition of 1851, Oxford, 1938–41; Research Fellow, Oxford, 1941–45; ICI Research Fellow, Oxford, 1945–48; Smithson Fellow of the Royal Society, Cambridge, 1949–52; Prof. of Organic Chemistry, University of Sydney, 1952–55; Prof. of Organic Chemistry, Manchester Univ., 1955–67; Dean, Research Sch. of Chemistry, ANU, Canberra, 1967–70, 1973–76; Newton Abraham Prof., Univ. of Oxford, 1980–81. Treas., Australian Acad. Science, 1969–73, Pres., 1982–86; Pres., RACI, 1978. Chairman: Ind. Enquiry into CSIRO, 1976–; Aust. Marine Sciences and Technologies Adv. Cttee, 1978–81. UNDP Consultant, People's Republic of China, 1980, 1982, 1984, 1986; OECD Examiner, Denmark, 1987. Foreign Mem., USSR Acad. of Science, 1976; Foreign Fellow, Indian Nat. Sci. Acad., 1990; Hon. FRCS 1980. Hon. DSc: Sydney, 1977; Manchester, 1982; Monash, 1982. Davy Medal, Royal Soc., 1972; Tetrahedron Prize, Tetrahedron Jl, 1987; ANZAAS Medal, 1990. *Publications:* How Chemistry Works, 1950; 426 original scientific communications, chiefly in Journal of Chemical Soc. and Australian Journal of Chemistry. *Address:* Department of Chemistry, Australian National University, PO Box 4, Canberra, ACT 0200, Australia.

BIRCH, Prof. Bryan John, FRS 1972; Professor of Arithmetic, University of Oxford, since 1985; Professorial Fellow of Brasenose College, Oxford, since 1985 (Fellow since 1966); *b* 25 Sept. 1931; *s* of Arthur Jack and Mary Edith Birch; *m* 1961, Gina Margaret Christ; two *s* one *d*. *Educ:* Shrewsbury Sch.; Trinity Coll., Cambridge (MA, PhD). Harkness Fellow, Princeton, 1957–58; Fellow: Trinity Coll., Cambridge, 1956–60; Churchill Coll., Cambridge, 1960–62; Sen. Lectr, later Reader, Univ. of Manchester, 1962–65; Reader in Mathematics, Univ. of Oxford, 1966–85. *Publications:* articles in learned jls, mainly on number theory; various editorships. *Recreations:* gardening (theoretical), opera, watching marmots. *Address:* Green Cottage, Boars Hill, Oxford OX1 5DQ. *T:* Oxford (01865) 735367; Mathematical Institute, 25–29 St Giles, Oxford. *T:* Oxford (01865) 273525.

BIRCH, Dennis Arthur, CBE 1977; DL; Councillor, West Midlands County Council, 1974–77; *b* 11 Feb. 1925; *s* of George Howard and Leah Birch; *m* 1948, Mary Therese Lyons; one *d*. *Educ:* Wolverhampton Municipal Grammar Sch. Wolverhampton County Borough Council: elected, 1952; served, 1952–74; Alderman, 1970–73; Mayor, 1973–74; Leader, 1967–73. Elected (following Local Govt reorganisation) Chm. West Midlands CC, 1974–76. DL West Midlands, 1979. MInstM. *Address:* 3 Tern Close, Wolverhampton Road East, Wolverhampton WV4 6AU. *T:* Sedgley (01902) 883837.

BIRCH, Frank Stanley Heath; public sector consultant; Chairman, Lifecare NHS Trust, since 1994; Commander, London District, St John Ambulance, since 1992 (Deputy Commander, 1990–92); *b* 8 Feb. 1939; *s* of late John Stanley Birch, CEng and Phyllis Edna Birch (*née* Heath), BA; *m* 1963, Diana Jacqueline Davies, BA; one *d*. *Educ:* Weston-super-Mare Grammar Sch. for Boys; Univ. of Wales (BA); Univ. of Birmingham (Inst. of Local Govt Studies). IPFA; MBIM. Entered local govt service, 1962; various appts, City Treasurer and Controller's Dept, Cardiff, 1962–69; Chief Internal Auditor, Dudley, 1969–73; Asst County Treasurer, 1973–74, Asst Chief Exec., 1974–76, W Midlands CC; Chief Exec., Lewisham, 1976–82; Town Clerk and Chief Exec., Croydon, 1982–90. Hon. Clerk, Gen. Purposes Cttee, 1982–90, Principal Grants Advr, 1983–86, London Boroughs Assoc.; Sec., London Co-ordinating Cttee, 1985–86. Dir, Croydon Business Venture Ltd, 1983–92. Freeman, City of London, 1980. FRSA 1980. CStJ 1992 (Mem. Council, London, 1986–); Vice-Pres., London SJAB, 1988–90. *Publications:* various articles on public admin and local govt management. *Recreations:* music, walking, caravanning, the countryside. *Address:* St John Ambulance, London (Prince of Wales's) District, Edwina Mountbatten House, 63 York Street, W1H 1PS.

BIRCH, Sir John (Allan), KCVO 1993; CMG 1987; HM Diplomatic Service, retired; Director, British Association for Central and Eastern Europe, since 1995; *b* 24 May 1935; *s* of late C. Allan Birch, MD, FRCP; *m* 1960, Primula Haselden; three *s* one *d*. *Educ:* Leighton Park Sch.; Corpus Christi Coll., Cambridge (MA). Served HM Forces, Middlesex Regt, 1954–56. Joined HM Foreign Service, 1959; served: Paris, 1960–63; Singapore, 1963–64; Bucharest, 1965–68; Geneva, 1968–70; Kabul, 1973–76; Royal Coll. of Defence Studies, 1977; Comprehensive Test Ban Treaty Negotiations, Geneva, 1977–80; Counsellor, Budapest, 1980–83; Hd of East European Dept, FCO, 1983–86; Ambassador and Dep. Perm. Rep. to UN, NY, 1986–89; Ambassador to Hungary, 1989–95. Mem. Council, SSEES, 1995–. *Recreations:* tennis, ski-ing, shooting, carpentry. *Address:* 185 Emery Hill Street, SW1P 1PD. *Club:* Athenæum.

BIRCH, John Anthony, MA, DMus; FRCM, FRCO(CHM), LRAM; Organist and Director of the Choir, Temple Church, since 1982; University Organist, University of Sussex, since 1967; Professor, Royal College of Music, since 1959; Organist: to the Royal Choral Society, since 1966; of the Royal Philharmonic Orchestra, since 1983; Curator-Organist, Royal Albert Hall, since 1984; *b* 9 July 1929; *s* of late Charles Aylmer Birch and Mabel (*née* Greenwood), Leek, Staffs; unmarried. *Educ:* Trent Coll.; Royal Coll. of Music (ARCM; Pitcher Schol. of RCO). Nat. Service, Royal Corps of Signals, 1949–50. Organist and Choirmaster, St Thomas's Church, Regent Street, London, 1950–53; Accompanist to St Michael's Singers, 1952–58; Organist and Choirmaster, All Saints Church, Margaret Street, London, 1953–58; Sub-Organist, HM Chapels Royal, 1957–58; Organist and Master of the Choristers, Chichester Cathedral, 1958–80. With the Cathedral Organists of Salisbury and Winchester re-established the Southern Cathedrals Festival, 1960; Musical Advr, Chichester Festival Theatre, 1962–80; Choirmaster, Bishop Otter Coll., Chichester, 1963–69. Rep., 1950–66, and Man. Dir, 1966–73, C. A. Birch Ltd, Staffs. Accompanist, Royal Choral Soc., 1965–70; Examr to Associated Bd, Royal Schs of Music, 1958–77; a Gen. Ed., Novello & Co., 1967–77; Vis. Lectr in Music, Univ. of Sussex, 1971–83. Special Comr, Royal Sch. of Church Music; Royal College of Organists: Mem. Council, 1964–; Pres., 1984–86. Fellow, Corp. of SS Mary and Nicolas (Woodard Schs), 1973–; Governor: Hurstpierpoint Coll., 1974–; St Catherine's, Bramley, 1981–89; Mem. Council, Corp. of Cranleigh and Bramley Schs, 1990. Trustee, Onseley Trust. Has made concert appearances in France, Belgium, Italy, Germany, Switzerland, Netherlands, Spain, Portugal, Scandinavia and Far East; recital tours: Canada and US, 1966 and 1967, Australia and NZ, 1969, S Africa, 1978. Freeman, City of London, 1991. DMus Lambeth, 1989; Hon. MA Sussex, 1971. *Address:* 13 King's Bench Walk, Temple, EC4Y 7EN. *T:* 0171–353 5115; Fielding House, The Close, Salisbury, Wilts SP1 2EB. *Clubs:* Garrick; New (Edinburgh).

BIRCH, Peter Gibbs, CBE 1992; Chief Executive, Abbey National plc (formerly Abbey National Building Society), since 1988 (Chief Executive, 1984–88); *b* 4 Dec. 1937; *m* 1962, Gillian (*née* Benge); three *s* one *d*. *Educ:* Allhallows Sch., Devon. Royal West Kent Regt, 1957–58 (2nd Lieut). Nestlé Co., 1958–65; Sales Manager, Gillette, 1965; Gen. Sales Manager, Gillette Australia, 1969; Man. Dir, Gillette, NZ, 1971; Gen. Manager, Gillette, SE Asia, 1973; Gp Gen. Manager, Gillette, Africa, ME, Eastern Europe, 1975; Man. Dir, Gillette UK, 1981. Director: Abbey National (formerly Abbey Nat. Building Soc.), 1984–; Hoskyns Gp, 1988–93; Argos, 1990–; Scottish Mutual Assurance, 1992–; Dalgety, 1993–. Chm., Council of Mortgage Lenders, 1991–92. FCBSI. Pres., Middlesex Assoc. of Boys' Clubs, 1988–. *Recreations:* active holidays, swimming. *Address:* Abbey House, Baker Street, NW1 6XL.

BIRCH, Philip Thomas; Director, Piccadilly Radio, 1973–90 (Founding Managing Director, 1973–83); *b* 23 April 1927; *s* of Thomas Stephen Birch and Ivy May Birch (*née* Bunyard); *m* 1979, Shiona Nelson Hawkins; four *s* one *d*. Commnd Queen's Own Royal W Kent Regt, BAOR, 1945–47. Space Buyer, Notley Advertising, 1948–49; Media and Account Dir, J. Walter Thompson Co., 1950–64; Founding Man. Dir, Radio London, 1964–68; Head of Broadcasting, Associated Newspapers Gp, 1969–73. Founding Chairman: Associated Indep. Radio Services, 1973–81; AIRC Pension Trust, 1974–83; Chm., Assoc. of Indep. Radio Contractors Ltd, 1976; Founding Chm., Indep. Radio Sales, 1981–86; Director: Associated Indep. Radio Gp, 1973–83; Indep. Radio News, 1983. *Recreations:* aviation, sailing, travel. *Club:* St James (Manchester).

BIRCH, Robert Edward Thomas, CBE 1979; Director General, Federation Against Copyright Theft, 1982–85; *b* 9 May 1917; *s* of late Robert Birch and Edith Birch; *m* 1946, Laura Pia Busini; two *d*. *Educ:* Dulwich Coll. Served RA, 1940–46; Africa, Italy, NW Europe; Major. Admitted solicitor, 1942; joined Solicitors' Dept, New Scotland Yard, 1946; Dep. Solicitor, 1968; Solicitor, 1976–82. *Recreations:* swimming, travel.

BIRCH, Robin Arthur, CB 1995; voluntary worker; civil servant, retired; *b* 12 Oct. 1939; *s* of Arthur and Olive Birch; *m* 1962, Jane Marion Irvine Sturdy; two *s*. *Educ:* King Henry VIII Sch., Coventry; Christ Church, Oxford (Marjoribanks Scholar, 1957; Craven Scholar, 1959; MA). Entered Min. of Health as Asst Principal, 1961; Private Sec. to Charles Loughlin, MP (Parly Sec.), 1965–66; Principal, 1966; seconded to: Interdeptl Social Work Gp, 1969–70; Home Office (Community Develt Project), 1970–72; Asst Sec., DHSS, 1973; Chm., Working Party on Manpower and Trng for Social Services, 1974–76 (Report, 1976); Principal Private Sec. to Rt Hon. Norman St John-Stevas, MP (Leader of the House of Commons), 1980–81; Under Sec., DHSS, 1982; Asst Auditor Gen., Nat. Audit Office, 1984–86, on secondment; Dir, Regl Orgn, 1988–90; Dep. Sec. (Policy), 1990–95, DSS. Hon. Sec., Friends of Christ Church Cathedral, Oxford, 1978–. Chm., Age Concern, 1995–. *Recreations:* family and friends; travel; music, mainly before 1809; byways of classical antiquity; model railway. *Address:* The Cathedral, Christ Church, Oxford OX1 1DP.

BIRCH, Sir Roger, Kt 1992; CBE 1987; QPM 1980; Chief Constable, Sussex Police, 1983–93; *b* 27 Sept. 1930; *s* of John Edward Lawrence Birch and Ruby Birch; *m* 1954, Jeanne Margaret Head; one *s*. *Educ:* King's Coll., Taunton. Cadet, Royal Naval Coll., Dartmouth, 1949–50; Pilot Officer, RAF, 1950–52. Devon Constabulary, 1954–72: Constable, uniform and CID; then through ranks to Chief Supt; Asst Chief Constable, Mid-Anglia Constab., 1972–74; Dep. Chief Constable, Kent Constab., 1974–78; Chief Constable, Warwickshire Constab., 1978–83. Dir, Police Extended Interviews, 1983–91; Pres., Assoc. of Chief Police Officers, 1987–88 (Vice-Pres., 1986–87; Chm., Traffic Cttee, 1983–86; Chm., Internat. Affairs Adv. Cttee, 1988–92); Vice Chm., Internat. Cttee, Internat. Assoc. of Chiefs of Police, 1989–93; Trustee: Police Dependants' Trust, 1981–93; Police Gurney Fund, 1983–91. Mem., St John Ambulance Council, Sussex, 1986–. UK Vice-Pres., Royal Life Saving Soc., 1985– (Chm., SE Region, 1983–93). Mem. Council, IAM, 1984–93. Hon. Fellow, Centre for Legal Studies, 1993. Hon. LLD Sussex, 1991. *Publications:* articles on criminal intelligence, breath measuring instruments and on the urban environment, in learned jls. *Recreations:* swimming, music. *Address:* c/o National Westminster Bank, 49 High Street, Uckfield, Sussex TN22 1AN. *Club:* Royal Air Force.

BIRCH, Prof. William; *b* 24 Nov. 1925; *s* of Frederick Arthur and Maude Olive Birch; *m* 1950, Mary Vine Stammers; one *s* one *d*. *Educ:* Ranelagh Sch.; Univ. of Reading. BA 1949, PhD 1957. Royal Navy, 1943–46, Sub-Lt RNVR. Lectr, Univ. of Bristol, 1950–60; Prof. of Geography, Grad. Sch. of Geog., Clark Univ., Worcester, Mass, USA, 1960–63; Prof., and Chm. of Dept of Geog., Univ. of Toronto, Canada, 1963–67; Prof., and Head of Dept of Geog., Univ. of Leeds, 1967–75; Dir, Bristol Polytechnic, 1975–86. Visiting Professor: Inst. of Educn, London Univ., 1986–88; Univ. of Bristol, 1990–94. Pres., Inst. of British Geographers, 1976–77; Chm., Cttee of Directors of Polytechnics, 1982–84. Mem., ESRC, 1985–88. Hon. DLitt CNAA, 1989. *Publications:* The Isle of Man: a study in economic geography, 1964; The Challenge to Higher Education: reconciling responsibilities to scholarship and society, 1988; contribs on higher educn policy and on geography and planning, Trans Inst. Brit. Geographers, Geog. Jl, Economic Geog., Annals Assoc. Amer. Geographers, Jl Environmental Management, Studies in Higher Educn, etc. *Recreations:* yachting, travel, gardening, pottery. *Address:* 3 Rodney Place, Clifton, Bristol BS8 4HY. *T:* Bristol (0117) 973 9719.

BIRCH, Rt. Hon. William (Francis); PC 1992; MP (Nat.) Pukekohe, New Zealand, since 1972; Minister of Finance, since 1993; *b* 9 April 1934; *s* of Charles William Birch and Elizabeth Alicia (*née* Wells); *m* 1953, Rosa Mitchell; three *s* one *d*. Surveyor. Borough Councillor 1965–74, Dep. Mayor 1968–74, Pukekohe. Jun. Opposition Whip, 1973–75; Sen. Govt Whip, 1975–78; Minister of: Energy, Science and Technol. and Nat. Develt, 1978–81; Energy, Regl Develt and Nat. Develt, 1981–84; Labour, Immigration and State Services, 1990–93; Employment, 1991–93; Health, 1993; Minister for Pacific Island Affairs, 1990–91. Chm., Internat. Energy Agency, 1983. *Recreation:* fishing. *Address:* Parliament Buildings, Wellington, New Zealand; 188 Kitchener Road, Pukekohe, New Zeland. *Clubs:* Rotary; Jaycee International.

BIRCHALL, Prof. (James) Derek, OBE 1990; FRS 1982; FRSC; FIM; Professor of Inorganic Chemistry, Keele University, since 1992; Non-executive Director, Ceram Research, since 1994; *b* 7 Oct. 1930; *s* of David Birchall and Dora Mary Birchall; *m* 1956, Pauline Mary Jones (*d* 1990); two *s*. ICI, 1956–92: Research Leader, 1965; Research Associate, 1970; Sen. Res. Associate, Mond Div., 1975–92. Visiting Professor: Univ. of Surrey, 1976–88; MIT, 1984–86; Univ. of Durham, 1987–; Univ. of Liverpool, 1991–; Professor Associate: Brunel Univ., 1983–; Sheffield Univ., 1989–; Industrial Fellow, Wolfson Coll., Oxford, 1977–79, Mem., Common Room, 1979–. Mem., Individual Merit Panel, HM Treasury, 1988–89. Lectures: John D. Rose Meml, SCI, 1983; Mellor Meml, Inst. of Ceramics, 1984; Hurter Meml, SCI, Univ. of Liverpool, 1989; Sir Eric Rideal Meml, SCI, 1989; Katritzky, UEA, 1991; Industrial Endowed Lectr, RSC, 1992–93; Orton Meml, American Ceramic Soc., 1993. Hon. ScD UEA, 1994. Ambrose Congreve Energy Award, 1983; RSC Award: for Solids and Materials Processing, 1990; for Materials Science, 1991; Royal Soc. Armourers and Braziers Award, 1993. *Publications:* A Classification of Fire Hazards, 1952, 2nd edn 1961; contribs to various encyclopedias and to learned jls, *ie* Nature, on inorganic chemistry and materials science. *Recreations:* old books, new cars. *Address:* Braeside, Stable Lane, Mouldsworth, Chester CH3 8AN. *T:* Manley (01928) 740320. *Club:* Athenæum.

BIRCHENOUGH, (John) Michael, BSc, PhD; Visiting Professor, School of Education, Open University, 1986–89; *b* 17 Jan. 1923; *s* of John Buckley Birchenough and Elsie Birchenough; *m* 1945, Enid Humphries; two *s*. *Educ:* Ashford Grammar Sch., Kent; Chiswick County Sch.; London Univ. Chemist, May & Baker Ltd, 1943–45; teaching posts, 1946–60; HM Inspector of Schools, 1960; Staff Inspector, 1966; Chief Inspector, 1968–72; Chief Inspector, ILEA, 1973–83; Res. Fellow, Sch. of Educn, Univ. of Bristol,

1983–86. Pres., Educn Section, BAAS Annual Meeting, Stirling, 1974. *Publications:* contribs to Jl of Chem. Soc. and other scientific jls. *Address:* 25 Somes Close, Greatford Road, Uffington, near Stamford, Lincs PE9 4UE.

BIRD, Prof. Adrian Peter, PhD; FRS 1989; Buchanan Professor of Genetics, Edinburgh University, since 1990; *b* 3 July 1947; *s* of Kenneth George Bird and Aileen Mary Bird; *m* 1st, 1976; one *s* one *d*; 2nd, 1993, Dr Catherine May Abbott; one *s*. *Educ:* Queen Elizabeth's Grammar School, Hartlebury; Univ. of Sussex (BSc(Hons)); Univ. of Edinburgh (PhD 1971). Damon Runyan Fellow, Yale, 1972–73; postdoctoral fellowship, Univ. of Zurich, 1974–75; Medical Research Council, Edinburgh: scientific staff, Mammalian Genome Unit, 1975–85, actg Dir, 1986–87; Hd of Structural Studies Sect., Clin. and Population Cytogenetics Unit, 1987; Sen. Scientist, Inst. for Molecular Pathol., Vienna, 1988–90. *Publications:* articles in Nature, Cell and other jls. *Recreations:* hill running, ball games, music, food. *Address:* Institute of Cell and Molecular Biology, University of Edinburgh, King's Buildings, Mayfield Road, Edinburgh EH9 3JR. *T:* 0131–667 1081.

BIRD, Rev. Dr Anthony Peter; General Medical Practitioner, since 1979; Principal of The Queen's College, Edgbaston, Birmingham, 1974–79; *b* 2 March 1931; *s* of late Albert Harry Bird and Noel Whitehouse Bird; *m* 1962, Sabine Boehmig; two *s* one *d*. *Educ:* St John's Coll., Oxford (BA LitHum, BA Theol, MA); Birmingham Univ. (MB, ChB, 1970). Deacon, 1957; Priest, 1958; Curate of St Mary's, Stafford, 1957–60; Chaplain, then Vice-Principal of Cuddesdon Theological Coll., 1960–64. General Medical Practitioner, 1972–73. Member: Home Office Policy Adv. Cttee on Sexual Offences, 1976–80; Parole Board, 1977–80. Freedom of Information Campaign Award, 1986. *Publication:* The Search for Health: a response from the inner city, 1981. *Recreations:* sailing, walking, music—J. S. Bach, innovation in primary health care, Wolverhampton Wanderers FC. *Address:* 93 Bournbrook Road, Birmingham B29 7BX.

BIRD, Ven. (Colin) Richard (Bateman); Archdeacon of Lambeth, since 1988; *b* 31 March 1933; *s* of Paul James Bird and Marjorie Bird (*née* Bateman); *m* 1963, Valerie Wroughton van der Bijl; two *d* one *s*. *Educ:* privately; County Technical Coll., Guildford; Selwyn Coll., Cambridge (MA); Cuddesdon Theol Coll. Curate: St Mark's Cathedral, George, S Africa, 1958–61; St Saviour's Claremont, Cape Town, 1961–64; Rector, Parish of Northern Suburbs, Pretoria, 1964–66; Rector, Tzaneen with Duiwelskloof and Phalaborwa, N Transvaal, 1966–70; Curate, Limpsfield, Surrey, 1970–75; Vicar of St Catherine, Hatcham, 1975–88; RD, Deptford, 1980–85; Hon. Canon of Southwark, 1982–88; Priest-in-Charge, St Saviour's, Brixton Hill, 1989–94. *Recreations:* theatre and concert going, walking, bird-watching. *Address:* 7 Hoadly Road, Streatham, SW16 1AE. *T:* 0181–769 4384; 5 Croft Terrace, Hastings, East Sussex TN34 3HG. *T:* Hastings (01424) 430432.

BIRD, Harold Dennis, (Dickie), MBE 1986; Test cricket umpire, since 1970; foundation Member, Independent International Panel of Umpires, 1993; *b* 19 April 1933; *s* of James Harold Bird and Ethel Bird; unmarried. *Educ:* Raley Sch., Barnsley. Played county cricket for Yorkshire, 1956–60, and Leicestershire, 1960–66; qualified MCC Advanced Cricket Coach, 1966; umpire of first-class cricket, 1970–; has umpired over 150 international matches: 66 Tests (world record in 1994), incl. Queen's Silver Jubilee Test, Lord's, 1977, Centenary Test, Lord's, 1980, Bi-Centenary Test, Lord's, 1987, 3 in Zimbabwe, and WI *v* Pakistan series, 1993, in NZ, Pakistan and India, 1994; 92 one-day internationals, 1973– (world record in 1994); 4 World Cup tournaments, 1975–87, and Final at Lord's, 1975, 1979, 1983; Women's World Cup, and Final, NZ, 1982; finals of Gillette, NatWest, and Benson & Hedges competitions, Lord's, 1974–; Rothmans Cup, 1983, 1985, Asia Cup, 1984, 1985, Champion's Cup, 1986, and Sharjah Tournament, 1993, UAE. Has travelled worldwide. Yorkshire Personality of the Year, 1977. *Publications:* Not Out, 1978; That's Out, 1985; From the Pavilion End, 1988. *Recreations:* watching football, listening to Barbra Streisand, Nat King Cole and Diana Ross records. *Address:* White Rose Cottage, 40 Paddock Road, Staincross, Barnsley, Yorks S75 6LE. *T:* Barnsley (01226) 384491. *Clubs:* MCC, Lord's Taverners; Yorkshire CC (Hon. Life Mem., 1994).

BIRD, James Gurth, MBE 1945; TD 1951; *b* 30 Jan. 1909; *s* of Charles Harold Bird and Alice Jane Bird (*née* Kirtland); *m* 1940, Phyllis Ellis Pownall; one *s* two *d*. *Educ:* King William's Coll., Isle of Man (Scholar); St Catharine's Coll., Cambridge (exhibnr). Classical Tripos Pts I and II, BA 1931, MA 1933. Asst Master, Rossall Sch., 1931–33; Asst Master and House Master, Denstone Coll., 1933–47 (interrupted by War Service); Head Master, William Hulme's Grammar Sch., Manchester, 1947–74. FRSA. *Recreations:* golf, gardening. *Address:* Ty Deryn, Ravenspoint Road, Trearddur Bay, Holyhead, Gwynedd LL65 2AX.

BIRD, John Alfred William; Member (Lab) Midlands West, European Parliament, March 1987–1994; *b* 4 Feb. 1924; *m* Gwen Davies; two *s*. Member: Wolverhampton BC, 1962–73; Wolverhampton Metropolitan BC, 1973–88 (Chm., Educn Cttee, 1972–80; Leader, 1973–87); W Midlands CC, 1973–81; Vice-Chm., W Midlands Police Cttee, 1973–77. Chm., W Midlands DCs, 1986–87; Vice-Pres., AMA, 1987– (Mem. Council, 1974–87); Member: W Midlands EDC, 1973–81; W Midlands Regl Econ. Forum, 1986–87; Pres., Norwest Midlands Br., Chartered Inst. of Marketing, 1990–91. European Parliament: Chm., British Lab Gp, 1989–90; Mem., Ext. Econ. Relations Cttee, 1987–92; Mem., Develt and Co-operation Cttee, 1992–94. Mem., AEU, 1950– (Shop Steward, 1953–63). Hon. Fellow, Faculty of Sci. and Technol., Wolverhampton Poly. Pres., W Mercia Scout Assoc., 1989–. *Address:* 5 Giffard Road, Bushbury, Wolverhampton WV10 8EG.

BIRD, Michael James; Regional Chairman of Industrial Tribunals for Wales, since 1992; *b* 11 Nov. 1935; *s* of Walter Garfield and Ireen Bird; *m* 1963, Susan Harris; three *d*. *Educ:* Lewis Sch., Pengam; King's Coll., Univ. of London (LLB Hons). Solicitor (Hons) 1961. Assistant solicitor, 1961–62; Partner, T. S. Edwards & Son, 1962–67, Sen. Partner, 1967–84. Deputy Registrar of County and High Court, 1976–77; Chairman of Industrial Tribunal, Cardiff (part-time), 1977–83; Chm. of Industrial Tribunal, Bristol, 1984–87, Cardiff, 1987–92. Chm., Gwent Italian Soc., 1978–86 (Sec., 1976–78); Member: Royal Life Saving Soc., 1976– (President's Commendation, 1984); Amateur Swimming Assoc. (Advanced Teacher, 1981–); Newport and Maindee ASC; Crawshays Welsh RFC. *Recreations:* water sports, opera. *Address:* 17 Allt-yr-yn Avenue, Newport, Gwent NP9 5DA. *T:* Newport (01633) 252000.

BIRD, Ven. Richard; *see* Bird, Ven. C. R. B.

BIRD, Richard; Director of Personnel, Department of Transport, since 1994; *b* 12 Feb. 1950; *s* of Desmond and late Betty Bird; *m* 1973, Penelope Anne Frudd; one *s* one *d*. *Educ:* King's Sch., Canterbury; Magdalen Coll., Oxford. Admin Trainee, DoE, 1971–73; Asst Private Sec. to Minister for Planning and Local Govt, 1974–75; Principal, Dept of Transport, 1975–78; First Sec., UK Rep. to EC, Brussels, 1978–82; Principal Private Sec. to Sec. of State for Transport, 1982–83; Asst Sec., 1983, Under Sec., 1990, Dept of Transport; Cabinet Office, 1992–94. Mem., Oxford Univ. Fencing Club, 1969–71 (represented Britain at World Youth Fencing Championship, 1970). *Recreations:* choral singing, summer sports. *Address:* Department of Transport, Lambeth Bridge House, SE1 7SB.

BIRD, Sir Richard (Geoffrey Chapman), 4th Bt *cr* 1922; *b* 3 Nov. 1935; *er surv. s* of Sir Donald Bird, 3rd Bt, and of Anne Rowena (*d* 1969), *d* of late Charles Chapman; *S* father, 1963; *m* 1st, 1957, Gillian Frances (*d* 1966), *d* of Bernard Haggett, Solihull; two *s* four *d*; 2nd, 1968, Helen Patricia, *d* of Frank Beaumont, Pontefract; two *d*. *Educ:* Beaumont. *Heir: s* John Andrew Bird, *b* 19 Jan. 1964. *Address:* 39 Ashleigh Road, Solihull, W Midlands B91 1AF.

BIRD, Richard Herries, CB 1983; Deputy Secretary, Department of Education and Science, 1980–90; *b* 8 June 1932; *s* of late Edgar Bird and Armorel (*née* Dudley-Scott); *m* 1963, Valerie, *d* of Edward and Mary Sanderson; two *d*. *Educ:* Winchester Coll.; Clare Coll., Cambridge. Min. of Transport and Civil Aviation, 1955; Principal Private Sec. to Minister of Transport, 1966–67; CSD 1969; DoE 1971; DES 1973. *Address:* 53 Kippington Road, Sevenoaks, Kent TN13 2LL.

BIRD, Rt. Hon. Vere Cornwall, PC 1982; Prime Minister of Antigua and Barbuda, 1981–94; *b* 7 Dec. 1910. *Educ:* St John's Boys' School, Antigua; Salvation Army Training School, Trinidad. Founder Mem. Exec., Antigua Trades and Labour Union, 1939 (Pres., 1943–67); Member: Antigua Legislative Council, 1945; Antigua Exec. Council, 1946 (Cttee Chm., 1951–56, land reform); Ministry of Trade and Production, 1956–60; first Chief Minister, 1960–67, first Premier, 1967–71; Founder (with reps from Barbados and Guyana), Caribbean Free Trade Assoc., 1965; led delegn to UK which achieved Associated Statehood for Antigua, 1966; re-elected to Parlt, 1976, Premier, 1976–81; Minister of Planning, External Affairs, Defence and Energy, 1981–82, of Finance and Defence, 1982–84; Leader, Antigua Labour Party, 1987. Hon. LLD St John Fisher Coll., Rochester, NY. *Address:* Tomlinsons, St John's, Antigua, West Indies.

BIRD-WILSON, Air Vice-Marshal Harold Arthur Cooper, CBE 1962; DSO 1945; DFC 1940 and Bar 1943; AFC 1946 and Bar 1955; *b* 20 Nov. 1919; *m* 1st, 1942, Audrey Wallace (*d* 1991); one *s* one *d*; 2nd, 1994, Mrs Margaret McGillivray Butler. *Educ:* Liverpool Coll. Joined RAF, Nov. 1937; No 17 Fighter Sqdn, Kenley, 1938. Served War of 1939–45 (France, Dunkirk, Battle of Britain): Flt Comdr No 234 Sqdn, 1941; Sqdn Comdr Nos 152 and 66, 1942 (despatches); Wing Leader, No 83 Gp, 1943; Comd and Gen. Staff Sch., Fort Leavenworth, Kansas, USA, 1944; Wing Leader, Harrowbeer, Spitfire Wing and then Bentwater Mustang Wing, 1944–45; CO, Jet Conversion Unit, 1945–46; CO, Air Fighting Development Sqdn, CFE, 1946–47; Op. Staff, HQ, MEAF, 1948; RAF Staff Coll., Bracknell, 1949; Personal Staff Officer to C-in-C, MEAF, 1949–50; RAF Flying Coll., Manby, 1951; OC Tactics, later CO AFDS, CFE, 1952–54; Staff, BJSM, Washington, USA, 1954–57; Staff, Air Sec. Dept., Air Min., 1957–59; CO, RAF Coltishall, 1959–61; Staff Intell., Air Min., 1961–63; AOC and Comdt, CFS, 1963–65; AOC Hong Kong, 1965–67; Dir of Flying (Research and Develt), Min. of Technology, 1967–70; AOC No 23 Gp, 1970–73; Comdr, S Maritime Air Region, RAF, 1973–74, retired. BAC, Saudi Arabia, then British Aerospace, 1974–84, retired. Czechoslovak Medal of Merit 1st class, 1945; Dutch DFC, 1945.

BIRDS, Prof. John Richard; Dibb Lupton Broomhead Professor of Commercial Law, University of Sheffield, since 1989; *b* 20 June 1948; *s* of John Sidney Birds and Katharine Charlotte Birds; *m* 1973, Margaret Rhona Richardson; two *s* one *d*. *Educ:* Chesterfield Grammar Sch.; University College London (LLB, LLM). Lectr in Law: Newcastle Polytechnic, 1970; QMC, Univ. of London, 1972; University of Sheffield: Lectr in Law, 1978–82; Sen. Lectr, 1982–85; Reader, 1985–89; Head of Dept of Law, 1987–. FRSA. *Publications:* Modern Insurance Law, 1982, 3rd edn 1993; (with A. J. Boyle) Company Law, 1983, 3rd edn 1995; (jtly) Secretarial Administration, 1984; (ed jtly) MacGillivray and Parkington on Insurance Law, 8th edn 1988; articles in learned jls. *Recreations:* music, gardening, walking. *Address:* 93 Millhouses Lane, Sheffield S7 2HD. *T:* Sheffield (0114) 236 0137.

BIRDSALL, Derek Walter, RDI; AGI; FCSD; freelance graphic designer; *b* 1 Aug. 1934; *s* of Frederick Birdsall and Hilda Birdsall (*née* Smith); *m* 1954, Shirley Thompson; three *s* one *d*. *Educ:* King's Sch., Pontefract, Yorks; Wakefield Coll. of Art, Yorks; Central Sch. of Arts and Crafts, London (NDD). National Service, RAOC Printing Unit, Cyprus, 1955–57. Lectr in Typographical Design, London Coll. of Printing, 1959–61; freelance graphic designer, working from his studio in Covent Garden, later Islington, 1961–; Founding Partner, Omnific Studios Partnership, 1983. Vis. Prof. of Graphic Art and Design, RCA, 1987–88. Consultant designer, The Independent Magazine, 1989–93; Tutor and designer of house-style for Prince of Wales's Inst. of Arch., 1991; Design Consultant, NACF, 1992–. Has broadcast on TV and radio on design subjects and his work; catalogue designs for major museums throughout the world have won many awards, incl. Gold Medal, New York Art Directors' Club, 1987. Mem., AGI, 1968–; FCSD (FSIAD 1964); RDI 1982; FRSA; Hon. FRCA 1988. *Publications:* (with C. H. O'D. Alexander) Fischer *v* Spassky, 1972; (with C. H. O'D. Alexander) A Book of Chess, 1974; (with Carlo M. Cippola) The Technology of Man—a visual history, 1978. *Recreations:* chess, poker. *Address:* 9 Compton Avenue, Islington, N1 2XD. *T:* 0171–359 1201. *Club:* Chelsea Arts.

BIRDSALL, Mrs Doris, CBE 1985; Lord Mayor of Bradford Metropolitan District, 1975–76; *b* 20 July 1915; *d* of Fred and Violet Ratcliffe; *m* 1940, James Birdsall; one *s* one *d*. *Educ:* Hanson Girls' Grammar School. Mem. Bradford City Council, 1958, Chm. of Educn Cttee, 1972–74; Mem. Bradford Univ. Council, 1963–. Hon. MA Bradford, 1975; Hon. LHD Lesley Coll., Mass, 1976. *Address:* 4 Flower Mount, Station Road, Baildon, Bradford, West Yorks BD17 6SB.

BIRDWOOD, family name of **Baron Birdwood.**

BIRDWOOD, 3rd Baron *cr* 1938, of Anzac and of Totnes; **Mark William Ogilvie Birdwood;** Bt 1919; Chairman: Martlet Ltd, since 1986; Worthington and Co. Ltd, since 1994; *b* 23 Nov. 1938; *s* of 2nd Baron Birdwood, MVO, and of Vere Lady Birdwood, CVO; *S* father, 1962; *m* 1963, Judith Helen, *e d* of late R. G. Seymour Roberts; one *d*. *Educ:* Radley Coll.; Trinity Coll., Cambridge. Commnd RHG. Director: Wrightson Wood Ltd, 1979–86; Du Pont Pixel Systems (formerly Benchmark Technology); Comac, 1988–92; Scientific Generics, 1989–. Liveryman, Glaziers' Co. *Address:* 5 Holbein Mews, SW1W 8NW; Russell House, Broadway, Worcs WR12 7BU. *Club:* Brooks's.
See also Earl of Woolton.

BIRK, family name of **Baroness Birk.**

BIRK, Baroness *cr* 1967 (Life Peer), of Regent's Park in Greater London; **Alma Birk,** JP; journalist; *d* of late Barnett and Alice Wilson; *m* Ellis Birk; one *s* one *d*. *Educ:* South Hampstead High Sch.; LSE. BSc Econ (Hons) London. Leader of Labour Group, Finchley Borough Council, 1950–53; contested (Lab): Ruislip-Northwood, 1950; Portsmouth West, 1951, 1955. Baroness in Waiting (Govt Whip), March-Oct. 1974; Parly Under-Sec. of State, DoE, 1974–79; Minister of State, Privy Council Office, 1979; Opposition frontbench spokesman H of L on: environment, 1979–86; arts, libraries, heritage and broadcasting, 1986–93. Associate Editor, Nova, 1965–69. Dir, New Shakespeare Co. Ltd, 1979–. Formerly Lectr and Prison Visitor, Holloway Prison. Mem., Youth Service Develt Council, 1967–71; Chm., Health Educn Council, 1969–72; President: Assoc. of Art

Instns, 1984–; Craft Arts Design Assoc., 1984–90; Vice-President: AMA, 1982–; Assoc. of District Councils, 1990–; Council for Children's Welfare, 1968–75; H. G. Wells Soc., 1967–; Stamford Hill Associated Clubs, 1967–70; Redbridge Jewish Youth Centre, 1970–; Playboard, 1984–; Member: Fabian Soc., 1946– (Sec., Fabian Soc. Res. Cttee on Marriage and Divorce, 1951–52); Howard League for Penal Reform, 1948– (Exec., 1980–); Hendon Group Hosp. Management Cttee, 1951–59; Panel, London Pregnancy Adv. Service, 1968–; RCOG working party on the unplanned pregnancy, 1969–72; Exec., Council of Christians and Jews, 1971–77; Hon. Cttee, Albany Trust; Ct of Governors, LSE, 1971–; Council, British Museum Soc., 1979–; Council, RSA, 1981–87; Adv. Cttee on Service Candidates, 1984–; All-party Penal Affairs Gp, 1983–; Council, Georgian Gp, 1985–; Chm. Arts Sub-Cttee, Holocaust Meml Cttee, 1979–. Trustee: Yorkshire Sculpture Park, 1980–; Health Promotion Res. Trust, 1983–; Stress Syndrome Foundn, 1983–88; Theatres Trust, 1990–; Governor: BFI, 1981–87; Mander Mitchenson Theatre Collection, 1981–. FRSA 1980. JP Highgate, 1952. *Publications:* pamphlets, articles. *Recreations:* travelling, theatre, reading, talking, grandchildren. *Address:* Flat 1, 34 Bryanston Square, W1H 7LQ.

BIRKENHEAD, Bishop Suffragan of, since 1993; **Rt. Rev. Michael Laurence Langrish;** *b* 1 July 1946; *s* of Douglas Frank and Brenda Florence Langrish; *m* 1968, Esther Vivien (*née* Rudd); one *s* two *d*. *Educ:* King Edward Sch., Southampton; Birmingham Univ. (BSocSc 1967; PGCE 1968); Fitzwilliam Coll., Cambridge (BA 1973; MA 1978); Ridley Hall, Cambridge. Lectr in Educn, Mid-West State Coll. of Educn, Nigeria, 1969–71. Ordained deacon, 1973, priest, 1974; Asst Curate, Stratford-upon-Avon with Bishopston, 1973–76; Chaplain, Rugby Sch., 1976–81; Vicar, Offchurch and Diocesan Dir of Ordinands, 1981–87; Team Rector, Rugby Team Ministry, 1987–93. Examining Chaplain to the Bishop of Coventry, 1982–89; Chm., ACCM Vocations Cttee, 1984–91; Dir, Diocesan Exploring Christian Ministry Scheme, 1984–87; Chaplain, Hosps of St Cross and St Luke, Rugby, 1987–93; Chm., House of Clergy, Coventry Diocesan Synod, 1988–93; Hon. Canon, Coventry Cathedral, 1990–93. Mem., UK Round Table on Sustainable Develt, 1995–. *Recreations:* walking, gardening, local history, theatre, railways (history, modelling and steam preservation), music. *Address:* Bishop's Lodge, 67 Bidston Road, Oxton, Birkenhead, Wirral L43 6TR. *T:* 0151–652 2741, *Fax:* 0151–651 2330. *Club:* Commonwealth Trust.

BIRKETT, family name of **Baron Birkett.**

BIRKETT, 2nd Baron *cr* 1958, of Ulverston; **Michael Birkett;** President, School for Performing Arts and Technology, British Record Industry Trust, since 1990; *b* 22 Oct. 1929; *s* of 1st Baron Birkett, PC and Ruth Birkett (*née* Nilsson, she *d* 1969); *S* father, 1962; *m* 1st, 1960, Junia Crawford (*d* 1973); 2nd, 1978, Gloria Taylor; one *s*. *Educ:* Stowe; Trinity Coll., Cambridge. Asst Dir at Ealing Studios and Ealing Films, 1953–59; Asst Dir, 1959–61, on films including: The Mark; The Innocents; Billy Budd; Associate Producer: Some People, 1961–62; Modesty Blaise, 1965; Producer: The Caretaker, 1962; Marat/Sade, 1966; A Midsummer Night's Dream, 1967; King Lear, 1968–69; Director: The Launching and The Soldier's Tale, 1963; Overture and Beginners, the More Man Understands, 1964; Outward Bound, 1971. Dep. Dir, National Theatre, 1975–77; Consultant to Nat. Theatre on films, TV and sponsorship, 1977–79; Dir for Recreation and Arts, GLC, 1979–86; Adviser to South Bank Bd, 1986–89; Exec. Dir, Royal Philharmonic Soc., 1989–90; Dir, Olympic Festival 1990, Manchester, 1990. A Vice-Pres., British Board of Film Classification, 1985–. Chairman: Children's Film & TV Foundn, 1981–; Theatres Adv. Council, 1986–; Adv. Cttee, Nat. Sound Archive, 1993–; Music Adv. Panel, British Council, 1994–. Chm., Management Cttee, Park Lane Gp, 1991–. Master, Curriers' Co., 1975–76. *Recreations:* music, printing, horticulture. *Heir: s* Hon. Thomas Birkett, *b* 25 July 1982. *Address:* House of Lords, SW1A 0PW.

BIRKETT, Peter Vidler; QC 1989; a Recorder, since 1989; *b* 13 July 1948; *s* of Neville Lawn Birkett, MA, MB BCh, FRES and Marjorie Joy Birkett; *m* 1976, Jane Elizabeth Fell; two *s*. *Educ:* Sedbergh School; Univ. of Leicester. Called to the Bar, Inner Temple, 1972; practice on SE Circuit, 1973–77, on N Circuit, 1977–. Asst Recorder, 1986–89. *Recreations:* golf, ski-ing, conversation, playing the piano. *Address:* 18 St John Street, Manchester M3 4EA. *T:* 0161–834 9843. *Club:* Wilmslow Golf.

BIRKIN, Sir Derek; *see* Birkin, Sir J. D.

BIRKIN, Sir John (Christian William), 6th Bt *cr* 1905, of Ruddington Grange, Notts; Director, Compound Eye Productions, since 1987; *b* 2 July 1953; *s* of Sir Charles Lloyd Birkin, 5th Bt and Janet (*d* 1983), *d* of Peter Johnson; *S* father, 1985; *m* 1994, Emma Gage. *Educ:* Eton; Trinity Coll., Dublin; London Film School. *Heir: cousin* James Francis Richard Birkin, *b* 27 Feb. 1957. *Address:* 23 St Luke's Street, Chelsea, SW3 3RP. *T:* 0171–351 4810.

BIRKIN, Sir (John) Derek, Kt 1990; TD 1965; Chairman, The RTZ Corporation PLC (formerly Rio Tinto-Zinc Corporation), since 1991 (Chief Executive and Deputy Chairman, 1985–91); *b* 30 Sept 1929; *s* of Noah and Rebecca Birkin; *m* 1952, Sadie Smith; one *s* one *d*. *Educ:* Hemsworth Grammar Sch. Managing Director: Velmar Ltd, 1966–67; Nairn Williamson Ltd, 1967–70; Dep. Chm. and Man. Dir, Tunnel Holdings Ltd, 1970–75; Chm. and Man. Dir, Tunnel Holdings, 1975–82; Dir, The RTZ Corporation (formerly Rio Tinto-Zinc Corp.), 1982–, Dep. Chief Exec., 1983–85. Director: Smiths Industries, 1977–84; British Gas Corp., 1982–85; George Wimpey, 1984–92; CRA Ltd (Australia), 1985–94; Rio Algom Ltd (Canada), 1985–92; The Merchants Trust PLC, 1986–; British Steel plc (formerly BSC), 1986–92; Barclays PLC, 1990–95; Merck & Co. Inc. (USA), 1992–; Carlton Communications Plc, 1992–; Unilever PLC, 1993–. Member: Review Body on Top Salaries, 1986–89; Council, Industrial Soc., 1985–. Dir, Royal Opera House, 1993– (Trustee, 1990–93). CIMgt (CBIM 1980); FRSA 1988. *Recreations:* opera, Rugby, cricket. *Address:* (office) 6 St James's Square, SW1Y 4LD. *Clubs:* Athenæum, MCC.

BIRKINSHAW, Prof. John Howard, DSc; FRSC; retired as Professor of Biochemistry and Head of Department of Biochemistry, London School of Hygiene and Tropical Medicine, University of London (1956–62), now Emeritus; *b* 8 Oct. 1894; *s* of John Thomas and Madeline Birkinshaw, Garforth, near Leeds; *m* 1929, Elizabeth Goodwin Guthrie, Ardrossan, Ayrshire; one *s* one *d*. *Educ:* Leeds Modern Sch.; Leeds Univ. War service, 1915, West Yorks Regt and Machine Gun Corps (POW); demobilised, 1919. BSc Hons 1920, MSc 1921, DSc 1929, Leeds. Research Biochemist to Nobel's Explosives Co. (later ICI), 1920–30; Research Asst to Prof. Raistrick, London Sch. of Hygiene and Tropical Medicine, 1931; Senior Lecturer, 1938; Reader, 1945. *Publications:* about 60 scientific papers in Biochemical Journal, Philos. Trans. Royal Society, etc. *Recreation:* photography. *Address:* 87 Barrow Point Avenue, Pinner, Mddx HA5 3HE. *T:* 0181–866 4784.

BIRKMYRE, Sir Archibald, 3rd Bt *cr* 1921, of Dalmunzie, Co. Perth; *b* 12 Feb. 1923; *s* of Sir Henry Birkmyre, 2nd Bt and Doris Gertrude Birkmyre (*née* Austen Smith); *S* father, 1992; *m* 1953, Gillian Mary, *o d* of late E. M. Downes, OBE; one *s* two *d*. *Educ:* Radley Coll. Served India and Burma, RA, 1942–45. Mem., London Stock Exchange, 1954–88. *Recreations:* golf, fishing, shooting. *Heir: s* James Birkmyre [*b* 29 Feb. 1956; *m* 1990, Leslie Amanda, *er d* of Richard Lyon, Seal Beach, Calif; one *s*]. *Address:* The Old Presbytery, Buckland, Faringdon, Oxon SN7 8QW. *T:* Faringdon (01367) 87253. *Clubs:* Boodle's; Huntercombe Golf.

BIRKS, Lt-Gen. Anthony Leonard, CB 1993; OBE 1985 (MBE 1977); Chief of Defence Force, New Zealand Defence Force, since 1995; *b* 30 Dec. 1941; *s* of Clifford Birks and Maisie Lola Gapes (*née* Brown); *m* 1964, Georgina May Ball, Bedfordshire; two *s* one *d*. *Educ:* St Andrew Coll., Christchurch; Nelson Coll.; RMA Sandhurst. Commissioned 1961; Platoon Comdr, 1 RNZIR, Mayala and Borneo, 1963–65; 1 Australian Task Force, Vietnam, 1968; 11 Field Force, Vietnam, 1970; Chief Instructor, Tactical Sch., 1977–78; Staff Coll., Australia, 1974; CO 2/1 RNZIR, 1979–81; Dir of Plans, Army, 1981–82; JSSC 1983; Comdr 3TF, 1985–87; Asst Chief Ops HQ, NZ Defence Force, 1988–89; RCDS 1990; Dep. Chief of Defence Staff HQ NZ Defence Force, 1991; CGS NZ Army, 1992–95. *Recreations:* golf, walking, driving. *Address:* 59 Pitt Street, Wadestown, Wellington, New Zealand. *Clubs:* Wellesley (Wellington); Wellington Golf.

BIRKS, Dr Jack, CBE 1975; FEng 1978; Chairman: North American Gas Investment Trust plc, since 1989; Midland & Scottish Resources, since 1994; *b* 1 Jan. 1920; *s* of late Herbert Horace Birks and of Ann Birks; *m* 1948, Vere Elizabeth Burrell-Davis; two *s* two *d*. *Educ:* Ecclesfield Grammar Sch.; Univ. of Leeds (BSc, PhD). Served with REME, Europe and India, 1941–46 (despatches, Captain). Exploration Research Div., Anglo Iranian Oil Co., 1948–57; Man., Petroleum Engrg Research, BP Research Centre, Sunbury, 1957–59; Vice-Pres. Exploration, BP North America, NY, 1959–62; various techn. and managerial appts, subseq. Dir and Gen. Man., Iranian Oil Exploration & Producing Co., Teheran and Masjid-i-Sulaiman, 1962–70; Gen. Man., Exploration and Production Dept, British Petroleum Co. Ltd, London, 1970–72; Technical Dir, BP Trading Ltd, and Dep. Chm., BP Trading Exec. Cttee, 1972–77; a Man. Dir, British Petroleum, 1978–82; Chairman: BP Coal, 1981–82; Selection Trust, 1981–82; BP Minerals International, 1981–82; NMI Ltd, 1982–85; Charterhouse Petroleum, 1982–86; Schroder Energy, subseq. LAE Energy Inc., 1981–88; British Maritime Technology, 1985–95; London American Energy NV, 1986–88 (Dir, 1981–88); Mountain Petroleum, 1988–90 (Dir, 1986–90); Director: Jebsens Drilling, subseq. Midland and Scottish Resources, 1982–; George Wimpey, 1982–90; Petrofina (UK), 1986–89; Bellwether Exploration Co., 1988–. Member: SRC, 1976–80; Meteorological Cttee, 1977–82; Adv. Council on R&D, Dept of Energy, 1978–82; Offshore Energy Technology Bd, Dept of Energy, 1978–82. Mem. Council, Royal Instn of GB, 1988–. President: Soc. for Underwater Technology, 1974; Pipeline Industries Guild, 1979–81; Inst. of Petroleum, 1984–86. Hon. FIMechE 1987. Hon. LLD Aberdeen, 1981; DU Surrey, 1981. *Publications:* contribs to technical internat. oil jls, sci. papers on oilfields develts and North Sea oil. *Recreations:* tennis, cricket, golf. *Address:* 1A Alwyne Road, Canonbury, N1 2HH. *T:* 0171–226 4905; High Silver, High Street, Holt, Norfolk NR25 6BN. *T:* Holt (01263) 712847. *Clubs:* Athenæum; Norfolk (Norwich).

BIRKS, His Honour Michael; a Circuit Judge, 1983–93; *b* 21 May 1920; *s* of late Falconer Moffat Birks, CBE, and Monica Katherine Lushington (*née* Mellor); *m* 1947, Ann Ethne, *d* of Captain Henry Stafford Morgan; one *d*. *Educ:* Oundle; Trinity Coll., Cambridge. Commissioned 22nd Dragoons, 1941; attached Indian Army, 1942, invalided out, 1943. Admitted Solicitor, 1946; Assistant Registrar: Chancery Div., High Court, 1953–60; Newcastle upon Tyne group of County Courts, 1960–61; Registrar: Birkenhead gp of County Courts, 1961–66; W London County Court, 1966–83; a Recorder of the Crown Court, 1979–83. Adv. Editor, Atkins Court Forms, 1966–91; Jt Editor, County Court Practice, 1976–83. Mem. County Court Rule Cttee, 1980–83. *Publications:* Gentlemen of the Law, 1960; Small Claims in the County Court, 1973; Enforcing Money Judgments in the County Court, 1980; contributed titles: County Courts and Interpleader (part), 4th edn Halsbury's Laws of England; Judgments and Orders (part), References and Inquiries (part), Service (part), and Transfer (part), County Courts Atkins Court Forms; contribs to legal jls. *Recreation:* painting.

BIRKS, Prof. Peter Brian Herrenden, FBA 1989; Regius Professor of Civil Law, University of Oxford, and Fellow of All Souls College, Oxford, since 1989; *b* 3 Oct. 1941; *e s* of Dr Peter Herrenden Birks and Mary (*née* Morgan); *m* 1984, Jacqueline S. Berrington (*née* Stimpson). *Educ:* Trinity Coll., Oxford (MA; Hon. Fellow, 1994); University Coll., London (LLM; Fellow, 1993). DCL Oxon, 1991; LLD Edin., 1991. Lectr in Laws, UCL, 1966–71; Law Fellow, Brasenose Coll., Oxford, 1971–81; Prof. of Civil Law, and Head of Dept of Civil Law, Edinburgh Univ., 1981–87; Prof. of Law, Southampton Univ., 1988–89. Wisselleerstoelhouder, Faculty of Law, Univ. of Nijmegen, 1994–Sept. 1996. Hon. Sec., SPTL, 1989– (Mem. Council, 1988–); Member: Lord Chancellor's Adv. Cttee on Legal Educn, 1989–91; Social Sciences Cttee, Schs Exams and Assessment Council, 1989–91 (Chm., Law Cttee, 1988–89); Sec., Standing Conf. on Legal Educn, 1991–94. Consultant Editor, Restitution Law Review, 1993–. Mem., Eur. Acad. of Private Lawyers, 1994–. Hon. QC 1995. FRSA 1992. *Publications:* Introduction to the Law of Restitution, 1985; (ed with D. N. MacCormick) The Legal Mind, 1986; (with G. McLeod) The Institutes of Justinian, 1987; (ed) New Perspectives on the Roman Law of Property, 1989; Restitution: the future, 1992; (ed) Frontiers of Liability, vols 1 and 2, 1994; (ed) Reviewing Legal Education, 1994; articles on Roman law, legal history, legal educn, and restitution. *Address:* Oak Trees, Sandy Lane, Boars Hill, Oxford OX1 5HN. *T:* Oxford (01865) 735625; All Souls College, Oxford OX1 4AL. *T:* Oxford (01865) 279338, *Fax:* (01865) 279299. *Club:* Athenæum.

BIRLEY, Anthony Addison, CB 1979; Clerk of Public Bills, House of Commons, 1973–82, retired; *b* 28 Nov. 1920; *s* of Charles Fair Birley and Eileen Mia Rouse; *m* 1951, Jane Mary Ruggles-Brise; two *d*. *Educ:* Winchester (exhibnr); Christ Church, Oxford (MA). Served War in RA (Ayrshire Yeomanry), 1940–45, in North Africa and Italian campaigns (wounded). Asst Clerk, House of Commons, 1948; Clerk of Standing Cttees, 1970. *Recreations:* gardening, walking, racing. *Address:* Holtom House, Paxford, Chipping Campden, Glos GL55 6XH. *T:* Paxford (0138678) 318. *Club:* Army and Navy.

BIRLEY, Sir Derek, Kt 1989; Vice-Chancellor, University of Ulster, 1984–91; *b* 31 May 1926; *s* of late Sydney John and late Margaret Birley; *m* 1990, Prof. Norma Reid. *Educ:* Hemsworth Grammar Sch.; Queens' Coll., Cambridge (BA 1950, MA 1954). Royal Artillery, 1944–48; Schoolmaster, Queen Elizabeth Grammar Sch., Wakefield, 1952–55; Admin. Asst, Leeds Educn Cttee, 1955–59; Asst Educn Officer: Dorset, 1959–61; Lancs, 1961–64; Dep. Dir of Educn, Liverpool, 1964–70; Rector, Ulster Polytechnic, 1970–84. Hon. Fellow, Sheffield Poly., 1991. Hon. LLD QUB, 1991. *Publications:* The Education Officer and his World, 1970; (with Anne Dufton) An Equal Chance, 1971; Planning and Education, 1972; The Willow Wand, 1979; Sport and the Making of Britain, 1993; Land of Sport and Glory, 1994; Playing the Game, 1995. *Recreations:* books, cricket, jazz. *Address:* Ferndown, Wall Hill Road, Coventry CV7 8AD.

BIRLEY, Prof. Eric, MBE 1943; FSA 1931; FBA 1969; Professor of Roman-British History and Archæology, University of Durham, 1956–71, now Professor Emeritus; *b* 12 Jan. 1906; *y s* of J. Harold Birley; *m* 1934, Margaret Isabel, *d* of Rev. James Goodlet; two *s. Educ:* Clifton Coll.; Brasenose Coll., Oxford (Hon. Fellow, 1987). Lecturer, University of Durham, 1931; Reader, 1943. War of 1939–45: Military Intelligence, Lt-Col, GSO1 Military Intelligence Research Section; Chief of German Military Document Section, War Dept. Vice-Master, Hatfield Coll., Durham, 1947–49, Master, 1949–56; first Dean of Faculty of Social Sciences, Univ. of Durham, 1968–70. President: Soc. of Antiquaries of Newcastle upon Tyne, 1957–59; Cumberland and Westmorland Antiquarian and Archaeological Soc., 1957–60; Architectural and Archæological Soc. of Durham and Northumberland, 1959–63; Member: German Archæological Inst.; Ancient Monuments Board for England, 1966–76; Hon. Member, Gesellschaft Pro Vindonissa (Switzerland); Hon. FSAScot, 1980; Chm., Vindolanda Trust, 1970–; Hon. Life Pres., Internat. Congress of Roman Frontier Studies, 1974. Hon. Dr Phil Freiburg i Br, 1970; Hon. DLitt Leicester, 1971; Dr *hc* Heidelberg, 1986. Polonia Restituta, 1944; Legion of Merit, 1947. *Publications:* The Centenary Pilgrimage of Hadrian's Wall, 1949; Roman Britain and the Roman Army, 1953; (ed) The Congress of Roman Frontier Studies 1949, 1952; Research on Hadrian's Wall, 1961; (jt ed) Roman Frontier Studies 1969, 1974; Fifty-one Ballades, 1980; The Roman Army: papers 1929–1986, 1988; numerous papers on Roman Britain and on the Roman army, excavation reports, etc. *Recreation:* archæology. *Address:* Carvoran House, Greenhead, Carlisle CA6 7JB. *T:* Gilsland (016977) 47594.

BIRLEY, James Leatham Tennant, CBE 1990; FRCP, FRCPsych, DPM; Consultant Psychiatrist, Bethlem Royal and Maudsley Hospitals, 1969–90, Emeritus Psychiatrist, 1990; President, British Medical Association, 1993–94; *b* 31 May 1928; *s* of late Dr James Leatham Birley and Margaret Edith (*née* Tennant); *m* 1954, Julia Davies; one *s* three *d. Educ:* Winchester Coll.; University Coll., Oxford; St Thomas' Hosp., London. Maudsley Hospital: Registrar, 1960; Sen. Registrar, 1963; Mem. Scientific Staff, MRC Social Psychiatry Research Unit, 1965; Dean, Inst. of Psychiatry, 1971–82. Dean, 1982–87, Pres., 1987–90, RCPsych. *Publications:* contribs to scientific jls. *Recreations:* music, gardening. *Address:* Upper Bryn, Longtown, Hereford HR2 0NA.

BIRLEY, Michael Pellew, MA (Oxon); Housemaster, 1970–80, Assistant Master, 1980–84, Marlborough College; *b* 7 Nov. 1920; *s* of late Norman Pellew Birley, DSO, MC, and Eileen Alice Morgan; *m* 1949, Ann Grover (*née* Street); two *s* two *d. Educ:* Marlborough Coll.; Wadham Coll., Oxford. 1st class Classical Honour Moderations, 1940; 1st class *Litterae Humaniores,* 1947; MA 1946. Served War of 1939–45 with the Royal Fusiliers; joined up, Sept. 1940; commissioned, April 1941; abroad, 1942–45 (despatches); demobilised, Jan. 1946. Taught Classics: Shrewsbury Sch., 1948–50; Eton Coll., 1950–56; Headmaster, Eastbourne College, 1956–70. Member Council: Ardingly Coll., 1981–90; Marlborough Coll., 1985–90. Fellow, Woodard Corp., 1983–90. *Recreations:* sailing, gardening, wine-making. *Address:* Long Summers, Cross Lane, Marlborough, Wilts SN8 1LA. *T:* Marlborough (01672) 512830.

BIRLEY, Prof. Susan Joyce, (Mrs David Norburn); Professor of Management, The Management School, Imperial College, since 1990; *m* 1st, 1964, Arwyn Hopkins (marr. diss. 1970); 2nd, 1975, Prof. David Norburn, *qv. Educ:* Nelson Grammar Sch.; University College London (BSc 1964); PhD London 1974. FSS. Teacher, Dunsmore Sch., 1964–66; Lectr, Lanchester Polytechnic, 1966–68; Lectr and Sen. Lectr, Poly. of Central London, 1968–72; Sen. Res. Fellow, City Univ., 1972–74; London Business School: Sen. Res. Fellow, 1974–79; Lectr in Small Business, 1979–82; University of Notre Dame, USA: Adjunct Associate Prof., 1978–82; Associate Prof. of Strategy and Entrepreneurship, 1982–85; Philip and Pauline Harris Prof. of Entrepreneurship, Cranfield Inst. of Technol., 1985–90. Academic Dir, European Foundn for Entrepreneurship Res., 1988–91. Member: CNAA, 1987–90; NI Economic Council, 1988–94; PCFC, 1988–92; Adv. Panel on Deregulation, DTI, 1989–91; Bd, LEDU, NI, 1992–93. Founder Director and Shareholder: Guidehouse Group, 1980–85; Greyfriars Ltd, 1982–85; Newchurch & Co., 1986– (Chm.). Governor, Harris City Technol. Coll., 1990–92. Freeman, City of London, 1964. Mem. Editl Bds, various business jls. *Publications:* From Private to Public (jtly), 1977; The Small Business Casebook, 1979; The Small Business Casebook: teaching manual, 1980; New Enterprises, 1982; (contrib.) Small Business and Entrepreneurship, ed Burns and Dewhurst, 1989; (jtly) Exit Routes, 1989; (jtly) The British Entrepreneur, 1989; (ed) European Entrepreneurship: emerging growth companies, 1989; (ed jtly) International Perspectives on Entrepreneurship, 1992; numerous contribs to learned jls. *Recreation:* gardening. *Address:* 10 Ripplevale Grove, N1 1HU. *T:* 0171–607 1566.

BIRMINGHAM, Archbishop of, (RC), since 1982; **Most Rev. Maurice Noël Léon Couve de Murville;** *b* 27 June 1929; *s* of Noël Couve de Murville and Marie, *d* of Sir Louis Souchon. *Educ:* Downside School; Trinity Coll., Cambridge (MA); STL (Institut Catholique, Paris); MPhil (Sch. of Oriental and African Studies, Univ. of London). Priest, 1957; Curate, St Anselm's, Dartford, 1957–60; Priest-in-Charge, St Francis, Moulsecoomb, 1961–64; Catholic Chaplain: Univ. of Sussex, 1961–77; Univ. of Cambridge, 1977–82. DUniv Open, 1994. *Publications:* (with Philip Jenkins) Catholic Cambridge, 1983; John Milner 1752–1826, 1986. *Recreations:* walking, gardening, local history. *Address:* 8 Shadwell Street, Birmingham B4 6EY. *Clubs:* Lansdowne; Birmingham (Birmingham).

BIRMINGHAM, Bishop of, since 1987; **Rt. Rev. Mark Santer,** MA; *b* 29 Dec. 1936; *s* of late Rev. Canon Eric Arthur Robert Santer and Phyllis Clare Barlow; *m* 1964, Henriette Cornelia Weststrate (*d* 1994); one *s* two *d. Educ:* Marlborough Coll.; Queens' Coll., Cambridge (Hon. Fellow, 1991); Westcott House, Cambridge. Deacon, 1963; priest 1964; Asst Curate, Cuddesdon, 1963–67; Tutor, Cuddesdon Theological Coll., 1963–67; Fellow and Dean of Clare Coll., Cambridge, 1967–72 (and Tutor, 1968–72; Hon. Fellow, 1987); Univ. Asst Lectr in Divinity, 1968–72; Principal of Westcott House, Cambridge, 1973–81; Hon. Canon of Winchester Cathedral, 1978–81; Area Bishop of Kensington, 1981–87. Co-Chm., Anglican Roman Catholic Internat. Commn, 1983–. *Publications:* (contrib.) The Phenomenon of Christian Belief, 1970; (with M. F. Wiles) Documents in Early Christian Thought, 1975; Their Lord and Ours, 1982; (contrib.) The Church and the State, 1984; (contrib.) Dropping the Bomb, 1985; articles in: Jl of Theological Studies; New Testament Studies; Theology. *Address:* Bishop's Croft, Old Church Road, Harborne, Birmingham B17 0BG. *T:* 0121–427 1163.

BIRMINGHAM, Auxiliary Bishops of, (RC); *see* Pargeter, Rt. Rev. P.; Brain, Rt. Rev. T. J.

BIRMINGHAM, Provost of; *see* Berry, Very Rev. P. A.

BIRMINGHAM, Archdeacon of; *see* Duncan, Ven. J. F.

BIRNBAUM, Michael Ian; QC 1992; a Recorder, since 1995; *b* 26 Feb. 1947; *s* of Samuel Birnbaum and Anne (*née* Zucker); *m* 1984, Aimee Dara Schachter. *Educ:* Southgate County Grammar Sch.; Christ Church, Oxford (BA Jurisp.). Called to the Bar, Middle Temple, 1969; practice mainly at Criminal Bar; Asst Recorder, 1990–95. *Recreations:* singing, opera, reading. *Address:* 1 Hare Court, Temple, EC4Y 7BE. *T:* 0171–353 5324.

BIRRELL, Sir James (Drake), Kt 1993; FCA; FCBSI; Chief Executive, Halifax Building Society, 1988–93; *b* 18 Aug. 1933; *s* of James Russell Birrell, MA and Edith Marion Birrell, BSc (*née* Drake); *m* 1958, Margaret Anne Pattison; two *d. Educ:* Belle Vue Grammar School, Bradford. FCA 1955; FCBSI 1989. Boyce Welch & Co. (articled clerk), 1949–55; Pilot Officer, RAF, 1955–57; chartered accountant, Price Waterhouse, 1957–60; Accountant, ADA Halifax, 1960–61; Management Accountant, Empire Stores, 1961–64; Dir and Co. Sec., John Gladstone & Co., 1964–68; Halifax Building Society, 1968–93. Non-executive Director: Securicor, 1993–; Wesleyan Gen. Assce Soc., 1993–. Mem., Building Societies Commn, 1994–. *Recreations:* golf, gardening, archaeology, local history. *Address:* Kinnesswood, Greenroyd Avenue, Skircoat Green, Halifax HX3 0JN.

BIRSE, Peter Malcolm; Chairman, Birse Group, since 1970; *b* 24 Nov. 1942; *s* of Peter A. M. Birse and Margaret C. Birse; *m* 1969, Helen Searle; two *s* one *d. Educ:* Arbroath High Sch.; St Andrews Univ. (BScEng). MICE. Engineer, John Mowlem, 1963–66; Site Manager: Cammon (Ghana), 1966–68; Cammon (UK), 1968–69; Engineer, Foster Wheeler, 1969–70; founded Birse Group, 1970. *Recreations:* sailing, ski-ing. *Address:* Birse Group, Humber Road, Barton-on-Humber, Humberside DN18 5BW. *Club:* Royal Ocean Racing.

BIRT, John; Director-General, BBC, since 1992 (Deputy Director-General, 1987–92); *b* 10 Dec. 1944; *s* of Leo Vincent Birt and Ida Birt; *m* 1965, Jane Frances (*née* Lake); one *s* one *d. Educ:* St Mary's Coll., Liverpool; St Catherine's Coll., Oxford (MA; Hon. Fellow 1992). Producer, Nice Time, 1968–69; Joint Editor, World in Action, 1969–70; Producer, The Frost Programme, 1971–72; Executive Producer, Weekend World, 1972–74; Head of Current Affairs, LWT, 1974–77; Co-Producer, The Nixon Interviews, 1977; Controller of Features and Current Affairs, LWT, 1977–81; Dir of Programmes, LWT, 1982–87. Vis. Fellow, Nuffield Coll., Oxford, 1991. Member: Wilton Park Academic Council, 1980–83; Media Law Gp, 1983–; Opportunity 2000 (formerly Women's Economic) Target Team, BITC, 1991–; Broadcasting Research Unit: Mem., Working Party on the new Technologies, 1981–83; Mem., Exec. Cttee, 1983–87. Vice-Pres., RTS, 1994– (Fellow, 1989). Hon. DLitt Liverpool John Moores, 1992. *Publications:* various articles in newspapers and journals. *Recreation:* walking. *Address:* c/o BBC, Broadcasting House, W1A 1AA.

BIRT, Prof. (Lindsay) Michael, AO 1986; CBE 1980; FTS; Vice-Chancellor, University of New South Wales, 1981–92; Chairman, Australian Science and Technology Council, since 1992; *b* 18 Jan. 1932; *s* of Robert Birt and Florence Elizabeth Chapman; *m* 1959, Jenny Tapfield; two *s. Educ:* Melbourne Boys' High Sch.; Univ. of Melbourne; Univ. of Oxford. BAgrSc, BSc and PhD (Melb), DPhil (Oxon). FTS 1992. Univ. of Melbourne: Lectr in Biochemistry, 1960–63, Sen. Lectr in Biochem., 1964; Sen. Lectr in Biochem., Univ. of Sheffield, 1964–67; Foundn Prof. of Biochemistry, ANU, 1967–73; Vice-Chancellor designate, Wollongong Univ. Coll., Nov. 1973; Vice-Chancellor, Univ. of Wollongong, 1975–81; Emer. Prof., ANU, 1974. Hon. DLitt Wollongong, 1981; Hon. LLD Sheffield, 1988; Hon. DSc: New South Wales, 1992; Queensland, 1992; DUniv Charles Sturt. *Publication:* Biochemistry of the Tissues (with W. Bartley and P. Banks), 1968 (London), 1970 (Germany, as Biochemie), 1972 (Japan). *Recreations:* music, reading. *Address:* 85 Florida Road, Palm Beach, NSW 2108, Australia. *T:* (2) 99744651. *Clubs:* Union, University and Schools (Sydney); Melbourne Cricket, Sydney Cricket.

BIRT, Michael Cameron St John; QC 1995; HM Attorney General, Jersey, since 1994; *b* 25 Aug. 1948; *s* of St John Michael Clive Birt and Mairi Araminta Birt (*née* Cameron); *m* 1973, Joan Frances Miller; two *s* one *d. Educ:* Marlborough Coll.; Magdalene Coll., Cambridge (MA Law). Called to the Bar, Middle Temple, 1970, to Jersey Bar, 1977; in practice: London, 1971–75; as Jersey advocate, with Ogier & Le Cornu, St Helier, 1976–93; Crown Advocate of Jersey, 1987–93. *Recreations:* ski-ing, yachting, golf. *Address:* Attorney General's Chambers, Royal Court House, Jersey JE1 1DD. *T:* Jersey (01534) 502200, *Fax:* (01534) 502299. *Clubs:* Royal Channel Islands Yacht; Royal Jersey Golf.

BIRT, Ven. Canon William Raymond; Archdeacon of Berkshire, 1973–77; Archdeacon Emeritus, since 1985; Hon. Canon of Christ Church Cathedral, Oxford, 1980; *b* 25 Aug. 1911; *s* of Rev. Douglas Birt, Rector of Leconfield with Scorborough, and Dorothy Birt; *m* 1st, 1936, Marie Louise Jeaffreson (*d* 1990); one *s* two *d*; 2nd, 1994, Diana Bronwen Warren (*née* Montgomery). *Educ:* Christ's Hospital; Ely Theological Coll. Journalist until 1940. Major, 22nd Dragoons (RAC), 1941–46 (despatches). Publisher, 1946–55. Deacon, 1956; priest, 1957; Curate, Caversham, 1956–59; Vicar, St George, Newbury, 1959–71; Rector of West Woodhay, 1971–81, Asst Rector, 1981–91; Rural Dean of Newbury, 1969–73. *Recreations:* gardens and gardening. *Address:* 1 The Old Bakery, George Street, Kingsclere, Newbury, Berkshire RG15 8NQ. *T:* Kingsclere (01635) 297426.

BIRTS, Peter William; QC 1990; a Recorder, since 1989; *b* 9 Feb. 1946; *s* of John Claude Birts and Audrey Lavinia Birts; *m* 1971, Penelope Ann Eyre; two *d* one *s. Educ:* Lancing College; St John's College, Cambridge (choral scholarship; MA). Called to the Bar, Gray's Inn, 1968; Mem., Gen. Council of the Bar, 1989– (Chm., Legal Aid and Fees Cttee, 1994–). Member: Judicial Studies Bd (Main Bd and Civil and Family Cttee), 1991–; County Court Rules Cttee, 1991–; Legal Mem., Mental Health Review Tribunals, 1994–. Asst Parly Boundary Comr, 1992–. Gov., Benenden Sch., 1990–93. Freeman, City of London, 1967; Liveryman, Carpenters' Co., 1967–. *Publications:* Trespass: summary procedure for possession of land (with Alan Willis), 1987; Remedies for Trespass, 1990. *Recreations:* music, shooting. *Address:* Farrar's Building, Temple, EC4Y 7BD. *T:* 0171–583 9241. *Club:* Hurlingham.

BIRTWISTLE, Maj.-Gen. Archibald Cull, CB 1983; CBE 1976 (OBE 1971); DL; Signal Officer in Chief (Army), 1980–83, retired; Master of Signals, since 1990; *b* 19 Aug. 1927; *s* of Walter Edwin Birtwistle and Eila Louise Cull; *m* 1956, Sylvia Elleray; two *s* one *d. Educ:* Sir John Deane's Grammar School, Northwich; St John's Coll., Cambridge (MA Mech. Sciences). CEng, MIEE. Commissioned, Royal Signals, 1949; served: Korea (despatches, 1952); UK; BAOR; CCR Sigs 1 (Br) Corps, 1973–75; Dep. Comdt, RMCS, 1975–79; Chief Signal Officer, BAOR, 1979–80. Col Comdt, Royal Corps of Signals, 1983–89, and 1990–; Hon. Colonel: Durham and South Tyne ACF, 1983–88; 34 (Northern) Signal Regt (Vol.), TA, 1988–90. DL N Yorks, 1991. *Recreations:* all sports, especially Rugby (former Chairman, Army Rugby Union), soccer and cricket; gardening. *Address:* c/o National Westminster Bank PLC, 97 High Street, Northallerton, North Yorks DL7 8PS.

BIRTWISTLE, Sir Harrison, Kt 1988; composer; Henry Purcell Professor of Composition, King's College London, since 1994; *b* 1934; *m* Sheila; three *s. Educ:* Royal Manchester Coll. of Music; RAM (Hon. FRAM). Dir of Music, Cranborne Chase Sch., 1962–65. Composer-in-residence, London Philharmonic Orch., 1993–. Vis. Fellow, Princeton Univ., 1966–68; Cornell Vis. Prof. of Music, Swarthmore Coll., 1973; Vis. Slee Prof., State Univ. of NY at Buffalo, 1974–75. An Associate Dir, NT, 1975–88. Mem., Akademie der Kunst, Berlin. Hon. DMus Sussex; Hon. DLitt Salford. Evening Standard Award for Opera, 1987, 1991. Chevalier des Arts et des Lettres (France), 1986. *Publications:* Refrains and Choruses, 1957; Monody for Corpus Christi, 1959; Précis, 1959; The World is Discovered, 1960; Chorales, 1962, 1963; Entre'actes and Sappho Fragments, 1964; Three Movements with Fanfares, 1964; Tragoedia, 1965; Ring a Dumb Carillon, 1965; Carmen Paschale, 1965; The Mark of the Goat, 1965, 1966; The Visions of Francesco Petrarca, 1966; Verses, 1966; Punch and Judy, 1966–67 (opera); Three Lessons in a Frame, 1967; Linoii, 1968; Nomos, 1968; Verses for Ensembles, 1969; Down by the Greenwood Side,

1969; Hoquetus David (arr. of Machaut), 1969; Cantata, 1969; Ut Hermita Solvs, 1969; Medusa, 1969–70; Prologue, 1970; Nenia on the Death of Orpheus, 1970; An Imaginary Landscape, 1971; Meridian, 1971; The Fields of Sorrow, 1971; Chronometer, 1971; Epilogue—Full Fathom Five, 1972; Tombeau, 1972; The Triumph of Time, 1972; La Plage: eight arias of remembrance, 1972; Dinah and Nick's Love Song, 1972; Chanson de Geste, 1973; The World is Discovered, 1973; Grimethorpe Aria, 1973; 5 Chorale Preludes from Bach, 1973; Chorales from a Toyshop, 1973; Interludes from a Tragedy, 1973; The Mask of Orpheus, 1973–84 (opera) (Grawemeyer Award, Univ. of Louisville, 1987); Melencolia I, 1975; Pulse Field, Bow Down, Silbury Air, 1977; For O, for O, the Hobby-horse is forgot, 1977; Carmen Arcardiae Mechanicae Perpetuum, 1978; agm, 1979; On the Sheer Threshold of the Night, 1980; Quintet, 1981; Pulse Sampler, 1981; Deowa, 1983; Yan Tan Tethera, 1984; Still Movement, 1984; Secret Theatre, 1984; Songs by Myself, 1984; Earth Dances, 1986; Fanfare for Will, 1987; Endless Parade, 1987; Gawain, 1990 (opera); Four Poems by Jaan Kaplinski, 1991; Gawain's Journey, 1991; Antiphonies, 1992; The Second Mrs Kong, 1994 (opera); Cry of Anubis, 1995. *Address:* c/o Allied Artists Agency, 42 Montpelier Square, SW7 1JZ.

BISCHOFF, Winfried Franz Wilhelm, (Win); Group Chief Executive, Schroders plc, since 1984 (Director, since 1983); Director: J. Henry Schroder Wagg & Co. Ltd, since 1978 (Chairman, 1983–94); Wertheim Schroder Holdings, NYC, since 1986; *b* 10 May 1941; *s* of Paul Helmut Bischoff and Hildegard (*née* Kühne); *m* 1972, Rosemary Elizabeth, *d* of Hon. Leslie Leathers; two *s*. *Educ:* Marist Brothers, Inanda, Johannesburg, S Africa; Univ. of the Witwatersrand, Johannesburg (BCom). Man. Dir, Schroders & Chartered Ltd, Hong Kong, 1971–82. Non-exec. Dir, Cable and Wireless, 1991–. *Recreations:* opera, music, golf. *Address:* 28 Bloomfield Terrace, SW1W 8PQ; J. Henry Schroder Wagg & Co. Ltd, 120 Cheapside, EC2V 6DS. *T:* 0171–382 6000. *Clubs:* Woking Golf, Frilford Heath Golf; 300 (Japan).

BISCOE, Rear-Adm. Alec Julian T.; *see* Tyndale-Biscoe.

BISCOE, Prof. Timothy John; Deputy Vice Chancellor, University of Hong Kong, since 1992; *b* 28 April 1932; *s* of late Rev. W. H. Biscoe and Mrs M. G. Biscoe; *m* 1955, Daphne Miriam (*née* Gurton); one *s* two *d*. *Educ:* Latymer Upper School; The London Hospital Medical College. BSc (Hons) Physiology, 1953; MB, BS 1957; DSc London, 1993; FRCP 1983. London Hospital, 1957–58; RAMC Short Service Commission, 1958–62; Physiologist, CDEE, Porton Down, 1959–62; ARC Inst. of Animal Physiology, Babraham, 1962–65; Res. Fellow in Physiology, John Curtin Sch. of Med. Res., Canberra, 1965–66; Associate Res. Physiologist, Cardiovascular Res. Inst., UC Medical Center, San Francisco, 1966–68; University of Bristol: Res. Associate, Dept of Physiology, 1968–70; 2nd Chair of Physiology, 1970–79; Head of Dept of Physiology, 1975–79. University College London: Jodrell Prof. of Physiology, 1979–92; Vice Provost, 1990–92. McLaughlin Vis. Prof., McMaster Univ., Ont, 1986; Hooker Distinguished Vis. Prof., McMaster Univ., 1990. Hon. Sec., Physiological Soc., 1977–82; Member Council: Harveian Soc., 1983–86; Research Defence Soc., 1983–90 (Hon. Sec., 1983–86). Mem., Academia Europaea, 1991. *Publications:* papers on neurophysiology in Journal of Physiology, etc. *Recreations:* looking, listening, reading. *Address:* University of Hong Kong, Pokfulam Road, Hong Kong. *T:* 8592103, *Fax:* 5470801. *Club:* Garrick.

BISHOP, family name of **Baroness O'Cathain**.

BISHOP, Alan Henry, CB 1989; HM Chief Inspector of Prisons for Scotland, 1989–94; *b* 12 Sept. 1929; *s* of Robert Bishop and May Watson; *m* 1959, Marjorie Anne Conlan; one *s* one *d*. *Educ:* George Heriot's Sch., Edinburgh; Edinburgh Univ. (MA 1st Cl. Hons Econ. Science, 1951, 2nd Cl. Hons History, 1952). Served RAF Educn Br., 1952–54. Asst Principal, Dept of Agric. for Scotland, 1954; Private Sec. to Parly Under-Secs of State, 1958–59; Principal, 1959; First Sec., Food and Agric., Copenhagen and The Hague, 1963–66; Asst Sec., Scottish Develt Dept, 1968; Asst Sec., Commn on the Constitution, 1969–73; Asst Under-Sec. of State, 1980–84, Principal Establishment Officer, 1984–89, Scottish Office. *Recreations:* contract bridge (Pres., Scottish Bridge Union, 1979–80), theatre, golf. *Address:* Beaumont Court, 19/8 Wester Coates Gardens, Edinburgh EH12 5LT. *T:* 0131–346 4641. *Clubs:* New, Melville Bridge (Edinburgh); Murrayfield Golf.

BISHOP, Dr Arthur Clive; Deputy Director, British Museum (Natural History), 1982–89, and Keeper of Mineralogy, 1975–89; *b* 9 July 1930; *s* of late Charles Henry Bishop and Hilda (*née* Clowes); *m* 1962, Helen (*née* Bennison); one *d*. *Educ:* Wolstanton County Grammar Sch., Newcastle, Staffs; King's Coll., Univ. of London (FKC 1985). BSc 1951, PhD 1954. Geologist, HM Geological Survey, 1954; served RAF Educn Br., 1955–57; Lectr in Geology, Queen Mary Coll., Univ. of London, 1958; Principal Sci. Officer, British Museum (Natural History), 1969, Deputy Keeper 1972. Geological Society: Daniel Pidgeon Fund, 1958; Murchison Fund, 1970; Vice-Pres., 1977–78; Mineralogical Society: Gen. Sec., 1965–72; Vice-Pres., 1973–74; Pres., 1986–87; Pres., Geologists' Assoc., 1978–80; Vice-Pres., Inst. of Science Technology, 1973–82. Mem. d'honneur, La Société Jersiaise, 1983. *Publications:* An Outline of Crystal Morphology, 1967; (with W. R. Hamilton and A. R. Woolley) Hamlyn Guide to Minerals, Rocks and Fossils, 1974; papers in various jls, mainly on geology of Channel Is and Brittany, and on dioritic rocks. *Recreations:* drawing and painting. *Address:* 4 Viewfield Road, Bexley, Kent DA5 3EE. *T:* 0181–302 9602.

BISHOP, Prof. David Hugh Langler, PhD, DSc; FIBiol; Fellow, St Cross College, Oxford, since 1984; Director, Natural Environment Research Council Institute of Virology and Environmental Microbiology (formerly Institute of Virology), 1984–95; *b* 31 Dec. 1937; *s* of late Reginald Samuel Harold Bishop and of Violet Rose Mary Langler; *m* 1st, 1963, Margaret Duthie; one *s* one *d*; 2nd, 1971, Polly Roy; one *s*. *Educ:* Liverpool Univ. (BSc 1959, PhD 1962); MA 1984, DSc 1988, Oxon. FIBiol 1989. Postdoctoral Fellow, CNRS, Gif-sur-Yvette, 1962–63; Research Associate, Univ. of Edinburgh, 1963–66, Univ. of Illinois, 1966–69; Asst Prof., 1969–70, Associate Prof., 1970–71, Columbia Univ.; Associate Prof., 1971–75, Prof., 1975, Rutgers Univ.; Prof., Univ. of Alabama in Birmingham, 1975–84 (Sen. Scientist, Comprehensive Cancer Center, 1975–84; Chm., Dept of Microbiology, 1983–84). Vis. Fellow, Lincoln Coll., Oxford, 1981–82; Vis. Prof. of Virology, Oxford Univ., 1984–. Nathaniel A. Young Award in Virology, 1981. *Publications:* Rhabdoviruses, 1979; numerous contribs to books and jls. *Recreation:* hill walking. *Address:* St Cross College, Oxford OX1 3LZ. *Club:* Athenæum.

BISHOP, Sir Frederick (Arthur), Kt 1975; CB 1960; CVO 1957; Director-General of the National Trust, 1971–75; *b* 4 Dec. 1915; *o s* of A. J. Bishop, Bristol; *m* 1940, Elizabeth Finlay Stevenson; two *s* one *d*. *Educ:* Colston's Hospital, Bristol. LLB (London). Inland Revenue, 1934. Served in RAF and Air Transport Auxiliary, 1942–46. Ministry of Food, 1947, where Principal Private Secretary to Ministers, 1949–52; Asst Secretary, Cabinet Office, 1953–55; Principal Private Secretary to the Prime Minister, 1956–59; Deputy Secretary: of the Cabinet, 1959–61; Min. of Agriculture, Fisheries and Food, 1961–64; Perm. Sec., Min. of Land and Natural Resources, 1964–65, resigned. Chm., Home Grown Timber Advisory Cttee, 1966–73; Member: BBC Gen. Adv. Council, 1971–75; Crafts Adv. Council, 1973–75. Director: S. Pearson & Son Ltd, 1965–70; Pearson Longman, 1970–77; English China Clays Ltd, 1975–86; Devon and Cornwall Bd, Lloyds Bank, 1976–86. *Address:* Manor Barn, Church Road, Bramshott, Liphook GU30 7SH.

BISHOP, George Robert, CBE 1993; DPhil; FRSE; CPhys, FInstP; Director General, Ispra Establishment, Joint Research Centre, European Commission, Ispra, Italy, 1983–92, retired (Director, 1982–83); *b* 16 Jan. 1927; *s* of George William Bishop and Lilian Elizabeth Garrod; *m* 1952, Adriana Giuseppina, *d* of Luigi Caberlotto and Giselda Mazzariol; two *s* one *d*. *Educ:* Christ Church, Oxford (MA, DPhil). ICI Research Fellow, Univ. of Oxford, 1951; Research Fellow, St Antony's Coll., Oxford, 1952; Chercheur, Ecole Normale Supérieure, Paris, 1954; Ingénieur-Physicien, Laboratoire de l'Accelerateur Linéaire, ENS, Orsay, 1958; Prof., Faculté des Sciences, Univ. de Paris, 1962; Kelvin Prof. of Natural Philosophy, Univ. of Glasgow, 1964–76; Dir, Dept of Natural and Physical Sciences, JRC, Ispra, 1974–82. Hon. DSc, Strathclyde, 1979. *Publications:* Handbuch der Physik, Band XLII, 1957; β and X-Ray Spectroscopy, 1960; Nuclear Structure and Electromagnetic Interactions, 1965; numerous papers in learned jls on nuclear and high energy physics. *Recreations:* literature, music, swimming, tennis, gardening, travel. *Address:* 3 Holly House, Sawyer's Hall Lane, Brentwood, Essex CM15 9BP. *T:* Brentwood (01277) 225530; via Favretti 23/A, Mogliano Veneto, 31021 (TV), Italy. *T:* (41) 455813.

BISHOP, Sir George (Sidney), Kt 1975; CB 1958; OBE 1947; Director, Booker McConnell Ltd, 1961–82 (Vice-Chairman, 1970–71, Chairman, 1972–79); Director: Barclays Bank International, 1972–83; Barclays Bank Ltd, 1974–83; Ranks Hovis McDougall, 1976–84; International Basic Economy Corporation, USA, 1980–83; *b* 15 Oct. 1913; *o s* of late J. and M. Bishop; *m* 1940, Marjorie Woodruff (marr. diss. 1961); one *d*; *m* 1961, Una Padel. *Educ:* Ashton-in-Makerfield Grammar Sch.; London Sch. of Economics. Social service work in distressed areas, 1935–38; SW Durham Survey, 1939; Ministry of Food, 1940; Private Secretary to Minister of Food, 1945–49; Under-Secretary, Ministry of Agriculture, Fisheries and Food, 1949–59, Dep. Secretary, 1959–61. Chm., Bookers Agricultural Holdings Ltd, 1964–70; Director: Nigerian Sugar Co. Ltd, 1966–70; Agricultural Mortgage Corp. Ltd, 1973–79. Chairman: Internat. Sugar Council, 1957; West India Cttee, 1969–71 (Pres., 1977–); Industry Co-operative Programme, 1976–78; Council, Overseas Develt Inst., 1977–84; Vice-Chm., Internat. Wheat Council, 1959; Member: Panel for Civil Service Manpower Review, 1968–70; Royal Commn on the Press, 1974–77; Council, CBI, 1973–80; Dir, Industry Council for Develt, USA (Chm., 1979); Governor, Nat. Inst. for Economic and Social Research, 1968–. President: RGS, 1983–87 (Mem. Council, 1980–; Hon. Fellow 1980; a Vice Pres., 1981); Britain-Nepal Soc., 1979–89; Mem., Management Cttee, Mount Everest Foundn, 1980– (Vice Chm. 1982; Chm. 1983). *Recreations:* mountaineering, motoring, photography. *Address:* Brenva, Eghams Wood Road, Beaconsfield, Bucks HP9 1JX. *T:* Beaconsfield (01494) 673096. *Clubs:* Reform, Travellers', Himalayan, Alpine, Royal Geographical Society, MCC.

BISHOP, James Drew; Chairman of Editorial Board, Natural World, since 1981; Editor-in-Chief, Illustrated London News Publications, 1987–94; Director, Illustrated London News & Sketch Ltd, 1973–94; *b* 18 June 1929; *s* of late Sir Patrick Bishop, MBE, MP, and Vera Drew; *m* 1959, Brenda Pearson; two *s*. *Educ:* Haileybury; Corpus Christi Coll., Cambridge. Reporter, Northampton Chronicle & Echo, 1953; joined editorial staff of The Times, 1954; Foreign Correspondent, 1957–64; Foreign News Editor, 1964–66; Features Editor, 1966–70; Editor, Illustrated London News, 1971–87. Dir, International Thomson Publishing Ltd, 1980–85. Chm., Assoc. of British Editors, 1987–. Mem. Adv. Bd, Annual Register, 1970– (contributor, Amer. sect., 1960–88). *Publications:* A Social History of Edwardian Britain, 1977; Social History of the First World War, 1982; (with Oliver Woods) The Story of The Times, 1983; (ed) The Illustrated Counties of England, 1985. *Recreations:* reading, walking, looking and listening. *Address:* 11 Willow Road, NW3 1TJ. *T:* 0171–435 4403, *Fax:* 0171–435 0778. *Clubs:* United Oxford & Cambridge University, MCC.

BISHOP, Dr John Edward; freelance musician; *b* 23 Feb. 1935; *s* of late Reginald John Bishop and of Eva Bishop (*née* Lucas). *Educ:* Cotham Sch., Bristol; St John's Coll., Cambridge (Exhibr); Reading and Edinburgh Univs. MA, MusB Cantab; DMus Edin.; FRCO (CHM); ADCM; Hon. FBSM. John Stewart of Rannoch Schol. (Univ. prize) 1954. Organist and Asst Dir of Music, Worksop Coll., Notts, 1958–69; Dir of Music, Worksop Coll., 1969–73; Birmingham School of Music: Dir of Studies, 1973–74; Sen. Lectr, 1974–79; Principal Lectr, Head of Organ Studies and Head of Admissions, 1979–87. Dir of Music, Cotham Parish Church, Bristol, 1976–90; Hon. Dir of Music, St Paul's Church, Birmingham, 1986; Dir, Bristol Highbury Singers, 1978–90; Consultant, Wells Cathedral Sch., 1986–93. Organ recitalist (incl. many broadcasts) and choral conductor, pianist, coach and adjudicator, 1960–. Former Pres., Sheffield, Birmingham and Bristol Organists' Assocs; Mem. Council, ISM, 1991–. *Publications:* various articles on history and practice of church music and 19th century organ design. *Recreations:* walking, ecclesiology, savouring the countryside, cities and towns, railways, architecture. *Address:* 98 High Kingsdown, Bristol BS2 8ER. *T:* Bristol (0117) 942 3373.

BISHOP, John Edward; His Honour Judge Bishop; a Circuit Judge, since 1993; *b* 9 Feb. 1943; *s* of Albert George Bishop and Frances Marion Bishop; *m* 1968, Elizabeth Ann Grover; two *d*. *Educ:* St Edward's Sch., Oxford. Articled to Messrs Oswald Hickson Collier & Co., WC2, 1962–66; admitted solicitor, 1966; Partner: Messrs Copley Clark & Co., Sutton, 1969–81; Messrs Tuck & Mann, Epsom, 1981–85; Registrar: Woolwich County Court, 1985–88; Croydon County Court, 1988–93 (District Judge, 1992–93); an Asst Recorder, 1987–90; a Recorder, 1990–93. Pres., Mid-Surrey Law Soc., 1980–81. *Recreations:* golf, walking, music, reading, garden, family. *Address:* Kingston-upon-Thames Crown Court, Canbury Park Road, Kingston-upon-Thames, Surrey KT1 2AA. *Club:* Walton Heath Golf.

BISHOP, Prof. (John) Michael, MD; Professor of Microbiology and Immunology, since 1972, and of Biochemistry and Biophysics, since 1982, and Director, G. W. Hooper Research Foundation, since 1981, University of California, San Francisco; *b* 22 Feb. 1936; *s* of John and Carrie Bishop; *m* 1959, Kathryn Putman; two *s*. *Educ:* Gettysburg Coll., Gettysburg (AB); Harvard Univ., Boston (MD). Intern/Asst Resident in Internal Med., Mass. Gen. Hosp., 1962–64; Res. Associate, NIAID, NIH, 1964–67; Vis. Scientist, Heinrich-Pette Inst., Hamburg, 1967–68; Asst Prof., Microbiology, 1968–70, Associate Prof., Microbiology, 1970–72, Univ. of California. Member: Nat. Acad. of Scis, 1980–; Amer. Acad. of Arts and Scis, 1984–. Hon. DSc Gettysburg, 1983. Albert Lasker Award for Basic Med. Res., 1982; Passano Foundn Award, 1983; Warren Triennial Prize, 1983; Armand Hammer Cancer Res. Award, 1984; Gen. Motors Cancer Res. Award, 1984; Gairdner Foundn Internat. Award, 1984; ACS Medal of Honor, 1985; (jtly) Nobel Prize in Physiology or Medicine, 1989. *Publications:* (ed jtly) Genes and Cancer, vol. 17, 1984; (ed jtly) Cancer Surveys — proteins encoded by oncogenes, vol. 5, 1986; over 240 pubns in refereed sci. jls. *Recreations:* music, reading, theatre. *Address:* 1542 HSW, University of California, San Francisco, CA 94143, USA. *T:* (415) 4763211.

BISHOP, Malcolm Leslie; QC 1993; *b* 9 Oct. 1944; *s* of late John Bishop and Irene Bishop (*née* Dunn). *Educ:* Ruabon Grammar Sch.; Regent's Park Coll., Oxford Univ. (Samuel Davies Prizeman; Hon. Mods in Theology, BA Jurisprudence, MA). Chm., OU

Dem. Lab. Club, 1966. Called to the Bar, Inner Temple, 1968; in practice on Wales and Chester Circuit. Circuit Rep., Bar Council, 1987–92; Mem., Exec. Cttee, Family Law Bar Assoc., 1985–. Contested (Lab), Bath, Feb. and Oct. 1974. *Recreations:* politics, wine. *Address:* 30 Park Place, Cardiff CF1 3BA. *T:* Cardiff (01222) 398421; 1 Gray's Inn Square, WC1R 5AA. *T:* 0171–405 3000. *Clubs:* United Oxford & Cambridge University; Cardiff and County (Cardiff).

BISHOP, Michael; *see* Bishop, J. M.

BISHOP, Sir Michael (David), Kt 1991; CBE 1986; Chairman: Airlines of Britain Holdings Plc, since 1978; British Midland Airways, Manx Airlines and Loganair, since 1978; Channel 4 Television Corporation, since 1993 (Deputy Chairman, 1991–93); *b* 10 Feb. 1942; *s* of Clive Leonard Bishop and Lilian Bishop (*née* Frost). *Educ:* Mill Hill School. Joined Mercury Airlines, Manchester, 1963; British Midland Airways Ltd, 1964–; Director: Airtours plc, 1987–; Williams Hldgs, 1993–. Member: E Midlands Electricity Bd, 1980–83; E Midlands Reg. Bd, Central Television, 1981–89; Chm., D'Oyly Carte Opera Trust Ltd, 1989–. Hon. Mem., Royal Soc. of Musicians of GB, 1989; CRAeS, 1989. Hon. DTech Loughborough Univ. of Technology, 1989; Hon. DLitt Univ. of Salford, 1991; Hon. LLD Nottingham, 1993; DUniv Central England, 1993; Hon. DLitt Coventry, 1994. *Recreation:* music. *Address:* Donington Hall, Castle Donington, near Derby DE74 2SB. *T:* Derby (01332) 854000. *Clubs:* Brooks's; St James's (Manchester).

BISHOP, Michael William; Director, Manchester Care Ltd, 1995; *b* 22 Oct. 1941; *s* of Ronald Lewis William and Gwendoline Mary Bishop; *m* Loraine Helen Jones; two *s* one *d*. *Educ:* Manchester Univ. (BA (Econs) IIi Hons); Leicester Univ. (CertAppSocStudies). Director of Social Services: Cleveland CC, 1981–89; Manchester City Council, 1989–95. Mem., Registered Homes Tribunal, 1995. *Recreations:* horse riding and competing. *Address:* 12 Higher Chisworth, Broadbottom, via Hyde, Cheshire SK14 6SA. *T:* Glossop (01457) 867837.

BISHOP, Prof. Peter Orlebar, AO 1986; DSc; FRS 1977; FAA; Professor Emeritus, Australian National University, since 1983; Visiting Scholar, Department of Anatomy, University of Sydney, since 1987; *b* 14 June 1917; *s* of Ernest John Hunter Bishop and Mildred Alice Havelock Bishop (*née* Vidal); *m* 1942, Hilare Louise Holmes; one *s* two *d*. *Educ:* Barker Coll., Hornsby; Univ. of Sydney (MB, BS, DSc). Neurol Registrar, Royal Prince Alfred Hosp., Sydney, 1941–42; Surgeon Lieut, RANR, 1942–46; Fellow, Postgrad. Cttee in Medicine (Sydney Univ.) at Nat. Hosp., Queen Square, London, 1946–47 and Dept Anatomy, UCL, 1947–50; Sydney University: Res. Fellow, Dept Surgery, 1950–51; Sen. Lectr, 1951–54, Reader, 1954–55, Prof. and Head, Dept Physiology, 1955–67; Prof. and Head of Dept of Physiology, John Curtin School of Medical Res., ANU, 1967–82; Vis. Fellow, ANU, 1983–87. Visiting Professor: Japan Soc. for Promotion of Science, 1974, 1982; Katholieke Universiteit Leuven, Belgium, 1984–85; Guest Prof., Zürich Univ., 1985; Vis. Fellow, St John's Coll., Cambridge, Jan.–Oct. 1986. FAA 1967; Fellow: Aust. Postgrad. Fedn in Medicine, 1969; Nat. Vision Res. Inst. of Australia, 1983. Hon. Member: Neurosurgical Soc. of Aust., 1970; Ophthalmol Soc. of NZ, 1973; Aust. Assoc. of Neurologists, 1977; Australian Neuroscience Soc., 1986; Aust. Physiol and Pharmacol Soc., 1987. Hon. MD Sydney, 1983. (Jtly) Australia Prize, 1993. *Publications:* contribs on physiological optics and visual neurophysiology. *Recreation:* bushwalking. *Address:* Department of Anatomy, University of Sydney, NSW 2006, Australia; 139 Cape Three Points Road, Avoca Beach, NSW 2251, Australia.

BISHOP, Stanley Victor, MC 1944; management consultant; *b* 11 May 1916; *s* of George Stanley Bishop, MA; *m* 1946, Dorothy Primrose Dodds, Berwick-upon-Tweed; two *s* one *d*. *Educ:* Leeds. Articled to Beevers & Adgie, Leeds; CA 1937. Served War of 1939–45: enlisted London Scottish (TA), 1938; commissioned, West Yorkshire Regt, 1940; served overseas, 1940–45, Middle East, India and Burma (MC) (Hon. Major). Joined Albert E. Reed and Co. Ltd, 1946; Brush Group, 1951; Massey Ferguson Ltd, 1959–79; Perkins Diesel Engine Group, 1963. Man. Dir, British Printing Corp., 1966–70; Chm. and Dir various cos, 1970–73 and 1979–92; Dir, Massey-Ferguson Europe Ltd, 1973–79. Has lectured to British Institute of Management, Institute of Chartered Accountants, Oxford Business Summer School, etc. *Publication:* Business Planning and Control, 1966. *Recreations:* golf, swimming, pottering. *Address:* Halidon, Rogers Lane, Ettington, Stratford-upon-Avon, Warwicks CV37 7SX.

BISHOP, Stephen; *see* Kovacevich, S.

BISHOP-KOVACEVICH, Stephen; *see* Kovacevich, S.

BISS, Adele, (Mrs R. O. Davies); Chairman, British Tourist Authority and English Tourist Board, since 1993; *b* 18 Oct. 1944; *d* of Robert and Bronia Biss; *m* 1973, Roger Oliver Davies, *qv*; one *s*. *Educ:* Cheltenham Ladies' Coll.; University Coll. London (BSc Econ). Unilever, 1968; Thomson Holidays, 1970; Chief Exec., Biss Lancaster, 1978–88; Director: Aegis plc, 1985–90; BR, 1987–92; European Passenger Services, 1990–; Bowthorpe, 1993–. FRSA. *Recreations:* piano, hiking, ski-ing. *Address:* British Tourist Authority, Thames Tower, Blacks Road, W6 9EL. *T:* 0181–746 9000.

BISSELL, Claude Thomas, CC 1969; MA, PhD; FRSC 1957; Professor, University of Toronto, since 1971 (President of the University, 1958–71); *b* 10 Feb. 1916; *m* 1945, Christina Flora Gray; one *d*. *Educ:* University of Toronto; Cornell Univ. BA 1936, MA 1937, Toronto; PhD Cornell, 1940. Instructor in English, Cornell, 1938–41; Lecturer in English, Toronto, 1941–42. Canadian Army, 1942–46; demobilised as Capt. University of Toronto: Asst Prof. of English, 1947–51; Assoc. Prof. of English, 1951–56; Prof. of English, 1962; Asst to Pres., 1948–52; Vice-Pres., 1952–56; Dean in Residence, University Coll., 1946–56; Pres., Carleton Univ., Ottawa, 1956–58; Chm., The Canada Council, 1960–62. President, Nat. Conference of Canadian Universities and Colleges, 1962–; Chairman, Canadian Universities Foundation, 1962–; President, World University Service of Canada, 1962–63. Visiting Prof. of Canadian Studies, Harvard, 1967–68. Aggrey-Fraser-Guggisberg Meml Lectr, Ghana Univ., 1976. Hon. DLitt: Manitoba, 1958; W Ontario, 1971; Lethbridge, 1972; Leeds, 1976; Toronto, 1977; Hon. LLD: McGill, 1958; Queen's, 1959; New Brunswick, 1959; Carleton, 1960; Montreal, 1960; St Lawrence, 1962; British Columbia, 1962; Michigan, 1963; Columbia, 1965; Laval, 1966; Prince of Wales Coll., 1967; Windsor, 1968; St Andrews, 1972. *Publications:* (ed) University College, A Portrait, 1853–1953, 1953; (ed) Canada's Crisis in Higher Education, 1957; (ed) Our Living Tradition, 1957; (ed) Great Canadian Writing, 1966; The Strength of the University, 1968; Halfway up Parnassus, 1974; The Humanities in the University, 1977; The Young Vincent Massey, 1981; The Imperial Canadian, 1986; Ernest Buckler Remembered, 1989; number of articles on literary subjects in Canadian and American jls. *Address:* 229 Erskine Avenue, Toronto, Ontario M4P 1Z5, Canada. *Clubs:* Arts and Letters, York (Toronto); Cercle Universitaire (Ottawa).

BISSELL, Frances Mary; The Times Cook, since 1987; *b* 19 Aug. 1946; *d* of Robert Maloney and Mary Maloney (*née* Kelly); *m* 1970, Thomas Emery Bissell; one step *d*. *Educ:* Univ. of Leeds (BA Hons French). VSO Nigeria, 1965–66; Assistante, Ecole Normale, Albi, 1968–69; British Council, 1970– (leave of absence, 1987–); food and cookery writer, cook and consultant, 1983–. Guest cook: Mandarin Oriental, Hong Kong, 1987, 1990, 1995; London Intercontinental, 1987 and 1988; Manila Peninsula, 1989; Colombo Hilton, Sri Lanka, 1991; The Dusit Thani, Bangkok, 1992; guest teacher: Bogotá Hilton, Colombia, 1988; Ballymaloe Cooking Sch., Ireland, 1990; The Times cookery evenings at Leith's Sch. of Food and Wine, 1991; Learning for Pleasure, Spain, 1995. Member judging panel: THF Hotels Chef of the Year, 1988 and 1990; Annual Catey Award Function Menu, 1989–94; A Fresh Taste of Britain, Women's Farming Union, 1989; UK Finals, Prix Taittinger, 1993, 1994; Roux Diners Club Scholarship, 1995. Founder Mem., Guild of Food Writers, 1985. Columnist, Caterer & Hotelkeeper, 1988–94. *Publications:* A Cook's Calendar, 1985; The Pleasures of Cookery, 1986; Ten Dinner Parties for Two, 1988; Sainsbury's Book of Food, 1989 (US edn, as The Book of Food, 1994); Oriental Flavours, 1990; The Real Meat Cookbook, 1992; The Times Cookbook, 1993; contrib. to Caterer and Hotelkeeper, Sunday Times Mag., Homes and Gardens, House & Garden, Country Living, Decanter, Country Life, Forte Magazine, Food and Entertaining. *Recreations:* travelling and reading. *Address:* c/o Peters, Fraser and Dunlop, 5th Floor, The Chambers, Chelsea Harbour, Lotts Road, SW10 0XS. *T:* 071–376 7676.

BISSON, Hon. Claude; Hon. Mr Justice Bisson; a Judge of the Court of Appeal, Quebec, since 1980; Chief Justice of Quebec, 1988–94; *b* 9 May 1931; *m* 1957, Louisette Lanneville; two *s* one *d*. *Educ:* Univ. de Laval, Quebec (BA 1950; LLL 1953). Called to Bar, Quebec, 1954. Superior Court Judge, Montreal, 1969–80. *Address:* Palais de Justice, Montreal, Quebec H2Y 1B6, Canada.

BISSON, Rt. Hon. Sir Gordon (Ellis), Kt 1991; PC 1987; Judge of the Court of Appeal, New Zealand, 1986–91; Chairman, New Zealand Banking Ombudsman Commission, since 1992; *b* 23 Nov. 1918; *s* of Clarence Henry Bisson and Ada Ellis; *m* 1948, Myra Patricia Kemp; three *d*. *Educ:* Napier Boys High Sch.; Victoria Coll., Wellington; Univ. of NZ. LLB. Served War of 1939–45, RN and RNZN, 1940–45 (mentioned in despatches); Lt Comdr RNZNVR. Partner, Bisson Moss Robertshawe & Co., Barristers and Solicitors, Napier, NZ, 1946–78; Crown Solicitor, Napier, 1961; Judge, Courts Martial Appeal Ct, 1976; Judge of Supreme Ct, 1978. Vice-President: NZ Law Soc., 1974–77; NZ Sect., Internat. Commn of Jurists, 1979–92. *Publication:* (jtly) Criminal Law and Practice in New Zealand, 1961. *Recreations:* tennis, fly-fishing. *Address:* 15 Golf Road, Heretaunga, Wellington 6007, New Zealand. *Clubs:* Wellington, Wellington Golf (Wellington, NZ).

BISZTYGA, Jan; Officer's Cross of the Order of Polonia Restituta 1970; Order of Merit 1973; Adviser on Foreign Trade Enterprise, EUROAMER, since 1991; expert in Office of President of the Polish Republic, since 1990; Adviser to Prime Minister's Office, since 1993; *b* 19 Jan. 1933; *s* of Kazimierz Biszytyga; *m* 1956, Otylia; one *s*. *Educ:* Jagiellonian Univ. (MSc Biochemistry). Asst Professor, Jagiellonian Univ., Cracow, 1954–57; political youth movement, 1956–59; Min. for Foreign Affairs, 1959–63; Attaché, New Delhi, 1963–64; Min. for Foreign Affairs, 1964–69; Head of Planning Dept, Min. for Foreign Affairs, 1969–71; Dep. Foreign Minister, 1972–75; Ambassador in Athens, 1975–78, to UK, 1978–81; Ideology Dept, Polish United Workers' Party. *Recreations:* game shooting, fishing, history. *Address:* (home) Jaworzyńska 11–18, Warsaw, Poland; (office) Al. Jerozolimskie 87, Warsaw 02–001, Poland. *T:* (22) 298940, *Fax:* (22) 218676.

BJELKE-PETERSEN, Hon. Sir Johannes, KCMG 1984; Premier of Queensland, 1968–87; *b* Dannevirke, NZ, 13 Jan. 1911; *s* of late C. G. Bjelke-Petersen, Denmark; *m* 1952, Florence Isabel (elected as Senator for Queensland in Commonwealth Parliament, 1981), *d* of J. P. Gilmour; one *s* three *d*. *Educ:* Taabinga Valley Sch.; corresp. courses, and privately. MLA National Party (formerly Country Party): for Nanango, 1947–50; for Barambah, 1950–87; Minister for Works and Housing, Qld, 1963–68. *Address:* Bethany, Kingaroy, Queensland 4610, Australia.

BJERREGAARD, Ritt Jytte; Member, European Commission, since 1995; *b* Copenhagen, 19 May 1941; *d* of Gudmund Bjerregaard and Rita (*née* Hærslev); *m* 1966, Prof. Søren Mørch. Qualified as teacher, 1964. MP (Social Dem.), Otterup (Fyn), Denmark, 1971–95; Minister for: Educn, 1973 and 1975–78; Social Affairs, 1979–81. Chm., Social Dem. Parly Gp, 1981–82 and 1987–91. Chm., Danish European Movt, 1992–94. Mem., Trilateral Commn, 1982–. Vice-Pres., Danish delgn, CSCE, 1992–94. *Publications:* books on educn and politics in Denmark, including: Strid, 1979; Til venner og fjender, 1982; I opposition, 1987; (with S. Mørch) Fyn med omliggende oor, 1989; Verden er saa stor, saa stor, 1990, etc; articles in Danish jls. *Recreation:* growing apples. *Address:* Rue de la Loi 200, Breydel 11/78, 1049 Brussels, Belgium.

BJØRNSON, Maria Elena; theatre designer, since 1969; *b* Paris, 16 Feb. 1949; *d* of Bjørn Bjørnson and Maria Prodan. *Educ:* Byam Shaw Sch. of Art (Pre-Dip); Central Sch. of Art and Design (MA). Ext. Examr, Central St Martin's Theatre Dept, 1993–. Designs include: *stage:* Scapino (costumes), NT, 1969; 13 productions for Citizens' Th., Glasgow; Antony and Cleopatra, Bankside Globe, 1973; Hedda Gabler, Duke of York's, 1977; Vieux Carre (costumes), Piccadilly, 1978; The Cherry Orchard, Chichester, 1981; The Lonely Road, Old Vic, 1985; Phantom of the Opera, Her Majesty's, 1986, NY and worldwide 1987 (numerous awards, UK and overseas, incl. Drama mag., 1987; Tony Award for Best Set and Best Costumes, 1987; Drama Critics' Award, LA, 1988); Follies, Shaftesbury, 1987 (Best Design award, Drama mag., 1988); Aspects of Love, Prince of Wales', 1989, NY, 1990; *Royal Shakespeare Co.:* The Way of the World, 1978; Hamlet, 1984; Measure for Measure, 1974, 1991; A Midsummer Night's Dream, 1981; The Tempest, 1982; Camille, 1984; The Blue Angel, 1991; *Royal Ballet:* Sleeping Beauty, 1994; *opera:* Katya Kabanova, 1971, The Gambler, 1974, Wexford Fest.; *Scottish Opera:* Rake's Progress (costumes), 1971; Tristan and Isolde (costumes), 1973; The Magic Flute (costumes), 1974; The Golden Cockerel (costumes), 1975; Die Meistersinger, 1976; Jenufa, Il Seraglio (costumes), The Bartered Bride (costumes), Hansel and Gretel (costumes), 1978; Don Giovanni, Katya Kabanova, 1979; The Cunning Little Vixen, 1980; House of the Dead, 1987; *Welsh National Opera:* Jenufa, 1975; Il Trovatore, 1976; The Makropulos Case, 1978; Ernani, 1979; Cunning Little Vixen, 1980; House of the Dead, 1982; *English National Opera:* Toussaint, 1977; Die Walkyrie, 1983; Carmen, 1986; Queen of Spades, 1987; Cunning Little Vixen, 1988; *Opera North:* Rigoletto, 1979; Don Giovanni, 1981; Werther, 1982; *Royal Opera:* Tales of Hoffman, 1980; Der Rosenkavalier (costumes), 1984; Donnerstag aus Licht, 1985; Katya Kabanova, 1994; *Glydebourne:* Così fan tutte, 1991; also for productions in Sydney, Kassel, Houston, Geneva, Florence, the Netherlands, Canada, and the provinces. *Recreations:* travel, running away. *Address:* c/o Judy Daish Associates, 83 Eastbourne Mews, W2 6LQ. *Club:* Peg's.

BLACH, Rolf Karl, MD; FRCS, FRCOphth; Ophthalmologist, St Dunstan's, since 1967; Consultant Surgeon, Moorfields Eye Hospital, 1970–91; *b* 21 Jan. 1930; *s* of Paul Samuel Blach and Hedwig Jeanette Blach; *m* 1960, Lynette Cecilia Sceales; two *s* one *d*. *Educ:* Berkhamsted Sch.; Trinity Coll., Cambridge (MA); St Thomas' Hosp. MD 1965; FRCS 1962; FRCOphth (FCOphth 1989). Capt. RAMC, 1957–58. Jun. medical appts, St Thomas' Hosp. and Moorfields Eye Hosp., 1955–62; Sen. Registrar, Middlesex Hosp., 1962–63; Consultant Ophthalmic Surgeon, St Mary's Hosp., 1963–70; Hon. Consultant Ophthalmologist, RPMS, Hammersmith, 1967–70; Dean, Inst. of Ophthalmology, Univ.

of London, 1985–91. *Publications:* articles on ophthalmology, esp. medical and surgical retina. *Recreations:* my family, aspects of history, a little sport. *Address:* 88A College Road, Dulwich, SE21 7NA. *T:* 0181–693 1917; 11 Wimpole Street, W1M 7AB. *T:* 0171–636 3407. *Club:* Royal Society of Medicine.

BLACK, Alastair Kenneth Lamond, CBE 1989; DL; Under Sheriff of Greater London, 1974–94; Clerk, Bowyers' Company, 1985–94; *b* 14 Dec. 1929; *s* of Kenneth Black and Althea Joan Black; *m* 1955, Elizabeth Jane (*d* 1995), *d* of Sir Henry Darlington, KCB, CMG, TD; one *s* two *d*. *Educ:* Sherborne Sch.; Law Soc. Coll. of Law. Admitted solicitor, 1953. Nat. Service, Intelligence Corps, 1953–55, Lieut. Partner in Messrs Burchell & Ruston, Solicitors, 1953–94. Dep. Sheriff, Co. of London, then Greater London, 1953–74; DL Greater London, 1978. Mem. Council, Shrievalty Assoc., 1985–91; Vice-Pres., Under Sheriffs Assoc., 1985–87, Pres., 1987–93. Member: House of Laity, Gen. Synod, 1982–; (a Chm., Gen. Synod, 1991); Dioceses Commn, 1986–91; Ecclesiastical Fees Adv. Commn, 1986–; Bd of Social Responsibility, 1992–. Lay Reader, 1983–. *Publications:* contributions to: Halsbury's Laws of England, 4th edn, vols 25, 1978 (rev. edn 1994), and 42, 1983; Atkin's Court Forms, 3rd edn, vols 19, 1972 (rev. edn 1985), 22, 1968, and 36, 1977 (rev. edn 1988); Enforcement of a Judgement, 8th edn, 1993. *Recreations:* horseracing, gardening, travel. *Address:* South Lodge, Effingham, Surrey KT24 5QE. *T:* Bookham (01372) 452862.

BLACK, Col Anthony Edward Norman, OBE 1981; Chief Executive Commissioner, Scout Association, since 1987; *b* 20 Jan. 1938; *s* of late Arthur Norman Black and Phyllis Margaret Ranicar; *m* 1963, Susan Frances Copeland; two *s*. *Educ:* Brighton College; RMA Sandhurst. Commissioned RE, 1957; served Kenya, Aden, Germany, Cyprus; Army Staff Course, Camberley, 1970; GSO1 Ghana Armed Forces Staff Coll., 1976–78; CO 36 Engr Regt, 1978–80; Col GS MGO Secretariat, 1980–82; Comd Engrs Falkland Islands, 1983; Comdt, Army Apprentices Coll., Chepstow, 1983–86; retired 1987. FIMgt (FBIM 1981); FRSA 1993. *Recreations:* walking, gardening, bird watching. *Address:* c/o Scout Association, Baden-Powell House, Queen's Gate, SW7 5JS. *T:* 0171–584 7030.

BLACK, Archibald Niel; Professor of Engineering, University of Southampton, 1968–72, retired; *b* 10 June 1912; *s* of late Steuart Gladstone Black, Glenormiston, Victoria, Australia, and Isabella McCance (*née* Moat); *m* 1940, Cynthia Mary Stradling; one *s* two *d*. *Educ:* Farnborough Sch.; Eton Coll.; Trinity Coll., Cambridge. 1st cl. hons with distinction in Applied Mechanics in Mech. Sciences Tripos, Cambridge, 1934; MA 1938. Lectr and Demonstrator in Engrg Science, Oxford Univ., 1935; Donald Pollock Reader in Engrg Science, Oxford Univ., 1945–50; Prof. of Mech. Engrg, Southampton Univ., 1950–67. Dep. Chm., Universities Central Council on Admissions, 1964–72. Hon. DSc Southampton, 1975. *Publications:* (with K. Adlard Coles) North Biscay Pilot, 1970, revd edn 1977; papers in Proc. Royal Soc. and technical jls. *Recreation:* sailing. *Address:* Little Pensbury, Compton Street, Compton, Winchester, Hants SO21 2AS. *T:* Twyford (01962) 712360. *Club:* Royal Cruising.

BLACK, Barrington (Malcolm); His Honour Judge Barrington Black; a Circuit Judge, since 1993; *b* 16 Aug. 1932; *s* of Louis and Millicent Black; *m* 1962, Diana Heller, JP; two *s* two *d*. *Educ:* Roundhay Sch.; Leeds Univ. (Pres. of Union, 1952; Vice-Pres., NUS, 1953–54; LLB). Admitted Solicitor, 1956. Served Army, 1956–58, commnd RASC. Partner, Walker, Morris & Coles, 1958–69; Sen. Partner, Barrington Black, Austin & Co., 1969–84. An Asst Recorder, 1987–91, a Recorder, 1991–93; a Metropolitan Stipendiary Magistrate, 1984–93. Chairman: Inner London Juvenile Court, 1985–93; Family Court, 1991–93. Mem. Court and Council, Leeds Univ., 1979–84. Councillor, Harrogate Bor. Council, 1964–67; contested (L) Harrogate, 1964. Mem., British Acad. of Forensic Science, 1976–. *Recreations:* ski-bobbing, opera, music. *Address:* Snaresbrook Crown Court, The Court House, 75 Holly Bush Hill, Snaresbrook, E11 1QW.

BLACK, Charles Stewart Forbes; Metropolitan Stipendiary Magistrate, since 1993 (Chairman, Youth Courts, since 1994); *b* 6 Feb. 1947; *s* of Roger Bernard Black and Mary Agnes (*née* Murray); *m* 1976, Mhairi Shuna Elspeth McNab; one *d*. *Educ:* Kent Coll., Canterbury; Council of Legal Educn. Called to the Bar, Inner Temple, 1970; *ad eundem* Gray's Inn, 1973; Head of Chambers, 1981–93. *Recreations:* scuba diving, ski-ing, reading, playing with computers. *Address:* c/o Horseferry Road Magistrates' Court, 70 Horseferry Road, SW1P 2AF.

BLACK, Colin Hyndmarsh; Chairman, Kleinwort Benson Investment Management Ltd, 1988–95; *b* 4 Feb. 1930; *s* of Daisy Louise (*née* Morris) and Robert Black; *m* 1955, Christine Fleurette Browne; one *s* one *d*. *Educ:* Ayr Acad.; Fettes Coll.; St Andrews Univ. (MA); Edinburgh Univ. (LLB). Brander and Cruickshank, Aberdeen, 1957–71 (Partner in charge of investment management); Globe Investment Trust, 1971–90, Dep Chm., 1983–90. Chairman: Scottish Widows' Fund and Life Assurance Soc., 1987–95; Assoc. of Investment Trust Cos, 1987–89; Non-Exec. Director: Temple Bar Investment Trust, 1963–; Clyde Petroleum, 1976–; Electra Investment Trust, 1975–94; Kleinwort Benson Gp plc, 1988–95; Scottish Power plc, 1990–95; East German Investment Trust, 1990–; Merchants Trust, 1992– (Chm., 1993–); Govett Asian Smaller Cos Investment Trust, 1994–. *Recreations:* golf, gardening, reading, watching cricket, walking Labradors. *Address:* 15 Tudor Close, Fairmile Park Road, Cobham, Surrey KT11 2PH. *T:* Cobham (01932) 865656. *Clubs:* New (Edinburgh); Wisley Golf (Mem. Bd, 1994–).

BLACK, Hon. Conrad Moffat, OC 1990; PC (Can.) 1992; Chairman and Chief Executive, Hollinger Inc., since 1985; *b* 25 Aug. 1944; *m* 1st, 1978, Joanna Catherine Louise Hishon (name changed by deed poll in 1990 from Shirley Gail Hishon) (marr. diss., 1992); two *s* one *d*; 2nd, 1992, Barbara Amiel. *Educ:* Carleton Univ. (BA); Laval Univ. (LLL); MA History McGill, 1973. Chm. and Chief Exec., Ravelston Corp., 1979–; Chm., 1979–, Chief Exec., 1985–, Argus Corp; Chairman: Saturday Night Magazine Inc., 1987–; The Telegraph plc, 1987–95 (Dir, 1985–95); Deputy Chairman: American Publishing Co., 1987–; John Fairfax Hldgs Ltd, 1992–; Director: Canadian Imperial Bank of Commerce, 1977–; Brascan, 1986–; Eaton's of Canada, 1976–; The Financial Post Company Ltd, 1988–; UniMédia Inc., 1987–; The Spectator (1828) Ltd, 1990–; Southam Inc., 1993–; Mem. Adv. Bd, Gulfstream Aerospace Corp. Member: Steering Cttee, Bilderberg Meetings, 1986; Adv. Bd, The National Interest, Washington DC, 1992–. Hon LLD: St Francis Xavier, 1979; McMaster, 1979; Carleton, 1989; Hon. LittD Univ. of Windsor, 1979. KLJ. *Publications:* Duplessis, 1977; Conrad Black: a life in progress (autobiog.), 1993. *Address:* c/o 10 Toronto Street, Toronto, Ont M5C 2B7, Canada. *T:* (416) 3638721; The Telegraph plc, 1 Canada Square, Canary Wharf, E14 5DT. *Clubs:* Everglades (Palm Beach); Toronto, York, Toronto Golf (Toronto); University, Mount Royal (Montreal).

BLACK, Sir David; *see* Black, Sir R. D.

BLACK, Don; lyric writer; *b* 21 June 1938; *s* of Betsy and Morris Blackstone; *m* 1958, Shirley Berg; two *s*. *Educ:* Hackney Central Sch. Professional lyric writer, 1960–; collaborates with Andrew Lloyd Webber, John Barry, Jule Styne, Elmer Bernstein and other leading composers; musicals include: Billy, 1974; Song and Dance, 1982; Aspects of Love, 1989; Sunset Boulevard, 1993. Numerous awards, UK and USA, incl. Academy Award, 1966, for song Born Free. *Recreations:* snooker, swimming. *Address:* c/o John Cohen, Clintons, 55 Drury Lane, WC2B 5SQ. *T:* 0171–379 6080. *Clubs:* Royal Automobile, Groucho, Tramp.

BLACK, Sir Douglas (Andrew Kilgour), Kt 1973; MD, FRCP; Professor of Medicine, Manchester University and Physician, Manchester Royal Infirmary, 1959–77, now Emeritus; Chief Scientist, Department of Health and Social Security, 1973–77; *b* 29 May 1913; *s* of late Rev. Walter Kilgour Black and Mary Jane Crichton; *m* 1948, Mollie Thorn; one *s* two *d*. *Educ:* Forfar Academy; St Andrews Univ. BSc 1933; MB, ChB 1936; MD 1940; MRCP 1939; FRCP 1952; FACP, FRACP, FRCPGlas, 1978; FRCPath, FRCPI, FRCPE, 1979; FRCPsych, 1982; FRCGP, FRCOG, FFPHM (FFCM 1983); FFOM 1984. MRC Research Fellow, 1938–40; Beit Memorial Research Fellow, 1940–42. Major RAMC, 1942–46. Lecturer, then Reader, in Medicine, Manchester Univ., 1946–58. Horder Travelling Fellow, 1967; Sir Arthur Sims Commonwealth Travelling Prof., 1971; Rock Carling Fellow, 1984. Lectures: Goulstonian, RCP, 1953; Bradshaw, RCP, 1965; Lumleian, RCP, 1970; Harben, RIPH&H, 1973; Crookshank, RCR, 1976; Harveian Orator, RCP, 1977; Maurice Bloch, Glasgow, 1979; Linacre, St John's Coll., Cambridge, 1980; Lloyd Roberts, RSM, 1980; John Locke, Soc. of Apothecaries, 1990; Thomas Young, St George's Hosp. Med. Sch., 1990; Annual, Office of Health Econs, 1994. Secretary, Manchester Medical Soc., 1957–59. Member: Medical Research Council, 1966–70 and 1971–77 (Chm., Clinical Res. Bd, 1971–73); Assoc. of Physicians; Medical Research Soc.; Renal Assoc., etc. President: RCP, 1977–83; Section X, British Assoc., 1977; Medical Protection Soc., 1982–85; BMA, 1984–85; Hon. Mem., Manchester Lit. and Phil. Soc., 1991. Trustee, 1968–77, Chm., 1977–83, Smith Kline & French Foundn. Chm., Research Working Group on Inequalities in Health, 1977–80. Hon. DSc: St Andrews, 1972; Manchester, 1978; Leicester, 1980; Cambridge, 1994; Hon. LLD Birmingham, 1984; Hon. MD Sheffield, 1984. KStJ 1989. *Publications:* Sodium Metabolism in Health and Disease, 1952; Essentials of Fluid Balance, 4th edn, 1967; The Logic of Medicine, 1968; (ed) Renal Disease, 4th edn, 1979; An Anthology of False Antitheses (Rock Carling Lecture), 1984; Invitation to Medicine, 1987; Recollections and Reflections, 1987; contributions to various medical journals. *Recreations:* reading and writing. *Address:* The Old Forge, Duchess Close, Whitchurch-on-Thames, near Reading, RG8 7EN. *T:* Pangbourne (01734) 844693. *Club:* Athenæum.

BLACK, Air Vice-Marshal George Philip, CB 1987; OBE 1967; AFC 1962 (Bar 1971); FIMgt; Royal Air Force, retired 1987; Director, Military Business Development, GEC-Marconi Defence Systems Ltd, since 1993; *b* 10 July 1932; *s* of William and Elizabeth Black; *m* 1954, Ella Ruddiman (*née* Walker); two *s*. *Educ:* Hilton Acad., Aberdeen. Joined RAF, 1950; flying trng in Canada, 1951; served, 1952–64: fighter pilot; carrier pilot (on exchange to FAA); Flying Instr; HQ Fighter Comd; commanded No 111 (Fighter) Sqdn, 1964–66; Mem., Lightning Aerobatic Team, 1965; commanded Lightning Operational Conversion Unit, 1967–69; commanded No 5 (Fighter) Sqdn, 1969–70 (Huddleston Trophy); JSSC, 1970; Air Plans, MoD, 1971–72; Stn Comdr, RAF Wildenwrath, and Harrier Field Force Comdr, RAF Germany, 1972–74; Gp Captain Ops HQ 38 Gp, 1974–76; RCDS, 1977; Gp Captain Ops HQ 11 (Fighter) Gp, 1978–80; Comdr Allied Air Defence Sector One, 1980–83; Comdt ROC, 1983–84; DCS (Ops), HQ AAFCE, 1984–87. Air ADC to the Queen, 1981–83. Sen. Defence Advr, subseq. Dir, Mil. Marketing, GEC-Ferranti, 1987–93. FIMgt (FBIM 1977). *Recreations:* philately, military aviation history, railways. *Address:* GEC-Marconi Defence Systems Ltd, The Grove, Warren Lane, Stanmore, Middx HA7 4LY. *Club:* Royal Air Force.

BLACK, Iain James, QC 1971; **His Honour Judge Black;** a Circuit Judge, since 1986. Called to the Bar, Gray's Inn, 1947, Bencher, 1985–86; Dep. Chm., Staffs QS, 1965–71; a Recorder, 1972–86. Member: Criminal Injuries Compensation Bd, 1975–86; Mental Health Review Tribunal, 1984–. *Address:* 3 Fountain Court, Steelhouse Lane, Birmingham B4 6DR. *T:* 0121–236 5854.

BLACK, James Walter, QC 1979; *b* 8 Feb. 1941; *s* of Dr James Black and Mrs Clementine M. Black (*née* Robb); *m* 1st, 1964, Jane Marie Keyden; two *s* one *d*; 2nd, 1985, Diana Marjorie Day (*née* Harris); one *d*. *Educ:* Harecroft Hall, Gosforth, Cumbria; Trinity Coll., Glenalmond, Perthshire; St Catharine's Coll., Cambridge (MA). Called to the Bar, Middle Temple, 1964, NSW Bar, 1986; a Recorder, 1976–87. *Recreations:* fishing, sailing, golf. *Address:* Edmund Barton Chambers, Level 44 MLC Centre, Martin Place, Sydney, NSW 2000, Australia.

BLACK, Sir James (Whyte), Kt 1981; FRCP; FRS 1976; Professor of Analytical Pharmacology, King's College Hospital Medical School, University of London, 1984–93, now Emeritus; Chancellor, Dundee University, since 1992; *b* 14 June 1924; *m* 1994, Rona McLeod Mackie. *Educ:* Beath High Sch., Cowdenbeath; Univ. of St Andrews (MB, ChB). Asst Lectr in Physiology, Univ. of St Andrews, 1946; Lectr in Physiology, Univ. of Malaya, 1947–50; Sen. Lectr, Univ. of Glasgow Vet. Sch., 1950–58; ICI Pharmaceuticals Ltd, 1958–64; Head of Biological Res. and Dep. Res. Dir, Smith, Kline & French, Welwyn Garden City, 1964–73; Prof. and Head of Dept of Pharmacology, University College, London, 1973–77; Dir of Therapeutic Research, Wellcome Res. Labs, 1978–84. Mem., British Pharmacological Soc., 1961–. Hon. FRSE 1986. Hon. Fellow, London Univ., 1990. Mullard Award, Royal Soc., 1978; (jtly) Nobel Prize for Physiology or Medicine, 1988. *Address:* Analytical Pharmacology Unit, Rayne Institute, 123 Coldharbour Lane, SE5 9NU; 3 Ferrings, Dulwich, SE21 7LU.

BLACK, Jill Margaret; QC 1994; *b* 1 June 1954; *d* of Dr James Irvine Currie and Margaret Yvonne Currie; *m* 1978, David Charles Black; one *s* one *d*. *Educ:* Penrhos Coll., Colwyn Bay; Durham Univ. (BA Hons Law). Called to the Bar, Inner Temple, 1976. *Publications:* Divorce: the things you thought you'd never need to know, 1982, 4th edn 1993; A Practical Approach to Family Law, 1986, 4th edn 1994; (with J. Bridge) The Working Mother's Survival Guide, 1988; (jtly) The Family Court Practice, 1994, 3rd edn 1995.

BLACK, Adm. Sir (John) Jeremy, GBE 1991 (MBE 1963); KCB 1987; DSO 1982; Stia Negara Brunei 1963; Commander-in-Chief, Naval Home Command, 1989–91; Flag Aide-de-Camp to the Queen, 1989–91; Chairman, Remy and Associates (UK) Ltd, since 1992; *b* 1932; *s* of Alan H. Black and G. Black; *m* 1958, Alison Pamela Barber; two *s* one *d*. *Educ:* Royal Naval College, Dartmouth (entered 1946). Korean War and Malayan Emergency, 1951–52; qualified in gunnery, 1958; commanded HM Ships: Fiskerton, 1960–62 (Brunei Rebellion, 1962); Decoy, 1969 (Comdr 1969, Captain 1974); Fife, 1977; RCDS 1979; Director of Naval Operational Requirements, Naval Staff, 1980–81; commanded HMS Invincible (Falklands), 1982–83; Flag Officer, First Flotilla, 1983–84; ACNS (Policy), Oct-Dec. 1984; ACNS, 1985–86; Dep. CDS (Systems), 1986–89. Director: Devonport Management Ltd, 1992–; Macallan-Glenlivet plc, 1993–; Global Emerging Markets Europe Ltd, 1993–; Consultant: Shorts, 1992–; British Aerospace, 1993–. Trustee, Imperial War Mus., 1991–. Mem. Council, RUSI, 1987–89. Gov., Wellington Coll., 1992–. Chairman: Whitbread Round the World Race Cttee, 1990–94; Royal Navy Club of 1765 and 1785, 1992–95; Governor, Ocean Youth Club, 1991–95 (Chm., World Voyage, 1994–). Life Vice Cdre, RNSA, 1991 (Cdre, 1989–91). *Recreations:* sailing, history. *Clubs:* Boodle's; Royal Yacht Squadron.

BLACK, John Newman, CEng, FICE, FIMarE; FRGS; Partner, Robert West and Partners, Chartered Consulting Engineers, 1988–90; *b* 29 Sept. 1925; *s* of late John Black and late Janet Black (*née* Hamilton); *m* 1952, Euphemia Isabella Elizabeth Thomson; two *d. Educ:* Cumberland and Medway Technical Colls. Civil and marine engrg naval stations and dockyards, UK and abroad, incl. Singapore, Hong Kong, Colombo, Gibraltar and Orkney Isles, 1941–64; joined PLA as Civil Engr, 1964; Planning and Construction, Tilbury Docks, 1964–66; Planning Manager, 1967; seconded to Thames Estuary Develt Co. Ltd, for work on Maplin Airport/Seaport Scheme, 1969; Asst Dir Planning, PLA, 1970; Director: Maplin, 1972; Tilbury Docks, 1974; all London Docks, 1977; Man. Dir, 1978–81; Bd Mem., 1978–86, Chief Exec., 1982–86, and Dep. Chm., 1985–86, PLA. Dep. Chm., PLA (Met. Terminals) Ltd, 1974; Director: PLACON Ltd (PLA's cons. subsid. co.), 1972; Orsett Depot Ltd, 1974; Port Documentation Services Ltd (Chm.), 1978; Chairman: Thames Riparian Housing Assoc., 1974; PLA Group Property Holdings, 1984. Member: Exec. Council, British Ports Assoc., 1982–86; Exec. Cttee, Nat. Assoc. of Port Employers, 1982–86 (Vice-Chm., 1984–86); British Nat. Cttee, Permt Internat. Assoc. of Navigation Congresses, 1981–; London Maritime Assoc., 1975; Council, ICHCA Internat., 1985–86; Nat. Exec. Cttee, ICHCA (UK), 1985–. Co-Adviser to Indian Govt on port ops and potential, 1968; lectures: for UN, Alexandria, 1975; for ESCAP (UN), Bangkok, 1983. FInstPet. Freeman: City of London, 1977; Watermen and Lightermen of River Thames, 1977. *Publications:* numerous articles and papers in Geographical Jl, Civil Engr and other learned jls. *Recreations:* shooting, fishing. *Address:* Westdene Cottage, Tanyard Hill, Shorne, near Gravesend, Kent DA12 3EN.

BLACK, John Nicholson, MA, DPhil, DSc; FRSE; Principal, Bedford College, University of London, 1971–81; *b* 28 June 1922; *e s* of Harold Black, MD, FRCP, and Margaret Frances Black (*née* Nicholson); *m* 1st, 1952, Mary Denise Webb (*d* 1966); one *s* one *d*; 2nd, 1967, Wendy Marjorie Waterston; two *s. Educ:* Rugby Sch.; Exeter Coll., Oxford. MA 1952, DPhil 1952, Oxford; DSc 1965, Adelaide; FRSE 1965. Served War, RAF, 1942–46. Oxford Univ., 1946–49; BA Hons Cl. 1 (Agri.) 1949; Agricl Research Council Studentship, 1949–52; Lectr, Sen. Lectr, Reader, Univ. of Adelaide (Waite Agricl Research Inst.), 1952–63; André Mayer Fellowship (FAO), 1958; Prof. of Forestry and Natural Resources, Univ. of Edinburgh, 1963–71. Dir and Sec., The Wolfson Foundn, 1981–87; Dir, The Wolfson Family Charitable Trust, 1987–89. Tutor in Ceramic Restoration, Missenden Abbey, 1993–. Mem., NERC, 1968–74; Mem. Council and Finance Cttee, RAF Benevolent Fund, 1989–. Conductor, City of Burnside Symphony Orch., SA, 1956–63; Chm., Donizetti Soc., 1984–87. *Publications:* The Dominion of Man, 1970; Donizetti's Operas in Naples, 1983; The Italian Romantic Libretto, 1984; (contrib. entries (26) on Italian librettists) The New Grove Dictionary of Opera, 1992; papers on: ecological subjects in scientific jls (70); Italian opera libretti (30); history of ceramics (1). *Recreations:* music, repair and restoration of porcelain and pottery. *Address:* Paddock House, Pyrton, near Watlington, Oxford OX9 5AP. *T:* Watlington (01491) 612600.

BLACK, Prof. Joseph, CBE 1980; PhD; FEng, FIMechE, FRAeS; Professor of Engineering, University of Bath, 1960–85, Head of School of Engineering, 1960–70 and 1973–85; *b* 25 Jan. 1921; *s* of Alexander Black and Hettie Black; *m* 1946, Margaret Susan Hewitt; three *s* one *d. Educ:* Royal Belfast Academical Instn; QUB (BScEng, MSc). PhD Bristol; FRAeS 1961, FIMechE 1964, FEng 1981. Scientific Officer, RAE, 1941–44; Res. Fellow, QUB, 1944–45; Aerodynamicist, de Havilland Aircraft, 1945–46; Lectr/Sen. Lectr in Engrg, Univ. of Bristol, 1946–59. Gillette Fellow, USA, 1963. Pro-Vice-Chancellor, Univ. of Bath, 1970–73. Member: UGC, 1964–74 (Chm. Educnl Technol. Cttee); (founder) Council for Educnl Technol., 1974–; A/M Cttee, SRC, 1975–79; Design Council, 1977–82 (Chm. Engrg Components Awards 1976, Engrg Products Awards 1977); Mech. Engrg and Machine Tool Requirement Bd, DoI, 1979–81. SERC/Design Council Engrg Design Co-ordinator, 1985–89. Hon. DTech Loughborough, 1990; Hon. DSc City, 1991. Silver Jubilee Medal, 1977. *Publications:* Introduction to Aerodynamic Compressibility, 1950; contrib. aeronaut. and mech. engrg jls (UK and Europe). *Recreations:* photography, antiquarian books, silversmithing. *Address:* 20 Summerhill Road, Bath BA1 2UR. *T:* Bath (01225) 423970. *Club:* Athenæum.

BLACK, Hon. Michael Eric John; Hon. Chief Justice Black; Chief Justice, Federal Court of Australia, since 1991; *b* 22 March 1940; *s* of Col E. R. E. Black, OBE; *m* 1963, Margaret Dungan; one *s* one *d. Educ:* St John's on the Hill; Wesley Coll., Melbourne; Univ. of Melbourne (LLB). Practice, Victorian Bar, 1964–90, ACT Bar, 1974–90; QC Victoria 1980, QC Tasmania 1984. Mem. Board, Royal Melbourne Hosp., 1986–90 (Chm., Ethics Cttee); Adviser, Chief of Defence Force, 1987–90. *Address:* Chief Justice's Chambers, Federal Court of Australia, 450 Little Bourke Street, Melbourne, Vic 3000, Australia.

BLACK, Michael Jonathan; QC 1995; *b* 31 March 1954; *s* of Samuel and Lillian Black; *m* 1984, Ann, *e d* of Keith and Rosa Pentol; two *s. Educ:* Stand Grammar Sch.; University College London (LLB). FCIArb. Called to the Bar, Middle Temple, 1978. *Address:* 25 Byrom Street, Manchester M3 4PF. *T:* 0161–834 5238.

BLACK, Neil Cathcart, OBE 1989; Principal Oboist, English Chamber Orchestra, since 1970; *b* 28 May 1932; *s* of Harold Black and Margaret Frances Black; *m* 1st, 1960, Jill (*née* Hemingsley); one *s* two *d*; 2nd, 1984, Janice Mary (*née* Knight). *Educ:* Rugby; Exeter College, Oxford (BA History). Entered musical profession, 1956; Principal Oboist: London Philharmonic Orch., 1959–61; in various chamber orchs, incl. London Mozart Players, Acad. of St Martin-in-the-Fields, 1965–72; oboe soloist internationally. Hon. RAM 1969. *Recreations:* wine, travel. *Address:* c/o English Chamber Orchestra, 2 Coningsby Road, W5 4HR. *T:* 0181–840 6565.

BLACK, Prof. Paul Joseph, OBE 1983; PhD; FInstP; Professor of Science Education, University of London, 1976–95 (in School of Education, King's College, 1985–95); *b* 10 Sept. 1930; *s* of Walter and Susie Black; *m* 1957, Mary Elaine Weston; four *s* one *d. Educ:* Rhyl Grammar Sch.; Univ. of Manchester (BSc); Univ. of Cambridge (PhD). FInstP 1986. Royal Society John Jaffé Studentship, 1953–56. Univ. of Birmingham: Lectr in Physics, 1956–66; Reader in Crystal Physics, 1966–74; Prof. of Physics (Science Education), 1974–76; Dir, Centre for Science and Maths Educn, Chelsea Coll., Univ. of London, 1976–85; subseq., following merger of colls, Head, Centre for Educnl Studies, KCL, 1985–89 (FKC 1990); Dean, Faculty of Educn, Univ. of London, 1978–82. Educnl Consultant: to Nuffield Chelsea Curriculum Trust, 1978–93; to OECD, 1988–; Consultant to: World Bank, 1991; US Nat. Sci. Foundn, 1992. Vice-Pres., Royal Instn of Great Britain, 1983–85; Chairman: National Curriculum Task Gp on Assessment and Testing, DES, 1987–88; Internat. Commn on Physics Educn, 1993– (Mem., 1987–93); Dep. Chm., Grubb Inst. for Behavioural Studies, 1990– (Mem. Council, 1983–; Chm., 1985–90); Member: School Curriculum Develt Cttee, 1984–88; Nat. Curriculum Council, 1988–91 (Dep. Chm., 1989–91); Exec., Univs Council for Educn of Teachers, 1982–86; Res. Grants Bd, ESRC, 1987–90; Exec., Editl Cttee for Nat. Sci. Educn Standards, Nat. Res. Council, USA, 1994–; President: Groupe Internat. de la Recherche sur l'Enseignement de la Physique, 1984–91; Educn Section, British Assoc., 1992–93; Hon. Pres., Assoc. for Science Educn, 1986 (Hon. Life Mem., 1986); Hon. Mem., Standing Conf. on Sch. Science and Technol., 1989. Trustee, Nat. Energy Foundn, 1992–. Hon. Mem., CGLI, 1989. FRSA 1990; Osher Fellow, San Francisco Exploratorium, 1993. DUniv Surrey, 1991. Bragg Medal, Inst. of Physics, 1973. Kt of St Gregory, 1973. *Publications:* (jtly) Nuffield Advanced Physics Project, 1972; (contrib.) Higher Education Learning Project Books, 1977; (jtly) Open Work in Science, 1992; Nuffield Primary Science books (for Key Stages 1 and 2), 1993; (ed jtly) Children's Informal Ideas in Science, 1993; (ed jtly) Teachers Assessing Pupils: lessons from science classrooms, 1995; (jtly) Primary SPACE Project Research Reports: Light, 1990, Electricity, 1991, Processes of Life, 1992, The Earth in Space, 1994; papers on crystallography, physics and science, technology education, and assessment in education. *Address:* 16 Wilton Crescent, SW19 3QZ. *T:* 0181–542 4178.

BLACK, Peter Blair, JP; Senior Partner, P. Blair Black & Partners, since 1948; *b* 22 April 1917; *s* of Peter Blair Black and Cissie Crawford Samuel; *m* 1952, Mary Madeleine Hilly, Philadelphia; one *s* three *d. Educ:* Sir Walter St John's, Battersea; Bearsden Acad.; Sch. of Building. CC 1949, Alderman 1961, Middlesex; Mem., GLC, 1963–86, Chm., 1970–71, Leader, Recreation and Community Services Policy Gp, 1977–81; motivator of Thames Barrier project; Chm., Cons. Group, GLC, 1982. Chm., Thames Water Authority, 1973–78; Pres., Pure Rivers Soc., 1976–. Leader: GLC group to Moscow and Leningrad, 1971; British delegn to Washington, Potomac/Thames River Conf., 1977; Mem. internat. team to Tokyo, Metropolitan Clean Air Conf., 1971. Mem. Exec. Cttee, Nat. Union of Cons. and Unionist Assocs, 1987–. Frequent performer on TV and radio. Former Member: Thames Conservancy Bd; Metrop. Water Bd; Jager Cttee on Sewage Disposal; PLA; Council, Nat. Fedn of Housing Socs; Founder Chm., Omnium Housing Assoc., 1962; Chm., 1972, Pres., 1983, Abbeyfield, London Region. JP Thames Div., 1961. Freeman: City of London; Tucson, Arizona. *Recreations:* small boats and fishing. *Address:* The New House, 101A Limmer Lane, Felpham, W Sussex PO22 7LP. *T:* Middleton-on-Sea (01243) 582054. *Clubs:* Middleton Sports; Sewers Synonymous (Dir).

BLACK, Prof. Robert; QC (Scot.) 1987; FRSE; Professor of Scots Law, University of Edinburgh, since 1981; *b* 12 June 1947; *s* of James Little Black and Jeannie Findlay Lyon. *Educ:* Lockerbie Acad.; Dumfries Acad.; Edinburgh Univ. (LLB); McGill Univ., Montreal (LLM); Lord Pres. Cooper Meml Prize, Univ. of Edinburgh, 1968; Vans Dunlop Scholarship, Univ. of Edinburgh, 1968; Commonwealth Scholarship, Commonwealth Scholarship Commn, 1968. Advocate, 1972; Lectr in Scots Law, Univ. of Edinburgh, 1972–75; Sen. Legal Officer, Scottish Law Commn, 1975–78; in practice at Scottish Bar, 1978–81; Temp. Sheriff, 1981–95. Chm., Inquiry into operations of Monklands DC, 1994–95. Gen. Editor, The Laws of Scotland: Stair Memorial Encyclopaedia, 1988– (Dep., then Jt, Gen. Editor, 1981–88). FRSA 1991; FRSE 1992. *Publications:* An Introduction to Written Pleading, 1982; Civil Jurisdiction: the new rules, 1983; articles in UK and S African legal jls. *Recreation:* baiting sociologists. *Address:* 6/4 Glenogle Road, Edinburgh EH3 5HW. *T:* 0131–557 3571. *Club:* Sloane.

BLACK, Sir Robert (Brown), (Sir Robin Black), GCMG 1962 (KCMG 1955; CMG 1953); OBE 1949 (MBE (mil.) 1948); *b* 3 June 1906; *s* of late Robert and Catherine Black, formerly of Blair Lodge, Polmont, Stirlingshire; *m* 1937, (Elsie) Anne Stevenson, CStJ (*d* 1986); two *d. Educ:* George Watson's Coll.; Edinburgh Univ. Colonial Administrative Service, 1930; served in Malaya, Trinidad, N Borneo, Hong Kong. Served War of 1939–45, commissioned in Intelligence Corps, 1942; 43 Special Military Mission; POW Japan, 1942–45. Colonial Secretary, Hong Kong, 1952–55; Governor and C-in-C: Singapore, 1955–57; Hong Kong, 1958–64. Chancellor: Hong Kong Univ., 1958–64; Chinese University of Hong Kong, 1963–64. Mem., Commonwealth War Graves Commn, 1964–82. Chm., Clerical, Medical and General Life Assurance Soc., 1975–78. Chm., Internat. Social Service of GB, 1965–73, Pres., 1973–82. LLD (*hc*): Univ. of Hong Kong; Chinese Univ. of Hong Kong. KStJ. Grand Cross Order of Merit, Peru. *Recreations:* walking, fishing. *Address:* Mapletons House, Ashampstead Common, near Reading, Berks RG8 8QN. *Club:* East India, Devonshire, Sports and Public Schools.

BLACK, Sir (Robert) David, 3rd Bt *cr* 1922; DL; *b* 29 March 1929; *s* of Sir Robert Andrew Stransham Black, 2nd Bt, ED, and Ivy (*d* 1980), *d* of late Brig.-Gen. Sir Samuel Wilson, GCMG, KCB, KBE; *S* father, 1979; *m* 1st, 1953, Rosemary Diana (marr. diss. 1972), *d* of Sir Rupert John Hardy, 4th Bt; two *d* (and one *d* decd); 2nd, 1973, Dorothy Maureen, *d* of Major Charles R. Eustace Radclyffe and *widow* of A. R. D. Pilkington. *Educ:* Eton. Lieut, Royal Horse Guards, 1949; Captain 1953; Major 1960; retired, 1961. Served with Berkshire and Westminster Dragoons, TA, 1964–67, and Berkshire Territorials, TAVR III, 1967–69; Vice-Chm., Berkshire, Eastern Wessex TAVRA, 1985–92. Joint Master, Garth and South Berks Foxhounds, 1965–73. Hon. Col, 94 (Berks Yeo.) Signal Sqn (TA), 1988–. DL Caithness, 1991; High Sheriff, Oxfordshire, 1993. *Recreations:* hunting, shooting, stalking and fishing. *Heir:* none. *Address:* Elvendon Priory, Goring, near Reading, Berks RG8 0LS. *T:* Goring-on-Thames (01491) 872160; Shurrery Lodge, Shebster, Thurso, Caithness KW14 7RB. *T:* Reay (0184781) 252. *Club:* Cavalry and Guards.

BLACK, Prof. Robert Denis Collison, FBA 1974; Professor of Economics, and Head of Department of Economics, Queen's University Belfast, 1962–85, now Emeritus; *b* 11 June 1922; *s* of William Robert Black and Rose Anna Mary (*née* Reid), Dublin; *m* 1953, Frances Mary, *o d* of William F. and Mary Weatherup, Belfast; one *s* one *d. Educ:* Sandford Park Sch.; Trinity Coll., Dublin (Hon. Fellow, 1982). BA 1941, BComm 1941, PhD 1943, MA 1945. Dep. for Prof. of Polit. Economy, Trinity Coll., Dublin, 1943–45; Asst Lectr in Economics, Queen's Univ., Belfast, 1945–46, Lectr, 1946–58, Sen. Lectr, 1958–61, Reader, 1961–62. Rockefeller Post-doctoral Fellow, Princeton Univ., 1950–51; Visiting Prof. of Economics, Yale Univ., 1964–65; Dean of Faculty of Economics and Social Sciences, QUB, 1967–70; Pro-Vice-Chancellor, 1971–75. President: Statistical & Social Inquiry Soc. of Ireland, 1983–86; Section F, BAAS, 1984–85. Distinguished Fellow, History of Economics Soc., USA, 1987. MRIA 1974. Hon. DSc(Econ) QUB, 1988. *Publications:* Centenary History of the Statistical Society of Ireland, 1947; Economic Thought and the Irish Question 1817–1870, 1960; Catalogue of Economic Pamphlets 1750–1900, 1969; Papers and Correspondence of William Stanley Jevons, Vol. I, 1972, Vol. II, 1973, Vols III–VI, 1977, Vol. VII, 1981; Ideas in Economics, 1986; Economic Theory and Policy in Context, 1995; articles in Economic Jl, Economica, Oxford Econ. Papers, Econ. History Review, etc. *Recreations:* travel, music. *Address:* Queen's University, Belfast, Northern Ireland BT7 1NN. *T:* Belfast (01232) 245133.

BLACK, Sir Robin; *see* Black, Sir R. B.

BLACK, Sheila (Psyche), OBE 1986; feature writer; Director, MAI plc (formerly Mills and Allen International), 1976–92; *b* 6 May 1920; *d* of Clement Johnston Black, CA, and Mildred Beryl Black; *m* 1st, 1939, Geoffrey Davien, Sculptor (marr. diss. 1951); one *d* (one *s* decd); 2nd, 1951, L. A. Lee Howard (marr. diss. 1973). *Educ:* Dorset; Switzerland; RADA. Actress, until outbreak of War of 1939–45; Asst to production manager of an electrical engineering factory. Post-war, in advertising; then in journalism, from the mid-fifties; Woman's Editor, Financial Times, 1959–72; specialist feature writer, The Times, 1972–79; Chm., Interflex Data Systems (UK) Ltd, 1975–83. Features writer for The Director, Financial Weekly, Punch, Mediaworld, and many newspapers and magazines.

Chairman: Nat. Gas Consumers' Council, 1981–86; Gas Consumers Council, 1986–88; Dir, Money Management Council, 1985–90; Member: Furniture Develt Council, 1967–70; Liquor Licensing Laws Special Cttee, 1971–72; (part-time) Price Commn, 1973–77; Nat. Consumer Council, 1981–91; Calcutt Cttee on Privacy and Related Matters, 1989–90. Dir, Countrywide Workshops Charitable Trust, 1982–88 and 1989–93. Mem. Council, Inst. of Directors, 1975–90. Freeman, City of London, 1985. *Publications:* The Black Book, 1976; Mirabelle: cuisine de qualité et tradition, 1979; The Reluctant Money Minder, 1980; various others. *Recreations:* gardening, grandchildren, football. *Address:* c/o National Westminster Bank, 195 Earls Court Road, SW5 9AP.

BLACK, Stewart; *see* Black, C. S. F.

BLACKADDER, Elizabeth Violet, OBE 1982; RA 1976; RSA 1972; artist; *b* 24 Sept. 1931; *m* 1956, John Houston. *Educ:* Falkirk High Sch.; Univ. of Edinburgh; Edinburgh Coll. of Art. Lectr, Sch. of Drawing and Painting, Edinburgh Coll. of Art, 1962–86. Exhibns, Mercury Gall., London, 1965–; retrospective exhibns, Scottish Arts Council, 1981, Aberystwyth Arts Centre, 1989. Work in collections including: Scottish Nat. Gall. of Modern Art; Scottish Nat. Portrait Gall.; Nat. Portrait Gall.; Government Art Collection; Kettle's Yard, Cambridge; Hunterian Art Gall., Glasgow. Hon. FRIAS; Hon. FRSE. Hon. Dr: Edinburgh; Heriot-Watt. *Address:* c/o Royal Scottish Academy, The Mound, Edinburgh EH2 2EL.

BLACKBOURN, Prof. David Gordon, PhD; FRHistS; Professor of History, Harvard University, since 1992; *b* 1 Nov. 1949; *s* of Harry Blackbourn and Pamela Jean (*née* Youngman); *m* 1985, Deborah Frances Langton; one *s* one *d*. *Educ:* Leeds Modern Grammar Sch.; Christ's Coll., Cambridge (BA Hons Hist. 1970); MA 1974, PhD 1976, Cambridge. Res. Fellow, Jesus Coll., Cambridge, 1973–76; Lectr in History, QMC, Univ. of London, 1976–79; Birkbeck College, University of London: Lectr, 1979–85; Reader, 1985–89; Prof. of Mod. European History, 1989–92. Research Fellow: Inst. of European Hist., Mainz, 1974–75; Alexander von Humboldt Foundn, Bonn-Bad Godesberg, 1984–85; John Simon Guggenheim Meml Foundn, NY, 1994–95; Vis. Kratter Prof. of European Hist., Stanford Univ., 1989–90. Mem., Editl Bd, Past and Present, 1988. Sec. 1979–81, Mem. Cttee 1981–86, German Hist. Soc.; Mem. Acad. Adv. Bd, German Hist. Inst., London, 1983–92. FRHistS 1987. *Publications:* Class, Religion and Local Politics in Wilhelmine Germany, 1980; (with Geoff Eley) Mythen Deutscher Geschichtsschreibung, 1980 (Japanese edn 1983); (with Geoff Eley) The Peculiarities of German History, 1984; Populists and Patricians, 1987; (ed with Richard J. Evans) The German Bourgeoisie, 1991; Marpingen: apparitions of the Virgin Mary in Bismarckian Germany, 1993. *Recreations:* reading, jazz and classical music, sport, family. *Address:* Minda de Gunzburg Center for European Studies, Harvard University, 27 Kirkland Street, Cambridge, MA 02138, USA. *T:* (617) 4954303, *Fax:* (617) 4958509.

BLACKBURN, Bishop of, since 1989; **Rt. Rev. Alan David Chesters;** *b* 26 Aug. 1937; *s* of Herbert and Catherine Rebecca Chesters; *m* 1975, Jennie Garrett; one *s*. *Educ:* Elland Grammar Sch., W Yorks; St Chad's Coll., Univ. of Durham (BA Mod. History); St Catherine's Coll., Oxford (BA Theol., MA); St Stephen's House, Oxford. Curate of St Anne, Wandsworth, 1962–66; Chaplain and Head of Religius Education, Tiffin School, Kingston-upon-Thames, 1966–72; Director of Education and Rector of Brancepeth, Diocese of Durham, 1972–84; Hon. Canon of Durham Cathedral, 1975–84; Archdeacon of Halifax, 1985–89. A Church Comr, 1982–89 (Mem., Bd of Governors, 1984–89, 1992–). Mem., General Synod, 1975– (Mem., Standing Cttee, 1985–89, 1990–). Pres., Woodard Corp., 1993–. *Recreations:* railways, hill walking, reading. *Address:* Bishop's House, Ribchester Road, Blackburn BB1 9EF.

BLACKBURN, Archdeacon of; *see* Robinson, Ven. W. D.

BLACKBURN, Provost of; *see* Frayne, Very Rev. David.

BLACKBURN, Rear-Adm. (David) Anthony (James), LVO 1978; Defence Attaché and Head of British Defence Staff, Washington, since 1994; *b* 18 Jan. 1945; *s* of late Lieut J. Blackburn, DSC, RN, and late Mrs M. J. G. Pickering-Pick; *m* 1973, Elizabeth Barstow; three *d*. *Educ:* Taunton Sch. RNC Dartmouth, 1963; HMS Kirkliston (in comd), 1972–73; Equerry-in-Waiting to the Duke of Edinburgh, 1976–78; Exec. Officer, HMS Antrim, 1978–81; MoD (Navy), 1981–83; Comdr, HMS Birmingham, 1983–84; MoD (Navy), 1984–86; HMS York (in comd) and Captain Third Destroyer Sqn, 1987–88; Dir, Naval Manpower and Trng (Seamen), MoD, 1988–90; Cdre, Clyde, and Naval Base Comdr, Clyde, 1990–92; HMS Cornwall (in comd) and Captain, Second Frigate Sqn, 1992–93. *Club:* Royal Cruising.

BLACKBURN, Prof. Elizabeth Helen, (Mrs J. W. Sedat), PhD; FRS 1992; Professor of Microbiology and Immunology and of Biochemistry and Biophysics, since 1990, Chair of Department of Microbiology and Immunology, since 1993, University of California, San Francisco; *b* 26 Nov. 1948; *d* of Harold Stewart Blackburn and Marcia Constance (*née* Jack); *m* 1975, John William Sedat; one *s*. *Educ:* Univ. of Melbourne (BSc Hons 1970; MSc 1972); Cambridge Univ. (PhD 1975). University of California, Berkeley: Asst Prof., Dept of Molecular Biol., 1978–83; Associate Prof., 1983–86; Prof. of Molecular Biology, 1986–90. Mem., Amer. Acad. Arts and Scis; For. Associate, Nat. Acad. of Scis, USA, 1993. Hon. DSc Yale, 1991. Award for Molecular Biol., Nat. Acad. Scis, USA, 1990. *Publications:* research and review articles in Nature, Science, Cell. *Recreations:* music, playing the piano. *Address:* Department of Microbiology and Immunology, University of California, Box 0414, San Francisco, CA 94143–0414, USA. *T:* (415) 4764912.

BLACKBURN, (Jeffrey) Michael; Director and Chief Executive, Halifax Building Society, since 1993; *b* 16 Dec. 1941; *s* of Jeffrey and Renee Blackburn; *m* 1987, Louise Clair Jouny; two *s*, and one *s* one *d* from a previous marriage. *Educ:* Northgate Grammar Sch., Ipswich. FCIB; CIMgt. Chief Manager, Lloyds Bank Business Adv. Service, 1979–83; Dir and Chief Exec., Joint Credit Card Co. Ltd, 1983–87; Dir and Chief Exec., Leeds Permanent Building Soc., 1987–93. Dir, RPO, 1985–. Mem. Court, Leeds Univ., 1989–. FRSA. *Recreations:* music, theatre. *Address:* Halifax Building Society, Trinity Road, Halifax, West Yorkshire HX1 2RG. *Club:* Oriental.

BLACKBURN, John; QC 1984; barrister; *b* 13 Nov. 1945; *s* of Harry and Violet Blackburn; *m* 1st, 1970, Alison Nield (marr. diss. 1978); 2nd, 1979, Elizabeth Parker; two *s*. *Educ:* Rugby Sch.; Worcester Coll., Oxford (Scholar, 1967; Gibbs Prize in Law, 1967). Called to the Bar, Middle Temple, 1969 (Astbury Law Scholar), Bencher, 1993. Practising barrister, 1970–. *Recreations:* cricket, golf, paintings, wine. *Address:* 1 Atkin Building, Gray's Inn, WC1R 5BQ.

BLACKBURN, Michael; *see* Blackburn, J. M.

BLACKBURN, Michael John, FCA; Chairman, Touche Ross & Co., 1990–92 (Managing Partner, 1984–90); *b* 25 Oct. 1930; *s* of Francis and Ann Blackburn; *m* 1955, Maureen (*née* Dale); one *s* two *d*. *Educ:* Kingston Grammar Sch. Joined Touche Ross, 1954; Partner, 1960. Chm., GEI International, 1990–; Deputy Chairman: Aerostructures Hamble Hldgs, 1992–; Blue Arrow Hldgs, 1992–; Director: Chubb Security, 1992–; William Hill Gp, 1992–; Steel, Burrill Jones, 1992–. Chm., Voices for Hospices, 1990–. *Recreations:* horse racing, the garden.

BLACKBURN, Michael Scott; His Honour Judge Blackburn; a Circuit Judge, since 1986; *b* 16 Jan. 1936; *m* 1961, Vivienne (*née* Smith); one *s* one *d*. *Educ:* Dame Allan's Sch., Newcastle upon Tyne; William Hulme's Grammar Sch., Manchester; Keble Coll., Oxford (MA). Notary Public. Recorder, 1981–86. President: Manchester Law Society, 1979–80; Manchester Medico-Legal Soc., 1986–88; Chairman, North Western Legal Services Cttee, 1981–85; Mem., Parole Bd, 1985–88. *Recreations:* squash rackets, hill walking, fishing, tennis. *Clubs:* Northern Lawn Tennis (Manchester), Bowdon Tennis, Cheshire Tally Ho.

BLACKBURN, Peter Hugh, FCA; Chairman and Chief Executive, Nestlé UK Ltd, since 1991; *b* 17 Dec. 1940; *s* of Hugh Edward Blackburn and Sarah Blackburn (*née* Moffatt); *m* 1967, Gillian Mary Popple; three *d*. *Educ:* Douai Sch., Reading; Leeds Univ. (BA Hons Philosophy and French); Poitiers Univ. (Dipl. French); Inst. of Chartered Accts; AMP, Harvard Business Sch., 1976. R. S. Dawson & Co., Bradford (articles), 1962–66; various positions within John Mackintosh and Rowntree Mackintosh, 1966–91; Chm., Rowntree UK, 1985–91; Head, Nestlé Chocolate, Confectionery and Biscuit Strategy Group, 1989–90. Mem. Exec. Cttee, FDF. Nat. Pres., Modern Languages Assoc., 1987–89; Chm., Council, Festival of Languages Young Linguist Competition, 1985–89. Mem., Council of Industry and Higher Educn, 1990–92. Mem. Council, York Univ., 1989–92. York Merchant Adventurers, 1989. FIGD 1991. Hon. FIL 1989. Hon. DLitt Bradford, 1991. Chevalier du Tastevin, 1984. *Recreations:* fell walking, swimming, photography. *Address:* Nestlé Holdings (UK), St George's House, Park Lane, Croydon CR9 1NR.

BLACKBURNE, Rt. Rev. Hugh Charles; *b* 4 June 1912; *s* of late Very Rev. Harry William Blackburne; *m* 1944, Doris Freda, *widow* of Pilot Officer H. L. N. Davis; two *s* one *d*. *Educ:* Marlborough; Clare Coll., Cambridge (MA); Westcott House, Cambridge. Deacon, 1937; Priest, 1938; Curate of Almondbury, Yorks, 1937–39. Chaplain to the Forces, 1939–47; served with 1st Guards Bde, 11th Armoured Div., HQ Anti-Aircraft Comd, and as Chaplain, RMC, Sandhurst. Rector, Milton, Hants, 1947–53; Vicar, St Mary's, Harrow, 1953–61. Rector of the Hilborough Group, 1961–72; Vicar of Ranworth and Chaplain for the Norfolk Broads, 1972–77; Hon. Canon of Norwich, 1965–77; Chaplain to the Queen, 1962–77. Bishop Suffragan of Thetford, 1977–80. *Recreations:* sailing, bird-watching. *Address:* 4 Goodrick Place, Swaffham, Norfolk PE37 7RP.

BLACKBURNE, Hon. Sir William (Anthony), Kt 1993; **Hon. Mr Justice Blackburne;** Judge of the High Court of Justice, Chancery Division, since 1993; *b* 24 Feb. 1944. *Address:* Royal Courts of Justice, Strand, WC2A 2LL.

BLACKER, Gen. Sir (Anthony Stephen) Jeremy, KCB 1992; CBE 1987 (OBE 1979); FIMechE; Master-General of the Ordnance, Ministry of Defence, 1991–95; *b* 6 May 1939; *s* of Kenneth Anthony Blacker, CBE and late Louise Margaret Blacker (*née* Band); *m* 1973, Julia Mary (*née* Trew); two *d*. *Educ:* Sherborne School; RMA Sandhurst; Corpus Christi Coll., Cambridge (BA Hons). FIMechE 1990. Commissioned Royal Tank Regt, 1959; Staff Coll., 1971; MA to VCGS, 1976–79; Comd 1 RTR, 1979–81; Mil. Dir of Studies, RMCS, 1981–82; Comd 11 Armd Brigade, 1982–84; Principal Staff Officer to Chief of Defence Staff, 1985–87; Comdt, RMCS, 1987–89; ACDS (Operational Requirements), Land Systems, MoD, 1989–91. Col Comdt, REME, 1987–92, RTR, 1988–95, RAC, 1993–95. *Recreations:* ski-ing, squash, tennis.

BLACKER, Dr Carmen Elizabeth, FBA 1989; Lecturer in Japanese, 1958–91, and Fellow of Clare Hall, since 1965, Cambridge University; *b* 13 July 1924; *d* of Carlos Paton Blacker, MC, GM, MA, MD, FRCP and Helen Maud Blacker (*née* Pilkington). *Educ:* Benenden School; School of Oriental Studies, London University; Somerville Coll., Oxford (Hon. Fellow, 1991). PhD London Univ., 1957. Visiting Professor: Columbia Univ., 1965; Princeton Univ., 1979; Ueno Gakuen Univ., Tokyo, 1991; Toronto Univ., 1992; Vis. Fellow, Kyoto Univ., 1986. Pres., Folklore Soc., 1982–84 (Hon. Mem., 1988). Order of the Precious Crown (Japan), 1988. *Publications:* The Japanese Enlightenment: a study of the writing of Fukuzawa Yukichi, 1964; The Catalpa Bow: a study of Shamanistic practices in Japan, 1975, rev. edn 1986; articles in Monumenta Nipponica, Folklore, Trans of Asiatic Soc. of Japan, Asian Folklore Studies, etc. *Recreations:* walking, comparative mythology. *Address:* Willow House, Grantchester, Cambridge CB3 9NF. *T:* Cambridge (01223) 840196. *Club:* University Women's.

BLACKER, Gen. Sir Cecil (Hugh), GCB 1975 (KCB 1969; CB 1967); OBE 1960; MC 1944; Adjutant-General, Ministry of Defence (Army), 1973–76, retired; ADC (General) to the Queen, 1974–76; *b* 4 June 1916; *s* of Col Norman Valentine Blacker and Olive Georgina (*née* Hope); *m* 1947, Felicity Mary, *widow* of Major J. Rew and *d* of Major I. Buxton, DSO; two *s*. *Educ:* Wellington Coll. Joined 5th Royal Inniskilling Dragoon Guards, 1936; Commanded 23rd Hussars, 1945; Instructor, Staff Coll., Camberley, 1951–54; Commanded 5th Royal Inniskilling Dragoon Guards, 1955–57; Military Asst to CIGS, 1958–60; Asst Commandant, RMA, Sandhurst, 1960–62; Commander, 39 Infantry Brigade Group, 1962–64; GOC 3rd Div., 1964–66; Dir, Army Staff Duties, MoD, 1966–69; GOC-in-C Northern Command, 1969–70; Vice-Chief of the General Staff, 1970–73. Colonel Commandant: RMP, 1971–76; APTC, 1971–76; Col, 5th Royal Inniskilling Dragoon Guards, 1972–81. Member: Jockey Club, 1954– (Dep. Sen. Steward, 1984–86); Horserace Betting Levy Bd, 1981–84; President: BSJA, 1976–80; BEF, 1980–84. *Publications:* The Story of Workboy, 1960; Soldier in the Saddle, 1963; Monkey Business, 1993. *Recreations:* painting; amateur steeplechase rider, 1947–54; represented GB in World Modern Pentathlon Championships, 1951; represented GB in Showjumping, 1959–61.

BLACKER, Captain Derek Charles, RN; Director of Personnel, Orion Royal Bank Ltd, 1984–88; *b* 19 May 1929; *s* of Charles Edward Blacker and Alexandra May Farrant; *m* 1952, Brenda Mary Getgood; one *s* one *d*. *Educ:* County Sch., Isleworth; King's Coll., Univ. of London (BSc Hons 1950). Entered RN, 1950; specialisations: navigation, meteorology, oceanography; HMS Birmingham, HMS Albion, BRNC Dartmouth, HMS Hermes, 1956–69; Comdr 1965; NATO Commands: SACLANT, 1969; CINCHAN, 1972; SACEUR, 1974; Captain 1975; Dir of Public Relations (RN), 1977–79; Bd Pres., Admiralty Interview Bd, 1980; staff of C-in-C, Naval Home Comd, 1980–81; Dir of Naval Oceanography and Meteorology, MoD, 1981–84. Naval ADC to the Queen, 1983–84. *Recreations:* music, tennis, golf, country pursuits. *Club:* Army and Navy.

BLACKER, Lt-Gen. Sir Jeremy; *see* Blacker, Lt-Gen. Sir A. S. J.

BLACKER, Norman; Executive Director, British Gas, since 1994; *b* 22 May 1938; *m* 1st, 1961, Jennifer Mary Anderson (*d* 1992); 2nd, 1994, Carol Anderson. *Educ:* Wolverton Grammar School. IPFA; CIGasE; CIMgt. British Gas: Dir of Finance, Northern Reg., 1976–80; Dir of Finance, 1980–84; Chm., N Eastern Region, then British Gas N Eastern, 1985–89; Managing Director: Eastern Regions, 1989–91; Regl Services, 1991–92; Gas Business, 1992–94. *Address:* British Gas plc, Rivermill House, 152 Grosvenor Road, SW1V 3JL. *T:* 0171–821 1444.

BLACKETT, Sir Hugh Francis, 12th Bt *cr* 1673, of Newcastle, Northumberland; *b* 11 Feb. 1955; *e s* of Major Sir Francis Hugh Blackett, 11th Bt and his 1st wife, Elizabeth Eily Barrie (*née* Dennison) (*d* 1982); *S* father, 1995; *m* 1982, Anna, *yr d* of J. St G. Coldwell; one *s* three *d*. *Educ:* Eton. *Heir: s* Henry Douglas Blackett, *b* 2 Feb. 1992.

BLACKETT-ORD, His Honour Andrew James, CVO 1988; a Circuit Judge, 1972–87; Vice-Chancellor, County Palatine of Lancaster, 1973–87; *b* 21 Aug. 1921; 2nd *s* of late John Reginald Blackett-Ord, Whitfield, Northumberland; *m* 1945, Rosemary Bovill; three *s* one *d*. *Educ:* Eton; New Coll., Oxford (MA). Scots Guards, 1943–46; called to Bar, 1947, Bencher, Lincoln's Inn, 1985; County Court Judge, 1971. Mem. Council, Duchy of Lancaster, 1973–87. Chancellor, dio. of Newcastle-upon-Tyne, 1971–. *Recreations:* reading, art, shooting, country life, travel. *Address:* Helbeck Hall, Brough, Kirkby Stephen, Cumbria CA17 4DD. *T:* Brough (017683) 41323. *Clubs:* Garrick, Lansdowne.

BLACKHAM, Rear-Adm. Jeremy Joe; Assistant Chief of Naval Staff, and Admiral President, Royal Naval College, Greenwich, since 1995; *b* 10 Sept. 1943; *s* of Rear-Adm. Joseph Leslie Blackham, *qv*; *m* 1971, Candy Carter. *Educ:* Bradfield Coll., Berks; Open Univ. (BA 1st Cl. Hons 1979); RN Staff Course, 1974. Joined RN, 1961; Spanish Interpreter, 1966; commanded HM Ships Beachampton, 1969–70, Ashanti, 1977–79, Nottingham, 1984–85; RCDS 1986; Commandant, RN Staff Coll., Greenwich, 1987–89; Dir of Naval Plans, 1989–92; Captain, HMS Ark Royal, 1992–93 (Comdr RN Task Group, Adriatic); DG, Naval Personnel Strategy and Support, 1993–95. Lectr, RUSI and defence organs. Member: Council, RUSI; RIIA. *Publications:* articles on defence, strategic affairs and walking. *Recreations:* cricket, music, theatre, language, travel, walking. *Address:* c/o Lloyds Bank, 15 The Village, Blackheath, SE3 9LH. *Club:* MCC.

BLACKHAM, Rear-Adm. Joseph Leslie, CB 1965; DL; *b* 29 Feb. 1912; *s* of Dr Walter Charles Blackham, Birmingham, and Margaret Eva Blackham (*née* Bavin); *m* 1938, Coreen Shelford Skinner, *er d* of Paym. Captain W. S. Skinner, CBE, RN; one *s* one *d*. *Educ:* West House Sch., Edgbaston; RNC Dartmouth. Specialised in Navigation; served war of 1939–45; JSSC 1950; Comdr, RNC Greenwich, 1953–54; Captain 1954; Admty, 1955–57; Sen. Officer, Reserve Fleet at Plymouth, 1957–59; Admty Naval Staff, 1959–61; Cdre. Supt, HM Dockyard, Singapore, 1962–63; Rear-Adm. 1963; Admiral Supt, HM Dockyard, Portsmouth, 1964–66; retired. Mem., IoW Hosp. Management Cttee, 1968–74; Vice-Chm., IoW AHA 1974–82; Chm., Family Practitioners Cttee, IoW, 1974–85; Mem., Bd of Visitors, HM Prison, Parkhurst, 1967–82 (Chm., 1974–77). CC Isle of Wight, 1967–77 (Chm., 1975–77); DL Hants and IoW, 1970–87; High Sheriff, IoW, 1975. Mentioned in despatches for service in Korea, 1951. SBStJ 1991. *Address:* Trinity Cottage, Love Lane, Bembridge, Isle of Wight PO35 5NH. *T:* Isle of Wight (01983) 874386.

See also Rear-Adm. J. J. Blackham, Rear-Adm. R. O. Irwin.

BLACKLEY, Air Vice-Marshal Allan Baillie, CBE 1983; AFC; BSc; Principal, Emergency Planning College, since 1993; *b* 28 Sept. 1937. Flight Lieut, 1961; Sqn Leader, 1968; Wing Comdr, 1974; Directorate of Air Staff Plans, Dept of CAS, Air Force Dept, 1977; Gp Capt., 1980; OC RAF Valley and ADC to the Queen, 1980–82; Gp Capt (Air Defence) RAF Strike Comd, 1982–83; Dir (Air Defence), MoD, 1984–85; Air Cdre, 1985; Comdt, RAF CFS, Scampton, 1985–87; SASO, No 11 Gp, 1987–89; Dep. COS (Ops), HQ AFCENT, 1989–91; AO Scotland and NI, 1991–93. *Address:* The Cottage, 52 Main Street, Dorrington, Lincoln LN4 3PX.

BLACKLEY, Ian Lorimer; HM Diplomatic Service; *b* 14 Dec. 1946; *s* of late John Lorimer Blackley and Christine Ferrier (*née* Aitken); *m* 1981, Pamela Ann Helena Belt; one *s*. *Educ:* Sedbergh Sch.; St Catharine's Coll., Cambridge (MA). Joined Diplomatic Service, 1969; MECAS, Lebanon, 1971–72; Third Sec., Tripoli, 1972–73; Second Sec., Berlin, 1973–74; First Sec., Damascus, 1974–77; FCO, 1977–80; Head of Chancery and HM Consul, Beirut, 1980–82; First Sec. (Agric.), The Hague, 1982–86; Asst Head, ME Dept, FCO, 1986–88; Counsellor, Kuwait, 1988–90; British Rep. to Govt of Occupied Kuwait in Exile, Aug. 1990–March 1991; Counsellor, Damascus, 1991–93. *Recreations:* fly fishing, Islamic art. *Address:* c/o Foreign and Commonwealth Office, King Charles Street, SW1A 2AH; Berscar, Closeburn, Thornhill, Dumfriesshire DG3 5JJ. *Club:* Naval and Military.

BLACKLOCK, Sir Norman (James), KCVO 1993 (CVO 1989); OBE 1974; FRCS; Professor and Head of Department of Urological Surgery, Victoria University of Manchester, at Withington Hospital, 1978–91, now Professor Emeritus; an Extra Gentleman Usher to the Queen, since 1993; *b* 5 Feb. 1928; 2nd *s* of Prof. John and Ella Blacklock; *m* 1956, Marjorie Dale Reid; one *s* one *d*. *Educ:* McLaren High Sch., Perthshire; Glasgow Univ. (MB ChB 1950). FRCS 1957. Jun. appts, Royal Inf. and Western Inf., Glasgow, 1950–51; Nat. Service, RN, 1951–54, Surg. Lieut, HMSs Theseus and Warrior; Surg. Registrar and Lectr, Glasgow Royal Inf., 1954–56; Surg. Registrar, Ipswich and St Bart's Hosps, 1956–58; Royal Navy: Surg. Specialist, then Cons. in Gen. Surg., serving in naval hosps at Chatham, Devonport, Malta and Portsmouth, 1958–70; Cons. in Surg. and Urol., and Dir of Surg. Res., 1970–78; retd in rank of Surg. Capt., 1978; Dir, Lithotripter Centre, Withington Hosp., 1987–91. Med. Advr to HM Queen on overseas visits, 1976–93; Hon. Cons. in Urol., RN, 1978–93. Former Ext. Examnr in Surgery, univs of Edinburgh, Newcastle upon Tyne and King Saud, Riyadh; Chm., Mil. Educn Cttee, Manchester Univ., 1986–91. Chm., Health Care Cttee, BSI, 1970–91 (mem. cttees concerned with safety of med. equipment etc). Member: Council, British Assoc. of Urolog. Surgs, 1975–78, 1987–91; Adv. Cttee in Urol., RCS, 1987–91. Gilbert Blane Medal, RCS and RCP, 1970; Errol Eldridge Prize, RN Med. Service, 1972. *Publications:* contributor to: Scientific Foundations of Urology, 1976, 3rd edn 1990; Urinary Infection, 1983; Textbook of Geriatric Medicine and Gerontology, 1985, 2nd edn 1991; Urinary Calculous Disease, 1979; Prostate Cancer, 1981; Western Diseases: their emergence and prevention, 1981; Recent Advances in Urology, 3rd edn 1981; Urolithiasis: clinical and basic research, 1982; Textbook of Genito-Urinary Surgery, 2 vols, 1985; Therapy of Prostatitis, 1986; Diagnostic Techniques in Urology, 1990; Tropical Urology and Renal Disease, 1992; many contribs to learned jls. *Recreations:* gardening, cookery, bread-making, pottering. *Address:* c/o Registrar, University of Manchester, Oxford Road, Manchester M13 9PT.

BLACKMAN, Sir Frank (Milton), KA 1985; KCVO 1985 (CVO 1975); OBE 1969 (MBE 1964); Ombudsman for Barbados, 1987–93; *b* 31 July 1926; *s* of late A. Milton Blackman and Winnifred Blackman (*née* Pile); *m* 1958, Edith Mary Knight (*d* 1994); one *s*. *Educ:* Wesley Hall Boys' Sch., Barbados; Harrison Coll., Barbados. Clerical Officer, Colonial Secretary's Office, 1944–56; Sec., Public Service Commn, 1956–57; Asst. Sec., Colonial Sec.'s Office, 1957; Cabinet Office/Premier's Office, 1958–66: Clerk of the Legislative Council, 1958–64; Perm. Sec./Cabinet Sec., 1966–86; Head of CS, 1981–86. *Recreation:* gardening. *Address:* Lausanne, Rendezvous Hill, Christ Church, Barbados. *T:* 4273463.

BLACKMAN, Gilbert Albert Waller, CBE 1978 (OBE 1973); FEng; FIMechE; Chairman, Central Electricity Generating Board, Jan.–March 1990, retired; *b* 28 July 1925; *s* of Ernest Albert Cecil Blackman and Amy Blackman; *m* 1948, Lilian Rosay. *Educ:* Wanstead County High Sch.; Wandsworth Tech. Coll. (CEng, FIMechE 1967). Hon. FInstE (FInstF 1964). Trainee Engr, London Div., Brit. Electricity Authority, 1948–50; various appts in power stns, 1950–63; Central Electricity Generating Board: Stn Supt, Belvedere, 1963–64; Asst Reg. Dir, E Midlands Div., 1964–67; Asst Reg. Dir, Midlands Reg., 1967–70; Dir of Generation, Midlands Reg., 1970–75; Dir Gen., N Eastern Reg., 1975–77; Mem., 1977–90; Dep. Chm. and Prodn Man. Dir, 1986–89; Chm., British Electricity Internat. Ltd, 1988–90; Dir, Nat. Power, 1990–94. *Recreations:* music, photography, walking. *Address:* Gryphon Lodge, 15 Norton Park, St Mary's Hill, Sunninghill, Berks SL5 9BW. *T:* Ascot (01344) 24374.

See also L. C. F. Blackman.

BLACKMAN, Dr Lionel Cyril Francis; Director, British American Tobacco Co. Ltd, 1980–84 (General Manager, Group Research and Development, 1978–80); *b* 12 Sept. 1930; *s* of Ernest Albert Cecil Blackman and Amy McBain; *m* 1955, Susan Hazel Peachey (marr. diss. 1983); one *s* one *d*. *Educ:* Wanstead High Sch.; Queen Mary Coll., London. BSc 1952; PhD 1955. Scientific Officer, then Senior Research Fellow, RN Scientific Service, 1954–57; ICI Research Fellow, then Lectr in Chemical Physics of Solids, Imperial Coll., London, 1957–60; Asst Dir (London), then Dir, Chemical Research Div., BR, 1961–64; Dir of Basic Research, then Dir Gen., British Coal Utilisation Research Assoc., 1964–71; Director: Fibreglass Ltd (subsid. of Pilkington Bros Ltd), 1971–78; Compocem Ltd, 1975–78; Cemfil Corp. (US), 1975–78; Vice-Pres., Cementos y Fibras SA (Spain), 1976–78. CEng; CChem; FRSC; DIC; SFInstE. *Publications:* (ed) Modern Aspects of Graphite Technology, 1970; Athletics World Records in the 20th Century, 1988; papers in various scientific and technical jls on dropwise condensation of steam, ferrites, sintering of oxides, graphite and its crystal compounds, glass surface coatings, glass reinforced cement. *Recreations:* gardening, music, wine. *Address:* Griffin House, Knowl Hill, The Hockering, Woking, Surrey GU22 7HL. *T:* Woking (01483) 766328.

See also G. A. W. Blackman.

BLACKMORE, (Edward) Anthony; Consultant, Simpson Curtis, solicitors, since 1993 (Partner, 1962–93); *b* 9 April 1933; *s* of Hilary Blackmore and Florence Olive Blackmore; *m* 1959, Caroline Ann Jones; two *s* one *d*. *Educ:* Winchester College; Emmanuel College, Cambridge (BA). Articled, Simpson Curtis, 1954; qualified (Hons), 1957; Asst Solicitor, Slaughter and May, 1952–59; Simpson Curtis: Asst Solicitor, 1959; Partner, 1962; Sen. Partner, 1988–92. Non-Exec. Dir, Liberty plc, 1970–. Vis. Prof. of Commercial Practice, Leeds Business School. *Recreations:* ski-ing, sailing, tennis, swimming, computers. *Address:* Simpson Curtis, 41 Park Square, Leeds LS1 2NS. *T:* Leeds (0113) 243 3433. *Club:* Leeds (Leeds).

BLACKMORE, Dr Stephen; Keeper of Botany, since 1990, and Associate Director, since 1992, Natural History Museum; *b* 30 July 1952; *s* of Edwin Arthur and Josephine Blackmore; *m* 1973, Patricia Jane Melrose Hawley; one *s* one *d*. *Educ:* Univ. of Reading (BSc 1973; PhD 1976). Botanist and Administrator, Royal Society Aldabra Research Station, Indian Ocean, 1976–77; Head of Nat. Herbarium and Lectr in Botany, Univ. of Malaŵi, 1977–80; Head of Palynology Section, Dept of Botany, BM (Natural Hist.), 1980–90. Vis. Prof., Reading Univ., 1995–. *Publications:* Bee Orchids, 1985; Buttercups, 1985; (ed jtly) Pollen and Spores: form and function, 1986; (ed jtly) Evolution, Systematics and Fossil History of the Hamamelidae, 2 vols, 1989; (ed jtly) Microspores: evolution and ontogeny, 1990; (ed jtly) Pollen and Spores: patterns of diversification, 1991; (ed jtly) An Atlas of Plant Sexual Reproduction, 1992; contribs to professional jls. *Recreations:* photography, blues guitar music. *Address:* Department of Botany, Natural History Museum, Cromwell Road, SW7 5BD. *T:* 0171–938 8992.

BLACKMUN, Hon. Harry A(ndrew); Associate Justice, United States Supreme Court, 1970–94; *b* Nashville, Illinois, 12 Nov. 1908; *s* of late Corwin Manning Blackmun and of Theo Huegely (*née* Reuter); *m* 1941, Dorothy E. Clark; three *d*. *Educ:* Harvard Univ.; Harvard Law Sch. AB, LLB. Admitted to Minnesota Bar, 1932; private legal practice with Dorsey, Colman, Barker, Scott & Barber, Minneapolis, 1934–50: Associate, 1934–38; Jun. Partner, 1939–42; General Partner, 1943–50; Instructor: St Paul Coll. of Law, 1935–41; Univ. of Minnesota Law Sch., 1945–47; Resident Counsel, Mayo Clinic, Rochester, 1950–59; Judge, US Ct of Appeals, 8th Circuit, 1959–70. Member: American Bar Assoc.; Amer. Judicature Soc.; Minnesota State Bar Assoc.; 3rd Judicial Dist (Minn) Bar Assoc.; Olmsted Co. (Minn) Bar Assoc.; Judicial Conf. Adv. Cttee on Judicial Activities, 1969–79; Rep. of Judicial Br., Nat. Historical Pubns and Records Commn, 1975–82 and 1986–; Mem., Bd of Mems, Mayo Assoc, Rochester, 1953–60; Bd of Dirs and Exec. Cttee, Rochester Methodist Hosp., 1954–70; Trustee: Hamline Univ., St Paul, 1964–70; William Mitchell Coll. of Law, St Paul, 1959–74. Mem. Faculty, Salzburg Seminar in Amer. Studies (Law), 1989 (Chm., 1977); Co-moderator: Seminar on Justice and Society, Aspen Inst., 1979–93; Seminar on Constitutional Justice and Society, Aspen Inst. Italia, Rome, 1986; participant, Franco-Amer. Colloquium on Human Rights, Paris, 1979; Vis. Instr on Constitutional Law, Louisiana State Univ. Law Sch's summer session, France, 1986 and 1992, Tulane Univ. Law Sch's summer session, Berlin, 1992. Hon. LLD: De Pauw Univ., Hamline Univ., and Ohio Wesleyan Univ., 1971; Morningside Coll., and Wilson Coll., 1972; Dickinson Sch. of Law, 1973; Drake Univ., 1975; Southern Illinois Univ., Pepperdine Univ., and Emory Univ., 1976; Rensselaer Polytech. Inst., 1979; Nebraska Univ., and New York Law Sch., 1983; McGeorge Sch. of Law, 1984; Vermont Law Sch., and Dartmouth Coll., 1985; Carleton Coll., and Luther Coll., 1986; Drury Coll., Tufts Univ., and Ill Inst. of Technol. Chicago-Kent Coll. of Law, 1987; Northern Ill Univ., and Brooklyn Law Sch., 1988; New York Univ., 1989; Claremont Graduate Sch., 1991; Columbia Univ., Franklin and Marshall Coll., Univ. of Dist of Columbia, and Shippensburg Univ., 1992; New England Sch. of Law, 1993; Hon. DLitt. Dickinson Sch. of Law, 1983; Hon. DPS Ohio Northern Univ., 1973; Hon. DHL: Oklahoma City, 1976; Massachusetts Sch. of Professional Psychology, 1984. *Publications:* contrib. legal and medical jls. *Recreations:* reading, music. *Address:* c/o Supreme Court Building, 1 First Street NE, Washington, DC 20543, USA.

BLACKSELL, Henry Oliver; QC 1994; a Recorder, since 1993; *b* 28 Nov. 1948; *s* of James Edward Blacksell, MBE and Joan Simmons Yates Blacksell (*née* Yates); *m* 1st, 1971, Diana Frances Mary Burton (marr. diss. 1985); 2nd, 1986, Miranda Jane Allardice; one *s* one *d*. *Educ:* Barnstaple Grammar Sch.; Exeter Univ. (LLB). Called to the Bar, Inner Temple, 1972. *Recreations:* family, theatre, ancient humour. *Address:* 3 Pump Court, Temple, EC4Y 7AJ. *T:* 0171–353 0711. *Club:* Harlequin Rugby Football.

BLACKSHAW, Alan, OBE 1992; VRD 1970; business consultant and author; Associate, Oakwood Environmental Ltd, since 1991; Chairman, Caledonian Career Consultants Ltd, since 1994; *b* 7 April 1933; *s* of late Frederick William Blackshaw and Elsie (*née* MacDougall); *m* 1st, 1956, Jane Elizabeth Turner (marr. diss. 1983); one *d*; 2nd, 1984, Dr Elspeth Paterson Martin, *d* of late Rev. Gavin C. Martin and Agnes Martin; one *s* two *d*. *Educ:* Merchant Taylors' Sch., Crosby; Wadham Coll., Oxford (MA). Royal Marines (commnd), 1954–56, and RM Reserve, 1956–76. Entered Home Civil Service, Min. of Power, 1956; 1st Sec., UK Delegn to OECD, Paris, 1965–66; Principal Private Sec. to Minister of Power, 1967–69; with Charterhouse Gp on loan, 1972–73; Dept of Energy:

Under Sec., 1974; Offshore Supplies Office, 1974–78 (Dir-Gen., 1977–78); Coal Div., 1978–79; Consultant, NCB, 1979–86. Consultant Dir, Strategy Internat., 1980–91. Member: Scottish Council for Develt and Industry, 1974–78; Offshore Energy Technol. Bd, 1977–78; Ship and Marine Technol. Requirements Bd, 1977–78; Scottish Sports Council, 1990–; Scottish Natural Heritage, 1992– (Chairman: Task Force on Access, 1992–94; Audit Cttee, 1994–). Libel damages against Daily Telegraph (upheld in Ct of Appeal, 1983) and Daily Mail, 1981. Pres., Oxford Univ. Mountaineering Club, 1953–54; Alpine Club: Editor, Alpine Jl, 1968–70; Vice-Pres., 1979–81; Trustee, 1980–90; Chm., Publications Sub-Cttee, 1986–92; British Mountaineering Council: Pres., 1973–76; Patron, 1979–; Chairman: Standing Adv. Cttee on Mountain Trng Policy, 1980–86 and 1990–; Ski Touring and Mountaineering Cttee, 1981–91. Chairman: Sports Council's Nat. Mountain Centre (formerly Nat. Centre for Mountain Activities), Plas y Brenin, 1986–; Mountaineering Cttee, UIAA, 1990– (Mem., 1985–; Dep. Chm., 1989–90); UIAA Gp on competitions in mountain areas, 1993–; UK Mountain Trng Bd, 1991–94; Scottish Nat. Ski Council, 1991–94 (Pres., 1994–); Interim Wkg Gp on Leadership in Outdoor Activities, Sports Council, 1990–91; Leader, British Alpine Ski Traverse, 1972; Hon. Advr, Mountaineering Council of Scotland, 1994–; Ski Club of Great Britain: Vice-Pres., 1977–80, 1983–85; Pery Medal, 1977; Hon. Mem., 1992; Pres., Eagle Ski Club, 1979–81 (Hon. Mem., 1982); British Ski Federation: Vice-Pres., 1983–84; Chm., 1984–86. Sec., Edinburgh Br., Oxford Soc., 1989–. Freeman, City of London. FRGS; FInstPet. *Publication:* Mountaineering, 1965, 3rd revision 1975. *Recreations:* mountaineering and ski-ing. *Address:* 2 Clark Road, Edinburgh EH5 3BD. *T:* 0131–467 3366; Les Autannes, Le Tour, Argentière, 74440, France. *T:* 50541220. *Clubs:* Royal Scottish Automobile, Alpine Ski (Hon. Mem.).

BLACKSHAW, William Simon; Headmaster of Brighton College, 1971–87; *b* 28 Oct. 1930; *s* of late C. B. Blackshaw, sometime Housemaster, Cranleigh School and Kathleen Mary (who *m* 1965, Sir Thomas McAlpine, 4th Bt); *m* 1956, Elizabeth Anne Evans; one *s* one *d* (and one *s* decd). *Educ:* Sherborne Sch.; Hertford Coll., Oxford. 2nd cl. hons Mod. Langs. Repton School: Asst Master, 1955–71; Head of Modern Languages Dept, 1961–66; Housemaster, 1966–71. Chm., Bankside Gall. Chm., Sussex Schs Cricket Assoc. *Publication:* Regardez! Racontez!, 1971. *Recreations:* philately, painting, cricket, golf. *Address:* Squash Court, The Green, Rottingdean, East Sussex BN2 7HA.

BLACKSTONE, Baroness *cr* 1987 (Life Peer), of Stoke Newington in Greater London; **Tessa Ann Vosper Blackstone,** PhD; Master, Birkbeck College, since 1987; *b* 27 Sept. 1942; *d* of late Geoffrey Vaughan Blackstone and of Joanna Blackstone; *m* 1963, Tom Evans (marr. diss.; he *d* 1985); one *s* one *d*. *Educ:* Ware Grammar Sch.; London School of Economics (BScSoc, PhD). Associate Lectr, Enfield Coll., 1965–66; Asst Lectr, then Lectr, Dept of Social Administration, LSE, 1966–75; Adviser, Central Policy Review Staff, Cabinet Office, 1975–78; Prof. of Educnl Admin, Univ. of London Inst. of Educn, 1978–83; Dep. Educn Officer (Resources), then Clerk and Dir of Education, ILEA, 1983–87. Fellow, Centre for Studies in Social Policy, 1972–74; Special Rowntree Visiting Fellow, Policy Studies Inst., 1987. Chm., Gen. Adv. Council of BBC, 1987–91; First Chm., Inst. for Public Policy Research, 1988–. Director: Project Fullemploy, 1984–91; Thames Television, 1991–92; Royal Opera House, 1987–, Chm. Ballet Bd, 1991–; Member: Planning Bd, Arts Council of GB, 1986–90; Management Cttee, King Edward's Hosp. Fund for London, 1990–; Gov. and Mem. of Council, Ditchley Foundn, 1990–. Opposition spokesman, House of Lords: on educn and science, 1988–92; on foreign affairs, 1992–. Trustee: Architecture Foundn, 1991–; Nat. Hist. Mus., 1992–. *Publications:* Students in Conflict (jtly), 1970; A Fair Start, 1971; Education and Day Care for Young Children in Need, 1973; The Academic Labour Market (jtly), 1974; Social Policy and Administration in Britain, 1975; Disadvantage and Education (jtly), 1982; Educational Policy and Educational Inequality (jtly), 1982; Response to Adversity (jtly), 1983; Testing Children (jtly), 1983; Inside the Think Tank (jtly), 1988; Prisons and Penal Reform, 1990. *Address:* 2 Gower Street, WC1E 6DP. *T:* 0171–631 6274.

BLACKWELL, Sir Basil (Davenport), Kt 1983; FEng; Chief Executive, 1974–85, and Chairman, 1985, Westland PLC (formerly Westland Aircraft Ltd) (Vice-Chairman, 1974–84, Deputy Chairman, 1984); retired; *b* Whitkirk, Yorks, 8 Feb. 1922; *s* of late Alfred Blackwell and late Mrs H. Lloyd; *m* 1948, Betty Meggs, *d* of late Engr Captain Meggs, RN; one *d*. *Educ:* Leeds Grammar Sch.; St John's Coll., Cambridge (MA; Hughes Prize); London Univ. (BScEng). FIMechE; FRAeS (Gold Medal, 1982); CBIM. Sci. Officer, Admiralty, 1942; Rolls-Royce Ltd, 1945; Engine Div., Bristol Aeroplane Co. Ltd, 1949; Bristol Siddeley Engines Ltd: Dep. Chief Engr, 1959; Sales Dir, 1963; Man. Dir, Small Engine Div., 1965 (subseq. Small Engines Div. of Rolls-Royce Ltd). Commercial Dir, Westland Aircraft Ltd, 1970–72; Westland Helicopters Ltd: Man. Dir, 1972; Chm., 1976–85; Chairman: British Hovercraft Corp., 1979–85; Normalair-Garrett Ltd, 1979–85. Member Council: BIM; CBI; NDIC; SBAC (Vice-Pres., 1978; Pres., 1979 and 1980; Dep. Pres., 1980); EEF (Vice-Pres., 1983–85); Bath Univ., 1986–. Pres., AECMA, 1984–85 (Président d'honneur 1985); Chm., Astrid Trust, 1986–93. Hon. DSc, Bath Univ., 1984. *Publications:* (jtly) The Global Challenge of Innovation, 1991; contrib. professional jls. *Recreations:* gardens and gardening. *Address:* High Newland, Newland Garden, Sherborne, Dorset DT9 3AF. *T:* Sherborne (01935) 813516. *Club:* United Oxford & Cambridge University.

BLACKWELL, Prof. Donald Eustace, MA, PhD; Savilian Professor of Astronomy, University of Oxford, 1960–88, now Emeritus; Fellow of New College, Oxford, 1960–88, now Emeritus; *b* 27 May 1921; *s* of John Blackwell and Ethel Bowe; *m* 1951, Nora Louise Carlton; two *s* two *d*. *Educ:* Merchant Taylors' Sch.; Sandy Lodge; Sidney Sussex Coll., Cambridge. Isaac Newton Student, University of Cambridge, 1947; Stokes Student, Pembroke Coll., Cambridge, 1948; Asst Director, Solar Physics Observatory, Cambridge, 1950–60. Various Astronomical Expeditions: Sudan, 1952; Fiji, 1955; Bolivia, 1958 and 1961; Canada, 1963; Manuae Island, 1965. Pres., RAS, 1973–75. *Publications:* papers in astronomical journals. *Address:* 4 Pullens Field, Headington, Oxford OX3 0BU.

BLACKWELL, Rt. Rev. Douglas Charles; a Suffragan Bishop of Toronto (Area Bishop of Trent-Durham), since 1988; *b* 3 June 1938; *s* of late William John Blackwell and Ethel N. Blackwell (*née* Keates); *m* 1963, Sandra Dianne Griffiths; one *s* two *d*. *Educ:* Wycliffe Coll., Univ. of Toronto (DipTh, LTh). Deacon 1963, priest 1964; Asst Curate, St Stephen's, Calgary, 1964; Vicar, Cochrane Mission, Diocese of Calgary, 1966; Rector, St Paul's, North Battleford, Diocese of Saskatoon, 1969; Regional Dean of Battleford, 1970; Archdeacon of Battlefords–Lloydminster, 1973; Asst Director, Aurora Conf. Centre, Diocese of Toronto, 1974; Executive Asst to Archbishop of Toronto, 1977; Canon of St James's Cathedral, Toronto, 1978; Archdeacon of York, 1986. Hon. DD Wycliffe Coll., Toronto, 1990. *Address:* 135 Adelaide Street East, Toronto, Ontario M5C 1L8, Canada. *T:* (416) 3636021.

BLACKWELL, Prof. Jenefer Mary; Glaxo Professor of Molecular Parasitology, Cambridge, since 1991; Professorial Fellow, Newnham College, Cambridge, since 1993; *b* 8 Dec. 1948; *d* of Frank Blackwell and Elsie Winifred Broadhurst; *m* 1973, Simon John Miles; one *s* one *d*. *Educ:* Univ. of Western Australia (BSc 1969 (1st Cl. Hons Zoology); PhD 1974 (Population Genetics)). Cons. Biologist and Res. Officer, WA Govt Depts, 1973–74; Lectr in Biol., Avery Hill Coll. of Educn, London, 1975–76; London School of Hygiene and Tropical Medicine: Res. Fellow, Ross Inst. of Tropical Hygiene, 1976–82; Wellcome Trust Sen. Lectr, Dept of Trop. Hygiene, 1982–88, Dept of Med. Parasitology, 1988–91 (and Head, Immunobiol. of Parasitic Diseases Unit); Reader, Univ. of London, 1989–91. Faculty Mem., Molecular Biol. of Parasitism Course, Marine Biol. Labs, Wood's Hole, Mass, 1988. *Publication:* (with D. Wakelin) Genetics of Resistance to Bacterial and Parasitic Infection, 1988. *Recreations:* music, walking. *Address:* Department of Medicine, Addenbrooke's Hospital, Hills Road, Cambridge CB2 2QQ. *T:* Cambridge (01223) 336947.

BLACKWELL, John Charles, CBE 1988; Development Adviser, British Council, since 1993; *b* 4 Nov. 1935; *s* of Charles Arthur Blackwell and Louisa Amy Blackwell (*née* Sellers); *m* 1st, 1961, Julia Rose; one *s*; 2nd, 1978, Inger Beatrice Lewin; one step *s*. *Educ:* Glynn Grammar Sch., Ewell; Dudley Coll. of Educn (Cert. in Educn); Bristol Univ. (BA, MEd, PhD). Metropolitan Police Cadet, 1952–53; RAF, 1954–56; teacher, Dempsey Secondary Sch., London, 1958–60; joined British Council, 1966; Asst Rep., Tanzania, 1966–70; Educn Officer, Calcutta, 1971–72; Asst Educn Adviser, New Delhi, 1973–75; Head, Schools and Teacher Educn Unit, 1976–78; attached British Embassy, Washington, 1979; Dir, Educn Contrasts Dept, 1980–83; Rep., Indonesia, 1983–89; Controller, later Dir, Sci. and Educn Div., 1989–92. *Recreations:* boating, fishing, reading. *Address:* British Council, 10 Spring Gardens, SW1A 2AH. *T:* 0171–389 4836.

BLACKWELL, Julian, (Toby); DL; President, Blackwell Ltd, since 1995; Chairman, The Blackwell Group Ltd, 1980–94; *b* 10 Jan. 1929; *s* of Sir Basil Henry Blackwell and late Marion Christine, *d* of John Soans; *m* 1953, Jennifer Jocelyn Darley Wykeham; two *s* one *d*. *Educ:* Winchester; Trinity Coll., Oxford. Served 5th RTR, 1947–49; 21st SAS (TA), 1950–59. Dir and Chm., various Blackwell companies, 1956–. Chm. Council, ASLIB, 1966–68 (Vice-Pres., 1982); Mem., Library and Inf. Services Council, 1981–84; Co-founder and Chm., Mail Users' Assoc., 1975–78 and 1987–90; Pres., Booksellers' Assoc., 1980–82; Chairman: Thames Business Advice Centre, 1986–; Heart of England TEC, 1989–94; Fox FM, 1989–.Chm., Son White Meml Trust, 1991–. DL Oxon 1987, High Sheriff, 1991–92. *Recreations:* sawing firewood, sailing. *Address:* c/o 50 Broad Street, Oxford OX1 3BQ. *T:* Oxford (01865) 792111. *Clubs:* Special Forces; Royal Yacht Squadron; Leander (Henley); Royal Southern Yacht (Southampton).

BLACKWOOD, family name of **Baron Dufferin and Clandeboye.**

BLACKWOOD, Wing Comdr George Douglas; Chairman, William Blackwood & Sons Ltd, publishers and printers, 1948–83; Editor of Blackwood's Magazine, and Managing Director of William Blackwood & Sons Ltd, 1948–76; *b* 11 Oct. 1909; *e s* of late James H. Blackwood and *g g g s* of Wm Blackwood, founder of Blackwood's Magazine; *m* 1936, Phyllis Marion, *y d* of late Sir John Caulcutt, KCMG; one *s* one *d*. *Educ:* Eton; Clare Coll., Cambridge. Short Service Commission in RAF, 1932–38; re-joined 1939. Formed first Czech Fighter Squadron, 1940–41; Battle of Britain (despatches); commanded Czech Wing of Royal Air Force 2nd TAF, 1944 (despatches); retired 1945. Czech War Cross, 1940; Czech Military Medal 1st class, 1944; Czech Medal of George of Podebrad, 1993. *Recreations:* countryside activities. *Address:* Airhouse, Oxton, Berwickshire TD2 6PX. *T:* Oxton (01578) 750225.

BLAIKLEY, Robert Marcel; HM Diplomatic Service, retired; *b* 1 Oct. 1916; *s* of late Alexander John Blaikley and late Adelaide Blaikley (*née* Miller); *m* 1942, Alice Mary Duncan; one *s* one *d*. *Educ:* Christ's Coll., Finchley; St John's Coll., Cambridge. Served HM Forces, 1940–46. Inland Revenue, 1946–48; General Register Office, 1948–65, Asst Secretary, 1958; transferred to Diplomatic Service as Counsellor, 1965; on loan to Colonial Office, 1965–66; Head of Aviation and Telecommunications Dept, CO, 1966–68; Counsellor, Jamaica, 1968–71, Ghana, 1971–73. *Recreations:* reading, growing shrubs. *Address:* Apartment 9, Pythouse, Tisbury, Wilts SP3 6PB.

BLAIN, Prof. Peter George, PhD; FRCP, FRCPE; CBiol, FIBiol; Professor of Environmental Medicine, University of Newcastle Upon Tyne, since 1986; *b* 15 March 1951; *s* of Reginald Blain and Margaret (*née* Graham); *m* 1977, Patricia Anne Crawford; two *s* one *d*. *Educ:* Univ. of Newcastle upon Tyne (BMed.Sci.; MB, BS; PhD 1988). MFOM 1990; FRCP 1990; FRCPE 1991; CBiol 1986; FIBiol 1989. Jun. hosp. doctor, Royal Victoria Infirmary, Newcastle upon Tyne, 1975–79; University of Newcastle upon Tyne: Lectr in Clinical Pharmacol., 1979–80; Wellcome Res. Fellow in Clinical Pharmacol. and Neurology, 1980–81; First Asst in Clinical Pharmacol., 1981–85; Hd, Biomed. Scis and Human Toxicol. Res., ICI plc, 1985–86. Consultant Physician, Freeman Gp of Hosps NHS Trust and Royal Victoria Infirmary NHS Trust, 1988–; Consultant in Envmtl Medicine and Toxicol., Northern and Yorks RHA, 1992–. *Publications:* contrib. to textbooks in toxicol. and medicine; res. papers in acad. jls in toxicol. *Recreation:* walking in the countryside. *Address:* Department of Environmental Medicine, Medical School, Newcastle upon Tyne NE2 4HH. *T:* (0191) 222 7195.

BLAIR, Sir Alastair Campbell, KCVO 1969 (CVO 1953); TD 1950; WS; JP; *b* 16 Jan. 1908; 2nd *s* of late William Blair, WS, and late Emelia Mylne Campbell; *m* 1933, Catriona Hatchard, *o d* of late Dr William Basil Orr; four *s*. *Educ:* Cargilfield; Charterhouse; Clare Coll., Cambridge (BA); Edinburgh Univ. (LLB). Writer to the Signet, 1932; retired 1977 as Partner, Dundas & Wilson, CS. RA (TA) 1939; served 1939–45 (despatches); Secretary, Queen's Body Guard for Scotland, Royal Company of Archers, 1946–59; appointed Captain 1982; retired 1984. Purse Bearer to The Lord High Commissioner to the General Assembly of the Church of Scotland, 1961–69. Chm., subseq. Vice-Pres., Edinburgh Area Scout Council, 1964– (Silver Wolf, 1990). JP Edinburgh, 1954. *Recreation:* golf. *Address:* 7 Abbotsford Court, Colinton Road, Edinburgh EH10 5EH. *T:* 0131–447 3095. *Club:* New (Edinburgh).

See also M. C. Blair.

BLAIR, Rt. Hon. Anthony Charles Lynton, (Tony); PC 1994; MP (Lab) Sedgefield, since 1983; Leader of the Labour Party, and Leader of the Opposition, since 1994; *b* 6 May 1953; *s* of Leo Charles Lynton Blair and late Hazel Blair; *m* 1980, Cherie Booth, *qv*; two *s* one *d*. *Educ:* Durham Choristers School; Fettes College, Edinburgh; St John's College, Oxford. Called to the Bar, Lincoln's Inn, 1976; Hon. Bencher, 1994. *Address:* Myrobella, Trimdon Station, Co. Durham TS29 6DU. *T:* Hartlepool (01429) 882202; (office) 0171–219 6937. *Clubs:* Trimdon Colliery and Deaf Hill Working Men's, Constituency Labour (Trimdon); Fishburn Working Men's.

See also W. J. L. Blair.

BLAIR, Bruce Graeme Donald; QC 1989; a Recorder, since 1995; *b* 12 April 1946; *s* of late Dr Donald Alexander Sangster Blair, MA, MD, DPM and Eleanor Violet Blair (*née* Van Ryneveld); *m* 1970, Susanne Blair (*née* Hartung); three *d* (and one *s* decd). *Educ:* Harrow School; Magdalene College, Cambridge. Called to the Bar, Middle Temple, 1969. *Publication:* Practical Matrimonial Precedents (jtly), 1989. *Recreations:* bridge, tennis, turf. *Address:* 1 Mitre Court Buildings, Temple, EC4Y 7BS. *T:* 0171–353 0434. *Club:* MCC.

BLAIR, Lt-Gen. Sir Chandos, KCVO 1972; OBE 1962; MC 1941 and bar, 1944; GOC Scotland and Governor of Edinburgh Castle, 1972–76; *b* 25 Feb. 1919; *s* of Brig.-Gen. Arthur Blair and Elizabeth Mary (*née* Hoskyns); *m* 1947, Audrey Mary Travers; one *s* one *d*. *Educ:* Harrow; Sandhurst. Commnd into Seaforth Highlanders, 1939; comd 4 KAR, Uganda, 1959–61; comd 39 Bde, Radfan and N. Ireland. GOC 2nd Division, BAOR, 1968–70; Defence Services Secretary, MoD, 1970–72. Col Comdt, Scottish Div., 1972–76; Col, Queen's Own Highlanders, 1975–83. *Recreations:* golf, fishing, shooting. *Club:* Naval and Military.

BLAIR, Cherie; *see* Booth, C.

BLAIR, Claude, OBE 1994; FSA 1956; Keeper, Department of Metalwork, Victoria and Albert Museum, 1972–82; *b* 30 Nov. 1922; *s* of William Henry Murray Blair and Lilian Wearing; *m* 1952, Joan Mary Greville Drinkwater; one *s*. *Educ:* William Hulme's Grammar Sch., Manchester; Manchester Univ. (MA). Served War, Army (Captain RA), 1942–46. Manchester Univ., 1946–51; Asst, Tower of London Armouries, 1951–56; Asst Keeper of Metalwork, V&A, 1956–66; Dep. Keeper, 1966–72. Hon. Editor, Jl of the Arms and Armour Soc., 1953–77. Consultant to Christie's, 1983–; Member: Arch. Adv. Panel, Westminster Abbey, 1979–; Council for the Care of Churches, 1991– (Mem. Exec. Cttee, 1983–91); Trustee, Churches Conservation Trust (formerly Mem., Redundant Churches Fund), 1982–.Vice-Pres., Soc. of Antiquaries, 1990–93; Hon. Pres., Meyrick Soc., 1979–94; Hon. Vice-President: Soc. for Study of Church Monuments, 1984– (Hon. Pres., 1978–84); Monumental Brass Soc. Hon. Liveryman, Cutlers' Co. Liveryman: Goldsmiths' Co.; Armourers and Brasiers' Co. Medal of Museo Militar, Barcelona, 1969; Medal of Arms and Armour Soc., 1986. *Publications:* European Armour, 1958 (2nd edn, 1972); European and American Arms, 1962; The Silvered Armour of Henry VIII, 1965; Pistols of the World, 1968; Three Presentation Swords in the Victoria and Albert Museum, 1972; The James A. de Rothschild Collection: Arms, Armour and Miscellaneous Metalwork, 1974; (ed) Pollard's History of Firearms, 1983; (ed) The History of Silver, 1987; numerous articles and reviews in Archaeological Jl, Jl of Arms and Armour Soc., Connoisseur, Waffen und Kostümkunde, etc. *Recreations:* travel, looking at churches, listening to music. *Address:* 90 Links Road, Ashtead, Surrey KT21 2HW. *T:* Ashtead (01372) 275532. *Club:* Civil Service.

BLAIR, Sir Edward Thomas H.; *see* Hunter-Blair.

BLAIR, Prof. Gordon Purves, CBE 1995; PhD, DSc; FEng 1982; FIMechE, FSAE; Professor of Mechanical Engineering, Queen's University of Belfast, since 1976; *b* 29 April 1937; *s* of Gordon Blair and Mary Helen Jones Blair; *m* 1964, Norma Margaret Millar; two *d*. *Educ:* Queen's Univ. of Belfast (BSc; PhD 1962; DSc 1978). CEng, FIMechE 1977; FSAE 1979. Asst Prof., New Mexico State Univ., 1962–64; Queen's University of Belfast: Lectr, 1964–71; Sen. Lectr, 1971–73; Reader, 1973–76; Head of Dept of Mechl and Industrial Engrg, 1982–89, and of Dept of Mechl and Manufacturing, Aeronautical and Chemical Engrg, 1987–89; Dean, Faculty of Engrg, 1985–88; Pro-Vice-Chancellor, 1989–94. Chm., Automobile Div., IMechE, 1991–. *Publications:* The Basic Design of Two-Stroke Engines, USA, 1990; wide pubn in IMechE and SAE Jls on design and develt of internal combustion engines. *Recreations:* golf, fishing, motorcycles. *Address:* 9 Ben Madigan Park South, Newtownabbey, N Ireland BT36 7PX. *T:* Belfast (01232) 773280. *Clubs:* Cairndhu Golf; Royal Portrush Golf.

BLAIR, Michael Campbell; Head of Policy and Legal Affairs, Securities and Investments Board, since 1993; *b* 26 Aug. 1941; *s* of Sir Alastair Blair, *qv*; *m* 1966, Halldóra Isabel (*née* Tunnard); one *s*. *Educ:* Rugby Sch.; Clare Coll., Cambridge (MA, LLM); Yale Univ., USA (Mellon Fellow; MA). Called to the Bar, Middle Temple, 1965 (Harmsworth Law Scholar); Bencher, 1995. Lord Chancellor's Dept, 1966–87: Private Sec. to the Lord Chancellor, 1968–71; Sec., Law Reform Cttee, 1977–79; Under Sec., 1982–87; Circuit Administrator, Midland and Oxford Circuit, 1982–86; Hd, Courts and Legal Services Gp, 1986–87. Attended Cabinet Office Top Management Programme, 1986. Dir of Legal Services, 1987–91, General Counsel, 1991–93, SIB. Chairman: Bar Assoc. for Commerce, Finance and Industry, 1990–91; Bar Conf., 1993; Member: Gen. Council of the Bar, 1989– (Chm., Professional Standards Cttee, 1994; Treas., 1995); Council of Legal Educn, 1992–. FRSA 1992. *Publications:* Sale of Goods Act 1979, 1980; Financial Services: the new core rules, 1991; legal articles in Modern Law Rev., Lancet, New Law Jl, Civil Justice Qly, Jl of Internat. Banking and Financial Law, etc. *Address:* 3 Burbage Road, SE24 9HJ. *T:* 0171–274 7614. *Club:* Athenæum.

BLAIR, Thomas Alexander, QC (NI) 1958; Chief Social Security (formerly National Insurance) Commissioner (Northern Ireland), 1969–83; *b* 12 Dec. 1916; *s* of late John Blair and Wilhelmina Whitla Blair (*née* Downey); *m* 1947, Ida Irvine Moore; two *s* one *d*. *Educ:* Royal Belfast Academical Instn; Queen's Univ. Belfast (BA, LLB). Served War, in Royal Navy, 1940–46 (commissioned, 1941). Called to Bar of N Ireland, 1946. Chairman: Wages Councils; War Pensions Appeal Tribunal. Sen. Crown Counsel for Co. Tyrone; Mem. Departmental Cttee on Legal Aid. Apptd Dep. Nat. Insurance Umpire, 1959; Pres., Industrial Tribunals (NI), 1967–69; Chief Nat. Insurance Commissioner (NI), 1969. *Recreation:* golf. *Address:* Lilac Cottage, Bowden, Melrose, Roxburghshire TD6 0SS. *T:* St Boswells (01835) 823680.

BLAIR, Tony; *see* Blair, A. C. L.

BLAIR, William James Lynton; QC 1994; *b* 31 March 1950; *s* of Leo Charles Lynton Blair and late Hazel Elizabeth (*née* Corscadden); *m* 1982, Katy Tse. *Educ:* Fettes Coll., Edinburgh; Balliol Coll., Oxford (BA 1971). Called to the Bar, Lincoln's Inn, 1972. Sen. Vis. Fellow, Centre for Commercial Law Studies, QMW, 1991–; Vis. Prof. of Law, LSE, 1994–. Consultant, World Bank and IMF, 1991–. Mem., Banking Law Sub-Cttee, Law Soc., 1988–. *Publications:* (ed) Encyclopaedia of Banking Law, 1982; (jtly) Banking and the Financial Services Act, 1993; contrib. other legal books and jls. *Recreations:* travel, walking.

See also A. C. L. Blair.

BLAIR-OLIPHANT, Air Vice-Marshal David Nigel Kington, CB 1966; OBE 1945; *b* 22 Dec. 1911; *y s* of Col P. L. K. Blair-Oliphant, DSO, Ardblair Castle, Blairgowrie, Perthshire, and Laura Geraldine Bodenham; *m* 1942, Helen Nathalie Donald (*d* 1983), *yr d* of Sir John Donald, KCIE; one *s* (and one *s* and one *d* decd). *Educ:* Harrow; Trinity Hall, Cambridge (BA). Joined RAF, 1934; Middle East and European Campaigns, 1939–45; RAF Staff Coll., 1945–48; Group Capt. 1949; Air Cdre 1958; Director, Weapons Engineering, Air Ministry, 1958–60; British Defence Staffs, Washington, 1960–63; Acting Air Vice-Marshal, 1963; Pres., Ordnance Board, 1965–66; Air Vice-Marshal, 1966. *Address:* 9 Northfield Road, Sherfield-on-Lodon, Basingstoke, Hants RG27 0DR. *T:* Basingstoke (01256) 882724. *Club:* Royal Air Force.

BLAIS, Hon. Jean Jacques, PC (Can.) 1976; QC (Can.) 1978; Partner, law firm of Lette McTaggart Blais Martin and Stein; *b* 27 June 1940; *m* 1968, Maureen Ahearn; two *s* one *d*. *Educ:* Secondary Sch., Sturgeon Falls; Univ. of Ottawa (BA, LLB). Professional lawyer. MP (L) Nipissing, Ontario, 1972, re-elected 1974, 1979, 1980; defeated Sept. 1984; Parliamentary Sec. to Pres. of Privy Council, 1975; Post Master General, 1976; Solicitor General, 1978; Minister of Supply and Services, and Receiver General, 1980; Minister of Nat. Defence, 1983–84. Lectr in Private Internat. Law, Ottawa Univ., 1986–88; joined Lette McTaggart Blais Martin, 1988. Chm., Ottawa Life Sci. Technol. Pk; Dir, Canada Israel Industrial R & D Foundn. Mem., Security and Intelligence Review Cttee, 1984–91. Chm., Canadian Inst. of Strategic Studies. Mem. Exec. Cttee, Bd of Govs, Univ. of Ottawa, 1988–. *Recreations:* squash, skiing, swimming. *Address:* (office) 10th Floor, 100 Sparks Street, Ottawa, Ontario K1P 5B7, Canada. *T:* (613) 2376430, *Fax:* (613) 5637671.

BLAKE, family name of **Baron Blake.**

BLAKE, Baron *cr* 1971 (Life Peer), of Braydeston, Norfolk; **Robert Norman William Blake,** FBA 1967; JP; Provost of The Queen's College, Oxford, 1968–87, Hon. Fellow, 1987; Pro-Vice-Chancellor, Oxford University, 1971–87; Joint Editor, Dictionary of National Biography, 1980–90; *b* 23 Dec. 1916; *er s* of William Joseph Blake and Norah Lindley Daynes, Brundall, Norfolk; *m* 1953, Patricia Mary (*d* 1995), *e d* of Thomas Richard Waters, Great Plumstead, Norfolk; three *d*. *Educ:* King Edward VI Grammar Sch., Norwich; Magdalen Coll., Oxford (MA), 1st Cl. Final Honour Sch. of Modern Greats, 1938; Eldon Law Scholar, 1938. Served War of 1939–45; Royal Artillery; North African campaign, 1942; POW in Italy, 1942–44; escaped, 1944; despatches, 1944. Student and Tutor in Politics, Christ Church, Oxford, 1947–68; Censor, 1950–55; Senior Proctor, 1959–60; Ford's Lectr in English History for 1967–68; Mem., Hebdomadal Council, 1959–81. Member: Royal Commn on Historical Manuscripts, 1975– (Chm., 1982–89); Bd of Trustees, BM, 1978–88; Bd, Channel 4, 1983–86. Chm., Hansard Soc. Commn on Electoral Reform, 1975–76; Pres., Electoral Reform Soc., 1986–93. Mem. (Conservative) Oxford City Council, 1957–64. Governor of Norwich Sch.; Rhodes Trustee, 1971–87 (Chm., 1983–87). Prime Warden, Dyers' Co., 1976–77. High Bailiff of Westminster Abbey and Searcher of the Sanctuary, 1988–89; High Steward of Westminster Abbey, 1989–. Hon. Student, Christ Church, Oxford, 1977; Hon. Fellow, Pembroke Coll., Cambridge, 1992. Hon. DLitt: Glasgow, 1972; East Anglia, 1983; Westminster Coll., Fulton, Mo, 1987; Buckingham, 1988. *Publications:* The Private Papers of Douglas Haig, 1952; The Unknown Prime Minister (Life of Andrew Bonar Law), 1955; Disraeli, 1966; The Conservative Party from Peel to Churchill, 1970, 2nd edn, The Conservative Party from Peel to Thatcher, 1985; The Office of Prime Minister, 1975; (ed with John Patten) The Conservative Opportunity, 1976; A History of Rhodesia, 1977; Disraeli's Grand Tour, 1982; (ed) The English World, 1982; The Decline of Power 1915–1964, 1985; (ed jtly) Salisbury: the man and his policies, 1987; (ed) Oxford Illustrated Encyclopaedia, Vol. 4, World History from 1800, 1989; (ed with Roger Louis) Churchill, 1993. *Address:* Riverview House, Brundall, Norfolk NR13 5LA. *T:* Norwich (01603) 712133. *Clubs:* Beefsteak, Brooks's, Pratt's, United Oxford & Cambridge University; Vincent's (Oxford); Norfolk County.

BLAKE, Sir Alfred (Lapthorn), KCVO 1979 (CVO 1975); MC 1945; DL; Director, The Duke of Edinburgh's Award Scheme, 1967–78; Consultant with Blake Lapthorn, Solicitors, Portsmouth and area, since 1985 (Partner, 1949–85, Senior Partner, 1983–85); *b* 6 Oct. 1915; *s* of late Leonard Nicholson Blake and Nora Woodfall Blake (*née* Lapthorn); *m* 1st, 1940, Beatrice Grace Nellthorp (*d* 1967); two *s*; 2nd, 1969, Alison Kelsey Dick, Boston, Mass, USA. *Educ:* Dauntsey's Sch. LLB (London), 1938. Qual. Solicitor and Notary Public, 1938. Royal Marines Officer, 1939–45: Bde Major 2 Commando Bde, 1944; Lieut-Col comdg 45 (RM) Commando and Holding Operational Commando, 1945 (despatches). Mem., Portsmouth CC, 1950–67 (Past Chm., Portsmouth Educn Cttee); Lord Mayor of Portsmouth, 1958–59. Mem., Youth Service Development Coun., 1960–66; Pres., Portsmouth Youth Activities Cttee, 1976–; Patron: Elizabeth Foundn, 1984–; Portsmouth Family Welfare, 1987–. Lay Canon, Portsmouth Cathedral, 1962–72. Hon. Fellow, Portsmouth Polytechnic, 1981. DL Hants, 1991. *Recreation:* golf. *Address:* 1 Kitnocks Cottages, Wickham Road, Curdridge, Southampton SO32 2HG. *T:* Botley (01489) 783660.

BLAKE, Prof. Christopher, CBE 1991; FRSE; Chairman, Glenrothes Development Corporation, since 1987; *b* 28 April 1926; *s* of George Blake and Eliza Blake; *m* 1951, Elizabeth McIntyre; two *s* two *d*. *Educ:* Dollar Academy; St Andrews Univ. MA St Andrews 1950, PhD St Andrews 1965. Served in Royal Navy, 1944–47. Teaching posts, Bowdoin Coll., Maine, and Princeton Univ., 1951–53; Asst, Edinburgh Univ., 1953–55; Stewarts & Lloyds Ltd, 1955–60; Lectr and Sen. Lectr, Univ. of St Andrews, 1960–67; Sen. Lectr and Prof. of Economics, 1967–74, Bonar Prof. of Applied Econs, 1974–88, Univ. of Dundee. Dir, Alliance Trust plc, 1974–94; Chm., William Low & Co. plc, 1985–90 (Dir, 1980–90). Member: Council for Applied Science in Scotland, 1978–86; Royal Commn on Envtl Pollution, 1980–86. Treasurer, RSE, 1986–89. *Publications:* articles in economic and other jls. *Recreation:* golf. *Address:* Westlea, 14 Wardlaw Gardens, St Andrews, Fife KY16 9DW. *T:* St Andrews (01334) 473840. *Clubs:* New (Edinburgh); Royal and Ancient (St Andrews).

BLAKE, Clifford Douglas, AM 1988; PhD; Vice-Chancellor, Charles Sturt University, since 1990; *b* 27 Aug. 1937; *s* of William Oscar Blake and Isobel Florence Blake (*née* Keown). *Educ:* Muswellbrook High Sch.; Univ. of Sydney (BScAgr); Univ. of London (PhD). FAIAS. Lectr and Sen. Lectr in Plant Pathology, Univ. of Sydney, 1963–70; foundation Principal, Riverina College of Advanced Educn, subseq. renamed Riverina-Murray Inst. of Higher Educn, 1971–90. Pres., Aust. Higher Educn Industrial Assoc., 1992–; Mem. Bd of Dirs, Open Learning Agency of Australia Pty, 1993–; Gov., Commonwealth of Learning, 1992–; Chm., Nat. Cttee on Distance Educn, 1994–. *Publication:* (ed) Fundamentals of Modern Agriculture, 1967, 3rd edn 1971. *Recreation:* travel. *Address:* The Chancellery, Charles Sturt University, Bathurst, NSW 2795, Australia. *T:* (63) 332209. *Clubs:* University and Schools (Sydney); Riverine (Wagga Wagga).

BLAKE, David Charles, Eur. Ing, CEng, FIMechE; Managing Director, Vendor Unit, British Rail Board, since 1993; *b* 23 Sept. 1936; *s* of Walter David John Blake and Ellen Charlotte Blake; *m* 1959, Della Victoria Stevenson; two *s*. *Educ:* South East Essex Technical Sch.; South East Essex Technical Coll. Engrg apprentice, Stratford Locomotive Works, 1953–57; Technical Management, BR Eastern Reg., 1957–69; Construction Engr, W Coast Main Line Electrification, 1969–74; Area Maintenance Engineer: Motherwell Scottish Reg., 1974–75; Shields Scottish Reg., 1975–76; Rolling Stock Engr, Scottish Reg., 1976–78; Electrical Engr, E Reg., 1978–80; Chief Mechanical and Electrical Engr, Southern Reg., 1980–82; Director: Manufacturing and Maintenance Policy, BRB, 1983–87; Mech. and Elec. Engrg, BRB, 1987–90; Man. Dir, Kings Cross Projects Gp, BRB, 1990–93. *Recreations:* gardening, hill walking. *Address:* Silverglade House, Oak Avenue, Thakeham Copse, Storrington, West Sussex RH20 3PW. *T:* Storrington (01903) 744671.

BLAKE, Prof. David Leonard; Professor of Music, University of York, since 1976; *b* 2 Sept. 1936; *s* of Leonard Blake and Dorothy Blake; *m* 1960, Rita Muir; two *s* one *d*. *Educ:* Latymer Upper School; Gonville and Caius College, Cambridge (BA 1960, MA 1963); Deutsche Akademie der Künste, Berlin, GDR. School teacher: Ealing Grammar Sch., 1961–62; Northwood Secondary Sch., 1962–63; University of York: Granada Arts Fellow, 1963–64; Lectr in Music, 1964; Sen. Lectr, 1971–76. *Recordings* (own compositions):

Violin concerto: In Praise of Krishna; Variations for Piano; The Almanack. *Publications* include: It's a Small War (musical for schools), 1963; Chamber Symphony, 1981; Lumina (Ezra Pound) (cantata for soprano, baritone, chorus and orch.), 1969; Metamorphoses for large orch., 1978; Nonet for wind, 1979; The Bones of Chuang Tzu (cantata for baritone and piano), 1976; In Praise of Krishna: Bengali lyrics, 1976; String Quartet No 2, 1977; Violin Concerto, 1979; Toussaint (opera), 1977; From the Mattress Grave (song cycle), 1981; Arias for clarinet, 1981; Cassation for wind, 1982; Sonata alla marcia, 1982; Clarinet Quintet, 1983; Rise Dove for bass and orch., 1983; Three choruses (Robert Frost), 1985; Capriccio for seven players, 1988; Fantasia for violin, 1989; The Plumber's Gift (opera), 1989; Mill Music for brass band, 1990; Seasonal Variants, 1992; Cello Concerto, 1992. *Recreations:* conservation (mills etc), political debate. *Address:* Mill Gill, Askrigg, near Leyburn, North Yorks DL8 3HR. *T:* Wensleydale (01969) 650364.

BLAKE, Sir Francis Michael, 3rd Bt *cr* 1907; *b* 11 July 1943; *o s* of Sir F. Edward C. Blake, 2nd Bt and Olive Mary (*d* 1946) *d* of Charles Liddell Simpson; *S* father, 1950; *m* 1968, Joan Ashbridge, *d* of F. C. A. Miller; two *s*. *Educ:* Rugby. *Heir: s* Francis Julian Blake, *b* 17 Feb. 1971. *Address:* The Dower House, Tillmouth Park, Cornhill-on-Tweed, Northumberland TD12 4UR. *T:* Coldstream (01890) 882443.

BLAKE, (Henry) Vincent; marketing consultant, retired; Secretary, Glassfibre Reinforced Cement Association, 1977–86; *b* 7 Dec. 1912; *s* of Arthur Vincent Blake and Alice Mabel (*née* Kerr); *m* 1938, Marie Isobel Todd; one *s*. *Educ:* King Edward's High Sch., Birmingham. Pupil apprentice, Chance Brothers, Lighthouse Engineers, Birmingham, 1931–34; subseq. Asst Sales Manager, 1937 and Sales Manager there, of Austinlite Ltd, 1945; Textile Marketing Manager, Fibreglass Ltd, 1951; Commercial Manager: Glass Yarns and Deeside Fabrics Ltd, 1960; BTR Industries Ltd, Glass and Resin Div., 1962–63, Plastics Group, 1963–66; Gen. Manager, Indulex Engineering Co. Ltd, 1966–71. Mem. Council and Chm., Reinforced Plastics Gp, British Plastics Fedn, 1959. Mem. Council, Royal Yachting Assoc., 1980– (Vice-Chm., Thames Valley Region, 1979–). *Publications:* articles in technical jls on reinforced plastics. *Recreations:* sailing, motoring, reading, and waiting for my wife. *Address:* Little Orchard, Fern Lane, Little Marlow, Bucks SL7 3SD. *T:* Bourne End (016285) 20252. *Clubs:* Datchet Water Sailing (Hon. Life Mem.), Cookham Reach Sailing (Hon. Life Mem.).

BLAKE, Howard David, OBE 1994; FRAM; composer, conductor and pianist; *b* 28 Oct. 1938; *s* of Horace C. Blake and Grace B. Blake (*née* Benson); *m* 1978, Patricia Rayment; one *s* one *d*. FRAM 1989. BFI, 1962–63; EMI recording artist, 1964–66; composed scores for The Avengers, 1967–68; feature film scores, 1969–86, ranging from The Duellists, 1977, to A Month in the Country, 1986 (BFI Anthony Asquith Award); ballet scores, 1976–93; music for RSC, 1984–89; television scores include: The Snowman, 1982; Granpa, 1988; concert works: Benedictus, 1979; Concerto for Clarinet, 1984; Shakespeare Songs, 1987; Festival Mass, 1987; Piano Concerto for Princess of Wales, 1990; Violin Concerto for City of Leeds, 1993; The Land of Counterpane, 1995. Dir, PRS, 1978–87; Founder Mem., Assoc. of Professional Composers, 1980. *Publications:* numerous musical pubns. *Recreations:* reading, walking, swimming. *Address:* Studio Flat 6, 18 Kensington Court Place, W8 5BJ. *T:* 0171–937 1966, *Fax:* 0171–938 1969. *Club:* Groucho.

BLAKE, John Michael; Managing Director, Blake Publishing, since 1991; *b* 6 Nov. 1948; *s* of late Major Edwin Blake, MBE, and of Joyce Blake; *m* 1968, Diane Sutherland Campbell; one *s* two *d*. *Educ:* Westminster City Grammar Sch.; North-West London Polytechnic. Reporter: Hackney Gazette, 1966; Evening Post, Luton, 1969; Fleet Street News Agency, 1970; Columnist: London Evening News, 1971; London Evening Standard, 1980; The Sun, 1982; Asst Editor, Daily Mirror, 1985; Editor, The People, 1988–89; Pres., Mirror Group Newspapers (USA), 1989; Exec. Producer, Sky Television, 1990. *Publications:* Up and Down with The Rolling Stones, 1978; All You Needed Was Love, 1981. *Recreations:* sailing, scuba diving, distance running, travel. *Address:* Blake Publishing Ltd, 3 Bramber Court, Bramber Road, W14 9PB.

BLAKE, Mary Netterville, MA; Headmistress, Manchester High School for Girls, 1975–83; *b* 12 Sept. 1922; *d* of John Netterville Blake and Agnes Barr Blake. *Educ:* Howell's Sch., Denbigh; St Anne's Coll., Oxford (MA). Asst Mistress, The Mount Sch., York, 1945–48; Head of Geography Dept, King's High Sch., Warwick, 1948–56; Associate Gen. Sec., Student Christian Movement in Schools, 1956–60; Head Mistress, Selby Grammar Sch., 1960–75. Pres., Assoc. of Headmistresses, 1976–77; first Pres., Secondary Heads Assoc., 1978. *Address:* 70A Guarlford Road, Malvern, Worcs WR14 3QT. *T:* Malvern (01684) 564359.

BLAKE, Nicholas John Gorrod; QC 1994; barrister; *b* 21 June 1949; *s* of Leslie Gorrod Blake and Jean Margaret (*née* Ballinger); *m* 1986, Clio Whittaker; one *s* two *d* (and one *s* decd). *Educ:* Cranleigh Sch.; Magdalene Coll., Cambridge (BA Hons Hist.); Inns of Court Sch. of Law. Called to the Bar, Middle Temple, 1974; Jun. Counsel in Birmingham Six, Guildford Four, Winchester Three, Judith Ward and Cardiff Three Appeals. Chm., Immigration Lawyers Practitioners Assoc., 1994–. Mem. Cttee, Haldane Soc. of Socialist Lawyers, 1979–87. *Publications:* Police Law and the People, 1974; (jtly) Wigs and Workers, 1980; (jtly) New Nationality Law, 1983; (jtly) Immigration Law and Practice, 1991. *Recreation:* the visual arts. *Address:* 2 Garden Court, Temple, EC4Y 9BL. *T:* 0171–353 1633.

BLAKE, Peter Thomas, CBE 1983; RA 1980 (ARA 1974); RDI 1987; ARCA; painter; *b* 25 June 1932; *s* of Kenneth William Blake; *m* 1963, Jann Haworth (marr. diss. 1982); two *d*; *m* 1987, Chrissy Wilson; one *d*. *Educ:* Gravesend Tech. Coll.; Gravesend Sch. of Art; RCA. Works exhibited: ICA, 1958, 1960; Guggenheim Competition, 1958; Cambridge, 1959; RA, 1960; Musée d'Art Moderne, Paris, 1968; Waddington Galls, 1970, 1972, 1977 and 1990; Stedlijk Mus., Amsterdam, 1973; Kunstverein, Hamburg, 1973; Gemeentemuseum, Arnhem, 1974; Palais des Beaux-Arts, Brussels, 1974; Galleria Documenta, Turin, 1982; retrospective exhibn, Tate Gall., 1983, Gal. Claude Bernard, Paris, 1984, Nishimura Gall., Tokyo, 1988; works in public collections: Trinity Coll., Cambridge; Carlisle City Gall.; Tate Gall.; Arts Council of GB; Mus. of Modern Art, NY; V & A Mus.; Mus. Boymans-van Beuningen, Rotterdam; Calouste Gulbenkian Foundn, London; RCA; Whitworth Art Gall., Univ. of Manchester; Baltimore Mus. of Art, Md. Third Associate Artist, Nat. Gall., 1994. *Publications:* illustrations for: Oxford Illustrated Old Testament, 1968; Roger McGough, Summer with Monica, 1978; cover illustration, Arden Shakespeare: Othello, 1980; Anthony and Cleopatra, 1980; Timon of Athens, 1980; contribs to: Times Educnl Supp.; Ark; Graphis 70; World of Art; Architectural Rev.; House and Garden; Painter and Sculptor. *Recreations:* sculpture, wining and dining, going to rock and roll concerts, boxing and wrestling matches; living well is the best revenge. *Address:* c/o Waddington Galleries Ltd, 11 Cork Street, W1X 2LT.

BLAKE, Quentin Saxby, OBE 1988; RDI 1981; FCSD; freelance artist and illustrator, since 1957; Visiting Professor, Royal College of Art, since 1989; *b* 16 Dec. 1932; *s* of William Blake and Evelyn Blake. *Educ:* Downing Coll., Cambridge (MA). Royal College of Art: Tutor, 1965–77; Head, Dept of Illustration, 1978–86; Vis. Tutor, 1986–89; Sen. Fellow, 1988. Exhibns of watercolour drawings, Workshop Gallery: Invitation to the Dance, 1972; Runners and Riders, 1973; Creature Comforts, 1974; Water Music, 1976; Retrospective exhibn of illustration work, Nat. Theatre, 1984; Chris Beetles Gall., 1993. *Publications:* (author and illustrator) for children: Patrick, 1968; Jack and Nancy, 1969; Angelo, 1970; Snuff, 1973; The Adventures of Lester, 1977; Mr Magnolia, 1980 (Fedn of Children's Bk Gps Award; Kate Greenaway Medal, 1981); Quentin Blake's Nursery Rhyme Book, 1983; The Story of the Dancing Frog, 1984; Mrs Armitage on Wheels, 1987; Quentin Blake's ABC, 1989; All Join In, 1990; Cockatoos, 1991; Simpkin, 1993; Clown, 1995; (ed and illus.) The Quentin Blake Book of Nonsense Verse, 1994; (ed and illus.) Custard and Company, by Ogden Nash, 1979; (illustrator) for children: Russell Hoban: How Tom Beat Captain Najork and his Hired Sportsmen, 1974 (Whitbread Lit. Award, 1975; Hans Andersen Honour Book, 1975); A Near Thing for Captain Najork, 1976; The Rain Door, 1986; Hilaire Belloc: Algernon and Other Cautionary Tales, 1991; Roald Dahl: The Enormous Crocodile, 1978; The Twits, 1980; George's Marvellous Medicine, 1981; Revolting Rhymes, 1982; The BFG, 1982; The Witches, 1983; Dirty Beasts, 1984; The Giraffe and the Pelly and Me, 1985; Matilda, 1988; Rhyme Stew, 1989; Esio Trot, 1990; Dahl Diary, 1991; My Year, 1993; Danny Champion of the World, 1994; Roald Dahl's Revolting Recipes, 1994; Charlie and the Chocolate Factory, 1995; Charlie and the Great Glass Elevator, 1995; James and the Giant Peach, 1995; The Magic Finger, 1995; John Yeoman: Featherbrains, 1993; The Singing Tortoise, 1993; The Family Album; The Do-It-Yourself House that Jack Built, 1994; Joan Aiken, The Winter Sleepwalker, 1994; books by Clement Freud, Sid Fleischman, Michael Rosen, Sylvia Plath, Margaret Mahy and Dr Seuss; (illustrator) for adults: Aristophanes, The Birds, 1971; Lewis Caroll, The Hunting of the Snark, 1976; Stella Gibbons, Cold Comfort Farm, 1977; Evelyn Waugh, Black Mischief, 1980, Scoop, 1981; George Orwell, Animal Farm, 1984; Cyrano de Bergerac, Voyages to the Sun and Moon, 1991. *Address:* 30 Bramham Gardens, SW5 0HF. *T:* 0171–373 7464.

BLAKE, Sir Richard; *see* Blake, Sir T. R. V.

BLAKE, Richard Frederick William; Editor, Whitaker's Almanack, 1981–86; *b* 9 April 1948; *s* of late Frederick William Blake and Doris Margaret Blake; *m* 1973, Christine Vaughan; one *d*. *Educ:* Archbishop Tenison's Grammar School. Joined J. Whitaker & Sons, Ltd (Whitaker's Almanack Dept), 1966; apptd Asst Editor of Whitaker's Almanack, 1974. *Recreations:* music, sport. *Address:* 118 Warren Drive, Elm Park, Hornchurch, Essex RM12 4QX.

BLAKE, Sir (Thomas) Richard (Valentine), 17th Bt *cr* 1622, of Menlough; *b* 7 Jan. 1942; *s* of Sir Ulick Temple Blake, 16th Bt, and late Elizabeth Gordon (she *m* 1965, Vice-Adm. E. Longley-Cook, CB, CBE, DSO); *S* father, 1963; *m* 1st, 1976, Mrs Jacqueline Hankey; 2nd, 1982, Bertice Reading (marr. diss. 1986; she *d* 1991); 3rd, 1991, Wendy, *widow* of Anthony Ronald Roberts. *Educ:* Bradfield Coll., Berks. Member, Standing Council of Baronets. *Recreations:* classic cars, horses, gardening. *Heir: kinsman* Anthony Telio Bruce Blake [*b* 5 May 1951; *m* 1988, Geraldine, *d* of Cecil Shnaps]. *Address:* Old Janes, River, near Petworth, West Sussex GU28 9AY. *Clubs:* Cowdray Park Polo, Gordon-Keeble Owners, Rolls-Royce Enthusiasts, Goodwood Racecourse.

BLAKE, Vincent; *see* Blake, H. V.

BLAKE-JAMES, Linda Elizabeth; *see* Sullivan, L. E.

BLAKEMORE, Prof. Colin (Brian), FRS 1992; Waynflete Professor of Physiology, Oxford University, since 1979; Fellow of Magdalen College, since 1979; *b* 1 June 1944; *s* of Cedric Norman Blakemore and Beryl Ann Smith; *m* 1965, Andrée Elizabeth Washbourne; three *d*. *Educ:* King Henry VIII Sch., Coventry; Corpus Christi Coll., Cambridge (Smyth Scholar; BA 1965; MA 1969; ScD 1988; Hon. Fellow, 1994); Univ. of Calif, Berkeley (PhD 1968); Magdalen Coll., Oxford (MA 1979; DSc 1989). Harkness Fellow, Neurosensory Lab., Univ. of Calif, Berkeley, 1965–68; Cambridge University: Fellow and Dir of Medical Studies, Downing Coll., 1971–79; Univ. Demonstr in Physiol., 1968–72; Univ. Lectr in Physiol., 1972–79; Leverhulme Fellow, 1974–75. Dir, McDonnell-Pew Centre for Cognitive Neuroscience, Oxford, 1989–; Associate Dir, MRC Oxford Res. Centre in Brain and Behaviour, 1991–. Royal Soc. Locke Res. Fellow, 1976–79. Chm., Neurobiology and Mental Health Bd Grants Cttee, MRC, 1977–79. Vis. Professor: NY Univ., 1970; MIT, 1971; Royal Soc. Study Visit, Keio Univ., Tokyo, 1974; Lethaby Prof., RCA, 1978; Storer Vis. Lectr, Univ. of Calif, Davis, 1980; Vis. Scientist, Salk Inst., 1982, 1983, 1992; Macallum Vis. Lectr, Univ. of Toronto, 1984; McLaughlin Vis. Prof., McMaster Univ., Ont, 1992. Vice-Pres., BAAS, 1990– (Pres., Gen. Section, 1989); Hon. Pres., World Cultural Council, 1983–. Founder and Mem., Bd of Govs, Internat. Brain Injury Assoc. (Nat. Head Injury Foundn Inc., Washington), 1993–; Member: Central Council, Internat. Brain Res. Org., 1973–92; BBC Science Consultative Group, 1975–79; British Nat. Cttee for Physiol. Scis, 1988–90; Professional Adv. Cttee, Schizophrenia: A National Emergency, 1989–. Hon. Associate, Rationalist Press Assoc., 1986–. BBC Reith Lectr, 1976; Presenter, The Mind Machine, BBC2 series, 1988; Lectures: Aubrey Lewis, Inst. of Psych., 1979; Lord Charnwood, Amer. Acad. of Optometry, 1980; Vickers, Neonatal Soc., 1981; Kershman, Eastern Assoc. of Electroencephalographers, NY, 1981; Harveian, Harveian Soc. of London, 1982; Christmas, Royal Instn, 1982; Earl Grey Meml, Newcastle Univ., 1982; George Frederic Still, BPA, 1983; Edridge-Green, RCS, 1984; Cyril Leslie Oakley Meml, Leeds Univ., 1984; Plenary, European Neuroscience Assoc., 1984; Mac Keith Meml, Brit. Paediatric Neurology Assoc., 1985; Faculty of Science, RHC, 1985; Halliburton, KCL, 1986; Cairns Meml, Cambridge Univ., 1986; Bertram Louis Abrahams, RCP, 1986; Norman McAlister Gregg (also Medal), RACO, 1988; Dietrich Bodenstein, Univ. of Va, 1989; Charnock Bradley, Univ. of Edinburgh, 1989; Doyne, Oxford Ophthalmol Congress, 1989 (also Medal); G. L. Brown, Physiol Soc., 1990; Sir Douglas Robb, Univ. of Auckland, 1991; Schs' Christmas, RSE, 1992; James Law, Cornell, 1994; Royal Soc., ASE, 1995. Foreign Mem., Royal Netherlands Acad. of Arts and Scis, 1993. Hon. DSc: Aston, 1992; Salford, 1994. Robert Bing Prize, Swiss Acad. of Med. Sciences, 1975; Richardson Cross Medal, S Western Opthalmol Soc., 1978; Copeman Medal, Corpus Christi Coll., Cambridge, 1976; Man of the Year, Royal Assoc. for Disability and Rehabilitation, 1978; Phi Beta Kappa Award in Sci., 1978; John Locke Medal, Apothecaries' Soc., 1983; Prix du Docteur Robert Netter, Acad. Nat. de Médecine, Paris, 1984; Cairns Medal, Cairns Meml Fund, 1986; Michael Faraday Award, Royal Soc., 1989; John P. McGovern Science and Soc. Medal, Sigma XI Scientific Soc., USA, 1990; Montgomery Medal, RCSI and Irish Ophthalmol Soc., 1991; Osler Medal, RCP, 1993; Ellison-Cliffe Medal, RSM, 1993; Annual Review Prize, Physiol Soc., 1994; Charles F. Prentice Award, Amer. Acad. of Optometry, 1994. *Publications:* Handbook of Psychobiology (with M. S. Gazzaniga), 1975; Mechanics of the Mind, 1977; (with S. A. Greenfield) Mindwaves, 1987; The Mind Machine, 1988, 2nd edn 1994; (with H. B. Barlow and M. Weston-Smith) Images and Understanding, 1990; Vision: coding and efficiency, 1990; res. reports in Jl of Physiol., Jl of Neuroscience, Nature, etc. *Recreation:* wasting time. *Address:* University Laboratory of Physiology, Parks Road, Oxford OX1 3PT. *Club:* Chelsea Arts (Hon. Mem.).

BLAKEMORE, Michael Howell; freelance director; *b* Sydney, NSW, 18 June 1928; *s* of late Conrad Blakemore and Una Mary Blakemore (*née* Litchfield); *m* 1st, 1960, Shirley (*née* Bush); one *s*; 2nd, 1986, Tanya McCallin; two *d*. *Educ:* The King's Sch., NSW; Sydney Univ.; Royal Academy of Dramatic Art. Actor with Birmingham Rep. Theatre, Shakespeare Memorial Theatre, etc, 1952–66; Co-dir, Glasgow Citizens Theatre (1st prod., The Investigation), 1966–68; Associate Artistic Dir, Nat. Theatre, 1971–76. Dir, Players, NY, 1978. Resident Dir, Lyric Theatre, Hammersmith, 1980. Best Dir, London Critics, 1972. *Productions include:* A Day in the Death of Joe Egg, Comedy, 1967, Broadway 1968; Arturo Ui, Saville, 1969, Israel, 1969; Forget-me-not Lane, Apollo, 1971; Design for Living, Phoenix, 1973; Knuckle, Comedy, 1974; Separate Tables, Apollo, 1976; Privates on Parade, Aldwych (RSC), transf. Piccadilly, 1977; Candida, Albery, 1977; All My Sons, Wyndam's, 1981; Benefactors, Vaudeville, 1984, NY, 1986; Made in Bangkok, Aldwych, 1986; Lettice and Lovage, Globe, 1987, NY, 1990; Uncle Vanya, Vaudeville, 1988; City of Angels, Broadway, 1989, Prince of Wales Th., 1993; Tosca, WNO, 1992; Here, Donmar Warehouse, 1993; The Sisters Rosensweig, Old Vic, 1994; *National Theatre:* The National Health, 1969; Long Day's Journey Into Night, 1971; The Front Page, Macbeth, 1972; The Cherry Orchard, 1973; Plunder, 1976; After the Fall, 1990; *Lyric Theatre, Hammersmith:* Make and Break, 1980; Travelling North, 1980; The Wild Duck, 1980; Noises off, 1982 (transf. to Savoy, 1982, NY, 1983 (Drama Desk Award, NY, 1983–84)); *foreign productions include:* The White Devil, Minneapolis, 1976; Hay Fever, 1976, The Seagull, 1979, Aarhus; Mourning Becomes Electra, Melbourne, 1980; Death Defying Acts, NY, 1995. *Films:* A Personal History of the Australian Surf, 1981; Privates on Parade, 1983; Country Life, 1995. *Publication:* Next Season, 1969 (novel). *Recreation:* surfing. *Address:* 18 Upper Park Road, NW3 2UP. *T:* 0171–483 2575, *Fax:* 0171–483 2476.

BLAKENEY, Hon. Allan Emrys, OC 1992; PC (Canada) 1982; Professor of Public Law, University of Saskatchewan, Saskatoon, since 1990; *b* Bridgewater, NS, 7 Sept. 1925; *m* 1st, 1950, Mary Elizabeth (Molly) Schwartz (*d* 1957), Halifax, NS; one *s* one *d*; 2nd, 1959, Anne Gorham, Halifax; one *s* one *d*. *Educ:* Dalhousie Univ. (BA, LLB); Queen's Coll., Oxford (MA). Univ. Medal for Achievement in Coll. of Law, Dalhousie; Rhodes Schol. Sec. and Legal Adviser, Saskatchewan Crown Corps, 1950; Chm., Saskatchewan Securities Commn, 1955–58; private law practice, 1958–60 and 1964–70. MLA, Saskatchewan, 1960–88; formerly Minister of Educn, Provincial Treas. and Health Minister; Chm., Wascana Centre Authority, 1962–64; Opposition Financial Critic, 1964–70; Dep. Leader, 1967–70; Federal New Democratic Party President, 1969–71; Saskatchewan NDP Leader and Leader of Opposition, 1970; Premier, 1971–82; Leader of Opposition, Sask, 1982–87. Prof. of Public Law, Osgoode Hall Law Sch., York Univ., Toronto, 1988–90. Hon. DCL Mount Allison; Hon. LLD: Dalhousie; York; Regina. *Recreations:* reading, swimming, formerly ice hockey and badminton. *Address:* 1752 Prince of Wales Avenue, Saskatoon, Sask S7K 3E5, Canada; College of Law, University of Saskatchewan, Saskatoon, Sask S7N 0W0.

BLAKENHAM, 2nd Viscount *cr* 1963, of Little Blakenham; **Michael John Hare;** Chairman, Pearson plc, since 1983; *b* 25 Jan. 1938; *s* of 1st Viscount Blakenham, PC, OBE, VMH, and Hon. Beryl Nancy Pearson (*d* 1994), *d* of 2nd Viscount Cowdray; *S* father, 1982; *m* 1965, Marcia Persephone, *d* of late Hon. Alan Hare, MC; one *s* two *d*. *Educ:* Eton College; Harvard Univ. (AB Econ.). National Service, 1956–57. English Electric, 1958; Harvard, 1959–61; Lazard Brothers, 1961–63; Standard Industrial Group, 1963–71; Royal Doulton, 1972–77; Pearson, 1977– (Man. Dir, 1978–83). Chairman: The Financial Times, 1983–93; MEPC, 1993– (Dir, 1990–); Partner, Lazard Partners, 1984–; Director: Lazard Bros, 1975–; Sotheby's Holdings Inc., 1987–; UK-Japan 2000 Group, 1990–; Mem., Internat. Adv. Bd, Lafarge Coppée, 1979–. Member, House of Lords Select Committee: on Science and Technol., 1985–88; on Sustainable Develt, 1994–95. Mem., Nature Conservancy Council, 1986–90; Pres., Sussex Wildlife Trust (formerly Sussex Trust for Nature Conservation), 1983–; Chm., RSPB, 1981–86, Vice-Pres., 1986–; Trustee, Royal Botanic Gardens, Kew, 1991–. *Address:* 3 Burlington Gardens, W1X 1LE. *T:* 0171–411 2000.

BLAKER, family name of **Baron Blaker.**

BLAKER, Baron *cr* 1994 (Life Peer), of Blackpool in the County of Lancashire, and of Lindfield in the County of West Sussex; **Peter Allan Renshaw Blaker,** KCMG 1983; PC 1983; MA; *b* Hong Kong, 4 Oct. 1922; *s* of late Cedric Blaker, CBE, MC; *m* 1953, Jennifer, *d* of late Sir Pierson Dixon, GCMG, CB; one *s* two *d*. *Educ:* Shrewsbury; Trinity Coll., Toronto (BA, 1st class, Classics); New Coll., Oxford (MA). Served 1942–46: Argyll and Sutherland Highlanders of Canada (Capt., wounded). Admitted a Solicitor, 1948. New Coll., Oxford, 1949–52; 1st Class, Jurisprudence, Pass degree in PPE. Pres. Oxford Union. Called to Bar, Lincoln's Inn, 1952. Admitted to HM Foreign Service, 1953; HM Embassy, Phnom Penh, 1955–57; UK High Commn, Ottawa, 1957–60; FO, 1960–62; Private Sec. to Minister of State for Foreign Affairs, 1962–64. Attended Disarmament Conf., Geneva; UN Gen. Assembly, 1962 and 1963; signing of Nuclear Test Ban Treaty, Moscow, 1963. MP (C) Blackpool South, 1964–92; an Opposition Whip, 1966–67; PPS to Chancellor of Exchequer, 1970–72; Parliamentary Under-Secretary of State: (Army), MoD, 1972–74; FCO, 1974; Minister of State: FCO, 1979–81; for the Armed Forces, MoD, 1981–83. Joint Secretary: Conservative Parly Foreign Affairs Cttee, 1965–66; Trade Cttee, 1967–70; Exec. Cttee of 1922 Cttee, 1967–70; Vice-Chm., All-Party Tourism Cttee, 1974–79; Member: Select Cttee on Conduct of Members, 1976–77; Public Accounts Commn, 1987–92; Chairman: Hong Kong Parly Gp, 1970–72, 1983–92; Cons. For. and Commonwealth Affairs Cttee, 1983–92 (Vice-Chm., 1974–79); Mem. Exec. Cttee, British-American Parly Gp, 1975–79; Hon. Sec., Franco-British Parly Relations Cttee, 1975–79. Chm., Bd, Royal Ordnance Factories, 1972–74; Chm. Governors, Welbeck Coll., 1972–74; Mem. Council: Chatham House, 1977–79, 1986–90; Council for Arms Control, 1983–; Freedom Assoc., 1984–; Vice-Chm., Peace Through NATO, 1983–93; Vice-Pres., Cons. Foreign and Commonwealth Council, 1983–; Mem. Council, Britain-Russia Centre (formerly GB-USSR Assoc.), 1974–79, and 1992– (Vice-Chm., 1983–92); Governor, Atlantic Inst., 1978–79; Trustee, Inst. for Negotiation and Conciliation, 1984–92. Chm., Maclean Hunter Cablevision Ltd, 1989–94; company director; farmer. *Publications:* Coping with the Soviet Union, 1977; Small is Dangerous: micro states in a macro world, 1984. *Recreations:* sailing, opera, shooting. *Address:* House of Lords, SW1A 0PW. *Clubs:* Garrick, Royal Automobile.

BLAKER, George Blaker, CMG 1963; Under-Secretary, HM Treasury, 1955–63, and Department of Education and Science, 1963–71 retired; *b* Simla, India, 30 Sept. 1912; *m* 1938, Richenda Dorothy Buxton (*d* 1987); one *d*. *Educ:* Eton; Trinity Coll., Cambridge. Private Sec. to Ministers of State in the Middle East, 1941–43; Cabinet Office, 1943; Private Sec. to Sec. of War Cabinet, 1944; Principal Private Sec. to Minister of Production and Presidents of the Board of Trade, 1945–47; accompanied Cabinet Mission to India, 1946; Sec. of UK Trade Mission to China, 1946; HM Treasury, 1947; UK Treasury Representative in India, Ceylon and Burma, 1957–63. President: Surrey Trust for Nature Conservation, 1969–80; Scientific and Medical Network, 1986– (Hon. Sec., 1973–86). Gold Medal, Royal Soc. for the Protection of Birds, 1934. *Address:* Lake House, Ockley, Surrey RH5 5NS.

BLAKER, Sir John, 3rd Bt *cr* 1919; *b* 22 March 1935; *s* of Sir Reginald Blaker, 2nd Bt, TD, and of Sheila Kellas, *d* of Dr Alexander Cran; *S* father, 1975; *m* 1st, 1960, Catherine Ann (marr. diss. 1965), *d* of late F. J. Thorold; 2nd, 1968, Elizabeth Katherine, *d* of late Col John Tinsley Russell, DSO. *Address:* Stantons Farm, East Chiltington, near Lewes, East Sussex BN7 3BB.

BLAKEY, David Cecil, QPM 1993; Chief Constable, West Mercia Constabulary, since 1991; *b* 1943; *s* of Cecil and Elsie Jane Blakey; *m* 1966, Wendy Margaret Cartwright; one *s* one *d*. *Educ:* Jarrow Grammar Sch.; Univ. of Newcastle upon Tyne (MBA). VSO, Sarawak, 1962; Constable, Durham Constabulary, 1963; Police National Computer, 1972–76; Supt, Durham, 1979; Chief Supt, Northumbria, 1984; Asst Chief Constable, West Mercia, 1986; RCDS, 1989; Deputy Chief Constable: Leics, 1989–90; West Mercia, 1990–91. *Recreations:* books, history, walking the dog. *Address:* Police HQ, PO Box 55, Hindlip Hall, Worcester WR3 8SP. *T:* Worcester (01905) 723000.

BLAKISTON, Sir Ferguson Arthur James, 9th Bt *cr* 1763; entrepreneur; *b* 19 Feb. 1963; *er s* of Sir Arthur Norman Hunter Blakiston, 8th Bt, and Mary Ferguson (*d* 1982), *d* of late Alfred Ernest Gillingham, Cave, S Canterbury, NZ; *S* father, 1977; *m* 1993, Linda Jane, *d* of late Robert John Key, Queenstown, NZ. *Educ:* Lincoln Coll., NZ (Diploma in Agriculture 1983); Auckland Inst. of Technology (Cert. in Marketing, 1993). *Heir: b* Norman John Balfour Blakiston, Executive Officer, *b* 7 April 1964. *Address:* 28 McKenzie Street, Geraldine, New Zealand.

BLAKSTAD, Michael Björn; Chief Executive, Workhouse Ltd, since 1984; Director, TEAM plc, since 1991; *b* 18 April 1940; *s* of late Clifford and Alice Blakstad; *m* 1965, Patricia Marilyn Wotherspoon; one *s* twin *d*. *Educ:* Ampleforth Coll.; Oriel Coll., Oxford (MA Lit. Hum.). General trainee, BBC, 1962–68; Producer, Yorkshire Television, 1968–71; freelance TV producer, 1971–74; Programme Editor, BBC, 1974–80; Dir of Programmes, TV South, 1980–84. Founder and Managing Director, Blackrod, 1980 (Chm., 1981–84); Chairman and Chief Executive: Workhouse Productions, 1984–88; Chrysalis Television Ltd, 1988–90; Chairman: Filmscreen Internat. Ltd, 1984–86; Friday Productions, 1984–88; Blackrod Interactive Services, 1988–90; Jt Chief Exec., Videodisc Co., 1984–88; Dir, Chrysalis Gp. Director: IPPA, 1986–90; Internat. Video Communications Assoc., 1988–90; Winchester Theatre Royal, 1988– (Chm., 1990–). Awards include: Radio Industries Club, 1975, 1977, 1979; RTS, 1976; BAFTA/Shell Prize, 1976; BIM/John Player, 1976; Nyon, 1978. Hon. MSc Salford, 1983; FRSA; MRI. *Publications:* The Risk Business, 1979; Tomorrow's World looks to the Eighties, 1979. *Recreations:* golf, writing. *Address:* The Tudor House, Workhouse Lane, East Meon, Hants GU32 1PD. *Club:* Reform.

BLAMEY, Norman Charles, RA 1975 (ARA 1970); Senior Lecturer, Chelsea School of Art, London, 1963–79; *b* 16 Dec. 1914; *s* of Charles H. Blamey and Ada Blamey (*née* Beacham); *m* 1948, Margaret (*née* Kelly); one *s*. *Educ:* Holloway Sch., London; Sch. of Art, The Polytechnic, Regent Street, London. ROI 1952; Hon. ROI 1974. Exhibited at: RA, RHA, ROI, RBA, NEAC, and provincial galleries; retrospective exhibn, Norwich Gall., Victoria Art Gall., Bath, and Fine Art Soc., London, 1992; *mural decorations in:* Anglican Church of St Luke, Leagrave, Beds, 1956; Lutheran Church of St Andrew, Ruislip Manor, Middx, 1964; *works in permanent collections:* Municipal Gall., Port Elizabeth, S Africa; Beaverbrook Gall., Fredericton, NB; Beecroft Art Gall., Southend-on-Sea; Towner Art Gall., Eastbourne; Preston Art Gall.; Pennsylvania State Univ. Mus of Art; La Salle Coll., Pa; V & A Museum; Tate Gall.; Chantry Bequest purchase, 1972, 1985; Govt Art Collection; Southampton Art Gall.; *portraits include:* Mrs Alison Munro; Dr Harry Pitt; Rev. Dennis Nineham; Sir Cyril Clarke; Prof. Graham Higman; Rt Hon. Bernard Weatherill, Speaker of H of C; Sir Alec Merrison, FRS; William Golding; Sir William Rees-Mogg; Sir Christopher Ball; George Richardson, Warden of Keble Coll., Oxford. Works in private collections in UK and USA. RA Summer Exhibitions: Rowney Bicentenary Award, 1983, Charles Wollaston Award, 1984. *Recreation:* walking. *Address:* 39 Lyncroft Gardens, NW6 1LB. *T:* 0171–435 9250.

BLAMIRE, Roger Victor; veterinary consultant; Director of Veterinary Field Services, Ministry of Agriculture, Fisheries and Food, 1979–83; *b* 9 July 1923; *s* of Thomas Victor Blamire and Anetta Elizabeth (*née* Lawson); *m* 1947, Catherine Maisie Ellis Davidson; two *d*. *Educ:* Kendal Sch.; Royal (Dick) Veterinary Coll., Edinburgh. MRCVS, DVSM. RAVC, 1945–48 (Captain); served India, Burma and Malaya. MAF, 1949; Asst Vet. Officer, City of London, 1949; Dep. Chief Advr on Meat Inspection, MOF, 1952; Dep. Dir, Vet. Field Services, MAFF, 1968. Hon. FRSH, 1979. *Recreations:* walking, gardening, listening to music. *Address:* 5 Atbara Road, Teddington, Middx TW11 9PA. *T:* 0181–943 4225.

BLAMIRE-BROWN, John, DL; County Clerk and Chief Executive, Staffordshire County Council, 1973–78; *b* 16 April 1915; *s* of Rev. F. J. Blamire Brown, MA; *m* 1945, Joyce Olivia Pearson; two *s*. *Educ:* Cheam Sch.; St Edmund's Sch., Canterbury. Solicitor 1937. Served War of 1939–45, Royal Marines (Captain). Asst Solicitor, Wednesbury, 1937; West Bromwich, 1946; Staffs CC, 1948; Deputy Clerk of County Council and of Peace, 1962; Clerk, Staffs CC, 1972; Clerk to Lieutenancy, 1972–78; Sec., Staffs Probation and After Care Cttee; Hon. Sec., W Mids Planning Authorities Conf., 1972–78. Dep. Chm., Manpower Services Commn Area Board, Staffs, Salop, W Midlands (North), 1978–83. Mem. Council, Beth Johnson Foundn, 1978–83; Governor, Newcastle-under-Lyme Endowed Schools, 1978–83; Chm., St Giles Hospice Ltd, 1979–84. Pres., Codsall Civic Soc., 1991–. DL Staffs, 1974. *Recreations:* local history, gardening, painting. *Address:* The Mount, Codsall Wood, Wolverhampton, West Midlands WV8 1QS. *T:* Wolverhampton (01902) 842044.

BLANC, Christian; President, Air France, since 1993; *b* Talence, Gironde, 17 May 1943; *s* of Marcel Blanc and Encarna (*née* Miranda); *m* 1973, Asa Birgitta Hagglund; two *d*. *Educ:* Institut d'Etudes Politiques, Bordeaux (Dip.). Asst Dir, Sopexa Scandinave, 1969; Dep. to Controller, Mission for Territorial Equipment, 1970–74; Hd of Bureau, Sec. of State for Youth and Sports, 1974–76; Asst Gen. Delegate, Tech. Interministerial Agency for Leisure and Fresh Air, 1976–80; Dir of Cabinet, Commn of EC, Brussels, 1981–83; Prefect: Commune of Haute-Pyrénées, 1983–84; Govt of New Caledonia, 1985; Seine and Marne, 1985–89; without portfolio, 1989–. Pres. and Dir-Gen., Régie Autonome des Transports Parisiens, 1989–92. Chevalier Légion d'Honneur (France), 1988; Officier, Ordre National du Merite (France), 1994. *Publication:* Le Lièvre et la Tortue, 1994. *Address:* Air France, 1 Square Max Hymans, 75757 Paris Cedex 15, France.

BLANC, Raymond René; chef; Patron and Chairman, Blanc Restaurants Ltd, since 1984; *b* 19 Nov. 1949; *m* 1st (marr. diss.); two *s*; 2nd, 1990, Katalin Szoke (separated). *Educ:* CEG de Valdahon; Lycée technique de horlogerie, Besançon. Chef de rang, 1971; Manager and chef de cuisine, 1976; proprietor and chef, Les Quat' Saisons, Summertown, 1977; Dir and Chm., Maison Blanc, 1978–88; proprietor, Le Petit Blanc, 1984–88; Chef/patron and Chairman, Le Manoir aux Quat' Saisons, 1984–. TV series, Blanc Mange, 1994. Academicien Mentor, Academie Culinaire de France. Master Chef Great Britain. Personalité de l'année, 1990. Commandeur de l'Assoc. Internat. des Maîtres Conseils en Gastronomie Française. *Publications:* Recipes from Le Manoir aux Quat' Saisons, 1988; Cooking for Friends, 1991; Blanc Mange, 1994. *Recreations:* reading, tennis, riding, classical and rock music. *Address:* Le Manoir aux Quat' Saisons, Church Road, Great Milton, Oxford OX44 7PD.

BLANCH, Mrs Lesley, (Madame Gary); FRSL; author; *b* 1907; *m* 2nd, 1945, Romain Kacew (Romain Gary) (marr. diss. 1962; he *d* 1980). *Educ:* by reading, and listening to conversation of elders and betters. FRSL 1969. *Publications:* The Wilder Shores of Love (biog.), 1954; Round the World in Eighty Dishes (cookery), 1956; The Game of Hearts (biog.), 1956; The Sabres of Paradise (biog.), 1960; Under a Lilac Bleeding Star (travels), 1963; The Nine Tiger Man (fict.), 1965; Journey into the Mind's Eye (autobiog.), 1968; Pavilions of the Heart (biog.), 1974; Pierre Loti: portrait of an escapist (biog.), 1983; From Wilder Shores: the tables of my travels (travel/autobiog.), 1989. *Recreations:* travel, opera, acquiring useless objects, animal welfare, gardening. *Address:* Roquebrune Village, 06190 Roquebrune-Cap-Martin, France. *Club:* Taharir (formerly Mahommed Ali) (Cairo).

BLANCHARD, Francis; Officier de la Légion d'Honneur; Member, French Economic and Social Council, since 1989; *b* Paris, 21 July 1916; *m* 1940, Marie-Claire Boué; two *s*. *Educ:* Univ. of Paris. French Home Office; Internat. Organisation for Refugees, Geneva, 1947–51; Internat. Labour Office, Geneva, 1951–89: Asst Dir-Gen., 1956–68; Dep. Dir-Gen., 1968–74; Dir-Gen., 1974–89. Dr *hc* Brussels, Cairo and Manila. *Recreations:* ski-ing, hunting, riding. *Address:* Prébailly, 01170 Gex, France. *T:* 50415170.

BLANCO WHITE, Thomas Anthony, QC 1969; *b* 19 Jan. 1915; *s* of late G. R. Blanco White, QC, and Amber Blanco White, OBE; *m* 1950, Anne Katherine Ironside-Smith; two *s* one *d*. *Educ:* Gresham's Sch.; Trinity Coll., Cambridge. Called to Bar, Lincoln's Inn, 1937, Bencher 1977, retired 1993. Served RAFVR, 1940–46. *Publications:* Patents for Inventions, 1950, 1955, 1962, 1974, 1983, etc. *Recreations:* gardening, photography. *Address:* 72 South Hill Park, NW3 2SN.

BLAND, Sir (Francis) Christopher (Buchan), Kt 1993; Chairman: Life Sciences International (formerly Phicom) plc, since 1987; NFC, since 1994; *b* 29 May 1938; *e s* of James Franklin MacMahon Bland and Jess Buchan Bland (*née* Brodie); *m* 1981, Jennifer Mary, Viscountess Enfield, *er d* of late Rt Hon. W. M. May, PC, FCA, MP, and of Mrs May, Mertoun Hall, Holywood, Co. Down; one *s* and two step *s* two step *d*. *Educ:* Sedbergh; The Queen's Coll., Oxford (Hastings Exhibnr). 2nd Lieut, 5th Royal Inniskilling Dragoon Guards, 1956–58; Lieut, North Irish Horse (TA), 1958–69. Dir, NI Finance Corp., 1972–76; Dep. Chm., IBA, 1972–80; Chairman: Sir Joseph Causton & Sons, 1977–85; LWT (Hldgs), 1984–94; Century Hutchinson Group, 1984–89; Director: Nat. Provident Instn, 1978–88; Storehouse plc, 1988–93. Mem. GLC, for Lewisham, 1967–70; Chm., ILEA Schs Sub-Cttee, 1970; Mem. Burnham Cttee, 1970; Chm., Bow Group, 1969–70; Editor, Crossbow, 1971–72; Mem., Prime Minister's Adv. Panel on Citizen's Charter, 1991–94. Chairman: NHS Rev. Gp on Nat. Trng Council and Nat. Staff Cttees, 1982; Hammersmith and Queen Charlotte's Hosps (formerly Hammersmith) SHA, 1982–94; Hammersmith Hosps NHS Trust, 1994–. Governor, Prendergast Girls Grammar Sch. and Woolwich Polytechnic, 1968–70; Mem. Council: RPMS, 1982–; St Mary's Med Sch., 1984–88. *Publications:* Bow Group pamphlet on Commonwealth Immigration; (with Linda Kelly) Feasts, 1987. *Recreations:* fishing, skiing; formerly: Captain, OU Fencing Team, 1961; Captain, OU Modern Pentathlon Team, 1959–60; Mem. Irish Olympic Fencing Team, 1960. *Address:* Blissamore Hall, Clanville, Andover, Hants SP11 9HL. *T:* Andover (01264) 772274; 10 Catherine Place, SW1E 6HF. *T:* 0171–834 0021. *Club:* Beefsteak.

BLAND, Sir Henry (Armand), Kt 1965; CBE 1957; *b* 28 Dec. 1909; *s* of Emeritus Prof. F. A. Bland, CMG, and Elizabeth Bates Jacobs; *m* 1933, Rosamund, *d* of John Nickal; two *d* (and one *d* decd). *Educ:* Sydney High Sch.; Univ. of Sydney. LLB (Hons) 1932. Admitted Solicitor Supreme Court of NSW, 1935. Entered NSW Public Service, 1927; Alderman, Ryde (NSW) Municipal Council, 1937–39; Acting Agent-Gen. for NSW in London, 1940–41; Adviser on Civil Defence to NSW and Commonwealth Govts, 1941; Princ. Asst to Dir-Gen. of Manpower, 1941–45; Asst Sec., First Asst Sec., 1946–51, Sec. 1952–67, Dept of Labour and National Service; Sec., Dept of Defence, Australia, 1967–70. Leader, Austr. Govt Delegns to Confs: 1948, 1953, 1957, 1960, 1962, 1963, 1964, 1966; Austr. Govt Rep. on the Governing Body of ILO, 1963–67; Adviser on industrial relations to Singapore Govt, 1958. Bd of Inquiry into Victorian Land Transport System, 1971; Chairman: Cttee on Administrative Discretions, 1972–73; Bd of Inquiry into Victorian Public Service, 1973–75; Commonwealth Admin. Rev. Cttee, 1976; ABC, 1976; Arbitrator between Aust. Nat. Railways and Tasmanian Govt, 1978. Chm. and Dir of numerous cos, 1970–90. *Address:* 54 Kenilworth Gardens, Kangaloon Road, Bowral, NSW 2576, Australia. *T:* (48) 613320. *Clubs:* Athenæum (Melbourne); Bowral Golf.

BLAND, Louise Sarah, (Mrs S. Bland); *see* Godfrey, L. S.

BLAND, Lt-Col Sir Simon (Claud Michael), KCVO 1982 (CVO 1973; MVO 1967); Extra Equerry to Princess Alice Duchess of Gloucester and the Duke and Duchess of Gloucester, since 1989 (Comptroller, Private Secretary and Equerry, 1972–89); *b* 4 Dec. 1923; *s* of late Sir Nevile Bland, KCMG, KCVO, and Portia (*née* Ottley); *m* 1954, Olivia, *d* of late Major William Blackett, Arbigland, Dumfries; one *s* three *d*. *Educ:* Eton College. Served War of 1939–45, Scots Guards, in Italy; BJSM, Washington, 1948–49; 2nd Bn, Scots Guards, Malaya, 1949–51; Asst Mil. Adviser at UK High Commn, Karachi, 1959–60; Comptroller and Asst Private Sec. to late Duke of Gloucester, 1961–74 and Private Sec. to late Prince William, 1968–72. Dir, West End Bd, Commercial Union, 1964–; Vice-Pres., Raleigh Internat. (formerly Operation Raleigh), 1989–. Chm., Coll. of St Barnabas, 1993–; Member Council: Pestalozzi Children's Village Trust, 1989–; Distressed Gentlefolk Aid Assoc., 1990–; Order of St John for Kent, 1990–; President: Friends of Edenbridge Hosp., 1990–; Lingfield Br., Riding for the Disabled, 1990–; Trustee, Grant Maintained Sch. Trust, 1990–. Freeman, City of London, 1988. KStJ 1988. *Recreation:* shooting. *Address:* Totties, Mill Hill, Edenbridge, Kent TN8 5DB. *T* and *Fax:* Edenbridge (01732) 862340. *Club:* Buck's.

BLANDFORD, Marquess of; Charles James Spencer-Churchill; Public Relations Director, Brodie Brittain Racing, since 1994; *b* 24 Nov. 1955; *e s* and *heir* of 11th Duke of Marlborough, *qv*; *m* 1990, Rebecca Mary, *d* of Peter Few Brown; one *s*. *Educ:* Pinewood; Harrow; RAC, Cirencester; Royal Berks Coll. of Agric. *Heir:* *s* Earl of Sunderland, *qv*. *Address:* Blenheim Palace, Woodstock, Oxon. *Clubs:* Turf, Tramp's, Annabel's; Racquet and Tennis (New York).

BLANDFORD, Eric George, CBE 1967; formerly a Judge of the Supreme Court of Aden; *b* 10 March 1916; *s* of George and Eva Blanche Blandford; *m* 1940, Marjorie Georgina Crane; one *s*. *Educ:* Bristol Grammar Sch. Admitted Solicitor Supreme Court, England, 1939; LLB (London) 1939. War Service, 1939–46 (despatches): India, Burma, Malaya; rank on release Temp. Major RA. Solicitor in London, 1946–51; Asst Comr of Lands, Gold Coast, 1951; Dist Magistrate, Gold Coast, 1952; called to the Bar, Inner Temple, 1955; Chief Registrar, Supreme Court, Gold Coast, 1956; Registrar of High Court of Northern Rhodesia, 1958; Judge, Supreme Court of Aden, 1961–68; Dep. Asst Registrar of Criminal Appeals, 1968–78; Asst Registrar of Criminal Appeals, Royal Courts of Justice, 1978–81. Chm. Aden Municipality Inquiry Commn, 1962. *Publication:* Civil Procedure Rules of Court, Aden, 1967. *Recreation:* local history research. *Address:* Hays Park, Sedgehill, Shaftesbury, Dorset SP7 9JR.

BLANDFORD, Heinz Hermann, CBE 1981; Fellow, Royal Postgraduate Medical School, Hammersmith Hospital, 1973 (Member Council, 1964–89; Treasurer, 1964–82; Vice Chairman, 1982–89); Chairman of Trustees, Blandford Trust for advancement of medical research and teaching, since 1964; *b* Berlin, Germany, 28 Aug. 1908; *s* of late Judge Richard Blumenfeld and Hedwig Kersten; *m* 1933, Hilde Kleczewer (*d* 1994); one *s* one *d*. *Educ:* Augusta Gymnasium; Univs of Berlin and Hamburg. Controller of continental cos in ceramic, pharmaceutical, iron and steel industries, 1933–39; Chm., Ulvir Ltd and various cos, 1936–76. Pioneered synthesis, manufacture and use of Liquid Fertilisers in the UK, 1945–60. School of Pharmacy, London University: Mem. Council, 1975–89; Treas., 1976–87; Vice-Chm., 1979–86; Hon. Fellow, 1988; British Postgraduate Medical Federation: Mem. Governing Body, 1969–86; Hon. Treas., 1969–84; Chm., 1977–79, Dep. Chm., 1980–85; Member: Management Cttee, Inst. of Ophthalmology, Moorfields, 1974–86; Court of Governors, LSHTM, 1982–89; Governor, London House for Overseas Graduates, 1977–80. Member: Org. Cttee, 6th World Congress of Cardiology, London, 1971; Board of Governors: Hammersmith and St Mark's Hospitals, 1972–74. *Recreations:* farming, gardening, walking. *Address:* Holtsmere Manor, Holtsmere End, Redbourn, Herts AL3 7AW. *T:* Redbourn (01582) 792206. *Club:* Farmers'.

BLANDFORD, Prof. Roger David, FRS 1989; Richard Chace Tolman Professor of Theoretical Astrophysics, California Institute of Technology, since 1989; *b* 28 Aug. 1949; *s* of Jack George and Janet Margaret Blandford; *m* 1972, Elizabeth Denise Kellett; two *s*. *Educ:* King Edward's Sch., Birmingham; Magdalene Coll., Cambridge Univ. (BA, MA, PhD; Bye Fellow 1973). Res. Fellow, St John's Coll., Cambridge, 1973–76; Inst. for Advanced Study, Princeton, 1974–75; CIT, 1976–. Fellow, Amer. Acad. of Arts and Scis, 1993. *Address:* 130–33 Caltech, Pasadena, CA 91125, USA. *T:* (818) 3564200.

BLANDY, Prof. John Peter, CBE 1995; MA, DM, MCh, FRCS, FACS; Consultant Surgeon: The Royal London (formerly London) Hospital, 1964–92, now Consulting Surgeon; St Peter's Hospital for the Stone, 1969–92, now Consulting Surgeon; Professor of Urology, University of London, 1969–92, now Emeritus; *b* 11 Sept. 1927; *s* of late Sir E. Nicolas Blandy, KCIE, CSI, ICS and Dorothy Kathleen (*née* Marshall); *m* 1953, Anne, *d* of Hugh Mathias, FRCS, Tenby; four *d*. *Educ:* Clifton Coll.; Balliol Coll., Oxford (Hon. Fellow, 1992); London Hosp. Med. Coll. BM, BCh 1951; MA 1953; FRCS 1956; DM 1963; MCh 1963; FACS 1980. House Phys. and House Surg., London Hosp., 1952; RAMC, 1953–55; Surgical Registrar and Lectr in Surgery, London Hosp., 1956–60; exchange Fellow, Presbyterian St Luke's Hosp., Chicago, 1960–61; Sen. Lectr, London Hosp., 1961; Resident Surgical Officer, St Paul's Hosp., 1963–64. McLaughlin-Gallie Vis. Prof., Royal Coll. of Physicians and Surgeons of Canada, 1988. Member: BMA; RSM; Council, RCS, 1982– (Hunterian Prof., 1964; Hunterian Orator, 1991; a Vice-Pres., 1992–94); GMC, 1992–; Internat. Soc. Pædiatric Urol. Surg.; Internat. Soc. of Urological Surgeons; British Assoc. Urological Surgeons (Pres., 1984); President: European Assoc. of Urology, 1986–88; European Bd of Urology, 1991–92. Chm., Nat. Confidential Enquiry into Perioperative Deaths, 1992. Fellow, Assoc. of Surgeons; Hon. FRCSI 1992; Hon. Fellow, Urological Society: of Australasia, 1973; of Canada, 1986; of Denmark, 1986; of Germany, 1987; of The Netherlands, 1990; of Romania, 1991; of Japan, 1991; Hon. Fellow: Mexican Coll. of Urology, 1974; Amer. Urol Assoc., 1989. Maurice Davidson Award, Fellowship of Postgrad. Med., 1980; St Peter's Medal, British Assoc. of Urol Surgs, 1982; Francisco Diaz Medal, Spanish Urol Assoc., 1988. *Publications:* (with A. D. Dayan and H. F. Hope-Stone) Tumours of the Testicle, 1970; Transurethral Resection, 1971; (ed) Urology, 1976; Lecture Notes on Urology, 1976; Operative Urology, 1978; (ed with B. Lytton) The Prostate, 1986; (with J. Moors) Urology for Nurses, 1989; (ed with R. T. D. Oliver and H. F. Hope-Stone) Urological and Genital Cancer, 1989; papers in surgical and urological jls. *Recreation:* painting. *Address:* 362 Shakespeare Tower, Barbican, EC2Y 8NJ. *T:* 0171–638 4095.

BLANK, Maurice Victor; Chairman, since 1991, and Chief Executive, since 1985, Charterhouse plc; Chairman and Chief Executive, Charterhouse Bank Ltd, since 1985; Chairman, Charterhouse European Holding, since 1993; *b* 9 Nov. 1942; *s* of Joseph Blank and Ruth Blank (*née* Levey); *m* 1977, Sylvia Helen (*née* Richford); two *s* one *d*. *Educ:* Stockport Grammar Sch.; St Catherine's Coll., Oxford (MA). Solicitor of the Supreme Court. Joined Clifford-Turner as articled clerk, 1964: Solicitor, 1966; Partner, 1969; Dir, and Head of Corporate Finance, Charterhouse Bank, 1981. Non-executive Director: Coats Viyella, 1989–; GUS, 1993–; Williams Hldgs, 1995–. Chm., Wellbeing, 1989–. Mem., RSA. *Publication:* (jtly) Weinberg and Blank on Take-Overs and Mergers, 3rd edn 1971 to 5th edn 1989. *Recreations:* family, cricket, tennis, theatre. *Address:* (office) 1 Paternoster Row, St Paul's, EC4M 7DH. *T:* 0171–248 4000.

BLANKS, Howard John; Under-Secretary, Highways Policy and Programme, Department of Transport, 1985–88; *b* 16 June 1932; *s* of Lionel and Hilda Blanks; *m* 1958, Judith Ann (*née* Hughes). *Educ:* Barking Abbey Sch.; Keble Coll., Oxford (BA 1st Cl. Hons Music). National Service, RAF (Pilot), 1956–58. Air Traffic Control Officer, Min. of Aviation, 1958–64; Principal, Min. of Aviation (later Min. of Technology and Aviation Supply), 1964–71; Private Sec. to Chief Executive, Min. of Defence (Procurement Executive), 1972; Assistant Secretary: MoD, 1972–75; Cabinet Office, 1975–77; Dept of Trade, 1977–79; Under-Secretary, Head of Civil Aviation Policy Div., Dept of Trade (subseq. Transport), 1980–85. *Recreations:* music, travel. *Address:* Withinlee, Hedgehog Lane, Haslemere, Surrey GU27 2PJ. *T:* Haslemere (01428) 652468.

BLANNING, Prof. Timothy Charles William, PhD; FBA 1990; Professor of Modern European History, University of Cambridge, since 1992; Fellow, Sidney Sussex College, Cambridge, since 1968; *b* 21 April 1942; *s* of Thomas Walter Blanning and Gwendolyn Marchant (*née* Jones); *m* 1988, Nicky Susan Jones. *Educ:* King's Sch., Bruton, Somerset; Sidney Sussex Coll., Cambridge (BA, MA; PhD 1967). University of Cambridge: Res. Fellow, Sidney Sussex Coll., 1965–68; Asst Lectr in History, 1972–76; Lectr in History, 1976–87; Reader in Modern European History, 1987–92. *Publications:* Joseph II and Enlightened Despotism, 1970; Reform and Revolution in Mainz 1740–1803, 1974; The French Revolution in Germany, 1983; The Origins of the French Revolutionary Wars, 1986; The French Revolution: aristocrats versus bourgeois?, 1987; Joseph II, 1994. *Recreations:* music, gardening. *Address:* Sidney Sussex College, Cambridge CB2 3HU. *T:* Cambridge (01223) 338800.

BLANTYRE, Archbishop of, (RC), since 1968; **Most Rev. James Chiona;** *b* 1924. *Educ:* Nankhunda Minor Seminary, Malaŵi; Kachebere Major Seminary, Malaŵi. Priest, 1954; Asst Parish Priest, 1954–57; Prof., Nankhunda Minor Seminary, 1957–60; study of Pastoral Sociology, Rome, 1961–62; Asst Parish Priest, 1962–65; Auxiliary Bishop of Blantyre and Titular Bishop of Bacanaria, 1965; Vicar Capitular of Archdiocese of Blantyre, 1967. *Recreation:* music. *Address:* Archbishop's House, PO Box 385, Blantyre, Malaŵi. *T:* (10)633516.

BLASHFORD-SNELL, Col John Nicholas, MBE 1969; Ministry of Defence consultant (on staff, 1983–91); Chairman, Discovery Expeditions Ltd, since 1992; *b* 22 Oct. 1936; *s* of late Rev. Prebendary Leland John Blashford Snell and Gwendolen Ives Sadler; *m* 1960, Judith Frances (*née* Sherman); two *d*. *Educ:* Victoria Coll., Jersey, CI; RMA, Sandhurst. Commissioned Royal Engineers, 1957; 33 Indep. Fd Sqdn RE Cyprus, 1958–61; comd Operation Aphrodite (Expedition) Cyprus, 1959–61; Instructor: Junior Leaders Regt RE, 1962–63; RMA Sandhurst, 1963–66; Adjt 3rd Div. Engineers, 1966–67; comd Great Abbai Expedn (Blue Nile), 1968; sc RMCS Shrivenham and Camberley, 1968–69; comd Dahlak Quest Expedn, 1969–70; GSO2 MoD, 1970–72; comd British Trans-Americas Expedn, 1971–72; OC 48 Fd Sqdn RE, service in Belize, Oman, Ulster, 1972–74; comd Zaire River Expedn, 1974–75; CO Junior Leaders Regt RE, 1976–78; Dir of Operations, Operation Drake, 1977–81; on staff (GSO1), MoD, 1978–82; in command, The Fort George Volunteers, 1982–83. Operation Raleigh: Operations Dir, 1982–88; Dir Gen., 1989–91. Hon. Chm., Scientific Exploration Soc., 1969–. Freeman, City of Hereford, 1984. Hon. DSc Durham, 1986. Darien Medal (Colombia), 1972; Livingstone Medal, RSGS, 1975; Patron's Medal, RGS, 1993; Gold Medal, Instn of RE, 1994. *Publications:* Weapons and Tactics (with Tom Wintringham), 1970; (with Richard Snailham) The Expedition Organiser's Guide, 1970, 2nd edn 1976; Where the Trails Run Out, 1974; In the Steps of Stanley, 1975, 2nd edn 1975; (with A. Ballantine) Expeditions the Experts' Way, 1977, 2nd edn 1978; A Taste for Adventure, 1978; (with Michael Cable) Operation Drake, 1981; Mysteries: Encounters with the Unexplained, 1983; Operation Raleigh, the Start of an Adventure, 1987; (with Ann Tweedy) Operation Raleigh, Adventure Challenge, 1988; (with Ann Tweedy) Operation Raleigh, Adventure Unlimited, 1990; Something lost behind the Ranges, 1994. *Recreations:* motoring, shooting, underwater diving, food, wine. *Address:* c/o Scientific Exploration Society, Expedition Base, Motcombe, Dorset SP7 9PB. *Fax:* Shaftesbury (01747) 853353. *Clubs:* Royal Automobile, Wig and Pen; Galley Hill Pistol (Hon. Pres.); Explorers' (New York) (Chm., British Chapter).

BLATCH, family name of **Baroness Blatch**.

BLATCH, Baroness *cr* 1987 (Life Peer), of Hinchingbrooke in the county of Cambridgeshire; **Emily May Blatch**, CBE 1983; PC 1993; Minister of State, Home Office, since 1994; *b* 24 July 1937; *d* of Stephen Joseph and Sarah Triggs; *m* 1963, John Richard Blatch, AFC; two *s* one *d* (of whom one *s* one *d* are twins) (and one *s* decd). *Educ:* Prenton, Birkenhead; Huntingdonshire College. WRAF, 1955–59; Ministry of Aviation, 1959–63. Member: Bd, Peterborough Develt Corp., 1984–89; Cambs CC, 1977–89 (Leader, 1981–85); ACC, 1981–85; European Econ. and Social Cttee, 1986–87; Cons. Nat. Local Govt Adv. Cttee, 1988–. Baroness in Waiting (Govt Whip), H of L, 1990; Parly Under-Sec. of State for the Envmt, 1990–91; Minister of State: DoE, 1991–92; DFE, 1992–94. Chm., Anglo-American Community Relations Cttee, RAF Alconbury, 1985–91. Pres., Nat. Benevolent Inst., 1989–. Paul Harris Fellow, Rotary Club, 1992. FRSA 1985. *Recreations:* music, theatre. *Address:* House of Lords, SW1A 0PW. *Club:* Royal Air Force.

BLATCHLEY, Geraldine; *see* James, G.

BLATCHLY, John Marcus, MA, PhD; FSA 1975; Headmaster, Ipswich School, 1972–93; *b* 7 Oct. 1932; *s* of late Alfred Ernest Blatchly and of Edith Selina Blatchly (*née* Giddings); *m* 1955, Pamela Winifred, JP, *d* of late Major and Mrs L. J. Smith; one *s* one *d*. *Educ:* Sutton Grammar Sch., Surrey; Christ's Coll., Cambridge (Natural Scis Triposes; BA, MA, PhD). Instr Lieut RN, 1954–57. Asst Master and Head of Science Dept: King's Sch., Bruton, 1957–62; Eastbourne Coll., 1962–66; Charterhouse, 1966–72 (PhD awarded 1967 publication of work carried out with Royal Society grants at these three schools). Pres., Suffolk Inst. of Archaeology and History, 1975–; Chm., Suffolk Records Soc., 1988–; Trustee, five county and town conservation trusts in Suffolk. Editor, Conference and Common Room (Journal of HMC Schools), 1987–92; Hon. Treas., 1990–92, Hon. Associate Mem., 1993, HMC. Co-ed., Bookplate Jl, 1994–. Hon. LittD UEA, 1993. *Publications:* Organic Reactions, vol. 19, 1972 (jtly, with J. F. W. McOmie); The Topographers of Suffolk, 1976, 5th edn 1988; (with Peter Eden) Isaac Johnson of Woodbridge, 1979; Eighty Ipswich Portraits, 1980; (ed) Davy's Suffolk Journal, 1983; The Town Library of Ipswich: a history and catalogue, 1989; many papers in chemical, educnl, archaeological and antiquarian jls. *Recreations:* East Anglian history, music, books. *Address:* 11 Burlington Road, Ipswich, Suffolk IP1 2HS.

BLATHERWICK, David Elliott Spiby, CMG 1990; OBE 1973; HM Diplomatic Service; Ambassador to Egypt, since 1995; *b* 13 July 1941; *s* of Edward S. Blatherwick; *m* 1964, (Margaret) Clare Crompton; one *s* one *d*. *Educ:* Lincoln Sch.; Wadham Coll., Oxford. Entered FO, 1964; Second Sec., Kuwait, 1968; First Sec., Dublin, 1970; FCO, 1973; Head of Chancery, Cairo, 1977; Head, Pol Affairs Dept, NI Office (Belfast), 1981; Hd, Energy, Science and Space Dept, FCO, 1983; sabbatical leave at Stanford Univ., Calif, 1985–86; Counsellor and Hd of Chancery, UK Mission to UN, NY, 1986–89; Prin. Finance Officer and Chief Inspector, FCO, 1989–91; Ambassador to Republic of Ireland, 1991–95. *Publication:* The International Politics of Telecommunications, 1987. *Recreations:* music, sailing, walking. *Address:* c/o Foreign and Commonwealth Office, King Charles Street, SW1A 2AH. *Club:* Athenæum.

BLAUG, Prof. Mark, PhD; FBA 1989; Professor of the Economics of Education, University of London Institute of Education, 1967–84, now Professor Emeritus; *b* 3 April 1927; *s* of Bernard Blaug and Sarah (*née* Toeman); *m* 1st, 1946, Rose Lapone (marr. diss.); 2nd, 1954, Brenda Ellis (marr. diss.); one *s*; 3rd, 1969, Ruth M. Towse; one *s*. *Educ:* Queen's Coll., NY (BA); Columbia Univ. (MA, PhD). Asst Prof., Yale Univ., 1954–62; Sen. Lectr, then Reader, Univ. of London Inst. of Educn, 1963–67; Lectr, LSE, 1963–78. Consultant Prof., Univ. of Buckingham, 1984–92, now Prof. Emeritus; Vis. Prof., Exeter Univ., 1989–. Guggenheim Foundn Fellow, 1958–59. Dist. Fellow, Hist. of Econs Soc., 1988. Dir, Edward Elgar Publishing, 1986–. Foreign Hon. Mem., Royal Netherlands Acad. of Arts and Scis, 1984. *Publications:* Ricardian Economics, 1958; Economic Theory in Retrospect, 1962, 4th edn 1985; (jtly) The Causes of Graduate Unemployment in India, 1969; Introduction to the Economics of Education, 1970; Education and the Employment Problem in Developing Countries, 1973; (jtly) The Practice of Manpower Forecasting, 1973; The Cambridge Revolution?, 1974; The Methodology of Economics, 1980, 2nd edn 1992; Who's Who in Economics, 1983, 2nd edn 1986; Great Economists Since Keynes, 1984; Great Economists Before Keynes, 1985; Economic History and the History of Economics, 1986; The Economics of Education and the Education of an Economist, 1987; Economic Theories: True or False?, 1990; Keynes: Life, Ideas and Legacy, 1990; (jtly) Appraising Economic Theories, 1991; (jtly) Quantity Theory of Money, 1995. *Recreations:* talking, walking, sailing. *Address:* Langsford Barn, Peter Tavy, Tavistock, Devon PL9 9LY. *T:* Tavistock (01822) 810562.

BLAYNEY, Elizabeth Carmel, (Eily Blayney); Head of Library and Records Department and Departmental Record Officer (Assistant Secretary), Foreign and Commonwealth Office, 1977–85, retired; *b* 19 July 1925; *d* of William Blayney, MRCS, LRCP, Medical Practitioner (previously County Inspector, RIC) of Harrold, Beds, and Mary Henrietta *d* of John Beveridge, sometime Town Clerk of Dublin. *Educ:* St Mary's Convent, Shaftesbury; The Triangle, S Molton Street. Chartered Librarian. Served War, WTS(FANY) in UK, India and Ceylon (Force 136), 1944–46. Library Asst, Hampstead Borough Libraries, 1947–50; Assistant Librarian: RSA, 1950–52; CO/CRO Jt Library, CRO, 1953; Head of Printed Library, FO, 1959–68; Librarian i/c, ODM, 1968–69; Librarian, FCO, 1969–77. *Address:* 6 Bamville Wood, East Common, Harpenden, Herts AL5 1AP. *T:* Harpenden (01582) 715067.

BLEACKLEY, David, CMG 1979; DPhil; Head, Overseas Division, and Assistant Director, Institute of Geological Sciences, 1975–80; *b* 1 Feb. 1919; *s* of Alfred Mason and Hilda Gertrude Bleackley; *m* 1st, 1945, Peggy Florence Chill (*d* 1966); one *s* one *d*; 2nd, 1973, Patricia Clavell Strakosch (*née* Hore); two step *s* one step *d*. *Educ:* City of Oxford Sch.; The Queen's Coll., Oxford (BA 1939, MA 1942, DPhil 1960). Served War, Royal Engineers, 1939–45. Geologist: Shell Oil Co., 1946–50; Geological Survey, British Guiana, 1954–57, Dep. Dir, 1957–60; Overseas Geological Surveys, 1960–65; Dep. Head, Overseas Div., Inst. of Geological Sciences, 1965–75. FIMM 1969; FGS 1943. *Publications:* papers in various jls. *Recreation:* country pursuits. *Address:* Well Farm, Dagnall, near Berkhamsted, Herts HP4 1QU. *T:* Little Gaddesden (0144284) 3232.

BLEAKLEY, Rt. Hon. David Wylie, CBE 1984; PC (NI) 1971; President, Church Mission (formerly Church Missionary) Society, since 1983; *b* 11 Jan. 1925; *s* of John Wesley Bleakley and Sarah Bleakley (*née* Wylie); *m* 1949, Winifred Wason; three *s*. *Educ:* Ruskin Coll., Oxford; Queen's Univ., Belfast. MA, DipEconPolSci (Oxon). Belfast Shipyard, 1940–46; Oxford and Queen's Univ., 1946–51; Tutor in Social Studies, 1951–55; Principal, Belfast Further Educn Centre, 1955–58; Lectr in Industrial Relations, Kivukoni Coll., Dar-es-Salaam, 1967–69; Head of Dept of Economics and Political Studies, Methodist Coll., Belfast, 1969–79; Chief Exec., Irish Council of Churches, 1980–92. MP (Lab) Victoria, Belfast, Parliament of N Ireland, 1958–65; contested: (Lab) East Belfast, General Elections, 1970, Feb. and Oct. 1974. Minister of Community Relations, Govt of NI, March-Sept. 1971; Member (NILP), E Belfast: NI Assembly, 1973–75; NI Constitutional Convention, 1975–76. Mem., Cttee of Inquiry on Police, 1978. Chm., NI Standing Adv. Commn on Human Rights, 1980–84. Irish Deleg. to Anglican Consultative Council, 1976; Delegate to World Council of Churches, to Conf. of European Churches. WEA and Open Univ. tutor; Vis. Sen. Lectr in Peace Studies, Univ. of Bradford, 1974–. Mem., Press Council, 1987–90. Hon. MA Open, 1975. *Publications:* Ulster since 1800: regional history symposium, 1958; Young Ulster and Religion in the Sixties, 1964; Peace in Ulster, 1972; Faulkner: a biography, 1974; Saidie Patterson, Irish Peacemaker, 1980; In Place of Work, 1981; The Shadow and Substance, 1983; Beyond Work—Free to Be, 1985; Will the Future Work, 1986; Europe: a Christian vision, 1992; Ageing and Ageism in a Technological Society, 1994; Peace in Ireland: two states, one people, 1995; regular contribs to BBC and to press on community relations and industrial studies. *Address:* 8 Thornhill, Bangor, Co. Down, Northern Ireland BT19 1RD. *T:* Bangor (01247) 454898, *Fax:* (01247) 274274.

BLEANEY, Prof. Brebis, CBE 1965; FRS 1950; MA, DPhil; Warren Research Fellow, Royal Society, 1977–80, Leverhulme Emeritus Fellow, 1980–82; Fellow, 1957–77, Senior Research Fellow, 1977–82, Wadham College, Oxford, now Emeritus Fellow; Dr Lee's Professor of Experimental Philosophy, University of Oxford, 1957–77, now Emeritus Professor; *b* 6 June 1915; *m* 1949, Betty Isabelle Plumpton; one *s* one *d*. *Educ:* Westminster City Sch.; St John's Coll., Oxford. Lecturer in Physics at Balliol Coll., Oxford, 1947–50. Research Fellow, Harvard Univ. and Mass Institute of Technology, 1949. University Demonstrator and Lectr in Physics, Univ. of Oxford, 1945–57; Fellow and Lectr in Physics, St John's Coll., Oxford, 1947–57; Tutor, 1950–57; Hon. Fellow, 1968. Visiting Prof. in Physics in Columbia Univ., 1956–57; Harkins Lectr, Chicago Univ., 1957; Kelvin Lectr, Instn Electrical Engineers, 1962; Morris Loeb Lectr, Harvard Univ., 1981; Cherwell Simon Meml Lectr, Oxford Univ., 1981–82; John and Abigail Van Vleck Lectr, Univ. of Minnesota, 1985; Visiting Professor: Univ. of California, Berkeley, 1961; Univ. of Pittsburgh, 1962–63; Manitoba, 1968; La Plata, Argentina, 1971; Amer. Univ. in Cairo, 1978; Univ. of NSW, 1981. Mem. Council for Scientific and Industrial Res., 1960–62; Chm., British Radiofrequency Spectroscopy Gp, 1983–85. FRSA 1971. Corr. Mem. Acad. of Sciences, Inst. of France, 1974, Associé Etranger, 1978; For. Hon. Mem., Amer. Acad. of Arts and Scis, 1978; Hon. Prof., Kazan Univ., 1994. DSc *hc* Porto, Portugal, 1987. Charles Vernon Boys Prize, Physical Soc., 1952; Hughes Medal, Royal Society, 1962; ISMAR Prize, Internat. Soc. for Magnetic Resonance, 1983; Holweck Medal and Prize, Inst. of Physics and Société Française de Physique, 1984; Zavoisky Prize, Kazan, Physical-Technical Inst., 1992. *Publications:* (with B. I. Bleaney) Electricity and Magnetism, 1957, 3rd edn, 1976, revd edn in 2 vols, 1989; (with A. Abragam) Electron Paramagnetic Resonance, 1970, revd edn 1986; over 200 papers in Proceedings of the Royal Society and Proceedings of the Physical Society, etc. *Recreations:* music and tennis. *Address:* Clarendon Laboratory, Parks Road, Oxford OX1 3PU.

BLEASDALE, Alan; playwright and novelist, since 1975; *b* 23 March 1946; *s* of George and Margaret Bleasdale; *m* 1970, Julia Moses; two *s* one *d*. *Educ:* St Aloysius RC Jun. Sch., Huyton; Wade Deacon Grammar Sch., Widnes; Padgate Teachers Trng Coll. (Teacher's Cert.). Schoolteacher, 1967–75. *TV series:* Boys from the Blackstuff, 1982 (BPG TV Award for Best Series, 1982; Best British TV Drama of the Decade, ITV Achievement of the Decade Awards, 1989); Scully, 1984; The Monocled Mutineer, 1986; GBH, 1992 (BPG TV Award for Best Drama Series, 1992). Hon. DLitt Liverpool Poly., 1991. BAFTA Writers Award, 1982; RTS Writer of the Year, 1982. *Publications: novels:* Scully, 1975; Who's been sleeping in my bed, 1977; *play scripts:* No more sitting on the Old School Bench, 1979; Boys from the Blackstuff, 1982; Are you lonesome tonight?, 1985 (Best Musical, London Standard Drama Awards, 1985); Having a Ball, 1986; It's a Madhouse, 1986; The Monocled Mutineer, 1986; On the Ledge, 1993; *film script:* No Surrender, 1986. *Recreation:* rowing. *Address:* c/o Harvey Unna & Stephen Durbridge Ltd, 24 Pottery Lane, Holland Park, W11 4LZ. *T:* 071–727 1346.

BLEASDALE, Cyril, OBE 1988; FCIT; MIMgt; FRSA; transport consultant; Chairman, Riverside Bakeries, Scotland; *b* 8 July 1934; *s* of Frederick and Alice Bleasdale; *m* 1970, Catherine; two *d*. *Educ:* Evered High Sch., Liverpool; Stanford Univ., Calif (Sen. Exec. Program). Man. Dir, Freightliner Ltd, 1975–82; Dir, Inter City British Rail, 1982–86; Gen. Manager, BR London Midland Region, 1986–90; Dir, Scotrail, 1990–94. Chm., Transaid. Exec. Cttee, Mediation UK. *Recreations:* music, fitness. *Address:* 8 Long Ridge, Aston, Stevenage SG2 7EY.

BLEASE, family name of **Baron Blease.**

BLEASE, Baron *cr* 1978 (Life Peer), of Cromac in the City of Belfast; **William John Blease**, JP; *b* 28 May 1914; *e s* of late William and Sarah Blease; *m* 1939, Sarah Evelyn Caldwell; three *s* one *d*. *Educ:* elementary and technical schs; Nat. Council of Labour Colls; WEA. Retail Provision Trade (apprentice), 1929; Retail Grocery Asst (Branch Manager), 1938–40; Clerk, Belfast Shipyard, 1940–45; Branch Manager, Co-operative Soc., Belfast, 1945–59; Divl Councillor, Union of Shop Distributive Workers, 1948–59; NI Officer, 1959–75, Exec. Consultant, 1975–76, Irish Congress of Trade Unions; Divl Chm. and Nat. Exec. Mem., Nat. Council of Labour Colls, 1948–61; Exec. Mem., NI Labour Party, 1949–59 (Dep. Chm., 1957–58); Trustee, LPNI, 1986–90. Labour Party Spokesman in House of Lords, on N Ireland, 1979–82; Trade Union Side Sec., NI CS

Industrial Jt Council, 1975–77. Member: NI Co-operative Develt Agency, 1987–92; NI Economic Council, 1964–75; Review Body on Local Govt, NI, 1970–71; Review Body on Ind. Relations, NI, 1970–73; Working Party on Discrimination in Employment, NI, 1972–73; NI Trng Res. Cttee, 1966–80; NI Regional Adv. Bd, BIM, 1971–80; NUU Vocational Guidance Council, 1974–83; Ind. Appeals Tribunals, 1974–76; Local Govt Appeals Tribunal, 1974–83; Irish Council of Churches Working Party, 1974–93; IBA, 1974–79; Standing Adv. Commn on Human Rights, NI, 1977–79; Police Complaints Bd, 1977–80; Conciliation Panel, Ind. Relations Agency, 1978–89; Security Appeal Bd, NI SC Commn, 1979–88; Chm., Community Service Order Cttee, 1979–80; Rapporteur, EEC Cross Border Communications Study on Londonderry/Donegal, 1978–80; President: NI Assoc., NACRO, 1982–85; NI Hospice, 1981–85; E Belfast Access Council for Disabled, 1982–88; NI Widows Assoc., 1985–89; Belfast Housing Aid, 1989–. Trustee: Belfast Charitable Trust for Integrated Educn, 1984–88; TSB Foundn, NI, 1986–. Mem., Management Bd, Rathgael Young People's Centre, 1989–93. Mem., Bd of Govs, St Mae Nissis Coll., 1981–90. Ford Foundn Travel Award, USA, 1959. Hon. Res. Fellow, Univ. of Ulster, 1976–83; Jt Hon. Res. Fellow, TCD, 1976–79. Hon. FBIM 1981 (MBIM 1970). JP Belfast, 1976–. Hon. DLitt New Univ. of Ulster, 1972; Hon. LLD QUB, 1982. *Publication:* Encyclopaedia of Labour Law, vol. 1: The Trade Union Movement in Northern Ireland, 1983. *Recreations:* gardening, reading.

BLECH, Harry, CBE 1984 (OBE 1962); Hon. RAM, 1963; Musical Director, Haydn-Mozart Society, and Founder and Conductor, London Mozart Players, 1949–84; *b* 2 March 1910; British; *m* 1935, Enid Marion Lessing (*d* 1977); one *s* two *d*; *m* 1957, Marion Manley, pianist; one *s* three *d*. *Educ:* Central London Foundation; Trinity Coll. of Music (Fellow); Manchester Coll. of Music (Fellow). Joined BBC Symphony Orchestra, 1930–36. Responsible for formation of: Blech Quartet, 1933–50; London Wind Players, 1942 (conductor); London Mozart Players, 1949 (Conductor Laureate); Haydn-Mozart Soc., 1949; London Mozart Choir, 1952. Dir of Chamber Orchestra, RAM, 1961–65. FRSA. *Address:* The Owls, 70 Leopold Road, Wimbledon, SW19 7JQ.

BLEDISLOE, 3rd Viscount *cr* 1935; **Christopher Hiley Ludlow Bathurst,** QC 1978; *b* 24 June 1934; *s* of 2nd Viscount Bledisloe, QC, and of Joan Isobel Krishaber; *S* father, 1979; *m* (marr. diss. 1986); two *s* one *d*. *Educ:* Eton; Trinity Coll., Oxford. Called to the Bar, Gray's Inn, 1959; Bencher, 1986. *Heir: s* Hon. Rupert Edward Ludlow Bathurst, *b* 13 March 1964. *Address:* Lydney Park, Glos GL15 6BT. *T:* Dean (01594) 842566; Fountain Court, Temple, EC4Y 9DH. *T:* 0171–583 3335.

BLEEHEN, Prof. Norman Montague, CBE 1994; Cancer Research Campaign Professor of Clinical Oncology, 1975–95, and Hon. Director of MRC Unit of Clinical Oncology and Radiotherapeutics, 1975–95, University of Cambridge (Director, Radiotherapeutics, and Oncology Centre, 1984–92); Fellow of St John's College, Cambridge, since 1976; *b* 24 Feb. 1930; *s* of Solomon and Lena Bleehen; *m* 1969, Tirza, *d* of Alex and Jenny Loeb. *Educ:* Manchester Grammar Sch.; Haberdashers' Aske's Sch.; Exeter Coll., Oxford (Francis Gotch medal, 1953); Middlesex Hosp. Med. School. BA 1951, BSc 1953, MA 1954, BM, BCh 1955, Oxon; MRCP 1957, FRCP 1973; FRCR 1964; DMRT 1962. MRC Res. Student, Biochem. Dept, Oxford, 1951; house appts: Middlesex Hosp., 1955–56; Hammersmith Hosp., 1957; Asst Med. Specialist Army, Hanover, 1957; Med. Specialist Army, Berlin, 1959 (Captain); Jun. Lectr in Medicine, Dept of Regius Prof. of Medicine, Oxford, 1959–60; Registrar and Sen. Registrar in Radiotherapy, Middlesex Hosp. Med. Sch., 1961–66; Lilly Res. Fellow, Stanford Univ., 1966–67; Locum Consultant, Middlesex Hosp., 1967–69; Prof. of Radiotherapy, Middlesex Hosp. Med. Sch., 1969–75. Consultant advr to CMO, DHSS, for radiation oncology, 1986–92. Cantor Lectr, RSA, 1979; Simon Lectr, RCR, 1986. Member: Jt MRC/CRC Cttee for jtly supported insts, 1971–74; Coordinating Cttee for Cancer Res., 1973–79, 1987–; Council, Imperial Cancer Res. Fund, 1973–76; Council, Brit. Inst. of Radiology, 1974–77; Sci. Cttee, Cancer Res. Campaign, 1976–90; MRC Cell Bd, 1980–84; UICC Fellowships Cttee, 1983–87; Council, European Organisation for Treatment of Cancer, 1983–88; Council, RCR, 1987–90; Vice-President: Bd of Dirs, Internat. Assoc. for Study of Lung Cancer, 1980–82, 1985–94; EEC Cancer Experts Cttee, 1987–; Pres., Internat. Soc. of Radiation Oncology, 1985–89; Chairman: MRC Lung Cancer Wkg Party, 1973–89; MRC Brain Tumour Wkg Party, 1978–89; MRC Cancer Therapy Cttee, 1972–88; British Assoc. for Cancer Res., 1976–79; Soc. for Comparative Oncology, 1983–86. Hon. FACR 1984. Hon. Dr, Faculty of Pharmacy, Bologna, 1990. Roentgen Prize, British Inst. of Radiology, 1986. *Publications:* (ed jtly) Radiation Therapy Planning, 1983; (Scientific Editor) British Medical Bulletin 24/1, The Scientific Basis of Radiotherapy, 1973; various on medicine, biochemistry cancer and radiotherapy. *Recreations:* gardening, television. *Address:* 21 Bentley Road, Cambridge CB2 2AW. *T:* Cambridge (01223) 354320. *Club:* Athenæum.

BLELLOCH, Sir John (Niall Henderson), KCB 1987 (CB 1983); Permanent Under-Secretary of State, Northern Ireland Office, 1988–90, retired; *b* 24 Oct. 1930; *s* of late Ian William Blelloch, CMG and Leila Mary Henderson; *m* 1958, Pamela, *d* of late James B. and E. M. Blair; one *s* (and one *s* decd). *Educ:* Fettes Coll.; Gonville and Caius Coll., Cambridge (BA). Nat. Service, RA, 1949–51 (commnd 1950). Asst Principal, War Office, 1954; Private Sec. to successive Parly Under Secs of State, 1956–58; Principal, 1958; MoD, 1964–80; London Business Sch. (EDP 3), 1967; Asst Sec., 1968; RCDS, 1974; Asst Under-Sec. of State (Air), Procurement Exec., 1976; Asst Under-Sec. of State, Defence Staff, 1979; Dep. Sec., NI Office, 1980–82; Dep. Under-Sec of State (Policy and Programmes), MoD, 1982–84; Second Permanent Under-Sec. of State, MoD, 1984–88. Member: Security Commn, 1991–; Adv. Council on Public Records, 1993–. Comr, Royal Hosp. Chelsea, 1988–94. Pres., Emergency Planning Soc., 1993–; Chm., Cttee for Monitoring Agreements on Tobacco Advertising and Sponsorship, 1991–94; Member: Cttee, GBA, 1992–; Cttee, AA, 1993–. Trustee, RAF Mus., 1994–; Gov., Fettes Coll., 1992–. *Recreations:* golf, skiing, learning the piano. *Address:* c/o Bank of Scotland, St James's Gate, 14–16 Cockspur Street, SW1 5BL. *Clubs:* Royal Mid-Surrey Golf, Sherborne Golf.

BLENKINSOP, Dorothy, CBE 1990; Regional Nursing Officer, Northern Regional Health Authority, 1973–89, retired; *b* 15 Nov. 1931; *d* of late Joseph Henry Blenkinsop, BEM, and Thelma Irene (*née* Bishop). *Educ:* South Shields Grammar Sch. for Girls. MA (Dunelm) 1978. SRN 1953; SCM 1954; Health Visitors Cert. 1962. Ward Sister, Royal Victoria Infirmary, Newcastle upon Tyne, 1955–61; Health Visitor, S Shields, 1962–64; Dep. Matron, Gen. Hosp., S Shields, 1964–67; Durham Hospital Management Committee: Prin. Nurse, Durham City Hosps, 1967–69; Prin. Nursing Officer (Top), 1969–71; Chief Nursing Officer, 1971–73. Chm., S Tyneside Health Care Trust, 1992–. Local Preacher, Methodist Church. Hon. MSc CNAA, 1990. *Publications:* (with E. G. Nelson): Changing the System, 1972; Managing the System, 1976; articles in nursing press. *Recreation:* gardening. *Address:* 143 Temple Park Road, South Shields, Tyne and Wear NE34 0EN. *T:* South Shields (091) 4561429.

BLENNERHASSETT, Sir (Marmaduke) Adrian (Francis William), 7th Bt, *cr* 1809; *b* 25 May 1940; *s* of Lieut Sir Marmaduke Blennerhassett, 6th Bt, RNVR (killed in action, 1940), and Gwenfra (*d* 1956), *d* of Judge Harrington-Morgan, Churchtown, Co. Kerry, and of Mrs Douglas Campbell; *S* father 1940; *m* 1972, Carolyn Margaret, *yr d* of late Gilbert Brown; one *s* one *d*. *Educ:* Michael Hall, Forest Row; McGill Univ.; Imperial Coll., Univ. of London (MSc); Cranfield Business Sch. (MBA). *Recreations:* flying (private pilot's licence), ocean racing (sailing), ski-ing. *Heir: s* Charles Henry Marmaduke Blennerhassett, *b* 18 July 1975. *Address:* 54 Staveley Road, Chiswick, W4 3ES. *Club:* Royal Ocean Racing.

BLESSLEY, Kenneth Harry, CBE 1974 (MBE 1945); ED; Valuer and Estates Surveyor, Greater London Council, 1964–77; *b* 28 Feb. 1914; *s* of Victor Henry le Blond Blessley and Ellen Mary Blessley; *m* 1946, Gwendeline MacRae; two *s*. *Educ:* Haberdashers' Aske's Hampstead Sch.; St Catharine's Coll., Cambridge (MA); Coll. of Estate Management. FRICS. Private practice, West End and London suburbs. Served War of 1939–45, TA Royal Engrs, Persia, Middle East, Sicily, Italy (despatches 1942 and 1944). Sen. Property Adviser, Public Trustee, 1946–50; Dep. County Valuer, Mddx CC, 1950–53; County Valuer, Mddx CC, 1953–65. Mem. Urban Motorways Cttee, 1970–72; Chm., Covent Garden Officers' Steering Gp, 1970–77; Chm., Thamesmead Officers' Steering Gp, 1971–76; Pres., Assoc. of Local Authority Valuers and Estate Surveyors, 1962 and 1972; Mem. Gen. Council, RICS, 1972–78, Pres., Gen. Practice Div., 1976–77. Pres., Old Haberdashers' Assoc., 1963 (Pres. RFC, 1966–68); Vice-Pres., Cambridge Univ. Land Soc., 1985–86. *Publications:* numerous articles and papers on compensation, property valuation and development. *Recreations:* music, drama, sport, motoring. *Address:* 99 Maplehurst Road, Summersdale, Chichester, West Sussex PO19 4RP. *T:* Chichester (01243) 528188.

BLEWETT, Hon. Neal, DPhil; FRHistS; High Commissioner for Australia in the United Kingdom, since 1994; *b* 24 Oct. 1933; *s* of James and Phyllis Blewett; *m* 1962, Jill Myford (*d* 1988); one *s* one *d*. *Educ:* Launceston High Sch.; Univ. of Tasmania (Dip Ed, MA); Jesus Coll., Oxford (MA); St Antony's Coll., Oxford (DPhil). FRHistS 1975. Oxford University: Sen. Schol., St Antony's Coll., 1959–61; Lectr, St Edmund Hall, 1961–63; Lectr in Politics, Univ. of Adelaide, 1964–69; Flinders University, S Australia: Reader, 1970–74; Prof., Dept of Pol Theory and Instns, 1974–77. MP (Lab) Bonython, SA, 1977–94; Mem., Jt Hse Cttee on Foreign Affairs and Defence, 1977–80; Deleg. to Australian Constitutional Convention, 1978; Opposition Spokesman on health and Tasmanian affairs, 1980–83; Minister for: Health, 1983–87; Community Services and Health, 1987–90; Trade and Overseas Develt, 1990–91; Social Security, 1991–93. Member Council: Univ. of Adelaide, 1972–74; Torrens Coll. of Advanced Educn, 1972–78. *Publications:* The Peers, the Parties and the People, 1972; (jtly) Playford to Dunstan: the politics of transition, 1971. *Recreations:* bush-walking, reading, cinema. *Address:* Australian High Commission, Australia House, Strand, WC2B 4LA. *T:* 0171–887 5220.

BLEWITT, Major Sir Shane (Gabriel Basil), KCVO 1989 (CVO 1987; LVO 1981); Keeper of the Privy Purse and Treasurer to the Queen, since 1988; Receiver-General, Duchy of Lancaster, since 1988; *b* 25 March 1935; *s* of late Col Basil Blewitt; *m* 1969, Julia Morrogh-Bernard, *widow* of Major John Morrogh-Bernard, Irish Guards, and *d* of late Mr Robert Calvert; one *s* one *d* (and one step *s* one step *d*). *Educ:* Ampleforth Coll.; Christ Church, Oxford (MA Hons Mod. Languages). Served Irish Guards, 1956–74; Antony Gibbs and Sons, 1974; Asst Keeper, 1975–85, Dep. Keeper, 1985–88, of the Privy Purse. *Recreations:* gardening, shooting. *Club:* White's.

BLIGH, family name of **Earl of Darnley.**

BLIN-STOYLE, Prof. Roger John, FRS 1976; Professor of Theoretical Physics, University of Sussex, 1962–90, now Emeritus; *b* 24 Dec. 1924; *s* of Cuthbert Basil St John Blin-Stoyle and Ada Mary (*née* Nash); *m* 1949, Audrey Elizabeth Balmford; one *s* one *d*. *Educ:* Alderman Newton's Boys' Sch., Leicester; Wadham Coll., Oxford (Scholar). MA, DPhil Oxon; FInstP; ARCM. Served Royal Signals, 1943–46 (Lieut). Pressed Steel Co. Res. Fellow, Oxford Univ., 1951–53; Lectr in Math. Physics, Birmingham Univ., 1953–54; Sen. Res. Officer in Theoret. Physics, Oxford Univ., 1952–62; Fellow and Lectr in Physics, Wadham Coll., Oxford, 1956–62, Hon. Fellow, 1987; Vis. Associate Prof. of Physics, MIT, 1959–60; Vis. Prof. of Physics, Univ. of Calif, La Jolla, 1960; Sussex University: Dean, Sch. of Math. and Phys. Sciences, 1962–68; Pro-Vice-Chancellor, 1965–67; Dep. Vice-Chancellor, 1970–72; Pro-Vice-Chancellor (Science), 1977–79. Chm., School Curriculum Develt Cttee, 1983–88. Member: Royal Greenwich Observatory Cttee, 1966–70; Nuclear Physics Bd, SRC, later SERC, 1967–70, 1982–84; Mem. Council, 1982–83, Chm. Educn Cttee, 1992–94, Royal Soc.; President: Inst. of Physics, 1990–92; Assoc. for Sci. Educn, 1993–94. Hon. DSc Sussex, 1990. Rutherford Medal and Prize, IPPS, 1976. Editor: Reports on Progress in Physics, 1977–82; Student Physics Series, 1983–87. *Publications:* Theories of Nuclear Moments, 1957; Fundamental Interactions and the Nucleus, 1973; Nuclear and Particle Physics, 1991; papers on nuclear and elementary particle physics in scientific jls. *Recreation:* making music. *Address:* 14 Hill Road, Lewes, E Sussex BN7 1DB. *T:* Lewes (01273) 473640.

BLISHEN, Anthony Owen, OBE 1968; HM Diplomatic Service, retired; Counsellor, Foreign and Commonwealth Office, 1981–92; *b* 16 April 1932; *s* of Henry Charles Adolphus Blishen and Joan Cecile Blishen (*née* Blakeney); *m* 1963, Sarah Anne Joscelyne (marr. diss.); three *s* one *d*; *m* 1994, Elizabeth Appleyard (*née* West). *Educ:* Clayesmore Sch., Dorset; SOAS, London Univ. Commnd Royal Hampshire Regt, 1951; Lt 1st Bn: BAOR, 1953; Malaya, 1953–55; Captain, GSO3 HQ 18 Inf. Bde, Malaya, 1955–56; attached HQ Land Forces, Hong Kong (language trng), 1957–59; GSO3 HQ Far East Land Forces, Singapore, 1960–62; FO, 1963–65; First Sec. and Consul, Peking, 1965–67; First Sec., FCO, 1968–70; Chargé d'Affaires (ad interim), Ulan Bator, 1970; Trade Comr (China trade), Hong Kong, 1971–73; First Sec., FCO, 1973–77; First Sec., 1977–78, Counsellor, 1978–81, Tokyo. *Recreations:* Renaissance music, oriental languages. *Address:* 331 Petersham Road, Ham, Richmond, Surrey TW10 7DB. *T:* 0181–948 6144.

BLISHEN, Edward; author; *b* 29 April 1920; *s* of William George Blishen and Elizabeth Anne (*née* Pye); *m* 1948, Nancy Smith; two *s*. *Educ:* Queen Elizabeth's Grammar Sch., Barnet. Weekly Newspaper reporter, 1937–40; agricultural worker, 1941–46. Teaching: Prep. Schoolmaster, 1946–49; Secondary Modern School Teacher, 1950–59. Presenter: Writers' Club, BBC African Service, 1959–72; The World of Books, BBC Topical Tapes, 1973–89; A Good Read, BBC Radio 4, 1989–. Carnegie Medal, 1970; Soc. of Authors Travelling Scholarship, 1979. FRSL 1989. DUniv Open, 1995. *Publications:* Roaring Boys, 1955; This Right Soft Lot, 1969; (with Leon Garfield) The God Beneath the Sea (Carnegie Medal), 1970; (with Leon Garfield) The Golden Shadow, 1972; *autobiography:* A Cackhanded War, 1972; Uncommon Entrance, 1974; Sorry, Dad, 1978; A Nest of Teachers, 1980; Shaky Relations, 1981 (J. R. Ackerley Prize); Lizzie Pye, 1982; Donkey Work, 1983; A Second Skin, 1984; The Outside Contributor, 1986; The Disturbance Fee, 1988; The Penny World, 1990; *edited:* Junior Pears Encyclopaedia, 1961–; Oxford Miscellanies, 1964–69; Blond Encyclopaedia of Education, 1969; The School that I'd Like, 1969; The Thorny Paradise, 1975; *compiled:* Oxford Book of Poetry for Children, 1964; Come Reading, 1967; (with Nancy Blishen) A Treasury of Stories for Five Year Olds, 1989; (with Nancy Blishen) The Kingfisher Treasury of Stories for Children, 1992.

Recreations: ambling, broadcasting, listening to music. *Address:* 12 Bartrams Lane, Hadley Wood, Barnet EN4 0EH. *T:* 0181–449 3252.

BLISS, Prof. Christopher John Emile, PhD; FBA 1988; Nuffield Professor of International Economics, Oxford University, since 1992, and Fellow of Nuffield College, Oxford, since 1977; *b* 17 Feb. 1940; *s* of John Llewlyn Bliss and Patricia Paula (*née* Dubern); *m* 1983, Ghada (*née* Saqf El Hait); one *s* two *d* by previous marr. *Educ:* Finchley Catholic Grammar Sch.; King's Coll., Cambridge (BA 1962, MA 1964, PhD 1966). Fellow of Christ's Coll., Cambridge, 1965–71; Asst Lectr, 1965–67, and Lectr, 1967–71, Cambridge Univ.; Prof. of Econs, Univ. of Essex, 1971–77; Nuffield Reader in Internat. Econs, Oxford Univ., 1977–92. Dir, General Funds Investment Trust Ltd, 1980–87. Fellow, Econometric Soc., 1978. Editor or Asst Editor, Rev. of Econ. Studies, 1967–71; Man. Editor, Oxford Economic Papers, 1989–. *Publications:* Capital Theory and the Distribution of Income, 1975; (with N. H. Stern) Palanpur: the economy of an Indian village, 1982; Economic Theory and Policy for Trading Blocks, 1994; papers and reviews in learned jls. *Recreation:* music. *Address:* Nuffield College, Oxford OX1 1NF. *T:* Oxford (01865) 278573.

BLISS, John Cordeux, QPM; retired as Deputy Assistant Commissioner, Metropolitan Police, 1971 (seconded as National Co-ordinator of Regional Crime Squads of England and Wales from inception, 1964–71); *b* 16 March 1914; *s* of late Herbert Francis Bliss and Ida Muriel (*née* Hays); *m* 1947, Elizabeth Mary, *d* of Charles Gordon Howard; one *s* two *d. Educ:* Haileybury Coll. Metropolitan Police Coll., Hendon, 1936–37. Served in RAF, 1941–45, Flt Lt, 227 Sqdn, MEF. Various ranks of Criminal Investigation Dept of Metropolitan Police, 1946–62; seconded as Dir of Criminal Law at Police Coll., Bramshill, 1962–63; Dep. Comdr, 1963–64. Barrister, Middle Temple, 1954. Mem., Parole Bd, 1973–76 and 1978–81. Liveryman, Merchant Taylors' Company. Churchill Memorial Trust Fellowship, 1967; Queen's Police Medal, 1969. *Recreations:* gardening; formerly: Rugby football, tennis. *Address:* Foxhanger Down, Hurtmore, Godalming, Surrey GU7 2RG. *T:* Guildford (01483) 422487. *Club:* Royal Air Force.

BLISS, Dr Timothy Vivian Pelham, FRS 1994; Head, Division of Neurophysiology and Neuropharmacology, National Institute for Medical Research, since 1988; *b* 27 July 1940; *s* of Pelham Marryat Bliss and Elizabeth Cotton Bliss (*née* Sproule); *m* 1st, 1975, Virginia Catherine Morton-Evans (*née* O'Rorke); one step *s* two step *d*; one *d* by Katherine Sarah Clough; 2nd, 1994, Isabel Frances Vasseur (*née* Wardrop); two step *s. Educ:* Dean Close Sch.; McGill Univ. (BSc 1963; PhD 1967). Mem., scientific staff, MRC, 1967–. Vis. Prof., Dept of Physiology, UCL, 1993–. Bristol Myers Squibb Award for Neuroscience, 1991; Feldberg Prize, 1994. *Publications:* numerous papers on the neural basis of memory and other aspects of the neurophysiology of the brain. *Recreation:* poring over fine wine catalogues. *Address:* 1 Southwood Park, Southwood Lawn Road, N6 5SG. *T:* 0181–341 1215, *Fax:* 0181–347 6046. *Club:* Academy.

BLIX, Hans, PhD, LLD; Director General, International Atomic Energy Agency, since 1981; *b* 28 June 1928; *s* of Gunnar Blix and Hertha Blix (*née* Wiberg); *m* 1962, Eva Margareta Kettis; two *s. Educ:* Univ. of Uppsala; Columbia Univ.; Univ. of Cambridge (PhD); Stockholm Univ. (LLD). Associate Prof. in International Law, 1960; Ministry of Foreign Affairs, Stockholm: Legal Adviser, 1963–76; Under-Secretary of State, in charge of internat. development co-operation, 1976; Minister for Foreign Affairs, 1978; Under-Secretary of State, in charge of internat. development co-operation, 1979. Member: Sweden's delegn to UN General Assembly, 1961–81; Swedish delegn to Conference on Disarmament in Geneva, 1962–78. Hon. doctorates: Moscow State Univ., 1987; Bucharest Univ., 1994. FORATOM Award, 1994. *Publications:* Treaty Making Power, 1959; Statsmyndigheternas Internationella Förbindelser, 1964; Sovereignty, Aggression and Neutrality, 1970; The Treaty-Maker's Handbook, 1974. *Recreations:* skiing, hiking. *Address:* International Atomic Energy Agency, POB 100, 1400 Vienna, Austria. *T:* (1) 2360, ext. 1111.

BLOCH, Prof. Konrad Emil; Higgins Professor of Biochemistry, Harvard University, since 1954; *b* 21 Jan. 1912; *s* of Frederick D. Bloch and Hedwig (*née* Striemer); *m* 1941, Lore Teutsch; one *s* one *d. Educ:* Technische Hochschule, Munich; Columbia Univ., New York. MA Oxon 1982. Instructor and Research Associate, Columbia Univ., 1939–46; Univ. of Chicago: Asst Prof., 1946–48; Associate Prof., 1948–50; Prof., 1950–54. Newton-Abraham Vis. Prof., and Fellow of Lincoln Coll., Oxford, 1982. Foreign Mem., Royal Soc., 1982. Nobel Prize for Medicine (jointly), 1964; US Nat. Medal of Science, 1988. *Publications:* Lipide Metabolism, 1961; numerous papers in biochemical journals. *Address:* 16 Moon Hill Road, Lexington, MA 02173, USA. *T:* (617) 8629076; Department of Chemistry, Harvard University, 12 Oxford Street, Cambridge, MA 02138, USA.

BLOCH, Prof. Maurice Émile Félix, PhD; FBA 1990; Professor of Anthropology, University of London at London School of Economics, since 1984; *b* 21 Oct. 1939; *s* of late Pierre Bloch and of Claude Kennedy; step *s* of John Stodart Kennedy, FRS; *m* 1963, Jean Helen Medlicott; one *s* one *d. Educ:* Lycée Carnot, Paris; Perse Sch., Cambridge; LSE (BA 1962); Fitzwilliam Coll., Cambridge (PhD 1968). Asst Lectr, Univ. of Wales, Swansea, 1968; Lectr, LSE, 1969; Reader, London Univ., 1977. Corresp. Mem., Académie Malgache, Madagascar, 1965. *Publications:* Placing the Dead, 1971; Marxism and Anthropology, 1983; From Blessing to Violence, 1986; Ritual, History and Power, 1989; Prey into Hunter, 1992. *Recreation:* book binding. *Address:* Department of Anthropology, London School of Economics, Houghton Street, WC2A 2AE. *T:* 0171–405 7686.

BLOCH, Dame Merle Florence; *see* Park, Dame Merle F.

BLOCK, Brig. David Arthur Kennedy William, CBE 1961; DSO 1945; MC 1943; retired; *b* 13 June 1908; *s* of late Col Arthur Hugh Block; *m* 1949, Elizabeth Grace (*d* 1975), *e d* of late Lieut-Col E. G. Troyte-Bullock, CMG, Zeals House, Wiltshire, and *widow* of Major G. E. Sebag-Montefiore, D'Anvers House, Culworth, near Banbury; no *c. Educ:* Blundell's; RMA, Woolwich. Served War of 1939–45 (despatches, MC, DSO); CO 152nd (Ayrshire Yeomanry) Field Regt, RA, 1943–45; Coll. Comdr, RMA Sandhurst, 1947–50. CO 2nd Regt RHA, 1950–53; GSO1 Secretariat, SHAPE, 1953–54; CRA, 7th Armoured Div., 1954–57; Comd 18th Trg Bde, RA, 1958–61; retired, 1961. ADC to the Queen, 1959. *Recreations:* hunting, shooting, golf. *Address:* Benville Manor Lodge, Corscombe, Dorchester, Dorset DT2 0NW. *T:* Corscombe (01935) 891205. *Club:* Army and Navy.

BLOCK, David Greenberg, AC 1988 (AO 1983); adviser and company director; *b* 21 March 1936; *s* of Emanuel Block and Hannah Greenberg; *m* 1959, Naomi Denfield; one *s* three *d. Educ:* King Edward VII Sch., Johannesburg; Univ. of Witwatersrand (BJuris cum laude). Joined Schroder-Darling & Co., 1964, Dir, 1967–72; Chairman: David Block & Associates, 1972–81; Trinity Properties, 1984–90; George Ward Group, 1986–89; Dep. Chm., Concrete Constructions, 1990; Director: CSR, 1977–88; Kalamazoo Holdings, 1986–94; Dep. Chm., Pacific Magazines & Publishing, 1991–; Dir, Lloyds Bank NZA, Chm., Lloyds Internat., Dir, Lloyds Merchant Bank (UK) and Adviser, Lloyds Merchant Bank Holdings, 1981–86; Consultant, Coudert Brothers, 1986–91; Adviser: Coopers & Lybrand, 1986–93; S. G. Warburg Group, 1987–. Consultant: to Prime Minister and Cabinet, 1986–89; to govts, cos and instns, 1986–; to Premier's Dept, NSW, 1987–88; Mem., Cttee of Enquiry into inflation and taxation, 1975; Chm., Efficiency Scrutiny Unit and Admin. Reform Unit, 1986–88. Comr, Aust. Film Commn, 1978–81; Chm., Sydney Opera House Trust, 1981–89; Trustee, Japanese Friends of Sydney Opera House Foundn, 1992–; Councillor, Asia-Australian Inst., 1991–; Gov., Aust. Nat. Gall. Foundn, 1992–. Dir, Univ. of NSW Foundn, 1989–. Fellow, Senate of Univ. of Sydney, 1983–87. Hon. LLD New South Wales, 1992. *Recreations:* swimming, squash, music, theatre. *Address:* David Block Pty, The Chifley Tower, 2 Chifley Square, Sydney, NSW 2000, Australia. *T:* (2) 2327199, *Fax:* (2) 2326908; (home) 30 Clarke Street, Vaucluse, NSW 2030, Australia. *T:* (2) 3376211. *Clubs:* American, University (Sydney).

BLOEMBERGEN, Prof. Nicolaas; Gerhard Gade University Professor, Harvard University, 1980–90, now Emeritus; *b* 11 March 1920; *m* 1950, Huberta Deliana Brink; one *s* two *d. Educ:* Univ. of Utrecht (BA, MA); Univ. of Leiden (PhD). Research Associate, Leiden, 1947–48; Harvard University: Associate Prof., 1951; Gordon McKay Prof. of Applied Physics, 1957; Rumford Prof. of Physics, 1974. Hon. DSc: Laval Univ., 1987; Connecticut Univ., 1988; Univ. of Hartford, 1990. Stuart Ballantine Medal, Franklin Inst., 1961; Nat. Medal of Science, 1974; Lorentz Medal, Royal Dutch Acad. of Science, 1978; Alexander von Humboldt Senior US Scientist Award, Munich, 1980; (jtly) Nobel Prize in Physics, 1981; IEEE Medal of Honor, 1983; Dirac Medal, Univ. of NSW, 1983. Commander, Order of Orange Nassau (Netherlands), 1983. *Publications:* Nuclear Magnetic Relaxation, 1948 (New York 1961); Nonlinear Optics, 1965, reprinted 1991; over 300 papers in scientific jls. *Address:* Pierce Hall, Harvard University, Cambridge, MA 02138, USA. *T:* (617) 4953336.

BLOEMFONTEIN, Bishop of, since 1982; **Rt. Rev. Thomas Shaun Stanage;** *b* 6 April 1932; *s* of late Robert and of Edith Clarice Stanage. *Educ:* King James I Grammar Sch., Bishop Auckland; Univ. of Oxford (MA, Hons Theology, 1956). Curate, St Faith, Great Crosby, 1958–61; Minister of Conventional District of St Andrews, Orford, 1961–63; Vicar, St Andrew, Orford, 1963–70; Rector, All Saints, Somerset West, 1970–75; Dean of Kimberley, 1975–78; Bishop Suffragan of Johannesburg, 1978–82. Liaison Bishop to Missions to Seamen, Southern Africa. Hon. DD, Nashotah Theol Sem., Wisconsin, 1986. *Recreations:* flying (private pilot); music (organ, violin and piano). *Address:* Bishop's House, 16 York Road, Bloemfontein, 9301, S Africa. *T:* (51) 314351. *Clubs:* Bloemfontein; Good Hope Flying, Cape Aero (Cape Town).

BLOFELD, Hon. Sir John Christopher Calthorpe, Kt 1991; DL; **Hon. Mr Justice Blofeld;** a Judge of the High Court of Justice, Queen's Bench Division, since 1990; Presiding Judge, South East Circuit, since 1993; *b* 11 July 1932; *s* of late T. R. C. Blofeld, CBE; *m* 1961, Judith Anne, *er d* of Alan Mohun and Mrs James Mitchell; two *s* one *d. Educ:* Eton; King's Coll., Cambridge. Called to Bar, Lincoln's Inn, 1956, Bencher, 1990; QC 1975; a Recorder of the Crown Court, 1975–82; a Circuit Judge, 1982–90. Inspector, Dept of Trade, 1979–81. Chancellor, Dio. St Edmundsbury and Ipswich, 1973. DL Norfolk, 1991. *Recreations:* cricket, gardening. *Address:* Royal Courts of Justice, Strand, WC2A 2LL. *Club:* Boodle's.

BLOIS, Sir Charles (Nicholas Gervase), 11th Bt, *cr* 1686; farming since 1965; *b* 25 Dec. 1939; *s* of Sir Gervase Ralph Edmund Blois, 10th Bt and Mrs Audrey Winifred Blois (*née* Johnson); *S* father, 1968; *m* 1967, Celia Helen Mary Pritchett; one *s* one *d. Educ:* Harrow; Trinity Coll., Dublin; Royal Agricultural Coll., Cirencester. Australia, 1963–65. FRGS. *Recreations:* yachting, shooting. *Heir:* *s* Andrew Charles David Blois, *b* 7 Feb. 1971. *Address:* Red House, Westleton, Saxmundham, Suffolk IP17 3EQ. *T:* Westleton (01728) 648200. *Clubs:* Cruising Association; Ocean Cruising.

BLOKH, Alexandre, PhD, (pen-name **Jean Blot**); writer, since 1956; International Secretary, PEN Club, since 1982; *b* Moscow, 31 March 1923; *s* of Arnold Blokh, man of letters, and Anne (*née* Berlinrote); *m* 1956, Nadia Ermolaiev. *Educ:* Bromsgrove Public Sch., Worcester; Univ. of Paris (PhD Law, PhD Letters). International Civil Servant, United Nations, 1947–62: New York, until 1956; Geneva, 1958–62; Director, Arts and Letters, UNESCO, Paris, 1962–81. Critic, arts and letters, in reviews: Arche, Preuves, NRF. Prix des Critiques, 1972; Prix Valéry Larbaud, 1977; Prix Cazes, 1982; Grand Prix de la Critique, 1986; Prix International de la Paix, 1990. *Publications: novels:* Le Soleil de Cavouri, 1956; Les Enfants de New York, 1959; Obscur Ennemi, 1961; Les Illusions Nocturnes, 1964; La Jeune Géante, 1969; La Difficulté d'aimer, 1971; Les Cosmopolites, 1976; Gris du Ciel, 1981; Tout l'été, 1985; Sainte Imposture, 1988; *essays:* Marguerite Yourcenar; Ossip Mandelstam; Là où tu iras; Sporade; Ivan Gontcharov; La Montagne Sainte; Albert Cohen; Si loin de Dieu et autres voyages; Bloomsbury; Retour en Asie; Vladimir Nabokov. *Address:* 34 Square Montsouris, 75014 Paris. *T:* 45893416; 9–10 Charterhouse Building, Goswell Road, EC1M 7AT. *T:* 0171–379 7939.

BLOM-COOPER, Sir Louis (Jacques), Kt 1992; QC 1970; Independent Commissioner for the Holding Centres, Northern Ireland, since 1993; a Judge of the Courts of Appeal, Jersey and Guernsey, since 1989; *b* 27 March 1926; *s* of Alfred Blom-Cooper and Ella Flesseman, Rotterdam; *m* 1952 (marr. diss. 1970); two *s* one *d*; *m* 1970, Jane Elizabeth, *e d* of Maurice and Helen Smither, Woodbridge, Suffolk; one *s* two *d. Educ:* Port Regis Prep. Sch.; Seaford Coll.; King's Coll., London (FKC 1994); Municipal Univ. of Amsterdam; Fitzwilliam Coll., Cambridge. LLB London, 1952; Dr Juris Amsterdam, 1954. HM Army, 1944–47: Capt., E Yorks Regt. Called to Bar, Middle Temple, 1952; Bencher, 1978. Mem., Home Secretary's Adv. Council on the Penal System, 1966–78. Chairman: Panel of Inquiry into circumstances surrounding the death of Jasmine Beckford, 1985; Cttee of Inquiry into complaints about Ashworth Hosp., 1991–92; Commissioner of Inquiry: into allegations of arson and political corruption in the Turks and Caicos Is, 1986 (report published, 1986); into the N Creek Develt Project, Turks and Caicos Is, 1986–87. Chairman: Indep. Cttee for the Supervision of Standards of Telephone Information Services, 1986–93; Mental Health Act Commn, 1987–94; Commn on the future of Occupational Therapy, 1988–89; Press Council, 1989–90; Review of Mental Health Services in S Devon, 1994; Georgina Robinson Inquiry Cttee, 1994. Vice-Pres., Howard League for Penal Reform, 1984– (Chm., 1973–84). Chm., BBC London Local Radio Adv. Council, 1970–73. Jt Dir, Legal Res. Unit, Bedford Coll., Univ. of London, 1967–82; Vis. Prof., QMC, London Univ., 1983–88. Trustee, Scott Trust (The Guardian Newspaper), 1982–88. Joint Editor, Common Market Law Reports. JP Inner London, 1966–79 (transf. City of London, 1969). FRSA 1984. Hon. DLitt Loughborough, 1991. *Publications:* Bankruptcy in Private International Law, 1954; The Law as Literature, 1962; The A6 Murder (A Semblance of Truth), 1963; (with T. P. Morris) A Calendar of Murder, 1964; Language of the Law, 1965; (with O. R. McGregor and Colin Gibson) Separated Spouses, 1970; (with G. Drewry) Final Appeal: a study of the House of Lords in its judicial capacity, 1972; (ed) Progress in Penal Reform, 1975; (ed with G. Drewry) Law and Morality, 1976; contrib. to Modern Law Review, Brit. Jl of Criminology, Brit. Jl of Sociology. *Recreations:* watching and reporting on Association football, reading, music, writing, broadcasting. *Address:* 2 Ripplevale Grove, N1 1HU. *T:* 0171–607 8045. *Clubs:* Athenæum, MCC.

BLOMEFIELD, Sir (Thomas) Charles (Peregrine), 6th Bt *cr* 1807; Fine Art Dealer; *b* 24 July 1948; *s* of Sir Thomas Edward Peregrine Blomefield, 5th Bt, and of Ginette, Lady

Blomefield; *S* father, 1984; *m* 1975, Georgina Geraldine, *d* of late Commander C. E. Over, Lugger End, Portscatho, Cornwall; one *s* two *d*. *Educ:* Wellington Coll., Berks; Mansfield Coll., Oxford. Christie's, 1970–75; Wildenstein and Co., 1975–76; Director, Lidchi Art Gallery, Johannesburg, 1976–78; Man. Director, Charles Blomefield and Co., 1980–. *Recreations:* travel, listening to music. *Heir: s* Thomas William Peregrine Blomefield, *b* 16 July 1983. *Address:* Attlepin Farm, Chipping Campden, Glos GL55 6PP.

BLOMQVIST, Leif; Commander, Order of the Lion of Finland; Knight, 1st Class, Order of White Rose of Finland; Ambassador of Finland to the Court of St James's, since 1991; *b* 20 March 1937; *s* of Viktor Hardy Blomqvist and Harriet Ellinor Blomqvist; *m* 1965, Marianne Sand, PhD. *Educ:* Univ. of Helsinki (LLM). Entered Finnish diplomatic service, 1965; Attaché, Addis Ababa, 1967–70; 2nd Sec., Tel Aviv, 1970–71; Dept of External Econ. Relns, Foreign Ministry, 1971–73; 1st Sec., Finnish Mission to CSCE, Geneva, 1973–75; Counsellor, Finnish Permanent Mission, Geneva, 1975–77; Vice-Chm., Finnish Delegn to CSCE follow-up meeting, Belgrade, 1977–78; Counsellor, Min. for Foreign Affairs, 1978–80; Dir and Dep. Dir Gen., External Econ. Relations, 1980–85; Ambassador to European Communities, Brussels, 1985–90; Ambassador, Min. for Foreign Affairs, 1990–91. Comdr, Order of North Star (Sweden); Grosses Verdienstkreutz (Germany); Kt Comdr, Order of White Falcon (Iceland). *Recreations:* oriental rugs, English furniture. *Address:* Embassy of Finland, 38 Chesham Place, SW1X 8HW. *T:* 0171–838 6200.

BLONDEL, Prof. Jean Fernand Pierre; Professor of Political Science, European University Institute, Florence, 1985–94; *b* Toulon, France, 26 Oct. 1929; *s* of Fernand Blondel and Marie Blondel (*née* Santelli); *m* 1st, 1954, Michèle (*née* Hadet) (marr. diss. 1979); two *d;* 2nd, 1982, Mrs Theresa Martineau. *Educ:* Collège Saint Louis de Gonzague and Lycée Henri IV, Paris; Institut d'Etudes Politiques and Faculté de Droit, Paris; St Antony's Coll., Oxford. Asst Lectr, then Lectr in Govt, Univ. of Keele, 1958–63; Vis. ACLS Fellow, Yale Univ., 1963–64; Prof. of Government, 1964–84, and Dean, Sch. of Comparative Studies, 1967–69, Univ. of Essex; Vis. Prof., Carleton Univ., Canada, 1969–70; Vis. Schol., Russell Sage Foundn, NY, 1984–85. Exec. Dir, European Consortium for Political Res., 1970–79. Member: Royal Swedish Acad. of Scis, 1990; Academia Europaea, 1993. Hon. DLitt Salford, 1990; Dr *hc* Essex, 1992; Univ. Catholique de Louvain, 1992. *Publications:* Voters, Parties and Leaders, 1963; (jtly) Constituency Politics, 1964; (jtly) Public Administration in France, 1965; An Introduction to Comparative Government, 1969; (jtly) Workbook for Comparative Government, 1972; Comparing Political Systems, 1972; Comparative Legislatures, 1973; The Government of France, 1974; Thinking Politically, 1976; Political Parties, 1978; World Leaders, 1980; The Discipline of Politics, 1981; The Organisation of Governments, 1982; (jtly) Comparative Politics, 1984; Government Ministers in the Contemporary World, 1985; Political Leadership, 1987; (ed jtly) Western European Cabinets, 1988; Comparative Government, 1990; (ed jtly) The Profession of Cabinet Minister in Western Europe, 1991; (ed jtly) Governing Together, 1993; articles in: Political Studies, Parliamentary Affairs, Public Administration, Revue Française de Science Politique, European Jl of Political Research, etc. *Recreation:* holidays in Provence. *Address:* 15 Marloes Road, W8 6LQ. *T:* 0171–370 6008; 9 rue Général de Partouneaux, Mourillon, Toulon, France.

BLOOD, Bindon, (Peter); Director, Western Marketing Consultants Ltd, since 1987; Senior Industrialist and Enterprise Counsellor for Department of Trade and Industry, 1986–94; *b* 24 Sept. 1920; *o s* of Brig. William Edmunds Robarts Blood, CBE, MC, Croix de Guerre, and Eva Gwendoline (*née* Harrison); *m* 1953, Elizabeth Ann, *d* of Harold Drummond Hillier, MC; one *s* one *d*. *Educ:* Imperial Service Coll., Windsor. Family public works and civil engineering business, 1938–41; served Royal Engineers, 1941–46 (despatches 1944); Engineering Div., Forestry Commn, 1946–48; regular commn, RE, 1948; Second i/c, RE Officer Training Unit, 1948–51; Staff Coll., Camberley, 1951; Sec., Army Bd, NATO Mil. Agency for Standardisation, 1952–53; invalided from service, 1953; Intelligence Co-ordination Staff, FO, 1953–58; Founder and formerly Managing Director: Isora Integrated Ceilings Ltd; Clean Room Construction Ltd; Mitchel and King (Sales) Ltd; Dep. Chm. and Group Marketing Dir, King Group. Institute of Marketing: Dir of Marketing Services, 1971; Dir-Gen., 1972–84. Chm., Industrial Market Research Ltd, 1984–87. Gov., Berks Coll. of Art and Design, 1975–89 (Chm. of Govs, 1981–86). FRSA, FInstM. *Recreations:* photography, furniture restoration, travel, music, local community activities. *Address:* Mallows, Berries Road, Cookham, Berks SL6 9SD. *T:* Bourne End (01628) 525319.

BLOOM, André Borisovich; *see* Anthony, Metropolitan.

BLOOM, Charles, QC 1987; a Recorder of the Crown Court, since 1983; *b* 6 Nov. 1940; *s* of Abraham Barnett Bloom and Freda Bloom (*née* Craft); *m* 1967, Janice Rachelle Goldberg; one *s* one *d*. *Educ:* Manchester Central Grammar School; Manchester University. LLB Hons 1962. Called to the Bar, Gray's Inn, 1963; practised on Northern Circuit, 1963–. Chm., Medical Appeal Tribunals, 1979–. *Recreations:* tennis, theatre. *Address:* 28 St John Street, Manchester M3 4DJ. *T:* 0161–834 8418. *Club:* Friedland Postmusaf Tennis (Cheadle).

BLOOM, Claire; *b* London, 15 Feb. 1931; *d* of late Edward Bloom and of Elizabeth Bloom; *m* 1st, 1959, Rod Steiger (marr. diss. 1969); one *d;* 2nd, 1969; 3rd, 1990, Philip Roth, *qv* (marr. diss. 1995). *Educ:* Badminton, Bristol; America and privately. First work in England, BBC, 1946. Stratford: Ophelia, Lady Blanche (King John), Perdita, 1948; The Damask Cheek, Lyric, Hammersmith, 1949; The Lady's Not For Burning, Globe, 1949; Ring Round the Moon, Globe, 1949–50. Old Vic: 1952–53: Romeo and Juliet; 1953: Merchant of Venice; 1954: Hamlet, All's Well, Coriolanus, Twelfth Night, Tempest; 1956: Romeo and Juliet (London, and N American tour). Cordelia, in Stratford Festival Company, 1955 (London, provinces and continental tour); Duel of Angels, Apollo, 1958; Rashomon, NY, 1959; Altona, Royal Court, 1961; The Trojan Women, Spoleto Festival, 1963; Ivanov, Phoenix, 1965; A Doll's House, NY, 1971; Hedda Gabler, 1971; Vivat! Vivat Regina!, NY, 1971; A Doll's House, Criterion, 1973 (filmed 1973); A Streetcar Named Desire, Piccadilly, 1974; Rosmersholm, Haymarket, 1977; The Cherry Orchard, Chichester Fest., 1981, Cambridge, Mass, 1994; These are Women, a portrait of Shakespeare's heroines, own one-woman perfs, 1981– (US tour, 1981–82); When We Dead Waken, Almeida, 1990. First film, Blind Goddess, 1947; *films include:* Limelight; The Man Between; Richard III; Alexander the Great; The Brothers Karamazov; The Buccaneers; Look Back in Anger; Three Moves to Freedom; The Brothers Grimm; The Chapman Report; The Haunting; 80,000 Suspects; Alta Infedelta; Il Maestro di Vigevano; The Outrage; The Spy Who Came in From The Cold; Charly; Three into Two won't go; A Severed Head; Red Sky at Morning; Islands In The Stream; The Clash of the Titans, 1979; Always, 1984; Sammy and Rosie Get Laid, 1987; Crimes and Misdemeanors, 1989. *Television:* first appearance on television programmes, 1952, since when she has had frequent successes on TV in the US: In Praise of Love, 1975; Anastasia, 1986; Queenie, 1986; BBC: A Legacy, 1975; The Ghost Writer, 1983; Shadowlands, 1985 (BAFTA award Best TV Actress); Time and the Conways, 1985; Oedipus the King, 1986; BBC Shakespeare: Katharine in Henry VIII, 1979; Gertrude in Hamlet, 1980; the Queen in Cymbeline, Lady Constance in King John, 1983; ITV: series: Brideshead Revisited, 1981; Intimate Contact, 1987; Shadow on the Sun, 1988; play, The Belle of Amherst, 1986; Channel Four: series, The Camomile Lawn, 1992; The Mirror Crack'd, 1992; Remember, 1993; A Village Affair, 1994. Distinguished Vis. Prof., Hunter Coll., NY, 1989. *Publication:* Limelight and After (autobiog.), 1982. *Recreations:* opera, music. *Address:* c/o Jeremy Conway, 18–21 Jermyn Street, SW1Y 6HB

BLOOMFIELD, Barry Cambray, MA, FLA; Director, Collection Development, Humanities and Social Sciences, British Library, 1985–90; *b* 1 June 1931; *s* of Clifford Wilson Bloomfield and Eileen Elizabeth (*née* Cambray); *m* 1958, Valerie Jean Philpot. *Educ:* East Ham Grammar Sch.; University College of the South-West, Exeter; University Coll. London; Birkbeck Coll., London. Served in Intelligence Corps, Malaya, 1952–54. Assistant, National Central Library, 1955; Librarian, College of S Mark and S John, Chelsea, 1956–61; Asst Librarian, London Sch. of Economics, 1961–63; Dep. Librarian, 1963–72, Librarian, 1972–78, School of Oriental and African Studies; Dir, India Office Library and Records, British Library (formerly FCO), 1978–85 and concurrently Keeper, Dept of Oriental MSS and Printed Bks, British Library, 1983–85. Chm., SCONUL Group of Orientalist Libraries, 1975–80; Pres., Bibliographical Soc., 1990–92 (Vice-Pres., 1979–90); Member: Council, Royal Asiatic Soc., 1980–84; British Assoc. for Cemeteries in S Asia, 1980–90; Britain-Burma Soc., 1980–90; Exec. Cttee, Friends of the Nat. Libraries, 1981–; Chm., Rare Books Gp, LA, 1991–95; International Federation of Library Associations: Chairman: Sect. on Bibliography, 1985–89; Div. of Bibliographic Control, 1985–89; Mem., Professional Bd, 1987–89. Trustee, Shakespeare Birthplace Trust, 1987–91. Vis. Professor, Univ. of Florida, 1963; Vis. Fellow, Univ. of Hawaii, 1977. *Publications:* New Verse in the '30s, 1960; W. H. Auden: a bibliography, 1964, 2nd edn 1972; ed, Autobiography of Sir J. P. Kay Shuttleworth, 1964; ed, (with V. J. Bloomfield, J. D. Pearson) Theses on Africa, 1964; ed, Theses on Asia, 1967; ed, The Acquisition and Provision of Foreign Books by National and University Libraries in the UK, 1972; An Author Index to Selected British 'Little' Magazines, 1976; Philip Larkin: a bibliography 1933–1976, 1979; (ed) Middle East Studies and Libraries, 1980; numerous articles in library and bibliog. jls. *Recreations:* reading, music. *Address:* Brambling, 24 Oxenturn Road, Wye, Kent TN25 5BE. *T:* Wye (01233) 813038. *Club:* Civil Service.

BLOOMFIELD, Keith George; HM Diplomatic Service; Counsellor (Political and Management), Rome, since 1994; *b* 2 June 1947; *s* of George William Bloomfield and Edith Joan Bloomfield; *m* 1976, Genevieve Charbonneau; three *d*. *Educ:* Kilburn Grammar Sch.; Lincoln Coll., Oxford (MA). Home Civil Service, 1969–80; Office of UK Rep. to EC, Brussels, 1980–85; Head of Chancery, Cairo, 1985–87; FCO, 1987–90; Dep. Head of Mission, Algiers, 1990–94. *Recreations:* music, tennis, reading. *Address:* c/o Foreign and Commonwealth Office, SW1A 2AH; Les Hommeaux, Combrée, 49520, France. *T:* (396) 4825411.

BLOOMFIELD, Sir Kenneth Percy, KCB 1987 (CB 1982); National Governor and Chairman of Broadcasting Council for Northern Ireland, BBC, since 1991; Head of Northern Ireland Civil Service, and Second Permanent Under Secretary of State, Northern Ireland Office, 1984–91; *b* 15 April 1931; *o c* of late Harry Percy Bloomfield and Doris Bloomfield, Belfast; *m* 1960, Mary Elizabeth Ramsey; one *s* one *d*. *Educ:* Royal Belfast Academical Instn; St Peter's Coll., Oxford (MA; Hon. Fellow, 1991). Min. of Finance, N Ireland, 1952–56; Private Sec. to Ministers of Finance, 1956–60; Dep. Dir, British Industrial Develt Office, NY, 1960–63; Asst and later Dep. Sec. to Cabinet, NI, 1963–72; Under-Sec., Northern Ireland Office, 1972–73; Sec. to Northern Ireland Executive, Jan.–May 1974; Permanent Secretary: Office of the Executive, NI, 1974–75; Dept of Housing, Local Govt and Planning, NI, 1975–76; Dept of the Environment, NI, 1976–81; Dept of Commerce, NI, 1981–82; Dept of Economic Develt, 1982–84. Review of Dental Remuneration, 1992. Chairman: Chief Executives' Forum for NI Public Services, 1991–; Higher Educn Council for NI, 1993–. Mem., NI Adv. Bd, Bank of Ireland, 1991–; Member of Board: Co-operation North, 1991–93; Opera, NI, 1992–; Member: Statute Law Adv. Cttee, 1992–; Nat. Steering Cttee, Give as You Earn, 1992–93. Chm., Children in Need Trust, 1992–; Mem. Bd, Green Park Hosp. Trust, 1993–; Patron, Belfast Improved Houses, 1992–. Senator (Crown nominee), QUB, 1991–93. Governor, Royal Belfast Academical Instn. Bass Ireland Lectr, Univ. of Ulster, 1991. Hon. LLD QUB, 1991. Dr Ben Wilson Trophy for Individual or Corporate Excellence, NI Chamber of Commerce and Industry, 1990. *Publication:* Stormont in Crisis (a memoir), 1994. *Recreations:* reading history and biography, swimming. *Address:* c/o Broadcasting House, Ormeau Avenue, Belfast BT2 8HQ. *T:* Belfast (01232) 338000.

BLOOR, Prof. David; Professor of Applied Physics, since 1989, and Chairman of Department of Physics, since 1993, University of Durham; *b* 25 July 1937; *s* of Alfred Edwin Bloor and Gladys Ellen Bloor (*née* Collins); *m* 1960, Margaret E. A. Avery; four *s* (and one *s* decd). *Educ:* Queen Mary College London (BSc, PhD). CPhys, FInstP. Lectr, Dept of Physics, Univ. of Canterbury, NZ, 1961–64; Queen Mary College London: Lectr, Dept of Physics, 1964; Reader, 1980–84; Prof. of Polymer Physics, 1984–89. Humboldt Fellow, Univ. of Stuttgart, 1975–76; Erskine Fellow, Univ. of Canterbury, NZ, 1983; Royal Society SERC Indust. Fellow, GEC Marconi Res. Centre, 1985–86. *Publications:* contribs to professional jls. *Recreations:* cycling, gardening. *Address:* Applied Physics Group, Department of Physics, University of Durham, South Road, Durham DH1 3LE. *T:* 0191–374 2393.

BLOSSE, Sir Richard Hely L.; *see* Lynch-Blosse.

BLOT, Jean; *see* Blokh, A.

BLOUNT, Bertie Kennedy, CB 1957; DrPhilNat; CChem, FRSC; *b* 1 April 1907; *s* of late Col G. P. C. Blount, DSO, and late Bridget Constance, *d* of Maj.-Gen. J. F. Bally, CVO; unmarried. *Educ:* Malvern Coll.; Trinity Coll., Oxford (MA 1932, BSc 1929); Univ. of Frankfurt (DrPhilNat 1931). Ramsay Memorial Fellow, 1931; 1851 Senior Student, 1933; Dean of St Peter's Hall, Oxford, 1933–37; Messrs Glaxo Laboratories Ltd: Head of Chemical Research Laboratory, 1937; Principal Technical Executive, 1938–40. Served Army (Intelligence Corps), War of 1939–45; Capt. 1940; Major 1942; Col 1945. Asst Director of Research, The Wellcome Foundation, 1947; Director of Research Branch, Control Commission for Germany, 1948, and subsequently also Chief of Research Div. of Military Security Board; Director of Scientific Intelligence, Min. of Defence, 1950–52; Dep. Secretary, DSIR, 1952; Min. of Technology, 1964; retired 1966. Member Exec. Cttee, British Council, 1957–66. Royal Society of Arts: Armstrong Lecturer, 1955; Cantor Lecturer, 1963. Member Parry Cttee to review Latin American Studies in British Universities, 1962; Pres., Exec. Cttee, Internat. Inst. of Refrigeration, 1963–71, Hon. Pres. 1971; Hon. Member: (British) Inst. of Refrigeration, 1971; Max-Planck-Ges. zur Förderung der Wissenschaften, 1984. Hon. Fellow, St Peter's Coll., Oxford, 1988. Golden doctorate, Frankfurt Univ., 1982. *Publications:* papers in scientific and other journals. *Recreations:* travel, walking, gardening. *Address:* Tarrant Rushton House, Blandford, Dorset DT11 8SD. *T:* Blandford (01258) 52256. *Club:* Athenæum.

BLOUNT, Sir Walter (Edward Alpin), 12th Bt *cr* 1642; DSC 1943 and two Bars 1945; farmer; *b* 31 Oct. 1917; *s* of Sir Edward Robert Blount, 11th Bt, and Violet Ellen (*d* 1969), *d* of Alpin Grant Fowler; *S* father, 1978; *m* 1954, Eileen Audrey, *d* of late Hugh B. Carritt; one *d*. *Educ:* Beaumont College; Sidney Sussex Coll., Cambridge (MA). Served RN, 1939–47 (MTBs). Qualified as Solicitor, 1950; practised Gold Coast, West Africa,

1950–52; London and Cambridge, 1952–76. Farmer, Tilkhurst, East Grinstead, Sussex, 1978–. *Recreation:* sailing. *Heir:* none. *Address:* 19 St Anns Terrace, St John's Wood, NW8 6PH. *T:* 0171–722 0802; Regent House, Seaview, IoW PO34 5ET; Tilkhurst, Imberhorne Lane, East Grinstead, Sussex RH19 1TY. *Clubs:* Bembridge Sailing, Seaview Yacht, Cambridge Cruising, RNVR Sailing, Island Sailing.

BLOW, Prof. David Mervyn, FRS 1972; Professor of Biophysics, Imperial College, University of London, 1977–94, now Emeritus; *b* 27 June 1931; *s* of Rev. Edward Mervyn and Dorothy Laura Blow; *m* 1955, Mavis Sears; one *s* one *d. Educ:* Kingswood Sch.; Corpus Christi Coll., Cambridge (MA, PhD). FInstP. Fulbright Scholar, Nat. Inst. of Health, Bethesda, Md, and MIT, 1957–59; MRC Unit for Study of Molecular Biological Systems, Cambridge, 1959–62; MRC Lab. of Molecular Biology, Cambridge, 1962–77; College Lectr and Fellow, Trinity Coll., Cambridge, 1968–77; Imperial College, London: Dean, Royal Coll. of Sci., 1981–84; Head, Dept of Physics, 1991–94. Pres., British Crystallographic Assoc., 1984–87. For. Associate Mem., Acad. des Scis, Paris, 1992. Mem. Governing Body, Imperial Coll., London, 1987–94. Biochem. Soc. CIBA Medal, 1967; (jtly) Charles Léopold Meyer Prize, 1979; (jtly) Wolf Foundn Prize for Chemistry, 1987. *Publications:* papers and reviews in scientific jls. *Recreations:* walking, sailing. *Address:* Blackett Laboratory, Imperial College of Science, Technology and Medicine, University of London, SW7 2BZ.

BLOW, Joyce, (Mrs Anthony Darlington), OBE 1994; FIPR; FIMgt; Chairman, Authority of the Direct Marketing Association, since 1992; *b* 4 May 1929; *d* of late Walter Blow and Phyllis (*née* Grainger); *m* 1974, Lt-Col J. A. B. Darlington, RE retd. *Educ:* Bell Baxter Sch., Cupar, Fife; Edinburgh Univ. (MA Hons). FIPR 1964. John Lewis Partnership, 1951–52; FBI, 1952–53; Press Officer, Council of Indust. Design, 1953–63; Publicity and Advertising Manager, Heal & Son Ltd, 1963–65; entered Civil Service on first regular recruitment of direct entry Principals from business and industry: BoT, 1965–67; Monopolies Commn (gen. enquiry into restrictive practices in supply of prof. services), 1967–70; DTI, 1970, Asst Sec. 1972; Dept of Prices and Consumer Protection, 1974–77; Under-Secretary: OFT, 1977–80; DTI, 1980–84; Chm., Mail Order Publishers' Authy, 1985–92. Chm., E Sussex FHSA, 1990–. Pres., Assoc. for Quality in Healthcare, 1991–94; Vice-Pres., Inst. of Trading Standards Admin, 1985–; Bd Mem., BSI, 1987– (Chm., Consumer Policy Cttee, 1987–93). Founder Mem. and Past Pres. Assoc. of Women in Public Relations. Trustee, Univ. of Edinburgh Develt Trust, 1990–94; Chm., PR Educn Trust, 1992–. Freeman, City of London. *Publication:* Consumers and International Trade: a handbook, 1987. *Recreations:* music, particularly opera; travel, France. *Address:* 17 Fentiman Road, SW8 1LD. *T:* 0171–735 4023; 9 Crouchfield Close, Seaford, E Sussex. *Clubs:* Arts, Reform.

BLOW, Sandra, RA 1978 (ARA 1971); *b* 14 Sept. 1925; *d* of Jack and Lily Blow. *Educ:* St Martin's School of Art; Royal Academy Sch.; Accademia di Belle Arti, Rome. Tutor, Painting School, Royal Coll. of Art, 1960–75. *Individual Exhibitions:* Gimpel Fils, 1952, 1954, 1960, 1962; Saidenburg Gallery, NY, 1957; New Art Centre, London, 1966, 1968, 1971, 1973; Francis Graham-Dixon, 1991; *retrospective:* Royal Acad's Sackler Galls, 1994. Represented in group exhibitions in Britain (including British Painting 74, Hayward Gall.; Tate, St Ives, 1995), USA, Italy, Denmark, France. Won British Section of Internat. Guggenheim Award, 1960; 2nd prize, John Moore's Liverpool Exhibition, 1961; Arts Council Purchase Award, 1965–66. *Official Purchases:* Peter Stuyvesant Foundation; Nuffield Foundation; Arts Council of Great Britain; Arts Council of N Ireland; Walker Art Gallery, Liverpool; Allbright Knox Art Gallery, Buffalo, NY; Museum of Modern Art, NY; Tate Gallery; Chantry Bequest; Gulbenkian Foundation; Min. of Public Building and Works; Contemp. Art Society; Victoria and Albert Museum; Fitzwilliam Museum, Cambridge; City of Leeds Art Gall.; Graves Art Gall., Sheffield; Heathrow Airport (glass screen). *Address:* c/o Royal Academy of Arts, Piccadilly, W1V 0DS.

BLOWERS, Dr Anthony John, CBE 1985; JP, DL; CBiol; FIMLS; Commissioner, Mental Health Act Commission, since 1987; Director of Corporate Affairs, Magellan Medical Communications, since 1990; *b* 11 Aug. 1926; *s* of Geoffrey Hathaway and Louise Blowers; *m* 1948, Yvonne Boiteux-Buchanan; two *s* one *d. Educ:* Sloane Sch., Chelsea; Sir John Cass Coll.; Univ. of London; Univ. of Surrey (PhD 1982). FIMLS 1983; CBiol 1984. served War, RCS, 1944–45; served: RAMC, 1945–46; RWAFF, 1946–48. Min. of Agriculture, 1948–59, Exptl Officer, 1953–54; Sandoz Pharmaceuticals, 1959–91; Sen. Res. Officer, 1973–87; Psychopharmacology Consultant, 1987–91; Consultant in Bacteriology, Mansi Labs, 1973–90. Actg Chief Exec., Parkinson's Disease Soc., 1995–. Chairman: W Surrey and NE Hants HA, 1981–86; Mental Health and Learning Disabilities Monitoring Gp, SW Surrey HA, 1991–; Member: Surrey AHA, 1973–80 (Vice Chm., 1976–77); SW Thames RHA, 1980–81; Mental Health Review Tribunal, 1975–; Nat. Standing Cttees on Consent to Treatment and Community Care, 1992–. Admin. Sec., All-Party Parly Gp on Reproductive Health, 1994–. Member: Chertsey UDC, 1964–74 (Chm., 1969–70, 1973–74); Runnymede BC, 1973–84 (Chm., 1973–74); Surrey CC, 1970–85 (Vice Chm., Social Services Cttee, 1973–77); Surrey Police Authority, 1973–90 (Chm., 1981–85); Chm., Runnymede and Elmbridge Police Community Liaison Cttee, 1983–94. Chm. SE Region, and Mem. Nat. Adv. Council, Duke of Edinburgh's Award, 1990–; Chm., Surrey Magistrates' Soc., 1988–94; Member: Council, Magistrates' Assoc., 1986–91; Bd of Visitors, Coldingley Prison, 1978–93; Court, Surrey Univ., 1986–; Surrey Scout Council, 1991–; Pres., Runnymede Scout Council, 1970–84. Vice-Pres., Hosp. Saving Assoc., 1994–; Mem. Council, 1986–, Trustee, 1995–, Psychiatry Res. Trust. Governor: Fullbrook Sch., 1967–85 (Chm., 1981–85); Ottershaw Sch., 1975–81 (Chm., 1979–81). Liveryman, Worshipful Soc. of Apothecaries, 1988 (Yeoman, 1983–88); Freeman, City of London, 1983; Hon. Freeman, Bor. of Runnymede, 1985. JP 1970, DL 1986, High Sheriff, 1990–91, Surrey. St John Ambulance: Asst Dir Gen., 1985–91; Dir Gen., 1991–94; Actg Chief Comdr, 1991–92; Comdr, Surrey, 1987–91; Chm., St John Fellowship, 1995–. KStJ 1991 (Mem., Chapter-Gen., 1991–). *Publications:* The Isolation of Salmonellae, 1978; Tardive Dyskinesia, 1982; contribs to med. and scientific books and jls. *Recreations:* fund-raising, gardening. *Address:* Westward, 12 Birch Close, Boundstone, Farnham, Surrey GU10 4TJ. *T:* Farnham (01252) 792769.

BLUCK, Duncan Robert Yorke, CBE 1990 (OBE 1984); Chairman: British Tourist Authority, 1984–90; English Tourist Board, 1984–90; Director, John Swire & Sons, since 1984; *b* 19 March 1927; *s* of Thomas Edward Bluck and Ida Bluck; *m* 1952, Stella Wardlaw Murdoch; one *s* three *d. Educ:* Taunton Sch. RNVR, 1944–47. Joined John Swire & Sons, 1948; Dir, 1964–, Chief Exec., 1971–84, Chm., 1980–84, Cathay Pacific Airways; Chairman: John Swire & Sons (HK) Ltd, 1980–84; Swire Pacific Ltd, 1980–84; Swire Properties Ltd, 1980–84. Dir, Hongkong and Shanghai Banking Corp., 1981–84. Chairman: English Schools Foundn (Hongkong), 1978–84; Hongkong Tourist Assoc., 1981–84; Kent Economic Develt Bd, 1986–91. Governor, Marlborough House Sch., 1986–; Mem. Ct, Univ. of Kent, 1991–. JP Hong Kong, 1981–84. *Recreations:* sailing, swimming. *Address:* Elfords, Hawkhurst, Kent TN18 4RP. *T:* Hawkhurst (01580) 752153. *Clubs:* Brooks's; Hongkong, Sheko (Hongkong).

BLUE, Rabbi Lionel, OBE 1994; Lecturer, Leo Baeck College, since 1967; Convener of the Beth Din (Ecclesiastical Court) of the Reform Synagogues of Great Britain, 1971–88; *b* 6 Feb. 1930; *s* of late Harry and Hetty Blue. *Educ:* Balliol Coll., Oxford (MA History); University Coll. London (BA Semitics); Leo Baeck Coll., London (Rabbinical Dip). Ordained Rabbi, 1960; Minister to Settlement Synagogue and Middlesex New Synagogue, 1960–63; European Dir, World Union for Progressive Judaism, 1963–66; Co-Editor, Forms of Prayer, 1967–; broadcaster, 1967–; Feature Writer: The Universe, 1979–; The Standard, 1985–86. Scriptwriter and presenter, TV series, In Search of Holy England, 1989. *Publications:* To Heaven with Scribes and Pharisees, 1975; (jtly) A Taste of Heaven, 1977; (ed jtly) Forms of Prayer (Sabbath and Daily), 1977; A Backdoor to Heaven, 1979, revd edn 1985; (ed jtly) Forms of Prayer (Days of Awe), 1985; Bright Blue, 1985; (jtly) Simply Divine, 1985; Kitchen Blues, 1985; Bolts from the Blue, 1986; Blue Heaven, 1987; (jtly) Daytrips to Eternity, 1987; (jtly) The Guide to the Here and Hereafter, 1988; Blue Horizons, 1989; Bedside Manna, 1991; (jtly) How to Get Up When Life Gets You Down, 1992; (jtly) The Little Blue Book of Prayer, 1993. *Recreations:* window shopping, package holidays, monasteries, cooking. *Address:* Leo Baeck College, 80 East End Road, N3 2SY. *T:* 0181–349 4525.

BLUGLASS, Prof. Robert Saul, CBE 1995; MD, FRCPsych; Professor of Forensic Psychiatry, University of Birmingham, since 1979 (Regional Postgraduate Clinical Tutor in Forensic Psychiatry, since 1967); Clinical Director, Reaside Clinic, Birmingham, since 1987; *b* 22 Sept. 1930; *s* of Henry Bluglass and Fay (*née* Griew); *m* 1962, Jean Margaret Kerry (*née* Montgomery); one *s* one *d. Educ:* Warwick Sch., Warwick; Univ. of St Andrews (MB, ChB 1957, MD 1967). DPM 1962; FRCPsych 1976 (MRCPsych 1971); MRCP 1994. Formerly, Sen. Registrar in Psych., Royal Dundee Liff Hosp. and Maryfield Hosp., Dundee; Consultant in Forensic Psychiatry: W Midlands RHA and the Home Office, 1967–94; S Birmingham Mental Health NHS Trust, 1994–. Consultant i/c Midland Centre for For. Psych., All Saints Hosp., Birmingham, 1967–93; Hon. Lectr in For. Psych., Univ. of Birmingham, 1968–75, Sen. Clin. Lectr in For. Psych., 1975–79; Jt Dir, Midland Inst. of For. Medicine, 1975–87. Dep. Regional Advr in Psychiatry, W Midlands RHA, 1985–87, Regional Advr, 1987–92; Specialist Advr, H of C Select Cttee on Social Services, 1985–87; Consultant Advr in Psych., RAF, 1992–. Member: Adv. Cttee on Alcoholism, DHSS, 1975–80; Adv. Council on Probation, Home Office, 1974–77; Mental Health Reveiw Tribunal, 1979–; Mental Health Act Commn, 1983–85; Forensic Psych. Res. Liaison Gp, DHSS; Rev. of Services for Mentally Disordered Offenders (Reed Cttee), DoH, 1991–. Royal College of Psychiatrists: Mem., Ct of Electors, 1976–79; Mem. Council, 1973–76, 1976–78, 1980–86, 1986–91; Vice-Pres., 1983–85; Chm., For. Psych. Specialist Section, 1978–82; Chm., Midlands Div., 1986–91. FRSocMed 1975; Past Pres., Sect. of Psych., Birmingham Med. Inst.; Mem., Brit. Acad. of For. Sciences. Baron ver Heyden de Lancey Law Prize, RSocMed, 1983. *Publications:* Psychiatry, The Law and The Offender, 1980; A Guide to the Mental Health Act 1983, 1983; (ed with Prof. Sir Martin Roth) Psychiatry, Human Rights and the Law, 1985; (ed with Dr Paul Bowden) The Principles and Practice of Forensic Psychiatry, 1990; articles in Brit. Jl of Hosp. Med., BMJ, and Med., Science and the Law. *Recreations:* water-colour painting, cooking, gardening, swimming. *Address:* Reaside Clinic, Bristol Road South, Rubery, Rednal, Birmingham B45 9BE.

BLUMBERG, Prof. Baruch Samuel, MD, PhD; Fox Chase Distinguished Scientist, Senior Adviser to the President, Fox Chase Cancer Center, since 1989; University Professor of Medicine and Anthropology, University of Pennsylvania, since 1970; *b* 28 July 1925; *s* of Meyer Blumberg and Ida Blumberg; *m* 1954, Jean Liebesman Blumberg; two *s* two *d. Educ:* Union Coll. (BS Physics, 1946); Columbia University Coll. of Physicians and Surgeons (MD 1951); Balliol Coll., Oxford Univ. (PhD Biochemistry, 1957); FRCP 1984. US Navy, 1943–46 (Lieut JG). US Public Health Service (rank of med. dir, col), and Chief, Geographic Medicine and Genetics Sect., Nat. Insts. of Health, Bethesda, Md, 1957–64; Associate Dir for Clinical Res., then Vice-Pres. for Population Oncology, Fox Chase Cancer Center, 1964–89; Clin. Prof., Dept of Epidemiology, Univ. of Washington Sch. of Public Health, 1983–89; Master of Balliol Coll., Oxford, 1989–94. George Eastman Vis. Prof., Oxford Univ., 1983–84. Mem. Nat. Acad. of Sciences, Washington, DC. Hon. Fellow: Balliol Coll., Oxford, 1977; Indian Acad. of Scis. Hon. DSc: Univ. of Pittsburgh, 1977; Union Coll., Schenectady, NY, 1977; Med. Coll. of Pa, 1977; Dickinson Coll., Carlisle, Pa, 1977; Hahnemann Med. Coll., Philadelphia, Pa, 1977; Elizabethtown Coll., Pa, 1988; Ball State Univ., Muncie, 1989; Dr *hc* Univ. of Paris VII, 1978. (Jt) Nobel Prize in Physiology or Medicine, 1976. *Publications:* (ed) Genetic Polymorphisms and Geographic Variations in Disease, 1961; (ed jtly) Medical Clinics of North America: new developments in medicine, 1970; (ed jtly) Hepatitis B: the virus, the disease and the vaccine, 1984; *chapters in:* McGraw-Hill Encyclopedia of Science and Technology Yearbook, 1962; The Genetics of Migrant and Isolate Populations, ed E. Goldschmidt, 1963; Hemoglobin: its precursors and metabolites, ed F. W. Sunderman and F. W. Sunderman, Jr, 1964; McGraw-Hill Yearbook of Science and Technology, 1970; (also co-author chapter) Viral Hepatitis and Blood Transfusion, ed G. N. Vyas and others, 1972; Hematology, ed W. J. Williams and others, 1972; Progress in Liver Disease, Vol. IV, ed H. Popper and F. Schaffner, 1972; Australia Antigen, ed J. E. Prier and H. Friedman, 1973; Drugs and the Liver, ed. W. Gerok and K. Sickinger, 1975 (Germany); (*jtly*) *chapters in:* Progress in Medical Genetics, ed A. G. Steinberg and A. G. Bearn, 1965 (also London); Viruses Affecting Man and Animals, ed M. Sanders and M. Schaeffer, 1971; Perspectives in Virology, 1971; Transmissable Disease and Blood Transfusion, ed T. J. Greenwalt and G. A. Jamieson, 1975; Physiological Anthropology, ed A. Damon, 1975; Hepatite a Virus B et Hemodialyse, 1975 (Paris); Onco-Developmental Gene Expression, 1976; contrib. symposia; over 420 articles in scientific jls. *Recreations:* rock climbing, cycling, canoeing, cattle raising. *Address:* Fox Chase Cancer Center, 7701 Burholme Avenue, Philadelphia, PA 19111, USA. *T:* (215) 7282203. *Clubs:* Athenæum; Explorers (NY).

BLUMENTHAL, W(erner) Michael, PhD; Senior Advisor, Lazard Frères & Co., since 1990; *b* Germany, 3 Jan. 1926. *Educ:* Univ. of California at Berkeley; Princeton Univ. Research Associate, Princeton Univ., 1954–57; Vice-Pres., Dir, Crown Cork Internat. Corp., 1957–61; Dep. Asst Sec. of State for Econ. Affairs, Dept of State, 1961–63; Dep. Special Rep. of the President (with rank Ambassador) for Trade Negotiations, 1963–67; Pres., Bendix Internat., 1967–70; Bendix Corp.: Dir, 1967–77; Vice-Chm., 1970–71; Pres. and Chief Operating Officer, 1971–72; Chm. and Chief Exec. Officer, 1972–77; US Secretary of the Treasury, 1977–79; Burroughs Corp. subseq. Unisys: Chief Exec. Officer, 1980–90; Vice-Chm., 1980; Chm., 1981–90. Director: Tenneco, Inc.; Daimler-Benz InterServices; Internat. Adv. Bd, Chemical Bank; Mem., Business Council. *Address:* (office) One Rockefeller Plaza, New York, NY 10020, USA.

BLUMER, Rodney Milnes, (Rodney Milnes); Editor, Opera magazine, since 1986; Chief Opera Critic, The Times, since 1992; *b* 26 July 1936; *s* of Charles Eric Milnes Blumer and Kathleen Bertha Croft. *Educ:* Rugby School; Christ Church, Oxford (BA Hons Hist.). Editorial Dir, Rupert Hart-Davis Ltd, 1966–68; Music Critic, Queen magazine, later Harpers and Queen, 1968–87; Opera Critic: The Spectator, 1970–90; Evening Standard, 1990–92; contribs to Opera, 1971–; Editl Bd, 1973; Associate Editor, 1976. Pres., Critics' Circle, 1988–90. Kt, Order of White Rose (Finland). *Publications:* numerous opera translations. *Recreation:* travel. *Address:* 3/23 Northwood Hall, N6 5PH.

BLUMFIELD, Clifford William, OBE 1976; Director, Dounreay Nuclear Power Development Establishment, 1975–87, and Deputy Managing Director, Northern Division, UKAEA, 1985–87; *b* 18 May 1922; *m* 1944, Jeanne Mary; three *c*. *Educ:* Ipswich Boys' Central Sch. CEng, FIMechE, FINucE. With Reavell & Co. Ltd, 1938–44; served REME, 1944–47 (Major); Min. of Supply, Harwell, 1947–54; UKAEA, Harwell, 1954–58; Atomic Energy Estabt, Winfrith, 1958–68 (Group Leader, Design Gp, and Head of Gen. Ops and Tech. Div.); Asst Dir, Ops and Engineering, later Dep. Dir, Dounreay, 1968–75. *Address:* Rosebank, Janet Street, Thurso, Caithness KW14 7EG.

BLUMGART, Prof. Leslie Harold, MD; FRCS, FRCSE, FRCSGlas, FACS; Enid A. Haupt Professor of Surgery, Memorial Sloane-Kettering Cancer Center, New York, since 1991 (Chief, Section of Hepato-Biliary Surgery; Director, Programme on Hepato-Biliary Diseases); Professor of Surgery, Cornell University Medical Center, since 1992; *b* 7 Dec. 1931, of S African parentage; *m* 1955, Pearl Marie Navias (decd); *m* 1968, Sarah Raybould Bowen; two *s* two *d*. *Educ:* Jeppe High Sch., Johannesburg, SA; Univ. of Witwatersrand (BDS); Univ. of Sheffield (MB, ChB Hons; MD 1969). Prize Medal, Clin. Med. and Surg.; Ashby-de-la-Zouche Prize, Surg., Med., Obst. and Gynaecol. FRCS 1966, FRCSGlas 1973, FRCSE 1976. General dental practice, Durban, SA, 1954–59; Sen. Surgical Registrar, Nottingham Gen. Hosp. and Sheffield Royal Infirmary, 1966–70; Sen. Lectr and Dep. Dir, Dept of Surgery, Welsh Nat. Sch. of Med., also Hon. Cons. Surg., Cardiff Royal Inf., 1970–72; St Mungo Prof. of Surgery, Univ. of Glasgow, and Hon. Cons. Surg., Glasgow Royal Inf., 1972–79; Prof. of Surgery, Royal Postgrad. Sch. of London and Dir of Surgery, Hammersmith Hosp., 1979–86; Prof. of Surgery, Univ. of Bern, 1986–91. Moynihan Fellow, Assoc. of Surgs of Gt Brit. and Ire., 1972; Mayne Vis. Prof., Univ. of Queensland, Brisbane, 1976; Vis. Prof., Univ. of Lund, Sweden, 1977; Nimmo Vis. Prof., Adelaide Univ., 1982; Purvis Oration, 1974; President's Oration, Soc. for Surgery of Aliment. Tract, Toronto, 1977; Lectures: Honyman Gillespie, Univ. of Edinburgh, 1978; Walton, RCPGlas, 1984; Monsarrat, Univ. of Liverpool, 1985; Legg Meml, KCH, 1985; Philip Sandblom, Lund Univ., Sweden, 1986; T. E. Jones Meml, Cleveland Clinic, USA, 1986; L. W. Edwards, Vanderbilt Univ., USA, 1987. Member: BMA, 1963–; Assoc. of Surgs of Gt Brit. and Ire., 1971–; Surgical Research Soc., 1971–; Brit. Soc. of Gastroenterology, 1972–; Swiss Surg. Soc., 1987; Internat. Hepato-Biliar Pancreatic Assoc.; Amer. Surgical Assoc., 1993–; Soc. Surgical Oncology, 1994–. Hon. Member: Soc. for Surgery of Aliment. Tract, USA, 1977; Soc. Amer. Endoscopic Surgs, 1986–; Danish Surg. Soc., 1988; Yugoslavian Surg. Soc., 1988; French Surg. Soc., 1990; Pres., Internat. Biliary Assoc., 1987. Acral Medal, Swedish Soc. Surgery, 1990. Order of Prasidda, Prabala-Gorkha-Dakshin Bahu, Nepal, 1984. *Publications:* (ed with A. C. Kennedy), Essentials of Medicine and Surgery for Dental Students, 3rd edn 1977, 4th edn 1982; (ed) The Biliary Tract, 1982; (ed) Surgery of the Liver and Biliary Tract, vols 1 and 2, 1988, 2nd edn 1994; chapters in books; numerous publications concerned with medical educn, gastrointestinal surgery and aspects of oncology with particular interests in surgery of the liver, pancreas and biliary tract and hepatic pathophysiology in med. and surgical jls. *Recreations:* water colour painting, wood carving. *Address:* Memorial Sloane-Kettering Cancer Center, 1275 York Avenue, New York, NY 10021, USA. *T:* (212) 6395526; 447 E 57th Street #3E, New York, NY 10022, USA.

BLUNDELL, Commandant Daphne Mary, CB 1972; Director, WRNS, 1970–73; *b* 19 Aug. 1916. *Educ:* St Helen's Sch., Northwood; Bedford Coll., London. Worked for LCC as Child Care Organiser. Joined WRNS, Nov. 1942; commnd 1943; served in Orkneys, Ceylon, E Africa; Malta, 1954–56; Staff of Flag Officer Naval Air Comd, 1964–67; Staff of C-in-C Portsmouth, 1967–69; Supt WRNS Training and Drafting, 1969–70. Supt 1967; Comdt 1970, retd 1973; Hon. ADC to the Queen, 1970–73. *Address:* 15 Northbrook Drive, Northwood, Mddx HA6 2YU.

BLUNDELL, Prof. Derek John; Professor of Environmental Geology, since 1975, and Head of Geology Department, since 1992, University of London; *b* 30 June 1933; *s* of Frank and Mollie Blundell; *m* 1960, Mary Patricia Leonard. *Educ:* Univ. of Birmingham (BSc); Imperial Coll., London (DIC, PhD). Res. Fellow 1957, Lectr 1959, in Geology, Univ. of Birmingham; Sen. Lectr 1970, Reader 1972, in Geophysics, Univ. of Lancaster; Royal Soc. Vis. Prof., Univ. of Ghana, 1974; Prof. of Environmental Geol., Univ. of London, first at Chelsea Coll. (Hd of Geol. Dept), 1975, then at Royal Holloway and Bedford New Coll., 1985–. Pres., Geological Soc., 1988–90. Mem., Academia Europaea, 1990. Coke Medal, Geological Soc., 1993. *Publications:* (jtly) A Continent Revealed: the European geotraverse, 1992; contribs to learned jls mainly relating to seismic exploration of the earth's crust, to earthquake hazards and, early on, to palæomagnetism. *Recreations:* travel, ski-ing. *Address:* Springwood, Tite Hill, Englefield Green, Surrey TW20 0NF. *T:* Egham (01784) 433170. *Club:* Athenæum.

BLUNDELL, Prof. Richard William; Professor of Economics, University College London, since 1984; Director of Research, Institute for Fiscal Studies, since 1987; *b* 1 May 1952; *s* of Horace Leon and Marjorie Blundell; *m* 1984, Anne Gaynor Aberdeen; one *s* one *d*. *Educ:* Univ. of Bristol (BSc 1st cl. Hons Econs with Stats); LSE (MSc Econometrics). Lectr in Econometrics, Univ. of Manchester, 1975–85; Head, Dept of Economics, UCL, 1988–92; Dir, ESRC Centre for Microecon. Analysis of Fiscal Policy, Inst. Fiscal Studies, 1991–. Visiting Professor: Univ. of BC, 1980–81; MIT, 1993; Berkeley, 1994. Council Mem., Royal Econ. Soc., 1989–; Programme Chm., European Econometric Soc. Meetings, 1992. Fellow, Econometric Soc., 1991. Member, Editorial Board: Rev. Econ. Studies, 1983–93 (Asst Ed, 1984–88); Manchester School, 1983–; Jl Applied Econometrics, 1986–89; Fiscal Studies, 1986–; Jl of Human Resources. Editor, Jl of Econometrics, 1991–. *Publications:* Unemployment, Search and Labour Supply, 1986; The Measurement of Household Welfare, 1994; contrib. Econometrica, Rev. Econ. Studies, Econ. Jl, Jl Econometrics. *Recreations:* saxophone, guitar, jazz music, African music, travel. *Address:* Department of Economics, University College London, Gower Street, WC1E 6BT. *T:* 0171–380 7863.

See also T. L. Blundell.

BLUNDELL, Prof. Thomas Leon, FRS 1984; Chief Executive and Deputy Chairman, Biotechnology and Biological Sciences Research Council, 1994–Oct. 1996 (on secondment); Sir William Dunn Professor of Biochemistry, and Fellow of Sidney Sussex College, Cambridge University, since 1995; *b* 7 July 1942; *s* of Horace Leon Blundell and Marjorie Blundell; one *s*; *m* 1987, Bancinyane Lynn Sibanda; two *d*. *Educ:* Steyning Grammar Sch.; Brasenose Coll., Oxford (BA, DPhil; Hon. Fellow, 1989). Postdoctoral Res. Fellow, Laboratory of Molecular Biophysics, Oxford Univ., 1967–72; Jun. Res. Fellow, Linacre Coll., Oxford, 1968–70; Lectr, Biological Scis, Sussex Univ., 1973–76; Prof. of Crystallography, Birkbeck Coll., Univ. of London, 1976–90; Dep. Chm. and Dir Gen., AFRC, 1991–94. Director, International Sch. of Crystallography, 1981–. Member: Council, SERC, 1989–90 (Mem., 1979–82, Chm., 1983–87, Biological Scis Cttee; Mem., Science Bd, 1983–87); Council, AFRC, 1985–90 (Member: Plants and Soils Res. Grants Cttee, 1986–90; Food Res. Cttee, 1987–90); MRC AIDS Res. Steering Cttee, 1987–90; ACOST, 1988–90; ABRC, 1991–94; Link Steering Gp, 1991–. Hon. Dir, ICRF Unit of Structural Molecular Biology, 1989–. Lectures: Plenary, Internat. Congress of Crystallography, 1969, 1978 and 1993; Gerhardt Schmidt, Weizman Inst., Israel, 1983; Plenary, Europ. Cryst. Meeting, 1983; Ferdinand Springer, Fedn of Europ. Biochemical Socs, 1984; Plenary, Asian and Ocean Biochemical Soc., 1986; Plenary, Fedn of European Biochemical Socs, 1987; Plenary, Internat. Juvenile Diabetes Congress, 1988; Plenary, Internat. Congress of Biochem., 1991. Councillor, Oxford CBC, 1970–73 (Chm. Planning Cttee, 1972–73). Industrial Consultant: CellTech, 1981–86; Pfizer Central Res., Groton, USA and Sandwich, UK, 1984–90; Abingworth Management Ltd, 1988–90. Governor, Birkbeck Coll., 1985–89. Hon. Fellow, Linacre Coll., Oxford, 1991. Hon. FRASE 1993; Hon. FIChemE 1995. Hon. doctorates: Edinburgh, East Anglia, 1993; Sheffield, Strathclyde, 1994; Warwick, Antwerp, 1995. Alcon Award for Dist. Work in Vision Research, 1985; Gold Medal, Inst. of Biotechnological Studies, 1987; Sir Hans Krebs Medal, Fedn of European Biochemical Socs, 1987; Ciba Medal, UK Biochemical Soc., 1988; Feldberg Prize for Biology and Medicine, 1988; Gold Medal, SCI, 1995. Jt Editor, Progress in Biophysics and Molecular Biology, 1979–; Member Editorial Advisory Board: Biochemistry, 1986–89; Protein Engineering, 1986–; Protein Science, 1992–; Structure, 1993–. *Publications:* Protein Crystallography, 1976; papers in Jl of Molecular Biology, Nature, European Jl of Biochemistry, etc. *Recreations:* playing jazz, listening to opera, walking, international travel. *Address:* (until Oct. 1996) BBSRC Central Office, Polaris House, North Star Avenue, Swindon SN2 1UH; Department of Biochemistry, Tennis Court Road, Cambridge CB2 1QW.

See also R. W. Blundell.

BLUNDEN, Sir George, Kt 1987; Deputy Governor, Bank of England, 1986–90 (Executive Director, 1976–84, Non-Executive Director, 1984–85); Joint Deputy Chairman, Leopold Joseph Holdings, 1984–85 and 1990–94; *b* 31 Dec. 1922; *s* of late George Blunden and Florence Holder; *m* 1949, Anne, *d* of late G. J. E. and Phyllis Bulford; two *s* one *d*. *Educ:* City of London Sch.; University Coll., Oxford (MA). Royal Sussex Regt, 1941–45. Bank of England, 1947–55; IMF, 1955–58; Bank of England: rejoined 1958; Dep. Chief Cashier, 1968–73; Chief of Management Services, 1973–74; Head of Banking Supervision, 1974–76. Director: Eagle Star Hldgs, 1984–85; Portals Hldgs, 1984–86; Grindlays Hldgs, 1984–85. Advr, Union Bank of Switzerland in London, 1990–94. Chairman: Group of Ten Cttees, BIS, Basle, on Banking Regulations and Supervisory Practices, 1974–77, on Payments Systems, 1981–83; cttee to oversee estabt and operation of Code of Banking Practice, 1990–94; London Pensions Fund Authy, 1989–92. Chm. Governors, St Peter's Gp of Hosps, 1978–82; Chm., St Peter's Hosps Special Trustees, 1982–; Chm., Inst. of Urology, 1982–88 (Hon. Treasurer, 1975–78); Mem. Council, Imperial Cancer Res. Fund, 1981–94 (Treas., 1988–91; Chm., 1991–94). Chairman: Samuel Lewis Housing Trust, 1985 (Trustee, 1980–85); St Peter's Trust for Kidney Res., 1988–90 (Trustee, 1971–91); Vice-Pres., Opportunities for the Disabled, 1980–90. President: Inst. of Business Ethics, 1994–. British-Malaysia Soc., 1989–94. Member: Court, Mermaid Theatre Trust, 1979–84; Council, RCM, 1983– (Dep. Chm., 1990–). Mem., Livery, Goldsmiths' Co., 1987. *Address:* Crossfield Farmhouse, Hindringham, Fakenham, Norfolk NR21 0PS. *T:* Fakenham (01328) 878509. *Clubs:* Reform, MCC; Norfolk (Norwich).

BLUNDEN, Sir Philip (Overington), 7th Bt *cr* 1766, of Castle Blunden, Kilkenny; artist and art restorer; *b* 27 Jan. 1922; *s* of Sir John Blunden, 5th Bt and Phyllis Dorothy (*d* 1967), *d* of Philip Crampton Creaghe; *S* brother, 1985; *m* 1945, Jeannette Francesca Alexandra, *e d* of Captain D. Macdonald, RNR; two *s* one *d*. *Educ:* Repton. Served RN, 1941–46 (1939–45 Star, Atlantic Star, Defence Medal). Estate Manager, Castle Blunden, 1947–60; engaged in marketing of industrial protective coatings, 1962–83; in art and art restoration, 1976–. *Recreations:* fishing, field sports, swimming, tennis, reading. *Heir: s* Hubert Chisholm Blunden [*b* 9 Aug. 1948; *m* 1975, Ellish O'Brien; one *s* one *d*]. *Club:* Royal Dublin Society (Life Mem.).

BLUNKETT, David; MP (Lab) Sheffield, Brightside, since 1987; *b* 6 June 1947; *m* (marr. diss.); three *s*. *Educ:* night sch. and day release, Shrewsbury Coll. of Technol. and Richmond Coll. of Further Educn, Sheffield; Nat. Cert. in Business Studies, E Midlands Gas Bd; Sheffield Univ. (BA Hons Pol Theory and Instns); Huddersfield Holly Bank Coll. of Educn (Tech.) (PGCFE). Tutor in Industrial Relns, Barnsley Coll. of Technol., 1974–87. Elected to Sheffield City Council (at age of 22), 1970; Chm., Family and Community Services Cttee, 1976–80; Leader, 1980–87; Dep. Chm., AMA, 1984–87. Joined Labour Party at age of 16; Chm., Labour Party NEC, 1993–94 (Dep. Chm., 1992–93; Mem., 1983–); Chm., Labour Party Cttee on Local govt, 1984–92. Front bench spokesman on the environment, with special responsibility for local govt and poll tax, 1988–92, on health, 1992–94, on educn, 1994– (Mem., Shadow Cabinet, 1992–). *Publications:* (jtly) Local Enterprise and Workers' Plans, 1981; (jtly) Building from the Bottom: the Sheffield Experience, 1983; (jtly) Democracy in Crisis: the town halls respond, 1987. *Address:* House of Commons, SW1A 0AA.

BLUNT, Charles William; Chief Executive Officer, American Chamber of Commerce in Australia, since 1990; *b* Sydney, 19 Jan. 1951; *s* of R. S. G. Blunt; *m* Gail; two *s*. *Educ:* Sydney Univ. (BEcon). AASA; CPA. Exec. appts in mining, finance and agricultural industries. MP (Nat. Party) Richmond, NSW, 1984–90; Leader, Parly Nat. Party, 1989–90; opposition Minister, 1984–90, variously for: Sport, Recreation and Tourism; Social Security; Transport and Communications; Community Services and Aged Care; Trade and Resources. Former Mem., parly cttees and official delegns. *Recreations:* tennis, reading. *Address:* PO Box 66, Wahroonga, NSW 2076, Australia; American Chamber of Commerce in Australia, Suite 4, Gloucester Walk, 88 Cumberland Street, Sydney, NSW 2000, Australia. *Clubs:* Union, American (Sydney).

BLUNT, David John; QC 1991; a Recorder of the Crown Court, since 1990; writer; *b* 25 Oct. 1944; *s* of late Vernon Egerton Rowland Blunt and of Catherine Vera Blunt; *m* 1976, Zaibonessa Ebrahim; one *s* one *d*. *Educ:* Farnham Grammar Sch.; Trinity Hall, Cambridge (MA Hons). Called to the Bar, Middle Temple, 1967. Asst Recorder, 1985–90. Contested (L): Lambeth Central, 1978, 1979; Cornwall SE, 1983. First TV play broadcast, 1976. *Recreations:* walking, running, cycling, reading, writing, old cars. *Address:* 4 Pump Court, Temple, EC4Y 7AN. *T:* 0171–353 2656.

BLUNT, Sir David Richard Reginald Harvey, 12th Bt *cr* 1720; *b* 8 Nov. 1938; *s* of Sir Richard David Harvey Blunt, 11th Bt and Elisabeth Malvine Ernestine, *d* of Comdr F. M. Fransen Van de Putte, Royal Netherlands Navy (retd); *S* father, 1975; *m* 1969, Sonia Tudor Rosemary (*née* Day); one *d*. *Heir: kinsman:* Robin Anthony Blunt, CEng, MIMechE [*b* 23 Nov. 1926; *m* 1st, 1949, Sheila Stuart (marr. diss. 1962), *d* of C. Stuart Brindley; one *s*; 2nd, 1962, June Elizabeth, *d* of Charles Wigginton; one *s*].

BLUNT, Oliver Simon Peter; QC 1994; a Recorder, since 1995; *b* 8 March 1951; *s* of Maj.-Gen. Peter Blunt, *qv* and Adrienne (*née* Richardson); *m* 1979, Joanna Margaret Dixon; one *s* three *d*. *Educ:* Bedford Sch.; Southampton Univ. (LLB 1973). Called to the Bar, Middle Temple, 1974; Asst Recorder, SE Circuit, 1991–95. *Recreations:* cricket, golf, ski-ing, swimming. *Address:* 171 Fleet Street, EC4A 2EA. *T:* 0171–583 0434. *Clubs:* Roehampton; Barnes Cricket.

BLUNT, Maj.-Gen. Peter, CB 1978; MBE 1955; GM 1959; *b* 18 Aug. 1923; *s* of A. G. Blunt and C. M. Blunt; *m* 1949, Adrienne, *o d* of Gen. T. W. Richardson; three *s*. Joined

Army aged 14 yrs, 1937; commnd Royal Fusiliers; served Duke of Cornwall's LI and Royal Scots Fusiliers, until 1946; foreign service, 1946–49; Staff Coll., 1957; Jt Services Staff Coll., 1963; RCDS, 1972; comd 26 Regt, Bridging, 1965; GSO 1 Def. Plans, FARELF, 1968; Comdr RCT 1 Corps, 1970; Dep. Transport Officer-in-Chief (Army), later Transp. Off.-in-Chief, 1973; Asst Chief of Personnel and Logistics (Army), MoD, 1977–78; Asst Chief of Defence Staff (Personnel and Logistics), MoD, 1978–79. Man. Dir, Earls Court Ltd, 1979–80; Exec. Vice-Chm., Brompton and Kensington Special Catering Co. Ltd, 1979–80; Jt Man. Dir, Angex-Watson, 1980–83; Dir, Associated Newspapers, 1984–90; Chm. and Man. Dir, Market Sensors, 1986–88; Man. Dir, 1980–88, non-exec. Chm., 1988–90, Angex Ltd; Chm., Argus Shield Ltd, 1988–89. Rep. Col Comdt, RCT, 1987–89 (Col Comdt, 1974–89). Specially apptd Comr, Royal Hosp., Chelsea, 1979–85. Exec. Mem., Caravan Club, 1989–. Liveryman,Co. of Carmen, 1973. *Recreations:* fishing, caravanning. *Address:* Harefield House, Crowood Lane, Ramsbury, Marlborough, Wilts SN8 2PT. *T:* Marlborough (01672) 20296. *Club:* RCT Luncheon (Pres.).

See also O. S. P. Blunt.

BLYE, Douglas William Alfred, CMG 1979; OBE 1973; company director and financial consultant; *b* 15 Dec. 1924; *s* of William Blye and Ethel Attwood; *m* 1955, Juanita, (June), Buckley. *Educ:* King's Road Sch., Herne Bay; Maidstone Polytechnic. ACMA. Served War, RAF, 1941–46. Various commercial and industrial appts in UK, 1947–55; Govt of Fedn of Malaya, 1955–58; Hong Kong Govt, 1958–85, Sec. for Monetary Affairs, 1977–85; Econ. and Financial Advr, Govt of Dubai, 1986–87. *Recreations:* squash, tennis. *Address:* Middlefield, The Street, Goodnestone, Canterbury, Kent CT3 1PG. *T:* Nonington (01304) 842196. *Club:* Royal Automobile.

BLYTH, family name of **Barons Blyth** and **Blyth of Rowington.**

BLYTH, 4th Baron *cr* 1907; **Anthony Audley Rupert Blyth;** Bt 1895; *b* 3 June 1931; *er s* of 3rd Baron Blyth and Edna Myrtle (*d* 1952), *d* of Ernest Lewis, Wellington, NZ; *S* father, 1977; *m* 1st, 1954, Elizabeth Dorothea (marr. diss., 1962), *d* of R. T. Sparrow, Vancouver, BC; one *s* two *d*; 2nd, 1963, Oonagh Elizabeth Ann, *yr d* of late William Henry Conway, Dublin; one *s* one *d*. *Educ:* St Columba's College, Dublin. *Heir: s* Hon. Riley Audley John Blyth, *b* 4 March 1955. *Address:* Blythwood Estate, Athenry, Co. Galway.

BLYTH OF ROWINGTON, Baron *cr* 1995 (Life Peer), of Rowington in the County of Warwickshire; **James Blyth;** Kt 1985; Director and Chief Executive, since 1987 and Deputy Chairman, since 1994, The Boots Company PLC; *b* 8 May 1940; *s* of Daniel Blyth and Jane Power Carlton; *m* 1967, Pamela Anne Campbell Dixon; one *d* (one *s* decd). *Educ:* Spiers Sch.; Glasgow Univ. Mobil Oil Co., 1963–69; General Foods Ltd, 1969–71; Mars Ltd, 1971–74; General Manager: Lucas Batteries Ltd, 1974–77; Lucas Aerospace Ltd, 1977–81; Head of Defence Sales, MoD, 1981–85; Managing Director: Plessey Electronic Systems, 1985–86; The Plessey Co plc, 1986–87. Non-exec. Director: Imperial Gp PLC, 1984–86; Cadbury-Schweppes PLC, 1986–90; British Aerospace, 1990–94. Chm., Adv. Panel on Citizen's Charter, 1991–. Pres., ME Assoc., 1988–93. Gov., London Business Sch., 1987–. FRAeS. Liveryman, Coachmakers' and Coach Harness Makers' Co. Hon. LLD Nottingham, 1992. *Recreations:* ski-ing, tennis, paintings, theatre. *Address:* The Boots Company PLC, Nottingham NG2 3AA. *Clubs:* East India, Queen's, Royal Automobile.

BLYTH, Charles, (Chay Blyth), CBE 1972; BEM; Managing Director, The Challenge Business Ltd (formerly Crownfields Ltd), since 1989; Organiser, BT Global Challenge Round the World Yacht Race 1996–97, since 1994; *b* 14 May 1940; *s* of Robert and Jessie Blyth; *m* 1962, Maureen Margaret Morris; one *d*. *Educ:* Hawick High School. HM Forces, Para. Regt, 1958–67. Cadbury Schweppes, 1968–69; Dir, Sailing Ventures (Hampshire) Ltd, 1969–73. Organiser, British Steel Challenge Round World Yacht Race 1992–93, 1989–93. Rowed North Atlantic with Captain John Ridgway, June–Sept. 1966; circumnavigated the world westwards solo in yacht British Steel, 1970–71; circumnavigated the world eastwards with crew of paratroopers in yacht Great Britain II, and Winner, Elapsed Time Prize Whitbread Round the World Yacht Race, 1973–74; Atlantic sailing record, Cape Verde to Antigua, 1977; won Round Britain Race in yacht Great Britain IV, 1978 (crew Robert James); won The Observer/Europe 1 doublehanded transatlantic race in record time, 1981 (crew Robert James); Number One to Virgin Atlantic Challenge II successful attempt on the Blue Riband, 1986. Yachtsman of the Year, 1971, Special Award for outstanding services to yachting, 1994, Yachting Journalists Assoc., Chichester Trophy, RYS, 1971. *Publications:* A Fighting Chance, 1966; Innocent Aboard, 1968; The Impossible Voyage, 1971; Theirs is the Glory, 1974; The Challenge, 1993. *Recreations:* sailing, horse-riding, hunting. *Address:* Trepen House, Menheniot, Liskeard, Cornwall PL14 3PN. *Clubs:* Special Forces, Royal Ocean Racing; Royal Southern Yacht, Royal Western Yacht.

BLYTH, John Douglas Morrison, CMG 1981; HM Diplomatic Service, retired; *b* 23 July 1924; *s* of late William Naismith Blyth and Jean (*née* Morrison); *m* 1st, 1949, Gabrielle Elodie (*née* Belloc) (*d* 1971); three *s* two *d*; 2nd, 1973, Lucy Anne (*née* Alcock); one *s* one *d*. *Educ:* Christ's Coll.; Lincoln Coll., Oxford (MA); Downing Coll., Cambridge (MA). Served War, RNVR, 1942–46. Editor, The Polar Record (publd by Scott Polar Res. Inst., Cambridge), 1949–54; joined FO, 1954; served: Geneva, 1955; Athens, 1959; Leopoldville, 1963; Accra, 1964; FO, 1966; Athens, 1968; FCO, 1972; Vienna, 1974; FCO, 1977. Pres., Hélène Heroys Literary Foundn, 1975–. Hon. Sec., Suffolk Preservation Soc., 1985–94. *Publications:* articles in The Polar Record. *Recreations:* gardening, military history, enjoying wine. *Address:* Crownland Hall, Walsham-le-Willows, Suffolk IP31 3BU. *T:* Walsham-le-Willows (01359) 259369. *Club:* Naval and Military.

BLYTHE, His Honour James Forbes, TD 1946; a Circuit Judge, 1978–92; Solicitor; *b* Coventry, 11 July 1917; *s* of J. F. Blythe and Dorothy Alice (*née* Hazlewood); *m* 1949, Margaret, *d* of P. D. Kinsey; two *d*. *Educ:* Wrekin Coll.; Birmingham Univ. (LLB). Commissioned TA, Royal Warwickshire Regt, 1936–53 (Major); served War of 1939–45 with BEF in France (Dunkirk), 1939–40; Central Mediterranean Force (Tunisia, Sicily, Corsica, S France and Austria), 1942–45; Air Liaison Officer GSO II (Ops) with RAF (Despatches). Admitted solicitor, 1947; private practitioner in partnership in Coventry and Leamington Spa, 1948. HM Deputy Coroner for City of Coventry and Northern Dist of Warwickshire, 1954–64; HM Coroner for City of Coventry, 1964–78; a Recorder of the Crown Court, 1972–78. Pres., Warwicks Law Soc., 1978–79. *Recreations:* shooting, sailing; past player and Sec. Coventry Football Club (RU). *Address:* Hazlewood, Upper Ladyes' Hill, Kenilworth, Warwickshire CV8 2FB. *Clubs:* Army and Navy; Drapers (Coventry); Tennis Court (Leamington Spa).

BLYTHE, Mark Andrew; Principal Assistant Solicitor, Treasury Solicitor's Department, since 1989; *b* 4 Sept. 1943; *s* of John Jarratt Blythe and Dorothy Kathleen Blythe; *m* 1972, Brigid Helen Frazer (*née* Skemp); two *s* one *d*. *Educ:* King Edward VII Grammar Sch., Sheffield; University Coll., Oxford (BCL, MA; Gibbs Prize in Law, 1963). Called to the Bar, Inner Temple, 1966; Attorney, NY Bar, 1980. Teaching Associate, Univ. of Pennsylvania Law Sch., 1965–66; Chancery Bar, 1967–77; Legal Consultant, NY, 1978–80; Treasury Solicitor's Dept, 1981–; Assistant Solicitor, European Div., 1986–89. *Address:* Queen Anne's Chambers, 28 Broadway, SW1H 9JS.

BLYTHE, Rex Arnold; Under-Secretary, Board of Inland Revenue, 1981–86, retired; *b* 11 Nov. 1928; *s* of late Sydney Arnold Blythe and Florence Blythe (*née* Jones); *m* 1953, Rachel Ann Best; one *s* two *d*. *Educ:* Bradford Grammar Sch.; Trinity Coll., Cambridge (MA Classics). Entered Inland Revenue as Inspector of Taxes, 1953; Sen. Inspector, 1962; Principal Inspector, 1968; Asst Sec., 1974. *Recreations:* golf, photography, walking. *Address:* 32 Townsend Lane, Harpenden, Herts AL5 2QS. *T:* Harpenden (01582) 715833. *Club:* MCC.

BLYTHE, Ronald George; writer, since 1953; *b* 6 Nov. 1922; *s* of Albert George Blythe and Matilda Elizabeth (*née* Elkins). *Educ:* St Peter's and St Gregory's Sch., Sudbury, Suffolk. Librarian, 1943–53. Soc. of Authors' Travel Scholarship, 1969. Editor, Penguin Classics, 1966–87. Assistant, Aldeburgh Fest., 1955–57; Member: Eastern Arts Lit. Panel, 1975–85; Cttee, Centre of E Anglian Studies, UEA, 1975–80; Soc. of Authors' Management Cttee, 1980–85; Chm., Essex Fest., 1981–84. Pres., John Clare Soc., 1981–. FRSL 1969. Hon. MA UEA, 1990. *Publications:* A Treasonable Growth, 1960; Immediate Possession, 1961; The Age of Illusion, 1963; William Hazlitt: selected writings, 1970; Akenfield (Heinemann Award), 1969; Aldeburgh Anthology, 1972; (ed jtly) Works of Thomas Hardy, 1978; The View in Winter, 1979; (ed) Writing in a War: stories, essays and poems of 1939–45, 1982; Places, 1982; From the Headlands, 1982; The Stories of Ronald Blythe (Angel Prize for Literature), 1985; Divine Landscapes, 1986; Each Returning Day: the pleasure of diaries, 1989; Private Words: letters and diaries of the Second World War, 1991. *Recreations:* walking, looking, listening. *Address:* Bottengoms Farm, Wormingford, Colchester, Essex CO6 3AP. *T:* Colchester (01206) 271308.

BOAG, Prof. John Wilson; Professor of Physics as Applied to Medicine, University of London, Institute of Cancer Research, 1965–76, now Emeritus; *b* Elgin, Scotland, 20 June 1911; *s* of John and Margaret A. Boag; *m* 1938, Isabel Petrie; no *c*. *Educ:* Universities of Glasgow, Cambridge and Braunschweig. Engineer, British Thomson Houston Co., Rugby, 1936–41; Physicist, Medical Research Council, 1941–52; Visiting Scientist, National Bureau of Standards, Washington, DC, 1953–54; Physicist, British Empire Cancer Campaign, Mount Vernon Hospital, 1954–64; Royal Society (Leverhulme) Visiting Prof. to Poland, 1964. President: Hosp. Physicists' Assoc., 1959; Assoc. for Radiation Res. (UK), 1972–74; Internat. Assoc. for Radiation Res., 1970–74; British Inst. of Radiology, 1975–76. L. H. Gray Medal, ICRU, 1973; Barclay Medal, BIR, 1975. *Publications:* (jtly) Kapitza in Cambridge and Moscow, 1990; papers on radiation dosimetry, statistics, radiation chemistry, radiodiagnosis. *Address:* 88 Craiglockhart Road, Edinburgh EH14 1EP.

BOAL, (John) Graham; QC 1993; a Recorder of the Crown Court, since 1985; *b* 24 Oct. 1943; *s* of late Surg. Captain Jackson Graham Boal, RN, and late Dorothy Kenley Boal; *m* 1978, Elizabeth Mary East; one *s*. *Educ:* Eastbourne Coll.; King's Coll. London (LLB). Called to the Bar, Gray's Inn, 1966, Bencher, 1991; Junior Treasury Counsel, 1977–85; Sen. Prosecuting Counsel to the Crown, 1985–91, First Sen. Treasury Counsel, 1991–93, CCC. Vice Chm., Criminal Bar Assoc., 1991–93. *Recreations:* theatre, golf, watching cricket. *Address:* Queen Elizabeth Building, Temple, EC4Y 9BS. *Clubs:* Garrick, MCC; Royal Wimbledon Golf.

BOAM, Maj.-Gen. Thomas Anthony, CB 1987; CBE 1978 (OBE 1973); Director, British Consultants Bureau, since 1988; *b* 14 Feb. 1932; *s* of late Lt-Col T. S. Boam, OBE, and of Mrs Boam; *m* 1961, Penelope Christine Mary Roberts; one *s* two *d*. *Educ:* Bradfield Coll.; RMA Sandhurst. Commissioned Scots Guards, 1952; Canal Zone, Egypt (with 1SG), 1952–54; GSO3, MO4 War Office, 1959–61; psc 1962, Kenya (with 2 Scots Guards), 1963–64; DAA&QMG 4 Guards Bde, 1964–65, Malaysia (with 1SG), 1966–67; BM 4 Guards Bde, 1967–69; GSO1 (DS) Staff Coll., Camberley, 1970–71; CO 2SG, 1972–74; RCDS 1974–75; Comd BAAT Nigeria, 1976–78; BGS (Trg) HQ UKLF, 1978; Dep. Comdr and COS Hong Kong, 1979–81; Hd of British Defence Staff Washington, and Defence Attaché, 1981–84, Mil. Attaché, 1981–83; Comdr, British Forces Hong Kong, and Maj.-Gen., Brigade of Gurkhas, 1985–87. Mem., Exec. Council, Hong Kong, 1985–87. *Recreations:* shooting, fishing, gardening, sport. *Address:* Bury Gate House, Pulborough, W Sussex RH20 1HA. *Clubs:* St Stephen's Constitutional, MCC.

BOARDMAN, family name of **Baron Boardman.**

BOARDMAN, Baron *cr* 1980 (Life Peer), of Welford in the County of Northamptonshire; **Thomas Gray Boardman,** MC 1944; TD 1952; DL; Chairman, National Westminster Bank, 1983–89 (Director, 1979–89; Chairman, Eastern Region, 1979–83); *b* 12 Jan. 1919; *s* of John Clayton Boardman, late of Daventry, and Janet Boardman, formerly Houston; *m* 1948, (Norah Mary) Deirdre, *widow* of John Henry Chaworth-Musters, Annesley Park, Nottingham, and *d* of late Hubert Vincent Gough; two *s* one *d*. *Educ:* Bromsgrove. Served Northants Yeomanry, 1939–45 and subsequently; Commanding Northants Yeomanry, 1956. Qualified as a Solicitor, 1947. MP (C) Leicester SW, Nov. 1967–74, Leicester South Feb.–Sept. 1974; Minister for Industry, DTI, 1972–74; Chief Sec. to Treasury, 1974. Jt Hon. Treas., Cons. Party, 1981–82. Chairman: Chamberlain Phipps Ltd, 1958–72; The Steetley Co. Ltd, 1978–83 (Dir, 1975–83); Heron Internat. NV, 1993–95; Director: Allied Breweries Ltd, 1968–72 and 1974–77 (Vice-Chm., 1975–76); MEPC, 1980–89; Mem. Adv. Bd, LEK Partnership, 1990–. Pres., Assoc. of British Chambers of Commerce, 1977–80. Chm., Cttee of London and Scottish Bankers, 1987–89. Mem., Exec. Assoc. of Cons. Peers, 1981–84, 1991–95. HM Lieut, City of London, 1989–; DL Northants, 1977–, High Sheriff, Northants, 1979. *Recreation:* riding. *Address:* 29 Tufton Court, Tufton Street, SW1P 3QH. *T:* 0171–222 6793; The Manor House, Welford, Northampton NN6 6HX. *T:* Welford (01858) 575235. *Club:* Cavalry and Guards.

See also Baron Ellenborough.

BOARDMAN, Sir John, Kt 1989; FSA 1957; FBA 1969; Lincoln Professor of Classical Archaeology and Art, and Fellow of Lincoln College, University of Oxford, 1978–94 (Hon. Fellow, 1995); *b* 20 Aug. 1927; *s* of Frederick Archibald Boardman; *m* 1952, Sheila Joan Lyndon Stanford; one *s* one *d*. *Educ:* Chigwell Sch.; Magdalene Coll., Cambridge (BA 1948, MA 1951, Walston Student, 1948–50; Hon. Fellow 1984). 2nd Lt, Intell. Corps, 1950–52. Asst Dir, British Sch. at Athens, 1952–55; Asst Keeper, Ashmolean Museum, Oxford, 1955–59; Reader in Classical Archaeology, Univ. of Oxford, 1959–78; Fellow of Merton Coll., Oxford, 1963–78, Hon. Fellow, 1978. Geddes-Harrower Prof., Aberdeen Univ., 1974; Vis. Prof., Australian Inst. of Archaeology, 1987; Prof. of Ancient History, Royal Acad., 1989–; Lectures: Andrew W. Mellon, Washington, 1993; Myres Meml, Oxford, 1993. Editor: Journal of Hellenic Studies, 1958–65; Lexicon Iconographicum, 1972–; Cambridge Ancient History, 1978–94. Conducted excavations on Chios, 1953–55, and at Tocra in Libya, 1964–65. Delegate, OUP, 1979–89. Pres. Fédn Internat. des Assocs d'Etudes Classiques, 1994–. Corr. Fellow, Bavarian Acad. of Scis, 1969; Fellow, Inst. of Etruscan Studies, Florence, 1983; Hon. Fellow, Archaeol Soc. of Athens, 1989; Foreign Mem., Royal Danish Acad., 1979; Mem. associé, Acad. des Inscriptions et Belles Lettres, Institut de France, 1991 (Correspondant, 1985); Hon. Mem., Archaeol Inst. of America, 1993. Hon. MRIA, 1986. Hon. Dr: Dept of Archaeology and

History, Univ. of Athens, 1991; Sorbonne, 1994. Cromer Greek Prize, 1959, Kenyon Medal, 1995, British Acad. *Publications:* Cretan Collection in Oxford, 1961; Date of the Knossos Tablets, 1963; Island Gems, 1963; Greeks Overseas, 1964, rev. edn 1980; Greek Art, 1964, rev. edns 1973, 1984; Excavations at Tocra, vol. I 1966, vol. II 1973; Pre-Classical, 1967, repr. 1978; Greek Emporio, 1967; Engraved Gems, 1968; Archaic Greek Gems, 1968; Greek Gems and Finger Rings, 1970; (with D. Kurtz) Greek Burial Customs, 1971; Athenian Black Figure Vases, 1974; Athenian Red Figure Vases, Archaic Period, 1975; Intaglios and Rings, 1975; Corpus Vasorum, Oxford, vol. 3, 1975; Greek Sculpture, Archaic Period, 1978; (with M. Robertson) Corpus Vasorum, Castle Ashby, 1978; (with M. L. Vollenweider) Catalogue of Engraved Gems, Ashmolean Museum, 1978; (with D. Scarisbrick) Harari Collection of Finger Rings, 1978; (with E. La Rocca) Eros in Greece, 1978; Escarabeos de Piedra de Ibiza, 1984; La Ceramica Antica, 1984; Greek Sculpture, Classical Period, 1985; (with D. Finn) The Parthenon and its Sculptures, 1985; (jtly) The Oxford History of the Classical World, 1986; Athenian Red Figure Vases, Classical Period, 1989; (jtly) The Oxford History of Classical Art, 1993; The Diffusion of Classical Art in Antiquity, 1994; Greek Sculpture, Later Classical, 1995; articles in jls. *Address:* 11 Park Street, Woodstock, Oxford OX20 1SJ. *T:* Woodstock (01993) 811259. *Club:* Athenæum.

BOARDMAN, Sir Kenneth (Ormrod), Kt 1981; DL; Founder Chairman, Planned Giving Ltd, 1959–93; *b* 18 May 1914; *s* of Edgar Nicholas Boardman and Emily Boardman; *m* 1939, Lucy Stafford; one *s* one *d* (and one *d* decd). *Educ:* St Peter's Sch., Swinton, Lancs. Trooper, Duke of Lancaster's Own Yeomanry, 1932–33; served War 1939–45, Major RA, 1942–46. Chm., K. O. Boardman Internat. Ltd, 1954–78. Hon. Treasurer, NW Area of Conservative Party, 1977–84; Member: Nat. Union of Cons. and Unionist Assocs, 1975–84 (Patron NW Area, 1984–93; Life Patron, Hazel Grove Cons. Assoc., 1975); NW Industrial Council, 1967–84; several Cons. constituency offices 1984. Pres., Manchester E Euro Constituency, 1984–. Dist Chm., NSPCC 100th Anniv. Appeal, 1984; President: Stockport & Dist NSPCC, 1985–; Stockport Cancer Res. Campaign, 1990–; Appeals Chm., John Charnley Trust, 1985–; Founder Mem., RA Heritage Appeal, 1991–; Patron, Hallé 125th Anniv. Appeal, 1984. Chm., Stockport Parish Church Restoration Fund, 1974–. Liveryman, Farriers Co., 1965–. *Recreations:* gardening, reading and writing, horse racing.

BOARDMAN, Norman Keith, AO 1993; PhD, ScD; FRS 1978; FAA; FTS; post-retirement Fellow, Commonwealth Scientific and Industrial Research Organization, since 1990 (Chief Executive, 1986–90); *b* 16 Aug. 1926; *s* of William Robert Boardman and Margaret Boardman; *m* 1952, Mary Clayton Shepherd; two *s* five *d*. *Educ:* Melbourne Univ. (BSc 1946, MSc 1949); St John's Coll., Cambridge (PhD 1954, ScD 1974). FAA 1972; FTS 1986. ICI Fellow, Cambridge, 1953–55; Fulbright Scholar, Univ. of Calif, LA, 1964–66. Res. Officer, Wool Res. Section, CSIRO, 1949–51; CSIRO Div. of Plant Industry: Sen. Res. Scientist, 1956; Principal Res. Scientist, 1961; Sen. Prin. Res. Scientist, 1966; Chief Res. Scientist, 1968; Mem. Exec., 1977–85, Chm. and Chief Exec., 1985–86, CSIRO. Member: Aust. Res. Grants Cttee, 1971–75; Council, ANU, 1979–89 and 1990–91; Bd, Aust. Centre for Internat. Agricl Research, 1982–88; Nat. Water Research Council, 1982–85; Prime Minister's Science Council, 1989–90. Director: Sirotech Ltd, 1986–90; Landcare Aust. Ltd, 1990–. Pres., Aust. Biochem. Soc., 1976–78; Sec. of Sci. Policy, Aust. Acad. of Sci., 1993– (Treas., 1978–81). Corresp. Mem., Amer. Soc. of Plant Physiologists. Hon. DSc Newcastle, NSW, 1988. David Syme Res. Prize, Melbourne Univ., 1967; Lemberg Medal, Aust. Biochem. Soc., 1969. *Publications:* scientific papers on plant biochemistry, partic. photosynthesis and structure, function and biogenesis of chloroplasts; papers on science and technology policy. *Recreations:* reading, tennis, listening to music. *Address:* 6 Somers Crescent, Forrest, ACT 2603, Australia. *T:* (6) 2951746. *Club:* Commonwealth (Canberra).

BOASE, Martin; Chairman, Omnicom UK plc, 1989–95; *b* 14 July 1932; *s* of Prof. Alan Martin Boase and Elizabeth Grizelle Boase; *m* 1st, 1960, Terry Ann Moir (marr. diss. 1971); one *s* one *d*; 2nd, 1974, Pauline Valerie Brownrigg; one *s* one *d*. *Educ:* Bedales Sch.; Rendcomb Coll.; New Coll., Oxford. MA; FIPA 1976. Executive, The London Press Exchange, Ltd, 1958–60; Pritchard Wood and Partners, Ltd: Manager, 1961–65; Dir, then Dep. Man. Dir, 1965–68; Founding Partner, The Boase Massimi Pollitt Partnership, Ltd, 1968; Chm., Boase Massimi Pollitt plc, 1977–89 (Jt Chm., 1977–79). Chairman: Maiden Outdoor, 1993–; Kiss 100 FM, 1993–; Herald Investment Trust, 1994–; Director: Omnicom Gp Inc., 1989–93; EMAP plc, 1991–; Taunton Cider plc, 1993–; Investment Trust of Investment Trusts, 1995–. Chairman: Advertising Assoc., 1987–92; British Television Advertising Awards Ltd, 1993–. Dir, Oxford Playhouse Trust, 1991–. *Recreation:* the Turf. *Address:* (office) 12 Bishop's Bridge Road, W2 6AA.

BOATENG, Prof. Ernest Amano, GM 1968; Environmental and Educational Consultant; Emeritus Professor of Geography, University of Ghana, since 1989; *b* 30 Nov. 1920; 2nd *s* of late Rev. Christian Robert and Adelaide Akonobea Boateng, Aburi, Ghana; *m* 1955, Evelyn Kensema Danso, *e d* of late Rev. Robert Opong Danso and of Victoria Danso, Aburi; four *d*. *Educ:* Achimota Coll.; St Peter's Hall, Oxford (Gold Coast Govt Schol.). Henry Oliver Beckit Meml Prize, 1949; BA (Geog.) 1949, MA 1953, MLitt 1954. UC Ghana: Lectr in Geography, 1950–57; Sen. Lectr, 1958–61; University of Ghana: Prof. of Geography, 1961–73; Dean, Faculty of Social Studies, 1962–69; Principal, 1969–71, Vice-Chancellor, 1972–73, Univ. Coll., Cape Coast, later Univ. of Cape Coast, Ghana. Vis. Asst Prof., Univ. of Pittsburgh and UCLA, 1960–61. Pres., Ghana Geographical Assoc., 1959–69; Foundn Fellow, Ghana Acad. of Arts and Sciences (Sec. 1959–62, Pres., 1973–76); Mem., Unesco Internat. Adv. Cttee on Humid Tropics Research, 1961–63; Mem., Scientific Council for Africa, 1963–80; Mem., Nat. Planning Commn of Ghana, 1961–64; Smuts Vis. Fellow, Univ. of Cambridge, 1965–66; Vis. Prof., Univ. of Pittsburgh, 1966; Deleg., UN Conf. on geographical names, Geneva, 1967; Mem., Council for Scientific and Industrial Research, Ghana, 1967–75; Dir, Ghana Nat. Atlas Project, 1965–77; Chm., Geographical Cttee, Ghana 1970 population census; Chm., Environmental Protection Council, Ghana, 1973–81; Member: Nat. Economic Planning Council of Ghana, 1974–78; Chm., Land Use Planning Cttee of Ghana, 1978–79; Pres., Governing Council of UNEP, 1979, Senior Consultant, 1980–; Member: Constituent Assembly for drafting constitution for third Republic of Ghana, 1978–79; Presidential Task Force on Investments, Ghana, 1980; Nat. Council for Higher Educn, 1975–82; Chm., W African Exams Council, 1977–85. Pres., Ghana Wildlife Soc., 1974–87. Alternate Leader, Ghana Delegn to UN Conf., Vancouver, 1976. Hon. Fellow, Ghana Inst. of Planners, 1984. FRSA 1973. Hon. DLitt: Ghana, 1979; Cape Coast, 1994. Nat. Book Award, Ghana, 1978. *Publications:* A Geography of Ghana, 1959; (contrib.) Developing Countries of the World, 1968; (contrib.) Population Growth and Economic Development in Africa, 1972; Independence and Nation Building in Africa, 1973; A Political Geography of Africa, 1978; African Unity: the dream and the reality (J. B. Danquah Memorial Lectures 1978), 1979; various pamphlets, Britannica and other encyclopaedia articles and articles in geographical and other jls and reference works. *Recreations:* photography, gardening. *Address:* Environmental Consultancy Services, PO Box 84, Trade Fair Site, Accra, Ghana. *T:* Accra 777875; (home) 3 Aviation Road, Airport Residential Area, Accra, Ghana.

BOATENG, Paul Yaw; MP (Lab) Brent South, since 1987; barrister-at-law; *b* 14 June 1951; *s* of Eleanor and Kwaku Boateng; *m* 1980, Janet Alleyne; two *s* three *d*. *Educ:* Ghana Internat. Sch.; Accra Acad.; Apsley Grammar Sch.; Bristol Univ. (LLB Hons); Coll. of Law. Admitted Solicitor, 1976; Solicitor, Paddington Law Centre, 1976–79; Solicitor and Partner, B. M. Birnberg and Co., 1979–87; called to the Bar, Gray's Inn, 1989. Legal Advr, Scrap Sus Campaign, 1977–81. Greater London Council: Mem. (Lab) for Walthamstow, 1981–86; Chm., Police Cttee, 1981–86; Vice-Chm., Ethnic Minorities Cttee, GLC, 1981–86. Contested (Lab) Hertfordshire W, 1983. Chairman: Afro-Caribbean Educn Resource Project, 1978–86; Westminster CRC, 1979–81. Opposition frontbench spokesman: on treasury and economic affairs, 1989–92; on legal affairs, LCD, 1992–. Mem., H of C Environment Cttee, 1987–89. Member: Home Sec.'s Adv. Council on Race Relations, 1981–86; WCC Commn on prog. to combat racism, 1984–91; Police Training Council, 1981–85; Exec., NCCL, 1980–86. Chm. Governors, Priory Park Sch., 1978–84; Governor, Police Staff Coll., Bramshill, 1981–84; Mem. Ct, Bristol Univ., 1994–. Mem. Bd, ENO, 1984–. Broadcaster. *Publication:* (contrib.) Reclaiming the Ground, 1993. *Recreations:* escapist. *Address:* House of Commons, SW1A 0AA. *Clubs:* Mangrove; Black and White Café (Bristol).

BOBROW, Prof. Martin, CBE 1995; FRCP, FRCPath; Professor of Medical Genetics, Cambridge University, since 1995; *b* 6 Feb. 1938; *s* of Joe and Bessie Bobrow; *m* 1963, Lynda Geraldine Strauss; three *d*. *Educ:* Univ. of the Witwatersrand (BSc Hons 1958; MB BCh 1963; DSc Med 1979). MRCPath 1978, FRCPath 1990; FRCP 1986. Clin. Sci. Officer MRC Population Genetics Res. Unit, 1965–72; Consultant in Clin. Genetics, Oxford, and Mem., MRC Ext. Sci. Staff, Genetics Lab., Oxford Univ., 1974–81; Prof. of Human Genetics, Univ. of Amsterdam, 1981–82; Prince Philip Prof. of Paediatric Res., UMDS of Guy's and St Thomas' Hosps, London Univ., 1982–95; Dir, SE Thames Regl Genetics Centre, Guy's Hosp., 1982–95. Mem. Council, 1988–92, 1993–94, Chm., Molecular and Cellular Medicine Bd, 1992–95, MRC; Chairman: Cttee on Med. Aspects of Radiation in the Envt, 1985–92; Unrelated Live Donor Transplant Regulatory Authy, 1990–; Res. Cttee, Muscular Dystrophy Gp, 1993– (Mem., 1980–; Chm. Nat. Council, 1995–); Steering Cttee, Cochrane Centre, Oxford, 1992–; Member: Internat. Standing Cttee on Human Cytogenetic Nomenclature, 1981–91; Black Adv. Gp on Possible Increased Incidence of Cancer in West Cumbria, 1983–84; Med. Adv. and Res. Cttees, Spastics Soc., 1983–89; Human Genome Orgn, 1989–; Cttee to examine the ethical implications of gene therapy, 1989–; NHS Central R&D Cttee, DoH, 1991–; Gene Therapy Adv. Cttee, 1993–; Lewisham NHS Trust Bd, 1994–95. Pres., 1993–95, Vice-Pres., 1992–93 and 1995–96, Clinical Genetics Soc. *Publications:* papers in sci. books and jls. *Address:* Department of Clinical Genetics, Addenbrooke's Hospital, Cambridge CB2 2QQ.

BOCK, Prof. Claus Victor, MA, DrPhil; Professor of German Language and Literature, Westfield College, University of London, 1969–84, now Emeritus; Hon. Research Fellow, Queen Mary and Westfield College (formerly Westfield College), since 1984, Fellow, 1993; *b* Hamburg, 7 May 1926; *o s* of Frederick Bock, merchant and manufacturer, and Margot (*née* Meyerhof). *Educ:* Quaker Sch., Eerde, Holland; Univs of Amsterdam, Manchester, Basle. DrPhil (insigni cum laude) Basle 1955. Asst Lectr in German, Univ. of Manchester, 1956–58; University of London: Lectr, Queen Mary Coll., 1958–69; Reader in German Lang. and Lit., 1964; Chm., Bd of Studies in Germanic Langs and Lit., 1970–73; Hon. Dir, Inst. of Germanic Studies, 1973–81 (Hon. Fellow, 1989); Dean, Fac. of Arts, 1980–84; Mem., Senate, 1981–83; Mem., Acad. Council, 1981–83; Mem., Central Research Fund (A), 1981–84. Mem. Council, English Goethe Soc., 1965–; Chm., Stichting Castrum Peregrini, 1984– (Mem., 1971–). Hon. Pres., Assoc. of Teachers of German, 1973–75. Mem., Maatschappij der Nederlandse Letteren, 1977. Mem. Editl Bd, Bithell Series of Dissertations, 1978–84. Officer, Order of Merit (FRG), 1984. *Publications:* Deutsche erfahren Holland 1725–1925, 1956; Q. Kuhlmann als Dichter, 1957; ed (with Margot Ruben) K. Wolfskehl Ges. Werke, 1960; ed (with G. F. Senior) Goethe the Critic, 1960; Pente Pigadia und die Tagebücher des Clement Harris, 1962; ed (with L. Helbing) Fr. Gundolf Briefwechsel mit H. Steiner und E. R. Curtius, 1963; Wort-Konkordanz zur Dichtung Stefan Georges, 1964; ed (with L. Helbing) Fr. Gundolf Briefe Neue Folge, 1965; A Tower of Ivory?, 1970; (with L. Helbing and K. Kluncker) Stefan George: Dokumente seiner Wirkung, 1974; (ed) London German Studies, 1980; (with K. Kluncker) Wolfgang Cordan: Jahre der Freundschaft, 1982; Untergetaucht unter Freunden, 1985, 3rd edn 1989; Besuch im Elfenbeinturm (selected essays), 1990; articles in English and foreign jls and collections. *Recreation:* foreign travel. *Address:* Queen Mary and Westfield College, Mile End Road, E1 4NS. *T:* 0171–975 5555; c/o Castrum Peregrini Presse, PB 645, 1000 AP Amsterdam, Netherlands. *T:* (20) 230043.

BOCK, Dieter; Chief Executive and Managing Director, Lonrho plc, since 1993; *b* 3 March 1939; *s* of Rudolf Bock and Helene (*née* Dannert); *m* 1985, Olga Giro; four *s*. *Educ:* Marburg; Munich Univ. Hon. Citizen, Houston, Texas. *Recreation:* sailing. *Address:* c/o Lonrho plc, Cheapside House, 138 Cheapside, EC2V 6B2. *T:* 0171–606 9898; c/o Anthony Cardew, Cardew & Co., 12 Suffolk Street, SW1Y 4HQ. *T:* 0171–930 0777. *Club:* Royal Cape Yacht (Cape Town).

BODDINGTON, Ewart Agnew, JP; DL; Chairman, Boddington Group PLC (formerly Boddington's Breweries), 1970–88, President, since 1989; *b* 7 April 1927; *m* 1954, Vine Anne Clayton (*d* 1989); two *s* one *d*. *Educ:* Stowe Sch., Buckingham; Trinity Coll., Cambridge (MA). Jt Man. Dir, Boddingtons', 1957, Man. Dir, 1980. Dir, Northern Bd, National Westminster Bank, 1977–92. Pres., Inst. of Brewing, 1972–74; Chm., Brewers' Soc., 1984–85; Mem., Brewers' Co., 1980–. JP Macclesfield, 1959; High Sheriff of Cheshire, 1978–79; DL Cheshire 1993. Hon. MA Manchester, 1977. *Recreations:* shooting, golf, fishing, music. *Address:* Fanshawe Brook Farm, Henbury, Macclesfield SK11 9PP. *T:* Marton Heath (01260) 244387.

BODDY, Jack Richard, MBE 1973; JP; Group Secretary, Agricultural and Allied Workers Trade Group, Transport and General Workers Union, 1982–87 (General Secretary, National Union of Agricultural and Allied Workers, 1978–82); *b* 23 Aug. 1922; *s* of Percy James Boddy and Lucy May Boddy, JP; *m* 1943, Muriel Lilian (*née* Webb) (*d* 1987); three *s* one *d*; *m* 1990, (Margaret) Joan Laws. *Educ:* City of Norwich Sch. Agricultural worker, 1939; farm foreman, 1943. District Organiser: Lincolnshire NUAAW, 1953; Norfolk NUAAW, 1960. Mem., TUC Gen. Council, 1978–83. Leader, Workers' side, Agricl Wages Bd, 1978–87. Member: Agricl Cttee, EDC, 1978–88; Economic and Social Cttee, EEC, 1980–90; Food and Drink Cttee, EDC, 1984–87; Industrial Injuries Adv. Cttee, DHSS, 1983–87. Member: Swaffham Town Council, 1987– (Dep. Mayor, 1990–91; Mayor, 1991–92); Breckland District Council, 1987–. Pres., Mid Norfolk Mencap, 1988–91. Freeman, City of Norwich. JP Swaffham, 1947. *Recreations:* caravanning, gardening. *Address:* The Brambles, 2b Spinners Lane, Swaffham, Norfolk PE37 7ND. *T:* Swaffham (01760) 722916.

BODEN, Leonard, RP; FRSA; portrait painter; *b* Greenock, Scotland; *s* of John Boden; *m* Margaret Tulloch (portrait painter, as Margaret Boden, PS, FRSA); one *d*. *Educ:* Sedbergh; Sch. of Art, Glasgow; Heatherley Sch. of Art, London. *Official portraits* include: HM Queen Elizabeth II; HRH The Prince Philip, Duke of Edinburgh; HM Queen Elizabeth the Queen Mother; HRH The Prince of Wales; The Princess Royal; HH Pope Pius XII; Field Marshals Lord Milne and Lord Slim, Margaret Thatcher, and many others. Vice-

President: Artists' Gen. Benevolent Instn; St Ives Soc. of Artists; Governor, Christ's Hospital. Freeman, City of London; Liveryman, Painter-Stainers Co. Gold Medal, Paris Salon, 1957. *Work reproduced in:* The Connoisseur, The Artist, Fine Art Prints. *Address:* 36 Arden Road, N3 3AN. *T:* 0181–346 5706. *Clubs:* Savage, Chelsea Arts.

BODEN, Prof. Margaret Ann, ScD, PhD; FBA 1983; Professor of Philosophy and Psychology, University of Sussex, since 1980; *b* 26 Nov. 1936; *d* of late Leonard Forbes Boden, OBE, LLB and Violet Dorothy Dawson; *m* 1967, John Raymond Spiers, *qv* (marr. diss. 1981); one *s* one *d. Educ:* City of London Sch. for Girls; Newnham Coll., Cambridge (Major schol. in Med. Scis; Sarah Smithson Scholar in Moral Scis; MA; Associate, 1981–93; ScD 1990); Harvard Grad. Sch. (Harkness Fellow; AM; PhD in Cognitive and Social Psychology). Asst Lectr, then Lectr, in Philosophy, Birmingham Univ., 1959–65; Sussex University: Lectr, 1965–72; Reader, 1972–80; Founding Dean, Sch. of Cognitive Sciences, later Cognitive and Computing Sciences, 1987. Vis. Scientist, Yale Univ., 1979. Lectures: Dacte, Cambridge, 1994; Templeton, Sydney, 1994; Sluckin, Leicester, 1994. Co-founder, Dir, 1968–85, Sec., 1968–79, Harvester Press. Founding Chm., Hist. and Philosophy of Psychology Sect., BPsS, 1983; Pres., Sect. X, BAAS, 1993; Vice-Pres., and Chm. of Council, Royal Instn of GB, 1993–95 (Mem. Council, 1992–95). Member: Council for Science and Society, 1986–91 (Trustee, 1990–91); ABRC, 1989–90 (Chm., Working Gp on Peer-Review, 1989–90); Animal Procedures Cttee, Home Office, 1994–; Council, Royal Inst. of Philosophy, 1987–; Council, British Acad., 1988– (Vice-Pres., 1989–91). Mem., Soc. of Authors, 1982–. Trustee, Eric Gill Trust, 1993–. Member: Academia Europaea, 1993; NY Acad. of Scis, 1994; Fellow, Amer. Assoc. for Artificial Intelligence, 1993; FRSA 1992. Leslie McMichael Premium, IERE, 1977. *Publications:* Purposive Explanation in Psychology, 1972; Artificial Intelligence and Natural Man, 1977; Piaget, 1979; Minds and Mechanisms, 1981; Computer Models of Mind, 1988; Artificial Intelligence in Psychology, 1989; The Philosophy of Artificial Intelligence, 1990; The Creative Mind: myths and mechanisms, 1990; (ed) Dimensions of Creativity, 1994; (ed) The Philosophy of Artificial Life, 1996; General Editor: Explorations in Cognitive Science; Harvester Studies in Cognitive Science; Harvester Studies in Philosophy; contribs to philosophical and psychological jls. *Recreations:* dress-making, dreaming about the South Pacific. *Address:* School of Cognitive and Computing Sciences, University of Sussex, Brighton BN1 9QH. *T:* Brighton (01273) 678386. *Club:* Reform.

BODEN, Thomas Bennion, OBE 1978; Deputy President, National Farmers' Union of England and Wales, 1979; Chairman, European Economic Community Advisory Committee on Questions of Agricultural Structure Policy, 1985–89; *b* 23 Oct. 1915; *s* of late Harry Bertram Boden and Florence Nellie Mosley; *m* 1939, Dorothy Eileen Ball; one *s* two *d. Educ:* Alleynes Grammar Sch., Uttoxeter; Nottingham Univ. BSc course up to final year, when moved into farming on death of father, 1936; became involved in agricultural politics through NFU, 1948; office holder of NFU, 1977. JP Staffs 1957–85. *Publications:* Memories of a Political Farmer, 1995; articles on agricultural taxation, farm structures in EEC, farm finance, young new entrants into farming. *Recreations:* cricket, tennis, swimming, hockey. *Address:* Denstone Hall, Denstone, Uttoxeter, Staffs ST14 5HF. *T:* Rocester (01889) 590243. *Clubs:* Farmers', NFU.

BODEY, David Roderick Lessiter; QC 1991; a Recorder, since 1993; *b* 14 Oct. 1947; *s* of late Reginald Augustus Bodey, FIA and Betty Francis Bodey; *m* 1976, Ruth (*née* MacAdorey); one *s* one *d. Educ:* King's Sch., Canterbury; Univ. of Bristol (LLB Hons 1969). Called to the Bar, Middle Temple, 1970 (Harmsworth Scholar, 1970). An Asst Recorder, 1989. Legal Assessor to UK Central Council for Nursing, Midwifery and Health Visiting, 1983. *Recreations:* music, marathon running. *Address:* Queen Elizabeth Building, Temple, EC4Y 9BS. *T:* 0171–797 7837. *Club:* Lansdowne.

BODGER; *see* Steele-Bodger.

BODILLY, Sir Jocelyn, Kt 1969; VRD; Chairman, Industrial Tribunals for London (South), 1976–86, retired; Chief Justice of the Western Pacific, 1965–75; *b* 1913; *m* 1st, 1936, Phyllis Maureen (*d* 1963), *d* of Thomas Cooper Gotch, ARA; 2nd, 1964, Marjorie, *d* of Walter Fogg. *Educ:* Munro Coll., Jamaica; Schloss Schule, Salem, Baden; Wadham Coll., Oxford. Called to Bar, Inner Temple, 1937; engaged in private practice until War; Royal Navy until 1946; RNVR, 1937–56 (Lt-Comdr (S)); Lt-Comdr, RNR, Hong Kong, 1961–65. High Court Judge, Sudan, 1946–55; Crown Counsel, Hong Kong, 1955, Principal Crown Counsel, 1961–65. *Address:* Myrtle Cottage, St Peters Hill, Newlyn, Penzance, Cornwall TR18 5EQ. *Club:* Royal Ocean Racing.

BODINHAM, Susan; Headmistress, St Mary's School, Wantage, since 1994; *b* 10 June 1951; *d* of Albert Henry Letley and Ethel May Letley; *m* 1973, Michael Geoffrey Bodinham (marr. diss. 1990); one *s* two *d. Educ:* Clarendon House Grammar Sch. for Girls, Ramsgate; King's Coll., London (BSc 2nd Cl. Hons; AKC; PGCE); Open Univ. (Adv. Dip Ed Man). Geography teacher, Peers Upper Comprehensive, Oxford, 1973–77 and 1984–85; Headington School, Oxford: Geog. teacher, 1985–87; Head of Dept, 1987; Housemistress, 1988; Head of Lower Sixth, 1991–93; Dep. Head, 1993–94. Sen. examng posts with EMREB, Southern Examng Gp and Northern Exams and Assessment Bd. Reader, Church of England, 1993–. *Publications:* articles in Britain and the British (pubd in Poland). *Recreations:* walking, reading, theatre, music. *Address:* 3 Post Office Lane, Wantage, Oxon OX12 8DR. *T:* Wantage (01235) 763571.

BODMER, Sir Walter (Fred), Kt 1986; FRCPath; FRS 1974; FIBiol; Director General, Imperial Cancer Research Fund, 1991–Sept. 1996 (Director of Research, 1979–91); Principal, Hertford College, Oxford, from Sept. 1996; *b* 10 Jan. 1936; *s* of late Dr Ernest Julius and Sylvia Emily Bodmer; *m* 1956, Julia Gwynaeth Pilkington; two *s* one *d. Educ:* Manchester Grammar Sch.; Clare Coll., Cambridge. BA 1956, MA, PhD 1959, Cambridge. FRCPath 1984; FIBiol 1990. Research Fellow 1958–61, Official Fellow 1961, Hon. Fellow 1989, Clare Coll., Cambridge; Demonstrator in Genetics, Univ. of Cambridge, 1960–61; Asst Prof. 1962–66, Associate Prof. 1966–68, Prof. 1968–70, Dept of Genetics, Stanford Univ.; Prof. of Genetics, Univ. of Oxford, 1970–79. Non-exec. Dir, Fisons plc, 1990–. Chm., BBC Sci. Consultative Gp, 1981–87; Member: BBC Gen. Adv. Council, 1981–91 (Chm., 1987); Council, Internat. Union Against Cancer, 1982–90; Adv. Bd for Res. Councils, 1983–88; Council, Found for Sci. and Technol., 1995–; Chairman: COPUS, 1990–93; Orgn of European Cancer Insts, 1990–93; President: Royal Statistical Soc., 1984–85 (Vice-Pres., 1983–84); BAAS, 1987–88 (Vice-Pres., 1989–); ASE, 1989–90; Human Genome Orgn, 1990–92; British Soc. for Histocompatibility and Immunogenetics, 1990–91 (Hon. Mem. 1992); EACR, 1994–; first Pres., Internat. Fedn of Assocs for Advancement of Sci. and Technol., 1992–94; Vice-President: Royal Instn, 1981–82; Parly and Scientific Cttee, 1990–93; Hon. Vice-Pres., Res. Defence Soc., 1990–. Trustee: BM (Natural History), 1983–93 (Chm., Bd of Trustees, 1989–93); Sir John Soane's Mus., 1982–. Hon. Member: British Soc. of Gastroenterology, 1989; Amer. Assoc. of Immunologists, 1985; For. Associate, US Nat. Acad. of Scis, 1981; For. Mem., Amer. Philosophical Soc., 1989; For. Hon. Mem., Amer. Acad. Arts and Scis, 1972; Fellow, Internat. Inst. of Biotechnology, 1989; Hon. Fellow: Keble Coll., Oxford, 1982; Green Coll., Oxford, 1993; Hon. FRCP 1985; Hon. FRCS 1986; Hon. FRSM 1994. Hon. DSc: Bath, Oxford, 1988; Hull, Edinburgh, 1990; Bristol, 1991; Loughborough, 1993; Lancaster, Aberdeen, 1994; DUniv Surrey, 1990; Laurea *hc* in Medicine and Surgery, Univ. of Bologna, 1987; Dr *hc:* Leuven, 1992; Masaryk, 1994; Hon. MD Birmingham, 1992; Hon. LLD Dundee, 1993. William Allan Meml Award, Amer. Soc. Human Genetics, 1980; Conway Evans Prize, RCP/Royal Soc., 1982; Rabbi Shai Shacknai Meml Prize Lectr, 1983; John Alexander Meml Prize and Lectureship, Univ. of Pennsylvania Med. Sch., 1984; Rose Payne Dist. Scientists Lectureship, Amer. Soc. for Histocompatibility and Immunogenetics, 1985; Bernal Lectr, Royal Soc., 1986; Neil Hamilton-Fairley Medal, RCP, 1990; Faraday Award, Royal Soc., 1994. *Publications:* The Genetics of Human Populations (with L. L. Cavalli-Sforza), 1971; (with A. Jones) Our Future Inheritance: choice or chance?, 1974; (with L. L. Cavalli-Sforza) Genetics, Evolution and Man, 1976; (with Robin McKie) The Book of Man, 1994; research papers in genetical, statistical and mathematical jls, etc. *Recreations:* playing the piano, riding, swimming. *Address:* (until Sept., 1996) Imperial Cancer Research Fund, Lincoln's Inn Fields, WC2A 3PX. *T:* 0171–242 0200; (from Sept. 1996) Hertford College, Oxford OX1 3BW. *Club:* Athenæum.

BODMIN, Archdeacon of; *see* Whiteman, Ven. R. D. C.

BODY, Sir Richard (Bernard Frank Stewart), Kt 1986; MP (C) Holland with Boston, since 1966; *b* 18 May 1927; *s* of Lieut-Col Bernard Richard Body, formerly of Hyde End, Shinfield, Berks; *m* 1959, Marion, *d* of late Major H. Graham, OBE; one *s* one *d.* Called to the Bar, Middle Temple, 1949. Underwriting Mem. of Lloyd's. Contested (C) Rotherham, 1950; Abertillery bye-election, 1950; Leek, 1951; MP (C) Billericay Div., Essex, 1955–Sept. 1959. Member: Jt Select Cttee on Consolidation of Law, 1975–91; Commons Select Cttee on Agric., 1979–87 (Chm., 1986–87). Chm., Open Seas Forum, 1971–. Jt Chm., Council, Get Britain Out referendum campaign, 1975. Chm. Trustees, Centre for European Studies, 1991–. Dir, New European Publications Ltd, 1986–. *Publications:* The Architect and the Law, 1954; (contrib.) Destiny or Delusion, 1971; (ed jtly) Freedom and Stability in the World Economy, 1976; Agriculture: The Triumph and the Shame, 1982; Farming in the Clouds, 1984; Red or Green for Farmers, 1987; Europe of Many Circles, 1990; Our Food, Our Land, 1991. *Address:* Jewell's Farm, Stanford Dingley, near Reading, Berks RG7 6LX. *T:* Reading (01734) 744295. *Clubs:* Athenæum, Carlton, Reform.

BOE, Norman Wallace; Deputy Solicitor to Secretary of State for Scotland, since 1987; *b* 30 Aug. 1943; *s* of Alexander Thomson Boe and Margaret Wallace Revans; *m* 1968, Margaret Irene McKenzie; one *s* one *d. Educ:* George Heriot's Sch., Edinburgh; Edinburgh Univ. LLB Hons 1965. Admitted Solicitor, 1967. Legal apprentice, Lindsays, WS, 1965–67; Legal Asst, Menzies & White, WS, 1967–70; Office of Solicitor to Sec. of State for Scotland, 1970–. *Recreations:* golf, gardening, dog-walking. *Address:* c/o Solicitor's Office, Scottish Office, New St Andrew's House, Edinburgh EH1 3TE. *T:* 0131–244 4884. *Club:* Edinburgh University Staff.

BOEGNER, Jean-Marc; Grand Officier, Légion d'Honneur; Commandeur, Ordre National du Mérite; Ambassadeur de France, 1973; *b* 3 July 1913; *s* of Marc and Jeanne Boegner; *m* 1945, Odilie de Moustier; three *d. Educ:* Lycée Janson-de-Sailly; Ecole Libre des Sciences Politiques; Paris University (LèsL). Joined French diplomatic service, 1939; Attaché: Berlin, 1939; Ankara, 1940; Beirut, 1941; Counsellor: Stockholm, 1945; The Hague, 1947; Ministry of Foreign Affairs, Paris, 1952–58; Counsellor to Charles de Gaulle, 1958–59; Ambassador to Tunisia, 1959–60; Permanent Representative of France: to EEC, 1961–72; to OECD, 1975–78. *Publication:* Le Marché commun de Six à Neuf, 1974. *Address:* 19 rue de Lille, 75007 Paris, France.

BOEVEY, Sir Thomas (Michael Blake) C.; *see* Crawley-Boevey.

BOGARDE, Sir Dirk; *see* Van den Bogaerde, Sir D. N.

BOGDANOR, Vernon Bernard; Reader in Government, since 1990, and Fellow of Brasenose College, Oxford University; *b* 16 July 1943; *s* of Harry Bogdanor and Rosa (*née* Weinger); *m* 1972, Judith Evelyn Beckett; two *s. Educ:* The Queen's College, Oxford (BA 1st Cl. PPE 1964; MA 1968). Sen. Tutor, Brasenose Coll., Oxford, 1979–85. Special Advr, H of L Select Cttee on European Communities, 1982–83; Advr on Constitutional and Electoral Matters to Czechoslovak, Hungarian, and Israeli Govts, 1988–; UK Delegn to CSCE Conf., Oslo, 1991. Member Council: Hansard Soc. for Parly Govt, 1981–; Inst. of Jewish Affairs, 1992–. FRSA 1992. *Publications:* (ed) Disraeli: Lothair, 1975; Devolution, 1979; The People and the Party System, 1981; Multi-Party Politics and the Constitution, 1983; (ed) Democracy and Elections, 1983; (ed) Coalition Government in Western Europe, 1983; What is Proportional Representation?, 1984; (ed) Parties and Democracy in Britain and America, 1984; (ed) Constitutions in Democratic Politics, 1988; (ed) The Blackwell Encyclopaedia of Political Science, 1992; (jtly) Comparing Constitutions, 1995; The Monarchy and the Constitution, 1995; contribs to learned jls. *Recreations:* music, walking, talking. *Address:* Brasenose College, Oxford OX1 4AJ. *T:* Oxford (01865) 277830.

BOGDANOV, Michael; Artistic Director, English Shakespeare Company, since 1986; *b* 15 Dec. 1938; *s* of Francis Benzion Bogdin and Rhoda Rees Bogdin; *m* 1966, Patsy Ann Warwick; two *s* one *d. Educ:* Lower School of John Lyon, Harrow; Univ. of Dublin Trinity Coll. (MA); Univs of the Sorbonne, and Munich. Writer, with Terence Brady, ATV series, Broad and Narrow, 1965; Producer/Director with Telefis Eireann, 1966–68; opening production of Theatre Upstairs, Royal Court, A Comedy of the Changing Years, 1969; The Bourgeois Gentilhomme, Oxford Playhouse, 1969; Asst Dir, Royal Shakespeare Theatre Co., 1970–71; Associate Dir, Peter Brook's A Midsummer Night's Dream, Stratford 1970, New York 1971, World Tour 1972; Dir, Two Gentlemen of Verona, São Paulo, Brazil, 1971; Associate to Jean Louis Barrault, Rabelais, 1971; Associate Director: Tyneside Th. Co., 1971–73; Haymarket Th., Leicester; Director: Phoenix Th., Leicester, 1973–77; Young Vic Th., London, 1978–80; an Associate Dir, Nat. Theatre, 1980–88; Intendant (Chief Exec.), Deutsche Schauspielhaus, Hamburg, 1989–92. Directed: The Taming of the Shrew, RSC, Stratford 1978, London 1979 (SWET Dir of the Year award, 1979); The Seagull, Toho Th. Co., Tokyo, 1980; Shadow of a Gunman, RSC, 1980; The Knight of the Burning Pestle, RSC, 1981; Hamlet, Dublin, 1983; Romeo and Juliet, Tokyo, 1983, RSC, 1986, Lyric, Hammersmith, 1993; The Mayor of Zalamea, Washington, 1984; Measure for Measure, Stratford, Ont., 1985; Mutiny (musical), 1985; Donnerstag aus Licht, Royal Opera House, 1985; Julius Caesar, Schauspielhaus, Hamburg, 1986 (also filmed by ZDF TV); Reineke Fuchs, Schauspielhaus, Hamburg, 1987; The Canterbury Tales, Prince of Wales, 1987; Montag, Stockhausen Opera, La Scala, Milan, 1988 (world première); Hamlet, Hamburg, 1989; The Venetian Twins, Swan, 1993; Hair, Old Vic, 1993; The Hostage, Barbican, 1994; National Theatre productions: Sir Gawain and the Green Knight, The Hunchback of Notre Dame, 1977–78; The Romans in Britain, Hiawatha, 1980; One Woman Plays, The Mayor of Zalamea, The Hypochondriac, 1981; Uncle Vanya, The Spanish Tragedy, 1982; Lorenzaccio, 1983; You Can't Take it With You, 1983; Strider, 1984; English Shakespeare Co. productions: Henry IV (Parts I and II), Henry V, UK tour, European tour, Old Vic, and Canada, 1986–87; The Wars of the Roses (7 play history cycle), UK, Europe and world tour, 1987–89 (Laurence Olivier Award, Dir of the Year, 1989); Coriolanus, The Winter's Tale, UK and world tour,

1990–91; Macbeth, UK tour, 1992; The Tempest, 1992. Deviser and Presenter, Shakespeare Lives, TV series, 1983. Co-author, plays, adaptations and children's theatre pieces. Hon. Prof., Univ. of Wales, 1993; Sen. Fellow, De Montfort Univ., 1992; Hon. FWCMD 1994. *Publication:* (jtly) The English Shakespeare Company, 1990. *Recreations:* cricket, wine, music, sheep. *Address:* English Shakespeare Company, 95 Palewell Park, SW14 8JJ. *T:* 0181–392 1958, *Fax:* 0181–392 1993.

BOGDANOVICH, Peter; American film director, writer, producer, actor; *b* Kingston, NY, 30 July 1939; *s* of Borislav Bogdanovich and Herma (*née* Robinson); *m* 1962, Polly Platt (marr. diss. 1970); two *d*; *m* 1988, L. B. Straten. Owner: Crescent Moon Productions, Inc., LA, 1986; Holly Moon Co. Inc., LA, 1992–. Member: Dirs Guild of America; Writers' Guild of America; Acad. of Motion Picture Arts and Sciences. *Theatre:* Actor, Amer. Shakespeare Fest., Stratford, Conn, 1956, NY Shakespeare Fest., 1958; Dir and producer, off-Broadway: The Big Knife, 1959; Camino Real, Ten Little Indians, Rocket to the Moon, 1961; Once in a Lifetime, 1964. *Films include:* The Wild Angels (2nd-Unit Dir, co-writer, actor), 1966; Targets (dir, co-writer, prod., actor), 1968; The Last Picture Show (dir, co-writer), 1971 (NY Film Critics' Award for Best Screenplay, British Acad. Award for Best Screenplay); Directed by John Ford (dir, writer, interviewer), 1971; What's Up, Doc? (dir, co-writer, prod.), 1972 (Writers' Guild of America Award for Best Screenplay); Paper Moon (dir, prod.), 1973 (Silver Shell Award, Spain); Daisy Miller (dir, prod.), 1974 (Brussels Festival Award for Best Director); At Long Last Love (dir, writer, prod.), 1975; Nickelodeon (dir, co-writer), 1976; Saint Jack (dir, co-writer, actor), 1979 (Pasinetti Award, Critics' Prize, Venice Festival); They All Laughed (dir, writer), 1981; Mask (dir), 1985; Illegally Yours (dir, prod.), 1988; Texasville (dir, prod., writer), 1990; Noises Off (dir, exec. prod.), 1992; The Thing Called Love (dir), 1993. *Television:* The Great Professional: Howard Hawks, BBC, 1967; CBS This Morning (weekly commentary), 1987–89. *Publications:* The Cinema of Orson Welles, 1961; The Cinema of Howard Hawks, 1962; The Cinema of Alfred Hitchcock, 1963; John Ford, 1968; Fritz Lang in America, 1969; Allan Dwan: the last pioneer, 1971; Pieces of Time: Peter Bogdanovich on the Movies (Picture Shows in the UK) 1961–85, 1973, enlarged 1985; The Killing of the Unicorn: Dorothy Stratten, 1960–1980, a Memoir, 1984; (ed with introd.) A Year and a Day Engagement Calendar, annually, 1991–; This is Orson Welles, 1992; features on films in Esquire, New York Times, Village Voice, Cahiers du Cinema, Los Angeles Times, New York Magazine, Vogue, Variety etc., 1961–. *Address:* c/o William Peiffer, 2040 Avenue of the Stars, Century City, CA 90067, USA; (agents) Martin Baum, Rick Nicita, CAA, 9830 Wilshire Boulevard, Beverly Hills, CA 90212, USA.

BOGGIS, Andrew Gurdon, MA; Warden of Forest School, since 1992; *b* 1 April 1954; *s* of Lt-Col (Edmund) Allan (Theodore) Boggis and Myrtle (Eirene) Boggis (*née* Donald); *m* 1983, Fiona Mary Cocke; two *d* one *s*. *Educ:* Marlborough Coll.; New Coll., Oxford (MA); King's Coll., Cambridge (PGCE). Asst Master, Hitchin Boys' Sch., 1978–79; Eton College: Asst Master, 1979–92; Master-in-College, 1984–92. Liveryman, Skinners' Co. Gov., King's Coll. Sch., Cambridge. *Recreations:* music, cookery, reading. *Address:* Forest School, College Place, Snaresbrook, E17 3PY. *T:* 0181–520 1744. *Club:* East India.

BOGGIS, John Graham; QC 1993; a Recorder, since 1994; *b* 2 April 1949; *s* of Robert Boggis and Joyce Meek; *m* 1976, Jennifer Coultas; three *s*. *Educ:* Whitgift Sch.; Univ. of London (LLB); Univ. of Keele (MA). Called to the Bar, Lincoln's Inn, 1972. Asst Boundary Comr, 1993–. Member: Chancery Bar Assoc., 1982–84; Senate of the Inns of Court and Bar, 1984–85. Staff Rep. Gov., Sherborne Sch., 1993–. *Recreation:* sailing. *Address:* 5 Stone Buildings, Lincoln's Inn, WC2A 3XT. *T:* 0171–242 6201.

BOGGIS-ROLFE, Hume, CB 1971; CBE 1962; farmer; *b* 20 Oct. 1911; *s* of Douglass Horace Boggis-Rolfe and Maria Maud (*née* Bailey); *m* 1941, Anne Dorothea, *e d* of Capt. Eric Noble, Henley-on-Thames; two *s* one *d*. *Educ:* Westminster Sch.; Freiburg Univ.; Trinity Coll., Cambridge. Called to Bar, Middle Temple, 1935. Army, Intelligence Corps, 1939–46 (Lieut-Col). Private Sec. to Lord Chancellor, 1949–50; Asst Solicitor in Lord Chancellor's Office, 1951–65; Sec. to Law Commn, 1965–68; Deputy Clerk of the Crown in Chancery, and Asst Perm. Sec. to Lord Chancellor, 1968–75, and Deputy Secretary, Lord Chancellor's Office, 1970–75. Master, Merchant Taylors' Co., 1971–72. Chm., Friends of the Elderly and Gentlefolks' Help, 1977–84. *Recreations:* gardening, travelling. *Address:* 22 Victoria Square, SW1W 0RB. *T:* 0171–834 2676; The Grange, Wormingford, Colchester, Essex. *T:* Bures (01787) 227303. *Club:* Athenæum.

BOGIE, David Wilson; Sheriff of Grampian, Highland and Islands at Aberdeen and Stonehaven, since 1985; *b* 17 July 1946; *o s* of late Robert T. Bogie, Edinburgh; *m* 1983, Lady Lucinda Mackay, *o d* of 3rd Earl of Inchcape. *Educ:* George Watson's Coll.; Edinburgh Univ. (LLB); Balliol Coll., Oxford (MA). FSAScot. Admitted to Faculty of Advocates, 1972; Temp. Sheriff, 1981. *Recreations:* architecture, heraldry, antiquities. *Address:* 50 Whitehall Road, Aberdeen AB2 4PR. *Clubs:* Brooks's; New (Edinburgh); Royal Northern and University (Aberdeen).

BOGLE, David Blyth, CBE 1967; WS; formerly Senior Partner, Lindsays, WS, Edinburgh; Member of Council on Tribunals, 1958–70, and Chairman of Scottish Committee, 1962–70; *b* 22 Jan. 1903; *s* of late Very Rev. Andrew Nisbet Bogle, DD and Helen Milne Bogle; *m* 1955, Ruth Agnes Thorley. *Educ:* George Watson's Coll., Edinburgh; Edinburgh Univ. (LLB). Writer to the Signet, 1927. Commissioned in the Queen's Own Cameron Highlanders, 1940, and served in UK and Middle East, 1942–45; demobilised, with rank of Major, 1945. *Recreation:* RNIB talking books. *Address:* 3 Belgrave Crescent, Edinburgh EH4 3AQ. *T:* 0131–332 0047. *Club:* New (Edinburgh).

BOGLE, Ellen Gray, CD 1987; Permanent Secretary, Ministry of Industry, Investment and Commerce (formerly of Industry, Tourism and Commerce), Jamaica, since 1993; *d* of late Victor Gray Williams and Eileen Avril Williams; *m* (marr. diss.); one *s* one *d*. *Educ:* St Andrew High Sch., Jamaica; Univ. of the West Indies, Jamaica (BA). Dir of For. Trade, Min. of For. Affairs, Jamaica, 1978–81; Dir, Jamaica Nat. Export Corp., 1978–81; High Comr to Trinidad and Tobago, Barbados, E Caribbean and Guyana, and Ambassador to Suriname, 1982–89; High Comr, UK, 1989–93, and Ambassador to Denmark, Norway, Sweden, Spain and Portugal, 1990–93. *Recreations:* gardening, reading, cooking, table tennis. *Address:* 36 Trafalgar Road, Kingston 10, Jamaica. *T:* 9298990.

BOGSCH, Arpad, Dr jur; Director General, World Intellectual Property Organization, since 1973 (Deputy Director General, 1963–73); *b* 24 Feb. 1919; *s* of Arpad Bogsch and Emilia Taborsky; *m* 1994, Adèle Fankhauser; one *s* one *d* by former marriage. *Educ:* Univ. of Budapest (Dr jur); Univ. of Paris (Dr jur); George Washington Univ. (LLM). Called to the Budapest Bar, 1940, to the Washington DC Bar, 1952. Private law practice, Budapest, 1940–48; Legal Officer, Unesco, Paris, 1948–54; Legal Adviser, Library of Congress, Washington DC, 1954–63. Hon. Prof. of Law, Peking Univ., 1991. LLD *hc* Jabalpur, 1978; George Washington, 1985; Colombo, 1987; Kyung Hee, Korea, 1991; Eötvös Lóránd, Budapest, 1991; Bucharest, 1991; Delhi, 1992; Charles Univ., Prague, 1994. Decorations from: Sweden, 1967; Austria, 1977; Spain, 1980; Senegal and Republic of Korea, 1981; Bulgaria, 1985; France, Japan and Thailand, 1986. *Address:* 34 chemin des Colombettes, 1211 Geneva, Switzerland. *T:* 022999111.

BOHAN, William Joseph, CB 1988; Assistant Under Secretary of State, Home Office, 1979–89, retired; *b* 10 April 1929; *s* of John and Josephine Bohan; *m* 1955, Brenda Skevington (*d* 1995); one *s* (one *d* decd). *Educ:* Finchley Catholic Grammar Sch.; Cardinal Vaughan Sch., Kensington; King's Coll., Cambridge (Chancellor's Classical Medallist, 1952). Home Office: Asst Principal, 1952; Principal, 1958; Sec., Cttee on Immigration Appeals, 1966–67; Asst Sec., 1967. Chm., European Cttee on Crime Problems, 1987–89. *Recreations:* languages and literature, walking. *Address:* 16 Mostyn Road, SW19 3LJ. *T:* 0181–542 1127.

BOHR, Prof. Aage Niels, DSc, DrPhil; physicist, Denmark; Professor of Physics, University of Copenhagen, 1956–92; *b* Copenhagen, 19 June 1922; *s* of late Prof. Niels Bohr and Margrethe Nørlund; *m* 1st, Marietta Bettina (*née* Soffer) (*d* 1978); two *s* one *d*; 2nd, 1981, Bente, *d* of late Chief Physician Johannes Meyer and Lone (*née* Rubow) and *widow* of Morten Scharff. *Educ:* Univ. of Copenhagen. Jun. Scientific Officer, Dept of Scientific and Industrial Research, London, 1943–45; Research Asst, Inst. for Theoretical Physics, Univ. of Copenhagen, 1946; Dir, Niels Bohr Inst. (formerly Inst. for Theoretical Physics), 1963–70. Bd Mem., Nordita, 1958–74, Dir, 1975–81. Member: Royal Danish Acad. of Science, 1955–; Royal Physiolog. Soc., Sweden, 1959–; Royal Norwegian Acad. of Sciences, 1962–; Acad. of Tech. Sciences, Copenhagen, 1963–; Amer. Phil. Soc., 1965–; Amer. Acad. of Arts and Sciences, 1965–; Nat. Acad. of Sciences, USA, 1971–; Royal Swedish Acad. of Sciences, 1974–; Yugoslavia Acad. of Sciences, 1976–; Pontificia Academia Scientiarum, 1978–; Norwegian Acad. of Sciences, 1979–; Polish Acad. of Sciences, 1980–; Finska Vetenskups-Societeten, 1980–; Deutsche Akademie der Naturforscher Leopoldina, 1981–. Awards: Dannie Heineman Prize, 1960; Pius XI Medal, 1963; Atoms for Peace Award, 1969; H. C. Ørsted Medal, 1970; Rutherford Medal, 1972; John Price Wetherill Medal, 1974; (jointly) Nobel Prize for Physics, 1975; Ole Rømer Medal, 1976. Dr *hc*: Manchester, 1961; Oslo, 1969; Heidelberg, 1971; Trondheim, 1972; Uppsala, 1975. *Publications:* Rotational States of Atomic Nuclei, 1954; (with Ben R. Mottelson) Nuclear Structure, vol. I, 1969, vol. II 1975. *Address:* Strandgade 34, 1st Floor, 1401 Copenhagen K, Denmark.

BOHUSZ-SZYSZKO, Dame Cicely (Mary Strode); *see* Saunders, Dame C. M. S.

BOILEAU, Sir Guy (Francis), 8th Bt *cr* 1838; sports administrator; *b* 23 Feb. 1935; *s* of Sir Edmond Charles Boileau, 7th Bt, and of Marjorie Lyle, *d* of Claude Monteath D'Arcy; *S* father, 1980; *m* 1962, Judith Frances, *d* of George Conrad Hannan; two *s* three *d*. *Educ:* Xavier College, Melbourne; Royal Military Coll., Duntroon, Australia. Lieut, Aust. Staff Corps, 1956; Platoon Comdr, 3rd Bn, Royal Aust. Regt, Malaysia, 1957–58; Observer, UN Mil. Observer Gp in India and Pakistan, 1959–60; Instructor, Aust. Army Training Team, Vietnam, 1963–64; attached US Dept of Defence, Washington, DC, 1966–68; Security Adviser, Dept of the Administrator, Territory of Papua-New Guinea, 1970–71; CO, Army Intelligence Centre, 1972–74; Directing Staff (Instructor), Aust. Staff Coll., 1975–76; SO1 Personnel, HQ Third Mil. Dist, 1979. *Recreations:* tennis, boating, fishing. *Heir:* *s* Nicolas Edmond George Boileau, *b* 17 Nov. 1964. *Address:* 14 Faircroft Avenue, Glen Iris, Victoria 3146, Australia. *T:* (3) 8228273. *Club:* The Heroes (Toorak, Victoria).

BOISSIER, Martin Scobell; Vice Lord-Lieutenant of Derbyshire, since 1992; Chairman, Derbyshire Family Health Services Authority, since 1990; *b* 14 May 1926; *s* of Ernest Gabriel Boissier, DSC and Doris Mary Boissier (*née* Bingham); *m* 1955, Margaret Jean Blair; one *s* one *d*. *Educ:* Bramcote Prep. Sch., Scarborough; RN Naval Coll., Dartmouth. Service in RN, 1943–58; qualified as Pilot, 1947; Lt-Comdr, retired 1958. Aiton & Co., Derby, 1958, Dir, 1976, retired 1988; Gp Personnel Controller and local Dir, Whessoe, 1980–88; former Director: Silkolene; ATV (Midlands). Mem., East Reg. Bd, Central ITV, 1982–92. Chm., Engrg Employers' Fedn Benevolent Fund. Chm., Arkwright Soc., Cromford; Pres., Royal Sch. for the Deaf, Derby; Vice-Pres., Derby Sea Cadet Corps. Freeman, City of London, 1978; Liveryman, Tinplate Workers alias Wire-workers' Co., 1978. DL 1977, High Sheriff, 1978–79, Derbys. *Recreations:* gardening; appreciation of art, music and wine; needlework, charity work, bon vivant. *Address:* Ithersay Cottage, Idridgehay, Belper, Derbyshire DE56 2SB. *T:* Cowers Lane (01773) 550210, *Fax:* (01773) 550225. *Clubs:* Army and Navy, MCC; County (Derby); Royal Naval Sailing Assoc. (Portsmouth); Carsington Sailing (Derbys).

See also R. H. Boissier.

BOISSIER, Roger Humphrey, CBE 1992; Chairman: Pressac Holdings PLC, since 1990; Kalon Group PLC, since 1992; *b* 30 June 1930; *y s* of late Ernest Boissier, DSC, CEng, FIEE and Doris Boissier (*née* Bingham), of Bingham's Melcombe; *m* 1965, (Elizabeth) Bridget (Rhoda), *e d* of Sir Gerald Ley, Bt, TD and Rosemary, Lady Ley; one *s* one *d*. *Educ:* Harrow. International Combustion, 1950–52; Cooper-Parry, Hall, Doughty & Co, 1952–53; Merz & McLellan, 1953–55; Aiton & Co, 1955–83, Man. Dir, 1975–83; Exec Dir, Whessoe, 1975–83; Non-Exec. Director: Pressac Holdings, 1984 (Dep. Chm., 1989); British Gas, 1986– (pt-time Mem., British Gas Corp., 1981–86); T & N, 1987–; Edward Lumley Holdings, 1988–; Severn Trent, 1989– (Severn Trent Water Authy, 1986–89); AMEC Power, 1992–94; AMEC Mechanical and Electrical Services, 1994–; Consultant, Allott & Lomax, 1984–; former Non-Executive Director: Derbyshire BS, 1972–81; Simmonds Precision NV, 1976–82; Ley's Foundries & Engineering, 1977–82. Mem. Exec., British Energy Assoc. (formerly Brit. Nat. Cttee, World Energy Council), 1975– (Chm., 1977–80); former Member: E Midlands Econ. Planning Council, 1972–75; CBI Central Council (selected Mem. from E Midlands regn), 1973–82. Mem. Court and Council, Loughborough Univ. of Technol., 1991–; Gov., Harrow Sch., 1976– (Dep. Chm., 1988). High Sheriff of Derbyshire, 1987–88. Master, Co. of Tin Plate Workers alias Wire Workers, 1988–89. CIGasE 1983; Companion, Inst. of Energy, 1991; FInstD 1984; FRSA 1987. *Recreations:* cars, foreign travel, reading, meeting people. *Address:* Easton House, The Pastures, Repton, Derby DE65 6GG. *T:* Burton-on-Trent (01283) 702274, *Fax:* (01283) 701489. *Clubs:* Brooks's, MCC; Surrey County Cricket; County (Derby).

See also M. S. Boissier.

BOIZOT, Peter James, MBE 1986; founded PizzaExpress Ltd, 1965; Chairman, PizzaExpress Plc, since 1993; *b* 16 Nov. 1929; *s* of Gaston Charles and late Susannah Boizot. *Educ:* King's Sch., Peterborough (chorister, Peterborough Cathedral); St Catharine's Coll., Cambridge. MA (BA (Hons) History). Captain, MV Yarvic, 1951. Various jobs, predominantly in sales field, 1953–64; Chm. and Man. Dir, PizzaExpress Ltd, 1965–93; Dir, Connoisseur Casino, 1970–82. Publisher BOZ (formerly Jazz Express), monthly magazine, 1983–. Proprietor: Pizza on the Park, 1976–; Kettners Restaurant, Soho, 1980–; Great Northern Railway Hotel, Peterborough, 1993–. Founder and Chm., Soho Restaurateurs Assoc., 1980–. Founder and Dir, Soho Jazz Fest., 1986–. Dir, CENTEC, 1990–93. Chm., Westminster Chamber of Commerce, 1992–94. Mem., Royal Acad. Adv. Bd, 1988–91. Contested (L) Peterborough, Feb. and Oct. 1974. Founder Mem., Soho Soc., 1972. Pres., Hampstead and Westminster Hockey Club, 1986–; a Vice-Pres., Hockey Assoc., 1990–. FHCIMA 1989. Bolla Award, 1983; Hotel and Caterer Food Service Award, 1989. Cavaliere Ufficiale, Al Merito della Repubblica Italiana, 1983. *Publication:* PizzaExpress Cook Book, 1976, rev. edn 1991. *Recreations:* hockey, presenting jazz, cabaret, dining out. *Address:* 10 Lowndes Square, SW1X 9HA. *T:* 0171–235 9100. *Clubs:* National Liberal, Royal Automobile.

BOJAXHIU, Agnes Gonxha; *see* Teresa, Mother.

BOK, Derek; Professor of Law, since 1961 and President, 1971–91, Harvard University; *b* Bryn Mawr, Pa, 22 March 1930; *s* of late Curtis and Margaret Plummer Bok (later Mrs William S. Kiskadden); *m* 1955, Sissela Ann Myrdal, *d* of Karl Gunnar and Alva Myrdal, *qqv*; one *s* two *d*. *Educ:* Stanford Univ., BA; Harvard Univ., JD; Inst. of Political Science, Univ. of Paris (Fulbright Scholar); George Washington Univ., MA in Economics. Served AUS, 1956–58. Asst Prof. of Law, Harvard Univ., 1958–61, Dean of Law Sch., 1968–71. *Publications:* The First Three Years of the Schuman Plan, 1955; (ed with Archibald Cox) Cases and Materials on Labor Law, 5th edn 1962, 6th edn 1965, 7th edn 1969, 8th edn 1977; (with John Dunlop) Labor and the American Community, 1970; Beyond the Ivory Tower, 1982; Higher Learning, 1986; Universities and the future of America, 1990; The Cost of Talent, 1993. *Recreations:* gardening, tennis, skiing. *Address:* c/o Harvard University, Cambridge, MA 02138, USA.

BOKHARY, Syed Kemal Shah; Hon. Mr Justice Bokhary; Justice of Appeal, Supreme Court of Hong Kong, since 1993; *b* 25 Oct. 1947; *s* of Syed Daud Shah Bokhary and Halima Bokhary (*née* Arculli); *m* 1977, Verina Saeeda Chung; three *d*. *Educ:* King George V Sch., Hong Kong. Called to the Bar, Middle Temple, 1970; QC (Hong Kong) 1983; practised in Hong Kong and before the Judicial Cttee of the Privy Council, London, 1971–89; Judge of High Court, Hong Kong, 1989–93. Mem., RSAA, 1988–. Mem., Welsh and W of England Bullmastiff Soc. *Publications:* articles in Hong Kong Law Jl and other learned jls. *Recreations:* dogs, opera, reading, walking, travel, shooting. *Address:* Supreme Court, 38 Queensway, Hong Kong. *T:* 8254310. *Clubs:* Royal Hong Kong Jockey, Hong Kong Country, Aberdeen Marina, Hong Kong Clay Target Shooting Association, Hong Kong Rifle Association, Hong Kong Kennel (President).

BOKSENBERG, Prof. Alexander, PhD; FRS 1978; FRAS; Director, Royal Observatories, since 1993: Royal Greenwich Observatory, Cambridge; Royal Observatory, Edinburgh; Isaac Newton Group of optical telescopes, Canary Islands; Joint Astronomy Centre, Hawaii; *b* 18 March 1936; *s* of Julius Boksenberg and Ernestina Steinberg; *m* 1960, Adella Coren; one *s* one *d*. *Educ:* Stationers' Co.'s Sch.; Univ. of London (BSc, PhD). Dept of Physics and Astronomy, University Coll. London: SRC Res. Asst, 1960–65; Lectr in Physics, 1965–75; Head of Optical and Ultraviolet Astronomy Res. Group, 1969–81; Reader in Physics, 1975–78; SRC Sen. Fellow, 1976–81; Prof. of Physics and Astronomy, 1978–81; Dir, Royal Greenwich Observatory, 1981–93. Sherman Fairchild Dist. Schol., CIT, 1981–82; Visiting Professor: Dept of Physics and Astronomy, UCL, 1981–; Astronomy Centre, Univ. of Sussex, 1981–89; Hon. Prof. of Experimental Astronomy, Univ. of Cambridge, 1991–. Chm., New Industrial Concepts Ltd, 1969–81. Chairman: SRC Astronomy II Cttee, 1980–81; Gemini Telescopes Project Expert Cttee, 1992 (Chm., UK Steering Cttee, 1992–93; Mem., USA Oversight Cttee, 1993–94); Mem. and Pres., Internat. Scientific Cttee, Canary Is Observatories, 1981–; Member: ESA Hubble Space Telescope Instrument Definition Team, 1973–; S African Astronomical Observatory Adv. Cttee, 1978–85; British Council Science Adv. Cttee, 1987–91; Anglo-Australian Telescope Bd, 1989–91 (Dep. Chm., 1991–92); Hubble Space Telescope Users Cttee, 1990–91; Fachbeirat, Max Planck Inst. für Astronomie, 1991–; European Southern Observatory Vis. Cttee, 1993–; formerly mem. or chm. of more than 30 other councils, boards, cttees, panels or courts, 1970–. Exec. Ed., Experimental Astronomy, 1995–. Pres., W London Astronomical Soc., 1978–; Hon. Pres., Astronomical Soc. of Glasgow, 1995–. Mem., Academia Europaea, 1989; Founding Mem., European Astronomical Soc., 1990. Fellow, UCL, 1991. FRAS 1965; FRSA 1984. Clockmakers' Co.: Freeman, 1984, Liveryman, 1989; Mem., Court of Assts, 1994–. Asteroid (3205) Boksenberg, named 1988. Dr *hc*, l'Observatoire de Paris, 1982; DSc *hc* Sussex, 1991. *Publications:* (ed jtly) Modern Technology and its Influence on Astronomy, 1990; over 200 contribs to learned jls. *Recreation:* ski-ing. *Address:* Royal Greenwich Observatory, Madingley Road, Cambridge CB3 0EZ. *T:* Cambridge (01223) 374886. *Club:* Athenæum.

BOLAM, James; actor; *b* Sunderland, 16 June 1938; *s* of Robert Alfred Bolam and Marion Alice Bolam (*née* Drury). *Educ:* Bede Grammar Sch., Sunderland; Bemrose Sch., Derby. First stage appearance, The Kitchen, Royal Court, 1959; later plays include: Events While Guarding the Bofors Gun, Hampstead, 1966; In Celebration, Royal Court, 1969; Veterans, Royal Court, 1972; Treats, Royal Court, 1976; Who Killed 'Agatha' Christie?, Ambassadors, 1978; King Lear (title rôle), Young Vic, 1981; Run for Your Wife!, Criterion, 1983; Arms and the Man, Cambridge; Who's Afraid of Virginia Woolf?, Birmingham, 1989; Victory, Chichester, 1989; Jeffrey Bernard is Unwell, Apollo, 1990; Glengarry Glen Ross, Donmar Warehouse, 1994. *Films:* Straight on till Morning, Crucible of Terror, Otley, A Kind of Loving, Half a Sixpence, Murder Most Foul, The Likely Lads, In Celebration, Whatever Happened to the Likely Lads?, The Great Question, Seaview Knights. *Television series:* The Likely Lads; Whatever Happened to the Likely Lads?; When the Boat Comes In; The Limbo Connection (Armchair Thriller Series); Only When I Laugh; The Beiderbecke Affair; Room at the Bottom; Andy Capp; The Beiderbecke Tapes; The Beiderbecke Connection; Second Thoughts; Eleven Men Against Eleven; also As You Like It, Macbeth, in BBC Shakespeare. *Address:* c/o Barry Burnett Organisation Ltd, Suite 42–43, Grafton House, 2–3 Golden Square, W1.

BOLAND, John Anthony; Public Trustee and Accountant General, 1987–91 (Public Trustee, 1980–87); *b* 23 Jan. 1931; *s* of late Daniel Boland, MBE, and Hannah Boland (*née* Barton), Dublin; *m* 1972, Ann, *d* of late James C. Doyle and Maureen Doyle. *Educ:* Castleknock Coll.; Xavier Sch.; Christian Brothers, Synge Street; Trinity Coll., Dublin (MA, LLB). Called to the Bar, Middle Temple, 1956; called to Irish Bar, 1967. Joined Public Trustee Office, 1956; Chief Administrative Officer, 1974–79; Asst Public Trustee, 1979–80. Mem., Royal Dublin Soc.; Hon. Member, College Historical Soc., TCD, 1954. Trustee of Trinity College Dublin (Univ. of Dublin) Trust, 1980–. Asst Editor, The Supreme Court Practice, 1984–91. *Recreations:* walking, foreign travel, trying to catch up on life. *Address:* c/o Lloyds Bank, 67 Kingsway, WC2B 6SX. *Club:* Kildare Street and University (Dublin).

BOLEAT, Mark John; Director-General, Association of British Insurers, since 1993; *b* 21 Jan. 1949; *s* of Paul Boleat and Peggy Boleat (*née* Still); *m* 1991, Elizabeth Ann Baker (*née* Barker). *Educ:* Victoria College, Jersey; Lanchester Polytechnic and Univ. of Reading (BA Econ, MA Contemp. European Studies). FCIB. Asst Master, Dulwich College, 1972; Economist, Indust. Policy Group, 1973; The Building Societies Association: Asst Sec., 1974; Under Sec., 1976; Dep. Sec., 1979; Dep. Sec.-Gen., 1981; Sec.-Gen., 1986; Dir-Gen., 1987. Sec.-Gen., Internat. Union of Housing Finance Instns (formerly Internat. Union of Building Socs and Savings Assocs), 1986–89; Mem. Bd, Housing Corp., 1988–93; Chm., Circle 33 Housing Trust, 1990–93. *Publications:* The Building Society Industry, 1982; National Housing Finance Systems: a comparative study, 1985; Housing in Britain, 1986; (with Adrian Coles) The Mortgage Market, 1987; Building Societies: the regulatory framework, 1988, 3rd edn 1992; articles on housing, insurance and finance. *Recreations:* reading, writing, squash, golf. *Address:* 26 Westbury Road, Northwood, Mddx HA6 3BU. *T:* Northwood (01923) 823684. *Clubs:* Carlton; Bushey Golf and Country; Moor Park Golf.

BOLES, Sir Jeremy John Fortescue, 3rd Bt, *cr* 1922; *b* 9 Jan. 1932; *s* of Sir Gerald Fortescue Boles, 2nd Bt, and Violet Blanche (*d* 1974), *er d* of late Major Hall Parlby, Manadon, Crown Hill, S Devon; *S* father 1945; *m* 1st, 1955, Dorothy Jane (marr. diss. 1970), *yr d* of James Alexander Worswick; two *s* one *d*; 2nd, 1970, Elisabeth Gildroy Willis Fleming, *yr d* of Edward Phillip Shaw; one *d*; 3rd, 1982, Marigold Aspey, *e d* of Donald Frank Seckington. *Heir: s* Richard Fortescue Boles, *b* 12 Dec. 1958. *Address:* Brook House, Stogumber, Taunton TA4 3SZ.

BOLES, Sir John Dennis, (Sir Jack), Kt 1983; MBE 1960; DL; Director General of the National Trust, 1975–83; *b* 25 June 1925; *s* of late Comdr Geoffrey Coleridge Boles and Hilda Frances (*née* Crofton); *m* 1st, 1953, Benita (*née* Wormald) (*d* 1969); two *s* three *d*; 2nd, 1971, Lady Anne Hermione, *d* of 12th Earl Waldegrave, KG, GCVO. *Educ:* Winchester Coll. Rifle Brigade, 1943–46. Colonial Administrative Service (later Overseas Civil Service), North Borneo (now Sabah), 1948–64; Asst Sec., National Trust, 1965, Sec., 1968; Mem., Devon and Cornwall Regl Cttee, Nat. Trust, 1985–. Dir, SW Region Bd, Lloyds Bank plc, 1984–91. Trustee, Ernest Cook Trust. Devon: DL 1991; High Sheriff 1993–94. *Address:* Rydon House, Talaton, near Exeter, Devon EX5 2RP. *Club:* Army and Navy.

See also J. D. Fishburn.

BOLGER, Rt. Hon. James B., (Rt. Hon. Jim Bolger); PC 1991; Prime Minister of New Zealand, since 1990; MP (Nat. Party) King Country, since 1972; Leader of National Party, New Zealand, since 1986; *b* 1935; *m* Joan Bolger; nine *c*. Sheep and cattle farmer, Te Kuiti. Parly Under-Sec., Min. of Agric. and Fisheries, Min. of Maori Affairs and Min. of Rural Banking and Finance, 1975; Minister of Fisheries and Associate Minister of Agric., 1977; Minister of Labour, 1978–84; Minister of Immigration, 1978–81; Leader of the Opposition, 1986–90. Pres., ILO, 1983. *Recreations:* tramping, fishing, reading. *Address:* Parliament Buildings, Wellington, New Zealand.

BOLINGBROKE, 7th Viscount *cr* 1712, **AND ST JOHN,** 8th Viscount *cr* 1716; **Kenneth Oliver Musgrave St John;** Bt 1611; Baron St John of Lydiard Tregoze, 1712; Baron St John of Battersea, 1716; Director, Italian importing companies; *b* 22 March 1927; *s* of Geoffrey Robert St John, MC (*d* 1972) and Katherine Mary (*d* 1958), *d* of late A. S. J. Musgrave; *S* cousin, 1974; *m* 1st, 1953, Patricia Mary McKenna (marr. diss. 1972); one *s*; 2nd, 1972, Jainey Anne McRae (marr. diss. 1987); two *s*. *Educ:* Eton; Geneva Univ. Chairman, A&P Gp of Cos, 1958–75; Director: Shaw Savill Holidays Pty Ltd; Bolingbroke and Partners Ltd; Wata Investment Inc., Panama. Pres., Travel Agents Assoc. of NZ, 1966–68; Dir, World Assoc. of Travel Agencies, 1966–75; Chm., Aust. Council of Tour Wholesalers, 1972–75. Fellow, Aust. Inst. of Travel; Mem., NZ Inst. of Travel. *Recreations:* golf, cricket, tennis, history. *Heir: s* Hon. Henry Fitzroy St John, *b* 18 May 1957. *Address:* PO Box 25.069, Christchurch, New Zealand; 5110 Conference Street, Christchurch, New Zealand. *Club:* Christchurch (Christchurch, NZ).

BOLLAND, Alexander; QC (Scot) 1992; *b* 21 Nov. 1950; *s* of James Bolland and Elizabeth Agnes (*née* Anderson); *m* 1973, Agnes Hunter, *d* of Dr George Pate Moffat, Crookedholm; one *s* two *d*. *Educ:* Kilmarnock Acad.; Univ. of St Andrews (BD 1973); Glasgow Univ. (LLB 1976). Admitted to Faculty of Advocates, 1978; Capt., Directorate of Army Legal Services, later Army Legal Corps, 1978–80; Standing Jun. Counsel to Dept of Employment in Scotland, 1988–92; Temp. Sheriff, 1988–; part-time Chm., Industrial Tribunals, 1993–. *Recreations:* Hellenistics, walking, reading. *Address:* The Old Dairy, 60 North Street, St Andrews, Fife KY16 9AH. *T:* St Andrews (01334) 74599. *Clubs:* Naval and Military; Royal Scottish Automobile (Glasgow).

BOLLAND, (David) Michael; Managing Director, Channel X Ltd, since 1990; *b* 27 Feb. 1947; *s* of Allan Bolland and Eileen Lindsay; *m* 1987, Katie Lander; one *s*, one *d*, and one *s* two *d* by former marrs. *Educ:* Hillhead High School, Glasgow. Film editor, BBC Scotland, 1965–73; TV Producer, BBC TV, 1973–81; Channel Four Television: Commissioning Editor, Youth, 1981–83; Senior Commissioning Editor, Entertainment, 1983–87; Asst Dir of Programmes, and Head of Art and Entertainment Gp, 1987–88; Controller Arts and Entertainment, and Dep. Dir of Progs, 1988–90; Man. Dir, Initial Films and Television, 1990; Project Dir, Channel X Broadcasting (Scotland) Ltd, 1991–95. Chairman: Edinburgh Internat. TV Fest., 1990; Producers' Alliance for Film and Television, 1995. Member: RTS; BAFTA. *Recreation:* catching up with the world. *Address:* 2c Belsize Park Gardens, NW3 4LD. *T:* 0171–586 9518.

BOLLAND, Sir Edwin, KCMG 1981 (CMG 1971); HM Diplomatic Service, retired; Ambassador to Yugoslavia, 1980–82; *b* 20 Oct. 1922; *m* 1948, Winifred Mellor; one *s* three *d* (and one *s* decd). *Educ:* Morley Grammar Sch.; University Coll., Oxford. Served in Armed Forces, 1942–45. Foreign Office, 1947; Head of Far Eastern Dept, FO, 1965–67; Counsellor, Washington, 1967–71; St Antony's Coll., Oxford, 1971–72; Ambassador to Bulgaria, 1973–76; Head of British delegn to Negotiations on MBFR, 1976–80. *Recreations:* walking, gardening. *Address:* Lord's Spring Cottage, Godden Green, Sevenoaks, Kent TN15 0JS. *T:* Sevenoaks (01732) 761105.

BOLLAND, Group Captain Guy Alfred, CBE 1943; Chief Intelligence Officer, British Joint Services Mission, Washington, DC, USA, 1949, and 1956–59, retired; *b* 5 Nov. 1909; 3rd *s* of late Capt. L. W. Bolland; *m* 1935, Sylvia Marguerite, 2nd *d* of late Oswald Duke, Cambridge; one *s* three *d*. *Educ:* Gilbert Hannam Sch., Sussex. Commissioned RAF, 1930, Pilot Officer; No 1 (Fighter) Sqdn, 1931; 84 (Bomber) Sqdn, Iraq, 1932; CFS, 1934; Flying Instr, 1934–36; RAF Navigation Sch., 1937; No 228 Flying Boat Sqdn, 1937–39; Commanding Officer: RAF Hooton Park, 1939–40 (Sqdn Ldr); 217 Sqdn, St Eval, 1940–41 (Wing Comdr); Fleet Aviation Officer on battleship King George V (when Bismarck sunk), 1941–42; Commanding Officer: RAF Gibraltar, 1942–43 (despatches (N African landings); Gp Capt.); RAF Pembroke Dock, 1943–44; RAF Staff Coll., 1945; Dep. Dir Orgn and Estabt, Air Min., 1946; USAF Air War Coll., 1948; CO RAF Ballykelly, 1952; Dep. Dir Ops (Maritime), 1954. *Recreations:* golf, bowls, travel. *Address:* The Oaks, Shaftesbury Road, Woking, Surrey GU22 7DU. *T:* Woking (01483) 760548.

BOLLAND, Mark William; Director, Press Complaints Commission, since 1992; *b* 10 April 1966; *s* of late Robert Arthur Bolland and of Joan Bolland (*née* Barker). *Educ:* Kings Manor Sch., Middlesbrough; Univ. of York (BSc Hons). Public Affairs Exec., Public Affairs Internat. Ltd, Toronto, 1985–87; Mkting Exec., IBM (UK) Ltd, 1987–88; Res. Manager, and Advr to Dir Gen., Advertising Standards Authy, 1988–91; Exec. Asst to Chm., Press Complaints Commn, 1991–92. *Address:* (office) 1 Salisbury Square, EC4Y 8AE. *T:* 0171–353 1248.

BOLLAND, Michael; *see* Bolland, D. M.

BOLLERS, Hon. Sir Harold (Brodie Smith), Kt 1969; CCH 1982; Chairman, Elections Commission, 1982; Chief Justice of Guyana, 1966–80; *b* 5 Feb. 1915; *s* of late John Bollers; *m* 1st, 1951, Irene Mahadeo (*d* 1965); two *s* one *d*; 2nd, 1968, Eileen Hanoman; one *s*. *Educ:* Queen's Coll., Guyana; King's Coll., London; Middle Temple. Called to the

Bar, Feb. 1938; Magistrate, Guyana, 1946, Senior Magistrate, 1959; Puisne Judge, Guyana, 1960. *Recreations:* reading, walking. *Address:* 252 South Road, Bourda, Georgetown, Guyana.

BOLLOBÁS, Dr Béla; Reader in Pure Mathematics, University of Cambridge, since 1985; Fellow and Director of Studies in Mathematics, Trinity College, Cambridge, since 1972; *b* 3 Aug. 1943; *s* of Béla Bollobás and Emma Varga; *m* 1969, Gabriella Farkas; one *s*. *Educ:* Univ. of Budapest (BA 1966; Dr rer nat 1967); Univ. of Cambridge (PhD 1972; DSc 1984). Res. Scientist, Hungarian Acad. of Scis, 1966–69; Vis. Scientist, Soviet Acad. of Scis, 1967–68; Vis. Fellow, Oxford, 1969; Cambridge University: Res. Fellow, Trinity Coll., 1970–72; Asst Lectr, 1971–74, Lectr in Mathematics, 1974–85. Foreign Mem., Hungarian Acad. of Scis, 1990. *Publications:* Extremal Graph Theory, 1978; Graph Theory, 1979; Random Graphs, 1985; Combinatorics, 1986; Linear Analysis, 1990; contribs to learned jls. *Recreations:* books, opera, theatre, tennis, swimming, jogging, windsurfing, riding, ski-ing. *Address:* Trinity College, Cambridge CB2 1TQ; 5 Selwyn Gardens, Cambridge CB3 9AX. *T:* Cambridge (01223) 354872.

BOLT, David Ernest, CBE 1984; FRCS; President, British Medical Association, 1987–88; *b* 21 Sept. 1921; *s* of Rev. E. A. J. Bolt and Hilda I. Bolt; *m* 1955, Phyllis Margaret, (Peggy), Fudge; two *d*. *Educ:* Queen Elizabeth's Hosp., Bristol; Univ. of Bristol. MB ChB 1945; FRCS 1950. Senior Surgical Registrar, W Middx Hosp. and St Mary's Hosp., Paddington, 1955–60; Consultant Surgeon, W Middx Hosp., 1960–82; Hon. Lectr, Charing Cross Hosp., 1972–82. British Medical Association: Mem., Central Cttee for Hosp. Med. Service (Dep. Chm., 1975–79; Chm., 1979–83); Dep. Chm., Jt Consultants' Cttee, 1979–83; Mem. Council, 1975–83. Mem., GMC, 1979–89 (Chm., Professional Conduct Cttee). *Publications:* articles on surgical subjects in professional jls. *Recreations:* motor boat cruising, tree planting, reading, walking. *Address:* Feniton House, Feniton, Honiton, Devon EX14 0BE. *T:* Honiton (01404) 850921. *Club:* Royal Society of Medicine.

BOLT, Air Marshal Sir Richard (Bruce), KBE 1979 (CBE 1973); CB 1977; DFC 1945; AFC 1959; Chairman, Pacific Aerospace Corp. of New Zealand, since 1982; *b* 16 July 1923; *s* of George Bruce Bolt and Mary (*née* Best); *m* 1st, 1946, June Catherine South (*d* 1984); one *s* one *d*; 2nd, 1987, Janice Caroline Tucker. *Educ:* Nelson Coll., NZ. Began service with RNZAF in mid 1942; served during 2nd World War in RAF Bomber Command (Pathfinder Force); Chief of Air Staff, NZ, 1974–76; Chief of Defence Staff, NZ, 1976–80. *Recreations:* fly fishing, golf, horse racing. *Address:* 14b Nikau Grove, Lower Hutt, Wellington, New Zealand. *Club:* Wellington (Wellington, NZ).

BOLTON, 7th Baron, *cr* 1797; **Richard William Algar Orde-Powlett;** *b* 11 July 1929; *s* of 6th Baron Bolton; *S* father, 1963; *m* 1st, 1951, Hon. Christine Helena Weld Forester (marr. diss. 1981), *e d* of 7th Baron Forester, and of Marie Louise Priscilla, CStJ, *d* of Sir Herbert Perrott, 6th Bt, CH, CB; two *s* one *d*; 2nd, 1981, Masha Anne (marr. diss. 1990), *d* of Major F. E. Hudson, Winterfield House, Hornby, Bedale, Yorks; 3rd, 1991, Mrs Lavinia Fenton. *Educ:* Eton; Trinity Coll., Cambridge (BA). Chairman, Richmond Div., Conservative Assoc., 1957–60; Chairman Yorkshire Div., Royal Forestry Soc., 1962–64; Member Council, Timber Growers' Organization. Director: Yorkshire Insurance Co., 1964–70; General Accident Life Assurance Ltd, 1970–. JP, North Riding of Yorkshire, 1957–80. FRICS. *Recreations:* shooting, fishing. *Heir:* *s* Hon. Harry Algar Nigel Orde-Powlett [*b* 14 Feb. 1954; *m* 1977, Philippa, *d* of Major P. L. Tapply; three *s*]. *Address:* Bolton Hall, Leyburn, North Yorkshire DL8 4UF. *T:* Wensleydale (01969) 22003.

BOLTON, Bishop Suffragan of, since 1991; **Rt. Rev. David Bonser;** *b* 1 Feb. 1934; *s* of George Frederick and Alice Bonser; *m* 1960, Shirley Wilkinson; one *s* two *d*. *Educ:* Hillhouse Secondary Sch., Huddersfield; King's Coll., London Univ. (AKC); Manchester Univ. (MA). Curate: St James's, Heckmondwike, 1962–65; St George's, Sheffield, 1965–68; Rector of St Clement's, Chorlton-cum-Hardy, 1968–82; Hon. Canon of Manchester Cathedral, 1980–82; Area Dean of Hulme, 1981–82; Archdeacon of Rochdale, 1982–91; Team Rector, Rochdale Team Ministry, 1982–91 (Vicar of St Chad's, 1982–86). *Recreations:* theatre, reading, walking, skiing, music, soup-making. *Address:* 4 Sandfield Drive, Lostock, Bolton BL6 4DU. *T:* Bolton (01204) 843400, *Fax:* (01204) 849652. *Club:* Commonwealth Trust.

BOLTON, Archdeacon of; *see* Davies, Ven. L. M.

BOLTON, Group Captain David; Chairman, Macbeth Associates, since 1994; *b* 15 April 1932; *o s* of late George Edward and Florence May Bolton; *m* 1955, Betty Patricia Simmonds; three *d*. *Educ:* Bede Sch., Co. Durham. Commnd RAF Regt, 1953; subsequent service in Egypt, Jordan, Singapore, Aden, Cyprus, Malta and Germany; RAF Staff Coll., 1969; National Def. Coll., 1972; Central Planning Staff, MoD, 1973–75; OC 33 Wing RAF Regt, 1975–77; Comdt RAF Regt Depot, Catterick, 1977–80; retd 1980; Dep. Dir, 1980–81, Dir, 1981–94, RUSI. Member: RUSI Council, 1973–79; IISS, 1964–90; RIIA, 1975–; Council, British Atlantic Cttee, 1981–91. Sen. Associate, CSIS, Washington, 1994–. Hon. Steward, Westminster Abbey, 1981–. Trench Gascoigne Essay Prize, RUSI, 1972. *Publications:* contrib. learned jls. *Recreations:* music, theatre, jogging, work. *Address:* c/o Royal United Services Institute for Defence Studies, Whitehall, SW1A 2ET. *Club:* Royal Air Force.

BOLTON, David Michael William; education consultant; Head Master, Dame Alice Owen's School, 1982–94; *b* 29 Feb. 1936; *s* of William Benedict Bolton and Edith Phyllis Bolton; *m* 1961, Janet Christine Fleming; two *s* one *d*. *Educ:* St Francis Xavier's Coll., Liverpool; St Edmund Hall, Oxford (BA 1960; MA 1964); DipEd London 1971. Nat. Service, RAF (Coastal Command), 1955–57. Reckitt & Colman Ltd, 1960–62; Alleyn's Sch., Dulwich, 1962–63; Housemaster, Highgate Sch., 1963–72; Dep. Head, Chancellor's Sch., Herts, 1972–74; Headmaster, Davenant Foundn Grammar Sch., 1974–82. Mem. Council, Secondary Heads Assoc., 1991–94 (Chm., Area Five). FRSA 1993. Freeman, City of London, 1994. *Publications:* articles and reviews in TES. *Recreations:* reading, music, jazz especially, travel, walking, sport. *Address:* 29 Normandy Avenue, Barnet, Herts EN5 2HU.

BOLTON, Prof. Eric James, CB 1987; Professor of Teacher Education, Institute of Education, University of London, since 1991; *b* 11 Jan. 1935; *s* of late James and Lilian Bolton; *m* 1960, Ann Gregory; one *s* twin *d*. *Educ:* Wigan Grammar Sch.; Chester Coll.; Lancaster Univ. MA. English teacher at secondary schs, 1957–68; Lectr, Chorley Teacher Training Coll., 1968–70; Inspector of Schs, Croydon, 1970–73; HM Inspector of Schs, 1973–79; Staff Inspector (Educnl Disadvantage), 1979–81; Chief Inspector of Schools, DES, 1981–83, Sen. Chief Inspector of Schools, 1983–91. *Publications:* Verse Writing in Schools, 1964; various articles in educnl jls. *Recreations:* reading, music and opera, fly fishing. *Address:* Institute of Education, 20 Bedford Way, WC1H 0AL.

BOLTON, Sir Frederic (Bernard), Kt 1976; MC; FIMarE; Chairman: The Bolton Group, 1953–91; Dover Harbour Board, 1982–88 (Member, 1957–62 and 1980–88); *b* 9 March 1921; *s* of late Louis Hamilton Bolton and late Beryl Dyer; *m* 1st, 1950, Valerie Margaret Barwick (*d* 1970); two *s*; 2nd, 1971, Vanessa Mary Anne Robarts; two *s* two *d*. *Educ:* Rugby. Served War, with Welsh Guards, 1940–46 (MC 1945, Italy); Northants Yeomanry, 1952–56. Member: Lloyd's, 1945–; Baltic Exchange, 1946–. Chm., Atlantic Steam Nav. Co. & Subs, 1960–71; Dir, B.P. Tanker Co., 1968–82; Mem., Brit. Rail Shipping & Int. Services Bd, 1970–82 (later Sealink UK Ltd). Pres., Chamber of Shipping of UK, 1966; Mem., Lloyd's Register of Shipping Gen. Cttee, 1961–86; Chairman: Ship & Marine Technol. Requirements Bd, 1977–81; British Ports Assoc., 1985–88; Pilots' Nat. Pension Fund, 1991–94; Member: PLA, 1964–71; Nat. Ports Council, 1967–74; President: Inst. of Marine Engineers, 1968–69 and 1969–70; British Shipping Fedn, 1972–75; Internat. Shipping Fedn, 1973–82; Gen. Council of British Shipping, 1975–76; British Maritime League, 1985–91. Hon. Treas., W Oxfordshire Cons. Assoc., 1991–. Hon. FNI. Grafton Hunt: Jt Master, 1956–67, Chm., 1967–72. *Recreations:* country sports. *Address:* Pudlicote, near Charlbury, Oxon OX7 3HX. *Clubs:* City of London, Cavalry and Guards.

BOLTON, Prof. Geoffrey Curgenven, AO 1984; DPhil; Professor of History, Edith Cowan University, since 1993; *b* 5 Nov. 1931; *s* of Frank and Winifred Bolton, Perth, W Australia; *m* 1958, (Ann) Carol Grattan; two *s*. *Educ:* North Perth State Sch.; Wesley Coll., Perth; Univ. of Western Australia; Balliol Coll., Oxford, (DPhil). FRHistS 1967; FAHA 1974; FASSA 1976. Res. Fellow, ANU, 1957–62; Sen. Lectr, Monash Univ., 1962–65; Prof. of Modern Hist., Univ. of Western Australia, 1966–73; Prof. of History, 1973–82 and 1985–89, and Pro-Vice-Chancellor, 1973–76, Murdoch Univ.; Prof. of Australian Studies, Univ. of London, 1982–85; Prof. of Australian Hist., Univ, of Queensland, 1989–93. Vis. Fellow, All Souls Coll., Oxford, 1995. Mem. Council, Australian Nat. Maritime Museum, Sydney, 1985–91. Deleg., Constitutional Convention, Sydney, 1991–. Boyer Lectr, Australian Broadcasting Corp., 1992. FRSA. General Editor, Oxford History of Australia, 1987–91. DUniv Murdoch, 1995. *Publications:* Alexander Forrest, 1958; A Thousand Miles Away, 1963; The Passing of the Irish Act of Union, 1966; Dick Boyer, 1967; A Fine Country to Starve In, 1972; Spoils and Spoilers: Australians Make Their Environment, 1981; Oxford History of Australia, vol. 5, 1990; articles in learned jls. *Recreation:* sleep. *Address:* 6 Melvista Avenue, Claremont, WA 6010, Australia. *Club:* Athenæum.

BOLTON, John Eveleigh, CBE 1972; DSC 1945; DL; Chairman and Managing Director, Growth Capital Ltd, since 1968; Chairman: Hall Bolton Estates Ltd; Atesmo Ltd; Riverview Investments Ltd; *b* 17 Oct. 1920; *s* of late Ernest and Edith Mary Bolton; *m* 1948, Gabrielle Healey Hall (*d* 1989), *d* of late Joseph and Minnie Hall; one *s* one *d*. *Educ:* Ilkley Sch.; Wolverhampton Sch.; Trinity Coll., Cambridge (Cassel Travelling Schol., 1948; BA Hons Econs 1948, MA 1953); Harvard Business School (Baker Schol., 1949; MBA with dist., 1950). Articled pupil to Chartered Acct, 1937–40; intermed. exam. of Inst. of Chartered Accts, 1940. Served War of 1939–45 (DSC): Destroyers, Lt RNVR, 1940–46. Research for Harvard in British Industry, 1950–51; Finance Dir, Solartron Laboratory Instruments Ltd, Kingston-upon-Thames, 1951–53 (Chm., 1953); Chm. and Man. Dir: Solartron Engineering Ltd, 1952; The Solartron Electronic Group Ltd, Thames Ditton and subseq. Farnborough, Hants, 1954–63 (Dep. Chm., 1963–65). Director: NCR Co. Ltd; Alphameric PLC; Black & Decker Group Inc.; Black & Decker Holdings Inc.; Black & Decker Investment Co.; Black & Decker Corp.; Plasmec PLC; Dawson International plc; Johnson Wax Ltd; Redland plc; Hoskyns plc; Business Advisers Ltd; Camperdowne Investment Holdings Ltd; Pres., Develt Capital Gp Ltd, 1984–88. A Gen. Comr of Income Tax, 1964–. British Institute of Management: Chm. Council, 1964–66; Bowie Medal 1969; CIMgt; Life Vice-Pres.; Pres., Engrg Industries Assoc., 1981–84; Chm. and Founder Subscriber: Advanced Management Programmes Internat. Trust; Foundn for Management Educn; Business Grads Assoc.; Dir, Management Publications Ltd, 1966–73 (Chm., 1969); Mem. Exec. Cttee, AA; Hon. Treasurer, Surrey Univ., 1975–82 (Past Chm.); Member: Sub-Cttee on Business Management Studies, UGC; Council of Industry for Management Educn; Harvard Business Sch. Vis. Cttee, 1962–75; Adv. Cttee on Industry, Cttee of Vice-Chancellors, 1984–; Business Educn Forum, 1969–74. Mem. Org. Cttee, World Research Hospital. Member: UK Automation Council, 1964–65; Adv. Cttee for Management Efficiency in NHS, 1964–65; Cttee for Exports to New Zealand, 1965–68; Adv. Cttee, Queen's Award to Industry, 1972–; Council, Inst. of Dirs; Chm., Economic Develt Cttee for the Rubber Industry, 1965–68; Vice-Chm., Royal Commn on Local Govt in England, 1966–69; Chm., Committee of Inquiry on Small Firms, 1969–71. Trustee, Small Business Research Trust. Life FRSA. DL Surrey, 1974; High Sheriff of Surrey, 1980–81. DUniv Surrey, 1982; Hon. DSc Bath, 1986. *Publications:* articles in newspapers and journals; various radio and TV broadcasts on industrial topics. *Recreations:* shooting, swimming, gardening, opera, antiques. *Address:* Sunnymead, Tite Hill, Englefield Green, Surrey TW20 0NH. *T:* Egham (01784) 35172. *Clubs:* Harvard Club of London, Institute of Directors.

BOLTON, Roger William; General Secretary, Broadcasting, Entertainment, Cinematograph and Theatre Union, since 1993; *b* 7 Sept. 1947; *s* of William and Honara Bolton; *m* 1974, Elaine Lewis; one *d*. *Educ:* St Thomas More's Sch., London. Photographic Asst, Boots The Chemists, 1960–64; photographer: Belgrave Press Bureau, 1964–69; BBC TV News, 1969–79; Trade Union Official: Assoc. of Broadcasting Staff, 1979–84; Broadcasting Entertainment Trades Alliance, 1984–93. Dir, Nat. Campaign for the Arts; Mem., British Screen Adv. Council. Gov., Nat. Film and TV Sch. *Address:* (office) 111 Wardour Street, W1V 4AY. *T:* 0171–437 8506.

BOMBAY, Archbishop of, (RC), since 1978; **His Eminence Simon Ignatius Cardinal Pimenta;** *b* 1 March 1920; *s* of late Joseph Anthony Pimenta and Rosie E. Pimenta. *Educ:* St Xavier's Coll., Bombay (BA with Maths); Propaganda Univ., Rome (Degree in Canon Law). Secretary at Archbishop's House, Bombay, 1954; also Vice-Chancellor and Defensor Vinculi; Vice Rector of Cathedral, 1960; Visiting Prof. of Liturgy, Bombay Seminary, 1960–65; Rector of Cathedral and Episcopal Vicar for Liturgy and Pastoral Formation of Junior Clergy, 1967; Rector of Seminary, 1971; Auxiliary Bishop, 1971; Coadjutor Archbishop with right of succession, 1977. Pres., Catholic Bishops' Conf. of India, 1982–88. Cardinal, 1988. *Publications:* (edited) The Catholic Directory of Bombay, 1960 and 1964 edns; Circulars and Officials of the Archdiocese of Bombay, 3 vols; booklet on the Cathedral of the Holy Name. *Address:* Archbishop's House, 21 Nathalal Parekh Marg, Bombay 400 001, India. *T:* 2021093, 2021193, 2021293.

BOMFORD, Nicholas Raymond, MA; Head Master of Harrow, since 1991; *b* 27 Jan. 1939; *s* of late Ernest Raymond Bomford and of Patricia Clive Bomford (*née* Brooke), JP; *m* 1966, Gillian Mary Reynolds; two *d*. *Educ:* Kelly Coll.; Trinity Coll., Oxford (MA, Mod. History). Teaching appts, 1960–64; Lectr in History and Contemp. Affairs, BRNC, Dartmouth, 1964–66, Sen. Lectr, 1966–68; Wellington Coll., 1968–76 (Housemaster, 1973–76); Headmaster: Monmouth Sch., 1977–82; Uppingham Sch., 1982–91. Chm., Jt Standing Cttee, HMC/IAPS, 1986–89; Nat. Rep., HMC Cttee, 1990–91. Mem. Navy Records Soc. (Councillor, 1967–70, 1973–76, 1984–88). Mem. Council, Roedean Sch.; Gov., Sherborne Sch. for Girls and five prep. schs. FRSA 1989. Freeman, Haberdashers' Co., 1992. *Publications:* Documents in World History, 1914–70, 1973; (contrib.) Dictionary of World History, 1973. *Recreations:* shooting (Captain OURC, 1959–60; England VIII (Elcho match), 1960), fishing, gardening, music, enjoying Welsh border country and Southern France. *Address:* Harrow School, Harrow-on-the-Hill, Middlesex HA1 3HW.

BOMPAS, Anthony George; QC 1994; *b* 6 Nov. 1951; *s* of Donald George Bompas, *qv*; *m* 1981, Donna Linda, *d* of J. O. Schmidt; two *s* one *d*. *Educ:* Merchant Taylors' Sch., Northwood; Oriel Coll., Oxford (Schol., MA). Called to the Bar, Middle Temple, 1975; Junior Counsel (Chancery), DTI, 1989–94. Liveryman, Merchant Taylors' Co., 1982–. *Address:* 4 Stone Buildings, Lincoln's Inn, WC2A 3XT. *T:* 0171–242 5524.

BOMPAS, Donald George, CMG 1966; Managing Executive, Philip and Pauline Harris Charitable Trust, since 1986; *b* 20 Nov. 1920; *yr s* of Rev. E. Anstie Bompas; *m* 1946, Freda Vice, *y d* of F. M. Smithyman, Malawi; one *s* one *d*. *Educ:* Merchant Taylors' Sch., Northwood; Oriel Coll., Oxford. MA Oxon, 1947. Overseas Audit Service, 1942–66, retired; Nyasaland, 1942–47; Singapore, 1947–48; Malaya, then Malaysia, 1948–66; Deputy Auditor-General, 1957–60; Auditor-General, Malaya, then Malaysia, 1960–66. Dep. Sec., Guy's Hosp. Med. and Dental Schools, 1966–69, Sec., 1969–82; Dep. Sec., 1982–83, Sec., 1984–86, UMDS of Guy's and St Thomas's Hosps. Chm., Univ. of London Purchasing Gp, 1976–82. Mem. Exec., Federated Pension Schemes, 1979–86. Mem. Council and Exec. Cttee, City Technology Colls Trust, 1990–; Trustee, Bacon's Coll., 1991–; Gov., St Olave's and St Saviour's Grammar Sch. Foundn, 1992–. Liveryman, Merchant Taylors' Co., 1951. JMN (Hon.) Malaya, 1961. *Address:* 8 Birchwood Road, Petts Wood, Kent BR5 1NY. *T:* Orpington (01689) 821661. *Club:* Commonwealth Trust.

See also A. G. Bompas.

BON, Christoph Rudolf; Partner, Chamberlin Powell & Bon, since 1952; *b* 1 Sept. 1921; *s* of Rudolf Bon and Nelly Fischbacher. *Educ:* Cantonal Gymnasium, Zürich; Swiss Federal Inst. of Technology, Zürich (DipArch ETH 1946). Prof. Holford's Office–Master Plan for City of London, 1946; Studio BBPR, Milan, 1949–50; teaching at Kingston Sch. of Art, 1950–52; Founder Partner, Chamberlin Powell & Bon, 1952. Work includes: Golden Lane Estate; Expansion of Leeds Univ.; schools, housing and commercial buildings; New Hall, Cambridge; Barbican. *Address:* 60 South Edwardes Square, W8 6HL. *T:* 0171–602 6462.

BON, Michel Marie; Directeur, Agence Nationale pour l'Emploi, France, since 1993; *b* 5 July 1943; *s* of Emmanuel Bon and Mathilde (*née* Aussedat); *m* 1971, Catherine de Sairigné; one *s* three *d*. *Educ:* Lycée Champollion, Grenoble; Ecole supérieure des scis économiques et commerciales, Paris; Inst. d'Etudes Politiques, Paris; Ecole Nat. d'Administration, Paris. Insp. of Finance, Min. of Finance, 1971–75; Crédit National, 1975–78; Caisse Nat. de Crédit Agricole, 1978–85; Carrefour, 1985–93 (Chm. and Chief Exec. Officer, 1990–93). *Address:* 4 avenue de Camoëns, 75116 Paris, France.

BONA, Sir Kina, KBE 1993; Public Prosecutor, Papua New Guinea, 1988–94; *b* 14 Feb. 1954; *m* 1990, Judith Lilian Sharples; one *d*. *Educ:* Univ. of Papua New Guinea (LLB 1976); Univ. of Paris II. Legal Officer, PNG, 1976–78; Teaching Fellow, Univ. of PNG, 1979; Sen. Legal Officer, 1980–82; Asst. Sec., Dept of Justice, 1985–87. *Address:* PO Box 622, Waigani, NCD, Papua New Guinea.

BONALLACK, Michael Francis, OBE 1971; Secretary, Royal and Ancient Golf Club of St Andrews, since 1983; *b* 31 Dec. 1934; *s* of Sir Richard (Frank) Bonallack, *qv*; *m* 1958, Angela Ward; one *s* three *d*. *Educ:* Chigwell; Haileybury. National Service, 1953–55 (1st Lieut, RASC). Joined family business, Bonallack and Sons Ltd, later Freight Bonallack Ltd, 1955; Director, 1962–74; Dir, Buckley Investments, 1976–84. Chairman: Golf Foundn, 1977–83; Professional Golfers' Assoc., 1976–82; Pres., English Golf Union, 1982. DUniv Stirling, 1994. *Recreation:* golf (British Amateur Champion, 1961, 1965, 1968, 1969, 1970; English Amateur Champion, 1962–63, 1965–67 and 1968; Captain, British Walker Cup Team, 1971; Bobby Jones Award for distinguished sportsmanship in golf, 1972). *Address:* Clatto Lodge, Blebo Craigs, Cupar, Fife KY15 5UF. *T:* Strathkinness (0133485) 600. *Clubs:* Chantilly (France); Pine Valley (USA), and 20 others.

BONALLACK, Sir Richard (Frank), Kt 1963; CBE 1955 (OBE (mil.) 1945); MIMechE; *b* 2 June 1904; *s* of Francis and Ada Bonallack; *m* 1930, Winifred Evelyn Mary Esplen (*d* 1986); two *s* one *d*. *Educ:* Haileybury. War service in TA, 1939–45; transferred to TA Reserve, 1946, with rank of Colonel. Bonallack and Sons Ltd, subseq. Freight Bonallack Ltd: Chm., 1953–74; Pres., 1974–87; Dir, Alcan Transport Products, 1979–85. Chm., Freight Container Section, SMMT, 1967–83; Mem., Basildon Development Corporation, 1962–77. Chm., Working Party, Anglo-Soviet Cttee for Jt Technical Collaboration, 1961–65. *Recreation:* golf. *Address:* 4 The Willows, Thorpe Bay, Southend on Sea, Essex SS1 3SH. *T:* Southend (01702) 588180.

See also M. F. Bonallack.

BOND, Alan, AO 1984; *b* 22 April 1938; *s* of Frank and Kathleen Bond; *m* 1956, Eileen Teresa Hughes (marr. diss. 1992); two *s* two *d*; *m* 1995, Diana Bliss. *Educ:* Perivale Sch., Ealing, UK; Fremantle Boys' Sch., W Australia. Chairman, Bond Corporation Holdings Ltd, 1969–90 (interests in property, brewing, electronic media, oil and gas, minerals, airships); Chairman: North Kalgurli Mines Ltd, 1985–89; Gold Mines of Kalgoorlie Ltd, 1987–89; Dallhold Investments Pty, 1987. Syndicate Head, America's Cup Challenge 1983 Ltd; Australia II Winners of 1983 America's Cup Challenge, following three previous attempts: 1974 Southern Cross, 1977 Australia, 1980 Australia. Australian of the Year, 1977. *Recreation:* yachting. *Address:* Dalkeith, Western Australia. *Clubs:* Royal Ocean Racing; Young Presidents Organisation, Royal Perth Yacht, Cruising Yacht, Western Australian Turf (WA).

BOND, Prof. Brian James, FRHistS; Professor of Military History, King's College, University of London, since 1986; *b* 17 April 1936; *s* of Edward Herbert Bond and Olive Bessie Bond (*née* Sartin); *m* 1962, Madeleine Joyce Carr. *Educ:* Sir William Borlase's Sch., Marlow; Worcester Coll., Oxford (BA Hist. 1959); King's Coll. London (MA Hist. 1962). FRHistS 1978. Nat. Service, 1954–56, commnd RA. Tutor in Mod. Hist., Univ. of Exeter, 1961–62; Lectr, Univ. of Liverpool, 1962–66; King's College London: Lectr in War Studies, 1966–78; Reader, 1978–86. Vis. Prof., Univ. of Western Ontario, 1972–73; Vis. Fellow, Brasenose Coll., Oxford, 1992–93. Mem. Council, RUSI, 1972–84. Pres., British Commn for Mil. Hist., 1986–. Member Editorial Board: Jl Contemp. Hist., 1988–; Jl Strategic Studies, 1978–; Jl Mil. Hist. (USA), 1992–; War in Hist., 1994–. *Publications:* (ed) Victorian Military Campaigns, 1967, 2nd edn 1994; The Victorian Army and the Staff College, 1972; (ed) Chief of Staff: the diaries of Lt-Gen. Sir Henry Pownall 1933–1944, vol. 1, 1972, vol. 2, 1974; Britain, France and Belgium, 1939–1940, 1975, 2nd edn 1990; Liddell Hart: a study of his military thought, 1977, 2nd edn 1991; British Military Policy between the Two World Wars, 1980; War and Society in Europe 1870–1970, 1984; (ed with S. Robbins) Staff Officer: the diaries of Lord Moyne 1914–1918, 1987; (ed) The First World War and British Military History, 1991; (ed) Fallen Stars: eleven studies of twentieth century military disasters, 1991; The Pursuit of Victory: from Napoleon to Saddam Hussein, 1996. *Recreations:* gardening, visiting country houses, observing and protecting wild animals (especially foxes). *Address:* Department of War Studies, King's College, Strand, WC2R 2LS. *T:* 0171–873 2178.

BOND, Rt. Rev. (Charles) Derek; appointed Bishop Suffragan of Bradwell, 1976, Area Bishop, 1984–92; Hon. Assistant Bishop, dioceses of Gloucester and Worcester, since 1992; *b* 4 July 1927; *s* of Charles Norman Bond and Doris Bond; *m* 1951, Joan Valerie Meikle; two *s* two *d*. *Educ:* Bournemouth Sch.; King's Coll., London. AKC (2nd hons). Curate of Friern Barnet, 1952; Midlands Area Sec. of SCM in Schools and Public Preacher, dio. Birmingham, 1956; Vicar: of Harringay, 1958; of Harrow Weald, 1962; Archdeacon of Colchester, 1972–76. Nat. Chm., CEMS, 1983–86. *Recreation:* travel. *Address:* Ambleside, 14 Worcester Road, Evesham, Worcs WR11 4JU. *T:* Evesham (01386) 446156.

BOND, Edward; playwright and director; *b* 18 July 1934; *m* 1971, Elisabeth Pablé. Northern Arts Literary Fellow, 1977–79. Hon. DLitt Yale, 1977. George Devine Award, 1968; John Whiting Award, 1968. *Opera Libretti:* We Come to the River (music by Hans Werner Henze), 1976; The English Cat (music by Hans Werner Henze), 1983; *ballet libretto:* Orpheus, 1982; *translations:* Chekhov, The Three Sisters, 1967; Wedekind, Spring Awakening, 1974; Wedekind, Lulu—a monster tragedy, 1992. *Publications:* Collected Poems 1978–1985, 1987; Notes on Post-Modernism, 1990; Selected Letters (4 vols), 1994–95; *plays:* Saved, 1965; Narrow Road to the Deep North, 1968; Early Morning, 1968; The Pope's Wedding, 1971; Passion, 1971; Black Mass, 1971; Lear, 1972; The Sea, 1973; Bingo, 1974; The Fool, 1976; A-A-merica! (Grandma Faust, and The Swing), 1976; Stone, 1976; The Woman, 1978; The Bundle, 1978; Theatre Poems and Songs, 1978; The Worlds and The Activist Papers, 1980; Restoration, 1981; Summer: a play for Europe, 1982; Derek, 1983; Human Cannon, 1984; The War Plays (part 1, Red Black and Ignorant; part 2, The Tin Can People; part 3, Great Peace), 1985; Jackets, 1989; The Company of Men, 1990; September, 1990; Olly's Prison (TV), 1992; Tuesday (TV), 1993; Coffee: a tragedy, 1995. *Recreation:* the study of physics, because in physics the problems of human motives do not have to be considered (for the benefit of newspaper reporters: this is a joke, as anyone who had attended a rehearsal with actors would know). *Address:* c/o Casarotto Ramsay, 60–66 Wardour Street, W1V 3HP.

BOND, Godfrey William; Public Orator, Oxford University, 1980–92; Emeritus Fellow, Pembroke College, Oxford, since 1992 (Dean, 1979–92); *b* 24 July 1925; *o s* of William Niblock Bond, MC of Newry and Janet Bond (*née* Godfrey) of Dublin; *m* 1959, Alison, *d* of Mr Justice T. C. Kingsmill Moore, Dublin; one *s* two *d*. *Educ:* Campbell Coll.; Royal Belfast Acad. Inst.; Trinity Coll. Dublin (Scholar 1946; Berkeley Medal 1948; BA 1st Cl. Classics (gold medal); 1st Cl. Mental and Moral Sci. 1949); St John's Coll., Oxford (MA). Served War Office and Foreign Office (GCHQ), 1943–45; Fellow and Classical Tutor, Pembroke Coll., Oxford, 1950–92; Senior Tutor, 1962–72; Oxford University: Lectr in Classics, 1952–92; Senior Proctor, 1964–65; Gen. Bd of Faculties, 1970–76; Visitor, Ashmolean Museum, 1972–81. Mem., Inst. for Advanced Study, Princeton, 1969–70. *Publications:* editions of Euripides, Hypsipyle, 1963, Heracles, 1981; orations (mostly Latin) in OU Gazette, 1980–; memorial addresses, articles and reviews. *Recreations:* people and places in Greece, France and Ireland; opera, dining, swimming. *Address:* Masefield House, Boars Hill, Oxford OX1 5EY. *T:* Oxford (01865) 735373. *Clubs:* Athenæum; Kildare Street and University (Dublin).

BOND, Maj.-Gen. Henry Mark Garneys, OBE 1993; JP; Vice Lord-Lieutenant of Dorset, since 1984; *b* 1 June 1922; *s* of W. R. G. Bond, Tyneham, Dorset; unmarried. *Educ:* Eton. Enlisted as Rifleman, 1940; commnd in Rifle Bde, 1941; served Middle East and Italy; seconded to Parachute Regt, 1947–50; ADC to Field Marshal Viscount Montgomery of Alamein, 1950–52; psc 1953; served in Kenya, Malaya, Cyprus and Borneo; Comd Rifle Bde in Cyprus and Borneo, 1964–66; Comd 12th Inf. Bde, 1967–68; idc 1969; Dir of Defence Operational Plans and Asst Chief of Defence Staff (Ops), 1970–72; retd 1972. President: Dorset Natural History and Archaeological Soc., 1972–75; Dorset Br., CPRE, 1990–; Dorset Community Council, 1988–; Dorset Assoc. of Parish Councils, 1990–; Chm., Dorset Police Authy, 1980–92. Mem., Dorset CC, 1973–85 (Vice-Chm., 1981–85). JP Dorset, 1972 (Chm., Wareham Bench, 1984–89). High Sheriff of Dorset, 1977, DL Dorset, 1977. Chm., Governors of Milton Abbey Sch., 1979–94 (Visitor, 1994–). *Recreations:* forestry, reading. *Address:* Moigne Combe, Dorchester, Dorset DT2 8JA. *T:* Warmwell (01305) 852265. *Club:* Boodle's.

BOND, John Reginald Hartnell; Group Chief Executive, HSBC Holdings plc, since 1993; *b* 24 July 1941; *s* of late Capt. R. H. A. Bond, OBE and of E. C. A. Bond; *m* 1968, Elizabeth Caroline Parker; one *s* two *d*. *Educ:* Tonbridge Sch., Kent; Cate Sch., Calif, USA (E-SU Scholar). Joined Hongkong & Shanghai Banking Corp., 1961; worked in Hong Kong, Thailand, Singapore, Indonesia and USA; Chief Exec., Wardley Ltd (Merchant Banking), 1984–87; Hongkong & Shanghai Banking Corporation: Exec. Dir, 1988–91; responsible for: Americas, 1988–89; commercial banking, based in Hong Kong, 1990–91; Pres. and Chief Exec., Marine Midland Banks Inc., Buffalo, USA, 1991–92. Chm., Hongkong Bank of Canada, 1987–; Director: Hongkong & Shanghai Banking Corp. Ltd, 1988–; Marine Midland Banks Inc., 1987–; Hang Seng Bank Ltd, 1990–; HSBC Hldgs, 1990–; Midland Bank, 1993–; non-executive Director: London Stock Exchange, 1994–; British Steel, 1994–. FCIB (FIB 1982). *Recreations:* golf, ski-ing. *Address:* HSBC Holdings plc, 10th Floor, 10 Lower Thames Street, EC3R 6AE. *T:* 0171–260 0497. *Clubs:* MCC; Hong Kong (Hong Kong); John's Island (Florida).

BOND, Sir Kenneth (Raymond Boyden), Kt 1977; Vice-Chairman, The General Electric Company plc, 1985–90 (Financial Director, 1962–66; Deputy Managing Director, 1966–85), retired; *b* 1 Feb. 1920; *s* of late James Edwin and Gertrude Deplidge Bond; *m* 1958, Jennifer Margaret, *d* of late Sir Cecil and Lady Crabbe; three *s* three *d*. *Educ:* Selhurst Grammar School. Served TA, Europe and Middle East, 1939–46. FCA 1960 (Mem. 1949). Partner, Cooper & Cooper, Chartered Accountants, 1954–57; Dir, Radio & Allied Industries Ltd, 1957–62. Member: Industrial Develt Adv. Bd, 1972–77; Cttee to Review the Functioning of Financial Instns, 1977–80; Audit Commn, 1983–86; Civil Justice Rev. Adv. Cttee, 1985–88. *Recreations:* golf, bowls. *Address:* Woodstock, Wayside Gardens, Gerrards Cross, Bucks SL9 7NG. *T:* Gerrards Cross (01753) 883513. *Club:* The Addington Golf.

BOND, Michael; author; *b* 13 Jan. 1926; *s* of Norman Robert and Frances Mary Bond; *m* 1950, Brenda Mary Johnson (marr. diss. 1981); one *s* one *d*; *m* 1981, Susan Marfrey Rogers. *Educ:* Presentation College, Reading. RAF and Army, 1943–47; BBC Cameraman, 1947–66; full-time author from 1966. Paddington TV series, 1976. *Publications: for children:* A Bear Called Paddington, 1958; More About Paddington, 1959; Paddington Helps Out, 1960; Paddington Abroad, 1961; Paddington at Large, 1962; Paddington Marches On, 1964; Paddington at Work, 1966; Here Comes Thursday, 1966; Thursday Rides Again, 1968; Paddington Goes to Town, 1968; Thursday Ahoy, 1969; Parsley's Tail, 1969; Parsley's Good Deed, 1969; Parsley's Problem Present, 1970; Parsley's Last Stand, 1970; Paddington Takes the Air, 1970; Thursday in Paris, 1970; Michael Bond's Book of Bears, 1971, 1992; Michael Bond's Book of Mice, 1972; The Day the Animals Went on Strike, 1972; Paddington Bear, 1972; Paddington's Garden, 1972; Parsley the Lion, 1972; Parsley Parade, 1972; The Tales of Olga da Polga, 1972; Olga Meets her Match, 1973; Paddington's Blue Peter Story Book, 1973; Paddington at the Circus, 1973; Paddington Goes Shopping, 1973; Paddington at the Sea-side, 1974; Paddington at the Tower, 1974; Paddington on Top, 1974; Windmill, 1975; How to make Flying Things, 1975; Eight Olga Readers, 1975; Paddington's Loose End Book,

1976; Paddington's Party Book, 1976; Olga Carries On, 1976; Paddington's Pop-up Book, 1977; Paddington Takes the Test, 1979; Paddington's Cartoon Book, 1979; J. D. Polson and the Liberty-Head Dime, 1980; J. D. Polson and the Dillogate Affair, 1981; Paddington on Screen, 1981; Olga Takes Charge, 1982; The Caravan Puppets, 1983; Paddington at the Zoo, 1984; Paddington and the Knickerbocker Rainbow, 1984; Paddington's Painting Exhibition, 1985; Paddington at the Fair, 1985; Oliver the Greedy Elephant, 1985; Paddington at the Palace, 1986; Paddington Minds the House, 1986; Paddington's Busy Day, 1987; Paddington and the Marmalade Maze, 1987; Paddington's Magical Christmas, 1988; with Karen Bond: Paddington Posts a Letter, 1986; Paddington at the Airport, 1986; Paddington's London, 1986; *for adults:* Monsieur Pamplemousse, 1983; Monsieur Pamplemousse and the Secret Mission, 1984; Monsieur Pamplemousse on the Spot, 1986; Monsieur Pamplemousse Takes the Cure, 1987; The Pleasures of Paris, 1987; Monsieur Pamplemousse Aloft, 1989; Monsieur Pamplemousse Investigates, 1990; Monsieur Pamplemousse Rests His Case, 1991; Monsieur Pamplemousse Stands Firm, 1992; Monsieur Pamplemousse on Location, 1992; Monsieur Pamplemousse takes the Train, 1993. *Recreations:* photography, travel, cars, wine. *Address:* 22 Maida Avenue, W2 1SR. *T:* 0171–262 4280. *Club:* Wig and Pen.

BOND, Sir Michael (Richard), Kt 1995; FRCPsych, FRCPGlas, FRCSE; Professor of Psychological Medicine, since 1973, Vice Principal, since 1986, Administrative Dean, Faculty of Medicine, since 1991, University of Glasgow; *b* 15 April 1936; *s* of Frederick Richard Bond and Dorothy Bond (*née* Gardner); *m* 1961, Jane Issitt; one *s* one *d*. *Educ:* Magnus Grammar Sch., Newark, Notts; Univ. of Sheffield (MD, PhD). Ho. Surg./Ho. Phys., Royal Inf., Sheffield, 1961–62; Asst Lectr/Res. Registrar, Univ. Dept of Surgery, Sheffield, 1962–64; Res. Registrar/Lectr, Univ. Dept of Psychiatry, Sheffield, 1964–67; Sen. Ho. Officer/Res. Registrar, Registrar/Sen. Registrar, Inst. of Neurological Scis, Glasgow, 1968–71; Lectr in Neurosurgery, Univ. Dept of Neurosurgery, Glasgow, 1971–73. Locum Cons. Neurosurgeon, Oxford, 1972; Hon. Cons. Psychiatrist, Greater Glasgow Health Bd, 1973–. Member: UFC, 1991–93; SHEFC, 1992–; Chm., Jt Med. Adv. Cttee, 1992–. Chm., Head Injuries Trust for Scotland, 1989–. FRSA 1992. *Publications:* Pain, its nature, analysis and treatment, 1979, 2nd edn 1984; (co-ed) Rehabilitation of the Head Injured Adult, 1983, 2nd edn 1989; papers on psychological and social consequences of severe brain injury, psychological aspects of chronic pain and cancer pain, 1963–, and others on similar topics. *Recreations:* painting, collecting antique books, forest walking, ornithology, gardening. *Address:* 33 Ralston Road, Bearsden, Glasgow G61 3BA. *T:* (home) 0141–942 4391; (work) 041–334 9826. *Club:* Athenæum.

BOND-WILLIAMS, Noel Ignace, CBE 1979; Director, National Exhibition Centre Ltd, 1970–89; *b* 7 Nov. 1914; *s* of late W. H. Williams, Birmingham; *m* 1939, Mary Gwendoline Tomey (*d* 1989); one *s* two *d*. *Educ:* Oundle Sch.; Birmingham Univ. (BSc). FIM, FBIM. Pres. Guild of Undergrads 1936–37, Pres. Guild of Grads 1947, Birmingham Univ. Various appts in metal industry; Director: Enfield Rolling Mills Ltd, 1957–65; Delta Metal Co. Ltd, 1967–77; Vice-Chm., 1978–79, Chm., 1979–83, Remploy Ltd; Dir, 1972–85, and Vice-Chm., 1979–85, Lucas (Industries) Ltd. Industrial Adviser, DEA, 1965–67. Pres., Birmingham Chamber of Commerce, 1969. Member: Commn on Industrial Relations, 1971–74; Price Commn, 1977–79. Mem. Council, Industrial Soc., 1947–78; Pres., Brit. Non-ferrous Metals Fedn, 1974–75. Pro-Chancellor, Univ. of Aston in Birmingham, 1970–81. Hon. DSc Aston, 1975. *Publications:* papers and articles on relationships between people in industry. *Recreation:* sailing. *Address:* Courtyard House, High Street, Lymington, Hants SO41 9AH. *T:* Lymington (01590) 672593. *Clubs:* Metallics; Royal Ocean Racing, Royal Cruising, Royal Lymington Yacht.

BONDI, Prof. Sir Hermann, KCB 1973; FRS 1959; FRAS; Master of Churchill College, Cambridge, 1983–90, Fellow, since 1990; Professor of Mathematics, King's College, London, since 1954 (titular since 1971, emeritus since 1985); *b* Vienna, 1 Nov. 1919; *s* of late Samuel and Helene Bondi, New York; *m* 1947, Christine M. Stockman, *d* of late H. W. Stockman, CBE; two *s* three *d*. *Educ:* Realgymnasium, Vienna; Trinity Coll., Cambridge (MA). Temporary Experimental Officer, Admiralty, 1942–45; Fellow Trinity Coll., Cambridge, 1943–49, and 1952–54; Asst Lecturer, Mathematics, Cambridge, 1945–48; University Lecturer, Mathematics, Cambridge, 1948–54. Dir-Gen., ESRO, 1967–71; Chief Scientific Advr, MoD, 1971–77; Chief Scientist, Dept of Energy, 1977–80; Chm. and Chief Exec., NERC, 1980–84. Research Associate, Cornell Univ., 1951; Visiting Prof. Cornell Univ., 1960. Lectures: Harvard Coll. Observatory, 1953; Lowell, Boston, Mass, 1953; Halley, Oxford, 1962; Tarner, Cambridge, 1965; Lees-Knowles, Cambridge, 1974; Conway Meml, London, 1992. Chairman: Space Cttee, MoD, 1964–65; Nat. Cttee for Astronomy, 1963–67; Adv. Council on Energy Conservation, 1980–82; IFIAS 1984–. Secretary, Royal Astronomical Soc., 1956–64; Mem., SRC, 1973–80. President: Inst. of Mathematics and its Applications, 1974–75; British Humanist Assoc., 1982; Assoc. of British Science Writers, 1981–85; Soc. for Res. into Higher Educn, 1981–; Assoc. for Science Educn, 1982; Hydrographic Soc., 1985–87; Rationalist Press Assoc., 1982–. Member: Science Policy Foundn; Mem., Ct, London Univ., 1963–67. FKC 1968. Hon. DSc: Sussex 1974; Bath 1974; Surrey 1974; York 1980; Southampton 1981; Salford, 1982; Birmingham, 1984; St Andrews, 1985; Plymouth, 1995; Dr *hc* Vienna, 1993. Hon. FIEE 1979; Hon. FInstP 1992; Hon. FIMA 1993. Einstein Soc. gold medal, 1983; Gold Medal, Inst. of Mathematics and its Applications, 1988; G. D. Birla Internat. Award for Humanism, 1990. *Publications:* Cosmology, 1952 (2nd edn, 1960); The Universe at Large, 1961; Relativity and Commonsense, 1964; Assumption and Myth in Physical Theory, 1968; (with Dame Kathleen Ollerenshaw) Magic Squares of Order Four, 1982; papers on astrophysics, etc, in Proc. Royal Society, Monthly Notices, Royal Astronomical Society, Proc. Cam. Phil. Society, etc. *Recreations:* walking, skiing, travelling. *Address:* Churchill College, Cambridge CB3 0DS; 60 Mill Lane, Impington, Cambridge CB4 4XN.

BONE, Charles, PPRI, ARCA, FRSA; President, Royal Institute of Painters in Water Colours, 1979–89; Governor, Federation of British Artists, 1976–81 and since 1983 (Member, Executive Council, 1983–84 and 1986–88); *b* 15 Sept. 1926; *s* of William Stanley and Elizabeth Bone; *m* Sheila Mitchell, FRBS, ARCA, sculptor; two *s*. *Educ:* Farnham Coll. of Art; Royal Coll. of Art (ARCA). FBI Award for Design. Consultant, COSIRA, 1952–70; Craft Adviser, Malta Inds Assoc., Malta, 1952–78; Lecturer, Brighton Coll. of Art, 1950–86; Director, RI Galleries, Piccadilly, 1965–70. Many mural paintings completed, including those in Eaton Square and Meretea, Italy; oils and water colours in exhibns of RA, London Group, NEAC and RBA, 1950–; 31 one-man shows, 1950–; works in private collections in France, Italy, Malta, America, Canada, Japan, Australia, Norway, Sweden, Germany. Designer of Stourhead Ball, 1959–69; produced Ceramic Mural on the History of Aerial Photography. Critic for Arts Review. Mem. Council, RI, 1964– (Vice-Pres. 1974). Hon. Member: Medical Art Soc.; Soc. Botanical Artists. Hon. FCA (Can.). Hunting Gp Prize for a British Watercolour, 1984. *Film:* Watercolour Painting: a practical guide, 1990. *Publication:* Waverley (author and illust.), 1991. *Address:* Winters Farm, Puttenham, Guildford, Surrey GU3 1AR. *T:* Guildford (01483) 810226.

BONE, Rt. Rev. John Frank Ewan; *see* Reading, Area Bishop of.

BONE, Quentin, JP; MA, DPhil; FRS 1984; zoologist; Hon. Research Fellow, Marine Biological Association UK; *b* 17 Aug. 1931; *s* of late Stephen Bone and Mary Adshead; *m* 1958, Susan Elizabeth Smith; four *s*. *Educ:* Warwick Sch.; St John's Coll., Oxon. Naples Scholarship, 1954; Fellow by examination, Magdalen Coll., Oxford, 1956. Zoologist at Plymouth Laboratory, 1959–91 (Marine Biol Assoc., DCSO). *Publications:* Biology of Fishes (with N. B. Marshall), 1983, new edn (with J. S. Blaxter also), 1994; papers on fish and invertebrates, mainly in Jl of Mar. Biol Assoc. UK. *Address:* Marchant House, 98 Church Road, Plymstock, Plymouth PL9 9BG.

BONE, Roger Bridgland; HM Diplomatic Service; Ambassador to Sweden, since 1995; *b* 29 July 1944; *s* of late Horace Bridgland Bone and of Dora R. Bone (*née* Tring); *m* 1970, Lena M. Bergman; one *s* one *d*. *Educ:* William Palmer's Sch., Grays; St Peter's Coll., Oxford (MA). Entered HM Diplomatic Service, 1966; UK Mission to UN, 1966; FCO, 1967; 3rd Sec., Stockholm, 1968–70; 2nd Sec., FCO, 1970–73; 1st Secretary: Moscow, 1973–75; FCO, 1975–78; 1st Sec., UK Perm. Representation to European Communities, Brussels, 1978–82; Asst Private Sec. to Sec. of State for Foreign and Commonwealth Affairs, 1982–84; Vis. Fellow, Harvard Univ. Center for Internat. Affairs, 1984–85; Counsellor, 1985–89, and Head of Chancery, 1987–89, Washington; Counsellor, FCO, 1989–91; Asst Under Sec. of State, FCO, 1991–95. *Recreations:* music, wine. *Address:* c/o Foreign and Commonwealth Office, SW1A 2AH.

BONE, Prof. Thomas Renfrew, CBE 1987; Deputy Principal, University of Strathclyde, since 1992; *b* 1935; *s* of James Renfrew Bone and Mary Williams; *m* 1959, Elizabeth Stewart; one *s* one *d*. *Educ:* Greenock High Sch.; Glasgow Univ. MA 1st cl. English 1956, MEd 1st cl. 1962, PhD 1967. Teacher, Paisley Grammar Sch., 1957–62; Lecturer: Jordanhill Coll. of Educn, 1962–63; Glasgow Univ., 1963–67; Jordanhill College of Education: Hd of Educn Dept, 1967–71; Principal, 1972–92. FCCEA 1984. *Publications:* Studies in History of Scottish Education, 1967; School Inspection in Scotland, 1968; *chapters in:* Whither Scotland, 1971; Education Administration in Australia and Abroad, 1975; Administering Education: international challenge, 1975; European Perspectives in Teacher Education, 1976; Education for Development, 1977; Practice of Teaching, 1978; World Yearbook of Education, 1980; The Management of Educational Institutions, 1982; The Effective Teacher, 1983; Strathclyde: changing horizons, 1985; The Changing Role of the Teacher, 1987; Teacher Education in Europe, 1990; Educational Leadership: challenge and change, 1992. *Recreation:* golf. *Address:* University of Strathclyde, 16 Richmond Street, Glasgow G1 1XQ. *T:* 0141–552 4400. *Clubs:* Western Gailes Golf; Paisley Burns.

BONELL, Carlos Antonio; guitarist; concert artist since 1969; *b* London, 23 July 1949; *s* of Carlos Bonell and Ana Bravo; *m* 1975, Pinuccia Rossetti; two *s*. *Educ:* William Ellis Sch., Highgate; Royal Coll. of Music (Hon. RCM 1973). Lectr, City Lit, 1970; Prof., RCM 1972. Début as solo guitarist, Purcell Room, 1971; GLAA Young Musician, 1973; resident guitarist, London Contemp. Dance Theatre, 1974; concert tours and recording with John Williams & Friends, 1975; first solo album, 1975; concerto début, RFH, 1977; NY début, 1978; Carlos Bonell Ensemble début, QEH, 1983, and tours in Europe and Far East; soloist with all major UK orchestras; commissioned and first performed Sonata by Stephen Oliver, 1981; recorded Rodrigo's Concierto de Aranjuez, 1981; numerous other records and awards. *Publications:* Spanish folk songs and dances, 1975; Gaspar Sanz airs and dances, 1977; A Tarrega collection, 1980; First Pieces for solo guitar, 1980; The romantic collection, 1983; The classical collection, 1983; Spanish folk songs for 3 guitars, 1984; Purcell: 3 pieces, 1984; Tarrega Fantasia, 1984. *Recreations:* cinema, reading, history, playing the guitar, listening to music. *Address:* Harold Holt, 31 Sinclair Road, W14 0NS. *T:* 0171–603 4600; 60 Burghley Road, NW5 1UN.

BONEY, Guy Thomas Knowles; QC 1990; a Recorder, since 1985; *b* 28 Dec. 1944; *o c* of Thomas Knowles Boney, MD and Muriel Hilary Eileen Long, FRCS; *m* 1976, Jean Harris Ritchie, *qv*; two *s*. *Educ:* Winchester College; New College, Oxford (BA 1966; MA 1987). Called to the Bar, Middle Temple, 1968 (Harmsworth Scholar); in practice on Western Circuit, 1969–. *Publications:* The Road Safety Act 1967, 1971; contribs to: Halsbury's Laws of England, 4th edn (Road Traffic); horological jls. *Recreations:* horology, music (Organist, King's Somborne Parish Church, 1980–), amateur theatre. *Address:* 3 Pump Court, Temple, EC4Y 7AJ. *Clubs:* Reform; Hampshire (Winchester).

BONEY, Jean Harris, (Mrs G. T. K. Boney); *see* Ritchie, J. H.

BONFIELD, Peter Leahy, CBE 1989; FEng 1993; Chairman and Chief Executive, ICL plc, since 1990; *b* 3 June 1944; *s* of George and Patricia Bonfield; *m* 1968, Josephine Houghton. *Educ:* Hitchin Boys Grammar School, Loughborough Univ. (BTech Hons; Hon. DTech, 1988). FIEE 1990, FBCS 1990, FCIM 1990. Texas Instruments Inc., Dallas, USA, 1966–81; Group Exec. Dir, ICL, 1981–84; Chm. and Man. Dir, STC Internat. Computers Ltd, 1984–90; Dir, 1985–90, and Dep. Chief Exec., 1987–90, STC plc; Dir, Zeneca Gp, 1995–. Chm., DESC, 1990–; Dir, BICC, 1992–. Mem., CS Coll. Adv. Council, 1993–. FRSA 1992. Freeman, City of London, 1990; Liveryman, Information Technologists' Co., 1992. *Recreations:* music, sailing, jogging. *Address:* ICL plc, ICL House, 1 High Street, Putney, SW15 1SW. *T:* 0181–788 7272. *Club:* Royal Automobile.

BONFIELD, Prof. William, PhD; FEng 1993; Professor of Materials, Queen Mary and Westfield (formerly Queen Mary) College, University of London, since 1974; Director, University of London Interdisciplinary Research Centre in Biomedical Materials, since 1991; *b* 6 March 1937; *s* of Cecil William Bonfield and Ellen Gertrude Bonfield; *m* 1960, Gillian Winifred Edith Cross; one *s* two *d*. *Educ:* Letchworth GS; Imperial College, London (Perry Meml and Bessemer Medals; BScEng, PhD, DIC, ARSM). CEng, FIM. Honeywell Res. Center, Hopkins, Minn, USA, 1961–68; Queen Mary, later Queen Mary and Westfield College, London: Reader in Materials Science, 1968; Head, Dept of Materials, 1980–90; Chm., Sch. of Engineering, 1981–88; Dean of Engineering, 1985–89. Vis. Prof., Chulalongkorn Univ., Bangkok, 1988; OCMR Dist. Vis. Prof., Univ. of Toronto, 1990; Vis. Prof., Henry Ford Hosp., Detroit, 1992; Hon. Prof., Univ. of Sichuan, 1992. Lectures: Royal Microscopical Soc., 1992; Mellor Meml, Inst. of Materials, 1993; Prof. Moore Meml, Univ. of Bradford, 1994; Dist. Scholar, QUB, 1994. Project Leader, EEC Concerted Action in Skeletal Implants, 1989. Chm., Med Engrg Cttee, 1989, Mem., Materials Cttee, later Materials Commn, 1983–88, SERC; Member: Jt Dental Cttee, 1984–89; DoH Cttee on Dental and Surgical Materials, 1986–; Directive Council, Internat. Soc. for Bio-analoging Skeletal Implants, 1988–; Materials Sci. Bd, Inst. of Materials, 1989–; Jl Cttee, Internat. Fedn for Med. and Biol Engrg, 1989–; Techl Cttee, BSI, 1992–. Chm., London Metallurgical Soc., 1991. Hon. Member: Canadian Ortho. Res. Soc., 1983; Materials Res. Soc. of India, 1993. Griffith Medal, Inst. of Metals, 1991; Royal Soc. Armourers' and Brasiers' Co. Medal, 1991; George Winter Award, Eur. Soc. for Biomaterials, 1994; Kelvin Medal, ICE, 1995. Freeman, Armourers' and Brasiers' Co., 1994. Chm., Editl Bd, Materials in Electronics, 1990–; Mem., Editl Bd, Jl of Applied Polymer Sci., 1992–; Editor, Jl of Materials Science, 1973–; Founding Editor: Jl of Materials Science Letters, 1981–; Materials in Medicine, 1990–. *Publications:* Bioceramics, 1991; research papers on biomaterials, biomechanics and physical metallurgy in sci. jls. *Recreations:* cycling, British Cycling Coaching Scheme coach. *Address:* Interdisciplinary Research Centre in Biomedical Materials, Queen Mary and Westfield College, Mile End Road, E1 4NS. *T:* 0171–975 5151. *Clubs:* Athenæum; North Road Cycling.

BONGERS, Paul Nicholas; Director, Local Government International Bureau, since 1988; *b* 25 Oct. 1943; *s* of Henry Bongers and late Marjorie Bongers (*née* Luxton); *m* 1968, Margaret Collins; two *s* two *d*. *Educ:* Bradfield Coll.; New Coll., Oxford (MA); DPA Univ. of London (external), 1968. Administrative Trainee, City of Southampton, 1965–68; Personal Asst to Chief Exec., City of Nottingham, 1968–69; Administrator, Council of Europe, 1969–71; Assistant Secretary: AMC, 1971–74; AMA, 1974–78; Exec. Sec., British Sections, IULA/CEMR, 1978–88. Founder and Dir, European Information Service, monthly bulletin, 1978–. *Publications:* Local Government and 1992, 1990, 2nd edn as Local Government and the European Single Market, 1992; articles in local govt jls. *Recreations:* family, music, countryside, travel, the arts. *Address:* Local Government International Bureau, 35 Great Smith Street, SW1P 3BJ. *Club:* Reform.

BONHAM, Major Sir Antony Lionel Thomas, 4th Bt, *cr* 1852; DL; late Royal Scots Greys; *b* 21 Oct. 1916; *o s* of Maj. Sir Eric H. Bonham, 3rd Bt, and Ethel (*d* 1962), *y d* of Col Leopold Seymour; *S* father 1937; *m* 1944, Felicity, *o d* of late Col. Frank L. Pardoe, DSO, Bartonbury, Cirencester; three *s*. *Educ:* Eton; RMC. Served Royal Scots Greys, 1937–49; retired with rank of Major, 1949. DL Glos 1983. *Heir: s* (George) Martin (Antony) Bonham [*b* 18 Feb. 1945; *m* 1979, Nenon Baillieu (marr. diss. 1992), *e d* of R. R. Wilson and Hon. Mrs Wilson, Durford Knoll, Upper Durford Wood, Petersfield, Hants; one *s* three *d*]. *Address:* Ash House, Ampney Crucis, Cirencester, Glos GL7 5RY. *T:* Poulton (01285) 851391.

BONHAM, Nicholas; Deputy Chairman, W. & F. C. Bonham & Sons Ltd, since 1987; *b* 7 Sept. 1948; *s* of late Leonard Charles Bonham and Diana Maureen (*née* Magwood); *m* 1977, Kaye Eleanor (*née* Ivett); two *d*. *Educ:* Trent College. Joined W. & F. C. Bonham & Sons Ltd, Fine Art Auctioneers, 1966; Dir, 1970; Man. Dir, 1975–87. Dir, Montpelier Properties, 1970–. *Recreations:* sailing, tobogganing, ski-ing, golf, swimming. *Address:* Montpelier Galleries, Montpelier Street, SW7 1HH. *T:* 0171–584 9161. *Clubs:* Kennel; Royal Thames Yacht, South West Shingles Yacht, Seaview Yacht; Berkshire Golf; St Moritz Tobogganing, St Moritz Sporting.

BONHAM CARTER, Helena; actress; *b* 26 May 1966; *d* of Hon. Raymond Bonham Carter, *qv* and Elena Bonham Carter (*née* Propper de Callejón). *Educ:* Hampstead High Sch. for Girls; Westminster Sch. *Films include:* Lady Jane, 1985; A Room with a View, 1986; A Hazard of Hearts, 1988; The Mask, 1988; St Francis of Assisi, 1989; Getting it Right, 1989; Hamlet, 1990; Where Angels Fear to Tread, 1990; Howard's End, 1992; Fatal Deception, 1993; Mary Shelley's Frankenstein, 1994; The Glace Bay Miner's Museum, 1994; *television includes:* Miami Vice, 1987; The Vision, 1988; Arms and the Man, 1988; Dancing Queen, 1993; A Dark Adapted Eye, 1994; *theatre includes:* Woman in White, Greenwich, 1988; The Chalk Garden, Windsor, 1989; House of Bernarda Alba, Nottingham Playhouse, 1991; The Barber of Seville, Palace, Watford, 1992; Trelawney of the Wells, Comedy, 1992; *radio:* The Reluctant Debutante; Marie Antoinette; The Seagull. *Recreation:* reading. *Address:* c/o Jeremy Conway, Conway van Gelder Ltd, 18/21 Jermyn Street, SW1Y 6HB. *T:* 0171–287 0077.

BONHAM-CARTER, John Arkwright, CVO 1975; DSO 1942; OBE 1967; ERD 1952; Chairman and General Manager, British Railways London Midland Region, 1971–75; *b* 27 March 1915; *s* of late Capt. Guy Bonham-Carter, 19th Hussars, and Kathleen Rebecca (*née* Arkwright); *m* 1939, Anne Louisa Charteris; two *s*. *Educ:* Winchester Coll.; King's Coll., Cambridge (Exhibitioner). 1st class hons Mech. Scis, Cantab, 1936; MA 1970. Joined LNER Co. as Traffic Apprentice, 1936; served in Royal Tank Regt, 1939–46 (despatches, 1940 and 1942); subsequently rejoined LNER; held various appointments; Asst General Manager, BR London Midland Region, 1963–65; Chief Operating Officer, BR Board, 1966–68; Chm. and Gen. Manager, BR Western Region, 1968–71. Lieut-Col, Engr and Transport (formerly Engr and Rly) Staff Corps RE (TA), 1966–71, Col 1971–. FCIT. KStJ 1984; Comdr, St John Ambulance, Dorset, 1984–87. *Recreations:* theatre, foreign travel, cabinet making and carpentry. *Address:* Redbridge House, Crossways, Dorchester, Dorset DT2 8DY. *T:* Warmwell (01305) 852669. *Club:* Army and Navy.

BONHAM CARTER, Hon. Raymond Henry; Executive Director, S. G. Warburg & Co. Ltd, 1967–77; retired in 1979 following disability; *b* 19 June 1929; *s* of Sir Maurice Bonham Carter, KCB, KCVO, and Lady Violet Bonham Carter, DBE (later Baroness Asquith of Yarnbury); *m* 1958, Elena Propper de Callejon; two *s* one *d*. *Educ:* Winchester Coll.; Magdalen Coll., Oxford (BA 1952); Harvard Business Sch. (MBA 1954). Irish Guards, 1947–49. With J. Henry Schröder & Co., 1954–58; acting Advr, Bank of England, 1958–63; Alternate Exec. Dir for UK, IMF, and Mem., UK Treasury and Supply Delegn, Washington, 1961–63; S. G. Warburg & Co. Ltd, 1964; Director: Transport Development Group Ltd, 1969–77; Banque de Paris et des Pays Bas NV, 1973–77; Mercury Securities Ltd, 1974–77; seconded as Dir, Industrial Develt Unit, DoI, 1977–79. Mem. Council, Internat. Inst. for Strategic Studies (Hon. Treasurer, 1974–84). *Address:* 7 West Heath Avenue, NW11 7QS.

See also H. Bonham Carter.

BONHAM-CARTER, Victor; Joint Secretary, Society of Authors, 1971–78, Consultant, 1978–82; Secretary, Royal Literary Fund, 1966–82; *b* 13 Dec. 1913; *s* of Gen. Sir Charles Bonham-Carter, GCB, CMG, DSO, and Gabrielle Madge Jeanette (*née* Fisher); *m* 1st, 1938, Audrey Edith Stogdon (marr. diss. 1979); two *s*; 2nd, 1979, Cynthia Claire Sanford. *Educ:* Winchester Coll.; Magdalene Coll., Cambridge (MA); Hamburg and Paris. Worked on The Countryman, 1936–37; Dir, School Prints Ltd, 1937–39, 1945–60; Army, R Berks Regt and Intell. Corps, 1939–45; farmed in W Somerset, 1947–59; historian of Dartington Hall Estate, Devon, 1951–66; on staff of Soc. of Authors, 1963–82. Active in Exmoor National Park affairs, 1955–; Pres., Exmoor Soc., 1975–; Partner, Exmoor Press, 1969–89. *Publications:* The English Village, 1952; (with W. B. Curry) Dartington Hall, 1958; Exploring Parish Churches, 1959; Farming the Land, 1959; In a Liberal Tradition, 1960; Soldier True, 1965; Surgeon in the Crimea, 1969; The Survival of the English Countryside, 1971; Authors by Profession, vol. 1 1978, vol. 2 1984; Exmoor Writers, 1987; The Essence of Exmoor, 1991; many contribs to jls, radio, etc on country life and work; also on authorship matters, esp. Public Lending Right. *Recreations:* music, conversation. *Address:* The Mount, Milverton, Taunton TA4 1QZ.

BONINGTON, Christian John Storey, CBE 1976; mountaineer, writer and photographer; *b* 6 Aug. 1934; *s* of Charles Bonington, journalist, and Helen Anne Bonington (*née* Storey); *m* 1962, Muriel Wendy Marchant; two *s* (and one *s* decd). *Educ:* University Coll. Sch., London. RMA Sandhurst, 1955–56; commnd Royal Tank Regt, 1956–61. Unilever Management Trainee, 1961–62; writer and photographer, 1962–. Climbs: Annapurna II, 26,041 ft (1st ascent) 1960; Central Pillar Freney, Mont Blanc (1st ascent), 1961; Nuptse, 25,850 ft (1st ascent), 1961; North Wall of Eiger (1st British ascent), 1962; Central Tower of Paine, Patagonia (1st ascent), 1963; Mem. of team, first descent of Blue Nile, 1968; Leader: successful Annapurna South Face Expedition, 1970; British Everest Expedition, 1972; Brammah, Himalayas (1st ascent), 1973; co-leader, Changabang, Himalayas (1st ascent), 1974; British Everest Expedition (1st ascent SW face), 1975; Ogre (1st ascent), 1977; jt leader, Kongur, NW China (1st ascent), 1981; Shivling West (1st ascent), 1983; Mt Vinson, highest point of Antarctica (1st British ascent), 1983; reached Everest summit, 1985; Panch Chuli II (W Ridge), Kumaon, Himalayas (1st ascent), 1992; Mejslen, Greenland (1st ascent), 1993; Rang Rik Rank, Kinnaur, Himalayas (1st ascent), 1994. President: British Mountaineering Council, 1988–91 (Vice-Pres., 1976–79, 1985–88); British Orienteering Fedn, 1985–; NT Lake Dist Appeal, 1989–; Council for National Parks, 1992–; Vice-Pres., Army Mountaineering Assoc., 1980–. Pres., LEPRA, 1983. FRGS (Founders' Medal, 1974). Hon. Fellow: UMIST, 1976; Lancashire Polytechnic, 1991. Hon. MA Salford, 1973; Hon. DSc: Sheffield, 1976; Lancaster, 1983. Lawrence of Arabia Medal, RSAA, 1986; Livingstone Medal, RSGS, 1991. *Publications:* I Chose to Climb (autobiog.), 1966; Annapurna South Face, 1971; The Next Horizon (autobiog.), 1973; Everest, South West Face, 1973; Everest the Hard Way, 1976; Quest for Adventure, 1981; Kongur: China's elusive summit, 1982; (jtly) Everest: the unclimbed ridge, 1983; The Everest Years, 1986; Mountaineer (autobiog.), 1989; The Climbers, 1992; (with Robin Knox-Johnston) Sea, Ice and Rock, 1992. *Recreations:* mountaineering, ski-ing, orienteering. *Address:* Badger Hill, Nether Row, Hesket Newmarket, Wigton, Cumbria CA7 8LA. *T:* Caldbeck (016974) 78286. *Clubs:* Alpine, Alpine Ski, Army and Navy, Climbers, Fell and Rock Climbing, Border Liners.

BONINO, Emma; Member, European Commission, since 1995; *b* 9 March 1948. *Educ:* Bocconi Univ., Milan (BA 1972). Mem., Italian Chamber of Deputies, 1976–94; posts include: Chm., Radical Party Gp, 1979–81; Mem., Bureau of Parlt, 1992–94; Mem., European Parlt, 1979–. Transnational Radical Party: Pres., 1991–93; Sec., 1993–95. *Recreations:* snorkling, scuba-diving. *Address:* European Commission, Breydel 7/16, Avenue d'Auderghem 45, 1040 Brussels, Belgium. *T:* (2) 956447.

BONNER, Frederick Ernest, CBE 1974; Deputy Chairman, Central Electricity Generating Board, 1975–86; *b* 16 Sept. 1923; *s* of late George Frederick Bonner and Mrs Bonner, Hammersmith; *m* 1st, 1957, Phyllis (*d* 1976), *d* of late Mr and Mrs H. Holder; 2nd, 1977, Mary, *widow* of Ellis Walter Aries, AFC, ARICS. *Educ:* St Clement Danes Holborn Estate Grammar Sch. BSc(Econ) London; DPA, JDipMA. Local Govt (Fulham and Ealing Borough Councils), 1940–49. Central Electricity Authority: Sen. Accountant, 1949–50; Asst Finance Officer, 1950–58; Central Electricity Generating Board: Asst Chief Financial Officer, 1958–61; Dep. Chief Financial Officer, 1961–65; Chief Financial Officer, 1965–69; Member, 1969–75. Member: UKAEA, 1977–86; Monopolies and Mergers Commn, 1987–93. Chm., British Airways Helicopters, 1983–85; Dir (non-exec.) Nuclear Electric, 1990–93. Hon. Treas., 1989–, Vice-Chm., 1993, Chm., 1994, BIEE. Mem., Public Finance Foundn, 1985–. Chm., Uranium Inst., 1985–87. Hon. Treas., Chichester Counselling Services, 1995. FCA, IPFA, CIMgt. *Recreations:* music, gardening, reading. *Address:* Joya, 20 Craigweil Manor, Aldwick, Bognor Regis, W Sussex PO21 4DJ.

BONNER, Paul Max; Director, Secretariat, ITV Network Centre, 1993–94; *b* 30 Nov. 1934; *s* of Jill and late Frank Bonner; *m* 1956, Jenifer Hubbard; two *s* one *d*. *Educ:* Felsted Sch., Essex. National Service commission, 1953–55. Local journalism, 1955; Radio production, BBC Bristol, 1955–57; Television production, BBC Bristol, 1957–59, BBC Lime Grove, 1959–62; Television Documentary prodn and direction, BBC Lime Grove and Kensington House, 1962–74; Editor, Community Programmes for BBC, 1974–77; Head of Science and Features Programmes for BBC, 1977–80; Channel Controller, Channel Four TV, 1980–83; Exec. Dir and Programme Controller, Channel Four TV, 1983–87; Dir, Programme Planning Secretariat, ITA, 1987–93. A Manager, Royal Instn, 1982–85; Governor, Nat. Film and TV School, 1983–88; Director: Broadcasting Support Services, 1982–93; House of Commons Broadcasting Unit Ltd, 1989–91; Parly Broadcasting Unit, 1991–94; Chm., Sponsorship and Advertising Cttee, EBU, 1991–94; Member: Bd, Children's Film Unit, 1989–; COPUS, 1986–92. FRTS 1989. *Publications: documentaries include.* Strange Excellency, 1964; Climb up to Hell, 1967; Lost: Four H Bombs, 1967; Search for the Real Che Guevara, 1971; Who Sank the Lusitania?, 1972. *Recreations:* photography, the theatre, sailing, walking, listening to good conversation. *Address:* North View, Wimbledon Common, SW19 4UJ. *Club:* Reform.

BONNET, C. M.; *see* Melchior-Bonnet.

BONNET, Maj.-Gen. Peter Robert Frank, CB 1991; MBE 1975; Colonel Commandant, Royal Regiment of Artillery, since 1990; *b* 12 Dec. 1936; *s* of James Robert and Phyllis Elsie Bonnet; *m* 1961, Sylvia Mary Coy; two *s*. *Educ:* Royal Military Coll. of Science, Shrivenham. BSc (Engrg). Commnd from RMA Sandhurst, 1958; RMCS Shrivenham, 1959–62; apptd to RHA, 1962; Staff trng, RMCS and Staff Coll., Camberley, 1969–70; Comd (Lt-Col), 26 Field Regt, RA, 1978–81; Comd RA (Brig.) 2nd Div., 1982–84; attendance at Indian Nat. Defence Coll., New Delhi, 1985; Dir RA, 1986–89 (Maj.-Gen. 1986); GOC Western Dist, 1989–91, retd 1992. Gen. Sec., Officers' Pensions Soc., 1995–; Dir, OPS Investment Co. Ltd, 1995–. Hon. Col, 26 Field Regt RA, 1992–. Vice-Pres., Nat. Artillery Assoc., 1989–; Member: Exec. Cttee, Army Benevolent Fund, 1992– (Chm., Grants Cttee, 1992–); RA Hist. Cttee, 1991–. *Publications:* International Terrorism, 1985; A Short History of the Royal Regiment of Artillery, 1994. *Recreations:* tennis, sculpture, painting. *T:* South Molton (01769) 572344. *Club:* Army and Navy.

BONNETT, Prof. Raymond, CChem, FRSC; Professor of Organic Chemistry, Queen Mary and Westfield (formerly Queen Mary) College, London, since 1976; *b* 13 July 1931; *s* of Harry and Maud Bonnett; *m* 1956, Shirley Rowe; two *s* one *d*. *Educ:* County Grammar Sch., Bury St Edmunds; Imperial Coll. (BSc, ARCS); Cambridge Univ. (PhD); DSc London 1972. Salters' Fellow, Cambridge, 1957–58; Res. Fellow, Harvard, 1958–59; Asst Prof., Dept of Chemistry, Univ. of British Columbia, 1959–61; Lectr in Organic Chem., 1961–66, Reader in Organic Chem., 1966–74, Prof. 1974–76, Hd of Dept of Chemistry, 1982–87, QMC, London Univ. *Publications:* sci. papers, esp. in Jls of Royal Soc. of Chemistry and Biochemical Soc. *Recreations:* theatre, private press books, gardening. *Address:* Elmbank, 19 Station Road, Epping, Essex CM16 4HG. *T:* Epping (01992) 573203.

BONNEY, George Louis William, MS, FRCS; Consulting Orthopædic Surgeon, St Mary's Hospital, London, since 1984; *b* 10 Jan. 1920; *s* of late Dr Ernest Bonney and Gertrude Mary Williams; *m* 1950, Margaret Morgan; two *d*. *Educ:* Eton (Scholar); St Mary's Hospital Medical Sch. MB, BS, MRCS, LRCP 1943; FRCS 1945; MS (London) 1947. Formerly: Surg.-Lieut RNVR; Research Assistant and Senior Registrar, Royal National Orthopædic Hospital; Consultant Orthopædic Surgeon: Southend Group of Hospitals; St Mary's Hosp., London, 1954–84 (Sen. Consultant, 1979–84). Travelling Fellowship of British Postgraduate Med. Fedn, Univ. of London, 1950. Watson-Jones Lectr, RCS, 1976. Sen. FBOA; Hon. Fellow, Medical Defence Union; Mem., SICOT. *Publications:* chapters in: Operative Surgery, 1957; Clinical Surgery, 1966; Clinical Orthopædics, 1983, 2nd edn 1995; Micro-reconstruction of Nerve Injuries, 1987; Current Therapy in Neurologic Disease, 1987; Medical Negligence, 1990, 2nd edn 1994; Clinical Neurology, 1991; papers in medical journals on visceral pain, circulatory mechanisms, nerve injuries and on various aspects of orthopædic surgery. *Recreations:* fishing, shooting, photography, music. *Address:* 6 Wooburn Grange, Grange Drive, Wooburn Green, Bucks HP10 0QU. *T:* Bourne End (01628) 525598. *Club:* Leander.

BONNICI, Carmelo M.; *see* Mifsud Bonnici.

BONSALL, Sir Arthur (Wilfred), KCMG 1977; CBE 1957; *b* 25 June 1917; *s* of late Wilfred Bonsall and Sarah Bonsall; *m* 1941, Joan Isabel Wingfield (*d* 1990); four *s* three *d*. *Educ:* Bishop's Stortford Coll.; St Catharine's Coll., Cambridge. 2nd Cl. Hons Mod. Langs. Joined Air Ministry, 1940; transf. to FO 1942; IDC, 1962; Dir, Govt Communications HQ, 1975–78. *Recreation:* coarse gardening. *Address:* 1 Coxwell Court, Coxwell Street, Cirencester, Glos GL7 2BQ.

See also F. F. Bonsall.

BONSALL, Prof. Frank Featherstone, FRS 1970; Professor of Mathematics, University of Edinburgh, 1965–84, now Emeritus; *b* 1920; *s* of late Wilfred Bonsall and Sarah Bonsall; *m* 1947, Gillian Patrick. *Educ:* Bishop's Stortford Coll.; Merton Coll., Oxford. *Publications* (all with J. Duncan): Numerical Ranges of Operators on Normed Spaces and of Elements of Normed Algebras, 1971; Numerical Ranges II, 1973; Complete Normed Algebras, 1973. *Recreation:* walking.

See also Sir A. W. Bonsall.

BONSER, Rt. Rev. David, *see* Bolton, Bishop Suffragan of.

BONSER, Air Vice-Marshal Stanley Haslam, CB 1969; MBE 1942; CEng, FRAeS; Director, Easams Ltd, 1972–81; *b* 17 May 1916; *s* of late Sam Bonser and late Phoebe Ellen Bonser; *m* 1941, Margaret Betty Howard (*d* 1994); two *s*. *Educ:* Sheffield University. BSc 1938; DipEd 1939. Armament Officer, Appts, 1939–44; British Air Commn, Washington, DC, 1944–46; Coll. of Aeronautics, 1946–47; RAE, Guided Weapons, 1947–51; Chief Instr (Armament Wing) RAF Techn. Coll., 1951–52; Staff Coll., Bracknell, 1953, psa 1953; Project Officer, Blue Streak, Min. of Technology, 1954–57; Asst Dir, GW Engineering, 1957–60; Senior RAF Officer, Skybolt Development Team, USA, 1960–62; Dir, Aircraft Mechanical Engineering, 1963–64; Dir, RAF Aircraft Development (mainly Nimrod), 1964–69; Dep. Controller: of Equipment, Min. of Technology and MoD, 1969–71; Aircraft C, MoD, 1971–72. *Recreations:* scout movement, gardening. *Address:* Chalfont, Waverley Avenue, Fleet, Hants GU13 8NW. *T:* Fleet (01252) 615835.

BONSOR, Sir Nicholas (Cosmo), 4th Bt *cr* 1925; MP (C) Upminster, since 1983 (Nantwich, 1979–83); Minister of State, Foreign and Commonwealth Office, since 1995; *b* 9 Dec. 1942; *s* of Sir Bryan Cosmo Bonsor, 3rd Bt, MC, TD, and of Elizabeth, *d* of late Captain Angus Valdimar Hambro; *S* father, 1977; *m* 1969, Hon. Nadine Marisa Lampson, *d* of 2nd Baron Killearn, *qv*; two *s* three *d* (including twin *d*). *Educ:* Eton; Keble College, Oxford (MA). Barrister-at-law, Inner Temple. Served Royal Buckinghamshire Yeomanry, 1964–69. Practised at the Bar, 1967–75. Mem., CLA Legal and Parly Sub-Cttee, 1978–82. Chm., Select Cttee on Defence, 1992–95; Sec., Cons. Africa Sub-Cttee, 1979–80; Vice-Chairman: Cons. Foreign Affairs Cttee, 1981–83; Cons. Defence Cttee, 1987–90. Chairman: Cyclotron Trust for Cancer Treatment, 1984–92; Food Hygiene Bureau, 1987–; British Field Sports Soc., 1988–; Standing Council of the Baronetage, 1990–93 (Vice-Chm., 1987–90); Baronets' Trust, 1993– (Trustee, 1986–); Trustee, Verdin Trust for Mentally Handicapped, 1983–92. Mem., Council of Lloyd's, 1987–. FRSA 1970. *Publications:* political pamphlets on law and trades unions and defence. *Recreations:* sailing, shooting, military history. *Heir: s* Alexander Cosmo Walrond Bonsor, *b* 8 Sept. 1976. *Address:* House of Commons, SW1A 0AA. *Clubs:* White's, Pratt's; Royal Yacht Squadron.

BONVIN, Jane Anne Marie, (Mrs S. M. Poulter); Her Honour Judge Bonvin; a Circuit Judge, since 1995; *b* 15 Dec. 1946; *d* of Jean Albert Bonvin and Phyllis Margaret (*née* Boyd); *m* 1972, Sebastian Murray Poulter. *Educ:* Putney High Sch.; Bristol Univ. (LLB Hons). Law Lectr, IVS, Lesotho, 1969–71; called to the Bar, Gray's Inn, 1971; barrister, Western Circuit, 1972–77 and 1979–95. Editor, Lesotho Law Reports, 1977–79. *Recreations:* gardening, tennis, travel. *Address:* c/o Bournemouth Combined Court Centre, Law Courts, Stafford Road, Bournemouth, Dorset BN1 1PN. *T:* Bournemouth (01202) 553701.

BONYNGE, Dame Joan; *see* Sutherland, Dame Joan.

BONYNGE, Richard, AO 1983; CBE 1977; opera conductor; *b* Sydney, 29 Sept. 1930; *s* of C. A. Bonynge, Epping, NSW; *m* 1954, Dame Joan Sutherland, *qv*; one *s*. *Educ:* Sydney Conservatorium (pianist). Official debut, as Conductor, with Santa Cecilia Orch. in Rome, 1962; conducted first opera, Faust, Vancouver, 1963. Has conducted in most leading opera houses in world, and in Edinburgh, Vienna and Florence Fests. Has been Princ. Conductor and Artistic/Musical Dir of cos, incl. Sutherland/Williamson Internat. Grand Opera Co., Aust., 1965; Vancouver Opera, 1974–78; Australian Opera, 1975–85. Many opera and ballet recordings; also recital discs with Sutherland, Tebaldi, Tourangeau and Pavarotti, and many orchestral and ballet anthologies. *Publication:* (with Dame Joan Sutherland) The Joan Sutherland Album, 1986. *Address:* c/o Ingpen and Williams, 14 Kensington Court, W8 5DN.

BOOKER, Christopher John Penrice; journalist and author; *b* 7 Oct. 1937; *s* of late John Booker and Margaret Booker; *m* 1979, Valerie, *d* of late Dr M. S. Patrick, OBE; two *s*. *Educ:* Dragon Sch., Oxford; Shrewsbury Sch.; Corpus Christi Coll., Cambridge (History). Liberal News, 1960; jazz critic, Sunday Telegraph, 1961; Editor, Private Eye, 1961–63, and regular contributor, 1965–; resident scriptwriter, That Was The Week That Was, 1962–63, and Not So Much A Programme, 1963–64; contributor to Spectator, 1962–, Daily Telegraph, 1972– (Way of the World column, as Peter Simple II, 1987–90), and to many other newspapers and jls; columnist, Sunday Telegraph, 1990–. Wrote extensively on property develt, planning and housing, 1972–77 (with Bennie Gray, Campaigning Journalist of the Year, 1973); City of Towers—the Rise and Fall of a Twentieth Century Dream (TV prog.), 1979. Mem., Cowgill enquiry into post-war repatriations from Austria, 1986–90. *Publications:* The Neophiliacs: a study of the revolution in English life in the 50s and 60s, 1969; (with Candida Lycett-Green) Goodbye London, 1973; The Booker Quiz, 1976; The Seventies, 1980; The Games War: a Moscow journal, 1981; (with Lord Brimelow and Brig. A. Cowgill) The Repatriations from Austria in 1945, 1990; (with Richard North) The Mad Officials: how the bureaucrats are strangling Britain, 1993; contrib. Private Eye anthologies, 1962–, incl. The Secret Diary of John Major, 1992. *Recreations:* the psychology of storytelling, nature, music, following Somerset cricket team. *Address:* The Old Rectory, Litton, Bath BA3 4PW. *T:* Mendip (01761) 241263.

BOOKER, Gordon Alan, FIWEM; Deputy Director General of Water Services, since 1990; *b* 17 Feb. 1938; *s* of Frederick William Booker and Beryl Booker; *m* 1957, Anne Christine Pike; two *s* one *d*. *Educ:* Dronfield Grammar Sch.; Sheffield Univ. (BEng (Hons) 1960). MICE 1963; FIWEM 1966. Sheffield Water, 1960–65; Birmingham Water, 1965–70; W Glam Water, 1970–74; Welsh Water, 1974–80; Chief Exec., E Worcester Water, 1980–89; Managing Director: Biwater Supply, 1987–90; Bournemouth and W Hants Water Cos, 1989–90. Mem., Council, Water Res. Centre, 1985–90; mem. and chm. of several water industry cttees on automation and leakage control. *Publications:* Water Distribution Systems, 1984; Telemetry and Control, 1986; contrib. Procs of ICE and of IWSA, reports for DoE and NWC, and Jls of IWEM and IAWPRC. *Recreations:* walking, painting. *Address:* 106 The Holloway, Droitwich, Worcs WR9 7AH. *T:* Droitwich (01905) 772432; Sheplegh Court, Blackawton, Devon TQ9 7AH.

BOOKER-MILBURN, Donald; Sheriff of Grampian, Highland and Islands, since 1983; *b* Dornoch, 20 May 1940; *s* of late Captain Booker Milburn, DSO, MC, Coldstream Guards, and late Betty Calthrop Calthrop; *m* 1963, Marjorie Lilian Elizabeth Burns; one *s* one *d*. *Educ:* Trinity College, Glenalmond; Grenoble Univ.; Jesus Coll., Cambridge (BA); Edinburgh Univ. (LLB). Admitted to Faculty of Advocates, 1968; Standing Junior Counsel to RAF, 1977–80; Sheriff of Lothian and Borders, 1980–83. *Recreations:* golf, skiing. *Address:* Clashmore House, Clashmore, Dornoch, Sutherland IV25 3RG. *Clubs:* Royal & Ancient Golf (St Andrews); Royal Dornoch Golf.

BOOLELL, Sir Satcam, Kt 1977; Attorney General, Minister of Justice and Minister of External Affairs and Emigration, Mauritius, 1986–90; *b* New Grove, Mauritius, 11 Sept. 1920; *s* of Sahadewoo Boolell and Cossilah Choony; *m* 1st, 1948, Inderjeet Kissoodaye (*d* 1986); two *s* one *d*; 2nd, 1987, Myrtha Poblete. *Educ:* primary and secondary schs in New Grove, Mare d'Albert, Rose Belle, and Port-Louis; LSE (LLB Hons 1951). Called to the Bar, Lincoln's Inn, 1952. Civil servant, Mauritius, 1944–48. Minister of Agric. and Natural Resources, 1959–82; Minister of Economic Planning, 1983–84. Mem. Central Exec., 1955–, Advr, 1990–, Mauritius Labour Party. Rep. Mauritius, internat. confs. Founder, French daily newspaper, The Nation. Hon. DCL Mauritius, 1986. Comdr, Légion d'Honneur (France), 1990. *Recreations:* travel books, walking in the countryside. *Address:* 4bis Bancilhon Street, Port Louis, Mauritius. *T:* 2080079, *Fax:* 2089207.

BOON, John Trevor, CBE 1968; Chairman, Mills & Boon Ltd, since 1972; *b* 21 Dec. 1916; 3rd *s* of Charles Boon and Mary Boon (*née* Cowpe); *m* 1943, Felicity Ann, *d* of Stewart and Clemence Logan; four *s*. *Educ:* Felsted Sch.; Trinity Hall, Cambridge (scholar). 1st Cl. Pts I and II History Tripos. Served War, 1939–45: with Royal Norfolk Regt and S Wales Borderers (despatches). Historical Section of War Cabinet, 1945–46. Joined Mills & Boon Ltd, 1938, Man. Dir, 1963, Chm., 1972–. Dir, Wood Bros Glass Works Ltd, 1968, Chm., 1973–75, Dep. Chm., 1975–78. Vice Chm., Harlequin Enterprises Ltd, Toronto, 1972–83. Chairman: Harlequin Overseas, 1978–; Marshall Editions, 1977–95; Director: Harmex, 1978–82; Harlequin France, 1980–82 (Chm., 1978–80); Torstar Corp., Toronto, 1981–85; Open University Educational Enterprises, 1977–79. President: Soc. of Bookmen, 1981; Internat. Publishers Assoc., 1972–76 (Hon. Mem., 1982); Chairman: Publishers Adv. Panel of British Council, 1977–81; Book Trade Res. Cttee, 1978–82; Director: Book Tokens Ltd, 1964–84; Book Trade Improvements Ltd, 1966–84; Publishers Association: Mem. Council, 1953, Treas., 1959–61, Pres., 1961–63, Vice-Pres., 1963–65. Over-seas missions: for British Council, to SE Asia, USSR (twice), Czechoslovakia; for Book Development Council, to Malaysia, Singapore, and New Zealand. Mem. Management Cttee, Wine Soc., 1971–77. Hon. MA, Open Univ., 1983. *Recreations:* wine, books, friends. *Address:* Mills & Boon Ltd, Eton House, 18–24 Paradise Road, Richmond, Surrey TW9 1SR. *Clubs:* Beefsteak, Garrick, Royal Automobile; Hawks (Cambridge).

BOON, Sir Peter Coleman, Kt 1979; Goodyear Professor of Business Administration, Kent State University, USA, 1983–86; *b* 2 Sept. 1916; *s* of Frank Boon and Evelyn Boon; *m* 1940, Pamela; one *s* one *d*. *Educ:* Felsted. Stock Exchange, 1933–34; Lloyds & National Provincial Foreign Bank, 1934–35; Dennison Mfg Co., USA, 1936–39; Armed Services, War of 1939–45, 1939–46; Dennison Mfg, 1946; graduate trainee, Hoover Ltd, 1946, Managing Dir (Australia), 1955–65; Managing Dir, Hoover Ltd, 1965–75, Chm., 1975–78. Dir, Belden & Blake UK Inc., 1985–. FIMgt; FRSA 1980. Hon. LLD Strathclyde, 1978. Chevalier de l'Ordre de la Couronne, Belgium. *Recreations:* horses, swimming, golf, theatre, economics, National Trust for Scotland, boys clubs, education. *Clubs:* Royal Wimbledon Golf; Western Racing, Australian, Imperial Services, American National, Royal Sydney Yacht Squadron, Australian Jockey, Sydney Turf (Australia).

BOORD, Sir Nicolas (John Charles), 4th Bt *cr* 1896; scientific translator; English training specialist; *b* 10 June 1936; *s* of Sir Richard William Boord, 3rd Bt, and of Yvonne, Lady Boord, *d* of late J. A. Hubert Bird; *S* father, 1975; *m* 1965, Françoise Renée Louise Mouret. *Educ:* Eton (Harmsworth Lit. Prize, 1952); Sorbonne, France; Societa Dante Alighieri, Italy; Univ. of Santander, Spain. *Publications:* (trans. jtly) The History of Physics and the Philosophy of Science—Selected Essays (Armin Teske), 1972; numerous translations of scientific papers for English and American scientific and technical jls. *Recreations:* English and French literature and linguistics. *Heir: b* Antony Andrew Boord [*b* 21 May 1938; *m* 1960, Anna Christina von Krogh; one *s* one *d*]. *Address:* 61 Traverse Le Mée, 13009 Marseille, France. *T:* 73.13.95.

BOORMAN, Lt.-Gen. Sir Derek, KCB 1986 (CB 1982); Lieutenant of the Tower of London, 1989–92; Chairman, Royal Hospitals NHS Trust, since 1994; *b* 13 Sept. 1930; *s* of late N. R. Boorman, MBE, and of Mrs A. L. Boorman (*née* Patman); *m* 1st, 1956, Jennifer Jane Skinner (*d* 1991); one *s* two *d*; 2nd, 1992, Mrs Nicola Cox. *Educ:* Wolstanton; RMA Sandhurst. Commnd N Staffords, 1950; Adjt 1 Staffords, 1958–59; Staff Coll., 1961; HQ 48 Gurkha Inf. Bde, 1962–64; Jt Services Staff Coll., 1968; CO 1 Staffords, 1969–71; Instr, Staff Coll., 1972–73; Comdr 51 Inf. Bde, 1975–76; RCDS, 1977; Dir, Public Relations (Army), 1978–79; Director of Military Operations, 1980–82; Comdr, British Forces Hong Kong, and Maj.-Gen. Bde of Gurkhas, 1982–85; Chief of Defence Intelligence, 1985–88. Colonel: 6th Queen Elizabeth's Own Gurkha Rifles, 1983–88; Staffordshire Regt (Prince of Wales's), 1985–90. Director: Tarmac Construction, 1988–95. Chm., KCH Trust, 1992–93. Mem., Security Commn, 1991–. *Recreations:* shooting, gardening, music. *Address:* c/o Royal Hospitals NHS Trust, Royal London Hospital, Whitechapel, E1 1BB. *Club:* Naval and Military.

BOORMAN, Edwin Roy Pratt; Chairman and Chief Executive, Kent Messenger Group, since 1986 (Managing Director, 1965–86); Chairman, Messenger Print Ltd; *b* 7 Nov. 1935; *s* of late H. R. P. Boorman, CBE and Enid (*née* Starke); *m* 1st, Merrilyn Ruth Pettit (marr. diss. 1982); four *d*; 2nd, 1983, Janine Craske; one *s*. *Educ:* Rydal; Queens' Coll., Cambridge (MA Econ. History). National Service, 1954–56. Cambridge Univ., 1956–59; Kent Messenger, 1959; Editor: South Eastern Gazette, 1960–62; Kent Messenger, 1962–65. Councillor, Newspaper Soc. Court Assistant, Livery, Worshipful Co. of Stationers and Newspapermakers; Pres., Dickens Area Newsagents' Benevolent Assoc.; Finance Dir, Royal British Legion Industries. Gov., Sutton Valence Sch. Vice-Pres., Age Concern, Kent; Chm., Kent Assoc. of Boys' Clubs, 1988–. Trustee, Chatham Historic Dockyard, 1992–. Tax Comr, Maidstone District 1. *Recreation:* sailing. *Address:* Redhill Farm, 339 Redhill, Wateringbury, Kent ME18 5LB. *Clubs:* Veteran Car, Kent CCC; Royal Yachting Association, Medway Yacht, Ocean Cruising.

BOORMAN, John, CBE 1994; film director; *b* 18 Jan. 1933; *m* 1956, Christel Kruse; one *s* three *d*. *Educ:* Salesian Coll., Chertsey. Film Editor, ITN, 1955–58; Dir and Producer, Southern TV, 1958–60; Head of Documentaries, BBC Bristol. *Films include:* Catch us if you Can, 1965; Point Blank, 1967; Hell in the Pacific, 1968; Leo the Last, 1969; Deliverance, 1970; Zardoz, 1973; The Heretic, 1976; Excalibur, 1981; The Emerald Forest, 1985; Hope and Glory, 1987; Where the Heart Is, 1989; I Dreamt I Woke Up, 1991; Beyond Rangoon, 1995. Gov., BFI, 1983–94. *Publications:* The Legend of Zardoz,

1973; Money into Light, 1985; Hope and Glory, 1987; Projections 1, 1992; Projections 2, 1993; Projections 3, 1994. *Address:* Merlin Films International, 16 Pembroke Street, Dublin 2, Ireland.

BOORSTIN, Dr Daniel J.; FRHistS; (12th) Librarian of Congress, 1975–87, now Emeritus; *b* 1 Oct. 1914; *s* of Samuel Boorstin and Dora (*née* Olsan); *m* 1941, Ruth Carolyn Frankel; three *s*. *Educ:* schs in Tulsa, Okla; Harvard Univ. (AB, summa cum Laude); Balliol Coll., Oxford (Rhodes Schol., BA Juris. 1st Cl. Hons, BCL 1st Cl. Hons); Yale Univ. Law Sch. (Sterling Fellow, JSD). Called to Bar, Inner Temple, 1937; admitted Mass Bar, 1942. Instr, tutor in history and lit., Harvard Univ. and Radcliffe Coll., 1938–42; Lectr, legal history, Law Sch., Harvard, 1939–42; Sen. Attorney, Office of Lend Lease Admin, Washington, DC, 1942–43; Office of Asst SG, USA, 1942–43; Asst Prof. of History, Swarthmore Coll., 1942–44; Univ. of Chicago, 1944–69: Asst Prof., 1944–49; Associate Prof., Preston and Sterling Morton Distinguished Prof. of Amer. History, 1956–69. During his 25 years tenure at Chicago, Visiting Lectr at Rome and Kyoto Univs, Sorbonne and Cambridge (Fellow, Trinity Coll., and Pitt Prof. of Amer. History and Instns; LittD 1968). Smithsonian Institution: Dir, Nat. Museum History and Techn., 1969–73; Sen. Historian, 1973–75. Many public service membership assignments, trusteeships, and active concern with a number of Amer. Assocs, esp. those relating to Amer. history, educn and cultural affairs. Past Pres., American Studies Assoc. Hon. FAGS. Hon. LittD Sheffield, 1979; Hon. DLitt: Cambridge, 1968; East Anglia, 1980; Sussex, 1983; numerous other hon. degrees. Watson-Davis Prize of the History of Science, Soc. for Discoverers, 1986; Charles Frankel Prize, Nat. Endowment for the Humanities, 1989; Nat. Book Award Medal for Distinguished Contribution to American Letters, 1989. Officier de L'Ordre de la Couronne, Belgium, 1980; Chevalier, Légion d'Honneur, France, 1984; Grand Officer, Order of Prince Henry the Navigator, Portugal, 1985; First Class Order of the Sacred Treasure, Japan, 1986. *Publications: include:* The Mysterious Science of the Law, 1941; The Lost World of Thomas Jefferson, 1948; The Genius of American Politics, 1953; The Americans: The Colonial Experience, 1958 (Bancroft Prize); America and the Image of Europe, 1960; The Image, 1962; The Americans: The National Experience, 1965 (Parkman Prize); The Decline of Radicalism, 1969; The Sociology of the Absurd, 1970; The Americans: The Democratic Experience, 1973 (Pulitzer Prize for History and Dexter Prize, 1974); Democracy and Its Discontents, 1974; The Exploring Spirit (BBC 1975 Reith Lectures), 1976; The Republic of Technology, 1978; (with Brooks M. Kelley) A History of the United States, 1980; The Discoverers, 1984 (Watson-Davis Prize), illustrated edn 1991; Hidden History, 1987; The Creators, 1992; Cleopatra's Nose, 1994; *for young readers:* Landmark History of the American People, vol. I, From Plymouth to Appomattox, 1968; vol. II, From Appomattox to the Moon, 1970; New Landmark History of the American People, 1987; *edited:* Delaware Cases 1792–1830, 1943; An American Primer, 1966; American Civilization, 1971; The Chicago History of American Civilization (30 vols). *Address:* (home) 3541 Ordway Street, NW, Washington, DC 20016, USA; (office) Library of Congress, Washington, DC 20540. *T:* (202) 9661853. *Clubs:* Cosmos (Washington); Elizabethan (Yale); International House (Japan).

BOOTE, Col Charles Geoffrey Michael, MBE 1945; TD 1943; DL; Vice Lord-Lieutenant of Staffordshire, 1969–76; *b* 29 Sept. 1909; *s* of Lt-Col Charles Edmund Boote, TD, The North Staffordshire Regt (killed in action, 1916); *m* 1937, Elizabeth Gertrude (*d* 1980), *er d* of Evan Richard Davies, Market Drayton, Salop; three *s*. *Educ:* Bedford Sch. 2nd Lt 5th Bn North Staffordshire Regt, 1927. Served 1939–45, UK and NW Europe; despatches, 1945; Lt-Col, 1947. Director, H. Clarkson (Midlands) Ltd, 1969–75. Dir, Brit. Pottery Manufacturers' Fedn (Trustee) Ltd, 1955, retd Dec. 1969; Pres., Brit. Pottery Manufacturers' Fedn, 1957–58; Vice-Chm., Glazed and Floor Tile Manufacturers' Assoc., 1953–57. Hon. Col 5/6 Bn North Staffordshire Regt, 1963–67; Mem. Staffs TAVR Cttee, retd 1976. JP, Stoke-on-Trent, 1955–65; DL, 1958, JP 1959, High Sheriff, 1967–68, Staffordshire. Chm., Eccleshall PSD, 1971–76; Mem. Court of Governors, Keele Univ., 1957. *Recreations:* salmon fishing; British Racing Drivers' Club (Life Mem.); North Staffordshire Hunt (Hon. Sec. 1948–59). *Address:* Morile Mhor, Tomatin, Inverness-shire IV13 7YN. *T:* Tomatin (01808) 511319. *Club:* Army and Navy.

BOOTE, Robert Edward, CVO 1971; first Director General, Nature Conservancy Council, 1973–80; *b* 6 Feb. 1920; *s* of Ernest Haydn Boote and Helen Rose Boote; *m* 1948, Vera (*née* Badian); one *s* one *d*. *Educ:* London Univ. (BSc Econ). DPA; FREconS 1953–61; AIPR 1957–61; FCIS 1960–81. War service, 1939–46, Actg Lt-Col, Hon. Major. Admin. Officer, City of Stoke-on-Trent, 1946–48; Chief Admin. Officer, Staffs County Planning and Develt Dept, 1948–54; Principal, 1954–64, Dep. Dir, 1964–73, Nature Conservancy. Sec. 1965–71, formerly Dep. Sec., Countryside in 1970 Confs, 1963, 1965, 1970 and numerous study groups; Mem., Pesticides Cttee, 1958–73; Chm., Broadland Report, 1963–65; UK Deleg. to Council of Europe Cttee for Conservation of Nature and Natural Resources, 1963–71; Mem., Countryside Review Cttee, 1977–79; a Chief Marshal to the Queen, 1970; various posts in meetings of UN, UNESCO, EEC and OECD, 1968–81; Chm. Preparatory Gp for Conservation Year 1970; Chm. Organising Cttee for European Conservation Conf. 1970 (Conf. Vice-Pres.); Chm. European Cttee, 1969–71; Consultant for European Architectural Heritage Year 1975; Advr, H of L Select Cttee on Europ. Communities, 1980–81. International Union for Conservation of Nature and Natural Resources: Treas., 1975–78; Mem., Governing Council and Bureau, 1975–81; a Vice-Pres., 1978–81; a Vice-Pres. and Chm., Euro Fedn of Nature and Nat. Parks, 1980–81; Rep., Internat. Conf. on Antarctic Marine Living Resources, 1980; Chm., Antarctica Resolution, 1981; Election Officer, 1984; Founder and Chm., 1974–80, Mem., 1980–85, UK Cttee. Council Member: FFPS, 1979–83; RGS, 1983–86; BTCV (Vice-Pres.) 1980–; RSNC (Vice-Pres.) 1980–95; RSNC Wildlife Appeal, 1983–87; WWF, 1980–86; Ecological Parks Trust, 1980–85; YPTES (Chm.), 1982–87; Friends of ENO, 1980–87; Common Ground Internat., 1981–85; Cttees for UK Conservation and Develt Prog., 1980–83; HGTAC, Forestry Commn, 1981–87; Conservator, Wimbledon and Putney Commons, 1981–; Patron, CSV, 1978–85; Chairman: Instn of Environmental Sciences, 1981–84; Seychelles Appeal Cttee, Royal Soc., 1980–87; Chm., Gp A, Ditchley Foundn Anglo/Amer. Conf. on Environment, 1970; Lead Speaker, Eurogespracht, Vienna, 1970; Mem., Entretiens Ecologiques de Dijon, 1981; UK Officer Rep., Eur. Environment Ministers Conf., 1976; Judge, Berlin world agro/environ films and TV competitions, 1970, 1972, 1974 and 1980. Initiator and Chm., Age Resource, 1988–; a Vice-Pres., Age Concern, 1990–. FRSA 1971. Hon. Associate, Landscape Inst., 1971; Hon. MRTPI, 1978. Greek Distinguished Service Medal, 1946; van Tienhoven European Prize, 1980; Merit Award, IUCN, 1984; Alfred Toepfer Prize for European nature protection, Goethe Foundn, 1995. Adviser: Macmillan Guide to Britain's Nature Reserves, 1980–94; Shell Better Britain Campaign, 1980–91. Member Editorial Boards: Internat. Jl of Environmental Studies, 1975–; Town Planning Review, 1979–85; Internat. Jl Environmental Educn and Information, 1981–83. Helped to prepare: Pacemaker (film), 1970 (also appeared in); Man of Action, BBC Radio, 1977. *Publications:* (as Robert Arvill) Man and Environment, 1967 (5th edn 1984); numerous papers, articles, addresses, TV and radio broadcasts, over 4 decades in UK and internat. professional confs in 50 countries. *Recreations:* travel, theatre, music, dancing. *Address:* 3 Leeward Gardens, SW19 7QR. *T:* 0181–946 1551.

BOOTH; *see* Gore-Booth.

BOOTH; *see* Sclater-Booth, family name of Baron Basing.

BOOTH, His Honour Alan Shore, QC 1975; a Circuit Judge, 1976–93; *b* Aug. 1922; 4th *s* of Parkin Stanley Booth and Ethel Mary Shore; *m* 1954, Mary Gwendoline Hilton; one *s* one *d*. *Educ:* Shrewsbury Sch.; Liverpool Univ. (LLB). Served War of 1939–45, RNVR, Fleet Air Arm, 1833 Sqdn (despatches 1944): Sub-Lt 1942; HMS Illustrious, Eastern and Pacific Fleets, 1943–45; Lieut 1944. Called to Bar, Gray's Inn, 1949. A Recorder of the Crown Court, 1972–76. Governor, Shrewsbury Sch., 1969. *Recreations:* golf, grandchildren, gardening. *Address:* 18 Abbey Road, West Kirby, Wirral L48 7EW. *T:* 0151–625 5796. *Clubs:* Royal Liverpool Golf; Royal and Ancient (St Andrews).

BOOTH, Rt. Hon. Albert Edward, PC 1976; CIMechE 1985; *b* 28 May 1928; *e s* of Albert Henry Booth and Janet Mathieson; *m* 1957, Joan Amis; three *s*. *Educ:* St Thomas's Sch., Winchester; S Shields Marine Sch.; Rutherford Coll. of Technology. Engineering Draughtsman. Election Agent, 1951 and 1955. County Borough Councillor, 1962–65. Exec. Dir, S Yorks Passenger Transport Exec., 1983–87. MP (Lab) Barrow-in-Furness, 1966–83; Minister of State, Dept of Employment, 1974–76; Sec. of State for Employment, 1976–79; Opposition spokesman on transport, 1979–83. Chm., Select Cttee on Statutory Instruments, 1970–74. Treasurer, Labour Party, 1984. Contested (Lab): Tynemouth, 1964; Barrow and Furness, 1983; Warrington South, 1987.

BOOTH, Anthony John, CBE 1993; CEng, FIEE; Chairman, Ericsson Ltd, since 1994; *b* 18 March 1939; *s* of Benjamin and Una Lavinia Booth; *m* 1965, Elspeth Marjorie (*née* Fraser); one *s* one *d*. *Educ:* Bungay Grammar Sch.; London Univ. (BScEng, DMS). Joined Post Office Res. Dept, 1957; Exec. Engr and Sen. Exec. Engr, Telecom HQ, 1965–71; Asst Staff Engr, Central HQ Appointments, 1971–74; Head of Section and Div., External Telecom Exec., 1974–78; Head of Div., THQ, 1978–79; Dir, Internat. Networks, 1979–80; Regional Dir, London Region, 1980–83; Corporate Dir, British Telecommunications PLC, 1984–94; Managing Director: BT International, 1983–91; Worldwide Networks, 1991; Business Communications, 1991–92; Special Businesses and Internat. Affairs Div., 1992–94. Gov., Ealing Coll., 1989–91; Gov., and Chm. Finance Cttee, Polytechnic of W London, 1991–92; Chm. of Govs, Thames Valley Univ., 1993–. Member, Guild of Freemen of City of London, 1982–. MInstD 1985; CIMgt (CBIM 1986); FRSA 1991. *Recreations:* opera, golf, synchronised swimming official. *Address:* 63 Hillsborough Park, Camberley, Surrey GU15 1HG.

BOOTH, Brian George, JP; FSS; Rector and Chief Executive, University of Central Lancashire (formerly Lancashire Polytechnic), since 1989; *b* 6 Sept. 1942; *s* of George and Ada Booth; *m* 1965, Barbara Ann (*née* Wright); two *d*. *Educ:* Univ. of Manchester (BA Econ 1964); Brunel Univ. (MTech 1972). FSS 1968. Asst Lectr in Statistics, High Wycombe Coll. of Technology, 1965–68; Lectr, Sen. Lectr, and Principal Lectr, Kingston Polytechnic, 1968–73; Head, Dept of Business and Admin, 1974–78, Dean, Faculty of Business and Management, 1978–82, Preston Polytechnic; Dep. Dir, Preston Polytechnic, later Lancashire Polytechnic, 1982–89. Chair of Bd, Preston Business Venture, 1983–92; Chair of Trustees, Preston Postgrad. Med. Centre, 1990–; non-exec. Dir, Preston Acute Hosps NHS Trust, 1993–. JP Preston, 1987. FRSA 1990. CIMgt 1992. *Recreations:* golf, watching Preston North End. *Address:* 9 Moorfield Close, Fulwood, Preston, Lancs PR2 4SW. *T:* Preston (01772) 864243.

BOOTH, Charles Leonard, CMG 1979; LVO 1961; HM Diplomatic Service, retired; re-employed in Foreign and Commonwealth Office, 1985–90; *b* 7 March 1925; *s* of Charles Leonard and Marion Booth; *m* 1958, Mary Gillian Emms; two *s* two *d*. *Educ:* Heywood Grammar Sch.; Pembroke Coll., Oxford Univ., 1942–43 and 1947–50. Served RA (Capt.), 1943–47. Joined HM Foreign Service, 1950; Foreign Office, 1950–51; Third and Second Secretary, Rangoon, 1951–55; FO, 1955–60 (Private Sec. to Parly Under-Sec. of State, 1958–60); First Sec., Rome, 1960–63; Head of Chancery, Rangoon, 1963–64, and Bangkok, 1964–67; FO, 1967–69. Counsellor, 1968; Deputy High Comr, Kampala, 1969–71; Consul-General and Counsellor (Administration), Washington, 1971–73; Counsellor, Belgrade, 1973–77; Ambassador to Burma, 1978–82; High Comr, Malta, 1982–85. Officer of Order of Merit of Italian Republic, 1961. *Recreations:* opera, gardening, walking. *Address:* 7 Queen Street, Southwold, Suffolk IP18 6EQ. *Club:* Travellers'.

BOOTH, Cherie, (Mrs A. C. L. Blair); QC 1995; *b* 23 Sept. 1954; *d* of Anthony and Gale Booth; *m* 1980, Rt Hon. Anthony Charles Lynton Blair, *qv*; two *s* one *d*. *Educ:* St Edmund's RC Primary Sch., Liverpool; Seafield Grammar Sch., Crosby; London Sch. of Economics (LLB). Called to the Bar, Lincoln's Inn, 1976; barrister specialisting in public law and employment law. Contested (Lab) Thanet North, 1983. *Publication:* (contrib.) Jordan's Employment Law Service, 1995. *Recreations:* theatre, the arts, keeping fit, enjoying my children. *Address:* 4/5 Gray's Inn Square, Gray's Inn, WC1R 5AY. *T:* 0171–404 5252.

BOOTH, Sir Christopher (Charles), Kt 1983; Harveian Librarian, Royal College of Physicians, since 1989; Convenor, History of 20th Century Group, Wellcome Institute for the History of Medicine, since 1990; *b* 22 June 1924; *s* of Lionel Barton Booth and Phyllis Petley Duncan; *m* 1st, 1959, Lavinia Loughridge, Belfast; one *s* one *d*; 2nd, 1970, Soad Tabaqchali; one *d*. *Educ:* Sedbergh Sch., Yorks; University of St Andrews; MB 1951, MD 1958 (Rutherford Gold Medal). Junior appointments at Dundee Royal Infirmary, Hammersmith Hosp. and Addenbrooke's Hosp., Cambridge; successively Medical Tutor, Lecturer in Medicine and Senior Lecturer, Postgraduate Medical School of London; Prof. and Dir of Dept of Medicine, RPMS, London Univ., 1966–77; Dir, Clin. Res. Centre, MRC, 1978–88. Member: Adv. Bd to Res. Councils, 1976–78; MRC, 1981–84; Chm., Medical Adv. Cttee, British Council, 1979–85; President: British Soc. of Gastroenterology, 1978–79; BMA, 1986–87; RSocMed, 1988; Johnson Soc., 1987–88; Soc. Social History of Medicine, 1990. Chm., Royal Naval Personnel Cttee, 1985–91. Trustee, Coeliac Soc., 1968–93 (Chm., 1968–83). FRCP 1964; FRCPEd 1967; Hon. FACP 1973; Hon. FRSM 1991. For. Mem., Amer. Philosophical Soc., 1981. Docteur (*hc*): Paris, 1975; Poitiers, 1981; Hon. LLD Dundee, 1982; Laurea (*hc*) Bologna, 1991. Dicke Gold Medal, Dutch Soc. of Gastroenterology, 1973; Ludwig Heilmeyer Gold Medal, German Soc. for Advances in Internal Medicine, 1982; Gold Medal, BMA, 1992. Chevalier de l'Ordre National du Mérite (France), 1977. *Publications:* (with Betsy C. Corner) Chain of Friendship: Letters of Dr John Fothergill of London, 1735–1780, 1971; (with G. Neale) Disorders of the Small Intestine, 1985; Doctors in Science and Society, 1987; papers in med. jls on relationship of nutritional disorders to disease of the alimentary tract, and on medical history. *Recreations:* fishing, history. *Address:* Royal College of Physicians, St Andrew's Place, NW1 4LE. *T:* 0171–935 1174.

BOOTH, Dr Clive; Vice-Chancellor, Oxford Brookes University, since 1992 (Director, Oxford Polytechnic, 1986–92); *b* 18 April 1943; *s* of Henry Booth and Freda Frankland; *m* 1969, Margaret Sardeson. *Educ:* King's Sch., Macclesfield; Trinity Coll., Cambridge (1st cl. Hons Nat Scis Tripos; MA 1969); Univ. of California, Berkeley (Harkness Fellow, 1973; MA 1974; PhD 1976). Joined DES, 1965; Prin. Pvte Sec. to Sec. of State for Educn and Science, 1975–77; Asst Sec., 1977–81; Dep. Dir, Plymouth Polytechnic, 1981–84; Mem., HM Inspectorate, DES, 1984–86. Asst Comr, Nat. Commn on Educn, 1992–.

Member: Governing Council, SRHE, 1981–90; Adv. Cttee, Brunel Univ. Educn Policy Centre, 1986–91; Computer Bd for Univs and Res. Councils, 1987–92; CNAA Cttee for Information and Develt Services, 1987–92; Fulbright Academic Administrators Selection Cttee, 1988–; British Council Cttee for Internat. Co-operation in Higher Educn, 1988– (Chm.); Council for Industry and Higher Educn, 1990–; Fulbright Commn, 1992–; Royal Soc. Study Gp on Higher Educn, 1991–; UFC Inf. Systems Cttee, 1991–93; Oxford Science Park Adv. Cttee, 1990–; Oxford Inst. of Nursing Bd, 1991–; Commonwealth Scholarships Commn, 1992–; UK ERASMUS Council, 1992– (Chm.); Oxford Trust Adv. Council; Chm., PCFC Steering Gp on Statistical Information, 1989–93; Vice-Chm., CVCP, 1992–. Director: Thames Action Resource Gp for Educn and Trng, 1986–; Thames Valley Technology Centre, 1989–; British Council, 1995–. Leverhulme Res. Fellow, 1983. Gov., Headington and Wheatley Park Schs. Jt Ed., Higher Educn Qly, 1986–; Mem., Editorial Bd, Oxford Review of Educn, 1990–. *Recreations:* cycling, walking, bridge, opera. *Address:* Oxford Brookes University, Gipsy Lane, Headington, Oxford OX3 0BP. *T:* Oxford (01865) 484801.

BOOTH, Sir Douglas Allen, 3rd Bt, *cr* 1916; writer and producer for television; *b* 2 Dec. 1949; *s* of Sir Philip Booth, 2nd Bt, and Ethel, *d* of Joseph Greenfield, NY, USA; *S* father 1960; *m* 1991, Yolanda Marcela (*née* Scantlebury); one *d. Educ:* Beverly Hills High Sch.; Harvard Univ. (Harvard Nat. Scholarship, Nat. Merit Scholarship, 1967); BA (*magna cum laude*) 1975. *Recreations:* music, back-packing. *Heir: b* Derek Blake Booth [*b* 7 April 1953; *m* 1981, Elizabeth Dreisbach; one *s* one *d*]. *Address:* 22933 Portage Circle Drive, Topanga, CA 90290, USA.

BOOTH, Eric Stuart, CBE 1971; FRS 1967; FEng 1976; Chairman, Yorkshire Electricity Board, 1972–79; *b* 14 Oct. 1914; *s* of Henry and Annie Booth; *m* 1945, Mary Elizabeth Melton (*d* 1987); two *d*; *m* 1988, Pauline Margaret Ford. *Educ:* Batley Grammar Sch.; Liverpool Univ. Apprentice, Metropolitan Vickers Electrical Co. Ltd, 1936–38; Technical Engineer, Yorks Electric Power Co., 1938–46; Dep., later City Electrical Engineer and Manager, Salford Corporation, 1946–48; various posts associated with construction of Power Stations with British, later Central Electricity Authority, 1948–57, Dep. Chief Engineer (Generation Design and Construction), 1957; Chief Design and Construction Engineer, 1958–59, Bd Mem. for Engrg, 1959–71, CEGB. Part-time Mem., UKAEA, 1965–72; Pres., IEE, 1976–77. Dir, British Electricity Internat., 1979–84; Consultant to Electricity Council, 1979–84. Hon. FIEE 1986. Hon. DTech Bradford, 1980. *Address:* Pinecroft, Upper Dunsforth, York YO5 9RU. *T:* Boroughbridge (01423) 322821.

BOOTH, Sir Gordon, KCMG 1980 (CMG 1969); CVO 1976; HM Diplomatic Service, retired; adviser on international trade and investment; Adviser, Hanson PLC, since 1989; Chairman: London Clubs International plc, since 1992; I-FAX Ltd, since 1992; Director, Allders International Ltd, since 1992; *b* 22 Nov. 1921; *s* of Walter and Grace Booth, Bolton, Lancs; *m* 1944, Jeanne Mary Kirkham; one *s* one *d. Educ:* Canon Slade Sch.; London Univ. (BCom). Served War of 1939–45: Capt. RAC and 13/18th Royal Hussars, 1941–46. Min. of Labour and Bd of Trade, 1946–55; Trade Comr, Canada and West Indies, 1955–65; Mem. HM Diplomatic Service, 1965–80; Counsellor (Commercial), British Embassy in Copenhagen, 1966–69; Dir, Coordination of Export Services, DTI, 1969–71; Consul-General, Sydney, 1971–74; HBM Consul-Gen., NY, and Dir-Gen. of Trade Develt in USA, 1975–80; Chm., SITPRO Bd, 1980–86. Director: Hanson PLC (formerly Hanson Trust), 1981–89; Bechtel Ltd, 1983–92. *Recreations:* golf, bridge. *Address:* Glade Lodge, The Glade, Kingswood, Surrey KT20 6LL. *T:* Tadworth (01737) 832156. *Club:* Walton Heath Golf.

BOOTH, Hartley; MP (C) Finchley, since 1992; *b* 17 July 1946; *s* of V. W. H. Booth and E. Morrow; *m* 1977, Adrianne Claire Cranefield; two *s* one *d. Educ:* Queen's Coll., Taunton; Bristol Univ. (LLB); Downing Coll., Cambridge (LLM, PhD). Called to the Bar, Inner Temple, 1970 (Scholar); in practice, 1970–84; Special Advr to Prime Minister and Mem., 10 Downing Street Policy Unit, 1984–88; Chief Exec., British Urban Develt, 1988–90; Consultant, Berwin Leighton (Solicitors), 1991–. PPS to Minister of State, FCO, 1992–94. Mem. Select Committees: Home Affairs, 1992; European Legislation, 1992. Vice President: Royal Life Saving Soc., 1990–; British Urban Regeneration Assoc., 1991–94 (Chm., 1990–91); AMA, 1992. European Editor, Current Law Year Books, 1974–84. *Publications:* British Extradition Law and Procedure, vol. I 1979, vol. II 1980; Return Ticket, 1994. *Recreations:* writing, swimming, delving into history, poetry. *Address:* House of Commons, SW1A 0AA. *T:* 0171–219 3000.

BOOTH, His Honour James; a Circuit Judge (formerly a County Court Judge), 1969–84; *b* 3 May 1914; *s* of James and Agnes Booth; *m* 1954, Joyce Doreen Mather; two *s* one *d. Educ:* Bolton Sch.; Manchester Univ. Called to Bar, Gray's Inn, 1936 (Arden Scholar, Gray's Inn). Town Clerk, Ossett, Yorks, 1939–41. RAFVR, 1941–46 (Flt-Lieut). Contested (L): West Leeds, 1945; Darwen, 1950. Recorder of Barrow-in-Furness, 1967–69. *Recreation:* fell walking. *Address:* Spinney End, Worsley, Lancs M28 2QN. *T:* 0161–790 2003.

BOOTH, John Antony W.; *see* Ward-Booth.

BOOTH, John Barton, FRCS; Consultant Otolaryngologist: Royal London Hospital (formerly London Hospital), since 1972; Royal Hospital of St Bartholomew, since 1995; Hon. Consultant, St Luke's Hospital for the Clergy, since 1983; Civil Consultant (Otology), Royal Air Force, since 1983; *b* 19 Nov. 1937; *s* of (Percy) Leonard Booth and Mildred Amy (*née* Wilson); *m* 1966, Carroll Griffiths; one *s. Educ:* Canford Sch., Dorset; King's Coll., London (AKC 1963); King's Coll. Hosp. Med. Sch. (MB, BS 1963). FRCS 1968. House Surgeon: Birmingham Accident Hosp., 1964; Hosp. for Sick Children, Gt Ormond St, 1965; House Surgeon, Registrar, Sen. Registrar, RNTNEH, 1966–70; Sen. Registrar, Royal Free Hosp., 1970–72; Clin. Assistant, Neuro-Otology, Nat. Hosp. for Nervous Diseases, 1968, 1971; Consultant Surgeon, RNTNEH, 1973–78; Hon. Consultant Laryngologist: Musicians Benevolent Fund, 1974–; Royal Coll. of Music, 1974–; Newspaper Press Fund, 1982–; Royal Opera House, Covent Gdn, 1983–; Royal Soc. of Musicians of GB, 1987–; Concert Artistes Assoc., 1987–; Webber-Douglas Acad. of Dramatic Art, 1987–. Hunterian Prof., RCS, 1980–81. Vice-Chm., 1960–61, Chm., 1961–62, Vice-Pres., 1962–63, Fedn of Univ. Conservatives; Mem., Gen. Purposes and Exec. Cttees, Cons. Party, 1961–62. FRSM 1967 (Mem. Council, 1980–88 and 1993–; Pres., Otology Sect., 1996–). MRAeS (Medical Aviation Gp) 1990. Howell Meml Prize (jtly), Univ. of London, 1988. Editor, Jl of Laryngology and Otology, 1987–92 (Asst Editor, 1979–87; Abstract Editor, 1987–94). *Publications:* (ed) Vol. 3, The Ear, of 5th edn of Scott-Brown's Otolaryngology, 1987, 6th edn 1995; chapters in: Rob and Smith, Operative Surgery, 3rd edn 1976; Audiology and Audiological Medicine, vol. I, 1981; Otologic Medicine and Surgery, 1988. *Recreations:* golf, the arts. *Address:* 18 Upper Wimpole Street, W1M 7TB. *T:* 0171–935 5631. *Clubs:* Royal Automobile, United and Cecil, MCC; New (St Andrews).

BOOTH, John Dick L.; *see* Livingston Booth.

BOOTH, Dame Margaret (Myfanwy Wood), DBE 1979; a Judge of the High Court, Family Division, 1979–94; *b* 1933; *d* of late Alec Wood Booth and Lilian May Booth; *m* 1st, 1982, Joseph Jackson, QC (*d* 1987); 2nd, 1993, Peter Glucksmann. *Educ:* Northwood Coll.; University Coll., London (LLM; Fellow, 1982). Called to the Bar, Middle Temple, 1956; Bencher, 1979. QC 1976. Chairman: Family Law Bar Assoc., 1976–78; Matrimonial Causes Procedure Cttee, 1982–85; Inner London Adv. Cttee on Justices of the Peace, 1990–93; Children Act Procedure Adv. Cttee, 1990; Children Act 1989 Adv. Cttee, 1991–93; Bar Central Selection Bd, 1993–; Family Law Cttee, Justice, 1993–. Pres., Family Mediators Assoc., 1994–. Vis. Prof. of Law, Liverpool Univ., 1994–. Governor, Northwood Coll., 1975–; Member, Council: Univ. Coll. London, 1980–84; Liverpool Univ., 1994–. Hon. LLD Liverpool, 1992. *Publications:* (co-ed) Rayden on Divorce, 10th-16th edns; (co-ed) Clarke Hall and Morrison on Children, 9th edn 1977, (cons. ed.) 10th edn 1985. *Address:* 15 Wellington House, Eton Road, NW3 4SY. *Club:* Reform.

BOOTH, Sir Michael Addison John W.; *see* Wheeler-Booth.

BOOTH, Peter John Richard; Textile National Trade Group Secretary, Transport and General Workers Union, since 1986; *b* 27 March 1949; *s* of Eric Albert and Edith Booth; *m* 1970, Edwina Ivy; three *s. Educ:* Little London Infant Sch.; Rawdon Littlemore Junior Sch., Rawdon; Benton Park Secondary Modern School. Dyers' Operative, 1964; National Union of Dyers, Bleachers and Textile Workers: District Officer, 1973; Nat. Research Officer, 1975; Nat. Organiser, 1980; transf. to TGWU, 1982; Nat. Trade Group Organiser, 1982. Director: Man-Made Fibres Industry Trng Adv. Bd, 1986–; Apparel, Knitting & Textiles Alliance, 1989–; Member: ITGLWF, 1986–; Confedn of British Wool Textiles Trng Bd, 1986–; Carpet Industry Trng Council, 1986– (Chm.); Nat. Textile Trng Gp, 1989– (Vice Pres.); Presidium, European TU Cttee, 1990–; Texiac, 1994–; Cotton & Allied Textiles Industry Adv. Cttee, 1986–. *Publication:* The Old Dog Strike, 1985. *Recreations:* walking, gardening, dominoes, chess. *Address:* Dye House, St John's Court, Yeadon, Leeds LS19 7NB. *T:* Leeds (0113) 250 2182. *Club:* Yeadon Trades Hall.

BOOTH, Richard George William Pitt; Chairman, Richard Booth (Bookshops) Ltd, Bookseller, since 1961; Chairman, Welsh Booksellers Association, since 1987; *b* 12 Sept. 1938; *m* 1987, Hope Estcourt Stuart (*née* Barrie). *Educ:* Rugby; Univ. of Oxford. *Publications:* Country Life Book of Book Collecting, 1976; Independence for Hay, 1977. *Recreations:* creating a monarchy in Hay (began home rule movement, 1 April 1977); gardening. *Address:* Hay Castle, Hay-on-Wye, via Hereford HR3.

BOOTH, Sir Robert (Camm), Kt 1977; CBE 1967; TD; Chairman, National Exhibition Centre Ltd, 1975–82 (Founder Director, 1970–82; Chief Executive, 1977–78); *b* 9 May 1916; *s* of late Robert Wainhouse and Gladys Booth; *m* 1939, Veronica Courtenay, *d* of late F. C. and Muriel Lamb; one *s* three *d. Educ:* Altrincham Grammar Sch.; Manchester Univ. (LLB). Called to Bar, Gray's Inn. War Service 8th (A) Bn Manchester Regt, France, Malta, Middle East, Italy, 1939–46. Manchester Chamber of Commerce, 1946–58; Sec., Birmingham Chamber of Industry and Commerce, 1958–65, Dir, 1965–78, Pres., 1978–79. Local non-exec. dir, Barclays Bank, 1977–84; Member: W Midlands Econ. Planning Council, 1974–77; BOTB Adv. Council, 1975–82; Midlands Adv. Bd, Legal and General Assurance Soc., 1979–86; Midlands and NW Bd, BR, 1979–85; Bd, Inst. of Occupational Health, 1980–90. Trustee, Nuffield Trust for the Forces of the Crown, 1977–. Life Mem., Court of Governors, 1969, Birmingham Univ. (Mem. Council, 1973–78); Governor, Sixth Form Coll., Solihull, 1974–77; Hon. Mem., British Exhbns Promotions Council, 1982. Overseas travel with 20 trade missions and author of marketing and economic publications. Marketor and Freeman, City of London, 1978. Hon. DSc Aston, 1975; Hon. FInstM; FRSA 1975. Midland Man of the Year Press Radio and TV Award, 1970. Officier de la Légion d'Honneur, 1982. *Address:* White House, 7 Sandal Rise, Solihull B91 3ET. *T:* 0121–705 5311.

BOOTH, Vernon Edward Hartley; *see* Booth, H.

BOOTH, Rev. William James; Sub-Dean of Her Majesty's Chapels Royal, Deputy Clerk of the Closet, Sub-Almoner and Domestic Chaplain to The Queen, since 1991; Priest-Vicar of Westminster Abbey, since 1987; *b* 3 Feb. 1939; *s* of William James Booth and Elizabeth Ethel Booth. *Educ:* Ballymena Acad., Co. Antrim; TCD (MA). Curate, St Luke's Parish, Belfast, 1962–64; Chaplain, Cranleigh Sch., Surrey, 1965–74. Priest-in-Ordinary to The Queen, 1976–91. Chaplain, Westminster School, London, 1974–91. Organiser, PHAB annual residential courses at Westminster (and formerly at Cranleigh). *Recreations:* music, hi-fi, cooking. *Address:* Marlborough Gate, St James's Palace, SW1A 1BG. *T:* 0171–930 6609.

BOOTH-CLIBBORN, Rt. Rev. Stanley Eric Francis; Bishop of Manchester, 1979–92; *b* 20 Oct. 1924; *s* of late Eric and Lucille Booth-Clibborn; *m* 1958, Anne Roxburgh Forrester, *d* of late Rev. William Roxburgh Forrester, MC; two *s* two *d. Educ:* Highgate School; Oriel Coll., Oxford (MA); Westcott House, Cambridge. Served RA, 1942–45; Royal Indian Artillery, 1945–47, Temp. Captain. Curate, Heeley Parish Church, Sheffield, 1952–54, The Attercliffe Parishes, Sheffield, 1954–56; Training Sec., Christian Council of Kenya, 1956–63; Editor-in-Chief, East African Venture Newspapers, Nairobi, 1963–67; Leader, Lincoln City Centre Team Ministry, 1967–70; Vicar, St Mary the Great, University Church, Cambridge, 1970–79. Hon. Canon, Ely Cathedral, 1976–79. Member: Div. of Internat. Affairs, BCC, 1968–80; Standing Cttee, General Synod, 1981–90; BCC delegn to Namibia, 1981; Chm., Namibia Communications Trust, 1983–95; Pres., St Ann's Hospice, 1979–92. Moderator, Movement for Ordination of Women, 1979–82. Introduced to House of Lords, 1985. Hon. Fellow, Manchester Polytechnic, 1989. Hon. DD Manchester, 1994. *Publication:* Taxes—Burden or Blessing?, 1991. *Recreations:* photography, tennis, listening to music. *Address:* 9 Kirkhill Drive, Edinburgh EH16 5DH. *T:* 0131–662 0443.

BOOTHBY, Sir Brooke (Charles), 16th Bt *cr* 1660, of Broadlow Ash, Derbyshire; *b* 6 April 1949; *s* of Sir Hugo Robert Brooke Boothby, 15th Bt and (Evelyn) Ann (*d* 1993), *d* of late H. C. R. Homfray; *S* father, 1986; *m* 1976, Georgiana Alexandra, *o d* of late Sir John Wriothesley Russell, GCVO, CMG; two *d. Educ:* Eton; Trinity Coll., Cambridge (BA Econs). Man. Dir, Fontygary Leisure, 1979–; Chairman: Tourism Quality Services Ltd, 1990–; Associated Quality Services, 1994–. Chairman: Historic Houses Assoc. Inheritance Cttee, 1984–86; Nat. Caravan Council Parks Div., 1987–90. Pres., Glamorgan Br., CLA, 1992–94. High Sheriff, South Glamorgan, 1986–87. *Recreation:* shooting. *Heir: kinsman* George William Boothby [*b* 18 June 1948; *m* 1977, Sally Louisa Thomas; three *d*]. *Address:* Fonmon Castle, Barry, South Glamorgan CF62 3ZN. *T:* Rhoose (01446) 710206, *Fax:* (01446) 711687.

BOOTHMAN, Campbell Lester; His Honour Judge Boothman; a Circuit Judge, since 1988; *b* 3 Sept. 1942; *s* of Gerald and Ann Boothman; *m* 1966, Penelope Evelyn Pepe; three *s. Educ:* Oundle; King's College, London. Called to the Bar, Inner Temple, 1965. A Recorder, 1985–88. *Recreations:* skiing, squash. *Address:* The Glen, Tower House Lane, Wraxall, Bristol BS19 1JX.

BOOTHMAN, Derek Arnold, FCA; Deputy Chairman, Central Manchester Development Corporation, since 1988; Non-Executive Director, Remploy Ltd, since 1987; *b* 5 June 1932; *s* of Eric Randolph Boothman and Doris Mary Boothman; *m* 1958,

Brenda Margaret; one *s* one *d*. *Educ:* William Hulme's Grammar Sch., Manchester. Articled to J. Needham & Co., 1948; Mem., ICA, 1954; National Service, RAF, 1954–56; Partner: J. Needham & Co. (now part of Binder Hamlyn), 1957; Binder Hamlyn, Chartered Accts, 1974–88. President: Manchester Chartered Accountants Students Soc., 1967–68; Manchester Soc. of Chartered Accountants, 1968–69; Institute of Chartered Accountants in England and Wales: Council Member, 1969–; Treasurer, 1981–83; Vice-Pres., 1983–85; Dep. Pres., 1985–86; Pres., 1986–87. Member, Accounting Standards Cttee, 1974–82. Chm. of Governors, William Hulme's Grammar Sch., 1988–; Mem. Ct, Univ. of Manchester, 1990–. Liveryman, Worshipful Company of Chartered Accountants, 1976–. *Publications:* contribs to professional press and lectures on professional topics, internationally. *Recreations:* cricket, skiing, gardening, travel. *Address:* Ashworth Dene, Wilmslow Road, Mottram St Andrew, Cheshire SK10 4QH. *T:* Prestbury (01625) 829101. *Clubs:* St James's (Manchester); Withington Golf (Manchester) (past Captain).

BOOTHMAN, Nicholas, CEng; Director of Technology, Metropolitan Police Service, since 1992; *b* 16 Dec. 1941; *s* of late Frederick Boothman and Sarah Ellen (*née* Kirk); *m* 1964, Ernestine Carole Jane Billings; one *d*. *Educ:* Threshfield Sch.; Ermysteds Grammar Sch., Skipton; Univ. of Birmingham (BSc Physics). CEng, MIEE 1972. Research at GEC Hirst Res. Centre, Wembley, 1963–72; project management of communication systems for RAF, MoD (PE), 1972–77; Project Manager, Metropolitan Police Office, 1977–88; Chief Engr, Metropolitan Police, 1988–92. *Recreations:* amateur musician, watching cricket, railways, unavoidable gardening. *Address:* Metropolitan Police Service, 1 Drummond Gate, SW1V 2JJ. *T:* 0171–230 8588.

BOOTHROYD, Rt. Hon. Betty, PC 1992; MP West Bromwich West; Speaker of the House of Commons, since 1992; *b* Yorkshire, 8 Oct. 1929; *d* of Archibald and Mary Boothroyd. *Educ:* Dewsbury Coll. of Commerce and Art. Personal/Political Asst to Labour Ministers. Delegate to N Atlantic Assembly, 1974. MP (Lab) West Bromwich, May 1973–1974, West Bromwich West, 1974–92 (when elected Speaker); an Asst Govt Whip, Oct. 1974–Nov. 1975; Dep. Chm. of Ways and Means, and Dep. Speaker, 1987–92. Member: Select Cttee on Foreign Affairs, 1979–81; Speaker's Panel of Chairmen, 1979–87; House of Commons Commn, 1983–87. Mem., European Parlt, 1975–77. Mem., Labour Party NEC, 1981–87. Contested (Lab): SE Leicester (by-elec.), 1957; Peterborough (gen. elec.), 1959; Nelson and Colne (by-elec.), 1968; Rossendale (gen. elec.), 1970. Chancellor, Open Univ., 1994–. Freeman: Borough of Sandwell, 1992; Borough of Kirklees, 1992; City of London, 1993. Hon. LLD: Birmingham, 1992; South Bank, 1992; Leicester, 1993; Cambridge, 1994; Hon. DLitt Bradford, 1993; DUniv: Leeds Metropolitan, 1993; North London, 1993; Hon. DCL Oxford, 1995. *Address:* Speaker's House, Westminster, SW1A 0AA.

BOOTLE-WILBRAHAM, family name of **Baron Skelmersdale.**

BOR, Walter George, CBE 1975; FRIBA, DistTP; FRTPI; FRSA; Consultant: Llewelyn-Davies Planning, since 1984; Llewelyn-Davies Weeks, 1976–84; Partner, Llewelyn-Davies Weeks Forestier-Walker & Bor, London, 1966–76; *b* 1916, Czech parentage; father chemical engineer; *m* Dr Muriel Blackburn; two *s* one *d*. *Educ:* Prague Univ. (degree of Arch.); Bartlett Sch. of Architecture and Sch. of Planning and Regional Research, London (Dip.). Private architectural practice, London, 1946–57; LCC Architect's Dept, 1947–62 (Dep. Planning Officer with special responsibility for civic design, 1960–62); Liverpool City Planning Officer, 1962–66. Mem. Minister's Planning Advisory Gp, 1964–65. In private practice as architect and planning consultant, 1966–. Pres., Town Planning Inst., 1970–71; Vice-Pres., Housing Centre Trust, 1971–. Visiting Professor: Princeton Univ., 1977–79; Rice Univ., Houston, 1980–81. Mem., Severn Barrage Cttee, 1978–81; Consultant, UNDP, Cyprus, 1982–83; Advr, Shenzhen City Planning Commn, China, 1987–89; Consultant to: municipalities of Prague, Vienna and Beijing, 1990–94; Prague strategic plan know-how Fund, 1994–. Pres., London Forum of Civic Socs, 1989–. *Publications:* Liverpool Planning Policy, 1965; Liverpool City Centre Plan (jt), 1966; Two New Cities in Venezuela (jt), 1967–69; The Milton Keynes Plan (jt), 1970; Airport City (Third London Airport urbanisation studies) (jt), 1970; The Making of Cities, 1972; Bogota Urban Development for UNDP (jt), 1974; Concept Plan for Tehran new city centre, 1974; Shetland Draft Structure Plan, 1975; (jtly) Unequal City: Birmingham Inner Area Study, 1977; (jtly) Shenzhen, China: airport and urban design reports, 1987; articles for jls of RTPI, RIBA, TCPA; Urbanistica, Habitat Internat.; Ekistics. *Recreations:* music, theatre, sketching, sculpting, pottery. *Address:* 99 Swains Lane, Highgate, N6 6PJ. *T:* 0181–340 6540. *Club:* Reform.

BORCHERDS, Prof. Richard Ewen, FRS 1994; Professor, Department of Mathematics, University of California at Berkeley, since 1993; *b* 29 Nov. 1959; *s* of Dr Peter Howard Borcherds and Margaret Elizabeth Borcherds (*née* Greenfield). *Educ:* Trinity Coll., Cambridge (BA, MA; PhD 1985). Research Fellow, Trinity Coll., Cambridge, 1983–87; Morrey Asst Prof., Univ. of California, Berkeley, 1987–88; Royal Society Univ Res. Fellow, Univ. of Cambridge, 1988–92; Lectr, Univ. of Cambridge, 1992–93. *Publications:* papers in math. jls. *Address:* Department of Mathematics, University of California, Berkeley, CA 94720–3840, USA. *T:* (510) 6428464.

BORDER, Allan Robert, AO 1989; with Castlemaine Perkins, since 1984; professional cricketer; Captain, Australian cricket team, 1984–94; *b* 27 July 1955; *s* of John and Sheila Border; *m* 1980, Jane, *d* of John and Eve Hiscox; two *d*. Educ: N Sydney Tech. Sch.; N Sydney High Sch. First class cricket début, for NSW, 1976; professional cricketer, Queensland State, 1977– (Captain, 1983–84); Test début, 1978; played 156 Test matches for Australia, with record of 93 as Captain, scored 27 centuries and 2 double centuries, record total of 11,174 Test runs, also took 39 wickets and record 156 catches; in all first-class cricket matches to 1994, has scored 25,551 runs incl. 68 centuries, and taken 102 wickets and 345 catches. With Ronald McConnell Hldgs, 1980–84. *Address:* c/o 90 Jolimont Street, Jolimont, Vic 3002, Australia.

BOREEL, Sir Francis (David), 13th Bt, *cr* 1645; Counsellor, Netherlands Foreign Service, 1966–87 (Attaché, 1956), retired; *b* 14 June 1926; *s* of Sir Alfred Boreel, 12th Bt and Countess Reiniera Adriana (*d* 1957), *d* of Count Francis David Schimmelpenninck; *S* father 1964; *m* 1964, Suzanne Campagne; three *d*. *Educ:* Utrecht Univ. *Recreations:* tennis, sailing. *Heir: kinsman* Stephen Gerard Boreel [*b* 9 Feb. 1945; *m* Francien P. Kooyman; one *s*]. *Address:* Kapellestraat 25, 4351 A. L. Veere, Netherlands.

BOREHAM, Sir Leslie Kenneth Edward, Kt 1972; a Judge of the High Court, Queen's Bench Division, 1972–92; Presiding Judge, North Eastern Circuit, 1974–80; Deputy Chairman, Agricultural Lands Tribunal; *b* 19 Oct. 1918; *o s* of Harry Edward and Mary Amelia Boreham; *m* 1941, Rachel, *o c* of T. M. Harding; one *s* one *d*. *Educ:* Bungay Grammar Sch. Served War of 1939–45, RAF. Called to the Bar at Lincoln's Inn, Nov. 1947, Bencher 1972; admitted to Bar of St Helena, 1962. Joined South-Eastern Circuit. Dep. Chm. 1962–65, Chm. 1965–71, East Suffolk QS; QC 1965; Recorder of Margate, 1968–71. Chm., Lord Chancellor's Cttee on Trng of Magistrates, 1974–82; Pres., Central Council of Probation Cttees, 1976–82; Parole Bd, 1979–81 (Vice Chm., 1981). *Recreations:* gardening, golf. *Address:* Royal Courts of Justice, Strand, WC2A 2LL.

BORG, Alan Charles Nelson, CBE 1991; PhD; FSA; Director, Victoria and Albert Museum, since 1995; *b* 21 Jan. 1942; *s* of late Charles John Nelson Borg and Frances Mary Olive Hughes; *m* 1st, 1964, Anne (marr. diss.), *d* of late Dr William Blackmore; one *s* one *d*; 2nd, 1976, Lady Caroline, *d* of late Captain Lord Francis Hill, *yr s* of 6th Marquess of Downshire; two *d*. *Educ:* Westminster Sch.; Brasenose Coll., Oxford (MA); Courtauld Inst. of Art (PhD). Lecteur d'anglais, Université d'Aix-Marseille, 1964–65; Lectr, History of Art, Indiana Univ., 1967–69; Asst Prof. of History of Art, Princeton Univ., 1969–70; Asst Keeper of the Royal Armouries, HM Tower of London, 1970–78; Keeper, Sainsbury Centre for Visual Arts, Univ. of E Anglia, 1978–82; Dir Gen., Imperial War Mus., 1982–95. Member: British Nat. Cttee for Hist. of Second World War, 1982–95; Bd of War Studies, KCL, 1982–95; COPUS, 1992–95; Council, Museums Assoc., 1992–95; Adv. Cttee on Public Records, 1993–; Chm., Nat. Inventory of War Memls, 1988–. President: Elizabethan Club, 1994–; Meyrick Soc., 1994–. Hon. FRCA 1991. *Publications:* Architectural Sculpture in Romanesque Provence, 1972; European Swords and Daggers in the Tower of London, 1974; Torture and Punishment, 1975; Heads and Horses, 1976; Arms and Armour in Britain, 1979; (ed with A. R. Martindale) The Vanishing Past: studies presented to Christopher Hohler, 1981; War Memorials, 1991; articles in learned jls. *Recreations:* fencing (Oxford blue, 1962, 1963), music, travel. *Address:* Telegraph House, 36 West Square, SE11 4SP. *Club:* Special Forces.

BORG, Björn Rune; tennis player; *b* 6 June 1956; *s* of Rune and Margaretha Borg; *m* 1980, Mariana Simionescu (marr. diss. 1984); one *s* by Jannike Bjorling; *m* 1989, Loredana Berte (marr. diss. 1992). *Educ:* Blombacka Sch., Södertälje. Started to play tennis at age of 9; won Wimbledon junior title, 1972; became professional player in 1972. Mem., Swedish Davis Cup team, annually 1972–80 (youngest player ever in a winning Davis Cup team, 1975). Championship titles: Italian, 1974, 1978; French, 1974, 1975, 1978, 1979, 1980, 1981; Wimbledon, record of 5 consecutive singles titles, 1976–80; World Champion, 1978, 1979, 1980; Masters, 1980, 1981. *Publication:* (with Eugene Scott) Björn Borg: my life and game, 1980. *Address:* c/o International Management Group, The Pier House, Strand on the Green, Chiswick, W4 3NN.

BORG COSTANZI, Prof. Edwin J.; Chairman, Public Service Commission, Malta, since 1992; *b* 8 Sept. 1925; 2nd *s* of late Michael Borg Costanzi and M. Stella (*née* Camilleri); *m* 1948, Lucy Valentino; two *s* one *d*. *Educ:* Lyceum, Malta; Royal University of Malta (BSc, BE&A); Balliol College, Oxford (BA 1946, MA 1952); Malta Rhodes Scholar, 1945. Professor of Mathematics, Royal University of Malta, 1950–64; Rector, Univ. of Malta, 1964–80 and 1988–90; Vis. Fellow, Univ. of Southampton, 1980–82; Professorial Res. Fellow, 1982–85, Hd of Dept of Computer Sci., 1985–87, Brunel Univ. Chm., 1976–77, Mem., 1965–66, 1968–69, 1972–74, 1977–78, Council of ACU. Chm., Public Service Reform Commn, 1990–. Hon. DLitt Malta, 1993. *Recreations:* fishing, photography. *Address:* 35 Don M. Rua Street, Sliema, SLM 10, Malta. *Club:* Casino (Valletta Malta).

BORGES, Thomas William Alfred; Managing Director, Thomas Borges & Partners, since 1949; Deputy Chairman, Phoenix Timber Group PLC, 1986–91; *b* 1 April 1923; *s* of Arthur Borges, Prague, and Paula Borges; *m* 1st (marr. diss.); 2nd, 1966, Serena Katherine Stewart (*née* Jamieson); two *s*. *Educ:* Dunstable Grammar Sch.; Luton Technical Coll. Served War, 1941–45. Trained in banking, shipping and industry, 1945–49; Dir, Borges Law & Co., Sydney and Melbourne, 1951; Chm., Smith Whitworth Ltd, 1974–80; Dir, Trust Co. of Australia (UK) Ltd, 1991–94. Governor, Royal National Orth. Hosp., 1968– (Dep. Chm., 1978–80, Chm., 1980–82); Dir, Inst. of Orths, Univ. of London, 1968– (Dep. Chm., 1978–80, Chm., 1980–82); Member: Grants Cttee, King Edward VII Hosp. Fund, 1975–80; Council, Professions Supp. to Medicine, 1980–88 (Dep. Chm., 1982–88); Sir Robert Menzies Centre for Australian Studies, 1993–; Treasurer, Riding for Disabled Assoc., 1977–84. Chm., Australian Art Foundn, 1984–. Trustee, Sir Robert Menzies Meml Trust, 1981–. FInstD. *Publication:* Two Expeditions of Discovery in North West and Western Australia by George Grey, 1969. *Recreations:* travel, collecting Australiana, riding, swimming. *Address:* Porchester Lodge, 70 Westbourne Park Road, W2 5PJ. *T:* 0171–229 5220. *Club:* Garrick.

BORINGDON, Viscount; Mark Lionel Parker; *b* 22 Aug. 1956; *s* and *heir* of 6th Earl of Morley, *qv*; *m* 1983, Carolyn Jill, *d* of Donald McVicar, Meols, Wirral, Cheshire; three *d*. *Educ:* Eton. Commissioned, Royal Green Jackets, 1976. *Address:* Pound House, Yelverton, Devon PL20 7LJ.

BORLAND, David Morton; former Chairman, Cadbury Ltd; Director, Cadbury Schweppes Ltd; *b* 17 Jan. 1911; *s* of David and Annie J. Borland; *m* 1947, Nessa Claire Helwig; one *s* one *d*. *Educ:* Glasgow Academy; Brasenose Coll., Oxford (BA). Management Trainee, etc., Cadbury Bros Ltd, Bournville, Birmingham, 1933. War service, Royal Marines (Lieut-Col), 1940–46. Sales Manager, J. S. Fry & Sons Ltd, Somerdale, Bristol, 1946; Sales Dir and a Man. Dir, J. S. Fry & Sons Ltd, 1948; a Man. Dir, British Cocoa & Chocolate Co. Ltd, 1959, and of Cadbury Bros Ltd, 1963. Mem. Govt Cttee of Inquiry into Fatstock and Meat Marketing and Distribution, 1962. Bristol University: Mem. Council, 1962–88; Pro-Chancellor, 1983–89; Hon. Fellow, 1989. Hon. LLD Bristol, 1980. *Recreation:* golf. *Address:* Garden Cottage, 3 Hollymead Lane, Stoke Bishop, Bristol BS9 1LN. *T:* Bristol (0117) 968 3978. *Clubs:* Achilles; Vincent's (Oxford).

BORLAUG, Norman Ernest, PhD; Consultant, International Center for Maize and Wheat Improvement; *b* 25 March 1914; *s* of Henry O. and Clara Vaala Borlaug; *m* 1937, Margaret Gibson; one *s* one *d*. *Educ:* Univ. of Minnesota; BS 1937; MS 1940; PhD 1942. US Forest Service (USDA), 1935–1937–1938; Biologist, Dupont de Nemours & Co, 1942–44; Plant Pathologist and Genetist, Wheat Improvement, employed by Rockefeller Foundn (Associate Dir of Agricultural Sciences) and Dir of Wheat Program, International Center for Maize and Wheat Improvement (CIMMYT), 1944–79. Dir, Population Crisis Cttee, 1971; Asesor Especial, Fundación para Estudios de la Población (Mexico), 1971–; Member: Adv. Council, Renewable Natural Resources Foundn, 1973–; Citizens' Commn on Science, Law and Food Supply, 1973–; Council for Agricl Science and Tech., 1973–; Commn on Critical Choices for Americans 1973–. Mem., Nat. Acad. of Scis (USA), 1968; Foreign Mem., Royal Soc., 1987. Outstanding Achievement Award, Univ. of Minnesota, 1959; Sitara-Imtiaz (Star of Distinction) (Pakistan), 1968, Hilal-I-Imtiaz 1978. Nobel Peace Prize, 1970. Holds numerous hon. doctorates in Science, both from USA and abroad; and more than 30 Service Awards by govts and organizations, including US Medal of Freedom, 1977. *Publications:* more than 70 scientific and semi-popular articles. *Recreations:* hunting, fishing, baseball, wrestling, football, golf. *Address:* c/o International Center for Maize and Wheat Improvement (CIMMYT), Apartado Postal 6–641, Lisboa 27, 06600 Mexico DF, Mexico. *T:* 7613311.

BORLEY, Lester, CBE 1993; Secretary General Europa Nostra, The Hague, since 1993; *b* 7 April 1931; *er s* of Edwin Richard Borley and Mary Dorena Davies; *m* Mary Alison, *e d* of Edward John Pearce and Kathleen Florence Barratt; three *d*. *Educ:* Dover Grammar Sch.; Queen Mary Coll. and Birkbeck Coll., London Univ. Pres. of Union, QMC, 1953; Dep. Pres., Univ. of London Union, 1954; ESU debating team tour of USA, 1955. Joined British Travel Assoc., 1955; Asst to Gen. Manager, USA, 1957–61; Manager: Chicago

Office, 1961–64; Australia, 1964–67; West Germany, 1967–69; Chief Executive: Scottish Tourist Bd, 1970–75; English Tourist Bd, 1975–83; Dir, Nat. Trust for Scotland, 1983–93. Member: Exec. Cttee, Scotland's Garden Scheme, 1970–75, 1983–93; Council, Nat. Gardens Scheme, 1975–83; Park and Gardens Cttee, Zool Soc. of London, 1979–83. Governor, Edinburgh Film House, 1987–. Founder Fellow, Tourism Soc., 1978. FRSA 1982. Hon. FRSGS 1989. Hon. DLitt Robert Gordon Inst. of Technology, Aberdeen, 1991. Honorable Kentucky Col, 1963. *Recreations:* listening to music, looking at pictures, gardening. *Address:* 4 Belford Place, Edinburgh EH4 3DH. *T:* and *Fax:* 0131–332 2364; The Old Schoolhouse, Wester Elchies, Morayshire AB3 9SD. *Club:* New (Edinburgh).

BORN, Prof. Gustav Victor Rudolf, FRCP 1976; FRS 1972; FKC; Professor of Pharmacology, King's College, University of London, 1978–86, now Emeritus; Director, The William Harvey Research Institute, St Bartholomew's Hospital Medical College, since 1989; *b* 29 July 1921; *s* of late Prof. Max Born, FRS; *m* 1st, 1950, Wilfrida Ann Plowden-Wardlaw (marr. diss., 1961); two *s* one *d*; 2nd, 1962, Dr Faith Elizabeth Maurice-Williams; one *s* one *d*. *Educ:* Oberrealschule, Göttingen; Perse Sch., Cambridge; Edinburgh Academy; University of Edinburgh. Vans Dunlop Scholar; MB, ChB, 1943; DPhil (Oxford), 1951, MA 1956. Med. Officer, RAMC, 1943–47; Mem. Scientific Staff, MRC, 1952–53; Research Officer, Nuffield Inst. for Med. Research, 1953–60 and Deptl Demonstrator in Pharmacology, 1956–60, University of Oxford; Vandervell Prof. of Pharmacology, RCS and Univ. of London, 1960–73; Sheild Prof. of Pharmacology, Univ. of Cambridge, and Fellow, Gonville and Caius Coll., Cambridge, 1973–78. Vis. Prof. in Chem., NW Univ., Illinois, 1970; William S. Creasy Vis. Prof. in Clin. Pharmacol., Brown Univ., 1977; Prof. of Fondation de France, Paris, 1982–84. Hon. Dir, MRC Thrombosis Res. Gp, 1964–73. Scientific Advr, Vandervell Foundn, 1967–; Pres., Internat. Soc. on Thrombosis and Haemostasis, 1977–79; Trustee, Heineman Med. Res. Center, Charlotte, NC, 1981–. Member: Editl Board, Handbook of Experimental Pharmacology; Cttee of Enquiry into Relationship of Pharmaceut. Industry with Nat. Health Service (Sainsbury Cttee), 1965–67; Kuratorium, Lipid Liga, Munich; Kuratorium, Ernst Jung Foundn, Hamburg, 1983–91; Forensic Science Adv. Gp, Home Office. Hon. Life Mem., New York Acad. of Scis. Lectures: Beyer, Wisconsin Univ., 1969; Sharpey-Schäfer, Edinburgh Univ., 1973; Cross, RCS, 1974; Wander, Bern Univ., 1974; Johnson Meml, Paris, 1975; Lo Yuk Tong Foundn, Hong Kong Univ., and Heineman Meml, Charlotte, NC, 1978; Carlo Erba Foundn, Milan, 1979; Sir Henry Dale, RCS, 1981; Rokitansky, Vienna, and Oration to Med. Soc., London, 1983. Mem., Akad. Leopoldina; Hon. Mem., German Physiological Soc.; Corresp. Member: German Pharmacological Soc.; Royal Belgian Acad. of Medicine; Rheinisch-Westfälische Akad. der Wissenschaften, Düsseldorf. Hon. Fellow, St Peter's Coll., Oxford, 1972; FKC 1988. Hon. D de l'Univ.: Bordeaux, 1978; Paris, 1987; Hon. MD: Münster, 1980; Leuven, 1981; Edinburgh, 1982; Munich, 1989; Hon. DSc: Brown Univ., 1987; Loyola Univ. Albrecht von Haller Medal, Göttingen Univ., 1979; Ratschow Medal, Internat. Kur. of Angiology, 1980; Auenbrugger Medal, Graz Univ., 1984; Royal Medal, Royal Soc., 1987; Morawitz Prize, German Soc. for Cardiovascular Res., 1990; Pfleger Prize, Robert Pfleger Foundn, Bamberg, 1990; Alexander von Humboldt Award, 1995. Chevalier de l'Ordre National de Mérite, France, 1980. *Publications:* articles in scientific jls and books. *Recreations:* music, history, being in the country. *Address:* William Harvey Research Institute, St Bartholomew's Hospital Medical College, Charterhouse Square, EC1M 6BQ. *T:* 0171–982 6070; 10 Woodland Gardens, N10 3UA. *Club:* Garrick.

BORODALE, Viscount; Sean David Beatty; *b* 12 June 1973; *s* and *heir* of 3rd Earl Beatty, *qv*.

BORODIN, George; *see* Sava, George.

BORRETT, Ven. Charles Walter; Archdeacon of Stoke-upon-Trent and Hon. Canon of Lichfield Cathedral, 1971–82, now Archdeacon Emeritus; Priest-in-charge of Sandon, Diocese of Lichfield, 1975–82; a Chaplain to the Queen, 1980–86; *b* 15 Sept. 1916; *s* of Walter George Borrett, farmer, and Alice Frances (*née* Mecrow); *m* 1941, Jean Constable, *d* of Charles Henry and Lilian Constable Pinson, Wolverhampton; one *s* two *d*. *Educ:* Framlingham Coll., Suffolk; Emmanuel Coll., Cambridge (MA); Ridley Hall, Cambridge. Deacon, 1941; Priest, 1943; Curate: of All Saints, Newmarket, 1941–45; of St Paul, Wolverhampton, 1945–48; of Tettenhall Regis, 1948–49; Vicar of Tettenhall Regis, 1949–71; Rural Dean of Trysull, 1958–71; Prebendary of Flixton in Lichfield Cathedral, 1964–71. Chm., C of E Council for Deaf, 1976–86. Fellow, Woodard Schs, 1972–86. *Address:* 34 Queensway, Mildenhall, Bury St Edmunds IP28 7JL. *T:* Mildenhall (01638) 712718. *Club:* Hawks (Cambridge).

BORRETT, Louis Albert Frank; a Chairman, Police Disciplinary Appeals, 1987–89; *b* 8 Aug. 1924; *e s* of late Albert B. Borrett and Louise Alfreda Eudoxie Forrestier; *m* 1946, Barbara Betty, *er d* of late Frederick Charles Bamsey and of Lily Gertrude Thompson. *Educ:* France and England; Folkestone Teachers' Trng Coll.; King's Coll., Univ. of London (LLB 1954). Called to the Bar, Gray's Inn, 1955. Served War, Army: volunteered, 1940; RASC, London Dist and South Eastern Comd; commnd Royal Sussex Regt, 1944; served India and Burma Border; Intell. Officer, 9th Royal Sussex, during invasion of Malaya, 1945; GSO III (Ops), ALFSEA, 1946 (Burma Star, Defence Medal, Victory Medal); demob., 1946 (Captain). Schoolmaster, 1947–53; barrister, in practice on South-Eastern circuit, 1955–86; a Recorder, 1980–89. Assist Comr, Boundary Commn, 1964–67. *Recreations:* music, the French language. *Address:* 54 Farm Close, East Grinstead, West Sussex RH19 3QG. *T:* East Grinstead (01342) 312350.

BORRETT, Neil Edgar; Director, Property Holdings, Department of the Environment, since 1990; *b* 10 March 1940; *m* 1965; two *d*. *Educ:* Coll. of Estate Management. FRICS 1969. Dir of property cos, 1963–90. *Address:* Property Holdings, St Christopher House, Southwark Street, SE1 0TE.

BORRIE, Sir Gordon (Johnson), Kt 1982; QC 1986; FCIArb; Director General of Fair Trading, 1976–92; *b* 13 March 1931; *s* of Stanley Borrie, Solicitor; *m* 1960, Dorene, *d* of Herbert Toland, Toronto, Canada; no *c*. *Educ:* John Bright Grammar Sch., Llandudno; Univ. of Manchester (LLB, LLM). Barrister-at-Law and Harmsworth Scholar of the Middle Temple; called to Bar, Middle Temple, 1952; Bencher, 1980. Nat. Service: Army Legal Services, HQ Brit. Commonwealth Forces in Korea, 1952–54. Practice as a barrister, London, 1954–57. Lectr and later Sen. Lectr, Coll. of Law, 1957–64; University of Birmingham: Sen. Lectr in Law, 1965–68; Prof. of English Law and Dir, Inst. of Judicial Admin, 1969–76; Dean of Faculty of Law, 1974–76; Hon. Prof. of Law, 1989–. Member: Parole Bd for England and Wales, 1971–74; CNAA Legal Studies Bd, 1971–76; Circuit Adv. Cttee, Birmingham Gp of Courts, 1972–74; Council, Consumers' Assoc., 1972–75; Consumer Protection Adv. Cttee, 1973–76; Equal Opportunities Commn, 1975–76; Chm., Commn on Social Justice, 1992–94. Director: Woolwich Building Soc., 1992–; Three Valleys Water, 1992–; Mirror Group, 1993–; UAPT/Infolink, 1993–94; TeleWest Communications Group, 1994–. Pres., Inst. of Trading Standards Admin, 1992– (Vice-Pres., 1985–92). Sen. Treasurer, Nat. Union of Students, 1955–58. Hon. Mem., SPTL, 1989. Contested (Lab): Croydon, NE, 1955; Ilford, S, 1959. Gov., Birmingham Coll. of Commerce, 1966–70. FCIArb 1992; FRSA 1982. Hon. LLD: City of London Polytechnic, 1989; Manchester Univ., 1990; Hull Univ., 1991; Dundee Univ., 1993. *Publications:* Commercial Law, 1962, 6th edn 1988; The Consumer, Society and the Law (with Prof. A. L. Diamond), 1963, 4th edn 1981; Law of Contempt (with N. V. Lowe), 1973, 3rd edn 1995; The Development of Consumer Law and Policy (Hamlyn Lectures), 1984. *Recreations:* gastronomy, piano playing, travel. *Address:* Manor Farm, Abbots Morton, Worcestershire WR7 4NA. *T:* Inkberrow (01386) 792330; 1 Plowden Buildings, Temple, EC4Y 9BU. *T:* 0171–353 4434. *Clubs:* Garrick, Reform (Chm., 1990–91).

BORTHWICK, family name of **Baron Borthwick.**

BORTHWICK, 23rd Lord *cr c* 1450 (Scot.); **John Henry Stuart Borthwick of That Ilk,** TD 1943; DL, JP; Baron of Heriotmuir and Laird of Crookston, Midlothian; Hereditary Falconer of Scotland to the Queen; Chairman: Heriotmuir Properties Ltd, since 1965; Heriotmuir Exporters Ltd, since 1972; *b* 13 Sept. 1905; *s* of Henry, 22nd Lord Borthwick (*d* 1937); claim to Lordship admitted by Lord Lyon, 1986; *m* 1938, Margaret Frances (*d* 1976), *d* of Alexander Campbell Cormack, Edinburgh; twin *s*. *Educ:* Fettes Coll., Edinburgh; King's Coll., Newcastle (DipAgric 1926). Formerly RATA, re-employed 1939; served NW Europe, Allied Mil. Govt Staff (Junior Staff Coll., SO 2), 1944; CCG (CO 1, Lt-Col), 1946. Dept of Agriculture for Scotland, 1948–50; farming own farms, 1950–71; Partner in Crookston Farms, 1971–79. National Farmers Union of Scotland: Mid and West Lothian Area Cttee, 1967–73 (Pres. 1970–72); Mem. Council, 1968–72; Member: Lothians Area Cttee, NFU Mutual Insurance Soc., 1969; Scottish Southern Regional Cttee, Wool Marketing Bd, 1966–87. Mem., Scottish Landowners' Fedn, 1937– (Mem., Land Use Cttee, 1972–83; Mem., Scottish Livestock Export Gp, 1972–83). Chm., Area Cttee, South of Scotland Electricity Bd Consultative Council, 1972–76. Chm., Monitoring Cttee for Scottish Tartans, 1976; Dir, Castles of Scotland Preservation Trust, 1985–. County Councillor, Midlothian, 1937–48; JP 1938; DL Midlothian (later Lothian Region), 1965; Member: Local Appeal Tribunal (Edinburgh and the Lothians), 1963–75; Midlothian Valuation Cttee, 1966–78. Member: Standing Council of Scottish Chiefs; The Committee of the Baronage of Scotland (International Delegate); Mem. Corresp., Istituto Italiano di Genealogia e Araldica, Rome and Madrid, 1964; Hon. Mem., Council of Scottish Clans Assoc., USA, 1975. Hon. Mem., Royal Military Inst. of Canada, 1976. Patron for Scotland and Dep. Patron for England, Normandy Veterans Assoc., 1985–. KLJ, GCLJ 1975; Comdr, Rose of Lippe, 1971; Niadh Nask, 1982. *Recreations:* shooting, travel, history. *Heir: s* Master of Borthwick, *qv*. *Address:* Crookston, Heriot, Midlothian EH38 5YS. *Clubs:* Carlton; New, Puffins (Edinburgh).

BORTHWICK, Master of; Hon. John Hugh Borthwick; farmer and landowner; *b* 14 Nov. 1940; *er twin s* and *heir* of Lord Borthwick, *qv*; *m* 1974, Adelaide, *d* of A. Birkmyre; two *d*. *Educ:* Gordonstoun; Edinburgh School of Agriculture (SDA, NDA). *Recreations:* wild trout fishing, stalking. *Address:* The Neuk, Heriot, Midlothian EH38 5YS. *T:* Heriot (01875) 835236. *Club:* New (Edinburgh).

BORTHWICK, Jason; *see* Borthwick, W. J. M.

BORTHWICK, Sir John Thomas, 3rd Bt *cr* 1908; MBE 1945; *b* 5 Dec. 1917; *S* to Btcy of uncle (1st and last Baron Whitburgh), 1967; *m* 1st, 1939; three *s*; 2nd, 1962; two *s*. *Heir: s* Antony Thomas Borthwick, *b* 12 Feb. 1941.

BORTHWICK, Kenneth W., CBE 1980; JP; DL; Rt Hon. Lord Provost of the City of Edinburgh, 1977–80; Lord Lieutenant of the City and County of Edinburgh, 1977–80; *b* 4 Nov. 1915; *s* of Andrew Graham Borthwick; *m* 1942, Irene Margaret Wilson, *d* of John Graham Wilson, Aberdeen; two *s* one *d*. *Educ:* George Heriot Sch., Edinburgh. Served War of 1939–45: Flying Officer, RAF. Elected Edinburgh Town Council, 1963; Lothian Regional Council, 1974–77; Edinburgh District Council, 1976. Judge of Police, 1972–75. Member: Lothians River Bd, 1969–73; Organising Cttee, Commonwealth Games, Edinburgh, 1970; Edinburgh and Lothian Theatre Trust, 1975–76; Lothian and Borders Police Bd, 1975–77; British Airports Authorities Consultative Cttee, 1977–80; Convention of Scottish Local Authorities, 1977; Scottish Council Develt and Industry, 1977; Chairman: Edinburgh Dist. Licensing Court, 1975–77; Edinburgh Internat. Festival Soc., 1977–80; Edinburgh Military Tattoo Policy Cttee, 1977–80; Queen's Silver Jubilee Edinburgh Appeal Fund, 1977; Organising Cttee, XIII Commonwealth Games, Scotland 1986, 1983–86. Dean, Consular Corps, Edinburgh and Leith, 1991–92. Curator of Patronage, Univ. of Edinburgh, 1977–80. Governor, George Heriot Sch., 1965–73. Vice-President (ex officio): RZS of Scotland, 1977–80; Lowland TA&VRA, 1977–80. DL City of Edinburgh, 1980. Hon. Consul for Malaŵi, 1982, Hon. Consul Gen., 1993–94. OStJ. Commander, Order of the Lion (Malaŵi), 1993. *Recreations:* golf, gardening. *Address:* 17 York Road, Edinburgh EH5 3EJ. *Club:* Caledonian (Hon. Mem.).

BORTHWICK, (William) Jason (Maxwell), DSC 1942; *b* 1 Nov. 1910; *er s* of late Hon. William Borthwick and Ruth (*née* Rigby); *m* 1937, Elizabeth Elworthy (*d* 1978), Timaru, NZ; one *s* three *d*. *Educ:* Winchester; Trinity Coll., Cambridge (BA). Called to Bar, Inner Temple, 1933. Commnd RNVR, 1940, Comdr (QO) 1945. Joined Thomas Borthwick & Sons Ltd, 1934, Dir 1946–76; Dir, International Commodities Clearing House Ltd and subsids, 1954–84; Dir, Commonwealth Develt Corp., 1972–78; Mem., Central Council of Physical Recreation, 1955–; Chm., Nat. Sailing Centre, 1965–79. *Recreations:* yachting, shooting. *Address:* North House, Brancaster Staithe, King's Lynn, Norfolk PE31 8BY. *T:* Brancaster (01485) 210475. *Clubs:* United Oxford & Cambridge University, Royal Thames Yacht.

BORWICK, family name of **Baron Borwick.**

BORWICK, 4th Baron, *cr* 1922; **James Hugh Myles Borwick;** Bt *cr* 1916; MC 1944; Major HLI retired; *b* 12 Dec. 1917; *s* of 3rd Baron and Irene Phyllis, *d* of late Thomas Main Paterson, Littlebourne, Canterbury; *S* father 1961; *m* 1954, Hyllarie Adalia Mary, *y d* of late Lieut-Col William Hamilton Hall Johnston, DSO, MC, DL, Bryn-y-Groes, Bala, N Wales; four *d*. *Educ:* Eton; RMC, Sandhurst. Commissioned as 2nd Lieut HLI, 1937; Capt. 1939; Major 1941; retired, 1947. *Recreations:* field sports, sailing. *Heir: half b* Hon. Robin Sandbach Borwick [*b* 22 March 1927; *m* 1950, Hon. Patricia Garnett, *o d* of Baron McAlpine of Moffat; two *s* one *d*]. *Address:* Leys Farm, Bircher, Leominster, Hereford HR6 0AZ. *T:* Leominster (01568) 780367. *Club:* Royal Ocean Racing.

BOSCAWEN, family name of **Viscount Falmouth.**

BOSCAWEN, Rt. Hon. Robert Thomas, MC 1944; PC 1992; *b* 17 March 1923; 4th *s* of 8th Viscount Falmouth and Dowager Viscountess Falmouth, CBE; *m* 1949, Mary Alice, JP London 1961, *e d* of Col Sir Geoffrey Ronald Codrington, KCVO, CB, CMG, DSO, OBE, TD; one *s* two *d*. *Educ:* Eton; Trinity College, Cambridge. Served Coldstream Guards, 1941–50 (with 1st (armoured) Bn Coldstream Guards, Normandy to N Germany, wounded 1945); NW Europe, 1944–45; attached to British Red Cross Civilian Relief Orgn in occupied Europe, 1946–47. Mem., London Exec. Council, Nat. Health Service, 1954–65; Underwriting Mem. of Lloyd's, 1952–. Contested Falmouth and Camborne (C), 1964, 1966; MP (C) Wells, 1970–83, Somerton and Frome, 1983–92. An Asst Govt Whip, 1979–81; a Lord Comr of HM Treasury, 1981–83; Vice-Chamberlain of HM Household, 1983–86, Comptroller, 1986–88. Mem., Select Cttee on Expenditure, 1974;

Vice-Chm., Conservative Parly Health and Social Security Cttee, 1974–79. Mem. Parly Delegns, USSR 1977, Nepal 1981; led Parly Delegn to UN Assembly, 1987, to Canada, 1991. *Recreation:* sailing. *Address:* 14 Tite Street, SW3 4HZ; Ivythorn Manor, Street, Somerset BA16 0TZ. *Clubs:* Pratt's; Royal Yacht Squadron.

BOSE, Mihir, FICA; freelance author and journalist, since 1987; *b* 12 Jan. 1947; *s* of Kiran Chandra Bose and Sova Rani Bose; *m* 1986, Kalpana; one *d*. *Educ:* St Xavier's High Sch.; St Xavier's Coll., Bombay (BSc Physics and Maths). Cricket Corresp., LBC, 1974–75; For. Corresp., Sunday Times, Spectator, New Society, 1975–78; freelance writer, 1979; Editor: Property Guide, 1980–81; International Fund Guide, 1980–81; Pensions, 1981–83; Financial Planning Ed. 1983–84, City Ed. 1984–86, Dep. Ed. 1985–86, Financial Weekly; City Features Ed., London Daily News, 1986–87; freelance writer, mainly on regular contract basis, specialising in finance, sports and feature writing for Sunday Times, Spectator, Mail on Sunday, Daily Telegraph, Independent, The Times, Guardian, 1987–. *Publications:* Keith Miller, 1979, 2nd edn 1980; The Lost Hero, 1982; All in a Day's Work, 1983; The Aga Khan, 1984; A Maidan View, 1986; The Crash, 1988, 3rd edn 1989, incl. Jap. edn; Insurance: are you covered?, 1988, 2nd edn 1991; Crash – a new money crisis, 1989; (jtly) Fraud, 1989; Cricket Voices, 1990; How to Invest in a Bear Market, 1990; History of Indian Cricket, 1990; Michael Grade: screening the image, 1992; (jtly) Behind Closed Doors, 1992; Sporting Colours, 1994. *Recreations:* running his own cricket team, reading, films, travelling. *Clubs:* Reform; Saturday (Calcutta).

BOSONNET, Paul Graham, CBE 1995; Deputy Chairman, British Telecommunications plc, since 1991; *b* 12 Sept. 1932; *s* of Edgar Raymond Bosonnet and Sylvia Gladys Cradock; *m* 1958, Joan Colet Cunningham; one *s* two *d*. *Educ:* St John's College, Southsea. FCA. Accountant, British Oxygen Co., 1957; Dir, BOC International, 1976; Dep. Chm., BOC Gp, 1985–92. Chm., Logica, 1990–; Director: MAM Gp, 1991–; Lucas Industries, 1993–. Vice Chm., Council, Royal Holloway (formerly RHBNC), Univ. of London, 1986–. *Recreations:* genealogy, walking. *Address:* The Old House Cottage, Pyrford Road, Pyrford, Surrey GU22 8UE. *T:* Byfleet (01932) 342991.

BOSSANO, Hon. Joseph; Chief Minister, Gibraltar, since 1988; MP (Gibraltar Socialist Labour Party); *b* 10 June 1939; *s* of Maria Teresa and Oscar Bossano; *m* (marr. diss.); three *s* one *d*; *m* 1988, Rose Torrilla. *Educ:* Gibraltar Grammar School; Univ. of London (BScEcon); Univ. of Birmingham (BA). Factory worker, 1958–60; Seaman, 1960–64; Health Inspector, 1964–68; student, 1968–72; building worker, 1972–74; Union leader, 1974–88; MP 1972–; Leader of Opposition, 1984–88. *Recreations:* thinking, cooking, gardening. *Address:* 6 Convent Place, Gibraltar. *T:* 70071.

BOSSOM, Hon. Sir Clive, 2nd Bt, *cr* 1953; *b* 4 Feb. 1918; *s* of late Baron Bossom (Life Peer); *S* to father's Baronetcy, 1965; *m* 1951, Lady Barbara North, *sister* of 9th Earl of Guilford, *qv*; three *s* one *d*. *Educ:* Eton. Regular Army, The Buffs, 1939–48; served Europe and Far East. Kent County Council, 1949–52; Chm. Council Order of St John for Kent, 1951–56; Mem. Chapter General, Order of St John (Mem., Jt Cttee, 1961–93; Chm., Ex-Services War Disabled Help and Homes Dept, 1973–87; Almoner, 1987–93). Contested (C) Faversham Div., 1951 and 1955. MP (C) Leominster Div., Herefordshire, 1959–Feb. 1974; Parliamentary Private Secretary: to Jt Parly Secs, Min. of Pensions and Nat. Insce, 1960–62; to Sec. of State for Air, 1962–64; to Minister of Defence for RAF, 1964; to Home Secretary, 1970–72. Chm., Europ Assistance Ltd, 1973–88. President: Anglo-Belgian Union, 1970–73, 1983–85 (Chm., 1967–70; Vice-Pres., 1974–82, 1985–); Anglo-Netherlands Soc., 1978–89; BARC, 1985–91; Vice-President: Industrial Fire Protection Assoc., 1981–88; Fédération Internationale de L'Automobile, 1975–81 (Vice-Pres. d'Honneur, 1982–); Internat. Social Service, 1989– (Internat. Pres., 1984–89); Chairman: RAC, 1975–78; RAC Motor Sports Council, 1975–81; RAC Motor Sports Assoc. Ltd, 1979–82; Iran Soc. 1973–76; Mem. Council, RGS, 1982–86. Trustee, Brooklands Museum Trust, 1987–. Liveryman of Worshipful Company of Grocers (Master, 1979). FRSA. KStJ 1961. Badge of Honour, British Red Cross, 1993. Comdr, Order of Leopold II; Order of Homayoun III (Iran), 1977; Comdr, Order of the Crown (Belgium), 1977; Kt Comdr, Order of Orange Nassau (Netherlands), 1980. *Recreation:* travel. *Heir:* *s* Bruce Charles Bossom, [*b* 22 Aug. 1952; *m* 1985, Penelope Jane, *d* of late Edward Holland-Martin and of Mrs Holland-Martin, Overbury Court, Glos; one *s* two *d*]. *Address:* 97 Cadogan Lane, SW1X 9DU. *T:* 0171–245 6531; Rotherdown, Grove Lane, Petworth, Sussex GU28 0LT. *T:* Petworth (01798) 42329. *Clubs:* Royal Automobile, Carlton.

BOSSY, Prof. John Antony, PhD; FRHistS; FBA 1993; Professor of History, University of York, since 1979; *b* 30 April 1933; *s* of Frederick James Bossy and Kate Louise Fanny Bossy (*née* White). *Educ:* St Ignatius' Coll., London; Queens' Coll., Cambridge (BA 1954; PhD 1961). FRHistS 1975. Res. Fellow, Queens' Coll., Cambridge, 1959–62; Lectr in Hist., Goldsmiths' Coll., London, 1962–66; Lectr, then Reader, in Mod. Hist., QUB, 1966–78. Mem., Editl Bd, Past and Present, 1972–. *Publications:* The English Catholic Community 1570–1850, 1976; Christianity in the West 1400–1700, 1984; Giordano Bruno and the Embassy Affair, 1991. *Recreations:* chess, piano, smoking. *Address:* 80 Stockton Lane, York YO3 0BS. *T:* York (01904) 424801.

See also Rev. M. J. F. Bossy.

BOSSY, Rev. Michael Joseph Frederick, SJ; Rector, Stonyhurst College, since 1993 (Headmaster, 1972–85); *b* 22 Nov. 1929; *s* of F. J. Bossy and K. Bossy (*née* White). *Educ:* St Ignatius Coll., Stamford Hill; Heythrop Coll., Oxon (STL); Oxford Univ. (MA). Taught at: St Ignatius Coll., Stamford Hill, 1956–59; St Francis Xavier's Coll., Liverpool, 1963–64; Stonyhurst Coll., 1965–85; Asst Priest, 1986–88, Rector and Parish Priest, 1988–92, Parish of St Aloysius, Glasgow; sabbatical leave, 1993. *Recreation:* watching games. *Address:* Stonyhurst College, Clitheroe, Lancashire BB7 9PZ.

See also J. A. Bossy.

BOSTOCK, David John; UK Deputy Permanent Representative to the European Union, since 1995; *b* 11 April 1948; *s* of John C. Bostock and Gwendoline G. (*née* Lee); *m* 1975, Beth Ann O'Byrne; one *s* one *d*. *Educ:* Cheltenham Grammar Sch.; Balliol Coll., Oxford (BA Mod. Hist. 1969); University Coll. London (MSc Econs of Public Policy 1978). VSO, Indonesia, 1970. Joined HM Treasury, 1971; Second Sec., Office of UK Permanent Rep. to EC, 1973–75; Principal: HM Treasury, 1975–81; Cabinet Office (Economic Secretariat), 1981–83; Asst Sec., HM Treasury, 1983–85; Financial and Econ. Counsellor, Office of UK Permanent Rep. to EC, 1985–89; Under Sec. and Head of EC Gp, HM Treasury, 1990–94. *Recreations:* choral singing, walking, looking at old buildings, drinking beer. *Address:* UK Permanent Representative to the European Union, Rond-Point Robert Schuman 6, 1040 Brussels, Belgium.

BOSTOCK, James Edward, RE 1961 (ARE 1947); ARCA London; painter and engraver; *b* Hanley, Staffs, 11 June 1917; *s* of William George Bostock, pottery and glass-worker, and Amy (*née* Titley); *m* 1939, Gwladys Irene (*née* Griffiths); three *s*. *Educ:* Borden Grammar Sch., Sittingbourne; Medway Sch. of Art, Rochester; Royal College of Art. War Service as Sgt in Durham LI and Royal Corps of Signals. Full-time Teacher, 1946–78; Vice-Principal, West of England Coll. of Art, 1965–70; Academic Develt Officer, Bristol Polytechnic, 1970–78. Elected Mem. of Soc. of Wood Engravers, 1950. Mem. Council. Soc. of Staffs Artists, 1963. Mem., E Kent Art Soc., 1980. Exhibited water-colours, etchings, wood engravings and drawings at RA, NEAC, RBA, RE, RI and other group exhibitions and in travelling exhibitions to Poland, Czechoslovakia, South Africa, Far East, New Zealand, USA, Sweden, Russia and Baltic States, and the provinces. One-man shows: Mignon Gall., Bath; Univ. of Bristol; Bristol Polytechnic; Margate Library Gall.; Deal Lib. Gall.; Broadstairs Lib. Gall.; Folkestone Lib. Gall.; Phillip Maslen Gall., Canterbury. Works bought by V & A Museum, British Museum, British Council, Hull, Swindon, Stoke-on-Trent and Bristol Education Cttees, Hunt Botanical Library, Pittsburgh, Hereford Mus., and private collectors. Commissioned work for: ICI Ltd, British Museum (Nat. Hist.), Odhams Press, and other firms and public authorities. *Publications:* Roman Lettering for Students, 1959; wood engraved illustrations to Poems of Edward Thomas, 1988; articles in: Times, Guardian, Staffordshire Sentinel, Studio, Artist; reproductions in: Garrett, History of British Wood Engraving, 1978; Garrett, British Wood Engraving of the Twentieth Century, 1980. *Address:* White Lodge, 80 Lindenthorpe Road, Broadstairs, Kent CT10 1DB. *T:* Thanet (01843) 869782.

BOSTOCK, Rev. Canon Peter Geoffrey, MA; Clergy Appointments Adviser, 1973–76; Deputy Secretary, Board for Mission and Unity, General Synod of Church of England, 1971–73; Canon Emeritus, Diocese of Mombasa, 1958; *b* 24 Dec. 1911; *s* of Geoffrey Bostock; *m* 1937, Elizabeth Rose; two *s* two *d*. *Educ:* Charterhouse; The Queen's Coll., Oxon; Wycliffe Hall, Oxon. Deacon, 1935; Priest, 1937; CMS Kenya, 1935–58; became Canon of Diocese of Mombasa, 1952; Archdeacon, 1953–58; Vicar-Gen., 1955–58. Examining Chaplain to Bishop of Mombasa, 1950–58; Chm., Christian Council of Kenya, 1957–58; Archdeacon of Doncaster and Vicar, High Melton, 1959–67; Asst Sec., Missionary and Ecumenical Council of Church Assembly, 1967–71. *Recreations:* home and family. *Address:* 6 Moreton Road, Oxford OX2 7AX. *T:* Oxford (01865) 515460. *Club:* Commonwealth Trust.

BOSTON, family name of **Baron Boston of Faversham.**

BOSTON, 10th Baron *cr* 1761; **Timothy George Frank Boteler Irby;** Bt 1704; *b* 27 March 1939; *s* of 9th Baron Boston, MBE, and Erica N. (*d* 1990), *d* of T. H. Hill; *S* father, 1978; *m* 1967, Rhonda Anne, *d* of R. A. Bate; two *s* one *d*. *Educ:* Clayesmore School, Dorset; Southampton Univ. (BSc Econ.). *Heir:* *s* Hon. George William Eustace Boteler Irby, *b* 1 Aug. 1971. *Address:* Cae'r Borth, Moelfre, Anglesey LL72 8NN. *T:* Moelfre (01248) 410249.

BOSTON OF FAVERSHAM, Baron *cr* 1976 (Life Peer), of Faversham, Kent; **Terence George Boston;** QC 1981; barrister; Chairman, TVS Entertainment plc, 1980–90; *b* 21 March 1930; *yr surv.* *s* of late George T. Boston and of Kate (*née* Bellati); *m* 1962, Margaret Joyce (Member: SE Metropolitan Regional Hospital Board, 1970–74; Mental Health Review Appeals Tribunal (SE Metropolitan area), 1970–74; market research consultant), *er d* of late R. H. J. Head and Mrs E. M. Winters, and step *d* of late H. F. Winters, Melbourne, Australia. *Educ:* Woolwich Polytechnic Sch.; King's Coll., University of London. Dep. President, University of London Union, 1955–56. Commnd in RAF during Nat. Service, 1950–52; later trained as pilot with University of London Air Sqdn. Called to the Bar, Inner Temple, 1960. BBC News Sub-Editor, External Services, 1957–60; Senior BBC Producer (Current Affairs), 1960–64; also Producer of Law in Action series (Third Programme), 1962–64. Joined Labour Party, 1946; contested (Lab) Wokingham, 1955 and 1959; MP (Lab) Faversham, Kent, June 1964–70; PPS to: Minister of Public Building and Works, 1964–66; Minister of Power, 1966–68; Minister of Transport, 1968–69; Asst Govt Whip, 1969–70; Minister of State, Home Office, 1979; opp. front bench spokesman on home affairs, 1979–84, on defence, 1984–86; Chm. of Cttees, H of L, 1994– (Prin. Dep. Chm., 1992–94; a dep. chm., 1991–94). UK Deleg. to UN Gen. Assembly, XXXIst, XXXIInd and XXXIIIrd Sessions, 1976–78. Member Executive Cttee, International Union of Socialist Youth, 1950; Select Cttee on Broadcasting Proceedings of Parliament, 1966; Speaker's Conference on Electoral Law, 1965–68. Trustee, Parly Lab. Party Benevolent Fund, 1967–70. Founder Vice-Chm., Great Britain—East Europe Centre, 1967–69; Chm., The Sheppey Gp, 1967–. *Recreations:* opera (going, not singing), fell-walking. *Address:* House of Lords, SW1A 0PW.

BOSTON, David Merrick, OBE 1976; MA; Director (formerly Curator), Horniman Public Museum and Public Park Trust (formerly Horniman Museum and Library), London, 1965–93; *b* 15 May 1931; *s* of late Dr H. M. Boston, Salisbury, Wilts; *m* 1961, Catharine, *d* of Rev. Prof. E. G. S. Parrinder, *qv*; one *s* two *d*. *Educ:* Rondebosch, Cape Town; Bishop Wordsworth's, Salisbury; Selwyn Coll., Cambridge; Univ. of Cape Town. BA History Cantab 1954; MA 1958. RAF, 1950–51; Adjt, Marine Craft Trng School. Field survey, S African Inst. of Race Relations, 1955; Keeper of Ethnology, Liverpool Museums, 1956–62; Asst Keeper, British Museum, New World archaeology and ethnography, 1962–65. Chm., British Nat. Cttee of Internat. Council of Museums, 1976–80; Vice-Chm., Internat. Cttee for Museums of Ethnography, 1989–95; Mem. Council: Museums Assoc., 1969; Royal Anthropological Inst., 1969 (Vice-Pres., 1972–75, 1977–80, 1995–, Hon. Sec., 1985–88, Hon. Librarian, 1992–). Visiting Scientist: National Museum of Man, Ottawa, 1970; Japan Foundation, Tokyo, 1986. Consultant, Prog. for Belize, 1994–. Gov., Dolmetsch Foundn, 1983–. Vice President: Dulwich Decorative & Fine Arts Soc., 1987–; Friends of the Horniman, 1995–. FMA; FRAS; FRGS; FRSA. Ordenom Jugoslavenske Zastave sa zlatnom zvezdom na ogrlici (Yugoslavia), 1981. *Publications:* Pre-Columbian Pottery of the Americas, 1980; contribs to learned jls and encyclopaedias and on Pre-European America, in World Ceramics (ed R. J. Charleston). *Address:* 51A Westcombe Park Road, Blackheath, SE3 7QZ. *T:* 0181–858 5603.

BOSTON, Richard; writer; *b* 29 Dec. 1938. *Educ:* Stowe; Regent Street Polytechnic School of Art; King's Coll., Cambridge (MA). Taught English in Sicily, Sweden and Paris; acted in Jacques Tati's Playtime. Glenfiddich Special Award, 1976. Editorial staff of Peace News, TLS, New Society; columnist and feature writer, The Guardian, at intervals, 1972–. Editor: The Vole, 1977–80; Quarto, 1979–82. *Publications:* The Press We Deserve (ed), 1969; An Anatomy of Laughter, 1974; The Admirable Urquhart, 1975; Beer and Skittles, 1976; Baldness Be My Friend, 1977; The Little Green Book, 1979; C. O. Jones's Compendium of Practical Jokes, 1982; Osbert: a portrait of Osbert Lancaster, 1989; Boudu Saved from Drowning, 1994. *Recreation:* procrastination. *Address:* The Old School, Aldworth, Reading, Berks RG8 9TJ. *T:* Compton (01635) 578587.

BOSVILLE MACDONALD OF SLEAT, Sir Ian Godfrey, 17th Bt, *cr* 1625; FRICS, MRSH; 25th Chief of Sleat; *b* 18 July 1947; *er s* of Sir (Alexander) Somerled Angus Bosville Macdonald of Sleat, 16th Bt, MC, 24th Chief of Sleat and of Mary, Lady Bosville Macdonald of Sleat; *S* father 1958; *m* 1970, Juliet Fleury, *o d* of late Maj.-Gen. J. M. D. Ward-Harrison, OBE, MC; one *s* two *d*. *Educ:* Pinewood Sch.; Eton Coll.; Royal Agricultural Coll. ARICS 1972; FRICS 1986. Member (for Bridlington South), Humberside CC, 1981–84. MRSH 1972; Mem., Econ. Res. Council, 1979–. Chm., Rural Develt Commn, Humberside, 1988–; President: British Food and Farming in Humberside, 1989; Humberside Br., British Red Cross, 1988–; Humberside Young Farmers, 1989–. High Sheriff, Humberside, 1988–89. *Heir:* *s* Somerled Alexander Bosville Macdonald, younger of Sleat, *b* 30 Jan. 1976. *Recreation:* ornithology. *Address:* Thorpe

Hall, Rudston, Driffield, East Yorkshire YO25 0JE. *T:* Bridlington (01262) 420239. *Clubs:* Lansdowne, White's; Puffin's (Edinburgh).

BOSWALL, Sir (Thomas) Alford H.; *see* Houstoun-Boswall.

BOSWELL, Lt-Gen. Sir Alexander (Crawford Simpson), KCB 1982; CBE 1974 (OBE 1971; MBE 1962); DL; Lieutenant-Governor and Commander-in-Chief, Guernsey, 1985–90; *b* 3 Aug. 1928; *s* of Alexander Boswell Simpson Boswell and Elizabeth Burns Simpson Boswell (*née* Park); *m* 1956, Jocelyn Leslie Blundstone Pomfret, *d* of Surg. Rear-Adm. A. A. Pomfret, CB, OBE; five *s*. *Educ:* Merchiston Castle Sch.; RMA, Sandhurst. Enlisted in Army, 1947; Commnd, Argyll and Sutherland Highlanders, Dec. 1948; regimental appts, Hong Kong, Korea, UK, Suez, Guyana, 1949–58; sc Camberley, 1959; Mil. Asst (GS02) to GOC Berlin, 1960–62; Co. Comdr, then Second in Comd, 1 A and SH, Malaya and Borneo, 1963–65 (despatches 1965); Directing Staff, Staff Coll., Camberley, 1965–68; CO, 1 A and SH, 1968–71; Col GS Trng Army Strategic Comd, 1971; Brig. Comdg 39 Inf. Bde, 1972–74; COS, 1st British Corps, 1974–76; NDC (Canada), 1976–77; GOC 2nd Armd Div., 1978–80; Dir, TA and Cadets, 1980–82; GOC Scotland and Governor of Edinburgh Castle, 1982–85. Chairman: Scottish Veterans' Residences, 1991–; Officers Assoc. (Scottish Br.), 1991–. Col, Argyll and Sutherland Highlanders, 1972–82; Hon. Col, Tayforth Univs OTC, 1982–86; Col Comdt, Scottish Div., 1982–86; Hon. Col, Scottish Transport Regt RLC(V), 1993–. Captain of Tarbet, 1974–82. KStJ 1985. DL East Lothian, 1993. *Address:* c/o Bank of Scotland, Palmerston Place Branch, 32 West Maitland Street, Edinburgh EH12 5DZ.

BOSWELL, Timothy Eric; MP (C) Daventry, since 1987; Parliamentary Secretary, Ministry of Agriculture, Fisheries and Food, since 1995; *b* 2 Dec. 1942; *s* of late Eric New Boswell and of Joan Winifred Caroline Boswell; *m* 1969, Helen Delahay, *d* of Rev. Arthur Rees; three *d*. *Educ:* Marlborough Coll.; New Coll., Oxford (MA; Dip. Agricl Econs). Conservative Res. Dept, 1966–73 (Head of Econ. Section, 1970–73); managed family farming business, 1974–87; part-time Special Adviser to Minister of Agriculture, Fisheries and Food, 1984–86. Chm., Leics, Northants and Rutland Counties Br., NFU, 1983; Mem. Council, 1966–90, Pres., 1984–90, Perry Foundn (for Agricl Res.); Mem., AFRC, 1988–90. PPS to Financial Sec. to the Treasury, 1989–90; an Asst Govt Whip, 1990–92; a Lord Comr of HM Treasury (a Govt Whip), 1992; Parly Under-Sec. of State, DFE, 1992–95. Member: Select Cttee for Agriculture, 1987–89; Sec., Cons. Backbench Cttee on Agriculture, 1987–89; Chm., All-Party Charity Law Review Panel, 1988–90. Treas., 1976–79, Chm., 1979–83, Daventry Constituency Cons. Assoc. Contested (C) Rugby, Feb. 1974. *Recreations:* the countryside, shooting, snooker, poetry. *Address:* House of Commons, SW1A 0AA. *T:* 0171–219 3520. *Club:* Farmers'.

BOSWOOD, Anthony Richard; QC 1986; *b* 1 Oct. 1947; *s* of Noel Gordon Paul Boswood and Cicily Ann Watson; *m* 1973, Sarah Bridget Alexander; three *d*. *Educ:* St Paul's Sch.; New Coll., Oxford (BCL, MA). Called to Bar, Middle Temple, 1970. *Recreations:* opera, tennis, gardening, olive farming. *Address:* Fountain Court, Temple, EC4Y 9DH. *T:* 0171–583 3335; Podere Casanuova, Pievasciata, Castelnuovo Berardenga (SI), Italy.

BOSWORTH, Prof. Clifford Edmund, FBA 1992; Professor of Arabic Studies, Manchester University, 1967–90, now Emeritus; Fellow, Manchester University, since 1990; *b* 29 Dec. 1928; *s* of Clifford Bosworth and Gladys Constance Gregory; *m* 1957, Annette Ellen Todd; three *d*. *Educ:* St John's College, Oxford (MA Mod. Hist.); Edinburgh Univ. (MA Arabic, Persian, Turkish; PhD). Dept of Agriculture for Scotland, 1952–54; Lectr in Arabic, St Andrews Univ., 1956–67. Vis. Associate Prof., Univ. of Toronto, 1965–66; Vis. Prof., UCLA, 1969; Center for Humanities Fellow, Princeton, 1984. Pres., British Soc. for Middle Eastern Studies, 1983–85. *Publications:* The Ghaznavids, 1963; The Islamic Dynasties, 1967; Sistan under the Arabs, 1968; The Book of Curious and Entertaining Information, 1968; The Medieval Islamic Underworld, 1976; The Later Ghaznavids, 1977; Al-Maqrizi's Book of contention and strife, 1981; Medieval Arabic Culture and Administration, 1982; The History of al-Tabari (annotated trans.), vols 30, 32–3, 1987–91. *Recreations:* walking, listening to music, collecting detective fiction. *Address:* 11 Prince's Road, Heaton Moor, Stockport, Cheshire SK4 3NQ. *T:* 0161–432 6464.

BOSWORTH, (John) Michael (Worthington), CBE 1972; FCA; Deputy Chairman, British Railways Board, 1972–83 (Vice-Chairman, 1968–72); *b* 22 June 1921; *s* of Humphrey Worthington Bosworth and Vera Hope Bosworth; *m* 1955, Patricia Mary Edith Wheelock; one *s* one *d*. *Educ:* Bishop's Stortford Coll. Served Royal Artillery, 1939–46. Peat, Marwick, Mitchell & Co., 1949–68, Partner, 1960. Chairman: British Rail Engineering Ltd, 1969–71; British Rail Property Bd, 1971–72; British Rail Shipping and International Services Ltd, now Sealink UK Ltd, 1976–84; BR Hovercraft Ltd, 1976–81; British Transport Hotels, 1978–83; British Rail Investments Ltd, 1981–84; British Rail Trustee Co., 1984–86; Director: Hoverspeed (UK) Ltd, 1981–89; British Ferries, 1984–90. Vice Pres., Société Belgo-Anglaise des Ferry-Boats, 1979–87. Dir, Compass Hotels Ltd, 1988–. *Recreations:* ski-ing, vintage cars. *Address:* Cross Farm, Yetminster, Sherborne, Dorset DT9 6LG. *Club:* Royal Automobile.

BOSWORTH, Sir Neville (Bruce Alfred), Kt 1987; CBE 1982; Consultant, Grove Tompkins Bosworth, Solicitors, Birmingham, since 1989; *b* 18 April 1918; *s* of W. C. N. Bosworth; *m* 1945, Charlotte Marian Davis; one *s* two *d*. *Educ:* King Edward's Sch., Birmingham; Birmingham Univ. LLB. Admitted Solicitor, 1941; Sen. Partner, Bosworth, Bailey Cox & Co., Birmingham, 1941–89. Birmingham City Council, 1950–; County Bor. Councillor (Erdington Ward), 1950–61; Alderman, 1961–74; Dist Councillor (Edgbaston Ward), 1973–; Lord Mayor of Birmingham, 1969–70; Dep. Mayor, 1970–71; Leader of Birmingham City Council, 1976–80, 1982–84; Leader of Opposition, 1972–76, 1980–82 and 1984–87; Cons. Gp Leader, 1972–87 (Dep. Gp Leader, 1971–72); Chairman: Gen. Purposes Cttee, 1966–69; Finance Cttee, 1976–80, 1982–84; National Exhibn Centre Cttee, 1976–80. Chm., W Midlands Police Bd, 1985–86. County Councillor (Edgbaston Ward), W Midlands CC, 1973–86; Chm., Legal and Property Cttee, 1977–79; Vice-Chm., Finance Cttee, 1980–81. Chm., Sutton Coldfield Cons. Assoc., 1963–66; Vice-Chm., Birmingham Cons. Assoc., 1972–87; Mem., Local Govt Adv. Cttee, National Union of Cons. and Unionist Assocs, 1973–; Pres., Edgbaston Constituency Cons. Assoc., 1992–. Vice Chm., Assoc. of Metropolitan Authorities, 1978–80, and Mem. Policy Cttee, 1976–80; Vice-Pres., Birmingham and Dist Property Owners Assoc.; Dir, Nat. Exhibn Centre Ltd, 1970–72, 1974–; Mem., W Midlands Econ. Council, 1978–79. Trustee, several charitable trusts; Mem. Council, Birmingham Univ., 1962–91; Governor, King Edward VI Schs, Birmingham, 1970–87 (Dep. Bailiff, 1979–80). Hon. Freeman, City of Birmingham, 1982. *Recreations:* politics, football, bridge. *Address:* Hollington, Luttrell Road, Four Oaks, Sutton Coldfield, Birmingham B74 2SR. *T:* 0121–308 0647; 54 Newhall Street, Birmingham B3 3QG. *T:* 0121–236 8091.

BOTHA, Matthys (Izak); South African Diplomat, retired; *b* 31 Oct. 1913; *s* of Johan Hendrik Jacobus Botha and Anna Botha (*née* Joubert); *m* 1940, Hester le Roux (*née* Bosman); two *s*. *Educ:* Selborne Coll.; Pretoria Univ. BA, LLB. Called to the Transvaal Bar, Dept of Finance, Pretoria, 1931–44; S African Embassy, Washington, 1944–51; S African Permanent Mission to UN, NY, 1951–54; Head, Political Div., Dept Foreign Affairs, Pretoria, 1955–59; Envoy Extraordinary and Minister Plenipoteniary, Switzerland, 1959–60; Minister, London, 1960–62; Ambassador and Permanent Rep., UN, NY, 1962–70; Ambassador to: Canada, 1970–73; Italy, 1973–77 (also to Costa Rica and El Salvador, 1973–74, and to Panama, 1973–76); Court of St James's, 1977–78; Ciskei, 1983–85. Member: Simon Vanderstel Foundn; South African Foundn; Huguenot Soc. Knight of Grand Cross, Order of Merit (Italy), 1977. *Recreations:* swimming, golfing, cycling. *Address:* 7 de Jongh Street, The Strand, Cape Province, 7140, South Africa. *Club:* Somerset West Country (near Cape Town).

BOTHA, Pieter Willem, DMS 1976; Star of South Africa, 1979; State President, Republic of South Africa, 1984–89 (Prime Minister, and Minister of National Intelligence Service, 1978–84); *b* 12 Jan. 1916; *s* of Pieter Willem and Hendriena Christina Botha; *m* 1943, Anna Elizabeth Rossouw; two *s* three *d*. *Educ:* Paul Roux; Bethlehem, Orange Free State; Univ. of Orange Free State, Bloemfontein. MP for George, 1948–84; Deputy Minister of the Interior, 1958; Minister of Community Development and of Coloured Affairs, 1961; Minister of Public Works, 1964; Minister of Defence, 1966–80. Leader of the National Party in the Cape Province, 1966–86; Chief Leader of Nat. Party, 1978–89. Hon. Doctorate in: Military Science, Stellenbosch Univ., 1976; Philosophy, Orange Free State Univ., 1981; DAdmin *hc* Pretoria Univ., 1985. Grand Cross of Military Order of Christ, Portugal, 1967; Order of Propitious Clouds with Special Grand Cordon, Taiwan, 1980; Grand Collar, Order of Good Hope, Republic of S Africa, 1985. *Recreations:* horseriding, walking, reading, small game hunting. *Address:* Die Anker, Wilderness 6560, South Africa.

BOTHA, Roelof Frederik, (Pik Botha), DMS 1981; Minister of Energy, South Africa, since 1994; MP (National Party) for Westdene, since 1977; Leader, Transvaal National Party, since 1992; *b* 27 April 1932; *m* 1953, Helena Susanna Bosman; two *s* two *d*. *Educ:* Volkskool, Potchefstroom; Univ. of Pretoria (BA, LLB). Dept of Foreign Affairs, 1953; diplomatic missions, Europe, 1956–62; Mem. team from S Africa, in SW Africa case, Internat. Court of Justice, The Hague, 1963–66, 1970–71; Agent for S African Govt, Internat. Court of Justice, 1965–66; Legal Adviser, Dept of Foreign Affairs, 1966–68; Under-Sec. and Head of SW Africa and UN Sections, 1968–70. National Party, MP for Wonderboom, 1970–74. Mem., SA Delegn to UN Gen. Assembly, 1967–69, 1971, 1973–74. Served on select Parly Cttees, 1970–74. South African Permanent Representative to the UN, NY, 1974–77; South African Ambassador to the USA, 1975–77. Minister of Foreign Affairs, 1977–94; Minister of Information, 1978–86. Grand Cross, Order of Good Hope, 1980; Order of the Brilliant Star with Grand Cordon, 1980. *Address:* House of Assembly, Cape Town, South Africa; c/o Department of Energy, Pretoria, South Africa.

BOTHAM, Ian Terence, OBE 1992; cricketer, retired 1993; *b* 24 Nov. 1955; *s* of Leslie and Marie Botham; *m* 1976, Kathryn Waller; one *s* two *d*. *Educ:* Milford Junior Sch.; Buckler's Mead Secondary Sch., Yeovil. Bowler and batsman; County Cricket Clubs: Somerset, 1974–87 (Captain, 1983–85; Hon. Life Mem., 1993); Worcestershire, 1987–91; Durham, 1992–93 (Hon. Life Mem.). England Test cricketer, 1977–92 (Captain, 1980–81); scored 1,000 runs and took 100 wickets in 21 Tests at age 23, 1979; scored 3,000 runs and took 300 wickets in Tests to 1982; first player to score a century and take 10 wickets in a Test match, Bombay, 1979; made 100 runs and took 8 wickets in 3 Tests, 1978, 1980, 1984; made 5,200 runs, took 383 wickets and 120 catches in 102 Tests; played cricket for Queensland, football for Scunthorpe and Yeovil. Marathon walks for leukaemia research incl. Land's End to John o'Groats and Alps; takes part in pantomimes; columnist, Daily Mirror. Team captain, A Question of Sport, BBC, 1989–. Mem., Sports Council for England, 1995–. *Publications:* Ian Botham on Cricket, 1980; (with Ian Jarrett) Botham Down Under, 1983; (with Kenneth Gregory) Botham's Bedside Cricket Book, 1983; (with Peter Roebuck) It Sort of Clicks, 1986, rev. edn 1987; (with Jack Bannister) Cricket My Way, 1989; Botham: my autobiography, 1994. *Address:* North Yorkshire. *Club:* MCC (Hon. Mem. 1994).

BOTHROYD, Shirley Ann, (Mrs Ian Mayes); barrister; First Prosecuting Counsel to the Inland Revenue at the Central Criminal Court and Inner London Crown Court, since 1991; *b* 23 July 1958; *d* of Reginald Bothroyd and Audrey (*née* Bryant); *m* 1986, Ian Mayes, *qv*; two *s*. Called to the Bar, Middle Temple, 1982; Second Prosecuting Counsel to Inland Revenue, 1989–91. *Recreations:* ski-ing, scuba diving, piano. *Address:* Littleton Chambers, 3 King's Bench Walk North, Temple, EC4Y 7HR. *T:* 0171–797 8600.

BOTHWELL, Rt. Rev. John Charles, DD; Archbishop of Niagara and Metropolitan of Ontario, 1985–91; *b* 29 June 1926; *s* of William Alexander Bothwell and Anne Bothwell (*née* Campbell); *m* 1951, Joan Cowan; three *s* two *d*. *Educ:* Runnymede Public School; Humberside Coll. Inst., Toronto; Trinity Coll., Univ. of Toronto (BA 1948, LTh 1951, BD 1952; DD 1972). Asst Priest, St James' Cathedral, Toronto, 1951–53; Sen. Assistant at Christ Church Cathedral, Vancouver, 1953–56; Rector: St Aidan's, Oakville, Ont, 1956–60; St James' Church, Dundas, Ont, 1960–65; Canon of Christ Church Cathedral, Hamilton, Ont, 1963; Dir of Programs for Niagara Diocese, 1965–69; Exec. Dir of Program, Nat. HQ of Anglican Church of Canada, Toronto, 1969–71; Bishop Coadjutor of Niagara, 1971–73; Bishop of Niagara, 1973–85. Chancellor, Trinity Coll., Univ. of Toronto, 1991–. Hon. Sen. Fellow, Renison Coll., Univ. of Waterloo, 1988. Hon. DD: Huron Coll., Univ. of Western Ont, 1989; Wycliffe Coll., Univ. of Toronto, 1989. *Publications:* Taking Risks and Keeping Faith, 1985; An Open View: keeping faith day by day, 1990; Old Time Religion or Risky Faith: the challenge and the vision, 1993. *Recreations:* golf, cross-country ski-ing, swimming. *Address:* 838 Glenwood Avenue, Burlington, Ont L7T 2J9, Canada. *T:* (416) 6348649.

BOTT, Catherine Jane; soprano; *b* 11 Sept. 1952; *d* of Maurice Bott and Patricia Bott (*née* Sherlock). *Educ:* King's High Sch. for Girls, Warwick; Guildhall Sch. of Music and Drama (GGSM). Concert singer specialising in baroque vocal music; worldwide concert engagements; radio broadcasts; numerous recordings with leading ensembles and orchestras, recital recordings and recordings of operatic roles, incl. Purcell's Dido, Messaggiera (l'Orfeo), Drusilla (l'Incoronazione di Poppaea), and Mandana (Artaxerxes). *Recreations:* reading, silent films, sea bathing. *Address:* c/o Magenta Music International, 4 Highgate High Street, N6 5JL.

BOTT, Ian Bernard, FEng 1985; Director, Admiralty Research Establishment, Ministry of Defence, 1984–88, retired; consultant engineer, since 1989; *b* 1 April 1932; *s* of late Edwin Bernard and Agnes Bott; *m* 1955, Kathleen Mary (*née* Broadbent); one *s* one *d*. *Educ:* Nottingham High Sch.; Southwell Minster Grammar Sch.; Stafford Technical Coll.; Manchester Univ. BSc Hon. Physics; FIEE, FInstP. Nottingham Lace Industry, 1949–53. Royal Air Force, 1953–55. English Electric, Stafford, 1955–57; Royal Radar Estabt, 1960–75 (Head of Electronics Group, 1973–75); Counsellor, Defence Research and Development, British Embassy, Washington DC, 1975–77; Ministry of Defence: Dep. Dir Underwater Weapons Projects (S/M), 1977–79; Asst Chief Scientific Advr (Projects), 1979–81; Dir Gen., Guided Weapons and Electronics, 1981–82; Principal Dep. Dir, AWRE, MoD, 1982–84. Mem. Council, Fellowship of Engrg, 1987–90. Hon. Chm., Portsmouth Area Hospice, 1989–94. Trustee, Panasonic Trust, 1993–. Freeman, City of London, 1985; Liveryman, Co. of Engineers, 1985. *Publications:* papers on physics and electronics subjects in jls of learned socs. *Recreations:* building, horology, music. *Club:* Royal Automobile.

BOTT, Prof. Martin Harold Phillips, FRS 1977; Professor, 1966–88, Research Professor, 1988–91, in Geophysics, University of Durham, now Professor Emeritus; *b* 12 July 1926; *s* of Harold Bott and Dorothy (*née* Phillips); *m* 1961, Joyce Cynthia Hughes; two *s* one *d*. *Educ:* Clayesmore Sch. Dorset; Magdalene Coll., Cambridge (Scholar). MA, PhD. Nat. Service, 1945–48 (Lieut, Royal Signals). Durham University: Turner and Newall Fellow, 1954–56; Lectr, 1956–63; Reader, 1963–66. Anglican Lay Reader. Mem. Council, Royal Soc., 1982–84. Murchison Medallist, Geological Soc. of London, 1977; Clough Medal, Geol Soc. of Edinburgh, 1979; Sorby Medal, Yorkshire Geol Soc., 1981; Wollaston Medal, Geol Soc. of London, 1992. *Publications:* The Interior of the Earth, 1971, 2nd edn 1982; papers in learned jls. *Recreations:* walking, mountains. *Address:* 11 St Mary's Close, Shincliffe, Durham DH1 2ND. *T:* Durham (0191) 3864021.

BOTTAI, Bruno; Ambassador of Italy to the Holy See, since 1994; *b* 10 July 1930; *s* of Giuseppe Bottai and Cornelia Ciocca. *Educ:* Univ. of Rome (law degree). Joined Min. for For. Affairs, 1954; Vice Consul, Tunis, 1956; Second Sec., Perm. Representation to EC, Brussels, 1958; Gen. Secretariat, Co-ord. Service, Min. for For. Affairs, 1961; Counsellor, London, 1966; Dep. Chef de Cabinet, Min. for For. Affairs, 1968; Minister-Counsellor, Holy See, 1969; Diplomatic Advr to Pres., Council of Ministers, 1970; Hd of Press and Inf. Dept 1972, Dep. Dir-Gen. of Political Affairs 1976, Min. for For. Affairs; Ambassador to Holy See and Sovereign Mil. Order of Malta, 1979; Dir-Gen. Pol. Affairs, Min. for For. Affairs, 1981; Ambassador to UK, 1985–87; Sec. Gen., Min. of Foreign Affairs, Italy, 1987–94. Numerous decorations from Europe, Africa, Latin Amer. countries, Holy See, Malta. *Publications:* political essays and articles. *Recreations:* modern paintings and modern sculpture, theatre, reading, walking. *Address:* via le Belle Arti, 2–00196 Rome, Italy.

BOTTING, Maj.-Gen. David Francis Edmund, CB 1992; CBE 1986; Director General of Ordnance Services, Ministry of Defence, 1990–93; *b* 15 Dec. 1937; *s* of Leonard Edmund Botting and Elizabeth Mildred Botting (*née* Stacey); *m* 1962, Anne Outhwaite; two *s*. *Educ:* St Paul's School, London. National Service, RAOC, 1956; commissioned Eaton Hall, 1957; Regular Commission, 1958; regtl appts, Kineton, Deepcut, Borneo, Singapore and Malaya, 1957–67; sc 1968; BAOR, 1972–74; 1 Div., 1974–75; 3rd Div., 1981–82; Col AQ 1 Div., 1982–85; Comd Sup. 1 (BR) Corps, 1987; ACOS HQ UKLF, 1987–90. Rep. Col Comdt, RAOC, 1993; Col Comdt, RLC, 1993–95. FILDM 1991; MInstPS 1991. Freeman, City of London, 1990; Liveryman, Co. of Gold and Silver Wyre Drawers, 1991. *Recreations:* sport, esp. golf, philately, furniture restoration. *Clubs:* Army and Navy; Tidworth Golf.

BOTTING, (Elizabeth) Louise, CBE 1993; broadcaster and financial journalist; Chairman, Douglas Deakin Young, since 1988 (Managing Director, 1982–88); *b* 19 Sept. 1939; *d* of Robert and Edith Young; marr. diss.; two *d*; *m* 1989, L. A. Carpenter, *qv*. *Educ:* Sutton Coldfield High School; London Sch. of Economics (BSc Econ.). Kleinwort Benson, 1961–65; Daily Mail, 1970–75; British Forces Broadcasting, 1971–83; Douglas Deakin Young, financial consultancy, 1975–. Director: Trinity International, 1991–; General Accident, 1992–; London Weekend Television, 1992–94. Presenter, BBC Moneybox, 1977–92. Mem. Top Salaries Review Body, 1987–94. *Address:* Douglas Deakin Young Ltd, 22 Sackville Street, W1X 2DH. *T:* 0171–439 3344.

See also *J. R. C. Young.*

BOTTINI, Reginald Norman, CBE 1974; General-Secretary, National Union of Agricultural and Allied Workers, 1970–78; Member, General Council of TUC, 1970–78; *b* 14 Oct. 1916; *s* of Reginald and Helena Teresa Bottini; *m* 1946, Doris Mary Balcomb; no *c*. *Educ:* Bec Grammar School. Apptd Asst in Legal Dept of Nat. Union of Agricultural Workers, 1945; Head of Negotiating Dept, 1954; elected Gen.-Sec., Dec. 1969. Member: Agricultural Wages Bd, 1963–78; Agricultural Economic Development Cttee, 1970–78; (part-time) SE Electricity Bd, 1974–83; Food Hygiene Adv. Council, 1973–83; BBC Agric. Adv. Cttee, 1973–78; Econ. and Soc. Cttee, EEC, 1975–78; Clean Air Council, 1975–80; Adv. Cttee on Toxic Substances, 1977–80; Meat and Livestock Commn, 1977–86 (and Chm. of its Consumers Cttee); Panel Mem., Central Arbitration Cttee, 1977–86; Commn on Energy and the Environment, 1978–81; Waste Management Adv. Council, 1978–81; Employees' Panel, Industrial Tribunals, 1984–85. Formerly: Secretary: Trade Union Side, Forestry Commn Ind. and Trades Council; Trade Union Side, British Sugar Beet Nat. Negotiating Cttee; Chairman: Trade Union Side, Nat. Jt Ind. Council for River Authorities; Market Harborough Volunteer Bureau, 1988– (Vice-Chm., 1986–87; Chm., 1989–); formerly Member: Central Council for Agric. and Hort. Co-operation; Nat. Jt Ind. Council for County Roadmen. *Recreations:* gardening, driving. *Address:* 43 Knights End Road, Great Bowden, Market Harborough, Leics LE16 7EY. *T:* Market Harborough (01858) 464229. *Clubs:* Farmers'; Probus (Market Harborough).

BOTTO DE BARROS, Adwaldo Cardoso; Director-General, International Bureau of Universal Postal Union, 1985–94; *b* 19 Jan. 1925; *s* of Julio Botto de Barros and Maria Cardoso Botto de Barros; *m* 1951, Neida de Moura; one *s* two *d*. *Educ:* Military Coll., Military Engineering Inst. and Higher Military Engineering Inst., Brazil. Railway construction, 1952–54; Dir, industries in São Paulo and Curitiba, 1955–64; Dir, Handling Sector, São Paulo Prefecture, Financial Adviser to São Paulo Engrg Faculty and Adviser to Suzano Prefecture, 1965–71; Regional Dir, São Paulo, 1972–74; Pres., Brazilian Telegraph and Post Office, Brasília-DF, 1974–84. Mem. and Head, numerous delegns to UPU and other postal assocs overseas, 1976–84. Numerous Brazilian and foreign hons and decorations. *Recreations:* philately, sports.

BOTTOMLEY, Baron *cr* 1984 (Life Peer), of Middlesbrough in the County of Cleveland; **Arthur George Bottomley,** OBE 1941; PC 1951; *b* 7 Feb. 1907; *s* of late George Howard Bottomley and Alice Bottomley; *m* 1936, Bessie Ellen Wiles (*see* Lady Bottomley); no *c*. *Educ:* Gamuel Road Council Sch.; Extension Classes at Toynbee Hall. London Organiser of National Union of Public Employees, 1935–45, 1959–62. Walthamstow Borough Council, 1929–49; Mayor of Walthamstow, 1945–46; Chairman of Emergency Cttee and ARP Controller, 1939–41. Dep. Regional Commissioner for S-E England, 1941–45. MP (Lab): Chatham Division of Rochester, 1945–50, Rochester and Chatham 1950–59; Middlesbrough East, 1962–74, Teesside, Middlesbrough, 1974–83. Parliamentary Under-Secretary of State for Dominions, 1946–47; Sec. for Overseas Trade, Board of Trade, 1947–51; Sec. of State for Commonwealth Affairs, 1964–66; Minister of Overseas Develt, 1966–67. Land Tax Comr, Becontree Div. of Essex; Special Govt Mission to Burma, 1947; Deleg. to UN, New York, 1946, 1947 and 1949; Leader: UK delegation to World Trade and Employment Conference, Havana, 1947; UK Delegn to Commonwealth Conference, Delhi, 1949; Trade Mission to Pakistan, 1950; Special Mission to West Indies, 1951; Member: Consultative Assembly, Council of Europe, 1952, 1953 and 1954; Leader: Parliamentary Labour Party Mission to Burma, 1962, to Malaysia, 1963; UK Delegation to CPA Conferences, Australia, Canada, Malawi, Malaysia, Mauritius; Member, Parliamentary Missions to: India, 1946; Kenya, 1954; Ghana, 1959; Cyprus, 1963; Hong Kong, 1964; China, 1983. Chairman: Commonwealth Relations and Colonies Group, Parly Labour Party, 1963; Select Parly Cttee on Race Relations and Immigration, 1969; Select Cttee on Cyprus, 1975; Special Parly Cttee on Admin and Orgn of House of Commons Services, 1976; House of Commons Commn, 1980–83; Treasurer, Commonwealth Parly Assoc., 1974 (Vice-Chm., UK Branch, 1968 and 1974–77). Chm., Attlee Foundn, 1978–; President: Britain-India Forum, 1981–; Britain-Burma Soc., 1981–. Hon. Fellow, Hunterian Soc., 1985. Hon. Freeman of Chatham, 1959; Freeman: City of London, 1975; Middlesbrough, 1976. Awarded title of Aung San Tagun, Burma, 1981. *Publications:* Why Britain should Join the Common Market, 1959; Two Roads to Colonialism, 1960; The Use and Abuse of Trade Unions, 1961; Commonwealth Comrades and Friends, 1986. *Recreations:* walking and theatre-going. *Address:* 19 Lichfield Road, Woodford Green, Essex IG8 9SU.

BOTTOMLEY, Lady; Bessie Ellen Bottomley, DBE 1970; *b* 28 Nov. 1906; *d* of Edward Charles Wiles and Ellen (*née* Estall); *m* 1936, Baron Bottomley, *qv*; no *c*. *Educ:* Maynard Road Girls' Sch.; North Walthamstow Central Sch. On staff of NUT, 1925–36. Member: Walthamstow Borough Council, 1945–48; Essex CC, 1962–65; Chm., Labour Party Women's Section, E Walthamstow, 1946–71, Chingford, 1973–. Mem., Forest Group Hosp. Man. Cttee, 1949–73; Mem., W Roding Community Health Council, 1973–76. Chm., Walthamstow Nat. Savings Cttee, 1949–65; Vice-Pres., Waltham Forest Nat. Savings Cttee, 1965– (Chm., 1975–). Mayoress of Walthamstow, 1945–46. Mem., WVS Regional Staff (SE England), 1941–45. Past Mem., Home Office Adv. Cttee on Child Care. Chm. of Govs of two Secondary Modern Schools, 1948–68, also group of Primary and Infant Schools; Chm. of Governors of High Schools. Mem., Whitefield Trust. JP 1955–76 and on Juvenile Bench, 1955–71; Dep. Chm., Waltham Forest Bench. *Recreations:* theatre, gardening. *Address:* 19 Lichfield Road, Woodford Green, Essex IG8 9SU.

BOTTOMLEY, Sir James (Reginald Alfred), KCMG 1973 (CMG 1965); HM Diplomatic Service, retired; *b* 12 Jan. 1920; *s* of Sir (William) Cecil Bottomley, KCMG, and Alice Thistle Bottomley (*née* Robinson), JP; *m* 1941, Barbara Evelyn Vardon (*d* 1994); two *s* two *d* (and one *s* decd). *Educ:* King's College Sch., Wimbledon; Trinity Coll., Cambridge. Served with Inns of Court Regt, RAC, 1940–46. Dominions Office, 1946; Pretoria, 1948–50; Karachi, 1953–55; Washington, 1955–59; UK Mission to United Nations, 1959; Dep. High Commissioner, Kuala Lumpur 1963–67; Assst Under-Sec. of State, Commonwealth Office (later FCO), 1967–70; Dep. Under-Sec. of State, FCO, 1970–72; Ambassador to South Africa, 1973–76; Perm. UK Rep. to UN and other Internat. Organisations at Geneva, 1976–78; Dir, Johnson Matthey plc, 1979–85. Mem., British Overseas Trade Bd, 1972. *Recreation:* golf. *Address:* 22 Beaufort Place, Thompson's Lane, Cambridge CB5 8AG. *T:* Cambridge (01223) 328760.

See also *P. J. Bottomley.*

BOTTOMLEY, Peter James; MP (C) Eltham, since 1983 (Greenwich, Woolwich West, June 1975–1983); *b* 30 July 1944; *er s* of Sir James Bottomley, *qv*; *m* 1967, Virginia Garnett (*see* Rt Hon. Virginia Bottomley); one *s* two *d*. *Educ:* comprehensive sch.; Westminster Sch.; Trinity Coll., Cambridge (MA). Driving, industrial sales, industrial relations, industrial economics. Contested (C) GLC elect., Vauxhall, 1973; (C) Woolwich West, Gen. Elecs, 1974. PPS to Minister of State, FCO, 1982–83, to Sec. of State for Social Services, 1983–84, to Sec. of State for NI, 1990; Parly Under Sec. of State, Dept of Employment, 1984–86, Dept of Transport, 1986–89, NI Office, 1989–90. Secretary: Cons. Parly Social Services Cttee, 1977–79; Cons. Parly For. and Commonwealth Cttee, 1979–81. Mem., Transport House Br., T&GWU, 1971–; Pres., Cons. Trade Unionists, 1978–80; Vice-Pres., Fedn of Cons. Students, 1980–82. Chairman: British Union of Family Orgns, 1973–80; Family Forum, 1980–82; Church of England Children's Soc., 1983–84. Mem. Council, MIND, 1981–82; Trustee, Christian Aid, 1978–84. Parly Swimming Champion, 1980–81, 1984–86; Captain, Parly Football Team. Castrol/Inst. of Motor Industry Road Safety Gold Medal, 1988. *Recreation:* children. *Address:* House of Commons, SW1A 0AA.

BOTTOMLEY, Rt. Hon. Virginia (Hilda Brunette Maxwell), PC 1992; JP; MP (C) Surrey South-West, since May 1984; Secretary of State for National Heritage, since 1995; *b* 12 March 1948; *d* of W. John Garnett, *qv*; *m* Peter Bottomley, *qv*; one *s* two *d*. *Educ:* Putney High Sch.; Univ. of Essex (BA); London Sch. of Econs and Pol Science (MSc). Research for Child Poverty Action Gp, 1971–73; psychiatric social worker, 1973–84. Vice Chm., National Council of Carers and their Elderly Dependants, 1982–88. Dir, Mid Southern Water Co., 1987–88. Mem., MRC, 1987–88. Contested (C) IoW, 1983. PPS to: Minister of State for Educn and Science, 1985–86; Minister for Overseas Develt, 1986–87; Sec. of State for Foreign and Commonwealth Affairs, 1987–88; Parly Under-Sec. of State, DoE, 1988–89; Minister for Health, 1989–92; Sec. of State for Health, 1992–95. Sec., Cons. Backbench Employment Cttee, 1985; Fellow, Industry Parlt Trust, 1987. Co-Chm., Women's Nat. Commn, 1991–92. Mem., Court of Govs, LSE, 1985–; Gov., Ditchley Foundn, 1991–. JP Inner London, 1975 (Chm., Lambeth Juvenile Court, 1981–84). Freeman, City of London, 1988. *Recreation:* family. *Address:* House of Commons, SW1A 0AA. *T:* 0171–219 6499. *Club:* Seaview Yacht.

BOTTOMS, Prof. Anthony Edward; Wolfson Professor of Criminology and Director of the Institute of Criminology, University of Cambridge, since 1984; Fellow of Fitzwilliam College, Cambridge, since 1984 (President, since 1994); *b* 29 Aug. 1939; *yr s* of James William Bottoms, medical missionary, and Dorothy Ethel Bottoms (*née* Barnes); *m* 1962, Janet Freda Wenger; one *s* two *d*. *Educ:* Eltham Coll.; Corpus Christi Coll., Oxford (MA); Corpus Christi Coll., Cambridge (MA); Univ. of Sheffield (PhD). Probation Officer, 1962–64; Research Officer, Inst. of Criminology, Univ. of Cambridge, 1964–68; Univ. of Sheffield: Lecturer, 1968–72; Sen. Lectr, 1972–76; Prof. of Criminology, 1976–84; Dean of Faculty of Law, 1981–84. Canadian Commonwealth Vis. Fellow, Simon Fraser Univ., BC, 1982. Member: Parole Bd for England and Wales, 1974–76; Home Office Res. and Adv. Gp on Long-Term Prison System, 1984–90. Trustee, Police Foundn, 1990–. Editor, Howard Journal of Penology and Crime Prevention, 1975–81. *Publications:* (jtly) Criminals Coming of Age, 1973; (jtly) The Urban Criminal, 1976; (jtly) Defendants in the Criminal Process, 1976; The Suspended Sentence after Ten Years (Frank Dawtry Lecture), 1980; (ed jtly) The Coming Penal Crisis, 1980; (ed jtly) Problems of Long-Term Imprisonment, 1987; (jtly) Social Inquiry Reports, 1988; (jtly) Intermediate Treatment and Juvenile Justice, 1990; Crime Prevention facing the 1990s (James Smart Lecture), 1990; various articles and reviews. *Address:* Institute of Criminology, 7 West Road, Cambridge CB3 9DT. *T:* Cambridge (01223) 335360.

BOTWOOD, Richard Price; Director-General, Chartered Institute of Transport, since 1989; *b* 1 June 1932; *s* of Allan Bertram and Hilda Amelia Botwood; *m* 1964, Victoria Sanderson; one *s* one *d*. *Educ:* Oundle School. Sec., Tozer Kemsley & Millbourn, 1952–56; Dir, International Factors, 1956–61; Asst Man. Dir, Melbray Group, 1961–73; Chm. and Man. Dir, W. S. Sanderson (Morpeth), wine and spirit merchants, 1973–85; Dir-Gen., Air Transport Users' Cttee, 1986–89. *Recreations:* opera, gardening, squash, golf. *Address:* 34 Brook Green, W6 7BL. *T:* 0171–603 5277.

BOUCHER, Prof. Robert Francis, PhD; FEng, FIMechE; Principal and Vice-Chancellor, University of Manchester Institute of Science and Technology, since 1995; *b* 25 April 1940; *s* of Robert Boucher and Johanna (*née* Fox); *m* 1965, Rosemary Ellen Maskell; two *s* one *d* (and one *s* decd). *Educ:* St Ignatius Coll.; Borough Poly.; Nottingham Univ. (PhD 1966). FEng 1994; FIMechE 1992; MASME; MIEE. ICI Post-doctoral Fellow, Nottingham Univ., 1966; Queen's University, Belfast: Res. Fellow, 1966–68; Lectr, 1968–70; University of Sheffield: Lectr, 1970–76; Sen. Lectr, 1976–85; Prof. of Mech. Engrg, 1985–95; Pro-Vice-Chancellor, 1992–95. Chm., Engrg Profs' Council, 1993–95. FRSA 1987. *Publications:* in engrg jls and confs incl. Proc. IMechE, Trans ASME, Trans IEEE, Inst. of Physics. *Recreations:* hill-walking, music, exercise. *Address:* University of Manchester Institute of Science and Technology, PO Box No 88, Manchester M60 1QD. *T:* 0161–200 3800. *Club:* Athenæum.

BOUCHIER, Prof. Ian Arthur Dennis, CBE 1990; Professor of Medicine, University of Edinburgh, since 1986; Chief Scientist, Scottish Office Home and Health Department, since 1992; *b* 7 Sept. 1932; *s* of E. A. and M. Bouchier; *m* 1959, Patricia Norma Henshilwood; two *s*. *Educ:* Rondebosch Boys' High Sch., Cape Town; Univ. of Cape Town. MB, ChB, MD, FRCP, FRCPE, FFPHM; FRSE, FIBiol. Groote Schuur Hospital: House Officer, 1955–58; Registrar, 1958–61; Asst Lectr, Royal Free Hosp., 1962–63; Instructor in Medicine, Boston Univ. Sch. of Medicine, 1964–65; Sen. Lectr 1965–70, Reader in Medicine 1970–73, Univ. of London; Prof. of Medicine, 1973–86, and Dean, Faculty of Medicine and Dentistry, 1982–86, Univ. of Dundee. Pres., World Organisation of Gastroenterology, 1990– (Sec. Gen., 1982–90). Member: Chief Scientist Cttee, Scotland, 1980–; MRC, 1982–86; Council, RCPE, 1984–90; Council, British Soc. of Gastroenterology, 1987–90 (Chm., Educn Cttee, 1987–90; Pres., 1994–95). Goulstonian Lectr, RCP, 1971; Sydney Watson Smith Lectr, RCPE, 1991. Visiting Professor of Medicine: Michigan Univ., 1979; McGill Univ., 1983; RPMS, 1984; Shenyang Univ., Hong Kong Univ., 1988. FRSA. Hon. FCP (SoAf); Hon. Mem., Japanese Soc. Gastroenterology; Corresp. Member: Soc. Italiana di Gastroenterologia; Royal Catalonian Acad. of Medicine. Chm., Editl Bd, Current Opinion in Gastroenterology, 1987–91; Member, Editorial Board: Baillière's Clinical Gastroenterology, 1987–; Hellenic Jl of Gastroenterology, 1988–; Internat. Gastroenterology, 1988–. *Publications:* (ed jtly) Bilirubin Metabolism, 1967; (ed) Clinical Investigation of Gastrointestinal Function, 1969, 2nd edn 1981; (ed) Seventh Symposium on Advanced Medicine, 1971; (ed) Diseases of the Biliary Tract, vol. 2, 1973; Gastroenterology, 1973, 3rd edn 1982; (jtly) Aspects of Clinical Gastroenterology, 1975; (ed jtly) Clinical Skills, 1976, 2nd edn 1982; (ed) Recent Advances in Gastroenterology 3, 1976, 4, 1980, 5, 1983; (ed jtly) Textbook of Gastroenterology, 1984; (ed jtly) Inflammatory Bowel Disease, 1986, 2nd edn 1993; (ed jtly) Davidson's Principles and Practice of Medicine, 15th edn 1987, 16th edn 1991; (ed jtly) Clinical Investigations in Gastroenterology, 1988; (ed) Jaundice, 1989; (ed jtly) Infectious Diarrhoea, 1993; (ed jtly) Gastroenterology Clinical Science and Practice, vols 1 and 2, 2nd edn 1993; (ed jtly) Quality Assurance in Medical Care, 1993; 500 scientific papers and communications. *Recreations:* history of whaling, music of Berlioz, cooking. *Address:* Department of Medicine, The Royal Infirmary, Edinburgh EH3 9YW. *T:* 0131–229 2477. *Club:* New (Edinburgh).

BOUGH, Francis Joseph; broadcaster; Presenter: London Broadcasting Co., since 1992; London News Radio, since 1994; *b* 15 Jan. 1933; *m*; three *s*. *Educ:* Oswestry; Merton College, Oxford (MA). With ICI, 1957–62; joined BBC, 1962; presenter of Sportsview, 1964–67, of Grandstand, 1967–82, of Nationwide, 1972–83, of breakfast television, 1983–87, of Holiday, 1987–88, of 6 o'clock Live, LWT, 1989–92, on Sky TV, 1989–90. Former Oxford soccer blue, Shropshire sprint champion. *Publications:* Cue Frank! (autobiog.), 1980; Frank Bough's Breakfast Book, 1984. *Address:* c/o Jon Roseman Agency, 46 Sutton Court Road, W4 4NL.

BOUGHEY, John Fenton C.; *see* Coplestone-Boughey.

BOUGHEY, Sir John (George Fletcher), 11th Bt *cr* 1798; medical practitioner; *b* 12 Aug. 1959; *s* of Sir Richard James Boughey, 10th Bt, and of Davina Julia (now the Lady Loch), *d* of FitzHerbert Wright; *S* father, 1978. *Educ:* Eton; Univ. of Zimbabwe (MB ChB 1984); LRCPE; LRCSE; LRCPSGlas 1990; MRCPI 1994. *Heir:* *b* James Richard Boughey [*b* 29 Aug. 1960; *m* 1989, Katy Fenwicke-Clennell; one *s* one *d*]. *Address:* Bratton House, Westbury, Wilts BA13 4RN.

BOULET, Gilles, OC 1985; Musée des arts et traditions populaires du Québec, since 1990; *b* 5 June 1926; *s* of Georges-A. Boulet and Yvonne Hamel; *m* 1971, Florence Lemire; one *s* one *d*. *Educ:* Coll. St Gabriel de St Tite; Séminaire St Joseph de Trois-Rivières; Laval Univ. (LTh 1951, DèsL 1954); Université Catholique de Paris (LPh, MA 1953). Prof. of Literature and History, Séminaire Ste Marie, Shawinigan, 1953–61; Centre d'Etudes Universitaires de Trois-Rivières: Founder, 1960; Dir, 1960–69; Prof. of Lit. and Hist., 1961–66; Laval University: Prof. of French, Faculty of Lit., 1955–62; Aggregate Prof., Fac. of Arts, 1959; Rector, Univ. du Québec à Trois-Rivières, 1969–78, Rector-Founder, 1979; Pres., Univ. of Quebec, 1978–88 (Asst to Pres., 1988–89). Founder and Pres., Inter-Amer. Orgn for Higher Educn, 1981–. Dr *hc* Universidade Federal de Rio Grande do Norte, Brazil, 1983; Univ. du Québec, 1992; Hon. Master of Administration, Univ. Autonoma de Guerrero, Mexico, 1984. Comdr, Assoc. Belgo-Hispanique, 1980; Comdr, Mérite et Dévouement Français, 1980; Officier de la Légion d'Honneur (France), 1988. Duvernay Award, Soc. St-Jean-Baptiste de Trois-Rivières (literature award), 1978; Gold Medal, Univ. Federal da Bahia, Brazil, 1983; Gold Medal of Merit (Sousandrade), Universidade Federal do Maranhão, Brazil, 1986; Medal, Gloire de l'Escolle, Laval Univ., 1988. Personality of the Year, CKTM/TV, 1988 . *Publications:* Nationalisme ou Séparatisme, Nationalisme et Séparatisme, 1961; (with Lucien Gagné) Le Français Parlé au Cours Secondaire, vols I and II, 1962, vols III and IV, 1963; Textes et Préceptes Littéraires, vol. I, 2nd edn, 1967, vol. II, 1964; (with others) Le Boréal Express, Album no 1, 1965, Album no 2, 1967; De la philosophie comme passion de la liberté, 1984; Going Global, 1988. *Recreations:* reading, skiing, skating. *Address:* 3021 de la Promenade, Ste Foy, Quebec G1W 2J5, Canada. *T:* (418) 6574266. *Club:* Saint-Maurice Hunting and Fishing (Quebec).

BOULEZ, Pierre; Hon. CBE 1979; composer; Director, Institut de Recherche et de Coordination Acoustique/Musique, 1976–91; *b* Montbrison, Loire, France, 26 March 1925. *Educ:* Saint-Etienne and Lyon (music and higher mathematics); Paris Conservatoire. Studied with Messiaen and René Leibowitz. Theatre conductor, Jean-Louis Barrault Company, Paris, 1948; visited USA with French Ballet Company, 1952. Has conducted major orchestras in his own and standard classical works in Great Britain, Europe and USA; also conducted Wozzeck in Paris and Frankfurt; Parsifal at Bayreuth, 1966–70; The Ring, at Bayreuth, 1976–80; Chief Conductor, BBC Symphony Orchestra, 1971–75; Music Dir, NY Philharmonic, 1971–77. Hon. DMus: Cantab, 1980; Oxon, 1987. Charles Heidsieck Award for Outstanding Contribution to Franco-British Music, 1989. Interested in poetry and aesthetics of Baudelaire, Mallarmé and René Char. *Compositions include:* Sonata No 1 (piano), 1946; Sonatine for flute and piano, 1946; Sonata No 2 (piano), 1948; Polyphonie X for 18 solo instruments, 1951; Visage nuptial (2nd version), 1951, rev. version, 1989; Structures for 2 pianos, 1952; Le Marteau sans Maître (voice and 6 instruments), 1954; Sonata No 3 (piano), 1956; Deux Improvisations sur Mallarmé for voice and 9 instruments, 1957; Doubles for orchestra, 1958; Poésie pour Pouvoir for voices and orchestra, 1958; Soleil des Eaux (text by René Char) for chorus and orchestra, 1958; Pli selon Pli: Hommage à Mallarmé, for voice and orchestra, 1960; Eclat, 1965; Domaines for solo clarinet, 1968; Cummings ist der Dichter (16 solo voices and instruments), 1970; Eclat/Multiples, 1970; Explosante Fixe (8 solo instruments), 1972; Rituel, for orchestra, 1975; Messagesquisses (7 celli), 1977; Notations, for orch., 1980; Répons, for orch. and live electronics, 1981–86; Mémoriale, 1984; Dérive, 1985; Dialogue de l'Ombre Double, 1986; Anthèmes, for violin solo, 1991; . . . explosaute/fixe . . . , for 3 flutes, large ensemble and electronics, 1993. *Publications:* Penser la musique d'aujourd'hui, 1966 (Boulez on Music Today, 1971); Relevés d'apprenti, 1967; Par volonté et par hasard, 1976; Points de Repère, 1981; Orientations, 1986; Jalons, 1989; Le pays fertile—Paul Klee, 1989. *Address:* IRCAM, 1 place Igor Stravinsky, 75004 Paris, France. *T:* 44781233.

BOULIND, Mrs (Olive) Joan, CBE 1975; Fellow, 1973–79, and Tutor, 1974–79, Hughes Hall, Cambridge; *b* 24 Sept. 1912; *e d* of Douglas Siddall and Olive Raby; *m* 1936, Henry F. Boulind (decd), MA, PhD; one *s* (and one *s* one *d* decd). *Educ:* Wallasey High Sch., Cheshire; Univ. of Liverpool (BA 1st class Hons History, Medieval and Modern; DipEd); MA Cantab 1974. Teacher: Wirral Co. Sch. for Girls, 1934–36; Cambridgeshire High Sch. for Girls, 1963. Nat. Pres., Nat. Council of Women, 1966–68 (Sen. Vice-Pres., 1964–66); Co-Chm., Women's Consultative Council, 1966–68; Leader, British delegn to conf. of Internat. Council of Women, Bangkok, 1970; Co-Chm., Women's Nat. Commn, 1973–75; Co-Chm., UK Co-ordinating Cttee for Internat. Women's Year, 1975; Chm., Westminster College Management Cttee, 1980–88. Member: Commn on the Church in the Seventies, Congregational Church in England and Wales, 1970–72 (Vice-Chm., 1971–72); Ministerial Trng Cttee, United Reformed Church, 1972–79 and 1982–86 (Chm., 1982–86); East Adv. Council, BBC, 1976–84 (Chm. 1981–84). Deacon, Emmanuel Congregational Ch., Cambridge, 1958–66. Trustee, Homerton Coll. of Educn, 1955–94. *Recreations:* reading, travel, music. *Address:* 28 Rathmore Road, Cambridge CB1 4AD.

BOULTER, Prof. Donald, CBE 1991; FIBiol; Head of Department of Biological Sciences, University of Durham, 1988–91 (Professor of Botany and Head of Department of Botany, 1966–88); Director of Durham University Botanic Garden, 1966–91; *b* 25 Aug. 1926; *s* of late George Boulter and of Vera Boulter; *m* 1956, Margaret Eileen Kennedy; four *d*. *Educ:* Portsmouth Grammar Sch.; Christ Church, Oxford (BA, MA, DPhil). FIBiol 1970. Served RAF, 1945–48. Sessel Fellow, Yale Univ., 1953–54; Asst Lectr in Botany, King's Coll., London, 1955–57; Lectr 1957–64, Sen. Lectr 1964–66, Liverpool Univ. Vis. Prof., Univ. of Texas, Austin, 1967. Chm., Plant Science Res. Ltd, 1992–96. Member: AFRC, 1985–89; Biological Scis Sub-Cttee, UFC (formerly UGC), 1988–89; Chm., Plants & Soils Res. Grant Bd, 1986–89; Pres., Sect. K, BAAS, 1981. Dep. Chm. Governing Body, AFRC Inst. of Horticultural Res., 1987–90; Member, Governing Body: Scottish Crop Res. Inst., 1986–92; AFRC Inst. of Plant Sci. Res., 1989–92. Mem., Exec. Cttee, Horticultural Res. Internat., 1990–96. FRSA 1972. Tate & Lyle Award for Phytochem., 1975. *Publications:* (ed) Chemotaxonomy of the Leguminosae, 1971; (ed) Encyclopedia of Plant Physiology, vol. 14B: Nucleic Acids and Proteins, 1982; papers in sci. jls on molecular evolution, genetic engrg of crops, biochem. and molecular biol of seed develt. *Recreation:* travel. *Address:* 5 Crossgate, Durham DH1 4PS. *T:* Durham (0191) 3861199.

BOULTER, Patrick Stewart, FRCSE, FRCS; Hon. Consultant Surgeon, Royal Surrey County Hospital and Regional Radiotherapy Centre, since 1991; President, Royal College of Surgeons of Edinburgh, 1991–94; *b* 28 May 1927; *s* of Frederick Charles Boulter, MC and Flora Victoria Boulter of Annan, Dumfriesshire; *m* 1946, Patricia Mary Eckersley Barlow, *d* of S. G. Barlow of Lowton, Lancs; two *d*. *Educ:* King's Coll. Sch.; Carlisle GS; Guy's Hosp. Med. Sch., Univ. of London (MB BS Hons and Gold Medal, 1955). FRCS 1958; FRCSE 1958; FRCPE 1993; FRCPSGlas 1993. Guy's Hospital and Medical School, University of London: House Surgeon, 1955–56; Res. Fellow, Dept of Surgery, 1956–57; Lectr in Anatomy, 1956–57; Sen. Surgical Registrar, 1959–62; Hon. Consultant Surgeon, 1963; Surgical Registrar, Middlesex Hosp., 1957–59; Consultant Surgeon, Royal Surrey County and St Luke's Hosps, Guildford, 1962–91; Vis. Surgeon, Cranleigh and Cobham Hosps, 1962–91. Chm., Conf. of Colls and Faculties (Scotland), 1992. Visiting Professor: Surrey Univ., 1986– (Hon. Reader, 1968–80); univs in USA, Australia, NZ, Pakistan and India. Examnr, Univs of Edinburgh, London, Nottingham and Newcastle. Royal College of Surgeons: Surgical Tutor, 1964; Regl Advr, 1975; Penrose May teacher, 1985–; Royal College of Surgeons of Edinburgh: Examnr, 1979; Mem. Council, 1984–; Vice-Pres., 1989–91. Hon. FRACS 1985; Hon. FCS(SA) 1992; Hon. FCSSL 1992; Hon. FRCSI 1993; Hon. FCSHK 1993; Mem., Acad. of Medicine of Malaysia, 1993; Hon. Member: Assoc. of Surgeons of India, 1993; Soc. of Surgeons of Nepal, 1994; Surgical Res. Soc., 1995; Fellow, Acad. of Medicine of Singapore, 1994. Hon. Citizen, State of Nebraska, USA, 1967. *Publications:* articles and book chapters on surgical subjects, esp. breast disease, surgical oncology and endocrine surgery. *Recreations:* mountaineering, skiing, fly-fishing. *Address:* Cairnsmore, Fairway, Merrow, Guildford, Surrey GU1 2XN. *T:* Guildford (01483) 504977; Quarry Cottage, Salkeld Dykes, Penrith, Cumbria CA11 9LL. *T:* Lazonby (01768) 898822. *Clubs:* Alpine, Caledonian; New (Edinburgh); Yorkshire Fly Fishers; Swiss Alpine.

BOULTING, Roy; Producer and Joint Managing Director, Charter Film Productions Ltd, since 1973; *b* 21 Nov. 1913; *s* of Arthur Boulting and Rose Bennett. *Educ:* HMS Worcester; Reading Sch. Formed independent film production company with twin brother John, 1937. Served War of 1939–45, RAC, finishing as Capt.; films for Army included Desert Victory and Burma Victory. Producer: Brighton Rock, 1947; Seven Days to Noon, 1950; Private's Progress, 1955; Lucky Jim (Edinburgh Festival), 1957; I'm All Right Jack, 1959; Heavens Above!, 1962. Director: Pastor Hall, 1939; Thunder Rock, 1942; Fame is the Spur, 1947; The Guinea Pig, 1948; High Treason, 1951; Singlehanded, 1952; Seagulls over Sorrento, Crest of the Wave, 1953; Josephine and Men, 1955; Run for the Sun, 1955; Brothers in Law, 1956; Happy is the Bride, 1958; Carlton-Browne of the FO, 1958–59; I'm All Right Jack, 1959; The Risk, 1960; The French Mistress, 1960; Suspect, 1960; The Family Way, 1966; Twisted Nerve, 1968; There's a Girl in My Soup, 1970; Soft Beds, Hard Battles, 1974; Danny Travis, 1978; The Last Word, 1979; The Moving Finger, 1984. *Play:* (with Leo Marks) Favourites, 1977. Dir, British Lion Films Ltd, 1958–72. Mem. Adv. Council, Dirs' and Producers' Rights Soc., 1988–. Hon. Dr RCA, 1990. *Address:* Charter Film Productions Ltd, Twickenham Film Studios, St Margarets, Twickenham, Middlesex TW1 2AW. *Club:* Lord's Taverners.

BOULTING, S. A.; *see* Cotes, Peter.

BOULTON, Sir Christian; *see* Boulton, Sir H. H. C.

BOULTON, Sir Clifford (John), GCB 1994 (KCB 1990; CB 1985); Clerk of the House of Commons, 1987–94; *b* 25 July 1930; *s* of Stanley Boulton and Evelyn (*née* Hey), Cocknage, Staffs; *m* 1955, Anne, *d* of Rev. E. E. Raven, Cambridge; one adopted *s* one adopted *d*. *Educ:* Newcastle-under-Lyme High School; St John's Coll., Oxford (exhibnr). MA (Modern History). National Service, RAC, 1949–50; Lt Staffs Yeomanry (TA). A Clerk in the House of Commons, 1953–94: Clerk of Select Cttees on Procedure, 1964–68 and 1976–77; Public Accounts, 1968–70; Parliamentary Questions, 1971–72; Privileges, 1972–77; Clerk of the Overseas Office, 1977–79; Principal Clerk, Table Office, 1979–83; Clerk Asst, 1983–87. A school Governor and subsequently board mem., Church Schools

Company, 1965–79. Trustee, Industry and Parliament Trust, 1991–95. Mem., Standing Cttee on Standards in Public Life, 1994–. Hon. LLD Keele, 1993. *Publications:* (ed) Erskine May's Parliamentary Practice, 21st edn, 1989; contribs to Halsbury's Laws of England, 4th edn, and Parliamentary journals. *Recreations:* visual arts, the countryside. *Address:* 2 Main Street, Lyddington, Oakham LE15 9LT. *T:* Uppingham (01572) 823487.

BOULTON, Prof. Geoffrey Stewart, FRS 1992; FRSE; Regius Professor of Geology and Mineralogy, since 1986, Provost and Dean, Faculty of Science and Engineering, since 1994, University of Edinburgh; *b* 28 Nov. 1940; *s* of George Stewart and Rose Boulton; *m* 1964, Denise Bryers Lawns; two *d*. *Educ:* Longton High Sch.; Birmingham Univ. BSc, PhD, DSc. FGS 1961; FRSE 1989. British Geol Survey, 1962–64; Demonstrator, Univ. of Keele, 1964–65; Fellow, Univ. of Birmingham, 1965–68; Hydrogeologist, Kenya, 1968; Lectr, then Reader, Univ. of E Anglia, 1968–86. Prof., Amsterdam Univ., 1980–86. Mem., Royal Commn on Envmtl Pollution, 1994–. NERC: Chairman: Polar Sci. Bd, 1992–; Earth Sci. and Technol. Bd, 1994–; Mem., Higher Educn Affairs Cttee and Earth Sci. Cttee, 1993–; Mem. Council, 1993–; Royal Society: Chm., Sect. Cttee 5 for Earth Sci. and Astronomy, 1993–95; Mem., Hooke Cttee, 1993–; Grants Cttee, 1993–; Exchange Prog. Cttee, 1994–. NCC Scotland, 1991–92; ESF Climate Change Cttee; Bd, Petroleum Sci. and Technology Inst., 1989–. President: Geol Soc. of Edinburgh, 1991–93; Quaternary Res. Assoc., 1991–94. *Publications:* numerous articles in learned jls on glaciology, quaternary, marine and polar geology. *Recreations:* violin, mountaineering. *Address:* 19 Lygon Road, Edinburgh EH16 5QD.

BOULTON, Sir (Harold Hugh) Christian, 4th Bt *cr* 1905; *b* 29 Oct. 1918; *s* of Sir (Denis Duncan) Harold (Owen) Boulton, 3rd Bt, and Louise McGowan (*d* 1978), USA; *S* father, 1968. *Educ:* Ampleforth College, Yorks. Late Captain, Irish Guards (Supplementary Reserve). *Address:* 37 Jay Avenue, Nepean, Ontario K29 0C1, Canada.

BOULTON, Prof. James Thompson, FBA 1994; Director, Institute for Advanced Research in the Humanities, University of Birmingham, since 1987 (Fellow, 1984); *b* 17 Feb. 1924; *e s* of Harry and Annie M. P. Boulton; *m* 1949, Margaret Helen Leary; one *s* one *d*. *Educ:* University College, Univ. of Durham; Lincoln Coll., Oxford. BA Dunelm 1948; BLitt Oxon 1952; PhD Nottingham 1960. FRSL 1968. Served in RAF, 1943–46 (Flt-Lt). Lectr, subseq. Sen. Lectr and Reader in English, Univ. of Nottingham, 1951–64; John Cranford Adams Prof. of English, Hofstra Univ., NY, 1967; Prof. of English Lit., Univ. of Nottingham, 1964–75, Dean, Faculty of Arts, 1970–73; University of Birmingham: Prof. of English Studies and Head of Dept of English Lang. and Lit., 1975–88, Prof. Emeritus, 1989; Dean of Faculty of Arts, 1981–84; Public Orator, 1984–88. Chm. of Govs, Fircroft Coll., Selly Oak, 1985–92. Editor, Renaissance and Modern Studies, 1969–75, 1985. General Editor: The Letters of D. H. Lawrence, 1973–; The Works of D. H. Lawrence, 1975–. Hon. DLitt: Dunelm, 1991; Nottingham, 1993. *Publications:* (ed) Edmund Burke: A Philosophical Enquiry into . . . the Sublime and Beautiful, 1958, rev. edn 1987; (ed) C. F. G. Masterman: The Condition of England, 1960; The Language of Politics in the Age of Wilkes and Burke, 1963, 2nd edn 1975; (ed) Dryden: Of Dramatick Poesy etc, 1964; (ed) Defoe: Prose and Verse, 1965, 2nd edn 1975; (with James Kinsley) English Satiric Poetry: Dryden to Byron, 1966; (ed) Lawrence in Love: Letters from D. H. Lawrence to Louie Burrows, 1968; (ed) Samuel Johnson: The Critical Heritage, 1971; (with S. T. Bindoff) Research in Progress in English and Historical Studies in the Universities of the British Isles, vol. 1, 1971, vol. 2, 1976; (ed) Defoe: Memoirs of a Cavalier, 1972, rev. edn 1991; (ed) The Letters of D. H. Lawrence, vol. 1, 1979, vol. 2 (jtly), 1982, vol. 3 (jtly), 1984, vol. 4 (jtly), 1987, vol. 5 (jtly), 1989, vol. 6 (jtly), 1991, vol. 7 (jtly), 1993; (contrib.) Renaissance and Modern Essays (ed G. R. Hibbard), 1966; (contrib.) The Familiar Letter in the 18th Century (ed H. Anderson), 1966; papers in Durham Univ. Jl, Essays in Criticism, Renaissance and Modern Studies, Modern Drama, etc. *Recreation:* gardening. *Address:* Institute for Advanced Research in the Humanities, University of Birmingham, Edgbaston, Birmingham B15 2TT.

See also P. H. Boulton.

BOULTON, Rev. Canon Peter Henry; Chaplain to the Queen, 1991–95; *b* 12 Dec. 1925; *s* of Harry Boulton and Annie Mary Penty Boulton; *m* 1955, Barbara Ethelinda Davies, SRN, SCM; three *s*. *Educ:* Lady Lumley's Grammar Sch., Pickering, N Yorks; St Chad's Coll., Univ. of Durham (BA Hons Theology); Ely Theol Coll., Cambs; Cardiff Law Sch. RNVR, 1943–46. Ordained deacon, 1950, priest, 1951 (Chester). Asst Curate: Coppenhall S Michael, Crewe, 1950–54; S Mark, Mansfield, 1954–55; Vicar: Clipstone Colliery Village, Notts, 1955–60, St John the Baptist, Carlton, Nottingham, 1960–67; Worksop Priory, 1967–87; Hon. Canon of Southwell, 1975–87; Canon Residentiary of Southwell Minster and Diocesan Dir of Educn, 1987–92, Canon Emeritus, 1993. C of E Delegate: ACC, 1972–80; WCC Assembly, Nairobi, 1975. Proctor in Convocation and Mem., Gen. Synod of C of E, 1959–92; Prolocutor of York Convocation and Jt Chm., House of Clergy, Gen. Synod, 1980–90; Member: Howick Commn on Crown Appts, 1962–64; Standing Cttee of Gen. Synod, 1974–90; Churches' Council for Covenanting, 1978–82; Crown Appts Commn, 1982–87 and 1988–92; Legal Adv. Commn of Gen. Synod, 1985–91; Gen. Synod Bd of Educn, 1991–92; Gen. Cttee, Ecclesiastical Law Soc., 1991–. Mem., Notts County Educn Cttee, 1987–92; County Gov., local primary sch., 1993–. *Publications:* articles in learned and ecclesiastical jls. *Recreations:* crosswords, bridge, local history, swimming. *Address:* 3 Grasmere Drive, Holmes Chapel, Cheshire CW4 7JT.

See also J. T. Boulton.

BOULTON, Sir William (Whytehead), 3rd Bt *cr* 1944; Kt 1975; CBE 1958; TD 1949; Secretary, Senate of the Inns of Court and the Bar, 1974–75; *b* 21 June 1912; *s* of Sir William Boulton, 1st Bt, and Rosalind Mary (*d* 1969), *d* of Sir John Davison Milburn, 1st Bt, of Guyzance, Northumberland; *S* brother, 1982; *m* 1944, Margaret Elizabeth, *o d* of late Brig. H. N. A. Hunter, DSO; one *s* two *d*. *Educ:* Eton; Trinity Coll., Cambridge. Called to Bar, Inner Temple, 1936; practised at the Bar, 1937–39. Secretary, General Council of the Bar, 1950–74. Served War of 1939–45: with 104th Regt RHA (Essex Yeo.) and 14th Regt RHA, in the Middle East, 1940–44; Staff Coll., Camberley, 1944. Control Commission for Germany (Legal Div.), 1945–50. Gazetted 2nd Lieut TA (Essex Yeo.), 1934; retired with rank of Hon. Lieut-Col. *Publications:* A Guide to Conduct and Etiquette at the Bar of England and Wales, 1st edn 1953, 6th edn, 1975. *Heir:* *s* John Gibson Boulton, *b* 18 Dec. 1946. *Address:* The Quarters House, Alresford, near Colchester, Essex CO7 8AY. *T:* Wivenhoe (01206) 822450.

BOUNDS, (Kenneth) Peter; Chief Executive, Liverpool City Council, since 1991; *b* 7 Nov. 1943; *s* of Rev. Kenneth Bounds and Doris Bounds; *m* 1965, Geraldine Amy Slee; two *s*. *Educ:* Ashville College, Harrogate. Admitted Solicitor, 1971. Dir of Admin, Stockport MBC, 1973–82; Chief Exec., Bolton MBC, 1982–91. Pres., Assoc. of Dist Secs, 1980–81; Company Secretary: Greater Manchester Econ. Develt Ltd, 1986–91; NW Tourist Bd, 1986–91. Dir, Royal Liverpool Philharmonic Soc., 1993–. Chairman: Liverpool City Challenge, 1991–95; Liverpool City of Learning, 1994–. Mem., President's Council, Methodist Church, 1981–84. Hon. Fellow, Bolton Inst. of Higher Educn, 1991. FRSA 1994. *Recreations:* music, theatre. *Address:* Municipal Buildings, Dale Street, Liverpool L69 2DH.

BOURASSA, Robert; Leader, Quebec Liberal Party, 1970–77 and 1983–94; Prime Minister of Québec, 1970–76 and 1985–94; Member of Québec National Assembly for St Laurent, 1986–94 (for Mercier, 1966–76 and for Bertrand, 1985); *b* 14 July 1933; *s* of Aubert Bourassa and Adrienne Courville; *m* 1958, Andrée Simard; one *s* one *d*. *Educ:* Jean-de-Brébeuf Coll.; Univs of Montreal, Oxford and Harvard. Gov.-Gen.'s Medal Montreal 1956. MA Oxford 1959. Admitted Quebec Bar 1957. Fiscal Adviser to Dept of Nat. Revenue and Prof. in Econs and Public Finance, Ottawa Univ., 1960–63; Sec. and Dir of Research of Bélanger Commn on Taxation, 1963–65; Special Adviser to Fed. Dept of Finance on fiscal and econ. matters, 1965–66; Prof. of Public Finance, Univs of Montreal and Laval, 1966–69; financial critic for Quebec Liberal Party; Minister of Finance, May–Nov. 1970; Minister of Inter-govtl Affairs, 1971–72. Lectr, Institut d'Etudes Européennes, Brussels, 1977–78; Prof., Center of Advanced Internat. Studies, Johns Hopkins Univ., 1978; Prof., Univ. de Laval, Univ. de Montréal, 1979; Visiting Professor: INSEAD, Fontainebleau, 1976; Univ. of Southern Calif., 1981; Yale Univ., 1982. Hon. DPhil Univ. of Tel-Aviv, 1987. *Publications:* Bourassa/Québec!, 1970; La Baie James, 1973 (James Bay, 1973); Les années Bourassa: l'intégrale des entretiens Bourassa–St Pierre, 1977; Deux fois la Baie James, 1981; Power from the North, 1985; L'Energie du Nord: la force du Québec, 1985; Le défi technologique, 1985.

BOURDEAUX, Rev. Canon Michael Alan; Director, Keston Institute, Oxford (formerly Keston College, Kent), since 1969; *b* 19 March 1934; *s* of Richard Edward and Lillian Myra Bourdeaux; *m* 1st, 1960, Gillian Mary Davies (*d* 1978); one *s* one *d*; 2nd, 1979, Lorna Elizabeth Waterton; one *s* one *d*. *Educ:* Truro Sch.; St Edmund Hall, Oxford (MA Hons Mod. Langs); Wycliffe Hall, Oxford (Hons Theology). Moscow State Univ., 1959–60; Deacon, 1960; Asst Curate, Enfield Parish Church, Mddx, 1960–64; researching at Chislehurst, Kent, on the Church in the Soviet Union, with grant from Centre de Recherches, Geneva, 1965–68. Vis. Prof., St Bernard's Seminary, Rochester, NY, 1969; Vis. Fellow, LSE, 1969–71; Research Fellow, RIIA, Chatham House, 1971–73; Dawson Lectr on Church and State, Baylor Univ., Waco, Texas, 1972; Chavasse Meml Lectr, Oxford Univ., 1976; Kathryn W. Davis Prof. in Slavic Studies, Wellesley Coll., Wellesley, Mass, 1981; Moorhouse Lectr, Melbourne, 1987; Vis. Fellow, St Edmund Hall, Oxford, 1989–90; Vis. Prof., Inst. for Econ., Political and Cultural Develt, Notre Dame Univ., Ind., 1993. Mem., High-Level Experts' Gp on For. Policy and Common Security, EC, 1993–94. Hon. Canon, Rochester Cathedral, 1990–. Founded Keston College, a research centre on religion in the Communist countries, 1969. Founder of journal, Religion in Communist Lands, 1973, retitled Religion, State and Society: the Keston Jl, 1992. Mem. Council, Britain–Russia Centre, 1991–. Templeton Prize for Progress in Religion, 1984. *Publications:* Opium of the People, 1965, 2nd edn 1977; Religious Ferment in Russia, 1968; Patriarch and Prophets, 1970, 2nd edn 1975; Faith on Trial in Russia, 1971; Land of Crosses, 1979; Risen Indeed, 1983; (with Lorna Bourdeaux) Ten Growing Soviet Churches, 1987; Gorbachev, Glasnost and the Gospel, 1990, rev. US edn, The Gospel's Triumph over Communism, 1991. *Recreations:* choral singing, officiating, as Member British Tennis Umpires Assoc., at Wimbledon and abroad. *Address:* Keston Institute, 4 Park Town, Oxford OX2 6SH. *T:* Oxford (01865) 311022; 101 Church Way, Iffley, Oxford OX4 4EG. *T:* Oxford (01865) 777276. *Club:* Athenæum.

BOURDILLON, Mervyn Leigh, JP; Lord-Lieutenant of Powys, since 1986; *b* 9 Aug. 1924; *s* of late Prebendary G. L. Bourdillon; *m* 1961, Penelope, *d* of late P. W. Kemp-Welch, OBE; one *s* three *d*. *Educ:* Haileybury. Served RNVR, 1943–46. Forestry Comr, 1973–76. Mem. Brecon County Council, 1962–73; DL 1962, JP 1970, High Sheriff 1970, Brecon; Vice Lord-Lieutenant, Powys, 1978–86. KStJ 1994. *Address:* Llwyn Madoc, Beulah, Llanwrtyd Wells, Powys LD5 4TU.

BOURDILLON, Peter John, FRCP; Grade 3, and Head of Health Care (Medical) Division, Department of Health, since 1993; Consultant in Clinical Physiology (Cardiology), Hammersmith Hospital, since 1974; *b* 10 July 1941; *s* of John Francis Bourdillon and Pamela Maud Bourdillon (*née* Chetham); *m* 1964, Catriona Glencairn-Campbell, FGA, *d* of Brig. W. Glencairn-Campbell, OBE and Lady Muir-Mackenzie; one *s* two *d*. *Educ:* Rugby Sch.; Middlesex Hosp. Med. Sch. (MB BS 1965). MRCP 1968, FRCP 1983. House physician and surgeon posts in London, 1965–68; Medical Registrar: Middlesex Hosp., 1969–70; Hammersmith Hosp., 1970–72; Sen. Registrar in Cardiol., Hammersmith Hosp., 1972–74; part-time MO, 1975–81, part-time SMO, 1981–91, Hd of Med. Manpower and Educn Div., 1991–93, DHSS, then DoH. Hon. Sen. Lectr, RPMS, London Univ., 1979–. *Publications:* contrib. to med. jls. *Recreations:* writing software, golf, ski-ing. *Address:* 13 Grove Terrace, NW5 1PH. *T:* 0171–485 6839. *Clubs:* Royal Society of Medicine; Highgate Golf.

BOURDON, Derek Conway, FIA; Director, 1981–84, and General Manager, 1979–84, Prudential Assurance Co. Ltd; Director, London and Manchester Group PLC, 1986–94; *b* 3 Nov. 1932; *s* of late Walter Alphonse Bourdon and Winifred Gladys Vera Bourdon; *m* 1st, Camilla Rose Bourdon (marr. diss.); one *s* one *d*; 2nd, Jean Elizabeth Bourdon. *Educ:* Bancroft's School. FIA 1957. RAF Operations Research (Pilot Officer), 1956–58. Joined Prudential, 1950; South Africa, 1962–65; Dep. General Manager, 1976–79. Chairman, Vanbrugh Life, 1974–79. Member, Policyholders Protection Board, 1980–84; Chm., Industrial Life Offices Assoc., 1982–84 (Vice-Chm., 1980–82). *Recreations:* golf, bridge. *Clubs:* Sloane; Crowborough Beacon Golf.

BOURKE, family name of **Earl of Mayo.**

BOURKE, Christopher John; Metropolitan Stipendiary Magistrate, since 1974; *b* 31 March 1926; *e s* of late John Francis Bourke of the Oxford Circuit and late Eileen Winifred Bourke (*née* Beddoes); *m* 1956, Maureen, *y d* of late G A. Barron-Boshell; two *s* one *d*. *Educ:* Stonyhurst; Oriel Coll., Oxford. Served Army, 1944–48: commnd Glos Regt; served BAOR and Jamaica (ADC to Governor). Called to Bar, Gray's Inn, 1953; Oxford Circuit, 1954–55; Dir of Public Prosecutions Dept, 1955–74. *Recreations:* history of art, water colour painting, music. *Address:* 61 Kingsmead Road, SW2 3HY. *T:* 0181–671 3977.

See also Baron Derwent.

BOURKE, Martin; HM Diplomatic Service; Governor, Turks and Caicos Islands, since 1993; *b* 12 March 1947; *s* of Robert Martin Bourke and Enid Millicent Bourke (*née* Love); *m* 1973, Anne Marie Marguerite Hottelet; four *s*. *Educ:* Stockport Grammar Sch.; University Coll. London (BA Hons 1969); King's Coll. London (MA 1970). Joined FCO, 1970; Brussels, 1971–73; Singapore, 1974–76; Lagos, 1978–80; on loan to DTI, 1980–84; Consul (Commercial), Johannesburg, 1984–88; Asst Head, Envmt, Sci. and Energy Dept, FCO, 1990–93. *Recreations:* walking, tennis, reading, theatre, amateur dramatics. *Address:* Government House, Grand Turk, West Indies. *T:* 9462308/9.

BOURKE, Rt. Rev. Michael; *see* Wolverhampton, Bishop Suffragan of.

BOURN, James; HM Diplomatic Service, retired; *b* 30 Aug. 1917; *s* of James and Sarah Gertrude Bourn; *m* 1st, 1944, Isobel Mackenzie (*d* 1977); one *s*; 2nd, 1981, Moya Livesey (*d* 1993). *Educ:* Queen Elizabeth's Grammar Sch., Darlington; Univ. of Edinburgh (MA Hons 1979). Executive Officer, Ministry of Health, 1936. War of 1939–45; served (Royal

Signals), in India, North Africa and Italy; POW; Captain. Higher Exec. Officer, Ministry of National Insurance, 1947; Asst Principal, Colonial Office, 1947; Principal, 1949; Secretary to the Salaries Commission, Bahamas, 1948–49; Private Sec. to Perm. Under-Sec., 1949; seconded to Tanganyika, 1953–55; UK Liaison Officer to Commn for Technical Co-operation in Africa (CCTA), 1955–57; Commonwealth Relations Office, 1961; seconded to Central African Office, 1962; Dar es Salaam, 1963; Deputy High Commissioner in Zanzibar, Tanzania, 1964–65; Counsellor and Dep. High Comr, Malawi, 1966–70; Ambassador to Somalia, 1970–73; Consul-General, Istanbul, 1973–75. *Address:* c/o National Westminster Bank, 20 Market Place, Richmond, North Yorks DL10 4QF. *Club:* Commonwealth Trust.

BOURN, Sir John (Bryant), KCB 1991 (CB 1986); Comptroller and Auditor General, since 1988; *b* 21 Feb. 1934; *s* of Henry Thomas Bryant Bourn and late Beatrice Grace Bourn; *m* 1959, Ardita Ann Fleming; one *s* one *d*. *Educ:* Southgate County Grammar Sch.; LSE. 1st cl. hons BScEcon 1954, PhD 1958. Air Min. 1956–63; HM Treasury, 1963–64; Private Sec. to Perm. Under-Sec., MoD, 1964–69; Asst Sec. and Dir of Programmes, Civil Service Coll., 1969–72; Asst Sec., MoD, 1972–74; Under-Sec., Northern Ireland Office, 1974–77; Asst Under-Sec. of State, MoD, 1977–82; Dep. Sec., Northern Ireland Office, 1982–84; Dep. Under Sec. of State (Defence Procurement), MoD, 1985–88. Vis. Prof., LSE, 1983–. *Publications:* articles and reviews in professional jls. *Recreations:* swimming, squash rackets. *Address:* National Audit Office, 157–197 Buckingham Palace Road, Victoria, SW1W 9SP.

BOURNE, Prof. Frederick John, CBE 1995; Director, Biotechnology and Biological Sciences (formerly Agricultural and Food) Research Council Institute for Animal Health, and Professor of Animal Health, University of Bristol, since 1988; *b* 3 Jan. 1937; *s* of Sidney John Bourne and Florence Beatrice Bourne; *m* 1959, Mary Angela Minter; two *s*. *Educ:* Univ. of London (BVetMed); Univ. of Bristol (PhD). MRCVS 1961. Gen. vet. practice, 1961–67; University of Bristol: Lectr in Animal Husbandry, 1967–76; Reader in Animal Husbandry, 1976–80; Prof. and Hd of Dept of Veterinary Medicine, 1980–88. Vis. Prof., Univ. of Reading, 1990–. *Publications:* over 200 contribs to variety of jls, incl. Immunology, Vet. Immunology and Immunopath., Res. in Vet. Sci., Infection and Immunity. *Recreations:* gardening, fishing, golf, cricket, music. *Address:* BBSRC Institute for Animal Health, Compton, near Newbury, Berks RG16 0NN. *T:* Newbury (01635) 578411.

BOURNE, Gordon Lionel, FRCS, FRCOG; Hon. Consultant, Department of Obstetrics and Gynæcology, St Bartholomew's Hospital, London; Hon. Consultant Gynæcologist to Royal Masonic Hospital, since 1986 (Consultant, 1972–86); *b* 3 June 1921; *s* of Thomas Holland Bourne and Lily Anne (*née* Clewlow); *m* 1948, Barbara Eileen Anderson; three *s* one *d*. *Educ:* Queen Elizabeth Grammar Sch., Ashbourne; St Bartholomew's Hosp.; Harvard Univ. MRCS, LRCP 1945, FRCS 1954; MRCOG 1956, FRCOG 1962; FRSocMed. Highlands Hosp., 1948; Derbs Royal Infirm., 1949; City of London Mat. Hosp., 1952; Hosp. for Women, Soho, 1954; Gynæcol Registrar, Middlesex Hosp., 1956; Sen. Registrar, Obsts and Gynae., St Bartholomew's Hosp., 1958; Nuffield Trav. Fellow, 1959; Res. Fellow, Harvard, 1959; Cons. Gynæcol., St Luke's Hosp., 1963. Arris and Gale Lectr, RCS, 1964; Mem. Bd of Professions Suppl. to Medicine, 1964; Regional Assessor in Maternal Deaths, 1974; Examr in Obsts and Gynae., Univs of London, Oxford and Riyadh, Jt Conjt Bd and RCOG, Central Midwives Bd; Mem. Ct of Assts, Haberdashers' Co., 1968, Master, 1984; Mem. Bd of Governors, 1971–83, Chm., 1980–83, Haberdashers' Aske's Schs, Hatcham; Mem., 1983–, Chm., 1987–, Bd of Governors, Haberdashers' Aske's Schs, Elstree. *Publications:* The Human Amnion and Chorion, 1962; Shaw's Textbook of Gynæcology, 9th edn, 1970; Recent Advances in Obstetrics and Gynæcology, 11th edn, 1966—13th edn, 1979; Modern Gynæcology with Obstetrics for Nurses, 4th edn, 1969 and 5th edn, 1973; Pregnancy, 1972, 5th edn 1989; numerous articles in sci. and professional jls. *Recreations:* ski-ing, water-ski-ing, shooting, swimming, writing, golf. *Address:* Oldways, Bishop's Avenue, N2 0BN. *T:* 0181–458 4788. *Club:* Carlton.

BOURNE, Sir (John) Wilfrid, KCB 1979 (CB 1975); QC 1981; Clerk of the Crown in Chancery, and Permanent Secretary, Lord Chancellor's Office, 1977–82; Barrister-at-Law; *b* 27 Jan. 1922; *s* of late Captain Rt Hon. R. C. Bourne, MP, and Lady Hester Bourne; *m* 1958, Elizabeth Juliet, *d* of late G. R. Fox, of Trewardreva, Constantine, Cornwall; two *s*. *Educ:* Eton; New Coll., Oxford (MA). Served War, Rifle Brigade, 1941–45. Called to Bar, Middle Temple, 1948, Bencher 1977; practised at Bar, 1949–56; Lord Chancellor's Office, 1956–82, Principal Assistant Solicitor, 1970–72, Deputy Sec., 1972–77. *Recreation:* gardening. *Address:* Povey's Farm, Ramsdell, Basingstoke, Hants RG26 5SN. *Club:* Leander (Henley-on-Thames).

BOURNE, Margaret Janet, OBE 1982; Chairman, CORDA Ltd, since 1992; *b* 18 Aug. 1931; *d* of Thomas William Southcott and Nora Annie Southcott (*née* Pelling); *m* 1960, George Brian Bourne. *Educ:* Twickenham Grammar Sch.; Royal Holloway Coll. (BSc). MRAeS. Fairey Engineering, 1953–62; Army Operational Res. Estabt, 1962–65; Defence Operational Analysis Estabt, 1965–76; Asst Dir, Scientific Adv. Gp Army, 1976–80; Hd of Assessments Div., ASWE, 1980–82; Hd of Weapon Dept, ASWE, 1982–84; Dep. Dir, Admiralty Res. Estabt, 1984–87; Asst Chief Scientific Advr (Capabilities), MoD, 1987–91. *Recreations:* playing early music, gardening, natural history. *Address:* c/o BAe SEMA Ltd, Biwater House, Portsmouth Road, Esher, Surrey KT10 9SJ.

BOURNE, (Rowland) Richard; Director, Commonwealth non-governmental office for South Africa and Director, Commonwealth Values in Education Project, Institute of Education, London University; *b* 27 July 1940; *s* of late Arthur Brittan and Edith Mary Bourne; *m* 1966, Juliet Mary, *d* of John Attenborough, CBE; two *s* one *d*. *Educ:* Uppingham Sch., Rutland; Brasenose Coll., Oxford (BA Mod. Hist.). Journalist, The Guardian, 1962–72 (Education correspondent, 1968–72); Asst Editor, New Society, 1972–77; Evening Standard: Dep. Editor, 1977–78; London Columnist, 1978–79; Founder Editor, Learn Magazine, 1979; Dep. Dir, Commonwealth Inst., 1983–89; Dir, Commonwealth Human Rights Initiative, 1990–92. Consultant: Internat. Broadcasting Trust, 1980–81; Adv. Council for Adult and Continuing Educn, 1982. Chm., Survival Internat. 1983–. Treas., Anglo-Portuguese Foundn, 1985–87. *Publications:* Political Leaders of Latin America, 1969; (with Brian MacArthur) The Struggle for Education, 1970; Getulio Vargas of Brazil, 1974; Assault on the Amazon, 1978; Londoners, 1981; (with Jessica Gould) Self-Sufficiency, 16–25, 1983; Lords of Fleet Street, 1990; News on a Knife-Edge, 1995. *Recreations:* theatre, fishing, supporting Charlton Athletic. *Address:* 36 Burney Street, SE10 8EX. *T:* 0181–853 0642. *Club:* Royal Automobile.

BOURNE, Sir Wilfrid; *see* Bourne, Sir J. W.

BOURNE-ARTON, Major Anthony Temple, MBE 1944; *b* 1 March 1913; 2nd *s* of W. R. Temple Bourne, Walker Hall, Winston, Co. Durham, and Evelyn Rose, 3rd *d* of Sir Frank Wills, Bristol; assumed surname of Bourne-Arton, 1950; *m* 1938, Margaret Elaine, *er d* of W. Denby Arton, Sleningford Park, Ripon, Yorks; two *s* two *d*. *Educ:* Clifton. Served Royal Artillery, 1933–48; active service, 1936, Palestine; 1939–45: France, N Africa, Sicily and Italy (despatches, MBE); Malaya, 1947–48. Gen. Commissioner Income Tax, 1952–80; has served on Bedale RDC, and N Riding County Agric. Cttee; County Councillor, N Riding of Yorks, 1949–61; CC, W Riding of Yorks, 1967–70; Chm., Yorkshire Regional Land Drainage Cttee, 1973–80. MP (C) Darlington, 1959–64; PPS to the Home Sec., 1962–64. JP N Riding of Yorks, 1950–80. *Recreations:* fishing and shooting. *Address:* The Old Rectory, West Tanfield, Ripon, N Yorks HG4 5JH. *T:* Bedale (01677) 470333.

See also S. N. Bourne-Arton.

BOURNE-ARTON, Simon Nicholas; QC 1994; a Recorder, since 1993; *b* 5 Sept. 1949; *s* of Major Anthony Temple Bourne-Arton, *qv*; *m* 1974, Diana Carr-Walker; two *s* one *d*. *Educ:* Aysgarth Prep. Sch.; Harrow; Teesside Poly. (HND Bus. Studies); Leeds Univ. (LLB Hons). Called to the Bar, Inner Temple, 1974. *Recreations:* living in the country, golf, tennis, being with family and friends, drinking wine. *Address:* Park Court Chambers, 40 Park Cross Street, Leeds LS1 2QH.

BOURNS, Prof. Arthur Newcombe, OC 1982; FRSC 1964; President and Vice-Chancellor, 1972–80, Professor of Chemistry 1953–81, now Emeritus, McMaster University; *b* 8 Dec. 1919; *s* of Evans Clement Bourns and Kathleen Jones; *m* 1943, Marion Harriet Blakney; two *s* two *d*. *Educ:* schs in Petitcodiac, NB; Acadia Univ. (BSc); McGill Univ. (PhD). Research Chemist, Dominion Rubber Co., 1944–45; Lectr, Acadia Univ., 1945–46; Asst Prof. of Chemistry, Saskatchewan Univ., 1946–47; McMaster HUniv.: Asst Prof., 1947–49; Associate Prof., 1949–53; Dean, Faculty of Grad. Studies, 1957–61; Chm., Chemistry Dept, 1965–67; Vice-Pres., Science and Engrg Div., 1967–72; Actg Pres., 1970. Nuffield Trav. Fellow in Science, University Coll., London, 1955–56. Chm., Gordon Res. Conf. on Chem. and Physics of Isotopes (Vice-Chm. 1959–60; Chm., 1961–62); Nat. Res. Council of Canada: Mem. Grant Selection Cttee in Chem., 1966–69 (Chm. 1968–69); Mem. Council, 1969–75; Mem. Exec. Cttee, 1969–75; Mem. or Chm. various other cttees; Natural Scis and Engrg Res. Council: Member: Council, 1978–85; Exec. Cttee, 1978–; Allocations Cttee, 1978–86; Cttee on Strategic Grants, 1978–83; Chm., Grants and Scholarships Cttee, 1978–83; Mem., Adv. Cttee on University/Industry Interface, 1979–83; Vis. Res. Officer, 1983–84. Member: Ancaster Public Sch. Bd, 1963–64; Bd, Royal Botanic Gdns, 1972–80 (Vice-Chm.); Cttee on Univ. Affairs, Prov. Ontario; Canadian Cttee for Financing Univ. Res., 1978–80; Council of Ontario Univs, 1972–80; Bd of Dirs and Exec. Cttee, Assoc. of Univs and Colleges of Canada, 1974–77; Mohawk Coll. Bd of Dirs, 1975–82; Council, Canadian Inst. for Advanced Research, 1983–89; Chm., Internat. Adv. Cttee, Chinese Univ. Develt Project, 1985–92; Pres. and Chm. Exec. Cttee, Canadian Bureau for Internat. Educn, 1973–76. McMaster Univ. Med. Centre: Member: Bd of Trustees, 1972–80; Exec. Cttee, 1972–80. Director: Nuclear Activation Services, 1978–80; Slater Steel Industries Ltd, 1975–79. British Council Lectr, 1963. Assoc. Editor, Canadian Jl Chemistry, 1966–69; Mem. Editorial Bd, Science Forum, 1967–73. FCIC 1954 (Chm. Hamilton Section, 1952–53; Mem. Educn Cttee, 1953–59; Mem. Council, 1966–69; Montreal Medal, 1976). Hon. Prof., Jiangxi Univ., China, 1989. Hon. DSc: Acadia, 1968; McGill, 1977; New Brunswick, McMaster, 1981; Hon. LLD Brock, 1980. *Address:* Unit 10, 2407 Woodward Avenue, Burlington, Ont L7R 1V2, Canada. *T:* (416) 6396964.

BOUTROS-GHALI, Boutros, PhD; Secretary-General, United Nations, since 1992; *b* Cairo, 14 Nov. 1922; *m* Maria Leia Nadler. *Educ:* Cairo Univ. (LLB 1946); Paris Univ. (PhD 1949). Prof. of Internat. Law and Internat. Relns, and Head, Dept of Political Scis, Cairo Univ., 1949–77; Minister of State for Foreign Affairs, Egypt, 1977–91; Dep. Prime Minister for Foreign Affairs, 1991–92. Mem., Secretariat, Nat. Democratic Party, 1980–92; MP 1987–92. Mem., UN Commn of Internat. Law, 1979–92. Founder and Editor: Al Ahram Iktisadi, 1960–75; Al-Siyassa Dawlya. *Publications:* Contribution à l'étude des ententes régionales, 1949; Cours de diplomatie et de droit diplomatique et consulaire, 1951; (jtly) Le problème du Canal de Suez, 1957; (jtly) Egypt and the United Nations, 1957; Le principe d'égalité des états et les organisations internationales, 1961; Contribution à une théorie générale des Alliances, 1963; Foreign Policies in a World of Change, 1963; L'Organisation de l'unité africaine, 1969; Le mouvement Afro-Asiatique, 1969; Les difficultés institutionelles du panafricanisme, 1971; La ligue des états arabes, 1972; Les Conflits de frontières en Afrique, 1973; also many books in Arabic and numerous contribs to periodicals and learned jls. *Address:* United Nations, New York, NY 10017, USA.

BOUVERIE; *see* Pleydell-Bouverie, family name of Earl of Radnor.

BOVELL, Hon. Sir (William) Stewart, Kt 1976; JP; Agent-General for Western Australia, in London, 1971–74; *b* 19 Dec. 1906; *s* of A. R. Bovell and Ethel (*née* Williams), Busselton, Western Australia. *Educ:* Busselton, WA. Banking, 1923–40. Served War, RAAF, 1941–45, Flt Lt. MLA: for Sussex, WA, 1947–50; for Vasse, WA, 1950–71. Minister: for Labour, WA, 1961–62; for Lands, Forests and Immigration, WA, 1959–71. Chief Govt Whip, WA, 1950–53; Opposition Whip, WA, 1953–57. Rep., Australian States Gen. Council, at British Commonwealth Parly Assoc., in Nairobi, Kenya, and Victoria Falls, S Rhodesia, 1954. Mem. Bd of Governors, Bunbury CofE Cathedral Grammar Sch., 1974 (Vice-Chm.). Hon. Lay Canon, St Boniface CofE Cathedral, Bunbury, WA, 1975. JP 1949, WA. Patron: Polocrosse Assoc. of WA; Geographe Bay Yacht Club. *Recreations:* swimming, tennis, walking. *Address:* Post Box 11, Busselton, WA 6280, Australia.

BOVENIZER, Vernon Gordon Fitzell, CMG 1948; Assistant Under-Secretary of State, Ministry of Defence, 1964–68, retired; *b* 22 July 1908; *s* of Rev. Michael Fitzell Bovenizer and Mary Gordon; *m* 1937, Lillian Cherry (*d* 1970), *d* of John Henry Rowe, Cork; two *s* two *d*. *Educ:* Liverpool Coll.; Sidney Sussex Coll., Cambridge (Scholar). War Office, 1931–45; Control Commission for Germany, 1945, until return to War Office, 1948; Asst Private Sec. to Secretaries of State for War, 1936, and 1940–42; Resident Clerk, 1934–37; Asst Sec., 1942, civilian liaison with US Armies in the UK; Establishment Officer and Dir of Organisation, CCG, 1945–47; Asst Sec. and Dep. Comptroller of Claims, War Office, 1948–58; Counsellor, UK Delegation to NATO, 1958–60; Asst Under-Sec. of State, War Office, 1960–68. US Medal of Freedom, 1945. *Address:* 6 Cambanks, Union Lane, Cambridge CB4 1PY; 9 The Square, Annalong, Co. Down BT34 4TS. *Club:* Reform.

BOVEY, Dr Leonard; Editor, Materials & Design, since 1985; Head of Technological Requirements Branch, Department of Industry, 1977–84; *b* 9 May 1924; *s* of late Alfred and Gladys Bovey; *m* 1943, Constance Hudson (*d* 1987); one *s* one *d*. *Educ:* Heles Sch., Exeter; Emmanuel Coll., Cambridge (BA, PhD). FInstP; CPhys. Dunlop Rubber, 1943–46; Post-doctoral Fellow, Nat. Res. Council, Ottawa, 1950–52; AERE Harwell, 1952–65; Head W Mids Regional Office, Birmingham, Min. of Technology, 1966–70; Regional Dir, Yorks and Humberside, DTI, 1970–73; Counsellor (Scientific and Technological Affairs), High Commn, Ottawa, 1974–77. Foreign correspondent, Soc. for Advancement of Materials and Processes Engineering (USA) Jl, 1987–. *Publications:* Spectroscopy in the Metallurgical Industry, 1963; papers on spectroscopy in Jl Optical Soc. Amer., Spectrochimica Acta, Jl Phys. Soc. London. *Recreations:* repairing neglected household equipment, work, reading (particularly crime novels), walking, theatre, music. *Address:* 32 Radnor Walk, Chelsea SW3 4BN. *T:* 0171–352 4142. *Club:* Civil Service.

BOVEY, Philip Henry; Under Secretary, Department of Trade and Industry, since 1985; *b* 11 July 1948; *s* of Norman Henry Bovey and Dorothy Yvonne Kent Bovey; *m* 1974, Jenet Alison, *d* of late Rev. Canon J. M. McTear and Margaret McTear; one *s* one *d*. Educ: Rugby; Peterhouse, Cambridge (schol.; MA). Solicitor. 3rd Sec., FCO, 1970–71; with Slaughter and May, 1972–75; Legal Assistant, 1976; Sen. Legal Assistant, 1976; Depts of Trade and Industry, 1976–77; Cabinet Office, 1977–78; Depts of Trade, Industry, Prices and Consumer Protection, then DTI, 1978–85; Asst Solicitor, 1982. Companies Act Inspector, 1984–88 (report published 1988). *Recreation:* photography. *Address:* 102 Cleveland Gardens, Barnes, SW13 0AH. *T:* 0181–876 3710.

BOWATER, Sir Euan David Vansittart, 3rd Bt *cr* 1939, of Friston, Suffolk; *b* 9 Sept. 1935; *s* of Sir Noël Vansittart Bowater, 2nd Bt, GBE, MC, and Constance Heiton (*d* 1993), *d* of David Gordon Bett; *S* father, 1984; *m* 1964, Susan Mary Humphrey, *d* of late A. R. O. Slater, FCA; two *s* two *d*. *Educ:* Eton; Trinity Coll., Cambridge (BA). *Recreations:* travel, golf. *Heir: s* Moray David Vansittart Bowater, *b* 24 April 1967.

BOWATER, Sir J(ohn) Vansittart, 4th Bt *cr* 1914; *b* 6 April 1918; *s* of Captain Victor Spencer Bowater (*d* 1967) (3rd *s* of 1st Bt) and Hilda Mary (*d* 1918), *d* of W. Henry Potter; *S* uncle, Sir Thomas Dudley Blennerhassett Bowater, 3rd Bt, 1972; *m* 1943, Joan Kathleen, (*d* 1982), *d* of late Wilfrid Scullard; one *s* one *d*. *Educ:* Branksome School, Godalming, Surrey. Served Royal Artillery, 1939–46. *Heir: s* Michael Patrick Bowater [*b* 18 July 1949; *m* 1968, Alison, *d* of Edward Wall; four *d*]. *Address:* 214 Runnymede Avenue, Bournemouth, Dorset BH11 9SP. *T:* Bournemouth (01202) 571782.

BOWCOCK, John Brown, FICE, FIMechE; Chairman, Sir Alexander Gibb & Partners Ltd, since 1993; *b* 25 Oct. 1931; *s* of John Brown Bowcock and Mabel Bowcock; *m* 1955, Pauline Mary Elizabeth Dalton; three *d*. *Educ:* Hastings Grammar Sch.; St Catherine's Coll., Oxford (MA). FICE 1971; FIMechE 1986. Nat. service, RAF, 1954–56. Joined Sir Alexander Gibb & Partners, 1957: worked on water resource projects overseas incl. Kariba (Zimbabwe), Roseires (Sudan) and Latiyan (Iran), 1957–70; responsible for major dam projects and Drakensberg pumped storage project, SA, 1970–78; Partner, 1978–89; Chief Exec., 1989–93. Chairman: British Dam Soc., 1992–93; British Consultants Bureau, 1991–92. Vice-Chm., ACE, 1994–. FRSA 1989. *Recreations:* golf, music, reading. *Address:* Lothlorien, Crowsley Road, Shiplake, Oxon RG9 3JU. *T:* Reading (01734) 404443. *Clubs:* Royal Air Force; Huntercombe Golf (Henley); Johannesburg Country.

BOWDEN, Rev. Andrew; *see* Bowden, Rev. R. A.

BOWDEN, Sir Andrew, Kt 1994; MBE 1961; MP (C) Kemptown Division of Brighton since 1970; *b* 8 April 1930; *s* of William Victor Bowden, Solicitor, and Francesca Wilson; *m* Benita Napier; one *s* one *d*. *Educ:* Ardingly College. Paint industry, 1955–68; Man. Dir, Personnel Assessments Ltd, 1969–71; Man. Dir, Haymarket Personnel Selection Ltd, 1970–71; Director: Sales Education & Leadership Ltd, 1970–71; Jenkin and Purser (Holdings) Ltd, 1973–77. Mem., Wandsworth Borough Council, 1956–62. Contested (C): N Hammersmith, 1955; N Kensington, 1964; Kemp Town, Brighton, 1966. Jt Chm., All Party Old Age Pensioners Parly Gp, 1972–; Chm., All Party BLESMA Gp; Mem. Select Cttee on Expenditure, 1973–74, on Abortion, 1975, on Employment, 1979–83. Mem., Council of Europe, 1987–. Nat. Chm., Young Conservatives, 1960–61. Internat. Chm., People to People, 1981–. Nat. Pres., Captive Animals Protection Soc., 1978–. Mem. School Council, Ardingly Coll., 1982–. *Recreations:* fishing, chess, golf. *Address:* House of Commons, SW1A 0AA. *T:* 0171–219 5047. *Club:* Carlton.

BOWDEN, Sir Frank Houston, 3rd Bt *cr* 1915; MA Oxon; retired industrialist and landowner; *b* 10 Aug. 1909; *o s* of Sir Harold Bowden, 2nd Bt, GBE, and of Vera, *d* of Joseph Whitaker, JP, FZS; *S* father 1960; *m* 1st, 1934, Marie-José, *d* of Charles Stiénon and Comtesse Laure de Messey; one *s*; 2nd, 1937, Lydia Eveline (*d* 1981), *d* of Jean Manolovici, Bucharest; three *s*; 3rd, 1989, Oriol Annette Mary, *d* of Charles Hooper Bath. *Educ:* Rugby; Merton Coll., Oxford. Served with RNVR, 1939–44. President: University Hall, Buckland, 1967–71; British Kendo Association, 1969; Thame Br., RN Assoc. Hon. Vice-Pres., 3rd World Kendo Championships, 1976. Vice-Pres., Oxfordshire County Scout Council, 1970–. *Recreation:* collecting weapons and armour, particularly Japanese (Vice-Chm. Japan Soc. of London, 1970–75, 1979–82, 1984–87, Vice-Pres., 1987–), photography, entomology. *Heir: s* Nicholas Richard Bowden, *b* 13 Aug. 1935. *Address:* The Old Vicarage, Winkfield, Windsor, Berks SL4 4SE. *Clubs:* White's, Royal Thames Yacht.

BOWDEN, Gerald Francis, TD 1971; barrister, chartered surveyor and university lecturer; *b* 26 Aug. 1935; *s* of Frank Albert Bowden and Elsie Bowden (*née* Burrill); *m* 1967, Heather Elizabeth Hill (*née* Hall) (*d* 1984); two *d*, and one step *s* one step *d*. *Educ:* Battersea Grammar School; Magdalen College, Oxford. MA; FRICS 1984 (ARICS 1971). Called to the Bar, Gray's Inn, 1963. Worked in advertising industry, 1964–68; property marketing and investment, 1968–72; Principal Lecturer in Law, Dept of Estate Management, Polytechnic of the South Bank, 1972–; Vis. Lectr, Kingston Univ., 1993–. Chm. Panel, Examination in Public of Suffolk Co. Structure Plan, 1993. Mem. GLC for Dulwich, 1977–81; a co-opted Mem., ILEA, 1981–84. MP (C) Dulwich, 1983–92; contested (C) Dulwich, 1992. PPS to Minister for Arts, 1990–92. Mem., Select Cttee on Educn, Sci. and Arts, 1990–92. Vice-Chairman: Cons. Backbench Educn Cttee, 1987–89; Cons. Backbench Arts and Heritage Cttee, 1987–92. Pres., Greater London Conservative Trade Unionists, 1985–88. Pres., Southwark Chamber of Commerce, 1986–. Chairman: Walcot Educn Foundn (formerly Soc.), 1978–; Lambeth and Southwark Housing Soc., 1973–84; London Rent Assessment Panel, 1994–; Magdalen Soc., 1991–; Trustee, Magdalen Develt Trust, 1991–. Mem. Council, Royal Albert Hall, 1994–. Estates Gov., Alleyn's Coll. of God's Gift, Dulwich, 1992–. After Nat. Service, continued to serve in TA until 1984 (Lt-Col). *Publications:* An Introduction to the Law of Contract and Tort (with Alan S. Morris), 1977; The Housing Act, 1988. *Recreations:* gardening, renovating old houses, books, pictures. *Address:* 2 Paper Buildings, Temple, EC4Y 7ET. *T:* 0171–936 2611; 130 Kennington Park Road, SE11 4DJ. *T:* 0171–582 7361. *Clubs:* United Oxford & Cambridge University, Chelsea Arts.

BOWDEN, Logan S.; *see* Scott Bowden.

BOWDEN, Rev. Canon (Robert) Andrew; Rector of Coates, Rodmarton and Sapperton with Frampton Mansell, since 1979; Chaplain to the Queen, since 1992; Local Ministry Officer, Diocese of Gloucester, since 1993; *b* 13 Nov. 1938; *s* of Charles Bowden and Miriam (*née* Howard-Tripp); *m* 1966, Susan (*née* Humpidge); three *d*. *Educ:* Clifton Coll., Bristol; Worcester Coll., Oxford (Scholar; BA 1962; DipTh 1963; MA 1967; BDQ 1968); Cuddesdon Coll., Oxford. Ordained deacon, 1965, priest, 1966. Curate: St George, Wolverhampton, 1965–69; St Luke's, Duston, 1969–72; Rector, Byfield, 1972–79. Chaplain, Royal Agricl Coll., Cirencester, 1979–93; Rural Advr to dio. of Gloucester, 1981–93; Mem., Archbp's Commn on Rural Areas, 1988–90. Hon. Canon, Gloucester Cathedral, 1990–. Hon. Res. Fellow, Capital Centre for Theology and Educn, Trinity Coll., Carmarthen, 1995–. *Publications:* Ministry in the Countryside, 1994; articles in Theology and Expository Times. *Recreations:* breeding old breeds of poultry, classical music. *Address:* Coates Rectory, Cirencester, Glos GL7 6NR. *T:* Cirencester (01285) 770235.

BOWDEN, Prof. Ruth Elizabeth Mary, OBE 1980; DSc London, MB, BS, FRCS; Professor of Anatomy, Royal Free Hospital School of Medicine, University of London, 1951–80, now Emeritus; Sir William Collins Professor of Human and Comparative Anatomy, Royal College of Surgeons of England, 1984–89; Hon. Research Fellow, Institute of Neurology, since 1980; *b* 21 Feb. 1915; *o c* of late Frank Harold and Louise Ellen Bowden. *Educ:* Westlands Sch.; St Paul's Girls' Sch.; London (Royal Free Hospital) Sch. of Medicine for Women, University of London. House Surg. and later House Physician, Elizabeth Garrett Anderson Hosp. (Oster House branch), 1940–42; House Surg., Royal Cancer Hosp., 1942; Grad. Asst in Nuffield Dept of Orthopædic Surgery, Peripheral Nerve Injury Unit, Oxford, 1942–45; Asst Lecturer in Anatomy, Royal Free Hospital Sch. of Medicine, 1945; later Lecturer, then University Reader in Human Anatomy, 1949; Rockefeller Travelling Fellowship, 1949–50; Hunterian Prof., RCS, 1950; part-time Lectr, Dept of Anatomy, St Thomas's Hosp. Med. Sch., 1980–83. WHO Consultant in anatomy, Khartoum Univ., 1972, 1974, 1977. President: Anat. Soc. of Gt Brit. and Ireland, 1970; Medical Women's Fedn, 1981. Member: Exec. Cttee, Women's Nat. Commn, 1984–89; Council and Exec. Cttee, N London Hospice Gp, 1986– (Chm., Professional Sub-Cttee, 1986–90); Exec. Cttee, 1988–, and Med. Adv. Bd, 1992, LEPRA. Member, later Convenor: Acad. Awards Cttee, British Fedn of University Women, 1956–94; Cttee for Awards and Fellowships, Internat. Fedn of University Women, 1986–92. FRSM; Fellow: Brit. Orthopædic Assoc.; Linnean Soc. Vice-President: Chartered Soc. of Physiotherapy (Chm., 1960–70); Inst. of Science Technology (Pres., 1960–65); Riding for the Disabled Assoc. DCLJ 1988, DMLJ 1984. Jubilee Medal, 1977; Wood Jones Medal, RCS, 1988. *Publications:* Peripheral Nerve Injuries, 1958; (contrib.) Surgery of the Spine, ed G. Findlay and R. Owen, 1992; contribs to Peripheral Nerve Injuries Report of Medical Research Council; contrib. to Oxford Companion to Medicine; contribs to medical and scientific jls. *Recreations:* reading, music, painting, walking, gardening, carpentry. *Address:* 6 Hartham Close, Hartham Road, N7 9JH. *T:* 0171–607 3464.

BOWE, Colette, PhD; Chief Executive, Personal Investment Authority, since 1994; *b* 27 Nov. 1946; *d* of Philip Bowe and Norah (*née* Hughes). *Educ:* Notre Dame High Sch., Liverpool; Queen Mary Coll., Univ. of London (BSc Econs, PhD); LSE (MSc Econs). Research Officer, LSE, 1969–70; Econ. Advr, Nat. Ports Council, 1971–73; Department of Industry: Econ. Advr, 1975–78; Principal, 1979–81; Department of Trade and Industry: Asst Sec., 1981–84; Dir of Information, 1984–87; Controller of Public Affairs, IBA, 1987–89; Dir, SIB, 1989–93. *Recreations:* gardening, music, films. *Address:* Personal Investment Authority, 1 Canada Square, E14 5AZ. *T:* 0171–538 8860. *Club:* Reform.

BOWE, David Robert; Member (Lab) Cleveland and Richmond (formerly Cleveland and Yorkshire North), European Parliament, since 1989; *b* Gateshead, 19 July 1955; *m* 1978, Helena Scattergood; one *s* one *d*. *Educ:* Sunderland Polytechnic; Bath Univ. BSc; PGCE. Former science teacher. Mem., Middlesbrough Borough Council, 1983–89 (Chm., Monitoring and Review Cttee). European Parliament: Mem., Cttee on Envmt, Public Health and Consumer Protection, 1989–; substitute Mem., Cttee on Econ. and Monetary Affairs. Mem., UNISON. *Address:* 10 Harris Street, Middlesbrough, Cleveland TS1 5EF.

BOWEN, Maj.-Gen. Bryan Morris, CB 1988; Paymaster-in-Chief and Inspector of Army Pay Services, 1986–89, retired; *b* 8 March 1932; *s* of Frederick Bowen and Gwendoline Bowen (*née* Morris); *m* 1955, Suzanne Rowena (*née* Howell); two *d*. *Educ:* Newport High Sch.; Exeter Univ. FCMA; ndc, psc†, sq, pfc. Joined RE, 1953, served UK and BAOR; transf. RAPC, 1958; Paymaster 1/6 QEO Gurkha Rifles, Malaya and UK, 1960–63; Army Cost and Management Accounting Services, 1963–68; DAAG, MoD, 1968–70; Exchange Officer, US Army, Washington, DC, 1970–72; Nat. Defence Coll., 1972–73; DS, RMCS Shrivenham, 1973–76; AAG, MOD, 1976–79; Col (Principal), MoD F4(AD), 1979–81; Chief Paymaster, Army Pay Office (Officers Accounts), 1981–82; Dep. Paymaster-in-Chief, 1982–85. Col Comdt, RAPC, 1990–92; Dep. Col Comdt, AGC, 1992–93. Mem. Council, CIMA, 1990–94; Chm., Oxfordshire Cttee, Army Benevolent Fund, 1990–92; Special Comr, Duke of York's Royal Mil. Sch., Dover, 1990– (Chm., 1992–); Dir, United Services Trustee, 1990–. Freeman, City of London, 1987. *Recreations:* golf, church affairs, gardening. *Address:* Yew Tree House, Claypits Lane, Shrivenham, Swindon, Wilts SN6 8AH.

BOWEN, Carolyn Elizabeth Cunningham, (Mrs S. J. Bowen); *see* Sinclair, C. E. C.

BOWEN, Charles John; Chief Executive, Booker, since 1993; *b* 11 December 1941; *s* of John and Millicent Bowen; *m* 1965, Naomi Stevens; one *s* one *d*. *Educ:* Exeter Univ. (BA Econs and Stats). Fellow, Royal Statistical Soc. Market Research Manager, ICI Paints Div., 1965–67; Product Manager, Unilever, 1967–73; Marketing Manager and Dir, General Foods UK, 1973–78; Gen. Manager, General Foods, Puerto Rico, 1978–82; Vice-Pres., General Foods Corp., USA, 1982–88; Exec. Dir, Hillsdown Holdings, 1988–93. *Address:* Isington Mill, Alton, Hants GU34 4PW. *T:* Alton (01420) 23126, *Fax:* (01420) 22508. *Club:* Travellers.

BOWEN, Prof. David Aubrey Llewellyn, FRCP, FRCPE, FRCPath; Professor of Forensic Medicine, University of London, 1977–89, now Emeritus; Head of Department of Forensic Medicine and Toxicology, Charing Cross Hospital Medical School, 1973–89 (Charing Cross and Westminster Medical School, 1985–89); Hon. Consultant Pathologist, Charing Cross Hospital, 1973–89; *b* 31 Jan. 1924; *s* of late Dr Thomas Rufus Bowen and Catherine (*née* Llewellyn); *m* 1st, 1950, Joan Rosemary Davis (*d* 1973); two *s* one *d*; 2nd, 1975, Helen Rosamund Landcastle. *Educ:* Caterham Sch.; Garw Secondary Sch., Pontycymmer; University College of Wales, Cardiff; Corpus Christi Coll., Cambridge (MA); Middlesex Hosp. Med. Sch. (MB BChir 1947); DipPath 1955; DMJ Soc. of Apoth. of London 1962. FRCPE 1971; FRCPath 1975; FRCP 1982. Ho. posts at W Middlesex Hosp. and London Chest Hosp., 1947 and 1950; RAMC, 1947–49; Jun. Resident Pathologist, Bristol Royal Inf., 1950–51; Registrar in Path., London Chest Hosp., 1951–52; Registrar and Sen. Registrar in Clin. Path., National Hosp. for Nervous Diseases, 1952–56; Asst Pathologist and Sen. Registrar, Royal Marsden Hosp., 1956–57; Demonstr 1957–63, Lectr 1963–66, in Forensic Medicine, St George's Hosp. Med. Sch.; Sen. Lectr 1966–73, Reader 1973–77, in Forensic Medicine, Vice-Dean 1974–78, Charing Cross Hosp. Med. Sch.; Lectr in Forensic Medicine, Oxford Univ., 1974–89. Chairman: Div. of Pathology, Charing Cross Hosp., 1976–78; Apptd and Recog. Teachers in Path., Charing Cross Hosp. Med. Sch., 1980–82; Examiner: Univ. of Riyadh, Saudi Arabia, 1978–81; on Forensic Med., RCPath, 1976–90; for Diploma of Med. Jurisprudence, Soc. of Apothecaries of London, 1970–93; for MD (Forensic Medicine) and Diploma in Legal Medicine, Univ. of Sri Lanka, 1985. Lectr, Metropolitan Police Trng Coll., Hendon, 1976–84; W. D. L. Fernando Oration to Medical Legal Soc. of Sri Lanka, 1985. Vice-President: Medico-Legal Soc., 1977–90; Medical Defence Union, 1979–91; President: British Assoc. in Forensic Med., 1977–79; W London Medico-Chirurgical Soc., 1987–88; Member: British Academy in Forensic Sci. and Forensic Sci. Soc., 1960–91 (Mem. Council, 1965–67); British Div. of Internat. Acad. of Path., 1974–93; Acad. Internat. de

Médicine Légale et de Méd. Sociale, 1976–90; RCPath Adv. Cttee on Forensic Path., 1973–76 and 1980–82. Vice-Pres., Old Caterhamians Assoc., 1987–88. *Publications:* sci. papers in numerous med., forensic med. and path. jls. *Recreations:* hockey, jogging. *Address:* 19 Letchmore Road, Radlett, Herts WD7 8HU. *T:* Radlett (01923) 856936.

BOWEN, Edward Farquharson, TD 1976; QC (Scot.) 1992; Advocate; *b* 1 May 1945; *s* of Stanley Bowen, *qv*; *m* 1975, Patricia Margaret Brown, *y d* of Rev. R. Russell Brown, Perth; two *s* two *d*. *Educ:* Melville Coll., Edinburgh; Edinburgh Univ. (LLB 1966). Enrolled as Solicitor in Scotland, 1968; admitted to Faculty of Advocates, 1970. Standing Jun. Counsel: to Scottish Educn Dept, 1977–79; to Home Office in Scotland, 1979; Advocate-Depute, 1979–83; Sheriff of Tayside Central and Fife, 1983–90; Partner, Thorntons, WS, 1990–91. Chm. (part-time), Industrial Tribunals, 1995–. Served RAOC (TA and T&AVR), 1964–80. *Recreation:* golf. *Address:* The Old Manse, Lundie, Angus DD2 5NW. *Clubs:* New (Edinburgh); Royal & Ancient Golf (St Andrews); Hon. Company of Edinburgh Golfers; Panmure Golf.

BOWEN, Maj.-Gen. Esmond John, CB 1982; Director, Army Dental Service, 1978–82; *b* 6 Dec. 1922; *s* of Major Leslie Arthur George Bowen, MC, and Edna Grace Bowen; *m* 1948, Elsie (*née* Midgley); two *s* two *d* (and one *d* decd). *Educ:* Clayesmore Sch.; Univ. of Birmingham. LDS Birmingham 1946. Commd Lieut, RADC, 1947; Captain 1948; Major 1955; Lt-Col 1962; Chief Instructor, Depot and Training Establishment RADC, 1966–69: CO Nos 2 and 3 Dental Groups, 1969–74; Asst Dir, Army Dental Service, 1974–76; Comdt, HQ and Training Centre, RADC, 1976–77; Brig. 1977; Dep. Dir, Dental Service, HQ BAOR, 1977–78. QHDS, 1977–82. Col Comdt, RADC, 1982–87. OStJ 1975. *Recreations:* target rifle and muzzle loading shooting. *Address:* 72 Winchester Road, Andover, Hants SP10 2ER. *T:* Andover (01264) 323252. *Club:* Lansdowne.

BOWEN, (Evan) Roderic, QC 1952; MA, LLD; Master Emeritus of the Middle Temple; *b* 6 Aug. 1913; 2nd *s* of late Evan Bowen, JP, and late Margaret Ellen Twiss, The Elms, Cardigan. *Educ:* Cardigan Schs; University Coll., Aberystwyth; St John's Coll., Cambridge. Practised at the bar with chambers in Cardiff until 1940; served in HM Forces, 1940–45, in the ranks and subsequently as an officer on staff of Judge Advocate-Gen. MP (L) County of Cardigan, 1945–66; Dep. Chm. of Ways and Means, House of Commons, 1965–66. Recorder of: Carmarthen, 1950; Merthyr Tydfil, 1953–60; Swansea, 1960–64; Cardiff, 1964–67; Chm., Montgomeryshire QS, 1959–71; Social Security (formerly Nat. Insurance) Comr, 1967–86. Chm. Welsh Parliamentary Party, 1955. Pres., St David's UC, Lampeter, 1977–92. Hon. Fellow, Trinity Coll., Carmarthen, 1992. Hon. LLD Wales, 1972. *Address:* 3 Maynard Court, Fairwater Road, Llandaff, Cardiff CF5 2LD. *T:* Cardiff (01222) 563207. *Club:* County (Cardiff).

BOWEN, Sir Geoffrey (Fraser), Kt 1977; Managing Director, Commercial Banking Company of Sydney Ltd, Australia, 1973–76, retired (General Manager, 1970–73); *m* 1st, Ruth (decd), *d* of H. E. Horsburgh; two *s* one *d*; 2nd, Isabel, *d* of H. T. Underwood. *Address:* Unit 56 The Cotswolds, 28 Curagul Road, North Turramurra, NSW 2074, Australia. *Clubs:* Union (Sydney); Warrawee Bowling.

BOWEN, John Griffith; playwright and novelist; freelance drama producer for television; *b* 5 Nov. 1924; *s* of Hugh Griffith Bowen and Ethel May Cook; unmarried. *Educ:* Queen Elizabeth's Grammar Sch., Crediton; Pembroke Coll., Oxford; St Antony's Coll., Oxford. Frere Exhibition for Indian Studies, Oxford, 1951–52 and 1952–53. Asst Editor, The Sketch, 1954–57; Advertising Copywriter and Copy Chief, 1957–60; Consultant on TV Drama, Associated TV, 1960–67; productions for Thames TV, LWT, BBC. *Publications:* The Truth Will Not Help Us, 1956; After the Rain, 1958; The Centre of the Green, 1959; Storyboard, 1960; The Birdcage, 1962; A World Elsewhere, 1965; The Essay Prize, 1965; Squeak, 1983; The McGuffin, 1984 (filmed for TV, 1986); The Girls, 1986; Fighting Back, 1989; The Precious Gift, 1992; No Retreat, 1994; *plays:* I Love You, Mrs Patterson, 1964; After the Rain, 1967; Fall and Redemption, 1967; Little Boxes, 1968; The Disorderly Women, 1968; The Corsican Brothers, 1970; The Waiting Room, 1970; Robin Redbreast, 1972; Heil Caesar, 1973; Florence Nightingale, 1975; Which Way Are You Facing?, 1976; Singles, 1977; Bondage, 1978; The Inconstant Couple (adaptation of Marivaux, L'Heureux Stratagème), 1978; Uncle Jeremy, 1981; The Geordie Gentleman (adaptation of Molière's Le Bourgeois Gentilhomme), 1987. *Address:* Old Lodge Farm, Sugarswell Lane, Edgehill, Banbury, Oxon OX15 6HP. *T:* Tysoe (01295) 680401.

BOWEN, Hon. Lionel Frost, AC 1991; MHR (Lab) Kingsford-Smith, NSW, 1969–90; Attorney-General of Australia, 1984–90; Chairman, National Gallery, Canberra, since 1990; *b* 28 Dec. 1922; *m* 1953, Claire Clement; five *s* three *d*. *Educ:* Sydney Univ. (LLB). Alderman, 1948, Mayor, 1949–50, Randwick Council; MLA, NSW, 1962–69; Postmaster Gen., 1972–74; Special Minister of State, 1974–75; Minister for Manufg Industry, 1975; Minister for Trade, 1983–84; Dep. Prime Minister, 1983–90. Dep. Leader, ALP, 1977–83. *Recreations:* surfing, reading. *Address:* 24 Mooramie Avenue, Kensington, NSW 2033, Australia.

BOWEN, Sir Mark Edward Mortimer, 5th Bt *cr* 1921, of Colworth, Co. Bedford; *b* 17 Oct. 1958; *s* of Sir Thomas Frederic Charles Bowen, 4th Bt and of Jill, *d* of Lloyd Evans; *S* father, 1989; *m* 1983, Kerry Tessa, *d* of Michael Moriarty; one *s* one *d*. *Heir: s* George Edward Michael Bowen, *b* 27 Dec. 1987. *Address:* 14 Pendarves Road, West Wimbledon, SW20 8TS.

BOWEN, Most Rev. Michael George; *see* Southwark, Archbishop and Metropolitan of, (RC).

BOWEN, Roderic; *see* Bowen, (Evan) Roderic.

BOWEN, Stanley, CBE 1972; Hon. Sheriff, Lothian and Borders, since 1975; *b* Carnoustie, Angus, 4 Aug. 1910; *s* of late Edward Bowen and Ellen Esther Bowen (*née* Powles), Birmingham; *m* 1943, Mary Shepherd Greig, *d* of late Alexander Greig and Mary Shand Greig (*née* Shepherd), Carnoustie; two *s* one *d*. *Educ:* Barry Sch., Angus; Grove Academy, Dundee; University Coll., Dundee. Enrolled Solicitor, in Scotland, 1932; entered Procurator Fiscal Service, in Scotland, 1933; Procurator Fiscal Depute at Hamilton, Lanarkshire, 1937; Interim Procurator Fiscal at Airdrie, Lanarkshire, 1938; Crown Office, Edinburgh: Legal Asst, 1941; Principal Asst, 1945; Crown Agent for Scotland, 1967–74. Chm., Sec. of State for Scotland's working party on forensic pathology services, 1975; Member: Sec. of State for the Environment's working party on drinking and driving offences, 1975; Sub-Cttee for legislation on transplantation of human tissues, Council of Europe, 1975–76; Police Adv. Bd for Scotland, 1976–83 (sub-cttee on police discipline, 1976, and working party on Cadet entry, 1979); Sec. of State for Scotland's working group on identification evidence in criminal cases, 1977; Council, Scottish Assoc. for Care and Resettlement of Offenders, 1978–83; Council, Corstorphine Trust, 1978–90 (Chm., 1982–90; Hon. Vice-Pres., 1990). *Recreations:* golf, gardening. *Address:* Achray, 20 Dovecot Road, Corstorphine, Edinburgh EH12 7LE. *T:* 0131–334 4096. *Clubs:* New, Press (Edinburgh); Carnoustie Golf.
See also E. F. Bowen.

BOWEN, Thomas Edward Ifor L.; *see* Lewis-Bowen.

BOWEN, Prof. William G(ordon), PhD; President, The Andrew W. Mellon Foundation, since 1988; Senior Fellow, Woodrow Wilson School of Public and International Affairs, Princeton University, since 1988 (President Emeritus of the University, 1988); *b* 6 Oct. 1933; *s* of Albert A. and Bernice C. Bowen; *m* 1956, Mary Ellen Maxwell; one *s* one *d*. *Educ:* Denison Univ. (AB); Princeton Univ. (PhD). Princeton University: Asst Prof. of Economics, Associate Prof. of Economics; Prof. of Econs, 1958–88; Provost, 1967–72; Pres., 1972–88. Director: NCR, 1975–91; Reader's Digest, 1985–; Merck, 1986–; American Express, 1988–. Trustee, Center for Advanced Study in the Behavioral Sciences, 1986–92; Regent, Smithsonian Instn, 1980–92; Mem. Bd of Dirs, Denison Univ., 1992–. Hon. LLD: Denison, Rutgers, Pennsylvania and Yale, 1972; Harvard, 1973; Jewish Theol Seminary, 1974; Seton Hall Univ., 1975; Dartmouth and Princeton, 1987; Brown, 1988. *Publications:* Economic Aspects of Education, 1964; (with W. J. Baumol) Performing Arts: the Economic Dilemma, 1966; (with T. A. Finegan) Economics of Labor Force Participation, 1969; Ever the Teacher, 1987; (with Julie Ann Sosa) Prospects for Faculty in the Arts & Sciences, 1989; (with N. L. Rudeustine) In Pursuit of the PhD, 1992; Inside the Boardroom: governance by directors and trustees, 1994; (jtly) The Charitable Nonprofits; contribs to Amer. Econ. Review, Economica, Quarterly Jl of Economics, etc. *Address:* 140 E 62 Street, New York, NY 10021, USA. *T:* (212) 8388400.

BOWER, Michael Douglas; Leader, Sheffield Metropolitan District Council; *b* 25 Aug. 1942; *s* of Stanley Arthur Bower and Rachael Farmer; *m*; two *d*. *Educ:* Colwyn Bay Grammar Sch.; Royal Coll. of Advanced Technol., Salford. Civil engr, 1961–64; journalist, 1965–77; with The Star, Sheffield, 1968–77; Regional Organiser, NUJ, 1977–81; Organiser, Sheffield Co-operative Develt Gp, 1981–94. Mem., Press Council, 1976–77. Mem., Sheffield Metropolitan DC, 1976– (Chm., Educn Cttee, 1983). Contested (Lab) Hallam Div. of Sheffield, 1979. *Recreations:* walking, golf. *Address:* 366 Walkley Bank Road, Sheffield S6 5AR. *T:* Sheffield (0114) 233 5753. *Club:* Carlton Working Men's (Gleadless, Sheffield).

BOWERING, Christine, MA; Headmistress, Nottingham High School for Girls (GPDST), since 1984; *b* 30 June 1936; *d* of Kenneth Soper and Florence E. W. Soper; *m* 1960, Rev. John Anthony Bowering; one *s* one *d*. *Educ:* St Bernard's Convent, Westcliff-on-Sea; Newnham Coll., Cambridge (MA). Assistant Teacher: St Bernard's Convent; Ursuline Convent, Brentwood; Sheffield High Sch. (GPDST). Mem., Engineering Council, 1988–91. Dir, Queen's Med. Centre, Nottingham, 1993–. Chairman: Educn Cttee, GSA, 1989–93; Indep. Schs Curriculum Cttee, 1992–94; Mem., Educn Cttee, Goldsmiths' Co., 1992–. Gov., Nottingham Trent Univ. (formerly Nottingham Poly.), 1989–. Assoc. Mem., Newnham Coll., Cambridge, 1991. FRSA. *Address:* The Vicarage, 2 Sunderland Street, Tickhill DN11 9QJ. *T:* Doncaster (01302) 742224. *Club:* University Women's.

BOWERING, Ven. Michael Ernest; Archdeacon of Lindisfarne, since 1987; *b* 25 June 1935; *s* of Hubert James and Mary Elizabeth Bowering; *m* 1962, Aileen (*née* Fox); one *s* two *d*. *Educ:* Barnstaple Grammar School; Kelham Theological Coll. Curate: St Oswald, Middlesbrough, 1959–62; Huntington with New Earswick, York, 1962–64; Vicar, Brayton with Barlow, 1964–72; RD of Selby, 1971–72; Vicar, Saltburn by the Sea, 1972–81; Canon Residentiary of York Minster and Secretary for Mission and Evengelism, 1981–87. *Recreations:* crosswords, walking the dog. *Address:* 12 Rectory Park, Morpeth, Northumberland NE61 2SZ. *T:* Morpeth (01670) 513207.

BOWERMAN, David Alexander; retired; *b* 19 April 1903; *s* of Frederick and Millicent Bowerman; *m* 1925, Constance Lilian Hosegood (*d* 1959); four *s* one *d*; *m* 1962, June Patricia Ruth Day. *Educ:* Queen's Coll., Taunton. Farmer, 1923–36; Wholesale Fruit and Potato Merchant (Director), 1936–60. Chairman, Horticultural Marketing Council, 1960–63. Director, 1963–75: Jamaica Producers Marketing Co. Ltd; JP Fruit Distributors Ltd; Horticultural Exports (GB) Ltd. *Publication:* Poems in time of war, 1991. *Recreations:* sailing, golf, gardens. *Address:* The Spinney, Brenchley, Kent TN12 7AE. *T:* Brenchley (01892) 722149. *Clubs:* Lamberhurst Golf; Isle of Purbeck Golf.

BOWERS, Michael John; Managing Director, TW Oil (UK) Ltd, since 1985; *b* 1 Oct. 1933; *s* of Arthur Patrick and Lena Frances Bowers; *m* 1959, Caroline (*née* Clifford); two *d*. *Educ:* Cardinal Vaughan Sch., Kensington. BP Group: various appts in Supply, Distribution Planning and Trading, 1951–73; Vice-Pres. and Dir, BP North America Inc. (NY), 1973–76; Man. Dir and Chief Exec. Officer, BP Gas, 1976–81; Dir, BP Shipping/BP Exploration, 1980–81; Regional Co-ordinator, Western Hemisphere, 1981–83; Chief Exec., International Petroleum Exchange of London Ltd, 1983–85. *Recreations:* gardening, tennis, bridge, chess. *Address:* Wood End, Warren Drive, Kingswood, Surrey KT20 6PZ. *T:* Mogador (01737) 832629.

BOWERS, Roger George, OBE 1984; PhD; Assistant Director-General (Manchester), and Director of Professional Services, British Council, since 1993; *b* 23 May 1942; *s* of George Albert Bowers and Hilda Mary Bowers (*née* Wells); *m* 1963, Gweneth Iris Pither (marr. diss.); one *s* one *d*. *Educ:* Royal Grammar Sch., Guildford; Wadham Coll., Oxford (BA); Reading Univ. (MPhil; PhD). Joined British Council, 1964; Tutor to Overseas Students, Univ. of Birmingham, 1965; Asst Regl Dir, Cape Coast, Ghana, 1965–69; seconded to Eng. Lang. Trng Inst., Allahabad, 1971–73; Asst Regl Educ. Advr, Calcutta, 1973–76; Eng. Lang. Consultancies Dept, 1978–80; seconded to Ain Shams Univ., Cairo, 1980–84; Dir, Eng. Lang. Services Dept, 1984–85; Dep. Controller, 1985–89, Controller, then Dir, 1989–93, Eng. Lang. and Lit. Div. Jt Editor, Cambridge Handbooks for Language Teachers, 1985–92; Member: Editorial Cttee, ELT Documents, 1984–; Bd of Management, ELT Jl, 1985–. FRSA 1993. *Publications:* In Passing, 1976; Talking About Grammar, 1987; Word Play, 1990. *Recreations:* fishing, cooking, eating. *Address:* 25 Hillbrow, Richmond Hill, Surrey TW10 6BH. *T:* 0181–948 6342; The British Council, Medlock Street, Manchester M15 4AA. *T:* 0161–957 7274, *Fax:* 0161–957 7277.

BOWERY, Prof. Norman George, PhD, DSc; Wellcome Professor of Pharmacology, The School of Pharmacy, University of London, since 1987; *b* 23 June 1944; *s* of George Bowery and Olga (*née* Beevers); *m* 1970, Barbara Joyce (*née* Westcott); one *s* two *d*. *Educ:* Christ's Coll., Finchley; NE Surrey Coll. of Technology; St Bartholomew's Med. Coll., Univ. of London (PhD 1974; DSc 1987). MIBiol 1970. Res. Asst, CIBA Labs, 1963–70; Res. Student, St Bart's Med. Coll., London, 1970–73; Postdoctoral Res. Fellow, Sch. of Pharmacy, London Univ., 1973–75; Lectr in Pharmacology, 1975–82, Sen. Lectr in Pharm., 1982–84, St Thomas's Hosp. Med. Sch.; Section Leader, Neuroscience Res. Centre, Merck, Sharp & Dohme, Harlow, 1984–87. Laurea in pharmacy *hc* Florence, 1992. Biological Council Medal, 1991. *Publications:* Actions and Interactions of GABA and Benzodiazepines, 1984; GABAergic Mechanisms in the Mammalian Periphery, 1986; GABA: basic mechanisms to clinical applications, 1989; $GABA_B$ Receptors in Mammalian Function, 1990. *Recreations:* gardening, socializing, walking, family life. *Address:* Department of Pharmacology, The School of Pharmacy, 29/39 Brunswick Square, WC1N 1AX. *T:* 0171–753 5899.

BOWES, Richard Noel; Deputy Chairman, Willis Faber plc and Chairman, Willis Faber and Dumas, 1985–88, retired; *b* 17 Dec. 1928; *m* 1961, Elizabeth Lyle; one *s* two *d*. *Educ:* Epsom College; Worcester Coll., Oxford (MA). Called to the Bar, Gray's Inn, 1950. RN,

1950–53. Willis Faber and Dumas, 1953–88. *Address:* Fairacre, Enton, Godalming, Surrey GU8 5AQ. *T:* Godalming (01483) 416544.

BOWES, Roger Norman; Chief Executive, Association for Information Management (Aslib), since 1989; *b* 28 Jan. 1943; *s* of late Russell Ernest Bowes and Sybil Caroline Rose Bowes (*née* Bell); *m* 1st, 1961, Denise Hume Windsor (marr. diss. 1974); one *d*; 2nd, 1977, Ann Rosemary O'Connor (*née* Hamstead) (marr. diss. 1988). *Educ:* Chiswick and Dorking Grammar Schools. Advertisement Executive: Associated Newspapers, 1962–67; IPC/Mirror Gp Newspapers, 1967–70; Marketing Exec./Sales Manager, Mirror Gp, 1970–75; Media Dir, McCann Erickson Advertising, 1976–78; Mirror Gp Newspapers: Adv. Dir, 1978–81; Dep. Chief Exec., 1982–83; Chief Exec., 1984; Man. Dir, Guinness Enterprises, 1985; Chief Exec., Express Gp Newspapers, 1985–86; Chm., Citybridge, 1987–. Member: British Liby Adv. Council; Adv. Cttee, Public Liby Develt Incentive Scheme; Europ. Council of Information Assocs; Adv. Cttee for Europ. Liby Plan; British Council Libraries Adv. Cttee; Treas., Internat. Fedn for Information and Documentation. FRSA. *Recreations:* political and military history, cookery, architectural restoration, classic cars. *Address:* Aslib, Information House, 20–24 Old Street, EC1V 9AP. *T:* 0171–253 4488, *Fax:* 0171–430 0514.

BOWES LYON, family name of **Earl of Strathmore.**

BOWES LYON, Simon Alexander, FCA; director of insurance and investment companies; Lord-Lieutenant of Hertfordshire, since 1986; *b* 17 June 1932; *s* of Hon. Sir David Bowes Lyon, KCVO, and of Rachel Bowes Lyon (*née* Spender Clay); *m* 1966, Caroline, *d* of Rt Rev. Victor Pike, CB, CBE, DD, and of Dorothea Pike; three *s* one *d*. *Educ:* Eton; Magdalen Coll., Oxford (BA). *Recreations:* botany, gardening, shooting, music. *Address:* St Paul's Walden Bury, Hitchin, Herts SG4 8BP. *T:* Whitwell (01438) 871218.

BOWETT, Prof. Derek William, CBE 1983; QC 1978; LLD; FBA 1983; Whewell Professor of International Law, Cambridge University, 1981–91; Professorial Fellow of Queens' College, Cambridge, 1982–91 (Hon. Fellow, 1991); *b* 20 April 1927; *s* of Arnold William Bowett and Marion Wood; *m* 1953, Betty Northall; two *s* one *d*. *Educ:* William Hulme's Sch., Manchester; Downing Coll., Cambridge. MA, LLB, LLD (Cantab), PhD (Manchester). Called to the Bar, Middle Temple, 1953, Hon. Bencher, 1975. Lectr, Law Faculty, Manchester Univ. 1951–59; Legal Officer, United Nations, New York, 1957–59; Cambridge University: Lectr, Law Faculty, 1960–76, Reader, 1976–81; Fellow of Queens' Coll., 1960–69, President 1969–82. Gen. Counsel, UNRWA, Beirut, 1966–68. Member: Royal Commn on Environmental Pollution, 1973–77; Internat. Law Commn, 1991–. Commander, Order of Dannebrog (Denmark), 1993; Grand Cross, Civil Order, Jose Cecilio del Valle (Honduras), 1993. *Publications:* Self-defence in International Law, 1958; Law of International Institutions, 1964; United Nations Forces, 1964; Law of the Sea, 1967; Search for Peace, 1972; Legal Régime of Islands in International Law, 1978. *Recreations:* music, cricket, tennis. *Address:* 228 Hills Road, Cambridge CB2 2QE. *T:* Cambridge (01223) 210688.

BOWEY, Prof. Angela Marilyn, PhD; Director, Pay Advice and Research Centre, Glasgow, 1986; Professor of Business Administration, Strathclyde Business School, University of Strathclyde, Glasgow, 1976–87; *b* 20 Oct. 1940; *d* of Jack Nicholas Peterson and Kathleen (*née* Griffin); *m* 1st, 1960, Miklos Papp; two *s* one *d*; 2nd, 1965, Gregory Bowey (marr. diss. 1980); one *s* one *d*. *Educ:* Withington Girls Sch., Manchester; Univ. of Manchester (BA Econ, PhD). Technical Asst, Nuclear Power Gp, 1961–62; Asst Lectr, Elizabeth Gaskell Coll. of Educn, 1967–68; Manchester Business School: Res. Associate, 1968–69; Res. Fellow, 1969–72; Lectr, 1972–76. Vis. Professor: Admin. Staff Coll. of India, 1975; Western Australian Inst. of Technology, 1976; Univ. of WA, 1977; Prahran Coll. of Advanced Educn, Australia, 1978; Massey Univ., NZ, 1978. ACAS Arbitrator, 1977–; Dir, Pay and Rewards Res. Centre, 1978–85; Comr, Equal Opportunities Commn, 1980–86; Member: Scottish Econ. Council, 1980–83; Police Adv. Bd (Scotland) (formerly Adv. Panel on Police), 1983–88. Gov., Scottish Police Coll., 1985–88. Editor, Management Decision, 1979–82. *Publications:* Job and Pay Comparisons (with Tom Lupton), 1973, 2nd edn 1974; A Guide to Manpower Planning, 1974, 2nd edn 1977; (with Tom Lupton) Wages and Salaries, 1974, 2nd edn 1982; Handbook of Salary and Wage Systems, 1975, 2nd edn 1982; The Sociology of Organisations, 1976; (with Richard Thorpe and Phil Hellier) Payment Systems and Productivity, 1986; Managing Salary and Wage Systems, 1987; articles in Brit. Jl of Indust. Relations, Jl of Management Studies, and Management Decision.

BOWEY, Olwyn, RA 1975 (ARA 1970); practising artist (painter); *b* 10 Feb. 1936, *o d* of James and Olive Bowey. *Educ:* West Hartlepool Sch. of Art; Royal Coll. of Art. One-man shows: Zwemmer Gall., 1961; New Grafton Gall., 1969; also exhibited at Leicester Gall., Royal Academy; work purchased through Chantrey Bequest for Tate Gall., Royal Academy, Min. of Works, etc.

BOWIE, Rev. (Alexander) Glen, CBE 1984; Principal Chaplain (Church of Scotland and Free Churches), Royal Air Force, 1980–84, retired; *b* 10 May 1928; *s* of Alexander Bowie and Annie (*née* McGhie); *m* 1952, Mary McKillop (*d* 1991); two *d*. *Educ:* Stevenston High Sch.; Irvine Royal Acad.; Glasgow Univ. (BSc 1951; Dip Theol 1954); BA Open Univ., 1977. Nat. Service, RAF, 1947–49. Assistant, Beith High Church, 1952–54; ordained, 1954; entered RAF Chaplains' Br., 1955; served: RAF Padgate, 1955–56; Akrotiri, 1956–59; Stafford, 1959–61; Butzweilerhof, 1961–64; Halton, 1964–67; Akrotiri, 1967–70; RAF Coll., Cranwell, 1970–75; Asst Principal Chaplain, 1975; HQ Germany, 1975–76; HQ Support Comd, 1976–80. Acting Chaplain to Moderator of Church of Scotland, in London, 1985–; Moderator, Ch of Scotland Presbytery of England, 1988–89. QHC 1980–84; Hon. Chaplain, Royal Scottish Corp., 1981–. Editor, Scottish Forces Bulletin, 1985–. *Recreations:* oil painting, travel, leading Holy Land tours. *Address:* 16 Weir Road, Hemingford Grey, Huntingdon, Cambs PE18 9EH. *T:* Huntingdon (01480) 381425. *Club:* Royal Air Force.

BOWIE, David; international recording artist and performer; film and stage actor; video and film producer; graphic designer; *b* 8 Jan. 1947; *s* of Hayward Stenton Jones and Margaret Mary Burns; *m* (marr. diss.); one *s*; *m* 1992, Iman Abdul Majid. *Educ:* Stansfield Road Sch., Brixton. Artiste from age of 16; many major recordings, 1970–, and video productions, 1979–; numerous live musical stage performances; guest appearances on television shows. Actor: *films:* The Man who Fell to Earth, 1976; Just a Gigolo, 1978; The Hunger, 1982; Merry Christmas, Mr Lawrence, 1983; Ziggy Stardust and the Spiders from Mars, 1983; Absolute Beginners, 1986; Labyrinth, 1986; Into the Night; The Last Temptation of Christ; *stage:* The Elephant Man, New York 1980; *television:* Baal, 1982. Recipient of internat. music and entertainment awards. *Recreations:* painting, skiing. *Address:* c/o Isolar, Suite 220, 641 5th Avenue, New York, NY 10022, USA.

BOWIE, Rev. Glen; *see* Bowie, Rev. A. G.

BOWIE, Graham Maitland, CBE 1992; Chief Executive, Lothian Regional Council, 1986–94; *b* 11 Nov. 1931; *s* of John Graham Bowie and Agnes Bowie; *m* 1962, Maureen Jennifer O'Sullivan; one *s* two *d*. *Educ:* Alloa Academy; Univ. of St Andrews (MA); Univ. of Glasgow (LLB). National Service, 1956–58. Asst Sec., Glasgow Chamber of Commerce, 1958–60; Product Planner, Ford Motor Co., 1960–64; Edinburgh Corp. Educn Dept, 1964–69; ILEA, 1969–75; Dir of Policy Planning, Lothian Regional Council, 1975–86. Mem., Nat. Lotteries Charities Bd. *Recreations:* walking, travel, the arts. *Address:* 8 Keith Crescent, Edinburgh EH4 3NH.

BOWIE, Prof. Malcolm McNaughtan, DPhil; FBA 1993; Marshal Foch Professor of French Literature, University of Oxford, since 1992; Fellow of All Souls College, Oxford, since 1992; *b* 5 May 1943; *s* of George Alexander Bowie and Beatrice Georgina Betty (*née* Strowger); *m* 1979, Alison Mary Finch; one *s* one *d*. *Educ:* Woodbridge Sch.; Univ. of Edinburgh (MA 1965); Univ. of Sussex (DPhil 1970); MA Cantab 1969; MA Oxon 1992. Asst Lectr in French, UEA, 1967–69; University of Cambridge: Asst Lectr, 1969–72; Lectr, 1972–76; Fellow and Dir of Studies, Clare Coll., 1969–76, Tutor, 1971–76; University of London: Prof. of French Lang. and Lit., 1976–92; Hd, Dept of French, QMC, 1976–89; Founding Dir, Inst. of Romance Studies, 1989–92 (Hon. Sen. Res. Fellow, 1993). Vis. Prof., Univ. of California, Berkeley, 1983; Vis. Dist. Prof., Grad. Center, CUNY, 1989; Andrew W. Mellon Lectr, Bucknell Univ., 1990; Vis. Fellow, Centre for Res. in Philosophy and Lit., Univ. of Warwick, 1991. Pres., Assoc. of Univ. Profs of French, 1982–84. Pres., Soc. for French Studies, 1994–. Mem. Exec. Cttee, Univs Council for Modern Langs, 1994–. Mem., Academia Europaea, 1989. Gen. Editor, French Studies, 1980–87; Founding Gen. Editor, Cambridge Studies in French, 1980–; Editor, Jl Inst. Romance Studies, 1992. Chevalier, L'Ordre des Palmes Académiques (France), 1987. *Publications:* Henri Michaux: a study of his literary works, 1973; Mallarmé and the Art of Being Difficult, 1978; Freud, Proust and Lacan: theory as fiction, 1987; Lacan, 1991; Psychoanalysis and the Future of Theory, 1993; contribs to learned jls and collective works. *Address:* All Souls College, Oxford OX1 4AL. *T:* Oxford (01865) 279379.

BOWIE, Stanley Hay Umphray, DSc; FRS 1975; FEng 1976; FRSE, FIMM, FMSA; FSAScot; Consultant Geologist; Assistant Director, Chief Geochemist, Institute of Geological Sciences, 1968–77; *b* 24 March 1917; *s* of Dr James Cameron and Mary Bowie; *m* 1948, Helen Elizabeth, *d* of Dr Roy Woodhouse and Florence Elizabeth Pocock; two *s*. *Educ:* Grammar Sch. and Univ. of Aberdeen (BSc, DSc). Meteorological Office, 1942; commissioned RAF, 1943; HM Geological Survey of Gt Britain: Geologist, Sen. Geologist and Principal Geologist, 1946–55; Chief Geologist, Atomic Energy Div., 1955–67; Chief Consultant Geologist to UKAEA, 1955–77. Visiting Prof. of Applied Geology, Univ. of Strathclyde, 1968–85; Vis. Prof., Imperial Coll., London, 1985–92. Principal Investigator, Apollo 11 and 12 lunar samples, 1969–71; Chairman: Internat. Mineralogical Assoc., Commn on Ore Microscopy, 1970–78; Royal Soc. Sectl Cttee 5, 1977–79; Royal Soc. Working Party on Envtl Geochem. and Health, 1979–81; DoE Res. Adv. Gp, Radioactive Waste Management, 1984–85; Mem., Radioactive Waste Management Adv. Cttee, 1978–82. Vice-Pres., Shetland Sheep Breeders Gp, 1992– (Chm., 1989–91). Vice-Pres., Geological Soc., 1972–74; Mem. Council, Mineralogical Soc., 1954–57, 1962–65 (Chairman: Applied Mineralogy Gp, 1969–72; Geochem. Gp, 1972–75). FGS 1959; FMSA 1963; FRSE 1970; FIMM 1972 (Pres. 1976–77), Hon. FIMM 1987; FSAScot 1992. Silver Medal, RSA, 1959; Team Mem., Queen's Award for Technol Achievement, 1990 (for develt of Inductively Coupled Plasma Mass Spectrometer). *Publications:* (ed jtly) Uranium Prospecting Handbook, 1972; (ed jtly) Mineral Deposits of Europe, Vol. 1: North-West Europe, 1978; (with P. R. Simpson) The Bowie-Simpson System for the Microscopic Determination of Ore Minerals, 1980; (ed jtly) Environmental Geochemistry and Health, 1985; (with C. Bowie) Radon and Health—The Facts, 1991; contributions to: Nuclear Geology, 1954; Physical Methods in Determinative Mineralogy, 1967, 2nd edn 1977; Uranium Exploration Geology, 1970; Proceedings of the Apollo Lunar Science Conference, 1970; Proceedings of the Second Lunar Science Conference, 1971; Uranium Exploration Methods, 1973; Recognition and Evaluation of Uraniferous Areas, 1977; Theoretical and Practical Aspects of Uranium Geology, 1979; Nuclear Power Technology, 1983; Applied Environmental Geochemistry, 1983; numerous papers in scientific and technical jls on uranium geology and economics, mineralogy, geophysics and geochemistry, and articles on rare breeds of domesticated animals. *Recreations:* farming, preservation of rare breeds, gardening, photography. *Address:* Tanyard Farm, Clapton, Crewkerne, Somerset TA18 8PS. *T:* Crewkerne (01460) 72093.

BOWIS, John Crocket, OBE 1981; MP (C) Battersea, since 1987; Parliamentary Under-Secretary of State, Department of Health, since 1993; *b* 2 Aug. 1945; *s* of Thomas Palin Bowis and Georgiana Joyce (*née* Crocket); *m* 1968, Caroline May (*née* Taylor); two *s* one *d*. *Educ:* Tonbridge Sch.; Brasenose Coll., Oxford (MA). Tutor, Cumberland Lodge, Windsor Great Park Student Conference Centre, 1966–67; Cons. Party Agent, Peterborough, Derby, Harborough and Blaby, 1968–72; Conservative Central Office: National Organiser, Fedn of Cons. Students, 1972–75; Nat. Organiser, Cons. Trade Unionists, 1975–79; Dir of Community Affairs, 1979–81; Campaign Dir, 1981–82, Public Affairs Dir, 1983–87, British Insurance Brokers Assoc.; Press and Parly Consultant, Nat. Fedn of Self-employed and Small Firms, 1982–83. Councillor (C) Royal Bor. of Kingston upon Thames, 1982–86 (Chm. of Educn, 1985–86). PPS to Minister for Local Govt and Inner Cities, DoE, 1989–90, to Sec. of State for Wales, 1990–93. Mem., Select Cttee on Members' Interests, 1987–90; Vice-Chm., All Party Gp on Social Sci., 1988–93; Chm., All Party Somali Gp, 1991–. Secretary: Cons. Inner Cities Cttee, 1987–89; Cons. Educn Cttee, 1988–89; Cons. Arts and Heritage Cttee, 1988–89; Parliamentary Adviser to: ACFHE, 1987–93; Assoc. for Coll. Management, 1990–93; ATL (formerly AMMA), 1992–93. Vice-Pres., Internat. Soc. for Human Rights, 1988–; Chm., Nat. Council for Civil Protection, 1992–93. Hon. Jt Pres., British Youth Council, 1987–93. Director: London Actors' Theatre Co., 1990–; Battersea Arts Centre, 1991–; Royal Nat. Theatre, 1992–; South Bank Centre, 1992–. *Recreations:* theatre, music, art, sport. *Address:* House of Commons, SW1A 0AA. *T:* 0171–219 3535, 0181–949 2555.

BOWKER, Prof. John Westerdale; Gresham Professor of Divinity, since 1992; Hon. Canon of Canterbury Cathedral, since 1985; Adjunct Professor of Religion, North Carolina State University, since 1986; Adjunct Professor of Religious Studies, University of Pennsylvania, since 1986; *b* 30 July 1935; *s* of Gordon Westerdale Bowker and Marguerite (*née* Burdick); *m* 1963, Margaret Roper; one *s*. *Educ:* St John's Sch., Leatherhead; Worcester Coll., Oxford (MA); Ripon Hall, Oxford. National Service, RWAFF, N Nigeria, 1953–55. Henry Stephenson Fellow, Sheffield Univ., 1961; Deacon, St Augustine's, Brocco Bank, Sheffield, 1961; Priest and Dean of Chapel, Corpus Christi Coll., Cambridge, 1962; Asst Lectr, 1965, Lectr, 1970, Univ. of Cambridge; Prof. of Religious Studies, Univ. of Lancaster, 1974–85; Dean, 1984–91 and Fellow, 1984–93, Trinity Coll., Cambridge. Lectures: Wilde, Univ. of Oxford, 1972–75; Staley, Rollins Coll., Florida, 1978–79; Public, Univ. of Cardiff, 1984; Riddell, Newcastle Univ., 1985; Boutwood, Univ. of Cambridge, 1985; Harris Meml, Toronto, 1986; Boardman, Univ. of Pa, 1988; Montefiore, Univ. of Southampton, 1989; Scott Holland, London Univ., 1989; Bicentary, Univ. of Georgetown, Washington, 1989. Member: Durham Commn on Religious Educn, 1967–70; Root Commn on Marriage and Divorce, 1967–71; Archbps' Commn on Doctrine, 1977–86; Patron, Marriage Research Inst.; Hon. Pres., Stauros; Vice-President: Inst. on Religion in an Age of Science, 1980; Culture and Animals Foundn, 1984–92; Pres., Christian Action on AIDS, 1987–91. Editor, Oxford Companion to Religions of the World, 1977–. *Publications:* The Targums and Rabbinic Literature,

1969, 2nd edn 1979; Problems of Suffering in Religions of the World, 1970, 3rd edn 1987; Jesus and the Pharisees, 1973; The Sense of God, 1973, 2nd edn 1995; The Religious Imagination and the Sense of God, 1978; Uncle Bolpenny Tries Things Out, 1973; Worlds of Faith, 1983; (ed) Violence and Aggression, 1983; Licensed Insanities: religions and belief in God in the contemporary world, 1987; The Meanings of Death, 1991 (HarperCollins Religious Book Award, 1993); A Year to Live, 1991; Hallowed Ground: the religious poetry of place, 1993; Voices of Islam, 1995; Is God a Virus? Genes, Culture and Religion, 1995. *Recreations:* walking, books, gardening, cooking, painting, poetry. *Address:* 14 Bowers Croft, Cambridge CB1 4RP.

BOWKETT, Alan John; Chief Executive, Berisford International, since 1992; *b* 6 Jan. 1951; *er s* of John and Margaret Bowkett; *m* 1975, Joy Dianne Neale; two *s* two *d. Educ:* King Charles I Grammar Sch., Kidderminster; University College London (BSc Econ); London Business Sch. (MSc Econ). Corporate Planning Manager, Lex Service, 1977–83; Corporate Develt Manager, BET, 1983–85; Man. Dir, Boulton & Paul, 1985–87; Chief Exec., United Precision Industries, 1987–91. Director: Anglian Group, 1992–94; Pallasinvest SA (Luxembourg), 1992–; Greene King, 1993–; Chm., Calder Gp Ltd, 1994–. Councillor (C) London Borough of Ealing, 1978–82 (Chm., Social Services); Dep. Chm., Ealing Acton Cons. Assoc., 1982–84. Council Mem., UEA, 1988– (Treasurer, 1990–94). FRSA 1993. *Recreations:* growing vegetables, shooting, opera, Italy. *Address:* Berisford International, 1 Baker Street, W1M 1AA. *T:* 0171–312 2500. *Club:* Carlton.

BOWLBY, Sir Richard Peregrine Longstaff, 3rd Bt *cr* 1923, of Manchester Square, St Marylebone; *b* 11 Aug. 1941; *s* of Edward John Mostyn Bowlby, CBE, MD (*d* 1990), 2nd *s* of Sir Anthony Alfred Bowlby, 1st Bt, KCB, KCMG, KCVO, and of Ursula, *d* of Dr T. G. Longstaff; *S* uncle, 1993; *m* 1963, Xenia, *o d* of R. P. A. Garrett; one *s* one *d. Heir: s* Benjamin Bowlby, *b* 2 Nov. 1966. *Address:* Boundary House, Wyldes Close, NW11 7JB.

BOWLBY, Rt. Rev. Ronald Oliver; Assistant Bishop, Diocese of Lichfield, since 1991; *b* 16 August 1926; *s* of Oliver and Helena Bowlby; *m* 1956, Elizabeth Trevelyan Monro; three *s* two *d. Educ:* Eton Coll.; Trinity College, Oxford (MA; Hon. Fellow, 1991); Westcott House, Cambridge. Curate of St Luke's, Pallion, Sunderland, 1952–56; Priest-in-charge and Vicar of St Aidan, Billingham, 1956–66; Vicar of Croydon, 1966–72; Bishop of: Newcastle, 1973–80; Southwark, 1980–91. Chairman: Hospital Chaplaincies Council, 1975–82; Social Policy Cttee, Bd for Social Responsibility, 1986–90; Mem., Anglican Consultative Council, 1977–85. President: Nat. Fedn of Housing Assocs, 1988–94; Churches' Nat. Housing Coalition, 1991–94. Hon. Fellow, Newcastle upon Tyne Polytechnic, 1980. *Publications:* contrib. Church without Walls, ed Lindars, 1969; contrib. Church and Politics Today, ed Moyser, 1985. *Recreations:* walking, gardening, music. *Address:* 4 Uppington Avenue, Bellevue, Shrewsbury SY3 7JL.

BOWLER, Geoffrey, FCIS; Chief General Manager, Sun Alliance & London Insurance Group, 1977–87; *b* 11 July 1924; *s* of James Henry Bowler and Hilda May Bowler. *Educ:* Sloane Sch., Chelsea. FCIS 1952. Dir, British Aviation Insurance Co., 1976–87 (Chm., 1977–83). Dep. Chm., British Insurance Assoc., 1977, Chm. 1979–80. *Address:* 13 Green Lane, Purley, Surrey CR8 3PP. *T:* 0181–660 0756.

BOWLER, Ian John, CBE 1971 (OBE 1957); President, Iranian Management & Engineering Group Ltd, since 1965; Chairman: International Management & Engineering Group Ltd, since 1973 (Managing Director, 1964–68); ICE, Moscow/London; *b* 1920; *s* of Major John Arthur Bowler; *m* 1963, Hamideh, *d* of Prince Yadollah Azodi, GCMG; two *d*, and one step *s* one step *d. Educ:* King's Sch., Worcester; privately; Oxford Univ. Director of Constructors, John Brown, 1961–64. Director: IMEG (Offshore) Ltd, 1974–; MMC Gas, Kuala Lumpur. Mem., RNLI, 1983–. Sec., Azerbaijan Foundn, 1992. MInstPet. *Publication:* Predator Birds of Iran, 1973. *Recreations:* ornithology, yachting. *Address:* 4 Kucheh, Bagh Bank, Golhak, Tehran, Iran. *Clubs:* Royal Thames Yacht, Ocean Cruising; S.R.R. (La Rochelle, France).

BOWLES, Rt. Rev. Cyril William Johnston; Hon. Assistant Bishop, diocese of Gloucester, since 1987; *b* Scotstoun, Glasgow, 9 May 1916; *s* of William Cullen Allen Bowles, West Ham, and Jeanie Edwards Kilgour, Glasgow; *m* 1965, Florence Joan, *d* of late John Eastaugh, Windlesham. *Educ:* Brentwood Sch.; Emmanuel Coll., Jesus Coll. (Lady Kay Scholar) and Ridley Hall, Cambridge. 2nd cl., Moral Sciences Tripos, Pt. I, 1936; 1st cl., Theological Tripos, Pt. I, and BA, 1938; 2nd cl., Theological Tripos, Pt. II, 1939; MA 1941. Deacon 1939, Priest 1940, Chelmsford; Curate of Barking Parish Church, 1939–41; Chaplain of Ridley Hall, Cambridge, 1942–44; Vice-Principal, 1944–51; Principal, 1951–63; Hon. Canon of Ely Cathedral, 1959–63; Archdeacon of Swindon, 1963–69; Bishop of Derby, 1969–87. Mem. of House of Lords, 1973–87. Select Preacher: Cambridge, 1945, 1953, 1958, 1963; Oxford, 1961; Dublin, 1961. Exam. Chaplain to Bishop of Carlisle, 1950–63; to Bishops of Rochester, Ely and Chelmsford, 1951–63; to Bishop of Bradford, 1956–61; to Bishop of Bristol, 1963–69. Hon. Canon, Bristol Cathedral, 1963–69; Surrogate, 1963–69; Commissary to Bishop of the Argentine, 1963–69. Mem., Archbishops' Liturgical Commn, 1955–75. Pres., St John's Coll., Durham, 1970–84 (Hon. Fellow, 1991); Visitor of Ridley Hall, 1979–87. *Publications:* contributor: The Roads Converge, 1963; A Manual for Holy Week, 1967; The Eucharist Today, 1974. *Address:* Rose Lodge, Tewkesbury Road, Stow-on-the-Wold, Cheltenham, Glos GL54 1EN. *T:* Cotswold (01451) 831965.

BOWLES, Godfrey Edward; Managing Director, Pearl Group, 1989–94; *b* 21 Dec. 1935; *s* of Llewellyn Crowley Bowles and Florence Jane Edwards; *m* 1958, Elizabeth Madge Dunning; two *s* two *d. Educ:* Commonweal Grammar Sch., Swindon; Exeter Coll., Oxford (MA). Emigrated to Australia, 1959; joined Australian Mutual Provident Society: Dep. Manager, Wellington, NZ, 1976; Manager, WA Br., Perth, 1980; Manager, Victoria Br., Melbourne, 1983; Chief Manager, Corporate Services, Sydney, 1986; Gen. Manager, AMP Corporate, Sydney, 1988; returned to UK after acquisition of Pearl Gp by AMP Soc., 1989. *Recreations:* running, including marathons, reading, music, theatre, cinema. *Address:* Priory Gardens, Church Road, Ketton, Stamford, Lincs PE9 3RD.

BOWLES, Peter; actor; *b* 16 Oct. 1936; *s* of Herbert Reginald Bowles and Sarah Jane (*née* Harrison); *m* 1961, Susan Alexandra Bennett; two *s* one *d. Educ:* High Pavement Grammar Sch., Nottingham; RADA (schol.; Kendal Prize 1955). London début in Romeo and Juliet, Old Vic, 1956; *theatre* includes: Happy Haven, Platonov, Royal Court, 1960; Bonne Soupe, Wyndham's, 1961; Afternoon Men, Arts, 1962; Absent Friends, Garrick, 1975; Dirty Linen, Arts, 1976; Born in the Gardens, Globe, 1980; Some of My Best Friends Are Husbands, nat. tour, 1985; The Entertainer, Shaftesbury, 1986; Canaries Sometimes Sing, Albery, 1987; Man of the Moment, Globe, 1990; Otherwise Engaged (also dir), nat. tour, 1992; Separate Tables, Albery, 1993; Pygmalion, Chichester, 1994; Present Laughter, nat. tour, 1994; In Praise of Love, Apollo, 1995; Gangster No 1, Almeida, 1995; *films* include: Blow Up, 1966; The Charge of the Light Brigade, 1967; Laughter in the Dark, 1968; A Day in the Death of Joe Egg, 1970; The Steal, 1994; *TV film:* Running Late (also co-prod), 1992; *television series* include: Rumpole of the Bailey, 1976–92; To the Manor Born, 1979–82; Only when I Laugh, 1979–82; The Bounder, 1982–83; The Irish RM, 1983–85; Lytton's Diary, 1984–86 (also co-created series); Executive Stress, 1987–88; Shadow on the Sun, 1988; Perfect Scoundrels, 1990–92 (also co-created series). Comedy Actor of the Year, Pye Awards, 1984; ITV Personality of the Year, Variety Club of GB, 1984. *Recreations:* motoring, physical jerks. *Address:* c/o ICM, 76 Oxford Street, W1N 0AX. *Clubs:* Garrick, Chelsea Arts, Groucho.

BOWLEY, Martin Richard; QC 1981; a Recorder of the Crown Court, 1979–88; *b* 29 Dec. 1936; *s* of late Charles Colin Stuart Bowley and Mary Evelyn Bowley. *Educ:* Magdalen Coll. Sch., Oxford; Queen's Coll., Oxford (Styring Exhibnr, 1955; MA; BCL 1961). National Service, 1955–57: commnd Pilot Officer as a Fighter Controller; served 2nd Tactical Air Force, 1956–57. Called to the Bar, Inner Temple, 1962, Bencher, 1994; Midland and Oxford Circuit; Member: Senate and Bar Council, 1985–86; Gen. Council of Bar, 1987–88, 1989–94 (Treas., 1992–94); Chm., Bar Cttee, 1987. Member: Lord Chancellor's Standing Commn on Efficiency, 1986–87; Marre Cttee on Future of Legal Profession, 1987–88. Pres., Bar Lesbian and Gay Gp, 1994–. Chm., Questors Theatre, 1972–84 and 1988–93 (Sec., 1963–72); Mem. Standing Cttee, Little Theatre Guild of GB, 1974–84 (Vice-Chm., 1979–81, Chm., 1981–84). *Recreations:* playing at theatre, watching cricket, island hopping, supporting Stonewall. *Address:* Flat E, 23/24 Great James Street, WC1N 3ES. *T:* 0171–831 1674; 1 King's Bench Walk, Temple, EC4Y 7DB. *T:* 0171–353 8436. *Clubs:* MCC, Questors.

BOWMAN; *see* Kellett-Bowman.

BOWMAN, Alan Keir, PhD; FBA 1994; Official Student of Christ Church, and Lecturer in Ancient History, University of Oxford, since 1977; *b* Manchester, 23 May 1944; *s* of late Cyril Bowman and of Freda (*née* Bowman); *m* 1966, Jacqueline Frayman; one *s* one *d. Educ:* Manchester Grammar Sch.; Queen's Coll., Oxford (MA); Univ. of Toronto (MA, PhD 1969). Canada Council Postdoctoral Fellow, 1969–70; Asst Prof. of Classics, Rutgers Univ., 1970–72; Lectr in Ancient Hist., Manchester Univ., 1972–77; Sen. Censor, Christ Church, Oxford, 1988–90. Vis. Mem., Inst. for Advanced Study, Princeton, 1976, 1981; British Acad. Res. Reader, 1991–93. Chm., Roman Res. Trust, 1990–. *Publications:* The Town Councils of Roman Egypt, 1971; Egypt after the Pharaohs, 1986, 2nd edn 1990; (jtly) The Vindolanda Writing-Tablets, 1994; Life and Letters on the Roman Frontier: Vindolanda and its people, 1994; (jtly) Literacy and Power in the Ancient World, 1994; contrib. learned jls. *Recreations:* photography, music, cricket, tennis, walking. *Address:* Christ Church, Oxford OX1 1DP. *T:* Oxford (01865) 276202. *Club:* Emeriti (Oxford).

BOWMAN, Claire Margaret; *see* Makin, C. M.

BOWMAN, (Edwin) Geoffrey, CB 1991; Parliamentary Counsel, since 1984; *b* Blackpool, Lancs, 27 Jan. 1946; *er s* of John Edwin Bowman and Lillian Joan Bowman (*née* Nield); *m* 1969, Carol Margaret, *er d* of late Alexander Ogilvie and of Ethel Ogilvie; two *s* one *d. Educ:* Roundhay Sch., Leeds; Trinity Coll., Cambridge (Senior Scholar; BA 1st cl., LLB 1st cl., MA, LLM). Called to Bar, Lincoln's Inn (Cassel Scholar), 1968; in practice, Chancery Bar, 1969–71; joined Parliamentary Counsel Office, 1971 (with Law Commission, 1977–79); Dep. Parly Counsel, 1981–84. *Publication:* The Elements of Conveyancing (with E. L. G. Tyler), 1972. *Recreations:* music (bassoon), English medieval history. *Address:* Parliamentary Counsel Office, 36 Whitehall, SW1A 2AY. *T:* 0171–210 6629. *Club:* Les Amis du Basson Français (Paris).

BOWMAN, Eric Joseph; consultant, since 1986; *b* 1 June 1929; *s* of late Joseph John Bowman and Lilley Bowman; *m* 1951, Esther Kay; one *d. Educ:* Stationers' Company's School; College of Estate Management. FRICS. Private practice, 1945–51; Royal Engineers, 1951–53; private practice, 1953–54; Min. of Works, 1954–63; Min. of Housing and Local Govt, 1963–73; Directorate of Diplomatic and Post Office Services, MPBW, later DoE, 1973–80; Directorate of Quantity Surveying Services, DoE, 1980–83; Dir of Building and Quantity Surveying Services, PSA, DoE, 1983–86. *Recreations:* fly fishing, walking, swimming, gardening, reading. *Address:* Mearsons Farm, Hubbersty Head, Crosthwaite, near Kendal, Cumbria LA8 8JB. *T:* Crosthwaite (015395) 68400.

BOWMAN, Geoffrey; *see* Bowman, E. G.

BOWMAN, James Thomas; counter-tenor; Teacher of Voice, Guildhall School of Music, since 1983; *b* Oxford, 6 Nov. 1941; *s* of Benjamin and Cecilia Bowman. *Educ:* Ely Cathedral Choir Sch.; King's Sch., Ely; New Coll., Oxford. MA (History) 1967; DipEd 1964. Schoolmaster, 1965–67. Many concert performances with Early Music Consort, 1967–76; operatic performances with: English Opera Gp, 1967; Sadler's Wells Opera, 1970–; Glyndebourne Festival Opera, 1970–; Royal Opera, Covent Gdn, 1972; Sydney Opera, Australia, 1978; Opéra Comique, Paris, 1979; Le Châtelet, Paris, 1982; Geneva, 1983; Scottish Opera, 1985; La Scala, Milan, 1988, 1991; La Fenice, Venice, 1991; Paris Opera, 1991; Badisches Staatsteater, Karlsruhe, 1984; in USA at Santa Fe and Wolf Trap Festivals, Dallas and San Francisco Operas; at Aix-en-Provence Fest., 1979; operatic roles include: Oberon, in A Midsummer Night's Dream; Endymion, in La Calisto; the Priest, in Taverner; Polinesso, in Ariodante; Apollo, in Death in Venice; Astron, in Ice Break; Ruggiero in Alcina; title rôles: Gulio Cesare; Tamerlano; Xerxes; Scipione; Giustino; Orlando; Ottone. Has made recordings of oratorio and Medieval and Renaissance vocal music. Lay Vicar, Westminster Abbey, 1969. *Recreations:* ecclesiastical architecture; collecting records. *Address:* 4 Brownlow Road, Redhill RH1 6AW.

BOWMAN, Sir Jeffery (Haverstock), Kt 1991; FCA; Chairman: Mid Essex Hospital Services NHS Trust, since 1993; Masthead Insurance Underwriting PLC, since 1993; *b* 3 April 1935; *s* of Alfred Haverstock Bowman and Doris Gertrude Bowman; *m* 1963, Susan Claudia Bostock; one *s* two *d. Educ:* Winchester Coll. (schol.); Trinity Hall, Cambridge (major schol.; BA Hons 1st cl. in Law). Served RHG, 1953–55 (commnd, 1954). Price Waterhouse: articled in London, 1958; NY, 1963–64; admitted to partnership, 1966; Mem., Policy Cttee, 1972–91; Dir of Tech. Services, 1973–76; Dir, London Office, 1979–81; Sen. Partner, 1982–91; Chm., Price Waterhouse Europe, 1988–93; Jt Chm., Price Waterhouse World Firm, 1992–93. Auditor, Duchy of Cornwall, 1971–93. Vice-Pres., Union of Indep. Cos, 1983–93; Member: Council, ICAEW, 1986–90 (Mem., Accounting Standards Cttee, 1982–87); Council, Industrial Soc., 1985–93; Economic and Financial Policy Cttee, CBI, 1987–93; City Capital Markets Cttee, 1989–93; Council, Business in the Community, 1985–91. Gov., Brentwood Sch., 1985–. FRSA 1989. *Recreations:* golf, opera, gardening, sailing. *Address:* The Old Rectory, Boreham, Chelmsford, Essex CM3 3EP. *T:* Chelmsford (01245) 467233. *Club:* Garrick.

BOWMAN, Dr John Christopher, CBE 1986; PhD; FIBiol; independent environmental consultant, since 1993; Managing Director (Europe and Africa), Brown & Root Environmental, 1991–93; *b* 13 Aug. 1933; *s* of M. C. Bowman and C. V. Simister; *m* 1961, S. J. Lorimer; three *d. Educ:* Manchester Grammar Sch.; Univ. of Reading (BSc); Univ. of Edinburgh (PhD). Geneticist, later Chief Geneticist, Thornbers, Mytholmroyd, Yorks, 1958–66. Post-doctoral Fellow, North Carolina State Univ., Raleigh, NC, USA, 1964–65; University of Reading: Prof. of Animal Production, 1966–81; Head of Dept of Agric., 1967–71; Dir, Univ. Farms, 1967–78; Dir, Centre for Agricl Strategy, 1975–81; Sec., NERC, 1981–89; Chief Exec., NRA, 1989–91. Chm., Sonning Parish Council, 1994–. Hon. DSc Cranfield, 1990. *Publications:* An Introduction to Animal Breeding, 1974; Animals for Man, 1977; (with P. Susmel) The Future of Beef Production in the

European Community, 1979; (jtly) Hammond's Farm Animals, 1983. *Recreations:* golf, tennis, gardening. *Address:* Farm House, Sonning, Reading, Berks RG4 0TH.

BOWMAN, Maj-Gen. John Francis, (Jack), CB 1986; Director of Army Legal Services, 1984–86; Chairman, Principles and Law Panel, British Red Cross, 1988–94; *b* 5 Feb. 1927; *s* of Frank and Gladys Bowman; *m* 1956, Laura Moore; one *s* one *d*. *Educ:* Queen Elizabeth Grammar Sch., Penrith; Hertford Coll., Oxford (MA Hons). Called to the Bar, Gray's Inn, 1955. Served RN, 1943–48. Journalist and barrister, 1951–56; Directorate of Army Legal Services, 1956–86. Dir, Concepts Financial, 1991–. Mem. Council, BRCS, 1988–91 and 1992–94. Life Vice-Pres., Army Boxing Assoc., 1986. *Recreations:* sailing, ski-ing, mountain walking. *Address:* c/o Midland Bank, Newmarket Street, Ulverston, Cumbria LA12 7LH.

BOWMAN, Sir Paul Humphrey Armytage, 5th Bt *cr* 1884, of Holmbury St Mary, Surrey; *b* 10 Aug. 1921; *s* of Major Humphrey Ernest Bowman, CMG, CBE (*d* 1965), and Frances Guinevere Armytage (*d* 1923), and *great nephew* of Sir William Paget Bowman, 2nd Bt; *S* cousin, 1994; *m* 1st, 1943, Felicité Anne Araminta MacMichael (marr. diss. 1947); 2nd, 1947, Gabrielle May Currie (marr. diss. 1974); one *d*; 3rd, 1974, Elizabeth Deirdre Churchill. *Educ:* Eton. Dir, Hill Samuel Co. Ltd, 1962–78. *Heir: cousin* Martin Ramsay Bowman, *b* 10 Nov. 1928.

BOWMAN, Sarah Meredith; District Judge, Principal Registry (Family Division), since 1993; *b* 24 May 1949; *d* of Alexander Dennis Bowman and Jean Bowman; *m* 1984, Jake Downey; three *s*. *Educ:* Notting Hill and Ealing High Sch.; Leeds Univ. (BA); Imperial Coll. of Science and Technol., Univ. of London. Called to the Bar, Middle Temple, 1976; Barrister, 1976–93. *Recreation:* my family.

BOWMAN, Dr Sheridan Gail Esther, FSA; Keeper, Department of Scientific Research, British Museum, since 1989; *b* Westlock, Alta, Canada, 11 March 1950; *o d* of late Otto Michael Bowman and of Eva (*née* McKnight). *Educ:* Whitehaven County Grammar Sch., Cumbria; St Anne's Coll., Oxford (Open Scholar; MA; DPhil Physics, 1976); Chelsea Coll., London (MSc Maths, 1981); (extramural) London Univ. (Dip. in Archaeol., 1985). FSA 1987 (a Vice Pres., 1993). Scientific Officer, BM, 1976. *Publications:* Radiocarbon Dating, 1990; (ed) Science and the Past, 1991; papers on scientific techniques, particularly dating, applied to archaeology. *Recreations:* heath and fell walking, gardening. *Address:* Department of Scientific Research, British Museum, WC1B 3DG. *T:* 0171–323 8669.

BOWMAN, William Powell, CBE 1995 (OBE 1972); Chairman, Covent Garden Market Authority, since 1988; *b* 22 Oct. 1932; *s* of George Edward and Isabel Conyers Bowman; *m* 1956, Patricia Elizabeth McCoskrie; two *s*. *Educ:* Uppingham School. MInstM 1964. Nat. Service, RAF, 1951–53; RAuxAF, 1953–57. Sales Manager: Goodall Backhouse & Co. Ltd, 1953–59; Cheeseboro Ponds Ltd, 1959–61; Marketing Manager, Dorland Advertising Ltd, 1961–63; United Biscuits UK Ltd: Marketing Manager, 1963–66; Man. Dir, Internat. Div., 1966–77; Gp Personnel Dir, 1977–84; Dir, The Extel Group PLC and Chm., Royds Advertising Gp, 1984–86; Chm., Royds McCann Ltd, 1986–87. Chairman: Trident Trust, 1985–94 (Hon. Life Vice Pres., 1994); Forum for Occupational Counselling and Unemployment Services Ltd, 1986–89; Van der Hass BV, 1987–89; Gibbson Blackthorn, 1989; Director: Harvey Bergenroth & Partners Ltd, 1987–89; Right Associates, 1989. Chairman: British Food Export Council, 1971–73; Cake and Biscuit Alliance, 1975–77; London Enterprise Agency, 1983–84; Industry and Parliament Trust, 1983–84; Flowers and Plants Assoc., 1989–; St Peter's Res. Trust, 1990–92; Dir, Nat. Assoc. of Fresh Produce, 1989–93; Mem., Develt Trust, Zool Soc. of London, 1987–91. UK Pres., European Catering Assoc., 1995. Freeman: City of London, 1989; Fruiterers' Co., 1990; Mem., Guild of Freemen, 1989–. FIPM 1980; FIMgt (FBIM 1984); FInstD 1984; FZS 1986. *Recreations:* gardening, music. *Address:* The Coach House, Shardeloes, Old Amersham, Bucks HP7 0RL. *T:* Amersham (01494) 724187. *Clubs:* Royal Air Force, Mosimann's.

BOWMAN-SHAW, Sir (George) Neville, Kt 1984; Chairman: Boss Trucks Ltd, since 1959; Lancer Boss Group Ltd, since 1966; FOREXIA (UK) Ltd, since 1994; Boss Trucks España SA, since 1987; *b* 4 Oct. 1930; *s* of George Bowman-Shaw and Hazel Bowman-Shaw (*née* Smyth); *m* 1962, Georgina Mary Blundell; three *s* one *d*. *Educ:* Caldicott Preparatory Sch.; then private tutor. Farming Trainee, 1947; Management Trainee in Engineering Co., 1948. Commissioned in 5th Royal Inniskilling Dragoon Guards, 1950. Sales Manager: Matling Ltd, Wolverhampton, 1953; Materials Handling Equipment (GB) Ltd, London, and Matbro Ltd, London, 1955; Chairman: Lancer Boss Ireland Ltd, 1966–94; Lancer Boss Fördergeräte Vertriebsges. (Austria), 1966–94; Boss France SA, 1967–94; Steinbock GmbH, 1983–94; Boss Trucks España SA, 1987–94. Member: Development Commn, 1970–77; Design Council, 1979–84; BOTB, 1982–85. Chm. of Governors, Hawtreys School. High Sheriff, Bedfordshire, 1987–88. *Recreations:* shooting, vintage tractors. *Address:* Toddington Manor, Toddington, Bedfordshire LU5 6HJ. *T:* Toddington (01525) 872576. *Clubs:* Carlton, Cavalry and Guards.

BOWMAR, Sir (Charles) Erskine, Kt 1984; QSO 1977; JP; *b* 6 May 1913; *s* of Erskine Bowmar and Agnes Julia (*née* Fletcher); *m* 1938, Kathleen Muriel Isobel McLeod (*d* 1993); one *s* four *d* (and one *s* decd). *Educ:* Gore Public Sch.; Gore High Sch.; Southland Tech Coll. Member: West Gore Sch. Cttee, 1952; Bd of Governors, Gore High Sch., 1961; Exec., NZ Counties Assoc. (former Vice-Pres.; PP, Otago and Southland Counties Assoc.); Nat. Roads Board; sometime Chairman: Southland County Council (Mem., 1953–86); Southland United Council; Mem., Gore Agricl and Pastoral Assoc., 1940, Life Mem., 1964. Mem., Southland Harbour, 1957–65; Vice-Pres., Southland Progress League; former Mem., NZ Territorial Local Govt Council. JP 1964. *Recreations:* mountaineering (Mem., NZ Alpine Club, 1933–), trout fishing, golf, gardening. *Address:* Waikaia Plains Station, RD6, Gore, Southland, New Zealand. *T:* (3) 2016201.

BOWMONT AND CESSFORD, Marquis of; Charles Robert George Innes-Ker; *b* 18 Feb. 1981; *s* and *heir* of Duke of Roxburghe, *qv*.

BOWN, Jane Hope, (Mrs M. G. Moss), CBE 1995 (MBE 1985); Photographer for The Observer, since 1950; *b* 13 March 1925; *d* of Charles Wentworth Bell and Daisy Bown; *m* 1954, Martin Grenville Moss, *qv*; two *s* one *d*. *Educ:* William Gibbs Sch., Faversham. Chart corrector, WRNS, 1944–46; student photographer, Guildford School of Art, 1946–50. Hon. DLitt Bradford, 1986. *Publications:* The Gentle Eye: a book of photographs, 1980; Women of Consequence, 1986; Men of Consequence, 1987; The Singular Cat, 1988; Pillars of the Church, 1991. *Recreations:* restoring old houses; chickens. *Address:* Parsonage Farm, Bentworth, near Alton, Hants GU34 5RB. *T:* Alton (01420) 562175.

BOWN, Prof. Lalage Jean, OBE 1977; FRSE; FEIS; FIPD; Hon. Professor, International Centre for Education in Development, University of Warwick, since 1992; Director, Department of Adult and Continuing Education, University of Glasgow, 1981–92, now Professor Emeritus; *b* 1 April 1927; *d* of Arthur Mervyn Bown, MC and Dorothy Ethel (*née* Watson); two foster *d*. *Educ:* Wycombe Abbey Sch.; Cheltenham Ladies' Coll.; Somerville Coll., Oxford (MA); Oxford Post-grad. Internship in Adult Education. FEIS 1990; FRSE 1991; FIPD 1993. Resident Tutor: University Coll. of Gold Coast, 1949–55; Makerere University Coll., Uganda, 1955–59; Asst Dir, then Dep. Dir, Extramural Studies, Univ. of Ibadan, Nigeria, 1960–66; Dir, Extramural Studies and Prof. (*ad personam*), Univ., of Zambia, 1966–70; Prof. of Adult Educn, Ahmadu Bello Univ., Nigeria, 1971–76, Univ. of Lagos, Nigeria, 1977–79; Dean of Educn, Univ. of Lagos, 1979–80; Vis. Fellow, Inst. of Development Studies, 1980–81. Member: Bd, British Council, 1981–89; Scottish Community Educn Council, 1982–88; Exec. Cttee, Scottish Inst. of Adult and Continuing Educn, 1982–88; Bd, Network Scotland, 1983–88; Bd of Trustees, Nat. Museums of Scotland, 1987–; Council, Insite Trust, 1987–; Bd of Trustees, Womankind, 1988–; Interim Trustee, Books for Develt, 1987–90; British Mem., Commonwealth Standing Cttee on Student Mobility and Higher Educn Co-operation, 1989–. Governor, Inst. of Develt Studies, 1982–91; President: Develt Studies Assoc., 1984–86; British Comparative and Internat. Educn Soc., 1985–86; Vice-President: WEA, 1989–95 (Hon. Vice-Pres., 1984–88); Commonwealth Assoc. for Educn and Trng of Adults, 1990–93; Hon. Pres., British Assoc. for Literacy in Develt, 1993–. Hon. Vice-Pres., Townswomen's Guilds, 1984–. Hon. Life Member: People's Educnl Assoc., Ghana, 1973; African Adult Educn Assoc., 1976. Hon. FITD 1993. DUniv: Open, 1975; Paisley, 1993; Stirling, 1994; Dr (*hc*) Edinburgh, 1993. William Pearson Tolley Medal, Syracuse Univ., USA, 1975; Meritorious Service Award, Nigerian Nat. Council for Adult Educn, 1979. *Publications:* (ed with Michael Crowder) Proceedings of First International Congress of Africanists, 1964; Two Centuries of African English, 1973; (ed) Adult Education in Nigeria: the next 10 years, 1975; A Rusty Person is Worse than Rusty Iron, 1976; Lifelong Learning: prescription for progress, 1979; (ed with S. H. O. Tomori) A Handbook of Adult Education for West Africa, 1980; (ed with J. T. Okedara) An Introduction to Adult Education: a multi-disciplinary and cross-cultural approach for developing countries, 1980; (ed) Towards a Commonwealth of Scholars: a new vision for the Nineties, 1994; numerous articles in learned jls. *Recreations:* travel, reading, entertaining friends. *Address:* 37 Partickhill Road, Glasgow G11 5BP. *T:* 0141–339 1714. *Club:* Royal Over-Seas League.

BOWNESS, Sir Alan, Kt 1988; CBE 1976; Director of the Tate Gallery, 1980–88; Director, Henry Moore Foundation, 1988–94 (Member, Committee of Management, 1984–88 and since 1994); *b* 11 Jan. 1928; *er s* of George Bowness and Kathleen (*née* Benton); *m* 1957, Sarah Hepworth-Nicholson, *d* of Ben Nicholson, OM, and Dame Barbara Hepworth, DBE; one *s* one *d*. *Educ:* University Coll. Sch.; Downing Coll., Cambridge (Hon. Fellow 1980); Courtauld Inst. of Art, Univ. of London (Hon. Fellow 1986). Worked with Friends' Ambulance Unit and Friends' Service Council, 1946–50; Reg. Art Officer, Arts Council of GB, 1955–57; Courtauld Inst., 1957–79, Dep. Dir, 1978–79; Reader, 1967–78, Prof. of Hist. of Art, 1978–79, Univ. of London. Vis. Prof., Humanities Seminar, Johns Hopkins Univ., Baltimore, 1969. Mem. Internat. Juries: Premio Di Tella, Buenos Aires, 1965; São Paulo Bienal, 1967; Venice Biennale, 1986; Lehmbruck Prize, Duisburg, 1970; Rembrandt Prize, 1979–88. Arts Council: Mem., 1973–75 and 1978–80; Mem., Art Panel, 1960–80 (Vice-Chm., 1973–75, Chm., 1978–80); Mem., Arts Film Cttee, 1968–77 (Chm., 1972–75). Member: Fine Arts Cttee, Brit. Council, 1960–69 and 1970–92 (Chm., 1981–92); Exec. Cttee, Contemp. Art Soc., 1961–69 and 1970–86; Cultural Adv. Cttee, UK National Commn for UNESCO, 1973–82. Governor, Chelsea Sch. of Art, 1965–93; Hon. Sec., Assoc. of Art Historians, 1973–76; Dir, Barbara Hepworth Museum, St Ives, Cornwall, 1976–88. Mem. Council, RCA, 1978– (Hon. Fellow 1984). Hon. Fellow, Bristol Polytechnic, 1980. Hon. FRIBA 1994. Hon. DLit Liverpool, 1988. Exhibitions arranged and catalogued include: 54:64 Painting and Sculpture of a Decade (with L. Gowing), 1964; Dubuffet, 1966; Sculpture in Battersea Park, 1966; Van Gogh, 1968; Rodin, 1970; William Scott, 1972; French Symbolist Painters (with G. Lacambre), 1972; Ceri Richards, 1975; Courbet (with M. Laclotte), 1977. Chevalier, l'Ordre des Arts et des Lettres, France, 1973. *Publications:* William Scott Paintings, 1964; Impressionists and Post Impressionists, 1965; (ed) Henry Moore: complete sculpture 1955–64 (vol. 3) 1965, 1964–73 (vol. 4) 1977, 1974–80 (vol. 5) 1983, 1949–54 (vol. 2) 1987, 1980–86 (vol. 6) 1988; Modern Sculpture, 1965; Barbara Hepworth Drawings, 1966; Alan Davie, 1967; Recent British Painting, 1968; Gauguin, 1971; Barbara Hepworth: complete sculpture 1960–70, 1971; Modern European Art, 1972; Ivon Hitchens, 1973; (contrib.) Picasso 1881–1973, ed R. Penrose, 1973; (contrib.) The Genius of British Painting, ed D. Piper, 1975; The Conditions of Success, 1989; articles in Burlington Magazine, TLS, Observer, and Annual Register. *Recreations:* listening to music; reading, especially poetry and 19th century fiction. *Address:* 91 Castelnau, SW13 9EL. *T:* 0181–846 8520; 16 Piazza, St Ives, Cornwall TR26 1NQ. *T:* Penzance (01736) 795444. *Club:* Athenæum.

BOWNESS, Sir Peter (Spencer), Kt 1987; CBE 1981; DL; Partner, Weightman, Sadler (formerly Horsley, Weightman, Richardson and Sadler), Solicitors, Purley, since 1970; Leader of the Opposition, Croydon Council, since 1994; *b* 19 May 1943; *s* of Hubert Spencer Bowness and Doreen (Peggy) Bowness; *m* 1969, Marianne Hall (marr. diss.); one *d*; *m* 1984, Mrs Patricia Jane Cook; one step *s*. *Educ:* Whitgift Sch., Croydon. Admitted Solicitor, 1966. Elected (C) Croydon Council, 1968, Leader, 1976–94; Mayor of Croydon, 1979–80; Chm., London Boroughs Assoc., 1978–94; Dep. Chm., Assoc. of Metropolitan Authorities, 1978–80. Member: Audit Commn, 1983–; London Residuary Body, 1985–93; Nat. Training Task Force, 1989–92; UK Delegn, CLRAE (Council of Europe), 1990–; UK Mem., Mem. Bureau, and Mem. Transportation and Telecommunications Commn, EC Cttee of the Regions, 1994–. Gov., Whitgift Foundn, 1982–. Hon. Col, 151 (Greater London) Transport Regt RCT (V), 1988–93. DL Greater London, 1981; Freeman, City of London, 1984. *Recreations:* travel, theatre. *Address:* 1/2 The Exchange, Purley Road, Purley, Surrey CR2 2YY. *T:* 0181–660 6455.

BOWRING, Edgar Rennie Harvey, MC 1945; Chairman, C. T. Bowring & Co. Ltd, 1973–78; Director, Marsh & McLennan Cos Inc., New York, 1980–88, Advisory Director, 1988–95; *b* 5 Nov. 1915; *y s* of Arthur Bowring; *m* 1940, Margaret Grace (*née* Brook); two *s* one *d*. *Educ:* Eastbourne Coll.; Clare Coll., Cambridge (MA); Berkeley Coll., Yale, USA (Mellon Fellow). War of 1939–45: commissioned Kent Yeomanry, RA, 1939; served in Iceland, France and Germany (despatches, 1944); demobilised, 1946. Solicitor, 1949; Partner in Cripps Harries Hall & Co., 1950–55. Member of Lloyd's, 1962. Joined C. T. Bowring & Co. (Insurance) Ltd, 1956 (Dir, 1960); Dep. Chm., 1966, Chief Exec., 1970, Chm., 1973–77, C. T. Bowring (Insurance) Holdings Ltd. Chairman: English & American Insurance Co. Ltd, 1965–71; Crusader Insurance Co. Ltd, 1973–77; Bowmaker Ltd, 1973–77. Pres., Insurance Inst. of London, 1971–72 (Dep. Pres., 1970–71); Vice-Pres., Corporation of Insurance Brokers, 1970–77; Mem., Insurance Brokers Registration Council, 1979–81. Chm., City Cttee for Electoral Reform, 1978–82. Comdt, West Kent Special Constab., 1965–71. Trustee, Meml Univ. of Newfoundland Harlow Campus, 1979–. CIMgt. *Recreations:* gardening, golf. *Address:* Leopards Mill, Horam, East Sussex TN21 0PD. *T:* Horam Road (01435) 812687. *Clubs:* City University; Rye Golf; Piltdown Golf.

BOWRING, Maj.-Gen. John Humphrey Stephen, CB 1968; OBE 1958; MC 1941; FICE; *b* 13 Feb. 1913; *s* of late Major Francis Stephen Bowring and late Mrs Maurice Stonor; *m* 1956, Iona Margaret (*née* Murray); two *s* two *d*. *Educ:* Downside; RMA Woolwich; Trinity Coll., Cambridge. MA 1936. Commissioned, 1933; Palestine, 1936; India, 1937–40; Middle East, 1940–42; India and Burma, 1942–46; British Military Mission to Greece, 1947–50; UK, 1951–55; CRE, 17 Gurkha Div., Malaya, 1955–58;

Col GS, War Office, 1958–61; Brig., Chief Engineer, Far East, 1961–64; Brig. GS, Ministry of Defence, 1964–65; Engineer-in-Chief, 1965–68. Col, The Gurkha Engineers, 1966–71; Col Comdt, RE, 1968–73. Dir, Consolidated Gold Fields, 1969–82. High Sheriff, Wiltshire, 1984. Kt SMO Malta, 1986. *Address:* The Manor, Coln St Aldwyns, Cirencester, Glos GL7 5AG. *T:* Coln St Aldwyns (01285) 750492. *Clubs:* Army and Navy, Royal Ocean Racing.

BOWRING, Air Vice-Marshal John Ivan Roy, CB 1977; CBE 1971; CEng, FRAeS; FIMgt; management consultant, aircraft maintenance, retired; Head of Technical Training and Maintenance, British Aerospace (formerly British Aircraft Corporation), Riyadh, Saudi Arabia, 1978–88, retired; *b* 28 March 1923; *s* of Hugh Passmore Bowring and Ethel Grace Bowring; *m* 1945, Irene Mary Rance; two *d. Educ:* Great Yarmouth Grammar Sch., Norfolk; Aircraft Apprentice, RAF Halton-Cosford, 1938–40; Leicester Tech. Coll.; commissioned, RAF, 1944; NW Europe, 1944–47; RAF, Horsham St Faith's, Engrg duties, 1947–48; RAF South Cerney, Pilot trng, 1949; Engr Officer: RAF Finningly, 1950–51; RAF Kai-Tak, 1951–53; Staff Officer, AHQ Hong Kong, ADC to Governor, Hong Kong, 1953–54; Sen. Engr Officer, RAF Coltishall, 1954–56; exchange duties with US Air Force, Research and Develt, Wright Patterson Air Force Base, Ohio, 1956–60; RAF Staff Coll., Bracknell, 1960; Air Min. Opl Requirements, 1961–64; OC Engrg Wing, RAF St Mawgan, 1964–67; Head of F111 Procurement Team, USA, 1967–68; OC RAF Aldergrove, NI, 1968–70; RCDS, 1971; Dir of Engrg Policy, MoD, 1972–73; AO Engrg, RAF Germany, 1973–74; SASO, RAF Support Comd, 1974–77; AO Maintenance, 1977. *Recreations:* sailing, golf. *Clubs:* Royal Air Force; Royal Air Force Yacht.

BOWRING, Peter, CBE 1993; Chairman, C. T. Bowring & Co. Ltd, 1978–82; Director, Marsh & McLennan Cos Inc., New York, 1980–85 (Vice-Chairman, 1982–84); *b* 22 April 1923; *e s* of Frederick Clive Bowring and Agnes Walker (*née* Cairns); *m* 1946, Barbara Ekaterina Brewis (marr. diss.); one *s* one *d*; *m* 1986, Mrs Carole Dear. *Educ:* Shrewsbury Sch. Served War, 1939–45: commnd Rifle Bde, 1942; served in Egypt, N Africa, Italy, Austria (mentioned in despatches, 1945); demobilised 1946. Joined Bowring Group of Cos, 1947: Dir, C. T. Bowring & Co. Ltd, 1956–84, Dep. Chm. 1973–78; Chairman: C. T. Bowring Trading (Holdings) Ltd, 1967–84; Bowmaker (Plant) Ltd, 1972–83; Bowring Steamship Co. Ltd, 1974–82; Bowmaker Ltd, 1978–82; C. T. Bowring (UK) Ltd, 1980–84. Director: City Arts Trust Ltd, 1984–94 (Chm., 1987–94); Independent Primary and Secondary Educn Trust, 1986–. Mem. of Lloyd's, 1968–. Chm., Help the Aged Ltd, 1977–87, Pres., 1988–. Dir, Centre for Policy Studies, 1983–88. Vice Pres., Aldeburgh Foundn, 1989– (Chm., 1982–89). Chairman: Inter-Action Social Enterprise Trust, 1989–91; Bd of Governors, St Dunstan's Educnl Foundn, 1977–91; Dulwich Picture Gall. Consultative Cttee, 1989–; Mem. Bd of Governors, Shrewsbury Sch., 1969–. Trustee: Ironbridge Gorge Mus. Develt Trust, 1989–93; Upper Severn Navigation Trust, 1989–; Third Age Challenge (formerly ReAction) Trust, 1991–; Wakefield (Tower Hill, Trinity Square) Trust, 1986–. Member: Guild of Freemen of City of London; Worshipful Co. of Insurers; Co. of World Traders (Master, 1989–90). FRSA; FZS; FInstD. *Recreations:* sailing, motoring, listening to music, photography, cooking, travel. *Address:* Flat 79, New Concordia Wharf, Mill Street, SE1 2BA. *T:* 0171-237 0818. *Clubs:* Royal Thames Yacht, Little Ship, Royal Green Jackets, City Livery.

BOWRING, Prof. Richard John; Professor of Modern Japanese Studies, and Fellow of Downing College, since 1985, and British Academy Reader, since 1995, University of Cambridge; *b* 6 Feb. 1947; *s* of late Richard Arthur Bowring and of Mabel Bowring (*née* Eddy); *m* 1970, Susan (*née* Povey); one *d. Educ:* Blundell's Sch.; Downing Coll., Cambridge (PhD 1973). Lectr in Japanese, Monash Univ., 1973–75; Asst Prof. of Japanese, Columbia Univ., NY, 1978–79; Associate Prof. of Japanese, Princeton Univ., NJ, 1979–84; Cambridge University: Lectr in Japanese, 1984; Chm, Faculty Bd of Oriental Studies, 1987–89. Trustee, Cambridge Foundn, 1989–. Advr, UFC, subseq. HEFCE, 1992–. Gov., SOAS, 1994–. *Publications:* Mori Ogai and the Modernization of Japanese Culture, 1979; trans., Murasaki Shikibu: her diary and poetic memoirs, 1982; Murasaki Shikibu: The Tale of Genji, 1988; An Introduction to Modern Japanese, 1992; (ed) Cambridge Encyclopedia of Japan, 1993. *Address:* Downing College, Cambridge CB2 1DQ.

BOWRON, John Lewis, CBE 1986; solicitor; Secretary-General, The Law Society, 1974–87; *b* 1 Feb. 1924; *e s* of John Henry and Lavinia Bowron; *m* 1950, Patricia, *d* of Arthur Cobby; two *d. Educ:* Grangefield Grammar Sch., Stockton-on-Tees; King's Coll., London (LLB, FKC 1976). Principal in Malcolm Wilson & Cobby, Solicitors, Worthing, 1952–74. Member of the Council of the Law Society, 1969–74. Chm. (part-time), Social Security Appeal Tribunals, 1988–; Agent (part-time) Crown Prosecution Service, 1988–93. *Recreations:* golf, music. *Address:* Hurworth, Sanctuary Lane, Storrington, Pulborough, West Sussex RH20 3JD. *T:* Storrington (01903) 746949.

BOWSER of Argaty and the King's Lundies, David Stewart, JP; a Forestry Commissioner, 1974–82; *b* 11 March 1926; *s* of late David Charles Bowser, CBE and Maysie Murray Bowser (*née* Henderson); *m* 1951, Judith Crabbe; one *s* four *d. Educ:* Harrow; Trinity Coll., Cambridge (BA Agric). Captain, Scots Guards, 1944–47. Member: Nat. Bd of Timber Growers Scotland Ltd (formerly Scottish Woodland Owners' Assoc.), 1960–82 (Chm. 1972–74); Regional Adv. Cttee, West Scotland Conservancy, Forestry Commn, 1964–74 (Chm. 1970–74). Chm., Scottish Council, British Deer Soc., 1989–94; Mem., Blackface Sheep Breeders' Assoc. (Vice-Pres., 1981–83; Pres., 1983–84); Pres., Highland Cattle Soc., 1970–72. Trustee, Scottish Forestry Trust, 1983–89. Mem. Perth CC, 1954–61; JP Co. Perth, 1956. *Recreations:* shooting, fishing, stalking. *Address:* Auchlyne, Killin, Perthshire FK21 8RG.

BOWSHER, Peter Charles, QC 1978; FCIArb; **His Honour Judge Bowsher;** an Official Referee and Circuit Judge, since 1987; *b* 9 Feb. 1935; *s* of Charles and Ellen Bowsher; *m* 1960, Deborah, *d* of Frederick Wilkins and Isobel Wilkins (*née* Copp), Vancouver; two *s. Educ:* Ardingly; Oriel Coll., Oxford (MA). FCIArb 1990. Commnd Royal Artillery, 1954; Territorial Army XX Rifle Team, 1957. Called to the Bar, Middle Temple, 1959, Bencher, 1985. A Recorder, 1983–87. Harmsworth Scholar; Blackstone Entrance Scholar. A Legal Assessor to GMC and GDC, 1979–87. Indep. Review Body, Modified Colliery Review Procedure, 1986–87; Adjudicator, Crown Prosecution Service (Transfer of Staff) Regulations, 1985, 1986–87. Mem. Council, Soc. for Computers and Law, 1990–95. Member: IT and the Courts Cttee, 1991–; Judicial Cttee, British Acad. of Experts, 1992–. *Recreations:* photography, music. *Address:* Royal Courts of Justice, Strand, WC2A 2LL. *Clubs:* Brooks's, Royal Automobile.

BOWTELL, Ann Elizabeth, CB 1989; Permanent Secretary, Department of Social Security, since 1995; *b* 25 April 1938; *d* of John Albert and Olive Rose Kewell; *m* 1961, Michael John Bowtell; two *s* two *d. Educ:* Kendrick Girls' Sch., Reading; Girton Coll., Cambridge (BA). Asst Principal, Nat. Assistance Board, 1960; Principal: Nat. Assistance Board, 1964; Min. of Social Security, 1966; DHSS, 1968; Asst Sec., 1973, Under Sec., 1980, DHSS; Dep. Sec., DHSS, later DSS, 1986; Principal Establishment and Finance Officer, DoH (on secondment), 1990–93; First Civil Service Comr and Dep. Sec., Cabinet Office, 1993–95; Dep. Sec., DSS, 1995. *Recreations:* tropical fish, music, walking. *Address:* Department of Social Security, Richmond House, 79 Whitehall, SW1A 2NS.

BOWYER, family name of **Baron Denham.**

BOWYER, Gordon Arthur, OBE 1970; RIBA; FCSD; Consultant, Bowyer Langlands Batchelor (formerly Gordon Bowyer & Partners), Chartered Architects (Partner, 1948–92); *b* 21 March 1923; *s* of Arthur Bowyer and Kathleen Mary Bowyer; *m* 1950, Ursula Meyer; one *s* one *d. Educ:* Dauntsey's Sch.; Polytechnic of Central London. Architect and designer in private practice, in partnership with Ursula Bowyer, Iain Langlands and Stephen Batchelor, 1948–92. Practice started with design of Sports Section, South Bank Exhibn, Fest. of Britain, 1951; schs and hostel for handicapped children in Peckham, Bermondsey and Dulwich, 1966–75; housing for Southwark, GLC, Family Housing Assoc., London & Quadrant Housing Assoc. and Greenwich Housing Soc., 1969–83; numerous office conversions for IBM (UK), 1969–89; Peckham Methodist Church, 1975; new offices and shops for Rank City Wall at Brighton, 1975 and Folkestone, 1976; Treasury at Gloucester Cathedral, 1976; conservation at Vanbrugh Castle, Greenwich, 1973, Charlton Assembly Rooms, 1980, Hill Hall, Essex, 1982; lecture theatre, library and accommodation, Jt Services Defence Coll., RNC, Greenwich, 1983; Cabinet War Rooms Museum, Whitehall (with Alan Irvine), 1984; refurbishment of Barry Rooms at Nat. Gall., Stuart & Georgian Galls at Nat. Portrait Gall. and East Hall of Science Museum; new Prints & Drawings and Japanese Gall. at BM; gall. for Japanese prints, Fitzwilliam Mus. Advisory architect: Science Mus., 1992–; Trustees' Buildings Cttee, Nat. Maritime Mus., 1993–. Hon. Sec., SIAD, 1957–58. Mem. Council, Friends of the Nat. Maritime Mus., 1985–; Trustee, Nat. Maritime Museum, 1977–93. *Address:* 111 Maze Hill, SE10 8XQ. *Club:* Arts.

BOWYER, William, RA 1981 (ARA 1974); RP, RBA, RWS; Head of Fine Art, Maidstone College of Art, 1971–82; *b* 25 May 1926; *m* 1951, Vera Mary Small; two *s* one *d. Educ:* Burslem School of Art; Royal College of Art (ARCA). Hon. Sec., New English Art Club. *Recreations:* cricket (Chiswick and Old Meadonians Cricket Clubs), snooker. *Address:* 12 Cleveland Avenue, Chiswick, W4 1SN. *T:* 0181-994 0346. *Club:* Dover Street Arts.

BOWYER-SMYTH, Sir T. W.; *see* Smyth.

BOX, Betty Evelyn, (Mrs P. E. Rogers), OBE 1958; Film Producer; *b* 25 Sept.; *m* 1949, Peter Edward Rogers; no *c. Educ:* home. Director: Welbeck Film Distributors Ltd, 1958–; Ulster Television, 1955–85. *Films include:* Dear Murderer; When the Bough Breaks; Miranda; Blind Goddess; Huggett Family series; It's Not Cricket; Marry Me; Don't Ever Leave Me; So Long at the Fair; Appointment with Venus; Venetian Bird; A Day to Remember; The Clouded Yellow; Doctor in the House; Mad About Men; Doctor at Sea; The Iron Petticoat; Checkpoint; Doctor at Large; Campbell's Kingdom; A Tale of Two Cities; The Wind Cannot Read; The 39 Steps; Upstairs and Downstairs; Conspiracy of Hearts; Doctor in Love; No Love for Johnnie; No, My Darling Daughter; A Pair of Briefs; The Wild and the Willing; Doctor in Distress; Hot Enough for June; The High Bright Sun; Doctor in Clover; Deadlier than the Male; Nobody Runs Forever; Some Girls Do; Doctor in Trouble; Percy; The Love Ban; Percy's Progress. *Address:* Pinewood Studios, Iver, Bucks.

BOX, Prof. George Edward Pelham, BEM 1946; FRS 1985; Emeritus Professor of Statistics and Engineering, since 1992, and Director of Research, Center for Quality and Productivity, since 1990, University of Wisconsin-Madison; *b* 18 Oct. 1919; *s* of Harry and Helen (Martin) Box; *m* 1st, 1945, Jessie Ward; 2nd, 1959, Joan G. Fisher; one *s* one *d*; 3rd, 1985, Claire Louise Quist. *Educ:* London University (BSc Maths and Statistics 1947, PhD 1952, DSc 1961). Served War of 1939–45 in Army; res. at Chemical Defence Exptl Station, Porton. Statistician and Head Statn, Statistical Res. Section, ICI, Blackley, 1948–56; Dir, Stats Tech. Res. Group, Princeton Univ., 1956–60; Prof. of Stats, 1960–92, and Vilas Res. Prof., Dept of Stats, 1980–92, Univ. of Wisconsin-Madison. Res. Prof., Univ. of N Carolina, 1952–53; Ford Foundn Vis. Prof., Harvard Business Sch., 1965–66; Vis. Prof., Univ. of Essex, 1970–71. President: Amer. Statistical Assoc., 1978; Inst. of Mathematical Statistics, 1979. Trustee, Biometrika Trust, 1985–. Fellow, Amer. Acad. of Arts and Scis, 1974; FAAAS, 1974. Hon. DSc: Univ. of Rochester, NY, 1975; Carnegie Mellon Univ., 1989; Don Carlos III Univ., Madrid, 1995. Numerous medals and awards. *Publications:* Statistical Methods in Research and Production, 1957; Design and Analysis of Industrial Experiments, 1959; Evolutionary Operation: a statistical method for process improvement, 1969; Time Series Analysis Forecasting and Control, 1970; Bayesian Inference in Statistical Analysis, 1973; Statistics for Experimenters, 1977; Empirical Model Building and Response Surfaces, 1986. *Address:* Center for Quality and Productivity Improvement, University of Wisconsin-Madison, 610 Walnut Street, Madison, WI 53705, USA. *T:* (608) 2632520.

BOX, John Allan Hyatt, RDI 1992; free-lance production designer of films; *b* 27 Jan. 1920; *s* of late Allan Cyril Box and of Bertha (*née* Storey); *m* 1st, 1944, Barbara Courtenay Linton; 2nd, 1953, Doris Lee; two *d. Educ:* Ceylon; Highgate Sch.; Sch. of Architecture, London Poly. ARIBA 1948. Served RAMC, 1940–46 (mentioned in despatches, Normandy, 1944). Entered film industry, 1948: films designed include: The Million Pound Note, 1954; The Inn of the Sixth Happiness, 1958; Our Man in Havana, 1959; The World of Suzie Wong, 1960; Lawrence of Arabia, 1962 (Academy Award); Doctor Zhivago, 1965 (Academy Award); A Man for All Seasons, 1967 (BAFTA Award); Oliver!, 1968 (Academy Award); Nicholas and Alexandra, 1971 (Academy Award); Travels with My Aunt, 1972; The Great Gatsby, 1974 (BAFTA Award); Rollerball, 1975 (BAFTA Award); A Passage to India, 1984; Black Beauty, 1994; First Knight, 1995; produced: The Looking Glass War, 1969. FRSA 1993. Award for special contribution to films, BAFTA, 1991. *Recreations:* painting, visiting art galleries and exhibitions, interest in cricket and Rugby. *Address:* 5 Elm Bank Mansions, The Terrace, Barnes, SW13 0NS. *T:* 0181-876 9125.

BOXALL, Barbara Ann, (Mrs Lewis Boxall); *see* Buss, Barbara Ann.

BOXER, Air Vice-Marshal Sir Alan (Hunter Cachemaille), KCVO 1970; CB 1968; DSO 1944; DFC 1943; *b* 1 Dec. 1916; *s* of late Dr E. A. Boxer, CMG, Hastings, Hawkes Bay, NZ; *m* 1941, Pamela Sword; two *s* one *d. Educ:* Nelson Coll., New Zealand. Commissioned in RAF, 1939; Trng Comd until 1942; flying and staff appts, Bomber Comd, 1942–45. RAF Staff Coll., 1945; Jt Staff, Cabinet Offices, 1946–47; Staff Coll., Camberley, 1948; Strategic Air Comd, USAF and Korea, 1949–51; Central Fighter Estabt, 1952–53; Mem. Directing Staff, RAF Staff Coll., 1954–56; OC No 7 Sqdn, RAF, 1957; Group Capt. and CO, RAF Wittering, 1958–59; Plans, HQ Bomber Comd, 1960–61; Air Cdre, idc, 1962; SASO: HQ No 1 Gp, RAF, 1963–65; HQ Bomber Comd, 1965–67; Defence Services Sec., MoD, 1967–70. Virtuti Militari (Polish), Bronze Star (US), Air Medal (US).

BOXER, Charles Ian; writer; *b* 11 Feb. 1926; *s* of Rev. William Neville Gordon Boxer and Margaret Boxer; *m* 1968, Hilary Fabienne Boxer. *Educ:* Glasgow High Sch.; Edinburgh Univ. (BL). Church of England ministry, 1950–54; apprentice to solicitors, 1954–58;

Mem., Dominican Order (RC), 1958–67; Sen. Community Relations Officer for Wandsworth, 1967–77; Dir, Community Affairs and Liaison Div., Commn for Racial Equality, 1977–81. Communicator of the Year, BAIE Awards, 1976. *Recreation:* music. *Address:* Parish Farmhouse, Hassell Street, Hastingleigh, near Ashford, Kent TN25 5JE. *T:* Elmsted (01233) 750219.

BOXER, Prof. Charles Ralph, FBA 1957; Emeritus Professor of Portuguese, University of London, since 1968; Fellow, King's Coll., 1967; *b* 8 March 1904; *s* of Col Hugh Boxer and Jane Boxer (*née* Patterson); *m* 1945, Emily Hahn; two *d*. *Educ:* Wellington Coll.; Royal Military Coll., Sandhurst. Commissioned Lincs Regt, 1923. Served War of 1939–45 (wounded, POW in Japanese hands, 1941–45). Retired with rank of Major, 1947. Camoens Prof. of Portuguese, London Univ., 1947–51; Prof. of the History of the Far East, London Univ., 1951–53; resigned latter post and re-apptd Camoens Prof., 1953–67; Prof. of History of Expansion of Europe Overseas, Yale, 1969–72. Visiting Research Prof., Indiana Univ., 1967–79; Emeritus Prof. of History, Yale, 1972–. Hon. Fellow, SOAS, 1974. A Trustee of National Maritime Museum, 1961–68. For. Mem., Royal Netherlands Acad. of Scis, 1976. Dr *hc* Universities of Utrecht (1950), Lisbon (1952), Bahia (1959), Liverpool (1966), Hong Kong (1971), Peradeniya (1980). Gold Medal, Institute Historico e Geografico Brasileiro, 1986. Order of Santiago da Espada (Portugal); Grand Cross of the Order of the Infante Dom Henrique (Portugal); Kt Order of St Gregory the Great, 1969. *Publications:* The Commentaries of Ruy Freyre de Andrade, 1929; The Journal of M. H. Tromp, *Anno* 1639, 1930; Jan Compagnie in Japan, 1600–1817, 1936 (2nd edn 1950); Fidalgos in the Far East, 1550–1770, 1948; The Christian Century in Japan, 1549–1640, 1951, 2nd edn 1967; Salvador de Sá and the Struggle for Brazil and Angola, 1952; South China in the 16th Century, 1953; The Dutch in Brazil, 1624–1654, 1957; The Tragic History of the Sea, 1589–1622, 1959; The Great Ship from Amacon, 1959; Fort Jesus and the Portuguese in Mombasa, 1960; The Golden Age of Brazil, 1695–1750, 1962; Race Relations in the Portuguese Colonial Empire, 1415–1825, 1963; The Dutch Seaborne Empire, 1600–1800, 1965; Portuguese Society in the Tropics, 1966; Further Selections from the Tragic History of the Sea, 1969; The Portuguese Seaborne Empire, 1415–1825, 1969; Anglo-Dutch Wars of the 17th Century, 1974; Mary and Misogyny, 1975; João de Barros: Portuguese humanist and historian of Asia, 1981; From Lisbon to Goa 1500–1750, 1984; Portuguese Conquest and Commerce in Southern Asia 1500–1750, 1985; Portuguese Merchants and Missionaries in Feudal Japan 1543–1640, 1986; Dutch Merchants and Mariners in Asia 1602–1795, 1988; numerous articles in learned periodicals. *Address:* Ringshall End, Little Gaddesden, Herts HP4 1NF.

BOXER, Air Cdre Henry Everard Crichton, CB 1965; OBE 1948; idc, ndc, psc; *b* 28 July 1914; *s* of late Rear-Adm. Henry P. Boxer; *m* 1938, Enid Anne Louise, *d* of late Dr John Moore Collyns; two *s* two *d*. *Educ:* Shrewsbury Sch.; RAF Coll., Cranwell. Commissioned RAF, 1935; No 1 Fighter Squadron, 1935–37; No 1 Flying Training Sch., 1937–39; Specialist Navigator, 1939. Served War of 1939–45, in UK, S Africa and Europe. BJSM, Washington, DC, 1945–48; directing Staff, RAF Staff Coll., 1949–50; Coastal Command, 1951–52; Nat. Defence Coll., Canada, 1952–53; Air Ministry, 1953–56; OC, RAF Thorney Island, 1956–58. ADC to the Queen, 1957–59; IDC, 1959; Sen. Air Liaison Officer and Air Adviser to British High Comr in Canada, 1960–62; AO i/c Admin, HQ Coastal Comd, 1962–65; Dir of Personnel (Air), MoD (RAF), 1965–67; retd, 1967. Counsellor (Defence Equipment), British High Commn, Ottawa, 1967–74; retd, 1975. *Address:* 42 Courtenay Place, Lymington, Hants SO41 3NQ. *T:* Lymington (01590) 672584. *Club:* Royal Air Force.

BOXSHALL, Dr Geoffrey Allan, FRS 1994; Senior Principal Scientific Officer, Natural History Museum, since 1991; *b* 13 June 1950; *s* of John Edward Boxshall and Sybil Irene Boxshall (*née* Baker); *m* 1972, Roberta Gabriel Smith; one *s* three *d*. *Educ:* Churcher's Coll., Petersfield; Leeds Univ. (BSc, PhD). British Museum (Natural History). Higher SO, 1974–76; SSO, 1976–80; PSO, 1980–91. *Publications:* (jtly) Dictionary of Ecology, Evolution and Systematics, 1982; (jtly) Cambridge Illustrated Dictionary of Natural History, 1987; (ed jtly) Biology of Copepods, 1988; (jtly) Copepod Evolution, 1991; (ed jtly) Pathogens of Wild and Farmed Fish: sea lice, 1993; numerous papers in scientific jls. *Recreations:* tennis, reading, lexicography, travel. *Address:* Department of Zoology, Natural History Museum, Cromwell Road, SW7 5BD. *T:* 0171–938 9489. *Club:* Zoological.

BOYCE, Graham Hugh, CMG 1991; HM Diplomatic Service; Counsellor, Foreign and Commonwealth Office, since 1993; *b* 6 Oct. 1945; *s* of Comdr Hugh Boyce, DSC, RN and Madeleine Boyce (*née* Manley); *m* 1970, Janet Elizabeth Spencer; one *s* three *d*. *Educ:* Hurstpierpoint Coll.; Jesus Coll., Cambridge (MA). VSO, Antigua, 1967; HM Diplomatic Service, 1968; Ottawa, 1971; MECAS, 1972–74; 1st Sec., Tripoli, Libya, 1974–77; FCO, 1977–81; Kuwait, 1981–85; Asst Hd of ME Dept, FCO, 1985–86; Counsellor and Consul-Gen., Stockholm, 1987–90; Ambassador and Consul-Gen., Doha, 1990–93. *Recreations:* tennis, golf, reading. *Address:* c/o Foreign and Commonwealth Office, King Charles Street, SW1A 2AH.

See also Vice-Adm. Sir M. C. Boyce.

BOYCE, Joseph Frederick, JP; FRICS; General Manager, Telford Development Corporation, 1980–86; *b* 10 Aug. 1926; *s* of Frederick Arthur and Rosalie Mary Boyce; *m* 1953, Nina Margaret, *o d* of A. F. Tebb, Leeds; two *s*. *Educ:* Roundhay Sch., Leeds; Leeds Coll. of Technology. Pupil and Asst Quantity Surveyor, Rex Procter & Miller, Chartered Quantity Surveyors, 1942–53; Sen. Quantity Surveyor, Bedford Corp., 1953–55; Group Quantity Surveyor, Somerset CC, 1955–60; Principal Asst Quantity Surveyor, Salop CC, 1960–64; Telford Development Corporation: Chief Quantity Surveyor, 1964–71; Technical Dir, 1971–76; Dep. Gen. Manager, 1976–80. JP Shrewsbury, 1975. *Publications:* technical articles and publications on new towns, in learned journals. *Recreations:* reading, travel, hill walking, France. *Address:* 6 College Hill, Shrewsbury, Shropshire SY1 1LZ; Provence, France.

BOYCE, Adm. Sir Michael (Cecil), KCB 1995; OBE 1982; Second Sea Lord, and Commander in Chief Naval Home Command, and Flag Aide-de-Camp to the Queen, since 1995; *b* 2 April 1943; *s* of Comdr Hugh Boyce, DSC, RN and Madeleine Boyce (*née* Manley); *m* 1971, Harriette Gail, *d* of late Surg. Capt. (D) Kenneth Fletcher, RN and Georgina Fletcher; one *s* one *d*. *Educ:* Hurstpierpoint Coll.; BRNC, Dartmouth. Joined RN, 1961; qualified Submarines, 1965 and TAS, 1970; served in HM Submarines Anchorite, Valiant, and Conqueror, 1965–72; commanded: HM Submarines: Oberon, 1973–74; Opossum, 1974–75; Superb, 1979–81; HMS Brilliant, 1983–84; Captain (SM), Submarine Sea Training, 1984–86; RCDS, 1988; Sen. Naval Officer, ME, 1989; Dir Naval Staff Duties, 1989–91; Flag Officer: Sea Training, 1991–92; Surface Flotilla, 1992–95; Comdr, Anti-Submarine Warfare Striking Force, 1992–94. *Recreations:* squash, tennis, photography, windsurfing. *Address:* c/o Naval Secretary, Victory Building, HM Naval Base, Portsmouth PO1 3LS.

See also G. H. Boyce.

BOYCE, Michael David; DL; Chief Executive, Cardiff Bay Development Corporation, since 1992; *b* 27 May 1937; *s* of Clifford and Vera Boyce; *m* 1962, Audrey May Gregory; one *s* one *d*. *Educ:* Queen Elizabeth's Sch., Crediton. DMA 1962; Dip. in French, UC Cardiff, 1984. Admitted Solicitor, 1968. Asst Solicitor, 1968–69, Sen. Asst Solicitor, and Asst Clerk of the Peace, 1969–71, Exeter CC; Dep. Town Clerk, 1971–73, Dep. Chief Exec., 1973–74, Newport, Gwent; County Solicitor, S Glam, 1974–87; Chief Exec., S Glam CC, and Clerk to Lieutenancy, 1987–92. Sec., Lord Chancellor's Adv. Cttee, 1987–92. Mem. Bd, S Glam TEC, 1987–95. Mem. Council, Univ. of Wales Coll. of Cardiff, 1987–93; Gov., Welsh Coll. of Music and Drama, 1992–. Chm., Cardiff City AFC, 1993–. DL S Glam, 1993. *Recreations:* France and French, Association Football, music, railways, travel. *Address:* 1 White Oaks Drive, Old St Mellons, Cardiff CF3 9EX. *T:* Cardiff (01222) 791927.

BOYCE, Peter John, AO 1995; PhD; Vice-Chancellor, Murdoch University, Western Australia, since 1985; *b* 20 Feb. 1935; *s* of Oswald and Marjorie Boyce; *m* 1962, Lorinne Peet; one *s* two *d*. *Educ:* Wesley Coll., Perth, WA; Univ. of Western Australia (MA); Duke Univ., USA (PhD). Res. Fellow, then Fellow, Dept of Internat. Relns, ANU, 1964–66; Nuffield Fellow, St Antony's Coll., Oxford, 1966–67; Sen. Lectr, then Reader, in Political Science, Tasmania Univ., 1967–75; Prof. of Pol. Science and Hd, Dept of Govt, Queensland Univ., 1976–79; Prof. of Politics and Hd of Dept, Univ. of W Australia, 1980–84. Vis. Fellow, Corpus Christi Coll., Cambridge, 1989. Exec. Mem., Aust.-NZ Foundn, 1979–83; Member: Aust. Human Rights Commn, 1981–86; Consultative Cttee on Relns with Japan, 1983–85; Asia Business Council of WA, 1993–. Lay Canon of St George's Cath., Perth. Editor, Australian Outlook, 1973–77. *Publications:* Malaysia and Singapore in International Diplomacy, 1968; Foreign Affairs for New States, 1977; (co-ord. ed.) Dictionary of Australian Politics, 1980; (co-ord. ed.) Politics in Queensland, 1980; (co-ord. ed.) The Torres Strait Treaty, 1981; (ed) Independence and Alliance, 1983; Diplomacy in the Market Place, 1991. *Recreations:* gardening, walking, church music. *Address:* 38 Clanmel Road, Floreat Park, WA 6014, Australia. *T:* (9) 3871992.

BOYCE, Dr Sir Robert (Leslie), 3rd Bt *cr* 1952; Senior House Officer in Ophthalmology, Manchester Royal Eye Hospital; *b* 2 May 1962; *s* of Sir Richard (Leslie) Boyce, 2nd Bt, and of Jacqueline Anne (who *m* 2nd, 1974, Christopher Boyce-Dennis), *o d* of Roland A. Hill; *S* father, 1968; *m* 1985, Fiona, second *d* of John Savage, Whitmore Park, Coventry; one *s*. *Educ:* Cheltenham Coll; Salford Univ. (BSc 1984, 1st cl. hons); Nottingham Univ. (BMedSci 1991, 1st cl. hons; BM BS 1993). Demonstrator of Anatomy, Manchester Univ. Med. Sch., 1994–95. *Heir: s* Thomas Leslie Boyce, *b* 3 Sept. 1993.

BOYCE, Walter Edwin, OBE 1970; Director of Social Services, Essex County Council, 1970–78; *b* 30 July 1918; *s* of Rev. Joseph Edwin Boyce and Alice Elizabeth Boyce; *m* 1942, Edna Lane (*née* Gargett); two *d*. *Educ:* High Sch. for Boys, Trowbridge, Wilts. Admin. Officer, Warwickshire CC, 1938–49. Served war, commnd RA; Gunnery sc, 1943; demob. rank Major, 1946. Dep. County Welfare Officer: Shropshire, 1949–52; Cheshire, 1952–57; Co. Welfare Officer, Essex, 1957–70. Adviser to Assoc. of County Councils, 1965–78; Mem., Sec. of State's Adv. Personal Social Services Council, 1973 until disbanded, 1980 (Chm., People with handicaps Gp); Mem., nat. working parties on: Health Service collaboration, 1972–74; residential accommodation for elderly and mentally handicapped, 1974–78; boarding houses, 1981. Pres., County Welfare Officers Soc., 1967–68. Governor, Queen Elizabeth's Foundn for the Disabled, 1980–. *Recreations:* sailing, golf, in sports, particularly Rugby and athletics, voluntary services, travel. *Address:* Highlanders Barn, Newmans Green, Long Melford, Suffolk CO10 0AD.

BOYCOTT, Prof. Brian Blundell, FRS 1971; Director, Medical Research Council Cell Biophysics Unit, 1980–89; Senior Research Fellow, Anatomy Department, Guy's Hospital, since 1990; Emeritus Professor of Biology, London University, 1990; *b* 10 Dec. 1924; *s* of Percy Blundell Boycott and Doris Eyton Lewis; *m* 1950, Marjorie Mabel Burchell; one *s* (and one *s* decd). *Educ:* Royal Masonic Sch. Technician, Nat. Inst. Medical Research, and undergraduate (BSc), Birkbeck Coll., London, 1942–46; University Coll., London: Asst Lectr, Zoology, 1946–47; Hon. Res. Asst, Anatomy, 1947–52; Lectr, Zoology, 1952–62; Reader in Zoology, Univ. of London, 1962, Prof. of Zoology, 1968–70, Prof. of Biology by title, 1971–89. Vis. Lectr, Harvard Univ., 1963. Dep. Chm., Neuroscis and Mental Health Bd, MRC, 1989–91. Member: Adv. Council, British Library Board, 1976–80; Council, 1975–87, Acad. Consultative Cttee, 1989–93, Open Univ.; Council, Royal Soc., 1976–78; Univ. of London Cttee on Academic Organization, 1980–82; Comr, 1851 Exhibition, 1974–84. FKC 1990. DUniv Open, 1988. Scientific medal, Zoological Soc. London, 1965. *Publications:* various articles in learned jls on structure and function of nervous systems. *Recreations:* nothing of special notability. *Address:* c/o Department of Anatomy, UMDS of Guy's and St Thomas's, Guy's Hospital, London Bridge, SE1 9RT. *T:* 0171–955 2991.

BOYCOTT, Geoffrey; cricket commentator; *b* 21 Oct. 1940; *s* of late Thomas Wilfred Boycott and Jane Boycott. *Educ:* Kinsley Modern Sch.; Hemsworth Grammar Sch. Played cricket for Yorkshire, 1962–86, received County Cap, 1963, Captain of Yorkshire, 1970–78. Played for England, 1964–74, 1977–82; scored 100th first-class hundred, England v Australia, 1977, 150th hundred, 1986; passed former world record no of runs scored in Test Matches, Delhi, Dec. 1981. Mem., General Cttee, Yorks CCC, 1984–93. Commentator: BBC TV; TWI; Channel 9; SABC. *Publications:* Geoff Boycott's Book for Young Cricketers, 1976; Put to the Test: England in Australia 1978–79, 1979; Geoff Boycott's Cricket Quiz, 1979; On Batting, 1980; Opening Up, 1980; In the Fast Lane, 1981; Master Class, 1982; Boycott, The Autobiography, 1987; Boycott on Cricket, 1990. *Recreations:* golf, tennis. *Address:* c/o Yorkshire County Cricket Club, Headingley Cricket Ground, Leeds, Yorks LS6 3BY.

BOYD, family name of **Baron Kilmarnock.**

BOYD OF MERTON, 2nd Viscount *cr* 1960, of Merton-in-Penninghame, Co. Wigtown; **Simon Donald Rupert Neville Lennox-Boyd;** Chairman, Stonham Housing, since 1992; *b* 7 Dec. 1939; *e s* of 1st Viscount Boyd of Merton, CH, PC, and of Lady Patricia Guinness, *d* of 2nd Earl of Iveagh, KG, CB, CMG, FRS; *S* father, 1983; *m* 1962, Alice Mary (JP, DL, High Sheriff of Cornwall, 1987–88), *d* of late Major M. G. D. Clive and of Lady Mary Clive; two *s* two *d*. *Educ:* Eton; Christ Church, Oxford. Dep. Chm., Arthur Guinness & Sons, 1981–86. Chm., SCF, 1987–92 (Vice-Chm., 1979–82). Trustee, Guinness Trust, 1974–. *Heir: s* Hon. Benjamin Alan Lennox-Boyd [*b* 21 Oct. 1964; *m* 1993, Sheila Carroll]. *Address:* Ince Castle, Saltash, Cornwall PL12 4QZ. *T:* Saltash (01752) 842672; 9 Warwick Square, SW1V 2AA. *T:* 0171–821 1618. *Club:* Royal Yacht Squadron.

BOYD, Sir Alexander Walter, 3rd Bt, *cr* 1916; *b* 16 June 1934; *s* of late Cecil Anderson Boyd, MC, MD, and Marjorie Catharine, *e d* of late Francis Kinloch, JP, Shipka Lodge, North Berwick; *S* uncle, 1948; *m* 1958, Molly Madeline, *d* of late Ernest Arthur Rendell; two *s* three *d*. *Heir: s* Ian Walter Rendell Boyd [*b* 14 March 1964; *m* 1986, LeeAnn Dillon; three *s*]. *Address:* Box 261, Whistler, BC V0N 1B0, Canada.

BOYD, Arthur Merric Bloomfield, AC 1992 (AO 1979); OBE 1970; painter; *b* Melbourne, 24 July 1920; *s* of William Merric Boyd and Doris Lucy Eleanor Gough; *m* 1945, Yvonne Hartland Lennie; one *s* two *d*. *Educ:* State Sch., Murrumbeena, Vic, Australia. Was taught painting and sculpture by parents and grandfather, Arthur Merric

Boyd; served in Australian Army, 1940–43. Exhibited first in Australia, 1937; has lived and exhibited in Europe and Australia since 1959; first one-man exhibn painting, London, 1960; retrospective exhibn, Whitechapel Gall., 1962; designed for ballet at Edinburgh Festival and Sadler's Wells Theatre, 1961, and at Covent Garden Royal Opera House, 1963; tapestry 30'×60' designed for new Parliament House, Canberra, installed 1988. *Publications:* include (illus.) Mars, by Peter Porter, 1988; *relevant publications:* Arthur Boyd, by Franz Philipp, 1967; Arthur Boyd Drawings, by Christopher Tadgell, 1973; Artist and River, by Sandra McGrath, 1983; Arthur Boyd—Seven Persistent Images, by Grazia Gunn, 1985; The Art of Arthur Boyd, by Ursula Hoff, 1986.

BOYD, Atarah, (Mrs Douglas Boyd); *see* Ben-Tovim, A.

BOYD, Christopher; *see* Boyd, T. C.

BOYD, (David) John; QC 1982; Director: Public Affairs and Communications, Digital Equipment Co. Ltd, since 1993 (Director, Legal Services, 1986–93); Digital Equipment Scotland Ltd, since 1987; *b* 11 Feb. 1935; *s* of David Boyd and Ellen Jane Boyd (*née* Gruer); *m* 1960, Raija Sinikka Lindholm, Finland; one *s* one *d. Educ:* Eastbourne Coll.; St George's Sch., Newport, USA (British-Amer. schoolboy schol.); Gonville and Caius Coll., Cambridge (MA). FCIArb 1979. Various secretarial posts, ICI, 1957–62; Legal Asst, Pfizer, 1962–66; called to the Bar, Gray's Inn, 1963, Bencher 1988; Sec. and Legal Officer, Henry Wiggin & Co., 1966; Asst Sec. and Sen. Legal Officer (UK), Internat. Nickel, 1968; Dir, Impala Platinum, 1972–78; Sec. and Chief Legal Officer, 1972–86, and Dir, 1984–86, Inco Europe; practising barrister, 1986. Gen. Comr of Income Tax, 1978–83. Chm., Bar Assoc. for Commerce, Finance and Industry, 1980–81; Mem., Senate of Inns of Court and Bar, 1978–81. Sec. Gen., Assoc. des Juristes d'Entreprise Européens (European Company Lawyers Assoc.), 1983–84. Dir, Centre for European Dispute Resolution, 1991–94. Legal Advisor to Review Bd for Govt Contracts, 1984–91. Chm., CBI Competition Panel, 1988–93; Mem., Monopolies and Mergers Commn, 1991–. Mem., Exec. Cttee, Royal Acad. of Dancing, 1991–. *Recreations:* theatre-going, holidaying in France, viticulture. *Address:* Beeches, Upton Bishop, Ross-on-Wye, Herefordshire HR9 7UD. *T:* Upton Bishop (01989) 780214. *Club:* Leander.

BOYD, Dennis Galt, CBE 1988; Chief Conciliation Officer, Advisory, Conciliation and Arbitration Service, 1980–92; *b* 3 Feb. 1931; *s* of late Thomas Ayre Boyd and Minnie (*née* Galt); *m* 1953, Pamela Mary McLean; one *s* one *d. Educ:* South Shields High School for Boys. National Service, 1949–51; Executive Officer, Civil Service: Min. of Supply/Min. of Defence, 1951–66; Board of Trade, 1966–69; Personnel Officer, Forestry Commission, 1969–75; Director of Corporate Services Health and Safety Executive, Dept of Employment, 1975–79; Director of Conciliation (ACAS), 1979–80. Hon. FIPM 1985. *Recreations:* golf, compulsory gardening. *Address:* Dunelm, Silchester Road, Little London, near Basingstoke RG26 5EW. *Club:* Civil Service.

BOYD, Sir Francis; *see* Boyd, Sir J. F.

BOYD, Ian Robertson; HM Stipendiary Magistrate, West Yorkshire, 1982–89; a Recorder of the Crown Court, 1983–88; *b* 18 Oct. 1922; *s* of Arthur Robertson Boyd, Edinburgh, and Florence May Boyd (*née* Kinghorn), Leeds; *m* 1952, Joyce Mary Boyd (*née* Crabtree); one *s* one *d. Educ:* Roundhay Sch.; Leeds Univ. (LLB (Hons)). Served Army, 1942–47: Captain Green Howards; Royal Lincolnshire Regt in India, Burma, Malaya, Dutch East Indies. Leeds Univ., 1947; called to Bar, Middle Temple, 1952; practised North Eastern Circuit, 1952–72; HM Stipendiary Magistrate, sitting at Hull, 1972–82. Sometime Asst/Dep. Recorder of Doncaster, Newcastle, Hull and York. *Recreation:* gardener manqué.

BOYD, James Edward, CA; Director and Financial Adviser, Denholm group of companies, since 1968; *b* 14 Sept. 1928; *s* of Robert Edward Boyd and Elizabeth Reid Sinclair; *m* 1956, Judy Ann Christey Scott; two *s* two *d. Educ:* Kelvinside Academy; The Leys Sch., Cambridge. CA Scot. (dist.) 1951. Director: Lithgows (Hldgs), 1962–87; Ayrshire Metal Products plc, 1965–93 (Chm., 1991–93); Invergordon Distillers (Holdings) plc, 1966–88; GB Papers plc, 1977–87; Jebsens Drilling plc, 1978–85; Scottish Widows' Fund & Life Assurance Soc., 1981–93 (Dep. Chm., 1988–93); Shanks & McEwan Gp Ltd, 1983–94; Scottish Exhibn Centre Ltd, 1983–89; British Linen Bank Ltd, 1983–94 (Gov., 1986–94); Bank of Scotland, 1984–94; Yarrow PLC, 1984–86 (Chm., 1985–86); Bank of Wales, 1986–88; Save and Prosper Gp Ltd, 1987–89; James River UK Hldgs Ltd, 1987–90; Chairman: London & Gartmore Investment Trust plc, 1978–91; English & Caledonian Investment plc, 1981–91. Partner, McClelland Ker & Co. CA (subseq. McClelland Moores & Co.), 1953–61; Finance Director: Lithgows Ltd, 1962–69; Scott Lithgow Ltd, 1970–78; Chm., Fairfield Shipbuilding & Engrg Co. Ltd, 1964–65; Man. Dir, Invergordon Distillers (Holdings) Ltd, 1966–67; Director: Nairn & Williamson (Holdings) Ltd, 1968–75; Carlton Industries plc, 1978–84. Dep. Chm., BAA plc (formerly British Airports Authority), 1985–94; Member: CAA (part-time), 1984–85; Clyde Port Authority, 1974–80; Working Party on Scope and Aims of Financial Accounts (the Corporate Report), 1974–75; Exec. Cttee, Accountants Jt Disciplinary Scheme, 1979–81; Mem. Council, Inst. of Chartered Accountants of Scotland, 1977–83 (Vice-Pres., 1980–82, Pres., 1982–83). Mem. Council, Glenalmond Coll., 1983–92. *Recreations:* tennis, golf, gardening. *Address:* Dunard, Station Road, Rhu, Dunbartonshire, Scotland G84 8LW. *T:* Rhu (01436) 820441.

BOYD, James Fleming, CB 1980; Member, Civil Service Appeal Board, 1984–90; *b* 28 April 1920; *s* of late Walter and late Mary Boyd; *m* 1949, Daphne Steer, Hendon; one *s* one *d. Educ:* Whitehill Sch., Glasgow. Tax Officer, Inland Revenue, 1937; served with HM Forces, RAF, 1940–46; Inspector of Taxes, 1950; Principal Inspector, 1964; Senior Principal Inspector, 1970; Dep. Chief Inspector of Taxes, 1973; Dir of Operations, Inland Revenue, 1975–77, Dir Gen. (Management), 1978–81. Financial Advr, B. & C. E. Holiday Management Scheme, 1981–86. *Recreations:* history, gardening. *Address:* 2A The Avenue, Potters Bar, Herts EN6 1EB.

BOYD, John; *see* Boyd, D. J.

BOYD, Sir John (Dixon Iklé), KCMG 1992 (CMG 1985); HM Diplomatic Service; Ambassador to Japan, since 1992; *b* 17 Jan. 1936; *s* of Prof. James Dixon Boyd and Amélie Lowenthal; *m* 1st, 1968, Gunilla Kristina Ingegerd Rönngren; one *s* one *d*; 2nd, 1977, Julia Daphne Raynsford; three *d. Educ:* Westminster Sch.; Clare Coll., Cambridge (BA; Hon. Fellow, 1994); Yale Univ. (MA). Joined HM Foreign Service, 1962; Hong Kong, 1962–64; Peking, 1965–67; Foreign Office, 1967–69; Washington, 1969–73; 1st Sec., Peking, 1973–75; secondment to HM Treasury, 1976; Counsellor: (Economic), Bonn, 1977–81; (Economic and Soc. Affairs), UK Mission to UN, 1981–84; Asst Under-Sec. of State, FCO, 1984; Political Advr, Hong Kong, 1985–87; Dep. Under-Sec. of State, FCO, 1987–89; Chief Clerk, FCO, 1989–92. *Recreations:* music, fly fishing. *Address:* c/o Foreign and Commonwealth Office, SW1A 2AH.

BOYD, Sir (John) Francis, Kt 1976; a Vice-President, Open Spaces Society, since 1982; *b* 11 July 1910; *s* of John Crichton Dick Boyd and Kate Boyd, Ilkley, Yorks; *m* 1946, Margaret, *d* of George Dobson and Agnes Dobson, Scarborough, Yorks; one *s* two *d. Educ:* Ilkley Grammar Sch.; Silcoates Sch., near Wakefield, Yorks. Reporter: Leeds Mercury, 1928–34; Manchester Guardian, 1934–37; Parly Correspondent, Manchester Guardian, 1937–39. Aux. Fire Service, London, 1939; Monitoring Unit, BBC, 1940; Army, 1940–45. Political Correspondent, Manchester Guardian and Guardian, 1945–72; Political Editor, 1972–75. Chm., Lobby Journalists, 1949–50. Hon. LLD Leeds, 1973. *Publications:* Richard Austen Butler, 1956; (ed) The Glory of Parliament, by Harry Boardman, 1960; British Politics in Transition, 1964. *Recreations:* reading, walking, gardening. *Address:* 7 Summerlee Avenue, N2 9QP. *T:* 0181–444 8601.

BOYD, John MacInnes, CBE 1990; QPM 1984; HM Chief Inspector of Constabulary for Scotland, since 1993; *b* 14 Oct. 1933; *s* of late F. Duncan Boyd and M. Catherine MacInnes; *m* 1957, Sheila MacSporran; two *s. Educ:* Oban High School. Paisley Burgh Police, 1956–67; Renfrew and Bute Constabulary, 1967–75; Strathclyde Police, 1975–84 (Asst Chief Constable, 1979–84); Chief Constable, Dumfries and Galloway Constabulary, 1984–89; HM Inspector of Constabulary for Scotland, 1989–93. Pres., Scotland, ACPO, 1988–89. *Recreations:* golf, gardening, reading, photography. *Address:* HM Inspectorate of Constabulary for Scotland, 2 Greenside Lane, Edinburgh EH1 3AH. *T:* 0131–244 5612.

BOYD, Dr (John) Morton, CBE 1987; FRSE; ecologist; Consultant: Scottish Hydro-Electric plc, since 1991 (North of Scotland Hydro-Electric Board, 1985–91); National Trust for Scotland, since 1985; Mirror Publishing, since 1989; Director, Scotland, Nature Conservancy Council, 1971–85; *b* Darvel, Ayrshire, 31 Jan. 1925; *s* of Thomas Pollock Boyd and Jeanie Reid Morton; *m* 1954, Winifred Isobel Rome; four *s. Educ:* Kilmarnock Acad.; Glasgow Univ. (BSc, PhD, DSc, DLitt). FRSE 1968. Served War, 1943–47: Flt Lieut RAF. Nature Conservancy Council: Reg. Officer, 1957–68; Asst Dir, 1969–70. Nuffield Trav. Fellow, ME and E Africa, 1964–65; Leader, British Jordan Expedn, 1966; Mem., Royal Soc. Aldabra Expedn, 1967. Member: Council, Royal Scottish Zool Soc., 1963–69, 1980–85, 1986–89, 1990–93; Council, Azraq Internat. Biol Stn, Jordan, 1967–69; Council, National Trust for Scotland, 1971–85; Seals Adv. Cttee, NERC, 1973–79; BBC Scottish Agr. Adv. Cttee, 1973–76; Exec. Bd, Internat. Waterfowl Res. Bureau, 1976–78; Council, Royal Soc. of Edinburgh, 1978–81; Consultative Panel on Conservation of the Line and Phoenix Islands (Central Pacific), 1981–86. Internat. Union for Conservation of Nature and Natural Resources: British Rep., Kinshasa, 1975, Geneva, 1977, Ashkhabad, 1978, Christchurch, 1981, and Madrid, 1985; Mem. Commn on Ecology, 1976–92; Confs, Senegal/Gambia and Switzerland, 1980, Holland, 1981, Catalonia and Indonesia, 1982, Malaysia, 1983, Bavaria, 1985. Co-Chm., Area VI Anglo-Soviet Environmental Protection Agreement, 1977–85; Chm., UK Internat. Conservation Cttee, 1980; Member: Council, Scottish Wildlife Trust, 1985–91; Cttee, Centre for Human Ecology, Edinburgh Univ., 1985–; Panel on Scottish Popular Mountain Areas, CCS, 1989; Adv. Cttee on SSSIs, SNH, 1992–; Vice-Pres., Scottish Conservation Projects Trust, 1985–. Church of Scotland Elder, 1959– (Rep., WCC Convocation on Justice, Peace and Integrity of Creation, Seoul, 1990). Hon. Consultant, Forestry Commn, 1992– (Consultant, 1985–92). Lectures: Keith Entwistle Meml, Cambridge, 1968; British Council, Amman, Nicosia and Ankara, 1972; East African Tours, Swan (Hellenic) Ltd, 1972–94; Meml in Agr. Zool., W of Scotland Agr. Coll., 1976; Sir William Weipers Meml, Glasgow Univ. Vet. Sch., 1980; Nat. Trust for Scotland Jubilee, 1981; British Council, Jakarta, 1982, Delhi and Kuala Lumpur, 1983; Serenissima Travel Ltd, 1990–94; Noble Caledonia Ltd, 1991–. Gen. Editor, Island Biology Series, Edinburgh Univ. Press, 1985–92. FRSA 1985; FRZSScot 1985; FRSGS 1987; CBiol 1987, FIBiol 1987. Neill Prize, Royal Soc. of Edinburgh, 1983. *Publications:* (with K. Williamson) St Kilda Summer, 1960; (with K. Williamson) Mosaic of Islands, 1963; (with F. F. Darling) The Highlands and Islands, 1964; Travels in the Middle East and East Africa, 1966; (with P. A. Jewell and C. Milner) Island Survivors, 1974; (ed) The Natural Environment of the Outer Hebrides, 1979; (ed with D. R. Bowes) The Natural Environment of the Inner Hebrides, 1983; Fraser Darling's Islands, 1986; (with I. L. Boyd) The Hebrides: a natural history, 1990; Fraser Darling in Africa, 1992; scientific papers on nature conservation and animal ecology. *Recreations:* travel, painting, photography. *Address:* 57 Hailes Gardens, Edinburgh EH13 0JH. *T:* 0131–441 3220; Balephuil, Tiree, Argyll PA77 6UE. *T:* Scarinish (01879) 220521. *Club:* New (Edinburgh).

BOYD, Leslie Balfour, CBE 1977; Courts Administrator, Central Criminal Court, 1972–77; *b* 25 Nov. 1914; *e s* of late Henry Leslie Boyd, Mem. of Lloyds, of Crowborough, Sussex, and Beatrix Boyd, *d* of Henry Chapman, for many years British Consul at Dieppe; *m* 1936, Wendy Marie, *d* of George and Nancy Blake, Oswestry, Salop; one *s* one *d. Educ:* Evelyn's; Royal Naval College, Dartmouth. Invalided out of Royal Navy, 1931. Called to the Bar, Gray's Inn, 1939; joined staff of Central Criminal Court, 1941; Dep. Clerk of Court, 1948; Clerk of the Court, 1955–71; Dep. Clerk of Peace, 1949–55, Clerk of the Peace, 1955–71, City of London and Town and Borough of Southwark. Master, Worshipful Company of Gold and Silver Wyre Drawers, 1969. *Publications:* contributor to Criminal Law and Juries titles, 3rd edn, Juries title, 4th edn, of Halsbury's Laws of England. *Recreations:* gardening and travel. *Address:* Flat G, Mulberry Court, 2 Highbury Hill, Islington, N5 1BA.

BOYD, Hon. Sir Mark Alexander L.; *see* Lennox-Boyd.

BOYD, Morgan Alistair, CMG 1990; Adviser, Commonwealth Development Corporation (Deputy Chief Executive, 1991–94); *b* 1 May 1934; *s* of Norman Robert Boyd and Kathleen Muriel Boyd; *m* 1959, Judith Mary Martin. *Educ:* Marlborough College; Wadham College, Oxford (BA, MA 1955). FRGS 1957. Management trainee, CDC, 1957; Exec., Malaysia, 1958–66; Manager, East Caribbean Housing, Barbados, 1967–70; Gen. Manager, Tanganyika Develt Finance Co., 1970–74; Advr, Industrial Develt Bank, Kenya, 1975; Regl Controller, Central Africa, 1976–80, East Africa, 1981–82; Dep. Gen. Manager, Investigations, London, 1983–84; Dir of Ops, 1985–89, Dep. Gen. Manager, 1989–91, Commonwealth Develt Corp. Director: Hub Power Co., Pakistan; EDESA Management, Switzerland. Member: RSA 1990–; Council, Royal African Soc., 1992–; Management Council, Africa Centre, 1995. *Publication:* Royal Challenge Accepted, 1962. *Recreations:* music, sailing, travel, *Address:* 7 South Hill Mansions, South Hill Park, NW3 2SL. *T:* 0171–435 1082. *Clubs:* Naval, English-Speaking Union.

BOYD, Morton; *see* Boyd, J. M.

BOYD, Sir Robert (Lewis Fullarton), Kt 1983; CBE 1972; FRS 1969; Professor of Physics in the University of London, 1962–83, now Emeritus; Director, Mullard Space Science Laboratory of Department of Physics and Astronomy of University College, London, 1965–83; *b* 1922; *s* of late William John Boyd, PhD, BSc; *m* 1949, Mary, *d* of late John Higgins; two *s* one *d. Educ:* Whitgift Sch.; Imperial Coll., London (BSc (Eng) 1943); University Coll., London (PhD 1949; Fellow 1988). FIEE 1967; FInstP 1972. Exp. Officer at Admty Mining Estabt, 1943–46; DSIR Res. Asst, 1946–49; ICI Res. Fellow, 1949–50, Maths Dept, UCL; ICI Res. Fellow, Physics Dept, UCL, 1950–52; Lectr in Physics, UCL, 1952–58, Reader in Physics, UCL, 1959–62. Prof. of Astronomy (part-time), Royal Institution, 1961–67; IEE Appleton Lectr, 1976; Bakerian Lectr, Royal Soc., 1978; Halley Lectr, Univ. of Oxford, 1981. Chairman: Meteorol Res. Cttee, MoD,

1972–75; Astronautics Cttee, MoD, 1972–77; Member: BBC Science Cons. Gp, 1970–79; SRC, 1977–81 (Chm., Astronomy, Space and Radio Bd, 1977–80); Council, Physical Soc., 1958–60; Council, RAS, 1962–66 (Vice-Pres., 1964–66); British Nat. Cttee on Space Res., 1976–87. Pres., Victoria Inst., 1965–76. Trustee, Nat. Maritime Museum, 1980–89. Governor: St Lawrence Coll., 1965–76; Croydon Coll., 1966–80; Southlands Coll., 1976–94; Chm., London Bible Coll., 1983–90. Hon. DSc Heriot-Watt, 1979. *Publications:* The Upper Atmosphere (with H. S. W. Massey), 1958; Space Research by Rocket and Satellite, 1960; Space Physics, 1975; papers in sci. jls on space sci. and other topics. *Recreations:* elderly Rolls Royce motors, model engineering. *Address:* Roseneath, 41 Church Street, Littlehampton, West Sussex BN17 5PU. *T:* Littlehampton (01903) 714438.

BOYD, Robert Stanley, CB 1982; Solicitor of Inland Revenue, 1979–86; *b* 6 March 1927; *s* of Robert Reginald Boyd (formerly Indian Police) and Agnes Maria Dorothea, *d* of Lt-Col Charles H. Harrison; *m* 1965, Ann, *d* of Daniel Hopkin. *Educ:* Wellington; Trinity Coll., Dublin (BA, LLB). Served RN, 1945–48. Called to Bar, Inner Temple, 1954. Joined Inland Revenue, 1959; Prin. Asst Solicitor, 1971–79. *Address:* Great Beere, North Tawton, Devon EX20 2BR.

BOYD, Stewart Craufurd, QC 1981; a Recorder, since 1994; *b* 25 Oct. 1943; *s* of Leslie Balfour Boyd and Wendy Marie Boyd; *m* 1970, Catherine Jay; one *s* three *d*. *Educ:* Winchester Coll.; Trinity Coll., Cambridge (MA). Called to the Bar, Middle Temple, 1967, Bencher, 1989. *Publications:* (ed) Scrutton, Charterparties, 18th edn 1972, 19th edn 1984; (with Sir Michael Mustill) The Law and Practice of Commercial Arbitration, 1982, 1989; contrib. Civil Justice Rev., Arbitration Internat., Lloyd's Commercial and Maritime Law Qly. *Recreations:* boats, pianos, gardens. *Address:* 1 Gayton Crescent, NW3 1TT. *T:* 0171–431 1581.

BOYD, (Thomas) Christopher; farmer; *b* 1916; *m*; one *s* two *d*. Army, 1940–44; civil servant, 1939 and 1944–48; MP (Lab) Bristol NW, 1955–59; Chelsea Borough Councillor, 1953–59. *Address:* Middlegill, Moffat, Dumfriesshire DG10 9SW. *T:* Beattock (016833) 415.

BOYD, Dame Vivienne (Myra), DBE 1986 (CBE 1983); Member: Advertising Standards Complaints Board (formerly Advertising Standards Council), since 1988; Environmental Choice Management Advisory Committee, since 1990; Vice Chairperson, Hutt Diabetic Foundation, since 1992; *b* 11 April 1926; *d* of Hugh France Lowe and Winifred May Lowe (*née* Shearer); *m* 1948, Robert Macdonald Boyd; one *s* three *d*. *Educ:* Eastern Hutt Sch.; Hutt Valley High Sch.; Victoria Coll., Univ. of New Zealand (MSc (Hons)). President: Dunedin Free Kindergarten Assoc., 1965; NZ Baptist Women's League, 1966; Nat. Council of Women of NZ, 1978–82; NZ Baptist Union of Churches and Missionary Soc., 1984–85; Wellington Br., NZ Epilepsy Assoc., 1994–. Member: Royal Commn on Nuclear Power Generation, 1976–78; Equal Opportunities Tribunal, 1979–89; chaired: Abortion Supervisory Cttee, 1979–80; Women and Recreation Conf., 1981; Review of Preparation and Initial Employment of Nurses, 1986–92; Consumer Council, NZ, 1983–88 (Mem., 1975–88); Consumers' Inst. of NZ Inc., 1988–89 (Mem. Bd, 1989–90); Convener, Internat. Council of Women Standing Cttee on Social Welfare, 1982–88. Mem., NZ Medic Alert Trust Bd, 1995–. Chm., Taita Home and Hosp. for the Elderly, 1989–92. Silver Jubilee Medal, 1977. *Recreations:* reading, gardening. *Address:* 1/38 Kings Cresent, Lower Hutt, New Zealand. *T:* (4) 5695028.

BOYD, William Andrew Murray, FRSL; author; *b* 7 March 1952; *s* of Dr Alexander Murray Boyd and Evelyn Boyd; *m* 1975, Susan Anne (*née* Wilson). *Educ:* Gordonstoun Sch.; Glasgow Univ. (MA Hons English and Philosophy); Jesus Coll., Oxford. Lecturer in English, St Hilda's Coll., Oxford, 1980–83; Television Critic, New Statesman, 1981–83. FRSL 1983. Chevalier de l'Ordre des Arts et des Lettres (France), 1991. *Publications:* A Good Man in Africa, 1981 (Whitbread Prize 1981, Somerset Maugham Award 1982); On the Yankee Station, 1981; An Ice-Cream War, 1982 (John Llewellyn Rhys Prize, 1982); Stars and Bars, 1984; School Ties, 1985; The New Confessions, 1987; Brazzaville Beach, 1990 (James Tait Black Meml Prize, 1990; McVitie's Prize, 1991); The Blue Afternoon (Sunday Express Book of the Year Award), 1993; The Destiny of Nathalie X, and Other Stories, 1995. *Screenplays:* Good and Bad at Games (TV), 1983; Dutch Girls (TV), 1985; Scoop (TV), 1987; Stars and Bars, 1988; Aunt Julia and the Scriptwriter, 1990; Mr Johnson, 1990; Chaplin, 1992; A Good Man in Africa, 1994; Cork, 1995. *Recreations:* tennis, strolling. *Address:* c/o Harvey Unna and Stephen Durbridge Ltd, 24 Pottery Lane, Holland Park, W11 4LZ.

BOYD-CARPENTER, family name of **Baron Boyd-Carpenter.**

BOYD-CARPENTER, Baron *cr* 1972 (Life Peer), of Crux Easton in the County of Southampton; **John Archibald Boyd-Carpenter,** PC 1954; *b* 2 June 1908; *s* of late Sir Archibald Boyd-Carpenter, MP; *m* 1937, Margaret, *e d* of Lieut-Col G. L. Hall, OBE; one *s* two *d*. *Educ:* Stowe; Balliol Coll., Oxford. Pres. Oxford Union, 1930; BA (History, 1930); Diploma in Economics, 1931; toured USA with Oxford Union Debating Team, 1931; Harmsworth Law Scholar, Middle Temple, 1933; Council of Legal Education's Prize for Constitutional Law, 1934; called to Bar, Middle Temple, 1934, and practised in London and SE Circuit. Contested (MR) Limehouse for LCC, 1934. Joined Scots Guards, 1940; held various staff appointments and served with AMG in Italy, retired with rank of Major. MP (C) for Kingston-upon-Thames, 1945–72; Financial Sec., to the Treasury, 1951–54; Minister of Transport and Civil Aviation, 1954–Dec. 1955; Minister of Pensions and National Insurance, Dec. 1955–July 1962; Chief Sec. to the Treasury and Paymaster-Gen., 1962–64; Opposition Front Bench Spokesman on Housing, Local Government and Land, 1964–66; Chm., Public Accounts Cttee, 1964–70. Chairman: Greater London Area Local Govt Cttee, Conservative Party, 1968; London Members Cttee, 1966–72; Pres. Wessex Area, Nat. Union of Conservative and Unionist Assocs, 1977–80. Chairman: CAA, 1972–77; Rugby Portland Cement, 1976–84 (Dir, 1970–76); Orion Insurance Co., 1969–72; CLRP Investment Trust, 1970–72; Dir, TR Far East Income (formerly Australia Investment) Trust, 1977–, and other cos; Mem. Council, Trust House Forte Ltd, 1977–. Governor, Stowe School; Chairman: Carlton Club, 1979–86; Assoc. of Cons. Peers, 1985–90 (Pres., 1991–); Mail Users' Assoc., 1986–90; Sort Out Sunday Cttee, 1986–. High Steward, Royal Borough of Kingston-upon-Thames, 1973–. DL Greater London, 1973–83. *Publications:* Way of Life, 1980; newspaper articles. *Recreations:* tennis and swimming. *Address:* 12 Eaton Terrace, SW1. *T:* 0171–730 7765; Crux Easton House, Crux Easton, near Newbury, Berks. *T:* Highclere (01635) 253037. *Club:* Carlton.
See also Lt-Gen. Hon. Sir T. P. J. Boyd-Carpenter, Baroness Hogg.

BOYD-CARPENTER, (Marsom) Henry, CVO 1994; Partner, Farrer & Co., Solicitors, since 1968; Private Solicitor to the Queen, since 1995; *b* 11 Oct. 1939; *s* of Francis Henry Boyd-Carpenter and Nina Boyd-Carpenter (*née* Townshend); *m* 1971, Lesley Ann Davies; one *s* one *d*. *Educ:* Charterhouse; Balliol Coll., Oxford (BA 1962; MA 1967). Admitted solicitor, 1966; Solicitor to Duchy of Cornwall, 1976–94. Law Society: Mem., 1966–; Hon. Auditor, 1979–81. Mem. Council, Prince of Wales's Inst. of Architecture, 1995–. Hon. Steward, Westminster Abbey, 1980–; Hon. Legal Advr, Canterbury Cathedral Appeal Fund, 1994–. Mem. Governing Body, Charterhouse Sch., 1981–; Gov., Sutton's Hosp. in Charterhouse, 1994–. Mem. Council, Chelsea Physic Garden, 1983–. *Recreations:* reading, listening to music, hill-walking. *Address:* 66 Lincoln's Inn Fields, WC2A 3LH; Guardswell House, Brockenhurst Road, South Ascot, Berks SL5 9HA. *Club:* Brooks's.

BOYD-CARPENTER, Lt-Gen. Hon. Sir Thomas (Patrick John), KBE 1993 (MBE 1973); Deputy Chief of Defence Staff (Programmes and Personnel), since 1992; *b* 16 June 1938; *s* of Baron Boyd-Carpenter, *qv*; *m* 1972, Mary-Jean (*née* Duffield); one *s* two *d*. *Educ:* Stowe. Commnd 1957; served UK, Oman, Malaya, Borneo and Germany; Instr, Staff Coll., 1975–77; Defence Fellowship, Aberdeen Univ., 1977–78; CO 1st Bn Scots Guards, 1979–81; Comdr 24 Inf. Brigade, 1983–84; Dir, Defence Policy, 1985–87; COS, HQ BAOR, 1988–89; ACDS (Programmes), 1989–92. *Publication:* Conventional Deterrence: into the 1990s, 1989. *Recreations:* reading, gardening. *Address:* c/o Barclays Bank, 6 Market Place, Newbury, Berks RG14 5AY.
See also Baroness Hogg.

BOYD de la GUARDIA, Aquilino; Ambassador of Panama to the Court of St James's, since 1994; *b* 30 March 1921; *m* Dora Brind; five *s*. *Educ:* Panama Univ. (Faculty of Law and Political Science); Holy Cross Coll., New Orleans. Ministry of Foreign Affairs, 1956–: served Cuba, Washington, Mexico, OAS, UN (Pres., Security Council, 1973; Panamanian Rep., 1976); Minister of Foreign Affairs, 1976; jointly drew up Boyd-Vance Memorandum of Understanding with USA on Panama Canal, 1977; Ambassador, Washington, 1982–85. Mem., Internat. Law Acad., Panama. Grand Cross, Order of Vasco Nuñez de Balboa and Order of Manuel Amador Guerrero, Panama; numerous foreign orders. *Address:* Embassy of Panama, 48 Park Street, W1Y 3PD.

BOYDE, Prof. Patrick, PhD; FBA 1987; Serena Professor of Italian, since 1981, and Fellow of St John's College, since 1965, University of Cambridge; *b* 30 Nov. 1934; *s* of Harry Caine Boyde and Florence Colonna Boyde; *m* 1956, Catherine Mavis Taylor; four *s*. *Educ:* Braintree County High Sch.; Wanstead County High Sch.; St John's Coll., Cambridge. BA 1956, MA 1960, PhD 1963. Nat. service, commnd RA, 1956–58. Research, St John's Coll., Cambridge, 1958–61; Asst Lectr in Italian, Univ. of Leeds, 1961–62; Asst Lectr, later Lectr, Univ. of Cambridge, 1962–81. Corresp. Fellow, Accademia Nazionale dei Lincei, 1986. *Publications:* Dante's Lyric Poetry (with K. Foster), 1967; Dante's Style in his Lyric Poetry, 1971; Dante Philomythes and Philosopher: Man in the Cosmos, 1981; Perception and Passion in Dante's 'Comedy', 1993. *Recreations:* walking, music.

BOYDELL, (The Worshipful Chancellor) Peter Thomas Sherrington, QC 1965; Leader, Parliamentary Bar, since 1975; Chancellor of Dioceses of Truro since 1957, Oxford since 1958 and Worcester since 1959; *b* 20 Sept. 1920; *s* of late Frank Richard Boydell, JP, and late Frances Barton Boydell, Blenheim Lodge, Whitegate Drive, Blackpool; unmarried. *Educ:* Arnold Sch., Blackpool; Manchester Univ. LLB Manchester 1940. Served War of 1939–45; Adjt, 17th Field Regt, RA, 1943; Bde Major, RA, 1st Armoured Div., 1944; Bde Major, RA, 10th Indian Div., 1945. Qualified as Solicitor, 1947. Called to Bar, Middle Temple, 1948, Bencher, 1970, Dep. Treas., 1988, Treas., 1989. Chm., Planning and Local Govt Cttee of the Bar, 1973–86; Founder Chm., Local Govt and Planning, Bar Assoc., 1986–90. Member: Legal Board of Church Assembly, 1958–71; Adv. Bd for Redundant Churches, 1993–. Contested (C) Carlisle, 1964. Associate (by invitation and election) RICS, 1982; ACIArb 1985. *Recreations:* mountaineering, music, travel. *Address:* 45 Wilton Crescent, SW1X 8RX. *T:* 0171–235 5505; 2 Harcourt Buildings, Temple, EC4Y 9DB. *T:* 0171–353 8415. *Clubs:* Garrick, Royal Automobile; Climbers.

BOYER, John Leslie, OBE 1982; Chief Executive, Zoological Society of London, 1984–88; *b* 13 Nov. 1926; *s* of Albert and Gladys Boyer; *m* 1953, Joyce Enid Thomasson; one *s* two *d*. *Educ:* Nantwich; Acton Grammar Sch. Served Army, 1944–48: commnd into South Lancashire Regt, 1946, and attached to Baluch Regt, then Indian Army. Joined Hongkong and Shanghai Banking Corp., 1948: served Hong Kong, Burma, Japan, India, Malaysia, Singapore; General Manager, Hong Kong, 1973; Director, March 1977; Dep. Chm., Sept. 1977–81; Chm., Antony Gibbs Hldgs Ltd, 1981–83. Director: Anglo and Overseas Trust (formerly Anglo and American Securities) PLC, 1981–; Overseas Investment Trust (formerly North Atlantic Securities), 1981–. *Recreations:* walking, swimming, bridge, reading. *Address:* Friars Lawn, Norwood Green Road, Norwood Green, Mddx UB2 4LA. *T:* 0181–574 8489. *Clubs:* Oriental; Shek O (Hong Kong); Tanglin (Singapore).

BOYERS, (Raphael) Howard, DFC 1945; Regional Chairman of Industrial Tribunals, Sheffield, 1984–87, retired 1988; *b* 20 Oct. 1915; *yr s* of late Bernard Boyers and Jennie Boyers; *m* 1st, 1949, Anna Moyra Cowan (*d* 1984); three *d*; 2nd, 1985, Estelle Wolman (*née* Davidson), JP; two step *s* one step *d*. *Educ:* King Edward VI Grammar School, Retford. Admitted Solicitor, 1939. Served War, RAF, 1940–45; 130 Sqdn, 10 Gp Fighter Comd, 1941; 51 Sqdn, 4 Gp Bomber Comd, 1944–45. Sen. Partner, Boyers Howson & Co., 1946–72. Clerk of the Peace, City of Sheffield, 1964–71; Chairman: VAT Tribunals, 1972–75; Industrial Tribunals, 1975–80; acting Regional Chm., 1980–84. Pres., Rep. Council of Sheffield and Dist Jews, 1963–67 and 1973–74. *Recreations:* theatre, music, watching football. *Address:* 49 Cortworth Road, Sheffield S11 9LN. *T:* Sheffield (0114) 236 2041. *Clubs:* Royal Air Force; Sheffield (Sheffield).

BOYES, Sir Brian Gerald B.; *see* Barratt-Boyes.

BOYES, James Ashley; Headmaster of City of London School, 1965–84; *b* 27 Aug. 1924; *s* of late Alfred Simeon Boyes and of Edith May Boyes; *m* 1st, 1949, Diana Fay (*née* Rothera), MA Cantab; two *d*; 2nd, 1973, April Tanner (*née* Rothery). *Educ:* Rugby Sch.; Clare Coll., Cambridge. Lieut RNVR; N Russian convoys and Brit. Pacific Fleet, 1942–46. Cambridge Univ., 1942, 1946–48; 1st class Hons Mod. Hist., 1948; Mellon Fellowship, Yale Univ., 1948–50; MA Yale, 1950. Asst Master, Rugby Sch., 1950–55; Headmaster, Kendal Grammar Sch., Westmorland, 1955–60; Dir of Studies, Royal Air Force Coll., Cranwell, 1960–65. Since retirement engaged in work for the mentally ill; Vice-Chair, Nat. Schizophrenia Fellowship, 1989–. *Recreations:* squash racquets, sailing. *Address:* 12 Linver Road, SW6 3RB. *Clubs:* Royal Automobile, Hurlingham; Harlequins RUFC (Hon. Mem.); Hawks (Cambridge); Royal Windermere Yacht.

BOYES, Kate Emily Tyrrell, (Mrs C. W. Sanders); Chairman, Civil Service Selection Boards, since 1978; *b* 22 April 1918; *e d* of S. F. Boyes, Sandiacre, Derbyshire; *m* 1944, Cyril Woods Sanders, *qv*; one *s* three *d*. *Educ:* Long Eaton Grammar Sch.; (Scholar) Newnham Coll., Cambridge. Economics Tripos, 1939; MA (Cantab). Administrative Class, Home Civil Service, 1939; Private Sec. to Parly Sec., 1942–45; Principal, 1945; Sec. to Council on Prices, Productivity and Incomes, 1958–60; Asst Sec., 1961; Speechwriter to President of Bd of Trade, 1963–64; Under-Sec., Europe, Industry and Technology Div., DTI, later Dept of Trade, 1972–78. Member: Council, National Trust, 1967–79; Exec., Keep Britain Tidy Gp, 1980–. *Recreations:* climbing, sailing, ski-ing, archæology. *Address:* 41 Smith Street, SW3 4EP. *T:* 0171–352 8053; Giles Point, Winchelsea, Sussex TN36 4AA. *T:* Rye (01797) 226431; Canower, Cashel, Connemara, Ireland. *Clubs:* Ski Club of Gt Britain; Island Cruising (Salcombe).

BOYES, Roland; MP (Lab) Houghton and Washington, since 1983; *m* 1962, Patricia James; two *s*. Member (Lab) Durham, European Parliament, 1979–84. An opposition frontbench spokesman on: Parly environment team, 1985–88; Parly defence team, 1988–92; Member, Select Committee: on Envmt, 1992–94; on Nat. Heritage, 1994–; Mem., Speaker's Panel of Chairmen, 1994–. Founder Chm., All Party Photography Gp, 1987–. Member GMB. Chm., Tribune Gp, 1985–86. Dir, Hartlepool United AFC, 1987–. *Publication:* People in Parliament, 1990. *Address:* (home) 12 Spire Hollin, Peterlee, Co. Durham SR8 1DA. *T:* 0191–586 3917; (office) 5A Grangewood Close, Shiney Row, Houghton-le-Spring, Tyne & Wear DH4 4SD. *T:* 0191–385 7825, *Fax:* 0191–385 4785; (House of Commons) 0171–219 3587, *Fax:* 0171–219 5657.

BOYLAN, Prof. Patrick John, PhD; FMA; FGS; Professor of Arts Policy and Management, City University, since 1990; *b* 17 Aug. 1939; *s* of Francis Boylan and Mary Doreen (*née* Haxby), Hull, Yorks. *Educ:* Marist Coll., Hull; Univ. of Hull (BSc 1960; PGCE 1961); Univ. of Leicester (PhD 1985). Museums Diploma (with Distinction), Museums Assoc., 1966. FMA 1972; FGS 1973. Asst Master, Marist Coll., Hull, 1961–63; Keeper of Geology and Natural History, Kingston upon Hull Museums, 1964–68; Dir of Museums and Art Gallery, Exeter City Council, 1968–72; Dir of Museums and Art Gall., Leicester City Council, 1972–74; Dir of Museums and Arts, Leics County Council, 1974–90. International Council of Museums: Chm., Internat. Cttee for Training of Personnel, 1983–89; Chm., UK Nat. Cttee, 1987–; Mem., Adv. Cttee, 1983–; Mem., Exec. Council, 1989–. Councillor, Museums Assoc., 1970–71 and 1986– (Centenary Pres., 1988–90); Chm., Library Cttee, Geol Soc., 1984–87. FIMgt (FBIM 1990; MBIM 1975); FRSA 1990. *Publications:* Ice Age in Yorkshire and Humberside, 1983; The Changing World of Museums and Art Galleries, 1986; Museums 2000: politics, people, professionals and profit, 1991; over 90 papers in learned jls and chapters in books on museums, prof. training, geology, natural history and history of science. *Recreations:* the arts (especially opera and contemporary arts and crafts), history of science research, avoiding gardening. *Address:* Department of Arts Policy and Management, City University, Frobisher Crescent, Barbican, EC2Y 8HB. *T:* 0171–477 8750, *Fax:* 0171–477 8887; The Deepings, Gun Lane, Knebworth, Herts SG3 6BJ. *T:* Stevenage (01438) 812658. *Club:* Leicester Rotary.

BOYLAND, Prof. Eric, (Dick), PhD London, DSc Manchester; Professor of Biochemistry, University of London, at Chester Beatty Research Institute, Institute of Cancer Research, Royal Marsden Hospital, 1948–70, now Emeritus Professor; Visiting Professor in Environmental Toxicology, London School of Hygiene and Tropical Medicine, 1970–76; *b* Manchester, 24 Feb. 1905; *s* of Alfred E. and Helen Boyland; *m* 1931, Margaret Esther (*d* 1985), *d* of late Maj.-Gen. Sir Frederick Maurice, KCMG, CB; two *s* one *d*. *Educ:* Manchester Central High Sch.; Manchester Univ. BSc Tech. 1926; MSc 1928; DSc 1936. Research Asst in Physiology, Manchester Univ., 1926–28; Grocers' Company Scholar and Beit Memorial Fellow for Med. Research at Lister Institute for Preventive Medicine, 1928–30, and Kaiser Wilhelm Institut für Medizinische Forschung, Heidelberg, 1930–31; Physiological Chemist to Royal Cancer Hosp., London, 1931; Reader in Biochemistry, University of London, 1935–47. Research Officer in Ministry of Supply, 1941–44; Ministry of Agriculture, 1944–45. Consultant to Internat. Agency for Research on Cancer, Lyon, 1970–72; Member WHO Panel on Food Additives. Hon. FFOM, RCP, 1982. Hon. PhD Frankfurt, 1982; Hon. MD Malta, 1985. Judd Award for Cancer Research, New York, 1948. *Publications:* The Biochemistry of Bladder Cancer, 1963; Modern Trends in Toxicology, vol. I, 1962, vol. II, 1974; scientific papers in biochemistry and pharmacology. *Recreations:* walking, painting and looking at paintings. *Address:* 42 Bramerton Street, SW3 5LA. *T:* 0171–352 2601; King's College London, Chelsea Campus, Manresa Road, SW3 6LX. *Clubs:* Athenæum; Rucksack (Manchester).

BOYLE, family name of **Earls of Cork, Glasgow,** and **Shannon.**

BOYLE, Viscount; Richard Henry John Boyle; *b* 19 Jan. 1960; *s* and *heir* of 9th Earl of Shannon, *qv*. *Educ:* Northease Manor School, Lewes. *Address:* Edington House, Edington, Bridgwater, Somerset TA7 9JS.

BOYLE, Alan Gordon; QC 1991; *b* 31 March 1949; *s* of Dr Michael Morris Boyle and Hazel Irene Boyle; *m* 1981, Claudine-Aimée Minne-Vercruysse; two *d*. *Educ:* Royal Shrewsbury Sch.; St Catherine's Coll., Oxford (BA). Called to the Bar, Lincoln's Inn, 1972. *Recreations:* walking, music. *Address:* 13 Old Square, Lincoln's Inn, WC2A 3UA. *T:* 0171–242 6105.

BOYLE, Archibald Cabbourn, MD; FRCP; Hon. Consultant Physician, King Edward VII, Midhurst, 1984–87; Director, Department of Rheumatology, Middlesex Hospital, 1954–83; Hon. Consultant Rheumatologist, King Edward VII Hospital for Officers, 1980–83; Hon. Clinical Adviser, Department of Rheumatological Research, Middlesex Hospital Medical School; *b* 14 March 1918; *s* of late Arthur Hislop Boyle and of Flora Ellen Boyle; *m* 1st, Patricia Evelyn Tallack (*d* 1944); one *d*; 2nd, Dorothy Evelyn (marr. diss. 1982), *widow* of Lieut G. B. Jones; one *s*; 3rd, 1983, June Rosemary Gautrey (*née* Pickett). *Educ:* Dulwich Coll.; St Bartholomew's Hospital. DPhysMed 1947; MD 1949; FRCP 1959. House Physician, St Bartholomew's Hosp., 1941–42. Served War of 1939–45 in Far East, and later as Command Specialist in Physical Medicine. Registrar and Sen. Asst, 1946–49, and Asst Physician, 1949–54, Mddx Hosp.; Consultant in Physical Medicine, Bromley Gp of Hosps, 1950–54; Physician, Arthur Stanley Inst. for Rheumatic Diseases, 1950–65. Member: Bd of Governors, Mddx Hosp.; Bd of Governors, Charterhouse Rheumatism Clinic; Bd of Studies in Medicine, Univ. of London; Council, British Assoc. for Rheumatology and Rehabilitation (Pres., 1973–74); British League against Rheumatism (Vice-Pres., 1972–77; Pres., 1977–81); Council, Section of Physical Medicine, RSM, 1950– (Pres., 1956–58; Vice-Pres., 1970–); Heberden Soc.; Cttee on Rheumatology and Rehabilitation, RCP. Ernest Fletcher Meml Lectr, RSM, 1971. Formerly: Examnr in Physical Medicine, RCP; Examnr to Chartered Soc. of Physiotherapy; Editor, Annals of Physical Medicine, 1956–63; Sec., Internat. Fedn of Physical Medicine, 1960–64; Chm., Physical Medicine Gp, BMA, 1956–58; Pres., London Br., Chartered Soc. of Physiotherapy. Former Member: Council, British Assoc. of Physical Medicine and Rheumatology, 1949–72 (Vice-Pres., 1965–68; Pres., 1970–72); Cttee on Chronic Rheumatic Diseases, RCP; Regional Scientific, and Educn, Sub-Cttees, Arthritis and Rheumatism Council; Physiotherapists Bd, Council for Professions Supplementary to Medicine; Central Consultants and Specialists Cttee, BMA; Med. Adv. Cttee, British Rheumatism and Arthritis Assoc. *Publications:* A Colour Atlas of Rheumatology, 1974; contribs to medical jls, mainly on rheumatic disease. *Recreation:* gardening. *Address:* Iping Barn, Iping, near Midhurst, West Sussex GU29 0PE. *T:* Midhurst (01730) 816467.

BOYLE, Leonard Butler, CBE 1977; Director and General Manager, Principality Building Society, Cardiff, 1956–78; *b* 13 Jan. 1913; *s* of Harold and Edith Boyle; *m* 1938, Alice Baldwin Yarborough (*d* 1989); two *s*. *Educ:* Roundhay Sch., Leeds. FCIB. Chief of Investment Dept, Leeds Permanent Building Soc., 1937; Asst Man., Isle of Thanet Bldg Soc., 1949; Jt Asst Gen. Man., Hastings and Thanet Bldg Soc., 1951, Sec. 1954. Building Socs Assoc.: Mem. Council, 1956–78 (Chm. Gen. Purposes Cttee, 1958–60; Chm. Develt Cttee, 1967–71); Chm. of Council, 1973–75 (Dep. Chm. 1971–73; Vice-Pres., 1978); Vice-Pres., CIB (formerly CBSI), 1982–. *Recreations:* gardening, walking, golf. *Address:* Northwick Cottage, Marlpit Lane, Seaton, Devon EX12 2HH. *T:* Seaton (01297) 22194.

BOYLE, Dr Nicholas; Reader in German Literary and Intellectual History, University of Cambridge, since 1993; Fellow, Magdalene College, Cambridge, since 1968; *b* 18 June 1946; *e s* of late Hugh Boyle and of Margaret Mary Faith (*née* Hopkins, now Mrs R. G. Boothroyd); *m* 1983, Rosemary Angela Devlin; one *s* two *d*. *Educ:* King's Sch., Worcester; Magdalene Coll., Cambridge (schol.; BA 1967; MA. PhD 1976). University of Cambridge: Res. Fellow in German, Magdalene Coll., 1968–72; Lectr in German, Magdalene and Girton Colls, 1972–74; Univ. Asst Lectr in German, 1974–79, Lectr, 1979–93; Sec., Faculty Bd of Mod. and Medieval Langs, 1982–85; Tutor, Magdalene Coll., 1984–93. Scholar, Alexander von Humboldt Foundn, 1978, 1980–81; British Acad. Res. Reader in Humanities, 1990–92; Res. Fellow, John Rylands Res. Inst., Univ. of Manchester, 1993; Fellow, Wissenschaftskolleg, Berlin, 1994–95. W. Heinemann Prize, RSL, 1992; J. G. Robertson Meml Prize, Univ. of London, 1994. *Publications:* (ed with M. Swales) Realism in European Literature: essays in honour of J. P. Stern, 1986; Goethe: Faust, Part One, 1987; Goethe: the poet and the age, Vol. 1, 1991; articles in New Blackfriars, German Life and Letters, French Studies, etc. *Recreations:* enjoying other people's gardens, thinking about the future. *Address:* Magdalene College, Cambridge CB3 0AG. *T:* Cambridge (01223) 332137; 20 Alpha Road, Cambridge CB4 3DG. *T:* Cambridge (01223) 64310.

BOYLE, Sir Stephen Gurney, 5th Bt *cr* 1904; *b* 15 Jan. 1962; *s* of Sir Richard Gurney Boyle, 4th Bt, and of Elizabeth Ann, *yr d* of Norman Dennes; *S* father, 1983. *Heir:* *b* Michael Desmond Boyle, *b* 16 Sept. 1963.

BOYLES, Edgar William; Under Secretary, Inland Revenue, 1975–81; *b* 24 March 1921; *s* of William John Boyles and Jessie Louisa Boyles; *m* 1950, Heather Iris Hobart, SRN; three *s* one *d*. *Educ:* Bedford Modern Sch. RAF, 1940–46. Tax Officer, Inland Revenue, 1939; Principal Inspector of Taxes, 1962; Sen. Principal Inspector, 1967. *Recreations:* chess, gardening, watching cricket. *Address:* The Keeley, 155 Bedford Road, Wootton, Bedford MK43 9BA. *T:* Bedford (01234) 851875.

BOYNE, 10th Viscount *cr* 1717; **Gustavus Michael George Hamilton-Russell,** KCVO 1995; DL; JP; Baron Hamilton, 1715; Baron Brancepeth, 1866; a Lord in Waiting, since 1981; Lord-Lieutenant of Shropshire, since 1994; *b* 10 Dec. 1931; *s* of late Hon. Gustavus Lascelles Hamilton-Russell and *g s* of 9th Viscount; *S* grandfather, 1942; *m* 1956, Rosemary Anne, 2nd *d* of Major Sir Dennis Stucley, 5th Bt; one *s* two *d* (and one *d* decd). *Educ:* Eton; Sandhurst; Royal Agricl Coll., Cirencester. Commissioned Grenadier Guards, 1952. Director: Nat. Westminster Bank, 1976–90 (Chm., W Midlands and Wales Regional Bd, 1976–90); Private Patients Plan Ltd, 1986–; Priplan Investments, 1987–; Chairman: Ludlow Race Club Ltd, 1987–; Harper Adams Agricl Coll., 1990–. Mem., 1963–83, Dep. Chm., 1975–82, Telford Develt Corp. Governor, Wrekin Coll., Telford, 1965–86. KStJ. JP 1961, DL 1965, Salop. *Heir:* *s* Hon. Gustavus Michael Stucley Hamilton-Russell [*b* 27 May 1965; *m* 1991, Lucy, *d* of George Potter; one *d*]. *Address:* Burwarton House, Bridgnorth, Salop WV16 6QH. *T:* Burwarton (01746) 787203. *Club:* White's.

See also Lord Forbes.

BOYNE, Donald Arthur Colin Aydon, CBE 1977; Director, 1974–85, Consultant, 1984–86, The Architectural Press; *b* 15 Feb. 1921; 2nd *s* of late Lytton Leonard Boyne and Millicent (*née* Nisbet); *m* 1947, Rosemary Pater; two *s* one *d*. *Educ:* Tonbridge Sch.; Architectural Assoc. School of Architecture, 1943–47. Indian Army, 8/13 FF Rifles, 1940–43. Editor, Architects' Jl, 1953–70; Chm., Editorial Bd, Architectural Review and Architects' Jl, 1971–74. Hon. FRIBA 1969. *Address:* Pound House, Southover, Wells, Somerset BA5 1UH. *T:* Wells (01749) 674704.

BOYNE, Sir Henry Brian, (Sir Harry Boyne), Kt 1976; CBE 1969; Political Correspondent, The Daily Telegraph, London, 1956–76; *b* 29 July 1910; 2nd *s* of late Lockhart Alexander Boyne, Journalist, Inverness, and late Elizabeth Jane Mactavish; *m* 1935, Margaret Little Templeton, Dundee; one *d*. *Educ:* High Sch. and Royal Academy, Inverness. Reporter, Inverness Courier, 1927; Dundee Courier and Advertiser, 1929. On active service, 1939–45, retiring with rank of Major, The Black Watch (RHR). Staff Correspondent, Glasgow Herald, at Dundee, 1945, and Edinburgh, 1949; Political Correspondent, Glasgow Herald, 1950. Dir of Communications, Conservative Central Office, 1980–82. Chairman: Parly Lobby Journalists, 1958–59 (Hon. Sec., 1968–71); Parly Press Gallery, 1961–62. Political Writer of Year, 1972. Mem., Police Complaints Bd, 1977–80; Chm., Bd of Visitors, HM Prison, Pentonville, 1980. Mem. Council, Savers' Union, 1982–86. *Publications:* The Houses of Parliament, 1981; Scotland Rediscovered, 1986. *Recreations:* reading, walking, watching cricket. *Address:* 122 Harefield Road, Uxbridge UB8 1PN. *T:* Uxbridge (01895) 255211.

BOYNE, Maj.-Gen. John, CB 1987; MBE 1965; CEng, FIMechE; FIMgt; company director, since 1988; *b* 7 Nov. 1932; *s* of John Grant Boyne and Agnes Crawford (*née* Forrester); *m* 1956, Norma Beech; two *s*. *Educ:* King's Sch., Chester; Royal Military Coll. of Science, Shrivenham (BScEng 1st Cl. Hons). CEng, FIMechE 1975; FBIM 1975. Served in Egypt, Cyprus, Libya and UK, 1951–62; Staff Coll., Camberley, 1963; DAQMG(Ops) HQ MEC, Aden, 1964–66; OC 11 Infantry Workshop, REME, BAOR, 1966–67; Jt Services Staff Coll., 1968; GSO2 MoD, 1968–70; GSO1 (DS), Staff Coll., 1970–72; Comdr REME, 2nd Div., BAOR, 1972–73; AAG MoD, 1973–75; CSO (Personnel) to CPL, MoD, 1975–76; Dep. Dir Elec. and Mech. Engrg, 1st British Corps, 1976–78; RCDS, 1979; Dep. Dir Personal Services (Army), MoD, 1980–82; Vice Adjutant Gen. and Dir of Manning (Army), MoD, 1982–85; Dir Gen., Electrical and Mechanical Engrg, Logistic Executive (Army), MoD, 1985–88. Col Comdt, REME, 1988–93 (Rep. Col Comdt, 1989–90). Trustee, Army Benevolent Fund, 1986–. *Recreations:* music, philately, football. *Address:* c/o Midland Bank, 48 High Street, Runcorn, Cheshire WA7 1AN.

BOYNTON, Sir John (Keyworth), Kt 1979; MC 1944; LLB; MRTPI; DL; Chief Executive, Cheshire County Council, 1974–79; Solicitor; *b* 14 Feb. 1918; *s* of late Ernest Boynton, Hull; *m* 1st, 1947, Gabrielle Stanglmaier, Munich (*d* 1978); two *d*; 2nd, 1979, Edith Laane, The Hague. *Educ:* Dulwich Coll. Served War, 15th Scottish Reconnaissance Regt, 1940–46 (despatches, MC). Dep. Clerk, Berks CC, 1951–64; Clerk, Cheshire CC, 1964–74. Member: Planning Law Cttee of Law Soc., 1964–88; Economic Planning Council for NW, 1965; Exec. Council of Royal Inst. of Public Admin., 1970; Council of Industrial Soc., 1974–93; Council, PSI, 1978–83. Pres., RTPI, 1976. Election Commissioner, Southern Rhodesia, 1979–80. DL Cheshire 1975. *Publications:* Compulsory Purchase and Compensation, 1964, 7th edn 1994; Job at the Top, 1986. *Recreation:* golf. *Address:* 1B Oakhill Avenue, NW3 7RD. *T:* 0171–435 0012. *Club:* Army and Navy.

BOYS, Rt Hon. Michael H.; *see* Hardie Boys.

BOYS, Penelope Ann, (Mrs D. C. H. Wright); Head of Personnel, Department of Trade and Industry, since 1993; *b* 11 June 1947; *d* of late Hubert John Boys and of Mollie Blackman Boys; *m* 1977, David Charles Henshaw Wright. *Educ:* Guildford County Sch. for Girls. Exec. Officer, DES, 1966–69; Asst Principal, Min. of Power, 1969–72; Private Sec., Minister without Portfolio, 1972–73; Principal, Dept of Energy, 1973–78; seconded to BNOC, 1978–80; Head of Internat. Unit, Dept of Energy, 1981–85; seconded to HM Treasury as Head, ST2 Div., 1985–87; Dir of Personnel, Dept of Energy, 1987–89; Dep. Dir Gen., Office of Electricity Regulation, 1989–93. *Recreations:* entertaining, racing, music. *Address:* Department of Trade and Industry, 1 Palace Street, SW1E 5HE.

BOYS-GREENE, Jenny; *see* Greene, J.

BOYS-SMITH, Captain Humphry Gilbert, DSO 1940; DSC 1943; RD; RNR, retired; *b* 20 Dec. 1904; *s* of late Rev. Edward Percy Boys-Smith, MA, Rural Dean of Lyndhurst, Hants, and Charlotte Cecilia, *d* of late Thomas Backhouse Sandwith, CB, HM Consular Service; *m* 1935, Marjorie Helen (*d* 1981), *d* of Capt. Matthew John Miles Vicars-Miles, JP; no *c. Educ:* Pangbourne Nautical Coll. Joined Royal Naval Reserve, 1921; Merchant Navy, 1922–35; Extra Master's Certificate, 1930; HM Colonial Service, 1935–40 (Palestine) and 1946–50 (Western Pacific High Commission as Marine Supt); Addnl Mem. RNR Advisory Cttee, 1949–51; War Course, Royal Naval Coll., Greenwich, 1950–51. Courtaulds Ltd, Central Staff Dept, 1951–68. Placed on Retired List of RNR, 1952; Younger Brother of Trinity House, 1944; Mem. of Hon Company of Master Mariners, 1946; Assoc. Instn Naval Architects, 1948; served War of 1939–45 (DSO and Bar, DSC, despatches and American despatches). *Address:* Dibben's, Semley, Shaftesbury, Dorset SP7 9BW. *T:* East Knoyle (01747) 830358.

BOYS SMITH, Stephen Wynn; Under Secretary, HM Treasury, since 1992; *b* 4 May 1946; *s* of late Rev. Dr John Sandwith Boys Smith and Gwendolen Sara Boys Smith (*née* Wynn); *m* 1971, Linda Elaine Price; one *s* one *d. Educ:* Sherborne Sch.; St John's Coll., Cambridge (MA); Univ. of British Columbia (MA). Home Office, 1968; Asst Private Sec. to Home Sec., 1971–73; Central Policy Review Staff, Cabinet Office, 1977; Home Office, 1979; Private Sec. to Home Sec., 1980–81; NI Office, 1981; Principal Private Sec. to Sec. of State for NI, 1981–82; Home Office, 1984; Principal Private Sec. to Home Sec., 1985–87; Asst Under Sec. of State, Home Office, 1989–92. *Recreations:* gardening, reading. *Address:* HM Treasury, Parliament Street, SW1P 3AG. *T:* 0171–270 4400.

BOYSE, Prof. Edward Arthur, MD; FRS 1977; Distinguished Professor, University of Arizona, Tucson, 1989–94, now Emeritus Professor; Member, Sloan-Kettering Institute for Cancer Research, New York, 1967–89; Professor of Biology, Cornell University, 1969–89; *b* 11 Aug. 1923; *s* of late Arthur Boyse, FRCO, and Dorothy Vera Boyse (*née* Mellersh); *m* 1951, Jeanette (*née* Grimwood) (marr. diss. 1987); two *s* one *d*; *m* 1987, Judith Bard. *Educ:* St Bartholomew's Hosp. Med. Sch., Univ. of London. MB BS 1952; MD 1957. Aircrew, RAF, 1941–46, commnd 1943. Various hospital appts, 1952–57; research at Guy's Hosp., 1957–60; research appts at NY Univ. and Sloan-Kettering Inst., 1960–89. Amer. Cancer Soc. Res. Prof., 1977. Member: Amer. Acad. of Arts and Scis, 1977; Nat. Acad. of Scis, USA, 1979. Cancer Research Institute Award in Tumor Immunology, 1975; Isaac Adler Award, Rockefeller and Harvard Univs, 1976. *Publications:* papers relating genetics and immunology to development and cancer. *Address:* Department of Microbiology and Immunology, University of Arizona Health Sciences Center, 1501 N Campbell Avenue, Tucson, AZ 85724, USA.

BOYSON, Rt. Hon. Sir Rhodes, Kt 1987; PC 1987; MP (C) Brent North, since Feb. 1974; *b* 11 May 1925; *s* of Alderman William Boyson, MBE, JP and Mrs Bertha Boyson, Haslingden, Rossendale, Lancs; *m* 1st, 1946, Violet Burletson (marr. diss.); two *d*; 2nd, 1971, Florette MacFarlane. *Educ:* Haslingden Grammar Sch.; UC Cardiff; Manchester Univ. (BA, MA); LSE (PhD); Corpus Christi Coll., Cambridge. Served with Royal Navy. Headmaster: Lea Bank Secondary Modern Sch., Rossendale, 1955–61; Robert Montefiore Secondary Sch., Stepney, 1961–66; Highbury Grammar Sch., 1966–67; Highbury Grove Sch., 1967–74. Chm., Nat. Council for Educnl Standards, 1974–79. Chm., Churchill Press and Constitutional Book Club, 1969–79. Councillor: Haslingden, 1957–61; Waltham Forest, 1968–74 (Chm. Establishment Cttee, 1968–71); Chm., London Boroughs Management Services Unit, 1968–70. Formerly Youth Warden, Lancs Youth Clubs. Contested (C) Eccles, 1970. Vice-Chm., Cons Parly Educn Cttee, 1975–76; Hon. Sec. Cons. Adv. Cttee on Educn, 1975–78; Opposition spokesman on educn, 1976–79; Parly Under-Sec. of State, DES, 1979–83; Minister of State: for Social Security, DHSS, 1983–84; NI Office, 1984–86; for Local Govt, DoE, 1986–87. Mem. Exec., 1922 Cttee, 1987–. Non-exec. Dir, Black's Leisure, 1987–. Consultant, Arc International, 1987–. Educnl columnist, Spectator, 1969. *Publications:* The North-East Lancashire Poor Law 1838–1871, 1965; The Ashworth Cotton Enterprise, 1970; (ed) Right Turn, 1970; (ed) Down with the Poor, 1971; (ed) Goodbye to Nationalisation, 1972; (ed) Education: Threatened Standards, 1972; (ed) The Accountability of Schools, 1973; Oversubscribed: the story of Highbury Grove, 1974; Crisis in Education, 1975; (jt ed) Black Papers on Education, 1969–77; (ed) 1985: An Escape from Orwell's 1984, 1975; Centre Forward, 1978; Speaking My Mind (autobiog.), 1995. *Recreations:* reading, writing, talk, hard work, meeting friends, inciting the millenialistic Left in education and politics. *Address:* House of Commons, SW1A 0AA. *T:* 0171–219 4507; 71 Paines Lane, Pinner, Middx HA5 3BX. *T:* 0181–866 2071. *Clubs:* Carlton, St Stephen's; Churchill (N Wembley), Wembley Conservative.

BOZZOLI, Guerino Renzo, DSc(Eng); Chairman, New Era (non-racial) Schools Trust, 1981–91; Vice-Chancellor and Principal, University of the Witwatersrand, Johannesburg, 1969–77; *b* Pretoria, 24 April 1911; *s* of late B. Bozzoli; *m* 1936, Cora Collins, *d* of late L. N. B. Collins; one *s* three *d. Educ:* Sunnyside Sch. and Boys' High Sch., Pretoria; Witwatersrand Univ. BSc(Eng) 1933, DSc(Eng) 1948; PrEng. Major, SA Corps of Signals, 1940–45 (commendation 1944). Asst Engr, African Broadcasting Co., 1934–36; Jun. Lectr, Dept of Electrical Engrg, Witwatersrand Univ., Lectr, 1939, Sen. Lectr, 1942; apptd Prof. and Head of Dept of Electrical Engineering, 1948. Dean, Univ. Residence, Cottesloe, 1948–56; Dean, Faculty of Engrg, 1954–57 and 1962–65; Senate Mem., Council of the Univ., 1957–68; Deputy Vice-Chancellor, 1965–68. Chm. Council, Mangosuthu Technikon, Kwa Zulu, 1978–85. Member: Straszacker Commn of Enquiry into Univ. Educn of Engineers, 1957–68; de Vries Commn of Enquiry into SA Univs, 1968–75; Nat. Educn Council, 1975–. President: SAIEE, 1955; AS&TS of SA, 1969–70; SA Assoc. for Advancement of Science, 1972. Hon. FSAIEE; Hon. FRSSAf 1976. Hon. LLD: Univ. of Cape Town, 1977; Univ. of Witwatersrand, 1978. *Publications:* numerous articles and papers on engineering education. *Recreations:* swimming, woodwork, electronics. *Address:* 121 Dundalk Avenue, Parkview, Johannesburg, 2193, South Africa. *T:* Johannesburg (11) 6461015. *Clubs:* 1926, Scientific and Technical (Johannesburg).

BRABAZON, family name of **Earl of Meath.**

BRABAZON OF TARA, 3rd Baron *cr* 1942; **Ivon Anthony Moore-Brabazon;** DL; *b* 20 Dec. 1946; *s* of 2nd Baron Brabazon of Tara, CBE, and Henriette Mary (*d* 1985), *d* of late Sir Rowland Clegg; *S* father, 1974; *m* 1979, Harriet Frances, *o d* of Mervyn P. de Courcy Hamilton, Salisbury, Zimbabwe; one *s* one *d. Educ:* Harrow. Mem., Stock Exchange, 1972–84. A Lord in Waiting (Govt Whip), 1984–86; Parly Under-Sec. of State, Dept of Transport, 1986–89; Minister of State: FCO, 1989–90; Dept of Transport, 1990–92. Mem., RAC Public Policy Cttee, 1992–. Dep. Chm., Foundn for Sport and the Arts, 1992–. President: UK Warehousing Assoc., 1992–; Natural Gas Vehicles Assoc., 1994–. DL Isle of Wight, 1993. *Recreations:* sailing, Cresta Run. *Heir: s* Hon. Benjamin Ralph Moore-Brabazon, *b* 15 March 1983. *Address:* House of Lords, SW1A 0PW. *Clubs:* White's; Royal Yacht Squadron; Bembridge Sailing, St Moritz Tobogganing.

BRABHAM, Sir John Arthur, (Sir Jack Brabham), Kt 1979; OBE 1966; retired, 1970, as Professional Racing Driver; Managing Director: Jack Brabham (Motors) Ltd; Jack Brabham (Worcester Park) Ltd; Engine Developments Ltd; *b* Sydney, Australia, 2 April 1926; *m* 1951, Betty Evelyn; three *s. Educ:* Hurstville Technical Coll., Sydney. Served in RAAF, 1944–46. Started own engineering business, 1946; Midget Speedway racing, 1946–52; several championships (Australian, NSW, South Australian); numerous wins driving a Cooper-Bristol, Australia, 1953–54; to Europe, 1955; Australian Grand Prix, 1955 and 1963 (debut of Repco Brabham); World Champion Formula II, 1958, also many firsts including Casablanca, Goodwood, Brands Hatch, NZ Grand Prix, Belgian Grand Prix; Formula II Champion of France, 1964. World Champion Driver: (after first full Formula I Season with 2½-litre car), 1959–60, 1960–61, 1966. First in Monaco and British Grandes Epreuves, 1959; won Grand Prix of: Holland, Belgium, France, Britain, Portugal, Denmark, 1960; Belgium, 1961. Elected Driver of the Year by Guild of Motoring Writers, 1959, 1966 and 1970, Sportsman of the Year by Australian Broadcasting Co., 1959; left Cooper to take up building own Grand Prix cars, 1961; debut, 1962; first ever constructor/driver to score world championship points, 1963; cars finished first: French GP; Mexican GP, 1964; Formula II and Formula III cars world-wide success, 1963; awarded Ferodo Trophy, 1964 and again, 1966; won French Grand Prix and British Grand Prix, 1966; won French Grand Prix, 1967. RAC Gold Medal, 1966; BARC Gold Medal, 1959, 1966, 1967; Formula I Manufacturers' Championship, 1966, 1967. *Publications:* Jack Brabham's Book of Motor Racing, 1960; When the Flag Drops, 1971; contribs to British journals. *Recreations:* photography, water ski-ing, under-water swimming, flying. *Address:* 33–45 Central Road, Worcester Park, Surrey KT4 8EG. *Clubs:* Royal Automobile, British Racing and Sports Car, British Racing Drivers'; Australian Racing Drivers'.

BRABOURNE, 7th Baron, *cr* 1880; **John Ulick Knatchbull,** CBE 1993; Bt 1641; film and television producer; Director, Thames Television, since 1978 (Chairman, 1990–93); *b* 9 Nov. 1924; *s* of 5th Baron and Lady Doreen Geraldine Browne (Order of the Crown of India; DStJ) (*d* 1979), *y d* of 6th Marquess of Sligo; *S* brother, 1943; *m* 1946, Lady Patricia Edwina Victoria Mountbatten (*see* Countess Mountbatten of Burma); four *s* two *d* (and one *s* decd). *Educ:* Eton; Oxford. *Films produced:* Harry Black, 1958; Sink the Bismarck!, 1959; HMS Defiant, 1961; Othello, 1965; The Mikado, 1966; Romeo and Juliet; Up the Junction, 1967; Dance of Death, 1968; Tales of Beatrix Potter, 1971; Murder on the Orient Express, 1974; Death on the Nile, 1978; Stories from a Flying Trunk, 1979; The Mirror Crack'd, 1980; Evil Under the Sun, 1982; A Passage to India, 1984; Little Dorrit, 1987. TV Series: National Gallery, 1974; A Much-Maligned Monarch, 1976; Leontyne, 1987. Chm.: Copyright Promotions Gp, 1974–; Dir, Thorn EMI, 1981–86. Governor: BFI, 1979–94 (Fellow, 1985); National Film Sch., 1980–; Mem., British Screen Adv. Council, 1985–; Trustee: BAFTA, 1975–; Science Museum, 1984–94; Nat. Mus. of Photography, Film and Television, 1984–94. Pres., Kent Trust for Nature Conservation. Chairman of Governors: Norton Knatchbull Sch.; Wye Coll.; Gordonstoun Sch., 1964–94; United World Colleges; Pro-Chancellor, Univ. of Kent. *Heir: s* Lord Romsey, *qv. Address:* Newhouse, Mersham, Ashford, Kent TN25 6NQ. *T:* Ashford (01233) 503636, *Fax:* (01233) 502244; Mersham Productions Ltd, 41 Montpelier Walk, SW7 1JH. *T:* 0171–589 8829, *Fax:* 0171–584 0024.

BRACEGIRDLE, Dr Brian, FSA, FRPS, FIBiol; Research Consultant in microscopy, and Fellow, Science Museum, since 1990; *b* 31 May 1933; *o c* of Alfred Bracegirdle; *m* 1st, 1958, Margaret Lucy Merrett (marr. diss. 1974); one *d*; 2nd, 1975, Patricia Helen Miles; no *c. Educ:* King's Sch., Macclesfield; Univ. of London (BSc, PhD). DipRMS 1975. FRPS 1969; FBIPP (FIIP 1970); FIBiol 1976; FSA 1981. Technician in industry, 1950–57; Biology Master, Erith Grammar Sch., 1958–61; Sen. Lectr in Biol., S Katharine's Coll., London, 1961–64; Head, Depts of Nat. Science and Learning Resources, Coll. of All Saints, London, 1964–77; Science Museum: Keeper, Wellcome Mus. of Hist. of Medicine, 1977; Head of Dept of Med. Scis, and Head of Collections, Management Div., 1987–89; Asst Dir, 1987–89. Hon. Lectr in History of Medicine, UCL; Hon. Res. Fellow in Hist. of Sci., Imperial Coll., 1990–. Hon. Treasurer, ICOM (UK), 1978–89. Chm., Inst. of Medical and Biological Illustration, 1983–84; President: Assoc. Européenne de Musées de l'Histoire des Sciences Medicales, 1983–90; Quekett Microscopical Club, 1985–88; Vice-Pres., Royal Microscopical Soc., 1988–90. *Publications:* Photography for Books and Reports, 1970; The Archaeology of the Industrial Revolution, 1973; The Evolution of Microtechnique, 1978, 1987; (ed) Beads of Glass: Leeuwenhoek and the early microscope, 1984; Scientific Photomacrography, 1994; (with W. H. Freeman): An Atlas of Embryology, 1963, 1978; An Atlas of Histology, 1966; An Atlas of Invertebrate Structure, 1971; An Advanced Atlas of Histology, 1976; (with P. H. Miles): An Atlas of Plant Structure, vol. I, 1971; An Atlas of Plant Structure, Vol. II, 1973; Thomas Telford, 1973; The Darbys and the Ironbridge Gorge, 1974; An Atlas of Chordate Structure, 1977; (with J. B. McCormick) The Microscopic Photographs of J. B. Dancer, 1993; papers on photography for life sciences, on scientific topics, and on history of science/medicine. *Recreations:* walking, music, travel. *Address:* Cold Aston Lodge, Cold Aston, Cheltenham, Glos GL54 3BN. *T:* Cotswold (01451) 820181. *Club:* Athenæum.

BRACEWELL, Hon. Dame Joyanne (Winifred), (Dame Joyanne Copeland), DBE 1990; **Hon. Mrs Justice Bracewell;** a Judge of the High Court of Justice, Family Division, since 1990; *b* 5 July 1934; *d* of Jack and Lilian Bracewell; *m* 1963, Roy Copeland; one *s* one *d. Educ:* Manchester Univ. (LLB, LLM). Called to Bar, Gray's Inn, 1955; pupillage at the Bar, 1955–56; Mem., Northern Circuit, 1956–; a Recorder of the Crown Court, 1975–83; QC 1978; a Circuit Judge, 1983–90. Family Div. Liaison Judge for London, 1990–. Chm., Children Act Adv. Cttee, 1993–. Consulting Editor: Butterworth's Family Law Service, 1989–; Family Practice, 1993–. FRSA 1994. Hon. LLD Manchester, 1991. *Recreations:* antiques, cooking, reading, walking, wildlife conservation. *Address:* Royal Courts of Justice, Strand, WC2A 2LL.

BRACEWELL-SMITH, Sir Charles, 4th Bt *cr* 1947, of Keighley; *b* 13 Oct. 1955; *s* of Sir George Bracewell Smith, 2nd Bt, MBE, and Helene Marie (*d* 1975), *d* of late John Frederick Hydock, Philadelphia, USA; *S* brother, 1983; *m* 1977, Carol Vivien Hough (*d* 1994). Founder, Homestead Charitable Trust. KM. *Publication:* On the Song of the Saints. *Recreations:* mysticism, theology, philosphy, psychology. *Heir:* none. *Address:* The Hermitage, 7 Clarence Gate Gardens, Glentworth Street, NW1 6AY. *Clubs:* Royal Automobile, Arsenal Football.

BRACK, Terence John, CB 1994; Assistant Under-Secretary of State (General Finance), Ministry of Defence, 1989–94; *b* 17 April 1938; *s* of Noël D. J. Brack and late Tertia Brack; *m* 1983, Christine Mary, *d* of late Douglas and Evelyn Cashin. *Educ:* Bradfield Coll., Berkshire; Caius Coll., Cambridge Univ. (BA Hist. (1st cl. Hons), MA). Pilot Officer, Secretarial Br., RAF, 1956–58. Entered Air Ministry, subseq MoD, 1961; Private Sec. to Parly Under-Sec. of State for Defence (RAF), 1964–66; Principal, 1966; seconded to HM Treasury, 1968–72; Asst Sec., 1973; Head, Finance and Sec. Div. for Controller of the Navy, 1975–78; Head, Defence Secretariat Div. for Equipment Requirements, 1978–81; RCDS, 1982; Head, Finance and Sec. Div. (Air Launched Guided Weapons and Electronics), 1983–84; Asst Under-Sec. of State (Naval Personnel), 1985–89. Vice-Chm., Management Bd, Royal Hosp. Sch., Holbrook, 1985–89. *Recreations:* walking, travel, family history projects.

BRACKENBURY, Ven. Michael Palmer; Archdeacon of Lincoln, 1988–95, now Emeritus; *b* 6 July 1930; *s* of Frank Brackenbury and Constance Mary (*née* Palmer); *m* 1953, Jean Margaret, *d* of Oscar Arnold Harrison and May (*née* Norton). *Educ:* Norwich School; Lincoln Theological Coll. ACII 1956. RAF, 1948–50. Asst Curate, South Ormsby Group, 1966–69; Rector of Sudbrooke with Scothern, 1969–77; RD of Lawres, 1973–78; Diocesan Dir of Ordinands, Lincoln, 1977–87; Personal Assistant to Bishop of Lincoln, 1977–88; Canon and Prebendary of Lincoln, 1979–95; Diocesan Lay Ministry Adviser, Lincoln, 1986–87. Mem., Gen. Synod of C of E, 1989–95. *Recreations:* music, reading, travel. *Address:* 2 Ashfield Road, Sleaford, Lincs NG34 7DZ.

BRADBEER, Sir (John) Derek (Richardson), Kt 1988; OBE 1973; TD 1965; DL; Partner, Wilkinson Maughan (formerly Wilkinson Marshall Clayton & Gibson), since 1961; President of the Law Society, 1987–88; *b* 29 Oct. 1931; *s* of late William Bertram Bradbeer and Winifred (*née* Richardson); *m* 1962, Margaret Elizabeth Chantler; one *s* one *d*. *Educ:* Canford Sch.; Sidney Sussex Coll., Cambridge (MA). Nat. Service, 2nd Lieut RA, 1951–52; TA, 1952–77: Lt-Col Comdg 101 (N) Med. Regt RA(V), 1970–73; Col, Dep. Comdr 21 and 23 Artillery Bdes, 1973–76; Hon. Col, 101 (N) Field Regt, RA(V), 1986–91. Admitted Solicitor, 1959. Mem., Criminal Injuries Compensation Bd, 1988–. Mem. Council, 1973–, Vice-Pres., 1986–87, Law Soc.; Pres., Newcastle upon Tyne Incorp. Law Soc., 1982–83; Gov., Coll. of Law, 1983– (Chm., 1990–). Director: Newcastle and Gateshead Water plc, 1978–; Sunderland and Shields Water plc, 1990–; Dir and Chm., R. B. Bolton (Mining Engrs), 1990–; Chm., North East Water, 1992–. UK Pres., Union Internationale des Grocats, 1988–. Chm., N of England TA&VRA, 1990– (Vice-Chm., 1988–90). DL Tyne and Wear, 1988. *Recreations:* reading, gardening, sport. *Address:* Forge Cottage, Shilvington, Ponteland, Newcastle upon Tyne NE20 0AP. *T:* Whalton (0167075) 214. *Clubs:* Army and Navy; Northern Counties (Newcastle upon Tyne).

BRADBURN, John; Chief Registrar of the High Court of Justice in Bankruptcy, 1984–88; Registrar of the Companies Court and Clerk of the Restrictive Practices Court, 1980–88; *b* 4 April 1915; *s* of Harold and Fanny Louise Bradburn; *m* 1948, Irène Elizabeth Norman, JP, *yr d* of Denham Grindley and Bertha Norman; two *s*. *Educ:* Repton; Trinity Coll., Oxford (MA). Served War, 1939–46; Oxfordshire and Bucks LI; Major. Called to the Bar, Inner Temple, 1939; practised at Chancery Bar, Lincoln's Inn, 1946–79 (Bencher, 1972–); a Conveyancing Counsel of the Supreme Court, 1977–80; Lord Chancellor's Legal Visitor, Ct of Protection, 1980–83. Mem., Gen. Council of the Bar, 1962–66. *Recreation:* freemasonry. *Address:* West Mews, 11 Calcot Court, Calcot Park, Reading, Berks RG3 5RW. *T:* Reading (01734) 425418. *Club:* MCC.

BRADBURY, family name of **Baron Bradbury.**

BRADBURY, 3rd Baron *cr* 1925, of Winsford, Co. Chester; **John Bradbury;** *b* 17 March 1940; *s* of 2nd Baron Bradbury and of his 1st wife, Joan, *o d* of W. D. Knight; *S* father, 1994; *m* 1968, Susan, *d* of late W. Liddiard; two *s*. *Educ:* Gresham's Sch.; Univ. of Bristol. *Heir: s* Hon. John Bradbury, *b* 16 Jan. 1973. *Address:* 10 Clifton Hill, NW8 0QG.

BRADBURY, Anita Jean, (Mrs Philip Bradbury); *see* Pollack, A. J.

BRADBURY, Anthony Vincent; His Honour Judge Bradbury; a Circuit Judge, since 1992; *b* 29 Sept. 1941; *s* of late Alfred Charles Bradbury, OBE and of Noreen Vincent Bradbury; *m* 1966, Rosalie Anne Buttrey; one *d*. *Educ:* Kent College, Canterbury; Univ. of Birmingham (Sir Henry Barber Law Scholar; LLB). Solicitor 1965; Principal, Bradbury & Co., 1970–81; Registrar, then Dist Judge, Ilford County Court, 1981–91; Dist Judge, Chelmsford County Court, 1991–92; a Recorder of the Crown Court, 1990. Chm., SE Circuit Gp of Registrars and Dist Judges, 1988–91. Wandsworth Mem., GLC and ILEA, 1967–70. Chm., Clapham Cons. Assoc., 1966–67. Contested (C): N Battersea, 1970; S Battersea, Feb. 1974. Chm. of Govs, Putney Coll. for Further Educn, 1968–75. *Publications:* contribs to Wisden Cricketers' Almanack and to cricketing periodicals. *Recreations:* walking, watching cricket, writing for pleasure. *Address:* c/o Chelmsford Court Administrator's Office, Steeple House, Church Lane, Chelmsford CM1 1NH. *Clubs:* MCC; Yorkshire CC.

BRADBURY, Edgar; Managing Director, Skelmersdale Development Corporation, 1976–85; *b* 5 June 1927; *s* of Edgar Furniss Bradbury and Mary Bradbury; *m* 1954, Janet Mary Bouchier Lisle; two *s* one *d*. *Educ:* Grove Park Sch., Wrexham; The High Sch., Newcastle, Staffs; King's Coll., Durham Univ. LLB (Hons). Solicitor. Asst Solicitor: Scarborough BC, 1952–54; St Helens CBC, 1954–57; Dep. Town Clerk, Loughborough, 1957–59; Town Clerk and Clerk of the Peace, Deal, 1960–63; Legal Dir, Skelmersdale Develt Corp., 1963–76. Vice-Chm., W Lancs Health Authority, 1984–94 (Mem., 1982–94). *Recreations:* tennis, bridge. *Address:* Overdale, 24 Granville Park, Aughton, Ormskirk, Lancs L39 5DU. *T:* Aughton Green (01695) 422308.

BRADBURY, Surgeon Vice-Adm. Sir Eric (Blackburn), KBE 1971; CB 1968; FRCS 1972; Medical Director-General of the Navy, 1969–72; Chairman, Tunbridge Wells District Health Authority, 1981–84; *b* 2 March 1911; *s* of late A. B. Bradbury, Maze, Co. Antrim; *m* 1939, Elizabeth Constance Austin (*d* 1991); three *d*. *Educ:* Royal Belfast Academical Instn; Queen's Univ., Belfast; MB, BCh 1934; DMRD (London) 1949; Hon. LLD 1973. Joined RN (Medical Service), 1934; served at sea in HMS Barham, HMS Endeavour, HMS Cumberland, 1935–38 and in HMS Charybdis and HMHS Oxfordshire, 1941–45; served in RN Hospitals: Haslar, Chatham, Plymouth and Malta; Med. Officer-in-Charge, RN Hosp., Haslar, and Comd MO, Portsmouth, 1966–69. QHP 1966–72. *Address:* 3 Lions Hall, St Swithun Street, Winchester, Hants SO23 9HW.

BRADBURY, Prof. Malcolm Stanley, CBE 1991; FRSL; Emeritus Professor, University of East Anglia, since 1995 (Professor of American Studies, 1970–94; Professorial Fellow, 1994–95); *b* 7 Sept. 1932; *s* of Arthur Bradbury and Doris Ethel (*née* Marshall); *m* 1959, Elizabeth Salt; two *s*. *Educ:* University Coll. of Leicester (BA); Queen Mary Coll., Univ. of London (MA; Hon. Fellow, 1984); Univ. of Manchester (PhD). Staff Tutor in Literature and Drama, Dept of Adult Education, Univ. of Hull, 1959–61; Lectr in English Language and Literature, Dept of English, Univ. of Birmingham, 1961–65; Lectr (later Sen. Lectr and Reader) in English and American Literature, Sch. of English and American Studies, Univ. of East Anglia, 1965–70. Visiting Professor: Univ. of Zürich, 1972; Washington Univ., St Louis, 1982; Univ. of Queensland, 1983; Sen. Vis. Res. Fellow, St John's Coll., Oxford, 1994. Chm. of Judges, Booker McConnell Prize for Fiction, 1981. Hon. DLitt: Leicester, 1986; Birmingham, 1989. Editor: Arnold Stratford-upon-Avon Studies series; Methuen Contemporary Writers series. Adapted for television: Tom Sharpe, Blott on the Landscape, 1985; Tom Sharpe, Porterhouse Blue, 1987 (Internat. Emmy Award); Alison Lurie, Imaginary Friends, 1987; Kingsley Amis, The Green Man, 1990; Stella Gibbons, Cold Comfort Farm, 1995; television serials: Anything More Would Be Greedy, 1989; The Gravy Train, 1990; The Gravy Train Goes East, 1991. *Publications: non-fiction:* Evelyn Waugh, 1962; E. M. Forster: a collection of critical essays (ed), 1965; What is a Novel?, 1969; A Passage to India: a casebook, 1970; (ed) Penguin Companion to Literature, vol. 3: American (with E. Mottram), 1971; The Social Context of Modern English Literature, 1972; Possibilities: essays on the state of the novel, 1973; (with J. W. McFarlane) Modernism, 1976; (ed) The Novel Today, 1977; (ed) An Introduction to American Studies (with H. Temperley), 1981; Saul Bellow, 1982; All Dressed Up And Nowhere To Go (humour), 1982; The Modern American Novel, 1983; Why Come to Slaka? (humour), 1986; No, Not Bloomsbury (essays), 1987; (ed) Penguin Book of Modern British Short Stories, 1987; Mensonge (humour), 1987; The Modern World: ten great writers, 1987; Unsent Letters (humour), 1988; (with R. Ruland) From Puritanism to Postmodernism: a history of American literature, 1991; (ed with Judy Cooke) New Writing, 1992; (ed with Andrew Motion) New Writing 2, 1993; The Modern British Novel, 1993; Present Laughter: an anthology of modern comic fiction, 1994; Dangerous Pilgrimages: transatlantic mythologies and the novel, 1995; Class Work (anthology of UEA fiction), 1995; *fiction:* Eating People is Wrong, 1959; Stepping Westward, 1965; The History Man, 1975; Who Do You Think You Are? (short stories), 1976; The After Dinner Game (television plays), 1982; Rates of Exchange, 1982 (shortlisted, Booker Prize); Cuts: a very short novel, 1987; Dr Criminale, 1992. *Recreations:* none. *Address:* School of English and American Studies, University of East Anglia, Norwich NR4 7TJ. *T:* Norwich (01603) 56161.

BRADBURY, Ray Douglas; author; *b* Waukegan, Ill, USA, 22 Aug. 1920; *s* of Leonard S. Bradbury and Esther Moberg; *m* 1947, Marguerite Susan McClure; four *d*. *Educ:* Los Angeles High Sch. First Science-Fiction stories, 1941–44; stories sold to Harpers', Mademoiselle, The New Yorker, etc., 1945–56. Stories selected for: Best American Short Stories, 1946, 1948, 1952, 1958; O. Henry Prize Stories, 1947, 1948; and for inclusion in numerous anthologies. *Screenplays:* Moby Dick, 1954; Icarus Montgolfier Wright, 1961; The Martian Chronicles, 1964; The Picasso Summer, 1968; The Halloween Tree, 1968; The Dreamers; And The Rock Cried Out. Benjamin Franklin Award for Best Story Published in an Amer. Magazine of General Circulation, 1954; 1000 dollar Grant from Inst. of Arts and Letters, 1954. *Publications: novels:* Dark Carnival, 1947; Fahrenheit 451, 1953 (filmed); (for children) Switch on the Night, 1955; Dandelion Wine, 1957; Something Wicked This Way Comes, 1962 (filmed 1983; adapted for stage, 1986); The Small Assassin, 1973; Mars and the Minds of Man, 1973; The Mummies of Guanajuato, 1978; The Ghosts of Forever, 1981; Death is a Lonely Business, 1986; The Toynbee Convector, 1989; A Graveyard for Lunatics, 1990; *short stories:* The Martian Chronicles, 1950 (English edn, The Silver Locusts, 1957); The Illustrated Man, 1951 (filmed with The Day It Rained Forever); The Golden Apples of the Sun, 1953; The October Country, 1955; A Medicine for Melancholy (English edn, The Day It Rained Forever), 1959; (for children) R Is For Rocket, 1962; (for children) S Is For Space, 1962; The Machineries of Joy, 1964; The Autumn People, 1965; The Vintage Bradbury, 1965; Tomorrow Midnight, 1966; Twice Twenty-Two, 1966; I Sing the Body Electric!, 1969; Long After Midnight, 1976; *general:* Zen and the Art of Writing, 1973; *poems:* When Elephants Last in the Dooryard Bloomed, 1973; Where Robot Mice and Robot Men Run Round in Robot Towns, 1977; This Attic where the Meadow Greens, 1980; The Haunted Computer and the Android Pope, 1981; *plays:* The Meadow, 1947; The Anthem Sprinters (one-act), 1963; The World of Ray Bradbury (one-act), 1964; The Wonderful Ice Cream Suit and Other Plays (one-act), 1965; Any Friend of Nicholas Nickleby's is a Friend of Mine, 1968; Pillar of Fire, 1975. *Recreations:* oil painting, ceramics, collecting native masks. *Address:* 10265 Cheviot Drive, Los Angeles, CA 90064, USA.

BRADBURY, Rear-Adm. Thomas Henry, CB 1979; *b* 4 Dec. 1922; *s* of Thomas Henry Bradbury and Violet Buckingham; *m* 1st, 1945, Beryl Doreen Evans (marr. diss. 1979; she *d* 1985); one *s* one *d*; 2nd, 1979, Sarah Catherine, *d* of Harley Hillier and Mrs Susan Hillier. *Educ:* Christ's Hosp. CO HMS Jufair, 1960–62; Supply Officer, HMS Hermes, 1965–67; Sec. to Controller of Navy, MoD, 1967–70; CO HMS Terror, 1970–71; RCDS, 1972; Dir, Naval Admin. Planning, MoD, 1974–76; Flag Officer, Admiralty Interview Bd, 1977–79. Gp Personnel Dir, Inchcape Gp of Cos, 1979–86; Gp Personnel Exec., Davy Corp., 1987–91. Non-exec. Dir, Eastbourne HA, 1990–93. *Recreation:* gardening in Sussex and Andalucia. *Address:* Padgham Down, Dallington, Heathfield, E Sussex TN21 9NS. *T:* Rushlake Green (01435) 830208; Las Colmenillas, Gaucin, Andalucia.

BRADBY, Prof. David Henry, PhD; Professor of Drama and Theatre Studies, University of London, at Royal Holloway (formerly Royal Holloway and Bedford New College), since 1988; *b* 27 Feb. 1942; *s* of Edward Lawrence Bradby, *qv*; *m* 1965, Rachel Anderson, writer; three *s* one *d*. *Educ:* Rugby Sch.; Trinity College, Oxford (MA); PhD Glasgow; CertEd Bristol. Lectr, Glasgow Univ., 1966–70; University of Kent at Canterbury: Lectr, 1971; Sen. Lectr, 1979–85; Reader in French Theatre Studies, 1985–88; Prof. of Theatre Studies, Univ. of Caen, 1983–84. Dir, Orange Tree Theatre, Richmond. FRSA. *Publications:* People's Theatre (with John McCormick), 1978; The Theatre of Roger Planchon, 1984; Modern French Drama 1940–1980, 1984, 2nd edn, as Modern French Drama 1940–1990, 1991; (with David Williams) Directors' Theatre, 1988; Le Théâtre Français Contemporain, 1990; The Theatre of Michael Vinaver, 1993. *Recreation:* forestry. *Address:* Department of Drama and Theatre Studies, Royal Holloway, University of London, Egham, Surrey TW20 0EX.

BRADBY, Edward Lawrence; Principal, St Paul's College, Cheltenham, 1949–72; *b* 15 March 1907; *y s* of late H. C. Bradby, Ringshall End, near Berkhamsted, Herts; *m* 1939, Bertha Woodall, *y d* of late Henry Woodall, Yotes Court, Mereworth, Maidstone; three *s* one *d*. *Educ:* Rugby Sch.; New College, Oxford (MA). Asst Master, Merchant Taylors' Sch., 1930–34; International Student Service, 1934–39; Secretary to Cttee for England and Wales, 1934–36; Asst General Secretary, Geneva, 1936–37; General Secretary, Geneva, 1937–39; Principal, Royal Coll., Colombo, Ceylon, 1939–46; Principal, Eastbourne Emergency Training Coll., 1946–49. Hon. MEd Bristol, 1972. *Publications:* Editor, The University Outside Europe, a collection of essays on university institutions in 14 countries, 1939; Seend, a Wiltshire Village Past and Present, 1981; The Book of Devizes, 1985; Seend Heritage, 1985. *Address:* 13 Hansford Square, Combe Down, Bath, Avon BA2 5LH. *T:* Bath (01225) 834092. *Club:* Commonwealth Trust.
See also D. H. Bradby.

BRADEN, Hugh Reginald, CMG 1980; DL; Mayor of Worthing, 1991–92; *b* 30 Jan. 1923; *s* of late Reginald Henry Braden and Mabel Braden (*née* Selby); *m* 1946, Phyllis Grace Barnes; one *d*. *Educ:* Worthing High School for Boys; Brighton College of Technology. Joined War Office, 1939; served War, Royal Navy, 1942–45; Far East Land Forces, 1946–50; British Army of the Rhine, 1953–56; War Office and Min. of Defence, 1956–66; jssc 1967; British Embassy, Washington, 1968–70; Min. of Defence, 1971–80 (Asst Under Sec. of State, 1978–80). Dir, A. B. Jay, 1981–90. Borough Councillor, Worthing, 1983–95; Chm., Worthing Cons. Assoc., 1992–95. DL W Sussex, 1993. *Address:* Field House, Honeysuckle Lane, High Salvington, Worthing, West Sussex BN13 3BT. *T:* Worthing (01903) 60203.

BRADFIELD, John Richard Grenfell, CBE 1986; PhD; Senior Bursar, Trinity College, Cambridge, 1956–92; Founder, and Manager, Cambridge Science Park, 1970–92; *b* 20 May 1925; *s* of Horace and Ada Bradfield; *m* 1951, Jane Wood; one *s*. *Educ:* Trinity Coll.,

Cambridge (schol. 1942; MA, PhD). Research Fellow in Cell Biology, Trinity Coll., Cambridge, 1947; Commonwealth (Harkness) Fellow, Chicago, 1948; Jun. Bursar, Trinity Coll., Cambridge, 1951. Director: Cambridge Water Co., 1965–; Cambridge Building Soc., 1968–; Biotechnology Investments, 1989–; Anglian Water, 1989–93 (Bd Mem., 1975–89); Chm., Abbotstone Agricl Property Unit Trust, 1975–. Chairman: Addenbrooke's NHS Trust, 1993–; Commn for the New Towns, 1995–. Darwin College, Cambridge: proposed foundn, 1963; Hon. Fellow, 1973. Hon. LLD Cambridge, 1992. FRSA 1990. *Publications:* scientific papers on cell biology. *Recreations:* walking, arboretum-visiting. *Address:* Trinity College, Cambridge CB2 1TQ. *T:* Cambridge (01223) 338400.

BRADFORD, 7th Earl of, *cr* 1815; **Richard Thomas Orlando Bridgeman;** Bt 1660; Baron Bradford, 1794; Viscount Newport, 1815; *b* 3 Oct. 1947; *s* of 6th Earl of Bradford, TD, and Mary Willoughby (*d* 1986), *er d* of Lt-Col T. H. Montgomery, DSO; *S* father, 1981; *m* 1979, Joanne Elizabeth, *d* of B. Miller; three *s* one *d. Educ:* Harrow; Trinity College, Cambridge. Owner of Porters Restaurant of Covent Garden. *Publications:* (compiled) My Private Parts and the Stuffed Parrot, 1984; The Eccentric Cookbook, 1985; Stately Secrets, 1994. *Heir: s* Viscount Newport, *qv. Address:* Woodlands House, Weston-under-Lizard, Shifnal, Salop TF11 8PX. *T:* (office) Weston-under-Lizard (01952) 850201; Weston Park, Shifnal, Salop TF11 8LE.

BRADFORD, Bishop of, since 1992; **Rt. Rev. David James Smith;** *b* 14 July 1935; *s* of Stanley James and Gwendolen Emie Smith; *m* 1961, Mary Hunter Moult; one *s* one *d. Educ:* Hertford Grammar School; King's College, London (AKC). Assistant Curate: All Saints, Gosforth, 1959–62; St Francis, High Heaton, 1962–64; Long Benton, 1964–68; Vicar: Longhirst with Hebron, 1968–75; St Mary, Monkseaton, 1975–81; Felton, 1982–83; Archdeacon of Lindisfarne, 1981–87; Bishop Suffragan of Maidstone, 1987–92; Bishop to the Forces, 1990–92. *Recreations:* fell walking, reading novels. *Address:* Bishopscroft, Ashwell Road, Bradford, West Yorkshire BD9 4AU. *T:* Bradford (01274) 545414.

BRADFORD, Archdeacon of; *see* Shreeve, Ven. D. H.

BRADFORD, Provost of; *see* Richardson, Very Rev. J. S.

BRADFORD, (Sir) Edward Alexander Slade, 5th Bt, *cr* 1902 (but does not use the title); *b* 18 June 1952; *s* of Major Sir Edward Montagu Andrew Bradford, 3rd Bt (*d* 1952) and his 2nd wife, Marjorie Edith (*née* Bere); *S* half-brother, Sir John Ridley Evelyn Bradford, 4th Bt, 1954. *Heir: uncle* Donald Clifton Bradford [*b* 22 May 1914; *m* 1949, Constance Mary Morgan; three *d*].

BRADFORD, Prof. Eric Watts, MDS (Sheffield); DDSc (St Andrews); Professor of Dental Surgery, 1959–85, now Emeritus, and Pro-Vice-Chancellor, 1983–85, University of Bristol; *b* 4 Nov. 1919; *e s* of E. J. G. and C. M. Bradford; *m* 1946, Norah Mary Longmuir; two *s* three *d. Educ:* King Edward VII Sch., Sheffield; High Storrs Grammar Sch., Sheffield; Univ. of Sheffield (Robert Styring Scholar). LDS, Sheffield, 1943; BDS, Sheffield, 1944; MDS, Sheffield, 1950; DDSc St Andrews, 1954. Lieut, Army Dental Corps, Nov. 1944; Capt. Nov. 1945. Lectr, Univ. of Sheffield, 1947–52; Senior Lectr, Univ. of St Andrews, 1952–59; Dean, Faculty of Medicine, Bristol University, 1975–79. Mem., Gen. Dental Council, 1979–85. *Publications:* many papers on dental anatomy in British and other journals. *Address:* 9 Cedar Court, Glenavon Park, Sneyd Park, Bristol BS9 1RL. *T:* Bristol (0117) 968 1849.

BRADFORD, Rt Hon. Roy Hamilton, PC (NI) 1969; Member (U) for East Belfast, Northern Ireland Assembly, 1973–75; Minister for the Environment, Northern Ireland Executive, 1974; Mayor of North Down; *b* 7 July 1921; *s* of Joseph Hamilton Bradford, Rockcorry, Co. Monaghan, and Isabel Mary (*née* McNamee), Donemana, Co. Tyrone; *m* 1946, Hazel Elizabeth, *d* of Capt. W. Lindsay, Belfast; two *s. Educ:* Royal Belfast Academical Institution; Trinity Coll., Dublin. Foundation Schol. 1940; First Class Hons (BA) German and French (with Gold Medal) 1942 (TCD). Army Intelligence, 1943–47 (France, Belgium, Germany). BBC and ITV Producer and Writer, 1950–. Dir, Geoffrey Sharp Ltd, 1962–. MP (U) for Victoria, Parlt of NI, 1965–73; Asst Whip (Unionist Party), 1966; Parly Sec., Min. of Educn, 1967; Chief Whip, Sept. 1968–April 1969; Minister of Commerce, NI, 1969–71; Minister of Develt, NI, 1971–72. Contested (Off U) North Down, 1974. Pres., NI European Movt, 1987–. *Publications:* Excelsior (novel), 1960; The Last Ditch (novel), 1981; Rogue Warrior of the SAS: the Life of Lt-Col R. B. "Paddy" Mayne, DSO, 1987. *Recreations:* golf, architecture. *Address:* Ardkeen, Carnalea, Bangor, Co. Down, N Ireland BT19 1EY. *T:* Bangor (01247) 465012. *Club:* Royal and Ancient Golf (St Andrews).

BRADING, Dr David Anthony, FBA 1995; Reader in Latin American History, University of Cambridge, since 1992; *b* 26 Aug. 1936; *s* of Ernest Arthur Brading and Amy Mary (*née* Driscol); *m* 1966, Celia Wu; one *s. Educ:* Pembroke Coll., Cambridge (BA; LittD 1991); UCL (PhD 1965). Asst. Prof., Univ. of Calif, Berkeley, 1965–71; Associate Prof., Yale Univ., 1971–73; University Lectr, Univ. of Cambridge, 1973–92. Hon. Prof., Univ. of Lima, 1993. *Publications:* Miners and Merchants in Bourbon Mexico, 1971; Haciendas and Ranchos in the Mexican Bajío, 1979; The Origins of Mexican Nationalism, 1985; The First America, 1991; Church and State in Bourbon Mexico, 1994. *Recreations:* music, walking. *Address:* 28 Storey's Way, Cambridge CB3 0DT. *T:* Cambridge (01223) 352098. *Club:* United Oxford & Cambridge University.

BRADING, Keith, CB 1974; MBE 1944; Chief Registrar of Friendly Societies and Industrial Assurance Commissioner, 1972–81; *b* 23 Aug. 1917; *s* of late Frederick C. Brading and late Lilian P. Brading (*née* Courtney); *m* 1949, Mary Blanche Robinson, *d* of late William C. and Blanche Robinson. *Educ:* Portsmouth Grammar Sch. Called to Bar, Gray's Inn, 1950. Entered Inland Revenue (Estate Duty Office), 1936. Served War, Royal Navy, 1941–46 (Lieut RNVR); Solicitor's Office, Inland Revenue, 1950; Asst Solicitor, 1962; Asst Registrar of Friendly Societies and Dep. Industrial Assurance Commissioner, 1969. Vice-President: CBSI, 1981–; Bldg Socs Assoc., 1982–. Pres., Soc. for Co-operative Studies, 1983–. Chairman: Kensington Housing Trust, 1987–92 (Vice Chm., 1992–); UK Co-operative Council, 1991–92 (Hon. Pres., 1992–). FRSA 1986. *Publications:* contrib. Halsbury's Laws of England and Atkins Court Forms and Precedents. *Address:* 35 Chiswick Staithe, W4 3TP. *T:* 0181–995 0517. *Club:* Savile.

BRADLEY, Anna Louise; Director, Institute for the Study of Drug Dependence Ltd, since 1993; *b* 29 July 1957; *d* of Donald Bradley and Angela Lucy Bradley (*née* Bradley, now Ratcliffe); partner, 1980, Norman Howard Jones; one *s* one *d. Educ:* Camden Sch. for Girls; Warwick Univ. (BA Phil, 1978; MBA 1994). Sen. Sub-Editor, Marshall Cavendish Partworks Ltd, 1978–82; Consumers' Association: Sen. Project Leader, 1982–87; Project Manager, Food and Health, 1987–88; Head, Food and Health, 1988–91; Dep. Research Dir, 1991–93. Jt Asst Sec., All Party Drugs Misuse Gp, 1994–. Mem., Mgt Cttee, Patients' Assoc., 1985–88. *Publications:* Healthy Eating, 1989; (ed) Understanding Additives, 1988; acad. and research papers in Lancet, Jl Human Nutrition, Dietetics, etc. *Address:* 87 Torbay Road, NW6 7DT. *T:* (office) 0171–928 1211.

BRADLEY, Anthony Wilfred; barrister and legal author; *b* 6 Feb. 1934; *s* of David and Olive Bradley (*née* Bonsey); *m* 1959, Kathleen Bryce; one *s* three *d. Educ:* Dover Grammar Sch.; Emmanuel Coll., Cambridge (BA 1957, LLB 1958, MA 1961). Solicitor of the Supreme Court, 1960 (Clifford's Inn Prize); called to the Bar, Inner Temple, 1989. Asst Lectr, 1960–64, Lectr, 1964–68, Cambridge, and Fellow of Trinity Hall, 1960–68; Prof. of Constitutional Law, 1968–89, Dean, Faculty of Law, 1979–82, Prof. Emeritus, 1990, Univ. of Edinburgh. Vis. Reader in Law, UC, Dar es Salaam, 1966–67; Vis. Prof. of Public Law, Univ. of Florence, 1984. Chairman: Edinburgh Council for Single Homeless, 1984–88; Social Security Appeal Tribunal, 1984–89; Sub-Cttee on Police Powers, ESRC, 1985–89; Member: Wolfenden Cttee on Voluntary Orgns, 1974–78; Social Scis and Law Cttee, SSRC, 1975–79; Social Studies Sub-Cttee, UGC, 1985–89; Cttee of Inquiry into Local Govt in Scotland, 1980; Cttee to review local govt in Islands of Scotland, 1983–84. Ed., Public Law, 1986–92. Hon. LLD Staffordshire, 1993. *Publications:* (with M. Adler) Justice, Discretion and Poverty, 1976; (with D. J. Christie) The Scotland Act 1978, 1979; (ed) Wade and Bradley, Constitutional and Administrative Law, 9th edn 1978, to 11th edn (ed with K. D. Ewing), 1993; Administrative Law (in Stair Meml Encyc. of the Laws of Scotland), 1987; (with J. S. Bell) Governmental Liability, 1991; articles in legal jls. *Recreation:* music. *Address:* Cloisters, 1 Pump Court, Temple, EC4Y 7AA. *T:* 0171–583 0303; 19 Grosvenor Road, Richmond, Surrey TW10 6PE. *T:* 0181–948 3127.

BRADLEY, Averil Olive, (Mrs J. W. P. Bradley); *see* Mansfield, A. O.

BRADLEY, Prof. Benjamin Arthur de Burgh, PhD; FRCPath; Director, University of Bristol Department of Transplantation Sciences, since 1992; *b* 17 Sept. 1942; *s* of Reuben Stephen Bradley and Elsie Marjorie Bradley (*née* Burke); *m* 1968, Anne White; four *d. Educ:* Silcoates Sch., Wakefield; Bilston Grammar Sch.; Birmingham Univ. Med. Sch. (MB ChB 1965); Birmingham Univ. (MSc 1967; PhD 1970). FRCPath 1986 (MRCPath 1974). House surgeon and house physician, United Birmingham Hosps, 1965–66; MRC Res. Fellow, Dept of Surgery and Exptl Pathology, Univ. of Birmingham, 1967–70; Asst Dir of Res., Dept of Surgery, Univ. of Cambridge, 1970–75; Asst Prof., Dept of Immunhaematology, Univ. of Leiden, 1975–79; Dir, UK Transplant Service, 1979–92. Member: Scientific Policy Adv. Cttee, Nat. Inst. for Biol Standards, 1991–; Bd, Jenner Educnl Trust, 1992–; Scientific Cttee, Foundn for Nephrology, 1992–. Med. Dir, British Bone Marrow Donor Appeal, 1992–. Chm., Editl Bd, European Jl Immunogenetics, 1989–. Hon. MA Cantab, 1974. *Publications:* (with S. M. Gore) Renal Transplantation: sense and sensitization, 1986; Editor and contributor to annual reports of: UK Transplant Service, 1979–90; Transplantation Services and Statistics in UK and Eire, 1991; contrib. textbooks and med. jls on clinical organ and tissue transplantation and immunology and genetics of transplantation. *Recreations:* competitive sailing, guitar, vacations with my family. *Address:* East Barn, The Pound, Lower Almondsbury, Bristol BS12 4EF; University of Bristol Department of Transplantation Sciences, Southmead Health Services, Westbury-on-Trym, Bristol BS10 5NB. *T:* Bristol (0117) 959 5340, *Fax:* (0117) 950 6277. *Club:* Royal Society of Medicine.

BRADLEY, Sir Burton Gyrth B.; *see* Burton-Bradley.

BRADLEY, Dr (Charles) Clive; Managing Director, Sharp Laboratories of Europe Ltd, since 1990; *b* 11 April 1937; *s* of late Charles William Bradley and Winifred Smith; *m* 1965, Vivien Audrey Godley; one *s* one *d. Educ:* Longton High Sch.; Birmingham Univ. (BSc Hons in Physics, 1958); Emmanuel Coll., Cambridge (PhD 1962). Nat. Phys. Lab., 1961–67; MIT, USA, 1967, 1969; Nat. Bureau of Standards, USA, 1968; Nat. Phys. Lab., 1969–75; DoI, 1975–82, SPSO and Head of Energy Unit, 1978–82; Counsellor (Science and Technology), British Embassy, Tokyo, 1982–88; Head of Secretariat, ACOST, Cabinet Office, 1988–90. Dep. Comr Gen. for Britain, Sci. Expo Tokyo, 1985. Mem., Oxford Univ. Adv. Council on Continuing Educn, 1993–. A. F. Bulgin Prize, IERE, 1972. *Publications:* High Pressure Methods in Solid State Research, 1969; contribs to jls on lasers, metals and semiconductors. *Recreations:* tennis, gardening. *Address:* Sharp Laboratories of Europe Ltd, Edmund Halley Road, Oxford Science Park, Oxford OX4 4GA. *Club:* Athenæum.

BRADLEY, (Charles) Stuart, CBE 1990; Managing Director, Associated British Ports, 1988–95; Chairman, Red Funnel Group, since 1989; Director, Associated British Ports Holdings, since 1988; *b* 11 Jan. 1936; *s* of Captain Charles Bradley, OBE and Amelia Jane Bradley; *m* 1959, Kathleen Marina (*née* Loraine); one *s* one *d* (and one *s* decd). *Educ:* Penarth County Sch.; University Coll. Southampton (Warsash). Master Mariner, 1961; FCIT 1978. Deck Officer, P&OSN Co., 1952–64; joined British Transport Docks Bd, subseq. Associated British Ports, 1964; Dock and Harbour Master, Silloth, 1968–70; Dock Master, 1970–74, Dock and Marine Superintendent, 1974–76, Plymouth; Docks Manager, Lowestoft, 1976–78; Port Manager, Barry, 1978–80; Dep. Port Manager, 1980–85, Port Manager, 1985–87, Hull; Asst Man. Dir (Resources), 1987–88. Younger Brother, Trinity House, 1994–. *Recreations:* Welsh Rugby football, cycling, walking, theatre. *Address:* c/o 150 Holborn, EC1N 2LR. *T:* 0171–430 1177. *Clubs:* Oriental, Honourable Company of Master Mariners; Cardiff Athletic.

BRADLEY, Clive; *see* Bradley, Charles C.

BRADLEY, Clive; Chief Executive, The Publishers Association (incorporating Book Development Council, Educational Publishers Council and Council of Academic and Professional Publishers), since 1976; Director, Confederation of Information Communication Industries, since 1984; *b* 25 July 1934; *s* of late Alfred and Kathleen Bradley. *Educ:* Felsted Sch., Essex; Clare Coll., Cambridge (Scholar; MA); Yale Univ. (Mellon Fellow). Called to the Bar, Middle Temple. Current Affairs Producer, BBC, 1961–63; Broadcasting Officer, Labour Party, 1963–64; Political Editor, The Statist, 1965–67; Gp Labour Adviser, IPC, 1967–69; Dep. Gen. Man., Daily and Sunday Mirror, 1969–71; Controller of Admin, IPC Newspapers, 1971–72; i/c IPC local radio applications, 1972–73; Dir i/c new prodn arrangements, The Observer, 1973–75. Dep. Chairman: Central London Valuation Tribunal; Member: Gen. Assembly, Organising Cttee, World Congress on Books, London, 1982; PA delegns to USSR, China, Australia/NZ, Southern Africa and Canada; IPA Congresses, Stockholm, 1980, Mexico City, 1984, London (also host), 1988, New Delhi, 1992. Governor, Felsted Sch. Contested (Lab) S Kensington, by-election, March 1968. *Publications:* Which Way?, 1970; (ed) The Future of the Book, 1982; articles on politics, economics, the press, television, industrial relations. *Recreations:* reading, travel. *Address:* 8 Northumberland Place, Richmond, Surrey TW10 6TS. *T:* 0181–940 7172; 19 Bedford Square, WC1B 3HJ. *T:* 0171–580 6321. *Clubs:* Reform, Groucho; Elizabethan (Yale).

BRADLEY, Prof. Daniel Joseph, PhD; FRS 1976; FInstP; Professor of Optical Electronics, Trinity College Dublin, since 1980; Emeritus Professor of Optics, London University, 1980; *b* 18 Jan. 1928; *s* of late John Columba Bradley and Margaret Mary Bradley; *m* 1958, Winefride Marie Therese O'Connor; four *s* one *d. Educ:* St Columb's Coll., Derry; St Mary's Trng Coll., Belfast; Birkbeck and Royal Holloway Colls, London (BSc Maths, BSc Physics, PhD). Primary Sch. Teacher, Derry, 1947–53; Secondary Sch. Teacher, London area, 1953–57; Asst Lectr, Royal Holloway Coll., 1957–60; Lectr, Imperial Coll. of Science and Technol., 1960–64; Reader, Royal Holloway Coll., 1964–66; Prof. and Head of Dept of Pure and Applied Physics, QUB, 1966–73; Prof. of Optics, 1973–80, and Head of Physics Dept, 1976–80, Imperial Coll., London. Vis.

Scientist, MIT, 1965; Consultant, Harvard Observatory, 1966. Lectures: Scott, Cambridge, 1977; Tolansky Meml, RSA, 1977. Chairman: Laser Facility Cttee, SRC, 1976–79; British Nat. Cttee for Physics, 1979–80; Quantum Electronics Commn, IUPAP, 1982–85; Member: Rutherford Lab. Estab. Cttee, SRC, 1977–79; Science Bd, SRC, 1977–80; Council, Royal Soc., 1979–80. Gov., Sch. of Cosmic Physics, DIAS, 1981–. MRIA 1969; Fellow, Optical Soc. of America, 1975. Hon. DSc: NUU, 1983; QUB, 1986. Thomas Young Medal, Inst. of Physics, 1975; Royal Medal, Royal Soc., 1983; C. H. Townes Award, Optical Soc. of America, 1989. *Publications:* papers on optics, lasers, spectroscopy, chronoscopy and astronomy in Proc. Roy. Soc., Phil. Mag., Phys. Rev., J. Opt. Soc. Amer., Proc. IEEE, Chem. Phys. Letts, Optics Communications. *Recreations:* television, walking, DIY. *Address:* Trinity College, Dublin 2, Ireland. *T:* Dublin (1) 6772941.

BRADLEY, Prof. David John, DM; FRCP; FRCPath; FFPHM; FIBiol; Professor of Tropical Hygiene, University of London and Director, Ross Institute, since 1974; *b* 12 Jan. 1937; *s* of late Harold Robert and of Mona Bradley; *m* 1961, Lorne Marie (marr. diss. 1989), *d* of late Major L. G. Farquhar and Marie Farquhar; two *s* two *d. Educ:* Wyggeston Sch., Leicester; Selwyn Coll., Cambridge (Scholar); University Coll. Hosp. Med. Sch. (Atchison Schol., Magrath Schol., Trotter Medal in Surgery, Liston Gold Medal in Surgery, BA Nat. Scis Tripos, Med. Scis and Zoology, 1st cl. Hons, Frank Smart Prize Zool.; MB, BChir, MA 1960); DM Oxon 1972. FIBiol 1974; FFPHM (FFCM 1979); FRCPath 1981; FRCP 1985. Med. Res. Officer, Ross Inst. Bilharzia Res. Unit, Tanzania, 1961–64; Lectr, 1964–66, Sen. Lectr, 1966–69, Makerere Univ. of East Africa, Uganda; Trop. Res. Fellow of Royal Soc., Sir William Dunn Sch. of Pathology, Oxford, 1969–73; Sen. Res. Fellow, Staines Med. Fellow, Exeter Coll., Oxford, 1971–74; Clinical Reader in Path., Oxford Clinical Med. Sch., 1973–74; Chm., Div. of Communicable and Tropical Diseases, LSHTM, 1982–88. Vis. Prof., Univ. of Wales Coll. of Medicine, 1994–. Co-Director, Malaria Ref. Lab., PHLS, 1974–; Hon. Specialist Community Physician, N Thames (formerly NW Thames and NE Thames) RHA, 1974–; Hon. Consultant in Trop. and Communicable Diseases, Bloomsbury DHA, 1983–; Dir, WHO Collaborating Centre Envtl Control of Vectors, 1983–; Mem., Bd of Trustees, Internat. Centre for Diarrhoeal Disease Res., Bangladesh, 1979–85 (Chm., 1982–83); Consultant Advisor to Dir, Royal Tropical Inst., Amsterdam, 1980–90; Advr, Indep. Internat. Commn on Health Res.; Res. Advr to Dean, LSHTM, 1989–; Member: WHO Expert Adv. Panel on Parasitic Diseases, 1972–; Tech. Adv. Gp, Diarrhoea Programme, 1979–85; Panel of Experts on Envtl Management, 1981–; External Review Gp on Trop. Diseases Programme, 1987; Task Force on Health Res. for Develt, 1991–93; Chm., Rev. Cttee, Swiss Tropical Inst., 1994–. For. Corresp. Mem., Royal Belgian Acad. of Medicine, 1984; Corresp. Mem., German Tropenmediziningesellschaft, 1980; Hon. FIWEM (Hon. FIPHE, 1981). Editor, Jl of Trop. Med. and Hygiene, 1981–. Chalmers Medal, RSTM&H, 1980. *Publications:* (with G. F. and A. U. White) Drawers of Water, 1972; (with O. V. Baroyan) Problems and Perspectives in Tropical Diseases (in Russian), 1979; (with E. E. Sabben-Clare and B. Kirkwood) Health in Tropical Africa during the Colonial Period, 1980; (with R. G. Feachem, D. D. Mara and H. Garelick) Sanitation and Disease, 1983; (jtly) Travel Medicine, 1989; (jtly) The Impact of Development Policies on Health, 1990; papers in learned jls. *Recreations:* natural history, landscape gardens, travel. *Address:* Ross Institute, London School of Hygiene and Tropical Medicine, Keppel Street, WC1E 7HT. *T:* 0171–927 2216; 11 Selwyn House, Lansdowne Terrace, WC1N 1DJ. *T:* 0171–278 3918.

BRADLEY, David Rice; Chief Executive, London Borough of Havering, since 1990; *b* 9 Jan. 1938; *s* of George Leonard Bradley and Evelyn Annie Bradley; *m* 1962, Josephine Elizabeth Turnbull Fricker (*née* Harries); two *s. Educ:* Christ Coll., Brecon; St Catharine's Coll., Cambridge (Exhibnr; MA English); Edinburgh Univ. (Dip. in Applied Linguistics). Nat. service commn, S Wales Borderers. British Council: served: Dacca, 1962–65; Allahabad, 1966–69; New Delhi, 1969–70; Dir of Studies, British Inst., Madrid, 1970–73; Department of the Environment: Principal, Res. Admin, 1973–76; Planning, Develt Control, 1976–78; Inner Cities, 1978–79; Rayner Study (develt of Management Inf. System for Ministers), 1979–80; Central Policy Planning Unit, 1980–81; Study of Local Govt Finance (Grade 5), 1981–82; on special leave, Gwilym Gibbon Res. Fellow, Nuffield Coll., Oxford, 1982–83; Finance, Envmtl Servs, 1983–86; London Urban Develt, sponsorship of LDDC, 1986–88; Dir (G3) Merseyside Task Force, DoE, 1988–90. Vis. Fellow, Nuffield Coll., Oxford, 1993. *Recreation:* gardening. *Address:* 27 Clare Lawn Avenue, SW14 8BE. *T:* 0181–876 2232.

BRADLEY, Prof. Donald Charlton, CChem, FRSC; FRS 1980; Professor of Inorganic Chemistry, 1965–87, and Head of Chemistry Department, 1978–82, Fellow, 1988, Queen Mary College, University of London; Emeritus Professor, University of London, since 1988; *b* 7 Nov. 1924; *m* 1st, 1948, Constance Joy Hazeldean (*d* 1985); one *s*; 2nd, 1990, Ann Levy (*née* MacDonald). *Educ:* Hove County School for Boys; Birkbeck Coll., Univ. of London (BSc 1st Cl. Hons Chemistry, PhD, DSc). Research Asst, British Electrical and Allied Industries Research Assoc., 1941–47; Asst Lectr in Chemistry, 1949–52, Lectr in Chemistry, 1952–59, Birkbeck Coll.; Prof. of Chemistry, Univ. of Western Ontario, Canada, 1959–64. Univ. of London: Chm., Bd of Studies in Chemistry and Chemical Industries, 1977–79; Mem. Senate, 1981–87. MRI 1979 (Mem. Council, 1987–93; Hon. Sec., 1988–93); Royal Society of Chemistry: Pres. Dalton Div., 1983–85; Ludwig Mond Lectr. Exec. Editor, Polyhedron, 1982–. FRSA 1982. *Publications:* (jtly) Metal Alkoxides, 1978; numerous pubns on synthesis and structure of metallo-organic compounds, co-ordination chemistry and inorganic polymers, mainly in Jl of Chemical Soc. *Recreations:* travelling, listening to music; amateur interest in archaeology. *Address:* Department of Chemistry, Queen Mary and Westfield College, Mile End Road, E1 4NS. *T:* 0171–975 5025.

BRADLEY, Edgar Leonard, OBE 1979; Metropolitan Stipendiary Magistrate, 1967–83; *b* 17 Nov. 1917; 2nd *s* of Ernest Henry and Letitia Bradley, W Felton, Oswestry; *m* 1942, Elsa, *o d* of Colin and Elizabeth Matheson, Edinburgh; two *s* three *d. Educ:* Malvern Coll.; Trinity Hall, Cambridge. BA 1939; MA 1944. Called to Bar, Middle Temple, 1940. Served 1940–46, RA; Capt. and Adjt, 1943–45; Major, GSO2, Mil. Govt of Germany, 1946. Practised at Bar, 1946–51, SE Circuit, Central Criminal Ct, S London and Surrey Sessions. Legal Dept of Home Office, 1951–54. Sec., Departmental Cttee on Magistrates' Courts Bill, 1952; Sec. of Magistrates' Courts Rule Cttee, 1952–54; Clerk to Justices: Wrexham and Bromfield, 1954–57; Poole, 1957–67. Justices' Clerks Society: Mem. Council, 1957–67; Hon. Sec., 1963–67. Mem., Nat. Adv. Council on Trng of Magistrates, 1965–67; Magistrates' Association: Vice Pres., 1984–; Mem. Council, 1968–84; Chm. Legal Cttee, 1973–82. Adv. tour of Magistrates' Courts in Ghana, 1970. *Publications:* (with J. J. Senior) Bail in Magistrates' Courts, 1977; articles in legal jls. *Recreations:* golf, music. *Address:* 55 St Germains, Bearsden, Glasgow G61 2RS. *T:* 0141-942 5831. *Clubs:* Army and Navy; Buchanan Castle Golf (Glasgow).

BRADLEY, Keith John Charles; MP (Lab) Manchester, Withington, since 1987; *b* 17 May 1950; *m*; one *s* one *d. Educ:* Manchester Polytechnic (BA Hons); York Univ. (MPhil). Former health service administrator, North West RHA. Mem., Manchester City Council, 1983–88. Opposition junior spokesman on social security, 1991–. Joined Labour Party, 1973; Mem., Manchester Withington Co-op Party. Member: MSF; COHSE. *Address:* House of Commons, SW1A 0AA. *T:* 0171–219 5124; 12 Meadow Bank, Chorltonville, Manchester M21 8FP. *T:* (constituency office) 0161-446 2047.

BRADLEY, Michael John, CMG 1990; QC (Cayman Islands) 1983; Law Revision Commissioner for the Cayman Islands, since 1994; *b* 11 June 1933; *s* of late Joseph Bradley and Catherine Bradley (*née* Cleary); *m* 1965, Patricia Elizabeth Macauley, MBE; one *s. Educ:* St Malachy's Coll., Belfast; Queen's Univ., Belfast (LLB Hons). Solicitor, Law Soc. of NI, 1964; Attorney, Supreme Ct, Turks and Caicos Is, 1980; Barrister-at-law, Eastern Caribbean Supreme Ct, 1982. Solicitor, NI, 1964–67; State Counsel, Malawi, 1967–69; Volume Editor, Halsbury's Laws, 1970; Sen., later Chief, Parly Draftsman, Botswana, 1970–72; UN Legal Advr to Govt of Antigua, 1973–76; Reg. Legal Draftsman to Govts of E Caribbean, British Develt Div. in the Caribbean, FCO, 1976–82; Attorney General: British Virgin Is, 1977–78; Turks and Caicos Is, 1980; Montserrat, 1981; Cayman Is, 1982–87; Gov., Turks and Caicos Is, 1987–93. British Dependent Territories Law Reform and Law Revision Consultant, 1993. *Recreations:* reading, philately, travel, good wine. *Address:* 25 Springfield, Bradford-on-Avon, Wilts BA15 1BA. *T:* and *Fax:* Bradford-on-Avon (01225) 865852; c/o Law Revision Commission, PO Box 907, Grand Cayman, Cayman Islands, West Indies. *T:* 9498047, *Fax:* 9475925. *Clubs:* Commonwealth Trust, Civil Service, Royal Over-Seas League.

BRADLEY, Maj.-Gen. Peter Edward Moore, CB 1968; CBE 1964 (OBE 1955); DSO 1946; Trustee, Vindolanda Trust, 1982–85 (Secretary, 1975–82); *b* 12 Dec. 1914; *s* of late Col Edward de Winton Herbert Bradley, CBE, DSO, MC, DL; *m* Margaret, *d* of late Norman Wardhaugh of Haydon Bridge, Northumberland; three *s. Educ:* Marlborough; Royal Military Academy, Woolwich. 2nd Lieut, Royal Signals, 1934. Served War of 1939–45; India, Middle East, Italy and North West Europe (DSO 6th Airborne Div.). Lieut-Col 1954; Col 1957; Brig. 1962; Maj.-Gen. 1965; Signal Officer in Chief (Army), Ministry of Defence, 1965–67; Chief of Staff to C-in-C Allied Forces Northern Europe, Oslo, 1968–70, retired. Dunlop Ltd, 1970–75. Col Comdt, Royal Signals, 1967–82, Master of Signals, 1970–82; Col Gurkha Signals, 1967–74. CEng, FIEE, 1966; FIMgt (FBIM 1970). *Address:* c/o RHQ Royal Signals, 56 Regency Street, SW1P 4AD.

BRADLEY, Richard Alan; Headmaster, Rivers Country Day School, Massachusetts, USA, 1981–91, retired; *b* 6 Oct. 1925; *s* of late Reginald Livingstone Bradley, CBE, MC, and of Phyllis Mary Richardson; *m* 1971, Mary Ann Vicary; one *s* two *d* by previous marriage. *Educ:* Marlborough Coll.; Trinity Coll., Oxford (Scholar). 2nd cl. hons Mod. History. Royal Marines, 1944–46; Oxford, 1946–48; Club Manager, Oxford and Bermondsey Club, 1949. Asst Master: Dulwich Coll., 1949–50; Tonbridge Sch., 1950–66 (Head of History Dept, 1957–66; Housemaster of Ferox Hall, 1961–66); Warden of St Edward's Sch., Oxford, 1966–71; Headmaster, Ridley Coll., Canada, 1971–81. *Recreations:* games, dramatics, mountains. *Address:* 10 Carver Hill, South Natick, MA 01760, USA. *Club:* Vincent's (Oxford).

BRADLEY, Prof. Richard John, FSA, FSAScot; FBA 1995; Professor of Archaeology, Reading University, since 1987; *b* 18 Nov. 1946; *s* of John Newsum Bradley and Margaret Bradley (*née* Saul); *m* 1976, Katherine Bowden. *Educ:* Portsmouth Grammar Sch.; Magdalen Coll., Oxford (MA). MIFA. Lectr in Archaeology, 1971–84, Reader, 1984–87, Reading Univ. Mem., Royal Commn on Historical Monuments of England, 1987–. *Publications:* (with A. Ellison) Rams Hill: a Bronze Age Defended Enclosure and its Landscape, 1975; The Prehistoric Settlement of Britain, 1978; (ed with J. Barrett) Settlement and Society in the British Later Bronze Age, 1980; The Social Foundations of Prehistoric Britain, 1984; (ed with J. Gardiner) Neolithic Studies, 1984; (with J. Barrett) Landscape, Monuments and Society, 1990; The Passage of Arms: an archæological analysis of prehistoric hoards and votive deposits, 1990; (ed with J. Barrett and M. Hall) Papers on the Prehistoric Archaeology of Cranborne Chase, 1991; Altering the Earth: the origins of monuments in Britain and Continental Europe, 1993; (with M. Edmonds) Interpreting the Axe Trade: production and exchange in Neolithic Britain, 1993; (jtly) Prehistoric Land Divisions on Salisbury Plain: the work of the Wessex Linear Ditches Project, 1994; contribs to learned jls. *Recreations:* literature, twentieth century music, watercolours, secondhand bookshops. *Address:* Department of Archaeology, The University, Whiteknights, Reading RG6 2AA. *T:* Reading (01734) 318130.

BRADLEY, Roger Thubron, FICFor; FIWSc; Head of Forestry Authority, Forestry Commission, since 1992; *b* 5 July 1936; *s* of Ivor Lewis Bradley and Elizabeth Thubron; *m* 1959, Ailsa Mary Walkden; one *s* one *d. Educ:* Lancaster Royal Grammar Sch.; St Peter's Coll., Oxford (MA). FICFor 1980; FIWSc 1985. Asst District Officer, Kendal, 1960; Mensuration Officer, Alice Holt, 1961; Working Plans Officer, 1967; District Officer, North Argyll, 1970; Asst Conservator, South Wales, 1974; Conservator, North Wales, 1977; Forestry Commission: Dir, and Sen. Officer for Wales, 1982–83; Dir, Harvesting and Marketing, Edinburgh, 1983–85; Forestry Comr, 1985–. Chm., Commonwealth Forestry Assoc., 1988–90. *Publications:* Forest Management Tables, 1966, 2nd edn 1971; Forest Planning, 1967; Thinning Control in British Forestry, 1967, 2nd edn 1971; various articles in Forestry, etc. *Recreation:* sailing. *Clubs:* Commonwealth Trust, Royal Over-Seas League.

BRADLEY, Stanley Walter; business consultant, since 1988; Director, W. Hart & Son (Saffron Walden) Ltd, since 1991; Director General, British Printing Industries Federation, 1983–88; *b* 9 Sept. 1927; *s* of Walter Bradley; *m* 1955, Jean Brewster; three *s* one *d. Educ:* Boys' British Sch., Saffron Walden. Joined Spicers Ltd, 1948: held posts in prodn, marketing and gen. management; Personnel Dir, 1973–83; Dir, Capital Spicers Ltd, Eire, 1971–83. Dir, Harman Gp, 1988–91. Chm., BPIF Manufg Stationery Industry Gp, 1977–81; Pres., E Anglian Printing Industries Alliance, 1978–79; Mem., Printing Industries Sector Working Party, 1979–87, Chm., Communications Action Team, 1980–85, NEDC. *Recreations:* painting, golf, fishing. *Address:* Dale House, Hogs Lane, Chrishall, Royston, Herts SG8 8RB. *T:* Royston (01763) 838820.

BRADLEY, Stuart; *see* Bradley, C. S.

BRADLEY, Thomas George; Director, British Section, European League for Economic Co-operation, 1979–91; *b* 13 April 1926; *s* of George Henry Bradley, Kettering; *m* 1953, Joy, *d* of George Starmer, Kettering; two *s. Educ:* Kettering Central Sch., Northants. Elected to Northants County Council, 1952, County Alderman, 1961; Mem., Kettering Borough Council, 1957–61. Transport Salaried Staffs' Association: Branch Officer, 1946–58; Mem. Exec. Cttee, 1958–77; Treasurer, 1961–64; Pres., 1964–77; Acting Gen. Sec., 1976–77. MP Leicester NE, July 1962–1974, Leicester E, 1974–83 (Lab, 1962–81, SDP, 1981–83); PPS: to Minister of Aviation, 1964–65; to Home Secretary, 1966–67; to Chancellor of the Exchequer, 1967–70; Chm., Select Cttee on Transport, 1979–83. Vice-Chm., Labour Party, 1974–75, Chm., 1975–76; Mem., Labour Party NEC, 1966–81. Contested: (Lab) Rutland and Stamford, 1950, 1951 and 1955; (Lab) Preston S, 1959; (SDP) Leicester E, 1983. *Address:* The Orchard, 111 London Road, Kettering, Northants NN15 7PH. *T:* Kettering (01536) 513019.

BRADLEY, William Ewart; Special Commissioner of Income Tax, 1950–75; *b* 5 Sept. 1910; *s* of W. E. Bradley, Durham City; *m* 1949, Mary Campbell Tyre; two *s*. *Educ:* Johnston Sch., Durham; LSE, London Univ. Inland Revenue, 1929–50. *Address:* 45 Spottiswoode Gardens, St Andrews, Fife KY16 8SB. *T:* St Andrews (01334) 476907.

BRADLEY GOODMAN, Michael; *see* Goodman, M. B.

BRADMAN, Sir Donald (George), AC 1979; Kt 1949; President of South Australian Cricket Association, 1965–73; Chairman, Australian Cricket Board, 1960–63 and 1969–72; *b* Cootamundra, NSW, 27 Aug. 1908; *s* of George and Emily Bradman; *m* 1932, Jessie, *d* of James Menzies, Mittagong, NSW; one *s* one *d*. *Educ:* Bowral Intermediate High Sch. Played for NSW 1927–34; for S Australia, 1935–49; for Australia 1928–48, Capt. 1936–48; records include: highest aggregate and greatest number of centuries in England *v* Australia test matches; highest score for Australia *v* England in test matches (334 at Leeds, 1930). Formerly stock and share broker and Mem. Stock Exchange of Adelaide Ltd. *Publications:* Don Bradman's Book, 1930; How to Play Cricket, 1935; My Cricketing Life, 1938; Farewell to Cricket, 1950, repr. 1988; The Art of Cricket, 1958; The Bradman Albums, 1988; *relevant publications:* Bradman: The Great, by B. J. Wakley, 1959; Sir Donald Bradman, by Irving Rosenwater, 1978; Bradman—The Illustrated Biography, by Michael Page, 1983. *Recreations:* cricket, golf, tennis, billiards, squash. *Address:* 2 Holden Street, Kensington Park, SA 5068, Australia. *Clubs:* MCC (Hon. Life Mem. and Hon. Life Vice-Pres.); Commerce (Adelaide).

BRADMAN, Godfrey Michael; Chairman: European Land and Property Corporation plc, since 1992; European Land and Property Investments Co., since 1993; Ashpest Finance Ltd, since 1993; Pondbridge Europe Ltd, since 1994; *b* 9 Sept. 1936; *s* of William Isadore Bradman and Anne Brenda Bradman (*née* Goldsweig); *m* 1975, Susan Clayton Bennett; two *s* three *d*. FCA 1961. Sen. Partner, Godfrey Bradman and Co. (Chartered Accountants), 1961; Chm. and Chief Exec., London Mercantile Corp. (Bankers), 1969; Chairman: Rosehaugh plc, 1979–91; Joint Chairman: Victoria Quay Ltd, 1993–; Welbeck Land and European Property Co., 1994–; Meco Investments Pondbridge Co., 1994–. Founder, CLEAR (Campaign for Lead-Free Air) Ltd, 1981–91; Jt Founder, 1983, and Pres., Campaign for Freedom of Information; Citizen Action, 1983–91 (Dir, AIDS Policy Unit, 1987–90); Chm., Friends of the Earth Trust, 1983–91; Council Mem., UN Internat. Year of Shelter for the Homeless, 1987; Pres., Soc. for the Protection of Unborn Children Educnl Res. Trust, 1987–. Founder of self-build housing schemes for unemployed and people on low incomes, 1987. Mem. governing body, LSHTM, 1988–91. *Recreations:* his children, reading, horseriding. *Address:* 15 Hanover Terrace, NW1 4RJ.

BRADNEY, John Robert; HM Diplomatic Service, retired; Oman Government Service, 1986–89; *b* 24 July 1931; *s* of Rev. Samuel Bradney, Canon Emeritus of St Alban's Abbey, and Constance Bradney (*née* Partington); *m* 1st, Jean Marion Halls (marr. diss. 1971); one *s* two *d*; 2nd, 1974, Sandra Cherry Smith, *d* of Richard Arthur Amyus Smith, MC. *Educ:* Christ's Hospital. HM Forces, 1949–51, Herts Regt and RWAFF; Colonial Police, Nigeria, 1953–65 (Chief Superintendent); HM Diplomatic Service, 1965; First Sec., Lagos, 1974; FCO, 1977–86 (Counsellor, 1985). DSM Oman, 1989. *Recreations:* salmon and trout fishing, gardening, ornithology. *Address:* Barclays Bank PLC, Penrith, Cumbria CA11 7YB. *Club:* Royal Over-Seas League.

BRADSHAW, Prof. Anthony David, PhD; FRS 1982; FIBiol; Holbrook Gaskell Professor of Botany, University of Liverpool, 1968–88, now Emeritus; *b* 17 Jan. 1926; *m* Betty Margaret Bradshaw; three *d*. *Educ:* St Paul's Sch., Hammersmith; Jesus Coll., Cambridge (BA 1947; MA 1951); PhD Wales 1959. FIBiol 1971. Lectr, 1952–63, Sen. Lectr, 1963–64, Reader in Agricl Botany, 1964–68, UCNW, Bangor. Member: Nature Conservancy Council, 1969–78; Natural Environment Res. Council, 1969–74; Bd of Management, Sports Turf Res. Inst., 1976– (Vice Pres., 1982–). President: British Ecological Soc., 1981–83; Inst. Ecology and Envmtl Management, 1991–94. Trustee, Nat. Museums and Galls on Merseyside, 1986–. Hon. Fellow, Indian Nat. Acad. Sci., 1990. FLS 1982; FIEEM 1994 (MIEEM 1991). *Publications:* (ed jtly) Teaching Genetics, 1963; (with M. J. Chadwick) The Restoration of Land, 1980; (with others) Quarry Reclamation, 1982; (with others) Mine Wastes Reclamation, 1982; (with R. A. Dutton) Land Reclamation in Cities, 1982; (with Alison Burt) Transforming our Waste Land: the way forward, 1986; (ed jtly) Ecology and Design in Landscape, 1986; (ed jtly) The Treatment and Handling of Wastes, 1992; (with B. Hunt and T. J. Walmsley) Trees in the Urban Landscape, 1995; contribs to symposia and learned jls. *Recreations:* sailing, gardening, appreciating land. *Address:* 60 Knowsley Road, Liverpool L19 0PG.

BRADSHAW, Sir Kenneth (Anthony), KCB 1986 (CB 1982); Administrator, Compton Verney Opera and Ballet Project (formerly Compton Verney Opera Project), since 1988; *b* 1 Sept. 1922; *s* of late Herbert and Gladys Bradshaw. *Educ:* Ampleforth Coll.; St Catharine's Coll., Cambridge (1st Cl. Hons History); MA 1947. War Service, 1942–45; served with Royal Ulster Rifles (2nd Bn), NW Europe (despatches). Temp. Asst Principal, Min. of Supply, Oct.–Dec. 1946; a Clerk in the House of Commons, 1947–87; seconded as Clerk of the Saskatchewan Legislature, 1966 session; Clerk of Overseas Office, 1972–76; Clerk of the House of Commons, 1983–87. Pres., Assoc. of Secs Gen. of Parls, IPU, 1986–87 (Jt Sec., 1955–71; Vice-Pres., 1984–86). *Publication:* (with David Pring) Parliament and Congress, 1972, new edn 1982. *Club:* Garrick.

BRADSHAW, Martin Clark; Director, Civic Trust, since 1987; *b* 25 Aug. 1935; *s* of late Cyril Bradshaw and Nina Isabel Bradshaw; *m* 1st, 1959, Patricia Anne Leggatt (*d* 1981); two *s* one *d*; 2nd, 1986, Gillian Rosemary Payne; three step *s* one step *d*. *Educ:* King's Sch., Macclesfield; St John's Coll., Cambridge (MA); Univ. of Manchester (DipTP); MRTPI. Staff Surveyor, Lands and Surveys Dept, Uganda Protectorate, 1958–63; Asst Planning Officer, Planning Dept, City of Manchester, 1963–67; Asst Dir, City of Toronto Planning Bd, 1967–70; Asst Chief Planner, Cheshire CC, 1970–72; Asst County Planning Officer, Leics CC, 1972–73; Exec. Dir, Planning and Transport, 1973–81, Dir of Planning, 1981–86, W Yorks MCC; DoE Local Plans Inspectorate, 1986–87. Mem. Council, 1989–, Pres., 1993, RTPI. Gen. Comr for Income Tax, Bedford, 1988–. FRSA 1985. *Recreations:* theatre, art, golf.

BRADSHAW, Prof. Peter, FRS 1981; Thomas V. Jones Professor of Engineering, Department of Mechanical Engineering, Stanford University, since 1988; *b* 26 Dec. 1935; *s* of Joseph W. N. Bradshaw and Frances W. G. Bradshaw; *m* 1968, Sheila Dorothy (*née* Brown). *Educ:* Torquay Grammar Sch.; St John's Coll., Cambridge (BA). Scientific Officer, Aerodynamics Div., National Physical Lab., 1957–69; Imperial College, London: Sen. Lectr, Dept of Aeronautics, 1969–71; Reader, 1971–78; Prof. of Experimental Aerodynamics, 1978–88. *Publications:* Experimental Fluid Mechanics, 1964, 2nd edn 1971; An Introduction to Turbulence and its Measurement, 1971, 2nd edn 1975; (with T. Cebeci) Momentum Transfer in Boundary Layers, 1977; (ed) Topics in Applied Physics: Turbulence, 1978; (with T. Cebeci and J. H. Whitelaw) Engineering Calculation Methods for Turbulent Flow, 1981; (with T. Cebeci) Convective Heat Transfer, 1984; author or co-author of over 100 papers in Jl of Fluid Mechanics, AIAA Jl, etc. *Recreations:* ancient history, walking. *Address:* Department of Mechanical Engineering, Stanford University, Palo Alto, CA 94305–3030, USA.

BRADSHAW, Lt-Gen. Sir Richard (Phillip), KBE 1977; Director General, Army Medical Services, 1977–81; *b* 1 Aug. 1920; *s* of late John Henderson Bradshaw and late May Bradshaw (*née* Phillips); *m* 1946, Estelle, *d* of late Emile Meyer; one *d*. *Educ:* Newport High Sch.; London Univ.; Westminster Hosp. MRCS, LRCP 1945; FRCPath 1967; FFCM 1977; DTM&H 1953; FRSocMed, FRSTM&H, Mem. BMA. House appts Westminster and Kent and Canterbury Hosps. Commnd RAMC, 1946; appts as Hosp. Pathologist, Mil. Hosps in UK and Ceylon; Staff appts in Path., WO, 1950–52; Comd Cons. Pathologist, E Africa, 1954–57; Exch. Officer, Armed Forces Inst. of Path., Washington, 1959–60; Demonstr in Path., Royal Army Med. Coll., Millbank, 1961–63; Asst Dir of Path., BAOR, 1966–69; Prof. of Path., Royal Army Med. Coll., Millbank, 1969–71; CO, Cambridge Mil. Hosp., Aldershot, 1971–73; Comdt RAMC Trng Centre, 1973–75; DMS, BAOR, 1975–77. QHP 1975–81. Member: Council, Sir Oswald Stoll Foundn, Fulham, 1977– (Chm., Management Cttee, 1983–); Council and Cttee, Phyllis Tuckwell Meml Hospice, Farnham, 1981–; formerly HM Comr, Royal Hosp., Chelsea. CStJ 1977. *Publications:* articles and reports in professional jls. *Recreations:* bird-watching, gardening, working with wood.

BRADSHAW, Prof. William Peter; Senior Research Fellow, Centre for Socio-Legal Studies, Wolfson College, Oxford, since 1985; *b* 9 Sept. 1936; *s* of Leonard Charles Bradshaw and Ivy Doris Bradshaw; *m* 1957, Jill Hayward; one *s* one *d*. *Educ:* Univ. of Reading (BA Pol. Economy, 1957; MA 1960). FCIT 1987 (MCIT 1966). Joined Western Region of British Railways as Management Trainee, 1959; various appts, London and W of England Divs; Divl Manager, Liverpool, 1973; Chief Operating Man., LMR, 1976, Dep. Gen. Man. 1977; Chief Ops Man., BR HQ, 1978; Dir, Policy Unit, 1980; Gen. Man., Western Region, BR, 1983–85; Prof. of Transport Mgt, Univ. of Salford, 1986–92; Chm., Ulsterbus and Citybus Ltd, 1987–93. Special Advr to Transport Select Cttee, H of C, 1992–. *Recreations:* growing hardy plants; playing member of a brass band. *Address:* Centre for Socio-Legal Studies, Wolfson College, Oxford OX2 6UD. *T:* Oxford (01865) 52967. *Club:* National Liberal.

BRADWELL, Area Bishop of, since 1993; **Rt. Rev. Dr Laurence Alexander, (Laurie), Green;** *b* 26 Dec. 1945; *s* of Leonard Alexander and Laura Elizabeth Green; *m* 1969, J. Victoria Bussell; two *d*. *Educ:* King's Coll. London (BD Hons, AKC); New York Theological Seminary, NY State Univ. (STM, DMin); St Augustine's Coll., Canterbury. Curate, St Mark, Kingstanding, Birmingham, 1970–73; Vicar, St Chad, Erdington, Birmingham, 1973–83; Industrial Chaplain, British Steel Corp., 1975–83; Lectr in Urban Studies, Urban Theol. Unit, Sheffield, 1976–82; Principal, Aston Training Scheme, 1983–89; Hon. Curate, Holy Trinity, Birchfield, Handsworth, 1983–89; Team Rector, All Saints, Poplar, 1989–93; Tutor in Urban Theology, Sheffield Univ., 1989–93. *Publications:* Power to the Powerless, 1987; Let's Do Theology, 1989; God in the Inner City, 1993; (jtly) A Thing Called Aston (ed Todd), 1987; contrib. St George's Windsor Review. *Recreations:* folk and jazz music, running. *Address:* Bishop's House, Orsett Road, Horndon-on-the-Hill, Essex SS17 8NS. *T:* Stanford-le-Hope (01375) 673806, *Fax:* (01375) 674222.

BRADY, Rev. Canon Ernest William; Dean of Edinburgh, 1976–82 and 1985–86; *b* 10 Nov. 1917; *s* of Ernest and Malinda Elizabeth Brady; *m* 1948, Violet Jeanne Louise Aldworth (*d* 1993); one *s* one *d*. *Educ:* Harris Academy, Dundee (Dux and Classics Medallist, 1936); Univ. of St Andrews; Edinburgh Theological Coll. (Luscombe Schol. 1942). LTh (Dunelm) 1942. Deacon 1942, Priest 1943; Asst Curate, Christ Church, Glasgow, 1942; Asst Curate, St Alphage, Hendon, 1946; Rector, All Saints, Buckie, 1949; Rector, All Saints, Edinburgh, 1957; Chaplain, Royal Infirmary of Edinburgh, 1959–74; Priest-in-Charge, Priory Church of St Mary of Mount Carmel, South Queensferry, 1974–82; Canon of St Mary's Cathedral, Edinburgh, 1967, Hon. Canon, 1983; Synod Clerk, Diocese of Edinburgh, 1969. Sub-dean, Collegiate Church of St Vincent, Edinburgh (Order of St Lazarus of Jerusalem), 1982–89. Kt of Holy Sepulchre of Jerusalem (Golden Cross with Crown), 1984. *Recreations:* Holy Land pilgrimage; choral music; ecclesiastical vestments and embroidery. *Address:* 44 Glendevon Place, Edinburgh EH12 5UJ. *T:* 0131–337 9528.

BRADY, Prof. (John) Michael, FEng 1992; BP Professor of Information Engineering, Oxford University, since 1985; Fellow of Keble College, Oxford; EPSRC Senior Fellow, since 1994; *b* 30 April 1945; *s* of John and Priscilla Mansfield; *m* 1967, Naomi Friedlander; two *d*. *Educ:* Manchester Univ. (BSc (1st Cl. Hons Mathematics) 1966; Renold Prize 1967; MSc 1968); Australian National Univ. (PhD 1970). FIEE 1992. Lectr, Computer Science, 1970, Sen. Lectr 1979, Essex Univ.; Sen. Res. Scientist, MIT, 1980. Member: ACOST, 1990–; Bd, UKAEA, 1994–; Chm., IT Adv. Bd, 1989–. *Publications:* Theory of Computer Science, 1975; Computer Vision, 1981; Robot Motion, 1982; Computational Theory of Discourse, 1982; Robotics Research, 1984; Artificial Intelligence and Robotics, 1984; Robotics Science, 1989; contribs to jls on computer vision, robotics, artificial intelligence, computer science. *Recreations:* squash, windsurfing, music, winetasting.

BRADY, Nicholas Frederick; Secretary of the US Treasury, 1988–93; Chairman: Templeton Emerging Markets Investment Trust, since 1994; Templeton Latin American Investment Trust, since 1994; *b* 11 April 1930; *s* of James Brady and Eliot Brady; *m* 1952, Katherine Douglas; three *s* one *d*. *Educ:* Yale Univ. (BA 1952); Harvard Univ. (MBA 1954). Joined Dillon Read & Co. Inc., 1954; Vice-Pres., 1961; Pres. and Chief Exec. Officer, 1971; Chm. and Chief Exec. Officer, 1982–88. Mem., US Senate, Apr.–Dec. 1982. Posts on federal commns include: Chairman: Commn on Executive, Legislative and Judicial Salaries, 1985; Task Force on Market Mechanisms, 1987–88; Mem., Central Amer. Study Commn, 1983. *Address:* c/o Darby Overseas Investments, 1155 21st Street North West, Suite 720, Washington, DC 20036, USA.

BRADY, Most Rev. Sean; Coadjutor Archbishop (RC) of Armagh, since 1995; *b* 1939. *Educ:* St Patrick's Coll., Cavan; St Patrick's Coll., Maynooth (BA 1960; HDipEd 1967); Irish Coll., Rome; Lateran Univ., Rome (STB 1964; DCL 1967). Ordained priest, 1964; teacher, High Sch., St Patrick's Coll., Cavan, 1967–80; Vice Rector, 1980–87, Rector, 1987–93, Pontifical Irish Coll., Rome; Parish priest, Castletara, Co. Cavan, 1993–95. *Address:* 48 Newry Road, Armagh BT60 1ER.

BRADY, Terence Joseph; playwright, novelist and actor, since 1962; *b* 13 March 1939; *s* of late Frederick Arthur Noel and Elizabeth Mary Brady; *m* Charlotte Mary Thérèse Bingham, *qv*; one *s* one *d*. *Educ:* Merchant Taylors', Northwood; TCD (BA Moderatorship, History and Polit. Science). Actor: Would Anyone who saw the Accident?, The Dumb Waiter, Room at the Top, 1962; Beyond the Fringe, 1962–64; Present from the Corporation, In the Picture, 1967; Quick One 'Ere, 1968; films include: Baby Love; Foreign Exchange; TV appearances include plays, comedy series and shows, incl. Nanny, 1981, and Pig in the Middle, 1981, 1982, 1983. Writer for *radio:* Lines from my Grandfather's Forehead (BBC Radio Writers' Guild Award, Best Radio Entertainment, 1972); *television:* Broad and Narrow; TWTWTW; with Charlotte Bingham: TV series: Boy Meets Girl; Take Three Girls; Upstairs Downstairs; Away From It All; Play for Today; Plays of Marriage; No—Honestly; Yes—Honestly; Thomas and Sarah; Pig in the Middle; The Complete Lack of Charm of the Bourgeoisie; Nanny; Oh Madeline! (USA

TV); Father Matthew's Daughter; Forever Green; TV Films: Love with a Perfect Stranger; Losing Control, 1987; The Seventh Raven, 1987; This Magic Moment, 1988; Riders, 1990; Polo, 1993; *stage:* (contrib.) The Sloane Ranger Revue, 1985; I wish I wish, 1989. Member: Soc. of Authors, 1988–; Point to Point Owners Assoc., 1988–. *Publications:* Rehearsal, 1972; The Fight Against Slavery, 1976; with Charlotte Bingham: Victoria, 1972; Rose's Story, 1973; Victoria and Company, 1974; Yes—Honestly, 1977; (with Michael Felton) Point-to-Point, 1990; regular contribs to Daily Mail, Living, Country Homes and Interiors, Punch, Sunday Express, Mail on Sunday. *Recreations:* painting, music, horse racing, training point to point, avoiding dinner parties. *Address:* c/o Peters, Fraser & Dunlop, 5th Floor, The Chambers, Chelsea Harbour, SW3 0XF. *Club:* PEN.

BRAGG, Melvyn; writer; Presenter and Editor, The South Bank Show, for ITV, since 1978; Controller of Arts, London Weekend Television, since 1990 (Head of Arts, 1982–90); Chairman, Border Television, since 1990 (Deputy Chairman, 1985–90); *b* 6 Oct. 1939; *s* of Stanley Bragg and Mary Ethel (*née* Parks); *m* 1st, 1961, Marie-Elisabeth Roche (decd); one *d*; 2nd, 1973, Catherine Mary Haste; one *s* one *d*. *Educ:* Nelson-Thomlinson Grammar Sch., Wigton; Wadham Coll., Oxford (MA). BBC Radio and TV Producer, 1961–67; writer and broadcaster, 1967–. Novelist, 1964–. Presenter: BBC TV series: 2nd House, 1973–77; Read all About It (also editor), 1976–77; Start the Week, Radio 4, 1988–. Mem. Arts Council, and Chm. Literature Panel of Arts Council, 1977–80. President: Cumbrians for Peace, 1982–; Northern Arts, 1983–87; Nat. Campaign for the Arts, 1986–. Domus Fellow, St Catherine's Coll., Oxford, 1990. FRSL; FRTS. Hon. FLA. Hon. Fellow, Lancashire Polytechnic, 1987. Hon. DLitt: Liverpool, 1986; Lancaster, 1990; CNAA, 1990; DUniv Open, 1987; Hon. LLD St Andrews, 1993; Hon. DCL Northumbria, 1994. *Plays:* Mardi Gras, 1976 (musical); Orion (TV), 1977; The Hired Man, 1984 (musical); King Lear in New York, 1992; *screenplays:* Isadora; Jesus Christ Superstar; (with Ken Russell) Clouds of Glory. *Publications:* Speak for England, 1976; Land of the Lakes, 1983 (televised); Laurence Olivier, 1984; Rich: the life of Richard Burton, 1988; The Seventh Seal: a study on Ingmar Bergman, 1993; *novels:* For Want of a Nail, 1965; The Second Inheritance, 1966; Without a City Wall, 1968; The Hired Man, 1969; A Place in England, 1970; The Nerve, 1971; Josh Lawton, 1972; The Silken Net, 1974; A Christmas Child, 1976; Autumn Manoeuvres, 1978; Kingdom Come, 1980; Love and Glory, 1983; The Maid of Buttermere, 1987; A Time to Dance, 1990 (televised 1992); Crystal Rooms, 1992; articles for various English jls. *Recreations:* walking, books. *Address:* 12 Hampstead Hill Gardens, NW3 2PL. *Clubs:* Garrick, Groucho, PEN.

BRAGG, Stephen Lawrence, MA, SM; FEng; FIMechE; FRAeS; Administrator, Cambridge Office, American Friends of Cambridge University, 1988–93; Fellow, Wolfson College, Cambridge, 1982–91, now Emeritus Fellow; *b* 17 Nov. 1923; *e s* of Sir Lawrence Bragg, CH, OBE, MC, FRS and Lady Bragg, CBE; *m* 1951, Maureen Ann (*née* Roberts); three *s*. *Educ:* Rugby Sch.; Cambridge Univ.; Massachusetts Inst. of Technology. BA 1945, MA 1949 (Cambridge); SM 1949 (MIT). FEng 1981. Rolls-Royce Ltd, 1944–48; Commonwealth Fund Fellow, 1948–49; Wm Jessop Ltd, Steelmakers, 1949–51; Rolls-Royce Ltd, 1951–71: Chief Scientist, 1960–63; Chief Research Engineer, 1964–68; Dir, Aero Div., 1969–71. Vice-Chancellor, Brunel Univ., 1971–81. Eastern Region Broker, SERC, 1981–83. Dir in Industrial Co-operation, Cambridge Univ., 1984–87. Chm., Cambridge DHA, 1982–86. Member: Univ. Grants Cttee, 1966–71; Aeronautical Research Council, 1970–73; Court of ASC, Henley, 1972–81; SRC Engineering Bd, 1976–79; Airworthiness Requirements Bd, 1979–81; Chm., Adv. Cttee on Falsework, 1973–75. Corres. Mem. Venezuelan Acad. Sci., 1975. Hon. DEng Sheffield, 1969; Hon. DTech Brunel, 1982. *Publications:* Rocket Engines, 1962; articles on Jet Engines, Research Management, University/Industry Collaboration, etc. *Recreation:* railway history. *Address:* 22 Brookside, Cambridge CB2 1JQ. *T:* Cambridge (01223) 362208. *Club:* Athenæum.
See also Sir Mark Heath, D. P. Thomson.

BRAGGINS, Maj.-Gen. Derek Henry, CB 1986; Director General, Transport and Movements, Army, 1983–86; *b* 19 April 1931; *s* of late Albert Edward Braggins and of Hilda Braggins; *m* 1953, Sheila St Clair (*née* Stuart); three *s*. *Educ:* Rothesay Academy; Hendon Technical College. FBIM 1979, FCIT 1983. Commissioned RASC, 1950; RCT, 1965; regtl and staff appts, Korea, Malaya, Singapore, Ghana, Aden, Germany and UK; student, Staff Coll., Camberley, 1962, JSSC, Latimer, 1970; CO 7 Regt RCT, 1973–75; Col AQ Commando Forces RM, 1977–80; Comd Transport and Movements, BAOR, 1981–83. Col Comdt, RCT, 1986–93; Pres., RASC/RCT Assoc., 1987–95. Freeman, City of London, 1983; Hon. Liveryman, Worshipful Co. of Carmen, 1983. *Recreations:* shooting, fishing, gardening.

BRAHAM, Allan John Witney, PhD; Keeper and Deputy Director, the National Gallery, 1978–92; *b* 19 Aug. 1937; *s* of Dudley Braham and Florence Mears; *m* 1963, Helen Clare Butterworth; two *d*. *Educ:* Dulwich Coll.; Courtauld Inst. of Art, Univ. of London (BA 1960, PhD 1967). Asst Keeper, National Gall., 1962, Dep. Keeper, 1973. Arts Council Exhibn (with Peter Smith), François Mansart, 1970–71; National Gall. Exhibitions: (co-ordinator and editor) The Working of the National Gallery, 1974; Velázquez, The Rokeby Venus, 1976; Giovanni Battista Moroni, 1978; Italian Renaissance Portraits, 1979; El Greco to Goya, 1981; Wright of Derby "Mr and Mrs Coltman", 1986. *Publications:* Dürer, 1965; Murillo (The Masters), 1966; The National Gallery in London: Italian Painting of the High Renaissance, 1971; (with Peter Smith) François Mansart, 1973; Funeral Decorations in Early Eighteenth Century Rome, 1975; (with Hellmut Hager) Carlo Fontana: The Drawings at Windsor Castle, 1977; The Architecture of the French Enlightenment, 1980 (Hitchcock Medal, Banister Fletcher Prize; French edn 1982); National Gall. catalogues: The Spanish School (revised edn), 1970, and booklets: Velázquez, 1972; Rubens, 1972; Architecture, 1976; Italian Paintings of the Sixteenth Century, 1985; contrib. prof. jls, etc. *Recreation:* history of architecture. *Address:* 15A Acol Road, NW6 3AA.

BRAHIMI, Lakhdar; Assistant Secretary-General, League of Arab States, Tunis, since 1984; *b* 1934; *m* 1964; two *s* one *d*. *Educ:* Faculté de Droit and Institut des Sciences Politiques, Algiers; then Paris. Permanent Rep. of FLN and later of Provisional Govt of Algeria, in SE Asia, 1956–61; Gen. Secretariat, Min. of External Affairs, 1961–63; Ambassador to Egypt and Sudan, and Permanent Rep. to Arab League, 1963–70; Ambassador to Court of St James's, 1971–79; Mem., Central Cttee, National Liberation Front, Algeria, 1979–84; Pol Advr to President Chadli, 1982–84. *Address:* The League of Arab States, Tunis, Tunisia.

BRAIDEN, Prof. Paul Mayo, PhD; FEng 1994; FIMechE, FIEE; CPhys; Sir James Woodeson Professor of Manufacturing Engineering, since 1983 and Head, Department of Mechanical, Materials and Manufacturing Engineering, since 1992, University of Newcastle upon Tyne; *b* 7 Feb. 1941; *s* of late Isaac Braiden and of Lilian Braiden (*née* Mayo); *m* 1st, 1967, Elizabeth Marjorie Spensley (marr. diss. 1993); 2nd, 1993, Lesley Howard. *Educ:* Univ. of Sheffield (BEng, PhD). CEng, FIMechE 1978; FIEE 1983; CPhys, MInstP 1973. Asst Prof., Carnegie Mellon Univ., Pittsburgh, 1968–70; Atomic Energy Research Establishment, Harwell: SSO, 1970–73; PSO, 1973–76; Lectr, then Sen. Lectr, Dept of Engrg, Univ. of Durham, 1976–83. Science and Engineering Research Council: Chm., Engrg Design Cttee, 1990–94; Member: Engrg Bd, 1990–91; Engrg Res. Commn, 1991–94; Cttee on Electro-Mechanical Engrg, 1989–91; Automotive Design Prog., 1989–91; Panel on the Innovative Manufg Initiative, 1993–94. Chm., DTI Working Party on Advanced Mfg Technol., 1987–89. Chm., Northern Reg. and Council Mem., IProdE, 1988–90. Mem. Bd, Entrust, 1984–91. Mem., Nat. Cttee for Revision of Methodist Hymn Book, 1979–82. *Publications:* articles on materials behaviour, stress analysis, manufacturing technol. and systems in various jls. *Recreations:* music, especially opera/oratorio (trained singer, tenor voice), cycling, ski-ing. *Address:* Department of Mechanical, Materials and Manufacturing Engineering, University of Newcastle upon Tyne, Stephenson Building, Claremont Road, Newcastle upon Tyne NE1 7RU. *T:* 0191–222 6210.

BRAIN, family name of **Baron Brain.**

BRAIN, 2nd Baron *cr* 1962, of Eynsham; **Christopher Langdon Brain;** Bt 1954; *b* 30 Aug. 1926; *s* of 1st Baron Brain, MA, DM, FRS, FRCP and Stella, *er d* of late Reginald L. Langdon-Down; *S* father 1966; *m* 1953, Susan Mary, *d* of George P. and Ethelbertha Morris; three *d*. *Educ:* Leighton Park Sch., Reading; New College, Oxford. MA 1956. Royal Navy, 1946–48. Liveryman, 1955, Upper Warden, 1974–75, Asst, 1980, Renter Bailiff, 1983–84, Upper Bailiff, 1984–85, Worshipful Co. of Weavers. Chm., Rhone-Alps Regional Council, British Chamber of Commerce, France, 1967. ARPS 1970. *Recreations:* bird watching, sailing, fly-fishing. *Heir:* *b* Hon. Michael Cottrell Brain, MA, DM, FRCP, FRCP Canada, Prof. of Medicine, McMaster Univ. [*b* 6 Aug. 1928; *m* 1960, Dr the Hon. Elizabeth Ann Herbert, *e d* of Baron Tangley, KBE; one *s* two *d*]. *Address:* The Old Rectory, 34 Cross Street, Moretonhampstead, Devon TQ13 8NL. *Club:* Oxford and Cambridge Sailing Society.

BRAIN, Albert Edward Arnold; Regional Director (East Midlands), Department of the Environment, and Chairman of Regional Economic Planning Board, 1972–77; *b* 31 Dec. 1917; *s* of Walter Henry and Henrietta Mabel Brain; *m* 1947, Patricia Grace Gallop; two *s* one *d*. *Educ:* Rendcomb Coll., Cirencester; Loughborough College. BSc (Eng) London, external; DLC hons Loughborough; CEng, MICE, MIMunE. Royal Engineers, 1940–46; Bristol City Corp., 1946–48; Min. of Transport: Asst Engr, London, 1948–54; Civil Engr, Wales, 1954–63; Sen. Engr, HQ, 1963–67; Asst Chief Engr, HQ, 1967–69; Divl Road Engr, W Mids, now Regional Controller (Roads and Transportation), 1969–72. Pres., Old Rendcombian Soc., 1986–91. *Recreations:* gardening, bridge, golf. *Address:* Withyholt Lodge, Moorend Road, Charlton Kings, Cheltenham GL53 9BW. *T:* Cheltenham (01242) 576264.

BRAIN, Sir (Henry) Norman, KBE 1963 (OBE 1947); CMG 1953; *b* 19 July 1907; *s* of late B. Brain, Rushall, Staffs; *m* 1939, Nuala Mary, *d* of late Capt. A. W. Butterworth; one *s* (and one *s* decd). *Educ:* King Edward's Sch., Birmingham; The Queen's Coll., Oxford (MA). Entered the Consular Service, 1930, and served at Tokyo, Kobe, Osaka, Tamsui, Manila, Mukden, Shanghai and Dairen; interned by Japanese, 1941–42; repatriated and served in Foreign Office, 1943; appointed to Staff of Supreme Allied Comdr, South-East Asia, 1944–46; Political Adviser to Saigon Control Commission, 1945; served with Special Commissioner in South-East Asia, at Singapore, 1946–48; Counsellor in Foreign Office, 1949; Inspector of HM Foreign Service Estabts, 1950–53; Minister, Tokyo, 1953–55; Ambassador to Cambodia, 1956–58; Asst Under-Sec. of State, FO, 1958–61; Ambassador to Uruguay, 1961–66, retired, 1966. Chairman: Royal Central Asian Soc., 1970–74; Japan Soc. of London, 1970–73; Pres., British Uruguayan Soc., 1974–. *Recreations:* music, golf. *Address:* St Andrews, Abney Court, Bourne End, Bucks SL8 5DL. *Club:* Canning.

BRAIN, Dame Margaret Anne, DBE 1994 (OBE 1989); President, Royal College of Midwives, 1987–94 (Member Council, since 1970); *b* 23 April 1932; *d* of late Charles and Leonora Brain; *m* 1985, Peter Wheeler (*d* 1988), MBE, FRCS, FRCOG. *Educ:* Northampton High Sch.; Westminster Hosp. (SRN 1953); Northampton and Epsom Hosps (SCM 1956); Sheffield Hosp. (MTD 1966). Med. Missionary, USPG St Columba's Hosp., Hazaribagh, Bihar, India, 1959–65; Dep. Matron, Barratt Maternity Home, Northampton, 1966–68; Prin. Midwifery Officer, Reading HMC, 1968–73; Dist Nursing Officer, W Berks DHA, 1974–77; Chief Admin. Nursing Officer, S Glamorgan HA, 1977–88, retd. Member: Nat. Staff Cttee for Nurses and Midwives, 1978–86; Maternity Services Adv. Cttee, 1981–85; Standing Midwifery Cttee, Welsh Nat. Bd, 1982–87; Perinatal Mortality Initiative Steering Gp for Wales, 1983–85; Standing Nursing and Midwifery Adv. Cttee, 1987–93; Women's Nat. Commn, 1990–92; Alternate Treas., 1972–78, Treas., 1978–90, Internat. Confedn of Midwives. *Address:* Squirrels, Castle Farm, Lower Broad Oak Road, West Hill, Ottery St Mary, Devon EX11 1UF. *T:* Ottery St Mary (01404) 812958.

BRAIN, Rt. Rev. Terence John; Auxiliary Bishop of Birmingham, (RC), since 1991; *b* 19 Dec. 1938; *s* of Reginald John Brain and Mary Cooney. *Educ:* Cotton Coll., North Staffordshire; St Mary's Coll., Oscott, Birmingham. Ordained priest, 1964; Asst Priest, St Gregory's, Longton, 1964–65; mem. of staff, Cotton Coll., 1965–69; Hosp. Chaplain, St Patrick's, Birmingham, 1969–71; Archbishop's Secretary, Birmingham, 1971–82; Parish Priest: Bucknall, Stoke-on-Trent, 1982–88; St Austin's, Stafford, 1988–91. Prelate of Honour, 1978. *Recreations:* crossword puzzles, water colour painting. *Address:* 84 St Bernard's Road, Olton, Solihull, West Midlands B92 7BS.

BRAINE, family name of **Baron Braine of Wheatley**.

BRAINE OF WHEATLEY, Baron *cr* 1992 (Life Peer), of Rayleigh in the County of Essex; **Bernard Richard Braine,** Kt 1972; PC 1985; DL; *b* Ealing, Middx, 24 June 1914; *s* of Arthur Ernest Braine; *m* 1935, Kathleen Mary Faun (*d* 1982); three *s*. *Educ:* Hendon County Grammar Sch. Served North Staffs Regt in War of 1939–45: West Africa, SE Asia, NW Europe; Staff Coll., Camberley, 1944 (sc); Lt-Col. Chm., British Commonwealth Producers' Organisation, 1958–60. MP (C) Billericay Div. of Essex, 1950–55, South East Essex, 1955–83, Castle Point, 1983–92; Father of the House of Commons, 1987–92. Parly Sec., Min. of Pensions and National Insurance, 1960–61; Parly Under-Sec. of State for Commonwealth Relations, 1961–62; Parly Sec., Min. of Health, 1962–64; Conservative front bench spokesman on Commonwealth Affairs and Overseas Aid, 1967–70; Chm., Select Cttees on Overseas Aid, 1970–71, on Overseas Devolt, 1973–74; Treasurer, UK Branch of Commonwealth Parly Assoc., 1974–77 (Dep. Chm., 1964 and 1970–74). Chairman: British-German Parly Group, 1970–92; British-Greek Parly Group, 1979–92; All-party Pro Life Cttee, to 1991; Inter-Parly Council Against Antisemitism, 1993–; Founder and Chm., All-party Misuse of Drugs Cttee, 1984–88; Nat. Council on Alcoholism, 1973–82; UK Chapter, Soc. of Internat. Devolt, 1976–83; Vice-Chm., Parly Human Rights Gp, 1979–92. President: UK Cttee for Defence of the Unjustly Prosecuted, 1980–88; River Thames Soc., 1981–87; Greater London Alcohol Adv. Service, 1983–; Falkland Is Assoc., 1993–. President, Cons. Clubs of Benfleet, Hadleigh and Canvey Is. Associate Mem., Inst. of Devolt Studies, Univ. of Sussex, 1971–; Vis. Prof., Baylor Univ., Texas, 1987–91. A Governor, Commonwealth Inst., 1968–81, Trustee, 1981–. FRSA 1971. DL Essex, 1978. Hon. DH Dallas Baptist Univ., 1993. KStJ 1985; KCSG 1987; GCLJ 1987; GCMLJ 1988. Europe Peace Cross, 1979; Knight Comdr's Cross with Star, German Order of Merit, 1984 (Comdr's Cross, 1974); Grand Comdr, Order of Honour (Greece), 1987; Grand Cross, Order of Polonia Restituta, 1990

(Comdr's Cross with Star, 1983). *Address:* King's Wood, 67 Great Wheatley Road, Rayleigh, Essex SS6 7AW.

BRAINE, Rear-Adm. Richard Allix, CB 1956; retired; *b* 18 Nov. 1900; *m* 1922, Lilian Violet (*d* 1985); one *s*. *Educ:* Dean Close Memorial Sch., Cheltenham. Joined RN as asst clerk, 1918; Comdr (S), Dec. 1938; Capt. (S), Dec. 1948; Rear-Adm. 1954. Command Supply Officer, Staff of Flag Officer Air (Home), 1954–56, Portsmouth, 1956–57. *Address:* The Old Cottage, Littlewick Green, near Maidenhead, Berks SL6 3RA. *T:* Littlewick Green (01628) 824484.

BRAININ, Norbert, OBE 1960; concert violinist; formed Amadeus Ensemble, incorporating Amadeus Trio, 1988; Professor of Chamber Music, Hochschule für Musik, Cologne, since 1976; Professor for Chamber Music, Royal Academy of Music, since 1986; *b* Vienna, 12 March 1923; *s* of Adolph and Sophie Brainin; *m* 1948, Kathe Kottow; one *d*. *Educ:* High Sch., Vienna. Commenced musical training in Vienna at age of seven and continued studies there until 1938; emigrated to London in 1938 and studied with Carl Flesch and Max Rostal; won Carl Flesch prize for solo violinists at the Guildhall Sch. of Music, London, 1946. Formed Amadeus String Quartet, 1947, Leader until disbanded in 1987. DUniv York, 1968. Grand Cross of Merit, 1st cl. Fed. Republic of Germany, 1972; Cross of Honour for Arts and Science (Austria), 1972. *Address:* 19 Prowse Avenue, Bushey Heath, Herts WD2 1JS. *T:* 0181–950 7379.

BRAITHWAITE, His Honour Bernard Richard; a Circuit Judge (formerly County Court Judge), 1971–88; *b* 20 Aug. 1917; *s* of Bernard Leigh Braithwaite and Emily Dora Ballard Braithwaite (*née* Thomas); unmarried. *Educ:* Clifton; Peterhouse, Cambridge. BA (Hons), Law. Served War: 7th Bn Somerset LI, 1939–43; Parachute Regt, 1943–46; Captain, Temp. Major. Called to Bar, Inner Temple, 1946. *Recreations:* hunting, sailing. *Address:* Summerfield House, Uley, Gloucestershire GL11 5BZ. *Club:* Boodle's.

BRAITHWAITE, Eustace Edward Adolph Ricardo; writer; Ambassador of Guyana to Venezuela, 1968–69; *b* 27 June 1922. *Educ:* New York Univ.; Cambridge Univ. Served War of 1939–45, RAF. Schoolteacher, London, 1950–57; Welfare Officer, LCC, 1958–60; Human Rights Officer, World Veterans Foundation, Paris, 1960–63; Lecturer and Education Consultant, Unesco, Paris, 1963–66; Permanent Rep. of Guyana to UN, 1967–68. Ainsfield-Wolff Literary Award, 1961; Franklin Prize. *Publications:* To Sir With Love, 1959; Paid Servant, 1962; A Kind of Homecoming, 1962; Choice of Straws, 1965; Reluctant Neighbours, 1972; Honorary White, 1976. *Recreations:* tennis, birdwatching.

BRAITHWAITE, Sir (Joseph) Franklin (Madders), Kt 1980; DL; CIMgt; Chairman: Baker Perkins Holdings plc, 1980–84; Peterborough Independent Hospital plc, 1981–87; *b* 6 April 1917; *s* of late Sir John Braithwaite and Martha Janette (*née* Baker); *m* 1939, Charlotte Isabel, *d* of late Robert Elmer Baker, New York; one *s* one *d*. *Educ:* Bootham Sch.; King's Coll., Cambridge, 1936–39 (BA 1939, MA 1955). Served Army, 1940–46 (Captain). Joined Baker Perkins Ltd, 1946, Director 1950, Vice-Chm. 1956; Chairman, Baker Perkins Exports Ltd, 1966; Man. Dir, Baker Perkins Holdings Ltd, 1971. Director, Lloyds Bank Ltd, Eastern Counties Regional Board, 1979–87. Member: Mech. Engrg Industry Economic Development Cttee, 1974–79; Management Board, 1978–82, Commercial and Econ. Cttee, 1977–84, Engrg Employers' Fedn; Board of Fellows, 1974–79, Economic and Social Affairs Cttee, 1979–84, BIM. Mem., Peterborough Develt Corp., 1981–88, Dep. Chm. 1982–88. President, Process Plant Assoc., 1977–79, Hon. life Vice-Pres., 1981. DL Cambs, 1983. *Recreations:* music, golf. *Address:* 7 Rutland Terrace, Stamford, Lincs PE9 2QD. *T:* Stamford (01780) 51244. *Club:* Army and Navy.

BRAITHWAITE, Sir Rodric (Quentin), GCMG 1994 (KCMG 1988; CMG 1981); HM Diplomatic Service, retired; Senior Advisor, Morgan Grenfell Group, since 1994; *b* 17 May 1932; *s* of Henry Warwick Braithwaite and Lorna Constance Davies; *m* 1961, Gillian Mary Robinson; three *s* one *d* (and one *s* decd). *Educ.* Bedales Sch.; Christ's Coll., Cambridge (1st cl. Mod. Langs, Pts I and II; Hon. Fellow, 1989). Mil. Service, 1950–52. Joined Foreign (subseq. Diplomatic) Service, 1955; 3rd Sec., Djakarta, 1957–58; 2nd Sec., Warsaw, 1959–61; FO, 1961–63; 1st Sec. (Commercial), Moscow, 1963–66; 1st Sec., Rome, 1966–69; FCO, 1969–72; Vis. Fellow, All Souls Coll., Oxford, 1972–73; Head of European Integration Dept (External), FCO, 1973–75; Head of Chancery, Office of Permanent Rep. to EEC, Brussels, 1975–78; Head of Planning Staff, FCO, 1979–80; Asst Under Sec. of State, FCO, 1981; Minister Commercial, Washington, 1982–84; Dep. Under-Sec. of State, FCO, 1984–88; Ambassador to Russia, 1988–92; Prime Minister's foreign policy advr, 1992–93. Mem., European Strategy Bd, ICL plc, 1994–. Chm. Council, Britain–Russia Centre, 1995–; Mem. Council, VSO, 1994–. Dir, ENO, 1992–. Mem., Governing Council, SSEES, 1993–; Gov., RAM, 1993–. Trustee, BBC Marshall Plan for the Mind, 1995–. *Recreations:* chamber music (viola), sailing, Russia.

BRAITHWAITE, William Thomas Scatchard; QC 1992; a Recorder, since 1993; *b* 20 Jan. 1948; *s* of late John Vernon Braithwaite and Nancy Phyllis Braithwaite; *m* 1972, Sheila Edgecombe; one *s* one *d*. *Educ:* Gordonstoun Sch.; Liverpool Univ. (LLB Hons). Called to the Bar, Gray's Inn, 1970; joined chambers in Liverpool, 1970; Asst Recorder of the Crown Court, 1990. *Recreations:* cars, wine. *Address:* Exchange Chambers, Pearl Assurance House, Derby Square, Liverpool L2 9XX. *Clubs:* Athenæum, Racquet (Liverpool).

BRAMALL, family name of **Baron Bramall.**

BRAMALL, Baron *cr* 1987 (Life Peer), of Bushfield in the County of Hampshire; **Field Marshal Edwin Noel Westby Bramall,** KG 1990; GCB 1979 (KCB 1974); OBE 1965; MC 1945; JP; HM Lord-Lieutenant of Greater London, since 1986; Chief of the Defence Staff, 1982–85; *b* 18 Dec. 1923; *s* of late Major Edmund Haselden Bramall and Mrs Katherine Bridget Bramall (*née* Westby); *m* 1949, Dorothy Avril Wentworth Vernon; one *s* one *d*. *Educ:* Eton College. Commnd into KRRC, 1943; served in NW Europe, 1944–45; occupation of Japan, 1946–47; Instructor, Sch. of Infantry, 1949–51; psc 1952; Middle East, 1953–58; Instructor, Army Staff Coll., 1958–61; on staff of Lord Mountbatten at MoD, 1963–64; CO, 2 Green Jackets, KRRC, Malaysia during Indonesian confrontation, 1965–66; comd 5th Airportable Bde, 1967–69; idc 1970; GOC 1st Div. BAOR, 1971–73; Lt-Gen., 1973; Comdr, British Forces, Hong Kong, 1973–76; Gen., 1976; C-in-C, UK Land Forces, 1976–78; Vice-Chief of Defence Staff (Personnel and Logistics), 1978–79; Chief of the General Staff, 1979–82; Field Marshal 1982. ADC (Gen.), 1979–82. Col Comdt, 3rd Bn Royal Green Jackets, 1973–84; Col, 2nd Goorkhas, 1976–86; President: Greater London TAVRA, 1986–; Gurkha Bde Assoc., 1987–. A Trustee, Imperial War Museum, 1983– (Chm., 1989–). JP London 1986. KStJ 1986. *Publication:* (jtly) The Chiefs, 1993. *Recreations:* cricket, painting, travel. *Address:* Lieutenancy Office, Westminster City Hall, PO Box 240, Victoria Street, SW1E 6QP. *Clubs:* Travellers', Army and Navy, Pratt's, MCC (Pres., 1988–89), I Zingari, Free Foresters.

See also Sir E. A. Bramall.

BRAMALL, Sir (Ernest) Ashley, Kt 1975; DL; Member (Lab), Greater London Council, Bethnal Green and Bow, 1973–86 (Tower Hamlets, 1964–73); Chairman: GLC, 1982–83; ILEA, 1965–67 and 1984–86 (Leader, 1970–81); *b* 6 Jan. 1916; *er s* of late Major E. H. Bramall and Mrs K. B. Bramall (*née* Westby); *m*; three *s*. *Educ:* Westminster and Canford Schs; Magdalen Coll., Oxford. Served in Army, 1940–46; Major; psc 1945. Contested Fareham Div. of Hants, 1945; MP (Lab) for Bexley, 1946–50; contested Bexley, 1950, 1951, 1959; Watford, 1955. Barrister, Inner Temple. Member: LCC (Lab) Bethnal Green, 1961; Westminster CC, 1959–68; Chm., Council of LEAs, 1975–76, 1977–78, Vice-Chm., 1976–77; Leader, Management Panel, Burnham Cttee (Primary and Secondary), 1973–78; Chm., Nat. Council for Drama Trng, 1981–89. Hon. Sec., Theatres Adv. Council, 1987–91. Mem. Council, City Univ., 1984–90; Chm., Westminster Further Educn Coll., 1992–. Governor, Museum of London, 1981–. DL Greater London, 1981. Grand Officer, Order of Orange Nassau, 1982. *Address:* 2 Egerton House, 59–63 Belgrave Road, SW1V 2BE. *T:* 0171–828 0973.

See also Field Marshal Baron Bramall.

BRAMALL, Margaret Elaine, OBE 1969; MA; JP; Vice-President, National Council for One Parent Families (formerly National Council for the Unmarried Mother and her Child) (Director, 1962–79); *b* 1 Oct. 1916; *d* of Raymond Taylor, MA and Nettie Kate Taylor, BA; *m* 1939, Sir Ashley Bramall (marr. diss.); two *s*. *Educ:* St Paul's Girls' Sch., Hammersmith; Somerville Coll., Oxford (BA 1939, MA 1942); LSE (Social Science Hon. Certif. 1950); Inst. of Almoners (Certif. 1951). Lectr, Applied Social Studies Course, Surrey Univ., 1979–89. Member: Probation Case Cttee; Management Cttee, Humming Bird Housing Assoc. Chm., Richmond on Thames Action for Southern Africa. JP Richmond 1965. *Publications:* contrib., One Parent Families, ed Dulan Barber, 1975; contrib. social work jls. *Recreations:* gardening, family. *Address:* 74 Fifth Cross Road, Twickenham, Mddx TW2 5LE. *T:* 0181–894 3998.

BRAMLEY, Prof. Sir Paul (Anthony), Kt 1984; FRCS, FDSRCS; Professor of Dental Surgery, University of Sheffield, 1969–88, now Emeritus; *b* 24 May 1923; *s* of Charles and Constance Bramley; *m* 1952, Hazel Morag Boyd, MA, MB ChB; one *s* three *d*. *Educ:* Wyggeston Grammar Sch., Leicester; Univ. of Birmingham. MB ChB, BDS. HS, Queen Elizabeth Hosp., Birmingham, 1945; Capt., RADC, 224 Para Fd Amb., 1946–48; MO, Church of Scotland, Kenya, 1952; Registrar, Rooksdown House, 1953–54; Consultant Oral Surgeon, SW Region Hosp. Bd, 1954–69; Dir, Dept of Oral Surgery and Orthodontics, Plymouth Gen. Hosp. and Truro Royal Infirmary, 1954–69; Civilian Consultant, RN, 1959–88, now Emeritus; Dean, Sch. of Clinical Dentistry, Univ. of Sheffield, 1972–75. Consultant Oral Surgeon, Trent Region, 1969–88. Chm., Dental Protection Ltd, 1989–95. Member: General Dental Council, 1973–89; Council, Medical Protection Soc., 1975–95; Council, RCS, 1975–83 (Tomes Lectr, 1980; Dean of Faculty of Dental Surgery, 1980–83; Colyer Gold Medal, 1988); Royal Commission on NHS; Dental Strategy Review Group; Chm., Standing Dental Adv. Cttee; Consultant Adviser, DHSS; Hon. Sec., British Assoc. of Oral Surgeons, 1968–72, Pres., 1975; President: S Yorks Br., British Dental Assoc., 1975; Oral Surgery Club of GB, 1985–86; Inst. of Maxillofacial Technol., 1987–89; BDA, 1988–89. Adviser, Prince of Songkla Univ., Thailand, 1982–; External Examiner to RCS, RCSI, RCSG, RACDS, Univs of Birmingham, Baghdad, Hong Kong, London, Singapore, Trinity College Dublin, Cardiff, NUI. Pres., Norman Rowe Educnl Trust, 1993–95; Chm., Cavendish Br., NADFAS, 1996–. Lay Reader, dios of Winchester and Exeter, 1953–68. Hon. FRACDS. Hon. DDS: Birmingham, 1987; Prince of Songkla Univ., 1989; Hon. MD Sheffield, 1994. Fellow, Internat. Assoc. of Oral and Maxillofacial Surgeons. Bronze Medal, Helsinki Univ., 1990. *Publications:* (with J. Norman) The Temporomandibular Joint: disease, disorders, surgery, 1989; scientific articles in British and foreign medical and dental jls. *Address:* Greenhills, Back Lane, Hathersage S30 1AR.

BRAMMA, Harry Wakefield, FRCO; Director, Royal School of Church Music, since 1989; Organist and Director of Music, All Saints', Margaret Street, since 1989; *b* 11 Nov. 1936; *s* of Fred and Christine Bramma. *Educ:* Bradford Grammar Sch.; Pembroke Coll., Oxford (MA). FRCO 1958. Dir of Music, King Edward VI Grammar Sch., Retford, Notts, 1961; Asst Organist, Worcester Cathedral, 1963; Dir of Music, The King's Sch., Worcester, 1965; Organist, Southwark Cathedral, 1976. Conductor, Kidderminster Choral Soc., 1972–79. Examnr, Associated Bd of Royal Schs of Music, 1978–89. Mem. Council, RCO, 1979, Hon. Treas., 1987–; Mem., Archbishops' Commn on Church Music, 1989–92; Organ Advr, Dio. of Southwark, 1976–93. Hon. Sec., Cathedral Organists' Assoc., 1989–. FGCM 1988; FRSCM 1994. Hon. DLitt Bradford, 1995. *Recreations:* travel, walking. *Address:* Addington Palace, Croydon, Surrey CR9 5AD. *T:* 0181-654 7676.

BRAMPTON, Sally Jane, (Mrs Jonathan Powell); freelance journalist; *b* 15 July 1955; *d* of Roy and Pamela Brampton; *m* 1981, Nigel Cole (marr. diss. 1990); *m* 1990, Jonathan Leslie Powell, *qv*; one *d*. *Educ:* Ashford Sch., Ashford, Kent; St Clare's Hall, Oxford; St Martin's School of Art, London. Fashion Writer, Vogue, 1978; Fashion Editor, Observer, 1981; Editor, Elle (UK), 1985–89; Associate Editor, Mirabella, 1990–91. *Publication:* Good Grief (novel), 1992. *Address:* 10a Wedderburn Road, NW3 5QG. *Club:* Groucho.

BRAMWELL, Richard Mervyn; QC 1989; *b* 29 Sept. 1944; *s* of Clifford and Dorothy Bramwell; *m* 1968, Susan Green; one *d*. *Educ:* Stretford Grammar Sch.; LSE (LLB, LLM). Called to the Bar, Middle Temple, 1967. *Publications:* Taxation of Companies and Company Reconstructions, 1973, 6th edn 1994; Inheritance Tax on Lifetime Gifts, 1987. *Recreations:* hunting, tennis. *Address:* 3 Temple Gardens, Temple, EC4Y 9AU. *T:* 0171–353 7884.

BRANAGH, Emma, (Mrs Kenneth Branagh); *see* Thompson, E.

BRANAGH, Kenneth Charles; actor and director; *b* 10 Dec. 1960; *s* of William and Frances Branagh; *m* 1989, Emma Thompson, *qv*. *Educ:* Meadway Comprehensive Sch., Reading; Royal Academy of Dramatic Art (Bancroft Gold Medalist). Mem. Bd, BFI, 1993–. *Theatre:* Another Country, Queen's, 1982 (SWET Award, Most Promising Newcomer; Plays and Players Award); The Madness; Francis; Henry V, Golden Girls, Hamlet, Love's Labours Lost, 1984–85; Tell Me Honestly (also author); Across the Roaring Hill; The Glass Maze; Hamlet, RSC, 1992; formed Renaissance Theatre Company, 1987: Romeo and Juliet (also dir); Public Enemy (also author); Much Ado About Nothing; As You Like It; Hamlet; Look Back in Anger (also televised); A Midsummer Night's Dream (also dir); King Lear (also dir); Coriolanus; *directed:* Twelfth Night (also televised); The Life of Napoleon; (with Peter Egan) Uncle Vanya; *films include:* A Month in the Country; High Season; Henry V (also dir) (Evening Standard Best Film of the Year, 1989; Oscar, Best Costume Design, 1990; BFI Award, Best Film and Technical Achievement, 1990; Young European Film of the Year, 1990; NY Critics Circle Award, Best New Dir; European Actor of the Year, 1990); Dead Again (also dir), 1991; Peter's Friends (also dir), Swan Song (dir), 1992; Swing Kids, Much Ado About Nothing (also dir), 1993; Mary Shelley's Frankenstein (also dir), 1994; *television includes:* Fortunes of War; Boy in the Bush; Billy Trilogy; To the Lighthouse; Strange Interlude; Ghosts; The Lady's Not for Burning; *radio includes:* Hamlet, and Romeo and Juliet (both also co-dir); King Lear; Anthem for the Doomed Youth; Diaries of Samuel Pepys; Mary Shelley's Frankenstein. *Publications:* Public Enemy (play), 1988; Beginning (autobiog.),

1989. *Recreations:* reading, playing guitar. *Address:* Shepperton Studios, Shepperton, Mddx TW17 0QD.

BRANCH, Prof. Michael Arthur, PhD; Director, School of Slavonic and East European Studies, since 1980, and Professor of Finnish, since 1986, University of London; *b* 24 March 1940; *s* of Arthur Frederick Branch and Mahala Parker; *m* 1963, Ritva-Riitta Hannele, *d* of Erkki Kari, Heinola, Finland; three *d. Educ:* Shene Grammar Sch.; Sch. of Slavonic and East European Studies, Univ. of London (BA 1963; PhD 1967). School of Slavonic and East European Studies: Asst Lectr and Lectr in Finno–Ugrian Studies, 1967–72; Lectr, 1972–77, and Reader in Finnish, 1977; Chm., Dept of East European Language and Literature, 1979–80. Corresponding Member: Finno–Ugrian Soc., 1977; Finnish Literature Soc. (Helsinki), 1980. Hon. PhD Oulu (Finland), 1983. Comdr, Lion of Finland, 1980; Comdr, Polish Order of Merit, 1992. *Publications:* A. J. Sjögren, 1973; (jtly) Finnish Folk Poetry: Epic, 1977; (jtly) A Student's Glossary of Finnish, 1980; (ed) Kalevala, 1985; (jtly) Edith Södergran, 1992; (jtly) The Great Bear, 1993; (jtly) Uses of Tradition, 1994. *Recreations:* gardening, walking. *Address:* 33 St Donatt's Road, SE14 6NU. *T:* 0171–637 4934. *Club:* Athenæum.

BRANCKER, Sir (John Eustace) Theodore, Kt 1969; President of the Senate, Barbados, 1971–76; *b* 9 Feb. 1909; *s* of Jabel Eustace and Myra Enid Vivienne Brancker; *m* 1967, Esme Gwendolyn Walcott (OBE 1987). *Educ:* Harrison Coll., Barbados; Grad., Inst. of Political Secretaries; LSE (Certificate in Colonial Admin, 1933). Called to Bar, Middle Temple, 1933; in private practice; QC (Barbados) 1961. Mem., House of Assembly, Barbados, 1937–71 (Leader of Opposition, 1956–61; Speaker, 1961–71). Mem., Medico-Legal Soc. Mem., CPA. Life Fellow, Royal Commonwealth Soc.; Life Mem., Barbados Mus. and Historical Soc. Chm., 1973, Hon. Awards Liaison Officer, 1978, Duke of Edinburgh Award Scheme. Mem., Soc. of Friends of Westminster Cathedral. Charter Pres., Rotary Club, Barbados. Mem. Adv. Bd, St Joseph Hosp. of Sisters of the Sorrowful Mother. Hon. LLD Soochow Univ., 1973. FZS; FRSA (Life Fellow). Queen's Coronation Medal, 1953; Silver Jubilee Medal, 1977. *Recreations:* classical music, chess, drama. *Address:* 16 East Charlemont, Paradise Heights, St James's, Barbados. *T:* 4325563. *Clubs:* Royal Over-Seas League (Life Mem.), Challoner (London); Empire, Bridgetown, Sunset Crest (Barbados); Rotary International.

BRAND, family name of **Viscount Hampden.**

BRAND, Hon. Lord; David William Robert Brand; a Senator of the College of Justice in Scotland, 1972–89; *b* 21 Oct. 1923; *s* of late James Gordon Brand, Huntingdon, Dumfries, and Frances (*née* Bull); *m* 1st, 1948, Rose Josephine Devlin (*d* 1968); four *d*; 2nd, Bridget Veronica Lynch (*née* Russell), *widow* of Thomas Patrick Lynch, Beechmount, Mallow, Co. Cork. *Educ:* Stonyhurst Coll.; Edinburgh Univ. Served War of 1939–45; Commissioned Argyll and Sutherland Highlanders, 1942; Capt. 1945. Admitted to Faculty of Advocates, 1948; Standing Junior Counsel to Dept of Education for Scotland, 1951; Advocate-Depute for Sheriff Court, 1953; Extra Advocate-Depute for Glasgow Circuit, 1955; Advocate-Depute, 1957–59; QC Scot. 1959; Senior Advocate-Depute, 1964; Sheriff of Dumfries and Galloway, 1968; Sheriff of Roxburgh, Berwick and Selkirk, 1970; Solicitor-General for Scotland, 1970–72; Judge of Appeal, High Court of Botswana, 1994. Chm., Medical Appeal Tribunal, 1959–70. Kt, SMO Malta. *Publications:* Joint Editor, Scottish Edn of Current Law, 1948–61; Scottish Editor, Encyclopedia of Road Traffic Law and Practice, 1960–64; contributor to Scots Law Times. *Recreation:* golf. *Address:* Ardgarten, Marmion Road, N Berwick, E Lothian EH39 4PG. *T:* North Berwick (01620) 3208. *Clubs:* New (Edinburgh); Highland Brigade; Honourable Company of Edinburgh Golfers.

BRAND, Alexander George, MBE 1945; *b* 23 March 1918; *s* of David Wilson Brand and Janet Ramsay Brand (*née* Paton); *m* 1947, Helen Constance Campbell; one *s* one *d. Educ:* Ayr Academy; Univ. of Glasgow. MA 1940, LLB 1948. Admitted Solicitor, 1948. Served in Royal Air Force, 1940–46 (Flt Lt). Legal Asst: Dumbarton CC, 1948; in Office of Solicitor to the Secretary of State for Scotland, 1949; Sen. Legal Asst, 1955; Asst Solicitor, 1964; Dep. Solicitor, 1972–79. Sec. of Scottish Law Commn, 1965–72. *Recreations:* golf, theatre, music, reading. *Address:* 16 Queen's Avenue, Edinburgh EH4 2DF. *T:* 0131–332 4472.

BRAND, Prof. Charles Peter, FBA 1990; Professor of Italian, 1966–88, and Vice-Principal, 1984–88, University of Edinburgh; *b* 7 Feb. 1923; *er s* of Charles Frank Brand and Dorothy (*née* Tapping); *m* 1948, Gunvor, *yr d* of Col I. Hellgren, Stockholm; one *s* three *d. Educ:* Cambridge High Sch.; Trinity Hall, Cambridge. War Service, Intelligence Corps, 1943–46. Open Maj. Scholar, Trinity Hall, 1940; 1st Class Hons. Mod. Languages, Cantab, 1948; PhD Cantab, 1951. Asst Lecturer, Edinburgh Univ., 1952; Cambridge University: Asst Lecturer, subsequently Lecturer, 1952–66; Fellow and Tutor, Trinity Hall, 1958–66. Pres., MHRA, 1995. Cavaliere Ufficiale, 1975, Commendatore, 1988, al Merito della Repubblica Italiana. General Editor, Modern Language Review, 1971–77; Editor, Italian Studies, 1977–. *Publications:* Italy and the English Romantics, 1957; Torquato Tasso, 1965; Ariosto: a preface to the Orlando Furioso, 1974; contributions to learned journals. *Recreations:* sport, travel, gardening. *Address:* 21 Succoth Park, Edinburgh EH12 6BX. *T:* 0131–337 1980.

BRAND, David William Robert; *see* Brand, Hon. Lord.

BRAND, Geoffrey Arthur; Under-Secretary, Department of Employment, 1972–85; *b* 13 June 1930; *s* of late Arthur William Charles Brand and Muriel Ada Brand; *m* 1954, Joy Trotman; two *d. Educ:* Andover Grammar Sch.; University Coll., London. Entered Min. of Labour, 1953; Private Sec. to Parly Sec., 1956–57; Colonial Office, 1957–58; Private Sec. to Minister of Labour, 1965–66; Asst. Sec., Industrial Relations and Research and Planning Divisions, 1966–72. Mem., Archbishop of Canterbury's Adv. Gp on Urban Priority Areas, 1986–. FRSA 1985. *Address:* Cedarwood, Seer Green, Beaconsfield, Bucks HP9 2UH. *T:* Beaconsfield (01494) 676637.

BRANDES, Lawrence Henry, CB 1982; Under Secretary and Head of the Office of Arts and Libraries, 1978–82; *b* 16 Dec. 1924; *m* 1950, Dorothea Stanyon; one *s* one *d. Educ:* Beltane Sch.; London Sch. of Economics. Min. of Health, 1950; Principal Private Sec. to Minister, 1959; Nat. Bd for Prices and Incomes, 1966; Dept of Employment and Productivity, 1969; Under-Sec., DHSS, 1970; HM Treasury, 1975. Chm., Textile Conservation Centre, 1993–; Mem., Museums and Galls Comm (Chm., Conservation Cttee), 1988–92. Trustee, SS Great Britain, 1987–. *Address:* 4 Hogarth Hill, NW11 6AX. *Club:* Arts.

BRANDO, Marlon; American actor, stage and screen; *b* Omaha, Nebraska, 3 April 1924; *s* of Marlon Brando; *m* 1957, Anna Kashfi (marr. diss., 1959); one *s. Educ:* Libertyville High Sch., Illinois; Shattuck Military Academy, Minnesota. Entered Dramatic Workshop of New School for Social Research, New York, 1943; has studied with Elia Kazan and Stella Adler. *Plays include:* I Remember Mama, Broadway, 1944; Truckline Café, 1946; Candida, 1946; A Flag is Born, 1946; The Eagle Has Two Heads, 1946; A Streetcar Named Desire, 1947. *Films include:* The Men, 1950; A Streetcar Named Desire, 1951; Viva Zapata!, 1952; Julius Cæsar, 1953; The Wild Ones, 1953; Désirée, 1954; On the Waterfront, 1954; Guys and Dolls, 1955; Tea House of the August Moon, 1956; Sayonara, 1957; The Young Lions, 1958; The Fugitive Kind, 1960; Mutiny on the Bounty, 1962; The Ugly American, 1963; Bedtime Story, 1964; The Saboteur, Code Name-Morituri, 1965; The Chase, 1966; Appaloosa, 1966; Southwest to Sonora, 1966; A Countess from Hong Kong, 1967; Reflections in a Golden Eye, 1967; Candy, 1968; The Night of the Following Day, 1969; Quiemad!, 1970; The Nightcomers, 1971; The Godfather, 1972; Last Tango in Paris, 1972; The Missouri Breaks, 1975; Apocalypse Now, 1977; Superman, 1978; The Formula, 1981; A Dry White Season, 1990; The Freshman, 1990; Christopher Columbus; Don Juan DeMarco, 1994. Directed, produced and appeared in One-Eyed Jacks, 1959. Academy Award, best actor of year, 1954, 1972. *Publication:* Songs My Mother Taught Me (autobiog.), 1994.

BRANDON, family name of **Baron Brandon of Oakbrook.**

BRANDON OF OAKBROOK, Baron *cr* 1981 (Life Peer), of Hammersmith in Greater London; **Henry Vivian Brandon;** Kt 1966; MC 1942; PC 1978; a Lord of Appeal in Ordinary, 1981–91; *b* 3 June 1920; *y s* of late Captain V. R. Brandon, CBE, RN, and late Joan Elizabeth Maud Simpson; *m* 1955, Jeanette Rosemary, *e d* of late J. V. B. Janvrin; three *s* one *d. Educ:* Winchester Coll. (Scholar); King's Coll., Cambridge (Scholar 1938, Stewart of Rannoch Scholar 1939). Commnd 2nd Lieut RA 1939; Major 1944; served UK, 1939–42, Madagascar, 1942, India and Burma, 1942–45. BA 1946. Barrister, Inner Temple, 1946 (Entrance and Yarborough Anderson Scholar); Member Bar Council, 1951–53; QC 1961; Judge of the High Court of Justice, Probate, Divorce and Admiralty Division, 1966–71, Family Division, 1971–78; Judge of the Admiralty Court, 1971–78; Judge of the Commercial Court, 1977–78; a Lord Justice of Appeal, 1978–81. Member panel of Lloyd's arbitrators in salvage cases, 1961–66; Member panel from which Wreck Commissioners chosen, 1963–66. Hon. LLD Southampton, 1984. *Recreations:* cricket, bridge, travelling. *Address:* 6 Thackeray Close, SW19 4JL. *T:* 0181–947 6344; House of Lords, SW1A 0PW. *Club:* MCC.

BRANDON, Bishop of, since 1992; **Rt. Rev. Malcolm Alfred Warden Harding;** *b* 28 June 1936; *s* of Henry Warden Harding and Grace (*née* Walker); *m* 1962, Marylou (*née* Richards); one *s* two *d. Educ:* Univ. of Western Ontario (BA 1959); Huron Coll. (LTh 1962); Univ. of Manitoba (BSW 1964, MSW 1966). Ordained deacon, 1962; i/c of five rural parishes, dio. of Fredericton, 1962–63; Child Welfare Worker, Children's Aid Soc., Ont., 1963–64; Social Worker, 1966–68, Supervisor, 1968–73, Manitoba Dept of Health and Social Devel t; ordained priest, 1973; Priest-in-charge, Birtle, Solsgirth, 1973–78; Rector, St George's, Brandon, 1978–92; Archdeacon of Brandon, 1986–92; Diocesan Administrator, Brandon, 1992. Hon. DD Huron, 1993. *Recreations:* model railroad, fishing, reading, railway enthusiast. *Address:* 3305 Rosser Avenue, Brandon, Manitoba R7B 0H1, Canada. *T:* (204) 7274750.

BRANDON, Prof. Peter Samuel, FRICS; Professor of Quantity and Building Surveying, since 1985, and Director of Research and Graduate College, since 1993, University of Salford; *b* 4 June 1943; *s* of Samuel Brandon and Doris Eileen Florence Brandon (*née* Downing); *m* 1968, Mary Ann Elizabeth Canham; one *s* two *d. Educ:* Bournemouth Grammar Sch.; Bristol Univ. (MSc Architecture). Private practice and local govt, 1963–69; Lectr, Portsmouth Poly., 1969–73; Prin. Lectr, Bristol Poly., 1973–81; Head of Dept, Portsmouth Poly., 1981–85; Salford University: Chm., Surveying Dept, 1985–93; Pro-Vice-Chancellor, 1993–. Royal Institution of Chartered Surveyors: Chm., Res. Cttee, 1987–91; Mem. Gen. Council representing Gtr Manchester, 1989–93; Mem., Exec. Bd, QS Div., 1991–; Science and Engineering Research Council: Chm., Construction Cttee, 1991–94; Chm., Building Design Technology and Management Sub-Cttee, 1990–91; Mem., Engrg Res. Commn, 1991–94. *Publications:* Cost Planning of Buildings, 1980, 6th edn 1990; (ed) Building Cost Techniques, 1982; Microcomputers in Building Appraisal, 1983; (ed) Quality and Profit in Building Design, 1984; Computer programs for Building Cost Appraisal, 1985; Building, Cost Modelling and Computers, 1987; Expert Systems: the strategic planning of construction projects, 1988; (ed) Investment, Procurement & Performance in Construction, 1991; (ed) Management, Quality and Economics in Building, 1991. *Recreations:* horse riding, walking, travel, modern art, swimming, caravanning. *Address:* Research and Graduate College, University of Salford, Salford M5 4WT. *T:* 0161–745 5839, *Fax:* 0161–745 5553. *Club:* Royal Over-Seas League.

BRANDON-BRAVO, Martin Maurice, FIMgt; *b* 25 March 1932; *s* of late Issac, (Alfred), and Phoebe Brandon-Bravo; *m* 1964, Sally Anne Wallwin; two *s. Educ:* Latymer Sch. FIMgt (FBIM 1980). Joined Richard Stump Ltd, later Richard Stump (1979), 1952; successively Floor Manager, Factory Manager, Production Dir and Asst Man. Dir; Man. Dir., 1979–83; non-exec. Dir, 1983–; Dir, Hall & Earl Ltd, 1970–83. Mem., Nottingham City Council, 1968–70 and 1976–87; Chm., 1970–73, Pres., 1975–83, Nottingham West Cons. Party Orgn; Dep. Chm., City of Nottingham Cons. Fedn. Contested (C): Nottingham East, 1979; Nottingham South, 1992. MP (C) Nottingham South, 1983–92; PPS to Minister of State for Housing and Urban Affairs, 1985–87, to Minister of State, Home Office, 1987–89, to Home Sec., 1989–90, to Lord Privy Seal and Leader of the House of Lords, 1990–92. Mem., Notts CC, 1993–. Contested (C) Nottingham and Leicestershire NW, Eur. Parly elecns, 1994. Mem., Nat. Water Sport Centre Management Cttee, 1972–83; President: Amateur Rowing Assoc., 1993–; Nottingham and Union Rowing Club. *Recreation:* rowing (Mem., Internat. Umpires' Commn; holder of Internat. Licence). *Address:* The Old Farmhouse, 27 Rectory Place, Barton-in-Fabis, Nottingham NG11 0AL. *T:* Nottingham (0115) 983 0459. *Clubs:* Carlton; Leander.

BRANDRETH, Gyles Daubeney; MP (C) City of Chester, since 1992; *b* 8 March 1948; *s* of late Charles Brandreth and of Alice Addison; *m* 1973, Michèle Brown; one *s* two *d. Educ:* Lycée Français de Londres; Betteshanger Sch., Kent; Bedales Sch., Hants; New Coll., Oxford (Scholar). Pres. Oxford Union, Editor of Isis. Chairman: Archway Productions Ltd, 1971–74; Victorama Ltd, 1974–93; Complete Editions Ltd, 1988–93; Director: Colin Smythe Ltd, 1971–73; Newarke Wools Ltd, 1988–92; J. W. Spear & Sons, 1992–. Dep. Chm., Unicorn Heritage, 1987–90. Freelance journalist, 1968–: contrib. Observer, Guardian, Daily Mail, Daily Mirror, Daily Telegraph, Evening Standard, Spectator, Punch, Homes & Gardens, She, Woman's Own; Columnist: Honey, 1968–69; Manchester Evening News, 1971–72; Woman, 1972–73, 1986–88; TV Times, 1989–92; Press Assoc. weekly syndicated column in USA, 1981–85; Ed., Puzzle World, 1989–92. PPS to Financial Sec. to Treasury, 1993–, to Sec. of State for Nat. Heritage, 1994–. Broadcaster, 1969–: TV series incl.: Child of the Sixties, 1969; Puzzle Party, 1977; Chatterbox, 1977–78; Memories, 1982; Countdown, 1983–90; TV-am, 1983–90; Railway Carriage Game, 1985; Catchword, 1986; (with Hinge and Bracket) Dear Ladies (TV script); (with Julian Slade) Now We Are Sixty (play); Theatrical producer, 1971–86: Through the Looking-Glass, 1972; Oxford Theatre Fest., 1974, 1976; The Dame of Sark, Wyndham's, 1974; The Little Hut, Duke of York's, 1974; Dear Daddy, Ambassador's, 1976; Cambridge Fest., 1996; also Son et Lumière. Founder: National Scrabble Championships, 1971; British Pantomime Assoc., 1971; Teddy Bear Mus., Stratford-upon-Avon, 1988. Dir, Europ. Movement's People for Europe campaign, 1975. Appeals Chm., 1983–89, Chm., 1989–93, Vice-Pres., 1993–, NPFA. Three times holder, world record for longest-ever after-dinner speech (4 hrs 19 mins, 1976; 11 hrs, 1978; 12 hrs 30 mins, 1982). *Publications:* over fifty books since Created in Captivity, 1972; most recent, Under the Jumper (autobiog.), 1993; over seventy books for children. *Address:* House of Commons, SW1A 0AA.

BRANDRICK, David Guy, CBE 1981; Secretary, British Coal Corporation (formerly National Coal Board), 1972–89, retired; Director: Coal Staff Superannuation Scheme Trustees Ltd; CMT Pension Trustee Services Ltd; *b* 17 April 1932; *s* of Harry and Minnie Brandrick; *m* 1956, Eunice Fisher; one *s* one *d.* *Educ:* Newcastle-under-Lyme High Sch.; St John's Coll., Oxford (MA). Joined National Coal Board, 1955; Chairman's Office, 1957; Principal Private Secretary to Chairman, 1961; Departmental Sec., Production Dept, 1963; Dep. Sec. to the Bd, 1967. *Recreation:* walking.

BRANDT, Paul Nicholas; His Honour Judge Brandt; a Circuit Judge, since 1987; *b* 21 Nov. 1937; *s* of late Paul Francis and of Barbara Brandt. *Educ:* St Andrew's Sch., Eastbourne; Marlborough Coll.; New Coll., Oxford (BA 2nd Cl. Hons Sch. of Jurisprudence). Called to the Bar, Gray's Inn, 1963; a Recorder, 1983–87. *Recreations:* sailing, shooting, Rugby football. *Address:* Colchester & Clacton County Court, Falkland House, 25 Southway, Colchester, Essex CO3 3EG. *Clubs:* Royal Harwich Yacht (Woolverstone, Suffolk), Bar Yacht.

BRANDT, Peter Augustus; Chairman, Atkins Fulford Ltd, since 1977; *b* 2 July 1931; *s* of late Walter Augustus Brandt and late Dorothy Gray Brandt (*née* Crane); *m* 1962, Elisabeth Margaret (*née* ten Bos); two *s* one *d.* *Educ:* Eton Coll.; Trinity Coll., Cambridge (MA). Joined Wm Brandt's Sons & Co. Ltd, Merchant Bankers, 1954; Mem. Bd, 1960; Chief Executive, 1966; resigned, 1972. Director: London Life Assoc., 1962–89; Corp. of Argentine Meat Producers (CAP) Ltd and affiliates, 1970; Edward Bates (Holdings) Ltd, 1972–77; Edward Bates & Sons Ltd, 1972–77 (Chm., 1974–77). Mem., Nat. Rivers Authy (formerly Nat. Rivers Adv. Cttee), 1988–95. *Recreations:* sailing, rowing, steam engines, wild fowl. *Address:* Spout Farm, Boxford, Suffolk CO10 5HA. *Clubs:* Carlton; Leander (Henley-on-Thames).

BRANIGAN, Sir Patrick (Francis), Kt 1954; QC; *b* 30 Aug. 1906; *e s* of late D. Branigan and Teresa, *d* of Thomas Clinton, Annagassan, Co. Louth; *m* 1935, Prudence, *yr d* of late Dr A. Avent, Seaton, Devon; one *s* one *d.* *Educ:* Newbridge Coll., Co. Kildare; Trinity Coll., Dublin. BA 1st Class Hons in Law and Political Science and gold medallist, 1928; called to Irish Bar, Certificate of Honour, 1928 (1st Victoria Prize, 1927); called to Bar, Gray's Inn, 1935. Practised at Irish Bar, 1928–30; Downing Coll., Cambridge, 1930–31; Colonial Administrative Service, Kenya, 1931; Crown Counsel, Tanganyika, 1934; Solicitor-General, N. Rhodesia, 1938; Chairman NR Man-power Cttee, 1939–41; Chairman Conciliation Board, Copperbelt Strike, 1940; Member NR Nat. Arbitration Tribunal, 1940–46; Member Strauss Arbitration Tribunal, Bulawayo, 1944; Chairman, Road Transport Services Board and Electricity Board of N. Rhodesia, 1939–46; Legal Secretary to Govt of Malta and Chairman Malta War Damage Commission, 1946–48; periodically acting Lieut-Governor of Malta, 1947–48. Minister of Justice and Attorney-General, Gold Coast, 1948–54; QC Gold Coast, 1949; retired, 1954. Chairman of Commission of inquiry into Copperbelt industrial unrest, 1956; Vice-Chm., and Ldr UK delgn to UN Seminar on Protection of Human Rights in Criminal Procedure, Vienna, 1960. Dep. Chm. Devon QS, 1958–71; a Recorder of the Crown Court, 1972–75. Chairman: Pensions Appeal Tribunal, 1955–81; Agricultural Land Tribunal for SW Area of England, 1955–79; Nat. Insurance Med. Appeal Tribunal, SW Reg., 1960–78; Mental Health Review Tribunal, SW England, 1960–78; Mem., Industrial Disputes Tribunal, 1955–59. Knight Commander of Order of St Gregory, 1956. *Address:* 17 Pyndar Court, Newland, near Malvern, Worcs WR13 5AX. *T:* Malvern (01684) 567761.

BRANN, Col William Norman, OBE 1967; ERD; Lord Lieutenant for County Down, 1979–90, retired; *b* 16 Aug. 1915; *s* of Rev. William Brann, BA, LLB, and Francesca Brann; *m* 1950, Anne Elizabeth Hughes; one *s* two *d.* *Educ:* Campbell Coll., Belfast. With Beck & Scott Ltd, Food Importers, Belfast, 1934–80, Chm., 1984–. Served War of 1939–45, Army, France and Far East; TA, 1947–53. Hon. ADC to HE the Governor of N Ireland, 1952–72. Belfast Harbour Comr, 1960–79. Chm., Somme Hosp. for Ex Service Men and Women, retd; Pres., Burma Star Assoc., NI. County Down: DL 1974–79; JP 1980; High Sheriff, 1982. KStJ 1991. *Recreations:* gardening, hunting. *Address:* 75 Ballymoney Road, Craigavad, Holywood, Co. Down BT18 0JJ. *T:* Holywood (01232) 422224. *Club:* Ulster Reform (Belfast).

BRANSON, Rear Adm. Cecil Robert Peter Charles, CBE 1975; *b* 30 March 1924; *s* of Cecil Branson and Marcelle Branson; *m* 1946, Sonia Moss; one *d.* *Educ:* RNC, Dartmouth. Served, HMS Dragon, W Africa, S Atlantic, Indian Ocean and Far East (present during time of fall of Singapore and Java), 1941–42; Sub-Lieut's Courses, 1942–43; qual. as submarine specialist, served in HM S/M Sea Rover, Far East, 1944–45; various appts in S/Ms, 1945–53; First Lieut, HMS Defender, 1953–55; jssc; CO, HMS Roebuck, Dartmouth Trng Sqdn, 1957; Staff, Flag Officer Flotillas Mediterranean, 1959–60; Jt Planning Staff, MoD, 1960–62; Exec. Officer, HMS Victorious, Far East, 1962–64; CO, HMS Rooke, Gibraltar, 1965; NATO Def. Coll., 1965; Defence Planning Staff, MoD, 1966–68; CO, HMS Phoebe, and Captain (D) Londonderry Sqdn, 1968–70; Naval Attaché, Paris, 1970–73; CO, HMS Hermes, 1973–74 (Hermes headed RN task force evacuating Brit. and foreign subjects from Cyprus beaches after Turkish invasion, 1973); Asst Chief of Naval Staff (Ops), MoD, 1975–77; retired. *Club:* Army and Navy.

BRANSON, Edward James, MA; financial consultant; a Metropolitan Stipendiary Magistrate, 1971–87; barrister-at-law; *b* 10 March 1918; *s* of late Rt Hon. Sir George Branson, PC, sometime Judge of High Court, and late Lady (Mona) Branson; *m* 1949, Evette Huntley, *e d* of late Rupert Huntley Flindt; one *s* two *d.* *Educ:* Bootham Sch., York; Trinity Coll., Cambridge. Served War, 1939–46, Staffordshire Yeomanry: Palestine, Egypt, and Western Desert 1941–42; GSO 3 (Ops) attd 2 NZ Div. for Alamein, 1942; GS02 (Ops), attd 6 (US) Corps for Salerno and Anzio landings, 1943–44; subseq. GSO2 (Ops) 53 (W) Div. in Germany. Called to the Bar, Inner Temple, 1950; practised London and SE Circuit. *Recreations:* shooting, fishing, archaeology. *Address:* Cakeham Manor, West Wittering, W Sussex PO20 8LG.

See also R. Branson.

BRANSON, Richard Charles Nicholas; Founder and Chairman, Virgin Retail Group, Virgin Communications, Virgin Travel Group, and Virgin Hotels Group; Life President, Virgin Music Group (sold to Thorn-EMI, 1992); *b* 18 July 1950; *s* of Edward James Branson, *qv*; *m* 1st, 1969 (marr. diss.); 2nd, 1989, Joan Templeman; one *s* one *d.* *Educ:* Stowe. Editor, Student magazine, 1968–69; set up Student Advisory Centre (now Help), 1970. Founded Virgin Mail-Order Co., 1969, followed by Virgin Retail, Virgin Record Label, Virgin Music Publishing, Virgin Recording Studios; estabd Virgin Record subsids in 25 countries, 1980–86; founded Virgin Atlantic Airways, 1984; Voyager Gp Ltd formed 1986, encompassing interests in travel, clubs and hotels; Virgin Records launched in US, 1987; founded Virgin Radio, 1993. Pres., UK 2000, 1988– (Chm., 1986–88); Dir, Intourist Moscow Ltd, 1988–. Launched charity, The Healthcare Foundn, 1987. Captain, Atlantic Challenger II, winner Blue Riband for fastest crossing of Atlantic by a ship, 1986; with Per Lindstrand, first to cross Atlantic in hot air balloon, 1987, and Pacific, 1991 (longest flight in hot air balloon, 6700 miles, and fastest speed, 200 mph, 1991). *Address:* c/o Virgin Group Ltd, 120 Campden Hill Road, W8 7AR. *T:* 0171–229 1282.

BRANSON, William Rainforth, CBE 1969; retired; *b* 2 Jan. 1905; *s* of late A. W. Branson, JP; *m* 1932, Dorothy Iris Green (*d* 1982); no *c.* *Educ:* Rydal Sch.; University of Leeds. BSc, 1st Class Hons (Fuel and Gas Engrg), 1927; MSc 1930. Asst Engineer, Gas Light & Coke Co., London, 1927–37; Asst Engineer, later Dep. Engineer, Cardiff Gas Light & Coke Co., 1937–45; Dep. Controller, later Controller, Public Utilities Br., Control Commn for Germany, 1945–49; Planning Engineer, Wales Gas Board, 1949–51; Technical Officer, E Midlands Gas Board, 1952–54; Dep. Chairman, W. Midlands Gas Board, 1954–65; Chm., Scottish Gas Bd, 1965–68; Dir, Woodall-Duckham Group Ltd, 1969–73. President, Instn of Gas Engineers, 1964–65. *Recreation:* music. *Address:* Sidmouth House West, Cotmaton Road, Sidmouth EX10 8ST.

BRANT, Colin Trevor, CMG 1981; CVO 1979; HM Diplomatic Service, retired; *b* 2 June 1929; *m* 1954, Jean Faith Walker; one *s* two *d.* *Educ:* Christ's Hospital, Horsham; Sidney Sussex Coll., Cambridge (MA). Served Army, 4th Queen's Own Hussars, active service, Malaya, 1948–49; Pilot, Cambridge Univ. Air Squadron, 1951–52. Joined Sen. Br., Foreign Office, 1952; MECAS, Lebanon, 1953–54; Bahrain, 1954; Amman, 1954–56; FO, 1956–59; Stockholm, 1959–61; Cairo, 1961–64; Joint Services Staff Coll., Latimer, Bucks, 1964–65 (jssc); FO, 1965–67; Head of Chancery and Consul, Tunis, 1967–68; Asst Head, Oil Dept, FCO, 1969–71; Counsellor (Commercial), Caracas, 1971–73; Counsellor (Energy), Washington, 1973–78; Ambassador to Qatar, 1978–81; FCO Fellow, St Antony's Coll., Oxford, 1981–82; Consul Gen., and Dir Trade Promotion for S Africa, Johannesburg, 1982–87. Consultant, Carmichael & Sweet, Portsmouth, 1990–93; Dir, Internat. Energy Management Ltd, 1994–. Donation Governor, Christ's Hosp., 1980, Almoner 1989. *Recreations:* music, painting, history. *Address:* The Old School House, Horcott, Fairford, Glos GL7 4BX. *Clubs:* Travellers', Royal Over-Seas League.

BRASH, Rev. Alan Anderson, OBE 1962; Moderator, Presbyterian Church of New Zealand, 1978–79; *b* 5 June 1913; *s* of Thomas C. Brash, CBE, New Zealand, and Margaret Brash (*née* Allan); *m* 1938, Eljean Ivory Hill; one *s* one *d.* *Educ:* Dunedin Univ., NZ (MA); Edinburgh Univ. (BD). Parish Minister in NZ, 1938–46 and 1952–56; Gen. Sec., NZ Nat. Council of Churches, 1947–52 and 1957–64, East Asia Christian Conf., 1958–68; Dir, Christian Aid, London, 1968–70; Dir, Commn on Inter-Church Aid, Refuge and World Service, WCC, 1970–73; Dep. Gen. Sec., WCC, 1974–78. Hon. DD Toronto, 1971. *Address:* 8 Gatonby Place, Avonhead, Christchurch, New Zealand.

BRASH, Robert, CMG 1980; HM Diplomatic Service, retired; Ambassador to Indonesia, 1981–84; *b* 30 May 1924; *s* of Frank and Ida Brash; *m* 1954, Barbara Enid Clarke; three *s* one *d.* *Educ:* Trinity Coll., Cambridge (Exhbnr). War Service, 1943–46. Entered Foreign Service, 1949; Djakarta, 1951–55; FO, 1955–58; First Sec., 1956; Jerusalem, 1958–61; Bonn, 1961–64; Bucharest, 1964–66; FCO, 1966–70; Counsellor, 1968; Canadian Nat. Defence Coll., 1970–71; Counsellor and Consul-Gen., Saigon, 1971–73; Counsellor, Vienna, 1974–78; Consul-Gen., Düsseldorf, 1978–81. Chm., Guildford Rambling Club, 1986–91. *Recreations:* walking, gardening, stained glass, golf. *Address:* Woodbrow, Woodham Lane, Woking, Surrey GU21 5SR.

BRASHER, Christopher William; President, London Marathon Ltd, since 1995 (Founder and Chairman, 1981–95); Chairman: Brasher Leisure Ltd, since 1977; The Brasher Boot Co., since 1992; Berghaus, since 1993; *b* 21 Aug. 1928; *s* of William Kenneth Brasher, CBE and Katie Howe Brasher; *m* 1959, Shirley Bloomer; one *s* two *d.* *Educ:* Rugby Sch.; St John's Coll., Cambridge (MA). Pres., Mountaineering Club and Athletic Club, Cambridge Univ. Management Trainee and Jun. Executive, Mobil Oil Co., 1951–57; Sports Editor, 1957–61, columnist and Olympic Corresp., 1961–91, The Observer; BBC Television: Reporter, Tonight, 1961–65; Editor, Time Out, and Man Alive, 1964–65, Head of Gen. Features, 1969–72; reporter/producer, 1972–81. Man. Dir, Fleetfoot Ltd, 1979–95; Chm., Reebok UK Ltd, 1990–93. Co-Founder and Chm., British Orienteering Fedn (formerly English Orienteering Assoc.), 1966–69. Trustee, London Marathon Charitable Trust, 1981–; Founder and Trustee, John Muir Trust, 1983–92; Chm., Chris Brasher Trust, 1988–. Rep. GB, Olympic Games, 1952 and 1956; Gold Medal for 3,000 metres Steeplechase, 1956. DUniv Stirling, 1989. OStJ 1995. National Medal of Honour, Finland, 1975; Sports Writer of the Year (British Press Awards), 1968, 1976. *Publications:* The Red Snows (with Sir John Hunt), 1960; Sportsmen of our Time, 1962; Tokyo 1964: a diary of the XVIIIth Olympiad, 1964; Mexico 1968: a diary of the XIXth Olympics, 1968; Munich 72, 1972; (ed) The London Marathon: the first ten years, 1991. *Recreations:* mountains, fishing, horse racing, orienteering, social running. *Address:* The Navigator's House, River Lane, Richmond, Surrey TW10 7AG. *T:* 0181–940 8822. *Clubs:* Alpine, Flyfishers', Hurlingham; Ranelagh Harriers (Petersham); Thames Hare and Hounds (Kingston Vale).

BRASNETT, John, CMG 1987; HM Diplomatic Service, retired; Deputy High Commissioner, Bombay, 1985–89; *b* 30 Oct. 1929; *s* of late Norman Vincent Brasnett and of Frances May Brasnett (*née* Hewlett); *m* 1956, Jennifer Ann Reid; one *s* one *d.* *Educ:* Blundells Sch.; Selwyn Coll., Cambridge (BA). Served Royal Artillery, 1948–49. Colonial Administrative Service, Uganda, 1953–65; retired from HM Overseas CS as Dep. Administrator, Karamoja District, 1965; entered HM Diplomatic Service, 1965; 1st Sec., OECD Delegn, 1968; Dep. High Comr, Freetown, 1970; FCO, 1973; Olympic Attaché, Montreal, 1975–76; Dep. High Comr, Accra, 1977–80; Counsellor (Econ. and Commercial), Ottawa, 1980–85). *Recreations:* reading, photography. *Address:* 8 Croft Way, Sevenoaks, Kent TN13 2JX. *Club:* Commonwealth Trust.

BRASS, John, CBE 1968; BSc, FEng, FIMinE; FRSA; Member, National Coal Board, 1971–73; *b* 22 Oct. 1908; 2nd *s* of late John Brass, Mining Engineer, and late Mary Brass (*née* Swainston); *m* 1934, Jocelyn Constance Cape, Stroud, Glos; three *s* (one *d* decd). *Educ:* Oundle Sch.; Birmingham Univ. (BSc Hons). Various appointments, all in mining; Chm., W Midlands Division, NCB, 1961–67; Regional Chm., Yorks and NW Areas, NCB, 1967–71. Chm., Amalgamated Construction Co., 1976–86. *Address:* Flat 6, The Old Mill, Scott Lane, Wetherby, W Yorks LS22 6NB.

BRASS, Prof. William, CBE 1981; FBA 1979; Professor of Medical Demography, 1972–88, now Emeritus, and Director of Centre for Population Studies, 1978–88, London School of Hygiene and Tropical Medicine; *b* 5 Sept. 1921; *s* of John Brass and Margaret Tait (*née* Haig); *m* 1948, Betty Ellen Agnes Topp; two *d.* *Educ:* Royal High Sch., Edinburgh; Edinburgh Univ. (MA Hons Maths and Nat. Phil., 1943). Scientific Officer, Royal Naval Scientific Service, 1943–46; E African Statistical Dept, Colonial Service, 1948–55; Lectr in Statistics, 1955–64, Sen. Lectr 1964, Aberdeen Univ.; London Sch. of Hygiene and Trop. Medicine: Reader in Med. Demography, 1965–72; Dir, Centre for Overseas Population Studies, 1974–78; Head, Dept of Med. Stats and Epidemiology, 1977–82. Pres., Internat. Union for the Scientific Study of Population, 1985–89. For. Associate, US Nat. Acad. of Scis, 1984. Mindel Sheps Award for distinguished contribn to demography, Population Assoc. of America, 1978. *Publications:* The Demography of Tropical Africa, 1968; Metodos para estimar la fecundidad y la mortalidad en poblaciones con datos Limitados: selección de trabajos, 1974; Methods of Estimating Fertility and Mortality from Limited and Defective Data, 1975; Advances in Methods for Estimating Fertility and Mortality from Limited and Defective Data, 1985; about 100 papers in learned jls. *Recreations:* travel, observing art and archaeology. *Address:* 3 Holt Close, N10 3HW. *T:* 0181–883 1195.

BRASSEY, family name of **Baron Brassey of Apethorpe.**

BRASSEY OF APETHORPE, 3rd Baron, *cr* 1938, of Apethorpe; **David Henry Brassey;** Bt 1922; OBE 1994; JP; DL; *b* 16 Sept. 1932; *er s* of 2nd Baron Brassey of Apethorpe, MC, TD, and late Lady Brassey of Apethorpe; *S* father, 1967; *m* 1st, 1958, Myrna Elizabeth (*d* 1974), *o d* of late Lt-Col John Baskervyle-Glegg; one *s*; 2nd, 1978, Caroline, *y d* of late Lt-Col G. A. Evill; two *d.* Commissioned, Grenadier Guards, 1951; Major, 1966, retired, 1967. JP 1970, DL 1972, Northants. *Heir: s* Hon. Edward Brassey, *b* 9 March 1964. *Address:* The Manor House, Apethorpe, Peterborough PE8 5DL. *T:* Stamford (01780) 470231.*Club:* White's.

BRATBY, Jean Esme Oregon; *see* Cooke, J. E. O.

BRATT, Guy Maurice, CMG 1977; MBE 1945; HM Diplomatic Service, retired; Counsellor, Foreign and Commonwealth Office, 1977–80; *b* 4 April 1920; *s* of late Ernst Lars Gustaf Bratt and late Alice Maud Mary Bratt (*née* Raper); *m* 1945, Françoise Nelly Roberte Girardet; two *s* one *d. Educ:* Merchant Taylors' Sch.; London Univ. (BA). Served Army, 1939–46 (MBE): Major, Royal Signals. Solicitor 1947. Asst Sec., Colonial Develt Corp.; joined HM Foreign (subseq. Diplomatic) Service, 1952; served FO, 1952–54; Berlin, 1954–56; Brussels, 1956–58; FO, 1958–62; Vienna, 1962–66; FCO, 1966–70; Geneva, 1970–72; FCO, 1972–74; Washington, 1974–77. *Publications:* The Bisses of Valais: man-made watercourses in Switzerland, 1995; articles in railway and model railway jls. *Recreations:* music, railways, mountaineering. *Address:* 2 Orchehill Rise, Gerrards Cross, Bucks SL9 8PR. *T:* Gerrards Cross (01753) 883106. *Club:* Travellers'.

BRATZA, Nicolas Dušan; QC 1988; a Recorder, since 1993; UK Member, European Commission of Human Rights, since 1993; *b* 3 March 1945; *s* of late Milan Bratza, concert violinist, and Hon. Margaret Bratza (*née* Russell). *Educ:* Wimbledon Coll.; Brasenose Coll., Oxford (BA 1st Cl. Hons, MA). Instructor, Univ. of Pennsylvania Law Sch., 1967–68; called to Bar, Lincoln's Inn, 1969 (Hardwicke and Droop Schol.), Bencher, 1993; Jun. Counsel to the Crown, Common Law, 1979–88. Vice-Chm., British Inst. of Human Rights, 1990–. *Publications:* (jtly) Contempt of Court, and Crown Proceedings, in Halsbury's Laws of England, 4th edn. *Recreations:* music, cricket. *Address:* 1 Hare Court, Temple, EC4Y 7BE. *T:* 0171–353 3171. *Clubs:* Garrick, MCC.

BRAVO, Martin Maurice B.; *see* Brandon-Bravo.

BRAY, Denis Campbell, CMG 1977; CVO 1975; JP; Chairman, Denis Bray Consultants Ltd, Hong Kong, since 1985; *b* 24 Jan. 1926; *s* of Rev. Arthur Henry Bray and Edith Muriel Bray; *m* 1952, Marjorie Elizabeth Bottomley; four *d* (one *s* decd). *Educ:* Kingswood Sch.; Jesus Coll., Cambridge (MA). BScEcon London. RN, 1947–49. Colonial Service Devonshire Course, 1949–50; Admin. Officer, Hong Kong, 1950; Dist Comr, New Territories, 1971; Hong Kong Comr in London, 1977–80; Sec. for Home Affairs, Hong Kong, 1973–77 and 1980–84, retd. Chairman: English Schools Foundn, Hong Kong, 1985–91; Jubilee Sports Centre, Hong Kong, 1985–89. Director: First Pacific Davies (Hldgs), 1986–; First Pacific Bancshares Hldgs, 1987–93; Herald (Hong Kong) Ltd, 1987–; Leighton Asia Ltd, 1990–; Exec. Dir, Community Chest of Hong Kong, 1985–92. Pres., Hong Kong Yachting Assoc., 1989–91. JP 1960–85, and 1987. *Recreations:* ocean racing and cruising. *Address:* 8A-7 Borrett Mansions, 8–9 Bowen Road, Hong Kong. *T:* 25263630. *Clubs:* Travellers', London Rowing, Royal Ocean Racing; Leander (Henley-on-Thames); Hong Kong, Royal Hong Kong Jockey, Royal Hong Kong Yacht; Tai Po Boat.
See also J. W. Bray.

BRAY, Jeremy William, PhD; MP (Lab) Motherwell South, since 1983 (Motherwell and Wishaw, Oct. 1974–1983); *b* 29 June 1930; *s* of Rev. Arthur Henry Bray and Mrs Edith Muriel Bray; *m* 1953, Elizabeth (*née* Trowell); four *d. Educ:* Aberystwyth Grammar Sch.; Kingswood Sch.; Jesus Coll., Cambridge (PhD 1956). Researched in pure mathematics at Cambridge, 1953–55; Choate Fellow, Harvard Univ., USA, 1955–56; Technical Officer, Wilton Works of ICI, 1956–62. Contested (Lab) Thirsk and Malton, General Election, 1959; MP (Lab) Middlesbrough West, 1962–70. Parly Sec., Min. of Power, 1966–67; Jt Parly Sec., Min. of Technology, 1967–69; Opposition spokesman on science and technology, 1983–92. Member: Select Cttee on Nationalised Industries, 1962–64; Estimates Cttee, 1964–66; Expenditure Cttee, 1978–79; Select Cttee on Treasury and Civil Service, 1979–83 (Chm., Sub-cttee, 1981–82); Select Cttee on Sci. and Technol., 1992–; Bd, Parly Office of Sci. and Technol., 1993–; Chairman: Labour, Science and Technol. Group, 1964–66; Economic Affairs Estimates Sub-Cttee, 1964–66; Parly Mental Health Gp, 1994–; Vice Pres., Parlt and Sci. Cttee, 1993–; Vice Chairman: Parly Engrg Gp, 1993–; British-Chinese Parly Gp, 1987–. Dir, Mullard Ltd, 1970–73; Consultant, Battelle Res. Centre, Geneva, 1973; Sen. Res. Fellow, 1974, Vis. Prof., 1975–79, Univ. of Strathclyde; Vis. Res. Fellow, Imperial Coll., 1989–. Mem. Adv. Council, Save British Science, 1993–. Dep. Chm., Christian Aid, 1972–84; Co-Dir, Programme of Res. into Econometric Methods, Imperial Coll., 1971–74. Chm., Fabian Soc., 1971–72. *Publications:* Decision in Government, 1970; Production Purpose and Structure, 1982; Fabian pamphlets and articles in jls. *Recreation:* sailing. *Address:* House of Commons, SW1A 0AA.
See also D. C. Bray.

BRAY, Prof. Kenneth Noel Corbett, PhD; FRS 1991; CEng; Hopkinson and Imperial Chemical Industries Professor of Applied Thermodynamics, Cambridge University, since 1985; *b* 19 Nov. 1929; *s* of Harold H. Bray and Effie E. Bray; *m* 1958, Shirley Maureen Culver; two *s* one *d. Educ:* Univ. of Cambridge (BA); Univ. of Southampton (PhD); MSE Princeton; CEng; MRAeS; MAIAA. Engr in Research Dept, Handley Page Aircraft, 1955–56; University of Southampton, 1956–85: Dean, Faculty of Engrg and Applied Science, 1975–78; Head, Dept of Aeronautics and Astronautics, 1982–85. Vis. appt, Avco-Everett Res. Lab., Mass, USA, 1961–62; Vis. Prof., MIT, 1966–67; Vis. Res. Engr, Univ. of California, San Diego, 1975, 1983. *Publications:* on topics in gas dynamics, chemically reacting flows, molecular energy transfer processes and combustion. *Recreations:* walking, wood carving, gardening. *Address:* 23 De Freville Avenue, Cambridge CB4 1HW.

BRAY, Maj.-Gen. Paul Sheldon, CB 1991; Paymaster-in-Chief and Inspector of Army Pay Services, 1989–92, now retired; *b* 31 Jan. 1936; *s* of Gerald Bray and Doris (*née* Holt); *m* 1958, Marion Diana Naden; one *s* two *d. Educ:* Purbrook Park County High Sch.; RMA Sandhurst; Southampton Univ. (BA 1995). FCIS, ndc, psc†, sq, pfc. Commissioned RA 1956; served BAOR, Cyprus, UK; transf. RAPC 1965; served Malaya, N Wales, MoD, HQ UKLF, HQ Scotland, HQ NE District; OC RAPC Training Centre, 1976–77; NDC 1978; DS RMCS Shrivenham, 1979–82; MoD 1982; Chief Paymaster, Army Pay Office (Officers' Accounts), 1982–83; Comdt, Defence ADP Training Centre, 1983–85; Chief Paymaster ADP, RAPC Computer Centre, 1985–89. Dep. Col Comdt, AGC, 1993–. Trustee, Winchester Children's Holiday Trust, 1989. Gov., King's Sch., Winchester, 1992–. *Recreations:* music, theatre, travel, oenology, rearranging the garden. *Address:* c/o Corps HQ, RAPC Worthy Down, Winchester, Hants SO21 2RG.

BRAY, Richard Winston Atterton; His Honour Judge Bray; a Circuit Judge, since 1993; *b* 10 April 1945; *s* of Winston Bray, *qv* and Betty Atterton (*née* Miller); *m* 1978, Judith Elizabeth Margaret Ferguson; one *s* three *d. Educ:* Rugby Sch.; Corpus Christi Coll., Oxford (BA). Called to the Bar, Middle Temple, 1970; practiced on Midland and Oxford Circuit; Asst Recorder, 1983–87; Recorder, 1987–93. *Recreations:* cricket, Real tennis, astronomy. *Address:* 1 King's Bench Walk, Temple, EC4Y 7DB. *T:* 0171–353 8436. *Clubs:* MCC, I Zingari, Frogs.

BRAY, Sir Theodor (Charles), Kt 1975; CBE 1964; Director, Queensland Arts Council, since 1976; Chancellor, Griffith University, Brisbane, 1975–85; *b* 11 Feb. 1905; *s* of Horace and Maude Bray; *m* 1931, Rosalie (*d* 1988), *d* of Rev. A. M. Trengove; three *s* two *d* (and one *s* one *d* decd). *Educ:* state schs; Adelaide Univ. Apprentice Printer, Reporter, Register, Adelaide; Sub-editor, Chief Sub-editor, The Argus, Melbourne; Editor (26 yrs), Editor-in-Chief, Jt Man. Dir, Queensland Newspapers Pty Ltd, 1936–70, Dir, 1956–80; Chm., Australian Associated Press, 1968–70; Mem., Austr. Council for the Arts, 1969–73; Austr. Chm., Internat. Press Inst., 1962–70; Chm., Griffith Univ. Council, 1970–75. *Recreations:* bowls, travel. *Address:* 10/64 Macquarie Street, St Lucia, Qld 4067, Australia. *T:* 8707442. *Clubs:* Queensland, Queensland University Staff (Brisbane).

BRAY, William John, CBE 1975; FEng 1978; Director of Research, Post Office, 1966–75 (Dep. Director, 1965); *b* 10 Sept. 1911; British; *m* 1936, Margaret Earp; one *d* (and one *d* decd). *Educ:* Imperial Coll., London Univ. Electrical engineering apprenticeship, Portsmouth Naval Dockyard, 1928–32; Royal and Kitchener Scholarships, Imperial Coll., 1932–34; entered PO Engineering Dept as Asst Engineer, 1934; Commonwealth Fund Fellowship (Harkness Foundation) for study in USA, 1956–57; Staff Engineer, Inland Radio Br., PO Engineering Dept, 1958. Vis. Prof., UCL, 1974–78. External Examr, MSc (Communications), Imperial Coll., London, 1976–80. Participation in work of International Radio Consultative Cttee of International Telecommunication Union and European Postal and Telecommunication Conferences; Consultant to UK Council for Educnl Technology, 1976–78. MSc(Eng), FCGI, DIC, FIEE; DUniv Essex, 1976. J. J. Thomson Medal, IEE, 1978. *Publications:* Memoirs of a Telecommunications Engineer, 1983; papers in Proc. IEE (IEE Ambrose Fleming Radio Sect. and Electronics Div. Premium Awards). *Recreation:* writing a book on pioneers of telecommunications. *Address:* The Pump House, Bredfield, Woodbridge, Suffolk IP13 6AH. *T:* Woodbridge (01394) 385838.

BRAY, Winston, CBE 1970; Deputy Chairman and Deputy Chief Executive, BOAC, 1972–74; Member Board, BOAC, 1971–74; Member Board, BAAC Ltd (formerly BOAC (AC Ltd), 1969–74; *b* 29 April 1910; *s* of late Edward Bray and Alice Walker; *m* 1937, Betty Atterton Miller; one *s* one *d* (and one *d* decd). *Educ:* Highgate Sch.; London Univ. (BCom). Missouri Pacific Railroad, USA, 1932; Asst to Traffic Manager, British Airways, 1938; Traffic Dept, BOAC, 1940; Sales Promotion Supt, 1946; Sales Manager, 1950; Sales Planning Manager, 1954; Dir of Planning, 1964; Planning Dir, 1969; Dep. Managing Dir, 1972. FCIT. *Recreations:* sailing, gardening. *Address:* Altenburg, Trafford Road, Great Missenden, Bucks HP16 0BT.
See also R. W. A. Bray.

BRAYBROOK, Edward John, CB 1972; *b* 25 Oct. 1911; *s* of late Prior Wormsley Braybrook and Kate Braybrook; *m* 1937, Eva Rosalin Thomas; one *s* two *d. Educ:* Edmonton Latymer Secondary Sch. Asst Naval Store Officer, Admty, Chatham, Malta and Devonport, 1930–37; Deputy Naval Store Officer, Admty, 1938–39; Naval Store Officer, Admty and Haslemere, 1940–43; Suptg Naval Store Officer, Levant, 1943; Comdr/Captain (SP) RNVR Suptg Naval Store Officer, Ceylon and Southern India, 1944–46; Supt, Perth, Scotland, 1946–47; Asst Director of Stores, Admty, 1947–53; Suptg Naval Store Officer, Chatham, 1953–55; Deputy Director of Stores, Admty, 1955–64; Director of Stores (Naval), MoD, 1964–70; Dir-Gen. Supplies and Transport (Naval), MoD, 1970–73. *Recreations:* gardening, photography, painting, handicrafts. *Address:* 22 Church Drive, North Harrow, Middlesex HA2 7NW. *T:* 0181–427 0838.

BRAYBROOKE, 10th Baron *cr* 1788; **Robin Henry Charles Neville;** Lord-Lieutenant of Essex, since 1992; Hereditary Visitor of Magdalene College, Cambridge; Patron of three livings; farmer and landowner; *b* 29 Jan. 1932; *s* of 9th Baron Braybrooke and Muriel Evelyn (*d* 1962), *d* of William C. Manning; *S* father, 1990; *m* 1st, 1955, Robin Helen Brockhoff (marr. diss. 1974); four *d* (inc. twins) (and one *d* decd); 2nd, 1974, Linda Norman; three *d. Educ:* Eton; Magdalene Coll., Cambridge (MA); RAC Cirencester. Commnd Rifle Bde, 1951; served 3rd Bn King's African Rifles in Kenya and Malaya, 1951–52. Dir of Essex and Suffolk Insurance Co. until amalgamation with Guardian Royal Exchange. Member: Saffron Walden RDC, 1959–69; for Stansted, Essex CC, 1969–72; Council of CLA, 1965–83; Agricl Land Tribunal, Eastern Area, 1975–. Chairman: Price Trust, 1983–95; Rural Develt Commn for Essex, 1984–90. Pres., Essex Show, 1990. DL Essex, 1980. *Recreations:* railway and airfield operating, flying, motorcycling. *Heir: kinsman* George Neville, *b* 23 March 1943. *Address:* Abbey House, Audley End, Saffron Walden, Essex CB11 4JB. *T:* Saffron Walden (01799) 522484. *Clubs:* Boodle's, Farmers'.

BRAYBROOKE, Rev. Marcus Christopher Rossi; non-stipendiary priest, Marsh and Toot Baldon, Dorchester Team Ministry, Oxford, since 1993; *b* 16 Nov. 1938; *s* of late Lt-Col Arthur Rossi Braybrooke and of Marcia Nona Braybrooke; *m* 1964, Mary Elizabeth Walker, JP, BSc, CQSW; one *s* one *d. Educ:* Cranleigh School; Magdalene College, Cambridge (BA, MA); Madras Christian College; Wells Theological College; King's College, London (MPhil). Curate, St Michael's, Highgate, 1964–67; Team Vicar, Strood Clergy Team, 1967–73; Rector, Swainswick, Langridge, Woolley, 1973–79; Dir of Training, Dio. of Bath and Wells, 1979–84; Hon. priest-in-charge, Christ Church, Bath, 1984–91; Exec. Director, Council of Christians and Jews, 1984–87; Preb., Wells Cathedral, 1990–93; Chaplain, Chapel of St Mary Magdalene, Bath, 1992–93. World Congress of Faiths: Chm., 1978–83 and 1992–; a Vice-Pres., 1986–; Chm., Internat. Cttee, 1988–93; Chm., Internat. Interfaith Orgns Co-ordinating Cttee, 1990–93. Examng Chaplain to Bishop of Bath and Wells, 1984–88. Sir Sigmund Sternberg Award for contributions to Christian-Jewish relations, 1992. Editor: World Faiths Insight, 1976–91; Common Ground, 1987–93. *Publications:* Together to the Truth, 1971; The Undiscovered Christ of Hinduism, 1973; Interfaith Worship, 1974; Interfaith Organizations: a historical directory, 1980; Time to Meet, 1990; Wide Embracing Love, 1990; Pilgrimage of Hope, 1992; Stepping Stones to a Global Ethic, 1992; Be Reconciled, 1992; (ed with Tony Bayfield) Dialogue with a Difference, 1992; contrib. to various theol books and jls incl. Theology, The Modern Churchman, The Tablet, The Expository Times. *Recreations:* gardening, tennis, swimming, travel, photography. *Address:* The Rectory, Marsh Baldon, Oxford OX44 9LS. *T:* Nuneham Courtney (01865) 343215, *Fax:* (01865) 343575.

BRAYBROOKE, Neville Patrick Bellairs; writer; *b* 30 May 1925; *s* of Patrick Philip William Braybrooke and Lettice Marjorie Bellairs; *m* 1953, June Guesdon Jolliffe (*d* 1994); one step *d. Educ:* Ampleforth. *Publications:* This is London, 1953; London Green: The

Story of Kensington Gardens, Hyde Park, Green Park and St James's Park, 1959; London, 1961; The Idler: novel, 1961; The Delicate Investigation (play for BBC), 1969; Four Poems for Christmas, 1986; Dialogue with Judas (long poem), 1989; *edited:* The Wind and the Rain: quarterly, 1941–1951; T. S. Eliot: a symposium for his 70th birthday, 1958, 7th edn 1986; A Partridge in a Pear Tree: a celebration for Christmas, 1960; Pilgrim of the Future: a Teilhard de Chardin symposium, 1966, 2nd edn, 1968; The Letters of J. R. Ackerley, 1975, 2nd edn 1977; Seeds in the Wind: 20th century juvenilia from W. B. Yeats to Ted Hughes, 1989, 3rd edn 1991; contrib. Independent, Guardian, New Statesman, New Yorker, Observer, The Tablet, Sunday Times, The Times, Times Lit. Suppl., Sunday Telegraph, Spectator. *Recreations:* animals, walking, reading little reviews, hats. *Address:* Grove House, Castle Road, Cowes, IoW PO31 7QZ. *T:* Cowes (01983) 293950; 10 Gardnor Road, NW3 1HA. *T:* 0171–435 1851. *Club:* PEN.

BRAYE, Baroness (8th in line) *cr* 1529, of Eaton Braye, Co. Bedford; **Mary Penelope Aubrey-Fletcher;** *b* 28 Sept. 1941; *d* of 7th Baron Braye and Dorothea (*d* 1994), *yr d* of late Daniel C. Donoghue, Philadelphia; *S* father, 1985; *m* 1981, Lt-Col Edward Henry Lancelot Aubrey-Fletcher, Grenadier Guards. *Educ:* Assumption Convent, Hengrave Hall; Univ. of Warwick. Pres., Blaby Cons. Assoc., 1986–; Dep. Pres., Northants Red Cross, 1983–92; Chm. School Cttee, St Andrew's Occupational Therapy School, 1988–93. Governor: St Andrew's Hosp., Northampton, 1978–; Three Shires Hosp., Northampton, 1983–. High Sheriff of Northants, 1983; JP South Northants, 1981–86. *Co-heiresses: cousins* Linda Kathleen Fothergill [*b* 2 May 1930, *née* Browne; *m* 1965, Comdr Christopher Henry Fothergill, RN; two *s*; Theresa Beatrice Browne, *b* 9 Aug. 1934]. *Address:* Stanford Hall, Lutterworth, Leics LE17 6DH.

BRAYNE, Richard Bolding, MBE 1957; Clerk of the Worshipful Company of Ironmongers, 1973–90 (Asst Clerk, 1971; Master, 1993–94); *b* 28 Oct. 1924; 3rd *s* of late Brig. Frank Lugard Brayne, MC, CSI, CIE, ICS, and late Iris Goodeve Brayne, K-i-H; *m* 1947, Anne Stoddart Forrest; one *s* two *d. Educ:* Sherborne Sch.; Pembroke Coll., Cambridge. Indian Army, 3rd (Peshawar) Indian Mountain Battery, FF, India, Burma and Far East, 1942–46. Entered Colonial Service as DO, Tanganyika, 1948; Staff Officer to HRH The Princess Margaret's tour of Tanganyika, 1956; Dist Comr, 1957; Principal, Admin. Trng Centre and Local Govt Trng Centre, 1960. Prin. Asst Sec., Min. of Educn, 1963; Mem., E African UGC and Makerere Univ. College Council, 1963; retd from Colonial Service, 1964. Sec., Brit. Paper and Board Makers' Assoc., 1964; Trng Adviser and Develt Manager, Construction Industry Trng Bd, 1966. Member: Exec. Cttee, Nat. Assoc. of Almshouses, 1972– (Chm., 1981–87); Council, Royal Surgical Aid Soc., 1972–95 (Chm., 1982–87). *Recreations:* shooting, golf, D-I-Y. *Address:* Thriftwood Cottage, Broomlands Lane, Limpsfield, Surrey RH8 0SP. *T:* Oxted (01883) 722300.

BRAYNE-BAKER, John, CMG 1957; Colonial Administrative Service, Nigeria (retired); *b* 13 Aug. 1905; *s* of Francis Brayne-Baker and Dorothea Mary Brayne-Baker (*née* Porcher); *m* 1947, Ruth Hancock; no *c. Educ:* Marlborough Coll.; Worcester Coll., Oxford. Nigeria: Asst District Officer, 1928; District Officer, 1938; Senior District Officer, 1948; Resident, 1953. Senior Resident and Deputy Commissioner of the Cameroons, 1954–56; retired 1956. Member, Tiverton RDC, 1959–74, Tiverton DC, 1973–76. *Address:* 48 Markers, Uffculme, Cullompton, Devon EX15 3DZ. *T:* Craddock (01884) 840236. *Club:* Tiverton Golf (Tiverton).

BRAYNE-NICHOLLS, Rear-Adm. (Francis) Brian (Price), CB 1965; DSC 1942; General Secretary, Officers Pensions Society, 1966–79; *b* 1 Dec. 1914; *s* of late Dr G. E. E. Brayne-Nicholls and *g s* of Sir Francis W. T. Brain; *m* 1st, 1939, Wendy (*née* Donnelly) (*d* 1983); one *d*; 2nd, 1986, Mimi M. Scott. *Educ:* RNC, Dartmouth. Sub-Lieut and Lieut, HMS Bee on Yangtse River, 1936–39; specialised in Navigation, 1939; Navigating Officer of: HM Ships Nelson, Rodney, Cardiff, 1939–41, Manxman (during many mining ops, Malta convoys and Madagascar op.), 1941–42; Combined Ops, taking part in Sicily (despatches), Salerno, and Normandy landings. Navigating Officer: HMS Glory, 1944–46; HMS Vanguard, 1948; Comdr 1948; Comdg Officer: HMS Gravelines, 1952–53; HMS St Kitts, 1953–54; Capt 1954; Naval Asst to First Sea Lord, 1954–55; Comdg Officer, HMS Apollo, 1955–57; NATO Standing Group, Washington, 1957–59; Captain of Navigation Direction Sch., HMS Dryad, 1959–61; Admiralty, 1961–63; Rear-Adm. 1963; Chief of Staff to Commander, Far East Fleet, 1963–65. Younger Brother, Trinity House. Mem., Nautical Inst. *Recreation:* golf. *Address:* 3 Tedworth Square, SW3 4DU. *T:* 0171–352 1681. *Club:* Naval and Military.

BRAZIER, Julian William Hendy, TD; MP (C) Canterbury, since 1987; *b* 24 July 1953; *s* of Lt-Col P. H. Brazier; *m* 1984, Katharine Elizabeth, *d* of Brig. P. M. Blagden; three *s* (inc. twins). *Educ:* Wellington Coll.; Brasenose Coll., Oxford (schol. in maths; MA); London Business Sch. Chm., Oxford Univ. Cons. Assoc., 1974. Management consultant to industry, H. B. Maynard, internat. management consultants. Contested (C) Berwick-upon-Tweed, 1983. PPS to Minister of State, HM Treasury, 1990–92, to Sec. of State for Employment, 1992–93. Vice Chm., Cons. Backbench Defence Cttee, 1993–; Sec., Cons. Backbench Finance Cttee, 1990. Served 13 yrs in TA, principally with airborne forces. *Publications:* pamphlets on defence, economic policy, social security and family issues. *Recreations:* science, philosophy, cross-country running. *Address:* House of Commons, SW1A 0AA.

BRAZIER-CREAGH, Maj.-Gen. Sir (Kilner) Rupert, KBE 1962 (CBE 1947); CB 1954; DSO 1944; Secretary of the Horse Race Betting Levy Board, 1961–65; Director of Staff Duties, War Office, 1959–61, retired; *b* 12 Dec. 1909; 2nd *s* of late Lt-Col K. C. Brazier-Creagh; *m* 1st, 1938, Elizabeth Mary (*d* 1967), *d* of late E. M. Magor; one *s* two *d*; 2nd, 1968, Mrs Marie Nelson. *Educ:* Rugby; RMA, Woolwich. 2nd Lieut, 1929; served War of 1939–45 (despatches, DSO); Bde Major, 9th Armoured Div., 1941; GSO1 12th Corps, 1943; Commanded 25th Field Regt, 1944; BGS 21st Army Group and BAOR, 1945–48 (CBE); idc 1949; DDRA, War Office, 1950; CRA 11th Armoured Div., 1951–52; Chief of Staff Malaya Command, 1952–55 (despatches, CB); Asst Comdt, Staff Coll., 1955–57; Chief of Staff, Eastern Command, 1957–59. Officer, American Legion of Merit, 1945. *Recreation:* racing. *Address:* Travis Corners Road, Garrison, NY 10524, USA.

BREACH, Gerald Ernest John; Director, Project Group, Export Credits Guarantee Department, 1988–90; *b* 14 March 1932; *s* of Ernest Albert Breach and Jane Breach; *m* 1st, 1958, Joan Elizabeth Eckford; one *s* one *d*; 2nd, 1988, Sylvia Eileen Harding. *Educ:* Roan Sch., Greenwich. Nat. Service, Royal Signals, 1950–52. Joined: ECGD, 1952; ECGD Management Bd, 1988. *Recreations:* boating, rambling. *Address:* Clunbury, Shropshire.

BREADALBANE AND HOLLAND, 10th Earl of, *cr* 1677; **John Romer Boreland Campbell;** Mac Chailein Mhic Dhonnachaidh (celtic designation); Viscount of Tay and Paintland; Lord Glenorchy, Benederaloch, Ormelie and Weik, 1677; Bt of Glenorchy; Bt of Nova Scotia, 1625; *b* 28 April 1919; *o s* of 9th Earl of Breadalbane and Holland, MC; *S* father, 1959; *m* 1949, Coralie (marr. diss.), *o d* of Charles Archer. *Educ:* Eton; RMC, Sandhurst; Basil Patterson Tutors; Edinburgh Univ. Entered Black Watch (Royal Highlanders), 1939; served France, 1939–41 (despatches); invalided, 1942. *Recreations:* piobaireachd, Scottish highland culture. *Heir:* none. *Address:* House of Lords, SW1A 0PW; 29 Mackeson Road, Hampstead, NW3 2LU.

BREADEN, Very Rev. Robert William; Dean of Brechin since 1984; Rector of St Mary's, Broughty Ferry, since 1972; *b* 7 Nov. 1937; *s* of Moses and Martha Breaden; *m* 1970, Glenice Sutton Martin; one *s* four *d. Educ:* The King's Hospital, Dublin; Edinburgh Theological Coll. Deacon 1961, priest 1962; Asst Curate, St Mary's, Broughty Ferry, 1961–65; Rector, Church of the Holy Rood, Carnoustie, 1965–72; Canon of St Paul's Cathedral, Dundee, 1977. *Recreations:* gardening, horse riding; Rugby enthusiast. *Address:* St Mary's Rectory, 46 Seafield Road, Broughty Ferry, Dundee DD5 3AN. *T:* Dundee (01382) 477477.

BREALEY, Prof. Richard Arthur; Tokai Bank Professor of Finance, London Business School, since 1993; *b* 9 June 1936; *s* of late Albert Brealey and of Irene Brealey; *m* 1967, Diana Cecily Brown Kelly; two *s. Educ:* Queen Elizabeth's, Barnet; Exeter Coll., Oxford (MA, 1st Cl. Hons PPE). Sun Life Assce Co. of Canada, 1959–66; Keystone Custodian Funds of Boston, 1966–68; London Business School: Prudential Res. Fellow, 1968–74; Sen. Lectr, 1972–74; Prof. of Finance, 1974–; Barclaytrust Prof. of Investment, 1974–82; Midland Bank Prof. of Corporate Finance, 1982–91; Dep. Prin., 1984–88; Governor, 1984–88. Director: Swiss Helvetia Fund Inc., 1987–; Sun Life Assurance Co. of Canada (UK) Ltd, 1994–; Tokai Derivative Products, 1995–. Pres., European Finance Assoc., 1975; Dir, Amer. Finance Assoc., 1979–81. *Publications:* An Introduction to Risk and Return from Common Stocks, 1969, 2nd edn 1983; (with S. C. Myers) Principles of Corporate Finance, 1981, 4th edn 1991; (with S. C. Myers and A. J. Marcus) Fundamentals of Corporate Finance, 1995; articles in professional jls. *Recreations:* ski-ing, rock climbing, pottery. *Address:* Haydens Cottage, The Pound, Cookham, Berks SL6 9QE. *T:* Bourne End (01628) 520143.

BREAM, Julian, CBE 1985 (OBE 1964); guitarist and lutenist; *b* 15 July 1933; *e s* of Henry G. Bream; *m* 1st, Margaret Williamson; one adopted *s*; 2nd, 1980, Isobel Sanchez. *Educ:* Royal College of Music (Junior Exhibition Award, 1945 and Scholarship, 1948). Began professional career at Cheltenham, 1947; London début, Wigmore Hall, 1950; subsequently has appeared in leading world festivals in Europe, USA, Australia and Far East. A leader in revival of interest in Elizabethan Lute music, on which he has done much research; has encouraged contemporary English compositions for the guitar. Formed Julian Bream Consort, 1960; inaugurated Semley Festival of Music and Poetry, 1971. DUniv Surrey, 1968. Villa-Lobos Gold Medal, 1976. *Recreations:* playing the guitar; cricket, table tennis, gardening, backgammon. *Address:* c/o Hazard Chase, 16–20 Regent Street, Cambridge CB2 1DB.

BREARLEY, Christopher John Scott, CB 1994; Deputy Secretary, Local Government and Planning, Department of the Environment, since 1994; *b* 25 May 1943; *s* of Geoffrey Brearley and Winifred (*née* Scott); *m* 1971, Rosemary Stockbridge; two *s. Educ:* King Edward VII Sch., Sheffield; Trinity Coll., Oxford. MA 1964, BPhil 1966. Entered Ministry of Transport, 1966; Private Sec. to Perm. Sec., 1969–70; Principal, DoE, 1970; Sec. to Review of Develt Control Procedures (Dobry), DoE, 1973–74; Private Sec. to the Secretary of the Cabinet, Cabinet Office, 1974–76; Asst Sec., 1977; Under Sec., 1981; Dir of Scottish Services, PSA, 1981–83; Cabinet Office, 1983–85; DoE, 1985–: Dep. Sec., Local Govt, 1990–94. Non-Exec. Dir, Housing Div., Tarmac plc, 1986–88. Mem. Bd, Public Finance Foundn, 1990–. Governor, Watford Grammar Sch. for Boys, 1988–; Trustee, Watford Grammar Schs, 1992–. FRSA 1991. *Recreations:* crosswords, walking. *Address:* Department of the Environment, 2 Marsham Street, SW1P 3EB. *T:* 0171–276 3479. *Club:* New (Edinburgh).

BREARLEY, (John) Michael, OBE 1978; psycho-analyst; *b* 28 April 1942; *s* of Horace and late Midge Brearley; lives with Mana Sarabhai; two *c. Educ:* City of London Sch.; St John's Coll., Cambridge (MA). Lectr in Philosophy, Univ. of Newcastle-upon-Tyne, 1968–71. Middlesex County Cricketer, intermittently, 1961–82, capped 1964, Captain, 1971–82, played first Test Match, 1976; Captain of England XI, 1977–80, 1981. *Publications:* (with Dudley Doust) The Return of the Ashes, 1978; (with Dudley Doust) The Ashes Retained, 1979; Phoenix: the series that rose from the ashes, 1982; The Art of Captaincy, 1985; (with John Arlott) Arlott in Conversation with Mike Brearley, 1986; articles for the Sunday Times and Observer. *Club:* MCC (Hon. Life Mem.).

BREARS, Peter Charles David, FMA, FSA; writer and museums consultant, since 1994; *b* 30 Aug. 1944; *s* of Charles Brears and Mary (*née* Fett). *Educ:* Castleford Technical High Sch.; Leeds Coll. of Art (DipAD 1967). FMA 1980; FSA 1980. Hon. Asst, Wakefield City Museum, 1957–66; Keeper of Folk Life, Hampshire CC, 1967–69; Curator: Shibden Hall, Halifax, 1969–72; Clarke Hall, Wakefield, 1972–75; Castle Museum, York, 1975–79; Dir, Leeds City Museums, 1979–94. Chm., Leeds Symposium for Food History, 1986–; Founder, 1975, and Mem., 1975–, Group for Regional Studies in Museums, subseq. Social Hist. Curators Gp, 1975; Mem., Social History and Industrial Classification Wkg Party, 1978–; Sec., Soc. for Folk Life Studies, 1984–. *Publications:* The English Country Pottery, 1971; Yorkshire Probate Inventories, 1972; The Collectors' Book of English Country Pottery, 1974; Horse Brasses, 1981; The Gentlewoman's Kitchen, 1984; Traditional Food in Yorkshire, 1987; North Country Folk Art, 1989; Of Curiosities and Rare Things, 1989; Treasures for the People, 1989; Images of Leeds, 1992; Leeds Describ'd, 1993; articles in Folk Life, Post-Medieval Archaeology, etc; museum guides and catalogues. *Recreations:* hill walking, drawing, history re-enactment, cookery. *Address:* 4 Woodbine Terrace, Headingley, Leeds LS6 4AF. *T:* Leeds (0113) 275 6537.

BRECHIN, Bishop of, since 1990; **Rt. Rev. Robert Taylor Halliday;** *b* 7 May 1932; *s* of James Halliday and Agnes Logan Halliday (*née* Scott); *m* 1960, Georgina Mabel, (Gena) (*née* Chadwin); one *d. Educ:* High Sch. of Glasgow; Univ. of Glasgow (MA, BD); Episcopal Theol Coll., Edinburgh. Deacon 1957; priest 1958. Assistant Curate: St Andrew's, St Andrews, 1957–60; St Margaret's, Newlands, Glasgow, 1960–63; Rector, Church of the Holy Cross, Davidson's Mains, Edinburgh, 1963–83; External Lectr in New Testament, Episcopal Theol Coll., Edin., 1963–74; Canon of St Mary's Cathedral, Edinburgh, 1973–83; Rector of St Andrew's, St Andrews, 1983–90; Tutor in Biblical Studies, Univ. of St Andrews, 1984–90. Hon. Canon, Trinity Cathedral, Davenport, Iowa, 1990. *Recreations:* walking, reading, gardening, uniting the Church. *Address:* The Bishop's Room, St Paul's Cathedral, Castlehill, Dundee DD1 1TD. *T:* Dundee (01382) 229230; Bishop's House, 35 Carlogie Road, Carnoustie DD7 6ER. *T:* Carnoustie (01241) 855781.

BRECHIN, Dean of; *see* Breaden, Very Rev. R. W.

BRECKENRIDGE, Prof. Alasdair Muir, CBE 1995; MD; FRCP; FRCPE; FRSE; Professor of Clinical Pharmacology, University of Liverpool, since 1974; *b* 7 May 1937; *s* of Thomas and Jane Breckenridge; *m* 1967, Jean Margaret Boyle; two *s. Educ:* Bell Baxter Sch., Cupar, Fife; Univ. of St Andrews (MB, ChB Hons 1961); Univ. of London (MSc 1968); Univ. of Dundee (MD Hons 1974). FRCP 1974; FRCPE 1988; FRSE 1991. House Phys. and Surg., Dundee Royal Infirm., 1961–62; Asst, Dept of Medicine, Univ. of St Andrews, 1962–63; successively House Phys., Registrar, Sen. Registrar, Tutor, Lectr and Sen. Lectr, Hammersmith Hosp. and RPMS, 1964–74. Non-exec. Dir, 1990–94, Vice Chm., 1993–94, Mersey RHA (Chm., Jan.–July 1993; Chm., Res. Cttee, 1987–91); Vice Chm., NW RHA, 1994– (Dir of R & D, 1994–). NHS Advr in Clin. Pharm. to

CMO, 1982–94; Mem., NHS Adv. Cttee on Drugs, 1985– (Vice Chm., 1986–). Committee on Safety of Medicines: Mem., 1982–; Chm., Adverse Reactions Subgroup, 1987–92; Chm., Adverse Reactions to Vaccination and Immunisation Sub Cttee, 1989–; Chm., Sub Cttee on Safety and Efficacy, 1993–. Medical Research Council: Mem., 1992–; Member: Clin. Trials Cttee, 1983–; Physiol Systems and Disorders Bd, 1987–91 (Vice Chm., 1990–91); AIDS Therapeutic Cttee, 1989– (Chm., 1993–). Royal College of Physicians: Mem. Council, 1983–86; Mem., Res. Cttee, 1983–88; Mem., Clin. Pharm. Cttee, 1990–; Mem. Adv. Res. Cttee, 1993–; Goulstonian Lectr, 1975. British Pharmacological Society: Mem., 1972–; Foreign Sec., 1984–91; Chm., Clin. Section, 1988–93; Lilly Medal, 1994; Chm. Editl Bd, British Jl of Clin. Pharmacol., 1983–87. Member: Panel on Tropical and Infectious Disease, Wellcome Trust, 1984–87; Res. Cttee, British Heart Foundn, 1977–82; Steering Cttee for Chemotherapy of Malaria, WHO, 1987–91; Exec. Cttee, Internat. Union of Pharm., 1981–87; Central R&D Cttee, NHS, 1991–94. Mem., Assoc. of Physicians, 1975–. Paul Martini Prize in Clin. Pharm., Paul Martini Foundn, 1974; Poulson Medal, Norwegian Pharmacol Soc., 1988. Exec. Editor, Pharmacology and Therapeutics, 1982–. *Publications:* papers on clinical pharmacology in various jls. *Recreations:* hill-walking, golf, music. *Address:* Cree Cottage, Feather Lane, Heswall, Wirral L60 4RL. *T:* 0151–342 1096.

BRECKNOCK, Earl of; James William John Pratt; *b* 11 Dec. 1965; *s* and *heir* of Marquess Camden, *qv*. *Educ:* Eton.

BRECON, Dean of; *see* Harris, Very Rev. J.

BREDIN, Maj.-Gen. Humphrey Edgar Nicholson, CB 1969; DSO 1944 (and bars, 1945 and 1957); MC 1938 (and bar, 1939); DL; Appeals Secretary, Cancer Research Campaign, Essex and Suffolk, 1971–83; *b* 28 March 1916; *s* of Lieut-Colonel A. Bredin, late Indian Army, and Ethel Bredin (*née* Homan); *m* 1st, 1947, Jacqueline Geare (marr. diss. 1961); one *d*; 2nd, 1965, Anne Hardie; two *d*. *Educ:* King's School, Canterbury; RMC, Sandhurst. Commissioned Royal Ulster Rifles, 1936; Commanded: 6th Royal Inniskilling Fusiliers, 1944; 2nd London Irish Rifles, 1945; Eastern Arab Corps, Sudan Defence Force, 1949–53; 2nd Parachute Regt, 1956–57; 99th Gurkha Infty Bde Group, 1959–62. Campaigns: Dunkirk, 1940; N Africa, 1943; Italy, 1943–45; Palestine, 1937–39 and 1946–47; Suez, 1956; Cyprus, 1956–57; Singapore-Malaya Internal Security, 1959–62; Chief of British Commander-in-Chief's Mission to Soviet Forces in Germany, 1963–65; Commanded 42nd Div. (TA), 1965–68. Brig. 1964; Maj.-Gen. 1965; Dir, Volunteers, Territorials and Cadets, 1968–71; retired 1971. Col Comdt, The King's Division, 1968–71; Col of the Regt, Royal Irish Rangers, 1979–85; Hon. Col D (London Irish Rifles) Co., 4th (V) Bn, The Royal Irish Rangers, 1980–86. Chm. Essex Co. Cttee, Army Benevolent Fund, 1983–92; President: Dunkirk Veterans Clacton and Colchester Assoc., 1983–; 78th Div. Battleaxe Club, 1991–. DL Essex, 1984. *Recreations:* shooting, fishing, gardening. *Address:* Bovills Hall, Ardleigh, Essex CO7 7RT. *T:* Colchester (01206) 230217. *Club:* Army and Navy.

BREDIN, James John; specialist in television archives; Contributing Editor, Industry Week, American management magazine, since 1991; *b* 18 Feb. 1924; *s* of late John Francis and Margaret Bredin; *m* 1958, Virginia Meddowes, *d* of John Meddowes and Mrs K. Thomas; one *s* two *d*. *Educ:* Finchley Catholic Grammar Sch.; London University. Served Fleet Air Arm, RNVR, S/Lieut, 1943–46. Scriptwriter, This Modern Age Film Unit, 1946–50; Producer, current affairs programmes, BBC TV, 1950–55; Sen. Producer, Independent Television News, 1955–59; Smith-Mundt Fellowship, USA, 1957; Producer of Documentaries, Associated Television, 1959–64; Man. Dir, Border TV Ltd, 1964–82. Chm., Guild of Television Producers and Directors, 1961–64. Director: Independent Television News Ltd, 1970–72; Independent Television Publications Ltd, 1965–82. FRTS 1983. Press Fellow, Wolfson Coll., Cambridge, 1987. *Address:* 25 Stack House, Cundy Street, SW1W 9JS. *T:* 0171–730 2689. *Club:* Beefsteak.

BREEN, Geoffrey Brian; Metropolitan Stipendiary Magistrate, since 1986; Chairman, Family Proceedings Courts, since 1991; a Recorder, since 1993 (an Assistant Recorder, 1989–93); *b* 3 June 1944; *s* of Ivor James Breen and Doreen Odessa Breen; *m* 1976, Lucy Bolaños; one *s* one *d*. *Educ:* Harrow High School. Articled to Stiles Wood & Co., Harrow, 1962–67; admitted Solicitor, 1967; Partner, Stiles, Wood, Head & Co, 1970–75; Sen. Partner, Stiles, Breen & Partners, 1976–86; Partner, Blaser Mills & Newman, Bucks and Herts, 1976–86. Chm., Youth Courts, 1989–93. Mem., British Acad. of Forensic Scis, 1989–. *Recreations:* classical guitar, reading, do-it-yourself, dog walking. *Address:* Horseferry Road Magistrates' Court, 70 Horseferry Road, SW1P 2AX.

BREEZE, Alastair Jon, CMG 1990; HM Diplomatic Service; Counsellor, Foreign and Commonwealth Office, since 1987; *b* 1 June 1934; *s* of Samuel Wilfred Breeze and Gladys Elizabeth Breeze; *m* 1960, Helen Burns Shaw; two *s* one *d*. *Educ:* Mill Hill School; Christ's College, Cambridge (Scholar; MA 1959). Served Royal Marines, 1953–55. Foreign Office, 1958; 3rd Sec., Jakarta, 1960–62; FO, 1962–64; 2nd Sec., seconded to Colonial Office for service in Georgetown, 1964–66; 1st Sec., Tehran, 1967–71; FCO, 1971–72; 1st Sec., Islamabad, 1972–75, Lagos, 1976–79; FCO, 1979–83; Counsellor, UK Mission to UN, NY, 1983–87. *Recreations:* sailing, ornithology. *Address:* c/o Foreign and Commonwealth Office, SW1A 2AH.

BREEZE, Dr David John, FSA, FSAScot, FRSE; Chief Inspector of Ancient Monuments, Historic Scotland, since 1989; *b* Blackpool, 25 July 1944; *s* of Reginald C. Breeze and Marian (*née* Lawson); *m* 1972, Pamela Diane Silvester; two *s*. *Educ:* Blackpool Grammar Sch.; University Coll., Durham Univ. (BA; PhD 1970). FSAScot 1970; FSA 1975; FRSE 1991; MIFA 1990. Inspector of Ancient Monuments, Scotland, 1969–88, Principal Inspector, 1988–89. Vis. Prof., Durham Univ., 1994–. Chm., Hadrian's Wall Pilgrimage, 1989; Member: Hadrian's Wall Adv. Cttee, English Heritage, 1977–; Internat. Cttee, Congress of Roman Frontier Studies, 1983–; President: South Shields Archaeol and Historical Soc., 1983–85; Soc. of Antiquaries of Scotland, 1987–90. Trustee, Senhouse Museum Trust, 1985–. Corresp. Mem., German Archaeol Inst., 1979. *Publications:* (with Brian Dobson) Hadrian's Wall, 1976, 3rd edn 1987; (with D. V. Clarke and G. Mackay) The Romans in Scotland, 1980; The Northern Frontiers of Roman Britain, 1982; Roman Forts in Britain, 1983, 2nd edn 1987; (ed) Studies in Scottish Antiquity, 1984; Hadrian's Wall, a Souvenir Guide, 1987, 2nd edn 1989; A Queen's Progress, 1987; The Second Augustan Legion in North Britain, 1989; (ed) Service in the Roman Army, 1989; (with Anna Ritchie) Invaders of Scotland, 1991; (with Brian Dobson) Roman Officers and Frontiers, 1993; contribs to British and foreign jls. *Recreations:* reading, walking, swimming, travel. *Address:* Historic Scotland, Longmore House, Salisbury Place, Edinburgh EH9 1SH. *T:* 0131–668 8724.

BREHONY, Dr John Albert Noel, CMG 1991; Director of Middle East Affairs, Rolls-Royce PLC, since 1992; *b* 11 Dec. 1936; *s* of Patrick Paul Brehony and Agnes Maher; *m* 1961, Jennifer Ann (*née* Cox); one *s* one *d*. *Educ:* London Oratory Sch.; Univ. of Durham (BA, PhD). Tutor, Durham Univ., 1960; Economist Intell. Unit, 1961; Res. Fellow, Jerusalem (Jordan), 1962; Lectr, Univ. of Libya, 1965–66; FO, 1966; Kuwait, 1967–69; Aden, 1970–71; Amman, 1973–77; Cairo, 1981–84; Counsellor, FCO, 1984–92. Res. Consultant, SOAS, 1992–. Chm., British Inst. at Amman for Archaeol. and Hist., 1992–. *Recreations:* Middle Eastern history, tennis, golf, opera. *Address:* (office) c/o 65 Buckingham Gate, SW1E 6AT. *Club:* Athenæum.

BREITMEYER, Brig. Alan Norman; DL; Lieutenant, HM Body Guard, Honourable Corps of Gentlemen at Arms, 1993–94 (Member, 1976–94; Harbinger, 1992–93); *b* 14 March 1924; *s* of Cecil Breitmeyer and Clare Herbert-Smith; *m* 1st, 1952, Hon. June Jane Barrie (marr. diss. 1977); one *s* one *d*; 2nd, 1978, Susan Irwin (*née* Lipscomb). *Educ:* Winchester Coll.; RMA Sandhurst. Commissioned Grenadier Guards, 1943; served NW Europe, 1944–45 (despatches 1945); ADC to Field Marshal Montgomery, 1948–50 (despatches, Palestine, 1948); Staff College, 1954; commanded 2nd Bn Grenadier Guards, 1964–66; commanding Grenadier Guards, 1966–69; Brig., 1971; Dep. Comdr, NE Dist, 1972–74, retired 1974. County Councillor, Cambs, 1977–85. DL Cambs, 1978; High Sheriff Cambs, 1984. *Recreation:* shooting. *Address:* Bartlow Park, Cambs CB1 6PP. *T:* Cambridge (01223) 891609. *Clubs:* Boodle's, Pratt's.

BRENCHLEY, Thomas Frank, CMG 1964; HM Diplomatic Service, retired; *b* 9 April 1918; *m* 1946, Edith Helen Helfand (*d* 1980); three *d*. *Educ:* privately and at Sir William Turner's Sch., Coatham; Merton Coll., Oxford (Modern History postmastership; Classical Hon. Mods, 1938; MA Philos. and Ancient Hist., 1946; Mem., Sen. Common Room, 1987; Hon. Fellow 1991); Open Univ. (BA in Science and Technol., 1986). CS quals in Arabic, Norwegian and Polish. Served with Royal Corps of Signals, 1939–46; Major on Staff of Military Attaché, Ankara, 1943–45; Director, Telecommunications Liaison Directorate, Syria and Lebanon, 1945–46. Civil Servant, GCHQ, 1947; transferred to Foreign Office, 1949; First Secretary: Singapore, 1950–53; Cairo, 1953–56; FO, 1956–58; MECAS, 1958–60; Counsellor, Khartoum, 1960–63; Chargé d'Affaires, Jedda, 1963; Head of Arabian Department, Foreign Office, 1963–67; Assistant Under-Secretary of State, Foreign Office, 1967–68; Ambassador to: Norway, 1968–72; Poland, 1972–74; Vis. Fellow, Inst. for Study of Conflict, 1974–75; Dep. Sec., Cabinet Office, 1975–76. Dep. Sec. Gen. and Chief Exec., Arab-British Chamber of Commerce, 1976–83; Chairman: Institute for Study of Conflict, 1983–89; Res. Inst. for Study of Conflict and Terrorism, 1989–94; Pres., Internat. Inst. for Study of Conflict, Geneva, 1989–91. Dir, Center for Security Studies, Washington DC, 1988–90. *Publications:* New Dimensions of European Security (ed), 1975; Norway and her Soviet Neighbour: NATO's Arctic Frontier, 1982; Diplomatic Immunities and State-sponsored Terrorism, 1984; Living With Terrorism: the problem of air piracy, 1986; Britain and the Middle East: an economic history 1945–87, 1989; Aegean Conflict and the Law of the Sea, 1990. *Recreation:* collecting (and sometimes reading) books. *Address:* 19 Ennismore Gardens, SW7 1AA. *Club:* Travellers' (Chm., 1991–94).

BRENDEL, Alfred, Hon. KBE 1989; concert pianist since 1948; *b* 5 Jan. 1931; *s* of Albert Brendel and Ida Brendel (*née* Wieltschnig); *m* 1960, Iris Heymann-Gonzala (marr. diss. 1972); one *d*; *m* 1975, Irene Semler; one *s* two *d*. Studied piano with: S. Deželić, 1937–43; L. V. Kaan, 1943–47; also under Edwin Fischer, P. Baumgartner and E. Steuermann; composition with Artur Michl, harmony with Franjo Dugan, Zagreb. Vienna State Diploma, 1947; Premio Bolzano Concorso Busoni, 1949. Hon. RAM; FRNCM 1990; Hon. Mem., Amer. Acad. of Arts and Sciences, 1984; Korrespondieren des Mitglied, Bayer. Akad. der Wissenschaften; Hon. Fellow, Exeter Coll., Oxford, 1987; Hon. DMus: London, 1978; Sussex, 1980; Oxford, 1983; Warwick, 1991; Yale, 1992. Busoni Foundn Award, 1990; Gold Medal, Royal Philharmonic Soc., 1993. Commandeur des Arts et des Lettres, 1985; Orden pour le Mérite für Wissenschaften und Künste, 1991. Concerts: most European countries, North and Latin America, Australia and New Zealand, also N and S Africa and Near and Far East. Many appearances Vienna and Salzburg Festivals, 1960–. Other Festivals: Athens, Granada, Bregenz, Würzburg, Aldeburgh, York, Cheltenham, Edinburgh, Bath, Puerto Rico, Barcelona, Prague, Lucerne, Dubrovnik, etc. Many long playing records (Bach to Schoenberg) incl. first complete recording of Beethoven's piano works (Grand Prix du Disque, 1965). Cycle of Beethoven Sonatas: London, 1962, 1977, 1982–83, 1992–95; Copenhagen, 1964; Vienna, 1965, 1982–83; Puerto Rico, 1968; BBC and Rome, 1970; Munich and Stuttgart, 1977; Amsterdam, Paris and Berlin, 1982–83; New York, 1983; Cycle of Schubert piano works 1822–28 in 19 cities, incl. London, Paris, Amsterdam, Berlin, Vienna, New York, Los Angeles, 1987–88. *Television (series):* Schubert Piano Music (13 films), Bremen, 1978; Alfred Brendel Masterclass, BBC, 1983; Liszt Années de Pèlerinage, BBC, 1986; Schubert Last Three Sonatas, BBC, 1988. *Publications:* Musical Thoughts and Afterthoughts (Essays), 1976; Music Sounded Out, 1990; essays on music, in: HiFi Stereophonie, Music and Musicians, Phono, Fono Forum, Osterreichische Musikzeitschrift, Gramophone, Die Zeit, New York Rev. of Books, Frankfurter Allgemeine, Neue Zürcher Zeitung, etc. *Recreations:* literature, art galleries, architecture, unintentional humour, "kitsch". *Address:* Ingpen & Williams, 14 Kensington Court, W8 5DN.

BRENIKOV, Prof. Paul, FRTPI; Professor and Head of Department of Town and Country Planning, University of Newcastle upon Tyne, 1964–86, now Professor Emeritus; *b* 13 July 1921; *o s* of Pavel Brenikov and Joyce Mildred Jackson, Liverpool; *m* 1943, Margaret, *e d* of Albert McLevy, Burnley, Lancs; two *s* one *d*. *Educ:* St Peter's Sch., York; Liverpool Coll.; Univ. of Liverpool (BA (Hons Geog.), MA, DipCD). War service with RNAS, 1941–46. Sen. Planning Officer, Lancs CC, 1950–55; Lectr, Dept of Civic Design, Univ. of Liverpool, 1955–64; Planning Corresp., Architect's Jl, 1957–63; Environmental Planning Consultant: in UK, for former Bootle CB, 1957–64; Govt of Ireland, 1963–67; overseas, for UN; Chile, 1960–61; E Africa, 1964; OECD; Turkey, 1968. Royal Town Planning Institute: Mem. Council, 1967–78; Chm., Northern Br., 1973–74. Member: Subject Cttee of UGC, 1975–86; DoE Local Plans Inspector's Panel, 1985–. FRSA 1979. *Publications:* contrib. Social Aspects of a Town Development Plan, 1951; contrib. Land Use in an Urban Environment, 1961; (jtly) The Dublin Region: preliminary and final reports, 1965 and 1967; other technical pubns in architectural, geographical, planning and sociological jls. *Recreations:* drawing, painting, listening to music, walking, reading. *Address:* 46 Mitchell Avenue, Jesmond, Newcastle upon Tyne NE2 3LA. *T:* 0191–281 2773.

BRENNAN, Anthony John Edward, CB 1981; Deputy Secretary, Northern Ireland Office, 1982–87; *b* 24 Jan. 1927; 2nd *s* of late Edward Joseph Brennan and Mabel Brennan (*née* West); *m* 1958, Pauline Margery, *d* of late Percy Clegg Lees; two *s* one *d*. *Educ:* St Joseph's; London Sch. of Economics (Leverhulme Schol.). BSc Econ 1946. Served Army, RA, RAEC, 1946–49; Asst Principal, Home Office, 1949; Private Sec. to Parly Under-Sec. of State, 1953–54; Principal, 1954; Principal Private Sec. to Home Sec., 1963; Asst Sec., 1963; Asst Under Sec. of State, Criminal Dept, 1971–75, Immigration Dept, 1975–77; Dep. Under-Sec. of State, Home Office, 1977–82. Sec., Royal Commn on Penal System, 1964–66; Mem., UN Cttee on Crime Prevention and Control, 1979–84; Chm., Bd of Visitors, Downview Prison, 1995–. *Recreations:* theatre, athletics. *Club:* Athenæum.

BRENNAN, Archibald Orr, (Archie Brennan), OBE 1981; Director, Edinburgh Tapestry Co., 1962; Visiting Artist, Papua New Guinea, 1978; *s* of James and Jessie Brennan; *m* 1956, Elizabeth Hewitt Carmichael (marr. diss.); three *d*. *Educ:* Boroughmuir Sch., Edinburgh; Edinburgh College of Art (DA). Training as tapestry weaver/student,

1947–62; Lectr, Edinburgh College of Art, 1962–78. Pres., Society of Scottish Artists, 1977–78; Chm., British Craft Centre, 1977–78; travelling lectr, UK, USA, Canada, Australia, Papua New Guinea, 1962–78. Fellow, ANU, 1974–75. *Publications:* articles in various jls.

BRENNAN, Brian John, MC 1944; Chairman, Lloyd's of London Press Ltd, 1985–88; Deputy Chairman of Lloyd's, 1981–83 (Underwriting Member, since 1951); *b* 17 May 1918; *s* of Alfred Eric Brennan and Jean (*née* Wallace); *m* 1950, Mary Patricia Newbould; one *s* two *d. Educ:* Dulwich College. Joined E. W. Payne, Lloyd's Brokers, 1936. Member, HAC, 1938; commnd Cameronians (Scottish Rifles), 1939; India, 1/Cameronians, 1940–45; Burma, 1942; Burma, 1944; commanded 26 Column 1/Cameronians 111 Bde Special Force; Lt-Col 1/Cameronians, 1944–45. Director, E. W. Payne, 1947, Chm., 1966–74; Director, Montagu Trust, 1967–74; Dep. Chm., Bland Payne Holdings, 1974–78; Chm., Bland Payne Reinsurance Brokers, 1974–78; Dir, Sedgwick Forbes Bland Payne Holdings, 1979; Chm., Sedgwick Payne, 1979; Dir, Sedgwick Gp Ltd, 1980. Mem., Cttee of Lloyd's, 1975–80, 1981–84. *Recreations:* Rugby (Old Alleynians, Kent, London, Barbarians); sailing, tennis, gardening. *Address:* Weybank House, Meadrow, Godalming, Surrey GU7 3BZ. *Clubs:* Alderney Sailing, Alderney Golf.

BRENNAN, Daniel Joseph; QC 1985; a Recorder of the Crown Court, since 1982; *b* 19 March 1942; *s* of late Daniel Brennan and Mary Brennan; *m* 1968, Pilar, *d* of late Luis Sanchez Hernandez; four *s. Educ:* St Bede's Grammar Sch., Bradford; Victoria University of Manchester (LLB Hons). President, University Union, 1964–65. Called to the Bar: Gray's Inn, 1967 (Bencher, 1993); King's Inns, Dublin, 1990. Legal Assessor, UK Nursing Council. Mem., Criminal Injuries Compensation Bd, 1989–. *Publications:* Provisional Damages, 1986; (contrib.) Bullen and Leake, Precedents of Pleading, 13th edn, 1990. *Address:* Brook House, Brook Lane, Alderley Edge SK9 7RU. *T:* Alderley Edge (01625) 585552; (chambers) 39 Essex Street, WC2R 3AT. *T:* 0171–583 1111.

BRENNAN, Edward A.; Chairman and Chief Executive Officer, 1986–95, and President, since 1989, Sears, Roebuck & Co.; *b* 16 Jan. 1934; *s* of Edward Brennan and Margaret (*née* Bourget); *m* 1955, Lois Lyon; three *s* three *d. Educ:* Marquette Univ., Wisconsin (BA). Joined Sears as salesman in Madison, Wisconsin, 1956; asst store manager, asst buyer, store manager, other positions in diff. locations, to 1969; Asst Manager, NY group, 1969–72; Gen. Manager, Sears Western NY group, 1972–75; Admin. Asst to Vice-Pres., Sears Eastern Territory, 1975; Gen. Manager, Boston group, 1976; Exec. Vice Pres., Southern Territory, 1978; Pres., Sears, Roebuck, 1980; Chm. and Chief Exec., Sears Merchandise Group, 1981; Pres. and chief operating officer, Sears, Roebuck & Co., 1984; dir of other cos. Member: President's Export Council; Business Roundtable; Conference Bd; business adv. council, Chicago Urban League; Civic Cttee, Commercial Club; Chm., Board of Governors, United Way of America; Member, Boards of Trustees: Savings and Profit Sharing Fund of Sears Employees; Univs of DePaul and Marquette; Chicago Museum of Science and Industry. *Address:* Sears, Roebuck and Co., Sears Tower, Chicago, IL 60684, USA. *T:* (312) 8751902.

BRENNAN, Hon. Sir (Francis) Gerard, AC 1988; KBE 1981; **Hon. Justice Brennan;** Justice of the High Court of Australia, since 1981; *b* 22 May 1928; *s* of Hon. Mr Justice (Frank Tenison) Brennan and Mrs Gertrude Brennan; *m* 1953, Patricia (*née* O'Hara); three *s* four *d. Educ:* Christian Brothers Coll., Rockhampton, Qld; Downlands Coll., Toowoomba, Qld; Univ. of Qld (BA, LLB). Called to the Queensland Bar, 1951; QC (Australia) 1965. Judge, Aust. Indust. Court, and Additional Judge of Supreme Court of ACT, 1976–81; Judge, Fed. Court of Australia, 1977–81. President: Admin. Appeals Tribunal, 1976–79; Admin. Review Council, 1976–79; Bar Assoc. of Qld, 1974–76; Aust. Bar Assoc., 1975–76; National Union of Aust. Univ. Students, 1949. Member: Exec. Law Council of Australia, 1974–76; Aust. Law Reform Commn, 1975–77. Hon. LLD TCD, 1988. *Recreation:* gardening. *Address:* 10 Kurundi Place, Hawker, ACT 2614, Australia. *T:* (62) 546794. *Club:* Commonwealth (Canberra).

BRENNAN, Hon. William Joseph, Jr; Legion of Merit, 1945; Associate Justice, Supreme Court of the US, 1956–90, retired; *b* 25 April 1906; *s* of William J. Brennan and Agnes McDermott; *m* 1st, 1928, Marjorie Leonard (*d* 1982); two *s* one *d;* 2nd, 1983, Mary Fowler. *Educ:* University of Pennsylvania; Harvard. BS Univ. of Pennsylvania, 1928; LLB Harvard, 1931. Admitted to New Jersey Bar, 1931; practised in Newark, New Jersey, 1931–49, Member Pitney, Hardin, Ward & Brennan; Superior Court Judge, 1949–50; Appellate Division Judge, 1950–52; Supreme Court of New Jersey Justice, 1952–56; served War of 1939–45 as Colonel, General Staff Corps, United States Army. Hon. LLD: Pennsylvania, Wesleyan, St John's, 1957; Rutgers, 1958; Notre Dame, Harvard, 1968; Princeton, Columbia, Brandeis, NY Law Sch., John Marshall Law Sch., 1986; Ohio State, Yale 1987; Glasgow, 1989; UC Dublin, 1990; Hon. DCL: New York Univ., Colgate, 1957; Hon. SJD Suffolk Univ., 1956. Hon. Bencher, Lincoln's Inn, 1985. US Medal of Freedom, 1993. *Address:* c/o US Supreme Court, 1 First Street NE, Washington, DC 20543, USA.

BRENNER, Sydney, CH 1987; DPhil; FRCP; FRS 1965; Member of Scientific Staff, MRC, 1957–92; Member, Scripps Research Institute, La Jolla, California, since 1992; Fellow of King's College, Cambridge, since 1959; *b* Germiston, South Africa, 13 Jan. 1927; *s* of Morris Brenner and Lena (*née* Blacher); *m* 1952, May Woolf Balkind; one *s* two *d* (and one step *s*). *Educ:* Germiston High School; University of the Witwatersrand, S Africa; Oxford University (Hon. Fellow, Exeter Coll., 1985). MSc 1947, MB, BCh 1951, Univ. of the Witwatersrand; DPhil Oxon, 1954; FRCP 1979; Hon. FRCPath 1990. Director: MRC Lab. of Molecular Biol., Cambridge, 1979–86; MRC Molecular Genetics Unit, Cambridge, 1986–92. Mem., MRC, 1978–82, 1986–90. Hon. Prof. of Genetic Medicine, Cambridge Univ., 1989–. Carter-Wallace Lectr, Princeton, 1966, 1971; Gifford Lectr, Glasgow, 1978–79; Dunham Lectr, Harvard, 1984; Croonian Lectr, Royal Soc., 1986. External Scientific Mem., Max-Planck Soc., 1988; Mem., Academia Europaea, 1989; Foreign Hon. Member, American Academy of Arts and Sciences, 1965; Foreign Associate: Nat. Acad. of Sciences, USA, 1977; Royal Soc. of S Africa, 1983; Académie des Sciences, Paris, 1992; Mem., Deutsche Akademie der Naturforscher, Leopoldina, 1975 (Gregor Mendel Medal, 1970); Foreign Member: Amer. Philosophical Soc., 1979; Real Academia de Ciencias, Spain, 1985; Correspondant Scientifique Emerite, Institut National de la Santé et de la Recherche Médicale, Paris, 1991; Hon. Member: Chinese Soc. of Genetics, 1989; Assoc. of Physicians of GB and Ireland, 1991. Hon. FRSE 1979. Hon. FIASc 1989. Hon. DSc: Dublin, 1967; Witwatersrand, 1972; Chicago, 1976; London, 1982; Leicester, 1983; Oxford, 1985; Hon. LLD Glasgow, 1981. Warren Triennial Prize, 1968; William Bate Hardy Prize, Cambridge Philosophical Soc., 1969; (jtly) Lasker Award for Basic Medical Research, 1971; Royal Medal, Royal Soc., 1974; (jtly) Prix Charles Leopold Mayer, French Acad. of Science, 1975; Gairdner Foundn Annual Award, 1978; Krebs Medal, FEBS, 1980; CIBA Medal, Biochem. Soc., 1981; Feldberg Foundn Prize, 1983; Neil Hamilton Fairley Medal, RCP, 1985; Rosenstiel Award, Brandeis Univ., 1986; Prix Louis Jeantet de Medecine, Switzerland, 1987; Genetics Soc. of America Medal, 1987; Harvey Prize, Technion-Israel Inst. of Technol., 1987; Hughlings Jackson Medal, RSocMed, 1987; Waterford Bio-Medical Sci. Award, Res. Inst. of Scripps Clinic, USA, 1988; Kyoto Prize, Inamori Foundn, 1990; Gairdner Foundn Internat. Award, Canada, 1991; Copley Medal, Royal Soc., 1991; King Faisal Internat. Prize for Science, King Faisal Foundn, Saudi Arabia, 1992; Bristol-Myers Squibb Award for Dist. Achievement in Neurosci. Res., NY, 1992. *Publications:* papers in scientific journals. *Recreation:* rumination. *Address:* Department of Medicine, University of Cambridge Clinical School, Addenbrooke's Hospital, Hills Road, Cambridge CB2 2QQ. *T:* Cambridge (01223) 244419; Scripps Research Institute, 10666 North Torrey Pines Road, La Jolla, CA 92037, USA. *T:* (619) 5548265.

BRENT, Prof. Leslie, FIBiol; Professor Emeritus, University of London, since 1990; *b* 5 July 1925; *s* of Charlotte and Arthur Baruch; *m* 1st, 1954, Joanne Elisabeth Manley (marr. diss. 1991); one *s* two *d*; 2nd, 1991, Carol Pamela Martin. *Educ:* Bunce Court Sch., Kent; Birmingham Central Technical Coll.; Univ. of Birmingham; UCL. BSc Birmingham, PhD London; FIBiol 1964. Laboratory technician, 1941–43; Army service, 1943–47, Captain; Lectr, Dept of Zoology, UCL, 1954–62; Rockefeller Res. Fellow, Calif Inst. of Technology, 1956–57; Res. scientist, Nat. Inst. for Med. Res., 1962–65; Prof. of Zoology, Univ. of Southampton, 1965–69; Prof. of Immunology, St Mary's Hosp. Med. Sch., London, 1969–90. European Editor, Transplantation, 1963–68; Gen. Sec., British Transplantation Soc., 1971–75 (Hon. Mem., 1988); Pres., The Transplantation Society, 1976–78 (Medawar Prize, 1994); Chairman: Wessex Br., Inst. of Biol., 1966–68; Organising Cttee, 9th Internat. Congress of The Transplantation Soc., 1978–82; Fellowships Cttee, Inst. of Biol., 1982–85; Art Cttee, St Mary's Hosp. Med. Sch., 1988–92. Pres., Guild of Undergrads, Birmingham Univ., 1950–51. Chairman: Haringey Community Relations Council, 1979–80; Haringey SDP, 1981–83. Hon. MRCP 1986. Hon. Mem., British Transplantation Soc., 1988; hon. mem. of several foreign scientific socs. Vice-Chancellor's Prize, Birmingham Univ., 1951; Scientific Medal, Zool Soc., 1963. Played hockey for UAU and Staffs, 1949–51. Co-editor, Immunology Letters, 1983–90. *Publications:* (ed jtly) Organ Transplantation: current clinical and immunological concepts, 1989; articles in scientific and med. jls on transplantation immunology. *Recreations:* music, singing (Crouch End Festival Chorus), fell-walking, chess, novels. *Address:* 30 Hugo Road, N19 5EU.

BRENT, Michael Leon; QC 1983; a Recorder, since 1990; a Deputy High Court Judge, since 1994; *b* 8 June 1936; *m* 1965, Rosalind Keller; two *d. Educ:* Manchester Grammar Sch.; Manchester Univ. (LLB Hons). Called to the Bar, Gray's Inn, 1961; practised on: Northern Circuit, 1961–67 (Circuit Junior, 1964); Midland and Oxford Circuit, 1967–. *Address:* 9 Gough Square, EC4A 3DE.

BRENTFORD, 4th Viscount *cr* 1929, of Newick; **Crispin William Joynson-Hicks;** Bt of Holmbury, 1919; Bt of Newick, 1956; Partner, Taylor Joynson Garrett (formerly Joynson-Hicks), 1961–95; *b* 7 April 1933; *s* of 3rd Viscount Brentford and Phyllis (*d* 1979), *o d* of late Major Herbert Allfrey, Tetbury, Glos; *S* father, 1983; *m* 1964, Gillian Evelyn, *er d* of Gerald Edward Schluter, OBE; one *s* three *d. Educ:* Eton; New College, Oxford. Admitted solicitor, 1960. Master, Girdlers' Co., 1983–84. *Heir: s* Hon. Paul William Joynson-Hicks, *b* 18 April 1971. *Address:* Cousley Place, Wadhurst, East Sussex TN5 6HF. *T:* Wadhurst (01892) 783737.

BRENTON, Anthony Russell; HM Diplomatic Service; Counsellor, Moscow, since 1994; *b* 1 Jan. 1950; *s* of Ivan Bernard Brenton and Jean Sylvia (*née* Rostgard); *m* 1981, Susan Mary Penrose; one *s* two *d. Educ:* Queens' Coll. Cambridge (BA); Open Univ. (MPhil). Joined HM Diplomatic Service, 1975; Cairo, 1978–81; European Communities Dept, FCO, 1981–85; with UK Perm. Repn to EC, 1985–86; Dep. Chef de Cabinet, EC, 1986–89; Counsellor, 1989; Head: UN Dept, FCO, 1989–90; Envmt, Sci. and Energy Dept, FCO, 1990–92; Fellow, Centre for Internat. Affairs, Harvard Univ., 1992–93. *Publication:* The Greening of Machiavelli, 1994. *Recreations:* history, ski-ing. *Address:* c/o Foreign and Commonwealth Office, King Charles Street, SW1A 2AH.

BRENTON, Howard; playwright; *b* 13 Dec. 1942; *s* of Donald Henry Brenton and Rose Lilian (*née* Lewis); *m* 1970, Jane Fry; two *s. Educ:* Chichester High Sch. for Boys; St Catharine's Coll., Cambridge (BA Hons English). *Full-length stage plays:* Revenge, 1969; Hitler Dances, and Measure for Measure (after Shakespeare), 1972; Magnificence, 1973; The Churchill Play, 1974; Government Property, 1975; Weapons of Happiness, 1976 (Evening Standard Award); Epsom Downs, 1977; Sore Throats, 1979; The Romans in Britain, 1980; Thirteenth Night, 1981; The Genius, 1983; Bloody Poetry, 1984; Greenland, 1988; H. I. D. (Hess is Dead), 1989; Berlin Bertie, 1992; *one-act stage plays:* Gum and Goo, Heads, The Education of Skinny Spew, and Christie in Love, 1969; Wesley, 1970; Scott of the Antartic, and A Sky-blue Life, 1971; How Beautiful with Badges, 1972; Mug, 1973; The Thing (for children), 1982; *collaborations:* (with six others) Lay-By, 1970; (with six others) England's Ireland, 1971; (with David Hare) Brassneck, 1973; (with Trevor Griffiths, David Hare and Ken Campbell), Deeds, 1978; (with Tony Howard) A Short Sharp Shock, 1980; (with Tunde Ikoli) Sleeping Policemen, 1983; (with David Hare) Pravda, 1985 (London Standard Award); (with Tariq Ali) Iranian Nights, 1989; (with Tariq Ali) Moscow Gold, 1990; Playing Away (opera), 1994 (score by Benedict Mason); One Once, 1995; *television plays:* Lushly, 1971; Brassneck (adaptation of stage play), 1974; The Saliva Milkshake, 1975 (also perf. theatre); The Paradise Run, 1976; Desert of Lies, 1984; Parental Guidance, 1995; *television series:* Dead Head, 1986; *translations:* Bertolt Brecht, The Life of Galileo, 1980; Georg Buchner, Danton's Death, 1982; Bertolt Brecht, Conversations in Exile, 1982; Goethe, Faust, 1995. *Publications:* Diving for Pearls (novel), 1989; Hot Irons: diaries, essays, journalism, 1995; many plays published. *Recreation:* painting. *Address:* c/o Casarotto Ramsay Ltd, 60–66 Wardour Street, W1V 3HP. *T:* 0171–287 4450.

BRENTWOOD, Bishop of, (RC), since 1980; **Rt. Rev. Thomas McMahon;** *b* 17 June 1936. *Address:* Bishop's House, Stock, Ingatestone, Essex CM4 9BU. *T:* Stock (01277) 840268.

BRERETON, Donald; Under Secretary, Social Security Policy Group, Department of Social Security, since 1993; *b* 18 July 1945; *s* of Clarence Vivian and Alice Gwendolin Brereton; *m* 1969, Mary Frances Turley; one *s* two *d. Educ:* Plymouth Coll.; Univ. of Newcastle upon Tyne (BA Hons Pol. and Soc. Admin). VSO, Malaysia, 1963–64. Asst Principal, Min. of Health, 1968; Asst Private Sec. to Sec. of State for Social Services, 1971; Private Sec. to Perm. Sec., DHSS, 1972; Prin., Health Services Planning, 1973; Private Sec. to Sec. of State for Social Services, 1979–82; Asst Sec., DHSS Policy Strategy Unit, 1982–83; Sec. to Housing Benefit Rev. Team, 1984; Asst Sec., Housing Benefit, 1985–89; Under Sec., Head of Prime Minister's Efficiency Unit, 1989–93. *Recreations:* squash, holidays, books, gardening, bridge. *Address:* Department of Social Security, The Adelphi, 1–11 John Adam Street, WC2N 6HT.

BRESSON, Robert, Officier, Légion d'Honneur, 1971; Grand Croix, Ordre National du Mérite, 1986; Commandeur, Arts et Lettres, 1974; film producer since 1934; *b* 25 Sept. 1901; *s* of Léon Bresson and Marie-Elisabeth Clausels; *m* 1st, 1926, Leidia van der Zee; 2nd, Marie-Madeleine van der Mersch. *Educ:* Lycée Lakanal, Sceaux. Started as painter; then producer of short films, Affaires Publiques. Full-length films produced include: Les Anges du Péché, 1943; Les Dames du Bois de Boulogne, 1948; Journal d'un Curé de Campagne, 1951 (Internat. Grand Prix, Venice); Un Condamné à Mort s'est Echappé,

1956; Pickpocket, 1960; Procès de Jeanne d'Arc, 1962 (Jury's special prize, Cannes); Au Hasard Balthazar, 1966; Mouchette, 1967; Une Femme Douce, 1969; Quatre nuits d'un rêveur, 1971; Lancelot du Lac, 1974; Le diable, probablement, 1977; L'Argent, 1983. *Publication:* Notes sur le cinématographe, 1976. *Address:* 49 quai de Bourbon, 75004 Paris, France.

BRETHERTON, James Russell; Secretary, and Director of Property Management and Services, Government Division, UKAEA, since 1994; *b* 28 March 1943; *y s* of Russell Frederick Bretherton, CB and Jocelyn Nina Mathews; *m* 1968, Harriet Grace Drew; two *s*. *Educ:* King's Sch., Canterbury; Wadham Coll., Oxford (MA History). Voluntary Service as Asst Dist Officer, Nigeria, 1965–66; Asst Principal, Min. of Fuel and Power, 1966–70; Principal, Min. of Technol., 1970–76; Principal Private Sec. to Sec. of State for Energy, 1976–78; Head of Oil Industry Div., Internat. Energy Agency, Paris, 1980–82; Asst Sec., Dept of Energy, 1983–86; Principal Finance and Programmes Officer, UKAEA, 1986–90; Sec., and Commercial and Planning Dir, AEA Technology (UKAEA), 1990–94. *Recreations:* gardening, walking, music (bassoon player). *Address:* Highview, 15 Hid's Copse Road, Cumnor Hill, Oxford OX2 9JJ. *T:* Oxford (01865) 863388; Authers Cottage, Cotleigh, Honiton, Devon EX14 9HD. *T:* Wilmington (01404) 831243.

BRETSCHER, Barbara Mary Frances, (Mrs M. S. Bretscher); *see* Pearse, B. M. F.

BRETSCHER, Mark Steven, PhD; FRS 1985; Head, Division of Cell Biology, Medical Research Council Laboratory of Molecular Biology, Cambridge, since 1984; *b* 8 Jan. 1940; *s* of late Egon Bretscher, CBE and Hanni (*née* Greminger); *m* 1978, Barbara Mary Frances Pearse, *qv*; one *s* one *d*. *Educ:* Abingdon Sch., Berks; Gonville and Caius Coll., Cambridge (MA, PhD). Res. Fellow, Gonville and Caius Coll., Cambridge, 1964–70; Mem., Scientific Staff, MRC Lab. of Molecular Biology, Cambridge, 1965–. Vis. Professor: Harvard Univ., 1975; Stanford Univ., 1984. Friedrich Miescher Prize, Swiss Biochemical Soc., 1979. *Publications:* papers in scientific jls on protein biosynthesis, membrane structure and cell locomotion. *Recreation:* gardening. *Address:* Ram Cottage, Commercial End, Swaffham Bulbeck, Cambridge CB5 0ND. *T:* Cambridge (01223) 811276.

BRETT, family name of **Viscount Esher.**

BRETT, Sir Charles (Edward Bainbridge), Kt 1990; CBE 1981; Consultant, L'Estrange & Brett, Solicitors, Belfast, since 1994 (Partner, 1954–94); *b* 30 Oct. 1928; *s* of Charles Anthony Brett and Elizabeth Joyce (*née* Carter); *m* 1953, Joyce Patricia Worley; three *s*. *Educ:* Rugby Sch.; New Coll., Oxford (Schol.; MA History). Solicitor, 1953. Journalist, Radiodiffusion Française and Continental Daily Mail, 1949–50. Member: Child Welfare Council of Northern Ireland, 1958–61; Northern Ireland Cttee, National Trust, 1956–83 and 1985–93 (Mem. Council, 1975–89); Board, Arts Council of N Ireland, 1970–76, and 1994– (Vice-Chm., 1994–); Chairman: N Ireland Labour Party, 1962; Ulster Architectural Heritage Soc., 1968–78 (Pres., 1979–); HEARTH Housing Assoc., 1978 and 1985–; NI Housing Exec., 1979–84 (Mem. Bd, 1971–77, Vice-Chm., 1977–78); Internat. Fund for Ireland, 1986–89. Mem. Bd, Irish Architectural Archive, Dublin, 1985–88. Hon. Mem., Royal Society of Ulster Architects, 1973; Hon. MRIAI 1988; Hon. FRIBA 1987. Hon. LLD QUB, 1989. *Publications:* Buildings of Belfast 1700–1914, 1967, rev. edn 1985; Court Houses and Market Houses of Ulster, 1973; Long Shadows Cast Before, 1978; Housing a Divided Community, 1986; lists and surveys for Ulster Architectural Heritage Soc., National Trusts of Guernsey and Jersey, and Alderney Soc; (as Albert Rechts) Handbook to a Hypothetical City, 1986. *Address:* 9 Chichester Street, Belfast BT1 4JG. *Club:* United Oxford & Cambridge University.

BRETT, John Alfred, MA; Headmaster, Durham School, Durham, 1958–67; retired; *b* 26 Oct. 1915; *s* of Alfred Brett, Harrogate, Yorks; *m* 1939, Margaret Coode; one *s* three *d*. *Educ:* Durham School; St Edmund Hall, Oxford. MA (Hons Modern History). Temp. teacher, Stowe School, 1938; Teacher, Diocesan College, Rondebosch, South Africa, 1939; restarted Silver Tree Youth Club for non-Europeans, Cape Town. Army: Gunner to Major, RA, 1940–44; Instructor 123 OCTU Catterick; invasion of Normandy, 1944 (lost right eye); Military testing officer, WOSBs, finally Senior Military Testing Officer, War Office Selection Centre. Returned to post at Diocesan College, Rondebosch, 1946; Housemaster, 1948; Temp. teacher, Canford School, Wimborne, Dorset, 1954; Headmaster, Shaftesbury Grammar School, 1954. Diocesan Lay Reader. Member Council: Brathay Hall Centre; McAlpine Educnl Endowments Ltd. Governor, Bernard Gilpin Society. *Recreations:* sport (Captain Oxford University Rugby Football Club, 1937, and Member British Touring XV to Argentina, 1936); travel; reading. *Address:* 32 Homefarris House, Bleke Street, Shaftesbury, Dorset SP7 8AU.

BRETT, Lionel; *see* Esher, 4th Viscount.

BRETT, Michael John Lee; freelance financial journalist, part-time lecturer and writer, since 1982; *b* 23 May 1939; *s* of late John Brett and of Margaret Brett (*née* Lee). *Educ:* King's Coll. Sch., Wimbledon; Wadham Coll., Oxford (BA Modern Langs). Investors Review, 1962–64; Fire Protection Assoc., 1964–68; Investors Chronicle, 1968–82: Dep. Editor, 1973–77; Editor, 1977–82. Past Director: Throgmorton Publications; Financial Times Business Publishing Div. Hon. Vis. Fellow, City Univ. *Publications:* Finance for Business: private sector finance; (contrib.) Valuation and Investment Appraisal; How to read the financial pages; Property and Money. *Recreations:* travelling, reading. *Address:* 134 Offord Road, N1.

See also S. A. L. Brett.

BRETT, Prof. Raymond Laurence; G. F. Grant Professor of English, University of Hull, 1952–82; *b* 10 January 1917; *s* of late Leonard and Ellen Brett; *m* 1947, Kathleen Tegwen, *d* of late Rev. C. D. Cranmer; one *s* (and two *s* decd). *Educ:* Bristol Cathedral School; University of Bristol (1st Class Hons BA, English and Philosophy, 1937; Taylor Prizeman, Hannam-Clark Prizeman, Haldane of Cloan Post-Grad. Studentship); University College, Oxford (BLitt 1940). Service in Admiralty, 1940–46; on Staff of First Lord; Lectr in English, Univ. of Bristol, 1946–52; Dean, Faculty of Arts, Hull Univ., 1960–62. Visiting Professor: Univ. of Rochester, USA, 1958–59; Kiel Univ., Osnabrück Univ., 1977; Baroda Univ., Jadavpur Univ., 1978; Univ. of Ottawa, 1981. Hon. DLitt Hull, 1983. *Publications:* The Third Earl of Shaftesbury: A Study in 18th Century Literary Theory, 1951; Coleridge's Theory of Imagination (English Essays), 1949; George Crabbe, 1956; Reason and Imagination, 1961; (with A. R. Jones) a critical edition of Lyrical Ballads by Wordsworth and Coleridge, 1963, 2nd edn 1991; Thomas Hobbes (The English Mind), 1964; (ed) Poems of Faith and Doubt, 1965; An Introduction to English Studies, 1965; Fancy and Imagination, 1969; (ed) S. T. Coleridge, 1971, 2nd edn 1978; William Hazlitt, 1978; (ed) Barclay Fox's Journal, 1979; (ed) Andrew Marvell, 1979; articles in: The Times, Time and Tide, Essays and Studies, Review of English Studies, Modern Language Review, Philosophy, English, South Atlantic Qly, Critical Qly, etc. *Address:* 19 Mill Walk, Cottingham, North Humberside HU16 4RP. *T:* Hull (01482) 847115.

BRETT, Richard John; Group Director, Finance and Management Services, Civil Aviation Authority, since 1988; *b* 23 October 1947; *s* of Henry William Brett and Dorothy Ada Brett; *m* 1st, 1972, Alison Elizabeth Lambert (marr. diss. 1991); one *d*; 2nd, 1991, Maria Antoinette Brown. *Educ:* Univ. of Bradford (MSc). FCA; Associate, Inst. of Taxation. Leonard C. Bye, Chartered Accountants, Middlesbrough, 1964; ICI Petrochemicals, 1971; Finance Director: Chloride Shires, 1976; Chloride Automotive Batteries, 1979; Westpark, 1981; Thorn EMI Datatech, 1985–88. *Recreation:* music. *Address:* CAA House, 45/59 Kingsway, WC2B 6TE. *T:* 0171–832 5770.

BRETT, Simon Anthony Lee; writer; *b* 28 Oct. 1945; *s* of late Alan John Brett and of Margaret Agnes Brett (*née* Lee); *m* 1971, Lucy Victoria McLaren; two *s* one *d*. *Educ:* Dulwich College; Wadham College, Oxford (BA Hons). Department store Father Christmas, 1967; BBC Radio Producer, 1968–77; LWT Producer, 1977–79. Radio and television scripts, incl. After Henry. *Publications: Charles Paris crime novels:* Cast, In Order of Disappearance, 1975; So Much Blood, 1976; Star Trap, 1977; An Amateur Corpse, 1978; A Comedian Dies, 1979; The Dead Side of the Mike, 1980; Situation Tragedy, 1981; Murder Unprompted, 1982; Murder in the Title, 1983; Not Dead, Only Resting, 1984; Dead Giveaway, 1985; What Bloody Man Is That?, 1987; A Series of Murders, 1989; Corporate Bodies, 1991; A Reconstructed Corpse, 1993; *Mrs Pargeter crime novels:* A Nice Class of Corpse, 1986; Mrs, Presumed Dead, 1988; Mrs Pargeter's Package, 1990; Mrs Pargeter's Pound of Flesh, 1992; *other crime novels:* A Shock to the System, 1984; Dead Romantic, 1985; The Three Detectives and the Missing Superstar, 1986; The Three Detectives and the Knight-in-Armour, 1987; The Christmas Crimes at Puzzel Manor, 1991; Singled Out, 1995; *crime short stories:* A Box of Tricks, 1985; *humorous books:* The Child-Owner's Handbook, 1983; Molesworth Rites Again, 1983; Bad Form, 1984; People-Spotting, 1985; The Wastepaper Basket Archive, 1986; How to Stay Topp, 1987; After Henry, 1987; The Booker Book, 1989; How to be a Little Sod, 1992; *anthologies:* The Faber Book of Useful Verse, 1981; (with Frank Muir) The Book of Comedy Sketches, 1982; Take a Spare Truss, 1983; The Faber Book of Parodies, 1984; The Faber Book of Diaries, 1987. *Recreations:* writing, reading, Real tennis, unreal fantasies. *Address:* Frith House, Burpham, Arundel, West Sussex BN18 9RR. *T:* Arundel (01903) 882257. *Clubs:* Groucho, Academy, Detection.

See also M. J. L. Brett.

BRETT, William Henry; General Secretary, Institution of Professionals, Managers and Specialists, since 1989; *b* 6 March 1942; *s* of William Joseph Brett and Mary Brett (*née* Murphy); *m* 1961, Jean Valerie (marr. diss. 1986); one *s* one *d*; lives with Janet Winters; two *d*. *Educ:* Radcliffe Secondary Technical College, Manchester. British Railways, 1958–64; TSSA, 1964–66; NW Organiser, NUBE (now BIFU), 1966–68; E Midlands Divl Officer, ASTMS, 1968–74; Asst Sec., IPCS later IPMS, Asst Gen. Sec., 1980, elected Gen. Sec., 1988. Mem., Gen. Council, TUC, 1989–. Exec. Sec., Internat. Fedn of Air Traffic Electronic Assocs, 1984–92; Mem. Public Services Internat. Exec. Cttee, 1989–. International Labour Organisation: Mem. Governing Body, Geneva, 1991– (Vice Pres., 1993); Pres., Worker Group, 1993. FRSA. *Publication:* International Labour in the 21st Century, 1994. *Recreations:* travelling, reading. *Address:* 36 Bassant Road, Plumstead, SE18 2NP. *T:* 0181–855 0596. *Clubs:* Plumstead Working Men's, Lydd War Memorial.

BRETTEN, George Rex, QC 1980; barrister-at-law; *b* 21 Feb. 1942; *s* of Horace Victor Bretten and Kathleen Edna Betty Bretten; *m* 1965, Maureen Gillian Crowhurst; one *d*. *Educ:* King Edward VII Sch., King's Lynn; Sidney Sussex Coll., Cambridge (MA, LLM). Lectr, Nottingham Univ., 1964–68; Asst Director, Inst. of Law Research and Reform, Alberta, Canada, 1968–70; called to the Bar, Lincoln's Inn, 1965, a Bencher 1989; in practice, 1971–. *Publication:* Special Reasons, 1977. *Recreations:* hobby farming, tennis. *Address:* Stonehill, Horam, Heathfield, East Sussex TN21 0JN. *T:* Chiddingly (01825) 872820.

BREW, Richard Maddock, CBE 1982; DL; Chairman, Budget Boilers Ltd, since 1984; *b* 13 Dec. 1930; *s* of late Leslie Maddock Brew and Phyllis Evelyn Huntsman; *m* 1953, Judith Anne Thompson Hancock; two *s* two *d*. *Educ:* Rugby Sch.; Magdalene Coll., Cambridge (BA). Called to the Bar, Inner Temple, 1955. After practising for short time at the Bar, joined family business, Brew Brothers Ltd, SW7, 1955, and remained until takeover, 1972. Chm., Monks Dormitory Ltd, 1979–; Regl Dir, Lloyds Bank, 1988–91. Mem., NE Thames RHA, 1982–90 (Vice-Chm., 1982–86); Chm., Tower Hamlets DHA, 1990–93. Farms in Essex. Member: Royal Borough of Kensington Council, 1959–65; Royal Borough of Kensington and Chelsea Council, 1964–70; Greater London Council: Mem., 1968–86; Alderman, 1968–73; Vice-Chm., Strategic Planning Cttee, 1969–71; Chm., Covent Garden Jt Development Cttee, 1970–71 and Environmental Planning Cttee, 1971–73; Mem. for Chingford, 1973–86; Dep. Leader of Council and Leader, Policy and Resources Cttee, 1977–81; Dep. Leader, Cons. Party and Opposition Spokesman on Finance, 1981–82; Leader of the Opposition, 1982–83. Mem., Nat. Theatre Bd, 1982–86. Mem., Pony Club Council, 1975–. High Sheriff, Greater London, 1988–89. DL Greater London, 1989. *Recreations:* hunting, gardening. *Address:* The Abbey, Coggeshall, Essex CO6 1RD. *T:* Coggeshall (01376) 561246. *Clubs:* Carlton, MCC.

BREWER, Prof. Derek Stanley, LittD; FSA; Master of Emmanuel College, Cambridge, 1977–90; Professor of English, University of Cambridge, 1983–90, now Professor Emeritus; *b* 13 July 1923; *s* of Stanley Leonard Brewer and Winifred Helen Forbes; *m* 1951, Lucie Elisabeth Hoole; three *s* two *d*. *Educ:* elementary school; The Crypt Grammar Sch.; Magdalen Coll., Oxford (Matthew Arnold Essay Prize, 1948; BA, MA 1948); Birmingham Univ. (PhD 1956). LittD Cantab 1980. Commnd 2nd Lieut, Worcestershire Regt, 1942; Captain and Adjt, 1st Bn Royal Fusiliers, 1944–45. Asst Lectr and Lectr in English, Univ. of Birmingham, 1949–56; Prof. of English, Internat. Christian Univ., Tokyo, 1956–58; Lectr and Sen. Lectr, Univ. of Birmingham, 1958–64; Lectr in English, Univ. of Cambridge, 1965–76, Reader in Medieval English, 1976–83; Fellow of Emmanuel Coll., Cambridge, 1965–77, Life Fellow 1990. Founder, D. S. Brewer Ltd, for the publication of academic books, 1972; now part of Boydell and Brewer Ltd (Dir, 1979–). Mem., Council of the Senate, Cambridge, 1978–83; Chairman: Fitzwilliam Museum Enterprises Ltd, 1978–90; Univ. Library Synd., 1980–93; English Faculty Bd, Cambridge, 1984–86, 1989. Sir Israel Gollancz Meml Lectr, British Academy, 1974; first William Matthews Lectr, Univ. of London, 1982; first Geoffrey Shepherd Meml Lectr, Univ. of Birmingham, 1983; Sandars Reader, Univ. of Cambridge, 1991. First British Council Vis. Prof. of English to Japan, 1987; Vis. Prof., Japan Soc. for Promotion of Science, 1988; Cline Distinguished Vis. Prof., Univ. of Texas at Austin, 1992. President: The English Assoc., 1982–83, 1987–90; Internat. Chaucer Soc., 1982–84; Chairman Trustees: Chaucer Heritage Trust, 1992–; British Taiwan Cultural Inst., 1990–; Trustee (Treas.), SOS Villages (UK), 1990–; Hon. Trustee, Osaka Univ. of Arts, 1987–. FSA 1977. Hon. Mem., Japan Acad., 1981; Corresp. Fellow, Medieval Soc. of America, 1987. Hon. LLD: Keio Univ., Tokyo, 1982; Harvard Univ., 1984; Hon. DLitt: Birmingham, 1985; Williams Coll., USA, 1990; DUniv: York, 1985; Sorbonne, 1988; Univ. of Liège, 1990. Seatonian Prize, Univ. of Cambridge, 1969, 1972, 1983, 1986 and 1988, (jtly) 1979, 1980, 1992 and 1993, (*prox. acc.*) 1985, 1990. Editor, The Cambridge Review, 1981–86. *Publications:* Chaucer, 1953, 3rd edn 1973; Proteus, 1958 (Tokyo); (ed) The Parlement of Foulys, 1960; Chaucer in his Time, 1963; (ed and contrib.) Chaucer and Chaucerians, 1966; (ed) Malory's Morte Darthur: Parts Seven and Eight, 1968; (ed and contrib.) Writers and their Backgrounds: Chaucer, 1974; (ed) Chaucer: the Critical

Heritage, 1978; Chaucer and his World, 1978; Symbolic Stories, 1980, 2nd edn 1988; (ed jtly) Aspects of Malory, 1981; English Gothic Literature, 1983; Tradition and Innovation in Chaucer, 1983; Chaucer: the Poet as Storyteller, 1984; Chaucer: an introduction, 1984; (ed) Beardsley's Le Morte Darthur, 1985; (with E. Frankl) Arthur's Britain: the land and the legend, 1985; (ed) Studies in Medieval English Romances, 1988; numerous articles in learned jls, reviews, etc. *Recreations:* reading, walking, looking at paintings and antiquities, travelling, publishing other people's books. *Address:* 240 Hills Road, Cambridge CB2 2QE; Emmanuel College, Cambridge CB2 3AP. *T:* Cambridge (01223) 334200.

BREWER, Rear-Adm. George Maxted Kenneth, CB 1982; Flag Officer Medway and Port Admiral Chatham, 1980–82; *b* Dover, 4 March 1930; *s* of Captain George Maxted Brewer and Cecilia Victoria (*née* Clark); *m* 1989, Betty Mary, *o d* of Comdr C. H. Welton, RN and Elsie Gwendoline (*née* Harris). *Educ:* Pangbourne College. In Command: HMS Carysfort, Far East and Mediterranean, 1964–65; HMS Agincourt, Home, 1967; HMS Grenville, Far East and Mediterranean, 1967–69; HMS Juno, and Captain Fourth Frigate Sqdn, Home and Mediterranean, 1973–74; rcds 1975; In Command: HMS Tiger, and Flag Captain to Flag Officer Second Flotilla, Far East, 1978; HMS Bulwark, NATO area, 1979–80. ADC to HM the Queen, 1980. *Recreation:* watercolour painting. *Address:* c/o National Westminster Bank, 2 West Street, Portchester, Fareham, Hants. *Club:* Royal Navy of 1765 and 1785.

BREWER, Rt. Rev. John; *see* Lancaster, Bishop of, (RC).

BREWSTER, (Elsie) Yvonne, OBE 1993; Artistic Director, Talawa Theatre Co., since 1986; *b* 7 Oct. 1938; *d* of Claude Noel Clarke and Kathleen Vanessa Clarke; *m* 1st, 1961, John Roger Francis Jones (marr. diss. 1965); 2nd, 1971, Starr Edmund Francis Home Brewster; one *s*. *Educ:* Rose Bruford Coll. of Speech and Drama (Dip.). LRAM. Stage, TV and radio actress, 1960–; theatre, film, TV and radio director, 1965–; Drama Officer, Arts Council of GB, 1982–84. Mem., London Arts Bd, 1993–; Trustee, Theatres Trust, 1992–. Non-exec. Dir, Riverside Mental Health NHS Trust, 1994–. FRSA 1992. *Publications:* Black Plays, Vol. 1, 1987, Vol. 2, 1989, Vol. 3, 1995. *Recreations:* reading, London. *Address:* 32 Buckley Road, NW6 7LU. *T:* 0171–372 6307.

BREYER, Stephen Gerald; Associate Justice, Supreme Court of the United States, since 1994; *b* 15 Aug. 1938; *s* of Irving Breyer and Anne (*née* Roberts); *m* 1967, Joanna Hare; one *s* two *d*. *Educ:* Stanford Univ. (AM 1959); Magdalen Coll., Oxford (Marshall Schol.; BA 1st Cl. Hons PPE 1961; Hon Fellow 1995); Harvard Law Sch. (LLB 1964). Law Clerk, US Supreme Court, 1964–65; Special Asst to Asst Attorney Gen., US Dept of Justice, 1965–67; Harvard University: Asst Prof. of Law, 1967–70; Prof. of Law, Harvard Law Sch., 1970–80, Lectr, 1981–; Prof., Kennedy Sch. of Govt, 1977–80; Asst Special Prosecutor, Watergate Special Prosecution Force, 1973; US Court of Appeals for First Circuit: Circuit Judge, 1980–94; Chief Judge, 1990–94. US Senate Judiciary Committee: Special Counsel, Admin. Practices Subcttee, 1974–75; Chief Counsel, 1979–80; Mem., US Sentencing Commn, 1985–89. Vis. Lectr, Coll. of Law, Sydney, Aust., 1975; Vis. Prof., Univ. of Rome, 1993. Fellow: Amer. Acad. of Arts and Scis; Amer Bar Foundn. *Publications:* (with P. MacAvoy) The Federal Power Commission and the Regulation of Energy, 1974; (with R. Stewart) Administrative Law and Regulatory Policy, 1979, 3rd edn 1992; Regulation and its Reform, 1982; Breaking the Vicious Circle: toward effective risk regulation, 1993; contrib. chapters in books; numerous articles in law jls and reviews. *Address:* Supreme Court Building, One First Street NE, Washington, DC 20543-0001, USA. *T:* (202) 4792977.

BRIAULT, Dr Eric William Henry, CBE 1976; Education Officer, Inner London Education Authority, 1971–76; Visiting Professor of Education, University of Sussex, 1977–81 and 1981–85; *b* 24 Dec. 1911; *s* of H. G. Briault; *m* 1935, Marie Alice (*née* Knight); two *s* one *d*. *Educ:* Brighton, Hove and Sussex Grammar Sch.; Peterhouse, Cambridge (Robert Slade Schol.). 1st cl. hons Geography, 1933; MA Cantab 1937; PhD London 1939. School teaching, 1933–47; Inspector of Schools, LCC, 1948–56; Dep. Educn Officer, ILEA, 1956–71. Dir, res. project on falling rolls in secondary schs, 1978–80. Hon. Sec., RGS, 1953–63. Freeman, City of London, 1935; Liveryman, Goldsmiths' Co., 1968–. Hon. DLitt Sussex, 1975. *Publications:* Sussex, East and West (Land Utilisation Survey report), 1942; (jtly) Introduction to Advanced Geography, 1957; (jtly) Geography In and Out of School, 1960; (jtly) Falling Rolls in Secondary Schools, Parts I and II, 1980; (ed jtly) Primary School Management, 1990. *Recreations:* travel, gardening, music, theatre and ballet; formerly athletics (Cambridge blue) and cross-country running (Cambridge half-blue). *Address:* Woodedge, Hampers Lane, Storrington, W Sussex RH20 3HZ. *T:* Storrington (01903) 743919.

BRICE, (Ann) Nuala, PhD; Deputy Special Commissioner of Taxes, since 1992; Chairman, VAT and Duties Tribunals (formerly VAT Tribunals), since 1992; *b* 22 Dec. 1937; *d* of William Connor and Rosaleen Gertrude Connor (*née* Gilmartin); *m* 1963, Geoffrey James Barrington Groves Brice, *qv*; one *s*. *Educ:* Loreto Convent, Manchester; University Coll. London. LLB (Hons), LLM 1976, PhD 1982, London. Admitted Solicitor of the Supreme Court, 1963 (Stephen Heelis Gold Medal and John Peacock Conveyancing Prize, 1963). The Law Society: Asst Solicitor, 1963; Asst Sec., 1964; Sen. Asst Sec., 1973; Deptl Sec., 1982; Asst Sec.-Gen., 1987–92. Sec., Revenue Law Cttee, 1972–82. Vis. Associate Prof. of Law, Tulane Univ., New Orleans, USA, 1990–. *Recreations:* reading, music, gardening. *Address:* Yew Tree House, Spring Coppice, Lane End, Bucks HP14 3NU. *T:* High Wycombe (01494) 881810; 15 Gayfere Street, Smith Square, SW1P 3HP. *T:* 0171–799 3807. *Club:* University Women's.

BRICE, Air Cdre Eric John, CBE 1971 (OBE 1957); CEng; AFRAeS; MBIM; RAF retd; stockbroker; *b* 12 Feb. 1917; *s* of Courtenay Percy Please Brice and Lilie Alice Louise Brice (*née* Grey); *m* 1942, Janet Parks, Roundhay, Leeds, Yorks; two *s* one *d*. *Educ:* Loughborough Coll. (DLC). Joined RAF, 1939; served War, MEAF, 1943–46 (Sqdn Ldr). Air Ministry, 1946–50; Parachute Trg Sch., 1950–52; Wing Comdr, 1952; RAE, Farnborough, 1952–58; Comd, Parachute Trg Sch., 1958–60; RAF Coll., Cranwell, 1960–61; Gp Capt., 1961; RAF Halton, 1961–64; Comd, RAF Innsworth, Glos, 1964–66; Dir, Physical Educn, RAF, MoD, 1966–68; Air Cdre, 1968; Dep. AOA, RAF Headqrs, Maintenance Comd, 1968–71; April 1971, retd prematurely. *Recreations:* athletics (Combined Services and RAF athletic blues); Rugby football (RAF trialist and Blackheath Rugby Club); captained Loughborough Coll. in three sports. *Address:* Durns, Boldre, Hampshire. *T:* Lymington (01590) 672196. *Clubs:* Royal Air Force; Royal Lymington Yacht.

BRICE, Geoffrey James Barrington Groves, QC 1979; barrister; a Recorder of the Crown Court, since 1980; *b* 21 April 1938; *s* of late Lt-Cdr John Edgar Leonard Brice, MBE and Winifred Ivy Brice; *m* 1963, Ann Nuala Brice, *qv*; one *s*. *Educ:* Magdalen Coll. Sch., Brackley; University Coll., London (LLB). Called to the Bar, Middle Temple, 1960, Bencher, 1986; Harmsworth Scholar and Robert Garraway Rice Prize, 1960. Vis. Prof. of Maritime Law, Tulane Univ., 1989–. Lloyd's Arbitrator, 1978–; Wreck Commissioner, 1979–. Chairman: London Bar Arbitration Scheme, 1986–; London Common Law and Commercial Bar Assoc., 1988–89; Member: UK Govt Delegn to IMO Legal Cttee, 1984–89; Gen. Council of the Bar, 1988–89. *Publications:* Maritime Law of Salvage, 1983, 2nd edn 1993; (contrib.) Limitation of Shipowners' Liability, 1986; articles in legal jls. *Recreations:* music, opera. *Address:* Yew Tree House, Spring Coppice, Newmer Common, Lane End, Bucks HP14 3NU. *T:* High Wycombe (01494) 881810; 15 Gayfere Street, Smith Square, SW1P 3HP. *T:* 0171–799 3807; Queen Elizabeth Building, Temple, EC4Y 9BS. *T:* 0171–353 9153. *Clubs:* Athenæum; Hampshire (Winchester).

BRICE, Nuala; *see* Brice, A. N.

BRICHTO, Rabbi Dr Sidney; Director, Joseph Levy Charitable Foundation, since 1989; Senior Vice-President, Union of Liberal and Progressive Synagogues, since 1992; Lecturer, Oxford Centre for Postgraduate Hebrew Studies, since 1991; *b* 21 July 1936; *s* of Solomon and Rivka Brichto; *m* 1st, 1959, Frances Goldstein (decd); one *s* one *d*; 2nd, 1971, Cathryn Goldhill; two *s*. *Educ:* New York Univ. (BA); Hebrew Union Coll., NY (MA, MHL, DD); University College London (Study Fellowship). Associate Minister, Liberal Jewish Synagogue, 1961–64; Founder and Principal, Evening Inst. for Study of Judaism, 1962–65; Exec. Vice-Pres. and Dir, ULPS, 1964–89. Chairman: Conf. of Rabbis, ULPS, 1969–70, 1974–75; Council of Reform and Liberal Rabbis, 1974–76; Chief Rabbi's Consultative Cttee on Jewish-non-Jewish Relations, 1976–78. Vice-Pres., Nat. Assoc. of Bereavement Services, 1992–. Founder and Chm., Adv. Cttee, Israel Diaspora Trust, 1982–; Mem. Exec. Council, Leo Baeck Coll., 1964–74; Mem. Exec. and Forum, Inst. of Jewish Affairs, 1992–. Gov., Oxford Centre for Hebrew and Jewish Studies, 1994–. *Publications:* Funny . . . you don't look Jewish, 1995; contribs to Service of the Heart (Liberal Jewish Prayer Book) and to national and Jewish jls. *Recreations:* pleasant lunches, writing letters to The Times. *Address:* c/o Joseph Levy Charitable Foundation, 37/43 Sackville Street, W1X 2DL. *T:* 0171–333 8111. *Club:* Athenæum.

BRICKELL, Christopher David, CBE 1991; VMH 1976; Director General, Royal Horticultural Society, 1985–93; *b* 29 June 1932; *s* of Bertram Tom Brickell and Kathleen Alice Brickell; *m* 1963, Jeanette Scargill Flecknoe; two *d*. *Educ:* Queen's College, Taunton; Reading Univ. (BSc Horticulture). Joined Royal Horticultural Society Garden, Wisley, 1958: Asst Botanist, 1958; Botanist, 1960; Sen. Scientific Officer, 1964; Dep. Dir, 1968; Dir, 1969–85. George Robert White Medal of Honor, Mass Hort. Soc., 1988. *Publications:* Daphne: the genus in cultivation, 1976; Pruning, 1979; The Vanishing Garden, 1986; An English Florilegium, 1987; (ed) The Gardener's Encyclopaedia of Plants and Flowers, 1989; (ed) The RHS Encyclopædia of Gardening, 1992; botanical papers in Flora Europaea, European Garden Flora, and Flora of Turkey; horticultural papers in RHS Jl and Alpine Garden Soc. Bulletin. *Recreations:* gardening, sailing, squash, tennis. *Address:* The Camber, Nutbourne, Pulborough, West Sussex RH20 2HE.

BRICKWOOD, Sir Basil (Greame), 3rd Bt *cr* 1927; *b* 21 May 1923; *s* of Sir John Brickwood, 1st Bt and Isabella Janet Gibson (*d* 1967), *d* of James Gordon; *S* half-brother, 1974; *m* 1956, Shirley Anne Brown; two *d*. *Educ:* King Edward's Grammar Sch., Stratford-upon-Avon; Clifton. Served War, RAF, 1940–46. *Club:* Royal Air Force.

BRIDEN, Prof. James Christopher, PhD, DSc; CGeol; FGS, FRAS; Visiting Professor (NERC Research Professor), University of Oxford, since 1994; Hon. Professor, University of Leeds, since 1986; *b* 30 Dec. 1938; *s* of Henry Charles Briden and Gladys Elizabeth (*née* Jefkins); *m* 1968, Caroline Mary (*née* Gillmore); one *s* one *d*. *Educ:* Royal Grammar Sch., High Wycombe; St Catherine's Coll., Oxford (MA); ANU (PhD 1965; DSc 1994). FGS 1962; CGeol 1990; FRAS 1962. Research Fellow: Univ. of Rhodesia, 1965–66; Univ. of Oxford, 1966–67; Univ. of Birmingham, 1967–68; University of Leeds: Lectr, 1968–73; Reader, 1973–75; Prof. of Geophysics, 1975–86; Head, Dept of Earth Sciences, 1976–79 and 1982–85; Dir of Earth Scis, NERC, 1986–94. Canadian Commonwealth Fellow and Vis. Prof., Univ. of Western Ontario, 1979–80. Mem., NERC, 1981–86; Chairman: Jt Assoc. for Geophysics, 1981–84 (Chm., Founding Cttee, 1978–79); Exec. Cttee, Ocean Drilling Prog., 1994–Sept. 1996; Member: Science and Engrg (formerly Science) Cttee, British Council, 1990–; Governing Council, Internat. Seismol Centre, 1978–83; Council: Eur. Geophysical Soc., 1976–84; RAS, 1978–79; Geol Soc., 1992–. Fellow, Amer. Geophysical Union, 1994. Murchison Medal, Geol Soc., 1984. Editor, Earth and Planetary Science Letters, 1971–. *Publications:* (with A. G. Smith) Mesozoic and Cenozoic Palaeocontinental World Maps, 1977; (with A. G. Smith and A. M. Hurley) Phanerozoic Palaeocontinental World Maps, 1981; over 80 papers on palaeomagnetism, palaeoclimates, tectonics and aspects of geophysics. *Recreations:* opera-, music-, theatre-going, various sports. *Address:* Department of Earth Sciences, University of Oxford, Parks Road, Oxford OX1 3PR. *T:* Oxford (01865) 376970. *Club:* United Oxford & Cambridge University.

BRIDGE, family name of **Baron Bridge of Harwich.**

BRIDGE OF HARWICH, Baron *cr* 1980 (Life Peer), of Harwich in the County of Essex; **Nigel Cyprian Bridge;** Kt 1968; PC 1975; a Lord of Appeal in Ordinary, 1980–92; *b* 26 Feb. 1917; *s* of late Comdr C. D. C. Bridge, RN; *m* 1944, Margaret Swinbank; one *s* two *d*. *Educ:* Marlborough College. Army Service, 1940–46; commnd into KRRC, 1941. Called to the Bar, Inner Temple, 1947; Bencher, 1964, Reader, 1985, Treasurer, 1986; Junior Counsel to Treasury (Common Law), 1964–68; a Judge of High Court, Queen's Bench Div., 1968–75; Presiding Judge, Western Circuit, 1972–74; a Lord Justice of Appeal, 1975–80. Mem., Security Commn, 1977–85 (Chm. 1982–85). Hon. Fellow, Amer. Coll. of Trial Lawyers, 1984. Hon. Fellow, Wolfson Coll., Cambridge, 1989. *Address:* House of Lords, SW1A 0PW.

See also Very Rev. A. C. Bridge.

BRIDGE, Very Rev. Antony Cyprian; Dean of Guildford, 1968–86; *b* 5 Sept. 1914; *s* of late Comdr C. D. C. Bridge, RN; *m* 1937, Brenda Lois Streatfeild (*d* 1995); one *s* two *d*. *Educ:* Marlborough College. Scholarship to Royal Academy School of Art, 1932. Professional painter thereafter. War of 1939–45: joined Army, Sept. 1939; commissioned Buffs, 1940; demobilised as Major, 1945. Ordained, 1955; Curate, Hythe Parish Church till 1958; Vicar of Christ Church, Lancaster Gate, London, 1958–68. Mem., Adv. Council V&A Museum, 1976–79. FSA 1987. *Publications:* Images of God, 1960; Theodora: portrait in a Byzantine landscape, 1978; The Crusades, 1980; Suleiman The Magnificent, 1983; One Man's Advent, 1985; Richard the Lionheart, 1989. *Recreations:* bird-watching, reading. *Address:* 34 London Road, Deal, Kent CT14 9TE.

See also Baron Bridge of Harwich.

BRIDGE, John, GC 1944; GM 1940 and Bar 1941; Director of Education for Sunderland Borough Council (formerly Sunderland County Borough Council), 1963–76, retired; *b* 5 Feb. 1915; *s* of late Joseph Edward Bridge, Culcheth, Warrington; *m* 1945, F. J. Patterson; three *d*. *Educ:* London Univ. BSc Gen. Hons, 1936 and BSc Special Hons (Physics), 1937; Teacher's Dip., 1938. Schoolmaster: Lancs CC, Sept.-Dec. 1938; Leighton Park, Reading, Jan.-Aug. 1939; Firth Park Grammar Sch., Sheffield, Sept. 1939–Aug. 1946 (interrupted by war service). Served War: RNVR June 1940–Feb. 1946, engaged on bomb and mine disposal; demobilised as Lt Comdr RNVR. *Recreations:* gardening, travel, fell walking, photography, fishing. *Address:* 37 Park Avenue, Roker, Sunderland SR6 9NJ. *T:* 0191–548 6356.

BRIDGE, Keith James; consultant; *b* 21 Aug. 1929; *s* of late James Henry Bridge and Lilian Elizabeth (*née* Nichols); *m* 1960, Thelma Ruby (*née* Hubble); three *d* (and one *s* decd). *Educ:* Sir George Monoux Grammar Sch., Walthamstow; Corpus Christi Coll., Oxford (MA). CIPFA 1959; CIMgt (CBIM 1978). Local govt service, 1953; Dep. City Treasurer, York, 1965; Borough Treas., Bolton, 1967; City Treas., Manchester, 1971; County Treasurer, Greater Manchester Council, 1973; Chief Exec., Humberside CC, 1978–83. Mem., W Yorks Residuary Body, 1985–91. Financial Adviser to Assoc. of Metrop. Authorities, 1971–78; Mem. Council, 1972–84, Pres., 1982–83, Chartered Inst. of Public Finance and Accountancy; Pres., Soc. of Metropolitan Treasurers, 1977–78. Member: Audit Commn for Local Authorities in Eng. and Wales, 1983–86; Exec. Council, Business in the Community, 1982–84; Bd, Public Finance Foundn, 1984–90; Educn Assets Bd, 1988–; Football Licensing Authy, 1990–. Dir, Phillips & Drew, 1987–89. Chm., York Diocesan Pastoral Cttee, 1989–94. Freeman, City of London, 1986. *Publications:* papers in professional jls. *Recreations:* gardening, literature, music. *Address:* 1 Fairlawn, Molescroft, Beverley, N Humberside HU17 7DD. *T:* Hull (01482) 887652.

BRIDGE, Ronald George Blacker, CBE 1990 (OBE 1985); Hong Kong Civil Service, retired; *b* 7 Sept. 1932; *s* of Blacker Frank Bridge and Aileen Georgina Edith (*née* Shaw); *m* 1956, Olive Tyrrell Brown; two *s* two *d*. *Educ:* Charterhouse; Lincoln Coll., Oxford (MA). National Service, 1954–56. Colonial Office Devonshire Course, 1956–57; Hong Kong Civil Service, 1957–89; language study, 1957–58; Resettlement Officer, 1958–61; Asst Sec. (Lands and Buildings), 1961–69; Asst Comr for Resettlement, 1969–72; Asst Colonial Sec. (Estabt), 1971–72; Dep. Sec. for the Civil Service, 1972–76; Dep. Sec. for Security, 1976–77; Sec. for the Civil Service, 1977–78; Dir of Immigration, 1978–83; Comr for Labour, 1983–86; Sec. for Educn and Manpower, 1986–89. Part-time: with Weltons & Morse, solicitors, 1989–94; with Nabarro Nathanson, solicitors, 1995–. *Recreations:* walking, reading. *Address:* 15 Lincoln Street, SW3 2TP. *T:* 0171–581 8090.

BRIDGEMAN, family name of **Earl of Bradford** and **Viscount Bridgeman.**

BRIDGEMAN, 3rd Viscount *cr* 1929, of Leigh; **Robin John Orlando Bridgeman,** CA; *b* 5 Dec. 1930; *s* of Hon. Geoffrey John Orlando Bridgeman, MC, FRCS (*d* 1974) (2nd *s* of 1st Viscount) and Mary Meriel Gertrude Bridgeman (*d* 1974), *d* of Rt Hon. Sir George John Talbot; *S* uncle, 1982; *m* 1966, (Victoria) Harriet Lucy, *d* of Ralph Meredyth Turton; four *s*. *Educ:* Eton. CA 1958. 2nd Lieut, Rifle Bde, 1950–51. Partner: Fenn & Crosthwaite, 1973; Henderson Crosthwaite & Co., 1975–86; Director: Nestor–BNA, 1988–; Guinness Mahon & Co. Ltd, 1988–90. Dir., Bridgeman Art Library Ltd, 1972–; Chm., Friends of Lambeth Palace Liby, 1992–; Special Trustee, Hammersmith Hosp., 1986–; Gov., Reed's Sch., 1994–. *Recreations:* shooting, ski-ing, gardening, music. *Heir:* *s* Hon. William Orlando Caspar Bridgeman, *b* 15 Aug. 1968. *Address:* 19 Chepstow Road, W2 5BP. *T:* 0171–727 4065; Watley House, Sparsholt, Winchester SO21 2LU. *T:* Sparsholt (01962) 776297. *Clubs:* Beefsteak, MCC; Pitt.

BRIDGEMAN, (John) Michael, CB 1988; Chief Registrar of Friendly Societies and Industrial Assurance Commissioner, 1982–91; First Commisioner (Chairman), Building Societies Commission, 1986–91; *b* 26 April 1931; *s* of late John Wilfred Bridgeman, CBE and Mary Bridgeman (*née* Wallace); *m* 1958, June Bridgeman, *qv*; one *s* four *d*. *Educ:* Marlborough Coll.; Trinity Coll., Cambridge. Asst Principal, BoT, 1954; HM Treasury, 1956–81, Under Sec., 1975–81. *Address:* Bridge House, Culverden Park Road, Tunbridge Wells, Kent TN4 9QX.

BRIDGEMAN, John Stuart, DL; Director-General of Fair Trading, since 1995; *b* 5 Oct. 1944; *s* of late James Alfred George Bridgeman and Edith Celia (*née* Watkins); *m* 1967, Lindy Jane Fillmore; three *d*. *Educ:* Whitchurch Sch., Cardiff; University Coll., Swansea (BSc); McGill Univ., Montreal. CIMgt 1995. Alcan Inds, 1966–69; Aluminium Co. of Canada, 1969–70; Alcan Australia, 1970; Commercial Dir, Alcan UK, 1971–80; Vice-Pres. (Europe), Alcan Basic Raw Materials, 1978–82; Divl Man. Dir, Alcan Aluminium (UK) Ltd, 1981–82; Managing Director: Extrusion Div., Brit. Alcan Aluminium plc, 1983–87; Brit. Alcan Enterprises, 1987–91; Dir, Corporate Planning, Alcan Aluminium Ltd, Montreal, 1992–93; Man. Dir, British Alcan Aluminium plc, 1993–95. Mem., Monopolies and Mergers Commn, 1990–95. Vis. Prof. of Mgt, Keele Univ., 1992–. Vice-Pres., Aluminium Fedn, 1995. Chairman: N Oxon Business Gp, 1984–92; Enterprise Cherwell Ltd, 1985–91. Commnd TA and Reserve Forces, 1978; QOY, 1981–84; Maj. REME (V), 1985–94; Staff Coll., 1986; Chm., TAVRA Oxon and E Wessex, 1985–. Member: Defence Science Adv. Council, 1991–94; Nat. Employer Liaison Cttee for Reserve Forces, 1992–. Mem., UK-Canada Colloquium, 1993–. Vice-Pres., UK-Canada Chamber of Commerce, 1995–. Gov., N Oxon Coll., 1985– (Chm., 1989). DL Oxon, 1989; High Sheriff, Oxon, 1995–96. US Aluminium Assoc. Prize, 1988. *Recreations:* education, gardening, public affairs, shooting, ski-ing, *Address:* Office of Fair Trading, Field House, Bream's Buildings, EC4A 1PR. *T:* 0171–269 8919. *Club:* Glamorgan County Cricket.

BRIDGEMAN, Mrs June, CB 1990; Deputy Chair, Equal Opportunities Commission, 1991–94; *b* 26 June 1932; *d* of Gordon and Elsie Forbes; *m* 1958, John Michael Bridgeman, *qv*; one *s* four *d*. *Educ:* variously, England and Scotland; Westfield Coll., London Univ. (BA; Fellow, QMW, 1993). Asst Principal, BoT, 1954; subseq. served in DEA, NBPI, Min. of Housing and Local Govt, DoE; Under Secretary: DoE 1974–76; Central Policy Review Staff, Cabinet Office, 1976–79; Dept of Transport, 1979–90. Mem., Central Bd of Finance, C of E, 1979–83; Bishops Selector for ACCM, 1974–89. Member of Council: PSI, 1984–90; NCOPF; GPDST. Vice-Pres., Fawcett Soc. Trustee, Rees Jeffreys Road Fund, 1992–. Governor: Skinners' Sch.; Bromley High Sch. FRSA 1991. *Recreations:* family, gardening, local history, opera. *Address:* Bridge House, Culverden Park Road, Tunbridge Wells TN4 9QX. *T:* Tunbridge Wells (01892) 525578.

BRIDGEMAN, Michael; *see* Bridgeman, J. M.

BRIDGER, Rev. Canon Gordon Frederick; Principal, Oak Hill Theological College, 1987–July 1996; *b* 5 Feb. 1932; *s* of late Dr John Dell Bridger and Hilda Bridger; *m* 1962, Elizabeth Doris Bewes; three *d*. *Educ:* Christ's Hospital, Horsham; Selwyn Coll., Cambridge (MA Hons Theology); Ridley Hall, Cambridge. Curate, Islington Parish Church, 1956–59; Curate, Holy Sepulchre Church, Cambridge, 1959–62; Vicar, St Mary, North End, Fulham, 1962–69; Chaplain, St Thomas's Episcopal Church, Edinburgh, 1969–76; Rector, Holy Trinity Church, Heigham, Norwich, 1976–87; RD Norwich (South), 1981–86; Exam. Chaplain to Bishop of Norwich, 1981–86; Hon. Canon, Norwich Cathedral, 1984–87, now Hon. Canon Emeritus. Dir, Open Theol Coll., 1993–. *Publications:* The Man from Outside, 1969, rev. edn 1978; A Day that Changed the World, 1975; A Bible Study Commentary (I Corinthians—Galatians), 1985; reviews in The Churchman, Anvil and other Christian papers and magazines. *Recreations:* music, sport, reading. *Address:* *(until Aug. 1996)* 10 Farm Lane, Oak Hill Theological College, Chase Side, Southgate, N14 4PP; *(from Aug. 1996)* 4 Common Lane, Sheringham, Norfolk.

BRIDGER, Pearl, MBE 1947; Director, Central Personnel, Post Office, 1968–72, retired; *b* 9 Dec. 1912; *d* of Samuel and Lottie Bridger. *Educ:* Godolphin and Latymer Girls' Sch., London, W6. BA (Hons) Open Univ., 1978. Entered Post Office as Executive Officer, 1931; Asst Telecommunications Controller, 1938; Principal, 1947; Asst Sec., 1954; Director, 1968. *Address:* Oakhill House, Eady Close, Horsham, W Sussex RH13 5LZ. *Club:* Civil Service.

BRIDGES, family name of **Baron Bridges.**

BRIDGES, 2nd Baron *cr* 1957; **Thomas Edward Bridges,** GCMG 1988 (KCMG 1983; CMG 1975); HM Diplomatic Service, retired; *b* 27 Nov. 1927; *s* of 1st Baron Bridges, KG, PC, GCB, GCVO, MC, FRS, and late Hon. Katharine Dianthe, *d* of 2nd Baron Farrer; *S* father, 1969; *m* 1953, Rachel Mary, *y d* of late Sir Henry Bunbury, KCB; two *s* one *d*. *Educ:* Eton; New Coll., Oxford. Entered Foreign Service, 1951; served in Bonn, Berlin, Rio de Janeiro and at FO (Asst Private Sec. to Foreign Secretary, 1963–66); Head of Chancery, Athens, 1966–68; Counsellor, Moscow, 1969–71; Private Sec. (Overseas Affairs) to Prime Minister, 1972–74; RCDS 1975; Minister (Commercial), Washington, 1976–79; Dep. Under Sec. of State, FCO, 1979–82; Ambassador to Italy, 1983–87. Mem., Select Cttee on Eur. Communities, H of L, 1988–92 and 1994–. Dir, Consolidated Gold Fields, 1988–89. Indep. Bd Mem., Securities and Futures Authority (formerly Securities Assoc.), 1989–. Chairman: UK Nat. Cttee for UNICEF, 1989–; British–Italian Soc., 1991–. Mem., E Anglian Regl Cttee, NT. Pres., Dolmetsch Foundn. *Heir:* *s* Hon. Mark Thomas Bridges [*b* 25 July 1954; *m* 1978, Angela Margaret, *er d* of J. L. Collinson, Mansfield, Notts; one *s* three *d*]. *Address:* 56 Church Street, Orford, Woodbridge, Suffolk IP12 2NT.

See also M. E. Aston.

BRIDGES, Brian; Under Secretary, HEF(A) Health Aspects of Environment and Food Division, Department of Health, since 1992; *b* 30 June 1937; 4th *s* of late William Ernest Bridges; *m* 1970, Jennifer Mary Rogers. *Educ:* Harrow Weald County Grammar Sch.; Univ. of Keele (BA 1961). Sec., Univ. of Keele Union, 1959–60. Joined Civil Service, 1961; Principal, 1967; Asst Sec. 1975; Under Sec., DHSS, 1985; Dir of Estabts and Personnel, DHSS, 1985–88; Under Sec. i/c of NHS dental, pharmaceutical and optical services and pharmaceutical industry, DoH, 1988–92. *Recreations:* reading, antiquarian, photography, long walks preferably in the tow of a dog.

BRIDGES, Rt. Rev. Dewi Morris; *see* Swansea and Brecon, Bishop of.

BRIDGES, Prof. James Wilfrid; Head, Institute of Health Sciences, since 1994; Research Director, Robens Institute of Industrial and Environmental Health and Safety, since 1978, and Professor of Toxicology, since 1979, University of Surrey; *b* 9 Aug. 1938; *s* of Wilfrid Edward Seymour Bridges and Mary Winifred Cameron. *Educ:* Bromley Grammar Sch.; Queen Elizabeth Coll., London Univ.; St Mary's Hosp. Med. Sch., London Univ. BSc, DSc, PhD; MRCPath; FRSC, CChem; FIBiol; FIOSH; MInstEnvSci. Lectr, St Mary's Hosp. Med. Sch., 1962–68; Senior Lectr then Reader, Dept of Biochemistry, 1968–78, and Dean, Faculty of Science, 1988–92, Univ. of Surrey. Visiting Professor: Univ. of Texas at Dallas, 1973, 1979; Univ. of Rochester, NY, 1974; Mexico City, 1991; Sen. Scientist, Nat. Inst. of Envtl Health Scis, N Carolina, 1976. Chm., British Toxicology Soc., 1980–81; First Pres., Fedn of European Toxicology Socs, 1985–88. Mem. Council, Inst. of Biology. FRSA. *Publications:* (ed jtly) Progress in Drug Metabolism, 10 vols, 1976–88; some 300 research papers and reviews in scientific jls. *Recreations:* theatre going, various sports. *Address:* Liddington Lodge, Liddington Hall Drive, Guildford GU3 3AE.

BRIDGES, Dame Mary (Patricia), DBE 1981; *b* 6 June 1930; *d* of Austin Edward and Lena Mabel Fawkes; *m* 1951, Bertram Marsdin Bridges; one step *s*. Chm., Honiton Div. Cons. Assoc., 1968–71; Pres., Western Provincial Area, Nat. Union of Cons. and Unionist Assocs, 1987–. Women's Section of Royal British Legion: Pres., Exmouth Br., 1965–; Chm., Devon County Women's Section, 1979–91; County Vice Pres., 1991; SW Area Rep. to Central Cttee, 1985–89; Nat. Vice-Chm., 1989–92; Nat. Chm., 1992–95; Nat. Council Rep., House Cttee, Dunkirk Meml House, 1994. Former Mem., Exe Vale HMC; Pres., Exmouth Council of Voluntary Service (Founder Chm., 1975). Member: Exec., Resthaven, Exmouth, 1970– (Chm., League of Friends, 1971–90); Devon FPC, 1985–91; President: Exmouth and Budleigh Salterton Br., CRUSE, 1980–88; Exmouth Campaign Cttee, Cancer Research, 1981– (Chm., 1975–81); Founder Pres., Exmouth Br., British Heart Foundn, 1984. Mem., SW Electricity Consultative Council, 1982–90 (Chm., Devon Cttee, 1986–90); Mem., Exmouth Cttee, LEPRA, 1962–87 (Hon. Sec., 1964–87); Dir, Home Care Trust, 1988–; Co-optative Trustee, Exmouth Welfare Trust, 1979–; Co-founder, and Trustee, Exmouth and Lympstone Hospiscare, 1986– (Pres., 1994); Trustee, Exmouth Adventure Trust for Girls, 1988–; Exec. Mem., St Loye's Coll. for Trng the Disabled for Commerce and Industry, 1988–; Governor, Rolle Coll., Exmouth, 1982–88. Hon. Life Mem., Retford Cricket Club, 1951; Pres., Exmouth Cricket Club, 1992– (Hon. Vice-Pres., 1981). *Recreations:* cricket, reading. *Address:* Walton House, Fairfield Close, Exmouth, Devon EX8 2BN. *T:* Exmouth (01395) 265317.

BRIDGES, Ven. Peter Sydney Godfrey; Archdeacon of Warwick, 1983–90, now Emeritus; Canon-Theologian of Coventry Cathedral, 1977–90, now Emeritus; *b* 30 Jan. 1925; *s* of Sidney Clifford Bridges and Winifred (*née* Livette); *m* 1952, Joan Penlerick (*née* Madge); two *s*. *Educ:* Raynes Park Grammar Sch.; Kingston upon Thames Sch. of Architecture; Lincoln Theol College. ARIBA 1950, Dip. Liturgy and Architecture 1967. Gen. and ecclesiastical practice, 1950–54; Lectr, Nottingham Sch. of Architecture, 1954–56. Deacon, 1958; Priest, 1959. Asst Curate, Hemel Hempstead, 1958–64; Res. Fellow, Inst. for Study of Worship and Religious Architecture, Univ. of Birmingham, 1964–67 (Hon. Fellow, 1967–72 and 1978); Warden, Anglican Chaplaincy and Chaplain to Univ. of Birmingham, 1965–68; Lectr, Birmingham Sch. of Arch., 1967–72; eccles. architect and planning consultant, 1968–75; Chm., New Town Ministers Assoc., 1968–72; Co-Dir, Midlands Socio-Religious Res. Gp, 1968–75; Dir, Chelmsford Diocesan R&D Unit, 1972–77; Archdeacon of Southend, 1972–77; Archdeacon of Coventry, 1977–83. Advr for Christian Spirituality, Dio. of Coventry, 1990–93. Mem., Cathedrals Advisory Commn for England, 1981–86. Chm., Painting and Prayer, 1989–94. *Publications:* Socio-Religious Institutes, Lay Academies, etc, 1967; contrib. Church Building, res. bulletins (Inst. for Study of Worship and Relig. Arch.), Clergy Review, Prism, Christian Ministry in New Towns, Cathedral and Mission, Church Architecture and Social Responsibility. *Recreations:* architecture, singing, painting. *Address:* Saint Clare, 25 Rivermead Close, Romsey, Hants SO51 8HQ. *T:* Romsey (01794) 512889. *Club:* Commonwealth Trust.

BRIDGES, Sir Phillip (Rodney), Kt 1973; CMG 1967; *b* 9 July 1922; *e s* of late Captain Sir Ernest Bridges and Lady Bridges; *m* 1st, 1951, Rosemary Ann Streeten (marr. diss. 1961); two *s* one *d*; 2nd, 1962, Angela Mary (*née* Dearden), *widow* of James Huyton. *Educ:* Bedford School. Military Service (Capt., RA) with Royal W African Frontier Force in W Africa, India and Burma, 1941–47; Beds Yeo., 1947–54. Admitted Solicitor (England), 1951; Colonial Legal Service, 1954; Barrister and Solicitor, Supreme Court of The Gambia, 1954; Solicitor-General of The Gambia, 1963; QC (Gambia) 1964; Attorney-General of The Gambia, 1964–68; Chief Justice of The Gambia, 1968–83. *Address:* Weavers, Coney Weston, Bury St Edmunds, Suffolk IP31 1HG. *T:* Coney Weston (01359) 221316. *Club:* Travellers'.

BRIDGES-ADAMS, John Nicholas William; a Recorder of the Crown Court, since 1972; *b* 16 Sept. 1930; *s* of late William Bridges-Adams, CBE; *m* 1962, Jenifer Celia Emily, *d* of David Sandell, FRCS. *Educ:* Stowe; Oriel Coll., Oxford (Scholar; MA, DipEd). Commnd Royal Artillery, 1949, transf. to RAFVR 1951 and served with Oxford and London Univ. Air Sqdn; Flying Officer, 2623 Sqdn RAuxAF Regt, 1980–82. Called to Bar, Lincoln's Inn, 1958 (Gray's Inn *ad eundem* 1979); Head of Chambers, 1979–92; Mem., Young Barristers Cttee, Bar Council, 1960–61; Actg Junior, Mddx Sessions Bar Mess, 1965–67. Mem., Exec. Cttee, Soc. of Cons. Lawyers, 1967–69 (Chairman: Rates of Exchange sub-cttee, 1967–70; Criminal Law sub-cttee, 1983–87; Criminal Justice and Sentencing sub-cttee, 1987–92); Mem., House of Lords Reform Cttee, CAER, 1982. Chm., panel from which Representations Cttees under Dumping at Sea Act 1974 drawn, 1976–85, and under Food and Environment Protection Act 1985, 1985–. Contested (C) West Bromwich West, Oct. 1974. Governor, St Benedict's Upper Sch., 1980–83. Member: RIIA; IISS; FCIArb. *Publication:* contrib. on collisions at sea, 3rd edn of Halsbury's Laws of England, Vol. 35. *Recreation:* doing some things better than others. *Address:* 2 Field Court, Gray's Inn, WC1R 5BB. *T:* 0171–405 6114; Fornham Cottage, Fornham St Martin, Bury St Edmunds, Suffolk IP31 1SP. *T:* Bury St Edmunds (01284) 755307. *Clubs:* Savile, Garrick.

BRIDGEWATER, Allan; Group Chief Executive, Norwich Union Insurance Group, since 1989; *b* 26 Aug. 1936; *m* 1960, Janet Bridgewater; three *d.* *Educ:* Wyggeston Grammar Sch., Leicester. ACII, FIPD, CIMgt. Asst Gen. Man., Norwich Union Insce Gp, 1979; Dep. Gen. Man. 1983, Gen. Man. 1984, Norwich Union Fire Insce Soc. Ltd; Norwich Union Insurance Group: Dir, 1985; Dep. Chief Gen. Man., 1988. Pres., Chartered Insurance Inst., 1989–90; Chm., Assoc. of British Insurers, 1993–. Chm., Endeavour Training. Trustee, Duke of Edinburgh's Commonwealth Study Conf. FRSA. *Address:* Norwich Union Insurance Group, 8 Surrey Street, Norwich, Norfolk NR1 3NG. *T:* Norwich (01603) 622200.

BRIDGEWATER, Bentley Powell Conyers; Secretary of the British Museum, 1948–73; *b* 6 Sept. 1911; *s* of Conyers Bridgewater, OBE, Clerk to Commissioners of Taxes for City of London, and Violet Irene, *d* of Dr I. W. Powell, Victoria, BC. *Educ:* Westminster School (King's Schol.); Christ Church, Oxford (Westminster Schol., BA 1933, MA 1965). Asst Keeper, British Museum, 1937; Asst Sec., 1940. Seconded to Dominions Office, 1941–42, and to Foreign Office, 1942–45; returned to British Museum, 1946; Deputy Keeper, 1950; Keeper, 1961; retired, 1973. *Recreation:* music. *Address:* 4 Doughty Street, WC1N 2PH. *Club:* Athenæum.

BRIDGLAND, Milton Deane, AO 1987; FTS, FRACI, FAIM; Chairman, ICI Australia Ltd, 1980–93; *b* 8 July 1922; *s* of late Frederick H. and Muriel E. Bridgland, Adelaide; *m* 1945, Christine L. Cowell; three *d.* *Educ:* St Peter's Coll., Adelaide; Adelaide Univ. (BSc). Joined ICI Australia Ltd, 1945; Technical Manager, Plastics Gp, 1955–62; Ops Dir, 1962–67, Man. Dir, 1967–71, Dulux Australia Ltd; Exec. Dir 1971, Man. Dir, 1978–84, ICI Australia Ltd. Chairman: Jennings Properties, later Centro Properties Ltd, 1985–92; ANZ Banking Group Ltd, 1989–92 (Dir, 1982–92; Dep Chm., 1987–89); Director: Jennings Group (formerly Industries) Ltd, 1984–92; Freeport-McMoRan Australia Ltd, 1987–89. President: Aust. Chemical Industry Council, 1977; Aust. Industry Develt Assoc., 1982–83. Vice President: Aust. Business Roundtable, 1983; Business Council of Australia, 1983–84; Dir, Aust. Inst. of Petroleum, 1980–84; Mem., National Energy Adv. Cttee, 1977–80. Member, Board of Management: Univ. of Melbourne Grad. Sch. of Management, 1983–86; Crawford Fund for Internat. Agricl Res., 1989–94. Chm. Adv. Bd, Salvation Army, Southern Territory, 1986–90. Mem., Cook Soc. *Recreations:* tennis, the arts, gardening. *Address:* 178 Barkers Road, Hawthorn, Vic 3122, Australia. *T:* (3) 98193939. *Club:* Athenæum (Melbourne).

BRIDGWATER, Prof. John, FEng 1987; FIChemE; Shell Professor and Head of Department of Chemical Engineering, and Professorial Fellow of St Catharine's College, Cambridge University, since 1993, *b* 10 Jan. 1938; *s* of Eric and Mary Bridgwater; *m* 1962, Diane Louise Tucker; one *s* one *d.* *Educ:* Solihull Sch.; St Catharine's Coll., Cambridge (Major Scholar; MA, PhD, ScD); Princeton Univ. (MSE). Chemical Engineer, Courtaulds, 1961–64; University of Cambridge: Demonstrator in Chem. Engrg, 1964–69; Univ. Lectr in Chem. Engrg and Fellow, St Catharine's Coll., 1969–71; Esso Res. Fellow in Chem. Engrg, Hertford Coll., Oxford, 1971–73; Univ. Lectr in Engrg Sci., Univ. of Oxford and Lubbock Fellow in Engrg, Balliol Coll., 1973–80; University of Birmingham: Prof., 1980–93; Head, Sch. of Chem. Engrg, 1983–89; Dean, Faculty of Engrg, 1989–92; Gp Leader in Inter-Disciplinary Res. Centre in Materials for High Performance Applications, 1989–93. Vis. Associate Prof., Univ. of British Columbia, 1970–71; Vis. Prof., Univ. of Calif at Berkeley, 1992–93. Mem., Engrg Bd, SERC, 1986–89; Chm., Process Engrg Cttee, SERC, 1986–89. Exec. Editor, Chem. Engrg Science, 1983–. *Publications:* (with J. J. Benbow) Paste Flow and Extrusion, 1993; papers on chem. and process engineering in professional jls. *Address:* Department of Chemical Engineering, University of Cambridge, Pembroke Street, Cambridge CB2 3RA. *T:* Cambridge (01223) 334799.

BRIDLE, Rear-Adm. Gordon Walter, CB 1977; MBE 1952; *b* 14 May 1923; *s* of Percy Gordon Bridle and Dorothy Agnes Bridle; *m* 1944, Phyllis Audrey Page; three *s.* *Educ:* King Edward's Grammar Sch., Aston, Birmingham; Northern Grammar Sch., Portsmouth; Royal Dockyard Sch., Portsmouth (Whitworth Scholar); Imperial Coll., London (ACGI). CEng, FIEE. jssc. Loan Service, Pakistan, 1950–52; served HM Ships: Implacable, St James, Gambia, Newfoundland, Devonshire; Proj. Manager, Sea Slug and Sea Dart, Mins of Aviation/Technol.; comd HMS Collingwood, 1969–71; Dir, Surface Weapons Projects, ASWE; Asst Controller of the Navy, 1974–77. *Address:* 25 Heatherwood, Midhurst, Sussex GU29 9LH. *T:* Midhurst (01730) 812838.

BRIDLE, Ronald Jarman, FEng 1979; private consultant and inventor, Cardiff University Industry Centre, since 1989, and Hon. Professor, Cardiff University, since 1991; Director, Key Resources International, since 1984; *b* 27 Jan. 1930; *s* of Raymond Bridle and Dorothy (*née* Jarman); *m* Beryl Eunice (*née* Doe); two *d.* *Educ:* West Monmouth Grammar Sch.; Bristol Univ. (BSc). FEng, FICE, FIHE. Graduate Asst, Monmouthshire CC, 1953–55; Exec. Engr, Gold Coast Govt, 1955–57; Sen. Engr, Cwmbran Develt Corp., 1957–60; Principal Designer, Cardiff City, 1960–62; Project Engr, Sheffield-Leeds Motorway, West Riding CC, 1962–65; Dep. County Surveyor II, Cheshire CC, 1965–67; Dir, Midland RCU, DoE, 1967–71; Dep. Chief Highway Engr, 1971–73, Under-Sec., Highways 1, 1973–75, Chief Highway Engr, 1975–76, DoE; Chief Highway Engr, Dept of Transport, 1976–80; Controller of R&D, Dept of Transport, and Dir, Transport and Road Res. Lab., 1980–84. Dir (Technology and Develt), Mitchell Cotts PLC, 1984–86; Chm., Permanent Formwork Ltd, 1987–89. FRSA. Former Member: Council, ICE; EDC for Civil Engrg; Past Pres., IHE; Mem. Bd., BSI, 1979–85; Chm., Building and Civil Engineering Council, BSI, 1979–85. *Publications:* papers in jls of ICE, IHE and internat. confs. *Recreations:* golf, painting. *Address:* Parsonage Farm, Kemeys Commander, Usk, Gwent NP5 1SU. *T:* Nantyderry (01873) 880929. *Club:* Royal Automobile.

BRIDPORT, 4th Viscount, *cr* 1868; **Alexander Nelson Hood;** Baron Bridport, 1794; 7th Duke of Bronte in Sicily (*cr* 1799); Managing Partner, Bridport & Cie SA, since 1991; *b* 17 March 1948; *s* of 3rd Viscount Bridport and Sheila Jeanne Agatha, *d* of Johann van Meurs; *S* father, 1969; *m* 1st, 1972, Linda Jacqueline Paravicini (marr. diss.), *d* of Lt-Col and Mrs V. R. Paravicini; one *s*; 2nd, 1979, Mrs Nina Rindt-Martyn; one *s.* *Educ:* Eton; Sorbonne. *Heir:* *s* Hon. Peregrine Alexander Nelson Hood, *b* 30 Aug. 1974. *Address:* Villa Jonin, 1261 Le Muids, Vaud, Switzerland. *T:* (22) 3661705, *Fax:* (22) 3661898. *Club:* Brooks's.

BRIEGEL, Geoffrey Michael Olver; Legacy Officer, The Institute of Cancer Research: Royal Cancer Hospital, since 1983; *b* 13 July 1923; *s* of late Roy C. Briegel, TD, and Veria Lindsey Briegel; *m* 1947, Barbara Mary Richardson; three *s* one *d.* *Educ:* Highgate Sch. Served War, RAF, 1942–46 (514 Sqdn Bomber Command). Called to Bar, Lincoln's Inn, 1950; Public Trustee Office, 1954; Clerk of the Lists, Queen's Bench Div., and Legal Sec. to Lord Chief Justice of England, 1963; Dep. Circuit Administrator, South Eastern Circuit, 1971; Dep. Master of the Court of Protection, 1977–83. *Recreations:* target rifle and pistol shooting, swimming, cricket, theatre. *Club:* Royal Air Force.

BRIEN, Alan; novelist and journalist; *b* 12 March 1925; *s* of Ernest Brien and Isabella Brien (*née* Patterson); *m* 1st, 1947, Pamela Mary Jones; three *d*; 2nd, 1961, Nancy Newbold Ryan; one *s* one *d*; 3rd, 1973, Jill Sheila Tweedie (*d* 1993). *Educ:* Bede Grammar Sch., Sunderland; Jesus Coll., Oxford. BA (Eng Lit). Served war RAF (air-gunner), 1943–46. Associate Editor: Mini-Cinema, 1950–52; Courier, 1952–53; Film Critic and Columnist, Truth, 1953–54; TV Critic, Observer, 1954–55; Film Critic, 1954–56, columnist, 1956–58, Evening Standard; Drama Critic and Features Editor, Spectator, 1958–61; Columnist, Daily Mail, 1958–62; Columnist, Sunday Dispatch, 1962–63; Political Columnist, Sunday Pictorial, 1963–64; Drama Critic, Sunday Telegraph, 1961–67; Columnist: Spectator, 1963–65; New Statesman, 1966–72; Punch, 1972–84; Diarist, 1967–75, Film Critic, 1976–84, Sunday Times. Foreign correspondent: NY (for Evening Standard), 1956–58; Moscow (for Sunday Times), 1974; Saigon (for Sunday Times, Punch), 1972. Regular broadcaster on radio, 1952–, and television, 1955–. Hannen Swaffer (now IPC) Critic of Year, 1966, 1967. *Publications:* Domes of Fortune (essays), 1979; Lenin: the novel (novel), 1987; And When Rome Falls (novel), 1996. *Recreations:* procrastination, empyromancy. *Address:* 15 Marlborough Yard, Holloway Road, N19 4ND. *T:* 0171–281 9640.

BRIERLEY, Christopher Wadsworth, CBE 1987; Senior Adviser, Natural Gas Development Unit, World Bank, Washington, USA, 1990–94; Managing Director, Resources and New Business, 1987–89, and Member of the Board, 1985–89, British Gas plc (formerly British Gas Corporation); *b* 1 June 1929; *s* of Eric Brierley and Edna Mary Lister; *m* 1st, Dorothy Scott (marr. diss. 1980); two *d*; 2nd, 1984, Dilwen Marie Srobat (*née* Morgan). *Educ:* Whitgift Middle School, Croydon. FCMA, ACIS. Branch Accountant, Hubert Davies & Co., Rhodesia, 1953–56; private business, N Rhodesia, 1956–59; Accountant, EMI, 1960; Chief Accountant, EMI Records, 1965; Dir of Finance, Long & Hambly, 1968; Chief Accountant, E Midlands Gas Bd, 1970; Director of Finance: Eastern Gas Bd, 1974; British Gas, 1977; Dir, 1980, Man. Dir, 1982, Economic Planning, British Gas. *Recreations:* golf, music, sailing. *Address:* 6 Stobarts Close, Knebworth, Herts SG3 6ND. *T:* Stevenage (01438) 814988. *Club:* Royal Automobile.

BRIERLEY, John David, CB 1978; retired Civil Servant; *b* 16 March 1918; *s* of late Walter George Brierley and late Doris Brierley (*née* Paterson); *m* 1956, Frances Elizabeth Davis; one (adopted) *s* one (adopted) *d.* *Educ:* elementary schools, London and Croydon; Whitgift Sch., Croydon; Lincoln Coll., Oxford. *Lit. Hum.*, BA Hons, 1940. Served War: Army, RASC, 1940–46. Ministry of Education: Asst Principal, 1946; Principal, 1949; Dept of Education and Science: Asst Sec., 1960; Under-Sec., 1969; Principal Finance Officer, 1969–75; Under Sec., DES, 1969–77. Dean of Studies, Working Mens' Coll., NW1, 1978–81 (Mem. Corp., 1980–94); Governor, Croydon High Sch. (GPDST), 1980–91. *Recreations:* fell-walking, cycling, photography, music. *Address:* Little Trees, Winterbourne, near Newbury, Berks RG16 8AS. *T:* Chieveley (01635) 248870.

BRIERLEY, Sir Ronald (Alfred), Kt 1988; Chairman, GPG plc, 1990; *b* Wellington, 2 Aug. 1937; *s* of J. R. Brierley. *Educ:* Wellington Coll. Editor, New Zealand Stocks and Shares, 1957–63; Chairman: Brierley Investments Ltd, 1961–89 (Founder, 1961, Pres. 1989–); Industrial Equity Ltd, 1966–89; Chm., Bank of New Zealand, 1987–88 (Dir, 1985–88; Dep. Chm., 1986). *Address:* Brierley Investments Ltd, 10 Eastcheap, EC3M 1DJ. *Clubs:* American National, City Tattersall's (NSW).

BRIERS, Richard David, OBE 1989; actor since 1955; *b* 14 Jan. 1934; *s* of Joseph Briers and Morna Richardson; *m* 1957, Ann Davies; two *d.* *Educ:* Rokeby Prep. Sch., Wimbledon; Ridgeway Sch., Wimbledon. RADA, 1954–56 (silver medal). First appearance in London in Gilt and Gingerbread, Duke of York's, 1959. *Plays:* (major parts in): Arsenic and Old Lace, Vaudeville, 1965; Relatively Speaking, Duke of York's, 1966; The Real Inspector Hound, Criterion, 1968; Cat Among the Pigeons, Prince of Wales, 1969; The Two of Us, Garrick, 1970; Butley, Criterion, 1972; Absurd Person Singular, Criterion, 1973; Absent Friends, Garrick, 1975; Middle Age Spread, Lyric, 1979; The Wild Duck, Lyric, Hammersmith, 1980; Arms and the Man, Lyric, 1981; Run for Your Wife, Shaftesbury, 1983; Why Me?, Strand, 1985; The Relapse, Chichester, 1986; Twelfth Night, Riverside Studios, 1987 (televised 1988); Midsummer Night's Dream, and King Lear, Renaissance Theatre world tour, 1990; Wind in the Willows, Nat. Theatre, 1991; Uncle Vanya, Lyric, Hammersmith, 1991; Coriolanus, Chichester, 1992; Home, Wyndham's, 1994. *Television series:* Brothers-in-Law; Marriage Lines; The Good Life; OneUpManShip; The Other One; Norman Conquests; Ever-Decreasing Circles; All In Good Faith; Down to Earth. *Films:* Henry V, 1989; Much Ado About Nothing, and Swan Song, 1993; Mary Shelley's Frankenstein, 1994. *Publications:* Natter Natter, 1981; Coward and Company, 1987; A Little Light Weeding, 1993. *Recreations:* reading, gardening. *Address:* c/o Lorraine Hamilton Management, 76 Oxford Street, W1N 0AT.

BRIGDEN, Wallace, MA, MD, FRCP; Consulting Physician: London Hospital, and Cardiac Department, London Hospital; National Heart Hospital; Consulting Cardiologist to the Royal Navy, now Emeritus; *b* 8 June 1916; *s* of Wallis Brigden and Louise Brigden (*née* Clarke); *m* 1st, 1942, Joan Mack (marr. diss. 1966); two *s* one *d*; 2nd, 1966, Everel Sankey; one *s*, and one step *s.* *Educ:* Latymer School; University of Cambridge; King's College Hospital; Yale University. Senior Scholar, King's College, Cambridge; First Class Natural Sciences Tripos, Parts I and II, 1936, 1937; Henry Fund Fellowship, Yale University, USA, 1937–38; Burney Yeo Schol., King's College Hospital, 1938. RAMC, 1943–47, Med. Specialist and O/C Medical Division. Lecturer in Medicine, Post-Grad. Med. School of London; Physician, Hammersmith Hospital, 1948–49; Asst Physician, later Consultant Physician, London Hospital and Cardiac Dept of London Hosp., 1949–81; Asst Physician, later Consultant Physician, National Heart Hospital, 1949–81; Cons. Cardiologist, Special Unit for Juvenile Rheumatism, Taplow, 1955–59; Director Inst. of Cardiology, 1962–66. Cons. Physician to Munich Re-Insurance Co., 1974–. Pres., Assurance Medical Society, 1987–89. St Cyres Lectr, 1956; R. T. Hall Lectr, Australia and New Zealand, 1961; Hugh Morgan Vis. Prof., Vanderbilt Univ., 1963. Late Assistant Editor, British Heart Journal. Mem. British Cardiac Society and Assoc. of Physicians. *Publications:* Section on Cardio-vascular disease in Price's Textbook of Medicine; Myocardial Disease, Cecil-Loeb Textbook of Medicine; contributor to the Lancet, British Heart Jl, British Medical Jl. *Recreation:* painting. *Address:* Willow House, 38 Totteridge Common, N20 8NE. *T:* 0181–959 6616.

BRIGGS, family name of **Baron Briggs.**

BRIGGS, Baron *cr* 1976 (Life Peer), of Lewes, E Sussex; **Asa Briggs,** MA, BSc (Econ); FBA 1980; Provost, Worcester College, Oxford, 1976–91; Chancellor, Open University, 1978–94; *b* 7 May 1921; *o s* of William Walker Briggs and Jane Briggs, Keighley, Yorks; *m* 1955, Susan Anne Banwell, *o d* of late Donald I. Banwell, Keevil, Wiltshire; two *s* two *d. Educ:* Keighley Grammar School; Sidney Sussex College, Cambridge (1st cl. History Tripos, Pts I and II, 1940, 1941; 1st cl. BSc (Econ.), Lond., 1941). Gerstenberg studentship in Economics, London, 1941. Served in Intelligence Corps, 1942–45. Fellow of Worcester College, Oxford, 1945–55; Reader in Recent Social and Economic History, Oxford, 1950–55; Member, Institute for Advanced Study, Princeton, USA, 1953–54; Faculty Fellow of Nuffield College, Oxford, 1953–55; Professor of Modern History, Leeds Univ., 1955–61; University of Sussex: Professor of History, 1961–76; Dean, School of Social Studies, 1961–65; Pro Vice-Chancellor, 1961–67; Vice-Chancellor, 1967–76. Chm. Bd of Governors, Inst. of Develt Studies, 1967–76. Visiting Professor: ANU, 1960; Chicago Univ., 1966, 1972; Sen. Gannett Fellow, Columbia Univ., 1988; Lectures: Gregynog, Univ. of Wales, 1981; Ford, Oxford Univ., 1991; Ellen McArthur, Cambridge Univ., 1992. Dep. Pres., WEA, 1954–58, Pres., 1958–67. Mem., UGC, 1959–67; Chm., Cttee on Nursing, 1970–72 (Cmnd 5115, 1972). Trustee: Glyndebourne Arts Trust, 1966–91; Internat. Broadcasting Inst., 1968–87 (Hon. Trustee, 1991); (Chm.) Heritage Educn Gp, 1976–86; Civic Trust, 1976–86; Chairman: Standing Conf. for Study of Local History, 1969–76; Council, European Inst. of Education, 1975–90; Commonwealth of Learning, 1988–93; Adv. Bd for Redundant Churches, 1983–89; Vice-Chm. of Council, UN Univ., 1974–80; Governor, British Film Institute, 1970–77; President: Social History Soc., 1976–; Victorian Soc., 1983–; The Ephemera Soc., 1984–; British Assoc. for Local History, 1984–86; Assoc. of Research Associations, 1986–88; Vice-Pres., Historical Assoc., 1986–. Mem., Ct of Governors, Administrative Staff Coll., 1971–91. Mem., Amer. Acad. of Arts and Sciences, 1970. Hon. Fellow: Sidney Sussex Coll., Cambridge, 1968; Worcester Coll., Oxford, 1969; St Catharine's Coll., Cambridge, 1977. Hon. DLitt: East Anglia, 1966; Strathclyde, 1973; Leeds, 1974; Cincinnati, 1977; Liverpool, 1977; Open Univ., 1979; Birmingham, 1989; Missouri, Teesside, 1993; Hon. DSc Florida Presbyterian, 1966; Hon. LLD: York, Canada, 1968; New England, 1972; Sussex, 1976; Bradford, 1978; Rochester, NY, 1980; Ball State, 1985; E Asia, 1987; George Washington, 1988. Marconi Medal for Communications History, 1975; Médaille de Vermeil de la Formation, Fondation de l'Académie d'Architecture, 1979; Snow Medal, Royal Coll. of Anaesthetists, 1991. *Publications:* Patterns of Peace-making (with D. Thomson and E. Meyer), 1945; History of Birmingham (1865–1938), 1952; Victorian People, 1954; Friends of the People, 1956; The Age of Improvement, 1959; (ed) Chartist Studies, 1959; (ed with John Saville) Essays in Labour History, Vol. I, 1960, Vol. II, 1971, Vol. III, 1977; (ed) They Saw it Happen, 1897–1940, 1961; A Study of the Work of Seebohm Rowntree, 1871–1954, 1961; History of Broadcasting in the United Kingdom: vol. I, The Birth of Broadcasting, 1961; vol. II, The Golden Age of Wireless, 1965; vol. III, The War of Words, 1970; vol. IV, Sound and Vision, 1979; vol. V, Competition 1955–1974, 1995; Victorian Cities, 1963; William Cobbett, 1967; How They Lived, 1700–1815, 1969; (ed) The Nineteenth Century, 1970; (ed with Susan Briggs) Cap and Bell, 1973; (ed) Essays in the History of Publishing, 1974; Iron Bridge to Crystal Palace: impact and images of the Industrial Revolution, 1979; Governing the BBC, 1979; The Power of Steam, 1982; Marx in London, 1982; A Social History of England, 1983, rev. edn, 1994; Toynbee Hall, 1984; Collected Essays, 2 vols, 1985, vol. III 1991; The BBC: the first fifty years, 1985; (with Joanna Spicer) The Franchise Affair, 1986; Victorian Things, 1988; Haut Brion, 1994; The Channel Islands, Occupation and Liberation 1940–1945, 1995. *Recreation:* travelling. *Address:* The Caprons, Keere Street, Lewes, Sussex BN7 1TY. *Clubs:* Beefsteak, United Oxford & Cambridge University.

BRIGGS, David John, FRCO; Organist, Gloucester Cathedral, since 1994; *b* 1 Nov. 1962; *s* of late J. R. Briggs and of J. A. Briggs (*née* Jones); *m* 1986, Elisabeth Anne Baker; one *d. Educ:* Solihull Sch. (Music Schol.); King's Coll., Cambridge (Organ Schol.; MA 1987). FRCO 1980; ARCM 1986. Asst Organist, Hereford Cathedral, 1985–88; Organist, Truro Cathedral, 1989–94. Has made numerous recordings. FRSA 1993. *Publication:* Improvisations on Alouette, gentille Alouette, 1993. *Recreation:* training for private pilot's licence. *Address:* 7 Miller's Green, Gloucester GL1 2BN. *T:* Gloucester (01452) 524764.

BRIGGS, Prof. Derek Ernest Gilmor, PhD; Professor of Palaeontology, University of Bristol, since 1994; *b* 10 Jan. 1950; *s* of John Gilmor Briggs and Olive Evelyn Briggs (*née* Scanlon); *m* 1972, Jennifer Olive Kershaw; three *s. Educ:* Sandford Park Sch., Dublin; Trinity Coll., Dublin (Foundn Scholar; BA Geology); Sidney Sussex Coll., Cambridge (MA, PhD). Res. Fellow, Cambridge, 1974–77; Goldsmiths' College, London University: Department of Geology: Lectr, 1977; Sen. Lectr, 1980; Principal Lectr and Dep. Dean of Sci. and Maths, 1982–85; University of Bristol, Department of Geology: Lectr, 1985; Reader, 1988; Asst Dir, Biogeochem. Res. Centre, 1990–. Res. Associate, Royal Ontario Mus., Toronto, 1983–; Vis. Scientist, Field Mus. of Nat. History, Chicago, 1983; Dist. Vis. Scholar, Univ. of Adelaide, 1994; Benedum Lectr, Univ. of W Virginia, 1994. Editor, Palaeontology and Special Papers in Palaeontology, 1982–86. *Publications:* (ed with K. C. Allen) Evolution and the Fossil Record, 1989; (ed with P. R. Crowther) Palaeobiology: a synthesis, 1990; (ed with P. A. Allison) Taphonomy: releasing the data locked in the fossil record, 1991; (jtly) The Fossils of the Burgess Shale, 1994; contribs to learned jls. *Recreations:* the outdoors, natural history, golf. *Address:* Department of Geology, University of Bristol, Wills Memorial Building, Queen's Road, Bristol BS8 1RJ. *T:* Bristol (0117) 928 7793; Longroof, All Saints' Lane, Clevedon, Avon BS21 6AU.

BRIGGS, Rt. Rev. George Cardell, CMG 1980; *b* Latchford, Warrington, Cheshire, 6 Sept. 1910; *s* of George Cecil and Mary Theodora Briggs; unmarried. *Educ:* Worksop Coll., Notts; Sidney Sussex Coll., Cambridge (MA); Cuddesdon Theological Coll. Deacon 1934; priest 1935; Curate of St Alban's, Stockport, 1934–37; Missionary priest, Diocese of Masasi, Tanzania, 1937; Archdeacon of Newala and Canon of Masasi, 1955–64; Rector of St Alban's, Dar-es-Salaam, 1964–69; Warden of St Cyprian's Theological Coll., Masasi, 1969–73; Bishop of Seychelles, 1973–79; Asst Bishop, Diocese of Derby, and Assistant Priest, parish of St Giles, Matlock, 1979–80. *Recreations:* walking, reading, music. *Address:* 1 Lygon Lodge, Newland, Malvern WR13 5AX. *T:* Malvern (01684) 572941. *Club:* Commonwealth Trust.

BRIGGS, Isabel Diana, (Mrs Michael Briggs); *see* Colegate, I. D.

BRIGGS, John; *see* Briggs, Peter J.

BRIGGS, Dr (Michael) Peter; Executive Secretary, British Association for the Advancement of Science, since 1990; *b* 3 Dec. 1944; *s* of late Hewieson Briggs and of Doris (*née* Habberley); *m* 1969, Jennifer Elizabeth Watts; one *s* one *d. Educ:* Abbeydale Boys' Grammar Sch., Sheffield; Univ. of Sussex (BSc, DPhil). Jun. Res. Fellow in Theoretical Chem., Univ. of Sheffield, 1969–71; Res. Assistant, Dept of Architecture, Univ. of Bristol, 1971–73; Deputation Sec., Methodist Church Overseas Div., 1973–77; Area Sec. (Herts and Essex), Christian Aid, BCC, 1977–80; British Association for the Advancement of Science: Educn Manager, 1980–86; Public Affairs Man., 1986–88; Dep. Sec., 1988–90. Mem. Council, Internat. Council for Advancement of Scientific Literacy, 1992–. Sec., Assoc. of British Science Writers, 1986–. Chairman: Management Cttee, Methodist Church Div. of Social Responsibility, 1983–86; Methodist Youth World Affairs Management Cttee, 1984–92. FRSA 1990. *Recreation:* walking. *Address:* British Association for the Advancement of Science, 23 Savile Row, W1X 2NB. *T:* 0171–973 3500.

BRIGGS, Michael Townley Featherstone; QC 1994; *b* 23 Dec. 1954; *s* of Capt. James William Featherstone Briggs, RN and Barbara Nadine Briggs (*née* Pelham Groom); *m* 1981, Beverly Ann Rogers; three *s* one *d. Educ:* Charterhouse; Magdalen Coll., Oxford (BA History). Called to the Bar, Lincoln's Inn, 1978; Jun. Counsel to Crown Chancery, 1990–94. *Recreations:* sailing, singing (solo and choral), cooking, garden railways. *Address:* 13 Old Square, Lincoln's Inn, WC2A 3UA. *T:* 0171–242 6105. *Clubs:* Bar Yacht; Emsworth Sailing.

BRIGGS, Patrick David, MA; Head Master, William Hulme's Grammar School, since 1987; *b* 24 Aug. 1940; *s* of late Denis Patrick Briggs and of Nancy Sylvester (*née* Jackson); *m* 1968, Alicia Dorothy O'Donnell; two *s* one *d. Educ:* Pocklington Sch.; Christ's Coll., Cambridge (MA). Bedford Sch., 1965–87 (Sen. Housemaster, 1983–87). Rugby Blue, Cambridge, 1962; England Rugby trialist, 1968 and 1969; Mem. Barbarians, 1968–69; RFU staff coach, 1973–; England Under-23 Rugby coach, 1975–80; Team Manager, England Students Rugby, 1988–. *Publication:* The Parents' Guide to Independent Schools, 1979. *Recreations:* cricket, Rugby, golf, fell walking, poetry, theatre. *Address:* Dunoon, 254 Wilbraham Road, Manchester M16 8PR. *T:* 0161–226 2058. *Clubs:* East India, Devonshire, Sports and Public Schools, XL; Hawks (Cambridge); Quidnuncs, Cheshire County Cricket, Lancashire County Cricket.

BRIGGS, Peter; *see* Briggs, M. P.

BRIGGS, (Peter) John; a Recorder of the Crown Court, since 1978; *b* 15 May 1928; *s* of late Percy Briggs and Annie M. Folker; *m* 1956, Sheila Phyllis Walton; one *s* three *d. Educ:* King's Sch., Peterborough; Balliol Coll., Oxford. MA, BCL. Called to the Bar, Inner Temple, 1953. Legal Member: Mersey Mental Health Review Tribunal, 1969 (Dep. Chm., 1971, Chm., 1981–94); North-West Mental Health Review Tribunal, 1994–; Pres., Merseyside Medico-Legal Soc., 1982–84. *Recreation:* music, particularly amateur operatics. *Address:* Third Floor, Peel House, Harrington Street, Liverpool L2 9XN. *T:* 0151–236 0718.

BRIGGS, Raymond Redvers, DFA; FCSD; freelance illustrator, since 1957; author, since 1961; *b* 18 Jan. 1934; *s* of Ernest Redvers Briggs and Ethel Bowyer; *m* 1963, Jean Taprell Clark (*d* 1973). *Educ:* Rutlish Sch., Merton; Wimbledon School of Art; Slade School of Fine Art. NDD; DFA London. Part-time Lecturer in Illustration, Faculty of Art, Brighton Polytechnic, 1961–87. *Publications:* The Strange House, 1961; Midnight Adventure, 1961; Ring-A-Ring O'Roses, 1962; Sledges to the Rescue, 1963; The White Land, 1963; Fee Fi Fo Fum, 1964; The Mother Goose Treasury, 1966 (Kate Greenaway Medal, 1966); Jim and the Beanstalk, 1970; The Fairy Tale Treasury, 1972; Father Christmas, 1973 (Kate Greenaway Medal, 1973); Father Christmas Goes On Holiday, 1975; Fungus The Bogeyman, 1977; The Snowman, 1978 (animated film, 1982); Gentleman Jim, 1980 (play, Nottingham Playhouse, 1985); When the Wind Blows, 1982 (play, BBC Radio and Whitehall Th., 1983; text publd 1983; cassette 1984; animated film, 1987); Fungus the Bogeyman Plop-Up Book, 1982; The Tin-Pot Foreign General and the Old Iron Woman, 1984; The Snowman Pop-Up, 1986; Unlucky Wally, 1987; Unlucky Wally Twenty Years On, 1989; The Man, 1992; The Bear, 1994. *Recreations:* gardening, reading, walking, second-hand bookshops. *Address:* Weston, Underhill Lane, Westmeston, Hassocks, Sussex BN6 8XG. *Clubs:* Groucho, Royal Over-Seas League.

BRIGGS, Rear-Admiral Thomas Vallack, CB 1958; OBE (mil.) 1945; DL (Retd); a Vice-Patron, Royal Naval Association (President, 1971–76); *b* 6 April 1906; *e s* of late Admiral Sir Charles John Briggs, and Lady Briggs (*née* Wilson); *m* 1947, Estelle Burland Willing, Boston, USA; one step *s. Educ:* The Grange, Stevenage, Herts; Imperial Service College, Windsor. Joined Royal Navy 1924; served HMS Thunderer, Hood, Wishart, Antelope, Wolsey, Nelson, Excellent, and Faulkner, 1924–37; Advanced Gunnery Specialist; served War of 1939–45: HMS Ark Royal, 1939–40; AA Comdr HMS Excellent, 1941–42; HMS Newcastle, 1943–44; staff of Flag Officer 2nd in Command, Eastern Fleet, 1944–45 (OBE and despatches twice); HMS Renown, Queen Elizabeth and Nelson; HMS Comus, 1945–46; US Naval War Coll., Newport, RI, 1946–47; Dep. Dir. of Naval Ordnance (G), 1947–49; commanded 5th Destroyer Flotilla, HMS Solebay, 1949–50, and HMS Cumberland, 1953–54; IDC, 1951; Chief of Staff: Plymouth, 1952–53, Home Fleet and Eastern Atlantic, 1956–57; Rear-Adm. 1956; Asst Controller of the Navy, 1958, retired. Director: Hugh Stevenson & Sons Ltd, 1958–69; Hugh Stevenson & Sons (North East) Ltd, 1964; Bowater-Stevenson Containers Ltd, 1969–71; Free-Stay Holidays Ltd, 1971; Internat. Consumer Incentives Ltd, 1974–83; Meru Group Ltd, 1978–83. Vice-Chm., City of Westminster Soc. for Mentally Handicapped Children, 1969; Mem., Management Cttee, Haileybury and ISC Junior Sch., Windsor, 1959–80 (Chm., 1978–80); Life Governor, Haileybury and Imperial Service Coll., 1959 (Mem. Council, 1959–80); Pres., Haileybury Soc., 1973–74. Fellow, Inst. of Marketing, 1970–83. Chm., Aldeburgh Festival Club, 1979–80. DL Greater London, 1970–82 (Representative DL, Kingston upon Thames, 1970–79). *Recreations:* golf, shooting, bowling. *Address:* 29 Twin Bridge Road, Madison, CT 06443, USA. *Clubs:* RN Golfing Society, Aldeburgh Golf (Captain, 1981–82); RN Sailing Association; RN Ski; Madison Winter, Madison Art.

BRIGHOUSE, Prof. Timothy Robert Peter; Chief Education Officer, Birmingham City Council, since 1993; Visiting Professor, Keele University, since 1993; *b* 15 Jan. 1940; *s* of Denison Brighouse and Mary Howard Brighouse; *m* 1st, 1962, Mary Elizabeth Demers (marr. diss. 1988); one *s* one *d*; 2nd, 1989, Elizabeth Ann (formerly Kearney). *Educ:* St Catherine's College, Oxford (MA Modern History); DipEd; DEd (CNAA) Oxford Poly, 1989. Head of History Dept, Cavendish Grammar Sch., Buxton, 1962–64; Dep. Head and Warden, Chepstow Comm. Coll., 1964–66; Asst Educn Officer, Monmouthshire Educn Dept, 1966–69; Sen. Asst Educn Officer, Bucks Educn Dept, 1969–74; Under-Sec., Educn, ACC, 1974–76; Dep. Educn Officer, ILEA, 1976–78; Chief Educn Officer, Oxon, 1978–89; Prof. of Educn and Hd of Dept, Keele Univ., 1989–93. *Publications:* Revolution in Education and Training (jt editor and author), 1986; Managing the National Curriculum (jt editor and author), 1990; What Makes a Good School, 1991; Successful Schooling, 1991. *Recreations:* gardening, politics. *Address:* Willowbank, Old Road, Headington, Oxford OX3 8ZA. *T:* Oxford (01865) 66995.

BRIGHT, Colin Charles; HM Diplomatic Service; Consul General, Frankfurt, since 1993; *b* 2 Jan. 1948; *s* of William Charles John Bright and Doris (*née* Sutton); *m* 1st, 1978, Helen-Anne Michie; 2nd, 1990, Jane Elizabeth Gurney Pease; one *s* one *d* (and one *d* decd). *Educ:* Christ's Hospital; St Andrews Univ. (MA Hons 1971). FCO, 1975–77; Bonn, 1977–79; FCO, 1979–83; seconded to Cabinet Office, 1983–85; British Trade Develt Office, NY, 1985–88; Dep. Head of Mission, Berne, 1989–93. *Address:* c/o Foreign and Commonwealth Office, SW1A 2AH.

BRIGHT, Sir Graham (Frank James), Kt 1994; MP (C) Luton South, since 1983 (Luton East, 1979–83); a Vice Chairman, Conservative Party, since 1994; *b* 2 April 1942; *s* of late

Robert Frank Bright and Agnes Mary (*née* Graham); *m* 1972, Valerie, *d* of late E. H. Woolliams; one *s*. *Educ:* Hassenbrook County Sch.; Thurrock Technical Coll. Marketing Exec., Pauls & White Ltd, 1958–70; Man. Dir, 1970–, and Chm., 1977–, Dietary Foods Ltd. PPS to Ministers of State, Home Office, 1984–87, DoE, 1988–89, to Paymaster Gen., 1989–90, to Prime Minister, 1990–94. Mem. Select Cttee on House of Commons Services, 1982–84. Jt Sec. to Parly Aviation Gp, 1984–90; Chm., Cons. Backbench Smaller Businesses Cttee, 1983–84, 1987–88 (Vice-Chm., 1980–83; Sec., 1979–80); Vice-Chairman: Cons. Backbench Food and Drink Sub-Cttee, 1983 (Sec., 1983–85); Backbench Aviation Cttee, 1987–88; former Sec., Space Sub-Cttee; Introduced Private Member's Bills: Video Recordings Act, 1984; Entertainment (Increased Penalties) Act, 1990. Member: Thurrock Bor. Council, 1966–79; Essex CC, 1967–70. Contested: Thurrock, 1970 and Feb. 1974; Dartford, Oct. 1974; Chm., Eastern Area CPC, 1977–79; Mem., Nat. CPC, 1980–; Vice Chm., YC Org., 1970–72; Pres., Eastern Area YCs, 1981–. Vice-Chm., Small Business Bureau, 1980–89, and 1991– (Dir, 1989–91). *Publications:* pamphlets on airports, small businesses, education. *Recreations:* golf, gardening. *Address:* House of Commons, SW1A 0AA. *T:* 0171–219 5156. *Club:* Carlton.

BRIGHTLING, Peter Henry Miller; Assistant Under Secretary of State, Ministry of Defence, 1973–81; *b* 12 Sept. 1921; *o s* of late Henry Miller Brightling and Eva Emily Brightling (*née* Fry); *m* 1951, Pamela Cheeseright; two *s* two *d*. *Educ:* City of London Sch.; BSc(Econ), London. War of 1939–45: Air Ministry, 1939–40; MAP, 1940–41; served in RAF, 1941–46. Ministry of: Supply, 1946–59; Aviation, 1959–67; Technology, 1967–70; Aviation Supply, 1970–71; MoD (Procurement Executive), 1971. *Address:* 5 Selwyn Road, New Malden, Surrey KT3 5AU. *T:* 0181–942 8014.

BRIGHTMAN, family name of **Baron Brightman.**

BRIGHTMAN, Baron *cr* 1982 (Life Peer), of Ibthorpe in the County of Hampshire; **John Anson Brightman;** Kt 1970; PC 1979; a Lord of Appeal in Ordinary, 1982–86; *b* 20 June 1911; 2nd *s* of William Henry Brightman, St Albans, Herts; *m* 1945, Roxane Ambatielo; one *s*. *Educ:* Marlborough College; St John's College, Cambridge (Hon. Fellow, 1982). Called to the Bar, Lincoln's Inn, 1932; Bencher 1966. QC 1961. Able Seaman, Merchant Navy, 1939–40; RNVR (Lieut-Commander), 1940–46; RNSC, 1944; Assistant Naval Attaché, Ankara, 1944. Attorney-General of the Duchy of Lancaster, and Attorney and Serjeant within the County Palatine of Lancaster, 1969–70; Judge of the High Court of Justice, Chancery Div., 1970–79; a Lord Justice of Appeal, 1979–82; Judge, Nat. Industrial Relns Court, 1971–74. Chairman, House of Lords Select Committee: on Charities, 1983–84; on Abortion Law, 1987–88; on City of Bristol Develt, 1988; on Spitalfields Market, 1989; on British Waterways, 1991; on Property Law, 1994; on Private Internat. Law, 1994–95. Member, General Council of the Bar, 1956–60, 1966–70. Chm., Tancred's Charities, 1982–. *Recreations:* sailing, cross-country ski-ing, mountain walking, Arctic travel. *Address:* House of Lords, SW1A 0PW. *T:* 0171–219 2034.

BRIGHTON, Peter, BSc; CEng, FIEE, FRAeS; independent consultant; *b* 26 March 1933; *s* of late Henry Charles Brighton and Ivy Irene Brighton (*née* Crane); *m* 1959, Anne Maureen Lewis Jones; one *d* (one *s* decd). *Educ:* Wisbech Grammar Sch.; Reading Univ. (BSc); RAF Technical Coll. and Staff Coll. CEng 1966; FIEE 1980; FRAeS 1981. Pilot, Engr and Attaché, RAF, 1955–71, retd as Wing Comdr. Man. Dir, Rockwell-Collins UK, 1974–77; Regional Man. Dir, Plessey Co., 1977–78; Man. Dir, Cossor Electronics Ltd, 1978–85; British Aerospace PLC: Divl Man. Dir, 1985–87; Co. Dir of Operations, 1988; Dir Gen., EEF, 1989–91. Pres., Electronic Engineering Assoc., 1984–85. Mem. Ct, Cranfield Inst. of Technology, 1989–92. CIMgt (CBIM 1984). Liveryman, Coachmakers and Coach Harness Makers Co., 1989; Freeman of City of London, 1989. *Publications:* articles on aviation topics in learned jls. *Recreations:* flying (current pilot's licence), bridge, golf. *Address:* St Andrew's Cottage, Church Lane, Much Hadham, Herts SG10 6DH. *T:* Much Hadham (01279) 842309. *Club:* Royal Air Force.

BRIGHTY, (Anthony) David, CMG 1984; CVO 1985; HM Diplomatic Service; Ambassador to Spain, and concurrently (non resident) to Andorra, since 1994; *b* 7 Feb. 1939; *s* of C. P. J. Brighty and Winifred (*née* Turner); *m* 1st, 1963, Diana Porteous (marr. diss. 1979; she *d* 1993); two *s* two *d*; 2nd, 1982, Jane Docherty (separated). *Educ:* Northgate Grammar Sch., Ipswich; Clare Coll., Cambridge (BA). Entered FO, 1961; Brussels, 1962–63; Havana, 1964–66; FO, 1967–69, resigned; joined S. G. Warburg & Co., 1969; reinstated in FCO, 1971; Saigon, 1973–74; UK Mission to UN, NY, 1975–78; RCDS, 1979; Head of Personnel Operations Dept, FCO, 1980–83; Counsellor, Lisbon, 1983–86; Dir, Cabinet of Sec.-Gen. of NATO, 1986–87; Resident Chm., CSSB, 1988; Ambassador to Cuba, 1989–91; Ambassador to Czech and Slovak Fed. Republic, later to Czech Republic and (non-resident) to Slovakia, 1991–94. *Address:* c/o Foreign and Commonwealth Office, SW1A 2AH.

BRIGSTOCKE, family name of **Baroness Brigstocke.**

BRIGSTOCKE, Baroness *cr* 1990 (Life Peer), of Kensington in the Royal Borough of Kensington and Chelsea; **Heather Renwick Brigstocke;** Chairman, English-Speaking Union of the Commonwealth, since 1993; High Mistress of St Paul's Girls' School, 1974–89; *b* 2 Sept. 1929; *d* of late Sqdn-Ldr J. R. Brown, DFC and Mrs M. J. C. Brown, MA; *m* 1952, Geoffrey Brigstocke (*d* 1974); three *s* one *d*. *Educ:* Abbey Sch., Reading; Girton Coll., Cambridge (MA, Pt I Classics, Pt II Archaeolog. and Anthropol.); Univ. Winchester Reading Prize, 1950. Classics Mistress, Francis Holland Sch., London, SW1, 1951–53; part-time Classics Mistress, Godolphin and Latymer Sch., 1954–60; part-time Latin Teacher, National Cathedral Sch., Washington, DC, 1962–64; Headmistress, Francis Holland Sch., London, NW1, 1965–74. Comr, Museums and Galls Commn, 1992–. Member: Council, London House for Overseas Graduates, 1965–91 (Vice-Chm., 1975–80); Council, Middlesex Hosp. Med. Sch., 1971–80; Cttee, AA, 1975–90; Council, RHC, 1977–85; Council, The City Univ., 1978–83; Pres., Girls' Schools Assoc., 1980–81; Vice Pres., C & G, 1993–. Member: Health Educn Authority, 1989–; Modern Foreign Langs Wkg Gp, 1989–90. Non-exec. Dir, 1982–90, Mem., Programme Adv. Bd, 1990–93, LWT; Ind. Dir, The Times, 1990–; Associate Dir, Great Universal Stores, 1993–; non-exec. Dir, Burberrys, 1993–. Member Council: RSA, 1983–87; St George's House, Windsor, 1984–90; Pres., Bishop Creighton House Settlement, Fulham, 1977–; Chairman: Thames LWT Telethon Trust, 1990; Menerva Educnl Trust, 1991–93; Mem. Council, Nat. Literacy Trust, 1993–; Chm. of Trustees, Geffrye Mus., 1990–; Trustee: Nat. Gall., 1975–82; Kennedy Meml Trust, 1980–85; City Technology Colleges Trust, 1987–; GB Sasakawa Foundn, 1994–. Governor: Mus. of London, 1986–92; Wellington Coll., 1975–87; Royal Ballet Sch., 1977–92; United World College of the Atlantic, 1980–85; Forest Sch., 1982–90; Imperial Coll., 1991–; Gordonstoun Sch., 1991–93; Chm. of Govs, Landau Forte Coll., Derby, 1993– (Gov., 1992–). Hon. Bencher, Inner Temple, 1992. *Address:* House of Lords, SW1A 0PW. *T:* 0171–219 3000.

BRIGSTOCKE, Vice-Adm. John Richard; Flag Officer, Surface Flotilla, since 1995; *b* 30 July 1945; *s* of late Rev. Canon George Edward Brigstocke and Mollie (*née* Sandford); *m* 1979, Heather Day; two *s*. *Educ:* Marlborough Coll.; BRNC, Dartmouth; RCDS. Joined RN, 1962; commands: HMS Upton; HMS Bacchante; HMS York; Capt. (D) 3rd Destroyer Squadron; BRNC Dartmouth; HMS Ark Royal; FO, Flotilla Two, subseq. Comdr, UK Task Gp, 1991–93; ACNS, 1993–95; Adm. Pres., RNC, Greenwich, 1994–95. Younger Brother, Trinity House, 1981. Freeman, City of London, 1995. *Recreations:* family, ski-ing, riding. *Address:* c/o Naval Secretary, Victory Building, HM Naval Base, Portsmouth PO1 3LS.

BRILLIANT, Fredda, (Mrs Herbert Marshall); sculptor; *m* 1935, Herbert P. J. Marshall (*d* 1991). *Educ:* The Gymnasium (High Sch.), Lodz, Poland; Chelsea Art Sch. (drawing). Sculptor, 1934–; actress and singer, USA, 1930–33; actress and script writer in England, 1937–50. Sculptures include: Nehru, Krishna Menon, Indira Gandhi, Paul Robeson, Herbert Marshall, Mahatma Gandhi (in Tavistock Square; Gandhi model now in the Queen's Collection in Reading Room of St George's, Windsor Castle, 1983), Buckminster Fuller, Carl Albert, Sir Maurice Bowra, Lord Elwyn-Jones, Sir Isaac Hayward, Tom Mann, Dr Delyte Morris, Elie Wiesel, Pope John Paul II (work in progress). Exhibns in London include: Royal Academy, Leicester Galls, Royal Watercolour Soc., Whitechapel Gall., St Paul's Cathedral; other exhibns in Melbourne, Moscow, Bombay and Washington. Work in permanent collections: Nat. Art Gall., New Delhi; Mayakovsky Mus. and Shevchenko Mus., USSR; Southern Illinois Univ. FRSA; FIAL. Mem. Soc. of Portrait Sculptors. *Publications:* Biographies in Bronze (The Sculpture of Fredda Brilliant), 1986; The Black Virgin, 1986; Women in Power, 1987; *short stories:* Truth in Fiction, 1986. *Recreations:* writing lyrics, composing songs and singing, attending classical concerts. *Address:* c/o Bonnie Owen, 816 East Main Street, Carbondale, IL 62901-3143, USA.

BRIMACOMBE, Prof. John Stuart, FRSE, FRSC; Roscoe Professor of Chemistry, University of Dundee, since 1969; *b* Falmouth, Cornwall, 18 Aug. 1935; *s* of Stanley Poole Brimacombe and Lillian May Kathleen Brimacombe (*née* Candy); *m* 1959, Eileen (*née* Gibson); four *d*. *Educ:* Falmouth Grammar Sch.; Birmingham Univ. (DSc). DSc Dundee Univ. Lectr in Chemistry, Birmingham Univ., 1961–69. Meldola Medallist, 1964. *Publications:* (co-author) Mucopolysaccharides, 1964; numerous papers, reviews, etc, in: Jl Chem. Soc., Carbohydrate Research, etc. *Recreations:* sport, swimming. *Address:* 29 Dalhousie Road, Barnhill, Dundee DD5 2SP. *T:* Dundee (01382) 779214.

BRINCKMAN, Sir Theodore (George Roderick), 6th Bt *cr* 1831; publisher; *b* 20 March 1932; *s* of Sir Roderick Napoleon Brinckman, 5th Bt, DSO, MC, and Margaret Wilson Southam; *S* father, 1985; *m* 1st, 1958, Helen Mary Anne Cook (marr. diss. 1983); two *s* one *d*; 2nd, 1983, Hon. Greta Sheira Bernadette Murray, formerly wife of Christopher Murray, and *d* of Baron Harvington, *qv*. *Educ:* Trinity College School, Port Hope, Ontario; Millfield; Christ Church, Oxford; Trinity Coll., Toronto (BA). *Heir: s* Theodore Jonathan Brinckman, *b* 19 Feb. 1960. *Address:* Hazleton Manor, Cirencester, Glos GL7 6PG. *T:* Cirencester (01285) 841241, 841297. *Clubs:* White's; University (Toronto).

BRIND, (Arthur) Henry, CMG 1973; HM Diplomatic Service, retired; *b* 4 July 1927; *o s* of late T. H. Brind and late N. W. B. Brind; *m* 1954, Barbara Harrison; one *s* one *d*. *Educ:* Barry; St John's Coll., Cambridge. HM Forces, 1947–49. Colonial Administrative Service: Gold Coast/Ghana, 1950–60; Regional Sec., Trans-Volta Togoland, 1959. HM Diplomatic Service, 1960–87: Acting High Comr, Uganda, 1972–73; High Comr, Mauritius, 1974–77; Ambassador to Somali Democratic Republic, 1977–80; Vis. Research Fellow, RIIA, 1981–82; High Comr, Malaŵi, 1983–87. Grand Comdr, Order of Lion of Malaŵi, 1985. *Recreations:* walking, swimming, books. *Address:* 20 Grove Terrace, NW5 1PH. *T:* 0171–267 1190. *Club:* Reform.

BRIND, Maj.-Gen. Peter Holmes Walter; CBE 1962 (OBE 1948); DSO 1945; DL; Vice President, Surrey Branch, British Red Cross Society, since 1984 (Deputy President, 1977–84); *b* 16 Feb. 1912; *yr s* of late General Sir John Brind, KCB, KBE, CMG, DSO; *m* 1942, Patricia Stewart Walker, *er d* of late Comdr S. M. Walker, DSC, RN, Horsalls, Harrietsham, Kent; three *s*. *Educ:* Wellington College; RMC, Sandhurst. Commissioned Dorset Regt, 1932. ADC to Governor of Bengal, 1936–39; Adjt, NW Europe, 1940; GSO 3 War Office, 1940–41; DAAG, HQ 12 Corps and Canadian Corps, 1941–42; Bde Major 1942; GSO 2 (MO) War Office, 1942; Comdt, Battle School, 1944, Comdg 2 Devons, NW Europe, 1944–45, GSO 1 (MT) War Office, 1946; GSO 1 (Ops), Palestine, 1948; GSO 1 (Plans), Egypt, 1949; GSO 1 (SD), War Office, 1950–54; Bt Lt-Col, 1952; Comdg 5th KAR (Kenya), 1954; Lt-Col, 1954; Col, 1955; Comdg 5 Inf. Bde Gp (BAOR), 1956; IDC 1959; Brig., 1960; Brig., AQ Middle East, 1960; BGS Eastern Comd, 1962; ADC to the Queen, 1964; Maj.-Gen., 1965; COS, Northern Comd, 1965–67. Dir, BRCS (Surrey Branch), 1968–77. Gov., public and preparatory schs, 1968–86. DL Surrey, 1970. *Recreations:* gardening, music. *Address:* Milestones, Hill Road, Haslemere, Surrey GU27 2JN.

BRINDLE, Ian; Senior Partner, Price Waterhouse, since 1991; *b* 17 Aug. 1943; *s* of John Brindle and Mabel Brindle (*née* Walsh); *m* 1967, Frances Elisabeth Moseby; two *s* one *d*. *Educ:* Blundells School; Manchester Univ. (BA Econ). FCA 1969. Price Waterhouse: articled in London, 1965; Toronto, 1971; admitted to partnership, 1976; Mem., Supervisory Cttee, 1988–; Dir, Audit and Business Advisory Services, 1990–91; Mem., UK Exec., 1990–. Member: Auditing Practices Cttee, CCAB, 1986–90 (Chm., 1990); Accounting Standards Bd, 1993– (Mem. Urgent Issues Task Force, 1991–93); Council, ICAEW, 1994–. Auditor, Duchy of Cornwall, 1993–. *Recreations:* tennis, golf. *Address:* Price Waterhouse, Southwark Towers, 32 London Bridge Street, SE1 9SY; Milestones, Packhorse Road, Bessels Green, Sevenoaks, Kent TN13 2QP.

BRINDLE, Michael John; QC 1992; *b* 23 June 1952; *s* of John Arthur Brindle and Muriel Jones; *m* 1988, Heather Mary (*née* Pearce); one *s* two *d*. *Educ:* Westminster Sch.; New Coll., Oxford (Ella Stephens Schol. in Classics; 1st Cl. Hons Mods, 1972; 1st Cl. Jurisprudence, 1974; MA). Called to the Bar, Lincoln's Inn, 1975 (Hardwicke Scholar). *Recreations:* classical music, travel, bridge. *Address:* 14 St Peter's Square, W6 9AB; Fountain Court, Temple, EC4Y 9DH.

BRINDLEY, Prof. Giles Skey, MA, MD; FRS 1965; FRCP; Partner, Brindley Surgical Implants, since 1991; Professor of Physiology in the University of London at the Institute of Psychiatry, 1968–91, now Emeritus; *b* 30 April 1926; *s* of late Arthur James Benet Skey and Dr Margaret Beatrice Marion Skey (*née* Dewhurst), later Brindley; *m* 1st, 1959, Lucy Dunk Bennell (marr. diss.); 2nd, 1964, Dr Hilary Richards; one *s* one *d*. *Educ:* Leyton County High School; Downing College, Cambridge (Hon. Fellow, 1969); London Hospital Medical College. Various jun. clin. and res. posts, 1950–54; Russian lang. abstractor, British Abstracts of Medical Sciences, 1953–56; successively Demonstrator, Lectr and Reader in Physiology, Univ. of Cambridge, 1954–68; Fellow: King's Coll., Cambridge, 1959–62; Trinity Coll., Cambridge, 1963–68. Hon. Dir, MRC Neurological Prostheses Unit, 1968–92; Hon. Consultant Physician, Maudsley Hosp., 1971–92. Chm. of Editorial Board, Journal of Physiology, 1964–66 (Member 1959–64). Visiting Prof., Univ. of California, Berkeley, 1968. Hon. FRCS 1988. Liebrecht-Franceschetti Prize, German Ophthalmological Soc., 1971; Feldberg Prize, Feldberg Foundn, 1974; St Peter's Medal, British Assoc. of Urological Surgeons, 1987. *Publications:* Physiology of the Retina and Visual Pathway, 1960, 2nd edn 1970; papers in scientific, musicological and medical journals. *Recreations:* ski-ing, orienteering, cross-country and track running (UK over-60 and over-65 record holder, 2000m and 3000m steeplechase, silver medallist, 2000m steeplechase and 800m (men over 65), World Veterans' Track and Field Championships,

Finland, 1991), designing, making and playing various musical instruments (inventor of the logical bassoon). *Address:* 102 Ferndene Road, SE24 0AA. *T:* 0171–274 2598. *Club:* Thames Hare and Hounds.

BRINDLEY, John Frederick; Circuit Administrator, South Eastern Circuit, since 1995; *b* 25 Sept. 1937; *s* of Harold and Eva Brindley; *m* 1960, Judith Ann Sherratt; one *d*. *Educ:* Leek Grammar Sch. Lord Chancellor's Department: Court Business Officer, Midland and Oxford Circuit, 1971; HQ Personnel Officer, 1976; Courts Administrator, Exeter Group, 1981; Head, Civil Business Div. HQ, 1987; Court Service Management Gp, 1988; Court Service Business Gp, 1991. *Recreations:* hockey, cricket, amateur theatricals. *Address:* South Eastern Circuit Office, New Cavendish House, 18 Maltravers Street, WC2R 3EU.

BRINDLEY, Stephen, FCIH; Chief Executive, North Hull Housing Action Trust, since 1991; *b* 18 April 1947; *s* of Bernard Patrick and Marjorie Yvonne Brindley; *m* 1969, Elaine Gillian Hill; two *d*. *Educ:* Wolverhampton Grammar Tech. Sch.; Univ. of Essex. FCIH 1981. Various local govt housing positions, 1969–81; Dir of Housing, Hull CC, 1981–91. *Recreation:* music. *Address:* North Hull Housing Action Trust, Pavilion, 536 Hall Road, Beverley Road, Hull HU6 9BS. *T:* Hull (01482) 856160.

BRINK, Prof. André Philippus, DLitt; Professor of English, University of Cape Town, since 1991; *b* 29 May 1935; *s* of Daniel Brink and Aletta Wilhelmina Wolmarans; three *s* one *d*. *Educ:* Potchefstroom Univ. (MA Eng. Lit. 1958, MA Afr. Lit. 1959); Rhodes Univ. (DLitt 1975). Rhodes University: Lectr, 1961; Sen. Lectr, 1975; Associate Prof., 1977; Prof. of Afrikaans and Dutch Literature, 1980–90. Hon. DLitt Witwatersrand, 1985. Prix Médicis étranger, 1981; Martin Luther King Meml Prize, 1981. Chevalier de la Légion d'honneur, 1982; Commandeur, l'Ordre des Arts et des Lettres, 1992. *Publications:* in Afrikaans: Die meul teen die hang, 1958; over 40 titles (novels, plays, travel books, literary criticism, humour); in English: Looking on Darkness, 1974; An Instant in the Wind, 1976; Rumours of Rain, 1978; A Dry White Season, 1979; A Chain of Voices, 1982; Mapmakers (essays), 1983; The Wall of the Plague, 1984; The Ambassador, 1985; (ed with J. M. Coetzee) A Land Apart, 1986; States of Emergency, 1988; An Act of Terror, 1991; The First Life of Adamastor, 1993; On the Contrary, 1993; Imaginings of Sand, 1995. *Address:* University of Cape Town, Rondebosch, 7700, South Africa.

BRINK, Prof. David Maurice, DPhil; FRS 1981; Professor of History of Physics, University of Trento, Italy, since 1993; *b* 20 July 1930; *s* of Maurice Ossian Brink and Victoria May Finlayson; *m* 1958, Verena Wehrli; one *s* two *d*. *Educ:* Friends' Sch., Hobart; Univ. of Tasmania (BSc); Univ. of Oxford (DPhil). Rhodes Scholar, 1951–54; Rutherford Scholar, 1954–58; Lectr, 1954–58, Fellow and Tutor, 1958–93, Balliol Coll., Oxford; Univ. Lectr, 1958–89, H. J. G. Moseley Reader in Physics, 1989–93, Oxford Univ., retd. Instructor, MIT, 1956–57. Rutherford Medal and Prize, Inst. of Physics, 1982. *Publications:* Angular Momentum, 1962, 2nd edn 1968; Nuclear Forces, 1965; Semi-classical Methods in Nucleus–Nucleus Scattering, 1985. *Recreations:* birdwatching, mountaineering. *Address:* Università degli Studi di Trento, Dipartimento di Fisica, Povo (Trento), Italy; 34 Minster Road, Oxford OX4 1LY. *T:* Oxford (01865) 246127.

BRINLEY JONES, Robert; *see* Jones.

BRINTON, Timothy Denis; self-employed broadcasting consultant, presentation tutor and communications adviser; *b* 24 Dec. 1929; *s* of late Dr Denis Hubert Brinton; *m* 1st, 1954, Jane-Mari Coningham; one *s* three *d*; 2nd, 1965, Jeanne Frances Wedge; two *d*. *Educ:* Summer Fields, Oxford; Eton Coll., Windsor; Geneva Univ.; Central Sch. of Speech and Drama. BBC staff, 1951–59; ITN, 1959–62; freelance, 1962–. Mem., Kent CC, 1974–81. Chm., Dartford Gravesham HA, 1988–90. MP (C): Gravesend, 1979–83; Gravesham, 1983–87. Member: Court, Univ. of London, 1978–; Med. Sch. Council, St Mary's Hosp., Paddington, 1983–88. Member: BAFTA; RTS. FRSA. Gov., Wye Coll., London Univ., 1989–. *Address:* Woodland Dane, Gibraltar Lane, Hawkinge, Folkestone, Kent CT18 7AE. *T:* Hawkinge (01303) 892341.

BRISBANE, Archbishop of, and Metropolitan of the Province of Queensland, since 1990; **Most Rev. Peter John Hollingworth,** AO 1988; OBE 1976; *b* 10 April 1935; *m* 1960, Kathleen Ann Turner; three *d*. *Educ:* Murrumbeena and Lloyd Street State Schools; Scotch Coll., Melbourne; Trinity Coll., Univ. of Melbourne (BA 1958; MA 1981); Australian Coll. of Theol. (ThL 1960); Univ. of Melbourne (Dip. Social Studies, 1969). Commercial Cadet, Broken Hill Pty, 1952–53. Ordained, 1961; Priest in charge, St Mary's, N Melbourne, 1960–64; Brotherhood of St Laurence: Chaplain and Dir of Youth Work, 1964–70; Assoc. Dir, 1970–79; Exec. Dir, 1980–90; Canon, St Paul's Cathedral, Melbourne, 1980; Bishop in the Inner City, dio. of Melbourne, 1985–90. Mem., Australian Assoc. of Social Workers, 1970–78. Hon. LLD: Monash, 1986; Melbourne, 1990; DUniv: Griffith, 1993; Qld Univ. of Technol., 1994. Australian of the Year, 1991. *Publications:* Australians in Poverty, 1978; The Powerless Poor, 1972; The Poor: victims of affluence, 1974. *Recreations:* writing, reading, swimming. *Address:* Bishopsbourne, 39 Eldernell Avenue, Hamilton, Qld 4007, Australia.

BRISBANE, Archbishop of, (RC), since 1992; **Most Rev. John Alexius Bathersby,** STD; *b* 26 July 1936; *s* of John Thomas Bathersby and Grace Maud Bathersby (*née* Conquest). *Educ:* Pius XII Seminary, Banyo, Qld, Australia; Gregorian Univ., Rome (STL, STD). Priest, 1961; Asst Priest, Goondiwindi, 1962–68; Spiritual Dir, Banyo Seminary, 1973–86; Bishop of Cairns, 1986–92. *Recreation:* bush walking. *Address:* Wynberg, 790 Brunswick Street, Brisbane, Qld 4005, Australia. *T:* (7) 32243364.

BRISBANE, Assistant Bishops of; *see* Noble, Rt Rev. J. A.; Williams, Rt Rev. R. J. C.; Wood, Rt Rev. C. M.

BRISCO, Sir Donald Gilfrid, 8th Bt *cr* 1782; JP; *b* 15 Sept. 1920; *s* of Sir Hylton (Musgrave Campbell) Brisco, 7th Bt and Kathleen (*d* 1982), *d* of W. Fenwick McAllum, New Zealand; *S* father, 1968; *m* 1945, Irene, *o d* of Henry John Gage, Ermine Park, Brockworth, Gloucestershire; three *d*. Served War of 1939–45 with Royal New Zealand Air Force and Royal Air Force (prisoner of war in Germany and Italy). Retired Farmer. JP Hawke's Bay, 1967. *Heir: cousin* Campbell Howard Brisco [*b* 1944; *m* 1969, Kay Janette, *d* of Ewan W. McFadzien; two *s* one *d*]. *Address:* 27a Chambers Street, PO Box 8165, Havelock North, Hawke's Bay, New Zealand.

BRISCOE, Brian Anthony; Chief Executive, Hertfordshire County Council, since 1990; *b* 29 July 1945; *s* of Anthony Brown Briscoe and Lily Briscoe; *m* 1969, Sheila Mary Cheyne; three *s*. *Educ:* Newcastle Royal Grammar Sch.; St Catharine's Coll., Cambridge (MA, DipTP). MRTPI, ARICS. Asst Planner, Derbyshire CC, 1967–71; Section Head, Herefordshire CC, 1971–74; Asst Chief Planner, W Yorks CC, 1974–79; Dep. County Planning Officer, Herts, 1979–88; County Planning Officer, Kent, 1988–90. FRSA. *Publications:* contribs to planning and property jls; chapter in English Structure Planning, 1982. *Recreations:* family, golf, Newcastle United FC. *Address:* County Hall, Hertford SG13 8DE. *T:* Hertford (01992) 555601.

BRISCOE, Sir John Geoffrey James, 6th Bt *cr* 1910, of Bourn Hall, Bourn, Cambridge; *b* (posthumously) 4 Nov. 1994; *o s* of Sir (John) James Briscoe, 5th Bt and of Felicity Mary, *e d* of David Melville Watkinson; *S* father, 1994. *Heir: uncle:* Edward Home Briscoe [*b* 27 March 1955; *m* 1st, 1979, Anne Lister (marr. diss. 1989); one *s* one *d*; 2nd, 1994, Sandy Elizabeth King (*née* Lloyd)].

BRISE; *see* Ruggles-Brise.

BRISON, Ven. William Stanley; Team Rector, Pendleton, Manchester, since 1995; *b* 20 Nov. 1929; *s* of William P. Brison and Marion A. Wilber; *m* 1951, Marguerite Adelia Nettleton; two *s* two *d*. *Educ:* Alfred Univ., New York (BS Eng); Berkeley Divinity School, New Haven, Conn (STM, MDiv). United States Marine Corps, Captain (Reserve), 1951–53. Engineer, Norton Co., Worcester, Mass, 1953–54. Vicar, then Rector, Christ Church, Bethany, Conn, 1957–69; Archdeacon of New Haven, Conn, 1967–69; Rector, Emmanuel Episcopal Church, Stamford, Conn, 1969–72; Vicar, Christ Church, Davyhulme, Manchester, 1972–81; Rector, All Saints', Newton Heath, Manchester, 1981–85; Area Dean of North Manchester, 1981–85; Archdeacon of Bolton, 1985–91, Archdeacon Emeritus, 1991; CMS Missionary, Nigeria, 1992–94; Lectr, St Francis of Assisi Theol Coll., Zaria, 1992–94. *Recreations:* squash, jogging, hiking. *Address:* Pendleton Rectory, 14 Eccles Old Road, Salford M6 7AF. *T:* 0161–737 2107.

BRISTER, William Arthur Francis, CB 1984; Deputy Director General of Prison Service, 1982–85; *b* 10 Feb. 1925; *s* of Arthur John Brister and Velda Mirandoli; *m* 1949, Mary Speakman; one *s* one *d* (and one *s* decd). *Educ:* Douai Sch.; Brasenose Coll., Oxford (MA 1949). Asst Governor Cl. II, HM Borstal, Lowdham Grange, 1949–52; Asst Principal, Imperial Trng Sch., Wakefield, 1952–55; Asst Governor II, HM Prison, Parkhurst, 1955–57; Dep. Governor, HM Prison: Camp Hill, 1957–60; Manchester, 1960–62; Governor, HM Borstal: Morton Hall, 1962–67; Dover, 1967–69; Governor II, Prison Dept HQ, 1969–71; Governor, HM Remand Centre, Ashford, 1971–73; Governor I, Prison Dept HQ, 1973–75, Asst Controller, 1975–79; Chief Inspector of the Prison Service, 1979–81; HM Dep. Chief Inspector of Prisons, 1981–82. Mem., Parole Board, 1986–89. Nuffield Travelling Fellow, Canada and Mexico, 1966–67. *Recreations:* shooting, music, Venetian history. *Clubs:* United Oxford & Cambridge University, English-Speaking Union.

BRISTOL, 7th Marquess of, *cr* 1826; **Frederick William John Augustus Hervey;** Baron Hervey of Ickworth, 1703; Earl of Bristol, 1714; Earl Jermyn, 1826; Hereditary High Steward of the Liberty of St Edmund; Governing Partner, Jermyn Shipping; Chairman, Estate Associates Ltd; *b* 15 Sept. 1954; *s* of 6th Marquess of Bristol and Pauline Mary, *d* of Herbert Coxon Bolton; *S* father, 1985; *m* 1984, Francesca (marr. diss.), *d* of Douglas Fisher. *Educ:* Harrow; Neuchâtel Univ. Director: Guided Properties Ltd; Flintlock Hldgs Ltd. MInstD. *Heir:* half-*b* Lord Frederick William Charles Nicholas Wentworth Hervey, *b* 26 Nov. 1961. *Clubs:* House of Lords Yacht, Royal Thames Yacht; Travellers' (Paris); Monte Carlo Country.

BRISTOL, Bishop of, since 1985; **Rt. Rev. Barry Rogerson;** *b* 25 July 1936; *s* of Eric and Olive Rogerson; *m* 1961, Olga May Gibson; two *d*. *Educ:* Magnus Grammar School; Leeds Univ. (BA Theology). Midland Bank Ltd, 1952–57; Leeds Univ. and Wells Theol Coll., 1957–62; Curate: St Hilda's, South Shields, 1962–65; St Nicholas', Bishopwearmouth,. Sunderland, 1965–67; Lecturer, Lichfield Theological Coll., 1967–71, Vice-Principal, 1971–72; Lectr, Salisbury and Wells Theol Coll., 1972–75; Vicar, St Thomas', Wednesfield, 1975–79; Team Rector, Wednesfield Team Ministry, 1979; Bishop Suffragan of Wolverhampton, 1979–85. Chm., ABM (formerly ACCM), 1987–93; Mem., Faith and Order Commn, 1987–, Central Cttee, 1991–, WCC. Hon. LLD Bristol, 1993. *Recreations:* cinema and stained glass windows. *Address:* Bishop's House, Clifton Hill, Bristol BS8 1BW.

BRISTOL, Dean of; *see* Carr, Very Rev. A. W.

BRISTOL, Archdeacon of; *see* Banfield, Ven. D. J.

BRISTOW, Alan Edgar, OBE 1966; Chairman: Briway Transit Systems, since 1985; Air & Ocean Aids Ltd, since 1985; *b* 3 Sept. 1923; *m* 1945; one *s* one *d*. *Educ:* Portsmouth Grammar School. Cadet, British India Steam Navigation Co., 1939–43; Pilot, Fleet Air Arm, 1943–46; Test Pilot, Westland Aircraft Ltd, 1946–49; Helicopair, Paris/Indo-China, 1949–51; Man. Dir, Air Whaling Ltd (Antarctic Whaling Expedns), 1951–54; Man. Dir, then Chm., Bristow Helicopters Ltd, 1954–85; Dir, British United Airways Ltd, 1960–70, Man. Dir 1967–70. Cierva Memorial Lectr, RAeS, 1967. FRAeS 1967. Croix de Guerre (France), 1950. *Publications:* papers to RAeS. *Recreations:* flying, shooting, sailing, farming, four-in-hand driving. *Address:* Baynards Park Estate, Cranleigh, Surrey GU6 8EE. *T:* Cranleigh (01483) 277170.

BRISTOW, Hon. Sir Peter (Henry Rowley), Kt 1970; a Judge of the High Court, Queen's Bench Division, 1970–85; *b* 1 June 1913; *s* of Walter Rowley Bristow, FRCS and Florence (*née* White); *m* 1st, 1940, Josephine Noel Leney (*d* 1969); one *s* one *d*; 2nd, 1975, Elsa, *widow* of H. B. Leney. *Educ:* Eton; Trinity College, Cambridge. Pilot, RAFVR, 1935–45. Called to the Bar, Middle Temple, 1936, Bencher 1961, Treasurer 1977; QC 1964; Mem., Inns of Court Senate, 1966–70 (Hon. Treas., 1967–70); Judge, Court of Appeal, Guernsey, and Court of Appeal, Jersey, 1965–70; Dep. Chm., Hants QS, 1964–71; Judge of the Commercial Court and Employment Appeals Tribunal, 1976–78; Vice-Chm., Parole Bd, 1977–78 (Mem. 1976); Presiding Judge, Western Circuit, 1979–82. *Publication:* Judge for Yourself, 1986. *Recreations:* fishing, gardening. *Address:* The Folly, Membury, Axminster, Devon EX13 7AG.

BRITISH COLUMBIA, Metropolitan of; *see* Kootenay, Archbishop of.

BRITTAIN, Clive Edward; racehorse trainer, since 1972; *b* 15 Dec. 1933; *s* of Edward John Brittain and Priscilla Rosalind (*née* Winzer); *m* 1957, Maureen Helen Robinson. *Educ:* Calne Secondary Mod. Sch. Winning horses trained include: Julio Mariner, St Leger, 1978; Pebbles, 1000 Guineas, 1984; Eclipse, Dubai Champion and Breeders Cup Turf, 1985; Jupiter Island, Japan Cup, Tokyo, 1986; Mystiko, 2000 Guineas, 1991; User Friendly, Oaks, Irish Oaks, Yorkshire Oaks, St Leger, 1992; Terimon, Juddmont Internat., 1991; Sayyedati, 1000 Guineas, 1993. *Recreation:* shooting. *Address:* Carlburg, 49 Bury Road, Newmarket, Suffolk CB8 7BY. *T:* Newmarket (01638) 664347. *Club:* Jockey Club Rooms (Newmarket).

BRITTAN, Diana, (Lady Brittan), CBE 1995; JP; Deputy Chairman: Human Fertilisation and Embryology Authority, since 1990; Equal Opportunities Commission, since 1994 (Member, since 1989); *b* 14 Oct. 1940; *d* of Leslie Howell Clemetson and Elizabeth Agnes Clemetson (*née* Leonard); *m* 1st, 1965, Dr Richard Peterson (marr. diss. 1979); two *d*; 2nd, 1980, Rt Hon. Sir Leon Brittan, *qv*. *Educ:* Westonbirt Sch., Tetbury. Man. Editor, Eibis Internat., London, 1977–89. JP City of London, 1984. *Recreations:* gardening, travel, cinema, cards, walking. *Address:* c/o Human Fertilisation and Embryology Authority, Paxton House, Artillery Lane, E1 7LS.

BRITTAN, Rt Hon. Sir Leon, Kt 1989; PC 1981; QC 1978; Member, since 1989, a Vice-President, 1989–93 and since 1995, European Commission (formerly Commission of the European Communities); *b* 25 Sept. 1939; *s* of late Dr Joseph Brittan and Mrs

Rebecca Brittan; *m* 1980, Diana Peterson (*see* Diana Brittan); two step *d*. *Educ:* Haberdashers' Aske's Sch.; Trinity Coll., Cambridge (MA); Yale Univ. (Henry Fellow). Chm., Cambridge Univ. Conservative Assoc., 1960; Pres., Cambridge Union, 1960; debating tour of USA for Cambridge Union, 1961. Called to Bar, Inner Temple, 1962; Bencher, 1983. Chm., Bow Group, 1964–65; contested (C) North Kensington, 1966 and 1970. MP (C): Cleveland and Whitby, Feb. 1974–1983; Richmond, Yorks, 1983–88. Editor, Crossbow, 1966–68; formerly Mem. Political Cttee, Carlton Club; Vice-Chm. of Governors, Isaac Newton Sch., 1968–71; Mem. European North American Cttee, 1970–78; Vice-Chm., Nat. Assoc. of School Governors and Managers, 1970–78; Vice-Chm., Parly Cons. Party Employment Cttee, 1974–76; opposition front bench spokesman on Devolution, 1976–79, on employment, 1978–79; Minister of State, Home Office, 1979–81; Chief Sec. to the Treasury, 1981–83; Sec. of State for Home Dept, 1983–85; Sec. of State for Trade and Industry, 1985–86. Chancellor, Univ. of Teesside, 1993–. Chm., Soc. of Cons. Lawyers, 1986–88. Hon. DCL: Newcastle, 1990; Durham, 1992; Hon. LLD Hull, 1990; Dr *hc* Edinburgh, 1991; Hon. DLitt Bradford, 1992. *Publications:* Hersch Lauterpacht Memorial Lectures, 1990; The Europe We Need, 1994; (contrib.) The Conservative Opportunity; pamphlets: Millstones for the Sixties (jtly), Rough Justice, Infancy and the Law, How to Save Your Schools, To spur, not to mould, A New Deal for Health Care, Discussions on Policy, Monetary Union. *Recreations:* opera, art, cricket, walking. *Address:* European Commission, 200 rue de la Loi, 1049 Brussels, Belgium. *Clubs:* Carlton, MCC.

See also Sir Samuel Brittan.

BRITTAN, Sir Samuel, Kt 1993; Principal Economic Commentator, since 1966, and Assistant Editor, since 1978, Financial Times; *b* 29 Dec. 1933; *s* of late Joseph Brittan, MD, and of Rebecca Brittan (*née* Lipetz). *Educ:* Kilburn Grammar Sch.; Jesus Coll., Cambridge (Hon. Fellow, 1988). 1st Class in Economics, 1955; MA Cantab. Various posts in Financial Times, 1955–61; Economics Editor, Observer, 1961–64; Adviser, DEA, 1965. Fellow, Nuffield Coll., Oxford, 1973–74, Vis. Fellow, 1974–82; Vis. Prof. of Economics, Chicago Law Sch., 1978; Hon. Prof. of Politics, Warwick Univ., 1987–92. Mem., Peacock Cttee on Financing the BBC, 1985–86. Hon. DLitt Heriot-Watt, 1985; DU Essex, 1994. Financial Journalist of the Year Award 1971; George Orwell Prize (for political journalism), 1980; Ludwig Erhard Prize (for economic writing), 1988. Chevalier de la Légion d'Honneur, 1993. *Publications:* The Treasury under the Tories, 1964, rev. edn, Steering the Economy, 1969, 1971; Left or Right: The Bogus Dilemma, 1968; The Price of Economic Freedom, 1970; Capitalism and the Permissive Society, 1973, rev. edn as A Restatement of Economic Liberalism, 1988; Is There an Economic Consensus?, 1973; (with P. Lilley) The Delusion of Incomes Policy, 1977; The Economic Consequences of Democracy, 1977; How to End the Monetarist Controversy, 1981; The Role and Limits of Government, 1983; There Is No Such Thing As Society, 1993; Capitalism with a Human Face, 1995; articles in various jls. *Address:* c/o Financial Times, Number One Southwark Bridge, SE1 9HL.

See also Rt Hon. Sir Leon Brittan.

BRITTEN, Alan Edward Marsh; Vice-President, Mobil Europe, since 1991 (Vice-President, Country Management, since 1993); Joint Managing Director, Mobil Services Co. Ltd, since 1993; *b* 26 Feb. 1938; *s* of Robert Harry Marsh Britten and Helen Marjorie (*née* Goldson); *m* 1967, Judith Clare Akerman; two *d*. *Educ:* Radley; Emmanuel Coll., Cambridge (MA English); Williams Coll., Mass (American Studies). Mobil Oil Co.: joined 1961; marketing and planning, UK, USA, Italy; Chief Exec., Mobil Cos in E Africa, 1975–77, Denmark, 1980–81, Portugal, 1982–84, Benelux, 1984–86; Managing Dir, Mobil Oil Co., 1987–89; Manager, Internat. Planning, Mobil Oil Corp., 1989–90. Member: Council for Aldeburgh Foundn; Council, Royal Warrant Holders' Assoc.; Adv. Board, Ten Days at Princeton. *Recreations:* music, travel, gardening, letter writing. *Address:* c/o Mobil Europe, Mobil Court, 3 Clements Inn, WC2A 2EB. *T.* 0171 412 1000. *Clubs:* Garrick, Noblemen & Gentlemen's Catch; Aldeburgh Golf.

BRITTEN, Brig. George Vallette, CBE 1947 (OBE 1942, MBE 1940); HM Diplomatic Service, retired; *b* 19 March 1909; *s* of John Britten, Bozeat Manor, Northamptonshire, and Elizabeth Franziska Britten (*née* Vallette); *m* 1937, Shirley Jean Stewart Wink; three *s*. *Educ:* Wellingborough; RMC Sandhurst. Regtl duty in UK, 1929–38; Staff Coll., Camberley, 1938–39. Served War: HQ 2 Corps, France and Belgium, 1939–40; Staff appts in UK, 1940–41; with 1st Airborne Div. in UK, N Africa and Sicily, 1942–43; DCS, 5(US) Army, N Africa and Italy, 1943–44; HQ, 21st Army Gp, NW Europe, 1944–45. DCS, Brit. Military Govt, Germany, 1945–47. Regtl Duty, Berlin and Austria, 1947–49; WO, 1949–51; Comdt, Sch. of Infty, Hythe, 1952–54; Instr, US Army Staff Coll., Kansas, 1954–56; Planning Staff, NATO, Fontainebleau, 1956–58; Mil. Attaché, Brit. Embassy, Bonn, 1958–61; retired from Army, 1961; Ghana Desk, Commonwealth Office, 1961–62; with British High Commissions, Enugu, Kaduna, and Bathurst, 1962–66; Head of Chancery, British Embassy, Berne, 1967–71. American Legion of Merit, 1946; W German Grosses Verdienst Kreuz, 1959. *Recreation:* gardening. *Address:* 41 Bosville Drive, Sevenoaks, Kent TN13 3JA.

BRITTEN, Rae Gordon, CMG 1972; HM Diplomatic Service, retired; *b* 27 Sept. 1920; *s* of Leonard Arthur Britten and Elizabeth Percival Taylor; *m* 1952, Valentine Alms (marr. diss. 1974); one *s* three *d*; *m* 1977, Mrs Joan Dorothy Bull. *Educ:* Liverpool Institute High School; Magdalen College, Oxford. Served War 1941–45 (artillery and infantry). Research Assistant with Common Ground Ltd, 1947; apptd Commonwealth Relations Office, 1948; 2nd Sec., Brit. High Commn in India (Calcutta, 1948–49, Delhi, 1949–50): 1st Sec. Brit. High Commn., Bombay, 1955–58, Karachi, 1961–62; Deputy High Commissioner: Peshawar, March 1962; Lahore, June 1962–July 1964; Kingston, Jamaica, 1964–68; Head of Trade Policy Dept, FCO, 1968–71; Dep. High Comr, Dacca, and British Rep. to Bangladesh, 1971–72; Counsellor and Head of Chancery, Oslo, 1973–76; Head of SW Pacific Dept, FCO, 1976–78; Counsellor on Special Duties, FCO, 1978–80. *Club:* Commonwealth Trust.

BRITTENDEN, (Charles) Arthur; Senior Consultant, Lowe Bell Communications Ltd, since 1988; Director of Corporate Relations, News International, 1981–87; General Manager (Editorial), Times Newspapers, 1982–87; Director, Times Newspapers Ltd, 1982–87; *b* 23 Oct. 1924; *o s* of late Tom Edwin Brittenden and Caroline (*née* Scrivener); *m* 1st, 1953, Sylvia Penelope Cadman (marr. diss., 1960); 2nd, 1966, Ann Patricia Kenny (marr. diss. 1972); 3rd, 1975, Valerie Arnison. *Educ:* Leeds Grammar School. Served in Reconnaissance Corps, 1943–46. Yorkshire Post, 1940–43, 1946–49; News Chronicle, 1949–55; joined Sunday Express, 1955: Foreign Editor, 1959–62; Northern Editor, Daily Express, 1962–63; Dep. Editor, Sunday Express, 1963–64; Exec. Editor, 1964–66, Editor, 1966–71, Daily Mail; Dep. Editor, The Sun, 1972–81. Dir, Harmsworth Publications Ltd, 1967–71; Man. Dir, Wigmore Cassettes, 1971–72. Dir, Dowson-Shurman Associates Ltd, 1990–. Mem., 1982–86, Jt Vice-Chm., 1983–86, Press Council. *Address:* 22 Park Street, Woodstock, Oxon OX20 1SP.

BRITTON, Andrew James Christie; Executive Secretary, Churches' Enquiry into Unemployment and the Future of Work, since 1995; *b* 1 Dec. 1940; *s* of late Prof. Karl William Britton and Sheila Margaret Christie; *m* 1963, Pamela Anne, *d* of His Honour Edward Sutcliffe, QC; three *d*. *Educ:* Royal Grammar Sch., Newcastle upon Tyne; Oriel Coll., Oxford (BA); LSE (MSc). Joined HM Treasury as Cadet Economist, 1966; Econ. Asst, 1968; Econ. Adviser, 1970; Sen. Econ. Adviser: DHSS, 1973; HM Treasury, 1975; London Business Sch., 1978–79; Under Sec., HM Treasury, 1980–82; Dir, NIESR, 1982–95. Mem., Treasury Panel of Indep. Forecasters, 1993–. Licensed Reader, Dio. of Southwark, 1986–. Mem., Industry and Econ. Affairs Cttee, 1989–, Bd for Social Responsibility, 1992–, Gen. Synod. *Publications:* (ed) Employment, Output and Inflation, 1983; The Trade Cycle in Britain, 1986; (ed) Policymaking with Macroeconomic Models, 1989; Macroeconomic Policy in Britain 1974–87, 1991. *Address:* 15 Hawthorn Road, Wallington, Surrey SM6 0SY. *Club:* United Oxford & Cambridge University.

BRITTON, Prof. Denis King, CBE 1978; Professor of Agricultural Economics at Wye College, 1970–83, now Emeritus Professor; Hon. Fellow, Wye College, 1986; *b* 25 March 1920; *s* of Rev. George Charles Britton and Harriet Rosa (*née* Swinstead); *m* 1942, Margaret Alice Smith; one *s* two *d*. *Educ:* Caterham School; London School of Economics, London University (BSc (Econ.)). Asst Statistician, Ministry of Agriculture and Fisheries, 1943–47; Lecturing and Research at University of Oxford, Agricultural Economics Res. Inst., 1947–52; MA Oxon 1948 (by decree); Economist, United Nations Food and Agriculture Organisation, Geneva, 1952–59; Gen. Manager, Marketing and Economic Res., Massey-Ferguson (UK) Ltd, 1959–61; Prof. of Agricultural Economics, Univ. of Nottingham, 1961–70; Dean, Faculty of Agriculture and Horticulture, Univ. of Nottingham, 1967–70. Member: EDC for Agriculture, 1966–83; Home Grown Cereals Authority, 1969–87; Adv. Council for Agriculture and Horticulture, 1973–80; Adv. Cttee, Nuffield Centre for Agric. Strategy, 1975–80; MAFF Gp to review Eggs Authority, 1985; Chairman: Council, Centre for European Agricl Studies, Wye Coll., 1974–79; Forestry Commn Rev. Gp on Integration of Farming and Forestry, 1983–84; President: Internat. Assoc. of Agric. Economists, 1976–79; British Agric. Economics Soc., 1977–78; Special Adviser, House of Commons Select Cttee on Agric., 1980–83. Vis. Prof., Uppsala, 1973; Winegarten Lecture, NFU, 1981. Farmers' Club Cup, 1966. FSS 1943; FRAgS 1970; FRASE 1980. Hon. DAgric, Univ. of Bonn, 1975; Hon. DEcon, Univ. of Padua, 1982. *Publications:* Cereals in the United Kingdom, 1969; (with Berkeley Hill) Size and Efficiency in Farming, 1975; (with H. F. Marks) A Hundred Years of British Food and Farming: a statistical survey, 1989; (ed) Agriculture in Britain: changing pressures and policies, 1990; articles in Jl of Royal Statistical Society, Jl of Agricultural Economics, Jl of RSA, etc. *Recreations:* music, golf, micro-computing. *Address:* 29 Chequers Park, Wye, Ashford, Kent TN25 5BB.

BRITTON, Sir Edward (Louis), Kt 1975; CBE 1967; General Secretary, National Union of Teachers, 1970–75; retired; *b* 4 Dec. 1909; *s* of George Edwin and Ellen Alice Britton; *m* 1936, Nora Arnald; no *c*. *Educ:* Bromley Grammar School, Kent; Trinity College, Cambridge. Teacher in various Surrey schools until 1951; Headmaster, Warlingham County Secondary School, Surrey, 1951–60; General Secretary, Association of Teachers in Technical Institutions, 1960–68. Pres., National Union of Teachers, 1956–57. Sen. Res. Fellow, Educn Div., Sheffield Univ., 1975–79; Mem. of staff, Christ Church Coll., Canterbury, 1979–86. Vice-Pres., NFER, 1979–; Member: TUC General Council, 1970–74; Beloe Cttee on Secondary Schs Exams, 1960; Schools Council, 1964–75; Adv. Cttee for Supply and Trng of Teachers, 1973–75; Burnham Primary and Secondary Cttee, 1956–75 (Jt Sec. and Leader of Teachers' Panel, 1970–75); Burnham Further Educn Cttee, 1959–69 (Jt Sec. and Leader of Teachers' Panel, 1961–69); Officers' Panel, Soulbury Cttee (and Leader), 1970–75; Staff Panel, Jt Negotiating Cttee Youth Leaders (and Leader), 1970–75; Warnock Cttee on Special Educn, 1974–78; Council and Exec., CGLI, 1974–77; Central Arbitration Cttee, 1977–83. Chm., Nat. Centre for Cued Speech for the Deaf, 1986–88. FCP, 1967; Hon. FEIS, 1974. Hon. DEd CNAA, 1969. *Publications:* many articles in educational journals. *Address:* 40 Nightingale Road, Guildford, Surrey GU1 1ER.

BRITTON, John William; independent consultant, since 1993; *b* 13 Dec. 1936; *s* of John Ferguson and Dinah Britton; *m* 1961, Maisie Rubython; one *s* one *d*. *Educ:* Bedlington Grammar Sch.; Bristol Univ. (BScEng 1st Cl. Hons). Royal Aircraft Establishment, Bedford, 1959–83: Hd, Flight Res. Div., 1978–80; Chief Supt and Hd, Flight Systems Bedford Dept, 1981–83; RCDS 1984; Dir, Avionic Equipment and Systems, MoD PE, 1985–86; Science and Technology Assessment Office, Cabinet Office, 1987; Dir Gen. Aircraft 3, MoD PE, 1987–90; Asst Chief Scientific Advr (Projects), MoD, 1990–92, retd. *Recreations:* wine, painting, motor racing (watching), gardening (especially dahlias and fuchsias). *Address:* 6 The Drive, Sharnbrook, Bedford MK44 1HU.

BRITTON, Paul John James; Director of Local Government Finance Policy, Department of the Environment, since 1991; *b* 17 April 1949; *s* of Leonard Britton and Maureen Britton (*née* Vowles); *m* 1972, Pauline Bruce; one *s* one *d*. *Educ:* Clifton Coll.; Magdalene Coll., Cambridge (BA 1971; MA 1974). Department of the Environment: Admin trainee, 1971–75; Private Sec. to Second Perm. Sec., 1975–77; Principal, 1977; Dept of Transport, 1979–81; DoE, 1981–: Private Sec. to Minister for Housing and Construction, 1983–84; Asst Sec., 1984; Grade 4, 1991; Under Sec., 1992. *Recreations:* architectural history, photography, topography. *Address:* Department of the Environment, 2 Marsham Street, SW1P 3EB. *T:* 0171–276 3162.

BRITZ, Jack; General Secretary, Clearing Bank Union, 1980–83; independent human resources consultant, since 1983; *b* 6 Nov. 1930; *s* of Alfred and Hetty Britz; *m* 1955, Thelma Salaver; one *s* two *d*. *Educ:* Luton Grammar School. Entered electrical contracting industry, 1944; various posts in industry; Director, Rolfe Electrical Ltd, 1964–65. National Recruitment Officer, EETPU, 1969–74; short period with Commission on Industrial Relations as sen. industrial relations officer, 1974; Personnel Manager, Courage Eastern Ltd, 1974–77; Gp Personnel Director, Bowthorpe Group Ltd, 1977–80. NVQ Assessor, 1992–. *Recreations:* walking, history, wargaming, etc. *Address:* West Wing, Longdown Hollow, Hindhead Road, Hindhead, Surrey GU26 6AY.

See also L. Britz.

BRITZ, Lewis; Executive Councillor, Electrical, Electronic, Telecommunication & Plumbing Union, since 1983; Member, Industrial Tribunals, since 1990; *b* 7 Jan. 1933; *s* of Alfred and Hetty Britz; *m* 1960, Hadassah Rosenberg; four *d*. *Educ:* Hackney Downs Grammar Sch.; Acton Technical Coll. (OND Elec. Engrg); Nottingham Univ. (BSc (Hons) Engrg). Head of Research, 1967–71, Nat. Officer, 1971–83, EETPU. Director: LEB, 1977–87; British Internat. Helicopters, 1987–; Esca Services, 1990–. Mem., Monopolies and Mergers Commn, 1986–92. Sat in Restrictive Practices Court, 1989. *Recreation:* philately. *Address:* 30 Braemar Gardens, West Wickham, Kent BR4 0JW. *T:* 0181–777 5986.

See also J. Britz.

BRIXWORTH, Bishop Suffragan of, since 1989; **Rt. Rev. Paul Everard Barber;** *b* 16 Sept. 1935; *s* of Cecil Arthur and Mollie Barber; *m* 1959, Patricia Jayne Walford; two *s* two *d* (and one *s* decd). *Educ:* Sherborne School; St John's Coll., Cambridge (BA 1958, MA 1966); Wells Theological College. Deacon 1960, priest 1961, dio. Guildford; Curate of St Francis, Westborough, 1960–66; Vicar: Camberley with Yorktown, 1966–73; St

Thomas-on-The Bourne, Farnham, 1973–80; Rural Dean of Farnham, 1974–79; Archdeacon of Surrey, 1980–89; Hon. Canon of Guildford, 1980–89. General Synod, 1979–85; Member, Council of College of Preachers, 1969–. Archbp of Canterbury's Advr to HMC, 1993–. *Recreations:* diocesan clergy cricket, theatre. *Address:* 4 The Avenue, Dallington, Northampton NN5 7AN. *T:* Northampton (01604) 759423.

BROACKES, Sir Nigel, Kt 1984; Hon. President, Trafalgar House PLC, since 1992; *b* Wakefield, 21 July 1934; *s* of late Donald Broackes and Nan Alford; *m* 1956, Joyce Edith Horne (*d* 1993); two *s* one *d*. *Educ:* Stowe. Nat. Service, commnd 3rd Hussars, 1953–54. Stewart & Hughman Ltd, Lloyds Underwriting agents, 1952–55; various property developments, etc, 1955–57; Trafalgar House Ltd: Man. Dir 1958; Dep. Chm. and Jt Man. Dir 1968; Chm. 1969–92. Chm., Ship and Marine Technology Requirements Bd, 1972–77; Dep. Chm., Offshore Energy Technology Bd, 1975–77; Chm. Designate, then Chm., London Docklands Develt Corp., 1979–84; British Chm., EuroRoute, 1984–86; non-exec. Director: Distillers Co., 1985–86; Eurotunnel plc, 1986–87; Channel Tunnel Gp Ltd, 1986–87. Mem. Council, Nat. Assoc. of Property Owners, 1967–73. Governor, Stowe Sch., 1974–81. Trustee: Royal Opera House Trust, 1976–81; National Maritime Museum, 1987–; Mem. Advisory Council, Victoria and Albert Museum, 1980–83. Dir, Horserace Totalisator Bd, 1976–81. Chm., Crafts Council, 1991–. Mem., European Round Table, 1990–92. Freeman, City of London; Liveryman, Worshipful Co. of Goldsmiths (Mem., Court of Assts, 1987–). Guardian Young Businessman of the Year, 1978. *Publication:* A Growing Concern, 1979. *Recreation:* silversmith. *Address:* 41 Chelsea Square, SW3 6LH; Checkendon Court, Checkendon, Oxon RG8 0SR.

BROADBENT, Sir Andrew George, 5th Bt *cr* 1893, of Brook Street, co. London and Longwood, co. Yorkshire; *b* 26 Jan. 1963; *s* of Sqn Ldr Sir George Broadbent, AFC, RAF, 4th Bt and of Valerie Anne, *o d* of Cecil Frank Ward; *S* father, 1992. *Educ:* Oakley Hall Prep. Sch., Cirencester; Monkton Combe Sch.; RMA, Sandhurst. Commnd, PWO Regt Yorks, 1984; retd 1994. *Recreations:* music, reading, walking, following sport. *Heir: uncle* Robert John Dendy Broadbent, *b* 4 Nov. 1938.

BROADBENT, Dr Edward Granville, FRS 1977; FEng, FRAeS, FIMA; Visiting Professor, Imperial College of Science and Technology (Mathematics Department), London University, since 1983; *b* 27 June 1923; *s* of Joseph Charles Fletcher Broadbent and Lucetta (*née* Riley); *m* 1949, Elizabeth Barbara (*née* Puttick). *Educ:* Huddersfield Coll.; St Catharine's Coll., Cambridge (State Scholarship, 1941; Eng Scholar; MA, ScD). FRAeS 1959; FIMA 1965. Joined RAE (Structures Dept), 1943; worked on aero-elasticity (Wakefield Gold Medal, RAeS, 1960); transf. to Aerodynamics Dept, 1960; worked on various aspects of fluid mechanics and acoustics; DCSO (IM), RAE, 1969–83, retired. FRSA 1984. Gold Medal, RAeS, 1991. *Publication:* The Elementary Theory of Aeroelasticity, 1954. *Recreations:* duplicate bridge, chess, music, theatre. *Address:* 11 Three Stiles Road, Farnham, Surrey GU9 7DE. *T:* Farnham (01252) 714621.

BROADBENT, (John) Michael; international wine auctioneer and wine writer; Director, Christie Manson & Woods, since 1967; *b* 2 May 1927; *s* of late John Fred Broadbent and of Hilary Louise Broadbent; *m* 1954, Daphne Joste; one *s* one *d*. *Educ:* Rishworth Sch., Yorks; Bartlett Sch. of Architecture, UCL (Cert. in Architecture 1952). Commissioned RA, 1945–48 (Nat. Service). Trainee, Laytons Wine Merchants, 1952–53; Saccone & Speed, 1953–55; John Harvey & Sons, Bristol, 1955–66 (Dir, 1963); Head, Wine Dept, Christie's, 1966–92; Chm., Christie's South Kensington, 1978–79. Wine Trade Art Society: Founder Mem., 1955; Chm., 1972–; Institute of Masters of Wine: Mem. Council, 1966–78; Chm., 1971–72; Chm., Central Panel MW Examn Bd, 1982–85. Distillers' Company: Liveryman, 1964–80; Mem. Council, 1981–; Master, 1990–91; International Wine and Food Society: Life Mem.; Mem. Council, 1969–92; Internat. Pres., 1985–92; Gold Medal, 1989; Chm., Wine and Spirit Benevolent Soc., 1991–92. Numerous awards from wine socs and other instns. Chevalier, Ordre National du Mérite, 1979; La Médaille de la Ville de Paris, Echelon Vermeil, 1989; Wine Spectator Annual Lifetime Achievement Award, 1991. Editor, Christie's Wine Publications, 1972–. *Publications:* Wine Tasting, 1st edn 1968 (numerous foreign edns); The Great Vintage Wine Book, 1980 (foreign edns); Pocket Guide to Wine Tasting, 1988; The Great Vintage Wine Book II, 1991; Pocket Guide to Wine Vintages, 1992; contribs to Decanter and other jls. *Recreations:* piano, painting. *Address:* Chippenham Lodge, Old Sodbury, Avon BS17 6RQ; 87 Rosebank, SW6 6LJ. *Clubs:* Brooks's, Saintsbury.

BROADBENT, Miles Anthony Le Messurier; Chief Executive, Norman Broadbent International Ltd, since 1987; *b* 1936; *m* 1980, Robin Anne Beveridge; two *s* two *d*. *Educ:* Shrewsbury Sch.; Magdalene Coll., Cambridge Univ. (MA); Harvard Bus. Sch. (MBA). *Recreations:* tennis, golf. *Address:* 65 Curzon Street, W1Y 8NA. *T:* 0171–629 9626. *Clubs:* Boodle's, Royal Automobile; St George's Hill Tennis; Burhill Golf, Wisley Golf.

BROADBENT, Ven. Peter Alan; Archdeacon of Northolt, since 1995; *b* 31 July 1952; *s* of Philip and Patricia Broadbent; *m* 1974, Sarah; one *s*. *Educ:* Merchant Taylors' Sch., Northwood, Middx; Jesus Coll., Cambridge (MA); St John's Coll., Nottingham (DipTh). Ordained deacon, 1977, priest 1978. Assistant Curate: St Nicholas, Durham City, 1977–80; Emmanuel, Holloway, 1980–83; Chaplain, Poly. of N London, 1983–89; Vicar, Trinity St Michael, Harrow, 1989–94. *Recreations:* football, theatre and film, railways. *Address:* 247 Kenton Road, Kenton, Harrow, Middx HA3 0HQ. *T:* 0181–907 5941, *Fax:* 0181–909 2368.

BROADBENT, Simon Hope; Chief Economic Adviser (formerly Head of Economic Advisers), Foreign and Commonwealth Office, 1984–93; *b* 4 June 1942; *s* of Edmund Urquhart Broadbent, CBE and Doris Hope; *m* 1966, Margaret Ann Taylor; two *s* one *d*. *Educ:* University College School; Hatfield College, Durham (BA); Magdalen College, Oxford (BPhil). Malawi Civil Service, 1964; Economic Adviser, FCO, 1971; First Sec., UK Treasury and Supply delegn, Washington, 1974; seconded to Bank of England, 1977; Senior Economic Adviser and Joint Head, Economists Dept, FCO, 1978; Institut Universitaire de Hautes Etudes Internationales, Geneva, 1984. *Address:* 40 Parliament Hill, NW3 2TN. *T:* 0171–435 4159, *Fax:* 0171–435 0752.

BROADBRIDGE, family name of **Baron Broadbridge.**

BROADBRIDGE, 3rd Baron *cr* 1945, of Brighton; **Peter Hewett Broadbridge;** Bt 1937; Deputy Speaker, House of Lords, since 1994; Manager, Guild of Master Craftsmen, since 1993; *b* 19 Aug. 1938; *s* of 2nd Baron Broadbridge and Mabel Daisy (*d* 1966), *o d* of Arthur Edward Clarke; *S* father, 1972; *m* 1st, 1967, Mary (marr. diss. 1980), *o d* of W. O. Busch; two *d*; 2nd, 1989, Sally Finn. *Educ:* Hurstpierpoint Coll., Sussex; St Catherine's Coll., Oxford (MA, BSc). Unilever Ltd, 1963–65; Colgate Palmolive Ltd, 1966; Gallaher Ltd, 1967–70; Management Consultant: Peat, Marwick Mitchell & Co., EC2, 1970–78; Coopers and Lybrand and Associates Ltd, 1979–80; Dir, London Venture Capital Market Ltd, 1980–86. Pres., Nat. Assoc. of Leisure Gardeners, 1978–81. Freeman, City of London, 1980; Liveryman, Worshipful Co. of Goldsmiths, 1983. *Recreations:* tennis, squash, antiques, silversmithing, watercolour painting, photography. *Heir: cousin* Martin Hugh Broadbridge [*b* 29 Nov 1929; *m* 1st, 1954, Norma, *d* of late Major Herbert Sheffield, MC; one *s* one *d*; 2nd, 1968, Elizabeth, *d* of J. E. Trotman]. *Address:* House of Lords, SW1A 0PW.

BROADFOOT, Prof. Patricia Mary, PhD; Professor, since 1992, and Head of School of Education, since 1993, University of Bristol; *b* 13 July 1949; *d* of late Norman John Cole, VRD, sometime MP and Margaret Grace Cole (*née* Potter); *m* 1971, John Ledingham Broadfoot; *m* 1980, David Charles Rockey; two *s* one *d*. *Educ:* Queen Elizabeth's Girls' Grammar Sch., Barnet; Leeds Univ. (BA 1970); Edinburgh Univ. (MEd 1977); Open Univ. (PhD 1984); PGCE London 1971. Teacher, Wolmer's Boys' Sch., Jamaica, 1971–73; Researcher, Scottish Council for Res. in Educn, 1973–77; Lectr and Sen. Lectr, Westhill Coll., Birmingham, 1977–81; Lectr, 1981–90, Reader, 1990–92, Univ. of Bristol. FRSA. *Publications:* Assessment, Schools and Society, 1979; (with J. D. Nisbet) The Impact of Research on Education, 1981; (with H. D. Black) Keeping Track of Teaching, 1982; (ed) Selection, Certification and Control, 1984; (ed) Profiles and Records of Achievement, 1986; Introducing Profiling, 1987; (with M. Osborn) Perceptions of Teaching, 1993; (jtly) The Changing English Primary School, 1994; Education, Assessment and Society, 1996. *Recreations:* gardening, travel. *Address:* Amercombe, Kingswood, Glos GL12 8RT. *T:* Wotton-under-Edge (01453) 844436.

BROADLEY, John Kenneth Elliott, CMG 1988; HM Diplomatic Service, retired; Ambassador to the Holy See, 1988–91; *b* 10 June 1936; *s* of late Kenneth Broadley and late Rosamund Venn (*née* Elliott); *m* 1961, Jane Alice Rachel (*née* Gee); one *s* two *d*. *Educ:* Winchester Coll.; Balliol Coll., Oxford (Exhibnr, MA). Served Army, 1st RHA, 1954–56. Entered HM Diplomatic Service, 1960; Washington, 1963–65; La Paz, 1965–68; FCO, 1968–73; UK Mission to UN, Geneva, 1973–76; Counsellor, Amman, 1976–79; FCO, 1979–84; Dep. Governor, Gibraltar, 1984–88. Non-Service Mem., Home Office Extended Interview Panel, 1994–. Mem. Assembly, CCBI, 1992–; Trustee, Overseas Bishopric Fund, 1993–. *Recreations:* sailing, gardening, tennis. *Address:* c/o Foreign and Commonwealth Office, SW1A 2AH. *Club:* Royal Automobile.

BROCAS, Viscount; Patrick John Bernard Jellicoe; *b* 29 Aug. 1950; *s* and *heir* of 2nd Earl Jellicoe, *qv*; *m* 1971, separated 1971, marr. diss. 1981; two *s* (*b* 1970, 1977). *Educ:* Eton. Profession, engineer.

BROCK, Michael George, CBE 1981; Warden of St George's House, Windsor Castle, 1988–93; *b* 9 March 1920; *s* of late Sir Laurence George Brock and Ellen Margery Brock (*née* Williams); *m* 1949, Eleanor Hope Morrison; three *s*. *Educ:* Wellington Coll. (Schol.); Corpus Christi Coll., Oxford (Open Schol.; First Cl. Hons Mod. Hist. 1948; MA 1948). FRHistS 1965; FRSL 1983. War service (Middlesex Regt), 1940–45. Corpus Christi Coll., Oxford: Jun. Res. Fellow, 1948–50; Fellow and Tutor in Modern History and Politics, 1950–66, Fellow Emeritus, 1977; Hon. Fellow, 1982; Oxford University: Jun. Proctor, 1956–57; Univ. Lectr, 1951–70; Mem., Hebdomadal Council, 1965–76, 1978–86; Vice Pres. and Bursar, Wolfson Coll., Oxford, 1967–76; Prof. of Educn and Dir, Sch. of Educn, Exeter Univ., 1977–78; Warden of Nuffield Coll., Oxford, 1978–88; Pro-Vice-Chancellor, Oxford Univ., 1980–88. Church Comr, 1990–93. FRSA 1987. Hon. Fellow: Wolfson Coll., Oxford, 1977; Nuffield Coll., Oxford, 1988; Hon FSRHE 1986. Hon. DLitt Exeter, 1982. *Publications:* The Great Reform Act, 1973; (ed with Eleanor Brock) H. H. Asquith: Letters to Venetia Stanley, 1982; many articles on historical topics and on higher education. *Address:* 11 Portland Road, Oxford OX2 7EZ. *Clubs:* Athenæum; Oxford Union.

BROCK, Dr Sebastian Paul, FBA 1977; Reader in Syriac Studies, University of Oxford, since 1991; Fellow of Wolfson College, Oxford, since 1974; *b* 1938; *m* 1966, Helen M. C. (*née* Hughes). *Educ:* Eton College; Univ. of Cambridge (BA 1962, MA 1965); MA and DPhil Oxon 1966. Asst Lectr, 1964–66, Lectr, 1966–67, Dept of Theology, Univ. of Birmingham; Lectr, Hebrew and Aramaic, Univ. of Cambridge, 1967–74; Lectr in Aramaic and Syriac, Univ. of Oxford, 1974–90. Corres. Mem., Syriac Section, Iraqi Acad., 1979. Hon. Dr Pontificio Istituto Orientale, Rome, 1992. Editor, JSS, 1987–90. *Publications:* Pseudepigrapha Veteris Testamenti Graece II; Testamentum Iobi, 1967; The Syriac Version of the Pseudo-Nonnos Mythological Scholia, 1971; (with C. T. Fritsch and S. Jellicoe) A Classified Bibliography of the Septuagint, 1973; The Harp of the Spirit: Poems of St Ephrem, 1975, 2nd edn 1983; The Holy Spirit in Syrian Baptismal Tradition, 1979; Sughyotho Mgabyotho, 1982; Syriac Perspectives on Late Antiquity, 1984; Turgome d'Mor Ya'qub da-Srug, 1984; The Luminous Eye: the spiritual world vision of St Ephrem, 1985, 2nd edn 1992; (with S. A. Harvey) Holy Women of the Syrian Orient, 1987; Vetus Testamentum Syriace III. 1: Liber Isaiae, 1987; The Syriac Fathers on Prayer and the Spiritual Life, 1987; Malpanuto d-abohoto suryoye d-'al ṣluto, 1988; St Ephrem: Hymns on Paradise, 1990; Studies in Syriac Christianity, 1992; Luqoṭo d-Mimre, 1993; contrib. Jl of Semitic Studies, JTS, Le Muséon, Oriens Christianus, Orientalia Christiana Periodica, Parole de l'Orient, Revue des études arméniennes. *Address:* Wolfson College, Oxford OX2 6UD; Oriental Institute, Pusey Lane, Oxford OX1 2LE.

BROCK, Timothy Hugh C.; *see* Clutton-Brock.

BROCK, Prof. William Ranulf, FBA 1990; Fellow of Selwyn College, Cambridge, since 1947; Professor of Modern History, University of Glasgow, 1967–81, now Emeritus; *b* 16 May 1916; *s* of Stewart Ernst Brock and Katherine Helen (*née* Temple Roberts); *m* 1950, Constance Helen (*née* Brown); one *s* one *d*. *Educ:* Christ's Hosp.; Trinity Coll., Cambridge (MA, PhD). Prize Fellow 1940 (in absentia). Military service (Army), 1939–45; Asst Master, Eton Coll., 1946–47. Commonwealth Fund Fellow, Berkeley, Calif, Yale and Johns Hopkins, 1952–53, 1958; Vis. Professor: Michigan Univ., 1968; Washington Univ., 1970; Maryland Univ., 1980; Charles Warren Fellow, Harvard Univ., 1976; Leverhulme Emeritus Fellow, 1981. *Publications:* Lord Liverpool and Liberal Toryism, 1941; The Character of American History, 1960; An American Crisis, 1963; The Evolution of American Democracy, 1970; Conflict and Transformation 1844–1877, 1973; The Sources of History: the United States 1790–1890, 1975; Parties and Political Conscience, 1979; Scotus Americanus, 1982; Investigation and Responsibility, 1985; Welfare, Democracy and the New Deal, 1988; (with P. H. M. Cooper) Selwyn College: a history, 1994; contrib. New Cambridge Mod. History, Vols VII and XI; articles and reviews in History, Jl Amer. Studies, Jl Amer. Hist., etc. *Recreation:* antiques. *Address:* 49 Barton Road, Cambridge CB3 9LG. *T:* Cambridge (01223) 313606.

BROCKBANK, (James) Tyrrell; solicitor; Vice Lord-Lieutenant of Durham, since 1990; *b* 14 Dec. 1920; *y s* of late James Lindow Brockbank; *m* 1950, Pamela, *yr d* of late Lt-Col J. Oxley Parker, TD, and Mary Monica (*née* Hills); four *s*. *Educ:* St Peter's Sch., York; St John's Coll., Cambridge (MA). Served War of 1939–45 with Sherwood Foresters and Inns of Court Regt. Asst Solicitor, Wolverhampton, 1949–51; Asst Clerk, Hertfordshire, 1951–54; Dep. Clerk, Nottinghamshire, 1954–61; Clerk of the Peace, Durham, 1961–71; Clerk of Durham CC, 1961–74; Clerk to the Lieutenancy, 1964–88; DL 1970, High Sheriff, 1989, Durham. Member, Local Govt Boundary Commn for England, 1976–85. *Recreations:* fishing, shooting, golf. *Address:* The Orange Tree, Shincliffe Village, Durham DH1 2NN. *T:* 0191–386 5569. *Clubs:* Travellers'; Durham County (Durham).

BROCKBANK, Maj.-Gen. John Myles, (Robin), CBE 1972; MC 1943; Vice Lord-Lieutenant of Wiltshire, since 1990; *b* 19 Sept. 1921; *s* of Col J. G. Brockbank, CBE, DSO, and Eireine Marguerite Robinson; *m* 1953, Gillian Findlay, *yr d* of Sir Edmund Findlay, 2nd Bt of Aberlour; three *s* one *d*. *Educ:* Eton Coll.; Oxford Univ. Commissioned into 12 Royal Lancers, 1941. Served War, North Africa, Italy, 1941–45. Served Germany: 1955–58, 1964–68 and 1970–72; Cyprus, 1959; USA, 1961–64; Staff Coll., 1950; IDC 1969; CO, 9/12 Royal Lancers; Comdr, RAC, HQ 1 Corps; Chief of Staff, 1 Corps; Dir, RAC, 1972–74; Vice-Adjutant General, MoD, 1974–76, retd. Col, 9/12 Lancers, 1982–85. Dir, British Field Sports Soc., 1976–84. DL Wilts 1982. *Recreations:* field sports, gardening, bird watching. *Address:* Manor House, Steeple Langford, Salisbury, Wilts SP3 4NQ. *T:* Salisbury (01722) 790353. *Club:* Cavalry and Guards.

BROCKBANK, Tyrrell; *see* Brockbank, J. T.

BROCKES, Prof. Jeremy Patrick, PhD; FRS 1994; Professor of Cell Biology, University College London, since 1991; Member, Ludwig Institute for Cancer Research, since 1991; *b* 29 Feb. 1948; *s* of Bernard A. Brockes and Edna (*née* Heaney). *Educ:* Winchester Coll.; St John's Coll., Cambridge (BA 1969); Edinburgh Univ. (PhD 1972). Muscular Dystrophy Assoc. of America Postdoctoral Fellow, Dept of Neurobiology, Harvard Med. Sch., 1972–75; Research Fellow, MRC Neuroimmunology Project, UCL, 1975–78; Asst, then Associate, Prof., Div. of Biology, CIT, 1978–83; Staff Mem., MRC Biophysics Unit, KCL, 1983–88; scientific staff, Ludwig Inst. for Cancer Res., UCL/Middlesex Hosp. Br., 1988–. Scientific Medal: Zool Soc. of London, 1986; Biol Council, 1990. *Publications:* Neuroimmunology, 1982; papers in scientific jls. *Recreations:* squash, soprano saxophone. *Address:* Ludwig Institute for Cancer Research, 91 Riding House Street, W1P 8BT. *T:* 0171–436 8441.

BROCKET, 3rd Baron, *cr* 1933; **Charles Ronald George Nall-Cain,** Bt 1921; proprietor, Brocket Hall conference venue and golf club; *b* 12 Feb. 1952; *s* of Hon. Ronald Charles Manus Nall-Cain (*d* 1961), and of Elizabeth Mary (who *m* 2nd, 1964, Colin John Richard Trotter), *d* of R. J. Stallard; *S* grandfather, 1967; *m* 1982, Isabell Maria Lorenzo (marr. diss. 1994), *o d* of Gustavo Lorenzo, New York; two *s* one *d*. *Educ:* Eton. 14/20 Hussars, 1970–75 (Lieut). Pres., Herts Chamber of Commerce and Industry, 1992–; Chm., Business Link Hertfordshire, 1994–. Chm., Trust for Information and Prevention (drug prevention initiatives), 1993–. Chm., British Motor Centenary Trust; Dir, De Havilland Museum Trust; Patron, Guild of Guide Lectrs, 1992–. *Heir: s* Hon. Alexander Christopher Charles Nall-Cain, *b* 30 Sept. 1984. *Address:* Brocket Hall, Welwyn, Herts AL8 7XG.

BROCKHOLES, Michael John F.; *see* Fitzherbert-Brockholes.

BROCKHOUSE, Dr Bertram Neville, OC 1982; FRS 1965; Professor of Physics, McMaster University, Canada, 1962–84, now Emeritus; *b* 15 July 1918; *s* of Israel Bertram Brockhouse and Mable Emily Brockhouse (*née* Neville); *m* 1948, Doris Isobel Mary (*née* Miller); four *s* two *d*. *Educ:* University of British Columbia (BA); University of Toronto (PhD). Served War of 1939–45 with Royal Canadian Navy. Lectr, University of Toronto, 1949–50; Research Officer, Atomic Energy of Canada Ltd, 1950–59; Branch Head, Neutron Physics Br., 1960–62. Foreign Member: Royal Swedish Acad. of Sciences, 1984; Amer. Acad. of Arts and Sciences, 1990. Hon. DSc: Waterloo, 1969; McMaster, 1984. Nobel Prize for Physics (jtly), 1994. *Publications:* some 75 papers in learned journals. *Address:* PO Box 7338, Ancaster, Ontario L9G 3N6, Canada. *T:* (416) 648 6329.

BROCKINGTON, Prof. Colin Fraser; Professor of Social and Preventive Medicine, Manchester University, 1951–64, Emeritus, 1964; *b* 8 Jan. 1903; *s* of late Sir William Brockington; *m* 1933, Dr Joyce Margaret Furze; three *s* one *d*. *Educ:* Oakham Sch.; Gonville and Caius Coll., Cambridge; Guy's Hosp., London. MD, MA, DPH, BChir Cantab, MSc Manchester, MRCS, MRCP; barrister-at-law, Middle Temple. Medical Superintendent, Brighton Infectious Diseases Hosp. and Sanatorium, 1929; Asst County Medical Officer, Worcs CC, 1930–33; general medical practice, Kingsbridge, Devon, 1933–36; Medical Officer of Health, Horsham and Petworth, 1936–38; Dep. County Medical Officer of Health, Warwickshire CC, 1938–42; County Medical Officer of Health: Warwickshire CC, 1942–46; West Riding CC, 1946–51. Member: Central Adv. Council for Educn (Eng.), 1945–56; Central Training Council in Child Care (Home Office), 1947–53; Adv. Council for Welfare of Handicapped (Min. of Health), 1949–54; Nursing Cttee of Central Health Services Council (Min. of Health), 1949–51; Council of Soc. of Med. Officers of Health, 1944–66; Public Health Cttee of County Councils Assoc., 1945–49. Chairman: WHO Expert Cttee on School Health, 1950; Symposium on "Mental Health-Public Health Partnership," 5th Internat. Congress on Mental Health, Toronto, 1954, WHO Research Study Group on Juvenile Epilepsy, 1955; UK Cttee of WHO, 1958–61. Took part as Expert in Technical Discussions on Rural Health at World Health Assembly, 1954; Far Eastern Lecture Tour for British Council, 1956–57; visited India, 1959, 1962, S America 1960, Jordan 1966–67, Spain 1967, Arabia 1968, Turkey 1955, 1969, 1970, 1972, Greece 1970, for WHO. Lecture Tour: S Africa and Middle East, 1964. *Publications:* Principles of Nutrition, 1952; The People's Health, 1955; A Short History of Public Health, 1956 (2nd edn 1966); World Health, 1958 (3rd edn 1975); The Health of the Community, 1955, 1960, 1965; Public Health in the Nineteenth Century, 1965; The Social Needs of the Over-Eighties, 1966; The Health of the Developing World, 1985; wide range of contribs to learned jls. *Recreations:* bookbinding, travel. *Address:* Werneth, Silverburn, Ballasalla, Isle of Man. *T:* Castletown (Isle of Man) (01624) 3465.

BROCKLEBANK, Sir Aubrey (Thomas), 6th Bt *cr* 1885; ACA; *b* 29 Jan. 1952; *s* of Sir John Montague Brocklebank, 5th Bt, TD, and of Pamela Sue, *d* of late William Harold Pierce, OBE; *S* father, 1974; *m* 1979, Dr Anna-Marie Dunnet (marr. diss. 1989); two *s*. *Educ:* Eton; University Coll., Durham (BSc Psychology). *Recreations:* deep sea tadpole wrestling, shooting, motor racing. *Heir: s* Aubrey William Thomas Brocklebank, *b* 15 Dec. 1980. *Address:* 120 Gloucester Terrace, W2 6HP.

BROCKLEBANK-FOWLER, Christopher; certified management consultant; *b* 13 Jan. 1934; 2nd *s* of Sidney Straton Brocklebank Fowler, MA, LLB; *m* 1st, 1957, Joan Nowland (marr. diss. 1975); two *s*; 2nd, 1975, Mrs Mary Berry (marr. diss. 1986). *Educ:* Perse Sch., Cambridge. Farm pupil on farms in Suffolk, Cambridgeshire and Norfolk, 1950–55. National service (submarines), Sub-Lt, RNVR, 1952–54. Farm Manager, Kenya, 1955–57; Lever Bros Ltd (Unilever Cos Management Trainee), 1957–59; advertising and marketing consultant, 1959–79; Chm., Overseas Trade and Develt Agency Ltd, 1979–83; Man. Dir, Cambridge Corporate Consultants Ltd, 1985–87. Mem. Bow Group, 1961–81 (Chm., 1968–69; Dir, Bow Publications, 1968–71). Mem. London Conciliation Cttee, 1966–67; Vice-Chm. Information Panel, Nat. Cttee for Commonwealth Immigrants, 1966–67; Mem. Exec. Cttee, Africa Bureau, 1970–74; Chm., SOS Childrens Villages, 1978–84. MP King's Lynn, 1970–74, Norfolk North West, 1974–83 (C, 1970–81, SDP, 1981–83); Chm., Conservative Parly Sub-Cttee on Horticulture, 1972–74; Vice-Chairman: Cons. Parly Cttee on Agriculture, 1974–75; Cons. Parly Foreign and Commonwealth Affairs Cttee, 1979 (Jt Sec., 1974–75, 1976–77); Cons. Parly Trade Cttee, 1979–80; SDP Agriculture Policy Cttee, 1982–83; Chairman: UN Parly Gp, 1979–83 (Jt Sec., 1971–78); Cons. Parly Overseas Develt Sub-Cttee, 1979–81; SDP Third World Policy Cttee, 1981–87; Member: Select Cttee for Overseas Develt, 1973–79; Select Cttee on Foreign Affairs, 1979–81; SDP Nat. Steering Cttee, 1981–82; SDP Nat. Cttee, 1982; SDP Parly spokesman on Agriculture, 1981–82, on Overseas Develt, 1981–83, on Foreign Affairs, 1982–83. Contested: (C) West Ham (North), 1964; (SDP) 1983, (SDP/Alliance) 1987, Norfolk North West; (Lib. Dem.) Norfolk South, 1992. Vice Chm., Centre for World Develt Educn, 1980–83; Governor, Inst. of Develt Studies, 1978–81. Fellow, De Montfort Univ., 1992–. FRGS; MCIM; MCAM; FInstD; FIMgt; MIMC; Hon. Fellow IDS. *Publications:* pamphlets and articles on race relations, African affairs, overseas development. *Recreations:* painting, fishing, shooting, swimming. *Address:* The Long Cottage, Flitcham, Norfolk PE31 6BU. *T:* Hillington (01485) 600255.

BROCKLEHURST, Major-General Arthur Evers, CB 1956; DSO 1945; late RA; *b* 20 July 1905; *m* 1940, Joan Beryl Parry-Crooke; twin *d*. *Educ:* King's School, Canterbury; RMA Woolwich. 2nd Lieut, RA, 1925; CRA 6th Armoured Div., 1951; IDC 1954; DDPS (B) 1955; Chief of Staff, Malaya Comd, 1956–57; GOC, Rhine Dist, BAOR, 1958–59; Dep. Comdr BAOR, 1959–61; retired 1961. Chm., Devizes Constituency Cons. Assoc., 1963–65. *Recreation:* painting watercolours. *Address:* Downland Cottage, Bottlesford, Pewsey, Wilts SN9 6LU. *Club:* Army and Navy.

BROCKLEHURST, Prof. John Charles, CBE 1988; FRCP, FRCPE, FRCPGlas; Professor of Geriatric Medicine, University of Manchester, 1970–89, now Emeritus; Associate Director, Research Unit, Royal College of Physicians, since 1989; *b* 31 May 1924; *s* of late Harold John Brocklehurst and of Dorothy Brocklehurst; *m* 1956, Susan Engle; two *s* one *d*. *Educ:* Glasgow High Sch.; Ayr Academy; Univ. of Glasgow (MB ChB 1947; MD Hons 1950). Christine Hansen Research Fellow, Glasgow Univ., 1948–49; RAMC (to rank of Major), 1949–51; Medical Registrar, Stobhill Hosp., and Asst Lectr, Dept of Materia Medica and Therapeutics, Glasgow Univ., 1952–53 and 1958–59; MO, Grenfell Mission, Northern Newfoundland and Labrador, 1955–57; Cons. Geriatrician, Bromley Hosp. Gp and Cray Valley and Sevenoaks Hosp. Gp, 1960–69; Cons. in Geriatric and Gen. Med., Guy's Hosp., London, 1969–70. Dir, Univ. of Manchester Unit for Biological Aging Research (formerly Geigy Unit for Res. in Aging), 1974–89. Chm., Age Concern England, 1973–77, Hon. Vice-Pres., 1980–; Governor, Research into Ageing (formerly British Foundn for Age Research), 1980–; President: Soc. of Chiropodists, 1977–83; British Geriatrics Soc., 1984–86; Trustee, Continence Foundn, 1992–. Vis. Professor of Geriatric Med. and Chm., Div. of Geriatric Med., Univ. of Saskatchewan, Canada, 1978–79. Hon. MSc Manchester 1974. Bellahouston Gold Medal, Univ. of Glasgow, 1950; Willard Thomson Gold Medal, Amer. Geriatrics Soc., 1978; Sandoz Prize, Internat. Assoc. of Gerontology, 1989; Founder's Medal, British Geriatrics Soc., 1990. *Publications:* Incontinence in Old People, 1951; The Geriatric Day Hospital, 1971; ed and part author, Textbook of Geriatric Medicine and Gerontology, 1973, 4th edn 1992; Geriatric Care in Advanced Societies, 1975; (jtly) Geriatric Medicine for Students, 1976, 3rd edn, 1986; (jtly) Progress in Geriatric Day Care, 1980; (jtly) Colour Atlas of Geriatric Medicine, 1983, 2nd edn 1991; (ed and part author) Urology: the elderly, 1985; Geriatric Pharmacology and Therapeutics, 1985; (jtly) British Geriatric Medicine in the 1980s, 1987. *Recreations:* painting, the mandoline. *Address:* 59 Stanneylands Road, Wilmslow, Cheshire SK9 4EX. *Clubs:* East India and Devonshire, Royal Society of Medicine.

BROCKLEHURST, Robert James, DM; Emeritus Professor of Physiology, University of Bristol, since 1965; *b* Liverpool, 16 Sept. 1899; *e s* of George and Sarah Huger Brocklehurst, Liverpool; *m* 1st, 1928, Sybille (*d* 1968), *y d* of Captain R. H. L. Risk, CBE, RN; two *s* one *d*; 2nd, 1970, Dora Millicent (*d* 1986), *y d* of late Alexander Watts. *Educ:* Harrow Sch.; University College, Oxford (Scholar; 1st Class Honours in Physiology); St Bartholomew's Hospital. BA 1921; MA, BM, BCh, 1924; DM, 1928; MRCS, LRCP, 1925; Demonstrator of Physiology, St Bartholomew's Hosp. Medical Coll., 1925–26; Radcliffe Travelling Fellow, 1926–28; Lecturer, 1928–29, and Senior Lecturer, 1929–30, in Dept of Physiology and Biochemistry, Univ. Coll., London; Prof. of Physiology, 1930–65, and Dean of Med. Fac., 1934–47, Univ. of Bristol, and Univ. Rep. on GMC, 1935–65 (Jt Treas., 1962–65); Long Fox Meml Lectr, 1952; Mem. Inter-departmental Cttee on Dentistry, 1943; Mem. Dental Bd of UK, 1945–56; Additional Mem., GDC, 1956–65; Pres., Bath, Bristol and Somerset Branch, BMA 1959; Fellow BMA, 1967; Pres. Bristol Medico-Chirurgical Society, 1960; Member Council, 1958–63, and President Sect. I (Physiology), 1950, British Association; Mem., S-W Regional Hosp. Bd, and Bd of Govs of United Bristol Hosps, 1947–66; Chm, Moorhaven Hosp. Management Cttee, 1966–71; a representative of Diocese of Bristol in the Church Assembly, 1945–65; Member, Central Board of Finance, 1957–65; Chm., Bristol Diocesan Bd of Finance, 1951–65. Mem., Council Westonbirt School, 1955–75 (Chm., 1956–68); Member Council, Christ Church College, Canterbury, 1961–73; Churchwarden, St Mary's, Stoke Bishop, 1939–60; a Vice-President Gloucester and Bristol Diocesan Association of Church Bell Ringers. Chm., Glos, Somerset and N Devon Regional Group, YHA, 1934–45. Served in Tank Corps, 1918–19. *Publications:* Papers on physiological, biochemical and educational subjects in medical and scientific jls. *Recreation:* gardening. *Address:* Cleeve, Court Road, Newton Ferrers, Plymouth, Devon PL8 1DE. *T:* Plymouth (01752) 872397. *Clubs:* Alpine, Commonwealth Trust, Royal Over-Seas League.

BROCKLESBY, Prof. David William, CMG 1991; FRCVS; Professor of Tropical Animal Health and Director of Centre for Tropical Veterinary Medicine, Royal (Dick) School of Veterinary Studies, University of Edinburgh, 1978–90, now Emeritus; *b* 12 Feb. 1929; *s* of late David Layton Brocklesby, AFC, and Katherine Jessie (*née* Mudd); *m* 1957, Jennifer Mary Hubble, MB, BS; one *s* three *d*. *Educ:* Terrington Hall Sch.; Sedbergh Sch.; Royal Vet. Coll., Univ. of London; London Sch. of Hygiene and Tropical Med. MRCVS 1954; FRCVS (by election) 1984; MRCPath 1964, FRCPath 1982; DrMedVet Zürich 1965. Nat. Service, 4th Queen's Own Hussars (RAC), 1947–49. Vet. Res. Officer (Protozoologist), E Afr. Vet. Res. Org., Muguga, Kenya, 1955–66; Hd of Animal Health Res. Dept, Fisons Pest Control, 1966–67; joined ARC Inst. for Res. on Animal Diseases, Compton, as Parasitologist, 1967; Hd of Parasitology Dept, IRAD, 1969–78. Member: Senatus Academicus, Univ. of Edinburgh, 1978–90; Governing Body, Animal Virus Res. Inst., Pirbright, 1979–86; Bd, Edinburgh Centre of Rural Economy, 1981–88; Council, RCVS, 1985–89. Mem. Editorial Board: Research in Veterinary Science, 1970–88; Tropical Animal Health and Production, 1978–90; British Vet. Jl, 1982–90. *Publications:* papers in sci. jls and chapters in review books, mainly on tropical and veterinary protozoa. *Recreations:* formerly squash and golf, now TV and The Times. *Address:* Lynwood, Honeyfield Road, Jedburgh, Borders TD8 6JN. *T:* Jedburgh (01835) 863472.

BROCKMAN, Rev. John St Leger, CB 1988; Permanent Deacon, St Joseph's RC Church, Epsom, since 1988; *b* 24 March 1928; *s* of late Prof. Ralph St Leger Brockman and Estelle Wilson; *m* 1954, Sheila Elizabeth Jordan; one *s* two *d* (and one *d* decd). *Educ:* Ampleforth; Gonville and Caius Coll., Cambridge. MA, LLB. Called to the Bar, Gray's Inn, 1952. Legal Asst, Min. of National Insurance, 1953; Sen. Legal Asst, Min. of Pensions and National Insurance, 1964; Asst Solicitor, DHSS, 1973; Under Sec. and Principal Asst Solicitor, DHSS, 1978; Solicitor to DHSS, to Registrar General and to OPCS, 1985–89. *Publications:* compiled and edited: The Law relating to Family Allowances and National Insurance, 1961; The Law relating to National Insurance (Industrial Injuries), 1961. *Address:* 304 The Greenway, Epsom, Surrey KT18 7JF. *T:* Epsom (01372) 812915.

BROCKMAN, Vice-Admiral Sir Ronald, KCB 1965; CSI 1947; CIE 1946; CVO 1979; CBE 1943; Extra Gentleman Usher to the Queen, since 1979 (Gentleman Usher, 1967–79); *b* 8 March 1909; *er s* of late Rear-Adm. H. S. Brockman, CB; *m* 1932, Marjorie Jean Butt (*d* 1994); one *s* three *d*. *Educ:* Weymouth Coll., Dorset. Entered Navy, 1927; Assistant Secretary to First Sea Lord, Admiral of the Fleet Sir Roger Backhouse, 1938–39; Lieut-Commander 1939; Admiral's Secretary to First Sea Lord, Admiral of the Fleet Sir Dudley Pound, 1939–43; Commander 1943; Admiral's Secretary to Admiral of the Fleet Lord Mountbatten in all appointments, 1943–59; Private Secretary to Governor-General of India, 1947–48. Principal Staff Officer to the Chief of Defence Staff, Min. of Defence, 1959–65. Captain, 1953; Rear-Admiral, 1959; Vice-Admiral, 1963; retired list, 1965. Mem., Rugby Football Union Cttee, 1956–. Asst in Court of Tin Plate Workers alias Wireworkers' Company. DL Devon. KStJ 1985; Mem. Chapter-Gen., Order of St John, 1979–93. Special Rosette of Cloud and Banner (China), 1946; Chevalier Legion of Honour and Croix de Guerre, 1946; Bronze Star Medal (USA), 1947. *Address:* 3 Raleigh Court, Budleigh Salterton, Devon EX9 6HR. *T:* Budleigh Salterton (01395) 442687. *Clubs:* Naval, MCC; Royal Western Yacht Club of England.

BRÖDER, Ernst-Günther, DEcon; German economist and financial executive; Chairman of Inspection Panel, World Bank, since 1994; *b* Cologne, 6 Jan. 1927. *Educ:* Univs of Cologne, Mayence, Freiburg and Paris. Corporate staff, Bayer AG Leverkusen, 1956–61; Projects Dept, World Bank, 1961–64; Kreditanstalt für Wiederaufbau, 1964–84: Manager, 1969–75; Mem., Bd of Management, 1975–84; Bd of Management Spokesman, 1980–84; European Investment Bank: a Dir, 1980–84; Pres., and Chm. of Bd of Dirs, 1984–93; Hon. Pres., 1993–. Member: Special Adv. Gp, Asian Develt Bank, 1981–82; Panel of Conciliators, Internat. Centre for Settlement of Investment Disputes, 1976–. *Address:* World Bank, 1818 H Street, NW, Washington, DC 20433, USA.

BRODIE, Sir Benjamin David Ross, 5th Bt *cr* 1834; *b* 29 May 1925; *s* of Sir Benjamin Collins Brodie, 4th Bt, MC, and Mary Charlotte (*d* 1940), *e d* of R. E. Palmer, Ballyheigue, Co. Kerry; *S* father, 1971; *m*; one *s* one *d*. *Educ:* Eton. Formerly Royal Corps of Signals. *Heir: s* Alan Brodie.

BRODIE, Colin Alexander, QC 1980; *b* 19 April 1929; *s* of Sir Benjamin Collins Brodie, 4th Bt, MC, and late Mary Charlotte, *e d* of R. E. Palmer, Ballyheigue, Co. Kerry; *m* 1955, Julia Anne Irene, *yr d* of Norman Edward Wates; two *s*. *Educ:* Eton; Magdalen Coll., Oxford. 2/Lieut 8th KRI Hussars, 1949–50. Called to the Bar, Middle Temple, 1954. Bencher, Lincoln's Inn, 1988. *Recreations:* polo, hunting. *Address:* 24 Old Buildings, Lincoln's Inn, WC2A 3UJ. *T:* 0171–404 0946.

BRODIE, Elizabeth, (Mrs S. E. Brodie); *see* Gloster, E.

BRODIE OF BRODIE, (Montagu) Ninian (Alexander), DL; JP; Chief of Clan Brodie; landowner since 1953; *b* 12 June 1912; *s* of I. A. M. Brodie of Brodie (*d* 1943) and C. V. M. Brodie of Brodie (*née* Hope) (*d* 1958); *m* 1939, Helena Penelope Mills Budgen (*d* 1972); one *s* one *d*. *Educ:* Eton. Stage, films, TV, 1933–40 and 1945–49. Served Royal Artillery, 1940–45. JP Morayshire, 1958; Hon. Sheriff-Substitute, 1958; DL Nairn, 1970. *Recreations:* shooting, collecting pictures. *Heir: s* Alastair Ian Ninian Brodie, Younger of Brodie [*b* 7 Sept. 1943; *m* 1968, Mary Louise Johnson (marr. diss. 1986); two *s* one *d*]. *Address:* Brodie Castle, Forres, Moray IV36 0TE, Scotland. *T:* Brodie (01309) 641202.

BRODIE, Philip Hope; QC (Scot) 1987; *b* 14 July 1950; *s* of Very Rev. Peter Philip Brodie and Constance Lindsay Hope; *m* 1983, Carol Dora McLeish; two *s* one *d*. *Educ:* Dollar Academy; Edinburgh Univ. (LLB Hons); Univ. of Virginia (LLM). Admitted Faculty of Advocates, 1976; called to the Bar, Lincoln's Inn, 1991; Standing Junior Counsel, MoD (Scotland) PE, and HSE, 1983–87. Mem., Mental Welfare Commn for Scotland, 1985–. Part-time Chairman: Industrial Tribunals, 1987–91; Medical Appeal Tribunals, 1991–. *Recreations:* fencing, walking, reading. *Address:* 2 Cobden Crescent, Edinburgh EH9 2BG. *T:* 0131–667 2651.

BRODIE, Robert, CB 1990; Solicitor to the Secretary of State for Scotland, since 1987; *b* 9 April 1938; *s* of Robert Brodie, MBE and Helen Ford Bayne Grieve; *m* 1970, Jean Margaret McDonald; two *s* two *d*. *Educ:* Morgan Acad., Dundee; St Andrews Univ. (MA 1959, LLB 1962). Admitted Solicitor, 1962. Office of Solicitor to the Sec. of State for Scotland: Legal Asst, 1965; Sen. Legal Asst, 1970; Asst Solicitor, 1975; Dep. Dir, Scottish Courts Admin, 1975–82; Dep. Solicitor to Sec. of State for Scotland, 1984–1987. *Recreations:* music, hill-walking. *Address:* 45 Stirling Road, Edinburgh EH5 3JB. *T:* 0131–552 2028.

BRODIE, Stanley Eric, QC 1975; a Recorder of the Crown Court, 1975–89; *b* 2 July 1930; *s* of Abraham Brodie, MB, BS and Cissie Rachel Brodie; *m* 1956, Gillian Rosemary Joseph; two *d*; *m* 1973, Elizabeth Gloster, *qv*; one *s* one *d*. *Educ:* Bradford Grammar Sch.; Balliol Coll., Oxford (MA). Pres., Oxford Univ. Law Soc., 1952. Called to Bar, Inner Temple, 1954; Bencher, 1984; Mem. NE Circuit, 1954; Lectr in Law, Univ. of Southampton, 1954–55. Mem., Bar Council, 1987–89. *Recreations:* opera, boating, winter sports, fishing. *Address:* Skeldon House, Dalrymple, Ayrshire KA6 6ED. *T:* Dalrymple (01292) 560223; 39 Clarendon Street, SW1V 4RE. *T:* 0171–821 0975. *Clubs:* Athenæum, Flyfishers'.

BRODIE-HALL, Sir Laurence (Charles), Kt 1982; AO 1993; CMG 1976; Director, 1962–82, Consultant, 1975–82, Western Mining Corporation; Chairman, West Australian Foundation for the Museum of Science and Technology; *b* 10 June 1910; *m* 1st, 1940, Dorothy Jolly (decd); three *s* two *d*; 2nd, 1978, Jean Verschuer. *Educ:* Sch. of Mines, Kalgoorlie (Dip. Metallurgy 1947, DipME 1948). Served War, RAE. Geologist, Central Norseman Gold Corp., 1948–49; Tech. Asst to Man. Dir, Western Mining Corp., 1950–51; Gen. Supt, Gt Western Consolidated, 1951–58; Gen. Supt, 1958–68, Exec. Dir, WA, 1967–75, Western Mining Corp.; Chairman: Gold Mines of Kalgoorlie (Aust.) Ltd, 1974–82; Central Norseman Gold Corp. NL, 1974–82; Westintech Innovation Corp. Ltd, 1984–88; Director: Ansett WA (formerly Airlines WA), 1983–93; Coolgardie Gold NL, 1985–93; former Chm. or Dir of many subsidiaries, and Dir, Alcoa of Australia Ltd, 1971–83. Pres., WA Chamber of Mines, 1970–75 (Life Mem.); Past Pres., Australasian Inst. of Mining and Metallurgy (Institute Medal, 1977, Hon. Life Mem., 1987); Chairman: WA State Cttee, CSIRO, 1971–81; Bd of Management, WA Sch. of Mines, to 1991. Hon. DTech, WA Inst. Technology, 1978. *Address:* (office) 2 Cliff Street, Perth, WA 6000, Australia. *Club:* Weld (Perth).

BRODRICK, family name of **Viscount Midleton.**

BRODRICK, Elizabeth Ann, JP; FCCA; Chairman, Southampton University Hospitals NHS Trust, since 1992; *b* 12 July 1942; *d* of William Henry Hornby and Aldwyth Mary Hornby (*née* Collins); *m* 1963, Derek John Brodrick; two *d*. *Educ:* Wimbledon County Sch. for Girls. FCCA 1987. Trainee accountant, Cable and Wireless Ltd, 1960–65; Asst Accountant, Condé Nast Pubns Ltd, 1966; Roffe Swayne & Co., Chartered Accountants: Audit Senior, 1966–68; one-off assignments, 1968–74; Accountant and Company Sec., Manitou (Site Life) Ltd, 1974–80; freelance financial consultant, 1980–85; Manager, Coopers & Lybrand, Southampton, 1985–92. Mem., Electricity Consumers' Cttee, Southern Region, 1991–93. JP Eastleigh, Southampton, 1984. *Recreations:* friends and family, pet cats, light-hearted bridge and badminton, going to the theatre and concerts, reading, travelling. *Address:* Southampton University Hospitals NHS Trust, Trust Management Offices, Southampton General Hospital, Tremona Road, Southampton SO9 4XY.

BRODRICK, Michael John Lee; His Honour Judge Brodrick; a Circuit Judge, since 1987; *b* 12 Oct. 1941; *s* of His Honour Norman John Lee Brodrick, QC and Ruth, *d* of Sir Stanley Unwin, KCMG; *m* 1969, Valerie Lois Stroud; one *s* one *d*. *Educ:* Charterhouse; Merton Coll., Oxford (2nd Jurisp.). Called to the Bar, Lincoln's Inn, 1965; Western Circuit; a Recorder, 1981–87. Judicial Mem., Transport Tribunal, 1986. Mem., Senate of Inns of Court and Bar, 1979, served 1979–82; Mem., Wine Cttee, Western Circuit, 1982–86. Liaison Judge to SE Hants Magistrates, 1989–93, to IoW Magistrates, 1989–94. Mem., Lord Chancellor's Adv. Cttee for the Appointment of Magistrates, for Portsmouth, 1990–93, for SE Hants, 1993–. Counsellor to Dean and Chapter, Winchester Cathedral, 1993–. *Recreation:* gardening. *Club:* Hampshire (Winchester).

BRODSKY, Joseph Alexandrovich; poet; *b* Leningrad, 24 May 1940; *s* of Alexander I. Brodsky and Maria M. Brodsky (*née* Volpert); one *s*. *Educ:* Leningrad. Began writing poetry 1955; imprisoned as dissident, Arkhangelsk region, 1964–65; left for Vienna, 1972; went on to London and USA; poet in residence, Univ. of Michigan, 1972–73 and 1974–80; John and Catherine MacArthur Foundn Grant, 1981; teaching poetry and literature: Columbia Univ. (Russian Inst.); NY Univ. (Fellow, Inst. of Humanities); Mt Holyoke, Smith, Amherst and Hampshire Colls; Queen's Coll., City Univ. of NY. Hon. DLitt Yale, 1978 and other awards. Nobel Prize for Literature, 1987. *Publications:* Elegy for John Donne and other poems, 1967; Selected Poems, 1973; A Part of Speech, 1980; Less Than One, 1981 (Nat. Book Critics' Award, USA); To Urania, 1988; Watermark, 1992. *Address:* c/o Farrar, Straus & Giroux Inc., 19 Union Square West, New York, NY 10003, USA.

BROERS, Prof. Alec Nigel, PhD, ScD; FRS 1986; FEng 1985; FIEE; FInstP; Professor of Electrical Engineering, since 1984, and Head of Department of Engineering, 1992–Sept. 1996, Cambridge University; Master of Churchill College, Cambridge, 1990–Sept. 1996; Vice-Chancellor, Cambridge University, from Oct. 1996; *b* 17 Sept. 1938; *s* of late Alec William Broers and of Constance Amy (*née* Cox); *m* 1964, Mary Therese Phelan; two *s*. *Educ:* Geelong Grammar School; Melbourne Univ. (BSc Physics 1958, Electronics 1959); Caius College, Cambridge Univ. (BA Mech Scis 1962; PhD Mech Scis 1965; ScD 1991). IBM Thomas Watson Research Center: Research Staff Mem., 1965–67; Manager, Electron Beam Technology, 1967–72; Manager, Photon and Electron Optics, 1972–80; IBM East Fishkill Laboratory: Manager, Lithography Systems and Technology Tools, 1981–82; Manager, Semiconductor Lithography and Process Develt, 1982–83; Manager, Advanced Develt, 1983–84; Mem., Corporate Tech. Cttee, IBM Corporate HQ, 1984; Cambridge University: Hd of Electrical Div., 1984–92; Fellow, Trinity Coll., 1985–90. Mem., EPSRC, 1994–. Mem. Council, Royal Acad. of Engineers, 1993–July 1996. Foreign Associate, Nat. Acad of Engrg, USA, 1994. IBM Fellow, 1977. Prize for Industrial Applications of Physics, Amer. Inst. of Physics, 1982; Cledo Brunetti Award, IEEE, 1985. *Publications:* patents and papers on electron microscopy, electron beam lithography, integrated circuit fabrication. *Recreations:* music, small-boat sailing, skiing, tennis. *Address:* (until Sept. 1996) The Master's Lodge, Churchill College, Cambridge CB3 0DS; (from Oct. 1996) The Old Schools, Trinity Lane, Cambridge CB2 1TN.

BROGAN, Prof. Denis Hugh Vercingetorix; R. A. Butler Professor of History, University of Essex, since 1992; *b* 20 March 1936; *s* of Prof. Sir Denis Brogan, FBA and late Olwen Brogan (*née* Kendall). *Educ:* St Faith's Sch., Cambridge; Repton Sch.; St John's Coll., Cambridge (BA Hist. 1959; MA 1964). Staff mem., The Economist, 1960–63; Harkness Fellow, 1962–64; Fellow, St John's Coll., Cambridge, 1963–74; Lectr, then Reader, Dept of Hist., Univ. of Essex, 1974–92. *Publications:* Tocqueville, 1973; The Times Reports The American Civil War, 1975; The Life of Arthur Ransome, 1984; The Longman History of the United States of America, 1985, repr. as The Penguin History of the United States of America, 1990; Mowgli's Sons: Kipling and Baden-Powell's Scouts, 1987; (with Anne P. Kerr) Correspondance et Conversations d'Alexis de Tocqueville et Nassau William Senior, 1991. *Recreation:* collecting English epitaphs. *Address:* Department of History, University of Essex, Colchester, Essex CO4 3SQ. *T:* Colchester (01206) 872307. *Clubs:* Reform, Academy.

BROINOWSKI, John Herbert, CMG 1969; FCA; finance and investment consultant; Senior Partner, J. H. Broinowski & Storey, Chartered Accountants, 1944–54; Founder/Chairman and Managing Director, Consolidated Metal Products Ltd, 1954–70; Chairman, Vielun Poll Hereford Stud, since 1955; *b* 19 May 1911; *s* of late Dr G. H. Broinowski and late Mrs Ethel Broinowski (*née* Hungerford); *m* 1939, Jean Gaerloch Broinowski, *d* of Sir Norman and Lady Kater; one *s* one step *s*. *Educ:* Sydney Church of England Grammar Sch. Served Australian Imperial Forces (Captain), 1940–44, New Guinea. Chief Exec. and Dep. Chm., Schroder Darling and Co. Ltd, 1963–73; Exec. Chm., Sims Consolidated Ltd, 1970–83; Chairman: Zip Heaters Ltd, 1987–93; Utilux Ltd, 1977–93; Allied Lyons Australia, 1982–92; Director: Electrical Equipment Ltd, 1954–77; Readers Digest Aust., 1955–77; Mount Morgan Ltd, 1962–67 (Chm.); Peko-Wallsend Ltd, 1962–83; South British United Insurance Gp, 1965–73; Hoyts Theatres Ltd, 1968–79 (Chm.); Compunet Ltd, 1969–77 (Chm.); Orient Lloyd Gp, Singapore, 1970–87 (Chm.); Doulton Aust. Ltd, 1972–77; Robe River Ltd, 1972–73; Aquila Steel Co. Ltd, 1973–81 (Chm.); Formfit Ltd, 1974–79 (Chm.); John Sands Ltd, 1974–77; Clive Hall Ltd, 1974–84 (Chm.); Castlemaine Tooheys Ltd, 1977–83 (Dep. Chm.); Hin Kong Ltd, 1977–86 (Chm.); Judson Steel Corp., San Francisco, 1979–83 (Chm.). Chm., Photographic Index of Australian Wildlife, 1980–93. Hon. Life Member: Aust. Council for Rehabilitation of the Disabled (Pres., 1964–68); NSW Soc. for Crippled Children (Pres., 1970–77); Vice-Pres., Internat. Soc. for Rehabilitation of the Disabled, 1966–72. *Address:* 1c Wentworth Place, Point Piper, Sydney, NSW 2027, Australia. *T:* 02/3287534. *Clubs:* Australian, Royal Sydney Golf (Sydney).

BROKE; *see* Willoughby de Broke.

BROKE, Col George Robin Straton, LVO 1977; Equerry-in-Waiting to the Queen, 1974–77; *b* 31 March 1946; *s* of Maj.-Gen. R. S. Broke, *qv*; *m* 1978, Patricia Thornhill Shann, *d* of Thomas Thornhill Shann; one *s*. *Educ:* Eton. Commissioned into Royal Artillery, 1965; CO 3 RHA, 1987–89. *Recreation:* country sports. *Address:* Ivy Farm, Holme Hale, Thetford, Norfolk IP25 7DJ. *T:* Holme Hale (01760) 440225. *Club:* Lansdowne.

BROKE, Maj.-Gen. Robert Straton, CB 1967; OBE 1946; MC 1940; *b* 15 March 1913; *s* of Rev. Horatio George Broke and Mary Campbell Broke (*née* Adlington); *m* 1939, Ernine Susan Margaret Bonsey; two *s*. *Educ:* Eton College (KS); Magdalene College, Cambridge (BA). Commissioned Royal Artillery, 1933. Commander Royal Artillery: 5th Division, 1959; 1st Division, 1960; 1st (British) Corps 1961; Northern Army Group, 1964–66, retired. Col Comdt, RA, 1968–78; Representative Col Comdt, 1974–75. Dir, Wellman Engrg Corp., later Wellman plc, and Chm. of six cos within the Group,

1968–88. Chm., Iron and Steel Plant Contractors Assoc., 1972, 1977. Pres., Metallurgical Plantmakers' Fedn, 1977–79. Treas., London Appeals, Cancer Relief Macmillan Fund, 1989–. *Recreations:* country sports. *Address:* Ivy Farm, Holme Hale, Thetford, Norfolk IP25 7DJ. *T:* Holme Hale (01760) 440225. *Club:* Army and Navy.

See also G. R. S. Broke.

BROME, Vincent; author; *s* of Nathaniel Gregory and Emily Brome. *Educ:* Streatham Grammar School; Elleston School; privately. Formerly: Feature Writer; Editor, Menu Magazines; Min. of Information; Asst Editor, Medical World. Since then author biographies, novels, plays and essays; broadcaster. Mem., British Library Adv. Cttee, 1975–82. *Plays:* The Sleepless One (prod. Edin), 1962; BBC plays. *Publications:* Anthology, 1936; Clement Attlee, 1947; H. G. Wells, 1951; Aneurin Bevan, 1953; The Last Surrender, 1954; The Way Back, 1956; Six Studies in Quarrelling, 1958; Sometimes at Night, 1959; Frank Harris, 1959; Acquaintance With Grief, 1961; We Have Come a Long Way, 1962; The Problem of Progress, 1963; Love in Our Time, 1964; Four Realist Novelists, 1964; The International Brigades, 1965; The World of Luke Jympson, 1966; Freud and His Early Circle, 1967; The Surgeon, 1967; Diary of A Revolution, 1968; The Revolution, 1969; The Imaginary Crime, 1969; Confessions of a Writer, 1970; The Brain Operators, 1970; Private Prosecutions, 1971; Reverse Your Verdict, 1971; London Consequences, 1972; The Embassy, 1972; The Day of Destruction, 1975; The Happy Hostage, 1976; Jung—Man and Myth, 1978; Havelock Ellis—philosopher of sex, 1981; Ernest Jones: Freud's alter ego, 1983; The Day of the Fifth Moon, 1984; J. B. Priestley, 1988; The Other Pepys, 1992; contrib. The Times, Sunday Times, Observer, Guardian, New Statesman, New Society, Encounter, Spectator, TLS etc. *Recreations:* writing plays and talking. *Address:* 45 Great Ormond Street, WC1N 3HZ. *T:* 0171–405 0550. *Club:* Savile.

BROMET, Air Comdt Dame Jean (Lena Annette), (Lady Bromet); *see* Conan Doyle, Air Comdt Dame J. L. A.

BROMHEAD, (Sir) John Desmond Gonville, (6th Bt *cr* 1806); *S* father, 1981, but does not use title. *Heir: cousin* John Edmund de Gonville Bromhead [*b* 10 Oct. 1939; *m* 1965, Janet Frances, *e d* of Harry Vernon Brotherton, Moreton-in-Marsh, Glos; one *s* one *d*].

BROMLEY, Archdeacon of; *see* Norman, Ven. G.

BROMLEY, Lance Lee, MA; MChir; FRCS; Director of Medical and Health Services, Gibraltar, 1982–85; Honorary Consultant Cardiothoracic Surgeon, St Mary's Hospital, W2; *b* 16 Feb. 1920; *s* of late Lancelot Bromley, MChir, FRCS, of London and Seaford, Sussex, and Dora Ridgway Bromley, Dewsbury, Yorks; *m* 1952, Rosemary Anne Holbrook; three *d*. *Educ:* St Paul's School; Caius Coll., Cambridge. Late Capt. RAMC. Late Travelling Fell. Amer. Assoc. for Thoracic Surgery. Consultant Thoracic Surgeon, St Mary's Hosp., 1953–80; Consultant Gen. Surgeon, Teddington Hosp., 1953–80. *Publications:* various contributions to medical journals. *Recreations:* sailing, golf. *Address:* 26 Molyneux Street, W1H 5HW. *T:* 0171–262 7175. *Club:* Royal Ocean Racing.

See also Sir Charles Knowles, Bt.

BROMLEY, Leonard John, QC 1971; **His Honour Judge Bromley;** a Circuit Judge, since 1984; *b* 21 Feb. 1929; 2nd *s* of George Ernest and Winifred Dora Bromley; *m* 1962, Anne (*née* Bacon); three *d*. *Educ:* City of Leicester Boys' Sch.; Selwyn Coll., Cambridge (exhibnr). MA, LLM (Cantab). National Service: 2nd Lt, RA, Hong Kong, 1947–49. Selwyn Coll., Cambridge, 1949–53; called to Bar, Lincoln's Inn, 1954 (Greenland Scholar); Bencher, 1978; in practice, Chancery Bar, 1954–84; a Recorder, 1980–84. Chief Social Security Comr, 1984–90. Gen. Council of the Bar: Mem., 1970–74; Chm., Law Reform Cttee, 1972–74; Mem., Exec. Cttee, 1972–74. Chm., Performing Right Tribunal, 1980–83. A Legal Assessor to: GMC, 1977–84; GDC, 1977–84. Governor, Latymer Sch., Edmonton, 1978–84. Chm., Selwyn Coll. Assoc., 1995–. Vice Cdre, Bar Yacht Club, 1971–75. *Recreations:* sailing, walking. *Address:* c/o South Eastern Circuit Office, Lord Chancellor's Department, 18 Maltravers Street, WC2R 3EU.

BROMLEY, Prof. Peter Mann; Professor of English Law, University of Manchester, 1985–86 (Professor of Law, 1965–85), now Professor Emeritus; *b* 20 Nov. 1922; *s* of Frank Bromley and Marion Maud (*née* Moy); *m* 1963, Beatrice Mary, *d* of Eric Charles Cassels Hunter and Amy Madeleine (*née* Renold). *Educ:* Ealing Grammar Sch.; The Queen's College, Oxford (MA 1948). Called to the Bar, Middle Temple, 1951. Served War, Royal Artillery, 1942–45. University of Manchester: Asst Lectr 1947–50, Lectr 1950–61, Sen. Lectr 1961–65; Dean, Faculty of Law, 1966–68, 1972–74 and 1981–83; Pro-Vice-Chancellor, 1977–81; Principal, Dalton Hall, 1958–65. Vis. Prof. of Law, Univ. of Buckingham, 1987–88. Chm., Cttee on Professional Legal Educn in NI, 1983–85; Member: Adv. Cttee on Legal Educn, 1972–75; University Grants Cttee, 1978–85 (Chm., Social Studies Sub-cttee, 1979–85); Commonwealth Scholarship Commn, 1986–92. Editor, Butterworths Family Law Service, 1983–. *Publications:* Family Law, 1957, 8th edn (with N. V. Lowe), 1992; (contrib.) Parental Custody and Matrimonial Maintenance, 1966; (contrib.) Das Erbrecht von Familienangehörigen, 1971; (contrib.) The Child and the Courts, 1978; (contrib.) Adoption, 1984; (contrib.) Children and the Law, 1990; (contrib.) Droit Sans Frontières, 1991; articles in various legal jls. *Recreations:* walking, listening to music. *Address:* Paddock Brow, Faulkners Lane, Mobberley, Cheshire WA16 7AL. *T:* Mobberley (01565) 872183. *Club:* United Oxford & Cambridge University.

BROMLEY, Sir Rupert Charles, 10th Bt, *cr* 1757; *b* 2 April 1936; *s* of Major Sir Rupert Howe Bromley, MC, 9th Bt, and Dorothy Vera (*d* 1982), *d* of late Sir Walford Selby, KCMG, CB, CVO; *S* father, 1966; *m* 1962, Priscilla Hazel, *d* of late Maj. Howard Bourne, HAC; three *s*. *Educ:* Michaelhouse, Natal; Rhodes Univ.; Christ Church, Oxford. *Recreations:* equestrian. *Heir: s* Charles Howard Bromley, *b* 31 July 1963. *Address:* PO Box 249, Rivonia, Transvaal, 2128, South Africa.

BROMLEY-DAVENPORT, William Arthur; landowner; chartered accountant; Lord-Lieutenant of Cheshire, since 1990; *b* 7 March 1935; *o s* of Lt-Col Sir Walter Bromley-Davenport, TD, DL and Lenette, *d* of Joseph Y. Jeanes, Philadelphia; *m* 1962, Elizabeth Watts, Oldwick, NJ; one *s* one *d*. *Educ:* Eton; Cornell Univ., NY. Mem. ICA, 1966. National Service, 2nd Batt. Grenadier Guards, 1953–54; Hon. Col 3rd (Vol.) Batt. 22nd (Cheshire) Regt, 1985. Owns land in UK and Norway. Mem. Cttee (past Chm.) Cheshire Br., CLA, 1962–. Pres., Cheshire Scout Council, 1990– (Chm., 1981–90). Chm. of Govs, King's Sch., Macclesfield, 1986–. JP 1975, DL 1982, High Sheriff 1983–84, Cheshire. *Address:* The Kennels, Capesthorne, Macclesfield SK11 9LB; Fiva, Aandalsnes, Norway.

BROMWICH, Prof. Michael; CIMA Professor of Accounting and Financial Management, London School of Economics and Political Science, since 1985; *b* 29 Jan. 1941; *s* of William James Bromwich and Margery (*née* Townley); *m* 1972, Christine Margaret Elizabeth Whitehead (OBE 1991). *Educ:* Wentworth High Sch., Southend; London School of Economics (BScEcon 1965); FCMA. Ford Motor Co., 1958–62 and 1965–66; Lectr, LSE, 1966–70; Professor: UWIST, 1971–77; Univ. of Reading, 1977–85. Mem. Council, ICMA, 1980–85; Vice Pres., ICMA, later CIMA, 1985–87, Pres., CIMA, 1987–88. Member: Accounting Standards Cttee, 1981–84; Monopolies and Mergers Commn, 1992–; Research Grants Bd, ESRC, 1992–. Hon. DEcon Lund Univ., Sweden, 1993. *Publications:* Economics of Capital Budgeting, 1976; Economics of Accounting Standard Setting, 1985; (jtly) Management Accounting: evolution not revolution, 1989; (jtly) Housing Association Accounting, 1990; Financial Reporting, Information and Capital Markets, 1992; Management Accounting: pathways to progress, 1994; co-ed others, incl. Essays in British Accounting Research; many articles. *Recreations:* working and eating in restaurants. *Address:* 14 Thornhill Road, N1 1HW. *T:* 0171–607 9323.

BRON, Prof. Anthony John, FRCS, FCOphth; Head of Department of Ophthalmology, since 1973, and Professor of Ophthalmology, since 1989, Nuffield Laboratory of Ophthalmology, and Fellow of Linacre College, since 1975, University of Oxford; *b* 3 Feb. 1936; *s* of late Sydney and Fagah Bron; *m* 1st, 1961, Sandra Ruth Shoot (*d* 1976); one *s* one *d* (and one *s* decd); 2nd, 1981, Diana S. Shortt; one step *s* three step *d*. *Educ:* London Univ. (BSc 1957; MB BS 1961); Guy's Hosp. (DO 1964). LRCP 1960; MRCS 1960, FRCS 1968; FCOphth 1989. Guy's Hosp., 1961–63; Clin. Fellow in Ophthalmol., Johns Hopkins Univ., 1964–65; Res. Assistant, Inst. of Ophthalmol., 1965; Moorfields Eye Hospital: Chief Clin. Assistant, 1965; Resident Surg. Officer, 1965–68; Lectr, 1968–70; Sen. Lectr and Hon. Consultant, 1970–73; Margaret Ogilvie's Reader in Ophthalmol., Oxford Univ., 1973–89; Hon. Consultant, Oxford Eye Hosp., 1989–. Pres., Ophthalmic Section, RSM, 1986; Vice Pres., Jt Eur. Meetings in Ophthal. and Vision; Chm., Assoc. for Eye Res., 1993–95. Mem., Soc. of Scholars, Johns Hopkins Univ., 1991. Hon. MA Oxon, 1973. *Publications:* (contrib.) The Inborn Errors of Metabolism, 1974; The Unquiet Eye, 1983, 2nd edn 1987; papers on the cornea, tears and crystalline lens. *Recreations:* drawing, photography, musing on Life. *Address:* Nuffield Laboratory of Ophthalmology, Walton Street, Oxford OX2 6AW. *T:* Oxford (01865) 248996. *Club:* Athenæum.

See also E. Bron.

BRON, Eleanor; actress and writer; *d* of late Sydney and Fagah Bron. *Educ:* North London Collegiate Sch., Canons, Edgware; Newnham Coll., Cambridge (BA Hons Mod. Langs). De La Rue Co., 1961. Dir, Actors Centre, 1982–93. Appearances include: revue, Establishment Nightclub, Soho, 1962, and New York, 1963; Not so much a Programme, More a Way of Life, BBC TV, 1964; several TV series written with John Fortune, and TV series: Making Faces, written by Michael Frayn, 1976; Pinkerton's Progress, 1983; *TV plays and films include:* Nina, 1978; My Dear Palestrina, 1980; A Month in the Country, 1985; Quartermaine's Terms, 1987; Changing Step, 1989; The Hour of the Lynx, 1990; The Blue Boy, 1994. *Stage roles include:* Jennifer Dubedat, The Doctor's Dilemma, 1966; Jean Brodie, The Prime of Miss Jean Brodie, 1967, 1984; title role, Hedda Gabler, 1969; Portia, The Merchant of Venice, 1975; Amanda, Private Lives, 1976; Elena, Uncle Vanya, 1977; Charlotte, The Cherry Orchard, 1978; Margaret, A Family, 1978; On Her Own, 1980; Goody Biddy Bean; The Amusing Spectacle of Cinderella and her Naughty, Naughty Sisters, 1980; Betrayal, 1981; Heartbreak House, 1981; Duet for One, 1982; The Duchess of Malfi, 1985; The Real Inspector Hound, and The Critic (double bill), 1985; Jocasta and Ismene, Oedipus and Oedipus at Colonus, 1987; Infidelities, 1987; The Madwoman of Chaillot, 1988; The Chalk Garden, 1989; The Miser, and The White Devils, 1991; opera, Die Glückliche Hand, Nederlandse Oper, Amsterdam, 1991; Desdemona—if you had only spoken! (one-woman show), 1992; Gertrude, Hamlet, 1993. *Films include:* Help!; Alfie; Two for the Road; Bedazzled; Women in Love; The National Health; The Day that Christ Died, 1980; Turtle Diary, 1985; Little Dorrit, 1987; The Attic, 1988; Deadly Advice, 1994; Black Beauty, A Little Princess, 1995. Author: song-cycle with John Dankworth, 1973; verses for Saint-Saens' Carnival of the Animals, 1975 (recorded). *Publications:* Is Your Marriage Really Necessary (with John Fortune), 1972; (contrib.) My Cambridge, 1976; (contrib.) More Words, 1977; Life and Other Punctures, 1978; The Pillow Book of Eleanor Bron, 1985; (trans.) Desdemona – if you had only spoken!, by Christine Brückner, 1992. *Address:* c/o Rebecca Blond Associates, 52 Shaftesbury Avenue, W1V 7DE. *T:* 0171–434 2010.

See also A. J. Bron.

BRONFMAN, Edgar Miles; Chairman: The Seagram Company Ltd, since 1975 (Chief Executive Officer, 1975–94); Joseph E. Seagram & Sons Inc.; *b* 20 June 1929; *s* of late Samuel Bronfman and of Saidye Rosner. *Educ:* Trinity College Sch., Port Hope, Ont., Canada; Williams Coll., Williamstown, Mass, US; McGill Univ., Montreal (BA 1951). President: Joseph E. Seagram & Sons, Inc, 1957; The Seagram Company Ltd, 1971; Dir, E. I. duPont de Nemours & Co. Pres., World Jewish Congress, 1980–. Hon. LHD Pace Univ., NY, 1982; Hon. Dr Laws Williams Coll., Williamstown, 1986. *Address:* 375 Park Avenue, New York, NY 10152, USA. *T:* (212) 5727000.

BROOK, Anthony Donald, FCA; Chairman: Advanced Media Group plc, since 1994; Ocean Sound Ltd, since 1994; *b* 24 Sept. 1936; *s* of Donald Charles Brook and Doris Ellen (*née* Emmett); *m* 1965, Ann Mary Reeves; two *d*. *Educ:* Eastbourne Coll. FCA 1970 (ACA 1960). Joined Associated Television Ltd, 1966; Financial Controller, ATV Network Ltd, 1969; Dir of External Finance, IBA, 1974; Finance Dir/Gen. Man., ITC Entertainment Ltd, 1978; Dep. Man. Dir, Television South plc, 1981; Man. Dir (Television), Television South, then TVS Entertainment, 1984–89, Man. Dir Broadcasting, 1989–91; Man. Dir, TVS Television Ltd, 1986–89; Dep. Chm. and Man. Dir, TVS Entertainment plc, 1991–93; Chm., SelecTV, 1993–95. *Recreations:* sailing, travel, golf. *Address:* 18 Brookvale Road, Highfield, Southampton SO17 1QP. *Clubs:* Royal Southern Yacht (Hamble, Hants); Tamesis (Teddington, Mddx).

BROOK, Air Vice-Marshal David Conway Grant, CB 1990; CBE 1983; Civil Emergencies Adviser, Home Office, 1989–93; *b* 23 Dec. 1935; *s* of late Air Vice-Marshal William Arthur Darville Brook, CB, CBE and of Jean Brook (now Jean Hamilton); *m* 1961, Jessica (*née* Lubbock); one *s* one *d*. *Educ:* Marlborough Coll.; RAF Coll. Pilot, Nos 263, 1 (Fighter) and 14 Sqdns, 1957–62 (Hunter aircraft; fighter combat leader); ADC to AOC-in-C Near East Air Force, 1962–64; CO No 1 (Fighter) Sqdn, 1964–66 (Hunter Mk 9); RN Staff Course, 1967 (psc); RAF Adviser to Dir Land/Air Warfare (MoD Army), 1968–69; Wing Comdr Offensive Support, Jt Warfare Estab., 1970–72; CO No 20 (Army Cooperation) Sqdn, 1974–76 (Harrier); Station Comdr, RAF Wittering, 1976–78 (Harrier); RCDS, 1979 (rcds); Principal Staff Officer to Chief of Defence Staff, 1980–82; SASO, HQ RAF Germany, 1982–85; Air Officer Scotland and NI, 1986–89. *Publications:* contrib. to Brasseys Annual. *Recreations:* golf, music, canal boating, walking. *Address:* c/o Lloyds Bank, 19 High Street, Evesham, Worcs WR11 4DQ.

BROOK, (Gerald) Robert, CBE 1981; Chief Executive, 1977–86, and Chairman, 1985–86, National Bus Company (Deputy Chairman, 1978–85); *b* 19 Dec. 1928; *s* of Charles Pollard Brook and Doris Brook (*née* Senior); *m* 1957, Joan Marjorie Oldfield; two *s* one *d*. *Educ:* King James Grammar Sch., Knaresborough. FCIS, FCIT. Served Duke of Wellington's Regt, 1947–49. Appointments in bus companies, from 1950; Company Secretary: Cumberland Motor Services Ltd, 1960; Thames Valley Traction Co. Ltd, 1963; General Manager: North Western Road Car Co. Ltd, 1968; Midland Red Omnibus Co. Ltd, 1972; Regional Director, National Bus Company, 1974; Director: Scottish Transport Gp; United Transport Internat. Plc; United Transport Buses Ltd; S Yorks Transport Ltd; Midland Fox Holdings Ltd. Pres., CIT, 1987–88. *Publications:* papers for professional instns and learned socs. *Recreation:* reading military history. *Address:* Middle Cottage, Manor

Fold, Follifoot, near Harrogate, N Yorks HG3 1UA. *T:* Harrogate (01423) 879789. *Club:* Army and Navy.

BROOK, Helen, (Lady Brook), CBE 1995; Founder, 1963, and President, Brook Advisory Centre for Young People (Chairman, 1964–74); *b* 12 Oct. 1907; *d* of John and Helen Knewstub; *m* 1937, Sir Robin Brook, *qv*; two *d* (and one *d* of previous marriage). *Educ:* Convent of Holy Child Jesus, Mark Cross, Sussex. Voluntary worker: Family Planning Association, 1949– (Mem. Exec., Nat. Council, 1954–; Vice-Pres., 1987–); Family Planning Sales, 1972– (Chm., 1974–81); Dir, Marie Stopes Meml Clinic, 1958–64; Vice-Pres., Nat. Assoc. of Family Planning Nurses, 1980–. Hon. DSc City, 1993. Galton Inst. Medal, 1994. *Recreations:* painting, gardening. *Address:* 31 Acacia Road, NW8 6AS. *T:* 0171–722 5844.

BROOK, Air Vice-Marshal John Michael, CB 1993; FRCGP; Director General, Royal Air Force Medical Services, 1991–94, retired; *b* 26 May 1934; *s* of late Norman Brook and Nellie Brook (*née* Burns); *m* 1959, Edna Kilburn; one *s* three *d*. *Educ:* Mirfield Grammar Sch.; Leeds Univ. (MB ChB 1957). MRCGP 1972, FRCGP 1992; Dip AvMed RCP 1974; MFOM 1981. Commissioned 1959; served Larbruch, Stafford, Muharraq, Watton, Linton-on-Ouse, MoD; SMO, RAF Finningley, 1974–76; MoD, 1976; SMO RAF Brize Norton, 1978–81; OC RAF Av. Med. Trng Centre, 1981–83; RAF Exchange Officer, USAF HQ Systems Command, 1983–86; OC Defence Services Med. Rehabilitation Unit, 1986–87; OC Central Med. Estabt, 1987–89; Dep. Principal MO, HQ Strike Comd, 1989–91; Dep. Surgeon Gen., Health Services, 1991–93. QHS 1991–94. OStJ 1980. *Recreations:* all music, travel, walking. *Address:* 2 Vicarage Fields, Hemingford Grey, Cambs PE18 9BY. *Club:* Royal Air Force.

BROOK, Leopold, BScEng, FICE, FIMechE; Director, Renishaw plc, since 1980; *b* 2 Jan. 1912; *s* of Albert and Kate Brook, Hampstead; *m* 1st, 1940, Susan (*d* 1970), *d* of David Rose, Hampstead; two *s*; 2nd, 1974, Mrs Elly Rhodes; two step *s* one step *d*. *Educ:* Central Foundation School, London; University College, London. L. G. Mouchel & Partners, Cons. Engineers, 1935–44; Simon Engineering Ltd, 1944–77 (Chief Exec., 1967–70; Chm., 1970–77); Chairman: Associated Nuclear Services Ltd, 1977–90; Brown & Sharpe Group (UK), 1979–88. Fellow, UCL, 1970–. CIMgt; FRSA 1973. *Recreations:* music, theatre, walking. *Address:* 55 Kingston House North, Prince's Gate, SW7 1LW. *T:* 0171–584 2041. *Clubs:* Athenæum, Hurlingham.

See also R. E. Rhodes.

BROOK, Peter Stephen Paul, CBE 1965; Producer; Co-Director, The Royal Shakespeare Theatre; *b* 21 March 1925; 2nd *s* of Simon Brook; *m* 1951, Natasha Parry, stage and film star; one *s* one *d*. *Educ:* Westminster; Greshams; Magdalen College, Oxford (Hon. Fellow, 1991). Productions include: The Tragedy of Dr Faustus, 1942; The Infernal Machine, 1945; Birmingham Repertory Theatre: Man and Superman, King John, The Lady from the Sea, 1945–46; Stratford: Romeo and Juliet, Love's Labour's Lost, 1947; London: Vicious Circle, Men Without Shadows, Respectable Prostitute, The Brothers Karamazov, 1946; Director of Productions, Royal Opera House, Covent Garden, 1947–50: Boris Godunov, La Bohème, 1948; Marriage of Figaro, The Olympians, Salome, 1949. Dark of the Moon, 1949; Ring Round the Moon, 1950; Measure for Measure, Stratford, 1950, Paris, 1978; The Little Hut, 1950; The Winter's Tale, 1951; Venice Preserved, 1953; The Little Hut, New York, Faust, Metropolitan Opera House, 1953; The Dark is Light Enough; Both Ends Meet, 1954; House of Flowers, New York, 1954; The Lark, 1955; Titus Andronicus, Stratford, 1955; Hamlet, 1955; The Power and the Glory, 1956; Family Reunion, 1956; The Tempest, Stratford, 1957; Cat on a Hot Tin Roof, Paris, 1957; View from the Bridge, Paris, 1958; Irma la Douce, London, 1958; The Fighting Cock, New York, 1959; Le Balcon, Paris, 1960; The Visit, Royalty, 1960; King Lear, Stratford and Aldwych, 1962; The Physicists, Aldwych, 1963; Sergeant Musgrave's Dance, Paris, 1963; The Persecution and Assassination of Marat..., Aldwych, 1964 (New York, 1966); The Investigation, Aldwych, 1965; US, Aldwych, 1966; Oedipus, National Theatre, 1968; A Midsummer Night's Dream, Stratford, 1970, NY, 1971; Timon of Athens, Paris, 1974 (Grand Prix Dominique, 1975; Brigadier Prize, 1975); The Ik, Paris, 1975, London, 1976; Ubu Roi, Paris, 1977; Antony and Cleopatra, Stratford, 1978, Aldwych, 1979; Ubu, Young Vic, 1978; Conference of the Birds, France, Australia, NY, 1980; The Cherry Orchard, Paris, 1981, NY, 1988; La tragédie de Carmen, Paris, 1981, NY, 1983 (Emmy Award, and Prix Italia, 1984); The Mahabharata, Avignon and Paris, 1985, Glasgow, 1988, televised, 1989 (Internat. Emmy Award 1990); Woza Albert, Paris, 1988; Carmen, Glasgow, 1989; The Tempest, Glasgow and Paris, 1990; Impressions de Pelléas, Paris, 1992; L'Homme Qui, Paris, 1993, The Man Who, Nat. Theatre, 1994, New York, 1995; work with Internat. Centre of Theatre Research, Paris, Iran, W Africa, and USA, 1971, Sahara, Niger and Nigeria, 1972–73. *Directed films:* The Beggar's Opera, 1952; Moderato Cantabile, 1960; Lord of the Flies, 1962; The Marat/Sade, 1967; Tell Me Lies, 1968; King Lear, 1969; Meetings with Remarkable Men, 1979; The Tragedy of Carmen, 1983. Hon. DLitt: Birmingham; Strathclyde, 1990; Oxford, 1994. SWET award, for outstanding contribn by UK theatre artist to US theatre season, 1983. Freiherr von Stein Foundn Shakespeare Award, 1973. Officier de l'Ordre des Arts et des Lettres; Legion of Honour (France), 1987. *Publications:* The Empty Space, 1968; The Shifting Point (autobiog.), 1988; Le Diable c'est l'Ennui, 1991; There Are No Secrets, 1993. *Recreations:* painting, piano playing and travelling by air. *Address:* c/o CICT, 56 rue de l'Université, 75007 Paris, France.

BROOK, Sir Ralph Ellis; *see* Brook, Sir Robin.

BROOK, Prof. Richard John, OBE 1988; ScD; Chief Executive, Engineering and Physical Sciences Research Council, since 1994; Professor of Materials Science, since 1995, and Professorial Fellow, St Cross College, since 1991, Oxford University (on leave of absence); *b* 12 March 1938; *s* of Frank Brook and Emily Sarah (*née* Lytle); *m* 1961, Elizabeth Christine Aldred; one *s* one *d*. *Educ:* Univ. of Leeds (BSc Ceramics); MIT (ScD Ceramics). Res. Asst, MIT, 1962–66; Asst Prof. of Materials Science, Univ. of S California, 1966–70; Gp Leader, AERE, 1970–74; Prof. and Head of Dept of Ceramics, Univ. of Leeds, 1974–88; Scientific Mem., Max Planck Soc. and Dir, Max Planck Inst. Metallforschung, Stuttgart, 1988–91; Cookson Prof. of Materials Sci., 1992–95, and Head, Dept of Materials, 1992–94, Oxford Univ. Chairman, Materials Cttee, 1985–88, Materials Commn, 1992–94, SERC; Ext. Mem., Res. Cttee, British Gas, 1989–. Pres., British Ceramic Soc., 1984–86; Vice-Pres., Inst. of Materials, 1993–; Fellow, Inst. of Ceramics, 1978 (Pres., 1984–86); Dist. Life Fellow, American Ceramic Soc., 1995; Mem. d'Honneur, Soc. Française Métall. Matériaux, 1995. Hon. Prof., Univ. of Stuttgart, 1990–. Mellor Meml Lectr, Swansea, 1989; Stuijts Meml Lectr, Maastricht, 1989. Editor, Jl of European Ceramic Soc., 1989–. *Publications:* Encyclopedia of Advanced Ceramic Materials, 1991; papers in publications of Inst. of Materials, Amer. Ceramic Soc., European Ceramic Soc. *Recreation:* Europe. *Address:* Engineering and Physical Sciences Research Council, Polaris House, North Star Avenue, Swindon SN2 1ET. *T:* Swindon (01793) 444170; 15 Rawlinson Road, Oxford OX2 6UE. *T:* Oxford (01865) 53394; Forststrasse 180, 70193 Stuttgart, Germany. *T:* (711) 6364112.

BROOK, Robert; *see* Brook, G. R.

BROOK, Sir Robin, Kt 1974; CMG 1954; OBE 1945; Member: City and E London Area Health Authority, 1974–82 (Vice Chairman, 1974–79); City and Hackney District Health Authority, 1982–86; *b* 19 June 1908; *s* of Francis Brook, Harley Street, and Mrs E. I. Brook; *m* 1937, Helen (*see* Helen Brook), *e d* of John Knewstub; two *d*. *Educ:* Eton; King's College, Cambridge. Served 1941–46; Brig., 1945 (OBE, despatches, Legion of Merit (Commander), Legion of Honour, Croix de Guerre and Bars, Order of Leopold (Officer), Belgian Croix de Guerre). Director, Bank of England, 1946–49. Formerly Chairman: Augustine Investments; Ionian Bank; Leda Inv. Trust; Jove Inv. Trust; W. E. Sykes; Carclo; Sir Joseph Causton; Gordon Woodroffe; Vice-Chm., United City Merchants. Chm., 1966–68, Pres., 1968–72, London Chamber of Commerce and Industry; Pres., Assoc. of British Chambers of Commerce, 1972–74; Pres., Assoc. of Chambers of Commerce of EEC, 1974–76; Leader of Trade Missions: for HM Govt to Libya and Romania; for London or British Chambers of Commerce to France, Iran, China, Greece, Finland and Hungary; HM Govt Dir, BP Co., 1970–73; Deputy Chairman: British Tourist and Holidays Board, 1946–50; Colonial Development Corp., 1949–53. Mem., Foundn for Management Educn, 1975–82. Sports Council: Mem., 1971–78; Vice-Chm., 1974; Chm., 1975–78; Chm., Sports Develt Cttee, 1971–74. Mem., Cttee on Invisible Exports, 1969–74; Mem. Court, Council, Finance and Hon. Degrees Cttees, City Univ.; Hon. Treasurer: Amateur Fencing Assoc., 1946–61; CCPR, 1961–77 (also Mem. Exec.); Family Planning Association, 1966–75. High Sheriff of County of London, 1950; Mem. Council, Festival of Britain. Mem. Council and Exec. Cttee, King Edward's Fund; Pres., London Homes for the Elderly, 1980–91 (Chm., 1973–80). St Bartholomew's Hospital: Governor, 1962–74; Treasurer and Chm., 1969–74; Chm., Special Trustees, 1974–88; Pres., St Bartholomew's Med. Coll., 1969–88; Governor, Royal Free Hosp., 1962–74; governor of schools; Mem. Governors and Exec. Cttee, Sports Aid Foundn, 1975–. Past Master, Wine Warden, Haberdashers' Co. Hon. DSc City, 1989. *Recreation:* British Sabre Champion, 1936; Olympic Games, 1936, 1948; Capt. British Team, 1933 (3rd in European Championship), etc. *Address:* 31 Acacia Road, NW8 6AS.

BROOK-PARTRIDGE, Bernard; Partner, Carsons, Brook-Partridge & Co. (Planning Consultants), since 1972; *b* Croydon, 1927; *o s* of late Leslie Brook-Partridge and late Gladys Vere Burchell (*née* Brooks), Sanderstead; *m* 1st, 1951, Enid Elizabeth (marr. diss. 1965), 2nd *d* of late Frederick Edmund Hatfield and Enid Hatfield; two *d*; 2nd, 1967, Carol Devonald, *o d* of late Arnold Devonald Francis Lewis and late Patricia (*née* Thomas), Gower, S Wales; two *s*. *Educ:* Selsdon County Grammar Sch.; Cambridgeshire Tech. Coll.; Cambridge Univ.; London Univ.; Gray's Inn. Military Service, 1945–48. Studies, 1948–50. Cashier/Accountant, Dominion Rubber Co. Ltd, 1950–51; Asst Export Manager, British & General Tube Co. Ltd, 1951–52; Asst Sec., Assoc. of Internat. Accountants, 1952–59; Sec.-Gen., Institute of Linguists, 1959–62; various teaching posts, Federal Republic of Germany, 1962–66; Special Asst to Man. Dir, M. G. Scott Ltd, 1966–68. Business consultancy work on own account, incl. various dirships with several client cos, 1968–72; Chairman: Brompton Troika Ltd, 1985–; Lucarne International (Bristol) Ltd, 1993–; St Albans Court Ltd; St Albans Court School Ltd; Daldorch Estates Ltd; Director: Edmund Nuttall Ltd, 1986–92; Kyle Stewart, 1989–92; PEG Management Consultants plc, 1989–94. Local Govt and Pol Advisor to Transmanche-Link UK, 1988 and 1989. Contested (C) St Pancras North, LCC, 1958; Mem. (C) St Pancras Metropolitan Borough Council, 1959–62. Prospective Parly Cand. (C), Shoreditch and Finsbury, 1960–62; contested (C) Nottingham Central, 1970. Greater London Council: Mem. for Havering, 1967–73, for Havering (Romford), 1973–85; Chm., 1980–81; Chairman: Planning and Transportation (NE) Area Bd, 1967–71; Town Develt Cttee, 1971–73; Arts Cttee, 1977–78; Public Services and Safety Cttee, 1978–79; Opposition spokesman: for Arts and Recreation, 1973–77; for Police Matters, 1983–85; Member: Exec. Cttee, Greater London Arts Assoc., 1973–78; Council and Exec., Greater London and SE Council for Sport and Recreation, 1977–78; GLC Leaders' Cttee with special responsibility for Law and Order and Police Liaison matters, 1977–79; Dep. Leader, Recreation and Community Services Policy Cttee, 1977–79. Vice-Pres., SPCK, 1993– (Gov. and Trustee, 1976–93); Member: BBC Radio London Adv. Council, 1974–79; Gen. Council, Poetry Soc., 1977–86 (Treas., 1982–84); Board Member: Peterborough Develt Corp., 1972–88 (Chm., Queensgate Management Services); London Festival Ballet (and Trustee), 1977–79; Young Vic Theatre Ltd, 1977–88 (Chm., 1983–87); London Orchestral Concert Bd Ltd, 1977–78; ENO, 1977–78; London Contemp. Dance Trust, 1979–84; Governor and Trustee, Sadler's Wells Foundn, 1977–79; Chairman: London Music Hall Trust, 1983–; London Symphony Chorus Develt Cttee, 1981–88; Samuel Lewis Housing Trust, 1985–92 (Trustee, 1976–94); Council, Royal Philharmonic Soc., 1991– (Chm., 1991–95); Pres., British Sch. of Osteopathy Appeal Fund, 1980–84. President: City of London Rifle League, 1980–; Gtr London Horse Show, 1982–85; Gtr London (County Hall) Br., Royal British Legion, 1988– . FCIS (Mem. Council, 1981–, Treas., 1984, Vice-Pres. 1985, Pres., 1986); MIMgt. Hon. FIET. Hon. PhD Columbia Pacific, 1982. Order of Gorkha Dakshina Bahu (2nd cl.), Nepal, 1981. *Publications:* Europe—Power and Responsibility: Direct Elections to the European Parliament (with David Baker), 1972; innumerable contribs to learned jls and periodicals on linguistics and translation, the use of language, political science and contemporary politics. *Recreations:* conversation, opera, classical music and being difficult. *Address:* 28 Elizabeth Road, Henley-on-Thames, Oxfordshire RG9 1RG. *T:* Henley-on-Thames (01491) 575505. *Clubs:* Athenæum, Sette of Odd Volumes.

BROOKE, family name of **Viscount Alanbrooke,** of **Baroness Brooke of Ystradfellte** and of **Viscount Brookeborough.**

BROOKE, Lord; Guy David Greville; *b* 30 Jan. 1957; *s* and *heir* of 8th Earl of Warwick, *qv* and of Mrs Harry Thomson Jones; *m* 1981, Susan McKinley Cobbold (marr. diss.); one *s*. *Educ:* Summerfields, Eton and Ecole des Roches. *Recreations:* girls, surfing. *Heir: s* Hon. Charles Fulke Chester Greville, *b* 27 July 1982. *Address:* 3A Brown Street, Claremont, WA 6010, Australia. *T:* (9) 3849940. *Club:* White's.

BROOKE OF YSTRADFELLTE, Baroness *cr* 1964 (Life Peer); **Barbara Brooke,** DBE 1960; *b* 14 Jan. 1908; *y d* of late Canon A. A. Mathews; *m* 1933, Henry Brooke, PC, CH (later Baron Brooke of Cumnor) (*d* 1984); two *s* two *d*. *Educ:* Queen Anne's School, Caversham. Joint Vice-Chm., Conservative Party Organisation, 1954–64. Member: Hampstead Borough Council, 1948–65; North-West Metropolitan Regional Hospital Board, 1954–66; Management Cttee, King Edward's Hospital Fund for London, 1966–71; Chairman: Exec. Cttee Queen's Institute of District Nursing, 1961–71; Governing Body of Godolphin and Latymer School, Hammersmith, 1960–78. Hon. Fellow, Queen Mary and Westfield College. *Address:* Romans Halt, Mildenhall, Marlborough, Wilts SN8 2LX.

See also Hon. Sir H. Brooke, Rt Hon. P. L. Brooke.

BROOKE, Sir Alistair Weston, 4th Bt *cr* 1919, of Almondbury; *b* 12 Sept. 1947; *s* of Major Sir John Weston Brooke, 3rd Bt, TD, and Rosemary (*d* 1979), *d* of late Percy Nevill, Birling House, West Malling, Kent; *S* father, 1983; *m* 1982, Susan Mary, *d* of Barry Charles Roger Griffiths, MRCVS, Church House, Norton, Powys; one *d*. *Educ:* Repton; Royal Agricultural Coll., Cirencester. *Recreations:* shooting, farming, racehorse training. *Heir: b* Charles Weston Brooke [*b* 27 Jan. 1951; *m* 1984, Tanya Elizabeth, *d* of Antony Thelwell Maurice; two *d*]. *Address:* Wootton Farm, Pencombe, Hereford. *T:* Pencombe (01885) 400615.

BROOKE, Arthur Caffin, CB 1972; Chairman, Arts Council of Northern Ireland, 1982–86 (Member, 1979–86); *b* 11 March 1919; *s* of late Rev. James M. Wilmot Brooke and Constance Brooke; *m* 1942, Margaret Florence Thompson; two *s*. *Educ:* Abbotsholme Sch.; Peterhouse, Cambridge (MA). Served War, Royal Corps of Signals, 1939–46. Northern Ireland Civil Service, 1946–79; Ministry of Commerce, 1946–73: Asst Sec., Head of Industrial Development Div., 1955; Sen. Asst Sec., Industrial Development, 1963; Second Sec., 1968; Permanent Sec., 1969; Permanent Sec., Dept of Educn, 1973–79. *Address:* 4 Camden Court, Brecon, Powys LD3 7RP. *T:* Brecon (01874) 625617.

BROOKE, Prof. Bryan Nicholas, MD, MChir, FRCS; Emeritus Professor (Professor of Surgery, University of London, at St George's Hospital 1963–80); lately consultant surgeon, St George's Hospital; *b* 21 Feb. 1915; *s* of George Cyril Brooke, LitD, FSA (numismatist) and Margaret Florence Brooke; *m* 1940, Naomi Winefride Mills; three *d*. *Educ:* Bradfield College, Berkshire; Corpus Christi College, Cambridge; St Bartholomew's Hospital, London. FRCSEng 1942; MChir (Cantab.) 1944; MD (Birm.) with hons 1954. Lieut-Colonel, RAMC, 1945–46. Lecturer in Surgery, Aberdeen Univ., 1946–47; Reader in Surgery, Birmingham Univ., 1947–63; Hunterian Prof. RCS, 1951 and 1979. Examiner in Surgery, Universities of: Birmingham, 1951–63; Cambridge, 1958–; Bristol, 1961–; London, 1962–; Glasgow, 1969; Oxford, 1970; Hong Kong, 1972; Nigeria, 1975; RCS, 1973; Chm., Ct of Examnrs, RCS, 1978. Member, Medical Appeals Tribunal, 1948–87. Founder Pres., Ileostomy Assoc. of GB, 1957–82. Chm., Malvern Girls' Coll., 1972–82. Copeman Medal for Scientific Research, 1960; Graham Award (Amer. Proctologic Soc.), 1961; Award of NY Soc., Colon and Rectal Surgeons, 1967. Hon. FRACS, 1977; Hon. Fellow, Colo-Proctological Sect., RSM, 1989; Hon. Mem., British Soc. of Gastroenterology, 1979. Consultant Editor, World Medicine, 1980–82. *Publications:* Ulcerative Colitis and its Surgical Treatment, 1954; You and Your Operation, 1957; United Birmingham Cancer Reports, 1953, 1954, 1957; (co-editor) Recent Advances in Gastroenterology, 1965; (co-author) Metabolic Derangements in Gastrointestinal Surgery, 1966; Understanding Cancer, 1971; Crohn's Disease, 1977; The Troubled Gut, 1986; (jtly) A Garden of Roses, 1987; Editor, Jl Clinics in Gastroenterology; contrib. to various surgical works. Numerous articles on large bowel disorder, medical education, steroid therapy. *Recreation:* painting. *Address:* The High House, 38 Kenley Lane, Kenley, Surrey CR8 5DD. *Club:* Athenæum.

BROOKE, Prof. Christopher Nugent Lawrence, CBE 1995; MA; LittD; FSA; FRHistS; FBA 1970; Dixie Professor of Ecclesiastical History, University of Cambridge, 1977–94, now Dixie Professor Emeritus; Fellow, Gonville and Caius College, Cambridge, 1949–56 and since 1977 (Life Fellow, 1994); *b* 23 June 1927; *y s* of late Professor Zachary Nugent Brooke and Rosa Grace Brooke; *m* 1951, Rosalind Beckford, *d* of Dr and Mrs L. H. S. Clark; three *s*. *Educ:* Winchester College (Scholar); Gonville and Caius College, Cambridge (Major Scholar). BA 1948; MA 1952; LittD 1973. Army service in RAEC, Temp. Captain 1949. Cambridge University: College Lecturer in History, 1953–56; Praelector Rhetoricus, 1955–56; Asst Lectr in History, 1953–54; Lectr, 1954–56; Prof. of Mediæval History, University of Liverpool, 1956–67; Prof. of History, Westfield Coll., Univ. of London, 1967–77. Member: Royal Commn on Historical Monuments (England), 1977–83; Reviewing Cttee on Export of Works of Art, 1979–82. Vice-Pres., Soc. of Antiquaries, 1975–79, Pres., 1981–84. Corresp. Fellow, Medieval Acad. of America, 1981; Corresp. Mem., Monumenta Germaniae Historica, 1988. DUniv York, 1984. Lord Mayor's Midsummer Prize, City of London, 1981. *Publications:* The Dullness of the Past, 1957; From Alfred to Henry III, 1961; The Saxon and Norman Kings, 1963; Europe in the Central Middle Ages, 1964, 2nd edn 1987; Time the Archsatirist, 1968; The Twelfth Century Renaissance, 1970; Structure of Medieval Society, 1971; Medieval Church and Society (sel. papers), 1971; (with W. Swaan) The Monastic World, 1974; (with G. Keir) London, 800–1216, 1975; Marriage in Christian History, 1977; (with R. B. Brooke) Popular Religion in the Middle Ages, 1000–1300, 1984; A History of Gonville and Caius College, 1985; The Church and the Welsh Border, 1986; (with J. R. L. Highfield and W. Swaan) Oxford and Cambridge, 1988; The Medieval Idea of Marriage, 1989; (jtly) David Knowles Remembered, 1991; A History of the University of Cambridge, vol. IV, 1870–1990, 1993; part Editor: The Book of William Morton, 1954; The Letters of John of Salisbury, vol. I, 1955, vol. II, 1979; Carte Nativorum, 1960; (with A. Morey) Gilbert Foliot and his letters, 1965 and (ed jtly) The Letters and Charters of Gilbert Foliot, 1967; (with D. Knowles and V. London) Heads of Religious Houses, England and Wales 940–1216, 1972; (with D. Whitelock and M. Brett) Councils and Synods, vol. I, 1981; (with Sir Roger Mynors) Walter Map, De Nugis Curialium (revision of M. R. James edn), 1983; (with M. Brett and M. Winterbottom) Hugh the Chanter, History of the Church of York (revision of C. Johnson edn), 1990; contributed to: A History of St Paul's Cathedral, 1957; A History of York Minster, 1977; general editor: Oxford (formerly Nelson's) Medieval Texts, 1959–87; Nelson's History of England, etc; articles and reviews in English Historical Review, Cambridge Historical Journal, Studies in Church History, Bulletin of Inst. of Historical Research, Downside Review, Traditio, Bulletin of John Rylands Library, Jl of Soc. of Archivists, etc. *Address:* Gonville and Caius College, Cambridge CB2 1TA.

BROOKE, (Christopher) Roger (Ettrick); Chairman, Candover Investments plc, since 1991; *b* 2 Feb. 1931; *s* of late Ralph Brooke and Marjorie (*née* Lee); *m* 1958, Nancy Belle Lowenthal; three *s* one *d*. *Educ:* Tonbridge; Trinity Coll., Oxford (MA). Served HM Diplomatic Service: Bonn, 1955–57; Southern Dept, FO, 1958–60; Washington, 1960–63; Tel Aviv, 1963–66. Dep. Man. Dir, IRC, 1966–69; Man. Dir, Scienta SA, 1969–71; Dir, Pearson Gp, 1971–79; Gp Man. Dir, EMI, 1979–80; Chief Exec., Candover Investments plc, 1980–90; Director: Slough Estates plc, 1980–; Lowndes Lambert Gp Holdings PLC, 1991–; Tarmac plc, 1994–, and various other cos. *Publication:* Santa's Christmas Journey, 1985. *Recreations:* golf, tennis, theatre, reading, travel. *Address:* c/o Candover Investments plc, 20 Old Bailey, EC4M 7LN; Water Meadow, Swarraton, near Alresford, Hants SO24 9TQ. *T:* Alresford (01962) 732259. *Club:* Woking Golf.

BROOKE, Clive; General Secretary, Inland Revenue Staff Federation, since 1988; *b* 21 June 1942; *s* of Mary Brooke (*née* Colbeck) and John Brooke; *m* 1967, Lorna Hopkin Roberts. *Educ:* Thornes House School, Wakefield. Asst Sec., 1964–82, Dep. Gen. Sec., 1982–88, Inland Revenue Staff Fedn. Trade Union Congress: Member: Gen. Council, 1989–; Exec. Cttee, 1993. Member: Council of Civil Service Unions (Mem., Major Policy Cttee); Inland Revenue Deptl Whitley Council, TUS, 1976–88 (Chm., 1986–88); H of C Speaker's Commn on Citizenship, 1988–; Exec. Cttee, Involvement and Participation Assoc., 1991–. Trustee: Duke of Edinburgh Study Conf., 1993 (Mem., Canada Conf., 1980); Community Services Volunteers, 1989–. Member: Labour Party; Fabian Soc. *Recreations:* opera, ballet, church affairs, speedway. *Address:* Inland Revenue Staff Federation, Douglas Houghton House, 231 Vauxhall Bridge Road, SW1V 1EH. *T:* 0171–834 8254.

BROOKE, Sir Francis (George Windham), 4th Bt *cr* 1903; *b* 15 Oct. 1963; *s* of Sir George Cecil Francis Brooke, 3rd Bt, MBE, and of Lady Melissa Brooke, *er d* of 6th Earl of Dunraven and Mount-Earl, CB, CBE, MC; *S* father, 1982; *m* 1989, Katharine Elizabeth, *o d* of Marmaduke Hussey, *qv* and Lady Susan Hussey, *qv*; one *s* one *d*. *Educ:* Eton; Edinburgh University (MA Hons). AIIMR. *Heir: s* George Francis Geoffrey Brooke, *b* 10 Sept. 1991. *Address:* 49 Masbro Road, W14 0LU; Glenbevan, Croom, Co. Limerick, Ireland. *Clubs:* Turf; Kildare Street and University (Dublin).

BROOKE, Hon. Sir Henry, Kt 1988; **Hon. Mr Justice Brooke;** Judge of the High Court of Justice, Queen's Bench Division, since 1988; Chairman, Law Commission, since 1993; *b* 19 July 1936; *s* of Lord Brooke of Cumnor, PC, CH and of Lady Brooke of Ystradfellte, *qv*; *m* 1966, Bridget Mary Kalaugher; three *s* one *d*. *Educ:* Marlborough College; Balliol Coll., Oxford. MA (1st Cl. Classical Hon. Mods, 1st Cl. Lit. Hum.). Called to the Bar, Inner Temple, 1963, Bencher, 1987; Junior Counsel to the Crown, Common Law, 1978–81; QC 1981; a Recorder, 1983–88; Counsel to the Inquiry, Sizewell 'B' Nuclear Reactor Inquiry, 1983–85; DTI Inspector, House of Fraser Hldgs plc, 1987–88. Mem., Bar Council, 1987–88 (Chairman: Professional Standards Cttee, 1987–88; Race Relations Cttee, 1989–91); Chairman: Computer Cttee, Senate of the Inns of Court and the Bar, 1985–86; London Common Law and Commercial Bar Assoc., 1988 (Vice-Chm., 1986–87); Ethnic Minority Adv. Cttee, Judicial Studies Bd, 1991–94; Member: Information Technology and the Courts Cttee, 1986–87, 1990–; Judicial Studies Bd, 1992–94. Pres., Soc. for Computers and Law, 1992–. *Publications:* Institute Cargo Clauses (Air), 1986; (contrib.) Halsbury's Laws of England, 4th edn. *Address:* Royal Courts of Justice, Strand, WC2A 2LL. *Club:* Brooks's.
See also Rt Hon. P. L. Brooke.

BROOKE, John Stephen P.; *see* Pitt-Brooke.

BROOKE, Michael Eccles Macklin; QC 1994; *b* 8 May 1942; *s* of late Reginald Eccles Joseph Brooke and Beryl Cicely Brooke (*née* Riggs); *m* 1972, Annie Sophie (marr. diss. 1985), *d* of André Vautier; three *s*. *Educ:* Froebel Sch., Datchet; Lycée Français de Londres; Edinburgh Univ. (LLB). Called to the Bar, Gray's Inn, and in practice, 1968–; admitted Avocat, Cour d'Appel, Paris, and in practice, 1987–. *Recreations:* boating, comparing England and France. *Address:* 2 Crown Office Row, Temple, EC4Y 7HJ. *T:* 0171–797 8000.

BROOKE, Rt. Hon. Peter Leonard, CH 1992; PC 1988; MP (C) City of London and Westminster South, since Feb. 1977; *b* 3 March 1934; *s* of Lord Brooke of Cumnor, PC, CH and of Lady Brooke of Ystradfellte, *qv*; *m* 1st, 1964, Joan Margaret Smith (*d* 1985); three *s* (and one *s* decd); 2nd, 1991, Lindsay Allinson. *Educ:* Marlborough; Balliol College, Oxford (MA); Harvard Business School (MBA). Vice-Pres., Nat. Union of Students, 1955–56; Chm., Nat. Conf., Student Christian Movement, 1956; Pres., Oxford Union, 1957; Commonwealth Fund Fellow, 1957–59. Research Assistant, IMEDE, Lausanne, 1960–61. Spencer Stuart & Associates, Management Consultants, 1961–79 (Director of parent company, 1965–79, Chairman 1974–79); lived in NY and Brussels, 1969–73. Mem., Camden Borough Council, 1968–69. Chm., St Pancras N Cons. Assoc., 1976–77. Contested (C) Bedwellty, Oct. 1974; an Asst Govt Whip, 1979–81; a Lord Comr of HM Treasury, 1981–83; Parly Under Sec. of State, DES, 1983–85; Minister of State, HM Treasury, 1985–87; Paymaster Gen., HM Treasury, 1987–89; Chm., Conservative Party, 1987–89; Secretary of State: for NI, 1989–92; for Nat. Heritage, 1992–94. Pres., IAPS, 1980–83; Mem. Council, Marlborough Coll., 1977–83, 1992–; Lay Adviser, St Paul's Cathedral, 1980–; Lay Mem., Univ. of London Council, 1994–. Chm., Churches Conservation Trust, 1995–. Trustee: Wordsworth Trust, 1975–; Cusichaca Project, 1978–; Conf. on Trng in Archtl Conservation, 1994–. Sen. Fellow, RCA, 1987; Presentation Fellow, KCL, 1989. *Recreations:* churches, conservation, cricket, visual arts. *Address:* c/o House of Commons, SW1A 0AA. *Clubs:* Beefsteak, Brooks's, City Livery, MCC, I Zingari, St George's (Hanover Square) Conservative.
See also Hon. Sir H. Brooke.

BROOKE, Sir Richard (Neville), 10th Bt *cr* 1662; *b* 1 May 1915; *s* of Sir Richard Christopher Brooke, 9th Bt, and Marian Dorothea (*d* 1965), *d* of late Arthur Charles Innes, MP, of Dromantine, Co. Down; *S* father, 1981; *m* 1st, 1937, Lady Mabel Kathleen Jocelyn (marr. diss. 1959; she *d* 1985), *d* of 8th Earl of Roden; two *s*; 2nd, 1960, Jean Evison, *d* of late Lt-Col A. C. Corfe, DSO. *Educ:* Eton. Served as Lieutenant, Scots Guards, 1939–46; prisoner of war (escaped). Chartered Accountant (FCA), 1946; Senior Partner, Price Waterhouse & Co., European Firms, 1969–75; retired, 1975. *Recreations:* racing, fishing. *Heir: s* Richard David Christopher Brooke [*b* 23 Oct. 1938; *m* 1st, 1963, Carola Marion (marr. diss. 1978), *d* of Sir Robert Erskine-Hill, 2nd Bt; two *s*; 2nd, 1979, Lucinda Barlow, *o d* of late J. F. Voelcker and of Jean Constance Voelcker, Lidgetton, Natal]. *Address:* Pond Cottage, Crawley, near Winchester, Hants SO21 2PR. *T:* Sparsholt (01962) 776272. *Club:* Boodle's.

BROOKE, Rodney George; DL; Secretary, Association of Metropolitan Authorities, since 1990; Visiting Fellow, Nuffield Institute for Health Service Studies, University of Leeds, since 1989; *b* 22 Oct. 1939; *s* of George Sidney Brooke and Amy Brooke; *m* 1967, Dr Clare Margaret Cox; one *s* one *d*. *Educ:* Queen Elizabeth's Grammar Sch., Wakefield. Admitted solicitor (hons), 1962. Rochdale County Bor. Council, 1962–63; Leicester CC, 1963–65; Stockport County Bor. Council, 1965–73; West Yorkshire Metropolitan County Council: Dir of Admin, 1973–81; Chief Exec. and Clerk, 1981–84; Clerk to W Yorks Lieutenancy, 1981–84; Chief Exec., Westminster City Council, 1984–89; Clerk to Gtr London Lieutenancy, 1987–89; Chm., Bradford HA, 1989–90. Secretary: Yorks and Humberside Tourist Board, 1974–84; Yorks and Humberside Develt Assoc., 1974–84; Hon. Sec., London Boroughs Assoc., 1984–90; Dir, Foundn for IT in Local Govt, 1988–92; Member: Action London, 1988–90; Exec., SOLACE, 1981–84, 1987–89; CS Final Selection Bd, 1991–. Vis. Res. Fellow, RIPA, 1989–92. Dir, Dolphin Square Trust, 1987–; Chm., London NE, Royal Jubilee and Prince's Trusts, 1984–91. Associate, Ernst & Young, 1989–90. Editl Advr, Longman Gp, 1989–90. Hon. Fellow, Inst. of Govt Studies, Birmingham Univ. FRSA. Freeman, City of London, 1993. DL Greater London, 1989. National Order of Merit (France), 1984; Nat. Order of Aztec Eagle (Mexico), 1985; Medal of Merit (Qatar), 1985; Order of Merit (Germany), 1986; Legion of Merit (Senegal), 1988. *Publications:* Managing the Enabling Authority, 1989; The Environmental Role of Local Government, 1990; (jtly) City Futures in Britain and Canada, 1990; (jtly) The Public Service Manager's Handbook, 1992; articles on local govt. *Recreations:* skiing, opera, Byzantium. *Address:* Stubham Lodge, Clifford Road, Middleton, Ilkley, West Yorks LS29 0AX. *T:* Ilkley (01943) 601869; 706 Grenville House, Dolphin Square, SW1V 3LR. *T:* 0171–798 8086. *Clubs:* Athenæum, Ski Club of Great Britain.

BROOKE, Roger; *see* Brooke, C. R. E.

BROOKE-LITTLE, John Philip Brooke, CVO 1984 (MVO 1969); Clarenceux King of Arms, since 1995; Norroy and Ulster King of Arms, and King of Arms, Registrar and Knight Attendant on the Most Illustrious Order of St Patrick, 1980–95; Librarian, 1974–94, and Treasurer, 1978–95, College of Arms; *b* 6 April 1927; *s* of late Raymond Brooke-Little, Unicorns House, Swalcliffe; *m* 1960, Mary Lee, *o c* of late John Raymond Pierce; three *s* one *d*. *Educ:* Clayesmore Sch; New Coll., Oxford (MA). Earl Marshal's staff, 1952–53; Gold Staff Officer, Coronation, 1953; Bluemantle Pursuivant of Arms, 1956–67; Richmond Herald, 1967–80; Registrar, Coll. of Arms, 1974–82. Dir, Heralds' Museum, 1991–; Adviser on heraldry: Nat. Trust, 1983–; Shrievalty Assoc., 1983–.

Founder of Heraldry Soc. and Chm., 1947–; Hon. Editor, The Coat of Arms, 1950–; Fellow, Soc. of Genealogists, 1969; Hon. Fellow, Inst. of Heraldic and Genealogical Studies, 1979. Chm., Harleian Soc., 1984–; Pres., English Language Literary Trust, 1985–. Governor Emeritus, Clayesmore Sch. (Chm., 1971–83). Freeman and Liveryman, Scriveners' Co. of London (Master, 1985–86). FSA 1961. KStJ 1975; Knight of Malta, 1955, Knight Grand Cross of Grace and Devotion, Order of Malta, 1974 (Chancellor, British Assoc., 1973–77); Comdr Cross of Merit of Order of Malta, 1964; Cruz Distinguida (1st cl.) de San Raimundo de Peñafort, 1955; Grand Cross of Grace, Constantinian Order of St George, 1975. *Publications:* Royal London, 1953; Pictorial History of Oxford, 1954; Boutell's Heraldry, 1970, 1973, 1978 and 1983 (1963 and 1966 edns with C. W. Scott-Giles); Knights of the Middle Ages, 1966; Prince of Wales, 1969; Fox-Davies' Complete Guide to Heraldry, annotated edn, 1969; (with Don Pottinger and Anne Tauté) Kings and Queens of Great Britain, 1970; An Heraldic Alphabet, 1973; (with Marie Angell) Beasts in Heraldry, 1974; The British Monarchy in Colour, 1976; Royal Arms, Beasts and Badges, 1977; Royal Ceremonies of State, 1979; genealogical and heraldic articles. *Recreations:* cooking, humming. *Address:* Heyford House, Lower Heyford, Bicester, Oxon OX6 3NZ. *T:* Steeple Aston (01869) 340337; College of Arms, EC4V 4BT. *T:* 0171–248 1310. *Club:* Chelsea Arts (Hon. Member).

BROOKE-ROSE, Prof. Christine; novelist and critic; Professor of English Language and Literature, University of Paris, 1975–88 (Lecturer, 1969–75). *Educ:* Oxford and London Univs. MA Oxon 1953, PhD London 1954. Research and criticism, 1955–. Reviewer for: The Times Literary Supplement, The Times, The Observer, The Sunday Times, The Listener, The Spectator, and The London Magazine, 1956–68; took up post at Univ. of Paris VIII, Vincennes, 1969. Has broadcast in book programmes on BBC, and on 'The Critics', and ABC Television. Hon. LittD East Anglia, 1988. Travelling Prize of Society of Authors, 1964; James Tait Black Memorial Prize, 1966; Arts Council Translation Prize, 1969. *Publications: novels:* The Languages of Love, 1957; The Sycamore Tree, 1958; The Dear Deceit, 1960; The Middlemen, 1961; Out, 1964; Such, 1965; Between, 1968; Thru, 1975; Amalgamemnon, 1984; Xorandor, 1986; Verbivore, 1990; Textermination, 1991; *criticism:* A Grammar of Metaphor, 1958; A ZBC of Ezra Pound, 1971; A Rhetoric of the Unreal, 1981; Stories, Theories and Things, 1991; *short stories:* Go when you see the Green Man Walking, 1969; short stories and essays in various magazines, etc. *Recreations:* people, travel. *Address:* c/o Cambridge University Press, PO Box 110, Cambridge CB2 3RL.

BROOKE TURNER, Alan, CMG 1980; HM Diplomatic Service, retired; Director, British Association for Central and Eastern Europe (formerly Great Britain/East Europe Centre), 1987–95; *b* 4 Jan. 1926; *s* of late Arthur Brooke Turner, MC; *m* 1954, Hazel Alexandra Rowan Henderson; two *s* two *d*. *Educ:* Marlborough; Balliol Coll., Oxford (Sen. Schol.). 1st cl Hon. Mods 1949; 1st cl. Lit. Hum. 1951. Served in RAF, 1944–48. Entered HM Foreign (subseq. Diplomatic) Service, 1951; FO, 1951; Warsaw, 1953; 3rd, later 2nd Sec. (Commercial), Jedda, 1954; Lisbon, 1957; 1st Sec., FO, 1959 (UK Delegn to Nuclear Tests Conf., Geneva, 1962); Cultural Attaché, Moscow, 1962; FO, 1965; Fellow, Center for Internat. Affairs, Harvard Univ., 1968; Counsellor, Rio de Janeiro, 1969–71; Head of Southern European Dept, FCO, 1972–73; Counsellor and Head of Chancery, British Embassy, Rome, 1973–76; Civil Dep. Comdt and Dir of Studies, NATO Defense Coll., Rome, 1976–78; Internat. Inst. for Strategic Studies, 1978–79; Minister, Moscow, 1979–82; Ambassador to Finland, 1983–85. Member: Council, Anglican Centre, Rome, 1976–77; Anglican Synod Wkg Gp on Peacemaking, 1986–88; Council, SSEES, 1987–95 (Chm., 1989–92). *Recreations:* sailing, skiing. *Address:* Poultons, Moor Lane, Dormansland, Lingfield, Surrey RH7 6NX; 11 Marsham Court, Marsham Street, SW1P 4JY. *Club:* Travellers'.

BROOKEBOROUGH, 3rd Viscount *cr* 1952, of Colebrooke; **Alan Henry Brooke;** Bt 1822; DL; farmer; *b* 30 June 1952; *s* of 2nd Viscount Brookeborough, PC and of Rosemary Hilda (*née* Chichester); *S* father, 1987; *m* 1980, Janet Elizabeth, *d* of J. P. Cooke, Doagh, Ballyclare. *Educ:* Harrow; Millfield. Commissioned 17th/21st Lancers, 1971; transferred 4th (County Fermanagh) Bn, UDR, 1977; Company Commander, 1981–83; Royal Irish Regt (Co. Comdr, 1988–93); Lt-Col, 1993, transf. to RARO. Now farms and runs an estate with a shooting/fishing tourist enterprise. Mem., EEC Agricl Sub-Cttee, House of Lords, 1988–92, 1993–. Non-exec. Dir, Green Park Unit Hosp. Trust, 1993–. DL 1987, High Sheriff 1995, Co. Fermanagh. *Recreations:* shooting, fishing. *Heir: b* Hon. Christopher Arthur Brooke [*b* 16 May 1954; *m* 1990, Amanda Hodges; one *s*]. *Address:* Colebrooke, Brookeborough, Co. Fermanagh, N Ireland BT94 4DW. *T:* Brookeborough (01365) 531402. *Club:* Cavalry and Guards.

BROOKER, Alan Bernard; JP, DL; FCA; Chairman: Kode International, since 1988; E. T. Heron & Co., since 1991; *b* 24 Aug. 1931; *s* of late Bernard John Brooker and of Gwendoline Ada (*née* Launchbury); *m* 1957, Diana (*née* Coles); one *s* two *d*. *Educ:* Chigwell School, Essex. FCA 1954. Served 2nd RHA (2nd Lieut), 1954–56. Articled, Cole, Dickin & Hills, Chartered Accountants, 1949–54, qualified 1954; Manager, Cole, Dickin & Hills, 1956–58; Accountant, Independent Dairies, 1958–59; Asst Accountant, Exchange Telegraph Co., 1959–64; Dir, 1964–87, Chm. and Chief Exec., 1980–87, Extel Group. Chm., Serif Cowells, then Serif, 1990–93; Vice-Chairman: Provident Financial, 1983–94; James Martin Associates, 1987–89; Non-exec. Director: Pauls plc, 1984–85; Aukett Associates, 1988–; Plysu, 1988–; PNA Holdings, 1988–89; Addison Worldwide, 1990–94; East Anglian Daily Times, 1990–. Member: Council, CBI London Region, 1980–83; Companies Cttee, CBI, 1979–83; Council, CPU, 1975–88. Appeal Chm., Newspaper Press Fund, 1985–86. Governor: Chigwell School, 1968– (Chm., 1978–); Felixstowe Coll., 1986–94. Freeman, City of London; Liveryman, Stationers and Newspapermakers' Co. (Court Asst, 1985–; Master, 1995–July 1996). Churchwarden, St Bride's, Fleet Street, 1986–. JP Essex 1972, DL Essex 1982. FInstD; FRSA 1980. *Recreations:* cricket, golf. *Address:* Plowlands, Laundry Lane, Little Easton, Dunmow, Essex CM6 2JW. *Clubs:* East India, MCC; Royal Worlington and Newmarket Golf.

BROOKES, family name of **Baron Brookes.**

BROOKES, Baron *cr* 1975 (Life Peer), of West Bromwich; **Raymond Percival Brookes,** Kt 1971; Life President, GKN plc (formerly Guest, Keen & Nettlefolds Ltd) (Group Chairman and Chief Executive, 1965–74); *b* 10 April 1909; *s* of William and Ursula Brookes; *m* 1937, Florence Edna Sharman; one *s*. Part-time Mem., BSC, 1967–68. First Pres., British Mechanical Engrg Confedn, 1968–70; a Vice-Pres., Engrg Employers' Fedn, 1967–75. Member: Council, UK S Africa Trade Assoc. Ltd, 1967–74; Council, CBI, 1968–75; BNEC, 1969–71; Wilberforce Ct of Inquiry into electricity supply industry dispute, Jan. 1971; Industrial Develt Adv. Bd, 1972–75. Member: Exec. Cttee, 1970–, Council, 1969–, Pres., 1974–75, Soc. of Motor Manufacturers & Traders Ltd; Court of Governors, Univ. of Birmingham, 1966–75; Council, Univ. of Birmingham, 1968–75. Pres., Motor Ind. Res. Assoc., 1973–75. Chm., Rea Bros (IoM) Ltd, 1976–89; Director: Plessey Co. Ltd, 1974–89; AMF Inc., 1975–78. *Recreations:* golf, fly-fishing. *Address:* GKN plc, PO Box 55, Redditch, Worcs B98 0TL; (private) Mallards, Santon, Isle of Man.

BROOKES, Beata; *b* 1931. *Educ:* Lowther College, Abergele; Univ. of Wales, Bangor; studied politics in USA (US State Dept Scholarship). Former social worker, Denbighshire CC; company secretary and farmer. Contested (C) Widnes, 1955, Warrington, 1963, Manchester Exchange, 1964. Contested (C) N Wales, European Parly Elecn, 1989. MEP (C) N Wales, 1979–89; Mem., Educn and Agricl Cttees. Member: Clwyd AHA, 1973–80 (Mem., Welsh Hosp. Bd, 1963–74); Clwyd Family Practitioner Cttee; Clwyd CC Social Services Cttee, 1973–81; Flintshire Soc. for Mentally Handicapped; N Wales Council for Mentally Handicapped; Council for Professions Supplementary to Medicine; Exec. Cttee, N Wales Cons. Group. Pres., N Wales Assoc. for the Disabled. *Address:* The Cottage, Wayside Acres, Bodelwyddan, near Rhyl, North Wales.

BROOKES, James Robert; Director, Information Services Organisation, Portsmouth University, since 1992; *b* 2 Sept. 1941; *s* of James Brookes and Hettie Brookes (*née* Colley); *m* 1964, Patricia Gaskell; three *d*. *Educ:* Manchester Grammar Sch.; Corpus Christi Coll., Oxford (MA Maths). FBCS; CEng 1990; Eur Ing, 1991. Various posts as systems and applications programmer in develt, tech. support and sales; Northern Branch Manager, Univs and Nat. Research Region, Ferranti/Internat. Computers, 1962–67; Computer Services Manager, Queen's Univ. Belfast, 1967–69; Operations Manager, Univ. of Manchester Regional Computer Centre, 1969–75; Director: SW Univs Regional Computer Centre, 1975–87; Bath Univ. Computer Service, 1983–87; Co-founder and non-exec Chm., Praxis Systems, 1983; Chief Exec., 1986–91, Consultant, 1991–92, BCS. Vis. Prof., Business Sch., Strathclyde Univ., 1991. Mem. Council, PITCOM; Hon. Sec., Council of European Professional Information Socs, 1991–93. FRSA 1988. Freeman, City of London, 1989; Liveryman, Information Technologists' Co. (Mem., 1988). *Recreations:* sailing, fellwalking, cycling, bridge, squash, badminton. *Address:* 29 High Street, Marshfield, Chippenham, Wilts SN14 8LR. *T:* (home) Bath (01225) 891294; (office) Portsmouth (01705) 843398. *Club:* United Oxford & Cambridge University.

BROOKES, John; landscape designer; *b* 11 Oct. 1933; *s* of Edward Percy Brookes and Margaret Alexandra Brookes. *Educ:* Durham; Dip. Landscape, UCL. Asst to Brenda Colvin, 1957, to Dame Sylvia Crowe, 1958–61; private practice, 1964–; Director: Inchbald Sch. of Garden Design, 1970–78; Inchbald Sch. of Interior Design, Tehran, 1978–80; founded Clock House Sch. of Garden Design, Sussex, 1980; gardening corresp., Evening Standard, 1988–89; Principal Lectr, Kew Sch. of Garden Design, 1990–93. Design workshops and lectures, UK and overseas, incl. annually at Henry Clewes Foundn, La Napoule; design and construction of gardens, and consultancies, UK, Europe, Japan, USA. *Publications:* Room Outside, 1969; Gardens for Small Spaces, 1970; Garden Design and Layout, 1970; Living in the Garden, 1971; Financial Times Book of Garden Design, 1975; Improve Your Lot, 1977; The Small Garden, 1977; The Garden Book, 1984; A Place in the Country, 1984; The Indoor Garden Book, 1986; Gardens of Paradise, 1987; The Country Garden, 1987; The New Small Garden Book, 1989; Garden Design Book, 1991. *Recreations:* reading, pottering, entertaining. *Address:* Clock House, Denmans, Fontwell, near Arundel, West Sussex BN18 0SU. *T:* Eastergate (01243) 542808; *Fax:* (01243) 544064.

BROOKES, Peter C.; *see* Cannon-Brookes, P.

BROOKES, Peter Derek; Political Cartoonist, The Times, since 1993; Cover Artist, The Spectator, since 1986; *b* 28 Sept. 1943; *s* of George Henry Brookes and Joan Elizabeth Brookes; *m* 1971, Angela Harrison; two *s*. *Educ:* Heversham Grammar Sch., Westmorland; RAF Coll., Cranwell (BA London Ext.); Central School of Art and Design (BA). Freelance illustrator, 1969–; contributor to: The Times, Sunday Times, Radio Times, New Statesman, The Listener, Spectator, TLS and Glyndebourne Fest. Opera Books. Illustration Tutor: Central Sch. of Art and Design, 1977–79; RCA, 1979–89. Mem., AGI, 1988–. *Recreations:* music (particularly opera), drawing, reading, football, arguing. *Address:* 30 Vanbrugh Hill, Blackheath, SE3 7UF. *T:* 0181–858 9022.

BROOKES, Sir Wilfred (Deakin), Kt 1979; CBE 1972; DSO 1944; AEA 1945; *b* 17 April 1906; *s* of Herbert Robinson Brookes and Ivy Deakin; *m* 1928, Betty (*d* 1968), *d* of A. H. Heal; one *s*. *Educ:* Melbourne Grammar Sch.; Melbourne Univ. Exec., later Alternate Dir, Aust. Paper Manufacturers Ltd, 1924–38; Exec. Dir, Box and Container Syndicate, 1938–39. War Service, 1939–45: Sqdn Officer, RAAF, 1939–41 (despatches); CO 24 Sqdn, 1942 (despatches); CO 22 Sqdn, 1942; CO 7 Fighter Section HQ; Comdr, 78th Fighter Wing, New Guinea Offensive, 1943–45; Dir of Postings, RAAF HQ, rank of Gp Captain, 1945. Chairman (retired): Associated Pulp and Paper Mills, 1952–78 (Dir, 1945–78); Colonial Mutual Life Soc., 1965–78 (Dir, 1955–78); Electrolytic Refining & Smelting Co. of Australia Ltd, 1956–80; Apsonor Pty Ltd, to 1983 (Dir, 1960–83); Collins Wales Pty Ltd, 1978–82 (Dir, 1974–82); Director (retired): BH South Group, 1956–82; North Broken Hill, 1970–82; Alcoa of Australia, 1961–83. Past Pres., Inst. of Public Affairs; Chm., Edward Wilson Charitable Trust (Trustee, 1960–); Patron, Deakin Foundn, 1988–. Hon. Dr of Letters Deakin, 1982. Dep. Chm., Corps of Commissionaires, 1979–88 (Governor, 1975–90). *Recreations:* swimming, walking. *Address:* 20 Heyington Place, Toorak, Vic 3142, Australia. *T:* (3) 98224553. *Clubs:* Melbourne, Australian (Melbourne).

BROOKING, Maj.-Gen. Patrick Guy, CB 1988; MBE 1975; Chief Executive, Worldwide Subsidiaries, KRONE AG (Berlin), since 1990; *b* 4 April 1937; *s* of late Captain C. A. H. Brooking, CBE, RN, and G. M. J. White (*née* Coleridge); *m* 1964, Pamela Mary Walford; one *s* one *d*. *Educ:* Charterhouse Sch. Dip. (French Lang.); Alliance Française, Paris, 1955. Commnd 5th Royal Inniskilling Dragoon Guards, 1956; early career served in England, W Germany, NI, Cyprus, with UN; sc 1969; Mil. Asst to Comdr 1st British Corps, 1970–71; Bde Major 39 Bde, Belfast, 1974–75; comd his regt, 1975–77; Instr Army Staff Coll., 1978; RCDS 1981; Comdr 33 Armd Bde, Paderborn Garrison, 1982–83; Commandant and GOC Berlin (British Sector), 1985–89; Dir Gen., Army Manning and Recruiting, 1989–90, retd. *Recreations:* ski-ing, tennis, golf, music (esp. choral singing). *Address:* c/o National Westminster Bank, 26 Haymarket, SW1Y 4ER. *Club:* Cavalry and Guards.

BROOKING, Trevor David, MBE 1981; football broadcaster, since 1984; *b* 2 Oct. 1948; *s* of Henry and Margaret Brooking; *m* 1970, Hilkka Helina Helakorpi; one *s* one *d*. *Educ:* Ilford County High Sch. Professional footballer with West Ham United, 1965–84: played 642 games; scored 111 goals; FA Cup winner, 1975, *v* Fulham, 1980, *v* Arsenal (scoring only goal); won Football League Div. 2, 1980–81; 47 appearances for England, 1974–82. Chm., Eastern Council for Sport and Recreation, 1986–; Mem., Sports Council for England (formerly Sports Council), 1989– (Vice-Chm., 1994–). *Publications:* Trevor Brooking (autobiog.), 1981; Trevor Brooking's 100 Great British Footballers, 1988. *Recreations:* golf, tennis.

BROOKMAN, (David) Keith; General Secretary, Iron and Steel Trades Confederation, since 1993; *b* 3 Jan. 1937; *s* of George Henry Brookman, MM and Blodwin Brookman (*née* Nash); *m* 1958, Patricia Worthington; three *d*. *Educ:* Nantyglo Grammar Sch., Gwent. Nat. Service, RAF, 1955–57. Crane driver, Richard Thomas & Baldwin, Ebbw Vale, 1953–55 and 1957–73; Iron & Steel Trades Confederation: Organiser, 1973–85; Asst Gen. Sec., 1985–93. Trades Union Congress: Member: Educn Adv. Cttee for Wales, 1976–82; Steel Cttee, 1985–90; Gen. Council, 1992–. Member: Brit. Steel Jt Accident Prevention Adv. Cttee, 1985–93; Brit. Steel Adv. Cttee on Educn and Trng, 1986–93; Nat. Steel Co-ordinating Cttee, 1991– (Chm., 1993–); Consultative Cttee, ECSC, 1993–;

Operatives' Secretary: Jt Ind. Council for Slag Ind., 1985–93; Brit. Steel Gen. Steels Jt Standing Cttee, 1993–; Brit. Steel Strip Trade Bd, 1993–; Mem. Bd, Brit. Steel (Ind.) Ltd, 1993–. Member Executive Council: European Metalworkers' Fedn, 1985– (Mem., Steel Cttee, 1994–); CSEU, 1989–; International Metalworkers' Federation: Hon. Sec., Brit. Section, 1993–; Pres., Iron and Steel and Non-Ferrous Metals Dept, 1993–. Labour Party: Member: Exec. Cttee, Wales, 1982–85; Nat. Constitutional Cttee, 1987–91; NEC, 1991–92. Trustee, Julian Melchett Trust, 1985–. Gov., Gwent Coll. of HE, 1980–84. *Recreations:* cricket, Rugby, reading, keep fit, golf. *Address:* Iron and Steel Trades Confederation, Swinton House, 324 Gray's Inn Road, WC1X 8DD. *T:* 0171–837 6691; 4 Bassett Close, Redbourn, Herts AL3 5JY. *T:* Redbourn (01582) 792066.

BROOKNER, Dr Anita, CBE 1990; Reader, Courtauld Institute of Art, 1977–88; *o c* of Newson and Maude Brookner. *Educ:* James Allen's Girls' Sch.; King's Coll., Univ. of London (FKC 1990); Courtauld Inst.; Paris. Vis. Lectr, Univ. of Reading, 1959–64; Slade Professor, Univ. of Cambridge, 1967–68; Lectr, Courtauld Inst. of Art, 1964. Fellow, New Hall, Cambridge. *Publications:* Watteau, 1968; The Genius of the Future, 1971; Greuze: the rise and fall of an Eighteenth Century Phenomenon, 1972; Jacques-Louis David, 1980; (ed) The Stories of Edith Wharton, Vol. 1, 1988, Vol. 2, 1989; *novels:* A Start in Life, 1981; Providence, 1982; Look at Me, 1983; Hotel du Lac, 1984 (Booker McConnell Prize; filmed for TV, 1986); Family and Friends, 1985; A Misalliance, 1986; A Friend from England, 1987; Latecomers, 1988; Lewis Percy, 1989; Brief Lives, 1990; A Closed Eye, 1991; Fraud, 1992; A Family Romance, 1993; A Private View, 1994; Incidents in the Rue Laugier, 1995; articles in Burlington Magazine, etc. *Address:* 68 Elm Park Gardens, SW10 9PB. *T:* 0171–352 6894.

BROOKS, family name of **Barons Brooks of Tremorfa** and **Crawshaw.**

BROOKS OF TREMORFA, Baron *cr* 1979 (Life Peer), of Tremorfa in the County of South Glamorgan; **John Edward Brooks,** DL; *b* 12 April 1927; *s* of Edward George Brooks and Rachel Brooks (*née* White); *m* 1948 (marr. diss. 1956); one *s* one *d*; *m* 1958, Margaret Pringle; two *s*. *Educ:* elementary schools; Coleg Harlech. Secretary, Cardiff South East Labour Party, 1966–84; Member, South Glamorgan CC, 1973–93 (Leader, 1973–77, 1986–92; Chm., 1981–82). Contested (Lab) Barry, Feb. and Oct. 1974; Parliamentary Agent to Rt Hon. James Callaghan, MP, Gen. Elections, 1970, 1979. Chm., Labour Party, Wales, 1978–79. Opposition defence spokesman, 1980–81. Steward, British Boxing Bd of Control, 1986–. DL S Glam, 1994. *Recreations:* reading, most sports. *Address:* 46 Kennerleigh Road, Rumney, Cardiff, S Glam CF3 9BJ.

BROOKS, Alan; Group Managing Director, BPB Gypsum Industries (formerly Gypsum Products, BPB Industries), since 1988; *b* 30 Dec. 1935; *s* of Charles and Annie Brooks; *m* 1959, Marie Curtis; one *s* two *d*. *Educ:* Leeds Univ. (BSc 1st Cl. Mining Engineering; 1st Cl. Cert. of Competency, Mines and Quarries). Asst Mine Manager, Winsford Salt Mine, ICI, 1961–66; British Gypsum: Dep. Mines Agent, 1966–71; Dir, Midland Region, 1971–74; Production Dir, 1974–77; Dep. Man. Dir, 1977–85; Man. Dir, 1985–88; Chairman: British Gypsum, 1988–; Westroc Industries, Canada, 1988–; Inveryeso, Spain, 1991. *Recreation:* fell walking. *Address:* Langley Park House, Uxbridge Road, Slough SL3 6DU. *T:* Slough (01753) 573273.

BROOKS, Diana D., (Dede); President and Chief Executive Officer: Sotheby's Holdings Inc., since 1994 (also Director); Sotheby's North and South America, since 1990; *m* Michael C. Brooks; one *s* one *d*. *Educ:* Miss Porter's Sch., Farmington; Yale Univ. (BA Amer. Studies, 1973). Lending officer, Nat. Banking Gp, Citibank, 1973–79; joined Sotheby's New York, 1979; Sotheby's North America: Sen. Vice Pres. and Chief Financial and Admin. Officer, 1982; Exec. Vice Pres., 1984; Chief Operating Officer, 1985; Pres., 1987; Chief Exec. Officer, 1990. Bd Mem., NY City Partnership; Advr to Bd, Old Westbury Gardens; Pres., Council of Associates, Frick Art Ref. Liby, NY. Trustee: Yale Univ.; Deerfield Acad., Mass; Allen-Stevenson Sch., NY. *Address:* (office) 34–35 New Bond Street, W1A 2AA. *T:* 0171–408 5263, *Fax:* 0171–408 5065.

BROOKS, Douglas; Consultant, Douglas Brooks Associates, since 1992; *b* 3 Sept. 1928; *s* of Oliver Brooks and Olive Brooks; *m* 1952, June Anne (*née* Branch); one *s* one *d*. *Educ:* Newbridge Grammar Sch.; University Coll., Cardiff (Dip. Soc. Sc.). CIPM. Girling Ltd: factory operative, 1951–53; Employment Officer, 1953–56; Hoover Ltd: Personnel Off., 1956–60; Sen. Personnel Off., 1960–63; Dep. Personnel Man., 1963–66; Indust. Relations Advr, 1966–69; Gp Personnel Man., 1969–73; Personnel Dir, 1973–78; Group Personnel Manager, Tarmac Ltd, 1979–80; Director: Walker Brooks and Partners Ltd, 1980–91; Flexello Castors & Wheels plc, 1987–91. Member: Council, SSRC, later ESRC, 1976–82; BBC Consultative Gp on social effects of television, 1978–80; Hon. Soc. Cymmrodorion, 1981– (Mem. Council, 1992–). Vis. Fellow, PSI, 1982–84. Vice-Pres., IPM, 1972–74. Chm., Wooburn Fest. Soc. Ltd, 1978–86. *Publications:* (with M. Fogarty) Trade Unions and British Industrial Development, 1986; various articles in professional jls. *Recreations:* talking, music, reading, gardening, cooking. *Address:* Old Court, Winforton, Hereford HR3 6EA. *T:* Eardisley (01544) 328425. *Club:* Reform.

BROOKS, Edwin, PhD; FAIM, FCIM; Director and Deputy Chairman, Riverina District Health Service, since 1994; Director, Wagga Wagga Base Hospital, since 1989 (Deputy Chairman, 1989–93); *b* Barry, Glamorgan, 1 Dec. 1929; *s* of Edwin Brooks and Agnes Elizabeth (*née* Campbell); *m* 1956, Winifred Hazel Soundie; four *s* one *d*. *Educ:* Barry Grammar Sch.; St John's Coll., Cambridge. PhD (Camb) 1958. National Service, Singapore, 1948–49. MP (Lab) Bebington, 1966–70. Univ. of Liverpool: Lectr, Dept of Geography, 1954–66 and 1970–72; Sen. Lectr, 1972–77; Dean, College Studies, 1975–77; Riverina College of Advanced Education, later Riverina-Murray Institute of Higher Education, then Charles Sturt University: Dean of Business and Liberal Studies, 1977–82; Dean of Commerce, 1982–88; Dir, Albury-Wodonga Campus, 1982; Dep. Principal, 1988–89; Dean Emeritus, 1990. Councillor, Birkenhead, 1958–67. Mem., Courses Cttee, Higher Educn Bd of NSW, 1978–82; Dir, Australian Business Educn Council, 1986–89. Pres., Wagga Wagga Chamber of Commerce, 1988–90. FAIM 1983; FCIM 1989. *Publications:* This Crowded Kingdom, 1973; (ed) Tribes of the Amazon Basin in Brazil, 1973. *Recreations:* gardening, listening to music, computing. *Address:* Inchnadamph, Gregadoo Road, Wagga Wagga, NSW 2650, Australia. *T:* (69) 226798.

BROOKS, Eric Arthur Swatton, MA; Head of Claims Department, Foreign Office, 1960 until retirement, 1967; *b* 9 Oct. 1907; *yr s* of late A. E. Brooks, MA, Maidenhead; *m* 1947, Daphne Joyce, *yr d* of late George McMullan, MD, FRCSE, Wallingford; one *s* one *d*. *Educ:* Reading Sch.; New Coll., Oxford (MA). 2nd cl. hons Jurisprudence, 1929. Solicitor, 1932; practised in London, 1932–39. Mem. Law Soc., 1934– (Mem. Overseas Relations Cttee, 1949–). Served War of 1939–45 in Admty and Min. of Aircraft Production, and in Operational Research as Hon. Ft-Lieut RAFVR until 1944; Disposal of Govt Factories of Min. of Aircraft Production, 1944–Dec. 1945. Foreign Office, 1946–. Served on Brit. Delegns in negotiations with: Polish and Hungarian Governments, 1953, 1954; Bulgarian Government, 1955; Rumanian Government, 1955, 1956, 1960; USSR, 1964, 1965, 1966, 1967. British Representative on Anglo-Italian Conciliation Commn, until 1967. Councillor: Borough of Maidenhead, 1972–74; Royal Borough of Windsor and Maidenhead, 1973–87. Pres., Maidenhead Civic Soc., 1989–94. *Publications:* The Foreign Office Claims Manual, 1968; Maidenhead and its Name, 1985; Earlier Days of Maidenhead Golf Club, 1985; articles in legal jls, and on local history, local education, town planning, and flood prevention. *Recreations:* golf (Oxford Univ. team *v* Cambridge Univ., 1929; various later Amateur European Championships); gardening. *Address:* Kitoha, 116b Grenfell Road, Maidenhead, Berks SL6 1HB. *T:* Maidenhead (01628) 21621.

BROOKS, Most Rev. Francis Gerard; *see* Dromore, Bishop of, (RC).

BROOKS, John Ashton, CBE 1989; FCIB; Director: Midland Bank plc, 1981–91; Hongkong and Shanghai Banking Corp., 1989–91; Thomas Cook Group Ltd, since 1983 (Chairman, 1988–93); *b* 24 Oct. 1928; *s* of Victor Brooks and Annie (*née* Ashton); *m* 1959, Sheila (*née* Hulse); one *s* one *d*. *Educ:* Merchant Taylors' Sch., Northwood. Joined Midland Bank, 1949; Manager: 22 Victoria Street Br., 1970; Threadneedle Street Br., 1972; Gen. Man., Computer Operations, 1975; Dep. Gp Chief Exec., Midland Group, 1981–89. President: Chartered Inst. of Bankers, 1987–89; Assoc. of Banking Teachers, 1990–. Trustee, Charities Aid Foundn, 1990–; Dir and Chm., Charities Aid Foundn Money Management Ltd, 1993–. *Recreations:* reading, walking. *Clubs:* Overseas Bankers', Institute of Directors.

BROOKS, Leslie James, CEng, FRINA; RCNC; Deputy Director of Engineering (Constructive), Ship Department, Ministry of Defence (Procurement Executive), 1973–76, retired; *b* 3 Aug. 1916; *yr s* of late C. J. D. Brooks and Lucy A. Brooks, Milton Regis, Sittingbourne, Kent; *m* 1941, Ruth Elizabeth Olver, Saltash, Cornwall; two *s*. *Educ:* Borden Grammar Sch., Sittingbourne, Kent; HM Dockyard Schs, Sheerness and Chatham; Royal Naval Engrg Coll., Keyham; RNC, Greenwich. War of 1939–45: Asst Constructor, Naval Construction Dept, Admty, Bath, 1941–44; Constr Lt-Comdr on Staff of Allied Naval Comdr, Exped. Force, and Flag Officer, Brit. Assault Area, 1944. Constr in charge Welding, Naval Constrn Dept, Admty, Bath, 1945–47; Constr Comdr, Staff of Comdr-in-Chief, Brit. Pacific Fleet, 1947–49; Constr in charge, No 2 Ship Tank, Admty Experiment Works, Haslar, Gosport, 1949–54. Naval Constrn Dept, Admty, Bath: Constr, Merchant Shipping Liaison, 1954–56; Chief Constr in charge of Conversion of First Commando Ships, and of Operating Aircraft Carriers, 1956–62; Dep. Supt, Admty Exper. Works, Haslar, 1962–64; Senior Officers War Course, RNC Greenwich, 1964–65; Ship Dept, Bath: Asst Dir of Naval Constrn, Naval Constrn Div., MoD(N), 1965–68; Asst Dir of Engrg (Ships), MoD(PE), 1968–73; Dep. Dir of Engrg/Constr., MoD(PE), 1973. Mem., Royal Corps of Naval Constructors. *Recreations:* walking, photography, natural history. *Address:* Merrymeet, Perrymead, Bath BA2 5AY. *T:* Bath (01225) 832856.

BROOKS, Mel; writer, director, actor; *b* Brooklyn, 1926; *m* Florence Baum; two *s* one *d*; *m* 1964, Anne Bancroft; one *s*. TV script writer for series: Your Show of Shows, 1950–54; Caesar's Hour, 1954–57; Get Smart, 1965. Films: (cartoon) The Critic (Academy Award), 1963; writer and director: The Producers (Academy Award), 1968; Young Frankenstein, 1974; writer, director and actor: The Twelve Chairs, 1970; Blazing Saddles, 1974; Silent Movie, 1976; writer, director, actor and producer: High Anxiety, 1977; History of the World Part 1, 1981; Spaceballs, 1987; writer, director and producer: Robin Hood: men in tights, 1993; actor, producer: To Be Or Not To Be, 1983; actor, director and producer: Life Stinks, 1991. Film productions include The Elephant Man, 1980. Several album recordings. *Address:* c/o Twentieth Century-Fox Film Corporation, Box 900, Beverly Hills, CA 90213, USA.

BROOKS, Prof. Nicholas Peter, DPhil; FSA, FRHistS; FBA 1989; Professor and Head of Department of Medieval History, University of Birmingham, since 1985; *b* 14 Jan. 1941; *s* of late W. D. W. Brooks, CBE; *m* 1967, Chloë Carolyn Willis; one *s* one *d*. *Educ:* Winchester Coll.; Magdalen Coll., Oxford (Demy; MA DPhil). FRHistS 1970; FSAScot 1970–85; FSA 1974. Lectr in Medieval Hist., 1964–78, Sen. Lectr, 1978–85, St Andrews Univ.; Birmingham University: Chm., Sch. of History, 1987–89; Chm., Jun. Year Abroad prog., 1988–; Dean, Faculty of Arts, 1992–. Chm., British Acad./RHistS Anglo-Saxon Charters Project, 1991–. Gen. Ed., Studies in the Early Hist. of Britain, 1978–. *Publications:* (ed) Latin and the Vernacular Languages in Early Medieval Britain, 1981; The Early History of the Church of Canterbury, 1984; numerous articles in festschriften, Medieval Archaeology, Anglo-Saxon England, Trans of RHistS, etc. *Recreations:* gardening, bridge, swimming, walking. *Address:* School of History, University of Birmingham, Edgbaston, Birmingham B15 2TT. *T:* 0121–414 5736.

BROOKS, Timothy Gerald Martin; JP; farmer; Lord-Lieutenant of Leicestershire, since 1989; *b* 20 March 1929; *s* of late Hon. Herbert William Brooks, *s* of 2nd Baron Crawshaw, and of Hilda Muriel (*née* Steel); *m* 1951, Hon. Ann Fremantle, *d* of Baron Cottesloe, GBE, TD and late Lady Elizabeth Harris; three *s* two *d*. *Educ:* Eton; RAC, Cirencester (NDA). Set up farm and market garden, Wistow, 1953; now farms 1100 acres; Director: Wistow Hall Gardens Ltd; Thomas Tapling & Co. Ltd. Mem., Harborough DC, 1975–89 (Chm., 1983–84). Chairman of Governors: Brooksby Agricl Coll., 1986–89; Wyggeston's Hosp., Leicester, 1988–. Churchwarden, St Wistan's, Wistow. JP 1960, High Sheriff, 1979–80, Leics. *Recreations:* arts, shooting, tennis. *Address:* Wistow Hall, near Great Glen, Leicester LE8 0QF.

BROOKSBANK, Sir (Edward) Nicholas, 3rd Bt *cr* 1919; with Christie's, since 1974; *b* 4 Oct. 1944; *s* of Sir Edward William Brooksbank, 2nd Bt, TD, and of Ann, 2nd *d* of Col T. Clitherow; *S* father, 1983; *m* 1970, Emma, *d* of Baron Holderness, *qv*; one *s* one *d*. *Educ:* Eton. Royal Dragoons, 1963–69; Blues and Royals, 1969–73; Adjutant, 1971–73. *Heir:* *s* (Florian) Tom (Charles) Brooksbank, *b* 9 Aug. 1982. *Address:* Ryton Grange, Malton, North Yorks.

BROOKSBANK, Sir Nicholas; *see* Brooksbank, Sir E. N.

BROOKSBY, John Burns, CBE 1973; FRS 1980; Director, Animal Virus Research Institute, Pirbright, 1964–79; *b* 25 Dec. 1914; *s* of George B. Brooksby, Glasgow; *m* 1940, Muriel Weir; one *s* one *d*. *Educ:* Hyndland Sch., Glasgow; Glasgow Veterinary Coll.; London University. MRCVS 1935; FRCVS 1978; BSc (VetSc) 1936; PhD 1947; DSc 1957; FRSE 1968; Hon. DSc Edinburgh, 1981. Research Officer, Pirbright, 1939; Dep. Dir, 1957; Dir, 1964. *Publications:* papers on virus diseases of animals in scientific jls. *Address:* The Burlings, 48 High Street, Swaffham Bulbeck, Cambridge CB5 0LX. *T:* Cambridge (01223) 812607.

BROOM, Prof. Donald Maurice; Colleen Macleod Professor of Animal Welfare, since 1986, Fellow, St Catharine's College, since 1987, University of Cambridge; *b* 14 July 1942; *s* of late Donald Edward Broom and of Mavis Edith Rose Broom; *m* 1971, Sally Elizabeth Mary Riordan; three *s*. *Educ:* Whitgift Sch.; St Catharine's Coll., Cambridge (MA, PhD); FIBiol 1986. Lectr, 1967, Sen. Lectr, 1979, Reader, 1982, Dept of Pure and Applied Zoology, Univ. of Reading. Vis. Asst Prof., Univ. of California, Berkeley, 1969; Vis. Lectr, Univ. of W Indies, Trinidad, 1972; Vis. Scientist, CSIRO Div. of Animal Prodn, Perth, WA, 1983. Invited Expert: EEC Farm Animal Welfare Expert Gp, 1981–89; Council of Europe Standing Cttee of Eur. Convention for Protection of Animals kept for Farming Purposes, 1987–; Chm., EU Scientific Veterinary Cttee on Animal Welfare, 1990–. Hon. Res. Associate, BBSRC Inst. of Grassland and Envmtl Res. (formerly AFRC Inst. for Grassland and Animal Production), 1985–. Member: Council, Assoc. for Study of

Animal Behaviour, 1980–83 (Hon. Treas., 1971–80); Internat. Ethological Cttee, 1976–79; Council, Soc. for Vet. Ethology, 1981–84 (Vice-Pres., 1986–87, 1989–91; Pres., 1987–89); NERC Special Cttee on Seals, 1986–; Farm Animal Welfare Council, 1991–; BSI Panel on ISO Animal (Mammal) Traps, 1993–; co-opted Mem. Adv. Council, RSPCA, 1993–. Trustee, Farm Animal Care Trust, 1986–. George Fleming Prize, British Vet. Jl, 1990. *Publications:* Birds and their Behaviour, 1977; Biology of Behaviour, 1981; (ed jtly) The Encyclopaedia of Domestic Animals, 1986; (ed) Farmed Animals, 1986; (with A. F. Fraser) Farm Animal Behaviour and Welfare, 1990; (with K. G. Johnson) Stress and Animal Welfare, 1993; numerous papers in behaviour, psychol, zool, ornithol, agricl and vet. jls. *Recreations:* squash, water-polo, modern pentathlon, ornithology. *Address:* Department of Clinical Veterinary Medicine, Madingley Road, Cambridge CB3 0ES. *T:* Cambridge (01223) 337697. *Club:* Hawks (Cambridge).

BROOM, Air Marshal Sir Ivor (Gordon), KCB 1975 (CB 1972); CBE 1969; DSO 1945; DFC 1942 (Bar to DFC 1944, 2nd Bar 1945); AFC 1956; international aerospace consultant, since 1977; Chairman: Gatwick Handling Ltd, 1982–93; Farnborough Aerospace Development Corporation, 1985–92; *b* Cardiff, 2 June 1920; *s* of Alfred Godfrey Broom and Janet Broom; *m* 1942, Jess Irene Broom (*née* Cooper); two *s* one *d.* *Educ:* West Monmouth Grammar Sch.; Pontypridd County Sch., Glam. Joined RAF, 1940; commissioned, 1941; 114 Sqdn, 107 Sqdn, 1941; CFS Course, 1942; Instructor on: 1655 Mosquito Trg Unit; 571 Sqdn, 128 Sqdn; commanded 163 Sqdn, 1943–45; HQ, ACSEA, 1945–46; commanded 28 (FR) Sqdn, 1946–48; RAF Staff Coll. Course, Bracknell, 1949; Sqdn Comdr, No 1 ITS, 1950–52; No 3 Flying Coll. Course, Manby, 1952–53; commanded 57 Sqdn, 1953–54; Syndicate Leader, Flying Coll., Manby, 1954–56; commanded Bomber Command Development Unit, Wittering, 1956–59; Air Secretary's Dept, 1959–62; commanded RAF Bruggen, 1962–64; IDC, 1965–66; Dir of Organisation (Establishments), 1966–68; Commandant, Central Flying School, 1968–70; AOC No 11 (Fighter) Gp, Strike Comd, 1970–72. Dep. Controller, 1972–74, Controller, 1974–77, Nat. Air Traffic Services; Mem., CAA Bd, 1974–77. Dir, Plessey Airports Ltd, 1982–86. Pres., Mosquito Aircrew Assoc., 1993–. Vice-Pres., RAFA, 1981–. President: Pathfinder Assoc., 1990–93; Blenheim Soc., 1990–. *Recreations:* golf, skiing. *Address:* Cherry Lawn, Bridle Lane, Loudwater, Rickmansworth, Herts WD3 4JB. *Clubs:* Royal Air Force; Moor Park Golf (Pres., 1993–).

BROOME, David, CBE 1995 (OBE 1970); farmer; British professional show jumper; *b* Cardiff, 1 March 1940; *s* of Fred and Amelia Broome, Chepstow, Gwent; *m* 1976, Elizabeth, *d* of K. W. Fletcher, Thirsk, N Yorkshire; three *s.* *Educ:* Monmouth Grammar Sch. for Boys. European Show Jumping Champion (3 times); World Show Jumping Champion, La Baule, 1970; Olympic Medallist (Bronze) twice, 1960, 1968; King George V Gold Cup 6 times (a record, in 1990). Mounts include: Sunsalve, Aachen, 1961; Mr Softee, Rotterdam, 1967, and Hickstead, 1969; Beethoven, La Baule, France, 1970, as (1st British) World Champion; Sportsman and Philco, Cardiff, 1974; Professional Champion of the World. *Publications:* Jump-Off, 1971; (with S. Hadley) Horsemanship, 1983. *Recreations:* hunting (MFH), shooting, golf. *Address:* Mount Ballan Manor, Crick, Chepstow, Gwent, Wales NP6 4XP. *T:* Caldicot (01291) 420778.

BROOME, John Lawson, CBE 1987; Founder and Chairman, Alton Towers Theme Park, since 1980 (Chief Executive, 1980–90); *b* 2 Aug. 1943; *s* of late Albert Henry and Mary Elizabeth Broome; *m* 1972, Jane Myott Bagshaw; one *s* two *d.* *Educ:* Rosall School. School master, 1960–65; Dir, JLB Investment Property Group, 1961–, and numerous other companies; Chief Exec., Carden Park Country Pursuits Resort, Cheshire, 1978–. Member: ETB and BTA, 1982–92; Internat. Assoc. of Amusement Parks and Attractions, USA, 1986–89 (Chm., Internat. Cttee; Chm., Internat. Council, 1986–89). Vice-Pres., Ironbridge Gorge Museum Trust. Governor, Staffordshire Univ. *Recreations:* ski-ing, travelling, antiques, old paintings, objects d'art, fine gardens. *Address:* Huntsmans House, Carden Park, Broxton, Cheshire CH3 9EP. *T:* (office) Tarparley (01829) 782135. *Clubs:* Grosvenor (Chester); Eaton Golf, Deeside Ramblers Hockey.

BROOMFIELD, Alexander Bryan; Chairman, Aberdeen Royal Hospitals NHS Trust, since 1992; *b* 13 Jan. 1937; *s* of late William P. Broomfield, OBE and Eliza M. Broomfield; *m* 1960, Morag Carruthers. *Educ:* Aberdeen Grammar Sch. 26 years with Town & Country Motor Garage Ltd; Man. Dir, retired 1992. Member: Grampian Health Bd, 1990–92; Bd, Scottish SHA, 1980–88; Council, Aberdeen Chamber of Commerce, to 1995 (Pres., 1978–79); Vice-Chm., Aberdeen Airport Consultative Cttee, 1990–. *Recreations:* walking, fishing, golf. *Address:* Aberdeen Royal Hospitals NHS Trust, Foresterhill House, Ashgrove Road West, Aberdeen AB9 8AQ.

BROOMFIELD, Sir Nigel (Hugh Robert Allen), KCMG 1993 (CMG 1986); HM Diplomatic Service; Ambassador to the Federal Republic of Germany, since 1993; *b* 19 March 1937; *s* of Arthur Allen Broomfield and Ruth Sheilagh Broomfield; *m* 1963, Valerie Fenton; two *s.* *Educ:* Haileybury Coll.; Trinity Coll., Cambridge (BA (Hons) English Lit.). Commnd 17/21 Lancers, 1959, retired as Major, 1968. Joined FCO as First Sec., 1969; First Secretary: British Embassy, Bonn, 1970–72; British Embassy, Moscow, 1972–74; European Communities Dept, London, 1975–77; RCDS, 1978; Political Advr and Head of Chancery, British Mil. Govt, Berlin, 1979–81; Head of Eastern European and Soviet Dept, 1981–83, and Head of Soviet Dept, 1983–85, FCO; Dep. High Comr and Minister, New Delhi, 1985–88; Ambassador to GDR, 1988–90; Dep. Under Sec. of State (Defence), FCO, 1990–92. Captain, Cambridge Squash Rackets and Real Tennis, 1957–58; British Amateur Squash Champion, 1958–59 (played for England, 1957–60). *Recreations:* tennis, cricket, gardening, reading, music. *Address:* c/o Foreign and Commonwealth Office, SW1A 2AH. *Clubs:* Royal Automobile, MCC; Hawks (Cambridge).

BROPHY, Michael John Mary; Executive Director, Charities Aid Foundation, since 1982; *b* 24 June 1937; *s* of Gerald and Mary Brophy; *m* 1962, Sarah Rowe; three *s* one *d.* *Educ:* Ampleforth Coll.; Royal Naval Coll., Dartmouth. Entered Royal Navy, 1955; retired as Lt-Comdr, 1966. Associate Dir, J. Walter Thompson, 1967–74; Appeals Dir, Spastics Soc., 1974–82. Dir, European Foundn Centre, 1989– (Chm., 1994–95). Sec., Council for Charitable Support, 1986–; Trustee, CAF America, 1993. FRSA 1986; FICFM 1990; CIMgt 1994. *Recreations:* travel, walking. *Address:* 8 Oldlands Hall, Herons Ghyll, Uckfield, E Sussex TN22 3DA. *Club:* Athenæum.

BROSAN, Dr George Stephen, CBE 1982; TD 1960; Director, North East London Polytechnic, 1970–82; *b* 8 Aug. 1921; *o s* of Rudolph and Margaret Brosan; *m* 1952, Maureen Dorothy Foscoe; three *d.* *Educ:* Kilburn Grammar Sch.; Faraday House; The Polytechnic; Birkbeck Coll., London. Faraday Scholar, 1939. PhD 1951; DFH 1957; FIMA 1966; CMath 1991; FIMechE 1971, CEng 1976, Eur Ing 1989, Hon. FIEE 1991 (FIEE 1964); MRIN 1983; CNI 1983. Teaching staff, Regent Street Polytechnic, 1950–58; Head of Dept, Willesden Coll. of Technology, 1958–60; Further Educn Officer, Middlesex CC, 1960–62; Principal, Enfield Coll. of Technology, 1962–70. Pres., Tensor Club of GB, 1973–82; Pres., IProdE, 1975–77 (Hon. FIProdE 1980–91); Mem. Council, BIM, 1975–79; Chairman: CEI Educn Cttee, 1978–79; Accountancy Educn Consultative Bd, 1979–82. Life Mem., ASME, 1977. Hon. MIED 1967; Hon. Mem., Council for Educn in the Commonwealth, 1983. CIMgt (FBIM 1975). Chevalier du Tastevin, 1976; Yachtmaster Ocean, 1986. *Publications:* (jtly) Advanced Electrical Power and Machines, 1966; (jtly) Patterns and Policies in Higher Education, 1971; numerous articles and papers in academic and professional press. *Recreation:* yachting. *Address:* High Orchard, Mark Way, Godalming, Surrey GU7 2BB; Tartagli Alti, Paciano 06060, Province of Perugia, Italy. *Club:* Reform.

See also Prof. N. J. Mackintosh.

BROTHERHOOD, Air Cdre William Rowland, CBE 1952; retired as Director, Guided Weapons (Trials), Ministry of Aviation (formerly Supply), 1959–61; *b* 22 Jan. 1912; *s* of late James Brotherhood, Tintern, Mon.; *m* 1939, Margaret (*d* 1981), *d* of late Ernest Sutcliffe, Louth, Lincs; one *s* one *d.* *Educ:* Monmouth School; RAF College, Cranwell. Joined RAF, 1930; Group Captain, 1943; Air Commodore, 1955; Director, Operational Requirements, Air Ministry, 1955–58. *Address:* Inglewood, Llandogo, Monmouth, Gwent NP5 4TQ. *T:* Dean (01594) 530333.

BROTHERS, Air Cdre Peter Malam, CBE 1964; DSO 1944; DFC 1940, and Bar, 1943; Managing Director, Peter Brothers Consultants Ltd, 1973–86; *b* 30 Sept. 1917; *s* of late John Malam Brothers; *m* 1939, Annette, *d* of late James Wilson; three *d.* *Educ:* N. Manchester Sch. (Br. of Manchester Grammar). Joined RAF, 1936; Flt-Lieut 1939; RAF Biggin Hill, Battle of Britain, 1940; Sqdn-Ldr 1941; Wing Comdr 1942; Tangmere Fighter Wing Ldr, 1942–43; Staff HQ No. 10 Gp, 1943; Exeter Wing Ldr, 1944; US Comd and Gen. Staff Sch., 1944–45; Central Fighter Estab., 1945–46; Colonial Service, Kenya, 1947–49; RAF Bomber Sqdn, 1949–52; HQ No. 3 Gp, 1952–54; RAF Staff Coll., 1954; HQ Fighter Comd, 1955–57; Bomber Stn, 1957–59; Gp Capt., and Staff Officer, SHAPE, 1959–62; Dir of Ops (Overseas), 1962–65; Air Cdre, and AOC Mil. Air Traffic Ops, 1965–68; Dir of Public Relations (RAF), MoD (Air), 1968–73; retired 1973. Freeman, Guild Air Pilots and Air Navigators, 1966 (Liveryman, 1968; Warden, 1971; Master, 1974–75); Freeman, City of London, 1967. Editorial Adviser, Defence and Foreign Affairs publications, 1973–76. Patron, Spitfire Assoc., Australia, 1971–; Vice-President: Spitfire Soc., 1984–; Devon Emergency Volunteers, 1986–93 (Chm., 1981–86). *Recreations:* golf, sailing, fishing, swimming, flying. *Address:* c/o National Westminster Bank, Topsham, Devon EX3 0HB. *Clubs:* Royal Air Force; Honiton Golf.

BROTHERTON, Ven. John Michael; Archdeacon of Chichester and Canon Residentiary of Chichester Cathedral, since 1991; *b* 7 Dec. 1935; *s* of late Clifford and Minnie Brotherton; *m* 1963, Daphne Margaret Yvonne, *d* of Sir Geoffrey Meade, KBE, CMG, CVO; three *s* one *d.* *Educ:* St John's Coll., Cambridge (MA); Cuddesdon Coll., Oxford; Univ. of London Inst. of Educn (PGCE). Ordained: deacon, 1961; priest, 1962; Asst Curate, St Nicolas, Chiswick, 1961–64; Chaplain, Trinity Coll., Port of Spain, Trinidad, 1965–69; Rector of St Michael's, Diego Martin, Trinidad, 1969–75; Vicar, St Mary and St John, Oxford, and Chaplain, St Hilda's Coll., Oxford, 1976–81; Rural Dean of Cowley, 1978–81; Vicar, St Mary, Portsea, 1981–91. Hon. Canon, St Michael's Cathedral, Kobe, Japan, 1986. *Recreations:* travel, walking. *Address:* 4 Canon Lane, Chichester, West Sussex PO19 1PX. *T:* Chichester (01243) 779134.

BROTHERTON, Michael Lewis; formed Michael Brotherton Associates, Parliamentary and Financial Consultants, 1986; *b* 26 May 1931; *s* of late John Basil Brotherton and Maud Brotherton; *m* 1968, Julia, *d* of Austin Gerald Comyn King and Katherine Elizabeth King, Bath; three *s* one *d.* *Educ:* Prior Park; RNC Dartmouth. Served RN, 1949–64: qual. Observer 1955; Cyprus, 1957 (despatches); Lt-Comdr 1964, retd. Times Newspapers, 1967–74. Chm., Beckenham Conservative Political Cttee, 1967–68; contested (C) Deptford, 1970; MP (C) Louth, Oct. 1974–1983. Pres., Hyde Park Tories, 1975. Mem., Select Cttee on violence in the family, 1975–76. *Recreations:* cricket, cooking, gardening, talking. *Address:* The Old Vicarage, Wrangle, Boston, Lincs PE22 9EP. *T:* Boston (01205) 870688. *Clubs:* Conservative Working Men's, Louth (Louth); Castaways; Cleethorpes Conservative; Immingham Conservative.

BROTHWOOD, Rev. John, MRCP, FRCPsych, FFOM; Hon. Curate, St Barnabas, Dulwich, since 1991; *b* 23 Feb. 1931; *s* of late Wilfred Cyril Vernon Brothwood and Emma Bailey; *m* 1957, Dr Margaret Stirling Meyer; one *s* one *d.* *Educ:* Marlborough Coll.; Peterhouse, Cambridge (Schol.); Middlesex Hosp. MB BChir (Cantab) 1955; MRCP 1960, DPM (London) 1964, FFCM 1972, FRCPsych 1976, FFOM 1988. Various posts in clinical medicine, 1955–64; joined DHSS (then Min. of Health) as MO, 1964; SPMO and Under Secretary, DHSS, 1975–78; CMO, Esso Petroleum (UK) and Esso, subseq. Exxon, Chemicals, 1979–90. Lay Reader, Parish of St Barnabas, Dulwich, 1982–91; Southwark Ordination Course, 1988–91; deacon, 1991; priest, 1992. *Publications:* various. *Recreations:* diverse. *Address:* 81 Calton Avenue, SE21 7DF. *T:* 0181–693 8273.

BROUCHER, David Stuart; HM Diplomatic Service; Counsellor, Foreign and Commonwealth Office, since 1994; *b* 5 Oct. 1944; *s* of Clifford Broucher and Betty Broucher (*née* Jordan); *m* 1971, Marion Monika Blackwell; one *s.* *Educ:* Manchester Grammar School; Trinity Hall, Cambridge (MA Modern Languages). Foreign Office, 1966; British Military Govt, Berlin, 1968; Cabinet Office, 1972; Prague, 1975; FCO, 1978; UK Perm. Rep. to EC, 1983; Counsellor, Jakarta, 1985–89; Economic Counsellor, Bonn, 1989–93. *Recreations:* music, golf, sailing. *Address:* c/o Foreign and Commonwealth Office, SW1A 2AL.

BROUGH, Dr Colin, FRCPE; FFCM; Chief Administrative Medical Officer, Lothian Health Board, 1980–88; *b* 4 Jan. 1932; *s* of Peter Brough and Elizabeth C. C. Chalmers; *m* 1957, Maureen Jennings; four *s* one *d.* *Educ:* Bell Baxter Sch., Cupar; Univ. of Edinburgh (MB ChB). DPH 1965; DIH 1965; FFCM 1978; MRCPE 1981; FRCPE 1982. House Officer, Leicester General Hosp. and Royal Infirmary of Edinburgh, 1956–57; Surg.-Lieut, Royal Navy, 1957–60; General Practitioner, Leith and Fife, 1960–64; Dep. Medical Supt, Royal Inf. of Edinburgh, 1965–67; ASMO, PASMO, Dep. SAMO, South-Eastern Regional Hosp. Board, Scotland, 1967–74; Community Medicine Specialist, Lothian Health Board, 1974–80. *Recreations:* golf, shooting, fishing, first aid. *Address:* The Saughs, Gullane, East Lothian EH31 2AL. *T:* Gullane (01620) 842179.

BROUGH, Edward; Chairman, Volker Stevin (UK) Ltd, 1980–82; *b* 28 May 1918; *s* of late Hugh and Jane Brough; *m* 1941, Peggy Jennings; two *s.* *Educ:* Berwick Grammar School; Edinburgh University (MA). Joined Unilever Ltd, 1938. War service, KOSB, 1939–46 (Captain). Rejoined Unilever, 1946; Commercial Dir, 1951, Man. Dir, 1954, Lever's Cattle Foods Ltd; Chairman, Crosfields (CWG) Ltd, 1957; Lever Bros & Associates Ltd: Development Dir, 1960; Marketing Dir, 1962; Chm., 1965; Hd of Unilever's Marketing Div., 1968–71; Dir of Unilever Ltd and Unilever NV, 1968–74, and Chm. of UK Cttee, 1971–74. Chm., Adriaan Volker (UK) Ltd, 1974–80. Mem., NBPI, 1967–70. FImgt (FBIM 1967). *Recreations:* flyfishing, golf. *Address:* Far End, The Great Quarry, Guildford, Surrey GU1 3XN. *T:* Guildford (01483) 504064; St John's, Chagford, Devon. *Club:* Farmers'.

BROUGH, Michael David, FRCS; Consultant Plastic Surgeon, University College Hospital, Royal Free, Whittington and Royal Northern Hospitals, since 1982; *b* 4 July 1942; *s* of late Kenneth David Brough and of Frances Elizabeth Brough (*née* Davies); *m* 1974, Dr Geraldine Moira Sleigh; two *s* two *d.* *Educ:* Westminster Sch.; Christ's Coll.,

Cambridge (MA); Middlesex Hosp. Med. Sch. (MB, BChir). Med. posts at Middlesex and Central Middlesex Hosps, 1968–71; Surgical trng posts, Birmingham Hosps, 1971–74; Plastic Surgery trng posts, Mount Vernon Hosp., London, Odstock Hosp., Salisbury, Whithington Hosp., Manchester, 1975–80; Cons. Plastic Surg., St Andrews Hosp., Billericay, Queen Elizabeth Hosp., Hackney, Whipps Cross Hosp., 1980–82. *Publications:* chapters in: Rob and Smith, Operative Surgery, 3rd edn 1976–79 and 4th edn 1988; Kirk and Williamson, General Surgical Operations, 2nd edn 1987; contribs to med. jls on plastic and reconstructive surgery. *Recreations:* family, ski-ing, Modern Pentathlon Half-Blue, 1964. *Address:* The Consulting Suite, 82 Portland Place, W1N 3DH. *T:* 0171–935 8910. *Club:* Hawks (Cambridge).

BROUGHAM, family name of **Baron Brougham and Vaux.**

BROUGHAM AND VAUX, 5th Baron *cr* 1860; **Michael John Brougham,** CBE 1995; *b* 2 Aug. 1938; *s* of 4th Baron and Jean (*d* 1992), *d* of late Brig.-Gen. G. B. S. Follett, DSO, MVO; *S* father, 1967; *m* 1st, 1963, Olivia Susan (marr. diss. 1968), *d* of Rear-Admiral Gordon Thomas Seccombe Gray; one *d*; 2nd, 1969, Catherine Gulliver (marr. diss. 1981), *d* of W. Gulliver; one *s*. *Educ:* Lycée Jaccard, Lausanne; Millfield School. Dep. Chm. of Cttees, H of L, 1992–. Pres., RoSPA, 1986–89. Chm., Tax Payers Soc., 1989–91. *Heir: s* Hon. Charles William Brougham, *b* 9 Nov. 1971. *Address:* 11 Westminster Gardens, Marsham Street, SW1P 4JA.

BROUGHAM, Christopher John; QC 1988; *b* 11 Jan. 1947; *s* of late Lt-Comdr Patrick Brougham and of Elizabeth Anne (*née* Vestey); *m* 1974, Mary Olwen (*née* Corker); one *s* three *d*. *Educ:* Radley Coll.; Worcester Coll., Oxford (BA Hons). Called to the Bar, Inner Temple, 1969; Dep. High Court Bankruptcy Registrar, 1984. Dep. Churchwarden, Christ Church, Kensington, 1980–. *Recreations:* music, crossword puzzles. *Address:* 3/4 South Square, Gray's Inn, WC1R 5HP. *T:* 0171–696 9900.

BROUGHSHANE, 2nd Baron (UK), *cr* 1945; **Patrick Owen Alexander Davison;** *b* 18 June 1903; *er s* of 1st Baron and Beatrice Mary, *d* of Sir Owen Roberts; *S* father, 1953; *m* 1929, Bettine (*d* 1994), *d* of Sir Arthur Russell, 6th Bt; (one *s* decd). *Educ:* Winchester; Magdalen College, Oxford. Barrister, Inner Temple, 1926. Served War of 1939–45: with Irish Guards, 1939–41; Assistant Secretary (Military), War Cabinet, 1942–45. Has US Legion of Merit. *Heir: b* Hon. (William) Kensington Davison, DSO, DFC, *b* 25 Nov. 1914. *Address:* 28 Fisher Street, Sandwich, Kent CT13 9EJ. *Club:* White's.

BROUGHTON, family name of **Baron Fairhaven.**

BROUGHTON, Air Marshal Sir Charles, KBE 1965 (CBE 1952); CB 1961; RAF retired; Air Member for Supply and Organization, Ministry of Defence, 1966–68; *b* 27 April 1911; *s* of Charles and Florence Gertrude Broughton; *m* 1939, Sylvia Dorothy Mary Bunbury (*d* 1995); one *d* (and one *d* decd). *Educ:* New Zealand; RAF College, Cranwell. Commissioned, 1932; India, 1933–37; Flying Instructor, 1937–40. Served War of 1939–45 in Coastal Command and Middle East (despatches four times). Flying Training Command, 1947–49; Air Ministry, 1949–51; Imperial Defence College, 1952; NATO, Washington DC, 1953–55; Far East, 1955–58; Transport Command, 1958–61; Dir-General of Organization, Air Min. (subseq. Min. of Defence), 1961–64; UK Representative in Ankara on Permanent Military Deputies Group of Central Treaty Organization (Cento), 1965–66.

BROUGHTON, Sir David (Delves), 13th Bt *cr* 1660, of Broughton, Staffordshire; *b* 7 May 1942; *s* of Lt-Comdr P. J. D. Broughton, RN, *g g g s* of Rev. Sir Henry Delves Broughton, 8th Bt, and of his 1st wife, Nancy Rosemary, *yr d* of J. E. Paterson; *S* kinsman, 1993; *m* 1969, Diane, *d* of R. L. Nicol. *Heir: half b* Geoffrey Delves Broughton, *b* 1962. *Address:* 25 Kings Road, Sandy, Beds SG19 1EJ.

BROUGHTON, Leonard, DL; Member, Lancashire County Council, 1974–89 (Chairman and Leader, 1974–81); *b* 21 March 1924; *s* of Charles Cecil Broughton and Florence (*née* Sunman); *m* 1949, Kathleen Gibson; one *d*. *Educ:* Kingston-upon-Hull. Served RASC, 1942–47. Estates Manager, Bedford Borough Council, 1957; business man. Member: Blackpool County Borough Council, 1961–74 (Leader, 1968–73); Blackpool Bor. Council, 1974–79; NW Co. Boroughs' Assoc., 1968–74; NW Economic Planning Council, 1970–72; Assoc. of Co. Councils, 1973–77; Board, Central Lancs Develt Corp., 1976–84. Mem. Courts, Lancaster and Salford Univs, 1974–81; Vice-President: Lancs Youth Clubs Assoc., 1974–81; NW Arts Assoc., 1974–81; Blackpool Social Service Council, 1974–84; Chm., Blackpool and Fylde Civilian Disabled Soc., 1964–84. Freeman, Co. Borough of Blackpool, 1973. DL Lancs, 1975; High Sheriff of Lancashire, 1983–84. *Recreations:* gardening, overseas travel. *Address:* 14 The Grove, Cleveleys, Blackpool, Lancs FY5 2JD.

BROUGHTON, Martin Faulkner, FCA; Group Chief Executive and Deputy Chairman, BAT Industries plc, since 1993; *b* 15 April 1947; *m* 1974, Jocelyn Mary Rodgers; one *s* one *d*. *Educ:* Westminster City Grammar Sch. FCA 1969. British-American Tobacco Co.: travelling auditor, 1971–74; Head Office, 1974–80; Souza Cruz, Brazil, 1980–85; BAT Industries: Chairman: Eagle Star, 1985–88 and 1992–93; Wiggins Teape Gp, 1989–90; Finance Dir, 1988–92; Mem., Chm.'s Policy Cttee, 1990–93; Man. Dir, Financial Services, 1992–. Dir, Whitbread, 1993–. Chairman: CBI Cos Cttee, 1995–; Urgent Issues Task Force, Accounting Standards Bd, 1991–. *Recreations:* theatre, golf. *Address:* c/o BAT Industries plc, Windsor House, 50 Victoria Street, SW1H 0NL. *T:* 0171–222 7979. *Club:* Hever Golf (Hever).

BROUN, Sir Lionel John Law, 12th Bt, *cr* 1686; *b* 25 April 1927; *s* of 11th Bt and Georgie, *y d* of late Henry Law, Sydney, NSW; *S* father 1962. *Heir: c* William Windsor Broun [*b* 1917; *m* 1952, D'Hrie King, NSW; two *d*]. *Address:* 23 Clanalpine Street, Mosman, NSW 2088, Australia.

BROWALDH, Tore; Grand Cross, Order of Star of the North, 1974; Kt Comdr's Cross, Order of Vasa, 1963; Hon. Chairman, Svenska Handelsbanken, since 1988; Deputy Chairman, Nobel Foundation, since 1966; *b* 23 Aug. 1917; *s* of Knut Ernfrid Browaldh and Ingrid Gezelius; *m* 1942, Gunnel Eva Ericson; three *s* one *d*. *Educ:* Stockholm Univ. (MA Politics, Economics and Law, 1941). Financial Attaché, Washington, 1943; Asst Sec., Royal Cttee of Post-War Econ. Planning, and Admin. Sec., Industrial Inst. for Econ. and Social Res., 1944–45; Sec. to Bd of Management, Svenska Handelsbanken, 1946–49; Dir of Econ., Social, Cultural and Refugee Dept, Secretariat Gen., Council of Europe, Strasbourg, 1949–51; Exec. Vice Pres., Confedn of Swedish Employers, 1951–54; Chief Gen. Man., Svenska Handelsbanken, 1955–66, Chm., 1966–78, Vice-Chm., 1978–88. Chairman: Svenska Cellulosa AB, 1965–88; Sandrew theater and movie AB, 1963–; Swedish IBM, 1978–; Swedish Unilever AB, 1977–; Industrivärden, 1976–88; Deputy Chairman: Beijerinvest AB, 1975–88; AB Volvo, 1977–81; Director: Volvo Internat. Adv. Bd, 1980–88; IBM World Trade Corp., Europe/ME/Africa, New York, 1979–88; Unilever Adv. Bd, Rotterdam and London, 1976–88. Member: Swedish Govt's Econ. Planning Commn, 1962–73 and Res. Adv. Bd, 1966–70; Consultative Cttee, Internat. Fedn of Insts for Advanced Study, 1972–; UN Gp of Eminent Persons on Multinational Corporations, 1973–74; Royal Swedish Acad. of Sciences; Hudson Inst., USA; Soc. of Scientists and Members of Parlt, Sweden; Royal Swedish Acad. of Engrg Sciences; Royal Acad. of Arts and Sciences, Uppsala. Dr of Technol. *hc* Royal Inst. of Technol., 1967; Dr of Econs *hc* Gothenburg, 1980. St Erik's Medal, Sweden, 1961; Gold Medal for public service, Sweden, 1981. *Publications:* Management and Society, 1961; (autobiography): vol. I, The Pilgrimage of a Journeyman, 1976; vol. II, The Long Road, 1980; vol. III, Against the Wind, 1984. *Recreations:* jazz, piano, golf, chess. *Address:* (office) Svenska Handelsbanken, Kungsträdgårdsgatan 2, 10670 Stockholm, Sweden. *T:* (8) 229220; (home) Sturegatan 14, 11436 Stockholm. *T:* (8) 6619643. *Club:* Sällskapet (Stockholm).

BROWN, Alan James; HM Diplomatic Service, retired; Deputy Commissioner-General, UN Relief and Works Agency for Palestine Refugees, 1977–84; *b* 28 Aug. 1921; *s* of W. Y. Brown and Mrs E. I. Brown; *m* 1966, Joy Aileen Key Stone (*née* McIntyre); one *s*, and two step *d*. *Educ:* Magdalene College, Cambridge (MA). Served with HM Forces, 1941–47; CRO 1948; 2nd Sec., Calcutta, 1948–50; CRO, 1951; Private Sec. to Parly Under-Secretary of State, 1951–52; 1st Secretary, Dacca, Karachi, 1952–55; CRO, 1955–57; Kuala Lumpur, 1957–62; CRO, 1962–63; Head of Information Policy Dept, 1963–64; Dep. High Comr, Nicosia, 1964; Head of Far East and Pacific Dept, CRO, 1964–66; Dep. High Comr, Malta, 1966–70; Dep High Comr, later Consul-Gen., Karachi, 1971–72; Ambassador to Togo and Benin, 1973–75; Head of Nationality and Treaty Dept, FCO, 1975–77. *Recreation:* sailing. *Address:* Lamerton Manor, Idless, near Truro, Cornwall TR4 9QT. *T:* Truro (01872) 73890. *Club:* United Oxford & Cambridge University.

BROWN, Alan Thomas, CBE 1978; DL; Chief Executive, Oxfordshire County Council, 1973–88; *b* 18 April 1928; *s* of Thomas Henry Brown and Lucy Lilian (*née* Betts); *m* 1962, Marie Christine East; two *d*. *Educ:* Wyggeston Grammar Sch., Leicester; Sidney Sussex Coll., Cambridge (Wrangler, Maths Tripos 1950, MA 1953). Fellow CIPFA, 1961. Asst, Bor. Treasurer's Dept, Wolverhampton, 1950–56; Asst Sec., IMTA, 1956–58; Dep. Co. Treas., Berks CC, 1958–61; Co. Treas., Cumberland CC, 1961–66; Town Clerk and Chief Exec., Oxford City Council, 1966–73. Member: SE Econ. Planning Council, 1975–79; Audit Commn, 1989–95. DL Oxon 1978. *Recreations:* chess, horticulture, music, reading. *Address:* 7 Field House Drive, Oxford OX2 7NT. *T:* Oxford (01865) 515809.

BROWN, Alan Winthrop, CB 1992; Head of Health Policy Division, Health and Safety Executive, 1992–94; *b* 14 March 1934; *s* of James Brown and Evelyn V. Brown (*née* Winthrop); *m* 1959, Rut Berit (*née* Ohlson); two *s* one *d*. *Educ:* Bedford Sch.; Pembroke Coll., Cambridge (BA Hons); Cornell Univ., NY (MSc). Joined Min. of Labour, 1959; Private Sec. to Minister, 1961–62; Principal, 1963; Asst Sec., 1969. Dir of Planning, Employment Service Agency, 1973–74; Under-Sec. and Head of Incomes Div., DoE, 1975; Chief Exec., Employment Service Div., 1976–79, Trng Services Div., 1979–82, MSC; Hd Electricity Div., Dept of Energy, 1983–85; Dir. Personnel and Management Services Div., Dept of Employment, 1985–89; Dir, Resources and Planning, HSE, 1989–92. *Publications:* papers on occupational psychology and industrial training. *Recreations:* reading history and poetry, gardening. *Address:* Groton, Ballfield Road, Godalming, Surrey GU7 2HE.

BROWN, Alexander Cosens Lindsay, CB 1980; Chief Veterinary Officer, Ministry of Agriculture, Fisheries and Food, 1973–80; *b* Glasgow, 30 Jan. 1920; *s* of William Tait Brown and Margaret Rae; *m* 1945, Mary McDougal Hutchison; two *s*. *Educ:* Hutchesons' Grammar Sch., Glasgow; Glasgow Veterinary Coll. Diploma of RCVS; FRCVS 1980. Ministry of Agriculture, Fisheries and Food: appointed Vet. Officer to Dorset, 1943; Divisional Vet. Officer, HQ Tolworth, 1955; Divisional Vet. Officer, Essex, 1958–62; Dep. Regional Vet. Officer, W Midland Region, Wolverhampton, 1962–63; Regional Vet. Officer, Eastern Region, Cambridge, 1963; HQ Tolworth, 1967; Dep. Dir, Veterinary Field Services, 1969–70, Dir, 1970–73. Mem. ARC, 1975–80. *Publications:* contribs to Jl of Royal Soc. of Medicine, Veterinary Record, State Veterinary Jl. *Recreations:* gardening, swimming, reading. *Address:* 29 Ashwood Park, Fetcham, Leatherhead, Surrey KT22 9NT. *T:* Bookham (01372) 457997.

BROWN, Alexander Douglas G.; *see* Gordon-Brown.

BROWN, Sir Allen (Stanley), Kt 1956; CBE 1953; MA; LLM; Australian Commissioner for British Phosphate Commissioners and Christmas Island Phosphate Commission, 1970–76; *b* 3 July 1911; *m* 1936, Hilda May Wilke; one *s* two *d*. Dir-Gen. of Post-War Reconstruction, 1948. Sec., PM's Dept and Sec. to Cabinet, Commonwealth Govt, 1949–58; Deputy Australian High Commissioner to UK, 1959–65; Australian Ambassador to Japan, 1965–70. *Address:* 2/28 Ridgeway Avenue, Kew, Victoria 3101, Australia. *Club:* Melbourne (Melbourne).

BROWN, Andrew William; Director General, Advertising Association, since 1993; *b* 3 March 1946; *s* of Harry Brown and Geraldine (*née* O'Leary); *m* 1977, Shelby Ann Hill. *Educ:* St Edmund's Coll., Ware, Herts. J. Walter Thompson Co. Ltd. 1965–93, Board Dir, 1982–93. *Recreations:* cricket, theatre, London. *Address:* Advertising Association, Abford House, 15 Wilton Road, SW1V 1NJ; 81 Westbourne Terrace, W2 6QS. *Clubs:* Reform, MCC; XL.

BROWN, Prof. Archibald Haworth, FBA 1991; Professor of Politics, University of Oxford, since 1989; Fellow, St Antony's College, Oxford, since 1971; *b* 10 May 1938; *s* of late Rev. Alexander Douglas Brown and of Mary Brown (*née* Yates); *m* 1963, Patricia Susan Cornwell; one *s* one *d*. *Educ:* Annan Acad.; Dumfries Acad.; City of Westminster Coll.; LSE (BSc Econ, 1st Cl. Hons 1962). MA Oxon 1972. Reporter, Annandale Herald and Annandale Observer, 1954–56. National Service, 1956–58. Lectr in Politics, Glasgow Univ., 1964–71; British Council exchange scholar, Moscow Univ., 1967–68; Lectr in Soviet Instns, Univ. of Oxford, 1971–89. Visiting Professor: of Political Science, Yale Univ. and Univ. of Connecticut, 1980; Columbia Univ., NY, 1985; Univ. of Texas, Austin, 1990–91; INSEAD, 1991; Henry L. Stimson Lectures, Yale Univ., 1980. Mem. Council, SSEES, Univ. of London, 1992–. *Publications:* Soviet Politics and Political Science, 1974; (ed jtly and contrib.) The Soviet Union since the Fall of Khrushchev, 1975, 2nd edn 1978; (ed jtly and contrib.) Political Culture and Political Change in Communist States, 1977, 2nd edn 1979; (ed jtly and contrib.) Authority, Power and Policy in the USSR: essays dedicated to Leonard Schapiro, 1980; (ed jtly and contrib.) The Cambridge Encyclopedia of Russia and the Soviet Union, 1982; (ed jtly and contrib.) Soviet Policy for the 1980s, 1982; (ed and contrib.) Political Culture and Communist Studies, 1984; (ed and contrib.) Political Leadership in the Soviet Union, 1989; (ed and contrib.) The Soviet Union: a biographical dictionary, 1990; (ed and contrib.) New Thinking in Soviet Politics, 1992; (ed jtly and contrib.) The Cambridge Encyclopedia of Russia and the Former Soviet Union, 1994; The Gorbachev Factor, 1995; papers in academic jls and symposia. *Recreations:* novels and political memoirs, opera, ballet, cricket (now as spectator). *Address:* St Antony's College, Oxford OX2 6JF. *T:* Oxford (01865) 59651.

BROWN, Gen. Arnold, OC 1982; International Leader, and General, Salvation Army, 1977–81; *b* 13 Dec. 1913; *s* of Arnold Rees Brown and Annie Brown; *m* 1939, Jean Catherine Barclay; two *d*. *Educ:* Belleville Collegiate, Canada. Commnd Salvation Army Officer, 1935; Editor, Canadian War Cry, 1937–47; Nat. Publicity Officer, Canada,

1947–62; Nat. Youth Officer, Canada, 1962–64; Head of Internat. Public Relations, Internat. HQ, London, 1964–69; Chief of Staff, 1969–74; Territorial Comdr, Canada and Bermuda, 1974–77. Freeman, City of London, 1978. Hon. LHD Asbury Coll., USA, 1972; Hon. DD Olivet Coll., USA, 1981. *Publications:* What Hath God Wrought?, 1952; The Gate and the Light, 1984; Fighting for His Glory, 1988; Yin: the mountain the wind blew here, 1988; With Christ at the Table, 1991; Occupied Manager—Unoccupied Tomb, 1994. *Recreations:* reading, writing, music. *Address:* 1200 Don Mills Road, Suite 416, North York, Ontario M3B 3N8, Canada. *Club:* Rotary of London and Toronto.

BROWN, Rt. Rev. Arthur Durrant; a Suffragan Bishop of Toronto, 1981–93 (Bishop of York-Scarborough); *b* 7 March 1926; *s* of Edward S. Brown and Laura A. Durrant; *m* 1949, Norma Inez Rafuse; three *d. Educ:* Univ. of Western Ontario (BA 1949); Huron College (LTh 1949). Ordained deacon, 1949; priest, 1950, Huron. Rector: of Paisley with Cargill and Pinkerton, 1948–50; of Glenworth and St Stephen, London, Ont., 1950–53; of St John, Sandwich, Windsor, Ont., 1953–63; of St Michael and All Angels, Toronto, 1963–80; Canon of Toronto, 1972–74; Archdeacon of York, Toronto, 1974–80. Member: Nat. Exec. Council, Anglican Church of Canada, 1969–81; Judicial Council of Ontario, 1978–85; Multi-Cultural Council of Ontario, 1985–87; Press Council of Ontario, 1986. Hon. Chm. Adv. Bd, Cdn Foundn on Compulsive Gambling (Ontario), 1983–; Chairman: Canadian Friends to West Indian Christians, 1982–; Royal Visit Children's Fund, 1984–. Columnist, Toronto Sunday Sun, 1974–86. Mem., Corp. of Huron Coll., 1961–86; Chancellor, Renison Coll., 1994–. City of Toronto Civic Award, 1981. Hon. DD: Huron Coll., 1979; Wycliffe Coll., 1981. *Address:* 45 Livingston Road # 810, Scarborough, Ontario M1E 1K8, Canada.

BROWN, Arthur Godfrey Kilner, MA; Headmaster, Worcester Royal Grammar School, 1950–78; *b* 21 Feb. 1915; *s* of Rev. Arthur E. Brown, CIE, MA, BSc, and Mrs E. G. Brown, MA, formerly of Bankura, India; *m* 1939, Mary Denholm Armstrong (*d* 1993); one *s* three *d. Educ:* Warwick Sch.; Peterhouse, Cambridge. BA Cantab 1938; MA 1950. Assistant Master, Bedford School, 1938–39; King's School, Rochester, 1939–43; Cheltenham College, 1943–50. Elected to Headmasters' Conference, 1950. Founder Mem., Worcester Civic Soc. (Chm., 1960–66); Foundn Trustee, Swan Theatre, Worcester (Chm., 1965–70 and 1977–82); Pres., Worcester Rotary Club, 1975. *Recreations:* athletics (Silver Medal, 400 metres, and Gold Medal, 1,600 metres relay, Olympic Games, 1936; Gold Medal, 400 metres, World Student Games, 1937, and European Championships, 1938); music, gardening, house maintenance, following sport, walking. *Address:* Palmer's Cottage, Coneyhurst, near Billingshurst, West Sussex RH14 9DN. *Clubs:* Achilles; Hawks (Cambridge) (Pres., 1937); Probus (Horsham Weald).

See also Hon. Sir R. K. Brown.

BROWN, A(rthur) I(vor) Parry, FFARCS; Anæsthetist: London Hospital, 1936–73; London Chest Hospital, 1946–73; Harefield Hospital, 1940–73; Royal Masonic Hospital, 1950–73; retired; *b* 23 July 1908; *s* of A. T. J. Brown; *m* Joyce Marion Bash. *Educ:* Tollington Sch., London; London Hospital. MRCS, LRCP, 1931; MB, BS London, 1933; DA, 1935; FFARCS, 1951. Member of the Board of the Faculty of Anæsthetists, RCS; Pres., Sect. of Anæsthetics, RSM, 1972–73; Fellow, Assoc. of Anæsthetists; Member, Thoracic Soc. *Publications:* chapter in Diseases of the Chest, 1952; contributions to: Thorax, Anæsthesia. *Address:* Long Thatch, Church Lane, Balsham, Cambridge CB1 6DS. *T:* Cambridge (01223) 893012.

BROWN, Sir (Arthur James) Stephen, KBE 1967; CEng, MIMechE; Chairman: Stone-Platt Industries Ltd, 1968–73 (Deputy Chairman, 1965–67); Molins Ltd, 1971–78; Deputy Chairman, Chloride Group, 1965–73; *b* 15 Feb. 1906; *s* of Arthur Mogg Brown, and Ada Kelk (*née* Upton); *m* 1935, Margaret Alexandra McArthur; one *s* one *d. Educ:* Taunton School; Bristol University (BSc(Eng.)). Apprenticed British Thomson-Houston Co. Ltd, 1928–32; joined J. Stone & Co. Ltd, 1932, Dir, 1945; Man. Dir J. Stone & Co. (Deptford) Ltd (on formation), 1951; Divisional Dir, Stone-Platt Industries Ltd (on formation), 1958; Director: Fairey Co., 1971–76; Porvair Ltd, 1971–87. Pres., Engineering Employers' Fedn, 1964–65; Pres., Confedn of British Industry, 1966–68; Founder Mem., Export Council for Europe, 1960 (Dep. Chm., 1962–63); Mem., NEDC, 1966–71. Hon. DSc Aston Univ., 1967. *Recreations:* fishing, golf. *Address:* Flat 20, Danny House, Hurstpierpoint, Sussex BN6 9BB. *T:* Hurstpierpoint (01273) 833755.

BROWN, Prof. Arthur Joseph, CBE 1974; FBA 1972; Professor of Economics, University of Leeds, 1947–79, now Emeritus; Pro-Vice-Chancellor, Leeds University, 1975–77; *b* 8 Aug. 1914; *s* of J. Brown, Alderley Edge, Cheshire; *m* 1938, Joan H. M., *d* of Rev. Canon B. E. Taylor, Holy Trinity, Walton Breck, Liverpool; two *s* (and one *s* decd). *Educ:* Bradford Grammar School; Queen's College, Oxford (Hon. Fellow, 1985). First Class Hons in Philosophy, Politics and Economics, 1936, MA, DPhil 1939. Fellow of All Souls College, Oxford, 1937–46; Lectr in Economics, Hertford College, Oxford, 1937–40; on staff of: Foreign Research and Press Service, 1940–43; Foreign Office Research Dept, 1943–45; Economic Section, Offices of the Cabinet, 1945–47. Head of Dept of Economics and Commerce, University of Leeds, 1947–65. Visiting Professor of Economics, Columbia University, City of New York, Jan.–June 1950. President Section F, British Assoc. for the Advancement of Science, 1958; Member: East African Economic and Fiscal Commn, 1960; UN Consultative Group on Economic and Social Consequences of Disarmament, 1961–62; First Secretary of State's Advisory Group on Central Africa, 1962; Hunt Cttee on Intermediate Areas, 1967–69; UGC, 1969–78 (Vice-Chm., 1977–78). Pres., Royal Economic Soc., 1976–78, Vice-Pres., 1978–. Chairman, Adv. Panel on Student Maintenance Grants, 1967–68. Vis. Prof. ANU, 1963; directing Regional Economics project, National Institute of Economic and Social Research, 1966–72. Hon. DLitt: Bradford, 1975; Kent, 1979; Hon. LLD Aberdeen, 1978; Hon. LittD Sheffield, 1979. *Publications:* Industrialisation and Trade, 1943; Applied Economics-Aspects of the World Economy in War and Peace, 1948; The Great Inflation, 1939–51, 1955; Introduction to the World Economy, 1959; The Framework of Regional Economics in the United Kingdom, 1972; (with E. M. Burrows) Regional Economic Problems, 1977; (with J. Darby) World Inflation since 1950: a comparative international study, 1985; articles in various journals. *Recreations:* gardening and walking. *Address:* 24 Moor Drive, Leeds LS6 4BY. *T:* Leeds (0113) 275 5799. *Club:* Athenæum.

See also W. A. Brown.

BROWN, Sir (Austen) Patrick, KCB 1995; Permanent Secretary, Department of Transport, since 1991; *b* 14 April 1940; *s* of late Austen K. and of Dorothy Mary Brown; *m* 1966, Mary (*née* Bulger); one *d. Educ:* Royal Grammar School, Newcastle upon Tyne; School of Slavonic and East European Studies, Univ. of London. Carreras Ltd, 1961–69 (Cyprus, 1965–66, Belgium, 1967–68); Management Consultant, Urwick Orr & Partners, UK, France, Portugal, Sweden, 1969–72; DoE, 1972; Asst. Sec., Property Services Agency, 1976–80, Dept of Transport, 1980–83; Under Sec., Dept of Transport, 1983–88; Dep. Sec., DoE, 1988–90; Second Perm. Sec., and Chief Exec., PSA, DoE, 1990–91. *Address:* c/o Department of Transport, 2 Marsham Street, SW1P 3EB.

BROWN, Barry; *see* Brown, James B. C.

BROWN, Dame Beryl P.; *see* Paston Brown.

BROWN, Adm. Sir Brian (Thomas), KCB 1989; CBE 1983; Chairman, P-E International plc, since 1995; Director, Cray Electronics plc, since 1991; *b* 31 Aug. 1934; *s* of late Walter Brown and Gladys (*née* Baddeley); *m* 1959, Veronica, *d* of late Wing Comdr and Mrs J. D. Bird; two *s. Educ:* Peter Symonds' School. Joined RN 1952; pilot in 898 and 848 Sqdns, 1959–62; Dep. Supply Officer, HMY Britannia, 1966–68; Supply Officer, HMS Tiger, 1973–75; Secretary to: VCNS, 1975–78; First Sea Lord, 1979–82; rcds 1983; CO HMS Raleigh, 1984–85; DGNPS, 1986; Dir Gen., Naval Manpower and Trng, 1986–88, and Chief Naval Supply and Secretariat Officer, 1987–88; Chief of Naval Personnel, Second Sea Lord and Admiral Pres., RNC, Greenwich, 1988–91, retired. Chm., King George's Fund for Sailors, 1993–; Pres., Victory Services Assoc., 1993–. CIMgt (CBIM 1989); FIPM 1990. Hon. DEd CNAA, 1990. Freeman, City of London, 1989; Liveryman, Gardeners' Co., 1991. *Recreations:* cricket, gardening, fishing. *Address:* The Old Dairy, Stoner Hill House, Froxfield, Petersfield, Hants GU32 1DX. *Club:* Army and Navy.

BROWN, Bruce; *see* Brown, John B.

BROWN, Bruce Macdonald; Director, New Zealand Institute of International Affairs, since 1993; *b* 1930; *s* of John Albert Brown and Caroline Dorothea Brown (*née* Jorgenson); *m* 1st, 1953, Edith Irene (*née* Raynor) (*d* 1989); two *s* one *d*; 2nd, 1990, Françoise Rousseau. *Educ:* Victoria University of Wellington (MA Hons). Private Secretary to Prime Minister, 1957–59; Second Sec., Kuala Lumpur, 1960–62; First Sec. (later Counsellor), New Zealand Mission to UN, New York, 1963–67; Head of Administration, Min. of Foreign Affairs, Wellington, 1967–68; Director, NZ Inst. of International Affairs, 1969–71; NZ Dep. High Commissioner, Canberra, 1972–75; Ambassador to Iran, 1975–78, and Pakistan, 1976–78; Asst Sec., Min. of Foreign Affairs, 1978–81; Dep. High Comr in London, 1981–85; Ambassador to Thailand, Vietnam and Laos, 1985–88, to Burma, 1986–88; High Comr to Canada, also accredited to Barbados, Guyana, Jamaica and Trinidad and Tobago, 1988–92. *Publications:* The Rise of New Zealand Labour, 1962; ed, Asia and the Pacific in the 1970s, 1971. *Recreations:* reading, golf. *Address:* New Zealand Institute of International Affairs, PO Box 600, Wellington, New Zealand.

BROWN, Carter; *see* Brown, John C.

BROWN, Cedric Harold, FEng 1990; FIGasE; FICE; Senior Managing Director, since 1991, Chief Executive, since 1992, British Gas plc; *b* 7 March 1935; *s* of late William Herbert Brown and Constance Dorothy Brown (*née* Frances); *m* 1956, Joan Hendry; one *s* three *d. Educ:* Sheffield, Rotherham and Derby Colleges of Technology. Pupil Gas Distribution Engineer, E Midlands Gas Bd, 1953–58, Tech. Asst, 1958–59; Engineering Asst, Tunbridge Wells Borough Council, 1959–60; engineering posts, E Midlands Gas Bd, 1960–75 (Chief Engineer, 1973–75); Dir of Engineering, E Midlands Gas, 1975–78; British Gas Corp., subseq. British Gas plc: Asst Dir (Ops) and Dir (Construction), 1978–79; Dir, Morecambe Bay Project, 1980–87; Regl Chm., British Gas W Midlands, 1987–89; Dir, Man. Dir, Exploration and Production, 1989; Man. Dir, Regl Services, 1989–91. Dir, Bow Valley Industries, 1988–. Mem., Adv. Council on Business and the Envmt, 1993–. Vice-Pres., IGasE, 1991–. Liveryman, Engineers' Co., 1988–. *Publications:* tech. papers to professional bodies. *Recreations:* sport, countryside, places of historic interest. *Address:* British Gas plc, The Adelphi, John Adam Street, WC2N 6JT.

BROWN, (Cedric Wilfred) George E.; *see* Edmonds-Brown.

BROWN, Charles Dargie, FEng 1981; consulting engineer, retired; Joint Chairman, Mott, Hay & Anderson, Consulting Engineers, 1981–89; *b* 13 April 1927; *s* of William Henry Brown and Jean Dargie; *m* 1952, Sylvia Margaret Vallis; one *s* one *d. Educ:* Harris Acad., Dundee; St Andrews Univ. (BScEng, 1st Cl. Hons.). FICE. Joined staff of Mott, Hay & Anderson, 1947; engaged on highways, tunnels and bridge works, incl. Tamar Bridge, Forth Road Bridge, George Street Bridge, Newport, Kingsferry and Queensferry Bridges, 1947–65; Partner and Director, 1965. Principally concerned with planning, design and supervision of major works, incl. Mersey Queensway tunnels and new London Bridge, and projects in Hong Kong, Malaysia, Singapore, Indonesia, Australia and USA, 1965–89. Member, Smeatonian Soc. of Civil Engrs, 1984–. Hon. LLD Dundee, 1982. *Publications:* papers to Instn of Civil Engrs, on Kingsferry Bridge, George St Bridge, London Bridge and Mersey tunnels; also various papers to engrg confs. *Recreations:* golf, gardening, bird watching, reading. *Address:* Mallards Mere, Russell Way, Petersfield, Hants GU31 4LD. *T:* Petersfield (01730) 267820. *Club:* Royal Automobile.

BROWN, Lt-Col Sir Charles Frederick Richmond, 4th Bt, *cr* 1863; TD; DL; *b* 6 Dec. 1902; *er s* of Frederick Richmond Brown (*d* 1933; 2nd *s* of 2nd Bt); *S* uncle, 1944; *m* 1st, 1933, Audrey (marr. diss., 1948), 2nd *d* of late Col Hon. Everard Baring, CVO, CBE, and late Lady Ulrica Baring; one *s* two *d*; 2nd, 1951, Hon. Gwendolen Carlis Meysey-Thomson (marr. diss. 1969; she *d* 1989), *y d* of 1st (and last) Baron Knaresborough; 3rd, 1969, Pauline (*d* 1994), *widow* of Edward Hildyard, Middleton Hall, Pickering, Yorks. *Educ:* Eton. Joined Welsh Guards, 1921; Captain 1932; retired with a gratuity, 1936; joined 5th Bn Green Howards, Territorial Army, as a Major, March 1939; Lieut-Colonel comdg 7th Bn Green Howards, July 1939, and proceeded to France with 7th Bn, April 1940. DL, North Riding of County of York, 1962. Hon. Alderman, after 27 years' service, of N Riding and N Yorks CC. *Heir: s* George Francis Richmond-Brown [*b* 3 Feb. 1938; *m* 1978, Philippa Jane, *d* of late E. J. Wilcox; two *s*]. *Recreations:* ornithology, growing species rhododendrons, country pursuits. *Address:* Wramghams, Middleton, Pickering, N Yorks YO18 8NX. *Clubs:* Cavalry and Guards, Pratt's; Yorkshire (York).

BROWN, Christina Hambley; *see* Brown, Tina.

BROWN, Christopher; Director and Chief Executive, National Society for Prevention of Cruelty to Children, since 1989; *b* 21 June 1938; *s* of Reginald Frank Greenwood Brown and Margaret Eleanor Brown; *m* 1968, Helen Margaret, *d* of George A. Woolsey and Hilda M. Woolsey; three *s* one *d. Educ:* Hertford Grammar Sch.; KCL. AKC; Home Office Cert. in Probation. Ordained Deacon, 1963, Priest, 1964; Assistant Curate, Diocese of Southwark: St Hilda's, Crofton Park, 1963; St Michael's, Wallington, 1964–67. Probation Officer, Nottingham, 1968–72; Sen. Probation Officer, W Midlands, 1972–74; Asst Dir, Social Services, Solihull, 1974–76; Asst Chief Probation Officer, Hereford and Worcester, 1976–79; Chief Probation Officer: Oxfordshire, 1979–86; Essex, 1986–89. Member: Parole Bd, 1985–87; Trng Cttee, Inst. for Study and Treatment of Delinquency, 1986–89; Professional Adv. Cttee, NSPCC, 1986–89; Chm., Social Issues Cttee, Assoc. of Chief Officers of Probation, 1985–87. Trustee, Nat. Council of Voluntary Childcare Orgns, 1995–. Mem., Green Coll., Oxford, 1981–86. Licensed to officiate, Dio. Chelmsford, 1986–. *Publications:* contribs to various jls on social work practice and community issues, 1971–. *Recreations:* walking, architecture, music, conversation, gardening. *Address:* (office) 42 Curtain Road, EC2A 3NH. *T:* 0171–825 2500. *Club:* Lansdowne.

BROWN, Christopher David, MA; Headmaster, Norwich School, since 1984; *b* 8 July 1944; *s* of E. K. Brown; *m* 1972, Caroline Dunkerley; two *d. Educ:* Plymouth College; Fitzwilliam College, Cambridge. MA. Assistant Master: The Leys School, Cambridge,

1967–71; Pangbourne College, 1971–73; Radley College, 1973–84 (Head of English, 1975–84). *Address:* 16 The Close, Norwich NR1 4DZ.

BROWN, Dr Christopher Paul Hadley; Chief Curator (formerly Keeper), National Gallery, since 1989; *b* 15 April 1948; *s* of late Arthur Edgar Brown and of Florence Marjorie Brown; *m* 1975, Sally Madeleine Stockton; one *s* one *d*. *Educ:* Merchant Taylors' Sch.; St Catherine's Coll., Oxford (BA Hons Modern History, Dip. History of Art); Courtauld Inst. of Art, Univ. of London (PhD). National Gallery: Asst Keeper, 1971, with responsibility for Dutch and Flemish 17th cent. paintings; Dep. Keeper, 1979. Trustee, Dulwich Coll. Picture Gall., 1993–. Lectures: Ferens Fine Art, Univ. of Hull, 1980; Cargill, Univ. of Glasgow, 1987; Jasper Walls, Pierpont Morgan Library, NY, 1991. Fellow, Netherlands Inst. for Advanced Study, Wassenaar, 1993–94. *Publications:* Carel Fabritius, 1981; Van Dyck, 1982; Scenes of Everyday Life: seventeenth-century Dutch genre painting, 1984; Dutch Landscape (catalogue), 1986; The Drawings of Anthony van Dyck, 1991; (jtly) Rembrandt: the master and his workshop (catalogue), 1991; National Gallery catalogues, incl. The Dutch School 1600–1900, 1990; contribs to art magazines, UK and overseas. *Recreations:* Italian art and architecture, travel, opera. *Address:* 61 Winterbrook Road, SE24 9HZ. *T:* 0171–274 7197; (office) 0171–389 1702.

BROWN, Craig Edward Moncrieff; freelance writer since 1977; *b* 23 May 1957; *s* of Peter Brown and Jennifer (*née* Bethell); *m* 1987, Frances, *d* of Colin Welch, *qv*; one *s* one *d*. *Educ:* Farleigh House; Eton Coll.; Bristol Univ. Drama Dept. Columnist on: Sunday Telegraph, Evening Standard, Private Eye, Independent on Sunday, Guardian (as Wallace Arnold, and Bel Littlejohn); specializing in parody and satire. *Publications:* The Marsh-Marlow Letters, 1984; A Year Inside, 1989; The Agreeable World of Wallace Arnold, 1990; Rear Columns, 1992; Welcome to My Worlds!, 1993; Craig Brown's Greatest Hits, 1993; The Hounding of John Thomas, 1994; The Private Eye Book of Craig Brown Parodies, 1995. *Recreations:* swimming in the sea, drinking, shopping. *Address:* c/o Private Eye, Carlisle Street, W1V 5RG. *Club:* Academy.

BROWN, Rev. Cyril James, OBE 1956; Rector of Warbleton, 1970–77; Chaplain to the Queen, 1956–74; *b* 12 Jan. 1904; *s* of late James Brown, Clifton, Bristol; *m* 1931, Myrtle Aufrère, *d* of late Mark Montague Ford, London; no *c*. *Educ:* Westminster Abbey Choir School; Clifton College; Keble College, Oxford; St Stephen's House, Oxford. Curate of St Gabriel's, Warwick Square, 1927–31; Chaplain, Missions to Seamen, Singapore, 1931–34, Hong Kong, 1934–41; Chaplain, Hong Kong RNVR, 1941–46; Youth Secretary, Missions to Seamen, 1946–47, Superintendent, 1947–51, General Superintendent, 1951–59, General Secretary, 1959–69; Prebendary of St Paul's, 1958–69. *Publications:* contributions to East and West Review, World Dominion, etc. *Recreation:* choral music. *Address:* Royal Alfred Seafarers Home, 5–11 Hartington Place, Eastbourne, East Sussex BN21 3BS.

BROWN, Sir (Cyril) Maxwell Palmer, (Sir Max), KCB 1969 (CB 1965); CMG 1957; Permanent Secretary, Department of Trade, March–June 1974; *b* 30 June 1914; *s* of late Cyril Palmer Brown; *m* 1940, Margaret May Gillhespy; three *s* one *d*. *Educ:* Wanganui College; Victoria University College, NZ; Clare College, Cambridge. Princ. Private Secretary to Pres. Board of Trade, 1946–49; Monopolies Commn, 1951–55; Counsellor (Commercial) Washington, 1955–57; returned to Board of Trade; Second Permanent Sec., 1968–70; Sec. (Trade), DTI, 1970–74; Mem., 1975–81, Dep. Chm., 1976–81, Monopolies and Mergers Commn. Director: John Brown & Co., 1975–82; ERA Technology Ltd, 1974–86; RHP Gp plc (formerly Ransome Hoffmann Pollard Ltd), 1975–88. *Address:* 20 Cottenham Park Road, Wimbledon, SW20 0RZ. *T:* 0181–946 7237.

BROWN, Dr Daniel McGillivray, BSc, PhD, ScD; FRS 1982; ARSC; Emeritus Reader in Organic Chemistry, Cambridge University, since 1983; Fellow of King's College, Cambridge, since 1953; Attached Fellow, Laboratory of Molecular Biology, Cambridge; *b* 3 Feb. 1923; *s* of David Cunninghame Brown and Catherine Stewart (*née* McGillivray); *m* 1953, Margaret Joyce Herbert; one *s* three *d*. *Educ:* Glasgow Acad.; Glasgow Univ. (BSc); London Univ. (PhD); Cambridge Univ. (PhD, ScD). Res. Chemist, Chester Beatty Res. Inst., 1945–53; Asst Dir of Res., 1953–58, Lectr, 1959–67, Reader in Org. Chem., 1967–83, Cambridge Univ.; Vice-Provost, King's Coll., Cambridge, 1974–81. Vis. Professor: Univ. of Calif, LA, 1959–60; Brandeis Univ., 1966–67. *Publications:* scientific papers, mainly in chemical jls. *Recreations:* modern art, gardening. *Address:* 60 Hartington Grove, Cambridge CB1 4UE. *T:* Cambridge (01223) 245304.

BROWN, Prof. David Anthony, PhD; FRS 1990; FIBiol; Professor of Pharmacology, Middlesex Hospital Medical School and University College London, since 1987; *b* 10 Feb. 1936; *s* of Alfred William and Florence Brown; *m* Susan Hames; two *s* one *d*. *Educ:* Univ. of London (BSc, BSc, PhD). Asst Lectr 1961–65, Lectr 1965–73, Dept of Pharmacology, St Bart's Hosp. Med. Coll.; Dept of Pharmacology, School of Pharmacy, Univ. of London: Sen Lectr, 1973–74; Reader, 1974–77; Professor, 1977–79; Wellcome Professor, 1979–87. Visiting Professor: Univ. of Chicago, 1970; Univ. of Iowa, 1971, 1973; Univ. of Texas, 1979, 1980, 1981; Vis. Scientist, Armed Forces Radiobiology Res. Inst., Bethesda, Md, 1976; Fogarty Schol.-in-Residence, NIH, Bethesda, 1985–86. Member: Physiological Soc., 1970; British Pharmacological Soc., 1965–; Biochemical Soc., 1969–; Academia Europaea, 1990. *Publications:* contribs to Jl of Physiology, British Jl of Pharmacology. *Recreation:* filling in forms. *Address:* Department of Pharmacology, University College London, Gower Street, WC1E 6BT.

BROWN, Prof. David Clifford; writer on music; Professor of Musicology, Southampton University, 1983–89, now Professor Emeritus; *b* 8 July 1929; *s* of Bertram and Constance Brown; *m* 1953, Elizabeth (*née* Valentine); two *d*. *Educ:* Sheffield Univ. (BA, MA, BMus); PhD Southampton Univ. LTCL. RAF 1952–54. Schoolmaster, 1954–59; Music Librarian, London Univ., 1959–62; Southampton University: Lectr in Music, 1962; Sen. Lectr, 1970; Reader, 1975. Many broadcast talks and scripts incl. series: Tchaikovsky and his World, 1980; Tchaikovsky: a fateful gift, 1984; A Sympathetic Person, 1989–90. Mem. Editl Cttee, Musica Britannica, 1980–. *Publications:* Thomas Weelkes, 1969; Mikhail Glinka, 1974; John Wilbye, 1974; Tchaikovsky, vol. 1, 1978, vol. 2, 1982 (Derek Allen Prize, British Acad.), vol. 3, 1986, vol. 4, 1991 (Yorkshire Post Music Book Award, 1992); Tchaikovsky Remembered, 1993; contribs to jls and periodicals. *Recreation:* walking. *Address:* Braishfield Lodge West, Braishfield, Romsey, Hants SO51 0PS. *T:* Braishfield (01794) 368163.

BROWN, David Colin, CMG 1995; HM Diplomatic Service; Head, Home Estates Department, Foreign and Commonwealth Office, since 1989; Project Director, Refurbishment of Foreign Office, Whitehall, since 1989; *b* 10 Aug. 1939; *yr s* of Alan James Brown and Catherine Mary Brown; *m* 1960, Ann Jackson; two *s* one *d*. *Educ:* Lymm Grammar Sch. Joined CRO, 1960; Tech. Aid Officer, Lagos, 1960–63; Admin Officer, Kingston, Jamaica, 1964–66; Diplomatic Service Admin Office, 1966–68; Second Sec., FCO, 1968; Vice-Consul (Commercial), Johannesburg, 1969–73; seconded to Commn on Rhodesian Opinion, Bulawayo, 1971; News Dept, FCO, 1974–77; Dep. High Comr, Port Louis, 1977–81; Overseas Inspectorate, 1981–83; Asst Hd, W Indian and Atlantic Dept, FCO, 1983–86; Dep. Consul Gen., Milan, 1986–89; Counsellor, 1989. *Recreations:* walking, gardening, building conservation. *Address:* c/o Foreign and Commonwealth Office, King Charles Street, SW1A 2AH.

BROWN, David John Bowes, CBE 1982; FCSD; Proprietor and Group Engineering and Market Research Director, Brown Group Holdings (Artix Ltd, and Brown Design Engineering Ltd); *b* 2 Aug. 1925; *s* of Matthew and Helene Brown; *m* 1st, 1954, Patricia Robson (marr. diss. 1982); two *s* two *d*; 2nd, 1986, Eve Watkinson. *Educ:* King James Grammar Sch., Knaresborough; Leeds College of Technology. Logging Contractor, UK and W Africa, 1946–60; joined Hunslet Engine Co. as Designer/Draughtsman, 1960–62; designed and patented transmission and exhaust gas conditioning systems for underground mines tractors; joined Chaseside as Chief Designer, 1962–65; designed and patented 4 wheel drive loading shovels; became Director and Chief Executive; joined Muir-Hill Ltd as Man. Dir, 1965–73; designed and patented 4 wheel drive tractors, cranes, steering systems, transmissions, axles; started DJB Engineering Ltd, 1973 (which became Artix Ltd, 1985); designed, manufactured and sold a range of off-highway articulated dump trucks in Peterlee, Co. Durham. The company has gained 4 Queen's Awards and 1 Design Council Award. Artix has exclusive design and manufg contracts with Caterpillar Inc.; Brown Design Engineering designs and builds Telescopic Handlers and the patented Multidrive system. FRSA. *Address:* Ravensthorpe Manor, Boltby, Thirsk, North Yorks YO7 2DX; Artix Ltd, Peterlee, Co Durham SR8 2HX. *T:* 0191–586 3333.

BROWN, David K.; *see* Kennett Brown.

BROWN, David Rodney H.; *see* Heath-Brown.

BROWN, Rev. Canon Prof. David William, PhD; Van Mildert Professor of Divinity, University of Durham and Canon of Durham Cathedral, since 1990; *b* 1 July 1948; *s* of David William Brown and Catherine Smith. *Educ:* Keil Sch., Dumbarton; Edinburgh Univ. (MA 1st cl. Classics 1970); Oriel Coll., Oxford (BA 1st cl. Phil. and Theol. 1972); Clare Coll., Cambridge (PhD 1976); Westcott House, Cambridge. Fellow, Chaplain and Tutor in Theol. and Phil., Oriel Coll., Oxford and Univ. Lectr in Theol., 1976–90. Vice-Chm., Doctrine Commn of C of E, 1990–95. *Publications:* Choices: ethics and the Christian, 1983; The Divine Trinity, 1985; Continental Philosophy and Modern Theology, 1987; Invitation to Theology, 1989; (ed) Newman: a man for our time, 1990; The Word To Set You Free, 1995. *Recreations:* gardening, reading, listening to music. *Address:* 14 The College, Durham DH1 3EQ. *T:* 0191–386 4657; Theology Department, Abbey House, Palace Green, Durham DH1 3RS. *T:* 0191–374 2064.

BROWN, Vice-Adm. Sir David (Worthington), KCB 1984; self-employed management consultant; *b* 28 Nov. 1927; *s* of late Captain J. R. S. Brown, RN and of Mrs D. M. E. Brown; *m* 1958, Etienne Hester Boileau; three *d*. *Educ:* HMS Conway. Joined RN, 1945; commanded HM Ships MGB 5036, MTB 5020, Dalswinton, Chailey, Cavendish, Falmouth, Hermione, Bristol; Dir, Naval Ops and Trade, 1971–72; Dir of Officers Appointments (Exec.), 1976–78; Asst Chief of Defence Staff (Ops), 1980–82; Flag Officer Plymouth, Port Adm. Devonport, 1982–85. Younger Brother of Trinity House. FIPD. *Recreations:* sailing, fishing. *Club:* Army and Navy.

BROWN, Hon. Dean Craig; MP (L) Finniss, South Australia, since 1993; Premier of South Australia and Minister for Multicultural and Ethnic Affairs, since 1993; *b* Adelaide, 5 Aug. 1943; *m* 1979, Rosslyn Judith Wadey; one *s* one *d*. *Educ:* Unley High Sch.; Univ. of New England, NSW (BRurSc, MRurSc); Australian Admin. Staff Coll.; S Australian Inst. of Technol. (Fellowship Dip. in Business Admin). MP (L) Davenport, 1973–85; Shadow Minister for Industrial Affairs, 1975–79; Minister for Industrial Affairs and for Public Works, 1979–82; Shadow Minister, 1982–85, for: Public Works; Transport; Technology; agricl consultant, 1985–92; MP (L) Alexandra, 1992–93; Leader of Opposition, 1992–93; Shadow Minister for Multicultural and Ethnic Affairs, 1992–93. *Publications:* contribs to political, technical and scientific jls. *Recreations:* jogging, fishing, gardening. *Address:* GPO Box 2343, Adelaide, SA 5000, Australia.

BROWN, Denise Lebreton, (Mrs Frank Waters), RE 1959 (ARE 1941); RWA 1986 (ARWA 1980); artist; *d* of Frederick Peter Brown and Jeanne Lebreton; *m* 1938, Frank William Eric Waters (*d* 1986); one *s*. *Educ:* Lyzeum Nonnenwerth im Rhein; Royal College of Art. British Instn Schol. in Engraving, 1932; ARCA 1935; RCA Travelling Schol., 1936; *prox. acc.* Rome Scholarship in Engraving, 1936. Has exhibited at: Royal Academy regularly since 1934; Royal Society of Painter-Etchers and Engravers; Royal West of England Acad.; also in Canada, USA and S Africa. Work represented in British, V&A, and Ashmolean Museums. *Publications:* books illustrated include: several on gardening; children's books, etc. *Recreations:* music, gardening. *Address:* 7 Priory Lodge, Nightingale Place, Rickmansworth, Herts WD3 2DG. *Club:* Royal Air Force.

BROWN, Denys Downing, CMG 1966; MM 1945; HM Diplomatic Service, retired; *b* 16 Dec. 1918; *s* of A. W. Brown, Belfast, and Marjorie Downing; *m* 1954, Patricia Marjorie, *e d* of Sir Charles Bartley; one *s* one *d*. *Educ:* Hereford Cathedral School; Brasenose College, Oxford (Scholar). Oxf. and Bucks LI, 1939–45 (prisoner-of-war, 1940; escaped, 1945). Entered Foreign Service, 1946; served in Poland, Germany, Egypt, Yugoslavia, Sweden, and FO; Minister (Economic), Bonn, retired 1971; Dir, P&O Steam Navigation Co., 1971–80. *Recreations:* reading, travel. *Address:* Step Cottage, Shadyhanger, Godalming, Surrey GU7 2HR. *T:* Godalming (01483) 416635.

BROWN, Sir Derrick H.; *see* Holden-Brown.

BROWN, Sir Douglas (Denison), Kt 1983; Chairman, 1981–87 and Managing Director, 1954–87, James Corson & Co. Ltd; *b* 8 July 1917; *s* of Robert and Alice Mary Brown; *m* 1941, Marion Cruickshanks Emmerson (*d* 1992); one *s* one *d*. *Educ:* Bablake Sch., Coventry. Served Army, 1940–46: RE, 1940–41; commnd RA, 1941; India, ME, N Africa, Italy; mentioned in despatches; retd in rank of Major. Member: Exec. Cttee, Clothing Manufrs of GB, 1967–82; Cttee, Wooltac, 1988– (Vice Chm., 1982–92); Exec., BCIA, 1988–90 (Hon. Mem., Yorks Humberside BCIA, 1990); Chairman: Leeds and Northern Clothing Assoc., 1975–77; Clothing Initiative, 1988–90; Leeds Clothing and Textile Centre, 1993–. Chairman: NW Leeds Cons. Assoc., 1961–74 (Pres. 1974); Yorks Area Cons. Assoc., 1978–83 (Treasurer, 1971–78); Mem., Nat. Exec. Cttee, Cons. and Unionist Assoc., 1971–90; Mem., Cons. Bd of Finance, 1971–78. Dir, Computer Internat., 1993–. Mem., Gas Consumer Council, NE Area, 1981–86; Bd Mem., Yorkshire Water Authority, 1983–86. President: Water Aid Yorkshire, 1988; Leeds Gardeners' Fedn, 1991–94; Vice-Chm., St Edmund's PCC, Roundhay, 1981–. Chm., Bd of Governors, Jacob Kramer Coll. of Further Educn, 1978–92 (Gov., 1975–93); Chm. Govs, Leeds Coll. of Art and Design, 1993–. *Recreations:* gardening, Rugby, cricket, golf. *Address:* Bankfield, 6 North Park Road, Leeds LS8 1JD. *T:* Leeds (0113) 266 2151.

BROWN, Hon. Sir Douglas (Dunlop), Kt 1989; **Hon. Mr Justice Douglas Brown;** a Judge of the High Court of Justice, Family Division, since 1989; *b* 22 Dec. 1931; *s* of late Robert Dunlop Brown, MICE, and Anne Cameron Brown; *m* 1960, June Margaret Elizabeth McNamara; one *s*. *Educ:* Ryleys Sch., Alderley Edge; Manchester Grammar Sch.; Manchester Univ. (LLB). Served in RN, 1953–55; Lieut, RNR. Called to Bar, Gray's Inn, 1953; Bencher, 1989; practised Northern Circuit from 1955; Mem. General

Council of Bar, 1967–71; Asst Recorder, Salford City QS, 1971; a Recorder of the Crown Court, 1972–80; QC 1976; a Circuit Judge, 1980–88; Family Div. Liaison Judge, Northern Circuit, 1990–95. Mem., Parole Bd for England and Wales, 1985–87. *Recreations:* cricket, golf, music. *Address:* Royal Courts of Justice, Strand, WC2A 2LL. *Club:* Wilmslow Golf.

BROWN, Edmund Gerald, Jr, (Jerry Brown); lawyer, writer and politician; Attorney with Fulbright Jaworski, 1986–91; *b* 7 April 1938; *s* of Edmund Gerald Brown and Bernice (*née* Layne). *Educ:* Univ. of California at Berkeley (BA 1961); Yale Law School (JD 1964). Admitted to California Bar, 1965; Research Attorney, Calif. Supreme Court, 1964–65; with Tuttle & Taylor, LA, 1966–70; Sec. of State, Calif., 1971–74; Governor of California, 1975–83; Democratic Candidate for US Senator from California, 1982; Chm., California Democratic Party, 1989–91; Candidate for Democratic Presidential Nomination, 1992. Founder, We the People, 1992. Trustee, Los Angeles Community Colls, 1969–70. *Address:* 295 Third Street, Oakland, CA 94607, USA.

BROWN, Prof. Edwin Thomas, PhD, DSc Eng; FEng; FTS; FIEAust; FIMM; Deputy Vice-Chancellor, University of Queensland, Australia, since 1990 (Dean of Engineering, 1987–90); *b* 4 Dec. 1938; *s* of George O. and Bessie M. Brown. *Educ:* Castlemaine High Sch.; Univ. of Melbourne (BE 1960, MEngSc 1964); Univ. of Queensland (PhD 1969); Univ. of London (DSc Eng 1985). MICE 1976; MASCE 1965; FIMM 1980; FIEAust 1987 (MIEAust 1965); FTS 1990. Engr, State Electricity Commn of Victoria, 1960–64; James Cook Univ. of North Queensland (formerly UC of Townsville): Lectr, 1965–69; Sen. Lectr, 1969–72; Associate Prof. of Civil Engrg, 1972–75; Imperial College, Univ. of London: Reader in Rock Mechanics, 1975–79; Prof. of Rock Mechanics, 1979–87; Dean, RSM, 1983–86; Hd, Dept of Mineral Resources Engrg, 1985–87. Res. Associate, Dept of Civil and Mineral Engrg, Univ. of Minnesota, 1970; Sen. Visitor, Dept of Engrg, Univ. of Cambridge, 1974; Vis. Prof., Dept of Mining and Fuels Engrg, Univ. of Utah, 1979. Chm., British Geotechnical Soc., 1982–83; Pres., Internat. Soc. for Rock Mechanics, 1983–87. Foreign Mem., Royal Acad. (formerly Fellowship) of Engrg, 1989. Instn of Mining and Metallurgy: Consolidated Gold Fields Gold Medal, 1984; Sir Julius Wernher Meml Lecture, 1985. Editor-in-Chief, Internat. Jl of Rock Mechanics and Mining Sciences, 1975–82. *Publications:* (with E. Hoek) Underground Excavations in Rock, 1980; (ed) Rock Characterization, Testing and Monitoring, 1981; (with B. H. G. Brady) Rock Mechanics for Underground Mining, 1985, 2nd edn 1993; (ed) Analytical and Computational Methods in Engineering Rock Mechanics, 1987; papers on rock mechanics in civil engrg and mining jls. *Recreations:* cricket, jazz. *Address:* J. D. Story Building, University of Queensland, St Lucia, Qld 4072, Australia. *T:* (7) 33651316.

BROWN, Elizabeth, (Mrs Ray Brown); *see* Vaughan, E.

BROWN, Prof. Eric Herbert, PhD; Professor of Geography, University College London, 1966–88, Honorary Research Fellow, since 1988; *b* 8 Dec. 1922; *s* of Samuel Brown and Ada Brown, Melton Mowbray, Leics; *m* 1945, Eileen (*née* Reynolds) (*d* 1984), Llanhowell, Dyfed; two *d*. *Educ:* King Edward VII Grammar Sch., Melton Mowbray; King's Coll., London (BSc 1st Cl. Hons). MSc Wales, PhD London. Served War: RAF Pilot, Coastal Comd, 1941–45. Asst Lectr, then Lectr in Geography, University Coll. of Wales, Aberystwyth, 1947–49; University College London: Lectr, then Reader in Geog., 1950–66; Dean of Students, 1972–75; Alumnus Dir, 1989–91; Mem. Senate, Univ. of London, 1981–86. Vis. Lectr, Indiana Univ., USA, 1953–54; Vis. Prof., Monash Univ., Melbourne, 1971. Mem., NERC, 1981–84. Geographical Adviser, Govt of Argentina, 1965–66, 1992–94; Hon. Mem., Geograph. Soc. of Argentina, 1968. Chairman: British Geomorphol Res. Group, 1971–72; British Nat. Cttee for Geog., 1985–90. Royal Geographical Society: Back Grant, 1961; Hon. Sec., 1977–87; Vice-Pres., 1988–89, Hon. Vice-Pres., 1989; Hon. Fellow, 1989; Pres., Inst. of British Geographers, 1978. Foreign Mem., Polish Acad. of Scis and Letters, 1992. *Publications:* The Relief and Drainage of Wales, 1961; (with W. R. Mead) The USA and Canada, 1962; (ed) Geography Yesterday and Tomorrow, 1980; contrib. Geog. Jl, Phil. Trans Royal Soc., Proc. Geologists' Assoc., Trans Inst. of British Geographers, and Geography. *Recreations:* watching Rugby football, wine. *Address:* Monterey, Castle Hill, Berkhamsted, Herts HP4 1HE. *T:* Berkhamsted (01442) 864077. *Clubs:* Athenæum, Geographical.

BROWN, Captain Eric Melrose, CBE 1970 (OBE 1945; MBE 1944); DSC 1942; AFC 1947; RN; Vice-President, European Helicopter Association, since 1992 (Chief Executive, 1980–92); *b* 21 Jan. 1919; *s* of Robert John Brown and Euphemia (*née* Melrose); *m* 1942, Evelyn Jean Margaret Macrory; one *s*. *Educ:* Royal High Sch., Edinburgh; Edinburgh University. MA 1947. Joined Fleet Air Arm as Pilot, 1939; Chief Naval Test Pilot, 1944–49 (RN Boyd Trophy, 1948); Resident British Test Pilot at USN Air Test Center, Patuxent River, 1951–52; CO No 804 Sqdn, 1953–54; Comdr (Air), RN Air Stn, Brawdy, 1954–56; Head of British Naval Air Mission to Germany, 1958–60; Dep. Dir (Air), Gunnery Div., Admty, 1961; Dep. Dir, Naval Air Warfare and Adviser on Aircraft Accidents, Admty, 1962–64; Naval Attaché, Bonn, 1965–67; CO, RN Air Stn, Lossiemouth, 1967–70. Chief Exec., British Helicopter Adv. Bd, 1970–87, Vice-Pres., 1988–. Chm., British Aviation Bicentenary Exec. Cttee, 1984. FRAeS 1964 (Pres., 1982–83; Chm., RAeS Rotorcraft Sect., 1973–76). Hon. FEng (Pakistan) 1984; Hon. Fellow, Soc. of Experimental Test Pilots, 1984. Liveryman, GAPAN, 1978. British Silver Medal for Practical Achievement in Aeronautics, 1949; Anglo-French Breguet Trophy, 1983; Bronze Medal, Fédération Aéronautique Internationale, 1986. *Publications:* Wings on My Sleeve, 1961; (jtly) Aircraft Carriers, 1969; Wings of the Luftwaffe, 1977; Wings of the Navy, 1980; The Helicopter in Civil Operations, 1981; Wings of the Weird and the Wonderful, vol. 1, 1982, vol. 2, 1985; Duels in the Sky, 1989; Testing for Combat, 1994. *Recreations:* travel, philately, bridge. *Address:* Carousel, New Domewood, Copthorne, W Sussex RH10 3HF. *T:* Copthorne (01342) 712610. *Clubs:* Naval and Military, City Livery; Explorers' (NY).

BROWN, Prof. Fred, FRS 1981; Adjunct Professor, School of Epidemiology and Public Health, Yale University, since 1990; Professorial Fellow, Queen's University, Belfast, since 1986; *b* 31 Jan. 1925; *m* 1948, Audrey Alice Doherty; two *s*. *Educ:* Burnley Grammar Sch.; Manchester Univ. BSc 1944, MSc 1946, PhD 1948. Asst Lectr, Manchester Univ., 1946–48; Lectr, Bristol Univ. Food Preservation Res. Station, 1948–50; Senior Scientific Officer: Hannah Dairy Res. Inst., Ayr, 1950–53; Christie Hosp. and Holt Radium Inst., Manchester, 1953–55; Head, Biochemistry Dept, 1955–83, and Dep. Dir, 1980–83, Animal Virus Res. Inst., Pirbright, Surrey; Hd of Virology Div., Wellcome Res. Labs, Beckenham, Kent, 1983–90; Prof. of Microbiology, Univ. of Surrey, 1989–90. Vis. Scientist, US Dept of Agric., Plum Is. Animal Disease Centre, NY, 1995–. Hon. DSc QUB, 1992. *Publications:* papers on viruses causing animal diseases, in scientific journals. *Recreations:* watching cricket, Association football, listening to classical music, fell walking. *Address:* Syndal, Glaziers Lane, Normandy, Surrey GU3 2DF. *T:* Guildford (01483) 811107.

BROWN, Sir (Frederick Herbert) Stanley, Kt 1967; CBE 1959; BSc; FEng, FIMechE, FIEE; retired; Chairman, Central Electricity Generating Board, 1965–72 (Deputy-Chairman, 1959–64); *b* 9 Dec. 1910; *s* of Clement and Annie S. Brown; *m* 1937, Marjorie Nancy Brown; two *d*. *Educ:* King Edward's School, Birmingham; Birmingham University. Corp. of Birmingham Electric Supply Dept, 1932–46; West Midlands Joint Electricity Authority, 1946–47; Liverpool Corporation Electricity Supply Department, 1947–48; Merseyside and N Wales Division of British Electricity Authority; Generation Engineer (Construction), 1948–49; Chief Generation Engineer (Construction), 1949–51; Deputy Generation Design Engineer of British Electricity Authority, 1951–54; Generation Design Engineer, 1954–57, Chief Engineer, 1957, of Central Electricity Authority; Member for Engineering, Central Elec. Generating Board, 1957–59. President: Instn of Electrical Engineers, 1967–68; EEIBA, 1969–70. Member: Council, City and Guilds of London Inst., 1969–; Court of Govs, Univ. of Birmingham, 1969–. Hon. DSc: Aston, 1971; Salford, 1972. *Publications:* various papers to technical institutions. *Recreation:* gardening. *Address:* Cobbler's Hill, Compton Abdale, Glos GL54 4DR. *T:* Withington (01242) 890233.

BROWN, Rev. Canon Geoffrey Harold; Vicar of St Martin-in-the-Fields, 1985–95; *b* 1 April 1930; *s* of Harry and Ada Brown; *m* 1963, Elizabeth Jane Williams; two *d*. *Educ:* Monmouth Sch.; Trinity Hall, Cambridge. MA. Asst Curate, St Andrew's, Plaistow, 1954–60; Asst Curate, St Peter's, Birmingham and Sub-Warden of Pre-Ordination Training Scheme, 1960–63; Rector: St George's, Newtown, Birmingham, 1963–73; Grimsby, 1973–85. Hon. Canon Lincoln Cathedral, 1978; Canon Emeritus, 1985. FRSA 1991. *Recreations:* the countryside, photography, theatre. *Address:* 32 Church Street, Hagley, near Stourbridge, W Midlands DY9 0NA.

BROWN, Geoffrey Howard; Film Critic, The Times, since 1990; *b* 1 March 1949; *s* of John Howard Brown and Nancy (*née* Fardoe); *m* 1985, Catherine Ann Surowiec. *Educ:* King Henry VIII Grammar Sch., Coventry; Pembroke Coll., Cambridge (BA); Royal Coll. of Art (Sch. of Film and TV, MA). Dep. Film Critic, Financial Times, 1977–81; Film Critic, Radio Times, 1981–89; Dep. Film Critic, The Times, 1981–90. *Publications:* Walter Forde, 1977; Launder and Gilliat, 1977; Der Produzent: Michael Balcon und der Englische Film, 1981; Michael Balcon: the pursuit of British cinema (essay), 1984; The Common Touch: the films of John Baxter, 1989. *Recreation:* music. *Address:* The Times, 1 Pennington Street, E1 9XN. *T:* 0171–782 5167.

BROWN, Geoffrey Robert C.; *see* Clifton-Brown.

BROWN, Hon. George Arthur, CMG; Governor, Bank of Jamaica, 1967–78 and 1989; *b* 25 July 1922; *s* of Samuel Austin Brown and Gertrude Brown; *m* 1964, Leila Leonie Gill; two *d* (and one *s* one *d* by previous marriage). *Educ:* St Simon's College, Jamaica; London School of Economics. Jamaica Civil Service: Income Tax Dept, 1941; Colonial Secretary's Office, 1951; Asst Secretary, Min. of Finance, 1954; Director, General Planning Unit, 1957; Financial Secretary, 1962; Dep. Administrator, 1978–84, Associate Administrator, 1984–89, UNDP. *Publications:* contrib. Social and Economic Studies (University College of the West Indies). *Recreations:* hiking, boating, fishing. *Address:* c/o Bank of Jamaica, PO Box 621, Kingston, Jamaica. *Club:* Jamaica (Jamaica).

BROWN, George Mackay, OBE 1974; FRSL 1977; author; *b* 17 Oct. 1921; *s* of John Brown and Mary Jane Mackay. *Educ:* Stromness Acad.; Newbattle Abbey Coll.; Edinburgh Univ. (MA). Hon. MA Open Univ., 1976; Hon. LLD Dundee, 1977; Hon. DLitt Glasgow, 1985. *Publications: fiction:* A Calendar of Love, 1967; A Time to Keep, 1969; Greenvoe, 1972; Magnus, 1973; Hawkfall, 1974; The Two Fiddlers, 1975; The Sun's Net, 1976; Pictures in the Cave, 1977; Six Lives of Frankle the Cat, 1980; Andrina, 1983; Time in a Red Coat, 1984; Christmas Stories, 1985; The Golden Bird, 1987; The Masked Fisherman, 1989; The Sea King's Daughter, 1991; Vinland, 1992; Beside the Ocean of Time, 1994; *plays:* A Spell for Green Corn, 1970; Three Plays, 1984; The Loom of Light, 1986; A Celebration for Magnus (son et lumière), 1987; *poetry:* Loaves and Fishes, 1959; The Year of the Whale, 1965; Fishermen with Ploughs, 1971; Winterfold, 1976; Selected Poems, 1977; Voyages, 1983; Christmas Poems, 1984; Tryst in Egilsay, 1989; The Wreck of the Archangel, 1989; Selected Poems 1954–1983, 1991; Forresterhill, 1992; The Lost Village, 1993; *essays, etc:* An Orkney Tapestry, 1969; Letters from Hamnavoe, 1975; Under Brinkie's Brae, 1979; Portrait of Orkney, 1981; (ed) Selected Prose of Edwin Muir, 1987; Letters to Gypsy, 1990; Rockpools and Daffodils, 1993. *Recreation:* reading. *Address:* 3 Mayburn Court, Stromness, Orkney KW16 3DH.

BROWN, Prof. Sir (George) Malcolm, Kt 1985; FRS 1975; consultant geologist; Director: British Geological Survey (formerly Institute of Geological Sciences), 1979–85; Geological Museum, 1979–85; Geological Survey of Northern Ireland, 1979–85; *b* 5 Oct. 1925; *s* of late George Arthur Brown and Anne Brown; *m* 1st, 1963 (marr. diss. 1977); 2nd, 1985, Sally Jane Marston, *e d* of A. D. Spencer, *qv*; two step *d*. *Educ:* Coatham Sch., Redcar; Durham Univ. (BSc, DSc); Oxford Univ. (MA, DPhil). RAF, 1944–47. FGS. Commonwealth Fund (Harkness) Fellow, Princeton Univ., 1954–55; Lectr in Petrology, Oxford Univ., 1955–66; Fellow, St Cross Coll., Oxford, 1965–67; Carnegie Instn Res. Fellow, Geophysical Lab., Washington DC, 1966–67; Prof. of Geology, 1967–79 (now Emeritus), Dean of Faculty of Science, 1978–79, and Pro-Vice-Chancellor, 1979, Durham Univ. Vis. Prof., Univ. of Berne, 1977–78; Adrian Vis. Fellow, Univ. of Leicester, 1983. NASA Principal Investigator, Apollo Moon Programme, 1967–75; Geol Advr to ODA, 1979–85; Chm., Internat. Geol Correlation Prog. (IUGS–UNESCO), 1993–. Member: Natural Environment Res. Council, 1972–75; Council, Royal Soc., 1980–81. Pres., Section C (Geology), British Assoc., 1987–88. Member: Council, RHBNC, Univ. of London, 1987–89; Adv. Bd, Sch. of Envmtl Scis, Univ. of E Anglia, 1991–94. UK Editor, Physics and Chemistry of the Earth, 1977–79. Hon. Foreign Fellow, Geol Soc. of America, 1993. Hon. DSc Leicester, 1984; DUniv Open, 1990. Daniel Pidgeon Fund Award, 1952, Wollaston Fund Award, 1963, Murchison Medal, 1981, Geol Soc. of London. *Publications:* (with L. R. Wager) Layered Igneous Rocks, 1968; (contrib.) Methods in Geochemistry, 1960; (contrib.) Basalts, 1967; (contrib.) Planet Earth, 1977; (contrib.) Origin of the Solar System, 1978; papers in several sci. jls. *Recreations:* travel and exploration, classical guitar playing. *Address:* Rose Dene, Shipton Road, Milton-under-Wychwood, Oxford OX7 6JT. *T:* Shipton (01993) 830812. *Club:* Royal Over-Seas League.

BROWN, Sir George (Noel), Kt 1991; **Hon. Chief Justice Brown;** Chief Justice, Belize, since 1990; Deputy Governor-General, since 1985; *b* 13 June 1942; *s* of late Noel Todd Brown and Elma Priscilla Brown; *m* 1974, Magdalene Elizabeth Bucknor; two *d*, and one *s* one *d* from previous marriage. *Educ:* St Michael's Coll., Belize City; Carlton Univ., Ottawa (Cert. in Public Admin); Univ. of WI (LLB Hons); Norman Manley Law Sch., Council of Legal Educn, Univ. of WI (Legal Educn Cert.); Nairobi Law Sch., Kenya (Cert. in Legislative Drafting). Customs Examiner, Customs and Excise Dept, 1960–67; Clerk of Courts, Magistracy Dept, 1967–69; Admin. Asst, Min. of Trade and Ind., 1970–72; Actg Magistrate, Belize Judicial Dist and Itinerant countrywide, 1972–73; Crown Counsel, Attorney General's Ministry, 1978–81; Solicitor General, 1981–84; Puisne Judge, Supreme Court Justice, 1984–85 and 1986–90; Actg Chief Justice, 1985–86. *Publication:* Consumer Society and the Law, 1976. *Recreations:* yachting, football (soccer), especially coaching and managing primary and secondary schools teams. *Address:* c/o Supreme Court, Belize City, PO Box 170, Belize, Central America. *T:* (2) 77256; PO Box 236, Belize City, Belize. *T:* (2) 77055. *Club:* Belize Yacht (Belize City).

BROWN, Prof. George William, OBE 1995; FBA 1986; Member, External Scientific Staff, Medical Research Council, since 1980; Hon. Professor of Sociology, Royal Holloway and Bedford New College, London University, since 1980; *b* 15 Nov. 1930; *s* of late William G. Brown and of Lily Jane (*née* Hillier); *m* 1st, 1954, Gillian M. Hole (marr. diss. 1970); one *s* one *d*; 2nd, 1978, Seija T. Sandberg (marr. diss. 1987); one *d*; 3rd, 1990, Elizabeth A. Davies; one *s*. *Educ:* Kilburn Grammar Sch.; University Coll. London (BA Anthropol. 1954); LSE (PhD 1961). Scientific Staff, DSIR, 1955–56; MRC Social Psychiatry Res. Unit, Inst. of Psychiatry, 1956–67; joined Social Res. Unit, Bedford Coll., London Univ., 1967; Prof. of Sociology, London Univ. and Jt Dir, Social Res. Unit, Bedford Coll., 1973–80. Mem., Academia Europaea, 1990. Hon.FRCPsych, 1987 *Publications:* (jtly) Schizophrenia and Social Care, 1966; (with J. K. Wing) Institutionalism and Schizophrenia, 1970; (with T. O. Harris) Social Origins of Depression, 1978; Life Events and Illness, 1989; numerous contribs to jls. *Address:* 40 Addington Square, SE5 7LB. *T:* 0171–703 2124.

BROWN, Prof. Gillian, CBE 1992; Professor of English as an International Language, University of Cambridge, since 1988; Fellow of Clare College, Cambridge, since 1988; *b* 23 Jan. 1937; *d* of Geoffrey Rencher Read and Elsie Olive Chapman; *m* 1959, Edward Keith Brown; three *d*. *Educ:* Perse Sch. for Girls; Girton Coll., Cambridge (MA); Univ. of Edinburgh (PhD 1971). Lectr, University Coll. of Cape Coast, Ghana, 1962–64; Lectr, 1965–81, Reader, 1981–83, Univ. of Edinburgh; Prof., Univ. of Essex, 1983–88 (Dean of Social Scis, 1985–88). Mem., ESRC Educn and Human Devlt Cttee, 1983–87; Chm., Research Grants Board, ESRC, 1987–90; Member: Kingman Cttee, 1987–88; UGC, subseq. UFC, 1988–91; Council, Philological Soc., 1988–93; British Council English Teaching Adv. Cttee, 1989–94; Cttee of Mgt, British Inst. in Paris, 1990–. Curator, Sch. of Advanced Studies, Univ. of London, 1994–. Gov., Bell Educnl Trust, 1987–92. Dr *hc* Univ. of Lyon, 1987. Member, Editorial Boards: Jl of Semantics; Jl of Applied Linguistics; Second Language Acquisition Res. *Publications:* Phonological Rules and Dialect Variation, 1972; Listening to Spoken English, 1977; (with George Yule) Discourse Analysis, 1983; articles in learned jls. *Address:* Clare College, Cambridge CB2 1TL.

BROWN, Dame Gillian (Gerda), DCVO 1981; CMG 1971; HM Diplomatic Service, retired; *b* 10 Aug. 1923; *er d* of late Walter Brown and late Gerda Brown (*née* Grenside). *Educ:* The Spinney, Gt Bookham; Stoatley Hall, Haslemere; Somerville Coll., Oxford (Hon. Fellow 1981). FO, 1944–52; 2nd Sec., Budapest, 1952–54; FO, 1954–59; 1st Sec., Washington, 1959–62; 1st Sec., UK Delegn to OECD, Paris, 1962–65; FO, 1965–66; Counsellor and Head of Gen. Dept, FO, subseq. Head of Aviation, Marine and Telecommunications Dept, later Marine and Transport Dept, FCO, 1967–70; Counsellor, Berne, 1970–74; Under Sec., Dept of Energy, 1975–78; Asst Under Sec. of State, FCO, 1978–80; Ambassador to Norway, 1981–83. Mem., Panel of Chairmen, CSSB, 1984–88. Council Mem., Greenwich Forum, 1985–. Chm., Anglo-Norse Soc., 1988–. Hon. LLD Bath, 1981. Grand Cross, Order of St Olav, 1981. *Address:* c/o Midland Bank plc, Central Hall, Westminster, SW1P 3AS.

BROWN, Prof. Godfrey Norman; Professor of Education, University of Keele, 1967–80, now Emeritus; Director, Betley Court Gallery, since 1980; *b* 13 July 1926; *s* of Percy Charles and Margaret Elizabeth Brown; *m* 1960, Dr Freda Bowyer; three *s*. *Educ:* Whitgift Sch.; School of Oriental and African Studies, London; Merton Coll., Oxford (MA, DPhil). Army service, RAC and Intelligence Corps, 1944–48. Social Affairs Officer, UN Headquarters, NY, 1953–54; Sen. History Master, Barking Abbey Sch., Essex, 1954–57; Lectr in Educn, University Coll. of Ghana, 1958–61; Sen. Lectr, 1961, Prof., 1963, Univ. of Ibadan, Nigeria; Dir, Univ. of Keele Inst. of Educn, 1967–80. Visiting Prof., Univ. of Rhodesia and Nyasaland, 1963; Chm., Assoc. for Recurrent Educn, 1976–77; Mem., Exec. Cttee and Bd of Dirs, World Council for Curriculum and Instruction, 1974–77. OECD Consultant on teacher education, Portugal, 1980. Vice-Pres., Community Council of Staffs, 1984–. Collector of the Year Award, Art and Antiques, 1981; Newcastle-under-Lyme Civic Award for Conservation, 1990. *Publications:* An Active History of Ghana, 2 vols, 1961 and 1964; Living History, 1967; Apartheid, a Teacher's Guide, 1981; Betley Through the Centuries, 1985; This Old House: a domestic biography, 1987; ed (with J. C. Anene) Africa in the Nineteenth and Twentieth Centuries, 1966; ed, Towards a Learning Community, 1971; ed (with M. Hiskett) Conflict and Harmony in Education in Tropical Africa, 1975; contrib. educnl and cultural jls. *Recreations:* family life; art history, conservation. *Address:* Betley Court, Betley, near Crewe, Cheshire CW3 9BH. *T:* Crewe (01270) 820652.

BROWN, Gordon; *see* Brown, James G.

BROWN, Harold, PhD; Counselor, Center for Strategic and International Studies, since 1992; *b* 19 Sept. 1927; *s* of A. H. Brown and Gertrude Cohen Brown; *m* 1953, Colene McDowell; two *d*. *Educ:* Columbia Univ. (AB 1945, AM 1946, PhD in Physics 1949). Res. Scientist, Columbia Univ., 1945–50, Lectr in Physics, 1947–48; Lectr in Physics, Stevens Inst. of Technol., 1949–50; Res. Scientist, Radiation Lab., Univ. of Calif, Berkeley, 1951–52; Gp Leader, Radiation Lab., Livermore, 1952–61; Dir, Def. Res. and Engrg, Dept of Def., 1961–65; Sec. of Air Force, 1965–69; Pres., Calif Inst. of Technol., Pasadena, 1969–77; Sec. of Defense, USA, 1977–81; Vis. Prof., 1981–84, Chm., 1984–92, Johns Hopkins Foreign Policy Inst., Sch. of Advanced Internat. Studies. Sen. Sci. Adviser, Conf. on Discontinuance of Nuclear Tests, 1958–59; Delegate, Strategic Arms Limitations Talks, Helsinki, Vienna and Geneva, 1969–77. Member: Polaris Steering Cttee, 1956–58; Air Force Sci. Adv. Bd, 1956–61; (also Consultant) President's Sci. Adv. Cttee, 1958–61. Hon. DEng Stevens Inst. of Technol., 1964; Hon. LLD: Long Island Univ., 1966; Gettysburg Coll., 1967; Occidental Coll., 1969; Univ. of Calif, 1969; Hon. ScD: Univ. of Rochester, 1975; Brown Univ., 1977; Univ. of the Pacific, 1978; Univ. of S Carolina, 1979; Franklin and Marshall Coll., 1982; Chung Ang Univ. (Seoul, Korea), 1983. Member: Amer. Phys. Soc., 1946; Nat. Acad. of Engrg, 1967; Amer. Acad. of Arts and Scis, 1969; Nat. Acad. of Scis, 1977. One of Ten Outstanding Young Men of Year, US Jun. Chamber of Commerce, 1961; Columbia Univ. Medal of Excellence, 1963; Air Force Exceptl Civil. Service Award, 1969; Dept of Def. Award for Exceptionally Meritorious Service, 1969; Joseph C. Wilson Award, 1976; Presidential Medal of Freedom, 1981. *Publication:* Thinking About National Security: defense and foreign policy in a dangerous world, 1983. *Address:* Center for Strategic and International Studies, Suite 400, 1800 K Street, NW, Washington, DC 20006, USA. *Clubs:* Bohemian (San Francisco); City Tavern (Washington, DC).

BROWN, Harold Arthur Neville, CMG 1963; CVO 1961; HM Diplomatic Service, retired; *b* 13 Dec. 1914; *s* of Stanley Raymond and Gladys Maud Brown; *m* 1939, Mary McBeath Urquhart (*d* 1994); one *s* one *d*. *Educ:* Cardiff High School; University College, Cardiff. Entered Ministry of Labour as 3rd Class Officer, 1939; Asst Principal, 1943; Private Sec. to Permanent Sec. of Min. of Labour and Nat. Service, 1944–46; Principal, 1946; Labour Attaché, Mexico City (and other countries in Central America and the Caribbean), 1950–54; transferred to Foreign Office, 1955; Head of Chancery, Rangoon, 1958 and 1959; British Ambassador in Liberia, 1960–63; Corps of Inspectors, Foreign Office, 1963–66; Ambassador to Cambodia, 1966–70; Consul-General, Johannesburg, 1970–73; Minister, Pretoria, Cape Town, 1973–74. Knight Great Band of the Humane Order of African Redemption, 1962. *Address:* 14 Embassy Court, King's Road, Brighton BN1 2PX.

BROWN, Harold James, AM 1979; BSc, ME; Hon. DSc; FIE(Australia); FIREE; retired; management consultant, Adelaide, South Australia, 1976–85; Technical Director, Philips Industries Holdings Ltd, Sydney, 1961–76; *b* 10 July 1911; *s* of Allison James and Hilda Emmy Brown; *m* 1936, Hazel Merlyn Dahl Helm; two *s* two *d*. *Educ:* Fort Street Boys' High Sch.; Univ. of Sydney, NSW, Australia. BSc 1933; BE (Univ. Medal) 1935; ME (Univ. Medal) 1945; Hon. DSc 1976. Research Engineer, Amalgamated Wireless Australasia Ltd, 1935–37; Electrical Engineer, Hydro-electric Commission of Tasmania, 1937–39; Research Officer and Principal Research Officer, Council for Scientific and Industrial Research, 1939–45; Chief Communications Engineer, Australian Nat. Airways Pty Ltd, 1945–47; Prof. of Electrical Engineering, Dean of Faculty of Engineering and Asst Director, NSW Univ. of Technology, 1947–52; Controller R&D, Dept of Supply, Melbourne, 1952–54; Controller, Weapons Research Establishment, Department of Supply, Commonwealth Government of Australia, 1955–58; Technical Director, Rola Co. Pty Ltd, Melbourne, 1958–61. Awarded Queen's Silver Jubilee Medal, 1977. *Publications:* numerous technical articles in scientific journals. *Recreations:* gardening, bowling. *Address:* 20 Woodbridge, 6 Island Drive, West Lakes, SA 5021, Australia.

BROWN, (Harold) Vivian (Bigley); Head of Small Firms and Business Link Division, Department of Trade and Industry, since 1994; *b* 20 Aug. 1945; *s* of Alec Sidney Brown and Joyce Brown (*née* Bigley); *m* 1970, Jean Josephine Bowyer, *yr d* of late Sir Eric Bowyer, KCB, KBE and Lady Bowyer (now Lady Caine); two *s*. *Educ:* Leeds Grammar Sch.; St John's Coll., Oxford (BA); St Cross Coll., Oxford (BPhil Islamic Philosophy). Min. of Technology, 1970; DTI, 1972–74 (Private Sec. to Permanent Sec., 1972–73); FCO, 1975–79 (First Sec. Commercial Jeddah); DTI, 1979–86; Hd of Sci. and Technol. Assessment Office, Cabinet Office, 1986–89; Hd of Competition Policy Div., 1989–91; Hd of Investigations Div., 1991–92, of Deregulation Unit, 1992–94, DTI. *Publication:* Islamic Philosophy and the Classical Tradition (with S. M. Stern and A. Hourani), 1972. *Recreations:* playing piano, cycling, cooking. *Address:* Department of Trade and Industry, 66–74 Victoria Street, SW1E 6SW.

BROWN, Henry Thomas C.; *see* Cadbury-Brown.

BROWN, Prof. Herbert Charles, PhD; R. B. Wetherill Research Professor Emeritus, Purdue University, 1978 (Professor, 1947–60, R. B. Wetherill Research Professor, 1960–78); *b* 22 May 1912; *s* of Charles Brown and Pearl (*née* Gorinstein); *m* 1937, Sarah Baylen; one *s*. *Educ:* Wright Jun. Coll., Chicago (Assoc. Sci. 1935); Univ. of Chicago (BS 1936; PhD 1938). Univ. of Chicago: Eli Lilly Postdoctoral Res. Fellow, 1938–39; Instr, 1939–43; Wayne University: Asst Prof., 1943–46; Associate Prof., 1946–47. Member: Nat. Acad. of Sciences, USA, 1957–; Amer. Acad. of Arts and Sciences, 1966–; Hon. Mem., Phi Lambda Upsilon, 1961–; Hon. Fellow, Chem. Soc., London, 1978– (Centenary Lectr, 1955; C. K. Ingold Medal, 1978); Foreign Fellow, Indian Nat. Science Acad., 1978–. Hon. Dr of Science: Univ. of Chicago, 1968; Wayne State Univ., 1980; Hebrew Univ. Jerusalem, 1980; Pontifica Univ. Catolica de Chile, 1980; Wales, 1982; Purdue, 1982, etc. (Jtly) Nobel Prize in Chemistry, 1979. Amer. Chemical Society: Harrison Howe Award, Rochester Sect., 1953; Nichols Medal, NY Sect., 1959; Linus Pauling Medal, Oregon and Puget Sound Sects, 1968; Roger Adams Medal, Organic Div., 1971; Priestley Medal, 1981. Award for Creative Res. in Org. Chem., Soc. of Organic Chem. Mfg Assoc., 1960; Herbert Newby McCoy Award, Purdue Univ., 1965 (1st co-recipient); Nat. Medal of Science, US Govt, 1969; Madison Marshall Award, 1975; Allied Chemical Award for Grad. Trng and Innovative Chem., 1978 (1st recipient); Perkins Medal, Amer. Sect., Soc. of Chemical Industry, 1982; Gold Medal, Amer. Inst. Chem., 1985; Chem. Sci. Award, Nat. Acad. of Scis, 1987; G. M. Kossolopoff Medal, Auburn Sect., Amer. Chem. Soc., 1987. Order of the Rising Sun, Gold and Silver Star (Japan), 1989. *Publications:* Hydroboration, 1962; Boranes in Organic Chemistry, 1972; Organic Syntheses via Boranes, 1975; The Non-classical Ion Problem, 1977; (with A. Pelter, K. Smith) Borane Reagents, 1988; over 1140 scientific articles in Jl Amer. Chem. Soc., Jl Org. Chem., Jl Organometal. Chem., and Synthesis. *Recreations:* travel, photography. *Address:* Department of Chemistry, Purdue University, West Lafayette, IN 47907, USA. *T:* (317) 4945316.

BROWN, Hugh Dunbar; *b* 18 May 1919; *s* of Neil Brown and Grace (*née* Hargrave); *m* 1947, Mary Glen Carmichael; one *d*. *Educ:* Allan Glen's School and Whitehill Secondary School, Glasgow. Formerly Civil Servant, Ministry of Pensions and National Insurance. Member of Glasgow Corporation, 1954; Magistrate, Glasgow, 1961. MP (Lab) Provan Div. of Glasgow, 1964–87. Parly Under-Sec. of State, Scottish Office, 1974–79. *Recreation:* golf. *Address:* 29 Blackwood Road, Milngavie, Glasgow G62 7LB.

BROWN, Col Hugh Goundry, TD 1968; FRCS; Vice Lord-Lieutenant, Tyne & Wear, since 1993; *b* 25 Feb. 1927; *s* of Charles Frank Brown and Edith Temple Brown (*née* Smithson); *m* 1961, Ann Mary Crump; one *s* two *d*. *Educ:* Durham Univ. (MB BS 1949). FRCS 1958. Nat. Service, RMO, 1 (N Yorks) Bn, KAR, 1950–52. TA 1 (N) Gen. Hosp., 1952–73; OC, 201 (N) Gen. Hosp., 1970–73, Hon. Col, 1982–87. Consultant Plastic Surgeon, Royal Victoria Inf., Newcastle upon Tyne and Sen. Lectr in plastic surgery, Univ. of Newcastle upon Tyne, 1968–92. President: Brit. Soc. for Surgery of the Hand, 1985; Brit. Assoc. Plastic Surgeons, 1988; Brit. Assoc. Clinical Anatomists, 1989. QHS 1972. Tyne & Wear: DL 1986; High Sheriff, 1992. *Publications:* contrib. Brit. Jl Plastic Surgery, Hand, Brit. Jl Anaesthesia. *Recreations:* family, fell-walking. *Address:* 12 Lindisfarne Road, Jesmond, Newcastle upon Tyne NE22 2HE. *T:* Newcastle upon Tyne (0191) 2814141. *Club:* Northern Counties (Newcastle).

BROWN, Ian James Morris, PhD; playwright; Reader in Drama, Queen Margaret College, Edinburgh, since 1994; *b* 28 Feb. 1945; *s* of Bruce Beveridge Brown and Eileen Frances Scott Carnegie; *m* 1968, Judith Ellen Sidaway; one *s* one *d*. *Educ:* Dollar Academy; Edinburgh Univ. MA Hons, MLitt, DipEd; Crewe and Alsager Coll. (PhD). Playwright, 1969–; Schoolmaster, 1967–69, 1970–71; Lectr in Drama, Dunfermline Coll., 1971–76; British Council: Asst Rep., Scotland, 1976–77; Asst Regional Dir, Istanbul, 1977–78; Crewe and Alsager College: Head of Drama, 1978–79; Head of Performance Arts, 1979–82; Programme Leader, BA Hons Drama Studies, 1982–86; Programme Dir, Alsager Arts Centre, 1980–86; Drama Dir, Arts Council of GB, 1986–94. Chm., Scottish Soc. of Playwrights, 1973–75, 1984–87; convenor, NW Playwrights' Workshop, 1982–85; British Theatre Institute: Vice-Chm., 1983–85; Chm., 1985–87. Chm., Dionysia (World Fest. of Contemp. Theatre), Chianti, Italy, 1991–93. Productions: Mother Earth, 1970; The Bacchae, 1972; Positively the Last Final Farewell Performance (ballet), 1972; Rune (choral work), 1973; Carnegie, 1973; The Knife, 1973; The Fork, 1976; New Reekie, 1977; Mary, 1977; Runners, 1978; Mary Queen and the Loch Tower, 1979; Joker in the Pack, 1983; Beatrice, 1989; (jtly) First Strike, 1990; The Scotch Play, 1991; Bacchai, 1991; Wasting Reality, 1992. FRSA 1991. *Publications:* articles on drama, theatre and arts policy. *Recreations:* theatre, sport, travel, cooking. *Address:* Queen Margaret College, Clerwood Terrace, Edinburgh EH12 8TS.

BROWN, Col James, CVO 1985; RNZAC (retd); *b* 15 Aug. 1925; *y s* of late John Brown and Eveline Bertha (*née* Cooper), Russells Flat, North Canterbury, NZ; *m* 1952, Patricia

Sutton; two *d*. *Educ:* Christchurch Boys' High Sch., NZ; Royal Military Coll., Duntroon, Australia (grad 1947). NZ Regular Army, 1947–71: active service, Korea, 1951–52; Reg. Comr of Civil Defence, Dept of Internal Affairs, NZ, 1971–77. Official Sec. to Governor-Gen. of NZ, 1977–85; Gen. Sec., Duke of Edinburgh's Award Scheme in NZ, 1986–94. Col Comdt, RNZAC, 1982–86; Pres., NZ Army Assoc., 1986–94. *Recreations:* fishing, shooting. *Address:* 7 Matenga Street, Waikanae, New Zealand. *Clubs:* Wellington, Wellesley (Wellington).

BROWN, Maj.-Gen. James, CB 1982; Assistant Director (Projects), Neumerical Algorithms Group Ltd, 1989–94; *b* 12 Nov. 1928; *s* of late James Brown; *m* 1952, Lilian May Johnson; two *s*. *Educ:* Methodist Coll., Belfast; RMA Sandhurst; psc, jssc, rcds. Commissioned RAOC 1948; served UK (attached 1 DWR), Egypt, Cyprus, War Office, 1948–58; Staff Coll., Camberley, 1959; BAOR, UK, 1960–64; JSSC, Latimer, 1964–65; HQ Gurkha Inf. Bde Borneo, 1965–66 (despatches); MoD, 1966–67; Comdr RAOC, 4 Div., 1967–70; AA&QMG (Ops/Plans), HQ 1 (BR) Corps, 1970–72; Central Ordnance Depots, Donnington and Bicester, 1972–75; Dep. Dir, Ordnance Services, MoD, 1975; RCDS, 1976; Dep. Dir, Personal Services, MoD, 1977–80; Dir Gen. of Ordnance Services, 1980–83. Col Comdt, RAOC, 1983–85. Sec., Computer Centre, 1983–85, Dir, Management Inf. Services Div., 1985–89, London Univ. *Address:* c/o Royal Bank of Scotland, Drummond's Branch, Kirkland House, Whitehall, SW1.

BROWN, James Alexander, TD 1948; QC 1956; Recorder of Belfast, 1978–82; *b* 13 June 1914; *s* of Rt Hon. Mr Justice (Thomas Watters) Brown and Mary Elizabeth Brown; *m* 1950, Shirley Wallace Sproule; one *s* two *d*. *Educ:* Campbell College, Belfast; Balliol College, Oxford (BA; Pres., Oxford Union Soc., 1936). Served 1/Royal Ulster Rifles, 1939–45 (wounded; Captain). Called Bar of NI, 1946; called English Bar (GI), 1950. County Court Judge, Co. Down, 1967–78.

BROWN, Dr (James) Barry (Conway), OBE 1978; Director, British Council, Poland, 1992–94; *b* 3 July 1937; *s* of Frederick Clarence and Alys Brown; *m* 1963, Anne Rosemary Clough; two *s* one *d*. *Educ:* Cambridge Univ. (BA Nat. Sci 1959; MA 1963); Birmingham Univ. (MSc 1960; PhD 1963). Research Officer, CEGB, Berkeley Nuclear Labs, 1963–67; British Council: Sen. Sci. Officer, Sci. Dept, 1967–69; Sci. Officer, Madrid, 1969–72, Paris, 1972–78; Head, Sci. and Technology Group, 1978–81; Rep. and Cultural Counsellor, Mexico, 1981–85; Dep. Controller (Higher Educn Div.), 1985–89; Dir, EC Liaison Unit (Higher Education), Brussels, 1989–91. *Recreations:* music, travel in (and study of) countries of posting, singing, reading. *Address:* 42 Hazel Road, Purley-on-Thames, Reading RG8 8BB. *T:* Reading (01734) 417581.

BROWN, (James) Gordon; MP (Lab) Dunfermline East, since 1983; *b* 20 Feb. 1951; *s* of Rev. Dr John Brown and J. Elizabeth Brown. *Educ:* Kirkcaldy High Sch.; Edinburgh Univ. MA 1972; PhD 1982. Rector, Edinburgh Univ., 1972–75; Temp. Lectr, Edinburgh Univ., 1976; Lectr, Glasgow Coll. of Technology, 1976–80; Journalist and Current Affairs Editor, Scottish TV, 1980–83. Member: NUJ; TGWU. Chm., Labour Party Scottish Council, 1983–84; Opposition Chief Sec. to the Treasury, 1987–89; Opposition Trade and Industry Sec., 1989–92; Opposition Treasury Sec., 1992–. Contested (Lab) S Edinburgh, 1979. *Publications:* (ed) The Red Paper on Scotland, 1975; (with H. M. Drucker) The Politics of Nationalism and Devolution, 1980; (ed) Scotland: the real divide, 1983; Maxton, 1986; Where There is Greed, 1989; (with J. Naughtie) John Smith: Life and Soul of the Party, 1994. *Recreations:* reading and writing, football and tennis. *Address:* House of Commons, SW1A 0AA.

BROWN, Jerry; *see* Brown, E. G.

BROWN, Joe, MBE 1975; freelance guide and climber, and film maker for television and cinema; *b* 26 Sept. 1930; *s* of J. Brown, Longsight, Manchester; *m* 1957, Valerie Gray; two *d*. *Educ:* Stanley Grove, Manchester. Started climbing while working as plumber in Manchester; pioneered new climbs in Wales in early 1950's; gained internat. reputation after climbing West Face of Petit Dru, 1954; climbed Kanchenjunga, 1955; Mustagh Tower, 1956; Mt Communism, USSR, 1962; Trango Tower, 1976; Cotaphxi, 1979; Mt Kenya, 1984; Mt McInley, 1986; other expdns: El Torro, 1970; Bramah 2, 1978; Thalaysagar, 1982; Everest NE Ridge, 1986 and 1988. Climbing Instructor, Whitehall, Derbs, 1961–65; opened climbing equipment shops, Llanberis, 1965, Capel Curig, 1970; Leader of United Newspapers Andean Expedn, 1970; Roraima Expedn, 1973. Hon. Fellow, Manchester Polytechnic, 1970. *Publication:* (autobiog.) The Hard Years, 1967. *Recreations:* mountaineering, ski-ing, fishing. *Address:* Menai Hall, Llanberis, Gwynedd LL55 4HA. *T:* Llanberis (01286) 870327. *Club:* Climbers'.

BROWN, John, CBE 1982; FEng 1984; FIEE; Part-time Dean of Technology, Brunel University, 1988–91; *b* 17 July 1923; *s* of George Brown and Margaret Ditchburn Brown; *m* 1st, 1947, Maureen Dorothy Moore (*d* 1991); one *d*; 2nd, 1992, Dr Helen Crawford Gladstone. *Educ:* Edinburgh University. Radar Research and Development Estab., 1944–51; Lectr, Imperial Coll., 1951–54; University Coll., London: Lectr, 1954–56; Reader, 1956–64; Prof., 1964–67; seconded to Indian Inst. of Technology as Prof. of Electrical Engrg, 1962–65; Prof. of Elect. Engineering, Imperial Coll. of Science and Technology, 1967–81 (Head of Dept, 1967–79); Tech. Dir, Marconi Electrical Devices Ltd, 1981–83; Dir, Univ. and Schs Liaison, GEC, 1983–88. Mem., SRC, 1977–81 (Chm., Engrg Bd, 1977–81); Chm., Joint ESRC-SERC Cttee, 1988–91; Member: Engrg Group, Nat. Advisory Bd, 1983–84; Engrg Cttee, CNAA, 1985–87; Accreditation Cttee, CNAA, 1987–89. Pres., IEE, 1979–80 (Vice-Pres., 1975–78; Dep. Pres., 1978–79); Pres., IEEIE, 1981–85 (Treasurer, 1989–). Governor: S Bank Polytechnic, 1985–90; Willesden Coll. of Technology, 1985–86. Hon. FIElecIE 1986. *Publications:* Microwave Lenses, 1953; (with H. M. Barlow) Radio Surface Waves, 1962; Telecommunications, 1964; (with R. H. Clarke) Diffraction Theory and Antennas, 1980; papers in Proc. IEE, etc. *Recreation:* gardening. *Address:* 28 Dale Side, Gerrards Cross, Bucks SL9 7JE.

BROWN, John, CMG 1989; HM Diplomatic Service, retired; *b* 13 July 1931; *s* of John Coultas Scofield Brown and Sarah Ellen Brown (*née* Brown); *m* 1955, Christine Ann Batchelor; one *d*. Export Credits Guarantee Dept, 1949; Nat. service, Grenadier Guards, 1949–51; Board of Trade, 1967; seconded to HM Diplomatic Service, 1969; Diplomatic Service, 1975; First Secretary and Head of Chancery, Accra, 1977; FCO, 1979, Counsellor, 1981; Counsellor (Commercial) and Dir of Trade Promotion, British Trade Develt Office, NY, 1984; Consul-Gen., Toronto, and Dir, Trade Promotion and Investment, 1989–91. *Recreation:* walking. *Club:* Royal Over-Seas League.

BROWN, John B.; *see* Blamire-Brown.

BROWN, (John) Bruce, FRICS; Chairman, Lambert Smith Hampton, since 1988; *b* 15 June 1944; *s* of late Bruce Brown and of Margaret Mary (*née* Roberts); *m* 1967, Daphne Jane Walker; one *s* two *d*. *Educ:* Acton Park, Wrexham; Grove Park, Wrexham; Coll. of Estate Management, London Univ. (BSc). FRICS 1977. Surveyor, Samuel Walker & Son, 1967–68; Estates Surveyor, Bracknell Develt Corp., 1968–69; Sen. Develt Surveyor, Town & City Properties, 1969–71; Sen. Partner, Anthony Brown Stewart, 1971–88. *Recreations:* motor-racing, vintage and veteran cars. *Address:* 6 Wimpole Mews, W1M 7TF. *T:* 0171–494 4000; Radnore Farm, Wappenham, Towcester, Northants NN12 8SX.

BROWN, Prof. John Campbell, PhD; DSc; Professor of Astrophysics, University of Glasgow, since 1984; Astronomer Royal for Scotland, since 1995; *b* 4 Feb. 1947; *s* of John Brown and Jane Livingston Stewart Brown (*née* Campbell); *m* 1972, Dr Margaret Isobel Logan; one *s* one *d*. *Educ:* Hartfield Primary; Dumbarton Acad.; Glasgow Univ. (BSc 1st Cl. Hons Physics and Astronomy 1968; PhD 1973; DSc 1984). University of Glasgow: Research Asst, 1968–70; Lectr, 1970–78; Sen. Lectr, 1978–80; Reader, 1980–84. Fellow: Univ. of Tubingen, 1971–72; Univ. of Utrecht, 1973–74; Vis. Fellow, Nat. Center for Atmospheric Res., Colorado, 1977; NASA Associate Prof., Univ. of Md, 1980; Nuffield/NSF Fellow, UCSD and Univ. of Amsterdam, 1984; Brittingham Prof., Univ. of Wisconsin-Madison, 1987. Vice Pres., RAS, 1986–87; Associate Mem., Brazilian Acad. of Scis, 1988. Kelvin Prize and Medal, Univ. of Glasgow, 1984. *Publications:* (with I. J. D. Craig) Inverse Problems in Astronomy, 1986; (ed with J. T. Schmeltz) The Sun: a laboratory for astrophysics, 1992; numerous papers in Astrophysical Jl, Astronomy and Astrophysics, Solar Physic, Nature, etc. *Recreations:* oil-painting, lapidary and silvercraft, woodwork, photography, conjuring, reading, cycling, hiking. *Address:* Department of Physics and Astronomy, University of Glasgow, Glasgow G12 8QQ. *T:* 0141–330 5182; 21 Bradfield Avenue, Glasgow G12 0QH. *T:* 0141–339 1688.

BROWN, (John) Carter, Hon. CBE 1993; Director, National Gallery of Art, Washington, DC, 1969–92, now Director Emeritus; Chairman, US Commission of Fine Arts, since 1971; Chairman, Ovation Inc., the Fine Arts Television Network, since 1993; *b* 8 Oct. 1934; *s* of John Nicholas Brown and Anne Kinsolving Brown; *m* 1976, Pamela Braga Drexel (marr. diss. 1991); one *s* one *d*. *Educ:* Harvard (AB *summa cum laude* 1956; MBA 1958); Inst. of Fine Arts, NY Univ. (Museum Trng Prog., Metropol. Museum of Art; MA 1961). Studied: with Bernard Berenson, Florence, 1958; Ecole du Louvre, Paris, 1958–59; Rijksbureau voor Kunsthistorische Documentatie, The Hague, 1960. National Gallery of Art: Asst to Dir, 1961–63; Asst Dir, 1964–68; Dep. Dir, 1968–69. Chm., Leadership Council, Nat. Cultural Alliance, 1992–; Vice-Chm., Design Cttee, Pennsylvania Avenue Develt Corp., 1982–; Mem., Federal Council on Arts and Humanities, 1971–. Treas., White House Historical Assoc., 1969–. Mem. Bd of Govs, John Carter Brown Liby; Trustee: Amer. Acad. in Rome; Amer. Fedn of Arts; Brown Univ.; John F. Kennedy Center for Performing Arts; Nat. Geographic Soc.; Storm King Art Center; World Monuments Fund. Mem., Amer. Philosophical Soc., 1992; Fellow, Amer. Acad. of Arts and Scis, 1993; Hon. Mem., Amer. Inst. of Architects, 1975; Hon. FRA 1991. Holds 15 hon. degrees. Gold Medal of Honor, National Arts Soc., 1972; Gold Medal of Honor, Nat. Inst. of Social Sciences, 1987; Nat. Medal of Arts, USA, 1991. Commandeur, l'Ordre des Arts et des Lettres, France, 1975; Chevalier de la Légion d'Honneur, France, 1976; Knight, Order of St Olav, Norway, 1979; Comdr, Order of the Republic, Egypt, 1979; Comdr, Order of Orange-Nassau, Netherlands, 1982; Commendatore, Order of Merit of Italian Republic, 1984; Kt Comdr, Order of Isabel la Católica, Spain, 1985; Austrian Cross of Honor for Arts and Letters, 1986; Comdr, Royal Order of the Polar Star, Sweden, 1988; Grande Oficial, Order of Prince Henry the Navigator, Portugal, 1992. Phi Beta Kappa, 1956. Author/Dir, (film), The American Vision, 1966. *Publications:* contrib. professional jls and exhibn catalogues. *Recreations:* sailing, riding, photography. *Address:* (office) 1201 Pennsylvania Avenue NW, Washington, DC 20004, USA. *Clubs:* Knickerbocker, New York Yacht (New York).

BROWN, Sir John (Douglas Keith), Kt 1960; Chairman, McLeod Russel plc, London, 1972–79 (Director, 1963–83), retired; Director of other companies; *b* 8 Sept. 1913; *s* of late Ralph Douglas Brown and Rhoda Miller Keith; *m* 1940, Margaret Eleanor (*d* 1995), *d* of late William Alexander Burnet; two *s*. *Educ:* Glasgow Acad. CA 1937. Joined Messrs. Lovelock & Lewes, Chartered Accountants, Calcutta, October 1937 (Partnership, 1946; retired 1948); joined Jardine Henderson Ltd as a Managing Director, 1949; Chairman, 1957–63. Pres. Bengal Chamber of Commerce and Industry and Associated Chambers of Commerce of India, 1958–60; Pres. UK Citizens' Assoc. (India), 1961. Mem. Eastern Area Local Bd, Reserve Bank of India, 1959–63; Mem. Advisory Cttee on Capital Issues, Govt of India, 1958–63; Mem. Technical Advisory Cttee on Company Law, 1958–63; Mem. Companies Act Amendment Cttee, 1957; Mem. Central Excise Reorganisation Cttee, 1960. *Recreations:* gardening, walking. *Address:* Glenyra, 60 Kingswood Firs, Grayshott, Hindhead, Surrey GU26 6ER. *T:* Hindhead (01428) 604173. *Clubs:* Oriental; Bengal (Calcutta).

BROWN, Rt Rev. John Edward; Bishop in Cyprus and the Gulf, 1987–95; Episcopal Canon, St George's Cathedral, Jerusalem, 1987–95; *b* 13 July 1930; *s* of Edward and Muriel Brown; *m* 1956, Rosemary (*née* Wood); one *s*. *Educ:* Wintringham Grammar Sch., Grimsby; Kelham Theological Coll., Notts. BD London. Deacon 1955, priest 1956; Master, St George's School, Jerusalem; Curate, St George's Cathedral, Jerusalem; Chaplain of Amman, Jordan, 1954–57; Curate-in-Charge, All Saints, Reading, 1957–60; Missionary and Chaplain, All Saints Cathedral, Khartoum, Sudan, 1960–64; Vicar: Stewkley, Buckingham, 1964–69; St Luke's, Maidenhead, 1969–73; Bracknell, Berkshire, 1973–77; Rural Dean of Sonning, 1974–77; Archdeacon of Berkshire, 1978–86. *Recreations:* walking; Middle East and African studies. *Address:* 130 Oxford Street, Cleethorpes, S Humberside DN35 0BP. *T:* Cleethorpes (01472) 698840.

BROWN, Sir John (Gilbert Newton), Kt 1974; CBE 1966; MA; Vice President, Blackwell Group Ltd, since 1987 (Director, 1980–87); *b* 7 July 1916; *s* of John and Molly Brown, Chilham, Kent; *m* 1946, Virginia, *d* of late Darcy Braddell and Dorothy Braddell; one *s* two *d*. *Educ:* Lancing Coll.; Hertford Coll., Oxford (MA Zoology). Bombay Branch Oxford University Press, 1937–40; commissioned Royal Artillery, 1941; served with 5th Field Regiment, 1941–46; captured by the Japanese at Fall of Singapore, 1942; prisoner of war, Malaya, Formosa and Japan, 1942–45; returned Oxford University Press, 1946; Sales Manager, 1949; Publisher, 1956–80; Chm., University Bookshops (Oxford) Ltd; Chm., 1980–83, Dep. Chm., 1983–87, Dir, 1980–87, B. H. Blackwell Ltd; Chm., 1983–85, Dir, 1983–87, Basil Blackwell Ltd (formerly Basil Blackwell Publisher Ltd); Director: Willshaw Booksellers Ltd, Manchester, 1966–89; Book Tokens Ltd, 1973–89; Archival Facsimiles Ltd, 1986–89; John Brown Publishing Ltd, 1989–. President, Publishers' Association, 1963–65. Member: Nat. Libraries Cttee; EDC for Newspapers, Printing and Publishing Industry, 1967–70; Adv. Cttee on Scientific and Technical Information, 1969–73; Communication Adv. Cttee for UK Nat. Cttee for UNESCO; Royal Literary Fund (Asst Treasurer); Bd of British Library, 1973–79; Royal Soc. Cttee on Scientific Information; Mem. Bd, British Council, 1968–81; Open Univ. Visiting Cttee. Professorial Fellow, Hertford Coll., Oxford, 1974–80. FRSA 1964. *Address:* Milton Lodge, Great Milton, Oxford OX44 7NJ. *T:* Great Milton (01844) 279217. *Club:* Garrick.

BROWN, (John) Michael, CBE 1986; HM Diplomatic Service, retired; *b* 16 Nov. 1929; *m* 1955, Elizabeth Fitton; one *s* one *d*. Served at: Cairo, 1954–55; Doha, 1956–57; FO, 1957–60; Havana, 1960–62; FO, 1962–64; Jedda, 1965–66; Maseru, 1966–67; Bogotá, 1967–69; FCO, 1969–71; Ankara, 1971–73; Tripoli, 1973–75; FCO, 1976–79; Ambassador to Costa Rica and Nicaragua, 1979–82; Consul-Gen., Geneva, 1983–85. *Address:* Springfield House, Donhead St Andrew, Shaftesbury, SP7 9DZ.

BROWN, Prof. John Russell; Professor of Theatre, University of Michigan, Ann Arbor, since 1985; *b* 15 Sept. 1923; *yr s* of Russell Alan and Olive Helen Brown, Coombe Wood, Somerset; *m* 1961, Hilary Sue Baker; one *s* two *d*. *Educ:* Monkton Combe Sch.; Keble Coll., Oxford. Sub-Lieut (AE) RNVR, 1944–46. Fellow, Shakespeare Inst., Stratford-upon-Avon, 1951–55; Lectr and Sen. Lectr, Dept of English, Birmingham Univ., 1955–63; Hd of Dept of Drama and Theatre Arts, Univ. of Birmingham, 1964–71; Prof. of English, Sussex Univ., 1971–82; Prof. of Theatre Arts, State Univ. of NY at Stony Brook, 1982–85; Artistic Dir, Project Theatre, Michigan Univ., 1985–89. Reynolds Lectr, Colorado Univ., 1957; Vis. Prof. Graduate Sch., New York Univ., 1959; Mellon Prof. of Drama, Carnegie Inst., Pittsburgh, 1964; Vis. Prof., Zürich Univ., 1969–70; Univ. Lectr in Drama, Univ. of Toronto, 1970. Robb Lectr, Univ. of Auckland, 1976; Lansdowne Visitor, Univ. of Victoria, BC, 1990. Associate, NT, 1973–88. Member: Adv. Council of Victoria and Albert Museum, 1980–83; Adv. Council of Theatre Museum, 1974–83 (Chm., 1979–83); Arts Council of GB, 1980–83, and Chm. Drama Panel, 1980–83 (formerly Dep. Chm.). *Theatre productions include:* Twelfth Night, Playhouse, Pittsburgh, 1964; Macbeth, Everyman, Liverpool, 1965; The White Devil, Everyman, 1969; Crossing Niagara, Nat. Theatre at the ICA, 1975; They Are Dying Out, Young Vic, 1976; Old Times, British Council tour of Poland, 1976; Judgement, Nat. Theatre, 1977; Hamlet (tour), 1978; Macbeth, Nat. Theatre (co-director), 1978; The Vienna Notes and The Nest, Crucible, Sheffield, 1979; Company, Nat. Theatre, 1980; Faith Healer, Nat. Theatre and Santa Fe, 1982, and, with Candida, British Council tour of India, 1983; The Double Bass, Nat. Theatre, 1984; The Daughter-in-Law, Antique Pink, Oedipus, Waiting for Godot, Don Juan, Every Good Boy, Project Theater, Ann Arbor, Mich, USA, 1985–89; Richard II, Nat. Theatre, Educn Project Tour, 1987; Much Ado About Nothing, Playhouse, Cincinnati, 1989; Burn This, 1989, On the Verge, 1991, Dunedin, NZ; Arden of Faversham, Empty Space, Seattle, 1991; Life Sentences, Group Theater of Mich, 1994. General Editor: Stratford-upon-Avon Studies, 1960–67; Stratford-upon-Avon Library, 1964–69; Theatre Production Studies, 1981–; Theatre Concepts, 1992–, Oxford Illustrated History of Theatre, 1992–95. *Publications:* (ed) The Merchant of Venice, 1955; Shakespeare and his Comedies, 1957; (ed) The White Devil, 1960; Shakespeare: The Tragedy of Macbeth, 1963; (ed) The Duchess of Malfi, 1965; (ed) Henry V, 1965; Shakespeare's Plays in Performance, 1966; Effective Theatre, 1969; Shakespeare's The Tempest, 1969; Shakespeare's Dramatic Style, 1970; Theatre Language, 1972; Free Shakespeare, 1974; Discovering Shakespeare, 1981; Shakespeare and his Theatre, 1982; A Short Guide to Modern British Drama, 1983; Shakescenes, 1993; articles in Shakespeare Survey, Critical Quarterly, Tulane Drama Review, Studies in Bibliography, etc. *Recreations:* gardening, travel. *Address:* Court Lodge, Hooe, Battle, Sussex TN33 9HJ. *Club:* Royal Over-Seas League.

BROWN, Joseph Lawler, CBE 1978; TD 1953; FMIC; CIMgt; DL; Chairman and Managing Director, The Birmingham Post & Mail Ltd, 1973–77; *b* 22 March 1921; *s* of late Neil Brown; *m* 1950, Mabel Smith, SRN, SCM; one *s* one *d*. *Educ:* Peebles; Heriot-Watt Coll., Edinburgh. BA Hons Open Univ. FCIM (FInstM 1976); CIMgt (FBIM 1978). Served War, The Royal Scots, 1939–46 (Major). The Scotsman Publications Ltd, 1947–60; Coventry Newspapers Ltd: Gen. Man., 1960; Jt Man. Dir, 1961; Man. Dir, 1964–69; The Birmingham Post & Mail Ltd: Dep. Man. Dir, 1970; Man. Dir, 1971. Director: Cambridge Newspapers Ltd, 1965–69; Press Assoc., 1968–75 (Chm. 1972); Reuters Ltd, 1972–75; BPM (Holdings) Ltd, 1973–81. Pres., Birmingham Chamber of Industry and Commerce, 1979–80. Exec. Chm., Birmingham Venture, 1981–85. Mem., Bromsgrove and Redditch DHA, 1982–84; Mem., Hereford and Worcester Family Practitioner Cttee, 1982–83. Mem. Council, Regular Forces Employment Assoc., 1983–87; Warden, Neidpath Castle, Peebles, 1983–84. Mem., Peebles Guildry Corp., 1991–. Life Mem., Court, Birmingham Univ., 1980; Bailiff, Schs of King Edward the Sixth in Birmingham, 1987–88. DL County of W Midlands, 1976. Kt, Mark Twain Soc., 1979. Commendatore, Order Al Merito Della Repubblica Italiana, 1973. *Publication:* (with J. C. Lawson) History of Peebles 1850–1990, 1990. *Recreations:* gardening, fishing, Japanese woodcuts. *Address:* Westerly, 37 Mearse Lane, Barnt Green, Birmingham B45 8HH. *T:* 0121–445 1231.

BROWN, Prof. Judith Margaret, (Mrs P. J. Diggle), FRHistS; Beit Professor of Commonwealth History, Oxford and Fellow of Balliol College, since 1990; *b* India, 9 July 1944; *d* of late Rev. Wilfred George Brown and of Joan M. Brown; *m* 1984, Peter James Diggle; one *s*. *Educ:* Sherborne Sch. for Girls; Girton Coll., Cambridge (BA 1965; PhD 1968; MA 1969); MA, DPhil Oxon 1990. Research Fellow, Official Fellow and Dir of Studies in History, Girton Coll., Cambridge, 1968–71; Lectr, Sen. Lectr, Reader Elect in History, Univ. of Manchester, 1971–90. *Publications:* Gandhi's Rise to Power: Indian politics 1915–1922, 1972; Gandhi and Civil Disobedience: the Mahatma in Indian politics 1928–1934, 1977; Men and Gods in a Changing World, 1980; Modern India: the origins of an Asian democracy, 1984, 2nd edn 1994; Gandhi: Prisoner of Hope, 1989; (ed with R. Foot) Migration: the Asian experience, 1994. *Recreations:* classical music, gardening, walking, ice-skating. *Address:* Balliol College, Oxford OX1 3BJ. *T:* Oxford (01865) 277736.

See also P. W. H. Brown.

BROWN, June P.; *see* Paterson-Brown.

BROWN, Prof. Lawrence Michael, ScD; FRS 1982; Professor of Physics, University of Cambridge, since 1990; Founding Fellow, Robinson College, Cambridge, since 1977; *b* 18 March 1936; *s* of Bertson Waterworth Brown and Edith Waghorne; *m* 1965, Susan Drucker; one *s* two *d*. *Educ:* Univ. of Toronto (BASc); Univ. of Birmingham (PhD); ScD Cantab 1992. Athlone Fellow, Univ. of Birmingham, 1957; W. M. Tapp Research Fellow, Gonville and Caius Coll., Cambridge, 1963; University Demonstrator, Cavendish Laboratory, 1965; Lectr, 1970–83, Reader, 1983–90, Cambridge Univ.; Lectr, Robinson Coll., Cambridge, 1977–90. *Publications:* many papers on structure and properties of materials and electron microscopy in Acta Metallurgica and Philosophical Magazine. *Address:* 74 Alpha Road, Cambridge CB4 3DG. *T:* Cambridge (01223) 337291.

BROWN, Leslie; Deputy Chairman, Prudential Assurance Co. Ltd, 1970–74 (a Director, 1965–77); *b* 29 Oct. 1902; *s* of late W. H. Brown and late Eliza J. Fiveash; *m* 1930, Frances Vernon (*d* 1995), *d* of T. B. Lever; two *s* one *d*. *Educ:* Selhurst Grammar School. Joined Prudential Assurance Co. Ltd, 1919; Secretary and Chief Investment Manager, Prudential Assurance Co. Ltd, 1955–64 (Joint Secretary 1942); Chairman: Prudential Unit Trust Managers Ltd, 1968–75; Prudential Pensions Ltd, 1970–75. Member, Jenkins Committee on Company Law Amendment, 1960. Deputy-Chairman, Insurance Export Finance Co. Ltd, 1962–65. Inst. of Actuaries: FIA 1929; Vice-Pres., 1949–51. *Recreation:* bowls. *Address:* 12 Park View, Christchurch Road, Purley, Surrey CR8 2NL.

BROWN, Rt. Rev. Leslie Wilfrid, CBE 1965; *b* 10 June 1912; *s* of Harry and Maud Brown; *m* 1939, Annie Winifred, *d* of Hon. R. D. Megaw, Belfast; one *d*. *Educ:* Enfield Gram. School; London College of Divinity (London Univ.). BD 1936, MTh 1944, DD 1957. MA Cantab. hon. causa, 1953. Deacon, Curate St James' Milton, Portsmouth, 1935; priest, 1936. Missionary, CMS, 1938 to Cambridge Nicholson Instn, Kottayam, Travancore, S India. Fellow Commoner and Chaplain, Downing College, Cambridge, 1943; Kerala United Theological Seminary, Trivandrum: tutor, 1945, Principal, 1946, and from 1951. Chaplain, Jesus Coll., Cambridge and Select Preacher before Univ. of Cambridge, 1950, 1967, 1979, Oxford, 1967. Archbishop of Uganda, Rwanda and Burundi, 1961–65; Bishop of Namirembe, 1960–65 (of Uganda, 1953–60; name of diocese changed); Bishop of St Edmundsbury and Ipswich, 1966–78. Chm., ACCM, 1972–76. Hon. Fellow, Downing Coll., Cambridge, 1966. DD (*hc*) Trinity Coll., Toronto, 1963. Chaplain and Sub-Prelate, Order of St John, 1968. *Publications:* The Indian Christians of St Thomas, 1956, 2nd edn 1982; The Christian Family, 1959; God as Christians see Him, 1961; Relevant Liturgy, 1965; Three Worlds, One Word, 1981; The King and the Kingdom, 1988. *Address:* 47 New Square, Cambridge CB1 1EZ. *Club:* Commonwealth Trust.

BROWN, Prof. L(ionel) Neville, OBE 1988; Professor of Comparative Law, University of Birmingham, 1966–90, Emeritus Professor, since 1990; Leverhulme Fellow, 1990– 92; *b* 29 July 1923; *s* of Reginald P. N. Brown and Fanny Brown (*née* Carver); *m* 1957, Mary Patricia Vowles; three *s* one *d*. *Educ:* Wolverhampton Grammar Sch.; Pembroke Coll., Cambridge (Scholar; MA, LLM); Lyons Univ. (Dr en Droit). RAF, 1942–45; Cambridge, 1945–48; articled to Wolverhampton solicitor, 1948–50; Rotary Foundn Fellow, Lyons Univ., 1951–52; Lectr in Law, Sheffield Univ., 1953–55; Lectr in Comparative Law, Birmingham Univ., 1956, Sen. Lectr, 1957; Sen. Res. Fellow, Univ. of Michigan, 1960. Mem., Council on Tribunals, 1982–88; Chm., Birmingham Social Security Appeal Tribunal, 1988–. Visiting Professor: Univ. of Tulane, New Orleans, 1968; Univ. of Nairobi, 1974; Laval, 1975, 1979, 1983, 1990; Limoges, 1986; Mauritius, 1988, 1989; Aix-en-Provence, 1991. Commonwealth Foundn Lectr (Caribbean), 1975–76. Dr *hc* Limoges, 1989; Hon. LLD Laval, 1992. Officier dans l'Ordre des Palmes Académiques, 1987. *Publications:* (with F. H. Lawson and A. E. Anton) Amos and Walton's Introduction to French Law, 2nd edn 1963 and 3rd edn 1967; (with J. F. Garner) French Administrative Law, 1967, 4th edn (with J. S. Bell) 1993; (with F. G. Jacobs) Court of Justice of the European Communities, 1977, 4th edn (with T. Kennedy), 1994. *Recreations:* landscape gardening, country walking, music. *Address:* Willow Rise, Waterdale, Compton, Wolverhampton, West Midlands WV3 9DY. *T:* Wolverhampton (01902) 26666. *Club:* United Oxford & Cambridge University.

BROWN, Sir Malcolm; *see* Brown, Sir G. M.

BROWN, (Marion) Patricia; Under-Secretary (Economics), Treasury, 1972–85; *b* 2 Feb. 1927; *d* of late Henry Oswald Brown and Elsie Elizabeth (*née* Thompson). *Educ:* Norwich High Sch. for Girls; Newnham Coll., Cambridge. Central Economic Planning Staff, Cabinet Office, 1947; Treasury, 1948–54; United States Embassy, London, 1956–59; Treasury, 1959–85. Mem. Council, Royal Holloway and Bedford New Coll., London Univ., 1985–. *Recreations:* bird watching, walking. *Address:* 28 The Plantation, SE3 0AB. *T:* 0181–852 9011.

BROWN, Martin; Commissioner, since 1993, and Director, Central Operations, since 1994, HM Customs and Excise; *b* 26 Jan. 1949; *s* of late Clarence Brown and of Anne Brown; *m* 1971, Frances Leithead; two *s*. *Educ:* Bolton Sch.; New Coll., Oxford (MA). Joined Customs and Excise as Admin. Trainee, 1971; Private Sec. to Minister of State and to Financial Sec., HM Treasury, 1974–76; Principal, HM Customs and Excise, 1976; Customs adviser to Barbados Govt, 1984–86; Asst Sec., 1987, Dir, Customs, 1993, HM Customs and Excise. *Recreations:* theatre, singing, walking, gardening, pottering. *Address:* HM Customs and Excise, Queen's Dock, Liverpool L74 4AA. *T:* 0151–703 8111. *Club:* Hale (Leigh Road) Tennis.

BROWN, Sir Max; *see* Brown, Sir C. M. P.

BROWN, Sir Mervyn, KCMG 1981 (CMG 1975); OBE 1963; HM Diplomatic Service, retired; *b* 24 Sept. 1923; *m* 1949, Elizabeth Gittings. *Educ:* Ryhope Gram. Sch., Sunderland, St John's Coll., Oxford. Served in RA, 1942–45. Entered HM Foreign Service, 1949; Third Secretary, Buenos Aires, 1950; Second Secretary, UK Mission to UN, New York, 1953; First Secretary, Foreign Office, 1956; Singapore, 1959; Vientiane, 1960; again in Foreign Office, 1963–67; Ambassador to Madagascar, 1967–70; Inspector, FCO, 1970–72; Head of Communications Operations Dept, FCO, 1973–74; Asst Under-Sec. of State (Dir of Communications), 1974; High Comr in Tanzania, 1975–78, and concurrently Ambassador to Madagascar; Minister and Dep. Perm. Representative to UN, 1978; High Comr in Nigeria, 1979–83, and concurrently Ambassador to Benin. Chairman: Visiting Arts Unit of GB, 1983–89; Anglo-Malagasy Soc., 1986–; Vice-Pres., Commonwealth Youth Exchange Council, 1984–87. *Publications:* Madagascar Rediscovered, 1978; A History of Madagascar, 1995. *Recreations:* music, tennis, history. *Address:* 195 Queen's Gate, SW7 5EU. *Clubs:* Commonwealth Trust, Hurlingham, All England Lawn Tennis.

BROWN, Michael; *see* Brown, J. M.

BROWN, Air Vice-Marshal Michael John Douglas; non-executive Director, Centre for Software Engineering Ltd, since 1993; consulting engineer; *b* 9 May 1936; *s* of late N. H. B. Brown, AMIERE; *m* 1961, Audrey (*d* 1994), *d* of late L. J. Woodward, Gidea Park, Essex; one *s*. *Educ:* Drayton Manor, W7; RAF Technical Coll., Henlow; Trinity Hall, Cambridge (MA). CEng; CMath; FIMA; MRAeS; MRIN. Commnd RAF Technical Br., 1954; Cambridge Univ. Air Sqdn, 1954–57; RAF pilot trng, 1958–59; served in Bomber Comd, 1959–61; signals duties in Kenya (also assisted with formation of Kenya Air Force), 1961–64; advanced weapons course, 1965–66; Defence Operational Analysis Estabt, 1966–69; RAF Staff Coll., 1970; MoD Operational Requirements Staff, 1971–73; RAF Boulmer, 1973–75; USAF Air War Coll., 1975–76; HQ RAF Strike Comd, 1976–78; Comdr, RAF N Luffenham, 1978–80; rcds 1981; Dir, Air Guided Weapons, MoD (PE), 1983–86; Dir Gen., Strategic Electronic Systems, MoD (PE), 1986–91. Vice-Pres., SSAFA, Powys, 1993–. *Club:* Royal Air Force.

BROWN, Ven. Michael René Warneford; Archdeacon of Nottingham, 1960–77, now Archdeacon Emeritus; *b* 7 June 1915; *s* of late George and Irene Brown; *m* 1978, Marie Joyce Chaloner, *d* of late Walter Dawson, and of Sarah Dawson, Burbage, Leics; three step *s*. *Educ:* King's School, Rochester; St Peter's College, Oxford; St Stephen's House, Oxford (MA). Deacon 1941; priest, 1942; Asst Master, Christ's Hospital, 1939–43; Curate of West Grinstead, 1941–43. Chap. RNVR, 1943–46; chaplain and Dean of St Peter's College and Curate of St Mary the Virgin, Oxford, 1946; Lecturer, RN College, Greenwich, 1946–47; Librarian, 1948–50 and Fellow, 1948–52, of St Augustine's Coll., Canterbury; Priest-in-charge of Bekesbourne, 1948–50; Asst Secretary, CACTM, 1950–60. Examining Chaplain: to Bishop of Southwell, 1954–77; to Archbishop of Canterbury, 1959–60; Commissary to Bishop of Waikato, 1958–70; Hon. Officiating Chaplain, RM, Deal, Kent, 1987–. Member: Church of England Pensions Board, 1966–84; Church Commissioners' Redundant Churches Cttee, 1978–88; Chm., Redundant Churches' Uses Cttee in Canterbury Dio., 1980–89; Vice-Chm., Diocesan Adv. Cttee for the Care of Churches, 1980–93; Church Commissioner, 1968–78. *Recreations:* antiquarian and aesthetic, especially English paintings and silver. *Address:* Faygate, 72 Liverpool Road, Walmer, Deal, Kent CT14 7LR. *T:* Deal (01304) 361326. *Club:* Athenæum.

BROWN, Michael Russell; MP (C) Brigg and Cleethorpes, since 1983 (Brigg and Scunthorpe, 1979–83); *b* 3 July 1951; *s* of Frederick Alfred Brown and Greta Mary Brown, OBE (*née* Russell). *Educ:* Andrew Cairns Secondary Modern Sch., Sussex; Univ. of York (BA (Hons) Economics and Politics). Graduate Management Trainee, Barclays Bank Ltd, 1972–74; Lecturer and Tutor, Swinton Conservative Coll., 1974–75; part-time Asst to Michael Marshall, MP, 1975–76; Law Student, 1976–77, Member of Middle Temple; Personal Asst to Nicholas Winterton, MP, 1976–79. PPS to Hon. Douglas Hogg, Minister of State, DTI, 1989–90, FCO, 1990–92; PPS to Sir Patrick Mayhew, Sec. of State for NI, 1992–93; an Asst Govt Whip, 1993–94. Mem., Energy Select Cttee, 1986–89; Sec., 1981–87, Vice-Chm., 1987–89, Conservative Parly N Ireland Cttee. *Recreations:* cricket, walking. *Address:* House of Commons, SW1A 0AA. *Clubs:* Reform; Scunthorpe Conservative, Cleethorpes Conservative.

BROWN, Prof. Michael Stuart, MD; Regental Professor, University of Texas; Professor of Internal Medicine and Genetics, University of Texas Southwestern Medical School at Dallas, since 1974; *b* 13 April 1941; *s* of Harvey and Evelyn Brown; *m* 1964, Alice Lapin; two *d. Educ:* Univ. of Pennsylvania (AB 1962, MD 1966). Resident in Internal Medicine, Mass. Gen. Hosp., Boston, 1966–68; Research Scientist, NIH, Bethesda, 1968–71; Asst Prof., Univ. of Texas Southwestern Med. Sch. at Dallas, 1971–74; Associate Prof., 1974–76. For, Mem., Royal Soc., 1991. Lounsbery Award, 1979; Albert D. Lasker Award, 1985; (jtly) Nobel Prize in Medicine or Physiology for the discovery of receptors for Low Density Lipoproteins, a fundamental advance in the understanding of cholesterol metabolism, 1985. *Publications:* numerous papers to learned jls. *Address:* Department of Molecular Genetics, University of Texas Southwestern Medical School, 5323 Harry Hines Boulevard, Dallas, TX 75235, USA.

BROWN, Prof. Morris Jonathan, FRCP; Professor of Clinical Pharmacology, Cambridge University, and Hon. Consultant Physician, Addenbrooke's Hospital, since 1985; Fellow of Gonville and Caius College, and Director of Clinical Studies, Cambridge, since 1989; *b* 18 Jan. 1951; *s* of Arnold and Irene Brown; *m* 1977, Diana Phylactou; three *d. Educ:* Harrow; Trinity College, Cambridge (MA, MD); MSc London. FRCP 1987. Lectr, Royal Postgraduate Medical School, 1979–82; Senior Fellow, MRC, 1982–85. Oliver-Sharpey Lectr, RCP, 1992. Chm., Med. Res. Soc., 1991–. *Publications:* Advanced Medicine 21, 1985; articles on adrenaline and cardiovascular disease. *Recreations:* violin and oboe playing, tennis. *Address:* 104 Grange Road, Cambridge CB3 9AA.

BROWN, Nicholas Hugh; MP (Lab) Newcastle upon Tyne East, since 1983; *b* 13 June 1950; *s* of late R. C. Brown and of G. K. Brown (*née* Tester). *Educ:* Swatenden Secondary Modern Sch.; Tunbridge Wells Tech. High Sch.; Manchester Univ. (BA 1971). Trade Union Officer, GMWU Northern Region, 1978–83. Mem., Newcastle upon Tyne City Council, 1980–83. Opposition front-bench spokesman: on legal affairs, 1987–92; on Treasury affairs, 1988–94; on health, 1994–. *Address:* House of Commons, SW1A 0AA. *Clubs:* Shieldfield Workingmen's, West Walker Social, Newcastle Labour (Newcastle).

BROWN, Patricia; *see* Brown, M. P.

BROWN, Sir Patrick; *see* Brown, Sir A. P.

BROWN, Paul G.; Executive Director, UK Retail Banking, Lloyds Bank plc, since 1991; *b* 10 Sept. 1942; *s* of Col E. G. Brown and Alice Brown (*née* Van Weyenberghe); *m* 1969, Jessica Faunce; one *s* two *d. Educ:* Belgium, Germany and UK. Management appts with Lloyds Bank plc in Germany, Switzerland, USA and UK, 1960–. *Recreations:* sailing, skiing. *Address:* Lloyds Bank, PO Box 112, Canons House, Canons Way, Bristol BS99 7LB.

BROWN, Prof. Peter Robert Lamont, FBA 1971; FRHistS; Rollins Professor of History, Princeton University since 1986 (Visiting Professor, 1983–86); *b* 26 July 1935; *s* of James Lamont and Sheila Brown, Dublin; *m* 1st, 1959, Friedl Esther (*née* Löw-Beer); two *d;* 2nd, 1980, Patricia Ann Fortini; 3rd, 1989, Elizabeth Gilliam. *Educ:* Aravon Sch., Bray, Co. Wicklow, Ireland; Shrewsbury Sch.; New Coll., Oxford (MA). Harmsworth Senior Scholar, Merton Coll., Oxford and Prize Fellow, All Souls Coll., Oxford, 1956; Junior Research Fellow, 1963, Sen. Res. Fellow, 1970–73, All Souls Coll.; Fellow, All Souls Coll., 1956–75; Lectr in Medieval History, Merton Coll. Oxford, 1970–75; Special Lectr in late Roman and early Byzantine History, 1970–73, Reader, 1973–75, Univ. of Oxford; Prof. of History, Royal Holloway Coll., London Univ., 1975–78; Prof. of History and Classics, Univ. of Calif. at Berkeley, 1978–86. Fellow, Amer. Acad. of Arts and Scis, 1978. Hon. DTheol Fribourg, 1975; Hon. DHL Chicago, 1978; Hon. DLitt: TCD, 1990; Wesleyan Univ., Conn, 1993. *Publications:* Augustine of Hippo: a biography, 1967; The World of Late Antiquity, 1971; Religion and Society in the Age of St Augustine, 1971; The Making of Late Antiquity, 1978; The Cult of the Saints: its rise and function in Latin Christianity, 1980; Society and the Holy in Late Antiquity, 1982; The Body and Society: men, women and sexual renunciation in Early Christianity, 1989; Power and Persuasion in Late Antiquity: towards a Christian Empire, 1992. *Address:* Department of History, Princeton University, Princeton, NJ 08544, USA.

BROWN, Peter Wilfred Henry; Secretary of the British Academy, since 1983; *b* 4 June 1941; *s* of late Rev. Wilfred George Brown and Joan Margaret (*née* Adams); *m* 1968, Kathleen Clarke (marr. diss.); one *d. Educ:* Marlborough Coll.; Jesus Coll., Cambridge (Rustat Schol.). Assistant Master in Classics, Birkenhead Sch., 1963–66; Lectr in Classics, Fourah Bay Coll., Univ. of Sierra Leone, 1966–68; Asst Sec., School of Oriental and African Studies, Univ. of London, 1968–75; Dep. Sec., British Academy, 1975–83 (Actg Sec., 1976–77). Member: British Library Adv. Council, 1983–88; Governing Body, British Assoc. for Central and Eastern Europe (formerly GB/E Europe Centre), 1983–; Conseil Internat. de la Maison Suger, Paris, 1988–; Council: Britain–Russia Centre (formerly GB/USSR Assoc.), 1983–; SSEES, Univ. of London, 1984–; Committee of Management: Inst. of Archaeol., Univ. of London, 1984–86; Inst. of Classical Studies, Univ. of London, 1984–; Warburg Inst., Univ. of London, 1987–; CNAA Cttee for Arts and Humanities, 1985–87; Cttee for Research, 1987–. Fellow, National Humanities Center, N Carolina, 1978. *Recreations:* travel on business, reading, listening to classical music, photography. *Address:* The British Academy, 20–21 Cornwall Terrace, NW1 4QP. *T:* 0171–487 5966; 34 Victoria Road, NW6 6PX.

See also J. W. Brown.

BROWN, Philip Anthony Russell, CB 1977; Director, National Provident Institution, 1985–90; *b* 18 May 1924; *e s* of late Sir William Brown, KCB, KCMG, CBE, and of Elizabeth Mabel (*née* Scott); *m* 1954, Eileen (*d* 1976), *d* of late J. Brennan; *m* 1976, Sarah Elizabeth Dean (*see* S. E. Brown). *Educ:* Malvern; King's Coll., Cambridge. Entered Home Civil Service, Board of Trade, 1947; Private Sec. to Perm. Sec., 1949; Principal, 1952; Private Sec. to Minister of State, 1953; Observer, Civil Service Selection Board, 1957; returned to BoT, 1959; Asst Sec., 1963; Head of Overseas Information Co-ordination Office, 1963; BoT, 1964; Under-Sec., 1969; Head of Establishments Div. 1, BoT, later DTI, 1969; Head of Cos Div., DTI, 1971; Dep. Sec., Dept of Trade, 1974–83. Head of External Relations, Lloyd's of London, 1983–85; Dir of Policy, IMRO, 1985–93. Mem., Disciplinary Cttee, ICA, 1985–. Mem., London Adv. Bd, Salvation Army, 1982–92. *Publications:* (contrib.) Multinational Approaches: corporate insiders, 1976; Poems from Square Mile, 1992; articles in various jls. *Recreations:* reading, gardening, music. *Address:* 32 Cumberland Street, SW1V 4LX. *Club:* United Oxford & Cambridge University.

BROWN, Ralph, RA 1972 (ARA 1968); FRBS; ARCA; sculptor; *b* 24 April 1928; *m* 1st, 1952, M. E. Taylor (marr. diss. 1963); one *s* one *d;* 2nd, 1964, Caroline Ann Clifton-Trigg; one *s. Educ:* Leeds Grammar School. ARCA 1955; FRBS 1992. Studied Royal College of Art, 1948–56; in Paris with Zadkine, 1954; travel scholarships to Greece 1955, Italy 1957. Tutor, RCA, 1958–64. Sculpture Prof., Salzburg Festival, Summer 1972. Work exhibited: John Moores, Liverpool (prizewinner 1957), Tate Gallery, Religious Theme 1958, Arnhem Internat. Open Air Sculpture, 1958; Middelheim Open Air Sculpture, 1959; Battersea Park Open Air Sculpture, 1960, 1963, 1966, 1977; Tokyo Biennale, 1963; British Sculptors '72, RA, 1972; Holland Park Open Air, 1975. One man Shows: Leicester Galls, 1961, 1963; Archer Gall., 1972; Salzburg 1972; Munich 1973; Montpellier 1974; Marseilles 1975; Oxford 1975; Taranman Gall., 1979; Browse & Darby Gall., 1979; Beaux Arts, Bath, 1983, 1987; Charles Foley Gall., Columbus, US, 1984; Lloyd Shine Gall., Chicago, 1984; Retrospective, Leeds City Art Gall. and Warwick Arts Centre, 1988. Work in Collections: Tate Gallery, Arts Council, Contemp. Art Society, Kröller-Müller, Gallery of NSW, Stuyvesant Foundation, City of Salzburg, Nat. Gallery of Wales, Allbright-Knox Gall., and at Leeds, Bristol, Norwich, Aberdeen, etc. *Address:* The Old House, Frampton-on-Severn, Glos GL2 7DY.

BROWN, Rt. Rev. Mgr Ralph, JCD; Vicar General, Archdiocese of Westminster, since 1976; *b* 30 June 1931; *s* of John William and Elizabeth Josephine Brown. *Educ:* Highgate Sch.; St Edmund's Coll., Old Hall Green, Herts; Pontifical Gregorian Univ., Rome. Licence in Canon Law, 1961, Doctorate, 1963. Commnd Middlesex Regt, 1949; Korea, 1950. Ordained priest, Westminster Cathedral, 1959; Vice-Chancellor, Vice Officialis, dio. of Westminster, 1964–69; Officialis, Westminster, 1969–76, 1988; Canonical Advr to British Mil. Ordinariate, 1987–. Pres., Canon Law Soc. of GB and Ireland, 1980–86, Sec., 1986–89. Apptd Papal Chamberlain, 1972; National Co-ordinator for Papal Visit to England and Wales, 1982; Prelate of Honour to HH the Pope, 1987; elected to Old Brotherhood of English Secular Clergy, 1987. Hon. Member: Canon Law Soc. of Aust. and NZ, 1975; Canadian Canon Law Soc., 1979; Canon Law Soc. of Amer., 1979. KHS 1985; KCHS 1991. *Publications:* Marriage Annulment, 1969, rev. edn 1990; (ed) Matrimonial Decisions of Great Britain and Ireland, 1969–; co-translator, The Code of Canon Law in English Translation, 1983; articles in Heythrop Jl, Studia Canonica, Theological Digest, The Jurist. *Address:* Flat 3, 8 Morpeth Mansions, Morpeth Terrace, SW1P 1EQ. *T:* (office) 0171–798 9035/9020. *Club:* Anglo-Belgian.

BROWN, Hon. Sir Ralph Kilner, Kt 1970; OBE (mil.) 1945; TD 1952; DL; a Judge of the High Court, Queen's Bench Division, 1970–84; a Judge of Employment Appeal Tribunal, 1976–84; *b* 28 Aug. 1909; *s* of Rev. A. E. Brown, CIE, MA, BSc; *m* 1943, Cynthia Rosemary Breffit; one *s* two *d. Educ:* Kingswood School; Trinity Hall, Cambridge (Squire Law Scholar; MA). Barrister, Middle Temple (Harmsworth Scholar; Bencher, 1964; Master Reader, 1982); Midland Circuit, 1934 and Northern Circuit, 1975. TA 1938; War Service, 1939–46; DAQMG NW Europe Plans; DAAG HQ53 (Welsh) Div.; AQMG (Planning), COSSAC; Col Q (Ops) and Brig. Q Staff HQ 21 Army Group (despatches, OBE); Hon. Col, TARO, 1952. QC 1958; Recorder of Lincoln, 1960–64; Recorder of Birmingham, 1964–65; Chairman, Warwicks QS, 1964–67 (Dep. Chm., 1954–64); a Judge of the Central Criminal Court, 1965–67; Recorder of Liverpool, and Judge of the Crown Court at Liverpool, 1967–69; Presiding Judge, N Circuit, 1970–75. Chairman, Mental Health Review Tribunal, Birmingham RHB Area, 1962–65. Contested (L) Oldbury and Halesowen, 1945 and 1950; South Bucks, 1959 and 1964; Pres., Birmingham Liberal Organisation, 1946–56; Pres., and Chm., W Midland Liberal Fedn, 1950–56; Mem., Liberal Party Exec., 1950–56. Pres., Birmingham Bn, Boys Bde, 1946–56; Mem., Exec., Boys Bde, 1950–55; Former Member: CCPR; Cttee of RNIB; Cttee of RNID. Former Mem., Governing Body, Kingswood Sch. DL Warwickshire, 1956. Guild of Freemen, City of London. *Publications:* The Office of Reader in the Middle Temple, 1982; Top Brass and No Brass, 1991. *Recreations:* watching athletics (represented Cambridge University and Great Britain; British AAA Champion 440 yds hurdles, 1934); cricket, Rugby football. *Address:* 174 Defoe House, Barbican, EC2Y 8ND. *Clubs:* Naval and Military; Hawks (Cambridge).

See also A. G. K. Brown.

BROWN, Rev. Raymond; *see* Brown, Rev. Robert R.

BROWN, Rev. Raymond, PhD; Senior Minister, Victoria Baptist Church, Eastbourne, 1987–93, retired; *b* 3 March 1928; *s* of Frank Stevenson Brown and Florence Mansfield; *m* 1966, Christine Mary Smallman; one *s* one *d. Educ:* Spurgeon's Coll., London (BD, MTh); Fitzwilliam Coll., Cambridge (MA, BD, PhD). Minister: Zion Baptist Church, Cambridge, 1956–62; Upton Vale Baptist Church, Torquay, 1964–71; Tutor in Church History, Spurgeon's Coll., London, 1971–73, Principal 1973–86. Pres., Evangelical Alliance, 1975–76; Trustee, Dr Daniel Williams's Charity, 1980–; Nat. Chaplain, Girls' Brigade, 1986–90. *Publications:* Their Problems and Ours, 1969; Let's Read the Old Testament, 1971; Skilful Hands, 1972; Christ Above All: the message of Hebrews, 1982; Bible Study Commentary: 1 Timothy-James, 1983; The English Baptists of the Eighteenth Century, 1986; The Bible Book by Book, 1987; Be My Disciple, 1992; The Message of Deuteronomy: not by bread alone, 1993; Collins Gem Bible Guide, 1993; contribs to: What the Bible Says, 1974; Dictionary of Christian Spirituality, 1983; My Call to Preach, 1986; Encyclopedia of World Faiths, 1987; New Dictionary of Theology, 1988; The Empty Cross, 1989; Dictionary of Evangelical Biography, 1995. *Recreations:* music, fell walking. *Address:* 5 The Paddock, Eaton Ford, Cambs PE19 3SA. *T:* Huntingdon (01480) 475136. *Club:* Penn.

BROWN, Richard George; His Honour Judge Richard Brown; a Circuit Judge, since 1992; *b* Durham, 10 April 1945; *s* of late Arthur Lawson Brown and of Ivy Abigail Brown (*née* Hathaway); *m* 1969, Ann Patricia Bridget Wade; one *s* one *d* (and one *s* decd). *Educ:* Bournville Grammar Sch.; Technical Sch., Birmingham; London Sch. of Economics (LLB Hons); Inns of Court Sch. of Law. Insurance clerk, 1961–62; shop assistant, 1962–63; bus conductor, 1963–64; Trainee Radio Officer, Merchant Navy, 1964–65; taxi driver, 1965–66; assistant, school for maladjusted children, 1966–67; driver, public service vehicle, 1967–68. Called to the Bar, Middle Temple, 1972 (Blackstone Entrance Exhibnr). Asst Recorder, 1986–90; a Recorder of the Crown Court, 1990–92. Chm., Bd of Govs, Farney Close Sch. for Maladjusted Children, 1984–86. *Recreations:* sport, travel, being with the family. *Address:* Lewes Crown Court, High Street, Lewes, East Sussex BN7 1YB. *T:* Lewes (01273) 480400.

BROWN, Prof. Robert, DSc London; FRS 1956; Regius Professor of Botany, Edinburgh University, 1958–77, now Emeritus Professor; *b* 29 July 1908; *s* of Thomas William and Ethel Minnie Brown; *m* 1940, Morna Doris Mactaggart. *Educ:* English School, Cairo; University of London. Assistant Lecturer in Botany, Manchester University, 1940–44; Lecturer in Botany, Bedford College, London, 1944–46; Reader in Plant Physiology, Leeds University, 1946–52; Professor of Botany, Cornell University, 1952–53; Director, Agricultural Research Council Unit of Plant Cell Physiology, 1953–58. *Publications:*

various papers on plant physiology in the Annals of Botany, Proceedings of Royal Society and Journal of Experimental Botany. *Recreation:* gardening. *Address:* 5 Treble House Terrace, Blewbury, Didcot, Oxfordshire OX11 9NZ. *T:* Blewbury (01235) 850415.

BROWN, Robert; His Honour Judge Robert Brown; a Circuit Judge, since 1988; *b* 21 June 1943; *s* of Robert and Mary Brown; *m* 1st, 1964, Susan (marr. diss. 1971); one *s* one *d*; 2nd, 1973, Carole; two step *s*. *Educ:* Arnold Sch., Blackpool; Downing Coll., Cambridge (Exhibnr; BA, LLB). Called to Bar, Inner Temple, 1968 (Major Schol.); a Recorder, 1983–88. *Recreation:* golf. *Address:* (chambers) 2 Old Bank Street, Manchester. *T:* 0161–832 3781. *Club:* Royal Lytham St Annes Golf.

BROWN, Robert Burnett; Under Secretary, Policy Group Division D, Department of Social Security, since 1993; *b* 10 Aug. 1942; *s* of late David Brown and of Isabella Dow; *m* 1972, Anne Boschetti. *Educ:* Kirkcaldy High Sch.; Edinburgh Univ. (1st cl. Hons BSc Chemistry). Min. of Social Security, 1967; DHSS, 1971–83; Cabinet Office and HM Treasury, 1983–87; DHSS and DSS, 1987–89; Under Sec., DSS, 1989–. *Recreations:* jazz, rock and roll, football, Greece. *Address:* Department of Social Security, The Adelphi, 1–11 John Adam Street, WC1N 6HT.

BROWN, Sir Robert C.; *see* Crichton-Brown.

BROWN, Robert Crofton; DL; Member, Newcastle City Council, since 1988; *b* 16 May 1921; *m* 1945, Marjorie Hogg, Slaithwaite, Yorks; one *s* one *d*. *Educ:* Denton Road Elementary School; Atkinson Road Technical School; Rutherford Coll. Apprenticed plumber and gasfitter, Newcastle & Gateshead Gas Co., 1937. War Service, 1942–46. Plumber from 1946; Inspector, 1949; in service of Northern Gas Board until 1966. Secretary of Constituency Labour Party and Agent to MP for 16 years. MP (Lab): Newcastle upon Tyne West, 1966–83; Newcastle upon Tyne North, 1983–87. Parly Sec., Ministry of Transport, 1968–70; Parly Under-Sec., Social Security, March-Sept. 1974; Parly Under-Sec. of State for Defence for the Army, 1974–79. Vice-Chairman: Trade Union Gp of MPs, 1970–74; PLP Transport Gp, 1970–74; PLP Defence Gp, 1981–83; Member: Select Cttee on Nationalised Inds, 1966–68; Speakers Conf., 1966–68. Member Newcastle Co. Borough Council (Chief Whip, Lab. Gp), retd 1968. Nat. Chm., Community Transport, 1987. Pres., Lemington Male Voice Choir, 1987. DL Tyne and Wear 1988. *Recreations:* walking, reading, gardening, watching Association football. *Address:* 1 Newsham Close, The Boltons, North Walbottle, Newcastle upon Tyne NE5 1QD. *T:* 0191–267 2199.

BROWN, Robert Glencairn; Director (formerly Deputy Chief Officer), Housing Corporation, 1986–91; *b* 19 July 1930; *s* of William and Marion Brown (*née* Cockburn); *m* 1957, Florence May Stalker; two *s*. *Educ:* Hillhead High Sch., Glasgow. Commnd, RCS, 1949–51. Forestry Commn, 1947–68; seconded to CS Pay Res. Unit, 1963–64 and to Min. of Land and Natural Resources, 1964–68; Min. of Housing and Local Govt, later DoE, 1968–71; seconded to Nat. Whitley Council, Staff Side, 1969; Asst Dir, Countryside Commn, 1971–77; Department of the Environment: Asst Sec., 1977–83; Under Sec., 1983–86. Chm., W Middx Centre, Nat. Trust, 1989–93. *Recreations:* golfing, gardening, ski-ing, reading. *Address:* 2 The Squirrels, Pinner, Middx HA5 3BD. *T:* 0181–866 8713. *Club:* Ski Club of Great Britain.

BROWN, Prof. Robert Hanbury, AC 1986; FRS 1960; Professor of Physics (Astronomy), in the University of Sydney, 1964–81, now Emeritus Professor; *b* 31 Aug. 1916; *s* of Colonel Basil Hanbury Brown and Joyce Blaker; *m* 1952, Hilda Heather Chesterman; two *s* one *d*. *Educ:* Tonbridge School; Brighton Technical College; City and Guilds College, London. BSc (Eng), London (external), 1935; DIC, 1936; DSc Manchester, 1960. MIEE, 1938. Air Ministry, Bawdsey Research Station, working on radar, 1936–42; British Air Commission, Washington, DC, 1942–45; Principal Scientific Officer, Ministry of Supply, 1945–47; Consulting Engineer, Sir Robert Watson-Watt and partners, 1947–49; ICI Research Fellow of Manchester University, 1949; Professor of Radio-Astronomy in the University of Manchester, 1960–63. Pres., Internat. Astronomical Union, 1982–85. ARAS 1986, FAA 1967. Hon. Mem., Aust. Optical Soc., 1987; Hon. FNA 1975, Hon. FASc 1975; Hon. Fellow, Royal Astronomical Soc. of Canada, Astronomical Soc. of India, 1987. Hon. DSc: Sydney, 1984; Monash, 1984. Holweck Prize, 1959; Eddington Medal, 1968; Lyle Medal, 1971; Britannica Australia Award, 1971; Hughes Medal, 1971; Michelson Medal, Franklin Inst., 1982; ANZAAS Medal, 1987. *Publications:* The Exploration of Space by Radio, 1957; The Intensity Interferometer, 1974; Man and the Stars, 1978; Photons, Galaxies and Stars, 1985; Wisdom of Science, 1986; Boffin, 1991; publications in Physical and Astronomical Journals. *Address:* White Cottage, Penton Mewsey, Andover, Hants SP11 0RQ.

BROWN, Rev. (Robert) Raymond; Principal Chaplain, Church of Scotland and Free Churches, Royal Air Force, 1990–94 (Assistant Principal Chaplain, 1987–90); *b* 24 March 1936; *s* of Robert Brown and Elsie (*née* Dudson); *m* 1959, Barbara (*née* Johnson); three *s* one *d*. *Educ:* Stockport Sch.; Univ. of Leeds (BA Hons Philosophy); Univ. of Manchester (BD Hons Theology). Ordained Methodist minister, 1959; Minister: Luton Industrial Coll. and Mission, 1959–64; Heald Green and Handforth, 1964–67; commnd RAF Chaplain, 1967; Vice Principal, RAF Chaplains' Sch., 1978–83; Comd Chaplain, RAF Germany, 1983–87. QHC 1990–94. *Recreations:* music and drama (amateur singer and actor), writing for pleasure. *Address:* Trinity Cottage, 6 Church Terrace, Melton Mowbray, Leics LE13 0PW. *T:* Melton Mowbray (01664) 61179. *Club:* Royal Air Force.

BROWN, Robert Ross Buchanan, CBE 1968; CEng, FIEE; Chairman, Southern Electricity Board, 1954–74; *b* 15 July 1909; 2nd *s* of Robert and Rhoda Brown, Sydney, Australia; *m* 1940, Ruth Sarah Aird; one *s* one *d*. *Educ:* The King's School, Sydney; Sydney University; Cambridge University. BA (Cantab.), BSc. Deputy Gen. Manager, Wessex Electricity Co., 1938. Captain 4th County of London Yeomanry, 1940–45. Gen. Manager, Wessex Electricity Co., 1945; Deputy Chairman, Southern Electricity Board, 1948. *Recreations:* gardening, golf. *Address:* Mumbery Lodge, School Hill, Wargrave, Reading, Berks RG10 8DY.

BROWN, Ven. Robert Saville; Archdeacon of Bedford, 1974–79, Archdeacon Emeritus since 1979; *b* 12 Sept. 1914; *s* of John Harold Brown and Frances May Brown; *m* 1947, Charlotte, *d* of late Percy John and Edith Furber; one *s*. *Educ:* Bedford Modern Sch.; Selwyn Coll., Cambridge (MA). Curate: Gt Berkhamsted, 1940–44; St Mary's, Hitchin, 1944–47; Vicar, Wonersh, 1947–53; Rector, Gt Berkhamsted, 1953–69; Canon of St Albans Cath., 1965; Vicar of St Paul's, Bedford, 1969–74; Priest-in-Charge of Old Warden, 1974–79. *Recreations:* reading, travel, chess. *Address:* The Rowans, 29 The Rise, Amersham, Bucks HP7 9AG. *T:* Amersham (01494) 728376.

See also F. R. Furber.

BROWN, Dr Roger John; Chief Executive, Higher Education Quality Council, since 1993; *b* 26 June 1947; *s* of John Richard Brown and Beatrice Anne (*née* Clamp); *m* 1st, 1971, Mary Elizabeth George (marr. diss. 1991); 2nd, 1992, Josephine Anne Titcomb. *Educ:* St Olave's Grammar Sch., Bermondsey; Queens' Coll., Cambridge (Haynes Exhibnr in History; MA); Inst. of Educn, Univ. of London (PhD). Admin. Officer, ILEA, 1969–75; Sec., William Tyndale Schs' Inquiry, 1975–76; Principal, Dept Industry, Dept Trade, Cabinet Office, OFT, DTI, 1976–84; Assistant Secretary: DoE, 1984–86; DTI, 1986–90; Sec., PCFC, 1990–91; Chief Exec., Cttee of Dirs of Polytechnics, 1991–93. *Publications:* Educational Policy Making: an analysis, 1983; contribs to educnl jls. *Recreations:* opera, cinema, jazz, collecting books about music. *Address:* c/o Higher Education Quality Council, 344–354 Gray's Inn Road, WC1X 8BP. *T:* 0171–837 2223.

BROWN, Roland George MacCormack; Legal Adviser, Technical Assistance Group, Commonwealth Secretariat, 1975–87; *b* 27 Dec. 1924; 2nd *s* of late Oliver and of Mona Brown; *m* 1964, Irene Constance, *d* of Rev. Claude Coltman; two *s* one *d*. *Educ:* Ampleforth College; Trinity College, Cambridge. Called to the Bar, Gray's Inn, Nov. 1949. Practised at the Bar, Nov. 1949–May 1961; Attorney-Gen., Tanganyika, later Tanzania, 1961–65; Legal Consultant to Govt of Tanzania, 1965–72; Fellow, Inst. of Develt Studies, Sussex Univ., 1973–75; on secondment as Special Adviser to Sec. of State for Trade, 1974. *Publication:* (with Richard O'Sullivan, QC) The Law of Defamation. *Recreation:* swimming.

BROWN, Rt. Rev. Ronald; Bishop Suffragan of Birkenhead, 1974–92; *b* 7 Aug. 1926; *s* of Fred and Ellen Brown; *m* 1951, Joyce Hymers (*d* 1987); one *s* one *d*. *Educ:* Kirkham Grammar Sch.; Durham Univ. (BA, DipTh). Vicar of Whittle-le-Woods, 1956; Vicar of St Thomas, Halliwell, Bolton, 1961; Rector and Rural Dean of Ashton-under-Lyne, 1970. *Publications:* Bishop's Brew, 1989; Good Lord, 1992. *Recreations:* antiques and golf. *Address:* Hurst Cottage, Moss Lane, Lathom, near Burscough, Lancs L40 4BA. *T:* Burscough (01704) 897314.

BROWN, Ronald, (Ron); *b* Edinburgh, 1940; *s* of James Brown and Margaret McLaren; *m* 1963, May Smart; two *s*. *Educ:* Pennywell Primary Sch., Edinburgh; Ainslie Park High Sch., Edinburgh; Bristo Technical Inst., Edinburgh. National Service, Royal Signals. Five yrs engrg apprenticeship with Bruce Peebles and Co. Ltd, East Pilton, Edinburgh. Chm., Pilton Br., AUEW; formerly: Chm. Works Cttee, Edinburgh Dist of SSEB; Convenor of Shop Stewards, Parsons Peebles Ltd, Edinburgh. Formerly Councillor for Central Leith, Edinburgh Town Council; Regional Councillor for Royston/Granton, Lothian Reg. Council, 1974–79. MP (Lab) Edinburgh Leith, 1979–92; contested (Ind. Lab) Edinburgh Leith, 1992. Member: Lothian and Borders Fire Bd, 1974–79; Central Scotland Water Develt Bd, 1974–79.

BROWN, Ronald William; JP; consultant, since 1991; Deputy Director General, Federation of Master Builders, 1987–91 (Director of Industrial Relations, 1984–87); *b* 7 Sept. 1921; *s* of George Brown; *m* 1944, Mary Munn; one *s* two *d*. *Educ:* Elementary School, South London; Borough Polytechnic. Sen. Lectr in Electrical Engineering, Principal of Industrial Training Sch. Leader of Opposition, Wanstead and Woodford BC, 1953–56; Leader, Camberwell Borough Council, 1956; Alderman and Leader, London Bor. of Southwark, 1964. MP Shoreditch and Finsbury, 1964–74, Hackney South and Shoreditch, 1974–83 (Lab, 1964–81, SDP, 1981–83); Asst Govt Whip, 1966–67; contested (SDP) Hackney South and Shoreditch, 1983. Member: Council of Europe Assembly and WEU, 1965–76; European Parlt, 1977–79. Chm., Energy Commn, Rapporteur on Science, Technology and Aerospace questions; Parly Advr to Furniture, Timber and Allied Trades Union, 1967–81. Member: Council of Europe, 1979–83; WEU, 1979–83. Member: Bldg Cttee, Construction ITB, 1985–90; NW Thames RHA, 1974–88; Bd of Govs, St Bartholomew's Hosp., 1964–74; College Gov., St Bartholomew's Hosp. Med. Coll., 1974–; St Bartholomew's Hosp. Local Res. and Ethics Cttee, 1980–94 (Vice-Chm., 1992–94); E London and City HA Local Res. and Ethics Cttee, 1994–. FIMgt. Assoc. Mem., Inst. of Engineering Designers. JP Co. London, 1961. *Address:* 45 Innings Drive, Pevensey Bay, E Sussex BN24 6BH.

BROWN, Ronald William; Deputy Legal Adviser and Solicitor to Ministry of Agriculture, Fisheries and Food, to Forestry Commission and to (EEC) Intervention Board for Agricultural Produce, 1974–82; *b* 21 April 1917; *o s* of late William Nicol Brown and Eleanor Brown (*née* Dobson); *m* 1958, Elsie Joyce (*d* 1983), *er d* of late Sir Norman Guttery, KBE, CB and Lady Guttery (*née* Crankshaw); two *s*. *Educ:* Dover Coll.; Corpus Christi Coll., Cambridge (MA). War service, 1939–45, King's Own Royal Regt (Lancaster), France, W Desert, Burma (Chindits) (Major). Called to Bar, Gray's Inn, 1946. Entered Legal Dept, Min. of Agric. and Fisheries, 1948; Asst Solicitor, MAFF, 1970. *Address:* 18 Tracery, Park Road, Banstead, Surrey SM7 3DD. *T:* Burgh Heath (01737) 358569. *Club:* Royal Automobile.

BROWN, Rowland Percival, OBE 1993; MA; JP; legal consultant, Secondary Heads Association, since 1993; Headmaster, Royal Grammar School, High Wycombe, 1975–93; *b* 8 Jan. 1933; *s* of late Percy and Gladys Mabel Brown; *m* 1959, Jessie Doig Connell; three *d*. *Educ:* Queen Mary's Sch., Basingstoke; Worcester Coll., Oxford (MA French and Russian, 1956). Called to the Bar, Inner Temple, 1966; ESU Walter Page Scholar, 1976. Intelligence Corps, 1951–53, Second Lieut. Hampton Sch., 1957–62; Head of Modern Langs, Tudor Grange Grammar Sch., Solihull, 1962–67; Head Master, King Edward VI Sch., Nuneaton, 1967–75. Legal Sec., Headmasters' Assoc. and SHA, 1975–85; Pres., SHA, 1985–86. Oxford Univ. Delegacy of Local Exams, 1986–; Mem., RAF OASC Selection Bd, 1970–. Liveryman, Feltmakers' Co., 1991–. JP Bucks, 1978. *Publications:* Heads Legal Guide, 1984; The School Management Handbook, 1993. *Recreations:* golf, walking, theatre, following sport. *Address:* Wildwood, Manor Road, Penn, Bucks HP10 8JA. *Club:* Phyllis Court (Henley).

BROWN, Roy Dudley; Director, Association of West European Shipbuilders, 1977–83; *b* 5 Aug. 1916; *y s* of late Alexander and Jessie Brown; *m* 1941, Maria Margaret Barry McGhee; one *s* one *d*. *Educ:* Robert Gordon's Coll., Aberdeen; Aberdeen Univ. (MA 1935, LLB 1937). In private law practice, Glasgow, 1937–38; joined Shipbldg Conf., London, 1938; War Service, RN; Jt Sec. on amalgamation of Shipbldg Conf., Shipbldg Employers Fedn, and Dry Dock Owners and Repairers Central Council into Shipbuilders and Repairers National Assoc., 1967; Dep. Dir, 1973, until dissolution of Assoc. on nationalization, 1977. Sec., Shipbldg Corp. Ltd, 1943–77. Liveryman, Worshipful Co. of Shipwrights. *Recreations:* golf, wine, gardening. *Address:* 109 Upper Selsdon Road, Sanderstead, Surrey CR2 0DP. *T:* 0181–657 7144.

BROWN, Rear-Adm. Roy S. F.; *see* Foster-Brown.

BROWN, Russell; *see* Brown, J. R.

BROWN, Sarah Elizabeth; Head of Companies Division, Department of Trade and Industry, since 1994; *b* 30 Dec. 1943; *d* of Sir Maurice Dean, KCB, KCMG and Anne (*née* Gibson); *m* 1976, Philip A. R. Brown, *qv*. *Educ:* St Paul's Girls' Sch.; Newnham Coll., Cambridge (BA Nat. Sci.). Joined BoT as Asst Principal, 1965; Private Sec. to Second Perm. Sec., 1968; Principal, 1970; DTI, 1971–; Asst. Sec., 1978; Sec. to Crown Agents Tribunal, 1978–82; Personnel Management Div., 1982–84; Head of Financial Services Bill team, 1984–86; Under Sec., 1986; Head of Companies Div., 1986–91; Head of Enterprise Initiative Div., 1991–93, and Small Firms Div., 1992–93; Head of Small Firms and Business Link Div., 1993–94. *Recreations:* travel, theatre, gardening. *Address:* c/o Department of Trade and Industry, 1–19 Victoria Street, SW1.

BROWN, Rt. Hon. Sir Simon Denis, Kt 1984; PC 1992; **Rt. Hon. Lord Justice Simon Brown;** a Lord Justice of Appeal, since 1992; *b* 9 April 1937; *s* of late Denis Baer Brown and of Edna Elizabeth (*née* Abrahams); *m* 1963, Jennifer Buddicom; two *s* one *d*. *Educ:* Stowe Sch.; Worcester Coll., Oxford (Hon. Fellow, 1993). Commnd 2nd Lt RA, 1955–57. Called to the Bar, Middle Temple, 1961 (Harmsworth Schol.); Master of the Bench, Hon. Soc. of Middle Temple, 1980; a Recorder, 1979–84; First Jun. Treasury Counsel, Common Law, 1979–84; a Judge of the High Court of Justice, QBD, 1984–92. President: Security Service Tribunal, 1989–; Intelligence Services Tribunal, 1995–. *Recreations:* golf, skiing, theatre, fishing, reading. *Address:* Royal Courts of Justice, Strand, WC2A 2LL. *Clubs:* Denham Golf; Lindrick Golf.

BROWN, Simon Staley; QC 1995; *b* 23 Aug. 1952; *s* of Peter Brown and Celia Rosamond Brown; *m* 1981, Kathleen Margaret Wain; one *s* one *d*. *Educ:* Harrow Sch.; Queen's Coll., Cambridge (MA). Called to the Bar, Inner Temple, 1976 (Governing Bencher, 1995). Bar Association: Mem., Professional Negligence; Official Referee; Mem., London Common Law and Commercial Bar Assoc. Mem., RHS. *Recreations:* gardening, cricket, golf. *Address:* One Paper Buildings, Temple, EC4Y 7EP. *Clubs:* Worcestershire County Cricket; Pavenham Park Golf.

BROWN, Sir Stanley; *see* Brown, Sir F. H. S.

BROWN, Sir Stephen; *see* Brown, Sir A. J. S.

BROWN, Rt. Hon. Sir Stephen, Kt 1975; PC 1983; a Lord Justice of Appeal, 1983–88; President of the Family Division, since 1988; *b* 3 Oct. 1924; *s* of Wilfrid Brown and Nora Elizabeth Brown, Longdon Green, Staffordshire; *m* 1951, Patricia Ann, *d* of Richard Good, Tenbury Wells, Worcs; two *s* (twins) three *d*. *Educ:* Malvern College; Queens' College, Cambridge (Hon. Fellow, 1984). Served RNVR (Lieut), 1943–46. Barrister, Inner Temple, 1949; Bencher, 1974; Treas., 1994. Dep. Chairman, Staffs QS, 1963–71; Recorder of West Bromwich, 1965–71; QC 1966; a Recorder, and Honorary Recorder of West Bromwich, 1972–75; a Judge of the High Court, Family Div., 1975–77, QBD, 1977–83; Presiding Judge, Midland and Oxford Circuit, 1977–81. Member: Parole Board, England and Wales, 1967–71; Butler Cttee on mentally abnormal offenders, 1972–75; Adv. Council on Penal System, 1977; Chairman: Adv. Cttee on Conscientious Objectors, 1971–75; Council of Malvern Coll., 1976–94. Hon. LLD Birmingham, 1985. *Recreation:* sailing. *Address:* Royal Courts of Justice, Strand, WC2A 2LL. *Clubs:* Garrick; Birmingham (Birmingham).

BROWN, Stephen David Reid; HM Diplomatic Service; Commercial Counsellor and Director of Trade Promotion, Peking, since 1994; *b* 26 Dec. 1945; *s* of Albert Senior Brown and Edna Brown; *m* 1965, Pamela Gaunt; one *s* one *d*. *Educ:* RMA Sandhurst; Univ. of Sussex (BA Hons). Served HM Forces, RA, 1966–76; FCO, 1976–77; 1st Sec., Nicosia, 1977–80; 1st Sec. (Commercial), Paris, 1980–85; FCO, 1985–89; DTI, 1989; Consul-Gen., Melbourne, 1989–94. *Recreations:* reading, ski-ing, sailing, motor sport. *Address:* c/o Foreign and Commonwealth Office, King Charles Street, SW1A 2AH.

BROWN, Stuart Christopher; QC 1991; a Recorder, since 1992; Visiting Teaching Fellow, Leeds Metropolitan University, since 1994; *b* 4 Sept. 1950; *s* of late Geoffrey Howard Brown and of Olive Baum; *m* 1973, Imogen Lucas; two *d*. *Educ:* Acklam High Sch., Middlesbrough; Worcester Coll., Oxford (BA, BCL). Called to the Bar, Inner Temple, 1974. Practises on NE Circuit; an Asst Recorder, 1988–92. *Recreations:* family, wind-surfing. *Address:* Cherry Hill, Staircase Lane, Leeds LS16 9JD; Pearl Chambers, 22 East Parade, Leeds LS1 5BT.

BROWN, Sir Thomas, Kt 1974; Chairman, Eastern Health and Social Services Board, Northern Ireland (formerly NI Hospitals Authority), 1967–84, retired; *b* 11 Oct. 1915; *s* of Ephraim Hugh and Elizabeth Brown; *m* 1988, Dr Eleanor A. Thompson. *Educ:* Royal Belfast Academical Institution. Admitted Solicitor, 1938. Mem., Royal Commn on NHS, 1976–79. *Recreation:* boating. *Address:* Westgate, Portaferry, Co. Down, Northern Ireland BT22 1PF. *T:* Portaferry (012477) 28309.

BROWN, Tina, (Christina Hambley Brown); Editor, The New Yorker, since 1992; *b* 21 Nov. 1953; *d* of Bettina Iris Mary Kohr Brown and George Hambley Brown; *m* 1981, Harold Matthew Evans, *qv*; one *s* one *d*. *Educ:* Univ. of Oxford (MA). Columnist for Punch, 1978; Editor, Tatler, 1979–83; Editor in Chief, Vanity Fair Magazine, 1984–92. Catherine Pakenham Prize, Most Promising Female Journalist (Sunday Times), 1973; Young Journalist of the Year, 1978. *Plays:* Under the Bamboo Tree (Sunday Times Drama Award), 1973; Happy Yellow, 1977. *Publications:* Loose Talk, 1979; Life as a Party, 1983. *Address:* New Yorker Magazine Inc., 20 W 43rd Street, New York, NY 10036, USA.

BROWN, Vivian; *see* Brown, H. V. B.

BROWN, William, CBE 1971; Chairman, Scottish Television plc, since 1991; *b* 24 June 1929; *s* of Robert C. Brown, Ayr; *m* 1955, Nancy Jennifer, 3rd *d* of Prof. George Hunter, Edmonton, Alta; one *s* three *d*. *Educ:* Ayr Academy; Edinburgh University. Lieut, RA, 1950–52. Scottish Television Ltd: London Sales Manager, 1958; Sales Dir, 1961; Dep. Man. Dir, 1963; Man. Dir, 1966–90; Dep. Chm., 1974–91. Chm., Scottish Amicable Life Assurance Soc., 1989–94 (Dir, 1981–); Director: ITN, 1972–77, 1987–90; Scottish Radio (formerly Radio Clyde) Holdings Ltd, 1973–; Channel Four Co. Ltd, 1980–84; GMTV Ltd, 1992–94. Dir, Scottish Opera Theatre Royal Ltd, 1974–91. Member: Royal Commn on Legal Services in Scotland, 1976–80; Arts Council of GB, 1992–94; Chm., Scottish Arts Council, 1992–. Chm., Council, Independent Television Cos Assoc., 1978–80. Trustee, Nat. Museums of Scotland, 1991–92. Dr *hc* Edinburgh, 1990; DUniv Strathclyde, 1992. Ted Willis Award (for outstanding services to television), 1982; Gold Medal, RTS, 1984. *Recreations:* gardening, golf, films. *Address:* Scottish Television plc, Cowcaddens, Glasgow G2 3PR. *T:* 0141–332 9999. *Clubs:* Caledonian; Prestwick Golf, Royal and Ancient Golf (St Andrews).

BROWN, Prof. William Arthur; Montague Burton Professor of Industrial Relations, University of Cambridge, since 1985; Chairman: Faculty of Economics and Politics, Cambridge, since 1992; School of Humanities and Social Sciences, Cambridge, since 1993; Fellow, Wolfson College, Cambridge, since 1985; *b* 22 April 1945; *s* of Prof. Arthur Joseph Brown, *qv*; *m* 1993, Kim Hewitt; two step *d*. *Educ:* Leeds Grammar Sch.; Wadham Coll., Oxford (BA Hons). Economic Asst, NBPI, 1966–68; Res. Associate, Univ. of Warwick, 1968–70; SSRC's Industrial Relations Research Unit, University of Warwick: Res. Fellow, 1970–79; Dep. Dir, 1979–81; Dir, 1981–85. *Publications:* Piecework Bargaining, 1973; The Changing Contours of British Industrial Relations, 1981; articles in industrial relations jls, etc. *Recreations:* walking, gardening. *Address:* Wolfson College, Cambridge CB3 9BB.

BROWN, Sir William B. P.; *see* Pigott-Brown.

BROWN, William Charles Langdon, CBE 1992 (OBE 1982); Deputy Group Chief Executive and Deputy Chairman, Standard Chartered PLC, 1988–91 (Director, since 1987); Deputy Chairman, Standard Chartered Bank, 1989–91; *b* 9 Sept. 1931; *s* of Charles Leonard Brown and Kathleen May Tizzard; *m* 1959, Nachiko Sagawa; one *s* two *d*. *Educ:* John Ruskin Sch., Croydon; Ashbourne Grammar Sch., Derbyshire. Joined Westminster Bank, 1947; transf. to Standard Chartered Bank (formerly Chartered Bank of India, Australia and China, the predecessor of Chartered Bank), 1954; Standard Chartered Bank: Tokyo, 1954–59; Bangkok, 1959–62; Hong Kong, 1962–69; Man., Singapore, 1969–72; Country Man., Bangkok, 1972–75; Area Gen. Man., Hong Kong, 1975–87; Dir, 1987–, Dep. Gp Chief Exec. and Dep. Chm., 1988–91, Standard Chartered PLC. Various additional positions in Hong Kong, 1975–87, include: MLC Hong Kong; Chm., Hong Kong Export Credit Insce Corp. Adv. Bd; Mem. Council, Hong Kong Trade Develt Council; Chm., Hong Kong Assoc. of Banks; Director: Mass Railway Corp.; Wing Lung Bank Ltd. Director: Hong Kong Investment Trust, 1991–; Kexim Bank (UK) Ltd, 1992–; Arbuthnot Latham & Co. Ltd, 1993–. Treas., Royal Commonwealth Soc. and Commonwealth Trust. FCIB 1984; FInstD 1988. Hon. DSSc Chinese Univ. of Hong Kong, 1987. *Recreations:* mountain walking, snow ski-ing, yoga, philately, photography, caligraphy, classical music. *Address:* Appleshaw, 11 Central Avenue, Findon Valley, Worthing, Sussex BN14 0DS. *T:* Worthing (01903) 873175; Penthouse B, 15 Portman Square, W1H 9HD. *T:* 0171–487 5741, *Fax:* 0171–486 3005. *Clubs:* Oriental, Royal Automobile; Hong Kong, Shek-O, Ladies Recreation (Hong Kong).

BROWN, Dr William Christopher, OBE 1966; RDI 1977; Founder, Brown Beech & Associates, 1987; *b* 16 Sept. 1928; *s* of William Edward Brown and Margaret Eliza Brown; *m* 1964, Celia Hermione Emmett. *Educ:* Monmouth Sch.; University Coll., Southampton (BScEng); Imperial Coll. of Science and Technol., London (DIC); FIC 1987. Partner, Freeman, Fox & Partners, 1970–85. Principal designer for major bridges, incl.: Volta River, 1956; Forth Road, 1964; Severn and Wye, 1966; Auckland Harbour, 1969; Erskine, 1971; Bosporus, 1973; Avonmouth, 1975; Humber, 1981; Bosporus 2, 1988. Holds patents on new concepts for long-span bridges. Designer for radio telescopes in Australia and Canada, and for other special structures. Master, Faculty of RDI, 1983–85. Hon. FRIBA 1978. McRobert Award, 1970; UK and European steel design awards, 1968, 1971, 1976. *Publications:* technical papers for engrg instns in UK and abroad. *Recreations:* archaeology, photography, motoring. *Address:* 1 Allen Mansions, Allen Street, W8 6UY. *T:* 0171–937 6550. *Club:* Royal Over-Seas League.

BROWN, William Eden T.; *see* Tatton Brown.

BROWN, Rev. William Martyn; *b* 12 July 1914; *s* of Edward Brown, artist; *m* 1939, Elizabeth Lucy Hill; one adopted *s*. *Educ:* Bedford School; Pembroke College, Cambridge (Scholar). 1st Class Honours in Modern Languages, 1936, MA 1947. Assistant Master, Wellington College, 1936–47; Housemaster 1943–47; Headmaster: The King's School, Ely, 1947–55; Bedford School, 1955–75. Commissioner of the Peace, 1954. Ordained 1976; Priest-in-charge, Field Dalling and Saxlingham, 1977–84; RD of Holt, 1984–88. *Recreation:* watercolour painting. *Address:* Lodge Cottage, Field Dalling, Holt, Norfolk NR25 7AS. *T:* Binham (01328) 830403.

BROWNE, family name of **Baron Kilmaine, Baron Oranmore, Marquess of Sligo.**

BROWNE, Andrew Harold; full-time Chairman of Industrial Tribunals, Nottingham Region, since 1983; *b* 2 Dec. 1923; *s* of late Harold and Ada Caroline Browne; *m* 1951, Jocelyn Mary Vade Ashmead; two *s* one *d*. *Educ:* Repton; Trinity Hall, Cambridge (MA). ACIArb 1983. Served Royal Navy, 1942–46; Lieut RNVR. Admitted Solicitor, 1950; Partner in firm of Wells & Hind, Nottingham, 1952–83. Dep. Clerk of the Peace, Nottingham City Sessions, 1951–55. Chairman, National Insurance Local Tribunal, Nottingham, 1965–83; Member, E Midland Rent Assessment Panel, 1966–83 (Vice-Pres., 1972–83). Part-time Chm. of Industrial Tribunals, 1975–83. Lay Chm., Bingham Deanery Synod, 1987–. Chm., Reserve Forces Reinstatement Cttee, 1991–93. *Recreations:* rural England, organ music. *Address:* The House in the Garden, Elton, near Nottingham NG13 9LA. *T:* Whatton (01949) 850419. *Club:* Aula.

BROWNE, Anthony Arthur Duncan M.; *see* Montague Browne.

BROWNE, Bernard Peter Francis K.; *see* Kenworthy-Browne.

BROWNE, Air Cdre Charles Duncan Alfred, CB 1971; DFC 1944; RAF, retired; *b* 8 July 1922; *m* 1946, Una Felicité Leader; one *s* decd. War of 1939–45: served Western Desert, Italy, Corsica and S France in Hurricane and Spitfire Sqdns; post war service in Home, Flying Training, Bomber and Strike Commands; MoD; CO, RAF Brüggen, Germany, 1966–68; Comdt, Aeroplane and Armament Exp. Estab., 1968–71; Air Officer i/c Central Tactics and Trials Orgn, 1971–72. *Club:* Royal Air Force.

BROWNE, Colin; *see* Browne, J. C. C.

BROWNE, Rt. Rev. Denis George; *see* Hamilton (NZ), Bishop of, (RC).

BROWNE, Desmond John Michael; QC 1990; Recorder, since 1994; *b* 5 April 1947; *s* of Sir Denis John Browne, KCVO, FRCS and of Lady Moyra Browne, *qv*; *m* 1973, Jennifer Mary Wilmore; two *d*. *Educ:* Eton College; New College, Oxford (Scholar). Called to the Bar, Gray's Inn, 1969. *Recreations:* Australiana, Venice, Sussex Downs. *Address:* 5 Raymond Buildings, Gray's Inn, WC1R 5BP. *T:* 0171–242 2902. *Clubs:* Brooks's, Beefsteak.

BROWNE, (Edmund) John (Phillip), FEng 1993; FIMM, FInstP; Managing Director, since 1991, and Chief Executive, since 1995, British Petroleum Co. plc; *b* 20 Feb. 1948; *s* of Edmund John Browne and Paula (*née* Wesz). *Educ:* King's Sch., Ely; St John's Coll., Cambridge (MA Hons); Stanford Grad. Sch. of Business (MS Business). FIMM 1987; FInstP 1993. Joined British Petroleum Co., 1966; Gp Treasurer and Chief Exec., BP Finance Internat., 1984–86; Executive Vice-President and Chief Financial Officer: Standard Oil Co., 1986–87; BP America, 1987–89; Chief Exec. Officer, Standard Oil Prodn Co., 1987–89; Chief Exec., BP Exploration Co., 1989–95. Dir, Redland plc, 1993–. Chm., Adv. Council, Stanford Grad. Sch. of Business, 1991–. *Recreations:* opera, photography, books, pre-Colombian art. *Address:* British Petroleum Co., Britannic House, 1 Finsbury Circus, EC2M 7BA. *T:* 0171–496 4488. *Club:* Athenæum.

BROWNE, Gillian Brenda B.; *see* Babington-Browne.

BROWNE, James Nicholas; QC 1995; a Recorder, since 1993; *b* 25 April 1947; *o s* of late James Christopher Browne, MC and Winifred Browne (*née* Pirie); *m* 1981, Angelica Elizabeth Mitchell, *o d* of Sir George Mitchell, CB, QC and Elizabeth (*née* Leigh Pemberton); two *d*. *Educ:* Cheltenham Coll.; Liverpool Univ. (LLB 1969). Called to the Bar, Inner Temple, 1971; Midland and Oxford Circuit, 1971–; Asst Recorder, 1990–93. Mem., Bar Council, 1992–94. *Recreations:* cricket, squash, theatre, spending time with family and friends. *Address:* 1 Serjeants' Inn, Fleet Street, EC4Y 1LL. *T:* 0171–353 9901. *Club:* Cumberland Lawn Tennis.

BROWNE, John; *see* Browne, E. J. P.

BROWNE, John Anthony; Stipendiary Magistrate for S Yorkshire, since 1992; *b* 25 Aug. 1948; *s* of George Henry Browne and Margaret Browne (now Wheeler); *m* 1971, Dr Jill Lesley Atfield; one *s* three *d*. *Educ:* St Peter's de la Salle, Bournemouth; Sheffield Univ.

(LLB Hons). Admitted solicitor, 1975; in private practice with Elliot Mather Smith, Chesterfield and Mansfield, 1975–92. *Recreations:* tennis, hill-walking, ski-ing, running (slowly), reading, supporting Sheffield Wednesday. *Address:* The Magistrates' Court, Castle Street, Sheffield S3 8LU. *T:* Sheffield (0114) 276 8535. *Club:* Sheffield.

BROWNE, (John) Colin (Clarke); Director of Corporate Affairs, BBC, since 1994; *b* 25 Oct. 1945; *s* of late Ernest Browne, JP and of Isobel Sarah Browne (*née* McVitie); *m* 1984, Karen Lascelles; one *s. Educ:* Wallace High Sch., Lisburn, Co. Antrim; Trinity Coll., Dublin (BA). Post Office, then British Telecommunications: Dir, Chairman's Office, 1980–85; Chief Exec., Broadband Services, 1985–86; Dir, Corporate Relations, 1986–94. *Recreations:* sport, music, reading. *Address:* BBC, Broadcasting House, W1A 1AA. *T:* 0171–765 5531. *Club:* Tulse Hill Hockey (Pres.).

BROWNE, John Ernest Douglas Delavalette; Managing Director, Falcon Finance Management Ltd, since 1978; *b* Hampshire, 17 Oct. 1938; *s* of late Col Ernest Coigny Delavalette Browne, OBE, and Victoria Mary Eugene (*née* Douglas); *m* 1st, 1965, Elizabeth Jeannette Marguerite Garthwaite (marr. diss.); 2nd, 1986, Elaine Schmid Boylen. *Educ:* Malvern; RMA Sandhurst; Cranfield Inst. of Technology (MSc); Harvard Business Sch. (MBA). Served Grenadier Guards, British Guiana (Battalion Pilot), Cyprus, BAOR, 1959–67; Captain 1963; TA, Grenadier Guards (Volunteers), 1981–91, Major 1985. Associate, Morgan Stanley & Co., New York, 1969–72; Pember & Boyle, 1972–74; Director: Middle East Operations, European Banking Co., 1974–78; Worms Investments, 1981–83; Scansat (Broadcasting) Ltd, 1988–; Internat. Bd, World Paper (Boston), 1988–; Tijari Finance Ltd, 1989–; Adviser: Barclays Bank Ltd, 1978–84; Trustees Household Div., 1979–83. Dir, Churchill Private Clinic, 1980–91. MP (C) Winchester, 1979–92; contested (Ind. C) Winchester, 1992, (C Rebel) Newbury, May 1993; introduced: Trades Description Act (Amendment) Bill, 1988; Protection of Animals (Amendment) Act, 1988; Protection of Privacy Bill, 1989; Armed Forces (Liability for Injury) Bill, 1991. Member: H of C Treasury Select Cttee, 1982–87; Social Services Select Cttee, 1991–92; Secretary: Conservative Finance Cttee, 1982–84; Conservative Defence Cttee, 1982–83; Chm., Conservative Smaller Business Cttee, 1984–87; UK deleg. to N Atlantic Assembly, 1986–92 (rapporteur on human rights, 1989–92). Councillor (C), Westminster Council, 1974–78; Mem., NFU. Mem., Winchester Preservation Trust, 1980–; Patron, Winchester Cadets Assoc., 1980–; Trustee, Winnall Community Assoc., 1981–. President: Winchester Gp for Disabled People, 1982–; Hursley Cricket Club, 1985. Mem. Court, Univ. of Southampton, 1979–; Governor, Malvern Coll. Liveryman, Goldsmiths' Co., 1982. OStJ. Interests include: economics, gold and internat. monetary affairs, defence, broadcasting. *Publications:* various articles on finance, gold (A New European Currency—The Karl, K, 1972), defence, Middle East, Soviet leadership. *Recreations:* riding, skiing, sailing, shooting, golf, tennis. *Address:* 40 South Eaton Place, SW1W 9JJ. *Clubs:* Boodle's, Turf.

BROWNE, Air Vice-Marshal John Philip Ravenscroft, CBE 1985; Director Systems, National Air Traffic Services, Civil Aviation Authority, since 1995 (Director Engineering, 1992–95); *b* 27 April 1937; *s* of late Charles Harold Browne and Lorna Browne (*née* Bailey); *m* 1962, Gillian Dorothy Smith; two *s. Educ:* Brockenhurst County High Sch.; Southampton Univ. (BSc(Eng)). CEng, FICE, FRAeS. Commissioned Airfield Construction Branch, RAF, 1958; appts in NEAF and UK, 1959–66; transf. to Engineer Branch, 1966; RAF Coll., Cranwell, 1966–67; aircraft engineering appts, RAF Valley and MoD, 1967–71; RAF Staff Coll., 1972; OC Engrg Wing, RAF Valley, 1973–75; staff appts, MoD and HQ RAF Germany, 1975–82; MoD (PE), 1982–89: Asst Dir, Harrier Projects, 1982–85, Dir, Electronics Radar Airborne, 1985–86, Dir, Airborne Early Warning, 1986–89; Dir Gen. Support Services (RAF), MoD, 1989–92; RAF retd, 1992. FIMgt. *Recreations:* reading, writing, aviation, military history, photography, music. *Address:* c/o Lloyds Bank, New Milton, Hants BH25 6HU. *Club:* Royal Air Force.

BROWNE, Mervyn Ernest, CBE 1976; ERD 1954; HM Diplomatic Service, retired 1976; *b* 3 June 1916; *s* of late Ernest Edmond Browne and of Florence Mary Browne; *m* 1st, 1942, Constance (*née* Jarvis) (*d* 1988); three *s*; 2nd, 1991, Cecily (*née* Baker). *Educ:* Stockport Sec. Sch.; St Luke's Coll., Exeter; University Coll., Exeter. BScEcon London; BA Exeter. RA, 1940–46; TA, 1947–53; AER, RASC, 1953–60. Distribution of industry res., BoT, 1948–56; HM Trade Comr Service: Trade Comr, Wellington, NZ, 1957–61 and Adelaide, 1961–64; Principal Trade Comr, Kingston, Jamaica, 1964–68; HM Diplomatic Service: Counsellor (Commercial), Canberra, 1968–70; Dir, Brit. Trade in S Africa, Johannesburg, 1970–73; Consul-Gen., 1974–76 and Chargé d'Affaires, 1974 and 1976, Brit. Embassy, Manila. *Recreations:* militaria, lepidoptery, squash rackets. *Address:* 32 Cydonia Court, Earlsdon Way, Highcliffe, Dorset BH23 5TD. *T:* Highcliffe (01425) 278529.

BROWNE, Lady Moyra (Blanche Madeleine), DBE 1977 (OBE 1962); Governor, Research into Ageing (formerly British Foundation for Age Research), since 1987 (National Chairman, Support Groups, 1987–93); *b* 2 March 1918; *d* of 9th Earl of Bessborough, PC, GCMG; *m* 1945, Sir Denis John Browne, KCVO, FRCS (*d* 1967); one *s* one *d. Educ:* privately. State Enrolled Nurse, 1946. Dep. Supt-in-Chief, 1964, Supt-in-Chief, 1970–83, St John Amb. Bde. Vice-Chm. Central Council, Victoria League, 1961–65; Vice-Pres., Royal Coll. of Nursing, 1970–85. Hon. Mem., British Assoc. of Paediatric Surgeons, 1990. GCStJ 1984. *Recreations:* music, fishing, travel. *Address:* 16 Wilton Street, SW1X 7AX. *T:* 0171–235 1419.

See also D. J. M. Browne.

BROWNE, Nicholas Walker; HM Diplomatic Service; Head of Middle East Department, Foreign and Commonwealth Office, since 1994; *b* 17 Dec. 1947; *s* of Gordon Browne and Molly (*née* Gray); *m* 1969, Diana Aldwinkle; two *s* two *d. Educ:* Cheltenham Coll.; University Coll., Oxford (Open Scholar) (BA). Third Sec., FCO, 1969–71; Tehran, 1971–74; Second, later First Sec., FCO, 1974–76; on loan to Cabinet Office, 1976–80; First Sec. and Head of Chancery, Salisbury, 1980–81; First Sec., FCO, 1981–84; First Sec. (Envmt), Office of UK Rep., Brussels, 1984–89; Chargé d'Affaires, Tehran, 1989; Counsellor, FCO, 1989–90; Counsellor (Press and Public Affairs), Washington, and Hd of British Information Services, NY, 1990–94. *Recreations:* travel, theatre, Match of the Day, keeping an eye on the children. *Address:* c/o Foreign and Commonwealth Office, King Charles Street, SW1A 2AH.

BROWNE, Rt. Hon. Sir Patrick (Reginald Evelyn), PC 1974; Kt 1965; OBE (mil.) 1945; TD 1945; a Lord Justice of Appeal, 1974–80, retired; *b* 28 May 1907; *er s* of Edward Granville Browne, Sir Thomas Adams's Prof. of Arabic, Fellow of Pembroke Coll., Cambridge, and Alice Caroline (*née* Blackburne-Daniell); *m* 1st, 1931, Evelyn Sophie Alexandra (*d* 1966), *o d* of Sir Charles and Lady Walston; two *d*; 2nd, 1977, Lena, *y d* of late Mr and Mrs James Atkinson. *Educ:* Eton; Pembroke Coll., Cambridge (Hon. Fellow, 1975). Barrister-at-law, Inner Temple, 1931; QC 1960; Bencher, 1962. Deputy Chairman of Quarter Sessions, Essex, Co. Cambridge and Isle of Ely, 1963–65; a Judge of the High Court of Justice, Queen's Bench Div., 1965–74. Pres., Cambs Branch, Magistrates' Assoc., 1972–85. A Controller, Royal Opera House Development Land Trust, 1981–84. Served Army, 1939–45; GSO 1, Lt-Col. *Publication:* Judicial Reflections, in Current Legal Problems 1982. *Address:* Thriplow Bury, Thriplow, Royston, Herts SG8 7RN. *T:* Fowlmere (01763) 208234. *Clubs:* Garrick; Cambridge County.

See also Prof. Sir H. P. F. Swinnerton-Dyer, Bt.

BROWNE, Percy Basil; DL; Chairman, Devon & Exeter Steeplechases Ltd, since 1990; *b* 2 May 1923; *s* of late Captain W. P. Browne, MC. *Educ:* The Downs, Colwall; Eton College. Served War of 1939–45 with Royal Dragoons in Italy and NW Europe. Rode in Grand National, 1953. MP (C) Torrington Division of Devon, 1959–64. Dir, Appledore Shipbuilders Ltd, 1965–72 (former Chm.); Chairman: N Devon Meat Ltd, 1982–86; Western Counties Bldg Soc., 1983–85; West of England Bldg Soc., 1987–89 (Vice-Chm., 1985–87); Vice-Chm., Regency & West of England Bldg Soc., 1989–90. Mem., SW Reg. Hosp. Bd, 1967–70. Chm., Minister of Agriculture's SW Regl Panel, 1985–88. High Sheriff, Devon, 1978; DL Devon, 1984. *Address:* Ford, Silverton, Exeter EX5 4DQ. *T:* Exeter (01392) 881496.

BROWNE, Peter K.; *see* Kenworthy-Browne.

BROWNE, Robert William M.; *see* Moxon Browne.

BROWNE, Sheila Jeanne, CB 1977; Principal, Newnham College, Cambridge, 1983–92; *b* 25 Dec. 1924; *d* of Edward Elliott Browne. *Educ:* Lady Margaret Hall, Oxford (MA; Hon. Fellow 1978); Ecole des Chartes, Paris. Asst Lectr, Royal Holloway Coll., Univ. of London, 1947–51; Tutor and Fellow of St Hilda's Coll., Oxford and Univ. Lectr in French, Oxford, 1951–61, Hon. Fellow, St Hilda's Coll., 1978; HM Inspector of Schools, 1961–70; Staff Inspector, Secondary Educn, 1970–72; Chief Inspector, Secondary Educn, 1972; Dep. Sen. Chief Inspector, DES, 1972–74, Senior Chief Inspector, 1974–83. Member: CNAA, 1985–93; Franco-British Council, 1987–; Marshall Aid Commemoration Comr, 1987–92. Trustee, Gladstone Meml Trust, 1991–. Chm. Council, Selly Oak Colls, 1992–93; Gov., Anglia Polytechnic Univ., 1993–. Hon. Fellow: Thames Valley Univ. (formerly Poly. of W London); Lancashire Polytechnic, 1989; Univ. (formerly Poly.) of N London, 1989. Hon. DLitt Warwick, 1981; Hon. LLD: Exeter, 1984; Birmingham, 1987. *Recreations:* medieval France, bell-ringing, mountains. *Address:* Hone House, Sheep Street, Charlbury, Oxford OX7 3RR. *T:* Charlbury (01608) 811214.

BROWNE-CAVE, Sir Robert C.; *see* Cave-Browne-Cave.

BROWNE-WILKINSON, family name of **Baron Browne-Wilkinson.**

BROWNE-WILKINSON, Baron *cr* 1991 (Life Peer), of Camden, in the London Borough of Camden; **Nicolas Christopher Henry Browne-Wilkinson;** Kt 1977; PC 1983; a Lord of Appeal in Ordinary, since 1991; *b* 30 March 1930; *s* of late Canon A. R. Browne-Wilkinson and Molly Browne-Wilkinson; *m* 1st, 1955, Ursula de Lacy Bacon (*d* 1987); three *s* two *d*; 2nd, 1990, Mrs Hilary Tuckwell. *Educ:* Lancing; Magdalen Coll., Oxford (BA; Hon. Fellow, 1993). Called to Bar, Lincoln's Inn, 1953 (Bencher, 1977); QC 1972. Junior Counsel: to Registrar of Restrictive Trading Agreements, 1964–66; to Attorney-General in Charity Matters, 1966–72; in bankruptcy, to Dept of Trade and Industry, 1966–72; a Judge of the Courts of Appeal of Jersey and Guernsey, 1976–77; a Judge of the High Court, Chancery Div., 1977–83; a Lord Justice of Appeal, 1983–85; Vice-Chancellor of the Supreme Court, 1985–91. Pres., Employment Appeal Tribunal, 1981–83. Pres., Senate of the Inns of Court and the Bar, 1984–86. Hon. Fellow, St Edmund Hall, Oxford, 1987. *Recreation:* gardening. *Address:* House of Lords, SW1A 0PW.

BROWNING, Angela Frances; MP (C) Tiverton, since 1992; Parliamentary Secretary, Ministry of Agriculture, Fisheries and Food, since 1994; *b* 4 Dec. 1946; *d* of late Thomas Pearson and of Linda Pearson; *m* 1968, David Browning; two *s. Educ:* Westwood Girls' Grammar Sch.; Reading Coll. of Technol.; Bournemouth Coll. of Technol. FInstSMM. Management Consultant. Mem. and Special Counsellor to Nat. Autistic Soc. *Recreations:* supporting family of keen oarsmen, theatre, opera. *Address:* House of Commons, SW1A 0AA. *T:* 0171–219 5067.

BROWNING, (David) Peter (James); CBE 1984; MA; Chief Education Officer, Southampton, 1969–73, Bedfordshire, 1973–89; *b* 29 May 1927; *s* of late Frank Browning and Lucie A. (*née* Hiscock); *m* 1953, Eleanor Berry, *d* of late J. H. Forshaw, CB, FRIBA; three *s. Educ:* Christ's Coll., Cambridge (Engl. and Mod. Langs Tripos); Sorbonne; Univs of Strasbourg and Perugia. Personal Asst to Vice-Chancellor, Liverpool Univ., 1952–56; Teacher, Willenhall Comprehensive Sch., 1956–59; Sen. Admin. Asst, Somerset LEA, 1959–62; Asst Dir of Educn, Cumberland LEA, 1962–66; Dep. Chief Educn Officer, Southampton LEA, 1966–69. Member: Schools Council Governing Council and 5–13 Steering Cttee, 1969–75; Council, Univ. of Southampton, 1970–73; C of E Bd of Educn Schools Cttee, 1970–75; Council, Nat. Youth Orch., 1972–77; Merchant Navy Trng Bd, 1973–77; British Educnl Administration Soc. (Chm., 1974–78; Founder Mem., Council of Management); UGC, 1974–79; Taylor Cttee of Enquiry into Management and Govt of Schs, 1975–77; Governing Body, Centre for Inf. on Language Teaching and Research, 1975–80; European Forum for Educational Admin (Founder Chm., 1977–84); Library Adv. Council (England), 1978–81; Bd of Governors, Camb. Inst. of Educn (Vice-Chm., 1980–89); Univ. of Cambridge Faculty Bd of Educn, 1983–92; Council of Management, British Sch. Tech., 1984–87, Trust Dir, 1987–92; Lancaster Univ. Council, 1988– (Treas., 1993–); Dir, Nat. Educnl Resources Inf. Service, 1988–91; Member: Carlisle Diocesan Bd of Educn, 1989– (Chm., 1992–); Council, Open Coll. of NW, 1991–94; Armitt (Liby) Trust, 1992– (Chm., 1994); Cumbria Arts in Educn Trust, 1992–95 (Chm., 1992–95); Carlisle DAC for Care of Churches, 1993– (Chm., 1993–). Governor: Gordonstoun Sch., 1985–92; Lakes Sch., Windermere, 1988–92; Charlotte Mason Coll. of Higher Educn, Ambleside, 1988–92; London Coll. of Dance, 1990–93. Consultant, Ministry of Education: Sudan, 1976; Cyprus, 1977; Italy, 1981. Sir James Matthews Meml Lecture, Univ. of Southampton, 1983. FRSA 1981–93. Cavaliere, Order of Merit (Republic of Italy), 1985; Médaille d'honneur de l'Oise, 1988; Commandeur, Ordre des Palmes Académiques (Republic of France), 1989 (Officier, 1985). *Publications:* Editor: Julius Caesar for German Students, 1957; Macbeth for German Students, 1959; contrib. London Educn Rev., Educnl Administration jl, and other educnl jls. *Recreations:* music, public affairs, travel. *Address:* Park Fell, Skelwith Bridge, near Ambleside, LA22 9NP. *T:* Ambleside (015394) 33978; 43/45 Chilkwell Street, Glastonbury BA6 8DE. *T:* Glastonbury (01458) 832514.

BROWNING, Most Rev. Edmond Lee; Presiding Bishop of the Episcopal Church in the United States, since 1986; *b* 11 March 1929; *s* of Edmond Lucian Browning and Cora Mae Lee; *m* 1953, Patricia A. Sparks; four *s* one *d. Educ:* Univ. of the South (BA 1952); School of Theology, Sewanee, Tenn (BD 1954). Curate, Good Shepherd, Corpus Christi, Texas, 1954–56; Rector, Redeemer, Eagle Pass, Texas, 1956–59; Rector, All Souls, Okinawa, 1959–63; Japanese Lang. School, Kobe, Japan, 1963–65; Rector, St Matthews, Okinawa, 1965–67; Archdeacon of Episcopal Church, Okinawa, 1965–67; first Bishop of Okinawa, 1967–71; Bishop of American Convocation, 1971–73; Executive for National and World Mission, on Presiding Bishop's Staff, United States Episcopal Church, 1974–76; Bishop of Hawaii, 1976–85. Chm., Standing Commn on World Mission, 1979–82. Member: Exec. Council, Episcopal Church, 1982–85; Anglican Consultative Council, 1982–. Hon. DD: Univ. of the South, Sewanee, Tenn, 1970; Gen. Theol Seminary, 1986; Church Divinity Sch. of the Pacific, 1987; Seabury Western Seminary, 1987; Hon. DHL: Chaminade Univ., Honolulu, 1985; St Paul's Coll., Lawrenceville, Va, 1987. *Publication:*

Essay on World Mission, 1977. *Address:* c/o Episcopal Church Center, 815 Second Avenue, New York, NY 10017, USA. *T:* (212) 9225322.

BROWNING, Rt. Rev. George Victor; *see* Canberra and Goulburn, Bishop of.

BROWNING, Ian Andrew; Chief Executive, Wiltshire County Council, since 1984; *b* 28 Aug. 1941; *m* 1967, Ann Carter; two *s*. *Educ:* Liverpool Univ. (BA Hons Pol Theory and Instns). Solicitor. Swindon BC, 1964–70; WR, Yorks, 1970–73; S Yorks CC, 1973–76; Wilts CC, 1976–. *Recreations:* golf, travel, ornithology. *Address:* Wiltshire County Council, County Hall, Trowbridge, Wilts BA14 8JN. *T:* Trowbridge (01225) 753641.

BROWNING, Prof. Keith Anthony, PhD; FRS 1978; Director, Joint Centre for Mesoscale Meteorology, since 1992, and Professor in Department of Meteorology, since 1995, University of Reading; *b* 31 July 1938; *s* of late Sqdn Ldr James Anthony Browning and Amy Hilda (*née* Greenwood); *m* 1962, Ann Muriel (*née* Baish), BSc, MSc; one *s* two *d*. *Educ:* Commonweal Grammar Sch., Swindon, Wilts; Imperial Coll. of Science and Technology, Univ. of London. BSc, ARCS, PhD, DIC. Research atmospheric physicist, Air Force Cambridge Research Laboratories, Mass, USA, 1962–66; in charge of Meteorological Office Radar Research Lab., RSRE, Malvern, 1966–85; Dep. Dir (Phys. Res.), Met. Office, Bracknell, 1985–89; Principal Research Fellow, 1966–69; Principal Scientific Officer, 1969–72; Sen. Principal Scientific Officer, 1972–79; Dep. Chief Scientific Officer, 1979–89; Chief Scientific Officer and Dir of Res., 1989–91. Ch. Scientist, Nat. Hail Res. Experiment, USA, 1974–75; Vis. Prof., Dept of Meteorology, Univ. of Reading, 1988–94. Member: Council, Royal Met. Soc., 1971–74 (Vice-Pres., 1979–81, 1987–88 and 1990–91; Pres., 1988–90; Mem., Accreditation Bd., 1993–; Chm., 1994–); Editing Cttee, Qly Jl RMetS, 1975–78; Inter-Union Commn on Radio Meteorology, 1975–78; Internat. Commn on Cloud Physics, 1976–84; British Nat. Cttee for Physics, 1979–84; British Nat. Cttee for Geodesy and Geophysics, 1983–89 (Chm., Met. and Atmos. Phys. Sub-Cttee, 1985–89, Vice-Chm., 1979–84); NERC, 1984–87; British Nat. Cttee for Space Res., 1986–89 (Remote Sensing Sub-Cttee, 1986–89); British Nat. Cttee, World Climate Res. Prog., 1988–89 (Scientific Steering Gp, Global Energy and Water Cycle Experiment, 1988– (Chm., Cloud System Sci. Panel, 1992–); WMO/ICSU Scientific Cttee of World Climate Res. Prog., 1990–94); Royal Soc. Interdisciplinary Sci. Cttee for Space Res., 1990–91. MAE, 1989; For. Associate, US Nat. Acad. of Engrg, 1992. UK Nat. Correspondent, Internat. Assoc. of Meteorology and Atmospheric Physics, 1991–94. L. F. Richardson Prize, 1968, Buchan Prize, 1972, William Gaskell Meml Medal, 1982, RMetS; L. G. Groves Meml Prize for Meteorology, Met. Office, 1969; Meisinger Award, 1974, Jule Charney Award, 1985, Amer. Met. Soc. (Fellow of the Society, 1975); Charles Chree Medal and Prize, Inst. of Physics, 1981. *Publications:* (ed) Nowcasting, 1982; meteorological papers in learned jls, mainly in Britain and USA. *Recreations:* home and garden.

BROWNING, Peter; *see* Browning, D. P. J.

BROWNING, Philip Harold Roger; Stipendiary Magistrate for Shropshire, since 1994; *b* 25 Aug. 1946; *s* of Harold and Barbara Browning; *m* 1972, Linda; two *s*. *Educ:* Hele's Sch., Exeter; Surbiton County Grammar Sch.; Windsor Grammar Sch.; Coll. of Law. Articled T. W. Stuchbery & Son, Windsor and Maidenhead, 1964–69; admitted solicitor, 1969; Asst Solicitor, Baily, Williams & Lucas, Saffron Walden, 1969–71; Prosecuting Solicitor, Devon, 1972–81; Clerk to Justices: Axminster, Exmouth, Honiton and Wonford, 1981–85; Norwich, 1985–94. *Recreations:* thinking, reading, writing, listening to music, choral singing, discovering Shropshire. *Address:* Telford Magistrates' Court, Telford Square, Malinsgate, Telford TF3 4HX. *T:* Telford (01952) 204500.

BROWNING, Rex Alan, CB 1984; Deputy Secretary, Overseas Development Administration, 1981–86, retired; *b* 22 July 1930; *s* of Gilbert H. W. Browning and Gladys (*née* Smith) *m* 1961, Paula McKain; three *d*. *Educ:* Bristol Grammar Sch.; Merton Coll., Oxford (Postmaster) (MA). HM Inspector of Taxes, 1952; Asst Principal, Colonial Office, 1957; Private Sec. to Parly Under-Sec. for the Colonies, 1960; Principal, Dept of Techn. Co-operation, 1961; transf. ODM, 1964; seconded to Diplomatic Service as First Sec. (Aid), British High Commn, Singapore, 1969; Asst Sec., 1971; Counsellor, Overseas Develt, Washington, and Alternate UK Exec. Dir, IBRD, 1973–76; Under-Secretary: ODM, 1976–78; Dept of Trade, 1978–80; ODA, 1980–81. *Address:* Taranaki House, Trusham, near Newton Abbot, Devon TQ13 0NR.

BROWNING, Prof. Robert, MA; FBA 1978; Professor Emeritus, University of London; *b* 15 Jan. 1914; *s* of Alexander M. Browning and Jean M. Browning (*née* Miller); *m* 1st, 1946, Galina Chichekova; two *d*; 2nd, 1972, Ruth Gresh. *Educ:* Kelvinside Academy, Glasgow; Glasgow Univ. (MA); Balliol Coll., Oxford. Served Army, Middle East, Italy, Balkans, 1939–46. Harmsworth Sen. Scholar, Merton Coll., Oxford, 1946; Lectr, University Coll. London, 1947, Reader, 1955; Prof. of Classics and Ancient History, Birkbeck Coll., Univ. of London, 1965–81. Fellow, Dumbarton Oaks, Washington, DC, 1973–74, 1982, Long-Term Fellow 1983–. President, Soc. for Promotion of Hellenic Studies, 1974–77; Life Vice-Pres., Assoc. Internat. des Etudes Byzantines, 1981; Chm., National Trust for Greece, 1985–. Corresponding Mem., Athens Acad., 1981. Hon. DLitt Birmingham, 1980; Hon. DPhil Athens, 1988. Gold Medal for Excellence in Hellenic Studies, Onassis Center for Hellenic Studies, NY Univ., 1990; Gold Medal, City of Athens, 1994. Comdr of the Order of the Phoenix, Greece, 1984. *Publications:* Medieval and Modern Greek, 1969, rev. edn 1983; Justinian and Theodora, 1971, rev. edn 1987; Byzantium and Bulgaria, 1975; The Emperor Julian, 1976; Studies in Byzantine History, Literature and Education, 1977; The Byzantine Empire, 1980, rev. edn 1992; (ed) The Greek World, Classical, Byzantine and Modern, 1985; History, Language and Literacy in the Byzantine World, 1989; (with C. N. Constantinides) Dated Greek Manuscripts from Cyprus, 1993; articles in learned jls of many countries. *Address:* 17 Belsize Park Gardens, NW3 4JG.

BROWNING, Rev. Canon Wilfrid Robert Francis; Canon Residentiary of Christ Church Cathedral, Oxford, 1965–87, Hon. Canon since 1987; *b* 29 May 1918; *s* of Charles Robert and Mabel Elizabeth Browning; *m* 1948, Elizabeth Beeston; two *s* two *d*. *Educ:* Westminster School; Christ Church, Oxford; Cuddesdon Coll., Oxford. MA, BD Oxon. Deacon 1941, priest 1942, dio. of Peterborough; on staff of St Deiniol's Library, Hawarden, 1946–48; Vicar of St Richard's, Hove, 1948–51; Rector of Great Haseley, 1951–59; Lectr, Cuddesdon Coll., Oxford, 1951–59 and 1965–70; Canon Residentiary of Blackburn Cath. and Warden of Whalley Abbey, Lancs, 1959–65; Director of Ordinands and Post-Ordination Trng (Oxford dio.), 1965–85; Dir of Trng for Non-Stipendiary Ordinands and Clergy, 1972–88; Examining Chaplain: Blackburn, 1960–70; Manchester, 1970–78; Oxford, 1965–89. Member of General Synod, 1973–85; Select Preacher, Oxford Univ., 1972, 1981. *Publications:* Commentary on St Luke's Gospel, 1960, 6th edn 1981; Meet the New Testament, 1964; ed, The Anglican Synthesis, 1965; Handbook of the Ministry, 1985. *Address:* 33 Dunstone Road, Plymstock, Plymouth PL9 8RJ. *T:* Plymouth (01752) 403039; 42 Alexandra Road, Oxford OX2 0DB. *T:* Oxford (01865) 723464.

BROWNLEE, Prof. George; Professor of Pharmacology, King's College, University of London, 1958–78, retired; now Emeritus Professor; *b* 1911; *s* of late George R. Brownlee and of Mary C. C. Gow, Edinburgh; *m* 1940, Margaret P. M. Cochrane (*d* 1970), 2nd *d* of Thomas W. P. Cochrane and Margaret P. M. S. Milne, Bo'ness, Scotland; three *s*; 2nd, 1977, Betty Jean Gaydon (marr. diss. 1981), *o d* of Stanley H. Clutterham and Margaret M. Fox, Sidney, Australia. *Educ:* Tynecastle Sch.; Heriot Watt Coll., Edinburgh, BSc 1936, DSc 1950, Glasgow; PhD 1939, London. Rammell Schol., Biological Standardization Labs of Pharmaceutical Soc., London; subseq. Head of Chemotherapeutic Div., Wellcome Res. Labs, Beckenham; Reader in Pharmacology, King's Coll., Univ. of London, 1949. Editor, Jl of Pharmacy and Pharmacology, 1955–72. FKC, 1971. *Publications:* (with Prof. J. P. Quilliam) Experimental Pharmacology, 1952; papers on: chemotherapy of tuberculosis and leprosy; structure and pharmacology of the polymyxins; endocrinology; toxicity of drugs; neurohumoral transmitters in smooth muscle, etc., in: Brit. Jl Pharmacology; Jl Physiology; Biochem. Jl; Nature; Lancet; Annals NY Acad. of Science; Pharmacological Reviews, etc. *Recreations:* collecting books, making things. *Address:* 602 Gilbert House, Barbican, EC2Y 8BD. *T:* 0171–638 9543. *Club:* Athenæum.

See also G. G. Brownlee.

BROWNLEE, Prof. George Gow, PhD; FRS 1987; E. P. Abraham Professor of Chemical Pathology, Sir William Dunn School of Pathology, University of Oxford, since 1980; Fellow of Lincoln College, Oxford, since 1980; *b* 13 Jan. 1942; *s* of Prof. George Brownlee, *qv*; *m* 1966, Margaret Susan Kemp; one *s* one *d*. *Educ:* Dulwich College; Emmanuel Coll., Cambridge (MA, PhD). Scientific staff of MRC at Laboratory of Molecular Biology, Cambridge, 1966–80. Fellow, Emmanuel Coll., Cambridge, 1967–71. Colworth Medal, 1977, Wellcome Trust Award, 1985, Biochemical Soc.; Owren Medal (Norway), 1987; Haemophilia Medal (France), 1988. *Publications:* Determination of Sequences in RNA (Vol. 3, Part I of Laboratory Techniques in Biochemistry and Molecular Biology), 1972; scientific papers in Jl of Molecular Biology, Nature, Cell, Nucleic Acids Research, etc. *Recreations:* gardening, cricket. *Address:* Sir William Dunn School of Pathology, South Parks Road, Oxford OX1 3RE. *T:* Oxford (01865) 275559.

BROWNLIE, Albert Dempster; Vice-Chancellor, University of Canterbury, Christchurch, New Zealand, since 1977; *b* 3 Sept. 1932; *s* of Albert Newman and Netia Brownlie; *m* 1955, Noelene Eunice (*née* Meyer); two *d*. *Educ:* Univ. of Auckland, NZ (MCom). Economist, NZ Treasury, 1954–55. Lecturer, Sen. Lectr, Associate Prof. in Economics, Univ. of Auckland, 1956–64; Prof. and Head of Dept of Economics, Univ. of Canterbury, Christchurch, 1965–77. Chairman: Monetary and Economic Council, 1972–78; Australia-NZ Foundn, 1979–83; UGC Cttee to Review NZ Univ. Educn, 1980–82; NZ Vice-Chancellors' Cttee, 1983–84, 1993; Member: Commonwealth Experts Group on New Internat. Economic Order, 1975–77; Commonwealth Experts Gp on Econ. Growth, 1980; Wage Hearing Tribunal, 1976. Silver Jubilee Medal, 1977. *Publications:* articles in learned jls. *Address:* University of Canterbury, Private Bag 4800, Christchurch 1, New Zealand. *T:* (3) 3667001.

BROWNLIE, Prof. Ian, CBE 1993; QC; DCL; FBA; International Law practitioner; Chichele Professor of Public International Law, and Fellow of All Souls College, University of Oxford, since 1980; *b* 19 Sept. 1932; *s* of John Nason Brownlie and Amy Isabella (*née* Atherton); *m* 1st, 1957, Jocelyn Gale; one *s* two *d*; 2nd, 1978, C. J. Apperley, LLM. *Educ:* Alsop High Sch., Liverpool; Hertford Coll., Oxford (Gibbs Scholar, 1952; BA 1953); King's Coll., Cambridge (Humanitarian Trust Student, 1955). DPhil Oxford, 1961; DCL Oxford, 1976. Called to the Bar, Gray's Inn, 1958, Bencher, 1987; QC 1979. Lectr, Nottingham Univ., 1957–63; Fellow and Tutor in Law, Wadham Coll., Oxford, 1963–76 and Lectr, Oxford Univ., 1964–76; Prof. of Internat. Law, LSE, Univ. of London, 1976–80. Reader in Public Internat. Law, Inns of Ct Sch. of Law, 1973–76. Dir of Studies, Internat. Law Assoc., 1982–91. Mem., Panel of Conciliators and Panel of Arbitrators, ICSID (World Bank), 1988–. Delegate, OUP, 1984–. Lectr, Hague Acad. of Internat. Law, 1979. Editor, British Year Book of International Law, 1974–. Mem., Inst. of Internat. Law, 1985 (Associate Mem., 1977). FBA 1979. Japan Foundn Award, 1978. Comdr, Royal Norwegian OM, 1993. *Publications:* International Law and the Use of Force by States, 1963; Principles of Public International Law, 1966, 4th edn 1990 (Russian edn, ed G. I. Tunkin, 1977; Japanese edn, 1989; Certif. of Merit, Amer. Soc. of Internat. Law, 1976); Basic Documents in International Law, 1967, 3rd edn 1983; The Law Relating to Public Order, 1968; Basic Documents on Human Rights, 1971, 3rd edn 1992; Basic Documents on African Affairs, 1971; African Boundaries, a legal and diplomatic encyclopaedia, 1979; State Responsibility, part 1, 1983; (ed jtly) Liber Amicorum for Lord Wilberforce, 1987. *Recreation:* travel. *Address:* 2 Hare Court, Temple, EC4Y 7BH. *T:* 0171–583 1770; All Souls College, Oxford OX1 4AL. *T:* Oxford (01865) 279342; 43 Fairfax Road, Chiswick, W4 1EN. *T:* 0181–995 3647.

BROWNLOW, 7th Baron *cr* 1776; **Edward John Peregrine Cust;** Bt 1677; Chairman and Managing Director of Harris & Dixon (Underwriting Agencies) Ltd, 1976–82; *b* 25 March 1936; *o s* of 6th Baron Brownlow and Katherine Hariot (*d* 1952), 2nd *d* of Sir David Alexander Kinloch, 11th Bt, CB, MVO; *S* father, 1978; *m* 1964, Shirlie Edith, 2nd *d* of late John Yeomans, The Manor Farm, Hill Croome, Upton-on-Severn, Worcs; one *s*. *Educ:* Eton. Member of Lloyd's, 1961–88, and 1993–; Director: Hand-in-Hand Fire and Life Insurance Soc. (branch office of Commercial Union Assurance Co. Ltd), 1962–82; Ermitage International Ltd, 1988–. High Sheriff of Lincolnshire, 1978–79. *Heir: s* Hon. Peregrine Edward Quintin Cust, *b* 9 July 1974. *Address:* La Maison des Prés, St Peter, Jersey JE3 7EL. *Clubs:* White's, Pratt's; United (Jersey).

BROWNLOW, Air Vice-Marshal Bertrand (John), CB 1982; OBE 1967; AFC 1962; Member, Civil Aviation Authority, since 1994; *b* 13 Jan. 1929; *s* of Robert John Brownlow and Helen Louise Brownlow; *m* 1958, Kathleen Shannon; two *s* one *d*. *Educ:* Beaufort Lodge Sch. Joined RAF, 1947; 12 and 101 Sqdns, ADC to AOC 1 Gp, 103 Sqdn, 213 Sqdn, Empire Test Pilots' Sch., OC Structures and Mech. Eng Flt RAE Farnborough, RAF Staff Coll., Air Min. Op. Requirements, 1949–64; Wing Comdr Ops, RAF Lyneham, 1964–66; Jt Services Staff Coll., 1966–67; DS RAF Staff Coll., 1967–68; Def. and Air Attaché, Stockholm, 1969–71; CO Experimental Flying, RAE Farnborough, 1971–73; Asst Comdt, Office and Flying Trng, RAF Coll., Cranwell, 1973–74; Dir of Flying (R&D), MoD, 1974–77; Comdt, A&AEE, 1977–80; Comdt, RAF Coll., Cranwell, 1980–82; Dir Gen., Trng, RAF, 1982–83, retired 1984. Exec. Dir, Marshall of Cambridge (Engineering), subseq. Dir, Marshall Aerospace, 1987–94. Silver Medal, Royal Aero Club, 1983, for servs to RAF gliding. *Recreations:* squash, tennis, golf, gliding (Gold C with two diamonds). *Address:* Woodside, Abbotsley Road, Croxton, Huntingdon, Cambs PE19 4SZ. *T:* Croxton (01480) 880663. *Club:* Royal Air Force.

BROWNLOW, James Hilton, CBE 1984; QPM 1978; Adviser on Ground Control, Football Association, 1990–94; HM Inspector of Constabulary for North Eastern England, 1983–89; *b* 19 Oct. 1925; *s* of late Ernest Cuthbert Brownlow and Beatrice Annie Elizabeth Brownlow; *m* 1947, Joyce Key; two *d*. *Educ:* Worksop Central School. Solicitor's Clerk, 1941–43; served war, RAF, Flt/Sgt (Air Gunner), 1943–47. Police Constable, Leicester City Police, 1947; Police Constable to Det. Chief Supt, Kent County Constabulary, 1947–69; Asst Chief Constable, Hertfordshire Constabulary, 1969–75; Asst to HM Chief Inspector of Constabulary, Home Office, 1975–76; Dep. Chief Constable, Greater Manchester Police, 1976–79; Chief Constable, S Yorks Police, 1979–82. Mem.,

Parole Bd, 1991–94. Queen's Commendation for Brave Conduct, 1972. Officer Brother OStJ 1981. *Recreations:* golf, gardening.

BROWNLOW, Air Vice-Marshal John; *see* Brownlow, Air Vice-Marshal B.

BROWNLOW, Kevin; author; film director; *b* 2 June 1938; *s* of Thomas and Niña Brownlow; *m* 1969, Virginia Keane; one *d. Educ:* University College School. Entered documentaries, 1955; became film editor, 1958, and edited many documentaries; with Andrew Mollo dir. feature films: It Happened Here, 1964; Winstanley, 1975; dir. Charm of Dynamite, 1967, about Abel Gance, and restored his classic film Napoleon (first shown London, Nov. 1980, NY, Jan. 1981). With David Gill produced and directed TV series: Hollywood, 1980; Thames Silents, 1981–90 (incl. The Big Parade); Unknown Chaplin, 1983; British Cinema—Personal View, 1986; Buster Keaton: a hard act to follow, 1987; Harold Lloyd—The Third Genius, 1990; D. W. Griffith, Father of Film, 1993; Cinema Europe—The Other Hollywood, 1995. *Publications:* The Parade's Gone By . . ., 1968; How it Happened Here, 1968; The War, the West and the Wilderness, 1978; Hollywood: the pioneers, 1979; Napoleon: Abel Gance's classic film, 1983; Behind The Mask of Innocence, 1991; many articles on film history. *Recreation:* motion pictures. *Address:* Photoplay Productions, 21 Princess Road, NW1 8JR.

BROWNLOW, Col William Stephen; Lord-Lieutenant of Co. Down, since 1990; *b* 9 Oct. 1921; *s* of late Col Guy J. Brownlow, DSO, DL, and Elinor H. G. Brownlow, *d* of Col George J. Scott, DSO; *m* 1961, Eveleigh, *d* of Col George Panter, MBE; one *s* two *d. Educ:* Eton; Staff Coll., Camberley (psc). Major, Rifle Bde, 1940–54 (wounded, despatches); Hon. Col 4 Bn Royal Irish Rangers, 1973–78. Member: Down CC, 1969–72; NI Assembly, 1973–75. Member: Irish Nat. Hunt Cttee, 1956–; Irish Turf Club, 1982–; Chairman: Downpatrick Race Club, 1960–90; NI Reg., British Field Sports Soc., 1971–90; Master, East Down Foxhounds, 1956–62. JP 1956, DL 1961, High Sheriff 1959, Co. Down. Comdr, Commandery of Ards, St Johns, 1990. *Recreation:* field sports. *Address:* Ballywhite House, Portaferry, Co. Down BT22 1PB. *T:* Portaferry (012477) 28325. *Club:* Army and Navy.

BROWNRIGG, Sir Nicholas (Gawen), 5th Bt, *cr* 1816; *b* 22 Dec. 1932; *s* of late Gawen Egremont Brownrigg and Baroness Lucia von Borosini, *o d* of Baron Victor von Borosini, California; *S* grandfather, 1939; *m* 1959, Linda Louise Lovelace (marr. diss. 1965), Beverly Hills, California; one *s* one *d*; *m* 1971, Valerie Ann, *d* of Julian A. Arden, Livonia, Michigan, USA. *Educ:* Midland Sch.; Stanford Univ. *Heir: s* Michael Gawen Brownrigg [*b* 11 Oct. 1961; *m* Margaret Dillon, *d* of Dr Clay Burchell; one *s*]. *Address:* PO Box 548, Ukiah, CA 95482, USA.

BROWNRIGG, Philip Henry Akerman, CMG 1964; DSO 1945; OBE 1953; TD 1945; *b* 3 June 1911; *s* of late Charles E. Brownrigg, Master of Magdalen Coll. Sch., Oxford; *m* 1936, Marguerite Doreen Ottley (*d* 1992); three *d. Educ:* Eton; Magdalen Coll., Oxford (BA). Journalist, 1934–52; Editor, Sunday Graphic, 1952. Joined Anglo American Corp. of S Africa, 1953: London Agent, 1956; Dir in Rhodesia, 1961–63; Dir in Zambia, 1964–65; retd, 1969. Director (apptd by Govt of Zambia): Nchanga Consolidated Copper Mines Ltd, 1969–80; Roan Consolidated Mines Ltd, 1969–80. Joined TA, 1938; served War of 1939–45 with 6 R Berks, and 61st Reconnaissance Regt (RAC); Lieut-Col 1944; CO 4/6 R Berks (TA) 1949–52. Insignia of Honour, Zambia, 1981. *Publication:* Kenneth Kaunda, 1989. *Recreations:* golf, sport on TV. *Address:* Wheeler's, Checkendon, near Reading, Berks RG8 0NJ. *T:* Checkendon (01491) 680328.

BROWNSWORD, Andrew; Chairman and Chief Executive Officer, Hallmark Cards/ Andrew Brownsword Group, since 1993; *s* of Douglas and Eileen Brownsword; *m* 1983, Christina Brenchley; two *d. Educ:* Harvey Grammar Sch., Folkestone. Formed A. Brownsword and Co., wholesale distributors of greetings cards and stationery, 1971; formed the Andrew Brownsword Collection Ltd, 1975; acquired Gordon Fraser Gallery, 1989; Hallmark Cards purchased Andrew Brownsword Group, 1993. *Recreations:* sailing, ski-ing, hill-walking. *Address:* Hallmark House, Station Road, Henley-on-Thames RG9 1LQ.

BROWSE, Lillian Gertrude; author; private archivist; *d* of Michael Browse and Gladys Browse (*née* Meredith); *m* 1st, 1934, Ivan H. Joseph; 2nd, 1964, Sidney H. Lines. *Educ:* Barnato Park, Johannesburg. Studied with Margaret Craske at Cecchetti Ballet Sch., London, 1928–30; joined Dolin-Nemtchinova ballet co., 1930; gave up ballet and worked at Leger Galls, London, 1931–39; organised war-time exhibns at Nat. Gall. and travelling exhibns for CEMA, 1940–45, also exhibns for Inst. of Adult Educn; Organising Sec., Red Cross picture sale, Christie's, 1942; founder partner, Roland, Browse & Delbanco, 1945; Founder Dir, Browse & Darby, 1977–81. Ballet Critic, Spectator, 1950–54. Organised: Sickert exhibn, Edinburgh, 1953; Sickert centenary exhibn, Tate Gall., 1960; exhibited own private collection at Courtauld Inst. Galls, 1983. Hon. Fellow, Courtauld Inst., 1986. *Publications:* Augustus John Drawings, 1941; Sickert, 1943; Degas Dancers, 1949; William Nicholson: Catalogue Raisonné, 1955; Sickert, 1960; Forain, the Painter, 1978; (ed) Ariel Books on the Arts, 1946; contribs to Apollo, Sunday Times, Country Life, Burlington Magazine and various articles. *Recreation:* gardening. *Address:* Little Wassell, Ebernoe, near Petworth, West Sussex GU28 9LD.

BROWSE, Sir Norman (Leslie), Kt 1994; MD; FRCS, FRCP; Professor of Surgery, St Thomas's Hospital Medical School, since 1981, and Consultant Surgeon, St Thomas' Hospital, since 1965; President, Royal College of Surgeons, 1992–95 (Member of Council, since 1986; Chairman, Joint Consultants Committee, since 1994); *b* 1 Dec. 1931; *s* of Reginald and Margaret Browse; *m* 1957, Dr Jeanne Menage; one *s* one *d. Educ:* St Bartholomew's Hosp. Med. Coll. (MB BS 1955); Bristol Univ. (MD 1961). FRCS 1959; FRCP 1993. Lectr in Surgery, Westminster Hosp., 1962–64; Harkness Fellow, Res. Associate, Mayo Clinic, Rochester, Minn, 1964–65. St Thomas's Hospital Medical School: Reader in Surgery, 1965–72; Prof. of Vascular Surgery, 1972–81. Hon. Consultant (Vascular Surgery) to: Army, 1980–; RAF, 1982–. President: European Soc. for Cardiovascular Surgery, 1982–84; Assoc. of Profs of Surgery, 1985–87; Surgical Res. Soc., 1990–92; Venous Forum, RSM, 1989–91; Vascular Surgical Soc. of GB and Ireland, 1991–92. Hon. FRCPGlas 1993; Hon. FSACM 1993; Hon. FRACS 1994; Hon. FRSCI 1995; Hon. FACS 1995. Distinguished Alumnus, Mayo Clinic, 1993. *Publications:* Physiology and Pathology of Bed Rest, 1964; Symptoms and Signs of Surgical Disease, 1978; Reducing Operations for Lymphoedema, 1986; Diseases of the Veins, 1988; papers on all aspects of vascular disease. *Recreations:* marine art, mediaeval history, sailing. *Address:* Department of Surgery, St Thomas' Hospital, SE1 7EH.

BRUBECK, David Warren; jazz musician, composer; *b* Concord, Calif, 6 Dec. 1920; *s* of Howard Brubeck and Elizabeth Ivey; *m* 1942, Iola Whitlock; five *s* one *d. Educ:* Univ. of the Pacific (BA); graduate study with Darius Milhaud, Mills Coll. Leader, Dave Brubeck Octet, Trio and Quartet, 1946–; formed Dave Brubeck Quartet, 1951; played colls, fests, clubs and symphony orchs; 3 month tour of Europe and Middle East (for US State Dept) and tours in Aust., Japan, USSR and S America. Numerous recordings. Has composed: *ballet:* Points on Jazz, 1962; Glances, 1976; *orchestral:* Elementals, 1963; They All Sang Yankee Doodle, 1976; *flute and guitar:* Tritonis, 1979; *piano:* Reminiscences of the Cattle Country, 1946; Four by Four, 1946; *oratorios:* The Light in the Wilderness, 1968; Beloved Son, 1978; The Voice of the Holy Spirit, 1985; *cantatas:* Gates of Justice, 1969; Truth is Fallen, 1971; La Fiesta de la Posada, 1975; In Praise of Mary, 1989; *chorus and orchestra:* Pange Lingua Variations, 1983; Upon This Rock Chorale and Fugue, 1987; Lenten Triptych, 1988; Joy in the Morning, 1991; *mass:* To Hope!, a celebration, 1980; *SATB Chorus:* I See Satie, 1987; Four New England Pieces, 1988; Earth is our mother (with chamber orch.), 1992; over 250 *jazz* compositions incl. Blue Rondo à la Turk; In Your Own Sweet Way; The Duke. Duke Ellington Fellow, Yale Univ., 1973. Hon. PhD: Univ. of Pacific; Fairfield Univ.; Bridgeport Univ., 1982; Mills Coll., 1982; Niagara Univ., 1989; Kalamazoo Coll., 1991. Hollywood Walk of Fame. Winner, jazz polls conducted by Downbeat, Melody Maker, Cashbox, Billboard and Playboy magazines, 1952–55; Broadcast Music Inc. Jazz Pioneer Award, 1985; Compostela Humanitarian award, 1986; Connecticut Arts award, 1987; American Eagle award, Nat. Music Council, 1988; Pantheon of the Arts, Univ. of the Pacific, 1989; Gerard Manley Hopkins Award, Fairfield Univ., 1990; Distinguished Achievement Award, Simon's Rock Coll., 1991; Connecticut Bar Assoc. Award, 1992. Officier de l'Ordre des Arts et des Lettres (France), 1990. *Address:* Derry Music, 601 Montgomery Street, Suite 800, San Francisco, CA 94111, USA; c/o Sutton Artists Corporation, 20 West Park Avenue, Suite 305, Long Beach, NY 11561, USA; Box 216, Wilton, CT 06897, USA.

BRUCE, family name of **Barons Aberdare,** and **Bruce of Donington,** of **Lord Balfour of Burleigh,** and of **Earl of Elgin.**

BRUCE; *see* Cumming-Bruce and Hovell-Thurlow-Cumming-Bruce.

BRUCE, Lord; Charles Edward Bruce; *b* 19 Oct. 1961; *s* and *heir* of 11th Earl of Elgin, *qv*; *m* 1990, Amanda, *yr d* of James Movius; two *s* one *d. Educ:* Eton College; Univ. of St Andrews (MA Hons). A Page of Honour to HM the Queen Mother, 1975–77. *Heir: s* Hon. James Andrew Charles Robert Bruce, *b* 16 Nov. 1991. *Address:* 11 Muschamp Road, SE15 4EG. *T:* 0171–639 9509. *Club:* Brooks's.

BRUCE OF DONINGTON, Baron *cr* 1974 (Life Peer), of Rickmansworth; **Donald William Trevor Bruce;** economist; Chartered Accountant, Casson Beckman; writer; *b* 3 Oct. 1912; *s* of late W. T. Bruce, Norbury, Surrey; *m* 1st, 1939, Joan Letitia Butcher (marr. diss.); one *s* two *d* (and one *d* decd); 2nd, 1981, Cyrena Shaw Heard. *Educ:* Grammar School, Donington, Lincs; FCA 1947. Re-joined Territorial Army, March 1939; commissioned, Nov. 1939; Major, 1942; served at home and in France until May 1945 (despatches). MP (Lab) for North Portsmouth, 1945–50; Parliamentary Private Sec. to Minister of Health, 1945–50; Member Min. of Health delegn to Sweden and Denmark, 1946, and of House of Commons Select Cttee on Public Accounts, 1948–50. MEP, 1975–79. Opposition spokesman on Treasury, economic and industrial questions, House of Lords, 1979–83, on trade and industry, 1983–86, on Treasury and economic questions, 1986–90. *Publications:* miscellaneous contributions on political science and economics to newspapers and periodicals. *Address:* 155 Gower Street, WC1E 6BH.

BRUCE, Christopher; dancer, choreographer, opera producer; Artistic Director, Rambert Dance Company, since 1994; Resident Choreographer, Houston Ballet, since 1989; *b* Leicester, 3 Oct. 1945; *m* Marian Bruce; two *s* one *d. Educ:* Ballet Rambert Sch. Joined Ballet Rambert Company, 1963; leading dancer with co. when re-formed as modern dance co., 1966; Associate Dir, 1975–79; Associate Choreographer, 1979; Associate Choreographer, London Fest. Ballet, later English Nat. Ballet, 1986–91. Leading roles include: Pierrot Lunaire, The Tempest (Tetley); L'Apres-Midi d'un Faune (Nijinsky); Cruel Garden (also choreographed with Lindsay Kemp); choreographed: for Ballet Rambert: George Frideric (1st work), 1969; Wings, 1970; For Those Who Die as Cattle, 1971; There Was a Time, 1972; Weekend, 1974; Ancient Voices of Children, 1975; Black Angels, 1976; Cruel Garden, 1977; Night with Waning Moon, 1977; Dancing Day, 1981; Ghost Dances, 1981; Berlin Requiem, 1982; Concertino, 1983; Intimate Pages, 1984; Sergeant Early's Dream, 1984; Ceremonies, 1986; Meeting Point, 1995; for London Festival Ballet, later English National Ballet: Land, 1985; The World Again, 1986; The Dream is Over, 1987; Swansong, 1988; Symphony in Three Movements, 1990; for Tanz Forum, Cologne: Cantata, 1981; for Nederlands Dans Theater: Village Songs, 1981; Curses and Blessings, 1983; Moonshine, 1993; for Houston Ballet: Gautama Buddha, 1989; Journey, 1990; Nature Dances, 1992; for Geneva: Rooster, 1991 (restaged for London Contemporary Dance Theatre, 1992); Kingdom, 1993; for London Contemporary Dance Theatre, Waiting, 1993; works for Royal Ballet, Batsheva Dance Co., Munich Opera Ballet, Gulbenkian Ballet Co., Australian Dance Theatre, Royal Danish Ballet, Royal Swedish Ballet. Kent Opera: choreographed and produced Monteverdi's Il Ballo delle Ingrate, and Combattimento di Tancredi e Clorinda, 1980; chor. John Blow's Venus and Adonis, 1980; co-prod Handel's Agrippina, 1982. Choreographed Mutiny (musical), Piccadilly, 1985. TV productions: Ancient Voices of Children, BBC, 1977; Cruel Garden, BBC, 1981–82; Ghost Dances, Channel 4, 1982, Danmark Radio, 1990; Requiem, Danish-German co-prodn, 1982; Silence is the end of our Song, Danish TV, 1984. Evening Standard's inaugural Dance Award, 1974. *Address:* c/o Rambert Dance Co., 94 Chiswick High Road, W4 7SH; Houston Ballet, 1916 West Gray, PO 13150, Houston, TX 77219-3150, USA.

BRUCE, David, CA; Partner, Deloitte Haskins & Sells, 1974–87; *b* 21 Jan. 1927; *s* of David Bruce and Margaret (*née* Gregson); *m* 1955, Joy Robertson McAslan; four *d. Educ:* High School of Glasgow. Commissioned, Royal Corps of Signals, 1947–49. Qualified as Chartered Accountant, 1955; Partner, Kerr McLeod & Co., Chartered Accountants, 1961 (merged with Deloitte Haskins & Sells, 1974); retired 1987. Vice-Pres., Inst. of Chartered Accountants of Scotland, 1978–79 and 1979–80, Pres. 1980–81. Mem., Council on Tribunals, 1984–90 (Mem., Scottish Cttee, 1984–90). *Recreations:* angling, curling, cooking. *Address:* 8 Beechwood Court, Bearsden, Glasgow G62 2RY.

BRUCE, Sir (Francis) Michael Ian; *see* Bruce, Sir Michael Ian.

BRUCE, George John Done, RP 1959; painter of portraits, landscapes, still life, flowers; *b* 28 March 1930; *s* of 11th Lord Balfour of Burleigh, Brucefield, Clackmannan, Scotland and Violet Dorothy, *d* of Richard Henry Done, Tarporley, Cheshire; *b* of 12th Lord Balfour of Burleigh, *qv. Educ:* Westminster Sch.; Byam Shaw Sch. of Drawing and Painting. Pres., Royal Soc. of Portrait Painters, 1991–94 (Hon. Sec., 1970–84; Vice-Pres., 1984–89). *Recreations:* hang-gliding, ski-ing, windsurfing. *Address:* 6 Pembroke Walk, W8 6PQ. *T:* 0171–937 1493. *Club:* Athenæum.

BRUCE, Sir Hervey (James Hugh), 7th Bt *cr* 1804; Major, The Grenadier Guards; *b* 3 Sept. 1952; *s* of Sir Hervey John William Bruce, 6th Bt, and Crista, (*d* 1984), *y d* of late Lt-Col Chandos De Paravicini, OBE; *S* father, 1971; *m* 1st, 1979, Charlotte (marr. diss. 1991), *e d* of Jack Gore; one *s* one *d*; 2nd, 1992, Joanna, *y d* of Frank Pope; one *s. Educ:* Eton; Officer Cadet School, Mons. *Recreations:* ice hockey, ski-ing, tapestry. *Heir: s* Hervey Hamish Peter Bruce, *b* 20 Nov. 1986. *Address:* 15 Wilmot Circle, Oromocto, New Brunswick, E2V 1J7, Canada. *Club:* Cavalry and Guards.

BRUCE, Ian Cameron; MP (C) Dorset South, since 1987; Chairman, Ian Bruce Associates Ltd, since 1975; *b* 14 March 1947; *s* of Henry Bruce and Ellen Flora Bruce (*née* Bingham);

m 1969, Hazel Bruce (*née* Roberts); one *s* three *d*. *Educ:* Chelmsford Tech. High Sch.; Bradford Univ.; Mid-Essex Tech. Coll. Mem., Inst. of Management Services. Student apprentice, Marconi, 1965–67; Work Study Engineer: Marconi, 1967–69; Pye Unicam, 1969–70; Haverhill Meat Products, 1970–71; Factory Manager and Work Study Manager, BEPI (Pye), 1971–74; Factory Manager, Sinclair Electronics, 1974–75; Chm. and Founder, gp of Employment Agencies and Management Consultants, 1975–. PPS to Social Security Ministers, 1992–. Mem., Employment Select Cttee, 1990–92; Jt Chm., All Party Street Children Gp, 1992–; Sec., Cons. Social Security Cttee, 1991–92; Vice Chm., Cons. Employment Cttee, 1992. Vice-Chm., European Informatics Market, 1993–. Parly Consultant to Telecommunication Managers Assoc., 1989–, to Trevor Gilbert Assoc., 1993–. *Publications:* numerous articles in press and magazines, both technical and political. *Recreations:* scouting, badminton, writing, sailing, camping. *Address:* House of Commons, SW1A 0AA. *T:* (home) Weymouth (01305) 833320; (office) 0171–219 5086.

BRUCE, Ian Waugh; Director-General, Royal National Institute for the Blind, since 1983; Visiting Professor, City University Business School, since 1991; *b* 21 April 1945; *s* of Thomas Waugh Bruce and Una (*née* Eagle); *m* 1971, Anthea Christine, (Tina), *d* of Dr P. R. Rowland, FRSC; one *s* one *d*. *Educ:* King Edward VI Sch., Southampton; Central High Sch., Arizona; Univ. of Birmingham (BSocSc Hons 1968). CIMgt (CBIM 1991; FBIM 1981; MBIM 1975). Apprentice Chem. Engr, Courtaulds, 1964–65; Marketing Trainee, then Manager, Unilever, 1968–70; Appeals and PR Officer, then Asst Dir, Age Concern England, 1970–74; Dir, The Volunteer Centre UK, 1975–81; Controller of Secretariat, then Asst Chief Exec., Bor. of Hammersmith and Fulham, 1981–83. Consultant, UN Div. of Social Affairs, 1970–72; Mem., Prime Minister's Gp on Voluntary Action, 1978–79; Sec., Volunteurope, Brussels, 1979–81; Adviser, BBC Community Progs Unit, 1979–81; Member: Educn Adv. Council, IBA, 1981–83; Exec. Cttee, NCVO, 1978–81, 1990–94; National Good Neighbour Campaign, 1977–79; Council, Retired Executives Action Clearing House, 1978–83; Adv. Council, Centre for Policies on Ageing, 1979–83; Disability Alliance Steering Cttee, 1985–93; Exec. Cttee, Age Concern England, 1986–92; Nat. Adv. Council on Employment of People with Disabilities, 1987–; DHSS Cttee on Inter-Agency Collaboration on Visual Handicap, 1987–88; Bd, Central London TEC, 1990–; Co-Chair, Disability Benefits Consortium, 1988–. Mem., Art Panel, Art Film Cttee and New Activities Cttee, Arts Council of GB, 1967–71; Spokesman, Artists Now, 1973–77. Chm., Coventry Internat. Centre, 1964. FRSA 1991. Sir Raymond Priestley Expeditionary Award, Univ. of Birmingham, 1968. *Publications:* Public Relations and the Social Services, 1972; (jtly) Patronage of the Creative Artist, 1974, 2nd edn 1975; Blind and Partially Sighted Adults in Britain, 1992; Meeting Need: successful charity marketing, 1994; papers on visual handicap, voluntary and community work, old people, contemporary art and marketing. *Recreations:* the arts, the countryside. *Address:* 54 Mall Road, W6 9DG. *Club:* ICA.

BRUCE, Hon. James Michael Edward, CBE 1992; JP; Founder and Chairman, Scottish Woodlands Ltd, 1967–93; *b* 26 Aug. 1927; *s* of 10th Earl of Elgin, KT, CMG, TD and Hon. Katherine Elizabeth Cochrane, Countess of Elgin, DBE (*d* 1989); *m* 1st, 1950, Hon. (Margaret) Jean Dagbjørt Coats (marr. diss.), *d* of 2nd Baron Glentanar; two *s* one *d* (and one *s* decd); 2nd, 1975, Morven-Anne Macdonald (*d* 1994); two *s* two *d*. *Educ:* Eton; RAC, Cirencester (Goldstand Medal). FInstD. Served Scots Guards, 2nd Lieut. Mem., Home Grown Timber Adv. Cttee, 1969–93; Dir, Forest Industry Cttee, 1989–93. Vice-Pres., Scottish Opera, 1985–94. FRSA (Council Mem., 1988–); Hon. Fellow: Game Conservancy, 1993; Scottish Council for Development and Industry, 1993. JP Perth, 1962. *Recreations:* gardens, boats, fishing, shooting. *Address:* Dron House, Balmanno, Perth PH2 9HG. *T:* Perth (01738) 812786. *Clubs:* Pratt's; New (Edinburgh).

BRUCE, Malcolm Gray; MP Gordon, since 1983 (L 1983–88, Lib Dem since 1988); *b* 17 Nov. 1944; *s* of David Stewart Bruce and Kathleen Elmslie (*née* Delf); *m* 1969, Veronica Jane Wilson (marr. diss. 1992); one *s* one *d*. *Educ:* Wrekin Coll., Shropshire; St Andrews Univ. (MA 1966); Strathclyde Univ. (MSc 1970). Liverpool Daily Post, 1966–67; Buyer, Boots Pure Drug Co., 1967–68; A. Goldberg & Son, 1968–69; Res. Information Officer, NE Scotland Develt Authority, 1971–75; Marketing Dir, Noroil Publishing House (UK), 1975–81; Jt Editor/Publisher/ Dir, Aberdeen Petroleum Publishing, 1981–84. Dep. Chm., Scottish Liberal Party, 1975–84 (Energy Spokesman, 1975–83); Liberal Parly Spokesman on Scottish Affairs, 1983–85, on Energy, 1985–87, on Trade and Industry, 1987–88; Alliance Parly Spokesman on Employment, 1987; Lib Dem Spokesman on Natural Resources (energy and conservation), 1988–90, on Trade and Industry, 1992–94, on Treasury affairs, 1994–. Mem., Select Cttee on Trade and Industry, 1992–94, Treasury and Civil Service, 1994–. Leader, Scottish Liberal Democrats, 1988–92. Rector of Dundee Univ., 1986–89. Vice-Pres., Nat. Deaf Children's Soc., 1990– (Pres., Grampian Br., 1985–). *Publications:* A New Life for the Country: a rural development programme for West Aberdeenshire, 1978; Putting Energy to Work, 1981; (with others) A New Deal for Rural Scotland, 1983; (with Paddy Ashdown) Growth from the Grassroots, 1985. *Recreations:* theatre, music, travel, fresh Scottish air. *Address:* Grove Cottage, Grove Lane, Torphins AB31 4HJ. *T:* Torphins (013398) 82386. *Club:* National Liberal.

BRUCE, Sir Michael Ian, 12th Bt, *cr* 1628; partner, Gossard-Bruce Co., from 1953; President, Newport Sailing Club Inc., since 1978; *b* 3 April 1926; *s* of Sir Michael William Selby Bruce, 11th Bt and Doreen Dalziel, *d* of late W. F. Greenwell; *S* father 1957; holds dual UK and US citizenship; has discontinued first forename, Francis; *m* 1st, 1947, Barbara Stevens (marr. diss., 1957), *d* of Frank J. Lynch; two *s*; 2nd, 1961, Frances Keegan (marr. diss., 1963); 3rd, 1966, Marilyn Ann (marr. diss., 1975), *d* of Carter Mulally; 4th, Patricia Gail (marr. diss. 1991), *d* of Frederich Root; 5th, 1994, Alessandro Conforto, MD. *Educ:* Forman School, Litchfield, Conn; Pomfret, Conn. Served United States Marine Corps, 1943–46 (Letter of Commendation); S Pacific area two years, Bismarck Archipelago, Bougainville, Philippines. Master Mariner's Ticket, 1968; Pres., Newport Academy of Sail, Inc., 1979–; Owner, American Maritime Co. Mem., US Naval Inst. *Recreations:* sailing, spear-fishing. *Heir: s* Michael Ian Richard Bruce, *b* 10 Dec. 1950. *Address:* 3424 Via Oporto #204, Newport Beach, CA 92663, USA. *T:* (714) 6757100. *Clubs:* Rockaway Hunt; Lawrence Beach; Balboa Bay (Newport Beach).

BRUCE, Michael Stewart Rae; *see* Marnoch, Hon. Lord.

BRUCE, Robert Nigel (Beresford Dalrymple), CBE 1972 (OBE (mil.) 1946); TD; CEng, Hon. FIGasE; *b* 21 May 1907; *s* of Major R. N. D. Bruce, late of Hampstead; *m* 1945, Elizabeth Brogden, *d* of J. G. Moore; twin *s* two *d*. *Educ:* Harrow School (Entrance and Leaving Scholar); Magdalen College, Oxford (Exhibitioner). BA (Hons Chem.) and BSc. Joined Territorial Army Rangers (KRRC), 1931; Major, 1939; served Greece, Egypt, Western Desert, 1940–42; Lt-Col Comdg Regt, 1942; GHQ, MEF, Middle East Supply Centre, 1943–45; Col, Dir. of Materials, 1944. Joined Gas, Light and Coke Co., as Research Chemist, 1929; Asst to Gen. Manager, 1937, Controller of Industrial Relations, 1946; Staff Controller, 1949, Dep. Chm., 1956, North Thames Gas Bd; Chm., S Eastern Gas Bd, 1960–72. President: British Road Tar Assoc., 1964 and 1965; Coal Tar Research Assoc., 1966; Institution of Gas Engineers, 1968; Mem. Bd, CEI, 1968–80. Chm. Governing Body, Westminster Technical Coll., 1958–76. Sec., Tennis and Rackets Assoc., 1974–81. *Publications:* Chronicles of the 1st Battalion the Rangers (KRRC), 1939–45; contribs to Proc. Royal Society, Jl Soc. Chemical Industry, Jl Chemical Society. *Recreations:* fishing, military history. *Address:* Fairway, 57 Woodland Grove, Weybridge, Surrey KT13 9EQ. *T:* Weybridge (01932) 852372. *Club:* Queen's (Hon. Mem.).

BRUCE, Prof. Victoria Geraldine, PhD, CPsychol, FBPsS; Professor of Psychology, University of Stirling, since 1992; *b* 4 Jan. 1953; *d* of Charles Frederick Bruce and Geraldine Cordelia Diane (*née* Giffard); *m* 1st, 1978, John Paul Fox (marr. diss.); 2nd, 1984, Anthony Michael Burton. *Educ:* Newcastle upon Tyne Church High Sch.; Newnham Coll., Cambridge (BA Nat. Scis 1974; MA, PhD Psychol. 1978). CPsychol, FBPsS 1989. University of Nottingham: Lectr, 1978–88; Reader, 1988–90; Prof. of Psychology, 1990–92. Member: Neuroscis Bd, MRC, 1989–92; ESRC, 1992–July 1996 (Chm., Res. Progs Bd, 1992–); SHEFC, 1995–(Mem., Chief Executive's Res. Adv. Gp, 1993–); Chm., Psychology Panel, Res. Assessment Exercise, HEFCE, 1996. Editor, British Jl of Psychology, 1995–. *Publications:* (with P. R. Green) Visual Perception: physiology, psychology and ecology, 1985, 2nd edn 1990; Recognising Faces, 1988; (with G. W. Humphreys) Visual Cognition: computational, experimental and neuropsychological perspectives, 1989; (ed) Face Recognition (special edn of European Jl of Cognitive Psychology), 1991; (ed jtly) Processing the Facial Image, 1992; (ed with A. M. Burton) Processing Images of Faces, 1992; (ed with G. W. Humphreys) Object and Face Recognition (special issue of Visual Cognition), 1994; (with I. Roth) Perception and Representation: current issues, 2nd edn 1995; numerous articles in learned jls and edited books. *Recreations:* dogs, walking, games. *Address:* Department of Psychology, University of Stirling, Stirling FK9 4LA. *T:* Stirling (01786) 467640.

BRUCE-GARDNER, Sir Douglas (Bruce), 2nd Bt, *cr* 1945; Director, Guest, Keen & Nettlefolds Ltd, 1960–82; *b* 27 Jan. 1917; *s* of Sir Charles Bruce-Gardner, 1st Bt; *S* father, 1960; *m* 1st, 1940, Monica Flumerfelt (marr. diss. 1964), *d* of late Sir Geoffrey Jefferson, CBE, FRS; one *s* two *d*; 2nd, 1964, Sheila Jane, *d* of late Roger and Barbara Stilliard, Seer Green, Bucks; one *s* one *d*. *Educ:* Uppingham; Trinity College, Cambridge. Lancashire Steel, 1938–51; Control Commn, Germany, 1945–46; joined GKN, 1951. Dir, GKN Ltd, 1960, Dep. Chm., 1974–77; Dep. Chm., GKN Steel Co. Ltd, 1962, Gen. Man. Dir, 1963–65, Chm., 1965–67; Chairman: GKN Rolled & Bright Steel Ltd, 1968–72; GKN (South Wales) Ltd, 1968–72; Exors of James Mills Ltd, 1968–72; Parson Ltd, 1968–72; Brymbo Steel Works Ltd, 1974–77; Miles Druce & Co. Ltd, 1974–77; Exec. Vice-Chm., UK Ops, Gen. Products, GKN Ltd, 1972–74; Dep. Chm., GKN (UK) Ltd, 1972–75; Director: Henry Gardner & Co. Ltd, 1952–68; Firth Cleveland Ltd, 1972–75; BHP-GKN Holdings Ltd, 1977–78; Dep.-Chm., Iron Trades Employers' Insurance Assoc., 1984–87 (Dir, 1977–87). President: Iron and Steel Inst., 1966–67; British Indep. Steel Producers' Assoc., 1972; Iron and Steel Employers' Assoc., 1963–64. Prime Warden, Blacksmiths' Co., 1983–4. *Recreations:* fishing, photography. *Heir: s* Robert Henry Bruce-Gardner [*b* 10 June 1943; *m* 1979, Veronica Ann Hand-Oxborrow, *d* of late Rev. W. E. Hand and of Mrs R. G. Oxborrow, Caterham; two *s*]. *Address:* Stocklands, Lewstone, Ganarew, near Monmouth NP5 3SS. *T:* Symonds Yat (01600) 890216.

BRUCE LOCKHART, Logie, MA; Headmaster of Gresham's School, Holt, 1955–82; *b* 12 Oct. 1921; *s* of late John Harold Bruce Lockhart; *m* 1944, Josephine Agnew; two *s* two *d* (and one *d* decd). *Educ:* Sedbergh School; St John's College, Cambridge (Schol. and Choral Studentship). RMC Sandhurst, 1941; served War of 1939–45; 9th Sherwood Foresters, 1942; 2nd Household Cavalry (Life Guards), 1944–45. Larmor Award, 1947; Asst Master, Tonbridge School, 1947–55. Sponsor, Nat. Council for Educnl Standards. *Publication:* The Pleasures of Fishing, 1981. *Recreations:* fishing, writing, music, natural history, games; Blue for Rugby football, 1945, 1946, Scottish International, 1948, 1950, 1953; squash for Cambridge, 1946. *Address:* Church Farm House, Lower Bodham, near Holt, Norfolk NR25 6PS. *T:* Holt (01263) 712137. *Club:* East India, Devonshire, Sports and Public Schools.

BRÜCK, Prof. Hermann Alexander, CBE 1966; DPhil (Munich); PhD (Cantab); Astronomer Royal for Scotland and Regius Professor of Astronomy in the University of Edinburgh, 1957–75; now Professor Emeritus; Dean of the Faculty of Science, 1968–70; *b* 15 Aug. 1905; *s* of late H. H. Brück; *m* 1st, 1936, Irma Waitzfelder (*d* 1950); one *s* one *d*; 2nd, 1951, Dr Mary T. Conway; one *s* two *d*. *Educ:* Augusta Gymnasium, Charlottenburg; Universities of Bonn, Kiel, Munich, and Cambridge. Astronomer, Potsdam Astrophysical Observatory, 1928; Lectr, Berlin University, 1935; Research Associate, Vatican Observatory, Castel Gandolfo, 1936; Asst Observer, Solar Physics Observatory, Cambridge, 1937; John Couch Adams Astronomer, Cambridge University, 1943; Asst Director, Cambridge Observatory, 1946; Director, Dunsink Observatory and Professor of Astronomy, Dublin Institute for Advanced Studies, 1947–57. Mem., Bd of Governors, Armagh Observatory, NI, 1971–84. MRIA, 1948; FRSE, 1958; Member Pontif. Academy of Sciences, Rome, 1955, Mem. Council, 1964–86; Corr. Member Academy of Sciences, Mainz, 1955. Hon. DSc: NUI, 1972; St Andrews, 1973. *Publications* (ed jtly) Astrophysical Cosmology, 1982; The Story of Astronomy in Edinburgh, 1983; (with Mary T. Brück) The Peripatetic Astronomer: a biography of Charles Piazzi Smyth, 1988; scientific papers in journals and observatory publications. *Recreations:* music, history of science. *Address:* Craigower, Penicuik, Midlothian EH26 9LA. *T:* Penicuik (01968) 75918.

BRUDENELL-BRUCE, family name of **Marquess of Ailesbury.**

BRÜGGEN, Frans; conductor; formerly recorder player; *b* Amsterdam, 1934. *Educ:* Conservatory and Univ. of Amsterdam. Prof., Royal Hague Conservatoire, 1955; formerly: Erasmus Prof., Harvard Univ.; Regents Prof., Univ. of Calif, Berkeley. Founder, Orch. of The Eighteenth Century, 1981; Artistic Dir, Stavanger Symphony Orch., 1990–94; guest conductor: Concertgebouw Orch., Amsterdam; Vienna Philharmonic Orch.; Rotterdam Philharmonic Orch.; Orch. of the Age of Enlightenment; Birmingham Philharmonic Orch. *Address:* c/o Lies Askonas Ltd, 6 Henrietta Street, WC2E 8LA.

BRUINVELS, Peter Nigel Edward; Principal, Peter Bruinvels Associates, media management and public affairs consultants, founded 1986; Managing Director, Bruinvels News & Media, since 1992; news broadcaster, political commentator and freelance journalist; *b* 30 March 1950; *er s* of Stanley and Ninette Maud Bruinvels; *m* 1980, Alison Margaret, *o d* of Major David Gilmore Bacon, RA retd; two *d*. *Educ:* St John's Sch., Leatherhead; London Univ. (LLB Hons). Bar Exams, Council of Legal Educn. Co. Sec., BPC Publishing, 1978–81; Sec./Lawyer, Amari PLC, 1981–82; Management Consultant and company director, 1982–. Chm., Dorking CPC, 1979–83; Mem., Cons. Nat. Union Exec., 1976–81. Contested (C) Leicester E, 1987. MP (C) Leicester E, 1983–87. Jt Chm., British Parly Lighting Gp; Vice-Chairman: Cons. Backbench Cttee on Urban Affairs and New Towns, 1984–87; Cons. Backbench Cttee on Education, 1986–87; Sec., Anglo-Netherlands Parly Gp, 1983–87; Chm., British-Malta Parly Gp, 1984–87; Member: Cons. Backbench Cttee on Home Affairs, 1983–87; Cons. Backbench Cttee on NI, 1983–87; Life Mem., British-Amer. Parly Gp, 1983. Promoter, Crossbows Act, 1987. Campaign Co-ordinator, Eastbourne, gen. election, 1992. Chm., Dorking Conservatives, 1992–. Director: Aalco Nottingham Ltd, 1983–88; Radio Mercury and Allied Radio, 1994–. Special Advr, DTI Deregulation Task Force on Pharmaceuticals and Chemicals, 1993.

Member: Social Security Appeals Tribunal, 1994–; Child Support Appeals Tribunal, 1995–. Inspector, Denominational Ch Schs, OFSTED, 1994–. Church Comr, 1992– (Mem., Pastoral and Houses Cttee, 1993–); Member: Guildford Dio. Synod 1979–; Gen. Synod, 1985–. Mem., Jersey Wildlife Preservation Trust. MIPR 1981; FRSA 1986; Hon. MCIM 1987; MJI 1988; Fellow, Industry and Parliament Trust. Granted Freedom, City of London, 1980. *Publications:* Zoning in on Enterprise, 1982; Light up the Roads, 1984; Sharing in Britain's Success—a Study in Widening Share Ownership, Through Privatisation, 1987; Investing in Enterprise—a Comprehensive Guide to Inner City Regeneration and Urban Renewal, 1989. *Recreations:* political campaigning, the media, Church of England. *Address:* 14 High Meadow Close, Dorking, Surrey RH4 2LG. *T:* and *Fax:* Dorking (01306) 887082. *Clubs:* Carlton, Inner Temple, Corporation of Church House.

BRUMFIT, Prof. Christopher John; Professor of Education, since 1984, Director, Centre for Language in Education, since 1986, University of Southampton; *b* 25 Oct. 1940; *s* of late John Raymond Brumfit and of Margaret May Brumfit (*née* Warner; she *m* 2nd, 1942, Frank Greenaway, *qv*); *m* 1st, 1965, Elizabeth Ann Sandars (marr. diss.); one *s*; 2nd, 1986, Rosamond Frances Mitchell; one *s*. *Educ:* Glyn Grammar Sch., Epsom; Brasenose Coll., Oxford (BA English Lang. and Lit.); Univ. of Essex (MA Applied Linguistics); PhD London 1983; Makerere Coll., Univ. of East Africa (DipEd). Head of English, Tabora Govt Sch., Tanzania, 1964–68; Lectr in Educn, Univ. of Dar es Salaam, 1968–71; Lectr in English and Linguistics, City of Birmingham Coll. of Educn, 1972–74; Lectr in Educn with ref. to English for Speakers of Other Languages, Univ. of London Inst. of Educn, 1974–80; Reader in Educn, Univ. of London, 1980–84; Head, Sch. of Educn, 1986–90, Dean, Faculty of Educnl Studies, 1990–93, Univ. of Southampton. Chairman: BAAL, 1982–85; British Council English Teaching Adv. Cttee, 1991–; British Assoc. of TESOL Qualifying Instns, 1991–94; Vice-Pres., Assoc. Internat. de Linguistique Appliquée, 1984–87. Editor: ELT Documents, 1982–90; Review of English Language Teaching, 1990–. *Publications:* (jtly) Teaching English as a Foreign Language, 1978; (with K. Johnson) The Communicative Approach to Language Teaching, 1979; Problems and Principles in English Teaching, 1980; English for International Communication, 1982; (with J. Roberts) An Introduction to Language and Language Teaching, 1983; (with M. Finocchiaro) The Functional-Notional Approach, 1983; Teaching Literature Overseas, 1983; Language Teaching Projects for the Third World, 1983; Communicative Methodology in Language Teaching, 1984; General English Syllabus Design, 1984; Language and Literature Teaching, 1985; (jtly) English as a Second Language in the UK, 1985; The Practice of Communicative Teaching, 1986; (with R. A. Carter) Literature and Language Teaching, 1986; Language in Teacher Education, 1988; (with R. Mitchell) Research in the Language Classroom, 1990; Literature on Language, 1991; Assessment in Literature Teaching, 1992; (with R. Bowers) Applied Linguistics and English Language Teaching, 1992; (with M. G. Benton) Teaching Literature, 1993; The Council of Europe and Language Teaching, 1995; (jtly) Language Education in the National Curriculum, 1995. *Recreations:* Russian literature, academic cricket, opera, walking. *Address:* 4 The Finches, Welbeck Avenue, Highfield, Southampton SO17 1SU. *T:* Southampton (01703) 557346. *Club:* Athenæum.

BRUNA, Dick; graphic designer; writer and illustrator of children's books; *b* 23 Aug. 1927; *s* of A. W. Bruna and J. C. C. Erdbrink; *m* 1953, Irene de Jongh; two *s* one *d*. *Educ:* Primary Sch. and Gymnasium, Utrecht, Holland; autodidact. Designer of book jackets, 1945–, and of posters, 1947– (many prizes); writer and illustrator of children's books, 1953– (1st book, The Apple); also designer of postage stamps, murals, greeting cards and picture postcards. Exhibn based on Miffy (best-known character in children's books): Gemeentemuseum, Arnhem, 1977; Frans Halsmus. Haarlem, 1989; Centre Pompidou, Paris, 1991. Member: Netherlands Graphic Designers; Authors League of America Inc.; PEN Internat.; Alliance Graphique Internat. *Publications:* 80 titles published and 80 million copies printed by 1994; children's books translated into 33 languages. *Address:* (studio) 3 Jeruzalemstraat, 3512 KW, Utrecht. *T:* (30) 316042. *Club:* Art Directors (Netherlands).

BRUNDIN, Clark Lannerdahl, PhD; Director, School of Management Studies, University of Oxford, since 1992; President, Templeton College, Oxford, since 1992; *b* 21 March 1931; *s* of late Ernest Walfrid Brundin and Elinor Brundin (*née* Clark); *m* 1959, Judith Anne (*née* Maloney); two *s* two *d*. *Educ:* Whittier High Sch., California; California Inst. of Technology; Univ. of California, Berkeley (BSc, PhD); MA Oxford. Electronics Petty Officer, US Navy, 1951–55. Associate in Mech. Engrg, UC Berkeley, 1956–57; Demonstr. Dept of Engrg Science, Univ. of Oxford, 1957–58; Res. Engr, Inst. of Engrg Res., UC Berkeley, 1959–63; Univ. Lectr, Dept of Engrg Sci., Univ. of Oxford, 1963–85, Vice-Chm., Gen. Bd of the Faculties, 1984–85; Jesus College, Oxford: Fellow and Tutor in Engrg, 1964–85; Sen. Tutor, 1974–77; Estates Bursar, 1978–84; Hon. Fellow, 1985; Vice Chancellor, Univ. of Warwick, 1985–92. Vis. Prof., Univ. of Calif Santa Barbara, 1978. Mem., CICHE, 1987–. Director: Cokethorpe Sch. Educnl Trust, 1983–; Heritage Projects (Oxford) Ltd, 1985–; Blackwell Scientific Publications Ltd, 1990–; Chm., Anchor Housing Assoc., 1985–91 (Bd Mem., 1985–94). Governor: Magdalen College Sch., 1987–; Coventry Sch. Foundn, 1991–. *Publications:* articles on rarefied gas dynamics in sci. lit. *Recreations:* sailing, mending old machinery, music of all sorts. *Address:* Templeton College, Oxford OX1 5NY. *T:* Oxford (01865) 735422. *Clubs:* Athenæum, Royal Fowey Yacht, Fowey Gallants Sailing (Fowey, Cornwall).

BRUNDTLAND, Gro Harlem, MD; Norwegian physician and politician; MP (Lab) Oslo, since 1977; Prime Minister of Norway, Feb.–Oct. 1981, 1986–89 and since 1990; *b* 20 April 1939; *d* of Gudmund and Inga Harlem; *m* 1960, Arne Olav Brundtland; two *s* one *d* (and one *s* decd). *Educ:* Oslo and Harvard Univs. MPH. MO, Directorate of Health, 1966–68; Asst Med. Dir, Oslo Bd of Health, 1968–74; Minister of Environment, 1974–79; Dep. Leader, Labour Party, 1975–81; Dep. Leader, Labour Parly Gp, 1979–81, Leader, 1981–90. Mem., Indep. Commn on Disarmament and Security Issues; Vice-Pres., Socialist Internat.; Chm., UN World Commn on Envmt and Develt. *Publications:* articles on preventive medicine, school health and growth studies, internat. issues. *Recreation:* cross-country ski-ing. *Address:* Office of the Prime Minister, PO Box 8001 Dep., 0030 Oslo 3, Norway. *T:* (2) 349090.

BRUNEI, HM Sultan of; *see* Negara Brunei Darussalam.

BRUNER, Jerome Seymour, MA, PhD; Watts Professor of Psychology, University of Oxford, 1972–80; G. H. Mead University Professor, New School for Social Research, New York, 1980–88; Research Professor of Psychology, New York University, since 1987; Fellow, New York Institute for the Humanities; *b* New York, 1 Oct. 1915; *s* of Herman and Rose Bruner; *m* 1st, 1940, Katherine Frost (marr. diss. 1956); one *s* one *d*; 2nd, 1960, Blanche Marshall McLane (marr. diss. 1984); 3rd, 1987, Carol Fleisher Feldman. *Educ:* Duke Univ. (AB 1937): Harvard Univ. (AM 1939, PhD 1941). US Intelligence, 1941; Assoc. Dir, Office Public Opinion Research, Princeton, 1942–44; govt public opinion surveys on war problems, 1942–43; political intelligence, France, 1943; Harvard University: research, 1945–72; Prof. of Psychology, 1952–72; Dir, Centre for Cognitive Studies, 1961–72. Lectr, Salzburg Seminar, 1952; Bacon Prof., Univ. of Aix-en-Provence, 1965. Editor, Public Opinion Quarterly, 1943–44; Syndic, Harvard Univ. Press, 1962–63. Member: Inst. Advanced Study, 1951; White House Panel on Educnl Research and Develt. Guggenheim Fellow, Cambridge Univ., 1955; Fellow: Amer. Psychol Assoc. (Pres., 1964–65; Distinguished Scientific Contrib. award, 1962); Amer. Acad. Arts and Sciences; Swiss Psychol Soc. (hon.); Soc. Psychol Study Social Issues (past Pres.); Amer. Assoc. Univ. Profs; Puerto Rican Acad. Arts and Sciences (hon.). Hon. DHL Lesley Coll., 1964; Hon. DSc: Northwestern Univ., 1965; Sheffield, 1970; Bristol, 1975; Hon. MA, Oxford, 1972; Hon. DSocSci, Yale, 1975; Hon. LLD: Temple Univ., 1965; Univ. of Cincinnati, 1966; Univ. of New Brunswick, 1969; Hon. DLitt: North Michigan Univ., 1969; Duke Univ., 1969; Dr *hc* Sorbonne, 1974; Leuven, 1976; Ghent, 1977; Madrid, 1987; Free Univ., Berlin, 1988; Columbia, 1988; Stirling, 1990; Rome, 1992. Internat. Balzan Prize, Fondazione Balzan, 1987. *Publications:* Mandate from the People, 1944; (with Krech) Perception and Personality: A Symposium, 1950; (with Goodnow and Austin) A Study of Thinking, 1956; (with Smith and White) Opinions and Personality, 1956; (with Bresson, Morf and Piaget) Logique et Perception, 1958; The Process of Education, 1960; On Knowing: Essays for the Left Hand, 1962; (ed) Learning about Learning: A conference report, 1966; (with Olver, Greenfield, and others) Studies in Cognitive Growth, 1966; Toward a Theory of Instruction, 1966; Processes of Cognitive Growth: Infancy, Vol III, 1968; The Relevance of Education, 1971; (ed Anglin) Beyond the Information Given: selected papers of Jerome S. Bruner, 1973; (with Connolly) The Growth of Competence, 1974; (with Jolly and Sylva) Play: its role in evolution and development, 1976; Under Five in Britain, 1980; Communication as Language, 1982; In Search of Mind: essays in autobiography, 1983; Child's Talk, 1983; Actual Minds, Possible Worlds, 1986; Acts of Meaning, 1990; contribs technical and professional jls. *Recreation:* sailing. *Address:* 200 Mercer Street, New York, NY 10012, USA. *Clubs:* Royal Cruising; Century (New York); Cruising Club of America.

BRUNNER, Adrian John Nelson; QC 1994; a Recorder, since 1990; *b* 18 June 1946; *s* of late Comdr Hugh Brunner, DSC, RN and of Elizabeth Brunner; *m* 1970, Christine Anne Hughes; one *s* four *d*. *Educ:* Ampleforth Coll.; BRNC; Coll. of Law. Served RN, 1963–66. Called to the Bar, Inner Temple, 1968 (Major Schol., 1967). *Recreations:* yachting, shooting. *Address:* 8 Acacia Road, NW8 6AB; Holborn Head Farm, Scrabster, Caithness KW14 7UW. *Clubs:* Royal Yacht Squadron, Bar Yacht.

BRUNNER, Dr Guido; Grand Cross, Order of Federal Republic of Germany; German diplomat and politician; Ambassador of the Federal Republic of Germany in Madrid, 1982–92; *b* Madrid, 27 May 1930; *m* 1958, Christa (*née* Speidel). *Educ:* Bergzabern, Munich; German Sch., Madrid; Univs of Munich, Heidelberg and Madrid (law and econs). LLD Munich; Licentiate of Law Madrid. Diplomatic service, 1955–74, 1981–; Private Office of the Foreign Minister, 1956; Office, Sec. of State for For. Affairs, 1958–60; German Observer Mission to the UN, New York, 1960–68; Min. for Foreign Affairs: Dept of scientific and technol relns, 1968–70; Spokesman, 1970–72; Head of Planning Staff, Ambassador and Head of Delegn of Fed. Rep. of Germany, Conf. for Security and Coop. in Europe, Helsinki/Geneva, 1972–74; Mem., Commn of the European Communities, (responsible for Energy, Research, Science and Educn), 1974–80; Mem., Bundestag, 1980–81; Mayor of Berlin and Minister of Economics and Transport, Jan.–May 1981; Ambassador, Min. of Foreign Affairs, Bonn, 1981–82. Corresp. Member: Spanish Acad. of History, 1986–; Spanish Royal Acad. of Arts, 1990–. Hon. DLitt Heriot-Watt, 1977; Dr *hc*, Technical Faculty, Patras Univ., Greece: City Univ., London, 1980. Melchett Medal, Inst. of Energy, 1978. Hon. Citizen, City of Madrid, 1993. Grand Cross, Order of Civil Merit, Spain, 1978; Grand Cross, Order of Leopold, Belgium, 1981; Grand Cross, Order of Merit, FRG, 1981; Grand Cross, Order of Isabel la Católica, Spain, 1986. *Publications:* Bipolarität und Sicherheit, 1965; Friedenssicherungsaktionen der Vereinten Nationen, 1968; Stolz wie Don Rodrigo, 1982; El Poder y la Unión, 1989; contrib. Vierteljahreshefte für Zeitgeschichte, Aussenpolitik, Europa-Archiv. *Address:* Paseo de Eduardo Dato 13, 7°A, 28010 Madrid, Spain.

BRUNNER, Sir John Henry Kilian, 4th Bt *cr* 1895; *b* 1 June 1927; *s* of Sir Felix John Morgan Brunner, 3rd Bt, and of Dorothea Elizabeth, OBE, *d* of late Henry Brodribb Irving; *S* father, 1982; *m* 1955, Jasmine Cecily, *d* of late John Wardrop Moore; two *s* one *d*. *Educ:* Eton; Trinity Coll., Oxford (BA 1950). Served as Lieut RA. On staff, PEP, 1950–53; Talks producer, 1953; Economic Adviser, Treasury, 1958–61; Asst Manager, Observer, 1961. *Heir:* *s* Nicholas Felix Minturn Brunner, *b* 16 Jan. 1960. *Address:* 138 Victoria Avenue, Dalkeith, WA 6009, Australia.

BRUNNING, David Wilfrid; His Honour Judge Brunning; a Circuit Judge, since 1988; *b* 10 April 1943; *s* of Wilfred and Marion Brunning; *m* 1967, Deirdre Ann Shotton; three *s*. *Educ:* Burton upon Trent Grammar Sch.; Worcester Coll., Oxford (BA 1965, DPA 1966). Midland and Oxford Circuit, 1970–88. Chairman: Kirk Lodge Probation Hostel, 1973–89; Leicester Anchor Club, 1983–89. *Recreations:* campanology, squash, walking, wine, music. *Address:* Leicester Combined Court Centre, Wellington Street, Leicester LE1 6HG.

BRUNO, Franklin Roy, (Frank), MBE 1990; professional boxer, since 1982; *b* 16 Nov. 1961; *s* of late Robert Bruno and of Lynette Bruno (*née* Campbell); *m* 1990, Laura Frances Mooney; one *s* two *d*. *Educ:* Oak Hall Sch., Sussex. Amateur boxer, Sir Philip Game Amateur Boxing Club, 1977–80: 21 contests, 20 victories; London ABA and Nat. ABA Heavyweight Champion, 1980; professional career, 1982–95: 40 contests, 37 victories; European Champion, 1985–86; WBC World Heavyweight Champion, 1995. Pantomime appearances: Aladdin, Dominion, 1989, Nottingham, 1990; Robin Hood, Bristol, 1991–92. Sports Personality of Year, Stars Orgn for Spastics, 1989, 1990. *Publications:* Know What I Mean?, 1987; Eye of the Tiger, 1992. *Recreations:* swimming, training, driving, eating, shopping for good clothes. *Address:* PO Box 2266, Brentwood, Essex CM15 0AQ. *Fax:* Brentwood (01277) 822209.

BRUNSDEN, Prof. Denys, PhD; Professor of Geography, Department of Geography, King's College, University of London, since 1983; *b* 14 March 1936; *s* of Francis Stephen Brunsden and Mabel Florence (*née* Martin); *m* 1961, Elizabeth Mary Philippa (*née* Wright); one *s* one *d*. *Educ:* Torquay Grammar Sch. for Boys; King's Coll., Univ. of London (BSc Hons Geography; PhD 1963). King's College, London: Tutorial Student, 1959–60; Asst Lectr, 1960–63; Lectr, 1963–75; Reader, 1975–83. Vis. Lectr, 1964–65, Erskine Fellow, 1988, Univ. of Canterbury, NZ; Vis. Associate Prof., Louisiana State Univ., 1971. Chairman: British Geomorphol Res. Gp, 1985–86; Wkg Pty for Collaboration in Internat. Geomorphology, 1985–; President: Geographical Assoc., 1986–87; Internat. Assoc. of Geomorphologists, 1989–93 (Sen. Past Pres., 1993–); Vice-Pres., RGS, 1984–87; Hon. Mem., Polish Assoc. of Geomorphologists, 1993. Gill Meml Award, RGS (for contribs to study of mass movement and fieldwork), 1977; Republic of China Award Lectr, 1988–89; Assoc. of American Geographers Honours, 1991; Linton Award, British Geomorphological Res. Gp, 1993. *Publications:* Dartmoor, 1968; Slopes, Forms and Process, 1970; (with J. C. Doornkamp) The Unquiet Landscape, 1971 (USA 1976, Australia 1976, Germany 1977); (with J. B. Thornes) Geomorphology and Time, 1977; (with C. Embleton and D. K. C. Jones) Geomorphology: present problems, future prospects, 1978; (with J. C. Doornkamp and D. K. C. Jones) The Geology, Geomorphology and Pedology of Bahrain, 1980; (with R. U. Cooke, J. C. Doornkamp and D. K. C. Jones) The Urban Geomorphology of Drylands, 1982; (with D. B. Prior) Slope Instability, 1984; (with R. Gardner, A. S. Goudie and D. K. C. Jones) Landshapes, 1989; Natural Disasters, 1990. *Recreations:* making walking sticks and shepherd's-crooks, painting, reading thrillers, watching TV, enjoying dinner parties and fine wine, talking, travelling to exotic places, eating, drinking and relaxing in the Drôme. *Address:* Department of Geography, King's College London, Strand, WC2R 2LS. *Club:* Geographical.

BRUNSDON, Norman Keith; Chairman: Anglican Retirement Villages, Diocese of Sydney, since 1991; Anglican Foundation for Aged Care, since 1993; Director, Arthur Yates & Co. Ltd, since 1993; *b* 11 Jan. 1930; *s* of late G. A. Brunsdon; *m* 1953, Ruth, *d* of late W. Legg; one *s* one *d. Educ:* Wagga Wagga High Sch., NSW. FCA. Price Waterhouse, Australia: joined, 1951; Partner, 1963; Mem. Policy Cttee (Bd), 1970–86; Partner-in-Charge, Sydney, 1975–81; Chm. and Sen. Partner, Australia, 1982–86; World Firm Policy Cttee (Bd) and Council of Firms, 1979–86; Agent Gen. for NSW in London, 1989–91. Chm., Aust. Govt's Taxation Adv. Cttee, 1979–83; Trustee, Econ. Develt of Aust. Cttee, 1977–86. Vice-Pres., Thai-Aust. Chamber of Commerce & Industry, 1982–85; Member: Pacific Basin Econ. Council, 1982–86; Aust. Japan Business Co-op. Cttee, 1982–86; Standing Cttee, C of E Dio. Sydney, 1969–74; C of E Children's Homes Cttee, 1974–84 (Treasurer, 1969–75; Acting Chm., 1972–73); Governor, King's Sch., Parramatta, 1977–86; Trustee, Bark Endeavour Foundn Pty Ltd, 1992–. Hon. Mem., Cook Soc. Freeman, City of London, 1989. FRSA; FAICD. *Recreations:* music, opera, theatre, reading, sailing, golf. *Address:* 71 Coolawin Road, Northbridge, NSW 2063, Australia. *T:* (2) 99580641, *Fax:* (2) 99672835. *Clubs:* Australian (Sydney); Royal Sydney Yacht Squadron.

BRUNSKILL, Prof. Ronald William, OBE 1990; MA, PhD; FSA; lecturer and author; Professor, School of the Built Environment, De Montfort University, since 1995; *b* 3 Jan. 1929; *s* of William Brunskill and Elizabeth Hannah Brunskill; *m* 1960, Miriam Allsopp; two *d. Educ:* Bury High Sch.; Univ. of Manchester (BA Hons Arch. 1951, MA 1952, PhD 1963). Registered Architect and ARIBA, 1951; FSA 1975. National Service, 2nd Lieut RE, 1953–55. Studio Asst in Arch., Univ. of Manchester, 1951–53; Architectural Asst, LCC, 1955; Asst in Arch., Univ. of Manchester, 1955–56; Commonwealth Fund Fellow (arch. and town planning), MIT, 1956–57; Architect to Williams Deacon's Bank, 1957–60; Manchester University: Lectr, 1960–73; Sen. Lectr, 1973–84; Reader in Architecture, 1984–89; Hon. Fellow, Sch. of Architecture, 1989–95; Architect in private practice, 1960–66; Partner, Carter, Brunskill & Associates, chartered architects, 1966–69, Consultant, 1969–73. Vis. Prof., Univ. of Florida, Gainesville, 1969–70; Hon. Vis. Prof., De Montfort Univ., 1994–95. President: Vernacular Arch. Gp, 1974–77; Cumberland and Westmorland Antiquarian and Archaeol Soc., 1990–93 (Vice-Pres., 1975–90); Vice-Pres., Weald and Downland Museum Trust, 1980–; Chairman: Ancient Monuments Soc., 1990– (Hon. Architect, 1983–88; Vice-Chm., 1988–90); Friends of Friendless Churches, 1990–; Member: Historic Bldgs Council for England, 1978–84; Royal Commn on Ancient and Historical Monuments of Wales, 1983– (Vice Chm., 1993–); Historic Buildings and Monuments Commn (English Heritage), 1989– (Mem., Historic Buildings Adv. Cttee and Ancient Monuments Adv. Cttee of Historic Buildings and Monuments Commn, 1984–90); Cathedrals Adv. Commn for England, 1981–91; Cathedrals Fabric Commn for England, 1991–; Manchester DAC for Care of Churches, 1973–79 and 1987–93; Manchester Cathedral Fabric Cttee, 1987–; Blackburn Cathedral Fabric Cttee, 1989– (Chm.); Chester Cathedral Fabric Cttee, 1989–94; Council, Soc. for Folk Life Studies, 1969–72 and 1980–83. Trustee, British Historic Buildings Trust, 1985–92. Neale Bursar, RIBA, 1962; President's Award, Manchester Soc. of Architects, 1977. *Publications:* Illustrated Handbook of Vernacular Architecture, 1971, 3rd edn (enlarged) 1987; Vernacular Architecture of the Lake Counties, 1974; (with Alec Clifton-Taylor) English Brickwork, 1977; Traditional Buildings of Britain, 1981, 2nd edn (enlarged) 1992; Houses (in series, Collins Archaeology), 1982; Traditional Farm Buildings of Britain, 1982, 2nd edn (enlarged) 1987; Timber Building in Britain, 1985, 2nd edn (enlarged) 1994; Brick Building in Britain, 1990; Houses and Cottages of Britain, 1996; articles and reviews in archaeol and architectural jls. *Recreation:* enjoying the countryside. *Address:* Three Trees, 8 Overhill Road, Wilmslow SK9 2BE. *T:* Wilmslow (01625) 522099; 159 Glan Gors, Harlech, Gwynedd LL46 2SA. *Club:* Athenæum.

BRUNSON, Michael John; Political Editor, ITN, since 1986; *b* 12 Aug. 1940; *s* of Geoffrey Brunson and Ethel (*née* Mills); *m* 1965, Susan Margaret Brown; two *s. Educ:* Bedford Sch.; Queen's Coll., Oxford (BA Theol. 1963). VSO, Sierra Leone, 1963–64; BBC General Trainee, 1964–65; Reporter, BBC SE Radio News, 1965–66; Asst Producer, BBC TV Current Affairs, 1966–68; Independent Television News: Reporter, 1968–72; Washington Corresp., 1972–77; Reporter, 1977–80; Diplomatic Editor, 1980–86; Campaign Reporter with Mrs Thatcher, 1979 and 1983 Gen. Elections. Columnist, The House Mag. (H of C), 1989–90. Chm., Parly Lobby Journalists, 1994. *Recreations:* growing geraniums, listening to Schubert. *Address:* c/o ITN, 200 Gray's Inn Road, WC1X 8XZ. *T:* 0171–833 3000.

BRUNT, Peter Astbury, FBA 1969; Camden Professor of Ancient History, Oxford University, and Fellow of Brasenose College, 1970–82; *b* 23 June 1917; *s* of Rev. Samuel Brunt, Methodist Minister, and Gladys Eileen Brunt. *Educ:* Ipswich Sch.; Oriel Coll., Oxford. Open Schol. in History, Oriel Coll., Oxford, 1935; first classes in Class. Mods, 1937, and Lit. Hum., 1939; Craven Fellowship, 1939. Temp. Asst Principal and (later) Temp. Principal, Min. of Shipping (later War Transport), 1940–45. Sen. Demy, Magdalen Coll., Oxford, 1946; Lectr in Ancient History, St Andrews Univ., 1947–51; Fellow and Tutor of Oriel Coll., Oxford, 1951–67, Dean, 1959–64, Hon. Fellow, 1973; Fellow and Sen. Bursar, Gonville and Caius Coll., Cambridge, 1968–70. Editor of Oxford Magazine, 1963–64; Chm., Cttee on Ashmolean Museum, 1967; Deleg., Clarendon Press, 1971–79; Mem. Council, British Sch. at Rome, 1972–87; Pres., Soc. for Promotion of Roman Studies, 1980–83. *Publications:* Thucydides (selections in trans. with introd.), 1963; Res Gestae Divi Augusti (with Dr J. M. Moore), 1967; Social Conflicts in the Roman Republic, 1971; Italian Manpower 225 BC-AD 14, 1971, rev. edn 1987; (ed) Arrian's Anabasis (Loeb Classical Library), vol. I, 1976, vol. II, 1983; The Fall of the Roman Republic and related essays, 1988; Roman Imperial Themes, 1990; Studies in Ancient Greek History and Thought, 1992; articles in classical and historical jls. *Address:* 37 Woodstock Close, Woodstock Road, Oxford OX2 8DB. *T:* Oxford (01865) 53024.

BRUNT, Peter William, OBE 1994; MD, FRCP, FRCPE; Physician to the Queen in Scotland, since 1983; Consultant Physician and Gastroenterologist, Grampian Health Board, Aberdeen, since 1970; Clinical Senior Lecturer in Medicine, University of Aberdeen, since 1970; *b* 18 Jan. 1936; *s* of late Harry Brunt and Florence J. J. Airey; *m* 1961, Dr Anne Lewis, *d* of Rev. R. H. Lewis; three *d. Educ:* Manchester Grammar Sch.; Cheadle Hulme Sch.; King George V Sch.; Univ. of Liverpool. MB, ChB 1959. Gen. Med. training, Liverpool Royal Infirmary and Liverpool Hosps, 1959–64; Research Fellow, Johns Hopkins Univ. Sch. of Medicine, 1965–67; Lectr in Medicine, Edinburgh Univ., 1967–68; Senior Registrar, Gastrointestinal Unit, Western Gen. Hosp., Edinburgh, 1968–69. Hon. Lectr in Medicine, Royal Free Hosp. Sch. of Medicine, Univ. of London, 1969–70. Mem., Assoc. of Physicians of GB and Ireland (Pres., 1995–96). *Publications:* (with M. Losowsky and A. E. Read) Diseases of the Liver and Biliary System, 1984; (with P. F. Jones and N. A. G. Mowat) Gastroenterology, 1984. *Recreations:* mountaineering, music, operatics, Crusaders' Union. *Address:* 17 Kingshill Road, Aberdeen AB2 4JY. *T:* Aberdeen (01224) 314204.

BRUNTISFIELD, 2nd Baron *cr* 1942, of Boroughmuir; **John Robert Warrender,** OBE 1963; MC 1943; TD 1967; DL; Bt 1715; *b* 7 Feb. 1921; *s* of 1st Baron Bruntisfield, MC and Dorothy (*d* 1975), *y d* of Col R. H. Rawson, MP; *S* father, 1993; *m* 1st, 1948, (Anne) Moireen Campbell (*d* 1976), 2nd *d* of Sir Walter Campbell, KCIE; two *s* two *d;* 2nd, 1977, Mrs Shirley Crawley (*d* 1981), *o d* of E. J. L. Ross; 3rd, 1985, Mrs (Kathleen) Joanna Graham, *o d* of David Chancellor. *Educ:* Eton; RMC, Sandhurst. Royal Scots Greys (2nd Dragoons), 1939–48; ADC to Governor of Madras, 1946–48; comd N Somerset Yeomanry/44th Royal Tank Regt, 1957–62; Dep. Brigadier RAC (TA), Southern and Eastern Commands, 1962–67. Mem., Queen's Body Guard for Scotland (Royal Co. of Archers) (Brigadier, 1973–85). DL Somerset 1965. *Recreations:* shooting, fishing. *Heir: s* Hon. Michael John Victor Warrender [*b* 9 Jan. 1949; *m* 1978, Baroness Walburga von Twickel]. *Address:* 18 Warriston Crescent, Edinburgh EH3 5LB. *T:* 0131–556 3701. *Clubs:* Puffin's, New (Edinburgh).

See also Hon. R. H. Warrender.

BRUNTON, Sir (Edward Francis) Lauder, 3rd Bt, *cr* 1908; Physician; *b* 10 Nov. 1916; *s* of Sir Stopford Brunton, 2nd Bt, and Elizabeth, *o d* of late Professor J. Bonsall Porter; *S* father 1943; *m* 1946, Marjorie, *o d* of David Sclater Lewis, MSc, MD, CM, FRCP (C); one *s* one *d. Educ:* Trinity College School, Port Hope; Bryanston School; McGill Univ. BSc 1940; MD, CM 1942; served as Captain, RCAMC. Hon. attending Physician, Royal Victoria Hosp., Montreal. Fellow: American Coll. of Physicians; Internat. Soc. of Hematology; Life Mem., Montreal Mus. of Fine Arts; Life Governor, Art Gall. of Nova Scotia. *Heir: s* James Lauder Brunton, MD, FRCP(C) [*b* 24 Sept. 1947; *m* 1967, Susan, *o d* of Charles Hons; one *s* one *d*]. *Address:* PO Box 140, Guysborough, Nova Scotia B0H 1N0, Canada. *Club:* Royal Nova Scotia Yacht Squadron.

BRUNTON, Sir Gordon (Charles), Kt 1985; Chairman: Communications and General Consultants, since 1985; The Racing Post plc, since 1985; Verity Group plc (formerly Wharfedale plc), since 1991; Green Field Leisure Group Ltd, since 1992; PhoneLink plc, since 1993; *b* 27 Dec. 1921; *s* of late Charles Arthur Brunton and late Hylda Pritchard; *m* 1st, 1946, Nadine Lucile Paula Sohr (marr. diss. 1965); one *s* two *d* (and one *s* decd); 2nd, 1966, Gillian Agnes Kirk; one *s* one *d. Educ:* Cranleigh Sch.; London Sch. of Economics. Commnd into RA, 1942; served Indian Army, Far East; Mil. Govt, Germany, 1946. Joined Tothill Press, 1947; Exec. Dir, Tothill, 1956; Man. Dir, Tower Press Gp of Cos, 1958; Exec. Dir, Odhams Press, 1961; joined Thomson Organisation, 1961; Man. Dir, Thomson Publications, 1961; Dir, Thomson Organisation, 1963; Chm., Thomson Travel, 1965–68; Man. Dir and Chief Exec., Internat. Thomson Orgn plc (formerly Thomson British Hldgs) and The Thomson Orgn Ltd, 1968–84; Pres., Internat. Thomson Orgn Ltd, 1978–84. Director: Times Newspapers Ltd, 1967–81; Sotheby Parke Bernet Group, 1978–83 (Chm., 1982–83, Chm. Emeritus, Sotheby's Holding Inc., 1983); Cable and Wireless plc, 1981–91; Yattendon Investment Trust, 1985–; Chairman: Bemrose Corp., 1978–91; Martin Currie Pacific Trust, 1985–92; Community Industry, 1985–92; Euram Consulting, 1985–92; Cavendish Shops, 1985–; Mercury Communications, 1986–90; Cavendish Retail, 1987–; Ingersoll Publications, 1988–91. President: Periodical Publishers Assoc., 1972–74, 1981–83; Nat. Advertising Benevolent Soc., 1973–75 (Trustee, 1980–); History of Advertising Trust, 1981–84; CPU, 1991–; Chm., EDC for Civil Engrg, 1978–84; Member: Printing and Publishing Ind. Trng Bd, 1974–78; Supervisory Bd, CBI Special Programmes Unit, 1980–84; Business in the Community Council, 1981–84; Chm., Independent Adoption Service, 1986–. Mem., South Bank Bd, Arts Council, 1985–92. Governor: LSE (Fellow, 1978); Ashridge Management Coll., 1983–86; Ct of Governors, Henley—The Management Coll., 1983–85; Mem. Council, Templeton College (formerly Oxford Centre for Management Studies), 1976–; Mem., Finance Cttee, OUP, 1985–91. *Recreations:* books, breeding horses. *Address:* (office) North Munstead, Godalming, Surrey GU8 4AX. *T:* Godalming (01483) 416313. *Club:* Garrick.

BRUNTON, Sir Lauder; *see* Brunton, Sir E. F. L.

BRUS, Prof. Wlodzimierz, PhD; Professor of Modern Russian and East European Studies, University of Oxford, 1985–88, now Emeritus Professor; Professorial Fellow, Wolfson College, 1985–88, now Emeritus Fellow; Senior Research Fellow, St Antony's College, Oxford, 1989–93; *b* 23 Aug. 1921; *s* of Abram Brus and Helena (*née* Askanas); *m* 1st, 1940, Helena Wolińska; 2nd, 1945, Irena Stergień; two *d;* 3rd, 1956, Helena Wolińska; one *s. Educ:* Saratov, USSR (MA Economic Planning); Warsaw, Poland (PhD Pol. Econ.). Polish Army, 1944–46. Junior Editor, Nowe Drogi (theoretical journal of Polish Workers' (later United Workers') Party), 1946–49; Asst (later Associate) Prof. of Political Economy, Central Sch. of Planning & Statistics, Warsaw, 1949–54; Hd of Dept of Political Economy, Inst. of Social Sciences attached to Central Cttee, Polish United Workers' Party, 1950–56; Prof. of Political Econ., Univ. of Warsaw, 1954–68; Dir, Research Bureau, Polish Planning Commn, 1956–68; Vice-Chm., Econ. Adv. Council of Poland, 1957–63; research worker, Inst. of Housing, Warsaw, 1968–72; Vis. Sen. Res. Fellow, Univ. of Glasgow, 1972–73; Sen. Res. Fellow, St Antony's Coll., Oxford, 1973–76; Univ. Lectr and Fellow, Wolfson Coll., Oxford, 1976–85. Visiting Professor (or Senior Fellow): Rome, 1971; Catholic Univ. of Louvain, 1973; Columbia, 1982; Johns Hopkins Bologna Centre, 1983; Siena, 1991. Consultant to World Bank, 1980–82, 1984. Officers' Cross, Order of Polonia Restituta, Poland, 1954; Polish and Soviet war medals, 1944, 1945. *Publications:* The Law of Value and Economic Incentives, 1956 (trans Hungarian, 1957); General Problems of Functioning of the Socialist Economy, 1961 (published in 10 langs); Economics and Politics of Socialism, 1973 (published in 6 langs); Socialist Ownership and Political Systems, 1975 (published in 8 langs); Economic History of Eastern Europe, 1983 (published in 6 langs); (with K. Laski) From Marx to the Market: socialism in search of an economic system, 1989; contribs to Soviet Studies, Jl of Comparative Economics, Cambridge Jl of Economics. *Recreations:* walking, swimming. *Address:* 21 Bardwell Court, Bardwell Road, Oxford OX2 6SX. *T:* Oxford (01865) 53790.

BRUTON, John (Gerard); TD (Fine Gael), Meath, Dáil Eireann (Parliament of Ireland), since 1969; Taoiseach (Prime Minister of Ireland), since 1994; Leader of Fine Gael, since 1990 (Deputy Leader, 1987–90); *b* 18 May 1947; *s* of Matthew Joseph Bruton and Doris Bruton (*née* Delany); *m* 1981, Finola Gill; one *s* three *d. Educ:* St Dominic's Coll., Dublin; Clongowes Wood Coll., Co. Kildare; University Coll., Dublin (BA, BL); King's Inns, Dublin; called to the Bar, 1972. National Secretary, Fine Gael Youth Group, 1966–69. Mem., Dáil Committee of Procedure and Privileges, 1969–73, 1982–; Fine Gael Spokesman on Agriculture, 1972–73; Parliamentary Secretary: to Minister for Education, 1973–77; to Minister for Industry and Commerce, 1975–77; Fine Gael Spokesman: on Agriculture, 1977–81; on Finance, Jan.–June 1981; Minister: for Finance, 1981–82, for Industry and Energy, 1982–83, for Industry, Trade, Commerce and Tourism, 1983–86, for Finance, 1986–87; Fine Gael Spokesman on Industry and Commerce, 1987–89, on education, 1989; Leader of the House, 1982–86. Pres., EEC Industry, Research and Internal Market Councils, July–Dec. 1984. Member: Parly Assembly, Council of Europe, 1989–90; British-Irish Parly Body, 1993–. Hon. Citizen of Sioux City, Iowa, USA, 1970;

Ambassador of Good Will, Hon. Dist. Citizen and Washington General, State of Washington, 1983; Calif. Legislature Assembly Rules Cttee and Calif. Senate Rules Cttee Commendations, 1983. *Publications:* Reform of the Dail, 1980; A Better Way to Plan the Nation's Finances, 1981; Industrial Policy—White Paper, 1984; Tourism Policy—White Paper, 1985; Fine Gael policy documents on 1992 and on televising of parliament; contrib. Furrow magazine. *Recreation:* reading history. *Address:* Cornelstown, Dunboyne, Co. Meath. *T:* (1) 6689333.

BRYAN, Sir Arthur, Kt 1976; Lord-Lieutenant of Staffordshire, 1968–93; President, Waterford Wedgwood Holdings plc and a Director, Waterford Glass Group plc, 1986–88 (Managing Director, 1963–85, Chairman, 1968–86, Wedgwood); *b* 4 March 1923; *s* of William Woodall Bryan and Isobel Alan (*née* Tweedie); *m* 1947, Betty Ratford; one *s* one *d.* *Educ:* Longton High Sch., Stoke-on-Trent. Served with RAFVR, 1941–45. Joined Josiah Wedgwood & Sons Ltd, 1947; London Man., 1953–57; General Sales Man., 1959–60; Director and President, Josiah Wedgwood & Sons Inc. of America, 1960–62; Director: Josiah Wedgwood & Sons Ltd, Barlaston, 1962; Josiah Wedgwood & Sons (Canada) Ltd; Josiah Wedgwood & Sons (Australia) Pty Ltd; Phoenix Assurance Co., 1976–85; Friends' Provident Life Office, 1985–92; Rank Organisation, 1985–94; United Kingdom Fund Inc., 1987–. Member: BOTB, 1978–82 (Chm., N American Adv. Gp, 1973–82); British-American Associates, 1988–; Marshall Aid Commem. Cttee, 1988–94. Pres., British Ceramic Manufacturers' Fedn, 1970–71; Mem., Design Council, 1977–82. Mem. Ct, Univ. of Keele. Fellow, Inst. of Marketing (grad. 1950); CIMgt (FBIM 1968); Comp. Inst. Ceramics. KStJ 1972. Hon. MUniv Keele, 1978; Hon. DLitt Staffordshire, 1993. *Recreations:* walking, reading. *Address:* Parkfields Cottage, Tittensor, Stoke-on-Trent, Staffs ST12 9HQ. *T:* Barlaston (01782) 372686.

BRYAN, Dora, (Mrs William Lawton); actress; *b* 7 Feb. 1924; *d* of Albert Broadbent and Georgina (*née* Hill); *m* 1954, William Lawton; one *s* (and one *s* one *d* adopted). *Educ:* Hathershaw Council Sch., Lancs. Pantomimes: London Hippodrome, 1936; Manchester Palace, 1937; Alhambra, Glasgow, 1938; Oldham Repertory, 1939–44; followed by Peterborough, Colchester, Westcliff-on-Sea. ENSA, Italy, during War of 1939–45. Came to London, 1945, and appeared in West End Theatres: Peace in our Time; Travellers' Joy; Accolade; Lyric Revue; Globe Revue; Simon and Laura; The Water Gypsies; Gentlemen Prefer Blondes; Six of One; Too True to be Good; Hello, Dolly!; They Don't Grow on Trees; Rookery Nook, Her Majesty's, 1979; The Merry Wives of Windsor, Regent's Park, 1984; She Stoops to Conquer, Nat. Theatre, 1985; The Apple Cart, Haymarket, 1986; Charlie Girl, Victoria Palace, 1986, Birmingham, 1988; Pygmalion, Plymouth, New York, 1987; 70, Girls, 70, Vaudeville, 1991; The Birthday Party, NT, 1994. Chichester Festival seasons, 1971–74 and 1995; London Palladium season, 1971; London Palladium Pantomime season, 1973–74. Has also taken parts in farces televised from Whitehall Theatre. *Films include:* The Fallen Idol, 1949; A Taste of Honey, 1961 (British Acad. Award); Two a Penny, 1968; Great St Trinian's Train Robbery, 1970; Apartment Zero, 1989. *TV series:* appearances on A to Z; Sunday Night at the London Palladium; According to Dora, 1968; Both Ends Meet, 1972; Mother's Ruin, 1994. Cabaret in Canada, Hong Kong and Britain. Has made recordings. *Publication:* According to Dora (autobiog.), 1987. *Recreations:* reading, patchwork quilts. *Address:* 119 Marine Parade, Brighton BN2 1DD. *T:* Brighton (01273) 603235.

BRYAN, Gerald Jackson, CMG 1964; CVO 1966; OBE 1960; MC 1941; Member, Lord Chancellor's Panel of Independent Inquiry Inspectors, 1982–91; *b* 2 April 1921; *yr s* of late George Bryan, OBE, LLD, and Ruby Evelyn (*née* Jackson), Belfast; *m* 1947, Georgiana Wendy Cockburn, OStJ, *d* of late William Barraud and Winnifred Hull; one *s* two *d.* *Educ:* Wrekin Coll.; RMA, Woolwich; New Coll., Oxford. Regular Commn, RE, 1940; served Middle East with No 11 (Scottish) Commando, 1941; retd 1944, Capt. (temp. Maj.). Apptd Colonial Service, 1944; Asst District Comr, Swaziland, 1944; Asst Colonial Sec., Barbados, 1950; Estabt Sec., Mauritius, 1954; Administrator, Brit. Virgin Is, 1959; Administrator of St Lucia, 1962–67, retired; Govt Sec. and Head of Isle of Man Civil Service, 1967–69; General Manager: Londonderry Develt Commn, NI, 1969–73; Bracknell Develt Corp., 1973–82. Director: Lovaux Engrg Co. Ltd, 1982–88; MDSL Estates Ltd, 1988–. Sec. Gen., Assoc. of Contact Lens Manufacturers, 1983–88. Mem. (C), Berks CC, 1983–85. Treasurer, Gordon Sch. (formerly Gordon Boys' Sch.), Woking, 1979–. Chm., St John Council for Berks, 1981–88. KStJ 1985, Mem., Chapter Gen., 1987–. FIMgt. *Recreation:* swimming. *Address:* Whitehouse, Murrell Hill Lane, Binfield, Berks RG12 5BY. *T:* Bracknell (01344) 425447.

BRYAN, Margaret, CMG 1988; HM Diplomatic Service, retired; Ambassador to Panama, 1986–89; *b* 26 Sept. 1929; *d* of late James Grant and Dorothy Rebecca Galloway; *m* 1952, Peter Bernard Bryan (marr. diss. 1981). *Educ:* Cathedral Sch., Shanghai; Croydon High Sch.; Girton Coll., Cambridge (MA Modern Languages). Second, later First, Secretary, FCO, 1962–80; Head of Chancery and Consul, Kinshasa, 1980–83; Counsellor, Havana, 1983–86. *Recreations:* theatre, travel, cookery, embroidery. *Address:* 10 Park Road, Blockley, Moreton-in-Marsh, Glos GL56 8BZ. *Club:* Royal Over-Seas League.

BRYAN, Sir Paul (Elmore Oliver), Kt 1972; DSO 1943; MC 1943; *b* 3 Aug. 1913; *s* of Rev. Dr J. I. Bryan, PhD; *m* 1st, 1939, Betty Mary (*née* Hoyle) (*d* 1968); three *d*; 2nd, 1971, Cynthia Duncan (*née* Ashley Cooper), *d* of late Sir Patrick Ashley Cooper and of Lady Ashley Cooper, Hexton Manor, Herts. *Educ:* St John's School, Leatherhead (Scholar); Caius College, Cambridge (MA). War of 1939–45; 6th Royal West Kent Regt; enlisted, 1939; commissioned, 1940; Lieut-Col, 1943; served in France, N Africa, Sicily, Italy; Comdt 164th Inf. OCTU (Eaton Hall), 1944. Sowerby Bridge UDC, 1947; contested Sowerby, By-Election, 1948, and General Elections, 1950 and 1951. MP (C): Howden Div. of ER Yorks, 1955–83; Boothferry, 1983–87. Assistant Government Whip, 1956–58; Parliamentary Private Secretary to Minister of Defence, 1956; a Lord Commissioner of the Treasury, 1958–61; Vice-Chairman, Conservative Party Organisation, 1961–65; Conservative Front Bench Spokesman on Post Office and broadcasting, 1965; Minister of State, Dept of Employment, 1970–72. Chm., All Party Hong Kong Parly Gp, 1974–87; Vice-Chm., Conservative 1922 Cttee, 1977–87. Chairman: Croydon Cable Television, subseq. United Artists Cables Internat. (London South), 1985–; Scottish Eagle Insce Co., 1990–93; Director: Granada TV Rental Ltd, 1966–70; Granada Television, 1972–83; Granada Theatres, 1973–83; Greater Manchester Independent Radio Ltd, 1972–84; Maritime Union Assurance Co. (Bermuda) Ltd, 1980–88; Scottish Lion Insurance Co. Ltd, 1981–95; Hewetson Holdings Ltd, 1983–91; (alternate) Port of Felixstowe, 1991–94; Dep. Chm., Furness Withy and Co. Ltd, 1984–89 (Dir, 1983–). *Publication:* Wool, War and Westminster, 1993. *Address:* Park Farm, Sawdon, near Scarborough, North Yorks YO13 9EB. *T:* Scarborough (01723) 859370; 5 Westminster Gardens, Marsham Street, SW1P 4JA. *T:* 0171–834 2050.

BRYAN, Robert Patrick, OBE 1980; security consultant; Police Adviser to Foreign and Commonwealth Office, and Inspector General of Dependent Territories Police, 1980–85, retired; *b* 29 June 1926; *s* of Maurice Bryan and Elizabeth (*née* Waite); *m* 1948, Hazel Audrey (*née* Braine) (*d* 1990); three *s.* *Educ:* Plaistow Secondary Sch.; Wanstead County High Sch. Indian Army (Mahratta LI), 1944–47. Bank of Nova Scotia, 1948–49; Metropolitan Police: Constable, 1950; Dep. Asst Commissioner, 1977, retired 1980. National Police College: Intermediate Comd Course, 1965; Sen. Comd Course, 1969; occasional lecturer. RCDS 1974. Chm., Food Distribn Security Assoc., 1988–. Gov., Corps of Commissionaires, 1993–. Governor, Hampton Sch., 1978–. *Publications:* contribs to police and related pubns, particularly on community relations and juvenile delinquency. *Address:* c/o National Westminster Bank, High Street, Teddington, Mddx TW11 8EP.

BRYANS, Dame Anne (Margaret), DBE 1957 (CBE 1945); DStJ; Chairman, Order of St John of Jerusalem and BRCS Service Hospitals Welfare and VAD Committee, 1960–89; Vice-Chairman, Joint Committee, Order of St John and BRCS, 1976–81; *b* 29 Oct. 1909; *e d* of late Col Rt Hon. Sir John Gilmour, 2nd Bt, GCVO, DSO, MP of Montrave and late Mary Louise Lambert; *m* 1932, Lieut-Comdr J. R. Bryans, RN, retired (*d* 1990); one *s.* *Educ:* privately. Joined HQ Staff British Red Cross Society, 1938; Deputy Commissioner British Red Cross and St John War Organisation, Middle East Commission, 1943; Commissioner Jan.-June 1945. Dep. Chm., 1953–64, Vice-Chm., 1964–76, Exec. Cttee, BRCS; Lay Mem., Council for Professions Supplementary to Med., 1973–79; Chm., Relief Cttee, Nations Fund for Nurses, 1980–. Member: Ethical practices Sub-Cttee, Royal Free Hosp., 1974–; Royal Free Hosp. Sch. Council, 1968–; Bd of Governors, Eastman Dental Hosp., 1973–79; Camden and Islington AHA, 1974–79; Vice-Pres., Open Sect., RSocMed, 1975, Pres. 1980–82; former Member: ITA, later IBA; Govt Anglo-Egyptian Resettlement Bd; BBC/ITA Appeals Cttee; Med. Sch. St George's Hosp.; Special Trustee and former Chm., Royal Free Hosp. and Friends of Royal Free Hosp.; former Chairman: Bd of Governors, Royal Free Hosp.; Council, Florence Nightingale Hosp.; Trustee, Florence Nightingale Aid in Sickness Trust, 1979–; Vice-Pres., Royal Coll. of Nursing; former Governor, Westminster Hosp. FRSM 1976; Hon. FRSM 1994. *Address:* 57 Elm Park House, Elm Park Gardens, SW10 9QD. *Clubs:* New Cavendish; Royal Lymington Yacht.

BRYANT, (Alan) Christopher, OBE 1995; Life President, Bryant Group plc (formerly Bryant Holdings Ltd), since 1992 (Managing Director, 1960–88; Chairman, 1962–92); *b* 28 July 1923; *s* of Ebenezer John Bryant and Ivy Maud Bryant (*née* Seymour); *m* 1951, Jean Mary Nock; four *d.* *Educ:* West House School, Birmingham; Malvern Coll.; Birmingham Univ. (BSc (Hons)). FCIOB 1958. Engineer Officer, Fleet Air Arm, 1944–47 (Sub-Lieut, RNVR); Project Manager, 1946–48, Director, 1948–86, C. Bryant & Son Ltd. Non-exec. Dir, BSG International plc, 1985–94. Chm., 1969–, Pres. and Chm., 1987–, Birmingham YMCA; Hon. Treas., Nat. Council of YMCAs, 1991–. Hon. DEng Birmingham, 1992. *Recreations:* sailing, shooting, walking. *Clubs:* Naval; South Caernarvonshire Yacht.

BRYANT, Christopher; *see* Bryant, A. C.

BRYANT, David John, CBE 1980 (MBE 1969); Director, Drakelite Ltd (International Bowls Consultants), since 1978; international bowler, 1958–92; *b* 27 Oct. 1931; *s* of Reginald Samuel Harold Bryant and Evelyn Claire (*née* Weaver); *m* 1960, Ruth Georgina (*née* Roberts); two *d.* *Educ:* Weston Grammar Sch.; St Paul's Coll., Cheltenham; Redland Coll., Bristol (teacher training colls). National Service, RAF, 1950–52; teacher trng, 1953–55; schoolmaster, 1955–71; company director, sports business, 1971–78. World Singles Champion, 1966, 1980 and 1988; World Indoor Singles Champion, 1979, 1980 and 1981; World Indoor Pairs Champion, 1986, 1987, 1989, 1990, 1991 and 1992; Kodak Masters International Singles Champion, 1978, 1979 and 1982; Gateway International Masters Singles Champion, 1984, 1985, 1986, 1987; Woolwich International Singles Champion, 1988, 1989; World Triples Champion, 1980; Commonwealth Games Gold Medallist: Singles: 1962, 1970, 1974 and 1978; Fours: 1962. Numerous national and British Isles titles, both indoor and outdoor. England Indoor Team Captain, 1993, 1994. *Publications:* Bryant on Bowls, 1966; Bowl with Bryant, 1984; Bryant on Bowls, 1985; The Game of Bowls, 1990; Bowl to Win, 1994. *Recreations:* angling, gardening. *Address:* 47 Esmond Grove, Clevedon, Avon BS21 7HP. *T:* Clevedon (01275) 875423. *Clubs:* Clevedon Bowling, Clevedon Conservative.

BRYANT, David Michael Arton; His Honour Judge Bryant; a Circuit Judge, since 1989; *b* 27 Jan. 1942; *s* of Lt-Col and Mrs A. D. Bryant; *m* 1969, Diana Caroline, *d* of Brig. and Mrs W. C. W. Sloan; two *s* one *d.* *Educ:* Wellington Coll.; Oriel Coll., Oxford (Open Scholar; BA). Called to the Bar, Inner Temple, 1964; practised North Eastern Circuit, 1965–89. A Recorder, 1985–89. *Recreations:* gardening, shooting, dining. *Address:* Sleningford Park, Ripon, N Yorks HG4 3JA. *Club:* Carlton.

BRYANT, Rt Rev. Denis William, DFC 1942; retired; *b* 31 Jan. 1918; *s* of Thomas and Beatrice Maud Bryant; *m* 1940, Dorothy Linda (*née* Lewis); one *d.* *Educ:* Clark's Coll., Ealing; Cardiff Techn. Coll. Joined RAF; Wireless Operator/Air Gunner, 1936; Navigator, 1939; France, 1940 (despatches); Pilot, 1943; commn in Secretarial Br., 1948; Adjt, RAF Hereford, 1950; Sqdn-Ldr i/c Overseas Postings Record Office, Gloucester, 1951; Sqdn-Ldr DP7, Air Min., 1953. Ordinand, Queen's Coll., Birmingham, 1956; Deacon, 1958; Priest, 1959; Rector of Esperance, 1961–67; Archdeacon of Goldfields, 1966–67; Bishop of Kalgoorlie, 1967 until 1973 when Kalgoorlie became part of Diocese of Perth; Asst Bishop of Perth, and Archdeacon and Rector of Northam, 1973–75; Rector of Dalkeith, WA, 1975–85. Hon. Chaplain, Anglican Homes, 1985–. *Recreations:* squash, tennis, oil painting. *Address:* U3 Dorothy Genders Village, 99 McCabe Street, Mosman Park, WA 6012, Australia. *T:* (9) 3854515.

BRYANT, Air Vice-Marshal Derek Thomas, CB 1987; OBE 1974; Air Officer Commanding, Headquarters Command and Staff Training and Commandant, Royal Air Force Staff College, 1987–89, retired; *b* 1 Nov. 1933; *s* of Thomas Bryant and Mary (*née* Thurley); *m* 1956, Patricia Dodge; one *s* one *d.* *Educ:* Latymer Upper Grammar Sch., Hammersmith. Fighter pilot, 1953; Qualified Flying Instructor, 1957; Sqdn Comdr, 1968–74; OC RAF Coningsby, 1976–78; SASO HQ 38 Gp, 1982–84; Dep. Comdr, RAF Germany, 1984–87; various courses and staff appts. *Recreations:* gardening, golf. *Address:* The Old Stables, Lower Swell, Fivehead, Taunton, Somerset TA3 6PH. *Club:* Royal Air Force.

BRYANT, Prof. Greyham Frank, PhD; FEng 1988; FIEE; FIMA; Professor of Control, Imperial College, London University, since 1982; *b* 3 June 1931; *s* of Ernest Noel Bryant and Florence Ivy (*née* Russell); *m* 1955, Iris Sybil Jardine; two *s.* *Educ:* Reading Univ.; Imperial Coll. (PhD). FIMA 1973; FIEE 1987. Sen. Scientific Officer, Iron and Steel Res., London, 1959–64; Imperial College: Res. Fellow, 1964–67; Reader in Industrial Control, 1975–82. Chm., Broner Consultants, 1979–88; Director: Greycon Consultants, 1985–; Circulation Research, 1989–. *Publications:* Automation of Tandem Mills (jtly), 1973; papers on design of management control schemes, multivariable control and modelling, in learned jls. *Recreation:* music. *Address:* 18 Wimborne Avenue, Norwood Green, Middlesex UB2 4HB. *T:* 0181–574 5648.

BRYANT, Judith Marie, (Mrs H. M. Hodkinson), SRN; retired; Fellow, King's Fund College, 1990–94 (part-time Fellow, 1986–90); *b* 31 Dec. 1942; *d* of Frederic John Bryant and Joan Marion (*née* Summerfield); *m* 1986, Prof. Henry Malcolm Hodkinson, *qv.* *Educ:* City of London Sch. for Girls; The London Hosp. (SRN 1964); Brunel Univ. (MPhil 1983). Ward Sister, UCH, 1965–69; Nursing Officer, subseq. Sen. Nursing Officer,

Northwick Park Hosp., Harrow, 1969–75; Divl Nursing Officer, Harrow, 1975–78; Dist Nursing Officer, Enfield, 1978–82, Victoria, 1982–85; Chief Nursing Officer and Dir of Quality Assurance, Riverside HA, 1985–86; Regl Nursing Officer, NE Thames RHA, 1986–90. Florence Nightingale Meml Scholar, USA and Canada, 1970. Adviser, DHSS Res. Liaison Cttee for the Elderly, 1977–83; Member: SW Herts DHA, 1981–86; NHS Training Authority, Nurses and Midwives Staff Training Cttee, 1986–89; 1930 Fund for Dist Nurses, 1985–. *Publication:* (with H. M. Hodkinson) Sherratt? A Natural Family of Staffordshire Figures, 1991. *Recreations:* opera, gardening. *Address:* 8 Chiswick Square, Burlington Lane, W4 2QG. *T:* 0181–747 0239.

BRYANT, Michael Dennis, CBE 1988; actor; Royal National Theatre player, since 1977; *b* 5 April 1928; *s* of William and Ann Bryant; *m* 1st, 1958, Josephine Martin (marr. diss. 1980); two *s* two *d*; 2nd, 1990, Judith Mary Coke. *Educ:* Battersea Grammar Sch. Merchant Navy, 1945; Army, 1946–49; drama sch., 1949–51; theatre and television, 1957–77; RSC, 1964–65. Rôles with National, subseq. Royal National, Theatre include: Hieronimo, in Spanish Tragedy; Iago, in Othello; Lenin, in State of Revolution (Best Actor, SWET awards, 1977); title rôle, in Mayor of Zalamea (Best Actor, British Theatrical Assoc. awards, 1981); Enobarbus, in Antony and Cleopatra, and Gloucester, in King Lear (Best Supporting Actor: Olivier awards, 1987; (for Enobarbus) London Critics awards, 1987); Prospero, in The Tempest, 1988; Polonius, in Hamlet, 1989; Racing Demon, 1990; The Wind in the Willows, 1990; Murmuring Judges, 1991; Doolittle, in Pygmalion, 1992; Trelawny of the Wells, 1993; The Absence of War, 1993; Johnny on a Spot, 1994; York, in Richard II, 1995. Council Mem., RADA, 1982–; Mem., Royal NT Foundn, 1990–. *Recreation:* rambling. *Address:* Willow Cottage, Kington Magna, Dorset SP8 5EW.

BRYANT, Prof. Peter Elwood, FRS 1991; Watts Professor of Psychology, Oxford University, since 1980; Fellow of Wolfson College, Oxford, since 1980; *b* 24 June 1937; *s* of Michael Bryant; *m* (marr. diss.); one *s* two *d*. *Educ:* Blundell's Sch.; Clare College, Cambridge (BA 1963; MA 1967); London Univ. (PhD). University Lecturer in Human Experimental Psychology, Oxford, 1967–80; Fellow, St John's Coll., Oxford, 1967–80. Editor, British Jl of Developmental Psychol., 1982–88. President's award, BPsS, 1984. *Publications:* Perception and Understanding in Young Children, 1974; (with L. Bradley) Children's Reading Problems, 1985; (with U. Goswami) Phonological Skills and Learning to Read, 1990. *Address:* Wolfson College, Oxford OX2 6UD.

BRYANT, Peter George Francis; Under Secretary, Department of Trade and Industry, 1989–92; *b* 10 May 1932; *s* of late George Bryant, CBE and Margaret Bryant; *m* 1961, Jean (*née* Morriss); one *s* one *d*. *Educ:* Sutton Valence Sch.; Birkbeck Coll., London Univ. (BA). Min. of Supply, 1953–55; BoT, 1955–69; 1st Sec. (Commercial), Vienna (on secondment), 1970–72; Dir of British Trade Drive in S Germany, 1973; Department of Trade (later Department of Trade and Industry), 1974–85; seconded to HM Diplomatic Service as Consul-Gen., Düsseldorf, 1985–88, and Dir-Gen. of Trade and Investment Promotion, FRG, 1988.

BRYANT, Richard Charles, CB 1960; Under-Secretary, Board of Trade, 1955–68; *b* 20 Aug. 1908; *s* of Charles James and Constance Byron Bryant, The Bounds, Faversham, Kent; *m* 1938, Elisabeth Ellington (*d* 1994), *d* of Dr. A. E. Stansfeld, FRCP; two *s* two *d*. *Educ:* Rugby; Oriel College, Oxford. Entered Board of Trade, 1932; Ministry of Supply, 1939–44. *Address:* Marsh Farm House, Brancaster, Norfolk PE31 8AE. *T:* Brancaster (01485) 210206. *Club:* Travellers'.

BRYANT, Thomas, CMG 1995; HM Diplomatic Service, retired; Consul General, Zürich, 1991–95; *b* 1 Nov. 1938; *s* of George Edward Bryant and Ethel May Bryant (*née* Rogers); *m* 1961, Vivien Mary Theresa Hill; twin *s* one *d*. *Educ:* William Ellis Sch., London; Polytechnic of Central London (DMS). Nat. service, Army, 1957–59. Entered FO, 1957; Hong Kong, 1963; Peking, 1963–65; Vice Consul, Frankfurt, 1966–68; Second Sec., Tel Aviv, 1968–72; First Sec., FCO, 1973–76; Vienna, 1976–80; FCO, 1980–84, Counsellor, 1982; Hd of Finance Dept, 1982–84; Consul-Gen., Munich, 1984–88; Dep. High Comr, Nairobi, 1988–91. *Recreations:* cricket, soccer, tennis, classical music, laughter. *Address:* The Old Surgery, Cottage Lane, Westfield, Sussex TN35 4RU.

BRYARS, Donald Leonard; Commissioner of Customs and Excise, 1978–84 and Director, Personnel, 1979–84, retired; *b* 31 March 1929; *s* of late Leonard and Marie Bryars; *m* 1953, Joan (*née* Yealand); one *d*. *Educ:* Goole Grammar Sch.; Leeds Univ. Joined Customs and Excise as Executive Officer, 1953, Principal, 1964, Asst Sec., 1971; on loan to Cabinet Office, 1976–78; Director, General Customs, 1978–79. Dir (non-exec.), The Customs Annuity Benevolent Fund Inc., 1986–. Trustee, Milton's Cottage Trust, 1993–. *Address:* 15 Ellwood Rise, Chalfont St Giles, Bucks HP8 4SU. *T:* Chalfont St Giles (01494) 875466. *Club:* Civil Service (Chm., 1981–85).

BRYARS, John Desmond, CB 1982; Deputy Under Secretary of State (Finance and Budget), Ministry of Defence, 1979–84, retired; *b* 31 Oct. 1928; *s* of William Bryars, MD and Sarah (*née* McMeekin); *m* 1964, Faith, *d* of Frederick Momber, ARCM and Anne Momber. *Educ:* St Edward's Sch., Oxford; Trinity Coll., Oxford (schol.; MA). Army, 1946–48. Entered Civil Service, Air Ministry, 1952; HM Treasury, 1960–62; Private Sec. to Sec. of State for Air, 1963–64, to Minister of Defence, RAF, 1964–65; Asst Sec., MoD, 1965–73; RCDS 1973; Asst Under-Sec. of State, MoD, 1973–75 and 1977–79; Under Sec., Cabinet Office, 1975–77. *Address:* 42 Osterley Road, Osterley, Isleworth, Middlesex TW7 4PN. *Club:* Commonwealth Trust.

BRYCE; *see* Graham Bryce and Graham-Bryce.

BRYCE, Gabe Robb, OBE 1959; Sales Manager (Operations) British Aircraft Corporation, 1965–75; occupied in breeding dogs and boarding cats, until retirement from animal world, 1987; *b* 27 April 1921; *m* 1943, Agnes Lindsay; one *s* one *d*. *Educ:* Glasgow High School. Served in RAF, 1939–46. Vickers-Armstrongs (Aircraft) Ltd, 1946–60 (Chief Test Pilot, 1951–60). Participated as First or Second Pilot, in Maiden Flights of following British Aircraft: Varsity; Nene Viking; Viscount 630, 700 and 800; Tay Viscount; Valiant; Pathfinder; Vanguard; VC-10; BAC 1–11; Chief Test Pilot, British Aircraft Corporation, 1960–64. Fellow Soc. of Experimental Test Pilots (USA), 1967. Sir Barnes Wallis Meml Medal, GAPAN, 1980. *Recreations:* squash, tennis. *Address:* 8 Rowan Green, Rosslyn Park, Weybridge, Surrey KT13 9NF. *T:* Weybridge (01932) 858996.

BRYCE, Sir Gordon; *see* Bryce, Sir W. G.

BRYCE, Gordon, RSA 1993 (ARSA 1976); RSW 1976; painter; Head of Fine Art, Gray's School of Art, Aberdeen, since 1986; *b* 30 June 1943; *s* of George and Annie Bryce; *m* 1st, 1966, Margaret Lothian (marr. diss. 1976); two *s*; 2nd, 1984, Hilary Duthie; one *s* two *d*. *Educ:* Edinburgh Acad.; George Watson's Coll., Edinburgh; Edinburgh Coll. of Art. Dip. in Art. Exhibited widely in UK, Europe and USA, 1965–; 30 one-man exhbns of painting, UK and overseas; paintings in public and private collections, UK, Europe, USA, Canada. *Recreation:* fly fishing. *Address:* Sylva Cottage, 2 Culter House Road, Milltimber, Aberdeen AB1 0EN. *T:* Aberdeen (01224) 733274.

BRYCE, Rt. Rev. Jabez Leslie; *see* Polynesia, Bishop in.

BRYCE, Sir (William) Gordon, Kt 1971; CBE 1963; Chief Justice of the Bahamas, 1970–73; *b* 2 Feb. 1913; *s* of James Chisholm Bryce and Emily Susan (*née* Lees); *m* 1940, Molly Mary, *d* of Arthur Cranch Drake; two *d*. *Educ:* Bromsgrove Sch.; Hertford Coll., Oxford (MA). Called to Bar, Middle Temple. War Service, 1940–46 (Major). Colonial Service: Crown Counsel, Fiji, 1949; Solicitor General, Fiji, 1953; Attorney General: Gibraltar, 1956; Aden, 1959; Legal Adviser, S Arabian High Commn, 1963; Attorney General, Bahamas, 1966. Comr, revised edn of Laws: of Gilbert and Ellice Islands, 1952; of Fiji, 1955; Comr, Bahamas Law Reform and Revision Commn, 1976. *Recreations:* riding, gardening. *Address:* Nevis, Broad Lane, Brancaster, Norfolk PE31 8AU.

BRYCE-SMITH, Prof. Derek, PhD, DSc; CChem, FRSC; Professor of Organic Chemistry, University of Reading, 1965–89, part-time, 1989–91, now Emeritus; *b* 29 April 1926; *s* of Charles Philip and Amelia Smith; *m* 1st, 1956, Marjorie Mary Anne Stewart (*d* 1966); two *s* two *d*; 2nd, 1969, Pamela Joyce Morgan; two step *d*. *Educ:* Bancrofts Sch., Woodford Wells; SW Essex Tech. Coll.; West Ham Municipal Coll.; Bedford Coll., London. Research Chemist: Powell Duffryn Res. Ltd, 1945–46; Dufay-Chromex Ltd, 1946–48; Inst. of Petroleum Student, Bedford Coll., 1948–51; ICI Post-doctoral Fellow, KCL, 1951–55; Asst Lectr in Chem., KCL, 1955–56; Lectr in Chem., 1956–63, Reader, 1963–65, Reading Univ. Founding Chm., European Photochem. Assoc., 1970–72; Founding Vice-Chm., UK Br., Internat. Solar Energy Soc., 1973–74; Chm., RSC Photochemistry Gp, 1981–92. John Jeyes Endowed Lectureship and Silver Medal, RSC, 1984–85. *Publications:* (with R. Stephens) Lead or Health, 1980, 2nd edn 1981; (with E. Hodgkinson) The Zinc Solution, 1986; (RSC Senior Reporter and contrib.) Photochemistry: a review of chemical literature, vols 1–25, 1970–94; contribs to learned jls in the fields of photochem., organometallic chem., environmental chem. and philosophy of sci. *Recreations:* gardening, making music. *Address:* Highland Wood House, Mill Lane, Kidmore End, Reading, Berks RG4 9HB. *T:* Kidmore End (01734) 723132.

BRYDEN, David John, PhD; FSA; Keeper, Department of Science, Technology and Working Life, National Museums of Scotland, since 1988; *b* 23 Nov. 1943; *s* of George Bryden and Marion (*née* Bellingham); *m* 1964, Helen Margaret Willison; two *s*. *Educ:* Univ. of Leicester (BSc(Engrg)); Linacre Coll., Oxford (Dip. in Hist. and Philos. of Sci.); Gonville and Caius Coll., Cambridge (MA 1973); St Edmund's Coll., Cambridge (PhD 1993). FSA 1993. Asst Keeper II, Royal Scottish Mus., 1966–70; Curator, Whipple Mus. of Hist. of Sci., Univ. of Cambridge, 1970–78; Fellow and Steward, St Edmund's House, 1977–78; Asst Keeper I, Science Mus. Library, 1979–87; Academic Administrator, Gresham Coll., 1987–88. *Publications:* Scottish Scientific Instrument Makers 1600–1900, 1972; Napier's Bones: a history and instruction manual, 1992; articles on early scientific instruments and history of science and technology. *Address:* Royal Museum of Scotland, Chambers Street, Edinburgh EH1 1JF. *T:* 0131–225 7534.

BRYDEN, William Campbell Rough, (Bill Bryden), CBE 1993; Associate Director, The Royal National Theatre, since 1975; Head of Drama Television, BBC Scotland, 1984–93; *b* 12 April 1942; *s* of late George Bryden and of Catherine Bryden; *m* 1971, Hon. Deborah Morris, *d* of Baron Killanin, *qv*; one *s* one *d*. *Educ:* Hillend Public Sch.; Greenock High Sch. Documentary writer, Scottish Television, 1963–64; Assistant Director: Belgrade Theatre, Coventry, 1965–67; Royal Court Th., London, 1967–69; Associate Dir, Royal Lyceum Th., Edinburgh, 1971–74; Dir, Cottesloe Theatre (Nat. Theatre), 1978–80. Director, Royal Opera House, Covent Garden: Parsifal, 1988; The Cunning Little Vixen, 1990. Director: Bernstein's Mass, GSMD, 1987; A Life in the Theatre, Haymarket, 1989; The Ship, Harland and Wolff Shipyard, Glasgow, 1990; Cops, Greenwich, 1991; A Month in the Country, Albery, 1994; The Big Picnic, Harland and Wolff Shipyard, Glasgow (also writer), 1994. BBC Television: Exec. Producer: Tutti Frutti, by John Byrne, 1987 (Best Series, BAFTA awards); The Play on 1 (series), 1989; Dir, The Shawl, by David Mamet, 1989. Member Board, Scottish Television, 1979–85. Dir of the Year, Laurence Olivier Awards, 1985, Best Dir, Brit. Th. Assoc. and Drama Magazine Awards, 1986, and Evening Standard Best Dir Award, 1985 (for The Mysteries, NT, 1985). *Publications: plays:* Willie Rough, 1972; Benny Lynch, 1974; Old Movies, 1977; *screenplay:* The Long Riders, 1980; *films:* (writer and director) Ill Fares The Land, 1982; The Holy City (for TV), 1985; Aria, 1987. *Recreation:* music. *Address:* The Royal National Theatre, South Bank, SE1 9PX. *T:* 0171–928 2033.

BRYDON, Donald Hood, OBE 1993; Deputy Chief Executive, Barclays de Zoete Wedd, since 1994; *b* 25 May 1945; *s* of James Hood Brydon and Mary Duncanson (*née* Young); *m* 1971, Joan Victoria; one *s* one *d*. *Educ:* George Watson's Coll., Edinburgh; Univ. of Edinburgh (BSc). Econs Dept, Univ. of Edinburgh, 1967–70; British Airways Pension Fund, 1970–77; Barclays Investment Manager's Office, 1977–81; Dep. Man. Dir, Barclays Investment Mgt Ltd, 1981–86; BZW Investment Management Ltd: Dir, 1986–88; Man. Dir, 1988–91; BZW Asset Management Ltd: Chm. and Chief Exec., 1991–94; Non-exec. Chm., 1994–95. *Publications:* (jtly) Economics of Technical Information Services, 1972; (jtly) Pension Fund Investment, 1988. *Recreation:* golf. *Club:* Caledonian.

BRYER, Prof. Anthony Applemore Mornington, FSA 1972; Professor of Byzantine Studies, since 1980 and Public Orator, since 1991, University of Birmingham; *b* 31 Oct. 1937; *e s* of late Group Captain Gerald Mornington Bryer, OBE and of Joan Evelyn (*née* Grigsby); *m* 1961, Elizabeth Lipscomb; three *d*. *Educ:* Canford Sch.; Sorbonne Univ.; Balliol Coll., Oxford (Scholar; BA, MA; DPhil 1967); Athens Univ. Nat. Service, RAF (Adjutant), 1956–58. University of Birmingham: Research Fellow, 1964–65, Lectr, 1965–73, Sen. Lectr, 1973–76, in Medieval History; Reader in Byzantine Studies, 1976–79; Dir of Byzantine Studies, 1969–76; Dir, Centre for Byzantine, Ottoman and Modern Greek Studies, 1976–94. Visiting Fellow: Dumbarton Oaks, Harvard, 1971–; Merton Coll., Oxford, 1985. Founder and Dir, annual British Byzantine Symposia, 1966–; Chm., British Nat. Cttee, Internat. Byzantine Assoc., 1989– (Sec., 1976–89); former Vice-Pres., Nat. Trust for Greece; Mem., Managing Cttees, British Sch. at Athens and British Inst. of Archaeology, Ankara; Consultant to Cyprus Govt on res. in humanities, 1988–89; field trips to Trebizond and Pontos, 1959–; Hellenic Cruise lectr, 1967–; British Council specialist lectr, Greece, Turkey and Australia; Loeb Lectr, Harvard, 1979; Vis. Byzantinist, Medieval Acad. of America, 1987; Wiles Lectr, QUB, 1990. Co-founder and publisher, Byzantine and Modern Greek Studies, 1975–. *Publications:* Byzantium and the Ancient East, 1970; Iconoclasm, 1977; The Empire of Trebizond and the Pontos, 1980; (with David Winfield) The Byzantine Monuments and Topography of the Pontos, 2 vols, 1985; (with Heath Lowry) Continuity and Change in late Byzantine and Early Ottoman Society, 1986; Peoples and Settlement in Anatolia and the Caucasus 800–1900, 1988; The Sweet Land of Cyprus, 1993; articles in learned jls. *Recreations:* travel, writing references. *Address:* Centre for Byzantine, Ottoman and Modern Greek Studies, University of Birmingham, Birmingham B15 2TT. *T:* 0121–414 5777. *Clubs:* Buckland (Birmingham); Lochaline Social (Morvern); Black Sea (Trabzon).

BRYER, Dr David Ronald William; Director, Oxfam, since 1992; *b* 15 March 1944; *s* of Ronald John William Bryer and Betty Gertrude Bryer (*née* Rawlinson); *m* 1980, Margaret Isabel, *e d* of Sir Eric Bowyer, KCB, KBE and Elizabeth (*née* Nicholls, who *m* 2nd, Sir Sydney Caine, KCMG); one *s* one *d*. *Educ:* King's Sch., Worcester; Worcester Coll., Oxford (MA, DPhil); Manchester Univ. (Dip. Teaching English Overseas). Teacher,

Shouf Nat. Coll., Baakleen, Lebanon, 1964–65; Teacher, later Principal, Oxford Acad. of English, 1967–74; Asst Keeper, Ashmolean Museum, 1972–74; Field Dir, Middle East, Oxfam, 1975–79; Principal, Malvern Sch. of English, 1979–81; Co-ordinator, Africa, 1981–84, Overseas Dir, 1984–91, Oxfam. Vis. Fellow, British Acad., 1972. Chm., Steering Cttee for Humanitarian Response, Geneva. Member: Council, VSO; Eurostep. *Publications:* The Origins of the Druze Religion, 1975; contrib. Der Islam. *Recreations:* family and friends, travel, esp. Eastern Mediterranean, walking. *Address:* 5 First Turn, Upper Wolvercote, Oxford OX2 8AG.

BRYMER, Jack, OBE 1960; Hon. RAM; Principal Clarinettist, London Symphony Orchestra, 1972–87; *b* 27 Jan. 1915; *s* of J. and Mrs M. Brymer, South Shields, Co. Durham; *m* 1939, Joan Richardson, Lancaster; one *s*. *Educ:* Goldsmiths' College, London University (FGCL 1991). Schoolmaster, Croydon, general subjects, 1935–40. RAF, 1940–45. Principal Clarinettist: Royal Philharmonic Orchestra, 1946–63; BBC Symphony Orchestra, 1963–72; Prof., Royal Acad. of Music, 1950–58; Prof., Royal Military Sch. of Music, Kneller Hall, 1969–73; Prof., Guildhall Sch. of Music and Drama, 1981–; Member of Wigmore, Prometheus and London Baroque ensembles; Director of London Wind Soloists. Has directed recordings of the complete wind chamber music of Mozart, Beethoven, Haydn and J. C. Bach. Presenter of several BBC music series, inc. At Home (nightly). Has taken a life-long interest in mainstream jazz, and in later life has toured and performed as soloist with many of finest British and American players in that field. Pres., ISM, 1993. Hon. RAM 1955; FGSM 1986; FRNCM 1992. Hon. MA Newcastle upon Tyne, 1973; Hon. DMus Kingston, 1993. Cobbett Medal, Worshipful Co. of Musicians, 1989. *Publications:* The Clarinet (Menuhin Guides), 1976; From Where I Sit (autobiog.), 1979; In the Orchestra, 1987. *Recreations:* golf, tennis, swimming, carpentry, gardening, music. *Address:* Underwood, Ballards Farm Road, South Croydon, Surrey CR2 7JA. *T:* 0181–657 1698. *Club:* Croham Hurst Golf.

BRYSON, Col (James) Graeme, OBE 1954; TD 1949; JP; Vice-Lord-Lieutenant of Merseyside, 1979–89; *b* 4 Feb. 1913; 3rd *s* of John Conway Bryson and Oletta Bryson; *m* Jean (*d* 1981), *d* of Walter Glendinning; two *s* four *d* (and one *s* decd). *Educ:* St Edward's Coll.; Liverpool Univ. (LLM); Open Univ. (BSc 1994). Admitted solicitor, 1935. Commnd 89th Field Bde RA (TA), 1936; served War, RA, 1939–45 (Lt-Col 1944); comd 470 (3W/Lancs) HAA Regt, 1947–52, and 626 HAA Regt, 1952–55; Bt-Col 1955; Hon. Col 33 Signal Regt (V), 1975–81. Sen. Jt Dist Registrar and Liverpool Admiralty Registrar, High Court of Justice, Liverpool, and Registrar of Liverpool County Court, 1947–78; Dep. Circuit Judge, Northern Circuit, 1978–82. President: Assoc. of County Court Registrars, 1969 (Hon. Life Pres., 1993); Liverpool Law Soc., 1969; City of Liverpool, 1965–, NW Area, 1979–90, Royal British Legion. Chm., Med. Appeal Tribunal, 1978–85; Member: Lord Chancellor's Cttee for enforcement of debts (Payne), 1965–69; IOM Commn to reform enforcement laws, 1972–74; Vice-Patron, Nat. Assoc. for Employment of Regular Sailors, Soldiers and Airmen, 1989– (Mem. Council, 1952–89). FRSA 1989. JP Liverpool, 1956; DL Lancs, 1965, later Merseyside. The Queen's Commendation for Brave Conduct, 1961. KHS 1974; KCHS 1990. *Publication:* (jtly) Execution, in Halsbury's Laws of England, 3rd edn 1976. *Recreations:* local history, boating. *Address:* Sunwards, Thirlmere Road, Hightown, Liverpool L38 3RQ. *T:* 0151–929 2652. *Clubs:* Athenæum (Liverpool; Pres., 1969); Lancashire County Cricket.

BRYSON, Adm. Sir Lindsay (Sutherland), KCB 1981; FRSE 1984; FEng; Chairman, ERA Technology, since 1990 (Director, since 1985); Lord Lieutenant of East Sussex, since 1989; *b* 22 Jan. 1925; *s* of James McAuslan Bryson and Margaret Bryson (*née* Whyte); *m* 1951, Averil Curtis-Willson; one *s* two *d*. *Educ:* Allan Glen's Sch., Glasgow; London Univ. (External) (BSc (Eng)); FIEE (Hon. FIEE 1991), FRAeS. Engrg Cadet, 1942; Electrical Mechanic, RN, 1944; Midshipman 1946; Lieut 1948; Comdr 1960; Captain 1967; comd HMS Daedalus, RNAS Lee-on-Solent, 1970–71; RCDS 1972; Dir, Naval Guided Weapons, 1973; Dir, Surface Weapons Project (Navy), 1974–76; Dir-Gen. Weapons (Naval), 1977–81; and Chief Naval Engr Officer, 1979–81; Controller of the Navy, 1981–84. Chm., Marine Technology Directorate, 1986–92; Dep. Chm., GEC-Marconi (formerly The Marconi Co. and GEC Avionics), 1987–90; Director (non-executive): Molins, 1988–; Elswick, 1990–94. Pres., Sussex Sci. and Technol. Regl Orgn, 1990–. Chairman: New Sussex Opera, 1990–; Brighton Festival Trust, 1991–. Institution of Electrical Engineers: Vice-Pres., 1982–84; Dep. Pres., 1984–85; Pres., 1985–86; Faraday Lectr, 1976–77. President: Soc. of Underwater Technol., 1989–91; Assoc. of Project Managers, 1991–95. Worshipful Co. of Cooks: Liveryman, 1964; Assistant, 1980; Warden, 1985; Second Master, 1986; Master, 1987; Liveryman, Worshipful Co. of Engrs, 1988. Chairman of Council: Sussex Univ., 1989–95 (Vice-Chm., 1988–89); Brighton Coll., 1990– (Governor, 1986–). Hon. Fellow, Paisley Coll. of Technology, 1986; Hon. FIMechE, 1991; Hon. DSc Strathclyde, 1987; Hon DSc(Eng) Bristol, 1988; Hon LLD Sussex, 1995. KStJ 1990. *Publications:* contrib. Jl RAeS, Jl IEE, Trans RINA, Seaford Papers, Control Engineering. *Recreations:* opera, fair weather sailing, gardening. *Address:* 74 Dyke Road Avenue, Brighton BN1 5LE. *T:* Brighton (01273) 553638, *Fax:* (01273) 562478. *Clubs:* Army and Navy, MCC; Sussex; Sussex CC.

BUCCLEUCH, 9th Duke of, *cr* 1663, **AND QUEENSBERRY,** 11th Duke of, *cr* 1684; **Walter Francis John Montagu Douglas Scott,** KT 1978; VRD; JP; Baron Scott of Buccleuch, 1606; Earl of Buccleuch, Baron Scott of Whitchester and Eskdaill, 1619; Earl of Doncaster and Baron Tynedale (Eng.), 1662; Earl of Dalkeith, 1663; Marquis of Dumfriesshire, Earl of Drumlanrig and Sanquhar, Viscount of Nith, Torthorwold, and Ross, Baron Douglas, 1684; Hon. Captain RNR; Captain, the Queen's Body Guard for Scotland, Royal Company of Archers; Lord-Lieutenant of Roxburgh, since 1974, of Ettrick and Lauderdale, since 1975; Chancellor, Order of the Thistle, since 1992; *b* 28 Sept. 1923; *o s* of 8th Duke of Buccleuch, KT, PC, GCVO, and Vreda Esther Mary (*d* 1993), *er d* of late Major W. F. Lascelles and Lady Sybil Lascelles, *d* of 10th Duke of St Albans; *S* father, 1973; *m* 1953, Jane, *d* of John McNeill, QC, Appin, Argyll; three *s* one *d*. *Educ:* Eton; Christ Church, Oxford. Served War of 1939–45, RNVR. MP (C) Edinburgh North, 1960–73; PPS to the Sec. of State for Scotland, 1962–64. Chairman: Buccleuch Heritage Trust, 1985–; Living Landscape Trust, 1986–; Assoc. of Lord Lieutenants, 1990–; President: Royal Highland & Agricultural Soc. of Scotland, 1969; St Andrew's Ambulance Assoc.; Royal Scottish Agricultural Benevolent Inst.; Scottish Nat. Inst. for War Blinded; Royal Blind Asylum & School; RADAR; Galloway Cattle Soc.; East of England Agricultural Soc., 1976; Commonwealth Forestry Assoc.; Royal Scottish Forestry Soc., 1994–; Vice-Pres., RSSPCC; Hon. President: Animal Diseases Research Assoc.; Scottish Agricultural Organisation Soc. DL, Selkirk 1955, Roxburgh 1962, Dumfries 1974; JP Roxburgh 1975. Countryside Award, Countryside Commn and CLA, 1983; Bledisloe Gold Medal, RASE, 1992. *Recreations:* country pursuits, painting, classical music, tormenting a French horn, works of art study, overseas travel. *Heir: s* Earl of Dalkeith, *qv*.

BUCHAN, family name of **Baron Tweedsmuir.**

BUCHAN, 17th Earl of, *cr* 1469; **Malcolm Harry Erskine;** JP; Lord Auchterhouse, 1469; Lord Cardross, 1610; Baron Erskine, 1806; *b* 4 July 1930; *s* of 16th Earl of Buchan and of Christina, Dowager Countess of Buchan (*d* 1994), *d* of late Hugh Woolner and adopted *d* of late Lloyd Baxendale; *S* father, 1984; *m* 1957, Hilary Diana Cecil, *d* of late Sir Ivan McLannahan Power, 2nd Bt; two *s* two *d*. *Educ:* Eton. JP Westminster. *Heir: s* Lord Cardross, *qv*. *Address:* Newnham House, Newnham, Basingstoke, Hants RG27 9AS. *Club:* Carlton.

BUCHAN OF AUCHMACOY, Captain David William Sinclair, JP; Chief of the Name of Buchan; *b* 18 Sept. 1929; *o s* of late Captain S. L. Trevor, late of Lathbury Park, Bucks, and late Lady Olivia Trevor, *e d* of 18th Earl of Caithness; *m* 1961, Susan Blanche Fionodbhar Scott-Ellis, *d* of Baron Howard de Walden and Seaford, *qv*; four *s* one *d*. *Educ:* Eton; RMA Sandhurst. Commissioned 1949 into Gordon Highlanders; served Berlin, BAOR and Malaya; ADC to GOC, Singapore, 1951–53; retired 1955. Member of London Stock Exchange. Sen. Partner, Messrs Gow and Parsons, 1963–72. Comr, Inland Revenue, 1974–76. Changed name from Trevor through Court of Lord Lyon King of Arms, 1949, succeeding 18th Earl of Caithness as Chief of Buchan Clan. Member: Queen's Body Guard for Scotland; The Pilgrims; Canada Club; Friends of Malta GC; Alexandra Rose Day Council; Cook Soc., 1982–; Council, Royal Sch. of Needlework, 1987–; Cons. Industrial Fund Cttee, 1988–. Gov., London Clinic, 1988–. Mem., Worshipful Company of Broderers (Master, 1992). Vice-President: Aberdeenshire CCC, 1962–; Bucks CCC, 1984–. JP Aberdeenshire, 1959–; JP London, 1972–. KStJ 1987 (OStJ 1981); Mem. Council for London, Order of St John. *Recreations:* cricket, tennis, squash. *Address:* 28 The Little Boltons, SW10 9LP. *T:* 0171–373 0654; Auchmacoy House, Ellon, Aberdeenshire AB41 8RB. *T:* Ellon (01358) 720229; Appt D-310, Puente Romano, Marbella, Spain. *Clubs:* White's, Royal Automobile, Turf, MCC, City of London, Pratt's, Pitt; Puffin's (Edinburgh).

BUCHAN, Ven. Eric Ancrum; Archdeacon of Coventry, 1965–77, Archdeacon Emeritus, since 1977; *b* 6 Nov. 1907; *s* of late Frederick Samuel and Florence Buchan. *Educ:* Bristol Grammar School; St Chad's College, University of Durham (BA). Curate of Holy Nativity, Knowle, Bristol, 1933–40. Chaplain RAFVR, 1940–45. Vicar of St Mark's with St Barnabas, Coventry, 1945–59; Hon. Canon of Coventry Cathedral, 1953; Chaplain Coventry and Warwickshire Hospital, 1945–59; Sec. Laymen's Appeal, Dio. of Coventry, 1951–53; Rural Dean of Coventry, 1954–63; Rector of Baginton, 1963–70. Member Central Board of Finance, 1953–80 (Chm., Develt and Stewardship Cttee, 1976–80; Mem., Church Commrs and CBF Joint Liaison Cttee, 1976–80); Mem. Schools Council, 1958–65; Chm. Dio. Board of Finance, 1958–77; Organiser of Bishop's Appeal, 1958–61; Dio. Director of Christian Stewardship, 1959–65; Domestic Chaplain to Bishop of Coventry, 1961–65; Church Commissioner, 1964–78; Member, Governing Body, St Chad's College, Durham University, 1966–83. Vice-Pres., Scouts of Wales, 1994. Awarded Silver Acorn for outstanding services to the Scout Movement, 1974. *Address:* 6B Millers Green, The Cathedral, Gloucester GL1 2BN. *T:* Gloucester (01452) 415944.

BUCHAN, Janey, (Jane O'Neil Buchan); Member (Lab) Glasgow, European Parliament, 1979–94; *b* 30 April 1926; *d* of Joseph and Christina Kent; *m* 1945, Norman Findlay Buchan, MP (*d* 1990); one *s*. *Educ:* secondary sch.; commercial coll. Housewife; Socialist; occasional scriptwriting and journalism. Mem., Strathclyde Regl Council, 1974–79 (Vice-Chm., Educn Cttee); Chm., local consumer gp; formerly Chm., Scottish Gas Consumers' Council. *Recreations:* books, music, theatre, watching television whenever and wherever I can and defending the freedom of action of viewers and programme makers. *Address:* 72 Peel Street, Glasgow G11 5LR. *T:* 0141–339 2583.

BUCHAN, Sir John, (Sir Thomas Johnston Buchan), Kt 1971; CMG 1961; FRAIA; Chairman, Buchan Laird International Planners, since 1982; Chairman and Chief Executive, Buchan, Laird and Buchan, Architects, 1957–82; *b* 3 June 1912; *s* of Thomas Johnston Buchan; *m* 1948, Virginia, *d* of William Ashley Anderson, Penn., USA; one *s* two *d*. *Educ:* Geelong Grammar School. Served Royal Aust. Engineers (AIF), 1940–44 (Capt.). Member Melbourne City Council, 1954–60. Member Federal Exec., Liberal Party, 1959–62, President, Liberal Party, Victorian Division, Australia, 1959–62, Treasurer, 1963–67, Pres., Australian American Assoc., Victoria, 1961–68, Federal Pres., Australian American Assoc., 1968–70, Vice-Pres., 1971–82. Member: Council, Latrobe University, 1964–72; Cttee of Management, Royal Melbourne Hosp., 1968–78. Founding Mem. and Dep. Chm., Nat. Cttee for Youth Employment, 1983–86; Co-Founder Apex Association of Australia. *Recreations:* golf, reading. *Address:* 14 Kent Court, Toorak, Vic 3142, Australia. *Club:* Melbourne (Melbourne).

BUCHAN, Dr Stevenson, CBE 1971; Chief Scientific Officer, Deputy Director, Institute of Geological Sciences, 1968–71; *b* 4 March 1907; *s* of late James Buchan and Christian Ewen Buchan (*née* Stevenson), Peterhead; *m* 1937, Barbara, *yr d* of late Reginald Hadfield, Droylsden, Lancs; one *s* one *d*. *Educ:* Peterhead Acad.; Aberdeen Univ. BSc 1st cl. hons Geology, James H. Hunter Meml Prize, Senior Kilgour Scholar, PhD; FRSE, FGS. Geological Survey of Great Britain: Geologist, 1931; Head of Water Dept, 1946; Asst Dir responsible for specialist depts in GB and NI, 1960; Chief Geologist, Inst. of Geological Sciences, 1967. Mem. various hydrological cttees; Founder Mem., Internat. Assoc. of Hydrogeologists (Pres., 1972–77; Advr, 1980–; Hon. Mem., 1985–); Pres., Internat. Ground-Water Commn of Internat. Assoc. of Hydrological Sciences, 1963–67; British Deleg. to Internat. Hydrological Decade; Scientific Editor, Hydrogeological Map of Europe; Vis. Internat. Scientist, Amer. Geol Inst.; Pres. Section C (Geology), Brit. Assoc., Dundee, 1968. Hon. FIWEM. Awarded Geol Soc.'s Lyell Fund, and J. B. Tyrell Fund for travel in Canada. *Publications:* Water Supply of County of London from Underground Sources; papers on hydrogeology and hydrochemistry. *Recreation:* oenology. *Address:* Southside Place, 122 The Street, Rockland St Mary, Norwich NR14 7HQ. *T:* Surlingham (01508) 538092.

BUCHAN, Sir Thomas Johnston; *see* Buchan, Sir John.

BUCHAN-HEPBURN, Sir (John) Alastair (Trant Kidd), 7th Bt *cr* 1815, of Smeaton Hepburn, Haddingtonshire; Director, Broughton Brewery Ltd, since 1986; *b* 27 June 1931; *s* of John Trant Buchan-Hepburn (*d* 1953), *g g s* of 2nd Bt, and Edith Margaret Mitchell (*née* Robb) (*d* 1980); *S* cousin, 1992; *m* 1957, Georgina Elizabeth, *d* of late Oswald Morris Turner, MC; one *s* three *d*. *Educ:* Charterhouse; St Andrews Univ.; RMA, Sandhurst. 1st King's Dragoon Guards, 1952–57; Captain, 1954; ADC to GOC-in-C, Malaya, 1954–57. Arthur Guinness & Son Co. Ltd, 1958–86. Life Mem., St Andrews Preservation Trust, 1984–; Mem., Baronets' Trust, 1992–. Mem., Inst. of Brewing, 1979. *Recreations:* golf, fishing, shooting, tennis, travel in Scottish Islands, antiquities. *Heir: s* (John) Christopher (Alastair) Buchan-Hepburn [*b* 9 March 1963; *m* 1990, Andrea Unwin]. *Address:* Chagford, 60 Argyle Street, St Andrews, Fife KY16 9BU. *T:* St Andrews (01334) 472161. *Club:* Royal and Ancient Golf (St Andrews).

BUCHANAN, Sir Andrew George, 5th Bt *cr* 1878; farmer; chartered surveyor; Lord-Lieutenant and Keeper of the Rolls for Nottinghamshire, since 1991; *b* 21 July 1937; *s* of Major Sir Charles Buchanan, 4th Bt, and Barbara Helen (*d* 1986), *o d* of late Lt-Col Rt Hon. Sir George Stanley, PC, GCSI, GCIE; *S* father, 1984; *m* 1966, Belinda Jane Virginia (*née* Maclean), JP, *widow* of Gresham Neilus Vaughan; one *s* one *d*, and one step *s* one step *d*. *Educ:* Eton; Trinity Coll., Cambridge; Wye Coll., Univ. of London. Nat. Service, 2nd Lieut, Coldstream Guards, 1956–58. Chartered Surveyor with Smith-Woolley & Co,

1965–70. Chm., Bd of Visitors, HM Prison Ranby, 1983 (Vice-Chm. 1982). Commanded A Squadron (SRY), 3rd Bn Worcs and Sherwood Foresters (TA), 1971–74; Hon. Col, B Sqn (SRY), Queen's Own Yeo., 1989–94. High Sheriff, Notts, 1976–77; DL Notts, 1985. KStJ 1991. *Recreations:* skiing, walking, forestry. *Heir: s* George Charles Mellish Buchanan, *b* 27 Jan. 1975. *Address:* Hodsock Priory, Blyth, Worksop, Notts S81 0TY. *T:* Blyth (Notts) (01909) 591204, *Fax:* (01909) 591578. *Club:* Boodle's.

BUCHANAN, Sir Charles Alexander James L.; *see* Leith-Buchanan.

BUCHANAN, Prof. Sir Colin (Douglas), Kt 1972; CBE 1964; Lieut-Colonel; consultant with Colin Buchanan & Partners, 47 Princes Gate, London; *b* 22 Aug. 1907; *s* of William Ernest and Laura Kate Buchanan; *m* 1933, Elsie Alice Mitchell (*d* 1984); two *s* one *d*. *Educ:* Berkhamsted School; Imperial College, London. Sudan Govt Public Works Dept, 1930–32; Regional planning studies with F. Longstreth Thompson, 1932–35; Ministry of Transport, 1935–39. War Service in Royal Engineers, 1939–46 (despatches). Ministry of Town and Country Planning (later Ministry of Housing and Local Govt), 1946–61; Urban Planning Adviser, Ministry of Transport, 1961–63; Prof. of Transport, Imperial Coll., London, 1963–72; Prof. of Urban Studies and Dir, Sch. for Advanced Urban Studies, Bristol Univ., 1973–75. Vis. Prof., Imperial Coll., London, 1975–78. Member: Commn on Third London Airport, 1968–70; Royal Fine Art Commn, 1972–74. Pres., CPRE, 1980–85. Pres., Friends of the Vale of Aylesbury, 1985–94. Hon. DCL Oxon, 1972; Hon. DSc: Leeds, 1972; City, 1972. *Publications:* Mixed Blessing, The Motor in Britain, 1958; Traffic in Towns (Ministry of Transport report), 1963, (paperback edn), 1964; The State of Britain, 1972; No Way to the Airport, 1981; numerous papers on town planning and allied subjects. *Recreations:* photography, carpentry, caravan touring. *Address:* Appletree House, Lincombe Lane, Boars Hill, Oxford OX1 5DU. *T:* Oxford (01865) 739458.
See also L. D. Reynolds.

BUCHANAN, Rt. Rev. Colin Ogilvie; Vicar of St Mark's, Gillingham, Kent, since 1991; Hon. Assistant Bishop, Diocese of Rochester, since 1989; *b* 9 Aug. 1934; *s* of late Prof. Robert Ogilvie Buchanan and of Kathleen Mary (*née* Parnell); *m* 1963, Diana Stephenie Gregory; two *d*. *Educ:* Whitgift Sch., S Croydon; Lincoln Coll., Oxford (BA, 2nd Cl. Lit. Hum., MA). Theological training at Tyndale Hall, Bristol, 1959–61; deacon, 1961; priest, 1962; Curate, Cheadle, Cheshire, 1961–64; joined staff of London Coll. of Divinity (now St John's Coll., Nottingham), 1964; posts held: Librarian, 1964–69; Registrar, 1969–74; Director of Studies, 1974–75; Vice-Principal, 1975–78; Principal, 1979–85; Hon. Canon of Southwell Minster, 1982–85; Bishop Suffragan of Aston, 1985–89. Member: Church of England Liturgical Commn, 1964–86; Doctrinal Commn, 1986–91; General Synod of C of E, 1970–85, 1990–; Assembly of British Council of Churches, 1971–80; Lambeth Conf., 1988; Steering Cttee, CCBI, 1990–92. Pres., Movt for Reform of Infant Baptism, 1988–. Vice-Pres., Electoral Reform Soc., 1987–. Grove Books: Proprietor, 1970–85; Hon. Manager, 1985–93; Chief Editor, 1993–. DD Lambeth, 1993. *Publications:* (ed) Modern Anglican Liturgies 1958–1968, 1968; (ed) Further Anglican Liturgies 1968–1975, 1975; (jtly) Growing into Union, 1970; (ed jtly) Anglican Worship Today, 1980; (ed) Latest Anglican Liturgies 1976–1984, 1985; (jtly) Reforming Infant Baptism, 1990; Open to Others, 1992; Infant Baptism and the Gospel, 1993; Cut the Connection, 1994; editor: Grove Booklets on Ministry and Worship, 1972–; Grove Liturgical Studies, 1975–86; Alcuin/Grove Joint Liturgical Studies, 1987– (regular author in these series); News of Liturgy, 1975–; contrib. learned jls. *Recreations:* interested in electoral reform, sport, etc. *Address:* St Mark's Vicarage, 173 Canterbury Street, Gillingham, Kent ME7 5UA. *T:* Medway (01634) 851818/855252, *Fax:* Medway (01634) 573549.

BUCHANAN, Prof. David Alan, PhD; Director, Loughborough University Business School, since 1992; *b* 26 July 1949; *s* of David Stewart and Harriet Buchanan; *m* 1974, Lesley Fiddes Fulton; one *s* one *d*. *Educ:* Heriot-Watt Univ. (BA Hons); Univ. of Edinburgh (PhD). Personnel Asst, Lothian Regl Council, Edinburgh, 1976–77; Lecturer in Organizational Behaviour: Napier Poly., Edinburgh, 1977–79; Univ. of Glasgow, 1979–86, Sen. Lectr, 1986–89; Prof. of Human Resource Management, Loughborough Univ. of Technology, 1989–. FRSA. *Publications:* The Development of Job Design Theories and Techniques, 1979; (with A. A. Huczynski) Organizational Behaviour: an introductory text, 1985, 2nd edn 1991, Student Workbook, 1994, Instructor's Manual, 1994; (ed jtly) The New Management Challenge: information systems for improved performance, 1988; (with J. McCalman) High Performance Work Systems: the digital experience, 1989; with D. Boddy: Organizations in the Computer Age: technological imperatives and strategic choice, 1983; Managing New Technology, 1986; The Technical Change Audit: action for results, 1987; Take the Lead: interpersonal skills for project managers, 1992; The Expertise of the Change Agent: public performance and backstage activity, 1992; numerous contribs to learned jls. *Recreations:* music, reading, photography, fitness. *Address:* 18 Ascott Gardens, West Bridgford, Nottingham NG2 7TH.

BUCHANAN, Sir Dennis; *see* Buchanan, Sir R. D.

BUCHANAN, Rev. Canon Eric; Vicar of St Mary's, Higham Ferrers, since 1990; Chaplain to the Queen, since 1992; *b* 2 Feb. 1932; *s* of Oswald Stanley Buchanan and Dorothy Aletta Buchanan (*née* Parkinson); *m* 1st, 1961, Julie Anne Taylor (*d* 1977); one *s* two *d*; 2nd, 1977, Julie Annette Howard (*née* Chamberlain); one step *s* two step *d*. *Educ:* Rotherham Grammar Sch.; Leeds Univ. (BA Hons Phil.); Coll. of the Resurrection, Mirfield. Ordained deacon, 1956, priest, 1957; Asst Curate, St Mark's, Coventry, 1956–59; Asst Chaplain, Univ. of London, 1959–64; Vicar: St Luke's, Duston, Northants, 1964–79; All Hallows, Wellingborough, 1979–90. Rural Dean of Wootton, 1974–79; Non-residentiary Canon of Peterborough Cathedral, 1977–. Chm., House of Clergy, Peterborough Diocesan Synod, 1978–91. *Recreations:* listening to classical music and jazz, gardening, theatre, detective fiction. *Address:* The Vicarage, Wood Street, Higham Ferrers, Northants NN10 8DL. *T:* Rushden (01933) 312433.

BUCHANAN, Rt. Rev. George Duncan; *see* Johannesburg, Bishop of.

BUCHANAN, Isobel Wilson, (Mrs Jonathan King); soprano; *b* 15 March 1954; *d* of Stewart and Mary Buchanan; *m* 1980, Jonathan Stephen Geoffrey King (otherwise Jonathan Hyde, actor); two *d*. *Educ:* Cumbernauld High Sch.; Royal Scottish Academy of Music and Drama (DRSAMD 1974). Australian Opera principal singer, 1975–78; freelance singer, 1978–; British debut, Glyndebourne, 1978; Vienna Staatsoper debut, 1978; American debut: Santa Fé, 1979; Chicago, 1979; New York, 1979; German debut, Cologne, 1979; French debut, Aix-en-Provence, 1981; ENO debut, 1985; Paris Opera debut, 1986. Performances also with Scottish Opera, Covent Garden, Munich Radio, Belgium, Norway, etc. Various operatic recordings. *Recreations:* reading, gardening, cooking, dressmaking, knitting, yoga. *Address:* c/o Marks Management Ltd, 14 New Burlington Street, W1X 1FF.

BUCHANAN, Prof. James McGill; Holbert L. Harris University Professor, since 1983 and Advisory General Director, Center for the Study of Public Choice, since 1988 (General Director, 1969–88), George Mason University; *b* 2 Oct. 1919; *s* of James Buchanan and Lila Scott; *m* 1945, Anne Bakke. *Educ:* Middle Tennessee State Coll. (BS 1940); Univ. of Tennessee (MA 1941); Univ. of Chicago (PhD 1948). Lieut, USNR, 1941–46. Professor of Economics: Univ. of Tennessee, 1950–51; Florida State Univ., 1951–56; Univ. of Virginia, 1956–62, 1962–68 (Paul G. McIntyre Prof.); UCLA, 1968–69; Virginia Polytechnic Inst., 1969–83 (Univ. Dist. Prof.). Fulbright Res. Scholar, Italy, 1955–56; Ford Faculty Res. Fellow, 1959–60; Fulbright Vis. Prof., Univ. of Cambridge, 1961–62. Fellow, Amer. Acad. of Arts and Scis; Dist. Fellow, Amer. Econ. Assoc. (Seidman Award, 1984). Hon. Dr, US and overseas Univs. Nobel Prize for Economics, 1986. *Publications:* Prices, Incomes and Public Policy (jtly), 1954; Public Principles of Public Debt, 1958; The Public Finances, 1960; Fiscal Theory and Political Economy, 1960; (with G. Tullock) The Calculus of Consent, 1962; Public Finance in Democratic Process, 1966; The Demand and Supply of Public Goods, 1968; Cost and Choice, 1969; (with N. Devletoglou) Academia in Anarchy, 1970; (ed jtly) Theory of Public Choice, 1972; (with G. F. Thirlby) LSE Essays on Cost, 1973; The Limits of Liberty, 1975; (with R. Wagner) Democracy in Deficit, 1977; Freedom in Constitutional Contract, 1978; What Should Economists Do?, 1979; (with G. Brennan) The Power to Tax, 1980; (ed jtly) Towards a Theory of the Rent-Seeking Society, 1980; (ed jtly) The Theory of Public Choice II, 1984; (with G. Brennan) The Reason of Rules, 1985; Liberty Market and State, 1985; (jtly) El Analisis Economico de lo Politico, 1985; (ed jtly) Deficits, 1987; Economics: between predictive science and moral philosophy, 1987; Economía y Política, 1987; Maktens Gränser, 1988; (ed) Explorations into Constitutional Economics, 1989; Essays on the Political Economy, 1989; Stato, mercato e libertà, 1989; The Economics and the Ethics of Constitutional Order, 1991; Constitutional Economics, 1991; Better than Plowing and Other Personal Essays, 1992. *Address:* Center for the Study of Public Choice, Buchanan House, George Mason University, Fairfax, VA 22030, USA; PO Drawer G, Blacksburg, VA 24060, USA.

BUCHANAN, John David, MBE 1944; ERD 1989; DL; Headmaster of Oakham School, Rutland, 1958–77; *b* 26 Oct. 1916; *e s* of late John Nevile Buchanan and Nancy Isabel (*née* Bevan); *m* 1st, 1946, Janet Marjorie (*d* 1990), *d* of late Brig. J. A. C. Pennycuick, DSO; three *s* four *d* (and one *s* decd); 2nd, 1992, Banoo Ramsamy. *Educ:* Stowe; Trinity College, Cambridge (MA). Served with Grenadier Guards, 1939–46; Adjutant, 3rd Bn Grenadier Guards, 1941–43 (despatches, 1943); Brigade Major, 1st Guards Bde, 1944–45; Private Secretary to Sir Alexander Cadogan, Security Council for the UN, 1946. Assistant Master, Westminster Under School, 1948; Assistant Master, Sherborne School, 1948–57. Administrator, Inchcape Educational Scholarship Scheme, 1978–; Educnl Consultant to Jerwood Foundn, 1978–. FRSA 1991. DL Leics, 1980. *Publications:* Operation Oakham, 1984; Oakham Overture to Poetry, 1985. *Recreation:* gardening. *Address:* Rose Cottage, Owston, Leics LE15 8DN.

BUCHANAN, John M.; *see* Macdonald-Buchanan.

BUCHANAN, Vice-Adm. Sir Peter (William), KBE 1980; *b* 14 May 1925; *s* of Lt-Col Francis Henry Theodore Buchanan and Gwendolen May Isobel (*née* Hunt); *m* 1953, Audrey Rowena Mary (*née* Edmondson); three *s* one *d*. *Educ:* Malvern Coll. Joined RN, 1943; served in HM Ships King George V, Birmingham, destroyers and frigates; comd HMS Scarborough 1961–63; Far East, 1963–65 (despatches); HMS Victorious, 1965–67; British Antarctic Survey, 1967–68; comd HMS Endurance, 1968–70; MoD, 1970–72; comd HMS Devonshire, 1972–74; MoD, 1974–76; Rear-Adm. 1976; Naval Sec., 1976–78; Vice-Adm., 1979; Chief of Staff, Allied Naval Forces Southern Europe, 1979–82. Lord Chancellor's Panel of Independent Inspectors, 1983–95. Younger Brother of Trinity House, 1963. Liveryman, Shipwrights' Co., 1984; Senior Warden, Guild of Freemen of City of London, 1995. MRIN; FNI. *Recreation:* sailing. *Clubs:* Caledonian; Royal Yacht Squadron.

BUCHANAN, Sir (Ranald) Dennis, Kt 1991; MBE 1976; Chairman and Managing Director, Talair Pty Ltd, since 1958; *b* Sydney, 6 Nov. 1932; *s* of Stanley Brisbane Buchanan and Jessica (*née* Hall); *m* 1956, Della Agnes Brown; four *s* five *d* (and one *s* decd). *Educ:* All Saints Coll., Bathurst, NSW. Joined Gibbes Sepik Airways Ltd, Wewak, PNG, 1949; purchased Territory Airlines Ltd, 1957 (renamed Talair Pty Ltd, 1975). *Recreation:* farming. *Address:* PO Box 108, Goroka, Eastern Highlands Province, Papua New Guinea. *T:* (office) 721408; (home) 721984. *Clubs:* Royal Automobile (Sydney); Aero (Goroka, PNG).

BUCHANAN, Richard, JP; *b* 3 May 1912; *s* of late Richard Buchanan and late Helen Henderson; *m* 1st, 1938, Margaret McManus (*d* 1963); six *s* two *d*; 2nd, 1971, Helen Duggan, MA, DipEd. *Educ:* St Mungo's Boys' School; St Mungo's Academy; Royal Technical Coll. Councillor, City of Glasgow, 1949–64 (Past Chm. Libraries, Schools and Standing Orders Cttees); Hon. City Treasurer, 1960–63. MP (Lab) Springburn, Glasgow, 1964–79; PPS to Treasury Ministers, 1967–70; Mem. Select Cttees: Public Accounts; Services. Chm., West Day School Management, 1958–64; Governor, Notre Dame College of Education, 1959–64, etc. Chm., Belvidere Hospital; Member Board of Managers, Glasgow Royal Infirmary; Hon. Pres., Scottish Library Assoc. (Pres., 1963); Life Mem., Scottish Secondary Teachers' Assoc., 1979; Chairman: Scottish Central Library; Adv. Cttee, Nat. Library of Scotland; Cttee on Burrell Collection; H of C Library Cttee; St Mungo's Old Folks' Day Centre, 1979–85; Director, Glasgow Citizens Theatre. Pres., Buchanan Soc., 1989–91. JP Glasgow, 1954. Hon. FLA, 1979. *Recreations:* theatre, walking, reading. *Address:* 18 Gargrave Avenue, Garrowhill, Glasgow G69 7LP. *T:* 0141–771 7234. *Club:* St Mungo's Centenary (Glasgow).

BUCHANAN, Prof. Robert Angus, OBE 1993; PhD; FSA; FRHistS; Founder and Director, Centre for the History of Technology, Science and Society, University of Bath, since 1964; Head of Humanities Group, School of Humanities and Social Sciences, since 1970; Professor of the History of Technology, since 1990; Director, National Cataloguing Unit for the Archives of Contemporary Scientists, since 1987; *b* 5 June 1930; *s* of Roy Graham Buchanan and Bertha (*née* Davis); *m* 1955, Brenda June Wade; two *s*. *Educ:* High Storrs Grammar Sch. for Boys, Sheffield; St Catharine's Coll., Cambridge (MA, PhD). FRHistS 1978; FSA 1990. Educn Officer to Royal Foundn of St Katharine, Stepney, 1956–60 (Co-opted Mem., LCC Educn Cttee, 1958–60); Asst Lectr, Dept of Gen. Studies, Bristol Coll. of Science and Technol. (now Univ. of Bath), 1960; Lectr, 1961; Sen. Lectr, 1966; Reader in Hist. of Technol., Univ. of Bath, 1981–90. Vis. Lectr, Univ. of Delaware, USA, 1969; Vis. Fellow, ANU, Canberra, 1981; Vis. Lectr, Huazhong (Central China) Univ. of Science and Tech., Wuhan, People's Repub. of China, 1983; Jubilee Chair in History of Technol., Chalmers Univ., Göteborg, Sweden, Autumn term, 1984. Royal Comr, Royal Commn on Historical Monuments (England), 1979–93; Sec., Res. Cttee on Indust. Archaeology, Council for British Archaeology, 1972–79; President: (Founding), Bristol Indust. Archaeology Soc., 1967–70; Assoc. for Indust. Archaeology, 1974–77; Newcomen Soc. for History of Engrg and Technol., 1981–83; Internat. Cttee for History of Technol., 1993– (Sec.-Gen., 1981–93); Chm., Water Space Amenity Commn's Working Party on Indust. Archaeology, 1982–83; Member: Properties Cttee, National Trust, 1974–; Technol Preservation Awards Cttee, Science Museum, 1973–81. FRSA 1993. Hon. Fellow, Science Mus., 1992. Hon. DSc (Engrg) Chalmers Univ., Göteborg, Sweden, 1986. Leonardo da Vinci Medal, Soc. for Hist. of Technol., 1989. *Publications:* Technology and Social Progress, 1965; (with Neil Cossons) Industrial Archaeology of the Bristol Region, 1969; Industrial Archaeology in Britain, 1972, 2nd edn 1982; (with George Watkins) Industrial Archaeology of the Stationary Steam Engine, 1976; History and Industrial Civilization, 1979; (with C. A. Buchanan) Industrial Archaeology of Central Southern England, 1980; (with Michael Williams) Brunel's Bristol, 1982; The Engineers: a history of the engineering profession in Britain, 1989; The Power of the Machine, 1992. *Recreations:* Cambridge Judo half-blue, 1955; rambling, travelling, exploring. *Address:* Centre for the History of Technology, Science and Society, University of Bath, Claverton Down, Bath BA2 7AY. *T:* Bath (01225) 826826, ext. 5833.

BUCHANAN, Sir Robert Wilson, (Sir Robin), Kt 1991; DL; CA; Chairman, NHS Supplies Authority, since 1991; *b* 28 Sept. 1930; *s* of Robert Downie and Mary Hobson Buchanan; *m* Naomi Pauline (*née* Lewis); three *d. Educ:* Dumbarton Acad.; Glasgow Acad. Mem., Inst. of Chartered Accts of Scotland, 1953. CA, Bath, 1965–; Lloyd's Underwriter, 1977–. Chairman: Bath DHA, 1982–88; Wessex RHA, 1988–93; Vice-Chm., NHS Training Authy, 1983–88; Mem., Bath City Council, 1978–86. Mem. Council, Bath Internat. Fest., 1970–88 (Chm., 1982–86, 1988); Trustee, Robin Buchanan Charitable Trust, 1985–. Mem., Court, 1984–, and Council, 1985–, Bath Univ.; Mem. Council, Southampton Univ., 1990–93; Gov., Millfield Sch., 1992– (Treas., 1963–92). DL Avon, 1992. *Recreations:* golf, beach walking. *Address:* Stonewalls, Beechwood Road, Combe Down, Bath BA2 5JS. *T:* Bath (01225) 833768; Settlers Beach, St James, Barbados. *T:* 4223025.

BUCHANAN-DUNLOP, Richard, QC 1966; *b* 19 April 1919; *s* of late Canon W. R. Buchanan-Dunlop and Mrs R. E. Buchanan-Dunlop (*née* Mead); *m* 1948, Helen Murray Dunlop; three *d. Educ:* Marlborough College; Magdalene College, Cambridge. Served in Royal Corps of Signals, 1939–46 (Hon. Major). BA (Hons) Law, Cambridge, 1949; Harmsworth Scholar, 1950. Called to the Bar, 1951. *Publications:* Skiathos and other Poems, 1984; Old Olive Men, 1986; Hie Paeeon: songs from the Greek Isles, 1989. *Recreations:* painting, writing. *Address:* Skiathos, Greece.

BUCHANAN-JARDINE, Sir A. R. J.; *see* Jardine.

BUCHTHAL, Hugo, FBA 1959; PhD; Ailsa Mellon Bruce Professor, 1970–75, Professor of Fine Arts, 1965–70, New York University Institute of Fine Arts; now Emeritus Professor; *b* Berlin, 11 Aug. 1909; *m* 1939, Amalia Serkin; one *d. Educ:* Universities of Berlin, Heidelberg, Paris and Hamburg. PhD, Hamburg, 1933; Resident in London from 1934; Lord Plumer Fellowship, Hebrew University, 1938; Librarian, Warburg Institute, 1941; Lecturer in History of Art, University of London, 1944; Reader in the History of Art, with special reference to the Near East, 1949; Professor of the History of Byzantine Art in the University of London, 1960. Visiting Scholarship, Dumbarton Oaks, Harvard University, 1950–51, 1965, 1974, 1978; Temp. Member Inst. for Advanced Study, Princeton, NJ, 1959–60, 1968, 1975–76; Visiting Professor Columbia University, New York, 1963. Prix Schlumberger, Académie des Inscriptions et Belles Lettres, 1958, 1981; Guggenheim Fellow, 1971–72; Corres. Mem., Oesterreichische Akad. der Wissenschaften, 1975; Hon. Fellow, Warburg Inst., 1975. *Publications:* The Miniatures of the Paris Psalter, 1938; (with Otto Kurz) A Handlist of illuminated Oriental Christian Manuscripts, 1942; The Western Aspects of Gandhara Sculpture, 1944; Miniature Painting in the Latin Kingdom of Jerusalem, 1957; Historia Trojana, studies in the history of mediaeval secular illustration, 1971; (jtly) The Place of Book Illumination in Byzantine Art, 1976; (with Hans Belting) Patronage in Thirteenth Century Constantinople: an atelier of late Byzantine illumination and calligraphy, 1978; The Musterbuch of Wolfenbüttel and its position in the art of the thirteenth century, 1979; Art of the Mediterranean World, AD 100 to AD 1400, 1983 (collected essays); numerous articles in learned journals. *Address:* 22 Priory Gardens, N6 5QS. *T:* 0181–348 1664.

BUCHWALD, Art, (Arthur); American journalist, author, lecturer and columnist; *b* Mount Vernon, New York, 20 Oct. 1925; *s* of Joseph Buchwald and Helen (*née* Kleinberger); *m* 1952, Ann McGarry, Warren, Pa; one *s* two *d. Educ:* University of Southern California. Sergeant, US Marine Corps, 1942–45. Columnist, New York Herald Tribune: in Paris, 1949–62; in Washington, 1962–. Syndicated columnist whose articles appear in 550 newspapers throughout the world. Mem., AAAL, 1986–. Pulitzer Prize for outstanding commentary, 1982. *Publications:* (mostly published later in England) Paris After Dark, 1950; Art Buchwald's Paris, 1954; The Brave Coward, 1957; I Chose Caviar, 1957; More Caviar, 1958; A Gift from the Boys, 1958; Don't Forget to Write, 1960; Art Buchwald's Secret List to Paris, 1961; How Much is That in Dollars?, 1961; Is it Safe to Drink the Water?, 1962; I Chose Capitol Punishment, 1963; . . . and Then I told the President, 1965; Son of the Great Society, 1966; Have I Ever Lied to You?, 1968; The Establishment is Alive and Well in Washington, 1969; Sheep on the Runway (Play), 1970; Oh, to be a Swinger, 1970; Getting High in Government Circles, 1971; I Never Danced at the White House, 1973; I Am not a Crook, 1974; Bollo Caper, 1974; Irving's Delight, 1975; Washington is Leaking, 1976; Down the Seine and up the Potomac, 1977; The Buchwald Stops Here, 1978; Laid Back in Washington, 1981; While Reagan Slept, 1984; You Can Fool All of the People All the Time, 1985; I Think I Don't Remember, 1987; Whose Rose Garden is it Anyway?, 1989; Lighten Up, George, 1991; Leaving Home: a memoir, 1994. *Recreations:* tennis, chess, marathon running. *Address:* 2000 Pennsylvania Avenue NW, Washington, DC 20006, USA. *T:* (202) 3936680.

BUCK, Prof. Kenneth William, PhD, DSc; Professor of Plant and Fungal Virology, since 1986, and Head, Plant and Microbial Sciences Section (formerly Microbiology and Plant Pathology Section), since 1986, Imperial College of Science, Technology and Medicine, University of London; *b* 16 Feb. 1938; *s* of William Buck and Nellie Sebra (*née* Turner); *m* 1961, Gwendoline Maureen Patterson; three *d. Educ:* Univ. of Birmingham (BSc 1st Cl. Hons 1959; PhD 1962; DSc 1983). Res. Fellow, Univ. of Birmingham, 1962–65; Imperial College, University of London: Lectr, Dept of Biochem., 1965–81; Reader, Dept of Biol., 1981–86; Chm., Sub-Bd of Examrs in Microbiol., 1981–; Chm. Panel of Vis. Examrs in Microbiol., London Univ., 1988–. Sec., Cttee on Non-Specific Immunity, MRC, 1968–71; Member: Plants and Envmt Res. Grants Bd, AFRC, 1992–94; Plant and Microbial Scis Cttee, BBSRC, 1994–. International Committee on Virus Taxonomy: Mem., Exec. Cttee, 1981–93; Chm., Fungal Virus Sub-cttee, 1981–87; Sec., 1984–90; Vice-Pres., 1990–93; Chm. of workshops on fungal virol. and plant virus replication, Internat. Congress of Virology, triennially, 1981–93; Mem., Soc. for Gen. Microbiol., 1975–. Editor, Jl of Gen. Virology, 1991– (Mem., Editl Bd, 1985–90). *Publications:* (ed) Fungal Virology, 1986; numerous papers in scientific jls and books. *Recreation:* genealogy. *Address:* Department of Biology, Imperial College of Science, Technology and Medicine, Prince Consort Road, SW7 2BB. *T:* 0171–594 5362.

BUCK, Prof. Margaret Ann; Head of College, Central Saint Martin's College of Art & Design, since 1991, and Assistant Rector, since 1989, The London Institute; *b* 23 Nov. 1948; *d* of William Ewart Buck and Winifred Annie Buck; *m* 1985, David Martin Burrows. *Educ:* Gloucestershire Coll. of Art and Design (DipAD Fine Art); Royal Coll. of Art (MA Furniture Design). Head of Dept, then Dep. Head of Sch., Central Sch. of Art and Design, 1986; Dep. Head of Sch., Camberwell Sch. of Arts and Crafts, 1987–89; Head, Camberwell Coll. of Arts, London Inst., 1989–91. *Address:* Central Saint Martin's College of Art & Design, Southampton Row, WC1B 4AP. *Club:* Chelsea Arts.

BUCK, Sir (Philip) Antony (Fyson), Kt 1983; QC 1974; Barrister-at-Law; *b* 19 Dec. 1928; *yr s* of late A. F. Buck, Ely, Cambs; *m* 1st, 1955, Judy Elaine (marr. diss. 1989), *o d* of late Dr C. A. Grant, Cottesloe, Perth, W Australia, and late Mrs Grant; one *d*; 2nd, 1990, Bienvenida Perez-Blanco (marr. diss. 1993); *m* 1994, Tamaro Norashkaryan. *Educ:* King's School, Ely; Trinity Hall, Cambridge. BA History and Law, 1951, MA 1954. Chm. Cambridge Univ. Cons. Assoc. and Chm. Fedn of Univ. Conservative and Unionist Associations, 1951–52. Called to the Bar, Inner Temple, 1954; Legal Adviser, Nat. Association of Parish Councils, 1957–59 (Vice-Pres., 1970–74). MP (C) Colchester, 1961–83, Colchester North, 1983–92. PPS to Attorney-General, 1963–64; Parly Under-Sec. of State for Defence (Navy), MoD, 1972–74. Chm., Select Cttee on Parly Comr for Admin (Ombudsman), 1977–92; Sec., Conservative Party Home Affairs Cttee, 1964–70, Vice-Chm., 1970–72, Chm. Oct./Nov. 1972; Chm., Cons. Parly Defence Cttee, 1979–89; Mem. Exec., 1922 Cttee, Oct./Nov. 1972, 1977–92. Sponsored and piloted through the Limitation Act, 1963. *Recreations:* most sports, reading. *Club:* United Oxford & Cambridge University.

BUCKHURST, Lord; William Herbrand Thomas Sackville; *b* 13 June 1979; *s* and *heir* of Earl De La Warr, *qv.*

BUCKINGHAM, Area Bishop of, since 1994; **Rt. Rev. Colin James Bennetts;** *b* 9 Sept. 1940; *s* of James Thomas Bennetts and Winifred Florence Bennetts (*née* Couldrey); *m* 1965, Veronica Jane Leat; two *s* two *d. Educ:* Battersea Grammar Sch.; Jesus Coll., Cambridge (Exhibnr); Ridley Hall, Cambridge. MA (Cantab); MA (Oxon) by incorporation. Assistant Curate: St Stephen, Tonbridge, 1965–69; St Aldate, Oxford, 1969–73; Chaplain to Oxford Pastorate, 1969–73; Chaplain, Jesus Coll., Oxford, 1973–80; Vicar, St Andrew, Oxford, 1980–90; RD of Oxford, 1984–90; Canon Residentiary of Chester Cathedral, 1990–94; Canon Librarian and Diocesan Director of Ordinands, 1990–94. *Recreations:* mediaeval music, woodcutting. *Address:* Sheridan, Grimms Hill, Great Missenden, Bucks HP16 9BD. *T:* Great Missenden (01494) 862173, *Fax:* 01494 890508.

BUCKINGHAM, Archdeacon of; *see* Morrison, Ven. J. A.

BUCKINGHAM, Amyand David, FRS 1975; Professor of Chemistry, University of Cambridge, since 1969, Fellow of Pembroke College, since 1970; *b* 28 Jan. 1930; 2nd *s* of late Reginald Joslin Buckingham and late Florence Grace Buckingham (formerly Elliot); *m* 1965, Jillian Bowles; one *s* two *d. Educ:* Barker Coll., Hornsby, NSW; Univ. of Sydney; Corpus Christi Coll., Cambridge (Shell Postgraduate Schol.). Univ. Medal 1952, MSc 1953, Sydney; PhD 1956, ScD 1985, Cantab. 1851 Exhibn Sen. Studentship, Oxford Univ., 1955–57; Lectr and subseq. Student and Tutor, Christ Church, Oxford, 1955–65; Univ. Lectr in Inorganic Chem. Lab., Oxford, 1958–65; Prof. of Theoretical Chem., Univ. of Bristol, 1965–69. Vis. Lectr, Harvard, 1961; Visiting Professor: Princeton, 1965; Univ. of California (Los Angeles), 1975; Univ. of Illinois, 1976; Univ. of Wisconsin, 1978; Vis. Fellow, ANU, 1979 and 1982; Vis. Erskine Fellow, Univ. of Canterbury, NZ, 1990. FRACI 1961 (Masson Meml Schol. 1952; Rennie Meml Medal, 1958); FRSC (formerly FCS) (Harrison Meml Prize, 1959; Tilden Lectr 1964; Theoretical Chemistry and Spectroscopy Prize, 1970; Member Faraday Div. (Pres., 1987–89; Mem. Council, 1965–67, 1975–83, 1987–)); FInstP (Harrie Massey Medal and Prize, 1995); Fellow: Optical Soc. of America; Amer. Phys. Soc.; Mem., Amer. Chem. Soc.; For. Associate, Nat. Acad. Scis, USA, 1992; For. Mem., Amer. Acad. of Arts and Scis, 1992; Mem., NY Acad. of Scis, 1994. Editor: Molecular Physics, 1968–72; Chemical Physics Letters, 1978–. Member: Chemistry Cttee, SRC, 1967–70; Adv. Council, Royal Mil. Coll. of Science, Shrivenham, 1973–87. Senior Treasurer: Oxford Univ. Cricket Club, 1959–64; Cambridge Univ. Cricket Club, 1977–90 (Pres., 1990–). Hon. Dr: Univ. de Nancy I, 1979; Sydney, 1993. *Publications:* The Laws and Applications of Thermodynamics, 1964; Organic Liquids, 1978; Principles of Molecular Recognition, 1993; papers in scientific jls. *Recreations:* walking, woodwork, cricket, tennis, travel. *Address:* The Old Rectory, Snailwell, Newmarket CB8 7LZ.

BUCKINGHAM, Ven. Hugh Fletcher; Archdeacon of the East Riding, since 1988; *b* 13 Sept. 1932; *s* of Rev. Christopher Leigh Buckingham and Gladys Margaret Buckingham; *m* 1967, Alison Mary Cock; one *s* one *d. Educ:* Lancing College; Hertford Coll., Oxford (MA Hons). Curate: St Thomas', Halliwell, Bolton, 1957–60; St Silas', Sheffield, 1960–65; Vicar of Hindolveston and Guestwick, dio. Norwich, 1965–70; Rector of Fakenham, 1970–88. Hon. Canon of Norwich Cathedral, 1985–88. *Publications:* How To Be A Christian In Trying Circumstances, 1985; Feeling Good, 1989. *Recreations:* pottery, gardening. *Address:* Brimley Lodge, 27 Molescroft Road, Beverley, North Humberside HU17 7DX. *T:* Hull (01482) 881659.

BUCKINGHAMSHIRE, 10th Earl of, *cr* 1746; **George Miles Hobart-Hampden;** Bt 1611; Baron Hobart 1728; company director; *b* 15 Dec. 1944; *s* of Cyril Langel Hobart-Hampden (*d* 1972) (*g g s* of 6th Earl), and Margaret Moncrieff Hilborne Hobart-Hampden (*née* Jolliffe) (*d* 1985); *S* cousin, 1983; *m* 2nd, 1975, Alison Wightman (*née* Forrest); two step *s. Educ:* Clifton College; Exeter Univ. (BA Hons History); Birkbeck Coll. and Inst. of Commonwealth Studies, Univ. of London (MA Area Studies). With Noble Lowndes and Partners Ltd, 1970–81; Dir, Scottish Pension Trustees Ltd, 1979–81, resigned; Director: Antony Gibbs Pension Services Ltd, 1981–86; Wardley Investment Services (UK) Ltd, 1986–91; Wardley Investment Services International Ltd (Man. Dir, 1988–91); Wardley Investment Services Ltd, 1988–91; Wardley Unit Trust Managers Ltd (Chm.), 1988–91; Wardley Fund Managers (Jersey) Ltd (Chm.), 1988–91; Wardley Investment Services (Luxembourg) SA, 1988–91; Wardley Asia Investment Services (Luxembourg) SA (Chm.), 1989–91; Wardley Global Selection, 1989–91; Gota Global Selection, 1988–; Korea Asia Fund, 1990–91; Wyatt Co. (UK) Ltd, 1991–95; Dir, Russian Pension Trust Co. Ltd, 1994–; Partner, Watson Wyatt Worldwide, 1995–. Member: Sub-Cttee C, 1985–90, Sub-Cttee A, 1990–93, H of L Select Cttee on European Affairs; H of L Sub-Cttee on Staffing of Community Instns, 1987–88. Pres., Buckingham Cons. Constituency Assoc., 1989–. Pres., John Hampden Soc., 1993–. FInstD 1983. Patron, Hobart Town (1804) First Settlers Assoc. *Recreations:* music, squash, fishing, Real tennis, Rugby football. *Heir:* Sir John Vere Hobart, Bt, *qv. Address:* House of Lords, SW1A 0PW. *Clubs:* Western (Glasgow); West of Scotland Football; Leamington Tennis.

BUCKLAND, Maj.-Gen. Ronald John Denys Eden, CB 1974; MBE 1956; DL; Chief Executive, Adur District Council, 1975–85; *b* 27 July 1920; *s* of late Geoffrey Ronald Aubert Buckland, CB and Lelgarde Edith Eleanor (*née* Eden); *m* 1968, Judith Margaret Coxhead, MBE, DL; two *d. Educ:* Winchester; New College, Oxford (MA). Commissioned into Coldstream Gds, Dec. 1940. Served War of 1939–45: NW Europe, with 4th Coldstream Gds, 1944–45 (wounded twice). GSO3, Gds Div., BAOR, 1946; Adjt, 1st Bn Coldstream Gds, Palestine and Libya, 1948; DAA&QMG, 2nd Guards Bde and 18th Inf. Bde, Malaya, 1950–52 (Dispatches); DAAG, 3rd Div., Egypt, 1954; jssc 1956; Bde Major, 1st Gds Bde, Cyprus, 1958; Bt Lt-Col 1959; Bde Major, 51st Inf. Bde, 1960; commanded 1st Bn, Coldstream Gds, 1961, British Guiana, 1962; GSO1, 4th Div., BAOR, 1963; Brig. 1966; Comdr, 133 Inf. Bde (TA), 1966; ACOS, Joint Exercises Div., HQ AFCENT, Holland, 1967; idc 1968; DA&QMG, 1st British Corps, BAOR, 1969;

Maj.-Gen. 1969; Chief of Staff, HQ Strategic Command, 1970; Maj.-Gen. i/c Admin, UKLF, 1972–75. DL W Sussex, 1986. *Recreations:* travel, watching cricket, bricklaying. *Clubs:* MCC; Leander; Sussex.

BUCKLAND, Ross; Chief Executive and Director, Unigate plc, since 1990; *b* 19 Dec. 1942; *s* of William Arthur Haverfield Buckland and Elizabeth Buckland; *m* 1966, Patricia Ann Bubb; two *s*. *Educ:* Sydney Boys' High Sch. Various positions in cos engaged in banking, engrg and food ind., 1958–66; Dir, Finance and Admin, Elizabeth Arden Pty Ltd, 1966–73; Kellogg (Australia) Pty Ltd, 1973–77, Man. Dir, 1978; Pres. and Chief Exec., Kellogg Salada Canada Inc., 1979–80; Chm., Kellogg Co. of GB Ltd and Dir, European Ops and Vice-Pres., Kellogg Co., USA, 1981–90. Fellow, Australian Soc. Certified Practising Accountants; FCIS; FIGD. *Recreation:* walking. *Address:* Unigate plc, Unigate House, Wood Lane, W12 7RP. *T:* 0181–749 8888. *Clubs:* Roehampton; Sydney Cricket.

BUCKLE, (Christopher) Richard (Sandford), CBE 1979; writer; critic; exhibition designer; Director, Theatre Museum Association, since 1978; *b* 6 Aug. 1916; *s* of late Lieut-Col C. G. Buckle, DSO, MC, Northamptonshire Regt, and Mrs R. E. Buckle (*née* Sandford). *Educ:* Marlborough; Balliol. Founded "Ballet", 1939. Served Scots Guards, 1940–46; in action in Italy (despatches, 1944). Started "Ballet" again, 1946; it continued for seven years. Ballet critic of the Observer, 1948–55: ballet critic of the Sunday Times, 1959–75; advised Canada Council on state of ballet in Canada, 1962; advised Sotheby & Co. on their sales of Diaghilev Ballet material, 1967–69. First play, Gossip Column, prod Q Theatre, 1953; Family Tree (comedy), prod Connaught Theatre, Worthing, 1956. *Organised:* Diaghilev Exhibition, Edinburgh Festival, 1954, and Forbes House, London, 1954–55; The Observer Film Exhibition, London, 1956; Telford Bicentenary Exhibition, 1957; Epstein Memorial Exhibition, Edinburgh Festival, 1961; Shakespeare Exhibition, Stratford-upon-Avon, 1964–65; a smaller version of Shakespeare Exhibition, Edinburgh, 1964; Treasures from the Shakespeare Exhibition, National Portrait Gallery, London, 1964–65; The Communities on the March area in the Man in the Community theme pavilion, Universal and Internat. Exhibition of 1967, Montreal; Exhibition of Beaton Portraits, 1928–68, National Portrait Gallery, 1968; Gala of ballet, Coliseum, 1971; exhibn of Ursula Tyrwhitt, Ashmolean Mus., Oxford, 1974; exhibn Omaggio ai Disegnatori di Diaghilev, Palazzo Grassi, Venice, 1975; exhibn of ballet, opera and theatre costumes, Salisbury Fest., 1975; exhibn Happy and Glorious, 130 years of Royal photographs, Nat. Portrait Gallery, 1977; presented Kama Dev in recital of Indian dancing, St Paul's Church, Covent Garden, 1970; *designed:* new Exhibition Rooms, Harewood House, Yorks, 1959; redesigned interior of Dundee Repertory Theatre, 1963 (burnt down 3 months later). *Publications:* John Innocent at Oxford (novel), 1939; The Adventures of a Ballet Critic, 1953; In Search of Diaghilev, 1955; Modern Ballet Design, 1955; The Prettiest Girl in England, 1958; Harewood (a guide-book), 1959 and (re-written and re-designed), 1966; Dancing for Diaghilev (the memoirs of Lydia Sokolova), 1960; Epstein Drawings (introd. only), 1962; Epstein: An Autobiography (introd. to new edn only), 1963; Jacob Epstein: Sculptor, 1963; Monsters at Midnight: the French Romantic Movement as a background to the ballet Giselle (limited edn), 1966; Nijinsky, 1971; Nijinsky on Stage: commentary on drawings of Valentine Gross, 1971; (ed) U and Non-U revisited, 1978; Diaghilev, 1979; (ed) Self Portrait with Friends, selected diaries of Cecil Beaton, 1979; Buckle at the Ballet, 1980; (with Roy Strong and others) Designing for the Dancer, 1981; (contrib.) The Englishman's Room, ed A. Lees-Milne, 1986; (contrib.) Sir Iain Moncreiffe of that Ilk, ed J. Jolliffe, 1986; L'Après-midi d'un faune, Vaslav Nijinski (introd. only), 1983; (with John Taras) George Balanchine, Ballet Master, 1988; *autobiography:* 1, The Most Upsetting Woman, 1981; 2, In the Wake of Diaghilev, 1982. *Recreations:* caricature, light verse. *Address:* Roman Road, Gutch Common, Semley, Shaftesbury, Dorset SP7 9BE.

BUCKLE, Richard; *see* Buckle, C. R. S.

BUCKLEY, family name of **Baron Wrenbury.**

BUCKLEY, Anthony James Henthorne; consultant; *b* 22 May 1934; *s* of late William Buckley, FRCS; *m* 1964, Celia Rosamund Sanderson, *d* of late C. R. Sanderson; one *s* two *d*. *Educ:* Haileybury and ISC; St John's Coll., Cambridge. MA, LLB, FCA. Peat Marwick Mitchell & Co., 1959–62; Rank Organisation Ltd, 1962–66; Slater Walker Securities Ltd, 1966–75, Man. Dir, 1972–75. *Address:* 2 St Mary's Grove, SW13 0JA.

BUCKLEY, Rt. Hon. Sir Denys (Burton), PC 1970; Kt 1960; MBE 1945; a Lord Justice of Appeal, 1970–81; *b* 6 Feb. 1906; 4th *s* of 1st Baron Wrenbury; *m* 1932, Gwendolen Jane (*d* 1985), *yr d* of late Sir Robert Armstrong-Jones, CBE, FRCS, FRCP; three *d*. *Educ:* Eton; Trinity College, Oxford. Called to the Bar, Lincoln's Inn, 1928, Bencher, 1949, Pro-Treasurer, 1967, Treasurer, 1969, Pres., Senate of the Inns of Court, 1970–72. Served War of 1939–45, in RAOC, 1940–45; Temporary Major; GSO II (Sigs Directorate), War Office. Treasury Junior Counsel (Chancery), 1949–60; Judge of High Court of Justice, Chancery Div., 1960–70. Member, Restrictive Practices Ct, 1962–70, President, 1968–70; Member: Law Reform Cttee, 1963–73; Cttee on Departmental Records, 1952–54; Advisory Council on Public Records, 1958–79. Hon. Fellow: Trinity Coll., Oxford, 1969; Amer. Coll. of Trial Lawyers, 1970. Master, Merchant Taylors' Co., 1972, First Upper Warden, 1986–87. CStJ 1966. Medal of Freedom (USA), 1945. *Address:* Flat 6, 105 Onslow Square, SW7 3LU. *T:* 0171–584 4735.

BUCKLEY, Eric Joseph, MA; FIOP; Printer to the University of Oxford, 1978–83; Emeritus Fellow of Linacre College, Oxford, 1983 (Fellow, 1979–83); *b* 26 June 1920; *s* of Joseph William Buckley and Lillian Elizabeth Major (*née* Drake); *m* 1st, 1945, Joan Alice Kirby (*d* 1973); one *s* one *d*; 2nd, 1978, Harriett, *d* of Judge and Mrs Robert Williams Hawkins, Caruthersville, Mo, USA. *Educ:* St Bartholomew's, Dover. MA Oxon 1979 (by special resolution; Linacre College). Served War, RAOC and REME, ME and UK, 1939–45. Apprentice, Amalgamated Press, London, 1935; Dir, Pergamon Press Ltd, 1956–74; joined Oxford Univ. Press as Dir, UK Publishing Services, 1974. Liveryman, Stationers and Newspaper Makers Co., 1981; Freeman, City of London, 1980. *Recreations:* reading, theatre, cats. *Address:* 43 Sandfield Road, Oxford OX3 7RN. *T:* Oxford (01865) 60588.

BUCKLEY, George Eric; Counsellor, Atomic Energy, British Embassy, Tokyo, 1976–81; *b* 4 Feb. 1916; *s* of John and Florence Buckley; *m* 1941, Mary Theresa Terry (*d* 1994); one *s* one *d*. *Educ:* Oldham High Sch.; Manchester Univ. BSc (Hons) Physics; MInstP. Lectr in Physics, Rugby Coll. of Technol., 1938. War service, Sqdn Ldr, RAF, 1940–46. Manager, Health Physics and Safety, Windscale Works, 1949; Works Manager, Capenhurst Works, 1952; Chief Ops Physicist, Risley, 1956; Chief Tech. Manager, Windscale and Calder Works, 1959; Superintendent: Calder Hall and Windscale Advanced Gas Cooled Reactors, 1964; Reactors, and Head of Management Services, 1974. *Recreations:* travel, good food, golf. *Address:* 12 Wast Water Rise, Seascale, Cumbria CA20 1LB. *T:* Seascale (019467) 28405.

BUCKLEY, James; Chief Executive, Baltic Exchange, since 1992; *b* 5 April 1944; *s* of late Harold Buckley and of Mabel Buckley; *m* 1972, Valerie Elizabeth Powles; one *d*. *Educ:* Sheffield City Grammar Sch.; Imperial College of Science and Technology (BSc, ARCS). RAF Operational Res., 1965. Principal Scientific Officer, 1971; Asst Sec., CSD; Private Secretary: to Lord Privy Seal, Lord Peart, 1979; to Lord President of Council, Lord Soames, 1979; to Chancellor of Duchy of Lancaster, Baroness Young, 1981; Sec., Civil Service Coll., 1982; Chief Exec., BVA, 1985–87; Dep. Dir Gen., GCBS, 1987–91. *Recreations:* photography, tennis. *Address:* Baltic Exchange, St Mary Axe, EC3A 8BH. *T:* 0171–623 5501.

BUCKLEY, James Arthur, CBE 1975; Senior Energy Consultant and Director, CIRS Ltd, Newmarket, since 1976; *b* 3 April 1917; *s* of late James Buckley and of Elizabeth Buckley; *m* 1939, Irene May Hicks; two *s*. *Educ:* Christ's Hosp., Horsham, Sussex; Westminster Technical Coll.; Bradford Technical Coll. RAFVR, 1940–46. Gas Light & Coke Co.; Gas Supply Pupil, 1934; Actg Service Supervisor, 1939; Service Supervisor, 1946; North Thames Gas Board: Divisional Man., 1954; Commercial Man., 1962; Commercial Man. and Bd Mem., 1964; East Midlands Gas Board: Dep. Chm., 1966–67; Chm., 1967–68; Mem., Gas Council, later British Gas Corp., 1968–76. Pres., IGasE, 1971–72. *Address:* Rosemary House, Lanwades Business Park, Newmarket CB8 7PW. *T:* Newmarket (01638) 751400.

BUCKLEY, Sir John (William), Kt 1977; Hon. FIChemE; FIEE; chairman and director of companies; Chairman, Davy Corporation (formerly Davy International Ltd), 1973–82, retired; *b* 9 Jan. 1913; *s* of John William and Florence Buckley; *m* 1st, 1935, Bertha Bagnall (marr. diss. 1967); two *s*; 2nd, 1967, Molly Neville-Clarke; one step *s* (and one step *s* decd). *Educ:* techn. coll. (Dipl. Engrg). MIEE. George Kent Ltd, 1934–50 (Gen. Man. 1945–50); Man. Dir, Emmco Pty Ltd, 1950–55; Man. Dir, British Motor Corp. Pty Ltd, 1956–60; Vice Chm. and Dep. Chm., Winget, Gloucester Ltd, 1961–68; Man. Dir and Dep. Chm., Davy International Ltd, 1968–73; Chm., Alfred Herbert Ltd, 1975–79; Chairman: Oppenheimer International, 1983–; Engelhard Industries, 1979–85; John Buckley Associates Ltd, 1983–; Harman Ltd, 1985–; Alexanders Laing & Cruickshank Mergers and Acquisitions Ltd, 1986–; Amchem Ltd, 1989–; Director: Engelhard Corp. Inc., USA, 1982–86; Fuerst Day Lawson, 1981–; AWD Ltd, 1989–91. Dir, British Overseas Trade Bd, 1973–76. Mem., BSC, 1978–81. Hon. FIChemE 1975. FRSA 1978. Order of the Southern Cross (Brazil), 1977. *Recreations:* gardening, music, photography, fishing, painting. *Address:* 49 Drayton Gardens, SW10 9RX. *T:* 0171–244 6486. *Club:* Boodle's.

BUCKLEY, Martin Christopher Burton; Registrar in Bankruptcy, Companies Court, High Court of Justice, and Clerk of Restrictive Practices Court, since 1988; *b* 5 Oct. 1936; *s* of late Hon. Dr Colin Burton Buckley and Evelyn Joyce Buckley (*née* Webster); *m* 1964, Victoria Gay, *d* of Dr Stanhope Furber; two *s* three *d*. *Educ:* Rugby School; Trinity College, Oxford (MA). Called to the Bar, Lincoln's Inn, 1961; practised at Chancery Bar, 1962–88. *Publication:* (ed jtly) Buckley on the Companies Acts, 14th edn 1981 (1st edn 1873—9th edn 1909 by grandfather, Henry Burton Buckley, later 1st Baron Wrenbury). *Recreations:* amateur theatre, choral singing. *Address:* Royal Courts of Justice, Strand, WC2A 2LL.

BUCKLEY, Michael Sydney; Chairman, Dartford and Gravesham NHS Trust, since 1995; *b* 20 June 1939; *s* of Sydney Dowsett Buckley and Grace Bew Buckley; *m* 1st, 1972, Shirley Stordy (*d* 1991); one *s* one *d*; 2nd, 1992, Judith Cartmell (*née* Cobb); two step *s* one step *d*. *Educ:* Eltham College; Christ Church, Oxford (MA; Cert. of Stats). Asst Principal, Treasury, 1962; Asst Private Sec. to Chancellor of Exchequer, 1965–66; Principal: Treasury, 1966–68 and 1971–74; CSD, 1968–71; Assistant Secretary: Treasury, 1974–77 and 1980–82; DoI, 1977–80; Under Secretary: Cabinet Office, 1982–85; Dept of Energy, 1985–91; Mem., CS Appeal Bd, 1991–. *Recreations:* photography, listening to music, reading. *Address:* 53 Bexley Road, SE9 2PE.

BUCKLEY, Peter Neville; Chief Executive, since 1987, and Chairman, since 1994, Caledonia Investments PLC (Deputy Chairman, 1987–94); *b* 23 Sept. 1942; *s* of Maj. Edward Richard Buckley and Ina Heather (*née* Cayzer); *m* 1967, Mary Barabel Stewart; two *d*. *Educ:* Eton; Manchester Business Sch. (DipBA). Served articles with McClelland Moores & Co. (later Ernst & Young); qualified as Chartered Accountant, 1966; joined Brit. & Commonwealth Shipping Co., later Brit. & Commonwealth Hldgs PLC, 1968; Exec. Dir, 1974–88. Chairman: Amber Ind. Hldgs, 1988–; English & Scottish Investors, 1988–; Sterling Inds, 1988–; Brit. Air Tspt (Hldgs), 1989–; Bristow Helicopter Gp, 1991–; Director: Cayzer Trust Co., 1982–; Clan Asset Mgmt, 1991–; Non-Executive Director: Provident Mutual Life Assce Assoc., 1980–; Société Générale de Surveillance Hldg SA, Geneva, 1991–; Exco Internat., 1992–; The Telegraph, 1992–; RHS Enterprises, 1993–. *Recreations:* gardening, golf, shooting. *Address:* Caledonia Investments PLC, Cayzer House, 1 Thomas More Street, E1 9AR. *T:* 0171–481 4343.

BUCKLEY, Lt-Comdr Sir (Peter) Richard, KCVO 1982 (CVO 1973; MVO 1968); *b* 31 Jan. 1928; 2nd *s* of late Alfred Buckley and Mrs E. G. Buckley, Crowthorne, Berks; *m* 1958, Theresa Mary Neve; two *s* one *d*. *Educ:* Wellington Coll. Cadet, RN, 1945. Served in HM Ships: Mauritius, Ulster, Contest, Defender, and BRNC, Dartmouth. Specialised in TA/S. Invalided from RN (Lt-Comdr), 1961. Private Sec. to the Duke and Duchess of Kent, 1961–89; Extra Equerry to the Duke of Kent, 1989–. Director: Vickers Internat., 1981–89; Malcolm McIntyre Consultancy, 1989–92. Governor: Wellington Coll., 1989–; Eagle House Sch., 1989– (Chm. of Govs, 1992–). *Recreations:* fishing, sailing, bee keeping. *Address:* Coppins Cottages, Iver, Bucks SL0 0AT. *T:* Iver (01753) 653004. *Clubs:* Army and Navy; All England Lawn Tennis and Croquet; Royal Yacht Squadron; Royal Dart Yacht.

BUCKLEY, Hon. Sir Roger (John), Kt 1989; **Hon. Mr Justice Buckley;** a Judge of the High Court of Justice, Queen's Bench Division, since 1989; *b* 26 April 1939; *s* of Harold and Marjorie Buckley; *m* 1965, Margaret Gillian, *d* of Robert and Joan Cowan; one *s* one *d*. *Educ:* Mill Hill Sch.; Manchester Univ. (LLB (Hons)). Called to the Bar, Middle Temple, 1962 (Harmsworth Schol.); Bencher, Middle Temple, 1987; QC 1979; a Recorder, 1986–89; a Judge of the Employment Appeal Tribunal, 1994–; Pres., Restrictive Practices Court, 1994–. *Recreations:* golf, theatre. *Address:* Royal Courts of Justice, WC2A 2LL. *Club:* Old Mill Hillians.

BUCKLEY, Major William Kemmis, MBE 1959; Vice Lord-Lieutenant of Dyfed, since 1989; President, Buckley's Brewery Ltd, 1983–86 (Director, 1960, Vice-Chairman, 1963–72, Chairman, 1972–83); *b* 18 Oct. 1921; *o s* of late Lt-Col William Howell Buckley, DL, and Karolie Kathleen Kemmis. *Educ:* Radley Coll.; New Coll., Oxford (MA). Commnd into Welsh Guards, 1941; served N Africa, Italy (despatches, 1945); ADC, 1946–47, Mil. Sec., 1948, to Governor of Madras; Staff Coll., Camberley, 1950; GSO2, HQ London Dist, 1952–53; OC Guards Indep. Para. Co., 1954–57; Cyprus, 1956; Suez, 1956; War Office, 1957; Mil. Asst to Vice-Chief of Imp. Gen. Staff, 1958–59; US Armed Forces Staff Coll., Norfolk, Va., 1959–60. Director: Rhymney Breweries Ltd, 1962–69; Whitbread (Wales) Ltd, 1969–81; Felinfoel Brewery Co., 1975–; Guardian Assurance Co. (S Wales), 1966–83 (Dep. Chm., 1967–83). Mem. Council, Brewers' Soc., 1967; Chm., S Wales Brewers' Assoc., 1971–74; Dep. Chm. and Treas., Nat. Trade Develt Assoc., 1966 (Chm., S Wales Panel, 1965); Lay Mem., Press Council, 1967–73. Chm., Council of St John of Jerusalem for Carms, 1966; Pres., Carms Antiquarian Soc.,

1971– (Chm., 1968); Mem., Nat. Trust Cttee for Wales, 1962–70; Mem., T&AFA (Carms), 1962–82 and T&AFA (S Wales and Mon.), 1967–83; Jt Master and Hon. Sec., Pembrokeshire and Carms Otter Hounds, 1962. High Sheriff of Carms, 1967–68, DL Dyfed (formerly Carms) 1969. KStJ 1984 (CStJ 1966). *Publications:* contributions in local history journals. *Recreations:* gardening, bee-keeping, tapestry work. *Address:* Briar Cottage, Ferryside, Dyfed, S Wales SA17 5UB. *T:* Ferryside (01267) 267359. *Clubs:* Brooks's; Cardiff and County (Cardiff).

BUCKMASTER, family name of **Viscount Buckmaster.**

BUCKMASTER, 3rd Viscount *cr* 1933, of Cheddington; **Martin Stanley Buckmaster,** OBE 1979; Baron 1915; HM Diplomatic Service, retired; *b* 11 April 1921; *s* of 2nd Viscount Buckmaster and Joan, Viscountess Buckmaster (*d* 1976), *d* of Dr Garry Simpson; *S* father, 1974. *Educ:* Stowe. Joined TA, 1939; served Royal Sussex Regt (Captain) in UK and Middle East, 1940–46. Foreign Office, 1946; Middle East Centre for Arab Studies, Lebanon, 1950–51; qualified in Arabic (Higher Standard); served in Trucial States, Sharjah (1951–53) and Abu Dhabi (Political Officer, 1955–58) and subsequently in Libya, Bahrain, FO, Uganda, Lebanon and Saudi Arabia, 1958–73; First Sec., FCO, 1973–77; Head of Chancery and Chargé d'Affaires, Yemen Arab Republic, 1977–81. Deputy Chairman: Council for the Advancement of Arab-British Studies; Christian Broadcasting Council. FRGS 1954. *Recreations:* walking, music, railways; Arab and African studies. *Heir:* *b* Hon. Colin John Buckmaster [*b* 17 April 1923; *m* 1946, May, *o d* of late Charles Henry Gibbon; three *s* two *d*]. *Address:* 90 Cornwall Gardens, SW7 4AX. *Club:* Travellers'.

BUCKS, Ven. Michael William, QHC 1993; Director General, Naval Chaplaincy Services, Chaplain of the Fleet and Archdeacon for the Royal Navy, since 1993; *b* 2 June 1940; *s* of William James Bucks and Dorothy Arkell Bucks (*née* Hill); *m* 1972, Maria Ines Currie; one *s* one *d*. *Educ:* Rossall Sch.; King's Coll. London (BD; AKC). Asst Curate, Workington Parish Church, 1964–68; Chaplain, Royal Navy, 1969–93: Temp. Addnl, HMS Victory and Eagle, 1969–70; Her Majesty's Ships: Raleigh, 1970–71; Albion, 1971–72; Neptune, 1972–74; Mauritius, 1974–76; Fearless, 1976–77; RNEC Manadon, 1977–81; Exchange Programme, US Navy, 1981–83; Staff Chaplain, MoD, London, 1983–86; HM Naval Base, Portsmouth, 1986–90; Staff Chaplain, C-in-C Fleet, HMS Warrior, 1990–93. *Recreations:* steam railways, model railways, country walking, organs and organ music, painting. *Address:* Room 205, Victory Building, HM Naval Base, Portsmouth PO1 3LS. *T:* Portsmouth (01705) 727900; Tamarin, Brodick, Isle of Arran KA27 8BE. *T:* Brodick (01770) 302132. *Club:* Brodick Golf (Isle of Arran).

BUCKWELL, Prof. Allan Edgar; Professor of Agricultural Economics, Wye College, University of London, since 1984; *b* 10 April 1947; *s* of George Alfred Donald Buckwell and Jessie Ethel Buckwell (*née* Neave); *m* 1967, Susan Margaret Hopwood (marr. diss. 1990); two *s*. *Educ:* Wye Coll., Univ. of London (BSc Agric.); Manchester Univ. (MA Econ.). Research Associate, Agricl Adjustment Unit, Newcastle Univ., 1970–73; Lectr in Agricl Economics, Newcastle Univ., 1973–84. Kellogg Res. Fellow, Univ. of Wisconsin, Madison, 1974–75; Vis. Prof., Cornell Univ., 1983. *Publications:* (jtly) The Cost of the Common Agricultural Policy, 1982; articles in Jl Agricl Economics. *Recreations:* walking, gardening, making boomerangs. *Address:* Greenways, The Street, Godmersham, Kent CT4 7DM. *T:* Canterbury (01227) 738713.

BUCZACKI, Dr Stefan Tadeusz; biologist, broadcaster and author; *b* 16 Oct. 1945; *o s* of late Tadeusz Buczacki and Madeleine Mary Buczacki (*née* Fry); *m* 1970, Beverley Ann Charman; two *s*. *Educ:* Ecclesbourne Sch., Duffield; Univ. of Southampton (BSc 1968); Linacre Coll., Oxford (DPhil 1971). FIHort 1986; CBiol, FIBiol; ARPS; FLS. Research Biologist, Nat. Vegetable Res. Station, 1971–84; freelance broadcaster and writer, 1984–. *Radio:* Gardeners' Question Time, 1982–94; Classic Gardening Forum, 1994–; The Gardening Quiz (originator and writer), 1988–93; *television:* Gardeners' Direct Line, 1983–85; That's Gardening, 1989–90, 1992; Bazaar, 1989–93; Gardeners' World, 1990–91; Chelsea Flower Show, 1990–91, Good Morning, 1992. Vice-Pres., British Mycological Soc., 1994. Mem. Council, Gardeners' Royal Benevolent Soc., 1990–. Trustee, Brogdale Horticultural Trust, 1990–. Patron: Parrs Wood Rural Trust, 1990–; Dawlish Gardens Trust, 1990–. Hon. Prof., Biomolecular Scis, Liverpool John Moores Univ., 1994–. *Publications:* (jtly) Collins Guide to the Pests, Diseases and Disorders of Garden Plants, 1981, shorter Guide, 1983; Gem Guide to Mushrooms and Toadstools, 1982; (ed) Zoosporic Plant Pathogens, 1983; Beat Garden Pests and Diseases, 1985; Gardeners' Questions Answered, 1985; (jtly) Three Men in a Garden, 1986; Ground Rules for Gardeners, 1986; Beginners Guide to Gardening, 1988; Creating a Victorian Flower Garden, 1988; Garden Warfare, 1988; New Generation Guide to the Fungi of Britain and Europe, 1989; A Garden for all Seasons, 1990; Understanding Your Garden, 1990; The Essential Gardener, 1991; Dr Stefan Buczacki's Gardening Hints, 1992; The Plant Care Manual, 1992; (ed) The Gardener's Handbook, 1993; The Budget Gardening Year, 1993; Stefan Buczacki's Best Gardening series: Climbers, 1994; Soft Fruit, 1994; Shade Plants, 1994; Foliage Shrubs, 1994; Herbs, 1995; Water Plants, 1995; articles in magazines and newspapers; numerous scientific papers in professional jls. *Recreations:* own garden, photography, riding, fishing, natural history, book collecting, theatre, fine music, travelling and then returning to appreciate the British countryside. *Address:* c/o Barbara Levy Literary Agency, 16 Jeffreys Place, NW1 9PP. *T:* 0171–485 6037.

BUDD, Alan Peter; Chief Economic Adviser to the Treasury and Head of Government Economic Service, since 1991; *b* 16 Nov. 1937; *s* of late Ernest and Elsie Budd; *m* 1964, Susan (*née* Millott); three *s*. *Educ:* Oundle Sch. (Grocers' Co. Schol.); London School of Economics (Leverhulme Schol.; BScEcon); Churchill Coll., Cambridge (PhD). Lectr, Southampton Univ., 1966–69; Ford Foundn Vis. Prof., Carnegie-Mellon Univ., Pittsburgh, 1969–70; Sen. Economic Advr, HM Treasury, 1970–74; Williams & Glyn's Sen. Res. Fellow, London Business Sch., 1974–78; High Level Cons., OECD, 1976–77; Special Advr, Treasury and CS Cttee, 1979–81; Dir, Centre for Economic Forecasting, 1980–88, Prof. of Econs, 1981–91, London Business Sch.; Gp Economic Advr, Barclays Bank, 1988–91. Reserve Bank of Aust. Vis. Prof., Univ. of New South Wales, 1983. Member: Securities and Investments Board, 1987–88; ABRC, 1991. Member: UK-Japan 2000 Gp, 1984–; Council, Inst. for Fiscal Studies, 1988–91; Council, REconS, 1988–93. Gov., LSE, 1994–. Econs columnist, The Independent, 1991. *Publications:* The Politics of Economic Planning, 1978; articles in professional jls. *Recreations:* music, gardening. *Address:* c/o HM Treasury, Parliament Street, SW1P 3AG. *T:* 0171–270 5203. *Club:* Reform.

BUDD, Bernard Wilfred, MA; QC 1969; *b* 18 Dec. 1912; *s* of late Rev. W. R. A. Budd; *m* 1944, Margaret Alison, MBE, *d* of late Rt Hon. E. Leslie Burgin, PC, LLD, MP; two *s*. *Educ:* Cardiff High Sch.; W Leeds High Sch.; Pembroke Coll., Cambridge (schol. in natural sciences). Joined ICS, 1935; various Dist appts incl. Dep. Comr, Upper Sind Frontier, 1942–43; Collector and Dist Magistrate, Karachi, 1945–46; cont. in Pakistan Admin. Service, 1947; Dep. Sec., Min. of Commerce and Works, Govt of Pakistan, 1947; Anti-corruption Officer and Inspector-Gen. of Prisons, Govt of Sind, 1949. Called to Bar, Gray's Inn, 1952; ceased English practice, 1982. Contested (L), Dover, 1964 and 1966, Folkestone and Hythe, Feb. and Oct. 1974 and 1979. Chm., Assoc. of Liberal Lawyers, 1978–82. Vice-Pres., Internat. Assoc. for the Protection of Industrial Property (British Group), 1978–92. Methodist Local (lay) Preacher, 1933–. *Recreations:* birds, hill walking. *Address* Highlands, Elham, Canterbury, Kent CT4 6UG. *T:* Elham (01303) 840350. *Clubs:* United Oxford & Cambridge University, National Liberal.

See also C. R. Budd.

BUDD, Colin Richard, CMG 1991; HM Diplomatic Service; Chef de Cabinet to Sir Leon Brittan, European Commission, since 1993 (on secondment); *b* 31 Aug. 1945; *s* of Bernard Wilfred Budd, *qv*; *m* 1971, Agnes Smit; one *s* one *d*. *Educ:* Kingswood Sch., Bath; Pembroke Coll., Cambridge. Entered HM Diplomatic Service, 1967; CO, 1967–68; Asst Private Sec. to Minister without Portfolio, 1968–69; Third Sec., Warsaw, 1969–72; Second Sec., Islamabad, 1972–75; FCO, 1976–80; First Sec., The Hague, 1980–84; Asst Private Sec. to Sec. of State for Foreign and Commonwealth Affairs, 1984–87; European Secretariat, Cabinet Office, 1987–88; Counsellor (Political), Bonn, 1989–92. *Recreations:* running, mountains, music (Mozart, chansons, Don McLean). *Address:* Rue de la Loi 200, 1049 Brussels, Belgium.

BUDD, Rt. Rev. Mgr. Hugh Christopher; *see* Plymouth, Bishop of, (RC).

BUDD, Prof. Malcolm John, PhD; FBA 1995; Professor of Philosophy, University College London, since 1990; *b* 23 Dec. 1941; *s* of Edward Charles Budd and Hilare (*née* Campbell). *Educ:* Latymer Upper Sch.; Jesus Coll., Cambridge (BA 1964; MA 1967; PhD 1968). William Stone Research Fellow, Peterhouse, Cambridge, 1966–70; University College London: Lectr in Philosophy, 1970–87; Reader, 1987–90. Editor, Aristotelian Soc., 1989–94. *Publications:* Music and the Emotions, 1985; Wittgenstein's Philosophy of Psychology, 1989; Values of Art, 1995. *Address:* Department of Philosophy, University College London, Gower Street, WC1E 6BT.

BUDDEN, Julian Medforth, OBE 1991; FBA 1987; *b* 9 April 1924; *s* of Prof. Lionel Bailey Budden and Dora Magdalene (*née* Fraser). *Educ:* Stowe Sch.; Queen's Coll., Oxford (MA); Royal Coll. of Music; Trinity Coll. of Music (BMus 1955). Joined BBC Music Dept, 1951, as clerk; Music Producer, 1956–70; Chief Producer, Opera (Radio), 1970–76; External Services Music Organiser, 1976–83. *Publications:* The Operas of Verdi, vol. I 1973, vol. II 1978, vol. III 1981; Verdi, 1985; contribs to various musicological periodicals. *Address:* (March, April, July–Sept.) 94 Station Road, N3 2SG. *T:* 0181–349 2954; (Oct.–Feb., May, June) Via Fratelli Bandiera, 9, 50137 Firenze, Italy. *T:* (55) 678471.

BUDDEN, Kenneth George, FRS 1966; MA, PhD; Reader in Physics, University of Cambridge, 1965–82, now Emeritus; Fellow of St John's College, Cambridge, since 1947; *b* 23 June 1915; *s* of late George Easthope Budden and Gertrude Homer Rea; *m* 1947, Nicolette Ann Lydia de Longesdon Longsdon; no *c*. *Educ:* Portsmouth Grammar Sch.; St John's College, Cambridge (MA, PhD). Telecommunications Research Establishment, 1939–41; British Air Commn., Washington, DC, 1941–44; Air Command, SE Asia, 1945. Research at Cambridge, 1936–39 and from 1947. *Publications:* Radio Waves in the Ionosphere, 1961; The Wave-Guide Mode Theory of Wave Propagation, 1961; Lectures on Magnetoionic Theory, 1964; The Propagation of Radio Waves, 1985; numerous papers in scientific jls, on the propagation of radio waves. *Recreation:* gardening. *Address:* 15 Adams Road, Cambridge CB3 9AD. *T:* Cambridge (01223) 354752.

BUDGE, Keith Joseph; Headmaster, Loretto School, since 1995; *b* 24 May 1957; *s* of William and Megan Budge; *m* 1983, Caroline Ann Gent; two *s* one *d*. *Educ:* Rossall Sch.; University Coll., Oxford (MA Hons English; PGCE). Asst Master, Eastbourne Coll., 1980–84; Marlborough College: Asst Master, 1984–88 and 1989–91; Housemaster, Cotton Hse, 1991–95; Instructor in English, Stevenson Sch., Pebble Beach, CA, 1988–89. *Recreations:* hill-walking, trout-fishing, gadgets, theatre. *Address:* Loretto School, Musselburgh, Midlothian EH21 7RE. *T:* 0131–665 5003. *Club:* Vincent's.

BUDGEN, Nicholas William; MP (C) Wolverhampton South-West, since Feb. 1974; *b* 3 Nov. 1937; *s* of Captain G. N. Budgen; *m* 1964, Madeleine E. Kittoe; one *s* one *d*. *Educ:* St Edward's Sch., Oxford; Corpus Christi Coll., Cambridge. Called to Bar, Gray's Inn, 1962; practised Midland and Oxford Circuit. An Asst Govt Whip, 1981–82. *Recreations:* hunting, racing. *Address:* Malt House Farm, Colton, near Rugeley, Staffs WS15 3LN. *T:* Rugeley (01889) 577059.

BUENO, Antonio De Padua Jose Maria; QC 1989; a Recorder, since 1989; *b* 28 June 1942; *s* of Antonio and Teresita Bueno; *m* 1966, Christine Mary Lees; three *d*. *Educ:* Downside School; Salamanca Univ. Called to the Bar, Middle Temple, 1964, and Gibraltar. An Asst Recorder, 1984–89. *Publications:* (ed jtly) Banking section, Atkin's Encyclopaedia of Court Forms, 2nd edn 1976; (Asst Editor, 24th edn 1979 and 25th edn 1983, Jt Editor, 26th edn 1988) Byles on Bills of Exchange; (Asst Editor) Paget's Law of Banking, 9th edn 1982. *Recreations:* fishing, shooting, flying. *Address:* 7 Pitt Street, W8 4NX. *T:* 0171–937 0403. *Clubs:* East India, Flyfishers'.

BUERK, Michael Duncan; foreign correspondent and newscaster, television; *b* 18 Feb. 1946; *s* of Betty Mary Buerk and Gordon Charles Buerk; *m* 1968, Christine Lilley; two *s*. *Educ:* Solihull School. Thomson Newspapers, Cardiff, 1967–69; reporter, Daily Mail, 1969–70; producer, BBC radio, 1970–71; reporter: HTV (West), 1971–72; BBC TV (South), 1972–73; BBC TV London, 1973–76; correspondent, BBC TV: industrial, 1976–77; energy, 1977–79; Scotland, 1979–81; special corresp. and newscaster, 1981–83; Southern Africa, 1983–87; presenter, BBC TV News, 1988–. Hon. MA Bath, 1991; Hon. LLD Bristol. RTS TV Journalist of the Year and RTS News Award, 1984; UN Hunger Award, 1984; numerous other awards, UK and overseas, 1984, 1985; BAFTA News Award, 1985; James Cameron Meml Award, 1988; Science Writer of the Year Award, 1989; Mungo Park Award, RSGS, 1994. *Recreations:* travel, oenophily. *Address:* c/o BBC Television, W12 7RJ. *T:* 0181–576 7771. *Club:* Reform.

BUFFET, Bernard; Chevalier de la Légion d'Honneur; painter; *b* Paris, 10 July 1928; *m* 1958, Annabel May Schwob de Lure; one *s* two *d*. *Educ:* Lycée Carnot; Ecole Nat. Supérieure des Beaux-Arts. Annual exhibitions: Galerie Drouant-David, 1949–56; Galerie David et Garnier, 1957–67; Galerie Maurice Garnier, 1968–. Retrospective exhibitions: Paris, 1958; Berlin, 1958; Belgium, 1959; Tokyo and Kyoto, 1963, Musée d'Unterlinden, Colmar, 1969; Wieger Deurne, Holland, 1977; Musée postal, Paris, 1978; Zurich, 1983; Toulouse, 1985; Musée Pouchkine, Moscow and Musée de l'Hermitage, Leningrad, 1991. Buffet Museum founded in Japan, 1973; large room of his mystic works in Vatican Museum. Illustrator of books, engraver, lithographer and state designer. Grand Prix de la Critique, 1948. Officier des Arts et des Lettres; Mem., Acad. des Beaux-Arts, 1974. *Address:* c/o Galerie Maurice Garnier, 6 avenue Matignon, 75008 Paris, France; Domaine de la Baume, Tourtour, 83690 Salernes, France.

BUFORD, William Holmes; Fiction and Literary Editor, The New Yorker, since 1995; *b* 6 Oct. 1954; *s* of William H. Buford and Helen Shiel; *m* 1991, Alicja Kobiernicka. *Educ:* Univ. of California, Berkeley (BA); King's College, Cambridge (MA). Editor, Granta, 1979–95; former Chm., Granta Publications Ltd. *Publications:* (as Bill Buford): Among the Thugs, 1991; (ed) The Best of Granta Travel, 1991; (ed) The Best of Granta Reportage, 1993; (ed) The Granta Book of the Family, 1995. *Address:* New Yorker Magazine, 20 W 43rd Street, New York, NY 10036, USA.

BUHARI, Alhaji Haroun Madani, High Commissioner for Sierra Leone in London, since 1995; *b* 23 Aug. 1945; *s* of Alhaji Mohammed Buhari and Haja Fatmatta M'balu (*née* Tejan-Sie); *m* 1st, 1975, Haja Sakinatu Onikeh Adams; three *s*; 2nd, 1990, Máriam Zainab Koroma; one *s* one *d*. *Educ:* St Helena Secondary Sch., Freetown; Islamic Missions Inst., Cairo; El Nasr Boys' Coll., Cairo; Univ. of Alexandria, Egypt (BA Hons 1970); Inst. of Social Studies, Univ. of Alexandria; SW London Coll.; Internat. Inst. for Journalism, W Berlin. Ministry of Information and Broadcasting, Sierra Leone: Inf. Officer, 1971–78; Sen. Inf. Officer, 1978–82 (Press. Sec., Office of Pres., 1981–82); Asst Controller/Principal Inf. Officer, 1982–90; Editor-in-Chief, Sierra Leone News Agency, 1986–87; Controller, Govt Inf. Services, 1990–91; Asst Dir of Inf., 1991–92 (Press Sec., Office of Pres., 1987–92); High Comr to Gambia and Ambassador to Senegal, Mauritania and Morocco, 1992–95. Founder Mem., Sierra Leone Assoc. of Journalists, 1971 (Chm., Interim Exec., 1992–93). Sec.-Gen., Sierra Leone Islamic Foundn, 1982–85; Exec. Sec. Federation of Sierra Leone Muslim Orgns, 1987. *Publications:* articles on literary, political, social and religious issues for Sierra Leone and internat. press. *Recreations:* football, reading, music. *Address:* Sierra Leone High Commission, 33 Portland Place, W1N 3AG. *T:* 0171–636 6483.

BUIST, John Latto Farquharson, (Ian), CB 1990; Under Secretary, Foreign and Commonwealth Office (Overseas Development Administration), retired; *b* 30 May 1930; *s* of late Lt-Col Thomas Powrie Buist, RAMC, and Christian Mary (*née* Robertson); partner, 1981, J. E. Regensburg, (Dennis Regensburg) (*d* 1988). *Educ:* Dalhousie Castle Sch.; Winchester Coll.; New Coll., Oxford (MA). Asst Principal, CO, 1952–54; seconded Kenya Govt, 1954–56; Principal, CO, 1956–61; Dept of Tech. Cooperation, 1961–62; Brit. High Commn, Dar-es-Salaam, 1962–64; Consultant on Admin, E African Common Services Org./Community, 1964–69; Sec., Commn on E African Cooperation and related bodies, 1966–69; Asst Sec., Min. of Overseas Develt, 1966–76; Under Sec., FCO (ODA), 1976–90. Director: PLAN International (UK), 1990–; Foster Parents PLAN Inc., 1991–. Co-founder, Classical Assoc. of Kenya; Member: Thames Philharmonic (formerly John Bate) Choir; United Reformed Church. *Recreations:* singing and other music-making. *Address:* 9 West Hill Road, SW18 1LH.

BUITER, Prof. Willem Hendrik, PhD; Professor of International Macroeconomics, and Fellow of Trinity College, University of Cambridge, since 1994; *b* 26 Sept. 1949; *s* of Harm Geert Buiter and Hendrien Buiter, *née* van Schooten; *m* 1973, Jean Archer; one *s*. *Educ:* Cambridge Univ. (BA 1971); Yale Univ. (PhD 1975). Asst Prof., Princeton Univ., 1975–76; Lectr, LSE, 1976–77; Asst Prof., Princeton Univ., 1977–79; Prof. of Economics, Univ. of Bristol, 1980–82; Cassel Prof. of Economics, LSE, Univ. of London, 1982–85; Prof. of Econs, 1985–90, Juan T. Trippe Prof. of Internat. Econs, 1990–94, Yale Univ. Consultant: IMF, 1979–80; World Bank, 1986–; Inter-American Develt Bank, 1992–; EBRD, 1994–; Specialist Adviser, House of Commons Select Cttee on the Treasury and CS, 1980–84; Adviser, Netherlands Min. of Educn and Science, 1985–86. Associate Editor, Econ. Jl, 1980–84. *Publications:* Temporary and Long Run Equilibrium, 1979; Budgetary Policy, International and Intertemporal Trade in the Global Economy, 1989; Macroeconomic Theory and Stabilization Policy, 1989; Principles of Budgetary and Financial Policy, 1990; International Macroeconomics, 1990; articles in learned jls. *Recreations:* tennis, poetry, music. *Address:* Faculty of Economics and Politics, University of Cambridge, Austin Robinson Building, Sidgwick Avenue, Cambridge CB3 9DD.

BUKHT, Mirza Michael John, (Michael Barry); food journalist; Programme Controller, Classic FM Radio, since 1992; *b* 10 Sept. 1941; *s* of Mirza Jawan Bukht and Lilian Ray Bukht (*née* Oaten); *m* 1964, Jennie Mary Jones; one *s* three *d*. *Educ:* Haberdashers' Aske's Sch.; King's Coll. London (BA Hons). BBC general trainee, 1963; Producer, Tonight prog., 1965; Prog. Controller, JBC, Jamaica, 1967; Dep. Editor, 24 Hours, BBC TV, 1969; Editor, Special Projects, BBC TV, 1970; Prog. Controller, Capital Radio, 1972; Principal, Nat. Broadcasting Sch., 1979; Man. Dir, Invicta Radio, 1985; Gp Prog. Dir, GWR Gp, 1988. *Publications:* (as Michael Barry) 5 Food and Drink books, 1984–89; Food Processor Cookery, 1985; Complete Crafty Cook Book, 1988; Exotic Food, 1989; Michael Barry's Cook Book, 1991; Big Food and Drink Book, 1993; Great House Cookery, 1993; Classic Recipes, 1993; The Radio Times Cookery Guide, 1994. *Recreations:* music, dance, sailing, gardening, military history, food. *Address:* The Manor House, St Stephen's, Canterbury, Kent CT2 7JT. *Clubs:* East India; Whitstable Yacht.

BULFIELD, Peter William, CA; Deputy Chairman, Yamaichi Bank (UK) PLC, 1991–94 (Managing Director and Chief Executive, 1988–91); *b* 14 June 1930; *s* of Wilfred Bulfield and Doris (*née* Bedford); *m* 1958, Pamela June Beckett; two *d*. *Educ:* Beaumont Coll., Old Windsor. Peat Marwick Mitchell & Co., 1947–59; J. Henry Schroder Wagg & Co., 1959–86, Dir, 1967–86; Director: Schroder Finance, 1966–73; Schroder Darling Hldgs, Sydney, 1973–80; Vice-Chm., Mitsubishi Trust & Banking Corporation (Europe) SA, 1973–84; Jt Dep. Chm., Schroder Internat., 1977–86; Dep. Chm., Crown Agents for Oversea Govts and Admin, 1982–85; Director: Yamaichi PLC, 1986–87; London Italian Bank, 1989–91. Member: Overseas Projects Board, 1983–86; Overseas Promotions Cttee, BIEC, 1984–86; Export Guarantees Adv. Council, 1985–88. Mem., Finance Cttee, CAFOD, 1994–. *Recreations:* sailing, music, painting. *Address:* The Mill House, Merrieweathers, Mayfield, Sussex TN20 6RJ. *T:* Mayfield (01435) 872177. *Club:* Royal Thames Yacht.

BULGER, His Honour Anthony Clare, BA, BCL; a Circuit Judge (formerly County Court Judge), 1963–86; *b* 5 Oct. 1912; *s* of Daniel Bulger; *m* Una Patricia Banks (*d* 1992); one *s* one *d*. *Educ:* Rugby; Oriel Coll., Oxford. Called to the Bar, Inner Temple, 1936. Oxford Circuit; Dep Chm., 1958–70, Chm. 1970–71, Glos QS; Dep. Chm. Worcs QS, 1962–71; Recorder of Abingdon, 1962–63. *Address:* The Dower House, Forthampton, Glos GL19 4QW. *T:* Tewkesbury (01684) 293257.

BULKELEY, Sir Richard Thomas W.; *see* Williams-Bulkeley.

BULL, Anthony, CBE 1968 (OBE 1944); Transport Consultant: Kennedy and Donkin, 1971–85; Freeman Fox and Partners, 1971–87; *b* 18 July 1908; 3rd *s* of Rt Hon. Sir William Bull, 1st Bt, PC, MP, JP, FSA (*d* 1931), and late Lilian, 2nd *d* of G. S. Brandon, Oakbrook, Ravenscourt Park; *m* 1946, Barbara (*d* 1947), *er d* of late Peter Donovan, Yonder, Rye, Sussex; one *d*. *Educ:* Gresham's Sch., Holt; Magdalene Coll., Cambridge (Exhibitioner; MA). Joined Underground Group of Cos, 1929; served in Staff, Publicity and Public Relations Depts and Chairman's Office. Sec. to Vice-Chm. London Passenger Transport Board, 1936–39. Served War, 1939–45; RE; Transportation Br., War Office, 1939–42; GHQ, Middle East, 1943; Staff of Supreme Allied Comdr, SE Asia (end of 1943); Col 1944; Transp. Div., CCG, 1945–46. Returned to London Transport as Chief Staff and Welfare Officer, 1946; Member: LTE, 1955–62; LTB, 1962–65; Vice-Chm., LTE (formerly LTB), 1965–71. Advr to House of Commons Transport Cttee, 1981–82. Inst. of Transport: served on Council, 1956–59; Vice-Pres., 1964–66; Hon. Librarian, 1966–69; Pres., 1969–70. Mem. Regional Advisory Council for Technological Educn, 1958–62 (Transp. Adv. Cttee, 1950–62; Chm. Cttee, 1953–62). CStJ 1969. Bronze Star (USA), 1946. *Publications:* contrib. to transport journals. *Recreation:* travel. *Address:* 35 Clareville Grove, SW7 5AU. *T:* 0171–373 5647. *Club:* United Oxford & Cambridge University.

See also Sir S. G. Bull, Bt, Sir Robin Chichester-Clark.

BULL, David Neill; Director, Amnesty International (British Section), since 1990; *b* 21 June 1951; *s* of Denis Albert and Doreen Lilian Bull; *m* 1978, Claire Grenger; one *d*. *Educ:* Sussex Univ. (BA Econ); Bath Univ. (MSc Develt Studies). Public Affairs Unit Officer, Oxfam, 1979–84; Dir, Environment Liaison Centre, Nairobi, 1984–87; Gen. Sec., World University Service (UK), 1987–90. Trustee: Refugee Council, 1987–90; Pesticides Trust, 1987–; Mem., Exec. Cttee, Assoc. of Chief Execs of Nat. Vol. Orgns, 1994–. *Publication:* A Growing Problem: pesticides and the Third World Poor, 1982. *Recreations:* swimming, walking, reading, esp. science fiction. *Address:* Amnesty International, 99–119 Rosebery Avenue, EC1R 4RE. *T:* 0171–814 6200.

BULL, George Anthony, OBE 1990; FRSL 1982; writer, translator and consultant; Director, Anglo-Japanese Economic Institute, since 1986; Editor, International Minds, since 1989; President, Central Banking Publications, since 1990; Publisher, Insight Japan, since 1992; *b* 23 Aug. 1929; *s* of George Thomas Bull and Bridget Philomena (*née* Nugent); *m* 1957, Doreen Marjorie Griffin; two *s* two *d*. *Educ:* Wimbledon Coll.; Brasenose Coll., Oxford (MA). National Service, Royal Fusiliers, 1947–49. Reporter, Financial Times, 1952–56, Foreign News Editor, 1956–59; News Editor, London Bureau, McGraw-Hill World News, 1959–60; The Director, 1960–84: successively Dep. Editor, Editor, Editor-in-Chief. Dir 1971–, and Trustee 1976–, The Tablet; Trustee, The Universe, 1970–86. Chm., Commn for Internat. Justice and Peace, Episcopal Conf. of England and Wales, 1971–74; Mem. Council, RSL, 1986– (Hon. Treas., 1992–); Mem., UK Cttee, European Cultural Foundn, 1987–; Hon. Treasurer, Soc. for Renaissance Studies, 1967–88; a Governor: St Mary's Coll., Strawberry Hill, 1976–87; Westminster Choir Sch., 1994–; Foundation Governor, St Thomas More Sch., 1980–87. *Publications:* (with A. Vice) Bid for Power, 1958, 2nd edn 1960; Vatican Politics, 1966; The Renaissance, 1968, new edn 1973; (ed) The Director's Handbook, 1969, 2nd edn 1978; (with E. D. Foster) The Director, his Money and his Job, 1970; (with Peter Hobday and John Hamway) Industrial Relations: the boardroom viewpoint, 1972; Venice: the most triumphant city, 1982, Folio Society 1980, USA 1982; Inside the Vatican, 1982, USA 1983, Italy 1983 (as Dentro il Vaticano), Germany and Japan 1987; Hungary, 1989; translations: Artists of the Renaissance, 1979–; (with Peter Porter) Life, Letters and Poetry of Michelangelo, 1987; The Travels of Pietro della Valle, 1989; translations for Penguin Classics: Life of Cellini, 1956; Machiavelli, The Prince, 1961; Vasari, Lives of the Artists, Vol. I, 1965, vol II, 1987; Castiglione, The Book of the Courtier, 1967; Aretino, Selected Letters, 1976. *Recreations:* book collecting, travelling. *Address:* 19 Hugh Street, SW1V 1QJ. *Clubs:* Garrick, Savile, Beefsteak.

BULL, George Jeffrey; Group Chief Executive, Grand Metropolitan PLC, since 1993; *b* 16 July 1936; *s* of late William Perkins Bull and of Hon. Noreen Bull (*née* Hennessy); *m* 1960, Jane Fleur Thérèse Freeland; four *s* one *d*. *Educ:* Ampleforth Coll.; IDV Ltd: Dir, 1972; Dep. Man. Dir, 1982–84; Chief Exec., 1984–92; Chm., 1988–92; Chm. and Chief Exec., Grand Metropolitan Food Sector, 1992–93. Non-Exec. Dir, United Newspapers, 1993–. Formerly Dir, BOTB. FRSA 1992. *Recreations:* golf, photography. *Address:* Grand Metropolitan PLC, 20 St James's Square, SW1Y 4RR; The Old Vicarage, Arkesden, Saffron Walden, Essex CB11 4HB. *T:* Saffron Walden (01799) 550445. *Clubs:* Cavalry and Guards; Royal Worlington and Newmarket Golf (Suffolk); Buckinghsmshire Golf (Denham).

BULL, John Michael; QC 1983; **His Honour Judge John Bull;** a Circuit Judge, since 1991; Resident Judge of the Crown Court at Guildford, since 1992; *b* 31 Jan. 1934; *s* of John Godfrey Bull and Eleanor Bull (*née* Nicholson); *m* 1959, Sonia Maureen, *d* of Frank Edward Woodcock; one *s* three *d*. *Educ:* Norwich Sch.; Corpus Christi Coll., Cambridge (Parker Exhibnr in Modern History; BA 1958; LLM 1959; MA 1963). Called to the Bar, Gray's Inn, 1960; Dep. Circuit Judge, 1972; Standing Counsel to the Board of Inland Revenue, Western Circuit, 1972–83; a Recorder, 1980–91. Judge, Employment Appeal Tribunal, 1993–.

BULL, Dr John Prince, CBE 1973; Director of MRC Industrial Injuries and Burns Unit, 1952–82; *b* 4 Jan. 1917; *s* of Robert James Bull and Ida Mary Bull; *m* 1939, Irmgard Bross; four *d*. *Educ:* Burton-on-Trent Grammar Sch.; Cambridge Univ.; Guy's Hospital. MA, MD, BCh Cantab; MRCS, FRCP; MFOM. Casualty Res. Officer, Min. of Home Security, 1941; RAMC, 1942–46; Mem. Research Staff 1947, Asst Dir 1948, MRC Unit, Birmingham Accident Hosp. Member: MRC, 1971–75; Med. Commn on Accident Prevention, 1975– (Chm., Transport Cttee, 1981–94); Chairman: Regional Res. Cttee, West Midlands RHA, 1966–82; Inst. of Accident Surgery, 1980–83. Mem., Med. Res. Soc. FRSocMed. *Publications:* contrib. scientific and med. jls. *Recreation:* bricolage. *Address:* 73 Reddings Road, Moseley, Birmingham B13 8LP. *T:* 0121–449 0474.

BULL, (Oliver) Richard (Silvester); Headmaster, Rugby School, 1985–90; *b* 30 June 1930; *s* of Walter Haverson Bull and Margaret Bridget Bull; *m* 1956, Anne Hay Fife; two *s* four *d*. *Educ:* Rugby Sch.; Brasenose Coll. Oxford (MA). Mil. Service (1st Beds and Herts), 1949–51. Asst Master, Eton Coll., 1955–77 (Housemaster, 1968–77); Headmaster, Oakham Sch., Rutland, 1977–84. *Recreations:* music, walking, reading, ball games. *Address:* Broken Bank Cottage, Gladestry, Kington, Herefords HR5 3NY.

BULL, Peter Anthony, JP; FRICS; Proprietor, Walter Bull & Co., since 1987; *b* 8 July 1937; *s* of Sir Walter Edward Avenon Bull, KCVO; *m* 1964, Susan Mary Battersby. *Educ:* Rugby Sch.; Coll. of Estate Management. Partner, Vigers, 1965–87. City of London: Mem., Court of Common Council, 1968–; Alderman, Ward of Cheap, 1984–. Church Comr, 1986–; Church Warden, St Lawrence Jewry, 1984–. Mem., ESU, 1984. Mem., Co. of Parish Clerks, 1993–; Liveryman: Merchant Taylors' Co., 1965; Chartered Surveyors' Co., 1977 (Master, 1990–91). JP City of London, 1984. *Recreations:* clocks, golf, wine, gardening, City of London. *Address:* PO Box 3533, SE12 8PS. *T:* 0181–297 8150. *Clubs:* Guildhall, City Livery, MCC.

BULL, Roger John; Vice-Chancellor and Chief Executive, University of Plymouth, since 1992 (Director and Chief Executive, Polytechnic South West, Plymouth, 1989–92); *b* 31 March 1940; *s* of William Leonard Bull and Margery Bull (*née* Slade); *m* 1964, Margaret Evelyn Clifton; one *s* one *d*. *Educ:* Churchers' Coll.; LSE (BSc Econ). FCCA. Research Fellow, DES/ICA, 1967–68; Principal Lectr in Accounting, Nottingham Poly., 1968–72; Head, Sch. of Accounting and Applied Econs, Leeds Poly., 1972–85; Dep. Dir (Academic), Plymouth Poly., 1986–89. Chm., Open Learning Foundn, 1994–; Dir, HEQC, 1994–; Hon. Treas., CVCP, 1994–. Non exec. Dir, Plymouth Hosps NHS Trust, 1993–; Dir, Plymouth Chamber of Commerce, 1994–. Member: Council, CNAA, 1981–87; Council for Industry and Higher Educn, 1993–. *Publications:* Accounting in Business, 1969, 6th edn 1990; articles in professional jls. *Recreations:* tennis, music. *Address:* c/o Office of the Vice-Chancellor, University of Plymouth, Drake Circus, Plymouth PL4 8AA. *T:* Plymouth (01752) 232000.

BULL, Sir Simeon (George), 4th Bt *cr* 1922, of Hammersmith; Senior Partner in legal firm of Bull & Bull; *b* 1 Aug. 1934; *s* of Sir George Bull, 3rd Bt and of Gabrielle, *d* of late Bramwell Jackson, MC; *S* father, 1986; *m* 1961, Annick Elizabeth Renée Geneviève, *d* of late Louis Bresson and Mme Bresson, Chandai, France; one *s* two *d*. *Educ:* Eton; Innsbruck; Paris. Admitted solicitor, 1959. *Heir:* *s* Stephen Louis Bull, *b* 5 April 1966. *Address:* Beech Hanger, Beech Road, Shepherd's Hill, Merstham, Surrey RH1 3AE; Pen Enez, Pont l'Abbé, France. *Clubs:* MCC; Royal Thames Yacht.

See also Anthony Bull.

BULL, Tony Raymond, FRCS; Consultant Surgeon: Charing Cross Hospital; Royal National Throat Nose and Ear Hospital; King Edward VII's Hospital for Officers; *b* 21 Dec. 1934; *m* 1958, Jill Rosemary Beresford Cook; one *s* two *d*. *Educ:* Monkton Combe School; London Hosp. (MB BS 1958). FRCS 1962. Pres., Section of Otology, RSocMed, 1993–94. Yearsley Lectr, RSocMed, 1982. Sir William Wilde Medal, Irish Otolaryngol Soc., 1993. Editor, Facial Plastic Surgery (Quarterly Monographs), 1983. *Publications:* Atlas of Ear, Nose and Throat Diagnosis, 1974, 2nd edn 1987; Recent Advances in Otolaryngology, 1978; Plastic Reconstruction in the Head and Neck, 1986; Diagnostic Picture Test, Ear, Nose and Throat, 1990. *Recreations:* tennis, golf. *Address:* 107 Harley Street, W1N 1DG. *T:* 0171–935 3171; 26 Scarsdale Villas, W8 6PR. *T:* 0171–937 3411. *Clubs:* MCC, Hurlingham, Queen's.

BULLARD, Sir Julian (Leonard), GCMG 1987 (KCMG 1982; CMG 1975); HM Diplomatic Service, retired; Fellow of All Souls College, Oxford, 1950–57 and since 1988; *b* 8 March 1928; *s* of late Sir Reader Bullard, KCB, KCMG, CIE, and late Miriam, *d* of late A. L. Smith, Master of Balliol Coll., Oxford; *m* 1954, Margaret Stephens; two *s* two *d*. *Educ:* Rugby; Magdalen Coll., Oxford. Army, 1950–52; HM Diplomatic Service, 1953–88: served at: FO, 1953–54; Vienna, 1954–56; Amman, 1956–59; FO, 1960–63; Bonn, 1963–66; Moscow, 1966–68; Dubai, 1968–70; Head of E European and Soviet Dept, FCO, 1971–75; Minister, Bonn, 1975–79; Dep. Under-Sec. of State, 1979–84 and Dep. to Perm. Under Sec. of State and Political Dir, 1982–84, FCO; Ambassador, Bonn, 1984–88. Birmingham University: Mem. Council, 1988–; Chm. Council and Pro-Chancellor, 1989–94. *Address:* 18 Northmoor Road, Oxford OX2 6UR. *T:* Oxford (01865) 512981.

BULLEN, Air Vice-Marshal Reginald, CB 1975; GM 1945; MA; Senior Bursar and Fellow, Gonville and Caius College, Cambridge, 1976–87, Life Fellow and Property Developments Consultant, since 1988; *b* 19 Oct. 1920; *s* of Henry Arthur Bullen and Alice May Bullen; *m* 1952, Christiane (*née* Phillips); one *s* one *d*. *Educ:* Grocers' Company School. 39 Sqdn RAF, 458 Sqdn RAAF, 1942–44; Air Min., 1945–50; RAF Coll. Cranwell, 1952–54; psa 1955; Exchange USAF, Washington, DC, 1956–58; RAF Staff Coll., Bracknell, 1959–61; Admin. Staff Coll., Henley, 1962; PSO to Chief of Air Staff, 1962–64; NATO Defence Coll., 1965; Adjutant General, HQ Allied Forces Central Europe, 1965–68; Dir of Personnel, MoD, 1968–69; idc 1970; Dep. AO i/c Admin, HQ Maintenance Comd, 1971; AOA Training Comd, 1972–75. Chm., Huntingdon DHA, 1981–92. MA Cantab, 1975. FIMgt (FBIM 1979; MBIM 1971). *Publications:* various articles. *Address:* Gonville and Caius College, Cambridge CB2 1TA. *Club:* Royal Air Force.

BULLER; *see* Manningham-Buller, family name of Viscount Dilhorne.

BULLER; *see* Yarde-Buller, family name of Baron Churston.

BULLER, Prof. Arthur John, ERD 1969; FRCP; Emeritus Professor of Physiology, University of Bristol, since 1982; *b* 16 Oct. 1923; *s* of Thomas Alfred Buller, MBE, and Edith May Buller (*née* Wager); *m* 1946, Helena Joan (*née* Pearson); one *s* one *d* (and one *d* decd). *Educ:* Duke of York's Royal Military Sch., Dover; St Thomas's Hosp. Med. Sch. (MB, BS); BSc; PhD 1992; FRCP 1976; FIBiol 1978; FRSA 1979. Kitchener Scholar, 1941–45; Lectr in Physiology, St Thomas' Hosp., 1946–49. Major, RAMC (Specialist in Physiology; Jt Sec., Military Personnel Research Cttee), 1949–53. Lectr in Medicine, St Thomas' Hosp., 1953–57. Royal Society Commonwealth Fellow, Canberra, Aust., 1958–59. Reader in Physiology, King's Coll., London, 1961–65; Gresham Prof. of Physic 1963–65; Prof. of Physiology, Univ. of Bristol, 1965–82, Dean, Fac. of Medicine, 1976–78, on secondment as Chief Scientist, DHSS, 1978–81. Res. Devel. Dir, subseq. Dir of Res. and Support Services, Muscular Dystrophy Gp of GB, 1982–90. Hon. Consultant in Clinical Physiology, Bristol Dist Hosp. (T), 1970–82. Vis. Scholar, UCLA, 1966; Visiting Prof., Monash Univ., Aust., 1972. Lectures: Long Fox Meml, Bristol, 1978; Milroy, RCP, 1983; Haig Gudenian Meml, Muscular Dystrophy Gp, 1993. Member: Bd of Governors, Bristol Royal Infirmary, 1968–74; Avon Health Authority (T), 1974–78; MRC, 1975–81; BBC, IBA Central Appeals Adv. Cttee, 1983–88; Neurosciences and Mental Health Bd, MRC, 1973–77 (Chm., 1975–77); Chm., DHSS Working Party on Clinical Accountability, Service Planning and Evaluation, 1981–86; Trustee, Health Promotion Res. Trust, 1983–90. External Scientific Advisor, Rayne Inst., St Thomas' Hosp., 1979–85. *Publications:* contribs to books and various jls on normal and disordered physiology. *Recreations:* clarets and conversation. *Address:* Lockhall Cottage, Cow Lane, Steeple Aston, Bicester, Oxon OX6 3SG. *T:* Steeple Aston (01869) 347502.

BULLERS, Ronald Alfred, CBE 1988; QFSM 1974; FIFireE, FIMgt; consultant fire prevention engineer; Chief Executive Officer, London Fire and Civil Defence Authority, 1986–87; *b* 17 March 1931; *m* 1954, Mary M. Bullers. *Educ:* Queen Mary's Grammar Sch., Walsall. Deputy Asst Chief Officer, Lancashire Fire Brigade, 1971; Dep. Chief Officer, Greater Manchester Fire Brigade, 1974, Chief Officer, 1977; Chief Officer, London Fire Bde, 1981–86. Adviser: Nat. Jt Council for Local Authority Fire Brigades, 1977–; Assoc. of Metropolitan Authorities, 1977–. OStJ. *Recreations:* gardening, travel. *Address:* 31 Pavillion Close, Aldridge, Walsall WA9 8LS.

BULLIMORE, John Wallace MacGregor; His Honour Judge Bullimore; a Circuit Judge, since 1991; *b* 4 Dec. 1945; *s* of late James Wallace Bullimore and of Phyllis Violet Emily Bullimore (*née* Brandt); *m* 1975, Christine Elizabeth Kinch; two *s* (one *d* decd). *Educ:* Queen Elizabeth Grammar School, Wakefield; Univ. of Bristol (LLB). Called to the Bar, Inner Temple, 1968; Chancellor, Diocese of Derby, 1980, of Blackburn, 1990. Mem., Gen. Synod of the Church of England, 1970–. *Address:* c/o North Eastern Circuit Administrator, West Riding House, Albion Street, Leeds LS1 5AA.

BULLMORE, (John) Jeremy David, CBE 1985; Chairman, J. Walter Thompson Co. Ltd, 1976–87; Director: The Guardian Media Group plc (formerly The Guardian and Manchester Evening News plc), since 1988; WPP Group plc, since 1988; *b* 21 Nov. 1929; *s* of Francis Edward Bullmore and Adeline Gabrielle Bullmore (*née* Roscow); *m* 1958, Pamela Audrey Green; two *s* one *d*. *Educ:* Harrow; Christ Church, Oxford. Military service, 1949–50. Joined J. Walter Thompson Co. Ltd, 1954: Dir, 1964; Dep. Chm., 1975; Dir, J. Walter Thompson Co. (USA), 1980–87. Mem., Nat. Cttee for Electoral Reform, 1978–. Chm., Advertising Assoc., 1981–87. *Publication:* Behind the Scenes in Advertising, 1991. *Address:* 17/20 Embankment Gardens, SW3 4LW. *T:* 0171–351 2197. *Club:* Arts.

BULLOCK, family name of **Baron Bullock.**

BULLOCK, Baron *cr* 1976 (Life Peer), of Leafield, Oxon; **Alan Louis Charles Bullock,** Kt 1972; FBA 1967; Founding Master, 1960, and Hon. Fellow, since 1980, St Catherine's College, Oxford (Master, 1960–80); Vice-Chancellor, Oxford University, 1969–73; *b* 13 Dec. 1914; *s* of Frank Allen Bullock; *m* 1940, Hilda Yates, *d* of Edwin Handy, Bradford; three *s* one *d* (and one *d* decd). *Educ:* Bradford Grammar Sch.; Wadham Coll., Oxford (Scholar). MA; 1st Class Lit Hum, 1936; 1st Class, Modern Hist., 1938. DLitt Oxon, 1969. Fellow, Dean and Tutor in Modern Hist., New Coll., 1945–52; Censor of St Catherine's Soc., Oxford, 1952–62; Chairman: Research Cttee of RIIA, 1954–78; Nat. Advisory Council on the Training and Supply of Teachers, 1963–65; Schools Council, 1966–69; Cttee on Reading and Other Uses of English Language, 1972–74 (Report, A Language for Life, published 1975); Trustees, Tate Gallery, 1973–80; Friends of Ashmolean Museum; Cttee of Enquiry on Industrial Democracy, 1976 (Report publ. 1977); Member: Arts Council of Great Britain, 1961–64; SSRC, 1966; Adv. Council on Public Records, 1965–77; Organising Cttee for the British Library, 1971–72. Joined Social Democratic Party, 1981. Sen. Fellow, Aspen Inst., USA; Trustee: Aspen Inst., Berlin; The Observer, 1957–69; Dir, The Observer, 1977–81. Raleigh Lectr, British Acad., 1967; Stevenson Meml Lectr, LSE, 1970; Leslie Stephen Lectr, Cambridge, 1976. Hon. Fellow: Merton Coll.; Wadham Coll.; Linacre Coll.; Wolfson Coll; New Coll. For. Mem., Amer. Acad. Arts and Sciences, 1972; Mem., Academia Europaea, 1990. Hon. Dr Univ. Aix-Marseilles; Hon. DLitt: Bradford; Reading; Newfoundland; Leicester; Sussex; Warwick; Essex; DUniv Open. Hon. FRIBA. Chevalier Légion d'Honneur, 1970. *Publications:* Hitler, A Study in Tyranny, 1952, rev. edn 1964; The Liberal Tradition, 1956; The Life and Times of Ernest Bevin, Vol. I, 1960, Vol. II, 1967, Vol III (Ernest Bevin, Foreign Secretary), 1983; (ed) The Twentieth Century, 1971; (ed with Oliver Stallybrass) Dictionary of Modern Thought, 1977, new edn (with S. Trombley), 1988; (ed) The Faces of Europe, 1980; (ed with B. R. Woodings) Fontana Dictionary of Modern Thinkers, 1983; The Humanist Tradition in the West, 1985; Hitler and Stalin: Parallel Lives, 1991, rev. edn 1993; Gen. Editor (with Sir William Deakin) of The Oxford History of Modern Europe. *Address:* St Catherine's College, Oxford OX1 3UJ; Gable End, 30 Godstow Road, Oxford OX2 8AJ. *T:* Oxford (01865) 513380.

BULLOCK, Edward Anthony Watson; HM Diplomatic Service, retired; *b* 27 Aug. 1926; *yr s* of late Sir Christopher Bullock, KCB, CBE, and late Lady Bullock (*née* Barbara May Lupton); *m* 1953, Jenifer Myrtle, *er d* of late Sir Richmond Palmer, KCMG, and late Lady Palmer (*née* Margaret Isabel Abel Smith); two *s* one *d*. *Educ:* Rugby Sch. (Scholar; Running VIII); Trinity Coll., Cambridge (Exhibitioner; MA). Chm., Cambridge Univ. Cons. Assoc. Served The Life Guards, 1944–47. Joined Foreign Service, 1950; served: FO, 1950–52; Bucharest, 1952–54; Brussels, 1955–58; FO, 1958–61; La Paz, 1961–65; ODM, 1965–67; FCO, 1967–69; Havana, 1969–72; HM Treasury, 1972–74; Head of Pacific Dependent Territories Dept, FCO, 1974–77; Consul-Gen., Marseilles, 1978–83; Counsellor, FCO, 1983–85. *Recreations:* walking, gardening, tree-planting, reading, charity work. *Address:* c/o National Westminster Bank, 36 St James's Street, SW1A 1JF. *Clubs:* United Oxford & Cambridge University; Union (Cambridge).

See also R. H. W. Bullock.

BULLOCK, Hugh, Hon. GBE 1976 (Hon. KBE 1957; Hon. OBE 1946); FRSA 1958; President, Pilgrims of the United States, since 1955; Chairman and Chief Executive Officer, Calvin Bullock Ltd; retired 1984; Head of Bullock Investment Advisory Co., since 1984; *b* 2 June 1898; *s* of Calvin Bullock and Alice Katherine (*née* Mallory); *m* 1933, Marie Leontine Graves (*d* 1986); two *d*. *Educ:* Hotchkiss Sch.; Williams Coll. (BA). Investment banker since 1921; President and Director: Calvin Bullock, Ltd, 1944–66; Bullock Fund, Ltd; Canadian Fund, Inc.; Canadian Investment Fund, Ltd; Dividend Shares, Inc.; Chairman and Director: Carriers & General Corp.; Nation-Wide Securities Co.; US Electric Light & Power Shares, Inc.; High Income Shares Inc.; Money Shares Inc.; Pres., Calvin Bullock Forum. Civilian Aide to Sec. of the Army, for First Army Area, United States, 1952–53 (US Army Certificate of Appreciation). Trustee: Roosevelt Hospital, 1949–69; Estate and Property of Diocesan Convention of New York; Williams Coll., 1960–68. Member Exec. Cttee, Marshall Scholarship Regional Cttee, 1955–58. Member: Amer. Legion; Academy of Political Science; Amer. Museum of Nat. History; Acad. of Amer. Poets (Dir.); Assoc. Ex-mems Squadron A (Gov. 1945–50); Council on Foreign Relations; Ends of the Earth; English-Speaking Union; Foreign Policy Assoc.; Investment Bankers Assoc. of Amer. (Gov. 1953–55); New England Soc.; Nat. Inst. of Social Sciences (Pres. 1950–53; Gold Medal, 1985); Newcomen Soc.; St George's Soc.; France America Assoc. Benjamin Franklyn Fellow, RSA. Hon. LLD; Hamilton Coll., 1954; Williams Coll., 1957. 2nd Lieut Infantry, European War, 1914–18; Lieut-Col, War of 1939–45 (US Army Commendation Ribbon). Distinguished Citizens' Award, Denver, 1958; Exceptional Service Award, Dept of Air Force, 1961; US Navy Distinguished Public Service Award, 1972. Assoc. KStJ 1961, and Vice-Pres. Amer. Society. Knight Comdr, Royal Order of George I (Greece), 1964. Is an Episcopalian. *Publication:* The Story of Investment Companies, 1959. *Address:* (office) 40th Floor, 1 Wall Street, New York, NY 10005, USA. *T:* (212) 8091920, (home) 1030 Fifth Avenue, New York, NY 10028. *T:* (212) 8795858. *Clubs:* White's (London); Bond (former Gov.), Century, Racquet and Tennis, Down Town Association, River, Union, Williams, Church, New York Yacht (New York); Denver County (Denver); Chevy Chase, Metropolitan (Washington); Edgartown Yacht (Cdre), Edgartown Reading Room (MA); West Side Tennis (Forest Hills, NY); Mount Royal (Montreal).

BULLOCK, John; Director: Kingfisher, since 1993; Nuclear Electric, since 1993; Brightreasons, since 1993; Joint Senior Partner and Deputy Chairman, Coopers & Lybrand (formerly Coopers & Lybrand Deloitte), 1989–92; Chairman, Coopers & Lybrand Europe, 1989–92; *b* 12 July 1933; *s* of Robert and Doris Bullock; *m* 1960, Ruth Jennifer (*née* Bullock); two *s* (and one *s* decd). *Educ:* Latymer Upper School. FCA; FCMA; FIMC. Smallfield Fitzhugh Tillet & Co., 1949–56 and 1958–61; RAF Commission, 1956–58; Robson Morrow, 1961, Partner, 1965–70; Robson Morrow merged with Deloitte Haskins & Sells; Partner in charge, Deloitte Haskins & Sells Management Consultants, 1971–79; Deloitte Haskins & Sells: Managing Partner, 1979–85; Dep. Senior Partner, 1984–85; Sen. Partner, 1985–90; Vice Chm., Deloitte Haskins & Sells Internat., 1985–89, Chm., Deloitte Europe, 1985–89. Mem., UKAEA, 1981–. Mem., Co. of Chartered Accountants' of England and Wales, 1989–. *Recreations:* ski-ing, opera, ballet. *Address:* Braddocks, Oak Avenue, Sevenoaks, Kent TN13 1PR.

BULLOCK, Richard Henry Watson, CB 1971; Consultant, Faulkbourn Consultancy Services; Director, Grosvenor Place Amalgamations Ltd; Director-General, Electronic Components Industry Federation, 1984–90 (Consultant Director, 1981–84); retired Civil Servant; *b* 12 Nov. 1920; *er s* of late Sir Christopher Bullock, KCB, CBE and late Lady Bullock (*née* Barbara May Lupton); *m* 1946, Beryl Haddan, *o d* of late Haddan J. Markes, formerly Malay Civil Service; one *s* one *d*. *Educ:* Rugby Sch. (Scholar); Trinity Coll., Cambridge (Scholar). Joined 102 OCTU (Westminster Dragoons), Nov. 1940; Commnd Westminster Dragoons (2nd County of London Yeo.), 1941; served in England, NW Europe (D-day), Italy, Germany, 1941–45; Instructor, Armoured Corps Officers' Training Sch., India, 1945–46; demobilized 1947, rank of Major. Established in Home Civil Service by Reconstruction Competition; joined Min. of Supply as Asst Principal, 1947; Principal, 1949; Asst Sec., 1956; on loan to War Office, 1960–61; Ministry of Aviation, 1961–64; Under-Sec., 1963; Min. of Technology, 1964–70, Head of Space Div., 1969–70, Dep.

Sec., 1970; DTI, 1970–74; Dept of Industry, 1974–80; retired Nov. 1980. Mem., BOTB, 1975–78. Dir, Berkeley Seventh Round Ltd, 1981–87. Vice-Pres. (and Chm. 1978–82), Westminster Dragoons Assoc.; Pres., Old Rugbeian Soc., 1984–86; Dir, Rugby Sch. Develt Campaign, 1981–86. *Recreations:* fly-fishing, hockey (President: Dulwich Hockey Club, 1962–91; Rugby Alternatives HC, 1976–; Civil Service Hockey Cttee/Assoc., 1978–84), lawn tennis, watching cricket. *Address:* 12 Peterborough Villas, SW6 2AT. *T:* 0171–736 5132. *Clubs:* MCC, Hurlingham; Union (Cambridge).

See also E. A. W. Bullock.

BULLOCK, Stephen Michael; Director, Civic Skills Consultancy, since 1994; *b* 26 June 1953; *s* of Fred George Bullock and Florence (*née* Gott); *m* 1992, Kristyne Margaret Hibbert. *Educ:* Sir William Turner's Sch., Redcar; Leeds Univ. (BA Hons); Goldsmiths' Coll. (PGCE). Greater London Council: Admin. Officer, 1977–79; Dep. Hd, Labour Gp Office, 1979–83; Asst Dir, Public Relns, 1983–86; Chief Officer, Greenwich CHC, 1986–90. London Borough of Lewisham: Councillor (Lab), 1982–; Leader of Council, 1988–93. Chm., ALA, 1992–93; Dep. Chm., AMA, 1992–94. Board Member: London Pension Fund Authy, 1989–; London First, 1993–; Chm., Deptford City Challenge Ltd, 1992–93; Vice-Chm., Local Govt Management Bd, 1994– (Chm., 1992–93); Non-Exec. Dir, Lewisham NHS Trust, 1993–; Mem., Commn for Local Democracy, 1994–. *Publications:* (contrib.) A Transatlantic Policy Exchange, 1993; contrib. Local Govt Chronicle, Municipal Jl. *Recreations:* inland waterways, waiting for Middlesbrough FC to get to the FA Cup Final, buying ties, seeking the "Moon under Water". *Address:* Garden Flat, 9 Tyson Road, Forest Hill, SE23 3AA. *T:* 0181–291 4484.

BULLOUGH, Prof. Donald Auberon, FSA, FRHistS; Professor of Mediaeval History, University of St Andrews, 1973–91, now Emeritus; *b* 13 June 1928; *s* of late William Bullough and of Edith Shirley (*née* Norman); *m* 1963, Belinda Jane Turland (marr. diss.); two *d*; *m* 1995, Dr Alice Harting-Correa. *Educ:* Newcastle-under-Lyme High Sch.; St John's Coll., Oxford (BA 1950, MA 1952). FRHistS 1958; FSA 1968; FRPSL 1993. National Service, 1946–48: commnd RA (attached RHA). Harmsworth Scholar, Merton Coll., Oxford, 1951; Medieval Scholar, British Sch. at Rome, 1951; Fereday Fellow, St John's Coll., Oxford, 1952–55; Lectr, Univ. of Edinburgh, 1955–66; Prof. of Med. History, Univ. of Nottingham, 1966–73; Dean, Faculty of Arts, Univ. of St Andrews, 1984–88. Vis. Prof., Southern Methodist Univ., Dallas, Tex, 1965–66; British Acad. Overseas Vis. Fellow, Max-Planck-Inst. für Gesch., 1972–73; Lilly Endowment Fellow, Pennsylvania Univ., 1980–81; Vis. Prof., Rutgers Univ., NJ, 1991–92, 1993–94; IAS, Princeton, 1994–95. Lectures: Ford's, in English Hist., Univ. of Oxford, 1979–80; Scott-Hawkins, Southern Methodist Univ., Dallas, 1980; Andrew Mellon, Catholic Univ., Washington, 1980; Raleigh, British Acad., 1985; (Inaugural) Hector Munro Chadwick, Univ. of Cambridge, 1990. Corresponding Fellow, Monumenta Germaniae Historica, 1983–. Mem. Council, Exec., Finance Cttee, British School at Rome, 1975–95 (Chm., Faculty of Hist., Archeol., and Letters, 1975–79, Acting Dir, 1984). Mem., Nottingham Univ. Hosp. Management Cttee, 1971–74. Dir, Paul Elek Ltd, 1968–79. Major RA (TA); seconded OTC, 1957–67. *Publications:* The Age of Charlemagne, 1965 (2nd edn 1974; also foreign trans); Alcuin: achievement and reputation, 1966; (ed with R. L. Storey) The Study of Medieval Records, 1971; Carolingian Renewal: sources and heritage, 1991; contrib. Settimane di Studi del Centro ital. di St. sull'Alto Medioevo, TLS, British and continental hist. jls, philatelic jls. *Recreations:* talk, looking at buildings, postal history, cooking. *Address:* 14 Queens Gardens, St Andrews, Fife KY16 9TA. *Club:* Athenæum.

BULLOUGH, Dr Ronald, FRS 1985; consultant in UK and USA; Chief Scientist, UK Atomic Energy Authority, 1988–93, and Director for Corporate Research, Harwell, 1990–93; *b* 6 April 1931; *s* of Ronald Bullough and Edna Bullough (*née* Morrow); *m* 1954, Ruth Corbett; four *s*. *Educ:* Univ. of Sheffield. BSc, PhD, DSc. FIM 1964; FInstP 1962. Res. Scientist, AEI Fundamental Res. Lab., Aldermaston Court, Aldermaston, 1956–63; Theoretical Physicist and Group Leader, Harwell Res. Lab., Didcot, Berks, 1963–84; Hd, Materials Develt Div., Harwell, 1984–88; Dir for Underlying Res., Harwell, 1988–90. Visiting Professor: Univ. of Illinois, USA, 1964, 1973, 1979; Univ. of Wisconsin, USA, 1978; Rensselaer Polytechnical Inst., USA, 1968; Visiting Scientist: Nat. Bureau of Standards, USA, 1965; Oak Ridge Nat. Lab., USA, 1969, 1979; Comisión Nacional de Energía Atómica, Buenos Aires, Argentina, 1977. Hon. Citizen of Tennessee, 1967. *Publications:* articles in learned jls such as Proc. Roy. Soc., Phil. Mag., Jl of Nucl. Materials etc., on defect properties in crystalline solids, particularly in relation to the irradiation and mechanical response of materials. *Recreations:* walking, reading, music. *Address:* 4 Long Meadow, Manor Road, Goring-on-Thames, Reading, Berkshire RG8 9EQ. *T:* Goring (01491) 873266.

BULLOUGH, Prof. William Sydney, PhD, DSc Leeds; Professor of Zoology, Birkbeck College, University of London, 1952–81, now Emeritus; *b* 6 April 1914; *o s* of Rev. Frederick Sydney Bullough and Letitia Anne Cooper, both of Leeds; *m* 1942, Dr Helena F. Gibbs (*d* 1975), Wellington, NZ; one *s* one *d*. *Educ:* William Hulme Grammar Sch., Manchester; Grammar Sch., Leeds; Univ. of Leeds. Lecturer in Zoology, Univ. of Leeds, 1937–44, McGill Univ., Montreal, 1944–46; Sorby Fellow of Royal Society of London, 1946–51; Research Fellow of British Empire Cancer Campaign, 1951–52; Hon. Fellow: Soc. for Investigative Dermatology (US); AAAS, 1981. Vice-Pres., Zoological Soc., 1983–84. *Publications:* Practical Invertebrate Anatomy, 1950; Vertebrate Sexual Cycles, 1951; (for children) Introducing Animals, 1953; Introducing Animals-with-Backbones, 1954; Introducing Man, 1958; The Evolution of Differentiation, 1967; The Dynamic Body Tissues, 1983; scientific papers on vertebrate reproductive cycles, hormones, and chalones published in a variety of journals. *Recreation:* gardening. *Address:* 75 Hillfield Court, Belsize Avenue, NW3 4BG. *T:* 0171–435 4558.

BULLUS, Wing Comdr Sir Eric (Edward), Kt 1964; journalist; *b* 20 Nov. 1906; 2nd *s* of Thomas Bullus, Leeds; *m* 1949, Joan Evelyn, *er d* of H. M. Denny; two *d*. *Educ:* Leeds Modern Sch.; Univ. of Leeds. Commnd RAFVR Aug. 1940; served War of 1939–45; Air Min. War Room, 1940–43; joined Lord Louis Mountbatten's staff in SE Asia, 1943; Wing Comdr, 1944; served India, Burma and Ceylon; demobilized, 1945. Journalist Yorkshire Post, Leeds and London, 1923–46. Mem. Leeds City Council, 1930–40; Sec., London Municipal Soc., 1947–50; Mem., Harrow UDC, 1947–50; Vice-Pres. Assoc. of Municipal Corps, 1953. MP (C) Wembley N, 1950–Feb. 1974; PPS to Secretary for Overseas Trade, and to Minister of State, 1953–56, to Minister of Aviation, 1960–62, to Secretary of State for Defence, 1962–64. FRGS, 1947; Fellow Royal Statistical Society, 1949. Foundation Mem. of Brotherton Collection Cttee of Univ. of Leeds, 1935; Member: Archdeaconry Council of Delhi, 1944; Management Board, Cambridge Mission to Delhi, 1954; House of Laity, Church Assembly, 1960. Ripon Diocesan Reader, 1929; London Diocesan Reader, 1947; St Alban's Diocesan Reader, 1960; Canterbury Diocesan Reader, 1967; Central Readers' Board, 1960; London Readers' Board, 1954; Council Westfield Coll., Univ. of London. Pres., Soc. of Yorkshiremen in London, 1969–70. *Publications:* History of Leeds Modern School, 1931; History of Church in Delhi, 1944; History of Lords and Commons Cricket, 1959. *Recreations:* played Headingley RU Football Club 15 years and Yorkshire Amateurs Assoc. Football Club; cricket and swimming (bronze and silver medallions). *Address:* Westway, Herne Bay, Kent CT6 8RL. *Clubs:* St Stephen's Constitutional, MCC.

BULMER, Esmond; *see* Bulmer, J. E.

BULMER, Dr Gerald; Rector of Liverpool Polytechnic, 1970–85 (sabbatical leave, 1984–85), retired; *b* 17 Nov. 1920; *s* of Edward and Alice Bulmer; *m* 1943, Greta Lucy Parkes, MA; two *d*. *Educ:* Nunthorpe Sch., York; Selwyn Coll., Cambridge. BA 1941; PhD 1944; MA 1945. Asst Master, King's Sch., Canterbury, 1945–49; Sen. Lecturer, Woolwich Polytechnic, 1949–53; Head of Dept of Science and Metallurgy, Constantine Technical Coll., Middlesbrough, 1954–57; Vice-Principal, Bolton Technical Coll., 1958–59; Principal, West Ham Coll. of Technology, 1959–64; Dir, Robert Gordon's Inst. of Technology, Aberdeen, 1965–70. Mem. Council CNAA, 1967–78. Freeman City of York, 1952. Hon. DSc CNAA, 1986. *Publications:* papers on organic sulphur compounds in Jl Chem. Soc. and Nature. *Address:* 11 Capilano Park, Winifred Lane, Aughton, Ormskirk, Lancs L39 5HA.

BULMER, (James) Esmond; Chairman, H. P. Bulmer Holdings plc, since 1982 (Director, since 1962, Deputy Chairman, 1980); *b* 19 May 1935; *e s* of late Edward Bulmer and Margaret Rye; *m* 1st, 1959, Morella Kearton; three *s* one *d*; 2nd, 1990, Susan Elizabeth Bower (*née* Murray). *Educ:* Rugby; King's Coll., Cambridge (BA); and abroad. Commissioned Scots Guards, 1954. Dir (non-exec.), Wales and W Midlands Regional Bd, National Westminster Bank PLC, 1982–92. Chm., Hereford DHA, 1987–94. MP (C): Kidderminster, Feb. 1974–1983; Wyre Forest, 1983–87. PPS to Minister of State, Home Office, 1979–81. Mem. Exec. Cttee, Nat. Trust, 1977–87. *Recreations:* gardening, fishing. *Club:* Boodle's.

BULMER-THOMAS, Prof. Victor Gerald, DPhil; Director, Institute of Latin American Studies, since 1992 and Professor of Economics, Queen Mary and Westfield College, since 1990, London University; *b* 23 March 1948; *s* of late Ivor Bulmer-Thomas, CBE and of Margaret Joan Bulmer-Thomas; *m* 1970, Barbara Ann Swasey; two *s* one *d*. *Educ:* Westminster Sch.; New Coll., Oxford (MA); St Antony's Coll., Oxford (DPhil). Research Fellow, Fraser of Allander Inst., Strathclyde Univ., 1975–78; Queen Mary College, London University: Lectr in Econs, 1978–87; Reader in Econs of Latin America, 1987–90. Dir, Latin America New Growth Fund, 1994–. Editor, Jl of Latin American Studies, 1986–. *Publications:* Input-Output Analysis for Developing Countries, 1982; The Political Economy of Central America since 1920, 1987; Studies in the Economics of Central America, 1988; (ed) Britain and Latin America, 1989; (jtly) Central American Integration, 1992; (ed jtly) Mexico and the North American Free Trade Agreement: Who Will Benefit?, 1994; The Economic History of Latin America since Independence, 1994; (jtly) Growth and Development in Brazil: Cordoso's real challenge, 1995. *Recreations:* tennis, hill-walking, canoeing, music (viola), underwater photography. *Address:* 55 Maze Hill, SE10 8XQ. *T:* 0181–858 5879. *Club:* Athenæum.

BULPITT, Cecil Arthur Charles, (Philip Bulpitt); Director, BIM Foundation Ltd, 1977–84 (Chairman, 1979–82); *b* 6 Feb. 1919; *s* of A. E. Bulpitt; *m* 1943, Joyce Mary Bloomfield; one *s* one *d*. *Educ:* Spring Grove Sch., London; Regent Street Polytechnic. Territorial Army, to rank of Staff Capt., RA, 1937–45. Carreras Ltd: joined firm, 1935; Gen. Manager, 1960; Asst Managing Dir, 1962; Dep. Chm. and Chief Exec., 1968; Chm. 1969–70. Dir, Thomas Tilling, 1973–81; Chairman: Tilling Construction Services Ltd, 1978–81; InterMed Ltd, 1978–81; Graham Building Services Ltd, 1979–81; Newey & Eyre Gp Ltd, 1979–81. Member: London Reg. Council, CBI, 1978–81; BBC Consultative Gp on Industrial and Business Affairs, 1980–84. MIPM 1955; CIMgt (FBIM 1963; Vice-Chm. Council, and Dir, Bd of Companions, BIM, 1979–83). Freeman, City of London, 1969. *Publication:* The Chief Executive, 1971. *Recreations:* golf, swimming, reading, travelling. *Address:* La Casa Tranquila, 35C, Calle 6D, Nueva Andalucia 29660, Málaga, Spain. *T:* (52) 811180. *Clubs:* El Madronal Country, Las Brisas Golf (Nueva Andalucia, Spain).

BULTEEL, Christopher Harris, MC 1943; Director, GAP Activity Projects (GAP) Ltd, 1982–88; *b* 29 July 1921; *er s* of late Major Walter Bulteel and Constance (*née* Gaunt), Charlestown, Cornwall; *m* 1958, Jennifer Anne, *d* of late Col K. E. Previté, OBE and of Frances (*née* Capper), Hindgaston, Marnhull, Dorset; one *s* two *d*. *Educ:* Wellington Coll.; Merton Coll., Oxford. Served War with Coldstream Guards, 1940–46 (MC). Assistant Master at Wellington Coll., 1949–61; Head of history dept, 1959–61; Hon. Sec., Wellington Coll. Mission, 1959–61; Headmaster, Ardingly Coll., 1962–80. *Recreations:* natural history, sailing. *Address:* 3 Coastguard Cottages, Mevagissey, St Austell, Cornwall PL26 6QP. *T:* St Austell (01726) 843928; Street Farm Cottage, Park Street, Charlton, near Malmesbury, Wilts SN16 9DF. *T:* Tetbury (01666) 823764.

BUMBRY, Grace; opera singer and concert singer; *b* St Louis, Mo, 4 Jan. 1937. *Educ:* Boston Univ.; Northwestern Univ.; Music Academy of the West (under Lotte Lehmann). Debut: Paris Opera, 1960; Vienna State Opera, 1963; Salzburg Festival, 1964; Metropolitan Opera, 1965; La Scala, 1964. Appearances also include: Bayreuth Festival, 1961–; Royal Opera Covent Garden, London, 1963–, and in opera houses in Europe, S America and USA. Film, Carmen, 1968. Richard Wagner Medal, 1963. Hon. Dr of Humanities, St Louis Univ., 1968; Hon. doctorates: Rust Coll., Holly Spring, Miss; Rockhurst Coll., Kansas City; Univ. of Missouri at St Louis. Has made numerous recordings. *Recreations:* psychology, entertaining. *Address:* Secretariat Grace Bumbry, Via Ceresio 9, 6926 Montagnola, Switzerland.

BUNBURY; *see* McClintock-Bunbury, family name of Baron Rathdonnell.

BUNBURY, Bishop of, since 1984; **Rt. Rev. Hamish Thomas Umphelby Jamieson;** *b* 15 Feb. 1932; *s* of Robert Marshall Jamieson and Constance Marzetti Jamieson (*née* Umphelby); *m* 1962, Ellice Anne McPherson; one *s* two *d*. *Educ:* Sydney C of E Grammar Sch.; St Michael's House, Crafers (ThL); Univ. of New England (BA). Deacon 1955; Priest 1956. Mem. Bush Brotherhood of Good Shepherd, 1955–62. Parish of Gilgandra, 1957; Priest-in-Charge, Katherine, NT, 1957–62; Rector, Darwin, 1962–67; Canon of All Souls Cathedral, Thursday Island, 1963–67; Royal Australian Navy Chaplain, 1967–74; HMAS Sydney, 1967–68; HMAS Albatross, 1969–71; Small Ships Chaplain, 1972; HMAS Cerberus, 1972–74; Bishop of Carpentaria, 1974–84. *Recreations:* reading, music, gardening. *Address:* Bishopscourt, PO Box 15, Bunbury, WA 6231, Australia.

BUNBURY, Sir Michael; *see* Bunbury, Sir R. D. M. R.

BUNBURY, Sir Michael (William), 13th Bt *cr* 1681, of Stanney Hall, Cheshire; Partner, Smith & Williamson; *b* 29 Dec. 1946; *s* of Sir John William Napier Bunbury, 12th Bt, and of Pamela, *er d* of late Thomas Alexander Sutton; *S* father, 1985; *m* 1976, Caroline Anne, *d* of Col A. D. S. Mangnall, OBE; two *s* one *d*. *Educ:* Eton; Trinity College, Cambridge (MA). *Heir:* *s* Henry Michael Napier Bunbury, *b* 4 March 1980. *Address:* Naunton Hall, Rendlesham, Woodbridge, Suffolk IP12 2RD. *T:* Eyke (01394) 460235. *Club:* Boodle's.

BUNBURY, Lt-Comdr Sir (Richard David) Michael (Richardson-), 5th Bt, *cr* 1787; RN; *b* 27 Oct. 1927; *er s* of Richard Richardson-Bunbury (*d* 1951) and Florence Margaret Gordon (*d* 1993), *d* of late Col Roger Gordon Thomson, CMG, DSO, late RA; *S* kinsman 1953; *m* 1961, Jane Louise, *d* of late Col Alfred William Pulverman, IA; one *s* (and one *s* decd). *Educ:* Royal Naval College, Dartmouth. Midshipman (S), 1945; Sub-

Lieut (S), 1947; Lieut (S), 1948; Lieut-Comdr, 1956; retd 1967. Dir, Sandy Laird Ltd, 1988–. Pres., HMS Sussex Assoc., 1991–. *Heir:* *s* Thomas William Richardson-Bunbury, *b* 4 Aug. 1965. *Address:* Upper House, Crowcombe, Somerset TA4 4AG. *T:* Watchet (01984) 618223.

BUNCE, Michael John; Executive Director, Royal Television Society, since 1991; *b* 24 April 1935; *er s* of late Roland John Bunce, ARIBA, and Dorrie Bunce (*née* Woods); *m* 1961, Tina Sims; two *s* two *d. Educ:* St Paul's Sch; Kingston Coll. Nat. Service, RAF. Joined BBC as engineer; subseq. Studio Manager; Producer, People and Politics (World Service); Dir, Gallery; Producer: A Man Apart—The Murderer, 1965; Minorities in Britain; The Younger Generation; Italy and the Italians; Editor: The Money Programme, 1968–70; Nationwide, 1970–75; Chief Asst, TV Current Affairs and Editor, Tonight, 1975–78; Head: Information Services TV, 1978–82; Information Div., 1982–83; Controller, Information Services, 1983–91. Member: Francis Cttee, 1977; EBU Working Party on Direct Elections, 1978; Adv. Bd, Univ. of Salford Media Centre, 1992–; Comité d'Honneur, Internat. Television Symposium and Technical Exhibn, Montreux; Chm., Nat. Industries PR Officers Group, 1991–92. Marshall Fund Vis. Fellow, USA, 1975; Vis. Editor in Residence, Univ. of Alabama, 1987–92. FRTS 1989. Shell Internat. Television Award, 1969. *Recreations:* gardening, visiting fine buildings, fishing. *Address:* Royal Television Society, Holborn Hall, 100 Gray's Inn Road, WC1X 8AL. *Club:* Groucho.

BUNCE, Very Rev. Michael John, FSAScot; Provost of St Paul's Cathedral, Dundee, since 1992; *b* 5 Dec. 1949; *s* of Harold Christopher and Kathleen June Bunce; *m* 1973, Frances Sutherland; one *s* one *d. Educ:* St Andrew's Univ. (MTh); Westcott House and Trinity Hall, Cambridge; Greenwich Univ. (PhD). Glazing clerk, Middleton Glass Merchant, 1965–69; Personnel Labour Controller, Bird's Eye Unilever, 1969–75. Ordained: deacon, 1980; priest, 1981; Curate, 1980–83, Hosp. Chaplain and Team Vicar, 1983–85, Grantham Parish Church; Rector, St Andrew's, Brechin with St Drostan's, Tarfside and St Peter's, Auchmithie (Angus), 1985–92. FRSA. *Recreations:* tennis, ski-ing, art, antiques. *Address:* St Paul's Cathedral Rectory, 4 Richmond Terrace, Dundee DD2 1BQ. *T:* Dundee (01382) 68548. *Club:* Edinburgh Angus.

BUNCH, Sir Austin (Wyeth), Kt 1983; CBE 1978 (MBE 1974); Vice-Patron, British Limbless Ex-Servicemen's Association, 1992 (National President, 1983–92); *b* 1918; *s* of Horace William and Winifred Ada Bunch; *m* 1944, Joan Mary Peryer; four *d. Educ:* Christ's Hospital. FCA. CompIEE. Deloitte, Plender, Griffiths, 1935–48; Southern Electricity Board, 1949–76: Area Man., Newbury, 1962; Area Man., Portsmouth, 1966; Dep. Chm., 1967; Chm., 1974; Dep. Chm., Electricity Council, 1976–81, Chm., 1981–83; Chm., British Electricity Internat. Ltd, 1977–83; retd. Chm., Queen Mary's Roehampton Hosp. Trust, 1983–89. *Recreation:* sports for the disabled. *Address:* Sumner, School Lane, Cookham, Berks SL6 9QJ.

BUNDY, Prof. Alan Richard, PhD; Professor of Automated Reasoning, Department of Artificial Intelligence, University of Edinburgh, since 1990; *b* 18 May 1947; *s* of Stanley Alfred Bundy and Joan Margaret Rose Bundy (*née* Wingfield); *m* 1967, D. Josephine A. Maule; one *d. Educ:* Univ. of Leicester (BSc 1st Cl. Maths 1968; PhD Mathematic Logic 1971). Teaching Asst, Dept of Maths, Univ. of Leicester, 1970–71; University of Edinburgh: Res. Fellow, Metamathematics Unit, 1971–74; Department of Artificial Intelligence: Lectr, 1974–84; Reader, 1984–87; Professorial Fellow, 1987–90. FAAAI 1990. FRSA 1988. *Publications:* Artificial Intelligence: an introductory course, 1978; The Computer Modelling of Mathematical Reasoning, 1983, 2nd edn 1986; The Benefits and Risks of Knowledge Based Systems, 1989; Eco-logic: logic based approaches to ecological modelling, 1991; Catalogue of Artificial Intelligence Techniques, 1984, 3rd edn 1990. *Recreations:* bridge, wine-making, valley walking. *Address:* Department of Artificial Intelligence, University of Edinburgh, 80 South Bridge, Edinburgh EH1 1HN. *T:* 0131–650 2716; 23a Lauder Road, Edinburgh EH9 2JG.

BUNDY, McGeorge; Professor of History, New York University, 1979–89, now Emeritus; *b* 30 March 1919; *s* of Harvey Hollister Bundy and Katharine Lawrence Bundy (*née* Putnam); *m* 1950, Mary Buckminster Lothrop; four *s. Educ:* Yale Univ. AB 1940. Political analyst, Council on Foreign Relations, 1948–49. Harvard University: Vis. Lectr, 1949–51; Associate Prof. of Government, 1951–54; Prof., 1954–61; Dean, Faculty of Arts and Sciences, 1953–61. Special Asst to the Pres. for National Security Affairs, 1961–66; President of the Ford Foundation, 1966–79. *Publications:* (with H. L. Stimson) On Active Service in Peace and War, 1948; (ed) Pattern of Responsibility, 1952; The Strength of Government, 1968; Danger and Survival, 1988. *Address:* 170 East 79th Street, New York, NY 10021, USA.

BUNGEY, Michael; Chairman and Chief Executive Officer: Bates Dorland Advertising Ltd (formerly Dorland Advertising), since 1987; Bates Worldwide (formerly BSB Worldwide), since 1994; *b* 18 Jan. 1940; *s* of William Frederick George and Irene Edith Bungey; *m* 1976, Darleen Penelope Cecilia Brooks; one *s* two *d. Educ:* St Clement Danes Grammar Sch.; LSE (BSc Econ). Marketing with Nestlé, 1961–65; Associate Dir, Crawfords Advertising, 1965–68; Account Dir, S. H. Benson Advertising, 1969–71; Chm., Michael Bungey & Partners, 1972–84; Dep. Chm., Dorland Advertising, 1984–; Chairman and Chief Executive Officer: DFS Dorland, 1987; Bates Dorland, 1988; Bates Europe, 1989; Pres. and Chief Operating Officer, BSB Worldwide, 1993–94; Chairman: Bates Dorland Gp; Bates Americas' Reg., 1993–; Bates USA, 1993–. Dir, Saatchi & Saatchi, 1995–. *Address:* Bates Dorland Advertising Ltd, 121–141 Westbourne Terrace, W2 6JR. *Club:* Hurlingham.

BUNKER, Albert Rowland, CB 1966; Deputy Under-Secretary of State, Home Office, 1972–75; *b* 5 Nov. 1913; *er* and *o* surv. *s* of late Alfred Francis Bunker and late Ethel Trudgian, Lanjeth, St Austell, Cornwall; *m* 1939, Irene Ruth Ella, 2nd *d* of late Walter and late Ella Lacey, Ealing; two *s. Educ:* Ealing Gram. Sch. Served in Royal Air Force, 1943–45. Service in Cabinet Office, HM Treasury, Ministry of Home Security and Home Office. *Recreation:* golf. *Address:* 35 Park Avenue, Ruislip HA4 7UQ. *T:* Ruislip (01895) 635331. *Clubs:* Royal Air Force; Denham Golf.

BUNKER, Very Rev. Michael; Dean of Peterborough, since 1992; *b* 22 July 1937; *s* of Murray Bunker and Nora Bunker; *m* 1957, Mary Helena Bunker; four *s. Educ:* Acton Technical Coll. and Brunel Coll., Acton (ONC and HNC in Engineering); Oak Hill Theol Coll. Work Study Engr, Napiers of Acton, London, 1956–60. Ordained deacon, 1963, priest, 1964; Assistant Curate: St James' Church, Alperton, Middlesex, 1963–66; Parish Church of St Helen, Merseyside, 1966–70; Incumbent: St Matthew's Church, Muswell Hill, London, 1970–78; St James with St Matthew, Muswell Hill, 1978–92. Prebendary of St Paul's Cathedral, 1990. *Publication:* The Church on the Hill, 1988. *Recreations:* flyfishing, walking. *Address:* The Deanery, Peterborough, Cambs PE1 1XS. *T:* Peterborough (01733) 62780.

BUNN, Douglas Henry David; Chairman: All England Jumping Course, Hickstead; White Horse Caravan Co. Ltd; *b* 1 March 1928; *s* of late George Henry Charles Bunn and Alice Ann Bunn; *m* 1st, 1952, Rosemary Pares Wilson; three *d*; 2nd, 1960, Susan Dennis-Smith; two *s* one *d*; 3rd, 1979, Lorna Kirk; one *s* two *d. Educ:* Chichester High Sch.; Trinity Coll., Cambridge (MA). Called to Bar, Lincoln's Inn; practised at Bar, 1953–59; founded Hickstead, 1960; British Show Jumping Team, 1957–68; Chm., BSJA, 1969, 1993– (Vice-Chm., 1969–93); Mem. British Equestrian Fedn; founded White Horse Caravan Co. Ltd, 1958; Chm., Southern Aero Club, 1968–72. Jt Master, Mid Surrey Drag Hounds, 1976–. *Recreations:* horses, flying, books, wine. *Address:* Hickstead Place, Sussex RH17 5NU. *T:* Hurstpierpoint (01273) 834666. *Clubs:* Saints and Sinners (Chm., 1989–90), Turf.

BUNTING, Prof. Arthur Hugh, CMG 1971; consultant in tropical agricultural research and development; Professor of Agricultural Development Overseas, Reading University, 1974–82, now Emeritus; *b* 7 Sept. 1917; *e s* of S. P. and R. Bunting; *m* 1941, Elsie Muriel Reynard; three *s. Educ:* Athlone High Sch., Johannesburg, S Africa; Univ. of the Witwatersrand, Johannesburg; Oriel Coll., University of Oxford. BSc 1937. BSc (Hons Botany), MSc 1938, Witwatersrand; Rhodes Scholar for the Transvaal, 1938; DPhil Oxford, 1941; CBiol, FIBiol; FLS 1993. Asst Chemist, Rothamsted Experimental Station, 1941–45; Member Human Nutrition Research Unit, Medical Research Council, 1945–47; Chief Scientific Officer, Overseas Food Corporation, 1947–51; Senior Research Officer, Sudan Min. of Agriculture, 1951–56; Prof. of Agricultural Botany, 1956–73, Dean, Faculty of Agriculture, 1965–71, Univ. of Reading. Pres., Assoc. of Applied Biologists, 1963–64, Hon. Mem., 1979–; Jt Editor, Journal of Applied Ecology, 1964–68. Foundn Mem., 1968–72, and Mem., 1974–80, Vice-Chm. 1975–77, and Chm. 1977–80, Board of Trustees, Internat. Inst. of Tropical Agriculture, Ibadan, Nigeria; Member: UK Council for Scientific Policy, 1970–72; UN Adv. Cttee on the Applications of Science and Technology to Develt (ACAST), 1972–75; Governing Bodies, Grassland Res. Inst., Hurley, 1959–77, Plant Breeding Inst., Cambridge, 1960–76; Consultant and then Mem., Scientific Cttee, Cotton Res. Corp., 1958–76 (Chm., 1972–76); Member: Panel of Scientific Advisers, CDC, 1967–94; Meteorological Cttee, MoD, 1973–88; Foundn Mem., Internat. Bd for Plant Genetic Resources, 1974–78. LLD *hc* Ahmadu Bello Univ., 1968. *Publications:* (ed) Change in Agriculture, 1970; (ed jtly) Policy and Practice in Rural Development, 1976; (ed jtly) Advances in Legume Science, 1980; (ed) Agricultural Environments, 1987; numerous papers in scientific and agricultural journals. *Recreation:* music. *Address:* 27 The Mount, Caversham, Reading, Berks RG4 7RU. *T:* Reading (01734) 472487; 4 Earley Gate, University of Reading, Berks RG6 2AR. *T:* Reading (01734) 318320.

BUNTING, John Reginald, CBE 1965; author and educational consultant, retired; *b* 12 Nov. 1916; *s* of John Henry and Jane Bunting, Mansfield; *m* 1940, May Hope Sturdy, Malvern, Jamaica; no *c. Educ:* Queen Elizabeth's Grammar Sch., Mansfield; Queen's Coll., Oxford (MA, DipEd). Sen. English Master and Housemaster, Munro Coll., Jamaica, 1939–42; Headmaster, Wolmer's Sch., Jamaica, 1943–49; Principal, King's Coll., Lagos, 1949–54; Actg Dir of Broadcasting, Nigeria, June-Oct. 1952; Actg Inspector of Educn, Western Region, Nigeria, April-Oct. 1954; Dep. Chief Federal Adviser on Educn, Nigeria, 1954–58; Chief Federal Adviser on Educn, Nigeria, 1958–61; Educn Adviser, W Africa, Brit. Council, 1961 and Head, Graduate VSO Unit, 1962; Asst Controller, Educn Div., 1964; Evans Bros Ltd: Editorial Consultant, 1965–68; Dir, Overseas Sales and Publications, 1969; Dir-Gen., Centre for Educnl Develt Overseas, 1970–74; Adviser on Educn to British Council, 1974–76. Hon. Jt Editor, W African Jl of Educn, 1956–61. *Publications:* Civics for Self-Government, 1956; New African English Course (Book 5), 1960; (jtly) Caribbean Civics, 1960; (jtly) Civics for East Africa, 1961; Primary English Course (Book 6): for Ghana, 1962, for Sierra Leone, 1969, for West Cameroon, 1971; Civics: a course in citizenship and character training, 1973; To Light a Candle, 1976. *Recreations:* golf, fishing, painting, bowls. *Address:* 8 Springhill Gardens, Lyme Regis, Dorset DT7 3HL. *T:* Lyme Regis (01297) 443726. *Clubs:* MCC; Lyme Regis Golf.

BUNTING, Martin Brian, FCA; company director; Chairman Marr Holdings Ltd, since 1991; *b* 28 Feb. 1934; *s* of late Brian and Renee Bunting; *m* 1959, Veronica Mary Cope; two *s* one *d. Educ:* Rugby School. Director, Courage Ltd, 1972, Man. Dir, later Dep. Chm., 1974–84; Dir, Imperial Group plc, 1975–84; Chief Executive, Clifford Foods PLC, 1990–93. Non-executive Director: George Gale & Co. Ltd, 1984–, Longman Cartermill Ltd, 1985–90; Norcros plc, 1986–93; Shepherd Neame Ltd, 1986–; Bluebird Toys, 1991–; NAAFI, 1993–; Hobson plc, 1994–. Member, Monopolies and Mergers Commission, 1982–88. *Address:* The Lodge, Basingstoke Road, Riseley, near Reading RG7 1QD. *T:* Reading (01734) 883234, 885414. *Club:* Travellers'.

See also Earl of Southesk.

BUNTON, George Louis, MChir (Cantab), FRCS; Consultant Surgeon to University College Hospital, London, 1955–84, to Metropolitan Hospital, 1957–70, and to Northwood Hospital, 1958–84, retired; Emeritus Consulting Surgeon to University College and Middlesex Hospitals, 1986; *b* 23 April 1920; *s* of late Surg. Capt. C. L. W. Bunton, RN, and Marjorie Denman; *m* 1st, 1948, Margaret Betty Edwards (*d* 1988); one *d*; 2nd, 1993, Louise Phillippa Brooks. Educ: Epsom; Selwyn Coll., Cambridge; UCH. MB, BChir Cantab 1951; MRCS, LRCP 1944; FRCS 1951; MChir Cantab 1955. Served in RNVR 1944–47. University of London: Examr in Surgery, 1974–78; Mem., Academic Council, 1975–77; University College Hospital, London: Chm., Med. Cttee, 1977–80; Mem., Academic Bd, Med. Sch., 1970–78; Mem., Sch. Council, Med. Sch., 1976–81; Mem., Bd of Governors, 1972–74; Mem., Bd of Trustees, UC Gp of Hosps, 1978–82. Chairman: Health Gp, Centre for Policy Studies, 1980–84; S Camden Dist Med. Cttee, 1980–83; Member: Exec., University Hosps Assoc. (England and Wales), 1975–89 (Treasurer, 1980–89); Court of Examiners, RCS, 1977–84 (Chm., 1984). Fellow, Assoc. of Surgeons; Fellow, British Assoc. of Pædiatric Surgeons. *Publications:* contribs. to journals and books on surgical subjects. *Recreations:* gardening, music. *Address:* Smarkham Orchard, Madgehole Lane, Shamley Green, Guildford, Surrey GU5 0SS. *T:* Guildford (01483) 892187.

BUNYAN, Dr Peter John; Chief Scientific Adviser to Ministry of Agriculture, Fisheries and Food, since 1990; *b* London, 13 Jan. 1936; *o s* of Charles and Jenny Bunyan; *m* 1961, June Rose Child; two *s. Educ:* Raynes Park County Grammar Sch.; University Coll., Durham Univ. (BSc, DSc); King's Coll., Univ. of London (PhD). FRSC; CChem; FIBiol; FIFST. Research at KCL, 1960–62, at UCL, 1962–63; Ministry of Agriculture, Fisheries and Food: Sen. Scientific Officer, Infestation Control Lab., 1963–69; PSO, Pest Infestation Control Lab., 1969–73, Head of Pest Control Chemistry Dept, 1973–80; Head of Food Science Div., 1980–84; Head of Agricl Sci. Service, ADAS, 1984–87; Dir of R & D Service, ADAS, 1987–90; Dir. Gen., ADAS and Regl Orgn, 1990–91. Member: AFRC, 1990–94; BBSRC, 1994–; NERC, 1991–. *Publications:* numerous scientific papers in wide variety of scientific jls. *Recreations:* gardening, jogging. *Address:* c/o Ministry of Agriculture, Fisheries and Food, Nobel House, 17 Smith Square, SW1P 3JR. *T:* 0171–238 5958. *Club:* Farmers'.

BUNYARD, Sir Robert (Sidney), Kt 1991; CBE 1986; QPM 1980; Commandant, Police Staff College, Bramshill and HM Inspector of Constabulary, 1988–93; *b* 20 May 1930; *s* of Albert Percy Bunyard and Nellie Maria Bunyard; *m* 1948, Ruth Martin; two *d. Educ:* Queen Elizabeth Grammar Sch., Faversham; Regent Street Polytechnic Management Sch. (Dip. in Man. Studies). BA (Hons) Open Univ. MIPD; CIMgt. Metropolitan Police,

1952; Asst Chief Constable, Leics, 1972; Dep. Chief Constable, 1977, Chief Constable, 1978–87, Essex Police. Man. Editor, Police Jl, 1981–88. Member: Royal Commn on Criminal Justice, 1991–93; Parole Bd, 1994–. Chm., Essex Reg., Royal Assoc. in Aid of Deaf People, 1994–. *Publications:* Police: organization and command, 1978; Police Management Handbook, 1979; contrib. police jls. *Recreations:* music, opera, painting. *Address:* Bellmans, Springfield, Essex CM2 6DB.

BURBIDGE, (Eleanor) Margaret, (Mrs Geoffrey Burbidge), FRS 1964; Professor of Astronomy, 1964–90, University Professor, 1984–90, now Emeritus, and Research Physicist, Department of Physics, since 1990, University of California at San Diego; *d* of late Stanley John Peachey, Lectr in Chemistry and Research Chemist, and of Marjorie Peachey; *m* 1948, Geoffrey Burbidge, *qv*; one *d. Educ:* Francis Holland Sch., London; University Coll., London (BSc); Univ. of London Observatory (PhD). Asst Director, 1948–50, Actg Director, 1950–51, Univ. of London Observatory; fellowship from Internat. Astron. Union, held at Yerkes Observatory, Univ. of Chicago, 1951–53; Research Fellow, California Inst. of Technology, 1955–57; Shirley Farr Fellow, later Associate Prof., Yerkes Observatory, Univ. of Chicago, 1957–62; Research Astronomer, 1962–64, Dir, Center for Astrophysics and Space Scis, 1979–88, Univ. of California at San Diego; Dir, Royal Greenwich Observatory, 1972–73. Abby Rockefeller Mauzé Vis. Prof., MIT, 1968. Member: American Acad. of Arts and Scis, 1969; US Nat. Acad. of Scis, 1978; Nat. Acad. of Scis Cttee on Science and Public Policy, 1979–81; Pres., Amer. Astronomical Soc., 1976–78; Chairwoman Bd of Dirs, Amer. Assoc. for Advancement of Science, 1983 (Pres., 1982); Mem., Amer. Philosophical Soc., 1980. Fellow University Coll., London, 1967; Hon. Fellow, Lucy Cavendish Collegiate Soc., 1971. Hon. DSc: Smith Coll., Massachusetts, USA, 1963; Sussex, 1970; Bristol, 1972; Leicester, 1972; City, 1974; Michigan, 1978; Massachusetts, 1978; Williams Coll., 1979; State Univ. of NY at Stony Brook, 1984; Rensselaer Poly. Inst., 1986; Notre Dame Univ., 1986; Chicago, 1991. Catherine Wolfe Bruce Medal, Astr. Soc. of the Pacific, 1982; Nat. Medal of Science (awarded by President of USA), 1984; Sesquicentennial Medal, Mt Holyoke Coll., 1987; Einstein Medal, World Cultural Council, 1988. *Publications:* Quasi-Stellar Objects (with Geoffrey Burbidge), 1967 (also USA, 1967); contribs to learned jls (mostly USA), Handbuch der Physik, etc. *Address:* Center for Astrophysics and Space Sciences, 0111, University of California, San Diego, La Jolla, CA 92093, USA. *T:* (619) 5344477. *Club:* University Women's.

BURBIDGE, Prof. Geoffrey, FRS 1968; Professor of Physics, University of California, San Diego, 1963–84 and since 1988 (Associate Professor, 1962–63, Emeritus Professor, 1984–88); *b* 24 Sept. 1925; *s* of Leslie and Eveline Burbidge, Chipping Norton, Oxon; *m* 1948, Margaret Peachey (*see* E. M. Burbidge); one *d. Educ:* Chipping Norton Grammar Sch.; Bristol University; Univ. Coll., London. BSc (Special Hons Physics) Bristol, 1946; PhD London, 1951. Asst Lectr, UCL, 1950–51; Agassiz Fellow, Harvard Univ., 1951–52; Research Fellow, Univ. of Chicago, 1952–53; Research Fellow, Cavendish Lab., Cambridge, 1953–55; Carnegie Fellow, Mount Wilson and Palomar Observatories, Caltech, 1955–57; Asst Prof., Dept of Astronomy, Univ. of Chicago, 1957–58; Assoc. Prof., 1958–62. Dir, Kitt Peak Nat. Observatory, Arizona, 1978–84. Phillips Vis. Prof., Harvard Univ., 1968. Elected Fellow: UCL, 1970; Amer. Acad. of Arts and Scis, 1970. Pres., Astronomical Soc. of the Pacific, 1974–76; Trustee, Assoc. Universities Inc., 1973–82; Editor, Annual Review Astronomy and Astrophysics, 1973–. *Publications:* (with Margaret Burbidge) Quasi-Stellar Objects, 1967; scientific papers in Astrophysical Jl, Nature, Rev. Mod. Phys, Handbuch der Physik, etc. *Address:* Department of Physics and Center for Astrophysics and Space Sciences, 0111, University of California, San Diego, La Jolla, CA 92093, USA. *T:* (619) 5346626.

BURBIDGE, Sir Herbert (Dudley), 5th Bt *cr* 1916; *b* 13 Nov. 1904; *s* of Herbert Edward Burbidge (*d* 1945) 2nd *s* of 1st Bt, and Harriet Georgina (*d* 1952), *d* of Henry Stuart Hamilton, Londonderry; *S* cousin, 1974; *m* 1933, Ruby Bly, *d* of Charles Ethelbert Taylor; one *s. Educ:* University Sch., Victoria, BC, Canada. Harrods Ltd, Knightsbridge, 1923–28; R. P. Clarke (Stock Brokers), Vancouver, BC, 1929–31; Merchandising Manager, Silverwood Industries of Vancouver, BC, 1931–70; retired 1970. President: Vancouver Executive Club, 1942; Vancouver Sales Executive Club, 1948. Mem. Bd of Referees, Workmen's Compensation Bd, 1943–61. *Recreation:* landscape gardening. *Heir: s* Peter Dudley Burbidge [*b* 20 June 1942; *m* 1967, Peggy Marilyn, *d* of Kenneth Anderson, Ladner, BC; one *s* one *d*]. *Address:* 3809 West 24th Avenue, Vancouver, BC V6S 1L9, Canada. *Club:* Vancouver Executive.

BURBIDGE, Margaret, (Mrs Geoffrey Burbidge); *see* Burbidge, E. M.

BURBRIDGE, Very Rev. (John) Paul, MA Oxon and Cantab; FSA; Dean of Norwich, 1983–95, now Emeritus; *b* 21 May 1932; *e s* of late John Henry Gray Burbridge and Dorothy Vera Burbridge; *m* 1956, Olive Denise Grenfell; four *d. Educ:* King's Sch., Canterbury; King's Coll., Cambridge; New Coll., Oxford; Wells Theolog. Coll. Nat. Service Commn in RA, 1957. Jun. Curate, 1959, Sen. Curate, 1961, Eastbourne Parish Church; Vicar Choral of York Minster, 1962–66; Chamberlain, 1962–76; Canon Residentiary, 1966–76; Succentor Canonicorum, 1966; Precentor, 1969–76; Archdeacon of Richmond and Canon Residentiary of Ripon Cathedral, 1976–83. *Recreation:* model engineering. *Address:* The Old School House, High Fremington, Richmond, N Yorks DL11 6AS. *T:* Richmond (01748) 884440.

See also S. N. Burbridge.

BURBRIDGE, Stephen Nigel, CB 1992; MA; Secretary, Monopolies and Mergers Commission, 1986–93; *b* 18 July 1934; *s* of late John Henry Gray Burbridge and late Dorothy Vera (*née* Pratt). *Educ:* King's Sch., Canterbury; Christ Church, Oxford. National Service, 2 Lieut, RA, 1953–55. Asst Principal, Bd of Trade, 1958–62; Trade Commissioner, Karachi, 1963–65; 1st Secretary (Economic), Rawalpindi, 1965–67; Principal, BoT, 1967–71; CS Selection Bd, 1971; Department of Trade and Industry: Asst Sec., 1971–80; Under Sec., 1980–86. *Recreations:* sports, books. *Address:* Chesil Cottage, Brede Hill, Brede, near Rye, E Sussex TN31 6HH. *Clubs:* Reform; Rye Golf; West Sussex Golf.

See also J. P. Burbridge.

BURBURY, Hon. Sir Stanley Charles, KCMG 1981; KCVO 1977; KBE 1958; Governor of Tasmania, 1973–82; *b* 2 Dec. 1909; *s* of Daniel Charles Burbury and Mary Burbury (*née* Cunningham); *m* 1934, Pearl Christine Barren; no *c. Educ:* Hutchins Sch., Hobart; The Univ. of Tasmania. LLB 1933; Hon. LLD 1970. Admitted to Bar, 1934; QC 1950; Solicitor-Gen. for Tasmania, 1952; Chief Justice, Supreme Court of Tasmania, 1956–73. Pres., Nat. Heart Foundn of Australia, 1967–73; Nat. Pres., Winston Churchill Memorial Trust, 1980–85. KStJ 1974. Hon. Col, Royal Tasmanian Regt, 1974–82. *Recreations:* music and lawn bowls. *Address:* 3 Mona Street, Kingston, Tasmania 7050, Australia. *Clubs:* Tasmanian, Athenæum, Royal Hobart Bowls (Hobart).

BURCH, Maj.-Gen. Keith, CB 1985; CBE 1977 (MBE 1965); Director Personnel, Defence Staff, Ministry of Defence, 1985, retired; Chapter Clerk, York Minster, 1985–95; *b* 31 May 1931; *s* of Christopher Burch and Gwendoline Ada (*née* James); *m* 1957, Sara Vivette Hales; one *s* two *d. Educ:* Bedford Modern Sch.; Royal Military Acad., Sandhurst. Commnd Essex Regt, 1951; DS Staff Coll., Camberley, 1968–69; Comd 3rd Bn Royal Anglian Regt, 1969–71; Asst Sec., Chiefs of Staff Cttee, MoD, 1972–75; Col GS HQ 2nd Armoured Div., 1975–78; Dir, Admin. Planning (Army), MoD, 1978–80; Indian National Defence Coll., New Delhi, 1981; Dep. Dir, Army Staff Duties, MoD, 1981–83; ACDS (Personnel and Logistics), 1984. *Recreations:* country pursuits. *Address:* Mayfield, Sandy Lane, Stockton on the Forest, York YO3 9US.

BURCH, Rt. Rev. William Gerald, DD; *b* Winnipeg, Manitoba, 5 March 1911; *m* 1942, Carroll Borrowman; four *d. Educ:* University of Toronto (BA); Wycliffe Coll., Toronto. Deacon, 1936; Priest, 1938. Curate, Christ Church, Toronto, 1936–40; Incumbent, Scarborough Junction with Sandown Park, 1940–42; Rector: St Luke, Winnipeg, 1942–52; All Saints, Windsor, 1952–56; Exam. Chaplain to Bishop of Huron, 1955–56; Canon of Huron, 1956; Dean and Rector, All Saints Cathedral, Edmonton, 1956–60; Suffragan Bishop of Edmonton, 1960–61; Bishop of Edmonton, 1961–76. *Address:* 901 Richmond Avenue, Victoria, BC V8S 3Z4, Canada. *T:* (604) 598 4369.

BURCHAM, Prof. William Ernest, CBE 1980; FRS 1957; Emeritus Professor of Physics, Birmingham University, since 1981; *b* 1 Aug. 1913; *er s* of Ernest Barnard and Edith Ellen Burcham; *m* 1st, 1942, Isabella Mary (*d* 1981), *d* of George Richard Todd and of Alice Louisa Todd; two *d*; 2nd, 1985, Patricia Newton, *er d* of Frank Harold Newton Marson and Miriam Eliza Marson. *Educ:* City of Norwich Sch.; Trinity Hall, Cambridge. Stokes Student, Pembroke Coll., Cambridge, 1937; Scientific Officer, Ministry of Aircraft Production, 1940, and Directorate of Atomic Energy, 1944; Fellow of Selwyn Coll., Cambridge, 1944; Univ. Demonstrator in Physics, Cambridge, 1945; Univ. Lecturer in Physics, Cambridge, 1946; Oliver Lodge Prof. of Physics, Univ. of Birmingham, 1951–80. Member: SRC, 1974–78; Council, Royal Soc., 1977–79. Hon. Life Fellow, Coventry Polytechnic, 1984. *Publications:* Nuclear Physics: an Introduction, 1963; Elements of Nuclear Physics, 1979; (with M. Jobes) Nuclear and Particle Physics, 1994; papers in Nuclear Physics A, Phys. Letters B, Phys. Rev. Letters. *Address:* 95 Witherford Way, Birmingham B29 4AN. *T:* 0121–472 1226.

BURCHFIELD, Dr Robert William, CBE 1975; Editor, A Supplement to the Oxford English Dictionary, 1957–86; Chief Editor, The Oxford English Dictionaries, 1971–84; Senior Research Fellow, St Peter's College, Oxford, 1979–90, now Emeritus Fellow (Tutorial Fellow, 1963–79); *b* Wanganui, NZ, 27 Jan. 1923; *s* of Frederick Burchfield and Mary Burchfield (*née* Blair); *m* 1949, Ethel May Yates (marr. diss. 1976); one *s* two *d*; *m* 1976, Elizabeth Austen Knight. *Educ:* Wanganui Technical Coll., New Zealand, 1934–39; Victoria University Coll., Wellington, NZ, 1940–41, 1946–48; MA (NZ) 1948; Magdalen Coll., Oxford, 1949–53; BA (Oxon) 1951, MA 1955. Served War, Royal NZ Artillery, NZ and Italy, 1941–46. NZ Rhodes Scholar, 1949. Junior Lectr in English Lang., Magdalen Coll., Oxford, 1952–53; Lectr in English Lang., Christ Church, Oxford, 1953–57; Lectr, St Peter's Coll., Oxford, 1955–63. Hon. Sec., Early English Text Society, 1955–68 (Mem. Council, 1968–80); Editor, Notes and Queries, 1959–62; Pres., English Assoc., 1978–79. Hon. For. Mem., American Acad. of Arts and Scis, 1977–; Hon. Fellow, Inst. of Linguists, 1984–. Hon. DLitt, Liverpool, 1978; Hon. LitD Victoria Univ. of Wellington, NZ, 1983. Freedom of City of Wanganui, 1986. Shakespeare Prize, FVS Foundn, Hamburg, 1994. *Publications:* (with C. T. Onions and G. W. S. Friedrichsen) The Oxford Dictionary of English Etymology, 1966; A Supplement to the Oxford English Dictionary, vol. I (A–G), 1972, vol. II (H–N), 1976, vol. III (O–Scz), 1982, vol. IV (Se–Z), 1986; (with D. Donoghue and A. Timothy) The Quality of Spoken English on BBC Radio, 1979; The Spoken Language as an Art Form, 1981; The Spoken Word, 1981; The English Language, 1985; The New Zealand Pocket Oxford Dictionary, 1986; (ed) Studies in Lexicography, 1987; Unlocking the English Language, 1989; Points of View, 1992; (ed) The Cambridge History of the English Language, vol. V, 1994; contribs to: Times Lit. Supp., Trans Philological Soc., Encounter, etc. *Recreations:* investigating English grammar, travelling, gardening. *Address:* The Barn, 14 The Green, Sutton Courtenay, Oxon OX14 4AE. *T:* Abingdon (01235) 848645. *Club:* Athenæum.

BURDEKIN, Prof. Frederick Michael, FRS 1993; FEng; Professor of Civil and Structural Engineering, University of Manchester Institute of Science and Technology, since 1977; *b* 5 Feb. 1938; *s* of Leslie and Gwendoline Burdekin; *m* 1965, Jennifer Meadley; two *s. Educ:* King's School, Chester; Trinity Hall, Cambridge (MA, PhD). MSc Manchester. FICE, FIMechE, FIStructE, FWeldI, FInstNDT. Welding Inst., 1961–68; Associate, Sandberg, Consulting Engineers, 1968–77. Vice-Principal External Affairs, UMIST, 1983–85. Chm., Manchester Science Park Ltd, 1988–. Mem., Engrg Council, 1990–93. *Publications:* numerous papers on fracture, fatigue and welded structures. *Recreations:* music, sport, countryside. *Address:* 27 Springbank, Bollington, Macclesfield, Cheshire SK10 5LQ.

BURDEN, family name of **Baron Burden.**

BURDEN, 3rd Baron, *cr* 1950, of Hazlebarrow, Derby; **Andrew Philip Burden;** *b* 20 July 1959; *e s* of 2nd Baron Burden and of Audrey Elsworth, *d* of Maj. W. E. Sykes; *S* father, 1995. *Heir: b* Hon. Fraser William Elsworth Burden, *b* 6 Nov. 1964. *Address:* 13 Langham Drive, Taunton TA1 4LJ.

BURDEN, Maj.-Gen. David Leslie, CBE 1988; Director-General, Army Manning and Recruiting, since 1995; *b* 14 July 1943; *s* of Jack Leslie Burden and Elizabeth Mary Burden (*née* Attkins); *m* 1974, Susan Stuart Watson; two *d. Educ:* Portsmouth Grammar School. FILDM. Commissioned RASC 1964, RAOC 1965. Served England, Berlin, W Germany, NI, Cyprus and Hong Kong; NDC, 1981; Chief, Personnel and Logistics, UN Force in Cyprus, 1981–83; CO, 1 Ordnance Bn, 1983–85; ACOS, British Forces, Hong Kong, 1985–87; RCDS, 1988; ACOS, BAOR, 1989–91; Dir-Gen., Resettlement, MoD, 1991–92; Dir-Gen., Logistic Support (Army), 1992–95. Freeman, City of London; Liveryman, Carmen's Co. *Recreations:* golf, cricket, walking. *Address:* c/o Barclays Bank, 54 Highgate High Street, N6 5JD. *Clubs:* Army and Navy, MCC; Walker's Cricket Circus; Tidworth Garrison Golf.

BURDEN, Derrick Frank; HM Diplomatic Service, retired; Counsellor and Head of Claims Department, Foreign and Commonwealth Office, 1973–78; *b* 4 June 1918; *s* of late Alfred Burden and Louisa Burden (*née* Dean); *m* 1942, Marjorie Adeline Beckley; two *d. Educ:* Bec Sch., London. Crown Agents, 1936. Served War, King's Royal Rifle Corps, 1939–41. Joined Foreign Office, 1945; Comr-Gen.'s Office, Singapore, 1950–53; 2nd Sec., Moscow, 1954–56; 2nd Sec., Tokyo, 1957–59; HM Consul, Lourenço Marques, 1959–61; FO, 1962–67 (Asst Head of Protocol Dept, 1965); HM Consul, Khorramshahr (Iran), 1967–69; 1st Sec., Nairobi, 1969–71; HM Consul, Luanda (Angola), 1972–73. *Recreations:* golf, gardening. *Address:* 12 Strathmore Drive, Charvil, Reading, Berks RG10 9QT. *T:* Twyford (Berks) (01734) 340564. *Clubs:* Travellers'; Nairobi (Nairobi); Phyllis Court (Henley-on-Thames).

BURDEN, Richard Haines; MP (Lab) Birmingham Northfield, since 1992; *b* 1 Sept. 1954; *s* of Kenneth Rodney Burden and late Pauline Langan Burden (*née* Ronnan); partner, 1981, Janis Taylor. *Educ:* Wallasey Technical Grammar Sch.; Bramhall Comprehensive Sch.; St John's Coll. of Further Educn, Manchester; York Univ. (BA Politics); Warwick Univ. (MA Indust. Relations). Pres., York Univ. Students' Union, 1976–77. Br. Organiser, 1979–81, Dist Officer, 1979–92, NALGO; whilst working for

NALGO led Midlands campaign against water privatisation. Founder and Sec., Joint Action for Water Services, 1985–90. Contested (Lab) Meriden, 1987. Vice-Chairman: PLP Trade and Industry Cttee, 1995–; Labour ME Council, 1994–. Mem., Labour Campaign for Electoral Reform. Mem., Austin Br., RBL. *Publications:* Tap Dancing: water, the environment and privatisation, 1988; contribs to Tribune, Chartist and other jls. *Recreations:* motor racing, cinema, reading, food. *Address:* House of Commons, SW1A 0AA. *T:* 0171–219 3000; 0121–475 9295. *Clubs:* Austin Sports and Social, Kingshurst Labour, 750 Motor.

BURDETT, Sir Savile (Aylmer), 11th Bt, *cr* 1665; Managing Director, Rapaway Energy Ltd; *b* 24 Sept. 1931; *s* of Sir Aylmer Burdett, 10th Bt; *S* father, 1943; *m* 1962, June E. C. Rutherford; one *s* one *d*. *Educ:* Wellington Coll.; Imperial Coll., London. *Heir: s* Crispin Peter Burdett, *b* 8 Feb. 1967. *Address:* Farthings, 35 Park Avenue, Solihull, West Midlands B91 3EJ. *T:* 0121–711 1454.

BURDUS, (Julia) Ann; Director: Dawson International, since 1992; BEM Ltd, since 1992; Chairman, The Marketing Triangle, since 1992; *b* 4 Sept. 1933; *d* of Gladstone Beaty and Julia W. C. Booth; *m* 1981, Ian B. Robertson. *Educ:* Durham Univ. (BA Psychology). Clinical psychologist, 1956–60; Res. Exec., Ogilvy, Benson & Mather, 1961–67; Res. Dir, McCann Erickson, 1971–75, Vice Chm., 1975–77; Senior Vice-Pres., McCann Internat., 1977–79; Chm., McCann & Co., 1979–81; Director: Strategic Planning and Development, Interpublic, 1981–83; Audits of Great Britain Ltd, 1983–86; AGB Research, 1986–89; Dir of Communications and Marketing, Olympia & York, Canary Wharf, 1989–92. Non-executive Director: Argyll Gp, 1993–; Next, 1993–. Chairman: Advertising Assoc., 1980–81; EDC for Distributive Trades, 1983–87. Jt Dep. Chm. and Mem., Health Educn Authority, 1987–90; Member: Sen. (formerly Top) Salaries Rev. Bd, 1991–; Adv. Council on Business and the Envmt, 1993–; part-time Mem., CAA, 1993–94. Mem. Council, Inst. of Dirs, 1995–. *Recreation:* home building.

BURFORD, Earl of; Charles Francis Topham de Vere Beauclerk; *b* 22 Feb. 1965; *s* and *heir* of Duke of St Albans, *qv*. *Educ:* Sherborne and Oxford. Created Brigadier-General of Louisiana, USA, on staff of Governor Edwin Edwards, 1986. Trustee, Shakespearean Authorship Trust; Chm., De Vere Soc.; Vice-Pres., Royal Stuart Soc., 1989–. Freeman, City of London 1986; Liveryman, Drapers' Co., 1990. *Address:* Canonteign, Exeter, Devon EX6 7RH. *Club:* Brooks's.

BURFORD, Jeremy Michael Joseph; QC 1987; **His Honour Judge Burford;** a Circuit Judge, since 1993; *b* 3 June 1942; *s* of Alexander Joseph Burford and Arlene Burford. *Educ:* Diocesan Coll., Cape Town; BA Cape Town; MA, LLB Cantab; LLM Harvard. Called to the Bar, Inner Temple, 1968; a Recorder, 1991–93.

BURG, Gisela Elisabeth, Hon. CBE 1987 (for services to exports); Managing Director, Expotus Ltd, since 1968; *b* 12 Oct. 1939; *d* of Friedrich and Gerda Schlüsselburg. *Educ:* Gymnasium Philippinum, Weilburg, Germany; Ladies Coll., Wetzlar, Germany; Polytechnic of Central London. Founded Expotus Ltd, 1968. Vice-Pres., Fedn of British Audio, 1979–85 (Chm., 1976); Member: NEDO, 1979–84 (Mem. Electronic Sector Working Party); BOTB, 1982–89. Non-exec. Dir, Royal Mint, 1993–. CIEx 1992. The Times/Veuve Clicquot Business Woman of the Year, 1981. *Recreations:* golf, horseracing. *Address:* 82 Kensington Heights, Campden Hill Road, W8 7BD. *T:* 0171–727 8884. *Club:* Woburn Golf and Country (Beds).

BURGE, Prof. Ronald Edgar, CPhys; FInstP; Wheatstone Professor of Physics, King's College, London, since 1989; Director, Leverhulme Trust Grant to Cavendish Laboratory, University of Cambridge, since 1994; *b* 3 Oct. 1932; *s* of John Henry Burge and Edith Beatrice Burge (*née* Thompson); *m* 1953, Janet Mary (*née* Pitts); two *s*. *Educ:* Canton High Sch., Cardiff; King's Coll. London (BSc, PhD; FKC 1989); DSc London 1975. FInstP 1963. King's College London: Asst Lectr in Physics, 1954–58; Lectr in Physics, 1958–62; Reader in Biophysics, 1962–63; Prof. and Head of Dept of Physics, Queen Elizabeth Coll., Univ. of London, 1963–84; Prof. of Physics, 1984–89, Head of Dept of Physics, 1984–92, Vice Principal, 1988–92, KCL. Vis. Fellow, 1992, Life Mem., 1993, Clare Hall, Cambridge. Member: Swinnerton-Dyer Cttee concerning Academic Governance of Univ. of London, 1979–82; Computer Bd for Univs and Res. Councils (responsible for computer develt in univs in Scotland and, latterly, SW England), 1978–82. MRI 1988. Rodman Medal, RPS, 1993. *Publications:* papers in sci. jls on theory of scattering (electrons, x-rays and radar) and develts in electron microscopy and x-ray microscopy. *Recreations:* gardening, music. *Address:* 5 Toft Lane, Great Wilbraham, Cambridge CB1 5JH. *T:* Cambridge (01223) 881378.

BURGE, Stuart, CBE 1974; freelance director and actor; *b* 15 Jan. 1918; *s* of late H. O. Burge and K. M. Haig; *m* 1949, Josephine Parker; three *s* two *d*. *Educ:* Eagle House, Sandhurst; Felsted Sch., Essex. Served War of 1939–45, Intell. Corps. Actor; trained Old Vic, 1936–37; Oxford Rep., 1937–38; Old Vic and West End, 1938–39; Bristol Old Vic, Young Vic, Commercial Theatre, 1946–49; 1st Dir, Hornchurch, 1951–53; productions for theatre and TV, 1953–; Dir, Nottingham Playhouse, 1968–74; Artistic Dir, Royal Court Theatre, 1977–80. *Theatre:* Lulu, 1970; Measure for Measure, The Devil is an Ass, Edinburgh Fest. and Nat. Theatre, 1977; Another Country, Greenwich 1981 and Queen's 1982; (actor) The Seagull, Royal Court, 1981; The London Cuckolds, Lyric Hammersmith, 1985; Curtains, Hampstead, 1987, Whitehall, 1988; The Black Prince, Aldwych, 1989; Sunsets and Glories, Leeds Fest., 1990; The Provoked Wife, Touring Partnership, 1994; *Opera:* La Colombe, Buxton and Sadler's Wells, 1983. *Television:* Bill Brand, Sons and Lovers, The Old Men at the Zoo, Much Ado About Nothing (BBC Shakespeare), Breaking Up, Naming the Names, The Rainbow, House of Bernarda Alba, After the Dance, The Wexford Trilogy, Seaforth, etc. Vis. Prof., UC Davis, USA; Hon. Prof. of Drama, Nottingham Univ. *Publication:* (ed) King John (Folio Society), 1973. *Address:* c/o Harriet Cruickshank, 97 Old South Lambeth Road, SW8 1XU.

BURGEN, Sir Arnold (Stanley Vincent), Kt 1976; FRCP 1969; FRS 1964; President, Academia Europaea, since 1988; Master of Darwin College, Cambridge, 1982–89; Deputy Vice-Chancellor, Cambridge University, 1985–89; *b* 20 March 1922; *s* of late Peter Burgen and Elizabeth Wolfers; *m* 1st, 1946, Judith Browne (*d* 1993); two *s* one *d*; 2nd, 1993, Dr Olga Kennard, *qv*. *Educ:* Christ's Coll., Finchley. Student, Middlesex Hospital Med. Sch., 1939–45; MRCP 1946. Ho. Phys., Middlesex Hospital, 1945; Demonstrator, 1945–48, Asst Lectr, 1948–49, in Pharmacology, Middlesex Hospital Med. Sch. Prof. of Physiology, McGill Univ., Montreal, 1949–62; Dep. Dir, Univ. Clinic, Montreal Gen. Hospital, 1957–62; Sheild Prof. of Pharmacology, Univ. of Cambridge, 1962–71; Fellow of Downing Coll., Cambridge, 1962–71, Hon. Fellow 1972; Dir, Nat. Inst. for Med. Res., 1971–82. Medical Research Council: Member, 1969–71, 1973–77; Hon. Dir, Molecular Pharmacology Unit, 1967–72; Chm., Tropical Medicine Res. Bd, 1977–81; Assessor, 1985–86. Pres., Internat. Union of Pharmacology, 1972–75; Member: Council, Royal Soc., 1972–73, 1980–86 (Vice Pres., 1980–86; Foreign Sec., 1981–86); Nat. Biol. Standards Bd, 1975–78; Med. Cttee, British Council, 1973–77; Gen. Cttee, ICSU, 1982–88; Exec. Cttee, Eur. Science Foundn, 1985–90; Chm., Adv. Cttee on Irradiated and Novel Foods, 1982–87. Dir, Amersham Internat., 1985–92. Trustee, CIBA Foundn, 1985–. Academico Correspondiente, Royal Acad. of Spain, 1983; Mem., Deutsche Akad. der Naturforscher Leopoldina, 1984; For. Associate, US Nat. Acad. of Scis, 1985. Hon. Fellow, Wolfson Coll., Oxford, 1990. Hon. DSc: Leeds, 1973; McGill, 1973; Liverpool, 1989; Hon. MD: Utrecht, 1983; Zûrich, 1983. DUniv. Surrey, 1983. Hon. FRCP (C); Hon. Mem., Amer. Assoc. of Physicians; Academician of Finland, 1990. *Publications:* Physiology of Salivary Glands, 1961; papers in Journals of Physiology and Pharmacology. *Address:* Keelson, 8a Hills Avenue, Cambridge CB1 4XA.

BURGES, Alan; *see* Burges, N. A.

BURGES, Mrs (Margaret) Betty (Pierpoint), MBE 1937; Headmistress, Staines Preparatory School, 1973–88; Chairman, Surrey County Council Conservative Group, 1981–84; *d* of Frederick Eales Hanson and Margaret Pierpoint Hanson (*née* Hurst); *m* 1937, Cyril Travers Burges, MA (*d* 1975). *Educ:* Edgbaston High Sch., Birmingham. Civil Service, 1929–37 and 1940–45. Councillor, Surrey County Council, 1967–85; Chairman, General Purposes Cttee, 1974–84. *Recreations:* walking, travel. *Address:* 7 Gresham Road, Staines, Mddx TW18 2BT. *T:* Staines (01784) 452852.

BURGES, (Norman) Alan, CBE 1980; MSc, PhD; FIBiol; FLS; Vice-Chancellor, New University of Ulster, Coleraine, Northern Ireland, 1966–76; *b* 5 Aug. 1911; *s* of late Lieut J. C. Burges, East Maitland, NSW; *m* 1940, Florence Evelyn (*née* Moulton); three *d*. *Educ:* Sydney Univ., Australia (represented Sydney and Combined Australian Univs at athletics, 1932); Emmanuel Coll., Cambridge. Graduated, Sydney, BSc Hons., 1931; MSc, 1932; PhD Cambridge, 1937. Senior 1851 Scholar, 1937. Research Fellow, Emmanuel Coll., 1938; Prof. of Botany, Sydney Univ., 1947–52; Dean of Faculty of Science and Fellow of Senate, 1949–52; Holbrook Gaskell Prof. of Botany, Univ. of Liverpool, 1952–66, Acting Vice-Chancellor, 1964–65; Pro-Vice-Chancellor, 1965–66. Hon. Gen. Sec., ANZAAS, 1947–52; President: British Ecological Soc., 1958, 1959; British Mycological Soc., 1962; Mem. Cttee, Nature Conservancy, England, 1959–66; Mem., Waste Management Adv. Council; Joint Editor, Flora Europæa Project, 1956–. Chm., NI Adv. Council for Education, 1966–75; Chairman: Ulster American Folk Park, 1975–88; NI American Bicentennial Cttee, 1975–77; Scots Irish Trust, 1977–92; Chm., Nat. Trust NI Cttee, 1978–81. Mem., Acad. Adv. Cttee, Loughborough Univ., 1967–71. Served War of 1939–45, RAF Bomber Command (despatches). Hon. LLD QUB, 1973; Hon. DTech Loughborough, 1975; Hon. DSc Ulster, 1977. *Publications:* Micro-organisms in the Soil, 1958; (with F. Raw) Soil Biology, 1967; reports: Primary Educn in Northern Ireland, 1968; Existing Selection Procedure for Secondary Educn in Northern Ireland, 1971; Reorganisation of Secondary Educn in Northern Ireland, 1973; various in scientific journals on plant diseases and fungi. *Recreation:* sailing. *Address:* Tokes Cottage, Semley, Wilts SP7 8BP. *T:* East Knoyle (01747) 830297. *Club:* Royal Air Force.

BURGES, Maj.-Gen. Rodney Lyon Travers, CBE 1963; DSO 1946; *b* 19 March 1914; *s* of Richard Burges and Hilda Christine Burges (*née* Lyon); *m* 1946, Sheila Marion Lyster Goldby (*d* 1991), *d* of H. L. Goldby; one *d* (one *s* decd). *Educ:* Wellington; RMA, Woolwich. 2nd Lieut RA, 1934; war service in Burma, 1942 and 1944–45; CO The Berkshire Yeomanry (145 Fd Regt, RA), 1945; Comdr, E Battery, RHA, 1949–51; Bt Lt-Col 1953; 2nd in comd, 1 RHA, 1954–55; CO 3 RHA, 1955–57; CRA 3 Div., 1958–59; IDC, 1960; Brig. Q (Ops) WO, 1961–63; CCRA, 1 Corps, BAOR, 1963–64; Maj.-Gen. 1964; GOC, Cyprus District, 1964–66; VQMG, MoD, 1966–67. Joined Grieveson, Grant & Co., 1968, Partner 1971, retd 1978; Consultant to Pat Simon Wines Ltd, 1978–85; Dir, Caroline Fine Wines Ltd, 1982–85. Freeman and Liveryman, Fishmongers' Co., 1974. *Recreations:* racing, drinking wine in the sun. *Address:* Freemantle, Over Wallop, Hants SO20 8JE. *Clubs:* Buck's, Army and Navy.

BURGES WATSON, Richard Eagleson Gordon; *see* Watson, R. E. G. B.

BURGESS, Anthony Reginald Frank, (Tony), CVO 1983; consultant on Third World development; HM Diplomatic Service, retired; *b* 27 Jan. 1932; *s* of Beatrice Burgess; *m* 1960, Carlyn Shawyer; one *s*. *Educ:* Ealing Grammar Sch.; University College London (BScEcon). National Service, 1953–55, TA, 16 Airborne Div., 1955–57. Journalism, 1955–62; European Community Civil Service, 1962–65, HM Diplomatic Service, 1966–: 1st Sec., European Economic Organisations Dept, FCO, 1966–67; 1st Sec. (Political), Dhaka, 1967–69; 1st Sec., SE Asia Dept, FCO, 1970–72; 1st Sec. (Economic), Ottawa, 1972–76; Head of Chancery and HM Consul, Bogota, 1976–79; 1st Sec., Rhodesia Dept, FCO, 1979–80; Asst Head of Information Dept, FCO, 1980–82; Dep. High Comr, Dhaka, 1982–86; Counsellor and Hd of Chancery, Havana, 1989–89. *Publication:* (jtly) The Common Market and the Treaty of Rome Explained, 1967. *Recreations:* travel, photography, shooting, riding. *Address:* c/o Barclays Bank, 23 St James's Street, SW1A 1HE. *Club:* Brooks's.

BURGESS, Averil, OBE 1994; Chairman: Camden and Islington Family Health Services Authority, 1993–April 1996; Independent Schools Joint Council Accreditation, Review and Consultancy Service, since 1993; *b* 8 July 1938; *d* of David and Dorothy Evans (*née* Owen); *m* 1959, Clifford Burgess (marr. diss. 1973). *Educ:* Ashby-de-la-Zouch Girls' Grammar Sch.; Queen Mary Coll., Univ. of London. BA Hons History. Assistant Mistress: Langleybury Secondary Modern Sch., 1959–60; Ensham Sch., 1960–62; Hatfield Sch., 1963–65; Fulham County Sch., 1965–69; Wimbledon High Sch., GPDST, 1969–74 (Head of History and Second Mistress); Headmistress, South Hampstead High School, GPDST, 1975–93. Chm., Policy Gp, ISJC, 1990–; Member: Council for Accreditation of Teacher Educn, 1990–93; Nat. Commn on Educn, 1991–93. Girls' Schools Association: Chm., Educn Sub-Cttee, 1984–88 (Mem., 1983–88); Mem., Exec. Cttee, 1984–91; Pres., 1988–89. Governor: Central Sch. of Speech and Drama, 1981–95; Mus. of London, 1994–. *Recreations:* visiting France, listening to music (especially opera), mountain walking in Wales and other forms of non-competitive exercise. *Address:* 123 North Hill, Highgate, N6 4DP.

BURGESS, Claude Bramall, CMG 1958; OBE 1954; Minister for Hong Kong Commercial Relations with the European Communities and the Member States, 1974–82; *b* 25 Feb. 1910; *s* of late George Herbert Burgess, Weaverham, Cheshire, and Martha Elizabeth Burgess; *m* 1952, Margaret Joan Webb (marr. diss. 1965); one *s*; *m* 1969, Linda Nettleton, *e d* of William Grothier Beilby, New York. *Educ:* Epworth Coll.; Christ Church, Oxford. Eastern Cadetship in HM Colonial Administrative Service, 1932. Commissioned in RA, 1940; POW, 1941–45; demobilized with rank of Lieut-Col, RA, 1946. Colonial Office, 1946–48. Attended Imperial Defence Coll., London, 1951. Various Government posts in Hong Kong; Colonial Secretary (and Actg Governor on various occasions), Hong Kong, 1958–63, retd; Head of Co-ordination and Develt Dept, EFTA, 1964–73. *Address:* 75 Chester Row, SW1W 8JL. *T:* 0171–730 8758.

BURGESS, Cyril Duncan, CB 1989; ERD 1970; Chairman, Council for Registered Gas Installers, 1991–94; *b* 18 Oct. 1929; *s* of John Arthur Burgess and Doris (*née* Sedgwick); *m* 1954, Jean Kathleen Whitney; one *s* one *d*. *Educ:* Southgate County Grammar Sch.; Univ. of London (BSc). CChem; MRSC. National Service, Royal Signals, 1950. Asst Engineer, English Electric Co., 1952; HM Factory Inspectorate, 1953; served in London and Huddersfield; Sup. Inspector, Scotland, 1974; Sec., Adv. Cttee on Asbestos, 1976; Dir, Hazardous Substances Div., HSE, 1978–89. Chm., Adv. Cttees on Dangerous Substances,

1982, on Toxic Substances, 1985. *Address:* 108 Gravel Lane, Hemel Hempstead, Herts HP1 1SB. *T:* Hemel Hempstead (01442) 392734.

BURGESS, Rev. David John, FSA; Guild Vicar of St Lawrence Jewry Next Guildhall, The Church of the Corporation of London, since 1987; a Chaplain to The Queen, since 1987; *b* 4 Aug. 1939; *e s* of Albert Burgess and Mary Burgess (*née* Kelsey); *m* 1976, Dr Kathleen Louise, *d* of Philip Lindsay Costeloe; one *s* one *d. Educ:* King's School, Peterborough; Trinity Hall, Cambridge; Cuddesdon Theological Coll. FSA 1992. Orthodox Studentship, Halki, Istanbul, 1963–64. Curate, All Saints, Maidstone, 1965; Assistant Chaplain, University Coll., Oxford, 1966; Fellow, 1969; Chaplain, 1970; Domestic Bursar, 1971; Canon of St George's Chapel, Windsor, 1978–87. Hon. Fellow, Inst. of Clerks of Works, 1978; Churchill Hon. Fellow, Westminster Coll., Fulton, Miss, 1989. *Publications:* articles and reviews. *Recreations:* opera, art, cooking. *Address:* The Vicarage, St Lawrence Jewry Next Guildhall, EC2V 5AA. *T:* 0171–600 9478.

BURGESS, Dilys Averil; *see* Burgess, A.

BURGESS, Gen. Sir Edward (Arthur), KCB 1982; OBE 1972; Deputy Supreme Allied Commander, Europe, 1984–87; Aide-de-Camp General to the Queen, 1985–87; *b* 30 Sept. 1927; *s* of Edward Burgess and Alice Burgess; *m* 1954, Jean Angelique Leslie Henderson; one *s* one *d. Educ:* All Saints Sch., Bloxham; Lincoln Coll., Oxford; RMA, Sandhurst. Commnd RA 1948; served Germany and ME, 1949–59; psc 1960; GSO 2 WO, 1961–63; served Germany and Far East, 1963–65; jssc 1966; Mil. Asst to C-in-C BAOR, 1966–67; GSO I (DS) Staff Coll., 1968–70; CO 25 Light Regt, RA, 1970–72; CRA 4th Div., 1972–74; Dir of Army Recruiting, 1975–77; Dir, Combat Development (Army), 1977–79; GOC Artillery Div., 1979–82; Comdr, UK Field Army, and Inspector Gen. TA, 1982–84. Gentleman Usher to the Sword of State, 1988–. Col Comdt, RA, 1982–92. Hon. Colonel: 6/7 (V) Bn Queen's Regt, 1991–92; 6/7 (V) Bn Princess of Wales's Royal Regt, 1992–. President: Royal British Legion, 1987–93; Army Football Assoc., 1982–88; Hon. Vice Pres., FA, 1982–88. Freeman, City of London, 1988; Liveryman, Glaziers' Co., 1989; Hon. Liveryman, Haberdashers' Co., 1990. *Publications:* articles in military jls. *Recreations:* sailing, fishing, music, reading, gardening. *Address:* c/o Lloyds Bank, Haslemere, Surrey. *Club:* Army and Navy.

BURGESS, Geoffrey Harold Orchard; Chief Scientist (Agriculture and Horticulture), Ministry of Agriculture, Fisheries and Food, 1982–86; *b* 28 March 1926; *s* of late Harold Frank and Eva M. F. Burgess, Reading; *m* 1952, Barbara Vernon, *y d* of late Rev. Gilbert Vernon Yonge; two *s. Educ:* Reading Sch.; Univ. of Reading; UC Hull. BSc Reading, 1951 (Colin Morley Prizewinner 1950); PhD London, 1955. Special research appt, Univ. of Hull, 1951; Sen. Scientific Officer, DSIR, Humber Lab., Hull, 1954; PSO, Torry Res. Stn, Aberdeen, 1960; Officer i/c, Humber Lab., Hull, 1962; Director, Torry Res. Station, 1969–79; Head of Biology Div., Agrictl Science Service, and Officer i/c Slough Lab., MAFF, 1979–82. Hon. Res. Lectr in Fish Technology, Univ. of Aberdeen, 1969–79; Buckland Lectr, 1964; Hon. Lectr in Fish Technology, Univ. of Leeds, 1966–69; Mem. Adv. Cttee on Food Science, Univ. of Leeds, 1970–86; Mem., Panel of Fish Technology Experts, FAO, 1962–79. *Publications:* Developments in the Handling and Processing of Fish, 1965; (with Lovern, Waterman and Cutting) Fish Handling and Processing, 1965; The Curious World of Frank Buckland, 1967; scientific and technical papers, reviews, reports etc concerning handling, processing, transport and preservation for food, of fish, from catching to consumption. *Recreations:* music, book collecting, walking. *Address:* Stoneleghe, Croxton, Stafford ST21 6NL. *T:* Wetwood (01630) 620202.

BURGESS, Geoffrey Kelsen; Chief Executive and Clerk, Cornwall County Council, 1982–93 (Deputy Clerk, 1969–82); *b* 4 June 1935; *s* of Monty and Edith Burgess; *m* 1959, Brenda (*née* Martin); three *s. Educ:* Central Foundn Boys' Grammar Sch.; London Sch. of Econs and Pol Science (LLB). Admitted solicitor, 1959. Articled with Simon, Haynes, Barlas & Cassels, London, 1956–59; Assistant Solicitor: East Ham CBC, 1960–62; Worcs CC, 1962–63; Northumberland CC, 1963–65; Asst Clerk, Berks CC, 1965–69; Clerk: Cornwall Magistrates' Courts Cttee, 1982–93; Cornwall Sea Fisheries Cttee, 1982–93; Devon and Cornwall Police Authy, 1988–93; Secretary: Adv. Cttee on appt of Magistrates in Cornwall, 1982–93; Cornwall Probation Cttee, 1982–93. *Recreations:* music, walking.

BURGESS, Rear-Adm. John, CB 1987; LVO 1975; CEng; Director, Rolls-Royce and Associates, since 1987; *b* 13 July 1929; *s* of Albert Burgess and Winifred (*née* Evans); *m* 1952, Avis (*née* Morgan); two *d. Educ:* RN Engineering College; Advanced Engineering RN College, Greenwich; nuclear courses, RN College. HM Ships Aisne, Maidstone, Theseus, Implacable, Cumberland, Caprice; Lectr in Thermodynamics, RNEC, 1962–65; HMS Victorious; nuclear reactor design and manufacture at Rolls Royce, 1968–70; Naval Staff, Washington, DC, 1970–72; Royal Yacht Britannia, 1972–75; Head, Forward Design Group, Ship Dept, 1975–77; Naval Asst to Controller of the Navy, 1977–79; in Command, HMS Defiance, 1979–81; in Command, HMS Sultan, 1981–83; Man. Dir, HM Dockyard, Rosyth, 1984–87. Chm., Maber and Rame Parish Council; occasional involvement with urban devlt and waterfront management cttees. *Publications:* papers to professional bodies. *Recreations:* golf, sailing.

BURGESS, Ven. John Edward; Archdeacon of Bath, since 1975; *b* 9 Dec. 1930; *s* of Herbert and Dorothy May Burgess; *m* 1958, Jonquil Marion Bailey; one *s* one *d. Educ:* Surbiton County Gram. Sch.; London Univ. (St John's Hall). BD (2nd Cl.), ALCD (1st Cl.). Shell Chemicals Ltd, 1947–53. Asst Curate, St Mary Magdalen, Bermondsey, 1957–60; Asst Curate, St Mary, Southampton, 1960–62; Vicar of Dunston with Coppenhall, Staffs, 1962–67; Chaplain, Staffordshire Coll. of Technology, 1963–67; Vicar of Keynsham with Queen Charlton and Burnett, Somerset, 1967–75; Rural Dean of Keynsham, 1971–74. *Recreation:* history of railways. *Address:* Birnfels, 56 Grange Road, Saltford, Bristol BS18 3AG. *T:* Saltford (01225) 873609, *Fax:* 01225 874110.

BURGESS, Sir (Joseph) Stuart, Kt 1994; CBE 1984; PhD; FRSC; Chairman, Anglia and Oxford Regional Health Authority, since 1994; Member, NHS Policy Board, since 1994; *b* 20 March 1929; *s* of late Joseph and Emma Burgess (*née* Wollerton); *m* 1955, Valerie Ann Street; one *s* one *d. Educ:* Barnsley Holgate Grammar School; University College London (1st Class Hons BSc Chem, PhD; Fellow, 1994). Amersham International plc (formerly The Radiochemical Centre), 1953–89: Gp Marketing Controller, 1977–79; Chief Exec., 1979–89; Pres., Amersham Corp. USA, 1975–77; Advr, Immuno Internat. AG, 1990–; Chm., Immuno UK Ltd, 1992–; Director: Haemonetics Corp. USA, 1992–; Anagen plc, 1993–. Chm., Oxford RHA, 1990–94. Dir, American Chamber of Commerce (UK), 1988–90. Member: Innovation Adv. Bd, DTI, 1988–93; ACOST Med. Res. and Health Cttee, 1991–92. CIMgt (CBIM 1986; Chm., Res. and Manufacturing Cttee, 1990–93; Mem., Nat. Manufacturing Council, 1991–92). *Recreations:* golf, music. *Address:* Barrington, Hearn Close, Penn, Bucks HP10 8JT. *T:* Penn (01494) 816387.

BURGESS, Sally, (Mrs N. S. Thornton); classical singer; *b* 9 Oct. 1953; *d* of Edna Rushton (formerly Burgess; *née* Sharman) and Douglas Burgess; *m* 1988, Neal Scott Thornton; one *s. Educ:* Royal College of Music. ARCM. Joined ENO 1977; for ENO as a soprano, rôles incl. Zerlina, Cherubino, Pamina, Mimi, Micaela; for ENO as a mezzo, rôles incl. Composer (Ariadne), Sextus (Julius Caesar), Charlotte (Werther), Carmen, Fennimore (Fennimore and Gerda), 1990; Judith (Duke Bluebeard's Castle), 1991; Octavian (Rosenkavalier), 1994; Mrs Begbick (Mahagonny), 1995; Opera North: Amneris (Aida), Dido (Trojans), Julie (Showboat), 1989–90; Orfeo (Glück), 1990; Laura (La Gioconda), 1993; Azucena (Trovatore), 1994; Royal Opera, Covent Garden: Siebel (Faust), Maddalena (Rigoletto), 1989; Scottish Opera: Fricka (Die Walküre), Amneris (Aida), 1991; New York Metropolitan: Carmen, 1995; Queen Isabella (The Voyage), 1996; Glyndebourne: Smeraldina (Love for Three Oranges); Amneris, Strasbourg, Wiesbaden, Lausanne and Nancy; Carmen, Oregon, Zürich, Berlin and NZ; Delilah, Nantes; numerous concert appearances; numerous recordings, incl. Liverpool Oratorio, and jazz. *Recreations:* family, cooking, walking, reading, singing jazz, theatre. *Address:* IMG Artists Europe, Media House, 3 Burlington Lane, Chiswick, W6 2TH.

BURGESS, Sir Stuart; *see* Burgess, Sir J. S.

BURGESS, Tony; *see* Burgess, A. R. F.

BURGH, 7th Baron, *cr* 1529 (title called out of abeyance, 1916; by some reckonings he is 9th Baron (from a *cr* 1487) and his father was 8th and grandfather 7th); **Alexander Peter Willoughby Leith;** *b* 20 March 1935; *s* of 6th (or 8th) Baron Burgh; *S* father 1959; *m* 1957, Anita Lorna Eldridge (marr. diss. 1982); two *s* one *d. Educ:* Harrow; Magdalene Coll., Cambridge (BA). *Heir: s* Hon. Alexander Gregory Disney Leith [*b* 16 March 1958; *m* 1984, Catherine Mary, *d* of David Parkes; one *s*].

BURGH, Sir John (Charles), KCMG 1982; CB 1975; President, Trinity College, University of Oxford, 1987–July 1996; Chairman, Associated Board of the Royal Schools of Music, 1987–94; Director-General, British Council, 1980–87; *b* 9 Dec. 1925; *m* 1957, Ann Sturge; two *d. Educ:* Friends' Sch., Sibford; London Sch. of Economics (BSc Econ.; Leverhulme post-intermediate Schol.; Pres. of Union, 1949; Hon. Fellow, 1983). Asst Principal, BoT, 1950; Private Sec. to successive Ministers of State, BoT, 1954–57; Colonial Office, 1959–62; Mem., UK Delegation to UN Conf. on Trade and Devlt, 1964; Asst Sec., DEA, 1964; Principal Private Sec. to successive First Secretaries of State and Secretaries of State for Econ. Affairs, 1965–68; Under-Sec., Dept of Employment, 1968–71; Dep.-Chm., Community Relations Commn, 1971–72; Deputy Secretary: Cabinet Office (Central Policy Rev. Staff), 1972–74; Dept of Prices and Consumer Protection, 1974–79; Dept of Trade, 1979–80. Member: Executive, PEP, 1972–78; Council, Policy Studies Inst., 1978–85; Council, RSA, 1982–85; Council, VSO, 1980–87; Acad. Council, Wilton Park, 1984–87; Exec. Cttee, Anglo-Austrian Soc., 1987–; Council, RIIA, 1993–95. Chairman: Nat. Opera Co-ordinating Cttee, 1991– (Sec., 1972–91); Oxford Educnl Trust for Develt of the Arts, 1990–95; Dir, English Shakespeare Co., 1988–94. Chm. Ct of Governors, LSE, 1985–87 (Gov., 1980–); Vice-Chm., Yehudi Menuhin Sch., 1994–. FRCM 1994. Hon. RNCM 1986. Hon. LLD Bath, 1987. *Recreations:* friends, music, the arts generally. *Address:* Trinity College, Oxford OX1 3BH.

BURGHLEY, Lord; Anthony John Cecil; *b* 9 Aug. 1970; *s* and *heir* of Marquess of Exeter, *qv. Educ:* Eton.

BURGNER, Thomas Ulric; Secretary, Committee of Vice Chancellors and Principals, 1989–95; *b* 6 March 1932; *s* of John Henry Burgner and Clara Doerte Burgner (*née* Wolff); *m* 1958, Marion (*née* Chasik); two *s. Educ:* Haberdashers' Aske's, Hampstead; St Catharine's Coll., Cambridge (BA (Hons), MA); Dip. Personnel Management. Flying Officer, RAF, 1954–55. National Coal Board, 1955–61; Assoc. of Chemical and Allied Employers, 1961–65; Principal, Dept of Economic Affairs, 1965–69; HM Treasury: Principal, 1969–72; Asst Secretary, 1972–76; Head of Exchange Control Div., 1972–74; Head of General Aid Div., 1974–76; Under Secretary, 1976; on secondment as Sec., NEDC, 1976–80; Head of Public Enterprises Gp, 1980–85; Head, Industry, Agric. and Employment Gp, 1985–89. Mem., BSC, 1980–83. Trustee, Anna Freud Centre, 1994–. Consultant, LTW. *Address:* 12 Kingsley Place, Highgate, N6 5EA.

BURGON, Geoffrey; composer; *b* 15 July 1941; *s* of Alan Wybert Burgon and Ada Vera Isom; *m* 1963, Janice Elizabeth Garwood (marr. diss.); one *s* one *d*; *m* 1992, Jacqueline Krofchak; one *s. Educ:* Pewley Sch., Guildford; Guildhall School of Music and Drama; studied composition with Peter Wishart, trumpet with Bernard Brown. Freelance trumpeter, 1964–71: Royal Opera House (stage band), Philomusica, London Mozart Players, Northern Sinfonia, Jacques and Capriol Orchestras, also session work, theatres and jazz bands. Full time composer and conductor, 1971–; work in almost every musical genre, particularly orchestral, choral, and music for dance, film & TV; commissions from many Festivals, incl. Bath, Edinburgh, Cheltenham, Southern Cathedrals, Three Choirs, and Camden; also many works for Dance, incl. Ballet Rambert and London Contemporary Dance Theatre; work performed internationally. *Major works:* Gending; Alleluia Nativitas; The World Again; Acquainted with Night; Think on Dreadful Domesday; Canciones del Alma; Requiem; Revelations; Title Divine; Short Mass; The Golden Eternity; The Fire of Heaven, Dos Coros; A Hymn to the Creatures; The Golden Fish; The Calm; Running Figures; Goldbergs Dream; Songs, Lamentations and Praises; Mass; The Trials of Prometheus; Hymn to Venus; Five Sonnets of John Donne; Four Guitars; Six Studies for Solo Cello; Worldes Blisse; Trumpet Concerto: the Turning World; First Was the World; *opera:* Hard Times; *film scores:* Life of Brian; Dogs of War; Turtle Diary; Robin Hood; *television scores:* Tinker, Tailor, Soldier, Spy; Brideshead Revisited; Bleak House; Happy Valley; Chronicles of Narnia; Children of the North; Martin Chuzzlewit. Prince Pierre of Monaco Award, 1969; Ivor Novello Award, 1979, 1981; Gold Disc for Brideshead record, 1986. *Recreations:* playing jazz, cricket, Bristol motor cars, sleeping. *Address:* c/o Chester Music, 8/9 Frith Street, W1V 5TZ. *T:* 0171–434 0066.

BURGOYNE, Rear-Adm. Robert Michael, CB 1982; *b* 20 March 1927; *s* of Robert and Elizabeth Burgoyne; *m* 1951, Margaret (Hilda) McCook; one *s* one *d. Educ:* Bradfield College; Magdalene College, Cambridge. Joined RN 1945; CO HMS Cleopatra, 1967–68; Captain 2nd Frigate Sqdn and CO HMS Undaunted, 1972–73; Dir, Maritime Tactical Sch., 1974–75; CO HMS Antrim, 1975–77; Comdr, British Navy Staff, Washington and UK Rep. to SACLANT, 1977–80; Senior Naval Member, Directing Staff, RCDS, 1980–82. Dir, RIN, 1983–92. Vice-Pres., Sea Safety Gp (UK), 1992–.

BURKE, Adm. Arleigh Albert; Navy Cross; DSM (3 Gold Stars); Legion of Merit (with 2 Gold Stars and Army Oak Leaf Cluster). Silver Star Medal, Purple Heart, Presidential Unit Citation Ribbon (with 3 stars), Navy Unit Commendation Ribbon; retired as Chief of Naval Operations, US Navy and Member of Joint Chiefs of Staff (1955–61); Member of Board of Directors, Freedoms Foundation, at Valley Forge; *b* 19 Oct. 1901; *s* of Oscar A. and Claire Burke; *m* 1923, Roberta Gorsuch; no *c. Educ:* United States Naval Academy; Univ. of Michigan (MSE). Commnd ensign, USN, 1923, advancing through grades to Admiral, 1955. USS Arizona, 1923–28; Gunnery Dept, US Base Force, 1928; Post-graduate course (explosives), 1929–31; USS Chester, 1932; Battle Force Camera Party, 1933–35; Bureau of Ordnance, 1935–37; USS Craven, 1937–39; USS Mugford, Captain, 1939–40; Naval Gun Factory, 1940–43; Destroyer Divs 43 and 44, Squadron 12 Comdg, 1943; Destroyer Squadron 23 Comdg, 1943–44; Chief of Staff to Commander Task Force 58 (Carriers), 1944–45; Head of Research and Development Bureau of Ordnance, 1945–46; Chief of Staff, Comdr Eighth Fleet and Atlantic Fleet, 1947–48; USS

Huntington, Captain, 1949; Asst Chief of Naval Ops, 1949–50; Cruiser Div. 5, Comdr, 1951; Dep. Chief of Staff, Commander Naval Forces, Far East, 1951; Director Strategic Plans Div., Office of the Chief of Naval Operations, 1952–53; Cruiser Division 6, Commanding, 1954; Commander Destroyer Force, Atlantic, 1955. Member: American Legion; American Soc. of Naval Engineers and numerous other naval assocs, etc.; National Geographic Society; also foreign societies, etc. Holds several hon. degrees. Ul Chi Medal (Korea), 1954; Korean Presidential Unit Citation, 1954. *Recreations:* reading, gardening. *Address:* The Virginian, Apt 323, 9229 Arlington Boulevard, Fairfax, VA 22031, USA. *Clubs:* Army-Navy Town, Metropolitan, Chevy Chase, Alfalfa, Circus Saints and Sinners, Ends of the Earth, etc (Washington, DC); Quindecum (Newport, US); The Brook, Lotos, Salmagundi, Inner Wheel, Seawanhaka Corinthian Yacht (New York); Bohemian (San Francisco).

BURKE, Most Rev. Austin-Emile; *see* Halifax (NS), Archbishop of, (RC).

BURKE, Hon. Brian Thomas, AC 1988; JP; Australian Ambassador to Republic of Ireland and to the Holy See, 1988–91; *b* 25 Feb. 1947; *s* of late Thomas Burke (Federal ALP Member for Perth, 1942–53), and Madeline Burke; *m* 1965, Susanne May Nevill; four *s* two *d*. *Educ:* Brigidine Convent; Marist Brothers' Coll.; Univ. of Western Australia. FAMI. Former journalist. MLA (Lab) Balga, WA, 1973–88; Opposition Shadow Minister, 1976–81; Leader of the Opposition, 1981–83; Premier and Treasurer of WA, 1983–88; Minister for: Women's Interests, 1983–87; Public Sector Management, 1987. Mem., numerous community and sporting orgns; former No 1 ticket holder, Perth FC; former Patron, Soccer Fedn of WA. Jaycees Outstanding Young W Australian Award, 1982. *Recreations:* reading, stamp-collecting, writing poetry, swimming, fishing. *Address:* PO Box 668, Scarborough, WA 6019, Australia.

BURKE, Prof. Derek Clissold, CBE 1994; DL; Vice-Chancellor, University of East Anglia, 1987–95; *b* 13 Feb. 1930; *s* of late Harold Burke and Ivy Ruby (*née* Clissold); *m* 1955, Mary Elizabeth Dukeshire, New York; one *s* three *d*. *Educ:* Univ. of Birmingham (BSc, PhD, Chemistry). Res. Fellow, Yale Univ., 1953–55; Scientist, Nat. Inst. for Med. Res., London, 1955–60; Lectr and Sen. Lectr, Dept of Biochemistry, Univ. of Aberdeen, 1960–69; Prof. of Biol Scis, 1969–82, Pro-Vice-Chancellor, 1971–73, Univ. of Warwick; Vice-Pres. and Scientific Dir, Allelix Inc., Toronto, 1982–86. Member: MRC Cell Bd, 1976–79; Scientific Cttee, Cancer Res. Campaign, 1979–82 and of CRC Council, 1987–; Europ. Molecular Biol Org., 1980–; Adv. Bd, AFRC Inst. of Food Res., 1989–; Adv. Cttee on Genetic Modification, HSE, 1987–95; Steering Gp, Technol. Foresight Initiative, OST, 1993–; Sci. and Engrg Bd, 1994–, Technol. Interaction Bd, 1994–, BBSRC. Chm., Adv. Cttee on Novel Foods and Processes, Dept of Health and MAFF, 1989–. Chm. Council, Paterson Inst. for Cancer Res., 1992–. Pres., Soc. for Gen. Microbiology, 1987–90. Editor and Editor in Chief, Journal of General Virology, 1976–87. Trustee, Norfolk and Norwich Fest., 1988–. Hon. LLD Aberdeen 1982; Hon. ScD UEA, 1995. DL Norfolk, 1992. *Publications:* Creation and Evolution (ed and contrib.), 1985; numerous sci. papers on interferon and animal viruses. *Recreations:* music, walking. *Address:* 13 Pretoria Road, Cambridge CB4 1HD. *Club:* Royal Over-Seas League.

BURKE, Rt. Rev. Geoffrey; Titular Bishop of Vagrauta; Auxiliary Bishop of Salford (RC), 1967–88; *b* 31 July 1913; *s* of Dr Peter Joseph Burke and Margaret Mary (*née* Coman). *Educ:* St Bede's Coll., Manchester; Stonyhurst Coll.; Oscott Coll., Birmingham; Downing Coll., Cambridge (MA). Taught History, St Bede's Coll., 1940–66; Prefect of Studies, 1950; Rector, 1966. Consecrated Bishop 29 June 1967. *Address:* St John's Cathedral, 250 Chapel Street, Salford, Lancashire M3 5LL. *T:* 0161–834 0333.

BURKE, Sir James (Stanley Gilbert), 9th Bt *cr* 1797 (Ire.), of Marble Hill, Galway; *b* 1 July 1956; *s* of Sir Thomas Stanley Burke, 8th Bt and Susanne Margaretha (*d* 1983), *er d* of Otto Salvisberg, Thun, Switzerland; *S* father, 1989; *m* 1980, Laura, *d* of Domingo Branzuela; one *s* one *d*. *Heir:* *s* Martin James Burke, *b* 22 July 1980. *Address:* Lindenbergstrasse 231, 5618 Bettwil, Switzerland.

BURKE, Jeffrey Peter, QC 1984; a Recorder of the Crown Court, since 1983; *b* 15 Dec. 1941; *s* of Samuel and Gertrude Burke; *m* 1994, Joanna Mary Heal. *Educ:* Shrewsbury Sch.; Brasenose Coll., Oxford (BA 1963). Called to the Bar, Inner Temple, 1964. Legal Mem., Mental Health Review Tribunal, 1994–. *Recreations:* sport, wine, charity triathlons, fighting stinging nettles. *Address:* Devereux Chambers, Devereux Court, Temple, WC2R 3JJ. *Clubs:* Economicals AFC; Caledon Cricket.

BURKE, John Joseph; Managing Director and Chief Executive, Bristol and West Building Society, since 1993; *b* 18 Sept. 1942; *m* 1967, Sally Elliott; three *s*. *Educ:* Bridlington Grammar Sch.; Sutton High Sch., Plymouth. Family retail business, 1958–64; Bristol & West Building Society, 1964–; Gen. Manager, Retail Ops, 1988–90, Business Develt, 1990–91; Main Bd Dir, 1991–; Business Develt Dir, 1991–93. *Recreations:* fishing, Rugby supporter. *Address:* Bristol & West Building Society, PO Box 27, Broad Quay, Bristol BS99 7AX; Applewood, Streamleaze, Chew Magna, Bristol BS18 8SE. *T:* Chew Magna (01275) 332105.

BURKE, John Kenneth; QC 1985; **His Honour Judge Burke;** a Circuit Judge, since 1995; *b* 4 Aug. 1939; *s* of Kenneth Burke and Madeline Burke; *m* 1962, Margaret Anne (*née* Scattergood); three *d*. *Educ:* Stockport Grammar Sch. Served Cheshire Regt, 1958–60; TA Parachute Regt, 1962–67. Called to the Bar, Middle Temple, 1965, Bencher, 1992. A Recorder, 1980–95. *Recreations:* painting and drawing, walking.

BURKE, Hon. Sir Kerry; *see* Burke, Hon. Sir T. K.

BURKE, Peter; *see* Burke, U. P.

BURKE, Prof. Philip George, CBE 1993; FRS 1978; MRIA 1974; Professor of Mathematical Physics, Queen's University of Belfast, since 1967; *b* 18 Oct. 1932; *s* of Henry Burke and Frances Mary Sprague; *m* 1959, Valerie Mona Martin; four *d*. *Educ:* Wanstead County High Sch.; Univ. Coll. of SW of England, Exeter (BSc London (ext.) 1953, 1st cl. Hons Physics); University Coll. London (PhD 1956, Fellow 1986). Res. Fellow, UCL, 1956–57; Asst Lectr, Univ. of London Computer Unit, 1957–59; Res. Associate, Alvarez Bubble Chamber Gp and Theory Gp, Lawrence Berkeley Lab., Calif, 1959–62; Res. Fellow, then Principal Scientific Officer, later SPSO, Theoretical Physics Div., AERE, Harwell, 1962–67; Queen's University of Belfast: Head, Dept of Applied Maths and Theoretical Physics, 1974–77; Dir, Sch. of Maths and Physics, 1988–90. Science, subseq. Science and Engineering, Research Council: Mem., Physics Cttee, 1967–71; Mem., Atlas Comp. Cttee, 1973–76; Hd, Div. of Theory and Computational Sci., Daresbury Lab., 1977–82; Chm., Science Bd Computer Cttee, 1976–77 and 1984–86; Chm., Scientific Computing Adv. Panel, 1989–94; Mem., 1989–94; Chairman: Internat. Conf. on Physics of Electronic and Atomic Collisions, 1973–75; Computational Physics Gp, Europ. Physical Soc., 1976–78; Atomic, Molecular and Optical Physics Div., Inst. of Physics, 1987–90; Allocations and Resources Panel, Jt Res. Councils Supercomputer Cttee, 1988–90; Supercomputing Management Cttee, 1991–94; Mem., ABRC Supercomputing Sub-cttee, 1991–94. Mem., Council, Royal Soc., 1990–92. Co-ordinator, EU HCM Network of nine European labs, 1993–; Hon. DSc Exeter, 1981. Guthrie Medal, Inst. of Physics, 1994. *Publications:* (with H. Kleinpoppen) series editor, Physics of Atoms and Molecules; principal editor, then hon. editor, Computer Physics Communications, 1969–; many papers in learned journals. *Recreations:* walking, swimming, reading. *Address:* Department of Applied Mathematics and Theoretical Physics, Queen's University of Belfast, Belfast BT7 1NN. *T:* Belfast (01232) 335047, *Fax:* (01232) 239182; 33 Leverogue Road, Lisburn, N Ireland BT27 5PP. *T:* Drumbo (01232) 826416.

BURKE, Richard; President, Canon Foundation in Europe, since 1988; *b* 29 March 1932; *s* of David Burke and Elisabeth Burke; *m* 1961, Mary Freeley; two *s* three *d*. *Educ:* University Coll., Dublin (MA). Called to the Bar, King's Inns. Mem., Dublin Co. Council, 1967–73 (Chm., 1972–73); Mem. Dail Eireann, for South County Dublin, 1969–77, for Dublin West, 1981–82; Fine Gael Chief Whip and spokesman on Posts and Telegraphs, 1969–73; Minister for Education, 1973–76. Commission of the European Communities: Member with special responsibility for Transport, Taxation, Consumer Protection, Relations with European Parlt, Research, Educ. and Sci., 1977–81, for Greenland, Greek Memorandum, Personnel and Admin, Jt Interpretation and Conf. Service, Statistical Office and Office of Publications, 1982–85; Vice Pres., 1984–85. Associate Fellow, Center for Internat. Affairs, Harvard Univ., 1980–81. Member: Conseil d'Administration, FIDEPS, UNESCO, 1990–; Develt Council, HEC, Paris, 1990–. Chieftain, Burke Clan, 1990, Hon. Life Pres., 1992. Pro Merito Europa Medal, 1980. Grand Croix, Leopold II (Belgium), 1981; Grand Croix, Phoenix (Greece), 1983. *Recreations:* music, golf, travel. *Address:* 67 Ailesbury Road, Dublin 4, Ireland. *T:* 2692520; (office) Canon Foundation, Rijnsbergerweg 3, 2334 BA Leiden, Netherlands. *T:* (71) 156555.

BURKE, Hon. Sir (Thomas) Kerry, Kt 1990; Speaker, New Zealand House of Representatives, 1987–90; *b* 24 March 1942; *m* 1st, 1968, Jennifer Shiel (marr. diss. 1984); two *s*; 2nd, 1984, Helen Paske (*d* 1989); one *s*. *Educ:* Linwood High Sch.; Univ. of Canterbury (BA); Christchurch Teachers' Coll. (Dip. Teaching). General labourer, Auckland, 1965–66; factory deleg., Auckland Labourers' Union; teacher: Rangiora High Sch., 1967–72; Greymouth High Sch., 1975–78. Chm., Rangiora Post-Primary Teachers' Assoc., 1969–71. MP (Lab) Rangiora, 1972–75, West Coast, 1978–90; Minister of Regional Develt, and of Employment and Immigration, 1984–87. *Recreations:* ski-ing, swimming.

BURKE, Tom; Special Adviser to Secretary of State for the Environment, since 1991; *b* 5 Jan. 1947; *s* of J. V. Burke, DSM, and Mary (*née* Bradley). *Educ:* St Boniface's, Plymouth; Liverpool Univ. (BA (Hons) Philosophy). Great George's Community Arts Project, 1969–70; Lecturer: West Cheshire Coll., 1970–71; Old Swan Technical Coll., 1971–73; Friends of the Earth: Local Groups Co-ordinator, 1973–75; Executive Director, 1975–79; Dir of Special Projects, 1979–80; Vice-Chm., 1980–81; Dir, The Green Alliance, 1982–92. Press Officer, European Environment Bureau, 1979–87; Sec., Ecological Studies Inst., 1987–92. Member: Bd of Dirs, Earth Resources Research, 1975–87; Waste Management Adv. Council, 1976–81; Packaging Council, 1978–82; Exec. Cttee, NCVO, 1984–89; UK Nat. Cttee, European Year of the Environment, 1986–88; Exec. Cttee, European Environment Bureau, 1987–91. Contested (SDP): Brighton Kemptown, 1983; Surbiton, 1987. Vis. Fellow, Cranfield, 1991–. Hon. Vis. Fellow, Manchester Business Sch., 1984. FRSA 1988 (Mem. Council, 1990–92). Royal Humane Society Testimonials: on Vellum, 1966; on Parchment, 1968; Global 500 Laureate, UNEP. *Publications:* Europe: environment, 1981; (jtly) Pressure Groups in the Global System, 1982; (jtly) Ecology 2000, 1984; (jtly) The Green Capitalists, 1987; (jtly) Green Pages, 1988. *Recreations:* photography, birdwatching. *Address:* 36 Crewdson Road, SW9 0LJ. *T:* 0171–735 9019. *Club:* Reform.

BURKE, (Ulick) Peter, FBA 1994; Reader in Cultural History, since 1988, and Fellow of Emmanuel College, since 1979, University of Cambridge; *b* 16 Aug. 1937; *s* of John Burke and Jennie Burke (*née* Colin); *m* 1st, 1972, Susan Patricia Dell (marr. diss. 1983); 2nd, 1989, Maria Lúcia Garcia Pallares. *Educ:* St John's Coll., Oxford; St Antony's Coll., Oxford (MA). Asst Lectr, then Lectr in History, subseq. Reader in Intellectual History, Sussex Univ., 1962–78. *Publications:* The Renaissance Sense of the Past, 1969; Culture and Society in Renaissance Italy, 1972, 3rd edn 1986; Venice and Amsterdam: a study of Seventeenth Century elites, 1974, 2nd edn 1994; Popular Culture in Early Modern Europe, 1978, 2nd edn 1994; Sociology and History, 1980; Montaigne, 1981; Vico, 1985; Historical Anthropology in Early Modern Italy: essays on perception and communication, 1987; The Renaissance, 1987; The French Historical Revolution: the Annales School 1929–89, 1990; The Fabrication of Louis XIV, 1992, 2nd edn 1994; History and Social Theory, 1992; Antwerp, a Metropolis in Europe, 1993; The Art of Conversation, 1993; The Fortunes of the Courtier, 1995. *Recreation:* travel. *Address:* Emmanuel College, Cambridge CB2 3AP. *T:* Cambridge (01223) 334272.

BURKE-GAFFNEY, John Campion; Director-General, The British Red Cross Society, 1985–90; *b* 27 Feb. 1932; *s* of late Dr Henry Joseph O'Donnell Burke-Gaffney, OBE and Constance May (*née* Bishop); *m* 1956, Margaret Mary Jennifer (*née* Stacpoole); two *s* two *d*. *Educ:* Douai School. Called to the Bar, Gray's Inn, 1956. Served: RAC, 1950–52; E Riding of Yorks Imperial Yeomanry (Wenlock's Horse), 1952–56. Shell-Mex and BP Ltd, 1956–75; Shell UK Ltd, 1976–77; Man. Dir, Shell and BP Zambia Ltd, 1977–81; Gp Public Affairs, Shell Internat. Petroleum Co. Ltd, 1981–85. *Address:* c/o Coutts & Co., Park Lane Branch, 1 Old Park Lane, W1A 4AL.

See also M. A. B. Burke-Gaffney.

BURKE-GAFFNEY, Michael Anthony Bowes, QC 1977; a Recorder, 1986–92; *b* Dar-es-Salaam, Tanzania, 1 Aug. 1928; *s* of late Henry Joseph O'Donnell Burke-Gaffney, OBE and Constance May (*née* Bishop); *m* 1961, Constance Caroline (*née* Murdoch); two *s* one *d*. *Educ:* Douai Sch.; RMA, Sandhurst. ACIArb. Commissioned Royal Irish Fusiliers, 1948; served with 1st Bn, Suez Canal Zone, Akaba, Gibraltar, BAOR and Berlin; served with Royal Ulster Rifles, Korean War, 1951, and in Hong Kong; qual. as interpreter in Turkish (studied at London Univ. and in Istanbul), 1955; Staff Captain, HQ 44 Div., 1956–58, when resigned commn and read for the Bar; joined Gray's Inn, 1956 (Lord Justice Holker Sen. Scholar); called to the Bar, 1959; Bencher, 1986. Jun. Counsel to HM Treasury in certain planning matters, 1974–77; a Legal Assessor to GMC and GDC, 1985–. Author, Three Lakes Inquiry Report, 1976; contrib. various articles in legal publications. *Recreations:* family, cricket, wildlife, viniculture. *Address:* Lamb Building, Temple, EC4Y 7AS. *T:* 0171–353 6701. *Club:* Naval and Military.

See also J. C. Burke-Gaffney.

BURKETT, Mary Elizabeth, OBE 1978; FRGS; FMA; Director of Abbot Hall Art Gallery, and Museum of Lakeland Life and Industry, 1967–86, and Borough Museum, Kendal, 1977–86; retired; *d* of Ridley Burkett and Mary Alice Gaussen. *Educ:* Univ. of Durham (BA, Teachers' Cert.). FRGS 1978; FMA 1980. Taught art, craft, maths, etc, at Wroxall Abbey, 1948–54; Art and Craft Lectr, Charlotte Mason Coll., Ambleside, 1954–62; seven months in Turkey and Iran, 1962; Asst Dir, Abbot Hall, 1963–66. Formerly part-time Teacher of Art, Bela River Prison. Member: numerous cttees including National Trust (NW Region), 1978–85; Carlisle Diocesan Adv. Cttee, 1980–; Carlisle

Cathedral Fabric Cttee, 1991–. Dir, Border Television, 1982–93. Round the World trip, lecturing in Hong Kong, Perth (WA), NY as well as seeing the Great Wall of China, 1986. FRSA 1983; Fellow, Huguenot Soc., 1986. Leverhulme Award (to continue research on Lake District portraits), 1986–88. *Publications:* The Art of the Felt Maker, 1979; Kurt Schwitters (in the Lake District), 1979; (with David Sloss) William Green of Ambleside, 1984; contrib. art and archaeol jls, and gall. and museum catalogues. *Recreations:* travel, bird watching, photography, writing, doing research into more Cumbrian artists, lecturing, picking up stones. *Address:* Isel Hall, Cockermouth, Cumbria CA13 0QG.

BURLAND, Prof. John Boscawen, FEng; Professor of Soil Mechanics in the University of London, at Imperial College of Science, Technology and Medicine (formerly Imperial College of Science and Technology), since 1980; *b* 4 March 1936; *s* of John Whitmore Burland and Margaret Irene Burland (*née* Boscawen); *m* 1963, Gillian Margaret, *d* of J. K. Miller; two *s* one *d*. *Educ:* Parktown Boys' High Sch., Johannesburg; Univ. of the Witwatersrand (BSc Eng, MSc Eng, DSc Eng); Univ. of Cambridge (PhD). MSAICE; FICE; MIStructE; FEng 1981. Res. Asst, Univ. of the Witwatersrand, 1960; Engineer, Ove Arup and Partners, London, 1961–63; Res. Student, Cambridge Univ., 63–66; Building Research Station: SSO and PSO, 1966–72; Head of Geotechnics Div., 1972–79; Asst Dir and Head of Materials and Structures Dept, 1979–80. Visiting Prof., Dept of Civil Engineering, Univ. of Strathclyde, 1973–82. Member: Adv. Panel to Sec. of State for Environment on Black Country Limestone, 1983–95; Italian Prime Minister's Commn for stabilising the Leaning Tower of Pisa, 1990–. Mem. Council, CIRIA, 1987–95; Official Visitor, BRE, 1990–. Mem. Council, Royal Acad. of Engrg, 1994–; Institution of Structural Engineers: Mem. of Council, 1979–82; Murray Buxton Silver Medal, 1977; Oscar Faber Bronze Medal, 1979; named in Special Award to DoE for Underground Car Park at Palace of Westminster, 1975; Oscar Faber Diploma, 1982; Instn of Civil Engineers: Telford Premium, 1972, 1985, 1987; Coopers Hill War Meml Medal, 1985; Baker Medal, 1986; Kelvin Medal, for outstanding contribn to engrg, 1989; Brit. Geotechnical Soc. Prize, 1968, 1971, 1974 and 1986; Kevin Nash Gold Medal, Internat. Soc. of Soil Mechanics and Foundn Engrs, 1994. Hon. DEng Heriot-Watt, 1994. *Publications:* numerous papers on soil mechanics and civil engineering. *Recreations:* sailing, golf, painting, classical guitar.

BURLEIGH, Thomas Haydon, CBE 1977; Director, John Brown & Co. Ltd, 1965–77; *b* 23 April 1911; *s* of late J. H. W. Burleigh, Great Chesterford; *m* 1933, Kathleen Mary Lenthall (*d* 1992), *d* of late Dr Gurth Eager, Hertford; two *s*. *Educ:* Saffron Walden Sch. RAF, short service commission, No 19 (F) Sqdn, 1930–35; Westland Aircraft Ltd, 1936–45; Thos. Firth & John Brown Ltd, 1945–48; Firth Brown Tools Ltd, 1948–77. Pres., Sheffield Chamber of Commerce, 1963–64; Pres. Nat. Fedn of Engineers' Tool Manufacturers, 1968–70; Master of Company of Cutlers in Hallamshire in the County of York, 1970–71. *Recreations:* golf, gardening. *Address:* Kirkgate, Holme next Sea, Hunstanton, Norfolk PE36 6LH. *T:* Holme (01485) 525387. *Clubs:* Royal Air Force; Royal and Ancient Golf (St Andrews).

BURLEY, Dr Jeffery, CBE 1991; Director, Oxford Forestry Institute, Oxford University, since 1985; Professorial Fellow, Green College, Oxford, since 1981; *b* 16 Oct. 1936; *s* of Jack Burley and Eliza Burley (*née* Creese); *m* 1961, Jean Shirley (*née* Palmer); two *s*. *Educ:* Portsmouth Grammar Sch.; New College, Oxford (BA 1961); Yale (MF 1962; PhD 1965). Lieut, Royal Signals, 1954–57. O i/c and Unesco Expert, Forest Genetics Res. Lab., ARC of Central Africa, 1965–69; Sen. Res. Officer, Commonwealth Forestry Inst., Oxford, 1969–76; Univ. Lectr, 1976–83, Head of Dept of Forestry, 1983–85, Oxford. *Publications:* (ed jtly) Multipurpose tree germplasm, 1984; (ed jtly) Increasing productivity of multipurpose species, 1985; many book chapters resulting from conference papers; many contribs to periodicals and learned jls on forestry, agroforestry and forest tree breeding. *Recreations:* beekeeping, cricket, gardening. *Address:* Oxford Forestry Institute, South Parks Road, Oxford OX1 3RB. *T:* Oxford (01865) 275050.

BURLEY, Sir Victor (George), Kt 1980; CBE 1969; FIE(Aust); FIMechE, FIProdE; Chairman, Advisory Council of Commonwealth Scientific and Research Organization (CSIRO), 1979–81; Chairman, Allied Industries Pty Ltd, since 1984; *b* 4 Dec. 1914; *s* of G. H. Burley and M. A. Luby; *m* 1941, Alpha Loyal Lord; one *s* three *d*. *Educ:* High Sch., Tasmania; Univ. of Tasmania (BE). MIEE, FIFST; FInstD, FAIM. Cadbury-Fry-Pascall Pty Ltd, Australia, 1938–71: Chief Engr, Director and Vice-Chm.; Director, Cadbury Schweppes Aust Ltd, 1971–78; Cons. Dir, Cadbury Fry Hudson NZ; Technical Cons., Cadbury Schweppes UK, 1978–82. Member, Adv. Council, CSIRO, 1961–78; Chm., State Cttee, Tas. CSIRO, 1964–78; Foundn Mem., Commonwealth Adv. Cttee on Advanced Educn, 1965–71; Foundn Chm., Council of Advanced Educn, Tasmania, 1968–76; Mem., Sci. and Industry Forum, Aust. Acad. of Science, 1967–81. Director: Productivity Promotion Council, Australia, 1983–88; University Research Co., 1985–. University of Tasmania: Warden of Convocation, 1964–74; Mem., Faculty of Engrg, 1968–; Mem. Council, 1982–84. *Recreations:* music, reading. *Address:* Montaigne, 553 Sandy Bay Road, Hobart, Tas 7005, Australia. *T:* (02) 252583. *Clubs:* Melbourne (Melbourne); Tasmanian (Hobart).

BURLIN, Prof. Terence Eric; Rector, University of Westminster (formerly Polytechnic of Central London), since 1984; *b* 24 Sept. 1931; *s* of Eric Jonas Burlin and Winifred Kate (*née* Thomas); *m* 1957, Plessey Pamela Carpenter; one *s* one *d*. *Educ:* Acton County School; University of Southampton (BSc); Univ. of London (DSc, PhD). CEng, FIEE 1976; CPhys, FInstP 1969; FIBiotech 1992. Physicist, Mount Vernon Hosp. and Radium Inst., 1953–57; Sen. Physicist, Hammersmith Hosp., 1957–62; Principal Physicist, St John's Hosp. for Diseases of the Skin, 1960–90; Polytechnic of Central London: Sen. Lectr, 1962; Reader, 1969; Pro-Director, 1971; Sen. Pro-Rector, 1974; Acting Rector, 1982. British Cttee on Radiation Units and Measurements: Mem., 1966–74 and 1979–; Vice-Chm., 1983–84; Chm., 1984–; Member: Council, Inst. for Study of Drug Dependence, 1974–86; various Boards, CNAA; Cttee on Practical Determination of Dose Equivalent, Internat. Commn on Radiation Units and Measurements (Chm.), 1979–87; Adv. Council on Adult and Continuing Educn, DES, 1980–83; Cttee on Effects of Ionising Radiation, Physics and Dosimetry Sub-Cttee, MRC, 1983–86; Science Bd, SERC, 1986–89. Mem. Council, BTEC, 1984–86. Member: Council, Westminster Chamber of Commerce, 1994–; Employment Affairs Cttee, London Chamber of Commerce and Industry, 1994–. Hon. FCP 1990. *Publications:* chapters in Radiation Dosimetry, 1968, 2nd edn 1972; papers on radiation dosimetry, radiological protection, biomechanical properties of skin, radiobiology. *Recreations:* music, tennis. *Address:* University of Westminster, 309 Regent Street, W1R 8AL. *T:* 0171–911 5000. *Club:* Athenæum.

BURLINGTON, Earl of; William Cavendish; *b* 6 June 1969; *s* and *heir* of Marquess of Hartington, *qv*. *Address:* Beamsley Hall, Skipton, North Yorks BD23 6HD.

BURLISON, Tom; Deputy General Secretary, GMB, since 1991; Treasurer, Labour Party, since 1992; *b* 23 May 1936; *s* of Robert Burlison and Georgina (*née* Doige); *m* 1981, Valerie Stephenson; two *s* one *d*. *Educ:* Edmondsley, Co. Durham. Panel beater, 1951–57; professional footballer, 1953–65; RAF, 1959–61; General and Municipal Workers' Union, then General, Municipal, Boilermakers and Allied Trades Union, later GMB: Regl Officer, 1965–78; Regl Sec., 1978–91. Exec. Mem., British North American Cttee, 1994–. *Recreation:* gardening. *Address:* c/o Labour Party, 150 Walworth Road, SE17 1JT; GMB, 22–24 Worple Road, SW19 4DD.

BURMAN, Sir (John) Charles, Kt 1961; DL; JP; *b* 30 Aug. 1908; *o s* of Sir John Burman, JP; *m* 1936, Ursula Hesketh-Wright, JP; two *s* two *d*. *Educ:* Rugby Sch. City Council, 1934–66 (Lord Mayor of Birmingham, 1947–49); General Commissioner of Income Tax, 1941–73; Indep. Chm., Licensing Planning Cttee, 1949–60; Chm. Birmingham Conservative and Unionist Assoc., 1963–72; County Pres. St John Ambulance Brigade, 1950–63; Member, Govt Cttee on Administrative Tribunals, 1955; Member Royal Commission on the Police, 1960. Director: Tarmac Ltd, 1955–71 (Chm., 1961–71); S Staffs Waterworks Co., 1949–82 (Chm. 1959–79). Life Governor, Barber Institute, at University of Birmingham (Trustee, 1936–90; Chm. Trustees, 1979–90). JP 1942; High Sheriff, Warwickshire, 1958, DL 1967. KStJ, 1961. Hon. LLD Birmingham, 1986. *Address:* Little Bickerscourt, Danzey Green, Tanworth-in-Arden, Warwickshire B94 5BL. *T:* Tanworth-in-Arden (01564) 742711.

BURMAN, Roger Stephen, CBE 1991; DL; Chairman, since 1976, and Managing Director, since 1973, Teledictor; *b* 3 April 1940; *s* of Sir Stephen France Burman, CBE and Lady (Joan Margaret) Burman; *m* 1964, Felicity Jane Crook; four *s*. *Educ:* Oundle Sch.; Univ. of Birmingham (BSc Hon.). Burman & Sons, 1961–72 (Dir, 1965–72); Teledictor, 1972–. Chm., Nat. Exhibn Centre, 1989– (Dir, 1984–); Dir, Black Country Develt Corp., 1992–. Gen. Tax Comr, 1973–. Member: British Hallmarking Council, 1980– (Chm., 1989–); BOTB, 1990–94; Council, ICC, 1990–; Pres., Birmingham Chamber of Commerce, 1984–85; Chm., Assoc. of British Chambers of Commerce, 1988–90. University of Birmingham: Life Governor, 1983–; Pro-Chancellor, 1994–. Liveryman, Goldsmiths' Co., 1993–. DL W Midlands, 1991. Hon. LLD Birmingham, 1994. *Recreation:* golf. *Address:* Morton Hall, Holberrow Green, Redditch, Worcs B96 6SJ. *T:* Inkberrow (01386) 793298.

BURN, Adrian; *see* Burn, B. A. F.

BURN, Angus Maitland P.; *see* Pelham Burn.

BURN, (Bryan) Adrian (Falconer); Managing Partner, Binder Hamlyn, since 1994; *b* 23 May 1945; *s* of Peter and Ruth Burn; *m* 1968, Jeanette Carol; one *s* three *d*. *Educ:* Abingdon Sch. FCA. Whinney Murray, 1963–72; joined Binder Hamlyn, 1972; seconded to DTI, 1975–77; Partner, 1977, London Managing Partner, 1988–94, Binder Hamlyn. Director: Sinclair-Stevenson Ltd, 1990–92; Brent Internat. plc, 1994–. Mem., Financial Adjudication Panel, Second Severn Crossing, 1991–. *Address:* Binder Hamlyn, 20 Old Bailey, EC4M 7BH; 13 Woodthorpe Road, Putney, SW15 6UQ. *T:* 0181–788 6383. *Club:* Roehampton.

BURN, Michael Clive, MC 1945; writer; *b* 11 Dec. 1912; *s* of late Sir Clive Burn and Phyllis Stoneham; *m* 1947, Mary Booker (*née* Walter) (*d* 1974); no *c*. *Educ:* Winchester; New Coll., Oxford (open scholar); Hons Degree in Soc. Scis, Oxford, 1945, with distinction in all subjects (awarded whilst POW at Colditz). Journalist, The Times, 1936–39; Lieut 1st Bn Queens Westminsters, KRRC, 1939–40; Officer in Independent Companies, Norwegian Campaign, 1940, subseq. Captain No. 2 Commando; taken prisoner in raid on St Nazaire, 1942; prisoner in Germany, 1942–45. Foreign Correspondent for The Times in Vienna, Jugoslavia and Hungary, 1946–49. Keats Poetry First Prize, 1973. *Plays:* The Modern Everyman (prod. Birmingham Rep., 1947); Beyond the Storm (Midlands Arts Co., and Vienna, 1947); The Night of the Ball (prod. New Theatre, 1956). *Publications: novels:* Yes, Farewell, 1946, repr. 1975; Childhood at Oriol, 1951; The Midnight Diary, 1952; The Trouble with Jake, 1967; *sociological:* Mr Lyward's Answer, 1956; The Debatable Land, 1970; *poems:* Poems to Mary, 1953; The Flying Castle, 1954; Out On A Limb, 1973; Open Day and Night, 1978; *play:* The Modern Everyman, 1948; *non-fiction:* Mary and Richard, 1988. *Address:* Beudy Gwyn, Minffordd, Gwynedd, N Wales LL48 6EN.

BURN, Rear Adm. Richard Hardy, CB 1992; AFC 1969; CEng; FRAeS; Director General Aircraft (Navy), Ministry of Defence, 1990–92; *b* 26 May 1938; *s* of Margaret (*née* Hardy) and Douglas Burn; *m* 1967, Judith Sanderson (*née* Tigg); one *s* one *d* and one step *s* one step *d*. *Educ:* Berkhamsted; BRNC Dartmouth; RNEC Manadon. MIMechE. HMS Broadsword 1958, fighter pilot, 890 Naval Air Sqdn, HMS Ark Royal, 1961–62; test flying work (incl. 3 years exchange, US Navy), NDC Latimer, to 1975; develt of Sea Harrier, MoD (PE), 1975–78; Ops Officer, A&AEE, 1978–79; Air Eng. Officer, RNAS Yeovilton, 1980; Asst Dir Eng. (N), MoD, 1981–84; RCDS 1985; Dir, Aircraft Maint. and Repair, MoD (N), 1986–87; Dir, Helicopter Projects, MoD (PE), and ADC, 1988–90. Mem., Soc. of Experimental Test Pilots. FIMgt. Commendation, US Navy, 1974; Médaille d'Honneur, Soc. d'Encouragement au Progrès, 1989. *Recreations:* skiing, golf, listening to music.

BURNE, Dr Yvonne Ann; Head, City of London School for Girls, since 1995; *b* 29 Aug. 1947; *d* of Archibald Ford and Florence Louise Ford (*née* Knott); *m* 1969, Anthony Richard Burne; one *s* one *d*. *Educ:* Redland High Sch. for Girls, Bristol; Westfield Coll., Univ. of London (BA Hons; PhD). School teacher: Harrow Co. Grammar Sch. for Girls, 1971–74; Lowlands Sixth Form Coll., 1974–77; Hd, Mod. Langs and Careers Guidance, Northwood Coll., 1984–87; Headmistress, St Helen's Sch. for Girls, Northwood, 1987–95. Editor: Educnl Challenges Inc. (VA, USA), 1978–82; Mary Glasgow Pubns, 1983–84; Heinemann Educnl Books, 1984. Mem., Hillingdon FHSA, 1990–. FRSA 1991. *Publications:* Tomorrow's News, 1979; The Circus comes to Town, 1979; articles for Nat. Geographic's World mag. *Recreations:* theatre, entertaining friends, walking. *Address:* City of London School for Girls, Barbican, EC2Y 8BB.

BURNELL, (Susan) Jocelyn B.; *see* Bell Burnell.

BURNET, George Wardlaw, LVO 1981; JP; Lord-Lieutenant of Midlothian, since 1992; *b* 26 Dec. 1927; *s* of late Sheriff John Rudolph Wardlaw Burnet, KC and Lucy Margaret Ord Burnet (*née* Wallace); *m* 1951, Jane Elena Moncrieff, *d* of late Malcolm Moncrieff Stuart, CIE, OBE; two *s* one *d*. *Educ:* Edinburgh Acad.; Lincoln Coll., Oxford (BA); Edinburgh Univ. (LLB). Served Black Watch (RHR) TA, retired as Captain, 1957. WS 1954; Partner, Murray Beith and Murray, 1956–90. County Councillor, Midlothian, 1967–76; Convener, Church of Scotland Gen. Finance Cttee, 1980–83; Chairman: Caledonian Res. Foundn; Life Assoc. of Scotland, 1985–93. Brig., Royal Company of Archers, Queen's Body Guard for Scotland, 1985–. Hon. FRIAS 1980. DL 1975, JP 1991, Midlothian. KStJ. *Recreations:* country pursuits, architecture, gardening. *Address:* Rose Court, Inveresk, Midlothian EH21 7TD. *T:* 0131–665 2689. *Club:* New (Edinburgh).

BURNET, Sir James William Alexander, (Sir Alastair Burnet), Kt 1984; journalist; *b* 12 July 1928; *s* of late Alexander and Schonaid Burnet, Edinburgh; *m* 1958, Maureen Campbell Sinclair. *Educ:* The Leys Sch., Cambridge; Worcester Coll., Oxford. Sub-editor and leader writer, Glasgow Herald, 1951–58; Commonwealth Fund Fellow, 1956–57; Leader writer, The Economist, 1958–62; Political editor, Independent Television News,

1963–64; Editor, The Economist, 1965–74; Editor, Daily Express, 1974–76; broadcaster with ITN, 1976–91; Assoc. Editor, News at Ten, 1982–91. Ind. Dir, Times Newspapers Hldgs Ltd, 1982–; Dir, United Racecourses Hldgs Ltd, 1985–94. Member: Cttee of Award, Commonwealth Fund, 1969–76; Cttee on Reading and Other Uses of English Language, 1972–75; Monopolies Commn specialist panel on newspaper mergers, 1973–91; Council, Banking Ombudsman, 1985–; Hon. Vice-Pres., Inst. of Journalists, 1990. Richard Dimbleby Award, BAFTA, 1966, 1970, 1979; Judges' Award, RTS, 1981. *Address:* 43 Hornton Court, Campden Hill Road, W8 7NT. *T:* 0171–937 7563; 33 Westbourne Gardens, Glasgow G12 9PF. *T:* 0141–339 8073.

BURNET, John Elliot; Chief Executive, Cumbria County Council, since 1991; *b* 13 Jan. 1947; *m* 1991, Deirdre Eleanor Elizabeth Burton. *Educ:* Barnard Castle Sch.; Nottingham Univ. (BA Law); College of Law, London. Articled, S Shields CBC (Clerk/Asst Solicitor), 1969–73; Sen. Asst Solicitor, S Tyneside MBC, 1973–74; Asst County Clerk, Tyne and Wear CC, 1974–82; Cumbria County Council: Sen. Asst Clerk and Dep. Co. Solicitor, 1982–86; Dir, Econ. Develt and Corporate Policy, 1986–90; Asst Chief Exec., 1990–91. *Recreations:* watching sport, archaeology, historic buildings. *Address:* Cumbria County Council, The Courts, Carlisle, Cumbria CA3 8NA. *T:* Carlisle (01228) 23456.

BURNETT, of Leys, Baronetcy of (unclaimed); *see under* Ramsay, Sir Alexander William Burnett, 7th Bt.

BURNETT, Dr Andrew Michael, FSA; Keeper of Coins and Medals, British Museum, since 1992; *b* 23 May 1952; *s* of Sir John (Harrison) Burnett, *qv*; *m* 1978, Susan Jennifer Allix; two *d*. *Educ:* Fettes Coll., Edinburgh; Balliol Coll., Oxford (BA, MA); Inst. of Archaeology, Univ. of London (PhD). Department of Coins and Medals, British Museum: Res. Assistant, 1974–79; Asst Keeper, 1979–90; Dep. Keeper, 1990–92. Secretary: RNS, 1982–89; Internat. Numismatic Commn, 1992–. Corresp. Mem., Amer. Numismatic Soc., 1982. FSA 1982. Norwegian Numismatic Soc. Medal, 1991; Silver Medal, RNS, 1993. *Publications:* Coinage in the Roman World, 1987; Interpreting the Past: Coins, 1991; Roman Provincial Coinage, Vol. 1, 1992; contrib. Numismatic Chronicle, Schweizerische Numismatisches Rundschau, Quaderni Ticinesi, Jl Roman Studies, Britannia, etc. *Address:* Department of Coins and Medals, British Museum, WC1B 3DG. *T:* 0171–323 8227; 19 Almorah Road, N1 3ER. *T:* 0171–359 2949.

BURNETT, Air Chief Marshal Sir Brian (Kenyon), GCB 1970 (KCB 1965; CB 1961); DFC 1942; AFC 1939; RAF, retired; Chairman, All England Lawn Tennis Club, Wimbledon, 1974–83; *b* 10 March 1913; *s* of late Kenneth Burnett and Anita Catherine Burnett (*née* Evans); *m* 1944, Valerie Mary (*née* St Ludger); two *s*. *Educ:* Charterhouse; Wadham Coll., Oxford (BA 1934; Hon. Fellow, 1974); Joined RAFO 1932; RAF 1934; Long Distance Record Flight of 7,158 miles from Egypt to Australia, Nov. 1938. Served War of 1939–45, in Bomber and Flying Training Commands; RAF Staff Coll. Course, 1944; Directing Staff, RAF Staff Coll., 1945–47; UN Military Staff Cttee, New York, 1947–48; Joint Planning Staff, 1949–50; SASO HQ No. 3 (Bomber) Group, 1951–53; CORAF Gaydon, 1954–55; ADC to the Queen, 1953–57; Director of Bomber and Reconnaissance Ops, Air Ministry, 1956–57; Imperial Defence Coll., 1958; Air Officer Administration, HQ Bomber Command, 1959–61; AOC No 3 Gp, Bomber Command, 1961–64; Vice-Chief of the Air Staff, 1964–67; Air Secretary, MoD, 1967–70; C-in-C, Far East Command, Singapore, 1970–71; retired 1972. Air ADC to the Queen, 1969–72. Pres., Squash Rackets Assoc., 1972–75. *Recreations:* tennis, golf, ski-ing. *Address:* Heather Hill, Littleworth Cross, Seale, Farnham, Surrey GU10 1JN. *Clubs:* Royal Air Force; Vincent's (Oxford); All England Lawn Tennis; Jesters Squash; International Lawn Tennis Club of Great Britain.

BURNETT, Charles John, FSAScot; Ross Herald, since 1988 (Dingwall Pursuivant, 1983); *b* 6 Nov. 1940; *s* of Charles Alexander Urquhart Burnett and Agnes Watt; *m* 1967, Aileen Elizabeth McIntyre; two *s* one *d*. *Educ:* Fraserburgh Academy; Gray's Sch. of Art, Aberdeen (DA); Aberdeen Coll. of Education (Teaching Cert.); MLitt Edinburgh 1992. AMA; FHS Scot. House of Fraser, 1963–64, COI, 1964–68; Asst Dir, Letchworth Mus., 1968–71; Head of Design, Nat. Mus. of Antiquities of Scotland, 1971–85; Curator of Fine Art, Scottish United Services Mus., Edinburgh Castle, 1985–. Heraldic Adviser, Girl Guide Assoc. in Scotland, 1978–; Vice-Patron, Geneal. Soc. of Queensland, 1986–; Vice-President: Heraldry Soc. of Scotland, 1987–; Soc. of Antiquaries of Scotland, 1992–. Trustee, Bield Retirement Housing Trust, 1992–. Convenor, Companions of the Order of Malta, 1991–94. KStJ 1991; Librarian, Priory of Order of St John in Scotland, 1987–. Hon. Citizen, Oklahoma, 1989. *Publications:* articles on Scottish heraldry. *Recreations:* reading, visiting places of historical interest. *Address:* 7 Spottiswoode Road, Edinburgh EH9 1BH. *T:* 0131–447 3111.

BURNETT, Sir David Humphery, 3rd Bt, *cr* 1913; MBE 1945; TD; one of HM Lieutenants of the City of London; *b* 27 Jan. 1918; *s* of Sir Leslie Trew Burnett, 2nd Bt, CBE, TD, DL, and Joan (*d* 1994), *d* of late Sir John Humphery; *S* father 1955; *m* 1948, Geraldine Elizabeth Mortimer, *d* of Sir Godfrey Arthur Fisher, KCMG; two *s* (and one *s* decd). *Educ:* Harrow; St John's Coll., Cambridge, MA. Served War of 1939–45 (despatches, MBE), in France, N Africa, Sicily and Italy; Temp. Lt-Col GSO1, 1945. Partner, David Burnett & Son, Chartered Surveyors, 1947–50; Director: Proprietors of Hay's Wharf Ltd, 1950–80 (Chm., 1965–80); Guardian Royal Exchange Assurance, 1967–88. Chairman: South London Botanical Institute, 1976–81 (Pres., 1985); London Assoc. of Public Wharfingers, 1964–71. Mem. PLA, 1962–75. Mem. Council, Brighton Coll., 1971–93. Master: Company of Watermen and Lightermen of the River Thames, 1964; Girdlers Company, 1970. FRICS 1970 (ARICS 1948); FIMgt (FBIM 1968); FLS 1979. *Heir:* *s* Charles David Burnett; [*b* 18 May 1951. *m* 1989, Victoria Joan, *d* of James Simpson]. *Address:* Tandridge Hall, near Oxted, Surrey RH8 9NJ; Twizel Millhouse, Cornhill-on-Tweed, Northumberland TD12 4UX. *Clubs:* Turf, United Oxford & Cambridge University.

BURNETT, Sir John (Harrison), Kt 1987; Chairman: Co-ordinating Commission for Biological Recording, since 1989; (and Founder), International Organization for Plant Information, since 1991; *b* 21 Jan. 1922; *s* of Rev. T. Harrison Burnett, Paisley; *m* 1945, E. Margaret, *er d* of Rev. Dr E. W. Bishop; two *s*. *Educ:* Kingswood Sch., Bath; Merton Coll., Oxford. BA, MA 1947; DPhil 1953; Christopher Welch Scholar, 1947. FRSE 1957; FIBiol 1969. Lecturer, Lincoln Coll., 1948–49; Fellow (by Exam.) Magdalen Coll., 1949–53; Univ. Lecturer and Demonstrator, Oxford, 1949–53; Lecturer, Liverpool Univ., 1954–55; Prof. of Botany: Univ. of St Andrews, 1955–60; King's Coll., Newcastle, Univ. of Durham, 1961–63, Univ. of Newcastle, 1963–68; Dean of Faculty of Science, St Andrews, 1958–60, Newcastle, 1966–68; Public Orator, Newcastle, 1966–68; Regius Prof. of Botany, Univ. of Glasgow, 1968–70; Oxford University: Sibthorpian Prof. of Rural Economy and Fellow, St John's Coll., 1970–79; Member: Gen. Bd of Faculties, 1972–77 (Vice-Chm, 1974–76); Hebdomodal Council, 1974–79; Prin. and Vice-Chancellor, Univ. of Edinburgh, 1979–87. Exec. Sec., World Council for the Biosphere, 1987–93. Lectures: Dalgarno, Univ. of Manitoba, 1979–80; Bewley Meml, 1982; Peacock Meml, Dundee Univ., 1982; St Leonard's, Univ. of St Andrews, 1988. Chm. Scottish Horticultural Research Inst., 1959–74; Member: Nature Conservancy Scottish Cttee, 1961–66, English Cttee, 1966–69; Nature Conservancy Council, 1987–89 (Dep. Chm. and Acting Chm., 1988–89; Mem. Scottish Cttee, 1980–87); Nuffield Foundn Biol. Project, 1962–68 (Chm., 1965–68); British Mycological Soc. (Pres., 1982–83); Trustee, The New Phytologist, 1962–85, Advr, 1985–; Member: Academic Adv. Council, Univs of St Andrews and Dundee, 1964–66; Council, Univ. of Buckingham, 1989–. Member: Newcastle Reg. Hosp. Bd, 1964–68; Kingswood Assoc. (Pres., 1989). Served 1942–46 as Lieut RNVR (despatches). Hon. Fellow: RCSE, 1983; Green Coll., Oxford, 1988. Hon. DSc: Buckingham, 1981; Pennsylvania, 1983; Hon. LLD: Dundee, 1982; Strathclyde, 1983; Glasgow, 1987; Dr *hc* Edinburgh, 1988. Commendatore, Order of Merit (Italy), 1990. *Publications:* Vegetation of Scotland, ed and contrib., 1964; Fundamentals of Mycology, 1968, 3rd edn 1994; Mycogenetics, 1975; Fungal Walls and Hyphal Growth, ed and contrib., 1979; Edinburgh University Portraits II, 1986; Speciation and Evolution in Fungi, 1989; (jt ed. and contrib.) The Maintenance of the Biosphere, 1989; Surviving with the Biosphere, 1994; papers in various books and scientific journals. *Recreations:* walking, writing, gardens. *Address:* 13 Field House Drive, Oxford OX2 7NT. *Clubs:* Athenæum, Royal Over-Seas League.

See also A. M. Burnett.

BURNETT, Rear-Adm. Philip Whitworth, CB 1957; DSO 1945; DSC 1943, and Bar, 1944; *b* 10 Sept. 1908; *s* of Henry Ridley Burnett; *m* 1947, Molly, *widow* of Brig. H. C. Partridge, DSO, and *d* of H. M. Trouncer; one *s* two *d*. *Educ:* Preparatory Sch., Seascale; Royal Naval Coll., Dartmouth. Served War of 1939–45; HMS Kelly, 1939–41; HMS Osprey, 1941–43; Western Approaches Escort Groups, 1943–45. Chief of Staff to Comdr-in-Chief, Portsmouth, 1955–57; retd list 1958. Lieut 1930; Comdr 1940; Capt. 1945; Rear-Adm. 1955.

BURNETT, Sir Walter (John), Kt 1988; President, Royal National Agricultural and Industrial Association of Queensland, since 1983; *b* 15 Jan. 1921; *s* of William Henry and Minna Anna Burnett; *m* 1945, Mabel Nestor Dalton; two *d*. *Educ:* Maleny Primary School; Church of England Grammar School; Pharmacy College, Queensland. Conducted own pharmacy business in Maleny for 32 years. Director: Geriatric Med. Foundn of Qld (also Founder Mem.); Sunshine Coast Hosps Bd, 1958–. Past Chm., Maleny Br., Qld Ambulance Transport Bde; Vice Patron, Schizophrenia Fellowship of S Qld, 1987. Mem., Electoral Re-distribution Commn, Brisbane City Council, 1984–85. Grand Master, United Grand Lodge of Qld, 1983–86. Past Pres., Maroochy Dist Bowls Assoc. *Recreation:* lawn bowls. *Address:* 28 Tamarind Street, Maleny, Qld 4552, Australia. *T:* (71) 942290. *Clubs:* Tattersall's, Masonic (Brisbane).

BURNETT-STUART, Joseph; Chairman, Robert Fleming Holdings Ltd, 1981–90 (Director, 1963–90); *b* 11 April 1930; *s* of late George Eustace Burnett-Stuart, CBE and Etheldreda Cecily (*née* Edge); *m* 1954, Mary Hermione, *d* of late John A. M. Stewart of Ardvorlich, TD; three *s* one *d*. *Educ:* Eton Coll.; Trinity Coll., Cambridge (BA). Bankers Trust Co., 1953–62. A Church Commissioner, 1984–94. *Recreations:* gardening, shooting, fishing. *Club:* New (Edinburgh).

BURNEY, Sir Cecil (Denniston), 3rd Bt *cr* 1921; *b* 8 Jan. 1923; *s* of Sir Charles Dennistoun Burney, 2nd Bt, CMG, and Gladys (*d* 1982), *d* of George Henry High; *S* father, 1968; *m* 1957, Hazel Marguerite de Hamel, *yr d* of late Thurman Coleman; two *s*. *Educ:* Eton; Trinity Coll., Cambridge. Man. Dir, 1951–68, Chm., 1968–72, Northern Motors Ltd; Chairman: Hampton Trust PLC, 1975–87; JMD, subseq. Rhino, Group plc, 1988–92; Director: Security Building Soc., 1959–71; Mount Martin Gold Mines NL, 1985–87. Member of Legislative Council, N Rhodesia, 1959–64; MP Zambia, 1964–68; Chairman, Public Accounts Cttee, Zambia, 1963–67. *Recreations:* tennis, skiing. *Heir:* *s* Nigel Dennistoun Burney [*b* 6 Sept. 1959; *m* 1992, Lucy Brooks; one *s*]. *Address:* PO Box 32037, Lusaka, Zambia; 5 Lyall Street, SW1X 8DW. *T:* 0171–235 4014. *Clubs:* White's, Carlton, Turf, Buck's; Leander; Harare, Bulawayo (Zimbabwe); Ndola (Zambia).

BURNHAM, 6th Baron *cr* 1903, of Hall Barn, Beaconsfield, Bucks; **Hugh John Frederick Lawson;** Bt 1892; *b* 15 Aug. 1931; *yr s* of 4th Baron Burnham, CB, DSO, MC, TD and (Marie) Enid Burnham, CBE (*d* 1979), *d* of Hugh Scott Robson, Buenos Aires; *S* brother, 1993; *m* 1955, Hilary Margaret, *yr d* of Alan Hunter, Perth; one *s* two *d*. *Educ:* Eton Coll.; Balliol Coll., Oxford (MA). Commissioned Scots Guards, 1950. Daily Telegraph, 1955–86 (Dep. Man. Dir, 1984–86). Dir Gen., King George's Fund for Sailors, 1988–93. *Recreations:* sailing, shooting. *Heir:* *s* Hon. Harry Frederick Alan Lawson, *b* 22 Feb. 1968. *Address:* Woodlands Farm, Beaconsfield, Bucks HP9 2SF. *Clubs:* Garrick, Pratt's; Royal Yacht Squadron.

BURNHAM, Rev. Anthony Gerald; General Secretary, United Reformed Church, since 1992; *b* 2 March 1936; *s* of Selwyn and Sarah Burnham; *m* 1961, Valerie Florence Cleaver; one *s* two *d*. *Educ:* Silcoates Sch.; Manchester Univ. (BA Admin); Northern Coll., Manchester. Minister: Brownhill Congregational Church, Blackburn, 1961–66; Poulton le-Fylde and Hambleton Congregational Churches, 1966–69; Lectr, Northern Coll., Manchester, 1969–77; Minister, SW Manchester United Reformed Churches, 1973–81; Provincial Moderator, NW Province, URC, 1981–92. *Publications:* In The Quietness, 1981; Say One For Me, 1990; scripts for radio and TV. *Recreations:* theatre, jazz. *Address:* 86 Tavistock Place, WC1H 9RT.

BURNINGHAM, John Mackintosh; free-lance author-designer; *b* 27 April 1936; *s* of Charles Burningham and Jessie Mackintosh; *m* 1964, Helen Gillian Oxenbury; one *s* two *d*. *Educ:* Summerhill School, Leiston, Suffolk; Central School of Art, Holborn, 1956–59 (Diploma). Now free-lance: illustration, poster design, exhibition, animated film puppets, and writing for children. Wall friezes: Birdland, Lionland, Storyland, 1966; Jungleland, Wonderland, 1968; Around the World, 1972. *Publications:* Borka, 1963 (Kate Greenaway Medal, 1963); John Burningham's ABC, 1964; Trubloff, 1964; Humbert, 1965; Cannonball Simp, 1966 (filmed, 1967); Harquin, 1967; The Extraordinary Tug-of-War, 1968; Seasons, 1969; Mr Gumpy's Outing, 1970 (Kate Greenaway Award, 1971); Around the World in Eighty Days, 1972; Mr Gumpy's Motor Car, 1973; "Little Books" series: The Baby, The Rabbit, The School, The Snow, 1974; The Blanket, The Cupboard, The Dog, The Friend, 1975; The Adventures of Humbert, Simp and Harquin, 1976; Come Away from the Water, Shirley, 1977; Time to Get Out of the Bath, Shirley, 1978; Would You Rather, 1978; The Shopping Basket, 1980; Avocado Baby, 1982; John Burningham's Number Play Series, 1983; First Words/Granpa, 1984 (filmed, 1989); Play and Learn Books: abc, 123, Opposites, Colours, 1985; Where's Julius, 1986; John Patrick Norman McHennessy—the Boy who is Always Late, 1987; Rhymetime: A Good Job, The Car Ride, 1988, Animal Chatter, A Grand Band, 1989; Oi! Get off our Train, 1989; Aldo, 1991; England, 1992; Harvey Slumfenburger's Christmas Present, 1993 (jt winner, W. H. Smith Award, 1994); Courtney, 1994; *illustrated:* Chitty Chitty Bang Bang, 1964; The Wind in the Willows, 1983. *Address:* c/o Jonathan Cape Ltd, 20 Vauxhall Bridge Road, SW1V 2FA.

BURNLEY, Bishop Suffragan of, since 1994; **Rt. Rev. Martyn William Jarrett;** *b* 25 Oct. 1944; *s* of Frederick and Ivy Jarrett, Bristol; *m* 1968, Betty, *d* of Frank and Mabel Wallis, Bristol; two *d*. *Educ:* Cotham GS, Bristol; King's Coll., London (BD 1967); Hull Univ. (MPhil 1991); St Boniface, Warminster. Ordained deacon, 1968, priest, 1969; Curate: St George, Bristol, 1968–70; Swindon New Town, 1970–74; St Mary, Northolt,

1974–76; Vicar: St Joseph the Worker, Northolt West End, 1976–81; St Andrew, Hillingdon, 1981–83; Priest-in-charge, Uxbridge Moor, 1982–83; Vicar, St Andrew with St John, Uxbridge, 1983–85; Selection Sec., 1985–88, Sen. Selection Sec., 1989–91, ACCM; Vicar, Our Lady and All Saints, Chesterfield, 1991–94. *Recreations:* psephology, vegetable gardening, reading. *Address:* Dean House, 449 Padiham Road, Burnley, Lancs BB12 6TE. *T:* Burnley (01282) 423564.

BURNLEY, Christopher John; Burnley and Evans, Chartered Accountants, Halesowen, since 1989; *b* 1 May 1936; *s* of John Fox Burnley and Helena Burnley; *m* 1960, Carol Joan Quirk; two *d*. *Educ:* King William's College, Isle of Man. Chartered Accountant. Articled Clerk, 1953–59; Military service, 1959–62; Computer Systems Analyst, IBM, 1962–66; Management Consultant, Peat Marwick, 1966–67; Systems Planning Manager, Castrol, 1967–68; Sen. Planner, IBM, 1969–72; Financial Dir, Foseco FS, 1972–74; Group Treasurer, Foseco Minsep, 1974–75; Financial Dir, BAA, 1975–86; Finance Dir, Dan Air Engrg, 1987–88. *Recreation:* railway enthusiast. *Address:* Thirlmere, 173 Worcester Road, West Hagley, West Midlands DY9 0PB. *T:* Hagley (01562) 883592.

BURNS, Andrew; *see* Burns, R. A.

BURNS, Mrs Anne, (Mrs D. O. Burns); British Gliding Champion, 1966; Principal Scientific Officer, Royal Aircraft Establishment, Farnborough, Hants, 1953–77; *b* 23 Nov. 1915; *d* of late Major Fleetwood Hugo Pellew, W Yorks Regt, and of late Violet Pellew (*née* Du Pré); *m* 1947, Denis Owen Burns; no *c*. *Educ:* The Abbey Sch., Reading; St Hugh's Coll., Oxford (BA). Joined Min. of Supply, 1940. Engaged in aircraft research at RAE, Farnborough, Hants, under various ministries, 1940–. Feminine International Records: 4 gliding records in S Africa, 1961; records, S Africa, 1963, 1965; Colorado USA, 1967. Queen's Commendation for Valuable Services in the Air, 1955 and 1963. (With Denis Burns) Britannia Trophy, Royal Aero Club, 1961; Lilienthal Medal, Fédération Aéronautique Internationale, 1966. *Publications:* contrib. scientific jls. *Recreations:* snooker, fishing. *Address:* Clumps End, Lower Bourne, Farnham, Surrey GU10 3HF.

BURNS, Dr B(enedict) Delisle, FRS 1968; Visitor, Divison of Neurobiology, University of Newcastle upon Tyne; *b* 22 Feb. 1915; *s* of C. Delisle Burns and Margaret Hannay; *m* 1st, 1938, Angela Ricardo; four *s*; 2nd, 1954, Monika Kasputis; one *d*. *Educ:* University Coll. Sch.; Tübingen Univ.; King's Coll., Cambridge; University Coll. Hospital. MRCS, LRCP 1939. Univ. extension lecturing for WEA, 1936–38; operational research, 1939–45; Research Asst, Nat. Inst. for Med. Research, 1945–49; Assoc. Prof of Physiology, McGill Univ., Canada, 1950–58; Scientific Advisor to Dept of Veterans' Affairs, 1950–67; Prof. of Physiology, 1958–67, Chm., Dept of Physiology, 1965–67, McGill Univ., Canada; Head, Div. of Physiology and Pharmacology, Nat. Inst. of Medical Research, 1967–76; MRC External Staff, Anatomy Dept, 1976–80, Hon. Prof. of Neurobiology, 1977–80, Univ. of Bristol. *Publications:* The Mammalian Cerebral Cortex, 1958; The Uncertain Nervous System, 1968; about 100 articles on neurophysiology in scientific jls. *Recreations:* painting, interior decoration. *Address:* Division of Neurobiology, University of Newcastle upon Tyne, NE2 4HH. *T:* 0191–222 6000, ext. 6948.

BURNS, David Allan, CMG 1993; HM Diplomatic Service; Ambassador to Finland, since 1995; *b* 20 Sept. 1937; *s* of Allan Robert Desmond Burns, GM, and Gladys Frances Dine; *m* 1971, Inger Ellen Kristiansson; one *s* one *d*. *Educ:* Sir Anthony Browne's Sch., Brentwood, Essex. Served HM Forces, 1956–58. Language student and Third Secretary, British Embassy, Belgrade, 1962–65; Second Secretary, Bangkok, 1966–68; First Secretary, Washington, 1969–72; Head of Chancery, Belgrade, 1973–76; Asst Head of Arms Control Dept, FCO, 1976–79; Counsellor, Bangkok, 1979–83; Consul General, Boston, 1983–87; Hd of N America Dept, FCO, 1988–91; Ambassador to Cambodia, 1991–94. Mem., Marshall Scholarships Selection Cttee for New England, 1983–87. *Recreation:* cinema. *Address:* c/o Foreign and Commonwealth Office, SW1A 2AH. *Club:* Travellers'.

BURNS, Maj.-Gen. Sir George; *see* Burns, Maj.-Gen. Sir W. A. G.

BURNS, Dr Henry James Gerard, FRCS; Director of Public Health, Greater Glasgow Health Board, since 1994; *b* 25 Jan. 1951; *s* of Henry Burns and Mary (*née* Boyle); *m* 1983, Agnes Capaldi; two *s* three *d*. *Educ:* St Aloysius Coll., Glasgow; Glasgow Univ. (MB, ChB). FRCS 1979. MPH 1990; MFPHM 1993. Glasgow University: Lectr in Surgery, 1975–83; Sen. Lectr, 1983–89. *Recreations:* participating in and, increasingly, watching sport. *Address:* Greater Glasgow Health Board, 112 Ingram Street, Glasgow G1 1ET. *T:* 0141–201 4602.

BURNS, Ian Morgan, CB 1990; Deputy Secretary and Head of Policy Group, Lord Chancellor's Department, since 1995; *b* 3 June 1939; *s* of late Donald George Burns and Margaret Brenda Burns; *m* 1965, Susan Rebecca (*née* Wheeler); two *d*. *Educ:* Bootham, York. LLB, LLM London. HM Forces, 1957–59. Examiner, Estate Duty Office, 1960; Asst Principal, 1965, Principal, 1969, Home Office; Principal, 1972, Asst Sec., 1974, NI Office; Asst Sec., Home Office, 1977; Under Sec., NI Office, 1979–84; Under Sec. (Finance), 1985, and Gen. Manager, Disablement Services, 1986, DHSS; Deputy Under Secretary of State: NI Office, 1987–90; Police Dept, Home Office, 1990–95. FRSA 1993. *Recreations:* listening to music, adventurous gardening, collecting siurells. *Address:* c/o Lord Chancellor's Department, Trevelyan House, Great Peter Street, SW1P 2BY. *Club:* Commonwealth Trust.

BURNS, James; JP; DL; Member, Strathclyde Regional Council, 1974–95 (Convener, 1982–86); *b* 8 Feb. 1931; *s* of late James Burns and of Mary Burns (*née* Magee); *m* 1959, Jean Ward; two *s*. *Educ:* St Patrick's Sch., Shotts; Coatbridge Tech. Coll. Engineer with NCB, 1966–71. Member: Lanark CC, 1967–75; Lanarks Health Bd, 1973–77; Strathclyde Regional Council: Chm., Gen. Purposes Cttee, 1975–82; Vice-Convener, 1978–82. Chm. Vis. Cttee, HM Prison, Shotts, 1980–; Member: Commonwealth Games Council for Scotland, 1982–86; Main Organising Cttee, Commonwealth Games 1986, 1982–86. Vice President: Glasgow Western St Andrew's Youth Club, 1982–86; St Andrew's Ambulance Assoc., 1984–86. Hon. President: Strathclyde CRC, 1982–86; Princess Louise Scottish Hosp. (Erskine Hosp.), 1982–86; Strathclyde Charities Band Assoc., 1982–86; Scottish Retirement Council, 1984–86; Hon. Vice Pres., SNO Chorus, 1982–86; Patron: Strathclyde Youth Club Assoc., 1982–86; YMCA Sports Centre, 1982–86; Scottish Pakistani Assoc., 1984–86. Trustee, The Pearce Institute, 1983–86. JP Motherwell, 1972. DL Monklands, Motherwell, Hamilton, E Kilbride and Clydesdale, 1989. *Recreations:* fishing, golf. *Address:* 57 Springhill Road, Shotts ML7 5JA. *T:* Shotts (01501) 20187. *Club:* Royal Scottish Automobile (Glasgow).

BURNS, Prof. James Henderson, FBA 1992; Professor of the History of Political Thought, University College London, 1966–86, now Emeritus; *b* 10 Nov. 1921; *yr s* of late William Burns and Helen Craig Tait Henderson; *m* 1947, Yvonne Mary Zéla Birnie, *er d* of late Arthur Birnie, MA, and of Yvonne Marie Aline Louis; two *s* (and one *d* decd). *Educ:* George Watson's Boys' Coll., Edinburgh; Univ. of Edinburgh; Balliol Coll., Oxford. MA (Edinburgh and Oxon), PhD (Aberdeen). Sub-Editor, Home News Dept, BBC, 1944–45; Lectr in Polit. Theory, Univ. of Aberdeen, 1947–60; Head of Dept of Politics, 1952–60; Reader in the History of Political Thought, University Coll. London, 1961–66; Head of History Dept, UCL, 1970–75. John Hinkley Vis. Prof., Dept of History, Johns Hopkins Univ., Baltimore, 1987; Lectures: Creighton, London Univ., 1986; Carlyle, Oxford Univ., 1988; Gifford, Aberdeen Univ., 1994. Gen. Editor, The Collected Works of Jeremy Bentham, 1961–79; Vice-Chm., Bentham Cttee, 1983–92 (Sec., 1966–78); Pres., Internat. Bentham Soc., 1986–92. FRHistS 1962; Hon. Vice-Pres., RHistS, 1986– (Hon. Sec., 1965–70; Vice-Pres., 1978–82). *Publications:* Scottish University (with D. Sutherland Graeme), 1944; Scottish Churchmen and the Council of Basle, 1962; Lordship, Kingship and Empire: the idea of monarchy 1400–1525, 1992; The True Law of Kingship: concepts of monarchy in early-modern Scotland, 1996; *contributor to:* (with S. Rose) The British General Election of 1951, by D. E. Butler, 1952; Essays on the Scottish Reformation, ed D. McRoberts, 1962; Mill: a collection of critical essays, ed J. B. Schneewind, 1968; Bentham on Legal Theory, ed M. H. James, 1973; Jeremy Bentham: ten critical essays, ed B. Parekh, 1974; Absolutism in Seventeenth Century Europe, ed J. Miller, 1990; The Church and Sovereignty c 590–1918, ed D. Wood, 1991; Political Discourse in Early Modern Britain, ed N. Phillipson and Q. Skinner, 1993; Politics, Ideology and the Law in Early Modern Europe, ed A. E. Baker, 1994; *edited* (with H. L. A. Hart): Jeremy Bentham, An Introduction in the Principles of Morals and Legislation, 1970; Jeremy Bentham, A Comment on the Commentaries and A Fragment on Government, 1977; (with F. Rosen) Jeremy Bentham, Constitutional Code, vol. I, 1983; (ed) The Cambridge History of Medieval Political Thought c350–c1450, 1988; (ed) The Cambridge History of Political Thought 1450–1700, 1991; articles and reviews in: English Historical Review, Scottish Historical Review, Innes Review, Political Studies, History, Trans of RHistSoc, Historical Jl, Jl of Eccles. History, etc. *Address:* 6 Chiltern House, Hillcrest Road, Ealing, W5 1HL. *T:* 0181–998 9515.

BURNS, Kevin Francis Xavier, CMG 1984; HM Diplomatic Service, retired; *b* 18 Dec. 1930; *m* 1st, 1963, Nan Pinto (*d* 1984); one *s* two *d*; 2nd, 1992, Elizabeth Hassell. *Educ:* Finchley Grammar Sch.; Trinity Coll., Cambridge (BA 1953). CRO, 1956–58; Asst Private Sec. to Sec. of State, 1958; 2nd Sec., 1959, 1st Sec., 1960–63, Colombo; CRO/FO, 1963–67; 1st Sec., Head of Chancery and Consul, Montevideo, 1967–70; FCO, 1970–73; Counsellor, UK Mission, Geneva, 1973–79; RCDS, 1979; Head of SE Asian Dept, FCO, 1980–83; High Commissioner: Ghana, 1983–86; Barbados, 1986–90.

BURNS, Michael; Chairman: Hatfield and Dunscroft Labour Party, 1965–86; South Yorkshire County Association, since 1986; *b* 21 Dec. 1917; *s* of Hugh Burns and Jane Ellin Burns; *m* 1939, Vera Williams (*d* 1984); two *d*. *Educ:* Thorne Grammar Sch. Served War, 1940–46: 1939–45 Star, France and Germany Star, War Medal, Defence Medal. Miner, Hatfield Main Colliery, 1934–40 and 1946–66; Thorpe Marsh Power Stn, 1966–70; Sch. Caretaker, Hatfield Travis Sch., 1970–81 (due to wife's illness); retd 1981. Mem., Nat. Cttee, NUPE, 1979–81; Chm., Health and Safety Local Govt Nat. Cttee, NUPE, 1979–81. Chairman: Goole CLP, 1977–83; Doncaster CVS, 1984–90 (Mem., 1977); Doncaster Victim Support Scheme, 1985–; Thorne No 2 Sub-Div., Police Community Liaison Forum, 1987–; Exec. Mem., Doncaster Intermediate Treatment Orgn, 1990–; Member: S Yorks CC, 1973–86 (Chm., 1982–83); S Yorks Valuation Panel, 1974–89; S Yorks Charity Information Service, 1983–90; Nat. Exec., CVSNA, 1985–87; Doncaster FPC, 1985–86; Doncaster Jt Consultative Cttee, 1985–89; Trustee, S Yorks Foundn Charity, 1986–90; Chm., Friends of S Yorks Training Trust, 1988–. Pres., Hatfield Br., Arthritic Care, 1980–86. Governor, Hatfield High Sch., 1974–88; Chairman: Hatfield Ash Hill Sch. Bd of Governors, 1974–88 and 1989– (Vice-Chm., 1988–89); Govs, Hatfield Sheepdip Lane Sch., 1974–; Hatfield Chase Sch. (ESNS), 1984–. Church Warden, Christ Church, Dunscroft, 1964–79. *Recreations:* DIY, oil painting, politics. *Address:* 15 Manor Road, Hatfield, Doncaster, South Yorks DN7 6SA. *T:* Doncaster (01302) 846666.

BURNS, (Robert) Andrew, CMG 1992; HM Diplomatic Service; Ambassador to Israel, since 1992; *b* 21 July 1943; *e s* of late Robert Burns, CB, CMG and Mary Burns (*née* Goodland); *m* 1973, Sarah Cadogan, JP; two *s* one *d*. *Educ:* Highgate Sch.; Trinity Coll., Cambridge. BA (Classics), MA. Entered Diplomatic Service, 1965; UK Mission to UN, NY, 1965; FO 1966; Sch. of Oriental and African Studies, 1966–67; Univ. of Delhi, 1967; served New Delhi, FCO, and UK Delegation to CSCE, 1967–76; First Secretary and Head of Chancery, Bucharest, 1976–78; Private Sec. to Perm. Under Sec. and Head of Diplomatic Service, FCO, 1979–82; Fellow, Center for Internat. Affairs, Harvard Univ., 1982–83; Counsellor (Information), Washington, and Head of British Information Services, NY, 1983–86; Head of S Asian Dept, FCO, 1986–88; Head of News Dept, FCO, 1988–90; Asst Under-Sec. of State (Asia), FCO, 1990–92. *Publication:* Diplomacy, War and Parliamentary Democracy, 1985. *Recreations:* music, theatre, country pursuits. *Address:* c/o Foreign and Commonwealth Office, SW1A 2AH. *Clubs:* Garrick, Royal Automobile.

BURNS, Sandra Pauline, CB 1989; Parliamentary Counsel, 1980–91, retired; *b* 19 June 1938; *d* of John Burns and Edith Maud Burns. *Educ:* Manchester Central High Sch.; Somerville Coll., Oxford (BCL, MA). Called to the Bar, Middle Temple, 1964. *Recreation:* photography. *Address:* 997 Finchley Road, Golders Green, NW11 7HB.

BURNS, Simon Hugh McGuigan; MP (C) Chelmsford, since 1987; a Lord Commissioner of HM Treasury (Government Whip), since 1995; *b* 6 Sept. 1952; *s* of late Brian Stanley Burns, MC, and of Shelagh Mary Nash; *m* 1982, Emma Mary Clifford; one *s* one *d*. *Educ:* Christ the King Sch., Accra, Ghana; Stamford Sch.; Worcester Coll., Oxford (BA Hons Modern History). Political Adviser to Rt Hon. Sally Oppenheim, 1975–81; Dir, What to Buy Ltd, 1981–83; Policy Exec., Inst. of Dirs, 1983–87. PPS to Minister of State: Dept of Employment, 1989–90; Dept of Educn, 1990–92; DTI, 1992–93; PPS to Minister of Agric., Fisheries and Food, 1993–94; an Asst Govt Whip, 1994–95. *Recreations:* American politics, reading, swimming, travelling. *Address:* House of Commons, SW1A 0AA. *T:* 0171–219 3000. *Club:* Chelmsford Conservative (Patron).

BURNS, Sir Terence, GCB 1995; Kt 1983; Permanent Secretary, HM Treasury, since 1991; *b* 13 March 1944; *s* of Patrick Owen and Doris Burns; *m* 1969, Anne Elizabeth Powell; one *s* two *d*. *Educ:* Houghton-Le-Spring Grammar Sch.; Univ. of Manchester (BAEcon Hons). London Business School: Research posts, 1965–70; Lecturer in Economics, 1970–74; Sen. Lectr in Economics, 1974–79; Prof. of Economics, 1979; Director, LBS Centre for Economic Forecasting, 1976–79, Fellow, 1989; Chief Econ. Advr to the Treasury and Hd of Govt Econ. Service, 1980–91. Member, HM Treasury Academic Panel, 1976–79. Vis. Fellow, Nuffield Coll., Oxford, 1989–. Vice-President: Soc. of Business Economists, 1985–; REconS, 1992–. CIMgt 1992. Bd Mem., Manchester Business Sch., 1992–. *Publications:* various articles in economic jls. *Recreations:* soccer spectator, music, golf. *Address:* c/o HM Treasury, Parliament Street, SW1P 3AG. *T:* 0171–270 5203. *Clubs:* Reform; Ealing Golf.

BURNS, Thomas Ferrier, OBE 1983; Editor of The Tablet, 1967–82; Chairman of Burns & Oates Ltd, 1948–67; Director, The Tablet Publishing Company, 1935–85; *b* 21 April 1906; *s* of late David Burns and late Clara (*née* Swinburne); *m* 1944, Mabel Marañon; three *s* one *d*. *Educ:* Stonyhurst. Press Attaché, British Embassy, Madrid, 1940–45. *Publication:* The Use of Memory, 1993. *Recreations:* painting and gardening. *Address:* Flat 7, 36 Buckingham Gate, SW1E 6PB. *T:* 0171–834 1385. *Club:* Garrick.

BURNS, Prof. Tom, FBA 1982; Professor of Sociology, University of Edinburgh, 1965–81; *b* 16 Jan. 1913; *s* of John and Hannah Burns; *m* 1944, Mary Elizabeth Nora Clark; one *s* four *d*. *Educ:* Hague Street LCC Elementary Sch.; Parmiters Foundation Sch.; Univ. of Bristol (BA). Teaching in private schools in Tunbridge Wells and Norwich, 1935–39. Friends' Ambulance Unit, 1939–45 (PoW, Germany, 1941–43). Research Asst, W Midland Gp on Post-war Reconstruction and Planning, 1945–49; Lectr, Sen. Lectr and Reader, Univ. of Edinburgh, 1949–65. Vis. Prof., Harvard, 1973–74. Mem., SSRC, 1969–70. *Publications:* Local Government and Central Control, 1954; The Management of Innovation (with G. M. Stalker), 1961; (ed) Industrial Man, 1969; (ed with E. Burns) Sociology of Literature and Drama, 1973; The BBC: Public Institution and Private World, 1977; Erving Goffman, 1991; Description, Explanation and Understanding, 1994; articles in a number of jls in Britain, USA, France, etc. *Recreations:* music, gardening. *Address:* Inchgarvie Lodge, South Queensferry, West Lothian EH30 9JS.

BURNS, Maj.-Gen. Sir (Walter Arthur) George, GCVO 1991 (KCVO 1962); CB 1961; DSO 1944; OBE 1953; MC 1940; retired; Lord-Lieutenant of Hertfordshire, 1961–86; *b* 29 Jan. 1911; *s* of late Walter Spencer Morgan and Evelyn Ruth Burns. *Educ:* Eton; Trinity Coll., Cambridge. BA Hons History. Commissioned Coldstream Guards 1932; ADC to Viceroy of India, 1938–40; Adjt 1st Bn, 1940–41 (MC); Brigade Major: 9 Inf. Bde, 1941–42; Sp. Gp Gds Armd Div., 1942; 32 Gds Bde, 1942–43; CO 3rd Bn Coldstream Gds, Italy, 1943–44 (DSO); Staff Coll., Camberley, 1945. Brigade Major, Household Bde, 1945–47; CO 3rd Bn Coldstream Gds, Palestine, 1947–50; AAG, HQ London Dist, 1951, 1952; Regimental Lt-Col Coldstream Gds, 1952–55; Comdg 4th Gds Bde, 1955–59. GOC London District and The Household Brigade, 1959–62; Col, Coldstream Guards, 1966–94. Steward, The Jockey Club, 1964–. Lay Canon, St Alban's Cathedral, 1992–. KStJ 1972. *Recreations:* shooting, racing. *Address:* Home Farm, North Mymms Park, Hatfield, Hertfordshire AL9 7TH. *T:* Potters Bar (01707) 645117. *Clubs:* Jockey, Pratt's, Buck's.

BURNS, Prof. William, CBE 1966; Emeritus Professor of Physiology, University of London; Professor of Physiology, Charing Cross Hospital Medical School, 1947–77; Hon. Consultant Otologist, Charing Cross Group of Hospitals; *b* 15 Oct. 1909; *e s* of late Charles Burns, MB, ChB, JP and Mary Sillars, lately of Stonehaven, Scotland; *m* 1936, Margaret, *o d* of late W. A. Morgan, Glasgow; one *s* one *d*. *Educ:* Mackie Acad., Stonehaven; Aberdeen Univ. BSc 1932, MB ChB 1935, DSc 1943 Aberdeen. FRCP 1973. Asst in Physiology, Aberdeen, 1935; Lectr in Physiology, Aberdeen, 1936; War-time duty with Admiralty, 1942; established in RN Scientific Service, 1946; Supt RN Physiological Laboratory, 1947; Chm., Flying Personnel Res. Cttee, RAF, 1978–80; Emeritus Civil Consultant to RN in Audiology; Hon. Consultant to RAF in Acoustic Science; pt-time activity for MRC, 1977–84. Member: Council, BAAS, 1956–61 (Pres., Sect. I, Cardiff, 1960); Noise Adv. Council, 1977–81; BMA; formerly Member: Physiol Soc.; British Inst. of Acoustics; Hon. Life Mem., British Soc. Audiology. *Publications:* Noise and Man, 1968, 2nd edn 1973; (with D. W. Robinson) Hearing and Noise in Industry, 1970; articles on various aspects of hearing, in Journal of the Acoustical Soc. of America, Annals of Occupational Hygiene, Proc. Assoc. of Industrial Med. Officers, etc. *Recreations:* working in wood and metal; interested in engineering in general.

BURNSTOCK, Prof. Geoffrey, FRS 1986; FAA 1971; Professor of Anatomy, University of London, and Head of Department of Anatomy and Developmental Biology (formerly Anatomy and Embryology), University College London, since 1975; Convener, Centre for Neuroscience, University College London, since 1979; *b* 10 May 1929; *s* of James Burnstock and Nancy Green; *m* 1957, Nomi Hirschfeld; three *d*. *Educ:* King's Coll., London; Melbourne Univ. BSc 1953, PhD 1957 London; DSc Melbourne 1971. National Inst. for Medical Res., Mill Hill, 1956–57; Dept of Pharmacology, Oxford Univ., 1957–59; Rockefeller Travelling Fellowship, Univ. of Ill, 1959; Dept of Zoology, Univ. of Melbourne: Sen. Lectr, 1959–62; Reader, 1962–64; Prof. of Zoology and Chm. of Dept, 1964–75; Associate Dean (Biological Sciences), 1969–72; Prof. Emeritus, Dept of Pharmacology, 1993. Vis. Prof., Dept of Pharmacology, Univ. of Calif, LA, 1970. Chm., Scientific Adv. Bd, Eisai London Ltd, 1990–. Vice-Pres., Anatomical Soc. of GB and Ireland, 1990. Member: Academia Europaea, 1992; Russian Soc. of Neuropathology, 1993. Hon. MRCP 1987. Hon. MSc Melbourne 1962. Silver Medal, Royal Soc. of Victoria, 1970; Special Award, NIH Conf., Bethesda, USA, 1989. *Publications:* (with M. Costa) Adrenergic Neurons: their Organisation, Function and Development in the Peripheral Nervous System, 1975; (with Y. Uehara and G. R. Campbell) An Atlas of the Fine Structure of Muscle and its Innervation, 1976; (ed) Purinergic Receptors, 1981; (ed with G. Vrbová and R. O'Brien) Somatic and Autonomic Nerve-Muscle Interactions, 1983; (ed with S. G. Griffith) Nonadrenergic Innervation of Blood Vessels, 1988; (ed with S. Bloom) Peptides: a target for new drug development, 1991; series editor, The Autonomic Nervous System, vols 1–14, 1992–96; papers on smooth muscle and autonomic nervous system, incl. purinergic nerves, in sci. jls. *Recreations:* tennis, wood sculpture. *Address:* Department of Anatomy and Developmental Biology, University College London, Gower Street, WC1E 6BT. *T:* 0171–387 7050.

BURNTON, Stanley Jeffrey; QC 1982; a Recorder, since 1994; *b* 25 Oct. 1942; *s* of Harry and Fay Burnton; *m* 1971, Gwenyth Frances Castle; one *s* two *d*. *Educ:* Hackney Downs Grammar Sch.; St Edmund Hall, Oxford. MA. Called to the Bar, Middle Temple, 1965, Bencher, 1991. *Recreations:* music, wine, travel, theatre. *Address:* 1 Essex Court, Temple, EC4Y 9AR. *T:* 0171–583 2000.

BURNYEAT, Prof. Myles Fredric, FBA 1984; Laurence Professor of Ancient Philosophy, Cambridge, since 1984; *b* 1 Jan. 1939; *s* of Peter James Anthony Burnyeat and Cynthia Cherry Warburg; *m* 1st, 1971, Jane Elizabeth Buckley (marr. diss. 1982); one *s* one *d*; 2nd, 1984, Ruth Sophia Padel; one *d*. *Educ:* Bryanston Sch.; King's Coll., Cambridge (BA). Assistant Lecturer in Philosophy 1964, Lecturer in Philosophy 1965, University Coll. London; Lectr in Classics, Cambridge Univ., 1978; Fellow and Lectr in Philosophy, Robinson Coll., Cambridge, 1978. For. Hon. Mem., Amer. Acad. of Arts and Scis, 1992. *Publications:* The Theaetetus of Plato, 1990; co-editor: Philosophy As It Is, 1979; Doubt and Dogmatism, 1980; Science and Speculation, 1982; (ed) The Skeptical Tradition, 1983; contribs to classical and philosophical jls. *Recreation:* travel. *Address:* Robinson College, Cambridge CB3 9AN.

BURR, Michael Rodney; His Honour Judge Burr; a Circuit Judge, since 1992; *b* 31 Aug. 1941; *s* of Edward Frank Burr and Aileen Maud Burr; *m* 1963, Rhoda Rule; four *s* one *d*. *Educ:* Brecon County Grammar Sch.; King Edward VI Sch., Chelmsford; Coll. of Law. Solicitor, 1964. Asst Solicitor, Hilliard & Ward, Chelmsford, 1964–69; Sen. Partner, Peter Williams & Co., Swansea, 1972–92; Asst Recorder, 1983; Recorder, 1988. Sec., Incorp. Law Soc. of Swansea and Dist, 1980–83; Law Society: non-Council Member: Professional Purposes Cttee, 1985–86; Adjudication Cttee, 1986–89. *Recreations:* flying, travel.

BURR, Timothy John; Assistant Auditor General, National Audit Office, since 1994; *b* 31 March 1950; *s* of Eric Cyril Burr and Myrtle Burr (*née* Waters); *m* 1975, Gillian Heather Croot; two *s*. *Educ:* Dulwich Coll. Entered HM Treasury, 1968; Cabinet Office, 1984; Asst Sec., HM Treasury, 1985; Under-Sec., Cabinet Office, 1990; Treasury Officer of Accounts, 1993–94. *Address:* c/o National Audit Office, Buckingham Palace Road, SW1W 9SP.

BURRELL, Derek William; DL; Headmaster, Truro School, 1959–86; Chairman, Methodist Day Schools' Committee, since 1988; *b* 4 Nov. 1925; *s* of late Thomas Richard Burrell and of Flora Frances Burrell (*née* Nash). *Educ:* Tottenham Grammar Sch.; Queens' Coll., Cambridge. Assistant Master at Solihull Sch. (English, History, Religious Instruction, Music Appreciation), 1948–52. Senior English Master, Dollar Academy, 1952–59. Vice-Pres., Methodist Conf., 1987–88. DL Cornwall, 1993. *Recreations:* music of any kind, theatre, wandering about London. *Address:* Flat 5, 2 Strangways Terrace, Truro, Cornwall TR1 2NY. *T:* Truro (01872) 77733. *Club:* East India, Devonshire, Sports and Public Schools.

BURRELL, Sir (John) Raymond, 9th Bt *cr* 1774; *b* 20 Feb. 1934; *s* of Sir Walter Raymond Burrell, 8th Bt, CBE, TD, and Hon. Anne Judith (OBE) (*d* 1987), *o d* of 3rd Baron Denman, PC, GCMG, KCVO; *S* father, 1985; *m* 1st, 1959, Rowena Frances (marr. diss. 1971), *d* of late M. H. Pearce; one *s*; 2nd, 1971, Margot Lucy, *d* of F. E. Thatcher, Sydney, NSW; one *s* one *d*. *Educ:* Eton; Royal Agricultural Coll., Cirencester. *Heir: s* Charles Raymond Burrell [*b* 27 Aug. 1962; *m* 1993, Isabella Elizabeth Nancy, adopted *d* of M. L. Tree]. *Address:* Rosemont, 14 Rosemont Avenue, Woollahra, NSW 2025, Australia. *Club:* Boodle's.

BURRELL, Mark William; Director, Pearson plc, since 1977; *b* 9 April 1937; *s* of Sir Walter Burrell, 8th Bt, CBE, TD and Hon. Anne Judith, OBE, *o d* of 3rd Baron Denham, PC, GCMG, KCVO; *m* 1966, Margot Rosemary Pearce; two *s* one *d*. *Educ:* Eton; Pembroke Coll., Cambridge (BA 1st Cl. Hons Engrg). With Sir Alexander Gibb & Partners, 1959, then Vickers, 1960–61; joined Pearson plc, 1963; Dir, Pearson Enterprises, 1991–; Whitehall Petroleum: Dir, 1964–88; Chm., 1987–88; joined Lazard Brothers, 1970; Dir, 1974; Man. Dir, 1984–86; Non-Exec. Dir, 1986–; Chm., Lazard Develt Capital Ltd, 1983–87; Director: BSB Holdings, 1987–; BSkyB Group plc, 1991–94; Dir, then Chm., Royal Doulton plc, 1993–; Chm., Millbank Financial Services Ltd, 1986–; Dir, Europe Online, 1994–. *Recreations:* hunting, polo, tennis, golf. *Address:* c/o Pearson plc, 3 Burlington Gardens, W1X 1LE. *Club:* Royal Automobile.

BURRELL, Peter, CBE 1957; Director, The National Stud, 1937–71; *b* 9 May 1905; *s* of Sir Merrik R. Burrell, 7th Bt; *m* 1st, 1929, Pamela Pollen (marr. diss., 1940); two *s*; 2nd, 1971, Mrs Constance P. Mellon (*d* 1980). *Educ:* Eton; Royal Agricultural Coll., Cirencester. *Recreations:* shooting, stalking. *Address:* Long Hill, Moulton Road, Newmarket, Suffolk CB8 8QQ. *T:* Newmarket (01638) 662280.

BURRELL, Sir Raymond; *see* Burrell, Sir J. R.

BURRENCHOBAY, Sir Dayendranath, KBE 1978; CMG 1977; CVO 1972; Governor-General of Mauritius, 1978–84; *b* 24 March 1919; *s* of Mohabeer Burrenchobay, MBE, and Anant Kumari Burrenchobay; *m* 1957, Oomawatee Ramphul; one *s* two *d*. *Educ:* Royal Coll., Curepipe, Mauritius; Imperial Coll., London (BScEng Hons); Inst. of Education, London (Postgrad. CertEd). Education Officer, Govt of Mauritius, 1951–60, Sen. Educn Officer, 1960–64, Chief Educn Officer, 1964; Permanent Secretary: Min. of Education and Cultural Affairs, 1964–68; Min. of External Affairs, Tourism and Emigration, also Prime Minister's Office, 1968–76; Secretary to Cabinet and Head of Civil Service, 1976–78. Attended various confs and seminars as Govt rep.; Chm., Central Electricity Bd, 1968–78. Hon. DCL, Univ. of Mauritius, 1978. Chevalier, Légion d'Honneur, 1975; Grand Cross, 1st Cl., Order of Merit, Fed. Republic of Germany, 1978. *Recreations:* swimming, walking. *Address:* S. Ramphul Street, Curepipe Road, Mauritius.

BURRETT, (Frederick) Gordon, CB 1974; Deputy Secretary, Civil Service Department, 1972–81; Member, Executive Committee, First Division Pensioners Group, since 1984; *b* 31 Oct. 1921; *s* of Frederick Burrett and Marion Knowles; *m* 1943, Margaret Joan Giddins; one *s* two *d*. *Educ:* Emanuel Sch.; St Catharine's Coll., Cambridge. Served in Royal Engrs, N Africa, Italy, Yugoslavia, Greece, 1942–45 (despatches). HM Foreign, subseq. Diplomatic, Service, 1946; 3rd Sec., Budapest, 1946–49; FO, 1949–51; Vice-Consul, New York, 1951–54; FO, 1954–57; 1st Sec., Rome, 1957–60; transf. to HM Treasury, 1960; Private Sec. to Chief Sec., Treasury, 1963–64; Asst Secretary: HM Treasury, 1964; Cabinet Office, 1967–68; Secretary: Kindersley Review Body on Doctors' and Dentists' Remuneration; Plowden Cttee on Pay of Higher Civil Service, 1967–68; Civil Service Dept, 1968, Under-Sec. 1969. Mem., Civil Service Pay Res. Unit Bd, 1978–81; conducted govt scrutiny of V&A and Sci. Museums, 1982; Adviser to Govt of Oman on CS reorganisation, 1984; led govt review of policies and operations of Commonwealth Inst., 1986; leader of review team to examine responsibilities and grading of dirs of nat. museums and galls, 1987; conducted review of sen. posts of Arts Council and BFI, 1987–88; Chm., Cttee of Inquiry into CS Pay, Hong Kong, 1988–89. Chairman: Redundant Churches Fund, later Churches Conservation Trust, 1982–95; Wagner Soc., 1984–88. FSA 1985. *Publication:* article on the watercolours of John Massey Wright (1777–1866) in vol. 54 of the Old Water-Colour Society's Club Annual. *Recreations:* music, books, walking, reading. *Address:* 14 Church Road, Claygate, Surrey KT10 0JP. *T:* Esher (01372) 462783. *Club:* Athenæum.

BURRIDGE, Alan; Certification Officer for Trade Unions and Employers' Associations, 1981–85; *b* 15 Feb. 1921; *m* 1961, Joan Edith Neale; one *s*. *Educ:* William Ellis Sch.; Bristol Univ. (BA 1st Cl. Hons 1950). Served War, Army, 1939–46. Northern Assurance Co., 1936–39; Bristol Univ., 1947–50; Swinton Coll., 1950–53; London Municipal Soc., 1953–56; General Electric Co., 1956–67; Dept of Employment, 1967–81. *Address:* 1 Castle Hill Avenue, Berkhamsted, Herts HP4 1HJ. *T:* Berkhamsted (01442) 865276.

BURRILL, Timothy; Managing Director, Burrill Productions, since 1966; Chairman, Film Asset Developments Plc, 1987–94; *b* 8 June 1931; *yr s* of L. Peckover Burrill, OBE and Marjorie S. Burrill; *m* 1st, 1959, Philippa (marr. diss. 1966), *o d* of Maurice and Margot Hare; one *d*; 2nd, 1968, Santa (marr. diss. 1993), *e d* of John and Betty Raymond; one *s* two *d*. *Educ:* Eton Coll.; Sorbonne Univ. Served Grenadier Guards, 1949–52: commnd 1950; served 2nd Bn, 1950–52. Jun. management, Cayzer Irvine & Co., 1952–56; entered film industry, 1956; joined Brookfield Prodns, 1965; Dir, World Film Services, 1967–69; first Prodn Administrator, National Film and TV Sch., 1972; Man. Dir, Allied Stars (resp. for Chariots of Fire), 1979–80; Director: Artistry Ltd, 1982–87 (resp. for Superman and Supergirl films); Fourth Protocol Films Ltd, 1985–; Chargeurs Productions, 1994–; Consultant: National Film Develt Fund, 1980–81; Really Useful Group, 1989–90. UK Rep., Eurimages, 1994–. Chairman: BAFTA, 1981–83 (Vice-Chm., 1979–81); First Film Foundn, 1989–; Producer Mem., Cinematograph Films Council, 1980–85; Member: Gen. Council, ACTT, 1975–76; Exec. Council, British Film and Television Producers Assoc., 1981–89; Exec. Council, The Producers Assoc., 1989–91; Exec. Council, Producers' Alliance for Cinema and Television, 1991– (Vice-Chm., 1993–). Chm., Impact Campaign, 1994–95. Governor: National Film and Television Sch., 1981–92; National

Theatre, 1982–88. Films include The Lover, and Bitter Moon, 1990–92. *Recreations:* theatre. *Address:* 19 Cranbury Road, SW6 2NS. *T:* 0171–736 8673, *Fax:* 0171–731 3921.

BURRINGTON, Ernest; Associate (formerly Deputy) Publisher, Globe Communications, USA, since 1993; Director, 1985–92, Chairman, 1991–92, Mirror Group Newspapers; *b* 13 Dec. 1926; *s* of late Harold Burrington and of Laura Burrington; *m* 1950, Nancy Crossley; one *s* one *d*. Self-educated. Reporter, Oldham Chronicle, 1941–43; Army service, 1943–47; reporter and sub-editor, Oldham Chronicle, 1947–49; sub-editor, Bristol Evening World, 1950; Daily Herald: sub-editor, Manchester, 1950, night editor, 1955; London night editor, 1957; IPC Sun: night editor, 1964; Asst Editor, 1965; Asst Editor and night editor, News International Sun, 1969; dep. night editor, Daily Mirror, 1970; Dep. Editor, 1971, Associate Editor, 1972, Sunday People; Editor, The People, 1985–88 and 1989–90; Dep. Chm. and Asst Publisher, 1988–91, Man. Dir, 1989–91, Mirror Gp Newspapers; Chm., Syndication Internat., 1989–92; Dep. Chm., Mirror Publishing Co., 1989–91; Director: Mirror Group Magazine and Newsday Ltd, 1989–92; Legionstyle Ltd, 1991–92; Mirror Colour Print Ltd, 1991–92; (non-exec.) Sunday Correspondent, 1990; The European, 1990–91; IQ Newsgraphics, 1990–92; Sygma Picture Agency, Paris, 1990–91. Member: Council, NPA, 1988–92; IPI (Mem., British Exec., 1988–92); Foreign Press Assoc.; Trustee, Internat. Centre for Child Studies, 1986–90. *Recreations:* travel, bridge. *Address:* c/o Globe, 5401 NW Broken Sound Boulevard, Boca Raton, FL 33487, USA. *T:* (407) 9977733; South Hall, Dene Park, Shipbourne, near Tonbridge TN11 9NS.

BURROUGH, Alan, CBE 1970; Director, 1946–87, President, 1983–87, James Burrough plc (Chairman, 1968–82); Chairman: London Tideway Harbour Co. Ltd, since 1988; Albion Quay (1992) Ltd, since 1992; *b* 22 Feb. 1917; *s* of Ernest James Burrough and Sophie (*née* Burston); *m* 1st, 1939, Rosemary June Bruce (*d* 1993); two *s* one *d*; 2nd, 1995, Sheila Vivien van Dam. *Educ:* St Paul's Sch., London; Jesus Coll., Cambridge Univ. (MA). Joined James Burrough Ltd, 1935. War of 1939–45: 91st Field Regt, RA, and 5th RHA (Captain). Rejoined James Burrough Ltd, 1945: Director, 1946; Deputy Chairman, 1967; Chairman, 1968; Director: Corby Distilleries Ltd, Montreal, 1968–82; Hawks Co. Ltd, 1989–. Dep. Pres., Oxon Br., British Red Cross, 1982–86. *Clubs:* Naval and Military; Hawks (Cambridge); Royal Channel Islands Yacht, Royal Lymington Yacht.

BURROUGH, John Outhit Harold, CB 1975; CBE 1963; *b* 31 Jan. 1916; *s* of Adm. Sir Harold M. Burrough, GCB, KBE, DSO, and late Nellie Wills Outhit; *m* 1944, Suzanne Cecile Jourdan; one *s* one *d*. *Educ:* Manor House, Horsham; RNC Dartmouth. Midshipman, 1934; Sub-Lt 1936; Lieut 1938; Lt-Comdr 1944; retd 1947. Foreign Office (GCHQ), 1946–65; IDC 1964; British Embassy, Washington, 1965–67; Under-Sec., Cabinet Office, 1967–69; an Under Sec., FCO (Govt Communications HQ), 1969–76. Director: Racal Communications Systems Ltd, 1976–79; Racal Communications Ltd, 1979–82. *Address:* The Old Vicarage, Guiting Power, Glos GL54 5TY. *T:* Guiting Power (01451) 850596. *Club:* Naval and Military (Chm., 1969–72).

BURROUGH, Rt. Rev. John Paul, MBE 1946; MA Oxon; *b* 5 May 1916; *s* of Canon E. G. Burrough; *m* 1962, Elizabeth (Bess) (*d* 1991), *widow* of Stephen John White; one step *d*. *Educ:* St Edward's Sch.; St Edmund Hall, Oxford; Ely Theol. College. Coach, Tigre Boat Club, Buenos Aires, 1938–39. Captain, Royal Signals, Malaya Campaign (POW), 1940–45. Asst, Aldershot Parish Church, 1946–51; Mission Priest, Dio. of Korea, 1951–59; Anglican Chaplain to Overseas Peoples in Birmingham, 1959–68; Canon Residentiary of Birmingham, 1967–68; Bishop of Mashonaland, 1968–81; Rector of Empingham and Hon. Asst Bishop, Diocese of Peterborough, 1981–85. Chaplain and Sub-Prelate, Order of St John of Jerusalem, 1969–. *Publications:* Lodeleigh, 1946; God and Human Chance, 1984; Angels Unawares, 1988. *Recreation:* rowing (Oxford crews, 1937 and 1938). *Address:* 6 Mill Green Close, Bampton, Oxon OX18 2HF. *T:* Bampton Castle (01993) 850952. *Clubs:* Leander (Henley); Vincent's (Oxford).

BURROW, Prof. John Anthony, FBA 1986; Winterstoke Professor of English, University of Bristol, since 1976; *b* 3 Aug. 1932; *s* of William and Ada Burrow; *m* 1956, Diana Wynne Jones; three *s*. *Educ:* Buckhurst Hill County High Sch., Essex; Christ Church, Oxford (BA, MA). Asst Lectr, King's Coll., London, 1955–57; Lectr in English, Christ Church, 1957–61, and Brasenose Coll., 1957–59, Oxford; Fellow in English, Jesus Coll., Oxford, 1961–75; Dean of Faculty of Arts, Univ. of Bristol, 1990–93. Vis. Prof., Yale Univ., 1968–69. Hon. Dir, EETS, 1983–. *Publications:* A Reading of Sir Gawain and the Green Knight, 1965; Geoffrey Chaucer (critical anthology), 1969; Ricardian Poetry, 1971; (ed) English Verse 1300–1500, 1977; Medieval Writers and their Work, 1982; Essays on Medieval Literature, 1984; The Ages of Man, 1986; (with Thorlac Turville-Petre) A Book of Middle English, 1992; Langland's Fictions, 1993; Thomas Hoccleve, 1994; articles and reviews in learned jls. *Recreation:* music. *Address:* 9 The Polygon, Clifton, Bristol BS8 4PW. *T:* Bristol (0117) 9277845.

BURROW, John Halcrow, CBE 1993 (OBE 1987); Chief Constable of Essex Police, since 1988; *b* 1935; *s* of John and Florence Burrow; *m* 1958, Ruth (*née* Taylor); two *s* one *d*. *Educ:* Ulverston Grammar School; University College London (LLB Hons). Lieut, 3rd Kenya Bn, King's African Rifles, 1953–55. Metropolitan Police, 1958–77; Asst/Dep. Chief Constable, Merseyside Police, 1977–88. Pres., ACPO, 1992–93; Chairman: Technical and Res. Cttee, ACPO, 1990–92; ACPO No 5 (SE) Region Cttee, 1991–; Shotley Training Centre Cttee, 1990–92. *Recreation:* walking. *Address:* Essex Police HQ, PO Box 2, Springfield, Chelmsford, Essex CM2 6DA. *T:* Chelmsford (01245) 491491.

BURROW, Prof. John Wyon, FBA 1986; FRHistS 1971; Flick Professor of European Thought, and Fellow of Balliol College, University of Oxford, since 1995; *b* 4 June 1935; *s* of Charles and Alice Burrow; *m* 1958, Diane Dunnington; one *s* one *d*. *Educ:* Exeter School; Christ's College, Cambridge (MA, PhD). Research Fellow, Christ's College, Cambridge, 1959–62; Fellow, Downing Coll., Cambridge, 1962–65; Lectr, Sch. of European Studies, Univ. of East Anglia, 1965–69; Reader in History, 1969–82, Prof. of Intellectual History, 1982–95, Univ. of Sussex. Vis. Prof., Univ. of California, Berkeley, 1981 and 1989; Visiting Fellow: History of Ideas Unit, ANU, 1983; All Souls Coll., Oxford, 1994–95. Carlyle Lectr, Oxford, 1985; Christian Gauss Seminars, Princeton Univ., 1988. Hon. Dr Scienze Politiche, Bologna, 1988. *Publications:* Evolution and Society, 1966; A Liberal Descent, 1981 (Wolfson Prize); (with S. Collini and D. Winch) That Noble Science of Politics, 1983; Gibbon, 1985; Whigs and Liberals, 1988. *Recreation:* cooking. *Address:* Balliol College, Oxford OX1 3BJ; 22 Bridge Street, Witney, Oxon OX8 6HY. *T:* Witney (01993) 700306.

BURROWES, Edmund Stanley Spencer, CMG 1959; Financial Secretary, Barbados, 1951–66; *b* 16 Dec. 1906; *m* 1st, 1934, Mildred B. Jackson (decd); one *s* three *d*; 2nd, 1965, Gwen Searson. *Educ:* Queen's Coll., British Guiana. British Guiana Colonial Secretariat, 1924; Inspector of Labour, 1940; Deputy Commissioner, 1945; Labour Commissioner, Barbados, 1947. *Publication:* Occupational Terms on Sugar Estates in British Guiana, 1945. *Recreation:* wild life watching. *Address:* 18B Butler's Way, Great Yeldham, Halstead, Essex CO9 4QN.

BURROWES, Norma Elizabeth; opera and concert singer; *d* of Henry and Caroline Burrowes; *m* 1st, 1969, Steuart Bedford, *qv* (marr. diss.); 2nd, 1987, Emile Belcourt; one *s* one *d*. *Educ:* Sullivan Upper Sch., Holywood, Co. Down; Queen's Univ., Belfast (BA); Royal Academy of Music (FRAM 1992). Operas include: Zerlina in Don Giovanni, Glyndebourne Touring Opera (début); Blöndchen in Die Entführung aus dem Serail, Salzburg Festival, and again Blöndchen, Paris Opera, 1976 (début); Fiakermili, Royal Opera House (début), also Oscar, Despina, Nanetta, Woodbird; Entführung aus dem Serail, Ballo in Maschera, Der Rosenkavalier, Metropolitan, NY; Daughter of the Regiment, Midsummer Night's Dream, Elisir d'Amore, Canada; Cosi Fan Tutte, Romeo and Juliet, France; Marriage of Figaro, Germany; Gianni Schicchi, Switzerland; Marriage of Figaro, La Scala. Television operas include: Nanetta in Falstaff; Susanna in Marriage of Figaro and Lauretta in Gianni Schicchi. Sings regularly with major opera companies, gives concerts and recitals, GB and abroad; many recordings. Hon. DMus Queen's Univ. Belfast, 1979. *Recreations:* swimming, gardening, needlework. *Address:* 56 Rochester Road, NW1 9JG. *T:* 0171–485 7322.

BURROWS, Prof. Andrew Stephen; Professor of English Law, University College London, since 1994; Law Commissioner for England and Wales, since 1994; *b* 17 April 1957; *s* of William George Burrows and Dora Burrows; *m* 1982, Rachel Jane Gent; three *s*. *Educ:* Prescot Grammar Sch.; Brasenose Coll., Oxford (Schol.; Martin Wronker Prize 1978; MA; BCL); Harvard Law Sch. (LLM). Called to the Bar, Middle Temple, 1985; Lectr in Law, Merton Coll., Oxford, 1979–80; Harkness Fellow, Harvard Law Sch., 1980–81; Lectr in Law, Univ. of Manchester, 1981–86; Fellow and CUF Lectr in Law, 1986–94, Hon. Res. Fellow, 1994–, LMH, Oxford. Jt winner, Prize for Outstanding Legal Scholarship, SPTL, 1993. *Publications:* Remedies for Torts and Breach of Contract, 1987, 2nd edn 1994; (ed jtly) Clerk and Lindsell on Torts, 16th edn 1989, 17th edn 1995; Essays on the Law of Restitution (ed Burrows), 1991; The Law of Restitution, 1993; (ed jtly) Chitty on Contracts, 27th edn 1994; numerous articles in legal jls. *Recreations:* sport (esp. football), mountain walking. *Address:* Law Commission, Conquest House, 37/38 John Street, Theobalds Road, WC1N 2BQ.

BURROWS, Sir Bernard (Alexander Brocas), GCMG 1970 (KCMG 1955; CMG 1950); *b* 3 July 1910; *s* of Edward Henry Burrows and Ione, *d* of Alexander Macdonald; *m* 1944, Ines, *d* of late John Walter; one *s* one *d*. *Educ:* Eton; Trinity Coll., Oxford. Entered HM Foreign Service (later Diplomatic Service), 1934; served at HM Embassy, Cairo, 1938–45; Foreign Office, 1945–50; Counsellor HM Embassy, Washington, 1950–53; Political Resident in the Persian Gulf, 1953–58; Ambassador to Turkey, 1958–62; Dep. Under-Secretary of State, FO, 1963–66; Permanent British Representative to N Atlantic Council, 1966–70, retired 1970. Dir-Gen., Federal Trust for Educn and Res., 1973–76. *Publications:* (with C. Irwin) Security of Western Europe, 1972; Devolution or Federalism, 1980; (with G. Edwards) The Defence of Western Europe, 1982; Footnotes in the Sand, 1990; contributed to: A Nation Writ Large, 1973; Federal Solutions to European Issues, 1978; The Third World War 1985, 1978; The Third World War: the untold story, 1982; articles and reviews in New Europe, etc. *Address:* Rubens West, East Dean, Chichester, West Sussex PO18 0JJ. *Club:* Travellers'.

BURROWS, General Eva, AC 1994 (AO 1986); General of the Salvation Army, 1986–93, retired; *b* 15 Sept. 1929; *d* of Robert John Burrows and Ella Maria Burrows (*née* Watson). *Educ:* Brisbane State High School; Queensland Univ. (BA); London Univ. (PGCE); Sydney Univ. (MEd). Salvation Army: Missionary Educator, Howard Inst., Zimbabwe, 1952–67; Principal, Usher Inst., Zimbabwe, 1967–69; Vice-Principal 1970–73, Principal 1974–75, Internat. Coll. for Officers, London; Leader, Women's Social Services in GB and Ireland, 1975–77; Territorial Commander: Sri Lanka, 1977–79; Scotland, 1979–82; Australia, 1982–86. Hon. Dr of Liberal Arts, Ewha Woman's Univ., Seoul, S. Korea, 1988; Hon. LLD Asbury Coll., USA, 1988; Hon DD Olivet Univ., USA, 1993; Hon. DPhil Queensland, 1993. *Recreations:* classical music, reading, travel. *Address:* Unit 102, 193 Domain Road, South Yarra, Melbourne, Vic 3141, Australia. *T:* (3) 98209701.

BURROWS, Fred, CMG 1981; PhD; international law consultant, since 1990; *b* 10 Aug. 1925; *s* of late Charles Burrows; *m* 1955, (Jennifer) Winsome Munt; two *s*. *Educ:* Altrincham Grammar Sch.; Trinity Hall, Cambridge (MA). PhD Cantab, 1988. Served in RAF, 1944–47. Called to Bar, Gray's Inn, 1950; Asst Legal Adviser, Foreign Office, 1956–65; Legal Adviser, British Embassy, Bonn, 1965–67; returned to FO, 1967; Legal Counsellor, FCO, 1968–77; Counsellor (Legal Adviser), Office of UK Perm. Rep. to European Communities, 1977–80; Legal Counsellor, FCO, 1980–85; Law Officer (Special Duties), then (International Law), Hong Kong, 1985–90. JP Hong Kong, 1986–90. *Publication:* Free Movement in European Community Law, 1985. *Recreations:* sailing, trombone. *Address:* c/o Foreign and Commonwealth Office, SW1A 2AL.

BURROWS, (George) Richard (William); Chief Executive since 1977, and Chairman, since 1991, Irish Distillers Group; *b* 16 Jan. 1946; *m* 1970, Sherril Dix; one *s* three d. Educ: Wesley College, Dublin; Rathmines College of Commerce. FICA. Articled Stokes Bros & Pim, 1963–70; Asst to Man. Dir, Edward Dillon & Co., 1970; Man. Dir, Old Bushmills Distillery Co., 1972; Gen. Manager, Irish Distillers, 1976; Man. Dir, Irish Distillers Group, 1978. *Recreations:* sailing, Rugby. Address: Irish Distillers Group, Bow Street Distillery, Smithfield, Dublin 7, Ireland.

BURROWS, Lionel John, CBE 1974; Chief Inspector of Schools, Department of Education and Science, 1966–73; Educational Adviser, Methodist Residential Schools, 1974–84; *b* 9 March 1912; *s* of H. L. Burrows, HM Inspector of Schools, and Mrs C. J. Burrows; *m* 1939, Enid Patricia Carter; one *s* one *d*. *Educ:* King Edward VI Sch., Southampton; Gonville and Caius Coll., Cambridge. BA Cantab (1st cl. hons Mod. Langs Tripos) 1933. West Buckland Sch., Devon, Tiffin Sch., Kingston-upon-Thames and primary schools in London and Surrey, 1934–41; HM Forces (RASC and Intell. Corps), 1941–46; Commendation from US Army Chief of Staff, 1945; HM Inspector of Schools, 1946; Divisional Inspector, Metropolitan Div., 1960. Vice-Pres., Nat. Assoc. for Gifted Children, 1975–88. *Publication:* The Middle School: high road or dead end?, 1978. *Recreations:* natural history, fell-walking. *Address:* 34 Groby Road, Ratby, Leicester LE6 0LJ. *Club:* English-Speaking Union.

BURROWS, Prof. Malcolm, FRS 1985; Professor of Neuroscience, University of Cambridge, since 1986, and Fellow of Wolfson College, Cambridge, since 1991; *b* 28 May 1943; *s* of William Roy Burrows and Jean Jones Burrows; *m* 1966, Christine Joan Ellis; one *s* one *d*. *Educ:* Cambridge Univ. (MA; ScD 1983); St Andrews Univ. (PhD 1967). Reader in Neurobiology, Univ. of Cambridge, 1983–86. Vis. Prof., Konstanz Univ., 1987; Cornelius Wiersma Vis. Prof., CIT, 1991; Distinguished Vis. Prof., Univ. of California, Davis, 1992. MAE 1992. Scientific Medal, Zoological Soc., 1980; Alexander von Humboldt award, 1993. *Address:* 6 Cherry Bounds Road, Girton, Cambridge CB3 0JT.

BURROWS, Margaret Ann; *see* Buck, M. A.

BURROWS, Reginald Arthur, CMG 1964; HM Diplomatic Service, retired; *b* 31 Aug. 1918; *s* of late Arthur Richard Burrows, first Dir of Programmes, BBC; *m* 1952, Jenny

Louisa Henriette Campiche (*d* 1985); one *s* one *d. Educ:* Mill Hill Sch.; St Catharine's Coll., Cambridge (Chancellor's Medal for English Verse, 1939). Served with Royal Air Force during War; comd No. 13 (bomber) Sqdn, 1945. Entered the Foreign Service (now the Diplomatic Service), 1947; served in: Paris; Karachi; Tehran; Saigon; The Hague; Istanbul; Foreign Office; Minister, Islamabad, 1970–72; Univ. of Leeds, 1972–73; on secondment as Under-Sec., Civil Service Selection Bd, 1974–75; Asst Under-Sec. of State, 1975–78. *Recreations:* walking, studying Roman history. *Address:* Flat 9, Summer Court, Summer Hill, Harbledown, near Canterbury, Kent CT2 8NP. *T:* Canterbury (01227) 457394.

BURROWS, Richard; *see* Burrows, G. R. W.

BURROWS, Rt. Rev. Simon Hedley; Bishop Suffragan of Buckingham, 1974–85, Area Bishop, 1985–94; *b* 8 Nov. 1928; *s* of late Very Rev. H. R. Burrows, and Joan Lumsden, *d* of Rt Rev. E. N. Lovett, CBE; *m* 1960, Janet Woodd; two *s* three *d. Educ:* Eton; King's Coll., Cambridge (MA); Westcott House, Cambridge. Curate of St John's Wood, 1954–57; Chaplain of Jesus Coll., Cambridge, 1957–60; Vicar of Wyken, Coventry, 1960–67; Vicar of Holy Trinity, Fareham, 1967–74, and Rector of Team Ministry, 1971–74. Hon. DLitt Buckingham, 1992. Sub-Prelate, Order of St John, 1992. *Address:* 8 Quarry Road, Winchester, Hants SO23 0JF. *T:* Winchester (01962) 853332.

BURSELL, Rev. Rupert David Hingston; QC 1986; **His Honour Judge Bursell;** a Circuit Judge, since 1988 (Official Referee, since 1992); *b* 10 Nov. 1942; *s* of Henry and Cicely Mary Bursell; *m* 1967, Joanna Ruth Gibb; two *s* one *d. Educ:* St John's School, Leatherhead; Univ. of Exeter (LLB); St Edmund Hall, Oxford (MA, DPhil). Called to the Bar, Lincoln's Inn, 1968; Sir Thomas More Bursary and Hubert Greenland Studentship, Lincoln's Inn, 1969; a Recorder, 1985–88. Chancellor, Vicar-General and Official Principal, Diocese of Durham, 1989–; Chancellor, Dio. of Bath and Wells, 1992; Chancellor, VG and Official Principal, Dio. of St Albans, 1992–; Dep. Chancellor, Dio. of York, 1994–. Mem., Legal Adv. Commn, Gen. Synod, 1990–. Deacon, 1968; Priest, 1969; Hon. Curate: St Marylebone, 1968–69; St Mary the Virgin, Almondsbury, 1969–71; St Francis, Bedminster, 1971–83; Christ Church, and St Stephen, Bristol, 1983–88; St Andrew, Cheddar, 1993–. *Publications:* (contrib.) Atkin's Court Forms, 1972, 2nd edn 1985; (contrib.) Halsbury's Laws of England, 1975; (jtly) Crown Court Practice, 1978; (contrib.) Principles of Dermatitis Litigation, 1985; articles in legal jls. *Recreations:* Church music, military history, archaeology of Greece, Turkey and Holy Land. *Address:* The Crown Court, Small Street, Bristol BS1 1DA. *Club:* MCC.

BURSTALL, Dr Clare, FBPsS; Director, National Foundation for Educational Research in England and Wales, 1983–93 (Deputy Director, 1972–83); *b* 3 Sept. 1931; *d* of Alfred and Lily Wells; *m* 1955, Michael Lyle Burstall (marr. diss. 1977); one *s* one *d. Educ:* King's Coll. and Birkbeck Coll., Univ. of London (BA Hons French, BA Hons Psychology, PhD Psychology); La Sorbonne, Paris. FBPsS 1975. Project Leader of team evaluating teaching of French in British primary schs, NFER, 1964–72. Charter Fellow, Coll. of Preceptors, 1988; FRSA 1990; Hon. Mem., CGLI, 1987. Hon. DSc Hull, 1988; Hon. DEd De Montford, 1993. *Publications:* French from Eight: a national experiment, 1968; French in the Primary School: attitudes and achievement, 1970; Primary French in the Balance, 1974; French from Age Eight or Eleven?, 1975; jl articles on various aspects of educnl research (eg, second language learning, large-scale assessment of achievement, class size, and management of educnl res.). *Recreations:* sailing, art collection, music, needlework. *Address:* 6 Jane's Court, The Packet Quays, Falmouth, Cornwall TR11 2BZ. *T:* Falmouth (01326) 212241, *Fax:* (01326) 314650. *Club:* Royal Over-Seas League.

BURSTEIN, Hon. Dame Rose; *see* Heilbron, Hon. Dame R.

BURSTON, Sir Samuel (Gerald Wood), Kt 1977; OBE 1966; Grazier at Noss Estate, Casterton, Victoria, since 1945; President, Australian Woolgrowers and Graziers Council, 1976–79; *b* 24 April 1915; *s* of Maj.-Gen. Sir Samuel Burston, KBE, CB, DSO, VD, late RAAMC, and late Lady Burston; *m* 1940, Verna Helen Peebles (*d* 1980); one *s* one *d. Educ:* St Peter's Coll., Adelaide (Sch. Captain, 1933). Major, AIF, 1939–45 (despatches). Chm., Country Fire Authority, Vic, 1964–65; Pres., Graziers Assoc. of Vic, 1973–76; Councillor, Nat. Farmers Fedn, 1979–82; Vice-Pres., Confedn of Aust. Industry, 1978–82; Member: Nat. Employers Policy Cttee, 1970–78; Australian Wool Industry Policy Cttee, 1976–78; Aust. Sci. and Technol. Council, 1976–85 (acting Chm., 1982); Aust. Stats Adv. Council, 1976–80; Aust. Govt Econ. Consultative Gp, 1976–82; Nat. Labour Consultative Council, 1976–82; Reserve Bank Bd, 1977–87. Aust. Trade Develt Council, 1979–85; Trade Practices Cons. Council, 1979–82; Aust. Manufacturing Council, 1979–84; Chm., Perpetual Executors & Trustee Co. of Australia, 1981–87. Mem., Victorian Selection Cttee, Winston Churchill Meml Trust, 1967–81; Chm., Aust. Pastoral Res. Trust, 1988–92. *Recreations:* golf, swimming. *Address:* 43/52 Brougham Place, North Adelaide, SA 5006, Australia. *T:* (8) 2673783. *Clubs:* Melbourne (Melbourne); Adelaide, Naval, Military and Air Force of South Australia (Adelaide); Royal Adelaide Golf.

BURT, Alistair James Hendrie; MP (C) Bury North, since 1983; Minister of State, Department of Social Security, since 1995; *b* 25 May 1955; *s* of James Hendrie Burt, med. practitioner and Mina Christie Robertson; *m* 1983, Eve Alexandra Twite; one *s* one *d. Educ:* Bury Grammar Sch.; St John's Coll., Oxford (BA Hons Jurisprudence, 1977). Pres., OU Law Soc., Michaelmas term, 1976. Articled Slater Heelis & Co., Manchester, 1978–80; solicitor, Watts, Vallance & Vallance, 1980–92; Consultant, Teeman, Levine and Co. (Solicitors), Leeds, 1992–. Councillor, Archway Ward, London Bor. of Haringey, 1982–84. Parliamentary Private Secretary: to Sec. of State for the Environment, 1985–86; to Sec. of State for Educn and Science, 1986–89; to Chancellor of Duchy of Lancaster and Chm. of Cons. Party, 1989–90; Parly Under-Sec. of State, DSS, 1992–95. Vice-Chm., Tory Reform Gp, 1985–88. Secretary: NW Cons. MPs Group, 1984–88; Parly Christian Fellowship, 1984–. *Recreations:* reading left-wing publications, sport (scored a goal at Wembley, playing for northern MPs football team, Nov. 1991), modern art, astronomy. *Address:* House of Commons, SW1A 0AA. *T:* 0171–219 3000.

BURT, Hon. Sir Francis (Theodore Page), AC 1988; KCMG 1977; QC 1960; Governor of Western Australia, 1990–93 (Lieutenant-Governor, 1977–90); *b* Perth, WA, 14 June 1918; *s* of A. F. G. Burt; *m* 1943, Margaret, *d* of Brig. J. E. Lloyd; two *s* two *d. Educ:* Guildford Grammar Sch.; Univ. of Western Australia (LLB, LLM); Hackett Schol., 1941; admitted to Bar of WA, 1941. Served War, RAN and RAAF, 1940–45. A Judge of Supreme Ct, WA, 1969–88; Chief Justice, WA, 1977–88. President: Law Soc. of WA, 1960–62; WA Bar Assoc., 1963–65. Visiting Lectr in Law, Univ. of WA, 1945–65. Chairman: Inst. of Radiotherapy, WA, 1960–62; Bd of Management, Sir Charles Gairdner Hosp., Hollywood, WA, 1962–72; Queen Elizabeth II Medical Centre Trust, 1966–85; Mem., Senate of Univ. of WA, 1968–76. Hon. LLD Univ. of WA, 1987. *Recreations:* tennis, fishing. *Address:* 64 Leake Street, Peppermint Grove WA 6011, Australia. *Club:* Weld (Perth).

BURT, Gerald Raymond, OBE 1984; BEM 1947; FCIT; Chief Secretary, British Railways Board, 1976–84; *b* 15 Feb. 1926; *s* of Reginald George Burt and Lilian May Burt; *m* 1948, Edna Ivy Elizabeth Sizeland; two *s. Educ:* Latymer Upper Sch. FCIT 1971. Joined GWR as Booking Clerk, 1942: RE (Movement Control), 1944–47; BR Management Trainee, 1951–54; Gen. Staff, British Transport Commn, 1956–59; Divl Planning Officer, Bristol, 1959–62; Planning Officer, LMR, 1962–64; Divl Man., St Pancras, 1965; Traffic Man., Freightliners, 1967–70; Principal Corporate Planning Officer, British Railways Bd, 1970–76. Member: Council, Chartered Inst. of Transport, 1967–70, 1981–84; British Transport Police Cttee, 1984–88. Governor, British Transport Staff Coll., 1976–82; Trustee, Rly Benevolent Instn, 1984–. FRSA 1983. Scouting Medal of Merit, 1978. *Recreations:* gardening, the countryside. *Address:* 36 Pound Lane, Marlow, Bucks SL7 2AY. *T:* Marlow (01628) 486200.

BURT, Maurice Edward; Deputy Director, Building Research Establishment, 1975–81, retired; *b* 17 Nov. 1921; *s* of Reginald Edward Burt and Bertha Winifred Burt; *m* 1947, Monica Evelyn Amy; one *s* three *d. Educ:* Victoria Coll., Jersey; Taunton's Sch., Southampton; BA Hons London, 1948. CEng, MICE; FRAeS. Aircraft industry, 1938–48; RAE, 1948–66 (Supt, Airworthiness, 1961–66); Head of Structures Dept, Transport and Road Res. Lab., 1966–73; Head of Res. Management, Dept of Environment, 1973–75. *Publications:* technical reports and articles. *Recreations:* golf, walking, gardening. *Address:* Roselle, Rue de Haut, St Lawrence, Jersey, CI JE3 1JQ. *T:* Jersey (01534) 35933.

BURT, Peter Alexander; Treasurer and Chief General Manager, Bank of Scotland, since 1988; *b* 6 March 1944; *s* of Robert W. Burt and May H. Rodger; *m* 1971, Alison Mackintosh Turner; three *s. Educ:* Merchiston Castle Sch., Edinburgh; Univ. of St Andrews (MA); Univ. of Pennsylvania (MBA). FCIBS (FIB (Scot.) 1987). Hewlett Packard Co., Palo Alto, 1968–70; CSL, Edinburgh, 1970–74; Edward Bates & Sons Ltd, Edinburgh, 1974; joined Bank of Scotland, 1975: Internat. Div., 1975–88; Asst Gen. Manager, 1979–84; Divisional Gen. Manager, 1984–85; Jt Gen. Manager, 1985–88. Mem., High Constables and Guard of Honour of Holyrood House, Edinburgh. *Recreations:* golf, ski-ing, gardening, reading. *Clubs:* New (Edinburgh); Hon. Co. of Edinburgh Golfers (Muirfield); Royal & Ancient (St Andrews); Gullane Golf (Gullane).

BURTON, 3rd Baron, *cr* 1897; **Michael Evan Victor Baillie;** *b* 27 June 1924; *er s* of Brig. Hon. George Evan Michael Baillie, MC, TD (*d* 1941) and *g s* of Baroness Burton (2nd in line); *S* grandmother, 1962; *m* 1st, 1948, Elizabeth Ursula Forster (marr. diss. 1977; she *d* 1993), *er d* of late Capt. A. F. Wise; two *s* four *d*; 2nd, 1978, Coralie Denise, 2nd *d* of late Claud R. Cliffe. *Educ:* Eton. Lieut, Scots Guards, 1944. Mem., CC, 1948–75, JP 1961–75, DL 1963–65, Inverness-shire; Mem., Inverness Dist Council, 1984–92. Grand Master Mason of Scotland, 1994–. *Heir: s* Hon. Evan Michael Ronald Baillie [*b* 19 March 1949; *m* 1970, Lucinda (marr. diss.), *e d* of Robert Law, Newmarket; two *s* one *d*]. *Address:* Dochfour, Inverness IV3 6JY. *T:* Dochgarroch (01463) 861252. *Clubs:* Cavalry and Guards; New (Edinburgh).

BURTON, (Anthony) David, CBE 1992; Chairman, Marshalls Finance Ltd; Director, LIFFE, 1981–94 (Chairman, 1988–92); *b* 2 April 1937; *s* of Leslie Mitchell Burton and Marion Burton (*née* Marsh); *m* 1964, Valerie (*née* Swire); one *s* two *d. Educ:* Arnold Sch., Blackpool. FCIB; FCT. Bank of America National Trust and Savings Assoc., 1966–72; S. G. Warburg & Co. Ltd, 1972–92. *Recreations:* antique glass, German pottery, music, opera, sport (participating and spectator). *Address:* c/o Marshalls Finance, Lloyds Chambers, 1 Portsoken Street, E1 8DF. *T:* 0171–488 4588. *Club:* MCC.

BURTON, Anthony George Graham; author and broadcaster, since 1968; *b* 24 Dec. 1934; *s* of Donald Graham Burton and Irene Burton; *m* 1959, Pip Sharman; two *s* one *d. Educ:* King James's Grammar Sch., Knaresborough; Leeds Univ. National Service, RAF, 1955–57. Research chemist, 1958–60; publishing, 1960–68. *Publications:* A Programmed Guide to Office Warfare, 1969; The Jones Report, 1970; The Canal Builders, 1972, 3rd edn 1993; Canals in Colour, 1974; Remains of a Revolution, 1975; Josiah Wedgwood, 1976; (jtly) Canal, 1976; The Miners, 1976; Back Door Britain, 1977; Industrial Archaeological Sites of Britain, 1977; (jtly) The Green Bag Travellers, 1978; The Past At Work, 1980; The Rainhill Story, 1980; The Past Afloat, 1982; The Changing River, 1982; The Shell Book of Curious Britain, 1982; National Trust Guide to Our Industrial Past, 1983; The Waterways of Britain, 1983; The Rise and Fall of King Cotton, 1984; (ed jtly) Canals: a new look, 1984; Walking the Line, 1985; Wilderness Britain, 1985; (jtly) Britain's Light Railways, 1985; The Shell Book of Undiscovered Britain and Ireland, 1986; (jtly) Landscape Detective, 1986; Britain Revisited, 1986; Opening Time, 1987; Steaming Through Britain, 1987; Walking Through History, 1988; Walk the South Downs, 1988; The Great Days of the Canals, 1989; Cityscapes, 1990; Astonishing Britain, 1990; Slow Roads, 1991; The Railway Builders, 1992; Canal Mania, 1993; (jtly) The Grand Union Canal Walk, 1993; The Railway Empire, 1994; The Rise and Fall of British Shipbuilding, 1994; The Cotswold Way, 1995; The Dales Way, 1995; *novels:* The Reluctant Musketeer, 1973; The Master Idol, 1975; The Navigators, 1976; A Place to Stand, 1977. *Recreations:* walking and travelling in search of steam engines and good beer; cinema. *Address:* 25 Cowper Road, Redland, Bristol BS6 6NZ.

BURTON, Rt Rev. Anthony John; *see* Saskatchewan, Bishop of.

BURTON, Sir Carlisle (Archibald), Kt 1979; OBE 1968; Barbados High Commissioner to the Bahamas, 1978–93; *b* 29 July 1921; *m* 1946, Hyacinth Marjorie Adelle Barker. *Educ:* Harrison Coll., Barbados, WI; Univ. of London (BA); School of Librarianship, Leeds (ALA); Univ. of Pittsburgh (MS). Assistant Master, Harrison Coll., Barbados, 1943–50; Sen. Asst Master, Bishop's High Sch., Tobago, 1950–51; Public Librarian, Barbados, 1953–58; Permanent Secretary: Min. of Educn, 1958–63; Min. of Health, 1963–71; Perm. Sec., Prime Minister's Office, and Head of Civil Service, 1972–81; Chm., Public Services Commn, Barbados, 1981–87, Turks and Caicos Islands, 1988–90. Member: Commonwealth Observer Gp at elections in Southern Rhodesia (Zimbabwe), 1980 and in Malaysia, 1990; Caribbean Community Review Team, 1989–91. Director: Barbados National Bank, 1978–86 (Dep. Chm., 1982–86); Insurance Corp. of Barbados, 1978–86 (Chm., 1981–86). Chm., Cave Hill Campus Council, Univ. of the WI, Barbados, 1984–94; Mem. Council, Barbados Mus. and Historical Soc. Life Mem., Barbados Nat. Trust. FRSA 1953. *Recreations:* (active) table tennis, swimming, bridge, reading; (spectator) cricket (Life Member, Barbados Cricket Assoc.), athletics (Life Member, Barbados Amateur Athletic Assoc.), soccer. *Address:* Caradelle, Mountjoy Avenue, Pine Gardens, St Michael, Barbados, West Indies. *T:* 4293724.

BURTON, David; *see* Burton, A. D.

BURTON, David Harold; Director, Product Quality, and Deputy Managing Director (South & East), British Railways Board, since 1994; *b* 28 Jan. 1947; *s* of George and Helen Burton; *m* 1973, Patricia Burton; one *s. Educ:* Bridlington Sch.; Leeds Univ. (BA (Hons) Geography). British Rail: Network Man., S Central Network SE, 1986; Dep. Gen. Man., Southern Region, 1988; Gen. Man., Anglia Region, 1989–91; Gp Dir North, Network SouthEast, 1991–92; Director: Express Parcels, BR Parcels, 1992–93; Restructuring, Network SouthEast, 1993–94. *Recreations:* spectator sport, lousy golf. *Address:* (office) Euston House, 24 Eversholt Street, NW1 1DZ.

BURTON, Sir George (Vernon Kennedy), Kt 1977; CBE 1972 (MBE (mil.) 1945); DL; Chairman, Fisons plc, 1973–84 (Chief Executive, 1966–76, Senior Vice-Chairman,

1966–71, Deputy Chairman, 1971–72); *b* 21 April 1916; *s* of late George Ethelbert Earnshaw Burton and Francesca (*née* Holden-White); *g s* of Sir Bunnell Burton, Ipswich; *m* 1st, 1945, Sarah Katherine Tcherniavsky (marr. diss.); two *s*; 2nd, 1975, Priscilla Margaret Gore, *d* of late Cecil H. King. *Educ:* Charterhouse; Germany. Served RA, 1939–45, N Africa, Sicily, Italy, Austria. Director: Barclays Bank Internat. plc, 1976–82; Thomas Tilling, 1976–83; Rolls-Royce Ltd, 1976–84. Member: Export Council for Europe, 1965–71 (Dep. Chm., 1967–71); Council, CBI, 1970–84 (Chm., CBI Overseas Cttee, 1975–81); BOTB, 1972–73 (BOTB European Trade Cttee, 1972–81; British Overseas Trade Adv. Council, 1975–79); Investment Insce Adv. Cttee, ECGD, 1971–76; Council on Internat. Develt of ODM, 1977–79; Council, BIM, 1968–70 (FBIM); NEDC, 1975–79; Whitford Cttee to Consider Law on Copyright and Designs, 1974–77; Ipswich County Borough Council, 1947–51; Ipswich Gp HMC; Assoc. for Business Sponsorship of the Arts, 1978–84; Governing Body, British National Cttee of Internat. Chamber of Commerce, 1979–86; Governor, Sutton's Hosp. in Charterhouse, 1979–92; Chm., Ipswich Conservative Assoc., 1982–84. FRSA 1978. DL Suffolk, 1980. Commander: Order of Ouissam Alaouite, Morocco, 1968; Order of Léopold II, Belgium, 1974. *Recreation:* music. *Address:* Aldham Mill, Hadleigh, Suffolk IP7 6LE.

BURTON, Graham Stuart, CMG 1987; HM Diplomatic Service; Ambassador to Indonesia, since 1994; *b* 8 April 1941; *s* of late Cyril Stanley Richard Burton and of Jessie Blythe Burton; *m* 1965, Julia Margaret Lappin; one *s* one *d*. *Educ:* Sir William Borlase's Sch., Marlow. Foreign Office, 1961; Abu Dhabi, 1964; Middle East Centre for Arabic Studies, 1967; Kuwait, 1969; FCO, 1972; Tunis, 1975; UK Mission to United Nations, 1978; Counsellor, Tripoli, 1981; Head, Security Co-ordination Dept, FCO, 1984; Consul General, San Francisco, 1987; Ambassador, UAE, 1990. *Recreations:* golf, watching all sport, opera. *Address:* c/o Foreign and Commonwealth Office, SW1A 2AH. *Club:* MCC.

BURTON, Humphrey McGuire; Consultant and Executive Producer, Covent Garden Pioneer (TV Productions), since 1994; *b* 25 March 1931; *s* of Harry (Philip) and Kathleen Burton; *m* 1st, 1957, Gretel (*née* Davis); one *s* one *d*; 2nd, 1970, Christina (*née* Hellstedt); one *s* one *d*. *Educ:* Long Dene Sch., Chiddingstone; Judd Sch., Tonbridge; Fitzwilliam House, Cambridge (BA). BBC Radio, 1955–58; BBC TV, 1958–67: Editor, Monitor, 1962; Exec. Producer Music Programmes, 1963; Head of Music and Arts Programmes, 1965–67, productions inc. Workshop, Master Class, In Rehearsal, Britten at 50, Conversations with Glenn Gould; Head of Music and Arts, 1975–81; Exec. Producer opera relays from Covent Garden and Glyndebourne (Capriccio, Così fan tutte); Producer: Omnibus at Santa Fe Opera; West Side Story (Omnibus documentary), 1985; Producer/Director: TV Proms with Giulini and Solti, 1981, and with others, 1982–94; Walton 80th Birthday Concert (Previn), Verdi Requiem (Abbado), and Call me Kiri (Te Kanawa), 1982; Candide, Scottish Opera, Glasgow, 1988 and Barbican (conducted by Leonard Bernstein), 1989; Covent Garden opera relays: Manon Lescaut, Die Fledermaus, 1983; Andrea Chénier, 1985; Turandot, 1987; Die Entführung aus dem Serail, 1988; Così fan tutte, Prince Igor, 1990; Die Fledermaus (Joan Sutherland farewell), 1990; La Traviata, 1994. Artistic Dir, 1988–90, Artistic Advr, 1990–93, Barbican Centre. *Host of BBC series:* Omnibus, 1976–78, 1984–85; Young Musician of the Year, biennially 1978–94; Wagner's Ring, 1982; In Performance, 1978–82; Opera Month, 1979; Cardiff Singer of the World, 1991; other arts and music programmes; *London Weekend TV:* Head of Drama, Arts and Music, 1967–69; Editor/Introducer, Aquarius, 1970–75, programmes incl. Mahler Festival, Verdi Requiem, Trouble in Tahiti, The Great Gondola Race, Anatomy of a Record, etc; *other ITV companies:* 5 Glyndebourne operas, adapted and produced, Southern, 1972–74; The Beach at Falesa, World Premiere, Harlech, 1974; dir. Eugene Onegin, Channel 4, 1994; UN Day Concert with Pablo Casals, 1971; *French TV:* Berlioz' Requiem at Les Invalides, 1975; many free-lance prodns in Austria, Czechoslovakia, Germany, Hungary, Italy, Israel, Poland, Russia and USA, including Mahler, Brahms, Schumann and Beethoven Cycles with Bernstein and Vienna Philharmonic; concerts with von Karajan and Berlin and Vienna Philharmonic, Giulini with LA Philharmonic, Mehta and NY Philharmonic, and Solti and Chicago SO; world première, Epitaph, by Charles Mingus, NY, 1989; Director: Boris Godounov, Kirov, 1990; War and Peace, Kirov, 1991; Mozart Requiem, Vienna Bicentennial 1991; Life of Leonard Bernstein (series, Classic FM). Producer: Leonard Bernstein's 70th Birthday Gala Season, Tanglewood, MA, 1988; Bernstein Meml Concert, Carnegie Hall, 1990. Guest Dir, Hollywood Bowl 1983 Summer Music Fest. Chairman: EBU Music Experts Gp, 1976–82; EBU TV Music Working Party, 1982–86; Mem., New Music Sub-Cttee, Arts Council, 1981–83; Advr, Manchester Olympic Fest., 1990; Administrator, Royal Philharmonic Soc.'s Music Awards, 1989–91. Hon. Professorial Fellow, University Coll., Cardiff, 1983–87. Hon. FCSD 1990. Desmond Davis Award, SFTA, 1966; Royal TV Soc. Silver Medal, 1971; Emmy, 1971 for 'Beethoven's Birthday' (CBS TV); Peabody Award, 1972; SFTA Best Specialised Series, 1974; Christopher Award, 1979; RAI Prize, Prix Italia and Robert Flaherty best documentary award, BAFTA (all for West Side Story), 1985; Emmy, 1988, for 'Celebrating Gershwin' (BBC TV). Chevalier de l'Ordre des Arts et des Lettres, 1975. *Publication:* Leonard Bernstein, 1994 (trans. German and Japanese). *Recreations:* music-making, tennis, travel. *Address:* 123 Oakwood Court, W14 8LA. *Club:* Garrick.

BURTON, Iris Grace; Editor-in-Chief: Woman's Realm, since 1991; Woman's Weekly, since 1992; *d* of Arthur Burton and late Alice Burton; *m*; one *s* two *d*. *Educ:* Roan Girls' Grammar Sch., Greenwich; City of London Coll. Local newspaper, SE London Mercury, until 1966; Writer, then Features Editor, Woman's Own, 1966–78; Asst Editor, TV Times, 1978–80; Editor, Woman's Own, 1980–86. Editor-in-Chief: Prima magazine, 1986–87; Best magazine, 1987–88; Editorial Dir, G+J of the UK publications, 1988–91. Mem., Press Complaints Commn, 1993–. *Address:* IPC Magazines, King's Reach Tower, Stamford Street, SE1 9LS; (home) Anerley, SE20.

BURTON, Prof. John Lloyd, MD; FRCP; Consultant Dermatologist, Bristol Royal Infirmary, since 1973; Professor of Dermatology, University of Bristol, since 1992; *b* 29 Aug. 1938; *s* of Lloyd Burton and Dorothy Mary Burton (*née* Pacey); *m* 1964, Patricia Anne Crankshaw; one *s* two *d*. *Educ:* Heanor Grammar Sch., Derbys; Manchester Univ. (BSc; MD 1971). FRCP 1978. Trng posts in hosps in Manchester, London, Edinburgh and Newcastle upon Tyne, 1964–73. Numerous guest lectures, including: Dowling Oration, 1980, Deville, 1995, RSM; Parkes-Weber, RCP, 1988; Long-Fox, Bristol Univ., 1994. Advr in Dermatol. to CMO, 1988–94. Examr, RCP, 1987–92. Chm., Dermatol. Cttee, RCP, 1993–95; President: Dermatol. Sect., RSocMed, 1994–95; Brit. Assoc. Dermatologists, 1995–96. Editor, Brit. Jl Dermatol., 1981–85. *Publications:* Aids to Postgraduate Medicine, 1970, 6th edn 1994; Aids to Undergraduate Medicine, 1973, 5th edn 1990; Essentials of Dermatology, 1979, 3rd edn 1990; (ed jtly) Textbook of Dermatology (4 Vols), 4th edn 1986, 5th edn 1992; numerous chapters and scientific papers. *Recreations:* safe mountaineering, adventurous book-binding. *Address:* Norland House, 33 Canynge Road, Clifton, Bristol BS8 3LD. *T:* Bristol (0117) 973 3933.

BURTON, Prof. Kenneth, FRS 1974; Professor of Biochemistry, 1966–88, now Emeritus, and Dean of Faculty of Science, 1983–86, University of Newcastle upon Tyne; *b* 26 June 1926; *s* of Arthur and Gladys Burton; *m* 1955, Hilda Marsden; one *s* one *d*. *Educ:* High Pavement Sch., Nottingham; Wath-upon-Dearne Grammar Sch.; King's Coll., Cambridge (MA, PhD). Asst Lectr in Biochem., Univ. of Sheffield, 1949, Lectr 1952; Res. Associate, Univ. of Chicago, 1952–54; MRC Unit for Research in Cell Metabolism, Oxford, 1954–66. Vis. Lectr in Medicine, Harvard, 1964; William Evans Vis. Prof., Univ. of Otago, 1977–78. *Publications:* scientific articles, especially on nucleic acids. *Recreations:* music, hill-walking. *Address:* 42 Cade Hill Road, Stocksfield, Northumberland NE43 7PU.

BURTON, Michael John; QC 1984; a Recorder, since 1989; *b* 12 Nov. 1946; *s* of late Henry Burton, QC, and Hilda Burton; *m* 1972, Corinne Ruth (*d* 1992), *d* of Dr Jack Cowan, MC, and late Dorothy Cowan; four *d*. *Educ:* Eton Coll. (KS, Captain of the School); Balliol Coll., Oxford (MA). President, Balliol JCR, 1967; First President, Oxford Univ. SRC, 1968. Called to Bar, Gray's Inn, 1970, Bencher, 1993; Law Lectr, Balliol Coll., Oxford, 1972–74. Head of Chambers, 1991–. Contested: (Lab) RBK&C (local elections), 1971; (Lab) Stratford upon Avon, Feb. 1974; (SDP) Putney, GLC, 1981. *Publication:* (contrib.) Bullen & Leake & Jacob's Precedents of Pleadings, 13th edn 1990. *Recreations:* amateur theatricals, lyric writing, singing, bridge, watching Wimbledon Football Club. *Address:* Littleton Chambers, 3 King's Bench Walk North, Temple, EC4Y 7HR. *T:* 0171–797 8600; High Trees, 63 Murray Road, Wimbledon, SW19 4PF.

BURTON, Sir Michael (St Edmund), KCVO 1992 (CVO 1979); CMG 1987; HM Diplomatic Service; Ambassador to the Czech Republic, since 1994; *b* 18 Oct. 1937; *s* of late Brig. G. W. S. Burton, DSO (and two Bars), and of Barbara Burton (*née* Kemmis Betty); *m* 1967, Henrietta Jindra Hones; one *s* one *d* (and one *d* decd). *Educ:* Bedford Sch.; Magdalen Coll., Oxford. MA. 2nd Lt, Rifle Brigade, 1955–57. Foreign Office, 1960; Asst Political Agent, Dubai, Trucial States, 1962–64; Private Sec. to Minister of State, FO, 1964–67; Second (later First) Sec. (Information), Khartoum, 1967–69; First Sec. (Inf.), Paris, 1969–72; Asst, Science and Technology Dept, FCO, 1972–75; First Sec. and Head of Chancery, Amman, 1975–77; Counsellor, Kuwait, 1977–79; Head of Maritime, Aviation and Environment Dept, FCO, 1979–81; Head of S Asian Dept, FCO, 1981–84; on secondment to BP as Head of Policy Rev. Unit, 1984–85; Berlin: Minister, 1985–92; Dep. Comdt, BMG, 1985–90; Head of Embassy Office, 1990–92; Asst Under-Sec. of State (ME), FCO, 1993. *Recreations:* tennis, opera, theatre, music, travel, wine. *Address:* c/o Foreign and Commonwealth Office, SW1A 2AH. *Clubs:* United Oxford & Cambridge University, Hurlingham.

BURTON, Richard Hilary; Chairman, Cable Authority, 1984–90; *b* 28 Dec. 1923; *s* of Robert Claud and Theodora Constance Helen Burton; *m* 1962, Priscilla Jane Coode-Adams; one *s* one *d*. *Educ:* Lancing; Brasenose Coll., Oxford (MA 2nd Cl. Hons Jurisprudence). Served War, 1942–46, 60th Rifles, Captain (mentioned in despatches); Mem., Military Courts, Palestine, 1946. Called to the Bar, Inner Temple, 1951; practised at Bar, 1951–54. Gillette Industries Ltd: Manager, Legal Dept, 1954–65; Legal Dir, 1965–78; Chm., 1978–84; Dep. to the Chm., The Gillette Company (USA), 1984–88; Chm., Nestor-BNA plc, 1986–89. Chm., W Mddx Arts Develt Trust, 1978–86. Freeman: City of London, 1974; Co. of Information Technologists, 1988. FRSA. *Recreations:* cricket, real tennis, shooting, ornithology, lepidoptery. *Address:* Danmoor House, Heckfield, near Basingstoke, Hants RG27 0JY. *T:* Heckfield (01734) 326233. *Clubs:* Boodle's, MCC (Mem. Cttee, 1989–92).

BURTON, Richard St John Vladimir; Partner, Ahrends Burton & Koralek, since 1961; *b* 3 Nov. 1933; *s* of Percy Basil Harmsworth Burton and Vera (*née* Poliakoff Russell); *m* 1956, Mireille, *d* of Joseph Dernbach-Mayen; three *s* one *d*. *Educ:* Bryanston; AA Sch. of Architecture (AA Dip Hons). ARIBA 1957. Founding Partner, Ahrends Burton & Koralek, 1961. Principal works: TCD Library and Arts Bldg, 1967 and 1979; Chalvedon and Northlands Housing, Basildon, 1968 and 1980; Templeton Coll., Oxford, 1969–; Nebenzahl House, 1972; extension, Keble Coll., Oxford, 1976; W. H. Smith Head Office Marketing, Swindon, 1985; Burton House, 1987, 1993; British Embassy, Moscow, 1988–; Hooke Park Coll., 1990; John Lewis, Kingston-on-Thames, 1991; St Mary's Isle of Wight Low Energy Hosp., 1991; Docklands Light Railway extension, 1993. Gov., Building Centre Trust, 1985–; Chairman: Arts Council Percent for Art Steering Gp, 1989; RIBA Steering Gp on Educn, 1991; Arts Council Adv. Gp on Architecture, 1994–. FRSA. *Publication:* Ahrends Burton and Koralek, 1991. *Recreations:* building, writing. *Address:* Ahrends Burton & Koralek, Unit 1, 7 Chalcot Road, NW1 8LH. *T:* 0171–586 3311.

BURTON, Roger; Director of Finance (formerly City Treasurer), Birmingham City Council, since 1990; *b* 12 Oct. 1946; *s* of Norman Burton and Marjorie Rose (*née* Burgin); *m* 1st, 1968, Dorothy May Hey (marr. diss.); one *s* one *d*; 2nd, 1984, Susan Jane Griffiths (marr. diss. 1988); 3rd, 1991, Janet Elizabeth Mauchlen (*née* Davies); two step *s* one step *d*. *Educ:* Doncaster Grammar Sch.; Lanchester Polytechnic (BSc Econs 1968). CIPFA 1972; IRRV 1990. Coventry CC, 1968–79; Birmingham CC, 1979–. *Recreations:* sport, walking, photography, Real Ale. *Address:* Council House, PO Box 50, Birmingham B3 3AB. *T:* 0121–235 3803.

BURTON, Sydney Harold, JP; FCIB; Director, Gateway Building Society, 1981–88 (Managing Director, 1975–81); *b* 6 April 1916; *s* of Sydney Collard Burton and Maud Burton; *m* 1st, 1941, Jean Cowling (*d* 1985); one *d*; 2nd, 1986, Irene Robertson. *Educ:* Belle Vue High Sch., Bradford. Various appts with Bradford Equitable Building Soc. (excl. war years), 1932–63; joined Temperance Permanent Building Soc., 1963; Jt Gen. Manager, 1965; Gen. Man. and Sec., 1972; following merger of Temperance Permanent and Bedfordshire Bldg Socs became Chief Gen. Man. and Sec. of Gateway Bldg Soc., 1974. Pres., Building Societies Inst., 1976–77; Mem. Council, Building Societies Assoc., 1971–81. JP Worthing, 1974. *Recreations:* music and theatre, social and religious work. *Address:* Cherry Trees, 52 Beehive Lane, Ferring, Sussex BN12 5NR. *T:* Worthing (01903) 244704.

BURTON, Victoria Geraldine, (Mrs A. M. Burton); *see* Bruce, V. G.

BURTON-BRADLEY, Sir Burton (Gyrth), Kt 1990; OBE 1982; MD; FRCPsych; Professor of Psychiatry, University of Papua New Guinea, since 1978 (Associate Professor, 1972–75); Clinical Professor of Psychiatry, University of Hawaii, since 1978; *b* 18 Nov. 1914; *s* of Alan Godfrey and Ruby Malvina Burton-Bradley; *m* 1950, Ingeborg Roeser (*d* 1972). *Educ:* Univs of Sydney, Melbourne, NSW; RCPsych. MD (NSW), BS. FRANZCP, FRACMA, DPM, DTM&H, DipAnth. MO, Western Suburbs Hosp., Sydney, 1945–46; GP, NSW, 1946–48; MO, Aust. Mil. Mission in Germany and Austria, 1949–50; Psychiatrist, Brisbane Mental Hosp., 1950–57; Colombo Plan Psychiatrist, Singapore, 1957–59; Lectr in Psychol Med., Univ. of Malaya, Singapore, 1957–59; Chief, Mental Health, Papua New Guinea, 1959–75. Wenner-Gren Res. Fellow in Psychol Anthropol., 1970; Travelling Fellow, Fund for Res. in Psych., 1975–76. Advr in Ethno-Psychiatry, S Pacific Commn, 1967–. World Health Organization: Mem., Expert Adv. Panel, 1978–; Advr, Solomon Is, 1979; Rockefeller Scholar, Italy, 1979. Abraham Flexner Lectr, Vanderbilt Univ., USA, 1973; Special Lectr, Pacific Rim Coll. of Psychiatrists, Tokyo, 1986; Ext. Examr, Dept of Tropical Medicine, Univ. of Sydney. Chm., first Conf., Asian Chapter of Internat. Coll. of Psychosomatic Medicine, Tokyo, 1984; Counsellor, Soc. Internat. de Psychopathologie de l'Expression, 1982–; Pres., PNGPsych. Assoc., 1978–; Vice Pres., Asian Chapter, Internat. Coll. of Psychosomatic Medicine, 1991. Fellow, Orgn

Internationale de Psychophysiologie, Montreal, 1981; Mem., NY Acad. of Scis; Hon. Mem., Sociedad Internat. de Nuevas de la Conducta Argentina, 1982. Mem. Editl Cttee, PNG Med. Jl, 1976–. Benjamin Rush Bronze Medal, APA, 1974; Sen. Organon Res. Award, RANCP, 1980. Papua New Guinea Independence Medal, 1975. *Publications:* Longlong, 1973; South Pacific Ethnopsychiatry, 1967; l'Examen Psychiatrique de Autochtone de Papuasie et Nouvelle Guinée, 1967; Mixed-race Society in Port Moresby, 1968; Psychiatry and the Law in the Developing Country, 1970; Stone Age Crisis, 1975; Crisis en la edad de piedra, 1988; (ed) History of Medicine in Papua New Guinea, 1990; Kavakava, the Irrational Vector: perspectives of trans-cultural psychiatry in Papua New Guinea, 1992; over 200 sci. papers in learned jls. *Recreations:* patrolling, historical research in PNG. *Address:* PO Box 111, Port Moresby, Papua New Guinea. *T:* 255245.

BURTON-CHADWICK, Sir Joshua (Kenneth), 3rd Bt *cr* 1935; Sales Manager/Trainer, Joshua Chadwick Marketing Developers; *b* 1 Feb. 1954; *s* of Sir Robert Burton-Chadwick, (Sir Peter), 2nd Bt, and of Beryl Joan, *d* of Stanley Frederick J. Brailsford; *S* father, 1983. *Heir:* none.

BURY, John, OBE 1979; designer for theatre, opera and film; *b* 27 Jan. 1925; *s* of C. R. Bury; *m* 1st, 1947, Margaret Leila Greenwood (marr. diss.); one *s*; 2nd, 1966, Elizabeth Rebecca Blackborrow Duffield; two *s* one *d*. *Educ:* Cathedral Sch., Hereford; University Coll., London. Served with Fleet Air Arm (RN), 1942–46. Theatre Workshop, Stratford, E15, 1946–63; Assoc. Designer, Royal Shakespeare Theatre, 1963–73; Head of Design: RSC, 1965–68; NT, 1973–85. Arts Council: Designers' Working Gp, 1962–78; Mem., Drama Panel, 1960–68 and 1975–77. Chairman: Soc. of British Theatre Designers, 1975–85; Scenographic Commn, Organisation Internationale des Scenographs, Techiciens et Architectes du Théâtre, 1990–. FRSA 1970. Hon. FRCA 1990. Co-winner, Gold Medal for Scene Design, Prague Quadrienale, 1975 and 1979; Antoinette Perry Awards (Best Set Design and Best Lighting), for Broadway prodn of Amadeus, 1981. *Address:* Burleigh House, Burleigh, Glos GL5 2PQ.

BURY, Lindsay Claude Neils; Chairman: Sharp Technology Fund, since 1985; SUMIT Equity Ventures, since 1992; South Staffordshire Waterworks Co., since 1992 (Dir, since 1981); *b* 13 Feb. 1939; *s* of Frank James Lindsay Bury and Diana Mary Lewis; *m* 1968, Sarah Ann Bury; one *s* one *d*. *Educ:* Eton; Trinity College, Cambridge (BA History). J. Henry Schroder Wagg, 1960–66; Singer & Friedlander, 1966–73; Dunbar & Co., 1973–83. Director: ACT (formerly Apricot Computers), 1968– (Chm., 1972–89); Portals Holdings, 1973–; Christie Group, 1989–; Planning Consultancy, 1990–; Tricom, 1991–; DataEase Sapphire Internat., 1991–; Roxboro Gp, 1993–. Dir, City of Birmingham Touring Opera, 1989–92. Chm. of Govs, Moor Park Sch.; Trustee, Millichope Foundn; WWF UK. *Recreations:* music, country pursuits. *Address:* Millichope Park, Munslow, Craven Arms, Shropshire SY7 9HA. *T:* Munslow (0158476) 234. *Clubs:* Turf, Pratt's.

BURY, Michael Oswell, OBE 1968; Consultant, Education and Training, Confederation of British Industry, 1986–87; *b* 20 Dec. 1922; *o s* of Lt-Col Thomas Oswell Bury, TD, and Constance Evelyn Bury; *m* 1954, Jean Threlkeld Wood, *d* of late William Threlkeld Wood; two *s* one *d*. *Educ:* Charterhouse; London Sch. of Economics. Served War of 1939–45: The Rifle Brigade (ranks of Rifleman to Captain), 1941–47. Steel Company of Wales, 1947–49; British Iron and Steel Fedn, 1949–64 (Dep. Dir, Labour and Trng, 1962–64); Dir, Iron and Steel Industry Trng Bd, 1964–70; Confederation of British Industry: Director, Educn, Trng and Technol., 1970–81; Dir, Corporate Affairs, 1981–84; Dir, Educn, Trng and Technol., 1985–86. Mem., Manpower Services Commn, 1974–81, 1985–87. *Recreations:* gardening, fishing, travel. *Address:* Springfield, Fingrith Hall Lane, Blackmore, Ingatestone, Essex CM4 0RU. *T:* Brentwood (01277) 821347. *Club:* Reform.

BURY, Shirley Joan, FSA; Keeper of Metalwork, Victoria and Albert Museum, 1982–85; *b* 1925; *d* of Ernest Leslie Saxton Watkin and Florence Keen; *m* 1947, John Morley Bury; one *s*. *Educ:* University of Reading. BA Fine Arts 1946, MA 1960; FSA 1972. Joined V & A 1948: Research Asst, 1948, Senior Research Asst, 1961, Circulation Dept; Asst Keeper, Library, 1962–68, Metalwork Dept, 1968–72; Dep. Keeper, Dept of Metalwork, 1972–82. Mem., British Hallmarking Council, 1974–85. Liveryman, Goldsmiths' Co., 1982–. *Publications:* Victorian Electroplate, 1972; V & A Jewellery Gallery Summary Catalogue, 1982; An Introduction to Rings, 1984; Sentimental Jewellery, 1985; Jewellery 1790–1910, 1988; (compiled and ed) Catalogue, Copy or Creation, Goldsmiths' Hall, 1967; (ed) Catalogue, Liberty's 1875–1975, V & A 1975; introd. to C. R. Ashbee, Modern English Silver, new edn 1974; contribs to Burlington Magazine, Connoisseur, Apollo, V & A Bulletin, Yearbook and Album. *Recreations:* theatre, walking, gardening.

BURY, Air Cdre Thomas Malcolm Grahame, CB 1972; OBE 1962; retired as Head of Technical Training and Maintenance, British Aircraft Corporation, Saudi Arabia; *b* 11 Sept. 1918; *s* of late Ernest Bury, OBE; *m* 1951, Dillys Elaine Jenkins, MBE, *d* of Dr Aneurin Jenkins, Swansea; two *s* one *d*. *Educ:* Forest Sch., E17. Served War, 1939–45, NW Europe, Arabia. Joined RAF, 1935; STSO, HQ, 1 Gp, 1961–64; DDME, MoD, 1965–66; Senior Engr Officer, Air Forces Gulf, 1967–68; Command Mech. Engr, HQ Strike Command, 1968–73; retired 1973. *Address:* Las Bayas, 71 Benimodo, Buzón T273, Moraira, Alicante 03724, Spain.

BUSCH, Constantinus Albertus Maria; Member: Board of Directors, Verenigde Nederlandse Uitgeversbedryven BV, since 1993; Supervisory Board: Cindu International NV, since 1992; Roto Smeets De Boer NV, since 1993; RTL SA, Luxembourg, since 1993; *b* 17 Aug. 1937; *m* 1963, Ingrid (*née* Haaksma); two *s* two *d*. *Educ:* in The Netherlands; Amsterdam Univ. (Economics degree). 1st Lieut, Dutch Army, 1962–64; Corporate Finance Dept, NV Philips Eindhoven, 1964–66; Manager, Philips Internat. Finance, Luxembourg, 1966–70; Naarden International NV: Treasurer, 1970–72; Dir of Finance and Mem. Bd of Management, 1973–80; Financial Dir, Philips Electronics UK, 1981–85; Corporate Finance Dir, NV Philips Eindhoven, 1985–87; UK Vice-Chm. and Financial Dir, Philips Electronics, 1988; Chm. and Man. Dir, Philips Electronics and Associated Industries, 1989–90; Corporate Finance Dir, Philips Internat. BV, 1991–92. *Recreations:* music, particularly piano, clarinet and saxophone; tennis, golf, ski-ing. *Address:* VNU BV, Ceylonpoort 5–25, Postbus 4028, 2003 EA Haarlem, Netherlands. *Club:* Foxhills (Addlestone).

BUSCH, Rolf Trygve; Comdr, Order of St Olav; Hon. GCVO 1988; Norwegian Ambassador to the Court of St James's, 1982–88; *b* 15 Nov. 1920; *s* of Aksel Busch and Alette (*née* Tunby); *m* 1950, Solveig Helle; one *s*. *Educ:* Oslo Univ. (degree in Law); National Defence Coll. Dep. Judge, 1946–47; entered Norwegian Foreign Service, 1947; Min. of For. Affairs, 1947–50; Sec., Cairo, 1950–52; Vice-Consul, New York, 1952–54; Min. of For. Affairs, 1954–56; National Def. Coll., 1956–57; First Sec., Norwegian Delegn to NATO, Paris, 1957–60; Min. of For. Affairs, 1960–65; Counsellor and Dep. Perm. Rep., Norwegian Delegn to NATO, Paris and Brussels, 1965–70; Dir-Gen., Min. of For. Affairs, 1970–71; Perm. Rep. to N Atlantic Council, 1971–77; Ambassador to Fed. Republic of Germany, 1977–82. Officer, Order of the Nile, Egypt; Comdr with Star, Order of the Falcon, Iceland; Grand Cross, Order of Merit, Fed. Republic of Germany. *Address:* 2 Hafrsfjords Gt, 0273 Oslo 2, Norway. *T:* 22431791.

BUSH, Alan; Composer; Conductor; Pianist; Professor of Composition, Royal Academy of Music, 1925–78; *b* 22 Dec. 1900; *s* of Alfred Walter Bush and Alice Maud (*née* Brinsley); *m* 1931, Nancy Rachel Head (*d* 1991); two *d* (and one *d* decd). *Educ:* Highgate Sch.; Royal Academy of Music; Univ. of Berlin. ARAM 1922; Carnegie Award 1924; FRAM 1938; BMus London, 1940; DMus London, 1968. Arts Council Opera Award, 1951; Händel Prize, City Council of Halle (Saale), 1962; Corresp. Member, Deutsche Akademie der Künste, 1955. FRSA 1966. Hon. DMus Dunelm, 1970. Appeared as piano-recitalist, London, Berlin, etc., 1927–33; played solo part in own Piano Concerto, BBC, 1938, with Sir Adrian Boult conducting. Toured Ceylon, India, Australia as Examiner for Assoc. Board of Royal Schools of Music, London, 1932–33; concert tours as orchestral conductor, introducing British Music and own compositions, to USSR, 1938, 1939, 1963, 1967, 1969, 1973, Czechoslovakia, Yugoslavia, Poland, Bulgaria, 1947, Czechoslovakia and Bulgaria again, 1949, Holland, 1950, Vienna, 1951, Berlin (German Democratic Republic) and Hungary, 1952, and Berlin again, 1958; Première of opera "Wat Tyler" at the Leipzig Opera House, 1953 (British première, 1974); Première of opera "Men of Blackmoor" at the German National Theatre, Weimar, 1956; Première of opera "The Sugar Reapers" at the Leipzig Opera House, 1966; Première of opera "Joe Hill (The Man Who Never Died)", German State Opera, Berlin, 1970. Musical Adviser, London Labour Choral Union, 1929–40; Chairman Workers' Music Assoc., 1936–41 (President 1941–). Chairman Composers' Guild of Great Britain, 1947–48. *Publications:* In My Eighth Decade and Other Essays, 1980; *operas:* Wat Tyler; Men of Blackmoor; The Sugar Reapers; Joe Hill (The Man Who Never Died); and children's operettas; *choral works:* The Winter Journey, Op. 29; Song of Friendship, Op. 34; The Ballad of Freedom's Soldier, Op. 44 (mixed voices); The Dream of Llewelyn ap Gruffydd, Op. 35 (male voices); The Alps and Andes of the Living World, Op. 66 (mixed chorus); Song for Angela Davis; Africa is my Name, Op. 85; Turkish Workers' Marching Song (chorus and piano), Op. 101; The Earth in Shadow (mixed chorus and orch.), Op. 102; Mandela Speaking, to text by Nelson Mandela (baritone solo, mixed chorus and orch.), Op. 110; Folksong arrangements; *song cycles:* Voices of the Prophets, for tenor and piano, Op. 41; Seafarers' Songs for baritone and piano, Op. 57; The Freight of Harvest, for tenor and piano, Op. 69; Life's Span, for mezzo-soprano and piano, Op. 77; Three Songs for baritone and piano, Op. 86; Woman's Life, for soprano and piano, Op. 87; Two Shakespeare Sonnets, Op. 91; *orchestral works:* Dance Overture, Op. 12; Piano Concerto, Op. 18; Symphony No 1 in C, Op. 21; Overture "Resolution", Op. 25; English Suite for strings, Op. 28; Piers Plowman's Day Suite, Op. 30; Violin Concerto, Op. 32; Symphony No 2 "The Nottingham", op. 33; Concert Suite for 'cello and orchestra, Op. 37; Dorian Passacaglia and Fugue, Op. 52; Symphony No 3 "The Byron Symphony", op. 53; Variations, Nocturne and Finale on an English Sea Song for piano and orchestra, Op. 60; Partita Concertante, Op. 63; Time Remembered for Chamber Orchestra, Op. 67; Scherzo for Wind Orchestra with Percussion, Op. 68; Africa: Symphonic Movement for piano and orchestra, Op. 73; Concert Overture for an Occasion, Op. 74; The Liverpool Overture, Op. 76; Lascaux Symphony, Op. 98; Meditation in Memory of Anna Ambrose, Op. 107; Song Poem and Dance Poem for string orch. and piano, Op. 109; Serenade and Duet for string orch. and piano, Op. 111; *chamber music:* String Quartet, Op. 4; Piano Quartet, Op. 5; Five Pieces for Violin, Viola, Cello, Clarinet and Horn, Op. 6; Dialectic for string quartet, Op. 15; Three Concert Studies for piano trio, Op. 31; Suite for Two Pianos, Op. 65; Serenade for String Quartet, Op. 70; Suite of six for String Quartet, Op. 81; Compass Points, Suite for Pipes, Op. 83; Trio for clarinet, cello and piano, Op. 91; Concertino for two violins and piano, Op. 94; Piano Quintet, Op. 104; Octet for flute, clarinet, horn, string quartet and piano, Op. 105; Canzona for flute, clarinet, violin, cello and piano, Op. 106; *instrumental solos and duos:* Prelude and Fugue for piano, Op. 9; Relinquishment for piano, Op. 11; Concert Piece for 'cello and piano, Op. 17; Meditation on a German song of 1848 for violin and String Orchestra or piano, Op. 22; Lyric Interlude for violin and piano, Op. 26; Le Quatorze Juillet for piano, Op. 38; Trent's Broad Reaches for horn and piano, Op. 36; Three English Song Preludes for organ, Op. 40; Northumbrian Impressions for oboe and piano, Op. 42a; Autumn Poem for horn and piano, Op. 45; Two Ballads of the Sea for piano, Op. 50; Two Melodies for viola with piano accompaniment, Op. 47; Suite for harpsichord or piano, Op. 54, Three African Sketches for flute with piano accompaniment, Op. 55; Two Occasional Pieces for organ, Op. 56; For a Festal Occasion for organ, Op. 58A; Prelude, Air and Dance for violin with accompaniment for string quartet and percussion, Op. 61; Two Dances for Cimbalom, Op. 64; Pianoforte Sonata in A flat, Op. 71; Corentyne Kwe-Kwe for piano, Op. 75; Sonatina for recorders and piano, Op. 82; Twenty-four Preludes for Piano, Op. 84; Sonatina for viola and piano, Op. 88; Rhapsody for cello and piano, Op. 89; Meditation and Scherzo for double-bass and piano, Op. 93; Scots Jigganspiel for piano, Op. 95; Six Short Pieces for piano, Op. 99; Summer Fields and Hedgerows, Two Impressions for clarinet and piano, Op.100; Serenade and Duet for violin and piano, Op. 111; Distant Fields for piano, Op. 112; Piano Sonata in G, Op. 114; Two Pieces for Nancy for piano solo, Op. 115; Prelude and Concert Piece for organ, Op. 116; Suite for organ, Op. 117; Three Five Beat First Year Pieces for piano, Op. 118; Sonata for Piano, Op. 119; Sonata for cello and piano, Op. 120; Two Preludes and Fugues for piano, Op. 121; The Six Modes for piano duet, Op. 122; A Heart's Expression for piano, Op. 123; *textbook:* Strict Counterpoint in Palestrina Style; *essays:* In My Eighth Decade and other essays, 1980. *Recreations:* walking, foreign travel. *Address:* 25 Christchurch Crescent, Radlett, Herts WD7 8AQ. *T:* Radlett (01923) 856422.

BUSH, Bryan; His Honour Judge Bush; a Circuit Judge, since 1983; *b* 28 Nov. 1936; *s* of Maurice and Hetty Bush; *m* 1963, Jacqueline (*née* Rayman); two *s* one *d*. *Educ:* Leeds Grammar Sch.; Keble Coll., Oxford (MA). Called to the Bar, Gray's Inn, 1961; practising on NE Circuit, 1961–83; a Recorder of the Crown Court, 1978–83. *Recreations:* theatre, lawn tennis. *Address:* c/o Leeds Crown Court, Leeds LS1 3BE.

BUSH, Charles Martin Peter, MA; Headmaster, Eastbourne College, since 1993; *b* 28 June 1952; *s* of late Dr John Peter Bush and of Edith Mary (*née* Farnsworth); *m* 1977, Rosalind Mary Nevin; three *s*. *Educ:* Melbourne C of E Grammar Sch.; Univ. of Melbourne; Trinity Coll., Oxford (MA). Aylesbury Grammar Sch., 1975–78, Hd of Pure Maths, 1977–78; Hd of Maths, Abingdon Sch., 1978–82; Marlborough College, 1982–93: Hd of Maths, 1982–89; Housemaster, B1 House, 1988–93. *Publication:* (co-author in SMP Team) Revised Advanced Mathematics (Book 1), 1988. *Recreations:* golf, cricket, mathematics, fell walking. *Address:* The Headmaster's House, Old Wish Road, Eastbourne, E Sussex BN21 4JX. *T:* Eastbourne (01323) 737655. *Clubs:* MCC; Melbourne Cricket.

BUSH, Geoffrey Hubert; Director General, Board of Inland Revenue, since 1994 (Under Secretary, 1988–94); *b* 5 April 1942; *s* of Sidney Arthur Bush and late Dorothy Elizabeth Bush; *m* 1965, Sylvia Mary Squibb; one *s* one *d*. *Educ:* Cotham Grammar Sch., Bristol. Tax Officer, 1959; Inspector of Taxes, 1968; Dist Inspector of Taxes, 1973; Principal Inspector of Taxes, 1981. *Recreation:* country week-ends. *Address:* (home) London and Devon; (office) c/o Board of Inland Revenue, Somerset House, WC2R 1LB. *Clubs:* Topsham Sailing (Devon); Knowle Lawn Tennis (Bristol).

BUSH, George Herbert Walker, Hon. GCB 1993; President of the United States of America, 1989–93; *b* Milton, Mass, 12 June 1924; *s* of late Prescott Sheldon Bush and Dorothy (*née* Walker); *m* 1945, Barbara, *d* of Marvin Pierce, NY; four *s* one *d*. *Educ:*

Phillips Acad., Andover, Mass; Yale Univ. (BA Econs 1948). Served War, USNR, Lieut, pilot (DFC, three Air Medals). Co-founder and Dir, Zapata Petroleum Corp., 1953–59; Founder, Zapata Offshore Co., Houston, 1954, Pres., 1956–64, Chm. Bd, 1964–66. Chm., Republican Party, Harris Co., Texas, 1963–64; Delegate, Republican Nat. Convention, 1964, 1968; Republican cand. US Senator from Texas, 1964, 1970; Mem., 90th and 91st Congresses, 7th District of Texas, 1967–71; US Perm. Rep. to UN, 1971–73; Chm., Republican Party Nat. Cttee, 1973–74; Chief, US Liaison Office, Peking, 1974–75; Dir, US Central Intelligence Agency, 1976–77; Vice-President of the USA, 1981–89. Cand. for Republican Presidential nomination, 1980. Hon. degrees from many colleges and univs. *Publication:* (with Victor Gold) Looking Foward: an autobiography, 1988. *Recreations:* tennis, jogging, golf, boating, fishing. *Address:* Suite 900, 10000 Memorial Drive, Houston, TX 77024, USA.

BUSH, Adm. Sir John (Fitzroy Duyland), GCB 1970 (KCB 1965; CB 1963); DSC 1941, and Bars, 1941, 1944; Vice-Admiral of the United Kingdom and Lieutenant of the Admiralty, 1979–84; *b* 1 Nov. 1914; *s* of late Fitzroy Bush, Beach, Glos; *m* 1938, Ruth Kennedy Horsey; three *s* two *d*. *Educ:* Clifton Coll. Entered Navy, 1933; served in Destroyers throughout War. Commanded HM Ships: Belvoir, 1942–44; Zephyr, 1944; Chevron, 1945–46. Comdr Dec. 1946; Plans Div., Admiralty, 1946–48; graduated Armed Forces Staff Coll., USA, 1949; Comd, HMS Cadiz, 1950–51; Capt. June 1952; Dep. Sec. Chiefs of Staff Cttee, 1953–55; Capt. (F) Sixth Frigate Sqdn, 1955–56; Cdre, RN Barracks, Chatham, 1957–59; Dir. of Plans, Admiralty, 1959–60; Rear-Adm. 1961; Flag Officer Flotillas (Mediterranean), 1961–62; Vice-Adm. 1963; Comdr, British Naval Staff and Naval Attaché, Washington, 1963–65; Vice-Chief of the Naval Staff, Ministry of Defence, 1965–67; C-in-C Western Fleet, C-in-C Eastern Atlantic, and C-in-C Channel (NATO), 1967–70; Admiral 1968; retd, 1970. Rear-Admiral of the UK, 1976–79. Dir, Gordon A. Friesen International Inc., Washington, DC, 1970–73. Adm., Texas (USA) Navy. Governor, Clifton Coll., 1973– (Chm. Council, 1978–81; Pres., 1982–87). Pres., Old Cliftonians Soc., 1967–69; Vice-Pres., Eighth Army Veterans Assoc., 1984–. Mem., E Hants District Council, 1974–76. *Recreations:* fishing, gardening. *Address:* Becksteddle House, Colemore, near Alton, Hants GU34 3PS. *T:* Tisted (01420) 588367.

BUSH, Maj.-Gen. Peter John, OBE 1968; Controller, Army Benevolent Fund, 1980–87; *b* 31 May 1924; *s* of Clement Charles Victor Bush and Kathleen Mabel Peirce; *m* 1948, Jean Mary Hamilton; two *s* one *d*. *Educ:* Maidenhead County Sch. Commnd Somerset LI, 1944; comd LI Volunteers, 1966; GSO 1 HQ 14 Div./Malaya Dist, 1968; Comdr 3 Inf. Bde, 1971 (mentioned in despatches, 1973); Asst Comdt RMA Sandhurst, 1974; Chief of Staff and Head of UK Delegn to Live Oak, SHAPE, 1977–79, retd. Col, The Light Infantry, 1977–82. *Recreations:* natural history, walking, reading. *Address:* c/o Barclays Bank, High Street, Maidenhead, Berks SL6 1PX.

BUSHBY, Frederick Henry; Director of Services, Meteorological Office, 1978–84; *b* 10 Jan. 1924; *s* of Mr and Mrs Frederick George Bushby; *m* 1945, Joan Janet (*née* Gates); one *s*. *Educ:* Portsmouth Southern Secondary Sch.; Imperial Coll. of Science and Technol. (BSc 1st Cl. Hons Special Maths). ARCS. Meteorol Br., RAF, 1944–48; Meteorol Office, 1948–84; Asst Dir (Forecasting Res.), 1965–74; Dep. Dir (Dynamical Res.), 1974–77, (Forecasting), 1977–78. *Recreations:* bridge, bowls. *Address:* 25 Holmes Crescent, Wokingham, Berks RG11 2SE. *T:* Wokingham (01734) 784930.

BUSHE, Frederick Joseph William, OBE 1994; RSA 1987 (ARSA 1977); Founder, 1979, and Director, 1979–March 1996, Scottish Sculpture Workshop; *b* 1 March 1939; *s* of Frederick M. C. Bushe and Kathleen Welch; *m* 1st, 1956, Rosemary R. Beattie; three *s* one *d*; 2nd, 1984, Fiona M. S. Marr; one *d*. *Educ:* Out Lady's High Sch., Motherwell; Glasgow Sch. of Art (DA). Temp. Captain RAEC, 1954–58. Art teacher, Midlothian, 1958–60, Berwickshire, 1960–62; Lectr in Art Educn, Notre Dame, Liverpool, 1962–69, Aberdeen Coll. of Educn, 1969–79. Curator, Scandex, 15th anniv. touring exhibn of Scottish sculpture, 1994–95. Governor, Edinburgh Coll. of Art, 1983–88. Invited Artist: Formaviva Internat. Symposium of Sculptors, Yugoslavia, 1988; Terra Internat. Symposium, Kikinda, Yugoslavia, 1990. Work in numerous public collections; one man exhibitions: Edinburgh, 1962, 1971, 1982; Liverpool, 1966; Glasgow, 1974; Manchester, 1975; Stirling, 1978; group exhibns. *Recreations:* listening to music, cooking. *Address:* Rose Cottage, Lumsden, Huntly, Aberdeenshire AB54 4JJ. *T:* Rhynie (01464) 861394.

BUSHELL, John Christopher Wyndowe, CMG 1971; HM Diplomatic Service, retired; Ambassador to Pakistan, 1976–79; *b* 27 Sept. 1919; *s* of late Colonel C. W. Bushell, RE, and Mrs Bushell, Netherbury, Dorset; *m* 1964, Mrs Theodora Todd, *d* of late Mr and Mrs Senior; one *s* (and one step *s* one step *d*). *Educ:* Winchester; Clare Coll., Cambridge. Served War of 1939–45, RAF. Entered FO, 1945; served in Moscow, Rome, FO; 1st Sec., 1950; NATO Defence Coll., Paris, 1953–54; Deputy Sec.-Gen., CENTO, 1957–59; Counsellor, 1961; Political Adviser to the Commander-in-Chief, Middle East, 1961–64; UK Delegn to NATO, Brussels, 1964–68; seconded to Cabinet Office, 1968–70; Minister and Deputy Commandant, British Mil. Govt, Berlin, 1970–74; Ambassador to Vietnam, 1974–75; FCO 1975–76. *Recreations:* varied. *Address:* 19 Bradbourne Street, SW6 3TF. *Club:* Travellers'.

BUSHNELL, Alexander Lynn, CBE 1962; County Clerk and Treasurer, Perth County Council, 1946–75, retired; *b* 13 Aug. 1911; *s* of William and Margaret Bushnell; *m* 1939, Janet Braithwaite Porteous; two *d*. *Educ:* Dalziel High Sch., Motherwell; Glasgow University. *Recreation:* golf. *Address:* 18 Fairies Road, Perth PH1 1NB. *T:* Perth (01738) 622675.

BUSK, Maj.-Gen. Leslie Francis Harry, CB 1990; Director General, British Heart Foundation, since 1990; *b* 12 Sept. 1937; *s* of late Lt-Col Charles William Francis Busk and Alice (*née* van Bergen); *m* 1st, 1960, Jennifer Helen Ring (*d* 1992); three *s*; 2nd, 1993, Glennis MacElwain. *Educ:* Wellington Coll.; RMA, Sandhurst; RMCS, Shrivenham (BSc (Eng) London Univ.). Commnd RE, 1957; served in UK, NI, BAOR, India and Singapore; Defence Services Staff Coll., India, 1969; OC 25 Field Sqn, 1971–73; Instr, Staff Coll., Camberley, 1975–77; CO 35 Engr Regt, 1977–79; C of S 2nd Armoured Div., 1979–81; Bde Comd 11 Engr Bde, 1981–83; RCDS, 1984; DMO, MoD, 1985–86; Army Pilots Course, 1986–87; Dir, AAC, 1987–89, retd. Hon. Col, RE Volunteers (Sponsored Units), 1986–91; Col Comdt, RE, 1990–95. Chm., Assoc. of Medical Res. Charities, 1991–. *Recreations:* golf, tennis. *Address:* British Heart Foundation, 14 Fitzhardinge Street, W1H 4DH. *Club:* Naval and Military.

BUSS, Barbara Ann, (Mrs Lewis Boxall); freelance journalist, since 1976; Editor-in-Chief, Woman magazine, 1974–75; Consultant, IPC Magazines Ltd, 1975–76; *b* 14 Aug. 1932; *d* of late Cecil Edward Buss and Victoria Lilian (*née* Vickers); *m* 1966, Lewis Albert Boxall (*d* 1983); no *c*. *Educ:* Lady Margaret Sch., London. Sec., Conservative Central Office, 1949–52; Sec./journalist, Good Taste magazine, 1952–56; Journalist: Woman and Beauty, 1956–57; Woman, 1957–59; Asst Editor, Woman's Illustrated, 1959–60; Editor, Woman's Illustrated, 1960–61; Journalist, Daily Herald, 1961; Associate Editor, Woman's Realm, 1961–62; Editor: Woman's Realm, 1962–64; Woman, 1964–74. *Recreations:* reading, theatre, cinema. *Address:* 1 Arlington Avenue, N1 7BE. *T:* 0171–226 3265.

BUSSELL, Darcey Andrea, OBE 1995; Principal Ballerina, Royal Ballet, since 1989; *b* 27 April 1969; *d* of Philip Michael Bussell and Andrea Pemberton (*née* Williams). *Educ:* Arts Educnl Sch.; Royal Ballet Sch. Joined Sadler's Wells Royal Ballet (later Birmingham Royal Ballet), 1987; joined Royal Ballet, 1988: soloist, 1988; first soloist, 1989. *Leading rôles in:* Giselle; Swan Lake; Sleeping Beauty; La Bayadère; Laurentia pas de six; Song of the Earth; Requiem; Galanteries; Spirit of Fugue; Pursuit; first Royal Ballet perf. of Ballanchine's Rubies; Cinderella; Enigma Variations; Nutcracker; McMillan's Elite Syncopations; Raymonda; Monotones; Symphony in C; first Royal Ballet perf. of Ballanchine's Stravinsky Violin Concerto; Agon; Bloodlines; Les Biches; Tchaikovsky pas de deux; first perf. of William Forsythe's In the middle somewhat elevated; Romeo and Juliet; *rôles created:* Princess Rose in Prince of the Pagodas, Royal Opera House, 1989; pas de deux (Farewell to Dreams) for HM Queen Mother's 90th Birthday Tribute, Palladium and Royal Opera House, 1990. Prix de Lausanne, 1986; Variety Club of GB Award for most promising newcomer, 1990; Dancer of Year Award, Dance and Dancers Mag., 1990; Evening Standard Award for dance, 1990. *Recreations:* art and painting, reading, swimming. *Address:* The Royal Opera House, Covent Garden, WC2E 9DD. *Club:* Caledonian.

BUSVINE, Prof. James Ronald; Professor of Entomology as applied to Hygiene in the University of London, 1964–76, Emeritus Professor 1977; *b* 15 April 1912; *s* of William Robert and Pleasance Dorothy Busvine; *m* 1960, Joan Arnfield; one *s* one *d*. *Educ:* Eastbourne Coll.; Imperial Coll. of Science and Technology, London Univ. BSc Special (1st Class Hons) 1933; PhD 1938; DSc 1948, London. Imperial Chemical Industries, 1936–39; MRC Grants, 1940–42; Entomological Adviser, Min. of Health, 1943–45; London Sch. of Hygiene and Tropical Medicine: Lecturer 1946; Reader 1954; Professor 1964. Member: WHO Panel of Experts on Insecticides, 1956– (Cttee Chm. 1959 and 1968); FAO Panel of Experts on Pest Resistance, 1967– (Cttee Rapporteur). Has travelled professionally in Malaya, Ceylon, Africa, USA, India, etc. *Publications:* Insects and Hygiene, 1951 (3rd edn 1980); A Critical Review of the Techniques for Testing Insecticides, 1957, 2nd edn 1971; Anthropod Vectors of Disease, 1975; Insects, Hygiene and History, 1976; I warmed both Hands, 1986; Discovery of Disease Transmission by Arthropods and 90 Years of Attempts to stop it, 1993; numerous scientific articles. *Recreations:* painting, golf. *Address:* Musca, 26 Braywick Road, Maidenhead, Berks SL6 1DA. *T:* Maidenhead (01628) 22888.

BUTCHER, Anthony John; QC 1977; a Recorder, since 1985; *b* 6 April 1934; *s* of late F. W. Butcher and O. M. Butcher (*née* Ansell); *m* 1959, Maureen Workman (*d* 1982); one *s* two *d*. *Educ:* Cranleigh Sch.; Sidney Sussex Coll., Cambridge (MA, LLB). Called to the Bar, Gray's Inn, 1957, Bencher, 1986; in practice at English Bar, 1957–. Mem., Bar Council, 1989–91, and 1993–; Chm., Official Referees Bar Assoc., 1986–92. *Recreations:* enjoying the arts and acquiring useless information. *Address:* Anthony Cottage, Polecat Valley, Hindhead, Surrey GU26 6BE. *T:* Hindhead (01428) 604155; 1 Atkin Building, Gray's Inn, WC1R 5BQ. *T:* 0171–404 0102. *Clubs:* Garrick, Beefsteak.

BUTCHER, John Patrick; MP (C) Coventry South West, since 1979; Chairman, Texas Instruments Ltd. *Educ:* Huntingdon Grammar Sch.; Birmingham Univ. (BSocSc). Marketing exec. and Product Manager, computer industry, 1968–79. Mem., Birmingham City Council, 1972–78 (Vice-Chm., Educn Cttee). Parly Under Sec. of State, DoI, 1982–83, DTI, 1983–88, DES, 1988–89. *Address:* c/o House of Commons, SW1A 0AA.

BUTCHER, Richard James; Under Secretary (Legal), Department of Health and Social Security, 1983–87, retired; *b* 5 Dec. 1926; *s* of late James Butcher, MBE and Kathleen Butcher; *m* 1954, Sheila Joan Windridge; one *s* two *d*. *Educ:* City of London Sch.; Peterhouse, Cambridge (BA 1948, MA 1961). Called to the Bar, Lincoln's Inn, 1950. Served Educn Br., RAF, 1948–50 (Flying Officer). Entered Legal Civil Service as Legal Asst, 1951; Sen. Legal Asst, 1960; Asst Solicitor, 1971. *Recreation:* gardening. *Address:* The Knoll, Park View Road, Woldingham, Surrey CR3 7DN. *T:*Woldingham (01883) 652275.

BUTCHER, Willard Carlisle; Chairman, and Chief Executive Officer, Chase Manhattan Bank (formerly Chase National Bank), New York City, 1981–90, retired; *b* Bronxville, NY, 25 Oct. 1926; *s* of Willard F. Butcher and Helen Calhoun; *m* 1st, 1949, Sarah C. Payne (*d* 1955); two *d*; 2nd, 1956, Elizabeth Allen (*d* 1978); one *s* one *d*; 3rd, 1979, Carole E. McMahon; one *s*. *Educ:* Scarsdale High School, New York; Middlebury Coll., Vermont; Brown Univ., Rhode Island (BA; Fellow, 1981, now Emeritus). Served with USNR, 1944–45. Joined Chase National Bank, 1947; Asst Vice-Pres., 1956; Vice-Pres., 1958; Sen. Vice-Pres., 1961; assigned Internat. Dept, 1968; Exec. Vice-Pres. in charge of Dept, 1969; Vice-Chm. 1972; Pres. 1972–81; Chief Exec. Officer, 1979. Trustee, Amer. Enterprise Inst. (Chm., 1986–90). Director: Texaco Inc., 1981–; Asarco Inc., 1974–; Lincoln Center for the Performing Arts, 1981– (Vice Chm., 1986–); International Paper, 1989–; Olympia & York Cos (USA), 1993–; MIM Hldgs, 1995–. Hon. LLD: Brown Univ.; Pepperdine Univ.; Tulane Univ.; Hon. HLD Pace Univ. *Address:* 101 Park Avenue, NY 10178, USA.

BUTE, 7th Marquess of, *cr* 1796; **John Colum Crichton-Stuart;** Viscount Ayr, 1622; Bt (NS), 1627; Earl of Dumfries, Lord Crichton of Sanquhar and Cumnock, 1633; Earl of Bute, Viscount Kingarth, Lord Mountstuart, Cumrae and Inchmarnock, 1703; Baron Mountstuart, 1761, Baron Cardiff, 1776; Earl of Windsor, Viscount Mountjoy, 1796; Hereditary Sheriff of Bute; Hereditary Keeper of Rothesay Castle; *b* 26 April 1958; *s* of 6th Marquess of Bute, KBE and of his 1st wife, Nicola (*née* Weld-Forester); *S* father, 1993; *m* 1984, Carolyn E. R. M., *d* of late Bryson Waddell; one *s* two *d*. British Formula Three Champion, 1984; European Formula Three Championship runner-up, 1984; Formula One Ferrari test driver, 1985; JPS Lotus Grand Prix Driver, 1986; Works Driver for World Champion Sports Prototype Team Silk Cut Jaguar, 1988 (Jt Winner, Le Mans sports car race, 1988); Lead Driver for Toyota GB, World Sports Prototype Championship, 1989, 1990. *Heir: s* Earl of Dumfries, *qv*.

BUTHELEZI, Mangosuthu Gatsha; Minister of Home Affairs, Republic of South Africa, since 1994; Chairman, Inkata Freedom Party; *b* 27 Aug. 1928; *s* of Chief Mathole Buthelezi and Princess Magogo; *m* 1952, Irene Audrey Thandekile Mzila; three *s* four *d*. *Educ:* Fort Hare Univ. (BA). Chief of Buthelezi Tribe, 1953–; involved in admin of Zulu people, 1953–68; Chief Minister, KwaZulu, 1976–94. Numerous foreign awards and orders. *Publication:* South Africa: my vision of the future, 1990. *Address:* Ministry of Home Affairs, Private Bag X741, Pretoria 0001, South Africa.

BUTLER, family name of **Earl of Carrick,** of **Baron Dunboyne,** of **Earl of Lanesborough,** of **Viscount Mountgarret,** and of **Marquess of Ormonde.**

BUTLER, Rt. Hon. Sir Adam (Courtauld), Kt 1986; PC 1984; DL; Director, H. P. Bulmer Holdings plc, since 1988; *b* 11 Oct. 1931; *s* of late Baron Butler of Saffron Walden, KG, CH, PC and late Sydney, *o c* of late Samuel Courtauld; *m* 1955, Felicity Molesworth-St Aubyn; two *s* one *d*. *Educ:* Eton; Pembroke College, Cambridge. National Service, 2nd Lieut KRRC, 1949–51. Cambridge (BA History/Economics), 1951–54. ADC to Governor-General of Canada, 1954–55; Courtaulds Ltd, 1955–73; Director: Aristoc Ltd, 1966–73; Kayser Bondor Ltd, 1971–73; Capital and Counties Property Co., 1973–79;

Dep. Chm., CMW Gp, 1989–93. MP (C) Bosworth, 1970–87. PPS to: Minister of State for Foreign Affairs, 1971–72; Minister of Agriculture, Fisheries and Food, 1972–74; PPS to Leader of the Opposition, 1975–79; an Asst Govt Whip, 1974; an Opposition Whip, 1974–75; Minister of State: DoI, 1979–81; NI Office, 1981–84; Defence Procurement, 1984–85. Mem. NFU. Mem. Court of Assistants, Goldsmiths' Co. 1987–. Chairman: Samuel Courtauld Trustees, 1989–; Airey Neave Trust, 1989–. Mem. Council, RSA, 1986–90. Pres., BHS, 1990–92. DL Warwicks, 1993. *Recreations:* field sports, music, pictures. *Address:* The Old Rectory, Lighthorne, Warwick CV35 0AR. *T:* Leamington Spa (01926) 651214.

See also Hon. Sir R. C. Butler.

BUTLER, Allan Geoffrey Roy; HM Diplomatic Service, retired; Director, Park South Management, since 1991; *b* 25 Aug. 1933; *s* of Frederick William Butler and Florence May Butler; *m* 1965, Pauline Rosalind Birch, SRN; three *d. Educ:* Chatham House School, Ramsgate. RAF, 1952–54. Colonial Office, 1954–66; served in Aden and Washington; Asst Private Sec. to Colonial Sec., 1965–66; HM Diplomatic Service, 1966; Birmingham University, 1966; Consul, Athens, 1967; First Sec., Athens, 1969, Georgetown, 1972, FCO, 1975; Head of Chancery, Dakar, 1977; Nat. Defence Coll., Latimer, 1981; Head of Parly Relations Unit, FCO, 1981; Ambassador to Mongolian People's Republic, 1984; Dep. Perm. Rep., UK Delegn to the Council of Europe, 1987–89. Director: Strategy, subseq. Saatchi & Saatchi Govt Communications, 1989–92; Hexagon Communications, 1991–93. Chm., Anglo-Mongolian Soc., 1990–93. *Recreations:* walking, listening to music. *Address:* Cringle Cottage, Snow Street, Roydon, Diss, Norfolk IP22 3SB.

BUTLER, Anthony John; Executive Director of Services (formerly of Personnel and Finance, then of Personnel), HM Prison Service, since 1990; *b* 30 Jan. 1945; *s* of Martin Edward and Freda Alice Butler; *m* 1967, Margaret Ann, *d* of George and Margaret Randon; one *s* one *d. Educ:* Maidstone Grammar Sch.; University Coll., Oxford (Exhibnr, Mod. Hist.; MA); Inst. of Criminology and Trinity Hall, Cambridge (Dip. Crim.); Cambridge–Columbia Fellow, Columbia Law Sch., NY. Joined Home Office as Asst Principal, 1969; Police and Criminal Depts, 1969–72; Private Sec. to Minister of State, Home Office, 1972–74; Principal, Gen. Dept, Sex Discrimination and Race Relations Legislation Units and Broadcasting Dept, 1974–79; Private Sec. to Sec. of State for the Home Dept, 1979–80; Asst Sec., Broadcasting, Finance and Prisons Depts, 1980–88; Asst Under-Sec. of State, seconded to DoE, 1988 as Dir, Inner Cities; Principal Finance Officer, Home Office, 1990. Trustee, University Coll. Oxford Old Members' Trust, 1988–94 (Chm. Trustees, 1991–94). *Recreations:* music, walking. *Address:* HM Prison Service Headquarters, Cleland House, Page Street, SW1P 4LN.

BUTLER, Arthur William, ERD 1964; consultant on parliamentary relations; Secretary, Parliamentary & Scientific Committee, 1979–95; *b* 20 Jan. 1929; *s* of late F. Butler and E. Butler; *m* 1958, Evelyn Mary Luetchford; one *d. Educ:* Wanstead High Sch.; LSE (BSc (Econ)). Universities' Prize Essayist, RAS, 1950. Nat. Service, India Cadet Co., Queen's Royal Regt, RAOC, 1946–48, 2nd Lt; Lt, AER, RAOC, 1953, Capt., 1957–64. Trainee, Kemsley Newspapers Graduate Trng Course, Middlesbrough Evening Gazette, 1951–55; Political Correspondent, News Chronicle, 1956–60; Political Ed., Reynolds News, 1960–62; Political Correspondent, Daily Express, 1963–69; Political Ed., Daily Sketch, 1969–71; Man. Dir, Partnerplan Public Affairs, 1971–74; Dir, Public Affairs Div., John Addey Associates, 1974–77; Vice-Chm., Charles Barker Watney & Powell, 1988–89 (Jt. Man. Dir, 1978–87). Dir, CSM Parly Consultants Ltd, 1995–. Secretary: Roads Campaign Council, 1974–86; All-Party Roads Study Gp, 1974–86; Founder Secretary: Parly All-Party Motor Industry Gp, 1978–90; Parly IT Cttee, 1981–84. Consultant on Parly Relns, McAvoy Wreford Bayley, 1989–92, GCI London, 1992–93. Jt Managing Editor, Science in Parliament, 1989–; Editor, Free Romanian (English edn), 1985–95. MRI. Freeman, City of London, 1976; Liveryman, Co. of Tobacco Pipe Makers, 1977. *Publications:* No Feet to Drag (with Alfred Morris, MP), 1972; (with C. Powell) The First Forty Years: a history of the Parliamentary & Scientific Committee, 1980; (with D. Smith) Lobbying in the British Parliament, 1986; articles in newspapers and various pubns. *Recreations:* travel, collecting books and militaria, gardening. *Address:* 30 Chester Way, Kennington, SE11 4UR. *T:* 0171–587 5170. *Club:* Royal Automobile.

BUTLER, Mrs Audrey Maude Beman, MA; Headmistress, Queenswood (GSA), Hatfield, Herts, 1981–Aug. 1996; *b* 31 May 1936; *d* of Robert Beman Minchin and Vivien Florence Fraser Scott; *m* 1959, Anthony Michael Butler (marr. diss. 1981); two *d. Educ:* Queenswood, Hatfield; St Andrews Univ., Scotland (1st Cl. MA Hons, Geography and Polit. Economy; Scottish Univs Medal, RSGS, 1957–58). Asst Geography Teacher, Queenswood, 1958–59; part-time teacher, Raines Foundn Sch. for Girls, Stepney, 1959–61; Head of Geography, S Michael's, Burton Park, 1970–73, VI Form Tutor/Geography asst, 1974–78; first House Mistress of Manor House, Lancing Coll., 1978–81. Chm., Boarding Schs Assoc., 1989–91; Mem. Exec. Cttee, GSA, 1987–90. Governor: Duncombe Sch., 1982–; Tockington Manor Sch., 1984– (Chm., 1995–); Aldenham Sch., 1987–; Maltman's Green Sch., 1988–. Vice-Chm., Bloxham Project, 1992–. Hon. Vice-Pres., Sussex County Ladies Golf Assoc., 1981–83; Vice-Pres., Herts LTA, 1986–. FRGS; MInstD 1986. *Recreations:* golf (Sussex County Colours, 1970), travel. *Address:* Queenswood, Shepherd's Way, Brookmans Park, Hatfield, Herts AL9 6NS. *T:* Potters Bar (01707) 652262.

BUTLER, Basil Richard Ryland, OBE 1976; FEng; FIMM; Chairman: Brown and Root Ltd, since 1993 (Director, since 1991); BP Solar International, since 1991; Director, Murphy Oil Corp., Arkansas, since 1991; *b* 1 March 1930; *s* of Hugh Montagu Butler and Annie Isabel (*née* Wiltshire); *m* 1954, Lilian Joyce Haswell; one *s* two *d. Educ:* Denstone Coll., Staffs; St John's Coll., Cambridge (MA). Reservoir Engr, Trinidad Leaseholds Ltd, 1954; Petroleum Engr to Chief Petroleum Engr and Supt Prodn Planning Div., Kuwait Oil Co., 1958–68; transf. to BP, Operations Man., Colombia, 1968; Ops Man., BP Alaska Inc., Anchorage, 1970; seconded to Kuwait Oil Co. as Gen. Man. Ops, 1972; Manager: Ninian Develts, BP Petroleum Development Co. Ltd, London, 1975; Sullom Voe Terminal, Shetland Is, 1976; BP Petroleum Development Ltd: Gen. Man., Exploration and Prodn, Aberdeen, 1978; Chief Exec., London, 1980; Dir, BP Internat. Ltd; Chm., BP Exploration Co. Ltd, 1986–89 (Man. Dir and Chief Exec., 1986); Man. Dir, British Petroleum Co. plc, 1986–91. Chm., Devonport Management, 1992–94. Chm., Europ. Council of Applied Scis and Engrg, 1992–. Mem., Cttee for ME Trade, 1985–93. Pres., Inst. of Petroleum, 1990–92; Mem. Council, Royal Acad. of Engng, 1994–. FInstPet 1965; Hon. FIChemE 1991. Liveryman, Shipwrights' Co., 1988. *Recreations:* sailing, music. *Address:* Brown and Root Ltd, 150 The Broadway, Wimbledon, SW19 1RX. *T:* 0181–544 6616.

BUTLER, (Christopher) David, CB 1995; Director, Department for National Savings, 1991–95 (Deputy Director, 1989–91); *b* 27 May 1942; *s* of Major B. D. Butler, MC (killed in action, 1944) and H. W. Butler (*née* Briggs); *m* 1967, Helen Christine, *d* of J. J. Cornwell and G. Cornwell (*née* Veysey); two *d. Educ:* Christ's Hospital; Jesus College, Oxford (BA). Joined HM Treasury, 1964; Asst Private Sec. to Chancellor of Exchequer, 1967–69; Sec., Cttee to Review Nat. Savings (Page Cttee), 1970–72; Head of public expenditure divs, HM Treasury, 1978–82; Head of corporate planning div., Central Computer and Telecoms Agency, 1982–85; HM Treasury: Under-Sec., 1985–89; Head of running costs, manpower and superannuation group, 1985–86; Principal Estabt and Finance Officer, 1987–89. Governor, Sadler's Wells Foundn, 1989–94; Dir, Sadler's Wells Trust Ltd, 1989–95. *Recreations:* ballet, opera, reading, family activities. *Club:* Civil Service (Chm., 1994–).

BUTLER, Christopher John; Director, Grandfield Public Affairs, since 1995; *b* 12 Aug. 1950; *s* of Dr John Lynn Butler and late Eileen Patricia Butler; *m* 1989, Jacqueline Clair, *d* of Mr and Mrs R. O. F. Harper, Lymm, Cheshire; one *s. Educ:* Emmanuel Coll., Cambridge (MA). Market Research Consultant, 1975–77; Cons. Res. Dept, 1977–80; Political Office, 10 Downing Street, 1980–83; Special Advr, Sec. of State for Wales, 1983–85; Market Res. Consultant, 1985–86; Special Advr, Minister for the Arts, and of the Civil Service, 1986–87; Consultant in Public Policy, Public Policy Unit, 1992–95. MP (C) Warrington South, 1987–92; contested (C) Warrington South, 1992. Mem., Select Cttee on Employment, 1990–92. Vice Chm., All Party Leasehold Reform Gp, 1989–92; Secretary: All Party Drugs Misuse Cttee, 1989–92; All Party Penal Affairs Cttee, 1990–92. Mem., Exec. Cttee, CPA, 1991–92. *Recreations:* writing, deltiology, book collecting. *Address:* 15B Connaught House, Clifton Gardens, W9 1AL.

BUTLER, Sir Clifford (Charles), Kt 1983; FRS 1961; BSc, PhD; Vice-Chancellor of Loughborough University of Technology, 1975–85; *b* 20 May 1922; *s* of C. H. J. and O. Butler, Earley, Reading; *m* 1947, Kathleen Betty Collins; two *d. Educ:* Reading Sch.; Reading Univ. BSc 1942, PhD 1946, Reading. Demonstrator in Physics, Reading Univ., 1942–45; Asst Lecturer in Physics, Manchester Univ., 1945–47, Lecturer in Physics, 1947–53; Imperial College of Science and Technology, London: Reader in Physics, 1953–57; Professor of Physics, 1957–63; Asst Dir, Physics Dept, 1955–62; Prof. of Physics and Head of Physics Dept, 1963–70; Dean, Royal Coll. of Science, 1966–69; Dir, Nuffield Foundn, 1970–75. Charles Vernon Boys Prizeman, London Physical Soc., 1956. Member: Academic Planning Board, Univ. of Kent, 1963–71; Schools Council, 1965–84; Nuclear Physics Board of SRC, 1965–68; University Grants Cttee, 1966–71; Council, Charing Cross Hosp. Med. Sch., 1970–73; Council, Open Univ., 1971–95 (Vice-Chm., 1986–94); Science Adv. Cttee, British Council, 1980–85; Chairman: Track Chamber Cttee, CERN, 1962–65; Standing Education Cttee, Royal Society, 1970–80; Council for the Educn and Training of Health Visitors, 1977–83; Adv. Council for Supply and Educn of Teachers, 1980–85; Steering Cttee, DES Educnl Counselling and Credit Transfer Information Service Project, 1983–89; ABRC/NERC Study Gp into Geol Surveying, 1985–87; Working Party on Res. Selectivity, Dept of Educn, NI, QUB and Univ. of Ulster, 1986–87. Pres., Internat. Union of Pure and Applied Physics, 1975–78 (Sec.-Gen., 1963–72; first Vice-Pres., 1972–75). Hon. DSc Reading, 1976; DUniv Open, 1986; Hon. DTech Loughborough, 1987. *Publications:* scientific papers on electron diffraction, cosmic rays and elementary particle physics in Proc. Royal Society and Physical Society, Philosophical Magazine, Nature, and Journal of Scientific Instruments, etc. *Address:* Low Woods Farm House, Belton, Loughborough, Leics LE12 9TR. *T:* Coalville (01530) 223125.

BUTLER, Dr Colin Gasking, OBE 1970; FRS 1970; retired as Head of Entomology Department, Rothamsted Experimental Station, Harpenden, 1972–76 (Head of Bee Department, 1943–72); *b* 26 Oct. 1913; *s* of Rev. Walter Gasking Butler and Phyllis Pearce; *m* 1937, Jean March Innes; one *s* one *d. Educ:* Monkton Combe Sch., Bath; Queens' Coll., Cambridge. MA 1937, PhD 1938, Cantab. Min. of Agric. and Fisheries Research Schol., Cambridge, 1935–37; Supt Cambridge Univ. Entomological Field Stn, 1937–39; Asst Entomologist, Rothamsted Exper. Stn, 1939–43. Hon. Treas., Royal Entomological Soc., 1961–69, Pres., 1971–72, Hon. FRES, 1984; Pres., Internat. Union for Study of Social Insects, 1969–73; Mem., NT Regional Cttee for Devon and Cornwall, 1982–89. FRPS 1957; FIBiol. Hon. Fellow, British Beekeepers' Assoc., 1983. Silver Medal, RSA, 1945. *Publications:* The Honeybee: an introduction to her sense physiology and behaviour, 1949; The World of the Honeybee, 1954; (with J. B. Free) Bumblebees, 1959; scientific papers. *Recreations:* nature photography, fishing. *Address:* 1 Redwood Lodge, Grange Road, Cambridge CB3 9AR. *T:* Cambridge (01223) 352455.

BUTLER, David; *see* Butler, C. D.

BUTLER, David; Chairman, Butler Cox & Partners, since 1977; *b* 1 Feb. 1936; *s* of James Charles Butler and Ethel Violet (*née* Newell); *m* 1st, 1956, Catherine Anita Harry (marr. diss. 1974); one *s* two *d*; 2nd, 1975, Frances Mary McMahon; one *d. Educ:* Mill Hill Sch.; Keble Coll., Oxford (BA Lit. Hum.). Management Trainee, Herts CC, 1960–64; Computer Manager, NW Metropolitan Hosp. Bd, 1964–65; Management Consultant, Urwick Gp, 1965–72; Dir, Diebold Europe, 1972–76; Chm., Butler Cox Foundn, 1977–92. Director: Istel, 1983–92; Octagon Services, 1986–92; JMI Advisory Services, 1986–92; Investment Advr, United Bank of Kuwait, 1985–92; Sen. Advr, Computer Scis Corp., 1994–. Mem., Fraud Trials Cttee, 1984–85; Vice Pres., BCS, 1981–83; Chm., Humanitec Foundn for the disabled, 1986–92. *Publications:* The Convergence of Technologies, 1977; Britain and the Information Society, 1981; A Director's Guide to Information Technology, 1982; Trends in Information Technology, 1984; Information Technology and Realpolitik, 1986; The Men who Mastered Time (novel), 1986; Senior Management IT Education, 1987; Measuring Progress in IT, 1995; numerous press articles. *Recreations:* cricket, Rugby, ancient history. *Address:* c/o Computer Sciences Corporation, 12 Bloomsbury Square, WC1A 2LL. *T:* 0171–344 7800.

BUTLER, David Edgeworth, CBE 1991; FBA 1994; Fellow of Nuffield College, Oxford, since 1954; *b* 1924; *yr s* of late Professor Harold Edgeworth Butler and Margaret, *d* of Prof. A. F. Pollard; *m* 1962, Marilyn Speers Evans (*see* M. S. Butler); three *s. Educ:* St Paul's; New Coll., Oxford (MA, DPhil). J. E. Procter Visiting Fellow, Princeton Univ., 1947–48; Student, Nuffield Coll., 1949–51; Research Fellow, 1951–54; Dean and Senior Tutor, 1956–64. Served as Personal Assistant to HM Ambassador in Washington, 1955–56. Hon. DUniv Paris, 1978; Hon. DSSc QUB, 1985; Dr *hc* Essex, 1993. Co-editor, Electoral Studies, 1982–92. *Publications:* The British General Election of 1951, 1952; The Electoral System in Britain 1918–51, 1953; The British General Election of 1955, 1955; The Study of Political Behaviour, 1958; (ed) Elections Abroad, 1959; (with R. Rose) The British General Election of 1959, 1960; (with J. Freeman) British Political Facts, 1900–1960, 1963; (with A. King) The British General Election of 1964, 1965; The British General Election of 1966, 1966; (with D. Stokes) Political Change in Britain, 1969; (with M. Pinto-Duschinsky) The British General Election of 1970, 1971; The Canberra Model, 1973; (with D. Kavanagh) The British General Election of February 1974, 1974; (with D. Kavanagh) The British General Election of October 1974, 1975; (with U. Kitzinger) The 1975 Referendum, 1976; (ed) Coalitions in British Politics, 1978; (ed with A. H. Halsey) Policy and Politics, 1978; (with A. Ranney), Referendums, 1978; (with A. Sloman) British Political Facts 1900–79, 1980; (with D. Kavanagh) The British General Election of 1979, 1980; (with D. Marquand) European Elections and British Politics, 1981; (with A. Ranney) Democracy at the Polls, 1981; (with V. Bogdanor) Democracy and Elections, 1983; Governing without a Majority, 1983; (with D. Kavanagh) The British General Election of 1983, 1984; A Compendium of Indian Elections, 1984; (with P. Jowett) Party

Strategies in Britain, 1985; (with G. Butler) British Political Facts 1900–85, 1986; (with D. Kavanagh) The British General Election of 1987, 1988; British Elections since 1945, 1989; (with P. Roy) India Decides, 1989, 2nd edn as India Decides 1952–1989, 1991; (with A. Low) Sovereigns and Surrogates, 1991; (with B. Cain) Congressional Redistricting, 1991; (with D. Kavanagh) The British General Election 1992, 1992; (with A. Ranney) Electioneering, 1992; Failure in British Government, 1994; (with G. Butler) British Political Facts 1900–94, 1994. *Address:* Nuffield College, Oxford OX1 1NF. *T:* Oxford (01865) 278500.

BUTLER, Denis William Langford; Comptroller and City Solicitor to the City of London, 1981–89; *b* 26 Oct. 1926; *s* of late William H. Butler, Shrewsbury and Kitty Butler; *m* 1953, Marna (*née* Taylor); three *d. Educ:* Repton. RM, 1945–47. Admitted Solicitor, 1951. Assistant Solicitor: Norfolk CC, 1953–54; Shropshire CC, 1954–57; Sen. Asst Solicitor, Lindsey (Lincs) CC, 1957–60; Dep. Clerk, 1960–74, County Solicitor and Clerk, 1974–81, Wilts CC. Chm., County Secs Soc., 1974–76. Freeman, City of London, 1981; Liveryman, City of London Solicitors' Co., 1983–. *Recreations:* travel, gardening. *Address:* Pipers Croft, 18 Riverside Close, Laverstock, Salisbury, Wilts SP1 1QW. *T:* Salisbury (01722) 339035. *Club:* Guildhall.

BUTLER, Edward Clive Barber, FRCS; Surgeon: The London Hospital, E1, 1937–69; Haroldwood Hospital, Essex, 1946–69; retired; *b* 8 April 1904; *s* of Dr Butler, Hereford; *m* 1939, Nancy Hamilton Harrison, Minneapolis, USA; two *s* one *d. Educ:* Shrewsbury Sch.; London Hospital. MRCS, LRCP 1928; MB, BS London, 1929; FRCS 1931. Resident posts London Hosp., 1928–32; Surgical Registrar, London Hosp., 1933–36; Surgeon, RMS Queen Mary, Cunard White Star Line, 1936. Hunterian Prof., RCS, 1939; examinerships at various times to London Univ. and Coll. of Surgeons. Pres. section of Proctology, Royal Soc. of Medicine, 1951–52; Member: Medical Soc. London; Royal Soc. Medicine. *Publications:* chapter on bacteraemia, in British Surgical Practice, 1948; on hand infections, in Penicillin (by Fleming), 1950; (jointly) on combined excision of rectum, in Treatment of Cancer and Allied Diseases (New York), 1952; articles on various surgical subjects in Lancet, BMJ, Proc. Royal Soc. Med., British Journal Surgery. *Recreations:* golf, gardening and yachting. *Address:* Flat 304, Enterprise House, Chingford, E4 7ND. *Club:* United Hospitals Sailing.

BUTLER, Air Vice-Marshal Eric Scott, CB 1957; OBE 1941; RAF; AOA HQ Fighter Command, 1957–61; *b* 4 Nov. 1907; *s* of Archibald Butler, Maze Hill, St Leonards-on-Sea, Sussex; *m* 1936, Alice Evelyn Tempest Meates (*d* 1985); three *s* one *d. Educ:* Belfast Academy. Commissioned RAF 1933; Bomber Command European War, 1939–45; idc 1952; Director of Organisation, Air Ministry, 1953–56. *Address:* Camden Cottage, High Street, Pevensey, Sussex BN24 5JP. *T:* Eastbourne (01323) 762353. *Club:* Royal Air Force.

BUTLER, Sir (Frederick Edward) Robin, GCB 1992 (KCB 1988); CVO 1986; Secretary of the Cabinet and Head of the Home Civil Service, since 1988; *b* 3 Jan. 1938; *s* of late Bernard Butler and of Nora Butler; *m* 1962, Gillian Lois Galley; one *s* two *d. Educ:* Harrow Sch.; University Coll., Oxford (BA Lit. Hum., 1961). Joined HM Treasury, 1961; Private Sec. to Financial Sec. to Treasury, 1964–65; Sec., Budget Cttee, 1965–69; seconded to Cabinet Office as Mem., Central Policy Rev. Staff, 1971–72; Private Secretary: to Rt Hon. Edward Heath, 1972–74; to Rt Hon. Harold Wilson, 1974–75; returned to HM Treasury as Asst Sec. i/c Gen. Expenditure Intell. Div., 1975; Under Sec., Gen. Expenditure Policy Gp, 1977–80; Prin. Establishments Officer, 1980–82; Principal Private Sec. to Prime Minister, 1982–85; Second Perm. Sec., Public Expenditure, HM Treasury, 1985–87. Governor, Harrow Sch., 1975–91 (Chm. of Govs, 1988–91). *Recreation:* competitive games. *Address:* Cabinet Office, SW1A 2AS. *Clubs:* Athenæum, Brooks's, Beefsteak, Royal Anglo-Belgian.

BUTLER, George, RWS 1958; RBA; NEAC; painter, principally in water-colour, in England and Provence; *b* 17 Oct. 1904; *s* of John George Butler; *m* 1933, Kcenia Kotliarevskaya (*d* 1992); one *s* one *d. Educ:* King Edward VII School, Sheffield; Central School of Art. Director and Head of Art Dept, J. Walter Thompson Co. Ltd, 1933–60. Vice Pres., Artists' General Benevolent Institution, 1977– (Mem. Council; Hon. Treas., 1957–77). Mem., Société des Artistes Indépendants Aixois. *Address:* Riversdale, Castle Street, Bakewell, Derbyshire DE4 1DU. *T:* Bakewell (01629) 813133. *Club:* Arts.

BUTLER, George William P.; *see* Payne-Butler.

BUTLER, Gerald Norman, QC 1975; **His Honour Judge Butler;** a Circuit Judge, since 1982; Senior Judge at Southwark Crown Court, since 1984; *b* 15 Sept. 1930; *s* of Joshua Butler and Esther Butler (*née* Lampel); *m* 1959, Stella, *d* of Harris and Leah Isaacs; one *s* two *d. Educ:* Ilford County High Sch.; London Sch. of Economics; Magdalen Coll., Oxford. LLB London 1952, BCL Oxon 1954. 2nd Lieut, RASC, 1956–57. Called to Bar, Middle Temple, 1955. A Recorder of the Crown Court, 1977–82. *Recreations:* Rugby, opera, Japanese pottery, walking. *Address:* Southwark Crown Court, SE1 2HU. *Club:* MCC.

BUTLER, Maj.-Gen. Hew Dacres George, CB 1975; DL; *b* 12 March 1922; *s* of late Maj.-Gen. S. S. Butler, CB, CMG, DSO; *m* 1954, Joanna, *d* of late G. M. Puckridge, CMG, ED; two *s* one *d. Educ:* Winchester. Commnd Rifle Bde, 1941; Western Desert, 1942–43; POW, 1943–45; psc 1951; BM 7th Armd Bde, 1951–53; Kenya, 1954–55; Instructor, Staff Coll., 1957–60; CO 1 RB, 1962–64; Cyprus (despatches, 1965); comd 24 Inf. Bde, Aden, 1966–67; idc 1969; ACOS G3 Northag, 1970–72; GOC Near East Land Forces, 1972–74. Chief of Staff (Contingencies Planning), SHAPE, 1975–76; retired 1977. Sec., Beit Trust, 1978–93. DL 1980, High Sheriff 1983, Hants. *Recreations:* shooting, racing, horticulture. *Address:* Bury Lodge, Hambledon, Hants PO7 6QL. *Clubs:* Boodle's, MCC.

BUTLER, Ian Geoffrey, CBE 1990; FCA; Chairman, Cookson Group, 1976–May 1990 and Nov. 1990–July 1991; and Director, Barclays Bank, 1985–91; *b* 12 April 1925; *s* of Hubert Desramaux Butler and Nita Butler (*née* Blake); *m* 1973, Anne Robertson; two *d. Educ:* Huyton Hill, Liverpool; Stowe Sch.; Trinity Coll., Oxford (MA). Commissioned Coldstream Guards, 1943–47. Tansley Witt & Co., 1948–55, Partner, 1951–55; Goodlass Wall & Lead Industries, 1956– (subseq. named Cookson Group): Finance Dir, 1965; Managing Dir, 1973. Chm., Tioxide Gp, 1987–90. Treasurer and Mem. Exec. Cttee, Internat. Yacht Racing Union, 1977–90; Mem. Council, Royal Yachting Assoc., 1960–91 (former Hon. Treasurer). *Recreations:* sailing, ski-ing, fell walking. *Address:* Wyke House, Ellanore Lane, West Wittering, West Sussex PO20 8AN. *T:* Birdham (01243) 513269. *Clubs:* Royal Thames Yacht; Royal Yacht Squadron, Itchenor Sailing.

BUTLER, James; *see* Butler, P. J.

BUTLER, James Walter, RA 1972 (ARA 1964); RWA; FRBS; *b* 25 July 1931; *m* (marr. diss.); one *d*; *m* 1975, Angela, *d* of Col Roger Berry, Johannesburg, South Africa; four *d. Educ:* Maidstone Grammar Sch.; Maidstone Coll. of Art; St Martin's Art Sch.; Royal Coll. of Art. National Diploma in Sculpture, 1950. Worked as Architectural Carver, 1950–53, 1955–60. Tutor, Sculpture and Drawing, City and Guilds of London Art School, 1960–75. Major commissions include: portrait statue of Pres. Kenyatta, Nairobi, 1973; Monument to Freedom Fighters of Zambia, Lusaka, 1974; statue, The Burton Cooper, Burton-on-Trent, 1977; memorial statue, Richard III, Leicester, 1980; memorial statue, Field Marshal Earl Alexander of Tunis, Wellington Barracks, London, 1985; portrait statue of Sir John Moore, Sir John Moore Barracks, Winchester, 1987; portrait statue of John Wilkes, New Fetter Lane, 1988; Dolphin Fountain, Dolphin Square, London, 1988; Skipping Girl, Harrow, 1988; The Leicester Seamstress, Leicester, 1990; The Stratford Jester, Stratford-upon-Avon; portrait statue, Thomas Cook, Leicester, 1994; statue, James Henry Greathead, Cornhill, 1994; meml statue, Reg Harris, Manchester, 1994; portrait bust, Sir Frank Whittle, RAF Club. Silver Medal, RBS, 1988. *Recreations:* interested in astronomy, golf. *Address:* Valley Farm, Radway, Warwick CV35 0UJ. *T:* Warwick (01926) 641938. *Club:* Arts.

BUTLER, John Manton, MSc; *b* 9 Oct. 1909; *m* 1940, Marjorie Smith, Melbourne; one *s* one *d. Educ:* Southland, NZ; Univ. of Otago (Sen. Schol., NZ, Physics; BSc 1929; Smeaton Schol. Chemistry, 1930, John Edmond Fellow, 1930; MSc 1st class Hons). Pres., Students' Union; Graduate Rep. Univ. Council. Joined Shell, NZ, 1934; served various Shell cos in UK, Australia and S Africa until 1957; Man. Dir, Lewis Berger (GB) Ltd, 1957; Dir, Berger, Jenson & Nicholson Ltd, 1969–74. Chm., BNEC Cttee for Exports to NZ, 1967 (Dep. Chm., 1965). Pres., NZ Soc., 1971. Member: Cttee, Spastics Soc.; St David's Cttee, Conservative Assoc., 1979–80; Aust. Inst. of Internat. Affairs, 1981–. Consultant. *Recreations:* travel, golf, photography. *Address:* Osborne, 28 Ranfurlie Crescent, Glen Iris, Victoria 3146, Australia. *T:* (3) 98859458. *Club:* Royal Melbourne Golf.

BUTLER, Prof. (John) Nicholas, (Nick), OBE 1988; RDI 1981; FCSD; industrial designer; Chairman and Joint Managing Director, BIB Design Consultants, since 1989; *b* 21 March 1942; *s* of William and Mabel Butler; *m* 1967, Kari Ann Morrison; two *s. Educ:* Leeds Coll. of Art (NDD); Royal Coll. of Art (DesRCA, 1st Cl. Hons). FCSD (FSIAD 1975). Founded BIB Design Consultants, 1967; Sen. Partner, 1967–89. Prof. of Industrial Design, RCA, 1987–90. Chm., British Design Export Gp, 1980–81; Member: Design Bd, RSA, 1987–; Design Council, 1988–93 (Mem., Chairman's Review Team, 1993–); Chairman's Design Bd, BAA, 1992–. Hon. Sec., SIAD, 1978–81, Treasurer 1981–84. FRSA 1983. *Recreations:* reading, music, country pursuits, watching Rugby, drawing. *Address:* BIB Design Consultants, The Mill, Whitchurch-on-Thames, Oxon RG8 7DG.

BUTLER, Keith Stephenson, CMG 1977; HM Diplomatic Service, retired; Appeal Director for various charities, since 1978; *b* 3 Sept. 1917; *s* of late Raymond R. Butler and Gertrude Stephenson; *m* 1st, 1952, Geraldine Marjorie Clark (*d* 1979); 2nd, 1979, Mrs Priscilla Wittels; no *c. Educ:* King Edward's Sch., Birmingham; Liverpool Coll.; St Peter's Coll., Oxford (MA). HM Forces, 1939–47 (despatches): served, RA, in Egypt, Greece and Crete; POW, Germany, 1941–45. Foreign Correspondent for Sunday Times and Kemsley Newspapers, 1947–50. Joined HM Foreign Service, 1950; served: First Sec., Ankara and Caracas; Canadian Nat. Defence Coll.; Paris; Montreal. HM Consul-General: Seville, 1968; Bordeaux, 1969; Naples, 1974–77. *Publications:* contrib. historical and political reviews. *Recreation:* historical research. *Address:* Sheilings, 10 Station Road, Kintbury, near Newbury, Berks RG15 0UP. *T:* Kintbury (01488) 658350.

BUTLER, Marilyn Speers, DPhil; Rector, Exeter College, University of Oxford, since 1993; *b* 11 Feb. 1937; *d* of Sir Trevor Evans, CBE and Margaret (*née* Gribbin); *m* 1962, David Edgeworth Butler, *qv*; three *s. Educ:* Wimbledon High Sch.; St Hilda's Coll., Oxford (MA; DPhil). Trainee and talks producer, BBC, 1960–62; Oxford University: full-time res. and teaching, 1962–70, Jun. Res. Fellow, 1970–73, St Hilda's Coll.; Fellow and Tutor, St Hugh's Coll., 1973–85; Lectr, 1985–86; King Edward VII Prof. of English Lit., 1986–93, and Fellow of King's Coll., 1988–93, Univ. of Cambridge. Pt-time Lectr, ANU, 1967; British Academy Reader, 1982–85. *Publications:* Maria Edgeworth: a literary biography, 1972; Jane Austen and the War of Ideas, 1975; Peacock Displayed, 1979; Romantics, Rebels and Reactionaries, 1981, 2nd edn 1985; (ed) Burke, Paine, Godwin and the Revolution Controversy, 1984; (ed with J. Todd) Works of Mary Wollstonecraft, 1989; (ed) Maria Edgeworth, Castle Rackrent, and Ennui, 1992; (ed) Frankenstein, the 1818 edition, 1993. *Address:* The Rector's Lodgings, Exeter College, Oxford OX1 3DP.

BUTLER, Sir Michael; *see* Butler, Sir R. M. T.

BUTLER, Sir Michael (Dacres), GCMG 1984 (KCMG 1980; CMG 1975); HM Diplomatic Service, retired; Director: Hambros PLC, since 1986; Hambros Bank Ltd, since 1986; Wellcome Foundation, since 1986; Eurosynergies (France), since 1990; Chairman: European Strategy Board, ICL, since 1988; Oriental Art Magazine, since 1988; *b* 27 Feb. 1927; *s* of T. D. Butler, Almer, Blandford, and Beryl May (*née* Lambert); *m* 1951, Ann, *d* of Rt Hon. Lord Clyde; two *s* two *d. Educ:* Winchester; Trinity Coll., Oxford. Joined HM Foreign Service, 1950; served in: UK Mission to UN, New York, 1952–56; Baghdad, 1956–58; FO, 1958–61 and 1965–68; Paris, 1961–65; Counsellor, UK Mission in Geneva, 1968–70; Fellow, Center for Internat. Affairs, Harvard, 1970–71; Counsellor, Washington, 1971–72; Head of European Integration Dept, FCO, 1972–74; Asst Under-Sec. in charge of European Community Affairs, FCO, 1974–76; Dep. Under-Sec. of State, FCO, 1976–79; Ambassador and Perm. UK Rep. to EC, Brussels, 1979–85. Advr, Govt of Ukraine, 1991–94. Chairman: City European Cttee, British Invisibles (formerly BIEC), 1988–93; European Unification Bd, Hercules Europe, 1989–94; Business Link–Dorset, 1994–; HALO Ltd, 1994–; Treasury Mgt Internat. Editl Adv. Panel, 1992–; Member: Standing Cttee on Internat. Relations, ACOST, 1987–90; Panel of Conciliators, Internat. Centre for the Settlement of Investment Disputes, 1987–94; Bank of Montreal Internat. Adv. Council, 1992–. Pro-Provost and Chm. Council, RCA, 1991–; Mem. Council, Oriental Ceramic Soc., 1977–80 and 1985–88; Dep. Chm., Bd of Trustees, V&A Museum, 1985–. *Publications:* Chinese Porcelain, The Transitional Period 1620–82: a selection from the Michael Butler Collection, 1986; Europe: More than a Continent, 1986; The Butler Family Collection, 17th Century Chinese Porcelain, 1990; contribs to Trans Oriental Ceramic Soc. *Recreations:* collecting Chinese porcelain, ski-ing, tennis. *Address:* 36A Elm Park Road, SW3 6AX. *Club:* Brooks's.

BUTLER, Michael Howard, FCA; Finance Director, British Coal (formerly National Coal Board), 1985–93, Member of the Board, 1986–93; Chairman: CIN Management Ltd, since 1993; British Investment Trust, since 1993; *b* 13 Feb. 1936; *s* of Howard Butler and Constance Gertrude Butler; *m* 1961, Christine Elizabeth Killer; two *s* one *d. Educ:* Nottingham High School. Articled pupil, H. G. Ellis Kennewell & Co., Nottingham, 1952–58; Stewarts & Lloyds Gp, 1960–62; National Coal Board: various posts, NCB HQ, W Midlands Div. and NE Area, 1962–68; Chief Accountant, Coal Products Div., 1968; Dep. Treas., NCB HQ, 1970; Treas. and Dep. Dir Gen. of Finance, 1978; Dir Gen. of Finance, 1981; Chm., British Fuels Co., 1992–93. Director: British Coal Enterprises, 1988–; Edinburgh Fund Managers, 1993–. Trustee, British Coal Pension Funds, 1981–. *Recreations:* gardening, listening to music, playing tennis. *Address:* Banstead Down, Chorleywood Road, Rickmansworth, Herts WD3 4EH. *T:* Rickmansworth (01923) 778001.

BUTLER, Prof. Neville Roy, MD; FRCP; FRCOG; Director, International Centre for Child Studies, since 1983; Professor of Child Health, Bristol University, 1965–85, Emeritus

Professor, since 1985; Hon. Consultant Paediatrician, Bristol & Weston Teaching District and Southmead District, 1965–85; *b* Harrow, 6 July 1920; *o s* of late Dr C. J. Butler, MRCS, LRCP and Ida Margaret Butler; *m* 1954, Jean Ogilvie (marr. diss.), *d* of late John McCormack; two *d*. *Educ:* Epsom Coll.; Charing Cross Hosp. Med. Sch. MB BS 1942, MD 1949; MRCP 1946, FRCP 1965; DCH 1949; FRCOG 1979. Served RAMC, 1942–44, temp. Captain. First Assistant to Paediatric Unit, UCH, 1950; Med. Registrar and Pathologist, Hosp. for Sick Children, Gt Ormond St, 1953; Consultant Paediatrician, Oxford and Wessex RHB, 1957–63; Dir, Perinatal Mortality Survey, Birthday Trust Fund, 1958; Consultant Physician, Hosp. for Sick Children, Gt Ormond St and Sen. Lectr, Inst. of Child Health, London Univ., 1963–65. Co-Dir, Nat. Child Develt Study (1958 cohort), 1965–69; Dir, Child Health and Educn Study (1970 cohort), and Youthscan UK, 1975–89. Harding Meml Lect., RIBA, 1983. Member: BPA, 1958–; Neonatal Soc., 1961–; Cuban Paediatric Soc., 1973–; Hungarian Paediatric Soc., 1979–. *Publications:* jointly: Perinatal Mortality, 1963; 11,000 Seven Year Olds, 1966; Perinatal Problems, 1969; From Birth to Seven, 1972; ABO Haemolytic Diseases of the Newborn, 1972; The Social Life of Britain's Five Year Olds, 1984; Ethnic Minority Children, 1985; The Health of Britain's Five Year Olds, 1986; papers in scientific and med. jls. *Address:* Vine Cottage, Seagry Road, Sutton Benger, Chippenham, Wilts SN15 4RX. *T:* Chippenham (01249) 720688; International Centre for Child Studies, Social Statistics Research Unit, City University, EC1V 0HB. *T:* 0171–477 8481. *Club:* Savage.

BUTLER, Nick; *see* Butler, J. N.

BUTLER, Norman John Terence, CBE 1993; Director of Social Services, Hampshire, since 1988; *b* 18 Feb. 1946; *s* of Arthur Reginald Butler and Lucy Mary Butler; *m* 1978, Bethan Mary Lewis; two *d*. *Educ:* Peveril Bilateral Sch., Nottingham; Trent Polytechnic, Nottingham (Cert. in Social Work); Nat. Inst. of Social Work, London; Brunel Univ. (MA Public and Social Admin). Mental Welfare Officer, Nottingham, 1965–71; Sen. Social Worker, Nottingham, 1971–73; Area Man., Haringey, 1974–81; Asst Dir of Social Services, Royal Bor. of Kingston upon Thames, 1981–83; Dep. Dir of Social Services, E. Sussex, 1983–88. Member: Firth Cttee, examining public expenditure on residential care, 1987; Algebra Gp, 1992–93; Adv. Bd for Restricted Patients, 1995–; Co-Leader, Community Care Support Force, providing practical support to local and health authorities in implementation of NHS and Community Care Act, 1992–93. *Publications:* articles in various jls, incl. Social Work Today, Insight and Community Care. *Recreations:* travel, tennis, soccer, entertaining, being entertained. *Address:* (office) Trafalgar House, The Castle, Winchester, Hants SO23 8UQ. *T:* Winchester (01962) 841841; Westwood, New Farm Road, New Alresford, Hants SO24 9QH. *T:* Alresford (01962) 2572. *Club:* Winchester Squash and Tennis.

BUTLER, (Percy) James, CBE 1981; DL; FCA; Chairman, European Passenger Services Ltd, since 1994; Senior Partner, KPMG Peat Marwick (formerly KPMG Peat Marwick McLintock), 1986–93; farmer, since 1974; *b* 15 March 1929; *s* of late Percy Ernest Butler and Phyllis Mary Butler (*née* Bartholomew); *m* 1954, Margaret Prudence Copland; one *s* two *d*. *Educ:* Marlborough Coll.; Clare Coll., Cambridge (MA). Joined Peat, Marwick, Mitchell & Co., 1952; qualified, 1955; Partner, 1965; Gen. Partner, 1971; Managing Partner, London Reg., 1981–85; Dep. Sen. Partner, 1985–86; Mem. of KPMG Exec. Cttee and Council, 1987–93; Chm., KPMG Internat., 1991–93. Director: Mersey Docks and Harbour Co., 1972–90 (Dep. Chm., 1987–90); Tompkins PLC, 1994–; Wadworth and Co. Ltd, 1994–; Camelot PLC, 1994–; Nicholson, Graham & Jones, 1994–. Mem. (part time), BRB, 1994–. Business Advr to Treasury and CS Cttee, 1980–82; Member: Cttee on review of Railway Finance, 1982; Cadbury Cttee on Financial Aspects of Corporate Governance, 1990–. Member: Council, Business in the Community, 1988–90; ICAEW Council, 1992–94; Council, CBI, 1989–94; Governing Body, City Res. Project, 1991–; Adv. Council, Prince's Youth Business Trust, 1993–; Council, SCF, 1994–. Treasurer, Pilgrims Soc., 1982–; Trustee, Royal Opera House Trust, 1991– (Chm., 1993–); Dir, Royal Opera House, 1994–. Mem., Marlborough Coll. Council, 1975– (Chm., 1992–). Liveryman: Worshipful Co. of Cutlers, 1965– (Mem. Court, 1985–; Master, 1995–July 1996); Worshipful Co. of Chartered Accountants in England and Wales, 1977–. DL Hants, 1994. *Recreations:* bridge, shooting, opera, ballet. *Address:* Littleton House, Crawley, near Winchester SO21 2QF. *T:* Winchester (01962) 880206; Flat 8, 3 Lennox Gardens, SW1 0DA. *T:* 0171–581 8759. *Club:* Carlton.

BUTLER, Peter; MP (C) Milton Keynes North East, since 1992; *b* 10 June 1951; *s* of late Kenneth Jonathan Butler and of Barbara Butler; *m* 1973, Peggy Mary, *d* of Richard Nott; three *d*. *Educ:* Adams Grammar Sch., Newport, Shropshire; St Edmund Hall, Oxford (MA English Lit.; PGCE 1974). Admitted Solicitor, 1978; Solicitor, Thames Valley Police, 1978–80; Partner, 1981–92, Consultant, 1992–, Linnells, solicitors, Oxford. Mem. (C) Oxfordshire CC, 1985–89. Nat. Chm., Trainee Solicitors, England and Wales, 1976. PPS to Minister of State, DoH, 1994–. Mem., Home Affairs Select Cttee, 1992–94. Sch. Gov., 1985–92. *Recreations:* music, three energetic children, avoiding organised exercise. *Address:* House of Commons, SW1A 0AA. *T:* 0171–219 6423. *Clubs:* Carlton; Frewen (Oxford); Vintage Sports Car.

BUTLER, Sir (Reginald) Michael (Thomas), 3rd Bt *cr* 1922; QC (Canada); Barrister and Solicitor, retired; sometime Partner of Butler, Angus, Victoria, BC; Director, Teck Corporation; *b* 22 April 1928; *s* of Sir Reginald Thomas, 2nd Bt, and Marjorie Brown Butler; *S* father, 1959; *m* Marja McLean (marr. diss.); three *s*; one *s* adopted; *m* Judith Anne Blackwell, LLB, *d* of Harold Blackwell. *Educ:* Brentwood Coll., Victoria, BC; Univ. of British Columbia (BA). Called to Bar (Hons) from Osgoode Hall Sch. of Law, Toronto, Canada, 1954. *Heir: s* (Reginald) Richard (Michael) Butler [*b* 3 Oct. 1953; *m* 1982, Dale Karen, *d* of Frederick William Piner, Vancouver; three *s*]. *Address:* Old Park Cottage, 634 Avalon Street, Victoria, BC V8V 1N7, Canada. *Club:* Vancouver (Vancouver).

BUTLER, Hon. Sir Richard (Clive), Kt 1981; DL; Chairman, County Natwest Investment Management, since 1989; Life Member, Council, National Farmers' Union, since 1962 (President, 1979–86); farmer since 1953; *b* 12 Jan. 1929; *e s* of late Baron Butler of Saffron Walden, KG, CH, PC and late Sydney, *o c* of late Samuel Courtauld; *m* 1952, Susan Anne Maud Walker; twin *s* one *d*. *Educ:* Eton Coll.; Pembroke Coll., Cambridge (MA). 2nd Lieut, Royal Horse Guards, 1947–49. Vice-Pres. 1970–71, Dep. Pres., 1971–79, NFU. Member: Agricultural Adv. Council, 1968–72; Central Council for Agricultural and Horticultural Co-operation, 1970–79. Director: National Westminster Bank, 1986–; Agroceres & Co. (formerly Ferruzzi Trading (UK)), 1986–; Agricola (UK), 1986–92; Barton Bendish Farms, 1986–92; County Natwest Group (formerly Natwest Investment Bank), 1989–92; National Farmers' Union Mutual Insurance Soc. Ltd, 1985–; Avon Insurance, 1990–. Mem. Ct of Assts, Farmers' Co.; Master, Skinners' Co., 1994–95. DL Essex, 1972. *Recreations:* hunting, shooting, DIY. *Address:* Penny Pot, Halstead, Essex CO9 1RY. *T:* Halstead (01787) 472828. *Club:* Farmers'.

See also Rt Hon. Sir A. C. Butler.

BUTLER, Richard Edmund, AM 1988; telecommunication policy adviser; Secretary-General, International Telecommunication Union, United Nations, Specialised Agency, Geneva, 1983–89 (Deputy Secretary-General, 1968–82); *b* 25 March 1926; *m* 1951, Patricia Carmel Kelly; three *s* two *d*. *Educ:* A, DPA; AASA; CPA; FRIPA. Posts in Australian Post Office, incl. Chief Industrial Officer, 1955–60; Exec. Officer, Dep. Asst Dir-Gen., 1960–68 (Ministerial and External Relations), 1960–68; apptd (in absentia) Sec., Aust. Telecommunications Commn, 1975 and later Dir, Corporate Planning Directorate. Formerly Member Australian delegations: for Internat. Telecommunication Satellite Consortium, Plenipotentiary Conf. 1965 (Dep. Leader; Mem. Administrative Council and Plan Cttees, 1962–68); to UN Conf. on Peaceful Uses of Outer Space, Vienna, 1968 (Dep. Leader). Mem., Admin. Cttee of Co-ordination for UN and Heads of Specialized Agencies; Chairman: Ad-Hoc UN Common System subsid. gps; ITU (Tripartite) Staff Pension Cttee, 1968–83; Member: Bd of Management, Centre for IT Res., Univ. of Wollongong, NSW, 1990–; Ministerial Adv. Cttee, Implementation of Australian Telecommns Reform decisions, 1990–; Centre for Internat. Res. on Communication and ITs, Melbourne, 1993– (Associate Mem., 1992; Dir, 1993–); Associate Mem., Austr. Telecommn Authy), 1990–91. Member, Advisory Board: Pacific Telecommns Council, Hawaii, 1993–; Telematics, India, 1994–; Advr and ITU Rep., Ind. Commn of ULCRA (Latin Amer. and Caribbean Broadcasting Union), 1990–. Governor, Internat. Computer Commns Conf., 1975–85; UN System co-ordinator, Develt of Commns Infrastructure prog., world commns year, 1983. Hon. Mem., Greek Soc. of Air and Space Law, 1984. FRIPA; Hon. Fellow, Instn of Electronic and Telecommunications Engrs, New Delhi, 1988. Philipp Reis Medal, Germany, 1987. Grand Insignia, Order of Merit for Telecommunications, Spain, 1983. *Publications:* papers on changing telecommunication environment and on multi-dimensional consequences of telecommunications for economic development of nations. *Recreations:* golf, reading. *Address:* 40 Barrington Avenue, Kew, Vic 3101, Australia. *Clubs:* Commonwealth Trust, Royal Over-Seas League; CTA Commerce (Vic); Melbourne Cricket.

BUTLER, Sir Richard (Pierce), 13th Bt *cr* 1628 (Ire.), of Cloughgrenan, Co. Carlow; *b* 22 July 1940; *s* of Col Sir Thomas Pierce Butler, 12th Bt, CVO, DSO, OBE and of Rosemary Liège Woodgate Davidson-Houston; *S* father, 1994; *m* 1965, Diana, *yr d* of Col S. J. Borg; three *s* one *d*. *Educ:* Eton; NY Univ. MBA. FCA 1963. Partner, Charles Wakeling & Co., 1964–66; Director: The First Boston Corp. (NY), 1967–78; PaineWebber Inc. (NY), 1978–88 (Management Council, 1985–88); PaineWebber International Bank, 1986–89; Emesco Industrial Equity Co. SA, 1987–; The Transportation Gp Ltd, 1989–94; Ibercapital SA, 1990–; Rauscher Pierce & Clark Inc., 1992–. Mem. Council, Pestalozzi Children's Village Trust, 1983– (Chm., 1985–94). Treas., GAPAN, 1963–66. *Heir: s* Thomas Pierce [*b* 9 Oct. 1966; *m* 1993, Lucinda Pamela Murphy]. *Address:* c/o Barclays Bank, 160 Piccadilly, W1A 2AB.

BUTLER, Sir Robin; *see* Butler, Sir F. E. R.

BUTLER, Dr Rohan D'Olier, CMG; MA; DLitt; FRHistS; Laureate, Institute of France; Fellow Emeritus of All Souls, Oxford, since 1984 (Fellow, 1938–84; Sub-Warden, 1961–63; representative at 12th International Historical Congress at Vienna, 1965, at 11th Anglo-American Conference of Historians, 1982); *b* St John's Wood, 21 Jan. 1917; surv. *s* of late Sir Harold Butler, KCMG, CB, MA, and Olive, Lady Butler, *y c* of late Asst Inspector-General S. A. W. Waters, RIC, JP; *m* Lucy Rosemary (Lady of the Manor of White Notley, Essex), *y c* of late Eric Byron. *Educ:* Eton; abroad and privately; Balliol Coll., Oxford (Hall Prizeman, 1938). BA (1st Class Hons in Modern History), 1938; on International Propaganda and Broadcasting Enquiry, 1939; on staff of MOI, 1939–41 and 1942–44, of Special Operations Executive, 1941; served with RAPC, 1941–42, with HG, 1942–44 (Defence Medal, War Medal); on staff of FO, 1944–45; Editor of Documents on British Foreign Policy (1919–39), 1945–65 (with late Sir Llewellyn Woodward, FBA, 1945–54; Senior Editor, 1955–65); Sen. Editor, Documents on British Policy Overseas, 1973–82. Leverhulme Res. Fellow, 1955–57, Emeritus Fellow, 1984–86. Governor, Felsted Sch., 1959–77, representative on GBA, 1964–77; Trustee, Felsted Almshouses, 1961–77; Noel Buxton Trustee, 1961–67. Historical Adviser to Sec. of State for Foreign Affairs, 1963–68, for Foreign and Commonwealth Affairs, 1968–82 (from 14th Earl of Home to 6th Baron Carrington). On management of Inst. of Hist. Research, Univ. of London, 1967–77; Mem., Lord Chancellor's Adv. Council on Public Records, 1982–86. Mem. Court, Univ. of Essex, 1971–91. *Publications:* The Roots of National Socialism (1783–1933); Documents on British Foreign Policy, 1st series, vols i–ix, 2nd series, vol. ix; The Peace Settlement of Versailles, 1918–33 (in New Cambridge Modern History); Paradiplomacy (in Studies in Diplomatic History in honour of Dr G. P. Gooch, OM, CH, FBA); Introduction to Anglo-Soviet historical exhibition of 1967; Choiseul (special award, Prix Jean Debrousse, Acad. des Sciences Morales et Politiques, 1982); Documents on British Policy Overseas, series I, vol. i; The Secret Compact of 1753 between the Kings of France and of Naples (in Sovereignty in Early Modern Europe). *Recreation:* idling. *Address:* White Notley Hall, near Witham, Essex CM8 1RX. *Club:* Beefsteak.

BUTLER, Rosemary Jane; Director of Statistics, Department of Health, since 1991; *b* 15 July 1946; *d* of Samuel Laight Medlar and Rosemary Peggy Medlar; *m* 1971, Anthony David Butler. *Educ:* Maynard School, Exeter; LSE (BSc Econ). Central Statistical Office, 1967–73; Unit for Manpower Studies, 1973–77; Dept of Employment, 1977–80; Statistician and Chief Statistician, MoD, 1980–85; Chief Statistician, HM Treasury, 1985–89; Asst Sec., DSS, 1989–91. FRSA 1993. *Recreations:* theatre, music, birdwatching. *Address:* Department of Health, Skipton House, 80 London Road, SE1 6LW.

BUTLER, Rt. Rev. Thomas Frederick; *see* Leicester, Bishop of.

BUTLER, Vincent Frederick, RSA 1977; RGI 1989; figurative sculptor; works in bronze; *b* Manchester, 1933; *m* 1961, Camilla Luisa Meazza; two *s*. *Educ:* Acad. of Fine Art, Milan. Regular exhibitor at major exhibitions in Scotland; work in RA and several private galleries in Edinburgh, Glasgow and London. *Address:* 17 Deanpark Crescent, Edinburgh EH4 1PH. *T:* 0131–332 5884.

BUTLER, Prof. William Elliott; Professor of Comparative Law in the University of London, since 1976; Director, Vinogradoff Institute (formerly Centre for the Study of Socialist Legal Systems), University College London, since 1982; *b* 20 Oct. 1939; *s* of William Elliott Butler and Maxine Swan Elmberg; *m* 1st, 1961, Darlene Mae Johnson (*d* 1989); two *s*; 2nd, 1991, Maryann Elizabeth Gashi. *Educ:* The American Univ. (BA); Harvard Law School (JD); The Johns Hopkins Univ. (MA, PhD); London Univ. (LLD). FSA 1989. Res. Asst, Washington Centre of Foreign Policy Res., Sch. of Advanced Internat. Studies, The Johns Hopkins Univ., 1966–68; Res. Associate in Law, and Associate, Russian Res. Centre, Harvard Univ., 1968–70; University of London: Reader in Comparative Law, 1970–76; Mem., SSEES, 1973–93 (Vice-Chm., 1983–88); Dean of Faculty of Laws, UCL, 1977–79; Vice Dean, 1986–88, Dean, 1988–90, Faculty of Laws, London Univ; Mem., Cttee of Management, Inst. of Advanced Legal Studies, 1985–88. Visiting Scholar: Faculty of Law, Moscow State Univ., 1972, 1980; Inst. of State and Law, USSR Acad. of Scis, 1976, 1981, 1983, 1984, 1988; Mongolian State Univ., 1979; Harvard Law Sch., 1982; Visiting Professor: NY Univ. Law Sch., 1978; Ritsumeikan Univ., 1985; Harvard Law Sch., 1986–87; Lectr, Hague Acad. of Internat. Law, 1985. Associé, Internat. Acad. of Comparative Law, 1982–; Member, Bar: Dist of Columbia; US Supreme Court; Union of Jurists, 1990. Chm., Civil Rights in Russia Adv. Panel,

Univ. of London, 1983–87; Co-ordinator, UCL-USSR Acad. of Sciences Protocol on Co-operation, 1981–; Special Counsel, Commn on Econ. Reform, USSR Council of Ministers, 1989–91; Of Counsel, Clifford Chance, London, Moscow and Almaty, 1992–94; Partner, White & Case, 1994–; Member: EC Joint Task Force on Law Reform in CIS, 1992–93; Working Gp on Commercial Law, Govt of Russian Fedn, 1992; Advr, State Property Fund, Rep. of Kyrgyzstan, 1992; Consultant, World Bank, 1992–. Mem., Secretariat, Internat. Assoc. of Mongolists (Ulan Bator), 1987–; Hon. Member: All-Union Soc. of Bibliophiles, USSR, 1989; Soviet Assoc. of Maritime Law, 1990. Mem., Court of Governors, City of London Polytechnic, 1985–89. Sec., The Bookplate Soc., 1978–86 (Foreign Sec., 1988–94); Exec. Sec., Féd. Internat. des Sociétés d'Amateurs d'Ex-Libris, 1988– (Vice-Pres., 1984–86). Academician: Internat. Acad. of the Book and Art of the Book, Russia, 1992; Russian Acad. of Natural Scis (Russian Encyclopedia Section), 1992; Acad. of Scis of Ukraine, 1992. Editor, Year Book on Socialist Legal Systems, 1985–90; Co-editor, The Bookplate Jl, 1989–91 (Editor, 1983–86); Editor, Bookplate Internat., 1994–; Mem., editorial bds of learned jls, incl. Marine Policy, 1988–, European Business Law Rev., 1990–; editor of looseleaf services and microfiche projects. FRSA 1986. *Publications:* more than 800 books, articles, translations, and reviews, including: The Soviet Union and the Law of the Sea, 1971; Russian Law, 1977; (with others) The Soviet Legal System, 3rd and 4th edns, 1977–84; A Source Book on Socialist International Organizations, 1978; Northeast Arctic Passage, 1978; International Law in Comparative Perspective, 1980; Basic Documents on Soviet Legal System, 1983, 2nd edn 1991; Chinese Soviet Republic 1931–1934, 1983; Soviet Law, 1983, 2nd edn 1988; Comparative Law and Legal System, 1985; The Law of the Sea and International Shipping, 1985; The Golden Era of American Bookplate Design, 1986; Justice and Comparative Law, 1987; International Law and the International System, 1987; The Non-Use of Force and International Law, 1989; Perestroika and International Law, 1990; The History of International Law in Russia 1647–1917, 1990; (with D. J. Butler) Modern British Bookplate Design, 1990; Sherlockian Bookplates, 1992; The Butler Commentaries: USSR Law on Ownership, 1991; USSR Fundamental Principles on Investment Activity, 1991; Foreign Investment Legislation in the Republic of the Former Soviet Union, 1993; (with M. E. Gashi-Butler) Doing Business in Russia, 1994; *translations of:* G. I. Tunkin, Theory of International Law, 1974; A. Kuznetsov, The Journey, 1984; Russian Civil Code, 1995. *Recreations:* book collecting, bookplate collecting. *Address:* 20 Ainger Road, NW3 3AS. *T:* 0171–586 2454. *Club:* Cosmos (Washington, DC).

BUTLER-SLOSS, Rt. Hon. Dame (Ann) Elizabeth (Oldfield), DBE 1979; PC 1988; **Rt. Hon. Lord Justice Butler-Sloss;** a Lord Justice of Appeal, since 1988; *b* 10 Aug. 1933; *d* of late Sir Cecil Havers, QC, and late Enid Snelling; *m* 1958, Joseph William Alexander Butler-Sloss, *qv*; two *s* one *d*. *Educ:* Wycombe Abbey Sch. Called to Bar, Inner Temple, Feb. 1955, Bencher, 1979; practice at Bar, 1955–70; Registrar, Principal Registry of Probate, later Family, Division, 1970–79; a Judge of the High Court, Family Div., 1979–88. Chm., Cleveland Child Abuse Inquiry, 1987–88. Contested (C), Lambeth, Vauxhall, 1959. Member: Medico-Legal Soc.; Judicial Studies Bd, 1985–89. Pres., Honiton Agricultural Show, 1985–86; Chancellor, Univ. of West of England, 1993–. Hon. Fellow, St Hilda's Coll., Oxford, 1988; Presentation Fellow, KCL, 1991. Hon. Mem., BPA, 1988. FRSM 1992; Hon. FRCP 1992; Hon. FRCPsych 1993. Hon. LLD: Hull, 1988; Keele, 1991; Bristol, 1991; Exeter, 1992; Brunel, 1992; Hon. DLitt Loughborough, 1992; DUniv Central England, 1994. *Publications:* Joint Editor: Phipson on Evidence (10th edn); Corpe on Road Haulage (2nd edn); a former Editor, Supreme Court Practice, 1976 and 1979. *Address:* c/o Royal Courts of Justice, Strand, WC2A 2LL. *Club:* Lansdowne.

BUTLER-SLOSS, Joseph William Alexander; Chairman, 1992 Delimitation Commission, Botswana, 1992–93; *b* 16 Nov. 1926; 2nd and *o* surv. *s* of late Francis Alexander Sloss and Alice Mary Frances Violet Sloss (*née* Patchell); *m* 1958, Ann Elizabeth Oldfield Havers (*see* Rt. Hon. Dame (Ann) Elizabeth (Oldfield) Butler-Sloss); two *s* one *d*. *Educ:* Bangor Grammar Sch., Co. Down; Hertford Coll., Oxford. Ordinary Seaman, RN, 1944; Midshipman 1945, Sub-Lieut 1946, RNVR. MA (Jurisprudence) Hertford Coll., Oxford, 1951. Called to Bar, Gray's Inn, 1952; joined Western Circuit, 1954; joined Inner Temple; a Recorder, 1972–84; a Judge of High Court, Kenya, 1984–90. Joint Master, East Devon Foxhounds, 1970–76. Hon. Editor, The Irish Genealogist, 1993–. *Recreations:* racing, the violin. *Address:* Higher Marsh Farm, Marsh Green, Rockbeare, Exeter EX5 2EX. *Clubs:* Carlton; Muthaiga; Nairobi.

BUTLIN, Martin Richard Fletcher, CBE 1990; FBA 1984; Keeper of Historic British Collection, Tate Gallery, 1967–89; Consultant, Christie's, since 1989; *b* 7 June 1929; *s* of Kenneth Rupert Butlin and Helen Mary (*née* Fletcher); *m* 1969, Frances Caroline Chodzko. *Educ:* Rendcomb Coll.; Trinity Coll., Cambridge (MA); Courtauld Inst. of Art, London Univ. (BA). DLit London 1984. Asst Keeper, Tate Gall., 1955–67. *Publications:* A Catalogue of the Works of William Blake in the Tate Gallery, 1957, 3rd edn 1990; Samuel Palmer's Sketchbook of 1824, 1962; Turner Watercolours, 1962; (with Sir John Rothenstein) Turner, 1964; (with Mary Chamot and Dennis Farr) Tate Gallery Catalogues: The Modern British Paintings, Drawings and Sculpture, 1964; The Later Works of J. M. W. Turner, 1965; William Blake, 1966; The Blake-Varley Sketchbook of 1819, 1969; (with E. Joll) The Paintings of J. M. W. Turner, 1977, 2nd edn 1984 (jtly, Mitchell Prize for the History of Art, 1978); The Paintings and Drawings of William Blake, 1981; Aspects of British Painting 1550–1800, from the Collection of the Sarah Campbell Blaffer Foundation, 1988; (with Mollie Luther and Ian Warrell) Turner at Petworth, 1989; (with Ted Gott and Irena Zdanowicz) William Blake in the Collection of the National Gallery of Victoria, 1989; selected paintings and prepared catalogues for following exhibitions: (with Andrew Wilton and John Gage) Turner 1775–1851, 1974; William Blake, 1978; (with Gert Schiff) William Blake, Tokyo, 1990; articles and reviews in Burlington Mag., Connoisseur, Master Drawings, Blake Qly, Blake Studies, Turner Studies. *Recreations:* music, travel. *Address:* 74c Eccleston Square, SW1V 1PJ.

BUTLIN, Robin Alan, DLitt; Principal, University College of Ripon and York St John, since 1995; *b* 31 May 1938; *s* of late Rowland Henry Butlin and Mona Butlin; *m* 1961, Norma Coroneo; two *s* one *d*. *Educ:* Liverpool Univ. (BA, MA); DLitt Loughborough, 1987. FRGS 1972. Demonstrator, University Coll. of N Staffordshire, 1961–62; Lectr in Geography, UC Dublin, 1962–71; Queen Mary College, University of London: Lectr in Geography, 1971; Sen. Lectr, 1975; Reader in Historical Geography, 1977–79; Loughborough University: Prof. of Geography, 1979–95; Hd of Dept, 1979–91; Dean, Sch. of Human and Environmental Studies, 1983–86. Vis. Associate Prof. of Geography, Univ. of Nebraska, 1969–70; Vis. Professorial Fellow and Leverhulme Res. Fellow, Wolfson Coll., Cambridge, 1986–87. *Publications:* (ed with A. R. H. Baker) Studies of Field Systems in the British Isles, 1973; (ed) The Development of the Irish Town, 1977; (ed with R. A. Dodgshon) An Historical Geography of England and Wales, 1978, 2nd edn 1990; (ed with H. S. A. Fox) Change in the Countryside: essays on rural England 1500–1900, 1979; The Transformation of Rural England c. 1580–1800, 1982; Historical Geography: through the gates of space and time, 1993. *Recreations:* music, swimming, reading. *Address:* University College of Ripon and York St John, Lord Mayor's Walk, York YO3 7EX. *T:* York (01904) 656771.

BUTROS, Prof. Albert Jamil; Istiqlal Order First Class, Jordan, 1987; Professor of English, University of Jordan, 1967–79 and since 1985; *b* 25 March 1934; *s* of Jamil Issa and Virginie Antoine (Albina); *m* 1962, Ida Maria Albina; four *d*. *Educ:* Univ. of London (BA Hons English 1958); Univ. of Exeter (BA *ad eundem* 1958); Columbia Univ. (PhD English 1963). Teacher, Amman, 1950–55; Instructor in English, Teacher's Coll., Amman, 1958–60; Lectr, Hunter Coll., City Univ., NY, 1961; Instructor, Miami Univ., Oxford, Ohio, 1962–63; University of Jordan: Asst Prof., English, 1963–65; Associate Prof., 1965–67; Acting Chm., Dept of English, 1964–67; Chm., Dept of English, 1967–73, 1974–76; Dean, Research and Graduate Studies, 1973–76; Ambassador to UK, 1987–91, and (non-res.) to Ireland, 1988–91, and to Iceland, 1990–91. Special Advr to HRH Crown Prince Hassan of Jordan, 1984–85. Dir Gen./Pres., Royal Sci. Soc., Amman, 1976–84. Vis. Prof., Ohio Wesleyan Univ., 1971–72; Sen. Res. Fellow, Internat. Develt Res. Centre, Canada, 1983–84. Member: Arab Thought Forum; World Affairs Council, Amman. Gov., Internat. Develt Res. Centre, Canada, 1986–; Mem., Bd of Trustees, Philadelphia Univ., Amman, 1995–. Fellow, World Acad. of Art and Sci., 1986. KStJ 1991. Order of Merit, Italy, 1983. *Publications:* Tales of the Caliphs, 1965; Leaders of Arab Thought, 1969; articles and translations. *Recreations:* reading, writing, translation, art, world affairs, application of science and technology to development, walking. *Address:* PO Box 309, Jubeiha, Jordan.

BUTT, Sir (Alfred) Kenneth (Dudley), 2nd Bt *cr* 1929; Underwriting Member of Lloyd's, 1931–74; farmer and bloodstock breeder; *b* 7 July 1908; *o s* of Sir Alfred Butt, 1st Bt and Lady Georgina Mary Butt (*née* Say); *S* father, 1962; *m* 1st, 1938, Kathleen Farmar (marr. diss., 1948); 2nd, 1948, Mrs Ivor Birts (*née* Bain), BA Oxon, *widow* of Lt-Col Ivor Birts, RA (killed on active service). *Educ:* Rugby; Brasenose Coll., Oxford. Lloyd's, 1929–39. Royal Artillery, 1939–45, Major RA. Chairman, Parker Wakeling & Co. Ltd, 1946–54; Managing Director, Brook Stud Co., 1962–81. Pres., Aberdeen-Angus Cattle Soc., 1968–69; Chm., Thoroughbred Breeders Assoc., 1973. *Recreations:* shooting, horse-racing, travelling, paintings. *Address:* Wheat Hill, Sandon, Buntingford, Herts SG9 0RB. *T:* Kelshall (01763) 287203. *Clubs:* Carlton, etc.

BUTT, Geoffrey Frank; Principal Assistant Solicitor, Inland Revenue, since 1993; *b* 5 May 1943; *s* of late Frank Thomas Woodman Butt and Dorothy Rosamond Butt; *m* 1972, Lee Anne Davey; two *s* one *d*. *Educ:* Royal Masonic Sch., Bushey; Univ. of Reading (BA). Solicitor 1970. Joined Solicitor's Office, HM Customs and Excise as Legal Asst, 1971; Sen. Legal Asst, 1974; Asst Solicitor, 1982; Prin. Asst Solicitor, 1986–93. *Recreations:* family life, classical music, literature and art, gardening.

BUTT, Sir Kenneth; *see* Butt, Sir A. K. D.

BUTT, Michael Acton; President and Chief Executive Officer: Mid Ocean Ltd, since 1994 (Director, since 1992; Vice Chairman, 1993); Mid Ocean Reinsurance Ltd, since 1994; Director, Phoenix Securities Ltd, since 1992; *b* Thruxton, 25 May 1942; *s* of Leslie Acton Kingsford Butt and Mina Gascoigne Butt; *m* 1st, 1964, Diana Lorraine Brook; two *s*; 2nd, 1986, Zoé Benson. *Educ:* Rugby; Magdalen Coll., Oxford (MA History); INSEAD, France (MBA 1967). Bland Welch Gp, 1964; Dir, Bland Payne Holdings, 1970; Chm., Sedgwick Ltd, 1983–87; Dep. Chm., Sedgwick Gp plc, 1985–87; Chm. and Chief Exec., Eagle Star Hldgs, 1987–91, Eagle Star Insce Co., 1987–91; Director: BAT Industries, 1987–91; Marceau Investissements, Paris, 1987–94. Board Mem., Internat. Adv. Council, INSEAD. *Recreations:* travel, tennis, opera, reading, family, the European movement. *Address:* Mid Ocean Reinsurance Co., PO Box HM 1066, Hamilton HM EX, Bermuda. *T:* (809) 2921358, *Fax:* (809) 2925226; Harrowby, 9 Cedarberry Drive, Hamilton Parish CR 04, Bermuda. *T:* (809) 2921378, *Fax:* (809) 2938511.

BUTT, Richard Bevan; Chief Executive, Rural Development Commission, since 1989; *b* 27 Feb. 1943; *s* of Roger William Bevan and Jean Mary (*née* Carter); *m* 1975, Amanda Jane Finlay; two *s*. *Educ:* Magdalen Coll., Oxford (BA Hist.); Lancaster Univ. (MA Regional Econs). Asst Principal, Min. of Housing, 1965–68; Sen. Res. Associate, Birmingham Univ., 1969–72; Consultant, 1972; HM Treasury: Principal, 1973–78; Asst Sec., 1978–86; seconded as Financial Counsellor, UK Perm. Repn to EC, 1981–84; Head of Conservation, English Heritage, 1986–89. *Recreations:* ceramics, architecture, gardening, travel. *Address:* 35 Gloucester Circus, SE10 8RY.

BUTTER, Major Sir David (Henry), KCVO 1991; MC 1941; JP; landowner and farmer; company director; HM Lord-Lieutenant of Perth and Kinross, 1975–95; *b* 18 March 1920; *s* of late Col Charles Butter, OBE, DL, JP, Pitlochry, and Agnes Marguerite (Madge), *d* of late William Clark, Newark, NJ, USA; *m* 1946, Myra Alice (CVO 1992), *d* of Hon. Maj.-Gen. Sir Harold Wernher, 3rd Bt, GCVO, TD; one *s* four *d*. *Educ:* Eton; Oxford. Served War of 1939–45: 2nd Lieut Scots Guards, 1940, Western Desert and North Africa, Sicily (Staff), 1941–43; Italy (ADC to GOC 8th Army, Gen. Sir Oliver Leese, 1944); Temp. Major, 1946; retd Army, 1948. Ensign, Queen's Body Guard for Scotland (Royal Company of Archers); Pres., Highland T&AVR, 1979–84. County Councillor, Perth, 1955–74; DL Perthshire, 1956, Vice-Lieutenant of Perth, 1960–71; HM Lieutenant of County of Perth, 1971–75, and County of Kinross, 1974–75. *Recreations:* shooting, golf, ski-ing, travel. *Address:* Cluniemore, Pitlochry, Scotland PH16 5NE. *T:* Pitlochry (01796) 2006; 64 Rutland Gate, SW7 1PJ. *T:* 0171–589 6731. *Clubs:* Turf; Royal and Ancient (St Andrews).

See also Lord Ramsay.

BUTTER, John Henry, CMG 1962; MBE 1946; Financial Director to Government of Abu Dhabi, 1970–83; *b* 20 April 1916; *s* of late Captain A. E. Butter, CMG, and late Mrs Baird; *m* 1950, Joyce Platt; three *s*. *Educ:* Charterhouse; Christ Church, Oxford. Indian Civil Service, 1939–47; Pakistan Admin. Service, 1947–50 (served in Punjab, except for period 1942–46 when was Asst to Political Agent, Imphal, Manipur State). HM Overseas Civil Service, Kenya, 1950–65 (Perm. Sec. to the Treasury, 1959–65); Financial Adviser, Kenya Treasury, 1965–69. *Publication:* Uncivil Servant, 1989. *Recreations:* golf, bridge. *Address:* PO Box 30181, Nairobi, Kenya; Whitehill, Gordon, Berwickshire TD3 6LQ. *Club:* East India.

See also Prof. P. H. Butter.

BUTTER, Neil (McLaren), QC 1976; **His Honour Judge Butter;** a Circuit Judge, since 1982; a Judge of Central London County Court, since 1994; *b* 10 May 1933; *y s* of late Andrew Butter, MA, MD and late Ena Butter, MB, ChB; *m* 1974, Claire Marianne Miskin. *Educ:* The Leys Sch.; Queens' Coll., Cambridge (MA). Called to Bar, Inner Temple, 1955, Bencher, 1994; an Asst and Dep. Recorder of Bournemouth, 1971; Recorder of the Crown Court, 1972–82; a Judge of Bow County Court, 1986–94. Member: Senate of the Inns of Court and the Bar, 1976–79; County Court Rule Cttee, 1993–. Inspector, for Dept of Trade, Ozalid Gp Hldgs Ltd, 1977–79. A Legal Assessor to GMC and GDC, 1979–82; Mem., Mental Health Review Tribunal, 1983–92. Trustee, Kingdon-Ward Speech Therapy Trust, 1980–87. *Recreations:* motoring, holidays, browsing through Who's Who. *Address:* c/o 3 Serjeants' Inn, EC4Y 1BQ. *Club:* Royal Over-Seas League.

BUTTER, Prof. Peter Herbert; Regius Professor of English, Glasgow University, 1965–86; *b* 7 April 1921; *s* of Archibald Butter, CMG, and Helen Cicely (*née* Kerr); *m* 1958, Bridget Younger; one *s* two *d*. *Educ:* Charterhouse; Balliol Coll., Oxford. Served in RA, 1941–46. Assistant, 1948, Lecturer, 1951, in English, Univ. of Edinburgh; Professor of English, Queen's Univ., Belfast, 1958–65. *Publications:* Shelley's Idols of the Cave, 1954; Francis Thompson, 1961; Edwin Muir, 1962; Edwin Muir: Man and Poet, 1966; (ed) Shelley's Alastor and Other Poems, 1971; (ed) Selected Letters of Edwin Muir, 1974; (ed) Selected Poems of William Blake, 1982; (ed) The Truth of Imagination: uncollected prose of Edwin Muir, 1988; (ed) Complete Poems of Edwin Muir, 1992; articles in periodicals. *Address:* Ashfield, Bridge of Weir, Renfrewshire PA11 3AW. *T:* Bridge of Weir (01505) 613139. *Club:* New (Edinburgh).

See also J. H. Butter.

BUTTER, Peter Joseph Michael, CB 1992; Deputy Managing Director, Property Services Agency, Building Management, Department of the Environment, 1992, retired; *b* 9 Dec. 1932; *s* of Joseph Butter and Kathleen (*née* Woodward); *m* 1956, Pamela Frances Roberts; three *s*. *Educ:* Brighton, Hove and Sussex Grammar School. Served Royal Signals, 1951–53. BR, 1953–67; Principal, Min. of Transport, 1967–73; Private Sec. to Minister of Transport, 1973; joined PSA, 1974: Hd, Defence Secretariat (Navy), 1974–79; Asst Dir, Estate Surveying Services, 1979–84; Dir, SE Region, 1984–88; Dir, Home Regional Services, 1988–90; Dir. of Ops, PSA, Bldg Management, DoE, 1990–91. *Recreations:* cricket umpiring, listening to music, exploring Britain. *Address:* 88 Bridger Way, Crowborough, East Sussex TN6 2XE. *Club:* Sussex CC.

BUTTERFIELD, family name of **Baron Butterfield.**

BUTTERFIELD, Baron *cr* 1988 (Life Peer), of Stechford in the County of West Midlands; **William John Hughes Butterfield;** Kt 1978; OBE 1953; DM; FRCP; Regius Professor of Physic, University of Cambridge, 1976–87 (Deputy, since 1987); Master of Downing College, Cambridge, 1978–87; *b* 28 March 1920; *s* of late William Hughes Butterfield and of Mrs Doris North; *m* 1st, 1946, Ann Sanders (decd); one *s*; 2nd, 1950, Isabel-Ann Foster Kennedy; two *s* one *d*. *Educ:* Solihull Sch.; Exeter Coll., Oxford (DM 1968; Hon. Fellow, 1978); Johns Hopkins Univ. (MD 1951); MA, MD Cantab 1975. Repr. Oxford Univ.: Rugby football, *v* Cambridge, 1940–41; hockey, 1940–42 (Captain); cricket, 1942 (Captain). Member, Scientific Staff, Medical Research Council, 1946–58: Major RAMC, Army Operational Research Group, 1947–50; Research Fellow, Medical Coll. of Virginia, Richmond, Va, USA, 1950–52; seconded to Min. of Supply, 1952; seconded to AEA, 1956; Prof. of Experimental Medicine, Guy's Hospital, 1958–63; Prof. of Medicine, Guy's Hosp. Med. Sch., and Additional Physician, Guy's Hosp., 1963–71; Vice-Chancellor, Nottingham Univ., 1971–75; Professorial Fellow, Downing Coll., Cambridge, 1975–78; Vice-Chancellor, Cambridge Univ., 1983–85. Chairman: Bedford Diabetic Survey, 1962; Woolwich/Erith New Town Medical Liaison Cttee, 1965–71; SE Met. Reg. Hospital Board's Clinical Research Cttee, 1960–71; Scientific Advisory Panel, Army Personnel Research Cttee, 1970–76; Council for the Education and Training of Health Visitors, 1971–76; East Midlands Economic Planning Council, 1974–75; Medicines Commn, 1976–81; Member: UGC Medical Sub-Cttee, 1966–71; Council, British Diabetic Assoc., 1963–74 (Chm. 1967–74, Vice-Pres. 1974–); DHSS Cttee on Medical Aspects of Food Policy, 1964–80; DHSS Panel on Medical Research, 1974–76; MRC Cttee on General Epidemiology, 1965–74; MRC Clinical Res. Grants Bd, 1969–71; MRC, 1976–80; Anglo-Soviet Consultative Cttee; Minister of Health's Long Term Study Group; Health Educn Council, DHSS, 1973–77; Trent RHA, 1973–75; IUC Council and Exec. Cttee, 1973–; British Council Med. Adv. Cttee, 1971–80; Northwick Park Adv. Cttee, 1971–76; Council, European Assoc. for Study of Diabetes, 1968–71 (Vice-Pres.); Hong Kong Univ. and Polytechnic Grants Cttee, 1975–83; House of Lords Sci. of Technology Cttee, 1987–88; St George's House Council, 1987–. Chairman: Jardine Educnl Trust, 1982–; Health Promotion Res. Trust, 1983–; Croucher Foundn, Hong Kong, 1989– (Trustee, 1979–89); GB-Sasakawa Foundn, 1992– (Trustee, 1985–92); Trustee, Ely Cathedral, 1986. Consultant, WHO Expert Cttee on Diabetes, 1964–80; Visitor, King Edward's Hospital Fund, 1964–71; Examiner in Medicine: Oxford Univ., 1960–66; Univ. of E Africa, 1966; Cambridge Univ., 1967–75; Pfizer Vis. Professor, NZ and Australia, 1965; Visiting Professor: Yale, 1966; Harvard, 1978. Rock Carling Fellow, RCP, 1968; Lectures: Oliver-Sharpey, RCP, 1967; Banting, BDA, 1970; Linacre, Cambridge, 1979; Roberts, Med. Soc. of London, 1981; Clayesmore, Blandford Forum, 1983; Northcott, Exeter, 1984; Cohen, Hebrew Univ. of Jerusalem, 1985. Dir, Prudential Corp., 1981–92. Member: Editorial Board, Diabetaloga, 1964–69; Jl Chronic Diseases, 1968–. Hon. Fellow: NY Acad. Science, 1962; NY Acad. of Medicine, 1987; Hughes Hall, Cambridge, 1988; Hon. FDS RCS, 1992; Corres. FACP, 1973. Hon. Med. Adviser, Leeds Castle. Patron, Richmond Soc., 1968–71. FRSA 1971. Hon. LLD Nottingham, 1977; Hon. DMedSci Keio Univ., Tokyo, 1983. Hon. DSc, Florida Internat. Univ., Miami, 1985; Hon. MD Chinese Univ., Hong Kong, 1989. *Publications:* (jointly) On Burns, 1953; Tolbutamide after 10 years, 1967; Priorities in Medicine, 1968; Health and Sickness: the choice of treatment, 1971; (ed) International Dictionary of Medicine and Biology, 1986; over 100 contribs to med. and allied literature incl. books, chapters, official reports and articles on diabetes, health care and educnl topics. *Recreations:* tennis (not lawn), cricket (village) and talking (too much). *Address:* 39 Clarendon Street, Cambridge CB1 1JX. *T:* Cambridge (01223) 328854. *Clubs:* Athenæum, MCC, Queen's; CURUFC (Pres., 1984–); CUCC (Pres., 1979–90).

BUTTERFIELD, Hon. Sir Alexander Neil Logie, Kt 1995; **Hon. Mr Justice Butterfield;** a Judge of the High Court of Justice, Queen's Bench Division, since 1995. *Educ:* Sidney Sussex Coll., Cambridge (BA 1964). Called to the Bar, Inner Temple, 1965; a Recorder, 1978–95; QC 1985. *Address:* Royal Courts of Justice, Strand, WC2A 2LL.

BUTTERFIELD, Charles Harris, QC (Singapore) 1952; HMOCS, retired; *b* 28 June 1911; 2nd *s* of William Arthur Butterfield, OBE, and Rebecca Butterfield; *m* 1st, 1938, Monica, *d* of Austin Harrison, London; one *d*; 2nd, by special permission of the Holy See, Ellen, *d* of Ernest John Bennett, Singapore and *widow* of J. E. King, Kuala Lumpur, Singapore and Hooe. *Educ:* Downside; Trinity Coll., Cambridge. Barrister-at-law, Middle Temple, 1934. Entered Colonial Legal Service, 1938; Crown Counsel, Straits Settlements, 1938. Served Singapore RA (Volunteer) and RA, 1941–46; POW, 1942–45. Solicitor-General, Singapore, 1948–55, Attorney-General, 1955–57; Legal Adviser's Dept CRO and FCO, 1959–69; DoE and Sec. of State's Panel of Inspectors (Planning), 1969–74. *Recreations:* beagling, swimming, walking. *Address:* 18 Kewhurst Avenue, Cooden, Bexhill on Sea, E Sussex TN39 3BJ.

BUTTERFIELD, John Michael; Chief Executive, National Association of Youth Clubs, 1975–86; *b* 2 July 1926; *s* of late John Leslie Butterfield and Hilda Mary Butterfield (*née* Judson); *m* 1955, Mary Maureen, *d* of John Martin; one *s* twin *d* (and one *s* decd). *Educ:* Leeds Modern Sch.; Leeds Univ. John Butterfield & Son, Leeds, 1949–60; John Atkinson & Sons (Sowerby Bridge) Ltd, 1960–61. Youth Officer, Coventry Cathedral, 1961–68; Liverpool Council of Social Service: Head of Youth and Community Dept, 1968–72; Operations Dir, 1972–75. Mem., BCC, 1954–73 (Mem., 1952–68; Chm., Exec. Cttee, 1962–67, Youth Dept); Vice-Chairman: Nat. Council for Voluntary Youth Services, 1977–83; UK Adv. Cttee, SCF, 1990–93; Chairman: Leics Council of Voluntary Youth Services, 1985–; Youthaid, 1986–90; Youth Club Leics, 1987–. Merseyside Advr, Baring Foundn, 1987–; UK Rep., Amer. Youth Work Center, 1987–. *Recreations:* music, reading, walking, railways. *Address:* 4 Church Farm Court, Aston Flamville, near Hinckley, Leics LE10 3AF. *T:* Hinckley (01455) 611027.

BUTTERFILL, John Valentine; MP (C) Bournemouth West, since 1983; *b* 14 Feb. 1941; *s* of George Thomas Butterfill and Elsie Amelia (*née* Watts); *m* 1965, Pamela Ross-Symons; one *s* three *d*. *Educ:* Caterham Sch.; Coll. of Estate Management. FRICS 1974. Valuer, Jones, Lang, Wootton, 1961–64; Sen. Exec., Hammerson Gp, 1964–69; Dir, Audley Properties Ltd (Bovis Gp), 1969–71; Man. Dir, St Paul's Securities Gp, 1971–76; Sen. Partner, Curchod & Co., 1977–91. Chm., Conservation Investments, 1984–; Director: Micro Business Systems, 1977–79; John Lelliott Developments, 1984–88; ISLEF Building and Construction, 1984–91; Pavilion Services Gp, 1992–94. Pres., European Property Associates, 1979–. Parliamentary Private Secretary: to Sec. of State for Energy, 1988–89; to Sec. of State for Transport, 1989–90; to Minister of State for NI, 1991–92. Mem., Trade and Industry Select Cttee, 1992–; Vice-Chairman: Backbench Tourism Cttee, 1986–88; Backbench Finance Cttee, 1992–; Backbench Europ. Affairs Cttee, 1992–; Sec., Backbench Trade and Industry Cttee, 1987–88, and 1991; Chm., All Party Gp on Occupational Pensions, 1992–; Vice Pres., Cons. Gp for Europe, 1992– (Chm., 1989–92). Mem., Council of Management, PDSA, 1990–. *Publications:* occasional contribs to property, insurance and financial publications. *Recreations:* ski-ing, riding, tennis, bridge, music. *Address:* House of Commons, SW1A 0AA. *Club:* Carlton.

BUTTERSS, Rt. Rev. Robert Leopold; Bishop of the Eastern Region (Assistant Bishop of the Diocese of Melbourne), 1985–94; *b* 17 Jan. 1931; *s* of A. L. Butterss; *m* 1956, Margaret (*née* Hayman); two *s* one *d*. *Educ:* Haileybury; Brighton and Ridley Coll., Melbourne. Ordained: deacon, 1955; priest, 1956; Curate, St Andrew's, Brighton, 1955–56; Vicar, Holy Trinity, Lara, 1956–60; Priest in charge, Popondetta, PNG, 1960–64; Vicar: Holy Trinity, Pascoe Vale, 1964–66; St Stephen's, Mt Waverley, 1970–76; Canon, St Peter and St Paul's Cathedral, PNG, 1976–83; Dean, St John's Cathedral, Brisbane, 1983–85. Chm., Australian Bd of Missions, Sydney, 1976–83. *Recreation:* music. *Address:* Dayspring, Stroud, NSW 2425, Australia.

BUTTERWORTH, family name of **Baron Butterworth.**

BUTTERWORTH, Baron *cr* 1985 (Life Peer), of Warwick in the County of Warwickshire; **John Blackstock Butterworth,** CBE 1982; JP; DL; Vice-Chancellor, University of Warwick, 1963–85; *b* 13 March 1918; *o s* of John William and Florence Butterworth; *m* 1948, Doris Crawford Elder; one *s* two *d*. *Educ:* Queen Elizabeth's Grammar Sch., Mansfield; The Queen's Coll., Oxford. Royal Artillery, 1939–46. MA 1946. Called to Bar, Lincoln's Inn, 1947, Hon. Bencher, 1989. New Coll., Oxford: Fellow, 1946–63; Dean, 1952–56; Bursar, 1956–63; Sub Warden, 1957–58. Junior Proctor, 1950–51; Faculty Fellow of Nuffield Coll., 1953–58; Member of Hebdomadal Council, Oxford Univ., 1953–63. Managing Trustee 1964–85, Trustee, 1985–, Nuffield Foundation; Chairman: Inter-Univ. Council for Higher Educn Overseas, 1968–77; Universities Cttee for Non-teaching Staffs, 1970–85; Inquiry into work of Probation Officers and Social Workers in Local Authorities and Nat. Service, 1971–73; Standing Cttee on Internat. Co-operation in Higher Educn, British Council, 1981–85; Inter-Univ. and Polytechnic Council, 1981–85; Council, Foundn for Sci. and Technol., 1990–. Univ. Comr (Under Educn Reform Act 1988), 1988–; Member: Royal Commn on the Working of the Tribunals of Inquiry (Act), 1921, 1966; Intergovernmental Cttee on Law of Contempt in relation to Tribunals of Inquiry, 1968; Jarratt Cttee on University Efficiency, 1986; Cttee on the review of UGC, 1987; Noise Advisory Council, 1974–81; Bd, British Council 1981–85; British delegn to Commonwealth Educn Conferences in Lagos, 1968, Canberra, 1971, Kingston, 1974, Accra, 1977, Colombo, 1980. Governor, Royal Shakespeare Theatre, 1964–. DL Warwickshire, 1967–74, DL West Midlands 1974–; JP City of Oxford, 1962, Coventry, 1963–. Hon. DCL Univ. of Sierra Leone, 1976; Hon. DSc Univ. of Aston, 1985; Hon. LLD Warwick, 1986. *Address:* The Barn, Barton, Guiting Power, Glos GL54 5US. *T:* Guiting Power (01451) 850297. *Club:* Athenæum.

See also Hon. A. E. B. Walker.

BUTTERWORTH, Prof. Anthony Edward, PhD; FRS 1994; MRC External Scientific Staff, since 1979; Hon. Professor of Medical Parasitology, University of Cambridge, since 1994; *b* 8 July 1945; *s* of Edward Alexander Butterworth and Sylvia (*née* Hardy); *m* 1972, Margot Lois Hudson (separated 1987); one *s* one *d*. *Educ:* Harrow Sch.; Trinity Hall, Cambridge (BA); St Mary's Hosp. Med. Sch., London (MB, BChir); Clare Coll., Cambridge (PhD). Wellcome Trust Research Fellow: Nairobi, Kenya, 1973–77; Harvard Med. Sch., Boston, 1977–79; University of Cambridge: Associate Lectr, 1980–89; Hon. Reader, 1989–93. Frederick Murgatroyd Prize, RCP, 1979; Bernhard Nocht Medal, 1987; King Faisal Internat. Prize in Medicine, 1990; Chalmers Medal, RSTM&H, 1990. *Publications:* papers and book chapters on immunology and parasitology. *Recreations:* travel, bird-watching, sailing, ski-ing. *Address:* Department of Pathology, Tennis Court Road, Cambridge CB2 1QP. *T:* Cambridge (01223) 333741.

BUTTERWORTH, Prof. George Esmond, DPhil; Professor of Psychology, University of Sussex, since 1991; *b* 8 Nov. 1946; *s* of late Reginald Esmond Butterworth and of Helen Butterworth; *m* 1st, 1970, Jonquil Delia Sandra Hale (*d* 1982); one *s* one *d*; 2nd, 1992, Margaret Harris; one *d*. *Educ:* Southern GS for Boys, Portsmouth; NE London Poly. (BSc London Ext. Psych.); Univ. of Birmingham (MSc Clinical Psych.); St John's Coll., Oxford (DPhil). FBPsS. Lectr and Sen. Lectr, Univ. of Southampton, 1974–85; Prof. of Psychology, Univ. of Stirling, 1985–91. Dist. Vis. Res. Fellow, La Trobe Univ., 1993. Editor, British Jl of Developmental Psych., 1988–94. *Publications:* (ed) The child's representation of the world, 1977; (ed) Infancy and epistemology, 1981; (ed jtly) Social cognition, 1982; (ed jtly) Evolution and developmental psychology, 1985; (ed) Infancy, 1985; (ed jtly) Causes of development, 1990; (ed jtly) Perspectives on the child's theory of mind, 1991; (jtly) Michotte's experimental phenomenology of perception, 1991; (ed jtly) Context and cognition, 1992; (with M. Harris) Principles of developmental psychology, 1994; papers in learned jls. *Recreation:* antique shops. *Address:* Division of Psychology, University of Sussex, Brighton, E Sussex BN1 9QN. *T:* Brighton (01273) 678501.

BUTTERWORTH, Henry, CEng, MIMechE; retired; Managing Director, Ammunition Division, (formerly Director General (Ammunition)), Royal Ordnance plc (formerly Royal Ordnance Factories), 1979–88; Chairman, Royal Ordnance (Speciality Metals) Ltd, 1986–88; *b* 21 Jan. 1926; *s* of late Henry and Wilhemena Butterworth; *m* 1948, Ann Smith; two *s*. *Educ:* St Mary's, Leyland, Lancs. DipProd Birmingham. Apprenticeship, 1940–47; Draughtsman, 1947–52; Technical Asst, 1952–53; progressively, Shop Manager, Asst Manager, Manager, 1953–71; Director ROF: Cardiff, Burghfield, Glascoed, 1971–79. *Recreation:* coarse fishing. *Address:* 5 Vicarsfield Road, Worden Park, Leyland, Lancs PR5 2BH. *T:* Leyland (01772) 436073.

BUTTERWORTH, Prof. Ian, CBE 1984; FRS 1981; Senior Research Fellow, Imperial College, since 1991; Professor of Physics, University of London, 1971–91, now Emeritus; *b* 3 Dec. 1930; *s* of Harry and Beatrice Butterworth; *m* 1964, Mary Therese (*née* Gough);

one *d*. *Educ:* Bolton County Grammar Sch.; Univ. of Manchester. BSc 1951; PhD 1954. Sen. Scientific Officer, UK Atomic Energy Authority, 1954–58; Lectr, Imperial Coll., 1958–64; Vis. Physicist, Lawrence Radiation Laboratory, Univ. of California, 1964–65; Sen. Lectr, Imperial Coll., 1965–68; Group Leader, Bubble Chamber Research Gp, Rutherford High Energy Laboratory, 1968–71; Professor, 1971–86, Head of Dept, 1980–83, Dept of Physics, Imperial Coll.; on leave of absence as Res. Dir, CERN, 1983–86; Principal, QMC, then QMW, 1986–91; Pro Vice-Chancellor for Eur. Affairs, London Univ., 1989–91. Science and Engineering Research Council (formerly Science Research Council): Mem., 1979–83 (Mem., Nuclear Physics Bd, 1972–75 and 1978–83, Chm., 1979–83; Mem., Particle Physics Cttee, 1978–79; Chm., Film Analysis Grants Cttee, 1972–75); UK deleg. on Council, CERN, 1979–82 (Mem., Research Bd, 1976–82; Chm., Super Proton Synchrotron Cttee, 1976–79). Member: Physics Res. Cttee, Deutsches Elektronen Synchroton, Hamburg, 1981–85; Sci. Policy Cttee, Stanford Linear Accelerator Center, Calif, 1984–88; Sci. Adv. Cttee, British Council, 1986–; Academia Europaea, 1989; Council Member: Royal Soc., 1989–90; Inst. of Physics, 1989–92 (Vice Pres., 1993–; Chm., IOP Publishing Ltd, 1993–); Hon. Mem., Manchester Lit. and Phil. Soc., 1987. Fellow, Imperial Coll., 1988. Dr *hc* Soka Univ., 1989. Glazebrook Prize and Medal, Inst. of Physics, 1993. *Publications:* numerous papers in learned jls (on experimental particle physics). *Recreations:* reading, history of art. *Address:* Blackett Laboratory, Imperial College, Prince Consort Road, SW7 2AZ; 1 Pierhead, Wapping High Street, E1 9PN.

BUTTFIELD, Dame Nancy (Eileen), DBE 1972; formerly Senator for South Australia; *b* 12 Nov. 1912; *d* of Sir Edward Wheewall Holden and Hilda May Lavis; *m* 1936, Frank Charles Buttfield; two *s*. *Educ:* Woodlands Church of England Girls' Grammar Sch., Adelaide; Composenea; Paris; Univ. of Adelaide, SA. Senator for South Australia, Oct. 1955–June 1965, re-elected July 1968–74. Exec. Mem., Commonwealth Immigration Adv. Council, 1955–; Vice-President: Good Neighbour Council of SA, 1956–62; Phoenix Soc. for the Physically Handicapped, 1959–. Dir, Co-operative Building Soc. of SA, 1959–. Mem. Council, Bedford Industries, 1965–. Mem., Nat. Council of Women of SA. *Recreations:* farming, dress-making, gourmet cooking, music. *Address:* 52 Strangeways Terrace, North Adelaide, SA 5006, Australia. *Clubs:* Queen Adelaide, Lyceum, Royal Adelaide Golf (all SA).

BUTTLE, Eileen, CBE 1995; PhD; FIBiol; Director, World Humanity Action Trust, since 1994; *b* 19 Oct. 1937; *d* of late George Ernest Linford and of Mary Stewart Linford; *m* 1970, Hugh Langley Buttle. *Educ:* Harrow Weald County Grammar Sch.; Univ. of Southampton (BSc (Hons); PhD). FIBiol 1990. Post-doctoral Res. Fellow, Univ. of Southampton, 1963–65; Research Scientist: Nat. Inst. of Res. in Dairying, 1965–71; Cattle Breeding Centre, MAFF, 1971–76; Policy Administrator, MAFF, 1976–89; Sec., NERC, 1989–94. Vis. Fellow, Green Coll., Oxford. Member: Scientific Cttee, European Envmt Agency; Planning and Resources Bd, BBSRC. Trustee: Buckland Foundn; Horniman Mus. of Gdns. *Recreations:* golf, fly fishing. *Address:* Willows Farm, Cleverton, Chippenham, Wilts SN15 5BT. *T:* Malmesbury (01666) 825618. *Club:* Farmers'.

BUTTON, Henry George; author; *b* 11 Aug. 1913; *e s* of late Rev. Frank S. and Bertha B. Button; *m* 1938, Edith Margaret Heslop (*d* 1972); two *d*. *Educ:* Manchester Grammar Sch.; Christ's Coll., Cambridge (Scholar). Mod. and Medieval Langs Tripos, Part II, 1st Class (with dist.) 1934; MLitt 1977; Tiarks German Scholar (research at Univ. of Bonn), 1934–35; Sen. Studentship of Goldsmiths' Company, 1935–36. Entered Civil Service, 1937; Board of Trade, 1937–57 (served in Min. of Production, 1942; Counsellor, UK Delegn to OEEC, Paris, 1952–55; on staff of Monopolies Commn, 1955–56); transf. Min. of Agriculture, Fisheries and Food, 1957; Under-Sec., Min. of Agriculture, Fisheries and Food, 1960–73 (Principal Finance Officer, 1965–73). Res. Student, 1974–76, Fellow-Commoner, 1982–, Christ's Coll., Cambridge. Mem. Agricultural Research Council, 1960–62. Leader of various UK Delegns to FAO in Rome. BBC Brain of Britain for 1962; rep. Great Britain in radio quiz in Johannesburg, 1966; Bob Dyer's TV show, Sydney, 1967. *Publications:* The Guinness Book of the Business World (with A. Lampert), 1976; contribs to various jls both learned and unlearned, and to newspapers. *Recreations:* reading, writing, studying old businesses (hon. review ed., Business Archives Council, 1966–75; Hon. Sec., Tercentenarians' Club, 1969–), showing visitors round the colleges. *Address:* 7 Amhurst Court, Grange Road, Cambridge CB3 9BH. *T:* Cambridge (01223) 355698. *Club:* Civil Service.

See also Air Marshal Sir T. Garden.

BUTTRESS, Donald Reeve, FSA; architect; Partner, Buttress Fuller Alsop, Manchester, since 1974; Surveyor of the Fabric of Westminster Abbey, since 1988; *b* 27 April 1932; *s* of Edward Crossley Buttress and Evelyn Edna Reeve-Whaley; *m* 1956, Elsa Mary Bardsley; two *s* three *d*. *Educ:* Stockport Sch.; Univ. of Manchester (MA, DipArch). ARIBA. Flying Officer, RAF, 1958–61. Lectr, Manchester Univ., 1964–78; Vis. Prof. and Fulbright Travelling Scholar, Univ. of Florida, 1967–68. Architect to: Bangor and Sheffield Cathedrals, 1978–88; Leeds (RC) Cathedral, 1983–; Llandaff Cathedral, 1986–; Surveyor to the Fabric, Chichester Cathedral, 1985–. Principal works: Stockport SS Community Centre, 1973; extn, St Matthew, Hayfield, 1978; St George's Chapel, Sheffield Cathedral, 1981; rebldg, St Matthew, Westminster, 1982; repair of spire, All Souls, Halifax, 1984; repair of nave and North transept, Chichester Cath., 1985–95; reconstruction, Tonbridge Sch. Chapel, 1992–95; restoration of West front and Henry VII Chapel, Westminster Abbey, 1989–95. Member: Cathedrals and Churches Adv. Cttee (formerly Churches Sub-Cttee, English Heritage), 1988–94; Council for the Care of Churches, 1976–86, 1991–; Council, Royal Archaeological Inst., 1991–94; Chester Dio. Adv. Cttee, 1970–88. President: Ecclesiol Soc., 1995– (Vice Pres., 1992–95); Surveyors' Club, 1994–95. Brother, Art Workers' Guild, 1989. Mem., Editl Bd, Church Building magazine, 1982–. *Publications:* Manchester Buildings, 1967; Gawthorpe Hall (NT guide), 1971; articles in learned jls. *Recreations:* ecclesiology, 18th Century furniture, stained glass, heraldry. *Address:* 2B Little Cloister, Westminster Abbey, SW1P 3PA. *T:* 0171–799 6893; 95 Fishpool Street, St Albans AL3 4RU. *Club:* Royal Air Force.

BUTTREY, Prof. Theodore Vern, PhD; Keeper, Department of Coins, Fitzwilliam Museum, Cambridge, 1988–91, now Keeper Emeritus; *b* 29 Dec. 1929; *s* of Theodore Vern Buttrey and Ruth Jeanette Scoutt; *m* 1st, 1954, Marisa Macina (marr. diss. 1967); three *s* one *d*; 2nd, 1967, Ann Elizabeth Johnston. *Educ:* Phillips Exeter Acad.; Princeton Univ. (BA 1950; PhD 1953). Instr, 1954–58, Asst Prof., 1958–64, Yale Univ.; University of Michigan: Associate Professor, 1964–67; Prof. of Greek and Latin, 1967–85; Prof. Emeritus, 1985–; Chm., Dept of Classical Studies, 1968–71, 1983–84; Dir, Kelsey Mus. of Archaeology, 1969–71. Member: Clare Hall, Cambridge, 1971–; Faculty of Classics, Cambridge Univ., 1975–. Pres., RNS, 1989–94; Sec., UK Numismatic Trust, 1994–. Medal, RNS, 1985. *Publications:* (jtly) Greek, Roman and Islamic Coins from Sardis, 1981; (jtly) Morgantina Studies: the coins, 1989; numerous publications in ancient and modern numismatics. *Recreations:* Ernest Bramah, P. G. Wodehouse, travel. *Address:* 6 de Freville Avenue, Cambridge CB4 1HR. *T:* Cambridge (01223) 351156.

BUXTON, family name of **Barons Buxton of Alsa** and **Noel-Buxton.**

BUXTON OF ALSA, Baron *cr* 1978 (Life Peer), of Stiffkey in the County of Norfolk; **Aubrey Leland Oakes Buxton,** MC 1943; DL; Director, Anglia Television, since 1958 (Chairman, 1986–88); *b* 15 July 1918; *s* of Leland Wilberforce Buxton and Mary, *d* of Rev. Thomas Henry Oakes; *m* 1st, 1946, Pamela Mary (*d* 1983), *d* of Sir Henry Birkin, 3rd Bt; two *s* four *d*; 2nd, 1988, Mrs Kathleen Peterson, Maine, USA. *Educ:* Ampleforth; Trinity Coll., Cambridge. Served 1939–45, RA; combined ops in Arakan, 1942–45 (despatches, 1944). Extra Equerry to Duke of Edinburgh. A Trustee of the British Museum (Natural History), 1971–73. Member: Countryside Commn, 1968–72; Royal Commission on Environmental Pollution, 1970–74; British Vice Pres., World Wildlife Fund; Trustee, Wildfowl Trust; Treasurer, London Zoological Soc., 1978–83; Former Pres., Royal Television Soc.; Chairman: Independent Television Cos Assoc., 1972–75; UPITN Inc., USA, 1981–83; ITN, 1981–86. Wildlife Film Producer, Anglia TV. Golden Awards, Internat. TV Festival, 1963 and 1968; Silver Medal, Zoological Society of London, 1967; Silver Medal, Royal TV Society, 1968; Queen's Award to Industry, 1974; Gold Medal, Royal TV Soc., 1977. High Sheriff of Essex 1972; DL Essex, 1975–85. *Publications:* (with Sir Philip Christison) The Birds of Arakan, 1946; The King in his Country, 1955. *Recreations:* travel, natural history, painting, sport. *Address:* Old Hall Farm, Stiffkey, Norfolk NR23 1QJ. *Club:* White's.

BUXTON, Adrian Clarence, CMG 1978; HM Diplomatic Service, retired; Ambassador to Bolivia, 1977–81, and to Ecuador, 1981–85; *b* 12 June 1925; *s* of Clarence Buxton and Dorothy (*née* Lintott); *m* 1st, 1958, Leonora Mary Cherkas (*d* 1984); three *s*; 2nd, 1985, June Samson. *Educ:* Christ's Hosp., Horsham; Trinity Coll., Cambridge. RNVR, 1944–46; FO, 1947; Bangkok, 1948–52; FO, 1952–53; Khartoum, 1953–55; Bonn, 1955–58; Bogota, 1958–62; FO, 1962–64; Saigon, 1964–67; Havana, 1967–69; Geneva, 1969–73; sabbatical, Univ. of Surrey, 1973–74; FCO, 1974–77. *Recreations:* golf, choral singing. *Address:* 7 Grove Road, Merrow, Guildford, Surrey GU1 2HR.

BUXTON, Andrew Robert Fowell; Chairman, Barclays Bank PLC, since 1992; *b* 5 April 1939; *m* 1965, Jane Margery Grant; two *d*. *Educ:* Winchester Coll.; Pembroke Coll., Oxford. Joined Barclays Bank Ltd, 1963; Dir, Barclays Bank UK Ltd, 1978; Barclays Bank PLC: Gen. Manager, 1980; Vice-Chm., 1984–91; Man. Dir, 1988–92; Dep. Chm., 1991–92; Chief Exec., 1992–93. *Club:* Royal Automobile.

BUXTON, Prof. John Noel, FBCS; CEng; Chairman, Room Underwriting Systems Ltd, since 1993; Professor of Information Technology, King's College, London, 1984–94; *b* 25 Dec. 1933; *s* of John William Buxton and Laura Frances Buxton; *m* 1958, Moira Jean O'Brien; two *s* two *d*. *Educ:* Bradford Grammar Sch.; Trinity Coll., Cambridge (BA 1955, MA 1959). FBCS 1968. Flight Trials Engr, De Havilland Propellers, 1955–59; Ops Res. Scientist, British Iron and Steel Res. Assoc., 1959–60; Applied Science Rep., IBM UK, 1960–62; Lectr, Inst. of Computer Science, Univ. of London, 1962–66; Chief Software Consultant, CEIR (now Scicon Ltd) 1966–68; Prof. of Computer Science, Univ. of Warwick, 1968–84. UNDP Proj. Manager, Internat. Computing Educn Centre, Budapest, 1975–77; Vis. Scholar, Harvard Univ., 1979–80; Dir of Systems Engrng, DTI, 1989–91 (on secondment). *Publications:* (ed) Simulation Programming Languages, 1968; (ed jtly) Software Engineering Concepts and Techniques (Procs of NATO Confs 1968 and 1969), 1976; (jtly) The Craft of Software Engineering, 1987; three computer programming languages; papers in professional jls. *Recreations:* mountaineering, music, ancient houses. *Address:* Bull's Hall, Yaxley, near Eye, Suffolk IP23 8BZ.

BUXTON, Hon. Margaret Evelyn; *see* Aston, Hon. M. E.

BUXTON, Prof. Neil Keith; Vice-Chancellor, University of Hertfordshire (formerly Director, Hatfield Polytechnic), since 1987; *b* 2 May 1940; *s* of William F. A. Buxton and Janet A. Buxton; *m* 1962, Margaret G. Buxton (*née* Miller); two *s* one *d*. *Educ:* Aberdeen Univ. (MA Hons Political Econs); PhD Heriot-Watt. Asst Lectr, Dept of Political Econ., Aberdeen Univ., 1962–64; Lectr, Dept of Econ., Univ. of Hull, 1964–69; Lectr and Sen. Lectr, 1969–78, Prof., 1979–83, Heriot-Watt Univ.; Depute Dir, Glasgow Coll. of Technology, 1983–87. Vis. Prof. in Econs and Public Admin, Lewis and Clark Coll., Oregon, 1982. Dir, Herts TEC; Mem. Bd, Businesslink, Herts. *Publications:* (with T. L. Johnston and D. Mair) Structure and Growth of the Scottish Economy, 1971; (with D. I. Mackay) British Employment Statistics, 1977; Economic Development of the British Coal Industry, 1978; (ed) British Industry Between the Wars, 1979; articles in professional jls. *Recreations:* hockey, swimming, bridge. *Address:* University of Hertfordshire, College Lane, Hatfield, Herts AL10 9AB. *T:* Hatfield (01707) 284000.

BUXTON, Paul William Jex; Northern Ireland Office, 1974–85 (Under Secretary, 1981–85); *b* 20 Sept. 1925; *s* of of late Denis Buxton and Emily Buxton (*née* Hollins); *m* 1st, 1950, Katharine Hull (marr. diss. 1971, she *d* 1977); two *s* one *d*; 2nd, 1971, Hon. Margaret Aston (*née* Bridges) (*see* M. E. Aston); two *d*. *Educ:* Rugby Sch.; Balliol Coll., Oxford (MA). Coldstream Guards, 1944–47. HM Foreign, later Diplomatic, Service, 1950–71; served Delhi, UN, Guatemala and Washington, latterly as Counsellor. Investment banking, 1972–74; on staff of Monopolies and Mergers Commn, 1985–91. Treasurer: Anti-Slavery International (formerly Anti-Slavery Soc.), 1986–; Howard League for Penal Reform, 1991– (Mem. Council, 1985–). *Address:* Castle House, Chipping Ongar, Essex CM5 9JT. *T:* Ongar (01277) 362642. *Club:* Brooks's.

BUXTON, Raymond Naylor, OBE 1975; BEM 1957; QPM 1971; *b* 16 Sept. 1915; *s* of late Tom Bird Buxton and Ethel Buxton, Rushall, Walsall; *m* 1939, Agatha, *d* of late Enoch and Elizabeth Price, Essington, Wolverhampton; three *s*. *Educ:* King Edward VI Grammar Sch., Stafford. Constable to Chief Supt in Staffordshire Co. Police. Served War, RAF, Navigator, 1943–45 (FO). Police Coll. Staff, 1958–61; Asst Chief Constable, then Dep. Chief Constable of Herts, 1963–69, Chief Constable, 1969–77; HM Inspector of Constabulary, 1977–79. *Address:* Mannicotts, Radford Rise, Weeping Cross, Stafford ST17 4PS.

BUXTON, Hon. Sir Richard (Joseph), Kt 1994; **Hon. Mr Justice Buxton;** FCIArb; a Judge of the High Court of Justice, Queen's Bench Division, since 1994; *b* 13 July 1938; *o s* of Bernard Buxton, DSO, chartered mechanical engineer, and Sybil (*née* Hurley), formerly of Burton-upon-Trent; *m* 1987, Mary, *y d* of late Donald Tyerman, CBE and of Margaret Tyerman. *Educ:* Brighton Coll. (Schol.); Exeter Coll., Oxford (Schol.; First Cl. Final Hon. Sch. of Jurisprudence 1961, First Cl. BCL 1962; Vinerian Schol. 1962; MA). FCIArb 1992. Lectr, Christ Church, 1962–63; Lectr 1963–64, Fellow and Tutor 1964–73, also Sub-Rector 1966–71, Exeter Coll., Oxford. Called to the Bar, Inner Temple, 1969; Bencher, 1992; in practice, 1972–88; QC 1983; a Recorder, 1987–93; a Law Comr, 1989–93. Second Lieut RAOC, 1957–58. Councillor, Oxford CC, 1966–69. Chm. of Governors, Penton I and JM Sch., 1986–91. *Publications:* Local Government, 1970, 2nd edn 1973; articles in legal periodicals. *Recreation:* walking. *Address:* Royal Courts of Justice, Strand, WC2A 2LL.

BUXTON, Ronald Carlile; MA Cantab; *b* 20 Aug. 1923; *s* of Murray Barclay Buxton and Janet Mary Muriel Carlile; *m* 1959, Phyllida Dorothy Roden Buxton; two *s* two *d*. *Educ:* Eton; Trinity Coll., Cambridge. Chartered Structural Engineer (FIStructE). Director of H. Young & Co., London and associated companies. MP (C) Leyton, 1965–66. *Recreations:* travel, music, riding. *Address:* Kimberley Hall, Wymondham, Norfolk; 67 Ashley Gardens, SW1P 1QG. *Club:* Carlton.

BUXTON, Sir Thomas Fowell Victor, 6th Bt *cr* 1840; *b* 18 Aug. 1925; *s* of Sir Thomas Fowell Buxton, 5th Bt, and Hon. Dorothy Cochrane (*d* 1927), *yr d* of 1st Baron Cochrane of Cults; *S* father, 1945; *m* 1955, Mrs D. M. Chisenhale-Marsh (*d* 1965). *Educ:* Eton; Trinity Coll., Cambridge. *Heir: cousin* Jocelyn Charles Roden Buxton [*b* 8 Aug. 1924; *m* 1960, Ann Frances, *d* of late Frank Smitherman, MBE; three *d*].

BUYERS, Thomas Bartlett, OBE 1975; HM Chief Inspector of Prisons for Scotland, 1985–89, retired; *b* 21 March 1926; *s* of Charles Stuart Buyers and Bessie Heywood Buyers; *m* 1951, Agnes Lodge Alexander; three *d*. *Educ:* Glasgow Acad., Glasgow; Glasgow Univ. (BSc). MIChemE. Res. Chemist, Shell, 1947–50; professional and management posts, BP Chemicals, Grangemouth and Baglan Bay, 1951–73; Dir, Scottish Petroleum Office, 1973–74; Dir of Engrg, Offshore Supplies Office, Dept of Energy, 1974–75; BP Rep./Commissioning Man., Sullom Voe Terminal, Shetland, 1975–80; Special Projects Man., BP Chemicals, London, 1980–84. *Recreations:* gardening, hill walking, voluntary work. *Address:* 24 Kinord Drive, Aboyne, Aberdeenshire AB34 5JZ.

BUZZARD, Sir Anthony (Farquhar), 3rd Bt *cr* 1929; Lecturer in Theology, Atlanta Bible (formerly Oregon Bible) College, since 1982; *b* 28 June 1935; *s* of Rear-Admiral Sir Anthony Wass Buzzard, 2nd Bt, CB, DSO, OBE, and Margaret Elfreda (*d* 1989), *d* of Sir Arthur Knapp, KCIE, CSI, CBE; *S* father, 1972; *m* 1970, Barbara Jean Arnold, Mendon, Michigan, USA; three *d*. *Educ:* Charterhouse; Christ Church, Oxford (MA 1960); Ambassador Coll., Pasadena, USA (BA); MA Th Bethany Theol Seminary, 1990. ARCM. Lecturer in French, Ambassador Coll., Pasadena, 1962–65; Peripatetic Music Teacher for Surrey County Council, 1966–68; Lectr in French and Hebrew, Ambassador Coll., Bricket Wood, Herts, 1969–74; teacher of mod. langs, American Sch. in London, 1974–81. Founded Restoration Fellowship, 1981. *Publications:* The Coming Kingdom of the Messiah: a Solution to the Riddle of the New Testament, 1988; The Doctrine of the Trinity: Christianity's Self-Inflicted Wound, 1994; Our Fathers who aren't in Heaven: the Christianity of Jesus the Jew, 1995; articles on eschatology and Christology in various jls. *Recreations:* tennis, squash, music. *Heir: b* Timothy Macdonnell Buzzard [*b* 28 Jan. 1939; *m* 1970, Jennifer Mary, *d* of late Peter Patching; one *s* one *d*]. *Address:* (home) 185 Summerville Drive, Brooks, GA 30205, USA; (office) Box 100,000, Morrow, GA 30260, USA. *T:* (404) 3620052.

BYAM SHAW, Nicholas Glencairn; Chairman, Macmillan Publishers Ltd, since 1990; *b* 28 March 1934; *s* of Lieut. Comdr David Byam Shaw, RN, OBE (killed in action, 19 Dec. 1941) and Clarita Pamela Clarke; *m* 1st, 1956, Joan Elliott; two *s* one *d*; 2nd, 1974, Suzanne Filer (*née* Rastello); 3rd, 1987, Constance Wilson (*née* Clarke). *Educ:* Royal Naval Coll., Dartmouth. Commnd RN, 1955 (Lieut). Joined William Collins Sons & Co. Ltd, Glasgow, as salesman, 1956; Sales Manager, 1960; Macmillan and Co., subseq. Macmillan Publishers Ltd: Sales Manager, 1964; Sales Dir, 1965; Dep. Man. Dir, 1967; Man. Dir, 1969–90. Director: St Martins Press, 1980–; Pan Books, 1983– (Chm., 1986–). *Recreations:* gardening, travel. *Address:* 9 Kensington Park Gardens, W11 3HB. *T:* 0171–221 4547.

BYATT, Antonia Susan, (Mrs P. J. Duffy), CBE 1990; FRSL 1983; writer; *b* 24 Aug. 1936; *d* of His Honour John Frederick Drabble, QC and late Kathleen Marie Bloor; *m* 1st, 1959, Ian Charles Rayner Byatt, *qv* (marr. diss. 1969); one *d* (one *s* decd); 2nd, 1969, Peter John Duffy; two *d*. *Educ:* Sheffield High Sch.; The Mount Sch., York; Newnham Coll., Cambridge (BA Hons); Bryn Mawr Coll., Pa, USA; Somerville Coll., Oxford. Extra-Mural Lectr, Univ. of London, 1962–71; Lectr in Literature, Central Sch. of Art and Design, 1965–69; Lectr in English, 1972–81, Sen. Lectr, 1981–83, UCL. Associate of Newnham Coll., Cambridge, 1977–. Member: Social Effects of Television Adv. Gp, BBC, 1974–77; Bd of Communications and Cultural Studies, CNAA, 1978–84; Bd of Creative and Performing Arts, CNAA, 1985–87; Kingman Cttee on English Language, 1987–88; PEN (Macmillan Silver Pen of Fiction, 1986); Management Cttee, Soc. of Authors, 1984–88 (Dep. Chm., 1986; Chm., 1986–88). Broadcaster, reviewer; judge of literary prizes (Hawthornden, Booker, David Higham, Betty Trask). FRSL. Hon. DLitt: Bradford, 1987; Durham, 1991; Nottingham, 1992; Liverpool, 1993; Portsmouth, 1994; DUniv York, 1991. *Publications:* Shadow of a Sun, 1964; Degrees of Freedom, 1965, repr. 1995; The Game, 1967; Wordsworth and Coleridge in their Time, 1970 (reprinted as Unruly Times: Wordsworth and Coleridge, Poetry and life, 1989); Iris Murdoch, 1976; The Virgin in the Garden, 1978; (ed) George Eliot, The Mill on the Floss, 1979; Still Life, 1985; Sugar and Other Stories, 1987; Possession: a romance, 1990 (Booker Prize, 1990; Irish Times/Aer Lingus Internat. Fiction Prize, 1990; Eurasian section of Best Book in Commonwealth Prize, 1991); (ed) George Eliot: Selected Essays, 1990; Passions of the Mind (essays), 1991; Angels and Insects (novellae), 1992; The Matisse Stories (short stories), 1994; The Djinn in the Nightingale's Eye: five fairy stories, 1995. *Address:* 37 Rusholme Road, SW15 3LF.

BYATT, Sir Hugh Campbell, KCVO 1985; CMG 1979; HM Diplomatic Service, retired; Director, EFM Japan Trust PLC, since 1992; Chairman: EFM Java Trust, since 1990; EFM Dragon Trust, since 1992 (Director, since 1987); *b* 27 Aug. 1927; *e s* of late Sir Horace Byatt, GCMG, and Lady Byatt (*née* Olga Margaret Campbell), MBE; *m* 1954, Fiona, *d* of Ian P. Coats, DL, and May Coats, MBE; two *s* one *d*. *Educ:* Gordonstoun; New College, Oxford (MA 1951). Served in Royal Navy, 1945–48 (Sub-Lieut RNVR); HMOCS Nigeria, 1952–57; Commonwealth Relations Office, 1958; Bombay, 1961–63; CRO, 1964–65; seconded to Cabinet Office, 1965–67; Head of Chancery, Lisbon, 1967–70; Asst Head, South Asian Dept, FCO, 1970–71; Consul-General, Mozambique, 1971–73; Inspector, HM Diplomatic Service, 1973–75; RCDS, 1976; Dep. High Comr, Nairobi, 1977–78; Ambassador to Angola, 1978–81, to São Tomé, 1980–81, to Portugal, 1981–86. Advr, RTZ, 1986–; Special Advr, Scottish Financial Enterprise, 1986–92. Mem., Parole Bd for Scotland, 1990–92. Chm., Cttee for Scotland, Malcolm Sargent Cancer Fund for Children, 1991–. Chm. of Govs, Centre for Inf. on Lang. Teaching and Res., 1986–90. FSAScot 1989. Hon. Sheriff, Campbeltown. Knight Grand Cross, Mil. Order of Christ (Portugal), 1985. *Recreation:* living in Argyll. *Address:* Leargnahension, Tarbert, Argyll PA29 6YB. *T:* Tarbert (01880) 820644. *Clubs:* Royal Ocean Racing; New (Edinburgh); Royal Highland Yacht (Oban).

See also R. A. C. Byatt.

BYATT, Ian Charles Rayner; Director General of Water Services, since 1989; *b* 11 March 1932; *s* of Charles Rayner Byatt and Enid Marjorie Annie Byatt (*née* Howat); *m* 1959, A. S. Byatt, *qv* (marr. diss. 1969); one *d* (one *s* decd). *Educ:* Kirkham Grammar Sch.; Oxford University. Commonwealth Fund Fellow, Harvard, 1957–58; Lectr in Economics, Durham Univ., 1958–62; Economic Consultant, HM Treasury, 1962–64; Lectr in Economics, LSE, 1964–67; Sen. Economic Adviser, Dept of Educn and Science, 1967–69; Dir of Econs and Stats, Min. of Housing and Local Govt, 1969–70; Dir Economics, DoE, 1970–72; Under Sec., 1972–78, Dep. Chief Econ. Advr, 1978–89, HM Treasury. Chm., Economic Policy Cttee of the European Communities, 1982–85 (Mem., 1978–89); Member: Central Council of Educn (England), 1965–66; Economics Cttee, CNAA, 1968–70; ESRC, 1983–89; Urban Motorways Cttee, 1970; Cttee on Water Services: Econ. and Financial Objectives, 1970–73; Chm., Adv. Cttee to HM Treasury on Accounting for Econ. Costs and Changing Prices, 1986. Member: Bd, Public Finance Foundn, 1984–89; Bd of Management, Internat. Inst. of Public Finance, 1987–90; Council, REconS, 1983–92 (Mem. Exec. Cttee, 1987–89); Vice-Pres., Strategic Planning Soc., 1993–. Treas., Holy Cross Centre Trust, 1988–. FRSA 1989; CIMgt 1993. DUniv Brunel. *Publications:* The British Electrical Industry 1875–1914, 1979; articles on economics in books and learned jls; official reports. *Recreation:* painting. *Address:* Office of Water Services, 7 Hill Street, Birmingham B5 4UA. *T:* 0121–625 1350. *Club:* United Oxford & Cambridge University.

BYATT, Ronald Archer Campbell, (Robin), CMG 1980; HM Diplomatic Service, retired; High Commissioner in New Zealand and concurrently to Western Samoa, and Governor (non-resident), Pitcairn Islands, 1987–90; *b* 14 Nov. 1930; *s* of late Sir Horace Byatt, GCMG and late Olga Margaret Campbell, MBE; *m* 1954, Ann Brereton Sharpe, *d* of C. B. Sharpe; one *s* one *d*. *Educ:* Gordonstoun; New Coll., Oxford; King's Coll., Cambridge. Served in RNVR, 1949–50. Colonial Admin. Service, Nyasaland, 1955–58; joined HM Foreign (now Diplomatic) Service, 1959; FO, 1959; Havana, 1961; FO, 1963; UK Mission to UN, NY, 1966; Kampala, 1970; Head of Rhodesia Dept, FCO, 1972–75; Vis. Fellow, Glasgow Univ., 1975–76; Counsellor and Head of Chancery, UK Mission to UN, NY, 1977–79; Asst Under Sec. of State, FCO, 1979–80; High Comr in Zimbabwe, 1980–83; Mem, Directing Staff, RCDS, 1983–84; Ambassador to Morocco, 1985–87. CSSB Chm., 1992–. Mem., HGTAC, 1993– (Chm., Envmt Sub-Cttee, 1993–). Trustee: Beit Trust, 1987–; UK Antarctic Heritage Trust, 1992–. Order of the Throne, 1st cl. (Morocco), 1987. *Recreations:* sailing, boating (OUBC 1953), bird-watching, gardening. *Address:* Drim-na-Vullin, Lochgilphead, Argyll PA31 8LE. *T:* Lochgilphead (01546) 602615. *Club:* United Oxford & Cambridge University.

See also Sir H. C. Byatt.

BYERS, Sir Maurice (Hearne), Kt 1982; CBE 1978; QC 1960; barrister; Solicitor-General of Australia, 1973–83; Chairman, Australian Constitutional Commission, 1986–88; *b* 10 Nov. 1917; *s* of Arthur Tolhurst Byers and Mabel Florence Byers (*née* Hearne); *m* 1949, Patricia Therese Davis; two *s* one *d*. *Educ:* St Aloysius Coll., Milson's Point, Sydney; Sydney Univ. LLB. Called to the Bar, 1944. Mem., Exec. Council, Law Council of Australia, 1966–68; Vice-Pres., NSW Bar Assoc., 1964–65, Pres., 1965–67. Leader, Australian delegations to: UN Commn on Internat. Trade Law, 1974, 1976–82; Diplomatic Conf. on Sea Carriage of Goods, Hamburg, 1979. Chm., Police Bd of NSW, 1984–88. Member: Council, ANU, 1975–78; Australian Law Reform Commn, 1984–85. *Address:* 14 Morella Road, Clifton Gardens, NSW 2088, Australia. *T:* (2) 99698257. *Club:* Commonwealth (Canberra).

BYERS, Dr Paul Duncan; Reader Emeritus in Morbid Anatomy, University of London; Head of Department of Morbid Anatomy, Institute of Orthopaedics, University of London, 1980–87, retired (Dean of Institute, 1971–79); *b* Montreal, 1922; *s* of A. F. Byers and Marion Taber; *m* 1959, Valery Garden. *Educ:* Bishops College Sch., PQ, Canada; McGill Univ. (BSc, MD, CM); Univ. of London (DCP, PhD). FRCPath. Alan Blair Memorial Fellow, Canadian Cancer Soc., 1955–57. Asst Morbid Anatomist, Inst. of Orthopaedics, 1960; Reader in Morbid Anatomy, Univ. of London, 1974. Hon. Consultant, Royal National Orthopaedic Hosp., 1965; Hon. Senior Lectr, Royal Postgrad. Med. Sch., 1969. Chm., Osteosarcoma Histopathol. Panel, MRC/EORTC, 1983–86; Member: Osteosarcoma Wkg Party, MRC, 1982–86; Soft Tissue Sarcoma Wkg Party, MRC, 1983–84. Mem., Management Cttee, Courtauld Inst. of Art, Univ. of London, 1979–82. *Publications:* (jtly) Diseases of Bones and Joints, 1994; articles in medical press on arthritis, metabolic bone disease, bone tumours, medical education. *Recreation:* arts. *Address:* 18 Wimpole Street, W1M 7AD. *T:* 0171–580 5206.

BYERS, Stephen John; MP (Lab) Wallsend, since 1992; *b* Wolverhampton, 13 April 1953; *s* of late Robert Byers. *Educ:* Chester City Grammar Sch.; Chester Coll. of Further Educn; Liverpool Polytechnic (LLB). Sen. Lectr in Law, Newcastle Polytechnic, 1977–92. Mem. (Lab) North Tyneside MBC, 1980–92 (Dep. Leader, 1985–92; Chm. Educn Cttee, 1982–85). Contested (Lab) Hexham, 1983. An Opposition Whip, 1994–. Mem., Select Cttee on Home Affairs, 1994. Chm., PLP Home Affairs Cttee, 1992–94. Leader, Council of Local Educn Authorities, 1990–92; Chairman: Nat. Employers' Orgn for Teachers, 1990–92; Educn Cttee, AMA, 1990–92; Mem., BTEC, 1985–89. FRSA 1991. *Address:* House of Commons, SW1A 0AA. *T:* 0171–219 4085.

BYFORD, Dame Hazel, DBE 1994; Vice President, National Union of Conservative and Unionist Associations, 1993–95; *b* 14 Jan. 1941; *d* of Sir Cyril Osborne, MP and Lady Osborne; *m* 1962, C. Barrie Byford, CBE; one *s* one *d*. *Educ:* St Leonard's Sch., St Andrews; Moulton Agricl Coll., Northampton. WRVS Leics, 1961–, County Organiser, 1972–76. Chm., Nat. Cttee, Conservative Women, 1990–93. Member: Transport Users' Consultative Cttee, 1989–94; Rail Users' Consultative Cttee, 1994–95. *Recreations:* golf, bridge, reading. *Club:* Farmers'.

BYFORD, Sir Lawrence, Kt 1984; CBE 1979; QPM 1973; DL; management consultant, since 1987; HM Chief Inspector of Constabulary, 1983–87; *b* 10 Aug. 1925; *s* of George Byford and Monica Irene Byford; *m* 1950, Muriel Campbell Massey; two *s* one *d*. *Educ:* Univ. of Leeds (LLB Hons). Barrister-at-Law. Joined W Riding Police, 1947; served on Directing Staff of Wakefield Detective Sch., 1959–62, and Police Staff Coll., Bramshill, 1964–66; Divl Comdr, Huddersfield, 1966–68; Asst Chief Constable of Lincs, 1968, Dep. Chief Constable 1970, Chief Constable, 1973–77; HM Inspector of Constabulary for: SE Region, 1977–78; NE Region, 1978–82. Lecture tour of univs, USA and Canada, 1976; Headed: British Police Mission to Turkey, 1978–79; official review into Yorkshire Ripper case, 1981. DL Lincs, 1987. Hon. LLD Leeds, 1987. *Recreations:* cricket, Pennine walking and travel. *Clubs:* Royal Over-Seas League (Chm., 1989–92, Vice-Pres., 1992–), MCC; Yorks County Cricket (Pres. and Chm., 1991–).

See also M. J. Byford.

BYFORD, Mark Julian; Deputy Managing Director, Regional Broadcasting, BBC, since 1994; *b* 13 June 1958; *s* of Sir Lawrence Byford, *qv*; *m* 1980, Hilary Bleiker; two *s* two *d*. *Educ:* Lincoln Sch.; Univ. of Leeds (LLB 1976). BBC Television: Look North, Leeds, 1979–82; producer, South Today and Inquiry, Southampton, 1982–87; editor, Points West, Bristol, 1987–88; Home Editor, BBC News and Current Affairs, 1988–89; Head of Centre, Leeds, 1989–90; Asst Controller, 1991, Controller, 1991–94, BBC Regl Broadcasting. Director: BARB, 1993–; Radio Joint Audience Research Ltd, 1993–. Trustee, BBC Children in Need Appeal, 1993–. *Recreations:* family, football (Leeds United and Southampton), cricket, Scarborough, the New Forest, cathedrals, fell-walking, rock music. *Address:* Bolberry House, 1 Clifton Hill, Winchester, Hants SO22 5BL. *T:* Winchester (01962) 860197, *Fax:* (01962) 860944; Room 702, Henry Wood House, BBC, W1A 1AA. *T:* 0171–765 2742, *Fax:* 0171–765 2812. *Club:* Yorkshire County Cricket.

BYGRAVES, Max Walter, OBE 1983; entertainer; *b* 16 Oct. 1922; *s* of Henry and Lilian Bygraves, Rotherhithe, SE16; *m* 1942, Gladys Blossom Murray; one *s* two *d*. *Educ:* St Joseph's, Rotherhithe. Began in advertising agency, carrying copy to Fleet Street, 1936. Volunteered for RAF, 1940; served 5 years as fitter. Performed many shows for troops; became professional, 1946; has appeared in venues all over English-speaking world, incl. 18 Royal Command Performances; best selling record artist. Host, Family Fortunes, TV,

1983–85. *Publications:* I Wanna Tell You a Story (autobiog.), 1976; The Milkman's on his Way (novel), 1977; After Thoughts (autobiog.), 1988; I Wanna Tell You a Funny Story, 1992. *Recreations:* golf, painting, reading, writing. *Address:* Roebuck House, Victoria, SW1E 5BE. *T:* 0171–828 4595. *Clubs:* St James's, East India.

BYNG, family name of **Earl of Strafford,** and of **Viscount Torrington.**

BYNOE, Dame Hilda Louisa, DBE 1969; in General Medical Practice, Port of Spain, Trinidad, 1974–89, retired; *b* Grenada, 18 Nov. 1921; *d* of late Thomas Joseph Gibbs, CBE, JP, Estate Proprietor, and Louisa Gibbs (*née* La Touche); *m* 1947, Peter Cecil Alexander Bynoe, ARIBA, Dip. Arch., former RAF Flying Officer; two *s*. *Educ:* St Joseph's Convent, St George's, Grenada; Royal Free Hospital Medical Sch., Univ. of London. MB, BS (London), 1951, MRCS, LRCP, 1951. Teacher, St Joseph's Convents, Trinidad and Grenada, 1939–44; hospital and private practice, London, 1951–53; public service with Govt of Trinidad and Tobago, 1954–55, with Govt of Guyana (then British Guiana), 1955–58, with Govt of Trinidad and Tobago, 1958–65; private practice, Trinidad, 1961–68; Governor of Associated State of Grenada, WI, 1968–74. Mem. YWCA. Patron: Caribbean Women's Assoc., 1970–; John Hayes Meml Kidney Foundn, 1979–; Music Foundn of Trinidad and Tobago, 1986–; African Assoc. of Trinidad and Tobago. *Recreations:* swimming, music, reading, poetry-writing. *Address:* 5A Barcant Avenue, Maraval, Trinidad. *Club:* Soroptimist (Port of Spain).

BYRNE, Douglas Norman; Head of Marine Directorate, Department of Transport (formerly Marine Division, Department of Trade), 1980–84; *b* 30 Jan. 1924; *s* of Leonard William Byrne and Clarice Evelyn Byrne; *m* 1949, Noreen Thurlby Giles; one *s* one *d*. *Educ:* Portsmouth Grammar Sch.; St John's Coll., Cambridge (MA). RAF, 1942–46. Asst Principal, Min. of Supply, 1949; BoT, 1956; Cabinet Office, 1961–64; Asst Sec., 1964; on staff of Monopolies Commn, 1966–68; Under-Sec., Dept of Industry, 1974–77; Hd of Fair Trading Div., Dept of Prices and Consumer Protection, 1977–79; Under-Sec., Dept of Trade, 1979–83, Dept of Transport, 1983–84. *Recreations:* hill walking, natural history. *Club:* Royal Air Force.

BYRNE, John Anthony; teacher and writer; Artistic Director and Chairman, Board of Examiners, Royal Academy of Dancing, 1991–93; *b* Sydney, Australia, 14 Dec. 1945; *s* of Reginald Thomas Byrne and Mary Ida (*née* Sinclair). *Educ:* Scully-Borovansky Sch. of Ballet, Sydney; Univ. of Sydney (BA); Polytechnic of Central London (Dip. Arts Admin 1977); Royal Acad. of Dancing (ARAD; Dip. PDTC 1979). Professional dancer with various companies in ballet, opera-ballet and musicals, Australia, NZ, Germany, UK and Hong Kong, 1970–76; teaching dance in Australia, 1979–90; Royal Academy of Dancing: Major Examr, 1987–; Tutor, Sydney and London HQ, 1990–91. *Publications:* (jtly) Body Basics, 1992; Classical syllabus for boys, 1992; contrib. articles on dance criticism, etc to Dance Australia Mag., 1981–90. *Recreations:* walking, reading, gardens. *Address:* 729 Forest Road, Bexley South, NSW 2207, Australia.

BYRNE, John Keyes; *see* Leonard, Hugh.

BYRNE, Rev. Father Paul Laurence, OMI; OBE 1976; Director, Irish Episcopal Commission for Emigrants, since 1994; *b* 8 Aug. 1932; *s* of late John Byrne and Lavinia Byrne. *Educ:* Synge Street Christian Brothers' Sch. and Belcamp Coll., Dublin; University Coll., Dublin (BA, Hons Phil.); Oblate Coll., Piltown. Ordained, 1958. Teacher, Belcamp Coll., 1959–65; Dean of Belcamp Coll., 1961–65; Dir, Irish Centre, Birmingham, 1965–68; Dir, Catholic Housing Aid Soc. (Birmingham) and Family Housing Assoc., Birmingham, 1965–69; Nat. Dir, Catholic Housing Aid Soc., and Dir, Family Housing Assoc., London, 1969–70; Dir, SHAC (a housing aid centre), 1969–76; Sec. Gen., Conf. of Major Religious Superiors of Ire., 1980–87; Provincial Superior, Anglo-Irish Prov. of Missionary OMI, 1988–94. Board Member: Threshold Centre; Servite Houses; SHAC; Housing Corp., 1974–77. Hon. Mem., Inst. of Housing, 1972. *Recreations:* golf, theatre-going. *Address:* 57 Parnell Square West, Dublin 1. *T:* Dublin 8723655. *Club:* Foxrock Golf.

BYRNE, Terence Niall; HM Diplomatic Service; Deputy High Commissioner, Kuala Lumpur, since 1994; *b* 28 April 1942; *e s* of late Denis Patrick Byrne and of Kathleen Byrne (*née* Carley); *m* 1st, 1966, Andrea Dennison (marr. diss. 1977); one *s* one *d*; 2nd, 1981, Susan Haddow Neill; two *d*. *Educ:* Finchley Catholic Grammar Sch.; Open Univ. (BA Hons). Min. of Housing and Local Govt, 1964–68; Prime Minister's Office, 1968–70; MAFF, 1971–78 (Private Sec. to Parly Sec., MAFF, 1974–75); First Sec. (Agriculture), The Hague, 1978–82; Commonwealth Co-ordination Dept, FCO, 1982–84; Asst Head, UN Dept, FCO, 1984–85; Head of Chancery and Consul, Quito, 1986–89; Counsellor and Dep. High Comr, Lusaka, 1990–93; Dir of Trade Promotion, Canberra, 1993–94. *Recreations:* running, golf, cinema. Address: c/o Foreign and Commonwealth Office, King Charles Street, SW1A 2AH.

BYROM, Peter Craig, OBE 1987; self-employed textile consultant, since 1985; non-executive Director, Parry Murray & Co. Ltd, since 1992; Lay Inspector of Schools, Office for Standards in Education, since 1993; *b* 4 Dec. 1927; *s* of Robert Hunter Byrom, Master Cotton Spinner and Winifred Agnes Byrom (*née* Goodwin); *m* 1st, 1952, Norma Frances Mawdesley Harris (marr. diss. 1984); three *s* three *d*; 2nd, 1984, Gillian Elizabeth Hoyte. *Educ:* Virginia Episcopal Sch., Lynchburg, USA; St Edward's Sch., Oxford; Univ. of Liverpool, Sch. of Architecture; Salford Royal Tech. Coll.; Admin. Staff Coll., Henley; Open Univ. (BA). CText; FTI 1986. RNVR, 1945–48. Asst Gen. Manager, Robert Byrom (Stalybridge), cotton spinners, 1951–59; Merchandising Manager, British Nylon Spinners, 1959–64; Marketing Manager and Adv. and Promotions Manager, ICI Fibres, 1964–71; Dir, Deryck Healey Internat., 1972–74; Man. Dir, Dartington Hall Tweeds, 1975–85. Consultant to: ODA, Nepal, 1980; Intermediate Tech. Gp, India, 1986; Chm., British Colour Council, 1971–73; Mem., Textile and Fashion Bd, CNAA, 1974–77; Chm. Council, RCA, 1981–86 (Mem., 1973–86; Sen. Fellow, 1983); Mem. Council, Textile Inst., 1986–; External Assessor, Manchester Metropolitan Univ., 1992–. Governor: Dartington Coll. of Arts, 1979–89; Loughborough Coll. of Art and Design, 1993–. FRSA 1970 (Mem. Council, 1987–93; Mem. Design Bd, 1986–91; Chm., Textiles, Young Designers into Industry, 1985–90). *Publications:* Textiles: product design and marketing, 1987; contrib. to Young Designers into the Textile Industry. *Recreations:* walking, cycling, swimming, theatre, music, books. *Address:* Barton House, Woodland, Ashburton, Devon TQ13 7LN. *T:* Ashburton (01364) 653926.

BYRON, 13th Baron *cr* 1643, of Rochdale, Co. Lancaster; **Robert James Byron;** Partner, Holman Fenwick & Willan, since 1984; *b* 5 April 1950; *o* surv. *s* of 12th Baron Byron, DSO and Dorigen Margaret (*d* 1985), *o d* of Percival Kennedy Esdaile; *S* father, 1989; *m* 1979, Robyn Margaret, *d* of John McLean, Hamilton, NZ; one *s* three *d*. *Educ:* Wellington Coll.; Trinity Coll., Cambridge (MA). Called to the Bar, Inner Temple, 1974; admitted solicitor, 1978. *Heir: s* Hon. Charles Richard Gordon Byron, *b* 28 July 1990. *Address:* Marlow House, Lloyds Avenue, EC3N 3AL.

BYRT, (Henry) John, QC 1976; **His Honour Judge Byrt;** a Circuit Judge, since 1983; *b* 5 March 1929; *s* of Dorothy Muriel Byrt and Albert Henry Byrt, CBE; *m* 1957, Eve Hermione Bartlett; one *s* two *d*. *Educ:* Charterhouse; Merton Coll., Oxford (BA, MA). Called to the Bar, Middle Temple, 1953; called within the Bar, 1976; a Recorder of the Crown Court, 1976–83. Pres., Social Security Appeal Tribunals and Medical Appeal Tribunals, 1983–90. Vice-Principal, Working Mens' Coll., London, 1978–82, Principal, 1982–87; Mem. Council, Queen's Coll., London, 1982–. *Recreations:* building, gardening, sailing, music. *Address:* 65 Gloucester Crescent, NW1 7EG. *T:* 0171–485 0341. *Club:* Leander.

BYWATER, Air Cdre David Llewellyn, FRAeS, FIMgt; Director, Airport and Flight Operations, Marshall Aerospace, since 1993; Commandant, Aeroplane and Armament Experimental Establishment, Boscombe Down, 1988–92, retired; *b* 16 July 1937; *s* of Stanley and Gertrude Bywater; *m* 1960, Shelagh May Gowling; one *s* one *d*. *Educ:* Liverpool Inst. High Sch.; RAF Coll., Cranwell. No XV Sqdn, 1958–63; Empire Test Pilots Sch., 1964; A&AEE Test Pilot, 1965–68; RAF Staff Coll., 1969; HQ Germany, 1970–73; Wing Comdr Flying, RAE Farnborough, 1974–78; MoD Operational Requirements, 1979–81; Gp Captain, Superintendent of Flying, A&AEE, 1982–85; RAF Staff Coll., Bracknell, 1985–88. *Recreations:* sailing, ski-ing. *Club:* Royal Air Force.

BYWATERS, Eric George Lapthorne, CBE 1975; MB (London); FRCP; Professor of Rheumatology, Royal Postgraduate Medical School, University of London, 1958–75, now Emeritus; Hon. Consultant Physician, Hammersmith Hospital and Wexham Park Hospital, Slough, Bucks; Hon. Librarian, Heberden Library, Royal College of Physicians, 1970–90; *b* 1 June 1910; *s* of George Ernest Bywaters and Ethel Penney; *m* 1935, Betty Euan-Thomas; three *d*. *Educ:* Sutton Valence Sch., Kent; Middx Hosp. (Sen. Broderip Schol., Lyell Gold Medallist). McKenzie McKinnon Fellow, RCP, 1935; Asst Clin. Pathologist, Bland Sutton Inst., 1936; Rockefeller Travelling Fellow and Harvard Univ. Research Fellow in Med., 1937–39; Beit Memorial Fellow, 1939; Actg Dir, MRC Clin. Res. Unit (Shock), 1943; Lectr in Med., Postgrad. Med. Sch., 1945; Dir, MRC Rheumatism Res. Unit, Taplow, 1958–75; Sen. MRC Res. Fellow, Bone and Joint Unit, London Hosp., 1977–. Pres., European League against Rheumatism, 1977 (Hon. Mem. 1981); Councillor, Internat. League against Rheumatism. Fellow, RPMS, 1993. Hon. Mem., Heberden Soc., 1977; Hon. FACP, 1973; Hon. FRCP&S (Canada), 1977; Hon. FRSM, 1983. Hon. MD Liège, 1973. Gairdner Foundation Medical Award, 1963; Heberden Orator and Medallist, 1966; Croonian Lectr, RCP, 1968; Bunim Lectr and Medallist, 1973; Ewart Angus Lectr, Toronto, 1974; Samuel Hyde Lectr, RSocMed, 1986. Hon. Mem. Dutch, French, Amer., German, Czech, Spanish, Portuguese, Aust., Indian, Canadian, Chilean, Peruvian, Jugoslav, Egyptian, Turkish, Greek, S African and Argentine Rheumatism Assocs. *Publications:* papers on rheumatism, Crush Syndrome, etc. *Recreations:* painting, gardening. *Address:* 53 Burkes Road, Beaconsfield, Bucks HP9 1PW.

C

CABALLÉ, Montserrat; Cross of Lazo de Dama of Order of Isabel the Catholic, Spain; opera and concert singer; *b* Barcelona, 12 April 1933; *d* of Carlos and Ana Caballé; *m* 1964, Bernabé Marti, tenor; one *s* one *d*. *Educ:* Conservatorio del Liceo, Barcelona. Continued to study singing under Mme Eugenia Kemeny. Carnegie Hall début as Lucrezia Borgia, 1965. London début in this role, with the London Opera Society, at the Royal Festival Hall, 1968. Has sung at Covent Garden, Glyndebourne, La Scala, Vienna, Metropolitan Opera, San Francisco and most major opera venues. Major roles include Maria Stuarda, Luisa Miller, Queen Elizabeth in Roberto Devereux, Imogene in Il Pirata, Violetta in La Traviata, Marguerite in Faust, Desdemona in Otello, Norma, Tosca, Turandot, Leonora in La Forza del Destino, Semiramide, Salome, Il Viaggio a Reims, Tristan und Isolde, and also those of contemporary opera. Over 120 roles sung and recorded. Numerous hon. degrees, awards and medals. *Address:* c/o Carlos Caballé, Via Augusta 59, 08006 Barcelona, Spain.

CABLE, Sir James (Eric), KCVO 1976; CMG 1967; HM Diplomatic Service, retired; writer; *b* 15 Nov. 1920; *s* of late Eric Grant Cable, CMG; *m* 1954, Viveca Hollmerus; one *s*. *Educ:* Stowe; CCC, Cambridge. PhD 1973. Served Royal Signals, 1941–46, Major. Entered Foreign (now Diplomatic) Service, 1947; 2nd Sec., 1948; Vice-Consul, Batavia, 1949; 2nd Sec., Djakarta, 1949; acted as Chargé d'Affaires, 1951 and 1952; Helsinki, 1952; FO, 1953; 1st Sec., 1953; Mem. of British Delegn to Geneva Conf. on Indo-China, 1954; 1st Sec. (Commercial), Budapest, 1956; Head of Chancery and Consul, Quito, 1959; acted as Chargé d'Affaires, 1959 and 1960; FO, 1961 and Head of SE Asia Dept, Dec. 1963; Counsellor, Beirut, 1966; acted as Chargé d'Affaires at Beirut, 1967, 1968 and 1969; Research Associate, Institute for Strategic Studies, 1969–70; Head of Western Organisations Dept, FCO, 1970–71; Counsellor, Contingency Studies, FCO, 1971; Head of Planning Staff, 1971–75, and Asst Under-Sec. of State, 1972–75, FCO; Ambassador to Finland, 1975–80; Leverhulme Res. Fellow, 1981–82. *Publications:* Britain in Tomorrow's World, 1969 (as Grant Hugo); Appearance and Reality in International Relations, 1970 (as Grant Hugo); Gunboat Diplomacy, 1971, 3rd edn 1994; The Royal Navy and the Siege of Bilbao, 1979; Britain's Naval Future, 1983; Diplomacy at Sea, 1985; The Geneva Conference of 1954 on Indochina, 1986; Political Institutions and Issues in Britain, 1987; Navies in Violent Peace, 1989; Intervention at Abadan, 1991; articles in British and foreign jls. *Address:* 8 Essex Close, Cambridge CB4 2DW.

CABLE-ALEXANDER, Lt-Col Sir Patrick (Desmond William), 8th Bt *cr* 1809, of the City of Dublin; Secretary to the Council and Bursar, Lancing College, since 1984; *b* 19 April 1936; *s* of Sir Desmond William Lionel Cable-Alexander, 7th Bt and of Mary Jane, *d* of James O'Brien, Enniskillen; *S* father, 1988; *m* 1st, 1961, Diana Frances Rogers (marr. diss. 1976); two *d*; 2nd, 1976, Jane Mary Weekes (*née* Lewis); one *s*. *Educ*. Downside School; RMA Sandhurst. Commnd 3rd Carabiniers (POWDG), 1956; Lt-Col Royal Scots Dragoon Guards, 1976; comd Duke of Lancaster's Own Yeomanry, 1978–80; Chief of Staff, HQ North West District, 1980–83; retd, 1984. *Recreations:* cricket, gardening, visiting France, art. *Heir:* *s* Fergus William Antony Cable-Alexander, *b* 19 June 1981. *Address:* Windrush House, Hoe Court, Lancing, West Sussex BN15 0QX. *T:* Lancing (01903) 754772. *Club:* Sloane.

CABORN, Richard George; MP (Lab) Sheffield, Central, since 1983; *b* 6 Oct. 1943; *s* of George and Mary Caborn; *m* 1966, Margaret Caborn; one *s* one *d*. *Educ:* Hurlfield Comprehensive Sch.; Granville Coll. of Further Educn; Sheffield Polytechnic. Engrg apprentice, 1959–64; Convenor of Shop Stewards, Firth Brown Ltd, 1967–79. Mem. (Lab) Sheffield, European Parlt, 1979–84. Chm., Select Cttee on Trade and Industry, 1992–. *Recreation:* amateur football. *Address:* 29 Quarry Vale Road, Sheffield S12 3EB. *T:* Sheffield (0114) 239 3802. *Club:* Carlton Working Men's (Sheffield).

CACHELIN, Commissioner Francy; International Evangelist, The Salvation Army, 1987–89, retired; *b* 4 Aug. 1923; *s* of Maurice Cachelin and France Hauswirth; *m* 1951, Geneviève Irène Catherine Booth; two *s* two *d*. *Educ:* Lausanne School of Arts. Commissioned Salvation Army Officer, 1944; served in Switzerland as Corps Officer; Editor, The War Cry, in Belgium, 1951; responsible for youth work, France, 1957; Field Secretary, Switzerland, 1966; Chief Secretary, France, 1975, British Territory, 1977; Territorial Commander, Germany, 1979; British Comr, 1984. Federal Cross of Merit (FRG), 1984. *Recreations:* reading, languages.

CACOYANNIS, Michael; director, stage and screen, since 1954; *b* 11 June 1922; *s* of late Sir Panayotis Cacoyannis and Angeliki, *d* of George M. Efthyvoulos and Zoe Constantinides, Limassol, Cyprus. *Educ:* Greek Gymnasium; Gray's Inn and Old Vic Sch., London. Radio Producer, BBC, Greek Service, 1941–50. Actor on English stage, 1946–51; parts included: Herod, in Salome, 1946; Caligula, in Caligula, 1949, etc. *Directed films:* Windfall in Athens, 1953; Stella, 1954; Girl in Black, 1956; A Matter of Dignity, 1958; Our Last Spring, 1960; The Wastrel, 1961; Electra, 1962; Zorba the Greek, 1964; The Day the Fish Came Out, 1967; The Trojan Women, 1971; Attila '74, 1975; Iphigenia, 1977; Sweet Country, 1986; Up, Down and Sideways, 1992; directed *plays:* produced several of these in Athens for Ellie Lambetti's Company, 1955–61; The Trojan Women, New York, 1963–65, Paris, 1965; Things That Go Bump in the Night, and The Devils, New York, 1965; Iphigenia in Aulis, New York, 1968; King Oedipus, Abbey Theatre, Dublin, 1973; Miss Margaria, Athens, 1975; The Bacchae, Comédie Française, 1977, New York, 1980; The Glass Menagerie, Nat. Theatre, Athens, 1978; Antony and Cleopatra, Athens, 1979; Zorba (musical), USA, 1983; Electra, Epidaurus, 1984; Naked, Athens, 1989; Henceforward, Athens, 1990; directed *operas:* Mourning Becomes Electra, Metropolitan Opera, NY, 1967; La Bohème, Juillard, NY, 1972; La Traviata, Athens, 1983; Iphigenia in Aulis and in Tauris, Frankfurt State Opera, 1987; La Clemenza di Tito, Aix-en-Provence, 1988. Hon. DH Columbia Coll., Chicago, 1981. Order of the Phœnix (Greece), 1965; Commandeur des Arts et des Lettres, 1987. *Publications:* Collected Writings, 1990; *translations:* (into English) The Bacchae, 1982; (into Greek) Antony and Cleopatra, 1980; Hamlet, 1985; Coriolanus, 1990. *Recreations:* walking, swimming. *Address:* 15 Mouson Street, Athens 117–41, Greece.

CADBURY, Sir Adrian; *see* Cadbury, Sir G. A. H.

CADBURY, Dominic; *see* Cadbury, N. D.

CADBURY, Sir (George) Adrian (Hayhurst), Kt 1977; a Director of the Bank of England, 1970–94; *b* 15 April 1929; *s* of late Laurence John Cadbury, OBE and Joyce, *d* of Lewis O. Mathews, Birmingham; *m* 1st, 1956, Gillian Mary (*d* 1992), *d* of late E. D. Skepper, Neuilly-sur-Seine; two *s* one *d*; 2nd, 1994, Susan Jacqueline, *d* of late D. B. Sinclair. *Educ:* Eton Coll.; King's Coll., Cambridge (MA Economics). Coldstream Guards, 1948–49; Cambridge, 1949–52. Cadbury Schweppes: Dep. Chm. and Man. Dir, 1969–74; Chm., 1975–89; Director: Cadbury Bros Ltd, 1958; IBM UK Ltd, 1975–94; Nat. Exhibition Centre, 1989–. Mem., Panel on Takeovers and Mergers, 1990–94. Chancellor, Univ. of Aston in Birmingham, 1979–. Chairman: West Midlands Economic Planning Council, 1967–70; CBI Econ. & Financial Policy Cttee, 1974–80; Food & Drink Industries Council, 1981–83; Promotion of Non-Exec. Dirs, 1984–; Cttee on Financial Aspects of Corporate Governance, 1991–95; Pres., Birmingham Chamber of Industry and Commerce, 1988–89. High Sheriff, W Midlands, 1994–95. Freeman, City of Birmingham, 1982. Hon. DSc: Aston, 1973; Cranfield, 1985; Hon. LLD: Bristol, 1986; Birmingham, 1989; Lancaster, 1993; Cambridge, 1994. *Publication:* The Company Chairman, 1990. *Fax:* Knowle (01564) 771130. *Clubs:* Athenæum, Boodle's; Hawks (Cambridge); Leander (Henley).

See also N. D. Cadbury.

CADBURY, (Nicholas) Dominic; Chairman, Cadbury Schweppes plc, since 1993 (Chief Executive, 1984–93); *b* 12 May 1940; *s* of late Laurence John Cadbury, OBE and Joyce Cadbury; *m* 1972, Cecilia Sarah Symes; three *d*. *Educ:* Eton Coll.; Trinity Coll., Cambridge; Stanford Univ. (MBA). Chm., Economist Gp, 1994– (Dir, 1990–); Dep. Chm., Guinness PLC, 1994–. Mem., President's Cttee, 1989–94, Chm., Educn and Trng Affairs Cttee, 1993–, CBI; Member: Royal Mint Adv. Cttee, 1986–94; Stanford Adv. Council, 1989–; Food Assoc., 1989–; NACETT, 1993–. Vice Pres., Edgbaston High Sch. for Girls, Birmingham, 1987–; Gov., Tudor Hall Sch., 1993–. CIMgt (CBIM 1984). *Recreations:* tennis, golf, shooting.

See also Sir G. A. H. Cadbury.

CADBURY, Peter (Egbert); Chairman, Preston Publications Ltd, since 1985; *b* Great Yarmouth, Norfolk, 6 Feb. 1918; *s* of late Sir Egbert Cadbury, DSC, DFC; *m* 1st, 1947, Eugenie Benedicta (marr. diss. 1968), *d* of late Major Ewen Bruce, DSO, MC and of Mrs Bruce; one *s* one *d*; 2nd, 1970, Mrs Jennifer Morgan-Jones (*see* J. M. V. d'Abo) (marr. diss. 1976), *d* of Major Michael Hammond Maude, Ramsden, Oxon; one *s*; 3rd, 1976, Mrs Jane Mead; two *s*. *Educ:* Leighton Park Sch.; Trinity Coll., Cambridge (BA, MA 1939). Called to Bar, Inner Temple, 1946; practised at Bar, 1946–54. Served Fleet Air Arm, 1940, until released to Ministry of Aircraft Production, 1942, as Prodn, Research and Experimental Test Pilot. Contested (L) Stroud (Glos), 1945. Member, London Travel Cttee, 1958–60; Chm. and Man. Dir, Keith Prowse Group, 1954–71; Chairman: Alfred Hays Ltd, 1955–71; Ashton & Mitchell Ltd and Ashton & Mitchell Travel Co. Ltd, 1959–71; Air Westward Ltd, 1977–79; Air West Ltd, 1977–79; Educational Video Index Ltd, 1981–83; Westward Travel Ltd, 1982–84; Exec. Chm., Westward Television Ltd, 1960–80; Chm., Preston Estates, 1973–90; Director: Independent Television News Ltd, 1972–79; Willett Investments Ltd, 1955–. Chm., George Cadbury Trust, 1979–; Trustee: Help the Aged, 1986–; Mus. of Army Flying, 1986–; Winchester Cathedral Trust, 1986–. Freeman of City of London, 1948. *Recreations:* theatre, racing, flying, golf, tennis, sailing. *Address:* Upton Grey Lodge, Upton Grey, near Basingstoke, Hants RG25 2RE. *T:* Basingstoke (01256) 862374, *Fax:* (01256) 862988; (car) 0836 220214. *Clubs:* Royal Thames Yacht, Buck's, XL (Forty), MCC (Hon. Life Mem.), Lord's Taverners; Hawks (Cambridge); Island Sailing, Royal Motor Yacht, RAF Yacht.

CADBURY-BROWN, Henry Thomas, OBE 1967; TD; RA 1975 (ARA 1971); FRIBA; Professor of Architecture, Royal Academy, 1975–88; architect, in partnership with John F. Metcalfe, 1962–84; *b* 20 May 1913; *s* of Henry William Cadbury-Brown and Marion Ethel Sewell; *m* 1953, Elizabeth Romeyn, *d* of Prof. A. Elwyn, Croton on Hudson, NY. *Educ:* Westminster Sch.; AA Sch. of Architecture (Hons Diploma). Architect in private practice since winning competition for British Railways Branch Offices, 1937. Work includes pavilions for "The Origins of the People", main concourse and fountain display at Festival of Britain; schools, housing, display and interiors. Architect for new civic centre at Gravesend and halls for residence for Birmingham Univ. and, with Sir Hugh Casson and Prof. Robert Goodden, for new premises for Royal College of Art; awarded London Architecture Bronze Medal, 1963; lecture halls for Univ. of Essex; for RBK & C: Tavistock Cres. housing; World's End redevelt (in gp partnership Eric Lyons, Cadbury-Brown, Metcalfe & Cunningham). Taught at Architectural Association Sch., 1946–49; Tutor at Royal Coll. of Art, 1952–61. Invited as Visiting Critic to Sch. of Architecture, Harvard Univ., 1956. Member: RIBA Council, 1951–53; MARS (Modern Architectural Research) group. Pres. Architectural Assoc., 1959–60. TA and military service, 1931–45; Major RA (TD). Hon. Fellow: RCA; Kent Inst. of Art and Design, 1992. DU Essex, 1989. *Recreations:* numerous, including work. *Address:* 3 Church Walk, Aldeburgh, Suffolk IP15 5DU. *T:* Aldeburgh (01728) 452591.

CADELL, Colin Simson, CBE 1944; Air Cdre RAF, retired; Vice Lieutenant for West Lothian, 1972–88; *b* 7 Aug. 1905; *s* of late Lt-Col J. M. Cadell, DL, Foxhall, Kirkliston, W Lothian; *m* 1939, Rosemary Elizabeth, *d* of Thomas Edward Pooley; two *s* one *d*. *Educ:* Merchiston; Edinburgh Univ.; Ecole Supérieur d'électricité, Paris. MA; AMIEE; Ingénieur

ESE. Commnd RAF, 1926; Dir of Signals, Air Min., 1944; retd 1947. Man. Dir, International Aeradio, 1947–58; Director: Carron Company, 1958–71; Royal Bank of Scotland, 1963–69. Mem., Edinburgh Airport Consultative Cttee, 1972– (Chm., 1972–82). Mem. Queen's Body Guard for Scotland (Royal Company of Archers). DL: Linlithgowshire, 1963–72. Officer, US Legion of Merit, 1945. *Address:* 2 Upper Coltbridge Terrace, Edinburgh EH12 6AD. *Club:* New (Edinburgh).

CADELL, Vice-Adm. Sir John (Frederick), KBE 1983; District General Manager, Canterbury and Thanet Health Authority, 1986–94; *b* 6 Dec. 1929; *s* of Henry Dunlop Mallock Cadell and Violet Elizabeth (*née* Van Dyke); *m* 1958, Jaquetta Bridget Nolan; one *s* two *d*. *Educ:* Britannia Royal Naval Coll., Dartmouth. Served in HMS Frobisher, 1946, then Mediterranean, Persian Gulf, North and Baltic Seas; 2 years with RNZN, to 1960; served in HMS Ashton, Dartmouth, HMS Leopard, 9th Minesweeping Sqdn, SACLANT, HMS Bulwark, 1960–70; Naval Asst to First Sea Lord, 1970–72; HMS Diomede, 1972–74; RCDS 1974–75; RN Presentation Team, 1975–76; Comd, Sch. of Maritime Ops, 1976–79; Dir Gen. Naval Personal Services, 1979–81; COS to Comdr, Allied Forces Southern Europe, 1982–85. *Recreations:* tennis, skiing, wind surfing. *Address:* Great Mongeham House, near Deal, Kent CT14 0HD.

CADELL, Patrick Moubray, FSAScot; Keeper of the Records of Scotland, since 1991; *b* 17 March 1941; *s* of Col H. M. Cadell of Grange, OBE and Christina Rose Nimmo; *m* 1968, Sarah Margaret Florence King; two *s* one *d*. *Educ:* Merchiston Castle Sch.; Trinity Coll., Cambridge (BA 1962); Toulouse Univ. FSAScot 1985. British Museum: guide lectr, Dept of Admin, 1964–66; Asst Keeper, Dept of Manuscripts, 1966–68; National Library of Scotland: Asst Keeper, Dept of Manuscripts, 1968–83; Keeper, Dept of Manuscripts, 1983–90. Bailie, Abbey Court of Holyrood. *Publications:* The Iron Mills at Cramond, 1973; (contrib.) The Water of Leith, 1984; The Abbey Court and High Constables of Holyrood, 1985; (contrib.) A Sense of Place: studies in Scottish Local history, 1988; (contrib.) For the Encouragement of Learning: Scotland's National Library 1689–1989, 1989; The Third Statistical Account of Scotland, Vol. for West Lothian, 1992; contribs on historical subjects to books and jls. *Recreations:* walking, the French language. *Address:* 11A Tipperlinn Road, Edinburgh EH10 5ET. *T:* 0131–447 6630.

CADELL, Simon John; actor; *b* 19 July 1950; *s* of John Cadell and Gillian (*née* Howell); *m* 1986, Rebecca Croft; two *s*. *Educ:* Bedales Sch., Petersfield. Bristol Old Vic Co., 1969–70; Nottingham Playhouse, 1971; Lloyd George Knew My Father, Savoy, 1972–73; Belgrade, Coventry, 1974; The Case in Question, Haymarket, 1975; Lies, Albery, 1975; Actors' Co., 1976, 1977; Private Lives, on tour, 1981; Noel and Gertie, King's Head, 1983; Hamlet, Birmingham Rep., 1984; Jumpers, Aldwych, 1985; Blythe Spirit, Vaudeville, 1985–86; Tons of Money, A Small Family Business, National, 1986–87; Double Act, Playhouse, 1988; Noel and Gertie, Comedy, 1989–90; Don't Dress for Dinner, Apollo, 1991; Travels with My Aunt, Wyndham's, 1992–93 (Olivier Award, Best Comedy Perf., 1993) . Work on radio and numerous TV appearances. *Recreations:* wine, travel. *Address:* c/o Caroline Renton, 23 Crescent Lane, SW4 9PT. *T:* 0171–498 7217. *Clubs:* Groucho, Tramps, MCC.

CADIEUX, Hon. Léo, PC 1965; OC 1975; Ambassador of Canada to France, 1970–75; *b* 28 May 1908; *s* of Joseph E. Cadieux and Rosa Paquette, both French Canadian; *m* 1962, Monique, *d* of Placide Plante; one *s*. *Educ:* Commercial Coll. of St Jerome and Seminary of Ste Thérèse de Blainville, Quebec. Editorial staff of La Presse, Montreal, Quebec, 1930–41; Associate Dir of Public Relations, Can. Army, 1941–44; War Corresp. for La Presse, Montreal, 1944; Mayor of St Antoine des Laurentides, Que., 1948. First elected to House of Commons, gen. elec., 1962; re-elected gen. elec., 1963, 1965, 1968; apptd Associate Minister of Nat. Defence, 1965; Minister of National Defence, Canada, 1967–70. *Address:* 20 Driveway, Appt 1106, Ottawa K2P 1C8, Canada.

CADMAN, family name of **Baron Cadman.**

CADMAN, 3rd Baron *cr* 1937, of Silverdale; **John Anthony Cadman;** farmer, 1964–85; *b* 3 July 1938; *s* of 2nd Baron Cadman and Marjorie Elizabeth Bunnis; *S* father, 1966; *m* 1975, Janet Hayes; two *s*. *Educ:* Harrow; Selwyn Coll., Cambridge; Royal Agricultural Coll., Cirencester. *Heir: s* Hon. Nicholas Anthony James Cadman, *b* 18 Nov. 1977. *Address:* c/o House of Lords, SW1A 0PW.

CADMAN, Surg. Rear-Adm. (D) (Albert) Edward; CB 1977; Director of Naval Dental Services, 1974–77; *b* 14 Oct. 1918; *m* 1st, 1946, Margaret Henrietta Tomkins-Russell (*d* 1974); one *s* one *d*; 2nd, 1975, Mary Croil Macdonald (*d* 1987), Superintendent, WRNS; 3rd, 1988, Irene Davies (*née* Lowther). *Educ:* Dover Grammar Sch.; Guy's Hosp. Dental Sch. LDS RCS 1941. Surg. Lieut (D) RNVR, 1942; transf. to RN, 1947; served as Asst to Dir, Naval Dental Services, 1967–70; Comd Dental Surgeon on staff of Flag Officer, Naval Air Comd, 1970–74. QHDS 1974–77. *Recreations:* music, gardening, golf. *Address:* Solent House, 2 Solent Way, Alverstoke, Hants PO12 2NS. *T:* Gosport (01705) 586648.

CADOGAN, family name of **Earl Cadogan.**

CADOGAN, 7th Earl, *cr* 1800; **William Gerald Charles Cadogan,** MC 1943; DL; Baron Cadogan, 1718; Viscount Chelsea, 1800; Baron Oakley, 1831; Lieut-Colonel Royal Wiltshire Yeomanry, RAC; Captain Coldstream Guards R of O until 1964 (retaining hon. rank of Lieut-Colonel); *b* 13 Feb. 1914; *s* of 6th Earl and Lilian Eleanora Marie (who *m* 2nd, 1941, Lt-Col H. E. Hambro, CBE; she *d* 1973), *d* of George Coxon, Craigleith, Cheltenham; *S* father, 1933; *m* 1st, 1936, Hon. Primrose Lillian Yarde-Buller (from whom he obtained a divorce, 1959), *y d* of 3rd Baron Churston; one *s* three *d*; 2nd, 1961, Cecilia, *y d* of Lt-Col H. K. Hamilton-Wedderburn, OBE. *Educ:* Eton; RMC Sandhurst. Served war of 1939–45 (MC). Mem. Chelsea Borough Council, 1953–59; Mayor of Chelsea, 1964. DL County of London, 1958. *Heir: s* Viscount Chelsea, *qv*. *Address:* 28 Cadogan Square, SW1X 0JH. *T:* 0171–584 2335; Snaigow, Dunkeld, Perthshire. *T:* Caputh (0173871) 223. *Club:* White's.

See also Baron Rockley.

CADOGAN, Prof. Sir John (Ivan George), Kt 1991; CBE 1985; PhD, DSc London; FRS 1976; FRSE, CChem, FRSC; first Director General, Research Councils, since 1993; Visiting Professor of Chemistry, Imperial College, since 1979; Professorial Fellow, University College of Swansea, University of Wales, since 1979; *b* Pembrey, Carmarthenshire, 8 Oct. 1930; *er s* of late Alfred Cadogan and of Dilys Cadogan; *m* 1955, Margaret Jeanne (*d* 1992), *d* of late William Evans, iron founder, Swansea; one *s* one *d*. *Educ:* Grammar Sch., Swansea; King's Coll., London (1st cl. Hons Chem. 1951). Research at KCL, 1951–54. Civil Service Research Fellow, 1954–56; Lectr in Chemistry, King's Coll., London, 1956–63; Purdie Prof. of Chemistry and Head of Dept, St Salvator's Coll., Univ. of St Andrews, 1963–69; Forbes Prof. of Organic Chemistry, Edinburgh Univ., 1969–79; Chief Scientist, BP Res. Centre, 1979–81; Dir of Res., BP, 1981–92. Chm., BP Vencap, 1988–92; Director: BP Gas International, 1983–87; BP Ventures, 1981–90 (Chief Exec., 1988–90); BP Chemicals, 1983–92; BP Solar International, 1988–92 (Chm., 1988–90); Chm., Kaldair Internat., 1988–90. Advr to EC Comr for Sci., R&D, 1993–94. Mem., Royal Commn on Criminal Justice, 1991–93. Member: Chemistry Cttee, SRC, 1967–71 (Chm. 1972–75); Council, SERC, 1981–85 (Chm., Science Bd, 1981–85; Mem., Science Bd, SRC, 1972–75); ACORD, Dept of Energy, 1987–89; HEFCW, 1992– (Chm., Res. Gp, 1992–94); HEFCE, 1994–; Hong Kong Technol. Review Bd, 1992–95. Member: Council, Chem. Soc., 1966–69, 1973–76; Council, RIC, 1979–80; Chem. Soc.-RIC Unification Cttee, 1975–80; Council, RSC, 1980–85, 1989–92 (Pres. RSC, 1982–84); Council of Management, Macaulay Inst. for Soil Res., Aberdeen, 1969–79; Council, St George's Sch. for Girls, 1974–79; Council, RSE, 1975–80 (Vice-Pres., 1978–80); Council, Royal Soc., 1989–91, 1993–95 (Mem., Royal Soc. Sci. Inquiry, 1990–92); COPUS, 1994–; Conseil d'Admin, Fondation de la Maison de la Chemie, 1994–; Vice-Pres., Royal Instn, 1986–87 (Mem. Council, 1984–87). Member: Bd of Trustees, Royal Observatory Trust, Edinburgh, 1979–86; Adv. Bd, RCDS, 1989–; Adv. Bd, Eur. Business Management Sch., UC Swansea, 1990–; Adv. Council, RMCS, 1992–; Res. Cttee, Univ. of Newcastle upon Tyne, 1992–94; Ind. Adv. Cttee, Univ. of Durham, 1992–94; Trustee, Overseas Students Trust, UC Swansea, 1989–. Gov., Jt Res. Centre, EC, 1994–. Pres., Chem. Sect., BAAS, 1981. Chemistry Advr, Carnegie Trust Univ. of Scotland, 1985–. Fellow: KCL, 1976 (Mem. Council, 1980–94; Vice-Chm., 1990–94); UC, Swansea, 1992; FIC 1992. Hon. FEng 1992. First RSE Schs Christmas Lectures, 1980; Lectures: Tilden, Chem. Soc., 1971; David Martin Royal Soc. BAYS, 1981; Humphry Davy, Royal Instn, 1982; Holroyd Meml, Soc. Chem. Ind., 1984; Salters' Co., Royal Instn, 1984; Philips, Royal Soc., 1985; Pedler, RSC, 1986; Dalton, RSC, 1989. Freeman and Liveryman, Salters' Co., 1993. Hon. DSc: St Andrews, 1983; Wales, 1984; Edinburgh, 1986; Aberdeen, 1991; Durham, 1992; Leicester, 1992; London, 1992; Sunderland, 1994; Cranfield, 1995; DUniv Stirling, 1984; Hon. Dr l'Univ Aix-Marseille, 1984. Samuel Smiles Prize, KCL, 1950; Millar Thomson Medallist, KCL, 1951; Meldola Medallist, Soc. of Maccabaeans and Royal Inst. of Chemistry, 1959; Corday-Morgan Medallist, Chem. Soc., 1965. *Publications:* Principles of Free Radical Chemistry, 1971; Organophosphorus Reagents in Organic Synthesis, 1979; about 280 scientific papers, mainly in Jl RSC, and patents. *Recreations:* being in France, music, supporting Rugby football (Vice-Pres., Crawshay's Welsh RFC, London Welsh RFC; Patron, Swansea RFCC). *Address:* Office of Science and Technology, Cabinet Office, Albany House, 84–86 Petty France, SW1H 9ST. *T:* 0171–271 2030, *Fax:* 0171–271 2018. *Club:* Athenæum.

CADOGAN, Peter William; lecturer, writer and campaigner; Secretary, Northern Ireland Project, Gandhi Foundation, since 1988; *b* 26 Jan. 1921; *s* of Archibald Douglas Cadogan and Audrey Cadogan (*née* Wannop); *m* 1949, Joyce (marr. diss. 1969), *d* of William Stones, MP; one *d*. *Educ:* Tynemouth Sch., Tynemouth; Univ. of Newcastle, 1946–51 (BA (Hons) History, DipEd; Joseph Cowen Meml Prize, 1951). Served War, Air Sea Rescue Service, RAF, 1941–46. Teaching, Kettering and Cambridge, 1951–65. Committed to the Far Left, 1945–60; broke with Marxism, 1960. Founding Secretary, East Anglian Committee of 100: exploring theory and practice of non-violent direct action, 1961; Sec., Internat. Sub-Cttee of Cttee of 100, 1962; Sec. (full-time), National Cttee of 100, 1965–68. Mem., Nat. Council of CND, mix-sixties; Founding Sec., Save Biafra Campaign, 1968–70; Gen. Sec., South Place Ethical Soc., 1970–81; Co-Founder: Turning Point, 1975; Peace Anonymous, Action '84 and Summit '84, 1983–84; Co-Chm., Anglo-Afghan Circle, 1987–92. Founder Mem., New Consensus/New Dialogue, 1990; Co-founder, Values and Vision, 1991. Chm., Blake Soc. of St James', 1988–94 (Vice-Pres., 1994). *Publications:* Extra-Parliamentary Democracy, 1968; Direct Democracy, 1974, rev. 1975; Early Radical Newcastle, 1975; Six Ballads for the Seventies, 1976; many articles in learned jls, periodicals and elsewhere. *Recreations:* reading, gardening, social invention. *Address:* 3 Hinchinbrook House, Greville Road, NW6 5UP. *T:* 0171–328 3709.

CADWALLADER, Air Vice-Marshal Howard George, CB 1974; RAF retd; Director of Purchasing, Post Office, 1978–79; *b* 16 March 1919; British; *m* 1950, Betty Ethel Samuels; no *c*. *Educ:* Hampton Sch., Mddx. Sen. Equipment Staff Officer: HQ Transport Comd, 1963–65; HQ FEAF Singapore, 1965–68; Dep. Dir of Equipment 14 MoD (Air), 1968–69; Comdt of RAF Supply Control Centre, Hendon, 1969–72; Dir of Movts (RAF), MoD (Air), 1972–73; SASO HQ Support Comd, RAF, 1973–74. Controller of Contracts, PO, 1974–78. *Recreations:* golf, sailing. *Address:* Spain.

CÆSAR, Rev. Canon Anthony Douglass, CVO 1991 (LVO 1987); an Extra Chaplain to the Queen, since 1991; *b* 3 April 1924; *s* of Harold Douglass and Winifred Kathleen Cæsar. *Educ:* Cranleigh School; Magdalene Coll., Cambridge; St Stephen's House, Oxford. MA, MusB, FRCO. Served War with RAF, 1943–46. Assistant Music Master, Eton Coll., 1948–51; Precentor, Radley Coll., 1952–59; Asst Curate, St Mary Abbots, Kensington, 1961–65; Asst Sec., ACCM, 1965–70; Chaplain, Royal School of Church Music, 1965–70; Deputy Priest-in-Ordinary to the Queen, 1967–68, Priest-in-Ordinary, 1968–70; Resident Priest, St Stephen's Church, Bournemouth, 1970–73; Precentor and Sacrist, Winchester Cathedral, 1974–79; Sub-Dean of HM Chapels Royal, Dep. Clerk of the Closet, Sub-Almoner and Domestic Chaplain to the Queen, 1979–91; Hon. Canon of Winchester Cathedral, 1975–76 and 1979–91, Residentiary Canon, 1976–79, Canon Emeritus, 1991–; Chaplain, St Cross Hosp., Winchester, 1991–93. *Publications:* (jt ed.) The New English Hymnal, 1986; part songs, church music. *Recreation:* other people. *Address:* Flat 2, Old Kiln, Yarbridge, Brading, Isle of Wight PO36 0BP. *T:* Isle of Wight (01983) 406435.

CÆSAR, Irving; author-lyrist; Past President of Songwriters' Protective Association; Member Board of Directors, American Society of Composers, Authors and Publishers; *b* New York, 4 July 1895; *s* of Rumanian Jews. *Educ:* public school; Chappaqua Quaker Inst.; City Coll. of New York. Protégé of Ella Wheeler Wilcox, who, when he was a boy of nine, became interested in bits of verse he wrote and published at the time; at twenty became attached to the Henry Ford Peace Expedition, and spent nine months travelling through neutral Europe (during the War) as one of the secretaries of the Ford Peace Conference; returned to America, and became interested in writing for the musical comedy stage. *Publications:* most important work up to present time, No, No, Nanette; has written hundreds of songs and collaborated in many other musical comedies; writer and publisher of Sing a Song of Safety, a vol. of children's songs in use throughout the public and parochial schools of USA; also Sing a Song of Friendship, a series of songs based on human rights; in England: The Bamboula, Swanee, Tea for Two (successive awards for being among the most performed ASCAP standards), I Want to be Happy, I Was So Young; author of "Peace by Wireless" proposal for freedom of international exchange of radio privilege between governments. *Recreations:* reading, theatre, swimming. *Address:* Irving Cæsar Music Corporation, 429 East 52nd Street, Apartment 31G, New York, NY 10022, USA. *Club:* Friars (New York).

CAFFERTY, Michael Angelo; HM Diplomatic Service; Consul-General, Melbourne, Australia, 1983–87; *b* 3 March 1927; *m* 1950, Eileen E. Geer; two *s* three *d*. *Educ:* Univ. of London. BoT, 1951; Asst Trade Comr, Johannesburg, 1955, Pretoria, 1957; seconded to FO, Buenos Aires, 1958; Trade Comr, Singapore, 1964; FCO, 1968; Consul (Commercial), Milan, 1974; First Sec. and Head of Chancery, Rome (Holy See), 1977; Ambassador and Consul-Gen., Santo Domingo, 1979–83. *Address:* 24 Phoenix Lodge Mansions, Brook Green, W6 7BG.

CAFFIN, A(rthur) Crawford; a Recorder of the Crown Court, 1971–82; solicitor since 1932; *b* 10 June 1910; *s* of Charles Crawford Caffin and Annie Rosila Caffin; *m* 1933, Mala Pocock; one *d.* *Educ:* King's Sch., Rochester. Asst Solicitor: to Norfolk CC, 1933–37; to Bristol Corporation, 1937–46. Partner in firm of R. L. Frank & Caffin, Solicitors, Truro, 1946–72; Consultant with that firm, 1972–84. Pres., Cornwall Law Soc., 1960; Mem. Council, the Law Society, 1966–76; Dep. Chm., Traffic Commissioners for Western Traffic Area, 1964–84. *Recreation:* swimming. *Address:* Cove Cottage, Portloe, Truro, Cornwall TR2 5QY. *Club:* Farmers' (Truro).

CAGIATI, Dr Andrea; Grand Cross, Italian Order of Merit, 1979; Hon. GCVO; Ambassador, retired 1988; *b* Rome, 11 July 1922; *m* 1968, Sigrid von Morgen; one *s* one *d.* *Educ:* University of Siena (Dr of Law). Entered Foreign Service, 1948. Served: Secretary, Paris, 1950; Principal Private Sec. to Minister of State, 1951; Vice-Consul-General, New York, 1953; Prin. Private Sec. to Minister of State and subsequently Dept of Political Affairs, 1955; Counsellor, Athens, 1957; Counsellor, Mexico City, 1960; Delegate, Disarmament Cttee, Geneva, March-Dec. 1962; Italian Delegation, UN, June 1962; Head, NATO Dept, Dec. 1962; Minister-Counsellor, Madrid, 1966; Ambassador, Bogotá, 1968; Inst for Diplomatic Studies, 1971; Diplomatic Adviser to Prime Minister, 1972; Ambassador, Vienna, 1973; Ambassador, Court of St James's, 1980; Ambassador to the Holy See and to the Order of Malta, 1985. Vice Chm., 1989–94, Dir, 1987–94, Alitalia. President: Circolo di Studi Diplomatici, 1989–; Centro Conciliazione Internazionale, 1989–; Fondazione Cagiati von Morgen, 1990–; Eurodéfence (Italia), 1994–; Vice-Pres., Fondazione De Gasperi, 1993–. Hon. GCVO during State Visit to Italy of HM The Queen, Oct. 1980; KM, 1953; Grand Cross: Order of Merit, Austria, 1980; Order of Merit, Malta, 1987; Order of Pius IX, Holy See, 1988. *Publications:* La Diplomazia dalle origini al XVII secolo, 1944; Verso quale avvenire?, 1958; I Sentieri della Vita, ricordi di un diplomato, 1990; Scritti di Politica Estera, 3 vols 1991–93; articles in quarterlies on foreign and defence affairs. *Recreations:* sculpture, golf, shooting. *Address:* Largo Olgiata, 15 (49D)–00123 Rome, Italy. *T:* and *Fax:* (6) 30888135. *Club:* Nuovo Circolo Scacchi (Rome).

CAHILL, John Conway; Chairman, Trans World Airlines, since 1995; *b* 8 Jan. 1930; *m* 1956, Giovanna Caterina, *d* of late Riccardo Lenardon; three *d.* Joined BTR Industries, 1955; Dep. Overseas Gen. Manager, 1963; Board of Directors, 1968; Dep. Managing Dir, 1976; Vice-Pres., BTR Inc., USA, 1978; Pres. and Chief Exec., BTR Inc., and Chm., BTR Pan American operations, 1979–86; non-exec. Chm., BTR Inc., 1987–92; Chief Exec., BTR plc, 1987–90; Chm., British Aerospace, 1992–94. *Recreations:* reading, gardening, music.

CAHILL, Michael Leo; Head of Central and Southern Africa Department, Overseas Development Administration, 1983–88, retired; *b* 4 April 1928; *s* of John and Josephine Cahill; *m* 1961, Harriette Emma Clemency, *e d* of late Christopher Gilbert Eastwood, CMG and Catherine Eastwood; two *d.* *Educ:* Beaumont Coll.; Magdalen Coll., Oxford (Demy). National Service, Intelligence Corps, Trieste, 1950–52, Lieut. FO, 1953; CO, 1955; Asst Private Sec. to Sec. of State, 1956–57; Private Sec. to Parly Under-Sec., 1957–58; Dept of Technical Co-operation, 1961; Asst Sec., ODM, 1969; UK Perm. Deleg. to Unesco, 1972–74. Chm., Woldingham Sch. Parents Assoc., 1981–83. *Recreations:* history of the arts, pianism. *Address:* 9 Murray Road, SW19 4PD. *T:* 0181–947 0568.
See also B. S. T. Eastwood.

CAHILL, Teresa Mary; opera and concert singer; *b* 30 July 1944; *d* of Florence and Henry Cahill; *m* 1971, John Anthony Kiernander (marr. diss. 1978). *Educ:* Notre Dame High Sch., Southwark; Guildhall School of Music and Drama; London Opera Centre (LRAM Singing, AGSM Piano). Glyndebourne début, 1969; Covent Garden début, 1970; La Scala Milan, 1976, Philadelphia Opera, 1981, specialising in Mozart, Strauss and Elgar; concerts: all London orchestras, Boston Symphony Orch., Chicago Symphony Orch., Rotterdam Philharmonic Orch., West Deutscher Rundfunk, Warsaw Philharmonic, RAI Turin, Frankfurt Radio Orch., Vienna Fest., 1983, Berlin Fest., 1987, Promenade concerts; BBC radio and TV; recordings, incl. Strauss, Elgar and Mahler, for all major companies; master classes, Dartington Fest., 1984, 1986; recitals and concerts throughout Europe, USA, Far East. Professor: Royal Northern Coll. of Music; Trinity Coll. of Music; Guildhall Sch. of Music and Drama. Silver Medal, Worshipful Co. of Musicians, 1966; John Christie Award 1970. *Recreations:* cinema, theatre, travel, reading, collecting antique furniture, photography. *Address:* 65 Leyland Road, SE12 8DW. *Club:* Royal Over-Seas League (Hon. Mem.).

CAHN, Sir Albert Jonas, 2nd Bt, *cr* 1934; company director; marital, sexual and family therapist; *b* 27 June 1924; *s* of Sir Julien Cahn, 1st Bt, and Phyllis Muriel, *d* of A. Wolfe, Bournemouth; *S* father, 1944; *m* 1948, Malka, *d* of late R. Bluestone; two *s* two *d.* *Educ:* Headmaster's House, Harrow. Dir, Elm Therapy Centre, New Malden, 1983–93. *Recreations:* cricket, horse riding, photography. *Heir: s* Julien Michael Cahn [*b* 15 Jan. 1951; *m* 1987, Marilynne Janelle, *d* of Frank Owen Blyth; one *s* one *d*]. *Address:* 10 Edgecoombe Close, Warren Road, Kingston upon Thames, Surrey KT2 7HP. *T:* 0181–942 6956.

CAHN, Andrew Thomas; Deputy Head, European Secretariat, Cabinet Office, since 1995; *b* 1 April 1951; *s* of Robert Wolfgang Cahn, *qv* and of Pat (*née* Hanson); *m* 1976, Virginia Beardshaw; two *s* one *d.* *Educ:* Bedales Sch.; Trinity Coll., Cambridge (BA 1st Cl. Hons). MAFF, 1973–77; FCO, 1977–78; Private Sec. to Perm Sec., MAFF, 1978–79; 1st Sec., Office of UK Perm. Repn to EC, FCO, 1981–84, Cabinet of Vice Pres., CEC, 1984–88; Asst Sec., MAFF, 1988–92; Principal Private Secretary to: Chancellor of Duchy of Lancaster, 1992–94; Minister of Agriculture, 1994–95. Non-exec. Dir, Cadbury Ltd, 1990–92. Gov., Bedales Sch., 1993–. FRSA 1979. *Recreations:* family, reading, mountains, squash. *Address:* Cabinet Office, Whitehall, SW1 2AS. *T:* 0171–270 0177; 91 Patshull Road, NW5 2LE. *Club:* Royal Automobile.

CAHN, Prof. Robert Wolfgang, PhD, ScD; FRS 1991; FIM; FInstP; Hon. Senior Associate, Department of Materials Science and Metallurgy, Cambridge University, since 1986; *b* 9 Sept. 1924; *s* of Martin and Else Cahn; *m* 1947, Patricia Lois Hanson; two *s* two *d.* *Educ:* Cambridge Univ. (BA 1945; PhD 1950; ScD 1963). FIM 1962; FInstP 1959. SO, later SSO, Harwell, 1947–51; Lectr, Sen. Lectr, then Reader, Physical Metallurgy Dept, Birmingham Univ., 1951–62; Professor of Materials Science: UCNW, 1962–64; Sussex Univ., 1965–81, now Prof. Emeritus (Dean of Engrg, 1973–78); Prof. of Physical Metallurgy, Université de Paris–Sud, 1981–83; Fairchild Distinguished Scholar, CIT, 1985–86. Commonwealth Vis. Prof., Monash Univ., Melbourne, 1976; Visiting Professor: Univ. of Surrey, 1986–92; Univ. Autónoma de Barcelona, 1993. Editor, several scientific jls and book series. Foreign Mem., Göttingen Acad. Arts and Scis, 1987; Mem., Academia Europaea, 1989. FRSA. Ste Claire Deville Medal, Société Française de Métallurgie, 1978; A. A. Griffith Medal, Materials Science Club, 1984. *Publications:* (ed) Physical Metallurgy, 1965, 4th edn 1996; (ed) Processing of Metals and Alloys, 1991; Artifice and Artefacts—100 Essays in Materials Science, 1992; (contrib.) Twentieth Century Physics, ed B. R. Pippard *et al*, 1995; contrib. scientific jls incl. Nature and Acta Metallurgica. *Recreations:* composing English prose, looking at and collecting pictures, mountains and alpine flowers, music. *Address:* Department of Materials Science and Metallurgy, Pembroke Street, Cambridge CB2 3QZ. *T:* and *Fax:* Cambridge (01223) 334381; 6 Storey's Way, Cambridge CB3 0DT. *T:* Cambridge (01223) 360143. *Clubs:* Fell and Rock Climbing (Lake District); Cambridge Gog Magog Golf.
See also A. T. Cahn.

CAIE, Andrew John Forbes; HM Diplomatic Service; Deputy High Commissioner, Islamabad, since 1993; *b* 25 July 1947; *s* of Norman Forbes Caie and Joan Margaret Caie (*née* Wise); *m* 1976, Kathie-Anne Williams; one *s* one *d.* *Educ:* St Dunstan's Coll., Catford; Sidney Sussex Coll., Cambridge (MA). Joined FCO, 1969; Manila, 1976–80; FCO, 1980–84; Dep. Head of Mission, Bogotá, 1984–88; FCO, 1988–93. *Address:* c/o Foreign and Commonwealth Office, SW1A 2AH.

CAILLARD, Air Vice-Marshal (Hugh) Anthony, CB 1981; retired 1982; Director General, Britain-Australia Society, and Hon. Secretary, Cook Society, 1982–89; *b* 16 April 1927; *s* of late Col F. Caillard, MC, and Mrs M. Y. Caillard; *m* 1957, Margaret-Ann Crawford, Holbrook, NSW, Australia; four *s.* *Educ:* Downside; Oriel Coll., Oxford. Cranwell, 1947–49; served, 1949–65: 13 Sqdn, Egypt; ADC to C-in-C MEAF, and to AOC-in-C Tech. Trng Comd; 101 Sqdn, Binbrook; RAAF No 2 Sqdn; 49 Sqdn (Sqdn Ldr) and 90 Sqdn; RN Staff Coll.; HQ Bomber Comd (Wg Cdr); OC 39 Sqdn, Malta, 1965–67; Jt Services Staff Coll., 1967; Planning Staffs, MoD, 1967–70; Asst Air Attaché, Washington (Gp Captain), 1970–73; OC Marham, 1974–75; Def. Intell. Staff (Air Cdre), 1975–79; Dep. Chief of Staff, Ops and Intelligence, HQ Allied Air Forces, Central Europe, 1979–82. Specialist Air Advr, H of C Defence Cttee, 1985–92. Chairman: Ex Forces Fellowship Centre, 1987–93; Ex Services Mental Welfare Soc., 1990–93; Member: Grants and Appeals Cttee, RAF Benevolent Fund, 1987–93; Britain-Australia Bicentennial Cttee, 1984–88; Council, British Atlantic Cttee, 1988–92; Trustee, Australian Arts Foundn, 1985–89. *Address:* 58 Hilltop Road, Clareville, NSW 2107, Australia. *Clubs:* Royal Air Force; Union (Sydney).

CAIN; *see* Nall-Cain, family name of Baron Brocket.

CAIN, Sir Edney; *see* Cain, Sir H. E. C.

CAIN, Sir Edward (Thomas), Kt 1972; CBE 1966; Commissioner of Taxation, Australia, 1964–76; retired; *b* Maryborough, Qld, Australia, 7 Dec. 1916; *s* of Edward Victor and Kathleen Teresa Cain; *m* 1942, Marcia Yvonne Cain (*née* Parbery); one *s* one *d.* *Educ:* Nudgee Coll., Queensland; Univ. of Queensland (BA, LLB). Commonwealth Taxation Office: in Brisbane, Sydney, Perth and Canberra, 1936–. Served War, 2/9th Bn, AIF, 1939–43. *Recreations:* golf, fishing. *Address:* 99 Buxton Street, Deakin, Canberra, ACT 2600, Australia. *T:* (62) 811462. *Clubs:* Commonwealth, Royal Canberra Golf (Canberra).

CAIN, Maj.-Gen. George Robert T.; *see* Turner Cain.

CAIN, Sir (Henry) Edney (Conrad), Kt 1986; OBE 1976 (MBE 1965); FCCA; CA (Belize); Governor, Central Bank of Belize, 1982–83, and 1991; *b* 2 Dec. 1924; *s* of Henry Edney Conrad I and Rhoda (*née* Stamp); *m* 1951, Leonie (*née* Locke). *Educ:* St George's Coll., Belize; St Michael's Coll., Belize; Balham and Tooting Coll. of Commerce, London. FCCA 1977 (ACCA 1961); CA Belize 1984. Belize Government Service, 1940–: Examr of Accts, Audit Dept, 1954; Auditor, Audit Dept, 1959; Asst Accountant Gen., 1961; Accountant Gen., 1963; Man. Dir, Monetary Authority of Belize, 1976; Ambassador to USA, 1983; High Comr to Canada (resident in Washington, DC), 1984; Financial Sec., Ministry of Finance, Belize, 1985–87; High Comr to UK, 1987–90. *Publication:* When the Angel says 'Write' (verse), 1948. *Recreations:* music, reading, current affairs. *Address:* PO Box 238, 936 Orchid Gardens, Belmopan, Belize. *T:* (501) 822492.

CAIN, James Crookall, FCA; Speaker, House of Keys, Isle of Man, since 1991; Deputy President of Tynwald, since 1992; *b* Douglas, IOM, 19 March 1927; *s* of James Mylchreest Cain, OBE, JP, formerly MHK and Jean (*née* Crookall); *m* 1959, Muriel Duckworth; two *d.* *Educ:* King William's Coll., IOM. Nat. Service, 1945–48, SSC, E Lancs, 1946. Qualified as Chartered Accountant with W. H. Walker & Co. (Liverpool), 1953; returned to Douglas office, 1954; Partner, 1959–71, Pannell Kerr Forster, 1971–86: Sen. IOM Partner, 1974; retd 1986. Mem., House of Keys, 1986–; Member: Treasury, 1986–88; Dept of Highways Posts & Properties, 1989; Minister for Health and Social Security, 1989–91. Pres., Hospice Care, 1990– (Chm., 1983–89). *Recreations:* walking, reading. *Address:* Maughold, Alexander Drive, Douglas, Isle of Man IM2 3QZ. *T:* Douglas (01624) 675068.

CAIN, Hon. John; MLA (Lab) for Bundoora, 1976–92; Premier of Victoria, 1982–90; Professorial Associate, Department of Political Science, University of Melbourne, since 1991; *b* 26 April 1931; *s* of late Hon. John Cain; *m* 1955, Nancye Williams; two *s* one *d.* *Educ:* Melbourne Univ. (LLB). Practised as barrister and solicitor. Mem., Law Reform Commn, 1975–77. Pres., Law Inst. of Victoria, 1972–73 (Treasurer, 1969–70; Chm. of Council, 1971–72); Mem. Exec., Law Council of Australia, 1973–76. Vice-Chm., Vic. Br., Australian Labor Party, 1973–75; Mem., Parly Labor Exec., 1977–90; Leader, State Labor Party, 1981–90; Leader of Opposition, 1981–82; Minister for Fed. Affairs, 1982; Attorney-General of Vic, 1982–83. Commonwealth Observer, S African elecns, Apr. 1994. *Address:* 9 Magnolia Road, Ivanhoe, Vic 3079, Australia.

CAIN, John Clifford; broadcasting research historian; Controller, Public Affairs, BBC, 1981–84; Hon. Vice-President, Broadcasting Support Services, since 1989 (Chairman, 1980–85; Trustee, 1985–89); *b* 2 April 1924; *s* of William John Cain and Florence Jessie (*née* Wood); *m* 1954, Shirley Jean Roberts; two *d.* *Educ:* Emanuel Sch.; Imperial Coll., Borough Road Coll., London Univ. (BSc); University Coll., London Univ. (MSc); BA (Hons) Open Univ., 1988. Served RAF (aircrew), 1944–47. Maths and science teacher in grammar, secondary modern and comprehensive schs and in polytechnic, 1950–59; Lectr, Science Museum, 1959–61; Asst Head of Sch. Broadcasting, Associated-Rediffusion, 1961–63; BBC Television: Producer, 1963–71; Asst Head of Further Educn Dept, 1971–72, Head, 1972–77; Asst Controller, Educn Br., BBC, 1977–80. Dir, Broadcasters' Audience Res. Bd, 1982–84. Mem., Health Educn Council, 1978–83. Mem., RTS, 1984–. FRSA 1990. *Publications:* Talking Machines, 1961; (jtly) Mathematics Miscellany, 1966; (contrib.) Culture, Education and the State, 1988; The BBC: 70 years of broadcasting, 1992; (jtly) In a Class of its Own: BBC education 1924–1994, 1994; articles in EBU Review, Adult Educn, etc. *Recreations:* reading, gardening, music, theatre. *Address:* 63 Park Road, Chiswick, W4 3EY. *T:* 0181–994 2712.

CAIN, Thomas William; QC 1989; Second Deemster, Isle of Man, since 1993 (HM Attorney-General, 1980–93); *b* 1 June 1935; *s* of late James Arthur Cain and Mary Edith Cunningham (*née* Lamb); *m* 1961, Felicity Jane, *d* of late Rev. Arthur Stephen Gregory; two *s* one *d.* *Educ:* King's College Choir Sch., Cambridge; Marlborough Coll.; Worcester Coll., Oxford (BA 1958, MA 1961). National Service, 2nd Lieut RAC, 1953–55. Called to the Bar, Gray's Inn, 1959; Advocate, Manx Bar, 1961. Pres., I of M Law Soc., 1985–89. *Recreations:* sailing; Chairman, Manx Nature Conservation Trust. *Address:* Ivie Cottage, Kirk Michael, Isle of Man. *T:* Kirk Michael (01624) 878266.

CAINE, Emma Harriet; *see* Nicholson, E. H.

CAINE, Michael, CBE 1992; actor; *b* Old Kent Road, London, 14 March 1933 (Maurice Joseph Micklewhite); *s* of late Maurice and of Ellen Frances Marie Micklewhite; *m* 1st,

1955, Patricia Haines (marr. diss.); one *d*; 2nd, 1973, Shakira Baksh; one *d*. *Educ:* Wilson's Grammar Sch., Peckham. Began acting in youth club drama gp. Served in Army, Berlin and Korea, 1951–53. Asst Stage Manager, Westminster Rep., Horsham, Sx, 1953; actor, Lowestoft Rep., 1953–55; Theatre Workshop, London, 1955; numerous TV appearances (over 100 plays), 1957–63; *play:* Next Time I'll Sing for You, Arts, 1963; *films:* A Hill in Korea, 1956; How to Murder a Rich Uncle, 1958; Zulu, 1964; The Ipcress File, 1965; Alfie, 1966; The Wrong Box, 1966; Gambit, 1966; Hurry Sundown, 1967; Woman Times Seven, 1967; Deadfall, 1967; The Magus, 1968; Battle of Britain, 1968; Play Dirty, 1968; The Italian Job, 1969; Too Late the Hero, 1970; The Last Valley, 1971; Get Carter, 1971; Zee & Co., 1972; Kidnapped, 1972; Pulp, 1972; Sleuth, 1973; The Black Windmill, Marseilles Contract, The Wilby Conspiracy, 1974; Fat Chance, The Romantic Englishwoman, The Man who would be King, Harry and Walter Go to New York, 1975; The Eagle has Landed, A Bridge Too Far, Silver Bears, 1976; The Swarm, 1977; California Suite, 1978; Ashanti, 1979; Beyond the Poseidon Adventure, 1979; The Island, 1979; Dressed to Kill, 1979; Escape to Victory, 1980; Death Trap, 1981; Jigsaw Man, 1982; Educating Rita, 1982; The Honorary Consul, 1982; Blame it on Rio, 1984; Water, 1985; The Holcroft Covenant, 1985; Hannah and Her Sisters (Academy Award), 1986; Half Moon Street, 1986; Mona Lisa, 1986; The Fourth Protocol, 1987; The Whistle Blower, 1987; Surrender, 1987; Jaws The Revenge, 1987; Without a Clue, 1989; Dirty Rotten Scoundrels, 1989; A Shock to the System, 1990; Bullseye, 1990; Mr Destiny, 1990; Noises Off, 1992; Blue Ice, 1992; The Muppet Christmas Carol, 1992; On Deadly Ground, 1993; *films for TV:* Jack The Ripper, 1988; Jekyll and Hyde, 1989; Then There Were Giants, 1993. *Recreations:* cinema, theatre, travel, gardening. *Address:* c/o Dennis Sellinger, International Creative Management, Oxford House, 76 Oxford Street, W1R 1RB.

CAINE, Sir Michael (Harris), Kt 1988; Chairman, 1979–93, Vice-Chairman, 1973–79, Chief Executive, 1975–84, Director, 1964–93, Booker plc; *b* 17 June 1927; *s* of Sir Sydney Caine, KCMG and Muriel Anne (*née* Harris); *m* 1st, 1952, Janice Denise (*née* Mercer) (marr. diss. 1987); one *s* one *d*; 2nd, 1987, Emma Harriet Nicholson, *qv*. *Educ:* Bedales; Lincoln Coll., Oxford; George Washington Univ., USA. Joined Booker McConnell Ltd, 1952; Chairman: Five TV Ltd, 1991–; Artisan Trust and Artisan Link Ltd, 1992–; Director: Arbor Acres Farm Inc., 1980–91; Booker Tate, 1993–; Commonwealth Equity Fund, 1990–95; Chm., African Emerging Markets Fund, 1993–. Chairman: Council for Technical Educn and Training for Overseas Countries, 1973–75; UK Council for Overseas Student Affairs, 1980–93. Member: Council, Inst. of Race Relations, 1969–72; Council, Bedford Coll., London, 1966–85; IBA, 1984–89; Commonwealth Develt Corp., 1985–94 (Dep. Chm., 1989–94); Governing Body: Inst. of Develt Studies, Sussex Univ., 1975–; NIESR, 1979–; Queen Elizabeth House, Oxford, 1983–; Chairman: Council, Royal African Soc., 1984–; Africa '95, 1993–; Commonwealth Scholarships Commn in the UK, 1987–; One World Broadcasting Trust, 1987–. *Address:* c/o Booker plc, Portland House, Stag Place, SW1E 5AY. *T:* 0171–411 5500. *Club:* Reform.

CAINES, Eric, CB 1993; Professor of Health Service Management, Nottingham University, since 1993; *b* 27 Feb. 1936; *s* of Ernest and Doris Caines; *m* 1st, 1958 (marr. diss. 1984); three *s;* 2nd, 1984, Karen Higgs; two *s*. *Educ:* Rothwell Grammar School, Wakefield; Leeds Univ. (LLB Hons). Dip. Hist. Art, London Univ., 1984. Short Service Commission, RAEC, 1958–61. NCB, 1961–65; BBC, 1965–66; as Principal, Min. of Health, Management Side Sec., General Whitley Council, 1966–70; Sec., NHS Reorganisation Management Arrangements Study, 1970–73; Assistant Sec., DHSS, 1973–77; IMF/World Bank, Washington, 1977–79; Under Sec., DHSS, 1979, Dir, Regl Organisation, 1981–84; Dir, Personnel and Finance, Prison Dept, Home Office, 1984–87; Dir, Operational Strategy, DHSS, then DSS, 1987–90; Dir of Personnel, NHS, DoH, 1990–93. Dir, Trebor Ltd, 1985–. FIPM; FRSA. *Recreation:* travelling on foot with a book. *Address:* Room C6, Portland Building, University Park, Nottingham NG7 2RD. *Club:* Athenæum.

CAINES, Sir John, KCB 1991 (CB 1983); Permanent Secretary, Department for Education (formerly of Education and Science), 1989–93; *b* 13 Jan. 1933; *s* of John Swinburne Caines and Ethel May Stenlake; *m* 1963, Mary Large; one *s* two *d*. *Educ:* Sherborne Prep. Sch.; Westminster Sch.; Christ Church, Oxford (MA). Asst Principal, Min. of Supply, 1957; Asst Private Sec., Min. of Aviation, 1960–61; Principal, Min. of Aviation, 1961–64; Civil Air Attaché in Middle East, 1964–66; Manchester Business Sch., 1967; Asst Sec., BoT, 1968; Sec., Commn on Third London Airport, 1968–71; Asst Sec., DTI, 1971–72; Principal Private Sec. to Sec. of State for Trade and Industry, 1972–74; Under-Sec., Dept of Trade, 1974–77; Sec., 1977–80, Mem. and Dep. Chief Exec., 1979–80, NEB; Dep. Sec., Dept of Trade, and Chief Exec., BOTB, 1980–82; Dep. Sec., Central Policy Review Staff, Cabinet Office, 1983; Dep. Sec., DTI, 1983–87; Permanent Sec., ODA, FCO, 1987–89. Director: Investors Compensation Scheme, 1993–; Norsk Hydro (UK) Ltd, 1994–; Chm., European Capital, 1995–. Member of Council: Southampton Univ., 1993–; Open Univ., 1993– (Chm., Audit Cttee, 1993–). DUniv Open, 1993. *Recreations:* travel, music, gardening, theatre. *Address:* 19 College Road, SE21 7BG.

CAIRD, Most Rev. Donald Arthur Richard; *see* Dublin, Archbishop of, and Primate of Ireland.

CAIRD, John Newport; theatre director and writer; Hon. Associate Director, Royal Shakespeare Company; *b* 22 Sept. 1948; *s* of late Rev. George Bradford Caird, DPhil, DD, FBA and of Viola Mary Newport, MA; *m* 1st, 1972, Helen Frances Brammer (marr. diss. 1982); 2nd, 1982, Ann Dorszynski (marr. diss. 1990); two *s* one *d*; 3rd, 1990, Frances Ruffelle; one *s* one *d*. *Educ:* Selwyn House Sch., Montreal; Magdalen Coll. Sch., Oxford; Bristol Old Vic Theatre Sch. Associate Dir, Contact Theatre, Manchester, 1974–76; directed, Contact: Look Back in Anger, Downright Hooligan, Twelfth Night; Resident Dir, 1977–82, Associate Dir, 1983–90, RSC; directed, RSC: Dance of Death, 1977; Savage Amusement, Look Out, Here Comes Trouble, 1978; Caucasian Chalk Circle, 1979; (co-dir, with Trevor Nunn) Nicholas Nickleby, London, New York and Los Angeles, 1980, 1982, 1986 (SWET Award, 1980, Tony Award, 1982, for Best Dir; televised, 1981, Emmy Award, 1983); Naked Robots, Twin Rivals, 1981; Our Friends in the North, 1982; Peter Pan (co-dir with Trevor Nunn), 1982–84; Twelfth Night, Romeo and Juliet, 1983; The Merchant of Venice, Red Star, 1984; Philistines, 1985; Les Misérables (co-dir with Trevor Nunn), London, Washington, NY, Boston, Oslo, LA, Tokyo, Paris and Sydney, 1985–91 (Tony Award for Best Dir, 1986, 1987); Every Man in his Humour, Misalliance, 1986; A Question of Geography, The New Inn, 1987; As You Like It, A Midsummer Night's Dream, 1989; Columbus and the Discovery of Japan, Antony and Cleopatra, 1992; directed, NT: Trelawny of the 'Wells', 1993; The Seagull, 1994. Directed: Song and Dance, London, 1982; As You Like It, Stockholm, 1984 (also for TV, 1985); Zaïde by Mozart, Battignano, 1991; Life Sentences, NY, 1993; The Millionairess, 1995. Devised and dir., Intimate Letters (a series of concerts for actors and string quartet); wrote and directed: The Kingdom of the Spirit, London, 1986; Siegfried & Roy at the Mirage, Las Vegas, 1989; Children of Eden, a musical (with music and lyrics by Stephen Schwartz), London, and Roanoke, Va, 1991; The Beggar's Opera (a new version with music by Ilona Sekacz), RSC, 1992; Jane Eyre, a musical (music by Paul Gordon). Hon. FWCMD. *Recreation:* music. *Address:* c/o Gloucester Mansions, Cambridge Circus, WC2H 8HD.

CAIRD, William Douglas Sime; Registrar, Family Division of High Court (formerly Probate, Divorce and Admiralty Division), 1964–82; *b* 21 Aug. 1917; *er s* of William Sime Caird and Elsie Amy Caird; *m* 1946, Josephine Mary, *d* of Peter and Elizabeth Seeney, Stratford on Avon; no *c*. *Educ:* Rutlish Sch., Merton. Entered Principal Probate Registry, 1937; Estabt Officer, 1954; Sec., 1959; Mem., Matrimonial Causes Rule Cttee, 1968–79. *Publications:* Consulting Editor, Rayden on Divorce, 10th edn 1967, 11th edn 1971, 12th edn 1974, 13th edn 1979. *Address:* 17 Pine Walk, Bookham, Surrey KT23 4AS. *T:* Bookham (01372) 456732.

CAIRNCROSS, Sir Alexander Kirkland, (Sir Alec Cairncross), KCMG 1967 (CMG 1950); FBA 1961; Chancellor, University of Glasgow, 1972–96; *b* 11 Feb. 1911; 3rd *s* of Alexander Kirkland and Elizabeth Andrew Cairncross, Lesmahagow, Scotland; *m* 1943, Mary Frances Glynn, *d* of Maj. E. F. Glynn, TD, Ilkley; three *s* two *d*. *Educ:* Hamilton Academy; Glasgow and Cambridge Univs. Univ. Lectr, 1935–39; Civil Servant, 1940–45; Dir of Programmes, Min. of Aircraft Production, 1945; Economic Advisory Panel, Berlin, 1945–46; Mem. of Staff of The Economist, 1946. Mem. of Wool Working Party, 1946; Economic Adviser to: BoT, 1946–49; Organisation for European Economic Co-operation, 1949–50; Prof. of Applied Economics, Univ. of Glasgow, 1951–61; Dir, Economic Development Inst., Washington DC, 1955–56; Economic Adviser to HM Govt, 1961–64; Head of Govt Economic Service, 1964–69; Master of St Peter's Coll., Oxford, 1969–78, Hon. Fellow, 1978; Supernumerary Fellow, St Antony's Coll., Oxford, 1978–89. Vis. Prof., Brookings Instn, Washington, DC, 1972; Leverhulme Vis. Prof., Inst. of Economic and Social Change, Bangalore, 1981; Leverhulme Emeritus Fellow, 1983–86. Chairman: independent advrs on reassessment of Channel Tunnel Project, 1974–75 (Adviser to Minister of Transport on Channel Tunnel Project, 1979–81); Commonwealth Secretariat Gp of Experts on Protectionism, 1982; Local Development Cttee, 1951–52; Member: Crofting Commn, 1951–54; Phillips Cttee, 1953–54; Anthrax Cttee, 1957–59; Radcliffe Cttee, 1957–59; Cttee on N Ireland, 1971; Cttee on Police Pay, 1978; Council of Management, Nat. Inst. of Economic and Social Research; Court of Governors, LSE, until 1989 (Hon. Fellow, 1980); Council, Royal Economic Soc. (Pres., 1968–70). President: Scottish Economic Soc., 1969–71; British Assoc. for Advancement of Science, 1970–71 (Pres. Section F, 1969); Vice Pres., GPDST, 1992– (Pres., 1972–92). Houblon-Norman Trustee, 1982–86. Editor, Scottish Journal of Political Economy, 1954–61. Hon. Mem., Amer. Econ. Assoc., 1989; For. Hon. Mem., Amer. Acad. of Arts and Scis, 1973. Hon. Fellow, St Antony's Coll., Oxford, 1989. Hon. LLD: Mount Allison, 1962; Glasgow, 1966; Exeter, 1969; Hon. DLitt: Reading, 1968: Heriot-Watt, 1969; Hon. DSc(Econ.): Univ. of Wales, 1971; QUB, 1972; DUniv Stirling, 1973. *Publications:* Introduction to Economics, 1944, 6th edn 1982; Home and Foreign Investment, 1870–1913, 1953; Monetary Policy in a Mixed Economy, 1960; Economic Development and the Atlantic Provinces, 1961; Factors in Economic Development, 1962; Essays in Economic Management, 1971; Control of Long-term International Capital Movements, 1973; Inflation, Growth and International Finance, 1975; Science Studies (Nuffield Foundn report), 1980; Snatches (poems), 1981; (with Barry Eichengreen) Sterling in Decline, 1983; Years of Recovery, 1985; The Price of War, 1986; Economics and Economic Policy, 1986; A Country to Play With, 1987; (ed) The Diaries of Robert Hall, Vol. I 1989, Vol. II 1991; (with Nita Watts) The Economic Section 1939–61, 1989; Planning in Wartime, 1991; The British Economy since 1945, 1992, 2nd edn 1995; (with K. Burk) Goodbye Great Britain, 1992; (ed with F. Cairncross) The Legacy of the Golden Age, 1992; Austin Robinson: the life of an economic adviser, 1993; Economic Ideas and Government Policy, 1995; Managing the British Economy in the 1960s, 1996. *Recreation:* writing. *Address:* 14 Staverton Road, Oxford OX2 6XJ. *T:* Oxford (01865) 52358.
See also F. A. Cairncross.

CAIRNCROSS, Frances Anne, (Mrs Hamish McRae); Media Editor, The Economist, since 1994; *b* 30 Aug. 1944; *d* of Sir Alexander Kirkland Cairncross, *qv*; *m* 1971, Hamish McRae, *qv*; two *d*. *Educ:* Laurel Bank Sch., Glasgow; St Anne's Coll., Oxford (MA History; Hon. Fellow 1993); Brown Univ., Rhode Island (MAEcon). On Staff of: The Times, 1967–69; The Banker, 1969; The Observer, 1970–73; Economics Correspondent 1973–81, Women's Page Editor 1981–84, The Guardian; Britain Ed., 1984–89, Envmt Ed., 1989–94, The Economist. Member: SSRC Economics Cttee, 1972–76; Newspaper Panel, Monopolies Commn, 1973–80; Council, Royal Economic Soc., 1980–85; Council, PSI, 1987–90; Cttee of Inquiry into Proposals to Amend the Shops Act, 1983–84; Inquiry into British Housing, 1984–85; School Teachers Review Body, 1991–94. Director: Prolific Gp plc, 1988–89; Alliance & Leicester Building Soc., 1990–. Hon. Treas., Nat. Council for One Parent Families, 1980–83; Trustee, Kennedy Memorial Trust, 1974–90; *Publications:* Capital City (with Hamish McRae), 1971; The Second Great Crash (with Hamish McRae), 1973; The Guardian Guide to the Economy, 1981; Changing Perceptions of Economic Policy, 1981; The Second Guardian Guide to the Economy, 1983; Guide to the Economy, 1987; Costing the Earth, 1991; Green, Inc, 1995. *Recreation:* home life. *Address:* 6 Canonbury Lane, N1 2AP. *T:* 0171–359 4612.

CAIRNCROSS, Neil Francis, CB 1971; Deputy Under-Secretary of State, Home Office, 1972–80; *b* 29 July 1920; *s* of late James and Olive Hunter Cairncross; *m* 1947, Eleanor Elizabeth Leisten; two *s* one *d*. *Educ:* Charterhouse; Oriel Coll., Oxford. Royal Sussex Regt, 1940–45. Called to the Bar, 1948. Home Office, 1948; a Private Sec. to the Prime Minister, 1955–58; Sec., Royal Commn on the Press, 1961–62; Dep. Sec., Cabinet Office, 1970–72; Dep. Sec., NI Office, March–Nov. 1972. Member: Parole Bd, 1982–85; Home Grown Timber Adv. Cttee, 1981–90; (co-opted) Avon Probation Cttee, 1983–89. *Recreation:* painting. *Address:* Little Grange, The Green, Olveston, Bristol BS12 3EJ. *T:* Almondsbury (01454) 613060. *Club:* United Oxford & Cambridge University.

CAIRNS, family name of **Earl Cairns.**

CAIRNS, 6th Earl *cr* 1878; **Simon Dallas Cairns,** CBE 1992; Baron Cairns 1867; Viscount Garmoyle 1878; Receiver-General of Duchy of Cornwall, since 1990; Chairman: BAT Industries, since 1996 (Director, since 1990); Commonwealth Development Corporation, since 1995; *b* 27 May 1939; *er s* of 5th Earl Cairns, GCVO, CB and of Barbara Jeanne Harrisson, *y d* of Sydney H. Burgess; *S* father, 1989; *m* 1964, Amanda Mary, *d* of late Major E. F. Heathcoat Amory, and of Mrs Roderick Heathcoat Amory, Oswaldkirk Hall, York; three *s*. *Educ:* Eton; Trinity Coll., Cambridge. Man. Dir, 1981–84, a Vice-Chm., 1984–86, Mercury Securities plc.; S. G. Warburg & Co.: Man. Dir, 1979–85; Dir, 1985–95; a Vice-Chm., 1985–87; Jt Chm., 1987–91; Chief Exec. and Dep. Chm., 1991–95. Mem., City Capital Markets Cttee, 1989–94. Treas., 1974–81, Chm., 1981–92, VSO. *Heir:* *s* Viscount Garmoyle, *qv*. *Address:* Bolehyde Manor, Allington, near Chippenham, Wilts SN14 6LW. *T:* Chippenham (01249) 652105; (office) Windsor House, 50 Victoria Street, SW1H 0NL. *Club:* Turf.

CAIRNS, David Adam; Music Critic, Sunday Times, since 1985; *b* 8 June 1926; *s* of Sir Hugh William Bell Cairns, KBE, FRCS and Barbara Cairns, *d* of A. L. Smith, sometime Master of Balliol; *m* 1959, Rosemary, *d* of Aubrey and Hilary Goodwin; three *s*. *Educ:* Trinity Coll., Oxford (1st Cl. Mod. History). Nat. Service, Intell. Corps, 1949–50. Co-Founder, Chelsea Opera Gp, 1950; Jane Eliza Procter Fellow, Princeton, 1950–51; Liby Clerk, H of C, 1951–53; TES, 1955–58; Music Critic: Evening Standard, and Spectator,

1958–62; Arts Editor, Spectator, 1961–62; Asst Music Critic, Financial Times, 1962–67; Music Critic, New Stateman, 1967–70; Classical Programme Co-ordinator, Philips Records, 1968–73; freelance music critic, 1973–85; founder and conductor, Thorington Players, 1983. Dist. Vis. Prof., Univ. of California, Davis, 1985; Vis. Scholar, Getty Center for History of Art and Humanities, 1992; Vis. Res. Fellow, Merton Coll., Oxford, 1993. Officier de l'Ordre des Arts et des Lettres, 1991 (Chevalier, 1975). *Publications:* The Memoirs of Hector Berlioz (ed and trans.), 1969, 4th edn 1990; Responses: musical essays and reviews, 1973; Berlioz: the making of an artist 1803–1832, 1989 (Yorkshire Post Prize; Royal Phil. Soc. Award; Derek Allen Meml Prize, British Acad.); (jtly) English National Opera Guides: The Magic Flute, 1980; Falstaff, 1982. *Recreations:* conducting, cinema, France and the French. *Address:* 49 Amerland Road, SW18 1QA. *T:* 0181–870 4931.

CAIRNS, Air Vice-Marshal Geoffrey Crerar, CBE 1970; AFC 1960; FRAeS 1979; Consultant, FLS Aerospace (Lovaux) Ltd, 1992–95; *b* 1926; *s* of late Dr J. W. Cairns, MD, MCh, DPH and Marion Cairns; *m* 1948, Carol (*d* 1985), *d* of H. I. F. Evernden, MBE; four *d. Educ:* Loretto School, Musselburgh; Cambridge Univ. Joined RAF, 1944; served: Sqdns 43 and 93, Italy; Sqdn 73, Malta, 1946–49; Sqdn 72, UK, 1949–51; Adjutant, Hong Kong Auxiliary Air Force; test pilot A&AEE, Boscombe Down, 1957–60; Jt Planning Staff, MoD, 1961; Chief Instructor, Helicopters, CFS, RAF Ternhill, 1963; JSSC 1966; Supt Flying A&AEE 1968; Dir, Defence Operational Requirements Staffs, MoD, 1970; Commandant, Boscombe Down, 1972–74; ACAS (Op. Requirements), MoD, 1974–76; Comdr, Southern Maritime Air Region, 1976–78; Chief of Staff No 18 Group, Strike Command, 1978–80. Consultant, Marconi Avionics, 1980–81. Dir, Trago Aircraft Ltd, 1982–87. *Recreations:* golf, railways. *Club:* Royal Air Force.

CAIRNS, Hugh John Forster; DM; FRS 1974; Professor of Microbiology, Harvard School of Public Health, 1980–91; *b* 21 Nov. 1922. *Educ:* Oxford Univ. BA 1943; BM, BCh 1946; DM 1952. Surg. Registrar, Radcliffe Infirmary, Oxford, 1945; Med. Intern, Postgrad. Med. Sch., London, 1946; Paediatric Intern, Royal Victoria Infirmary, Newcastle, 1947; Chem. Pathologist, Radcliffe Infirmary, 1947–49; Virologist, Hall Inst., Melbourne, Aust., 1950–51; Virus Research Inst., Entebbe, Uganda, 1952–54; Research Fellow, then Reader, Aust. Nat. Univ., Canberra, 1955–63; Rockefeller Research Fellow, California Inst. of Technology, 1957; Nat. Insts of Health Fellow, Cold Spring Harbor, NY, 1960–61; Dir, Cold Spring Harbor Lab. of Quantitative Biology, 1963–68 (Staff Mem., 1968–); Prof of Biology (Hon.), State Univ. of New York, Stony Brook, 1968–73, Amer. Cancer Soc. Prof. 1968–73; Head of Imperial Cancer Research Fund Mill Hill Laboratories, 1973–80. *Address:* Holly Grove House, Wilcote, Chipping Norton, Oxon OX7 3EA. *T:* Ramsden (01993) 868706.

CAIRNS, Dr James Ford; MHR (ALP) for Lalor, 1969–78 (for Yarra, 1955–69); *b* 4 Oct. 1914; *s* of James John Cairns and Letitia Cairns (*née* Ford); *m* 1939, Gwendolyn Olga Robb; two *s. Educ:* Melton/Sunbury State Sch.; Northcote High Sch.; Melbourne Univ. MComm and PhD (Melb.). Australian Estates Co. Ltd, 1932; Victoria Police Force, 1935. Served War, AIF, 1945. Melbourne University: Sen. Tutor, Lectr, Sen. Lectr (Economic Hist.), 1946–55; Nuffield Dominion Fellow, Oxford Univ., 1951–52. Minister for Overseas Trade, 1972–74; Treasurer of Australia, 1974–75; Dep. Prime Minister, 1974–75; Minister for the Environment, Australia, 1975. *Publications:* Australia, 1951 (UK); Living with Asia, 1965; The Eagle and the Lotus, 1969; Tariffs or Planning, 1970; Silence Kills, 1970; The Quiet Revolution, 1972; Oil in Troubled Waters, 1976; Vietnam: Scorched Earth Reborn, 1976; Growth to Freedom, 1979; Survival Now, the Human Transformation, 1983; Human Growth: its source . . . and potential, 1985; Strength Within: towards an end to violence, 1988; The Untried Road, 1990; Towards a New Society: a new day has begun, 1993; numerous articles in jls and press, incl. title Australia: History in Enc. Brit. *Recreations:* sleeping, reading.

CAIRNS, James George Hamilton Dickson; Chief Architect and Director of Works, Home Office, 1975–80; *b* 17 Sept. 1920; *s* of Percival Cairns and Christina Elliot Cairns; *m* 1944, G. Elizabeth Goodman; one *d. Educ:* Hillhead High Sch., Glasgow; London Polytechnic. ARIBA. Served War, Royal Corps of Signals (Intell.), 1941–46. Architects' Dept, GLC, 1946–75. Divisional Architect, Thamesmead New Town, awarded Sir Patrick Abercrombie Prize by Internat. Union of Architects, 1969. *Recreations:* golf, sailing. *Address:* Elmsleigh, 12 Elmstead Park Road, West Wittering, W Sussex PO20 8NQ. *T:* Birdham (01243) 513316. *Clubs:* Goodwood Golf; West Wittering Sailing.

CAITHNESS, 20th Earl of, *cr* 1455; **Malcolm Ian Sinclair,** PC 1990; FRICS; Lord Berriedale, 1455; Bt 1631; consultant to various companies, since 1994; *b* 3 Nov. 1948; *s* of 19th Earl of Caithness, CVO, CBE, DSO, DL, JP; *S* father, 1965; *m* 1975, Diana Caroline (*d* 1994), *d* of Major Richard Coke, DSO, MC, DL; one *s* one *d. Educ:* Marlborough; Royal Agricl Coll., Cirencester. Savills, land and estate agents, 1972–78; Brown and Mumford, 1978–80; property developer and other small businesses, 1980–84. A Lord in Waiting (Govt Whip), 1984–85; parly spokesman on health and social security, 1984–85, on Scotland, 1984–86; Parly Under-Sec. of State, Dept of Transport, 1985–86; Minister of State: Home Office, 1986–88; DoE, 1988–89; Paymaster Gen. and Minister of State, HM Treasury, 1989–90; Minister of State: FCO, 1990–92; Dept of Transport, 1992–94. *Heir: s* Lord Berriedale, *qv. Address:* c/o House of Lords, SW1A 0PW.

CALATRAVA-VALLS, Dr Santiago; architect; *b* Valencia, 28 July 1951; *m* 1976, Robertina Calatrava-Maragoni; three *s. Educ:* art sch., Valencia; Escuela Technica Superior de Arquitectura de Valencia; Swiss Fed. Inst. of Technol., Zürich (studies in civil engrg; Dr Tech. Sci.). Asst, Inst. for Bldg Statics and Construction and for Aerodynamics and Light Weight Constructions, Zürich, 1979–81; Founder: architectural and civil engrg practice, Zürich, 1981; architectural practice, Paris, 1989, and Valencia, 1991. Major projects include: Stadelhofen Rly Stn, Zürich, 1983–90; Lucerne Stn Hall, 1983–89; BCE Place, Toronto, 1987–92; Alamillo Bridge and La Cartuja Viaduct, Seville, 1987–92; Lusitania Bridge, Merida, 1988–91; Montjuic Communication Tower, Barcelona, 1989–92; Lyon Airport Rly Stn, 1989–94; Kuwait Pavilion, Expo '92, Seville, 1991–92. Exhibitions of work include: Mus. of Architecture, Basel, 1987; Design Mus., Zürich, 1991; Mus. of Modern Art, NY, 1992; retrospective, RIBA, London, 1992; Deutsches Mus., Munich, 1993; Valencia, Lübeck and Copenhagen, 1993. Member: Union of Swiss Architects, 1987; Internat. Acad. of Architecture, 1987; European Acad., 1992. Hon. FRIBA 1993. Hon. Mem., Union of German Architects, 1989. Dr *hc*: Valencia, 1993; Seville, 1994. Numerous international prizes and awards including: Internat. Assoc. for Bridge and Structural Engrg Award, 1988; Gold Medal, IStructE, 1992. *Address:* Höschgasse 5, 8008 Zürich, Switzerland. *T:* (1) 4227500, *Fax:* (1) 4225600.

CALCUTT, Sir David (Charles), Kt 1991; QC 1972; Chairman: City Panel on Takeovers and Mergers, since 1989; Institute of Actuaries' Appeal Board, since 1985; Council of the Banking Ombudsman, since 1994; President, Lloyd's of London Appeal Tribunal, since 1987 (Deputy President, 1983–87); a Judge of the Courts of Appeal of Jersey and Guernsey, since 1978; Chancellor of the Dioceses of Exeter and of Bristol, since 1971 and of Gibraltar in Europe, since 1983; *b* 2 Nov. 1930; *s* of late Henry Calcutt; *m* 1969, Barbara, JP and Freeman, City of London, *d* of late Vivian Walker. *Educ:* Christ Church, Oxford (chorister); Cranleigh Sch. (music schol.); King's Coll., Cambridge (choral schol.; Stewart of Rannoch Schol., 1952; prizeman; MA, LLB, MusB). Called to the Bar, Middle Temple, 1955 (Bencher, 1981); Harmsworth Law Schol., Garraway Rice Prize, 1956; Chm. of the Bar, 1984–85 (Vice-Chm., 1983–84). Dep. Chm., Somerset QS, 1970–71; a Recorder, 1972–89. Fellow Commoner, 1980–85, Master, 1986–94, Magdalene Coll., Cambridge (Hon. Fellow, 1994–). Dept of Trade Inspector, Cornhill Consolidated Gp Ltd, 1974–77; Chm., CS Arbitration Tribunal, 1979–94; Member: Criminal Injuries Compensation Bd, 1977–; Council on Tribunals, 1980–86; Chm., Falkland Is Commn of Enquiry, 1984; conducted: Cyprus Service Police Inquiry, 1985–86; Colin Wallace Inquiry, 1990; Review of Press Self-Regulation, 1992–93; Member: Colliery Indep. Review Body, 1985–88; Interception of Communications Tribunal, 1986–; Arbitrator, Internat. Centre for the Settlement of Investment Disputes, Washington DC; Indep. Mem., Diplomatic Service Appeal Bd, 1986–92; Home Office and MoD Assessor of Compensation for Miscarriages of Justice, 1989–; Chm., Cttee on Privacy and Related Matters, 1989–90; Judicial Chm., City Disputes Panel, 1994–. UK Deleg., Consultative Cttee, Bars and Law Socs, EEC, 1979–83. Gresham Prof. of Law, 1992–95. Fellow, Internat. Acad. of Trial Lawyers (NY), 1978–; Hon. Member: American Bar Assoc., 1985–; Canadian Bar Assoc., 1985–; Cambridge Union Soc., 1994–. Dir, Edington Music Fest., 1956–64. Dep. Chm., RCM, 1988–90 (FRCM 1988). Chairman: Council, Cranleigh and Bramley Schs, 1987–93 (Vice-Chm., 1983–87); Septemviri, Cambridge Univ., 1988–; Gov., Ditchley Foundn, 1992–. Fellow, Winchester Coll., 1992. *Recreation:* hill-farming on Exmoor. *Address:* 35 Essex Street, Temple, WC2R 3AR. *Clubs:* Athenæum; New (Edinburgh); Hawks (Cambridge).

CALCUTTA, Archbishop of, (RC), since 1986; **Most Rev. Henry Sebastian D'Souza;** *b* 20 Jan. 1926; *s* of George William and Aurelia Clotilde D'Souza. *Educ:* Papal Atheneum, Kandy (LPH, LD); Urban Univ., Rome (DCL). Nominated Archbishop of Cuttack-Bhubaneswar, 1974. Secretary General: Catholic Bishops' Conference of India, 1979–82; Federation of Asian Bishops' Confs, 1983–93. Pres., Conf. of Catholic Bishops of India (Latin Rite), 1988–94. *Address:* Archbishop's House, 32 Park Street, Calcutta 700016, India. *T:* (33) 441960, (33) 444666.

CALCUTTA, Bishop of, since 1982; **Rt. Rev. Dinesh Chandra Gorai;** *b* 15 Jan. 1934. *Educ:* Calcutta Univ. (BA 1956); Serampore Theological Coll. (BD 1959). Ordained, 1962; Methodist Minister in Calcutta/Barrackpore, 1968–70; first Bishop, Church of N India Diocese of Barrackpore, 1970–82; Dep. Moderator, 1980, Moderator, 1983–86, Church of N India. Hon. DD: Bethel Coll., 1985; Serampore Coll., 1991. *Publications:* Society at the Cross Road, 1968; (ed) Transfer of Vision: a leadership development programme for the Church of North India 1983–1986, 1984; New Horizons in Christian Ministry, 1993. *Address:* Bishop's House, 51 Chowringhee Road, Calcutta 700 071, India. *T:* (33) 2425259, *Fax:* (33) 242634.

CALDECOTE, 2nd Viscount *cr* 1939, of Bristol; **Robert Andrew Inskip,** KBE 1987; DSC 1941; DL; FEng 1977; Chairman: Delta Group plc (formerly Delta Metal Co.), 1972–82; Investors in Industry (formerly Finance for Industry), 1980–87; *b* 8 Oct. 1917; *o s* of Thomas Walker Hobart Inskip, 1st Viscount Caldecote, PC, CBE, and Lady Augusta Orr Ewing (*d* 1967), *widow* of Charles Orr Ewing, MP for Ayr Burghs and *e d* of 7th Earl of Glasgow; *S* father, 1947; *m* 1942, Jean Hamilla, *d* of late Rear-Adm. H. D. Hamilton; one *s* two *d. Educ:* Eton Coll.; King's Coll., Cambridge. BA Cantab 1939; MA 1944; Hon. LLD 1983. RNVR, 1939–45; RNC Greenwich, 1946–47; an Asst Manager, Vickers-Armstrong Naval Yard, Walker-on-Tyne, 1947–48; Fellow, King's Coll., and Lectr, Engineering Dept, Cambridge Univ., 1948–55; Dir, English Electric Co., 1953–69; Man. Dir, English Electric Aviation, 1960–63; Dep. Man. Dir, British Aircraft Corp., 1961–67 (Dir, 1960–69); Chm., Legal and General Gp, 1977–80. Chairman: EDC Movement of Exports, 1965–72; Export Council for Europe, 1970–71. Mem., H of L Select Cttee for Sci. and Technol., 1988–92. President: Soc. of British Aerospace Cos, 1965–66; Internat. Assoc. of Aeronautical and Space Equipment Manufacturers, 1966–68; Parliamentary and Scientific Cttee, 1966–69; Fellowship of Engineering, 1981–86; RINA, 1987–90 (FRINA 1987). Director: Consolidated Gold Fields, 1969–78; Lloyds Bank, 1975–88; Lloyds Bank International, 1979–85; Equity Capital for Industry, 1980–85; W. S. Atkins Ltd, 1985–92; Industry Ventures Ltd, 1989–93. Member: Review Bd for Govt Contracts, 1969–76; Inflation Accounting Cttee, 1974–75; Engineering Industries Council, 1975–82; British Railways Bd, 1979–85; Adv. Council for Applied R & D, 1981–84; Engrg Council, 1981–85. Chairman: Design Council, 1972–80; BBC Gen. Adv. Council, 1982–85; Mary Rose Trust, 1983–92; Crown Appts Commn, 1990. Pro-Chancellor, Cranfield Inst. of Technology, 1976–84. Mem., Church Assembly, 1950–55. Mem. UK Delegn to UN, 1952. Pres., Assoc. Sail Training Orgns, 1988–. Fellow, Eton Coll., 1953–72; Pres., Dean Close Sch., 1960–90. DL Hants, 1991. Hon. FICE, 1981; Hon. FIMechE, 1982; Hon. FIEE, 1984; Hon. FIM 1984; Hon. FCSD (FSIAD 1976). Hon. DSc: Cranfield, 1976; Aston, 1979; City, 1982; Bristol, 1982. Hon. LLD: London, 1981; Cambridge, 1985. *Recreations:* sailing, shooting, golf. *Heir: s* Hon. Piers James Hampden Inskip [*b* 20 May 1947; *m* 1st, 1970, Susan Bridget, *d* of late W. P. Mellen; 2nd, 1984, Kristine Elizabeth, *d* of Harvey Holbrooke-Jackson; one *s*]. *Address:* Orchard Cottage, South Harting, Petersfield, Hants GU31 5NR. *T:* Harting (01730) 825529. *Clubs:* Pratt's, Athenæum, Royal Ocean Racing; Royal Yacht Squadron.

CALDECOTT, Andrew Hilary; QC 1994; *b* 22 June 1952; *s* of Andrew Caldecott, CBE and Zita (*née* Belloc); *m* 1977, Rosamond Ashton Shuttleworth; two *s* two *d. Educ:* Eton Coll.; New Coll., Oxford (BA Hons Mod. Hist.). Called to the Bar, Inner Temple, 1975. *Address:* 1 Brick Court, Temple, EC4Y 9BY. *T:* 0171–353 8845.

CALDER, Elisabeth Nicole; Publishing Director, Bloomsbury Publishing, since 1986; *b* 20 Jan. 1938; *d* of Florence Mary Baber and Ivor George Baber; *m* 1958, Richard Henry Calder (marr. diss. 1972); one *d* one *s. Educ:* Broadfields, Edgware; Palmerston North Girls' High Sch., NZ; Canterbury Univ., NZ (BA 1958). Reader, Metro-Goldwyn-Mayer story dept, 1969–70; Publicity Manager, Victor Gollancz, 1971–74; Editorial Director: Victor Gollancz, 1975–78; Jonathan Cape, 1979–86. *Recreations:* reading, thinking about gardening, junking. *Address:* Bloomsbury Publishing, 2 Soho Square, W1V 5DE. *T:* 0171–494 2111. *Club:* Groucho.

CALDER, Dr Ian Maddison, TD 1973; MD; FFOM; FCPath (HK); consultant adviser on occupational medicine to Ministry of Defence, since 1994; *b* 22 March 1937; *s* of late Walter James Calder, MIMechE, and Alice (*née* Maddison); *m* 1964, Dorothy Joan Hubbard, RGN; one *s* one *d. Educ:* Norwich Sch.; Univ. of St Andrews (MB ChB 1962; State Scholar); Univ. of Dundee (MD 1977; DSc 1992). MRCPath 1981; FFOM 1990; FCPath (HK) 1993. Served RA, 1955 (2nd Lieut); Hon. Col, 254 Field Ambulance, RAMC (V), 1991–; Mem., E Anglia TAVRA Cttee, 1990. Lectr in Forensic Medicine, St George's Hosp. Med. Sch., Univ. of London, 1972–76. Visiting Fellow: St Edmund's Coll., Cambridge, 1978–; Wellcome Inst. of Comparative Neurology, Univ. of Cambridge, 1978–; Travelling Scholar, UCLA, 1976; Advr to Nat. Undersea Res. Centre, Univ. of N Carolina. Ext. Examnr, Univ. of Hong Kong, 1985–90; Advr to Labour Dept, Hong Kong, 1991–94. Member: MoD Ethical Cttee, 1983–; MRC Hyperbaric Scis Panel; MRC Long Term Health Effects Cttee; DoH Dangerous Pathogens Working Party.

Mem., Physicians for Human Rights. *Publications:* chapters in textbooks of pathology and occupational medicine; papers on diving and hyperbaric medicine research. *Recreations:* sailing, boat-building, antique furniture and cabinet making, rowing, church music. *Address:* Thorpe, Huntingdon Road, Girton, Cambridge CB3 0LG. *T:* Cambridge (01223) 277220. *Club:* Athenæum.

CALDER, John Mackenzie; Managing Director: John Calder (Publishers) Ltd, 1950–91; Calder Publications Ltd, since 1991; President, Riverrun Press Inc., New York, since 1978; *b* 25 Jan. 1927; *e s* of James Calder, Ardargie, Forgandenny, Perthshire, and Lucianne Wilson, Montreal, Canada; *m* 1st, 1949, Mary Ann Simmonds; one *d*; 2nd, 1960, Bettina Jonic (marr. diss. 1975); one *d*. *Educ:* Gilling Castle, Yorks; Bishops College Sch., Canada; McGill Univ.; Sir George Williams Coll.; Zürich Univ. Studied political economy; subseq. worked in Calders Ltd (timber co.), Director; founded John Calder (Publishers) Ltd, 1949; Man. Dir, Calder & Boyars, 1964–75. Organiser of literary confs for Edinburgh Festival, 1962 and 1963, and Harrogate Festival, 1969. Founded Ledlanet Nights, 1963, in Kinross-shire (music and opera festival, closed 1974). Active in fields related to the arts and on many cttees; Co-founder, Defence of Literature and the Arts Society; Chm., Fedn of Scottish Theatres, 1972–74. Contested (L): Kinross and W Perthshire, 1970; Hamilton, Oct. 1974; (European Parlt) Mid Scotland and Fife, 1979. FRSA 1974. Chevalier des Arts et des Lettres, 1975; Chevalier de l'Ordre nationale de mérite, 1983. *Publications:* (ed) A Samuel Beckett Reader, 1967; (ed) Beckett at 60, 1967; (ed) William Burroughs Reader, 1982; (ed) New Samuel Beckett Reader, 1983; (ed) Henry Miller Reader, 1985; (ed) The Nouveau Roman Reader, 1986; (ed) As No Other Dare Fail: for Samuel Beckett on his 80th birthday, 1986; The Garden of Eros, 1994; (ed) Gambit International Drama Review, etc; articles in many jls. *Recreations:* writing (several plays, stories; criticism, etc; translations); music, theatre, opera, reading, chess, lecturing, conversation; travelling, promoting good causes, fond of good food and wine. *Address:* c/o Calder Publications Ltd, 179 King's Cross Road, WC1X 9BZ. *Clubs:* Caledonian; Scottish Arts (Edinburgh).

CALDER, Julian Richard; Head of Division, Government Statistical Service and General Division, Central Statistical Office, since 1994; *b* 6 Dec. 1941; *s* of Donald Alexander and Ivy O'Nora Calder; *m* 1965, Avril Tucker; two *s*. *Educ:* Dulwich College; Brasenose College, Oxford; Birkbeck College, London. Statistician, 1973, Chief Statistician, 1978, Central Statistical Office; Chief Statistician, 1981, Dir of Stats, 1985–94, Board of Inland Revenue. *Recreations:* cycling, listening to music. *Address:* Central Statistical Office, PO Box 1333, Millbank Tower, Millbank, SW1P 4QQ. *T:* 0171–217 4362.

CALDER, Nigel David Ritchie, MA; science writer; *b* 2 Dec. 1931; *e s* of Baron Ritchie-Calder, CBE; *m* 1954, Elisabeth Palmer; two *s* three *d*. *Educ:* Merchant Taylors' Sch.; Sidney Sussex Coll., Cambridge. Physicist, Mullard Research Laboratories, 1954–56; Editorial staff, New Scientist, 1956–66; Science Editor, 1960–62; Editor, 1962–66. Science Correspondent, New Statesman, 1959–62 and 1966–71; Chairman, Assoc. of British Science Writers, 1962–64. Member: Initiative Group, Foundn Scientific Europe, 1987–90; Orgng Group, Cosmorama Exhibn (Europe), 1991–92. FRAS; FRGS. (Jtly) UNESCO Kalinga Prize for popularisation of science, 1972. *Publications:* Electricity Grows Up, 1958; Robots, 1958; Radio Astronomy, 1958; (ed) The World in 1984, 1965; The Environment Game, 1967; (ed) Unless Peace Comes, 1968; Technopolis: Social Control of the Uses of Science, 1969; Living Tomorrow, 1970; (ed) Nature in the Round: a Guide to Environmental Science, 1973; Timescale, 1983; 1984 and After, 1983; The English Channel, 1986; The Green Machines, 1986; (ed) Future Earth, 1988; (ed) Scientific Europe, 1990; Giotto to the Comets, 1992; Hubble Space Telescope, 1993; (ed) World Treasury of the New Life Sciences, 1995; Out of this World, 1995; *books of own TV programmes:* The Violent Universe, 1969; The Mind of Man, 1970; The Restless Earth, 1972; The Life Game, 1973; The Weather Machine, 1974; The Human Conspiracy, 1975–76; The Key to the Universe, 1977; Spaceships of the Mind (TV series), 1978; Einstein's Universe, 1979; Nuclear Nightmares, 1979; The Comet is Coming!, 1980; Spaceship Earth, 1991 (TV series). *Recreation:* sailing. *Address:* 26 Boundary Road, Northgate, Crawley, W Sussex RH10 2BT. *T:* Crawley (01293) 549969. *Club:* Cruising Association (Vice-Pres., 1981–84).

CALDERWOOD, Sir Robert, Kt 1990; Chairman, Greater Glasgow Health Board, since 1993; Chief Executive, Strathclyde Regional Council, 1980–92; Director, GEC (Scotland) Ltd, since 1991; *b* 1 March 1932; *s* of Robert Calderwood and Jessie Reid (*née* Marshall); *m* 1958, Meryl Anne (*née* Fleming); three *s* one *d*. *Educ:* William Hulme's Sch., Manchester; Manchester Univ. (LLB (Hons)). Admitted solicitor, 1956; Town Clerk: Salford, 1966–69; Bolton, 1969–73; Manchester, 1973–79. Dir, Glasgow Garden Fest. 1988 Ltd, 1985–88; Chm., Strathclyde Buses, 1989–93. Member: Parole Bd for England and Wales, 1971–73; Soc. of Local Authority Chief Execs, 1974–92 (Pres., 1989–90); Scottish Consultative Cttee, Commn for Racial Equality, 1981–88; Employers Panel, Industrial Tribunals in Scotland, 1992–; Local and Central Govt Relations Res. Cttee, Joseph Rowntree Foundn, 1992–. Director: European Summer Special Olympic Games 1990 (Strathclyde) Ltd, 1989–90; Scottish Opera, 1991– (Dep. Chm., 1992–); Quality Scotland Foundn, 1991–92. Mem. Council, Industrial Soc., 1983–92. Hon. FIWEM 1992. *Recreations:* theatre, watching Rugby. *Address:* 6 Mosspark Avenue, Milngavie, Glasgow G62 8NL.

CALDICOTT, Dr Fiona, FRCP, FRCPsych; Consultant Psychotherapist, Uffculme Clinic, Birmingham, since 1979; Senior Clinical Lecturer in Psychotherapy, University of Birmingham, since 1982; Medical Director, South Birmingham Mental Health Trust, since 1994; *b* 12 Jan. 1941; *d* of Joseph Maurice Soesan and Elizabeth Jane (*née* Ransley); *m* 1965, Robert Gordon Woodruff Caldicott; one *d* (one *s* decd). *Educ:* City of London Sch. for Girls; St Hilda's Coll., Oxford (MA, BM, BCh); DPM. House Surgeon and Physician, Coventry Hosps, 1966–67; General Practice, Family Planning and Child Welfare, 1968–70; training in Psychiatry, Walsgrave Hosp., Coventry and Central Hosp., Warwick, 1970–76; Sen. Registrar in Psychiatry, W Midlands Regl Trng Scheme, 1977–79; Consultant Psychiatrist, Univ. of Warwick, 1979–85; Unit General Manager, Mental Health, Central Birmingham, 1989–91; Clin. Dir, Adult Psychiatric and Psychotherapy Service, Mental Health Unit, S Birmingham, 1991–94. Mem., Sec. of State's Standing Adv. Cttee, on Med. Manpower Planning, 1991–, on Postgrad. Med. Educn, 1993–; Secretary: Monospecialist Cttee for Psychiatry, 1991–, European Bd of Psychiatry, 1992–, Union of European Med. Specialists. Sub-Dean 1987–90, Dean 1990–93, Pres., 1993–July 1996, RCPsych; Chm., Conf. of Med. Royal Colls, 1995–96. Fellow, Acad. of Medicine, Singapore, 1994; Mem., Czech Psychiatric Soc., 1994. Chevalier du Tastevin, 1991. *Publications:* contrib. Discussing Doctors' Careers (ed Isobel Allen), 1988; papers in Bull. RCPsych, Current Opinion in Psychiatry, Postgraduate Psychiatry. *Recreations:* family, friends, reading, theatre, wine. *Address:* King's Hill, King's Hill Lane, Finham, Coventry CV3 6PS. *T:* Coventry (01203) 415346. *Clubs:* Reform, Royal Society of Medicine.

CALDOW, William James, CMG 1977; Consultant, ICI plc, 1981–86; *b* 7 Dec. 1919; *s* of William Caldow and Mary Wilson Grier; *m* 1950, Monique Henriette Hervé, *d* of Gaétan Hervé, Chevalier de la Légion d'Honneur and Croix de Guerre (member of French Resistance, executed 1944); one *s* (and one *s* decd). *Educ:* Marr College (Dux Medallist); Glasgow University (Scholar; MA Hons); Sorbonne. Captain, Intelligence Corps, 1940–45. Colonial Administrative Service, Gold Coast, later Ghana, 1947–59; War Office, later Ministry of Defence, 1959–80. *Recreations:* reading, music, bird watching. *Address:* 3 Pilgrims Way, Guildford, Surrey GU4 8AB. *T:* Guildford (01483) 62183.

CALDWELL, Surg. Vice-Adm. Sir Dick; *see* Caldwell, Surg. Vice-Adm. Sir E. D.

CALDWELL, Edward George, CB 1990; Parliamentary Counsel, since 1981; *b* 21 Aug. 1941; *s* of Arthur Francis Caldwell and Olive Caldwell (*née* Riddle); *m* 1st, 1965, Bronwen Crockett (marr. diss. 1992); two *d*; 2nd, 1992, Dr Helen Beynon. *Educ:* St Andrew's, Singapore; Clifton College; Worcester College, Oxford. Law Commission, 1967–69, 1975–77, 1986–88; joined Office of Parly Counsel, 1969. *Address:* Office of the Parliamentary Counsel, 36 Whitehall, SW1A 2AY. *T:* 0171–210 6611.

CALDWELL, Surg. Vice-Adm. Sir (Eric) Dick, KBE 1969; CB 1965; MD; FRCP, FRCPE; Medical Director-General of the Royal Navy, 1966–69; Executive Director, Medical Council on Alcoholism, 1970–79; *b* 6 July 1909; *s* of late Dr John Colin Caldwell; *m* 1942, Margery Lee Abbott (*d* 1991). *Educ:* Edinburgh Acad.; Edinburgh Univ. MB, ChB Edinburgh 1933; MD Edinburgh 1950; MRCP 1956; FRCP(Edin) 1962; FRCP(London) 1967. Joined Royal Navy, 1934. Served War of 1939–45 in Atlantic, Mediterranean and Pacific; survivor from torpedoeing of HMS Royal Oak and HMS Prince of Wales. Medical Specialist, RN Hosp., Hong Kong, 1947; Sen. Med. Specialist at RN Hosp., Haslar, 1956–58; Surg. Captain 1957; MO i/c of RN Hosp., Plymouth, 1963–66. RN Consultant in Medicine, 1962; Surg. Rear-Adm. 1963; Surg. Vice-Adm. 1966. QHP 1963–69. Gilbert Blane Gold Medal, 1962; FRSocMed. CStJ. *Recreations:* reading, travelling, trying to write. *Address:* Flat 10 Woodsford, 14 Melbury Road, Kensington, W14 8LS. *T:* 0171–602 2225.

CALDWELL, Maj.-Gen. Frank Griffiths, OBE 1953 (MBE 1945); MC 1941 and Bar 1942; retired; *b* 26 Feb. 1921; *s* of William Charles Francis and Violet Marjorie Kathleen Caldwell; *m* 1945, Betty, *d* of Captain Charles Palmer Buesden; one *s* one *d*. *Educ:* Elizabeth Coll., Guernsey. Commnd Royal Engrs, 1940; served Western Desert RE, 1940–43 (MC and Bar); Special Air Service NW Europe, 1944–45 (MBE); Malaya, 1951–53 (OBE); Comdr RE, 2 Div. BAOR, 1961–63; Corps Comdr RE, 1 (BR) Corps, 1967–68; Dir Defence Operational Plans, MoD, 1970; Engineer in Chief (Army), 1970–72; Asst CGS (Operational Requirements), 1972–74. Col Comdt, RE, 1975–80. President: RBL, Guernsey, 1986–; La Société Guernesiaise, 1994–; Chm., Guernsey Scout Council, 1987–. Belgian Croix de Guerre, 1940, and Croix Militaire, 1945. *Recreation:* ornithology. *Address:* Le Courtil Tomar, Rue des Pres, St Pierre du Bois, Guernsey.

CALDWELL, Prof. John Bernard, OBE 1979; PhD; FEng 1976; FRINA; Emeritus Professor of Naval Architecture, University of Newcastle upon Tyne, since 1991; *b* 26 Sept. 1926; *s* of John Revie Caldwell and Doris (*née* Bolland); *m* 1955, Jean Muriel Frances Duddridge; two *s*. *Educ:* Bootham Sch., York; Liverpool Univ. (BEng); Bristol Univ. (PhD). CEng; FRINA 1963. Res. Fellow, Civil Engrg, Bristol Univ., 1953; Sen. Scientific Officer 1955, Principal Sci. Off. 1958, Royal Naval Scientific Service; Asst Prof. of Applied Mechanics, RNC Greenwich, 1960–66; Newcastle upon Tyne University: Prof. of Naval Architecture, 1966–91; Hd of Dept of Naval Architecture, 1966–83; Hd, Sch. of Marine Technol., 1975–80, 1986–88; Dean of Faculty of Engrg, 1983–86. Director: Nat. Maritime Inst. Ltd, 1983–85; Marine Design Consultants Ltd, 1985–89; Newcastle Technology Centre, 1985–90; Northern Engrg Centre, 1989–92. Vis. Prof. of Naval Arch., MIT, 1962–63. President: N-E Coast Instn of Engrs and Shipbuilders, 1976–78; RINA, 1984–87 (Vice-Pres., 1977–84). Mem., Engineering Council, 1988–94 (Chm., Bd for Engrs' Registration, 1990–92). FRSA 1982. Hon. DSc Gdansk Tech. Univ., 1985. Froude Medal, RINA, 1984; and David W. Taylor Medal, SNAME, 1987. *Publications:* numerous papers on research and educn in naval arch. *Address:* Barkbooth, Winster, Windermere, Cumbria LA23 3NZ. *T:* Crosthwaite (01539) 568222. *Club:* National Liberal.

CALDWELL, Philip; Senior Managing Director, Shearson Lehman Brothers Inc., since 1985; *b* Bourneville, Ohio, 27 Jan. 1920; *s* of Robert Clyde Caldwell and Wilhelmina (*née* Hemphill); *m* 1945, Betsey Chinn Clark; one *s* two *d*. *Educ:* Muskingum Coll. (BA Econs 1940); Harvard Univ. Graduate Sch. of Business (MBA Indust. Management, 1942). Served to Lieut, USNR, 1942–46. With Navy Dept, 1946–53, as civilian (Dep. Dir, Procurement Policy Div., 1948–53); joined Ford Motor Co., 1953: Vice Pres. and Gen. Man. Truck Ops, 1968–70; Pres. and Dir, Philco-Ford Corp. (subsid. of Ford Motor Co.), 1970–71; Vice Pres. Manufg Gp, N Amer. Automotive Ops, 1971–72; Chm. and Chief Exec. Officer, Ford of Europe, Inc., 1972–73; Dir, Ford Motor Co., 1973–90; Exec. Vice Pres., Internat. Automotive Ops, 1973–77; Vice Chm. of Bd, 1977–79; Dep. Chief Exec. Officer, 1978–79; Pres., 1978–80; Chief Exec. Officer, 1979–85 and Chm. of Bd, 1980–85, retd; Director: Ford of Europe, 1972–85; Ford Latin America, 1973–85; Ford Mid-East and Africa, 1973–85; Ford Asia-Pacific, 1973–85; Ford Motor Credit Co., 1977–85; Ford of Canada, 1977–85; Mem., Eur. Adv. Council, 1976–88 (Chm., 1987–88). Director: Digital Equipment Corp., 1980–; Chase Manhattan Corp., and Chase Manhattan Bank, NA, 1982–85 (Mem., Chase Manhattan Bank Internat. Adv. Cttee, 1979–85); Federated Dept Stores, 1984–88; Russell Reynolds Associates, Inc., 1984–; Kellogg Co., 1985–92; Shearson Lehman Brothers Hldgs Inc., 1985–87, and 1990–; Amer. Guarantee and Liability Insce Co., 1986–; Zurich Reinsurance Co. of New York, 1987–90; Zurich Hldg Co. of America Inc., 1989–; Mexico Fund, 1991–; Specialty Coatings Internat., 1991–; Detroit Symphony Orch., 1974–85; Harvard Business Sch. Associates, 1977–. Vice Chairperson, New Detroit, Inc., 1977–85; Vice Chm., Japan Soc., 1987–89 (Mem., 1983–89; Chm. Exec. Cttee, 1987–89); Member: US Chamber of Commerce Transportation Cttee, 1968–77; US Council, Internat. Chamber of Commerce, 1973–77; US Council for Internat. Business, 1977–85; Soc. of Automotive Engrs, 1969–85; Engrg Soc. of Detroit, 1970–85; Motor Vehicle Manufrs Assoc. of US, 1978–85 (Chm., 1978 and 1983; Mem., Motor Truck Cttee, 1964–70); Econ. Club of Detroit, 1977–86; Highway Users Fedn, 1977–85; INSEAD, 1978– (Chm., US Adv. Bd, 1979–84; Mem., Internat. Council, 1983–); Conf. Bd, 1979–; Cttee for Econ. Develt, 1979–; (Charter Mem.) Business Higher Educn Forum, 1979–83; Business Council, 1980–; Policy Cttee, Business Roundtable, 1980–85; Trilateral Commn, 1980–86; Citizens Res. Council of Mich, 1980–85; Adv. Council on Japan–US Econ. Relations, 1981–85; US Trade Representative Adv. Cttee for Trade Negotiations, 1983–85; President's Export Council, 1985–89; Council on Foreign Relations, 1985–; Mexico-US Bus. Com., 1985–. Bd of Advrs, Jerome Levy Econs Inst., 1988–. Trustee: Muskingum Coll., 1967–; Winterthur Mus. and Gdns, 1986–. Philip Caldwell Professorship of Business Admin, Harvard Business Sch., established 1989. Hon. HHD Muskingum, 1974; Hon. DBA Upper Iowa Univ., 1978; Hon. LLD: Boston Univ. and Eastern Mich Univ., 1979; Miami Univ., 1980; Davidson Coll., 1982; Univ. of Mich, 1984; Ohio Univ., 1984; Lawrence Inst. of Technol., 1984. 1st William A. Jump Meml Award, 1950; Meritorious Civilian Service Award, US Navy, 1953; Muskingum Coll. Alumni Dist. Service Award, 1978; Brigham Young Univ. Sch. of Management Internat. Exec. of the Year Award, 1983; Automotive Industry Leader of the Year, 1984; Harvard Business School: Clubs of Greater NY Business Statesman Award, 1984; Alumni Achievement Award, 1985; Businessman of the Year, Columbus, Ohio, 1984; Automotive Hall of Fame, 1990; Statesman of the Year, Detroit,

1991. *Address:* Shearson Lehman Brothers Inc., World Financial Center, American Express Tower, 200 Vesey Street, New York, NY 10285-1900, USA. *Clubs:* Links, River (New York).

CALDWELL-MOORE, Patrick; *see* Moore, P. C.

CALEDON, 7th Earl of, *cr* 1800; **Nicholas James Alexander;** Baron Caledon, 1790; Viscount Caledon, 1797; Lord Lieutenant of County Armagh, since 1989; *b* 6 May 1955; *s* of 6th Earl of Caledon, and Baroness Anne (*d* 1963), *d* of late Baron Nicolai de Graevenitz; *S* father, 1980; *m* 1st, 1979, Wendy (marr. diss.), *d* of Spiro Coumantaros and Mrs Suzanne Dayton; 2nd, 1989, Henrietta, *d* of John Newman, Compton Chamberlayne, Wilts; one *s* one *d*. *Educ:* Sandroyd School, Gordonstoun School (Round-Square House). *Recreations:* ski-ing, tennis, swimming, photography, travel. *Heir: s* Viscount Alexander, *qv*. *Address:* Caledon Castle, Caledon, Co. Tyrone, Northern Ireland. *T:* Caledon (0861) 568232.

CALEDONIA, Bishop of, since 1981; **Rt. Rev. John Edward Hannen;** *b* 19 Nov. 1937; *s* of Charles Scott Hannen and Mary Bowman Hannen (*née* Lynds); *m* 1977, Alana Susan Long; two *d*. *Educ:* McGill Univ. (BA); College of the Resurrection, Mirfield (GOE). Asst Curate, St Alphege's, Solihull, Warwicks, 1961–64; Priest in Charge, Mission to the Hart Highway, Diocese of Caledonia, BC, 1965–67; Priest, St Andrew's, Greenville, BC, 1967–68; Priest in Charge, Church of Christ the King, Port Edward, BC, 1969–71; Rector, Christ Church, Kincolith, BC, 1971–81; Regional Dean of Metlakatla, 1972–78. *Recreations:* music, Irish wolfhounds. *Address:* Bishop's Lodge, 208 Fourth Avenue West, Prince Rupert, BC V8J 1P3, Canada. *T:* (604) 6246013.

CALGARY, Archbishop of, since 1994; **Most Rev. John Barry Curtis;** Metropolitan of Rupert's Land, since 1994; *b* 19 June 1933; *s* of Harold Boyd Curtis and Eva B. Curtis (*née* Saunders); *m* 1959, Patricia Emily (*née* Simpson); two *s* two *d*. *Educ:* Trinity Coll., Univ. of Toronto (BA 1955, LTh 1958); Theological Coll., Chichester, Sussex. Deacon 1958, priest 1959; Asst Curate, Holy Trinity, Pembroke, Ont, 1958–61; Rector: Parish of March, Kanata, Ont, 1961–65; St Stephen's Church, Buckingham, Que, 1965–69; Church School Consultant, Diocese of Ottawa, 1969; Rector, All Saints (Westboro), Ottawa, 1969–78; Director of Programme, Diocese of Ottawa, 1978–80; Rector, Christ Church, Elbow Park, Calgary, Alta, 1980–83; Bishop of Calgary, 1983–. Hon. DD Trinity Coll., Toronto, 1985. *Recreations:* reading, hiking, skiing, cycling. *Address:* 3015 Glencoe Road SW, Calgary, Alberta T2S 2L9, Canada. *T:* (403) 2433673; (home) 12 Varanger Place NW, Calgary, Alta T3A 0E9. *T:* (403) 2865127. *Club:* Ranchmen's (Calgary, Alta).

CALIGARI, Prof. Peter Douglas Savaria, PhD, DSc; Professor of Agricultural Botany, since 1986, and Head of Department of Agricultural Botany, since 1987, University of Reading; *b* 10 Nov. 1949; *s* of Kenneth Vane Savaria Caligari, DFM, RAF retd, and Mary Annetta (*née* Rock); *m* 1973, Patricia Ann (*née* Feeley); two *d*. *Educ:* Hereford Cathedral Sch.; Univ. of Birmingham (BSc Biol Sci., 1971; PhD Genetics, 1974; DSc Genetics, 1989). Res. Asst, 1971–74, Res. Fellow, 1974–81, Dept of Genetics, Univ. of Birmingham; SSO, 1981–84, PSO, 1984–86, Scottish Crop Res. Inst. Member: Exec. Cttee, XVIIth Internat. Congress of Genetics, 1991–93; Governing Body, Plant Science Research Ltd, 1991–94; Governing Council, John Innes Centre, 1994–. FRSA 1990. Editor, Heredity, 1987–90 (Jun. Editor, 1985–87); Mem. Editl Bd, Euphytica, 1991–. *Publications:* (contrib.) The Potato Crop, 1991; (contrib.) Applications of Synthetic Seeds to Crop Improvement, 1992; (jtly) Selection Methods in Plant Breeding, 1995; scientific papers and reports on genetics, plant breeding and biotechnology (*c* 150 papers, *c* 22 reports). *Address:* Department of Agricultural Botany, School of Plant Sciences, University of Reading, Whiteknights, PO Box 221, Reading RG6 2AS. *T:* Reading (01734) 318091, *Fax:* (01734) 316577.

CALLADINE, Prof. Christopher Reuben, ScD; FRS 1984; FEng 1994; Professor of Structural Mechanics, University of Cambridge, since 1986; Fellow of Peterhouse, since 1960; *b* 19 Jan. 1935; *s* of Reuben and Mabel Calladine (*née* Boam); *m* 1964, Mary R. H. Webb; two *s* one *d*. *Educ:* Nottingham High Sch.; Peterhouse, Cambridge; Massachusetts Inst. of Technology. Development engineer, English Electric Co., 1958; Demonstrator in Engrg, Univ. of Cambridge, 1960, Lectr, 1963; Reader, 1978. Vis. Research Associate, Brown Univ., 1963; Vis. Prof., Stanford Univ., 1969–70. *Publications:* Engineering Plasticity, 1969; Theory of Shell Structures, 1983; (with H. R. Drew) Understanding DNA, 1992; papers in engrg and biological jls. *Address:* 25 Almoners Avenue, Cambridge CB1 4NZ. *T:* Cambridge (01223) 246742.

CALLAGHAN, family name of **Baron Callaghan of Cardiff.**

CALLAGHAN OF CARDIFF, Baron *cr* 1987 (Life Peer), of the City of Cardiff in the County of South Glamorgan; **Leonard James Callaghan,** KG 1987; PC 1964; *b* 27 March 1912; *s* of James Callaghan, Chief Petty Officer, RN; *m* 1938, Audrey Elizabeth Moulton; one *s* two *d*. *Educ:* Elementary and Portsmouth Northern Secondary Schs. Entered Civil Service as a Tax Officer, 1929; Asst Sec., Inland Revenue Staff Fed., 1936–47 (with an interval during the War of 1939–45, when served in Royal Navy). Joined Labour Party, 1931. MP (Lab): S Cardiff, 1945–50; SE Cardiff, 1950–83; Cardiff S and Penarth, 1983–87. Parly Sec., Min. of Transport, 1947–50; Chm. Cttee on Road Safety, 1948–50; Parliamentary and Financial Sec., Admiralty, 1950–51; Opposition Spokesman: Transport, 1951–53; Fuel and Power, 1953–55; Colonial Affairs, 1956–61; Shadow Chancellor, 1961–64; Chancellor of the Exchequer, 1964–67; Home Secretary, 1967–70; Shadow Home Sec., 1970–71; Opposition Spokesman on Employment, 1971–72; Shadow Foreign Sec., 1972–74; Sec. of State for Foreign and Commonwealth Affairs, 1974–76; Minister of Overseas Develt, 1975–76; Prime Minister and First Lord of the Treasury, 1976–79; Leader, Labour Party, 1976–80; Leader of the Opposition, 1979–80. Father, House of Commons, 1983–87. Deleg. to Council of Europe, Strasburg, 1948–50 and 1954. Mem., Labour Party NEC, 1957–80; Treasurer, Labour Party, 1967–76, Vice-Chm. 1973, Chm. 1974. Consultant to Police Fedn of England and Wales and to Scottish Police Fedn, 1955–64. President: Adv. Cttee on Pollution of the Sea, 1963– (Chm., 1952–63); United Kingdom Pilots Assoc., 1963–76; Jt Pres., RIIA, 1983–. Hon. Pres., Internat. Maritime Pilots Assoc., 1971–76. Pres., Univ. of Wales, Swansea (formerly UC Swansea), 1986– (Hon. Fellow, 1993). Visiting Fellow, Nuffield Coll., Oxford, 1959–67, Hon. Life Fellow, 1967; Hon. Fellow: UC Cardiff, 1978; Portsmouth Polytechnic, 1981; Cardiff Inst. of Higher Educn, 1991. Hon. LLD: Wales, 1976; Sardar Patel Univ., India, 1978; Birmingham, 1981; Sussex, 1989; Westminster, 1993. Hon. Bencher, Inner Temple, 1976. Freeman: City of Portsmouth, 1991; City of Swansea, 1993; Hon. Freeman: City of Cardiff, 1974; City of Sheffield, 1979. Hubert H. Humphrey Internat. Award, 1978. Grand Cross, 1st class, Order of Merit of Federal Republic of Germany, 1979. *Publications:* A House Divided: the dilemma of Northern Ireland, 1973; Time and Chance (autobiog.), 1987. *Address:* House of Lords, SW1A 0PW.

See also Baroness Jay of Paddington.

CALLAGHAN, Rev. Brendan Alphonsus, SJ; Principal of Heythrop College, University of London, since 1985; *b* 29 July 1948; *s* of Dr Kathleen Callaghan (*née* Kavanagh) and Dr Alphonsus Callaghan. *Educ:* Stonyhurst; Heythrop, Oxon; Campion Hall, Oxford (MA 1977); Univ. of Glasgow (MPhil 1976); Heythrop Coll., Univ. of London (MTh 1979). FRSM; AFBPsS; CPsychol. Joined Society of Jesus, 1967; Clinical Psychologist, Glasgow, 1974–76; Middx Hosp., 1976–79; ordained priest, 1978; curate, St Aloysius, Glasgow, 1979–80; Lectr in Psychology, Heythrop, 1980–, Allen Hall, Chelsea, 1981–87. Superior, Brixton Jesuit Community, 1993–94. University of London: Chm., Bd of Examrs, Theol and Religious Studies, 1987–89; Schools Examn Bd, 1987–; Collegiate Council and Senate, 1989–94; Council, 1994–; Institute of Medical Ethics: Hon. Asst/Associate Dir, 1976–89; Governing Body, 1989–. Visiting Lecturer: Oblate Sch. of Theology, Natal, 1987; KCL, 1991–; Vis. Prof., Fordham Univ., NY, 1990; Vis. Scholar, Weston Sch. of Theol., Cambridge, Mass, 1992. Member: Ethics Cttee, W Lambeth HA, 1990–; Higher Educn Cttee, RC Bps Conf. of England and Wales, 1986–; Academic Adv. Cttee, Jews' Coll., 1993–. Member, Advisory Boards: Campion Hall, Oxford, 1985–; Syon House, Angmering, 1985–; Centre for the Study of Communication and Culture (Chm.), 1990–; Inst. of St Anselm, Westgate, 1991–; Mem., Management Cttee, Family Res. Trust, 1991–. Vice Pres., Catholic Students Trust Appeal. Consultant Psychologist to Catholic Marriage Adv. Council, 1981–, and to religious congregations and orders. Member: Catholic Inst. for Internat. Relations; Amnesty; CND. Broadcaster, BBC and World Service radio, Channel Four. Mem. Editl Bd, Law and Justice. *Publications:* Life Before Birth (with K. Boyd and E. Shotter), 1986; articles, reviews and verse in Br. JL Psych, Jl Med. Ethics, Heythrop Jl and magazines. *Recreations:* photography, long distance walking, poetry. *Address:* Heythrop College, Kensington Square, W8 5HQ. *T:* 0171–795 6600, *Fax:* 0171–795 4200.

CALLAGHAN, Rear-Adm. Desmond Noble, CB 1970; FRSA; Director-General, National Supervisory Council for Intruder Alarms, 1971–77; *b* 24 Nov. 1915; *s* of Edmund Ford Callaghan and Kathleen Louise Callaghan (*née* Noble): *m* 1948, Patricia Munro Geddes; one *s* two *d*. *Educ:* RNC Dartmouth. HMS Frobisher, 1933; RNEC Keyhan, 1934; HM Ships: Royal Oak, 1937; Iron Duke, 1938; Warspite, 1939; Hereward, 1941; Prisoner of War, 1941; HMS Argonaut, 1945; HMS Glory, 1946; RNC Dartmouth, 1947; Admiralty, 1949; C-in-C Med. Staff, 1950; HMS Excellent, 1953; HMS Eagle, 1956; RN Tactical Sch., 1958; Admiralty, 1960; HMS Caledonia, 1962; Admiralty, 1965; Vice-Pres. and Pres., Ordnance Board, 1968–71, retired 1971. *Recreations:* Rugby, tennis, swimming. *Address:* Bridge End, Abbotsbrook, Bourne End, Bucks SL8 5RE. *T:* Bourne End (01628) 520519.

CALLAGHAN, James; MP (Lab) Heywood and Middleton (Middleton and Prestwich, Feb. 1974–1983); *b* 28 Jan. 1927. Lectr, Manchester Coll., 1959–74. Metropolitan Borough Councillor, 1971–74. *Recreations:* sport and art. *Address:* 17 Towncroft Avenue, Middleton, Manchester.

CALLAN, Ivan Roy, CMG 1990; HM Diplomatic Service; High Commissioner, Brunei, since 1994; *b* 6 April 1942; *s* of Roy Ivan Callan and (Gladys) May Callan (*née* Coombe); *m* 1st, 1965, Hilary Flashman; one *d*; 2nd, 1987, Mary Catherine Helena Williams; two step *s* one step *d*. *Educ:* Reading Sch.; University Coll., Oxford. BA, Dip. Soc. Anthrop., BLitt, MA. Entered FCO, 1969; Middle East Centre for Arab Studies, 1970–71; Second, later First Sec., Beirut, 1971–75; FCO, 1975–80; First Sec. and Head of Chancery, Ottawa, 1980–83; Counsellor, Hd of Chancery and Consul-General, Baghdad, 1983–87; Consul-General, Jerusalem, 1987–90; Counsellor, FCO, 1991–94. *Recreations:* fine arts, painting, craftsmanship. *Address:* c/o Foreign and Commonwealth Office, King Charles Street, SW1A 2AH. *Club:* Reform.

CALLAN, Maj.-Gen. Michael, CB 1979; President, and Chairman of Board of Trustees, Royal Army Ordnance Corps Charitable Trust, since 1993; *b* 27 Nov. 1925; *s* of Major John Callan and Elsie Dorothy Callan (*née* Fordham); *m* 1948, Marie Evelyn Farthing; two *s*. *Educ:* Farnborough Grammar Sch., Hants. rcds, jssc, psc. Enlisted Hampshire Regt, 1943; commnd 1st (KGV's Own) Gurkha Rifles (The Malaun Regt), 1944; resigned commn, 1947; re-enlisted, 1948; re-commnd, RAOC, 1949; overseas service: India, Burma, French Indo China, Netherlands East Indies, 1944–47; Kenya, 1950–53; Malaya/Singapore, 1958–61; USA, 1966–68, Hong Kong, 1970–71; Comdr, Rhine Area, BAOR, 1975–76; Dir Gen., Ordnance Services, 1976–80. Col Comdt, RAOC, 1981–89; Hon. Col, SW London ACF, 1982–89. Registrar, Corporation of the Sons of the Clergy, 1982–83; consultant in defence logistics and admin, 1984–89. *Recreations:* sailing, DIY, gardening. *Address:* c/o Royal Bank of Scotland, Drummonds Branch, 49 Charing Cross, SW1A 2DX.

CALLARD, Sir Eric John, (Sir Jack Callard), Kt 1974; FEng; Chairman, British Home Stores Ltd, 1976–82 (Director 1975–82); *b* 15 March 1913; *s* of late F. Callard and Mrs A. Callard; *m* 1938, Pauline M., *d* of late Rev. Charles Pengelly; three *d*. *Educ:* Queen's Coll., Taunton; St John's Coll., Cambridge. 1st cl. Hons Mech. Sci. Tripos; BA 1935; MA 1973; Harvard Business Sch. (Adv. Management Programme, 1953). Joined ICI Ltd, 1935; seconded to Min. of Aircraft Prodn, 1942; ICI Paints Div., 1947 (Jt Man. Dir, 1955–59; Chm., 1959–64); Chairman: Deleg. Bd, ICI (Hyde) Ltd, 1959; ICI (Europa) Ltd, 1965–67; ICI Ltd, 1971–75 (Dir, 1964–75; Dep. Chm., 1967–71); Director: Pension Funds Securities Ltd, 1963–67; Imp. Metal Industries Ltd, 1964–67; Imp. Chemicals Insurance Ltd, 1966–70; Midland Bank Ltd, 1971–87; Ferguson Industrial Holdings, 1975–86; Commercial Union Assurance Co., 1976–83; Equity Capital for Industry, 1976–84. Member Council: BIM, 1964–69; Manchester Univ. Business Sch., 1964–71; Export Council for Europe, 1965–71; Member: CBI Steering Cttee on Europe, 1965–71; Cambridge Univ. Appointments Bd, 1968–71; CBI Overseas Cttee, 1969–71; Council of Industry for Management Educn, 1967–73; Royal Instn of GB, 1971–; Vice-Pres., Manchester Business Sch. Assoc., 1971– (Hon. Mem., 1966–; Pres., 1969–71); Pres., Industrial Participation Assoc., 1971–76 (Chm., 1967–71). Member: Hansard Soc. Commn on Electoral Reform, 1975–76; Cttee of Inquiry into Industrial Democracy, 1976–77. Trustee, Civic Trust, 1972–75; Governor, London Business Sch., 1972–75. Mem. Court, British Shippers' Council, 1972–75. FRSA 1970; CIMgt (FBIM 1966); Hon. FIMechE. Hon. DSc Cranfield Inst. of Technology, 1974. *Recreations:* games, fishing. *Address:* Crookwath Cottage, High Row, Dockray, Penrith, Cumbria CA11 0LG. *Club:* Flyfishers'.

CALLAWAY, Betty; *see* Callaway-Fittall, B. D.

CALLAWAY, Sir Frank (Adams), Kt 1981; AO 1995; CMG 1975; OBE 1970; Professor and Head of Department of Music, University of Western Australia, 1959–84, Professor Emeritus, since 1985; *b* 16 May 1919; *s* of Archibald Charles Callaway and Mabel Callaway (*née* Adams); *m* 1942, Kathleen Jessie, *d* of R. Allan; two *s* two *d*. *Educ:* West Christchurch High Sch.; Dunedin Teachers' Coll., NZ; Univ. of Otago, NZ (MusB); Royal Academy of Music. FRAM, ARCM, FTCL; FACE. Head, Dept of Music, King Edward Tech. Coll., Dunedin, NZ, 1942–53; Reader in Music, Univ. of WA, 1953–59. Mem., RNZAF Band, 1940–42. Conductor: King Edward Tech. Coll. Symphony Orchestra, 1945–53; Univ. of WA Orchestral Soc., 1953–64; Univ. of WA Choral Soc., 1953–79; Guest Conductor: WA Symphony Orchestra; S Australia Symphony Orchestra; Adelaide Philharmonic Choir; Orpheus Choir, Wellington, NZ. Member: Australian Music Exams Bd, 1955–84 (Chm., 1964–66 and 1977–79); Adv. Bd, Commonwealth Assistance to Australian Composers, 1966–72; Australian Nat. Commn for UNESCO, 1968–82; Exec. Bd, Internat. Music Council of UNESCO, 1976–82 (Pres., 1980–81; Individual Mem.,

1982–85, Life Mem. of Honour, 1986); Music Bd, Australia Council, 1969–74; Chairman: WA Arts Adv. Bd, 1970–73; WA Arts Council, 1973–79; Organizing Cttees, Aust. Nat. Eisteddfod 1979, Indian Ocean Fests, 1979, 1984; Indian Ocean Arts Assoc., 1980–85 (Pres., 1985–). Founding Pres. and Life Mem., Australian Soc. for Music Educn, 1966–71; Mem., Bd of Dirs, Internat. Soc. for Music Educn, 1958– (Pres., 1968–72, Treasurer, 1972–88, Hon. Pres., 1988–). Chm., Bd of Dirs, Internat. Acad. of Music, Nairobi, Kenya, 1985–; External Examiner (Music), Kenyatta Univ., Nairobi, 1985–87; Consultant, Frank Callaway Internat. Resource Centre for Music Educn (Univ. of WA), 1988–. Patron, Music Council of Australia, 1994. Foundn Mem., 1983, Pres., 1984–, WA Br., Lord's Taverners Australia. Founding Editor: Australian Jl of Music Educn, 1967–82; Studies in Music, 1967–84; Internat. Jl of Music Educn, 1983–85; also General Editor, Music Series and Music Monographs. W Australian Citizen of the Year, 1975. Hon. MusD: W Australia, 1975; Melbourne, 1982. Aust. Nat. Critics' Circle Award for Music, 1977; Sir Bernard Heinze Award for Service to Australian Music, 1988; Internat. Percy Grainger Medal, 1991. *Publications:* (General Editor) Challenges in Music Education, 1975; (ed with D. E. Tunley) Australian Composition in the Twentieth Century, 1978. *Recreations:* reading, gardening, cricket. *Address:* 1 Sambell Close, Churchlands, WA 6018, Australia. *T:* (9) 2443733.

CALLAWAY-FITTALL, Betty Daphne, (Betty Callaway), MBE 1984; trainer of skaters; skating consultant to Ice Arena, Slough, since 1986; *b* 22 March 1928; *d* of William A. Roberts and Elizabeth T. Roberts; *m* 1st, 1949, E. Roy Callaway; 2nd, 1980, Captain W. Fittall (*d* 1990), British Airways, retd. *Educ:* Greycoat Sch., and St Paul's Convent, Westminster. Started teaching, Richmond Ice Rink, 1952; Nat. Trainer, W Germany, 1969–72; retired from full-time teaching, 1972. Commentator, ITV, 1984–. Pupils include: Angelika and Erich Buck (European Champions and 2nd in World Championship, 1972); Chrisztine Regoczy and Andras Sally (Hungarian and World Champions and Olympic silver medallists, 1980); Jayne Torvill and Christopher Dean (World Champions, 1981, 1982, 1983, 1984, European Champions, 1981, 1982, and Olympic gold medallists, 1984). Pres., British Ice Teachers Assoc., 1985–. Hon. Citizen, Ravensburg, Germany, 1972. Gold Medal, Nat. Skating Assoc., 1955; Hungarian Olympic Medal, 1980; Coach of the Year Award, Nat. Coaching Foundn, 1995. *Recreations:* music, water ski-ing, gardening. *Address:* 35 Long Grove, Seer Green, Beaconsfield, Bucks HP9 2YN.

CALLBECK, Hon. Catherine Sophia; Premier and President of Executive Council, Prince Edward Island, since 1993; MLA (L) First District of Queens, since 1993; *b* 25 July 1939; *d* of Ralph Callbeck and Ruth Callbeck (*née* Campbell), Central Bedeque, PEI. *Educ:* Mt Allison Univ. (BComm 1960); Dalhousie Univ. (BEd 1963); Syracuse Univ. Prince Edward Island: MLA (L) Fourth Dist, 1974–78; Minister of Health and Social Services and Minister responsible for Disabled, 1974–78; with family business, Callbeck's Ltd, 1978–88; MP (L) Malpeque, 1988–93; Official Opposition Critic for Consumer and Corporate Affairs, Energy, Mines and Resources and Financial Instns, 1988–93; Associate Critic for Privatization and Regulatory Affairs; Vice-Chm., Caucus Cttee on sustainable develt. Leader, Liberal Party of PEI, 1993–. *Address:* (office) 95 Rochford Street, PO Box 2000, Charlottetown, Prince Edward Island C1A 7N8, Canada. *T:* (902) 3684400; Central Bedeque, Prince Edward Island C0B 1G0, Canada. *T:* (902) 8872988.

CALLENDER, Dr Maurice Henry; Ministry of Defence, 1977–80; retired, 1980; *b* 18 Dec. 1916; *s* of Harry and Lizbeth Callender; *m* 1941, Anne Kassel; two *s*. *Educ:* Univ. of Durham (MA, PhD). FSA. Commissioned: Royal Northumberland Fusiliers, 1939–41; RAF, 1941–45. Lectr, Huddersfield Technical Coll., 1945–47; Research, Univ. of Durham, 1947–49; Lectr, Bristol Univ. Extra-Mural Dept, 1949–53; MoD, 1953–62; Joint Services Staff Coll., 1959–60; Cabinet Office, 1962–64; MoD, 1964–70; Cabinet Office, 1970–73; Counsellor, Canberra, 1973–77. *Publications:* Roman Amphorae, 1965; various articles in archaeological jls. *Recreations:* oil painting, golf, bridge. *Address:* 24 Glanleam Road, Stanmore, Mddx HA7 4NW. *T:* 0181–954 1435. *Club:* Aldenham Golf and Country.

CALLER, Maxwell Marshall; Chief Executive, London Borough of Barnet, since 1989; *b* 9 Feb. 1951; *s* of Abraham Leon Caller and Cynthia Rachel Caller; *m* 1972, Linda Ann Wohlberg; three *s* one *d*. *Educ:* Newport High Sch.; University Coll. London (BSc Hons Engrg). CEng, MICE; MIWEM; CDipAF. GLC, 1972–74; Thames Water Authority, 1974–75; London Boroughs of: Hammersmith, 1975–78; Newham, 1978–81; Merton, 1981–85 (Asst Dir of Development); Barnet: Controller of Engrg Services, 1985–87; Dir of Technical Services, 1987–89. Technical Advr, N London Waste Authy, 1985–87; Adviser, Highways Cttee 1987–89, Public Works Cttee 1990–, AMA; Founder Mem. and Vice Chm., Steering Cttee, Barnet Crime Reduction Partnership, 1991–. *Recreations:* watching Welsh Rugby Union, work. *Address:* Town Hall, The Burroughs, Hendon, NW4 4BG. *T:* 0181–202 8282.

CALLEY, Sir Henry (Algernon), Kt 1964; DSO 1945; DFC 1943; DL; Owner and Manager of a stud, since 1948; *b* 9 Feb. 1914; *s* of Rev. A. C. M. Langton and Mrs Langton (*née* Calley); changed surname to Calley, 1974; unmarried. *Educ:* St John's Sch., Leatherhead. Taught at Corchester. Corbridge-on-Tyne, 1933–35; Bombay Burmah Trading Corp., 1935–36; teaching, 1936–38; Metropolitan Police Coll., and Police Force, 1938–41; Royal Air Force, 1941–48; Pilot in Bombers, Actg Wing Comdr, 1944. Mem. Wiltshire CC, 1955; Chm. Finance Cttee, 1959–68; Chm. of Council, 1968–73; Chm. Wessex Area Conservative Assoc., 1963–66. DL Wilts, 1968.

CALLIL, Carmen Thérèse; Chairman, Virago Press, 1972–95; *b* 15 July 1938; *d* of Frederick Alfred Louis Callil and Lorraine Clare Allen. *Educ:* Star of the Sea Convent, Gardenvale, Melbourne; Loreto Convent, Mandeville Hall, Melbourne; Melbourne Univ. (BA). Buyer's Asst, Marks & Spencer, 1963–65; Editorial Assistant: Hutchinson Publishing Co., 1965–66; B. T. Batsford, 1966–67; Publicity Manager, Panther Books, later also of Granada Publishing, 1967–70; André Deutsch, 1971–72; publicity for Ink newspaper, 1972; founded Carmen Callil Ltd, book publicity co., 1972; founded Virago Press, 1972, incorp. as co., 1973, Man. Dir, 1972–82. Man. Dir, Chatto & Windus: The Hogarth Press, 1983–93; Publisher-at-Large, Random House UK, 1993–94; Ed.-at-Large, Knopf, NY, 1993–94. Mem. Bd, Channel 4, 1985–91. FRSA. Hon. LittD Sheffield, 1994; DUniv York, 1995. *Recreations:* friends, reading, animals, television, politics, films, gardening. *Club:* Groucho (Dir).

CALLMAN, Clive Vernon; His Honour Judge Callman; a Circuit Judge, since 1973, assigned to South-Eastern Circuit; a Deputy High Court Judge, since 1976; *b* 21 June 1927; *o s* of Felix Callman, DMD, LDS, RCS and Edith Callman, Walton-on-Thames, Surrey; *m* 1967, Judith Helen Hines, BA, DipSocStuds (Adelaide), *o d* of Gus Hines, OBE, JP, and Hilde Hines, St George's, Adelaide, S Aust.; one *s* one *d*. *Educ:* Ottershaw Coll.; St George's Coll., Weybridge; LSE, Univ. of London. BSc(Econ), Commercial Law. Called to the Bar, Middle Temple, 1951; Blackstone Pupillage Prizeman, 1951; practised as Barrister, London and Norwich, 1952–73 (Head of London chambers, 1963), South-Eastern Circuit; Hon. Mem., Central Criminal Court Bar Mess; Dep. Circuit Judge in Civil and Criminal Jurisdiction, 1971–73. Dir, Woburn Press, Publishers, 1971–73; dir of finance cos, 1961–73. University of London: Fac. Mem., Standing Cttee of Convocation, 1954–79; Senator, 1978–; Mem. Careers Adv. Bd, 1979–92; Mem., Commerce Degree Bureau Cttee, 1980; Mem., Adv. Cttee for Magistrates' Courses, 1979; Vice-Pres., Graduates' Soc.; Governor: Birkbeck Coll., 1982–; LSE, 1990–; Hebrew Univ. of Jerusalem, 1992–; Mem. Court, City Univ., 1991–. Mem. Exec. Cttee, Soc. of Labour Lawyers, 1958; Chm., St Marylebone Constituency Labour Party, 1960–62. Mem. Council, Anglo-Jewish Assoc., 1956–. Editor, Clare Market Review, 1947; Member Editorial Board: Media Law and Practice, 1980–; Professional Negligence, 1985–; Jl of Child Law, 1989–. *Recreations:* reading, travelling, the arts. *Address:* 11 Constable Close, NW11 6UA. *T:* 0181–458 3010. *Club:* Bar Yacht.

CALLOW, His Honour Henry William, CBE 1994; HM Second Deemster, Isle of Man, 1988–93; *b* 16 May 1926; 2nd *s* of Frederick Henry Callow and Elizabeth Callow (*née* Cowley); *m* 1952, Mary Elaine Corlett. *Educ:* Douglas High Sch.; King William's Coll., IOM. Served Army, 1945–48. Advocate, Manx Bar, 1950; High Bailiff and Coroner of Inquests, IOM, 1969–88; Chairman: IOM Criminal Injuries Compensation Tribunal, 1988–93; IOM Licensing Appeal Court, 1988–93. Mem., Police Complaints Commn, 1994–. Chairman of Trustees: Noble's Hosp., IOM, 1987–; Ellan Vannin Home, 1988–. *Recreations:* music, walking. *Address:* 8 Marlborough Crescent, Clifton Park, Ramsey, Isle of Man. *T:* IOM (01624) 81–5929. *Clubs:* Manx Automobile (Douglas); Laxey Sailing (Laxey), Ramsey Golf.

CALLOW, Prof. James Arthur, PhD; CBiol, FIBiol; Mason Professor of Botany, University of Birmingham, since 1983; *b* 17 Jan. 1945; *s* of James and Olive Callow; *m* 1968, Dr Maureen Elizabeth Wood; one *s*. *Educ:* Barrow-in-Furness Grammar Sch. for Boys; Univ. of Sheffield (BSc 1st cl. Hons Botany 1966; PhD 1969). Lectr in Botany, Univ. of Leeds, 1969–83. *Publications:* numerous, including books, professional academic jl articles. *Recreations:* golf, gardening, antiques, photography, travel. *Address:* School of Biological Sciences, University of Birmingham, Birmingham B15 2TT. *T:* 0121–414 5559.

CALLOW, Simon Phillip Hugh; actor and director; *b* 15 June 1949; *s* of Neil Callow and Yvonne Mary Callow. *Educ:* London Oratory Grammar Sch.; Queen's Univ. Belfast; Drama Centre. London productions include: Schippel, 1975; A Mad World My Masters, 1977; Arturo Ui, Mary Barnes, 1978; As You Like It, Amadeus, NT, 1979; The Beastly Beatitudes of Balthazar B, Total Eclipse, Restoration, 1981; The Relapse, 1983; On the Spot, 1984; Kiss of the Spider Woman, 1985; Faust I and II, Lyric, Hammersmith, 1988; Single Spies (double bill: A Question of Attribution (also dir); An Englishman Abroad), NT, 1988, Queen's, 1989; *directed:* Loving Reno, Bush, 1984; The Passport, 1985, Nicolson Fights, Croydon, 1986, Offstage; Amadeus, Theatr Clwyd, 1986; The Infernal Machine, 1986; Così fan Tutte, Switzerland, 1987; Jacques and his Master, LA, 1987; Shirley Valentine, Vaudeville, 1988, NY, 1989; Die Fledermaus, Theatre Royal, Glasgow, 1988, 1989; Stevie Wants to Play the Blues, LA Theater Center, 1990; Carmen Jones, Old Vic, 1991; Ballad of the Sad Café, 1991; Shades, 1992; My Fair Lady, 1992. *Films:* Amadeus, 1983; A Room with a View, 1986; The Good Father, 1986; Maurice, 1987; Manifesto, 1988; Mr & Mrs Bridge, 1991; Postcards from the Edge, 1991; Crucifer of Blood, 1991; Soft Top, Hard Shoulder, 1993; Don't Look Away, 1993; Four Weddings and a Funeral, 1994; Jefferson in Paris, 1995. *Television series:* Chance in a Million, 1983, 1985–86; David Copperfield, 1986; *other television includes:* Cariani and the Courtesans, 1987; Charles Laughton (documentary), 1987; Old Flames, 1989; Revolutionary Witness, 1989; Femme Fatale, 1993. *Publications:* Being an Actor, 1984; A Difficult Actor: Charles Laughton, 1987; trans. Jacques et son Maître, by Kundera, 1986; trans. The Infernal Machine, by Jean Cocteau, 1987; Shooting the Actor, 1990; Orson Welles: the road to Xanadu, 1995. *Address:* c/o Marina Martin, 6a Danbury Street, N1 8JU. *T:* 0171–359 3646.

CALLWAY, Eric Willi; HM Diplomatic Service; Deputy High Commissioner, Karachi, since 1994; *b* 30 Jan. 1942; *s* of Edward and Auguste Callway; *m* 1965, Gudrun Viktoria Granström; two *s*. Joined HM Foreign, later Diplomatic, Service, 1960: FO, 1960–61; CRO, 1961–63; New Delhi, 1963–66; Georgetown, Guyana, 1966–70; Second Sec., FCO, 1970–72; RAF Staff Coll., Bracknell, 1972; UK Mission, Geneva, 1973–77; First Secretary: FCO, 1977–79; on loan to MoD, 1979–80; FCO, 1980–81; (Commercial), E Berlin, 1981–84; (Labour), 1984–86, then (Commercial), Stockholm, 1986–88; on loan to ODA, 1988; FCO, 1989–94. *Address:* c/o Foreign and Commonwealth Office, King Charles Street, SW1A 2AH.

CALMAN, Prof. Kenneth Charles, MD; FRCP, FRCS; FRSE; Chief Medical Officer (at Department of Health), Department for Education and Employment (formerly Department of Education and Science, then Department for Education), since 1991; *b* 25 Dec. 1941; *s* of Arthur McIntosh Calman and Grace Douglas Don; *m* 1967, Ann Wilkie; one *s* two *d*. *Educ:* Allan Glen's Sch., Glasgow; Univ. of Glasgow (BSc, MD, PhD). FRCSGlas 1971; FRCP 1985, FRCPE 1989; FRCGP 1989; FRCR 1990; FRCSE 1991; FFPHM 1992; FRCPath 1992; FRSE 1979. Hall Fellow in Surgery, Western Infirmary, Glasgow, 1968; Lectr in Surgery, Univ. of Glasgow, 1969; MRC Clinical Res. Fellow, Inst. of Cancer Res., London, 1972; University of Glasgow: Prof. of Clinical Oncology, 1974; Dean of Postgrad. Medicine and Prof. of Postgrad. Med. Educn, 1984–88; Chief Med. Officer, Scottish Office Home and Health Dept, 1989–91. DUniv Stirling, 1992; Hon. DSc Strathclyde, 1993; Hon. MD: Nottingham, 1994; Newcastle, 1995. *Publications:* Basic Skills for Clinical Housemen, 1971, 2nd edn 1983; Basic Principles of Cancer Chemotherapy, 1982; Invasion, 1984; Healthy Respect, 1987, 2nd edn 1994. *Recreations:* gardening, golf, collecting cartoons, Scottish literature. *Address:* Department of Health, 79 Whitehall, SW1A 2NS.

CALNAN, Prof. Charles Dermod, MA, MB, BChir Cantab; FRCP; Director, Department of Occupational Dermatoses, St John's Hospital for Diseases of the Skin, 1974–82, retired; Honorary Consultant Dermatologist: Royal Free Hospital, 1958–82; St John's Hospital for Diseases of the Skin, London, 1958–82; *b* 14 Dec. 1917; *s* of James Calnan, Eastbourne, Sussex; *m* 1950, Josephine Gerard Keane, *d* of late Lt-Col Michael Keane, RAMC; three *s* one *d*. *Educ:* Stonyhurst Coll.; Corpus Christi Coll., Cambridge; London Hospital. 1st Cl. Hons Nat. Sci. Trip., Cambridge 1939. RAMC Specialist in Dermatology, Major, 1942–46; Marsden Prof., Royal Free Hosp., 1958; Visiting Research Associate, Univ. of Pennsylvania, 1959; Prof. of Dermatology, Inst. of Dermatology, 1960–74. WHO Cons. Adviser to Nat. Inst. of Dermatology of Thailand, 1971–. Editor: Transactions of the St John's Hosp. Dermatological Soc., 1958–75; Contact Dermatitis, 1975–. Mem. Brit. Assoc. of Dermatology. FRSocMed (Mem. Dermatological Section). Order of the White Elephant (Thailand), 1986. *Publications:* Atlas of Dermatology, 1974; The Life and Times of Geoffrey Barrow Dowling, 1992; various papers in med. and dermatological jls. *Recreations:* squash, books, theatre. *Address:* 80 Harley Street, W1N 1AE.

CALNAN, Prof. James Stanislaus, FRCP; FRCS; Professor of Plastic and Reconstructive Surgery, University of London, at the Royal Postgraduate Medical School and Hammersmith Hospital, 1970–81, now Emeritus; *b* 12 March 1916; *e s* of James and Gertrude Calnan, Eastbourne, Sussex; *m* 1949, Joan (formerly County Councillor for

Great Berkhamsted and Dacorum District Councillor, and Town Councillor, Berkhamsted), *e d* of George Frederick and Irene Maud Williams, Roath Park, Cardiff; one *d*. *Educ:* Stonyhurst Coll.; Univ. of London at London Hosp. Med. Sch. LDS RCS 1941; MRCS, LRCP 1943; DA 1944; DTM&H 1948; MRCP (London and Edinburgh) 1948; FRCS 1949; FRCP 1971. Served War of 1939–45, F/Lt RAF, UK, France, India. RMO, Hosp. for Tropical Diseases, 1948; Sen. Lectr, Nuffield Dept of Plastic Surgery, Oxford, 1954; Hammersmith Hospital and Royal Postgraduate Med. Sch.: Lectr in Surgery, 1960; Reader, 1965; Professor, 1970. Hunterian Prof. RCS, 1959. Vis. Prof. in Plastic Surgery, Univ. of Pennsylvania, 1959. Member: BMA, 1941–82; British Assoc. of Plastic Surgeons, 1949–71; Sen. Mem., Surgical Research Soc., 1962–. Fellow, Royal Soc. of Medicine, 1943; FCST 1966. Mem., Soc. of Authors, 1985–. Clemson Award for Bioengineering, 1980. *Publications:* Speaking at Medical Meetings, 1972, 2nd edn 1981; Writing Medical Papers, 1973; How to Speak and Write: a practical guide for nurses, 1975; One Way to do Research, 1976; Talking with Patients, 1983; Coping with Research: the complete guide for beginners, 1984; The Hammersmith 1935–1985: the first 50 years of the Royal Postgraduate Medical School, 1985; Principles of Surgical Research, 1989; contribs to medical and scientific jls and chapters in books, on cleft palate, wound healing, lymphatic diseases, venous thrombosis, research methods and organisation. *Recreations:* gardening, carpentry, reading and writing. *Address:* White Haven, 23 Kings Road, Berkhamsted, Herts HP4 3BH. *T:* Berkhamsted (01442) 862320; Royal Postgraduate Medical School, Ducane Road, W12 0HS. *T:* 0181–743 2030.

See also Prof. C. D. Calnan.

CALNE, Sir Roy (Yorke), Kt 1986; MA, MS; FRCS; FRS 1974; Professor of Surgery, University of Cambridge, since 1965; Fellow of Trinity Hall, Cambridge, since 1965; Hon. Consulting Surgeon, Addenbrooke's Hospital, Cambridge, since 1965; *b* 30 Dec. 1930; *s* of Joseph Robert and Eileen Calne; *m* 1956, Patricia Doreen Whelan; two *s* four *d*. *Educ:* Lancing Coll.; Guy's Hosp. Med. Sch. MB, BS London with Hons (Distinction in Medicine), 1953. House Appts, Guy's Hosp., 1953–54; RAMC, 1954–56 (RMO to KEO 2nd Gurkhas); Deptl Anatomy Demonstrator, Oxford Univ., 1957–58; SHO Nuffield Orthopædic Centre, Oxford, 1958; Surg. Registrar, Royal Free Hosp., 1958–60; Harkness Fellow in Surgery, Peter Bent Brigham Hosp., Harvard Med. Sch., 1960–61; Lectr in Surgery, St Mary's Hosp., London, 1961–62; Sen. Lectr and Cons. Surg., Westminster Hosp., 1962–65. Royal Coll. of Surgeons: Hallet Prize, 1957; Jacksonian Prize, 1961; Hunterian Prof., 1962; Cecil Joll Prize, 1966; Mem. Ct of Examiners, 1970–76; Mem. Council, 1981–90; Vice-Pres., 1986–89; Hunterian Orator, 1989. Fellow Assoc. of Surgeons of GB; Mem. Surgical Research Soc.; Pres., European Soc. for Organ Transplantation, 1983–84; Corresp. Fellow, Amer. Surgical Assoc., 1972, Hon. Fellow 1981; Hon. FRCP 1989; Hon. FRCS Thailand, 1992; Hon. FRCSE 1993. Hon. MD: Oslo, 1986; Athens, 1990; Hanover, 1991; QUB, 1994; Karachi, 1994. Prix de la Société Internationale de Chirurgie, 1969; Faltin Medal, Finnish Surgical Soc., 1977; Lister Medal, 1984; Fothergill Gold Medal, Med. Soc. of London, 1989; Cameron Prize, Edinburgh Univ., 1990; Ellison-Cliffe Medal, 1990; Ernst Jung Preis, 1992; Medawar Prize, Transplantation Soc., 1992; Medal of Helsinki Univ., 1993. *Publications:* Renal Transplantations, 1963, 2nd edn 1967; (with H. Ellis) Lecture Notes in Surgery, 1965, 7th edn 1987; A Gift of Life, 1970; (ed and contrib.) Clinical Organ Transplantation, 1971; (ed and contrib.) Immunological Aspects of Transplantation Surgery, 1973; (ed and contrib.) Liver Transplantation, 1983; (ed and contrib.) Transplantation Immunology, 1984; Surgical Anatomy of the Abdomen in the Living Subject, 1988; (ed) Operative Surgery, 1992; Too Many People, 1994; papers on tissue transplantation and general surgery; sections in several surgical text-books. *Recreations:* tennis, squash, painting. *Address:* 22 Barrow Road, Cambridge CB2 2AS. *T:* Cambridge (01223) 59831.

CALNE AND CALSTONE, Viscount; Simon Henry George Petty-Fitzmaurice; *b* 24 Nov. 1970; *s* and *heir* of Earl of Shelburne, *qv*. *Educ:* Eton; Jesus Coll., Cambridge.

CALTHORPE; *see* Anstruther-Gough-Calthorpe, and Gough-Calthorpe.

CALTHORPE, 10th Baron *cr* 1796; **Peter Waldo Somerset Gough-Calthorpe;** Bt 1728; *b* 13 July 1927; *s* of late Hon. Frederick Somerset Gough-Calthorpe and Rose Mary Dorothy, *d* of late Leveson William Vernon-Harcourt; *S* brother, 1945; *m* 1st, 1956, Saranne (marr. diss. 1971; she *d* 1984), *o d* of James Harold Alexander, Ireland; 2nd, 1979, Elizabeth, *d* of James and Sibyl Young, Guildford, Surrey. *Heir:* none. *Address:* c/o Isle of Man Bank, 2 Athol Street, Douglas, Isle of Man.

CALVERLEY, 3rd Baron *cr* 1945; **Charles Rodney Muff;** Member of the West Yorkshire Metropolitan Police; *b* 2 Oct. 1946; *s* of 2nd Baron Calverley and of Mary, *d* of Arthur Farrar, Halifax; *S* father, 1971; *m* 1972, Barbara Ann, *d* of Jonathan Brown, Kelbrook, nr Colne; two *s*. *Educ:* Fulneck School for Boys. *Heir:* *s* Hon. Jonathan Edward Muff, *b* 16 April 1975. *Address:* 110 Buttershaw Lane, Wibsey, Bradford, W Yorks BD6 2DA.

CALVERT, Barbara Adamson, (Lady Lowry), QC 1975; barrister-at-law; a Recorder of the Crown Court, since 1980; *b* 30 April 1926; *d* of late Albert Parker, CBE; *m* 1st, 1948, John Thornton Calvert, CBE (*d* 1987); one *s* one *d*; 2nd, 1994, Baron Lowry, *qv*. *Educ:* St Helen's, Northwood; London Sch. of Economics (BScEcon). Called to Bar: Middle Temple, 1959 (Bencher 1982); NI, 1978 (Hon. Bencher, 1995). Admin. Officer, City and Guilds of London Inst., 1961; practice at Bar, 1962–. Full-time Chm., Industrial Tribunals, London, 1986– (part-time Chm., 1974–86); Mem., Matrimonial Causes Rules Cttee, 1983–85. Freeman, City of London, 1989. *Recreations:* gardening, swimming, poetry. *Address:* (home) 158 Ashley Gardens, SW1P 1HW; (chambers) 4 Brick Court, Temple, EC4Y 7AN. *Clubs:* Sloane; Royal Fowey Yacht.

CALVERT, Denis; *see* Calvert, L. V. D.

CALVERT, Florence Irene, (Mrs W. A. Prowse); Principal, St Mary's College, University of Durham, 1975–77; *b* 1 March 1912; *d* of Ernest William Calvert and Florence Alice (*née* Walton), *m* 1977, William Arthur Prowse (*d* 1981). *Educ:* Univ. of Sheffield (BA, 1st Cl. Hons French and Latin, MA). Asst Language Teacher, Accrington Grammar Sch., 1936–39; Head, Modern Langs Dept, Accrington Girls' High Sch., 1939–48; Univ. of Durham: Lectr in Educn, 1948; Sen. Lectr, 1964–75. *Publications:* French Plays for the Classroom, 1951; L'Homme aux Mains Rouges, 1954; Contes, 1957; French by Modern Methods in Primary and Secondary Schools, 1965. *Address:* 7 St Mary's Close, Shincliffe, Durham DH1 2ND. *T:* Durham (0191) 3865502.

CALVERT, John Raymond, FIPD; Managing Director, Tyne Tees Television, since 1993; *b* 14 June 1937; *s* of Matthew and Eva Mary Calvert; *m* 1962, Elspeth Sarah Naish; one *s* one *d*. *Educ:* Bootham, York; Manchester Univ. (BA Econs). FIPD (FIPM 1986). Cadbury Schweppes Ltd, 1961–70; Delta Metals Ltd, 1970–73; Pilkington Bros Ltd, 1973–84: Personnel Dir, Triplex Safety Glass Ltd, 1973–80; Dir, Chance Bros Ltd, 1973–80; Gp Employee Relations Manager, 1980–84; Dir, Industrial Relations, ITCA, 1984–88; Gp Personnel Dir, Yorkshire Tyne Tees TV Hldgs plc, 1988–93. Director: Northern Sinfonia, 1993–; Newcastle Initiative, 1994–. Council Member: Industrial Soc., 1994–; NE Chamber of Commerce, 1995–. Mem., Mgt Cttee, Childrens' Foundn, 1993. Gov., Newcastle Coll., 1994–. FRSA 1989. *Recreations:* church organist and choirmaster, fell walking, tennis. *Address:* Tyne Tees Television Ltd, The Television Centre, City Road, Newcastle upon Tyne NE1 2AL. *T:* 0191–261 0181; 3 Love Lane, Pandon Quays, Quayside, Newcastle upon Tyne NE1 3DW. *T:* 0191–233 0635. *Club:* Northern Counties (Newcastle).

CALVERT, (Louis Victor) Denis, CB 1985; Comptroller and Auditor General for Northern Ireland, 1980–89, retired; *b* 20 April 1924; *s* of Louis Victor Calvert, Belfast and Gertrude Cherry Hobson, Belfast; *m* 1949, Vivien Millicent Lawson; two *s* one *d*. *Educ:* Belfast Royal Academy; Queen's Univ., Belfast (BScEcon); Admin. Staff Coll., Henley-on-Thames. Served with RAF, 1943–47, navigator (F/O). Northern Ireland Civil Service, 1947–80: Min. of Agriculture, 1947–56; Dep. Principal 1951; Principal, Min. of Finance, 1956–63; Min. of Health and Local Govt, 1963–65; Asst Sec. 1964; Min. of Development, 1965–73; Sen. Asst Sec. 1970; Dep. Sec. 1971; Min. of Housing, Local Govt and Planning, 1973–76; DoE for NI, 1976–80. Mem. Bd, Internat. Fund for Ireland, 1989–92. *Recreations:* gardening, golf, reading.

CALVERT, Norman Hilton; retired; Deputy Secretary, Departments of the Environment and of Transport, 1978–80; *b* 27 July 1925; *s* of Clifford and Doris Calvert; *m* 1st, 1949, May Yates (*d* 1968); one *s* one *d*; 2nd, 1971, Vera Baker. *Educ:* Leeds Modern Sch.; Leeds Univ.; King's Coll., Durham Univ. BA Hons 1st cl. Geography, 1950. Served Royal Signals, 1943–47: 81 (W African) Div., India, 1945–47. Min. of Housing and Local Govt: Asst Principal, 1950–55; Principal, 1956–64; Asst Sec., 1964–71; Sec., Water Resources Bd, 1964–68; Principal Regional Officer, Northern Region, 1969–71; Regional Dir, Northern Region, and Chm, Northern Econ. Planning Bd, 1971–73; Under Sec., DoE, 1971–78. *Recreations:* fell walking, listening to music, motoring. *Address:* 6 Monmouth Gardens, Beaminster, Dorset DT8 3BT. *T:* Beaminster (01308) 863366.

CALVERT, Phyllis; actress; *b* 18 Feb. 1915; *d* of Frederick and Annie Bickle; *m* 1941, Peter Murray Hill (*d* 1957); one *s* one *d*. *Educ:* Margaret Morris Sch.; Institut Français. Malvern Repertory Company, 1935; Coventry, 1937; York, 1938. First appeared in London in A Woman's Privilege, Kingsway Theatre, 1939; Punch Without Judy, Embassy, 1939; Flare Path, Apollo, 1942; Escapade, St James's, 1953; It's Never Too Late, Strand, 1954; River Breeze, Phoenix, 1956; The Complaisant Lover, Globe, 1959; The Rehearsal, Globe, 1961; Ménage à Trois, Lyric, 1963; Portrait of Murder, Savoy, Vaudeville, 1963; A Scent of Flowers, Duke of York's, 1964; Present Laughter, Queen's, 1965; A Woman of No Importance, Vaudeville, 1967; Blithe Spirit, Globe, 1970; Crown Matrimonial, Haymarket, 1973; Dear Daddy, Ambassadors, 1976; Mrs Warren's Profession, Worcester, 1977; She Stoops to Conquer, Old World, Exeter, 1978; Suite in Two Keys, tour, 1978; Before the Party, Queen's, 1980; Smithereens, Theatre Royal, Windsor, 1985; The Heiress, Chichester Fest., 1989. Started films, 1939. *Films include:* Kipps, The Young Mr Pitt, Man in Grey, Fanny by Gaslight, Madonna of the Seven Moons, They were Sisters, Time out of Mind, Broken Journey, My Own True Love, The Golden Madonna, A Woman with No Name, Mr Denning Drives North, Mandy, The Net, It's Never Too Late, Child in the House, Indiscreet, The Young and The Guilty, Oscar Wilde, Twisted Nerve, Oh! What a Lovely War, The Walking Stick. *Television* series and serials: Kate, 1970; Cover her Face, 1985; All Passion Spent, 1986; A Killing on the Exchange, 1987; Boon, 1987; Sophia and Constance, 1988; The Woman He Loved, 1988; Capsticks Law, 1989; Victoria Wood, 1989; After Henry, 1990; Lime Grove, 1991; Jute City, 1991; Woof, 1991; House of Elliot, 1993; Sherlock Holmes, 1994; plays: Death of a Heart, 1985; Across the Lake, 1988. *Recreations:* swimming, gardening, collecting costume books. *Address:* Hill House, 118 High Street, Waddesdon, Bucks HP18 0JF.

CALVERT-SMITH, David; First Senior Treasury Counsel, since 1995; a Recorder of the Crown Court, since 1986; *b* 6 April 1945; *s* of Arthur and late Stella Calvert-Smith; *m* 1971, Marianthe Phoca. *Educ:* Eton; King's Coll., Cambridge (MA). Called to the Bar, Middle Temple, 1969, Bencher, 1994; Jun. Treasury Counsel, 1986; Sen. Treasury Counsel, 1991. *Recreations:* music, sports. *Address:* Queen Elizabeth Building, Temple, EC4Y 7EH. *T:* 0171-583 5766.

CALVET, Jacques; President, Peugeot SA, since 1984; Referendary Councillor, Cour des Comptes (Audit Office), since 1963; *b* 19 Sept. 1931; *s* of Prof. Louis Calvet and Yvonne Calvet (*née* Olmières); *m* 1956, Françoise Rondot; two *s* one *d*. *Educ:* Lycée Janson-de-Sailly; Law Faculty, Paris (Licencié en droit; Dipl. Inst. d'Etudes Politiques; Dipl. d'Etudes Supérieures d'Economie Politique et des Sciences Economiques). Trainee, l'Ecole Nationale d'Administration, 1955–57; Audit Office, 1957–59; Office of Sec. of State for Finance, 1959–62, of Minister of Finance, 1962–66; Dep. Dir, 1964, Head of Dept, 1967, Central Finance Admin; Head of Finance Dept, Paris Préfecture, 1967–69; Asst Dir, later Dir, Office of Minister of Economy and Finance, 1969–74; Dir in Ministry of Finance, 1973; Asst Dir Gen., 1974, Dir Gen., 1976, Pres., 1979–82, Banque Nationale de Paris; Vice-Prés. du Conseil d'Administration, 1984, Prés, 1990, Automobile Peugeot; Président du Conseil d'Administration: Automobiles Citroën, 1983–; Publicité Française, 1991–. Administrator: Compagnie Génèrale des Eaux; Chaussures André; Galeries Lafayette; Société Générale; Athéna; Consulting Advr, Banque de France; Member: Internat. Council, Morgan Bank; Internat. Adv. Council, Allianz. Officier de la Légion d'Honneur; Officier de l'ordre National du Mérite et du Mérite Agricole; Chevalier des Palmes académiques. *Address:* Peugeot SA, 75 avenue de la Grande Armée, 75116 Paris, France. *T:* 40665511; Automobiles Citroën, 62 boulevard Victor Hugo, 92208 Neuilly-sur-Seine, France. *T:* 47484141; 31 avenue Victor Hugo, 75116 Paris, France.

CALVIN, Prof. Melvin; University Professor of Chemistry, University of California, since 1971; Professor of Molecular Biology, 1963–80; *b* 8 April 1911; *s* of Rose and Elias Calvin; *m* 1942, Marie Genevieve Jemtegaard; one *s* two *d*. *Educ:* Univ. of Minnesota, Minneapolis (PhD). Fellow, Univ. of Manchester, 1935–37. Univ. of California, Berkeley: Instr., 1937; Asst Prof., 1941–45; Assoc. Prof., 1945–47; Prof., 1947–71; Dir, Laboratory of Chemical Biodynamics, 1960–80; Associate Dir, Lawrence Berkeley Lab., 1967–80. Foreign Mem., Royal Society, 1959. Member: Nat. Acad. of Sciences (US); Royal Netherlands Acad. of Sciences and Letters; Amer. Philos. Society. Nobel Prize in Chemistry, 1961; Davy Medal, Royal Society, 1964; Virtanen Medal, 1975; Gibbs Medal, 1977; Priestley Medal, 1978; Amer. Inst. Chemists Gold Medal, 1979; Nat. Medal of Science, US, 1989; John Ericsson Award in Renewable Energy, US Dept. of Energy, 1991. Hon. Degrees: Michigan Coll. of Mining and Technology, 1955; Univ. of Nottingham, 1958; Oxford Univ., 1959; Northwestern Univ., 1961; Univ. of Notre Dame, 1965; Brooklyn Polytechnic Inst., 1969; Rijksuniversiteit-Gent, 1970; Columbia Univ., 1979. *Publications:* very numerous, including (8 books): Theory of Organic Chemistry (with Branch), 1941; Isotopic Carbon (with Heidelberger, Reid, Tolbert and Yankwich), 1949; Chemistry of Metal Chelate Compounds (with Martell), 1952; Path of Carbon in Photosynthesis (with Bassham), 1957; Chemical Evolution, 1961; Photosynthesis of Carbon Compounds (with Bassham), 1962; Chemical Evolution, 1969; Following the Trail of Light: a scientific odyssey, 1992. *Address:* University of California, Berkeley, CA 94720, USA; (home) 2683 Buena Vista Way, Berkeley, CA 94708, USA. *T:* (510) 8484036.

CALVO, Roberto Q.; *see* Querejazu Calvo.

CALVOCORESSI, Peter (John Ambrose); author; *b* 17 Nov. 1912; *s* of Pandia Calvocoressi and Irene (Ralli); *m* 1938, Barbara Dorothy Eden, *d* of 6th Baron Henley; two *s*. *Educ:* Eton (King's Scholar); Balliol Coll., Oxford. Called to Bar, 1935. RAF Intelligence, 1940–45; Wing Comdr. Trial of Major War Criminals, Nuremberg, 1945–46. Contested (L) Nuneaton, 1945. Staff of Royal Institute of International Affairs, 1949–54 (Mem. Council, 1955–70); Dir of Chatto & Windus Ltd and The Hogarth Press Ltd, 1954–65; Editorial Dir, 1972–76, Publisher and Chief Exec., 1973–76, Penguin Books. Chm., Open Univ. Educnl Enterprises Ltd, 1979–88. Reader (part time) in International Relations, Univ. of Sussex, 1965–71; Member: Council, Inst. for Strategic Studies, 1961–71; Council, Inst. of Race Relations, 1970–71; UN Sub-Commn on the Prevention of Discrimination and Protection of Minorities, 1962–71; Chm., The Africa Bureau, 1963–71; Mem., Internat. Exec., Amnesty International, 1969–71; Chm., The London Library, 1970–73; Dep. Chm., N Metropolitan Conciliation Cttee, 1967–71. DUniv Open, 1990. *Publications:* Nuremberg: The Facts, the Law and the Consequences, 1947; Surveys of International Affairs, vol. 1, 1947–48, 1950; vol. 2, 1949–50, 1951; vol. 3, 1951, 1952; vol. 4, 1952, 1953; vol. 5, 1953, 1954; Middle East Crisis (with Guy Wint), 1957; South Africa and World Opinion, 1961; World Order and New States, 1962; World Politics since 1945, 1968, 6th edn 1991; (with Guy Wint) Total War, 1972, 2nd rev. edn 1989; The British Experience 1945–75, 1978; Top Secret Ultra, 1980; Independent Africa and the World, 1985; A Time for Peace, 1987; Who's Who in the Bible, 1987; Resilient Europe 1870–2000, 1991; Threading My Way (memoirs), 1994. *Recreation:* walking. *Address:* 1 Queen's Parade, Bath BA1 2NJ. *T:* Bath (01225) 333903. *Club:* Garrick.

CALVOCORESSI, Richard Edward Ion; Keeper, Scottish National Gallery of Modern Art, since 1987; *b* 5 May 1951; *s* of Ion Melville Calvocoressi and Katherine (*née* Kennedy); *m* 1976, Francesca Temple Roberts; one *s* two *d*. *Educ:* Eton; Brooke House, Market Harborough; Magdalen Coll., Oxford (Exhibnr; BA (Hons) English Lang. and Lit.); Courtauld Inst. of Art (MA Hist. of Art, 19th and 20th centuries). Research Assistant: Scottish Nat. Gall. of Modern Art, Edinburgh, 1977–79; Modern Collection, Tate Gall., 1979–82; Asst Keeper, Tate Gall., 1982–87. Art Advr, Chelmsford Mus., 1980–86; Member: Cttee, British Council, Scotland, 1989–; Visual Arts Adv. Cttee, British Council, 1991–; Visual Arts Cttee, Scottish Arts Council, 1993–. Dir, Grimsthorpe and Drummond Castle Trust, 1993–. Governor, Glasgow Sch. of Art, 1988–91. *Publications:* Magritte, 1979, 4th edn 1994; numerous exhibn catalogues, reviews and articles. *Address:* Scottish National Gallery of Modern Art, Belford Road, Edinburgh EH4 3DR.

CAMBELL, Rear-Adm. Dennis Royle Farquharson, CB 1960; DSC 1940; *b* 13 Nov. 1907; *s* of Dr Archibald Cambell and Edith Cambell, Southsea; *m* 1933, Dorothy Elinor Downes; two *d*. *Educ:* Westminster Sch. Joined RN, 1925, HMS Thunderer Cadet Training; trained as FAA pilot, 1931; 1st Capt. of HMS Ark Royal IV, 1955–56; retired, 1960. *Address:* c/o National Westminster Bank, High Street, Petersfield, Hants GU32 3JF.

CAMBRIDGE, Alan John; HM Diplomatic Service, retired; *b* 1 July 1925; *s* of Thomas David Cambridge and Winifred Elizabeth (*née* Jarrett); *m* 1947, Thelma Elliot; three *s* one *d*. *Educ:* Beckenham Grammar Sch. Served War, FAA and RAFVR, 1943–47 (Air Gunner, Bomber Comd). War Pensions Office and MPNI, 1948–55; entered CRO, 1955; Chief Clerk: Madras, 1956–58; Kuala Lumpur, 1959–62; 2nd Sec., Salisbury, Fedn of Rhodesia and Nyasaland, 1962–65; 1st Sec. (Political), Freetown, 1965–66; UN Dept, FCO, 1966–68; 1st Sec., Prague, 1969; 1st Sec. (Consular/Aid), Suva, 1970–72; HM Consul, Milan, 1972–74; Asst Head of Inf. Dept, FCO, 1974–78; 1st Sec., Ankara, 1978–81; Asst Head, 1981–82, Head and Counsellor, 1983–85, Migration and Visa Dept, FCO; Assessor, FCO, 1985–90. *Recreations:* photography, swimming, tennis. *Address:* 9 The Ferns, Carlton Road, Tunbridge Wells TN1 2JT. *T:* Tunbridge Wells (01892) 531223. *Club:* Civil Service.

CAMBRIDGE, Sydney John Guy, CMG 1979; CVO 1979; HM Diplomatic Service, retired; *b* 5 Nov. 1928; *o s* of late Jack and Mona Cambridge; unmarried. *Educ:* Marlborough; King's Coll., Cambridge. Entered HM Diplomatic Service, Sept. 1952; Oriental Sec., British Embassy, Jedda, 1953–56; Foreign Office, 1956–60; First Sec., UK Delegn to United Nations, at New York, 1960–64; Head of Chancery, British Embassy, Djakarta, 1964–66; FO, 1966–70; Counsellor, British Embassy, Rome, 1970–73; Head of Financial Relations Dept, FCO, 1973–75; Counsellor, British High Commn, Nicosia, 1975–77; Ambassador: to Kuwait, 1977–82; to Morocco, 1982–84. *Address:* Saint Peter's House, Filkins, Lechlade, Glos GL7 3JQ.

CAMDEN, 6th Marquess *cr* 1812; **David George Edward Henry Pratt;** Baron Camden, 1765; Earl Camden, Viscount Bayham, 1786; Earl of Brecknock, 1812; *b* 13 Aug. 1930; *o s* of 5th Marquess Camden and Marjorie, Countess of Brecknock, DBE (*d* 1989); *S* father, 1983; *m* 1961, Virginia Ann (marr. diss. 1984), *o d* of late F. H. H. Finlaison, Arklow Cottage, Windsor, Berks; one *s* one *d* (and one *s* decd). Late Lieutenant, Scots Guards. *Educ:* Eton. Dir, Clive Discount Co. Ltd, 1958–69. *Heir: s* Earl of Brecknock, *qv*. *Address:* Wherwell House, Andover, Hants SP11 7JP. *T:* Andover (01264) 860020.

CAMDEN, John; President, RMC Group plc (Chairman, 1974–93; Managing Director, 1966–85); *b* 18 Nov. 1925; *s* of late Joseph Reginald Richard John Camden and Lilian Kate McCann; *m* 1972, Diane Mae Friese; two *d* (and one *s* two *d* of former *m*). *Educ:* Worcester Royal Grammar Sch.; Birmingham Univ. (BSc). Royal Tank Corps and Intell. Corps, 1943–47. Joined RMC Group (formerly Ready Mixed Concrete Group), 1952; Dir responsible for Group's ops in Europe, 1962. Grand Decoration of Honour in Silver (Austria), 1978. *Recreations:* golf, gardening. *Address:* RMC Group plc, RMC House, Coldharbour Lane, Thorpe, Egham, Surrey TW20 8TD.

CAMDESSUS, Michel; Managing Director, International Monetary Fund, since 1987; *b* 1 May 1933; *s* of Alfred Camdessus and Madeleine Camdessus (*née* Cassembon); *m* 1957, Brigitte d'Arcy; two *s* four *d*. *Educ:* Inst. of Political Studies, Paris; Diploma, Nat. Sch. of Administration. Administrateur Civil, French Treasury, 1960; Financial Attaché, Permt French Delegn to European Communities, 1966–68; Asst Dir, Treasury, 1971, Dep. Dir, 1974, Dir, 1982; Dep. Governor, Bank of France, Aug. 1984, Governor, Nov. 1984. Chm., Paris Club, 1978–84. Chevalier de la Légion d'Honneur; Chevalier de l'Ordre National du Mérite; Croix de la valeur militaire. *Address:* International Monetary Fund, 700 19th Street NW, Washington, DC 20431, USA. *T:* (202) 6237000.

CAME, Nicholas John Gard, FICS; Director, Australian British Chamber of Commerce (UK), since 1993; *b* Swansea, 10 March 1937; *s* of Victor Henry Thomas Came and Dorothy Edith Came (*née* Prestidge); *m* 1961, Edelgard Elise Irma Meyer; two *d*. *Educ:* Bromsgrove Sch. FICS 1984; MCIT 1988. Officer Cadet Trng Vessel, Rakaia, 1954–57; Bethell Gwyn & Co., 1958–59; Nat. Service, commnd RA, 1959–61; Exec., Dowie & Marwood Ltd, 1961–66; Manager: NZ Shipping Co. Ltd, London, 1967–71; P&OSN Co., 1971–78; Dir, Shipping Corp. of NZ (UK) Ltd, 1978–91. Pres., NZ Soc., 1990–91. *Recreations:* walking, music, languages, travel. *Address:* 11 Silverdale, Fleet, Hants GU13 9TT. *T:* Fleet (01252) 623691. *Club:* Royal Over-Seas League.

CAMERON, family name of **Baron Cameron of Lochbroom**.

CAMERON, Hon. Lord; John Cameron, KT 1978; Kt 1954; DSC; HRSA; FRSGS; a Senator of The College of Justice in Scotland and Lord of Session 1955–85; *b* 1900; *m* 1st, 1927, Eileen Dorothea (*d* 1943), *d* of late H. M. Burrell; one *s* two *d*; 2nd, 1944, Iris, *widow* of Lambert C. Shepherd. *Educ:* Edinburgh Acad.; Edinburgh Univ. Served European War, 1918–19, with RNVR. Advocate, 1924; Advocate-Depute, 1929–36; QC (Scotland), 1936. Served with RNVR, Sept. 1939–44 (despatches, DSC); released to reserve, Dec. 1944. Sheriff of Inverness, Elgin and Nairn, 1945; Sheriff of Inverness, Moray, Nairn and Ross and Cromarty, 1946–48; Dean of Faculty of Advocates, 1948–55. Member: Cttee on Law of Contempt of Court, 1972–; Royal Commn on Civil Liability and Compensation for Personal Injury, 1973–78. DL Edinburgh, 1953–84. Hon. FRSE 1983; Hon. FBA 1983. DUniv Edinburgh, 1983; Hon. LLD: Aberdeen; Glasgow; Edinburgh; Hon. DLitt Heriot-Watt. *Address:* 28 Moray Place, Edinburgh EH3 6BX. *T:* 0131–225 7585. *Clubs:* New, Scottish Arts (Edinburgh); Royal Forth Yacht.

See also Baron Cameron of Lochbroom, Hon. Lord Weir.

CAMERON OF LOCHBROOM, Baron *cr* 1984 (Life Peer), of Lochbroom in the District of Ross and Cromarty; **Kenneth John Cameron;** PC 1984; a Senator of the College of Justice in Scotland, since 1989; *b* 11 June 1931; *s* of Hon. Lord Cameron, *qv*; *m* 1964, Jean Pamela Murray; two *d*. *Educ:* The Edinburgh Academy; Corpus Christi Coll., Oxford (MA 1955; Hon. Fellow, 1989); Edinburgh Univ. (LLB). Served RN, 1950–52; commissioned RNVR, 1951 (Lt). Admitted Faculty of Advocates, 1958; QC (Scot.) 1972; Standing Junior to Dept of Transport, 1964–71; to DoE, 1971–72; Chairman of Industrial Tribunals in Scotland, 1966–81; Advocate Depute, 1981–84; Lord Advocate, 1984–89. Chm. of Pensions Appeal Tribunal (Scotland), 1975, Pres. 1976–84. Chairman: Cttee for Investigation in Scotland of Agricultural Marketing Schemes, 1980–84; Scottish Civic Trust, 1989–95; Edinburgh New Town Conservation Cttee, 1991–; Royal Fine Art Commn for Scotland, 1995–. Pres., Scottish Council for Voluntary Orgns, 1989–. Hon. Bencher, Lincoln's Inn, 1984. FRSE 1990. Hon. FRIAS 1994. *Recreations:* fishing, sailing, music. *Address:* 10 Belford Terrace, Edinburgh EH4 3DQ. *T:* 0131–332 6636. *Clubs:* Scottish Arts, New (Edinburgh).

CAMERON, Prof. Alan Douglas Edward, FBA 1975; Anthon Professor of Latin Language and Literature, Columbia University, New York, since 1977; *b* 13 March 1938; *er s* of A. D. Cameron, Egham; *m* 1962, Averil Sutton (marr. diss. 1980; *see* Averil Cameron); one *s* one *d*. *Educ:* St Paul's Sch. (Schol.); New Coll., Oxford (Schol.). Craven Scholar 1958; 1st cl. Hon. Mods 1959; De Paravicini Scholar 1960; Chancellor's Prize for Latin Prose 1960; 1st cl. Lit. Hum. 1961; N. H. Baynes Prize 1967; John Conington Prize 1968. Asst Master, Brunswick Sch., Haywards Heath, 1956–57; Asst Lectr, then Lectr, in Humanity, Glasgow Univ., 1961–64; Lectr in Latin, 1964–71, Reader, 1971–72, Bedford Coll., London; Prof. of Latin, King's Coll., London, 1972–77. Visiting Professor: Columbia Univ., NY, 1967–68; UCLA, 1989; Visiting Fellow: Humanities Research Centre, ANU, 1985; Inst. for Advanced Study, Princeton, 1990. Fellow: Amer. Acad. of Arts and Sciences, 1979; Amer. Phil Soc., 1992. *Publications:* Claudian: Poetry and Propaganda at the Court of Honorius, 1970; (contrib.) Prosopography of the Later Roman Empire, ed Jones, Morris and Martindale, i, 1971, ii, 1980; Porphyrius the Charioteer, 1973; Bread and Circuses, 1974; Circus Factions, 1976; Literature and Society in the Early Byzantine World, 1985; (jtly) The Consuls of the Later Roman Empire, 1985; (with J. Long) Barbarians and Politics at the Court of Arcadius, 1993; The Greek Anthology: from Meleager to Planudes, 1993; Callimachus and his Critics, 1995; articles and reviews in learned jls. *Recreation:* the cinema. *Address:* Columbia University, Morningside Heights, New York, NY 10027, USA.

CAMERON, Alan John; Chairman, Australian Securities Commission, since 1993; *b* 9 Feb. 1948; *s* of John and Norma Cameron; *m* 1971, Susan Patricia Sanders; two *s*. *Educ:* Sydney Univ. (BA, LLB, LLM). Principal Solicitor, NSW Aboriginal Legal Service, 1973–75; Lectr in Law, Univ. of N Sumatra, 1975–77; Dawson Waldron, Solicitors, later Blake Dawson Waldron: Partner, 1979–91; Man. Partner, 1982–85, 1989–91; Commonwealth Ombudsman (Australia), 1991–92. *Recreations:* tennis, walking, reading. *Address:* GPO Box 4866, Sydney, NSW 2001, Australia. *T:* (2) 9112001.

CAMERON, Major Allan John, MBE 1988; JP; Vice Lord-Lieutenant, Highland Region (Ross and Cromarty), 1977–92; *b* 25 March 1917; *s* of Col Sir Donald Cameron of Lochiel, KT, CMG (*d* 1951), and Lady Hermione Cameron (*d* 1978), *d* of 5th Duke of Montrose; *m* 1945, Mary Elizabeth Vaughan-Lee, Dillington, Somerset; two *s* two *d* (and one *s* decd). *Educ:* Harrow; RMC Sandhurst. Served QO Cameron Highlanders, 1936–48; Major, Retd (POW Middle East, 1942). County Councillor, Ross-shire, 1955–75 (Chm. Educn Cttee, 1962–75); Councillor, 1975–, Convener, 1991–, Ross and Cromarty DC. Former Member: Red Deer Commn; Countryside Commn for Scotland; Broadcasting Council for Scotland. *Recreations:* curling (Past Pres. Royal Caledonian Curling Club), gardening, golf. *Address:* Allangrange, Munlochy, Ross-shire IV8 8NZ. *T:* Munlochy (01463) 811249. *Club:* Naval and Military.

See also Col Sir Donald Cameron of Lochiel.

CAMERON, Rt. Rev. Andrew Bruce; *see* Aberdeen and Orkney, Bishop of.

CAMERON, Averil Millicent, MA, PhD; FBA 1981; FSA 1982; Warden, Keble College, Oxford, since 1994; *b* 8 Feb. 1940; *d* of T. R. Sutton, Leek, Staffs; *m* 1962, Alan Douglas Edward Cameron, *qv* (marr. diss. 1980); one *s* one *d*. *Educ:* Westwood Hall Girls' High Sch., Leek, Staffs; Somerville Coll., Oxford (Passmore Edwards Schol. 1960; Rosa Hovey Schol. 1962; MA); Univ. of Glasgow; University Coll. London (PhD; FKC 1987). King's College London: Asst Lectr, 1965; Lectr, 1968; Reader in Ancient History, 1970; Prof. of Ancient History, 1978–89; Head of Dept of Classics, 1984–89; Prof. of Late Antique and Byzantine Studies, and Dir, Centre for Hellenic Studies, 1989–94. Visiting Professor: Columbia Univ., 1967–68; Collège de France, 1987; Sather Prof., Univ. of Calif. at Berkeley, 1985–86; Vis. Member, Inst. of Advanced Study, Princeton, 1977–78; Summer Fellow, Dumbarton Oaks Center for Byzantine Studies, 1981; British Acad. Wolfson Res. Reader in Hist., 1990–92. Chm., British Nat. Byzantine Cttee, 1983–89; Vice-President: Roman Soc., 1983–; British Acad. Council, 1983–86. Editor, Jl of Roman Studies, 1985–90. *Publications:* Procopius, 1967; Agathias, 1970; Corippus: In laudem Iustini minoris, 1976; Change and Continuity in Sixth-Century Byzantium, 1981; (ed jtly) Images of Women in Antiquity, 1983, 2nd edn 1993; (ed jtly) Constantinople in the Eighth Century: the Parastaseis Syntomoi Chronikai, 1984; Procopius and the Sixth Century, 1985; (ed) History as Text: the writing of ancient history, 1989; Christianity and the Rhetoric of Empire, 1991; (ed jtly) The Byzantine and Early Islamic Near East, vol. I: problems in the literary source material, 1992; The Later Roman Empire, 1993; The Mediterranean World in Late Antiquity, AD 395–600, 1993; (ed jtly) The Byzantine and Early Islamic Near East, vol. II: land use and settlement patterns, 1994; numerous articles in learned jls. *Address:* Keble College, Oxford OX1 3PG.

CAMERON, Dr Clive Bremner; Dean, Institute of Cancer Research, London, 1978–82; *b* 28 Sept. 1921; *s* of Clive Rutherford and Aroha Margaret Cameron; *m* 1958, Rosalind Louise Paget; two *s* one *d*. *Educ:* King's Coll., Auckland, NZ; Otago Univ., NZ (MD). Consultant in Clinical Pathology, Royal Marsden Hospital, 1961–82; Chairman, SW

Thames Regional Cancer Council, 1976–81. Mem. Bd of Governors, Royal Marsden Hosp., 1977–82. *Publications:* papers on steroid biochemistry, biochemical and other aspects of cancer. *Recreation:* country pursuits. *Address:* East Kennett Manor, Marlborough, Wilts SN8 5ET. *T:* Lockeridge (01672) 861239.

CAMERON, Colin Neil; Head of Television, BBC Scotland, since 1991; *b* 30 March 1950; *s* of Hector MacDonald Cameron and Frances (*née* Majury); *m* 1978, Christine Welsh Main; two *s*. *Educ:* Glasgow Acad.; Duke of York, Nairobi; Poly. of Central London (Dip. Communication Studies). Journalist, BBC Scotland, 1973–76; BBC TV: Film Dir, That's Life, 1976–77; Producer/Dir, Everyman and Heart of the Matter, 1977–85; Editor, Features and Documentaries, BBC North, 1985–88; Hd, Documentary Features, BBC TV, 1988–91. Chm., BAFTA Scotland, 1993–95; Mem. Bd, Scottish Film Prodn Fund, 1992–. Mem., Adv. Gp, Glasgow Common Purpose. Judge, CRE Race in the Media Awards. Trustee, Television Trust for the Envmt, 1989–95. Mem., RTS, 1984–. UNA Media Peace Prize, 1984. *Recreations:* sailing, cycling, cinema, Scottish art. *Address:* BBC Scotland, Queen Margaret Drive, Glasgow G12 8DG. *T:* 0141–338 2424.

CAMERON OF LOCHIEL, Colonel Sir Donald (Hamish), KT 1973; CVO 1970; TD 1944; JP; 26th Chief of the Clan Cameron; Lord-Lieutenant of County of Inverness, 1971–85 (Vice-Lieutenant, 1963–70); Chartered Accountant; *b* 12 Sept. 1910; *s* of Col Sir Donald Walter Cameron of Lochiel, KT, CMG, 25th Chief of the Clan Cameron, and Lady Hermione Emily Graham (*d* 1978), 2nd *d* of 5th Duke of Montrose; *S* father, as 26th Chief, 1951; *m* 1939, Margaret, *o d* of Lieut-Col Hon. Nigel Gathorne-Hardy, DSO; two *s* two *d*. *Educ:* Harrow; Balliol Coll., Oxford. Joined Lovat Scouts, 1929; Major 1940; Lieut-Col 1945; Lieut-Col comdg 4/5th Bn (TA) QO Cameron Highlanders, 1955–57; Col 1957 (TARO). Hon. Colonel: 4/5th Bn QO Cameron Highlanders, 1958–67; 3rd (Territorial) Bn Queen's Own Highlanders (Seaforth and Camerons), 1967–69; 2nd Bn, 51st Highland Volunteers, 1970–75. Member (part-time): British Railways Bd, 1962–64; Scottish Railways Bd, 1964–72 (Chm. Scottish Area Bd, BTC, 1959–64); Transport Holding Co., 1962–65; Director: Royal Bank of Scotland, 1954–80 (Vice-Chm., 1969–80); Save & Prosper Gp, 1968–84; Culter Guard Bridge Holdings Ltd, 1970–77 (Chm., 1970–76); Scottish Widows Life Assurance Soc., 1955–81 (Chm., 1964–67). Crown Estate Comr, 1957–69. Chm., Scottish Cttee, Malcolm Sargent Cancer Fund for Children, 1975–91. President: Scottish Landowners Fedn, 1979–84; Royal Highland and Agricultural Soc. of Scotland, 1971, 1979 and 1987. Governor, Harrow Sch., 1967–77. *Heir: s* Donald Angus Cameron, younger of Lochiel [*b* 2 Aug. 1946; *m* 1974, Lady Cecil Kerr, *d* of Marquess of Lothian, *qv*; one *s* three *d*]. *Address:* Achnacarry, Spean Bridge, Inverness-shire PH34 4EJ. *T:* Spean Bridge (01397) 712708. *Clubs:* Pratt's; New (Edinburgh).

See also A. J. Cameron.

CAMERON, Donald William; Canadian Consul General to New England, since 1993; *b* 20 May 1946; *m* 1969, Rosemary Simpson; one *s* two *d*. *Educ:* East Pictou Rural High Sch.; Nova Scotia Agricl Coll.; McGill Univ. (BSc). Dairy farmer; MLA (PC) Pictou East, 1974–93; Minister of: Recreation, 1978–79; Fisheries, 1978–80; Industry, Trade and Technology, 1988–91; Leader, Nova Scotia Progressive Cons. Party, 1991; Premier of Nova Scotia, 1991–93. *Recreations:* ski-ing, boating, hockey, tennis. *Address:* Canadian Consulate General, 3 Copley Place, Suite 400, Boston, MA 02116, USA.

CAMERON, Rt. Rev. Douglas Maclean; *see* Argyll and the Isles, Bishop of.

CAMERON, Ellen; *see* Malcolm, E.

CAMERON, Sir (Eustace) John, Kt 1977; CBE 1970; MA Cantab; Tasmanian pastoralist, since 1946; *b* 8 Oct. 1913; *s* of Eustace Noel Cameron and Alexina Maria Cameron; *m* 1934, Nancie Ailsa Sutherland (OBE 1983) (*d* 1988); one *d*. *Educ:* Geelong Grammar Sch.; Trinity Coll., Cambridge. Served RANVR, 1942–46. ICI, 1938–41. State Pres., Liberal Party, 1948–52. Pres., Tasmanian Stockowners Assoc., 1965–68; Vice-Pres., Aust. Graziers, 1968–71. University of Tasmania: Mem. Council, 1956–82; Dep. Chancellor, 1964–72; Chancellor, 1973–81. Member: Selection Cttee, Winston Churchill Fellowship, 1965–74; CSIRO Adv. Cttee, 1959–77; Housing Loan Insurance Corp., 1970–73. Hon. LLD Tasmania, 1982. *Publications:* contrib. Australian Dictionary of Biography. *Recreations:* Australiana, gardening, pottering. *Address:* Lochiel, Ross, Tas 7209, Australia. *T:* Ross (03) 815253. *Clubs:* Tasmanian (Hobart); Launceston (Launceston).

CAMERON, Rt. Rev. Ewen Donald; Assistant Bishop, Diocese of Sydney, 1975–93; *b* 7 Nov. 1926; *s* of Ewen Cameron, Balranald, NSW, and Dulce M. Cameron, Sydney, NSW; *m* 1952, Joan R., *d* of T. Wilkins, Mosman, NSW; one *s* two *d*. *Educ:* Sydney C of E Grammar Sch., N Sydney; Moore Theological Coll., Sydney. ACA (Aust.); BD (London), ThSchol (Aust. Coll. of Theol.). Public Accountancy, 1945–57. Lectr, Moore Theological Coll., 1960–63; Rector, St Stephen's, Bellevue Hill, 1963–65; Federal Secretary, CMS of Aust., 1965–72; Archdeacon of Cumberland with Sydney, 1972–75; Bishop of North Sydney, 1983–90; Registrar, dio. of Sydney, 1990–93. Mem., ARCIC, 1983–90. *Address:* 114 Bent Street, Lindfield, NSW 2070, Australia. *T:* (2) 4168423. *Club:* Union (Sydney).

CAMERON, Francis (Ernest), MA, DipEth (Oxon); FRCO(CHM), ARAM; organist and ethnomusicologist; Choirmaster and Organist, City Church of St Michael at the North Gate, Oxford, 1988–94; *b* London, 5 Dec. 1927; *er s* of Ernest and Doris Cameron; *m* 1952, Barbara Minns; three *d*. *Educ:* Mercers' Sch.; Caerphilly Boys' Secondary Sch.; Royal Acad. of Music; University Coll., Oxford. Henry Richards Prizewinner, RAM, 1946. Organist, St Peter's, Fulham, 1943; Pianist, Canadian Legion, 1944; Organist, St Luke's, Holloway, 1945; Sub-organist, St Peter's, Eaton Square, 1945; Organist, St James-the-Less, Westminster, 1946; commissioned RASC, 1948; Organ Scholar, University Coll., Oxford, 1950; Organist: St Anne's, Highgate, 1952; St Barnabas', Pimlico, 1953; St Mark's, Marylebone Road, 1957–58, Choirmaster, St Aloysius, Somers Town, 1959; Master of Music, Westminster Cathedral, 1959; Visiting Organist, Church of St Thomas of Canterbury, Rainham, Kent, 1961; Organist and Choirmaster, Church of Our Lady of the Assumption and St Gregory, Warwick Street, W1, 1962–68. Travel for UNESCO, 1952–55; Dep. Dir of Music, LCC (subsequently GLC), 1954–68; Asst-Dir of Music, Emanuel Sch., 1954; Music Master, Central Foundation Boys' Grammar Sch., 1956; Prof. of Organ and Composition, RAM, 1959–68; *locum tenens* Dir of Music, St Felix Sch., Southwold, 1963 and 1964; Asst Dir, 1968, Chm. of Musicology, 1974–79, NSW State Conservatorium of Music; Organist, Church of St Mary the Virgin, Iffley, 1980–88; Sen. Lectr, Musical Studies, Oxford Poly., 1982–86. Inaugural Conductor, Witan Operatic Soc., 1957–58; Conductor: "I Cantici", 1961–65; Francis Cameron Chorale, 1965–68; Singers of David, 1973–76; British Adjudicator, Fedn of Canadian Music Festivals, 1965; Examr Associated Bd of Royal Schools of Music, 1965–68; Dep. Chm., NSW Adv. Bd, Aust. Music Exams Bd, 1969–74. Field Officer, Deep Creek Aboriginal Monuments res. and recording prog., 1973; Mem., Lancefield Archaeol Expedn, 1975. President: "Open Score", 1946–68; Musicol Soc. of Aust., 1971–75 (jt leader, ethnomusicol expedn to New Hebrides, 1971–72); Sydney Univ. Anthropol Soc., 1974–75; Phoenix Photographic Circle, 1977–79; Conservatorium Professional Staff Assoc., 1978–79; Vice-Pres., Aust. Chapter, Internat. Soc. for Contemporary Music, 1970–77; Ed., INFO, European Seminar in Ethnomusicology, 1986–90. Beethoven Commemorative Medal, Fed. Repub. of Germany, 1970. *Publications:* editor (with John Steele) Musica Britannica vol. xiv (The Keyboard Music of John Bull, part I), 1960; Old Palace Yard, 1963; Eight dances from Benjamin Cosyn's Second Virginal Book, 1964; I Sing of a Maiden, 1966; John Bull, ausgewählte Werke, 1967; I Believe, 1969; incidental music for film The Voyage of the New Endeavour, 1970; songs and incidental music for Congreve's Love for Love, 1972; Alleluia, 1990; contributor to: Church Music; Composer; The Conductor; Liturgy; Musical Times; Australian Jl of Music Education; Studies in Music; Music in Tertiary Educn; Con Brio; Musicology IV; Aust. Nat. Hist.; Nation Review; Quanta; ICTM (UK) Bulletin; Eur. Studies in Ethnomusicol. *Address:* 17A East Saint Helen Street, Abingdon, Oxford OX14 5EE. *T:* Abingdon (01235) 530627.

CAMERON, George Edmund, CBE 1970; retired; *b* 2 July 1911; *s* of William Cameron and Margaret Cameron (*née* Craig); *m* 1939, Winifred Audrey Brown; two *s*. *Educ:* Ballymena Academy. Chartered Accountant, 1933; Partner, Wright Fitzsimons & Cameron, 1937–79. Pres., Inst. of Chartered Accountants in Ireland, 1960–61. *Recreations:* golf, gardening. *Address:* Ardavon, Glen Road, Craigavad, Co. Down BT18 0HB. *T:* Holywood (01232) 422232. *Clubs:* Royal County Down Golf, Royal Belfast Golf.

CAMERON, Prof. Iain Thomas, MD; Regius Professor of Obstetrics and Gynaecology, University of Glasgow, since 1993; *b* 21 Feb. 1956; *s* of late James David Cameron and of Stella (*née* Turner); *m* 1st, 1983, Sally Herries (marr. diss.); two *d*; 2nd, 1992, Heidi Wade; one *s*. *Educ:* Hutton Grammar Sch.; Univ. of Edinburgh (BSc Med. Sci. 1977; MB ChB 1980; MD 1988); MA Cantab 1992. MRCOG 1986; MRACOG 1987. House Officer and Sen. House Officer, Western Infirmary, Glasgow, Royal Infirmary, Edinburgh and Simpson Meml Maternity Pavilion, Edinburgh, 1980–82; University of Edinburgh: Research Fellow, Dept of Obstetrics and Gynaecology, 1982–84; Lectr and Registrar, 1984–86; Monash University: Clinical Res. Fellow, 1986–88; Lectr, 1987–88; Sen. Registrar, Royal Women's Hosp., Melbourne, 1988–89; University of Cambridge: Lectr, 1989–92; Sen. Registrar, 1989–91; Consultant, 1991–92. *Publications:* articles and other contribs on menstrual disorders, oocyte donation, endometrium, prostaglandins and endothelins. *Recreation:* solo piping. *Address:* Department of Obstetrics and Gynaecology, The Queen Mother's Hospital, Yorkhill, Glasgow G3 8SJ. *T:* 0141–201 0568.

CAMERON, Ian Alexander; Sheriff of Grampian, Highland and Islands at Wick, Dornoch and Stornoway, since 1993; *b* 5 Nov. 1938; *s* of late James Cameron and of Isabella Cameron; *m* 1968, Dr Margaret Anne Innes; one *s*. *Educ:* Elgin Acad.; Edinburgh Univ. (MA); Aberdeen Univ. (LLB with dist.). Qualified as solicitor, 1961; Partner, Stewart & McIsaac, Solicitors, Elgin, 1962–87; Sheriff of Lothian and Borders at Edinburgh, 1987–93. *Recreations:* travel, railway history, hillwalking. *Address:* Achnacarry, Elgin IV30 1NU. *T:* Elgin (01343) 542731; 19/4 Damside, Dean Village, Edinburgh EH4 3BB. *T:* 0131–220 1548.

CAMERON, Prof. Ian Rennell, FRCP; Provost and Vice-Chancellor, University of Wales College of Medicine, since 1994; *b* 20 May 1936; *s* of James and Frances Mary Cameron; *m* 1st, 1964, Jayne Bustard (marr. diss.); one *s* one *d*; 2nd, 1980, Jennifer, *d* of Stewart and Josephine Cowin. *Educ:* Westminster Sch.; Corpus Christi Coll., Oxford (BA 1958 1st Cl. Hons Animal Physiol; MA 1961; DM 1969); St Thomas's Hosp. Med. Sch. (BM BCh 1961). FRCP 1976. Jun. med. appts, St Thomas' Hosp., 1961–64; Res. Asst, Dept of Physiol., UCL, 1966–68; Lectr 1967, Sen. Lectr 1969, Reader 1975, St Thomas's Hosp. Med. Sch.; Prof. of Medicine, UMDS of Guy's and St Thomas' Hosps, 1979–94 (Dean, St Thomas', 1986–89; Principal, UMDS, 1989–92); Hon. Consultant Physician, St Thomas' Hosp., 1970–94. NIH Postdoctoral Fellowship at Cedars-Sinai Med. Center, LA, and Asst Prof., Dept of Physiol, UCLA, 1968–69. Mem., Medway HA, 1981–86. Dir, R & D, SE Thames RHA, 1993–94. Examiner, Univ. of London Final MB, 1980–94; Mem. Senate, Univ. of London, 1989–92. Member: Med. Res. Soc., 1966–; Physiol Soc., 1974–; Assoc. of Physicians of GB and Ire., 1979–; Council, RCP, 1992–. Mem. Council, KCL, 1993–. FRSA 1990. *Publications:* Respiratory Disorders (with N. T. Bateman), 1983; papers in various med. and physiol jls. *Recreation:* collecting (books, paintings and ceramics). *Address:* University of Wales College of Medicine, Heath Park, Cardiff CF4 4XN. *Club:* Athenæum.

CAMERON, Ivor Gill S.; *see* Smith-Cameron.

CAMERON, Prof. J(ames) Malcolm, MD, PhD; FRCSGlas, FRCPath, DMJ; Professor of Forensic Medicine, University of London, at The London Hospital Medical College, 1973–92, now Professor Emeritus, and Director, Department of Forensic Medicine; Hon. Medical Adviser to Amateur Swimming Association; Editor of Medicine, Science and Law, since 1970; *b* 29 April 1930; *s* of late James Cameron and Doris Mary Robertson; *m* 1956, Primrose Agnes Miller McKerrell, MCST; one *d*. *Educ:* The High Sch. of Glasgow; Univ. of Glasgow (MB, ChB, MD, PhD). The London Hospital Medical College: Lectr in Forensic Med., 1963–65; Sen. Lectr in Forensic Med., 1965–70; Reader in Forensic Med., 1970–72; Sen. Lectr in Forensic Med. at St Bartholomew's Hosp. Med. Coll., 1971–92; Ver Heyden De Lancey Reader in Forensic Medicine, Council of Legal Educn, 1978–92. Hon. Consultant: London, subseq. Royal London Hosp., 1967–92; in Forensic Medicine, to Army, 1971–92, and RN, 1972–92; RAF, 1990–92; Lectr to Metropolitan Police Detective Trng Sch., SW Detective Trng Sch., Bristol, and Special Investigation Br. of RMP, 1969–92; former Examiner in Forensic Med. to Univ. of Dublin; Convenor for Exams of Dip. in Med. Jurisp. of Honourable Soc. of Apothecaries of London; former Mem. Council, Royal Coll. of Pathologists. Chm. and Hon. Sec., Med. Cttee, Ligue Européenne de Natation, 1990–. Member: BMA; Council, Brit. Assoc. in Forensic Med. (Pres., 1985–87); British Acad. of Forensic Sciences (Sec. Gen., 1970–85; Pres., 1978–79); FINA Med. Cttee (Hon. Sec., 1986–); Assoc. of Police Surgeons of GB (Hon. Fellow); Forensic Science Soc.; Assoc. of Clinical Pathologists; Pathological Soc. of GB and Ire.; Research Defence Soc., Fellow, Amer. Acad. of Forensic Sciences; Mem., Academic Internationalis Medicinae Legalis et Medicinae Socialis. Hon. D For. Odont. *Publications:* scientific papers in numerous learned jls, both med. and forensic. *Recreations:* sports medicine and legal medicine. *Address:* c/o Department of Forensic Medicine, The London Hospital Medical College, Turner Street, E1 2AD. *Clubs:* Savage, Royal Naval Medical.

CAMERON, Prof. James Munro; University Professor, St Michaels College, University of Toronto, 1971–78, now Emeritus; *b* 14 Nov. 1910; *o s* of Alan and Jane Helen Cameron; *m* 1933, Vera Shaw (*d* 1985); one *d* (one *s* decd). *Educ:* Central Secondary Sch., Sheffield; Keighley Grammar Sch.; Balliol Coll., Oxford (Scholar). Tutor, Workers' Educational Assoc., 1931–32; Staff Tutor, Univ. Coll., Southampton, 1932–35; Staff Tutor, Vaughan Coll., Leicester (Dept of Adult Education, Univ. Coll., Leicester), 1935–43. Univ. of Leeds: Staff Tutor for Tutorial Classes, 1943–47; Lectr in Philosophy, 1947–60 (Sen. Lectr from 1952); Acting Head of Dept of Philosophy, 1954–55 and 1959–60; Prof. of Philosophy, 1960–67; Master of Rutherford Coll., and Prof. of Philosophy, Univ. of Kent at Canterbury, 1967–71. Vis. Prof., Univ. of Notre Dame, Indiana, 1957–58, 1965; Terry Lectr, Yale Univ., 1964–65. Newman Fellow, Univ. of Melbourne, 1968; Christian Culture Award, Univ. of Windsor, Ont, 1972. Hon. DLittS St Michael's Coll., Univ. of Toronto, 1990. *Publications:* Scrutiny of Marxism, 1948; (trans.

with Marianne Kuschnitzky) Max Picard, The Flight from God, 1951; John Henry Newman, 1956; The Night Battle, 1962; Images of Authority, 1966; (ed) Essay on Development (1845 edn), by J. H. Newman, 1974; On the Idea of a University, 1978; The Music is in the Sadness (poems), 1988; Nuclear Catholics and other Essays, 1990; articles and papers in many periodicals. *Address:* 360 Bloor Street E, Apt 409, Toronto, Ontario M4W 3M3, Canada.

CAMERON, Sir John; *see* Cameron, Hon. Lord.

CAMERON, Sir John; *see* Cameron, Sir E. J.

CAMERON, John Alastair; *see* Abernethy, Hon. Lord.

CAMERON, John Bell, CBE 1982; Chairman, British Rail (Scotland), and Scottish Member, British Rail Board, 1988–93; Chairman, World Meats Group, International Federation of Agricultural Producers, since 1984; *b* 14 June 1939; *s* of John and Margaret Cameron; *m* 1964, Margaret (*née* Clapperton). *Educ:* Dollar Academy. AIAgrE; FRAgS. Studied agriculture in various countries, Scandinavia, S America and Europe, 1956–61; farmed in Scotland, 1961–64. National Farmers' Union of Scotland: Mem. National Council, 1964; Vice-Pres., 1976; Pres., 1979–84 (first long-term Pres.). Mem., Agricultural Praesidium of EEC, 1979–89; Chairman: EEC Adv. Cttee for Sheep Meat, 1982–89; UK Sheep Consultative Cttee, 1986–87. Chm. Governors, Dollar Acad., 1984–. Winner: George Headley Award to the UK Sheep Industry, 1986; Sir William Young Award to the Scottish Livestock Industry, 1986. *Recreations:* flying, shooting, travelling. *Address:* Balbuthie Farm, By Leven, Fife, Scotland KY9 1EX. *T:* St Monans (01333) 730210.

CAMERON, John Charles Finlay; *b* 8 Feb. 1928; *s* of Robert John and Nancy Angela Cameron; *m* 1st, Ruth Thompson, Sydney, Australia; two *s* two *d*; 2nd, Nancy Foy, author, Redlands, Calif. *Educ:* privately; University Coll., Southampton. CEng, MICE, FCIT, CIMgt. Royal Marines, 1946–48. British Railways, Southern Region, Civil Engineering, 1948; BR Transport Commn, 1957; BR Rlys Workshops, 1962; Rank Organisation, 1968–75. Mem., LTE, 1975–84. Dir-Gen. and Sec., CIT, 1983–88 (Hon. Vice Pres., 1988–91; Vice Chm., Scot. Sect., 1994–95); Dir, BURA, 1989–93; Chm., Highland Perthshire Develt Co., 1990–94. Member: Management Cttee, Abbotstone, Ag. Prop. Unit Trust, 1982–91; Westminster Br., IMgt (Chm., 1985–88; Vice-Pres., 1988–91). Gov., Pitlochry Fest. Theatre. Major, Engr and Transport Staff Corps, RE (TA). Liveryman, Carmen's Co. *Recreations:* book collecting, binding and dealing, building, garden construction. *Address:* Clunemore Farm, Killiecrankie, Pitlochry, Perthshire PH16 5LS. *T:* Pitlochry (01796) 473470, *Fax:* (01796) 473030. *T:* 0171–249 1177. *Club:* Oriental.

CAMERON, Prof. John Robinson; Regius Professor of Logic, University of Aberdeen, since 1979; *b* 24 June 1936; *s* of Rev. George Gordon Cameron and Mary Levering (*née* Robinson); *m* 1st, 1959, Mary Elizabeth Ranson (*d* 1984); one *s* two *d*; 2nd, 1987, Barbara Elizabeth Blair. *Educ:* Dundee High Sch.; Univ. of St Andrews (MA 1st Cl. Hons Maths, BPhil Philosophy); Univ. of Calif, Berkeley; Cornell Univ. Harkness Fellow, Berkeley and Cornell, USA, 1959–61; University of Dundee (formerly Queen's College): Asst in Phil., 1962–63; Lectr in Phil., 1963–73; Sen. Lectr in Phil., 1973–78. *Publications:* articles in phil jls. *Recreation:* bricolage. *Address:* 70 Cornhill Road, Aberdeen AB2 5DH. *T:* Aberdeen (01224) 486700.

CAMERON, John Taylor; *see* Coulsfield, Hon. Lord.

CAMERON, Sir John (Watson), Kt 1981; OBE 1960; President, J. W. Cameron & Co., since 1977; *b* 16 Nov. 1901; *s* of Captain Watson Cameron and Isabel Mann; *m* 1930, Lilian Florence Sanderson; one *s* two *d*. *Educ:* Lancing Coll. Commnd Durham RGA, 1920. Joined J. W. Cameron & Co., brewery co., 1922; Man. Dir, 1940; Chm., 1943–75. Mem., Northern Area, Economic League, 1950–80. Chm., 1964–69, Treasurer, 1967–72, Northern Area Cons. Party; Hartlepool Conservative Party: Chm., 1942–45; Pres., 1945–76; Patron, 1976–78; Pres. and Patron, 1978–. Chm., Hartlepools Hosp. Trust, 1973–80. *Recreations:* gardening, shooting, fishing. *Address:* Cowesby Hall, near Thirsk, N Yorks YO7 2JJ.

CAMERON, Prof. Kenneth, CBE 1987; FBA 1976; Professor of English Language, 1963–87, now Professor Emeritus, and Head of Department of English Studies, 1984–87, University of Nottingham; *b* Burnley, Lancs, 21 May 1922; *s* of late Angus W. Cameron and E. Alice Cameron, Habergham, Burnley; *m* 1947, Kathleen (*d* 1977), *d* of late F. E. Heap, Burnley; one *s* one *d*. *Educ:* Burnley Grammar Sch.; Univ. of Leeds (BA Hons, Sch. of English Language and Literature); PhD Sheffield. Served War, 1941–45; Pilot, RAF. Asst Lectr in English Language, Univ. of Sheffield, 1947–50; Nottingham University: Lectr in English Language, 1950–59; Sen. Lectr, 1959–62; Reader, 1962–63. External Prof., Loughborough Univ., 1990–93; Leverhulme Emeritus Fellow, 1990–91. Sir Israel Gollancz Meml Lecture, British Academy, 1976; O'Donnell Lectr, 1979. Pres., Viking Soc., 1972–74; Hon. Dir, 1966–93, Hon. Sec., 1972–93, English Place-Name Soc. Gen. Editor, English Place-Name Survey, 1966–93; Editor, Jl of the English Place-Name Soc., 1972–90. FRHistS 1970; FSA 1984. Hon. FilDr Uppsala, 1977; Hon. LittD Sheffield, 1991. Sir Israel Gollancz Meml Prize, British Academy, 1969; Jöran Sahlgren prize, Royal Gustaf Adolfs Acad., Sweden, 1990. *Publications:* The Place-Names of Derbyshire, 1959; English Place-Names, 1961, rev. edn 1995; Scandinavian Settlement in the Territory of the Five Boroughs: the place-name evidence, 1965; The Meaning and Significance of OE *walh* in English Place-Names, 1980; The Place-Names of the County of the City of Lincoln, 1985; The Place-Names of Lincolnshire: Yarborough Wapentake, 1991; The Wapentake of Walshcroft, 1992; Stenton and Place-Names, 1994; The Wapentakes of Ludborough and Haverstoe, 1995; *festschrift:* Studies in Honour of Kenneth Cameron, 1987; contribs to: Nottingham Medieval Studies; Medium Ævum; Mediaeval Scandinavia; Festschrifts, etc. *Recreations:* sports (supporting), home, "The Queens". *Address:* 16 The Cloisters, Beeston, Nottingham NG9 2FR. *T:* Nottingham (0115) 9254303.

CAMERON, Lewis; Sheriff of South Strathclyde, Dumfries and Galloway at Hamilton, since 1994; *b* 12 Aug. 1935; *s* of James Aloysius Cameron and Marie Isobel McKenzie; *m* 1962, Sheila Colette Gallacher; two *s* two *d*. *Educ:* Blairs Coll., Aberdeen; St Sulpice, Paris; Glasgow Univ. (MA, LLB). Admitted Solicitor, 1962. RAF (Nat. Service), 1954–56. Chm., Social Security Appeal Tribunals, 1983–88; Mem., Legal Aid Central Cttee, 1970–80; Legal Aid Sec., Airdrie, 1978–87; Dean, Airdrie Soc. of Solicitors, 1984–85; Tutor, Strathclyde Univ., 1981–88; Sheriff of S Strathclyde, Dumfries and Galloway at Dumfries, 1988–94. Treas., Monklands Victim Support Scheme, 1983–88; Chairman: Dumfries and Galloway Family Conciliation Service, 1988–92; Dumfries and Galloway Scottish Assoc. for Study of Delinquency, 1989–92. Mem., Scotland Cttee, Nat. Children's Home, 1991–94; Chm., Phew (Parental Help Evenings/Weekends, Mentally Handicapped), 1994–. Trustee, Oscar Marzaroli Trust, 1990–93. *Publications:* occasional articles and journalism. *Recreations:* cinema, theatre, tennis, travel. *Address:* Sheriff Court House, 4 Beckford Street, Hamilton ML3 6AA. *T:* Hamilton (01698) 282957. *Clubs:* New (St Andrews); Royal Scottish Automobile (Glasgow); Ross Priory (Gartocharn, Loch Lomond).

CAMERON, Roy James, CB 1982; PhD; Australian Statistician, 1977–85; *b* 11 March 1923; *s* of Kenneth Cameron and Amy Jean (*née* Davidson); *m* 1951, Dorothy Olive Lober; two *s* one *d*. *Educ:* Univ. of Adelaide (BEc 1st Cl. Hons, MEc); PhD Harvard. Lecturer in Economics, Canberra University College, 1949–51; Economist, World Bank, 1954–56; Australian Treasury official, 1956–73; Australian Ambassador to OECD, Paris, 1973–77. Chairman: ACT Taxi Fares Adv. Cttee, 1987–89; Cttee of Inquiry into Distribution of Federal Roads Grants, 1985–86. Associate Comr, Industries Assistance Commn, 1989–90. Mem. Council, Canberra Coll. of Advanced Educn, 1986–89. *Recreation:* lawn bowls. *Address:* PO Box 305, Curtin, ACT 2605, Australia. *T:* (6) 2814522.

CAMERON, Sheila Morag Clark, (Mrs G. C. Ryan); QC 1983; a Recorder, since 1985; Vicar-General of the Province of Canterbury, since 1983; *b* 22 March 1934; *d* of Sir James Clark Cameron, CBE, TD, and Lady (Irene M.) Cameron; *m* 1960, Gerard Charles Ryan, *qv*; two *s*. *Educ:* Commonweal Lodge Sch., Purley; St Hugh's Coll., Oxford (MA). Called to the Bar, Middle Temple, 1957, Harmsworth Law Scholar, 1958, Bencher, 1988; Part-time Lectr in Law, Southampton Univ., 1960–64; part-time Tutor, Council of Legal Educn, 1966–71. Mem., Bar Council, 1967–70. Comr, Boundary Commn for England, 1989– (Asst Comr, 1981–89). Official Principal, Archdeaconry of Hampstead, 1968–86; Chancellor: Dio. of Chelmsford, 1969–; Dio. of London, 1992–. Chm., Archbishops' Group on the Episcopate, 1986–90; Member: Legal Adv. Commn, Gen. Synod of C of E, 1975–; Gen. Synod Marriage Commn, 1975–78; Council on Tribunals, 1986–90. Mem. Council, Wycombe Abbey Sch., 1972–86. *Address:* 2 Harcourt Buildings, Temple, EC4Y 9DB. *T:* 0171–353 8415.

CAMERON, Stuart Gordon, MC 1943; *b* 8 Jan. 1924; *s* of late James Cameron and Dora Sylvia (*née* Godsell); *m* 1946, Joyce Alice, *d* of Roland Ashley Wood; three *s* one *d*. *Educ:* Chigwell School, Essex. Served War, 2nd Gurkha Rifles, 1942–46 (MC). Managing Dir, 1976–78, Dep. Chm., 1978–80, Chm. and Chief Exec., 1980–89, Gallaher Ltd. Director: American Brands Inc., 1980–89; Royal Mint, 1989–94. *Club:* Royal Thames Yacht.

CAMERON, Thomas Anthony, (Tony); Under Secretary, Agriculture, Scottish Office, since 1992; *b* 3 Feb. 1947; *o s* of late Thomas Alexander and Olive Cameron; *m* 1970, Elizabeth Christine Sutherland; two *s*. *Educ:* Stranraer High Sch. Dept of Agric. and Fisheries for Scotland, Scottish Office, 1966–72; Private Secretary: to Dep. Under Sec. of State, 1972; to Perm. Under Sec. of State, 1973–74; Department of Agriculture and Fisheries for Scotland: HEO(D), 1974–77; Principal, 1977–82; Asst Sec., 1982–87; Scottish Office Finance Div., 1987–92. Mem., Duke of Edinburgh's Sixth Commonwealth Study Conf., Australia, 1986. *Recreations:* reading, mountaineering, cycling. *Address:* Scottish Office, Pentland House, 47 Robb's Loan, Edinburgh EH14 1TW. *T:* 0131–244 6032.

CAMERON-RAMSAY-FAIRFAX-LUCY; *see* Fairfax-Lucy.

CAMERON WATT, Prof. Donald, FBA 1990; Stevenson Professor of International History in the University of London, 1981–93, now Professor Emeritus; *b* 17 May 1928; *s* of late Robert Cameron Watt and Barbara, *d* of late Rt Rev. E. J. Bidwell, former Bishop of Ontario; *m* 1st, 1951, Marianne Ruth Grau (*d* 1962); one *s*; 2nd, 1962, Felicia Cobb Stanley; one step *d*. *Educ:* Rugby Sch.; Oriel Coll., Oxford (BA 1951; MA 1954; DLitt 1991). FRHistS. Asst Editor, Documents on German Foreign Policy, 1918–1945, in Foreign Office, 1951–54; Asst Lectr, Lectr, Sen. Lectr in Internat. History, LSE, 1954–66; Reader in Internat. History in Univ. of London, 1966; Titular Prof. of Internat. History, 1972–81. Editor, Survey of Internat. Affairs, Royal Inst. of Internat. Affairs, 1962–71; Rockefeller Research Fellow in Social Sciences, Inst of Advanced Internat. Studies, Washington, 1960–61; Official Historian, Cabinet Office Historical Section, 1978–. Sec., 1967, Chm., 1976–87, Assoc. of Contemporary Historians; Mem. Bd, Inst. of Contemporary British History, 1987–; Chm., Greenwich Forum, 1974–84; Sec.-Treasurer, Internat. Commn for the Hist. of Internat. Relations, 1982–. Member Editorial Board: Political Quarterly, 1969–; Marine Policy, 1978–94; International History, 1984–94; Intelligence and National Security, 1986–; Review of Internat. Studies, 1989–; Gen. Ed. British Documents on Foreign Affairs, 1985–. FRSA 1990. Foreign Mem., British Acad. of Arts and Scis, Krakow, 1993. *Publications:* Britain and the Suez Canal, 1956; (ed) Documents on the Suez Crisis, 1957; Britain looks to Germany, 1965; Personalities and Policies, 1965; (ed) Survey of International Affairs 1961, 1966; (ed) Documents on International Affairs 1961, 1966; (ed, with K. Bourne) Studies in International History, 1967; A History of the World in the Twentieth Century, Pt I, 1967; (ed) Contemporary History of Europe, 1969; (ed) Hitler's Mein Kampf, 1969, 2nd edn 1992; (ed) Survey of International Affairs 1962, 1969; (ed, with James Mayall): Current British Foreign Policy 1970, 1971; Current British Foreign Policy 1971, 1972; Current British Foreign Policy 1972, 1973; Too Serious a Business, 1975; (ed) Survey of International Affairs 1963, 1977; Succeeding John Bull: America in Britain's place 1900–1975, 1984; How War Came, 1989; (ed with Guido Di Tella): Argentina between the Great Powers, 1990. *Recreations:* exploring London, cats. *Address:* c/o London School of Economics and Political Science, Houghton Street, WC2A 2AE. *Club:* Players Theatre.

CAMILLERI, Victor; Ambassador and Permanent Representative for Malta to the United Nations, since 1991; *b* 8 Oct. 1942; *s* of John Camilleri and Esther (*née* Casingena); *m* 1967, Elizabeth Bernadette Heaney; two *s*. *Educ:* Lyceum, Malta; Birmingham Univ. (BA Hons English). Joined Min. of Foreign Affairs, Malta, 1968: 2nd Sec., 1968–74; 1st Sec., 1974–86; Counsellor, 1986–90; 1st Counsellor, 1990; postings in Rome, Brussels, NY and London; Ambassador; to UNIDO and UNESCO, 1981–85; to CSCE, 1985–86; Actg Sec., Min. of Foreign Affairs, 1986–87; Dep. High Comr, 1987–90, High Comr, 1991, London. *Recreations:* reading, swimming. *Address:* Permanent Mission of Malta to UN, 249 East 35th Street, New York, NY 10016, USA.

CAMM, Prof. A(lan) John, MD; FRCP, FACC, FESC; QHP; Prudential Professor of Clinical Cardiology, since 1986, and Chairman, Department of Medicine, 1991–94, St George's Hospital Medical School, London University; *b* 11 Jan. 1947; *s* of John Donald and Joan Camm; *m* 1987, Joy-Maria Frappell; one *s* one *d*. *Educ:* Guy's Hosp. Med. Sch., London Univ. (BSc 1968; MB BS 1971; MD 1981). LRCP, MRCS 1971; FACC 1981; FRCP 1984; FESC 1988. Guy's Hospital: House Surgeon, 1971; House Physician, 1971–72; Jun. Registrar, 1972; Jun. Lectr in Medicine, 1972–73; Registrar in Cardiology, 1973–74; Clin. Fellow in Cardiology, Univ. of Vermont, USA, 1974–75; St Bartholomew's Hospital: British Heart Foundn Res. Registrar, 1975–76, Sen. Registrar 1977–79; Wellcome Sen. Lectr and Hon. Consultant Cardiologist, 1979–83; Sir Ronald Bodley Scott Prof. of Cardiovascular Medicine, 1983–86. Mem. Council, RCP, 1994–. QHP 1992–. Freeman, City of London, 1984. CStJ 1990. *Publications:* First Aid, Step by Step, 1978; Pacing for Tachycardia Control, 1983; Heart Disease in the Elderly, 1984, 2nd edn 1994; Clinical Electrophysiology of the Heart, 1987; Heart Disease in Old Age, 1988; Clinical Aspects of Cardiac Arrhythmias, 1988; Diseases of the Heart, 1989; Heart Disease in Old Age, 1990; approx. 600 papers in major jls. *Recreations:* collector of prints, watercolours and other antiques, model railway enthusiast. *Address:* St George's Hospital Medical School, Cranmer Terrace, Tooting, SW17 0RE. *Club:* Athenæum.

CAMMELL, John Ernest; Consultant, Warwick Manufacturing Group, Warwick University, since 1993; a Director, British Standards Institution, since 1992; *b* 14 Nov. 1932; *s* of Ernest Alfred Cammell and Gladys Clara (*née* Burroughes); *m* 1976, Janis Linda Moody. *Educ:* Highfield Coll., Leigh-on-Sea, Essex. Mil. Service, Royal Signals. Joined Victualling Dept, Admiralty, 1952; DSIR, 1963; Min. of Technology, 1964; DTI, 1967; Dept of Industry, 1973; Dir, National Maritime Inst., 1981–84; Hd, Mech. Engrg and Manufg Technol. Div., subseq. Manufg Technol. Div., DTI, 1986–92. CompIEE (Companion, IProdE, 1988); FRSA. *Recreations:* amateur theatre, golf, cricket, eating. *Address:* 41 Cunnington Street, Chiswick, W4 5ER. *T:* 0181–995 6937.

CAMOYS, 7th Baron *cr* 1264 (called out of abeyance, 1839); **Ralph Thomas Campion George Sherman Stonor;** DL; a Lord in Waiting, since 1992; Deputy Chairman: Barclays de Zoete Wedd (BZW), since 1987 (Chief Executive, 1986–88); Sotheby's, since 1993; *b* 16 April 1940; *s* of 6th Baron Camoys and Mary Jeanne (*d* 1987), *d* of late Captain Herbert Marmaduke Joseph Stourton, OBE; *S* father, 1976; *m* 1966, Elisabeth Mary Hyde, *d* of Sir William Stephen Hyde Parker, 11th Bt; one *s* three *d. Educ:* Eton Coll.; Balliol Coll., Oxford (MA). Chm., Jacksons of Piccadilly, 1968–85; Gen. Manager and Director, National Provincial and Rothschild (London) Ltd, 1968; Man. Director, Rothschild Intercontinental Bank Ltd, 1969; Chief Exec. Officer and Man. Dir, 1975–77, Chm., 1977–78, Amex Bank Ltd; Man. Dir, 1978–84, Exec. Vice-Chm., 1984–86, Barclays Merchant Bank; Director: Barclays Bank Internat. Ltd, 1980–84; Barclays Bank PLC, 1984–94; Mercantile Credit Co. Ltd, 1980–84; National Provident Instn, 1982–; Administrative Staff Coll., 1989–; 3i Group, 1991–; Perpetual, 1994–. Pres., Mail Users' Assoc., 1977–84; Member: House of Lords EEC Select Cttee, 1979–81; Historic Bldgs and Monuments Commn for England, 1985–87; Royal Commn on Historical MSS, 1987–94. Consultor, Extraordinary Section of Administration of Patrimony of Holy See, 1991–. Mem. Court of Assistants, Fishmongers' Co., 1980– (Prime Warden, 1992–93). DL Oxfordshire, 1993. Order of Gorkha Dakshina Bahu, 1st class (Nepal), 1981. *Recreations:* the arts, shooting. *Heir: s* Hon. (Ralph) William (Robert Thomas) Stonor, *b* 10 Sept. 1974. *Address:* Stonor Park, Henley-on-Thames, Oxon RG9 6HF. *Clubs:* Boodle's, Pratt's; Leander (Henley-on-Thames).

CAMP, Anthony John; Director, Society of Genealogists, since 1979; *b* 27 Nov. 1937; *s* of late Henry Victor Camp and Alice Emma Camp (*née* Doidge); *m* 1976, Deborah Mary (marr. diss. 1978), *d* of D. J. Jeavons; one *s. Educ:* Alleyne's Sch., Stevenage; University College London (BA Hons). Society of Genealogists: Res. Assistant, 1957; Librarian, 1959; Dir of Res., 1962; Hon. Fellow, 1982. Member Council: Assoc. of Genealogists and Record Agents, 1968–75 (Chm., 1973–75; Vice-Pres., 1980–); British Record Soc., 1967–71, 1983–; British Records Assoc. (Record Preservation Sect.), 1980–83, 1985–88; English Genealogical Congress, 1975–90 (Pres., 1991–92); Friends of Public Record Office, 1988–94; Marc Fitch Fund, 1991–; Fedn of Family History Socs, 1992–; Pres., Herts Family and Population Hist. Soc., 1982. Lecturer: yearly Nat. Geneal. Soc. Confs, USA, 1981–; Australasian Congress, Canberra, 1986; Sesquicentennial Conf., Auckland, 1990; First Irish Genealogical Congress, 1991. Fellow, Utah Geneal. Assoc., 1989. Freeman, City of London, 1984. Award of Merit, Nat. Geneal. Soc., USA, 1984. *Publications:* (with P. Spufford) Genealogists Handbook, 1961; Wills and their Whereabouts, 1963; Tracing Your Ancestors, 1964; Everyone has Roots, 1978; Index to Wills proved in the Prerogative Court of Canterbury 1750–1800, 6 vols, 1976–92; (contrib.) My Ancestor series, 1987–; (contrib.) The Records of the Nation, 1990; articles to Family Tree and other jls. *Recreation:* genealogy. *Address:* 65 Fursecroft, George Street, W1H 5LG. *T:* 0171–723 3758; Society of Genealogists, 14 Charterhouse Buildings, Goswell Road, EC1M 7BA. *T:* 0171–251 8799.

CAMP, Jeffery Bruce, RA 1984 (ARA 1974); artist; Lecturer, Slade School of Fine Art, 1963–88; *b* 1923. *Educ:* Edinburgh Coll. of Art. DA (Edin.). One-man exhibitions include: Galerie de Seine, 1958; Beaux Arts Gallery, 1959, 1961, 1963; New Art Centre, 1968; S London Art Gall., 1973 (retrospective); Serpentine Gall., 1978; Bradford City Art Gallery, 1979; Browse and Darby, 1984, 1993; Aldeburgh Fest., 1986; Nigel Greenwood Gall., 1986, 1990, 1993; Royal Acad., 1988 (retrospective); other exhibitions include: Hayward Annual, 1974, 1982, 1985; Serpentine Gall., 1974, 1987; Narrative Painting, ICA and Arts Council tour, 1979; British Council touring exhibns to China and Edinburgh, 1982, to India, 1985, to Kuala Lumpur, 1988; Chantrey Bicentenary, Tate Gall., 1981; The Hardwon Image, Tate Gall., 1984; group exhibn, Twining Gall., NY, 1985; Peter Moores exhibn, Liverpool, 1986; Athena Art Awards, 1987; represented in public collections including Arts Council, British Council, Tate Gall. and Royal Acad. *Publication:* Draw, 1981. *Address:* c/o Nigel Greenwood Gallery, 4 New Burlington Street, W1X 1FE. *T:* 0171–434 3795.

CAMP, William Newton Alexander; writer and political and corporate adviser; *b* 12 May 1926; *s* of I. N. Camp, OBE, Colonial Administrative Service, Palestine, and Freda Camp; *m* 1st, 1950, Patricia Cowan (marr. diss. 1973); two *s* one *d*; 2nd, 1975, Juliet Schubart, *d* of late Hans Schubart, CBE; four step *s. Educ:* Bradfield Coll.; Oriel Coll., Oxford (Classical Scholar, MA). Served in Army, 1944–47. Asst Res. Officer, British Travel and Holidays Assoc., 1950–54; Asst Sec., Consumer Adv. Council, BSI, 1954–59; Asst Sec., Gas Council, 1960–63; Public Relations Adviser, Gas Council (British Gas Corp.), 1963–67; Dir of Information Services, British Steel Corp., 1967–71; Mem., British Nat. Oil Corp., 1976–78. Special Adviser: milling and baking industries, 1972–90; British Leyland Motor Corp., 1975; railway trades unions, 1975–76; C. A. Parsons & Co. Ltd, 1976–77; Prudential Corp. (formerly Prudential Assurance Co.), 1978–88; Northern Engineering Industries plc, 1978–84; Corporate Advr, British Railways Bd, 1977–90. Director: Quartet Books, 1973–76; Westminster Communications Gp Ltd, 1989–90; Chm., Camden Consultants Ltd, 1975–91. Chm., Oxford Univ. Labour Club, 1949; contested (Lab) Solihull, 1950; Mem., Southwark Borough Council, 1953–56; Press Adviser (unpaid) to Prime Minister, Gen. Election, 1970. Founder Mem., Public Enterprise Group. *Publications: novels:* Prospects of Love, 1957; Idle on Parade, 1958 (filmed, 1959); The Ruling Passion, 1959; A Man's World, 1962; Two Schools of Thought, 1964; Flavour of Decay, 1967; The Father Figures, 1970; Stroke Counterstroke, 1986; *biography:* The Glittering Prizes (F. E. Smith), 1960. *Address:* 61 Gloucester Crescent, NW1 7EG. *T:* 0171–482 5112; Keeper's Cottage, Marshfield, near Chippenham, Wilts SN14 8PD. *T:* Bath (01225) 891211. *Clubs:* Garrick, Beefsteak.

CAMPBELL, family name of **Duke of Argyll,** of **Earl of Breadalbane,** of **Earl Cawdor,** and of **Barons Campbell of Alloway, Campbell of Croy, Colgrain** and **Stratheden.**

CAMPBELL OF ALLOWAY, Baron *cr* 1981 (Life Peer), of Ayr in the District of Kyle and Carrick; **Alan Robertson Campbell,** QC 1965; a Recorder of the Crown Court, 1976–89; *b* 24 May 1917; *s* of late J. K. Campbell; *m* 1957, Vivien, *y d* of late Comdr A. H. de Kantzow, DSO, RN. *Educ:* Aldenham; Ecole des Sciences Politiques, Paris; Trinity Hall, Cambridge. Called to Bar, Inner Temple, 1939, Bencher, 1972; Western Circuit. Commissioned RA (Suppl. Res.), 1939; served France and Belgium, 1939–40; POW, 1940–45. Consultant to sub-cttee of Legal Cttee of Council of Europe on Industrial Espionage, 1965–74; Chm., Legal Res. Cttee, Soc. of Conservative Lawyers, 1968–80. Member: Law Adv. Cttee, British Council, 1974–82; Management Cttee, UK Assoc. for European Law, 1975–90. *Publications:* (with Lord Wilberforce) Restrictive Trade Practices and Monopolies, 1956, 2nd edn, 1966, Supplements 1 and 2, 1973; Restrictive Trading Agreements in the Common Market, 1964, Supplement, 1965; Common Market Law, vols 1 and 2, 1969, vol. 3, 1973 and Supplement, 1975; Industrial Relations Act, 1971; EC Competition Law, 1980; Trade Unions and the Individual, 1980. *Address:* 2 King's Bench Walk, Temple, EC4Y 7DE. *T:* 0171–353 9276. *Clubs:* Carlton (Mem., Political Cttee, 1967–79), Pratt's, Beefsteak.

CAMPBELL OF CROY, Baron *cr* 1974 (Life Peer), of Croy in the County of Nairn; **Gordon Thomas Calthrop Campbell,** PC 1970; MC 1944, and Bar, 1945; DL; Vice-Lord-Lieutenant, Highland Region (Nairn), since 1988; *b* 8 June 1921; *s* of late Maj.-Gen. J. A. Campbell, DSO and bar; *m* 1949, Nicola Elizabeth Gina Madan; two *s* one *d. Educ:* Wellington and Hospital. War of 1939–45: commissioned in Regular Army, 1939; Captain, 1940; instructor OCTU, Larkhill; RA, Major, 1942; commanded 320 Field Battery in 15 Scottish Div.; wounded and disabled, 1945. Entered HM Foreign Service, 1946; served, until 1957, in FO, UK Delegn to the UN (New York), Cabinet Office (Private Sec. to Sec. of Cabinet) and Vienna. MP (C) Moray and Nairn, 1959–Feb. 1974; Asst Govt Whip, 1961–62; a Lord Comr of the Treasury and Scottish Whip, 1962–63; Joint Parly Under-Sec. of State, Scottish Office, 1963–64; Opposition Spokesman on Defence and Scottish Affairs, 1966–70; Sec. of State for Scotland, 1970–74. Vice-Pres., Parly Maritime Gp, 1986–. Oil industry consultant, 1975–; Partner in Holme Rose Farms and Estate, 1969–; Chm., Scottish Bd, 1976–94, Dir, 1983–91, Alliance and Leicester (formerly Alliance) Building Soc.; Chm., Stoic Financial Services (formerly Stoic Insurance Services), 1979–93; Advisory Committee on Pollution of Sea: Vice-Pres., 1976–84; Acting Chm., 1980–82; Chm., 1987–89. Chm., Scottish Cttee, Internat. Year of Disabled, 1981; Mem., RA Council, Scotland, 1980–91; Pres., Anglo-Austrian Soc., 1991–. Trustee, Thomson Foundn, 1980–; First Fellow, Nuffield Provincial Hospitals Trust Queen Elizabeth The Queen Mother Fellowship, 1980. DL Nairn, 1985. *Publication:* Disablement: Problems and Prospects in the UK, 1981. *Recreations:* music, birds. *Address:* Holme Rose, Cawdor, Nairnshire IV12 5XT. *T:* Croy (01667) 493223.

CAMPBELL, Sir Alan (Hugh), GCMG 1979 (KCMG 1976; CMG 1964); HM Diplomatic Service, retired; *b* 1 July 1919; *y s* of late Hugh Campbell and Ethel Campbell (*née* Warren); *m* 1947, Margaret Taylor; three *d. Educ:* Sherborne Sch.; Caius Coll., Cambridge. Served in Devonshire Regt, 1940–46. 3rd Sec., HM Foreign (now Diplomatic) Service, 1946; appointed to Lord Killearn's Special Mission to Singapore, 1946; served in Rome, 1952, Peking, 1955; UK Mission to UN, New York, 1961; Head of Western Dept, Foreign Office, 1965; Counsellor, Paris, 1967; Ambassador to Ethiopia, 1969–72; Asst Under-Sec. of State, FCO, 1972–74; Dep. Under-Sec. of State, FCO, 1974–76; Ambassador to Italy, 1976–79; Foreign Affairs adviser to Rolls Royce Ltd, 1979–81. Director: National Westminster Bank, 1979–89; Mercantile and General Reinsurance Co., 1979–89; H. Clarkson (Hldgs), 1979–89; Agricola (UK) Ltd, 1987–92. Chairman: Soc. of Pension Consultants, 1982–87; British-Italian Soc., 1983–90; British Sch. at Rome, 1987–94 (Mem. Council, 1982–94); Mem. Council, London Philharmonic Orchestra, 1982–90. Governor, Sherborne Sch., 1973–87 (Chm. of Governors, 1982–87). *Publications:* Colleagues and Friends (autobiog.), 1988; articles in Internat. Affairs. *Recreation:* painting in watercolour. *Address:* 45 Carlisle Mansions, Carlisle Place, SW1P 1HY. *Clubs:* Brooks's, Beefsteak.

CAMPBELL, Alastair John; Press Secretary to Leader of Opposition, since 1994; *b* 25 May 1957; *s* of Donald Campbell and Elizabeth (*née* Caldwell); partner, Fiona Millar; two *s* one *d. Educ:* City of Leicester Boys Sch.; Gonville and Caius Coll., Cambridge (MA). Trainee reporter, Tavistock Times and Sunday Independent, 1980–82; freelance reporter, London, 1982–83; reporter, Daily Mirror, 1982–85; news editor, Sunday Today, 1985–86; reporter, Daily Mirror, 1986; Sunday Mirror: Political Corresp., 1986–87; Political Editor, 1987–89; Columnist, 1989–91; Daily Mirror: Political Editor, 1989–93; Columnist, 1991–93; Asst Editor and Columnist, Today, 1993–95. *Recreations:* family, bagpipes, Burnley Football Club. *Address:* Office of Leader of Opposition, House of Commons, SW1A 0AA. *T:* 0171–219 3000. *Club:* Burnley Football Supporters' (Pres., Keighley Branch).

CAMPBELL, Hon. Alexander Bradshaw, PC (Canada) 1967; Judge, Supreme Court of Prince Edward Island, 1978–94; *b* 1 Dec. 1933; *s* of Dr Thane A. Campbell and late Cecilia B. Campbell; *m* 1961, Marilyn Gilmour; two *s* one *d. Educ:* Dalhousie Univ. (BA, LLB). Called to Bar of Prince Edward Island, 1959; practised law with Campbell & Campbell, Summerside, PEI, 1959–66; QC (PEI) 1966. MLA, Prince Edward Island, 1965–78; Leader of Liberal Party, Dec. 1966–78; Premier, 1966–78; served (while Premier) as Attorney-Gen., 1966–69, Minister of Development, 1969–72, Minister of Agriculture, 1972–74, and Minister of Justice, 1974–78. Dir, Inst. of Man and Resources, 1976–80. Pres., Summerside YMCA, 1981–91; Founder Pres., Summerside Area Historical Soc., 1983; Founder Chm., PEI Council, Duke of Edinburgh Awards (Canada), 1984. Elder of Trinity United Church, Summerside. Sigma Chi Fraternity. Hon. LLD: McGill 1967; PEI, 1978. *Recreations:* curling, skiing, golf, boating, gardening. *Address:* 330 Beaver Street, Summerside, PEI C1N 2A3, Canada. *T:* 4362714. *Club:* Y's Men's (Summerside).

CAMPBELL, Alexander Buchanan, ARSA; FRIBA; architect; Senior Partner, A. Buchanan Campbell and Partners, Glasgow, 1949–90; *b* 14 June 1914; *s* of Hugh Campbell and Elizabeth Flett; *m* 1939, Sheila Neville Smith; one *s* one *d. Educ:* Royal Technical Coll., Glasgow; Glasgow School of Art; Univ. of Strathclyde (BArch). ARSA 1973; PPRIAS. Assistant: Prof. T. Harold Hughes, 1937; G. Grey Wornum, 1938; City Architect, Glasgow, 1939; served War, Royal Engineers, 1940–46; Inspector, Inspectorate of Elect. and Mech. Equipment, 1947; Chief Technical Officer, Scottish Building Centre, 1948, Dep. Dir, 1949. Principal works include: Dollan Swimming Baths and Key Youth Centre, East Kilbride; Whittingehame Court, Ascot; Flats, Great Western Road, Glasgow; St Christopher's Church, Glasgow; Priesthill Church, Glasgow; St James Primary Sch., Renfrew; Callendar Park Coll. and Craigie College of Education at Falkirk and Ayr (Civic Trust Awards); High Rise Flats, Drumchapel. President: Glasgow Inst. of Architects, 1974–76; Royal Incorporation of Architects in Scotland, 1977–79. *Recreations:* music, art, golf, exhibiting show dogs. *Address:* 19 Lochan Avenue, Kirn, Dunoon, Argyll PA23 8HT. *T:* Dunoon (01369) 703674. *Club:* Glasgow Art (President, 1972–74).

CAMPBELL, Prof. (Alexander) Colin (Patton), FRCPath, FRCPE; Procter Professor of Pathology and Pathological Anatomy, University of Manchester, 1950–73, now Professor Emeritus (formerly Dean, Faculty of Medicine and Pro-Vice Chancellor); formerly Director of Studies, Royal College of Pathologists; *b* 21 Feb. 1908; *s* of late A. C. Campbell, Londonderry; *m* 1943, Hon. Elisabeth Joan Adderley, 2nd *d* of 6th Baron Norton; one *s* one *d* (and one *s* decd). *Educ:* Foyle Coll., Londonderry; Edinburgh Univ. MB, ChB (Hons) Edinburgh 1930; FRCPE 1939. Rockefeller Fellow and Research Fellow in Neuropathology, Harvard Univ., 1935–36; Lectr in Neuropathology, Edinburgh Univ., 1937–39; Lectr in Pathology, Edinburgh Univ., and Pathologist, Royal Infirmary, Edinburgh, 1939–50. War service, 1940–46, RAFVR (Wing-Comdr). Hon. MSc Manchester, 1954. *Publications:* papers on pathological subjects in various medical and scientific jls. *Recreations:* carpentry and cabinet-making. *Address:* The Priory House, Ascott-under-Wychwood, Oxford OX7 6AW.

CAMPBELL, Prof. Alexander Elmslie, PhD; FRHistS; Professor of American History, University of Birmingham, 1972–87 (part-time, 1984–87; Director of American Studies, 1972–84); now Emeritus Professor; *b* 12 May 1929; *s* of Rev. John Young Campbell and Emma (*née* Wickert); *m* 1st, 1956, Sophia Anne Sonne (*d* 1972); one *s* one *d*; 2nd, 1983, Juliet Jeanne d'Auvergne Collings (*see* J. J. d'A. Campbell). *Educ:* Paisley Grammar Sch.; Perse Sch., Cambridge; St John's Coll., Cambridge (MA; PhD 1956). MA Oxon 1959. FRHistS 1970. Smith-Mundt Student, Harvard Univ., 1953–54; Fellow, King's Coll., Cambridge, 1955–59; Second Sec., HM Foreign Service, 1958–60; Fellow and Tutor in Mod. Hist., Keble Coll., Oxford, 1960–72, Emeritus Fellow 1981–. Vis. Professor: Hobart and William Smith Colls, NY, 1970; Columbia Univ., 1975; Univ. of Kansas, 1976; Stanford Univ., 1977. Mem., Inst. for Advanced Study, Princeton, 1975. *Publications:* Great Britain and the United States, 1895–1903, 1960; (ed) Expansion and Imperialism, 1970; America Comes of Age: the era of Theodore Roosevelt, 1971; (ed) The USA in World Affairs, 1974; articles and reviews in collections and jls. *Address:* 3 Belbroughton Road, Oxford OX2 6UZ. *T:* Oxford (01865) 58685. *Clubs:* Athenæum; Cosmos (Washington, DC).

CAMPBELL, Andrew Neville; QC 1994; a Recorder, since 1989; *b* 17 June 1949; *s* of Archibald Campbell, CMG and of Peggie Campbell (*née* Hussey); *m* 1980, Rebecca Thornton; two *s* one *d*. *Educ:* Berkhamsted Sch.; New Coll., Oxford (BA Hons Jurisprudence). Called to the Bar, Middle Temple, 1972. *Recreations:* fishing, shooting, cricket, squash, ski-ing, walking. *Address:* 10 Park Square, Leeds, W Yorks LS21 2NJ. *T:* Leeds (0113) 2455438. *Club:* Harrogate Cricket.

CAMPBELL, Anne, FIS; MP (Lab) Cambridge, since 1992; *b* 6 April 1940; *d* of late Frank Lucas and Susan (*née* Chadwick); *m* 1963, Archibald MacRobert Campbell; one *s* two *d*. *Educ:* Newnham Coll., Cambridge (Maths Tripos Pt II, 1962; MA 1965). FSS 1985; FIS 1985. Sen. Lectr in Statistics, Cambs Coll. of Arts and Technol., 1970–83; Head of Stats and Data Processing, Nat. Inst. of Agricl Botany, Cambridge, 1983–92. Mem., Cambs CC, 1985–89. FRSA 1992. *Publication:* Calculation for Commercial Students, 1972. *Recreations:* tennis, ski-ing, jogging, gardening. *Address:* Alex Wood Hall, Norfolk Street, Cambridge CB1 2LD. *T:* Cambridge (01223) 300991.

CAMPBELL, Hon. Sir Anthony; *see* Campbell, Hon. Sir W. A.

CAMPBELL, Arthur McLure, CBE 1990; Principal Clerk of Session and Justiciary, Scotland, 1982–89, retired; *b* 15 Aug. 1932; *s* of late Hector Brownlie Campbell, MBE, AIPA and Catherine Smylie (*née* Renwick). *Educ:* Queen's Park Sch., Glasgow. Deptl Legal Qual., Scottish Court Service, 1956. National Service, FAA, 1950–52. Admiralty Supplies Directorate, 1953–54; entered Scottish Court Service (Sheriff Clerk Br.), 1954; Sheriff Clerk Depute, Kilmarnock, 1957–60; Sheriff Clerk of Orkney, 1961–65; seconded HM Treasury (O & M), 1965–69; Principal Sheriff Clerk Depute, Glasgow, 1969; Sheriff Clerk, Airdrie, 1969–72; Principal, Scottish Court Service Staff Trng Centre, 1973–74; Asst Sheriff Clerk of Glasgow, 1974–81. Clerk of Cttees, H of L (temp.), 1991. Secretary: Lord Chancellor's Cttee on Re-sealing of Probates and Confirmations, 1967–68; Scottish Office Cttee on Money Transfer Services, 1968–69; Chm., Simplified Divorce (Scotland) Implementation Gp, 1981–82 (Scottish Consumer Council Champion Award, 1983); Mem., Review Body on Use of Judicial Time in Superior Courts in Scotland, 1985–86. Chm., Sheriff Clerks' Assoc., 1971–72. *Recreation:* opsimathy. *Address:* c/o Bank of Scotland, 56 Albert Street, Kirkwall, Orkney KW15 1HJ; Calle Maestro Nicolau 8, Palma Nova-Calvia, Mallorca. *Clubs:* National Liberal, Civil Service.

CAMPBELL, Maj.-Gen. (Charles) Peter, CBE 1977; Director, Quicks (formerly H. & J. Quick) Group Plc, 1982–91; *b* 25 Aug. 1926; *s* of late Charles Alfred Campbell and Blanche Campbell; *m* 1st, 1949, Lucy Kitching (*d* 1986); two *s*; 2nd, 1986, Elizabeth Tristram. *Educ:* Gillingham Grammar Sch.; Emmanuel Coll., Cambridge. FIMgt. Commnd RE, 1945 (despatches, Palestine, 1948); psc 1957; DAA&QMG Trng Bde, RE, 1958–60; OC 11 Indep. Field Sqdn, RE, 1960–62; Jt Services Staff Coll., 1963; DAAG WO, 1963–65; Co. Comd, RMA Sandhurst, 1965–67; CO 21 Engr Regt, 1967–70; GSO1 MoD, 1970–71; CRE 3 Div., 1971; Comd 12 Engr Bde, 1972–73; RCDS, 1974; COS HQ NI, 1975–77; Engineer-in-Chief (Army), 1977–80. Col Comdt, RE, 1981–86, Rep. Col Comdt, 1982; Hon. Colonel: RE (Vol.) (Explosive Ordnance Disposal), 1986–88; 101 (London) Engr Regt (Explosive Ordnance Disposal) (V), 1988–91. Chm., RE Assoc., 1983–89. Foundn Mem., 1991–, Governor, 1993–, Gordon's Sch. *Recreations:* painting and collecting militaria. *Club:* Naval and Military.

CAMPBELL, Cheryl (Anne); actress; *b* 22 May 1949. *Educ:* Francis Bacon Grammar Sch., St Albans; London Acad. of Music and Dramatic Art (Rodney Millington Award). Formerly: student and acting Asst Stage Manager, Watford Palace Theatre; acted at Glasgow Citizens Theatre, Watford Rep., Birmingham Rep., King's Head and National Theatre; Nora in A Doll's House (SWET Award, 1983, for best actress of 1982 in a revival), and Diana in All's Well That Ends Well, RSC; title role in Miss Julie, Lyric, Hammersmith, and Duke of York's, 1983; Asta in Little Eyolf, Lyric, Hammersmith, 1985; title rôle in Daughter-in-Law, Hampstead, 1985; The Sneeze, Aldwych, 1988; Betrayal, Almeida, 1991; Merry Wives of Windsor, The Changeling, RSC, 1992; Misha's Party, Macbeth, RSC, 1993; The Strip, Royal Court, 1995. *Television* serials: Pennies from Heaven; Testament of Youth (Best Actress Award, BAFTA, and British Broadcasting Press Guild Award, 1979); Malice Aforethought; A Winter Harvest; Centrepoint; The Secret Agent, 1992. *Films* include Chariots of Fire, 1981; Greystoke, 1983; The Shooting Party, 1985. *Address:* c/o Michael Whitehall Ltd, 125 Gloucester Road, SW7 4TE. *T:* 0171–244 8466.

CAMPBELL, Christopher James, CBE 1993; Vice-Chairman, British Railways Board, since 1994; Chairman, British Shipbuilders, since 1989; Director: Harrods Bank Ltd, since 1991; Riverside Mental Health Trust, since 1993; *b* 2 Jan. 1936; *s* of David Heggie Campbell and Nettie Phyllis (*née* Burgess). *Educ:* Epsom College. FCA. Served RAPC, 1959–61. Debenhams and subsidiaries, 1966–86, incl. Man. Dir, Hardy Amies, 1978–79; former Director: Debenhams dept stores; Harvey Nichols; Lotus; Debenhams Finance; Debenhams (M & S). Mem., and chief negotiator, 1986–88, non-exec. Mem., 1988–91, National Bus Co.; Finance Dir, Nat. Rivers Authy Adv. Cttee, 1988–89. Treas., Bow Gp, 1966. Gov., United World Coll. of the Atlantic, 1993–. Captain Paymaster, HAC Inf. Bn, 1960–63. *Recreations:* reading, listening to music, entertaining, bridge, visual arts. *Address:* 19 Morpeth Mansions, Morpeth Terrace, SW1P 1ER. *T:* 0171–630 7527. *Club:* Brooks's.

CAMPBELL, Colin; *see* Campbell, A. C. P.

CAMPBELL, Colin Malcolm; QC (Scot.) 1990; *b* 1 Oct. 1953; *s* of Malcolm Donald Campbell and Annabella Ferguson or Campbell; *m* 1977, Fiona Anderson; one *s* one *d* (and one *d* decd). *Educ:* Grove Acad., Broughty Ferry; Univ. of Dundee (LLB). Passed Advocate, 1977. Lectr, Dept of Scots Law, Univ. of Edinburgh, 1977–79; Standing Junior Counsel: to Scottish Devalt Dept (all matters other than Planning), 1984–86; to Scottish Develt Dept (Planning), 1986–90. *Publications:* articles in Scots Law Times and Jl of Law Soc. of Scotland. *Recreation:* golf. *Address:* Advocates' Library, Parliament House, Edinburgh EH1 1RF. *T:* 0131-226 5071. *Clubs:* New, Bruntsfield Links (Edinburgh).

CAMPBELL, Sir Colin Moffat, 8th Bt *cr* 1667, of Aberuchill and Kilbryde, Dunblane, Perthshire; MC 1945; Director, James Finlay plc, 1971–92 (Chairman, 1975–90); *b* 4 Aug. 1925; *e s* of Sir John Campbell, 7th Bt and Janet Moffat (*d* 1975); *S* father, 1960; *m* 1952, Mary Anne Chichester Bain, *er d* of Brigadier G. A. Bain, Sandy Lodge, Chagford, Devon; two *s* (one *d* decd). *Educ:* Stowe. Scots Guards, 1943–47, Captain. Employed with James Finlay & Co. Ltd, Calcutta, 1948–58, Nairobi, 1958–71, Dep. Chm., 1973–75. President Federation of Kenya Employers, 1962–70; Chairman: Tea Board of Kenya, 1961–71; E African Tea Trade Assoc., 1960–61, 1962–63, 1966–67. Member: Scottish Council, CBI, 1979–85; Council, CBI, 1981–92; Commonwealth Develt Corp., 1981–89 (Dep. Chm., 1983–89). CIMgt (CBIM 1980); FRSA 1982. *Recreations:* gardening, racing, cards, travel. *Heir: s* James Alexander Moffat Bain Campbell, [*b* 23 Sept. 1956; *m* 1993, Carola Jane, *yr d* of George Denman; one *d*]. *Address:* Kilbryde Castle, Dunblane, Perthshire FK15 9NF. *T:* Dunblane (01786) 823104. *Clubs:* Boodle's; Western (Glasgow); Royal Calcutta Turf, Tollygunge (Calcutta); Nairobi (E Africa).

CAMPBELL, Sir Colin (Murray), Kt 1994; Vice-Chancellor, University of Nottingham, since 1988; Professor Emeritus, Queen's University, Belfast; *b* 26 Dec. 1944; *s* of late Donald Campbell and of Isobel Campbell; *m* 1974, Elaine Carlisle; one *s* one *d*. *Educ:* Robert Gordon's Coll., Aberdeen; Univ. of Aberdeen (LLB 1st Cl. Hons). Lecturer: Faculty of Law, Univ. of Dundee, 1967–69; Dept of Public Law, Univ. of Edinburgh, 1969–73; Prof. of Jurisprudence, 1974–88, Dean of Faculty of Law, 1977–80, Pro-Vice-Chancellor, 1983–87, QUB. Member: Council, Soc. for Computers and Law, 1973–88; Standing Adv. Commn on Human Rights, 1977–80; Legal Aid Adv. Cttee, NI, 1978–82; Mental Health Legislation Rev. Cttee, NI, 1978–82; UGC, 1987–88; Nottingham Develt Enterprise, 1988–91; UFC Scottish Cttee, 1989–93; HEFCE, 1992–; Inquiry into Police Responsibilities and Rewards, 1992–93; Trent RHA, 1992–. Chairman: QUBIS Ltd, 1983–88; Zeton Ltd, 1990; Ind. Adv. Gp on Consumers Protection in NI, 1984; NI Economic Council, 1987–94 (Mem., 1985–94); Lace Market Develt Co., 1989–; Human Fertilisation and Embryology Authy, 1990–94; Med. Manpower Standing Adv. Cttee, 1991–; Food Adv. Cttee, 1994–. *Publications:* (ed jtly) Law and Society, 1979; (ed) Do We Need a Bill of Rights?, 1980; (ed) Data Processing and the Law, 1984; numerous articles in books and jls. *Recreations:* sport, walking, music, reading. *Address:* University of Nottingham, Nottingham NG7 2RD.

CAMPBELL, Sir Donald, Kt 1994; CBE 1987; FRCA; FRCS; FRCSE; FFARCSI; FRCPGlas; FRCPE; Professor of Anaesthesia, University of Glasgow, 1976–92, now Emeritus (Dean of Faculty of Medicine, 1987–91); President, Royal College of Physicians and Surgeons of Glasgow, 1992–94; *b* 8 March 1930; *s* of Archibald Peter and Mary Campbell; *m* 1st, 1954, Nancy Rebecca McKintosh (decd); one *s* one *d*; 2nd, 1975, Catherine Conway Bradburn; two *d*. *Educ:* Hutchesons' Boys' Grammar Sch.; Univ. of Glasgow (MB, ChB). Lectr in Anaesthesia, 1959–60, Cons. Anaesthetist, 1960–76, Royal Inf., Glasgow. Vice-Dean, 1981–82, Dean, 1982–85, Faculty of Anaesthetists, RCS; Vice-Pres., RCS, 1985–87; Visitor, RCPSG, 1990–92. Chm., Scottish Council for Postgrad. Med. Educn, 1985–90. FACP; FRACP. *Publications:* A Nurse's Guide to Anaesthetics, Resuscitation and Intensive Care, 1964, 7th edn 1983; Anaesthetics, Resuscitation and Intensive Care, 1965, 7th edn 1990; contribs to med. jls, mainly on anaesthesia and intensive therapy. *Recreations:* angling, curling. *Address:* Novar, 27 Tannoch Drive, Milngavie, Glasgow G62 8AR. *T:* 0141–956 1736.

CAMPBELL, Donald le Strange, MC; *b* 16 June 1919; *s* of late Donald Fraser Campbell and Caroline Campbell, Heacham, Norfolk; *m* 1952, Hon. Shona Catherine Greig Macpherson, *y d* of 1st Baron Macpherson of Drumochter; one *s* one *d*. *Educ:* Winchester Coll.; Clare Coll., Cambridge. Served War, 1939–45, Major RA (MC). EFCO Ltd, 1947–55; MEECO Ltd, 1955–61; Davy-Ashmore Ltd, 1961–67. Chm., BNEC Latin America, 1967. *Recreations:* farming, sailing, field sports. *Address:* Little Dartmouth House, Dartmouth, Devon TQ6 0JP. *Clubs:* Boodle's; Royal Yacht Squadron.

CAMPBELL, Duncan; Director of Communications, Scottish Natural Heritage, since 1992; *b* 23 Sept. 1935; *s* of late Duncan Campbell, sometime Manager, Chartered Bank of India and Australasia, and Mary Beryl Campbell; *m* 1959, Morny Key; two *s*. *Educ:* Merchiston Castle Sch., Edinburgh; Edinburgh Univ.; Newcastle upon Tyne Univ. Nat. service, RHA, 1954–56. Forestry Commission: Forest Manager, 1960–73; Landscape Architect, 1973–80; Head of Design and Recreation Br., 1980–85; Head of Environment Br., 1985–88; Dir, CCS, 1988–92. *Publications:* articles in Landscape Design and Jl of RASE. *Recreations:* landscape appreciation, fishing. *Address:* (office) 12 Hope Terrace, Edinburgh EH9 2AS.

CAMPBELL, Graham Gordon, CB 1984; Under-Secretary, Department of Energy, 1974–84; *b* 12 Dec. 1924; *s* of late Lt-Col and Mrs P. H. Campbell; *m* 1955, Margaret Rosamond Busby; one *d*. *Educ:* Cheltenham Coll.; Caius Coll., Cambridge (BA Hist.). Served War, Royal Artillery, 1943–46. Asst Principal, Min. of Fuel and Power, 1949; Private Sec. to Parly Sec., Min. of Fuel and Power, 1953–54; Principal, 1954; Asst Sec., Min. of Power, 1965; Under-Sec., DTI, 1973. *Recreations:* watching birds, music, hill-walking, clearing scrub. *Address:* 3 Clovelly Avenue, Warlingham, Surrey CR6 9HZ. *T:* Upper Warlingham (01883) 624671.

CAMPBELL, Harold Edward; Director, Greater London Secondary Housing Association, 1978–83; Chairman, Sutton (Hastoe) Housing Association, 1975–85; *b* 28 Feb. 1915; *s* of Edward Inkerman Campbell and Florence Annie Campbell. *Educ:* Southbury Road Elementary Sch.; Enfield Central Sch. Asst Sec., 1946–64, Sec., 1964–67, Cooperative Party; Mem., 1967–73, Dep. Chm., 1969–73, Housing Corp. Gen. Manager, Newlon Housing Trust, 1970–76; Chairman: Cooperative Planning Ltd, 1964–74; Co-Ownership Develt Soc. Ltd, 1966–76; Sutton Housing Trust, 1973–80 (Trustee, 1967–86); Dir, Co-op. Housing Centre, and S British Housing Assoc., 1976–78; Dep. Chm., Stevenage Develt Corp., 1968–80; Mem., Cooperative Develt Agency, 1978–81; Pres., Enfield Highway Cooperative Soc. Ltd, 1976–85 (Dir, 1965–85); Dir, CWS Ltd, 1968–73. Chairman: DoE Working Party on Cooperative Housing, 1973–75; DoE Working Group on New Forms of Housing Tenure, 1976–77; Housing Assoc. Registration Adv. Cttee, 1974–79; Hearing Aid Council, 1970–71. Borough Councillor, Enfield, 1959–63. *Recreations:* music, theatre, cinema.

CAMPBELL, Hugh, PhD; Industrial Adviser, Department of Trade and Industry, 1971–74, retired; *b* 24 Oct. 1916; *s* of Hugh Campbell and Annie C. Campbell (*née* Spence); *m* 1946, Sybil Marian Williams, MB, ChB (*d* 1988), *y d* of Benjamin and Sarah Williams; two *s*. *Educ:* University College Sch., London; St John's Coll., Cambridge (MA, PhD). Research, Dept of Colloid Science, Cambridge, 1938–45; Head of Physical Chem., Research Gp, May and Baker Ltd, 1945–61; Lectr, West Ham Techn. Coll., 1949–54; Research Manager, Chloride Electrical Storage Co. Ltd, 1961–65; Managing Dir: Alkaline Batteries Ltd, 1965–67; Electric Power Storage Ltd, 1968–71; Dir, Chloride Electrical Storage Co. Ltd, 1968–71. Career Consultant in Paris and London, 1974–78. *Publications:*

papers on various subjects in scientific jls. *Recreations:* skiing, theatre, travelling. *Address:* 25 Kittiwake Drive, Kidderminster, Worcs DY10 4RS. *T:* Kidderminster (01562) 829626.

CAMPBELL, Hugh Hall, QC (Scot.) 1983; FCIArb; *b* 18 Feb. 1944; *s* of William Wright Campbell and Marianne Doris Stuart Hutchison or Campbell; *m* 1969, Eleanor Jane Hare; three *s*. *Educ:* Glasgow Acad.; Trinity Coll., Glenalmond (Alexander Cross Scholar); Exeter Coll., Oxford (Open Scholar in Classics; BA Hons, MA); Edinburgh Univ. (LLB Hons). FCIArb 1986. Called to the Scottish Bar, 1969; Standing Jun. Counsel to Admiralty, 1976. *Recreations:* music, hill-walking, golf. *Address:* 12 Ainslie Place, Edinburgh EH3 6AS. *T:* 0131–225 2067. *Club:* Hon. Company of Edinburgh Golfers.

CAMPBELL, Prof. Iain (Donald), PhD; FRS 1995; Professor of Structural Biology, University of Oxford, since 1992; Tutorial Fellow in Biochemistry, St John's College, Oxford, since 1989; *b* 24 April 1941; *s* of Daniel Campbell and Catherine Campbell (*née* Lauder); *m* 1967, Karin C. Wehle; one *s* two *d*. *Educ:* Perth Acad.; St Andrews Univ. (BSc 1963; PhD 1967); MA Oxon 1987. University Lectr, Dept of Biochem., Oxford, 1976–92. Member: Molecular and Cellular Medicine Bd, MRC, 1992–; EMBO, 1990–. Mem., various editl bds of scientific jls. Education in Partnership with Industry Award, DTI, 1982; BDH Medal, Biochem. Soc., 1990. *Publications:* numerous scientific papers and reviews. *Address:* Department of Biochemistry, Oxford University, South Parks Road, Oxford OX1 3QU. *T:* Oxford (01865) 275346, *Fax:* (01865) 275253.

CAMPBELL, Ian, JP; CEng, MIMechE; national and local government consultant; Director, Dumbarton District Enterprise Trust, since 1987; *b* 26 April 1926; *s* of William Campbell and Helen Crockett; *m* 1950, Mary Millar; two *s* three *d*. *Educ:* Dumbarton Academy; Royal Technical Coll., Glasgow (now Strathclyde Univ.). Engineer with South of Scotland Electricity Board for 17 years. Councillor, Dumbarton, 1958–70; Provost of Dumbarton, 1962–70. MP (Lab): Dunbartonshire W, 1970–83; Dumbarton, 1983–87. PPS to Sec. of State for Scotland, 1976–79. Mem., Strathclyde Region Local Valuation Panel, 1988–. *Address:* The Shanacles, Gartocharn, Alexandria, Dunbartonshire G83 8NB. *T:* Alexandria (01389) 52286.

CAMPBELL, Ian Burns; His Honour Judge Ian Campbell; a Circuit Judge, since 1984; *b* 7 July 1938; *s* of late James Campbell and of Laura W. Campbell; *m* 1967, Mary Elisabeth Poole, BArch, MCD Liverpool; two *s* one *d*. *Educ:* Tiffin Boys' Sch.; Cambridge Univ. (MA, LLM, PhD); Diplôme d'Etudes Supérieures de Droit Comparé, Strasbourg, 1964. Called to the Bar, Middle Temple, 1966. French Govt Scholar, Univ. of Paris, 1961–62; Asst Lectr in Law, Liverpool Univ., 1962–64, Lectr 1964–69; a Recorder, 1981–84. *Publication:* Essay in Legal Visions of the New Europe, 1993. *Recreation:* journeying.

CAMPBELL, Ian Dugald, QHP 1977; FRCPE, FFCM; Treasurer, Royal College of Physicians of Edinburgh, 1981–85; *b* Dornie, Kintail, 22 Feb. 1916; *s* of John Campbell and Margaret Campbell; *m* 1943, Joan Carnegie Osborn; one *s* two *d*. *Educ:* Dingwall Acad.; Edinburgh Univ. (MB, ChB 1939). FRCPE 1973, FFCM 1974. Served War, 1941–46: UK, BAOR, MEF, RAMC; final appt OC Field Amb. (Lt-Col). Med. Supt, St Luke's Hosp., Bradford, 1946–49; Asst SMO, Leeds Reg. Hosp. Bd, 1949–57; Dep. Sen. Admin. MO, S-Eastern Reg. Hosp. Bd, Scotland, 1957–72, Sen. Admin. MO, 1972–73; Chief Admin. MO, Lothian Health Bd, 1973–80. WHO assignments, SE Asia, 1969, 1971, 1975. *Publications:* various medical. *Recreations:* fishing, shooting, golf. *Address:* 5 Succoth Park, Edinburgh EH12 6BX. *T:* 0131–539 5965. *Clubs:* New (Edinburgh); Hon. Company of Edinburgh Golfers (Muirfield); Royal Burgess Golfing Society (Barnton, Edinburgh).

CAMPBELL, Ian James; Director General Research Maritime, Ministry of Defence, 1978–81; *b* 9 June 1923; *s* of Allan and Elizabeth Campbell; *m* 1946, Stella Margaret Smith. *Educ:* George Heriot's Sch.; Edinburgh Univ. (MA Hons, Maths and Natural Phil.). Op. Res. Sect., HQ Bomber Comd, 1943–46; Asst Lectr in Astronomy, St Andrews Univ., 1946–48, joined Royal Naval Scientific Service, 1948; Dept of Aeronaut. and Eng Res., Admiralty, 1948–49, Admiralty Res. Lab., 1949–59; Admiralty Underwater Weapons Estab., 1959–68 (leader of res. team which established concept and technol. base for Stingray torpedo, 1962–68); Chief Scientist, Naval Construction Res. Estab., 1969–73; Head of Weapons Dept, Admiralty Underwater Weapons Estab., 1973–76; Ministry of Defence: Dir of Res. (Ships), 1976–78; Scientific Advr to Ship Dept, 1976–81. Defence sci. consultant, 1982–92; Technical Dir, CAP Scientific, 1983–87; Dir of Studies, Centre for Operational Res. and Defence Analysis, 1987–88. Chm., Res. Adv. Cttee, Electronic Engrg Assoc., 1989–91. *Publications:* papers on fluid mechanics in scientific jls. *Address:* 6 Queens Avenue, Dorchester, Dorset DT1 2EW. *T:* Dorchester (01305) 264270. *Club:* Sloane.

CAMPBELL, Air Vice-Marshal Ian Robert, CB 1976; CBE 1964; AFC 1948; *b* 5 Oct. 1920; *s* of late Major and Hon. Mrs D. E. Campbell; *m* 1st, 1953, Beryl Evelyn Newbigging (*d* 1982); one *s*; 2nd, 1984, Elisabeth Lingard-Guthrie. *Educ:* Eton; RAF Coll., Cranwell. Anti-Shipping Ops, 1940–42; POW, Italy and Germany, 1942–45; 540 Sqdn, Benson, 1946; psa 1949; PSO to C-in-C Far East, 1950; 124 (F) Wing Oldenburg, 1953; OC, RAF Sandwich, 1956; pfc 1957; OC 213 Sqdn, Bruggen, 1958; ACOS Plans HQ 2ATAF, 1959; OC, RAF Marham, 1961; MoD (Air) DASB, 1964; SASO, HQ No 1 Group, 1965; Air Attaché, Bonn, 1968; Dir of Management and Support Intell., MoD, 1970–73; C of S, No 18 (M) Group, Strike Command, 1973–75, retired. *Recreations:* shooting, travel. *Address:* Pike Farm, Fossebridge, Cheltenham, Glos GL54 3JR. *Clubs:* Boodle's, Royal Air Force.

CAMPBELL, Maj.-Gen. Ian Ross, CBE 1954; DSO and Bar, 1941; *b* 23 March 1900; *m* 1927, Patience Allison Russell (*d* 1961); one *d*; *m* 1967, Irene Cardamatis. *Educ:* Wesley Coll., Melbourne; Scots Coll., Sydney; Royal Military College, Duntroon, Canberra (Sword of Honour, 1922). psc Camberley, 1936–37. Served War of 1939–45, Middle East Campaigns, Libya, Greece and Crete (DSO and bar, Cross of Kt Comdr, Greek Order of Phœnix; pow 1941–45); comd Aust. forces in Korean War, 1951–53 (CBE); Comdt, Australian Staff Coll., 1953–54; Comdt, Royal Mil. Coll. Duntroon, 1954–57; retired, 1957, Mem. Federal Exec., RSL, 1955–56. Chm., NSW Div., Aust. Red Cross Soc., 1967–74. Pres., Great Public Schs Athletic Assoc., NSW, 1966–69. Hon. Col, NSW Scottish Regt, 1957–60. *Recreation:* reading. *Address:* 15/17 Wylde Street, Potts Point, Sydney, NSW 2011, Australia. *Clubs:* Australian, Royal Sydney Golf (Sydney).

CAMPBELL, Sir Ian (Tofts), Kt 1988; CBE 1984; VRD 1961; JP; Director, Conservative Board of Finance, 1978–90; Director of Finance and Administration, Scottish Conservative Party, 1988–90; *b* 3 Feb. 1923; *o s* of John Walter Campbell and Mary Hardie Campbell (*née* Scott); *m* 1961, Marion Kirkhope Paterson (*née* Shiel); one *d*. *Educ:* Daniel Stewart's College, Edinburgh. FInstD 1964. RN 1942–46, RNR 1946–65 (Comdr). Man. Dir, MacGregor Wallcoverings, 1966–78. Chm., Select Assured Properties, Glasgow, 1989–95; Dep. Chm., Heath (Scotland) Ltd, 1988– (Dir, 1987–); Director: Travel System, 1987–89; Hermiston Securities, 1990–. Mem., Transport Users' Cons. Cttee for Scotland, 1981–87. Councillor, City of Edinburgh District Council, 1984–88. JP Edinburgh, 1987. Freeman, City of Glasgow, 1992. OStJ 1987. KLJ 1984. *Recreations:* golf, water colour painting, vintage cars. *Address:* Merleton, 10 Boswall Road, Edinburgh EH5 3RH. *T:* 0131–552 4825. *Clubs:* Caledonian, New (Edinburgh).

CAMPBELL of Succoth, Sir Ilay (Mark), 7th Bt *cr* 1808, of Succoth, Dunbartonshire; *b* 29 May 1927; *o s* of Sir George Ilay Campbell, 6th Bt; *S* father, 1967; *m* 1961, Margaret Minette Rohais, *o d* of J. Alasdair Anderson; two *d*. *Educ:* Eton; Christ Church, Oxford. BA 1952; MA 1970. Chm., Christie's Scotland. Dir., High Craigton Farming Co. Member: Historic Buildings Council for Scotland, 1989–; Gardens Cttee, Nat. Trust for Scotland, 1994–. Pres., Assoc. for Protection of Rural Scotland, 1978–90. Mem., C of S Cttee for Artistic Matters, 1984–91 (Covener, 1987–91); Convener, Church Bldgs Renewal Trust, Glasgow, 1995–. Hon. Vice Pres., Scotland's Gardens Scheme, 1960–; Trustee, Crarae Gardens Charitable Trust, 1978–. *Recreations:* heraldry, collecting heraldic bookplates, horticulture. *Heir:* none. *Address:* Crarae Lodge, Inveraray, Argyll PA32 8YA. *T:* Minard (01546) 86274. *Club:* Turf.

See also Sir Gregor MacGregor of MacGregor, Bt.

CAMPBELL, James, FBA 1984; FSA 1971; Fellow of Worcester College, since 1957 and Reader in Medieval History, since 1990, Oxford University; *b* 26 Jan. 1935. *Educ:* Mill Road Mixed Infants, Clowne, Derbyshire and other primary schools; Lowestoft Grammar School; Magdalen College (Exhibitioner; BA 1955, MA). Oxford University: Junior Research Fellow, Merton College, 1956–57; Tutorial Fellow, 1957, Fellow Librarian, 1977–, Sen. Tutor, 1989–93, Worcester College; Lectr in Modern History, 1958–90; Senior Proctor, 1973–74. Visiting Professor: Univ. of South Carolina, 1969; Univ. of Rochester, 1986–87. *Publications:* Norwich, 1975; (ed) The Anglo-Saxons, 1982; Essays in Anglo-Saxon History, 1986; articles in learned jls. *Recreation:* topography. *Address:* Worcester College, Oxford OX1 2HB. *T:* Oxford (01865) 278340. *Club:* United Oxford & Cambridge University.

CAMPBELL, James Hugh; Consultant, Bird Semple Fyfe Ireland, WS, Glasgow, Edinburgh and London, 1991–93; *b* 13 Nov. 1926; *s* of William Campbell and Agnes Wightman Campbell; *m* 1953, Iris Burnside (*née* Hercus); two *s* one *d*. *Educ:* Univ. of Glasgow, 1944–45 and 1948–50 (BL). Service in RAF, Japan, 1946–48. Solicitor; Partner, Bird Son & Semple, 1952–73, Sen. Partner, 1965–73; Sen. Partner, Bird Semple & Crawford Herron, subseq. Bird Semple Fyfe Ireland, 1973–91. President: Glasgow Juridical Soc., 1951–52; Law Soc. of Scotland, 1991–92 (Mem. Council, 1986–95; Vice-Pres., 1990–91). *Recreations:* music, reading, golf. *Address:* 24 Woodvale Avenue, Giffnock, Glasgow G46 6RQ. *T:* 0141–638 2630. *Clubs:* Royal Scottish Automobile, Western (Glasgow); East Renfrewshire Golf, Glasgow Golf.

CAMPBELL, John Davies, CVO 1980; CBE 1981 (MBE 1957); MC 1945, and bar 1945; company director; HM Diplomatic Service, retired; Consul-General, Naples, 1977–81; *b* 11 Nov. 1921; *s* of late William Hastings Campbell and of late The Hon. Mrs Campbell (Eugenie Anne Westenra, subsequently Harbord), *d* of 14th Baron Louth; *m* 1959, Shirley Bouch; one *s* two *d*. *Educ:* Cheltenham Coll.; St Andrews Univ. Served War, HM Forces, Argyll and Sutherland Highlanders and Popski's Private Army, 1940–46. HM Colonial Service (subseq. HMOCS), 1949–61 (despatches, 1957); HM Foreign (subseq. HM Diplomatic) Service, 1961; First Secretary, 1961; Counsellor, 1972; Counsellor (Information) Ottawa, 1972–77. Commendatore dell'ordine al merito della Repubblica Italiana, 1980. *Recreations:* travel, walking. *Address:* Townsend House, Luston, Leominster, Herefordshire HR6 0DZ. *T:* Leominster (01568) 612446. *Clubs:* Special Forces; Muthaiga Country (Nairobi) (Life Mem.); Mombasa.

CAMPBELL, John L., OBE 1990; owner of Heiskeir and Humla, of the Small Isles; formerly owner of Isle of Canna, which he presented to National Trust for Scotland, 1981; farmer (retired) and author; *b* 1 Oct. 1906; *e s* of late Col Duncan Campbell of Inverneill and Ethel Harriet, *e d* of late John I. Waterbury, Morristown, NJ; *m* 1935, Margaret Fay (author of Folksongs and Folklore of South Uist), *y d* of Henry Clay Shaw, Glenshaw, Pennsylvania (US); no *c*. *Educ:* Cargilfield; Rugby; St John's Coll., Oxford (Dipl. Rural Economy 1930; MA 1933, DLitt 1965). Sec., Barra Sea League, 1933–38. Curator of Woods on Isle of Canna for Nat. Trust for Scotland. FRSE 1989. Hon. LLD, St Francis Xavier Univ., Antigonish, NS, 1953; Hon. DLitt Glasgow Univ., 1965. KSG 1992. *Publications include:* Highland Songs of the Forty-Five, 1933, 2nd edn 1984; The Book of Barra (with Compton Mackenzie and Carl Hj. Borgstrom), 1936; Act Now for the Highlands and Islands (with Sir Alexander MacEwen, in which creation of Highland Develt Bd suggested for first time), 1939; Gaelic in Scottish Education and Life, 1945, 2nd edn 1950; Fr Allan McDonald of Eriskay, Priest, Poet and Folklorist, 1954; Tales from Barra, told by the Coddy, 1960; Stories from South Uist, 1961; The Furrow Behind Me, 1962; Edward Lhuyd in the Scottish Highlands (with Prof. Derick Thomson), 1963; A School in South Uist (memoirs of Frederick Rea), 1964; Gaelic Poems of Fr. Allan McDonald, 1965; Strange Things (story of SPR enquiry into Highland second sight, with Trevor H. Hall), 1968; Hebridean Folksongs (waulking songs from South Uist and Barra) (with F. Collinson), vol. i, 1969, vol. ii, 1977, vol. iii, 1981; Canna, the Story of a Hebridean Island, 1984; Songs Remembered in Exile, traditional Gaelic songs from Nova Scotia, 1990; (contrib.) DNB; other pubns and articles on Highland history and Gaelic oral tradition, also on Hebridean entomology. *Recreations:* entomology, sea fishing, listening to old Gaelic stories. *Address:* Canna House, Isle of Canna, Scotland PH44 4RS.

CAMPBELL, (John) Quentin; Metropolitan Stipendiary Magistrate, since 1981; a Recorder, since 1989; *b* 5 March 1939; *s* of late John McKnight Campbell, OBE, MC, and late Katharine Margaret Campbell; *m* 1st, Penelope Jane Redman (marr. diss. 1976); three *s* one *d*; 2nd, 1977, Ann Rosemary Beeching; one *s* one *d*. *Educ:* Loretto Sch., Musselburgh, Scotland; Wadham Coll., Oxford (MA). Admitted as Solicitor, 1965; private practice, Linnell & Murphy, Oxford (Partner, 1968–80). Chm., Inner London Youth Courts, 1985–. Chairman, Bd of Governors, Bessels Leigh Sch., near Oxford, 1979–. *Recreations:* opera, gardening. *Address:* Marlborough Street Magistrates' Court, 21 Great Marlborough Street, W1A 4EY. *T:* 0171–287 4525. *Clubs:* Travellers', Chelsea Arts; Frewen (Oxford).

CAMPBELL, Juliet Jeanne d'Auvergne, CMG 1988; HM Diplomatic Service, retired; Mistress of Girton College, Cambridge, since 1992; Deputy Vice-Chancellor, Cambridge University, since 1993; *b* 23 May 1935; *d* of Maj.-Gen. Wilfred d'Auvergne Collings, CB, CBE and of Nancy Draper Bishop; *m* 1983, Prof. Alexander Elmslie Campbell, *qv*. *Educ:* a variety of schools; Lady Margaret Hall, Oxford (BA; Hon. Fellow, 1992). Joined Foreign Office 1957; Common Market Delegation, Brussels, 1961–63; FO, 1963–64; Second, later First Secretary, Bangkok, 1964–66; News Dept, FO, 1967–70; Head of Chancery, The Hague, 1970–74; European Integration Dept, FCO, 1974–77; Counsellor (Inf.), Paris, 1977–80; RCDS, 1981; Counsellor, Jakarta, 1982–83; Head of Training Dept, FCO, 1984–87; Ambassador to Luxembourg, 1988–91. Member: Cambridge Univ. Council of Senate (later Council), 1993–; Wilton Park Academic Council, 1993–. Trustee: Changing Faces, 1992–; Cambridge European Trust, 1994–; Kurt Hahn Trust, 1995–; Cambridge Overseas Trust, 1995–. Gov., Queen's Coll., Harley St, 1992–. *Address:* Girton College, Cambridge CB3 0JG. *Club:* United Oxford & Cambridge University.

CAMPBELL, Air Vice-Marshal Kenneth Archibald, CB 1989; consulting engineer; Air Officer Maintenance, RAF Support Command, 1987–89; *b* 3 May 1936; *s* of John McLean and Christina Campbell; *m* 1959, Isobel Love Millar; two *d*. *Educ:* George Heriot's Sch.; Glasgow Univ. (BSc); College of Aeronautics, Cranfield (MSc). Various engrg appts, RAF, 1959–90; Air Officer, Wales, 1977–79; Dir, Engrg Policy (RAF), 1981–83; AO, Engrg and Supply, RAF Germany, 1983–85; DG Personal Services (RAF), 1985–87. *Recreations:* golf, skiing. *Club:* Royal Air Force.

CAMPBELL, Rt Hon. Kim, PC 1989; QC (BC) 1990; Prime Minister of Canada, 1993; *b* 10 March 1947. *Educ:* Univ. of British Columbia (BA 1965; LLB 1983); LSE (Hon. Fellow, 1994). Called to the Bar of BC, 1984. Lectr in Pol Sci., Univ. of BC, 1975–78; Lectr in Pol Sci. and Hist., Vancouver Community Coll., 1978–81; Articled student, 1983–84, Associate, Gen. Litigation, 1984–85, Ladner Downs Vancouver; Exec. Dir, Office of Premier of BC, 1985–86; MLA Vancouver Point Grey, 1986–88; MP (PC) Vancouver Centre, 1988–93; Minister of State, Indian Affairs and Northern Develt, 1989–90; Minister of Justice and Attorney Gen., 1990–93; Minister of Nat. Defence and Minister of Veterans' Affairs, 1993. Fellow, John F. Kennedy Sch. of Govt, Harvard Univ., 1994. *Address:* 963 West 8th Avenue, Vancouver, BC V52 1E4, Canada.

CAMPBELL, Sir Lachlan (Philip Kemeys), 6th Bt *cr* 1815; *b* 9 Oct. 1958; *e s* of Col Sir Guy Campbell, 5th Bt, OBE, MC and of Lizbeth Webb, *d* of late Frederick Holton; *S* father, 1993; *m* 1986, Harriet Jane Sarah, *o d* of F. E. J. Girling; one *s* one *d*. *Educ:* Temple Grove; Eton; RMA Sandhurst. Commnd The Royal Greenjackets (Lieut); served NI. *Recreations:* golf, Rugby, cricket, painting. *Heir: s* Archibald Edward FitzGerald Campbell, *b* 13 June 1990. *Address:* 20 Rush Hill Road, SW11 5NW. *Clubs:* Army and Navy, MCC; London Scottish Golf.

CAMPBELL, Rev. Laurence Jamieson; Methodist Minister, supernumerary; Minister, Trinity Church, Newport, Gwent Circuit, 1987–94; *b* 10 June 1927; *er s* of George S. Campbell and Mary P. Paterson; *m* 1954, Sheena E. Macdonald; two *s* one *d*. *Educ:* Hillhead High Sch., Glasgow; Aberdeen Univ., Edinburgh Univ. (MA). Lieut RA, 1945–48. Housemaster, Alliance High Sch., Kenya, 1952–56; Presbyterian Church of E Africa, 1957–61: Tumutumu Coll., 1957–60; Supervisor of Schs, 1960–61; Educn Sec., Christian Council of Kenya, 1962; Headmaster: Alliance High Sch., Kenya, 1963–70; Kingswood Sch., Bath, 1970–87. Methodist minister, ordained 1988. Contested North Kenya Constituency, Kenya General Election, 1961. Mem. Council, Univ. of East Africa, 1963–69; Chm., Heads Assoc. of Kenya, 1965–69; Official of Kenya Commonwealth Games Team, 1970. Schoolmaster Fellow, Balliol Coll., Oxford, 1970. Chairman: Christians Abroad, 1977–81; Bloxham Project, 1981–84. *Recreations:* golf, athletics, church. *Address:* 1A Edward VII Avenue, Newport, Gwent NP9 4NF.

CAMPBELL, Sir Matthew, KBE 1963; CB 1959; FRSE; Deputy Chairman, White Fish Authority, and Chairman, Authority's Committee for Scotland and Northern Ireland, 1968–78; *b* 23 May 1907; *s* of late Matthew Campbell, High Blantyre; *m* 1939, Isabella, *d* of late John Wilson, Rutherglen; two *s*. *Educ:* Hamilton Academy; Glasgow Univ. Entered CS, 1928, and after service in Inland Revenue Dept and Admiralty joined staff of Dept of Agriculture for Scotland, 1935; Principal, 1938; Assistant Sec., 1943; Under Sec., 1953; Sec., Dept of Agriculture and Fisheries for Scotland, 1958–68. *Address:* 10 Craigleith View, Edinburgh EH4 3JZ. *T:* 0131–337 5168.

CAMPBELL, Menzies; *see* Campbell, W. M.

CAMPBELL, Sir Niall (Alexander Hamilton), 8th Bt *cr* 1831, of Barcaldine and Glenure; 15th Chieftain, Hereditary Keeper of Barcaldine Castle; Clerk to Justices of N Devon Divisions of Barnstaple, Bideford and Great Torrington and South Molton, 1976–90; *b* 7 Jan. 1925; *o s* of Sir Ian Vincent Hamilton Campbell, 7th Bt, CB, and Madeline Lowe Reid (*d* 1929), *e d* of late Hugh Anglin Whitelocke, FRCS; *S* father, 1978; *m* 1st, 1949, Patricia Mary (marr. diss. on his petition, 1956), *d* of R. G. Turner; 2nd, 1957, Norma Joyce, *d* of W. N. Wiggin; two *s* two *d* (including twin *s* and *d*). *Educ:* Cheltenham College (Scholar); Corpus Christi Coll., Oxford. Called to the Bar, Inner Temple. Served War, 1943–46, Lieut Royal Marines; in Inf. bn, NW Europe campaign and on staff of Comdr RM training bde. Appts as Hosp. Administrator, 1953–70, inside and outside NHS, including St Mary's, Paddington, London Clinic, and Royal Hosp. and Home for Incurables, Putney (Chief Exec.); Dep. Chief Clerk, Inner London Magistrates' Courts, 1970–76, and Dep. Coroner, Inner London (South), Southwark. Mem. Exec. Cttee, N Devon Community Health Council; Governor, Grenville Coll., Bideford; Mem. Management Cttee, N Devon Cheshire Home. *Publication:* Making the Best Use of Bed Resources—monograph based on lecture sponsored by King Edward's Hospital Fund, 1965. *Recreations:* garden labour; writing letters to the Times, with little success; keeping a golden retriever; birds. *Heir: er s* Roderick Duncan Hamilton Campbell, of Barcaldine, Younger [*b* 24 Feb. 1961; *m* 1989, Jean Caroline, *d* of Laurie Bicknell, Braunton, Devon; two *d*]. *Address:* The Old Mill, Milltown, Muddiford, Barnstaple, Devon EX31 4HG. *T:* Shirwell (01271) 850341; (seat) Barcaldine Castle, Benderloch via Connel, Argyllshire. *Club:* Marshalls (Barnstaple).

CAMPBELL, Niall Gordon; Under Secretary, Social Work Services Group, Scottish Office Home and Health Department, since 1989; *b* 9 Nov. 1941; *s* of Ian M. Campbell and Jean G. Sanderson; *m* 1975, Alison Margaret Rigg; three *s*. *Educ:* Edinburgh Academy; Merton College, Oxford (BA). Entered Scottish Office, 1964; Asst Sec., 1978; posts in Scottish Educn and Scottish Develt Depts. *Address:* 15 Warriston Crescent, Edinburgh EH3 5LA. *T:* 0131–556 2895.

CAMPBELL, Maj.-Gen. Peter; *see* Campbell, Maj.-Gen. C. P.

CAMPBELL, Prof. Peter Nelson; Courtauld Professor of Biochemistry, and Director of the Courtauld Institute, Middlesex Hospital Medical School, London University, 1976–87, now Emeritus Professor; Editor in Chief, Biotechnology and Applied Biochemistry, since 1981; *b* 5 Nov. 1921; *s* of late Alan A. Campbell and Nora Nelson; *m* 1946, Mollie (*née* Manklow); one *s* one *d* (and one *s* decd). *Educ:* Eastbourne Coll.; Univ. Coll. London (Fellow, 1981). BSc, PhD, DSc, London; FIBiol. Research and Production Chemist with Standard Telephones and Cables, Ltd, 1942–46; PhD Student, UCL, 1946–47; Asst Lectr UCL, 1947–49; staff of Nat. Inst. for Med. Research, Hampstead and Mill Hill, 1949–54; Asst, Courtauld Inst. of Biochem., Middx Hosp. Med. Sch., 1954–57; Sen. Lectr, Middx Hosp. Med. Sch., 1957–64; Reader in Biochem., Univ. of London, 1964–67; Prof. and Head of Dept of Biochem., Leeds Univ., 1967–75. Hon. Consulting Chemical Pathologist to Middlesex Hosp., 1987–. Butland Vis. Prof., Univ. of Auckland, 1988. Chm., Assoc. of Researchers in Medicine and Sci., 1987–95. Hon. Lectr, Dept of Biochem., UCL, 1954–67. Hon. Mem., Biochemical Soc., 1988. Convenor, FEBS Scientific Apparatus Recycling Scheme, 1990–. Diplôme d'Honneur, Fedn of European Biochemical Socs., 1981. *Publications:* Structure and Function of Animal Cell Components, 1966; (ed with B. A. Kilby) Basic Biochemistry for Medical Students, 1975; (ed) Biology in Profile, 1981; (with A. D. Smith) Biochemistry Illustrated, 1982, 3rd edn 1994; many scientific papers in Biochem. Jl. *Recreations:* theatre, travelling, conversation. *Address:* Department of Biochemistry and Molecular Biology, University College London, WC1E 6BT. *T:* 0171–380 7777.

CAMPBELL, Prof. Peter (Walter); Professor of Politics, Reading University, 1964–91, now Emeritus; *b* 17 June 1926; *o s* of late W. C. H. and L. M. Campbell. *Educ:* Bournemouth Sch.; New Coll., Oxford. 2nd class PPE, 1947; MA 1951; Research Student, Nuffield Coll., Oxford, 1947–49. Asst Lecturer in Govt, Manchester Univ., 1949–52; Lectr, 1952–60; Vice-Warden Needham Hall, 1959–60; Visiting Lectr in Political Science, Victoria Univ. Coll., NZ, 1954; Prof. of Political Economy, 1960–64, Dean, Faculty of Letters, 1966–69, Chm., Graduate Sch. of Contemporary European Studies, 1971–73, Reading University. Hon. Sec. Political Studies Assoc., 1955–58; Chm., Inst. of Electoral Research, 1959–65; Mem. Council, Hansard Soc. for Parly Govt, 1962–77; Editor of Political Studies, 1963–69; Hon. Treas., Joint Univ. Council for Social and Public Administration, 1965–69; Chm., Reading Romilly Assoc., 1965–69; Vice-Chm., Reading and District Council of Social Service, 1966–71; Vice-Pres., Electoral Reform Soc., 1972–; Mem., Nat. Cttee for Electoral Reform, 1976–93; Trustee, Ballot Services (ERS) Ltd, 1988–92; Hon. Treas., CAER, 1990–94. Member: Adv. Panel, Commonwealth Scholarship Commn, 1964–73; Political Science Cttee, SSRC, 1968–72; CNAA Bds and Panels, 1971–78; Social Studies Sub-Cttee, UGC, 1973–83. Co-Pres., Reading Univ. Cons. Assoc., 1961–91. Mem. Council, Campaign for Homosexual Equality, 1978–79; Convenor, Reading CHE, 1979–80; Mem. Council of Management, Albany Soc., 1988–91; Vice-Pres., Conservative Gp for Homosexual Equality, 1988– (Chm., 1982–88); Chm., Exec. Cttee, Soc. for Individual Freedom, 1992–93; Trustee, Civic Educn and Res. Trust, 1993–95. Patron, Univ. of Buckingham, 1984–. *Publications:* (with W. Theimer) Encyclopædia of World Politics, 1950; French Electoral Systems and Elections, 1789–1957, 1958; (with B. Chapman) The Constitution of the Fifth Republic, 1958. Articles in British, French and New Zealand Jls of Political Science. *Recreations:* ambling, idling. *Address:* 6 Treyarnon Court, 37 Eastern Avenue, Reading RG1 5RX. *T:* Reading (01734) 661888. *Clubs:* Athenæum, United Oxford & Cambridge University.

CAMPBELL, Quentin; *see* Campbell, J. Q.

CAMPBELL, Robert, MSc; FICE; Management Consultant; Chairman and Chief Executive, Rem Campbell Management Ltd, since 1987; *b* 18 May 1929; *s* of Robert Stewart Campbell and Isobella Frances Campbell; *m* 1950, Edna Maud Evans. *Educ:* Emmanuel IGS; Loughborough Univ. (DLC (Hons), MSc). MIWES. Member of Gray's Inn, 1960. Contracts Engineer, Wyatts, Contractors, 1954–56; Chief Asst Engr, Stirlingshire and Falkirk Water Board, 1956–59; Water Engr, Camborne, 1959–60; Chief Asst City Water Engr, Plymouth, 1960–65; Civil Engr, Colne Valley Water Co., 1965–69; Engrg Inspector, Min. of Housing and Local Govt/DoE, 1969–74; Asst Dir, Resources, Planning, Anglian Water Authority, 1974–77; Chief Executive, Epping Forest Dist Council, 1977–79; Sec., ICE, 1979–81, and Man. Dir, Thomas Telford Ltd, Dir, Watt Cttee on Energy, and Hon. Sec., ICE Benevolent Fund, 1979–81; Chm., Rem Campbell Internat., 1981–87. Freeman of City of London, 1977; Liveryman of Horners' Co. 1977–. *Publication:* The Pricing of Water, 1973. *Recreations:* golf, music, caravanning, cricket. *Address:* Bronafon, Pen-y-Banc, Llechryd, near Cardigan, Dyfed SA43 2NR. *Club:* MCC.

CAMPBELL, Sir Robin Auchinbreck, 15th Bt *cr* 1628 (NS); *b* 7 June 1922; *s* of Sir Louis Hamilton Campbell, 14th Bt and Margaret Elizabeth Patricia (*d* 1985), *d* of late Patrick Campbell; *S* father, 1970; *m* 1st, 1948, Rosemary, (Sally) (*d* 1978), *d* of Ashley Dean, Christchurch, NZ; one *s* two *d*; 2nd, 1978, Mrs Elizabeth Gunston, *d* of Sir Arthur Colegate, Bembridge, IoW. Formerly Lieut (A) RNVR. *Heir: s* Louis Auchinbreck Campbell [*b* 17 Jan. 1953; *m* 1976, Fiona Mary St Clair, *d* of Gordon King; two *d*]. *Address:* 287A Waikawa Road, Picton, New Zealand.

CAMPBELL, Ronald, (Ronnie); MP (Lab) Blyth Valley, since 1987; *b* 14 Aug. 1943; *m* Deirdre (*née* McHale); five *s* one *d*. *Educ:* Ridley High Sch., Blyth. Former miner. Member: Blyth Borough Council, 1969–74; Blyth Valley Council, 1974–88 (Chm., Environmental Health Cttee; Vice-Chm., Housing Cttee). Mem., NUM. *Address:* 68 Broadway, Blyth, Northumberland NE24 2PR; House of Commons, SW1A 0AA.

CAMPBELL, Ronald Francis Boyd, MA; *b* 28 Aug. 1912; *o s* of Major Roy Neil Boyd Campbell, DSO, OBE and Effie Muriel, *y d* of Major Charles Pierce, IMS; *m* 1939, Pamela Muriel Désirée, *o d* of H. L. Wright, OBE, late Indian Forest Service; one *s* two *d*. *Educ:* Berkhamsted Sch.; Peterhouse, Cambridge. Asst Master, Berkhamsted Sch., 1934–39. War of 1939–45: Supplementary Reserve, The Duke of Cornwall's Light Infantry, Sept. 1939; served in England and Italy; DAQMG, HQ 3rd Div., 1943; demobilized with hon. rank of Lt-Col, 1945. Housemaster and OC Combined Cadet Force, Berkhamsted Sch., 1945–51; Headmaster, John Lyon Sch., Harrow, 1951–68. Dir, Public Sch. Appointments Bureau, later Independent Schs Careers Orgn, 1968–78. Hon. Assoc. Mem., HMC, 1969–. Walter Hines Page Travelling Scholarship to USA, 1960. 1939–45 Star, Italy Star, Defence and Victory Medals; ERD (2 clasps). *Recreations:* sailing, fishing. *Address:* 30 Marine Drive, Torpoint, Cornwall PL11 2EH. *T:* Plymouth (01752) 813671. *Clubs:* East India, Devonshire, Sports and Public Schools, Royal Cruising.

CAMPBELL, Ross, DSC 1944; Senior Partner, InterCon Consultants, Ottawa, since 1983; *b* 4 Nov. 1918; *s* of late William Marshall Campbell and of Helen Isabel Harris; *m* 1945, Penelope Grantham-Hill; two *s*. *Educ:* Univ. of Toronto Schs; Trin. Coll., Univ. of Toronto. BA, Faculty of Law, 1940. Served RCN, 1940–45. Joined Dept. of Ext. Affairs, Canada, 1945; Third Sec., Oslo, 1946–47; Second Sec., Copenhagen, 1947–50; European Div., Ottawa, 1950–52; First Sec., Ankara, 1952–56; Head of Middle East Div., Ottawa, 1957–59; Special Asst to Sec. of State for Ext. Aff., 1959–62; Asst Under-Sec. of State for Ext. Aff., 1962–64; Adviser to Canadian Delegns to: UN Gen. Assemblies, 1958–63; North Atlantic Coun., 1959–64; Ambassador to Yugoslavia, 1964–67, concurrently accredited Ambassador to Algeria, 1965–67; Ambassador and Perm. Rep. to NATO, 1967–73 (Paris May 1967, Brussels Oct. 1967); Ambassador to Japan, 1973–75, and concurrently to Republic of Korea, 1973. Chm., Atomic Energy of Canada Ltd, 1976–79; President: Atomic Energy of Canada International, 1979–80; Canus Technical Services Corp., Ottawa, 1981–83; Dir, Adopac Ltd, 1992–. *Recreation:* gardening. *Address:* Rivermead House, 890 Aylmer Road, Aylmer, Que J9H 5T8, Canada; (office) Suite 1003, 275 Slater Street, Ottawa K1P 5H9, Canada. *Clubs:* Rideau (Ottawa); Country (Lucerne).

CAMPBELL, Ross; Director, International Military Services Ltd, 1979–83, retired; *b* 4 May 1916; 2nd *s* of George Albert Campbell and Jean Glendinning Campbell (*née* Ross); *m* 1st, 1939, Emmy Zoph (marr. diss. 1948); one *s* one *d*; 2nd, 1952, Dr Diana Stewart (*d* 1977); one *d* (and one *d* decd); 3rd, 1979, Jean Margaret Turner (*née* Ballinger) (marr. diss. 1984). *Educ:* Farnborough Grammar Sch.; Reading Univ. CEng, FICE. Articled to Municipal Engr; Local Authority Engr, 1936–39; Air Min. (UK), 1939–44; Sqdn Ldr, RAF, Middle East, 1944–47; Air Min. (UK), 1947–52; Supt Engr, Gibraltar, 1952–55; Air Min. (UK), 1955–59; Chief Engr, Far East Air Force, 1959–62 and Bomber Comd, 1962–63; Personnel Management, MPBW, 1963–66; Chief Resident Engr, Persian Gulf, 1966–68; Dir Staff Management, MPBW, 1968–69; Dir of Works (Air), 1969–72; Under-Sec., and Dir of Defence Services II PSA, DoE, 1972–75. Dir, 1975–77, Dep. Chief

Exec., 1977–79, Internat. Military Services Ltd. *Publications:* papers on professional civil engrg and trng in ICE Jl. *Recreations:* golf, music. *Address:* 41 Nightingale Road, Rickmansworth, Herts WD3 2DA. *T:* Rickmansworth (01923) 773744. *Clubs:* Royal Air Force; Denham Golf.

CAMPBELL, Sir Thomas C.; *see* Cockburn-Campbell.

CAMPBELL, Hon. Sir Walter (Benjamin), AC 1989; Kt 1979; QC (Qld) 1960; Governor of Queensland, Australia, 1985–92; *b* 4 March 1921; *s* of Archie Eric Gordon Campbell and Leila Mary Campbell; *m* 1942, Georgina Margaret Pearce; one *s* one *d* (and one *s* decd). *Educ:* Univ. of Queensland (MA, LLB; Hon. LLD 1980). Served War, RAAF, 1941–46 (pilot). Called to the Qld Bar, 1948; Judge, Supreme Court, Qld, 1967; Chief Justice, Qld, 1982–85. Chairman: Law Reform Commn of Qld, 1969–73; Remuneration Tribunal (Commonwealth), 1974–82; sole Mem., Academic Salaries Tribunal (Commonwealth), 1974–78. President: Qld Bar Assoc., 1965–67; Australian Bar Assoc., 1966–67; Mem. Exec., Law Council of Aust., 1965–67. Dir, Winston Churchill Meml Trust, 1969–80; Chm., Utah Foundn, 1977–85. Mem. Senate 1963–85, and Chancellor 1977–85, Univ. of Qld. Trustee, Gowrie Scholarship Trust Fund, 1984–. Fellow Aust. Inst. Judicial Admin., 1986. KStJ 1986. Freeman, City of London, 1987; Liveryman, GAPAN, 1988. Hon. DLitt James Cook Univ., 1988; DUniv: Queensland Univ. of Technology, 1991; Griffith Univ., 1992. *Recreations:* golf, reading. *Address:* 6 Dennison Street, Ascot, Qld 4007, Australia. *Clubs:* Queensland, Brisbane (Hon. Life Mem.), Royal Queensland Golf (Brisbane); Australasian Pioneers (Sydney).

CAMPBELL, (Walter) Menzies, CBE 1987; QC (Scot.) 1982; MP Fife North East, since 1987 (L 1987–88, Lib Dem since 1988); *b* 22 May 1941; *s* of George Alexander Campbell and Elizabeth Jean Adam Phillips; *m* 1970, Elspeth Mary Urquhart or Grant-Suttie, *d* of Maj.-Gen. R. E. Urquhart, CB, DSO. *Educ:* Hillhead High School, Glasgow; Glasgow Univ. (MA 1962, LLB 1965; President of the Union, 1964–65); Stanford Univ., Calif. Advocate, Scottish Bar, 1968; Advocate Depute, 1977–80; Standing Jun. Counsel to the Army, 1980–82. Member: Clayson Cttee on licensing reform, 1971; Legal Aid Central Cttee, 1983–87; Scottish Legal Aid Bd, 1987; Broadcasting Council for Scotland, 1984–87. Part-time Chairman: VAT Tribunal, 1984–87; Medical Appeal Tribunal, 1985–87. Chm., Scottish Liberal Party, 1975–77; contested (L): Greenock and Port Glasgow, Feb. 1974 and Oct. 1974; E Fife, 1979; NE Fife, 1983; Lib. spokesman on arts, broadcasting and sport, 1987–88; Lib Dem spokesman on arts, broadcasting and sport, 1988, on defence and sport, 1988–94, on Foreign Affairs, 1994–. Member: Select Cttee on Members Interests, 1987–90; Select Cttee on Trade and Industry, 1990–92; Defence Select Cttee, 1992–. Member: UK Delegn to N Atlantic Assembly, 1989–; UK Delegn to Parly Assembly, CSCE, 1992–. Chm., Royal Lyceum Theatre Co., Edinburgh, 1984–87. Member: UK Sports Council, 1965–68; Scottish Sports Council, 1971–81. Governor, Scottish Sports Aid Foundn, 1981–90; Trustee, Scottish Internat. Educn Trust, 1984–. AAA 220 Yards Champion, 1964 and 1967; UK 100 Metres Record Holder, 1967–74; competed at Olympic Games, 1964 and Commonwealth Games, 1966; Captain, UK Athletics Team, 1965 and 1966. *Recreations:* all sports, reading, music, theatre. *Address:* c/o House of Commons, SW1A 0AA. *T:* 0171–219 4446. *Clubs:* Reform; Scottish Liberal (Edinburgh).

CAMPBELL, Hon. Sir (William) Anthony; Kt 1988; **Hon. Mr Justice Campbell;** a Judge of the High Court of Justice, Northern Ireland, since 1988; *b* 30 Oct. 1936; *s* of late H. E. Campbell and of Marion Wheeler; *m* 1960, Gail, *e d* of F. M. McKibbin; three *d*. *Educ:* Campbell Coll., Belfast; Queens' Coll., Cambridge. Called to the Bar, Gray's Inn, 1960; called to the Bar of NI, 1960 (Bencher, 1983; Chm., Exec. Council, 1985–87). Jun. Counsel to Attorney-Gen. for NI, 1971–74; QC (NI) 1974; Senior Crown Counsel in NI, 1984–88. Chm., Council of Legal Educn in NI, 1994–. Governor, Campbell Coll., 1976– (Chm., 1984–86); Mem. Council, St Leonards Sch., St Andrews, 1985–94. *Recreations:* sailing, hill walking. *Address:* Royal Courts of Justice, Belfast BT1 3JY. *Clubs:* New (Edinburgh); Royal Ulster Yacht.

See also J. E. P. Grigg.

CAMPBELL, Maj.-Gen. William Tait, CBE 1945 (OBE 1944); retired; *b* 8 Oct. 1912; *s* of late R. B. Campbell, MD, FRCPE, Edinburgh; *m* 1942, Rhoda Alice, *y d* of late Adm. Algernon Walker-Heneage-Vivian, CB, MVO, Swansea; two *d*. *Educ:* Cargilfield Sch.; Fettes Coll.; RMC Sandhurst. 2nd Lieut, The Royal Scots (The Royal Regt), 1933; served War of 1939–45: 1st Airborne Div. and 1st Allied Airborne Army (North Africa, Sicily, Italy and Europe). Lieut-Col Commanding 1st Bn The Royal Scots, in Egypt, Cyprus, UK and Suez Operation (despatches), 1954–57; Col, Royal Naval War Coll., Greenwich, 1958; Brig. i/c Admin. Malaya, 1962; Maj.-Gen., 1964; DQMG, MoD (Army Dept), 1964–67; Col, The Royal Scots (The Royal Regt), 1964–74. Dir, The Fairbridge Soc., 1969–78. US Bronze Star, 1945. *Recreations:* gardening, golf, shooting, fishing. *Address:* Ashwood, Boarhills, St Andrews, Fife KY16 8PR.

CAMPBELL-GRAY, family name of **Lord Gray.**

CAMPBELL-JOHNSON, Alan, CIE 1947; OBE 1946; Officer of US Legion of Merit, 1947; MA Oxon; FRSA, MRI; public relations consultant; *b* 16 July 1913; *o c* of late Lieut-Col James Alexander Campbell-Johnson and late Gladys Susanne Campbell-Johnson; *m* 1938, Imogen Fay de la Tour Dunlap; one *d* (one *s* decd). *Educ:* Westminster; Christ Church, Oxford (scholar). BA 2nd Cl. Hons Mod. Hist., 1935. Political Sec. to Rt Hon. Sir Archibald Sinclair, Leader of Parl. Lib. Party, 1937–40; served War of 1939–45, RAF; COHQ, 1942–43; HQ SACSEA (Wing Comdr i/c Inter-Allied Records Section), 1943–46. Contested (L) Salisbury and South Wilts. Div., Gen. Elections, 1945 and 1950. Press Attaché to Viceroy and Gov.-Gen. of India (Earl Mountbatten of Burma), 1947–48. Chm., Campbell-Johnson Ltd, Public Relations Consultants, 1953–78; Dir, Hill and Knowlton (UK) Ltd, 1976–85. Hon. Fellow Inst. of Public Relations, Pres. 1956–57. Hon. DLitt Southampton, 1990. *Publications:* Growing Opinions, 1935; Peace Offering, 1936; Anthony Eden: a biography, 1938, rev. edn 1955; Viscount Halifax: a biography, 1941; Mission with Mountbatten, 1951, repr. 1972. *Recreations:* watching cricket, listening to music. *Address:* 21 Ashley Gardens, Ambrosden Avenue, SW1P 1QD. *T:* 0171–834 1532. *Clubs:* Brooks's, National Liberal, MCC.

CAMPBELL-JOHNSTON, Very Rev. Michael Alexander Ninian, SJ; Provincial, British Province of the Society of Jesus, 1987–93; *b* 27 Sept. 1931; *s* of Ninian Campbell-Johnston and Marguerite Antoinette Shakespear. *Educ:* Beaumont College; Séminaire Les Fontaines, France (Lic Phil); LSE (BSc Econ, DipEd); Col. Max. Christi Regis, Mexico (STL). Dir, Guyana Inst. for Social Research and Action, 1967–75; Dir, Social Secretariat, Jesuit Generalate, Rome, 1975–84; Regional Co-ordinator, Jesuit Refugee Service for Mexico and Central America, El Salvador, 1984–87. Editor: Gisra; Promotio Justitiae. *Recreations:* reading, motorbike riding. *Address:* Apartado Postal 01-34, San Salvador, El Salvador. *T:* 981640, *Fax:* 981056.

CAMPBELL-ORDE, Sir John A.; *see* Orde.

CAMPBELL-PRESTON, Dame Frances (Olivia), DCVO 1990 (CVO 1977); Woman of the Bedchamber to HM Queen Elizabeth the Queen Mother, since 1965; *b* 2 Sept. 1918; *d* of Lt-Col Arthur Grenfell and Hilda Margaret Grenfell (*née* Lyttelton); *m* 1938, Lt-Col George Patrick Campbell-Preston (*d* 1960), The Black Watch; two *s* two *d*. *Educ:* St Paul's Girls' Sch. WRNS, 1941–43. Mem., Argyll CC, 1960–64; Chm., Children's Panel, Argyle and Argyll and Bute, 1970–80. *Address:* The Turret Cottage, Inverawe, Taynuilt, Argyll PA35 1HU.

CAMPBELL-PRESTON of Ardchattan, Robert Modan Thorne, OBE 1955; MC 1943; TD; DL; Vice-Lieutenant, Argyll and Bute, 1976–90; *b* 7 Jan. 1909; *s* of Colonel R. W. P. Campbell-Preston, DL, JP, of Ardchattan and Valleyfield, Fife, and Mary Augusta Thorne, MBE; *m* 1950, Hon. Angela Murray (*d* 1981), 3rd *d* of 2nd Viscount Cowdray and *widow* of Lt-Col George Anthony Murray, OBE, TD (killed in action, Italy, 1945); one *d*. *Educ:* Eton; Christ Church, Oxford (MA). Lt Scottish Horse, 1927; Lt-Col 1945. Hon. Col, Fife-Forfar Yeo./Scottish Horse, 1962–67. Member Royal Company of Archers, Queen's Body Guard for Scotland. Joint Managing Director, Alginate Industries Ltd, 1949–74. DL 1951, JP 1950, Argyllshire. Silver Star (USA), 1945. *Recreations:* shooting, fishing, gardening. *Address:* Ardchattan Priory, by Oban, Argyll PA37 1RQ. *T:* Bonawe (0163175) 274. *Club:* Puffin's (Edinburgh).

See also Duke of Atholl.

CAMPBELL-SAVOURS, Dale Norman; MP (Lab) Workington, Cumbria, since 1979; *b* 23 Aug. 1943; *s* of late John Lawrence and of Cynthia Lorraine Campbell-Savours; *m* 1970, Gudrun Kristin Runolfsdottir; three *s*. *Educ:* Keswick Sch.; Sorbonne, Paris. Dir, manufacturing co., 1969–77. Member, Ramsbottom UDC, 1972–73. Mem., TGWU and COHSE, 1970–. Contested (Lab): Darwen Division of Lancashire, gen. elections, Feb. 1974, Oct. 1974; Workington, by-election, 1976. *Address:* House of Commons, SW1A 0AA.

CAMPBELL-WHITE, Martin Andrew; Chief Executive, Harold Holt Ltd, since 1992; *b* 11 July 1943; *s* of John Vernon Campbell-White and Hilda Doris (*née* Ash); *m* 1969, Dr Margaret Mary Miles; three *s*. *Educ:* Dean Close Sch., Cheltenham; St John's Coll., Oxford; Univ. of Strasbourg. Thomas Skinner & Co. Ltd (Publishers), 1964–66; Ibbs & Tillett Ltd (Concert Agents), 1966–72, Dir, 1969–72; Harold Holt Ltd (Concert Agents), 1972–: Dir, 1973–; Dep. Chm., 1989–92. Chm., Brit. Assoc. of Concert Agents, 1978–81. Council Mem., London Sinfonietta, 1973–86; Dir, Chamber Orchestra of Europe, 1983–93; Mem. Bd, Première Ensemble, 1991–. Asst Dir, Fest. of German Arts, 1987; Founding Dir, Japan Fest. 1991, 1991. Trustee, Abbado Trust for Young Musicians, 1987–; Mem. Bd, Riverside Studios, 1988–. FRSA 1980. *Recreations:* tennis, watching cricket, classical music, travel. *Address:* c/o Harold Holt Ltd, 31 Sinclair Road, W14 0NS. *T:* 0171–603 4600. *Club:* MCC.

CAMPDEN, Viscount; Anthony Baptist Noel; *b* 16 Jan. 1950; *s* and *heir* of 5th Earl of Gainsborough, *qv*; *m* 1972, Sarah Rose, *er d* of Col T. F. C. Winnington; one *s*. *Educ:* Ampleforth; Royal Agricultural Coll., Cirencester. *Heir:* *s* Hon. Henry Robert Anthony Noel, *b* 1 July 1977. *Address:* Exton Park, Oakham, Rutland, Leics LE15 8AN. *T:* Oakham (01572) 812209; 105 Earls Court Road, W8 6QH. *T:* 0171–370 5650. *Clubs:* White's, Pratt's.

See also Sir F. S. W. Winnington, Bt.

CAMPION, Sir Harry, Kt 1957; CB 1949; CBE 1945; MA; retired as Director of Central Statistical Office, Cabinet Office, 1967; *b* 20 May 1905; *o s* of John Henry Campion, Worsley, Lancs. *Educ:* Farnworth Grammar Sch.; Univ. of Manchester. Rockefeller Foundation Fellow, United States, 1932; Robert Ottley Reader in Statistics, Univ. of Manchester, 1933–39. Dir. of Statistical Office, UN, 1946–47; Mem. of Statistical Commission, United Nations, 1947–67; Pres.: International Statistical Institute, 1963–67; Royal Statistical Society, 1957–59; Hon. LLD, Manchester, 1967. *Publications:* Distribution of National Capital; Public and Private Property in Great Britain; articles in economic and statistical journals. *Address:* Rima, Priory Close, Stanmore, Mddx HA7 3HW. *T:* 0181–954 3267. *Club:* Reform.

CAMPION, Peter James, DPhil; FInstP; technical consultant; *b* 7 April 1926; *s* of Frank Wallace Campion and Gertrude Alice (*née* Lambert); *m* 1950, Beryl Grace Stanton, *e d* of John and Grace Stanton; one *s* one *d* (and one *s* decd). *Educ:* Westcliff High Sch., Essex; Exeter Coll., Oxford (MA, DPhil). FInstP 1964. RNVR, 1943. Nuffield Res. Fellow, Oxford, 1954; Chalk River Proj., Atomic Energy of Canada Ltd, 1955; National Physical Lab., Teddington, 1960–86: Supt, Div. of Radiation Science, 1964; Supt, Div. of Mech. and Optical Metrology, 1974; Dep. Dir, 1976. Mem., Comité Consultatif pour les Etalons de Mesure des Rayonnements Ionisante, 1963–79; Chm., Sect. II, reconstituted Comité Consultatif, Mesure des radionucléides, 1970–79; Mem., NACCB, 1984–86. Editor, Internat. Jl of Applied Radiation and Isotopes, 1968–71. *Publications:* A Code of Practice for the Detailed Statement of Accuracy (with A. Williams and J. E. Burns), 1973; technical and rev. papers in learned jls on neutron capture gamma rays, measurement of radioactivity, and on metrology generally. *Recreation:* winemaking and wine drinking.

CAMPLING, Very Rev. Christopher Russell; Dean of Ripon, 1984–95; *b* 4 July 1925; *s* of Canon William Charles Campling; *m* 1953, Juliet Marian Hughes; one *s* two *d*. *Educ:* Lancing Coll.; St Edmund Hall, Oxford (MA; Hons Theol. cl. 2); Cuddesdon Theol. Coll. RNVR, 1943–47. Deacon 1951, priest 1952; Curate of Basingstoke, 1951–55; Minor Canon of Ely Cathedral and Chaplain of King's School, Ely, 1955–60; Chaplain of Lancing Coll., 1960–67; Vicar of Pershore with Pinvin and Wick and Birlingham, 1968–76; RD of Pershore, 1970–76; Archdeacon of Dudley and Director of Religious Education, Diocese of Worcester, 1976–84. Mem., General Synod of Church of England, 1970–95; Chm., House of Clergy, Diocese of Worcester, 1981–84; Chm., Council for the Care of Churches, 1988–94. Lectr, Leeds Parish Church, 1988–. *Publications:* The Way, The Truth and The Life: Vol. 1, The Love of God in Action, 1964; Vol. 2, The People of God in Action, 1964; Vol. 3, The Word of God in Action, 1965; Vol. 4, God's Plan in Action, 1965; also two teachers' volumes; Words of Worship, 1969; The Fourth Lesson, Vol. 1 1973, Vol. 2 1974. *Recreations:* music, drama, golf. *Address:* Pebble Ridge, Aglaia Road, Worthing, West Sussex. *Club:* Naval.

CAMPORA, Dr Mario; Argentine Ambassador to the Court of St James's, 1990–94; *b* 3 Aug. 1930; *m* 1972, Magdalena Teresa María Díaz Gavier; one *s* two *d*. *Educ:* Nat. Univ. of Rosario, Argentina (Dr in Diplomacy). Argentine Foreign Service, 1955–71 and 1973–75; Internat. Orgns Dept, Foreign Policy Bureau, and Legal Dept, Ministry for Foreign Affairs; has served in Geneva, Washington, The Hague, New Delhi, and as deleg. to UN and OAS; Mem., Justicialist Party, active in politics, 1971–73, 1975–; Ambassador Extraordinary, Argentine Special Mission for Disarmament, Geneva, 1985; Sec. of State, Ministry for Foreign Affairs, 1989–90. *Publications:* articles on foreign policy and international relations. *Address:* c/o Ministry of Foriegn Affairs, Reconquista 1088, 1003 Buenos Aires, Argentina.

CAMPOS, Prof. Christophe Lucien, OBE 1994; Director, British Institute in Paris, since 1978; *b* 27 April 1938; *s* of Lucien Antoine Campos and Margaret Lilian (*née* Dunn); *m* 1977, Lucy Elizabeth Mitchell; one *s* four *d*. *Educ:* Lycée Lamoricière, Oran; Lycée Français de Londres; Lycée Henri IV, Paris; Gonville and Caius Coll., Cambridge. LèsL

(Paris), PhD (Cantab). Lector in French, Gonville and Caius Coll., 1959; Lecturer in French: Univ. of Maryland, 1963; Univ. of Sussex, 1964; Lectr in English, Univ. i Oslo, 1969; Prof. of French, University Coll., Dublin, 1974. Gen. Editor, Franco-British Studies, 1988–. Chevalier de l'Ordre des Arts et des Lettres (France), 1988. *Publications:* The View of France, 1964; L'Enseignement de la civilisation française, 1988; contribs to Th. Qly, TLS, Univs Qly, Franco-British Studies. *Recreations:* bees, football, gastronomy, navigation. *Address:* 53 Houndean Rise, Lewes, Sussex BN7 1EH; L'Hocherie, Saint-Gervais-les-trois-clochers, Vienne, France.

CAMPOS, Roberto de Oliveira, Hon. GCVO 1976; Deputy, Rio de Janeiro, House of Congress, Brazil; *b* Cuiabá, Mato Grosso, 17 April 1917. *Educ:* Catholic Seminaries: Guaxupé and Belo Horizonte, Brazil (grad. Philosophy and Theol.); George Washington Univ., Washington (MA Econs); Columbia Univ., NYC (Hon. Dr). Entered Brazilian Foreign Service, 1939; Economic Counsellor, Brazil-US EDC, 1951–53; Dir 1952, Gen. Man. 1955, Pres. 1959, Nat. Economic Develt Bank; Sec. Gen., Nat. Develt Council, 1956–59; Delegate to internat. confs, incl. ECOSOC and GATT, 1959–61; Roving Ambassador for financial negotiations in W Europe, 1961; Ambassador of Brazil to US, 1961–63; Minister of State for Planning and Co-ord., 1964–67; Ambassador to UK, 1975–82; Senator, House of Congress, Brazil, 1982. Prof., Sch. of Econs, Univ. of Brazil, 1956–61. Mem. or past Mem., Cttees and Bds on economic devclt (particularly inter-Amer. econ. develt). *Publications:* Ensaios de História Econômica e Sociologia; Economia, Planejamento e Nacionalismo; A Moeda, o Govêrno e o Tempo; A Técnica e o Riso; Reflections on Latin American Development; Do outro lado da cerca; Temas e Sistemas; Ensaios contra a maré; Política Econômica e Mitos Políticos (jtly); Trends in International Trade (GATT report); Partners in Progress (report of Pearson Cttee of World Bank); A Nova Economia Brasileira; Formas Criativas do Desenvolvimento Brasileiro; Omundo que vejo e não desejo; Reflexões do Crepúsculo; O Século Esquisito; Guia Para os Perplexos; Ensaios Imprudentes; Além do Cotidiano; techn. articles and reports on develt and internat. econs, in jls. *Address:* House of Congress, Praça dos Tres Poderes, 70160 Brasilia DF, Brazil; Rua Francisco Otaviano 140, Ipanema 22080, Rio de Janeiro, Brazil.

CAMPS, William Anthony; Master of Pembroke College, Cambridge, 1970–81; *b* 28 Dec. 1910; *s* of P. W. L. Camps, FRCS, and Alice, *d* of Joseph Redfern, Matlock; *m* 1953, Miriam Camp, Washington, DC, *d* of Prof. Burton Camp, Wesleyan Univ., Connecticut. *Educ:* Marlborough Coll.; Pembroke Coll., Cambridge (Schol.). Fellow, Pembroke Coll., 1933; Univ. Lectr in Classics, 1939; Temp. Civil Servant, 1940–45; Asst Tutor, Pembroke Coll., 1945; Senior Tutor, 1947–62; Tutor for Advanced Students, 1963–70; Pres., 1964–70. Mem., Inst. for Advanced Study, Princeton, 1956–57; Vis. Assoc. Prof., UC Toronto, 1966; Vis. Prof., Univ. of North Carolina at Chapel Hill, 1969. *Publications:* edns of Propertius I, 1961, IV, 1965, III, 1966, II, 1967; An Introduction to Virgil's Aeneid, 1969; An Introduction to Homer, 1980; sundry notes and reviews in classical periodicals. *Recreations:* unremarkable. *Address:* c/o Pembroke College, Cambridge CB2 1RF. *T:* Cambridge (01223) 338100.

CAMRE, Henning Niels Juel; Director, National Film and Television School, since 1992; *b* 15 Nov. 1938; *s* of Sigfred N. J. Camre and Carna (*née* Petersen); *m* 1st, 1967, Merete Friis (marr. diss.); one *d*; 2nd, 1978, Janne Giese (marr. diss.); one *d* and one adopted *d*; partner, Regitze Oppenhejm. *Educ:* Univ. of Copenhagen; Nat. Film Sch. of Denmark (Dip. in Cinematography). Dir of Photography (feature and documentary film), 1968–88; Dir, Nat. Film Sch. of Denmark, 1975–92. Chairman: Nordic Film Council, 1979–89; Danish State Film Studio, 1989–92; Centre International de Liaison des Ecoles de Cinéma et de Télévision: Mem., Exec. Council, 1980–86; Chm., Programme for Developing Countries, 1982–; Vice-Pres., 1986–. Chevalier de l'Ordre des Arts et des Lettres (France), 1990. *Publications:* Bridging the Gap, 1982; Film and Television Training in Indonesia, 1985; Asia-Pacific Film and Television Schools, 1991. *Recreation:* cycling. *Address:* 11 King Henry's Road, NW3 3QP. *T:* 0171–722 1133.

CAMROSE, Viscountcy of (*cr* 1941, of Hackwood Park); title disclaimed by 3rd Viscount (see under Baron Hartwell).

CANADA, Primate of All; *see* Peers, Most Rev. M. G.

CANADA, Primate of; *see* Quebec, Archbishop of, (RC).

CANADA, Metropolitan of the Ecclesiastical Province of; *see* Newfoundland, Western, Archbishop of.

CANAVAN, Dennis Andrew; MP (Lab) Falkirk West, since 1983 (West Stirlingshire, Oct. 1974–1983); *b* 8 Aug. 1942; *s* of Thomas and Agnes Canavan. *Educ:* St Columba's High Sch., Cowdenbeath; Edinburgh Univ. (BSc Hons, DipEd). Head of Maths Dept, St Modan's High Sch., Stirling, 1970–74; Asst Head, Holy Rood High Sch., Edinburgh, 1974. District Councillor, 1973–74; Leader of Labour Gp, Stirling District Council, 1974; Member: Stirling Dist Educn Sub-cttee, 1973–74; Stirlingshire Youth Employment Adv. Cttee, 1972–74. Sec., W Stirlingshire Constituency Labour Party, 1972–74; Labour Party Agent, Feb. 1974; Treasurer, Scottish Parly Lab. Gp, 1976–79, Vice-Chm., 1979–80, Chm., 1980–81. Sponsored by UNISON; Parly spokesman for Scottish Cttee on mobility for the disabled, 1977–; Mem., H of C Select Cttee on For. Affairs, 1982–; Chair: PLP NI Cttee, 1989–; Parly Br, EIS, 1983–; Founder and Convener, All-Party Parly Scottish Sports Gp, 1987–. *Publications:* contribs to various jls on educn and politics. *Recreations:* hill walking, marathon running, swimming, reading, football (Scottish Univs football internationalist, 1966–67 and 1967–68; Hon. Pres., Milton Amateurs FC). *Address:* Ardsonas, Sauchieburn, Bannockburn, Stirlingshire FK7 9PZ. *T:* Bannockburn (01786) 812581; House of Commons, SW1A 0AA. *T:* 0171–219 3000. *Clubs:* Bannockburn Miners' Welfare (Bannockburn); Camelon Labour (Falkirk).

CANAVAN, Vincent Joseph; Sheriff of South Strathclyde, Dumfries and Galloway at Hamilton, since 1987; *b* 13 Dec. 1946; *s* of James Canavan and Catherine Ludivine Brogan; *m* 1973, Mary Allison; three *s* three *d*. *Educ:* St Aloysius Coll., Glasgow; Univ. of Glasgow (LLB Hons 1968). Qualified as Solicitor, 1970; passed Advocate, 1980. Mem., Victim Support (Scotland) Hamilton Court Project Working Party, 1990–94. Chm., Lanarks Br., Scottish Assoc. for Study of Delinquency, 1992–95 (Vice-Chm., 1991–92). *Recreations:* reading history, Italian cuisine, visiting art exhibitions. *Address:* Sheriff Court, Almada Street, Hamilton, Lanarks ML3 0HF. *Club:* Edinburgh University Staff.

CANBERRA AND GOULBURN, Archbishop of, (RC), since 1983; **Most Rev. Francis Patrick Carroll;** *b* 9 Sept. 1930; *s* of P. Carroll. *Educ:* De La Salle Coll., Marrickville; St Columba's Coll., Springwood; St Patrick's Coll., Manly; Pontifical Urban Univ. De Propaganda Fide. Ordained priest, 1954; Asst Priest, Griffith, NSW, 1955–59; Asst Inspector of Catholic Schs, dio. of Wagga, 1957–61; Asst Priest, Albury, 1959–61; Bishop's Sec., Diocesan Chancellor, Diocesan Dir of Catholic Educn, 1965–67; consecrated Co-Adjutor Bishop, 1967; Bishop of Wagga Wagga, 1968–83. Chm., Nat. Catholic Educn Commn, 1974–78; Mem., Internat. Catechetical Council, Rome, 1974–93. Hon. DLitt Charles Sturt Univ., NSW, 1994. *Publication:* The Development of Episcopal Conferences, 1965. *Address:* Archbishop's House, GPO Box 89, Canberra, ACT 2601, Australia.

CANBERRA AND GOULBURN, Bishop of, since 1993; **Rt. Rev. George Victor Browning;** *b* 28 Sept. 1942; *s* of John and Barbara Browning; *m* 1965, Margaret Rowland; three *s*. *Educ:* Ardingly Coll.; Lewes County Grammar Sch., Sussex; St John's Coll., Morpeth, NSW (ThL 1st cl. Hons 1965). Curate: Inverell, 1966–68; Armidale, 1968–69; Vicar, Warialda, 1969–73; Vice Warden and Lectr in Old Testament Studies and Pastoral Theol., St John's Coll., Morpeth, 1973–75 (Acting Warden, 1974); Rector of Singleton, Rural Dean and Archdeacon of the Upper Hunter, 1976–84; Rector of Woy Woy and Archdeacon of the Central Coast, 1984–85; Bishop of the Northern Reg., Brisbane, 1985–92; Principal, St Francis' Theol Coll., 1988–92; Bishop of the Coastal Reg., and Asst Bishop, dio. of Brisbane, 1992–93. *Recreations:* reading, running (anything that presents a challenge). *Address:* 51 Rosenthal Street, Campbell, Canberra, ACT 2601, Australia. *T:* (62) 480716, 480811, *Fax:* (62) 476829.

CANDELA OUTERINO, Felix; engineer and architect; Professor, Escuela Nacional de Arquitectura, University of Mexico, since 1953 (on leave of absence); *b* Madrid, 27 Jan. 1910; *s* of Felix and Julia Candela; *m* 1940, Eladia Martin Galan (*d* 1964); four *d*; *m* 1967, Dorothy H. Davies. *Educ:* Univ. of Madrid, Spain. Architect, Escuela Superior de Arquitectura de Madrid, 1935. Captain of Engineers, Republican Army, Spanish Civil War, 1936–39. Emigrated to Mexico, 1939; Mexican Citizen, 1941; USA citizen, 1978. General practice in Mexico as Architect and Contractor. Founded (with brother Antonio) Cubiertas ALA, SA, firm specializing in design and construction of reinforced concrete shell structures. Work includes Sports Palace for Mexico Olympics, 1968. Founding Mem., Internat. Acad. of Architecture, Sofia, 1986; Hon. Member: Sociedad de Arquitectos Colombianos, 1956; Sociedad Venezolana de Arquitectos, 1961; International Assoc. for Shell Structures, 1962; Acad. de Arquitectura de Mexico, 1983. Charles Elliot Norton Prof. of Poetry, Harvard Univ., for academic year, 1961–62; Jefferson Meml Prof., Univ. of Virginia, 1966; Andrew D. White Prof., Cornell Univ., 1969–74; Prof., Dept of Architecture, Univ. of Illinois at Chicago, 1971–78; Prof. Honorario: Escuela Tecnica Superior de Arquitectura de Madrid, 1969; Univ. Nacional Federico Villareal, Peru, 1977; William Hoffman Wood Prof., Leeds Univ., 1974–75. Gold Medal, Instn Structural Engineers, England, 1961; Auguste Perret Prize of International Union of Architects, 1961; Alfred E. Lindau Award, Amer. Concrete Inst., 1965; Silver Medal, Acad. d'Architecture, Paris, 1980; Gold Medal, Consejo Superior de Arquitectos de España, 1981; Silver Medal, Union des Architects Bulgares, 1983; Gold Medal, Premio Antonio Camuñas, Madrid, 1985. Hon. Fellow American Inst. of Architects, 1963; Hon. Corr. Mem., RIBA, 1963; Plomada de Oro, Soc. de Arquitectos Mexicanos, 1963; Doctor in Fine Arts (*hc*): Univ. of New Mexico, 1964; Univ. of Illinois, 1979; Dr Ing *hc* Univ. de Santa Maria, Caracas, 1968; Dr *hc*: Univ. of Sevilla, Spain, 1990; Univ. Politécnica of Madrid, Spain, 1994. Order of Civil Merit, Spain, 1978. *Publications:* En Defensa del Formalismo, 1985; several articles in architectural and engineering magazines all around the world; *relevant publication:* Candela, the Shell Builder, by Colin Faber, 1963. *Address:* 6109 Bayberry Lane, Raleigh, NC 27612, USA. *T:* (919) 8483303, *Fax:* (919) 6762498; Avenida America 14–7, Madrid 2, Spain. *T:* 3560096, *Fax:* 2556365.

CANDLIN, Prof. Christopher Noel; Professor and Chairman of Linguistics Department, Macquarie University, Sydney, Australia, since 1987; Executive Director, National Centre for English Language Teaching and Research, since 1988 and Director, Centre for Language in Social Life, since 1993, Macquarie University; *b* 31 March 1940; *s* of Edwin Frank Candlin and Nora Candlin (*née* Letts); *m* 1964, Sally (*née* Carter); one *s* three *d*. *Educ:* Jesus Coll., Oxford (MA); Univ. of London (PGCE); Yale Univ. (MPhil). Research Associate, Univ. of Leeds, 1967–68; University of Lancaster: Lectr, 1968, later Sen. Lectr; Prof. of Linguistics and Modern English Language, 1981–87. Visiting Professor: Univ. of Giessen, 1975; Ontario Inst. for Studies in Educn, Toronto, 1983; East–West Centre, Honolulu, 1978; Univ. of Hawaii at Manoa, 1984; Univ. of Melbourne, 1985; Jyväskylä Univ., Finland, 1993; Univ. of Wales, Cardiff, 1995. FRSA. General Editor: Applied Linguistics and Language Study; Language in Social Life; Language Teacher Educn Scheme; Language Teaching Methodology Series. *Publications:* Challenges, 1978; The Communicative Teaching of English, 1981; Computers in English Language Teaching and Research, 1985; Language Learning Tasks, 1986; Language, Learning and Community, 1989; English at Work, vol. 1, 1991, vol. 2, 1992; Australian Learners' Dictionary, 1993. *Recreations:* theatre, concerts, sailing, cooking. *Address:* School of English, Linguistics and Media, Macquarie University, Sydney, NSW 2109, Australia.

CANDLISH, Thomas Tait, FEng 1980; Chairman, Historic Cars Ltd, since 1988; consultant, construction industry, since 1989; *b* 26 Nov. 1926; *s* of John Candlish and Elizabeth (*née* Tait); *m* 1964, Mary Trinkwon; two *s*. *Educ:* Perth Acad.; Glasgow Univ. (BSc Eng). FICE 1971. Served RE, 1946–49 (commnd). Student Engr, George Wimpey & Co. Ltd, 1944–46; rejoined Wimpey, 1951; served in: Borneo, 1951–54; Papua New Guinea, 1955–57; Arabian Gulf area, 1958–62; W Africa, 1962–65; Director: George Wimpey PLC, 1973–85 (Man. Dir, 1978–85); Wimpey Internat., 1973–85 (Chm., 1979–85); Wimpey ME & C, 1973–85; Wimpey Marine Ltd, 1975–85 (Chm., 1979–85); Brown & Root-Wimpey Highlands Fabricators, 1974–89 (Chm., 1981–86); British Smelter Constructions Ltd, 1977–83 (Chm., 1977–83); Hill Samuel Developments, 1978–85; A & P Appledore Holdings, 1979–85; Brown & Root (UK) Ltd, 1985–89; Chm., Howard Humphreys Gp Ltd, 1987–89. Chm., Export Gp for Constructional Industries, 1983–85; Member: EDC for Civil Engrg, 1979–82; British Overseas Trade Bd, 1984–87. *Recreations:* motor sport, ski-ing, golf. *Address:* Tithe Cottage, Dorney Wood Road, Burnham, Bucks SL1 8EQ. *Club:* Royal Automobile.

CANDY, Elizabeth Mary; Head Mistress, The Lady Eleanor Holles School, Hampton, since 1981; *b* 12 Oct. 1942; *d* of late Donald Glen Candy and of Phyllis Mary Candy (*née* Denbury). *Educ:* Merrywood Grammar Sch., Bristol; Westfield Coll., London (BSc 1965). Chemistry Mistress then Jt Head of Science, Bromley High Sch., 1965–71; Head of Science then Second Mistress, Putney High Sch., 1971–81. FRSA 1994. *Recreations:* opera, reading, France and French wine, photography, cycling, tennis, golf. *Address:* The Lady Eleanor Holles School, Hanworth Road, Hampton, Middx TW12 3HF. *T:* 0181–979 1601. *Club:* Cripplegate Ward.

CANE, Prof. Violet Rosina; Professor of Mathematical Statistics, University of Manchester, 1971–81, now Emeritus; *b* 31 Jan. 1916; *d* of Tubal George Cane and Annie Louisa Lansdell. *Educ:* Newnham Coll., Cambridge (MA, Dipl. in Math. Stats). BoT, 1940; Univ. of Aberdeen, 1941; FO, 1942; Min. of Town and Country Planning, 1946; Statistician to MRC Applied Psychol. Unit, 1948; Queen Mary Coll., London, 1955; Fellow, Newnham Coll., Cambridge, 1957; Lectr, Univ. of Cambridge, 1960. Mem., UGC, 1974–79. Mem., Cambridge CC, 1965–72, 1982–90. Hon. MSc Manchester, 1974. *Publications:* (contrib.) Current Problems in Animal Behaviour, 1961; (contrib.) Perspectives in Probability and Statistics, 1975; papers in Jl of Royal Stat. Soc., Animal Behaviour, and psychol jls. *Recreation:* supporting old houses. *Address:* 13/14 Little St Mary's Lane, Cambridge CB2 1RR. *T:* Cambridge (01223) 357277; Statistical Laboratory, University of Cambridge, 16 Mill Lane, Cambridge CB2 1SB.

CANET, Maj.-Gen. Lawrence George, CB 1964; CBE 1956; BE; Master General of the Ordnance, Australia, 1964–67, retired; *b* 1 Dec. 1910; *s* of late Albert Canet, Melbourne,

Victoria; *m* 1940, Mary Elizabeth Clift, *d* of Cecil Clift Jones, Geelong, Victoria; one *s*. *Educ:* RMC Duntroon; Sydney Univ. (BE). Served War of 1939–45 with 7th Australian Div. (Middle East and Pacific). GOC Southern Command, 1960–64. Brigadier 1953; Maj.-Gen. 1957. *Address:* 37 The Corso, Isle of Capri, Surfers Paradise, Qld 4217, Australia.

CANHAM, Paul George, LVO 1991; JP; Official Secretary to Governor-General of New Zealand, 1985–90; *b* 25 Oct. 1933; *s* of George Ernest Canham and Ella Mary (*née* Mackenzie); *m* 1964, Diane Alderton; one *s* one *d*. *Educ:* Timaru Boys' High Sch.; Victoria Univ. of Wellington (BA, MA Hons History). Teacher: Pomfret Sch., Conn., 1957; Matamata Coll., NZ, 1960; Hauraki Plains Coll., 1967; Heretaunga Coll., 1969; Dep. Prin., Hutt Valley High Sch., 1973; Prin., Wanganui High Sch., 1979. JP Hawkes Bay, 1991. *Recreations:* bridge, golf. *Address:* 59C Avondale Road, Taradale, Hawkes Bay, New Zealand. *T:* (6) 8445823.

CANN, Charles Richard; Deputy Secretary, Ministry of Agriculture, Fisheries and Food, since 1991; *b* 3 Feb. 1937; *s* of Charles Alfred Cann and Grace Elizabeth Cann; *m* 1979, Denise Ann Margaret Love; two *s*. *Educ:* Merchant Taylors' Sch., Northwood, Mddx; St John's Coll., Cambridge (MA). Asst Principal, MAFF, 1960, Principal 1965; Cabinet Office, 1969–71; Asst Sec., MAFF, 1971; Under Sec., 1981; Fisheries Sec., MAFF, 1987–91. *Address:* c/o Ministry of Agriculture, Fisheries and Food, Whitehall Place East, SW1A 2HH.

CANN, James Charles; MP (Lab) Ipswich, since 1992; *b* 28 June 1946; *s* of Charles George Cann and Brenda Julia Cann; *m* 1970, Rosemary Lovitt; two *s*. *Educ:* Barton on Humber Grammar Sch.; Kesteven Coll. of Education. Schoolteacher, 1967–92; Dep. Head, Handford Hall Primary Sch., Ipswich, 1981–92. Leader, Ipswich Council, 1979–91. *Recreations:* snooker, squash, badminton, walking, reading, history. *Address:* 79 Woodbridge Road East, Ipswich IP4 5QL. *T:* Ipswich (01473) 726670. *Clubs:* various Ipswich sports and social.

CANN, Prof. Johnson Robin, ScD; FRS 1995; Professor of Earth Sciences, University of Leeds, since 1989; *b* 18 Oct. 1937; *er s* of Johnson Ralph Cann and (Ethel) Mary (*née* Northmore); *m* 1963, Janet (*d* 1994), *d* of late Prof. Charles John Hamson, QC; two *s*. *Educ:* St Alban's Sch.; St John's Coll., Cambridge (MA, PhD, ScD). Research fellow, St John's Coll., 1962–66; post-doctoral work in Depts of Mineralogy and Petrology, and Geodesy and Geophysics, Cambridge, 1962–66; Dept of Mineralogy, British Museum (Natural History), 1966–68; Lectr, then Reader, School of Environmental Sciences, Univ. of East Anglia, 1968–77; J. B. Simpson Prof. of Geology, Univ. of Newcastle upon Tyne, 1977–89; current research in hot springs of mid-ocean ridges, seafloor volcanoes, rocks of ocean floor, creation of oceanic crust, obsidian in archaeology. Member, then Chm., ocean crust panel, 1975–78, UK rep. on planning cttee, 1978–84, Jt Oceanographic Instns for Deep Earth Sampling; co-chief scientist on Glomar Challenger, 1976 and 1979; Adjunct Scientist, Woods Hole Oceanographic Instn, 1987–; Chief Scientist, British Mid-Ocean Ridge Initiative, 1992–. Chm., UK Ocean Drilling Program Grants Cttee, 1987–90. Mem., UGC physical sciences sub-cttee, 1982–88. Murchison Medal, Geol Soc. of London, 1990. *Publications:* papers in jls of earth science and archaeology. *Recreations:* gathering, music, local politics. *Address:* Department of Earth Sciences, University of Leeds, Leeds LS2 9JT. *T:* Leeds (0113) 2335200.

CANNADINE, Prof. David Nicholas, DPhil, LittD; FRHistS; Moore Collegiate Professor of History, Columbia University, since 1992 (Professor of History, 1988–92); *b* 7 Sept. 1950; *s* of Sydney Douglas Cannadine and Dorothy Mary Cannadine (*née* Hughes); *m* 1982, Linda Jane Colley, *qv*; one *d* decd. *Educ:* King Edward's Five Ways Sch., Birmingham; Clare Coll., Cambridge (schol.; BA 1st cl. Hons 1972; MA 1975; LittD 1993); Princeton Univ. (Jane Eliza Procter Vis. Fellow); St John's Coll., Oxford (Sen. Schol.; DPhil 1975). FRHistS 1981. Cambridge University: Res. Fellow, St John's Coll., 1975–77; Asst Lectr, 1976–80, Lectr, 1980–88, in Hist.; Christ's College: Fellow, 1977–88; Dir of Studies in Hist., 1977–83; Tutor, 1979–81. Vis. Mem., Inst. for Advanced Study, Princeton, 1980–81; Vis. Prof., Birkbeck Coll., London Univ., 1995–; Vis. Fellow, Whitney Humanities Center, Yale Univ., 1995–. Lectures: first Leonard Hastings Schoff, Columbia Univ., 1993; Hayes Robinson, RHC, 1994. Fellow: Berkeley Coll., Yale Univ., 1985; ACLS, 1990–91; J. P. Morgan Liby, NY, 1992. Regular broadcaster on wireless and television. Gov., Ipswich Sch., 1982–88. General Editor: Studies in Modern Hist., 1979–; Penguin Hist. of Britain, 1989–; Penguin Hist. of Europe, 1991–; Member, Editorial Board: Urban Hist. Yearbook, 1979–83; Past and Present, 1983–; Midland Hist., 1985–88; Twentieth Century British Hist., 1990–; Rural Hist., 1995–. T. S. Ashton Prize, Econ. Hist. Soc., 1977. Silver Jubilee Prize, Agricl Hist. Soc., 1977. *Publications:* Lords and Landlords: the aristocracy and the towns 1774–1967, 1980; (ed and contrib.) Patricians, Power and Politics in Nineteenth-Century Towns, 1982; (ed jtly and contrib.) H. J. Dyos, Exploring the Urban Past, 1982; (ed jtly and contrib.) Rituals of Royalty: power and ceremonial in traditional societies, 1987; The Pleasures of the Past, 1989; (ed and contrib.) Winston Churchill's Famous Speeches, 1989; (ed jtly and contrib.) The First Modern Society: essays in English history in honour of Lawrence Stone, 1989; The Decline and Fall of the British Aristocracy (Lionel Trilling Prize), 1990; G. M. Trevelyan: a life in history, 1992; Aspects of Aristocracy: grandeur and decline in modern Britain, 1994; (ed jtly and contrib.) History and Biography: essays in honour of Derek Beales, 1996; numerous contribs to other books and learned jls. *Recreations:* life, laughter. *Address:* Department of History, Columbia University, New York, NY 10027, USA. *T:* (212) 8544646; c/o Curtis Brown, Haymarket House, 28–29 Haymarket, SW1Y 4SP. *T:* 0171–396 6600. *Club:* Century (New York).

CANNAN, Denis; dramatist and script writer; *b* 14 May 1919; *s* of late Captain H. J. Pullein-Thompson, MC, and late Joanna Pullein-Thompson (*née* Cannan); *m* 1st, 1946, Joan Ross (marr. diss.); two *s* one *d*; 2nd, 1965, Rose Evansky; he changed name to Denis Cannan, by deed poll, 1964. *Educ:* Eton. A Repertory factotum, 1937–39. Served War of 1939–45, Queen's Royal Regt, Captain (despatches). Actor at Citizens' Theatre, Glasgow, 1946–48. *Publications: plays:* Max (prod. Malvern Festival), 1949; Captain Carvallo (Bristol Old Vic and St James's Theatres), 1950; Colombe (trans. from Anouilh), New Theatre, 1951; Misery Me!, Duchess, 1955; You and Your Wife, Bristol Old Vic, 1955; The Power and The Glory (adaptation from Graham Greene), Phoenix Theatre, 1956, and Phœnix Theatre, New York, 1958; Who's Your Father?, Cambridge Theatre, 1958; US (original text), Aldwych, 1966; adapted Ibsen's Ghosts, Aldwych, 1966; One at Night, Royal Court, 1971; The Ik (adaptation and collaboration), 1975; Dear Daddy, Oxford Festival and Ambassadors, 1976 (Play of the Year award, 1976); the screenplays of several films; plays for TV and radio, adaptations for TV series. *Address:* 43 Osmond Road, Hove, Sussex BN3 1TF.

See also D. L. A. Farr, J. M. W. Pullein-Thompson.

CANNELL, Prof. Robert Quirk; Director, Virginia Agricultural Experiment Station and Associate Dean for Research, Virginia Polytechnic Institute and State University, since 1994; *b* 20 March 1937; *s* of William Watterson Cannell and Norah Isabel Corjeag; *m* 1962, Edwina Anne Thornborough; two *s*. *Educ:* King's Coll., Newcastle upon Tyne; Univ. of Durham (BSc, PhD). FIBiol 1986. Shell Chemical Co., London, 1959; School of Agriculture, Univ. of Newcastle upon Tyne, 1961; Dept of Agronomy and Plant Genetics, Univ. of Minnesota, 1968–69; Letcombe Lab., AFRC, Oxon, 1970; Dir, Welsh Plant Breeding Station, Aberystwyth, 1984–87; Head of Crop and Soil Envmtl Scis Dept, Virginia Polytech. Inst. and State Univ., 1987–94. *Publications:* papers in agricultural science jls. *Address:* College of Agriculture and Life Sciences, Virginia Polytechnic Institute and State University, Blacksburg, VA 24061, USA. *T:* (703) 2316305. *Club:* Farmers.

CANNING, family name of **Baron Garvagh.**

CANNON, Prof. John Ashton, CBE 1985; PhD; Professor of Modern History, University of Newcastle upon Tyne, 1976–92, now Professor Emeritus; Pro-Vice Chancellor, 1983–86; *b* 8 Oct. 1926; *s* of George and Gladys Cannon; *m* 1st, 1948, Audrey Elizabeth, *d* of G. R. Caple (marr. diss. 1953); one *s* one *d*; 2nd, 1953, Minna, *d* of Frederick Pedersen, Denmark; one *s* two *d*. *Educ:* Hertford Grammar Sch.; Peterhouse, Cambridge (MA 1955). PhD Bristol, 1958. Served RAF, 1947–49 and 1952–55. History of Parlt Trust, 1960–61; Univ. of Bristol: Lectr, 1961; Sen. Lectr, 1967; Reader, 1970; Dean, Faculty of Arts, Univ. of Newcastle upon Tyne, 1979–82. Member: UGC, 1983–89 (Vice-Chm., 1986–89; Chm., Arts Sub-Cttee, 1983–89); Open Univ. Vis. Cttee, 1988–92. Lectures: Wiles, Queen's Univ. Belfast, 1982; Raleigh, British Acad., 1982; Prothero, RHistS, 1985; Stenton, Reading Univ., 1986. Chm., Radio Bristol, 1970–74. FRHistS 1980; FRSA 1990. *Publications:* The Fox-North Coalition: crisis of the constitution, 1970; Parliamentary Reform, 1640–1832, 1973; (ed with P. V. McGrath) Essays in Bristol and Gloucestershire History, 1976; (ed) The Letters of Junius, 1978; (ed) The Historian at Work, 1980; (ed) The Whig Ascendancy, 1981; Aristocratic Century, 1984; (ed jtly) The Blackwell Dictionary of Historians, 1988; (with R. Griffiths) The Oxford Illustrated History of the British Monarchy, 1988; Samuel Johnson and the politics of Hanoverian England, 1994. *Recreations:* music, losing at tennis. *Address:* 35a Osborne Road, Jesmond, Newcastle upon Tyne NE2 2AH. *T:* Tyneside (0191) 2814096.

CANNON, John Francis Michael; Keeper of Botany, Natural History Museum (formerly British Museum (Natural History)), 1978–90; *b* 22 April 1930; *s* of Francis Leslie Cannon and Aileen Flora Cannon; *m* 1954, Margaret Joy (*née* Herbert); two *s* one *d*. *Educ:* Whitgift Sch., South Croydon, Surrey; King's Coll., Newcastle upon Tyne, Univ. of Durham (BSc 1st Cl. Hons Botany). Dept of Botany, British Museum (Nat. History), 1952, Dep. Keeper 1972. President: Botanical Soc. of the British Isles, 1983–85; Ray Soc., 1986–88. *Publications:* papers in scientific periodicals and similar pubns. *Recreations:* travel, music, gardening. *Address:* Barn Croft, Rodmell, near Lewes, E Sussex BN7 3HF.

CANNON, Richard Walter, CEng, FIEE; Joint Managing Director, 1977–83, Managing Director, 1983, Cable and Wireless plc; retired; *b* 7 Dec. 1923; *s* of Richard William Cannon and Lily Harriet Cannon (*née* Fewins); *m* 1949, Dorothy (formerly Jarvis); two *d*. *Educ:* Eltham Coll. Joined Cable and Wireless Ltd, 1941; Exec. Dir, 1973. Director: Batelco (Bahrain), 1981–90; Teletswana (Botswana), 1984–86. *Publications:* telecommunications papers for IEE and IERE.

CANNON, Thomas; Chief Executive, MDE Services; Associate Rector, Hajioannion University; *b* 20 Nov. 1945; *s* of Albert and Bridget Cannon; *m* 1971, Frances Cannon (*née* Constable); one *s* one *d*. *Educ:* St Francis Xavier's Grammar Sch., Liverpool; Borough Polytechnic. BSc (Hons) Sociology (London Univ. external degree). Res. Associate, Warwick Univ., 1969–71; Lectr, Middlesex Poly., 1971–72; Products Man., Imperial Gp, 1972–74; Lectr, Durham Univ., 1975–81; Prof., Univ. of Stirling, 1981–89; Dir, 1989–92, Vis. Prof., 1992–, Manchester Business Sch. Dir, Stirling Gp. Member: ESRC; Industry, Environment and Economy R&D Gp, 1990–92; Jt Cttee, ESRC/SERC, 1990–94; Business Links Gp, 1993–94; Chm., Jt Working Party, Scottish Examinations Bd, 1988–90; Dep. Chm., Management Develt to the Millenium, Inst. of Management, 1992. Mem., Internat. Adv. Bd, Lahore Univ. of Management Scis. FIEx, FIPDM; FRSA; FCIM; CIMgt (Pres., N Cheshire Br.). *Publications:* Advertising Research, 1972; Distribution Research, 1973; Advertising: the economic implications, 1974; Basic Marketing, 1976, 3rd edn 1991; How to Win Profitable Business, 1983; How to Win Business Overseas, 1984; Enterprise, 1991; The World of Business, 1991; Women as Entrepreneurs, 1992; Corporate Responsibility, 1993; (ed jtly) The Times Good University Guide, 1994; How to Get Ahead in Business, 1994; papers in learned jls. *Recreations:* soccer, supporting Everton FC, walking, writing. *Address:* 13 Old Broadway, Manchester M20 9DH. *T:* 0161–434 2989.

CANNON-BROOKES, Peter, PhD; FMA, FIIC; international museum consultant; *b* 23 Aug. 1938; *s* of Victor Montgomery Cannon Brookes and late Nancy Margaret (*née* Markham Carter); *m* 1966, Caroline Aylmer, *d* of John Aylmer Christie-Miller; one *s* one *d*. *Educ:* Bryanston; Trinity Hall, Cambridge (MA); Courtauld Inst. of Art, Univ. of London (PhD). FMA 1975. Gooden and Fox Ltd, London, 1963–64; Keeper, Dept of Art, City Museums and Art Gall., Birmingham, 1965–78; Sessional Teacher in History of Art, Courtauld Inst. of Art, London, 1966–68; Keeper of Dept of Art, Nat. Mus. of Wales, Cardiff, 1978–86; Mus. Services Dir, STIPPLE Database Services, 1986–90. Internat. Council of Museums: Mem. Exec. Bd, UK Cttee, 1973–81; Pres., Internat. Art Exhibns Cttee, 1977–79 (Dir, 1974–80; Sec., 1975–77); Dir, Conservation Cttee, 1975–81 (Vice Pres., 1978–81). Member: Town Twinning Cttee, Birmingham Internat. Council, 1968–78; Birm. Diocesan Synod, 1970–78; Birm. Diocesan Adv. Cttee for Care of Churches, 1972–78; Edgbaston Deanery Synod, 1970–78 (Lay Jt Chm., 1975–78); Society of Authors, 1972–; Art and Design Adv. Panel, Welsh Jt Educn Cttee, 1978–86; Welsh Arts Council, 1979–84 (Member: Art Cttee, 1978–84; Craft Cttee, 1983–87); Projects and Orgns Cttee, Crafts Council, 1985–87. President: Welsh Fedn of Museums and Art Galleries, 1980–82; S Wales Art Soc., 1980–87. Trustee, Welsh Sculpture Trust, 1981–94; Consultant Curator, Tabley House Collection, 1988–. Editor, Museum Management and Curatorship, 1981–. Freeman 1969, Liveryman 1974, Worshipful Co. of Goldsmiths. FRSA. JP Birmingham, 1973–78, Cardiff, 1978–82. *Publications:* (with H. D. Molesworth) European Sculpture, 1964; (with C. A. Cannon-Brookes) Baroque Churches, 1969; Lombard Painting, 1974; After Gulbenkian, 1976; The Cornbury Park Bellini, 1977; Michael Ayrton, 1978; Emile Antoine Bourdelle, 1983; Ivor Roberts-Jones, 1983; Czech Sculpture 1800–1938, 1983; Paintings from Tabley, 1989; The Painted Word, 1991; contrib. Apollo, Art Bull., Arte Veneta, Burlington Mag., Connoisseur, Internat. Jl of Museum Management and Curatorship, and Museums Jl. *Recreations:* photography, growing vegetables, cooking. *Address:* Thrupp House, Abingdon, Oxon OX14 3NE. *T:* Abingdon (01235) 520595, *Fax:* Abingdon (01235) 534817. *Clubs:* Athenæum; Birmingham (Birmingham).

CANT, Rev. Harry William Macphail; Minister of St Magnus Cathedral, Kirkwall, Orkney, 1968–90; Chaplain to the Queen in Scotland, 1972–91, and Extra Chaplain, since 1991; *b* 3 April 1921; *s* of late J. M. Cant and late Margaret Cant; *m* 1951, Margaret Elizabeth Loudon; one *s* two *d*. *Educ:* Edinburgh Acad.; Edinburgh Univ. (MA, BD); Union Theological Seminary, NY (STM). Lieut, KOSB, 1941–43; Captain, King's African Rifles, 1944–46; TA Chaplain, 7th Argyll and Sutherland Highlanders, 1962–70. Asst Minister, Old Parish Church, Aberdeen, 1950–51; Minister of Fallin Parish Church,

Stirling, 1951–56; Scottish Sec., Student Christian Movt, 1956–59; Minister of St Thomas' Parish Church, 1960–68. *Publications:* Preaching in a Scottish Parish Church: St Magnus and Other Sermons, 1970; Springs of Renewal in Congregational Life, 1980; (ed jtly) Light in the North, 1989. *Recreations:* angling, golf. *Address:* Quoylobs, Holm, Orkney KW17 2RY.

CANT, Robert (Bowen); *b* 24 July 1915; *s* of Robert and Catherine Cant; *m* 1940, Rebecca Harris Watt; one *s* two *d*. *Educ:* Middlesbrough High Sch. for Boys; London Sch. of Economics. BSc (Econ.) 1945. Lecturer in Economics, Univ. of Keele, 1962–66. Member: Stoke-on-Trent City Council, 1953–76; Staffs CC, 1973–93 (Chm., Educn Cttee, 1981–89). Contested (Lab) Shrewsbury, 1950, 1951; MP (Lab) Stoke-on-Trent Central, 1966–83. *Publication:* American Journey. *Recreation:* bookbinding. *Address:* (home) 119 Chell Green Avenue, Stoke-on-Trent, Staffordshire ST6 7LA. *Club:* Chell Working Men's.

CANTACUZINO, Sherban, CBE 1988; FRIBA; Secretary, Royal Fine Art Commission, 1979–94; *b* 6 Sept. 1928; *s* of late Georges M. Cantacuzino and Sanda Stirbey; *m* 1954, Anne Mary Trafford; two *d* (one *s* decd). *Educ:* Winchester Coll.; Magdalene Coll., Cambridge (MA). Partner, Steane, Shipman & Cantacuzino, Chartered Architects, 1956–65; private practice, 1965–73; Asst Editor, Architectural Review, 1967–73, Exec. Editor, 1973–79. Sen. Lectr, Dept of Architecture, College of Art, Canterbury, 1967–70. Trustee: Thomas Cubitt Trust, 1978–; Design Museum, 1981–; Member: Arts Panel, Arts Council, 1977–80; Steering Cttee, Aga Khan Award for Architecture, 1980–83 (Mem., Master Jury, 1980); Council, RSA, 1980–85; Design Cttee, London Transport, 1981–82; Adv. Panel, Railway Heritage Trust, 1985–; Fabric Cttee, Canterbury Cathedral, 1987–; Adv. Cttee, Getty Grant Prog., 1993–; Design Panel, Plymouth Develt Corp., 1994–; Bd, Landscape Foundn, 1995–. Advr, Earth Centre, 1995–. Dir, Taylor Warren Ltd, 1995–. Pres., UK Cttee, ICOMOS, 1993– (Mem., Exec. Cttee, 1990–). Chm., Princess Margarita of Roumania Trust, 1995–; Trustee, Wallingford Arts Park Gallery Trust, 1995–. *Publications:* Modern Houses of the World, 1964, 3rd edn 1966; Great Modern Architecture, 1966, 2nd edn 1968; European Domestic Architecture, 1969; New Uses for Old Buildings, 1975; (ed) Architectural Conservation in Europe, 1975; Wells Coates, a monograph, 1978; (with Susan Brandt) Saving Old Buildings, 1980; The Architecture of Howell, Killick, Partridge and Amis, 1981; Charles Correa, 1984; (ed) Architecture in Continuity: building in the Islamic world today, 1985; Re/Architecture: old buildings/New uses, 1989; What makes a good building?: an inquiry by Royal Fine Art Commission, 1994; articles in Architectural Rev. *Recreations:* music, cooking. *Address:* 140 Iffley Road, W6 0PE. *T:* 0181–748 0415. *Club:* Garrick.

CANTER, Prof. David Victor, PhD; FBPsS; Professor of Psychology, University of Liverpool, since 1994; *b* 5 Jan. 1944; *s* of late Hyman Victor Canter and Coralie Lilian Canter (*née* Hyam); *m* 1967, Sandra Lorraine Smith; one *s* two *d*. *Educ:* Liverpool Collegiate Grammar Sch.; Liverpool Univ. (BA Hons 1964; PhD 1969). Research Associate, Liverpool Univ., 1964–65; Strathclyde University: Res. Associate, 1966; Res. Fellow, Building Performance Res. Unit, 1967–70; Lectr, 1971–72; University of Surrey: Lectr, 1972–78; Reader, 1978–83; Prof. of Applied Psychology, 1983–87; Prof. of Psychology, 1987–94; Hd of Dept of Psychology, 1987–91. CPsychol 1988; FBIM; FAPA. Mem., Forensic Sci. Soc. Hon. Mem., Japanese Inst. of Architects, 1971. Man. Ed., Jl of Envmtl Psychology, 1981–. *Publications:* Architectural Psychology, 1970; Psychology for Architects, 1974; (ed jtly) Psychology and the Built Environment, 1974; Environmental Interaction, 1975; (with P. Stringer) Psychology of Place, 1977; (ed jtly) Designing for Therapeutic Environments, 1979; (ed) Fires and Human Behaviour, 1980, 2nd edn 1990; (ed jtly) Psychology in Practice, 1982; (ed) Facet Theory, 1985; (ed jtly) The Research Interview, 1985; (ed jtly) Environmental Perspectives, 1988; (ed jtly) Environmental Policy, Assessment and Communication, 1988; (ed jtly) New Directions in Environmental Participation, 1988; (ed jtly) Environmental Social Psychology, 1988; (with M. Comber and D. Uzzell) Football in its Place, 1989; (ed jtly) Empirical Approaches to Social Representations, 1992; Criminal Shadows: inside the mind of the serial killer, 1994; (jtly) The Faces of Homelessness, 1995; Psychology in Action, 1996; contribs to learned jls, newspapers, radio, TV. *Recreations:* clarinet, collage. *Address:* Department of Psychology, University of Liverpool, Liverpool L69 3BX. *T:* 0151–794 3910.

CANTERBURY, Archbishop of, since 1991; **Most Rev. and Rt. Hon. George Leonard Carey;** PC 1991; *b* 13 Nov. 1935; *s* of George and Ruby Carey; *m* 1960, Eileen Harmsworth Hood, Dagenham, Essex; two *s* two *d*. *Educ:* Bifrons Secondary Modern Sch., Barking; London College of Divinity; King's College, London. BD Hons, MTh; PhD London. National Service, RAF Wireless Operator, 1954–56. Deacon, 1962; Curate, St Mary's, Islington, 1962–66; Lecturer: Oak Hill Coll., Southgate, 1966–70; St John's Coll., Nottingham, 1970–75; Vicar, St Nicholas' Church, Durham, 1975–82; Principal, Trinity Coll., Stoke Hill, Bristol, 1982–87; Hon. Canon, Bristol Cathedral, 1983–87; Bishop of Bath and Wells, 1987–91. FKC, 1994. Hon. doctorates from UK and USA univs. *Publications:* I Believe in Man, 1975; God Incarnate, 1976; (jtly) The Great Acquittal, 1980; The Meeting of the Waters, 1985; The Gate of Glory, 1986, 2nd edn 1992; The Message of the Bible, 1988; The Great God Robbery, 1989; I Believe, 1991; Sharing a Vision, 1993; Spiritual Journey, 1994; contributor to numerous jls. *Recreations:* reading, writing, walking. *Address:* Lambeth Palace, SE1 7JU. *T:* 0171–928 8282.

CANTERBURY, Dean of; *see* Simpson, Very Rev. J. A.

CANTERBURY, Archdeacon of; *see* Till, Ven. M. S.

CANTY, Brian George John, CBE 1993 (OBE 1988); HM Diplomatic Service, retired; Governor of Anguilla, 1989–92; *b* 23 Oct. 1931; *s* of George Robert Canty and Phœbe Charlotte Canty (*née* Cobb); *m* 1954, Maureen Kathleen Kenny; one *s* one *d*. *Educ:* South West Essex Technical College; external student, London University (Social Studies); RAF Staff College (psc 1970). RN 1950; Air Ministry, 1957; Financial Adviser's Office, Cyprus, 1960; MoD (Air), 1963; FCO, 1971; served Oslo, 1973, Kingston, 1977, Vienna, 1979; FCO, 1984; Dep. Governor, Bermuda, 1986. JP Bermuda, 1986. *Recreations:* sailing, skiing, DIY. *Clubs:* Royal Automobile; Beefsteak (Vienna); Royal Bermuda Yacht.

CAPE, Donald Paul Montagu Stewart, CMG 1977; HM Diplomatic Service, retired; Ambassador and UK Permanent Representative to the Council of Europe, Strasbourg, 1978–83; *b* 6 Jan. 1923; *s* of late John Scarvell and Olivia Millicent Cape; *m* 1948, Cathune Johnston; four *s* one *d*. *Educ:* Ampleforth Coll.; Brasenose Coll., Oxford. Scots Guards, 1942–45. Entered Foreign Service, 1946. Served: Belgrade, 1946–49; FO, 1949–51; Lisbon, 1951–55; Singapore, 1955–57; FO, 1957–60; Bogota, 1960–61; Holy See, 1962–67; Head of Information Administration Dept, FCO, 1968–70; Counsellor, Washington, 1970–73; Counsellor, Brasilia, 1973–75; Ambassador to Laos, 1976–78. Administrator, Anglo-Irish Encounter, 1983–; Chm., Anglo-Portuguese Soc., 1988–91. *Recreations:* tennis, walking, swimming, skiing. *Address:* Hilltop, Wonersh, Guildford, Surrey GU5 0QT.

CAPE, Maj.-Gen. Timothy Frederick, CB 1972; CBE 1966; DSO; idc, jssc, psc; FAIM; *b* Sydney, 5 Aug. 1915; *s* of C. S. Cape, DSO, Edgecliff, NSW; *m* 1961, Elizabeth (*d* 1985), *d* of Brig. R. L. R. Rabett; one *d*. *Educ:* Cranbrook Sch., Sydney; RMC Duntroon. Served with RAA, 1938–40; Bde Major Sparrow Force, Timor, 1942; GS01: (Air) New Guinea Force, 1942–43; (Ops) Melbourne, 1944; (Air) Morotai, 1945; (Ops) Japan, 1946–47; (Plans) Melbourne, 1948–49; Instructor, Staff Coll., Camberley, UK, 1950–52; Comdt, OCS, Portsea, 1954–56; Dep. Master-Gen. Ordnance, 1957–59; COS Northern Comd, Brisbane, 1961; Dir of Staff Duties, Army HQ, Canberra, 1962–63; Comdr, Adelaide, 1964; GOC Northern Comd, Brisbane, 1965–68; Master-General of the Ordnance, 1968–72; retd 1972. Nat. Chm., Royal United Services Inst. of Australia, 1980–83; Chm., Nat. Disaster Relief Cttee and Mem., Nat. Council, Australian Red Cross Soc., 1975–85. Bronze Star (US). *Address:* PO Box E2, Queen Victoria Terrace, ACT 2600, Australia. *Clubs:* Melbourne (Melbourne); Commonwealth (Canberra); Union (Sydney); Royal Sydney Golf.

CAPE TOWN, Archbishop of, and Metropolitan of Southern Africa, since 1986; **Most Rev. Desmond Mpilo Tutu;** *b* Klerksdorp, Transvaal, 7 Oct. 1931; *s* of Zachariah and Aletta Tutu; *m* 1955, Leah Nomalizo Shenxane; one *s* three *d*. *Educ:* Johannesburg Bantu High Sch.; Bantu Normal Coll., Pretoria (Higher Teachers' Dip. 1953); Univ. of S Africa (BA 1954); St Peter's Theol Coll., Johannesburg (LTh 1960); King's Coll. London (BD 1965, MTh 1966; FKC 1978). Schoolmaster: Madibane High Sch., Johannesburg, 1954; Munsieville High Sch., Krugersdorp, 1955–57. Theological coll. student, 1958–60; deacon 1960, priest 1961, St Mary's Cathedral, Johannesburg. Curate: St Alban's Church, Benoni, 1960–61; St Philip's Church, Alberton, 1961–62; St Alban's, Golder's Green, London, 1962–65; St Mary's, Bletchingley, Surrey, 1965–66. Lecturer: Federal Theol Seminary, Alice, CP, 1967–69; Univ. of Botswana, Lesotho and Swaziland, Roma, Lesotho, 1970–72; Associate Dir, Theol Education Fund (WCC) based in Bromley, Kent, and Hon. Curate, St Augustine's, Grove Park, 1972–75; Dean of Johannesburg, 1975–76; Bishop of Lesotho, 1976–78; Gen. Sec., South African Council of Churches, 1978–85; Rector, St Augustine's Parish, Soweto, 1981–85; Bishop of Johannesburg, 1985–86. Chancellor, Univ. of Western Cape, Cape Town, 1988–. Pres., All Africa Conference of Churches, 1987–. Trustee, Phelps Stoke Fund, New York. Holds over fifty hon. degrees from academic institutions in UK, Europe and USA. Athena Prize, Onassis Foundation, 1980; Nobel Peace Prize, 1984; Albert Schweitzer Humanitarian Award, Emmanuel Coll., Boston, 1988. Order of Southern Cross (Brazil), 1987; Order of Merit of Brasilia (Brazil), 1987. *Publications:* Crying in the Wilderness, 1982; Hope and Suffering, 1983; The Words of Desmond Tutu, 1989; The Rainbow People of God, 1994; articles and reviews. *Recreations:* music, reading, jogging. *Address:* Bishopscourt, Claremont, 7700, South Africa.

CAPE TOWN, Bishops Suffragan of; *see* Castle, Rt Rev. M. E.; Quinlan, Rt Rev. A. G.

CAPEL CURE, (George) Nigel, TD; JP; DL; *b* 28 Sept. 1908; *o s* of late Major George Edward Capel Cure, JP, Blake Hall, Ongar; *m* 1935, Nancy Elizabeth, *d* of late William James Barry, Great Witchingham Hall, Norwich; two *s* one *d*. *Educ:* Eton; Trinity Coll., Cambridge. DL and JP, 1947, High Sheriff, 1951, Essex; Vice-Lieutenant, later Vice Lord-Lieutenant, Essex, 1958–78; late of Blake Hall, Ongar. *Recreations:* shooting, cricket. *Address:* Ashlings, Moreton Road, Ongar, Essex CM5 0EZ. *T:* Ongar (01277) 362634. *Clubs:* MCC, City University.

CAPELL, family name of **Earl of Essex.**

CAPEY, Montague Martin; Director of Establishments and Organisation, Department for Education (formerly Department of Education and Science), 1988–93; *b* 16 July 1933; *s* of Ernest Paton Capey and Lettice Isabel Capey; *m* 1960, Diana Mary Barnes; one *s* one *d*. *Educ:* The Leys Sch., Cambridge; Clare Coll., Cambridge (MA); Didsbury Coll., Bristol; Univ. of Bristol (BA). Methodist Minister, 1958–71. Principal 1971–76, Asst Sec. 1976–88, DES. *Recreations:* gardening, music, enjoying Cornwall. *Address:* Bramble Cottage, West Kitty, St Agnes, Cornwall TR5 0SU.

CAPLAN, Hon. Lord; Philip Isaac Caplan; a Senator of the College of Justice in Scotland, since 1989; *b* 24 Feb. 1929; *s* of Hyman and Rosalena Caplan; *m* 1st, 1953; two *s* one *d*; 2nd, 1974, Joyce Ethel Stone; one *d*. *Educ:* Eastwood Sch., Renfrewshire; Glasgow Univ. (MA, LLB). Solicitor, 1952–56; called to Bar, 1957; Standing Junior Counsel to Accountant of Court, 1964–70; QC (Scot.) 1970; Sheriff of Lothian and Borders, 1979–83; Sheriff-Principal of North Strathclyde, 1983–89. Member: Sheriff Court Rules Council, 1984–89; Adv. Council on Messengers-at-Arms and Sheriff Officers, 1987–89. Chairman: Plant Varieties and Seeds Tribunal, Scotland, 1977–79; Scottish Assoc. for Study of Delinquency, 1985–89 (Hon. Vice-Pres., 1990–); Family Mediation Scotland (formerly Scottish Assoc. of Family Conciliation Services), 1989–; Bd of Trustees, James Powell UK Trust, 1992–. Hon. Pres., Scottish Photographic Circle, 1995– (Mem., 1986–95). FRPS 1988; AFIAP 1985. *Recreations:* photography, reading, music. *Address:* Parliament House, Parliament Square, Edinburgh EH1 1RQ. *Club:* New (Edinburgh).

CAPLAN, Daniel; Under-Secretary, Department of the Environment, 1970–71; *b* 29 July 1915; *y s* of Daniel and Miriam Caplan; *m* 1945, Olive Beatrice Porter; no *c*. *Educ:* Elem. and Secondary Schools, Blackpool; St Catharine's Coll., Cambridge. Asst Principal, Import Duties Adv. Cttee, 1938; Private Secretary to three Permanent Secretaries, Ministry of Supply, 1940; Principal, 1942; Ministry of Supply Representative and Economic Secretary to British Political Representative in Finland, 1944–45; Asst Secretary, Board of Trade, 1948; Adviser to Chancellor of Duchy of Lancaster, 1957–60; Under-Secretary, Scottish Development Dept, 1963–65; Under-Secretary, National Economic Development Office, 1966; Asst Under-Sec. of State, DEA, 1966–69; Under-Sec., Min. of Housing and Local Govt, 1969–70; Consultant to Minister for Housing for Leasehold Charges Study, 1972–73. Indep. Review of Royal Commn on Historical Manuscripts, for HM Govt, 1980. *Publications:* People and Homes (indep. report on Landlord and Tenant Relations in England for British Property Fedn), 1975; Border Country Branch Lines, 1981; Report on the Work of the Royal Commission on Historical Manuscripts, 1981; The Waverley Route, 1985; The Royal Scot, 1987; The West Highland Line, 1988; numerous papers on religious and economic history in learned journals. *Recreations:* railways, historical research, gardening. *Address:* Knowle Wood, London Road, Cuckfield, West Sussex RH17 5ES. *T:* Haywards Heath (01444) 454301.

CAPLAN, Jonathan Michael; QC 1991; a Recorder, since 1995; *b* 11 Jan. 1951; *s* of Dr Malcolm Denis Caplan and late Jean Hilary Caplan, JP; *m* 1993, Selena Lennard (*née* Peskin); one *s*, and one step *s* one step *d*. *Educ:* St Paul's Sch.; Downing Coll., Cambridge (MA). Called to Bar, Gray's Inn, 1973; Asst Recorder, 1989–95. Mem., General Council of Bar, 1986–90; Chairman: Bar Council Report on Televising the Courts, 1989; Public Affairs Cttee, Bar Council, 1991–92. FRSA 1992. Mem. Editl Bd, Jl of Criminal Law, 1988–. *Publications:* The Confait Confessions, 1977; (contrib.) Disabling Professions, 1978. *Recreations:* writing, tennis, collecting historical newspapers and manuscripts, Khmer and Thai sculpture, cinema, books. *Address:* 5 Paper Buildings, Temple, EC4Y 7HB. *T:* 0171–583 6117. *Club:* Queen's.

CAPLAN, Leonard, QC 1954; *b* 28 June 1909; *s* of late Henry Caplan, Liverpool; *m* 1st, 1942, Tania Finklestein, LLB (Lond), BLitt (Oxon) (*d* 1974); two *d*; 2nd, 1977, Mrs

Herskovits (marr. diss. 1989), NY. Served War of 1939–45, Royal Artillery (Anti-Tank): Staff Captain, 47th Div.; Staff Captain ("Q" Operations), Southern Command, engaged in D-Day Planning; passed Staff Coll., Camberley; Major, DAAG and Lt-Col, AAG, HQ Allied Land Forces, South East Asia. Called to the Bar, Gray's Inn, 1935; Master of the Bench, 1964; Vice-Treasurer, 1978; Treasurer, 1979; Master of the Library, 1980–86; joined South Eastern Circuit; Middle Temple, 1949; sometime Dep. High Ct Judge. Conservative candidate: Pontypool, 1935; N Hammersmith, 1945; N Kensington, 1950–51. Chm., Coll. Hall (Univ. of London), 1958–67. Chm., Mental Health Review Tribunal, SE Region, 1960–63; Vice-Chm., NI Detention Appeals Tribunal, 1973–75; Senate of Inns of Court and the Bar, 1975–81. Pres., Medico-Legal Soc., 1979–81. *Publications:* (with late Marcus Samuel, MP) The Great Experiment: a critical study of Soviet Five Year Plans, 1935; numerous historico-legal articles. *Recreation:* yachting. *Address:* 1 Pump Court, Temple, EC4Y 7AB. *T:* 0171–353 9332; Skol, Marbella, S Spain. *Clubs:* Savage, Authors', Arts, Royal Automobile.

CAPLAN, Philip Isaac; *see* Caplan, Hon. Lord.

CAPLAT, Moran Victor Hingston, CBE 1968; General Administrator, Glyndebourne Festival Opera, retired; *b* 1 Oct. 1916; *s* of Roger Armand Charles Caplat and Norah Hingston; *m* 1943, Diana Murray Downton; one *s* two *d* (and one *s* decd). *Educ:* privately; Royal Acad. of Dramatic Art. Actor, etc., 1934–39. Royal Navy, 1939–45. Glyndebourne: Asst to Gen. Man., 1945; Gen. Man., later known as Gen. Administrator, 1949–81. *Publication:* Dinghies to Divas (autobiog.), 1985. *Address:* Mermaid Cottage, 6 Church Road, Newick, Lewes, East Sussex BN8 4JU. *T:* Newick (01825) 722964. *Clubs:* Garrick, Royal Ocean Racing; Royal Yacht Squadron (Cowes).
See also D. N. O. Sekers.

CAPLIN, Dianne; *see* Hayter, D.

CAPPER, Rt. Rev. Edmund Michael Hubert, OBE 1961; LTh (Dur.); Auxiliary Bishop in the Diocese of Gibraltar in Europe, since 1973; Assistant Bishop of Southwark, since 1981; *b* 12 March 1908; *e s* of Arthur Charles and Mabel Lavinia Capper; unmarried. *Educ:* St Joseph's Academy, Blackheath; St Augustine's College, Canterbury. Deacon, 1932, Priest, 1933. Royal Army Chaplains' Dept, 1942–46 (EA); Archdeacon of Lindi and Canon of Masasi Cathedral, 1947–54; Archdeacon of Dar es Salaam, 1954–58. Provost of the Collegiate Church of St Alban the Martyr, Dar es Salaam, Tanganyika, 1957–62; Canon of Zanzibar, 1954–62; Member, Universities' Mission to Central Africa, 1936–62; Chairman, Tanganyika British Legion Benevolent Fund, 1956–62; President, Tanganyika British Legion, 1960–62; Chaplain, Palma de Mallorca, 1962–67; Bishop of St Helena, 1967–73; Chaplain of St George's, Malaga, 1973–76. *Recreations:* swimming and walking. *Address:* Morden College, Blackheath, SE3 0PW. *T:* 0181–858 9169. *Club:* Travellers'.

CAPRON, (George) Christopher; independent television producer; Director, Capron Productions, since 1987; *b* 17 Dec. 1935; *s* of late Lt-Col George Capron and Hon. Mrs (Edith) Christian Capron (*née* Hepburne-Scott); *m* 1958, Edna Naomi Goldrei; one *s* one *d*. *Educ:* Wellington Coll.; Trinity Hall, Cambridge (BA Hons Mod. Langs). Served Army, 12th Royal Lancers (Prince of Wales's), 1954–56. British Broadcasting Corporation: radio producer, 1963–67; television producer, 1967–76; Editor, Tonight, 1976–77; Editor, Panorama, 1977–79; Asst Head, 1979–81, Head, 1981–85, TV Current Affairs Programmes; Head of Parly Broadcasting, 1985–87. *Recreations:* village cricket, tennis. *Address:* 32 Amerland Road, SW18 1PZ; Southwick Hall, Oundle, Northants PE8 5BL.

CAPSTICK, Brian Eric, QC 1973; **His Honour Judge Capstick;** a Circuit Judge, since 1985; *b* 12 Feb. 1927; *o s* of late Eric and Betty Capstick; *m* 1960, Margaret Harrison; one *s* one *d*. *Educ:* Sedbergh; Queen's Coll., Oxford (Scholar) (MA). Served HM Forces, 1945–48: 17/21st Lancers, Palestine, 1947–48. Tancred Student, and called to Bar, Lincoln's Inn, 1952; Bencher, 1980; a Recorder, 1980–85. Dep. Chm., Northern Agriculture Tribunal, 1976–; Asst Boundary Comr, 1978–85. Appeal Steward, British Board of Boxing Control, 1985–. *Recreations:* shooting, reading, cooking. *Address:* c/o Central Criminal Court, Old Bailey, EC4M 7EH. *Club:* Garrick.

CAPSTICK, Charles William, CB 1992; CMG 1972; Deputy Secretary, Food Safety Directorate, Ministry of Agriculture, Fisheries and Food, 1989–94; *b* 18 Dec. 1934; *s* of late William Capstick and Janet Frankland; *m* 1962, Joyce Alma Dodsworth; two *s*. *Educ:* King's Coll., Univ. of Durham (BSc (Hons)); Univ. of Kentucky, USA (MS). MAFF: Asst Agricl Economist, 1961; Principal Agricl Economist, 1966; Senior Principal Agricl Economist, 1968; Sen. Econ. Advr and Head, Milk and Milk Products Div., 1976; Under Sec., 1977, Dir of Econs and Statistics, 1977. Pres., Agricultural Economics Soc., 1983. *Recreations:* gardening, golf. *Address:* 7 Dellfield Close, Radlett, Herts WD7 8LS.

CARBERY, 11th Baron *cr* 1715; **Peter Ralfe Harrington Evans-Freke;** Bt 1768; *b* 20 March 1920; *o s* of Major the Hon. Ralfe Evans-Freke, MBE (*yr s* of 9th Baron) (*d* 1969), and Vera (*d* 1984), *d* of late C. Harrington Moore; *S* uncle, 1970; *m* 1941, Joyzelle Mary, *o d* of late Herbert Binnie; three *s* two *d*. *Educ:* Downside School. MICE. Served War of 1939–45, Captain RE, India, Burmah. Member of London Stock Exchange, 1955–68. *Recreations:* hunting, tennis, winter sports. *Heir: e s* Hon. Michael Peter Evans-Freke [*b* 11 Oct. 1942; *m* 1967, Claudia Janet Elizabeth, *o d* of Captain P. L. C. Gurney; one *s* three *d*]. *Address:* 2 Hayes Court, Sunnyside, Wimbledon, SW19 4SH.

CARBERY, Prof. Thomas Francis, OBE 1983; Emeritus Professor, University of Strathclyde, since 1990; Chairman, South of Scotland Electricity Consumers' Committee, since 1990; *b* 18 Jan. 1925; *o c* of Thomas Albert Carbery and Jane Morrison; *m* 1954, Ellen Donnelly; one *s* two *d*. *Educ:* St Aloysius Coll., Glasgow; Univ. of Glasgow and Scottish Coll. of Commerce. Cadet Navigator and Meteorologist, RAFVR, 1943–47; Min. of Labour, 1947–61; Lectr, then Sen. Lectr, in Govt and Econs, Scottish College of Commerce, Glasgow, 1961–64; University of Strathclyde: Sen. Lectr in Govt-Business Relations, 1964–75; Head of Dept of Office Organisation, 1975–79, and Prof., 1979–85; Prof., Dept of Inf. Science, 1985–88, and Chm. of Dept, 1985–86; Prof. (part-time), Dept. of Marketing, 1988–90. Member: IBA (formerly ITA), 1970–79 (Chm., Scottish Cttee, 1970–79); Royal Commn on Gambling, 1976–78; Central Transport Users' Consultative Cttee, 1976–80 (Chm., Scottish Transport Users' Consultative Cttee, 1976–80); European (later International) Adv. Council, Salzburg Seminar, 1980–91; Broadcasting Complaints Commn, 1981–86; Data Protection Tribunal, 1984–; Scottish Legal Aid Bd, 1986–92; Press Council, 1987–90; Dep. Chm., Scottish Consumer Council, 1980–84 (Mem. 1977–80); Chm., Scottish Cttee, Information Technology, 1982–85; Ombudsman to Mirror Gp Newspapers Scottish titles, 1990–91; Special Adviser, H of C Select Cttee on Scottish Affairs, 1982. Academic Governor, Richmond Coll., 1983–; Governor, 1984–, Trustee, 1991–, St Aloysius' Coll., Glasgow. Editor, Approaches to Information Technology (Plenum Press series), 1984–90. *Publications:* Consumers in Politics, 1969; (jtly) An Introduction to Office Management and Automation, 1991. *Recreations:* golf, conversation, spectating at Association football, listening to Radio 4, watching television. *Address:* 24 Fairfax Avenue, Glasgow G44 5AL. *T:* 0141–637 0514. *Clubs:* University of Strathclyde, Glasgow Art, Ross Priory (Glasgow).

CARDEN, (Sir) Christopher Robert, (5th Bt *cr* 1887, of Molesley, Surrey; but does not use the title); tropical forest management consultant; conservationist; *b* 24 Nov. 1946; *o s* of Sir Henry Carden, 4th Bt, OBE and of his 1st wife, Jane St Clare Daniell; *S* father, 1993; *m* 1st, 1972, Sainimere Rokotuibau (marr. diss. 1979), Suva, Fiji; 2nd, 1981, Clarita Eriksen, Manila, Philippines. *Educ:* Eton; Univ. of Aberdeen (BSc Forestry, 1970). Guide, Internat. Raëlian Movement. *Address:* Casilla 1341, Santa Cruz, Bolivia.

CARDEN, Derrick Charles, CMG 1974; HM Diplomatic Service, retired; HM Ambassador, Sudan, 1977–79; *b* 30 Oct. 1921; *s* of Canon Henry Craven Carden and Olive (*née* Gorton); *heir pres.* to Sir John Craven Carden, 7th Bt, *qv*; *m* 1952, Elizabeth Anne Russell; two *s* two *d*. *Educ:* Marlborough; Christ Church, Oxford. Sudan Political Service, 1942–54. Entered HM Diplomatic Service, 1954; Foreign Office, 1954–55; Political Agent, Doha, 1955–58; 1st Sec., Libya, 1958–62; Foreign Office, 1962–65; Head of Chancery, Cairo, 1965; Consul-General, Muscat, 1965–69; Dir, ME Centre of Arab Studies, 1969–73; Ambassador, Yemen Arab Republic, 1973–76. Governor, IDS, Sussex Univ., 1981–87. Mem. Bd, CARE Britain, 1988–90. JP Fareham, 1980–91. *Recreation:* pleasures of the countryside. *Address:* Cottage 38, Headbourne Worthy House, Winchester SO23 7JG. *Club:* Vincent's (Oxford).

CARDEN, Sir John Craven, 7th Bt, *cr* 1787; *b* 11 March 1926; *s* of Capt. Sir John V. Carden, 6th Bt and Dorothy Mary, *d* of Charles Luckrart McKinnon; *S* father, 1935; *m* 1947, Isabel Georgette, *y d* of late Robert de Hart; one *d*. *Educ:* Eton. *Heir: cousin* Derrick Charles Carden, *qv*. *Address:* PO Box 66, St Helier, Jersey, CI. *Club:* White's.

CARDEN, Richard John Derek; Deputy Secretary, Food Safety Directorate, Ministry of Agriculture, Fisheries and Food, since 1994; *b* 12 June 1943; *s* of late John and Hilda Carden; *m* 1971, Pamela Haughton; one *s* one *d*. *Educ:* Merchant Taylors' Sch., Northwood; St John's Coll., Oxford (Craven Scholar, 1964; Derby Scholar, 1966; MA Lit. Hum. 1969; DPhil 1970); Freie Universität, Berlin. Research for Egypt Exploration Soc., 1969–70; entered Civil Service, MAFF, 1970; HM Treasury, 1977–79; MAFF, 1979–: Chief Regional Officer, Midlands and Western Region, 1983–86; Under Sec., European Community and Ext. Trade Policy, 1987–91; Fisheries Sec., 1991–93; Under Sec., Cabinet Office (on secondment), 1993–94. Dir (non-exec.), Golden Wonder Ltd, 1985–86. *Publications:* The Papyrus Fragments of Sophocles, 1974; (contrib.) The Oxyrhynchus Papyri, vol. LIV, 1987; articles on Greek literature. *Address:* Ministry of Agriculture, Fisheries and Food, Whitehall Place, SW1A 2HH.

CARDIFF, Archbishop of, (RC), since 1983; **Most Rev. John Aloysius Ward,** OFM Cap; *b* 24 Jan. 1929; *s* of Eugene Ward and Hannah Ward (*née* Cheetham). *Educ:* Prior Park College, Bath. Received as Capuchin Franciscan Friar, 1945; solemn profession as Friar, 1950; ordained Priest, 1953; Diocesan Travelling Mission, Menevia, 1954–60; Guardian and Parish Priest, Peckham, London, 1960–66; Provincial Definitor (Councillor), 1963–69; Provincial Dir of Vocations, 1963–69; Provincial Deleg. to Secular Order of Franciscans, 1966–69; Minister Provincial, 1969–70; General Definitor (Councillor), Rome, 1970–80; Bishop Coadjutor of Menevia, 1980–81; Bishop of Menevia, 1981–83. *Address:* Archbishop's House, 41–43 Cathedral Road, Cardiff, S Glamorgan CF1 9HD. *T:* Cardiff (01222) 220411.

CARDIFF, Jack; film director and cameraman; *b* 18 Sept. 1914; *s* of John Joseph and Florence Cardiff; *m* 1940, Julia Lily (*née* Mickleboro); three *s*. *Educ:* various schools, incl. Medburn Sch., Herts. Started as child actor, 1918; switched to cameras, 1928. World travelogues, 1937–39. Photographed, MOI Crown Film Unit: Western Approaches, 1942; best known films include: A Matter of Life and Death, Black Narcissus, The Red Shoes, Scott of the Antarctic, Under Capricorn, Pandora and the Flying Dutchman, African Queen, War and Peace. Started as Director, 1958. *Films include: directed:* Sons and Lovers, My Geisha, The Lion, The Long Ships, Young Cassidy, The Mercenaries, The Liquidator, Girl on a Motorcycle, The Mutation; *photographed:* Ride a Wild Pony, The Prince and the Pauper, Behind the Iron Mask, Death on the Nile, Avalanche Express, The Awakening, The Dogs of War, Ghost Story, The Wicked Lady, Scandalous, The Far Pavilions, The Last Days of Pompeii, Conan II, First Blood II, Catseyes. Awards: Academy Award (Oscar) Photography, Black Narcissus, 1947; Golden Globe Award, 1947; Coup Ce Soir (France), 1951; Film Achievement Award, Look Magazine; BSC Award, War and Peace; New York Critics Award for best film direction, Golden Globe Award, outstanding directorial award (all for Sons and Lovers); Internat. Award for Outstanding Achievement, Amer. Soc. of Cinematographers, 1994; six Academy Award nominations. Hon. Dr of Art, Rome, 1953; Hon. Mem., Assoc. Française de Cameramen, 1971. *Recreations:* tennis, cricket, painting. *Club:* MCC.

CARDIGAN, Earl of; David Michael James Brudenell-Bruce; Manager, since 1974, owner, since 1987, and 31st Hereditary Warden, Savernake Forest; *b* 12 Nov. 1952; *s* and *heir* of 8th Marquess of Ailesbury, *qv*; *m* 1980, Rosamond Jane, cookery author, *er d* of Captain W. R. M. Winkley, Wyke Champflower Manor, near Bruton, Somerset, and of Mrs Jane Winkley, Kepnal Cottage, Kepnal, Marlborough; one *s* one *d*. *Educ:* Eton; Rannoch; Royal Agricultural Coll., Cirencester. Sec., Marlborough Conservatives, 1985–; Mem. Exec., Devizes Constituency Cons. Assoc., 1988–. *Heir: s* Viscount Savernake, *qv*. *Address:* Savernake Lodge, Savernake Forest, Marlborough, Wilts SN8 3HP.

CARDIN, Pierre; Chevalier de la Légion d'Honneur, 1983; couturier; *b* 2 July 1922. Designer: Paquin, Paris, 1945–46; Dior, Paris, 1946–50; founded own fashion house, 1950. Founder and Dir, Théâtre des Ambassadeurs, now Espace Pierre Cardin complex, 1970–; Chm., Maxim's Restaurant, 1981–. Designed costumes for films, including: Cocteau's La Belle et la Bête, 1946; The Yellow Rolls Royce, 1965. Retrospective exhibition, V & A, 1990. Dé d'Or, 1977, 1979, 1982; Fashion Oscar, 1985; prize of Foundn for Advancement of Garment and Apparel Res., Japan, 1988. Grand Officer, Order of Merit (Italy), 1988. *Address:* 59 rue du Faubourg Saint-Honoré, 75008 Paris, France.

CARDOSO E CUNHA, António José Baptista; Commissioner General, EXPO '98, since 1993; Chairman, PARQUE EXPO '98 SA, since 1993; *b* 28 Jan. 1934; *s* of Arnaldo and Maria Beatriz Cardoso e Cunha; *m* 1958, Dea Cardoso e Cunha; four *s*. *Educ:* Instituto Superior Tecnico; Lisbon Univ. MSc Chem. Engrg. Professional engineer, Lisbon, 1957–65; Man. Dir/Chief Exec. Officer of private cos, Sa da Bandeira, Angola, 1965–77; in business, director of private cos, Lisbon, 1977–78 and 1982–85. Mem. Portuguese Parlt, 1979–83 and 1985–89; Mem. Portuguese Government: Sec. of State for Foreign Trade, 1978, for Industry, 1979; Minister for Agriculture/Fisheries, 1980–82; Mem., European Commn, 1986–92. Grand Croix, Leopold II, Belgium, 1980; Gran Cruz, Merito Agricola, Spain, 1981; Grã-Cruz, Ordem Infant D. Henrique, Portugal, 1993. *Address:* EXPO '98, Av. Marechal Gomes da Costa 37, 1800 Lisbon, Portugal. *T:* 8370101.

CARDROSS, Lord; Henry Thomas Alexander Erskine; *b* 31 May 1960; *s* and *heir* of 17th Earl of Buchan, *qv*; *m* 1987, Charlotte, *d* of Hon. Matthew Beaumont and Mrs Alexander Maitland; two *s*.

CARDY, Prof. John Lawrence, PhD; FRS 1991; Senior Research Fellow, All Souls College, Oxford, since 1993; *b* 19 March 1947; *s* of late George Laurence Cardy and Sarah

Cardy; *m* 1985, Mary Ann Gilreath. *Educ:* Downing Coll., Cambridge (BA 1968; PhD 1971). Research Associate: European Orgn for Nuclear Res., Geneva, 1971–73; Daresbury Lab., 1973–74; Res. Associate, 1974–76, Prof. of Physics, 1977–93, Univ. of California, Santa Barbara; Fellow: European Orgn for Nuclear Res., 1976–77; Alfred P. Sloan Foundn, 1978; Guggenheim Foundn, 1986. *Publications:* Finite-Size Scaling, 1988; contrib. to learned jls. *Recreation:* mountaineering. *Address:* All Souls College, Oxford OX1 4AL.

CAREW, 7th Baron (UK) *cr* 1838; **Patrick Thomas Conolly-Carew;** Baron Carew (Ire.) 1834; *b* 6 March 1938; *er s* of 6th Baron Carew, CBE and Lady Sylvia Maitland (*d* 1991), *o d* of 15th Earl of Lauderdale; *S* father, 1994; *m* 1962, Celia Mary, *d* of Col Hon. (Charles) Guy Cubitt, CBE, DSO, TD; one *s* three *d*. *Educ:* Harrow Sch.; RMA Sandhurst. RHG (The Blues), 1958–65 (Captain); served UK, Cyprus, Germany. Mem., Irish Olympic Three Day Event Team, Mexico 1968, Munich 1972, Montreal 1976. Pres., Equestrian Fedn of Ireland, 1979–84. Mem. Bureau, Fédération Equestre Internationale, 1989– (Chm., 3 Day Event Cttee, 1989–). *Recreations:* all equestrian sports, cricket, shooting, bridge. *Heir: s* Hon. William Patrick Conolly-Carew, *b* 27 March 1973. *Address:* Donadea House, Naas, near Donadea, Co. Kildare, Ireland. *T:* Naas (45) 68204. *Club:* Kildare Street and University (Dublin).

CAREW, Sir Rivers (Verain), 11th Bt *cr* 1661; journalist; *b* 17 Oct. 1935; *s* of Sir Thomas Palk Carew, 10th Bt, and Phyllis Evelyn (*d* 1976), *o c* of Neville Mayman; *S* father, 1976; *m* 1st, 1968, Susan Babington (marr. diss. 1991), *yr d* of late H. B. Hill, London; one *s* three *d* (and one *s* decd); 2nd, 1992, Siobhán, 2nd *d* of late C. MacCárthaigh, Cork. *Educ:* St Columba's Coll., Rathfarnham, Co. Dublin; Trinity Coll., Dublin. MA, BAgr (Hort.). Asst Editor, Ireland of the Welcomes (Irish Tourist Bd magazine), 1964–67; Joint Editor, The Dublin Magazine, 1964–69; Irish Television, 1967–; BBC World Service, 1987–93. *Publication:* (with Timothy Brownlow) Figures out of Mist (verse). *Recreations:* reading, music, reflection. *Heir: s* Gerald de Redvers Carew, *b* 24 May 1975. *Address:* Undercliffe Cottage, Clarence Street, Dartmouth TQ6 9NW.

CAREW POLE, Sir (John) Richard (Walter Reginald), 13th Bt *cr* 1628, of Shute House, Devonshire; DL; farmer and chartered surveyor; *b* 2 Dec. 1938; *s* of Sir John Gawen Carew Pole, 12th Bt, DSO, TD and Cynthia Mary (*d* 1977), OBE, *o d* of Walter Burns; *S* father, 1993; *m* 1st, 1966, Hon. Victoria Marion Ann Lever (marr. diss. 1974), *d* of 3rd Viscount Leverhulme, *qv*; 2nd, 1974, Mary (MVO 1983), *d* of Lt-Col Ronald Dawnay; two *s*. *Educ:* Eton Coll.; Royal Agricultural Coll., Cirencester. ARICS 1967. Lieut, Coldstream Guards, 1958–63. Asst Surveyor, Laws & Fiennes, Chartered Surveyors, 1967–72. Dir, South West Venture Capital, 1985–87; Mem. Regional Bd, West of England, subseq. Portman, Bldg Soc., 1989–91. Chm., Devon and Cornwall Police Authority, 1985–87 (Mem., 1973–89); Member: SW Area Electricity Bd, 1981–90; NT Cttee for Devon and Cornwall, 1979–83. President: Surf Life Saving Assoc. of GB, 1976–86; Royal Cornwall Agricultural Show, 1981; Trustee: Nat. Heritage Meml Fund, 1991–; Countryside Commission, 1991–; Tate Gall., 1993–. Governor: Seale Hayne Agric. Coll., 1979–89; Plymouth Coll., 1985–; Mem. Bd, Theatre Royal, Plymouth, 1985–. County Councillor, Cornwall, 1973–93 (Chairman: Planning Cttee, 1980–84; Finance Cttee, 1985–89; Property Cttee, 1989–93); High Sheriff of Cornwall, 1979; DL Cornwall, 1988. Liveryman, Fishmongers' Co., 1960 (Mem. Court of Assistants, 1993–). *Recreations:* gardening, daydreaming, contemporary art. *Heir: s* Tremayne John Carew Pole, *b* 22 Feb. 1974. *Address:* Antony House, Torpoint, Cornwall PL11 2QA. *T:* Plymouth (01752) 814914. *Club:* Pratt's.

CAREY, Group Captain Alban M., CBE 1943; owner/farmer Church Farm, Great Witchingham, since 1973; *b* 18 April 1906; *m* 1934, Enid Morten Bond; one *s*. *Educ:* Bloxham. Commissioned RAF 1929; served in night bombers, flying boats and as flying boat and landplane instructor; Pilots Cert. no 5283 for Public Transport; Navigator's Licence no 175, 1936; Sen. Op. Trng Officer, Coastal Command, 1939–42; Station Commander: Pembroke Dock, 1942–43; Gibraltar, 1943–45; Haverfordwest, 1945; St Eval, 1945–46. Chairman: Shaw & Sons Ltd, 1946–79; Jordan & Sons Ltd, 1953–68; Hadden Best Ltd, 1957–72; Shaw & Blake Ltd, 1960–68; H. T. Woodrow & Co., 1961–68; Chirit Investment Co., 1970–; Leutromedia Computers Internat., 1971–; Maden Park Property Investment Co., 1975–; East Coast Plastics, 1984–; Viking Opticals, 1986–; Dep. Chm., Trident Group Printers plc 1972–78; Sen. Partner, Park Farm Syndicate, Snettisham, 1988–. Pres., Nat. Assoc. of Engravers and Die Stampers, 1954; Pres., Central London Br., British Fedn of Printing Industries, 1963; Chm., Nat. Assoc. of Law Stationers, 1963–68; Pres., Egham and Thorpe, Royal Agr. Assoc., 1961, 1962; Chm., Egham and Dist Abbeyfield Assoc., 1970–82. Trustee: Pensthorpe Waterfowl Trust, 1986–; Thursford Collection of Steam Engines, 1990–. *Recreations:* shooting, fishing, yachting. *Address:* Church Farm, Great Witchingham, Norfolk NR9 5PQ. *T:* Norwich (01603) 872511. *Clubs:* Royal Air Force; Royal Air Force Yacht.

CAREY, Charles John, CMG 1993; Member, European Communities' Court of Auditors, 1983–92; *b* 11 Nov. 1933; *s* of Richard Mein Carey and Celia Herbert Amy (*née* Conway); *m* 1990, Elizabeth Dale (*née* Slade). *Educ:* Rugby; Balliol Coll., Oxford. HM Treasury: Asst Principal, 1957; Principal, 1962; Asst Sec., 1971; seconded to HM Diplomatic Service as Counsellor (Econs and Finance), Office of UK Perm. Rep. to EEC, Brussels, 1974–77; Under Sec., HM Treasury, 1978–83. Chm., EC Conciliation Body for clearance of European Agricl Guidance and Guarantee Fund accounts, 1994–. Mem., CIPFA, 1988. Grand Croix de l'ordre de Merite (Luxembourg), 1992. *Recreations:* mountaineering, Bavarian baroque churches, Trollope novels. *Club:* United Oxford & Cambridge University.

CAREY, Brig. Conan Jerome; Director General, The Home Farm Trust, since 1988; *b* 8 Aug. 1936; *s* of Dr James J. Carey and Marion Carey; *m* 1966, Elizabeth Gay Docker, *d* of late Lt-Col L. R. Docker, OBE, MC, TD and Cynthia (*née* Washington); one *s* two *d*. *Educ:* Belvedere College, Dublin; RMA Sandhurst; RMCS Shrivenham; Staff Coll., Camberley (psc). FIPM. Enlisted Royal Hampshire Regt, 1954; Commissioned RASC, 1956; qualified aircraft pilot, 1960; seconded Army Air Corps, 1960–65; flying duties Malaya, Brunei, Borneo, Hong Kong, BAOR; transf. to RCT, 1965; Comdr 155 (Wessex) Regt RCT(V), 1976–78; Defence Staff, British Embassy, Washington DC, 1979–82; HQ BAOR, 1982; Dep. Dir-Gen., Transport and Movements, MoD, 1985; Comdr Training Gp, RCT, 1988. MInstD; FRSA. *Recreations:* golf, tennis. *Address:* Home Farm Trust, Merchants House, Bristol BS1 4RW. *Clubs:* Army and Navy; Tracy Park Golf and Country (Bath).

CAREY, D(avid) M(acbeth) M(oir), CBE 1983; MA, DCL Oxon; Joint Registrar to Faculty Office of Archbishop of Canterbury, since 1982; Legal Secretary to the Archbishop of Canterbury and Principal Registrar to the Province of Canterbury, 1958–82; Legal Secretary to the Bishops of Ely, 1953–82 and Gloucester, 1957–82; Registrar to the Diocese of Canterbury, 1959–82; *b* 21 Jan. 1917; *s* of Godfrey Mohun Carey, Sherborne, Dorset, and Agnes Charlotte Carey (*née* Milligan); *m* 1949, Margaret Ruth (*née* Mills), Highfield Sch., Liphook, Hants; three *s* one *d*. *Educ:* Westminster Sch. (King's Scholar); St Edmund Hall, Oxford. Articled Clerk, Messrs Lee, Bolton & Lee, 1938–40. Lt-Cdr (S) RNVR, 1940–46. Qualified Solicitor, 1947; Partnership with Lee, Bolton & Lee, 1948–82, Consultant, 1982–. Gov., Westminster Sch., 1960–92. *Recreation:* fishing. *Address:* Two Trees, 30 Shepherds Way, Liphook, Hants GU30 7HF. *T:* Liphook (01428) 723452. *Club:* Army and Navy.

CAREY, de Vic Graham; Deputy Bailiff of Guernsey, since 1992; *b* 15 June 1940; *s* of Victor Michael de Vic Carey and Jean Burnett (*née* Bullen); *m* 1968, Bridget Lindsay Smith; two *s* two *d*. *Educ:* Cheam Sch.; Bryanston Sch.; Trinity Hall, Cambridge (BA 1962; MA 1967). Admitted Solicitor, 1965; Advocate, Royal Court of Guernsey, 1966; QC (Guernsey) 1989. People's Dep., States of Guernsey, 1976; Solicitor-Gen. for Guernsey, 1977–82; Attorney-Gen., 1982–92; Receiver-Gen., 1985–92. Mem., Gen. Synod of C of E, 1982–; Chm., House of Laity, Winchester Dio. Synod, 1993–. *Address:* Les Padins, St Saviours, Guernsey. *T:* Guernsey (01481) 64587.

CAREY, Most Rev. and Rt. Hon. George Leonard; *see* Canterbury, Archbishop of.

CAREY, Godfrey Mohun Cecil; QC 1991; a Recorder of the Crown Court, since 1986; *b* 31 Oct. 1941; *s* of Dr Godfrey Fraser Carey, MVO and Prudence Loveday (*née* Webb); *m* 1st, 1965, Caroline Jane Riggall (marr. diss. 1975); one *s* one *d* (and one *s* decd); 2nd, 1978, Dorothy May Sturgeon (marr. diss. 1983); one *d*. *Educ:* Highfield, Liphook; Eton. Legal Advr, Small Engine Div., Rolls Royce Ltd, 1964–70. Called to the Bar, Inner Temple, 1969; in practice at the Bar, 1971–. *Recreations:* music, tennis, Woodruff. *Address:* 5 Paper Buildings, EC4Y 7HB. *T:* 0171–583 6117. *Club:* Lansdowne.

CAREY, Hugh Leo; Executive Vice-President, W. R. Grace and Co.; *b* Brooklyn, NY, 11 April 1919; *s* of Denis Carey and Margaret (*née* Collins); *m* 1947, Helen Owen Twohy (*d* 1974); seven *s* four *d* one step *d* (and two *s* decd). *Educ:* St Augustine's Academy and High School, Brooklyn; St John's Coll.; St John's Law School. JD 1951. Served War of 1939–45 (Bronze Star, Croix de Guerre with Silver Star); with US Army in Europe, 1939–46, rank of Lt-Col. Joined family business (petrochemicals), 1947. Called to Bar, 1951. Member US House of Reps, rep. 12th District of Brooklyn, 1960–75 (Democrat); Deputy Whip; Governor of New York State, 1974–83. *Address:* W. R. Grace & Co., 919 18th Street, NW, Suite 400, Washington, DC 20006, USA.

CAREY, Prof. John; FRSL 1982; Merton Professor of English Literature, Oxford University, since 1976; *b* 5 April 1934; *s* of Charles William Carey and Winifred Ethel Carey (*née* Cook); *m* 1960, Gillian Mary Florence Booth; two *s*. *Educ:* Richmond and East Sheen County Grammar Sch.; St John's Coll., Oxford (MA, DPhil; Hon. Fellow, 1991). 2nd Lieut, East Surrey Regt, 1953–54; Harmsworth Sen. Scholar, Merton Coll., Oxford, 1957–58; Lectr, Christ Church, Oxford, 1958–59; Andrew Bradley Jun. Research Fellow, Balliol, Oxford, 1959–60; Tutorial Fellow: Keble Coll., Oxford, 1960–64; St John's Coll., Oxford, 1964–75. Principal book reviewer, Sunday Times, 1977–. Chm., Booker Prize Judges, 1982; W. H. Smith Prize Judge, 1990–; Irish Times Lit. Prize Judge, 1993. Mem. Council, RSL, 1989–. Hon. Fellow, Balliol Coll., Oxford, 1992. *Publications:* The Poems of John Milton (ed with Alastair Fowler), 1968; Milton, 1969; (ed) Andrew Marvell, 1969; (ed) The Private Memoirs and Confessions of a Justified Sinner, by James Hogg, 1969, 2nd edn 1981; The Violent Effigy: a study of Dickens' imagination, 1973, 2nd edn 1991; (trans.) Milton, Christian Doctrine, 1973; Thackeray: Prodigal Genius, 1977; John Donne: Life, Mind and Art, 1981, 2nd edn 1990; (ed) William Golding—the Man and his Books: a tribute on his 75th birthday, 1986; Original Copy: selected journalism and reviews, 1987; (ed) The Faber Book of Reportage, 1987; (ed) Donne, 1990; The Intellectuals and the Masses, 1992; (ed) Saki, Short Stories, 1994; (ed) The Faber Book of Science and Discovery, 1995; articles in Rev. of English Studies, Mod. Lang. Rev., etc. *Recreations:* swimming, gardening, bee-keeping. *Address:* Brasenose Cottage, Lyneham, Oxon OX7 6QL; 57 Stapleton Road, Headington, Oxford OX3 7LX. *T:* Oxford (01865) 64304.

CAREY, Dr Nicholas Anthony Dermot; Director General, City and Guilds of London Institute, since 1993; *b* 4 May 1939; *s* of Eustace Dermot Carey and Audrey Mabel Carey (*née* Grenfell); *m* 1964, Helen Margaret Askey; two *s*. *Educ:* Shrewsbury Sch.; Trinity Coll., Dublin (BA, MA); King's Coll., Cambridge (PhD). ICI, 1968–93: Gen. Manager, Chlorine and derivatives, 1980–87; Man. Dir, Petrochemicals and Plastics, 1987–92; Planning Manager, Millbank, 1992–93. Director: Nalfloc, 1981–89; Phillips Imperial Petroleum, 1987–92; Teeside Power, 1991–92. Chm., Sir Isaac Pitman Ltd, 1993–. Gov., Imperial Coll., 1993–; Mem. Council, City Tech. Colls Trust, 1993–. Liveryman: Vintners' Co., 1960–; Tallow Chandlers' Co., 1995–. *Recreations:* opera, reading, an occasional game of golf. *Address:* City and Guilds of London Institute, 1 Giltspur Street, EC1A 9DD. *T:* 0171–294 2468. *Club:* MCC.

CAREY, Peter Philip, FRSL; writer; *b* 7 May 1943; *s* of Percival Stanley Carey and Helen Jean Carey; *m* 1st, 1964, Leigh Weetman; 2nd, Alison Margaret Summers; two *s*. *Educ:* Geelong Grammar Sch., Vic., Aust. FRSL 1988. Hon. DLitt Queensland, 1989. *Publications:* Fat Man in History, 1980; Bliss, 1981; Illywhacker, 1985; Oscar and Lucinda, 1988 (Booker Prize, 1988); The Tax Inspector, 1991; The Unusual Life of Tristan Smith, 1994; Collected Stories, 1995. *Recreation:* sleeping. *Address:* c/o Rogers, Coleridge & White, Powis Mews, W11 1JN.

CAREY, Sir Peter (Willoughby), GCB 1982 (KCB 1976; CB 1972); Senior Adviser, Morgan Grenfell Group, since 1990; Chairman, Dalgety PLC, 1986–92 (Director, 1983–92); Director: BPB Industries PLC, since 1983; NV Philips Electronics, since 1984; *b* 26 July 1923; *s* of Jack Delves Carey and Sophie Carey; *m* 1946, Thelma Young; three *d*. *Educ:* Portsmouth Grammar Sch.; Oriel Coll., Oxford; Sch. of Slavonic Studies. Served War of 1939–45: Capt., Gen. List, 1943–45. Information Officer, British Embassy, Belgrade, 1945–46; FO (German Section), 1948–51; Bd of Trade, 1953; Prin. Private Sec. to successive Presidents, 1960–64; IDC, 1965; Asst Sec., 1963–67, Under-Sec., 1967–69, Bd of Trade; Under-Sec., Min. of Technology, 1969–71; Dep. Sec., Cabinet Office, 1971–72; Dep. Sec., 1972–73, Second Permanent Sec., 1973–74, DTI; Second Permanent Sec., 1974–76, Permanent Sec., 1976–83, DoI. Director: Morgan Grenfell Hldgs, then Morgan Grenfell Gp, 1983–90 (Chm., 1987–89); Cable and Wireless, 1984–94; Westland Gp, 1986–88. Hon. LLD Birmingham, 1983; Hon. DSc Cranfield Inst. of Tech., 1984; Hon. DCL City, 1991. *Recreations:* music, theatre, travel. *Address:* 5 Rushmere Place, Marryat Road, Wimbledon, SW19 5RP. *T:* 0181–947 5222. *Club:* United Oxford & Cambridge University.

CAREY EVANS, David Lloyd, OBE 1984; JP; DL; farmer; *b* 14 Aug. 1925; *s* of Sir Thomas Carey Evans, MC, FRCS and Lady Olwen Carey Evans, DBE; *m* 1959, Annwen Williams; three *s* one *d*. *Educ:* Rottingdean Sch.; Oundle Sch.; Univ. of Wales, Bangor. BSc (Agric) 1950. Sub-Lieut, RNVR, 1943–46; farming 1947–; Chm., Welsh Council, NFU, 1976–79; Welsh Representative and Chm., Welsh Panel, CCAHC, 1974; Chm., WAOS. JP Portmadoc, Gwynedd, 1969. DL Gwynedd 1988. *Address:* Eisteddfa, Criccieth, Gwynedd LL52 0PT. *T:* Criccieth (01766) 522104. *Club:* Sloane.

CAREY JONES, Norman Stewart, CMG 1965; Director, Development Administration, Leeds University, 1965–77; *b* 11 Dec. 1911; *s* of Samuel Carey Jones and Jessie Isabella Stewart; *m* 1946, Stella Myles (*d* 1990); two *s*. *Educ:* Monmouth Sch.; Merton Coll., Oxford. Colonial Audit Service: Gold Coast, 1935; Northern Rhodesia, 1939; British Honduras, 1946; Kenya, 1950; Asst Financial Sec., Treasury, Kenya, 1954; Dep. Sec.,

Min. of Agric., Kenya, 1956; Perm. Sec., Min. of Lands and Settlement, Kenya, 1962. *Publications:* The Pattern of a Dependent Economy, 1952; The Anatomy of Uhuru, 1966; Politics, Public Enterprise and The Industrial Development Agency, 1974; articles and reviews for: Journal of Rhodes-Livingstone Inst.; E African Economics Review; Africa Quarterly; Geog. Jl. *Address:* Mawingo, Welsh St Donats, near Cowbridge, S Glam CF7 7SS. *Club:* Commonwealth Trust.

CARINE, Rear-Adm. James; Chief of Staff to Commander-in-Chief Naval Home Command, 1989–91; Registrar, Arab Horse Society, since 1992; *b* 14 Sept. 1934; *s* of Amos Carine and Kathleen Prudence Carine (*née* Kelly); *m* 1961, (Carolyn) Sally Taylor; three *s* one *d* (and two *s* decd). *Educ:* Victoria Road Sch., Castletown, IoM; King William's Coll., IoM. FCIS 1971. Joined Royal Navy 1951; Captain 1980; Sec., Second Sea Lord, 1979–82; SACLANT HQ, Norfolk, Va, 1982–85; Naval Home Staff, 1985–88; Commodore in Comd, HMS Drake, 1988–89. Pres., RN Assoc. (IOM), 1992–. London Campaign Cttee for Multiple Sclerosis, 1993–. Liveryman, 1988, Mem., Court of Assistants, 1989, Chartered Secretaries' Co. KSG. *Recreations:* dinghy sailing, horse racing. *Address:* (office) Windsor House, Ramsbury, Wilts SN8 2PE.

CARINGTON, family name of **Baron Carrington.**

CARLESS, Hugh Michael, CMG 1976; HM Diplomatic Service, retired; Executive Vice President, Hinduja Foundation, since 1986; Vice Chairman, South Atlantic Council, since 1987; *b* 22 April 1925; *s* of late Henry Alfred Carless, CIE, and Gwendolen Pattullo; *m* 1956, Rosa Maria, *e d* of Martino and Ada Frontini, São Paulo; two *s*. *Educ:* Sherborne; Sch. of Oriental Studies, London; Trinity Hall, Cambridge. Served in Paiforce and BAOR, 1943–47; entered Foreign (subseq. Diplomatic) Service, 1950; 3rd Sec., Kabul, 1951; 2nd Sec., Rio de Janeiro, 1953; Tehran, 1956; 1st Sec., 1957; FO, 1958; Private Sec. to Minister of State, 1961; Budapest, 1963; Civil Service Fellow, Dept of Politics, Glasgow Univ., 1966; Counsellor and Consul-Gen., Luanda, 1967–70; Counsellor, Bonn, 1970–73; Head of Latin American Dept, FCO, 1973–77; Minister and Chargé d'Affaires, Buenos Aires, 1977–80; on secondment to Northern Engineering Industries International Ltd, 1980–82; Ambassador to Venezuela, 1982–85. Chm. British Cttee, Argentine-British Confs, 1994–. An Hon. Vice Pres., RSAA, 1992–. *Recreations:* golf, history. *Address:* 15 Bryanston Square, W1H 7FF. *Clubs:* Travellers'; Royal Mid Surrey Golf.

CARLESS, Prof. John Edward, BPharm, MSc, PhD; Professor and Head of Department of Pharmaceutics, School of Pharmacy, London University, 1977–83, Emeritus Professor, since 1984; *b* 23 Nov. 1922; *s* of Alfred Edward Carless and Frances Mary (*née* Smith); *m* 1950, Dorothy Litherland; one *d* and two step *d*. *Educ:* Leominster Grammar Sch.; Leicester Coll. of Science and Technol. (BPharm); FPS 1947; Univ. of Manchester (MSc, PhD). FRPharmS. Asst Lectr in Pharmacy, Univ. of Manchester, 1947–54; Chelsea College: Sen. Lectr in Pharmaceutics, 1954–61; Reader, 1961–67; Prof. of Pharmaceutics, 1967–77. Member: Cttee on Safety of Medicines, 1976–78 (Mem., Sub-Cttee on Chemistry, Pharmacy and Standards, 1973–92); Veterinary Products Cttee, 1978–85; Cttee on Review of Medicine, 1980–92; UK Working Gp on iodine prophylaxis following nuclear accidents, 1989–90; Chm., Pharmacy Bd, CNAA, 1978–85. Chm., Reigate Photographic Soc., 1984–86; Governor, Reigate Sixth Form Coll., 1986–93. Harrison Meml Medal, 1980. *Publications:* (ed jtly) Advances in Pharmaceutical Sciences: Vol. 1, 1964–vol. 5, 1982; (contrib.) Bentley's Text Book of Pharmaceutics, 1977. *Recreations:* photography, listening to records, bowls. *Address:* Manton, Colley Manor Drive, Reigate, Surrey RH2 9JS. *T:* Reigate (01737) 43670.

CARLETON, Air Vice-Marshal Geoffrey Wellesley; Director, Royal Air Force Legal Services, Ministry of Defence, since 1992; *b* 22 Sept. 1935; *s* of Gp Capt. Cyril Wellesley Carleton and Francis Beatrice (*née* Hensman); *m* 1985, Dianne Margaret Creswick; one *s*. *Educ:* Sherborne Sch. Admitted solicitor, 1959; commnd RAF, 1959, Pilot Officer, 1959–61; Asst Solicitor, Herbert Smith & Co., 1961–65; re joined RAF, 1965 as Flt Lieut; Legal Officer, HQ MEAF, Aden, HQ NEAF, Cyprus, HQ FEAF, Singapore, HQ RAF, Germany, 1965–78; Deputy Director of Legal Services: HQ RAF, Germany, 1979–82 and 1985–88; MoD, 1988–92. *Publications:* articles in professional and service jls and pubns. *Recreations:* sailing, ski-ing, equitation, opera. *Address:* c/o National Westminster Bank, 8 Christchurch Road, Bournemouth BH1 3LZ. *Clubs:* Royal Air Force, Royal Ocean Racing.

CARLETON, Janet (Buchanan), (Mrs John Carleton); *see* Adam Smith, J. B.

CARLETON-SMITH, Maj.-Gen. Michael Edward, CBE 1980 (MBE 1966); DL; Director-General, Marie Curie Memorial Foundation, since 1985; Chairman, Marie Curie Trading Co. Ltd, since 1990; *b* 5 May 1931; *s* of late Lt-Col D. L. G. Carleton-Smith and Mrs B. L. C. Carleton-Smith (*née* Popham); *m* 1963, Helga Katja Stoss (*d* 1993); three *s*. *Educ:* Radley Coll.; RMA, Sandhurst. Graduate: Army Staff Coll.; JSSC; NDC; RCDS. Commissioned into The Rifle Brigade, 1951; Rifle Bde, Germany, 1951–53; active service: Kenya, 1954–55; Malaya, 1957; Exchange PPCLI, Canada, 1958–60; GSO2 General Staff, HQ1(BR) Corps, 1962–63; Rifle Brigade: Cyprus, Hong Kong, active service, Borneo, 1965–66; Sch. of Infantry Staff, 1967–68; Comd Rifle Depot, 1970–72; Directing Staff NDC, 1972–74; Col General Staff, HQ BAOR, 1974–77; Commander Gurkha Field Force, Hong Kong, 1977–79; Dep. Director Army Staff Duties, MoD, 1981; Defence Advr and Head of British Defence Liaison Staff, Canberra, Australia, also Mil. Advr, Canberra, and Wellington, NZ, and Defence Advr, PNG, 1982–85, retd. Vice-Chm., Nat. Council for Hospice and Specialist Palliative Care Services, 1992–. DL Leics, 1992. *Recreations:* riding, travel. *Address:* 28 Belgrave Square, SW1X 8QG.

CARLIER, Maj.-Gen. Anthony Neil, CB 1992; OBE 1982; Director: Haig Homes, since 1992; Housing Association for Officers' Families, since 1992; *b* 11 Jan. 1937; *s* of Geoffrey Anthony George and Sylvia Maude Carlier; *m* 1974, Daphne Kathleen Humphreys; one *s* one *d*. *Educ:* Highgate Sch.; RMA Sandhurst; RMCS. BSc(Eng) London. Troop Comdr, Cyprus, 1962–64; GSO3, 19 Inf. Bde, Borneo, 1965–66; Instructor, RMA Sandhurst, 1967–70; Staff Course: RMCS Shrivenham, 1971; BRNC Greenwich, 1972; GSO2, Staff of Flag Officer, Carriers and Amphibious Ships, 1973–74; Sqn Comdr, 1975–76; Regtl Comdr, 1977–80; Mil. Asst to Army Bd Mem., 1980–83; Engr Gp Comdr, 1983–85; rcds, 1986; Comdr British Forces, Falkland Is, 1987–88; Chief, Jt Services Liaison Organisation, Bonn, 1989–90; Team Leader, QMG's Logistic Support Review, 1991–92. President: Officers' Christian Union, 1992–; Mission to Mil. Garrisons, 1992–; Chm., UK Appeal Cttee for Christ Church Cathedral, Falkland Is., 1989–. Trustee: Cornelius Trust; Royal Engineer Yacht Club, 1992–. *Recreations:* offshore sailing, fishing, gardening, DIY. *Club:* International Association of Cape Horners (St Malo).

CARLILE, Alexander Charles, QC 1984; MP Montgomery, since 1983 (L 1983–88, Lib Dem since 1988); a Recorder, since 1986; *b* 12 Feb. 1948; *s* of Erwin Falik, MD and Sabina Falik; *m* 1968, Frances, *d* of Michael and Elizabeth Soley; three *d*. *Educ:* Epsom Coll.; King's Coll., London (LLB; AKC). Called to the Bar, Gray's Inn, 1970, Bencher, 1992. Chm., Welsh Liberal Party, 1980–82; Leader, Welsh Lib Dems, 1992–. Lib. spokesman, 1983–88, Soc & Lib Dem spokesman, 1988, on Home Office and legal affairs; Alliance spokesman on legal affairs, 1987; Lib Dem spokesman on foreign affairs, 1988–89, on legal affairs, 1989–90, on trade and industry, 1990–92, on Wales, and on employment, 1992–94, on health and welfare, 1994–. Contested (L) Flint East, Feb. 1974, 1979. Member: Adv. Council on Public Records, 1989–; GMC, 1989–; Council, Howard League, 1989–; Council, Justice, 1993–. *Recreations:* reading, theatre. *Address:* 4 Paper Buildings, Temple, EC4Y 7EX. *Club:* Reform.

CARLILE, Rev. Edward Wilson; Liaison Officer, East Africa Church Army Appeal, 1981–84; *b* 11 June 1915; *s* of Victor Wilson and Elsie Carlile; *m* 1946, Elizabeth (*née* Bryant); two *s* one *d*. *Educ:* Epsom Coll.; King's Coll., London (BD). Chartered Accountant, 1939. Deacon, 1943; priest, 1944; Curate, All Saints, Queensbury, 1943–46; Hon. Asst Sec. of Church Army, 1946–49; Chief Sec. of Church Army, 1949–60; Vicar of St Peter's with St Hilda's, Leicester, 1960–73; Rector of Swithland, Leicester, 1973–76; Priest in Charge of St Michael and All Angels, Belgrave, Leicester, 1976–81. *Recreations:* race relations, evangelism, walking, travel, photography. *Address:* 120A Mount View Road, Sheffield S8 8PL. *T:* Sheffield (0114) 258 1098.

CARLILE, Thomas, CBE 1975; FEng; Chairman, Burnett and Hallamshire Holdings, 1985–88; *b* 9 Feb. 1924; *s* of late James Love Carlile and Isobel Scott Carlile; *m* 1955, Jessie Davidson Clarkson; three *d*. *Educ:* Minchenden County Sch.; City & Guilds Coll., London. Joined Babcock & Wilcox Ltd, 1944; Man. Dir, 1968–84, Dep. Chm., 1978–84, Babcock Internat. plc. Chm., Shipbuilding Industry Training Board, 1967–70; Dep. Chm., Police Negotiating Bd, 1987–. Mem., Energy Commn, 1977–79. Pres., Engineering Employers' Fedn, 1972–74, a Vice-Pres., 1979–84. Director: Chubb & Son plc, 1976–84; French Kier Hldgs Plc, 1985–86. FCGI 1978; FEng 1979. *Address:* 8 Aldenham Grove, Radlett, Herts WD7 7BW. *T:* Radlett (01923) 857033.

CARLILL, Rear Adm. John Hildred, OBE 1969; DL; Royal Navy, retired 1982; *b* 24 Oct. 1925; *o s* of late Dr and Mrs H. B. Carlill; *m* 1955, (Elizabeth) Ann, *yr d* of late Lt Col and Mrs W. Southern; three *d*. *Educ:* RNC Dartmouth. psc 1961; jssc 1967. Served War 1939–45. Joined RN as Exec. Cadet 1939, transferred to Accountant Branch 1943; HMS Mauritius 1943–45. Comdr 1963, Captain 1972 (Sec. to FO Naval Air Comd, Dir Naval Manning and Training (S), Sec. to Second Sea Lord, Admty Interview Board, Cdre HMS Drake); Rear Admiral 1980; Adm. President, RNC Greenwich, 1980–82. Sec., Engineering Council, 1983–87. Chm., Guildford Sea Cadet Cttee, 1987; Pres., Guildford Br., RN Assoc., 1989–. Freeman: City of London, 1980; Drapers' Co., 1983. DL Surrey, 1994. *Recreations:* walking, short story writing, water colour painting. *Address:* Crownpits Barn, Crownpits Lane, Godalming, Surrey GU7 1NY. *T:* Godalming (01483) 415022.

CARLILL, Vice-Admiral Sir Stephen Hope, KBE 1957; CB 1954; DSO 1942; *b* Orpington, Kent, 23 Dec. 1902; *s* of late Harold Flamank Carlill; *m* 1928, Julie Fredrike Elisabeth Hildegard, *o d* of late Rev. W. Rahlenbeck, Westphalia; two *s*. *Educ:* Royal Naval Colleges, Osborne and Dartmouth. Lieut RN, 1925; qualified as Gunnery Officer, 1929; Commander 1937; Commanded HM Destroyers Hambledon, 1940, and Farndale, 1941–42; Captain 1942; Captain (D), 4th Destoyer Flotilla, HMS Quilliam, 1942–44 (despatches); Admiralty, 1944–46; Chief of Staff to C-in-C British Pacific Fleet, 1946–48; Captain, HMS Excellent, 1949–50; Commanded HMS Illustrious, 1950–51; Rear-Admiral, 1952; Senior Naval Member, Imperial Defence Coll., 1952–54; Vice-Admiral, 1954; Flag Officer, Training Squadron, 1954–55; Chief of Naval Staff, Indian Navy, 1955–58, retired. Representative in Ghana of West Africa Cttee 1960–66; Adviser to W Africa Cttee, 1966–67. *Recreations:* walking and gardening. *Address:* Evendine House, Colwall, Malvern, Worcs WR13 6DT. *Club:* Naval and Military.

CARLING, William David Charles, OBE 1991; Captain of England, Rugby Football, since 1988 (centre three-quarter); *b* 12 Dec. 1965; *s* of Pamela and Bill Carling; *m* 1994, Julia, *o d* of H. B. Smith. *Educ:* Sedbergh School; Durham Univ. (BA Psych.). Played for Harlequins, 1987–; 1st cap for England, 1988; 60 caps to 1995, 53 as Captain; captained: two Grand Slam sides, 1991, 1992; World Cup final, 1991; Barbarians, in Hong Kong 7's, 1991; England tour, South Africa, 1994; World Cup, South Africa, 1995; Mem., British Lions, NZ tour, 1993. *Publications:* Captain's Diary, 1991; Will Carling (autobiog.), 1994; (with R. Heller) The Way to Win, 1995. *Recreations:* theatre, sketching, golf. *Address:* c/o Insights Ltd, 106 Dawes Road, Fulham, SW6 7EG. *Club:* Harlequins.

CARLISLE, family name of **Baron Carlisle of Bucklow.**

CARLISLE, 13th Earl of *cr* 1661; **George William Beaumont Howard;** Viscount Howard of Morpeth, Baron Dacre of Gillesland 1661; Lord Ruthven of Freeland 1651; *b* 15 Feb. 1949; *s* of 12th Earl of Carlisle, MC, and of Hon. Ela Hilda Aline Beaumont, *o d* of 2nd Viscount Allendale, KG, CB, CBE, MC; *S* father, 1994. *Educ:* Eton Coll.; Balliol Coll., Oxford. 9th/12th Royal Lancers, 1967–87; Lieut 1970, Captain 1974, Major 1981. Contested: (L/Alliance) Easington, 1987; (Lib Dem) Northumbria, European parly elecn, 1989. *Recreations:* reading, travel. *Heir: b* Hon. Philip Charles Wentworth Howard, *b* 25 March 1963. *Address:* 8 Mill Terrace, Easington, Co. Durham. *Clubs:* Beefsteak, Brooks's.

CARLISLE OF BUCKLOW, Baron *cr* 1987 (Life Peer), of Mobberley in the County of Cheshire; **Mark Carlisle,** PC 1979; QC 1971; DL; a Recorder of the Crown Court, 1976–79 and since 1981; a Judge of the Courts of Appeal, Jersey and Guernsey, since 1990; *b* 7 July 1929; 2nd *s* of late Philip Edmund and Mary Carlisle; *m* 1959, Sandra Joyce Des Voeux; one *d*. *Educ:* Radley Coll.; Manchester Univ. LLB (Hons) Manchester, 1952. Called to the Bar, Gray's Inn, 1953, Bencher 1980; Northern Circuit. Member Home Office Advisory Council on the Penal System, 1966–70. MP (C): Runcorn, 1964–83; Warrington S, 1983–87. Joint Hon. Secretary, Conservative Home Affairs Cttee, 1965–69; Conservative Front Bench Spokesman on Home Affairs, 1969–70; Parly Under-Sec. of State, Home Office, 1970–72; Minister of State, Home Office, 1972–74; Sec. of State for Educn and Science, 1979–81. Chairman: Cons. Home Affairs Cttee, 1983–87; Parole Review Cttee, 1987–88; Prime Minister's Adv. Cttee on Business Appts of Crown Servants, 1988–; Criminal Injuries Compensation Bd, 1989–. Treas., CPA, 1982–85, Dep. Chm., UK Br., 1985–87. Mem., Adv. Council, BBC, 1975–79. DL Cheshire, 1983. *Recreation:* golf. *Address:* Queen Elizabeth Building, Temple, EC4Y 9BS. *T:* 0171-583 5766; 3 Holt Gardens, Mobberley, Cheshire WA16 7LH. *T:* Mobberley (0156587) 2275. *Club:* Garrick.

CARLISLE, Bishop of, since 1989; **Rt. Rev. Ian Harland;** *b* 19 Dec. 1932; *s* of late Canon Samuel James Harland and of Brenda Gwendolyn Harland; *m* 1967, Susan Hinman; one *s* three *d*. *Educ:* Dragon School, Oxford; Haileybury; Peterhouse, Cambridge (MA); Wycliffe Hall, Oxford. Teaching at Sunningdale School, 1956–58; Curate, Melton Mowbray, 1960–63; Vicar, Oughtibridge, Sheffield, 1963–72; Member, Wortley RDC, 1969–73; Vicar, St Cuthbert, Fir Vale, Sheffield, 1972–75; Priest-in-charge, All Saints, Brightside, 1973–75; RD of Ecclesfield, 1973–75; Vicar of Rotherham, 1975–79; RD of Rotherham, 1976–79; Archdeacon of Doncaster, 1979–85; Bishop Suffragan of Lancaster, 1985–89. Proctor in Convocation, 1975–85. *Recreations:* politics, sport. *Address:* Rose Castle, Dalston, Carlisle CA5 7BZ. *T:* Raughton Head (016974) 76274.

CARLISLE, Dean of; *see* Stapleton, Very Rev. H. E. C.

CARLISLE, Archdeacon of; *see* Turnbull, Ven. D. C.

CARLISLE, Brian Apcar, CBE 1974; DSC 1945; Chairman, Saxon Oil PLC, 1980–85; *b* 27 Dec. 1919; 2nd *s* of Captain F. M. M. Carlisle, MC; *m* 1953, Elizabeth Hazel Mary Binnie, 2nd *d* of Comdr J. A. Binnie, RN; one *s* three *d*. *Educ:* Harrow Sch.; Corpus Christi Coll., Cambridge. Royal Navy, 1940–46, served in N Atlantic, Channel and Mediterranean in HMS Hood and destroyers; Sudan Political Service, 1946–54, served in Kassala, Blue-Nile and Bahr-el-Ghazal Provinces; Royal Dutch/Shell Group, 1955–74: served in India with Burmah Shell, 1960–64; Regional Co-ordinator, Middle East, and Dir, Shell International Petroleum, 1970–74; participated in pricing negotiations with OPEC states, 1970–73; Dir, Home Oil Co. Ltd, 1977–80; Oil Consultant to Lloyds Bank International, 1975–81. Chm., Bd of Governors, Gordon's Sch. (formerly Gordon Boys' Sch.), 1985–95. Chm., Sudan Church Assoc., 1982–. *Recreations:* gardening, crosswords, golf. *Address:* Heath Cottage, Hartley Wintney, Hants RG27 8RE. *T:* Hartley Wintney (01252) 842224.

CARLISLE, Hugh Bernard Harwood, QC 1978; a Recorder of the Crown Court, since 1983; *b* 14 March 1937; *s* of late W. H. Carlisle, FRCS (Ed), FRCOG, and Joyce Carlisle; *m* 1964, Veronica Marjorie, *d* of G. A. Worth, MBE; one *s* one *d*. *Educ:* Oundle Sch.; Downing Coll., Cambridge. Nat. Service, 2nd Lt, RA. Called to the Bar, Middle Temple, 1961, Bencher, 1985. Jun. Treasury Counsel for Personal Injuries Cases, 1975–78. Dept of Trade Inspector: Bryanston Finance Ltd, 1978–87; Milbury plc, 1985–87. Member: Criminal Injuries Compensation Bd, 1982–; Bar Council, 1989–92 (Chm., Professional Conduct Cttee, 1991–92). *Recreations:* fishing, croquet. *Address:* 1 Temple Gardens, EC4Y 9BB. *T:* 0171-583 1315. *Clubs:* Garrick, Hurlingham (Chm., 1982–85).

CARLISLE, Sir James (Beethoven), GCMG 1993; Governor-General of Antigua and Barbuda, since 1993; *b* 5 Aug. 1937; *s* of late James Carlisle and of Jestina Jones; *m* 1st, 1963, Umilta Mercer (marr. diss. 1973); one *s* one *d*; 2nd, 1973, Anne Jenkins (marr. diss. 1984); one *d*; 3rd, 1984, Nalda Amelia Meade; one *s* one *d*. *Educ:* Univ. of Dundee (BDS). General Dentistry, 1972–92. Chief Scout of Antigua and Barbuda. Chm., Nat. Parks Authority, 1986–90. Member: BDA; Amer. Acad. of Laser Dentistry; Internat. Assoc. of Laser Dentistry; Vice Pres., Antigua and Barbuda Dental Assoc. Hon. FDSRCSE 1995. *Recreation:* gardening. *Address:* Governor-General's Residence, St John's, Antigua, West Indies. *T:* (809) 4620003.

CARLISLE, Sir (John) Michael, Kt 1985; CEng, FIMechE, FIMarE; Director, Torday & Carlisle plc, 1981–94 (non-executive, 1989–94); Chairman, Community Health Sheffield NHS Trust, since 1994; *b* 16 Dec. 1929; *s* of John Hugh Carlisle and Lilian Amy (*née* Smith); *m* 1957, Mary Scott Young; one *s* one *d*. *Educ:* King Edward VII Sch., Sheffield; Sheffield Univ. (BEng). Served Royal Navy (Lieut), 1952–54. Production Engr, Lockwood & Carlisle Ltd, 1954–57, Man. Dir, 1958–70, Chm. and Man. Dir, 1970–81; Dir of several overseas subsid. cos; Director: Eric Woodward (Electrical) Ltd, 1965–85; Diesel Marine Internat., 1981–89. Chairman: N Sheffield Univ. HMC, 1971–74; Sheffield AHA(T), 1974–82; Trent RHA, 1982–94; Member: Sheffield HMC, 1969–71; Bd of Governors, United Sheffield Hosps, 1972–74; MRC, 1991–95; NHS Policy Bd, 1993–94. Member Council: Sheffield Chamber of Commerce, 1967–78; Production Engrg Res. Assoc., 1968–73; Chm., Sheffield Productivity Assoc., 1970; Pres., Sheffield Jun. Chamber of Commerce, 1967–68; non-exec. Director: Fenchurch Midlands Ltd, 1986–94; Norhomes plc, 1989–; Welpac plc, 1991–; Residences at York plc, 1992–; York Science Park Ltd, 1992–; York Science Park (Innovation) Centre Ltd; Headrow Northern plc, 1992–; Headrow Western plc, 1993–. Governor: Sheffield City Polytechnic, 1979–82 (Hon. Fellow, 1977); Sheffield High Sch., 1977–87; Member: Sheffield Univ. Court, 1968–; Sheffield Univ. Careers Adv. Bd, 1974–82; Nottingham Univ. Court, 1982–94; Council and Court, York Univ., 1991–. Hon. LLD: Sheffield, 1988; Nottingham, 1992. Freeman, City of London, 1989; Freeman, Co. of Cutlers in Hallamshire. CIMgt. *Recreations:* golf, country walking, water colour painting, genealogy. *Address:* 7 Rushley Avenue, Dore, Sheffield S17 3EP. *T:* Sheffield (0114) 2365988; St Ovin, Lastingham, N Yorks YO6 6TL. *T:* Lastingham (01751) 417341. *Clubs:* Royal Society of Medicine; Sickleholme Golf; Kirbymoorside Golf.

CARLISLE, John Russell; MP (C) Luton North, since 1983 (Luton West, 1979–83); *b* 28 Aug. 1942; *s* of Andrew and Edith Carlisle; *m* 1964, Anthea Jane Lindsay May; two *d*. *Educ:* Bedford Sch.; St Lawrence Coll.; Coll. of Estate Management, London. Sidney C. Banks Ltd, Sandy, 1964–78; Consultant: Louis Dreyfus plc, 1982–87; Barnet Devanney & Co. Ltd, 1987–; Barry Simmons PR, 1987–; non-exec. Dir, Bletchley Motor Gp, 1988–; Member: London Corn Exchange, 1987–; Baltic Exchange, 1991–. Chm., Mid Beds Cons. Assoc., 1974–76. Chm., Cons Parly Cttee on Sport, 1981–82, 1983–84, 1985–; Vice Chm., All-Party Football Cttee, 1987–; Mem., Commons Select Cttee on Agriculture, 1985–88. Chm., British–S Africa Gp, 1987 (Sec., 1983–87); Treas., Anglo-Gibraltar Gp, 1981–82. Governor, Sports Aid Foundn (Eastern), 1985–. President: Luton 100 Club; Luton Band; Bedfordshire CCC, 1993–. *Recreations:* sport, music. *Address:* House of Commons, SW1A 0AA. *T:* 0171–219 4571. *Clubs:* Farmers', MCC, Rugby.

CARLISLE, Sir Kenneth (Melville), Kt 1994; MP (C) Lincoln, since 1979; *b* 25 March 1941; *s* of late Kenneth Ralph Malcolm Carlisle, TD and of Hon. Elizabeth Mary McLaren, *d* of 2nd Baron Aberconway; *m* 1986, Carla, *d* of A. W. Heffner, Md, USA; one *s*. *Educ:* Harrow; Magdalen Coll., Oxford (BA History). Called to Bar, Inner Temple, 1965. Brooke Bond Liebig, 1966–74; farming in Suffolk, 1974–. PPS to: Minister of State for Energy, 1981–83; Minister of State for Home Office, 1983–84; Sec. of State for NI, 1984–85; Home Secretary, 1985–87; an Asst Govt Whip, 1987–88; a Lord Comr of HM Treasury, 1988–90; Parly Under-Sec. of State, MoD, 1990–92, Dept of Transport, 1992–93. *Recreations:* botany, gardening, walking, history. *Address:* House of Commons, SW1A 0AA.

CARLISLE, Sir Michael; *see* Carlisle, Sir J. M.

CARLOW, Viscount; Charles George Yuill Seymour Dawson-Damer; *b* 6 Oct. 1965; *s* and *heir* of 7th Earl of Portarlington, *qv*. *Educ:* Eton College; Univ. of Edinburgh (MA Hons 1988). A Page of Honour to the Queen, 1979–80. *Address:* c/o John Swire & Sons (HK) Ltd, GPO Box 1, Hong Kong. *Club:* Royal Sydney Golf (Sydney).

CARLTON, Viscount; Reed Montagu Stuart Wortley; *b* 5 Feb. 1980; *s* and heir of Earl of Wharncliffe, *qv*.

CARLYLE, Joan Hildred; soprano; *b* 6 April 1931; *d* of late Edgar James and Margaret Mary Carlyle; *m*; two *d*. *Educ:* Howell's Sch., Denbigh, N Wales. Became Principal Lyric Soprano, Royal Opera House, Covent Garden, 1955; Oscar in Ballo in Maschera, 1957–58 season; Sophie in Rosenkavalier, 1958–59; Micaela in Carmen, 1958–59; Nedda in Pagliacci (new Zeffirelli production), Dec. 1959; Mimi in La Bohème, Dec. 1960; Titania in Gielgud production of Britten's Midsummer Night's Dream, London première, Dec. 1961; Pamina in Klemperer production of The Magic Flute, 1962; Countess in Figaro, 1963; Zdenko in Hartman production of Arabella, 1964; Sœur Angelica (new production), 1965; Desdemona in Otello, 1965, 1967; Sophie in Rosenkavalier (new production), 1966; Pamina in Magic Flute (new production), 1966; Arabella in Arabella, 1967; Marschallin in Rosenkavalier, 1968; Jenifer, Midsummer Marriage (new prod.), 1969; Donna Anna, 1970; Reiza, Oberon, 1970; Adrianna Lecouvreur, 1970; Russalka, for BBC, 1969; Elizabeth in Don Carlos, 1975. Roles sung abroad include: Oscar, Nedda, Mimi, Pamina, Zdenko, Micaela, Desdemona, Donna Anna, Arabella, Elizabeth. Has sung in Buenos Aires, Belgium, Holland, France, Monaco, Naples, Milan, Berlin, Capetown, Munich. Has made numerous recordings; appeared BBC, TV (in film). *Recreations:* gardening, cooking, interior decorating, countryside preservation. *Address:* The Griffin, Ruthin, Clwyd, N Wales.

CARMAN, George Alfred, QC 1971; a Recorder of the Crown Court, 1972–84; *b* 6 Oct. 1929; *o s* of late Alfred George Carman and Evelyn Carman; *m* 1960, Cecilia Sparrow (marr. diss. 1976); one *s*; *m* 1976, Frances Elizabeth Venning (marr. diss. 1984). *Educ:* St Joseph's Coll., Blackpool; Balliol Coll., Oxford. First Class, Final Hons Sch. of Jurisprudence, 1952. Captain RAEC, 1948–49. Called to the Bar (King George V Coronation Schol.) Lincoln's Inn, 1953, Bencher 1978; practised on Northern Circuit. *Address:* New Court, Temple, EC4Y 9BE. *Club:* Garrick.

CARMICHAEL, family name of **Baron Carmichael of Kelvingrove.**

CARMICHAEL OF KELVINGROVE, Baron *cr* 1983 (Life Peer), of Camlachie in the District of the City of Glasgow; **Neil George Carmichael;** *b* Oct. 1921; *m* 1948, Catherine McIntosh Rankin (*see* C. M. Carmichael) (marr. diss.); one *d*. *Educ:* Estbank Acad.; Royal Coll. of Science and Technology, Glasgow. Employed by Gas Board in Planning Dept. Past Member Glasgow Corporation. MP (Lab) Glasgow, Woodside, 1962–74, Glasgow, Kelvingrove, 1974–83; contested (Lab) Glasgow, Hillhead, 1983. PPS to Minister of Technology, 1966–67; Jt Parly Sec., Min. of Transport, 1967–69; Parly Sec., Min. of Technology, 1969–70; Parliamentary Under-Secretary of State: DoE, 1974–75; DoI, 1975–76; Mem., Select Cttee on Transport, 1980–83; Hon. Sec., Scottish Labour Gp of MPs, 1979–83. *Address:* House of Lords, SW1A 0PW; 53 Partick Hill Road, Glasgow G11 5AB.

CARMICHAEL, Catherine McIntosh, (Kay); social worker; *b* 22 Nov. 1925; *d* of John D. and Mary Rankin; *m* 1948, Neil George Carmichael (now Baron Carmichael of Kelvingrove, *qv*) (marr. diss.); one *d*; *m* 1987, David Vernon Donnison, *qv*. *Educ:* Glasgow and Edinburgh. Social worker, 1955–57; psychiatric social work, 1957–60; Dep. Dir, Scottish Probation Training Course, 1960–62; Lectr, 1962, Sen. Lectr, 1974–80, Dept of Social Administration and Social Work, Univ. of Glasgow. Mem., 1969–75, Dep. Chm., 1975–80, Supplementary Benefits Commn. *Recreation:* Alexander technique. *Address:* 23 Bank Street, Glasgow G12 8JQ. *T:* 0141–334 5817.

CARMICHAEL, Sir David William G. C.; *see* Gibson-Craig-Carmichael.

CARMICHAEL, Ian (Gillett); *b* 18 June 1920; *s* of Arthur Denholm Carmichael, Cottingham, E Yorks, and Kate Gillett, Hessle, E Yorks; *m* 1st, 1943, Jean Pyman Maclean (*d* 1983), Sleights, Yorks; two *d*; 2nd, 1992, Kathryn Ann Fenton. *Educ:* Scarborough Coll.; Bromsgrove Sch. Studied at RADA, 1938–39. Served War of 1939–45 (despatches). First professional appearance as a Robot in "RUR", by Karel and Josef Capek, The People's Palace, Stepney, 1939; *stage appearances* include: The Lyric Revue, Globe, 1951; The Globe Revue, Globe, 1952; High Spirits, Hippodrome, 1953; Going to Town, St Martin's, 1954; Simon and Laura, Apollo, 1954; The Tunnel of Love, Her Majesty's, 1958; The Gazebo, Savoy, 1960; Critic's Choice, Vaudeville, 1961; Devil May Care, Strand, 1963; Boeing-Boeing, Cort Theatre, New York, 1965; Say Who You Are, Her Majesty's, 1965; Getting Married, Strand, 1968; I Do! I Do!, Lyric, 1968; Birds on the Wing, O'Keefe Centre, Toronto, 1969; Darling I'm Home, S African tour, 1972; Out on a Limb, Vaudeville, 1976; Overheard, Theatre Royal, Haymarket, 1981; Pride and Prejudice, Theatre Royal, York and nat. tour, 1987; The Circle, nat. tour, 1990; The School for Scandal, Chichester, 1995. *Films* include: (from 1955) Simon and Laura; Private's Progress; Brothers in Law; Lucky Jim; Happy is the Bride; The Big Money; Left, Right and Centre; I'm All Right Jack; School for Scoundrels; Light Up The Sky; Double Bunk; The Amorous Prawn; Hide and Seek; Heavens Above!; Smashing Time; The Magnificent Seven Deadly Sins; From Beyond the Grave; The Lady Vanishes. *TV series* include: The World of Wooster; Bachelor Father; Lord Peter Wimsey; All For Love; Obituaries; Strathblair. Hon. DLitt Hull, 1987. *Publication:* Will the Real Ian Carmichael . . . (autobiog.), 1979. *Recreations:* cricket, gardening, photography and reading. *Address:* c/o London Management, 2–4 Noel Street, W1V 3RB. *Club:* MCC.

CARMICHAEL, Sir John, KBE 1955; Chairman, St Andrews Links Trust, 1984–88; *b* 22 April 1910; *s* of late Thomas Carmichael and Margaret Doig Coupar; *m* 1940, Cecilia Macdonald Edwards; one *s* three *d*. *Educ:* Madras Coll., St Andrews; Univ. of St Andrews; Univ. of Michigan (Commonwealth Fund Fellow). Guardian Assurance Co., Actuarial Dept, 1935–36; Sudan Govt Civil Service, 1936–59; Member, Sudan Resources Board and War Supply Dept, 1939–45; Secretary, Sudan Development Board, 1944–48; Asst Financial Secretary, 1946–48; Dep. Financial Secretary, 1948–53; Director, Sudan Gezira Board, 1950–54; Chm., Sudan Light and Power Co., 1952–54; Acting Financial Secretary, then Permanent Under Secretary to Ministry of Finance, 1953–55; Financial and Economic Adviser to Sudan Government, 1955–59. Member: UK delegation to General Assembly of UN, 1959; Scottish Gas Board, 1960–70; Scottish Industrial Develt Adv. Bd, 1973–80; Dep. Chm., ITA, 1960–64, Acting Chm., ITA, 1962–63; Chm., Herring Industry Bd, 1962–65; Director: Fisons Ltd, 1961–80 (Chief Executive, 1962–66, Dep. Chm., 1965–71); Grampian Television, 1965–72; Jute Industries Ltd, later Sidlaw Industries Ltd, 1966–80 (Dep. Chm., 1969; Chm., 1970–80); Royal Bank of Scotland, 1966–80; Adobe Oil and Gas Corp., Texas, 1973–85; Mem., Social and Economic Cttee, EEC, 1972–77. Pres., Senior Golfers' Soc., 1982–85. *Recreations:* golf, gardening. *Address:* Hayston Park, Balmullo, St Andrews, Fife KY16 0AN. *T:* Balmullo (01334) 870268. *Clubs:* Honourable Company of Edinburgh Golfers; Royal and Ancient Golf (St Andrews) (Captain, 1974–75); Augusta National Golf, Pine Valley Golf.

CARMICHAEL, Kay; *see* Carmichael, C. M.

CARMICHAEL, Keith Stanley, CBE 1981; FCA; Managing Partner, Longcrofts, 1981–90; *b* 5 Oct. 1929; *s* of Stanley and Ruby Dorothy Carmichael; *m* 1958, Cynthia Mary (née Jones); one *s*. *Educ:* Charlton House Sch.; Bristol Grammar Sch.; qualified as Chartered Accountant, 1951; FTII 1951, FCA 1961. Partner, Wilson Bigg & Co., 1957–69; Dir, H. Foulks Lynch & Co. Ltd, 1957–69; Dir, Radio Rentals Ltd, 1967–69; sole practitioner, 1969–81, 1990–. Mem., Monopolies and Mergers Commn, 1983–92; Lloyd's Underwriter, 1976–90. Pres., Hertsmere Cons. Assoc. Chm. Bd of Governors, and Trustee, Rickmansworth Masonic Sch., 1984–. Freeman, City of London, 1960; Mem., Ct of Assistants, Co. of Chartered Accountants in England and Wales, 1986–. FInstD. Mem., Editl Bd, Simon's Taxes, 1970–82. *Publications:* Spicer and Pegler's Income Tax (ed), 1965; Corporation Tax, 1966; Capital Gains Tax, 1968; Ranking Spicer and Pegler's Executorship Law and Accounts (ed), 1969, 1987; (with P. Wolstenholme) Taxation of Lloyd's Underwriters, 1980, 4th edn 1993; contribs to Accountancy. *Recreations:* gardening, reading, golf. *Address:* 117 Newberries Avenue, Radlett, Herts WD7 7EN. *T:* Radlett (01923) 855098. *Clubs:* Carlton (Dep. Chm., 1989–), MCC, Lord's Taverners.

CARMICHAEL, Peter, CBE 1981; retired; self-employed consultant and horological specialist; *b* 26 March 1933; *s* of Robert and Elizabeth Carmichael; *m* 1st; two *s* four *d*; 2nd, 1980, June Carmichael (*née* Philip). *Educ:* Glasgow Univ. (BSc 1st Cl. Hons Physics). Design Engineer with Ferranti Ltd, Edinburgh, 1958–65; Hewlett-Packard: Project Leader, 1965–67 (Leader of Project Team which won Queen's Award to Industry for Technical Innovation, 1967); Production Engrg Manager, 1967–68; Quality Assurance Manager, 1968–73; Engrg Manager, 1973–75; Manufacturing Manager, 1975–76; Division Gen. Man., 1976–82, and Jt Managing Director, 1980–82. Scottish Development Agency: Dir, Small Business and Electronics, 1982–88; Gp Dir (East), 1988–89. Chairman: Strathclyde Fabricators, 1989–93; Wolfson Microelectronics, 1990–93. Chm., Esmée Fairbairn Res. Centre, Heriot-Watt Univ., 1990–. Hon. DSc Heriot-Watt, 1984. *Recreations:* fishing, antique clock restoration. *Address:* 86 Craiglea Drive, Edinburgh EH10 5PH. *T:* 0131–447 6334; Marchbank Cottage, Ballantrae KA26 0LR. *T:* Ballantrae (01465) 83355.

CARNAC; *see* Rivett-Carnac.

CARNARVON, 7th Earl of, *cr* 1793; **Henry George Reginald Molyneux Herbert,** KCVO 1982; KBE 1976; DL; Baron Porchester 1780; *b* 19 Jan. 1924; *o s* of 6th Earl of Carnarvon and of Catherine, *d* of late Jacob Wendell, New York; *S* father, 1987; *m* 1956, Jean Margaret, *e d* of Hon. Oliver Wallop, Big Horn, Sheridan Co., Wyoming, USA; two *s* one *d*. Late Lieut RHG; retired pay, 1947. Hon. Col, Hampshire Fortress Regt, RE (TA) 1963–67, retaining rank of Hon. Col. Racing Manager to the Queen, 1969–. Chairman: South East Economic Planning Council, 1971–79; Agricultural Research Council, 1978–82; Game Research Assoc., 1960–67 (Vice-Pres., 1967–); Stallion Adv. Cttee to Betting Levy Bd, 1974–86; Standing Conf. on Countryside Sports, 1978–; Newbury Racecourse plc, 1985–; Standing Conf. on London and SE Regl Planning Authys, 1989–; President: Thoroughbred Breeders' Assoc., 1969–74, 1986–91 (Chm. 1964–66); RASE, 1980–81. Member: Hampshire Agriculture Exec. Cttee, 1955–65; Nature Conservancy, 1963–66; Sports Council, 1965–70 (Chm., Planning Cttee, 1965–70); Forestry Commission, 1967–70; Pres., Hampshire and IoW Naturalist Trust, 1987–; President: Amateur Riders' Assoc., 1969–75; Hampshire County Cricket Club, 1966–68; Mem., Jockey Club, 1964– (Chm., Flat Pattern Cttee, 1967–85). CC Hants, 1954; County Alderman, 1965–74; Vice-Chm. County Council, 1971–74, Chm., New County Council, 1973–77; Vice-Chm., CC Assoc., 1972–74 (Chm. Planning Cttee, 1968–74); Member: Basingstoke Town Develt Jt Cttee, 1960–73; Andover Town Develt Jt Cttee, 1960–65. Verderer of the New Forest, 1961–65. DL Hants 1965. High Steward of Winchester, 1977. Hon. Fellow, Portsmouth Polytech., 1976. Hon. DSc Reading, 1980. *Heir: s* Lord Porchester, *qv. Address:* Milford Lake House, Burghclere, Newbury, Berks RG16 9EL. *T:* Highclere (01635) 253387. *Clubs:* White's, Portland.

CARNE, Dr Stuart John, CBE 1986 (OBE 1977); FRCGP; Senior Partner, Grove Health Centre, 1967–91; *b* 19 June 1926; *s* of late Bernard Carne and Millicent Carne; *m* 1951, Yolande (*née* Cooper); two *s* two *d*. *Educ:* Willesden County Grammar Sch.; Middlesex Hosp. Med. Sch. MB BS; MRCS; LRCP; DCH. House Surgeon, Middlesex Hosp., 1950–51; House Physician, House Surgeon and Casualty Officer, Queen Elizabeth Hosp. for Children, 1951–52; Flight Lieut, Med. Branch, RAF, 1952–54; general practice in London, 1954–91; Sen. Tutor in General Practice, RPMS, 1970–91. DHSS appointments: Chm., Standing Med. Adv. Cttee, 1982–86 (Mem., 1974–86); Member: Central Health Services Council, 1976–79; Children's Cttee, 1978–81; Personal Social Services Council, 1976–80; Chm., Jt Cttee on Contraception, 1983–86 (Mem., 1975–86). Hon. Civil Consultant in Gen. Practice to RAF, 1974–. Royal College of General Practitioners: Mem. Council, 1961–91; Hon.Treasurer, 1964–81; Pres., 1988–91; President: Section of General Practice, 1973–74, United Services Sect., 1985–87, RSocMed; Mem. Council, World Orgn of Nat. Colls and Acads of Gen. Practice and Family Medicine,1970–80 (Pres., 1976–78); Mem. Exec. Council, British Diabetic Assoc., 1981–87. Examnr in medicine, Soc. of Apothecaries, 1980–88. Chm., St Mary Abbots Court Ltd, 1981–. Hon. MO, 1959–89, Vice-Pres., 1989–, Queen's Park Rangers FC. Hon. Mem., BPA, 1982. *Publications:* Paediatric Care, 1976; (jtly) DHSS Handbook on Contraceptive Practice, 3rd edn 1984, 4th edn 1988; numerous articles in Lancet, BMJ and other jls. *Recreations:* music, theatre, photography, philately. *Address:* 5 St Mary Abbots Court, Warwick Gardens, W14 8RA. *T:* 0171–602 1970. *Club:* Royal Air Force.

CARNEGIE, family name of **Duke of Fife** and **Earl of Northesk.**

CARNEGIE, Lord; Charles Duff Carnegie; *b* 1 July 1989; *s* and *heir* of Earl of Southesk, *qv*.

CARNEGIE, Lt-Gen. Sir Robin (Macdonald), KCB 1979; OBE 1968; DL; Director General of Army Training, 1981–82, retired; *b* 22 June 1926; *yr s* of late Sir Francis Carnegie, CBE; *m* 1955, Iona, *yr d* of late Maj.-Gen. Sir John Sinclair, KCMG, CB, OBE; one *s* two *d*. *Educ:* Rugby. Commnd 7th Queen's Own Hussars, 1946; comd The Queen's Own Hussars, 1967–69; Comdr 11th Armd Bde, 1971–72; Student, Royal Coll. of Defence Studies, 1973; GOC 3rd Div., 1974–76; Chief of Staff, BAOR, 1976–78; Military Secretary, 1978–80. Col, The Queen's Own Hussars, 1981–87. Non-Service Mem., Police, Prison and Fire Service Selection Bds, 1987–. DL Wilts, 1990.

CARNEGIE, Sir Roderick (Howard), Kt 1978; FTS; Chairman: Hudson Conway Ltd, since 1987; GIO Australia Holdings Ltd, since 1992; Valiant Consolidated Ltd, since 1993; *b* 27 Nov. 1932; *s* of Douglas H. Carnegie and Margaret F. Carnegie, AO; *m* 1959, Carmen, *d* of W. J. T. Clarke; three *s*. *Educ:* Geelong Church of England Grammar Sch.; Trinity Coll., Univ. of Melbourne; New Coll., Oxford Univ.; Harvard Business Sch., Boston. BSc; Dip. Agricl Economics, MA Oxon; MBA Harvard; FTS 1985. McKinsey & Co., New York, 1954–70: Principal, 1964–68, Director, 1968–70; Man. Dir, 1971–83, Chm. and Chief Exec., 1974–86, CRA Ltd. Director: Comalco Ltd, 1970–; Aust. Mining Industry Council, 1974– (a Sen. Vice-Pres., 1985–); Aust. and NZ Banking Gp Ltd; Mem., IBM Asia Pacific Gp. Member: General Motors Aust. Adv. Council, 1979–; Chm., Consultative Cttee on Relations with Japan, 1984–; Pres., Business Council of Aust., 1987–88; International Councillor: Morgan Guaranty Trust; The Brookings Instn. Mem., CSIRO Bd, 1987. Hon. DSc Newcastle, 1985. *Recreations:* surfing, tennis, reading. *Address:* The Domain, 1 Albert Road, South Melbourne, Vic 3205, Australia. *Clubs:* Melbourne (Victoria, Aust.); Links (New York).

CARNEGY OF LOUR, Baroness *cr* 1982 (Life Peer), of Lour in the District of Angus; **Elizabeth Patricia Carnegy of Lour;** DL; formerly a farmer; *b* 28 April 1925; *e d* of late Lt Col U. E. C. Carnegy, DSO, MC, DL, JP, 12th of Lour, and Violet Carnegy, MBE. *Educ:* Downham Sch., Essex. Served Cavendish Lab., Cambridge, 1943–46. With Girl Guides Association, 1947–89: County Comr, Angus, 1956–63; Trng Adviser, Scotland, 1958–62; Trng Adviser, Commonwealth HQ, 1963–65; Pres. for Angus, 1971–79, for Scotland, 1979–89. Co-opted to Educn Cttee, Angus CC, 1967–75; Tayside Regional Council: Councillor, 1974–82; Convener: Recreation and Tourism Cttee, 1974–76; Educn Cttee, 1977–81. Chairman: Working Party on Prof. Trng for Community Education in Scotland, 1975–77; Scottish Council for Community Educn, 1981–88 (Mem., 1978–88); Tayside Cttee on Med. Res. Ethics, 1990–93. Member: MSC, 1979–82 (Chm., Cttee for Scotland, 1981–83); Council for Tertiary Educn in Scotland, 1979–84; Scottish Economic Council, 1981–93; H of L Select Cttee on European Communities, 1983–; Council, Open Univ., 1984–; Admin. Council, Royal Jubilee Trusts, 1985–88; Court, St Andrews Univ., 1991–; Trustee, Nat. Museums of Scotland, 1987–91. Hon. Sheriff, 1969–84; DL Angus, 1988. Hon. LLD Dundee, 1991. *Address:* Lour, by Forfar, Angus DD8 2LR. *T:* Inverarity (01307) 820237; 33 Tufton Court, Tufton Street, SW1P 3QH. *Club:* Lansdowne.

CARNELL, Rev. Canon Geoffrey Gordon; Chaplain to The Queen, 1981–88; Non-Residentiary Canon of Peterborough Cathedral, 1965–85, Canon Emeritus since 1985; *b* 5 July 1918; *m* 1945, Mary Elizabeth Boucher Smith; two *s*. *Educ:* City of Norwich Sch.; St John's Coll., Cambridge (Scholar, 1937; BA 1940; Naden Divinity Student, 1940; Lightfoot Scholar, 1940; MA 1944); Cuddesdon Coll., Oxford. Ordained deacon, Peterborough Cathedral, 1942; priest, 1943. Asst Curate, Abington, Northampton, 1942–49; Chaplain and Lectr in Divinity, St Gabriel's Coll., Camberwell, 1949–53; Rector of Isham with Great and Little Harrowden, Northants, 1953–71; Rector of Boughton, Northampton, 1971–85. Examining Chaplain to Bishop of Peterborough, 1962–86; Dir, Post-Ordination Trng and Ordinands, 1962–86. Chaplain: to High Sheriff of Northants, 1972–73; to Mayor of Kettering, 1988–89. Member: Ecclesiastical History Soc., 1979–; Church of England Record Soc., 1992–; a Vice-Chm., Northants Record Soc., 1982–89. *Publication:* The Bishops of Peterborough 1541–1591, 1993. *Recreations:* walking, music, art history, local history. *Address:* 52 Walsingham Avenue, Barton Woods, Kettering, Northamptonshire NN15 5ER. *T:* Kettering (01536) 511415.

CARNELLEY, Ven. Desmond; Archdeacon of Doncaster, 1985–94, now Archdeacon Emeritus; *b* 28 Nov. 1929; *m* 1st, 1954, Dorothy Frith (*d* 1986); three *s* one *d*; 2nd, 1988, Marjorie Freeman. *Educ:* St John's Coll., York; St Luke's Coll., Exeter; William Temple Coll., Rugby; Ripon Hall, Oxford. BA (Open Univ.); Cert. Ed. (Leeds); Cert. Rel. Ed. (Exon). Curate of Aston, 1960–63; Priest-in-charge, St Paul, Ecclesfield, 1963–67; Vicar of Balby, Doncaster, 1967–72; Priest-in-charge, Mosborough, 1973; Vicar of Mosborough, 1974–85; RD of Attercliffe, 1979–84; acting Dir of Educn, dio. of Sheffield, 1991–92. *Recreations:* reading, theatre, walking in Derbyshire. *Address:* 7 Errwood Avenue, Buxton, Derbyshire SK17 9BD. *T:* Buxton (01298) 71460.

CARNEY, Michael; Secretary, Water Services Association (formerly Water Authorities Association), 1987–92; *b* 19 Oct. 1937; *s* of Bernard Patrick Carney and Gwyneth (*née* Ellis); *m* 1963, Mary Patricia (*née* Davies); two *s* one *d*. *Educ:* University College of North Wales, Bangor (BA). Administrative Officer, NCB, 1962–65; Staff Officer to Dep. Chm., NCB, 1965–68; Electricity Council: Administrative Officer, 1968–71; Asst Sec. (Establishments), 1971–74; Sec., S Western Region, CEGB, 1974–80, Personnel Man., Midlands Region, 1980–82; Personnel Dir, Oxfam, 1982–87. *Publication:* Britain in Pictures: a history and bibliography, 1995. *Recreations:* reading, book collecting, music, theatre. *Address:* 3 College Fields, Clifton, Bristol BS8 3HP. *T:* Bristol (0117) 973 6558.

CARNLEY, Most Rev. Peter Frederick; *see* Perth (Australia), Archbishop of.

CARNOCK, 4th Baron *cr* 1916, of Carnock; **David Henry Arthur Nicolson;** Bt (NS) of that Ilk and Lasswade 1629, of Carnock 1637; Chief of Clan Nicolson; solicitor; *b* 10 July 1920; *s* of 3rd Baron Carnock, DSO, and Hon. Katharine (*d* 1968), *e d* of 1st Baron Roborough; *S* father, 1982. *Educ:* Winchester; Balliol Coll., Oxford (MA). Admitted Solicitor, 1949; Partner, Clifford-Turner, 1953–86. Served War of 1939–45, Royal Devon Yeomanry and on staff, Major. *Recreations:* shooting, fishing, gardening. *Heir: cousin* Nigel Nicolson, *qv. Address:* 90 Whitehall Court, SW1A 2EL; Ermewood House, Harford, Ivybridge, S Devon PL21 0JE. *Clubs:* Travellers', Beefsteak.

CARNWATH, Sir Andrew Hunter, KCVO 1975; DL; a Managing Director, Baring Brothers & Co. Ltd, 1955–74; Chairman, London Multinational Bank, 1971–74; *b* 26 Oct. 1909; *s* of late Dr Thomas Carnwath, DSO, Dep. CMO, Min. of Health, and Margaret Ethel (*née* McKee); *m* 1st, 1939, Kathleen Marianne Armstrong (*d* 1968); five *s* one *d*; 2nd, 1973, Joan Gertrude Wetherell-Pepper (Joan Alexander, author). *Educ:* Eton (King's Scholar; Hon. Fellow 1981). Served RAF (Coastal Comd Intelligence), 1939–45. Joined Baring Bros & Co. Ltd, 1928; rejoined as Head of New Issues Dept, 1945. Chm., Save and Prosper Group Ltd, 1961–80 (Dir, 1960–80); Director: Equity & Law Life Assurance Soc. Ltd, 1955–83; Scottish Agricultural Industries Ltd, 1969–75; Great Portland Estates Ltd, 1977–89. Member: London Cttee, Hongkong and Shanghai Banking Corp., 1967–74; Council, Inst. of Bankers, 1955– (Dep. Chm., 1969–70, Pres., 1970–72, Vice-Pres., 1972–); Cttee on Consumer Credit; Central Bd of Finance of Church of England (Chm., Investment Management Cttee), 1960–74; Chm., Chelmsford Diocesan Bd of Finance, 1969–75 (Vice-Chm., 1967–68). Member: Council, King Edward's Hosp. Fund for London, 1962–89 (Treasurer, 1965–74; Governor, 1976–85); Royal Commn for Exhibn of 1851, 1964–85; Council, Friends of Tate Gall., 1962–84 (Treasurer, 1966–82). Trustee: Imp. War Graves Endowment Fund, 1963–74, Chm., 1964–74; Thalidomide Children's Trust, 1980–85; Chairman: Manor Charitable Trustees, 1969–88; Baring Foundn, 1982–85. A Governor, Felsted Sch., 1965–81; Treasurer, Essex Univ., 1973–82 (DU Essex, 1983). Pres., Saffron Walden Conservative Assoc. until 1977. Musicians Company: Mem., Ct of Assts, 1973–; Master, 1981–82. Mem., Essex CC, 1973–77; High Sheriff, 1965, DL Essex, 1972–85. FCIB; FRSA. DU Essex, 1983. *Recreations:* crosswords, struggling with the piano, pictures. *Address:* 37 Riverview Gardens, Barnes, SW13 9QY. *T:* 0181–748 8927. *Club:* Athenæum.

See also Hon. Sir R. J. A. Carnwath.

CARNWATH, Hon. Sir Robert John Anderson, Kt 1994; CVO 1995; **Hon. Mr Justice Carnwath;** a Judge of the High Court of Justice, Chancery Division, since 1994; *b* 15 March 1945; *s* of Sir Andrew Carnwath, *qv*; *m* 1974, Bambina D'Adda. *Educ:* Eton; Trinity Coll., Cambridge (MA, LLB). Called to the Bar, Middle Temple, 1968, Bencher 1991; QC 1985. Junior Counsel to Inland Revenue, 1980–85; Attorney Gen. to the Prince of Wales, 1988–94. Chairman: Shepherds Bush Housing Assoc., 1988–93; Administrative Law Bar Assoc., 1993–94. Governor, RAM, 1989– (Hon. Fellow 1994). *Publications:* Knight's Guide to Homeless Persons Act, 1977; (with Rt Hon. Sir Frederick Corfield) Compulsory Acquisition and Compensation, 1978; Enforcing Planning Control (report commnd for DoE), 1989; various legal texts and reports on planning and local govt law. *Recreations:* violin, singing (Bach Choir), tennis, etc. *Address:* Royal Courts of Justice, Strand, WC2A 2LL. *Club:* Garrick.

CARO, Sir Anthony (Alfred), Kt 1987; CBE 1969; sculptor; *b* 8 March 1924; *s* of Alfred and Mary Caro; *m* 1949, Sheila May Girling; two *s*. *Educ:* Charterhouse; Christ's Coll., Cambridge (Hon. Fellow, 1981); Regent Street Polytechnic; Royal Acad. Schs, London (Landseer Schol., 1st Landseer Award). Served FAA, 1944–46. Asst to Henry Moore, 1951–53; taught part-time, St Martin's Sch. of Art, 1953–79; taught sculpture at Bennington Coll., Vermont, 1963, 1965. Initiated and taught at Triangle Workshop, Pine Plains, NY, 1982–89. Visiting Artist, 1989: Univ. of Alberta; Red Deer Coll., Alberta. *One-man exhibitions include:* Galleria del Naviglio, Milan, 1956; Gimpel Fils, London, 1957; Whitechapel Art Gall., 1963; Andre Emmerich Gall., NY, 1964, 1966, 1968, 1970, 1972, 1973, 1974, 1977, 1978, 1979, 1982, 1984, 1986, 1988, 1989; Washington Gall. of

Modern Art, Washington, DC, 1965; Kasmin Ltd, London, 1965, 1967, 1971, 1972; David Mirvish Gall., Toronto, 1966, 1971, 1974; Galerie Bischofberger, Zurich, 1966; Rijkmuseum, Kroller-Muller, Holland, 1967; Hayward Gall., 1969; British Section, X Bienal de São Paulo, 1969; Norfolk and Norwich Triennial Fest., 1973; Kenwood House, Hampstead, 1974, 1981, 1994; Galleria dell'Ariete, Milan, 1974; Galerie Andre Emmerich, Zurich, 1974, 1978, 1985; Mus. of Modern Art, NY, 1975 (toured to Walker Art Center, Minn, Mus. of Fine Arts, Houston, Mus. of Fine Arts, Boston); Richard Gray Gall., Chicago, 1976, 1978, 1986, 1989; Watson/de Nagy Gall., Houston, 1976; Lefevre Gall., London, 1976; Galerie Wentzel, Hamburg, 1976, 1978, Cologne, 1982, 1984, 1985, 1988; Galerie Piltzer-Rheims, Paris, 1977; Waddington & Tooth Galls, London, 1977; Waddington Galls, London, 1983, 1986; Harkus Krackow Gall., Boston, 1978, 1981, 1985; Knoedler Gall., London, 1978, 1982, 1983, 1984, 1986, 1989, 1991; Ace Gall., Venice, Calif, 1978, Vancouver, 1979; Kunsthalle Mannheim, 1979; Kunstverein Braunschweig, 1979; Kunstverein Frankfurt, 1979; Stadtische Galerie im Lenbachhaus, Munich, 1979; Gall. Kasahara, Osaka, Japan, 1979, 1990; York Sculptures, Christian Science Center, Boston, 1980; Acquavella Galls, NY, 1980, 1984, 1986; Galerie Andre, Berlin, 1980; Downstairs Gall., Edmonton, Alta, 1981; Storm King Art Center, Mountainville, NY, 1981; Stadtische Galerie im Stadel, Frankfurt, 1981; Saarland Mus., Saarbrucken, 1982; Gallery One, Toronto, 1982, 1985, 1987–88, 1990; Galerie de France, Paris, 1983; Martin Gerard Gall., Edmonton, 1984; Serpentine Gall., 1984; Whitworth Art Gall., Manchester, 1984; Leeds City Art Gall., 1984; Ordrupgaard Samlingen, Copenhagen, 1984; Kunstmuseum Düsseldorf, 1985; Joan Miró Foundn, Barcelona, 1985; C. Grimaldis Gall., Baltimore, 1985, 1987, 1989; Galerie Blanche, Stockholm , 1985; Galleri Lang, Malmö, 1985; Galerie Artek, Helsinki, 1985; Galleria Stendhal, Milan, 1985; Norrkipings Kunstmuseum, Sweden, 1985; Richard Galerie Joan Prats, Barcelona, 1986; Comune di Bogliasco, Genoa, 1986; Iglesia de San Esteban, Spain, 1986; La Lonja, Spain, 1987; Soledad Lorenzo Galerie, Madrid, 1987; Northern Centre for Contemp. Art, Sunderland, 1987; Sylvia Cordish Fine Art, Baltimore, 1988; Elisabeth Franck Gall., Belgium, 1988; Galerie Renée Ziegler, Zurich, 1988; Annely Juda Fine Art, 1989, 1991, 1994 (retrospective); Walker Hill Art Center, Seoul, 1989; Galeria Fluxis, Porto, 1989; Galerie Lelong, Paris, 1990; Baugre Palace, Antwerp, 1990; Tate Gall., 1991. British Council touring exhibn, 1977–79: Tel Aviv, NZ and Australia. *Exhibited:* Venice Biennale, 1958, 1966; 1st Paris Biennale, 1959 (Sculpture Prize); Battersea Park Open Air Exhibns, 1960, 1963, 1966; Gulbenkian Exhibn, London, 1964; Documenta III, Kassel, 1965; Primary Structures, Jewish Mus., NY, 1966 (David Bright Prize); Pittsburgh Internat., 1967, 1968; Univ. of Pennsylvania, 1969; Everson Mus., Syracuse, 1976. Sculpture commnd by Nat. Gall. of Art, Washington, 1978. Member: Council, RCA, 1981–83 (Hon. Fellow 1986); Council, Slade Sch. of Art, 1982–; Trustee, Tate Gall., 1982–89. Hon. Mem., Amer. Acad. and Inst. of Arts and Letters, 1979; For. Hon. Mem., Amer. Acad. of Arts and Sciences, 1988. Lectures: William Townsend Meml, UCL, 1982; Delia Heron Meml, Falmouth Sch. of Art, 1985; Annual, Clore Gall., London, 1987. Hon. Fellow, Wolfson Coll., Oxford, 1992. Hon. DLitt: East Anglia; York Univ., Toronto; Brandeis Univ., Mass; Hon. LittD Cambridge, 1985; DUniv Surrey, 1987; Hon. DFA Yale, 1989. Given key to City of New York, 1974. *Relevant publications:* Anthony Caro, by R. Whelan *et al*, 1974; Anthony Caro, by W. S. Rubin, 1975; Anthony Caro, by D. Waldman, 1982; Anthony Caro, by Terry Fenton, 1986. *Recreation:* listening to music. *Address:* 111 Frognal, Hampstead, NW3 6XR.

CARO, Prof. David Edmund, AO 1986; OBE 1977; MSc, PhD; FInstP, FAIP, FACE; Vice-Chancellor: University of Melbourne, 1982–87; (interim), Northern Territory University, 1988–89; *b* 29 June 1922; *s* of George Alfred Caro and Alice Lillian Caro; *m* 1954, Fiona Macleod; one *s* one *d*. *Educ:* Geelong Grammar Sch.; Univ. of Melbourne (MSc); Univ. of Birmingham (PhD). FInstP 1960, FAIP 1963, FACE 1982. Served War, RAAF, 1941–45. Demonstrator, Univ. of Melbourne, 1947–49; 1851 Overseas Res. Scholar, Birmingham, 1949–51; University of Melbourne: Lectr, 1952; Sen. Lectr, 1954; Reader, 1958; Foundn Prof. of Exper. Physics, 1961; Dean, Faculty of Science, 1970; Dep. Vice-Chancellor, 1972–77; Vice-Chancellor, Univ. of Tasmania, 1978–82. Chairman: Antarctic Res. Policy Adv. Cttee, 1979–85; Aust. Vice-Chancellors Cttee, 1982–83; Melbourne Theatre Co., 1982–87; Pres., Victorian Coll. of the Arts, 1989–91. Chairman: SSAU Nominees Ltd, 1984–89; UniSuper Ltd, 1990–94; Sarou Pty Ltd, 1991–. Member: Management Cttee, Royal Melbourne Hosp., 1982–92; Council, Univ. of South Australia, 1990–94; Council, Univ. of Ballarat, 1994–. Hon. LLD: Melbourne, 1978; Tasmania, 1982; Hon. DSc Melbourne, 1987. *Publication:* (jtly) Modern Physics, 1961 (3rd edn 1978). *Recreations:* skiing, gardening, theatre. *Address:* 17 Fairbairn Road, Toorak, Vic 3142, Australia. *Clubs:* Melbourne (Melbourne); Peninsula Golf (Vic); Tasmanian (Hobart).

CAROE, Martin Bragg, FSA; conservation architect, specialising in the care of historic buildings; Partner, Caroe & Partners, since 1963; *b* 15 Nov. 1933; *s* of Alban Douglas Rendall Caroe and Gwendolen Mary (*née* Bragg); *m* 1962, Mary Elizabeth Roskill; one *s* three *d* (and one *s* decd). *Educ:* Amesbury Sch.; Winchester Coll.; Trinity Coll., Cambridge (BA); Kingston Sch. of Art (DipArch). Joined family firm of Caroe & Partners, 1961. *Works include:* St Davids Cathedral, 1966–; Wells Cathedral West Front sculpture conservation, 1981–86; Kingston Lacy on accession to NT, 1982–84; Rochester Cathedral, 1982–; Chatham Dockyard, Masthouse and Mould Loft, 1988–89; HM Tower of London, 1991. Pres., Ecclesiastical Architects and Surveyors Assoc., 1978–79; Mem., Exec. Cttee, Council for Care of Churches, 1986–89; Commissioner: Faculty Jurisdiction Commn, 1980–84; English Heritage, 1989–92; Commn on Faculties (Church in Wales), 1991–92; Cathedrals and Churches Commn, 1994–. FSA 1988. Master, Plumbers' Co., 1986. *Publications:* articles on conservation of Wells Cathedral West Front in Bull. of Assoc. of Preservation Technology (USA), preprints of Bologna Conf. of Internat. Inst. of Conservators, Trans ASCB; on Kingston Lacy in Trans ASCHB. *Recreations:* care and presentation to the public of a Jekyll garden, punting. *Address:* (office) 1 Greenland Place, NW1 0AP. *T:* 0171–267 9348; Vann, Hambledon, near Godalming, Surrey. *T:* Haslemere (01428) 683413.

CAROL, Sister; *see* Griese, Sr Carol.

CAROLIN, Prof. Peter Burns, ARIBA; Professor of Architecture, University of Cambridge, and Fellow of Corpus Christi College, since 1989; *b* 11 Sept. 1936; *s* of late Joseph Sinclair Carolin and of Jean Bell Carolin (*née* Burns); *m* 1964, Anne-Birgit Warning; three *d*. *Educ:* Radley Coll.; Corpus Christi Coll., Cambridge (MA); University Coll. London (MA Architecture). Served RNR, Lieut, 1955–61. Asst to John Voelcker, 1960–63; Architect: with Colin St John Wilson, 1965–70; with Sir John Burnet, Tait and Partners, 1970–71; Associate, 1971–73, and Partner, 1973–80, Colin St John Wilson and Partners; Partner, Cambridge Design, 1980–81; Technical Ed., 1981–84, Editor, 1984–89, Architects' Jl; Co-founder, Facilities Newsletter, 1983. Magazine of Year Award (jtly), 1985; (jtly) numerous publishing awards, 1985–87. *Publications:* articles in professional jls in UK and Germany. *Recreation:* sailing. *Address:* 34 Selwyn Gardens, Cambridge CB3 9AY. *T:* Cambridge (01223) 352723; University of Cambridge Department of Architecture, 1 Scroope Terrace, Cambridge CB2 1PX. *T:* Cambridge (01223) 332958/9.

CARON, Leslie (Claire Margaret); film and stage actress; *b* 1 July 1931; *d* of Claude Caron and Margaret Caron (*née* Petit); *m* 1st, 1951, George Hormel (marr. diss.); 2nd, 1956, Peter Reginald Frederick Hall (marr. diss. 1965); one *s* one *d*; 3rd, 1969, Michael Laughlin (marr. diss.). *Educ:* Convent of the Assumption, Paris. With Ballet des Champs Elysées, 1947–50, Ballet de Paris, 1954. *Films include:* American in Paris, 1950; subsequently, Lili; The Glass Slipper; Daddy Long Legs; Gaby; Gigi; The Doctor's Dilemma; The Man Who Understood Women; The Subterraneans; Fanny; Guns of Darkness; The L-Shaped Room; Father Goose; A Very Special Favour; Promise Her Anything; Is Paris Burning?; Head of the Family; Madron; QB VII; Valentino; Sérail; L'homme qui aimait les femmes; The Contract; The Unapproachable; Master of the Game; Damage, 1993. *Plays:* Orvet, Paris, 1955; Gigi, London, 1956; Ondine, London, 1961; The Rehearsal, UK tour, 1983; On Your Toes, US tour, 1984. *Musical:* Grand Hotel, Berlin. *Television:* Tales of the Unexpected, 1982. *Publication:* Vengeance (short stories), 1982. *Recreation:* collecting antiques. *Address:* c/o Maureen Vincent, Peters, Fraser & Dunlop, 5th Floor, The Chambers, Chelsea Harbour, Lots Road, SW10 0XF. *T:* 0171–352 4446.

CARPENTER; *see* Boyd-Carpenter.

CARPENTER, Rev. Dr Edward Frederick, KCVO 1985; Dean of Westminster, 1974–85; Lector Theologiae of Westminster Abbey, 1958; *b* 27 Nov. 1910; *s* of Frederick James and Jessie Kate Carpenter; *m* Lilian Betsy Wright; three *s* one *d*. *Educ:* Strodes Sch., Egham; King's Coll., University of London. BA 1932, MA 1934, BD 1935, PhD 1943; AKC 1935; FKC 1951; Hon. DD London, 1976. Deacon, 1935; Priest, 1936; Curate, Holy Trinity, St Marylebone, 1935–41; St Mary, Harrow, 1941–45; Rector of Great Stanmore, 1945–51; Canon of Westminster, 1951; Treasurer, 1959–74; Archdeacon, 1963–74. Fellow of King's Coll., London University, 1954 (AKC 1935). Chairman Frances Mary Buss Foundation, 1956–; Chairman Governing Body of: North London Collegiate Sch.; Camden Sch. for Girls, 1956–; Chairman of St Anne's Soc., 1958–; Joint Chm., London Soc. of Jews and Christians, 1960–; Chm., CCJ, 1986–; Member, Central Religious Advisory Cttee serving BBC and ITA, 1962–67; Chairman: Recruitment Cttee, ACCM, 1967; Religious Adv. Cttee of UNA, 1969–; President: London Region of UNA, 1966–67; Modern Churchmen's Union, 1966–91; World Congress of Faiths, 1966, 1992–. Chm., Christian Consultative Council for Welfare of Animals, 1981–. *Publications:* Thomas Sherlock, 1936; Thomas Tenison, His Life and Times, 1948; That Man Paul, 1953; The Protestant Bishop, 1956; (joint author) of Nineteenth Century Country Parson, 1954, and of History of St Paul's Cathedral, 1957; Common Sense about Christian Ethics, 1961; (jtly) From Uniformity to Unity, 1962; (jtly) The Church's Use of the Bible, 1963; The Service of a Parson, 1965; (jtly) The English Church, 1966; (jtly) A House of Kings, 1966; Cantuar: the Archbishops in their office, 1971; contrib. Man of Christian Action, ed Ian Henderson, 1976; (with David Gentleman) Westminster Abbey, 1987; Archbishop Fisher: his life and times, 1991. *Recreations:* walking, conversation, Association football. *Address:* 6 Selwyn Avenue, Richmond, Surrey TW9 2HA.

CARPENTER, Ven. Frederick Charles; Archdeacon of the Isle of Wight, 1977–86, Archdeacon Emeritus since 1986; Chaplain, Godolphin School, Salisbury, since 1989; *b* 24 Feb. 1920; *s* of Frank and Florence Carpenter; *m* 1952, Rachel Nancy (*d* 1994), *widow* of Douglas H. Curtis. *Educ:* Sir George Monoux Grammar Sch., Walthamstow; Sidney Sussex Coll., Cambridge (BA 1947, MA 1949); Wycliffe Hall, Oxford; MPhil Exeter, 1993. Served with Royal Signals, 1940–46; Italy, 1944 (despatches). Curate of Woodford, 1949–51; Assistant Master and Chaplain, Sherborne School, Dorset, 1951–62; Vicar of Moseley, Birmingham, 1962–68; Director of Religious Education, Diocese of Portsmouth, 1968–75; Canon Residentiary of Portsmouth, 1968–77; Priest-in-charge of the Holy Cross, Binstead, IoW, 1977–86. *Recreations:* music, gardening. *Address:* Gilston, Mount Pleasant, Stoford, Salisbury SP2 0PP. *T:* Salisbury (01722) 790335.

CARPENTER, Harry Leonard, OBE 1991; sports commentator, BBC, 1949–94; *b* 17 Oct. 1925; *s* of Harry and Adelaide May Carpenter; *m* 1950, Phyllis Barbara Matthews; one *s*. *Educ:* Ashburton School, Shirley; Selhurst Grammar School, Croydon. Greyhound Express, 1941; RN, 1943–46; Greyhound owner, 1946–48; Speedway Gazette, 1948–50; Sporting Record, 1950–54; Daily Mail, 1954–62; BBC TV, full-time 1962–94. Sports Personality of the Year, TV and Radio Industries, 1989; Internat. Award, Amer. Sportscasters' Assoc., 1989. *Publications:* Masters of Boxing, 1964; Illustrated History of Boxing, 1975; The Hardest Game, 1981; Where's Harry? My Story, 1992. *Recreations:* golf, chess, classical music. *Address:* Sommerfield Holdings plc, 35 Old Queen Street, SW1H 9JD.

CARPENTER, Humphrey William Bouverie, FRSL; author, broadcaster, musician; *b* 29 April 1946; *s* of late Rt Rev. Harry James Carpenter and of Urith Monica Trevelyan; *m* 1973, Mari Christina Prichard; two *d*. *Educ:* Dragon Sch., Oxford; Marlborough Coll.; Keble Coll., Oxford (MA, DipEd). FRSL 1983. BBC general trainee, 1968–70; staff producer, BBC Radio Oxford, 1970–74; freelance writer and broadcaster, 1975–. Founded: 1983, the band Vile Bodies, playing 1920s and 1930s dance music and jazz, resident at the Ritz Hotel, London, 1987–; 1984, Mushy Pea Theatre Co., children's theatre group. Prog. dir, Cheltenham Fest. of Lit., 1994–. *Plays:* Father Ignatius, Edinburgh Fest. fringe, 1974; Mr Majeika, the Musical, Oxford, 1991, Shaw Theatre, 1993; Secret Gardens trilogy, BBC Radio, 1992; Babes (musical), Oxford, 1992, Shaw Theatre, 1993; Over the Rainbow, BBC Radio, 1995. *Publications:* A Thames Companion (with Mari Prichard), 1975; J. R. R. Tolkien: a biography, 1977; The Inklings (Somerset Maugham Award), 1978; Jesus (Past Masters series), 1980; (ed with Christopher Tolkien) The Letters of J. R. R. Tolkien, 1981; W. H. Auden: a biography, 1981 (E. M. Forster Award, Amer. Acad. of Arts and Letters, 1984); (with Mari Prichard) The Oxford Companion to Children's Literature, 1984; OUDS: a centenary history of the Oxford University Dramatic Society, 1985; Secret Gardens: the golden age of children's literature, 1985; Geniuses Together: American writers in Paris, 1987; A Serious Character: the life of Ezra Pound (Duff Cooper Meml Prize), 1988; The Brideshead Generation: Evelyn Waugh and his friends, 1989; Benjamin Britten: a biography, 1992; *children's books:* The Joshers, 1977; The Captain Hook Affair, 1979; Mr Majeika, 1984; Mr Majeika and the Music Teacher, 1986; Mr Majeika and the Haunted Hotel, 1987; The Television Adventures of Mr Majeika, 1987; More Television Adventures of Mr Majeika, 1988; Mr Majeika and the Dinner Lady, 1989; Further Television Adventures of Mr Majeika, 1990; Mr Majeika and the School Play, 1991; Mr Majeika and the School Book Week, 1992 (Mr Majeika books serialised on television, 1988–90); (with Jenny McDade) Wellington and Boot, 1991; What Did You Do At School Today?, 1992; Charlie Crazee's Teevee, 1993; Mr Majeika and the School Inspector, 1993; Mr Majeika amd the Ghost Train, 1994; Shakespeare Without the Boring Bits, 1994; Mr Majeika and the School Inspector, 1995; (ed) The Puffin Book of Classic Children's Stories, 1996. *Recreation:* sleep. *Address:* 6 Farndon Road, Oxford OX2 6RS. *T:* Oxford (01865) 56673.

CARPENTER, John; *see* Carpenter, V. H. J.

CARPENTER, Leslie Arthur; Director, Reed International PLC, since 1974 (Chief Executive, 1982–86; Chairman, 1985–87); *b* 26 June 1927; *s* of William and Rose Carpenter; *m* 1st, 1952; one *d*; 2nd, 1989, Louise Botting, *qv*. *Educ:* Hackney Techn. Coll. Director: Country Life, 1965; George Newnes, 1966; Odhams Press Ltd (Managing), 1968; International Publishing Corp., 1972; Reed International Ltd, 1974; IPC (America)

Inc., 1975; Chairman: Reed Hldgs Inc. (formerly Reed Publishing Hldgs Inc.), 1977; Reed Publishing Hldgs Ltd, 1981; Chm. and Chief Exec., IPC Ltd, 1974; Chief Exec., Publishing and Printing, Reed International Ltd, 1979. Dir, Watmoughs (Hldgs) plc, 1988–. *Recreations:* racing, gardening. *Address:* 10 Park Square Mews, Upper Harley Street, NW1 4PP.

CARPENTER, Louise, (Mrs L. A. Carpenter); *see* Botting, Louise.

CARPENTER, Maj.-Gen. (Victor Harry) John, CB 1975; MBE 1945; FCIT; Senior Traffic Commissioner, Western Traffic Area and Licensing Authority, 1990–91; *b* 21 June 1921; *s* of Harry and Amelia Carpenter; *m* 1946, Theresa McCulloch; one *s* one *d*. *Educ:* Army schools; Apprentice Artificer RA; RMC Sandhurst. Joined the Army, Royal Artillery, 1936; commissioned into Royal Army Service Corps as 2nd Lieut, 1939. Served War of 1939–45 (Dunkirk evacuation, Western Desert, D-Day landings). Post-war appts included service in Palestine, Korea, Aden, and Singapore; also commanded a company at Sandhurst. Staff College, 1951; JSSC, 1960; served WO, BAOR, FARELF, 1962–71; Transport Officer-in-Chief (Army), MoD, 1971–73; Dir of Movements (Army), MoD, 1973–75; Chm., Traffic Comrs, NE Traffic Area (formerly Yorks Traffic Area), 1975–85; Traffic Comr, W Traffic Area, 1985–90. Col Comdt, 1975–87, Representative Col Comdt, 1976, 1978 and 1985, RCT; Nat. Pres., 1940 Dunkirk Veterans Assoc.; Pres., Artificers Royal Artillery Assoc.; Pres., RASC/RCT Assoc., 1977–87; Chm., Yorkshire Section, CIT, 1980–81. Hon. FIRTE 1987. Commander, Order of Leopold II (Belgium), 1992. *Recreation:* gardening. *Club:* Royal Over-Seas League.

CARR, family name of **Baron Carr of Hadley.**

CARR OF HADLEY, Baron *cr* 1975 (Life Peer), of Monken Hadley; **(Leonard) Robert Carr,** PC 1963; FIC; *b* 11 Nov. 1916; *s* of late Ralph Edward and of Katie Elizabeth Carr; *m* 1943, Joan Kathleen, *d* of Dr E. W. Twining; two *d* (and one *s* decd). *Educ:* Westminster Sch. (Hon. Fellow, 1991); Gonville and Caius Coll., Cambridge, BA Nat. Sci. Hons, 1938; MA 1942. FIM 1957. Joined John Dale Ltd, 1938 (Dir, 1948–55; Chm., 1958–63); Director: Metal Closures Group Ltd, 1964–70 (Dep. Chm., 1960–63 and Jt Man. Dir, 1960–63); Carr, Day & Martin Ltd, 1947–55; Isotope Developments Ltd, 1950–55; Metal Closures Ltd, 1959–63; Scottish Union & National Insurance Co. (London Bd), 1958–63; S. Hoffnung & Co., 1963, 1965–70, 1974–80; Securicor Ltd and Security Services PLC, 1961–63, 1965–70, 1974–85; SGB Gp PLC, 1974–86; Prudential Assurance Co., 1976–85 (Dep. Chm., 1979–80, Chm., 1980–85); Prudential Corporation PLC, 1978–89 (Dep. Chm., 1979–80, Chm., 1980–85); Cadbury Schweppes PLC, 1979–87; Chm., Strategy Ventures, 1988–; Mem., London Adv. Bd, Norwich Union Insurance Gp, 1965–70, 1974–76; Member, Advisory Board: PA Strategy Partners, 1985–87; LEK Partnership, 1987–95. Mem. Council, CBI, 1976–87 (Chm., Educn and Trng Cttee, 1977–82); Chm., Business in the Community, 1984–87. MP (C) Mitcham, 1950–74, Sutton, Carshalton, 1974–76; PPS to Sec. of State for Foreign Affairs, Nov. 1951–April 1955, to Prime Minister, April–Dec. 1955; Parly Sec., Min. of Labour and Nat. Service, Dec. 1955–April 1958; Sec. for Technical Co-operation, 1963–64; Sec. of State for Employment, 1970–72; Lord President of the Council and Leader of the House of Commons, April–Nov. 1972; Home Secretary, 1972–74. Governor: St Mary's Hosp., Paddington, 1958–63; Imperial Coll. of Science and Technology, 1959–63 and 1976–87 (Fellow 1985); St Mary's Medical Sch. Council, 1958–63; Hon. Treas., Wright Fleming Inst. of Microbiology, 1960–63. Duke of Edinburgh Lectr, Inst. of Building, 1976. Pres., Surrey CCC, 1985–86. CIMgt (CBIM 1982); CIPD (CIPM 1975). *Publications:* (jt) One Nation, 1950; (jt) Change is our Ally, 1954; (jt) The Responsible Society, 1958; (jt) One Europe, 1965; articles in technical jls. *Recreations:* lawn tennis, music, gardening. *Address:* 14 North Court, Great Peter Street, SW1P 3LL. *Club:* Brooks's.

CARR, Alan Michael; Senior Partner, Simmons & Simmons, since 1992; *b* 1 Sept. 1936; *m* 1963, Dalia Lebhar; two *s* one *d*. *Educ:* Gresham's Sch., Holt; King's Coll., Cambridge (MA). Articled Simmons & Simmons; admitted solicitor, 1961; Partner, 1966–. *Recreation:* oriental travel. *Address:* Simmons & Simmons, 21 Wilson Street, EC2M 2TQ. *T:* 0171–628 2020.

CARR, Sir (Albert) Raymond (Maillard), Kt 1987; DLitt (Oxon); FRHistS; FRSL; FBA 1978; Warden of St Antony's College, Oxford, 1968–87 (Sub-Warden, 1966–68); Fellow since 1964; *b* 11 April 1919; *s* of Reginald and Marion Maillard Carr; *m* 1950, Sara Strickland; three *s* one *d*. *Educ:* Brockenhurst Sch.; Christ Church, Oxford (Hon. Student 1986). Gladstone Research Exhnr, Christ Church, 1941; Lectr, UCL, 1945–46; Fellow of All Souls' Coll., 1946–53; Fellow of New Coll., 1953–64. Director, Latin American Centre, 1964–68. Chm. Soc. for Latin American Studies, 1966–68. Prof. of History of Latin America, Oxford, 1967–68. Distinguished Prof., Boston Univ., 1980; King Juan Carlos Prof. of Spanish History, NY Univ., 1992. Mem., Nat. Theatre Bd, 1968–77. Hon. Fellow: Exeter Univ., 1987; St Antony's Coll., Oxford, 1988. Corresp. Mem., Royal Acad. of History, Madrid. Award of Merit, Soc. for Spanish Hist. Studies of the US, 1987; Leimer Award for Spanish Studies, Univ. of Augsburg, 1990. Grand Cross of the Order of Alfonso el Sabio (Spain), 1983; Order of Infante Dom Henrique (Portugal), 1989. *Publications:* Spain 1808–1939, 1966; Latin America (St Antony's Papers), 1969; (ed) The Republic and the Civil War in Spain, 1971; English Fox Hunting, 1976; The Spanish Tragedy: the Civil War in Perspective, 1977; (jtly) Spain: Dictatorship to Democracy, 1979; Modern Spain, 1980; (with Sara Carr) Fox-Hunting, 1982; Puerto Rico: a colonial experiment, 1984; (ed) The Spanish Civil War, 1986; articles on Swedish, Spanish and Latin American history. *Recreation:* fox hunting. *Address:* Burch, North Molton, South Molton EX36 3JU. *T:* Bishops Nympton (01769) 550267. *Clubs:* Beefsteak, United Oxford & Cambridge University, Academy.

CARR, Very Rev. Arthur Wesley, PhD; Dean of Bristol, since 1987; *b* 26 July 1941; *s* of Arthur and Irene Carr; *m* 1968, Natalie Gill; one *d*. *Educ:* Dulwich College; Jesus Coll., Oxford (MA); Jesus Coll., Cambridge (MA); Ridley Hall, Cambridge; Univ. of Sheffield (PhD). Curate, Luton Parish Church, 1967–71; Tutor, Ridley Hall, Cambridge, 1970–71, Chaplain 1971–72; Sir Henry Stephenson Fellow, Dept of Biblical Studies, Univ. of Sheffield, 1972–74; Hon. Curate, Ranmoor, 1972–74; Chaplain, Chelmsford Cathedral, 1974–78; Dep. Director, Chelmsford Cathedral Centre for Research and Training, 1974–82; Dir of Training, Diocese of Chelmsford, 1976–82; Canon Residentiary, Chelmsford Cathedral, 1978–87. Mem., Gen. Synod of C of E, 1980–87, 1989–. Select Preacher, Univ. of Oxford, 1984–85; Hon. Fellow, New Coll., Edinburgh, 1986. *Publications:* Angels and Principalities, 1977; The Priestlike Task, 1985; Brief Encounters, 1985; The Pastor as Theologian, 1989; Ministry and the Media, 1990; Lost in Familiar Places, 1991; Manifold Wisdom, 1991; Say One for Me, 1992; articles in Theology, etc. *Recreations:* music, reading, writing, gardening. *Address:* The Deanery, 20 Charlotte Street, Bristol, Avon BS1 5PZ. *T:* Bristol (0117) 926 2443; (office) Bristol (0117) 926 4879, *Fax:* (0117) 925 3678.

CARR, Christopher; QC 1983; barrister; *b* 30 Nov. 1944; *s* of Edwin Wilfred Carr and Kathleen Carr; *m*; two *d* one *s*. *Educ:* Skegness Grammar Sch.; London Sch. of Economics; Clare Coll., Cambridge. Called to the Bar, Lincoln's Inn, 1968, Bencher, 1991. Lectr in Law, LSE, 1968–69 and 1972–73; Asst Prof. of Law, Univ. of British Columbia, 1969–72; Associate Prof. of Law, Univ. of Toronto, 1973–75; part-time Lectr, QMC, London, 1975–78; in practice at the Bar, 1975–. *Publications:* articles and notes in English and Canadian law jls. *Recreations:* mixed. *Address:* 1 Essex Court, Temple, EC4Y 9AR. *Club:* Athenæum.

CARR, Donald Bryce, OBE 1985; Secretary, Cricket Council and Test and County Cricket Board, 1974–86, retired; *b* 28 Dec. 1926; *s* of John Lillingston Carr and Constance Ruth Carr; *m* 1953, Stella Alice Vaughan Simpkinson; one *s* one *d*. *Educ:* Repton Sch.; Worcester Coll., Oxford (MA). Served Army, 1945–48 (Lieut Royal Berks Regt). Asst Sec., 1953–59, Sec., 1959–62, Derbyshire CCC; Asst Sec., MCC, 1962–74. *Recreations:* golf, following most sports. *Address:* 28 Aldenham Avenue, Radlett, Herts WD7 8HX. *T:* Radlett (01923) 855602. *Clubs:* MCC, British Sportsman's, Lord's Taverners; Vincent's, Oxford University Cricket (Oxford).

CARR, Edward Arthur John, CBE 1995; heritage and tourism consultant, since 1995; Chief Executive, CADW, Welsh Historic Monuments Executive Agency, 1991–95 (Director, 1985–91); *b* 31 Aug. 1938; *s* of Edward Arthur Carr, CMG and Margaret Alys Carr (*née* Willson); *m* 1st, 1960, Verity Martin (marr. diss.); two *d*; 2nd, 1980, Patrice Metro; one *s* one *d*. *Educ:* Leys Sch., Cambridge; Christ's Coll., Cambridge (BA 1960; MA 1963). Journalist: Thomson Regional Newspapers, 1960–65; Financial Times, 1965–67; Sunday Times, 1967–70; Manager, Times Newspapers, 1970–81; Chief Executive, Waterlow & Sons, 1981; Dir, Neath Develt Partnership, 1982–84. *Recreations:* family, newspapers. *Address:* 2 East Cliff, Southgate, Swansea SA3 2AS. *T:* Swansea (01792) 232800.

CARR, Dr Eric Francis, FRCP, FRCPsych; Lord Chancellor's Medical Visitor, 1979–89; Member: Mental Health Act Commission, since 1983; Parole Board, since 1988; *b* 23 Sept. 1919; *s* of Edward Francis Carr and Maude Mary Almond; *m* 1954, Janet Gilfillan (marr. diss. 1980); two *s* one *d*. *Educ:* Mill Hill Sch.; Emmanuel Coll., Cambridge. MA, MB BChir; FRCP, 1971, FRCPsych, 1972; DPM. Captain, RAMC, 1944–46. Consultant Psychiatrist: St Ebba's Hosp., 1954–60; Netherne Hosp., 1960–67; Epsom and West Park Hosps, 1967–76; Hon. Consultant Psychiatrist, KCH, 1960–76; SPMO, DHSS, 1976–79. Fellow, RSocMed. *Recreations:* reading, listening to music, cooking. *Address:* 116 Holly Lane East, Banstead, Surrey SM7 2BE. *T:* Burgh Heath (01737) 353675.

CARR, Glyn; *see* Styles, F. S.

CARR, Air Marshal Sir John Darcy B.; *see* Baker-Carr.

CARR, John Roger, CBE 1991; JP; Chairman, Countryside Commission for Scotland, 1986–92 (Member, 1979–84; Vice-Chairman, 1984–85); *b* 18 Jan. 1927; *s* of James Stanley Carr and Edith Carr (*née* Robinson); *m* 1951, Catherine Elise Dickson-Smith; two *s*. *Educ:* Ackworth and Ayton (Quaker Schools). FRICS. Royal Marines, 1944–47; Gordon Highlanders (TA), 1950–54. Factor, Walker Scottish Estates Co., 1950–54; Factor, 1954–67, Dir and Gen. Man., 1967–88, Dir, 1988–90, Moray Estates Develt Co. Dir, Strathearn Tourism Develt Co., 1959–. Mem., Wkg Party, Management Training for Leisure and Recreation in Scotland, 1986; Chm., Countryside around Towns Forum, 1991–; Vice Pres., Farming and Wildlife Adv. Gp for Scotland, 1992–; Director: Macaulay Land Use Res. Inst., 1987–; UK 2000 Scotland, 1991–93. Mem., Moray DC, 1974–80. JP Moray, 1975. *Recreations:* most countryside pursuits. *Address:* Bradbush, Darnaway, Forres, Moray IV36 0SU. *T:* Brodie (01309) 641249. *Club:* Royal Findhorn Yacht.

CARR, Maurice Chapman; His Honour Judge Carr; a Circuit Judge, since 1986; *b* 14 Aug. 1937; *s* of John and Elizabeth Carr; *m* 1959, Caryl Olson; one *s* one *d*. *Educ:* Hookergate Grammar Sch.; LSE (LLB); Harvard Univ. (LLM). Lectr in Law, 1960–62, Asst Prof. of Law, 1963–64, Univ. of British Columbia; Lecturer in Law: UCW, 1964–65; Univ. of Newcastle upon Tyne, 1965–69. Called to the Bar, Middle Temple, 1966. *Recreations:* walking, music. *Address:* 33 Broad Chare, Newcastle upon Tyne NE1 3DQ. *T:* Tyneside (0191) 2320541.

CARR, Michael; *b* 31 Jan. 1946; *s* of James and Sheila Mary Carr; *m* 1st (wife *d* 1979); one *s*; 2nd, 1980, Georgina Clare; four *s* two *d*. *Educ:* St Joseph's Coll., Blackpool; Catholic Coll., Preston; Margaret McMillan Coll. of Educn, Bradford (CertEd); Bradford and Ilkley Community Coll. (DPSE). Engrg apprentice, 1962–63; Local Govt Officer, 1964–68; partner in family retail newsagency, 1968–70; Teacher of Geography: Brookside Sec. Sch., Middlesbrough, 1973–74; Stainsby Sch., Middlesbrough, 1974–75; Head of Geog., St Thomas Aquinas RC High Sch., Darwen, Lancs, 1975–82; Head of Gen. Studies, Blackthorn County Sec. Sch. and Blackthorn Wing of Fearns CS Sch., Bacup, 1982–87; Mem., Lancs Educn Cttee Sch. Support Team (Disruptive Behaviour), 1988–91. Mem., Sabden Parish Council, 1976–78, 1979–83; Mem. (C 1979–81, SDP 1981–83), Ribble Valley BC, 1979–83. Joined SDP, 1981; contested (SDP/Lib Alliance) Ribble Valley, 1983, 1987; MP (Lib Dem) Ribble Valley, March 1991–1992; contested (Lib Dem) Ribble Valley, 1992. Mem., NAS/UWT (Dist Sec., Rossendale Assoc., 1983–87; Press Officer, Lancs Fedn, 1983–87, 1988–90). *Recreations:* hill walking, cooking, music.

CARR, Peter Derek, CBE 1989; Chairman: Occupational Pensions Board, since 1994; County Durham Development Co., since 1990; Northern Screen Commission, since 1990; Durham County Waste Management Co., since 1993; *b* 12 July 1930; *s* of George William Carr and Marjorie (*née* Tailby); *m* 1958, Geraldine Pamela (*née* Ward); one *s* one *d*. *Educ:* Fircroft Coll., Birmingham; Ruskin Coll., Oxford. National Service, RAF, 1951–53. Carpenter and joiner, construction industry, 1944–51 and 1953–56; college, 1956–60; Lectr, Percival Whitley Coll., Halifax, 1960–65; Sen. Lectr in Indust. Relations, Thurrock Coll., and part-time Adviser, NBPI, 1965–69; Director: Commn on Industrial Relations, 1969–74; ACAS, 1974–78; Diplomatic Service, Washington, 1978–83; Regl Dir, Northern Regl Office, Dept of Employment, and Leader, City Action Team, 1983–89; Chm., Northern RHA, 1990–94. Vis. Fellow, Durham Univ., 1989–. *Publications:* directed study for CIR on worker participation and collective bargaining in Europe, and study for ACAS on industrial relations in national newspaper industry. *Recreations:* cycling, cooking, furniture-making. *Address:* 4 Corchester Towers, Corbridge, Northumberland NE45 5NR. *T:* Hexham (01434) 632841, *Fax:* (01434) 633726; Occupational Pensions Board, PO Box 2EE, Newcastle upon Tyne NE99 2EE.

CARR, Sir Raymond; *see* Carr, Sir A. R. M.

CARR, Hon. Robert John; MP (ALP) Maroubra, NSW, since 1983; Premier of New South Wales, and Minister for the Arts and for Ethnic Affairs, since 1995; *b* 28 Sept. 1947; *s* of Edward and Phyllis Carr; *m* 1973, Helena John. *Educ:* Univ. of NSW (BA Hons). Journalist, ABC Current Affairs Radio, 1969–72; Educn Officer, Labour Council, NSW, 1972–78; Journalist, The Bulletin, 1978–83. Minister for: Planning and Envmt, 1984–88; Consumer Affairs, 1986; Heritage, 1986–88; Leader of the Opposition, NSW, 1988–95. *Address:* Governor Macquarie Lower, 1 Ferrer Place, Sydney, NSW 2000, Australia. *T:* (2) 2285239, *Fax:* (2) 2283935.

CARR, Dr Thomas Ernest Ashdown, CB 1977; part-time medical referee, Department of Health and Social Security, 1979–87; retired; *b* 21 June 1915; *s* of late Laurence H. A.

Carr, MScTech, MIEE, ARPS, Stockport, and late Norah E. V. Carr (*née* Taylor); *m* 1940, Mary Sybil (*née* Dunkey); one *s* two *d*. *Educ:* County High Sch. for Boys, Altrincham; Victoria Univ. of Manchester (BSc). MB, ChB 1939; FRCGP 1968; FFCM 1972; DObstRCOG. Jun. hosp. posts, Manchester and Ipswich, 1939–41; RAMC, UK and NW Europe, 1941–46 (Hon. Major, 1946). GP, Highcliffe, Hants, 1947; Mem. Hants Local Med. Cttee, 1952–55; Min. of Health: Regional Med. Officer, Southampton, 1956; Sen. Med. Officer, 1963; Principal Med. Officer, 1966; SPMO in charge of GP and Regional Med. Service, DHSS, 1967–79. Founder Mem., 1953, Provost of SE England Faculty 1962–64, Mem. Council 1964–66, RCGP; Chm., Guildford Div., BMA, 1988–89 (Mem. Exec. Cttee, Lambeth and Southwark Div., 1975–79). FRSocMed (Mem. Council, Gen. Practice Section, 1977–79). Member: Camping Club of GB and Ireland, 1976–83; Southampton Gramophone Soc., 1956–63 (Chm., 1957–58); Guildford Philharmonic Soc., 1964–89; Guildford Soc., 1968–89; Putney Music, 1989–; Putney Soc., 1989–; Consumers' Assoc., 1974–; Nat. Soc. of Non-Smokers (QUIT), 1981– (Chm., 1982–86, Vice-Pres., 1987–93); British Humanist Assoc., 1965–; Fabian Soc., 1989–. *Publications:* papers on NHS practice organisation in Medical World, Practitioner, Update, Health Trends, faculty jls of RCGP, Proc. of RSM. *Recreations:* playing and listening to music, photography, country walks, foreign travel. *Address:* 17 Westpoint, Putney Hill, SW15 6RU. *T:* 0181–788 9969. *Club:* Civil Service.

CARR, William Compton; *b* 10 July 1918; *m*; two *s* one *d*. *Educ:* The Leys Sch., Cambridge. MP (C) Barons Court, 1959–64; PPS to Min. of State, Board of Trade, 1963; PPS to Financial Sec. to the Treasury, 1963–64. *Recreations:* reading, theatre-going, skin diving, eating, dieting.

CARR-ELLISON, Sir Ralph (Harry), Kt 1973; TD; Chairman, Tyne Tees Television Ltd, since 1974 (Director since 1966); Director, Yorkshire–Tyne Tees Television Holdings plc, since 1992; Lord-Lieutenant of Tyne and Wear, since 1984; *b* 8 Dec. 1925; *s* of late Major John Campbell Carr-Ellison; *m* 1951, Mary Clare, *d* of late Major Arthur McMorrough Kavanagh, MC; three *s* one *d*. *Educ:* Eton. Served Royal Glos Hussars and 1st Royal Dragoons, 1944–49; Northumberland Hussars (TA), (Lt-Col Comdg), 1949–69; TAVR Col, Northumbrian Dist, 1969–72; Col, Dep. Comdr (TAVR), NE Dist, 1973; Chm., N of England TA&VRA, 1976–80, Pres. 1987–90; ADC (TAVR) to HM the Queen, 1970–75; Hon. Colonel: Northumbrian Univs OTC, 1982–86; QOY, 1988–90 (Northumberland Hussars Sqn, 1986–88); Col Comdt, Yeomanry RAC TA, 1990–94. Co. Comr, Northumberland Scouts, 1958–68; Mem. Cttee of Council, 1960–67, Mem. Council, 1982–, Scout Assoc. Chm., Berwick-on-Tweed Constituency Cons. Assoc., 1959–62, Pres., 1973–77; Northern Area Cons. Assocs: Treas., 1961–66, Chm., 1966–69; Pres., 1974–78; Vice Chm., Nat Union of Cons. and Unionist Assocs, 1969–71. Director: Newcastle & Gateshead Water Co., 1964–73; Trident Television, 1972–81 (Dep. Chm., 1976–81); Chairman: Northumbrian Water Authority, 1973–82; North Tyne Area, Manpower Bd, MSC, 1983–84; Automobile Assoc., 1986–95 (Vice-Chm., 1985–86). Mem. Council, The Wildfowl Trust, 1981–88. Chm., Newcastle Univ. Develt Trust, 1978–81 (Mem., 1992–); Mem. Ct, Newcastle Univ., 1979–; Governor, Swinton Conservative College, 1967–81. FRSA 1983. High Sheriff, 1972, JP 1953–75, DL 1981–85, Vice Lord-Lieut, 1984, Northumberland. Hon. DCL Newcastle, 1989. KStJ 1984. *Recreation:* Jt Master, West Percy Foxhounds, 1950–90. *Address:* Hedgeley Hall, Powburn, Alnwick, Northumberland NE66 4HZ. *T:* Powburn (0166578) 273; (office) Newcastle upon Tyne (0191) 2610181. *Clubs:* Cavalry and Guards, White's, Pratt's; Northern Counties (Newcastle upon Tyne).

CARR-GOMM, Richard Culling, OBE 1985; Consultant to the Carr-Gomm Society and Morpeth Society (charity societies); *b* 2 Jan. 1922; *s* of Mark Culling Carr-Gomm and Amicia Dorothy (*née* Heming); *m* 1957, Susan, *d* of Ralph and Dorothy Gibbs; two *s* three *d*. *Educ:* Stowe School. Served War: commnd Coldstream Guards, 1941; served 6th Guards Tank Bde, NW Europe (twice wounded, mentioned in despatches); Palestine, 1945; ME; resigned commn, 1955. Founded: Abbeyfield Soc., 1956; Carr-Gomm Soc., 1965; Morpeth Soc., 1972. Templeton UK Project Award, 1984. Croix de Guerre (Silver Star), France, 1944. KStJ. *Publications:* Push on the Door (autobiog.), 1979; Loneliness—the wider scene, 1987. *Recreations:* golf, backgammon, painting. *Address:* 9 The Batch, Batheaston, Avon BA1 7DR. *T:* Bath (01225) 858434.

CARR LINFORD, Alan, RWS 1955 (ARWS 1949); ARE 1946; ARCA 1946; *b* 15 Jan. 1926; *m* 1948, Margaret Dorothea Parish; one *s* one *d*. *Educ:* Royal College of Art, and in Rome. Was awarded the Prix de Rome, 1947. *Recreation:* shooting.

CARR-SMITH, Maj.-Gen. Stephen Robert; Chief Policy and Plans Division, NATO Communications and Information Systems Agency, Brussels, 1992–95; *b* 3 Dec. 1941; *s* of Charles Carr-Smith and Elizabeth Carr-Smith (*née* Marsh); *m* 1967, Nicole Bould; two *s* one *d*. *Educ:* Welbeck College; RMA; RMCS; BA Open Univ., 1992. Commissioned Royal Signals, 1962; served in UK, Germany, Aden and Belgium; Mil. Sec., 1973–74, Operational Requirements, 1978–79, MoD; CO, 1st Armoured Div. HQ and Signal Regt, 1979–82; Instructor, Army Staff Coll., 1982–84; Comdt, Army Apprentices Coll., Harrogate, 1984–86; Col MGO Secretariat, MoD, 1986–88; SHAPE, 1988–92. FIMgt. *Recreations:* cricket, golf, bridge, politics, international affairs. *Address:* c/o Lloyds Bank, 23 Old Woking Road, West Byfleet, Surrey KT14 6LN.

CARREL, Philip, CMG 1960; OBE 1954; *b* 23 Sept. 1915; *s* of late Louis Raymond Carrel and Lucy Mabel (*née* Cooper); *m* 1948, Eileen Mary Bullock (*née* Hainworth); one *s* one *d*. *Educ:* Blundell's; Balliol. Colonial Admin. Service, 1938, Zanzibar Protectorate. EA Forces, 1940. Civil Affairs, 1941–47 (OETA); Civilian Employee Civil Affairs, GHQ MELF, 1947–49 (on secondment from Som. Prot.); Colonial Admin. Service (Somaliland Protectorate), 1947; Commissioner of Somali Affairs, 1953; Chief Sec. to the Government, Somaliland Protectorate, 1959–60. Cttee Sec., Overseas Relns, Inst. of Chartered Accountants in England and Wales, 1961–77; retired. *Address:* Lych Gates, 51 Chiltley Lane, Liphook, Hants GU30 7HJ. *T:* Liphook (01428) 722150.

CARRELL, Prof. Robin Wayne, FRSNZ 1980; FRCP; Professor of Haematology, University of Cambridge, since 1986; Fellow of Trinity College, Cambridge, since 1987; *b* 5 April 1936; *s* of Ruane George Carrell and Constance Gwendoline Carrell (*née* Rowe); *m* 1962, Susan Wyatt Rogers; two *s* two *d*. *Educ:* Christchurch Boys' High School, NZ; Univ. of Otago (MB ChB 1959); Univ. of Canterbury (BSc 1965); Univ. of Cambridge (MA, PhD 1968). FRACP 1973; FRCPath 1976; MRCP 1985, FRCP 1990. Mem., MRC Abnormal Haemoglobin Unit, Cambridge, 1965–68; Dir, Clinical Biochemistry, Christchurch Hosp., NZ, 1968–75; Lectr and Consultant in Clinical Biochem., Addenbrooke's Hosp. and Univ. of Cambridge, 1976–78; Prof. of Clinical Biochem., Christchurch Sch. of Clinical Medicine, Univ. of Otago, 1978–86. Mem., Gen. Bd, Univ. of Cambridge, 1989–92. Commonwealth Fellow, St John's Coll. and Vis. Scientist, MRC Lab. of Molecular Biol., 1985. Pharmacia Prize for biochem. res., NZ, 1984; Hector Medal, Royal Soc., NZ, 1986. *Publications:* articles in sci. jls, esp. on genetic abnormalities of human proteins. *Recreations:* gardening, walking. *Address:* 19 Madingley Road, Cambridge CB3 0EG. *T:* Cambridge (01223) 312970.

CARRERAS, José; tenor; *b* 5 Dec. 1947; *s* of José and Antonia Carreras; *m*; one *s* one *d*. Opera début as Gennaro in Lucrezia Borgia, Barcelona, 1970; US début in Madama Butterfly, NY City Opera, 1972; Tosca, NY Met, 1974; Covent Garden début in La Traviata, 1974; Un Ballo In Maschera, La Scala, 1975; after break owing to illness, concerts in Barcelona, 1988, Covent Gdn, 1989; Music Dir, Barcelona Olympics, 1992; first UK perf., Stiffelio, Covent Gdn, 1993; appears at all major opera houses and festivals in Europe, USA and S America; has made many recordings. *Films:* Don Carlos, 1980; West Side Story (TV), 1985. RAM 1990. Personality of the Year, Classical Music Awards, 1994. *Address:* c/o Carlos Caballé, Via Augusta 59, 08006 Barcelona, Spain.

CARRICK, 10th Earl of *cr* 1748; **David James Theobald Somerset Butler;** Viscount Ikerrin 1629; Baron Butler (UK) 1912; *b* 9 Jan. 1953; *s* of 9th Earl of Carrick, and his 1st wife, (Mary) Belinda (*d* 1993), *e d* of Major David Constable-Maxwell, TD; *S* father, 1992; *m* 1975, Philippa V. J., *yr d* of Wing Commander L. V. Craxton; three *s* (including twin *s*). *Educ:* Downside. *Heir: s* Viscount Ikerrin, *qv*.

CARRICK, Edward; *see* Craig, E. A.

CARRICK, Hon. Sir John (Leslie), KCMG 1982; Senator, Commonwealth Parliament of Australia, 1971–87, retired; *b* 4 Sept. 1918; *s* of late A. J. Carrick and of E. E. Carrick; *m* 1951, Diana Margaret Hunter; three *d*. *Educ:* Univ. of Sydney (BEc; Hon. DLitt 1988). Res. Officer, Liberal Party of Aust., NSW Div., 1946–48, Gen. Sec., 1948–71; Minister: for Housing and Construction, 1975; for Urban and Regional Develt, 1975; for Educn, 1975–79; Minister Assisting Prime Minister in Fed. Affairs, 1975–78; Minister for Nat. Develt and Energy, 1979–83; Dep. Leader, 1978, Leader, 1978–83, Govt in the Senate. Vice-Pres., Exec. Council, 1978–82. Chairman: NSW Govt Cttee of Review of Schs, 1988–89; Gas Council of NSW, 1990–. Pres., Univ. of Sydney Dermatology Res. Foundn, 1989–. Hon. FACE 1994. *Recreations:* swimming, reading. *Address:* 8 Montah Avenue, Killara, NSW 2071, Australia. *T:* (2) 4986326. *Clubs:* Australian (Sydney); Commonwealth (Canberra).

CARRICK, Sir Roger John, KCMG 1995 (CMG 1983); LVO 1972; HM Diplomatic Service; High Commissioner to Australia, since 1994; *b* 13 Oct. 1937; *s* of John H. and Florence M. Carrick; *m* 1962, Hilary Elizabeth Blinman; two *s*. *Educ:* Isleworth Grammar Sch.; Sch. of Slavonic and East European Studies, London Univ. Served RN, 1956–58. Joined HM Foreign (subseq. Diplomatic) Service, 1956; SSEES, 1961; Sofia, 1962; FO, 1965; Paris, 1967; Singapore, 1971; FCO, 1973; Counsellor and Dep. Head, Personnel Ops Dept, FCO, 1976; Vis. Fellow, Inst. of Internat. Studies, Univ. of Calif, Berkeley, 1977–78; Counsellor, Washington, 1978; Hd, Overseas Estate Dept, FCO, 1982; Consul-Gen., Chicago, 1985–88; Asst Under-Sec. of State (Economic), FCO, 1988–90; Ambassador, Republic of Indonesia, 1990–94. Churchill Fellow (Life), Westminster Coll., Fulton, Missouri, 1987. Member: Royal Commonwealth Soc., ACT; Australia–Britain Soc.; Cook Soc. *Publication:* East-West Technology Transfer in Perspective, 1978. *Recreations:* sailing, music, reading, avoiding gardening. *Address:* c/o Foreign and Commonwealth Office, SW1A 2AH. *Clubs:* Royal Over-Seas League, Pilgrims; Australian (Sydney); Melbourne; Canberra; Lord's Taverners (Australia).

CARRICK, Maj-Gen. Thomas Welsh, OBE 1959; retired; Specialist in Community Medicine, Camden and Islington Area Health Authority (Teaching), 1975–78; *b* 19 Dec. 1914; *s* of late George Carrick and late Mary Welsh; *m* 1948, Nan Middleton Allison; one *s*. *Educ:* Glasgow Academy; Glasgow Univ.; London Sch. of Hygiene and Tropical Med. MB, ChB 1937, FFPHM (FFCM 1972), DPH 1951, DIH 1961. House appts in medicine, surgery and urological surgery at Glasgow Royal Infirmary, 1937–38; Dep. Supt, Glasgow Royal Infirmary, 1939–40. Commissioned, RAMC, 1940. Later service appts include: Asst Dir, Army Health, 17 Gurkha Div., Malaya, 1961–63; Asst Dir, Army Health, HQ Scotland, 1964–65; Dir Army Personnel Research Estabt, 1965–68; Dep. Dir, Army Health, Strategic Command, 1968–70; Prof. of Army Health, Royal Army Med. Coll., 1970; Dir of Army Health and Research, MoD, 1971–72; Comdt and Postgraduate Dean, Royal Army Medical Coll., Millbank, 1973–75, retd. Col Comdt, RAMC, 1975–79. Blackham Lectr, RIPH, 1977. QHS 1973. Pres., Blackmore Vale and Yeovil Centre, National Trust, 1979–85. OStJ 1946. *Publications:* articles in Jl of RAMC, Army Review, Community Health. *Recreations:* gardening, theatre.

CARRINGTON, 6th Baron (Ireland) *cr* 1796, (Great Britain) *cr* 1797; **Peter Alexander Rupert Carington,** KG 1985; GCMG 1988 (KCMG 1958); CH 1983; MC 1945; PC 1959; Director: Christies International plc, since 1988 (Chairman, 1988–93); The Telegraph plc, since 1990; Chancellor, Order of the Garter, since 1994; *b* 6 June 1919; *s* of 5th Baron and Hon. Sibyl Marion (*d* 1946), *d* of 2nd Viscount Colville; *S* father, 1938; *m* 1942, Iona, *yr d* of late Sir Francis McClean; one *s* two *d*. *Educ:* Eton Coll.; RMC Sandhurst. Served NW Europe, Major Grenadier Guards. Parly Sec., Min. of Agriculture and Fisheries, 1951–54; Parly Sec., Min. of Defence, Oct. 1954–Nov. 1956; High Comr for the UK in Australia, Nov. 1956–Oct. 1959; First Lord of the Admiralty, 1959–63; Minister without Portfolio and Leader of the House of Lords, 1963–64; Leader of the Opposition, House of Lords, 1964–70 and 1974–79; Secretary of State: for Defence, 1970–74; for Energy, 1974; for For. and Commonwealth Affairs, 1979–82; Minister of Aviation Supply, 1971–74. Chm., Cons. Party Organisation, 1972–74. Chm., GEC, 1983–84; Sec.-Gen., NATO, 1984–88. Chm., EC Conf. on Yugoslavia, 1991–92. Sec. for Foreign Correspondence and Hon. Mem., Royal Acad. of Arts, 1982–; Chm., Bd of Trustees, V & A Museum, 1983–88. Chancellor, Univ. of Reading, 1992–. President: The Pilgrims, 1983–; VSO, 1993–. Hon Bencher, Middle Temple, 1983; Hon. Elder Brother of Trinity House, 1984. Chancellor, Order of St Michael and St George, 1984–94. JP 1948, DL Bucks. Fellow of Eton Coll., 1966–81; Hon. Fellow, St Antony's Coll., Oxford, 1982. Hon. LLD: Cambridge, 1981; Leeds, 1981; Aberdeen, 1985; Nottingham, 1993; Birmingham, 1993; Hon. Dr Laws: Univ. of Philippines, 1982; Univ. of S Carolina, 1983; Harvard, 1986; Reading, 1989; Sussex, 1989; DUniv: Essex, 1983; Buckingham, 1989; Hon. DSc Cranfield, 1988. *Publication:* Reflect on Things Past (autobiog.), 1988. *Heir: s* Hon. Rupert Francis John Carington [*b* 2 Dec. 1948; *m* 1989, Daniela, *d* of Mr and Mrs Flavio Diotallevi; one *s* two *d*]. *Address:* 32a Ovington Square, SW3 1LR. *T:* 0171–584 1476; The Manor House, Bledlow, Princes Risborough, Bucks HP27 9PB. *T:* Princes Risborough (01844) 343499. *Clubs:* Pratt's, White's.

CARRINGTON, Prof. Alan, FRS 1971; Royal Society Research Professor, Southampton University, 1979–84 and since 1987, Oxford University, 1984–87; *b* 6 Jan. 1934; *o s* of Albert Carrington and Constance (*née* Nelson); *m* 1959, Noreen Hilary Taylor; one *s* two *d*. *Educ:* Colfe's Grammar Sch.; Univ. of Southampton. BSc, PhD; MA Cantab., MA Oxon. FRSC 1989; FInstP 1993. Univ. of Cambridge: Asst in Research, 1960; Fellow of Downing Coll., 1960; Asst Dir of Res., 1963; Prof. of Chemistry, Univ. of Southampton, 1967; Fellow, Jesus Coll., Oxford, 1984–87. Tilden Lectr, Chem. Soc., 1972; Sen. Fellowship, SRC, 1976. Foreign Hon. Mem., Amer. Acad. of Arts and Scis, 1987; Foreign Associate, Nat. Acad. of Scis, USA, 1994. Hon. DSc Southampton, 1985. Harrison Mem. Prize, Chem. Soc., 1962; Meldola Medal, Royal Inst. of Chemistry, 1963; Marlow Medal, Faraday Soc., 1966; Corday Morgan Medal, Chem. Soc., 1967; Chem. Soc. Award in Structural Chemistry, 1970; Faraday Medal, RSC, 1985; Davy Medal, Royal Soc., 1992.

Publications: (with A. D. McLachlan) Introduction to Magnetic Resonance, 1967; Microwave Spectroscopy of Free Radicals, 1974; numerous papers on topics in chemical physics in various learned jls. *Recreations:* family, music, fishing, golf, sailing. *Address:* 46 Lakewood Road, Chandler's Ford, Hants SO53 1EX. *T:* Chandler's Ford (01703) 265092.

CARRINGTON, Maj.-Gen. Colin Edward George, CB 1991; CBE 1983; Commander, Army Security Vetting Unit, since 1991; *b* 19 Jan. 1936; *s* of Edgar John Carrington and Ruth Carrington (*née* West); *m* 1967, Joy Bracknell; one *s* one *d*. *Educ:* Royal Liberty Sch.; RMA Sandhurst. FCIT 1988. Troop Comdr, BAOR, 1956–59; Air Despatch duties, 1960–64; Instructor, RMA, 1964–68; Sqdn Comdr, BAOR, 1972–74; Directing Staff, Staff Coll., 1975–77; CO 1 Armd Div. Transport Regt, 1977–79; DCOS 1 Armd Div., 1979–82; RCDS 1983; Dir, Manning Policy (Army), 1984–86; Comd Transport 1 (BR) Corps, 1986–88; Dir Gen. Transport and Movements (Army), MoD, 1988–91, retd. *Recreations:* gardening, reading.

CARRINGTON, Matthew Hadrian Marshall; MP (C) Fulham, since 1987; *b* 19 Oct. 1947; *s* of Walter and Dilys Carrington; *m* 1975, Mary Lou Darrow; one *d*. *Educ:* London Lycée; Imperial Coll. of Science and Technol., London (BSc Physics); London Business Sch. (MSc). Prodn Foreman, GKN Ltd, 1969–72; banker: with The First National Bank of Chicago, 1974–78; with Saudi Internat. Bank, 1978–87. PPS to Rt Hon. John Patten, MP, 1990–94. Mem., Treasury and Civil Service Select Cttee, 1994–. *Recreations:* cooking, political history. *Address:* House of Commons, SW1A 0AA.

CARROL, Charles Gordon; Director, Commonwealth Institute, Scotland, since 1971; *b* 21 March 1935; *s* of Charles Muir Carrol and Catherine Gray Napier; *m* 1970, Frances Anne, *o d* of John A. and Flora McL. Sinclair; three *s*. *Educ:* Melville Coll., Edinburgh; Edinburgh Univ. (MA); Moray House Coll. (DipEd). Education Officer: Govt of Nigeria, 1959–65; Commonwealth Inst., Scotland, 1965–71. Lay Member, Press Council, 1978–82. *Recreations:* walking, reading, cooking. *Address:* 11 Dukehaugh, Peebles, Scotland EH45 9DN. *T:* Peebles (01721) 21296.

CARROLL, Ven. Charles William Desmond; Archdeacon of Blackburn, 1973–86; Archdeacon Emeritus since 1986; Vicar of Balderstone, 1973–86; *b* 27 Jan. 1919; *s* of Rev. William and Mrs L. Mary Carroll; *m* 1945, Doreen Daisy Ruskell; three *s* one *d*. *Educ:* St Columba Coll.; Trinity Coll., Dublin. BA 1943; Dip. Ed. Hons 1945; MA 1946. Asst Master: Kingstown Grammar Sch., 1943–45; Rickerby House Sch., 1945–50; Vicar of Stanwix, Carlisle, 1950–59; Hon. Canon of Blackburn, 1959; Dir of Religious Education, 1959; Hon. Chaplain to Bishop of Blackburn, 1961; Canon Residentiary of Blackburn Cathedral, 1964. *Publication:* Management for Managers, 1968. *Address:* 11 Assheton Road, Blackburn BB2 6SF. *T:* Blackburn (01254) 51915. *Club:* Rotary (Blackburn).

CARROLL, Maj.-Gen. Derek Raymond, OBE 1958; retired; *b* 2 Jan. 1919; *er s* of late Raymond and Edith Lisle Carroll; *m* 1946, Bettina Mary, *d* of late Leslie Gould; one *s* two *d*. Enlisted TA, 1939; commnd into Royal Engineers, 1943; served Western Desert, 1941–43, Italy, 1943–44; psc 1945; various appts, 1946–66, in War Office (2), Germany (2), Sudan Defence Force, Libya, Malaya; CRE 4 Div., 1962–64; comd 12 Engr Bde, 1966–67; idc 1968; Dir, MoD, 1969–70; Chief Engr, BAOR, 1970–73; RARO, 1973.

CARROLL, Most Rev. Francis Patrick; *see* Canberra and Goulburn, Archbishop of, (RC).

CARROLL, Prof. John Edward, FEng 1985; Professor of Engineering, since 1983, and Head of Electrical Division, since 1992, University of Cambridge; Fellow of Queens' College, Cambridge, since 1967; *b* 15 Feb. 1934; *s* of Sydney Wentworth Carroll and May Doris Carroll; *m* 1958, Vera Mary Jordan; three *s*. *Educ:* Oundle Sch.; Queens' Coll., Cambridge (Wrangler; Foundn Schol., 1957). BA 1957; PhD 1961; FIEE; ScD 1982. Microwave Div., Services Electronic Res. Lab., 1961–67; Cambridge University: Lectr, 1967–76, Reader, 1976–83, Dep. Hd of Engrg Dept, 1986–90. Vis. Prof., Queensland Univ., 1982. Editor, IEE Jl of Solid State and Electron Devices, 1976–82. *Publications:* Hot Electron Microwave Generators, 1970; Physical Models of Semiconductor Devices, 1974; Solid State Devices (Inst. of Phys. vol. 57), 1980; Rate Equations in Semiconductor Electronics, 1986; contribs on microwaves, semiconductor devices and optical systems to learned jls. *Recreations:* swimming, piano, walking, reading thrillers, carpentry. *Address:* Engineering Department, Cambridge University, Trumpington Street, Cambridge CB2 1PZ. *T:* Cambridge (01223) 332799, *Fax:* Cambridge (01223) 332662.

CARROLL, Rt. Rev. Mgr. Philip; General Secretary, Catholic Bishops' Conference of England and Wales, since 1992; *b* 30 Nov. 1946; *s* of Joseph Carroll and Jean Carroll (*née* Graham). *Educ:* Venerable English College, Rome (PhL, STL). Ordained 1971; Assistant Priest, Our Blessed Lady Immaculate, Washington, 1972–78; Hexham and Newcastle Diocesan Religious Educn Service, 1979–88; Asst Gen. Sec., Catholic Bishops' Conf., 1988–91. *Recreations:* cricket, squash, fell walking. *Address:* Catholic Bishops' Conference Secretariat, 39 Eccleston Square, SW1V 1BX. *T:* 0171–630 8220. *Clubs:* Ryton Cricket, Old Hendon Cricket.

CARROLL, Terence Patrick, (Terry); Treasury Director, National & Provincial Building Society, since 1990; Chairman, Bradford Breakthrough Ltd, since 1990; *b* 24 Nov. 1948; *s* of George Daniel Carroll and Betty Doreen Carroll (*née* Holmes); *m* 1st, 1971, Louise Mary (*née* Smith) (marr. diss. 1984); one *s*; 2nd, 1984, Penelope Julia, (Penny) (*née* Berry). *Educ:* Gillingham Grammar Sch.; Univ. of Bradford (BSc Business Studies). FCA 1980; MCT 1985; FCBSI 1986. Auditor and Computer Auditor, Armitage & Norton, 1970–76; Management Accountant, Bradford & Bingley Building Soc., 1976–80; Exec. and Mem. Stock Exchange, Sheppards & Chase, 1980–82; Treasurer, Halifax Building Soc., 1982–85; National & Provincial Building Society: Gen. Manager Finance, 1985–88 (acting Chief Exec., 1985–86); Finance Dir, 1987–90. MIMgt. *Recreations:* golf, hockey, bridge. *Address:* National & Provincial Building Society, Provincial House, Bradford, West Yorks BD1 1NL. *T:* Bradford (01274) 842502, *Fax:* (01274) 304353. *Clubs:* Bradford; Ilkley Golf.

CARRUTHERS, Alwyn Guy; Director of Statistics, Department of Employment, 1981–83 (Deputy Director, 1972–80); *b* 6 May 1925; *yr s* of late John Sendall and of Lily Eden Carruthers, Grimsby; *m* 1950, Edith Eileen, *o d* of late William and Edith Addison Lumb; no *c*. *Educ:* Wintringham Grammar Sch., Grimsby; King's Coll., London Univ. BA First Cl. Hons in Mathematics, Drew Gold Medal and Prize, 1945. RAE, Farnborough, 1945–46; Instructor Lieut, RN, 1946–49; Rothamsted Experimental Station, 1949. Postgraduate Diploma in Mathematical Statistics, Christ's Coll., Cambridge, 1951. Bd of Trade and DTI Statistics Divisions, 1951–72. Lay Reader, Church of England, 1994–. *Publications:* articles in official publications and learned jls. *Recreations:* gardening, music. *Address:* 24 Red House Lane, Bexleyheath, Kent DA6 8JD. *T:* 0181–303 4898.

CARRUTHERS, Colin Malcolm, CMG 1980; HM Diplomatic Service, retired; Government and International Relations Consultant, World Vision International, since 1985; *b* 23 Feb. 1931; *s* of Colin Carruthers and late Dorothy Beatrice Carruthers; *m* 1954, Annette Audrey Buckton; three *s* one *d*. *Educ:* Monkton Combe School; Selwyn College, Cambridge (MA). Royal Signals, 1950–51; joined HMOCS Kenya, 1955; District Officer, Kenya, 1955–63; Dep. Civil Sec., Rift Valley Region, Kenya, 1963–65 (retired on Africanisation of post); Field Dir, Oxfam, Maseru, Lesotho, 1965–67; joined HM Diplomatic Service, 1968; First Sec. (Economic), Islamabad, 1969–73; First Sec., Ottawa, 1973–77; Counsellor and Hd of Chancery, Addis Ababa, 1977–80 (Chargé d'Affaires, 1978–79); Asst Election Comr, Zimbabwe-Rhodesia elecns, 1980; Head of South Pacific Dept, FCO, 1980–83, retired. UK Comr, British Phosphate Comrs, 1981–87. Governor, Monkton Combe Sch., 1984–91. Churchwarden, St Alban's, Frant, 1992–. *Recreations:* golf, family. *Address:* Thornbury, Frant, near Tunbridge Wells, Kent TN3 9DH. *T:* Frant (01892) 750238. *Clubs:* Commonwealth Trust; Hawks (Cambridge).

CARRUTHERS, Prof. Ian Douglas, PhD; Professor of Agrarian Development, Wye College, University of London, since 1984; Director, Wye External Programme, since 1988; *b* 30 Aug. 1938; *s* of William Walker Carruthers and late Kathleen Carruthers (*née* Irvin); *m* 1st, 1961, Barbara Price (marr. diss.); two *s* one *d*; 2nd, 1993, Sarah Ladbury. *Educ:* Chislehurst and Sidcup Grammar Sch.; Wye Coll., Univ. of London (BSc 1961); St Edmund Hall, Oxford (DipAgEcon 1962); Univ. of London (PhD 1976). Agricl Economist, Pakistan, 1963–67; Wye College: ODA Home-based Lectr, 1967–72 (Res. Fellow, Makerere Univ. Coll., Uganda, 1968–69; Res. Officer, Min. of Agric., Nairobi, 1971–72); Lectr in Agricl Econs, 1972–76; Reader in Agrarian Develt, 1976–84. Member: Council, ODI, 1991–; Bd, Commonwealth Develt Corp., 1992–. Consultant/adviser on rural develt and water resource economics: World Bank; FAO; ILO; UNDP; WHO; OECD; Commonwealth Secretariat; ODA; USAID; German Technical Assistance in Africa, ME and Asia. *Publications:* (with C. Clark) The Economics of Irrigation, 1981; (with L. Small) Farmer Financed Irrigation, 1991; (ed) Aid for Irrigation, 1986. *Recreation:* horticulture. *Address:* Wye College, Ashford, Kent TN25 5AH. *T:* Ashford (01233) 812401. *Club:* Railway (Lahore, Pakistan).

CARRUTHERS, James Edwin; Assistant Secretary, Royal Hospital Chelsea, 1988–94; *b* 19 March 1928; *er s* of James and Dollie Carruthers; *m* 1955, Phyllis Williams; one *s*. *Educ:* George Heriot's Sch.; Edinburgh Univ. (MA; Medallist in Scottish Hist.). FSAScot. Lieut, The Queen's Own Cameron Highlanders, 1949–51, and TA, 1951–55. Air Ministry: Asst Principal, 1951; Private Sec. to DCAS, 1955; Asst Private Sec. to Sec. of State for Air, 1956; Principal, 1956; Min. of Aviation, 1960–62; Private Secretary: to Minister of Defence for RAF, 1965–67; to Parly Under Sec. of State for RAF, 1967; Asst Sec., 1967; Chief Officer, Sovereign Base Areas Admin, Cyprus, 1968–71; Dep. Chief of Public Relations, MoD, 1971–72; Private Sec. to Chancellor of Duchy of Lancaster, Cabinet Office, 1973–74; Sec., Organising Cttee for British Aerospace, DoI, 1975–77; Under-Sec., 1977; seconded as Asst to Chm., British Aerospace, 1977–79; Dir Gen., Royal Ordnance Factories (Finance and Procurement), 1980–83; Chm., C S Selection Bd, 1983–84; Asst Under Sec. of State, MoD, 1984–88. *Recreations:* painting, travel. *Address:* 10 The Burren, Tudor Park, Amersham, Bucks HP6 5HQ.

CARRUTHERS, Hon. Norman Harry; Hon. Mr Justice Carruthers; Chief Justice of the Supreme Court of Prince Edward Island, since 1985; *b* 25 Oct. 1935; *s* of Lorne C. H. Carruthers and Jean R. Webster; *m* 1970, Diana C. Rodd; one *s* two *d*. *Educ:* Prince of Wales Coll.; Mount Allison Univ. (BSc, BEd); Dalhousie Law Sch. (LLB). Canadian Industries Ltd, 1956–59; schoolteacher, 1961–64; Lawyer, Foster, MacDonald and Carruthers, 1968–80; Chief Judge, Provincial Court, PEI, 1980–85. *Address:* 16 Trafalgar Street, Charlottetown, PEI C1A 3Z1, Canada. *T:* (902) 5663007; (office) (902) 3686023.

CARRUTHERS, William Buttrick; Regional Chairman, Industrial Tribunals, Bedford, 1990–95; *b* 1 Aug. 1929; *s* of Alexander Norman and Olive Carruthers; *m* 1961, Jennifer Stevens; one *s* two *d*. *Educ:* Middlesex School, Concord, Mass; Radley College; Clare College, Cambridge (BA Hons, LLB). Called to the Bar, Lincoln's Inn, 1954; practised in N Rhodesia (later Zambia), 1956–70; part time Chm., Industrial Tribunals, 1970; Chm., Industrial Tribunals, Bedford, 1975. *Recreations:* tennis, walking. *Address:* Worditch Hall, Kimbolton, Huntingdon, Cambs PE18 0JW. *T:* Huntingdon (01480) 860203.

CARSBERG, Sir Bryan (Victor), Kt 1989; Secretary-General, International Accounting Standards Committee, since 1995; *b* 3 Jan. 1939; *s* of Alfred Victor Carsberg and Maryllia (*née* Collins); *m* 1960, Margaret Linda Graham; two *d*. *Educ:* Berkhamsted Sch.; London Sch. of Econs and Polit. Science (MScEcon; Hon. Fellow, 1990). Chartered Accountant, 1960. Sole practice, chartered accountant, 1962–64; Lectr in Accounting, LSE, 1964–68; Vis. Lectr, Grad. Sch. of Business, Univ. of Chicago, 1968–69; Prof. of Accounting, Univ. of Manchester, 1969–81 (Dean, Faculty of Econ. and Social Studies, 1977–78); Arthur Andersen Prof. of Accounting, LSE, 1981–87; Dir of Res., ICA, 1981–87; Dir Gen. of Telecommunications, 1984–92; Dir Gen. of Fair Trading, 1992–95. Visiting Professor: of Business Admin, Univ. of Calif, Berkeley, 1974; of Accounting, LSE, 1988–89. Asst Dir of Res. and Technical Activities, Financial Accounting Standards Bd, USA, 1978–81; Mem., Accounting Standards Bd, 1990–94 (Vice-Chm., 1990–92). Mem. Council, ICA, 1975–79. Director: Economists Adv. Gp, 1976–84; Economist Bookshop, 1981–91; Philip Allan (Publishers), 1981–92; Mem. Bd, Radiocommunications Agency, 1990–92. Mem., Council, Univ. of Surrey, 1990–92. Hon. MAEcon Manchester, 1973; Hon. ScD UEA, 1992; Hon. DLitt Loughborough, 1994. Chartered Accountants Founding Societies Centenary Award, 1988. *Publications:* An Introduction to Mathematical Programming for Accountants, 1969; (with H. C. Edey) Modern Financial Management, 1969; Analysis for Investment Decisions, 1974; (with E. V. Morgan and M. Parkin) Indexation and Inflation, 1975; Economics of Business Decisions, 1975; (with A. Hope) Investment Decisions under Inflation, 1976; (with A. Hope) Current Issues in Accountancy, 1977, 2nd edn 1984; (with J. Arnold and R. Scapens) Topics in Management Accounting, 1980; (with S. Lumby) The Evaluation of Financial Performance in the Water Industry, 1983; (with M. Page) Current Cost Accounting, 1984; (with M. Page *et al*) Small Company Financial Reporting, 1985. *Recreations:* road running, theatre, music, opera. *Address:* International Accounting Standards Committee, 167 Fleet Street, EC4A 2ES. *T:* 0171–353 0565.

CARSON, John, CBE 1981; Draper; Member (OUP) for Belfast North, Northern Ireland Assembly, 1982–86; *b* 1934. Member of the Orange Order; Member, Belfast District Council, (formerly Belfast Corporation), 1971–; Official Unionist Councillor for Duncairn; Lord Mayor of Belfast, 1980–81, 1985–86. MP (UU) Belfast North, Feb. 1974–1979. Dir, Laganside Corp., 1989; Vice-Chm., NI Youth Council, 1985. High Sheriff, Belfast, 1978. *Address:* 16A Cardy Road, Greyabbey, Co. Down, N Ireland BT22 2LS.

CARSON, Robert Andrew Glendinning, FBA 1980; Keeper, Department of Coins and Medals, British Museum, 1978–83; *b* 7 April 1918; *s* of Andrew and Mary Dempster Carson; *m* 1949, Meta Fransisca De Vries; one *s* one *d*. *Educ:* Kirkcudbright Acad.; Univ. of Glasgow (MA (1st Cl. Hons Classics) 1940; Foulis Schol. 1940; Hon. DLitt 1983). FSA 1965. Served War, RA, 1940–46, NW Europe; 2nd Lieut 1941, Captain 1945. Asst Keeper, 1947, Dep. Keeper, 1965, Dept of Coins and Medals, British Museum. Pres., Internat. Numismatic Commn, 1979–86. Editor, Numismatic Chronicle, 1966–73; Mem., Adv. Cttee on Historic Wreck Sites, 1973–80; Pres., Royal Numismatic Soc., 1974–79 (Medallist, 1972; Hon. Fellow, 1980); Patron, Australian Numismatic Soc., 1984–. Hon. Vis. Fellow, Univ. of Tasmania, 1990. Hon. Assoc., Powerhouse Mus., Sydney, 1986. Hon. Member: Romanian Numismatic Soc., 1977; British Numismatic Soc., 1979; Corresponding Member: Amer. Numismatic Soc., 1967; Austrian Numismatic Soc., 1971;

Foreign Mem., Finnish Soc. of Science and Letters, 1986. Medallist: Soc. française de Numismatique, 1970; Luxembourg Museum, 1971; Amer. Numismatic Soc., 1978. Silver Jubilee Medal, 1977. *Publications:* (with H. Mattingly and C. H. V. Sutherland) Roman Imperial Coinage, 1951–; ed, Essays in Roman Coinage presented to Harold Mattingly, 1956; (with P. V. Hill and J. P. C. Kent) Late Roman Bronze Coinage, 1960; Coins, ancient, mediæval and modern, 1962, 2nd edn 1972; Catalogue of Roman Imperial Coins in the British Museum, vol. VI, 1962; ed, Mints, Dies and Currency, 1971; Principal Coins of the Romans, vol. I, 1978, vol. II, 1980, vol. III, 1981; ed, Essays presented to Humphrey Sutherland, 1978; History of the Royal Numismatic Society, 1986; Coins of the Roman Empire, 1990; articles in Numismatic Chron., Rev. Numismatique, etc. *Address:* 2/2A Queen's Parade, Newport, NSW 2106, Australia.

CARSON, William Hunter Fisher, OBE 1983; jockey; *b* 16 Nov. 1942; *s* of Thomas Whelan Carson and Mary Hay; *m* 1963, Carole Jane Sutton (marr. diss. 1979); three *s*; *m* 1982, Elaine Williams. *Educ:* Riverside, Stirling, Scotland. Apprenticed to Captain G. Armstrong, 1957; trans. to Fred Armstrong, 1963–66; First Jockey to Lord Derby, 1967; first classic win, High Top, 1972; Champion Jockey, 1972, 1973, 1978, 1980 and 1983; became First Jockey to W. R. Hern, 1977; also appointed Royal Jockey, riding Dunfermline to the Jubilee Oaks and St Leger wins in the colours of HM the Queen; won the 200th Derby on Troy, trained by W. R. Hern, 1979; the same combination won the 1980 Derby, with Henbit, and the 1980 Oaks, with Bireme; also won King George VI and Queen Elizabeth Stakes, on Troy, 1979, on Ela-Mana-Mou, 1980, on Petoski, 1985, on Nashwan, 1989; 1983 Oaks and St Leger, with Sun Princess; Ascot Gold Cup, on Little Wolf, 1983; St Leger, on Minster Son, 1988 (only jockey ever to breed and ride a Classic winner); Derby, on Nashwan, 1989; 1,000 Guineas, Oaks and Irish Derby, on Salsabil, 1990; Derby, on Erhaab, 1994. During the 1989 season rode 50th Group One winner in England. *Recreation:* hunting. *Address:* Minster House, Barnsley, Cirencester, Glos GL7 5DZ.

CARSTEN, Prof. Francis Ludwig, DPhil, DLitt Oxon; FBA 1971; Masaryk Professor of Central European History in the University of London, 1961–78; *b* 25 June 1911; *s* of Prof. Paul Carsten and Frida Carsten (*née* Born); *m* 1945, Ruth Carsten (*née* Moses); two *s* one *d*. *Educ:* Heidelberg, Berlin and Oxford Univs. Barnett scholar, Wadham Coll., Oxford, 1939; Senior Demy, Magdalen Coll., Oxford, 1942; Lectr in History, Westfield Coll., Univ. of London, 1947; Reader in Modern History, Univ. of London, 1960. Co-Editor, Slavonic and East European Review, 1966–84. *Publications:* The Origins of Prussia, 1954; Princes and Parliaments in Germany from the 15th to the 18th Century, 1959; The Reichswehr and Politics, 1918–1933, 1966; The Rise of Fascism, 1967, rev. edn, 1980; Revolution in Central Europe, 1918–1919, 1972; Fascist Movements in Austria, 1977; War against War: British and German Radical Movements in the First World War, 1982; Britain and the Weimar Republic, The British Documents, 1984; Essays in German History, 1985; The First Austrian Republic, 1986; A History of the Prussian Junkers, 1988; August Bebel und die Organisation der Massen, 1991; Eduard Bernstein, 1993; The German Workers and the Nazis, 1995; ed and contributor, The New Cambridge Modern History, vol. V: The Ascendancy of France, 1961; articles in English Historical Review, History, Survey, Historische Zeitschrift, etc. *Recreations:* gardening, climbing, swimming. *Address:* 11 Redington Road, NW3 7QX. *T:* 0171–435 5522.

CARSWELL, John Patrick, CB 1977; FRSL; Secretary, British Academy, 1978–83, now emeritus; Honorary Research Fellow, Department of History, University College London, since 1983; *b* 30 May 1918; *s* of Donald Carswell, barrister and author, and Catherine Carswell, author; *m* 1944, Ianthe Elstob; two *d*. *Educ:* Merchant Taylors' Sch.; St John's Coll., Oxford (MA). Served in Army, 1940–46. Entered Civil Service, 1946. Joint Sec., Cttee on Economic and Financial Problems of Provision for Old Age (Phillips Cttee), 1953–54; Asst Sec., 1955; Principal Private Sec. to Minister of Pensions and Nat. Insurance, 1955–56; Treasury, 1961–64; Under-Sec., Office of Lord Pres. of the Council and Minister for Science, 1964, Under-Sec., DES and Ministry of Health, 1964–74; Sec., UGC, 1974–77. Life Mem., Inst. of Historical Research, Univ. of London, 1984; FRSL 1984. *Publications:* The Prospector, 1950; The Old Cause, 1954; The South Sea Bubble, 1960, 2nd edn 1993; (ed with L. A. Dralle) The Diary and Political Papers of George Bubb Dodington, 1965; The Civil Servant and his World, 1966; The Descent on England, 1969; From Revolution to Revolution: English Society 1688–1776, 1973; Lives and Letters, 1978; The Exile: a memoir of Ivy Litvinov, 1983; Government and the Universities in Britain, 1986; The Porcupine: a life of Algernon Sidney, 1989; The Saving of Kenwood and the Northern Heights, 1992; contribs to Times Literary Supplement and other periodicals. *Address:* 5 Prince Arthur Road, NW3 6AX. *T:* 0171–794 6527. *Club:* Garrick.

CARSWELL, Rt. Hon. Sir Robert (Douglas), Kt 1988; PC 1993; **Rt. Hon. Lord Justice Carswell;** Lord Justice of Appeal, Supreme Court of Judicature, Northern Ireland, since 1993; *b* 28 June 1934; *er s* of late Alan E. Carswell and of Nance E. Carswell; *m* 1961, Romayne Winifred Ferris, OBE, *o d* of late James Ferris, JP, Greyabbey, Co. Down, and of Eileen Ferris, JP; two *d*. *Educ:* Royal Belfast Academical Instn; Pembroke Coll., Oxford (Schol.; 1st Cl. Honour Mods, 1st Cl. Jurisprudence, MA; Hon. Fellow, 1984); Univ. of Chicago Law Sch. (JD). Called to Bar of N Ireland, 1957 (Bencher, 1979), and to English Bar, Gray's Inn, 1972 (Hon. Bencher, 1993); Counsel to Attorney-General for N Ireland, 1970–71; QC (NI), 1971; Sen. Crown Counsel in NI, 1979–84; Judge of High Court of Justice, NI, 1984–93. Chancellor, Dios of Armagh and of Down and Dromore, 1990–. Chairman: Council of Law Reporting for NI, 1987–; Law Reform Adv. Cttee for NI, 1989–. Pres., NI Scout Council, 1993–. Governor, Royal Belfast Academical Instn, 1967–, Chm. Bd of Governors, 1986–; Pro-Chancellor and Chm. Council, Univ. of Ulster, 1984–94. Hon. DLitt Ulster, 1994. *Publications:* Trustee Acts (Northern Ireland), 1964; articles in legal periodicals. *Recreations:* golf, hill walking. *Address:* Royal Courts of Justice, Belfast BT1 3JF. *Club:* Ulster Reform (Belfast).

CARTER; *see* Bonham-Carter and Bonham Carter.

CARTER, family name of **Baron Carter.**

CARTER, Baron *cr* 1987 (Life Peer), of Devizes in the County of Wiltshire; **Denis Victor Carter;** agricultural consultant and farmer, since 1957; *b* 17 Jan. 1932; *s* of Albert William and Annie Julia Carter; *m* 1957, Teresa Mary Greengoe; one *d* (one *s* decd). *Educ:* Xaverian Coll., Brighton; East Sussex Inst. of Agriculture; Essex Inst. of Agriculture (NDA, Queen's Prize); Oxford Univ. (BLitt). Nat. Service, Canal Zone, GHQ MELF, 1950–52. Audit clerk, 1949–50 and 1952–53; farmworker, 1953–54; student of agriculture, 1954–57. Founded AKC Ltd, Agricultural Accounting and Management, 1957; commenced farming, Oxfordshire, Hants and Wilts, 1975. Sen. Research Fellowship in Agricultural Marketing, MAFF, 1970–72. Dep. Chief Opposition Whip, H of L, 1990–92. Opposition frontbench spokesman on agric. and rural affairs, 1987–, also on social security, 1988–90, and health, 1989–92. Contested (Lab) Basingstoke, 1970. Chairman: UK Co-operative Council, 1993–; BBC Rural Affairs and Agricl Adv. Cttee, 1987–90; President: British Inst. of Agricl Consultants, 1992–; Guild of Agricl Journalists, 1994–. Trustee: Rural Housing Trust, 1992–; John Arlott Meml Trust, 1993–. Vice-Pres., Shaw Trust, 1991–. *Recreations:* walking, reading, supporting Southampton Football Club. *Clubs:* Farmers' (Chm., 1982); Turners (Stockbridge); Grasshoppers (Amesbury).

CARTER, Andrew, CMG 1995; HM Diplomatic Service; Minister, Moscow, since 1995; *b* 4 Dec. 1943; *s* of Eric and Margaret Carter; *m* 1st, 1973, Anne Caroline Morgan (marr. diss. 1986); one *d*; 2nd, 1988, Catherine Mary Tyler; one *s* one *d*. *Educ:* Latymer Upper Sch., Hammersmith; Royal Coll. of Music; Jesus Coll., Cambridge (Scholar 1962; MA). FRCO; LRAM; ARCM. Asst Master, Marlborough Coll., 1965–70. Joined HM Diplomatic Service, 1971; Warsaw, 1972; Geneva, 1975; Bonn, 1975; FCO, 1978; Brussels, 1986; Dep. Gov., Gibraltar, 1990–95. *Recreation:* music. *Address:* c/o Foreign and Commonwealth Office, SW1A 2AH.

CARTER, Bernard Thomas; Hon. RE 1975; full-time artist (painter and etcher), since 1977; *b* 6 April 1920; *s* of Cecil Carter and Ethel Carter (*née* Darby); *m* Eugenie Alexander, artist and writer; one *s*. *Educ:* Haberdashers' Aske's; Goldsmith's College of Art, London Univ. NDD, ATD. RAF, 1939–46. Art lectr, critic and book reviewer, 1952–68; National Maritime Museum: Asst Keeper (prints and drawings), 1968; Dep. Keeper (Head of Picture Dept), 1970; Keeper (Head of Dept of Pictures and Conservation), 1972–77. One-man exhibns in London: Arthur Jeffress Gall., 1955; Portal Gall., 1963, 1965, 1967, 1969, 1974, 1978, 1979, 1981, 1984, 1987, 1990 and 1993; mixed exhibns: Royal Academy, Arts Council, British Council and galleries in Europe and USA; works in public collections, galleries abroad and British educn authorities, etc. TV and radio include: Thames at Six, Pebble Mill at One, Kaleidoscope, London Radio, etc. *Publication:* Art for Young People (with Eugenie Alexander), 1958. *Recreations:* reading, listening to music, gardening, theatre. *Address:* 56 King George Street, Greenwich, SE10 8QD. *T:* 0181–858 4281.

CARTER, Dr Brandon, FRS 1981; Directeur de Recherche (Centre National de la Recherche Scientifique), Observatoire de Paris-Meudon, since 1986; *b* Sydney, Australia, 26 May 1942; *s* of Harold Burnell Carter and Mary (*née* Brandon Jones); *m* 1969, Lucette Defrise; three *d*. *Educ:* George Watson's Coll., Edinburgh; Univ. of St Andrews; Pembroke Coll., Cambridge (MA, PhD 1968, DSc 1976). Res. Student, Dept of Applied Maths and Theoretical Physics, Cambridge, 1964–67; Res. Fellow, Pembroke Coll., Cambridge, 1967–68; Staff Mem., Inst. of Astronomy, Cambridge, 1968–73; Univ. Asst Lectr, 1973–74, Univ. Lectr, 1974–75, Dept of Applied Maths and Theoretical Physics, Cambridge; Maître de Recherche, co-responsable Groupe d'Astrophysique Relativiste (CNRS), Paris-Meudon, 1975–86. *Recreation:* wilderness. *Address:* 19 rue de la Borne au Diable, 92310 Sèvres, France. *T:* (Paris) 45344677.

CARTER, Bruce; *see* Hough, R. A.

CARTER, Sir Charles (Frederick), Kt 1978; FBA 1970; Joint President, Policy Studies Institute, since 1991 (President, 1989–91); Vice-Chancellor, University of Lancaster, 1963–79; *b* Rugby, 15 Aug. 1919; *y s* of late Frederick William Carter, FRS; *m* 1944, Janet Shea; one *s* two *d*. *Educ:* Rugby Sch.; St John's Coll., Cambridge. Friends' Relief Service, 1941–45; Lectr in Statistics, Univ. of Cambridge, 1945–51; Fellow of Emmanuel Coll., 1947–51 (Hon. Fellow, 1965–); Prof. of Applied Economics, The Queen's Univ., Belfast, 1952–59; Stanley Jevons Prof. of Political Economy and Cobden Lectr, Univ. of Manchester, 1959–63. Chairman: Science and Industry Cttee, RSA, British Assoc. and Nuffield Foundn, 1954–59; Schools' Broadcasting Council, 1964–71; Joint Cttee of the Univs and the Accountancy Profession, 1964–70; Adv. Bd of Accountancy Educn, 1970–76; North-West Economic Planning Council, 1965–68; Centre for Studies in Social Policy, 1972–78; PO Rev. Cttee, 1976–77; NI Economic Council, 1977–87; Sec.-Gen., Royal Econ. Soc., 1971–75; Member: UN Expert Cttee on Commodity Trade, 1953; Capital Investment Advisory Cttee, Republic of Ireland, 1956; British Assoc. Cttee on Metric System, 1958; Council for Scientific and Industrial Research, 1959–63; Commn on Higher Education, Republic of Ireland, 1960–67; Heyworth Cttee on Social Studies, 1963; Advisory Council on Technology, 1964–66; North Western Postal Bd, 1970–73; President: Manchester Statistical Soc., 1967–69; BAAS, 1981–82. Joint Editor: Journal of Industrial Economics, 1955–61; Economic Journal, 1961–70; Editor, Policy Studies, 1980–88. Chm. Council, Goldsmiths' Coll., Univ. of London, 1988–94. Fellow, Internat. Acad. of Management; Hon. MRIA; Comp OR; Trustee: Joseph Rowntree Meml Trust, 1966–94 (Vice-Chm., 1981–94); Sir Halley Stewart Trust, 1969– (Chm., 1986–); Chairman: Rosehill Theatre Trust, 1984–94; Learning from Experience Trust, 1986–92 and 1994–. Hon. DEconSc, NUI, 1968; Hon. DSc: NUU, 1979; Lancaster, 1979; QUB, 1980; Hon. LLD: TCD, 1980; Liverpool, 1982. *Publications:* The Science of Wealth, 1960, 3rd edn 1973; (with W. B. Reddaway and J. R. N. Stone) The Measurement of Production Movements, 1948; (with G. L. S. Shackle and others) Uncertainty and Business Decisions, 1954; (with A. D. Roy) British Economic Statistics, 1954; (with B. R. Williams) Industry and Technical Progress, 1957; Investment in Innovation, 1958; Science in Industry, 1959; (with D. P. Barritt) The Northern Ireland Problem, 1962, 2nd edn 1972; Wealth, 1968; (with G. Brosan and others) Patterns and Policies in Higher Education, 1971; On Having a Sense of all Conditions, 1971; (with J. L. Ford and others) Uncertainty and Expectation in Economics, 1972; Higher Education for the Future, 1980; (with J. H. M. Pinder) Policies for a Constrained Economy, 1982; (with P. John) A New Accord, 1992; articles in Economic Journal, etc. *Recreation:* gardening. *Address:* 1 Gosforth Road, Seascale, Cumbria CA20 1PU. *T:* Seascale (019467) 28359. *Club:* National Liberal.
See also C. P. Carter.

CARTER, (Christopher) Peter, MBE 1971; Deputy Director-General, Office of Electricity Regulation, since 1993; *b* 10 Dec. 1945; *s* of Sir Charles Frederick Carter, *qv*; *m* 1st, 1971, Pamela Joy Waddilove (marr. diss. 1985); two *s* one *d*; 2nd, 1986, Andrea Rigby; one *s* one *d*. *Educ:* Methodist Coll., Belfast; Manchester Grammar Sch.; St Catharine's Coll., Cambridge (BA Geography 1967). HM Diplomatic Service, 1967–78; served MECAS, Amman, Copenhagen and European Integration Dept, FCO; Department of Energy: Community and Internat. Policy Div., 1978–80; Energy Conservation Div., 1980–81; Coal Div., 1981–85; Gas Div., 1985–86; Dir, R&D, Offshore Supplies Office, 1986–93; Dep. Dir-Gen. (Scotland), Office of Electricity Regulation, 1993. *Recreations:* playing the violin, gardening, recreational cycling. *Address:* Office of Electricity Regulation, Hagley House, Hagley Road, Birmingham B16 8QG. *T:* 0121–456 6213.

CARTER, David; *see* Carter, R. D.

CARTER, Dr David, CVO 1995; HM Diplomatic Service; Counsellor and Deputy Head of Mission, British High Commission (formerly Embassy), South Africa, since 1992; *b* 4 May 1945; *s* of John Carter and Kathleen Carter (*née* Oke); *m* 1968, Susan Victoria Wright; one *s* one *d*. *Educ:* Zambia; Univ. of Wales (BA Jt Hons); Univ. of Durham (PhD 1978). Joined HM Diplomatic Service, 1970; FCO, 1970–71; Accra, 1971–75; FCO, 1975–80; Hd of Chancery, Manila, 1980–83; 1st Sec., S Africa Desk, later Asst Hd, SE Asia Dept, FCO, 1983–86; Dep. High Comr and Counsellor, Lusaka, 1986–90; Counsellor and Overseas Inspector, FCO, 1990–92. *Publications:* contrib. jls on Southern Africa. *Recreations:* distant travel, music, reading, walking, manual labour. *Address:* c/o Foreign and Commonwealth Office, King Charles Street, SW1A 2AH. *Club:* Commonwealth Trust.

CARTER, Prof. David Craig, FRCSE, FRCSGlas, FRCPE; Regius Professor of Clinical Surgery, Edinburgh University, since 1988; Hon. Consultant Surgeon: Royal Infirmary, Edinburgh, since 1988; Scottish Liver Transplantation Unit, since 1992; Surgeon to the Queen in Scotland, since 1993; *b* 1 Sept. 1940; *s* of Horace Ramsay Carter and Mary Florence Carter (*née* Lister); *m* 1967, Ilske Ursula Luth; two *s*. *Educ:* Cockermouth Grammar Sch.; St Andrews Univ. (MB ChB, MD). FRCSE 1967; FRCSGlas 1980; FRCPE 1993. British Empire Cancer Campaign Fellow, 1967; Lecturer in Surgery: Edinburgh Univ., 1969; Makerere Univ., Uganda, 1972; Wellcome Trust Sen. Lectr, Edinburgh Univ., 1974, seconded for 12 months to Center for Ulcer Res. and Educn, LA, 1976; Sen. Lectr in Surgery, Edinburgh Univ., 1974–79; St Mungo Prof. of Surgery, Glasgow Univ., 1979–88. External Examiner at univs incl. London, Oxford, Leeds, Dundee, Nairobi, Penang and Kuwait. Chairman: Scottish Foundn for Surgery in Nepal, 1988–; Scottish Council for Postgrad. Med. Educn, 1990–; Mem., Jt Med. Adv. Cttee, HEFC, 1993–. Pres., Internat. Hepatobiliary-Pancreatic Assoc., 1988–89. Member: Council, RCSE, 1980–90; James IV Assoc. of Surgeons, 1981–; Internat. Surgical Gp, 1984–. Mem., Broadcasting Council, BBC Scotland, 1989–94. Non-exec. Dir, Lothian Health Bd, 1994–. Company Sec., British Jl of Surgery Soc., 1991–; Co-Editor, British Journal of Surgery, 1986–91; General Editor, Operative Surgery, 1983–. Hon. Fellow, Deutsche Ges. für Chirurgie, 1994; Hon. Mem., Soc. of Surgeons of Nepal, 1994. William Leslie Prize in Surgery, Univ. of Edinburgh, 1968; Moynihan Prize in Surgery, Assoc. of Surgeons of GB and Ire., 1973. *Publications:* Peptic Ulcer, 1983; Principles and Practice of Surgery, 1985; Pancreatitis, 1988; Surgery of the Pancreas, 1993; numerous contribs to surgical and gastroenterological jls. *Recreations:* music, golf. *Address:* 19 Buckingham Terrace, Edinburgh EH4 3AD. *T:* 0131–332 5554. *Clubs:* New (Edinburgh); Royal & Ancient Golf (St Andrews); Luffness Golf.

CARTER, Sir Derrick (Hunton), Kt 1975; TD 1952; Vice-Chairman, Remploy Ltd, 1976–78 (Chairman, 1972–76; Director, 1967–79); *b* 7 April 1906; *s* of Arthur Hunton Carter, MD and Winifred Carter, Sedbergh; *m* 1st, 1933, Phyllis, *d* of Denis Best, Worcester; one *s* one *d*; 2nd, 1948, Madeline (*d* 1992), *d* of Col D. M. O'Callaghan, CMG, DSO; one *d*. *Educ:* Haileybury Coll.; St John's Coll., Cambridge (MA). 2nd Lieut, 27th (LEE) Bn RE, TA, 1936, mobilised Aug. 1939; in AA until Dec. 1941; 1st War Advanced Class; Major RA, Dept Tank Design; comd Armament Wing of DTD, Lulworth, 1942–45 (Lt-Col). Civil Engr, Dominion Bridge Co., Montreal, 1927–28; Res. Engr, Billingham Div., ICI, 1928–33; Asst Sales Controller, ICI, London, 1933–38; Asst Sales Man., ICI, 1938–39 and 1945–47; Gen. Chemicals Div., ICI: Sales Control Man., 1947; Commercial Dir, 1951; Man. Dir, 1953; Chm., 1961; also Chm. Alkali Div., 1963; Chm. (of merged Divs as) Mond Div., 1964; retd from ICI, 1967. Chm., United Sulphuric Acid Corp. Ltd, 1967–71; Chm., Torrance & Sons Ltd, 1971–79; Director: Avon Rubber Co. Ltd, 1970–81; Stothert & Pitt Ltd, 1971–79; BICERI Ltd, 1967–90. Mem. Exec. Cttee, Gloucestershire Council for Small Industries in Rural Areas, 1970–86. Mem. Council of Management, Nat. Star Centre for Disabled Youth, 1977–82; Vice-Pres., Glos Assoc. of Boys' Clubs. Freeman of City of London, 1973; Liveryman, Worshipful Co. of Coachmakers and Coach Harness Makers, 1973. *Recreations:* shooting, gardening. *Address:* Withington House, Withington, Cheltenham, Glos GL54 4BB. *T:* Withington (01242) 890286. *Club:* Army and Navy.

CARTER, Douglas, CB 1969; Under-Secretary, Department of Trade and Industry, 1970–71; *b* 4 Dec. 1911; 3rd *s* of Albert and Mabel Carter, Bradford, Yorks; *m* 1935, Alice (*d* 1986), *d* of Captain C. E. Le Mesurier, CB, RN; three *s* one *d*. *Educ:* Bradford Grammar Sch.; St John's Coll., Cambridge (Scholar). First Cl. Hons, Historical Tripos Part I and Economics Tripos Part II. Wrenbury Research Scholarship in Economics, Cambridge, 1933. Asst Principal, Board of Trade, 1934; Sec., Imperial Shipping Cttee, 1935–38; Princ. BoT, 1939; Asst Sec., BoT, 1943; Chm., Cttee of Experts in Enemy Property Custodianship, Inter-Allied Reparations Agency, Brussels, 1946; Controller, Import Licensing Dept, 1949; Distribution of Industry Div., BoT, 1954; Industries and Manufactures Div., 1957; Commercial Relations and Exports Div., 1960; Under-Sec., 1963; Tariff Div., 1965. *Publications:* articles in bridge magazines. *Recreations:* reading, golf, bridge, travel. *Address:* 12 Garbrand Walk, Ewell Village, Epsom, Surrey KT17 1UQ. *T:* 0181–394 1316. *Club:* Walton Heath Golf.

CARTER, (Edward) Graydon; Editor in Chief, Vanity Fair, since 1992; *b* 14 July 1949; *s* of E. P. Carter and Margaret Ellen Carter; *m* 1982, Cynthia Williamson; three *s* one *d*. *Educ:* Carleton Univ. (incomplete); Univ. of Ottawa (incomplete). Editor, The Canadian Review, 1973–77; writer, Time, 1978–83; Writer, Life, 1983–86; Founder and Editor, Spy, 1986–91; Editor, New York Observer, 1991–92. Hon. Editor, Harvard Lampoon, 1989. *Recreation:* fly fishing. *Address:* Condé Nast Building, 350 Madison Avenue, New York, NY 10017, USA. *Club:* Washington (Washington, Connecticut).

CARTER, Elizabeth Angela; *see* Shaw, E. A.

CARTER, Elliott (Cook), DrMus; composer; *b* New York City, 11 Dec. 1908; *m* 1939, Helen Frost-Jones; one *s*. *Educ:* Harvard Univ. (MA); Ecole Normale, Paris (DrMus). Professor of Greek and Maths, St John's Coll., Annapolis, 1940–42; Professor of Music: Columbia Univ., 1948–50; Yale Univ., 1960–61. *Compositions include:* First Symphony, 1942–43; Quartet for Four Saxophones, 1943; Holiday Overture, 1944; Ballet, The Minotaur, 1946–47; Woodwind Quintet, 1947; Sonata for Cello and Piano, 1948; First String Quartet, 1950–51; Sonata for Flute, Oboe, Cello and Harpsichord, 1952; Variations for Orchestra, 1953; Second String Quartet, 1960 (New York Critics' Circle Award; Pulitzer Prize; Unesco 1st Prize); Double Concerto for Harpsichord and Piano, 1961 (New York Critics' Circle Award); Piano Concerto, 1967; Concerto for Orchestra, 1970; Third String Quartet, 1971 (Pulitzer Prize); Duo for Violin and Piano, 1973–74; Brass Quintet, 1974; A Mirror on which to Dwell (song cycle), 1976; A Symphony of Three Orchestras, 1977; Syringa, 1979; Night Fantasies (for piano), 1980; In Sleep in Thunder, 1982; Triple Duo, 1983; Penthode, 1985; Fourth String Quartet, 1986; Oboe Concerto, 1988; Three Occasions for Orchestra, 1989; Violin Concerto, 1991; Partita, 1992; Adagio Tenebroso, 1993. Member: Nat. Inst. of Arts and Letters, 1956 (Gold Medal for Music, 1971); Amer. Acad. of Arts and Sciences (Boston), 1962; Amer. Acad. of Arts and Letters, 1971; Akad. der Kunste, Berlin, 1971. Hon. degrees incl. MusD Cantab, 1983. Sibelius Medal (Harriet Cohen Foundation), London, 1961; Premio delle Muse, City of Florence, 1969; Handel Medallion, New York City, 1978; Mayor of Los Angeles declared Elliott Carter Day, 27 April 1979; Ernst Von Siemens Prize, Munich, 1981; Gold Medal, MacDowell Colony, 1983; National Medal of Arts, USA, 1985. Commander, Order of Merit, (Italy), 1991. *Publication:* The Writings of Elliott Carter, 1977; *relevant publication:* The Music of Elliott Carter, by David Schiff, 1983.

CARTER, Eric Bairstow, BSc(Eng); CEng, FIMechE, FRAeS, FIEE; Director-General (Engine Research and Development), Ministry of Technology, later Ministry of Defence (Aviation Supply), 1969–72; *b* 26 Aug. 1912; *s* of John Bolton Carter and Edith Carter (*née* Bairstow); *m* 1st, 1934, Lily (*d* 1981), *d* of John Charles and Ethel May Roome (*née* Bates); one *d*; 2nd, 1981, Olive Hicks Wright, *d* of Major William George and Olive Theresa Groombridge (*née* Hicks). *Educ:* Halifax Technical Coll. Staff appt, Halifax Tech. Coll., 1932; Supt and Lectr, Constantine Technical Coll., Middlesbrough, 1936; apptd to Air Min. (Engine Directorate), Sept. 1939; subseq. Air Min. appts to engine firms and at HQ. Asst Dir (Research and Develt, Ramjets and Liquid Propellant Rockets), Dec. 1955; Dir (Engine Prod.), 1960; Dir (Engine R&D), 1963. Chm., Gas Turbine Collaborative Cttee, 1969–70. *Recreations:* Spain, aviation history, bowls. *Address:* 15 Colyford Road, Seaton, Devon EX12 2DP.

CARTER, Eric Stephen, CBE 1986; Convener, Standing Conference on Countryside Sports, since 1988; *b* 23 June 1923; *s* of Albert Harry Carter, MBE and Doris Margaret (*née* Mann); *m* 1948, Audrey Windsor; one *s*. *Educ:* Grammar Sch., Lydney; Reading Univ. BSc (Agric) 1945. Techn. Officer, Gloucester AEC, 1945–46; Asst District Officer, Gloucester NAAS, 1946–49, Dist Off. 1949–57; Sen. Dist Off., Lindsey (Lincs) NAAS, 1957–63, County Agric. Off. 1963–69; Yorks and Lancs Region: Dep. Regional Dir, NAAS, 1969–71; Regional Agric. Off., ADAS, 1971–73; Regional Off. (ADAS), 1973–74; Chief Regional Off., MAFF, 1974–75; Dep. Dir-Gen., Agricl Develt and Advisory Service, 1975–81; Adviser, Farming and Wildlife Adv. Gp, 1981–88. Member: Nuffield Farming Scholarships Trust Selection Cttee, 1981–92 (Hon. Nuffield Farming Scholar, 1992); Adv. Cttee, Welsh Plant Breeding Station, 1987–89; Governing Body, AFRC Inst. for Grassland and Envmtl Res., 1989–91. FIBiol 1974, CBiol 1974 (Vice-Pres., 1993–); FRAgS 1985; Hon. FRASE 1988. Editor, Jl of Royal Agricl Soc. of England, 1985–94. *Publications:* (with M. H. R. Soper) Modern Farming and the Countryside, 1985, 2nd edn (with M. H. R. Soper) as Farming and the Countryside, 1991; (with J. M. Stansfield) British Farming: changing policies and production systems, 1994; contrib. agric. and techn. jls. *Recreations:* travel, reading, music, countryside. *Address:* 15 Farrs Lane, East Hyde, Luton, Beds LU2 9PY. *T:* Harpenden (01582) 760504. *Club:* Farmers'.

CARTER, Francis Jackson, CMG 1954; CVO 1963; CBE 1946; Under-Secretary of State of Tasmania and Clerk of Executive Council, 1953–64; also permanent head of Premier's and Chief Secretary's Department; *b* Fremantle, W Australia, 9 Sept. 1899; *s* of late Francis Henry Carter, formerly of Bendigo, Victoria; *m* 1926, Margaret Flora, *d* of late William Thomas Walker, Launceston; two *s* one *d*. *Educ:* Hobart High Sch.; Univ. of Tasmania. Entered Tasmanian Public Service, 1916; transferred to Hydro-Electric Dept, 1925; Asst Secretary, Hydro-Electric Commn, 1934; Secretary to Premier, 1935–39; Dep. Under-Secretary of State, 1939–53; served War of 1939–45 as State Liaison Officer to Commonwealth Dept of Home Security; Official Secretary for Tasmania in London, 1949–50; State Director for Royal Visits, 1954, 1958, 1963, and Thai Royal Visit, 1962. Executive Member, State Economic Planning Authority, 1944–55; Chairman, Fire Brigades Commn of Tasmania, 1945–70. Grand Master GL of Tasmania, 1956–59. FCIS, FCIM. JP 1939. *Recreations:* music, golf and lawn bowls. *Address:* Bowditch Hostel, 3 Wellington Road, Lindisfarne, Tas 7015, Australia. *T:* (02) 435975. *Clubs:* Royal Automobile of Tasmania, Masonic (Hobart).

CARTER, Frederick Brian; QC 1980; **His Honour Judge Carter;** a Circuit Judge, since 1985; *b* 11 May 1933; *s* of late Arthur and Minnie Carter; *m* 1960, Elizabeth Hughes, JP, *d* of late W. B. Hughes and Mrs B. M. Hughes; one *s* three *d* (and one *s* decd). *Educ:* Stretford Grammar Sch.; King's Coll., London (LLB). Called to Bar, Gray's Inn, 1955, practised Northern Circuit, 1957–85; Prosecuting Counsel for Inland Revenue, Northern Circuit, 1973–80; a Recorder, 1978–85. *Recreations:* golf, travel. *Address:* 23 Lynton Park Road, Cheadle Hulme, Cheadle, Cheshire SK8 6JA. *Clubs:* Big Four (Manchester); Chorlton-cum-Hardy Golf.

CARTER, George; *see* Carter, W. G. K.

CARTER, His Eminence G(erald) Emmett, Cardinal, CC 1983; Archbishop Emeritus of Toronto (Archbishop, 1978–90); *b* Montreal, Quebec, 1 March 1912; *s* of Thomas Carter and Mary Kelty. *Educ:* Univ. of Montreal (BA, MA, PhD); Grand Seminary of Montreal (STL). Founder, Director and Teacher at St Joseph's Teachers' Coll., Montreal, 1939–61; Auxiliary Bishop of London, Ont., 1961; Bishop of London, 1964. Cardinal, 1979. Chairman, Internat. Cttee for English in the Liturgy, 1971; President, Canadian Catholic Conf. of Bishops, 1975–77. Elected Member, Permanent Council of the Synod of Bishops in Rome, 1977. Hon. LLD: Univ. of W Ontario, 1964; Concordia Univ., 1976; Univ. of Windsor, 1977; McGill Univ., Montreal, 1980; Notre Dame Univ., 1981; Hon. DD, Huron Coll., Univ. of W Ont., 1978; Hon. DHL, Duquesne Univ., Pittsburg, 1965; Hon. DLitt, St Mary's Univ., Halifax, 1980. *Publications:* The Catholic Public Schools of Quebec, 1957; Psychology and the Cross, 1959; The Modern Challenge, 1961. *Recreations:* tennis, skiing. *Address:* Chancery Office, 355 Church Street, Toronto, Ontario M5B 1Z8, Canada. *T:* (416) 9771500.

CARTER, Godfrey James, CBE 1984; Parliamentary Counsel, 1972–79; *b* 1 June 1919; *s* of Captain James Shuckburgh Carter, Grenadier Guards (killed in action, 1918), and Diana Violet Gladys Carter (*née* Cavendish); *m* 1946, Cynthia, *e d* of Eric Strickland Mason; three *s*. *Educ:* Eton (KS); Magdalene Coll., Cambridge. BA 1945, LLM 1946. War Service (Rifle Bde), Middle East, 1940–43 (twice wounded). Called to Bar, Inner Temple, 1946; Asst Parly Counsel, 1949–56; commercial dept, Bristol Aeroplane Co. Ltd, and Bristol Siddeley Engines Ltd, 1956–64; re-joined Parly Counsel Office, 1964; Dep. Counsel, 1970. *Address:* Old Bournstream House, Wotton-under-Edge, Glos GL12 7PA. *T:* Dursley (01453) 843246. *Club:* Travellers'.

CARTER, Graydon; *see* Carter, E. G.

CARTER, James Earl, Jr, (Jimmy); President of the United States of America, 1977–81; *b* Plains, Georgia, USA, 1 Oct. 1924; *s* of late James Earl Carter and Lillian (*née* Gordy); *m* 1946, Rosalynn Smith; three *s* one *d*. *Educ:* Plains High Sch.; Georgia Southwestern Coll.; Georgia Inst. of Technology; US Naval Acad. (BS); Union Coll., Schenectady, NY (post grad.). Served in US Navy submarines and battleships, 1946–53; Ensign (commissioned, 1947); Lieut (JG) 1950, (SG) 1952; retd from US Navy, 1953. Became farmer and warehouseman, 1953, farming peanuts at Plains, Georgia, until 1977. Member: Sumter Co. (Ga) School Bd, 1955–62 (Chm. 1960–62); Americus and Sumter Co. Hosp. Authority, 1956–70; Sumter Co. (Ga) Library Bd, 1961; President: Plains Develt Corp., 1963; Georgia Planning Assoc., 1968; Chm., W Central Georgia Area Planning and Develt Commn, 1964; Dir, Georgia Crop Improvement Assoc., 1957–63 (Pres., 1961). State Chm., March of Dimes, 1968–70; Dist Governor, Lions Club, 1968–69. State Senator (Democrat), Georgia, 1963–67; Governor of Georgia, 1971–75. Chm., Congressional Campaign Cttee, Democratic Nat. Cttee, 1974; Democratic Candidate for the Presidency of the USA, 1976. Founder, Carter Center, Emory Univ, 1982. Mem., Bd of Dirs, Habitat for Humanity, 1984–87; Chairman, Board of Trustees: Carter Center, Inc., 1986–; Carter-Menil Human Rights Foundn, 1986–; Global 2000 Inc., 1986–; Chairman: Council of Freely-Elected Heads of Government, 1986–; Council of Internat. Negotiation Network, 1991–. Distinguished Prof., Emory Univ., 1982–. Baptist. Hon. LLD: Morehouse Coll., and Morris Brown Coll., 1972; Notre Dame, 1977; Emory Univ., 1979; Kwansei Gakuim Univ., Japan, and Georgia Southwestern Coll., 1981; New York Law Sch., and Bates Coll., 1985; Centre Coll., and Creighton Univ., 1987; Hon. DE Georgia Inst. Tech., 1979; Hon. PhD: Weizmann Inst. of Science, 1980; Tel Aviv Univ., 1983; Haifa Univ., 1987; Hon. DHL Central; Connecticut State Univ., 1985. Awards include: Gold Medal, Internat. Inst. for Human Rights, 1979; Internat. Mediation Medal,

American Arbitration Assoc., 1979; Harry S. Truman Public Service Award, 1981; Ansel Adams Conservation Award, Wilderness Soc., 1982; Distinguished Service Award, Southern Baptist Convention, 1982; Human Rights Award, Internat. League for Human Rights, 1983; Albert Schweitzer Prize for Humanitarianism, 1987; Jefferson Award, Amer. Inst. of Public Service, 1990. *Publications:* Why Not the Best?, 1975; A Government as Good as its People, 1977; Keeping Faith: memoirs of a President, 1982; The Blood of Abraham, 1985; (with Rosalynn Carter) Everything to Gain: making the most of the rest of your life, 1987; An Outdoor Journal, 1988; Always a Reckoning (poetry), 1995. *Address:* (office) The Carter Center, One Copenhill, Atlanta, GA 30307, USA.

CARTER, Sir John, Kt 1966; QC (Guyana) 1962; Guyana Diplomatic Service, retired; *b* 27 Jan. 1919; *s* of Kemp R. Carter; *m* 1959, Sara Lou (formerly Harris); two *s* three *d*. *Educ:* University of London and Middle Temple, England. Called to English Bar, 1942; admitted to Guyana (late British Guiana) Bar, 1945; Member of Legislature of Guyana, 1948–53 and 1961–64; Pro-Chancellor, Univ. of Guyana, 1962–66; Ambassador of Guyana to US, 1966–70; High Comr for Guyana in UK, 1970–76; Ambassador to China and Korea, 1976–81 and to Japan, 1979–81; High Comr to Jamaica, 1981–83. *Recreations:* cricket, swimming. *Address:* 3603 East West Highway, Chevy Chase, Maryland 20815, USA. *Clubs:* MCC; Georgetown (Guyana).

CARTER, Sir John (Alexander), Kt 1989; Chairman, Stock Land & Estates Ltd, since 1987; *b* 2 Nov. 1921; *s* of Allan Randolph Carter and Beatrice Alice Carter; *m* 1954; two *d*. *Educ:* Duke of York's Royal Military Sch., Dover, Kent. Served Territorial Army, 1939–45: Warwicks Yeo., RA and Loyal N Lancs Regt. Founder Chm., Carter Holdings PLC, 1964–89. Co-opted Mem., Conservative Central Bd of Finance, 1983–87; Conservative Party, East of England: Chm., Industrial Council, 1983–87; Chm., Property Adv. Bd, 1986–87. KStJ 1992; Chm. Council, Order of St John for Essex, 1988–94. *Recreations:* golf, swimming, reading. *Address:* Cobblers, Mill Road, Stock, near Ingatestone, Essex CM4 9RG. *T:* Stock (01277) 840580. *Clubs:* Carlton, Institute of Directors.

CARTER, John Gordon Thomas, FIA; Chief Executive, Commercial Union plc, since 1994; *b* 28 Dec. 1937; *s* of Gordon Percival Carter and Mary Ann Carter (*née* Edgington); *m* 1961, Margaret Elizabeth Dobson; three *s*. *Educ:* City of Oxford High Sch.; Jesus Coll., Oxford (Lawrence Exhibnr; MA Maths). FIA 1966. Nat. Service, MEAF, 1956–58. Joined Commercial Union, 1961: Life Manager, 1978–80; Dep. Gen. Manager, 1981–82; Gen. Manager, 1983–86; Dir, 1987–. Director: Trade Indemnity plc, 1991–; Credito Italiano Bank, 1994–. Mem., Council for Industry and Higher Educn, 1993–. Chairman: Mgt Cttee, Motor Insurers Bureau, 1985–90; Loss Prevention Council, 1991–94; Assoc. of British Insurers, 1995–. *Recreations:* golf, ski-ing, hill walking, opera, theatre. *Address:* Commercial Union plc, St Helens, 1 Undershaft, EC3P 3DQ. *T:* 0171–283 7500. *Club:* Moor Park Golf.

CARTER, Dr (John) Timothy, FRCP, FFOM; Director of Field Operations Division, Health and Safety Executive, since 1992; *b* 12 Feb. 1944; *s* of Reginald John Carter and Linda Mary (*née* Briggs); *m* 1967, Judith Ann Lintott; one *s* two *d*. *Educ:* Dulwich Coll.; Corpus Christi Coll., Cambridge (MB, MA); University Coll. Hosp., London. FFOM 1984; FRCP 1987. London Sch. of Hygiene, 1972–74 (MSc). MO, British Petroleum, 1974–78; SMO, BP Chemicals, 1978–83; Dir of Med. Services, 1983–92, and of Health Policy, 1989–92, HSE. Member: MRC, 1983–; Bd, Faculty of Occupnl Medicine, 1982–88; Hon. Sec., Occupnl Medicine Section, RSM, 1979–83; Pres., British Occupnl Hygiene Soc., 1987–88. *Publications:* articles on investigation and control of occupnl health hazards and med. history. *Recreation:* history—natural, medical and local. *Address:* 41 Clarence Road, St Albans, Herts AL1 4NP.

CARTER, Peers Lee, CMG 1965; HM Diplomatic Service, retired; Member Committee, Afghanaid, since 1984 (Trustee, 1984–92; Chairman, 1989–92); *b* 5 Dec. 1916; *s* of Peers Owen Carter; *m* 1940, Joan Eleanor Lovegrove; one *s*. *Educ:* Radley; Christ Church, Oxford. Entered HM Foreign Service, 1939. Joined the Army in 1940; served in Africa (with Gen. Leclerc) and Europe (SOE). HM Embassy, Baghdad, 1945; First Secretary, Commissioner-General's Office, Singapore, 1951; Counsellor HM Embassy, Washington, 1958; (Temp. duty) UK Delegation to UN, New York, 1961; Head of UK Permanent Mission, Geneva, 1961; Inspector of Foreign Service Establishments, 1963–66; Chief Inspector of HM Diplomatic Service, 1966–68; Ambassador to Afghanistan, 1968–72; Ministerial Interpreter and Asst Under-Sec. of State, FCO, 1973–76. Dir, Afghanistan Support Cttee, 1981–84; Member: Bureau Internat. Afghanistan, Paris, 1985–; Internat. Assoc. of Conference Interpreters, 1976–87. Sardar-e A'ala, Afghanistan, 1971. *Address:* Dean Land Shaw, by Jobes, Balcombe, Sussex RH17 6HZ. *T:* Balcombe (01444) 811205. *Clubs:* Special Forces, Travellers'.

CARTER, Peter; *see* Carter, C. P.

CARTER, Peter; QC 1995; *b* 8 Aug. 1952; *s* of Tom Carter and Winifred (*née* Fox); *m* 1973, Caroline Ann Adams; one *s*. *Educ:* University Coll. London (LLB 1973). Called to the Bar, Gray's Inn, 1974. *Publication:* Offences of Violence, 1991, supplement 1994. *Recreations:* poetry, cricket, walking. *Address:* 5 King's Bench Walk, Temple, EC4Y 7DN. *T:* 0171–797 7600.

CARTER, Peter Basil; QC 1990; Emeritus Fellow, Wadham College, Oxford, since 1988 (Fellow, 1949–88); *b* 10 April 1921; *s* of Albert George Carter and Amy Kathleen FitzGerald (*née* Arthur); *m* 1st, 1960, Elizabeth Maxwell (*née* Ely) (decd); 2nd, 1982, Lorna Jean (*née* Sinclair). *Educ:* Loughborough GS; Oriel Coll., Oxford (BA 1st Cl. Hons Jurisprudence; BCL 1st Cl. Hons; Vinerian Scholar, 1949; MA). War Service, RAC, 1941–46 (Croix de Guerre, 1944). Called to the Bar, Middle Temple, 1947; Hon. Bencher, 1981. Curator, Bodleian Library, Oxford, 1963–90; Sen. Bursar, Wadham Coll., Oxford, 1965–77. Inns of Court School of Law: Lectr in Conflict of Laws, 1960–89; Lectr in Evidence, 1971–95; Hon. Reader, 1985–. Visiting Professor of Law: Univ. of Melbourne, 1953; Univ. of Florida, 1955; New York Univ., 1961 and 1969; Osgoode Hall Law Sch., Ont, 1971, 1973, 1978 and 1982; Walter S. Owen Prof., Univ. of British Columbia, 1986; Canada Commonwealth Vis. Fellow, Faculty of Law, Univ. of Toronto, 1970; delivered Gen. Course of Lectures on Private Internat. Law, The Hague Acad. of Internat. Law, 1981. Rapporteur, Cttee on Transnational Recognition and Enforcement of Foreign Public Laws, Internat. Law Assoc., 1984–88. Gen. Comr for Income Tax Appeals, E Oxfordshire, 1965–95 (Chm., 1991–95). Dir (non-exec.), University Life Assurance Soc., 1969–91 (Chm., 1980–91). FInstD 1984. JP Oxon, 1959–88. Jt Editor, International and Comparative Law Qly, 1961–. *Publications:* Essays on the Law of Evidence (with Sir Zelman Cowen), 1956; Cases and Statutes on Evidence, 1981, 2nd edn 1990, supplement 1992; articles, mostly on private internat. law or law of evidence, in British Yearbook of Internat. Law, Internat. and Comparative Law Qly, Law Qly Rev., Cambridge Law Jl, Modern Law Rev., etc. *Recreation:* appreciating architecture. *Address:* Wadham College, Oxford OX1 3PN. *T:* Oxford (01865) 277900; Fountain Court, Temple, EC4Y 9DH. *T:* 0171–583 3335. *Club:* United Oxford & Cambridge University.

CARTER, Sir Philip (David), Kt 1991; CBE 1982; Managing Director, Littlewoods Organisation, 1976–83; *b* 8 May 1927; *s* of Percival Carter and Isobell (*née* Stirrup); *m* 1946, Harriet Rita (*née* Evans); one *s* two *d*. *Educ:* Waterloo Grammar Sch., Liverpool. Volunteered for Fleet Air Arm, 1945. Professional career in Littlewoods Organisation, 1948–83. Chm., Mail Order Traders Assoc. of GB, 1979–83; Pres., European Mail Order Traders Assoc., 1983; Chm., Man Made Fibres Sector Wkg Party, 1980–; Member: Jt Textile Cttee, NEDO, 1979–; Distributive Trades EDC, 1980–; Merseyside Develt Corp., 1981–91 (Chm., 1987–91); Merseyside Residuary Body, 1986–. Chm., Merseyside Tourism Bd, 1986–93. Vice-Chm., 1980–86, Chm., 1986–, Empire Theatre Trust, Liverpool; Chm., Liverpool John Moores Univ. Trust, 1993–; Pro-Chancellor, and Vice-Chm. Bd of Govs, Liverpool John Moores Univ., 1994–. Chm., Liverpool Conservative Assoc., 1985–. Dir, Everton FC, 1975– (Chm., 1978–91); Pres., Football League, 1986–88. *Recreations:* football, private flying, music, theatre. *Address:* Oak Cottage, Noctorum Road, Noctorum, Wirral, Merseyside L43 9UQ. *T:* 0151–652 4053.

CARTER, Raymond John, CBE 1991; Executive, since 1980, Director, since 1983, Marathon Oil Co.; *b* 17 Sept. 1935; *s* of John Carter and Nellie Carter (*née* Woodcock); *m* 1959, Jeanette Hills; one *s* two *d*. *Educ:* Mortlake Co. Secondary Sch.; Reading Technical Coll.; Staffordshire Coll. of Technology. National Service, Army, 1953–55. Sperry Gyroscope Co.: Technical Asst, Research and Development Computer Studies, 1956–65. Electrical Engineer, Central Electricity Generating Bd, 1965–70, Mem., CEGB Management, 1979–80. Mem., Gen. Adv. Council, BBC, 1974–76. Mem., Interim Adv. Cttee (Teachers' Pay and Conditions), DES, 1987–91; Dep. Chm., School Teachers' Review Body, 1991–93. Mem. Easthampstead RDC, 1963–68. Contested: Wokingham, Gen. Elec., 1966; Warwick and Leamington, By-elec., March 1968; MP (Lab) Birmingham, Northfield, 1970–79; Parly Under-Sec. of State, Northern Ireland Office, 1976–79. Member: Public Accounts Cttee, 1973–74; Parly Science and Technology Cttee, 1974–76; author of Congenital Disabilities (Civil Liability) Act, 1976. Delegate: Council of Europe, 1974–76; WEU, 1974–76. Trustee: BM (Nat. Hist.), 1986–; Guild of Handicraft Trust, 1991–. Co-cataloguer and exhibitor, works of Sir John Betjeman, 1983. *Recreations:* running, reading, book collecting. *Address:* 1 Lynwood Chase, Warfield Road, Bracknell, Berkshire RG12 2JT. *T:* Bracknell (01344) 420237.

CARTER, Sir Richard (Henry Alwyn), Kt 1992; Chairman: Ports of Auckland Ltd, since 1993; Carter Holt Harvey Ltd, 1984–92; *b* 24 April 1935; *s* of Kenneth Clifford Alwyn Carter, OBE and Stella Grace (*née* Dedman); *m* 1960, June Doreen White; one *d*. *Educ:* Waitaki Boys' High Sch.; Auckland Univ. FCA. With Carter Consolidated, subseq. Carter Holt Hldgs, then Carter Holt Harvey Ltd, 1953–92: Gen. Manager, Admin, 1960; Associate Dir, 1961; Dir, 1966; Jt Man. Dir, 1974. Chm., Council, NZ Timber Industry, 1976–78; Member: NZ Timber Merchants Fedn Inc., 1960–78 (Pres., 1976–78); NZ Business Roundtable, 1974–92. *Recreations:* field shooting, farming. *Address:* Waytemore Farm, Ararimu Road, Drury RD 3, S Auckland, New Zealand. *T:* (9) 2925892.

CARTER, Air Commodore Robert Alfred Copsey, CB 1956; DSO 1942; DFC 1943; Royal Air Force, retired; *b* 15 Sept. 1910; *s* of S. H. Carter and S. Copsey; *m* 1947, Sally Ann Peters, Va, USA; two *s* one *d*. *Educ:* Portsmouth Grammar Sch.; RAF Coll., Cranwell. Cranwell Cadet, 1930–32; commissioned in RAF, 1932; served in India, 1933–36; grad. RAF School of Aeronautical Engineering, 1938; served in Bomber Command, 1940–45; commanded 103 and 150 Sqdns; Station Comdr, RAF, Grimsby; grad. RAF Staff Coll., 1945; attended US Armed Forces Staff Coll., Norfolk, Va, USA, 1947; attached to RNZAF, 1950–53; comd. RAF Station, Upwood, 1953–55; SASO, RAF Transport Command, 1956–58; Director of Personal Services, Air Ministry, 1958–61; AO i/c Admin, HQ, RAF Germany, 1961–64; retired 1964. MRAeS 1960; CEng, 1966. *Club:* Royal Air Force.

CARTER, Robert William Bernard, CMG 1964; HM Diplomatic Service, retired; *b* 1913; 3rd *s* of late William Joseph Carter and late Lucy (*née* How); *m* 1945, Joan Violet, *o d* of Theodore and Violet Magnus; one *s* two *d* (and one *d* decd). *Educ:* St Bees Sch., Cumberland; Trinity Coll., Oxford (Scholar). Asst Master, Glenalmond, Perthshire, 1936. Served with the Royal Navy, 1940–46; Lieut, RNVR. Administrative Assistant, Newcastle upon Tyne Education Cttee, 1946; Principal, Board of Trade, 1949; Trade Commissioner: Calcutta, 1952; Delhi, 1955; Accra, 1956; Principal Trade Commissioner, Colombo (Assistant Secretary), 1959; Senior British Trade Commissioner in Pakistan, 1961; Minister (Commercial), Pakistan, and Dep. High Comr, Karachi, 1967–68; Dep. High Comr, 1969–73 and Consul-Gen., 1973, Melbourne. *Recreations:* reading, travelling, collecting beer-mugs. *Address:* The Old Parsonage, Heywood, Westbury, Wilts BA13 4NB. *T:* Westbury (01373) 822194. *Club:* Oriental.

CARTER, Roland; retired; Visiting Fellow, 1990–91, Visiting Senior Research Fellow, 1991–92, Institute for Research in the Social Sciences, York University; *b* 29 Aug. 1924; *s* of Ralph Carter; *m* 1950, Elisabeth Mary Green; one *s* two *d*. *Educ:* Cockburn High Sch., Leeds; Leeds Univ. Served War of 1939–45: Queen's Royal Regt, 1944; 6th Gurkha Rifles, 1945; Frontier Corps (South Waziristan and Gilgit Scouts), 1946. Seconded to Indian Political Service, as Asst Political Agent, Chilas, Gilgit Agency, 1946–47; Lectr, Zurich Univ. and Finnish Sch. of Economics, 1950–53. Joined Foreign Service, 1953: FO, 1953–54; Third Sec., Moscow, 1955; Germany, 1956–58; Second Sec., Helsinki, 1959 (First Sec., 1962); FO, 1962–67; Kuala Lumpur, 1967–69; Ambassador to People's Republic of Mongolia, 1969–71; seconded to Cabinet Office, 1971–74; Counsellor: Pretoria, 1974–77; FCO, 1977–80, retired. Area Appeals Manager, N and NE England, Nat. Soc. for Cancer Relief, 1981–89. *Publication:* Näin Puhutaan Englantia (in Finnish; with Erik Erämetsä), 1952. *Recreations:* music, linguistics, Iranian history and culture. *Address:* Post Cottage, Langton, Malton, N Yorks YO17 9QP.

CARTER, (Ronald) David, CBE 1980; RDI 1975; Founder and Chairman, DCA Design International Ltd, since 1975; Professor of Industrial Design Engineering, Royal College of Art, and Imperial College of Science, Technology and Medicine, since 1991; *b* 30 Dec. 1927; *s* of H. Miles Carter and Margaret Carter; *m* 1953, Theo (Marjorie Elizabeth), *d* of Rev. L. T. Towers; two *s* two *d*. *Educ:* Wyggeston Sch., Leicester; Central Sch. of Art and Design, London. Served RN, 1946–48. Appts in industry, 1951–60; Principal, David Carter Associates, 1960–75. Visiting Lectr, Birmingham Coll. of Art and Design, 1960–65. Examnr, RCA, 1976–79 and 1987–90. Mem., Design Council, 1972–84 (Dep. Chm., 1975–84; Chm., Report on Industrial Design Educn in UK, 1977). Pres., Soc. of Industrial Artists and Designers, 1974–75; Chm., DATEC, 1977–82; Royal Fine Arts Comr, 1986–. Vice-Chm., Design Mus. (formerly Conran Foundn), 1992– (Chm., 1986–92; Trustee, 1981–); Moderator, Hong Kong Polytechnic, 1981–86; Mem., Prince of Wales Award for Indust. Innovation, 1981–85. Governor, London Inst., 1988–91. Design Awards, 1961, 1969, 1983; Duke of Edinburgh Prize for Elegant Design, 1967. FSIA 1967; FRSA 1975. Hon. DDes De Montfort, 1993. *Recreations:* dry stone walling, boats, County Cork. *Address:* The Old Parsonage, Compton Abdale, near Cheltenham, Glos GL54 4DS. *T:* Cheltenham (01242) 890340. *Club:* Reform.

CARTER, Ronald Louis, DesRCA; RDI 1971; FCSD (FSIAD 1961); private consultancy design practice, since 1974; *b* 3 June 1926; *s* of Harry Victor Carter and Ruth Allensen; *m* 1st (marr. diss.); three *d*; 2nd, 1985, Ann McNab; one step *s* two step *d*. *Educ:* Birmingham Central College of Art: studied Industrial and Interior Design (NDD; Louisa Anne Ryland

Schol. for Silver Design), 1946–49; Royal College of Art: studied Furniture Design (1st Cl. Dip.; Silver Medal for work of special distinction; Travelling Schol. to USA), 1949–52; DesRCA; Fellow, RCA, 1966; Hon. Fellow, 1974; Sen. Fellow, 1994. Staff Designer with Corning Glass, 5th Avenue, NY City, 1952–53; freelance design practice, Birmingham and London, 1954; Tutor, School of Furniture, RCA, 1956–74; Partner: Design Partners, 1960–68; Carter Freeman Associates, 1968–74; Dir, Miles-Carter, 1980–. *Recreations:* fishing, cabinet making, wood carving, painting, cooking, walking. *Address:* 35 Great Queen Street, WC2B 5AA. *T:* 0171–242 2291.

CARTER, Timothy; *see* Carter, J. T.

CARTER, Air Vice-Marshal Wilfred, CB 1963; DFC 1943; international disaster consultant; *b* 5 Nov. 1912; *s* of late Samuel Carter; *m* 1950, Margaret Enid Bray; one *d* (one *s* decd). Educ: Witney Grammar Sch. RAF, 1929. Served War of 1939–45 with Bomber Command in UK and Middle East. Graduate, Middle East Centre for Arab Studies, 1945–46. Air Adviser to Lebanon, 1950–53; with Cabinet Secretariat, 1954–55; OC, RAF, Ternhill, 1956–58; Sen. RAF Dir, and later Commandant, Jt Services Staff Coll.; Asst Chief of Staff, Cento, 1960–63; Asst Commandant, RAF Staff Coll., 1963–65; AOA, HQ Bomber Command, 1965–67; Dir, Austr. Counter Disaster Coll., 1969–78. Gordon Shephard Memorial Prize (for Strategic Studies), 1955, 1956, 1957, 1961, 1965, 1967. Officer, Order of Cedar of Lebanon, 1953. *Publications:* Disaster Preparedness and Response, 1985; Disaster Management, 1991. *Recreations:* walking, swimming. *Address:* Blue Range, Macedon, Vic 3440, Australia.

CARTER, (William) George (Key), CBE 1994; FCA; Chairman, Black Country Development Corporation, since 1994; *b* 29 Jan. 1934; *s* of late William Tom Carter, OBE, JP and Georgina Margaret Carter (*née* Key); *m* 1965, Anne Rosalie Mary Flanagan; one *s* one *d*. *Educ:* Warwick School. FCA 1957. Articled with Loarridge Beaven & Co., 1951–56; joined Price Waterhouse, 1956; Nat. Service, 2nd Lieut, 16/5th Queen's Royal Lancers, 1958–60; returned to Price Waterhouse, 1960: Manager, 1963–66; Partner, London, 1966–82; Dir of Finance, 1966–70; Sen. Partner, W Midlands, 1982–94. Dir, W Midlands Develt Agency, 1989–95 (Chm., 1991–95); Mem., NW Worcs HA, 1994–. Mem., Pharmacists Rev. Panel, 1981–. Member: CBI W Midlands Regl Council, 1988–; DTI Industry '96 Steering Gp, 1993–. Pres., Birmingham Chamber of Industry and Commerce, 1993–94; Vice-Chm., Birmingham Mkting Partnership, 1993–95; Non-exec. Dir, Birmingham Econ. Develt Partnership, 1991–95. Institute of Chartered Accountants: Member: Insce Industry Cttee (Chm., 1974–80); Parly and Law Cttee, 1978–83; Co-Chm., Auditors and Actuaries Cttee, 1975–80; Courses Cttee 1978–81. Member: Birmingham Univ. Business Sch. Adv. Bd, 1989–; Council, Aston Univ., 1995–. Chm., Council, Order of St John, W Midlands, 1994–. Gov. and Feoffee, Old Swinford Hosp. Sch., 1986–. FRSA 1993. *Publication:* (jtly) Institute of Chartered Accountants Guide to Investigations, 1978. *Recreations:* gardening, golf, shooting. *Address:* The Old Rectory, Elmley Lovett, Droitwich, Worcs WR9 0PS. *T:* Stourport (01299) 851459; 28 Westmoreland Terrace, Pimlico, SW1V 4AF. *T:* 0171–630 0597. *Club:* Cavalry and Guards.

CARTER, William Nicholas, (Will Carter),OBE 1984; Senior Partner, Rampant Lions Press, since 1967; *b* 24 Sept. 1912; *s* of Thomas Buchanan Carter and Margaret Theresa Stone; *m* 1939, Barbara Ruth Digby; one *s* three *d*. *Educ:* Sunningdale Sch.; Radley. Served War, RN, 1941–46: S Atlantic, Coastal Forces Eastern Med.; commnd 1943. Gen. career in printing, advertising, typography and inscriptional letter-carving; founded Rampant Lions Press, 1949. Artist-in-Residence, Dartmouth Coll., NH, USA, 1969. Member: Royal Mint Adv. Cttee, 1971–91; Arch. Adv. Panel, Westminster Abbey, 1979–92. Hon. Fellow, Magdalene Coll., Cambridge, 1977. Frederick W. Goudy Award, Rochester Inst. of Technol., New York State, 1975; Silver Jubilee Medal, 1977. *Publication:* (with Wilfrid Blunt) Italic Handwriting, 1954. *Address:* 12 Chesterton Road, Cambridge CB4 3AB. *T:* Cambridge (01223) 357553. *Club:* Double Crown (Pres., 1961).

CARTER, Sir William (Oscar), Kt 1972; Consultant, Eversheds, Daynes, Hill & Perks, Solicitors, Norwich; *b* 12 Jan. 1905; *s* of late Oscar Carter and Alice Carter; *m* 1934, Winifred Thompson. *Educ:* Swaffham Grammar Sch.; City of Norwich Sch. Admitted Solicitor of Supreme Court of Judicature, 1931. Served War, 1940–45, RAF (Wing Comdr), UK and Middle East. Mem. Council, The Law Society, 1954–75, Vice-Pres. 1970, Pres. 1971–72; President: East Anglian Law Soc., 1952–80; Norfolk and Norwich Incorporated Law Soc., 1959; Internat. Legal Aid Assoc., 1974–80; Life Mem. Council, Internat. Bar Assoc. (first Vice-Pres., 1976–78). Member: County Court Rules Cttee, 1956–60; Supreme Court Rules Cttee, 1960–75; Criminal Injuries Compensation Board, 1967–82 (Dep. Chm., 1977–82). Former Chm., Mental Health Review Tribunals for E Anglian and NE Thames RHA Areas. Upper Warden, 1984, Master, 1985–86, Worshipful Co. of Glaziers; Hon. Mem., The Fellows of American Bar Foundn. *Recreations:* swimming, walking, foreign travel. *Address:* 83 Newmarket Road, Norwich NR2 2HP. *T:* Norwich (01603) 53772. *Clubs:* Army and Navy; Norfolk (Norwich).

CARTER-JONES, Lewis, CBE 1995; *b* Gilfach Goch, S Wales, 17 Nov. 1920; *s* of Tom Jones, Kenfig Hill, Bridgend, Glam.; *m* 1945, Patricia Hylda, *d* of late Alfred Bastiman, Scarborough, Yorks; two *d*. *Educ:* Bridgend County Sch.; University Coll. of Wales, Aberystwyth (BA; Chm. Student Finance Cttee; Capt, Coll., Univ. and County Hockey XI). Served War of 1939–45 (Flight Sergeant Navigator, RAF). Head of Business Studies, Yale Grammar Technical Sch., Wrexham, 1950–64. Contested (Lab) Chester, by-election, 1956, and general election, 1959. MP (Lab) Eccles, 1964–87. Chairman: Cttee for Research for Apparatus for Disabled, 1973–80; Anglo-Columbian Gp, 1975–87; PLP Disablement Gp, 1975–81; PLP Aviation Gp, 1978–87. Exec. Mem., UK Br., CPA, 1983–87; Secretary: Indo-British Parly Gp, 1966–87; All-Party BLESMA Gp, 1973–87; All Party Aviation Gp, 1980–87. Hon. Parliamentary Adviser: RNIB, 1973–87; British Assoc. of Occupational Therapists; Soc. of Physiotherapists, until 1987. Mem., Gen. Adv. Council, IBA, 1982–87. Chairman: British Cttee, Rehabilitation International, 1978–92; Adv. Gp on Artificial Limbs to DoH, 1993–; Vice-President. Wales Council for the Disabled, 1981–; RADAR, 1987– (Chm., Access to the Skies Cttee, 1992–); Member: Disablement Services Authority, 1987–91; Disabled Persons Transport Adv. Cttee, Dept of Transport, 1988– (Chm., Airport Sub Cttee, 1988–); Adv. Gp on Rehabilitation to Sec. of State for Health, 1991–; Trustee, Granada Telethon, 1987–. Dir, Possum Controls Ltd, 1974–. *Address:* Cader Idris, 5 Cefn Road, Rhosnesni, Wrexham, Clwyd LL13 9NF.

CARTER-MANNING, Jeremy James; QC 1993; a Recorder, since 1993; *b* 25 Dec. 1947; *s* of Landon and Nancie Carter-Manning; *m* 1970, Bridget Mary Simpson; one *s* one *d*. *Educ:* St Paul's Sch. Solicitor 1971; called to the Bar, Middle Temple, 1975. *Recreation:* tennis. *Address:* 9–12 Bell Yard, WC2A 2LF. *T:* 0171–400 1800.

CARTER-RUCK, Peter Frederick; Senior Partner, Peter Carter-Ruck and Partners, Solicitors, since 1981 (Senior Partner, Oswald Hickson, Collier & Co., 1945–81); *b* 26 Feb. 1914; *s* of Frederick Henry Carter-Ruck and Nell Mabel Carter-Ruck; *m* 1940, Pamela Ann, *o d* of late Gp Capt. Reginald Stuart Maxwell, MC, DFC, AFC, RAF; one *d* (one *s* decd). *Educ:* St Edward's, Oxford; Law Society; Solicitor of the Supreme Court (Hons). Admitted Solicitor, 1937; served RA, 1939–44, Captain Instr in gunnery. Specialist Member, Council of Law Soc., 1971–84; Chairman: Law Soc. Law Reform Cttee, 1980–83; Media Cttee, Internat. Bar Assoc., 1983–85; Mem., Council of Justice (Internat. Commn of Jurists), 1968–; President: City of Westminster Law Soc., 1975–76; Council, Media Soc., 1981–82 and 1984–86 (Hon. Life Vice Pres., 1988). Governor, St Edward's Sch., Oxford, 1950–78; past Chm. and Founder Governor, Shiplake Coll., Henley, 1960–73; Mem. Livery, City of London Solicitors' Co., 1949–. *Publications:* Libel and Slander, 1953, 4th edn 1992; (with Ian Mackrill) The Cyclist and the Law, 1953; (with Edmund Skone James) Copyright: modern law and practice, 1965; Memoirs of a Libel Lawyer, 1990. *Address:* 75 Shoe Lane, EC4A 3BQ. *T:* 0171–353 5005; Latchmore Cottage, Great Hallingbury, Bishop's Stortford, Herts CM22 7PJ. *T:* Bishop's Stortford (01279) 654357; Eilagadale, N Ardnamurchan, Argyll PH36 4LG. *T:* Kilchoan (01972) 510267. *Clubs:* Garrick, Press; Royal Yacht Squadron, Lloyd's Yacht, Law Society Yacht (past Commodore), Royal Ocean Racing, Ocean Cruising (past Commodore).

CARTIER-BRESSON, Henri; photographer; *b* France, 22 Aug. 1908. Studied painting with André Lhote, 1927–28. Asst Dir to Jean Renoir, 1936–39; Co-founder, Magnum Photos, 1947. Photographs exhibited: Mexico; Japan; Mus. of Modern Art, NY, 1947, 1968, 1987; Villa Medicis, Rome; Louvre, 1955, 1967, Grand Palais, 1970, Paris; V&A, 1969; Manege, Moscow, 1972; Edinburgh Festival, 1978; Hayward Gall., London, 1978; drawings exhibited: Carlton Gall., NY, 1975; Bischofberger Gall., Zürich, 1976; Forcalquier Gall., France, 1976; Mus. of Modern Art, Paris, 1981; Mus. of Modern Art, Mexico, 1982; French Inst., Stockholm, 1983; Pavilion of Contemporary Art, Milan, 1983; Mus. of Modern Art, Oxford, 1984; Palace Liechtenstein, Vienna, Salzburg, 1985; Herstand Gall., NY, 1987; Ecole des Beaux Arts, Paris, 1989; le Printemps, Tokyo, 1989; Fondation Gianadda, Switzerland, 1990; Villa Medici, Rome, 1990; Musée de Louvain, Belgium, 1991; Mus. of Modern Art, Taiwan, 1991; Palazzo Sanvitale, Parma, 1992; Museo Camon Aznar, Zaragoza, 1992. Collection of 390 photographs at DeMenil Foundn, Houston, USA, V&A, Univ. of Fine Arts, Osaka, Japan, Bibliothèque Nationale, Paris. Documentary films: on hosps, Spanish Republic, 1937; (with J. Lemare) Le Retour, 1945; (with J. Boffety) Impressions of California, 1969; (with W. Dombrow) Southern Exposures, 1970. Mem., Amer. Acad. of Arts and Scis, 1974. Hon. DLitt Oxon, 1975. Awards: US Camera, 1948; Overseas Press Club of America, 1949; Amer. Soc. of Magazine Photography, 1953; Photography Soc. of America, 1958; Overseas Press Club, 1954 (for Russia), 1960 (for China), 1964 (for Cuba); German Photographic Soc.; Hasselblad, 1983; Novecento, Palermo, 1986; Japanese Photographic Soc., 1989. *Publications:* (ed) Images à la Sauvette (The Decisive Moment), 1952; The Europeans, Moscow, 1955; From One China to the Other, 1956; Photographs by Cartier-Bressons; Flagrants Délits (The World of Henri Cartier-Bresson, 1968); (with F. Nourrissier) Vive la France, 1970; Cartier-Bresson's France, 1971; (jtly) L'Homme et la Machine, 1972 (Man and Machine, 1969) for IBM; Faces of Asia, 1972; A Propos de l'URSS, 1973 (About Russia, 1974); Henri Cartier-Bresson Pocket Book, 1985; Henri Cartier-Bresson in India, 1988; Traits pour Traits (Line by Line, 1989) (drawings); L'Amérique Furtivement (America in Passing), 1991; A Propos de Paris, 1994 (also German, American and Japanese edns); Carnets mexicains (text by Carlos Fuentes), 1995 (also German and Italian edns); André Breton, roi soleil, 1995; *relevant publications:* Yves Bonnefoy, Henri Cartier-Bresson, Photographer, 1979, rev. edn 1992; André P. de Mandiargues, Photoportrait, 1985; Peter Galassi, Early Work, USA 1987 (French edn 1991); Jean Pierre Montier, L'Art sans Art, 1995. *Address:* c/o Magnum Photos, 5 impasse Piver, 75011 Paris, France; c/o Helen Wright, 135 East 74th Street, New York, NY 10021, USA.

CARTLAND, Dame Barbara (Hamilton), DBE 1991; authoress and playwright; *b* 9 July 1901; *d* of late Major Bertram Cartland, Worcestershire Regiment; *m* 1st, 1927, Alexander George McCorquodale (whom she divorced, 1933; he *d* 1964), of Cound Hall, Cressage, Salop; one *d*; 2nd, 1936, Hugh (*d* 1963), 2nd *s* of late Harold McCorquodale, Forest Hall, Ongar, Essex; two *s*. Published first novel at the age of twenty-one, which ran into five editions; designed and organised many pageants in aid of charity, including Britain and her Industries at British Legion Ball, Albert Hall, 1930; carried the first aeroplane-towed glider-mail in her glider, the Barbara Cartland, from Manston Aerodrome to Reading, June 1931; 2 lecture tours in Canada, 1940; Hon. Junior Commander, ATS and Lady Welfare Officer and Librarian to all Services in Bedfordshire, 1941–49; Certificate of Merit, Eastern Command, 1946; County Cadet Officer for St John Ambulance Brigade in Beds, 1943–47, County Vice-Pres. Cadets, Beds, 1948–50; organised and produced the St John Ambulance Bde Exhibn, 1945–50; Chm., St John Ambulance Bde Exhibn Cttee, 1944–51; County Vice-Pres.: Nursing Cadets, Herts, 1951 (instigated a govt enquiry into the housing conditions of old people, 1955); Nursing Div., Herts, 1966; CC Herts (Hatfield Div.), 1955–64; Pres., St John Council, Herts, 1992–; Pres., Herts Br. of Royal Coll. of Midwives, 1961. Had Law of England changed with regard to sites for gypsies so that their children can go to school; founded Cartland Onslow Romany Trust, with private site in Hatfield for family of Romany Gypsies. Founder and Pres., Nat. Assoc. for Health, 1964–. DStJ 1972 (Mem. Chapter Gen.). FRSA. Bishop Wright Air Industry Award for contrib. to aviation in 1931, Kennedy Airport, 1984; Médaille de Vermeil de la Ville de Paris (Gold Medal of City of Paris) for Achievement, for sales of 25 million books in France, 1988. Bestselling author in the world (Guinness Book of Records); broke world record for last 18 years, by writing an average of 23 books a year. *Publications: novels:* Jigsaw, 1923; Sawdust, 1926; If the Tree is Saved, 1929; For What?, 1930; Sweet Punishment, 1931; A Virgin in Mayfair, 1932; Just off Piccadilly, 1933; Not Love Alone, 1933; A Beggar Wished, 1934; Passionate Attainment, 1935; First Class, Lady?, 1935; Dangerous Experiment, 1936; Desperate Defiance, 1936; The Forgotten City, 1936; Saga at Forty, 1937; But Never Free, 1937; Bitter Winds of Love, 1938; Broken Barriers, 1938; The Gods Forget, 1939; Stolen Halo, 1940; Now Rough—Now Smooth, 1941; Open Wings, 1942; The Leaping Flame, 1942; A Heart is Broken, 1944; The Dark Stream, 1944; Sleeping Swords, 1944; Escape From Passion, 1945; Towards the Stars, 1945; Armour Against Love, 1945; Out of Reach, 1945; The Hidden Heart, 1946; Against the Stream, 1946; Again This Rapture, 1947; The Dream Within, 1947; Where is Love?, 1947; No Heart is Free, 1948; A Hazard of Hearts, 1949; A Duel of Hearts, 1949; The Enchanted Moment, 1949; The Knave of Hearts, 1950; The Little Pretender, 1950; A Ghost in Monte Carlo, 1951; Love is an Eagle, 1951; Love is Mine, 1952; The Passionate Pilgrim, 1952; Love is the Enemy, 1952; Cupid Rides Pillion, 1952; Blue Heather, 1953; Love me Forever, 1953; Elizabethan Lover, 1953; Wings on My Heart, 1954; Desire of The Heart, 1954; The Enchanted Waltz, 1955; The Kiss of the Devil, 1955; The Kiss of Paris, 1956; The Captive Heart, 1956; The Coin of Love, 1956; Love Forbidden, 1957; The Thief of Love, 1957; Stars in my Heart, 1957; Sweet Adventure, 1957; Lights of Love, 1958; The Sweet Enchantress, 1958; The Golden Gondola, 1958; The Kiss of Silk, 1959; Love in Hiding, 1959; The Smuggled Heart, 1959; The Price is Love, 1960; Love Under Fire, 1960; The Runaway Heart, 1961; The Messenger of Love, 1961; A Light to the Heart, 1962; The Wings of Love, 1962; Love is Dangerous, 1963; The Hidden Evil, 1963; Danger by the Nile, 1964; The Fire of Love, 1964; The Unpredictable Bride, 1964; The Magnificent Marriage, 1964; Love on the Run, 1965; Love Holds the Cards, 1965; Theft of a Heart, 1966; A Virgin in Paris, 1966; Love to the Rescue, 1967; Love is Contraband, 1968; The Enchanting Evil, 1968; The Unknown Heart, 1969; The Secret Fear, 1970; The Reluctant Bride, 1970; The Black Panther, 1970; The Pretty Horse-

Breakers, 1971; The Audacious Adventuress, 1972; Halo for the Devil, 1972; The Irresistable Buck, 1972; Lost Enchantment, 1972; The Complacent Wife, 1972; The Odious Duke, 1973; The Wicked Marquis, 1973; The Daring Deception, 1973; The Little Adventure, 1974; No Darkness for Love, 1974; Lessons in Love, 1974; The Ruthless Rake, 1974; Journey to Paradise, 1974; The Karma of Love, 1974; The Dangerous Dandy, 1974; The Bored Bridegroom, 1974; The Penniless Peer, 1974; The Cruel Count, 1974; The Castle of Fear, 1974; Love is Innocent, 1975; The Mask of Love, 1975; A Sword to the Heart, 1975; Bewitched, 1975; The Impetuous Duchess, 1975; The Shadow of Sin, 1975; The Tears of Love, 1975; The Devil in Love, 1975; The Frightened Bride, 1975; The Flame is Love, 1975; A Very Naughty Angel, 1975; Call of the Heart, 1975; As Eagles Fly, 1975; Say Yes, Samantha, 1975; An Arrow of Love, 1975; A Gamble with Hearts, 1975; A Kiss for the King, 1975; A Frame of Dreams, 1975; The Glittering Lights, 1975; Fire on the Snow, 1975; Fragrant Flowers, 1976; The Elusive Earl, 1976; Moon Over Eden, 1976; The Golden Illusion, 1976; No Time for Love, 1976; The Husband Hunters, 1976; The Slaves of Love, 1976; Passions in the Sands, 1976; An Angel in Hell, 1976; The Wild Cry of Love, 1976; The Blue-Eyed Witch, 1976; The Incredible Honeymoon, 1976; A Dream from the Night, 1976; Never Laugh at Love, 1976; The Secret of the Glen, 1976; The Dream and the Glory, 1976; The Proud Princess, 1976; Hungry for Love, 1976; The Heart Triumphant, 1976; The Disgraceful Duke, 1976; Conquered by Love, 1977; The Taming of Lady Lorinda, 1977; Vote for Love, 1977; The Mysterious Maidservant, 1977; The Magic of Love, 1977; Kiss the Moonlight, 1977; Love Locked In, 1977; The Marquis Who Hated Women, 1977; Rhapsody of Love, 1977; Look, Listen and Love, 1977; Duel with Destiny, 1977; The Wild Unwilling Wife, 1977; Punishment of a Vixen, 1977; The Curse of the Clan, 1977; The Outrageous Lady, 1977; The Love Pirate, 1977; The Dragon and the Pearl, 1977; The Naked Battle, 1977; The Hell-Cat and the King, 1977; No Escape from Love, 1977; A Sign of Love, 1977; A Touch of Love, 1978; The Temptation of Torilla, 1978; The Passion and the Flower, 1978; Love, Lords and Ladybirds, 1978; Love and the Loathsome Leopard, 1978; The Castle Made for Love, 1978; The Saint and the Sinner, 1978; A Fugitive from Love, 1978; Love Leaves at Midnight, 1978; The Problems of Love, 1978; The Twists and Turns of Love, 1978; Magic or Mirage, 1978; The Ghost Who Fell in Love, 1978; The Chieftain Without a Heart, 1978; Lord Ravenscar's Revenge, 1978; A Runaway Star, 1978; A Princess in Distress, 1978; The Irresistible Force, 1978; Lovers in Paradise, 1978; The Serpent of Satan, 1978; Love in the Clouds, 1978; The Treasure is Love, 1978; Imperial Splendour, 1978; Light of the Moon, 1978; The Prisoner of Love, 1978; Love in the Dark, 1978; The Duchess Disappeared, 1978; Love Climbs In, 1978; A Nightingale Sang, 1978; Terror in the Sun, 1978; Who Can Deny Love?, 1978; Bride to the King, 1978; The Judgement of Love, 1979; The Race for Love, 1979; Flowers for the God of Love, 1979; The Duke and the Preacher's Daughter, 1979; The Drums of Love, 1979; Alone in Paris, 1979; The Prince and the Pekinese, 1979; Only Love, 1979; The Dawn of Love, 1979; Love Has His Way, 1979; The Explosion of Love, 1979; Women Have Hearts, 1979; A Gentleman in Love, 1979; A Heart is Stolen, 1979; The Power and the Prince, 1979; Free From Fear, 1979; A Song of Love, 1979; Love for Sale, 1979; Little White Doves of Love, 1979; The Perfection of Love, 1979; Lost Laughter, 1979; Punished with Love, 1979; Lucifer and the Angel, 1979; Ola and the Sea Wolf, 1979; The Prude and the Prodigal, 1979; The Goddess and the Gaiety Girl, 1979; Signpost to Love, 1979; Money, Magic and Marriage, 1979; From Hell to Heaven, 1980; Pride and The Poor Princess, 1980; The Lioness and The Lily, 1980; A Kiss of Life, 1980; Love At The Helm, 1980; The Waltz of Hearts, 1980; Afraid, 1980; The Horizons of Love, 1980; Love in the Moon, 1980; Dollars for the Duke, 1981; Dreams Do Come True, 1981; Night of Gaiety, 1981; Count the Stars, 1981; Winged Magic, 1981; A Portrait of Love, 1981; River of Love, 1981; Gift of the Gods, 1981; The Heart of the Clan, 1981; An Innocent in Russia, 1981; A Shaft of Sunlight, 1981; Love Wins, 1981; Enchanted, 1981; Wings of Ecstasy, 1981; Pure and Untouched, 1981; In the Arms of Love, 1981; Touch a Star, 1981; For All Eternity, 1981; Secret Harbour, 1981; Looking for Love, 1981; The Vibration of Love, 1981; Lies for Love, 1981; Love Rules, 1981; Moments of Love, 1981; Lucky in Love, 1981; Poor Governess, 1981; Music from the Heart, 1981; Caught by Love, 1981; A King in Love, 1981; Winged Victory, 1981; The Call of the Highlands, 1981; Love and the Marquis, 1981; Kneel for Mercy, 1981; Riding to the Moon, 1981; Wish for Love, 1981; Mission to Monte Carlo, 1981; A Miracle in Music, 1981; A Marriage Made in Heaven, 1981; From Hate to Love, 1982; Light of the Gods, 1982; Love on the Wind, 1982; The Duke Comes Home, 1982; Journey to a Star, 1983; Love and Lucia, 1983; The Unwanted Wedding, 1983; Gypsy Magic, 1983; Help from the Heart, 1983; A Duke in Danger, 1983; Tempted to Love, 1983; Lights, Laughter and a Lady, 1983; The Unbreakable Spell, 1983; Diona and a Dalmatian, 1983; Fire in the Blood, 1983; The Scots Never Forget, 1983; A Rebel Princess, 1983; A Witch's Spell, 1983; Secrets, 1983; The Storms of Love, 1983; Moonlight on the Sphinx, 1983; White Lilac, 1983; Revenge of the Heart, 1983; Bride to a Brigand, 1983; Love Comes West, 1983; Theresa and a Tiger, 1983; An Island of Love, 1983; Love is Heaven, 1983; Miracle for a Madonna, 1984; A Very Unusual Wife, 1984; The Peril and the Prince, 1984; Alone and Afraid, 1984; Temptation for a Teacher, 1984; Royal Punishment, 1984; The Devilish Deception, 1984; Paradise Found, 1984; Love is a Gamble, 1984; A Victory for Love, 1984; Look with Love, 1984; Never Forget Love, 1984; Helga in Hiding, 1984; Safe at Last, 1984; Haunted, 1984; Crowned with Love, 1984; Escape, 1984; The Devil Defeated, 1985; The Secret of the Mosque, 1985; A Dream in Spain, 1985; The Love Trap, 1985; Listen to Love, 1985; The Golden Cage, 1985; Love Casts Out Fear, 1985; A World of Love, 1985; Dancing on a Rainbow, 1985; Love Joins the Clans, 1985; An Angel Runs Away, 1985; Forced into Marriage, 1985; Bewildered in Berlin, 1985; Wanted—a Wedding Ring, 1985; Starlight Over Tunis, 1985; The Earl Escapes, 1985; The Love Puzzle, 1985; Love and Kisses, 1985; Sapphires in Siam, 1985; A Caretaker of Love, 1985; Secrets of the Heart, 1985; Riding to the Sky, 1986; Lovers in Lisbon, 1986; Love is Invincible, 1986; The Goddess of Love, 1986; An Adventure of Love, 1986; A Herb for Happiness, 1986; Only a Dream, 1986; Saved by Love, 1986; Little Tongues of Fire, 1986; A Chieftain Finds Love, 1986; The Lovely Liar, 1986; The Perfume of the Gods, 1986; A Knight in Paris, 1987; Revenge is Sweet, 1987; The Passionate Princess, 1987; Solita and the Spies, 1987; The Perfect Pearl, 1987; Love is a Maze, 1987; A Circus for Love, 1987; The Temple of Love, 1987; The Bargain Bride, 1987; The Haunted Heart, 1987; Real Love or Fake, 1987; A Kiss from a Stranger, 1987; A Very Special Love, 1987; A Necklace of Love, 1987; No Disguise for Love, 1987; A Revolution of Love, 1988; The Marquis Wins, 1988; Love is the Key, 1988; Free as the Wind, 1988; Desire in the Desert, 1988; A Heart in the Highlands, 1988; The Music of Love, 1988; The Wrong Duchess, 1988; The Taming of a Tigress, 1988; Love Comes to the Castle, 1988; The Magic of Paris, 1988; Stand and Deliver Your Heart, 1988; The Scent of Roses, 1988; Love at First Sight, 1988; The Secret Princess, 1988; Heaven in Hong Kong, 1988; Paradise in Penang, 1988; A Game of Love, 1988; The Sleeping Princess, 1988; A Wish Comes True, 1988; Loved for Himself, 1988; Two Hearts in Hungary, 1988; A Theatre of Love, 1988; A Dynasty of Love, 1988; Magic from the Heart, 1988; Windmill of Love, 1988; Love Strikes Satan, 1988; The Earl Rings a Belle, 1988; The Queen Saves the King, 1988; Love Lifts the Curse, 1988; Beauty or Brains, 1988; Too Precious to Lose, 1988; Hiding, 1988; A Tangled Web, 1988; Just Fate, 1988; A Miracle in Mexico, 1988; Warned by a Ghost, 1988; Terror from the Throne, 1988; The Cave of Love, 1988; The Peaks of Ecstasy, 1988; A Kiss in Rome, 1988; Hidden by Love, 1988; Walking to Wonderland, 1988; Lucky Logan Finds Love, 1988; Born of Love, 1988; The Angel and the Rake, 1988; The Queen of Hearts, 1988; The Wicked Widow, 1988; To Scotland and Love, 1988; Love and War, 1988; Love at the Ritz, 1989; The Dangerous Marriage, 1989; Good or Bad, 1989; This is Love, 1989; Seek the Stars, 1989; Escape to Love, 1989; Look with the Heart, 1989; Safe in Paradise, 1989; Love in the Ruins, 1989; A Coronation of Love, 1989; A Duel of Jewels, 1989; The Duke is Trapped, 1989; Just a Wonderful Dream, 1989; Love and a Cheetah, 1989; Drena and the Duke, 1989; A Dog, a Horse and a Heart, 1989; Never Lose Love, 1989; The Eyes of Love, 1989; The Duke's Dilemma, 1989; Saved by a Saint, 1989; Beyond the Stars, 1990; The Spirit of Love, 1991; The Innocent Imposter, 1991; The Incomparable, 1991; The Dare-Devil Duke, 1991; A Royal Rebuke, 1991; Love Runs in, 1991; Love Light of Apollo, 1991; Love, Lies and Marriage, 1991; In Love in Lucca, 1991; Fascination in France, 1992; Something to Love, 1992; Three Days to Love, 1992; A Magical Moment, 1992; A Secret Passage to Love, 1992; An Icicle in India, 1992; Running from Russia, 1992; The Loveless Marriage, 1992; The Protection of Love, 1992; The Patient Bridegroom, 1992; A Train to Love, 1992; The Unbroken Dream, 1992; A Challenge of Hearts, 1993; The Man of her Dreams, 1993; The White Witch, 1993; Saved by the Duke, 1993; Captured by Love, 1993; Danger to the Duke, 1993; The King without a Heart, 1993; A Battle of Love, 1993; Lovers in London, 1993; Love or Money, 1993; Love Wins in Berlin, 1993; Learning to Love, 1993; One Minute to Love, 1993; Saved by an Angel, 1993; The Marquis is Deceived, 1993; A Princess Runs Away, 1993; A Change of Hearts, 1993; Love by the Lake, 1993; A Heart of Stone, 1993; Journey to Love, 1993; Love finds a Treasure, 1993; The Mountain of Love, 1993; Follow your Heart, 1993; A Kiss in the Desert, 1993; Love for Eternity, 1993; The Duke Disappears, 1993; The Earl Elopes, 1993; The King Wins, 1993; A Beauty Betrayed, 1993; Rivals for Love, 1993; The Earl's Revenge, 1993; A Golden Lie, 1993; Love and Apollo, 1993; A Princess Prays, 1993; The Battle of Brains, 1993; Ruled by Love, 1993; Wanted a Royal Wife, 1993; A Kiss of Love, 1993; Money or Love, 1993; The Marquis is Trapped, 1993; Pray for Love, 1993; Hide and Seek for Love, 1993; A Teacher of Love, 1993; The Gates of Paradise, 1993; The Tree of Love, 1993; Search for Love, 1993; Love is Magic, 1993; The Prince is Saved, 1993; Secret Love, 1993; Search for Love, 1994; Love is Magic, 1994; The Prince is Saved, 1994; Secret Love, 1994; Love in Egypt, 1994; The Kingdom of Love, 1994; The Healing Hand, 1994; A Miracle for Love, 1994; A Virgin Bride, 1994; A Royal Love Match, 1994; A Steeplechase for Love, 1994; Search for a Wife, 1994; A Shooting Star, 1994; The Duke is Deceived, 1994; The Queen Wins, 1994; Love and the Clans, 1994; The Winning Post is Love, 1994; Love and the Gods, 1994; Love Conquers War, 1994; A Sacrifice for Love, 1994; A Call of Love, 1994; A Heart Finds Love, 1994; She Wanted Love, 1994; A Prayer for Love, 1994; Wish Upon a Star, 1994; A Road to Romance, 1994; Soft, Sweet and Gentle, 1994; The Viscount's Revenge, 1994; An Archangel Called Ivan, 1994; Wanted a Bride, 1994; A Prisoner in Paris, 1994; Rescued by Love, 1994; Danger in the Desert, 1994; The Bride Runs Away, 1994; The Duke is Captured, 1994; Crowned by Music, 1995; Love Solves the Problem, 1995; *philosophy:* Touch the Stars; *sociology:* You in the Home; The Fascinating Forties; Marriage for Moderns; Be Vivid, Be Vital; Love, Life and Sex; Look Lovely, Be Lovely; Vitamins for Vitality; Husbands and Wives; Etiquette; The Many Facets of Love; Sex and the Teenager; Charm; Living Together; Woman the Enigma; The Youth Secret; The Magic of Honey; Health Food Cookery Book; Book of Beauty and Health; Men are Wonderful; The Magic of Honey Cookbook; Food for Love; Recipes for Lovers; The Romance of Food; Getting Older, Growing Younger; (jtly) Keep Young and Beautiful; The Etiquette of Romance, 1985; *biography:* Ronald Cartland, 1942; Bewitching Women; The Outrageous Queen; Polly, My Wonderful Mother, 1956; The Scandalous Life of King Carol; The Private Life of Charles II; The Private Life of Elizabeth, Empress of Austria; Josephine, Empress of France; Diane de Poitiers; Metternich, the Passionate Diplomat; *historical:* A Year of Royal Days, 1988; Royal Jewels, 1989; Royal Lovers, 1989; Royal Eccentrics, 1989; *autobiography:* The Isthmus Years, 1943; The Years of Opportunity, 1947; I Search for Rainbows, 1967; We Danced All Night, 1919–1929, 1971; I Seek the Miraculous, 1978; I Reach for the Stars, 1994; *general:* Useless Information (foreword by Earl Mountbatten of Burma); Light of Love (prayers), 1978; Love and Lovers (pictures), 1978; Barbara Cartland's Book of Celebrities, 1982; Barbara Cartland's Scrapbook, 1980; Romantic Royal Marriages, 1981; (ed) Written with Love, 1981; (ed) The Library of Love; (ed) The Library of Ancient Wisdom; How to Write like Barbara Cartland, vols 1 and 2, 1994; *for children:* Princess to the Rescue; *verse:* Lines on Love and Life; *plays:* Blood Money, 1925; French Dressing (with Bruce Woodhouse), 1943; *revue:* The Mayfair Revue; *radio play:* The Caged Bird; *television:* Portrait of Successful Woman, 1957; This is Your Life, 1958 and 1989; Success Story, 1959; Midland Profile, 1961; No Looking Back-a Portrait of Barbara Cartland, 1967; The Frost Programme, 1968; The Time of Your Life (programme about the first glider air mail, 1931), BBC1, 1985; *radio:* The World of Barbara Cartland, 1970, and many other radio and television appearances. Editor of the Common Problem, by Ronald Cartland, 1943. *Address:* Camfield Place, Hatfield, Herts AL9 6JE. *T:* Potters Bar (01707) 642612, 642657.

See also Comtesse de Chambrun.

CARTLAND, Sir George (Barrington), Kt 1963; CMG 1956; BA; Vice-Chancellor of the University of Tasmania, 1968–77; Chairman, Australian National Accreditation Authority for Translators and Interpreters, 1977–83; *b* 22 Sept. 1912; *s* of William Arthur and Margaret Cartland, West Didsbury; *m* 1937, Dorothy Rayton (*d* 1993); two *s*. *Educ:* Manchester Central High Sch.; Manchester Univ.; Hertford Coll., Oxford. Entered Colonial Service, Gold Coast, 1935; served Colonial Office, 1944–49; Head of African Studies Br. and Ed. Jl of Afr. Adminis., 1945–49; Sec. London Afr. Conf., 1948; Admin. Sec., Uganda, 1949; Sec. for Social Services and Local Govt, Uganda, 1952; Min. for Social Services, Uganda, 1955; Min. of Education and Labour, Uganda, 1958; Chief Sec., Uganda, 1960; Deputy Gov. of Uganda, 1961–62 (Acting Gov., various occasions, 1952–62); Registrar of Univ. of Birmingham, 1963–67. Part-time Mem., West Midlands Gas Bd, 1964–67. Member: Exec. Cttee, Inter Univ. Council for Higher Educn Overseas (UK), 1963–67; Commonwealth Scholarship Commn (UK), 1964–67. Dep. Chm., Australian Vice-Chancellors' Cttee, 1975 and 1977. Chairman: Adv. Cttee on National Park in SW Tasmania, 1976–78; Tasmanian Council of Australian Trade Union Trng Authority, 1979. Appointed to review: Library and Archives Legislation of Tasmania, 1978; Tasmanian Govt Admin, 1979. Mem., Australian Nat. Cttee of Hoover Awards for Marketing, 1968–82. Chm., St John Council, Uganda, 1958–59; Pres., St John Council, Tasmania, 1969–78. Member Council: Makerere Coll., 1952–60; Royal Tech. Coll., Nairobi, 1952–60; UC of Rhodesia, 1963–67; Univ. of S Pacific, 1972–76. FACE 1970. Hon. LLD Univ. of Tasmania, 1978. KStJ 1972; awarded Belgian Congo medal, 1960. *Publication:* (jtly) The Irish Cartlands and Cartland Genealogy, 1978. *Recreation:* fly fishing. *Address:* 5 Aotea Road, Sandy Bay, Hobart, Tasmania 7005. *Clubs:* Athenæum; Tasmanian, Royal Tasmanian Yacht (Hobart).

CARTLEDGE, Sir Bryan (George), KCMG 1985 (CMG 1980); Principal of Linacre College, Oxford, 1988–Sept. 1996; *b* 10 June 1931; *s* of Eric Montague George Cartledge and Phyllis (*née* Shaw); *m* 1st, 1960, Ruth Hylton Gass (marr. diss. 1994), *d* of John Gass;

one *s* one *d*; 2nd, 1994, Dr Freda Gladys Newcombe. *Educ:* Hurstpierpoint; St John's Coll., Cambridge (Hon. Fellow, 1985). Queen's Royal Regt, 1950–51. Commonwealth Fund Fellow, Stanford Univ., 1956–57; Research Fellow, St Antony's Coll., Oxford, 1958–59 (Hon. Fellow, 1987). Entered HM Foreign (subseq. Diplomatic) Service, 1960; served in FO, 1960–61; Stockholm, 1961–63; Moscow, 1963–66; DSAO, 1966–68; Tehran, 1968–70; Harvard Univ., 1971–72; Counsellor, Moscow, 1972–75; Head of E European and Soviet Dept, FCO, 1975–77; Private Sec. (Overseas Affairs) to Prime Minister, 1977–79; Ambassador to Hungary, 1980–83; Asst Under-Sec. of State, FCO, 1983–84; Dep. Sec. of the Cabinet, 1984–85; Ambassador to the Soviet Union, 1985–88. *Publications:* (ed) Monitoring the Environment, 1992; (ed) Energy and the Environment, 1993; (ed) Health and the Environment, 1994; (ed) Population and the Environment, 1995; (ed) Transport and the Environment, 1996. *Address:* (until Sept. 1996) Linacre College, Oxford OX1 3JA; (from Sept. 1996) Jasmine House, Holton, Oxon OX33 1PU. *Club:* Reform.

CARTTISS, Michael Reginald Harry; MP (C) Great Yarmouth, since 1983; *b* Norwich, 11 March 1938; *s* of Reginald Carttiss and Doris Culling. *Educ:* Filby County Primary Sch.; Great Yarmouth Tech. High Sch.; Goldsmiths' Coll., London Univ. (DipEd); LSE (part time, 1961–64). Nat. Service, RAF, 1956–58. Teacher: Orpington, Kent, and Waltham Cross, Herts, 1961–64; Oriel Grammar Sch., 1964–69; Cons. Party Agent, Gt Yarmouth, 1969–82. Member: Norfolk CC, 1966–85 (Vice-Chm., 1972, Chm., 1980–85, Educn Cttee); Gt Yarmouth BC, 1973–82 (Leader, 1980–82). Chm., Norfolk Museums Service, 1981–85; Mem., E Anglian RHA, 1981–85; Comr, Gt Yarmouth Port and Haven Commn, 1982–86. *Recreations:* reading, writing, talking, walking, theatre. *Address:* c/o House of Commons, SW1A 0AA; Main Road, Filby, Great Yarmouth, Norfolk NR29 3HN; (office) 13/14 South Quay, Great Yarmouth, Norfolk NR30 2QX.

CARTWRIGHT, David Edgar, DSc; FRS 1984; Assistant Director, Institute of Oceanographic Sciences, Bidston Observatory, Birkenhead, 1973–86, retired; *b* 21 Oct. 1926; *s* of Edgar A. Cartwright and Lucienne Cartwright (*née* Tartanson); *m* 1952, Anne-Marie Guerin; two *s* two *d*. *Educ:* St John's Coll., Cambridge (BA); King's Coll., London (BSc, DSc). Dept of Naval Construction, Admiralty, Bath, 1951–54; Nat. Inst. of Oceanography (later Inst. of Oceanographic Sciences), Wormley, Surrey: Sci. Officer, rising to Individual Merit SPSO, 1954–73; Research Associate, Univ. of California, La Jolla, 1964–65; Sen. Res. Associate, NASA–Goddard Space Flight Center, Greenbelt, Md, 1987–89; Consultant, NASA, 1990–92. Mem., Royal Astronomical Soc., 1976–; Fellow, Amer. Geophysical Union, 1991–. Dr (*hc*) Toulouse, 1992. *Publications:* over 80 papers on marine sci. research; reviews, etc, in various learned jls. *Recreations:* music, walking, travel. *Address:* 3 Borough House, Borough Road, Petersfield, Hants GU32 3LF. *T:* Petersfield (01730) 267195.

CARTWRIGHT, Rt. Rev. (Edward) David; *b* 15 July 1920; *o c* of John Edward Cartwright, master butcher and grazier, and Gertrude Cartwright (*née* Lusby), North Somercotes and Grimsby, Lincs; *m* 1946, Elsie Irene, *o c* of Walter and Jane Elizabeth Rogers, Grimsby; one *s* two *d*. *Educ:* Grimsby Parish Church Choir Sch.; Lincoln Sch.; Selwyn Coll. and Westcott House, Cambridge. 2nd Cl. Hons Hist. Tripos Pt 1, 1940; 2nd Cl.Hons Theol Tripos Pt 1, 1942; Steel Univ. Student in Divinity, 1941; BA 1941, MA 1945; Pres., SCM in Cambridge, 1941–42. Deacon, 1943; Priest, 1944; Curate of Boston, 1943–48; Vicar: St Leonard's, Redfield, Bristol, 1948–52; Olveston with Aust, 1952–60; Bishopston, 1960–73; Secretary, Bristol Diocesan Synod, 1967–73; Hon. Canon of Bristol Cathedral, 1970–73; Archdeacon of Winchester and Vicar of Sparsholt with Lainston, 1973–84; Hon. Canon of Winchester Cathedral, 1973–88; Bishop Suffragan of Southampton, 1984–88. Dir of Studies, Bristol Lay Readers, 1956–72; Proctor in Convocation, Mem. of Church Assembly and General Synod, 1956–73, 1975–83. Member: Central Bd of Finance of C of E, 1970–73; C of E Pensions Bd, 1980–84. Church Commissioner, 1973–83 (Mem. Board of Governors, 1978–83); Member: Dilapidations Legislation Commn, 1958–64; Working Party on Housing of Retired Clergy, 1972–73; Differential Payment of Clergy, 1976–77. Secretary, Bristol Council of Christian Churches, 1950–61; Chm., Winchester Christian Council, 1976–77; Pres., Southampton Council of Churches, 1984–88. Chm., Christian Aid Cttee: Bristol, 1956–73; Winchester, 1974–81. Anglican-Presbyterian Conversations, 1962–66; Convocations Jt Cttees on Anglican-Methodist Union Scheme, 1965. *Recreations:* book-hunting and rose-growing. *Address:* Bargate House, 25 Newport, Warminster, Wilts BA12 8RH. *T:* Warminster (01985) 216298.

CARTWRIGHT, Frederick; *see* Cartwright, W. F.

CARTWRIGHT, Harry, CBE 1979 (MBE 1946); MA, CEng, MIMechE, MIEE; Director, Atomic Energy Establishment, Winfrith, 1973–83; *b* 16 Sept. 1919; *s* of Edwin Harry Cartwright and Agnes Alice Cartwright (*née* Gillibrand); *m* 1950, Catharine Margaret Carson Bradbury; two *s*. *Educ:* William Hulme's Grammar Sch., Manchester; St John's Coll., Cambridge (Schol.). 1st cl. Mechanical Sciences Tripos, 1940. Served War, RAF, 1940–46: Flt Lt, service on ground radar in Europe, India and Burma. Decca Navigator Co., 1946–47; English Electric Co., 1947–49; joined Dept of Atomic Energy, Risley, as a Design and Project Engr, 1949; Chief Engr, 1955; Dir in charge of UKAEA consultancy services on nuclear reactors, 1960–64; Dir, Water Reactors, 1964–70, and as such responsible for design and construction of Winfrith 100 MW(e) SGHWR prototype power station; Dir, Fast Reactor Systems, 1970–73. Pres., British Nuclear Energy Soc., 1979–82; Pres., European Nuclear Soc., 1983–85 (Vice-Pres., 1980–83). Chm. of Trustees, Corfe Castle Charities, 1991–. Chm. of Govs, Purbeck Sch., 1985–88. *Publications:* various techn. papers. *Recreations:* walking, gardening, golf. *Address:* Tabbit's Hill House, Corfe Castle, Wareham, Dorset BH20 5HZ. *T:* Corfe Castle (01929) 480582. *Club:* United Oxford & Cambridge University.

CARTWRIGHT, John Cameron; JP; Deputy Chairman, Police Complaints Authority, since 1993 (Member, since 1992); *b* 29 Nov. 1933; *s* of Aubrey John Randolph Cartwright and Ivy Adeline Billie Cartwright; *m* 1959, Iris June Tant; one *s* one *d*. *Educ:* Woking County Grammar School. Exec. Officer, Home Civil Service, 1952–55; Labour Party Agent, 1955–67; Political Sec., RACS Ltd, 1967–72; Director, RACS Ltd, 1972–74. Leader, Greenwich Borough Council, 1971–74. Mem., Labour Party Nat. Exec. Cttee, 1971–75 and 1976–78. MP Greenwich, Woolwich East, Oct. 1974–1983, Woolwich, 1983–92 (Lab, 1974–81; SDP, 1981–90; Soc. Dem., 1990–92); contested (Soc. Dem.) Woolwich, 1992. PPS to Sec. of State for Education and Science, 1976–77; Chm., Parly Labour Party Defence Group, 1979–81; Mem., Select Cttee on Defence, 1979–82 and 1986–92; SDP party spokesman on environment, 1981–87, on defence and foreign affairs, 1983–87; SDP/Liberal Alliance spokesman on defence, 1987; SDP Parly Whip, 1983–92; Vice Pres., SDP, 1987–88, Pres., 1988–91. Jt Chm., Council for Advancement of Arab British Understanding, 1983–87; Vice-Chm., GB-USSR Assoc., 1983–91. Mem., Calcutt Cttee on Privacy and Related Matters, 1989–90. Vice-Pres., Assoc. of Metropolitan Authorities, 1974–. Trustee, Nat. Maritime Museum, 1976–83. JP Inner London, 1970. *Publication:* (jtly) Cruise, Pershing and SS20, 1985. *Recreations:* do-it-yourself, listening to jazz, supporting Lincoln City FC. *Address:* 17 Commonwealth Way, SE2 0JZ. *T:* 0181–311 4394.

CARTWRIGHT, Dame Mary Lucy, DBE 1969; FRS 1947; ScD Cambridge 1949; MA Oxford and Cambridge; DPhil Oxford; Hon. LLD (Edin.) 1953; Hon. DSc: Leeds, 1958; Hull, 1959; Wales, 1962; Oxford, 1966; Brown (Providence, RI), 1969; Fellow of Girton College, Cambridge, 1930–49, and since 1968; *b* 1900; *d* of late W. D. Cartwright, Rector of Aynhoe. *Educ:* Godolphin Sch., Salisbury, and St Hugh's Coll., Oxford. Asst Mistress, Alice Ottley Sch., Worcester, 1923–24, Wycombe Abbey Sch., Bucks, 1924–27; read for DPhil, 1928–30; Yarrow Research Fellow of Girton Coll., 1930–34; Univ. Lectr in Mathematics, Cambridge, 1935–59; Mistress of Girton Coll., Cambridge, 1949–68; Reader in the Theory of Functions, Univ. of Cambridge, 1959–68, Emeritus Reader, 1968–; Visiting Professor: Brown Univ., Providence, RI, 1968–69; Claremont Graduate Sch., California, 1969–70; Case Western Reserve, 1970; Polish Acad. of Sciences, 1970; Univ. of Wales, 1971; Case Western Reserve, 1971. Consultant on US Navy Mathematical Research Projects at Stanford and Princeton Universities, Jan.-May 1949. Comdt, British Red Cross Detachment, Cambs 112, 1940–44. Fellow of Cambridge Philosophical Soc.; President: London Math. Soc., 1961–63; Mathematical Assoc., 1951–52 (now Hon. Mem.). Hon. FIMA, 1972; Hon. FRSE. Sylvester Medal, Royal Soc., 1964; De Morgan Medal, London Mathematical Soc., 1968; Medal of Univ. of Jyväskylä, Finland, 1973. Commander, Order of the Dannebrog, 1961. *Publications:* Integral Functions (Cambridge Tracts in Mathematics and Mathematical Physics), 1956; math. papers in various journals. *Address:* Midfield Nursing Home, Cambridge Road, Oakington, Cambridge CB4 5BG.
See also W. F. Cartwright.

CARTWRIGHT, Rt. Rev. Richard Fox; Assistant Bishop, Diocese of Exeter, since 1988; *b* 10 Nov. 1913; *s* of late Rev. George Frederick Cartwright, Vicar of Plumstead, and Constance Margaret Cartwright (*née* Clark); *m* 1947, Rosemary Magdalen, *d* of Francis Evelyn Bray, Woodham Grange, Surrey; one *s* three *d*. *Educ:* The King's School, Canterbury; Pembroke Coll., Cambridge (BA 1935, MA 1939); Cuddesdon Theological Coll. Deacon, 1936; Priest, 1937; Curate, St Anselm, Kennington Cross, 1936–40; Priest-in-Charge, Lower Kingswood, 1940–45; Vicar, St Andrew, Surbiton, 1945–52; Proctor in Convocation, 1950–52; Vicar of St Mary Redcliffe, Bristol (with Temple from 1956 and St John Bedminster from 1965), 1952–72; Hon. Canon of Bristol, 1960–72; Suffragan Bishop of Plymouth, 1972–81; Asst Bishop, dio. of Truro, 1982–91. Sub-Chaplain, Order of St John, 1957–; Director: Ecclesiastical Insurance Office Ltd, 1964–85; Allchurches Trust Ltd, 1985–91. Chm. Governors, Kelly Coll., 1973–88. Hon. DD Univ. of the South, Tennessee, 1969. *Recreations:* fly-fishing, gardening, water-colour painting. *Address:* 5 Old Vicarage Close, Ide, near Exeter, Devon EX2 9RT. *T:* Exeter (01392) 211270. *Club:* Army and Navy.

CARTWRIGHT, Dame Silvia (Rose), DBE 1989; **Hon. Justice Dame Silvia Cartwright;** Judge of the High Court of New Zealand, since 1993; *b* 7 Nov. 1943; *d* of Monteith Poulter and Eileen Jane Poulter, both of Dunedin, NZ; *m* 1969, Peter John Cartwright. *Educ:* Univ. of Otago, NZ (LLB). Partner, Harkness Henry & Co., Barristers and Solicitors, Hamilton, NZ, 1971–81; Dist Court and Family Court Judge, 1981–89; Chief Dist Court Judge, 1989–93. Mem., Commn for the Future, 1975–80; conducted Inquiry into: Soc. Sci. Funding in NZ, 1986–87; Treatment of Cervical Cancer at Nat. Women's Hosp., Auckland, NZ, 1987–88. Mem. Cttee, UN Human Rights Convention to eliminate discrimination against women, 1992–96. F. W. Guest Meml Lectr, Univ. of Otago, 1993. Hon. LLD: Otago, 1993; Waikato, 1994. *Publications:* UNESCO Monograph, 1985; Report of the Cervical Cancer Inquiry, 1988; contrib. Jl of Assoc. of Family and Conciliation Courts (US). *Recreations:* reading, gardening, boating. *Address:* Judge's Chambers, Box 60, Auckland, New Zealand. *T:* (9) 3797577, *Fax:* (9) 3734223.

CARTWRIGHT, Sonia Rosemary Susan, (Mrs C. Cartwright); *see* Proudman, S. R. S.

CARTWRIGHT, (William) Frederick, CBE 1977; DL; MIMechE; Director, BSC (International) Ltd; a Deputy Chairman, British Steel Corporation, 1970–72; Group Managing Director, S Wales Group, British Steel Corporation, 1967–70; Chairman, The Steel Co. of Wales Ltd, 1967 (Managing Director, 1962–67); *b* 13 Nov. 1906; *s* of William Digby Cartwright, Rector of Aynhoe; *m* 1937, Sally Chrystobel Ware; two *s* one *d*. *Educ:* Rugby Sch. Joined Guest, Keen and Nettlefold, Dowlais, 1929; gained experience at steelworks in Germany, Luxembourg and France, 1930; Asst Works Manager, 1931, Tech. Asst to Managing Director, 1935, Dir and Chief Engineer, 1940, Dir and General Manager, 1943, Guest, Keen and Baldwin, Port Talbot Works; Dir and General Manager, Steel Co. of Wales, 1947; Asst Man. Dir and General Manager of the Steel Div., The Steel Co. of Wales Ltd, 1954. Pres., Iron and Steel Inst., 1960. Dir, Lloyds Bank, 1968–77 (Chm., S Wales Regional Bd, 1968–77). Dir, Develt Corp for Wales. Freeman of Port Talbot, 1970. DL, County of Glamorgan; High Sheriff, Glamorgan, 1961. OStJ. Hon. LLD Wales, 1968. Bessemer Gold Medal, 1958; Frederico Giolitti Steel Medal, 1960. *Recreations:* riding and yachting. *Address:* Castle-upon-Alun, St Brides Major, near Bridgend, Mid Glam CF32 0TN. *T:* Southern-down (01656) 880298. *Clubs:* Royal Ocean Racing, Royal Cruising; Royal Yacht Squadron.
See also Dame Mary Cartwright.

CARTWRIGHT SHARP, Michael; *see* Sharp, J. M. C.

CARTY, Hilary; Director of Dance, Arts Council, since 1994; *b* 26 May 1962; *d* of Solomon Carty and Catherine (*née* Bailey). *Educ:* Poly. of Central London (MBA); Leicester Poly. (BA Hons Performing Arts); Cultural Trng Centre, Jamaica (Cert. in Dance Educn). Community Arts Officer, Leics Expressive Arts, 1985; Community Arts Develt Officer, The Cave, Birmingham, 1985; Arts Officer (Dance and Mime), E Midlands Arts, 1986–90; Gen. Manager, Adzido Pan African Dance Ensemble, 1990–94. *Publication:* Folk Dances of Jamaica, 1988. *Recreations:* squash, badminton, theatre, dance. *Address:* 296 Crystal Palace Road, Dulwich, SE22 9JJ. *T:* 0171–973 6489.

CARUS, Louis Revell, Hon. RAM, FRSAMD, FRCM, FBSM; Artistic Director, International String Quartet Week, since 1985; Principal, Birmingham School of Music, 1975–87; *b* Kasauli, India, 22 Oct. 1927; *s* of Lt-Col Martin and Enid Carus-Wilson; *m* 1951, Nancy Reade Noell; two *s* one *d*. *Educ:* Rugby Sch.; Brussels Conservatoire (Premier Prix); Peabody Conservatory, USA. LRAM. Scottish National Orchestra, 1950; solo violinist and chamber music specialist, 1951–; Head of Strings, Royal Scottish Academy of Music, 1956; Scottish Trio and Piano Quartet, New Music Group of Scotland, 1956–75; Northern Sinfonia, Monteverdi Orchestras, 1963–73; Orchestra Da Camera, 1975; Adjudicator, 1960–; Examr, Associated Bd of Royal Schs of Music, 1976–. Pres., ISM, 1986–87; FRSAMD 1976; Hon. RAM 1977; FRCM 1983; FBSM 1988. Fellow, Birmingham Polytechnic (now Univ. of Central England in Birmingham), 1988. *Publications:* various musical journalism, eg, daily press, Strad Magazine, ISM Jl, Gulbenkian Report. *Recreations:* painting, gardening, travel. *Address:* 15 Kings End Road, Powick, Worcester WR2 4RA. *T:* Worcester (01905) 831715. *Clubs:* Royal Society of Musicians, Incorporated Society of Musicians, European String Teachers Association; Rotary (Worcester).

CARUS, Roderick; QC 1990; a Recorder, since 1990; *b* 4 June 1944; *s* of Anthony and Kathleen Carus; *m* 1972, Hilary Mary (*née* Jones); two *s* two *d*. *Educ:* Wirral GS,

Merseyside; University Coll., Oxford (BA Law); Manchester Business Sch. (Postgrad. Diploma in Advanced Business Studies). Called to the Bar, Gray's Inn, 1971. Merchant bank, investments, 1966–70. Asst Recorder, 1987–90. *Recreations:* chess, crosswords, fishing, gardening. *Address:* Yealand House, Park Road, Hale, Cheshire WA15 9LQ. *Club:* Hale Conservative.

CARVER, family name of **Baron Carver.**

CARVER, Baron *cr* 1977 (Life Peer); **Field-Marshal (Richard) Michael (Power) Carver,** GCB 1970 (KCB 1966; CB 1957); CBE 1945; DSO 1943 and Bar 1943; MC 1941; designated British Resident Commissioner in Rhodesia, 1977–78; *b* 24 April 1915; 2nd *s* of late Harold Power Carver and late Winifred Anne Gabrielle Carver (*née* Wellesley); *m* 1947, Edith, *d* of Lt-Col Sir Henry Lowry-Corry, MC; two *s* two *d. Educ:* Winchester Coll.; Sandhurst. 2nd Lieut Royal Tank Corps, 1935; War of 1939–45 (despatches twice); GSO1, 7th Armoured Div., 1942; OC 1st Royal Tank Regt, 1943; Comdr 4th Armoured Brigade, 1944; Tech. Staff Officer (1), Min. of Supply, 1947; Joint Services Staff Coll., 1950; AQMG, Allied Land Forces, Central Europe, 1951; Col GS, SHAPE 1952; Dep. Chief of Staff, East Africa, 1954 (despatches); Chief of Staff, East Africa, 1955; idc 1957; Dir of Plans, War Office, 1958–59; Comdr 6th Infty Brigade, 1960–62; Maj.-Gen. 1962; GOC, 3 Div., 1962–64, also Comdr Joint Truce Force, Cyprus, and Dep. Comdr United Nations' Force in Cyprus, 1964; Dir, Army Staff Duties, Min. of Defence, 1964–66; Lt-Gen. 1966; comd FE Land Forces, 1966–67; Gen., 1967; C-in-C, Far East, 1967–69; GOC-in-C, Southern Command, 1969–71; Chief of the General Staff, 1971–73; Field-Marshal 1973; CDS, 1973–76. Col Commandant: REME 1966–76; Royal Tank Regt, 1968–72; RAC, 1974–77; ADC (Gen.) 1969–72. Hon. DLitt Southampton, 1991. *Publications:* Second to None (History of Royal Scots Greys, 1919–45), 1954; El Alamein, 1962; Tobruk, 1964; (ed) The War Lords, 1976; Harding of Petherton, 1978; The Apostles of Mobility, 1979; War Since 1945, 1980; A Policy for Peace, 1982; The Seven Ages of the British Army, 1984; Dilemmas of the Desert War, 1986; Twentieth Century Warriors, 1987; Out of Step: memoirs of Field-Marshal Lord Carver, 1989; Tightrope Walking: British defence policy since 1945, 1992. *Address:* Wood End House, Wickham, Fareham, Hants PO17 6JZ. *T:* Wickham (01329) 832143. *Club:* Anglo-Belgian.

CARVER, James, CB 1978; CEng, FIMinE; consulting mining engineer; *b* 29 Feb. 1916; *s* of late William and Ellen Carver; *m* 1944, Elsie Sharrock; one *s* two *d* (of whom one *s* one *d* are twins). *Educ:* Wigan Mining and Technical Coll. Certificated Mine Manager. Asst Mine Manager, Nos 5, 6 and 7 mines, Garswood Hall, Lancs, 1941–43; HM Jun. Inspector Mines and Quarries, W Midlands Coalfields, 1943; Dist Inspector, Mines and Quarries, N Staffordshire, 1951; Senior District Inspector: M&Q, London Headquarters, 1957; M&Q, Doncaster Dist (in charge), 1962; Principal Inspector, M&Q, London Headquarters, 1967; Dep. Chief, M&Q, 1973; Chief Inspector, M&Q, 1975–77; Member, Health and Safety Exec., 1976–77. *Publications:* author or co-author, papers in Trans IMinE; several papers to internat. mining confs. *Recreation:* golf. *Address:* 196 Forest Road, Tunbridge Wells, Kent TN2 5JB. *T:* Tunbridge Wells (01892) 526748. *Club:* Nevill Golf (Tunbridge Wells).

CARVILL, Patrick, CB 1994; Permanent Secretary, Department of Education for Northern Ireland, since 1990; *b* 13 Oct. 1943; *s* of Bernard and Susan Carvill; *m* 1965, Vera Abbott; two *s. Educ:* St Mary's Christian Brothers Grammar School, Belfast; Queen's Univ., Belfast (BA Hons). Min. of Fuel and Power, Westminster, 1965; Min. of Development, Stormont, 1967; Min. of Community Relations, 1969; Asst Sec., Dept. of Educn, 1975–83; Under-Secretary: Dept of Finance and Personnel, 1983–88; Dept. of Econ. Develt, 1988–89; Dept. of Finance and Personnel, 1989–90. *Recreations:* reading, hill-walking, diving. *Address:* c/o Department of Education for Northern Ireland, Rathgael House, Balloo Road, Bangor, Co. Down BT19 2PR.

CARY, family name of **Viscount Falkland.**

CARY, Sir Roger Hugh, 2nd Bt *cr* 1955; a consultant to BBC's Director-General, since 1986; *b* 8 Jan. 1926; *o s* of Sir Robert (Archibald) Cary, 1st Bt, and Hon. Rosamond Mary Curzon (*d* 1985), *d* of late Col Hon. Alfred Nathaniel Curzon; *S* father, 1979; *m* 1st, 1948, Marilda (marr. diss. 1951), *d* of Major Pearson-Gregory, MC; one *d*; 2nd, 1953, Ann Helen Katharine, *e d* of Hugh Blair Brenan, OBE (formerly Asst Sec., Royal Hosp., Chelsea); two *s* one *d. Educ:* Ludgrove; Eton; New Coll., Oxford (BA Mod. Hist. 1949). Enlisted Grenadier Guards, 1943; Lieut 1945; Staff Captain and Instr, Sch. of Signals, Catterick, 1946; Signals Officer, Guards Trng Bn, 1946–47; R of O 1947. Sub-editor and Leader-writer, The Times, 1949–50; Archivist, St Paul's Cathedral, 1950; joined BBC, 1950: attached Home Talks, 1951; Producer, Overseas Talks, 1951–56; Asst, European Talks, 1956–58; Dep. Editor, The Listener, 1958–61; Man. Trng Organiser, 1961–66; Asst, Secretariat, 1966–72, Sen. Asst, 1972–74; Sec., Central Music Adv. Cttee, 1966–77, 1982–83; Special Asst (Public Affairs), 1974–77; Special Asst to Alasdair Milne, when Man. Dir, BBC TV, 1977–82; Chief Asst to Sec., BBC, 1982–83; Chief Asst to Dir of Progs, BBC TV, 1983–86; Research, Richard Cawston's documentary film, Royal Family, 1969; Secretary: Sims Cttee on portrayal of violence on TV, 1979, Wyatt Cttee revision 1983; Wenham Cttee on Subscription Television, 1980–81; Cotton Cttee on Sponsorship and BBC TV, 1981; British Deleg., Internat. Art-Historical Conf., Amsterdam, 1952; Salzburg Scholar in Amer. Studies, 1956. Associate, RHistS. Trustee, Kedleston, 1988–. *Recreations:* looking at pictures, collecting books. *Heir: s* Nicolas Robert Hugh Cary [*b* 17 April 1955; *m* 1979, Pauline Jean, *d* of Dr Thomas Ian Boyd; three *s*]. *Address:* 23 Bath Road, W4 1LJ. *Clubs:* Pratt's, First Guards; The Bushmen.

CASALONE, Carlo D.; *see* Dionisotti-Casalone.

CASE, Anthea Fiendley, (Mrs D. C. Case); Assistant Director, Budget & Public Finances Directorate, HM Treasury, since 1995; *b* 7 Feb. 1945; *d* of Thomas Fiendley Stones and of late Bess Stones (*née* Mackie); *m* 1967, David Charles Case; two *d. Educ:* Christ's Hospital, Hertford; St Anne's Coll., Oxford (BA). HM Treasury: Asst Principal, 1966–70; Private Sec. to Financial Sec., 1970–71; Principal, 1971–79; Asst Sec., 1980–88; Under Sec., 1988–95 (with Fiscal Policy Gp, 1993–95). *Address:* HM Treasury, Parliament Street, SW1P 3AG. *T:* 0171–270 4419.

CASE, Humphrey John; Keeper, Department of Antiquities, Ashmolean Museum, 1973–82; *b* 26 May 1918; *s* of George Reginald Case and Margaret Helen (*née* Duckett); *m* 1st, 1942, Margaret Adelia (*née* Eaton); 2nd, 1949, Jean Alison (*née* Orr); two *s*; 3rd, 1979, Jocelyn (*née* Herickx). *Educ:* Charterhouse; St John's Coll., Cambridge (MA); Inst. of Archaeology, London Univ. Served War, 1939–46. Ashmolean Museum: Asst Keeper, 1949–57; Sen. Asst Keeper, 1957–69; Dep. Keeper, Dept of Antiquities, 1969–73. Vice-Pres., Prehistoric Soc., 1969–73; has directed excavations in England, Ireland and France. FSA 1954. *Publications:* in learned jls (British and foreign): principally on neolithic in Western Europe, prehistoric metallurgy and regional archaeology. *Recreations:* drawing, reading, music, gardening. *Address:* Pitt's Cottage, 187 Thame Road, Warborough, Wallingford, Oxon OX10 7DH.

CASE, Richard Ian, FEng, FRAeS; Managing Director, Westland Helicopters Ltd, since 1992; *b* 14 June 1945; *m* 1975, Denise Margaret Mills; one *s* one *d. Educ:* Cranfield Inst. of Technology (MSc Aircraft Propulsion). MIMechE 1973; FRAeS 1985; FEng 1993. Technical Manager, Arab British Helicopters, Egypt, 1978–82; Westland Helicopters Ltd: Chief Designer, 1982–85; Engrg Dir, 1985–88; EH101 Project Dir and Engrg Dir, 1988–92. *Recreations:* golf, opera. *Address:* Westland Helicopters Ltd, Yeovil, Somerset BA20 2YB. *T:* Yeovil (01935) 702505.

CASEY, Most Rev. Eamonn, DD; RC Bishop of Galway and Kilmacduagh, 1976–92; Apostolic Administrator of Kilfenora, 1976–92; *b* Firies, Co. Kerry, 23 April 1927; *s* of late John Casey and late Helena (*née* Shanahan). *Educ:* St Munchin's Coll., Limerick; St Patrick's Coll., Maynooth. LPh 1946; BA 1947. Priest, 1951. Curate, St John's Cath., Limerick, 1951–60; Chaplain to Irish in Slough, 1960–63; set up social framework to re-establish people into new environment; started social welfare scheme; set up lodgings bureau and savings scheme; invited by Cardinal Heenan to place Catholic Housing Aid Soc. on national basis; founded Family Housing Assoc., 1964; Dir, British Council of Churches Housing Trust; Trustee, Housing the Homeless Central Fund; Founder-Trustee of Shelter (Chm. 1968); Mem. Council, Nat. Fedn of Housing Socs; Founder Mem., Marian Employment Agency; Founder Trustee, Shelter Housing Aid Soc., 1963–69; Bishop of Kerry, 1969–76. Exec. Chm., Trocaire, 1973–92; Mem. Bd, Siamsa Tire, Nat. Folk Th. of Ireland. Launched Meitheal, 1982; estab. Galway Adult Educn Centre, 1985, Galway Family Guidance Inst., 1986. Chm., Nat. Youth Resource Gp, 1979–86. Member: Commn for Social Welfare, 1971–74; Maynooth Coll. Exec. Council, 1974–84; Episcopal Commn for Univs, 1976–92; Governing Body, University Coll., Galway, 1976–92. *Publications:* (with Adam Ferguson) A Home of Your Own; Housing—A Parish Solution; contribs to journals, etc. *Recreations:* music, theatre, concerts, films when time, conversation, motoring.

CASEY, Rt. Hon. Sir Maurice (Eugene), Kt 1991; PC 1986; **Rt. Hon. Mr Justice Casey;** Judge of Court of Appeal of New Zealand, since 1986; *b* 28 Aug. 1923; *s* of Eugene Casey and Beatrice Casey; *m* 1948, Stella Katherine Wright (*see* Dame Stella Casey); three *s* six *d. Educ:* St Patrick's Coll., Wellington; Victoria Univ. (LLM Hons). Served War, Naval Officer, 1943–45. Barrister and Solicitor, 1946; Vice Pres., Auckland Dist Law Soc., 1974; Judge, Supreme (now High) Court, 1974. Chm., Penal Policy Review Cttee, 1981. *Publication:* Hire Purchase Law in New Zealand, 1961. *Address:* 5/144 Oriental Parade, Wellington, New Zealand. *T:* (4) 3843258. *Clubs:* Wellington; Northern (Auckland).

CASEY, Michael Bernard; Chairman, Michael Casey & Associates; *b* 1 Sept. 1928; *s* of late Joseph Bernard Casey, OBE, and Dorothy (*née* Love); *m* 1963, Sally Louise, *e d* of late James Stuart Smith; two *s* two *d. Educ:* Colwyn Bay Grammar Sch.; LSE (Scholar in Laws, 1952; LLB 1954). RAF, 1947–49. Principal, MAFF, 1961; Office of the Minister for Science, 1963–64; Asst Sec., DEA, 1967; DTI (later Dept of Prices and Consumer Protection), 1970; Under Sec., DoI, 1975–77; a Dep. Chm. and Chief Exec., British Shipbuilders, 1977–80; Chm. and Man. Dir, Mather & Platt, 1980–81; Chm., Sallingbury Casey Ltd, later Rowland Sallingbury Casey, 1982–92. *Recreations:* golf, chess, bridge. *Address:* 19 Warwick Gardens, Kensington, W14 8PH. *T:* 0171–603 1641. *Club:* Reform.

CASEY, Michael Vince, OBE 1990; BSc(Eng), FEng 1985; FIMechE; Chief Engineer, Channel Tunnel Rail Link, British Rail, 1989–90; *b* 25 May 1927; *s* of Charles John Casey and May Louise Casey; *m* 1954, Elinor Jane (*née* Harris) (*d* 1987); two *s* two *d. Educ:* Glossop Grammar Sch.; The College, Swindon. BSc(Eng) Hons London. Premium Apprentice, GWR Locomotive Works, Swindon, 1944–49; Univ. of London External Degree Course, 1949–52; British Rail Western Region: Locomotive Testing and Experimental Office, Swindon, 1952–58; Supplies and Contracts Dept, Swindon, 1958–61; Chief Mechanical and Electrical Engr's Dept, Paddington, 1961–63; Area Maintenance Engr, Old Oak Common, 1963–66; Chief Mech. and Elec. Engr's Dept, Paddington, 1966–71; Chief Mech. and Elec. Engineer: Scottish Region, Glasgow, 1971–76; Eastern Region, York, 1976–78; Engrg Dir, British Rail Engrg Ltd, 1978–82; Dir, Mechanical and Electrical Engrg, BRB, 1982–87; Project Dir (BR Engrg), 1987–89. *Recreations:* gardening, philately. *Address:* Anakiwa, Wards Road, Chipping Norton, Oxon OX7 5BU. *T:* Chipping Norton (01608) 642644.

CASEY, Rt. Rev. Patrick Joseph; Former Bishop of Brentwood; *b* 20 Nov. 1913; *s* of Patrick Casey and Bridget Casey (*née* Norris). *Educ:* St Joseph's Parochial Sch., Kingsland; St Edmund's Coll., Ware. Ordained priest, 1939; Asst, St James's, Spanish Place, 1939–61; Parish Priest of Hendon, 1961–63; Vicar Gen. of Westminster, 1963; Domestic Prelate, and Canon of Westminster Cathedral, 1964; Provost of Westminster Cathedral Chapter, 1967; Auxiliary Bishop of Westminster and Titular Bishop of Sufar, 1966–69; Bishop of Brentwood, 1969–79, then Apostolic Administrator; Parish Priest, Our Most Holy Redeemer and St Thomas More, Chelsea, 1980–89. *Address:* 7 Cliffsea Grove, Leigh-on-Sea, Essex SS9 1NG.

CASEY, Dr Raymond, FRS 1970; retired; Senior Principal Scientific Officer (Special Merit), Institute of Geological Sciences, London, 1964–79; *b* 10 Oct. 1917; *s* of Samuel Gardiner Casey and Gladys Violet Helen Casey (*née* Garrett); *m* 1943, Norah Kathleen Pakeman (*d* 1974); two *s. Educ:* St Mary's, Folkestone; Univ. of Reading. PhD 1958; DSc 1963. Geological Survey and Museum: Asst 1939; Asst Exper. Officer 1946; Exper. Officer 1949; Sen. Geologist 1957; Principal Geologist 1960. *Publications:* A Monograph of the Ammonoidea of the Lower Greensand, 1960–80; (ed, with P. F. Rawson) The Boreal Lower Cretaceous, 1973; numerous articles on Mesozoic palaeontology and stratigraphy in scientific press. *Recreation:* research into early Russian postal and military history (Past Pres., British Soc. of Russian Philately). *Address:* 38 Reed Avenue, Orpington, Kent. BR6 9RX. *T:* Farnborough (Kent) (01689) 851728.

CASEY, Dame Stella (Katherine), DBE 1990; *b* 22 May 1924; *d* of William Wright and Stella Hickey; *m* 1948, Maurice Eugene Casey (*see* Rt Hon. Sir M. E. Casey); three *s* six *d. Educ.* Rahotu Sch.; Opunake Dist High Sch.; Victoria Univ. (BA). Voluntary service: Catholic Women's League of NZ, 1967–; Nat. Council of Women of NZ, 1976–; NZ Fedn of Univ. Women, 1969–; World Union of Catholic Women's Organisations, 1975–79; Hato Petra Coll. Assoc., 1968–73; Girl Guides Assoc., 1968–75; Bd of Governors, Sacred Heart Coll., 1976–82; Banking Ombudsman Commn, 1992–. Member: Cttee on Secondary Educn, 1975–76; Working Party, Teacher Training Review, 1977–78; Christchurch Polytechnic Council, 1979–82; Nat. Adv. Cttee on Women and Educn, 1982–83; Dep. Chm., Adv. Cttee on Women's Affairs, 1981–84. Chm. Trustees, Natural Family Planning Foundn, 1992–. Chm. Dirs, Dorchester Apartments, 1992–. *Publications:* Drugs and the Young New Zealander, 1968. *Address:* 5/144 Oriental Parade, Wellington, New Zealand. *T:* (4) 3843258.

CASH, Sir Gerald (Christopher), GCMG 1980; GCVO 1985 (KCVO 1977); OBE 1964; JP; Governor-General, Commonwealth of the Bahamas, 1979–88 (Acting Governor-General, 1976–79); Consultant Counsel, Cash, Fountain & Co., Nassau, since 1989; *b* Nassau, Bahamas, 28 May 1917; *s* of late Wilfred Gladstone Cash and of Lillian Cash; *m* Dorothy Eileen (*née* Long); two *s* one *d. Educ:* Govt High Sch., Nassau. Called to the Bar,

Middle Temple, 1948. Counsel and Attorney, Supreme Court of Bahamas, 1940. Member: House of Assembly, Bahamas, 1949–62; Exec. Council, 1958–62; Senate, 1969–73 (Vice-Pres., 1970–72; Pres., 1972–73). Chm., Labour Bd, 1950–52. Member: Bd of Educn, 1950–62; Police Service Commn, 1964–69; Immigration Cttee, 1958–62; Road Traffic Cttee, 1958–62. Rep. Bahamas, Independence Celebrations of Jamaica, Trinidad and Tobago, 1962. Chairman: Vis. Cttee, Boys Indust. Sch., 1952–62; Bd of Governors, Govt High Sch., 1949–63 and 1965–76; Bahamas National Cttee, United World Colls, 1977–. Formerly: Hon. Vice-Consul for Republic of Haiti; Vice-Chancellor, Anglican Dio.; Admin. Adviser, Rotary Clubs in Bahamas to Pres. of Rotary Internat.; Treasurer and Dir, YMCA; Treas., Bahamas Cricket Assoc.; Chm., Boy Scouts Exec. Council; Mem. Board: Dirs of Central Bank of Bahamas; Dirs of Bahamas Assoc. for Mentally Retarded. Formerly: President: Rotary Club of E Nassau; Gym Tennis Club; Florida Tennis Assoc.; Bahamas Lawn Tennis Assoc.; Bahamas Table Tennis Assoc.; Vice-President: Boy Scouts Assoc.; Olympic Assoc., Amateur Athletic Assoc., Swimming Assoc., Football Assoc., Bahamas. JP Bahamas, 1940. Coronation Medal, 1953; Silver Jubilee Medal, 1977; Silver Medal, Olympic Order, 1983. *Recreations:* golf, tennis, table tennis, swimming. *Address:* 4 Bristol Street, PO Box N-476, Nassau, Bahamas. *T:* 3934767, 3932062. *Clubs:* Commonwealth Trust; Kingston Cricket (Jamaica); Lyford Cay, Paradise Island Golf, South Ocean Golf, Ambassador Golf, Gym Tennis (Nassau).

CASH, Prof. John David, PhD; FRCPE, FRCPath, FRCSE, FRCPGlas; National Medical and Scientific Director, Scottish National Blood Transfusion Service, since 1988; *b* 3 April 1936; *s* of John Henry Cash and May Annie Cash (*née* Taylor); *m* 1962, Angela Mary Thomson; one *s* one *d*. *Educ:* Ashville College, Harrogate; Edinburgh Univ. (BSc, MB ChB, PhD). Regional Transfusion Centre Dir, Edinburgh and SE Scotland, 1974–79; Nat. Med. Dir, Scottish Nat. Blood Transfusion Service, 1979–88. Pres., RCPE, 1994– (Vice-Pres., 1992–94). Hon. Prof., Edinburgh Univ., 1986. *Publication:* Progress in Transfusion Medicine, 1988. *Recreations:* fishing, gardening, golf. *Address:* 1 Otterburn Park, Edinburgh EH14 1JX; Scottish National Blood Transfusion Service, Ellen's Glen Road, Edinburgh EH17 7QT. *T:* 0131–664 2317.

CASH, William Nigel Paul; MP (C) Stafford, since 1984; *b* 10 May 1940; *s* of Paul Trevor Cash, MC (killed in action Normandy, July 13, 1944) and Moyra Roberts (*née* Morrison); *m* 1965, Bridget Mary Lee; two *s* one *d*. *Educ:* Stonyhurst Coll.; Lincoln Coll., Oxford (MA History). Qualified as Solicitor, 1967; William Cash & Co. (constitutional and administrative lawyer), 1979–; Consultant, Radcliffes & Co. Chairman: Cons. Backbench Cttee on European Affairs, 1989–91; All Party Cttee on E Africa, 1988–; Joint Chairman: All Party Parly Gp on Complementary and Alternative Medicine, 1984–; All Party Jazz Gp, 1991–; Mem., Select Cttee on European Legislation, 1985–. Founder, and Chm., European Foundn, 1993–. Vice Pres., Cons. Small Business Bureau, 1986–. Dir, Ironbridge Gorge Museum Trust, 1980–. *Publications:* Against a Federal Europe—The Battle for Britain, 1991; Europe: the crunch, 1992. *Recreations:* history, cricket, jazz. *Address:* Upton Cressett Hall, near Bridgnorth, Shropshire WV16 6UH. *T:* Morville (01746) 714307. *Clubs:* Carlton, Beefsteak; Vincent's (Oxford); Free Foresters CC; Lords and Commons Cricket.

CASHEL AND EMLY, Archbishop of, (RC), since 1988; **Most Rev. Dermot Clifford,** DD; *b* 25 Jan. 1939. *Educ:* St Brendan's Coll., Killarney, Co. Kerry; St Patrick's Coll., Maynooth (BSc 1960); Irish Coll., Rome; Lateran Coll., Rome (STL 1964); NUI (HDipE 1966); LSE (MSc 1974); Loughborough (PhD 1989). Ordained priest, Rome, 1964; Dean of Studies, St Brendan's Coll., Killarney, 1964–72; Diocesan Sec., Kerry, 1974–86; Lectr, Univ. Coll., Cork, 1975–81; Chaplain, St Mary of the Angels Home for Handicapped Children, Beaufort, Co. Kerry, 1976–86; ordained Archbishop, Thurles, 1986; Coadjutor Archbishop of Cashel and Emly, 1986–88. Chm., Council for R&D of Irish Episcopal Commn, 1991–. Patron, Gaelic Athletic Assoc., 1989–. *Publication:* The Social Costs and Rewards of Caring, 1990. *Recreations:* reading, walking, sport. *Address:* Archbishop's House, Thurles, Co. Tipperary, Ireland.

CASHEL AND OSSORY, Bishop of, since 1980; **Rt. Rev. Noel Vincent Willoughby;** *b* 15 Dec. 1926; *s* of George and Mary Jane Willoughby; *m* 1959, Valerie Moore, Dungannon, Tyrone; two *s* one *d*. *Educ:* Tate School, Wexford; Trinity Coll., Dublin (Scholar, Moderator and Gold Medallist in Philosophy). Deacon 1950, priest 1951, Armagh Cathedral; Curate: Drumglass Parish, 1950–53; St Catherine's, Dublin, 1953–55; Bray Parish, 1955–59; Rector: Delgany Parish, 1959–69; Glenageary Parish, 1969–80; Hon. Sec., General Synod, 1976–80; Treasurer, St Patrick's Cathedral, Dublin, 1976–80; Archdeacon of Dublin, 1979–80. *Recreations:* gardening, golf, tennis, fishing. *Address:* The Palace, Kilkenny, Ireland. *T:* Kilkenny (56) 21560.

CASHMAN, John Prescott; Under-Secretary, Department of Health (formerly of Health and Social Security), 1973–88; *b* 19 May 1930; *s* of late John Patrick Cashman and late Mary Cashman (*née* Prescott). *Educ:* Balliol Coll., Oxford. MA (English Lang. and Lit.). Army (Intell. Corps), 1948–49. Entered Min. of Health, 1951; Principal 1957; Private Sec. to Minister, 1962–65; Asst Sec. 1965; Nuffield Foundn Trav. Fellow, 1968–69; Private Sec. to Sec. of State, 1969. Trustee, Macfarlane Trust, 1989–; Mem. Exec. Council, Hospital Saving Assoc., 1989–. *Address:* 3 Paul Gardens, Croydon, Surrey CR0 5QL. *T:* 0181–681 6578.

CASHMORE, Prof. Roger John, DPhil; FInstP; Professor of Experimental Physics, since 1991, and Fellow of Balliol College, since 1979, Oxford University; *b* 22 Aug. 1944; *e s* of C. J. C. and E. M. Cashmore; *m* 1971, Elizabeth Ann, *d* of Rev. S. J. C. Lindsay; one *s*. *Educ:* Dudley Grammar Sch.; St John's Coll., Cambridge (schol.; BA 1965; MA); Balliol Coll., Oxford (DPhil 1969). FInstP 1985. Weir Jun. Res. Fellow, University Coll., Oxford, 1967–69; 1851 Res. Fellow, 1968; Res. Associate, Stanford Linear Accelerator Centre, Calif, 1969–74; Oxford University: Res. Officer, 1974–79; Lectr, Christ Church, 1976–78; Sen. Res. Fellow, Merton Coll., 1977–79; Tutor, Balliol Coll., and Univ. Lectr in Physics, 1979–90; Reader in Experimental Physics, 1990–91. SERC Sen. Res. Fellow, 1982–87; Vis. Prof., Vrije Univ., Brussels, 1982; Guest Scientist, Fermilab, Chicago, 1986. Mem., policy and prog. cttees, CERN, Deutsches Electronen–Synchrotron, Hamburg, and SERC. C.V. Boys Prize, Inst. of Physics, 1983. *Publications:* contrib. Nuclear Physics, Physics Letters, Phys. Rev., Phys. Rev. Letters. *Recreations:* sports, wine. *Address:* Balliol College, Oxford OX1 3BJ.

CASKEN, Prof. John, DMus; composer; Professor of Music, University of Manchester, since 1992; *b* 15 July 1949. *Educ:* Birmingham Univ. (BMus, MA); Durham Univ. (DMus). Polish Govt Scholarship, Warsaw, 1971–72. Lectr, Birmingham Univ., 1973–79; Res. Fellow, Huddersfield Poly., 1980–81; Lectr, Durham Univ., 1981–92. Northern Electric Arts Award, 1990. *Compositions include: orchestral:* Tableaux des Trois Ages, 1977; Masque, 1982; Orion over Farne, 1984; Cello Concerto, 1991; Still Mine, 1992 (Prix de Composition Musicale, Prince Pierre de Monaco, 1993); Second String Quartet, 1993; Infanta Marina, 1994; Violin Concerto, 1995; *vocal:* Firewhirl, 1980; To Fields We Do Not Know, 1984; *opera:* Golem, 1988 (first Britten Award, 1990; Gramophone Award for best contemp. recording, 1991); *electronic:* Piper's Linn, 1984; also chamber, instrumental, choral and ensemble works. *Address:* Department of Music, University of Manchester, Denmark Road, Manchester M15 6HY.

CASLEY, Henry Roberts; Chief Executive, Southern Electric plc, since 1993; *s* of Benjamin Rowe Casley and May Casley; *m* 1960, Sheila Laity; one *s* one *d*. MCIM. Eastern Electricity: Energy Mkting Manager, 1975–78; Supplies Manager, 1978–82; Mkting Dir, 1982–86; Southern Electric plc: Dep. Chm., 1986–89; Man. Dir, 1989–93. *Recreations:* sport, gardening. *Address:* Southern Electric plc, Westacott Way, Littlewick Green, Maidenhead, Berks SL6 3QB; Dogmore Cottage, Stoke Row, Henley-on-Thames, Oxon RG9 5PD. *T:* Henley-on-Thames (01491) 680877. *Club:* Phyllis Court (Henley-on-Thames).

CASS, Edward Geoffrey, CB 1974; OBE 1951; Alternate Governor, Reserve Bank of Rhodesia, 1978–79; *b* 10 Sept. 1916; *s* of Edward Charles and Florence Mary Cass; *m* 1941, Ruth Mary Powley; four *d*. *Educ:* St Olave's; Univ. Coll., London (Scholar); BSc (Econ.) London (1st Cl.) 1937; The Queen's Coll., Oxford (Scholar); George Webb Medley Scholarship, 1938; BA Oxon (1st Cl. PPE) 1939, MA 1987. Lecturer in Economics, New Coll., Oxford, 1939. From 1940 served in Min. of Supply, Treasury, Air Ministry, MoD; Private Sec. to the Prime Minister, 1949–52; Chief Statistician, Min. of Supply, 1952; Private Sec. to Min. of Supply, 1954; Imperial Defence Coll., 1958; Asst Under-Sec. of State (Programmes and Budget), MoD, 1965–72; Dep. Under-Sec. of State (Finance and Budget), MoD, 1972–76. Mem., Review Bd for Govt Contracts, 1977–84; Chm., Verbatim Reporting Study Gp, 1977–79. *Address:* 60 Rotherwick Road, NW11 7DB. *T:* 0181–455 1664.

CASS, Sir Geoffrey (Arthur), Kt 1992; MA; CIMgt; Chairman: Royal Shakespeare Company, since 1985; Royal Shakespeare Theatre Trust, since 1983; Fellow of Clare Hall, Cambridge, since 1979; Chief Executive, Cambridge University Press, 1972–92 (Secretary of the Press Syndicate, 1974–92; University Printer, 1982–83, 1991–92); *b* 11 Aug. 1932; *o c* of late Arthur Cass and Jessie Cass (*née* Simpson), Darlington and Oxford; *m* 1957, Olwen Mary, *o c* of late William Leslie Richards and of Edith Louisa Richards, Llanelli and Brecon; four *d*. *Educ:* Queen Elizabeth Grammar Sch., Darlington (Head of Sch.); Jesus Coll., Nuffield Coll., and Dept of Social and Admin. Studies, Oxford Univ. (BA 1954; MA 1958); MA Cantab, 1972. FInstD 1968; FIWM, FIIM 1979; CIMgt (CBIM 1980). Commnd RAFVR, fighter control, 1954; served RAF, 1958–60: Air Min. Directorate of Work Study; Pilot Officer, 1958; Flying Officer, 1960. Consultant: PA Management Consultants Ltd, 1960–65; British Communications Corp., and Controls and Communications Ltd, 1965; Dir, Controls and Communications Ltd, 1966–69; Managing Director, George Allen and Unwin Ltd, 1967–71; Director: Weidenfeld (Publishers) Ltd, 1972–74; Chicago Univ. Press (UK), 1971–86; Mem., Jesus Coll., Cambridge, 1972–. Member: Univ. of Cambridge Cttee of Management of Fenner's (and Exec. Cttee), 1976–; Univ. of Cambridge Careers Service Syndicate (formerly Appts Bd), 1977– (Exec. Cttee, 1982–); Governing Syndicate, Fitzwilliam Mus., Cambridge, 1977–78; Chm. Governors, Perse Sch. for Girls, Cambridge, 1978–88 (Governor, 1977–). Founder Mem. Council, Royal Shakespeare Theatre Trust, 1967–; Gov. and Mem. Council, RSC, 1975– (Mem. 1976–, Chm. 1982–, Exec. Cttee, Council); Trustee and Guardian, Shakespeare Birthplace Trust, 1982–94 (Life Trustee, 1994). Director: Newcastle Theatre Royal Trust, 1984–89; American Friends of the Royal Shakespeare Theatre, 1985–; Method & Madness (formerly Cambridge Theatre Co.), 1986–; Theatres Trust, 1991–; Cambridgeshire LTA: Mem. Exec., 1974–84; Chm., F and GP Cttee 1982–84; Captain 1974–78; Pres., 1980–82; Hon. Life Vice-Pres., 1982–; The Lawn Tennis Association of GB: Dep. Pres., 1993–; Member: Council, 1976–; Management Bd, 1985–90, 1993–; Nat. Trng and Internat. Match Cttee (Davis Cup, Fedn Cup, Wightman Cup, etc), 1982–90, 1992–93 (Chm., 1985–90); Internat. Events Cttee, 1991–93; Chm., Nat. Ranking Cttee, 1990–; Wimbledon Championships: Member: Cttee of Management, 1990–; Jt Finance Bd, 1989–93; Jt Finance Cttee, 1993–; British Jun. Championships Cttee of Management, 1983–90 (Chm., 1985–90); Nat. Championships Cttee of Management, 1988–89; Rules and Internat. Cttee, 1980–81; Re-orgn Wkg Party, 1984–85; Chm., Reconstruction Wkg Gp, 1994–. Tennis singles champion: Durham County, 1951; Cambridgeshire, 1975; Oxford University: tennis Blue, 1953, 1954, 1955 (Sec., 1955); badminton, 1951, 1952 (Captain, 1952); Chm., Cambridge Univ. Lawn Tennis Club, 1977– (Hon. Cambridge tennis Blue, 1980); played in Wimbledon Championships, 1954, 1955, 1956, 1959; played in inter-county lawn tennis championships for Durham County, then for Cambridgeshire, 1952–82; represented RAF, 1958–59; Brit. Veterans (over 45) singles champion, Wimbledon, 1978; Mem., Brit. Veterans' Internat. Dubler Cup Team, Barcelona, 1978, Milano Marittima, 1979 (Captain). FRSA 1991. Chevalier, Ordre des Arts et des Lettres (France), 1982. *Recreations:* lawn tennis, theatre. *Address:* Middlefield, Huntingdon Road, Cambridge CB3 0LH. *Clubs:* Hurlingham, Queen's, Institute of Directors, All England Lawn Tennis and Croquet, International Lawn Tennis of GB, The 45, Veterans' Lawn Tennis of GB; Cambridge University Lawn Tennis.

CASS, John, QPM 1979; National Co-ordinator of Regional Crime Squads, 1981–84; Security Consultant; *b* 24 June 1925; *m* 1948, Dilys Margaret Hughes, SRN; three *d*. *Educ:* Nelson Sch., Wigton, Cumbria. Served no 40 RM Commando, 1944–45. Joined Metropolitan Police, 1946; Comdt, Detective Training Sch., Hendon, 1974; Commander: CID, New Scotland Yard, 1975; Complaints Bureau, 1978; Serious Crime Squads, New Scotland Yard, 1980. UK Rep., Interpol Conf. on crime prediction, Paris, 1976. Student in Criminology, Cambridge Univ., 1966. Adviser, Police Staff Coll., on multi-Force major investigations, 1982–83; Chief Investigator, War Crimes Inquiry, Home Office, 1988–89. Mem., British Acad. of Forensic Scis, 1965. Member: Association of Chief Police Officers; Metropolitan Police Commanders' Assoc.; Internat. Police Assoc. Freeman, City of London, 1979. *Recreations:* Lakeland, walking, wild life; and Janet (BA), Anne (BDS), Sarah (LLB), James, Gwilym, Bryn and Elizabeth. *Address:* 30 Latchingdon Court, Forest Road, E17 6JT. *T:* 0181–521 1580; Carmarthen (01267) 236918. *Club:* Special Forces.

CASS, Sir John (Patrick), Kt 1978; OBE 1960; Director: Farmers and Graziers Co-operative Co., since 1962; The Land Newspaper Ltd, since 1964; Queensland Country Life Newspaper, since 1977; *b* 7 May 1909; *s* of Phillip and Florence Cass; *m* 1932, Velma Mostyn; two *s*. *Educ:* Christian Brothers College, Young, NSW. Gen. Pres., Farmers and Settlers Assoc. of NSW, 1954–59; Senior Vice-Pres., Aust. NFU, 1960–70; Chm., NSW Wheat Research Cttee, 1954–72; Mem., Aust. Wheat Board, 1952–77, Chm., 1972–77. Agricultural Man of the Year in Australia, 1977. *Address:* Stoney Ridge, Crowther, NSW 2692, Australia. *Clubs:* Royal Automobile of Australia, Royal Automobile of Victoria.

CASSAR, Francis Felix Anthony; Director, Omnirace Ltd, since 1990; *b* 10 May 1934; *s* of Carmelo and Filomena Cassar; *m* 1969, Doreen Marjorie; two *s*. *Educ:* Primary Sch., Malta; Lyceum, Malta. Emigrated to UK, 1953. Studied mech. engrg, 1953–58; Man. Dir of own motor engrg co., 1959–74; Co. Sec., Malta Drydocks (UK) Ltd, 1975–80. Represented Malta Labour Party in the UK, also at meetings of the Bureau of the Socialist International, 1960–80; Acting High Comr for Malta in London and Cyprus, 1981–85, High Comr, 1985–87; Chargé d'Affaires, Baghdad, 1988–90. Mem., Inst of Management,

1977. JP: Brentford and Ealing, Tottenham, 1972–80; Enfield, 1990. *Recreations:* music, football, DIY, cooking.

CASSEL, family name of **Baroness Mallalieu.**

CASSEL, His Honour Sir Harold (Felix), 3rd Bt *cr* 1920; TD 1975; QC 1970; a Circuit Judge, 1976–88; *b* 8 Nov. 1916; 3rd *s* of Rt Hon. Sir Felix Cassel, 1st Bt, PC, QC (*d* 1953), and Lady Helen Cassel (*d* 1947); *S* brother, 1969; *m* 1st, 1940, Ione Jean Barclay (marr. diss. 1963); three *s* one *d*; 2nd, 1963, Mrs Eileen Elfrida Smedley. *Educ:* Stowe; Corpus Christi Coll., Oxford. Served War of 1939–45, Captain, 1941, Royal Artillery. Called to Bar, Lincoln's Inn, 1946. Recorder of Great Yarmouth, 1968–71, Hon. Recorder, 1972–. JP Herts, 1959–62; Dep. Chm., Herts QS, 1959–62. Mem. Council, British Commonwealth Ex-Services League, 1988–. *Recreations:* shooting, scuba diving, travelling. *Heir:* *s* Timothy Felix Harold Cassel, *qv*. *Address:* 49 Lennox Gardens, SW1X 0DF. *T:* 0171–584 2721.

CASSEL, Timothy Felix Harold; QC 1988; *b* 30 April 1942; *s* of Sir Harold Cassel, Bt, *qv*; *m* 1st, 1971, Jenifer Puckle (marr. diss. 1976); one *s* one *d*; 2nd, 1979, Ann Mallalieu (*see* Baroness Mallalieu); two *d*. *Educ:* Eton College. Called to the Bar, Lincoln's Inn, 1965, Bencher, 1994; Jun. Prosecuting Counsel at Central Criminal Court, 1978, Sen. Prosecuting Counsel, 1986–88; Asst Boundaries Comr, 1979–85. *Address:* Studdridge Farm, Stokenchurch, Bucks HP14 3XS. *T:* High Wycombe (01494) 482303. *Club:* Garrick.

CASSELL, Frank, CB 1987; Member, Board of Crown Agents, since 1991; Economic Minister, Washington, and UK Executive Director, International Monetary Fund and World Bank, 1988–90; *b* 21 August 1930; *s* of Francis Joseph Cassell and Ellen Blanche Cassell (*née* Adams); *m* 1957, Jean Seabrook; two *s* one *d*. *Educ:* Borden Grammar School; LSE (BSc Econ). Asst City Editor, News Chronicle, 1953–58; Dep. Editor, The Banker, 1958–65; HM Treasury: Economic Adviser, 1965; Senior Economic Adviser, 1968; Under Sec., 1974; Deputy Sec., 1983–88. Chm., Stats Cttee, British Invisibles. Vis. Scholar, Federal Reserve Bank of Minneapolis, 1970. *Publications:* Gold or Credit?, 1965; articles on economic policy, 1953–65. *Recreations:* walking, watching cricket, reading history. *Address:* Crown Agents, St Nicholas House, Sutton, Surrey SM1 1EL.

CASSELL, Michael Robert; Financial Times Business Correspondent, since 1990; *b* 2 June 1946; *s* of Donald and Joyce Cassell. *Educ:* Lode Heath High Sch.; Solihull Coll. Reporter, W Midlands Press, 1964–67; Business Reporter, Birmingham Post, 1967–69; City Reporter, Daily Express, 1969–70; Financial Times, 1970–: Property and Political Correspondent. *Publications:* One Hundred Years of Co-operation, 1984; Readymixers, 1986; Dig it, Burn it, Sell it!, 1990; Long Lease, 1991. *Recreations:* horse riding, walking, watercolours. *Address:* Gunridge House, Clunton, Shropshire SY7 0HX.

CASSELS, Field-Marshal Sir (Archibald) James (Halkett), GCB 1961 (CB 1950); KBE 1952 (CBE 1944); DSO 1944; Chief of the General Staff, Ministry of Defence, 1965–68; *b* 28 Feb. 1907; *s* of late General Sir Robert A. Cassels, GCB, GCSI, DSO; *m* 1st, 1935, Joyce (*d* 1978), *d* of late Brig.-Gen. Henry Kirk and Mrs G. A. McL. Sceales; one *s*; 2nd, 1978, Joy (Mrs Kenneth Dickson). *Educ:* Rugby Sch.; RMC, Sandhurst. 2nd Lieut Seaforth Highlanders, 1926; Lieut 1929; Capt. 1938; Major 1943; Col 1946; temp. Maj.-Gen. 1945; Maj.-Gen. 1948; Lieut-Gen. 1954; Gen. 1958. Served War of 1939–45 (despatches twice): BGS 1944; Bde Comd 1944; GOC 51st Highland Div., 1945; GOC 6th Airborne Div., Palestine, 1946 (despatches); idc, 1947; Dir Land/Air Warfare, War Office, 1948–49; Chief Liaison Officer, United Kingdom Services Liaison Staff, Australia, 1950–51; GOC 1st British Commonwealth Div. in Korea (US Legion of Merit), 1951–52; Comdr, 1st Corps, 1953–54; Dir-Gen. of Military Training, War Office, 1954–57; Dir of Emergency Operations Federation of Malaya, 1957–59; PMN (Panglima Mangku Negara), 1958; GOC-in-C, Eastern Command, 1959; C-in-C, British Army of the Rhine and Comdr NATO Northern Army Group, 1960–63; Adjutant-Gen. to the Forces, 1963–64; Field-Marshal, 1968. ADC Gen. to the Queen, 1960–63. Col Seaforth Highlanders, 1957–61; Col Queen's Own Highlanders, 1961–66; Colonel Commandant: Corps of Royal Military Police, 1957–68; Army Physical Training Corps, 1961–65. Pres., Company of Veteran Motorists, 1970–73. *Recreations:* follower of all forms of sport. *Address:* Hamble End, Barrow, Bury St Edmunds, Suffolk IP29 5BE. *Club:* Cavalry and Guards (Hon. Mem.).

CASSELS, Sir John (Seton), Kt 1988; CB 1978; Director General, National Economic Development Office, 1983–88; Director, National Commission on Education, since 1991; *b* 10 Oct. 1928; *s* of Alastair Macdonald Cassels and Ada White Cassels (*née* Scott); *m* 1956, Mary Whittington; two *s* two *d*. *Educ:* Sedbergh Sch., Yorkshire; Trinity Coll., Cambridge (1st cl. Hons, Classics, 1951). Rome Scholar, Classical Archaeology, 1952–54. Entered Ministry of Labour, 1954; Secretary of the Royal Commission on Trade Unions and Employers' Associations, 1965–68; Under-Sec., NBPI, 1968–71; Managing Directors' Office, Dunlop Holdings Ltd, 1971–72; Chief Exec., Training Services Agency, 1972–75; Dir, Manpower Services Commn, 1975–81; Second Permanent Sec., MPO, 1981–83. Member Council: Inst. of Manpower Studies, subseq. Inst. of Employment Studies, 1982– (Pres., 1989–95); Policy Studies Inst., 1983–88; Industrial Soc., 1984–93; Assoc. for Consumer Res., 1989–94; NIESR, 1993–. Dir, Volunteers (PTP) Trust, 1990– (Chm., 1990–91); Chm., UK Skills, 1990–. Non-exec. Dir, Ealing HA, 1990–91. Dist. Vis. Fellow, 1989, Sen. Fellow, 1990, PSI. CIMgt; FIPD; FRSA. Hon. CGIA 1989. *Publication:* Britain's Real Skill Shortage—and what to do about it, 1990. *Address:* 10 Beverley Road, Barnes, SW13 0LX. *T:* 0181–876 6270; National Commission on Education, 344–354 Gray's Inn Road, WC1X 8BP. *T:* 0171–278 4411. *Club:* Reform.

CASSELS, Prof. John William Scott, FRS 1963; FRSE 1981; MA, PhD; Sadleirian Professor of Pure Mathematics, Cambridge University, 1967–84; Head of Department of Pure Mathematics and Mathematical Statistics, 1969–84; *b* 11 July 1922; *s* of late J. W. Cassels (latterly Dir of Agriculture in Co. Durham) and late Mrs M. S. Cassels (*née* Lobjoit); *m* 1949, Constance Mabel Merritt (*née* Senior); one *s* one *d*. *Educ:* Neville's Cross Council Sch., Durham; George Heriot's Sch., Edinburgh; Edinburgh and Cambridge Univs. MA Edinburgh, 1943; PhD Cantab, 1949. Fellow, Trinity, 1949–; Lecturer, Manchester Univ., 1949; Lecturer, Cambridge Univ., 1950; Reader in Arithmetic, 1963–67. Mem. Council, Royal Society, 1970, 1971 (Sylvester Medal, 1973); Vice Pres., 1974–78, Mem. Exec., 1978–82, Internat. Mathematical Union; Pres., London Mathematical Soc., 1976–78. Dr (*hc*) Lille Univ., 1965; Hon. ScD Edinburgh, 1977. De Morgan Medal, London Mathematical Soc., 1986. *Publications:* An Introduction to Diophantine Approximation, 1957; An Introduction to the Geometry of Numbers, 1959; Rational Quadratic Forms, 1978; Economics for Mathematicians, 1981; Local Fields, 1986; Lectures on Elliptic Curves, 1991; papers in diverse mathematical journals on arithmetical topics. *Recreations:* arithmetic (higher only), gardening (especially common vegetables). *Address:* 3 Luard Close, Cambridge CB2 2PL. *T:* Cambridge (01223) 246108; (office) Cambridge (01223) 337975.

CASSELS, Adm. Sir Simon (Alastair Cassillis), KCB 1982; CBE 1976; *b* 5 March 1928; *o s* of late Comdr A. G. Cassels, RN, and Clarissa Cassels (*née* Motion); *m* 1962, Jillian Francies Kannreuther; one *s* one *d*. *Educ:* RNC, Dartmouth. Midshipman 1945; Commanding Officer: HM Ships Vigilant, Roebuck, and Tenby, 1962–63; HMS Eskimo, 1966–67; HMS Fearless, 1972–73; Principal Staff Officer to CDS, 1973–76; CO HMS Tiger, 1976–78; Asst Chief of Naval Staff (Op. Requirements), 1978–80; Flag Officer, Plymouth, Port Adm. Devonport, Comdr Central Sub Area Eastern Atlantic and Comdr Plymouth Sub Area Channel, 1981–82; Second Sea Lord, Chief of Naval Personnel and Adm. Pres., RNC, Greenwich, 1982–86. Dir Gen., TSB Foundn for Eng. and Wales, 1986–90. Younger Brother of Trinity House, 1963. Pres., Regular Forces Employment Assoc., 1990–93 (Chm., 1989). Freeman, City of London, 1983; Liveryman, Shipwrights' Co., 1984. FRGS 1947. *Publication:* Peninsular Portrait 1811–1814, 1963. *Recreations:* archaeology, historical research, water colours. *Address:* c/o Lloyds Bank, Bishop's Waltham, Hants. *Club:* Army and Navy.

CASSEN, Prof. Robert Harvey; Director, Queen Elizabeth House, International Development Centre, University of Oxford, and Professorial Fellow, St Antony's College, since 1986; *b* 24 March 1935; *s* of John and Liliane Cassen; *m* 1989, Sun Shuyun. *Educ:* Bedford School; New Coll., Oxford (BA LitHum, MA); Univ. of California, Berkeley; Harvard (PhD Econ). Dept of Economics, LSE, 1961–69; Sen. Economist, ODM, 1966–67; First Sec. (Econ.), New Delhi, 1967–68; Sen. Economist, World Bank, Washington, 1969–72 and 1980–81; Fellow, Inst. of Develt Studies, Sussex Univ., 1972–86; Sen. Res. Fellow, Centre for Population Studies, LSHTM, 1976–77. Special Adviser, H of C Select Cttee on Overseas Develt, 1973–74; Secretariat, Brandt Commn, 1978–79 and 1981–82; Mem., Bd of Trustees, Population Council, NY, 1978–87; UK Mem., UN Cttee for Develt Planning, 1982–84. *Publications:* India: Population, Economy, Society, 1978; (ed and contrib.) Planning for Growing Populations, 1979; (ed and contrib.) World Development Report, 1981; (ed and contrib.) Rich Country Interests and Third World Development, 1982; (ed) Soviet Interests in the Third World, 1985; Does Aid Work? (report), 1986; (ed) Poverty in India, 1992; contribs to learned jls. *Recreations:* music and other pursuits. *Address:* Queen Elizabeth House, 21 St Giles, Oxford OX1 3LA. *T:* Oxford (01865) 273600.

CASSIDI, Adm. Sir (Arthur) Desmond, GCB 1983 (KCB 1978); President, Royal Naval Association, since 1987; Deputy Grand President, British Commonwealth Ex-Services League, since 1986; *b* 26 Jan. 1925; *s* of late Comdr Robert A. Cassidi, RN and late Clare F. (*née* Alexander); *m* 1st, 1950, Dorothy Sheelagh Marie (*née* Scott) (*d* 1974); one *s* two *d*; 2nd, 1982, Dr Deborah Marion Pollock (*née* Bliss), FRCS. *Educ:* RNC Dartmouth. Qual. Pilot, 1946; CO, 820 Sqdn (Gannet aircraft), 1955; 1st Lieut HMS Protector, 1955–56; psc 1957; CO, HMS Whitby, 1959–61; Fleet Ops Officer Home Fleet, 1962–64; Asst Dir Naval Plans, 1964–67; Captain (D) Portland and CO HMS Undaunted, 1967–68; idc 1969; Dir of Naval Plans, 1970–72; CO, HMS Ark Royal, 1972–73; Flag Officer Carriers and Amphibious Ships, 1974–75; Dir-Gen., Naval Manpower and Training, 1975–77; Flag Officer, Naval Air Command, 1978–79; Chief of Naval Personnel and Second Sea Lord, 1979–82; C-in-C Naval Home Comd, 1982–85; Flag ADC to the Queen, 1982–85. Mem. Adv. Council, Science Museum, 1979–84, Trustee, 1984–92; Pres., FAA Museum, 1985–. FRSA 1986. *Recreation:* country pursuits. *Address:* c/o Barclays Bank, 22/25 Northumberland Avenue, WC2N 5BH.

CASSIDY, Bryan Michael Deece; Member (C) European Parliament, Dorset and East Devon, since 1994 (Dorset East and Hampshire West, 1984–94); *b* 17 Feb. 1934; *s* of late William Francis Deece Cassidy and Kathleen Selina Patricia Cassidy (*née* Geraghty); *m* 1960, Gillian Mary Isobel Bohane; one *s* two *d*. *Educ:* Ratcliffe College; Sidney Sussex College, Cambridge. MA (Law). Commissioned RA, 1955–57 (Malta and Libya); HAC, 1957–62. With Ever Ready, Beecham's and Reed International (Dir, European associates). Mem. Council, CBI, 1981–84. Dir Gen., of a trade assoc., 1981–84. Contested (C) Wandsworth Central, 1966; Mem. GLC (Hendon North), 1977–86 (opposition spokesman on industry and employment, 1983–84). *Recreations:* history, country sports, theatre. *Address:* 11 Esmond Court, Thackeray Street, W8 5HB. *T and Fax:* 0171–937 3558; (office) The Stables, White Cliff Gardens, Blandford DT11 7BU. *T:* Blandford (01258) 452420, *Fax:* (01258) 693253.

CASSIDY, Most Rev. Edward; *see* Cassidy, Most Rev. I. E.

CASSIDY, Ven. George Henry; Archdeacon of London and Canon Residentiary of St Paul's Cathedral, since 1987; *b* 17 Oct. 1942; *s* of Joseph Abram Cassidy and Ethel McDonald; *m* 1966, Jane Barling Stevens; two *d*. *Educ:* Belfast High School; Queen's Univ., Belfast (BSc 1965; Cert. Bib. Studies 1968); University Coll., London (MPhil 1967); Oak Hill Theological College. MRTPI 1969. Civil Servant: N Ireland, 1967–68; Govt of Kenya, 1968–70. Curate, Christ Church, Clifton, Bristol, 1972–75; Vicar: St Edyth, Sea Mills, Bristol, 1975–82; St Paul's, Portman Square, W1, 1982–87. Trustee, City Parochial Foundn, 1987–. Freeman, Tylers' & Bricklayers' Co., 1988; Hon. Chaplain, Chartered Accountants' Co., 1990; Hon. Liveryman, Founders' Co., 1994. *Recreations:* Rugby football, art, chamber music, Classic FM fan, walking in the Quantocks. *Address:* 2 Amen Court, EC4M 7BU. *T:* 0171–248 3312. *Club:* National.

CASSIDY, Very Rev. Herbert; Dean of Armagh and Keeper of the Library, since 1989; *b* 25 July 1935; *s* of Herbert Cassidy and Fredericka Jane Summerville; *m* 1961, Elizabeth Ann Egerton; one *s* two *d*. *Educ:* Cork Grammar Sch.; Trinity Coll., Dublin (BA 1957; MA 1965). Curate Assistant: Holy Trinity, Belfast, 1958–60; Christ Church, Londonderry, 1960–62; Rector: Aghavilly and Derrynoose, 1962–65; St Columba's, Portadown, 1965–85; Dean of Kilmore, 1985–89. Hon. Sec., Gen. Synod, Ch. of Ireland, 1990–. *Publications:* various pamphlets. *Recreations:* music, travel. *Address:* The Library, Abbey Street, Armagh BT61 7DY. *T:* Armagh (01861) 523142.

CASSIDY, His Eminence Cardinal (Idris) Edward, AC 1990; President, Pontifical Council for Promoting Christian Unity, and Commission for Religious Relations with the Jews, since 1989; *b* 5 July 1924; *s* of Harold George Cassidy and Dorothy May Philipps. *Educ:* Parramatta High Sch.; St Columba Seminary, Springwood; St Patrick's Coll., Manly; Lateran Univ., Rome (DCnL 1955); Diploma of Pontifical Eccl. Acad., Rome, 1955. Ordained priest, 1949; Asst Priest, Parish of Yenda, NSW, Australia, 1950–52; Secretary, Apostolic Nunciature, India, 1955–62 and Ireland, 1962–67; El Salvador, 1967–69; Counsellor, Apostolic Nunciature, Argentina, 1969–70; ordained bishop, Rome, 1970; Apostolic Pro-Nuncio: to Republic of China, 1970–79; to Bangladesh, 1973–79; to Lesotho, 1979–84, and Apostolic Delegate to Southern Africa; to the Netherlands, 1984–88; Substitute of Vatican Secretariat of State, 1988–89. Cardinal, 1991. Orders from El Salvador, China, Netherlands, Italy, France, Sweden and Germany. *Recreations:* tennis, golf. *Address:* Pontifical Council for Christian Unity, 00120 Vatican City, Rome, Italy. *T:* (6698) 84181.

CASSIDY, Most Rev. Joseph; *see* Tuam, Archbishop of, (RC).

CASSIDY, Michael John; Chairman, Policy and Resources Committee, Corporation of London, since 1992; Senior Partner, Maxwell Batley, solicitors, since 1991; *b* 14 Jan. 1947; *s* of Frank and Vera Cassidy; *m* 1974, Amanda (marr. diss. 1988); one *s* two *d*. *Educ:* Downing Coll., Cambridge (BA); MBA (with distinction), City Univ. Business Sch.,

1985. Qualified Solicitor, 1971; Partner, Maxwell Batley, 1971–; Dir, London American Growth Trust, 1992–. Mem., Common Council, Corp. of London, 1980 (Chm., Planning Cttee, 1986–89). Liveryman: Fletchers' Co.; Solicitors' Co. *Publications:* articles on City matters and pension fund investment. *Recreations:* boating, Barbican concerts. *Address:* 202 Cromwell Tower, Barbican EC2Y 8DD. *T:* 0171–628 5687. *Club:* City Livery.

CASSIDY, Dr Sheila Anne; Palliative Care Physician, Plymouth General Hospital, since 1993; *b* 18 Aug. 1937; *d* of late Air Vice-Marshal John Reginald Cassidy and Barbara Margaret Cassidy. *Educ:* Univ. of Sydney; Somerville Coll., Oxford (BM BCh 1963; MA). Worked in Oxford and Leicester to 1971; went to Chile to work, 1971; arrested for treating wounded revolutionary, 1975; tortured and imprisoned 2 months, released Dec. 1975; lectured on human rights; in monastic religious order, 1978–80; returned to medicine, 1980; Medical Dir, St Luke's Hospice, Plymouth, 1982–93; lecturer in UK and overseas, preacher, writer, broadcaster. Hon. DSc Exeter, 1991; Hon. DLitt CNAA, 1992. Valiant for Truth Media Award, 1977. *Publications:* Audacity to Believe, 1977; Prayer for Pilgrims, 1979; Sharing the Darkness, 1988; Good Friday People, 1991 (Collins Religious Book Award Special Prize, 1991); Light from the Dark Valley, 1994. *Recreations:* writing, sewing, creative pursuits, reading, TV. *Address:* 6 The Esplanade, The Hoe, Plymouth PL1 2PJ.

CASSILLY, Prof. Richard; operatic tenor; Professor, School of Fine Arts, Boston University, since 1986; *b* Washington, DC, 14 Dec. 1927; *s* of Robert Rogers Cassilly and Vera F. Swart; *m* 1st, 1951, Helen Koliopoulos; four *s* three *d*; 2nd, 1985, Patricia Craig. *Educ:* Peabody Conservatory of Music, Baltimore, Md. New York City Opera, 1955–66; Chicago Lyric, 1959–; Deutsche Oper, Berlin, 1965–; Hamburgische Staatsoper, 1966–; San Francisco Opera, 1966–; Covent Garden, 1968–; Staatsoper, Vienna, 1969–; La Scala, Milan, 1970–; Staatsoper, Munich, 1970–; Paris Opera, 1972–; Metropolitan Opera, NY, 1973–; *Television:* Otello, Peter Grimes, Fidelio, Wozzeck, Die Meistersinger; numerous recordings. Kammersänger, Hamburg, 1973; Distinguished Alumni Award, Peabody, 1977; Gold Medal, Acad. of Vocal Arts, Philadelphia, 1984. *Address:* c/o Boston University School of Fine Arts, 855 Commonwealth Avenue, Boston, Mass 02215, USA.

CASSIRER, Nadine, (Mrs Reinhold Cassirer); *see* Gordimer, N.

CASSON, (Frederick) Michael, OBE 1983; self-employed potter, since 1945 (first workshop, 1952); *b* 2 April 1925; *s* of William and Dorothy Casson; *m* 1955, Sheila Wilmot; one *s* two *d*. *Educ:* Tollington Grammar Sch.; Hornsey Coll. of Art (Art Teachers Dip.). First pots made 1945; has continued to make functional pots from opening of first workshop, 1952; at present making stoneware and porcelain pots fired with wood. Teaches part-time, all ages, 1946–; at present teaching history of ceramics and lecturing in USA. Founder member: Craftsmen Potters Assoc., 1958 (Chm., 1963–67); Harrow Studio Pottery Course, 1963; Vice-Chm., Crafts Council of GB, 1986–88. Presenter, The Craft of the Potter, BBC TV series, 1975. Trustee, Holburne Mus. and Craft Centre, Bath, 1993–. Gold Medal, Prague Internat. Acad. of Ceramic Art, 1964. *Publications:* Pottery in Britain Today, 1967; The Craft of the Potter, 1976, 2nd edn, 1980; many articles in Crafts, Ceramic Review, Ceramics Monthly (USA). *Recreation:* history - particularly the history of crafts. *Address:* Wobage Farm, Upton Bishop, near Ross-on-Wye, Herefordshire HR9 7QP. *T:* Upton Bishop (0198985) 233.

CASSON, Sir Hugh (Maxwell), CH 1985; KCVO 1978; Kt 1952; RA 1970; RDI 1951; MA Cantab; RIBA, FCSD; President of the Royal Academy, 1976–84; Professor of Environmental Design, 1953–75, Provost, 1980–86, Royal College of Art; Member, Royal Mint Advisory Committee, since 1972; *b* 23 May 1910; *s* of late Randal Casson, ICS; *m* 1938, Margaret Macdonald Troup (*see* Margaret MacDonald Casson); three *d*. *Educ:* Eastbourne Coll.; St John's Coll., Cambridge. Craven Scholar, British Sch. at Athens, 1933; in private practice as architect since 1937 with late Christopher Nicholson; served War of 1939–45, Camouflage Officer in Air Ministry, 1940–44; Technical Officer Ministry of Town and Country Planning, 1944–46; private practice, Sen. Partner, Casson Conder & Partners, 1946–76; Dir. of Architecture, Festival of Britain, 1948–51. Master of Faculty, RDI, 1969–71. Mem., Royal Fine Art Commn, 1960–83; Trustee: British Museum (Nat. Hist.), 1976–86; Nat. Portrait Gall., 1976–84; Mem. Bd, British Council, 1977–81. Mem., Royal Danish Acad., 1954; Hon. Associate, Amer. Inst of Architects, 1968; Hon. Mem., Royal Canadian Acad. of Arts, 1980. Hon. Dr: RCA 1975; Southampton, 1977; Hon. LLD, Birmingham, 1977; Hon. DLitt Sheffield, 1986. Hon. Fellow University Coll. London, 1983. Albert Medal, RSA, 1984. Italian Order of Merit, 1980. Regular contributor as author and illustrator to technical and lay Press. *Publications:* New Sights of London (London Transport), 1937; Bombed Churches, 1946; Homes by the Million (Penguin), 1947; (with Anthony Chitty) Houses-Permanence and Prefabrication, 1947; Victorian Architecture, 1948; Inscape: the design of interiors, 1968; (with Joyce Grenfell) Nanny Says, 1972; Diary, 1981; Hugh Casson's London, 1983; Hugh Casson's Oxford, 1988; Japan Observed, 1991; Hugh Casson's Cambridge, 1992; The Tower of London: an artist's portrait, 1993. *Recreation:* drawing. *Address:* 6 Hereford Mansions, Hereford Road, W2 5BA. *T:* (office) 0171–221 7774.

See also A. G. Moses.

CASSON, Margaret MacDonald, (Lady Casson); architect, designer; Senior Tutor, School of Environmental Design, Royal College of Art, retired 1974; *b* 26 Sept. 1913; 2nd *d* of James MacDonald Troup, MD, and Alberta Davis; *m* 1938, Hugh Maxwell Casson, *qv*, three *d*. *Educ:* Wychwood Sch., Oxford; Bartlett Sch. of Architecture, University Coll. London; Royal Inst. of British Architecture. Office of late Christopher Nicholson, 1937–38; private practice, S Africa, 1938–39; Designer for Cockade Ltd, 1946–51; Tutor, Royal Coll. of Art, 1952–72; private practice as Architect and Designer for private and public buildings and interiors, also of china, glass, carpets, furniture, etc. Design consultant to various cos; Member: Council for Design Council, 1967–73 (Chm. Panel for Design Council Awards for Consumer Goods, 1972); Three-Dimensional Design Panel of NCDAD, 1962–72 (Ext. Assessor for NCDAD, 1962–65); Council of RCA, 1970; Arts Council, 1972–75; Adv. Council of V&A Museum, 1975–80; Craft Adv. Cttee, 1976–82; Royal Soc. of Arts, 1977–82; Stamp Adv. Cttee, PO, 1980–; Design Cttee, London Transport, 1980–88; Council, Zoological Soc. of London, 1983–86. Mem. Bd of Governors: Wolverhampton Coll. of Art, 1964–66; West of England Coll. of Art, 1965–67; BFI, 1973–79. FSIAD; Sen. Fellow RCA; Hon. Fellow, Royal Acad., 1985. Art photographer (as Margaret MacDonald): exhibited: London 1984, 1985, 1986, 1993; RPS, Bath, 1989; Tokyo, 1989; NY, 1988, 1990, 1994. *Address:* 6 Hereford Mansions, Hereford Road, W2 5BA. *T:* 0171–727 2999.

See also A. G. Moses.

CASSON, Prof. Mark Christopher; Professor of Economics, University of Reading, since 1981; *b* 17 Dec. 1945; *s* of Stanley Christopher Casson and Dorothy Nowell Barlow; *m* 1975, Janet Penelope Close; one *d*. *Educ:* Manchester Grammar Sch.; Univ. of Bristol (BA 1st cl. hons 1966); Churchill Coll., Cambridge (graduate student). University of Reading: Lecturer in Economics, 1969; Reader, 1977; Head, Dept of Econs, 1987–94. Mem. Council, REconS, 1985–90. Fellow, Acad. of Internat. Business, 1993. *Publications:* Introduction to Mathematical Economics, 1973; (jtly) The Future of the Multinational Enterprise, 1976; Alternatives to the Multinational Enterprise, 1979; Youth Unemployment, 1979; Unemployment: a disequilibrium approach, 1981; The Entrepreneur: an economic theory, 1982; Economics of Unemployment: an historical perspective, 1983; (ed) The Growth of International Business, 1983; (jtly) The Economic Theory of the Multinational Enterprise: selected papers, 1985; (jtly) Multinationals and World Trade: vertical integration and the division of labour in world industries, 1986; The Firm and the Market: studies in multinational enterprise and the scope of the firm, 1987; Enterprise and Competitiveness: a systems view of international business, 1990; (ed) Entrepreneurship, 1990; (ed) Multinational Corporations, 1990; Economics of Business Culture: game theory, transaction costs and economic performance, 1991; (ed) Global Research Strategy and International Competitiveness, 1991; (ed) International Business and Global Integration, 1992; (ed jtly) Multinational Enterprise in the World Economy: essays in honour of John Dunning, 1992; (ed jtly) Industrial Concentration and Economic Inequality: essays in honour of Peter Hart, 1993; Entrepreneurship and Business Culture, 1995; The Organization of International Business, 1995. *Recreations:* collecting old books, studying old railways, visiting old churches. *Address:* 6 Wayside Green, Woodcote, Reading RG8 0QJ. *T:* (home) Checkendon (01491) 681483; (office) Reading (01734) 318227.

CASSON, Michael; *see* Casson, F. M.

CASTALDI, Dr Peter; Chief Medical Advisor, Department of Social Security and Director of Medical Services, Benefits Agency, since 1992; *b* 13 Jan. 1942; *s* of Frank and Sarah Jane Castaldi; *m* 1967, Joan Sherratt; one *s* one *d*. *Educ:* Grammar Sch. for Boys, Neath; Welsh Nat. Sch. of Medicine (MB, BCh 1966). Resident hosp. posts, N Wales, 1966–69; Principal in General Practice, Bangor, Gwynedd, 1969–79; MO 1979–84, SMO 1984–86, DHSS; PMO, DSS, 1986–92. CStJ 1993. *Recreations:* squash, swimming, armchair Rugby critic, St John Ambulance Brigade. *Address:* Room 4E 31, Quarry House, Leeds LS2 7UA. *T:* Leeds (0113) 232 4258.

CASTELL, William Martin, FCA; Chief Executive, Amersham International plc, since 1990; *b* 10 April 1947; *s* of William Gummer Castell and Gladys (*née* Doe); *m* 1971, Renice Mendelson; one *s* two *d*. *Educ:* St Dunstan's Sch.; City of London Coll. (BA). ACA 1974, FCA 1980. Various posts in marketing, finance and admin, Wellcome Foundn, 1975–86; Co-founding Dir, Biomedical Res. Centre, Vancouver, 1983; Man. Dir, Wellcome Biotech., 1984–87; Commercial Dir, Wellcome plc, 1987–89. Chm., Cttee on Design Bursaries Health and Envmt, RSA, 1986–88; Dep. Chm., 1988–94, Chm., 1994–, Design Dimension. Vis. Fellow, Green Coll., Oxford, 1993–. *Recreations:* international affairs, shooting, ski-ing, tennis. *Address:* Amersham International plc, Amersham Place, Little Chalfont, Bucks HP7 9NA. *T:* Little Chalfont (01494) 542000. *Club:* Athenæum.

CASTILLO, Rudolph Innocent, MBE 1976; first resident High Commissioner for Belize in Canada, 1990–93; Representative to International Civil Aviation Organisation, 1991–93; business consultant; *b* 28 Dec. 1927; *s* of late Justo S. and Marcelina Castillo; *m* 1947, Gwen Frances Powery; three *s* four *d*. *Educ:* St John's Coll., Belize. Training Assignments with BBC and COI, London. Lectr in Maths, Spanish and Hist., St John's Coll., 1946–52; Radio Belize: Announcer, 1952–53; Sen. Announcer, 1953–55; Asst Prog. Organizer, 1955–59; Govt Information Services: Information Officer, 1959–62; Chief Information Officer, 1962–74; Permanent Secretary: Agriculture, 1974–76; Education, 1976–79; Sec. to Cabinet, 1980–83; Chief of Protocol, 1981–83; first High Comr for Belize in London, and first Belize Ambassador to France, Fed. Republic of Germany, Holy See, EEC and Unesco, 1983–85; retired from public service, 1985. TV Commercial Productions (script writing, shooting supervision, voicing commentary). *Recreations:* photography, theatre, watercolour painting. *Address:* 29 Mahogany Street, Belmopan, Belize, Central America.

CASTLE, family name of **Baroness Castle of Blackburn.**

CASTLE OF BLACKBURN, Baroness *cr* 1990 (Life Peer), of Ibstone in the County of Buckinghamshire, **Barbara Anne Castle;** PC 1964; BA; Member (Lab) Greater Manchester West, European Parliament, 1984–89 (Greater Manchester North, 1979–84); Leader, British Labour Group, 1979–85, Vice-Chairman of Socialist Group, 1979–86, European Parliament; *b* 6 Oct. 1910; *d* of Frank and Annie Rebecca Betts; *m* 1944, Edward Cyril Castle (later Baron Castle (*d* 1979); no *c*. *Educ:* Bradford Girls' Grammar Sch.; St Hugh's Coll., Oxford. Elected to St Pancras Borough Council, 1937; Member Metropolitan Water Board, 1940–43; Editor, Town and County Councillor, 1936–40; Administrative Officer, Ministry of Food, 1941–44; Housing Correspondent and Affairs Adviser, Daily Mirror, 1944–45. MP (Lab) Blackburn, 1945–50, Blackburn East, 1950–55, Blackburn, 1955–79. Member of National Executive Cttee of Labour Party, 1950–79; Chm., Labour Party, 1958–59 (Vice-Chm. 1957–58). Minister of: Overseas Development, 1964–65; Transport, 1965–68; First Secretary of State and Sec. of State for Employment and Productivity, 1968–70; Sec. of State for Social Services, 1974–76. Hon. Fellow: St Hugh's Coll., Oxford, 1966; Bradford and Ilkley Community Coll., 1985; UMIST, 1991; Humberside Poly., 1991; York Univ., 1992. Hon. DTech: Bradford, 1968; Loughborough, 1969; Hon. LLD: Lancaster, 1991, Manchester, 1993. Cross of Order of Merit (FRG), 1990. *Publications:* part author of Social Security, edited by Dr Robson, 1943; The Castle Diaries 1974–76, 1980, vol. II, 1964–70, 1984, repr. in one vol., 1990; Sylvia and Christabel Pankhurst, 1987; Fighting All the Way (autobiog.), 1993. *Recreations:* poetry and walking. *Address:* House of Lords, SW1A 0PW.

CASTLE, Enid; JP; Principal, The Cheltenham Ladies' College, since 1987; *b* 28 Jan. 1936; *d* of Bertram and Alice Castle. *Educ:* Hulme Grammar Sch. for Girls, Oldham; Royal Holloway Coll., Univ. of London. BA Hons History. Colne Valley High Sch., Yorks, 1958–62; Kenya High Sch., Nairobi, 1962–65; Queen's Coll., Nassau, Bahamas, 1965–68; Dep. Head, Roundhill High Sch., Leicester, 1968–72; Headmistress: High Sch. for Girls, Gloucester, 1973–81; Red Maids' Sch., Bristol, 1982–87. Pres., GSA, 1990–91. JP Glos, 1989. *Recreations:* tennis, squash, bridge, choral music. *Address:* The Cheltenham Ladies' College, Cheltenham, Glos GL50 3EP.

CASTLE, Rt Rev. Merwyn Edwin; Bishop Suffragan of Cape Town, Southern Region, since 1994; *b* 2 Nov. 1942; *s* of Ernest Edwin and Catherine Castle. *Educ:* Federal Theol Seminary, Alice (DipTh). Ordained deacon, 1969, priest, 1970; Rector, Christ the King, Coronationville, 1977–82; Dean, Johannesburg, 1982–87; Rector: Gambleville, Uitenhage, 1987–90; Matroosfontein, Cape Town, 1990–92; Chaplain, Archbishop of Cape Town, 1992–93; Rector, St Saviour's, Claremont, 1993–94. *Recreations:* gardening, music, reading. *Address:* Bishopsholme, 18 Rue Ursula, Glenhaven 7530, S Africa. *T:* (21) 9514277, *Fax:* (21) 9514314.

CASTLE STEWART, 8th Earl, *cr* 1800 (Ireland); **Arthur Patrick Avondale Stuart;** Viscount Stuart, 1793; Baron, 1619; Bt 1628; *b* 18 Aug. 1928; 3rd but *e* surv. *s* of 7th Earl Castle Stewart, MC, and Eleanor May (*d* 1992), *er d* of late S. R. Guggenheim, New York; *S* father, 1961; *m* 1952, Edna Fowler; one *s* one *d*. *Educ:* Brambletye; Eton; Trinity Coll., Cambridge (BA). Lieut Scots Guards, 1949. FIMgt. *Heir:* *s* Viscount Stuart, *qv*. *Address:* Manor Farm, Babcary, Somerton, Somerset TA11 7DT. *T:* Somerton (01458)

223040; Stuart Hall, Stewartstown, Co. Tyrone BT71 5AE. *T:* Stewartstown (01868) 738208. *Club:* Carlton.

CASTLEMAINE, 8th Baron *cr* 1812; **Roland Thomas John Handcock,** MBE (mil.) 1981; *b* 22 April 1943; *s* of 7th Baron Castlemaine and Rebecca Ellen (*d* 1978), *o d* of William T. Soady, RN; *S* father, 1973; *m* 1st, 1969, Pauline Anne (marr. diss.), *e d* of John Taylor Bainbridge; 2nd, 1989, Lynne Christine, *e d* of Maj. Justin Michael Gurney, RAEC; one *s*. *Educ:* Campbell Coll., Belfast. psc, ph (cfs). Lt-Col, AAC, retd 1992. *Heir:* *s* Hon. Ronan Michael Edward Handcock, *b* 27 March 1989.

CASTLEMAN, Christopher Norman Anthony; corporate adviser; Executive Director, Financial Services, Standard Chartered Bank, since 1991; *b* 23 June 1941; *s* of late S. Phillips and of Mrs Joan S. R. Pyper; *m* 1st, 1965, Sarah Victoria (*née* Stockdale) (*d* 1979); one *s* one *d*; 2nd, 1980, Caroline Clare (*née* Westcott) (marr. diss. 1990); two *d*; 3rd, 1990, Suzy M. Diamond (*née* Twycross); one *s*. *Educ:* Harrow; Clare Coll., Cambridge (MA Law). Joined M. Samuel & Co. Ltd, 1963; General Manager, Hill Samuel Australia Ltd, 1970–72; Director, Hill Samuel & Co. Ltd, 1972; Man. Dir, Hill Samuel Group (SA) Ltd and Hill Samuel (SA) Ltd, 1978–80; Chief Executive: Hill Samuel Gp Plc, 1980–87; Blue Arrow PLC, 1987–88; Director: Macquarie Bank Ltd, 1985–92; Consolidated Gold Fields plc, 1988–89; Chairman: Nat. Investment Hldgs, 1988–90; Johnson Fry (formerly LIT) Holdings, 1991– (Chief Exec., 1989–91); ABP Holdings, 1991–. *Recreations:* sport, travel. *Address:* 1 Aldermanbury Square, EC2V 7SB. *T:* 0171–280 7008.

CASTLEREAGH, Viscount; Frederick Aubrey Vane-Tempest-Stewart; *b* 6 Sept. 1972; *s* and *heir* of 9th Marquess of Londonderry, *qv*.

CASTON, Geoffrey Kemp, CBE 1990; Vice-Chancellor, University of the South Pacific, 1983–92; *b* 17 May 1926; *s* of late Reginald and Lilian Caston, West Wickham, Kent; *m*; two *s* one *d*; *m* Judy Roizen, Berkeley, Calif. *Educ:* St Dunstans Coll.; (Major Open Scholar) Peterhouse, Cambridge (MA). First Cl. Pt 1 History; First Cl. Pt II Law (with distinction) and Geo. Long Prize for Jurisprudence, 1950; Harvard Univ. (Master of Public Admin. 1951; Frank Knox Fellow, 1950–51). Sub-Lt, RNVR, 1945–47. Colonial Office, 1951–58; UK Mission to UN, New York, 1958–61; Dept of Techn. Co-op., 1961–64; Asst Sec., Dept of Educn and Sci. (Univs and Sci. Branches), 1964–66; Jt Sec., Schools Council, 1966–70; Under-Secretary, UGC, 1970–72; Registrar of Oxford Univ. and Fellow of Merton Coll., Oxford, 1972–79; Sec.-Gen., Cttee of Vice-Chancellors and Principals, 1979–83. Sec., Assoc. of First Div. Civil Servants, 1956–58; Adv. to UK Delegn to seven sessions of UN Gen. Assembly, 1953–63; UK Rep. on UN Cttee on Non-Self-Governing Territories, 1958–60; UN Techn. Assistance Cttee, 1962–64; Mem., UN Visiting Mission to Trust Territory of Pacific Islands, 1961; Consultant, Commonwealth Secretariat, 1992–. Chm., SE Surrey Assoc. for Advancement of State Educn, 1962–64; UK Delegn to Commonwealth Educn Conf., Ottawa, 1964. Ford Foundn travel grants for visits to schools and univs in USA, 1964, 1967, 1970. Vis. Associate, Center for Studies in Higher Educn, Univ. of Calif, Berkeley, 1978–. Chairman: Planning Cttee, 3rd and 4th Internat. Curriculum Confs, Oxford, 1967, New York, 1968; Ford Foundn Anglo-American Primary Educn Project, 1968–70; Library Adv. Council (England), 1973–78; Nat. Inst. for Careers Educn and Counselling, 1975–83; DES/DHSS Working Gp on Under 5s Res., 1980–82; Vice-Chm., Educnl Res. Bd, SSRC, 1973–77; Member: Steering Gp, OECD Workshops on Educnl Innovation, Cambridge 1969, W Germany, 1970, Illinois 1971; Exec. Cttee, Inter-Univ. Council for Higher Educn Overseas, 1977–83; Council, Univ. of Papua New Guinea, 1984–92; Council, ACU, 1987–88; Governor, Centre for Educnl Development Overseas, 1969–70; Dep., Admin. Bd, Internat. Assoc. of Univs, 1990–. Bank of Hawaii Distinguished Lectr, 1992. Hon. LLD Dundee, 1982; Hon. DLitt Deakin, 1991. *Publications:* contribs to educnl jls. *Address:* 29 Kings Road, Uxbridge, Middx UB8 2NW. *T:* Uxbridge (01895) 252529.

CASTRO, Rev. Emilio Enrique; Pastor, Methodist Church, Montevideo; *b* Uruguay, 2 May 1927; *s* of Ignacio Castro and Maria Pombo; *m* 1951, Gladys Nieves; one *s* one *d*. *Educ:* Union Theol. Seminary, Buenos Aires (ThL); University of Basel (post graduate work, 1953–54); University of Lausanne (ThD 1984). Ordained, 1948; Pastor: Durazno and Trinidad (Uruguay), 1951–53; Central Methodist Church, La Paz, 1954–56; Central Methodist Church, Montevideo, 1957–65; concurrently Prof. of Contemp. Theol. Thought, Mennonite Seminary, Montevideo; Coordinator, Commn for Evangelical Unity in Latin America, 1965–72; Exec. Sec., S American Assoc. of Theol. Schools, 1966–69; Pres., Methodist Church in Uruguay, 1970–72; Dir, WCC Commn on World Mission and Evangelism, 1973–83; Gen. Sec., WCC, 1985–92. Chm., Fellowship of Christians and Jews in Uruguay, 1962–66; Moderator, Conf. on future of CCIA, Netherlands, 1967; Chm., WCC's Agency for Christian Literature Develt, 1970–72. Hon. DHL: Westmar Coll., USA, 1984; Holy Cross, Boston, 1988; Hon. DTh Geneva, 1992. *Publications:* Jesus the Conqueror, 1956; When Conscience Disturbs, 1959; Mission, Presence and Dialogue, 1963; A Pilgrim People, 1965; Reality and Faith, 1966; Amidst Evolution, 1975; Towards a Latin American Pastoral Perspective, 1973; Sent Free: Mission and Unity in the Perspective of the Kingdom, 1985; When we pray together, 1989; (ed and contrib.) Christian Century, 1971–75; (ed and contrib.) International Review of Mission, 1973–83; (ed) To the Wind of God's Spirit: Reflections on the Canberra Theme, 1990; A Passion for Unity, 1992; numerous articles in several languages. *Recreation:* basket ball. *Address:* Avenida 8 de Octubre 2739, CP 11600, Montevideo, Uruguay. *Fax:* (2) 472181.

CATCHPOLE, Nancy Mona, OBE 1987; Vice-Chairman of Governors, since 1992, and Chairman of Awards Committee, British Federation of Women Graduates Charitable Foundation (formerly Crosby Hall); *b* 6 Aug. 1929; *d* of George William Page and Mona Dorothy Page (*née* Cowin), New Eltham; *m* 1959, Geoffrey David Arthur Catchpole; one *s* one *d*. *Educ:* Haberdashers' Aske's Hatcham Girls' Sch.; Bedford Coll., Univ. of London. BA Hons (History). Asst mistress, Gravesend Grammar Sch. for Girls, 1952–56; i/c History, Ipswich High Sch. GPDST, 1956–62; part time lectr in History and General Studies, Bath Tech. Coll., 1977–. Sec., Bath Assoc. of University Women, 1970–75; Regional Rep. on Exec., BFUW, 1975–77, Vice-Pres., 1977–80, Pres., 1981–84. Women's National Commission: Co-Chairman, 1983–85; Immediate Past Co-Chairman, 1985–86; part-time Sec. with special responsibility for Women's Trng Roadshow prog., 1985–88; Actg Sec., March–Dec. 1988; Consultant to Industry Matters, 1989, and to RSA, 1989–94, for Women's Trng Roadshow prog. Vice-Chm., RSA Women's Adv. Gp, (formerly Women's Working Group for Industry Year 1986), 1985–. Chm., Bath Branch, Historical Assoc., 1993– (Sec., 1975–79); a Governor, Weston Infants' Sch., Bath, 1975–85 (Chm., 1981–83; Vice-Chm., 1983–86). Member: Managers, Eagle House Community Sch., Somerset CC, 1979–82; Case Cttee, Western Nat. Adoption Soc., 1975–77; Wessex RHA, 1986–90; Avon FHSA Service Cttee, 1990–. FRSA 1986. *Recreations:* listening, viewing, talking, writing. *Address:* 66 Leighton Road, Weston, Bath, Avon BA1 4NG. *T:* Bath (01225) 423338.

CATER, Antony John E., *see* Essex-Cater.

CATER, Douglass; writer and educator in USA, since 1968; President, Washington College, Chestertown, Maryland, 1982–90; Founding Fellow, and Trustee since 1982, Aspen Institute (Director, Programme on Communications and Society, 1970–76); *b* Montgomery, Ala, 24 Aug. 1923; *s* of Silas D. Cater and Nancy Chesnutt; *m* 1950, Libby Anderson; two *s* two *d*. *Educ:* Philip Exeter Acad. (grad.); Harvard Univ. (AB, MA). Served War, 1943–45, with OSS. Washington Editor, The Reporter (Magazine), 1950–63; Nat. Affairs Editor, 1963–64; Special Assistant: to Sec. of Army, 1951; to the President of the United States, 1964–68. Vice-Chm., The Observer, 1976–81. Consultant to Dir, Mutual Security Agency, 1952. Visiting Professor, 1959–: Princeton Univ.; Weslyan Univ., Middletown, Conn; Stanford Univ., etc. Guggenheim Fellow, 1955; Eisenhower Exchange Fellow, 1957; George Polk Meml Award, 1961; NY Newspaper Guild, Page One Award, 1961. Mem., Delta Sigma Chi. *Publications:* (with Marquis Childs) Ethics in a Business Society, 1953; The Fourth Branch of Government, 1959; Power in Washington, 1963; The Irrelevant Man, 1970. *Address:* c/o Washington College, Chestertown, Md 21620, USA.

CATER, Sir Jack, KBE 1979 (CBE 1973; MBE 1956); JP; Consultant, Hong Kong Nuclear Investment Co., since 1990 (Managing Director, 1987–89); Director, Guangdong Nuclear Power Joint Venture Co. Ltd, 1986–89 (First Deputy General Manager, 1985–86); *b* 21 Feb. 1922; *yr s* of Alfred Francis Cater and Pamela Elizabeth Dukes; *m* 1950, Peggy Gwenda Richards; one *s* two *d*. *Educ:* Sir George Monoux Grammar Sch., Walthamstow. Served War of 1939–45, Sqdn Ldr, RAFVR; British Military Administration, Hong Kong, 1945; joined Colonial Administrative Service, 1946, appointed Hong Kong; attended 2nd Devonshire Course, Oxford (The Queen's Coll.), 1949–50; various appts, incl. Registrar of Co-operative Societies and Director of Marketing, Dir of Agriculture and Fisheries, Dep. Economic Sec.; IDC 1966; Defence Sec./Special Asst to Governor/Dep. Colonial Sec. (Special Duties), 1967; Executive Dir, HK Trade Development Council, 1968–70; Director, Commerce and Industry, 1970–72; Secretary for Information, 1972; for Home Affairs and Information, 1973; Founding Commissioner, Independent Commn Against Corruption, 1974–78; Chief Secretary, Hong Kong, 1978–81; actg Governor and Dep. Governor on several occasions; MEC and MLC, variously 1970–81; Hong Kong Comr in London, 1982–84; Adviser to Consultative Cttee for the Basic Law, Hong Kong, 1986–90. Chairman: HG (Asia) Ltd, 1992– (Dir, Hoare Govett (Asia), 1990–92); Oriental Develt Co. Ltd, 1992–; Director: Hong Kong Cable Communications Ltd, 1990–92; The Scottish Asian Development Co. Ltd, 1990–; Hong Kong Inst. of Biotechnol./Syntex Ltd, 1991–; Television Broadcasts Ltd, 1992–; Television Entertainment (Holdings) Ltd, 1992–; Springfield Bank and Trust, 1994–; Consultant: Philips & Co., China and Hong Kong, 1990–92; Internat. Bechtel Inc., 1990–. Pres., Agency for Volunteer Service, Hong Kong, 1982–; Member: Internat. Bd of Dirs, United World Colls, UK, 1981–92; Court, Univ. of Hong Kong, 1982–; Bd of Govs, Hong Kong Baptist Univ., 1991–; Dir, Li Po Chun United World Coll. of Hong Kong, 1991–. Hon. DSSc Univ. of Hong Kong, 1982. *Recreations:* work, walking, bridge, reading, watching television. *Address:* (office) Hong Kong Nuclear Investment Co. Ltd, 147 Argyle Street, Kowloon, Hong Kong. *T:* Hong Kong 27608058; (home) 97 Kadoorie Avenue, Kowloon, Hong Kong. *T:* Hong Kong 27154004. *Clubs:* Hong Kong, Royal Hong Kong Jockey (Hong Kong).

CATER, Sir John Robert, (Sir Robin), Kt 1984; Chairman, Distillers Co. Ltd, 1976–83; *b* 25 April 1919; *s* of Sir John Cater; *m* 1945, Isobel Calder Ritchie; one *d*. *Educ:* George Watson's Coll., Edinburgh; Cambridge Univ. (MA). Trainee, W. P. Lowrie & Co. Ltd, 1946; James Buchanan & Co. Ltd, 1949: Dir 1950; Prodn Dir 1959; Prodn Asst, Distillers Co. Ltd, Edinburgh: Prodn Asst, 1959; Dir, 1967–83 (Mem., Management Cttee); Dep. Chm., 1975–76; Man. Dir, John Haig & Co. Ltd, 1965–70; Non-Exec. Dir, United Glass, 1969, Chm. 1972. *Recreations:* music, theatre, fishing, golf (Walker Cup team, 1955; played for Scotland, 1952–56). *Address:* Avernish, Elie, Fife, Scotland KY9 1DA. *Clubs:* New (Edinburgh); Royal and Ancient (St Andrews); The Golf House (Elie).

CATFORD, Sir (John) Robin, KCVO 1993; CBE 1990; Secretary for Appointments to the Prime Minister and Ecclesiastical Secretary to the Lord Chancellor, 1982–93; *b* 11 Jan. 1923; *er s* of late Adrian Leslie Catford and Ethel Augusta (*née* Rolfe); *m* 1948, Daphne Georgina, *o d* of late Col J. F. Darby, CBE, TD; three *s* one *d*. *Educ:* Hampton Grammar Sch.; Univ. of St Andrews (BSc); St John's Coll., Cambridge (DipAgric). Sudan Civil Service: Dept of Agriculture and Forests: Kordofan Province, 1946; Equatoria Province, 1948; Blue Nile Province (secondment to White Nile Schemes Bd), 1952–55; various posts in industry and commerce, mainly in UK, 1955–66; Home Civil Service: Principal, MAFF, 1966; sec. to Cttee of Inquiry on Contract Farming, 1971; Asst Sec., 1972; Under-Sec. (Agricultural Resources Policy and Horticulture), 1979; transferred to PM's Office, 1982. Member: Economic Development Cttee for Hotels and Catering, 1972–76; EDC for Agriculture, 1979–82. Mem. Chichester Dio. Synod, 1979–84 and 1988–90. Crafts Advr, Radcliffe Trust, 1993–. *Recreations:* sailing, theatre, avoiding gardening. *Address:* Priory Cottage, Priory Road, Chichester, West Sussex PO19 1NS. *T:* Chichester (01243) 783197. *Club:* United Oxford & Cambridge University.

CATHCART, family name of **Earl Cathcart.**

CATHCART, 6th Earl *cr* 1814; **Alan Cathcart,** CB 1973; DSO 1945; MC 1944; Viscount Cathcart, 1807; Baron Greenock (United Kingdom) and 15th Baron Cathcart (Scotland), 1447; Major-General; *b* 22 Aug. 1919; *o s* of 5th Earl and Vera, *d* of late John Fraser, of Cape Town; *S* father, 1927; *m* 1st, 1946, Rosemary (*d* 1980), *yr d* of late Air Commodore Sir Percy Smyth-Osbourne, CMG, CBE; one *s* two *d*; 2nd, 1984, Marie Isobel Lady Weldon. *Educ:* Eton; Magdalene Coll., Cambridge. Served War of 1939–45 (despatches, MC, DSO). Adjt RMA Sandhurst, 1946–47; Regimental Adjt Scots Guards, 1951–53; Brigade Major, 4th Guards Brigade, 1954–56; Commanding Officer, 1st Battalion Scots Guards, 1957; Lt-Col comd Scots Guards, 1960; Colonel AQ Scottish Command, 1962–63; Imperial Defence Coll., 1964; Brigade Comdr, 152 Highland Brigade, 1965–66; Chief, SHAPEX and Exercise Branch SHAPE, 1967–68; GOC Yorkshire District, 1969–70; GOC and British Comdt, Berlin, 1970–73; retd. A Dep-Chm. of Cttees and Dep. Speaker, House of Lords. Ensign, Queen's Body Guard for Scotland, Royal Company of Archers. Pres., ACFA, 1975–82; Dep. Grand Pres., British Commonwealth Ex-Services League, 1976–86. Pres., RoSPA, 1982–86. Cdre, RYS, 1974–80. GCStJ 1986 (KStJ 1985); Lord Prior, Order of St John of Jerusalem, 1986–88 (Vice Chancellor, 1984–86). *Heir:* *s* Lord Greenock, *qv*. *Address:* Moor Hatches, West Amesbury, Salisbury, Wilts SP4 7BH. *Clubs:* Brooks's; Royal Yacht Squadron (Cowes).

CATHERWOOD, Sir (Henry) Frederick (Ross), Kt 1971; Member (C) Cambridge and North Bedfordshire, European Parliament, 1984–94 (Cambridgeshire, 1979–84); *b* 30 Jan. 1925; *s* of late Stuart and of Jean Catherwood, Co. Londonderry; *m* 1954, Elizabeth, *er d* of late Rev. Dr D. M. Lloyd Jones, Westminster Chapel, London; two *s* one *d*. *Educ:* Shrewsbury; Clare Coll., Cambridge (Hon. Fellow, 1992). Articled Price, Waterhouse & Co.; qualified as Chartered Accountant, 1951; Secretary, Laws Stores Ltd, Gateshead, 1952–54; Secretary and Controller, Richard Costain Ltd, 1954–55; Chief Executive, 1955–60; Asst Managing Director, British Aluminium Co. Ltd, 1960–62; Managing Director, 1962–64; Chief Industrial Adviser, DEA, 1964–66; Dir-Gen., NEDC, 1966–71; Managing Dir and Chief Executive, John Laing & Son Ltd, 1972–74. European Parliament: Chm., Cttee for External Economic Relations, 1979–84; Dep. Chm., EDG, 1983–87; a Vice-Pres., 1989–91; Vice Pres., Foreign Affairs Cttee, 1992–94. British Institute of

Management, subseq. Institute of Management: Mem. Council, 1961–66, 1969–79; Vice-Chm., 1972; Chm., 1974–76; Vice-Pres., 1976–. Member of Council: NI Development Council, 1963–64; RIIA, 1964–77; BNEC, 1965–71; NEDC, 1964–71; Chm., BOTB, 1975–79. Vice-Pres., 1976, Pres., 1977, Fellowship of Independent Evangelical Churches; Chm. of Council, 1971–77, Pres., 1983–84, Univs and Colls Christian Fellowship (formerly Inter-Varsity Fellowship); Pres., Evangelical Alliance, 1992–; Mem., Central Religious Adv. Cttee to BBC and IBA, 1975–79. Hon. DSc Aston, 1972; Hon. DSc (Econ.) QUB, 1973; Hon. DUniv Surrey, 1979. *Publications:* The Christian in Industrial Society, 1964, rev. edn 1980 (On the Job, USA, 1983); The Christian Citizen, 1969; A Better Way, 1976; First Things First, 1979; God's Time God's Money, 1987; Pro Europe?, 1991; David: Poet, Warrior, King, 1993; At the Cutting Edge (memoirs), 1995. *Recreations:* music, gardening, reading. *Address:* Sutton Hall, Balsham, Cambridgeshire CB1 6DX. *T:* Cambridge (01223) 894017. *Club:* United Oxford & Cambridge University.

CATHERWOOD, Herbert Sidney Elliott, CBE 1979; former Chairman of Ulsterbus and Citybus; *b* 1929. *Educ:* Belfast Royal Academy, N Ireland. Chairman, Ulsterbus Ltd, from inception, 1967; Member, NI Transport Holding Co., 1968; became Director of Merger of Belfast Corporation Transport with Ulsterbus, 1972. Director: RMC Catherwood; Sea Ferry Parcels. Member: NE Area Board, Ulster Bank, 1976. *Address:* Boulderstone House, 917 Antrim Road, Templepatrick, Co. Antrim, N Ireland.

CATLIN, Brian Ernest Frederick; His Honour Judge Catlin; a Circuit Judge, since 1995; *b* 7 Feb. 1937; *s* of Ernest William Catlin and Winifred May Catlin (*née* White); *m* 1962, Patricia Ann Wheeldon; two *s* one *d*. *Educ:* Welwyn Garden City Grammar Sch. Served RN, 1955–57. Clerk, Bown Cotton & Bown, 1953–60; Clerk, Kidd Rapinet, 1960–67; admitted solicitor, 1967; Partner, Kidd Rapinet, 1969–84; Dist Judge, 1984–95; a Recorder, 1991–95. *Recreations:* golf, grandchildren, gardening, steeplechasing. *Address:* c/o Uxbridge County Court, 114 High Street, Uxbridge UB8 1DF. *T:* Uxbridge (01895) 230441. *Club:* Donnington Valley Golf.

CATLIN, John Anthony; Deputy Solicitor, Department of the Environment, since 1989 (Assistant Solicitor, 1984–89); *b* 25 Nov. 1947; *s* of John Vincent Catlin and Kathleen Glover Catlin (*née* Brand); *m* 1974, Caroline Jane Goodman; one *s* two *d*. *Educ:* Ampleforth Coll., York; Birmingham Univ. (LLB 1969). Solicitor of the Supreme Court, 1972. Articled Clerk, 1970–72, Asst Solicitor, 1972–75, Gregory Rowcliffe & Co.; Legal Asst, 1975–78, Sen. Legal Asst, 1978–84, Treasury Solicitor's Dept. *Recreations:* music, travel. *Address:* Department of the Environment, 2 Marsham Street, SW1P 3EB. *T:* 0171–276 4702.

CATLING, Hector William, CBE 1989 (OBE 1980); MA, DPhil, FSA; Director of the British School at Athens, 1971–89, retired; *b* 26 June 1924; *s* of late Arthur William Catling and Phyllis Norah Catling (*née* Vyvyan); *m* 1948, Elizabeth Anne (*née* Salter); two *s* one *d*. *Educ:* The Grammar Sch., Bristol; St John's Coll., Oxford (Hon. Fellow 1986). Casberd Exhbr, 1948, BA 1950, MA 1954, DPhil 1957. Served War, RNVR, 1942–46. At Univ.: undergrad. 1946–50, postgrad. 1950–54. Goldsmiths' Travelling Schol., 1951–53. Archaeological Survey Officer, Dept of Antiquities, Cyprus, 1955–59; Asst Keeper, Dept of Antiquities, Ashmolean Museum, Univ. of Oxford, 1959–64, Sen. Asst Keeper, 1964–71. Fellow, 1967–71, Supernumerary Fellow, 1991–, Linacre Coll., Oxford. Sanders Meml Lectr, Sheffield, 1979; Myres Meml Lectr, Oxford, 1987; Mitford Meml Lectr, St Andrews, 1989. Corresp. Mem., German Archaeological Inst., 1961; Hon. Mem., Greek Archaeological Soc., 1975 (Counsellor, 1987–). Hon. Dr Athens, 1987. *Publications:* Cypriot Bronzework in the Mycenaean World, 1964; contribs to jls concerned with prehistoric and classical antiquity in Greek lands. *Recreation:* ornithology. *Address:* Dunford House, Langford, Lechlade, Glos GL7 3LN. *Club:* Athenæum.

CATLING, Sir Richard (Charles), Kt 1964; CMG 1956; OBE 1951; KPM 1945; *b* 22 Aug. 1912; *y s* of late William Catling, Leiston, Suffolk; *m* 1951, Mary Joan Feyer (*née* Lewis) (*d* 1974). *Educ:* The Grammar School, Bungay, Suffolk. Palestine Police, 1935–48; Federation of Malaya Police, 1948–54; Commissioner of Police, Kenya, 1954–63 (despatches); Inspector General of Police, Kenya, 1963–64, Police Advr to Jordan Govt, 1971–75. Security/Safety Consultant to Guthrie Corp., London, 1965–88. Officer Brother, OStJ, 1956. Freeman, City of London, 1979. *Recreations:* reading, gardening. *Address:* Hall Fen House, Irstead, Norfolk NR12 8XT. *Club:* East India.

CATLOW, Prof. Charles Richard Arthur; Wolfson Professor of Natural Philosophy at Royal Institution of Great Britain, since 1989; *b* 24 April 1947; *s* of Rolf M. Catlow and Constance Catlow (*née* Aldred); *m* 1978, Carey Anne Chapman; one *s*. *Educ:* Clitheroe Royal Grammar School; St John's College, Oxford (MA, DPhil). Research Fellow, Oxford Univ., 1973–76; Lectr, Dept of Chemistry, UCL, 1976–85; Prof. of Physical Chemistry, Univ. of Keele, 1985–89. *Publications:* (jtly) Point Defects in Materials, 1988; ed jtly and contrib. to works on computational and materials sciences; papers in learned jls. *Recreations:* reading, music, walking. *Address:* Royal Institution of Great Britain, 21 Albemarle Street, W1X 4BS. *T:* 0171–409 2992. *Club:* Athenæum.

CATO, Sir Arnott Samuel, KCMG 1983; Kt 1977; President of the Senate of Barbados, 1976–86; *b* St Vincent, 24 Sept. 1912. *Educ:* St Vincent Grammar Sch. (St Vincent Scholar, 1930); Edinburgh Univ. (MB, ChB). Returned to St Vincent; Asst Resident Surgeon, Colonial Hosp., 1936–37; Ho. Surg., Barbados Gen. Hosp., 1937–41; private practice from 1941; Vis. Surgeon, Barbados Gen. Hosp., later Queen Elizabeth Hosp., and Chm. Med. Staff Cttee 1965–70. Past Pres., Barbados Br. BMA. Chm., Barbados Public Service Commn, 1972–76; (Prime Minister's Nominee) Senate of Barbados, following Gen. Election of Sept. 1976; Actg Governor Gen. for periods in 1976, 1980, 1981, 1983, 1984, 1985 and 1986. PC (Barbados) 1976–87. Hon. LLD, Univ. of West Indies, 1978. *Address:* Little Kent, Kent, Christ Church, Barbados.

CATO, Brian Hudson; Full-time Chairman of Industrial Tribunals, 1975–92, Regional Chairman, Newcastle upon Tyne, 1989–92; *b* 6 June 1928; *s* of Thomas and Edith Willis Cato; *m* 1963, Barbara Edith Myles; one *s*. *Educ:* LEA elem. and grammar schs; Trinity Coll., Oxford; RAF Padgate. MA Oxon, LLB London. RAF, 1952–54. Called to Bar, Gray's Inn, 1952; in practice NE Circuit, 1954–75; a Recorder of the Crown Court, 1974–75. Special Lectr (part-time) in Law of Town and Country Planning, King's Coll., now Univ. of Newcastle, 1956–75; Hon. Examnr, Inst. of Landscape Architects, 1960–75. Pres., N of England Medico-legal Soc., 1973–74. Corresp. Sec., Berwickshire Naturalists Club, 1992–. Freeman of City of Newcastle upon Tyne by patrimony; Mem. Plumbers', Hostmen's, Goldsmiths' and Colliers' Companies; Founder Mem. Scriveners' Co. (Clerk, 1992–). Freeman, City of London, 1985. Hon. ALI. *Recreations:* bibliomania, antiquarian studies, family life. *Address:* 2 Croft Place, Newton-by-the-Sea, Alnwick, Northumberland NE66 3DL. *T:* Embleton (01665) 576334.

CATO, Rt. Hon. (Robert) Milton, PC 1981; Barrister; Leader of the Opposition, St Vincent and the Grenadines, since 1984 (Prime Minister, 1979–84); *b* 3 June 1915; *m* Lucy Claxton. *Educ:* St Vincent Grammar Sch. Called to the Bar, Middle Temple, 1948; in private practice. Served War of 1939–45, Canadian Army. Leader, St Vincent Labour Party; Premier of St Vincent, 1967–72, 1974–79; former Minister of Finance. Mem., Kingstown Town Bd, 1952–59 (Chm., 1952–53); former Mem., Public Service Commn. A Governor, Caribbean Reg. Devlt Bank for St Vincent. Former Pres., St Vincent Cricket Assoc. *Address:* PO Box 138, Kingstown, St Vincent and the Grenadines. *Club:* Kingstown.

CATON, Dr Valerie, (Mrs D. M. Harrison); HM Diplomatic Service; Deputy Head of Mission, Stockholm, since 1993; *b* 12 May 1952; *d* of Robert Caton and Florence Amy Caton (*née* Aspden); *m* 1987, David Mark Harrison; one *s* one *d*. *Educ:* Blackburn High Sch. for Girls; Bristol Univ. (BA, PhD); Grad. Sch. of European Studies, Univ. of Reading (MA). Lectrice, Univ. of Sorbonne, Paris, 1977–78; Tutor in French, Exeter Univ., 1978–80; joined HM Diplomatic Service, 1980: FCO, 1980–82; second, later First Sec., EC Affairs, Brussels, 1982–84; (First Sec. (Chancery),) Paris, 1988–92. *Publications:* various articles in jls on works of French writer, Raymond Queneau. *Recreations:* reading, theatre, collecting humorous books, walking, riding. *Address:* c/o Foreign and Commonwealth Office, King Charles Street, SW1A 2AH.

CATOVSKY, Prof. Daniel, MD, DSc; FRCP, FRCPath; Professor of Haematology, Institute of Cancer Research, since 1988; Hon. Consultant, Royal Marsden Hospital, since 1988; *b* 19 Sept. 1937; *s* of Felix Catovsky and Ana Kabanchik; *m* 1960, Julia Margarita Polak, *qv*; two *s* one *d*. *Educ:* Faculty of Medicine, Buenos Aires Univ. (MD 1961); London Univ. (DSc Med. 1985). FRCPath 1986; FRCP 1990. Royal Postgraduate Medical School: Fellow, 1967–76; Hon. Sen. Lectr in Haematol. and Medicine, 1976–87; Prof. of Haematol Oncology, 1987–88; Consultant, Hammersmith Hosp., 1976–88. Vis. Prof., Mount Sinai Med. Sch., NY, 1981. Ham–Wasserman Lecture (first annual), Amer. Soc. of Hematology, 1984. *Publications:* The Leukemic Cell, 1981, 2nd edn 1991; (with A. Polliack) Chronic Lymphocytic Leukaemia, 1988; (with R. Foa) The Lymphoid Leukaemias, 1990. *Recreations:* walking, squash, films, theatre. *Address:* Royal Marsden Hospital, Fulham Road, SW3 6JJ. *T:* 0171–352 8171.

CATOVSKY, Julia Margaret, (Mrs Daniel Catovsky); *see* Polak, J. M.

CATTANACH, Bruce Macintosh, PhD, DSc; FRS 1987; Head of Genetics Division, MRC Radiobiology Unit, Chilton, since 1987; *b* 5 Nov. 1932; *s* of James and Margaretta Cattanach; *m* 1966, Margaret Bouchier Crewe; two *d*. *Educ:* King's Coll., Univ. of Durham (BSc, 1st Cl. Hons); Inst. of Animal Genetics, Univ. of Edinburgh (PhD, DSc). Scientific Staff, MRC Induced Mutagenesis Unit, Edinburgh, 1959–62, 1964–66; NIH Post Doctoral Res. Fellow, Biology Div., Oak Ridge Nat. Lab., Tenn, USA, 1962–64; Sen. Scientist, City of Hope Med. Centre, Duarte, Calif, 1966–69; Scientific Staff, MRC Radiobiology Unit, Chilton, Oxon, 1969–86. *Publications:* contribs to several learned jls on X-chromosome inactivation, sex determination, mammalian chromosome imprinting, and genetics generally. *Recreations:* squash; breeding, showing and judging pedigree dogs. *Address:* Down's Edge, Reading Road, Harwell, Oxon OX11 0JJ. *T:* Abingdon (01235) 835410.

CATTELL, George Harold Bernard; Group Managing Director, FMC, 1978–84; Chief Executive, NFU Holdings Ltd, since 1978; Director, Agricultural Credit Corporation, since 1980; *b* 23 March 1920; *s* of H. W. K. Cattell; *m* 1951, Agnes Jean Hardy; three *s* one *d*. *Educ:* Royal Grammar Sch., Colchester. Served Regular Army, 1939–58; psc 1954; despatches, Malaya, 1957; retired as Major, RA. Asst Director, London Engineering Employers' Assoc., 1958–60; Group Industrial Relations Officer, H. Stevenson & Sons, 1960–61; Director, Personnel and Manufacturing, Rootes Motors Ltd, 1961–68; Managing Director, Humber Ltd, Chm., Hills Precision Diecasting Ltd, Chm., Thrupp & Maberly Ltd, 1965–68; Dir, Manpower and Productivity Services, Dept of Employment and Productivity, 1968–70; Dir-Gen., NFU, 1970–78. Member Council: Industrial Soc. 1965–84; CBI, 1970–84. FRSA; FIMgt. AMN Federation of Malaya, 1958. *Recreations:* tennis, fishing. *Address:* Little Cheveney, Yalding, Kent ME18 6DY. *T:* Hunton (01622) 820365. *Club:* Institute of Directors.

CATTERALL, Dr John Ashley, OBE 1995; FIM, FInstP; Secretary and Chief Executive, The Institute of Materials, since 1991 (Secretary, Institute of Metals, 1988–91); *b* 26 May 1928; *s* of John William Catterall and Gladys Violet Catterall; *m* 1960, Jennifer Margaret Bradfield; two *s*. *Educ:* Imperial Coll. of Science and Technol., London (BSc, PhD, DIC). ARSM; FIM 1964; FInstP 1968; CEng 1978. National Physical Lab., 1952–74; Dept of Industry, 1974–81; Head, Energy Technology Div., and Dep. Chief Scientist, Dept of Energy, 1981–83; Sec., SERC, 1983–88. Inst. of Metals Rosenhain Medal for Physical Metallurgy, 1970. *Publications:* (with O. Kubaschewski) Thermochemical Data of Alloys, 1956; contrib. Philos. Mag., Jl Inst. of Physics, Jl Inst. of Metals. *Recreation:* reading. *Address:* 65 Hamilton Avenue, Pyrford, Woking, Surrey GU22 8RU. *T:* Byfleet (019323) 46707.

CATTERALL, John Stewart; Managing Director, Conferences and Training Ltd, since 1993; *b* 13 Jan. 1939; *s* of John Bernard and Eliza Catterall; *m* 1965, Ann Beryl Hughes; two *s*. *Educ:* Blackpool Tech. Coll. and Sch. of Art. Mem. CIPFA. Posts in local authorities, 1961–70; Management Accountant, Cambridgeshire and Isle of Ely CC, 1970–72, Chief Accountant, 1972–73; Asst County Treasurer, Financial Planning and Accounting, Cambs CC, 1973–76; Dist. Treasurer, Southampton and SW Hants DHA, 1976–78, Area Treasurer, 1978–82; Regional Treasurer, NE Thames RHA, 1982–85; Dep. Dir, Finance, NHS Mgt Bd, 1985–89; Head of Health Services, 1985–89, Head of Health Adv. Services, 1989, CIPFA. Chm. and Chief Exec., C International Ltd, 1990–92; Dir, Capita PLC, 1992–93. *Publications:* contribs to professional jls. *Recreations:* golf, swimming, reading. *Address:* Birkdale, Green Lane, Chilworth, Southampton SO1 7JW. *T:* Southampton (01703) 769402.

CATTERMOLE, Joan Eileen, (Mrs J. Cattermole); *see* Mitchell, Prof. J. E.

CATTO, family name of **Baron Catto.**

CATTO, 2nd Baron, *cr* 1936, of Cairncatto; Bt *cr* 1921; **Stephen Gordon Catto;** President, Morgan Grenfell Group plc, since 1987 (Chairman, Morgan Grenfell Group plc, 1980–87); Chairman, Yule Catto & Co. plc, since 1971; Director: News International plc, since 1969; Times Newspapers Holdings Ltd, since 1981, and other companies; *b* 14 Jan. 1923; *o s* of 1st Baron Catto and Gladys Forbes (*d* 1980), *d* of Stephen Gordon; *S* father 1959; *m* 1st, 1948, Josephine Innes (marr. diss. 1965), *er d* of G. H. Packer, Alexandria, Egypt; two *s* two *d*; 2nd, 1966, Margaret, *d* of J. S. Forrest, Dilston, Tasmania; one *s* one *d*. *Educ:* Eton; Cambridge Univ. Served with RAFVR, 1943–47. Dir, 1957, Chief Exec., 1973–74, and Chm., 1973–79, Morgan Grenfell & Co. Ltd; Chairman: Australian Mutual Provident Soc. (UK branch) 1972–91; Pearl Gp, 1989–91; Dir, The General Electric Co. plc, 1959–93. Member, Advisory Council, ECGD, 1959–65; part-time Mem., London Transport Bd, 1962–68; Mem., London Adv. Cttee, Hong Kong & Shanghai Banking Corp., 1966–80. Chm. Council, RAF Benevolent Fund, 1978–91; Trustee and Chm., Exec. Cttee, Westminster Abbey Trust, 1973–. *Heir: s* Hon. Innes Gordon Catto, *b* 7 Aug. 1950. *Address:* Morgan Grenfell Group plc, 23 Great Winchester Street, EC2P 2AX; 41 William Mews, Lowndes Square, SW1X 9HQ. *Clubs:* Oriental; Melbourne (Australia).

CATTO, Prof. Henry Edward; Professor of Political Science, University of Texas (San Antonio), since 1993; *b* 6 Dec. 1930; *s* of Henry E. Catto and Maurine H. Catto; *m* 1958, Jessica Hobby; two *s* two *d*. *Educ:* Williams Coll. (BA). Businessman, San Antonio, Texas, 1952–69; Dep. US Rep., Orgn of American States, 1969–71; US Ambassador to El Salvador, 1971–73; US Chief of Protocol, 1974–76; Consultant, Washington DC, 1977–81; Asst Sec. of Defense, 1981–83; Vice-Chm., H & C Communications, 1983–89; US Ambassador to UK, 1989–91; Dir, US Inf. Agency, 1991–93. *Recreations:* tennis, hiking, running, ski-ing, golf. *Address:* 110 East Crockett Street, San Antonio, TX 78205, USA.

CAULCOTT, Thomas Holt; management consultant; *b* 7 June 1927; *s* of late L. W. Caulcott and Doris Caulcott; *m* 1st, 1954, C. Evelyn Lowden (marr. diss. 1987); one *d* (and one *s* decd); 2nd, 1988, Jane Marguerite Allsopp. *Educ:* Solihull Sch.; Emmanuel Coll., Cambridge. Asst Principal, Central Land Bd and War Damage Commn, 1950–53; transferred to HM Treasury, 1953; Private Sec. to Economic Sec. to the Treasury, 1955; Principal, Treasury supply divs, 1956–60; Private Sec. to successive Chancellors of the Exchequer, Sept. 1961–Oct. 1964; Principal Private Sec. to First Sec. of State (DEA), 1964–65; Asst Sec., HM Treasury, 1965–66; Min. of Housing and Local Govt, 1967–69; Civil Service Dept, 1969–70; Under-Sec., Machinery of Govt Gp, 1970–73; Principal Finance Officer, Local Govt Finance Policy, DoE, 1973–76; Sec., AMA, 1976–82; Chief Exec., Birmingham City Council, 1982–88. Mem., S Shropshire DC, 1991–95 (Chm., Policy and Resources Cttee, 1993–94). Mem. Cttee of Mgt, Hanover Housing Assoc., 1988–94. Harkness Fellowship, Harvard and Brookings Instn, 1960–61; Vis. Fellow, Dept of Land Economy, Univ. of Cambridge, 1984–85; Hon. Fellow: Inst. of Local Govt Studies, Univ. of Birmingham, 1979–; Univ. of Central England (formerly Birmingham Polytechnic), 1990–. *Address:* 37 Lower Broad Street, Ludlow, Shropshire SY8 1PH. *T:* Ludlow (01584) 875154.

CAULFEILD, family name of **Viscount Charlemont.**

CAULFIELD, Ian George; Clerk of the Council and Chief Executive, Warwickshire County Council, and Clerk to the Warwickshire Lieutenancy, since 1986; *b* 14 Dec. 1942; *s* of William and Elizabeth Caulfield; *m* 1967, Geraldine Mary Hind; three *s*. *Educ:* Liverpool Inst. High Schs for Boys; Univ. of Manchester (BA Hons Geography); Liverpool Poly. (DipTP). Jun. Planning Assistant, Liverpool City, 1964–65; Planning Assistant, Lancs CC, 1965–69; Sen. Planning Officer, Hants CC, 1969–74; Asst Hd, Res. and Intelligence Unit, 1974–76, Prin. Assistant to Chief Exec., 1976–78, Oxford CC; Asst Exec., 1978–83, Dep. Clerk and Asst Chief Exec., 1983–86, Warwicks CC. *Publication:* (jtly) Planning for Change: strategic planning and local government, 1989. *Recreation:* sport, particularly soccer. *Address:* 52 Northumberland Road, Leamington Spa, Warwicks CV32 6HB. *T:* Leamington Spa (01926) 423625.

CAULFIELD, Patrick, RA 1993; artist; *b* London, 29 Jan. 1936; *s* of Patrick and Annie Caulfield; *m* 1968, Pauline Jacobs; three *s*. *Educ:* Acton Central Secondary Modern Sch.; Chelsea Sch. of Art; RCA (Sen. FRCA 1993). Served RAF, 1953–56. Taught at Chelsea Sch. of Art, 1963–71. First exhibited, FBA Galls, 1961; group exhibitions include: Whitechapel, Tate, Hayward, Waddington and Tooth Galls, and ICA, in London; Walker Art Gall., Liverpool; and exhibns in Paris, Brussels, Milan, NY, São Paulo, Berlin, Lugano, Dortmund, Bielefeld and Helsinki. One-man exhibitions include: Robert Fraser Gall., London, 1965, 1967; Robert Elkon Gall., NY, 1966, 1968; Waddington Galls, 1969, 1971, 1973, 1975, 1979, 1981, and 1985; Tate Gall. (retrospective), 1981; Serpentine Gall. (retrospective), 1992; also in Italy, France, Australia, Belgium, USA and Japan. Design for Party Game (ballet), Covent Garden, 1984. Work in public collections incl. Tate Gall.; V&A; Walker Art Gall., Liverpool; Whitworth Art Gall., and Manchester City Art Gall.; and museums and galls in GB, Australia, USA, W Germany and Japan. *Address:* c/o Waddington Galleries, 2 Cork Street, W1X 1PA; 6 Primrose Hill Studios, Fitzroy Road, NW1.

CAUSEY, Prof. Gilbert, FRCS; retired; Sir William Collins Professor of Anatomy, Royal College of Surgeons, Professor of Anatomy, University of London, and Conservator of Hunterian Museum, 1952–70; *b* 8 Oct. 1907; 2nd *s* of George and Ada Causey; *m* 1935, Elizabeth, *d* of late F. J. L. Hickinbotham, JP, and of Mrs Hickinbotham; two *s* three *d*. *Educ:* Wigan Grammar Sch.; University of Liverpool. MB, ChB (1st Hons.), 1930; MRCS, LRCP, 1930; FRCS 1933; DSc 1964; FDSRCS 1971. Gold Medallist in Anatomy, Surgery, Medicine, and Obstetrics and Gynæcology; Lyon Jones Scholar and various prizes. Member of Anatomical and Physiological Societies. Asst Surgeon, Walton Hospital, Liverpool, 1935; Lecturer in Anatomy, University College, London, 1948; Rockefeller Foundation Travelling Fellow, 1950. John Hunter Medal, 1964; Keith Medal, 1970. *Publications:* The Cell of Schwann, 1960; Electron Microscopy, 1962; contributions to various scientific texts and journals. *Recreation:* music. *Address:* Orchard Cottage, Bodinnick-by-Fowey, Cornwall PL23 1LX. *T:* Polruan (01726) 870433.

CAUSLEY, Charles Stanley, CBE 1986; poet; broadcaster; *b* Launceston, Cornwall, 24 Aug. 1917; *o s* of Charles Causley and Laura Bartlett. *Educ:* Launceston National Sch.; Horwell Grammar Sch.; Launceston Coll.; Peterborough Training Coll. Served on lower-deck in Royal Navy (Communications Branch), 1940–46. Literary Editor, 1953–56, of BBC's West Region radio magazines Apollo in the West and Signature. Awarded Travelling Scholarships by Society of Authors, 1954 and 1966. Mem., Arts Council Poetry Panel, 1962–66. Hon. Vis. Fellow in Poetry, Univ. of Exeter, 1973. FRSL 1958. Hon. DLitt Exeter, 1977; Hon. MA Open, 1982. Awarded Queen's Gold Medal for Poetry, 1967; Cholmondeley Award, 1971; Kurt Maschler Award, 1987; Ingersoll Prize, 1990. *Publications:* Hands to Dance (short stories), 1951, rev. edn as Hands to Dance and Skylark, 1979; *poetry:* Farewell, Aggie Weston, 1951; Survivor's Leave, 1953; Union Street, 1957; Peninsula (ed), 1957; Johnny Alleluia, 1961; Dawn and Dusk (ed), 1962; Penguin Modern Poets 3 (with George Barker and Martin Bell), 1962; Rising Early (ed), 1964; Modern Folk Ballads (ed), 1966; Underneath the Water, 1968; Figure of 8, 1969; Figgie Hobbin, 1971; The Tail of the Trinosaur, 1973; (ed) The Puffin Book of Magic Verse, 1974; Collected Poems 1951–1975, 1975; The Hill of the Fairy Calf, 1976; (ed) The Puffin Book of Salt-Sea Verse, 1978; The Animals' Carol, 1978; (ed) Batsford Book of Stories in Verse for Children, 1979; (trans.) 25 Poems by Hamdija Demirović, 1980; (ed) The Sun, Dancing, 1982; Secret Destinations, 1984; 21 Poems, 1986; (trans.) Kings' Children, 1986; Early in the Morning, 1986; Jack the Treacle Eater, 1987; A Field of Vision, 1988; The Young Man of Cury, 1991; Bring in the Holly, 1992; Collected Poems, 1992; All Day Saturday, 1994; Going to the Fair, 1994; Collected Poems for Children, 1995; *children's stories:* Three Heads made of Gold, 1978; The Last King of Cornwall, 1978; *verse plays:* The Gift of a Lamb, 1978; The Ballad of Aucassin and Nicolette, 1981; *libretti:* Jonah (music by William Mathias), 1990; St Martha and the Dragon (music by Phyllis Tate), 1991; contrib. to many anthologies of verse in Great Britain and America. *Recreations:* the theatre; European travel; the re-discovery of his native town; playing the piano with expression. *Address:* 2 Cyprus Well, Launceston, Cornwall PL15 8BT. *T:* Launceston (01566) 772731.

CAUTE, (John) David, MA, DPhil; writer; *b* 16 Dec. 1936; *m* 1st, 1961, Catherine Shuckburgh (marr. diss. 1970); two *s*; 2nd, 1973, Martha Bates; two *d*. *Educ:* Edinburgh Academy; Wellington; Wadham Coll., Oxford. Scholar of St Antony's Coll., 1959. Spent a year in the Army in the Gold Coast, 1955–56, and a year at Harvard Univ. on a Henry Fellowship, 1960–61. Fellow of All Souls Coll., Oxford, 1959–65; Visiting Professor, New York Univ. and Columbia Univ., 1966–67; Reader in Social and Political Theory, Brunel Univ., 1967–70. Regents' Lectr, Univ. of Calif., 1974; Vis. Prof., Bristol Univ., 1985. Literary Editor, New Statesman, 1979–80. Co-Chm., Writers' Guild, 1981–82; Chm., Sinclair Fiction Prize, 1984. *Plays:* Songs for an Autumn Rifle, staged by Oxford Theatre Group at Edinburgh, 1961; The Demonstration, Nottingham Playhouse, 1969; The Fourth World, Royal Court, 1973; Brecht and Company, BBC TV, 1979; BBC Radio: Fallout, 1972; The Zimbabwe Tapes, 1983; Henry and the Dogs, 1986; Sanctions, 1988. *Publications:* At Fever Pitch (novel), 1959 (Authors' Club Award and John Llewelyn Rhys Prize, 1960); Comrade Jacob (novel), 1961; Communism and the French Intellectuals, 1914–1960, 1964; The Left in Europe Since 1789, 1966; The Decline of the West (novel), 1966; Essential Writings of Karl Marx (ed), 1967; Fanon, 1970; The Confrontation: a trilogy, 1971 (consisting of The Demonstration (play), 1970; The Occupation (novel), 1971; The Illusion, 1971); The Fellow-Travellers, 1973, rev. edn 1988; Collisions, 1974; Cuba, Yes?, 1974; The Great Fear: the anti-communist purge under Truman and Eisenhower, 1978; Under the Skin: the Death of White Rhodesia, 1983; The K-Factor (novel), 1983; The Espionage of the Saints, 1986; News from Nowhere (novel), 1986; Sixty Eight: the year of the barricades, 1988; Veronica or the Two Nations (novel), 1989; The Women's Hour (novel), 1991; Joseph Losey, 1994; Dr Orwell and Mr Blair (novel), 1994; *as John Salisbury: novels:* The Baby-Sitters, 1978; Moscow Gold, 1980. *Address:* 41 Westcroft Square, W6 0TA.

CAUTHEN, Stephen Mark; jockey; *b* Covington, Kentucky, 1 May 1960; *e s* of Ronald (Tex) Cauthen and Myra Cauthen; *m* Amy Kathrine Roth Fuss; one *d*. Apprentice jockey, 1976, Churchill Downs, Kentucky; first win, Red Pipe, 1976; raced at Aqueduct and Santa Anita; champion jockey, USA, 1977; won US Triple Crown on Affirmed, 1978; moved to Lambourn, 1979; champion jockey, UK, 1984, 1985, 1987; races won include: with Tap on Wood, 2,000 Guineas, 1979; with Slip Anchor, Derby, 1985; with Oh So Sharp, Oaks, 1,000 Guineas and St Leger, 1985; with Reference Point, Derby, St Leger and King George V and Queen Elizabeth Diamond Stakes, 1987; with Diminuendo, Oaks, 1988; with Michelozzo, St Leger, 1989; with Old Vic, French Derby and Irish Derby, 1989; Champion Stakes 3 times (Cormorant Wood, Indian Skimmer, In the Groove); Grand Prix de St Cloud (Atcatanango, Diamond Shoal); Prix de Diane (Indian Skimmer). *Address:* 167 S Main Street, Walton, KY 41094, USA.

CAVALIERO, Roderick; Deputy Director General, British Council, 1981–88 (Assistant Director General, 1977–81); *b* 21 March 1928; *s* of Eric Cavaliero and Valerie (*née* Logan); *m* 1957, Mary McDonnell; one *s* four *d*. *Educ:* Tonbridge School; Hertford Coll., Oxford. Teaching in Britain, 1950–52; teaching in Malta, 1952–58; British Council Officer, 1958–88 (service in India, Brazil, Italy). Chm., Educnl and Trng Export Cttee, 1979–88; Dir, Open Univ. Educnl Enterprises, 1980–88; Pres., British Educnl Equipment Assoc., 1987–92. Mem., British Section, Franco-British Council, 1981–88. Trustee, Charles Wallace India Trust, 1981–. Mem. Council, British Sch. at Rome, 1989– (Chm., Management Cttee, 1991–); Trustee, St George's English Sch., Rome, 1979–. *Publications:* Olympia and the Angel, 1958; The Last of the Crusaders, 1960; The Independence of Brazil, 1993; Admiral Satan: the life and campaigns of Suffren, 1994. *Address:* 10 Lansdowne Road, Tunbridge Wells, Kent TN1 2NJ. *T:* Tunbridge Wells (01892) 533452.

CAVALLERA, Rt. Rev. Charles; *b* Centallo, Cuneo, Italy, 1909. *Educ:* International Missionary College of the Consolata of Turin; Pontifical Univ. of Propaganda Fide of Rome (degree in Missionology). Sec. to Delegate Apostolic of British Africa, 1936–40; Vice-Rector, then Rector, of Urban Coll. of Propaganda Fide of Rome, 1941–47; formerly Titular Bishop of Sufes; Vicar-Apostolic of Nyeri (Kenya), 1947–53; RC Bishop of Nyeri, 1953–64; RC Bishop of Marsabit, 1964–81. *Address:* Missioni Consolata, Viale Mura Aurelie 12, 00165 Rome, Italy.

CAVAN, 13th Earl of, *cr* 1647 (Ire.); **Roger Cavan Lambart;** Baron Cavan 1618; Baron Lambart 1618; Viscount Kilcoursie 1647; *b* 1 Sept. 1944; *s* of Frederick Cavan Lambart (*d* 1963) and Audrey May, *d* of Albert Charles Dunham. *Educ:* Wilson's School, Wallington, Surrey. *Address:* 34 Woodleigh Gardens, SW16.

Has not yet established his right to the peerage.

CAVANAGH, John Bryan; Dress Designer; Chairman and Managing Director, John Cavanagh Ltd, retired 1974; *b* 28 Sept. 1914; *s* of Cyril Cavanagh and Anne (*née* Murphy). *Educ:* St Paul's School. Trained with Captain Edward Molyneux in London and Paris, 1932–40. Joined Intelligence Corps, 1940, Captain (GS, Camouflage), 1944. On demobilisation, 1946, travelled throughout USA studying fashion promotion. Personal Assistant to Pierre Balmain, Paris, 1947–51; opened own business, 1952; opened John Cavanagh Boutique, 1959. Elected to Incorporated Society of London Fashion Designers, 1952 (Vice-Chm., 1956–59). Took own complete Collection to Paris, 1953; designed clothes for late Princess Marina and wedding dresses for the Duchess of Kent and Princess Alexandra. Gold Medal, Munich, 1954. *Recreations:* the theatre, swimming, travelling. *Address:* 10 Birchlands Avenue, SW12 8ND.

CAVE, Alexander James Edward, MD, DSc, FRCS, FLS; Emeritus Professor of Anatomy, University of London; *b* Manchester, 13 Sept. 1900; *e s* of late John Cave and Teresa Anne d'Hooghe; *m* 1st, 1926, Dorothy M. Dimbleby (*d* 1961); one *d*; 2nd, 1970, Catherine Elizabeth FitzGerald. *Educ:* Manchester High Sch.; Victoria University of Manchester. MB, ChB (distinction Preventive Medicine) 1923; MD (commendation) 1937; DSc, 1944; FRCS, 1959; DSc London, 1967. Senior Demonstrator (later Lecturer) in Anatomy, University of Leeds, 1924–34; Senior Demonstrator of Anatomy and Curator of Anatomical Museum, University College, London, 1934–35; Asst Conservator of Museum (1935–46), Arnott Demonstrator (1936–46), Arris and Gale Lectr (1932, 1941), Professor of Human and Comparative Anatomy (1941–46), and Wood Jones Medalist 1978, Royal College of Surgeons of England; Prof. of Anatomy, St Bartholomew's Hospital Medical Coll., University of London, 1946–67, now Mem., Bd of Govs. Mem., Bd of Trustees, Hunterian Collection. Stopford Lectr, 1967; Morrison Watson Research Fellow, 1961–72. Late Examiner in Anatomy, Universities of Cambridge, Malta, London and Ireland, Primary FRCS and English Conjoint Board; Fellow *hc* (formerly Council Mem. and Pres.), Linnean Society; Fellow and Hon. Res. Associate (late Vice-Pres. and Council Mem.) and Silver Medallist Zoological Society; Life-Member (late Council Mem., Hon. Secretary and Recorder, Vice-Pres.) Anatomical Soc.; Hon. Associate BM (Nat. Hist.). Liveryman, Soc. of Apothecaries. *Publications:* papers on human and mammalian morphology. *Address:* 18 Orchard Avenue, Church End, Finchley, N3 3NL. *T:* 0181–346 3340. *Club:* Athenæum.

CAVE, Sir Charles (Edward Coleridge), 4th Bt, *cr* 1896; JP; DL; *b* 28 Feb. 1927; *o s* of Sir Edward Charles Cave, 3rd Bt, and Betty (*d* 1979), *o d* of late Rennell Coleridge, Salston, Ottery St Mary; *S* father 1946; *m* 1957, Mary Elizabeth, *yr d* of late John Francis Gore, CVO, TD; four *s*. *Educ:* Eton. Lieut The Devonshire Regt, 1946–48. CC Devon, 1955–64; High Sheriff of Devonshire, 1969. JP Devon 1972, DL Devon 1977. FRICS.

Heir: *s* John Charles Cave [*b* 8 Sept. 1958; *m* 1984, Carey D., *er d* of John Lloyd, Langport, Somerset; two *s* one *d*]. *Address:* Sidbury Manor, Sidmouth, Devon EX10 0QE. *T:* Sidmouth (01395) 597207.

CAVE, Sir (Charles) Philip H.; *see* Haddon-Cave.

CAVE, John Arthur, FCIB; Chairman: Midland Bank Finance Corporation Ltd, 1975–79; Midland Montagu Leasing Ltd, 1975–79; Forward Trust Ltd, 1975–79; Director, Midland Bank Ltd, 1974–79; *b* 30 Jan. 1915; *s* of Ernest Cave and Eva Mary Cave; *m* 1937, Peggy Pauline, *y d* of Frederick Charles Matthews Browne; two *s* two *d*. *Educ:* Loughborough Grammar Sch. FCIB (FIB 1962). Served War, Royal Tank Regt, 1940–46. Entered Midland Bank, Eye, Suffolk, 1933; Manager, Threadneedle Street Office, 1962–64; Jt Gen. Man., 1965–72; Asst Chief Gen. Man., 1972–74; Dep. Chief Gen. Man., 1974–75. Dir, Midland Bank Trust Co. Ltd, 1972–76. Mem. Council, Inst. of Bankers, 1967–75 (Dep. Chm., 1973–75). Hon. Captain and Founder, Midland Bank Sailing Club (Cdre, 1967–75). *Recreation:* sailing. *Address:* Dolphin House, Centre Cliff, Southwold, Suffolk IP18 6EN. *T:* Southwold (01502) 722232. *Club:* Royal Norfolk and Suffolk Yacht (Lowestoft).

CAVE, Prof. Terence Christopher, FBA 1991; Professor of French Literature, Oxford University, since 1989; Fellow and Tutor in French, St John's College, Oxford, since 1972; *b* 1 Dec. 1938; *s* of Alfred Cyril Cave and Sylvia Norah (*née* Norman); *m* 1965, Helen Elizabeth Robb (marr. diss. 1990); one *s* one *d*. *Educ:* Winchester Coll.; Gonville and Caius Coll., Cambridge (MA; PhD). University of St Andrews: Assistant, 1962–63; Lectr, 1963–65; University of Warwick: Lectr, 1965–70; Sen. Lectr, 1970–72. Visiting Professor: Cornell Univ., 1967–68; Univ. of California, Santa Barbara, 1976; Univ. of Virginia, Charlottesville, 1979; Univ. of Toronto, 1991; Univ. of Alberta, 1992; Visiting Fellow: All Souls Coll., Oxford, 1971; Princeton Univ., 1984; Royal Norwegian Soc. of Scis and Letters, Trondheim, 1991 (Mem., 1993); Hon. Sen. Res. Fellow, Inst. of Romance Studies, Univ. of London, 1990. Mem., Academia Europaea, 1990. *Publications:* Devotional Poetry in France, 1969; Ronsard the Poet, 1973; The Cornucopian Text: problems of writing in the French Renaissance, 1979; Recognitions: a study in poetics, 1988; (trans.) Madame de Lafayette, The Princesse de Clèves, 1992; articles and essays in learned jls, collective vols, etc. *Recreations:* music, languages. *Address:* St John's College, Oxford OX1 3JP. *T:* Oxford (01865) 277345.

CAVE-BROWNE-CAVE, Sir Robert, 16th Bt, *cr* 1641; President of Seaboard Chemicals Ltd; *b* 8 June 1929; *s* of 15th Bt, and Dorothea Plewman, *d* of Robert Greene Dwen, Chicago, Ill; *S* father 1945; *m* 1st, 1954, Lois Shirley, (marr. diss. 1975), *d* of John Chalmers Huggard, Winnipeg, Manitoba; one *s* one *d*; 2nd, 1977, Joan Shirley, d of Dr Kenneth Ashe Peacock, West Vancouver, BC. *Educ:* University of BC (BA 1951). KSJ 1986. *Heir:* *s* John Robert Charles Cave-Browne-Cave, *b* 22 June 1957. *Address:* 20901–83 Avenue, RR11, Langley, BC V3A 6Y3, Canada.

CAVELL, John James; His Honour Judge Cavell; a Circuit Judge, since 1994; *b* 1 Oct. 1947; *s* of Eric Essery Cavell and Edith Emma Doreen (*née* Jose); *m* 1977, Philippa Julia Frances (*née* Kelly); one *s* one *d*. *Educ:* King Edward's Sch., Stourbridge; Churchill Coll., Cambridge (MA). Called to the Bar, Middle Temple, 1971. Practising Barrister on Midland and Oxford Circuit, 1971–94; a Recorder, 1991–94. *Recreations:* playing the piano, music generally, walking, bridge, gardening. *Address:* c/o Courts Administrator's Office, Kemley House, 2 Victoria Road, Stafford ST16 2AE.

CAVELL, Rt. Rev. John Kingsmill; Assistant Bishop, Diocese of Salisbury, since 1988; Hon. Canon, Salisbury Cathedral, since 1988; *b* 4 Nov. 1916; *o s* of late William H. G. Cavell and Edith May (*née* Warner), Deal, Kent; *m* 1942, Mary Grossett (*née* Penman) (*d* 1988), Devizes, Wilts; one *d*. *Educ:* Sir Roger Manwood's Sch., Sandwich; Queens' Coll., Cambridge (MA; Ryle Reading Prize); Wycliffe Hall, Oxford. Ordained May 1940; Curate: Christ Church, Folkestone, 1940; Addington Parish Church, Croydon, 1940–44; CMS Area Secretary, dio. Oxford and Peterborough, and CMS Training Officer, 1944–52; Vicar: Christ Church, Cheltenham, 1952–62, St Andrew's, Plymouth, 1962–72; Rural Dean of Plymouth, 1967–72; Prebendary of Exeter Cathedral, 1967–72; Bishop Suffragan of Southampton, 1972–84; Bishop to HM Prisons and Borstals, 1975–85. Hon. Canon, Winchester Cathedral, 1972–84. Proctor in Convocation; Member of General Synod (Mem., Bd for Social Responsibility, 1982–84); Surrogate. Chm., Home Cttee, CMS London; Chm., Sarum Dio. Readers' Bd, 1984–88. Chaplain, Greenbank and Freedom Fields Hosps, Plymouth; Member: Plymouth City Educn Cttee, 1967–72; City Youth Cttee; Plymouth Exec. Council NHS, 1968–72; Chairman: Hants Assoc. for the Deaf, 1972–84; Salisbury Diocesan Assoc. for the Deaf, 1988–91; Pres., Hants Genealogical Soc., 1979–84; Vice-Pres., Soc. of Genealogists. Life Fellow, Pilgrim Soc., Massachusetts, 1974. Patron, Southampton RNLI Bd, 1976–84. Governor: Cheltenham Colls of Educn; King Alfred's College of Educn, 1973–84; Croft House Sch., Shillingstone, 1986–88; Chairman: St Mary's Coll. Building Cttee, 1957–62; Talbot Heath Sch., Bournemouth, 1975–84; Queensmount Sch., Bournemouth, 1980–84. *Recreations:* historical research, genealogy, philately. *Address:* Strathmore, 5 Constable Way, West Harnham, Salisbury, Wilts SP2 8LN. *T:* Salisbury (01722) 334782.

CAVENAGH, Prof. Winifred Elizabeth, OBE 1977; JP; PhD, BScEcon; Professor of Social Administration and Criminology, University of Birmingham, 1972–76, now Emeritus; Barrister-at-Law; *d* of Arthur Speakman and Ethel Speakman (*née* Butterworth); *m* 1938, Hugh Cavenagh; one step *s*. *Educ:* London Sch. of Economics, Univ. of London. BSc Econ (London); PhD (Birm.). Called to the Bar, Gray's Inn, 1964. With Lewis's Ltd, 1931–38; Min. of Labour, 1941–45. Univ. of Birmingham, 1946–. Birmingham: City Educn Cttee (co-opted expert), 1946–66; City Magistrate, 1949– (Dep. Chm., 1970–78); Police Authority, 1970–78. Governor, Birmingham United Teaching Hosps (Ministerial appt, 1958–64); W Midlands Economic Planning Council, 1967–71; Indep. Mem. of Wages Councils; Home Office Standing Advisory Cttee on Probation, 1958–67; Lord Chancellor's Standing Adv. Cttee: on Legal Aid, 1960–71; on Training of Magistrates, 1965–73. Nat. Chm., Assoc. of Social Workers, 1955–57; Council, Magistrates Assoc. (co-opted expert), 1965–78; BBC Gen. Adv. Council, 1977–80; Chm., Industrial Tribunal, 1974–77; Hon. Mem., Internat. Assoc. of Juvenile and Family Courts (Vice-Pres., 1978–91). Visiting Prof., Univ of Ghana, 1971; Eleanor Rathbone Meml Lectr, 1976; Moir Cullis Lectr Fellowship, USA, 1977, Canada, 1980. *Publications:* Four Decades of Students in Social Work, 1953; The Child and the Court, 1959; Juvenile Courts, the Child and the Law, 1967; contrib. articles to: Public Administration, Brit. Jl Criminology, Justice of the Peace, Social Work To-day, etc. *Recreations:* theatre, music, films. *Address:* 25 High Point, Richmond Hill Road, Edgbaston, Birmingham B15 3RU. *T:* 0121–454 0109. *Club:* University Women's.

CAVENAGH-MAINWARING, Captain Maurice Kildare, DSO 1940; Royal Navy; Simpson (Piccadilly) Ltd, 1961–91; *b* 13 April 1908; *yr s* of Major James Gordon Cavenagh-Mainwaring, Whitmore Hall, Whitmore, Staffordshire; *m* Iris Mary, *d* of late Colonel Charles Denaro, OBE; one *s*. *Educ:* RN College, Dartmouth. Joint Services Staff College, 1951–52; HMS St Angelo and Flag Captain to Flag Officer, Malta, 1952–54; President, Second Admiralty Interview Board, 1955–56; Naval Attaché, Paris, 1957–60. ADC to the Queen, 1960. Retired from RN, 1960. Cross of Merit Sovereign Order, Knights of Malta, 1955; Comdr Légion d'Honneur, 1960. *Address:* 47 Cadogan Gardens, SW3 2TH. *T:* 0171–584 7870. *Club:* Naval and Military.

CAVENDISH, family name of **Barons Cavendish of Furness, Chesham,** of **Duke of Devonshire,** and of **Baron Waterpark.**

CAVENDISH OF FURNESS, Baron *cr* 1990 (Life Peer), of Cartmel in the County of Cumbria; **Richard Hugh Cavendish;** Chairman, Holker Estate Group of Companies (interests including agricultural and urban property, leisure, mineral extraction, export, construction and forestry), since 1971; *b* 2 Nov. 1941; *s* of late Richard Edward Osborne Cavendish and of Pamela J. Lloyd Thomas; *m* 1970, Grania Mary Caulfeild; one *s* two *d*. *Educ:* Eton. International banking, 1961–71. Dir, UK Nirex Ltd, 1993–. A Lord in Waiting (Govt Whip), 1990–92. Mem., Hist. Buildings and Monuments Commn for England, 1992–. Chm., Lancs & Cumbria Foundn for Med. Res., 1994–. Chm., Morecambe and Lonsdale Conservative Assoc., 1975–78. Chm. Governors, St Anne's Sch., Windermere, 1983–89. Mem., Cumbria CC, 1985–90. High Sheriff 1978, DL 1988, Cumbria. FRSA. *Recreations:* gardening, National Hunt racing, collecting drawings, reading, travel. *Address:* Holker Hall, Cark-in-Cartmel, Cumbria LA11 7PL. *T:* Flookburgh (015395) 58220. *Clubs:* Brooks's, Pratt's, White's, Beefsteak.

CAVENDISH, Lady Elizabeth (Georgiana Alice), LVO 1976; Extra Lady-in-Waiting to Princess Margaret, since 1951; Chairman, Cancer Research Campaign, since 1981; Member, Press Complaints Commission, since 1991; *b* 24 April 1926; *d* of 10th Duke of Devonshire, KG, and Lady Mary Cecil, GCVO, CBE (*d* 1988), *d* of 4th Marquess of Salisbury, KG, GCVO. *Educ:* private. Member: Advertising Standards Authority, 1981–91; Marre Cttee on Future of Legal Profession, 1986–89; Lay Mem., Disciplinary Cttee of Gen. Council of the Bar (formerly Senate of Inns of Court's Professional Conduct Cttee of Bar Council and Disciplinary Cttee Tribunal), 1983–. Chm., Bd of Visitors, Wandsworth Prison, 1970–73; Mem. Council, St Christopher's Hospice, Sydenham, 1991–. JP London, 1961; Chairman: N Westminster Magistrates' Court PSD, 1980–83; Inner London Juvenile Courts, 1983–86. *Address:* 19 Radnor Walk, SW3 4BP. *T:* 0171–352 0774; Moor View, Edensor, Bakewell, Derbyshire DE4 1PH. *T:* Baslow (01246) 2204.

See also Duke of Devonshire.

CAVENDISH, Maj.-Gen. Peter Boucher, CB 1981; OBE 1969; DL; retired; Chairman, Military Agency for Standardisation and Director, Armaments Standardisation and Interoperability Division, International Military Staff, HQ NATO, 1978–81; *b* 26 Aug. 1925; *s* of late Brig. R. V. C. Cavendish, OBE, MC (killed in action, 1943) and Helen Cavendish (*née* Boucher); *m* 1952, Marion Loudon (*née* Constantine); three *s*. *Educ:* Abberley Hall, Worcester; Winchester Coll.; New Coll., Oxford. Enlisted 1943; commnd The Royal Dragoons, 1945; transf. 3rd The King's Own Hussars, 1946; Staff Coll., Camberley, 1955; served Palestine, BAOR, Canada and N Africa to 1966; CO 14th/20th King's Hussars, 1966–69; HQ 1st British Corps, 1969–71; Comdt RAC Centre, 1971–74; Canadian Defence Coll., 1975; Sec. to Mil. Cttee and Internat. Mil. Staff, HQ NATO, 1975–78. Colonel, 14th/20th King's Hussars, 1976–81; Hon. Col, The Queen's Own Mercian Yeomanry, TAVR, 1982–87; Col Comdt, Yeomanry RAC TA, 1986–90. Mem., Peak Park Jt Planning Bd, 1982–91 (Vice-Chm., 1987–91). Chm., SSAFA/FHS Derbyshire, 1987–. FIMgt (FBIM 1979). High Sheriff, 1986–87, DL 1989, Derbys. *Recreations:* shooting, country pursuits, DIY. *Address:* The Rock Cottage, Middleton-by-Youlgrave, Bakewell, Derbys DE4 1LS. *T:* Matlock (01629) 636225.

CAWDOR, 7th Earl *cr* 1827; **Colin Robert Vaughan Campbell;** Baron Cawdor, 1796; Viscount Emlyn, 1827; *b* 30 June 1962; *s* of 6th Earl and of his 1st wife, Cathryn, *d* of Maj.-Gen. Sir Robert Hinde, KBE, CB, DSO; *S* father, 1993; *m* 1994, Lady Isabella Stanhope, *y d* of Earl of Harrington, *qv*. *Educ:* Eton; St Peter's College, Oxford. Member, James Bridal Meml Soc., London. *Heir:* *b* Hon. Frederick William Campbell, *b* 29 July 1965. *Address:* Cawdor Castle, Nairn, Scotland.

CAWDRON, George Edward; Provincial Stipendiary Magistrate for North East London, since 1993; *b* 24 Feb. 1943; 3rd *s* of William Edward Cawdron and Louise Kathleen (*née* Walker); *m* 1965, Linda Margaret Preest; two *d*. *Educ:* Arnos Sch. Called to the Bar, Inner Temple, 1974. Dep. Clerk to the Justices, Willesden Div., London, 1975–77; Clerk to the Justices, Dacorum Div., 1977–91, Dacorum and Watford Divs, 1991–93, Herts; County Trng Officer for magistrates and staff, Herts, 1980–93. *Recreations:* classic cars, swimming, golf, gardening. *Address:* Croft End, 23 Barncroft Road, Berkhamsted, Herts HP4 3NL. *T:* Berkhamsted (01442) 871112.

CAWLEY, family name of **Baron Cawley.**

CAWLEY, 3rd Baron, *cr* 1918; **Frederick Lee Cawley,** 3rd Bt, *cr* 1906; *b* 27 July 1913; *s* of 2nd Baron and Vivienne (*d* 1978), *d* of Harold Lee, Broughton Park, Manchester; *S* father 1954; *m* 1944, Rosemary Joan, *y d* of late R. E. Marsden; six *s* one *d*. *Educ:* Eton; New Coll., Oxford. BA Nat. Science (Zoology), 1935, MA 1942. Called to the Bar, Lincoln's Inn, 1938; practised at the Patent Bar, 1946–73. Served War of 1939–45 in Europe; Capt. RA Leicestershire Yeomanry (wounded). Mem. Woking UDC, 1949–57. Dep.-Chm. of Cttees, House of Lords, 1958–67; Mem., Jt Parly Cttees: Consolidation Bills, 1956–73; Delegated Legislation, 1972–73; Ecclesiastical, 1974; Chm. of many Private Bill Select Cttees. *Recreations:* gardening, shooting. *Heir:* *s* Hon. John Francis Cawley [*b* 28 Sept. 1946; *m* 1979, Regina Sarabia, *e d* of late Marqués de Hazas, Madrid; three *s* one *d*]. *Address:* Bircher Hall, Leominster, Herefordshire HR6 0AX. *T:* Yarpole (01568) 780218.

CAWLEY, Sir Charles (Mills), Kt 1965; CBE; Chief Scientist, Ministry of Power, 1959–67; a Civil Service Commissioner, 1967–69; *b* 17 May 1907; *s* of John and Emily Cawley, Gillingham, Kent; *m* 1934, Florence Mary Ellaline, *d* of James Shepherd, York; one *d*. *Educ:* Sir Joseph Williamson's Mathematical Sch., Rochester; Imperial Coll. of Science and Technology (Royal College of Sci.). ARCS, BSc (First Cl. Hons in Chem.), DIC; MSc; PhD; FRSC; DSc(London); SFInstF; FRSA; Fellow, Imperial Coll. of Science and Technology. Fuel Research Station, DSIR, 1929–53. Imperial Defence Coll., 1949. A Dir, Headquarters, DSIR, 1953–59. Chm., Admiralty Fuels and Lubricants Advisory Cttee, 1957–64. Melchett Medal, Inst. of Fuel, 1968. *Publications:* Papers in various scientific and technical journals. *Address:* 8 Glen Gardens, Ferring-by-Sea, Worthing, West Sussex BN12 5HG.

CAWLEY, Prof. Robert Hugh, PhD; FRCP, FRCPsych; Professor of Psychological Medicine, University of London, at King's College School of Medicine and Dentistry (formerly King's College Hospital Medical School), and Institute of Psychiatry, and Consultant Psychiatrist, King's College Hospital, 1975–89; now Emeritus Professor; *b* 16 Aug. 1924; *yr s* of Robert Ernest Cawley and Alice Maud (*née* Taylor); *m* 1985, Elizabeth Ann, *d* of Eugene Malachy Doris and Mary Doris (*née* Crummie). *Educ:* Solihull Sch.; Univ. of Birmingham (BSc Hons Zool., PhD, MB, ChB); Univ. of London (DPM). FRCP 1975; FRCPsych 1971, Hon. FRCPsych 1990. Univ. of Birmingham: Res. Scholar, 1947; Res. Fellow, 1949; Halley Stewart Res. Fellow, 1954; House Phys. and Surg., Queen Elizabeth Hosp., Birmingham, 1956–57; Registrar, then Sen. Registrar,

Bethlem Royal and Maudsley Hosps, 1957–60; Clin. Lectr, Inst. of Psych., 1960–62; Sen. Lectr and First Asst in Psych., Univ. of Birmingham, and Hon. Consultant, United Birm. Hosps and Birm. RHB, 1962–67; Phys., 1967–75, and Consultant Psychiatrist, 1967–89, Bethlem Royal and Maudsley Hosps. Consultant Advr (Psychiatry) to DHSS, 1984–89; Civilian Advr in Psychiatry to RAF, 1986–89. Mem., MRC, 1979–83 (Chm., Neurosciences Bd, 1979–81). Chief Examr, Royal Coll. of Psychiatrists, 1981–88. *Publications:* papers on biological, medical and psychiatric subjects in scientific books and jls. *Club:* Athenæum.

CAWS, Genevra Fiona Penelope Victoria, (Mrs J. W. O. Curtis); QC 1991; *b* 21 Feb 1949; *d* of Richard Byron Caws and Fiona Ruth Muriel Elton Caws; *m* 1985, James William Ockford Curtis, *qv*; one *d*. *Educ:* Notting Hill and Ealing High School; Lady Margaret Hall, Oxford (MA Jurisp.). Called to the Bar, Inner Temple, 1970. *Recreations:* fishing, ski-ing, sheep breeding. *Address:* 4/5 Gray's Inn Square, Gray's Inn, WC1R 5AY. *T:* 0171–404 5252.

CAWS, Richard Byron, CBE 1984; FRICS; Chairman, Caws & Morris Ltd, Chartered Surveyors, London, since 1987; Senior Property Adviser, BZW Property Advisory Group, since 1993; *b* 9 March 1927; *s* of Maxwell and Edith S. Caws; *m* 1948, Fiona Muriel Ruth Elton Darling; one *s* two *d* (and one *s* decd). FRICS 1949. Partner, Chartered Surveyors: Nightingale Page & Bennett, Kingston upon Thames, 1944–60; Debenham Tewson & Chinnocks, 1961–87. Sen. Consultant (Real Estate), Goldman Sachs Internat. Corp. (London), 1987–93. Crown Estate Comr, 1971–. Member: Commn for the New Towns, 1976– (Chm., Property Cttee, 1978–94; Dep. Chm., CNT Land, 1994–); Dobry Cttee on Review of the Dev. Control System, 1973–75; DoE Adv. Gp on Commercial Property Dev., 1973–77; DoE Property Adv. Gp, 1978–88. Dir, British Sailors' Soc., 1965–. Gov., Royal Agricl Coll., 1985–88; Mem. Council, Queen's Coll., Harley St, 1984–. Master, Worshipful Co. of Chartered Surveyors, 1982–83; Chm., Jun. Orgn, RICS, 1959–60. *Recreations:* sailing, travel. *Address:* 36 Mount Park Road, Ealing, W5 2RS. *Clubs:* Boodle's, Royal Thames Yacht, Little Ship.

See also G. F. P. V. Caws.

CAWSON, Prof. Roderick Anthony, MD; FDS, RCS and RCPS Glasgow; FRCPath; Professor (Hon. Consultant) and Head of Department of Oral Medicine and Pathology, United Medical and Dental Schools, Guy's Hospital, 1966–86, now Emeritus; *b* 23 April 1921; *s* of Capt. Leopold Donald Cawson and Ivy Clunies-Ross; *m* 1949, Diana Hall, SRN; no *c*. *Educ:* King's College Sch. Wimbledon; King's College Hosp. Med. Sch. MD (London); MB, BS, BDS (Hons) (London); FDS, RCS; FDS, RCPS Glasgow; MRCPath; LMSSA. Served RAF, 1944–48; Nuffield Foundn Fellow, 1953–55; Dept of Pathology, King's Coll. Hosp., Sen. Lectr in Oral Pathology, King's Coll. Hosp. Med. Sch., 1955–62; Sen. Lectr in Oral Pathology, Guy's Hosp. Med. Sch., 1962–66. Examinerships: Pathology (BDS) London, 1965–69; Univ. of Wales, 1969–71; Dental Surgery (BDS), Glasgow, 1966–70; BChD Leeds, 1966–70; Newcastle, 1967–71; FDS, RCPS Glasgow, 1967–86; BDS Lagos, 1975–; RCPath, 1984–87. Chairman: Dental Formulary Sub-cttee (BMA); Dental and Surgical Materials Cttee, Medicines Division, 1976–80; recently First Chm, Univ. Teachers' Gp (BDA). *Publications:* Essentials of Dental Surgery and Pathology 1962, 5th edn 1991; Medicine for Dental Students (with R. H. Cutforth), 1960; (with R. G. Spector) Clinical Pharmacology in Dentistry, 1975, 5th edn 1989; Aids to Oral Pathology and Diagnosis, 1981; (with C. Scully) Medical Problems in Dentistry, 1982, 3rd edn 1993; (with A. W. McCracken and P. B. Marcus) Pathology: the mechanisms of disease, 1982, 2nd edn 1989; (with A. W. McCracken) Clinical and Oral Microbiology, 1982; (with J. W. Eveson) Oral Disease: clinico-pathological correlations, 1987, 2nd edn 1993; numerous papers, etc, in med. and dental jls. *Recreations:* reading, music, gardening (reluctantly). *Address:* 40 Court Lane, Dulwich, SE21 7DR. *T:* 0181–693 5781.

CAWTHRA, Rear-Adm. Arthur James, CB 1966; Admiral Superintendent, HM Dockyard, Devonport, 1964–66; *b* 30 Sept. 1911; *s* of James Herbert Cawthra, MIEE, and Margaret Anne Cawthra; *m* 1959, Adrien Eleanor Lakeman Tivy, *d* of Cecil B. Tivy, MCh, Plymouth; one *s* (and one *s* decd). *Educ:* abroad. Joined Royal Navy, 1930; Imperial Defence Course, 1956; HMS Fisgard, 1958–59; Dir Underwater Weapons, Admiralty, 1960–63. Capt. 1955; Rear-Adm. 1964.

CAWTHRA, David Wilkinson, FEng, FICE; FIHT; Chief Executive, Miller Group Ltd, 1992–94; *b* 5 March 1943; *s* of Jack and Dorothy Cawthra; *m* 1967, Maureen Williamson; one *s* one *d*. *Educ:* Heath Grammar Sch., Halifax; Univ. of Birmingham (BSc Hons). Mitchell Construction Co., 1963–73; Tarmac Construction, 1973–78; Balfour Beatty Ltd, 1979–91; Chief Exec., Balfour Beatty, 1988–91. Dir, BICC, 1988–91. CIMgt. *Recreation:* hill walking. *Address:* Redhurst, 68 Ravelston Dykes, Edinburgh EH12 6HF. *Club:* Royal Automobile.

CAYFORD, Dame Florence Evelyn, DBE 1965; JP; Mayor, London Borough of Camden, 1969; *b* 14 June 1897; *d* of George William and Mary S. A. Bunch; *m* 1923, John Cayford (*d* 1989); two *s*. *Educ:* Carlton Road Sch.; St Pancras County Secondary Sch., Paddington Technical Institute. Alderman, LCC, 1946–52; Member: LCC for Shoreditch and Finsbury, 1952–64; GLC (for Islington) and ILEA, 1964–67. Chairman: Hospital and Medical Services Cttee LCC, 1948; (Health Cttee). Division 7, 1948–49, Division 2 in 1949; Health Cttee, 1953–60; Welfare Cttee, 1965, of LCC; Metropolitan Water Bd, 1966–67 (Vice-Chm., 1965–66). Mem. Hampstead Borough Council, 1937–65 (Leader of Labour Group, 1945–58), Councillor for Kilburn until 1945, Alderman, 1945–65; Chm., LCC, 1960–61; Chairman: (Hampstead), Maternity and Child Welfare Cttee, 1941–45, Juvenile Court Panel, 1950–62; Dep. Mayoress, Camden Borough Council, 1967–68. Probation Cttee, 1959–; Leavesden Hosp. Management Cttee, 1948–63; Harben Secondary Sch., 1946–61. Member: Co-operative Political Party (ex-Chm. and Sec.); Co-operative Soc.; Labour Party; National Institute for Social Work Training, 1962–65; Min. of Health Council for Training of Health Visitors, 1962–65; Min. of Health Council for Training in Social Work, 1962–65. Chm., YWCA Helen Graham Hse, 1972–. JP, Inner London, 1941–. Freeman, London Borough of Camden (formerly Borough of Hampstead), 1961. Noble Order, Crown of Thailand, 3rd Class, 1964. *Address:* 26 Hemstal Road, Hampstead, NW6 2AL. *T:* 0171–624 6181.

CAYGILL, Hon. David Francis; MP (Lab) St Albans, New Zealand, since 1978; Deputy Leader of the Opposition, since 1994; *b* 15 Nov. 1948; *s* of Bruce Allott Caygill and Gwyneth Mary Caygill; *m* 1974, Eileen Ellen Boyd; one *s* three *d*. *Educ:* St Albans Primary Sch.; Christchurch Boys' High Sch.; Univ. of Canterbury (BA, LLB). Pres., Univ. of Canterbury Students' Assoc., 1971. Barrister and Solicitor, 1974–78; Christchurch City Councillor, 1971–80; Minister of Trade and Industry, Minister of Nat. Develt, Associate Minister of Finance, 1984–87; Minister of Health, Dep. Minister of Finance, 1987–88; Minister of Finance, 1988–90. *Recreations:* collecting and listening to classical records, following American politics. *Address:* Parliament House, Wellington, New Zealand. *T:* (4) 719930. *Club:* St Albans Shirley.

CAYLEY, Sir Digby (William David), 11th Bt *cr* 1661; MA; Assistant Classics Master and Master i/c Shooting, Marlborough College, since 1994; *b* 3 June 1944; *s* of Lieut-Comdr W. A. S. Cayley, RN (*d* 1964) (*g g s* of 7th Bt), and Natalie Maud Cayley, BA (*d* 1994); *S* kinsman, 1967; *m* 1st, 1969, Christine Mary Gaunt (marr. diss. 1987); two *d*; 2nd, 1993, Cathryn Mary Russell, BA Cantab. *Educ:* Malvern Coll.; Downing Coll., Cambridge (MA). Assistant Classics Master: Portsmouth Grammar Sch., 1968–73; Stonyhurst Coll., 1973–81; dealer in antiques, 1981–89; Assistant Classics Master: Marlborough Coll., 1989–90; Abingdon Sch., 1990–94. *Recreations:* antique furniture, travel. *Heir: cousin* George Paul Cayley [*b* 23 May 1940; *m* 1967, Shirley Southwell, *d* of Frank Woodward Petford; two *s*]. *Address:* Morris House, Marlborough College, Marlborough, Wilts SN8 1PA. *T:* Marlborough (01672) 513188.

CAYLEY, Michael Forde; Director, Capital and Valuation Division, since 1991, and Financial Institutions Division, since 1994, Inland Revenue; *b* 26 Feb. 1950; *s* of Forde Everard De Wend Cayley and Eileen Lilian Cayley; *m* 1987, Jennifer Athalie Jeffcoate Lytle. *Educ:* Brighton Coll.; St John's Coll., Oxford (MA English). Admin Trainee, Inland Revenue, 1971–73; Private Sec. to Chm., Price Commn, 1973–75; Inland Revenue: Principal, 1975; Asst Sec., 1982; Under Sec., 1991. *Publications: poems:* Moorings, 1971; (ed) Selected Poems of Richard Crashaw, 1972; The Spider's Touch, 1973; poems and articles on modern poets in various mags. *Recreations:* piano-playing, choral singing, languages, walking, art, history, crosswords. *Address:* Inland Revenue, Somerset House, Strand, WC2R 1LB. *T:* 0171–438 7739.

CAYZER, family name of **Barons Cayzer** and **Rotherwick.**

CAYZER, Baron *cr* 1982 (Life Peer), of St Mary Axe in the City of London; **William Nicholas Cayzer;** Bt 1921; Chairman: British and Commonwealth Shipping Co. Ltd, 1958–87; Caledonia Investments PLC, 1958–94; *b* 21 Jan. 1910; *s* of Sir August Cayzer, 1st Bt, and Ina Frances (*d* 1935), 2nd *d* of William Stancombe, Blounts Ct, Wilts; *S* to father's baronetcy, 1943; *m* 1935, Elizabeth Catherine, *d* of late Owain Williams and *g d* of Morgan Stuart Williams, Aberpergwm, Glamorgan; two *d*. *Educ:* Eton; Corpus Christi Coll., Cambridge. Director: Clan Line Steamers Ltd, 1938–87 (Chm.); Cayzer, Irvine & Co. Ltd, 1939–87 (Chm.); Union-Castle Mail Steamship Co. Ltd and associated cos, 1956–87 (Chm.); Air Hldgs Ltd, 1962–87 (Chm.); Meldrum Investment Trust, 1971– (Chm.). Chm. Liverpool Steamship Owners Association, 1944–45; Pres. Chamber of Shipping of the UK, 1959; Pres. Inst. of Marine Engineers, 1963. Chairman: Gen. Council of Brit. Shipping, 1959; Chamber of Shipping's British Liner Cttee, 1960–63; Mem., MoT Shipping Adv. Panel, 1962–64; sometime Mem. Mersey Dock and Harbour Board; sometime Mem. National Dock Labour Board. Prime Warden, Shipwrights Company, 1969. *Heir* (to baronetcy): none. *Address:* The Grove, Walsham-le-Willows, Suffolk IP31 3AD. *T:* Walsham-le-Willows (01359) 259263; 95j Eaton Square, SW1W 9AQ. *T:* 0171–235 5551. *Club:* Brooks's.

See also M. K. B. Colvin.

CAYZER, Sir James Arthur, 5th Bt, *cr* 1904; *b* 15 Nov. 1931; *s* of Sir Charles William Cayzer, 3rd Bt, MP (*d* 1940), and Beatrice Eileen (*d* 1981), *d* of late James Meakin and Emma Beatrice (later wife of 3rd Earl Sondes); *S* brother, 1943. *Educ:* Eton. *Heir: cousin,* Baron Cayzer, *qv*. *Address:* Kinpurnie Castle, Newtyle, Angus PH12 8TW. *T:* Newtyle (01828) 650207. *Club:* Carlton.

CAZALET, Hon. Lady; Camilla Jane; *b* 12 July 1937; *d* of 6th Viscount Gage, KCVO, and Hon. Alexandra Imogen Clare Grenfell (*d* 1969); *m* 1965, Edward Stephen Cazalet, *qv*; two *s* one *d*. *Educ:* Benenden Sch. Dir, Lumley Cazalet, 1967–. Trustee, Glyndebourne Arts Trust, 1978–; Mem., Royal Nat. Theatre Bd, 1991–. *Recreations:* theatre, music, tennis. *Address:* 58 Seymour Walk, SW10 1NF. *T:* 0171–352 0401; Shaw Farm, Plumpton Green, near Lewes, Sussex BN7 3DG. *T:* Lewes (01273) 890207.

CAZALET, Hon. Sir Edward (Stephen), Kt 1988; DL; **Hon. Mr Justice Cazalet;** a Judge of the High Court of Justice, Family Division, since 1988; *b* 26 April 1936; *s* of late Peter Victor Ferdinand Cazalet and Leonora Cazalet (*née* Rowley); *m* 1965, Camilla Jane (*née* Gage) (*see* Hon. Lady Cazalet); two *s* one *d*. *Educ:* Eton Coll. (Fellow, 1989); Christ Church, Oxford (MA Jurisprudence). Called to the Bar, Inner Temple, 1960, Bencher, 1985. QC 1980; a Recorder, 1985–88; Family Division Liaison Judge for SE Circuit, 1990–. Chairman: Horserace Betting Levy Appeal Tribunal, 1977–88; Sussex Assoc. for Rehabilitation of Offenders, 1991–; CAB, Royal Courts of Justice, 1992–. Chm. Trustees, Charles Douglas-Home Award, 1986–. Trustee, Injured Jockeys' Fund, 1987–. DL E Sussex, 1989. *Recreations:* riding, ball games, chess. *Address:* Royal Courts of Justice, Strand, WC2A 2LL. *Clubs:* White's, Garrick, Wig and Pen.

CAZALET, Sir Peter (Grenville), Kt 1989; Chairman, APV plc, since 1989; Deputy Chairman, GKN, since 1989; *b* 26 Feb. 1929; *e s* of Vice-Adm. Sir Peter (Grenville Lyon) Cazalet, KBE, CB, DSO, DSC, and of Lady (Elise) Cazalet (*née* Winterbotham); *m* 1957, Jane Jennifer, *yr d* of Charles and Nancy Rew, Guernsey, CI; three *s*. *Educ:* Uppingham Sch., Uppingham, Rutland; Magdalene Coll., Cambridge (Schol.; MA Hons). General Manager, BP Tanker Co. Ltd, 1968; Regional Co-ordinator, Australasia and Far East, 1970; Pres., BP North America Inc., 1972–75; Director: Standard Oil Co. of Ohio, 1973–75; BP Trading Ltd, 1975; Peninsular & Oriental Steam Navigation Co., 1980–; Man. Dir, 1981–89, Dep. Chm., 1986–89, BP; Chm., BP Oil International, 1981–89. Dir, De La Rue Co., 1983–. Chm., Armed Forces Pay Review Body, 1989–93; Mem., Top Salaries Review Body, 1989–93. Vice-Pres., China British Trade Gp, 1993–; a Vice-Pres., ME Assoc.; Hon. Sec., King George's Fund for Sailors; Gov., Wellcome Trust Ltd, 1992– (Trustee, Wellcome Trust, 1989–92); Trustee, Uppingham Sch., 1976–; Mem., Gen. Cttee, Lloyd's Register of Shipping, 1981– (Mem. Bd, 1981–86). CBIM 1982. Liveryman: Tallow Chandlers' Co. (Master, 1991–92); Shipwrights' Co. *Recreations:* theatre, fishing. *Address:* APV plc, 1 Lygon Place, SW1W 0JR. *T:* 0171–730 7244. *Clubs:* Brooks's, Royal Wimbledon Golf, MCC.

CECIL, family name of **Baron Amherst of Hackney, Marquess of Exeter, Baron Rockley,** and **Marquess of Salisbury.**

CECIL, Baron; *see* Viscount Cranborne.

CECIL, Henry Richard Amherst; Trainer of Racehorses; *b* 11 Jan. 1943; *s* of late Hon. Henry Kerr Auchmuty Cecil and of Elizabeth Rohays Mary (who *m* 2nd, Sir Cecil Boyd-Rochfort, KCVO), *d* of Sir James Burnett, 13th Bt, CB, CMG, DSO; *m* 1st, 1966, Julia (marr. diss. 1990), *d* of Sir Noel Murless; one *s* one *d*; 2nd, 1992, Natalie Payne. *Educ:* Canford School. Commenced training under flat race rules, 1969; previously Assistant to Sir Cecil Boyd-Rochfort. Leading Trainer, 1976, 1978, 1979, 1982, 1984, 1985, 1987, 1988, 1990, 1993. *Publication:* On the Level (autobiog.), 1983. *Recreation:* gardening. *Address:* Warren Place, Newmarket, Suffolk CB8 8QQ. *T:* Newmarket (01638) 662387.

CECIL, Rear-Adm. Sir (Oswald) Nigel Amherst, KBE 1979; CB 1978; *b* 11 Nov. 1925; *s* of Comdr the Hon. Henry M. A. Cecil, OBE, RN, and the Hon. Mrs Henry Cecil; *m* 1961, Annette (CStJ 1980), *d* of Maj. Robert Barclay, TD, Bury Hill, near Dorking, Surrey; one *s*. *Educ:* Royal Naval Coll., Dartmouth. Joined Navy, 1939; served during War, 1939–45. In comd, HM MTB 521, 1946–48; Flag Lieut to Admiral, BJSM, Washington, 1950–52; Comdr, 1959; Chief Staff Officer, London Div. RNR, 1959–61; in comd: HMS Corunna, 1961–63; HMS Royal Arthur, 1963–66; Captain 1966; Staff of

Dep. Chief of Defence Staff (Operational Requirements), 1966–69; Captain (D) Dartmouth Trng Sqdn and in comd HMS Tenby and HMS Scarborough, 1969–71; Senior British Naval Officer, S Africa, Naval Attaché, Capetown, and in command HMS Afrikander, as Cdre, 1971–73; Dir, Naval Operational Requirements, 1973–75; Naval ADC to the Queen, 1975; Rear-Adm., 1975; NATO Comdr SE Mediterranean, 1975–77; Comdr British Forces Malta, and Flag Officer Malta, 1975–79; Lieut Gov., Isle of Man, and Pres. of Tynwald, 1980–85. County Pres. (IoW), St John Ambulance, 1991–; Vice Pres., RUKBA, 1991–; Vice Patron, Naval Officers Assoc. of S Africa, 1973–. FIMgt (FBIM 1980). KStJ 1980 (OStJ 1971). *Recreations:* racing, cricket, tennis. *Address:* c/o C. Hoare & Co., 37 Fleet Street, EC4P 4DQ. *Clubs:* White's, MCC.

CELA, Camilo José; Grand Cross, Order of Isabel la Católica; Spanish writer; *b* 11 May 1916; *s* of Camilo Cela and Camila (*née* Trulock Bertorini); *m* 1944, Maria del Rosario Conde Picavea (separated); one *s*. *Educ:* Univ. of Madrid. Has held various jobs including those of actor, bull fighter, painter, journalist and civil servant. Senator, Cortés, 1977–78. Founder, 1956, and Editor, 1956–79, Papeles de Son Armadans (literary jl). Asturias Prize, 1987; Nobel Prize for Literature, 1989. Grand Cross, Order of the Sun (Peru). *Publications: fiction:* La familia de Pascal Duarte, 1942; Pabellón de reposo, 1943; Nuevas andanzas y desventuras del Lazarillo de Tormes, 1944; La colmena, 1951; Timoteo el incomprendido, 1952; Santa Balbina, 37, gas en cada piso, 1952; Mrs Cadwell habla con su hijo, 1952; Café des artistas, 1953; La catira, 1955; El molino de viento, 1956; Tobogán de hambrientos, 1962; El ciudadano Iscariote Reclús, 1965; La familia del héroe o Discurso histórico de los últimos restos, 1965; Víspera, festividad y octava de San Camilo 1936 en Madrid, 1969; Oficio de tinieblas 5, 1973; Mazurca para dos muertos, 1983 (Nat. Literature Prize, 1984); Cristo Versus Arizona, 1988; Los Caprichos de Francisco de Goya y Lucientes, 1989; El asesinato del perdedor, 1994; La cruz de San Andrés, 1994; *short stories:* Esas nubes que pasan, 1945; El gallego y su cuadrilla, 1949; Nuevo retablo de Don Cristobita, 1957; Los viejos amigos, 1960; Gavillas de fábulas sin amor, 1962; Toreo de salón: farsa con acompañamiento de clamor y murga, 1963; El solitario y los sueños de Quesada de Rafael Zabaleta, 1963; Once cuentos de fútbol, 1963; Izas, rabizas y colipoterras: drama con acompañamiento de cachondeo y dolor de corazón, 1964; Nuevas escenas matritenses, 1965; Rol de cornudos, 1976; El espejo y otros cuentos, 1981; La bandada de palomas, 1987; El hombre y el mar, 1990; La sima de las penúltimas inocencias, 1993; *poetry:* Pisando la dudosa luz del día, 1945; Reloj de arena, reloj de sol, reloj de sangre, 1989; *plays:* Maria Sabina, 1967; El carro de heno o el inventor de la guillotina, 1969; *travel:* Viaje a la Alcarria, 1948; Del Miño al Bidasoa, 1952; Judíos, moros y cristianos, 1956; Primer viaje andaluz, 1959; Viaje al Pirineo de Lérida, 1965; Nuevo viaje a la Alcarria, 1986; Galicia, 1990; *non-fiction:* Diccionario secreto, 1968; *essays:* Mesa revuelta, 1945; Cajón de sastre, 1957; Cuatro figuras del 98, 1959; Garito de hospicianos o guirigay de imposturas y bambollas, 1963; Las compañías convenientes y otros fingimientos y cegueras, 1963; Al servicio de algo, 1969; Enciclopedia del erotismo, 1976; Los sueños vanos, los ángeles curiosos, 1979; Vuelta de hoja, 1981; Los vasos comunicantes, 1981; El juego de los tres madroños, 1983; El asno de Buridán, 1986; Cachondeos, escarceos y otros meneos, 1991; Desde el palomar de Hita, 1991; El camaleón soltero, 1992; El huevo del juicio, 1993; *memoirs:* Memorias, entendimientos y voluntades, 1993. *Address:* c/o Agencia Literaria Carmen Balcells, Diagonal 580, 08021 Barcelona, Spain.

CELAC, Sergiu; Ambassador of Romania to the Court of St James's, since 1990, and to Ireland, since 1991; *b* Bucharest, 26 May 1939; *s* of Nicolae and Elena Celac; *m* 1964, Rea-Silvia Casu. *Educ:* Bucharest Univ. Joined Foreign Service, 1961; Private Sec. to Dep. Foreign Minister, 1963–69; Dep. Dir, then Dir, Policy Planning, Min. of Foreign Affairs, 1969–74; interpreter at Presidency, 1974–78; reader, Scientific and Encyclopaedic Publishing House, 1978–89; Minister of Foreign Affairs, Dec. 1989–June 1990. Member: Nat. Council, Romanian Writers' Union, 1990–; Journalists' Soc. of Romania, 1991–; European Atlantic Gp, 1991–; Atlantic Council of UK, 1993–; IISS, 1994. Mem. Nat. Exec., Romanian Shooting and Fishing Sports Union, 1990 (Past Pres.). Mem., Rotary Club, London. *Publications:* studies and essays on political sci.; trans. novels and poetry from and into Russian and English. *Recreation:* shooting. *Address:* Romanian Embassy, 4 Palace Green, W8 4QD. *T:* 0171–937 9666; 1 Belgrave Square, SW1 8PH. *Club:* Arts.

CELIBIDACHE, Sergiu; Chief Conductor, Munich Philharmonic Orchestra, since 1979; Composer and Guest Conductor to leading orchestras all over the world; *b* Rumania, 28 June 1912; *s* of Demosthene Celibidache; *m* Maria Celibidache. *Educ:* Jassy; Berlin. Doctorate in mathematics, musicology, philosophy and Buddhist religion. Conductor and Artistic Dir, Berlin Philharmonic Orchestra, 1946–51. Member: Royal Acad. of Music, Sweden; Acad. of Music, Bologna. German Critics' Prize, 1953; Berlin City Art Prize, 1955; Grand Cross of Merit, Federal Republic of Germany, 1954. *Recreations:* skiing, water-skiing. *Address:* Munich Philharmonic Orchestra, 8000 Munich 2, Rindermarkt 3–4, Germany.

CENTRAL AFRICA, Archbishop of, since 1980; **Most Rev. Walter Paul Khotso Makhulu;** Bishop of Botswana, since 1979; *b* Johannesburg, 1935; *m* 1966, Rosemary Sansom; one *s* one *d*. *Educ:* St Peter's Theological Coll., Rosettenville; Selly Oak Colls, Birmingham. Deacon 1957, priest 1958, Johannesburg; Curate: Johannesburg, 1957–60; Botswana, 1961–63; St Carantoc's Mission, Francistown, Botswana, 1961–63; St Andrew's Coll., Selly Oak, Birmingham, 1963–64; Curate: All Saints, Poplar, 1964–66; St Silas, Pentonville, with St Clement's, Barnsbury, 1966–68; Vicar of St Philip's, Battersea, 1968–75; Secretary for E Africa, WCC, 1975–79; a President: WCC, 1983–91; All Africa Conf. of Churches, 1981–86. Hon. DD: Kent, 1988; Gen. Theol Seminary, NY, 1990. Officier, Ordre des Palmes Académiques (France), 1981. *Address:* PO Box 769, Gaborone, Botswana.

CHABAN-DELMAS, Jacques Pierre Michel; Commander Légion d'Honneur; Compagnon de la Libération; Deputy, Department of Gironde, 1946–93; Mayor of Bordeaux, 1947–93; *b* Paris, 7 March 1915; *s* of Pierre Delmas and Georgette Delmas (*née* Barrouin); *m* 1947 (2nd marr.), Mme Geoffray (*née* Marie Antoinette Iõn) (*d* 1970); two *s* two *d*; *m* 1971, Mme Micheline Chavelet. *Educ:* Lycée Lakanal, Sceaux; Faculté de Droit, Paris; Ecole Libre des Sciences Politiques (Dip.). Licencié en droit. Journalist with l'Information, 1933. Served War of 1939–45: Army, 1939–40 (an Alpine Regt); joined the Resistance; *nom de guerre* of Chaban added (Compagnon de la Libération, Croix de Guerre); attached to Min. of Industrial Production, 1941; Inspector of Finance, 1943; Brig.-Gen., 1944; Nat. Mil. Deleg. (co-ord. mil. planning) Resistance, 1944; Inspector Gen. of Army, 1944; Sec.-Gen., Min. of Inf., 1945. Deputy for Gironde (Radical), 1946. Leader of Gaullist group (Républicans Sociaux) in Nat. Assembly, 1953–56; also Mem. Consultative Assembly of Council of Europe; Minister of State, 1956–57; Minister of Nat. Defence, 1957–58; Pres., Nat. Assembly, France, 1958–69, 1978–81 and 1986–88; Prime Minister, June 1969–July 1972. Président: Communauté urbain de Bordeaux, 1983–; Conseil régional d'Aquitaine, 1985–. *Publications:* L'ardeur, 1975; De Gaulle, 1980; La Libération, 1984; Les Compagnons, 1986; Aliénor d'Aquitaine, 1987; Montaigne, 1992. *Address:* 1 rue de Sille, Paris 7e, France.

CHACKSFIELD, Air Vice-Marshal Sir Bernard, KBE 1968 (OBE 1945); CB 1961; CEng, FRAeS 1968; *b* 13 April 1913; *s* of Edgar Chacksfield, Ilford, Essex; *m* 1st, 1937, Myrtle, (*d* 1984), *d* of Walter Matthews, Rickmansworth, Herts; two *s* two *d* (and one *s* decd); 2nd, 1985, Mrs Elizabeth Beatrice Ody. *Educ:* Co. High Sch., Ilford; RAF, Halton; RAF Coll., Cranwell. Service: NW Frontier, 1934–37; UK, India, Burma, Singapore, 1939–45 (OBE); Air Min., 1945–48; Western Union (NATO), Fontainebleau, 1949–51; RAF Staff Coll., 1951–53; Fighter Command, 1954–55; Director, Guided Weapons (trials), Min. of Supply, 1956–58; IDC, 1959; SASO, Tech. Trg Comd, RAF, 1960; AOC No. 22 Group RAF Technical Training Command, 1960–62; Comdt-Gen., RAF Regiment and Inspector of Ground Defence, 1963–68; retired 1968. Chm., Burma Star Assoc. Council, 1977– (Vice-Chm., 1974–76). Chm., Bd of Management, Royal Masonic Hosp., 1988–92 (Mem., 1987–88); Chairman of Governors: Bedstone College, 1978–90 (Governor, 1970; Pres., 1991–); Wye Valley Sch. (formerly Deyncourt Sch.), 1978–89 (Governor, 1977). Order of Cloud and Banner with special rosette (Chinese), 1941. *Recreations:* scouting (HQ Comr, Air Activities, 1959–72; Chief Comr for England, 1968–77), sailing, fencing (Pres. RAF Fencing Union, 1963–68), gliding, travel, model aircraft (Pres. British Model Flying Assoc. (formerly Soc. Model Aircraft Engrs, GB), 1965–), modern Pentathlon (Pres., RAF Pentathlon Assoc., 1963–68), shooting (Chm. RAF Small Arms Assoc., 1963–68); swimming; youth work, amateur dramatics. *Address:* 8 Rowan House, Bourne End, Bucks SL8 5TG. *T:* Bourne End (01628) 520829. *Club:* Royal Air Force.

CHADWICK, Charles McKenzie, CBE 1992 (OBE 1984); British Council Director (formerly Representative), Poland, 1989–92; *b* 31 July 1932; *s* of late Trevor McKenzie Chadwick and of Marjorie Baron; *m* 1965, Evelyn Ingeborg Ihlenfeldt; one *s*. *Educ:* Charterhouse School; Trinity Coll., Toronto (BA). Army service, 1950–52; HMOCS Provincial Administration, Northern Rhodesia, 1958–64; Lectr, 1964–66, and Head, Administrative Training, 1966–67, Staff Trng Coll., Lusaka; British Council Officer, 1967–92; service in Kenya, Nigeria, Brazil, London; British Election Supervisor, Zimbabwe, 1980; British Council Rep., Canada, 1981–88. Member: Commonwealth Observer Gp, Ghanaian Presidential elections, 1992, Pakistan National elections, 1993; EU observer team, S African election, 1994. Chm., BBC English Summer Sch. Cttee, 1992–; Gov., Hampstead Sch., 1992–. *Address:* 25A Denning Road, NW3 1ST.

CHADWICK, Derek James, DPhil; CChem, FRSC; Director, Ciba Foundation, since 1988; *b* 9 Feb. 1948; *s* of Dennis Edmund and Ida Chadwick; *m* 1980, Susan Reid; two *s*. *Educ:* St Joseph's Coll., Blackpool; Keble Coll., Oxford (BA, BSc, MA, DPhil). FRSC 1982; MACS 1989. ICI Fellow, Cambridge Univ., 1972–73; Prize Fellow, Magdalen Coll., Oxford, 1973–77; Lectr and Sen. Lectr, Liverpool Univ., 1977–88. Member: Sci. Cttee, Louis Jeantet Foundn, Geneva, 1989–; Hague Club of European Foundn Dirs, 1989– (Sec., 1993–); Sci. Adv. Cttee, 1990–, Exec. Council, 1991– (Vice-Chm., 1994–), Assoc. of Med. Res. Charities. Mem., Soc. of Apothecaries, 1990. *Publications:* chapters in: Aromatic and Heteroaromatic Chemistry, 1979; Comprehensive Heterocyclic Chemistry, 1984; The Research and Academic Users' Guide to the IBM PC, 1988; Pyrroles, Pt 1, 1990; ed many vols in Ciba Foundn symposium series; many papers in chemistry jls, eg, Jl Chem. Soc., Tetrahedron, Tet. Letters, etc. *Recreations:* music, gardening. *Address:* 4 Bromley Avenue, Bromley, Kent BR1 4BQ. *T:* 0181–460 3332; The Ciba Foundation, 41 Portland Place, W1N 4BN. *T:* 0171–636 9456.

CHADWICK, Gerald William St John, (John Chadwick), CMG 1961; HM Diplomatic Service, retired; *b* 28 May 1915; *s* of late John F. Chadwick, Solicitor; *m* 1938, Madeleine Renée Boucheron (*d* 1991); two *s* one *d*. *Educ:* Lancing; St Catharine's Coll., Cambridge (open Exhibitioner). Asst Principal, Colonial Office, 1938; transf. Dominions Office, following demobilisation, 1940; Sec., Parl. Mission to Newfoundland, 1943; further missions to Newfoundland and Bermuda, 1946 and 1947; attended United Nations, 1949; Office of UK High Commission, Ottawa, 1949–52; Counsellor, British Embassy, Dublin, 1952–53; UK Delegn to NATO, Paris, 1954–56; Asst Sec., CRO, 1956; Asst Under-Sec. of State, CRO, 1960–66; first Dir, Commonwealth Foundn, 1966–80. Governor, Commonwealth Inst., 1967–80. Certificate of Merit, Canadian Historical Soc., 1968. *Publications:* The Shining Plain, 1937; Newfoundland: Island into Province, 1967; International Organisations, 1969; (ed jtly) Professional Organisations in the Commonwealth, 1976; The Unofficial Commonwealth, 1982; contrib. to A Decade of the Commonwealth 1955–64, 1966; numerous reviews and articles. *Recreation:* travel.

CHADWICK, Rt. Rev. Graham Charles; Assistant Bishop of Liverpool, since 1990; *b* 3 Jan. 1923; *s* of William Henry and Sarah Ann Chadwick; *m* 1955, Jeanne Suzanne Tyrell; one *s*. *Educ:* Swansea Grammar School; SOAS; Keble Coll., Oxford (MA); St Michael's Coll., Llandaff. RNVR, 1942–46. Deacon 1950, priest 1951; Curate, Oystermouth, Dio. Swansea and Brecon, 1950–53; Diocese of Lesotho, 1953–63; Chaplain, University Coll., Swansea, 1963–68; Senior Bursar, Queen's Coll., Birmingham, 1968–69; Diocesan Missioner, Lesotho, and Warden of Diocesan Training Centre, 1970–76; Bishop of Kimberley and Kuruman, 1976–82; Chaplain, St Asaph Cathedral, and Advr on Spirituality, Dio. of St Asaph, 1983–90. *Address:* 423 Eaton Road, West Derby, Liverpool L12 2AJ. *T:* 0151–228 2891.

CHADWICK, Helen; artist; *b* 18 May 1953. *Educ:* Brighton Poly.; Chelsea Sch. of Art. Solo exhibitions, 1990– include: Meat Lamps, Chicago and NY, 1990; Viral Landscapes, Canada, Germany and Mus. of Modern Art, Oxford, 1990; De Light, Philadelphia, 1991; Im Fleischgarten, Germany, 1992; Trophies, Austria, 1993; Effluvia, Germany, Spain and Serpentine Gall., 1994; Poesies, Austria, 1994; Bad Blooms, NY, 1995. *Address:* c/o Zelda Cheatle Gallery, 8 Cecil Court, WC2N 4HE. *T:* 0171–836 0506.

CHADWICK, Professor Henry, KBE 1989; DD; FBA 1960; MRIA; Master of Peterhouse, Cambridge, 1987–93 (Hon. Fellow, 1993); Regius Professor Emeritus of Divinity, University of Cambridge, 1983 (Regius Professor, 1979–83); *b* 23 June 1920; 3rd *s* of late John Chadwick, Barrister, Bromley, Kent, and Edith (*née* Horrocks); *m* 1945, Margaret Elizabeth, *d* of late W. Pemell Brownrigg; three *d*. *Educ:* Eton (King's Scholar); Magdalene Coll., Cambridge (Music Schol.). John Stewart of Rannoch Scholar, 1939. MusB. Asst Master, Wellington Coll., 1945; University of Cambridge: Fellow of Queens' Coll., 1946–58; Hon. Fellow, 1958; Junior Proctor, 1948–49. Regius Professor of Divinity and Canon of Christ Church, Oxford, 1959–69; Dean of Christ Church, Oxford, 1969–79 (Hon. Student, 1979); Pro-Vice-Chancellor, Oxford Univ., 1974–75; Delegate, OUP, 1960–79; Fellow, Magdalene Coll., Cambridge, 1979–87 (Hon. Fellow 1962). Fellow, Eton, 1976–79; Hon. Fellow: St Anne's Coll., Oxford, 1979; Trinity Coll., Cambridge, 1987. Gifford Lectr, St Andrews Univ., 1962–64; Birkbeck Lectr, Cambridge, 1965; Burns Lectr, Otago, 1971; Sarum Lectr, Oxford, 1982–83. Editor, Journal of Theological Studies, 1954–85. Member, Anglican-Roman Catholic International Commn, 1969–81 and 1983–90. Mem., Amer. Philosophical Soc.; For. Hon. Mem., Amer. Acad. Arts and Sciences; Correspondant de l'Académie des Inscriptions et des Belles Lettres, Institut de France; Mem., Société des Bollandistes, Brussels; Corresponding Member: Göttingen Acad. of Scis; Rhineland Acad. of Scis. Hon. DD, Glasgow, Yale, Leeds, Surrey, Manchester and Rome (Augustinianum); Hon. Teol Dr, Uppsala; D Humane Letters, Chicago. Humboldt Prize, 1983; Lucas Prize, Tübingen, 1991. Pour le mérite, Bonn, 1993. *Publications:* Origen, Contra Celsum, 1953, 3rd edn 1980; Alexandrian Christianity (with J. E. L. Oulton), 1954; Lessing's Theological Writings, 1956; The Sentences of

Sextus, 1959; Early Christian Thought and the Classical Tradition, 1966; The Early Church (Pelican), 1967, 2nd edn 1993; The Treatise on the Apostolic Tradition of St Hippolytus of Rome, ed G. Dix (rev. edn), 1968; Priscillian of Avila, 1976; Boethius, 1981; History and Thought of the Early Church, 1982; Augustine, 1986; (ed) Atlas of the Christian Church, 1987; Augustine's Confessions, 1991; Heresy and Orthodoxy in the Early Church, 1991; Tradition and Exploration, 1994; (contrib.) Oxford History of the Classical World, 1986; (contrib.) Oxford Illustrated History of Christianity, 1990. *Recreation:* music. *Address:* 46 St John's Street, Oxford OX1 2LH. *T:* Oxford (01865) 512814.

See also W. O. Chadwick.

CHADWICK, John; *see* Chadwick, G. W. St J.

CHADWICK, John, FBA 1967; MA; LittD; Perceval Maitland Laurence Reader in Classics, University of Cambridge, 1969–84; Hon. Fellow, Downing College, Cambridge, since 1984 (Collins Fellow, 1960–84); *b* 21 May 1920; *yr s* of late Fred Chadwick; *m* 1947, Joan Isobel Hill; one *s. Educ:* St Paul's Sch.; Corpus Christi Coll., Cambridge. Editorial Asst, Oxford Latin Dictionary, Clarendon Press, 1946–52; Asst Lectr in Classics, 1952–54, Lectr in Classics, 1954–66, Reader in Greek Language, 1966–69, Univ. of Cambridge. Corresponding Member: Deutsches Archäologisches Inst., 1957; Austrian Acad. of Scis, 1974; Associé étranger, Acad. des Inscriptions et Belles-Lettres, Institut de France, 1985; Pres., Swedenborg Soc., 1987–88. Hon. Councillor, Athens Archaeol Soc., 1988 (Hon. Fellow, 1974); For. Mem., Accademia Nazionale dei Lincei, 1992. Hon. Dr of Philosophical Sch., University of Athens, 1958; Hon. DLitt, Trinity Coll., Dublin, 1971; Hon. Dr: Université Libre de Bruxelles, 1969; Euskal Herriko Unibertsitatea, Vitoria, Spain, 1985; Univ. of Salzburg, 1990. Medal of J. E. Purkyně Univ., Brno, 1966; Ehrenzeichen für Wissenschaft und Kunst, Austria, 1992. Comdr, Order of the Phoenix, Greece, 1984. *Publications:* (jtly) The Medical Works of Hippocrates, 1950; (jtly) Documents in Mycenaean Greek, 1956, rev. edn 1973; The Decipherment of Linear B, 1958, 2nd edn 1967 (trans. into 12 languages); The Pre-history of the Greek Language (in Camb. Ancient History), 1963; The Mycenaean World, 1976 (trans. into 6 languages); (ed jtly) Corpus of Mycenaean Inscriptions from Knossos, Vol. I, 1986, Vol. II, 1990; Linear B and Related Scripts, 1987; (trans.) E. Swedenborg, The True Christian Religion, 1988; articles in learned jls on Mycenaean Greek. *Recreation:* travel. *Address:* 75 Gough Way, Cambridge CB3 9LN. *T:* Cambridge (01223) 356864.

CHADWICK, Hon. Sir John (Murray), Kt 1991; ED; **Hon. Mr Justice Chadwick;** a Judge of the High Court of Justice, Chancery Division, since 1991; *b* 20 Jan. 1941; *s* of Hector George Chadwick and Margaret Corry Laing; *m* 1975, Diana Mary Blunt; two *d. Educ:* Rugby School; Magdalene Coll., Cambridge (MA). Called to the Bar, Inner Temple, 1966, Bencher, 1986; QC 1980; Judge of Courts of Appeal of Jersey and Guernsey, 1986–93; a Recorder, 1989–91; Chancery Supervising Judge, Birmingham, Bristol and Cardiff, 1995–. *Recreation:* sailing. *Address:* Royal Courts of Justice, Strand, WC2A 2LL. *Clubs:* Athenæum, Beefsteak; Royal Yacht Squadron (Cowes).

CHADWICK, Sir Joshua Kenneth B.; *see* Burton-Chadwick.

CHADWICK, Lynn Russell, CBE 1964; sculptor since 1948; *b* 24 Nov. 1914; *s* of late Verner Russell Chadwick and Margery Brown Lynn; *m* 1942, Charlotte Ann Secord; one *s*; *m* 1959, Frances Mary Jamieson (*d* 1964); two *d*; *m* 1965, Eva Reiner; one *s. Educ:* Merchant Taylors' Sch. Architectural Draughtsman, 1933–39; Pilot, FAA, 1941–44. Exhibitions have been held in London, in various galleries, by the Arts Council and British Council; his works have also been shown in numerous international exhibitions abroad, including Venice Biennale, 1956 (Internat. Sculpture Prize). *Works in public collections:* Great Britain: Tate Gallery, London; British Council, London; Arts Council of Great Britain; Victoria and Albert Museum; Pembroke Coll., Oxford; City Art Gallery, Bristol; Art Gallery, Brighton; Whitworth Art Gallery, University of Manchester; France: Musée National D'Art Moderne, Paris; Holland: Boymans van Beuningen Museum, Rotterdam; Germany: Municipality of Recklinghausen; Staatliche Graphische Sammlung, Munich; Staatische Kunstmuseum, Duisburg; Sweden: Art Gallery, Gothenburg; Belgium: Musées Royaux des Beaux-Arts de Belgique, Brussels; Italy: Galleria D'Arte Moderna, Rome; Museo Civico, Turin; Australia: National Gallery of SA, Adelaide; Canada: National Gallery of Canada, Ottawa; Museum of Fine Arts, Montreal; USA: Museum of Modern Art, New York; Carnegie Institute, Pittsburgh; University of Michigan; Albright Art Gallery, Buffalo; Art Institute, Chicago; Chile: Inst. de Artes Contemporáneas, Lima. Commandeur des Arts et des Lettres (France), 1992; Order of Andres Bello, First Class (Venezuela), 1988. *Address:* Lypiatt Park, Stroud, Glos GL6 7LL.

CHADWICK, Owen; *see* Chadwick, W. O.

CHADWICK, Peter, PhD, ScD; FRS 1977; Professor of Mathematics, University of East Anglia, 1965–91, now Emeritus; *b* 23 March 1931; *s* of late Jack Chadwick and Marjorie Chadwick (*née* Castle); *m* 1956, Sheila Gladys Salter, *d* of late Clarence F. and Gladys I. Salter; two *d. Educ:* Huddersfield Coll.; Univ. of Manchester (BSc 1952); Pembroke Coll., Cambridge (PhD 1957, ScD 1973). Scientific Officer, then Sen. Scientific Officer, Atomic Weapons Res. Estabt, Aldermaston, 1955–59; Lectr, then Sen. Lectr, in Applied Maths, Univ. of Sheffield, 1959–65; Dean, Sch. of Maths and Physics, 1979–82, Leverhulme Emeritus Fellow, 1991–93, UEA. Vis. Prof., Univ. of Queensland, 1972. Member: Exec. Cttee, Internat. Soc. for Interaction of Mechanics and Maths, 1983–88; British Nat. Cttee for Theoretical and Applied Mechanics, 1969–75, 1985–89. Hon. Mem., British Soc. of Rheology, 1991. Jt Exec. Editor, Qly Jl of Mechanics and Applied Maths, 1965–72, Trustee, 1977–91. Hon. DSc Glasgow, 1991. *Publications:* Continuum Mechanics, 1976; numerous papers on theoretical solid mechanics and the mechanics of continua in various learned journals and books. *Address:* 8 Stratford Crescent, Cringleford, Norwich NR4 7SF. *T:* Norwich (01603) 451655.

CHADWICK, Robert Everard; Director, Leeds Permanent Building Society, 1974–86 (President, 1983–85); *b* 20 Oct. 1916; *s* of Robert Agar Chadwick and Aline Chadwick; *m* 1948, Audrey Monica Procter; two *s* one *d. Educ:* Oundle; Leeds Univ. (LLB). Served RA, 1939–46. Solicitor, 1938–82; Director: J. Hepworth & Son, 1946–81 (Chm., 1956–81); John Waddington, 1954–77 (Chm., 1969–77); Magnet Joinery, 1969–77; Robert Glew & Co., 1969–77; W Riding Reg. Bd, Barclays Bank, 1972–82. *Recreations:* hill walking, fishing. *Address:* Baxters Fold, Cracoe, Skipton, N Yorks BD23 6LB. *T:* Cracoe (01756) 730233. *Club:* Leeds (Leeds).

CHADWICK, (William) Owen, OM 1983; KBE 1982; FBA 1962; *b* 20 May 1916; 2nd *s* of John Chadwick and Edith (*née* Horrocks); *m* 1949, Ruth, *e d* of B. L. Hallward, *qv*; two *s* two *d. Educ:* Tonbridge; St John's Coll., Cambridge, and took holy orders. Fellow of Trinity Hall, Cambridge, 1947–56; Master of Selwyn Coll., Cambridge, 1956–83; Dixie Professor of Ecclesiastical History, 1958–68; Regius Prof. of Modern History, 1968–83; Vice-Chancellor, Cambridge Univ., 1969–71; Chancellor, UEA, 1985–94. Pres., British Academy, 1981–85. Chm., Archbishops' Commn on Church and State, 1966–70; Mem., Royal Commn on Historical MSS, 1984–91. Trustee, Nat. Portrait Gall., 1978–94 (Chm., 1988–94). Hon. Mem., American Acad. of Arts and Scis, 1977. Hon. FRSE. Hon. DD: St Andrews; Oxford; Wales; Hon. DLitt: Kent; Bristol; London; Leeds; Hon. LittD: UEA; Cambridge; Hon. Dr of Letters, Columbia; Hon. LLD Aberdeen. *Publications include:* John Cassian, 1950; From Bossuet to Newman, 1957; Victorian Miniature, 1960; The Reformation, 1964; The Victorian Church, 1966, 1971; The Secularization of the European Mind in the 19th Century, 1976; The Popes and European Revolution, 1981; Britain and the Vatican during the Second World War, 1986; Michael Ramsey, 1990; The Spirit of the Oxford Movement, 1990; The Christian Church in the Cold War, 1992. *Address:* 67 Grantchester Street, Cambridge CB3 9HZ.

See also Henry Chadwick.

CHADWICK-JONES, Prof. John Knighton, PhD, DSc(Econ); Professor of Psychology, Saint Mary's University, Halifax, Canada, since 1974; *b* 26 July 1928; *s* of Thomas Chadwick-Jones and Cecilia Rachel (*née* Thomas); *m* 1965, Araceli Carceller y Bergillos, PhD; two *s* one *d. Educ:* Bromsgrove Sch.; St Edmund Hall, Oxford (MA). PhD Wales, 1960; DSc(Econ) Wales, 1981. FBPsS. Scientific Staff, Nat. Inst. of Industrial Psychol., London, 1957–60; Lectr, then Sen. Lectr, in Industrial Psychol., UC, Cardiff, 1960–66; Reader in Social Psychol., Flinders Univ. of South Australia, 1967–68; Dir, Occupational Psychol. Res. Unit, UC, Cardiff, 1968–74; Mem., Exec. Cttee, Bd of Governors, Saint Mary's Univ., 1975–78. Canada Soc. Scis and Humanities Res. Council Leave Fellow: Darwin Coll., Cambridge, 1980–81; MRC Unit on Develt and Integration of Behaviour, Cambridge, 1984–85; Visiting Fellow: Clare Hall, Cambridge, 1982; Wolfson Coll., Cambridge, 1984–85; Wolfson Coll., Oxford, 1988–89; St Edmund's Coll., Cambridge, 1990–91. Dir, Cambridge Canadian Trust (Toronto), 1988–. Fellow: Amer. Psychol Assoc.; Canadian Psychol Assoc. *Publications:* Automation and Behavior: a social psychological study, 1969; Social Exchange Theory: its structure and influence in social psychology, 1976; (jtly) Brain, Environment and Social Psychology, 1979; Absenteeism in the Canadian Context, 1979; (jtly) Social Psychology of Absenteeism, 1982; articles in academic jls. *Address:* 1105 Belmont-on-the-Arm, Halifax, Nova Scotia B3H 1J2, Canada.

CHADWYCK-HEALEY, Sir Charles (Edward), 5th Bt *cr* 1919, of Wyphurst, Cranleigh, Co. Surrey and New Place, Luccombe, Somerset; Chairman, Chadwyck-Healey Ltd, since 1973; President: Chadwyck-Healey Inc., since 1975; Chadwyck-Healey France SA, since 1985; *b* 13 May 1940; *s* of Sir Charles Arthur Chadwyck-Healey, 4th Bt, OBE, TD, and of Viola, *d* of late Cecil Lubbock; *S* father, 1986; *m* 1967, Angela Mary, *e d* of late John Metson; one *s* two *d. Educ:* Eton; Trinity Coll., Oxford (MA). Hon. Pres., European Information Assoc., 1991–. *Heir: s* Edward Alexander Chadwyck-Healey, *b* 2 June 1972. *Address:* Manor Farm, Bassingbourn, Cambs SG8 5NX. *T:* Royston (01763) 242447. *Club:* Brooks's.

CHAILLY, Riccardo; conductor; Principal Conductor: Royal Concertgebouw Orchestra, Amsterdam, since 1988; *b* 20 Feb. 1953; *m* 1987, Gabriella Terragni; two *s. Educ:* Conservatory of Music, Perugia; St Cecilia, Rome; Giuseppe Verdi, Milan. Principal Conductor and Music Dir, Teatro Comunale, Bologna, 1986–93; has conducted world's leading orchestras, including Vienna and Berlin Philharmonic, Chicago Symphony and Cleveland; has performed in major opera houses, including: La Scala, Milan, Vienna State Opera, Covent Garden, Munich, Metropolitan Opera, NY. Numerous recordings. Grand Prix du Disque, Acad. Charles Cros, 1984, 1985, 1987, 1992, and other recording awards. *Address:* c/o IMG Artists Europe, Media House, 3 Burlington Lane, W4 2TH.

CHAIR, Somerset de; *see* de Chair.

CHAKAIPA, Most Rev. Patrick; *see* Harare, Archbishop of, (RC).

CHALDECOTT, John Anthony; Keeper, Science Museum Library, South Kensington, 1961–76; *b* 16 Feb. 1916; *o s* of Wilfrid James and Mary Eleanor Chaldecott; *m* 1940, Kathleen Elizabeth Jones; one *d. Educ:* Latymer Upper Sch., Hammersmith; Brentwood Sch.; Borough Road Coll., Isleworth; University College, London. BSc 1938, MSc 1949, PhD 1972. FInstP; CPhys. Meteorological Branch, RAFVR, 1939–45 (despatches). Lecturer, Acton Technical Coll., 1945–48; entered Science Museum as Asst Keeper, Dept of Physics, 1949; Deputy Keeper and Secretary to Advisory Council, 1957. Pres., British Society for the History of Science, 1972–74. *Publications:* Josiah Wedgwood: the arts and sciences united (with J. des Fontaines and J. Tindall), 1978; Science Museum handbooks; papers on the history of science. *Address:* 7 Ravens Court, St John's Road, Eastbourne, E Sussex BN20 7HY.

CHALFONT, Baron, *cr* 1964 (Life Peer); **Alun Arthur Gwynne Jones,** PC 1964; OBE 1961; MC 1957; Chairman: VSEL plc (formerly VSEL Consortium), since 1987; Marlborough Stirling Group, since 1994; Chairman, All Party Defence Group, House of Lords, since 1980; *b* 5 Dec. 1919; *s* of Arthur Gwynne Jones and Eliza Alice Hardman; *m* 1948, Dr Mona Mitchell, MB ChB; one *d* decd. *Educ:* West Monmouth Sch. Commissioned into South Wales Borderers (24th Foot), 1940; served in: Burma 1941–44; Malayan campaign 1955–57; Cyprus campaign 1958–59; various staff and intelligence appointments; Staff Coll., Camberley, 1950; Jt Services Staff Coll., 1958; Russian interpreter, 1951; resigned commission, 1961, on appt as Defence Correspondent, The Times; frequent television and sound broadcasts and consultant on foreign affairs to BBC Television, 1961–64; Minister of State, Foreign and Commonwealth Office, 1964–70; UK Permanent Rep. to WEU, 1969–70; Foreign Editor, New Statesman, 1970–71. Dep. Chm., IBA, 1989–90; Chm., Radio Authy, 1991–94. Director: W. S. Atkins International, 1979–83; IBM UK Ltd, 1973–90 (Mem. IBM Europe Adv. Council, 1973–90); Lazard Bros & Co. Ltd, 1983–90; Shandwick plc, 1985–; Triangle Holdings, 1986–90; Chairman: Industrial Cleaning Papers, 1979–86; Peter Hamilton Security Consultants Ltd, 1984–86; President: Abington Corp. (Consultants) Ltd, 1981–; Nottingham Bldg Soc., 1983–90. President: Hispanic and Luso Brazilian Council, 1975–80; RNID, 1980–87; Llangollen Internat. Music Festival, 1979–90; Freedom in Sport, 1982–88; Chairman: UK Cttee for Free World, 1981–89; Eur. Atlantic Gp, 1983–; Member: Nat. Defence Industries Council, 1992–; IISS; Bd of Governors, Sandle Manor Sch. MRI; MInstD. FRSA. Hon. Fellow UCW Aberystwyth, 1974. Hon. Col, Univ. of Wales OTC, 1991–94. Liveryman, Worshipful Co. of Paviors. Freeman, City of London. *Publications:* The Sword and The Spirit, 1963; The Great Commanders, 1973; Montgomery of Alamein, 1976; (ed) Waterloo: battle of three armies, 1979; Star Wars: suicide or survival, 1985; Defence of the Realm, 1987; By God's Will: a portrait of the Sultan of Brunei, 1989; contribs to The Times, and other national and professional journals. *Recreations:* formerly Rugby football, cricket, lawn tennis; now music and theatre. *Address:* House of Lords, SW1A 0PW. *Clubs:* Garrick, MCC, Lord's Taverners, City Livery.

CHALKER OF WALLASEY, Baroness *cr* 1992 (Life Peer), of Leigh-on-Sea in the County of Essex; **Lynda Chalker;** PC 1987; Minister of State, since 1986 and Minister for Overseas Development, since 1989, Foreign and Commonwealth Office; *b* 29 April 1942; *d* of late Sidney Henry James Bates and Marjorie Kathleen Randell; *m* 1st, 1967, Eric Robert Chalker (marr. diss. 1973); no *c*; 2nd, 1981, Clive Landa. *Educ:* Heidelberg Univ.; London Univ.; Central London Polytechnic. Statistician with Research Bureau Ltd (Unilever), 1963–69; Dep. Market Research Man. with Shell Mex & BP Ltd, 1969–72; Chief Exec. of Internat. Div. of Louis Harris International, 1972–74. MP (C) Wallasey, Feb. 1974–1992; Opposition Spokesman on Social Services, 1976–79; Parly Under-Sec.

of State, DHSS, 1979–82, Dept of Transport, 1982–83; Minister of State, Dept of Transport, 1983–86. Jt Sec., Cons. Health and Social Services Cttee, 1975–76; Chm., Greater London Young Conservatives, 1969–70; Nat. Vice-Chm., Young Conservatives, 1970–71. Member: BBC Gen. Adv. Cttee, 1975–79; RIIA, 1977–. Hon. Col, 156(NW) Transport Regt, RLC(V), 1995. *Publications:* (jtly) Police in Retreat (pamphlet), 1967; (jtly) Unhappy Families (pamphlet), 1971; (jtly) We are Richer than We Think, 1978; Africa: turning the tide, 1989. *Recreations:* music, cooking, theatre, driving. *Address:* House of Lords, SW1A 0PW.

CHALLEN, Rt. Rev. Michael Boyd, AM 1988; Executive Director, Brotherhood of St Laurence, since 1991; *b* 27 May 1932; *s* of late B. Challen; *m* 1961, Judith, *d* of A. Kelly; two *d*. *Educ:* Mordialloc High School; Frankston High School; Univ. of Melbourne (BSc 1955); Ridley College, Melbourne (ThL 1956). Deacon 1957, priest 1958; Curate of Christ Church, Essendon, 1957–59; Member, Melbourne Dio. Centre 1959–63; Director, 1963–69; Priest-in-charge, St Luke, Fitzroy, 1959–61; St Alban's, N Melbourne, 1961–65; Flemington, 1965–69; Dir, Anglican Inner-City Ministry, 1969; Dir, Home Mission Dept, Perth, 1971–78; Priest-in-charge, Lockridge with Eden Hill, 1973; Archdeacon, Home Missions, Perth, 1975–78; Asst Bp, dio. of Perth, WA, 1978–91; Exec. Dir, Anglican Health and Welfare Service, Perth, 1977–78. *Address:* 67 Brunswick Street, Fitzroy, Vic 3065, Australia. *T:* (3) 4197055, *Fax:* (3) 4172691.

CHALLENS, Wallace John, CBE 1967 (OBE 1958); Director, Atomic Weapons Research Establishment, Aldermaston, 1976–78; *b* 14 May 1915; *s* of late Walter Lincoln Challens and Harriet Sybil Challens (*née* Collins); *m* 1st, 1938, Winifred Joan Stephenson (*d* 1971); two *s*; 2nd, 1973, Norma Lane. *Educ:* Deacons Sch., Peterborough; University Coll., Nottingham; BSc (Hons) London. Research Dept, Woolwich, 1936; Projectile Develt Estabt, Aberporth, 1939. British Commonwealth Scientific Office, Washington, 1946; Armament Research Estabt, Fort Halstead, 1947; Atomic Weapons Research Estabt: Fort Halstead, 1954; Aldermaston, 1955–78. Scientific Dir of trials at Christmas Island, 1957. Appointed: Chief of Warhead Develt, 1959; Asst Dir, 1965; Dep. Dir, 1972. FInstP 1944. US Medal of Freedom (Bronze) 1946. *Recreation:* golf. *Address:* Far End, Crossborough Hill, Basingstoke, Hampshire RG21 2AG. *T:* Basingstoke (01256) 464986.

CHALLIS, Dr Anthony Arthur Leonard, CBE 1980; Chief Scientist, Department of Energy, 1980–83; *b* 24 Dec. 1921; *s* of Leonard Hough Challis and Dorothy (*née* Busby); *m* 1947, L. Beryl Hedley; two *d*. *Educ:* Newcastle upon Tyne Royal Grammar Sch.; King's Coll., Univ. of Durham. 1st cl. hons BSc Chemistry; PhD. Imperial Chemical Industries: joined Billingham Div., 1946; Research Man., HOC Div., 1962; Research Dir, Mond Div., 1966; Head of Corporate Lab., 1967; Gen. Man. Planning, 1970; Sen. Vice-Pres., ICI Americas Inc., 1975–76; Dir, Polymer Engrg, SRC, subseq. SERC, 1976–80. Dir, Wyvern Waste Services, 1992–. Mem., SERC (formerly SRC), 1973–83; Pres., PRI, 1985–87 (Chm. Council, 1983–85). Associate Prof., Wolfson Unit on Processing Materials, Brunel Univ., 1968. Mem. Court, Univ. of Stirling, 1968–74. Mem., Horners' Co. *Publications:* contrib. chem, energy and managerial jls. *Recreations:* music, walking, narrow boat. *Address:* Classeys, Low Ham, Langport, Somerset TA10 9DP.

CHALMERS, Ian Pender, CMG 1993; OBE 1980; HM Diplomatic Service; Counsellor, Foreign and Commonwealth Office, since 1987; *b* 30 Jan. 1939; *s* of John William Pender Chalmers and Beatrice Miriam Emery; *m* 1962, Lisa Christine Hay; two *s* two *d* (and one *d* decd). *Educ:* Hordle House, Harrow; Trinity College Dublin. Joined HM Diplomatic Service, 1963; Second Sec., Beirut, 1966–68; FCO, 1968–70; First Sec., Warsaw, 1970–72; FCO, 1972–76; First Sec., Paris, 1976–80; FCO, 1980–84; Counsellor, UK Mission to UN, Geneva, 1984–87. *Recreations:* golf, reading, walking, ski-ing. *Address:* c/o Foreign and Commonwealth Office, SW1A 2AH. *Club:* Frilford Heath Golf.

CHALMERS, Prof. John Philip, AC 1991; FAA; Foundation Professor of Medicine, Flinders University, since 1975; *b* 12 Jan. 1937; *m* 1977, Dr Alexandra Bune; four *s* one *d*. *Educ:* King's Sch., Parramatta; St Paul's Coll., Univ. of Sydney (BSc, MB BS); Univ. of NSW (PhD); MD Queensland 1991. FRCP, FRCPG, FRCPE, FACP, FRACP, FRACMA. Medical appts, Royal Prince Alfred Hosp., to 1968; Research Fellow: Nat. Heart Foundn, Univ. of NSW, 1965–66; MIT, 1969–70; RPMS, 1970–71; University of Sydney: Sen. Lectr, 1971–72; Assoc. Prof. of Medicine, 1973–75. Hon. Physician, Royal Prince Alfred Hosp., 1971–75; Vis MO, Repatriation Gen. Hosp., Concord, 1972–75; Mem., Bd of Management, Flinders Med. Centre, 1977–; Dean, Sch. of Medicine, Flinders Univ., 1991–92. Royal Australian College of Physicians: Chm., State Cttee for SA, 1982–86; Chm., Bd of Censors, 1984–88; Vice-Pres., 1988–90; Pres., 1990–92; Pres., Internat. Soc. of Hypertension, 1992–; former mem. and chm., numerous sci. adv. cttees and govt med. bodies. FAA 1987; Hon. FRACS. Wellcome Medal for contrib. to Med. Res., 1981. Mem., editl bds of learned jls. *Publications:* numerous contribs to medical jls, on pharmacology, physiology, blood pressure, hypertension and other medical research. *Recreations:* cricket, cooking, theatre, travel. *Address:* Department of Medicine, Flinders Medical Centre, Bedford Park, SA 5042, Australia; 22 Ayr Avenue, Torrens Park, SA 5042, Australia. *T:* (8) 2721855.

CHALMERS, Neil Robert, PhD; Director, The Natural History Museum (formerly British Museum (Natural History)), since 1988; *b* 19 June 1942; *s* of William King and Irene Margaret Chalmers (*née* Pemberton); *m* 1970, Monica Elizabeth Byanjeru (*née* Rusoke); two *d*. *Educ:* King's College Sch., Wimbledon; Magdalen Coll., Oxford (BA); St John's Coll., Cambridge (PhD). Lectr in Zoology, Makerere University Coll., Kampala, 1966–69; Scientific Dir, Nat. Primate Res. Centre, Nairobi, 1969–70; Open University: Lectr, subseq. Sen. Lectr, then Reader in Biology, 1970–85; Dean of Science, 1985–88. *Publications:* Social Behaviour in Primates, 1979; numerous papers on animal behaviour in Animal Behaviour and other learned jls. *Recreations:* music, squash. *Address:* The Natural History Museum, Cromwell Road, SW7 5BD.

CHALMERS, Patrick Edward Bruce; Director: Hutchvision News Ltd, since 1992; Scottish Ensemble, since 1995; *b* Chapel of Garioch, Aberdeenshire, 26 Oct. 1939; *s* of L. E. F. Chalmers, farmer, Lethenty, Inverurie, and Helen Morris Campbell; *m* 1963, Ailza Catherine Reid, *d* of late William McGibbon, Advocate in Aberdeen; three *d*. *Educ:* Fettes Coll., Edinburgh; N of Scotland Coll. of Agriculture (NDA); Univ. of Durham (BScA). Joined BBC as radio talks producer, BBC Scotland, 1963; television producer, 1965; sen. producer, Aberdeen, 1970; Head of Television, Scotland, 1979–82; Gen. Man., Co-Productions, London, 1982; Controller, BBC Scotland, 1983–92; Dir, BBC World Service Television, Asia, 1992; retd from BBC, 1994. President: Edinburgh Television Fest., 1984–92; BAFTA, Scotland, 1990–92. Dir, Scottish Film Production Fund, 1988–91. Mem., Grampian Region Children's Panel, 1974–79. Councillor, Aberdeenshire CC, 1995– (Chm., Lib Dem Gp). FRSA 1990. Bailie of Bennachie, 1975. *Recreations:* skiing, gardening. *Address:* Corblelack, Logie Coldstone, Aboyne, Aberdeenshire AB34 5PR. *T:* and *Fax:* Tarland (013398) 81439. *Clubs:* New (Edinburgh); Royal Northern (Aberdeen); Foreign Correspondents (Hong Kong); Kandahar Ski.

CHALMERS, William Gordon, CB 1980; MC 1944; Crown Agent for Scotland, 1974–84; *b* 4 June 1922; *s* of Robert Wilson Chalmers and Mary Robertson Chalmers (*née* Clark); *m* 1948, Margaret Helen McLeod; one *s* one *d*. *Educ:* Robert Gordon's Coll., Aberdeen; Aberdeen Univ. (BL). University, 1940–42 and 1947–48; served with Queen's Own Cameron Highlanders, 1942–47; Solicitor in Aberdeen, 1948–50; Procurator Fiscal Depute at Dunfermline, 1950–59; Senior Procurator Fiscal Depute at Edinburgh, 1959–63; Asst in Crown Office, 1963–67; Deputy Crown Agent, 1967–74. Jt Hd, War Crimes Enquiry in UK, 1988–89. *Recreations:* golf, bridge. *Address:* 3/4 Rocheid Park, East Fettes Avenue, Edinburgh EH4 1RP. *T:* 0131–332 7937.

CHALONER, family name of Baron Gisborough.

CHALONER, Prof. William Gilbert, FRS 1976; Hildred Carlile Professor of Botany and Head of School of Life Sciences, Royal Holloway (formerly Royal Holloway and Bedford New College), University of London, 1985–94 (at Bedford College, 1979–85), Emeritus Professor, 1994, and in Department of Geology, since 1994; *b* London, 22 Nov. 1928; *s* of late Ernest J. and L. Chaloner; *m* 1955, Judith Carroll; one *s* two *d*. *Educ:* Kingston Grammar Sch.; Reading Univ. (BSc, PhD). 2nd Lt RA, 1955–56. Lectr and Reader, University Coll., London, 1956–72. Visiting Prof., Pennsylvania State Univ., USA, 1961–62; Prof. of Botany, Univ. of Nigeria, 1965–66; Prof. of Botany, Birkbeck Coll., Univ. of London, 1972–79. Wilmer D. Barrett Prof. of Botany, Univ. of Mass, 1988–91. Member: Senate, Univ. of London, 1983–91; Bd of Trustees, Royal Botanic Gardens, Kew, 1983–. Mem., NERC, 1991–94. President: Palaeontological Assoc., 1976–78; Internat. Orgn of Palaeobotany, 1981–87; Linnean Soc., 1985–88; Vice-Pres., Geol Soc. London, 1985–86. Corresponding Mem., Botanical Soc. of Amer., 1987–. Associé Etranger de l'Acad. des Scis, Inst. de France, 1989. Linnean Medal (Botany), Linnean Soc., 1991. *Publications:* papers in Palaeontology and other scientific jls, dealing with fossil plants. *Recreations:* swimming, tennis, visiting USA. *Address:* 20 Parke Road, SW13 9NG. *T:* 0181–748 3863.

CHALSTREY, (Leonard) John, MD; FRCS; JP; Lord Mayor of London, 1995–Nov. 1996; Consultant Surgeon, St Bartholomew's Hospital, since 1969; Senior Lecturer, St Bartholomew's Hospital Medical College, University of London, since 1969; *b* 17 March 1931; *s* of late Leonard Chalstrey and of Frances Mary (*née* Lakin); *m* 1958, Aileen Beatrice Bayes; one *s* one *d*. *Educ:* Dudley Sch., Worcs; Queens' Coll., Cambridge (BA Hons 1954; MA 1958); Med. Coll., St Bartholomew's Hosp. (MB, BChir 1957; MD 1967). MRCS, LRCP 1957; FRCS 1962. Nat. Service, RAEC, 1949–51. Jun. med. and surgical posts, St Bartholomew's Hosp., 1958–59; Lectr in Anatomy, Middx Hosp. Med. Sch., 1959–61; Jun. Surgical Registrar, St Bartholomew's Hosp., 1962; Registrar, then Sen. Surgical Registrar, Royal Free Hosp., 1963–69; Hon. Consultant Surgeon, St Luke's Hosp. for Clergy, 1975–93. Examiner in Surgery: Univ. of London, 1976–; Univ. of Cambridge, 1989–94. Non-exec. Mem., City and Hackney HA, 1992–93. Mem., Court, 1986–92, Council, 1992–, City Univ. Maj., 357 Field Surgical Team., RAMC(V), TA; Member: City of London TAVRA, 1992–; Gtr London TAVRA, 1992–. Governor, Corp. of Sons of the Clergy, 1992–. Mem., Court of Common Council, City of London Corp., 1981–84; Alderman (Vintry Ward), City of London, 1984–; Sheriff, City of London, 1993–94; HM Lieut, City of London, 1995; JP 1984. Member, Court of Assistants: Soc. of Apothecaries (Sen. Warden, 1992–93 and 1993–94; Master, 1994–95); Barbers' Co. (Middle Warden, 1993–94); Mem., Parish Clerks' Co., 1993–. Vice-Pres., City of London Sect., BRCS, 1992–. KStJ 1995 (Mem., Chapter-Gen., 1994–); Surgeon-in-Chief, and Chm., Med. Bd, St John Ambulance, 1993–. *Publications:* (with Coffman and Smith-Laing) Gastro-Intestinal Disorders, 1986; (contrib.) Cancer in the Elderly, 1990; (contrib.) Maingot's Abdominal Operations, 7th edn 1980, 8th edn 1986; papers on surgical subjects in Brit. Jl Surgery, Brit. Jl Cancer and Jl RSM. *Recreations:* painting in oils, history of City of London. *Address:* 116 Harley Street, W1N 1AG. *T:* 0171–935 7413; Danebury, 113 The Chine, N21 2EG. *T:* 0181–360 8921. *Clubs:* United Oxford & Cambridge University, City Livery.

CHAMBERLAIN, Prof. Geoffrey Victor Price, RD 1974; MD; FRCS, FRCOG; Professor and Chairman, Obstetrics and Gynaecology, St George's Hospital Medical School, 1982–95; *b* 21 April 1930; *s* of late Albert Chamberlain and Irene Chamberlain (*née* Price); *m* 1956, Jocelyn Olivia Kerley, *d* of late Sir Peter Kerley, KCVO, CBE; three *s* two *d*. *Educ:* Llandaff Cathedral Sch.; Cowbridge; University Coll. and UCH, London (Goldsmith Schol. 1948; MB 1954; Fellow, UCL, 1987); MD 1968; FRCS 1960; FRCOG 1978. Residencies at RPMS, Gt Ormond St, Queen Charlotte's and Chelsea Hosps, KCH, 1955–69; Tutor, George Washington Med. Sch., Washington DC, 1965–66; Consultant Obstetrician and Gynaecologist, Queen Charlotte's and Chelsea Hosps, 1970–82. RNR, 1955–74, Surgeon Comdr. Member: Council, RSocMed, 1977–84 (Council, Obst. Sect., 1970–87; Council, Open Sect., 1987–); Council, RCOG, 1971–77, 1982–87, 1990–94 (Vice-Pres., 1984–87; Pres., 1993–94); Chairman: Med. Cttee, Nat. Birthday Trust, 1982–; Blair Bell Res. Soc., 1977–80; Assoc. of Profs of Obstetrics and Gynaecology, 1989–92; Fulbright Fellow, RCOG, 1966; Thomas Eden Fellow, RCOG, 1966; Vis. Professor: Beckman, USA, 1984; Daphne Chung, Hong Kong, 1985; Edwin Tooth, Brisbane, 1987; Peshwar, Pakistan, 1993. S African Representative Cttee, 1988. Hon. FACOG 1990; Hon. FSLCOG 1994. Hon. Mem., Polish Acad. of Medicine, 1992. Freeman, City of London, 1982. Foundn Prize, Amer. Assoc. of Obstetricians, 1967; James Simpson Gold Medal, RCSE, 1993. Editor: Contemporary Reviews in Obstetrics and Gynaecology, 1987–; British Jl of Obstetrics and Gynaecology, 1992–. *Publications:* Safety of the Unborn Child, 1969; Lecture Notes in Obstetrics, 1975, 5th edn 1985; British Births, 1970; Placental Transfer, 1979; Clinical Physiology in Obstetrics, 1980; Tubal Infertility, 1982; Pregnant Women at Work, 1984; Prepregnancy Care, 1985; (ed) Obstetrics by Ten Teachers, 14th edn, 1985, to 16th edn, 1994; (ed) Gynaecology by Ten Teachers, 14th edn, 1985, to 16th edn, 1994; Birthplace, 1987; Lecture Notes in Gynaecology, 1988; Manual of Obstetrics, 1988; ABC of Antenatal Care, 1991; Pregnancy in the 1990s, 1992; contribs to BMJ, Lancet, UK and overseas Jls of Obst. and Gyn. *Recreations:* travel, labouring in wife's garden. *Address:* Sycamores, Llanmadoc, Gower, Glamorgan SA3 1DB.

CHAMBERLAIN, Rev. George Ford, (Leo), OSB; Headmaster, Ampleforth College, since 1993; *b* 13 Aug. 1940; *s* of Brig. Noel Joseph Chamberlain, CBE and Sarah (Sally) (*née* Ford). *Educ:* Ampleforth Coll.; University Coll., Oxford (BA 1961; MA 1965). Novitiate, Ampleforth Abbey, 1961, solemn profession, 1964; ordained priest, 1968; Housemaster, St Dunstan's House, 1972–92; Sen. History Master, Ampleforth Coll., 1974–92. Member: Council of Management, Keston Inst. (formerly Keston Coll.), 1985–; Catholic Bishops' Cttee for European Affairs, 1992–; HMC. *Recreation:* assisting Christians in Central and Eastern Europe. *Address:* Ampleforth College, York YO6 4ER. *T:* Ampleforth (01439) 788224.

CHAMBERLAIN, Air Vice-Marshal George Philip, CB 1946; OBE 1941; RAF, retired; *b* 18 Aug. 1905; *s* of G. A. R. Chamberlain, MA, FLAS, FRICS, Enville, Staffordshire; *m* 1930, Alfreda Rosamond Kedward; one *s* one *d*. *Educ:* Denstone Coll.; Royal Air Force Coll., Cranwell. Commissioned RAF, 1925. On loan to Min. of Civil Aviation, 1947–48; Imperial Defence Coll., 1949; AOA 205 Group, MEAF, 1950; AOC Transport Wing, MEAF, 1951–52; Commandant, RAF Staff Coll., Andover, 1953–54; AO i/c A, HQ Fighter Command, 1954–57; Dep. Controller of Electronics, Min. of Supply, 1957–59, Min. of Aviation, 1959–60; Managing Director, Collins Radio Co. of

England, 1961–66, non-executive director, 1967–75. *Recreations:* gardening, walking. *Address:* Little Orchard, 12 Adelaide Close, Stanmore, Middlesex HA7 3EL. *T:* 0181–954 0710. *Club:* Royal Air Force.

CHAMBERLAIN, Kevin John, CMG 1992; Deputy Legal Adviser, Foreign and Commonwealth Office, since 1990; *b* 31 Jan. 1942; *s* of Arthur James Chamberlain and Gladys Mary (*née* Harris); *m* 1967, Pia Rosita Frauenlob; one *d. Educ:* Wimbledon Coll.; King's Coll., London (LLB). Called to the Bar, Inner Temple, 1965. Asst Legal Adviser, FCO, 1965–74; Legal Adviser: British Mil. Govt, Berlin, 1974–76; British Embassy, Bonn, 1976–77; Asst Legal Adviser, FCO, 1977–79; Legal Counsellor, FCO, 1979–83; Counsellor (Legal Advr), Office of UK Perm. Rep. to EC, Brussels, 1983–87; Legal Counsellor, FCO, 1987–90. *Recreations:* opera, tennis, skiing. *Address:* c/o Foreign and Commonwealth Office, SW1A 2AH.

CHAMBERLAIN, (Leslie) Neville, CBE 1990; Chief Executive, British Nuclear Fuels plc, since 1986; *b* 3 Oct. 1939; *s* of Leslie Chamberlain and Doris Anne Chamberlain (*née* Thompson); *m* 1971, Joy Rachel Wellings; one *s* three *d. Educ:* King James Grammar School, Bishop Auckland; King's College, Univ. of Durham. UKAEA, 1962–71; Urenco Ltd, 1971–77; British Nuclear Fuels: Fuel Production, 1977–81; Enrichment Business Manager, 1981–84; Dir, Enrichment Div., 1984–86. *Recreations:* horse racing, swimming, music. *Address:* British Nuclear Fuels plc, Risley, Warrington, Cheshire WA3 6AS. *T:* Warrington (01925) 835006.

CHAMBERLAIN, Michael Aubrey, FCA; Consultant, KPMG, Leicester, since 1994; *b* 16 April 1939; *s* of George Thomas Everard Chamberlain and Doris (*née* Arden). *Educ:* Repton Sch., Derbys. FCA 1963. Sen. partner, KPMG Peat Marwick, 1974–93. Pres., Inst. of Chartered Accountants in England and Wales, 1993–94 (Vice-Pres., 1991–92; Dep. Pres., 1992–93). Chm., Leicester Diocesan Bd of Finance, 1983–. Mem. Court, Univ. of Leicester, 1995–. Hon. LLD Leicester, 1993. *Address:* 1 Waterloo Way, Leicester LE1 6LP. *T:* Leicester (0116) 256 6000. *Club:* Savile.

CHAMBERLAIN, Neville; *see* Chamberlain, L. N.

CHAMBERLAIN, Prof. Owen, AB, PhD; Professor of Physics, University of California, 1958–89, now Emeritus; *b* San Francisco, 10 July 1920; *s* of W. Edward Chamberlain and Genevieve Lucinda Owen; *m* 1943, Babette Copper (marr. diss. 1978); one *s* three *d*; *m* 1980, June Greenfield Steingart (*d* 1991). *Educ:* Philadelphia; Dartmouth Coll., Hanover, NH (AB). Atomic research for Manhattan District, 1942, transferred to Los Alamos, 1943; worked in Argonne National Laboratory, Chicago, 1947–48, and studied at University of Chicago (PhD); Instructor in Physics, University of California, 1948; Asst Professor, 1950; Associate Professor, 1954. Guggenheim Fellowship, 1957; Loeb Lecturer in Physics, Harvard Univ., 1959. Fellow: American Phys. Soc.; Amer. Acad. of Arts and Scis; Mem., Nat. Acad. of Sciences, 1960; Berkeley Fellow, 1992. Nobel Prize (joint) for Physics, 1959; Berkeley Citation, 1989. *Publications:* papers in Physical Review, Physical Review Letters, Nature, Nuovo Cimento. *Address:* Department of Physics, University of California, Berkeley, CA 94720, USA.

CHAMBERLAIN, Peter Edwin, FEng; FRINA; Engineering Director, System and Services Division, British Aerospace Defence Company, since 1992; *b* 25 July 1939; *s* of Dr Eric Alfred Charles Chamberlain, OBE, FRSE, and Winifred Louise (Susan) (*née* Bone); *m* 1963, Irene May Frew; two *s* one *d. Educ:* Royal High Sch.; Edinburgh Univ. (Keasby Schol., BSc); RN Colls Manadon and Greenwich. RCNC. Asst Constructor, ship and submarine design, ME and Bath, 1963–68; Constructor: submarine design, Bath, 1968–69; submarine construction, Birkenhead, 1969–72; ship structures R&D, Dunfermline, 1972–74; postgrad. programmes in Naval Architecture, UCL, 1974–77; ship design, Bath, 1977–78; Chief Constructor: Hd of Secretariat, Bath, 1978–80; Surface Ship Forward Design, Bath, 1980–82; RCDS 1983; Asst Sec., Hd of Secretariat to Master Gen. of Ordnance, London, 1984–85; Under Sec., Dir Gen. Future Material Programmes (Naval), London, 1985–87; Dep. Controller Warship Equipments, MoD, 1987–88; Chief Underwater Systems Exec., MoD, 1988–89; creation of Defence Res. Agency, MoD, 1989–92. Mem., Nat. Council on Systems Engrg, 1995–. FEng 1988. *Recreations:* jogging, music, visual arts, poetry, computing. *Address:* W 295, Warton Aerodrome, Preston PR4 1AX. *T:* Preston (01772) 856323.

CHAMBERLAIN, Richard, TD 1949; Chief Master of the Supreme Court, Chancery Division, 1985–86 (Master, 1964–84); *b* 29 Jan. 1914; *o s* of late John Chamberlain and Hilda (*née* Poynting); *m* 1938, Joan, *d* of late George and Eileen Kay; two *s* one *d. Educ:* Radley Coll.; Trinity Coll., Cambridge (MA). Admitted Solicitor, 1938. Served War, 1939–45: Devon Regt, TJFF, Staff Coll., Haifa. Partner, Kingsford Dorman & Co., 1948–64. Asst, Worshipful Co. of Solicitors of the City of London, 1966, Warden, 1973–74, Master, 1975. *Publication:* Asst Editor, Supreme Court Practice, 1967. *Recreations:* gardening, photography, travel, grandparental duties. *Address:* 3 Fitzwarren House, Highgate, N6 5LX. *T:* 0171–281 2289. *Club:* Garrick.
See also P. A. Penney.

CHAMBERLAIN, William Richard Frank, DL; Chairman: Cricket Council, since 1990; Test and County Cricket Board, 1990–94; *b* 13 April 1925; *s* of Lt-Comdr Richard Chamberlain and Elizabeth Chamberlain (*née* Robson); *m* 1960, Gillian Diarmid Castle; one *s* one *d. Educ:* Uppingham School. Served Fleet Air Arm 1943–46. Played cricket for Northants CCC, 1946. Joined W. W. Chamberlain (Assoc. Cos) Ltd, subseq. Chamberlain Phipps, 1947: Dir, 1953; Jt Man. Dir, 1957; Chm. and Jt Man. Dir, 1963–69; Dep. Chm. and Man. Dir, 1969, Chm. and Man. Dir, 1972, Chm., 1975–87, Chamberlain Phipps Ltd; Chm., Stead & Simpson, 1984–89; Regional Dir, Nat. Westminster Bank, 1983–90; Dir, Kingsgrange, 1989–91; Mem. Council, CBI, 1982–87. Pres., Northants CCC, 1990– (Chm., 1985–90). Freeman, City of London; Master, Patternmaker's Co., 1987. High Sheriff, 1990, DL 1991, Northants. *Recreations:* cricket, shooting. *Address:* Manor House, Swineshead, Bedford MK44 2AF. *T:* Bedford (01234) 708283. *Clubs:* Naval & Military, MCC.

CHAMBERLEN, Nicholas Hugh; Chairman, Clive Discount Company, 1977–93; *b* 18 April 1939; *s* of Rev. Leonard Saunders Chamberlen, MC, and Lillian Margaret (*née* Webley); *m* 1962, Jane Mary Lindo; three *s* one *d. Educ:* Sherborne Sch.; Lincoln Coll., Oxford (BA Hons). Nat. Cash Register Co., 1962–67; Clive Discount Co. Ltd, 1967–93. *Recreations:* shooting, golf, cricket. *Address:* Ryders Wells House, Ringmer, East Sussex BN8 5RN. *Clubs:* Turf; Royal and Ancient Golf (St Andrews).

CHAMBERS, Prof. Andrew David; Chief Executive, Management Audit Ltd, since 1991; Professor of Audit and Control, University of Hull, since 1994; *b* 7 April 1943; *s* of Lewis Harold and Florence Lilian Chambers; *m* 1st, 1969, Mary Elizabeth Ann Kilbey (marr. diss. 1984); two *s*; 2nd, 1987, Celia Barrington (*née* Pruen); two *s* two *d* (incl. twin *s* and *d*), and one step *s. Educ:* St Albans Sch.; Hatfield Coll., Univ. of Durham (BA Hons). CEng; FCA, FBCS, FCCA, FIIA. Arthur Andersen & Co., 1965–69; Barker & Dobson, 1969–70; United Biscuits, 1970–71; City University Business School: Lectr in Computer Applications in Accountancy, 1971–74; Leverhulme Sen. Res. Fellow in Internal Auditing, 1974–78; Sen. Lectr in Audit and Management Control, 1978–83; Prof. of Internal Auditing, 1983–93; Prof. Emeritus, 1993–; Administrative Sub-Dean, 1983–86; Acting Dean, 1985–86; Dean, 1986–91; Head of Dept of Business Studies, 1986–89. Warden, Northampton Hall, City Univ., 1983–86 (Dep. Warden, 1972–76). Vis. Prof. in Computer Auditing, Univ. of Leuven, Belgium, 1980–81, 1992–93. Consultant: MacIntyre Hudson, Chartered Accountants, 1987–89; BBHW, Chartered Accountants, 1990–92; Director: Council of Univ. Management Schs, 1988–92; Nat. Home Loans Hldgs, 1991–; Nat. Mortgage Bank, 1991–92; Management Audit, 1991–; IIA Inc., 1993– (Mem. Internat. Standards Bd, 1992–). Member Council: BCS, 1979–82 (Mem., Tech. Bd; Chm., Meetings Cttee); IIA–UK, 1985–86 (Chairman: Res. Cttee; Professional Standards and Guidelines Cttee, 1991–); Member: IT Cttee, ICA, 1986–91; Educn, Training and Technol. Transfer Cttee, British Malaysian Soc., 1987–90; MBA Adv. Bd, Ashridge Management Coll., 1986–92; British Acad. of Management, 1990–. Hon. Auditor, RSAA, 1986–91. MInstD 1986; FRSA. Gov., Islington Green Comprehensive Sch., 1989–91. Member, Editorial Board: Computer Fraud and Security, 1981–87; Managerial Auditing Jl, 1986–. *Publications:* (with O. J. Hanson) Keeping Computers Under Control, 1975; (ed) Internal Auditing: developments and horizons, 1979; Internal Auditing: theory and practice, 1981, 2nd edn (with G. M. Selim and G. Vinten) 1987; Computer Auditing, 1981, 3rd edn (with J. M. Court) 1991; Effective Internal Audits: how to plan and implement, 1992; (with G. Rand) Auditing the IT Environment, 1994; papers in learned jls. *Recreations:* family, conservation. *Address:* Management Audit Ltd, The Water Mill, Moat Lane, Old Bolingbroke, Spilsby, Lincs PE23 4EU. *T:* Spilsby (01790) 763350. *Clubs:* Reform, Travellers.

CHAMBERS, Dr Douglas Robert; HM Coroner, City of London, since 1994; *b* 2 Nov. 1929; *s* of Douglas Henry Chambers and Elizabeth Paterson; *m* 1955, Barbara June Rowe; one *s* two *d. Educ:* Shene Grammar Sch.; King's College, London. MB BS; AKC 1953; LLB 1960; MA Univ. of Wales, 1989. FIBiol 1992. Called to the Bar, Lincoln's Inn, 1965. RAF Med. Br., 1955–58; Med. Advr, Parke Davis, 1959–61, Nicholas Laboratories, 1961–63, Pharmacia, 1964–65; Med. Dir, Hoechst Pharmaceuticals, 1965–70; Dep. Coroner, West London, 1969–70; HM Coroner, Inner North London, 1970–94. Vis. Lectr, City Univ., 1976–; Hon. Sen. Clin. Lectr in med. law, UCL, 1978–; Hon. Sen. Lectr, medical law, Royal Free Hosp., 1978–. Chairman: Richmond Div., BMA, 1969–70; Animal Research and Welfare Panel, Biological Council, 1986–92; Animal Welfare in Res. and Educn Cttee, Inst. of Biology, 1992–95; Pres., Library (sci. research) section, RSocMed, 1979–80; Pres., British sect., Anglo-German Med. Soc., 1980–84; Pres., Coroners' Soc., 1985–86. Hon. Mem., British Micro-circulation Soc., 1986 (Hon. Treas., 1968–86). Dist Comr, Richmond & Barnes Dist Scouts, 1976–85 (Silver Acorn 1984). Pres., Kensington Rowing Club, 1973–78. Baron C. ver Heyden de Lancey Prize for services to law and medicine, RSocMed, 1990. *Publications:* (jtly) Coroners' Inquiries, 1985; (consultant editor with Dr J. Burton) Jervis on Coroners, 11th edn, 1993; papers on medico-legal subjects. *Recreation:* local history of coroners and of scouting. *Address:* 4 Ormond Avenue, Richmond, Surrey TW10 6TN. *T:* (home) 0181–940 7745, (court) 0171–332 1598. *Club:* Auriol-Kensington Rowing.

CHAMBERS, Fredrick Rignold H.; *see* Hyde-Chambers.

CHAMBERS, George Michael; MP (People's National Movement), St Ann's, 1966–86; Prime Minister and Minister of Finance and Planning, Trinidad and Tobago, 1981–86; *b* 4 Oct. 1928; *m* 1956, Juliana; one *d. Educ:* Nelson Street Boys' RC Sch.; Burke's Coll.; Osmond High Sch.; Wolsey Hall, Oxford. Parly Sec., Min. of Finance, 1966; Minister of Public Utilities and Housing, 1969; Minister of State in Min. of National Security and Minister of State in Min. of Finance, Planning and Develt, 1970; Minister of National Security, Nov. 1970; Minister of Finance, Planning and Development, 1971–73; Minister of Finance, 1973–75; Minister of Educn and Culture, 1975–76; Minister of Industry and Commerce and Minister of Agriculture, Lands and Fisheries, 1976–81. Formerly, Asst Gen. Sec. and Mem. Central Exec., Gen. Council, and Res. and Disciplinary Cttees, People's National Movement. Chm. Bd of Governors, World Bank and IMF, 1973; Governor, Caribbean Develt Bank, 1981.

CHAMBERS, Harry Heyworth; Assistant Secretary, Ministry of Defence, 1988–91, retired; *b* 7 Nov. 1926; *s* of Francis Charles Chambers and Margaret Chambers; *m* 1st, 1955, Stella Howard (decd); 2nd, 1965, Elizabeth Mary Sansom; one *d. Educ:* Liverpool Collegiate Sch.; Liverpool Univ. (BComm). RAF 1945–48. Joined Automotive Products Co. Ltd, 1951, Manager, Service Div., 1956; Principal, 1971, Asst Sec., 1976, MoD; Counsellor (Defence Supply), British Embassy, Bonn, 1984–88. *Recreations:* mountaineering, translating.

CHAMBERS, Nicholas Mordaunt; QC 1985; a Recorder, since 1987; a Deputy High Court Judge, since 1994; *b* 25 Feb. 1944; *s* of Marcus Mordaunt Bertrand Chambers and Lona Margit Chambers (*née* Gross); *m* 1966, Sarah Elizabeth, *er d* of T. H. F. (Tony) Banks; two *s* one *d. Educ:* King's School, Worcester; Hertford College, Oxford (BA 1965). Called to the Bar, Gray's Inn, 1966, Bencher, 1994. *Recreation:* sketching. *Address:* Brick Court Chambers, 15/19 Devereux Court, WC2R 3JJ. *Clubs:* Garrick, Lansdowne.

CHAMBERS, Robert Alexander H.; *see* Hammond-Chambers.

CHAMBERS, Prof. Robert Guy; Professor of Physics, University of Bristol, 1964–90, Emeritus 1990; *b* 8 Sept. 1924; *s* of A. G. P. Chambers; *m* 1st, 1950, Joan Brislee (marr. diss. 1981); one *d*; 2nd, 1988, Susan Eden. *Educ:* King Edward VI Sch., Southampton; Peterhouse, Cambridge. Work on tank armament (Ministry of Supply), 1944–46; Electrical Research Association, 1946–47; Royal Society Mond Laboratory, Cambridge, 1947–57; Stokes Student, Pembroke Coll., 1950–53; PhD 1952; ICI Fellow, 1953–54; NRC Post-doctoral Fellow, Ottawa, 1954–55; University Demonstrator, Cambridge, 1955–57; Bristol University: Sen. Lectr, 1958–61; Reader in Physics, 1961–64; Dean of Science, 1973–76, 1985–88; Pro-Vice-Chancellor, 1978–81. Member: Physics Cttee, 1967–71, Nuclear Physics Bd, 1971–74, Sci. Bd, 1975–78, SRC; Physical Sci. Sub-Cttee, UGC, 1974–81. Institute of Physics: Mem., Publications Cttee, 1969–81 (Chm., 1977–81); Vice-Pres., 1977–81. Chm., Standing Conf. of Physics Profs, 1987–89. Chairman: SLS (Information Systems) Ltd, 1986–89; Track Analysis Systems Ltd, 1986–92. Hon. Fellow, Univ. of Bristol, 1994. Hughes Medal, Royal Soc., 1994. *Publications:* Electrons in Metals and Semiconductors, 1990; various papers in learned journals on the behaviour of metals at low temperatures. *Recreation:* hill-walking. *Address:* 9 Apsley Road, Clifton, Bristol BS8 2SH. *T:* Bristol (0117) 973 9833.

CHAMBERS, Dr Timothy Lachlan, JP; FRCP; Consultant Physician, Royal Hospital for Sick Children, Bristol, Department of Paediatrics, Southmead Hospital, and Weston-super-Mare General Hospital, since 1979; Deputy Medical Director, Southmead Health Services NHS Trust, since 1994; *b* 11 Feb. 1946; adopted *s* of late Victor Lachlan Chambers and Elsie Ruth (*née* Reynolds); *m* 1971, (Elizabeth) Joanna Ward, FRCR; one *s* two *d. Educ:* Wallington County Grammar Sch.; King's College London; King's Coll. Hosp. Med. Sch. (MB BS 1969). MRCP 1972; FRCP 1983; FRCPE 1985; FRCPI 1995. Jun. med. posts, London and SE England, 1969–73; Tutor in paed. and child health, Univ. of Leeds, 1973–76 (Sen. Registrar in medicine, St James's Hosp., Leeds, 1974–75); Physician, Derbyshire Children's Hosp. and other Derby and Nottingham Hosps, 1976–79;

University of Bristol: Clinical Lectr in Child Health, 1979–; Clinical Dean, Southmead Hosp., 1983–90; Mem. Governing Body, Inst. of Child Health, 1987–; Mem. Court, 1994–. Consultant in paediatrics: MoD, 1985–; RN, 1993–. Royal College of Physicians: Mem. Council, 1979–80, 1981–82, 1990–92; Mem., Paed. Bd, 1991–94; Pro Censor, 1992–93, Censor, 1993–94; Member: BPA, 1976 (Hon. Asst Sec., 1981–84; Hon. Sec., 1984–89); BMA, 1979 (Chm., Paed. Sub-Cttee, Central Consultants and Specialists Cttee, 1989–94); Council, Paed. Sect., RSM, 1992– (Pres., Paed. Sect., 1994–95); Pres., Union of Nat. Eur. Paed. Socs and Assocs, 1990–94. Past and present Examnr to med. bodies and univs in UK and abroad; past and present Chm. and Mem., local, regl, nat. and European prof. and govtl cttees and adv. bodies. Member: Bristol Medico-Legal Soc.; Philosophical Soc., Oxford; British Assoc. for Paed. Nephrology; Corresp. Mem., Société Française de pédiatrie, 1994. Patron, Lifeline Charity, 1985–; Trustee, St John's Home, Bristol, 1985–93; Mem. Bd of Govs, Hosps for Sick Children, (London) SHA, 1993–94. Major, RAMC(V), 1989–. Eucharistic Minister and Reader, Cathedral Church of SS Peter and Paul, Clifton, 1991–. FRSocMed 1977. Freeman, City of London; Liveryman, Apothecaries' Soc., 1985. JP Bristol, 1993. *Publications:* Fluid Therapy in Childhood, 1987; contribs to med. and lay jls and collective works. *Recreation:* Quixotry. *Address:* 4 Clyde Park, Bristol BS6 6RR. *T:* Bristol (0117) 974 2814. *Clubs:* Athenæum; Clifton (Bristol).

CHAMIER, Anthony Edward Deschamps; Under Secretary, Department of Education and Science, 1980–92; *b* 16 Aug. 1935; *s* of late Brig. George Chamier, OBE and of Marion (*née* Gascoigne), Achandunie, Alness, Ross-shire; *m* 1962, Anne-Carole Tweeddale Dalling, *d* of William and Kathleen Dalling, Transvaal, S Africa; one *s* one *d*. *Educ:* Stowe, Buckingham; Trinity Hall, Cambridge; Yale Univ. (Henry Fellow). Military service, 1st Bn Seaforth Highlanders, 1953–55. HM Foreign (later Diplomatic) Service, 1960; Third Secretary, Foreign Office, 1960–62; Second Sec., Rome, 1962–64; Asst Political Adviser, HQ Middle East Comd, Aden, 1964–66; First Sec., FCO, 1966–71; Head of Chancery, Helsinki, 1971–72; seconded, later transf. to Dept of Educn and Science; Principal, 1972–73; Principal Private Sec. to Sec. of State for Educn and Science, 1973–74; Asst Sec., 1974–79; Prin. Estabt Officer, 1980–84. *Recreations:* walking, shooting, gardening. *Address:* Achandunie House, Ardross, by Alness, Ross-shire IV17 0YB. *T:* Alness (01349) 883255. *Club:* Army and Navy.

CHAMPERNOWNE, David Gawen, MA; FBA 1970; Professor of Economics and Statistics, Cambridge University, 1970–78, now Emeritus; Fellow of Trinity College at Cambridge, since 1959; *b* Oxford, 9 July 1912; *s* of late F. G. Champernowne, MA, Bursar of Keble Coll., Oxford; *m* 1948, Wilhelmina Dullaert; two *s*. *Educ:* The College, Winchester; King's Coll., Cambridge. Asst Lecturer at London Sch. of Economics, 1936–38; Fellow of King's Coll., Cambridge, 1937–48; University Lecturer in Statistics at Cambridge, 1938–40; temp. Civil Servant, 1940–45; Dir of Oxford Univ. Institute of Statistics, 1945–48; Fellow of Nuffield Coll., Oxford, 1945–59; Prof. of Statistics, Oxford Univ., 1948–59; Reader in Economics, Cambridge Univ., 1959–70. Editor, Economic Jl, 1971–76. *Publications:* Uncertainty and Estimation in Economics (3 vols), 1969; The Distribution of Income between Persons, 1973; sundry articles on mathematics, statistics and economics in learned jls, 1933–. *Address:* 20 Manor Court, Grange Road, Cambridge CB3 9BE. *T:* Cambridge (01223) 328477; Trinity College, Cambridge CB2 1TQ.

CHAN, Cho-chak John, CBE 1993 (OBE 1985); LVO 1986; JP; Managing Director, The Kowloon Motor Bus Co. (1933) Ltd, since 1993; *b* 8 April 1943; *s* of late Kai Kit Chan and of Yuk Ying Wong; *m* 1965, Wai-chun Agnes Wong; one *s* one *d*. *Educ:* St Rose of Lima's Sch.,; Wah Yan Coll., Kowloon; La Salle Coll., Univ. of Hong Kong (BA (Hons), DMS). Commerce and Industry Dept, 1964; Economic Br., Govt Secretariat, 1970; Private Sec. to Gov., 1973; City Dist Comr (Hong Kong), 1975; Asst Dir of Home Affairs, 1976; Dep. Dir of Trade, 1977; Exec. Dir and Gen. Man., Sun Hung Kai Finance Co. Ltd, 1978; Principal Assistant Secretary: for Security, Govt Secretariat, 1980; for CS, 1982; Dep. Dir of Trade, 1983; Dep. Sec. (Gen. Duties), 1984; Dir of Inf. Services, 1986; Dep. Chief Sec., 1987; Sec. for Trade and Industry, 1989; Sec. for Educn and Manpower, 1991. JP Hong Kong, 1984. *Recreations:* swimming, ten-pin bowling, music, reading. *Address:* The Kowloon Motor Bus Co. (1933) Ltd, 1 Po Lun Street, Lai Chi Kok, Kowloon, Hong Kong. *T:* 27868833. *Clubs:* Royal Hong Kong Jockey; Hong Kong.

CHAN, Chun Hung Jerome; Hon. Mr Justice Jerome Chan; Judge of the High Court of Hong Kong, since 1993; *b* 14 July 1951; *s* of Tan Thye Poh and Chih Pui Fan; *m* 1977, Tang Yiu Kin Grace; two *s* one *d*. *Educ:* Univ. of Hong Kong (LLB, PCLL Dist.). Demonstrator, Dept of Law, Hong Kong Univ., 1974–75; Barrister in private practice, 1976–85; Permanent Magistrate, 1985–87; Presiding Officer, Labour Tribunal, 1987–89; Judge of Dist Court, 1989; Dep. Registrar of Supreme Court, 1990–93. Hong Kong University: Visitor, Faculty of Law, 1991; Hon. Lectr, Dept of Professional Legal Educn, 1992–; Chief Ext. Examr, Hong Kong and City Univs, 1995. *Recreations:* music, photography, sports. *Address:* High Court, Hong Kong.

CHAN FANG, Anson Maria Elizabeth, (Mrs Anson Chan), CBE 1992; JP; Chief Secretary, Hong Kong, since 1993; *b* 17 Jan. 1940; *d* of Howard Fang and Fang Zhao Ling; *m* 1963, Archibald John Chan Tai-wing, MBE, QPM, CPM; one *s* one *d*. *Educ:* Univ. of Hong Kong (BA Hons). Admin. Officer, Hong Kong Govt, 1962–70; Asst Financial Sec., 1970–72; Asst Sec. for New Territories, 1972–75; Principal Asst Sec. for Social Services, 1975–79; Dep. Dir, 1979–84, Dir, 1984–87, Social Welfare; Sec. for Econ. Services, 1987–93; Sec. for CS, April–Nov. 1993. JP Hong Kong, 1975. *Recreation:* music. *Address:* Chief Secretary's Office, Central Government Offices, Main Wing, Lower Albert Road, Hong Kong. *T:* 8102406. *Clubs:* Zonta (Hong Kong East); Hong Kong, Royal Hong Kong Jockey, American (Hong Kong).

CHAN, Rt. Hon. Sir Julius, GCMG 1994; KBE 1980 (CBE 1975); PC 1981; MP 1968; Parliamentary Leader, People's Progress Party, Papua New Guinea, since 1970; Prime Minister, 1980–82 and since 1994; *b* 29 Aug. 1939; *s* of Chin Pak and Tingoris Chan; *m* 1966, Stella Ahmat. *Educ:* Marist Brothers Coll., Ashgrove, Qld; Univ. of Queensland, Australia (Agricl Science). Co-operative Officer, Papua New Guinea Admin, 1960–62; private business, coastal shipping and merchandise, 1963–70. Minister for Finance, 1972–77; Dep. Prime Minister and Minister for Primary Industry, 1977–78; Minister for Finance and Planning, 1985–86; Dep. Prime Minister, 1985–88; Minister for Trade and Industry, 1986–88; Dep. Opposition Leader, 1988–92; Dep. Prime Minister and Minister for Finance and Planning, 1992–94. Governor: World Bank/IMF, 1976, 1992–; Asian Development Bank, 1977, 1992. Fellow, Internat. Bankers Assoc., USA, 1976. Attended meetings and conferences worldwide as rep. of PNG, latterly as leader of PNG delegn, 1970–; made State and official visits to Australia, Rep. of Korea, China, Vanuatu, Indonesia, UK, France, Italy, NZ, USA. Hon. DEc Dankook (Republic of Korea) 1978; Hon. Dr Technol., Univ. of Technol., PNG, 1983. *Recreations:* swimming, walking, boating. *Address:* PO Box 717, Rabaul, Papua New Guinea.

CHAN, Nai Keong, (Kenneth), CBE 1985; JP; FEng 1986; Chairman Emeritus, Parsons Brinckerhoff (Asia) Ltd, since 1992; *b* 17 Nov. 1931; two *s* one *d*. FICE, FIStructE, FHKIE. Public Works Dept, Hong Kong: pupil engineer, Roads Office, 1952; Civil Engineering Office, 1960; Senior Engineer, 1964; Highways Office, 1969; Principal Govt Engineer, 1973, i/c Tuen Mun New Town develt; Dir, Engineering Dept, 1980; Dep. Dir, Public Works, 1981; Dep. Sec. for Lands and Works, 1982; Sec. for Lands and Works, 1983–86; Gp Man. Dir, Cavendish Internat. Holdings Ltd, 1987–89; Dir, Parsons Brinckerhoff (Asia) Ltd, 1989–92. JP Hong Kong, 1972. Hon. DTech Loughborough, 1984. *Recreations:* bridge, swimming, yoga, music. *Address:* c/o Parsons Brinckerhoff (Asia) Ltd, 7th Floor, Devon House, Taikoo Place, 979 King's Road, Quarry Bay, Hong Kong. *T:* 25798899, *Fax:* 28569902. *Clubs:* Hongkong; Royal HK Jockey, Pacific, Chinese, HK Country, Chinese Recreation.

CHAN, Siu-Oi, Patrick; Hon. Mr Justice Chan; Judge of the High Court, Hong Kong, since 1992; *b* 21 Oct. 1948; *s* of late Chan Chu-Yau and of Li Man-Yee; *m* 1990, Lisa Chiang Miu-Chu. *Educ:* Univ. of Hong Kong (LLB 1974; PCLL 1975). Barrister in private practice, 1977–87; Judge of District Court, 1987–91; Dep. Registrar of Supreme Court, 1991–92. *Address:* Supreme Court, Queensway, Hong Kong. *T:* 28254530.

CHANCE, Sqdn Ldr Dudley Raymond, FRGS; a Recorder of the Crown Court, 1980–86; *b* 9 July 1916; *s* of Captain Arthur Chance, Sherwood Foresters, and Byzie Chance; *m* 1958, Jessie Maidstone, widow, *d* of John and Alice Dewing. *Educ:* Nottingham High Sch.; London Univ. (BA Oriental Religions and Philosophies, LLB 1969); BA Hons Internat. Politics and For. Policy, Open Univ., 1980. Called to Bar, Middle Temple, 1955; Dep. Circuit Judge, 1973–80. Commissioned in Royal Air Force, 1936; served Egypt, Transjordan, 1936–37; Bomber Comd (4 Gp), 1938; served in Bomber Comd Nos 97 and 77 Sqdns; took part in first raids on Norway; crashed off Trondheim; picked up later from sea by HMS Basilisk, later sunk at Dunkirk; Air Ministry, Whitehall, 1941–42, later in 2 Group, Norfolk, 21 Sqdn; also served in SEAC, Bengal/Burma. Sqdn Ldr, RAFO, until March 1961; gazetted to retain rank of Sqdn Ldr from that date. Member: panel of Chairmen of Medical Appeal Tribunals (DHSS), 1978–88; panel of Independent Inspectors for motorway and trunk road inquiries for DoE, 1978–83. Contested (C) Norwich North, 1959. FRGS 1979. *Recreations:* violin, painting. *Address:* Lamb Buildings, Temple, EC4Y 7AS; Fenners Chambers, 4 Madingley Road, Cambridge CB3 0EE. *Club:* Goldfish (RAF aircrew rescued from sea).

CHANCE, Sir (George) Jeremy (ffolliott), 4th Bt *cr* 1900, of Grand Avenue, Hove; retired; *b* 24 Feb. 1926; *s* of Sir Roger James Ferguson Chance, 3rd Bt, MC and Mary Georgina (*d* 1984), *d* of Col William Rowney; *S* father, 1987; *m* 1950, (cousin) Cecilia Mary Elizabeth, *d* of Sir William Hugh Stobart Chance, CBE; two *s* two *d*. *Educ:* Gordonstoun School; Christ Church, Oxford (MA). Sub-Lieut RNVR, 1944–47. Harry Ferguson Ltd, 1950–53; Massey-Ferguson, 1953–78; Director, Massey-Ferguson (UK) Ltd, 1973–78; farmer, 1978–87. *Recreations:* making lakes, planting trees, choral singing, painting. *Heir:* *s* (John) Sebastian Chance [*b* 2 Oct. 1954; *m* 1977, Victoria Mary, *d* of Denis McClean; two *s* one *d*]. *Address:* Rhosgyll Fawr, Chwilog, Pwllheli, Gwynedd LL53 6TQ. *T:* Chwilog (01766) 810584.

CHANCE, Michael Edward Ferguson; counter-tenor; *b* Penn, Bucks, 7 March 1955; *s* of John Wybergh Chance and Wendy Muriel (*née* Chance); *m* 1991, Irene, *d* of Hon. Francis Edward Noel-Baker, *qv*; one *s*. *Educ:* St George's Sch., Windsor; Eton Coll.; King's Coll., Cambridge (MA English 1977; Mem., King's Coll. Choir, 1974–77). Stockbroker, Mullens & Co., 1977–80. Founder Mem., The Light Blues, 1977–83; Mem., Monteverdi Choir, 1980–83; solo career, 1983–: operatic débuts: Buxton Fest., 1983; Kent Opera, Opéra de Lyon, Göttingen Handel Fest., 1985; Paris Opera, 1988; Glyndebourne Fest., 1989; Netherlands Opera, 1991; Covent Garden, ENO, Scottish Opera, 1992; Australian Opera, 1993; rôles include: Oberon in A Midsummer Night's Dream; Apollo in Death in Venice; Julius Caesar; Andronico in Tamerlano; Bertarido in Rodelinda; Orfeo in Orfeo ed Euridice; Ottone in Agrippina; Ottone in L'incoronazione di Poppea; Military Governor in A Night at the Chinese Opera; Orpheus in The Second Mrs Kong; concert performances in Europe, USA and Japan. Numerous recordings of oratorio, opera and recitals. *Recreations:* many sports, fly-fishing, hill-walking, bridge. *Address:* c/o IMG Artists, Media House, 3 Burlington Lane, Chiswick, W4 2TH. *T:* 0181–233 5800.

CHANCE, Michael Spencer; Executive Counsel, Joint Disciplinary Scheme, since 1993; *b* 14 May 1938; *s* of Florence and Ernest Horace Chance; *m* 1962, Enid Mabel Carter; three *d*. *Educ:* Rossall School. Solicitor. With Challinor & Roberts, Warley, 1962–70; Senior Asst Prosecuting Solicitor, Sussex Police Authy, 1970–72; Office of Director of Public Prosecutions, 1972–86: Asst Dir, 1981–86; Chief Crown Prosecutor, North London, 1986–87; Asst Head of Legal Services, Crown Prosecution Service, 1987; Dep. Dir, Serious Fraud Office, 1987–90; Consultant, Cameron Markby Hewitt, 1991–93. *Address:* 8 Seaview Bay, Pier Road, Seaview, Isle of Wight PO34 5BP.

CHANCELLOR, Alexander Surtees; Associate Editor, The Sunday Telegraph, since 1994; *b* 4 Jan. 1940; *s* of Sir Christopher Chancellor, CMG and of Sylvia Mary, OBE, *e d* of Sir Richard Paget, 2nd Bt and Lady Muriel Finch-Hatton, *d* of 12th Earl of Winchilsea and Nottingham; *m* 1964, Susanna Elisabeth Debenham; two *d*. *Educ:* Eton College; Trinity Hall, Cambridge. Reuters News Agency, 1964–74; ITN, 1974–75; Editor: The Spectator, 1975–84; Time and Tide, 1984–86; Dep. Editor, Sunday Telegraph, 1986; US Editor, The Independent, 1986–88; Editor: The Independent Magazine, 1988–92; The New Yorker's Talk of the Town, 1992–93. Columnist, The Times, 1992–93. Comr, English Heritage, 1990–92. *Address:* 1 Souldern Road, W14 0JE. *Club:* Garrick.

CHANDLER, Sir Colin (Michael), Kt 1988; FRAeS; Managing Director, since 1990, Chief Executive, since 1992, Vickers PLC; *b* 7 Oct. 1939; *s* of Henry John Chandler and Mary Martha (*née* Bowles); *m* 1964, Jennifer Mary Crawford; one *s* one *d*. *Educ:* St Joseph's Acad.; Hatfield Polytechnic. FCMA; FRAeS 1994. Commercial Apprentice, De Havilland Aircraft Co., 1956; Hawker Siddeley Aviation, later British Aerospace, Kingston: Commercial Manager, 1967–72; Exec. Dir, Commercial, 1973–78; Divl Man. Dir., 1978–82; Gp Marketing Dir, 1983–85; Hd of Defence Export Services, MoD, 1985–89. Non-Exec. Director: Siemens Plessey Electronic Systems, 1990–; TI Group, 1992–. Vice Pres., EEF, 1991; Member: NDIC, 1992–; Cttee, DTI Priority Japan Campaign, 1992–; Chm., Overseas Project Bd, Healthcare Sector Gp. Trustee, RAF Museum, 1992–. Commander, Order of the Lion of Finland, 1982. *Recreations:* playing tennis, reading, listening to music. *Address:* c/o Vickers PLC, Millbank Tower, Millbank, SW1P 4RA. *T:* 0171–828 7777. *Clubs:* Reform, Mark's; Vanderbilt Racquet; Harbour.

CHANDLER, Sir Geoffrey, Kt 1983; CBE 1976; Chairman, National Council for Voluntary Organisations, since 1989; *b* 15 Nov. 1922; *s* of Frederick George Chandler, MD, FRCP, and Marjorie Chandler; *m* 1955, Lucy Bertha Buxton; four *d*. *Educ:* Sherborne; Trinity Coll., Cambridge (MA History). Military Service, 1942–46: Captain 60th Rifles; Political Warfare Exec., Cairo; Special Ops Exec. (Force 133), Greece; Anglo-Greek Information Service, W Macedonia, 1945; Press Officer, Volos and Salonika, 1946. Cambridge Univ., 1947–49; Captain, Univ. Lawn Tennis, 1949. BBC Foreign News Service, 1949–51; Leader Writer and Features Editor, Financial Times, 1951–56; Commonwealth Fund Fellow, Columbia Univ., New York, 1953–54; Shell Internat. Petroleum Co.: Manager, Econs Div., 1957–61; Area Co-ordinator, W Africa, 1961–64; Chm. and Man. Dir, Shell Trinidad Ltd, 1964–69; Shell Internat. Petroleum Co.: Public

Affairs Co-ordinator, 1969–78; Dir, 1971–78; Dir, Shell Petroleum Co.; and Shell Petroleum NV, 1976–78; Dir Gen., NEDO, and Mem., NEDC, 1978–83; Dir, Industry Year 1986, 1984–86; Leader, RSA Industry Matters team, 1987–89; Industry Advr, RSA, 1987–92. Pres., Inst. of Petroleum, 1972–74. Member: Council and Exec. Cttee, Overseas Develt Inst., 1969–78; British Overseas Trade Adv. Council, 1978–82; Council and Exec. Cttee, VSO. Chm., BBC Consultative Group on Industrial and Business Affairs, and Mem. BBC Gen. Adv. Council, 1983–88; Chm., Consultative Council, Soc. of Educn Officers Schools Curriculum Award, 1984–; Member: Wilton Park Academic Council, 1983–87; Council for Charitable Support, 1990–; Associate, Ashridge Management Coll., 1983–89; Pres., Assoc. for Management & Business Educn, 1986–90; Chm., Amnesty Internat. British Section Business Gp, 1992–; Trustee, Charities Aid Foundn, 1990–; Dir, Blackheath Preservation Trust. FRSA. Hon. Mem., CGLI, 1988. Hon. Fellow: Sheffield City Polytechnic, 1981; Girton Coll., Cambridge, 1986; Hon. FInstPet 1982. Hon. DBA Internat. Management Centre from Buckingham, 1986; Hon. DSc: CNAA, 1986; Bradford, 1987; Aston, 1987; Hon. CGIA 1987. *Publications:* The Divided Land: an Anglo-Greek Tragedy, 1959, 2nd edn 1994; (jtly) The State of the Nation: Trinidad & Tobago in the later 1960s, 1969; (contrib.) Britain's Economic Performance, 1994; articles on oil, energy, trans-national corporations, and development; numerous speeches, urging employee participation, coherent British indust. policy and the need for clearly articulated business principles. *Recreations:* working in woodland, gardening, music. *Address:* (office) 8 John Adam Street, WC2N 6EZ. *T:* 0171–930 5115; (home) 46 Hyde Vale, Greenwich, SE10 8HP. *T:* 0181–692 5304. *Clubs:* Athenæum; Hawks (Cambridge).

CHANDLER, Tony John; Hon. Research Fellow, University College London, since 1989; *b* 7 Nov. 1928; *s* of Harold William and Florence Ellen Chandler; *m* 1954, Margaret Joyce Weston; one *s* one *d*. *Educ:* King's Coll., London. MSc. PhD, AKC, MA. Lectr, Birkbeck Coll., Univ. of London, 1952–56; University Coll. London: Lectr, 1956–65; Reader in Geography, 1965–69; Prof. of Geography, 1969–73; Prof. of Geography, Manchester Univ., 1973–77; Master of Birkbeck Coll., Univ. of London, 1977–79. Sec., Royal Meteorological Soc., 1969–73, Vice-Pres., 1973–75. Member: Council, NERC; Health and Safety Commn; Cttee of Experts on Major Hazards; Royal Soc. Study Gp on Pollution in the Atmosphere, 1974–77; Clean Air Council; Royal Commn on Environmental Pollution, 1973–77; Standing Commn on Energy and the Environment 1978. *Publications:* The Climate of London, 1965; Modern Meteorology and Climatology, 1972, 2nd edn 1981; contribs to: Geographical Jl, Geography, Weather, Meteorological Magazine, Bulletin of Amer. Meteorological Soc., etc. *Recreations:* horology, music, reading, travel. *Address:* Charnwood, 44 Knoll Rise, Orpington, Kent BR6 0EL. *T:* Orpington (01689) 832880.

CHANDLEY, Peter Warren, OBE 1995; MVO 1981; HM Diplomatic Service, retired; Deputy Head of Mission, Bogotá, Colombia, 1992–95; *b* 24 Nov. 1934; *s* of Samuel and Freda Chandley; *m* 1961, Jane Williams. *Educ:* Manchester Warehousemen and Clerks Orphan School, Cheadle Hulme. Clerk, Min. of Fuel and Power, 1953; Nat. Service, RAF, 1953–55; FO, 1955; served Tripoli, 1955; Kabul, 1958; Havana, 1960; Phnom Penh, 1962; Madagascar, 1966; FCO, 1969; Nairobi, 1972; Kampala, 1976; Oslo, 1977; FCO, 1981; Chargé d'Affaires, Libreville, Gabon, 1984–85; Abidjan, 1986; Amb. to People's Republic of the Congo, 1990–91. Ridder 1st Class, Order of St Olav (Norway), 1981. *Recreations:* bird-watching, reading, conservation activities.

CHANDOS, 3rd Viscount *cr* 1954, of Aldershot; **Thomas Orlando Lyttelton;** Director, Botts Co. Ltd, since 1993; *b* 12 Feb. 1953; *s* of 2nd Viscount Chandos and of Caroline Mary (who *m* 1985, Hon. David Hervey Erskine), *d* of Rt Hon. Sir Alan Lascelles, GCB, GCVO, CMG, MC; *S* father, 1980; *m* 1985, Arabella Sarah, *d* of Adrian Bailey and Lady Mary Russell; two *s* one *d*. *Educ:* Eton; Worcester College, Oxford (BA). Banker, 1974–93, Dir, 1985–93, Kleinwort Benson. Director: Capital and Regl Properties; Chrysalis Gp; Lopex. *Heir: s* Hon. Oliver Antony Lyttelton, *b* 21 Feb. 1986. *Address:* 149 Gloucester Avenue, NW1 8LA. *T:* 0171–722 8329.

CHANDRACHUD, Hon. Yeshwant Vishnu; Chief Justice of India, 1978–85; *b* Poona (Maharashtra), 12 July 1920; *s* of Vishnu Balkrishna Chandrachud and Indira; *m* Prabha; one *s* one *d*. *Educ:* Bombay Univ. (BA, LLB). Advocate of Bombay High Court, 1943, civil and criminal work; part-time Prof. of Law, Government Law Coll., Bombay, 1949–52; Asst Govt Pleader, 1952; Govt Pleader, 1958; Judge, Bombay High Court, 1961–72; one-man Pay Commn for Bombay Municipal Corporation officers, later Arbitrator in dispute between Electricity Supply and Transport Undertaking and its employees' union; one-man Commn to inquire into circumstances leading to death of Deen Dayal Upadhyaya; Judge, Supreme Court of India, 1972–78. President: Internat. Law Assoc. (India Branch), 1978–; Indian Law Inst., 1978–. *Address:* (official) 7–B Samata, General Bhosale Marg, Bombay 400021, India. *T:* (22) 2042474.

CHANDRASEKHAR, Prof. Sivaramakrishna, FRS 1983; Director, Centre for Liquid Crystal Research, Bangalore, since 1991; *b* 6 Aug. 1930; *s* of S. Sivaramakrishnan and Sitalaxmi; *m* 1954, Ila Pinglay; one *s* one *d*. *Educ:* Nagpur Univ. (MSc, DSc); Pembroke Coll., Cambridge (PhD 1958; ScD 1987). Res. Schol., Raman Res. Inst., Bangalore, 1950–54; 1851 Exhibn Schol., Cavendish Lab., Cambridge, 1954–57; DSIR Fellow, Dept of Crystallography, UCL, 1957–59; Res. Fellow, Davy Faraday Res. Lab., Royal Instn, 1959–61; Prof. and Hd of Dept of Physics, Univ. of Mysore, 1961–71; Prof., Raman Res. Inst., Bangalore, 1971–90. Nehru Vis. Prof., and Fellow Pembroke Coll., Cambridge, 1986–87; Bhatnagar Fellow, CSIR, 1990–. India Corresp., Royal Soc., 1987–. *Publications:* Liquid Crystals, 1977, 2nd edn, 1992; editor of several books; contrib. scientific papers to learned jls. *Address:* Centre for Liquid Crystal Research, PO Box 1329, Jalahalli, Bangalore 560013, India.

CHANEY, Hon. Sir Frederick (Charles), KBE 1982 (CBE 1969); AFC 1945; Chairman, Home Building Society, 1974–87; *b* 12 Oct. 1914; *s* of Frederick Charles Chaney and Rose Templar Chaney; *m* 1938; four *s* three *d*. *Educ:* Aquinas Coll.; Claremont Coll. Served War, RAAF, 1940–45. Teacher, 1936–40 and 1946–55. MHR (L) Perth, 1955–69; Govt Whip, 1961–63; Minister for the Navy, 1963–66; Administrator, Northern Territory, 1970–73. Lord Mayor of Perth, WA, 1978–82. Dep. Pres., King's Park Bd, 1981–84. *Recreation:* golf. *Address:* 9A Melville Street, Claremont, WA 6010, Australia. *T:* 3840596. *Clubs:* West Australian Cricket Assoc., East Perth Football (Perth); Mount Lawley Golf (WA).

CHANG-HIM, Rt Rev. French Kitchener; *see* Seychelles, Bishop of.

CHANNON, Prof. Derek French, DBA; FCIM; Professor of Management, Imperial College of Science, Technology and Medicine, since 1990; *b* 4 March 1939; *s* of John French and Betty Blanche Channon; *m* 1963, Ann Lesley (marr. diss. 1986); one *s* one *d*. *Educ:* University Coll. London (BSc); Manchester Business Sch. (MBA); Harvard Graduate Sch. of Business (DBA). FCIM 1985. Marketing management, Royal Dutch Shell Gp, 1960–68; Lectr in Marketing, Manchester Business Sch., 1968–70; Ford Foundn European Doctoral Fellow, Harvard Bus. Sch., 1968–71; Manchester Business School: Sen. Res. Fellow, 1971–76; Prof. of Strategic Management and Marketing, 1977–89; Associate Dir, 1985–87. Jt Man. Dir, Evode Holdings PLC, 1976–77. Director: Strategic Management Soc., 1982– (Pres. 1985–88); Bray Technologies, 1983–; Royal Bank of Scotland, 1988–. *Publications:* Strategy and Structure of British Enterprise, 1973; (with J. Stopford and B. Norburn) British Business Policy, 1975; British Banking Strategy and the International Challenge, 1977; The Service Industries, 1978; (with R. M. Jalland) Multi-national Strategic Planning, 1979; British Transnational Bank Strategy, 1979; (with J. Stopford and J. Constable) Cases in Strategic Management, 1980; (with P. Rushton) Retail Electronic Banking and Point of Sale, 1982; Bank Strategic Management and Marketing, 1986; Global Banking Strategy, 1988. *Recreations:* golf, tennis. *Address:* Imperial College, 53 Prince's Gate, Exhibition Road, SW7 2PG.

CHANNON, Rt. Hon. (Henry) Paul (Guinness); PC 1980; MP (C) for Southend West, since Jan. 1959; *b* 9 Oct. 1935; *o s* of late Sir Henry Channon, MP, and of late Lady Honor Svejdar (*née* Guinness), *e d* of 2nd Earl of Iveagh, KG; *m* 1963, Ingrid Olivia Georgia Guinness (*née* Wyndham); one *s* one *d* (and one *d* decd). *Educ:* Lockers Park, Hemel Hempstead; Eton Coll., Christ Church, Oxford. 2nd Lieut Royal Horse Guards (The Blues), 1955–56. Pres. of Oxford Univ. Conservative Association, 1958. Parly Private Sec. to: Minister of Power, 1959–60; Home Sec., 1960–62; First Sec. of State, 1962–63; PPS to the Foreign Sec., 1963–64; Opposition Spokesman on Arts and Amenities, 1967–70; Parly Sec., Min. of Housing and Local Govt, June-Oct. 1970; Parly Under-Sec. of State, DoE, 1970–72; Minister of State, Northern Ireland Office, March-Nov. 1972; Minister for Housing and Construction, DoE, 1972–74; Opposition Spokesman on: Prices and Consumer Protection, March-Sept. 1974; environmental affairs, Oct. 1974–Feb. 1975; Minister of State, CSD, 1979–81; Minister for the Arts, 1981–83; Minister for Trade, 1983–86; Sec. of State for Trade and Industry, 1986–87; Sec. of State for Transport, 1987–89. Chairman: Finance and Services Cttee, H of C, 1992–; Transport Select Cttee, 1993–. Dep. Leader, Cons. Delegn to WEU and Council of Europe, 1976–79. Chm., British Assoc. for Central and Eastern Europe, 1991–. Mem., Gen. Adv. Council to ITA, 1964–66. *Address:* House of Commons, SW1A 0AA.

CHANT, (Elizabeth) Ann; Chief Executive, Child Support Agency, Department of Social Security, since 1994; *b* 16 Aug. 1945; *d* of late Capt. Harry Charles Chant and Gertrude Chant (*née* Poel). *Educ:* Blackpool Collegiate Sch. for Girls. Nat. Assistance Bd, Lincoln, 1963–66; Min. of Social Security, Lincoln, 1966–70; NHS Whitley Council, DHSS London, 1970–72; DHSS, Lincoln, 1972–74; DHSS Regl Office, Nottingham, 1974–82; Manager, DHSS Sutton-in-Ashfield, 1982–83; DHSS HQ, London, 1983–85; Prin. Private Sec. to Permanent Sec., DHSS, 1985–87; Head: Records Br., DSS, Newcastle upon Tyne, 1987–89; Contribns Unit, 1990–91; Chief Exec., Contributions Agency, DSS, 1991–94. Exec. Council Mem., Industrial Soc., 1993–. FRSA 1991. *Recreations:* friends, music (especially opera), theatre. *Address:* Child Support Agency, Millbank Tower, 21–24 Millbank, SW1 4QU.

CHANTLER, Prof. Cyril, MD; FRCP; Professor of Paediatric Nephrology, since 1980, and Principal, since 1992, United Medical and Dental Schools of Guy's and St Thomas' Hospitals; *b* 12 May 1939; *s* of Fred Chantler and Marjorie Chantler (*née* Clark); *m* 1963, Shireen Saleh; two *s* one *d*. *Educ:* Wrekin Coll.; St Catharine's Coll., Cambridge (BA 1960; MB BChir 1963; MD 1973); Guy's Hosp. Med. Sch. MRC Travelling Fellow, Univ. of California, 1971; Guy's Hospital: Sen. Lectr and Consultant Paediatrician, 1972–80; General Manager, 1985–88; Clinical Dean, UMDS, Guy's and St Thomas' Hosps, 1989–92. Mem., NHS Policy Bd, 1989–. Chm., Sci. Adv. Cttee, Foundn for the Study of Infant Deaths, 1988–90; Non-Executive Director: Guy's and Lewisham NHS Trust, 1991–92; Guy's and St Thomas' NHS Trust, 1993–; Inst. of Health Management Consultants, 1990–94; Pres., British Assoc. of Medical Managers, 1991–. Teale Lectr, 1987, Censor, 1989–90, RCP. Hon. Mem., Amer. Paed. Assoc., 1992. Co-Editor, Pediatric Nephrology Jl, 1986–. *Recreations:* golf, opera, squash, reading. *Address:* UMDS, Guy's Hospital, SE1 9RT. *T:* 0171–955 4222; 60 Herne Hill, SE24 9QP. *Club:* Athenæum.

CHANTRY, Dr George William, CEng, FIEE; CPhys; FInstP; Senior Vice-President Europe, Carnahan & Associates, since 1994 (Director, European Operations, 1990–93); Consultant to Ministry of Defence on Strategic Defence Initiative Technology Transfer, since 1990; *b* 13 April 1933; *s* of George William Chantry and Sophia Veronica (*née* Johnston); *m* 1956, Diana Margaret Rhodes (*née* Martin); two *s* one *d*. *Educ:* Christ Church, Oxford (DPhil 1959, MA 1960). CEng, FIEE 1976; FInstP 1974. Res. Associate, Cornell Univ., 1958; National Physical Lab., Dept of Industry: Sen. Res. Fellow, 1960; Sen. Scientific Officer, 1962; Principal Sci. Officer, 1967; Sen. Principal Sci. Officer, 1973; Dep. Chief Sci. Officer, DoI HQ, 1982, seconded to FCO; Counsellor (Sci. and Tech.), Bonn and Berne, 1982; Res. and Technol. Policy Div., DTI, 1985; seconded to MoD as Asst Dir for Industry in SDI Participation Office, 1985. Past Chm., European Molecular Liquids Gp; Mem., Science Educn and Technol. Bd, IEE, 1980–82. Editor, Proc. IEE, Part A, 1981–. *Publications:* Submillimetre Spectroscopy, 1971; High-Frequency Dielectric Measurement, 1972; Submillimetre Waves and their Applications, 1978; Modern Aspects of Microwave Spectroscopy, 1980; Long-Wave Optics, 1983; papers in learned literature. *Recreations:* philately, bridge, gardening, music. *Address:* 42 Cranwell Grove, Shepperton, Mddx TW17 0JR. *T:* Chertsey (01932) 560524.

CHAPLAIS, Pierre Théophile Victorien Marie; Médaille de la Résistance, 1946; FBA 1973; Reader in Diplomatic in the University of Oxford, 1957–87, now Reader Emeritus; Professorial Fellow, Wadham College, Oxford, 1964–87, now Emeritus Fellow; *b* Châteaubriant, Loire-Atlantique, France, 8 July 1920; *s* of late Théophile Chaplais and Victorine Chaplais (*née* Roussel); *m* 1948, Mary Doreen Middlemast; two *s*. *Educ:* Collège St-Sauveur, Redon, Ille-et-Vilaine; Univ. of Rennes, Ille-et-Vilaine (Licence en Droit, Licence ès-Lettres); Univ. of London (PhD). Editor, Public Record Office, London, 1948–55; Lectr in Diplomatic, Univ. of Oxford, 1955–57; Literary Dir, Royal Hist. Soc., 1958–64. Corresp. Fellow, Mediaeval Acad. of America, 1979. *Publications:* Some Documents regarding . . . The Treaty of Brétigny, 1952; The War of St Sardos, 1954; Treaty Rolls, vol. I, 1955; (with T. A. M. Bishop) Facsimiles of English Royal Writs to AD 1100 presented to V. H. Galbraith, 1957; Diplomatic Documents, vol. I, 1964; English Royal Documents, King John-Henry VI, 1971; English Medieval Diplomatic Practice, Part II, 1975, Part I, 1983; Essays in Medieval Diplomacy and Administration, 1981; Piers Gaveston, Edward II's Adoptive Brother, 1994; articles in Bulletin of Inst. of Historical Research, English Hist. Review, Jl of Soc. of Archivists, etc. *Recreations:* gardening, fishing. *Address:* Lew Lodge, Lew, Bampton, Oxfordshire OX18 2BE. *T:* Bampton Castle (01993) 850613.

CHAPLIN, Arthur Hugh, CB 1970; Principal Keeper of Printed Books, British Museum, 1966–70; *b* 17 April 1905; *er s* of late Rev. Herbert F. Chaplin and Florence B. Lusher; *m* 1938, Irene Marcousé (*d* 1990). *Educ:* King's Lynn Grammar Sch.; Bedford Modern Sch.; University Coll., London. Asst Librarian: Reading Univ. 1927–28; Queen's Univ., Belfast, 1928–29; Asst Keeper, Dept of Printed Books, British Museum, 1930–52; Dep. Keeper, 1952–59; Keeper, 1959–66. Exec. Sec., Organizing Cttee of Internat. Conf. on Cataloguing Principles, Paris, 1961; Mem. Council, Library Assoc. 1964–70; Pres., Microfilm Assoc. of GB, 1967–71; Mem. Senate, Univ. of London, 1973–79. Fellow UCL, 1969. *Publications:* contributions to Jl Documentation, Library Assoc. Record, Library Quarterly, and to Cataloguing Principles and Practice (ed M. Piggott), 1954; Tradition and Principle in Library Cataloguing, 1966; GK: 150 Years of the General Catalogue of Printed Books, 1987. *Address:* 41 Ridgmount Gardens, WC1E 7AT. *T:* 0171–636 7217.

CHAPLIN, John Cyril, CBE 1988; FEng 1987; FRAeS; Member, Civil Aviation Authority and Group Director, Safety Regulation (formerly Safety Services), 1983–88; *b* 13 Aug. 1926; *s* of late Ernest Stanley Chaplin and Isabel Chaplin; *m* 1949, Ruth Marianne Livingstone; two *s* two *d*. *Educ:* Keswick School. Miles Aircraft, 1946; Vickers-Supermarine, 1948; Handley Page, 1950; Somers-Kendall Aircraft, 1952; Heston Aircraft, 1956; Air Registration Board, 1958; Civil Aviation Authority, 1972, Dir-Gen. Airworthiness, 1979. *Publications:* papers to RAeS. *Recreations:* sailing, photography. *Address:* Norman Croft, Mattingley, Basingstoke, Hants RG27 8LF. *T:* Reading (01734) 326207. *Club:* Cruising Association.

CHAPLIN, Sir Malcolm Hilbery, Kt 1991; CBE 1984; Senior Partner, Hilbery Chaplin. *Educ:* Rugby Sch.; Trinity Hall, Cambridge (MA 1961). FRICS. Freeman, City of London. *Address:* Hilbery Chaplin, 4 Eastern Road, Romford RM1 3PL.

CHAPMAN, family name of **Baron Northfield.**

CHAPMAN, Angela Mary, (Mrs I. M. Chapman); Headmistress, Central Newcastle High School (GPDST), since 1985; *b* 2 Jan. 1940; *d* of Frank Dyson and Mary Rowe; *m* 1959, Ian Michael Chapman; two *s*. *Educ:* Queen Victoria High Sch., Stockton; Univ. of Bristol (BA Hons French); Sorbonne (Dip. de Civilisation Française). Teacher of French, Bede Sch., Sunderland, 1970–80; Dep. Headmistress, Newcastle-upon-Tyne Church High Sch., 1980–84. FRSA. *Recreations:* military history, walking, tennis. *Address:* 14 Alpine Way, Sunderland, Tyne and Wear SR3 1TN.

CHAPMAN, Ben; *see* Chapman, J. K.

CHAPMAN, Charles Cyril Staplee; consultant; Member for Corporate Development and Finance, UK Atomic Energy Authority, 1988–90; *b* 9 Aug. 1936; *s* of Thomas John Chapman and Gertrude Gosden Chapman; *m* 1963, Lorraine Dorothy Wenborn; two *s*. *Educ:* St Peter's Sch., York; Univ. of Sheffield (BSc Hons). British Petroleum Co., 1958, Manager, Chemicals, Corporate Planning, Minerals, 1962–85; Senior Strategy Advisor, British Telecom, 1986–88. *Recreation:* growing rhododendrons.

CHAPMAN, Prof. Christopher Hugh; Scientific Advisor, Schlumberger Cambridge Research, since 1991; *b* 5 May 1945; *s* of John Harold Chapman and Margaret Joan Weeks; *m* 1974, Lillian Tarapaski; one *s* one *d*. *Educ:* Latymer Upper School; Christ's College, Cambridge (MA); Dept of Geodesy and Geophysics, Cambridge (PhD). Asst Prof., Univ. of Alberta, 1969–72, Associate Prof., 1973–74; Asst Prof., Univ. of California, Berkeley, 1972–73; University of Toronto: Associate Prof., 1974–80; Prof., 1980–84; Killam Research Fellow, 1981–83; Adjunct Prof., 1984–88; Prof. of Physics, 1988–90; Prof. of Geophysics, Dept of Earth Scis, and Fellow, Christ's Coll., Cambridge, 1984–88. Green Scholar, Univ. of California, San Diego, 1978–79, 1986. *Publications:* research papers in sci. jls. *Recreations:* sailing, photography, woodwork. *Address:* Schlumberger Cambridge Research, High Cross, Madingley Road, Cambridge CB3 0EL. *T:* Cambridge (01223) 315576.

CHAPMAN, His Honour Cyril Donald, QC 1965; a Circuit Judge, 1972–86; *b* 17 Sept. 1920; *s* of Cyril Henry Chapman and Frances Elizabeth Chapman (*née* Braithwaite); *m* 1st, 1950, Audrey Margaret Fraser (*née* Gough) (marr. diss., 1959); one *s*; 2nd, 1960, Muriel Falconer Bristow; one *s*. *Educ:* Roundhay Sch., Leeds; Brasenose Coll., Oxford (MA). Served RNVR, 1939–45. Called to Bar, 1947; Harmsworth Scholar, 1947; North Eastern Circuit, 1947; Recorder of Huddersfield, 1965–69, of Bradford, 1969–71. Contested (C) East Leeds 1955, Goole 1964, Brighouse and Spenborough, 1966. *Recreation:* walking. *Address:* Hill Top, Collingham, Wetherby, W Yorks LS22 5BB. *T:* Collingham Bridge (01937) 572813. *Club:* Leeds (Leeds).

CHAPMAN, Daniel Ahmling, *see* Chapman Nyaho.

CHAPMAN, Sir David (Robert Macgowan), 3rd Bt *cr* 1958, of Cleadon, Co. Durham; Director, Wise Speke Ltd, Stock and Share Brokers, Newcastle upon Tyne, since 1987 (Partner, 1971–87); *b* 16 Dec. 1941; *s* of Sir Robert Macgowan Chapman, 2nd Bt, CBE, TD and of Barbara May, *d* of Hubert Tonks; *S* father, 1987; *m* 1965, Maria Elizabeth de Gosztonyi-Zsolnay, *o d* of Dr N. de Mattyasovsky-Zsolnay; one *s* one *d*. *Educ:* Marlborough; McGill Univ., Montreal (BCom). Chm., Team General Partner Ltd, 1994–; Director: Northern Rock (formerly North of England) Building Soc., 1974–; Breathe North Ltd, 1988–95; British Lung Foundation Ltd, 1989–95; Montfort Press Ltd, 1994–95; Gordon Durham & Co. Ltd, 1994–. Stock Exchange: Mem. Council, 1979–88; Chairman: Northern Unit, 1988–91; NE Reg. Adv Gp, 1991–. MSI 1991. Chm., Northumbria Coalition Against Crime, 1995–. Gov., St Aidan's Coll., Durham, 1987–. High Sheriff, Tyne and Wear, 1993–94. *Heir: s* Michael Nicholas Chapman, *b* 21 May 1969. *Address:* Westmount, 14 West Park Road, Cleadon, Sunderland, Tyne and Wear SR6 7RR; Wise Speke Ltd, Commercial Union House, 39 Pilgrim Street, Newcastle upon Tyne NE1 6RQ.

CHAPMAN, Prof. Dennis, FRS 1986; Professor of Biophysical Chemistry, since 1977, Head of Department of Protein and Molecular Biology, since 1988, and Vice Dean, since 1990, Royal Free Hospital School of Medicine, University of London; *b* 6 May 1927; *s* of George Henry Chapman and Katherine Magnus; *m* 1st, 1949, Elsie Margaret Stephenson (*d* 1989); two *s* one *d*; 2nd, 1993, Françoise Nioukleen Ng. *Educ:* London Univ. (BSc; DSc); Liverpool Univ. (PhD); Cambridge Univ. Comyns Berkeley Fellow, Gonville and Caius Coll., Cambridge, 1960–63; Head of Gen. Research Div., Unilever Ltd, Welwyn, 1963–69; Professor Associate, Biophysical Chem., Sheffield Univ., 1968–76; Sen. Wellcome Trust Research Fellow, Dept of Chemistry, Chelsea Coll., Univ. of London, 1976–77; Head of Div. of Basic Med. Scis, Royal Free Hosp. Sch. of Medicine, London Univ., 1988–89. Associate Dir, IRC (Medical Biomaterials), Univ. of London, 1991–. Langmuir Lectr, US, 1992. Founder, Biocompatibles Ltd, 1984. Hon. MRCP 1988; First Hon. Mem., Spanish Biophysical Soc., 1991. Hon. DSc: Utrecht, 1976; Meml, Canada, 1980; Pais Vasco, Spain, 1994. Royal Free Hosp. Sch. of Medicine Medal, 1987; Interdisciplinary Award, 1992; Harden Medal, 1995. *Publications:* Biological Membranes, vol. I–vol. V, 1968–84; 430 scientific publications in biochemical jls. *Recreations:* golf, walking. *Address:* IRC (Medical Biomaterials) Unit, Royal Free Hospital School of Medicine, Rowland Hill Street, NW3 2PF. *T:* 0171–794 0500, ext. 3246.

CHAPMAN, (Francis) Ian, CBE 1988; Deputy Chairman, Orion Publishing Group, 1993–94; Chairman: Scottish Radio Holdings (formerly Radio Clyde) PLC, 1972–95; Guinness Publishers Ltd, since 1991; *b* 26 Oct. 1925; *s* of late Rev. Peter Chapman and Frances Burdett; *m* 1953, Marjory Stewart Swinton; one *s* one *d*. *Educ:* Shawlands Academy, Glasgow. Served RAF, 1943–44; worked in coal mines as part of national service, 1945–47. Joined Wm Collins Sons & Co. Ltd, 1947 as management trainee; Sales Manager, 1955; Gp Sales Dir, 1960; Jt Man. Dir, 1968–76; Dep. Chm., William Collins Hldgs, 1976–81; Chm., William Collins Publishers Ltd, 1979–81; Chm. and Gp Chief Exec., William Collins plc, 1981–89. Chairman: Harvill Press Ltd, 1976–89; Hatchards Ltd, 1976–89; Ancient House Bookshop (Ipswich) Ltd, 1976–89; Co-Chm. and Actg Chief Exec., Harper & Row, NY, 1987–89; Chm. and Man. Dir, Chapmans Publishers, 1989–94. Chm., The Listener Publications PLC, 1988–93; Director: Independent Radio News, 1984–85; Pan Books Ltd, 1962–84 (Chm., 1974–76); Book Tokens Ltd, 1981–94; Stanley Botes Ltd, 1985–89; (non-exec.) Guinness PLC, 1986–91; (non-exec.) United Distillers PLC, 1987–91. Mem. Council, Publishers' Assoc., 1963–76, 1977–82 (Vice Pres., 1978–79 and 1981–82; Pres., 1979–81); Member: Bd, Book Develt Council, 1967–73; Governing Council, Scottish Business in the Community, 1983–; Dir, Scottish Opera, Theatre Royal Ltd, 1974–79; Trustee, Book Trade Benevolent Soc., 1982–. Chm. Council, Strathclyde Univ. Business School, 1985–88. FRSA 1985; CBIM 1982. Hon. DLitt Strathclyde, 1990. Scottish Free Enterprise Award, 1985. *Publications:* various articles on publishing in trade jls. *Recreations:* music, golf, reading, grandchildren. *Address:* (business) Guinness Publishers Ltd, 33 London Road, Enfield, Middlesex EN2 6DJ. *T:* 0181–367 4567, *Fax:* 0181–367 5912; Kenmore, 46 The Avenue, Cheam, Surrey SM2 7QE. *T:* 0181–642 1820. *Clubs:* Garrick, Groucho, MCC; Royal Wimbledon Golf; Prestwick Golf; Walton Heath Golf.

CHAPMAN, Frank Arthur; His Honour Judge Chapman; a Circuit Judge, since 1992; *b* 28 May 1946; *s* of Dennis Arthur Chapman and Joan Chapman; *m* 1968, Mary Kathleen Jones; one *s* one *d*. *Educ:* Newton-le-Willows Grammar School; University College London (LLB, LLM). Called to the Bar, Gray's Inn, 1968; practice at Birmingham. Practising Anglican. *Recreations:* travel, mountaineering, angling.

CHAPMAN, Frederick John; Treasurer, since 1989, and Vice-President, since 1990, Varity Corporation (Treasurer (Europe), 1988–89); Principal Establishment and Finance Officer (Under Secretary), Export Credits Guarantee Department, 1985–88; *b* 24 June 1939; *s* of late Reginald John Chapman and Elizabeth Chapman; *m* 1964, Paula Brenda Waller; one *s* two *d*. *Educ:* Sutton County Grammar Sch. Joined ECGD, 1958; Principal, 1969; Asst Sec., 1977; Under Sec., 1982. *Recreations:* reading, music. *Address:* c/o Varity Europe Ltd, 9 Upper Belgrave Street, SW1X 8BD. *T:* 0171–465 0610.

CHAPMAN, Prof. Garth; Professor of Zoology, Queen Elizabeth College, University of London, 1958–82, now Emeritus (Vice Principal, 1974–80; Acting Principal, Sept. 1977–March 1978; Fellow, 1984); *b* 8 Oct. 1917; *o s* of E. J. Chapman and Edith Chapman (*née* Attwood); *m* 1941, Margaret Hilda Wigley; one *s* one *d* (and one *s* decd). *Educ:* Royal Grammar Sch., Worcester; Trinity Hall, Cambridge (Major Scholar); ScD Cantab 1977. FIBiol 1963; FKC 1985. Telecommunications Research Establishment, Ministry of Aircraft Production, 1941–45; Asst Lectr in Zoology, 1945–46, Lectr in Zoology, 1946–58, QMC, Univ. of London; Dean, Faculty of Science, Univ. of London, 1974–78. Vis. Prof., Univ. of California, Berkeley, 1967, Los Angeles, 1970–71. Member: Cttee for Commonwealth Univ. Interchange, British Council, 1978–80; Inter-Univ. Council for Higher Educn Overseas, 1973–83; Council, Westfield Coll., Univ. of London, 1978–84; Central Research Fund Cttee B, 1978–82; Management Cttee of Univ. Marine Biological Station, Millport, 1975–82. *Publications:* Zoology for Intermediate Students (with W. B. Barker), 1964; Body Fluids and their Functions, 1967; various on structure and physiology of marine invertebrates. *Recreations:* gardening; wood-engraving. *Address:* The Grove, Callis Street, Clare, Suffolk CO10 8PX. *T:* Clare (01787) 277235. *Club:* Athenæum.

CHAPMAN, Geoffrey Lloyd; Vice Judge Advocate General, 1984–94; *b* 20 Oct. 1928; *o s* of Sydney Leslie Chapman and Dora Chapman (*née* Lloyd); *m* 1958, Jean, *er d* of Valentine Harry Coleman and Marjorie Coleman (*née* Poston); one *s* two *d*. *Educ:* Latymer Upper School; Christ Church, Oxford (MA, BCL). National Service, 1947–49 (commissioned RASC). Called to the Bar, Inner Temple, 1953; practised London and Western Circuit; Legal Asst, Min. of Labour and Nat. Service, 1957; Legal Asst, JAG's Office, 1958; Dep. Judge Advocate, 1961 (Germany, 1963–66, Cyprus, 1969–72); Asst JAG, 1971 (Germany, 1972–76); Dep. JAG, British Forces in Germany, 1979–82. *Recreations:* beagling, reading. *Address:* The Myrtles, Alma Road, Reigate, Surrey RH2 0DH. *T:* Reigate (01737) 247860.

CHAPMAN, Sir George (Alan), Kt 1982; FCA; FCIS; Senior Partner, Chapman Ross & Co., Chartered Accountants; *b* 13 April 1927; *s* of late Thomas George Chapman and of Winifred Jordan Chapman; *m* 1950, Jacqueline Sidney (*née* Irvine); two *s* five *d*. *Educ:* Trentham Sch.; Hutt Valley High Sch.; Victoria University. Fellow, Chartered Inst. of Secretaries, 1969 (Mem., 1948–); Fellow, NZ Soc. of Accountants, 1969 (Mem., 1948–). Joined Chapman Ross & Co., 1948. Chairman: Norwich Union General Insurance (formerly Norwich Winterthur) (NZ), 1985–92 (Dir, 1982–92); BNZ Finance, 1979–88 (Dir, 1977–88); Mitel Telecommunications, 1984–91; Pilkington (formerly Pilkington Brothers) (NZ), 1989–94 (Dir, 1982–94); Director: Bank of New Zealand, 1968–86 (Dep. Chm., 1976–86); Maui Developments Ltd, 1979–85; Offshore Mining Co. Ltd, 1979–85; Liquigas Ltd, 1981–85 (Chm., 1982–84); NZ Bd, Norwich Union Life Insurance Soc., 1982–92; Skellerup Industries Ltd, 1982–90 (Dep. Chm., 1984–87); Skellerup Industries, Malaysia, 1986–90; State Insurance Ltd, 1990– (Vice Chm., 1992–); Norwich Union Holdings (NZ) Ltd, 1990– (Vice Chm., 1992–); Vice Chm., Norwich Union Life Insurance (NZ) Ltd, 1993–. Chairman: NZ Building Industry Authority, 1992–; Housing New Zealand Ltd, 1992– (Chm. Housing Corp. of NZ and Housing NZ Estabt Bd, April–July 1992). NZ National Party: Member, 1948–; Vice-Pres., 1966–73; Pres., 1973–82. Councillor, Upper Hutt Bor. Council, 1952–53, Deputy Mayor, Upper Hutt, 1953–55; Member: Hutt Valley Drainage Bd, 1953–55; Heretaunga Bd of Governors, 1953–55; Pres., Upper Hutt Chamber of Commerce, 1956–57. MInstD 1979. *Publication:* The Years of Lightning, 1980. *Recreations:* golf, reading, tennis. *Address:* 53 Barton Avenue, Heretaunga, Wellington, New Zealand. *T:* (4) 5283512. *Clubs:* Wellington Golf, Wellington Racing.

CHAPMAN, Ian; *see* Chapman, F. I.

CHAPMAN, James Keith, (Ben); Director, Trade and Industry, Government Office for the North West, since 1994; *b* 8 July 1940; *s* of John Hartley and Elsie Vera Chapman; *m* (marr. diss); three *d*. *Educ:* Appleby Grammar Sch., Appleby in Westmorland. Pilot Officer, RAFVR, 1959–61. Min. of Pensions and Nat. Insce, 1958–62; Min. of Aviation/BAA, 1962–67; Rochdale Cttee of Inquiry into Shipping, 1967–70; BoT, 1970–74; First Sec. (Commercial), Dar es Salaam, 1974–78; First Sec. (Econ.), Accra, 1978–81; Asst Sec., DTI, 1981–87; Commercial Counsellor, Peking, 1987–90; Dep. Regl Dir, NW, and Dir, Merseyside, 1991–93, Regl Dir, Northwest, 1993–94, DTI. FIMgt. *Recreations:* opera, theatre, music, walking. *Address:* 18 The Keep, Pond Road, Blackheath, SE3 0AF; 14 Murton View, Appleby in Westmorland, Cumbria CA16 6RF; (office) Sunley Tower, Piccadilly Plaza, Manchester M1 4BA. *Clubs:* St James's, Portico Library (Manchester).

CHAPMAN, John Henry Benjamin, CB 1957; CEng; FRINA; RCNC; *b* 28 Dec. 1899; *s* of Robert Henry Chapman and Edith Yeo Chapman (*née* Lillicrap); *m* 1929, Dorothy Rowlerson (*d* 1991); one *s* one *d*. *Educ:* HM Dockyard Sch., Devonport; RNC Greenwich. Dir of Naval Construction, Admiralty, 1958–61. Dir, Fairfield S & E Co. Ltd, 1962–66; Consultant, Upper Clyde Shipbuilders, 1966–68. Mem. of Royal Corps of

Naval Constructors, 1922–61; Hon. Vice-Pres., RINA. *Address:* Lordington Park, near Chichester, W Sussex PO18 9DX. *T:* Emsworth (01243) 377273. *Club:* Bosham Sailing.

CHAPMAN, Kathleen Violet, CBE 1956; RRC 1953 (ARRC 1945); QHNS 1953–56; Matron-in-Chief, Queen Alexandra's Royal Naval Nursing Service, 1953–56, retired; *b* 30 May 1903; *d* of late Major H. E. Chapman, CBE, DL Kent, Chief Constable of Kent, and Mrs C. H. J. Chapman. *Educ:* Queen Anne's, Caversham. Trained St Thomas's Hospital, 1928–32.

CHAPMAN, Leslie Charles; Founder and Chairman, Campaign to Stop Waste in Public Expenditure, since 1981; *b* 14 Sept. 1919; *e s* of Charles Richard Chapman and Lilian Elizabeth Chapman; *m* 1947, Beryl Edith England; (one *s* decd). *Educ:* Bishopshalt Sch. Served War, Army, 1939–45. Civil Service, 1939 and 1945–74; Regional Dir, Southern Region, MPBW and PSA, 1967–74. Chm. and mem., various cttees; Mem. (pt-time), LTE, 1979–80. *Publications:* Your Disobedient Servant, 1978, 2nd revised edn 1979; Waste Away, 1982. *Recreations:* reading, music, gardening. *Address:* Cae Caradog, Ffarmers, Llanwrda, Dyfed SA19 8NQ. *T:* Pumpsaint (015585) 504.

CHAPMAN, Mark Fenger, CVO 1979; HM Diplomatic Service, retired; Member, Police Complaints Authority, since 1991; *b* 12 Sept. 1934; *er s* of late Geoffrey Walter Chapman and of Esther Maria Fenger; *m* 1959, Patricia Mary Long; three *s* (and one *s* decd). *Educ:* Cranbrook Sch.; St Catharine's Coll., Cambridge. Entered HM Foreign Service, 1958; served in: Bangkok, 1959–63; FO, 1963–67; Head of Chancery, Maseru, 1967–71; Asst Head of Dept, FCO, 1971–74; Head of Chancery, Vienna, 1975–76; Dep. High Comr and Counsellor (Econ. and Comm.), Lusaka, 1976–79; Diplomatic Service Inspector, 1979–82; Counsellor, The Hague, 1982–86; Ambassador to Iceland, 1986–89. *Address:* c/o Barclays Bank, Holt, Norfolk NR25 6BQ. *Club:* Commonwealth Trust.

CHAPMAN, Ven. Michael Robin; Archdeacon of Northampton, since 1991; *b* 29 Sept. 1939; *s* of Frankland and Kathleen Chapman; *m* 1973, Bernadette Taylor; one *s* one *d.* *Educ:* Lichfield Cathedral Sch.; Ellesmere Coll.; Leeds Univ. (BA 1961); Coll. of the Resurrection, Mirfield. Ordained, dio. of Durham, deacon, 1963, priest, 1964; curate, St Columba, Sunderland, 1963–68; Chaplain, RN, 1968–84; Vicar, St John the Evangelist, Farnham, 1984–91; Rural Dean of Farnham, 1988–91. *Recreations:* flying light aircraft, music, hill walking. *Address:* 11 The Drive, Northampton NN1 4RZ. *T:* Northampton (01604) 714015.

CHAPMAN, Nicholas John; Director, BBC Worldwide Ltd, since 1994; Managing Director, BBC Worldwide Publishing, since 1994; Director, BBC Americas Inc., since 1994; *b* 17 June 1947; *s* of Frank and Elizabeth Chapman; *m* 1974, Susan Barrow (marr. diss. 1981); *m* 1995, Louise Shaxson. *Educ:* Merchant Taylors' Sch.; Clare Coll., Cambridge (MA). With Hodder and Stoughton: Graduate Trainee, 1969; European Sales, 1970; Editor, 1973; Publishing Dir, Associated Business Press, 1975; Editor-in-Chief, Futura Paperbacks, 1979; Publishing Director: Macdonald Futura, 1980; Macmillan London, 1983; Head of BBC Books and Education, BBC Enterprises, 1986–89; Dir, Consumer Products Gp, BBC Enterprises, 1989–94; Mem., BBC Bd of Management, 1994–. Pres., Publishers Assoc., 1994–April 1996. *Recreations:* walking, reading, history, tennis. *Address:* BBC Worldwide Publishing, Woodlands, 80 Wood Lane, W12 0TT. *T:* 0181–576 2615.

CHAPMAN, Prof. Norman Bellamy, MA, PhD; CChem, FRSC; G. F. Grant Professor of Chemistry, Hull University, 1956–82, now Emeritus; Pro-Vice-Chancellor, 1973–76; *b* 19 April 1916; *s* of Frederick Taylor Chapman and Bertha Chapman; *m* 1949, Fonda Maureen Bungey; one *s* one *d.* *Educ:* Barnsley Holgate Grammar Sch.; Magdalene Coll., Cambridge (Entrance Scholar). 1st Cl. Parts I and II Nat. Sciences Tripos, 1937 and 1938; BA 1938, MA 1942, PhD 1941. Bye-Fellow, Magdalene Coll., 1939–42; Univ. Demonstrator in Chemistry, Cambridge, 1945; Southampton Univ.: Lectr, 1947; Senior Lectr, 1949; Reader in Chemistry, 1955. R. T. French Visiting Prof., Univ. of Rochester, NY, 1962–63; R. J. Reynolds Vis. Prof., Duke Univ., N Carolina, 1971; Cooch Behar Prof., Calcutta, 1982. Universities Central Council on Admissions: Dep. Chm., 1979–83; Chm., Technical Cttee, 1974–79; Chm., Statistics Cttee, 1983–89. Hon. DSc Hull, 1984. *Publications:* (ed with J. Shorter) Advances in Free Energy Relationships, 1972; (ed) Organic Chemistry, Series One, vol. 2: Aliphatic Compounds (MTP Internat. Review of Science), 1973, Series Two, vol 2, 1976; Correlation Analysis in Chemistry: recent advances, 1978; contribs to Jl Chem. Soc., Analyst, Jl Medicinal Chem., Tetrahedron, Jl Organic Chemistry, Chemistry and Industry. *Recreations:* music, gardening, cricket, Rugby football. *Address:* 5 The Lawns, Molescroft, Beverley HU17 7LS. *T:* Hull (01482) 860553.

CHAPMAN, Hon. Rhiannon Elizabeth, FIPM; Member, Welsh Development Agency, since 1994; *b* 21 Sept. 1946; *d* of 2nd Viscount St Davids and Doreen Guinness Jowett; *m* 1974, Donald Hudson Chapman (marr. diss. 1992); two step *s.* *Educ:* Tormead Sch., Guildford; King's Coll., London Univ. (LLB Hons 1967; AKC). FIPM 1972. Industrial Soc., 1968; LWT, 1968–70; Philips Electronics Industries, 1970–77; CPI Data Peripherals Ltd, 1977–80; Personnel Dir, London Stock Exchange, 1980–90; business consultant, 1990–91; Dir, Industrial Soc., 1991–93. Chm., National Australia CIF Trustee Ltd; non-exec. Dir, S. R. Gent plc, 1994–. Member: UFC, 1989–93; Employment Appeal Tribunal, 1991–; Council, PSI, 1993–. Governor, London Guildhall Univ., 1992–; Council, London Lighthouse, 1994–. CIMgt. *Recreations:* tennis, circuit training, handcrafts, opera, travel. *Address:* 39 Spice Court, Asher Way, E1 9JD. *T:* 0171–709 0226. *Club:* New Cavendish.

CHAPMAN, Roy de Courcy; Headmaster of Malvern College, since 1983; *b* 1 Oct. 1936; *s* of Edward Frederic Gilbert Chapman and Aline de Courcy Ireland; *m* 1959, Valerie Rosemary Small; two *s* one *d.* *Educ:* Dollar Academy; St Andrews Univ. (Harkness Schol.: MA 1959); Moray House Coll. of Educn, Edinburgh. Asst Master, Trinity Coll., Glenalmond, 1960–64; Marlborough College: Asst Master, 1964–68; Head of Mod. Langs, 1968–75; OC CCF, 1969–75; Rector of Glasgow Acad., 1975–82. Chairman: Common Entrance Bd, 1988–93; HMC, 1994. *Publications:* Le Français Contemporain, 1971; (with D. Whiting) Le Français Contemporain: Passages for translation and comprehension, 1975. *Recreations:* France, snorkelling. *Address:* Headmaster's House, Malvern College, Worcs WR14 3HW. *T:* Malvern (01684) 574472.

CHAPMAN, Roy John, FCA; Chairman, Post Office Pension Fund, since 1995; Director, Halifax Building Society, since 1994; Senior Partner, Arthur Andersen, 1989–93; *b* 30 Nov. 1936; *s* of William George Chapman and Frances Harriet Chapman; *m* 1961, Janet Gibbeson Taylor; two *s* one *d.* *Educ:* Kettering Grammar Sch.; St Catharine's Coll., Cambridge (Athletics Blue; MA). CIMgt, FIMC, FBPICS, FRSA. Joined Arthur Andersen & Co., Chartered Accountants, 1958; consulting, UK and abroad, incl. France, USA, Algeria, Greece, Turkey, Thailand and Switzerland, 1964–84; admitted to Partnership, 1970; Hd of Financial Services Practice, 1970–84; Man. Partner, London, 1984–89; Mem., Internat. Bd, 1988–93. Member: Adv. Council, London Enterprise Agency, 1985–88; Jt Disciplinary Scheme for Accounting Profession, 1994–. Mem. Governing Body, SOAS, London, 1990–. Council Mem., BITC, 1991–93. London Marathon, 1983 (Save the Children). Pres., St Catherine's Coll. Cambridge Soc., 1994–95. Liveryman, Farriers' Co., 1992–. *Publications:* contribs to professional jls. *Recreations:* cricket, walking, reading, travel. *Address:* 9 Chislehurst Road, Bickley, Kent BR1 2NN. *T:* 0181–467 3749. *Clubs:* United Oxford & Cambridge University, MCC; Hawks (Cambridge).

CHAPMAN, Sir Sydney (Brookes), Kt 1995; RIBA; FRTPI; MP (C) Chipping Barnet, since 1979; Chartered Architect and Chartered Town and Country Planner; private planning consultant (non-practising); freelance writer; *b* 17 Oct. 1935; *m* 1976, Claire Lesley McNab (*née* Davies); two *s* one *d.* *Educ:* Rugby Sch.; Manchester University. DipArch 1958; ARIBA 1960; DipTP 1961; AMTPI 1962; FFB 1980. Nat. Chm., Young Conservatives, 1964–66 (has been Chm. and Vice-Chm. at every level of Movt); Sen. Elected Vice-Chm., NW Area of Nat. Union of C and U Assocs, 1966–70. Contested (C) Stalybridge and Hyde, 1964; MP (C) Birmingham, Handsworth, 1970–Feb. 1974; PPS to Sec. of State for Transport, 1979–81, to Sec. of State for Social Services, 1981–83; an Asst Govt Whip, 1988–90; a Lord Comr of HM Treasury (Govt Whip), 1990–92; Vice-Chamberlain of HM Household, 1992–95. Member: Select Cttee on Environment, 1983–87; House of Commons Services Cttee, 1983–87; Jt Cttee on Private Bill Procedure, 1987–88. Chm., Parly Consultants Gp, British Consultants Bureau, 1980–88. Lectr in Arch. and Planning at techn. coll., 1964–70; Dir (Information), British Property Fedn, 1976–79; Dir (non-exec.), Capital and Counties plc, 1980–88; consultant to YJ Lovell (Holdings) plc, 1982–88. Originator of nat. tree planting year, 1973; President: Arboricultural Assoc., 1983–89; London Green Belt Council, 1985–89; Chm., Queen's Silver Jubilee London Tree Group, 1977; Vice-Chm., Wildlife Link, 1985–89; Patron, Tree Council. RIBA: Vice-Pres., 1974–75; Chm., Public Affairs Bd, 1974–75; Mem. Council, 1972–77. President: Friends of Barnet Hosps, 1981–; Friends of Tamarisk Trust (formerly Peter Pan Homes), 1981–; Barnet Soc., 1990–. Hon. Assoc. Mem., BVA, 1983–; Hon. ALI; FRSA; Hon. FIAAS 1987; Hon. FFB 1989. *Publications:* Town and Countryside: future planning policies for Britain, 1978; regular contributor to bldg and property jls and to political booklets. *Recreation:* tree spotting. *Address:* House of Commons, SW1A 0AA.

CHAPMAN, Maj.-Gen. Timothy John G.; *see* Granville-Chapman.

CHAPMAN NYAHO, Daniel Ahmling, CBE 1961; Director: Pioneer Tobacco Co. Ltd, Ghana (Member of British-American Tobacco Group), 1967–89; Standard Bank Ghana Ltd, 1970–75; *b* 5 July 1909; *s* of William Henry Chapman and Jane Atsiamesi (*née* Atriki); *m* 1941, Jane Abam (*née* Quashie); two *s* four *d* (and two *d* decd). *Educ:* Bremen Mission Schs, Gold Coast and Togoland; Achimota Coll., Ghana; St Peter's Hall, Oxford. Postgraduate courses at Columbia Univ. and New York Univ.; Teacher, Government Senior Boys' School, Accra, 1930; Master, Achimota Coll., 1930–33, 1937–46. Area Specialist, UN Secretariat, Lake Success and New York, 1946–54; Sec. to Prime Minister and Sec. of Cabinet, Gold Coast/Ghana, 1954–57; Ghana's Ambassador to USA and Permanent Representative at UN, 1957–59; Headmaster, Achimota Sch., Ghana, 1959–63; Dir, UN Div. of Narcotic Drugs, Geneva, 1963–66; Ambassador (Special Duties), Min. of External Affairs, Ghana, 1967. Gen. Sec., All-Ewe Conf., 1944–46; Commonwealth Prime Ministers' Conf., 1957; Mem., Ghana delegn to the conf. of indep. African States, Accra, 1958. First Vice-Chm., Governing Council of UN Special Fund, 1959; Chairman: Mission of Indep. African States to Cuba, Dominican Republic, Haiti, Venezuela, Bolivia, Paraguay, Uruguay, Brazil, Argentina, Chile, 1958; Volta Union, 1968–69. Vice-Chairman: Commn on Univ. Educn in Ghana, 1960–61; Ghana Constituent Assembly, 1978–79. Member: Board of Management, UN Internat. Sch., New York, 1950–54, 1958–59; UN Middle East and N. Africa Technical Assistance Mission on Narcotics Control, 1963; Dir, UN Consultative Gp on Narcotics Control in Asia and Far East, Tokyo, 1964; Member: Political Cttee of Nat. Liberation Council, 1967; Board of Trustees of General Kotoka Trust Fund, 1967–83; Chairman: Arts Council of Ghana, 1968–69; Council of Univ. of Science and Technology, Kumasi, 1972; Bd. of Directors, Ghana Film Industry Corporation, 1979–80; Ghana National Honours and Awards Cttee, 1979–80. Darnforth Vis. Lectr, Assoc. Amer. Colls, 1969, 1970. Hon. LLD Greenboro Agric. and Techn. Coll., USA, 1958. Fellow, Ghana Acad. of Arts and Sciences. *Publications:* Human Geography of Eweland, 1946; Our Homeland—Book I: South-East Gold Coast, 1945; (Ed.) The Ewe News-Letter, 1945–46. *Recreations:* music, gardening, walking. *Address:* 7 Tenth Avenue, Tesano, Accra, Ghana. *T:* 227180.

CHAPPLE, family name of **Baron Chapple.**

CHAPPLE, Baron *cr* 1985 (Life Peer), of Hoxton in Greater London; **Francis Joseph Chapple;** General Secretary, Electrical, Electronic, Telecommunication and Plumbing Union, 1966–84; *b* Shoreditch, 1921; *m*; two *s.* *Educ:* elementary school. Started as Apprentice Electrician; Member ETU, 1937–83; Shop Steward and Branch Official; Member Exec. Council, 1958; Asst General Secretary, 1963–66. Mem., Gen. Council of TUC, 1971–83, Chm. 1982–83; Gold Badge of Congress, 1983. Member: National Exec. Cttee of Labour Party, 1965–71; Cttee of Inquiry into Shipping, 1967; Royal Commn on Environmental Pollution, 1973–77; Horserace Totalisator Bd, 1976–90; Energy Commn, 1977–79; NEDC, 1979–83; Nat. Nuclear Corp., 1980–86; Southern Water Authority, 1983–89; Director: Inner City Enterprises, 1983–88; N. G. Bailey Orgn, 1989–. *Publication:* (autobiog.) Sparks Fly, 1984. *Recreation:* racing pigeons. *Address:* c/o Amalgamated Engineering and Electrical Union, Hayes Court, West Common Road, Bromley BR2 7AU.

CHAPPLE, Field Marshal Sir John, GCB 1988 (KCB 1985); CBE 1980 (MBE 1969); Governor and Commander-in-Chief, Gibraltar, since 1993; *b* 27 May 1931; *s* of C. H. Chapple; *m* 1959, Annabel Hill; one *s* three *d.* *Educ:* Haileybury; Trinity Coll., Cambridge (MA). Joined 2nd KEO Goorkhas, 1954; served Malaya, Hong Kong, Borneo; Staff Coll., 1962; jssc 1969; Commanded 1st Bn 2nd Goorkhas, 1970–72; Directing Staff, Staff Coll., 1972–73; Commanded 48 Gurkha Infantry Bde, 1976; Gurkha Field Force, 1977; Principal Staff Officer to Chief of Defence Staff, 1978–79; Comdr, British Forces Hong Kong, and Maj.-Gen., Brigade of Gurkhas, 1980–82; Dir of Military Operations, 1982–84; Dep. Chief of Defence Staff (Progs and Personnel), 1985–87; C-in-C, UKLF, 1987–88; CGS, 1988–92. ADC Gen. to the Queen, 1987–92. Col, 2nd Goorkhas, 1986–94. Hon. Col, Oxford Univ. OTC, 1988–95. Services Fellow, Fitzwilliam Coll., Cambridge, 1973. President: Soc. for Army Historical Res., 1991–; Military History Soc, 1991–. FZS (Pres., 1992–94), FLS, FRGS (Mem. Council). OStJ. *Club:* Beefsteak.

CHAPPLE, Keith, FIEE; Chairman and Managing Director, Intel Corporation (UK) Ltd, since 1972; *b* 11 Aug. 1935; *s* of Reginald Chapple and Gladys Evelyn (*née* Foster); *m* 1962, Patricia Margaret Aitchison; one *s* two *d.* *Educ:* City of Bath Boys' Sch.; Rugby Coll. of Technol. FIEE 1984; MIMgt 1976. Engrg Manager, Gen. Precision Systems Ltd, 1961–66; Sales Engr, SGS-Fairchild Ltd, 1966–69; Mktg Manager, SGS-Fairchild SpA (Italy), 1969–70; Sales Manager, Intel Corp. (Belgium), 1970–72. Dep. Pres., 1995–96, Pres., May 1996–, Fedn of Electronics Industry; Vice Pres., Swindon Chamber of Commerce, 1994–. Mem., Oxford Isis Br., Rotary Club. Hon. DTech Loughborough, 1986. *Recreations:* music, family. *Address:* Intel Corporation (UK) Ltd, Pipers Way, Swindon, Wilts SN3 1RJ. *T:* Swindon (01793) 403000. *Club:* Clarendon (Oxford).

CHAPPLE, Air Vice-Marshal Robert, CB 1994; Principal Medical Officer, Royal Air Force Support Command, 1991–94, retired; *b* 2 May 1934; *s* of Kevin Chapple and

Florence Elsie (*née* Cann); *m* 1960, Barbara Ann (*née* Webster); one *s* one *d*. *Educ:* Finchley Catholic Grammar Sch.; St Mary's Hosp. Med. Sch. (MB, BS 1958). MRCS, LRCP 1958; DPH 1973; MFPHM 1978; MFOM 1980. Joined RAF Med. Br., 1960; served in UK, Singapore, Gibraltar, Germany and Cyprus; Officer Commanding: Princess Mary Hosp., Cyprus, 1982–85; Princess Mary's RAF Hosp., Halton, 1987–89; Princess Alexandra Hosp., Wroughton, 1989–91; Commandant, RAF Central Med. Estabt, 1991. QHP, 1992–94. MIMgt (MBIM 1974). *Recreations:* golf, watching most sports, archaeology, visiting old churches, matters of general interest. *Address:* Hazel House, Withington, Cheltenham, Glos GL54 4DA.

CHARD, Prof. Timothy, MD; FRCOG; Professor of Reproductive Physiology, St Bartholomew's Hospital Medical College, since 1973; *b* 4 June 1937; *s* of Henry Francis and Dorothea Elaine Chard; *m* 1977, Linda Kay Elmore; two *s*. *Educ:* Merchant Taylors' School; St Thomas's Hosp. Med. Sch. Junior med. posts, 1960–65; MRC Clinical Research Fellow, 1965–68; Sen. Lectr, St Bartholomew's Hosp., 1968–73. *Publications* (jointly): Radioimmunoassay, 1978, 3rd edn 1987; Placental Function Tests, 1982; Basic Sciences for Obstetrics, 1984, 2nd edn 1987; Computing for Clinicians, 1988. *Recreations:* fine arts, venture capital. *Address:* 509 Mountjoy House, Barbican, EC2Y 8BP. *T:* 0171–628 4570.

CHARING CROSS, Archdeacon of; *see* Fulham, Bishop of.

CHARKHAM, Jonathan Philip; director of companies; Adviser to the Governors, Bank of England, 1988–93 (Chief Advr, 1985–88); *b* 17 Oct. 1930; *s* of late Louis Charkham and Phoebe Beatrice Barquet (*née* Miller); *m* Moira Elizabeth Frances, *d* of late Barnett A. Salmon and of Molly Salmon; twin *s* one *d*. *Educ:* St Paul's Sch. (scholar); Jesus Coll., Cambridge (Exhibitioner). BA 1952. Called to Bar, Inner Temple, 1953. Morris Charkham Ltd, 1953–63 (Man. Dir, 1957–63); Div. Dir, Rest Assured Ltd, 1963–68. Civil Service Department: Principal, Management Services, later Pay, 1969–73; Asst Sec., 1973–78, Personnel Management, 1973–75; Dir, Public Appts Unit, 1975–82; Under Sec., 1978, Management and Organisation, 1980–82; on secondment from Bank of England as Dir, PRO NED, 1982–85. Director: Great Universal Stores, 1993–; CrestaCare, 1993–; CLM, 1993–; Leopold Joseph Hldgs, 1994–; Consultant, Pensions and Investment Research Consultants, 1994–. Member: Council, Royal Inst. of Public Admin., 1981–82; Industry and Finance Cttee, NEDC, 1988–90; Steering Cttee, Corporate Takeovers Inquiry, 1990–91; Instnl Investors Project Adv. Bd, Columbia Univ. of NY Center for Law and Econ. Studies, 1989–; City Transportation Task Force, 1990–; Cttee on Financial Aspects of Corporate Governance, 1991–; US subcouncil on Corporate Governance and Financial Mkts, 1992–; CIT Working Party on Financing Transport Infrastructure, 1992–93; Steering Cttee on Corporate Governance in NHS, 1993–94. Member: Duke of Edinburgh's 7th Commonwealth Study Conf., 1990–92; Cttee, Knightsbridge Assoc., 1989–. Chm., CU Labour Club, 1952. Master, Worshipful Co. of Upholders, 1979–80, 1980–81. Sheriff, City of London, 1994–95. FRSA; CIMgt. *Publications:* Keeping Good Company: a survey of corporate governance in five countries, 1994; booklets and pamphlets on non-executive directors, boards and shareholders. *Recreations:* music, playing golf, antique furniture, wine. *Address:* The Yellow House, 22 Montpelier Place, SW7 1HL. *T:* 0171–589 9879, *Fax:* 0171–581 8520. *Clubs:* Athenæum, MCC, City Livery.

CHARKIN, Richard Denis Paul; Executive Director, since 1988, and Chief Executive, since 1994, Reed Books International; *b* 17 June 1949; *s* of Frank Charkin and Mabel Doreen Charkin (*née* Rosen); *m* 1972, Susan Mary Poole; one *s* two *d*. *Educ:* Haileybury and ISC; Trinity College, Cambridge (MA); Harvard Bus. Sch. (AMP). Science Editor, Harrap & Co., 1972; Sen. Publishing Manager, Pergamon Press, 1973; Oxford University Press: Medical Editor, 1974; Head of Science and Medicine, 1976; Head of Reference, 1980; Managing Dir, Academic and General, 1984; Octopus Publishing Group (Reed International Books), 1988; Chief Exec., Reed Consumer Books, 1989–94. Vis. Fellow, Green College, Oxford, 1987. *Recreations:* music, cricket. *Address:* 3 Redcliffe Place, SW10 9DB.

CHARLEMONT, 14th Viscount *cr* 1665 (Ire.); **John Day Caulfeild;** Baron Caulfeild of Charlemont 1620 (Ire.); *b* 19 March 1934; *s* of Eric St George Caulfeild (*d* 1975) and of Edith Evelyn, *d* of Frederick William Day, Ottawa; *S* uncle, 1985; *m* 1st, 1964, Judith Ann (*d* 1971), *d* of James E. Dodd; one *s* one *d*; 2nd, 1972, Janet Evelyn, *d* of Orville R. Nancekivell. *Heir:* *s* Hon. John Dodd Caulfeild, *b* 15 May 1966. *Address:* 39 Rossburn Drive, Etobicoke, Ontario M9C 2P9, Canada.

CHARLES, Rt. Rev. Adrian Owen, AM 1994; RFD 1983; ED 1976; Bishop of Western Region (Assistant Bishop of Diocese of Brisbane), 1984–92; Bishop to Australian Defence Force, since 1989; *b* 31 July 1926; *s* of Robert Charles and Alice (*née* Donovan); *m* 1955, Leonie Olive (*née* Robinson); one *s* one *d*. *Educ:* Slade Sch., Warwick, Qld; St Francis Coll., Univ. of Qld; Anglican Central Coll., Canterbury (ThL, Diploma in Divinity). Ordained priest, 1952; Royal Australian Army Chaplains Dept, 1955–83; Rector: Christ Church, St Lucia, Brisbane, 1958–66; St Paul's, Ipswich, 1966–71; Dir, Religious Studies, Christ Church Grammar Sch., Perth, 1971–72; Dean, St James' Cathedral, Townsville, 1972–77; Rector, St David's, Chelmer, Brisbane, 1977–83; Sen. Chaplain, 1st Mil. Dist, 1981–83; Archdeacon and Chaplain to Archbishop of Brisbane, 1981–83; Bishop of Southern Region, 1983–84. *Recreations:* reading, cricket, golf, theatre. *Address:* c/o Diocesan Registry, St Martin's House, Ann Street, Brisbane, Qld 4001, Australia. *Clubs:* United Service (Brisbane); Middle Ridge Golf (Toowoomba); Officers Mess, Aviation Regiment (Oakey).

CHARLES, Arthur William Hessin; First Junior Counsel to HM Treasury on Chancery Matters, since 1989; *b* 25 March 1948; *s* of Arthur Attwood Sinclair Charles and May Davies Charles (*née* Westerman); *m* 1974, Lydia Margaret Ainscow; one *s* one *d*. *Educ:* Malvern College; Christ's College, Cambridge (MA Hons). Called to the Bar, Lincoln's Inn, 1971; Junior Counsel to the Crown (Chancery), 1986. *Recreations:* golf, tennis. *Address:* 13 Old Square, Lincoln's Inn, WC2 3UA. *T:* 0171–404 4800. *Clubs:* Hawks (Cambridge); Denham Golf.

CHARLES, (Bernard) Leopold, QC 1980; **His Honour Judge Charles;** a Circuit Judge, since 1990; *b* 16 May 1929; *s* of Chaskiel Charles and Mary Harris; *m* 1st, 1958, Margaret Daphne Abel (marr. diss. 1993); one *s* two *d*; 2nd, 1994, Judith Linda Orns. *Educ:* King's Coll., Taunton. Called to the Bar, Gray's Inn, 1955. Practised in London and on South Eastern Circuit, 1956–90; a Recorder, 1985–90. *Recreations:* music, politics. *Address:* Lamb Building, Temple, EC4Y 7AS. *T:* 0171–353 6701; 12 East 41st Street, New York, NY 10017, USA.

CHARLES, Caroline, (Mrs Malcolm Valentine); fashion designer; Founder, Caroline Charles, 1963; *b* 18 May 1942; *m* 1966, Malcolm Valentine; one *s* one *d*. *Educ:* Sacred Heart Convent, Woldingham; Swindon Art Sch. *Recreations:* gardening, tennis, theatre, travel. *Address:* 56/57 Beauchamp Place, SW3 1NY. *T:* 0171–225 3197.

CHARLES, Dame Eugenia; *see* Charles, Dame M. E.

CHARLES, Hampton; *see* Martin, R. P.

CHARLES, Jack; Director of Establishments, Greater London Council, 1972–77, retired; *b* 18 Jan. 1923; *o s* of late Frederick Walter Charles and Alice Mary Charles; *m* 1959, Jean (*d* 1991), *d* of late F. H. Braund, London; one *s* one *d*. *Educ:* County High Sch., Ilford. Air Min., 1939–42; RAF, 1942–46; Min. of Supply, 1947–59 (Private Sec. to Minister of Supply, 1952–54); War Office, 1959–60; UKAEA, 1960–68 (Authority Personnel Officer, 1965–68); Dep. Dir of Estabs, GLC, 1968–72. *Recreations:* gardening, walking. *Address:* Kings Warren, Enborne Row, Wash Water, Newbury, Berks RG15 0LY. *T:* Newbury (01635) 30161.

CHARLES, James Anthony, ScD; FEng 1983; Reader in Process Metallurgy, University of Cambridge, 1978–90, now Emeritus; Fellow, St John's College, Cambridge, since 1963; *b* 23 Aug. 1926; *s* of John and Winifred Charles; *m* 1951, Valerie E. King; two *s*. *Educ:* Imperial College of Science and Technology, Royal School of Mines (BScEng, ARSM); MA, ScD Cantab; FIM; FRSA. J. Stone & Co. Ltd, 1947–50; British Oxygen Ltd, 1950–60; Dept of Metallurgy and Materials Science, Univ. of Cambridge, 1960–90. Vis. Prof., UCL (Inst. of Archaeology), 1991–; Special Prof., Univ. of Nottingham, 1993–. Syndic, Fitzwilliam Museum, 1986–. Sir George Beilby Medal and Prize, RIC, Soc. Chem. Ind. and Inst. of Metals, 1965; Sir Robert Hadfield Medal, Metals Soc., 1977; Kroll Medal, Inst. of Metals, 1989; Elegant Work Prize, Inst. of Materials, 1992. *Publications:* Oxygen in Iron and Steel Making, 1956; Selection and Use of Engineering Materials, 1984, 2nd edn 1989; numerous papers on the science and technology of metals and archaeometallurgy. *Recreations:* gardening, listening to music, archaeology. *Address:* New Lodge, 22 Mingle Lane, Stapleford, Cambridge CB2 5BG. *T:* Cambridge (01223) 843812.

CHARLES, Leopold; *see* Charles, B. L.

CHARLES, Leslie Stanley Francis; Director, Birmid Qualcast plc, 1981–88, retired; *b* 28 July 1917; *s* of Samuel Francis Charles and Lena Gwendolyn (*née* Reed); *m* 1941, Henrietta Elizabeth Calvin Thomas; one *s*. *Educ:* Cardiff High Sch.; University Coll. of S Wales and Mon, Univ. of Wales (BScEng London, 1st Cl. Hons). Grad. Engr, Metropolitan Vickers Ltd, 1936–39; Regular Officer, REME, 1939–54; Consultant, Urwick Orr & Partners Ltd, 1954–60; Chief Engr Ops, UKAEA, 1960–63; Dir of Factories, Raleigh Industries Ltd, 1963–66; Man. Dir, Aluminium Wire & Cable Co. Ltd, 1966–68; British Aluminium Co. Ltd: Dep. Man. Dir, 1968–79; Man. Dir, 1979–82. Chm., European Aluminium Assoc., 1981–84. *Recreations:* golf, bridge, music. *Address:* Crana, Claydon Lane, Chalfont St Peter, Bucks SL9 8JU. *T:* Gerrards Cross (01753) 884290.

CHARLES, Dame (Mary) Eugenia, DBE 1991; Prime Minister and Minister of Finance, Commonwealth of Dominica, 1980–95; MP (Dominica Freedom Party) Roseau, 1970–95 (Nominated MP, 1970–75); *b* 15 May 1919; *d* of John Baptiste Charles and Josephine (*née* Delauney). *Educ:* Convent High Sch., Roseau, Dominica; St Joseph's Convent, St George's, Grenada; University Coll., Univ. of Toronto (BA); London Sch. of Econs and Pol. Science. Called to the Bar, Inner Temple, 1947; admitted to practice, Dominica, 1949. Entered Parlt, 1970; Leader of the Opposition, 1975–79; Minister of Foreign Affairs, 1980–90. *Recreations:* reading, gardening, travelling. *Address:* PO Box 121, 1 Cross Lane, Roseau, Commonwealth of Dominica. *T:* 4482855.

CHARLES, Michael Geoffrey A.; *see* Audley-Charles.

CHARLESWORTH, Arthur Leonard, FCIOB; Joint Managing Director, John Mowlem Co., 1978–89; Non-Executive Director, John Mowlem Group, 1989–95; *b* 11 June 1927; *s* of William Henry and Florence Alice Charlesworth; *m* 1948, June Edith (*née* Sims); one *s* two *d*. *Educ:* Wandsworth Grammar Sch. Joined John Mowlem Co., 1941; Dir, Mowlem (Building), 1965, John Mowlem & Co., 1969; Man. Dir, John Mowlem & Co., 1978; Jt Man. Dir, Mowlem Group, 1986. FRSA. *Recreation:* golf. *Address:* 61 Vicarage Road, SW14 8RY. *T:* 0181–876 6724. *Club:* Richmond Golf.

CHARLESWORTH, Prof. Brian, PhD; FRS 1991; G. W. Beadle Distinguished Service Professor, Department of Ecology and Evolution, University of Chicago, since 1992; *b* 29 April 1945; *s* of Francis Gustave Charlesworth and Mary (*née* Ryan); *m* 1967, Deborah Maltby; one *d*. *Educ:* Queens' Coll., Cambridge (BA Natural Scis; PhD Genetics). Post-Doctoral Fellow, Univ. of Chicago, 1969–71; Lectr in Genetics, Univ. of Liverpool, 1971–74; Lectr, 1974–82, Reader, 1982–84, in Biology, Univ. of Sussex; Prof., 1985–92, Chm., 1986–91, Dept of Ecology and Evolution, Univ. of Chicago. *Publications:* Evolution in Age-Structured Populations, 1980, 2nd edn 1994; papers in Nature, Science, Genetics, Genetical Res., Evolution, Amer. Naturalist, Procs Roy. Soc. *Recreations:* reading, listening to classical music, walking. *Address:* Department of Ecology and Evolution, University of Chicago, 1101 E 57th Street, Chicago, IL 60637, USA. *T:* (312) 7028942.

CHARLESWORTH, Peter James; His Honour Judge Charlesworth; a Circuit Judge, since 1989; *b* 24 Aug. 1944; *s* of late Joseph William Charlesworth and Florence Mary Charlesworth; *m* 1967, Elizabeth Mary Postill; one *s* one *d*. *Educ:* Hull Grammar Sch.; Leeds Univ. (LLB 1965, LLM 1966). Called to the Bar, Inner Temple, 1966. In practice on North-Eastern Circuit, 1966–89; a Recorder, 1982–89. Mem., Rugby Football League Adv. Panel, 1994–. *Recreations:* tennis, reading, Rugby League football (spectating), walking in the Yorkshire dales. *Address:* Daleswood, Creskeld Gardens, Bramhope, Leeds LS16 9EN. *T:* Leeds (0113) 267 4377. *Clubs:* Hull Rugby League Football (Vice-Pres.); Leeds YMCA Tennis.

CHARLISH, Dennis Norman; Panel Chairman, Civil Service Selection Board, 1978–88 (Resident Chairman, 1975–78); *b* 24 May 1918; *s* of Norman Charlish and Edith (*née* Cherriman); *m* 1941, Margaret Trevor (*d* 1995), *o d* of William Trevor and Margaret Ann Williams, Manchester; one *d*. *Educ:* Brighton Grammar Sch.; London Sch. of Economics. Rosebery Schol., 1947; BSc (Econ) 1st class hons., 1951. Joined Civil Service as Tax Officer, Inland Revenue, 1936; Exec. Officer, Dept of Overseas Trade, 1937; Dep. Armament Supply Officer, Admty, 1941; Principal, BoT, 1949; Asst Secretary, 1959; Imperial Defence Coll., 1963; Under-Sec., BoT, 1967–69; Min. of Technology, 1969–70; Head of Personnel, DTI, 1971–74, Dept of Industry, 1974–75. *Address:* 28 Multon Road, SW18 3LH.

CHARLTON, Sir Bobby; *see* Charlton, Sir Robert.

CHARLTON, (Foster) Ferrier (Harvey), CBE 1986; DFC 1945; Partner, 1953–88, Senior Partner, 1985–88, Linklaters & Paines, Solicitors; *b* 26 March 1923; *s* of Foster Ferrier Charlton and Esther Naomi French Charlton (*née* Brown); *m* 1950, Doris Winnifred (Lola) Marson; one *s* three *d*. *Educ:* Rugby Sch.; Wadham Coll., Oxford (MA, PPE 1st Cl. 1947). RAFVR (Pilot), 1941–53; served W Africa, India, Ceylon, 8 Sqdn and 200 Sqdn, RAF, 1944–45. Articles with Linklaters & Paines, 1948; qualified as solicitor, 1950. Director: Short Bros, 1958–89; Law Debenture Corp., 1988–95. Member: City/Industry Task Force, CBI, 1987; DTI Companies Acts Wkg Party, 1993–95. *Publications:* legal and gardening articles. *Recreation:* gardening (Pres., Alpine Garden Soc., 1988–91). *Address:* 28 Witches Lane, Riverhead, Sevenoaks, Kent TN13 2AX. *T:* Sevenoaks (01732) 453370.

CHARLTON, (Frederick) Noel, CB 1961; CBE (mil.) 1946; *b* 4 Dec. 1906; *s* of late Frederick William Charlton and Marian Charlton; *m* 1932, Maud Helen Rudgard; no *c*. *Educ:* Rugby School; Hertford Coll., Oxford Univ. (MA). Admitted a Solicitor, 1932; in private practice as Solicitor in London, 1932–39. War Service, 1939–46 (attained rank of Colonel, Gen. List). Joined Treasury Solicitor's Dept, 1946; Principal Asst Solicitor (Litigation), Treasury Solicitor's Dept, 1956–71; Sec., Lord Chancellor's Cttee on Defamation, 1971–74; with Dept of Energy (Treasury Solicitor's Branch), 1975–81, retired. Chairman, Coulsdon and Purley UDC, 1953–54 and 1964–65; Hon. Alderman, London Borough of Croydon. Bronze Star (USA), 1945. *Recreations:* golf, travel. *Address:* 4 Newton Road, Purley, Surrey CR8 3DN. *T:* 0181–660 2802. *Club:* Army and Navy.
See also T. A. G. Charlton.

CHARLTON, Graham; *see* Charlton, T. A. G.

CHARLTON, Prof. Graham, MDS; FDSRCSE; Professor of Conservative Dentistry, University of Edinburgh, 1978–91, now Emeritus Professor (Dean of Dental Studies, 1978–83); *b* 15 Oct. 1928; *s* of Simpson R. Charlton and Georgina (*née* Graham); *m* 1956, Stella Dobson; two *s* one *d*. *Educ:* Bedlington Grammar Sch., Northumberland; St John's Coll., York (Teaching Cert.); King's Coll., Univ. of Durham (BDS); Univ. of Bristol (MDS). Teacher, Northumberland, 1948–52; National Service, 1948–50; Dental School, 1952–58; General Dental Practice, Torquay, 1958–64; University of Bristol: Lecturer, 1964–72; Cons. Sen. Lectr, 1972–78; Dental Clinical Dean, 1975–78. *Address:* 7A Thorn Road, Bearsden, Glasgow G61 4PP. *T:* 0141–942 9188.

CHARLTON, Henry Marshall, DPhil; FRS 1994; Reader in Neuroendocrinology, since 1990, and Fellow of Linacre College, since 1970, University of Oxford; *b* 10 March 1939; *s* of Joseph Douglass Charlton and Lilian Charlton; *m* 1965, Margaret Jeffrey; one *s* one *d*. *Educ:* Corpus Christi Coll., Oxford (MA, DPhil). Mem., MRC Neuroendocrinology Unit, Oxford, 1964–68; Lectr, Oxford Univ., 1968–90. *Publications:* contrib. scientific jls. *Recreations:* Real tennis, hill walking, gardening. *Address:* 61 Plantation Road, Oxford OX2 6JE. *T:* Oxford (01865) 54248.

CHARLTON, John, (Jack Charlton), OBE 1974; Manager, Republic of Ireland Football Team, since 1986; broadcaster; *b* 8 May 1935; *s* of Robert and Elizabeth Charlton; *m* 1958, Patricia; two *s* one *d*. *Educ:* Hirst Park Sch., Ashington. Professional footballer, Leeds United, 1952–73; Manager: Middlesbrough, 1973–77; Sheffield Wednesday FC, 1977–83; Newcastle United FC, 1984–85. Mem., Sports Council, 1977–82. *Publication:* Jack Charlton's American World Cup Diary, 1994. *Recreations:* shooting, fishing, gardening. *Address:* c/o Football Association of the Republic of Ireland, 8 Merrion Square, Dublin 2, Ireland.
See also Sir Robert Charlton.

CHARLTON, Prof. Kenneth; Emeritus Professor of History of Education, King's College, University of London, since 1983; *b* 11 July 1925; 2nd *s* of late George and Lottie Charlton; *m* 1953, Maud Tulloch Brown, *d* of late P. R. Brown, MBE and M. B. Brown; one *s* one *d*. *Educ:* City Grammar Sch., Chester; Univ. of Glasgow. MA 1949, MEd 1953, Glasgow. RNVR, 1943–46. History Master, Dalziel High Sch., Motherwell, and Uddingston Grammar Sch., 1950–54; Lectr in Educn, UC N Staffs, 1954–64; Sen. Lectr in Educn, Keele Univ., 1964–66; Prof. of History and Philosophy of Educn, Birmingham Univ., 1966–72; Prof. of History of Educn and Head of Dept of Educn, King's Coll., Univ. of London, 1972–83. *Publications:* Recent Historical Fiction for Children, 1960, 2nd edn 1969; Education in Renaissance England, 1965; contrib. Educnl Rev., Brit. Jl Educnl Psych., Year Bk of Educn, Jl Hist. of Ideas, Brit. Jl Educnl Studies, Internat. Rev. of Educn, Trans Hist. Soc. Lancs and Cheshire, Irish Hist. Studies, Northern Hist., Hist. of Educn, Hist. of Educn Quarterly. *Recreations:* gardening, listening to music. *Address:* 128 Ridge Langley, Sanderstead, Croydon CR2 0AS.
See also P. Charlton.

CHARLTON, Philip, OBE 1987; FCIB; CIMgt; Co-Founder, and Chairman since 1991, Charlton Associates; *b* 31 July 1930; *s* of George and Lottie Charlton; *m* 1953, Jessie Boulton; one *s* one *d*. *Educ:* Chester Grammar School. Entered service of Chester Savings Bank, 1947; Gen. Manager, Chester, Wrexham and N Wales Savings Bank, 1966–75; Gen. Manager, TSB Wales & Border Counties, 1975–81; TSB Group Central Executive: Dep. Chief Gen. Manager, 1981–82; Chief Gen. Manager, 1982–85; Gp Man. Dir, 1986–88; Chief Exec., 1988–89; Dep. Chm., 1990–91; Mem., TSB Central Bd, 1976–77, 1981–90; Director: TSB Computer Services (Wythenshawe) Ltd, 1976–81; TSB Trust Co. Ltd, 1979–82; TSB Gp Computer Services Ltd, 1981–86; Central Trustee Savings Bank, later TSB Bank, 1982–89; TSB (Holdings) Ltd, 1982–86; Hill Samuel Gp, 1987–89. Council Mem., 1968–71, Hon. Treasurer, 1975–77, Savings Bank Inst.; Vice Pres., Internat. Savings Banks Inst. (Geneva), 1988–91; Mem., Bd of Admin, European Savings Banks Gp, Brussels, 1989–91. Chm., TSB Nat. Sports Council, 1979–82. FCIB (FIB 1977; Mem. Council, 1982–; Dep. Chm., 1989–91; Pres., 1990–92); CIMgt (CBIM 1983). *Recreations:* music, swimming, sport. *Address:* 62 Quinta Drive, Arkley, near Barnet, Herts EN5 3BE. *T:* 0181–440 4477. *Clubs:* Royal Automobile; City (Chester).
See also Prof. K. Charlton.

CHARLTON, Richard McKenzie, FTS; FInstPet; Chairman: South East Water, since 1995; Chart Roads, since 1995; Sino-Australian Business Corporation, since 1995; Chairman, Art Foundation, Victoria, since 1994 (Deputy Chairman, 1992–94); *b* 20 March 1935; *s* of Richard Rutherford Charlton and Yvonne Gladys Charlton (*née* McKenzie); *m* 1978, Pauline Joyce Wright; two *s* two *d*. *Educ:* Sydney Univ. (BE Mining 1957; MESc 1959). Joined Shell as trainee petroleum engr, 1959: various posts in The Hague, UK, Nigeria, Kuwait, Trinidad and Brunei, 1959–75; Shell Australia: Gen. Manager, Exploration & Prodn, 1975–76; Exec. Dir, NW Shelf Project, 1976–80; Dir Ops, Shell UK Exploration & Prodn, Aberdeen, 1980–83; Chm., Shell Cos in Malaysia, 1983–86; Hd, Exploration & Prodn Ops & Liaison, The Hague, 1986–91; Chm. and Chief Exec. Officer, Shell Gp of Cos in Australia, 1991–95, retd. Chancellor, Univ. of Newcastle, NSW, 1994–. Mem., Soc. Petroleum Engrs, 1971; FAICD; FInstD; FAIM. *Publications:* papers on petroleum industry. *Recreations:* horse racing, Rugby, snow ski-ing, surfing, tennis. *Address:* c/o Level 5, 1 Spring Street, Melbourne, Vic 3000, Australia. *T:* (3) 96668850. *Clubs:* Melbourne, Australia (Melbourne); Victoria Racing, Moonee Valley Racing.

CHARLTON, Sir Robert, (Sir Bobby Charlton), Kt 1994; CBE 1974 (OBE 1969); Director, Manchester United Football Club, since 1984; *b* 11 Oct. 1937; *s* of Robert and Elizabeth Charlton; *m* 1961, Norma; two *d*. *Educ:* Bedlington Grammar Sch., Northumberland. Professional Footballer with Manchester United, 1954–73, for whom he played 751 games and scored 245 goals; FA Cup Winners Medal, 1963; FA Championship Medals, 1956–57, 1964–65 and 1966–67; World Cup Winners Medal (International), 1966; European Cup Winners medal, 1968. 100th England cap, 21 April 1970; 106 appearances for England, 1957–73. Manager, Preston North End, 1973–75. Hon. Fellow, Manchester Polytechnic, 1979. Hon. MA Manchester Univ. *Publications:* My Soccer Life, 1965; Forward for England, 1967; This Game of Soccer, 1967; Book of European Football, Books 1–4, 1969–72. *Recreation:* golf. *Address:* Garthollerton, Chelford Road, Ollerton, near Knutsford, Cheshire WA16 8RY.
See also John Charlton.

CHARLTON, (Thomas Alfred) Graham, CB 1970; Secretary, Trade Marks, Patents and Designs Federation, 1973–84; *b* 29 Aug. 1913; 3rd *s* of late Frederick William and Marian Charlton; *m* 1940, Margaret Ethel, *yr d* of A. E. Furst; three *d*. *Educ:* Rugby School; Corpus Christi Coll., Cambridge. Asst Principal, War Office, 1936; Asst Private Secretary to Secretary of State for War, 1937–39; Principal, 1939; Cabinet Office, 1947–49; Asst Secretary, 1949; International Staff, NATO, 1950–52; War Office, later MoD, 1952–73; Asst Under-Sec. of State, 1960–73. Coronation Medal, 1953. *Recreations:* golf, gardening. *Address:* 2A Sandelswood End, Beaconsfield, Bucks HP9 2NY. *T:* Beaconsfield (01494) 672837.
See also Frederick Noel Charlton.

CHARLTON, Prof. Thomas Malcolm, FRSE 1973; historian of engineering science; Jackson Professor of Engineering, University of Aberdeen, 1970–79, now Emeritus; *b* 1 Sept. 1923; *s* of William Charlton and Emily May Charlton (*née* Wallbank); *m* 1950, Valerie, *d* of late Dr C. McCulloch, Hexham; two *s* (and one *s* decd). *Educ:* Doncaster Grammar Sch.; Derby Tech. Coll.; UC, Nottingham. BSc (Eng) London, 1943; MA Cantab, 1954. Junior Scientific Officer, Min. of Aircraft Prodn, TRE, Malvern, 1943–46; Asst Engr, Merz & McLellan, Newcastle upon Tyne, 1946–54; Univ. Lectr in Engrg, Cambridge, 1954–63; Fellow and Tutor, Sidney Sussex Coll., 1959–63; Prof. of Civil Engrg, Queen's Univ., Belfast, 1963–70; Dean, Faculty of Applied Science, QUB, 1967–70. Vis. Prof. of Civil Engineering, Univ. of Newcastle upon Tyne, 1982–89. FICE, 1964–83; Mem. Council, Instn of Civil Engrs of Ireland, 1965–69. For. Mem., Finnish Acad. of Technical Sciences, 1967. Personal Symposium, Turin Politecnico, 1989. Mem., Bd of Finance, Hereford Dio., 1980–82. *Publications:* Model Analysis of Structures, 1954, new edn 1966; (contrib.) Hydro-electric Engineering Practice, 1958; Energy Principles in Applied Statics, 1959; Analysis of Statically-indeterminate Frameworks, 1961; Principles of Structural Analysis, 1969, new edn 1977, Arabic edn 1983; Energy Principles in Theory of Structures, 1973; (contrib.) The Works of I. K. Brunel, 1976; A History of Theory of Structures in the Nineteenth Century, 1982; (contrib.) Encyclopaedia of Building Technology, 1986; Professor Emeritus (autobiog.), 1991; (contrib.) Rendicanti Lincei, 1991; contrib. Children's Britannica; papers on energy principles, hist. of structures. *Recreations:* ecclesiastical history, golf. *Address:* The Old School House, 72 North Street, Burwell, Cambridge CB5 0BB. *T:* Newmarket (01638) 741351. *Club:* Royal Northern and University (Aberdeen).

CHARNLEY, Sir (William) John, Kt 1981; CB 1973; MEng, FEng, FRAeS, FRIN; consultant in advanced technology; *b* 4 Sept. 1922; *s* of George and Catherine Charnley; *m* 1945, Mary Paden; one *s* one *d*. *Educ:* Oulton High Sch., Liverpool; Liverpool Univ. MEng 1945; FEng 1982; FRIN 1963; FRAeS 1966. Aerodynamics Dept, RAE Farnborough, 1943–55; Supt. Blind Landing Experimental Unit, 1955–61; Imperial Defence Coll., 1962; Head of Instruments and Electrical Engineering Dept, 1963–65, Head of Weapons Dept, 1965–68, RAE Farnborough; Head of Research Planning, 1968–69, Dep. Controller, Guided Weapons, Min. of Technology, later MoD, 1969–72; Controller, Guided Weapons and Electronics, MoD (PE), 1972–73; Chief Scientist (RAF), 1973–77, and Dep. Controller, R&D Establishments and Res. C, MoD, 1975–77; Controller, R&D Establishments and Res., MoD, 1977–82. Director: Fairey Holdings Ltd, 1983–86; Winsdale Investments Ltd, 1985–88. Technical Advr, Monopolies and Mergers Commn, 1982; Specialist Advr to House of Lords Select Cttee on Science and Technology, 1986. Chm., Civil Aviation Res. and Develt Programme Bd, 1984–92; Mem., Air Traffic Control Bd, 1985–. Pres., Royal Inst. of Navigation, 1987–90. Trustee, Richard Ormonde Shuttleworth Remembrance Trust, 1987–. Hon. FRAeS 1992. Hon. DEng Liverpool, 1988. Bronze Medal, RIN, 1960; Silver Medal, 1973, Gold Medal, 1980, RAeS. *Publications:* papers on subjects in aerodynamics, aircraft all weather operation, aircraft navigation, defence R&D. *Address:* Kirkstones, 29 Brackendale Close, Camberley, Surrey GU15 1HP. *T:* Camberley (01276) 22547. *Club:* Royal Air Force.

CHARNOCK, Henry, CBE 1992; FRS 1976; Professor of Physical Oceanography, 1966–71 and 1978–86, now Emeritus, Deputy Vice-Chancellor, 1982–84, Southampton University; *b* 25 Dec. 1920; *s* of Henry Charnock and Mary Gray McLeod; *m* 1946, Eva Mary Dickinson; one *s* two *d*. *Educ:* Queen Elizabeth's Grammar Sch., Municipal Techn. Coll., Blackburn; Imperial Coll., London. Staff, Nat. Inst. of Oceanography, 1949–58 and 1959–66; Reader in Physical Oceanography, Imperial Coll., 1958–59; Dir, Inst. of Oceanographic Scis (formerly Nat. Inst. of Oceanography), 1971–78. President: Internat. Union of Geodesy and Geophysics, 1971–75; RMetS, 1982–84; Vice-Pres., Scientific Cttee on Oceanic Res., 1980–82 (Sec., 1978–80); Mem., Royal Commn on Environmental Pollution, 1985–94. *Publications:* papers in meteorological and oceanographic jls. *Address:* 5 Links View Way, Southampton SO16 7GR. *T:* Southampton (01703) 769629.

CHARPAK, Georges; Physicist, Organisation européene pour la recherche nucléaire (CERN); *b* Poland, 1 Aug. 1924; *s* of Anne Szapiro and Maurice Charpak; *m* 1953, Dominique Vidal; three *c*. *Educ:* Ecole des Mines de Paris. Went to France at age 7; served in French Resistance; imprisoned for 1 year in Dachau. Centre national de la recherche scientifique (CNRS), 1948; CERN, Geneva, 1959; in 1968 invented multiwire proportional chamber (linked to computers) for detecting particles in atom smashers. Mem., Acad des Sciences, France, 1985; Foreign Associate of Nat. Acad. of Sciences, USA, 1986. Nobel Prize for Physics, 1992. *Recreations:* ski-ing, travel, music. *Address:* CERN, 1211 Geneva 23, Switzerland. *T:* (22) 7672144, *Fax:* (22) 7677555.

CHARTERIS, family name of **Baron Charteris of Amisfield** and of **Earl of Wemyss.**

CHARTERIS OF AMISFIELD, Baron *cr* 1978 (Life Peer), of Amisfield, E Lothian; **Martin Michael Charles Charteris,** GCB 1977 (KCB 1972; CB 1958); GCVO 1976 (KCVO 1962; MVO 1953); QSO 1978; OBE 1946; PC 1972; Royal Victorian Chain, 1992; Hon. RA 1981; Provost of Eton, 1978–91; Chairman of Trustees, National Heritage Memorial Fund, 1980–92; *b* 7 Sept. 1913; 2nd *s* of Hugo Francis, Lord Elcho (killed in action, 1916); *g s* of 11th Earl of Wemyss; *m* 1944, Hon. Mary Gay Hobart Margesson, *yr d* of 1st Viscount Margesson, PC, MC; two *s* one *d*. *Educ:* Eton; RMC Sandhurst. Lieut KRRC, 1933; served War of 1939–45; Lieut-Colonel, 1944. Private Secretary to Princess Elizabeth, 1950–52; Asst Private Secretary to the Queen, 1952–72; Private Secretary to the Queen and Keeper of HM's Archives, 1972–77. A Permanent Lord in Waiting to the Queen, 1978–. Director: Claridge's Hotel, 1978–; Connaught Hotel, 1978–; De La Rue Co., 1978–85; Rio Tinto Zinc Corp., 1978–84. Trustee, BM, 1979–89. Hon. DCL Oxon, 1978; Hon. LLD London, 1981. *Recreation:* sculpting. *Address:* Wood Stanway House, Wood Stanway, Cheltenham, Glos GL54 5PG. *T:* Stanton (01368) 584480; 11 Kylestrome House, Cundy Street, SW1W 9JT. *T:* 0171–730 2959. *Club:* White's.
See also Baron Pearson of Rannoch.

CHARTRES, Rt Rev. and Rt Hon. Richard John Carew; *see* London, Bishop of.

CHARVET, Richard Christopher Larkins, RD 1972; JP; Consultant, Alexander Howden Marine Ltd, since 1994; General Manager, Morline Ltd (formerly Associate

Director, Anglo Soviet Shipping Co. Ltd), 1988–94; *b* 12 Dec. 1936; *s* of late Patrice and Eleanor Charvet; *m* 1990; two *s* one *d* by a previous marriage. *Educ:* Rugby. FITT, ACIArb; FCIS; FBIM; MIFF; MIEx. FRSA 1985. National Service, Royal Navy, 1955–57; Mem., London Div., RNR, 1955–. Union Castle Line, 1957–58; Killick Martin & Co. Ltd, Shipbrokers, 1958–81; Vogt and Maguire Ltd, Shipbrokers, 1981–88. Mem., Court of Common Council for Aldgate Ward, City of London, 1970–76; Alderman, Aldgate Ward, 1976–85; Sheriff, 1983–84. Prime Warden, Worshipful Co. of Shipwrights, 1985–86 (Renter Warden, 1984–85); Master, Guild of World Traders, 1991. President: City of London Sea Cadet Corps, 1994; NE Area, St John Ambulance, London (POW) Dist, 1995; Chairman: City Br., St John Ambulance Appeal, 1985–92; City Br., RNLI, 1986–. JP 1976. CStJ 1989. Hon. JSM, Malaysia, 1974. *Publication:* Peter and Tom in the Lord Mayor's Show, 1982. *Recreations:* gardening, travel, sailing. *Clubs:* Aldgate Ward, Lime Street Ward, Little Ship.

CHASE, Robert John; HM Diplomatic Service; Consul-General, Chicago, since 1993; *b* 13 March 1943; *s* of late Herbert Chase and of Evelyn Chase; *m* 1966, Gillian Ann Chase (*née* Shelton); one *s* two *d*. *Educ:* Sevenoaks Sch.; St John's Coll., Oxford. MA (Mod. Hist.). Entered HM Diplomatic Service, 1965; Third, later Second Sec., Rangoon, 1966–69; UN Dept, FCO, 1970–72; First Sec. (Press Attaché), Brasilia, 1972–76; Hd Caribbean Section, Mexico and Caribbean Dept, FCO, 1976–80; on secondment as a manager to Imperial Chemical Industries PLC, 1980–82; Asst Hd, S American Dept, FCO, 1982–83; Asst Hd, Maritime, Aviation and Environment Dept, FCO, 1983–84; Counsellor (Commercial), Moscow, 1985–88; Overseas Inspector, FCO, 1988–89; Hd, Resource Mgt Dept, FCO, 1989–92. *Recreations:* military history, visiting historic sites, swimming, tennis. *Address:* c/o Foreign and Commonwealth Office, King Charles Street, SW1A 2AH. *T:* 0171–210 4722; Forest House, Bishops Down Park Road, Tunbridge Wells, Kent. *T:* Tunbridge Wells (01892) 521623.

CHASE, Rodney Frank; Managing Director, British Petroluem Co. plc, since 1992; *b* 12 May 1943; *s* of Norman Maxwell Chase and Barbara Chase (*née* Marshall); *m* 1968, Diana Mary Lyle; one *s* one *d*. *Educ:* Liverpool Univ. (BA Hons Hist.). Joined British Petroleum, 1964: various posts in marketing, oil trading and shipping distribn, 1964–81; Dir (Exploration and Prodn), BP Australia, 1982–85; Gp Treas, BP Co. plc, 1986–89; Chief Exec. Officer, BP Exploration (USA) Inc., 1989–92; Chm. and Chief Exec. Officer, BP America Inc., 1992–94. *Recreations:* golf, ski-ing. *Address:* British Petroleum Co. plc, Britannic House, 1 Finsbury Circus, EC2M 7BA. *T:* 0171–496 4000.

CHASE, Roger Robert, FIPM; Director of Personnel, BBC, 1989–91; *b* 19 Sept. 1928; *s* of Robert Joseph Chase and Lillian Ada (*née* Meredith); *m* 1958, Geraldine Joan Whitlamsmith; three *d*. *Educ:* Gosport Grammar Sch. Served RN, 1947–49. Joined BBC, 1944; Engrg Div., 1944–47 and 1949–67; Television Personnel Dept, 1967–74; Head, Central Services Dept, 1974–76; Controller, Personnel, Television, 1976–82; Dep. Dir of Personnel, 1982–89. Chm., BBC Club, 1979–91. *Recreation:* sailing. *Address:* Vernons, Vernons Road, Chappel, Colchester, Essex CO6 2AQ. *T:* Colchester (01206) 240143. *Club:* Royal Naval Sailing Association.

CHATAWAY, Rt Hon. Sir Christopher (John), Kt 1995; PC 1970; Chairman, Civil Aviation Authority, since 1991; *b* 31 Jan. 1931; *m* 1st, 1959, Anna Lett (marr. diss. 1975); two *s* one *d*; 2nd, 1976, Carola Walker; two *s*. *Educ:* Sherborne Sch.; Magdalen Coll., Oxford (BA Hons PPE). Rep. Great Britain, Olympic Games, 1952 and 1956; briefly held world 5,000 metres track record in 1954. Arthur Guinness Son & Co., 1953–55; Independent Television News, 1955–56; BBC Television, 1956–59. Elected for N Lewisham to LCC, 1958–61; Leader, Educn Cttee, ILEA, 1967–69. MP (C): Lewisham North, 1959–66; Chichester, May 1969–Sept. 1974; PPS to Minister of Power, 1961–62; Joint Parly Under-Secretary of State, Dept of Education and Science, 1962–64; Minister of Posts and Telecommunications, 1970–72; Minister for Industrial Develt, DTI, 1972–74. Man. Dir, Orion Royal Bank, 1974–88; Director: BET, 1974–; Credito Italiano Internat., 1992–; Macquarie Securities Ltd, 1994–; Chm., LBC, 1981–93; 1975–92: Chm., United Med. Enterprises, Isola 2000, Kitcat & Aitken, RBC CI, Crown Communications; Dir, Fisons, Plessey Telecommunications, Dorchester Hotel, UK subsids of Honeywell, GE of America and Petrofina. Treasurer, Nat. Cttee for Electoral Reform, 1976–84; Chairman: Action in Distress then Action Aid, 1986–92 (Treas., 1976–86); Groundwork Foundn, 1985–90. Hon. DLitt Loughborough, 1985; Hon. DSc Cranfield, 1994. Nansen Medal, 1960. *Address:* CAA House, Kingsway, WC2.

CHATER, Dr Anthony Philip John; Editor, Morning Star, since 1974; parents both shoe factory workers; *m* 1954, Janice (*née* Smith); three *s*. *Educ:* Northampton Grammar Sch. for Boys; Queen Mary Coll., London. BSc (1st cl. hons Chem.) 1951, PhD (Phys.Chem.) 1954. Fellow in Biochem., Ottawa Exper. Farm, 1954–56; studied biochem. at Brussels Univ., 1956–57; Teacher, Northampton Techn. High Sch., 1957–59; Teacher, Blyth Grammar Sch., Norwich, 1959–60; Lectr, subseq. Sen. Lectr in Phys. Chem., Luton Coll. of Technology, 1960–69; Head of Press and Publicity of Communist Party, 1969–74; Nat. Chm. of Communist Party, 1967–69. Contested (Com) Luton, Nov. 1963, 1964, 1966, 1970. Mem. Presidential Cttee, World Peace Council, 1969–. *Publications:* Race Relations in Britain, 1966; numerous articles. *Recreations:* walking, swimming, music, camping.

CHATER, Prof. Keith Frederick, PhD; FRS 1995; Deputy Head, Department of Genetics, John Innes Centre, since 1989; *b* 23 April 1944; *s* of Frederick Ernest Chater and Marjorie Inez Chater (*née* Palmer); *m* 1966, Jean Wallbridge; three *s* one *d*. *Educ:* Trinity Sch. of John Whitgift, Croydon; Univ. of Birmingham (BSc 1st Cl. Hons Bacteriol. 1966; PhD Genetics 1969). Research scientist in Streptomyces genetics, John Innes Inst., later John Innes Centre, 1969–. Fulbright Scholar, Harvard Univ., 1983; Hon. Prof., UEA, 1988–. Member, Editorial Board: Jl of Bacteriology, 1983–; Gene, 1983–. *Publications:* (jtly) Genetic Manipulation of Streptomyces: a laboratory manual, 1985; (ed jtly) Genetics of Bacterial Diversity, 1989. *Recreations:* painting, gardening, bird-watching. *Address:* John Innes Centre, Norwich Research Park, Colney, Norwich NR4 7UH. *T:* Norwich (01603) 452571.

CHATER, Nancy, CBE 1974; Headmistress, Stanley Park Comprehensive School, Liverpool, 1964–75, retired; *b* 18 July 1915; *d* of William John and Ellen Chater. *Educ:* Northampton Sch. for Girls; Girton Coll., Cambridge (Math. Schol., Bell Exhibr, MA); Cambridge Trng Coll. for Women (CertifEd). Asst Mistress, Huddersfield College Grammar Sch. for Boys, 1940–42; Asst Mistress, Fairfield High Sch. for Girls, Manchester, 1942–45; Sen. Maths Mistress, Thistley Hough High Sch., Stoke-on-Trent, 1945–49; Sen. Lectr, Newland Park Trng Coll. for Teachers, 1949–55; Dep. Head, Whitley Abbey Comprehensive Sch., Coventry, 1955–63. *Publications:* contrib. Math. Gazette. *Address:* c/o Priory Comprehensive School, Priory Road, Liverpool L4 2SL. *T:* 0151–263 5665. *Clubs:* Soroptimist International, Business and Professional Women's.

CHATFIELD, family name of **Baron Chatfield.**

CHATFIELD, 2nd Baron *cr* 1937, of Ditchling; **Ernle David Lewis Chatfield;** *b* 2 Jan. 1917; *s* of 1st Baron Chatfield, PC, GCB, OM, KCMG, CVO (Admiral of the Fleet Lord Chatfield), and Lillian Emma St John Matthews (*d* 1977); *S* father, 1967; *m* 1969, (Felicia Mary) Elizabeth, *d* of late Dr John Roderick Bulman, Hereford. *Educ:* RNC Dartmouth; Trinity Coll., Cambridge. ADC to Governor-General of Canada, 1940–44. *Heir:* none. *Address:* 535 Island Road, Victoria, BC V8S 2T7, Canada.

CHATFIELD, Sir John (Freeman), Kt 1993; CBE 1982; DL; Chairman, Association of County Councils, 1989–92; Consultant Solicitor in private practice, 1989–95; *b* 28 Oct. 1929; *s* of Cecil Freeman Chatfield and Florence Dorothy Chatfield; *m* 1954, Barbara Elizabeth Trickett. *Educ:* Southdown Coll., Eastbourne; Roborough Sch., Eastbourne; Lawrence Sheriff Sch., Rugby; Lewes Grammar Sch.; Law Soc. Sch. (Final, 1951). Solicitor, 1952; Sen. Partner, Hart Reade & Co., Eastbourne, 1976–89; Dep. Registrar, County Court, 1965–78. Mem., E Sussex CC, 1972–93 (Leader, 1981–85; Chm., 1985–87); Chairman: Sussex Police Authy, 1982–85; Police Cttee, ACC, 1982–85; Official Side, Police Negotiating Bd, 1982–85; Mem., Police Adv. Bd, England and Wales, 1980–85; Vice-Chm., ACC, 1986–89; Chm., UK Local Authorities Internat. Bureau, 1989–92; first Chm., Internat. Council for Local Envmt Initiatives, 1990–93; Pres., Consultative Council of Local and Regional Authorities in Europe, 1990–93; a Vice-President: CEMR, 1989–93; British Section, IULA/CEMR, 1993–; Leader, UK Delegn, 1989–92, Mem., Standing Cttee, 1990–93, CLRAE. Mem. Ct and Council, Sussex Univ., 1981–85 and 1991–. Pres., Eastbourne Law Soc., 1972–73. Freeman, City of London, 1994. DL E Sussex, 1986. *Recreations:* music, theatre, travel. *Address:* Underhill House, East Dean, Eastbourne, E Sussex BN20 0DB. *T:* Eastbourne (01323) 423397.

CHATTEN, Harold Raymond Percy, CB 1975; RCNC; Chief Executive, Royal Dockyards, 1975–79, and Head of Royal Corps of Naval Constructors, Apr.-Sept. 1979, Ministry of Defence. Production Manager, HM Dockyard, Chatham, 1967–70; General Manager, HM Dockyard, Rosyth, Fife, 1970–75. MA Cambridge 1946.

CHATTERJEE, Dr Satya Saran, OBE 1971; JP; FRCP, FRCPE; Consultant Chest Physician and Physician in Charge, Department of Respiratory Physiology, Wythenshawe Hospital, Manchester, 1959–88; *b* 16 July 1922; *m* 1948, Enid May (*née* Adlington); one *s* two *d*. *Educ:* India, UK, Sweden and USA. MB, BS; FCCP (USA). Asst Lectr, Dept of Medicine, Albany Med. Coll. Hosp., NY, 1953–54; Med. Registrar, Sen. Registrar, Dept of Thoracic Medicine, Wythenshawe Hosp., Manchester, 1954–59. Mem., NW RHA, 1976–. Chairman: NW Conciliation Cttee, Race Relations Board, 1972–77; Overseas Doctors Assoc., 1975–81 (Pres., 1981–87); Manchester Area Cttee on Ethnic Minority Health, 1993–94; Member: Standing Adv. Council on Race Relations, 1977–86; GMC, 1979–92; NW Adv. Council, BBC, 1987–92; Vice-Pres., Manchester Council for Community Relations, 1974–. President: Rotary Club, Wythenshawe, 1975–76; Indian Assoc., Manchester, 1962–71. *Publications:* research papers in various projects related to cardio/pulmonary disorders. *Address:* March, 20 Macclesfield Road, Wilmslow, Cheshire SK9 2AF. *T:* Wilmslow (01625) 522559.

CHATTO, Beth, VMH 1988; Creator and Managing Director of The Beth Chatto Gardens; *b* 27 June 1923; *d* of William George and Bessie Beatrice Little; *m* 1943, Andrew Edward Chatto; two *d*. *Educ:* Colchester County High Sch.; Hockerill Training Coll. for Teachers. No formal horticultural educn; parents enthusiastic gardeners; husband's lifelong study of natural associations of plants was original inspiration in use of species plants in more natural groupings; Sir Cedric Morris' knowledge and generosity with many rare plants from his rich collection at Benton End, Suffolk, became basis for gdns at Elmstead Market; began career demonstrating flower arranging; Beth Chatto Gardens, 1960–, Nursery, 1967–; a keen advocate of organic gardening and diet for over 40 yrs. Founder Mem., Colchester Flower Club (2nd Flower Club in England). Lectures throughout UK; lecture tours and talks: USA, 1983, 1984 and 1986; Holland and Germany, 1987; Australia and Toronto, 1989. DUniv Essex, 1988. Lawrence Meml Medal, RHS, 1988. *Publications:* The Dry Garden, 1978; The Damp Garden, 1982; Plant Portraits, 1985; The Beth Chatto Garden Notebook, 1988; The Green Tapestry, 1989 (also USA); articles in Popular Gardening, Englishwoman's Garden, Horticulture, Amer. Jl of Hort., Sunday Telegraph, and Hortus. *Recreations:* family, cooking, entertaining, music, reading—and always creating the garden. *Address:* The Beth Chatto Gardens, Elmstead Market, Colchester, Essex CO7 7DB. *T:* Colchester (01206) 822007.

CHATWANI, Jaswanti; Vice President, Immigration Appeal Tribunal, since 1992; *b* 23 Nov. 1933; *d* of Keshavji Ramji Tanna and Shantaben Tanna; *m* 1953, Rajnikant Popatlal Chatwani; one *s* one *d*. *Educ:* Government Sch., Dar-es-Salaam, Tanzania. Called to the Bar, Lincoln's Inn, 1959; attached to Chopra & Chopra, Legal Practice, Mwanza, Tanzania, 1959–60; in private practice, Zanzibar, 1960–65; Sec. and Legal Aid Counsel, Tanganyika Law Soc., 1965–68; in private practice, Dar-es-Salaam, Tanzania, 1968–70; Sen. Immigration Counsellor, UKIAS, 1971–78; Legal Officer, then Sen. Complaints Officer, CRE, 1979–87; part-time Adjudicator, Immigration Appeals, 1980–87, full-time Adjudicator 1987–92. Mem., Judicial Studies Bd, Ethnic Minorities Adv. Cttee, 1991–94. *Recreations:* walking, travel, reading. *Address:* 2 Hartshill Close, North Hillingdon, Uxbridge, Middx UB10 9LH. *T:* Uxbridge (01895) 270253.

CHATWIN, (John) Malcolm, CEng, FIEE; Chief Executive, Yorkshire Electricity Group, since 1992; *b* 19 July 1945; *s* of John Edward Chatwin and Louie Valery Chatwin; *m* 1969, Elizabeth Joy West; one *s* two *d*. *Educ:* City of London Sch.; University College London (BSc(Eng) Elect. Eng.). Operations Engr, LEB, 1969–73; Commercial Economist, Seeboard, 1973–77; Pricing Policy Manager, Electricity Council, 1977–79; Dep. Commercial Dir and Commercial Dir, N of Scotland Hydro-Electric Bd, 1980–87; Yorkshire Electricity: Dir, Business Planning, 1987–90; Commercial Dir, 1990–92. Dir, Electricity Assoc., 1992–; Chm., Regional Power Generators, 1992–94. Dir, Century Inns, 1995–. CIMgt. *Recreations:* ski-ing, sailing. *Address:* Yorkshire Electricity Group, Scarcroft, Leeds LS14 3HS. *T:* Leeds (0113) 289 5042.

CHAUDHURI, Prof. Kirti Narayan, PhD; FBA 1990; Vasco da Gama Professor of the History of European Expansion, European University Institute, Florence, since 1991; *b* 8 Sept. 1934; *s* of Nirad C. Chaudhuri, *qv*; *m* 1961, Surang Chaudhuri; one *s*. *Educ:* privately in India; London Univ. (BA Hons Hist., 1959; PhD 1961). Derby Postgrad. Schol., London Univ., 1959–61; School of Oriental and African Studies, London University: Res. Fellow in Econ. Hist., 1961–63; Lectr in Econ. Hist. of Asia, 1963–74; Reader, 1974–81; Prof. of Econ. Hist. of Asia, 1981–91; Chairman: S Asia Area Studies Centre, 1982–85; History Exam. Bd, 1982–87. D. João de Castro Internat. History Prize. *Publications:* The English East India Company: the study of an early joint-stock company 1600–1640, 1965; The Economic Development of India under the East India Company 1814–58: a selection of contemporary writings, 1971; The Trading World of Asia and the English East India Company 1660–1760, 1978; Trade and Civilisation in the Indian Ocean: an economic history from the rise of Islam to 1750, 1985; Asia before Europe: the economy and civilisation in the Indian Ocean from the rise of Islam to 1750, 1990; contribs to Econ. Hist. Rev., Eng. Histl Rev., Jl of European Econ. Hist., Jl of RAS, Modern Asian Studies, TLS. *Recreations:* mountain walking, sailing, exploration, collecting modern prints and vintage watches, photography, wine tasting. *Address:* Istituto Universitario Europeo, CP No 2330, 50100 Firenze, Italy. *Club:* Athenæum.

CHAUDHURI, Nirad Chandra, Hon. CBE 1992; FRSL; FRAS; author and broadcaster; *b* Bengal, 23 Nov. 1897; *s* of Upendra Narayan Chaudhuri and Sushila, of Banagram, Bengal; *m* 1932, Amiya Dhar (*d* 1994); three *s*. *Educ:* Calcutta University. BA (Hons) 1918. Resident in UK, 1970–. University Lectures include: Chicago; Texas Univ. at Austin; Pennsylvania; Potsdam; Boston; Oxford; Canadian Univs. DUniv Stirling, 1978; Hon. DLitt Oxon, 1990. Broadcasting on radio and TV; television appearances include: A Brown Man in Search of Civilization (feature on life), 1972; Everyman, 1983; Springing Tiger, 1984. *Publications:* The Autobiography of an unknown Indian, 1951; A Passage to England, 1959; The Continent of Circe, 1965 (Duff Cooper Meml Prize, 1966); The Intellectual in India, 1967; Woman in Bengali Life, 1967 (in Bengali language); To Live or not to Live, 1970; Scholar Extraordinary: life of F. Max Muller, 1974; Clive of India, 1975; Culture in the Vanity Bag, 1976; Hinduism, 1979, Italian trans. 1980, Japanese trans. 1985; Thy Hand, Great Anarch!, 1987; contribs to The Times, TLS, The Daily Telegraph, Guardian, London Magazine, Encounter, The New English Review, Spectator, The Atlantic Monthly (USA), Pacific Affairs (USA), major Indian newspapers and magazines. *Recreations:* music, gardening, walks. *Address:* 20 Lathbury Road, Oxford OX2 7AU. *T:* Oxford (01865) 57683.

See also K. N. Chaudhuri.

CHAUVIRÉ, Yvette, Commandeur de la Légion d'Honneur, 1988 (Officier, 1974); Commandeur des Arts et des Lettres, 1975; Commandeur, Ordre National du Mérite, 1981 (Officier, 1972); ballerina assoluta, since 1950; *b* Paris, 22 April 1917. *Educ:* Ecole de la Danse de l'Opéra, Paris. Paris Opera Ballet, 1931; first major rôles in David Triomphant and Les Créatures de Prométhée; Danseuse étoile 1942; danced Istar, 1941; Monte Carlo Opera Ballet, 1946–47; returned to Paris Opera Ballet, 1947–49. Has appeared at Covent Garden, London; also danced in the USA, and in cities of Rome, Moscow, Leningrad, Berlin, Buenos Aires, Johannesburg, Milan, etc; official tours: USA 1948; USSR 1958, 1966, 1969; Canada 1967; Australia. Leading rôles in following ballets: Les Mirages, Lac des Cygnes, Sleeping Beauty, Giselle, Roméo et Juliette, Suite en Blanc, Le Cygne (St Saens), La Dame aux Camélias, etc; Giselle, Moscow, 1966 (guest for 150th annivesary celebration); acting rôle, Reine Léda, Amphitryon 38, Paris, 1976–77; La Comtessa de Doris in Raymonda, Paris, 1983. Choreographer: La Péri, Roméo et Juliette, Le Cygne; farewell performances: Paris Opera, Giselle, Nov. 1972, Petrouchka and The Swan, Dec. 1972; Berlin Opera, Giselle, 1973; Artistic and Tech. Adviser, Paris Opera, 1963–72, teacher of dance for style and perfection, 1970–; Acad. Internat. de la Danse, Paris, 1972–76; Artistic Dir, Acad. ARIMA, Kyoto, Japan, 1980–81. *Films:* La Mort du Cygne, 1937 (Paris); Carrousel Napolitain, 1953 (Rome); Dominique Delouche présente un grand portrait sur Yvette Chauviré, une Etoile pour l'exemple, 1988. *Publication:* Je suis Ballerine. *Recreations:* painting and drawing, collections of swans. *Address:* 21 Place du Commerce, Paris 75015, France.

CHAVASSE, Christopher Patrick Grant, MA; Clerk to the Worshipful Company of Grocers, 1981–88; *b* 14 March 1928; *s* of late Grant Chavasse and of Maureen Shingler (*née* Whalley); *m* 1955, Audrey Mary Leonard; two *s* one *d*. *Educ:* Bedford Sch.; Clare Coll., Cambridge (Exhibitioner). Commissioned The Rifle Brigade, 1947; served in Palestine (despatches), 1948; RAFVR 1949. Admitted Solicitor, 1955; Partner: Jacobs & Greenwood, 1960; Woodham Smith, 1970; President, Holborn Law Soc., 1977–78. Chairman: NADFAS Tours Ltd, 1986–92; Totnes DFAS, 1993–95; Vice-President: NADFAS, 1992–; Chiltern DFAS, 1986–. Hon. Steward of Westminster Abbey, 1950–; Treasurer, St Mary-le-Bow Church, 1981–88. Secretary: Governing Body of Oundle and Laxton Schs, 1981–88; The Grocers' Charity, 1981–88. Mem. Ct, Corp. of Sons of the Clergy, 1985–. *Publications:* Conveyancing Costs, 1971; Non-Contentious Costs, 1975; The Discretionary Items in Contentious Costs, 1980; various articles in Law Society's Gazette, New Law Jl, Solicitors Jl, and others. *Address:* Duncannon House, Stoke Gabriel, Totnes, Devon TQ9 6QY. *T:* Stoke Gabriel (01803) 782291. *Clubs:* Royal Air Force; Leander.

CHAYTOR, Sir George Reginald, 8th Bt *cr* 1831; *b* 28 Oct. 1912; *s* of William Richard Carter Chaytor (*d* 1973) (*g s* of 2nd Bt) and Anna Laura (*d* 1947), *d* of George Fawcett; *S* cousin, Sir William Henry Clervaux Chaytor, 7th Bt, 1976. *Heir: cousin* (Herbert) Gordon Chaytor [*b* 15 June 1922; *m* 1947, Mary Alice, *d* of Thomas Craven; three *s*]. *Address:* 103–9372 Fletcher Avenue, Chilliwack, BC V2P 4Z2, Canada.

CHAZOT, Georges Christian; Group Chief Executive, Eurotunnel, since 1994; *b* 19 March 1939; *s* of late Raymond Chazot, banker and Suzanne Monnet; *m* 1962, Marie-Dominique Tremois, painter; one *s* two *d*. Educ: Lycée Gauthier; Lycée Bugeaud Algiers; Ecole Polytechnique, Paris; Univ. of Florida (MSEE 1964); Internat. Marketing Inst., Harvard. FCIT. Joined Schlumberger Group, 1962; Electro-Mechanical Research, USA, 1962–65; Schlumberger Instrument and Systems, 1965–76; Alcatel Alsthom, 1977–92; Saft, 1977–88; Chairman and Chief Executive Officer: Saft, 1984; Alcatel Business Systems, 1990; Adia France, 1992–93. Director: BVA, Paris; Actim, Paris; Fondn Franco Japonaise Sasakawa; Dir and former Dir, internat. cos. Mem., Adv. Council, World Economic Forum, Switzerland. Chevalier, Légion d'honneur. *Recreation:* sailing. *Address:* Eurotunnel, The Adelphi, John Adam Street, WC2N 6JT. *T:* 0171–747 6747, *Fax:* 0171–747 6666.

CHECKETTS, Sir David (John), KCVO 1979 (CVO 1969; MVO 1966); Squadron Leader, retired; an Extra Equerry to the Prince of Wales, since 1979; *b* 23 Aug. 1930; 3rd *s* of late Reginald Ernest George Checketts and late Frances Mary Checketts; *m* 1958, Rachel Leila Warren Herrick; one *s* three *d*. Flying Training, Bulawayo, Rhodesia, 1948–50; 14 Sqdn, Germany, 1950–54; Instructor, Fighter Weapons Sch., 1954–57; Air ADC to C-in-C Malta, 1958–59; 3 Sqdn, Germany, 1960–61; Equerry to Duke of Edinburgh, 1961–66, to the Prince of Wales, 1967–70; Private Sec. to the Prince of Wales, 1970–79. Dir, Alpine Consultants Ltd. Chm., Rainbow Boats Trust. *Recreation:* ornithology. *Address:* Church Cottage, Winkfield, Windsor, Berks SL4 4SF. *T:* Winkfield Row (01344) 882289. *Club:* Whitefriars.

CHECKETTS, Guy Tresham, CBE 1982; Deputy Chairman and Managing Director, Hawker Siddeley International, 1975–90, retired; *b* 11 May 1927; *s* of John Albert and Norah Maud Checketts; *m* 1957, Valerie Cynthia Stanley; four *s*. *Educ:* Warwick Sch.; Birmingham Univ. (BScEng Hons). British Thompson Houston Co., Rugby, 1948–51; Brush Group, 1951–57; Hawker Siddeley International, 1957–90. Chm., SE Asia Trade Adv. Gp, 1979–83; Mem., BOTB, 1981–84. *Recreation:* sailing. *Club:* Royal Over-Seas League.

CHECKLAND, Sir Michael, Kt 1992; Director-General, BBC, 1987–92; *b* 13 March 1936; *s* of Leslie and Ivy Florence Checkland; *m* 1st, 1960, Shirley Frances Corbett (marr. diss. 1983); two *s* one *d*; 2nd, 1987, Sue Zetter. *Educ:* King Edward's Grammar Sch., Fiveways, Birmingham; Wadham Coll., Oxford (BA Modern History; Hon. Fellow, 1989). FCMA; CIMgt. Accountant: Parkinson Cowan Ltd, 1959–62; Thorn Electronics Ltd, 1962–64; BBC: Senior Cost Accountant, 1964; Head of Central Finance Unit, 1967; Chief Accountant, Central Finance Services, 1969; Chief Accountant, Television, 1971; Controller, Finance, 1976; Controller, Planning and Resource Management, Television, 1977; Director of Resources, Television, 1982; Dep. Dir-Gen., 1985; Director: BBC Enterprises, 1979–92 (Chm., 1986–87); Visnews, 1980–85. Nynex Cable Communications, 1995–. President: Commonwealth Broadcasting Assoc., 1987–88; Birmingham & Midland Inst., 1994; Vice-President: RTS, 1985–94 (FRTS 1987); EBU, 1991–92. Chairman: NCH Action for Children, 1991–; Brighton Internat. Fest., 1993–; Dep. Chm., CBSO, 1994–; Dir, Nat. Youth Music Theatre, 1992–; Trustee, Reuters, 1994–. Governor: Westminster Coll., Oxford, 1993–; Birkbeck Coll., 1993–. *Recreations:* sport, music, travel. *Address:* Orchard Cottage, Park Lane, Maplehurst, near Horsham, West Sussex RH13 6LL.

CHECKLEY, Dr Stuart Arthur, FRCPsych; Consultant Psychiatrist, Maudsley Hospital, since 1981; Dean, since 1989, and Professor of Psychoneuroendocrinology, since 1994, Institute of Psychiatry; *b* 15 Dec. 1945; *s* of Arthur William George Checkley and Hilda Dorothy Checkley; *m* 1971, Marilyn Jane Evans, BA; one *s* one *d*. *Educ:* St Albans Sch.; Brasenose Coll., Oxford (BA, BM BCh). FRCP, FRCPsych. House appts, London Hosp. and St Charles Hosp., 1970–73; Registrar in Psych., London Hosp., 1973–74; Maudsley Hospital: Registrar, 1974–76; Hon. Sen. Registrar, 1977–78; Hon. Consultant, 1980–81; research worker, supported by Wellcome Trust, 1978–81; Mapother Travelling Fellow, USA, 1979; Institute of Psychiatry: Sen. Lectr, 1979–81; Sen. Lectr, Metabolic Unit, 1985–94. Chm., Biol Psych. Special Interest Gp, RCPsych, 1995–. *Publications:* papers on treatment of depression and hormones in relation to depression. *Recreation:* bird watching. *Address:* Institute of Psychiatry, De Crespigny Park, SE5 8AF. *T:* 0171–703 5411.

CHEDLOW, Barry William, QC 1969; a Recorder of the Crown Court, since 1974; Member, Criminal Injuries Compensation Board, since 1976; *b* Macclesfield, 8 Oct. 1921; *m* Anne Sheldon, BA; one *s* one *d*. *Educ:* Burnage High Sch.; Manchester Univ. Served RAF, 1941–46: USAAF, Flying Instructor, 1942; Flt-Lt 1943. Called to Bar, Middle Temple, 1947, Bencher, 1976; Prizeman in Law of Evidence. Practises in London, Midland and Oxford Circuit. *Publications:* author and editor of various legal text-books. *Recreations:* flying (private pilot's licence, singles, twins, helicopters), languages, sailing. *Address:* 12 King's Bench Walk, Temple, EC4Y 7EL. *T:* 0171–583 0811; Little Kimblewick Farm, Finch Lane, Amersham, Bucks HP7 9NB. *T:* Little Chalfont (01494) 762156.

CHEESEMAN, Prof. Ian Clifford, PhD; ARCS; CEng, FRAeS; Professor of Helicopter Engineering, University of Southampton, 1970–82, now Emeritus; consultant in aeronautical, acoustic and general engineering matters; *b* 12 June 1926; *s* of Richard Charles Cheeseman and Emily Ethel Clifford; *m* 1957, Margaret Edith Pither; one *s* two *d*. *Educ:* Andover Grammar Sch.; Imperial Coll. of Science and Technology. Vickers Supermarine Ltd, 1951–53; Aeroplane and Armament Estab., 1953–56; Atomic Weapons Res. Estab., 1956–58; Nat. Gas Turbine Estab., 1958–70. Res. Dir, 1983–87, Dir and Consultant, 1987–88, Stewart Hughes Ltd, Southampton. Pres., Airship Assoc., 1986–94. *Publications:* contribs to Jl RAeS, Jl CIT, Jl Sound and Vibration, Procs Phys. Soc. 'A', Vertica. *Recreations:* dog breeding, gardening, photography, historical research. *Address:* Abbey View, Tarrant Keynston, Blandford Forum, Dorset DT11 9JE. *T:* Blandford (01258) 456877.

CHEETHAM, Anthony John Valerian; Chairman, Orion Publishing Group (formerly Orion Books), since 1991; *b* 12 April 1943; *s* of Sir Nicolas Cheetham, *qv*; *m* 1st, 1969, Julia Rollason (marr. diss.); two *s* one *d*; 2nd, 1979, Rosemary de Courcy; two *d*. *Educ:* Eton Coll.; Balliol Coll., Oxford (BA Hons Modern History). Editorial Dir, Sphere Books, 1968; Managing Director: Futura Publications, 1973; Macdonald Futura, 1979; Chm., Century Publishing, 1982–85; Man. Dir, Century Hutchinson, 1985; Chm. and Chief Exec., Random Century Gp, 1989–91. *Publication:* Richard III, 1972. *Recreations:* walking, tennis, gardening. *Address:* 20 Grove Park, SE5 8LH. *T:* 0171–733 8204.

CHEETHAM, Prof. Anthony Kevin, FRS 1994; FRSC; Director, Materials Research Laboratory, since 1992, Professor of Materials, since 1991, and Professor of Chemistry, since 1992, University of California at Santa Barbara; Professor of Solid State Chemistry, Royal Institution, since 1986; Emeritus Student, Christ Church, Oxford, since 1991; *b* 16 Nov. 1946; *s* of Norman James Cheetham and Lilian Cheetham; *m* 1984, Janet Clare (*née* Stockwell); one *s* one *d*, and one *s* one *d* from a previous marriage. *Educ:* Stockport Grammar Sch.; St Catherine's Coll., Oxford (Hon. Scholar); Wadham Coll., Oxford (Sen. Scholar). BA (Chem.) 1968; DPhil 1971. University of Oxford: Cephalosporin Fellow, Lincoln Coll., 1971–74; Lectr in Inorganic Chem., St Hilda's Coll., 1971–85; Lectr in Chemical Crystallography, 1974–90; Tutor in Inorganic Chem., Christ Church, 1974–91; Reader in Inorganic Materials, 1990–91. Visiting Professor: Arizona State Univ., 1977; Univ. of California, Berkeley, 1979; Vis. Foreign Scientist, Amer. Chem. Soc., 1981. Mem. Scientific Council, Institut Laue-Langevin, Grenoble, 1988–90. Dir, Gen. Funds Investment Trust plc, 1984–87. Corday-Morgan Medal and Prize, RSC, 1982; Solid State Chemistry Award, RSC, 1988. *Publications:* Solid State Chemistry: techniques (with P. Day), 1986; Solid State Chemistry: compounds (with P. Day), 1992; contribs to sci. jls. *Recreations:* cricket, stock market. *Address:* 1695 East Valley Road, Montecito, CA 93108, USA. *T:* (805) 565 1211.

CHEETHAM, Francis William, OBE 1979; FMA; Director, Norfolk Museums Service, 1974–90; *b* 5 Feb. 1928; *s* of Francis Cheetham and Doris Elizabeth Jones; *m* 1954, Monica Fairhurst; three *s* one *d*. *Educ:* King Edward VII Sch., Sheffield; Univ. of Sheffield (MA). Dep. Art Dir and Curator, Castle Museum, Nottingham, 1960–63; Dir, City of Norwich Museums, 1963–74. Winston Churchill Fellow, 1967. Member: Management Cttee, Norfolk and Norwich Triennial Fest., 1966–89; Crafts Council, 1978–81; Management Cttee, Eastern Arts Assoc., 1978–79, 1987–89; Bd, Norwich Puppet Theatre, 1981–87; Founder Mem., National Heritage, 1970; Chairman: Norfolk and Norwich Film Theatre, 1968–70; Norfolk Contemporary Crafts Soc., 1972–85 and 1991–94 (Life Pres., 1985); Melton Arts Trust, 1990–92. Museums Association: AMA 1959; FMA 1966; Hon. Treasurer, 1970–73; Vice-Pres., 1977–78, 1979–80; Pres., 1978–79; Chm., Soc. of County Museum Dirs, 1974–77; Museum Advr to ACC, 1976–84. Member: Exec. Bd, ICOM (UK), 1981–84; Bd, Radio Broadland (ILR Station), 1983–. FRSA 1986. *Publications:* Medieval English Alabaster Carvings in the Castle Museum, Nottingham, 1962, revd edn 1973; English Medieval Alabasters, 1984; contrib. Jl of Museums Assoc. *Recreations:* hill-walking, listening to music, especially early and baroque. *Address:* 25 St Andrew's Avenue, Thorpe St Andrew, Norwich NR7 0RG. *T:* Norwich (01603) 34091.

CHEETHAM, John Frederick Thomas, CB 1978; Secretary, Exchequer and Audit Department, 1975–79; *b* 27 March 1919; *s* of late James Oldham Cheetham, MA, BCom; *m* 1943, Yvonne Marie Smith; one *s* one *d*. *Educ:* Penarth Grammar Sch.; Univ. of Wales. Entered Exchequer and Audit Dept, 1938; War Service, Royal Artillery, 1939–46; Office of Parly Comr for Administration, 1966–69; Dep. Sec., Exchequer and Audit Dept, 1973–74. *Recreations:* tennis, food and wine. *Address:* 70 Chatsworth Road, Croydon, Surrey CR0 1HB. *T:* 0181–688 3740. *Club:* MCC.

CHEETHAM, Juliet, OBE 1995; Professor and Director, Social Work Research Centre, Stirling University, since 1986; *b* 12 Oct. 1939; *d* of Harold Neville Blair and Isabel (*née* Sanders); *m* 1965, Christopher Paul Cheetham; one *s* two *d*. *Educ:* St Andrews Univ.

(MA); Oxford Univ. (Dip. in Social and Admin. Studies). Qual. social worker. Probation Officer, Inner London, 1960–65; Lectr in Applied Social Studies, and Fellow of Green Coll., Oxford Univ., 1965–85. Member: Cttee of Enquiry into Immigration and Youth Service, 1966–68; Cttee of Enquiry into Working of Abortion Act, 1971–74; NI Standing Adv. Commn on Human Rights, 1974–77; Central Council for Educn and Trng in Social Work, 1973–89; Commn for Racial Equality, 1977–84; Social Security Adv. Cttee, 1983–88; CNAA Social Scis Cttee, 1989–91; ESRC Res. Resources Bd, 1993–. *Publications:* Social Work with Immigrants, 1972; Unwanted Pregnancy and Counselling, 1977; Social Work and Ethnicity, 1982; Social Work with Black Children and their Families, 1986; (jtly) Evaluating Social Work Effectiveness, 1992; contrib. collected papers and prof. jls. *Recreation:* canal boats. *Address:* Peffermill House, 91 Peffermill Road, Edinburgh EH16 5UX. *T:* 0131–661 0948; Social Work Research Centre, Department of Applied Social Science, University of Stirling, Stirling FK9 4LA. *T:* Stirling (01786) 67724.

CHEETHAM, Sir Nicolas (John Alexander), KCMG 1964 (CMG 1953); *b* 8 Oct. 1910; *s* of late Sir Milne Cheetham, KCMG, and late Mrs Nigel Law, CBE, DStJ; *m* 1st, 1937, Jean Evison Corfe (marr. diss. 1960); two *s*; 2nd, 1960, Lady Mabel Brooke (*née* Jocelyn). *Educ:* Eton College; Christ Church, Oxford. Entered HM Diplomatic Service, 1934; served in Foreign Office and at Athens, Buenos Aires, Mexico City and Vienna; UK Deputy Permanent Representative on North Atlantic Council, 1954–59; HM Minister to Hungary, 1959–61; Assistant Under-Secretary, Foreign Office, 1961–64; Ambassador to Mexico, 1964–68. *Publications:* A History of Mexico, 1970; New Spain, 1974; Mediaeval Greece, 1981; Keepers of the Keys: the Pope in history, 1982. *Address:* 50 Cadogan Square, SW1X 0JW. *T:* 0171–589 5624. *Club:* Travellers'.
See also A. J. V. Cheetham.

CHEEVERS, William Harold; Director of Engineering, Granada Television, 1970–73, retired; *b* 20 June 1918; *m* 1964, Shirley Cheevers; one *s*. *Educ:* Christ's Coll., London. Engineer, BBC Television, 1938–39. War Service, Army, PoW, 1941–45. Sen. Engr, BBC Television, 1946–54; Planning Engr, Radio-Corp. of America, in USA and Canada, 1954–55; Head of Engineering, Associated Rediffusion, 1955–60; Gen. Manager, Westward Television, Jt Man. Dir, 1963–67, Man. Dir, 1967–70; Dir, ITN News, 1967–70, and of IT Publications; also Director: Keith Prowse, 1963–70; Direct Line Services, 1964–87; Prowest, 1967–70; Penwell Ltd, 1971–88. Chm., British Regional Television Assoc., 1968–69. Fellow British Kinematograph Soc.; MInstD; MBIM; AssIEE. *Publications:* articles for most TV Jls, and Symposiums, at home and abroad. *Recreations:* boating, golf, reading. *Address:* 52 Preston Down Road, Paignton, Devon TQ3 1DU. *T:* Paignton (01803) 524455. *Club:* Royal Western Yacht Club of England (Plymouth).

CHELMER, Baron *cr* 1963 (Life Peer), of Margaretting; **Eric Cyril Boyd Edwards,** Kt 1954; MC 1944; TD; JP; DL; *b* 9 Oct. 1914; *s* of Col C. E. Edwards, DSO, MC, TD, DL, JP, and Mrs J. Edwards; *m* 1939, Enid, *d* of F. W. Harvey; one *s*. *Educ:* Felsted Sch. Solicitor, 1937; LLB (London) 1937. Served Essex Yeomanry, 1940–54 (MC), Lieut-Col Commanding, 1945–46. Chm., Provident Financial Gp, 1976–83 (Dir, 1970–83); Chm. and Dir, Greycoat Group, 1977–85; Director: NEM Group, 1970–86; NEL Assurance, 1970–86. National Union of Conservative Associations: Chm., 1956; Pres., 1967; Chm., Review Cttee, 1970–73; Chm., Nat. Exec. Cttee of Conservative and Unionist Assoc., 1957–65; Conservative Party: Jt Treas., 1965–77; Mem. Adv. Cttee on Policy, 1956–85. Member: Political Cttee, Carlton Club, 1961; Cttee of Musicians' Benevolent Fund; Ralph Vaughan Williams Trust. JP Essex, 1950; DL Essex 1971. *Recreation:* "improving". *Address:* Peacocks, Margaretting, Essex CM4 9HY. *Clubs:* Carlton, Royal Ocean Racing.
See also D. Edwards, J. T. Edwards.

CHELMSFORD, 3rd Viscount *cr* 1921, of Chelmsford; **Frederic Jan Thesiger;** Baron Chelmsford, 1858; Lloyd's Insurance Broker, retired; Director, Willis Faber plc, 1979–91; *b* 7 March 1931; *s* of 2nd Viscount Chelmsford and of Gilian (*d* 1978), *d* of late Arthur Nevile Lubbock; *S* father, 1970; *m* 1958, Clare Rendle, *d* of Dr G. R. Rolston, Haslemere; one *s* one *d*. Formerly Lieut, Inns of Court Regt. *Publication:* L is for Limnet, 1992. *Heir: s* Hon. Frederic Corin Piers Thesiger, *b* 6 March 1962. *Address:* 26 Ormonde Gate, SW3 4EX.

CHELMSFORD, Bishop of, 1986–April 1996; **Rt. Rev. John Waine;** Clerk of the Closet to the Queen, since 1989; *b* 20 June 1930; *s* of late William and Ellen Waine; *m* 1957, Patricia Zena Haikney; three *s*. *Educ:* Prescot Grammar Sch.; Manchester Univ. (BA); Ridley Hall, Cambridge. Deacon 1955, Priest 1956; Curate of St Mary, West Derby, 1955–58; Curate in Charge of All Saints, Sutton, 1958–60; Vicar of Ditton, 1960–64; Vicar of Holy Trinity, Southport, 1964–69; Rector of Kirkby, 1969–75; Bishop Suffragan of Stafford, 1975–78; Bishop of St Edmundsbury and Ipswich, 1978–86. Chm., Churches Main Cttee, 1991–. ChStJ 1983 (Sub-Prelate, 1991). *Recreations:* music, gardening. *Address:* Bishopscourt, Margaretting, Ingatestone, Essex CM4 0HD; (from April) Broadmere, Ipswich Road, Grundisburgh, Woodbridge, Suffolk IP13 6TJ. *Club:* Royal Air Force.

CHELMSFORD, Provost of; *see* Moses, Very Rev. J. H.

CHELSEA, Viscount; Charles Gerald John Cadogan; *b* 24 March 1937; *o s* of 7th Earl Cadogan, *qv*; *m* 1st, 1963, Lady Philippa Wallop (*d* 1984), *d* of 9th Earl of Portsmouth; two *s* one *d*; 2nd, 1989, Jennifer Jane Greig Rae (marr. diss. 1994), *d* of J. E. K. Rae and Mrs S. Z. de Ferranti; 3rd, 1994, Dorothy Ann Shipsey, MVO, *yr d* of late Dr W. E. Shipsey. *Educ:* Eton. Chm., Leukaemia Research Fund, 1985–. Freeman, City of London, 1979; Liveryman, GAPAN. *Heir: s* Hon. Edward Charles Cadogan [*b* 10 May 1966; *m* 1990, Katharina Johanna Ingeborg, *d* of Rear-Adm. D. P. A. Hülsemann; one *d*]. *Clubs:* White's, Royal Automobile.

CHELTENHAM, Archdeacon of; *see* Lewis, Ven. J. A.

CHELTON, Captain Lewis William Leonard, RN; Secretary, Engineering Council, since 1987; *b* 19 Dec. 1934; *s* of Lewis Walter Chelton and Doris May Chelton (*née* Gamblin); *m* 1957, Daphne Joan Landon; three *s*. *Educ:* Royal Naval College, Dartmouth. Called to the Bar, Inner Temple, 1966. Entered RN as Cadet, 1951; served in ships and shore estabts, home and abroad; Fleet Supply Officer, 1979–81; Captain, 1981; Chief Naval Judge Advocate, 1982–84; retired (voluntarily), 1987. Trustee, R. S. Surtees Soc. *Recreations:* shooting, gardening, country life. *Address:* Palmers Green House, Hatch Beauchamp, near Taunton, Som TA3 6AE. *T:* Hatch Beauchamp (01823) 480221. *Club:* Farmers'.

CHENERY, Peter James; Secretary, since 1990, and Head of Public Affairs, British Council; *b* 24 Oct. 1946; *s* of Dudley James Chenery and Brenda Dorothy (*née* Redford); *m* 1979, Alice Blanche Faulder; three *d*. *Educ:* Forest Sch.; Christ Church, Oxford (MA). Teacher, Ghana Teaching Service, 1967–70; joined British Council, 1970: Amman, 1971–73; Middle East Dept, 1973–76; Riyadh, 1977; Freetown, 1978–80; Jedda, 1981–84; Sana'a, 1984–88; Munich, 1988–90. *Recreations:* amusing conversation, beers of the world, early English coins. *Address:* The British Council, 10 Spring Gardens, SW1A 2BN. *T:* 0171–930 8466. *Club:* Leander.

CHENEY, Richard Bruce; Senior Fellow, American Enterprise Institute, since 1993; *b* 30 Jan. 1941; *s* of Richard H. Cheney and Marjorie Dickey Cheney; *m* 1964, Lynne Ann Vincent; two *d*. *Educ:* Casper Elementary Sch.; National County High Sch.; Univ. of Wyoming (BA 1965; MA 1966); Univ. of Wisconsin. Public service, Wyoming, 1965–69; Federal service, 1969–73; Vice-Pres., Bradley Woods, 1973–74; Dep. Asst to Pres. Ford, 1974–75; Asst to Pres. Ford and White House Chief of Staff, 1975–77; Mem. (Republican) for Wyoming House of Representatives, 1978–89; Chm., Repub. Policy Cttee, 1981, Repub. House Conf., 1987; Repub. House Whip, 1988; Sec. of Defense, USA, 1989–93; Mem., Cttees on Interior and Insular Affairs, Intelligence, Iran Arms Deals. *Publication:* (with Lynne V. Cheney) Kings of the Hill, 1983. *Recreation:* tennis. *Address:* Suite 1100, 1150 17th Street NW, Washington, DC 20034, USA.

CHERKASSKY, Shura; pianist; *b* 7 Oct. 1911; *s* of late Isaac and Lydia Cherkassky; *m* 1946, Genia Ganz (marr. diss. 1948). *Educ:* Curtis Institute of Music, Pa, USA (diploma). Plays with the principal orchestras and conductors of the world and in all the major series and festivals in Asia, America, Australia and Europe. Has made numerous recordings. *Address:* c/o Lies Askonas, 6 Henrietta Street, WC2E 8LA.

CHERMAYEFF, Serge, FRIBA, FRSA; architect; author; abstract painter; *b* 8 Oct. 1900; *s* of Ivan and Rosalie Issakovitch; changed surname by deed poll to Chermayeff and adopted British nationality, 1927; became US citizen, 1945; *m* 1928, Barbara Maitland May; two *s*. *Educ:* Harrow Sch. Journalist, 1918–22; studied architecture, 1922–25; principal work in England, studios for BBC; Modern Exhibitions; Gilbey's Offices; ICI Laboratories; in Partnership: Bexhill Pavilion. Professor, Brooklyn Coll., 1942–46; Pres. and Dir, Inst. of Design, Chicago, 1946–51; Prof., Harvard Univ., 1953–62; Prof., Yale Univ., 1962–71, now Emeritus. Hon. Fellow, Assoc. of Columbian Architects. Hon. Dr of Fine Art, Washington Univ., 1964; Hon. Dr of Humanities, Ohio State Univ., 1980. Gold Medal, Royal Architectural Inst., Canada, 1974; AIA and Assoc. of Collegiate Schs 1980 Award for excellence in educn; Misha Black Meml Medal for significant contribn to design educn, SIAD, 1980; Gold Medal, NY State Univ. at Buffalo, 1982. *Publications:* Art and Architectural Criticism; ARP, 1939; Community and Privacy, 1963; Shape of Community, 1970; Design and the Public Good (Collected Works), 1982. *Address:* Box 1472, Wellfleet, MA 02667, USA.

CHERRY, Bridget Katherine, FSA; Editor: Buildings of England, since 1983; Buildings of Scotland, Ireland and Wales, since 1991; *b* 17 May 1941; *d* of Norman Stayner Marsh, *qv*; *m* 1966, John Cherry, *qv*; one *s* one *d*. *Educ:* Oxford High Sch. for Girls; Lady Margaret Hall, Oxford (BA Modern Hist.); Courtauld Inst. of Art, Univ. of London (Dip. Hist. of Art). FSA 1980. Asst Librarian, Conway Library, Courtauld Inst., 1964–68; Res. Asst to Sir Nikolaus Pevsner, Buildings of England, 1968–83. Mem., Royal Commn on Historical Monuments of England, 1987–94; English Heritage: Comr, 1992–; Mem., London Adv. Cttee, 1985–; Mem., Historic Buildings Adv. Cttee, 1986–. Trustee, Sir John Soane's Mus., 1994–. Hon. FRIBA 1993. *Publications:* reviser or part author, 2nd edns, Buildings of England series, incl. London I, 3rd edn 1973, Wiltshire, 1975, Hertfordshire, 1977, London 2: South, 1983, Devon, 1989; London 3: North West, 1991; articles and reviews on arch. subjects in learned jls. *Recreation:* walking. *Address:* Buildings of England, Penguin Books, 27 Wrights Lane, W8 5TZ. *T:* 0171–416 3201.

CHERRY, Colin; Director of Operations, Inland Revenue, 1985–90; *b* 20 Nov. 1931; *s* of late Reginald Cherry and Dorothy (*née* Brooks); *m* 1958, Marjorie Rose Harman; two *d*. *Educ:* Hymers Coll., Hull. Joined Inland Revenue, 1950; HM Inspector of Taxes, 1960; Under Sec., 1985. Fiscal Advr, IMF, 1994–. Chm., CS Retirement Fellowship, 1992–94. *Recreations:* music, chrysanthemums, photography. *Address:* 13 Wathen Road, Dorking, Surrey RH4 1JZ. *Club:* Reform.

CHERRY, Prof. Gordon Emanuel; Professor of Urban and Regional Planning, University of Birmingham, 1976–91, now Emeritus Professor; *b* 6 Feb. 1931; *s* of Emanuel and Nora Cherry; *m* 1957, Margaret Mary Loudon Cox; one *s* two *d*. *Educ:* Holgate and District Grammar Sch., Barnsley; QMC, Univ. of London (BA(Hons) Geog. 1953). Variously employed in local authority planning depts, 1956–68; Research Officer, Newcastle upon Tyne City Planning Dept, 1963–68; University of Birmingham: Sen. Lectr and Dep. Dir, Centre for Urban and Regional Studies, 1968–76; Dean, Fac. of Commerce and Social Science, 1981–86; Head, Sch. of Geography, 1987–91. Member: Local Govt Boundary Commn for England, 1979–89; Adv. Cttee on Landscape Treatment of Trunk Roads, 1984–94; Adv. Bd, Nat. Forest, 1991–94; Trustee, Bournville Village Trust, 1979–91 (Chm., 1992–). President: RTPI, 1978–79; Internat. Planning History Soc., 1993–. FRICS; FRSA 1991. Hon. DSc Heriot-Watt, 1984. *Publications:* Town Planning in its Social Context, 1970, 2nd edn 1973; (with T. L. Burton) Social Research Techniques for Planners, 1970; Urban Change and Planning, 1972; The Evolution of British Town Planning, 1974; Environmental Planning, Vol. II: National Parks and Recreation in the Countryside, 1975; The Politics of Town Planning, 1982; (with J. L. Penny) Holford: a study in planning, architecture and civic design, 1986; Cities and Plans, 1988; Birmingham: a study in geography, history and planning, 1994; (with A. W. Rogers) Rural Change and Planning, 1995; Editor: Urban Planning Problems, 1974; Rural Planning Problems, 1976; Shaping an Urban World, 1980; Pioneers in British Planning, 1981; (with A. R. Sutcliffe) Planning Perspectives, 1986–. *Recreations:* work, professional activities, church ecumenism, reading, music, enjoyment of family life. *Address:* Quaker Ridge, 66 Meriden Road, Hampton in Arden, West Midlands B92 0BT. *T:* Hampton in Arden (01675) 443200.

CHERRY, John, FSA, FRHistS; Deputy Keeper, Department of Medieval and Later Antiquities, British Museum, since 1981 (Acting Keeper, 1991–92); *b* 5 Aug. 1942; *s* of Edwin Lewis Cherry and Vera Edith Blanche (*née* Bunn); *m* 1966, Bridget Katherine Marsh (*see* B. K. Cherry); one *s* one *d*. *Educ:* Portsmouth Grammar Sch.; Christ Church, Oxford (Open Scholar 1960, MA). British Museum: Asst Keeper, Dept of British and Medieval Antiquities, 1964–69; Asst Keeper, Dept of Medieval and Later Antiquities, 1969–81. Dir, British Archaeological Assoc., 1977–82; Sec., Soc. of Antiquaries of London, 1986–. *Publications:* (jtly) The Ring from Antiquity to the 20th Century, 1981; (ed with I. H. Longworth) Archaeology in Britain since 1945, 1986; Medieval Decorative Art, 1991; Goldsmiths, 1992; The Middleham Jewel and Ring, 1994; articles in learned jls on topics of archaeology and collecting. *Address:* 58 Lancaster Road, N4 4PT. *T:* 0171–272 0578.

CHERRY, John Mitchell; QC 1988; a Recorder, since 1987; *b* 10 Sept. 1937; *s* of John William and Dorothy Mary Cherry; *m* 1972, Eunice Ann Westmoreland; two *s* two *d*. *Educ:* Cheshunt Grammar Sch.; Council of Legal Education. Called to the Bar, Gray's Inn, 1961. Mem., Criminal Injuries Compensation Bd, 1989–. *Recreations:* cricket, Rugby, food, wine. *Address:* Winterton, Turkey Street, Enfield, Middx EN1 4RJ. *T:* Lea Valley (01992) 719018.

CHERRYMAN, John Richard, QC 1982; a Recorder, since 1992; *b* 7 Dec. 1932; *s* of Albert James and Mabel Cherryman; *m* 1963, Anna Greenleaf Collis; three *s* one *d*. *Educ:* Farnham Grammar Sch.; London School of Economics (LLB Hons); Harvard Law Sch. Called to Bar, Gray's Inn, 1955, Bencher, 1988. *Recreation:* splitting hairs. *Address:* 4 Breams Buildings, EC4A 1AQ.

CHESHAM, 6th Baron, *cr* 1858; **Nicholas Charles Cavendish;** Captain of the Yeoman of the Guard (Deputy Government Chief Whip), since 1995; *b* 7 Nov. 1941; *s* of 5th Baron Chesham, TD, PC and of Mary Edmunds, *d* of late David G. Marshall; *S* father, 1989; *m* 1st, 1965, Susan Donne Beauchamp (marr. diss. 1969); 2nd, 1973, Suzanne Adrienne, *d* of late Alan Gray Byrne; two *s*. *Educ:* Eton. Chartered Accountant. *Recreations:* tennis, ski-ing, shooting. *Heir: s* Hon. Charles Gray Compton Cavendish, *b* 11 Nov. 1974. *Address:* Manor Farm, Preston Candover, Basingstoke, Hants RG25 2EN. *Clubs:* Pratt's; Australian (Sydney); Royal Sydney Golf.

CHESHIRE, Air Marshal Sir John (Anthony), KBE 1995 (CBE 1991; OBE 1982); CB 1994; UK Military Representative, HQ NATO, since 1995; *b* 4 Sept. 1942; *s* of Air Chief Marshal Sir Walter Cheshire, GBE, KCB and of Lady Cheshire; *m* 1964, Shirley Ann Stevens; one *s* one *d*. *Educ:* Ipswich Sch.; Worksop Coll.; RAF Coll., Cranwell. Operational Flying Duties, UK and Singapore, 1964–70; Air Ops Officer, Special Forces, 1971–73; Canadian Forces Staff Coll., 1973–74; Operational Flying Duties, Special Forces, 1975–76; Air Plans, MoD, 1976–79; Commander: Air Wing, Brunei, 1980–82; RAF Lyneham, 1983–85; Plans Br., HQ Strike Command, 1986–87; Defence and Air Attaché, Moscow, 1988–90; Dep. Comdt, RAF Staff Coll., 1991–92; ACOS (Policy), SHAPE, 1992–94. *Recreations:* squash, tennis, golf, field shooting. *Club:* Royal Air Force.

CHESSELLS, Sir Arthur David, (Sir Tim Chessells), Kt 1993; Chairman, Legal Aid Board, since 1995; *b* 15 June 1941; *s* of late Brig. Arthur Chessells and Carmel (*née* McGinnis); *m* 1966, Katharine, *d* of Dick and Rachel Goodwin; two *s* two *d*. *Educ:* Stonyhurst Coll. CA 1965. Partner, Arthur Young, 1972–89; Mem., Kent AHA, 1979–82; Vice-Chm., Tunbridge Wells HA, 1982–88; Mem., SE Thames RHA, 1988–90; Chairman: NE Thames RHA, 1990–92; London Implementation Gp, 1992–95. Non-exec. Mem., NHS Policy Bd, 1992–95. Dir, Odgers and Co. Ltd, 1989–95, Price and Pierce Inc., 1993–, and other cos; Mem. Council, St Christopher's Hospice, 1989–92. Trustee: Kent Community Housing Trust, 1990–; Stonyhurst Charitable Fund, 1980–93; Chatham Historic Dockyard, 1992–. *Recreations:* reading, shooting, gardening. *Address:* Legal Aid Board, 85 Gray's Inn Road, WC1X 8AA. *T:* 0171–813 1000. *Club:* Carlton.

CHESSHYRE, (David) Hubert (Boothby), LVO 1988; FSA; Norroy and Ulster King of Arms, since 1995; Secretary, Most Noble Order of the Garter, since 1988; Registrar of the College of Arms, since 1992; *b* 22 June 1940; *e s* of late Col Hubert Layard Chesshyre and Katharine Anne (*née* Boothby), Canterbury, Kent. *Educ:* King's Sch., Canterbury; Trinity Coll., Cambridge (MA); Christ Church, Oxford (DipEd 1967). FSA 1977; FHS 1990. Taught French in England and English in France, at intervals 1962–67; wine merchant (Moët et Chandon and Harvey's of Bristol), 1962–65; Hon. Artillery Co., 1964–65 (fired salute at funeral of Sir Winston Churchill, 1965); Green Staff Officer at Investiture of the Prince of Wales, 1969; Rouge Croix Pursuivant, 1970–78, and on staff of Sir Anthony Wagner, Garter King of Arms, 1971–78; Chester Herald of Arms, 1978–95. Mem., Westminster Abbey Architectural Adv. Panel, 1985–. Member: Council, Heraldry Soc., 1973–85; Bach Choir, 1979–93; Madrigal Soc., 1980–. Hon. Genealogist to Royal Victorian Order, 1987–. Lectr, NADFAS, 1982–. Lay Clerk, Southwark Cathedral, 1971–. Freeman: City of London, 1975; Musicians' Co., 1994. *Publications:* (Eng. lang. editor) C. A. von Volborth, Heraldry of the World, 1973; The Identification of Coats of Arms on British Silver, 1978; (with A. J. Robinson) The Green: a history of the heart of Bethnal Green, 1978; (with Adrian Ailes) Heralds of Today, 1986; (ed with T. Woodcock) Dictionary of British Arms, vol. I, 1992; genealogical and heraldic articles in British Heritage and elsewhere. *Recreations:* singing, gardening, mountain walking, motorcycling. *Address:* Hawthorn Cottage, 1 Flamborough Walk, E14 7LS. *T:* 0171–790 7923; College of Arms, Queen Victoria Street, EC4V 4BT. *T:* 0171–248 1137.

CHESTER, Bishop of, 1982–Aug. 1996; **Rt. Rev. Michael Alfred Baughen;** *b* 7 June 1930; *s* of Alfred Henry and Clarice Adelaide Baughen; *m* 1956, Myrtle Newcomb Phillips; two *s* one *d*. *Educ:* Bromley County Grammar Sch.; Univ. of London; Oak Hill Theol Coll. BD (London). With Martins Bank, 1946–48, 1950–51. Army, Royal Signals, 1948–50. Degree Course and Ordination Trng, 1951–56; Curate: St Paul's, Hyson Green, Nottingham, 1956–59; Reigate Parish Ch., 1959–61; Candidates Sec., Church Pastoral Aid Soc., 1961–64; Rector of Holy Trinity (Platt), Rusholme, Manchester, 1964–70; Vicar of All Souls, Langham Place, W1, 1970–75; Rector, 1975–82; Area Dean of St Marylebone, 1978–82; a Prebendary of St Paul's Cathedral, 1979–82. Hon. LLD Liverpool, 1994. *Publications:* Moses and the Venture of Faith, 1979; The Prayer Principle, 1981; II Corinthians: a spiritual health-warning to the Church, 1982; Chained to the Gospel, 1986; Evidence for Christ, 1986; Getting through to God, 1992; (with Myrtle Baughen) Your Marriage, 1994; Editor: Youth Praise, 1966; Youth Praise II, 1969; Psalm Praise, 1973; consultant editor, Hymns for Today's Church, 1982. *Recreations:* music, railways, touring. *Address:* Bishop's House, Chester CH1 2JD. *T:* Chester (01244) 350864.

CHESTER, Dean of; *see* Smalley, Very Rev. S. S.

CHESTER, Archdeacon of; *see* Hewetson, Ven. C.

CHESTER, Maj.-Gen. John Shane, OBE 1982; Secretary, Chartered Institute of Management Accountants, since 1995; *b* 21 April 1944; *s* of Hugh Chester and Stella Florence Mary Chester (*née* Turner); *m* 1970, Amanda Gay, *d* of late Wing Comdr Stanley Graham Pritchard; two *s*. *Educ:* St Joseph's Coll., Ipswich. 2nd Lieut, RM, 1963; served 40, 41, 43 and 45 Commandos RM (Borneo, Norway, NI), 1964–88 (despatches 1981); BM, 3 Commando Brigade, 1981–83 (incl. Falklands Campaign); CO 40 Commando RM, 1987–89 (despatches 1988); COS, HQ Special Forces, 1989–91; Brig. Comdg Training and Reserve Forces, RM, 1991–92; Sen. Directing Staff (Navy), RCDS, 1993–95. FIPD, FIMgt. *Recreations:* sailing, golf, ski-ing, military history. *Address:* c/o Lloyds Bank, Budleigh Salterton, Devon EX9 6NQ. *Clubs:* Army and Navy; Royal Marines Sailing.

CHESTER, Dr Peter Francis, FEng; FInstP; FIEE; Chairman, National Wind Power Ltd, since 1991; *b* 8 Feb. 1929; *s* of late Herbert and of Edith Maud Chester (*née* Pullen); *m* 1953, Barbara Ann Collin; one *s* four *d*. *Educ:* Gunnersbury Grammar Sch.; Queen Mary College, London. BSc 1st Physics 1950; PhD London 1953. Post-doctoral Fellow, Nat. Research Council, Ottawa, 1953–54; Adv. Physicist, Westinghouse Res. Labs, Pittsburgh, 1954–60; Head of Solid State Physics Section, CERL, 1960–65; Head of Fundamental Studies Section, CERL, 1965–66; Res. Man., Electricity Council Res. Centre, 1966–70; Controller of Scientific Services, CEGB NW Region, 1970–73; Dir, Central Electricity Res. Labs, 1973–82; a Dir, Technol. Planning and Res., Div., CEGB, 1982–86; Dir, Environment, CEGB, 1986–89; Exec. Dir, Technology and Environment, Nat. Power, 1990–92. Science Research Council: Mem., 1976–80; Mem., Science Bd, 1972–75; Chm., Energy Round Table and Energy Cttee, 1975–80. Mem., ACORD, DTI, 1992–93. Vice-Pres., Inst. of Physics, 1972–76. A Dir, Fulmer Res. Inst., 1976–83. Faraday Lectr, IEE, 1984–85. Robens Coal Science Medal, 1985. *Publications:* original papers in solid state and low temperature physics, reports on energy and the environment, and acid rain. *Address:* National Wind Power Ltd, Riverside House, Furlong Road, Bourne End SL8 5AJ.

CHESTER JONES, Prof. Ian, DSc; Professor of Zoology, University of Sheffield, 1958–81, now Emeritus Professor; Independent Research Worker, Pathology, Sheffield Medical School, since 1987; *b* 3 Jan. 1916; *s* of late H. C. Jones; *m* 1942, Nansi Ellis Williams; two *s* one *d*. *Educ:* Liverpool Institute High Sch. for Boys; Liverpool Univ. BSc 1938; PhD 1941; DSc 1958. Served in Army, 1941–46 (despatches). Commonwealth Fund Fellow, Harvard Univ., 1947–49; Senior Lecturer in Zoology, Univ. of Liverpool, 1955. Milton Fellow, Harvard Univ., 1960; Vis. Prof., Coll. of William and Mary, Virginia, 1968–69. Ian Chester Jones Internat. Lectureship for Distinction in Comparative Endocrinology, triennium. Chm., Soc. for Endocrinology, 1966 (Sir Henry Dale medal, 1976, Hon. Fellow): Hon. FZS; Hon. FIBiol; Hon. Fellow: Amer. Soc. of Zoologists; NY Acad. of Scis. Dr de l'Université de Clermont (*hc*), 1967. *Publications:* The Adrenal Cortex, 1957; Integrated Biology, 1971; General, Comparative and Clinical Endocrinology of the Adrenal Cortex, vol. 1, 1976, vol. 2, 1978, vol. 3, 1980; Fundamentals of Comparative Vertebrate Endocrinology, 1987. *Address:* 36 Sale Hill, Sheffield S10 5BX.

CHESTERFIELD, Archdeacon of; *see* Phizackerley, Ven. G. R.

CHESTERMAN, Sir Ross, Kt 1970; MSc, PhD; DIC; Warden of Goldsmiths' College (University of London), 1953–74; Hon. Fellow, 1980; Master of the College of Design, Craft and Technology (formerly College of Craft Education), since 1982 (Vice-Master, 1960–82; Dean, 1958–60); *b* 27 April 1909; *s* of late Dudley and Ettie Chesterman; *m* 1st, 1938, Audrey Mary Horlick (*d* 1982); one *s* one *d*; 2nd, 1985, Patricia Burns Bell. *Educ:* Hastings Grammar Sch.; Imperial College of Science, London (scholar). Acland English Essay Prizeman, 1930; 1st class hons BSc (Chem.), 1930; MSc 1932; Lecturer in Chemistry, Woolwich Polytechnic; PhD 1937; Science master in various grammar schools; Headmaster, Meols Cop Secondary Sch., Southport, 1946–48. Chief County Inspector of Schools, Worcestershire, 1948–53. Educnl Consultant to numerous overseas countries, 1966–73. Ford Foundation Travel Award to American Univs, 1966. Chairman: Standing Cttee on Teacher Trng; Nat. Council for Supply and Trng of Teachers Overseas, 1971; Adv. Cttee for Teacher Trng Overseas, FCO (ODA), 1972–74. Fellow *hc* of Coll. of Handicraft, 1958. Liveryman and Freeman of Goldsmiths' Co., 1968. *Publications:* The Birds of Southport, 1947; chapter in The Forge, 1955; chapter in Science in Schools, 1958; Teacher Training in some American Universities, 1967; scientific papers in chemical journals and journals of natural history; articles in educational periodicals. *Recreations:* writing, music, painting, travel, natural history. *Address:* The Garden House, 6 High Street, Lancaster LA1 1LA. *T:* Lancaster (01524) 65687.

CHESTERS, Rt. Rev. Alan David; *see* Blackburn, Bishop of.

CHESTERTON, David; Head of Heritage and Tourism Group, Department of National Heritage, since 1992; *b* 30 Nov. 1939; *s* of Raymond and Joyce Chesterton; *m* 1st, 1965, Ursula Morgan; one *s* three *d*; 2nd, 1977, Lindsay Fellows; three step *d*. *Educ:* Reading Sch.; St Catherine's Coll., Oxford (BA). Editorial Assistant: Financial World, 1961–62; Fleet Street Letter, 1962–65; Producer, BBC External Services, 1965–68, Exec. Producer, 1968–74; Northern Ireland Office: Principal, 1974–80; Asst Sec., 1980–85; Under Sec., 1985–92. *Recreation:* walking. *Address:* Department of National Heritage, 2–4 Cockspur Street, SW1Y 5DH.

CHESTERTON, Dame Elizabeth (Ursula), DBE 1987 (OBE 1977); architect and town planner; *b* 12 Oct. 1915; *d* of late Maurice Chesterton, architect, and Dorothy (*née* Deck). *Educ:* King Alfred Sch.; Queen's Coll., London; Architectural Assoc. Sch. of Architecture, London. AA Dipl. (Hons) 1939; ARIBA 1940; DistTP 1968; FRTPI 1967 (AMTPI 1943). Asst County Planning Officer, E Suffolk CC, 1940–47; Develt Control Officer, Cambs CC Planning Dept, 1947–51; Mem. Staff: Social Res. Unit, Dept of Town Planning, UCL, 1951–53; Architectural Assoc. Sch. of Architecture, 1954–61. Member: Council, Architectural Assoc., 1964–67; Royal Fine Art Commn, 1970–93; Historic Buildings Council, 1973–84; Royal Parks Review Gp, 1991–. English Heritage: Member: Historic Bldgs Adv. Cttee, 1984–88, Historic Areas Adv. Cttee, 1984–91; Historic Bldgs and Areas Adv. Cttee, 1991–95; British Rail: Member: Envmt Panel, 1983–88; Architecture Panel, 1988–91; Architecture and Design Panel, 1991–93; National Trust: Member: Architecture Panel, 1978–90; Council, 1984–90. FRSA 1982. Reports prepared: Report on Local Land Use for the Dartington Hall Trustees, 1957; (jtly) The Historic Core of King's Lynn: study and plan, 1964; Plan for the Beaulieu Estate, 1966; North West Solent Shore Estates Report, 1969; Snowdon Summit Report for Countryside Commission, 1974; Plans for Quarries and Rail Distribution Depots, Foster Yeoman and Yeoman (Morvern), 1974–81; Central Area Study, Chippenham, for North Wiltshire District Council, 1975–80; The Crumbles, Eastbourne, for Chatsworth Settlement, 1976; Aldeburgh, Suffolk, for Aldeburgh Soc., 1976; Old Market Conservation and Redevelopment Study, for City of Bristol and Bristol Municipal Charities, 1978; Uplands Landscape Study, for Countryside Commission, 1980. *Recreations:* gardening, travel. *Address:* 12 The Mount, NW3 6SZ. *T:* 0171–435 0666.

CHESTERTON, Sir Oliver (Sidney), Kt 1969; MC 1943; Consultant, Chestertons, Chartered Surveyors, London, since 1980 (Partner, 1936, Senior Partner, 1945–80); *b* 28 Jan. 1913; *s* of Frank and Nora Chesterton; *m* 1944, Violet Ethel Jameson; two *s* one *d*. *Educ:* Rugby Sch. Served War of 1939–45, Irish Guards. Director: Woolwich Equitable Building Soc., 1962–86 (Chm., 1976–83); Property Growth Assurance, 1972–85; London Life Assoc., 1975–84; Estates Property Investment Co., 1979–88. Vice-Chm., Council of Royal Free Med. Sch., 1964–77; Crown Estate Comr, 1969–82. Past Pres., Royal Instn of Chartered Surveyors, Hon. Sec., 1972–79; Pres., Commonwealth Assoc. Surveying and Land Economy, 1969–77; first Master, Chartered Surveyors' Co., 1977–78. Governor, Rugby Sch., 1972–88. *Recreations:* golf, fishing, National Hunt racing. *Address:* Hookfield House, Abinger Common, Dorking, Surrey RH5 6JF. *Club:* New Zealand Golf.

CHESWORTH, Air Vice-Marshal George Arthur, CB 1982; OBE 1972; DFC 1954; Lord-Lieutenant of Morayshire, since 1994; Deputy Chairman, Moray, Badenoch and Strathspey Enterprise Co., since 1991; *b* 4 June 1930; *s* of Alfred Matthew Chesworth and Grace Edith Chesworth; *m* 1951, Betty Joan Hopkins; two *d* (one *s* decd). *Educ:* Carshalton and Wimbledon. Joined RAF, 1948; commissioned, 1950; 205 Flying boat Sqdn, FEAF, 1951–53 (DFC 1954); RAF Germany, RAF Kinloss, RAF St Mawgan, 1956–61; RN Staff Coll., 1963; MoD, 1964–67; OC 201 Nimrod Sqdn, 1968–71 (OBE); OC RAF Kinloss, 1972–75; Air Officer in Charge, Central Tactics & Trials Orgn, 1975–77; Director, RAF Quartering, 1977–80; C of S to Air Comdr CTF 317 during Falkland Campaign, Apr.-June 1982 (CB); C of S, HQ 18 Gp, RAF, 1980–84. Chief Exec., Glasgow Garden Fest. (1988), 1985–89; Dir, SEC Ltd, 1989–95. Hon. Col, 76 Engr Regt (Vols), 1992–. Chm., ATC Council for Scotland and NI, 1989–95; Vice Chm. (Air), Highland TAVR, 1990–. Develt Dir, Military and Aerospace Mus. (Aldershot) Trust, 1990–91; Trustee, MacRobert Trusts, 1994–; Mem. Management Bd, RAF Benevolent Fund Home, Alastrean House, Tarland, Aberdeenshire, 1990– (Chm., 1994–). DL Morayshire, 1992. *Address:* Pindlers Croft, Lower Califer, Forres, Moray IV36 0RN. *T:* Forres (01309) 674136. *Club:* Royal Air Force.

CHETWODE, family name of **Baron Chetwode.**

CHETWODE, 2nd Baron *cr* 1945, of Chetwode; **Philip Chetwode;** Bt, 1700; *b* 26 March 1937; *s* of Capt. Roger Charles George Chetwode (*d* 1940; *o s* of Field Marshal Lord Chetwode, GCB, OM, GCSI, KCMG, DSO) and Hon. Molly Patricia Berry, *d* of 1st Viscount Camrose (she *m* 2nd, 1942, 1st Baron Sherwood, from whom she obtained a divorce, 1948, and *m* 3rd, 1958, late Sir Richard Cotterell, 5th Bt, CBE); *S* grandfather, 1950; *m* 1st, 1967, Mrs Susan Dudley Smith (marr. diss. 1979); two *s* one *d*; 2nd, 1990, Mrs Fiona Holt. *Educ:* Eton. Commissioned Royal Horse Guards, 1956–66. *Heir: s* Hon. Roger Chetwode, *b* 29 May 1968. *Address:* The Mill House, Chilton Foliat, Hungerford, Berks RG17 0TG. *Club:* White's.

CHETWOOD, Sir Clifford (Jack), Kt 1987; FCIOB, FRSH; Chairman: Chetwood Associates Ltd, since 1988; Broadgate Properties PLC, since 1994 (Director, 1993–94); *b* 2 Nov. 1928; *s* of Stanley Jack Chetwood and Doris May Palmer; *m* 1953, Pamela Phyllis Sherlock; one *s* three *d*. George Wimpey & Co. Ltd, later George Wimpey PLC: Director, 1969; Chm., Bd of Management, 1975–79; a Gp Man. Dir, 1978–82; Chief Exec., 1982–90; Chm., 1984–92; Chairman: Wimpey Construction UK, 1979–83; Wimpey Homes Holdings, 1981–83. Pres., Building Employers' Confedn, 1989–92; Chm., Construction ITB, 1990–. Mem. Council, Imperial Soc. of Knights Bachelor, 1988–95; Trustee: V&A Museum, 1985–; London Zoological Soc. Develt Trust, 1986–90; Chm. of Trustees, Develt Trust, ICE, 1988–; Pres., Bldg Industry Youth Trust, 1990–; Vice-President: C&G, 1992–; Tennis and Rackets Assoc., 1992–. Master, Guild of Freemen, City of London, 1993–94. FRSA; Hon. FICE 1990; Hon. FCGI 1991. Prince Philip Medal, CGLI, 1987. Man of the Year, Architects and Surveyors Inst., 1989. *Recreations:* Real tennis (Pres., Royal Court Club, 1991–), lawn tennis. *Address:* Wineberry House, The Drive, Eaton Park, Cobham, Surrey KT11 2JQ.

CHETWYN, Robert; *b* 7 Sept. 1933; *s* of Frederick Reuben Suckling and Eleanor Lavinia (*née* Boffee). *Educ:* Rutlish, Merton, SW; Central Sch. of Speech and Drama. First appeared as actor with Dundee Repertory Co., 1952; subseq. in repertory at Hull, Alexandra Theatre, Birmingham, 1954; Birmingham Repertory Theatre, 1954–56; various TV plays, 1956–59; 1st prodn, Five Finger Exercise, Salisbury Playhouse, 1960; Dir of Prodns, Opera Hse, Harrogate, 1961–62; Artistic Dir, Ipswich Arts, 1962–64; Midsummer Night's Dream, transf. Comedy (London), 1964; Resident Dir, Belgrade (Coventry), 1964–66; Assoc. Dir, Mermaid, 1966, The Beaver Coat, three one-act plays by Shaw; There's a Girl in My Soup, Globe, 1966 and Music Box (NY), 1967; A Present for the Past, Edinburgh Fest., 1966; The Flip Side, Apollo, 1967; The Importance of Being Earnest, Haymarket, 1968; The Real Inspector Hound, Criterion, 1968; What the Butler Saw, Queens, 1968; The Country Wife, Chichester Fest., 1968; The Bandwaggon, Mermaid, 1968 and Sydney, 1970; Cannibal Crackers, Hampstead, 1969; When We are Married, Strand, 1970; Hamlet, in Rome, Zurich, Vienna, Antwerp, Cologne, then Cambridge (London), 1971; Parents Day, Globe, 1972; Restez Donc Jusq'au Petit Dejeuner, Belgium, 1973; Who's Who, Fortune, 1973; At the End of the Day, Savoy, 1973; Chez Nous, Globe, 1974; Qui est Qui, Belgium, 1974; The Doctor's Dilemma, Mermaid, 1975; Getting Away with Murder, Comedy, 1976; Private Lives, Melbourne, 1976; It's All Right If I Do It, Mermaid, 1977; A Murder is Announced, Vaudeville, 1977; Arms and The Man, Greenwich, 1978; LUV, Amsterdam, 1978; Brimstone and Treacle, Open Space, 1979; Bent, Royal Court and Criterion, 1979; Pygmalion, National Theatre of Belgium, 1979; Moving, Queen's, 1980; Eastward Ho!, Mermaid, 1981; Beethoven's 10th, Vaudeville, 1983 (also Broadway, New York); Number One, Queen's, 1984; Why Me?, Strand, 1985; Selling The Sizzle, Hampstead, 1988. Has produced and directed for BBC (incl. series Private Shulz, by Jack Pullman, film, That Uncertain Feeling, Born In the Gardens) and ITV (Irish RM first series, Small World, Case of the Late Pig). Trustee, Dirs' Guild of GB, 1984–. *Publication:* (jtly) Theatre on Merseyside (Arts Council report), 1973. *Recreations:* tennis, films, gardening. *Address:* 1 Wilton Court, Eccleston Square, SW1V 1PH.

CHETWYND, family name of **Viscount Chetwynd.**

CHETWYND, 10th Viscount *cr* 1717 (Ireland); **Adam Richard John Casson Chetwynd;** Baron Rathdowne, 1717 (Ireland); Life Assurance Agent, Liberty Life Association of Africa Ltd, Sandton Branch, Johannesburg; *b* 2 Feb. 1935; *o s* of 9th Viscount and Joan Gilbert (*d* 1979), *o c* of late Herbert Alexander Casson, CSI, Ty'n-y-coed, Arthog, Merioneth; *S* father, 1965; *m* 1st, 1966, Celia Grace (marr. diss. 1974), *er d* of Comdr Alexander Robert Ramsay, DSC, RNVR, Fasque, Borrowdale, Salisbury, Rhodesia; twin *s* one *d*; 2nd, 1975, Angela May, *o d* of Jack Payne McCarthy, 21 Llanberis Grove, Nottingham. *Educ:* Eton. Fellow, Inst. of Life and Pension Advrs, 1982. 2nd Lieut Cameron Highlanders, 1954–56. With Colonial Mutual Life Assurance Soc. Ltd, Salisbury, Rhodesia, then Johannesburg, 1968–78; Liberty Life Assoc. of Africa (formerly Prudential Assurance Co. of South Africa), 1978–. Liveryman, GAPAN. Qualifying Mem., Million Dollar Round Table, 1979–94; qualified Top of the Table, 1984–92; Holder, Internat. Quality Award, 1979–94. *Recreations:* astronomy, travel. *Heir: s* Hon. Adam Douglas Chetwynd, *b* 26 Feb. 1969. *Address:* c/o J. G. Ouvry Esq., Lee Bolton & Lee, 1 The Sanctuary, Westminster, SW1P 3JT. *Club:* Rotary (Morningside).

CHETWYND, Sir Arthur (Ralph Talbot), 8th Bt *cr* 1795; President: Brocton Hall Communications Ltd, Toronto, 1978–88; Post Productions Inc.; Chairman, Board of Directors, Chetwynd Films Ltd, Toronto, since 1977 (Founder, President and General Manager, 1950–76); *b* Walhachin, BC, 28 Oct. 1913; *o s* of Hon. William Ralph Talbot Chetwynd, MC, MLA (*d* 1957) (*b* of 7th Bt), and Frances Mary (*d* 1986), *d* of late James Jupe; *S* uncle, 1972; *m* 1940, Marjory May McDonald, *er d* of late Robert Bruce Lang, Vancouver, BC, and Glasgow, Scotland; two *s*. *Educ:* Vernon Preparatory School, BC; University of British Columbia (Physical Education and Recreation). Prior to 1933, a rancher in interior BC; Games Master, Vernon Prep. School, BC, 1933–36, also Instructor, Provincial Physical Education and Recreation; Chief Instructor, McDonald's Remedial Institute, Vancouver, 1937–41; Director of Remedial Gymnastics, British Columbia Workmen's Compensation Board, 1942; RCAF, 1943–45; Associate in Physical and Health Education, Univ. of Toronto, also Publicity Officer, Univ. of Toronto Athletic Assoc., 1946–52. Former Dir, NZ Lamb Co. Ltd. Former Chairman: Canterbury Cathedral Appeal in Canada; Codrington Coll. (Barbados) Appeal in Canada; Toronto Branch, Royal Commonwealth Soc.; Pres., Empire Club of Canada, 1974–75; Member: Monarchist League of Canada; Military and Hospitaller Order of St Lazarus of Jerusalem, Canada. KCLJ. Hon. Mem., Order of Barbados (SCM), 1984. *Recreations:* photography, travelling, swimming. *Heir: er s* Robin John Talbot Chetwynd [*b* 21 Aug. 1941; *m* 1st, 1967, Heather Helen (marr. diss. 1986), *d* of George Bayliss Lothian; one *s* one *d*; 2nd, 1986, Donna Preece]. *Address:* #3–117 King Street East, Cobourg, Ont K9A 1L2, Canada. *Clubs:* Albany, Toronto Hunt (Toronto).

CHETWYND-TALBOT, family name of **Earl of Shrewsbury and Waterford.**

CHEUNG, Sir Oswald (Victor), Kt 1987; CBE 1976 (OBE 1972); QC (Hong Kong) 1965; Member, Executive Council, Hong Kong, 1974–86; *b* 22 Jan. 1922; *s* of Cheung U Pui and Elizabeth Ellis; *m* 1963, Pauline Cheng; one *s*. *Educ:* Diocesan Boys' Sch.; Hong Kong Univ.; University Coll., Oxford (BA 1949, MA 1963). Called to the Bar, Lincoln's Inn, 1951; Bencher, 1987. Magistrate, 1951–52; Hong Kong Bar, 1952–; Mem., Legislative Council, Hong Kong, 1970–81 (Senior Unofficial Mem., 1978–81); Chairman: Criminal Injuries Compensation Bd; Law Enforcement Injuries Compensation Bd. Director: Mass Transit Railway Corp., 1975–89; Hong Kong Electric (Holdings) Ltd, 1985–94; Ciba-Geigy (HK) Ltd; Wing On Company Internat. Ltd. Member: Univ. and Polytechnic Grants Cttee, 1970–78; Court, Hong Kong Univ. Trustee, Croucher Foundn, 1986–92; Chm., Children's Meals Soc., 1966–81; Steward, Royal Hong Kong Jockey Club, 1977–92 (Chm. of Stewards, 1986–89). Captain, Royal Hong Kong Regt, 1956–62, Hon. Col, 1977–82. Fellow, Internat. Acad. of Trial Lawyers. Hon. LLD Hong Kong, 1979. *Recreations:* photography, racing, travel. *Address:* New Henry House, 10th Floor, 10 Ice House Street, Hong Kong. *T:* 524–2156. *Clubs:* Turf, Oriental; Royal Hong Kong Jockey, Hong Kong, Royal Hong Kong Golf, Country, Chinese.

CHEW, (Victor) Kenneth, TD 1958; Research Fellow of the Science Museum, London; *b* 19 Jan. 1915; *yr s* of Frederick and Edith Chew. *Educ:* Christ's Hospital; Christ Church, Oxford (Scholar). 1st class, Final Honours School of Natural Science (Physics), 1936; BA (Oxon) 1936, MA 1964. Asst Master, King's Sch., Rochester, 1936–38; Winchester Coll., 1938–40. Served War: Royal Signals, 1940–46. Asst Master, Shrewsbury Sch., 1946–48 and 1949–58; Lecturer in Education, Bristol Univ., 1948–49. Entered Science Museum as Asst Keeper, 1958; Deputy Keeper and Sec. to Advisory Council, 1967; Keeper, Dept of Physics, 1970–78. *Publications:* official publications of Science Museum. *Recreations:* hill walking, photography. *Address:* 701 Gilbert House, Barbican, EC2Y 8BD.

CHEWTON, Viscount; Edward Robert Waldegrave; *b* 10 Oct. 1986; *e s* of 13th Earl Waldegrave, *qv*.

CHEYNE, Major Sir Joseph (Lister Watson), 3rd Bt *cr* 1908; OBE 1976; Curator, Keats Shelley Memorial House, Rome, 1976–90; *b* 10 Oct. 1914; *e s* of Sir Joseph Lister Cheyne, 2nd Bt, MC, and Nelita Manfield (*d* 1977), *d* of Andrew Pringle, Borgue; *S* father, 1957; *m* 1st, 1938, Mary Mort (marr. diss. 1955; she *d* 1959), *d* of late Vice-Adm. J. D. Allen, CB; one *s* one *d*; 2nd, 1955, Cicely, *d* of late T. Metcalfe, Padiham, Lancs; two *s* one *d*. *Educ:* Stowe Sch.; Corpus Christi Coll., Cambridge. Major, The Queen's Westminsters (KRRC), 1943; Italian Campaign. 2nd Sec. (Inf.), British Embassy, Rome, 1968, 1st Sec., 1971, 1st Sec. (Inf.), 1973–76. *Heir: s* Patrick John Lister Cheyne [*b* 2 July 1941; *m* 1968, Helen Louise Trevor, *yr d* of Louis Smith, Southsea; one *s* three *d*]. *Address:* Leagarth, Fetlar, Shetland; The Haa, Gloup, Cullivoe, Yell, Shetland ZE2 9DD. *Clubs:* Boodle's; Circolo della Caccia (Rome).

CHEYSSON, Claude, Commander Legion of Honour; Croix de Guerre (5 times); Hon. GCMG 1984; Member, European Parliament, 1989–94; *b* 13 April 1920; *s* of Pierre Cheysson and Sophie Funck-Brentano; *m* 1969, Danièle Schwarz; one *s* two *d* (and two *s* one *d* by former marrs). *Educ:* Coll. Stanislas, Paris; Ecole Polytechnique; Ecole Nationale d'Administration. Escaped from occupied France, 1943; Tank Officer, Free French Forces, France and Germany, 1944–45. Liaison Officer with German authorities, Bonn, 1948–52; Political Adviser to Viet Nam Govt, Saigon, 1952–53; Personal Adviser: to Prime Minister of France, Paris, 1954–55; to French Minister of Moroccan and Tunisian Affairs, 1956; Sec.-Gen., Commn for Techn. Cooperation in Africa, Lagos, Nairobi, 1957–62; Dir-Gen., Sahara Authority, Algiers, 1962–66; French Ambassador in Indonesia, 1966–69; Pres., Entreprise Minière et Chimique, 1970–73; European Comr (relations with Third World), 1973–81, 1985–89; Minister for External Relations, 1981–84. Bd Mem., Le Monde, 1978–92. President: Institut Pierre Mendes-France, 1988–91; Arche de la Fraternité, 1989–93. Town Councillor, Bargemon, 1983–89. Grand Cross, Grand Officer and Comdr of many national orders; US Presidential Citation. Dr *hc* Univ. of Louvain; Joseph Bech Prize, 1978; Luderitz Prize, 1983. *Publications:* Une idée qui s'incarne, 1978; articles on Europe, and develt policies. *Recreation:* ski-ing. *Address:* 52 rue de Vaugirard, 75006 Paris, France. *T:* 43264665, *Fax:* 40518774.

CHIANG KAI-SHEK, Madame (Mayling Soong Chiang); Chinese sociologist; *y d* of C. J. Soong; *m* 1927, Generalissimo Chiang Kai-Shek (*d* 1975). *Educ:* Wellesley Coll., USA. LHD, John B. Stetson Univ., Deland, Fla, Bryant Coll., Providence, RI, Hobart and William Smith Colls, Geneva, NY; LLD, Rutgers Univ., New Brunswick, NJ, Goucher Coll., Baltimore, MD, Wellesley Coll., Wellesley, Mass, Loyola Univ., Los Angeles, Cal., Russell Sage Coll., Troy, NY, Hahnemann Medical Coll., Philadelphia, Pa, Wesleyan Coll., Macon, Ga, Univ. of Michigan, Univ. of Hawaii; Hon. FRCS. First Chinese woman appointed Mem. Child Labor Commn; Inaugurated Moral Endeavor Assoc.; established schools in Nanking for orphans of Revolutionary Soldiers; former Mem. Legislative Yuan; served as Sec.-General of Chinese Commission on Aeronautical Affairs; formerly: Member Chinese Commission on Aeronautical Affairs; Director-General of the New Life Movement and Chairman of its Women's Advisory Council; Founder and Director: National Chinese Women's Assoc. for War Relief; National Assoc. for Refugee Children; Chinese Women's Anti-Aggression League; Huashing Children's Home; Cheng Hsin Medical Rehabilitation Center for Post Polio Crippled Children. Chm., Fu Jen Catholic University. Governor, Nat. Palace Museum. Frequently made inspection tours to all sections of Free China where personally trained girl workers carry on war area and rural service work; accompanied husband on military campaigns; first Chinese woman to be decorated by National Govt of China. Recipient of highest military and Civil decorations; formerly: Hon. Chm., British United Aid to China Fund, China; Hon. Chm., Soc. for the Friends of the Wounded; Hon. President, American Bureau for Medical Aid to China; Patroness, International Red Cross Commn; Hon. President, Chinese Women's Relief Assoc. of New York; Hon. Chairman, Canadian Red Cross China Cttee; Hon. Chairman, Board of Directors, India Famine Relief Cttee; Hon. Mem., New York Zoological Soc.; Hon. Pres., Cttee for the Promotion of the Welfare of the Blind; Life Mem., San Francisco Press Club and Associated Countrywomen of the World; Mem., Phi Beta Kappa, Eta Chapter; first Hon. Member, Bill of Rights Commemorative Society; Hon. Member: Filipino Guerrillas of Bataan Assoc.; Catherine Lorillard Wolf Club. Medal of Honour, New York City Federation of Women's Clubs; YWCA Emblem; Gold Medal, New York Southern Soc.; Chi Omega Nat. Achievement Award for 1943; Gold Medal for distinguished services, National Institute for Social Sciences; Distinguished Service Award, Altrusa Internat. Assoc.; Churchman Fifth Annual Award, 1943; Distinguished Service Citation, All-American Conf. to Combat Communism, 1958; Hon. Lieut-Gen. US Marine Corps. *Publications:* China in Peace and War, 1939; China Shall Rise Again, 1939; This is Our China, 1940; We Chinese Women, 1941; Little Sister Su, 1943; Ten Eventful Years, for Encyclopædia Britannica, 1946; Album of Reproduction of Paintings, vol. I, 1952, vol. II, 1962; The Sure Victory, 1955; Madame Chiang Kai-Shek Selected Speeches, 1958–59; Madame Chiang Kai-shek Selected Speeches, 1965–66; Album of Chinese Orchid Paintings, 1971; Album of Chinese Bamboo Paintings, 1972; Album of Chinese Landscape Paintings, 1973; Album of Chinese Floral Paintings, 1974; Conversations with Mikhail Borodin, 1977; Religious Writings 1934–63, 1964.

CHIASSON, Most Rev. Donat; *see* Moncton, Archbishop of, (RC).

CHIBA, Kazuo; Counselor, Mitsui & Co. Ltd, since 1991; Director, Foreign & Colonial Pacific Investment Trust, London, since 1993; *b* 19 April 1925; *s* of Shin-ichi and Miyoko

Chiba; *m* 1954, Keiko Okamoto; one *s* one *d*. *Educ:* Univ. of Tokyo (LLB 1949); Fletcher Sch. of Law and Diplomacy, Medford, Mass, USA (MA 1951). Joined Min. of Foreign Affairs, Tokyo, 1948; Geneva, 1956; Iran, 1958; Min. of For. Affairs, 1959; Washington, DC, 1964; Dir, N America Div., N American Affairs Bureau, Min. of For. Affairs, 1967; Minister, Moscow, 1972; Consul-Gen., Atlanta, Ga, 1974; Consul-Gen., West Berlin, 1976; Dir Gen., Middle Eastern and African Affairs Bureau, Min. of For. Affairs, 1978; Ambassador: to Sri Lanka, 1980; in Geneva (Perm. Mission of Japan to internat. orgns), 1982–87; to UK, 1988–91. Chairman: GATT Council, 1984–85; GATT Contracting Parties, 1985–86. Advr, Toshiba Corp., 1991–. Vis. Centennial Prof., LSE, 1992–94. *Recreations:* reading (history), travel. *Address:* Mitsui & Co. Ltd, 2-1 Ohtemachi 1-Chome, Chiyoda-ku, Tokyo 100, Japan.

CHIBNALL, Marjorie McCallum, MA, DPhil; FSA; FBA 1978; Fellow of Clare Hall, Cambridge, since 1975; *b* 27 Sept. 1915; *d* of J. C. Morgan, MBE; *m* 1947, Prof. Albert Charles Chibnall, FRS (*d* 1988); one *s* one *d* and two step *d*. *Educ:* Shrewsbury Priory County Girls' Sch.; Lady Margaret Hall, Oxford; Sorbonne, Paris. BLitt, MA, DPhil (Oxon); PhD (Cantab). Amy Mary Preston Read Scholar, Oxford, 1937–38; Goldsmiths' Sen. Student, 1937–39; Nursing Auxiliary, 1939; Susette Taylor Research Fellow, Lady Margaret Hall, Oxford, 1940–41; Asst Lectr, University Coll., Southampton, 1941–43; Asst Lectr, 1943–45, Lectr, 1945–47, in Medieval History, Univ. of Aberdeen; Lectr in History, later Fellow of Girton Coll., Cambridge, 1947–65; Research Fellow, Clare Hall, Cambridge, 1969–75; Leverhulme Emeritus Fellowship, 1982. Dir, Battle Conf. on Anglo-Norman Studies, 1989–93. Prothero Lectr, RHistS, 1987. Vice-Pres., Selden Soc., 1987–90. Corresp. Fellow, Medieval Acad. of America, 1983. Hon. Fellow, Girton Coll., Cambridge, 1988. Hon. DLitt Birmingham, 1979. *Publications:* The English Lands of the Abbey of Bec, 1946; Select Documents of the English Lands of the Abbey of Bec, 1951; The *Historia Pontificalis* of John of Salisbury, 1956; The Ecclesiastical History of Orderic Vitalis, 6 vols, 1969–80; Charters and Custumals of the Abbey of Holy Trinity Caen, 1982; The World of Orderic Vitalis, 1984; Anglo-Norman England 1066–1166, 1986; (ed) Anglo-Norman Studies, XII, 1990, XIII, 1991, XIV, 1992, XV, 1993, XVI, 1994; The Empress Matilda, 1991; (ed with Leslie Watkiss) The Waltham Chronicle, 1994; numerous articles and reviews, principally in English and French historical jls. *Address:* Clare Hall, Cambridge CB3 9AL. *T:* Cambridge (01223) 353923. *Club:* University Women's.

CHICHESTER, family name of **Marquess of Donegall.**

CHICHESTER, 9th Earl of, *cr* 1801; **John Nicholas Pelham;** Bt 1611; Baron Pelham of Stanmer, 1762; *b* (posthumous) 14 April 1944; *s* of 8th Earl of Chichester (killed on active service, 1944) and Ursula (*d* 1989) (she *m* 2nd, 1957, Ralph Gunning Henderson; marr. diss. 1971), *o d* of late Walter de Pannwitz, de Hartekamp, Bennebroek, Holland; *S* father, 1944; *m* 1975, Mrs June Marijke Hall; one *d*. *Recreations:* music, flying. *Heir: kinsman* Richard Anthony Henry Pelham [*b* 1 Aug. 1952; *m* 1987, Georgina, *d* of David Gilmour; two *s*]. *Address:* Little Durnford Manor, Salisbury, Wilts SP4 6AH.

CHICHESTER, Viscount; James Chichester; *b* 19 Nov. 1990; *s* and *heir* of Earl of Belfast, *qv*.

CHICHESTER, Bishop of, since 1974; **Rt. Rev. Eric Waldram Kemp,** MA Oxon, DD; *b* 27 April 1915; *o c* of Tom Kemp and Florence Lilian Kemp (*née* Waldram), Grove House, Waltham, Grimsby, Lincs; *m* 1953, Leslie Patricia, 3rd *d* of late Rt Rev. K. E. Kirk, sometime Bishop of Oxford; one *s* four *d*. *Educ:* Brigg Grammar Sch., Lincs; Exeter Coll., Oxford; St Stephen's House, Oxford. Deacon 1939; Priest 1940; Curate of St Luke, Southampton, 1939–41; Librarian of Pusey House, Oxford, 1941–46; Chaplain of Christ Church Oxford, 1943–46; Actg Chap., St John's Coll., Oxford, 1943–45; Fellow, Chaplain, Tutor, and Lectr in Theology and Medieval History, Exeter Coll., Oxford, 1946–69; Dean of Worcester, 1969–74. Exam. Chaplain: to Bp of Mon, 1942–45; to Bp of Southwark, 1946–50; to Bp of St Albans, 1946–69; to Bp of Exeter, 1949–69; to Bp of Lincoln, 1950–69. Proctor in Convocation for University of Oxford, 1949–69. Bp of Oxford's Commissary for Religious Communities, 1952–69; Chaplain to the Queen, 1967–69. Canon and Prebendary of Caistor in Lincoln Cathedral, 1952; Hon. Provincial Canon of Cape Town, 1960–; Bampton Lecturer, 1959–60. FRHistS 1951. Hon. DLitt Sussex, 1986; Hon. DD Berne, 1987. *Publications:* (contributions to) Thy Household the Church, 1943; Canonization and Authority in the Western Church, 1948; Norman Powell Williams, 1954; Twenty-five Papal Decretals relating to the Diocese of Lincoln (with W. Holtzmann), 1954; An Introduction to Canon Law in the Church of England, 1957; Life and Letters of Kenneth Escott Kirk, 1959; Counsel and Consent, 1961; The Anglican-Methodist conversations: A Comment from within, 1964; (ed) Man: Fallen and Free, 1969; Square Words in a Round World, 1980; contrib. to English Historical Review, Jl of Ecclesiastical History. *Recreations:* music, travel. *Address:* The Palace, Chichester, W Sussex PO19 1PY. *T:* Chichester (01243) 782161. *Club:* National Liberal (Pres., 1994–).

CHICHESTER, Dean of; *see* Treadgold, Very Rev. J. D.

CHICHESTER, Archdeacon of; *see* Brotherton, Ven. J. M.

CHICHESTER, Sir (Edward) John, 11th Bt *cr* 1641; *b* 14 April 1916; *s* of Comdr Sir Edward George Chichester, 10th Bt, RN, and late Phyllis Dorothy, *d* of late Henry F. Compton, Minstead Manor, Hants; *S* father, 1940; *m* 1950, Hon. Mrs Anne Rachel Pearl Moore-Gwyn, *widow* of Capt. Howel Moore-Gwyn, Welsh Guards, and *d* of 2nd Baron Montagu of Beaulieu and of Hon. Mrs Edward Pleydell-Bouverie; two *s* two *d* (and one *d* decd). *Educ:* Radley; RMC Sandhurst. Commissioned RSF, 1936. Patron of one living. Served throughout War of 1939–45. Was employed by ICI Ltd, 1950–60. A King's Foreign Service Messenger, 1947–50. Formerly Capt., Royal Scots Fusiliers and Lieut RNVR. *Heir: s* James Henry Edward Chichester [*b* 15 Oct. 1951; *m* 1990, Anne, *d* of late Major J. W. Chandos-Pole; two *s*]. *Address:* Battramsley Lodge, Boldre, Lymington, Hants SO41 8PT. *Club:* Naval.

CHICHESTER, Giles Bryan; Member (C) Devon and East Plymouth, European Parliament, since 1994; *b* 29 July 1946; *s* of Sir Francis Chichester, KBE and Sheila Mary (*née* Craven); *m* 1979, Virginia Ansell; two *s* one *d*. *Educ:* Westminster Sch.; Christ Church, Oxford (BA Hons Geography; MA). FRGS 1972. Trainee, Univ. of London Press and Hodder & Stoughton, publishers, 1968–69; Francis Chichester Ltd: Production Manager, 1969–71; Co. Sec., 1970–89; Dir, 1971–; Man. Dir, 1983–; Chm., 1989–. Chm., Foreign Affairs Forum, 1987–90. Cons. spokesman on research, Technol Develt Cttee, EP, 1994–. *Publication:* pamphlet on nuclear energy. *Recreations:* rowing, sailing, snooker, vegetarian cooking. *Address:* (office) 9 St James's Place, SW1A 1PE. *T:* 0171–493 0931; Longridge, West Hill, Ottery St Mary, Devon EX11 1UX. *Clubs:* Carlton (Chm., Political Cttee, 1992–95), Pratt's, United and Cecil; London Rowing; Royal Western Yacht (Plymouth).

CHICHESTER, Sir John; *see* Chichester, Sir E. J.

CHICHESTER-CLARK, family name of **Baron Moyola.**

CHICHESTER-CLARK, Sir Robert, (Sir Robin Chichester-Clark), Kt 1974; Director, Welbeck Group Ltd; management consultant; *b* 10 Jan. 1928; *s* of late Capt. J. L. C. Chichester-Clark, DSO and Bar, DL, MP, and Mrs C. E. Brackenbury; *m* 1st, 1953, Jane Helen Goddard (marr. diss. 1972); one *s* two *d*; 2nd, 1974, Caroline, *d* of Anthony Bull, *qv*; two *s*. *Educ:* Royal Naval Coll.; Magdalene Coll., Cambridge (BA Hons Hist. and Law). Journalist, 1950; Public Relations Officer, Glyndebourne Opera, 1952; Asst to Sales Manager, Oxford Univ. Press, 1953–55. MP (UU) Londonderry City and Co., 1955–Feb. 1974; PPS to Financial Secretary to the Treasury, 1958; Asst Government Whip (unpaid), 1958–60; a Lord Comr of the Treasury, 1960–61; Comptroller of HM Household, 1961–64; Chief Opposition Spokesman on N Ireland, 1964–70, on Public Building and Works and the Arts, 1965–70; Minister of State, Dept of Employment, 1972–74. Dir, Instn of Works Managers, 1968–72. Chm., Restoration of Appearance and Function Trust, 1988–; Trustee, Royal Philharmonic Orchestra Develt Trust, 1993–. FIPM. Hon. FIWM 1972. *Recreations:* fishing, reading. *Club:* Brooks's.

See also P. Hobhouse, Baron Moyola.

CHICK, John Stephen; public affairs consultant; HM Diplomatic Service, retired; *b* 5 Aug. 1935; *m* 1966, Margarita Alvarez de Sotomayor; one *s* three *d*. *Educ:* St John's Coll., Cambridge (BA 1959); Univ. of Pennsylvania (MA 1960). Entered FO, 1961; Madrid, 1963–66; First Sec., Mexico City, 1966–69; FCO, 1969–73; First Sec. and Head of Chancery, Rangoon, 1973–76; Head of Chancery, Luxembourg, 1976–78; Commercial Counsellor and Consul-Gen., Buenos Aires, 1978–81; Head of Arms Control Dept, FCO, 1981–83; Head of S Pacific Dept, FCO, 1983–85. Consul-Gen., Geneva, 1985–89. Dir of Internat. Affairs, Sallingbury Casey Ltd, 1990–91; Associate Dir, Rowland Public Affairs, 1991. *Address:* 24 Beverley Road, SW13 0LX. *T:* 0181–876 5916.

CHIDGEY, David William George, CEng, FICE, FIHT; MP (Lib Dem) Eastleigh, since June 1994; *b* 9 July 1942; *s* of Cyril Cecil Chidgey and Winifred Hilda Doris Chidgey (*née* Weston); *m* 1965, April Carolyn Idris-Jones; one *s* two *d*. *Educ:* Royal Naval Coll., Portsmouth; Portsmouth Poly. CEng 1971; MCIT 1985; FIHT 1990; FIEI 1990; FICE 1993; MConsEI 1993. Mech. and aeronautical engr, Admiralty, 1958–64; Highways and Civil Engr, Hants CC, 1965–72; Brian Colquhoun and Partners: Chartered Engr and Project Manager, UK, ME and W Africa, 1973–80; Associate Partner and Man. Dir, Ireland, 1981–88; Associate Partner, Central Southern England, 1988–93; Thorburn Colquhoun: Associate Dir, Southern England and Project Dir, Engrg Facilities Management, mil. estabts in Hants, 1994. *Publications:* papers in technical jl, Traffic Engineering and Control. *Recreations:* golf, reading. *Address:* c/o House of Commons, SW1A 0AA. *Club:* National Liberal.

CHIENE, John; Deputy Chairman, County NatWest Ltd, 1989–90; *b* 27 Jan. 1937; *s* of John and Muriel Chiene; *m* 1st, 1965, Anne; one *s* one *d*; 2nd, 1986, Carol; one *d*. *Educ:* Rugby; Queen's Coll., Cambridge (BA). Wood Mackenzie: joined, 1962; Man. Partner, 1969; Sen. Partner, 1974; Jt Chief Exec., Hill Samuel & Co. Ltd (who had merged with Wood Mackenzie), 1987; Chm., County NatWest Securities, on their merger with Wood Mackenzie, 1988–89. *Recreations:* golf, opera, ski-ing. *Address:* 7 St Leonard's Terrace, SW3 4QB. *Clubs:* Cavalry and Guards, City of London; New (Edinburgh).

CHIEPE, Hon. Gaositwe Keagakwa Tibe, PMS 1975; MBE 1962; FRSA; Minister for External Affairs, Botswana, since 1984; *b* 20 Oct. 1922; *d* of late T. Chiepe. *Educ:* Fort Hare, South Africa (BSc, EdDip); Bristol Univ., UK (MA (Ed)). Asst Educn Officer, 1948–53; Educn Officer and Schools Inspector, 1953–62; Sen. Educn Officer, 1962–65; Dep. Dir of Educn, 1965–67; Dir of Educn, 1968–70; Diplomat, 1970–; High Comr to UK and Nigeria, 1970–74; Ambassador: Denmark, Norway, Sweden, France and Germany, 1970–74; Belgium and EEC, 1973–74; Minister of Commerce and Industry, 1974–77; Minister for Mineral Resources and Water Affairs, 1977–84. Chairman: Africa Region, CPA, 1981–83; Botswana Branch, CPA, 1981–. Member: Botswana Society; Botswana Girl Guide Assoc.; Internat. Fedn of University Women. Hon. Pres., Kalahari Conservation Soc.; Patron, Botswana Forestry Assoc. Hon. LLD Bristol, 1972. FRSA 1973. *Recreations:* gardening, a bit of swimming (in Botswana), reading. *Address:* Department of External Affairs, Private Bag 001, Gabarone, Botswana.

CHIKETA, Stephen Cletus; High Commissioner for Zimbabwe in London, 1990–93; *b* 16 Sept. 1942; *s* of Mangwiro S. Chiketa and Mary Magdalene (*née* Chivero); *m* 1976, Juliet Joalane; one *s* two *d*. *Educ:* Univ. of South Africa (BA Hons); Univ. of Basutoland, Botswana and Swaziland (BA, PGCE). Asst Teacher, Swaziland schs, 1967–73; part-time Lectr, Univ. of Botswana, Lesotho and Swaziland, 1972–73; Principal, High School in Lesotho, 1974–80; Under Sec., Min. of Foreign Affairs, 1982; Dep. Perm. Rep., UN, 1982–86; Dep. Sec., Min. of Foreign Affairs, 1986–87; Ambassador to Romania and Bulgaria, 1987–90. *Publications:* history articles in Swaziland weekly newspapers. *Recreations:* photography, tennis, reading, table tennis, cards. *Address:* c/o Ministry of Foreign Affairs, Box 4240, Harare, Zimbabwe.

CHILCOT, Sir John (Anthony), KCB 1994 (CB 1990); Permanent Under Secretary of State, Northern Ireland Office, since 1990; *b* 22 April 1939; *s* of Henry William Chilcot and Catherine Chilcot (*née* Ashall); *m* 1964, Rosalind Mary Forster. *Educ:* Brighton Coll. (Lyon Scholar); Pembroke Coll., Cambridge (Open Scholar; MA). Joined Home Office, 1963; Asst Private Sec. to Home Secretary (Rt Hon. Roy Jenkins), 1966; Private Sec. to Head of Civil Service (late Baron Armstrong of Sanderstead), 1971–73; Principal Private Secretary to Home Secretary (Rt Hon. Merlyn Rees; Rt Hon. William Whitelaw), 1978–80; Asst Under-Sec. of State, Dir of Personnel and Finance, Prison Dept, 1980–84; Under-Sec., Cabinet Office (MPO), 1984–86; Asst Under Sec. of State, 1986 (seconded to Schroders, 1986–87), Dep. Under Sec. of State, 1987–90, Home Office. Dir, RTZ Pillar, 1986–90. *Recreations:* reading, music and opera, travel. *Address:* c/o Northern Ireland Office, Whitehall, SW1A 2AZ. *Club:* Travellers'.

CHILD, Christopher Thomas; National President, Bakers' Union, 1968–77; former Consultant to Baking Industry, Industrial Relations Officer and Training Officer, Baking Industry and Health Food Products, 1970–85; *b* 8 Jan. 1920; *s* of late Thomas William and Penelope Child; *m* 1943, Lilian Delaney; two *s* one *d*. *Educ:* Robert Ferguson Sch., Carlisle; Birmingham Coll. of Food and Domestic Science. Apprenticed baker, 1936; gained London City and Guilds final certificates in Breadmaking, Flour Confectionery and Bakery Science, 1951, and became Examiner in these subjects for CGLI. Full-time trade union official in Birmingham, 1958. Member: Birmingham Trades Council Exec., 1958–68; Adv. Council, Midland Regional TUC, 1959–68; Disablement Adv. Cttee, Birmingham, 1959–68. Former Chairman: Nat. Council Baking Education; Nat. Joint Apprenticeship Council for Baking. Mem., Industrial Training Bd, Food, Drink and Tobacco, 1968–78; former Vice-Pres., EEC Food Group and Mem., EEC Cttees on Food Products, Vocational Training, and Food Legislation; former Sec., Jt Bakers' Unions of England, Scotland and Ireland. Mem., TEC C4 programme Cttee, Hotel, Food, Catering and Institutional Management. *Recreations:* fishing, gardening, climbing in English Lake District. *Address:* 200 Bedford Road, Letchworth, Herts SG6 4EA. *T:* Letchworth (01462) 672170.

CHILD, Sir (Coles John) Jeremy, 3rd Bt *cr* 1919; actor; *b* 20 Sept. 1944; *s* of Sir Coles John Child, 2nd Bt, and Sheila (*d* 1964), *e d* of Hugh Mathewson; *S* father, 1971; *m* 1971, Deborah Jane (*née* Snelling) (marr. diss. 1976); one *d*; *m* 1978, Jan (marr. diss. 1986), *y d* of B. Todd, Kingston upon Thames; one *s* one *d*; *m* 1987, Libby Morgan; one *s* one *d*. *Educ:* Eton; Univ. of Poitiers (Dip. in French). Trained at Bristol Old Vic Theatre Sch., 1963–65; Bristol Old Vic, 1965–66; repertory at Windsor, Canterbury and Colchester; Conduct Unbecoming, Queen's, 1970; appeared at Royal Court, Mermaid and Bankside Globe, 1973; Oh Kay, Westminster, 1974; Donkey's Years, Globe, 1977; Hay Fever, Lyric, Hammersmith, 1980; *films include:* Privilege, 1967; Oh What a Lovely War!, 1967; The Breaking of Bumbo, 1970; Young Winston, 1971; The Stud, 1976; Quadrophenia, 1978; Sir Henry at Rawlinson's End, 1979; Chanel Solitaire, 1980; High Road to China, 1982; Give my Regards to Broad Street, 1983; Taffin, 1987; A Fish called Wanda, 1989; *television includes:* T'is Pity She's a Whore; Diana, Her True Story; *series:* Father, Dear Father, Edward and Mrs Simpson, The Jewel in the Crown, Bergerac, The Glittering Prizes, Wings, Fairly Secret Army, Oxbridge Blues, Edge of Darkness, First Among Equals, Game, Set and Match, Lovejoy, Perfect Scoundrels, Gravy Train Goes East, Headhunters, Harnessing Peacocks, Sharpe's Enemy, Frank Stubbs promotes. *Recreations:* gardening, cooking, travel. *Heir: s* Coles John Alexander Child, *b* 10 May 1982. *Club:* Garrick.

CHILD, Denis Marsden, CBE 1987; Chairman: Lombard North Central PLC, since 1991; IBM UK Pensions Trust, since 1994 (Member, since 1984); *b* 1 Nov. 1926; *s* of late Percival Snowden Child and Alice Child (*née* Jackson); *m* 1973, Patricia Charlton; two *s* one *d* by previous marr. *Educ:* Woodhouse Grove Sch., Bradford. Joined Westminster Bank, Leeds, 1942; RN, 1944–48; rejoined Westminster Bank; National Westminster Bank: Asst Area Manager, Leeds, 1970; Area Manager, Wembley, 1972; Chief Manager, Planning and Marketing, 1975; Head, Management Inf. and Control, 1977; Gen. Manager, Financial Control Div., 1979; Director, 1982–, NatWest Bank and subsids; Dep. Gp Chief Exec., 1982–87. Chairman: Exec. Cttee, BBA, 1986–87; Council, Assoc. for Payment Clearing Services, 1985–86; Financial Markets Cttee, Fedn Bancaire, EC, 1985–87; Director: Internat. Commodities Clearing House, 1982–86 (Chm., 1990–93); Eurotunnel Gp, 1985–; Investors Compensation Scheme Ltd, 1988–92. Bd Mem., CAA, 1986–90. Member: Accounting Standards Cttee, 1985–90; Securities and Investments Bd, 1986–92. FCIB; FCT; FIMgt. *Recreations:* golf, gardening. *Address:* Hill House, Ascott, Shipston on Stour, Warwicks CV36 5PP. *T:* Long Compton (01608) 684268. *Club:* Stoke Poges Golf.

CHILD, Sir Jeremy; *see* Child, Sir C. J. J.

CHILD, Prof. John; Guinness Professor of Management Studies, University of Cambridge, and Fellow of St John's College, Cambridge, since 1991; *b* 10 Nov. 1940; *s* of late Clifton James Child, OBE and of Hilde Child (*née* Hurwitz); *m* 1965, Elizabeth Anne Mitchiner; one *s* one *d*. *Educ:* St John's College, Cambridge (scholar; MA, PhD, ScD). Rolls-Royce, 1965–66; Aston Univ., 1966–68; London Business Sch., 1968–73; Prof. of Organizational Behaviour, Aston Univ., 1973–91 (Dean, Aston Business Sch., 1986–89); Dean and Dir, China-Europe Management Inst., Beijing, 1989–90. Vis. Fellow, Nuffield Coll., Oxford, 1973–78. FIMgt. Editor-in-Chief, Organization Studies, 1992–. *Publications include:* British Management Thought, 1969; The Business Enterprise in Modern Industrial Society, 1969; Organization, 1977; (jtly) Lost Managers, 1982; (ed) Reform Policy and the Chinese Enterprise, 1990; (jtly) Reshaping Work, 1990; (jtly) New Technology in European Services, 1990; Management in China, 1994; numerous contribs to learned jls. *Recreations:* sailing, mountain walking, bridge. *Address:* St John's College, Cambridge CB2 1TP. *T:* (college) Cambridge (01223) 338743; (dept) Cambridge (01223) 337054. *Club:* Earlswood Sailing.

CHILD, Prof. Mark Sheard, PhD; FRS 1989; Coulson Professor of Theoretical Chemistry, University of Oxford, since 1994, and Fellow of University College, Oxford, since 1994; *b* 17 Aug. 1937; *s* of George Child and Kathleen (*née* Stevenson); *m* 1964, Daphne Hall; one *s* two *d*. *Educ:* Pocklington Sch., Yorks; Clare Coll., Cambridge (BA, PhD). Vis. Scientist, Berkeley, California, 1962–63; Lectr in Theoretical Chem., Glasgow Univ., 1963–66; Oxford University: Lectr in Theoretical Chem., 1966–89; Aldrichian Praelector in Chemistry, Oxford Univ., 1989–92; Prof. of Chemical Dynamics, 1992–94; Fellow, St Edmund Hall, 1966–94. *Publications:* Molecular Collision Theory, 1974; Semiclassical Methods with Molecular Applications, 1991. *Recreations:* gardening, walking. *Address:* University College, Oxford OX1 4BH. *T:* Oxford (01865) 271532.

CHILD VILLIERS, family name of **Earl of Jersey.**

CHILE, Bishop of, since 1977; **Rt Rev. Colin Frederick Bazley;** *b* 27 June 1935; *s* of Reginald Samuel Bazley and Isabella Davies; *m* 1960, Barbara Helen Griffiths; three *d*. *Educ:* Birkenhead School; St Peter's Hall, Oxford (MA); Tyndale Hall, Bristol. Deacon 1959, priest 1960; Assistant Curate, St Leonard's, Bootle, 1959–62; Missionary of S American Missionary Society in Chile, 1962–69; Rural Dean of Chol-Chol, 1962–66; Archdeacon of Temuco, 1966–69; Assistant Bishop for Cautin and Malleco, Dio. Chile, Bolivia and Peru, 1969–75; Assistant Bishop for Santiago, 1975–77; Bishop of Chile, Bolivia and Peru, 1977; diocese divided, Oct. 1977; Bishop of Chile and Bolivia until Oct. 1981, when diocese again divided; Presiding Bishop of the Anglican Council for South America, 1977–83; Primate, Province of S Cone of America, 1989–95. *Recreations:* football (Liverpool supporter) and fishing on camping holidays. *Address:* Iglesia Anglicana, Casilla 50675, Correo Central, Santiago, Chile. *T:* (2) 8212478.

CHILSTON, 4th Viscount *cr* 1911, of Boughton Malherbe; **Alastair George Akers-Douglas;** Baron Douglas of Baads, 1911; film producer; *b* 5 Sept. 1946; *s* of Ian Stanley Akers-Douglas (*d* 1952) (*g s* of 1st Viscount) and of Phyllis Rosemary (who *m* 2nd, John Anthony Cobham Shaw, MC), *d* of late Arthur David Clere Parsons; *S* cousin, 1982; *m* 1971, Juliet Anne, *d* of Lt-Col Nigel Lovett, Glos Regt; three *s*. *Educ:* Eton College; Madrid Univ. *Recreation:* sailing. *Heir: s* Hon. Oliver Ian Akers-Douglas, *b* 13 Oct. 1973. *Address:* The Old Rectory, Twyford, near Winchester, Hants SO21 1NS. *T:* Twyford (01962) 712300.

CHILTON, Brig. Sir Frederick Oliver, Kt 1969; CBE 1963 (OBE 1957); DSO 1941 and bar 1944; Chairman, Repatriation Commission, Australia, 1958–70; *b* 23 July 1905. *Educ:* Univ. of Sydney (BA, LLB). Solicitor, NSW, 1929. Late AIF; served War of 1939–45, Libya, Greece, New Guinea and Borneo (despatches, DSO and bar); Controller of Joint Intelligence, 1946–48; Asst Sec., Dept of Defence, Australia, 1948–50; Dep. Sec., 1950–58. *Address:* 30 Hudson Parade, Clareville Beach, NSW 2107, Australia. *Clubs:* Melbourne, Union, Naval and Military (Melbourne).

CHILTON, John James; jazz musician, since 1958; *b* 16 July 1932; *s* of Thomas William Chilton and Eileen Florence (*née* Burke); *m* 1963, Teresa McDonald; two *s* one *d*. *Educ:* Yardley Gobion Sch., Northants; Claremont Sch., Kenton, Middx. Nat. Service, RAF, 1950–52. Worked in an advertising agency and for nat. newspaper before becoming professional musician, leading own band, 1958; played in a ship's orchestra, 1960; with Bruce Turner's Jump Band, 1960–63; jt-leader with Wally Fawkes, 1969–72; formed The Feetwarmers, 1972, regular accompanists for George Melly, 1972–93. Recording, composing and arranging, 1972–. Grammy Award, USA, for best album notes, 1983; ARSC Award, USA, for best researched jazz or blues book, 1992. *Publications:* Who's Who of Jazz, 1970, 5th edn 1989; Billie's Blues, 1974, 5th edn 1990; McKinney's Music, 1978; Teach Yourself Jazz, 1979; 2nd edn 1980; A Jazz Nursery, 1980; Stomp Off, Let's Go, 1983; Sidney Bechet: the wizard of jazz, 1987; The Song of the Hawk, 1990; Let the Good Times Roll, 1992; articles on jazz in books and newspapers. *Recreations:* watching cricket, soccer, collecting modern first editions. *Address:* 3 Great Ormond Street, WC1N 3RA.

CHILVER, family name of **Baron Chilver.**

CHILVER, Baron *cr* 1987 (Life Peer), of Cranfield in the County of Bedfordshire; **Henry Chilver;** Kt 1978; FRS 1982; FEng 1977; CIMgt; Chairman: RJB Mining, since 1993; *b* 30 Oct. 1926; *e s* of A. H. Chilver and A. E. Mack; *m* 1959, Claudia M. B. Grigson, MA, MB, BCh, *o d* of Sir Wilfrid Grigson; three *s* two *d*. *Educ:* Southend High Sch.; Bristol Univ. (Albert Fry Prize 1947). Structural Engineering Asst, British Railways, 1947; Asst Lecturer, 1950, Lecturer, 1952, in Civil Engineering, Bristol Univ.; Demonstrator, 1954, Lectr, 1956, in Engineering, Cambridge Univ.; Fellow of Corpus Christi Coll., Cambridge, 1958–61 (Hon. Fellow, 1981); Chadwick Prof. of Civil Engineering, UCL, 1961–69; Vice-Chancellor, Cranfield Inst. of Technology, 1970–89; Director: Centre for Environmental Studies, 1967–69; Node Course (for civil service and industry), 1974–75. Chm., English China Clays, 1989–95 (Dir, 1973–95); Director: SKF (UK), 1972–80; De La Rue Co., 1973–81; SE Reg., Nat. Westminster Bank, 1975–83; Delta Gp, 1977–84; Powell Duffryn, 1979–89; TR Technology Investment Trust, 1982–88; Hill Samuel Gp, 1983–87; Britoil, 1986–88; ICI, 1990–93; Zeneca Group, 1993–95. Chm., Milton Keynes Develt Corp., 1983–92. Chairman: PO, 1980–81; Higher Educn Review Body, NI, 1978–81; Univs' Computer Bd, 1975–78; RAF Trng and Educn Adv. Cttee, 1976–80; Adv. Council, RMCS, Shrivenham, 1978–83; Working Gp on Advanced Ground Transport, 1978–81; Electronics EDC, 1980–85; ACARD, 1982–85; Interim Adv. Cttee on Teachers' Pay, 1987–91; UFC, 1988–91; Innovation Adv. Bd, DTI, 1989–93. Member: Ferrybridge Enquiry Cttee, 1965; Management Cttee, Inst. of Child Health, 1965–69; ARC, 1967–70 and 1972–75; SRC, 1970–74; Beds Educn Cttee, 1970–74; Planning and Transport Res. Adv. Council, 1972–79; Cttee for Ind. Technologies, 1972–76; ICE Special Cttee on Educn and Trng, 1973 (Chm.); CNAA, 1973–76; Royal Commn on Environmental Pollution, 1976–81; Standing Commn on Energy and the Environment, 1978–81; Adv. Bd for Res. Councils, 1982–85; Bd, Nat. Adv. Body for Local Authority Higher Educn, 1983–85. Dep. Pres., Standing Conf. on Schools Sci. and Technol.; Assessor, Inquiry on Lorries, People and the Envt, 1979–80. President: Inst. of Management Services, 1982–; Inst. of Logistics, 1993–; Vice-Pres., ICE, 1981–83; Mem., Smeatonian Soc. of Civil Engrs. Member Council: Birkbeck Coll., 1980–82; Cheltenham Coll., 1980–88. Lectures: STC Communications, 1981; O'Sullivan, Imperial Coll., 1984; Lady Margaret Beaufort, Bedford, 1985; Fawley, Southampton Univ., 1985; Lubbock, Oxford, 1990. Telford Gold Medal, ICE, 1962; Coopers Hill War Meml Prize, ICE, 1977. Hon. DSc: Leeds, 1982; Bristol, 1983; Salford, 1983; Strathclyde, 1986; Bath, 1986; Cranfield, 1989; Buckingham, 1990; Compiègne, 1990. *Publications:* Problems in Engineering Structures (with R. J. Ashby), 1958; Strength of Materials (with J. Case), 1959, 3rd edn as Strength of Materials and Structures (with J. Case and C. T. Ross), 1993; Thin-walled Structures (ed), 1967; papers on structural theory in engineering journals. *Clubs:* Athenæum, United Oxford & Cambridge University.

CHILVER, Brian Outram; Chairman, Seafield, since 1990; *b* 17 June 1933; *s* of late Bertram Montagu Chilver and of Edith Gwendoline Chilver; *m* 1956, Erica Mary; two *s* two *d*. *Educ:* University College Sch. FCA 1965; ACMA 1966. Temple Gothard & Co., 1949–55 (articled clerk); National Service, RAF, 1955–57; Barton Mayhew & Co., 1957–59; Temple Gothard & Co., 1959–85 (Partner, 1960, Senior Partner, 1975); Chairman: Laing Properties, 1987–90; Eskmuir Properties plc, 1990–; Forward Technology Industries plc, 1991–; Dir (non-exec.), John Laing plc, 1988–. Chm., Tear Fund, 1990–. *Recreations:* walking, swimming, reading, music. *Address:* Bretaye, Limbourne Lane, Fittleworth, West Sussex RH20 1HR; (office) 8 Queen Anne Street, W1M 9LD.

CHILVER, Elizabeth Millicent, (Mrs R. C. Chilver); Principal of Lady Margaret Hall, Oxford, 1971–79, Honorary Fellow, 1979; *b* 3 Aug. 1914; *o d* of late Philip Perceval Graves and late Millicent Graves (*née* Gilchrist); *m* 1937, Richard Clementson Chilver, CB (*d* 1985). *Educ:* Benenden Sch., Cranbrook; Somerville Coll., Oxford (Hon. Fellow, 1977). Journalist, 1937–39; temp. Civil Servant, 1939–45; Daily News Ltd, 1945–47; temp. Principal and Secretary, Colonial Social Science Research Council and Colonial Economic Research Cttee, Colonial Office, 1948–57; Director, Univ. of Oxford Inst. of Commonwealth Studies, 1957–61; Senior Research Fellow, Univ. of London Inst. of Commonwealth Studies, 1961–64; Principal, Bedford Coll., Univ. of London, 1964–71, Fellow, 1974. Mem. Royal Commn on Medical Education, 1965–68. Trustee, British Museum, 1970–75; Mem. Governing Body, SOAS, Univ. of London, 1975–80. Médaille de la Reconnaissance française, 1945. *Publications:* articles on African historical subjects. *Address:* 47 Kingston Road, Oxford OX2 6RH. *T:* Oxford (01865) 53082.

CHILVERS, Prof. Clair Evelyn Druce; Professor of Epidemiology, University of Nottingham Medical School, since 1990; *b* 8 Feb. 1946; *d* of Air Cdre Stanley Edwin Druce Mills, *qv* and Joan Mary Mills (*née* James); *m* 1965, Antony Stuart Chilvers, MA, MChir, FRCS; one *s* one *d*. *Educ:* Cheltenham Ladies' Coll.; LSE (BSc Econ); LSHTM (MSc). Scientist, Inst. of Cancer Res., 1979–90; Vice-Dean (Res.), Fac. of Med. and Health Scis, Nottingham Univ., 1994–; Director: Trent Inst. for Health Services Res., Nottingham, 1994–; Trent Cancer Registry, 1994–. Mem., Royal Commn on Envmtl Pollution, 1994–. Mem., Cttee on Carcinogenicity of Chemicals in Food, Consumer Products and Envmt, DoH, 1993–. Non-Exec. Dir, Nottingham Community Health NHS Trust, 1991–. Mem. Council, Nottingham Univ., 1994–. Hon. MFPHM 1991. *Publications:* numerous in learned jls, mainly in field of cancer epidemiology. *Recreations:* music, walking, theatre, collecting 20th Century prints. *Address:* Department of Public Health Medicine and Epidemiology, University of Nottingham Medical School, Queen's Medical Centre, Nottingham NG7 2UH. *T:* Nottingham (0115) 970 9300. *Club:* Royal Society of Medicine.

CHILWELL, Hon. Sir Muir Fitzherbert, Kt 1989; **Hon. Mr Justice Chilwell;** Judge of the Court of Appeal, Cook Islands, since 1990; Judge of the High Court, Cook Islands, 1991–94; *b* 12 April 1924; *s* of Benjamin Charles Chilwell and Loris Madeleine Chilwell; *m* 1947, Lynette Erica Frances Cox; two *d* (one *s* decd). *Educ:* Auckland University Coll., Univ. of New Zealand (LLB 1949; LLM Hons 1950). Law Clerk, 1941–49; admitted Barrister and Solicitor, 1949; Partner, Haddow, Haddow & Chilwell, later Haddow Chilwell Pain & Palmer, 1949–65; QC 1965; admitted Victorian Bar (Aust.) and QC Vict. 1970; Judge of the Supreme, later High, Court of NZ, 1973–91; Admin. Div., High Court, 1982–91. Lectr, Univ. of Auckland, 1950 and 1953–60. Member: Contracts and Commercial Law Reform Cttee, 1966–68 (Chm., 1968–73); Law Revision Commn, 1968–73; Disciplinary Cttee, NZ Law Soc., 1971–73; Council, Legal Educn, NZ, 1985–91 (Assessor in Law of Contract, 1964–67); Chm., Legal Res. Foundn, 1977–81; Mem. Council, Auckland Dist Law Soc., 1960–67, Pres., 1967–68; Pres., Auckland

Medico-Legal Soc., 1969–70, Life Mem., 1989. Silver Jubilee Medal, 1977; Commemoration Medal, NZ, 1990. *Recreation:* boating. *Address:* 87 St Heliers Bay Road, Auckland 5, New Zealand. *T:* (9) 5757999. *Club:* Royal New Zealand Yacht Squadron.

CHING, Henry, CBE 1982; Secretary General, Caritas–Hong Kong, 1990–91; *b* 2 Nov. 1933; *s* of Henry Ching, OBE and Ruby Irene Ching; *m* 1963, Eileen Frances Peters; two *d. Educ:* Diocesan Boys' School, Hong Kong; Hong Kong Univ. (BA Hons); Wadham Coll., Oxford (MA, DipEd). Schoolmaster, 1958–61; Hong Kong Civil Service: various appts, 1961–73; Principal Asst Financial Sec., 1973–76; Dep. Financial Sec., 1976–83; Sec. for Health and Welfare and MLC, Hong Kong, 1983–85, retired. Chief Administrator, Hong Kong Foundn, 1989. *Recreations:* cricket, rowing. *Address:* 39 Saiala Road, East Killara, NSW 2071, Australia.

CHINN, Sir Trevor (Edwin), Kt 1990; CVO 1989; Chairman and Chief Executive, Lex Service PLC, since 1973 (Managing Director, 1968–73); *b* 24 July 1935; *s* of Rosser and Susie Chinn; *m* 1965, Susan Speelman; two *s. Educ:* Clifton Coll.; King's Coll., Cambridge. Dir, Lex Service, 1959–. Chm., Robins Cinemas Ltd, 1990–. Pres., Joint Israel Appeal; Chm., Britain/Israel Public Affairs Centre. Vice Chm., Wishing Well Appeal, Gt Ormond St Hosp. for Sick Children, 1985–89. Trustee, Royal Acad. Trust, 1989–; Dir, Hampstead Theatre, 1990–. Freeman of the City of London. Chief Barker, Variety Club of GB, 1977, 1978. *Address:* Lex House, 17 Connaught Place, W2 2EL. *T:* 0171–705 1212.

CHINNERY, (Charles) Derek; Controller, Radio 1, BBC, 1978–85; *b* 27 April 1925; *s* of Percy Herbert and Frances Dorothy Chinnery; *m* 1953, Doreen Grace Clarke. *Educ:* Gosforth Grammar School. Youth in training, BBC, 1941; RAF Cadet Pilot, 1943. BBC: Technical Asst, 1947; Programme Engineer, 1948; Studio Manager, 1950; Producer, 1952; Executive Producer, 1967; Head of Radio 1, 1972. *Recreations:* DIY, sailing. *Address:* 2 Meads Brow, Eastbourne BN20 7UP.

CHINO, Yoshitoki, Hon. KBE 1992; Hon. Chairman, Daiwa Securities Co. Ltd, since 1991; *b* 18 March 1923; *s* of Hisakichi Chino and Tokiyo Chino; *m* 1950, Sachiko Kawabata; one *s* one *d. Educ:* Keio Univ. (BA Law 1946). Joined Daiwa Securities Co. Ltd, 1946: Gen. Manager, Sales and Foreign Depts, 1959–61; Dir, 1961–65; Man. Dir, 1966–70; Sen. Man Dir, 1970–72; Exec. Vice-Pres., 1972–81; Vice-Chm., 1981–82; Chm., 1982–91. Commendatore dell'Ordine al Merito (Italy), 1994. *Publication:* Internationalization by Feel, 1988. *Recreations:* personal computer, reading books, fishing. *Address:* Daiwa Securities Co. Ltd, 6–4 Otemachi 2-chome, Chiyoda-ku, Tokyo 100, Japan.

CHIONA, Most Rev. James; *see* Blantyre, Archbishop of, (RC).

CHIPIMO, Elias Marko Chisha; MP (MMD) Kantanshi, Zambia, since 1991; *b* 23 Feb. 1931; *s* of Marko Chipimo, Zambia (then Northern Rhodesia); *m* 1959, Anna Joyce Nkole Konie; four *s* three *d. Educ:* St Canisius, Chikuni, Zambia; Munali; Fort Hare Univ. Coll., SA; University Coll. of Rhodesia and Nyasaland; Univ. of Zambia (LLB 1985). Schoolmaster, 1959–63; Sen. Govt Administrator, 1964–67; High Comr for Zambia in London, and Zambian Ambassador to the Holy See, 1968–69; Perm. Sec., Min. of Foreign Affairs, 1969; Hon. Minister, Lusaka Province, 1991–; Nat. Chm., 1991–, and Mem., Nat. Exec. Cttee, MMD. Chairman: Zambia Stock Exchange Council, 1970–72; Zambia Nat. Bldg Soc., 1970–71; Dep. Chm., Development Bank of Zambia Ltd, 1973–75; Dep. Chm., 1975, Chm., 1976–80, Standard Bank Zambia Ltd; Director: Zambia Airways Corp., 1975–81; Zambia Bata Shoe Co. Ltd, 1977–92. Mem., Nat Council for Sci. Res., 1977–80. Pres., Zambia Red Cross, 1990–95 (Vice-Pres., 1976–90; Life Mem., 1995; Pres., Lusaka Br., 1970–75); Mem., Zambia Univ. Council, 1970–76; Dir, Internat. Sch. of Lusaka, 1970–76. Cllr, Lusaka City Council, 1974–80. Representative: Knights of Malta, 1978–; Commonwealth Soc., 1979–88. *Publications:* Our Land and People, 1966; Tied Loans and the Role of Banks (vol. 2 of International Financing of Economic Development), 1978; articles in Univ. of Zambia Jl. *Recreations:* rose gardening, reading, general literature, linguistics, philosophy, politics, economics, discussions, chess, growing roses. *Address:* PO Box 32115, 10101 Lusaka, Zambia.

CHIPMAN, Dr John Miguel Warwick; Director, International Institute for Strategic Studies, since 1993; *b* 10 Feb. 1957; *s* of Lawrence Carroll Chipman and Maria Isabel (*née* Prados). *Educ:* Harvard Coll. (BA Hons); London Sch. of Economics (MA Dist.); Balliol Coll., Oxford (MPhil, DPhil). Research Associate: IISS, 1983–84; Atlantic Inst. for Internat. Affairs, Paris, 1985–87; International Institute for Strategic Studies: Asst Dir for Regl Security, 1987–91; Dir of Studies, 1991–93. *Publications:* Vième République et Défense de l'Afrique, 1986; (ed and jt author) NATO's Southern Allies, 1988; French Power in Africa, 1989; numerous contribs to edited vols and learned jls. *Recreations:* tennis, ski-ing, scuba diving, collecting travel books. *Address:* International Institute for Strategic Studies, 23 Tavistock Street, WC2E 7NQ. *T:* 0171–379 7676. *Club:* Harvard (New York).

CHIPP, David Allan; Editor in Chief, Press Association, 1969–86; *b* 6 June 1927; *s* of late Thomas Ford Chipp and late Isabel Mary Ballinger; unmarried. *Educ:* Geelong Grammar Sch., Australia; King's Coll., Cambridge (MA). Served with Middlesex Regt, 1944–47; Cambridge, 1947–50. Joined Reuters as Sports Reporter, 1950; Correspondent for Reuters: in SE Asia, 1953–55; in Peking, 1956–58; various managerial positions in Reuters, 1960–68; Editor of Reuters, 1968. An Indep. Dir, The Observer, 1985–93; Director: Reuter Foundn, 1986–90; TV-am News Co., 1986–92; Lloyds of London Press, 1990–93; Teletext UK, 1992–; Talk Radio UK, 1994–; Chm., News World, 1994–. Mem., Press Complaints Commn, 1991–93. *Recreations:* reading, opera. *Address:* 2 Wilton Court, 59/60 Eccleston Square, SW1V 1PH. *T:* 0171–834 5579. *Clubs:* Garrick, Beefsteak; Leander (Henley-on-Thames); Hawks (Cambridge).

CHIPPERFIELD, Sir Geoffrey (Howes), KCB 1992 (CB 1985); Director, South West Water plc, since 1993; *b* 20 April 1933; *s* of Nelson Chipperfield and Eleanor Chipperfield; *m* 1959, Gillian James; two *s. Educ:* Cranleigh; New Coll., Oxford. Called to the Bar, Gray's Inn, 1955. Joined Min. of Housing and Local Govt, 1956; Harkness Fellow, Inst. of Govtl Studies, Univ. of Calif, Berkeley, 1962–63; Principal Private Sec., Minister of Housing, 1968–70; Sec., Greater London Develt Plan Inquiry, 1970–73; Under Sec., 1976, Dep. Sec., 1982–87, DoE; Dep. Sec., Dept of Energy, 1987–89; Perm. Under-Sec. of State, Dept of Energy, 1989–91; Perm. Sec. and Chief Exec., PSA Services, 1991–93. *Recreations:* reading, gardening. *Club:* United Oxford & Cambridge University.

CHIPPINDALE, Christopher Ralph, PhD; FSA; Editor, Antiquity, since 1987; Senior Assistant Curator, Cambridge University Museum of Archaeology, since 1993 (Assistant Curator, 1988–93); Bye-Fellow, Girton College, Cambridge, since 1988; *b* 13 Oct. 1951; *s* of Keith and Ruth Chippindale; *m* 1976, Anne Lowe; two *s* two *d. Educ:* Sedbergh School; St John's College, Cambridge (BA Hons); Girton Coll., Cambridge (PhD). FSA 1991; MIFA. Editor, freelance, Penguin Books, Hutchinson Publishing Group, 1974–82; Res. Fellow in Archaeology, Girton Coll., Cambridge, 1985–88. *Publications:* Stonehenge Complete, 1983; (ed jtly) The Pastmasters, 1989; (jtly) Who owns Stonehenge?, 1990; articles in jls. *Recreations:* work, worrying. *Address:* 85 Hills Road, Cambridge CB2 1PG.

CHIRAC, Jacques René; President of the French Republic, since 1995; *b* Paris, 29 Nov. 1932; *s* of François Chirac, company manager and Marie-Louise (*née* Valente); *m* 1956, Bernadette Chodron de Courcel; two *d. Educ:* Lycée Carnot and Lycee Louis-le-Grand, Paris; Diploma of Inst. of Polit. Studies, Paris, and of Summer Sch., Harvard Univ., USA. Served Army in Algeria. Ecole Nat. d'Admin, 1957–59; Auditor, Cour des Comptes, 1959; Head Dept: Sec.-Gen. of Govt, 1962; Private Office of Georges Pompidou, 1962–67; Counsellor, Cour des Comptes, 1965; State Secretary: Employment Problems, 1967–68; Economy and Finance, 1968–71; Minister for Parly Relations, 1971–72; Minister for Agriculture and Rural Development, 1972–74; Home Minister, March–May 1974; Prime Minister, 1974–76 and 1986–88. Deputy from Corrèze, elected 1967, 1968, 1973, 1976 (UDR), 1978 (RFR), 1981, 1986, 1988 and 1993; Sec.-Gen., UDR, Dec. 1974–June 1975; Pres., Rassemblement pour la République, 1976–81 and 1982–94. Mayor of Paris, 1977–95. Member from Meymac, Conseil Général of Corrèze, 1968–, Pres. 1970–79. Mem., European Parlt, 1979–80. Treasurer, Claude Pompidou Foundn (charity for elderly and for handicapped children), 1969–. Grand-Croix, Ordre national du Mérite; Croix de la valeur militaire; Chevalier du Mérite agricole, des Arts et des Lettres, de l'Etoile noire, du Mérite sportif, du Mérite touristique; Médaille de l'Aéronautique. *Publications:* a thesis on development of Port of New Orleans, 1954; Discours pour la France à l'heure du choix, la lueur d'espérance: réflexion du soir pour le matin, 1978; Une Nouvelle France, 1994; La France pour Tous, 1995. *Address:* Palais de l'Elysée, 75008 Paris, France.

CHISHOLM, Prof. Alexander William John; Professor Emeritus, University of Salford, since 1994; *b* 18 April 1922; *s* of Thomas Alexander Chisholm and Maude Mary Chisholm (*née* Robinson); *m* 1945, Aline Mary (*née* Eastwood); one *s* one *d. Educ:* Brentwood Sch., Essex; Northampton Polytechnic; Manchester Coll. of Science and Technology; Royal Technical Coll., Salford (BSc(Eng) London). CEng, FIMechE, FIEE. Section Leader, Res. Dept, Metropolitan Vickers Electrical Co. Ltd, 1944–49; Sen. Scientific Officer, then Principal Scientific Officer, Nat. Engrg Lab., 1949–57; UK Scientific Mission, British Embassy, USA, 1952–54; Head of Dept of Mechanical Engrg, then Prof. of Mechanical Engrg, Royal Coll. of Advanced Technology, Salford, 1957–67; University of Salford: Prof. of Mech. Engineering, 1967–82; Research Prof. in Engrg., 1982–87; Professorial Fellow, 1987–94; Chm., Salford Univ. Industrial Centre, subseq. Salford Univ. Industrial Centre Ltd, 1968–82. Visitor, Cambridge Univ. Engrg Dept and Vis. Fellow, Wolfson Coll., 1973–74. Chm., Engrg Profs Conf., 1976–80; Dir, Prog. for Improvement of Quality of Engrg Educn, 1990–. Chm., Industrial Admin and Engrg Prodn Gp, IMechE, 1960–62. Nat. Council for Technological Awards: Chm., Mechanical/Prodn Engrg Cttee, 1960–63; Vice-Chm., Bd of Studies in Engrg and Governor, 1963–65. Member: Technology Cttee, UGC, 1969–74; Engrg Processes Cttee, SERC, 1980–83. Pres., CIRP, 1983–84 (Chm., UK Bd, 1977–88; Hon. Life Mem. 1987). Mem., Court, Cranfield Inst. of Technology, 1974–91. Whitworth Prize, IMechE, 1965. *Publications:* numerous on production process technology, manufacturing systems, industrial research, educn and training of engineers, human factors in manufacturing. *Recreations:* hill walking, sailing, tree planting. *Address:* 12 Legh Road, Prestbury, Macclesfield, Cheshire SK10 4HX. *T:* Prestbury (01625) 829412. *Club:* Athenæum.

CHISHOLM, John Alexander Raymond, CEng; Chief Executive, Defence Evaluation and Research (formerly Defence Research) Agency, since 1991; *b* 27 Aug. 1946; *s* of Ruari Ian Lambert Chisholm and Pamela Harland Chisholm; *m* 1969, Catherine Alexandra (*née* Pana); one *s* one *d. Educ:* Univ. of Cambridge (MA). CEng 1974; FIEE 1995. Vauxhall Motors, 1964–69; Scicon Ltd, 1969–79; Cap Scientific Ltd, 1979–91: Man. Dir, 1981–86; Chm., 1986–91; Chm., Yard Ltd, 1986–91; UK Man. Dir, Sema Group plc, 1988–91. Non-exec. Dir, Expro Internat. plc, 1994–. Pres., Electronic and Business Equipment Assoc., 1989–90. *Recreations:* participative sports, old cars. *Address:* 13 The Green, Woughton-on-the-Green, Milton Keynes, Bucks MK6 3BE. *T:* Milton Keynes (01908) 670714.

CHISHOLM, Malcolm; MP (Lab) Edinburgh, Leith, since 1992; *b* 7 March 1949; *s* of Olive and George Chisholm; *m* 1975, Janet Broomfield, writer; two *s* one *d. Educ:* Edinburgh Univ. (MA Hons, Dip Ed). Formerly Teacher of English, Castlebrae High School and Broughton High School. *Recreations:* reading, football. *Address:* House of Commons, SW1A 0AA. *T:* 0171–219 4613.

CHISHOLM, Prof. Malcolm Harold, PhD; FRS 1990; Distinguished Professor of Chemistry, Indiana University, since 1985; *b* 15 Oct. 1945; *s* of Angus and Gweneth Chisholm; *m* 1st, 1969, Susan Sage (marr. diss.); one *s*; 2nd, 1982, Cynthia Brown; two *s. Educ:* London Univ. (BSc 1966; PhD 1969). Sessional Lectr, Univ. of W Ontario, 1970–72; Asst Prof. of Chemistry, Princeton Univ., 1972–78; Associate Prof., 1978–80, Prof., 1980–85, Indiana Univ. Guggenheim Fellow, 1985–86. FAAAS 1987. Hon. DSc London, 1980. RSC Award for Chem. and Electrochem. of Transition Elements, 1987; Alexander von Humboldt Sen. Scientist Award, 1988; (jtly) ACS Nobel Laureate Signature Award, 1988; ACS Award in Inorganic Chm., 1989. *Publications:* Reactivity of Metal-Metal Bonds, 1982; Inorganic Chemistry: towards the 21st century, 1983; Early Transition Metal Clusters with π-Donor Lizards, 1995; numerous articles, mostly in chem. jls. *Recreations:* squash, gardening. *Address:* 515 Hawthorne, Bloomington, IN 47405, USA. *T:* (812) 8556606; 38 Norwich Street, Cambridge CB2 1NE. *T:* Cambridge (01223) 312392.

CHISHOLM, Prof. Michael Donald Inglis; Professor of Geography, University of Cambridge, since 1976; Professorial Fellow, St Catharine's College, Cambridge, since 1976; *b* 10 June 1931; *s* of M. S. and A. W. Chisholm; *m* 1st, 1959, Edith Gretchen Emma (*née* Hoof) (marr. diss. 1981); one *s* two *d*; 2nd, 1986, Judith Carola Shackleton (*née* Murray). *Educ:* St Christopher Sch., Letchworth; St Catharine's Coll., Cambridge (MA). MA Oxon. Nat. Service Commn, RE, 1950–51. Deptl Demonstrator, Inst. for Agric. Econs, Oxford, 1954–59; Asst Lectr, then Lectr in Geog., Bedford Coll., London, 1960–64; Vis. Sen. Lectr in Geog., Univ. of Ibadan, 1964–65; Lectr, then Reader in Geog., Univ. of Bristol, 1965–72; Prof. of Economic and Social Geography, Univ. of Bristol, 1972–76. Associate, Economic Associates Ltd, consultants, 1965–77; Mem. SSRC, and Chm. of Cttees for Human Geography and Planning, 1967–72; Member: Local Govt Boundary Commn for England, 1971–78; Rural Develt Commn, 1981–90; English Adv. Cttee on Telecommunications, 1990–92; Local Govt Commn for England, 1992–. Mem. Council, Inst. of British Geographers, 1961 and 1962, Junior Vice-Pres., 1977, Sen. Vice-Pres., 1978, Pres. 1979. Conservator of River Cam, 1979– (Chm., 1991–). Gill Memorial Prize, RGS, 1969. Geography Editor for Hutchinson Univ. Lib., 1973–82. *Publications:* Rural Settlement and Land Use: an essay in location, 1962; Geography and Economics, 1966; (ed jtly) Regional Forecasting, 1971; (ed jtly) Spatial Policy Problems of the British Economy, 1971; Research in Human Geography, 1971; (ed) Resources for Britain's Future, 1972; (jtly) Freight Flows and Spatial Aspects of the British Economy, 1973; (jtly) The Changing Pattern of Employment, 1973; (ed jtly) Studies in Human Geography, 1973; (ed jtly) Processes in Physical and Human Geography: Bristol Essays, 1975; Human Geography: Evolution or Revolution?, 1975; Modern World Development, 1982; Regions in Recession and Resurgence, 1990; (ed jtly) Shared Space: Divided Space, 1990;

Britain on the Edge of Europe, 1995; papers in Farm Economist, Oxford Econ. Papers, Trans Inst. British Geographers, Geography, Geographical Jl, Applied Statistics, Area, etc. *Recreations:* gardening, theatre, opera, interior design. *Address:* Department of Geography, Downing Place, Cambridge CB2 3EN.

CHISLETT, Derek Victor; Warden, Sackville College, since 1988; *b* 18 April 1929; *s* of Archibald Lynn Chislett and Eva Jessie Chislett (*née* Collins); *m* 1954, Joan Robson; two *d*. *Educ:* Christ's Hospital. Admiralty, 1946–53; HM Forces, 1947–49; Nat. Assistance Board, 1953–66; Min. of Social Security, 1966–68; Department of Health and Social Security, 1968–88: Under Sec., 1983; Controller, Newcastle Central Office, 1983–86; Dir of Finance (Social Security), 1986–88. Mem. Exec. Cttee, Nat. Assoc. of Almshouses, 1989–. Trustee: Motability Tenth Anniversary Trust, 1989–; Independent Living Fund, 1990–93. *Publication:* Sackville College: a short history and guide, 1995. *Recreations:* opera, playing and listening to the 'cello, bee-keeping. *Address:* Sackville College, East Grinstead, W Sussex RH19 3AZ. *T:* East Grinstead (01342) 326561.

CHISWELL, Rt. Rev. Peter; *see* Armidale, Bishop of.

CHISWELL, Maj.-Gen. Peter Irvine, CB 1985; CBE 1976 (OBE 1972; MBE 1965); DL; Director, Buckland Leadership Development Centre, since 1989; *b* 19 April 1930; *s* of late Col Henry Thomas Chiswell, OBE (late RAMC) and of Gladys Beatrice Chiswell; *m* 1958, Felicity Philippa, *d* of R. F. Martin; two *s*. *Educ:* Allhallows School; RMA Sandhurst. Commissioned Devonshire Regt, 1951; transf. Parachute Regt, 1958; DAAG HQ Berlin Inf. Bde, 1963–65; Brigade Major, 16 Para Bde, 1967–68; GSO1 (DS), Staff Coll., 1968–69; CO 3 PARA, 1969–71; Col GS (Army Training), 1971–74; Comd British Contingent DCOS UN Force Cyprus, 1974–76; Comd, 44 Para Bde, 1976–78; ACOS (Operations), HQ Northern Army Gp, 1978–81; Comd, Land Forces NI, 1982–83; GOC Wales, 1983–85. Vice-Chm., ACFA, 1988–. Gov., Christ Coll., Brecon, 1987–. DL Powys, 1994. *Recreations:* travel, sailing.

CHITNIS, family name of **Baron Chitnis.**

CHITNIS, Baron *cr* 1977 (Life Peer), of Ryedale, N Yorks; **Pratap Chidamber Chitnis;** Chairman, British Refugee Council, 1986–89; *b* 1 May 1936; *s* of late Chidamber N. Chitnis and Lucia Mallik; *m* 1964, Anne Brand; one *s* decd. *Educ:* Penryn Sch.; Stonyhurst Coll.; Univs of Birmingham (BA) and Kansas (MA). Admin. Asst, Nat. Coal Board, 1958–59; Liberal Party Organisation: Local Govt Officer, 1960–62; Agent, Orpington Liberal Campaign, 1962; Trng Officer, 1962–64; Press Officer, 1964–66; Head of Liberal Party Organisation, 1966–69. Sec., 1969–75, Chief Exec. and Dir, 1975–88, Joseph Rowntree Social Service Trust. Mem., Community Relations Commn, 1970–77; Chm., BBC Immigrants Programme Adv. Cttee, 1979–83 (Mem., 1972–77). Chm., Refugee Action, 1981–86. Reported on elections in: Zimbabwe, 1979; (jtly) Guyana, 1980; El Salvador, 1982, 1984, 1988 and 1989; Nicaragua, 1984. *Address:* Quartier des Trois Fontaines, 84490 Vaucluse, France.

CHITTY, Alison Jill; theatre designer; *b* 16 Oct. 1948; *d* of late Ernest Hedley Chitty, Prebendary of St Paul's Cathedral and of Irene Joan Waldron. *Educ:* King Alfred School, London; St Martin's School of Art; Central School of Art and Design (Degree in Theatre Design); Arts Council Scholarship. Victoria Theatre, Stoke-on-Trent, 1970–79 (designed over 40 productions; Head of Design 4 years); designer, 1970–, for *theatre:* Hampstead Theatre, Riverside studios, Sheffield, RSC, NT, Haymarket, Stratford East, Playhouse (Rose Tattoo, 1991; Khovanshchina, 1994); for *opera:* Opera North, Houston Grand Opera, Glyndebourne, Royal Opera House (Gawain, 1991); Opera Theatre, St Louis (The Vanishing Bridegroom, 1992); Gotenborg Music Theatre (Falstaff, 1993); Dallas Opera (Jenufa, 1993); Geneva Opera (Billy Budd, 1994); Santa Fe Opera (Blond Eckbert); for *films:* Blue Jean, Aria, Life is Sweet, 1991; A Sense of History, 1992; Naked, 1993. *Address:* c/o Curtis Brown Group, 4th Floor, Haymarket House, 28/29 Haymarket, SW1Y 4SP.

CHITTY, Dr Anthony; retired; Director of Corporate Engineering, Rolls-Royce Power Engineering Ltd (formerly Northern Engineering Industries, R R Industrial Power Group), 1989–93 (Deputy Director, 1988–89); *b* 29 May 1931; *s* of Ashley George Chitty and Doris Ellen Mary Buck; *m* 1956, Audrey Munro; two *s* one *d*. *Educ:* Glynn Grammar Sch., Epsom; Imperial Coll., London. BSc, PhD, DIC; CEng. GEC Res. Labs, 1955; Hd, Creep of Steels Lab., ERA, 1959; GEC Power Gp, 1963; Chief Metallurgist (Applications), C. A. Parsons, 1966; Dir, Advanced Technol. Div., Clarke Chapman-John Thompson, 1973; Internat. Res. and Develt, 1978; Gen. Manager, Engrg Products, N.E.I. Parsons, 1979; Regional Industrial Adviser, NE Region, DTI, 1984–88. Vis. Prof., Univ. of Aston in Birmingham, 1977–84. Chairman: Bd of Newcastle Technol. Centre, 1988–90 (Dep. Chm., 1985–88); Centre for Adhesive Technol, 1990–93; Member, Board: Newcastle Univ. New Ventures Ltd, 1989–93; Newcastle Polytechnic Products Ltd, 1989–93. *Publications:* research publications in the fields of materials and welding for power generation. *Recreations:* hill walking, gardening. *Address:* 1 Willow Way, Darras Hall, Ponteland, Northumberland NE20 9RJ. *T:* Ponteland (01661) 23899.

CHITTY, (Margaret) Beryl, (Mrs Henry Fowler), CMG 1977; HM Diplomatic Service, retired; *b* 2 Dec. 1917; *d* of Wilfrid and Eleanor Holdgate; *m* 1st, 1949, Keith Chitty, FRCS (*d* 1958); 2nd, 1989, Henry Fowler, CD, Kingston, Jamaica. *Educ:* Belvedere Sch. (GPDST), Liverpool; St Hugh's Coll., Oxford (BA, MA; Hon. Fellow, 1982). Dominions Office, 1940; Private Sec. to Parly Under-Sec. of State, 1943–45; Principal, 1945; CRO, 1947–52; First Sec., Commonwealth Office, 1958; UK Mission to UN, New York, 1968–70; FCO, 1970–71; Dep. (and Acting) British High Comr in Jamaica, 1971–75; Head of Commonwealth Co-ord. Dept, FCO, 1975–77. Appeal Sec., St Hugh's Coll., Oxford, 1978–81; Appeal Dir, St Peter's Coll., Oxford, 1982–88. Non-Press Mem., Press Council, 1978–80. Mem., Governing Body, Queen Elizabeth House, Oxford, 1977–80. *Address:* 79 Bainton Road, Oxford OX2 7AG. *T:* Oxford (01865) 53384.

CHITTY, Susan Elspeth, (Lady Chitty); author; *b* 18 Aug. 1929; *d* of Rudolph Glossop and Mrs E. A. Hopkinson; *m* 1951, Sir Thomas Willes Chitty, Bt, *qv*; one *s* three *d*. *Educ:* Godolphin Sch., Salisbury; Somerville Coll., Oxford. Mem. editorial staff, Vogue, 1952–53; subseq. journalist, reviewer, broadcaster and lecturer. *Publications: novels:* Diary of a Fashion Model, 1958; White Huntress, 1963; My Life and Horses, 1966; *biographies:* The Woman who wrote Black Beauty, 1972; The Beast and the Monk, 1975; Charles Kingsley and North Devon, 1976; Gwen John 1876–1939, 1981; Now to My Mother, 1985; That Singular Person Called Lear, 1988; *non-fiction:* (with Thomas Hinde) On Next to Nothing, 1976; (with Thomas Hinde) The Great Donkey Walk, 1977; The Young Rider, 1979; *edited:* The Intelligent Woman's Guide to Good Taste, 1958; The Puffin Book of Horses, 1975; As Once in May, by Antonia White, 1983; Antonia White: Diaries 1926–1957, vol. I, 1991, vol. II, 1992. *Recreations:* riding, travel. *Address:* Bow Cottage, West Hoathly, Sussex RH19 4QF. *T:* Sharpthorne (01342) 810269.

CHITTY, Sir Thomas Willes, 3rd Bt *cr* 1924; author (as Thomas Hinde); *b* 2 March 1926; *e s* of Sir (Thomas) Henry Willes Chitty, 2nd Bt, and Ethel Constance (*d* 1971), *d* of S. H. Gladstone, Darley Ash, Bovingdon, Herts; *S* father, 1955; *m* 1951, Susan Elspeth (*see* S. E. Chitty); one *s* three *d*. *Educ:* Winchester; University Coll., Oxford. Royal Navy, 1944–47. Shell Petroleum Co., 1953–60. Granada Arts Fellow, Univ. of York, 1964–65; Visiting Lectr, Univ. of Illinois, 1965–67; Vis. Prof., Boston Univ., 1969–70. *Publications: novels:* Mr Nicholas, 1952; Happy as Larry, 1957; For the Good of the Company, 1961; A Place Like Home, 1962; The Cage, 1962; Ninety Double Martinis, 1963; The Day the Call Came, 1964; Games of Chance, 1965; The Village, 1966; High, 1968; Bird, 1970; Generally a Virgin, 1972; Agent, 1974; Our Father, 1975; Daymare, 1980; *non-fiction:* (with wife, as Susan Hinde) On Next to Nothing, 1976; (with Susan Chitty) The Great Donkey Walk, 1977; The Cottage Book, 1979; Stately Gardens of Britain, 1983; Forests of Britain, 1985; (ed) The Domesday Book: England's heritage, then and now, 1986; Courtiers: 900 years of court life, 1986; Tales from the Pumproom: an informal history of Bath, 1988; Imps of Promise: a history of the King's School, Canterbury, 1990; Looking Glass Letters, 1991; Paths of Progress: a history of Marlborough College, 1993; A History of Highgate School, 1993; A History of King's College School, 1994; Carpenter's Children: a history of the City of London School, 1995; *autobiography:* Sir Henry and Sons, 1980; *biography:* A Field Guide to the English Country Parson, 1983; Capability Brown, 1986; *anthology:* Spain, 1963. *Heir: s* Andrew Edward Willes Chitty, *b* 20 Nov. 1953. *Address:* Bow Cottage, West Hoathly, Sussex RH19 4QF. *T:* Sharpthorne (01342) 810269.

CHOLERTON, Frederick Arthur, CBE 1978; *b* 15 April 1917; *s* of Frederick Arthur Cholerton and Charlotte (*née* Wagstaffe); *m* 1939, Ethel (*née* Jackson); one *s* decd. *Educ:* Penkhull Secondary Sch., Stoke-on-Trent. Locomotive driver, British Rail, 1934–77; Trade Union work with ASLEF, 1934–71. City of Stoke-on-Trent: Councillor, 1951–87; Leader of Council, 1976–81; Lord Mayor, 1971–72; Staffordshire County Council: Councillor, 1973–89; Vice-Chm., 1973–76; Chm., 1977 and 1981–89; Opposition Leader, 1977–81. Chm., Poplars Resource Management Co. Ltd, 1992–; Director: North Staffordshire South Cheshire Broadcasting (Signal Radio), Ltd, 1982–88; Longton Enterprise Ltd, 1980–87; 1986 Nat. Garden Festival, Stoke-on-Trent, Staffordshire Ltd, 1983–88; W Midlands Industrial Develt Bd, 1983–89; Staffordshire Cable, 1988–. Chairman: Bereavement Care Centre, Potteries and N Staffs, 1988–; Staffs Sports for Disabled Trust, 1992–; Trustee, Central Telephon, 1990–. JP Stoke-on-Trent, 1956–74. MUniv Keele, 1988. *Recreations:* sports, gardening, politics, voluntary work for charities. *Address:* 12 Werburgh Drive, Trentham, Stoke-on-Trent ST4 8JP. *T:* Stoke-on-Trent (01782) 657457.

CHOLMELEY, John Adye, FRCS; Surgeon, Royal National Orthopædic Hospital, 1948–70, Hon. Consulting Surgeon, since 1970; Chairman of Joint Examining Board for Orthopædic Nursing, 1959–83; *b* 31 Oct. 1902; *s* of Montague Adye Cholmeley and Mary Bertha Gordon-Cumming; unmarried. *Educ:* St Paul's Sch.; St Bartholomew's Hosp. MRCS, LRCP 1926; MB, BS London 1927; FRCS 1935; Resident appts St Bart's Hosp., 1928–30; Asst MO: Lord Mayor Treloar Cripples' Hosp., Alton, 1930–32; Alexandra Orth. Hosp., Swanley, 1933–34; Resident Surg. and Med. Supt, Country Br., Royal Nat. Orth. Hosp., Stanmore, 1940–48 (Asst Res. Surg., 1936–39); former Orthopædic Surg., Clare Hall Hosp., Neasden Hosp. Mem. Internat. Soc. of Orthopædic Surgery and Trauma (Société Internationale de Chirurgie Orthopédique et de Traumatologie, SICOT); FRSocMed (Pres. Orthopædic Sect., 1957–58); Fellow Brit. Orth. Assoc. *Publications:* History of the Royal National Orthopaedic Hospital, 1985; articles on orthopædic subjects, particularly tuberculosis and poliomyelitis in med. jls. *Address:* 14 Warren Fields, Valencia Road, Stanmore, Mddx HA7 4JQ. *T:* 0181–954 6920.

CHOLMELEY, Sir Montague (John), 6th Bt *cr* 1806; *b* 27 March 1935; *s* of 5th Bt and Cecilia, *er d* of W. H. Ellice; *S* father, 1964; *m* 1960, Juliet Auriol Sally Nelson; one *s* two *d*. *Educ:* Eton. Grenadier Guards, 1954–64. *Heir: s* Hugh John Frederick Sebastian Cholmeley [*b* 3 Jan. 1968; *m* 1993, Ursula, *d* of H. P. D. Bennett, *qv*]. *Address:* Church Farm, Burton le Coggles, Grantham, Lincs. *T:* Corby Glen (0147684) 329. *Clubs:* White's, Cavalry and Guards.

CHOLMONDELEY, family name of **Marquess of Cholmondeley,** and of **Baron Delamere.**

CHOLMONDELEY, 7th Marquess of, *cr* 1815; **David George Philip Cholmondeley;** DL; Bt 1611; Viscount Cholmondeley (Ire.), 1661; Baron Cholmondeley of Namptwich (Eng.), 1689; Earl of Cholmondeley, Viscount Malpas, 1706; Baron Newborough (Ire.), 1715; Baron Newburgh (Gt Brit.), 1716; Earl of Rocksavage, 1815; Joint Hereditary Lord Great Chamberlain of England (acting for the reign of Queen Elizabeth II); *b* 27 June 1960; *s* of 6th Marquess of Cholmondeley, GCVO, MC and of Lavinia Margaret, *d* of late Col John Leslie, DSO, MC; *S* father, 1990. DL Cheshire, 1992. *Heir: cousin* Charles George Cholmondeley, *b* 18 March 1959. *Address:* Cholmondeley Castle, Malpas, Cheshire.

CHOLMONDELEY CLARKE, Marshal Butler; Master of the Supreme Court of Judicature (Chancery Division), 1973–92; *b* 14 July 1919; *s* of Major Cecil Cholmondeley Clarke and Fanny Ethel Carter; *m* 1947, Joan Roberta Stephens; two *s*. *Educ:* Aldenham. Admitted a solicitor, 1943; Partner, Burton Yeates & Hart, Solicitors, London, WC2, 1946–72. Pres., City of Westminster Law Soc., 1971–72; Mem. Council, Law Soc., 1966–72; Chm., Family Law Cttee, 1970–72; Chm., Legal Aid Cttee, 1972; Chancery Procedure Cttee, 1968–72. *Publication:* The Supreme Court Practice (Chancery ed.), 1985, 1991, 1993. *Recreations:* reading, genealogy. *Address:* 16 Cheyne Court, SW3 5TP. *Club:* Turf.

CHOMSKY, Prof. (Avram) Noam, PhD; Institute Professor, Massachusetts Institute of Technology, since 1976 (Ferrari P. Ward Professor of Modern Languages and Linguistics, 1966–76); *b* Philadelphia, 7 Dec. 1928; *s* of late William Chomsky and of Elsie Simonofsky; *m* 1949, Carol Doris Schatz; one *s* two *d*. *Educ:* Central High Sch., Philadelphia; Univ. of Pennsylvania (PhD); Society of Fellows, Harvard, 1951–55. Massachusetts Institute of Technology: Asst Prof., 1955–58; Associate Prof., 1958–61; Prof. of Modern Langs, 1961–66. Res. Fellow, Harvard Cognitive Studies Center, 1964–65. Vis. Prof., Columbia Univ., 1957–58; Nat. Sci. Foundn Fellow, Inst. for Advanced Study, Princeton, 1958–59; Linguistics Soc. of America Prof., Univ. of Calif, LA, 1966; Beckman Prof., Univ. of Calif, Berkeley, 1966–67; Vis. Watson Prof., Syracuse Univ., 1982; Lectures: Shearman, UCL, 1969; John Locke, Oxford, 1969; Bertrand Russell Meml, Cambridge 1971; Nehru Meml, New Delhi, 1972; Whidden, McMaster Univ., 1975; Huizinga Meml, Leiden, 1977; Woodbridge, Columbia, 1978; Kant, Stanford, 1979. Member: Nat. Acad. of Scis; Amer. Acad. of Arts and Scis; Linguistic Soc. of America; Amer. Philosophical Assoc.; Bertrand Russell Peace Foundn; Utrecht Soc. of Arts and Scis; Deutsche Akademie der Naturforscher Leopoldina; Corresp. Mem., British Acad., 1974; Hon. Mem., Ges. für Sprachwissenschaft, Germany, 1990. Fellow, Amer. Assoc. for Advancement of Science; William James Fellow, Amer. Psychological Assoc., 1990. Hon. FBPsS; Hon. FRAI 1990. Hon. DLitt: London, 1967; Visva-Bharati, West Bengal, 1980; Hon. DHL: Chicago, 1967; Loyola Univ., Chicago, 1970; Swarthmore Coll., 1970; Bard Coll., 1971; Delhi, 1972; Massachusetts, 1973; Pennsylvania, 1985; Maine, 1992; Gettysburg Coll., 1992; Distinguished Scientific Contribution Award, Amer. Psychological Assoc., 1984; Kyoto

Prize in Basic Science, Inamori Foundn, 1988; Orwell Award, Nat. Council of Teachers of English, 1987, 1989; Killian Award, MIT, 1992; Lannan Literary Award, for non-fiction, 1992; Homer Smith Award, New York Univ. Sch. of Medicine, 1994; Loyola Mellon Humanities Award, Loyola Univ., Chicago, 1994. *Publications:* Syntactic Structures, 1957; Current Issues in Linguistic Theory, 1964; Aspects of the Theory of Syntax, 1965; Cartesian Linguistics, 1966; Topics in the Theory of Generative Grammar, 1966; Language and Mind, 1968; (with Morris Halle) Sound Pattern of English, 1968; American Power and the New Mandarins, 1969; At War with Asia, 1970; Problems of Knowledge and Freedom, 1971; Studies on Semantics in Generative Grammar, 1972; For Reasons of State, 1973; The Backroom Boys, 1973; Peace in the Middle East?, 1974; (with Edward Herman) Bains de Sang, 1974; Reflections on Language, 1975; The Logical Structure of Linguistic Theory, 1975; Essays on Form and Interpretation, 1977; Human Rights and American Foreign Policy, 1978; Language and Responsibility, 1979; (with Edward Herman) Political Economy of Human Rights, 1979; Rules and Representations, 1980; Radical Priorities, 1981; Lectures on Government and Binding, 1981; Towards a New Cold War, 1982; Some Concepts and Consequences of the Theory of Government and Binding, 1982; Fateful Triangle: the United States, Israel and the Palestinians, 1983; Modular Approaches to the Study of the Mind, 1984; Turning the Tide, 1985; Barriers, 1986; Pirates and Emperors, 1986; Knowledge of Language: its nature, origin and use, 1986; Generative Grammar: its basis, development and prospects, 1987; On Power and Ideology, 1987; Language in a Psychological Setting, 1987; Language and Problems of Knowledge, 1987; The Chomsky Reader, 1987; The Culture of Terrorism, 1988; (with Edward Herman) Manufacturing Consent, 1988; Necessary Illusions, 1989; Deterring Democracy, 1991; Chronicles of Dissent, 1992; Year 501: the conquest continues, 1993; Rethinking Camelot: JFK, the Vietnam war, and US political culture, 1993; Letters from Lexington: reflections on propaganda, 1993; World Orders, Old and New, 1994. *Recreation:* gardening. *Address:* Department of Linguistics and Philosophy, Massachusetts Institute of Technology, 20D-219, 77 Massachusetts Avenue, Cambridge, Mass 02139, USA. *T:* (617) 2537819.

CHOPE, Christopher Robert, OBE 1982; barrister; Consultant, Ernst & Young, since 1992; *b* 19 May 1947; *s* of late His Honour Robert Charles Chope and of Pamela Durell; *m* 1987, Christo Hutchinson; one *s* one *d. Educ:* St Andrew's Sch., Eastbourne; Marlborough Coll.; St Andrews Univ. (LLB Hons). Called to the Bar, Inner Temple, 1972. Mem., Wandsworth Borough Council, 1974–83; Chm., Housing Cttee, 1978–79; Leader of Council, 1979–83. MP (C) Southampton, Itchen, 1983–92; contested (C) Southampton, Itchen, 1992. PPS to Minister of State, HM Treasury, 1986; Parly Under-Sec. of State, DoE, 1986–90; Parly Under-Sec. of State (Minister for Roads and Traffic), Dept of Transport, 1990–92. Jt Sec., Cons. Backbench Environment Cttee, 1983–86; Mem., Select Cttee on Procedure, 1984–86. Member: HSC, 1993–; Local Govt Commn for England, 1994–. Mem. Exec. Cttee, Soc. of Cons. Lawyers, 1983–86. *Address:* 63 Roupell Street, Waterloo, SE1 8SS. *T:* 0171–633 9129. *Clubs:* Royal Southampton Yacht; Bitterne Conservative.

CHORLEY, family name of **Baron Chorley.**

CHORLEY, 2nd Baron *cr* 1945, of Kendal; **Roger Richard Edward Chorley,** FCA; Chairman, National Trust, since 1991; *b* 14 Aug. 1930; *er s* of 1st Baron Chorley, QC, and Katharine Campbell (*d* 1986), *d* of late Edward Hopkinson, DSc; *S* father, 1978; *m* 1964, Ann, *d* of late A. S. Debenham; two *s. Educ:* Stowe Sch.; Gonville and Caius Coll., Cambridge (BA). Pres., CU Mountaineering Club. Expedns to Himalayas, 1954 (Rakaposhi), 1957 (Nepal); joined Cooper Brothers & Co. (later Coopers & Lybrand), 1955; New York office, 1959–60; Pakistan (Indus Basin Project), 1961; Partner, 1967–89; Hon. Sec., Climbers Club, 1963–67; seconded to Nat. Bd for Prices and Incomes as accounting adviser, 1965–68; Mem. Management Cttee, Mount Everest Foundn, 1968–70; Visiting Prof., Dept of Management Sciences, Imperial Coll. of Science and Technology, Univ. of London, 1979–82. Dep. Chm., British Council, 1990– (Mem. Bd, 1981–). National Trust: Member: Finance Cttee, 1970–90; Exec. Cttee, 1989–; Council, 1989–. Member: Royal Commn on the Press, 1974–77; Finance Act 1960 Tribunal, 1974–79; Ordnance Survey Rev. Cttee, 1978–79; British Council Rev. Cttee, 1979–80; Nat. Theatre Bd, 1980–91; Top Salaries Review Body, 1981–90; Ordnance Survey Adv. Bd, 1983–85; H of L Select Cttee on Sci. and Technology, 1983, 1987, 1988, 1989, 1993, 1994, and Select Cttee on Sustainable Devlt, 1994–95; NERC, 1988–94; Council, City and Guilds of London Inst., 1977–90; Council, RGS, 1984– (Pres., 1987–90); Council, RSA, 1987–89; Chm., Cttee into Handling of Geographic Information, 1985–87. Pres., Alpine Club, 1983–85. Hon. Fellow, Central Lancs Univ., 1993. Hon. DSc: Reading, 1990; Kingston, 1992. *Recreation:* mountains. *Heir: s* Hon. Nicholas Rupert Debenham Chorley, *b* 15 July 1966. *Address:* House of Lords, SW1A 0PW. *Club:* Alpine.

CHORLEY, Prof. Richard John; Professor of Geography, University of Cambridge, 1974–94, now Emeritus; Fellow of Sidney Sussex College, Cambridge, 1962–94, now Emeritus (Vice-Master, 1990–93); *b* 4 Sept. 1927; *s* of Walter Joseph Chorley and Ellen Mary Chorley; *m* 1965, Rosemary Joan Macdonald More; one *s* one *d. Educ:* Minehead Grammar Sch.; Exeter Coll., Oxford. MA (Oxon), ScD (Cantab). Lieut, RE, 1946–48. Fulbright Schol., Columbia Univ., 1951–52; Instructor: in Geography, Columbia Univ., 1952–54; in Geology, Brown Univ., 1954–57; Cambridge University: Demonstrator in Geography, 1958–62; Lectr in Geography, 1962–70, Reader, 1970–74. British rep. on Commn on Quantitative Techniques of Internat. Geographical Union, 1964–68; Dir, Madingley Geog. Courses, 1963–78. First Hon. Life Mem., British Geomorphological Res. Gp, 1974; Corresponding Mem., Italian Geographical Soc. Gill Meml Medal, 1967, Patron's Medal, 1987, RGS; Hons Award, Assoc. of Amer. Geographers, 1981; David Linton Award, 1984. *Publications:* co-author of: The History of the Study of Landforms, Vols I, II and III, 1964, 1973, 1991; Atmosphere, Weather and Climate, 1968, 6th edn 1992; Network Analysis in Geography, 1969; Physical Geography, 1971; Environmental Systems, 1978; Geomorphology, 1984; co-editor of: Frontiers in Geographical Teaching, 1965; Models in Geography, 1967; editor of: Water, Earth and Man, 1969; Spatial Analysis in Geomorphology, 1972; Directions in Geography, 1973; contribs to: Jl of Geology, Amer. Jl of Science, Bulletin of Geolog. Soc. of Amer., Geog. Jl, Geol. Magazine, Inst. of Brit. Geographers, etc. *Recreations:* gardening, theatre, grave renovation. *Address:* 76 Grantchester Meadows, Newnham, Cambridge CB3 9JL.

CHOUFFOT, Geoffrey Charles, CBE 1983 (MBE 1965); Director and Treasurer, St Wilfrid's Hospice (South Coast) Ltd, 1987–93; Deputy Chairman, Civil Aviation Authority, 1980–83, retired; *m* 1941, June Catherine, *d* of Rev. W. Peebles Fleming; one *s* two *d*. Group Director, Safety Services, Civil Aviation Authority, 1978–80. *Club:* Royal Air Force.

CHRÉTIEN, Rt. Hon. Jean, PC (Canada); QC (Canada) 1980; MP (L) Beauséjour, New Brunswick, since 1990; Prime Minister of Canada, since 1993; *b* 11 Jan. 1934; *s* of Wellie Chrétien and Marie Boisvert Chrétien; *m* 1957, Aline Chaîné; two *s* one *d. Educ:* Trois-Rivières; Joliette; Shawinigan; Laval Univ. (BA, LLL). Called to the Bar, and entered Shawinigan law firm of Chrétien, Landry, Deschênes, Trudel and Normand, 1958; Counsel, Lang Michener Lawrence and Shaw, 1986–90; Director: Shawinigan Sen. Chamber of Commerce, 1962; Bar of Trois-Rivières, 1962–63. Govt of Canada: MP (L) St Maurice, 1963–86; Parly Sec. to Prime Minister, 1965, and to Minister of Finance, 1966; Minister of State, 1967; Minister of National Revenue, Jan. 1968; Minister of Indian and Northern Affairs, July 1968; Pres., Treasury Bd, 1974; Minister of Industry, Trade and Commerce, 1976; Minister of Finance, 1977–79; Minister of Justice, responsible for constitutional negotiations, Attorney General, Minister of State for Social Develt, 1980–82; Minister of Energy, 1982–84; Deputy Prime Minister and External Affairs Minister, 1984; External Affairs Critic for official Opposition, 1984–86; Leader of the Opposition, 1990–93. Elected Leader, Liberal Party of Canada, June 1990. Hon LLD: Wilfred Laurier Univ., 1981; Laurentian Univ., 1982; Univ. of W Ontario, 1982; York Univ., Ont., 1986; Univ. of Alberta, 1987; Lakehead Univ., 1988. *Recreations:* skiing, fishing, golf, reading, classical music. *Address:* Office of the Prime Minister, Langevin Block, Parliament Buildings, Ottawa, Ont K1A 0A2, Canada.

CHRIMES, Henry Bertram, DL; Chairman, Liverpool Daily Post and Echo Ltd, 1976–85; *b* 11 March 1915; *s* of Sir Bertram Chrimes, CBE, and Mary (*née* Holder); *m* 1946, Suzanne, *d* of W. S. Corbett-Lowe, Sodylt Hall, Ellesmere; one *s* three *d. Educ:* Oundle; Clare Coll., Cambridge. Served War of 1939–45: RA, India and Burma, Bde Major (despatches). Cooper & Co.'s Stores Ltd, 1945–60 (Man. Dir, 1954–60); Ocean Transport & Trading Ltd, 1960–85 (Dep. Chm., 1971–75); Liverpool Daily Post & Echo Ltd, 1963–85; Member, Liverpool Bd, Barclays Bank Ltd, 1972–83. Member: Council, Univ. of Liverpool, 1951–87 (Pres., 1975–81; Pro-Chancellor, 1981–Nov. 1987); Univ. Authorities Panel, 1976–87; Dir, Univs Superannuation Scheme Ltd, 1980–85; Vice-Pres., Liverpool Sch. of Tropical Medicine, 1981–87; Mem., 1951–, Vice-Pres., 1973–, Liverpool Council of Social Service (Chm., 1964–70); President: Merseyside Pre-Retirement Assoc., 1977–87; Royal Liverpool Seamen's Orphan Instn, 1980–86. DL 1974, High Sheriff 1978–79, Merseyside. Hon. LLD Liverpool, 1987. *Recreations:* books, gardening. *Address:* Bracken Bank, Heswall, Merseyside L60 4RP. *T:* 0151–342 2397. *Clubs:* Reform; Racquet (Liverpool).

See also E. Toulson, R. G. Toulson.

CHRIMES, Neil Roy; Deputy UK Permanent Representative, and Counsellor (Economic and Financial), Organization for Economic Co-operation and Development, Paris, since 1994; *b* 10 June 1954; *s* of Geoffrey Richard Chrimes and Dorothy Enid Chrimes (*née* Wyatt); *m* 1982, Anne Margery Barnes; one *s* one *d. Educ:* Queen Mary's Grammar Sch., Basingstoke; Univ. of Exeter (BA 1975); MIT (SM 1979). Economic Assistant, MAFF, 1975–77; Harkness Fellow, MIT, 1977–79; Sen Economic Assistant, MAFF, 1979–81; Economic Advr, FCO, 1981–87; Economist, Res. Dept, IMF, Washington DC, 1987–89; Sen. Econ. Advr, FCO, 1989–94. *Address:* c/o Foreign and Commonwealth Office, SW1A 2AH. *Club:* MCC.

CHRIST CHURCH, Dublin, Dean of; *see* Salmon, Very Rev. T. N. D. C.

CHRIST CHURCH, Oxford, Dean of; *see* Heaton, Very Rev. E. W.

CHRISTCHURCH, Bishop of, since 1990; **Rt. Rev. David John Coles;** *b* 23 March 1943; *s* of Samuel Arthur and Evelyn Ann Coles; *m* 1970, Ceridwyn Mary Parr; one *s* one *d. Educ:* Auckland Grammar Sch.; Univ. of Auckland (MA Hons 1967); Univ. of Otago (BD 1969; MTh 1971); Univ. of Manchester (PhD 1974); Melbourne Coll. of Divinity (Dip. Religious Educn). Deacon 1968, priest 1969; Curate, St Mark, Remuera, Auckland, 1968–70; Asst Chaplain, Selwyn Coll., Dunedin, 1970–71; Curate, Fallowfield, 1972–73; Chaplain, Hulme Hall, Univ. of Manchester, 1973–74; Vicar of: Glenfield, 1974–76; Takapuna, 1976–80; Examining Chaplain to Bp of Auckland, 1974–80; Dean and Vicar of St John's Cathedral, Napier, dio. Waiapu, 1980–84; Dean of Christchurch and Vicar-General, dio. Christchurch, 1984–90. Pres., Conf. of Churches of Aotearoa–NZ, 1991. *Recreations:* music, ski-ing, tramping. *Address:* Bishop's House, 80 Bealey Avenue, Christchurch 8001, New Zealand. *T:* (3) 3662653.

CHRISTENSEN, Jayne, (Mrs P. L. Christensen); *see* Torvill, J.

CHRISTENSEN, Jens; Commander First Class, Order of the Dannebrog; Hon. GCVO; Ambassador of Denmark to Organization for Economic Co-operation and Development, 1989–91; *b* 30 July 1921; *s* of Christian Christensen and Sophie Dorthea Christensen; *m* 1st, 1950, Tove (*née* Jessen) (*d* 1982); one *s* two *d*; 2nd, 1983, Vibeke Pagh. *Educ:* Copenhagen Univ. (MPolSc 1945). Joined Danish Foreign Service, 1945; Head of Section, Econ. Secretariat of Govt, 1947; Sec. to OECD Delegn in Paris, 1949 and to NATO Delegn, 1952; Hd of Sect., Min. of Foreign Affairs, 1952, Actg Hd of Div., 1954; Chargé d'Affaires *a.i.* and Counsellor of Legation, Vienna, 1957; Asst Hd of Econ.-Polit. Dept, Min. of For. Affairs, 1960; Dep. Under-Sec., 1961; Under-Sec. and Hd of Econ.-Polit. Dept, 1964–71; Hd of Secretariat for Europ. Integration, 1966; Ambassador Extraord. and Plenipotentiary, 1967; State Sec. for Foreign Econ. Affairs, 1971; Ambassador to the Court of St James's, 1977–81; Pres., Danish Oil and Natural Gas Co., 1980–84; Ambassador to Austria, 1984–89. Governor for Denmark, The Asian Development Bank, 1967–73. Knight Grand Cross: Order of Icelandic Falcon; Order of Northern Star, Sweden; Order of St Olav, Norway; Royal Victorian Order; Austrian Order of Honour. *Address:* Strandvejen 647, 2930 Klampenborg, Denmark.

CHRISTIAN, Clifford Stuart, CMG 1971; consultant in environmental matters, retired; *b* 19 Dec. 1907; *s* of Thomas William and Lily Elizabeth Christian; *m* 1933, Agnes Robinson; four *d. Educ:* Univ. of Queensland (BScAgr); Univ. of Minnesota (MS). Officer-in-charge: Northern Australia Regional Survey Section, 1946–50; Land Research and Regional Survey Section, CSIRO, 1950–57; Chief, Div. of Land Research, CSIRO, 1957–60; Mem. Executive, CSIRO, 1960–72. Adviser, Ranger Uranium Environmental Inquiry, 1975–76. Farrer Memorial Medal, 1969. FAIAS; FWA; Fellow, Aust. Acad. of Technological Sciences and Engrg. Hon. DScAgr Queensland, 1978. *Publications:* A Review Report, Alligator Rivers Study (with J. Aldrick), 1977; chapter contribs to books; articles in various pubns mainly concerning natural resources and regional surveying. *Recreation:* photography. *Address:* 6 Baudin Street, Forrest, ACT 2603, Australia. *T:* (62) 952495.

CHRISTIAN, Prof. John Wyrill, FRS 1975; Professor of Physical Metallurgy, Oxford University, 1967–88, now Emeritus; Fellow of St Edmund Hall, Oxford, 1963–93, now Emeritus; *b* 9 April 1926; *e s* of John Christian and Louisa Christian (*née* Crawford); *m* 1949, Maureen Lena Smith; two *s* one *d. Educ:* Scarborough Boys' High Sch.; The Queen's Coll., Oxford. BA 1946, DPhil 1949, MA 1950. Pressed Steel Co. Ltd Research Fellow, Oxford University, 1951–55; Lectr in Metallurgy, 1955–58; George Kelley Reader in Metallurgy, 1958–67. Visiting Prof.: Univ. of Illinois, 1959; Case Inst. of Technology, USA, 1962–63; MIT and Stanford Univ., 1971–72; Hon. Prof., Beijing Univ. of Sci. and Tech., 1987–. Lectures: Williams, MIT, 1971; Hume-Rothery Meml, 1976; Inst. of Metals, AIME, 1981; Campbell Meml, ASM, 1982. Hon. Member: India Materials Res. Soc., 1991–; Japan Inst. of Metals, 1991–. Rosenhain medallist of Inst. of Metals, 1969; Mehl Medallist of AIME, 1981; Platinum Medallist of Metals Soc., 1984; Gold Medallist Acta Metallurgica, 1984. Editor: Progress in Materials Science, 1970–; Jl Less Common Metals, 1976–85. *Publications:* Metallurgical Equilibrium Diagrams (with others), 1952; The Theory of Transformations in Metals and Alloys, 1965, 2nd rev. edn, 1975; contribs to scientific jls. *Address:* 11 Charlbury Road, Oxford OX2 6UT. *T:* Oxford (01865) 58569.

CHRISTIAN, Prof. Reginald Frank; Professor of Russian, St Andrews University, 1966–92, Emeritus Professor 1992; *b* Liverpool, 9 Aug. 1924; *s* of late H. A. Christian and late Jessie Gower (*née* Scott); *m* 1952, Rosalind Iris Napier; one *s* one *d.* *Educ:* Liverpool Inst.; Queen's Coll., Oxford (Open Scholar; MA). Hon. Mods Class. (Oxon), 1943; 1st cl. hons Russian (Oxon), 1949. Commnd RAF, 1944; flying with Atlantic Ferry Unit and 231 Sqdn, 1943–46. FO, British Embassy, Moscow, 1949–50; Lectr and Head of Russian Dept, Liverpool Univ., 1950–55; Sen. Lectr and Head of Russian Dept, Birmingham Univ., 1956–63; Vis. Prof. of Russian, McGill Univ., Canada, 1961–62; Prof. of Russian, Birmingham Univ., 1963–66; Exchange Lectr, Moscow, 1964–65. Mem. Univ. Ct, 1971–73 and 1981–85, Associate Dean, Fac. of Arts, 1972–73, Dean, Fac. of Arts, 1975–78, St Andrews Univ. Pres., British Univs Assoc. of Slavists, 1967–70; Member: Internat. Cttee of Slavists, 1970–75; UGC Atkinson Cttee, 1978–81. *Publications:* Korolenko's Siberia, 1954; (with F. M. Borras) Russian Syntax, 1959, 2nd rev. edn, 1971; Tolstoy's War and Peace: a study, 1962; (with F. M. Borras) Russian Prose Composition, 1964, 2nd rev. edn, 1974; Tolstoy: a critical introduction, 1969; (ed and trans.) Tolstoy's Letters, 2 vols, 1978; (ed and trans.) Tolstoy's Diaries, 2 vols, 1985, abridged edn, Tolstoy's Diaries, 1994; numerous articles and reviews in Slavonic and E European Review, Slavonic and E European Jl, Mod. Languages Review, Survey, Forum, Birmingham Post, Times Lit. Supp., Oxford Slavonic Papers, etc. *Recreations:* fell-walking, violin. *Address:* Culgrianach, 48 Lade Braes, St Andrews KY16 9DA. *T:* (01334) 474407; Scioncroft, Knockard Road, Pitlochry, Perthshire PH16 5HJ. *T:* Pitlochry (01796) 472993.

CHRISTIANSON, Alan, CBE 1971; MC 1945; Deputy Chairman, South of Scotland Electricity Board, 1967–72; retired; *b* 14 March 1909; *s* of Carl Robert Christianson; *m* 1936, Gladys Muriel Lewin, *d* of William Barker; two *d.* *Educ:* Royal Grammar Sch., Newcastle upon Tyne; FCA, CompIEE. Served as Major, RA, 1939–45: comd Field Battery, 1943–45. Central Electricity Bd, 1934–48; Divisional Sec., British Electricity Authority, SW Scotland Div., 1948–55; Dep. Sec., S of Scotland Electricity Bd, 1955–62; Chief Financial Officer, 1962–65; Gen. Man., Finance and Administration, 1965–67. *Recreation:* golf. *Address:* Tynedale, Lennox Drive East, Helensburgh, Dunbartonshire G84 9JD. *T:* Helensburgh (01436) 74503.

CHRISTIE, Ann Philippa; *see* Pearce, A. P.

CHRISTIE, Campbell; General Secretary, Scottish Trades Union Congress, since 1986; *b* 23 Aug. 1937; *s* of Thomas Christie and Johnina Rolling; *m* 1962, Elizabeth Brown Cameron; two *s.* *Educ:* Albert Sen. Secondary Sch., Glasgow. Civil Service, 1954–72: Admiralty, 1954–59; DHSS, 1959–72; Society of Civil and Public Servants, 1972–85: Asst Sec., 1972–73; Asst Gen. Sec., 1973–75; Dep. Gen. Sec., 1975–85. Dir, Scottish Coal Co. Ltd, 1994–. Director: Glasgow Develt Agency, 1991–; Edinburgh Fest. Theatre Trust, 1993–; Falkirk Royal Infirmary NHS Trust, 1994–. Chm., Falkirk FC, 1993–94. *Address:* 31 Dumyat Drive, Falkirk, Stirlingshire FK1 5PA. *T:* Falkirk (01324) 24555.

CHRISTIE, Elizabeth Mary, (Mrs Stuart Christie); *see* Steel, E. M.

CHRISTIE, Sir George (William Langham), Kt 1984; DL; Chairman, Glyndebourne Productions Ltd; *b* 31 Dec. 1934; *o s* of John Christie, CH, MC, and Audrey Mildmay Christie; *m* 1958, Patricia Mary Nicholson; three *s* one *d.* *Educ:* Eton. Asst to Sec. of Calouste Gulbenkian Foundation, 1957–62. Chm. of Glyndebourne Productions, 1956–, and of other family companies. Mem., Arts Council of GB, 1988–92 (Chm., Adv. Panel on Music, 1988–92). Founder Chm., The London Sinfonietta, 1968–88. DL E Sussex, 1983. Hon. FRCM 1986; Hon. FRNCM 1986; Hon. GSM 1991. DUniv Sussex, 1990; Hon. DMus: Keele, 1993; Exeter, 1994. Cavaliere al Merito della Repubblica Italiana, 1977. *Address:* Glyndebourne, Lewes, E Sussex BN8 5UU. *T:* Ringmer (01273) 812250.

CHRISTIE, Herbert; Director, Research Department, European Investment Bank, since 1983; *b* 26 Sept. 1933; *s* of Brig.-Gen. H. W. A. Christie, CB, CMG, and Mary Ann Christie; *m* 1982, Gilberte F. M. V. Desbois; one *s.* *Educ:* Methodist Coll., Belfast; Univ. of St Andrews (MA). Asst Lectr, Univ. of Leeds, 1958–60; Econ. Asst, HM Treasury, 1960–63; First Sec., Washington, DC, 1963–66; Econ. Adviser, J. Henry Schroder Wagg and Co. Ltd, 1966–71, with secondment as Econ. Adviser, NBPI, 1967–71; Sen. Econ. Adviser, Min. of Posts and Telecommunications, 1971–74, and Dept of Prices and Consumer Protection, 1974–76; Econ. Adviser, EEC Commn, Brussels, 1976–78; Under Sec., HM Treasury, 1978–83. *Publications:* contrib. to books and learned jls. *Recreations:* languages, foreign travel. *Address:* c/o European Investment Bank, 100 boulevard Konrad Adenauer, 2950 Luxembourg. *T:* Luxembourg 4379.

CHRISTIE, Ian Leslie, FBA 1994; Visiting Lecturer in Film, Oxford University, and Fellow, Magdalen College, Oxford, since 1995; *b* 23 Feb. 1945; *s* of Robert Christie and late Ethel Christie; *m* 1989, Patsy Nightingale; one *s* three *d.* *Educ:* Belfast Royal Acad.; Queen's Univ., Belfast (BA 1966). Lectr in Complementary Studies, Derby Coll. of Art, 1969–73; Sen. Lectr in Art Hist. and Film Studies, Derby Coll. of Higher Educn, 1973–75; British Film Institute: Regl Prog. Advr, then Hd of Programming, 1976–84; Hd of Distbn, 1984–92; Head of Special Projects, 1993–94; Associate Ed., Sight and Sound, 1995–. Vis. Dir, Film Centre, Art Inst. of Chicago, 1985–86; Vis. Prof., Univ. of S Florida, 1989. Dir, Connoisseur Video, 1990–. Vice-Pres., Europa Cinemas, 1993–; founder Mem., Espace Video Européen, 1990. Mem. Exec. Cttee, GB-USSR Assoc., 1983–89. Frequent radio and television broadcaster on cinema. *Publications:* Powell, Pressburger and Others, 1978; Arrows of Desire: the films of Michael Powell and Emeric Pressburger, 1985, 2nd edn 1994; (ed) The Life and Death of Col Blimp, 1994; The Last Machine, 1995; *edited jointly:* FEKS, Formalism, Futurism, 1978; The Film Factory, 1988, 2nd edn 1994; Eisenstein at 90, 1988; Scorsese on Scorsese, 1989, 2nd edn 1995; Inside the Film Factory, 1991; Eisenstein Rediscovered, 1993, Protazanov and the Continuity of Russian Cinema, 1993; A Matter of Life and Death, 1996. *Recreations:* children, carpentry, photography. *Address:* 131 Mount View Road, N4 4JH. *T:* 0181–348 3656.

CHRISTIE, Prof. Ian Ralph, FBA 1977; Astor Professor of British History, University of London at University College, 1979–84, now Professor Emeritus; Hon. Research Fellow, University College London, since 1984; *b* 11 May 1919; *s* of John Reid Christie and Gladys Lilian (*née* Whatley); *m* 1992, Ann (*née* Hastings). *Educ:* privately; Worcester Royal Grammar Sch.; Magdalen Coll., Oxford, 1938–40 and 1946–48 (MA). Served War, RAF, 1940–46. University Coll. London: Asst Lectr in Hist., 1948; Lectr, 1951; Reader, 1960; Prof. of Modern British History, 1966; Dean of Arts, 1971–73; Chm. History Dept, 1975–79. Ford Lectr, Oxford Univ., 1983–84. Jt Literary Dir, Royal Hist. Soc., 1964–70, Mem. Council, 1970–74. Mem. Editorial Bd, History of Parliament Trust, 1973–. *Publications:* The End of North's Ministry, 1780–1782, 1958; Wilkes, Wyvill and Reform, 1962; Crisis of Empire: Great Britain and the American Colonies, 1754–1783, 1966; (ed) Essays in Modern History selected from the Transactions of the Royal Historical Society, 1968; Myth and Reality in late Eighteenth-century British Politics, 1970; (ed) The Correspondence of Jeremy Bentham, vol. 3, 1971; (with B. W. Labaree) Empire or Independence, 1760–1776, 1976; (with Lucy M. Brown) Bibliography of British History, 1789–1851, 1977; Wars and Revolutions: Britain, 1760–1815, 1982; Stress and Stability in Late Eighteenth Century Britain: reflections on the British avoidance of revolution, 1984; The Benthams in Russia 1780–1791, 1993; British 'Non-élite' MPs 1715–1820, 1995; contrib. to jls. *Recreation:* walking. *Address:* 10 Green Lane, Croxley Green, Herts WD3 3HR. *T:* Rickmansworth (01923) 773008. *Club:* Commonwealth Trust.

CHRISTIE, John Belford Wilson, CBE 1981; Sheriff of Tayside, Central and Fife (formerly Perth and Angus) at Dundee, 1955–83; *b* 4 May 1914; *o s* of late J. A. Christie, Advocate, Edinburgh; *m* 1939, Christine Isobel Syme, *o d* of late Rev. J. T. Arnott; four *d.* *Educ:* Merchiston Castle Sch.; St John's Coll., Cambridge; Edinburgh Univ. Admitted to Faculty of Advocates, 1939. Served War of 1939–45, in RNVR, 1939–46. Sheriff-Substitute of Western Div. of Dumfries and Galloway, 1948–55. Mem., Parole Bd for Scotland, 1967–73; Mem., Queen's Coll. Council, Univ. of St Andrews, 1960–67; Mem. Univ. Court, 1967–75, and Hon. Lectr, Dept of Private Law, Univ. of Dundee. Hon. LLD Dundee, 1977. KCHS 1994 (KHS 1988). *Recreations:* curling, golf. *Address:* Glebe House, Ashlar Lane, Cupar, Fife KY15 5BA. *T:* Cupar (01334) 653999. *Clubs:* New (Edinburgh); Royal and Ancient (St Andrews).

CHRISTIE, John Rankin, CB 1978; Deputy Master and Comptroller of the Royal Mint, 1974–77; *b* 5 Jan. 1918; *s* of Robert Christie and Georgina (*née* Rankin); *m* 1941, Constance May, *d* of Henry Gracie; one *s* two *d.* *Educ:* Ormskirk Gram. Sch.; London Sch. of Economics. Royal Ordnance Factories, 1936–43; Royal Artillery, 1943–47; Min. of Supply, 1947; Admin. Staff Coll., 1949; Air Ministry, 1954; Private Sec. to Ministers of Supply, 1955–57; Asst Sec., 1957; British Defence Staffs, Washington, 1962–65; Under-Sec., Min. of Aviation, 1965–67, Min. of Technology, 1967–70, Min. of Aviation Supply, 1970–71; Asst Under-Sec. of State, MoD, 1971–74. *Recreations:* travel, bird-watching. *Address:* Twitten Cottage, East Hill, Oxted, Surrey RH8 9AA. *T:* Oxted (01883) 713047.

CHRISTIE, Julie (Frances); actress; *b* 14 April 1940; *d* of Frank St John Christie and Rosemary Christie (*née* Ramsden). *Educ:* Convent; Brighton Coll. of Technology; Central Sch. of Speech and Drama. *Films:* Crooks Anonymous, 1962; The Fast Lady, 1962; Billy Liar, 1963; Darling, 1964 (Oscar, NY Film Critics Award, Br. Film Academy Award, etc); Young Cassidy, 1964; Dr Zhivago, 1965 (Donatello Award); Fahrenheit 451, 1966; Far from the Madding Crowd, 1966; Petulia, 1967; In Search of Gregory, 1969; The Go-Between, 1971; McCabe and Mrs Miller, 1972; Don't Look Now, 1973; Shampoo, 1974; Heaven Can Wait, 1978; Memoirs of a Survivor, 1981; The Animals Film, 1982; Return of the Soldier, 1982; Heat and Dust, 1983; The Gold Diggers, 1984; Power, 1987; Miss Mary, 1987; The Railway Station Man, 1992; *stage:* Old Times, Wyndham's, 1995. Motion Picture Laurel Award, Best Dramatic Actress, 1967; Motion Picture Herald Award, Best Dramatic Actress, 1967. *Address:* c/o ICM Ltd, 76 Oxford Street, W1R 1RB.

CHRISTIE, Linford, MBE 1990; athlete; *b* Jamaica, 2 April 1960; *s* of James and late Mabel Christie. *Educ:* Wandsworth Tech. Coll. Has competed over 50 times for Great Britain, 1980–. *European indoor championships:* Gold medal (200 m), 1986; Gold medal (60 m), 1988 and 1990; *European championships:* Gold medal (100 m), 1986 and 1990; *Commonwealth Games:* Silver medal (100 m), 1986; Gold medal (100 m), 1990 and 1994; *European Cup:* Gold medals (100 and 200 m), 1987; Gold medal (100 m), 1991, 1992 and 1994; *Olympic Games:* Silver medal (100 m), 1988; Gold medal (100 m), 1992 (British Men's Team Captain); *World indoor championships:* Silver medals (60 and 200 m), 1991; *World Cup:* Silver medal (200 m), 1992; Gold medal (100 m), 1989 and 1992; *World championships:* Gold medal (100 m), 1993; Silver medal (100 m relay), 1993. British and European 100 m record (9.92 seconds), and British 200 m record (20.09 seconds), 1988; British 100 yards record (9.30 seconds), Edinburgh, 1994; European 60 m record (6.47 seconds) and World indoor 200 m record (20.25 seconds), 1995. British Athletics Writers' Assoc., Male Athlete of the Year, 1988 and 1992. Hon. MSc Portsmouth Univ., 1993. *Publication:* Linford Christie (autobiog), 1989. *Address:* Nuff Respect, Rosedale House, Rosedale Road, Richmond, Surrey TW9 2SZ. *T:* 0181–940 0033. *Club:* Thames Valley Harriers.

CHRISTIE, Sir William, Kt 1975; MBE 1970; JP; Lord Mayor of Belfast, 1972–75; a Company Director; *b* 1 June 1913; *s* of Richard and Ellen Christie, Belfast; *m* 1935, Selina (*née* Pattison); one *s* two *d* (and one *s* decd). *Educ:* Ward Sch., Bangor, Northern Ireland. Belfast City Councillor, 1961, High Sheriff of Belfast, 1964–65, Deputy Lord Mayor, 1969; Alderman, 1973–77. JP Belfast, 1951; DL Belfast, 1977. Freeman, City of London, 1975. Salvation Army Order of Distinguished Auxiliary Service, 1973. *Recreations:* travel, walking, boating, gardening.

CHRISTIE, William James; Sheriff of Tayside, Central and Fife at Kirkaldy, since 1979; *b* 1 Nov. 1932; *s* of William David Christie and Mrs Anne Christie; *m* 1957, Maeve Patricia Gallacher; three *s.* *Educ:* Holy Cross Acad., Edinburgh; Edinburgh Univ. LLB. Nat. Service, 1954–56; commnd Royal Scots. Private Practice, 1956–79. Mem. Council, Law Soc. of Scotland, 1975–79; President: Soc. of Procurators of Midlothian, 1977–79; Soc. of Solicitors in the Supreme Court, 1979. *Recreations:* music, reading, shooting. *Address:* Sheriff Court House, Whytescauseway, Kirkcaldy, Fife KY1 1XQ. *Club:* New (Edinburgh).

CHRISTODOULOU, Anastasios, CBE 1978; Secretary-General, Association of Commonwealth Universities, since 1980; Secretary-General (formerly Joint Secretary), UK Commonwealth Scholarship Commission, since 1980; Executive Secretary, Marshall Scholarships Commemoration Commission, since 1980; *b* Cyprus, 1 May 1932; *s* of Christodoulos and Maria Haji Yianni; *m* 1955, Joan P. Edmunds; two *s* two *d.* *Educ:* St Marylebone Grammar Sch.; The Queen's Coll., Oxford (MA). Colonial Administrative Service, Tanganyika (Tanzania), 1956–62; served as District Commissioner and Magistrate. Univ. of Leeds Administration, 1963–68: Asst Registrar, 1963–65; Dep. Sec., 1965–68; Secretary, Open Univ., 1969–80. Chm., Surrey Univ. Centre for Commonwealth and European Educnl Develt, 1990–; Vice-Chm., Commonwealth Inst., 1981–89; Member: Bd of Trustees, Harlow Campus, Meml Univ. of Newfoundland, 1980–; Exec. Cttee, Council for Educn in Commonwealth, 1980–; Fulbright Commn, 1980–; Bd of Trustees, Richmond Coll., London, 1988–; Bd of Govs, Commonwealth of Learning, 1988–93. Member, Court: Exeter Univ., 1980–; Hull Univ., 1980–; RCA, 1980–. FRSA. Hon. Prof., Univ. of Mauritius, 1986; Hon. Vis. Prof., Surrey, 1991. DUniv: Open, 1981; Athabasca, 1981; Hon. LLD Auckland, 1992; Hon. DCL Acadia, 1992. Univ. of Lesotho 50th Anniversary Award for Distinguished Service to African Educn, 1995. *Recreations:* sport, music, bridge; international and Commonwealth relations. *Address:* 246 Lauderdale Mansions, Lauderdale Road, W9 1NQ. *T:* 0171–286 0011. *Club:* Commonwealth Trust.

CHRISTOPHER, Ann, RA 1989 (ARA 1980); RWA; FRBS; sculptor; *b* 4 Dec. 1947; *d* of William and Phyllis Christopher; *m* 1969, Kenneth Cook. *Educ:* Harrow School of Art (pre-Diploma); West of England College of Art (DipAD Sculpture). RWA 1983; FRBS 1992. Prizewinner, Daily Telegraph Young Sculptors Competition, 1971; Arts Council grants, 1973–76. *Exhibitions include:* Oxford Gallery, Oxford, 1973, 1974, 1978; London Group exhibns, 1975, 1977; Park Street Gall., Bristol, 1978, 1980; Dorset County Mus.

and Art Gall. (retrospective), 1989; Victoria Art Gall., Bath, 1992; RWEA, 1992; Royal Academy, Summer Exhibns, 1971–. *Work in Collections:* Bristol City Art Gallery; Contemporary Arts Soc.; Chantrey, London; Glynn Vivian Art Gall., Swansea; RWEA. *Commissions:* 3½m bronze, Tower Bridge Rd, London, 1990; 4½m bronze, Castle Park, Bristol, 1993. *Recreation:* cinema. *Address:* The Stable Block, Hay Street, Marshfield, near Chippenham, Wilts SN14 8PF.

CHRISTOPHER, Anthony Martin Grosvenor, CBE 1984; Chairman, TU Fund Managers Ltd (formerly Trades Union Unit Trust), since 1983 (Director, since 1981); General Secretary, Inland Revenue Staff Federation, 1976–88; *b* 25 April 1925; *s* of George Russell Christopher and Helen Kathleen Milford Christopher (*née* Rowley); *m* 1962, Adela Joy Thompson. *Educ:* Cheltenham Grammar Sch.; Westminster Coll. of Commerce. Articled Pupil, Agric. Valuers, Gloucester, 1941–44; RAF, 1944–48; Inland Revenue, 1948–57; Asst Sec. 1957–60, Asst Gen. Sec. 1960–74, Jt Gen. Sec. 1975, Inland Revenue Staff Fedn; Member: TUC General Council, 1976–89 (Chm., 1988–89); TUC Economic Cttee, 1977–89; TUC Education Cttee, 1977–85; TUC Educn and Training Cttee, 1985–86; TUC Employment Policy and Orgn Cttees, 1985–89; TUC International Cttee, 1982–89; TUC Finance and General Purposes Cttee, 1983–89; TUC Media Working Group, 1979–89 (Chm., 1985–89); TUC Employment Policy and Orgn Cttee, 1979–85; TUC Social Insurance Cttee, 1986–89; Mems Auditor, ICFTU, 1984–. Member: Tax Reform Cttee, 1974–80; Tax Consultative Cttee, 1980–88; Royal Commn on Distribution of Income and Wealth, 1978–79; IBA, 1978–83; Council, Inst. of Manpower Studies, 1984–89; ESRC, 1985–88; GMC, 1989–94. Chm., Tyre Industry EDC, 1983–86; Vice Pres., Building Socs Assoc., 1985–90; Director: Civil Service Building Soc., 1958–87 (Chm., 1978–87); Birmingham Midshires Building Soc., 1987–88; Policy Studies Inst. Council, 1983–91; Member: Bd, Civil Service Housing Assoc., 1958– (Vice-Chm., 1988); Council, NACRO, 1956– (Chm., 1973–); Home Sec.'s Adv. Council for Probation and After-care, 1967–77; Inner London Probation and After-care Cttee, 1966–79; Audit Commn, 1989–; Broadcasting Complaints Commn, 1989–95; Council, 1985–90, Assembly, 1990–, SCF; Chm., Alcoholics Recovery Project, 1970–76; Member: Home Sec.'s Working Party on Treatment of Habitual Drunken Offenders, 1969–71; Inquiry into Rover Cowley Works Closure, 1990. Trustee: Commonwealth Trades Union Council Charitable Trust, 1985–89; Inst. for Public Policy Res., 1989–94 (Treas., 1990–94). Vis. Fellow, Univ. of Bath, 1981–; Mem. Council, Royal Holloway and Bedford New Coll., 1985–89. FRSA 1989. *Publications:* (jtly) Policy for Poverty, 1970; (jtly) The Wealth Report, 1979; (jtly) The Wealth Report 2, 1982. *Recreations:* gardening, reading, walking dogs. *Address:* c/o TU Fund Managers Ltd, Congress House, Great Russell Street, WC1B 3LQ. *Club:* Wig and Pen.

CHRISTOPHER, Colin Alfred; National Secretary, Construction, Furniture, Timber and Allied Section, GMB, since 1993; *b* 6 Nov. 1932; *s* of Alfred and Ivy Christopher; *m* 1952, Mary (*née* Wells); one *s* one *d*. *Educ:* Woodland Secondary Modern Sch., Gillingham, Kent. Apprentice upholsterer, furniture industry, 1947–52. Nat. Service, RAOC, 1952–54. Furniture, Timber and Allied Trades Union: Dist Organiser for Kent/Sussex/Hampshire area, 1968; Nat. Trade Organiser for Soft Furnishing and Bedding Sect., 1978; Gen. Sec., 1986–93. Mem. Bd, FIRA, 1986–; Member: Furniture EDC, 1986–; Exec. Cttee, IFBWW, 1989–. Active Mem, British Labour Party, at Constituency and Nat. Level, 1960–. *Recreations:* gardening, reading, classical music, ballet. *Address:* GMB, 22–24 Worple Road, Wimbledon, SW19 4DD.

CHRISTOPHER, (Duncan) Robin (Carmichael); HM Diplomatic Service; Ambassador to Ethiopia, since 1994; *b* 13 Oct. 1944; *m* 1980, Merril Stevenson; two *d*. FCO, 1970; Second, then First, Sec., New Delhi, 1972; First Sec., FCO, 1976; Hd of Chancery, Lusaka, 1980; First Sec., FCO, 1983; on secondment to Cabinet Office, 1985; Counsellor: Madrid, 1987; FCO, 1991. *Recreation:* family life. *Address:* c/o Foreign and Commonwealth Office, SW1A 2AH.

CHRISTOPHER, John Anthony, CB 1983; BSc; FRICS; Chief Valuer, Valuation Office, Inland Revenue, 1981–84, retired; *b* 19 June 1924; *s* of John William and Dorothy Christopher; *m* 1947, Pamela Evelyn Hardy; one *s* one *d* (and one *s* decd). *Educ:* Sir George Monoux Grammar Sch., Walthamstow; BSc Estate Management (London). Chartered Surveyor; LCC Valuation Dept, 1941. Served War, RAF, 1943–47. Joined Valuation Office, 1952; District Valuer and Valuation Officer, Lincoln, 1965; Superintending Valuer, Darlington, 1972; Asst Chief Valuer, 1974; Dep. Chief Valuer, Valuation Office, Inland Revenue, 1978. *Recreation:* golf. *Address:* 40 Svenskaby, Orton Wistow, Peterborough, Cambs PE2 6YZ. *T:* Peterborough (01733) 238199.

CHRISTOPHER, Robin; *see* Christopher, D. R. C.

CHRISTOPHER, Warren; lawyer; Secretary of State, United States of America, since 1993; *b* 27 Oct. 1925; *s* of Ernest and Catharine Christopher; *m* 1956, Marie Wyllis; three *s* one *d*. *Educ:* Univ. of Southern California; Stanford Law Sch. USNR, 1943–45. Joined O'Melveny and Myers, LA, 1950, partner, 1958–67, 1969–76, 1981–92. Dep. Attorney-Gen., USA, 1967–69; Dep. Sec. of State, 1977–81. US Medal of Freedom, 1981. *Address:* Department of State, 2201 C Street NW, Washington, DC 20520, USA. *T:* (202) 6474000.

CHRISTOPHERS, Richard Henry Tudor, (Harry); conductor; *b* 26 Dec. 1953; *s* of Richard Henry Christophers and Constance Clavering Christophers (*née* Thorp); *m* 1979, Veronica Mary Hayward; two *s* two *d*. *Educ:* Canterbury Cathedral Choir Sch.; King's Sch., Canterbury; Magdalen Coll., Oxford (Mods Classics, BA Music). Founder and Conductor, The Sixteen Choir and Orchestra, 1977–; BBC Prom. concert début, 1990; Salzburg Fest. début, 1989; Lisbon Opera début, 1994; freelance conductor: Scottish Chamber Orch., Avanti!, BBC Philharmonic, City of London Sinfonia, Concertgebouw Chamber Orch., etc. Numerous recordings. Grand Prix du Disque, 1988; Deutschen Schallplattenkritik, 1992 and 1993; Gramophone Award, 1992. *Recreations:* cooking, Arsenal FC. *Address:* c/o Magenta Music International Ltd, 4 Highgate High Street, N6 5JL.

CHRISTOPHERSEN, Henning; a Vice-President, European Commission (formerly Commission of the European Communities), 1985–95; *b* Copenhagen, 8 Nov. 1939; *m* Jytte Christophersen; three *c*. *Educ:* Copenhagen University (graduated in economics, 1965). Head, Economic Div., Danish Fedn of Crafts and Smaller Industries, 1965–70; economics reporter for periodical NB, 1970–71, for weekly Weekendavisen, 1971–78. MP (L) for Hillerød, 1971–85; Nat. Auditor, 1976–78; Minister for Foreign Affairs, 1978–79; Pres., Liberal Party Parly Gp, 1979–82; Dep. Prime Minister and Minister for Finance, 1982–84. Mem., parly finance and budget cttee, 1972–76 (Vice-Chm., 1975); Chm., parly foreign affairs cttee, 1979–81; Mem., Nordic Council, 1981–82. Dep. Leader, Danish Liberal Party, Venstre, 1972–77; Political spokesman of Liberal MPs, 1973–78; Acting Leader, Liberal Party, 1977, Party Leader, 1978–84. Vice-Pres., Fedn of European Liberals and Democrats, 1980–84. *Publications:* books and articles on political and economic subjects. *Address:* Avenue des Biches, 1930 Kraainem, Belgium.

CHRISTOPHERSON, Sir Derman (Guy), Kt 1969; OBE 1946; FRS 1960; FEng 1976; DPhil (Oxon) 1941; MICE, FIMechE; Master, Magdalene College, Cambridge, 1979–85; *b* 6 Sept. 1915; *s* of late Derman Christopherson, Clerk in Holy Orders, formerly of Blackheath, and Edith Frances Christopherson; *m* 1940, Frances Edith (*d* 1988), *d* of late James and Martha Tearle; three *s* one *d*. *Educ:* Sherborne Sch.; University Coll., Oxford (Hon. Fellow, 1977). Henry Fellow at Harvard Univ., 1938; Scientific Officer, Research and Experiments Dept, Ministry of Home Security, 1941–45; Fellow, Magdalene Coll., Cambridge, 1945 (Hon. Fellow 1969), Bursar, 1947; University Demonstrator, Cambridge Univ. Engineering Dept, 1945, Lecturer, 1946; Professor of Mechanical Engineering, Leeds Univ., 1949–55; Prof. of Applied Science, Imperial Coll. of Science and Technology, 1955–60; Vice-Chancellor and Warden, Durham Univ., 1960–78. Mem. Council of Institution of Mechanical Engineers, 1950–53; Clayton Prize, Instn of Mechanical Engineers, 1963. Chairman: Cttee of Vice-Chancellors and Principals, 1967–70; Central Council for Educn and Training in Social Work, 1971–79; CNAA (Chm., Educn Cttee), 1966–74; Board of Washington New Town Develt Corp., 1964–78; SRC, 1965–70; Jt Standing Cttee on Structural Safety, Instns of Civil and Structural Engrs, 1983–88. Member: Council, Royal Soc., 1975; British Library Adv. Council, 1984–; Chm., Royal Fine Art Commn, 1980–85 (Mem., 1978). Fellow, Imperial Coll. of Science and Technology, 1966. Hon. DCL: Kent, 1966; Newcastle, 1971; Durham, 1986; Hon DSc: Aston, 1967; Sierra Leone, 1970; Cranfield Inst. of Technology, 1985; Hon. LLD: Leeds, 1969; Royal Univ. of Malta, 1969; DTech Brunel, 1979. *Publications:* The Engineer in The University, 1967; The University at Work, 1973; various papers in Proc. Royal Soc., Proc. IMechE, Jl of Applied Mechanics, etc. *Address:* c/o 10 Hallam Road, Mapperley, Nottingham NG3 6HA.

CHRISTOPHERSON, Harald Fairbairn, CMG 1978; Commissioner of Customs and Excise, 1970–80, retired; *b* 12 Jan. 1920; *s* of late Captain H. and Mrs L. G. L. Christopherson; *m* 1947, Joyce Winifred Emmett (*d* 1979); one *s* two *d*. *Educ:* Heaton Grammar Sch., Newcastle upon Tyne; King's Coll., Univ. of Durham (BSc and DipEd). Served in RA, 1941–46, Captain 1945. Teacher and lecturer in mathematics, 1947–48. Entered administrative class, Home CS, Customs and Excise, 1948; seconded to Trade and Tariffs Commn, W Indies, 1956–58; Asst Sec., 1959; seconded to Treasury, 1965–66; Under Sec., 1969. Senior Clerk, Committee Office: House of Commons, 1980–85; House of Lords, 1985–86. Mem. Cttee for Southern Region, Nat. Trust, 1986–94. *Recreations:* music, museums and galleries, books, travel. *Address:* 57a York Road, Sutton, Surrey SM2 6HN. *T:* 0181–642 2444. *Club:* Reform.

CHRISTOPHERSON, Romola Carol Andrea; Director of Information, Department of Health (formerly of Health and Social Security), since 1986; *b* 10 Jan. 1939; *d* of Albert Edward Christopherson and Kathleen Christopherson (*née* Marfitt). *Educ:* Collegiate School for Girls, Leicester; St Hugh's College, Oxford (BA Hons English). DSIR, Min. of Technology, 1962; DoE, 1970; Min. of Agriculture, Fisheries and Food, 1978; N Ireland Office, 1981; Dep. Press Sec. to Prime Minister, 1983; Head of Inf., Dept of Energy, 1984. *Recreations:* amateur dramatics, antiques. *Address:* Department of Health, Richmond House, 79 Whitehall, SW1A 2NS.

CHRUSZCZ, Charles Francis; QC 1992; a Recorder, since 1990; *b* 19 Nov. 1950; *s* of Janick Francis Chruszcz and Kathleen Whitehurst Chruszcz; *m* 1972, Margaret Olivia Chapman; three *s*. *Educ:* Queen Mary Coll., London (LLB Hons). Called to the Bar, Middle Temple, 1973; Asst Recorder, 1985. *Recreations:* reading, music, building renovation, the outdoors. *Address:* 28 St John Street Chambers, Manchester M3 4DJ. *T:* 0161–834 8418.

CHUA, Nam-Hai, FRS 1988; Andrew W. Mellon Professor and Head of Laboratory of Plant Molecular Biology, Rockefeller University, since 1981; *b* 8 April 1944; *m* 1970, Suat Choo Pearl; two *d*. *Educ:* Univ. of Singapore (BSc Botany and Biochem.); Harvard Univ. (AM, PhD Biol.). Lectr, Biochem. Dept, Univ. of Singapore, 1969–71; Rockefeller University, Cell Biology Department: Res. Associate, 1971–73; Asst Prof., 1973–77; Associate Prof., 1977–81. Fellow, Acad. Sinica, Taipei, 1988; Associate Fellow, Third World Acad. of Scis, 1988; Hon. Mem., Japanese Biochemical Soc., 1992. *Publications:* Methods in Chloroplast Molecular Biology, 1982; Plant Molecular Biology, 1987; Methods in Arabidopsis Research, 1992; 230 pubns in professional jls. *Recreations:* squash, skiing. *Address:* Rockefeller University, 1230 York Avenue, New York, NY 10021–6399, USA. *T:* (212) 3278126, *Fax:* (212) 3278327.

CHUBB, family name of **Baron Hayter.**

CHUBB, Anthony Gerald Trelawny, FCA; Chairman, Foseco (formerly Foseco Minsep) PLC, 1986–90; *b* 6 April 1928; *s* of Ernest Gerald Trelawny Chubb and Eunice Chubb; *m* 1951, Beryl Joyce (*née* Cross); two *s*. *Educ:* Wylde Green Coll., Sutton Coldfield. FCA 1962 (ACA 1951); ACMA 1956. CBIM 1981. Joined Foundry Services Ltd, 1951; Man. Dir, Foseco UK, 1964–69; Dir, Foseco Ltd, 1966; Man. Dir, Foseco International, 1969–78; Dep. Gp Man. Dir, 1974–79, Gp Man. Dir, 1979–86, Foseco Minsep PLC; Chm., Electrocomponents PLC, 1986–90 (Dep. Chm., 1983–86; Dir, 1980–90). *Recreations:* golf, gardening, reading.

CHUBB, Dr Frederick Basil, MA, DPhil, LittD; Professor of Political Science, 1960–91, now Fellow Emeritus, Trinity College, Dublin; *b* 8 Dec. 1921; *s* of late Frederick John Bailey Chubb and Gertrude May Chubb, Ludgershall, Wilts; *m* 1st, 1946, Margaret Gertrude Rafther (*d* 1984); no *c*; 2nd, 1985, Orla, *d* of Seán and Veronica Sheehan; one *d*. *Educ:* Bishop Wordsworth's Sch., Salisbury; Merton Coll., Oxford. BA 1946; MA Oxon; MA Dublin; DPhil Oxon 1950; LittD Dublin 1976. Lecturer in Political Science, Trinity Coll., Dublin, 1948; Fellow in Polit. Sci., 1952; Reader in Polit. Sci., 1955; Bursar, 1957–62. Chm., Comhairle na n-Ospidéal, 1972–78; Chm., Employer-Labour Conf., 1970–. MRIA 1969. *Publications:* The Control of Public Expenditure, 1952; (with D. E. Butler (ed) and others) Elections Abroad, 1959; A Source Book of Irish Government, 1964, 2nd edn 1983; (ed with P. Lynch) Economic Development and Planning, 1969; The Government and Politics of Ireland, 1970, 3rd edn 1992; Cabinet Government in Ireland, 1974; The Constitution and Constitutional Change in Ireland, 1978; The Politics of the Irish Constitution, 1991; articles in learned jls. *Recreation:* fishing. *Address:* 19 Clyde Lane, Ballsbridge, Dublin 4. *T:* 6684625.

CHUBB, John Oliver, CMG 1976; HM Diplomatic Service, retired; Counsellor, Foreign and Commonwealth Office, 1973–80; *b* 21 April 1920; *s* of Clifford Chubb and Margaret Chubb (*née* Hunt); *m* 1945, Mary Griselda Robertson (marr. diss. 1980); one *s* two *d*. *Educ:* Rugby; Oxford (MA). Served War, Scots Guards, 1940–46. Joined Diplomatic Service, 1946; Beirut, 1947; Bagdad, 1948–49; Canal Zone, 1950–52; Cyprus, 1953; FO, 1954–56; Tokyo, 1957–61; FO, 1961–63; Hong Kong, 1964–66; FO, 1967. Chm., St John's Wood Soc., 1978–83. *Recreations:* reading, spectator sports, golf, gardening, sailing. *Address:* Clayhill House, Clayhill, Beckley, near Rye, East Sussex TN31 6SQ. *T:* Northiam (01797) 252268. *Clubs:* Athenæum, MCC; Rye Golf, Senior Golfers' Society.

CHUMAS, Henry John, CMG 1991; TD 1969; Director General, Directorate General for Customs Union and Indirect Taxation, Commission of the European Communities,

1989–90 (Director, 1986–89); retired; *b* 21 Dec. 1933; *s* of Charles Savel Chumas and Bertha Emily Pratley; *m* 1956, Maureen Audry Collin; one *s* two *d* (and one *d* decd). *Educ:* Ealing Grammar Sch. for Boys; Sch. of Slavonic Studies, Cambridge Univ. Intelligence Corps, TA, 1957–71, Major and Co. Comdr, Intelligence and Security Gp, 1969–71. Immigration Officer, Home Office, 1955–61; HM Customs and Excise: Asst Principal, 1962–64; Principal, 1964–69; Sloan Fellow, London Grad. Sch. of Business Studies, 1969–70; Asst Sec., 1970–73; Dir, Customs Union service, Commn of EC, 1973–86. *Recreation:* ski-ing, sailing. *Address:* Les Peupliers, Chemin Perrey, 27680 Trouville la Haule, France. *T:* 32428831.

CHUNG, Kyung-Wha, Korean Order of Merit; concert violinist; *b* 26 March 1948; *d* of Chun-Chai Chung and Won-Sook (Lee) Chung; *m*; two *s*. *Educ:* Juilliard Sch. of Music, New York. Moved from Korea to New York, 1960; 7 years' study with Ivan Galamian, 1960–67; New York début with New York Philharmonic Orch., 1967; European début with André Previn and London Symphony Orch., Royal Festival Hall, London, 1970. First prize, Leventritt Internat. Violin Competition, NY, 1967. *Address:* c/o Harrison/Parrott Ltd, 12 Penzance Place, W11 4PA.

CHUNG, Sir Sze-yuen, GBE 1989 (CBE 1975; OBE 1968); Kt 1978; PhD; FEng, JP; Founding Chairman, Hong Kong University of Science and Technology, since 1987; Founding Chairman, Hong Kong Hospital Authority, since 1990; Adviser to the Government of People's Republic of China on Hong Kong affairs, since 1992; *b* 3 Nov. 1917; *m* 1942, Nancy Cheung (*d* 1977); one *s* two *d*. *Educ:* Hong Kong Univ. (BScEng 1st Cl. Hons, 1941); Sheffield Univ. (PhD 1951). FEng 1983; FIMechE 1957, Hon. FIMechE 1983; Hon. FHKIE 1976; FIEE (FIProdE 1958); CBIM (FBIM 1978). Consulting engr, 1952–56; Gen. Man., Sonca Industries (now Sonca Products), 1956–60, Man. Dir 1960–77, Chm. 1977–88. Director: China Light & Power Co., 1968–; World Internat. Hldgs, 1983–; Hong Kong Telecommunications, 1988–. Mem., Hong Kong Legislative Council, 1965–74, Sen. Mem., 1974–78; Mem., Hong Kong Exec. Council, 1972–80, Sen. Mem., 1980–88. Chairman: Standing Commn on CS Salaries and Conditions of Service, 1980–88; Hong Kong Provisional Hosp. Authy, 1988–90; Hong Kong Productivity Council, 1974–76; Asian Product. Orgn, 1969–70; Hong Kong Industrial Design Council, 1969–75; Fedn of Hong Kong Industries, 1966–70 (Hon. Life Pres. 1974); Hong Kong Metrication Cttee, 1969–73; Hong Kong–Japan Business Co-operation Cttee, 1983–88; Hong Kong–US Econ. Co-operation Cttee, 1984–88. Founding Chairman: Hong Kong Polytechnic, 1972–86; City Polytechnic of Hong Kong, 1984 (Founding Fellow, 1986). Pres., Engrg Soc. of Hong Kong, 1960–61. LLD (*hc*): Chinese Univ. of Hong Kong, 1983; Sheffield, 1985; DSc (*hc*) Hong Kong Univ., 1976; DEng (*hc*) Hong Kong Polytechnic, 1989; DBA (*hc*) City Polytechnic of Hong Kong, 1989. JP Hong Kong, 1964. Man of the Year, Hong Kong Business Today magazine, 1985. Defence Medal, 1948; Silver Jubilee Medal, 1977; Gold Medal, Asian Productivity Orgn, 1980. Japanese Order of Sacred Treasure (3rd cl.), 1983. *Publications:* contrib. Proc. IMechE, Jl Iron and Steel Inst., and Jl Engrg Soc. of Hong Kong. *Recreations:* swimming, hiking, badminton, windsurfing. *Address:* House 25, Bella Vista, Silver Terrace Road, Clear Water Bay, Kowloon, Hong Kong. *T:* Hong Kong 7610281, 7192857, *Fax:* Hong Kong 7607493, 3580689. *Clubs:* Hong Kong, Royal Hong Kong Jockey, Kowloon Cricket (Hong Kong); Pacific (Kowloon).

CHURCH, Ian David; Editor, Official Report (Hansard), House of Commons, since 1989; *b* 18 Oct. 1941; *s* of John Jasper and Violet Kathleen Church; *m* 1964, Christine Stevenson; one *d*. *Educ:* Roan School. Journalist with Press Association, 1964; The Scotsman, 1966; The Times, 1968; joined Hansard, 1972; Dep. Editor, 1988. Sec., Commonwealth Hansard Editors Assoc., 1990– (Pres., 1989–90). *Recreations:* photography, writing fiction. *Address:* Department of the Official Report, House of Commons, SW1A 0AA.

CHURCH, James Anthony; *see* Church, Tony.

CHURCH, John Carver, CMG 1986; CVO 1988; MBE 1970; HM Diplomatic Service, retired; consultant, human resources, Barcelona, since 1990; *b* 8 Dec. 1929; *s* of Richard Church, CBE, FRSL, and Catherina Church; *m* 1953, Marie-Geneviève Vallette; two *s* two *d*. *Educ:* Cranbrook Sch., Kent; Ecole Alsacienne, Paris; Christ's Coll., Cambridge (MA 1953). Reuters News Agency, 1953–59; Central Office of Information, 1959–61; Commonwealth Relations Office: Information Officer, Calcutta, 1961–65; Foreign and Commonwealth Office: Second Secretary (Commercial) Rio de Janeiro, 1966–69; First Sec. (Information) Tel Aviv, 1969–74; First Sec., News Dept, FCO, 1974–77; Consul (Commercial) Milan, 1977–78; Consul-General: São Paulo, 1978–81; Naples, 1981–86; Barcelona, 1986–89. *Address:* Barón de la Barre 26–28, 08023 Barcelona, Spain. *T:* (3) 2193965; La Métairie, Le Maine, 24510 Ste Alvère, France.

CHURCH, John George, FCA; Managing Director, since 1976, and Chairman, since 1991, Church & Co. plc; *b* 14 May 1936; *s* of Dudley Ross Church and Louise Elizabeth Church; *m* 1965, Rhona Elizabeth Gibson; one *s* one *d*. *Educ:* Stowe Sch. FCA 1959. Mgt Consultant, Annan Impey Morrish, 1961–64; joined Church & Co. plc, 1964: Asst Co. Sec., 1964–67; Co. Sec., 1967–76; Dir, 1968–. Non Executive Director: James Southall and Co. Ltd, 1985–; Start Rite Ltd, 1985–; St Matthew's Hosp. Ltd, 1981–. Pres., British Footwear Mfrs Fedn, 1988–89. Mem., Bd of Mgt, Cordwainers' Coll. Liveryman, Cordwainers' Co., 1958–. FRSA 1995. High Sheriff, Northants, 1993–94. *Recreation:* country pursuits. *Address:* The Old Rectory, Farthingstone, Towcester, Northants NN12 8EZ. *T:* Northampton (01604) 361227. *Club:* Metropolitan (New York).

CHURCH, Judith Ann; MP (Lab) Dagenham, since June 1994; *b* 19 Sept. 1953; *d* of late Edmund Church and of Helen Church; two *s*. *Educ:* Leeds Univ. (BA Hons Maths and Phil.); Huddersfield Poly. (PGCE Technical); Aston Univ. (Postgrad. Dip. Occupational Health and Safety); Thames Valley Coll. (DMS). Teacher, VSO, 1975–77; Process Research, Mars UK, 1979–80; HM Inspector of Factories, HSE, 1980–86; Nat. Health and Safety Officer, MSF, 1986–94. *Recreation:* keeping fit. *Address:* House of Commons, SW1A 0AA.

CHURCH, Prof. Ronald James H.; *see* Harrison-Church.

CHURCH, Tony, (James Anthony Church); Dean of the National Theatre Conservatory, Denver, USA, since 1989; *b* 11 May 1930; *s* of Ronald Frederic and Margaret Fanny Church; *m* 1958, Margaret Ann Blakeney; one *s* two *d*. *Educ:* Hurstpierpoint Coll.; Clare Coll., Cambridge. MA 1954. First perf. as professional, Arts Theatre, London, 1953; frequent television, radio, regional theatre perfs; founder mem., RSC, 1960, and Associate Artist, 1960–; roles there include: Henry IV; Polonius (twice); King Lear; John of Gaunt; Friar Laurence; Ulysses; Pandarus; York in Richard II; Trelawney in Maydays; Horsham in Waste; Director of Nuclear Plant in Sarcophagus; Wizard in Wizard of Oz, 1987; Cymbeline, Gonzalo and Antigonus in the late Shakespeares, NT, 1988. Extensive tours of USA, 1974–: King Lear, 1982; Falstaff (Santa Cruz), 1984; Prospero, Shylock (Colorado), 1987; Denver Center Theatre Company: Scrooge, 1990; Malvolio, 1991; Uncertainty, 1992; The Quick Change Room, King Lear, 1995. Recorded 26 Shakespeare roles, 1956–66. Founder dir, Northcott Theatre, Exeter, 1967–71; Dir of Drama, GSMD, 1982–88; Drama Advr, Hong Kong Govt, 1982–85. Member: Arts Council 1982–85 (Chm., Drama Panel, 1982–85); British Council Drama Cttee, 1985–88. Hon. MA Exeter, 1971. *Recreations:* listening to music, narrowboats, travel. *Address:* 1050 13th Street, Denver, CO 80204, USA. *T:* (303) 8934200; 38 Rosebery Road, N10 2LJ.

CHURCHER, Maj.-Gen. John Bryan, CB 1952; DSO 1944, Bar 1946; retired; Director and General Secretary, Independent Stores Association, 1959–71; *b* 2 Sept. 1905; *s* of late Lieut-Col B. T. Churcher, Wargrave, Berks, and Beatrice Theresa Churcher; *m* 1937, Rosamond Hildegarde Mary (*d* 1993), *y d* of late Frederick Parkin, Truro Vean, Truro, Cornwall; one *s* two *d*; *m* 1995, Mrs Pauline Thompson. *Educ:* Wellington Coll., Berks; RMC Sandhurst. Commissioned DCLI, 1925; Lieut, 1927; Capt. KSLI, 1936; Staff Coll., 1939; served War of 1939–45 (despatches, DSO and Bar); commanded: 1 Bn Hereford Regt, 1942–44; 159 Inf. Bde, 1944–46; 43 Div., 1946; Northumbrian Dist., 1946; 2 Div., 1946; 3 Div., 1946–47; 5 Div., 1947–48; Brig., Imperial Defence Coll., 1948; BGS, Western Command, 1949–51; Chief of Staff, Southern Comd, 1951–54; GOC, 3rd Inf. Div., 1954–57; Dir of Military Training at the War Office, 1957–59; retired, 1959. ADC to King George VI, 1949–52; ADC to the Queen to 1952. *Address:* 34 Oaks Drive, Colchester, Essex CO3 3PS. *T:* Colchester (01206) 574525.

CHURCHHOUSE, Prof. Robert Francis, CBE 1982; PhD; Professor of Computing Mathematics, University of Wales, College of Cardiff (formerly University College, Cardiff), since 1971; *b* 30 Dec. 1927; *s* of Robert Francis Churchhouse and Agnes Howard; *m* 1954, Julia McCarthy; three *s*. *Educ:* St Bede's Coll., Manchester; Manchester Univ. (BSc 1949); Trinity Hall, Cambridge (PhD 1952). Royal Naval Scientific Service, 1952–63; Head of Programming Gp, Atlas Computer Lab., SRC, 1963–71. Vis. Fellow, St Cross Coll., Oxford, 1972–90. Chm., Computer Bd for Univs and Res. Councils, 1979–82; Mem., Welsh Cttee, UFC, 1989–93. Pres., IMA, 1986–87. Hon. DSc South Bank, 1993. KSG 1988. *Publications:* (ed jtly) Computers in Mathematical Research, 1968; (ed jtly) The Computer in Literary and Linguistic Studies, 1976; Numerical Analysis, 1978; papers in math. and other jls. *Recreations:* cricket, astronomy. *Address:* 15 Holly Grove, Lisvane, Cardiff CF4 5UJ. *T:* Cardiff (01222) 750250.

CHURCHILL; *see* Spencer-Churchill.

CHURCHILL, 3rd Viscount *cr* 1902; **Victor George Spencer;** Baron 1815; Investment Manager, Central Board of Finance of the Church of England and Charities Official Investment Fund; Director, CCLA Investment Management Ltd; *b* 31 July 1934; *s* of 1st Viscount Churchill, GCVO, and late Christine Sinclair (who *m* 3rd, Sir Lancelot Oliphant, KCMG, CB); *S* half-brother, 1973. *Educ:* Eton; New Coll., Oxford (MA). Lieut, Scots Guards, 1953–55. Morgan Grenfell & Co. Ltd, 1958–74. Director: Local Authorities' Mutual Investment Trust; Kleinwort Charter Investment Trust; Schroder Split Fund; Foreign & Colonial Income and Growth Investment Trust. *Heir* (to Barony only): Richard Harry Ramsay Spencer [*b* 11 Oct. 1926; *m* 1958, Antoinette Rose-Marie de Charrière; two *s*]. *Address:* 6 Cumberland Mansions, George Street, W1H 5TE.

CHURCHILL, Caryl, (Mrs David Harter); playwright; *b* 3 Sept. 1938; *d* of Robert Churchill and Jan (*née* Brown); *m* 1961, David Harter; three *s*. *Educ:* Trafalgar Sch., Montreal; Lady Margaret Hall, Oxford (BA 1960). Student prodns of early plays, 1958–61; *radio plays:* The Ants, 1962; Lovesick, 1966; Identical Twins, 1968; Abortive, 1971; Not... not... not... not... not enough oxygen, 1971; Schreber's Nervous Illness, 1972; Henry's Past, 1972; Perfect Happiness, 1973; *television plays:* The Judge's Wife, 1972; Turkish Delight, 1973; The After Dinner Joke, 1978; The Legion Hall Bombing, 1978; Crimes, 1981; (with Ian Spink) Fugue, 1987; *stage plays:* Owners, 1972; Moving Clocks Go Slow, 1975; Objections to Sex and Violence, 1975; Light Shining in Buckinghamshire, 1976; Vinegar Tom, 1976; Traps, 1977; (contrib.) Floorshow, 1977; Cloud Nine, 1979; Three More Sleepless Nights, 1980; Top Girls, 1982; Fen, 1983; Softcops, 1983; (collaborator) Midday Sun, 1984; (with David Lan and Ian Spink) A Mouthful of Birds, 1986; Serious Money, 1987; Ice cream, 1989; Hot Fudge, 1989; Mad Forest, 1990; (with Ian Spink and Orlando Gough) Lives of the Great Poisoners, 1991; The Skriker, 1994. *Publications:* Owners, 1973; Light Shining, 1976; Traps, 1977; Vinegar Tom, 1978; Cloud Nine, 1979; Top Girls, 1982; Fen, 1983; Fen and Softcops, 1984; A Mouthful of Birds, 1986; Serious Money, 1987; Plays I, 1985; Plays II, 1988; Objections to Sex and Violence in Plays by Women, vol 4, 1985; Light Shining, 1989; Traps, 1989; Cloud Nine, 1989; Ice cream, 1989; Mad Forest, 1990; Lives of the Great Poisoners, 1992; The Skriker, 1994; anthologies. *Address:* c/o Casarotto Ramsay Ltd, National House, 60–66 Wardour Street, W1V 3HP. *T:* 0171–287 4450.

CHURCHILL, Winston Spencer; MP (C) Davyhulme, Manchester, since 1983 (Stretford, Lancs, 1970–83); author; journalist; *b* 10 Oct. 1940; *s* of late Randolph Frederick Edward Spencer Churchill, MBE and of Hon. Mrs Averell Harriman (*see* Hon. Pamela Harriman); *m* 1964, Mary Caroline, (Minnie), d'Erlanger, *d* of late Sir Gerard d'Erlanger, CBE, Chairman of BOAC; two *s* two *d*. *Educ:* Eton; Christ Church, Oxford (MA). Correspondent in Yemen, Congo and Angola, 1963; Presenter, This Time of Day, BBC Radio, 1964–65; Correspondent: Borneo and Vietnam, 1966; Middle East, 1967; Chicago, Czechoslovakia, 1968; Nigeria, Biafra and Middle East, for The Times, 1969–70; Special Correspondent, China, 1972, Portugal, 1975. Lecture tours of the US and Canada, 1965, 1969, 1971, 1973, 1975, 1978, 1980, 1981, 1984, 1985, 1989, 1990, annually 1992–. Contested Gorton Div. of Manchester in Bye-election, Nov. 1967. PPS to Minister of Housing and Construction, 1970–72, to Minister of State, FCO, 1972–73; Sec., Cons. Foreign and Commonwealth Affairs Cttee, 1973–76; Conservative Party front-bench spokesman on Defence, 1976–78. Member: Select Cttee on Defence, 1983–; Select Cttee on H of C (Services), 1985–86. Vice-Chm., Cons. Defence Cttee, 1979–83; Cons. Party Co-ordinator for Defence and Multilateral Disarmament, 1982–84; Mem. Exec., 1922 Cttee, 1979–85, Treas., 1987–88. Sponsored Motor Vehicles (Passenger Insce) Act 1972, Crown Proceedings (Armed Forces) Act 1987. Pres., Trafford Park Indust. Council, 1971–. Member, Council: Consumers' Assoc., 1990–93; British Kidney Patients Assoc., 1990–. Trustee: Winston Churchill Meml Trust, 1968–; Nat. Benevolent Fund for the Aged, 1974–; Governor, English-Speaking Union, 1975–80; Vice-Pres., British Technion Soc., 1976, Chm., 1994. Hon. Fellow, Churchill Coll., Cambridge, 1969. Hon. FSE 1989. Hon. LLD Westminster Coll., Fulton, Mo, USA, 1972. *Publications:* First Journey, 1964; Six Day War, 1967; Defending the West, 1981; Memories and Adventures, 1989. *Recreations:* tennis, sailing, ski-ing. *Address:* House of Commons, SW1A 0AA. *Clubs:* White's, Buck's, Press.

CHURSTON, 5th Baron *cr* 1858; **John Francis Yarde-Buller;** Bt 1790; *b* 29 Dec. 1934; *s* of 4th Baron Churston, VRD and Elizabeth Mary (*d* 1951), *d* of late W. B. du Pre; *S* father, 1991; *m* 1973, Alexandra Joanna, *d* of A. G. Contomichalos; one *s* two *d*. *Educ:* Eton Coll. 2nd Lt RHG, 1954. *Heir:* *s* Hon. Benjamin Anthony Francis Yarde-Buller, *b* 13 Sept. 1974. *Address:* Yowlestone House, Puddington, Tiverton, Devon EX16 8LN. *T:* Tiverton (01884) 860328. *Clubs:* Buck's, White's.

CHYNOWETH, David Boyd; Chief Executive, Universities Superannuation Scheme Ltd, since 1994; *b* 26 Dec. 1940; *s* of Ernest and Blodwen Chynoweth; *m* 1968, Margaret

Slater; one *s* two *d*. *Educ:* Simon Langton Sch., Canterbury; Univ. of Nottingham (BA). IPFA 1966; FCCA 1983. Public Finance posts with Derbs CC, 1962 and London Borough of Ealing, 1965; Asst County Treas., Flints CC, 1968; Dep. County Treas., West Suffolk CC, 1970; County Treasurer, S Yorks CC, 1973; Dir of Finance, Lothian Regl Council, 1985. Mem. Council, CIPFA, 1983– (Vice Pres., 1991–92; Pres., 1992–93); Mem. Investment Protection Cttee, Nat. Assoc. of Pension Funds; Pres., Assoc. of Public Service Finance Officers, 1981–82. *Recreations:* sailing, photography. *Address:* (office) Richmond House, Rumford Place, Liverpool L3 9FD. *T:* 0151–227 4711. *Club:* Royal Over-Seas League.

CHYNOWETH, Rt. Rev. Neville James, ED 1966; *b* 3 Oct. 1922; *s* of Percy James and Lilian Chynoweth; *m* 1951, Joan Laurice Wilson; two *s* two *d*. *Educ:* Manly High School; Sydney Univ. (MA); Melbourne Coll. of Divinity (BD); Moore Theological Coll. (ThL). Assistant, St Michael's, Sydney, 1950; Rector, Kangaroo Valley, 1951–52; Chaplain, Royal Prince Alfred Hospital, 1952–54; Rector: St John's, Deewhy, 1954–63; St Anne's, Strathfield, 1963–66; All Saints, Canberra, 1966–71; St Paul's, Canberra, 1971–74; Archdeacon of Canberra, 1973–74; Assistant Bishop of Canberra and Goulburn, 1974–80; Bishop of Gippsland, 1980–87. *Address:* 10 Fortitude Street, Red Hill, Canberra, ACT 2603, Australia. *T:* (6) 2397056.

CICUTTO, Francis John; Director and Chief Executive, Clydesdale Bank PLC, since 1994; *b* 9 Nov. 1950; *s* of Francesco Cicutto and Ultima (*née* Margaritta); *m* 1982, Christine Bates; one *s*. *Educ:* Univ. of NSW. Chief Manager, Central Business Dist, Victoria Nat. Australia Bank Ltd, 1986–88; Exec. Vice Pres., Americas, NAB, USA, 1988–89; NAB Australia: Gen. Manager, Credit Bureau, 1989–92; State Manager, NSW and ACT, 1992–94. *Recreations:* Rugby, golf, cricket, theatre. *Address:* Clydesdale Bank PLC, 30 St Vincent Place, Glasgow G1 2HL. *T:* 0141–248 7070. *Clubs:* Union, Killara Golf (Sydney); Ranfurly Castle Golf.

CITARELLA, Victor Thomas; Director of Social Services, City of Liverpool, since 1991; *b* 8 May 1951; *s* of Thomas and Evelyn R. M. Citarella; *m* 1975, Jacqueline Hopley; three *s* one *d*. *Educ:* Sweyne Grammar Sch., Essex; University Coll., Cardiff (BSc Hons Econs 1973, Cert. Social Work 1978). Residential Child Care Officer, S Glamorgan, 1974–80; Team Manager, Hillingdon Social Services, 1980–82; Day and Residential Care Officer, W Sussex, 1982–85; Area Manager, Bristol, Avon, 1985–88; Dep. Dir of Social Services, Liverpool, 1988–91. Pres., Social Care Assoc., 1992. *Address:* Liverpool Social Services Department, 26 Hatton Garden, Liverpool L3 2AW. *T:* 0151–225 3800.

CITRINE, family name of **Baron Citrine.**

CITRINE, 2nd Baron *cr* 1946, of Wembley; **Norman Arthur Citrine,** LLD; solicitor in general practice, retired 1984; author, editor, lecturer, advocate; *b* 27 Sept. 1914; *er s* of 1st Baron Citrine, GBE, PC, and Doris Helen (*d* 1973), *d* of Edgar Slade; *S* father, 1983; *m* 1939, Kathleen Alice (*d* 1993), *d* of George Thomas Chilvers; one *d*. *Educ:* University Coll. Sch., Hampstead; Law Society's Sch., London. Admitted solicitor of Supreme Court (Hons), 1937; LLB (London), 1938; LLD (London), 1993. Articled Clerk, Shaen, Roscoe, Massey & Co., 1934–37. Served War of 1939–45, Lieut RNVR, 1940–46. Legal Adviser to Trades Union Congress, 1946–51; re-entered general legal practice, 1951. Pres., Devon and Exeter Law Soc., 1971. Fellow, Inst. of Diagnostic Engrs, 1990. *Publications:* War Pensions Appeal Cases, 1946; Guide to Industrial Injuries Acts, 1948; Citrine's Trade Union Law, 1950, 3rd edn, 1967; Citrine's ABC of Chairmanship, 1952–82. *Recreations:* yachting, camping, hiking, music, literature, art and numerous creative pursuits. *Heir: b* Dr the Hon. Ronald Eric Citrine [*b* 19 May 1919; *m* 1945, Mary, *d* of Reginald Williams]. *Address:* Casa Katrina, The Mount, Opua, Bay of Islands, New Zealand.

CLAES, Willy; Secretary General, NATO, since 1994; *b* Hasselt, Belgium, 24 Nov. 1938; *m* 1965, Suzanne Meynen; one *s* one *d*. *Educ:* Free Univ., Brussels. Asst Sec., then Provincial Sec., De Voorzorg, 1962–65; Local Councillor, Hasselt, 1964–94; MHR (Socialist), Hasselt, 1968–94; Minister of: Nat. Educn, Flemish Reg., 1972–73; Econ. Affairs, 1973–74 and 1977–79; Deputy Prime Minister and Minister of: Econ. Affairs, 1979–81; Econ. Affairs and Planning and Nat. Educn, 1987; Foreign Affairs, 1992–94. Belgian Socialist Party: Mem., Exec. Cttee, 1965–94; Co-Pres., 1975–77. Numerous decorations from Europe, Mexico and Bolivia. *Publications:* Tussen droom en werkelijkheid: bouwstenen voor en ander Europa, 1979; La Chine et l'Europe, 1980; Livre Blanc de l'Energie, 1980; Quatre Années aux Affaires Economiques, 1980; Elementen voor een nieuw energiebeleid, 1980; Belgie . . . quo vadis?: un conte monderne, 1980; De Derde Weg: beschouwingen over de Wereldcrisis, 1987. *Recreations:* piano music, conducting orchestras. *Address:* NATO, 1110 Brussels, Belgium. *T:* (2) 7284916.

CLAGUE, Joan; Director of Nursing Services, Marie Curie Memorial Foundation, 1986–90; *b* 17 April 1931; *d* of James Henry Clague and Violet May Clague (*née* Johnson). *Educ:* Malvern Girls' Coll.; Guy's Hosp.; Hampstead Gen. Hosp.; Simpson Meml Maternity Pavilion. Asst Regional Nursing Officer, Oxford Regional Hosp. Bd, 1965–67; Principal, then Chief Nursing Officer, St George's Hosp. Bd of Governors, 1967–73; Area Nursing Officer, Merton, Sutton and Wandsworth AHA, 1973–81; Regl Nursing Officer, NE Thames RHA, 1981–86. Pres., Assoc. of Nurse Administrators, 1983–85. Trustee, WRVS Trustees Ltd, 1991–. WHO Fellow, 1969; Smith and Nephew EEC Scholar, 1981. *Recreations:* walking, domestic pursuits. *Address:* 7 Tylney Avenue, SE19 1LN. *T:* 0181–670 5171.

CLAMAGERAN, Alice Germaine Suzanne; Director, School of Social Workers, Centre Hospitalier Universitaire de Rouen, 1942–73; President, International Council of Nurses, 1961–65; *b* 5 March 1906; *d* of William Clamageran, shipowner at Rouen and of Lucie Harlé. *Educ:* Rouen. Nursing studies: Red Cross School of Nurses, Rouen; Ecole Professionnelle d'Assistance aux Malades, Paris. Tutor, Red Cross Sch. for Nurses, Rouen, 1931–42 (leave, for course in Public Health at Florence Nightingale Internat. Foundn, London, 1934–35). War service (6 months), 1939–40. President: Bd of Dirs, Fondation Edith Seltzer (Sanatorium Chantoiseau, Briançon) for Nurses, Social Workers and Medical Auxiliaries; Assoc. Médico-Sociale Protestante de Langue Française; Hon. Pres. Nat. Assoc. of Trained Nurses in France. Hon. Fellow, Royal Coll. of Nursing of UK, 1977. Médaille de Bronze de l'Enseignement Technique, 1960; Officier dans l'Ordre de la Santé Publique, 1961; Chevalier, Légion d'Honneur, 1962. *Address:* Hautonne, 27310 Bourg-Achard, France.

CLANCARTY, 9th Earl of, *cr* 1803; **Nicholas Power Richard Le Poer Trench;** Baron Kilconnel 1797; Viscount Dunlo 1801; Baron Trench (UK) 1815; Viscount Clancarty (UK) 1823; Marquess of Heusden (Kingdom of the Netherlands) 1818; *b* 1 May 1952; *o s* of Hon. Power Edward Ford Le Poer Trench (*d* 1975), *y s* of 5th Earl of Clancarty, and Jocelyn Louise Courtney (*d* 1962); S uncle, 1995. *Educ:* Ashford Grammar Sch.; Plymouth Polytech.; Univ. of Colorado. *Address:* c/o House of Lords, SW1A 0PW.

CLANCHY, Joan Lesley, (Mrs Michael Clanchy); Headmistress, North London Collegiate School, since 1986; *b* 26 Aug. 1939; *d* of Leslie and Mary Milne; *m* 1962, Dr Michael Clanchy; one *s* one *d*. *Educ:* St Leonard's Sch., St Andrews; St Hilda's Coll., Oxford. MA; DipEd. Schoolteacher: Woodberry Down Sch., London, 1962–63; The Park Sch., Glasgow, 1967–76; Headmistress, St George's Sch., Edinburgh, 1976–85. *Address:* 28 Hillfield Road, NW6 1PZ.

CLANCY, His Eminence Cardinal Edward Bede; *see* Sydney, Archbishop of, (RC).

CLANFIELD, Viscount; Ashton Robert Gerard Peel; *b* 16 Sept. 1976; *s* and *heir* of 3rd Earl Peel, *qv*. *Educ:* Ampleforth.

CLANMORRIS, 8th Baron *cr* 1800 (Ire.); **Simon John Ward Bingham,** MA; FCA; *b* 25 Oct. 1937; *s* of 7th Baron Clanmorris and of Madeleine Mary, *d* of late Clement Ebel; *S* father, 1988; *m* 1971, Gizella Maria, *d* of Sandor Zverkó; one *d*. *Educ:* Downside; Queens' College, Cambridge (MA). ACA 1965, FCA 1975. *Heir: cousin* Robert Derek de Burgh Bingham [*b* 29 Oct. 1942; *m* 1969, Victoria Mary, *yr d* of P. A. Pennant-Rea; three *d*]. *Address:* 19 Old Court Place, W8 4PL.

See also Hon. Charlotte Bingham.

CLANWILLIAM, 7th Earl of, *cr* 1776 (Ire.); **John Herbert Meade;** Bt 1703; Viscount Clanwilliam, Baron Gilford 1766; Baron Clanwilliam (UK) 1828; *b* 27 Sept. 1919; 2nd *s* of Adm. Hon. Sir Herbert Meade-Fetherstonhaugh, GCVO, CB, DSO (*d* 1964) (3rd *s* of 4th Earl) and Margaret Ishbel Frances (*d* 1977), *d* of Rt. Rev. Hon. Edward Carr Glyn, DD; *S* cousin, 1989; *m* 1956, Maxine, *o d* of late J. A. Hayden-Scott; one *s* two *d*. *Educ:* RNC Dartmouth. *Heir: s* Lord Gilford, *qv*. *Address:* House of Lords, SW1A 0PW. *Club:* Turf.

CLAPHAM, His Honour Brian Ralph; arbitrator; a Circuit Judge, South East Circuit, 1974–85; *b* 1 July 1913; *s* of Isaac Clapham and Laura Alice Clapham (*née* Meech); *m* 1961, Margaret Warburg; two *s*. *Educ:* Tonbridge Sch.; Wadham Coll., Oxford; University Coll. London (LLB; LLM 1976); BA Open, 1981. FCIArb 1988. Called to Bar, Middle Temple, 1936. Contested (Lab): Tonbridge, 1950; Billericay, 1951, 1955; Chelmsford, 1959. Councillor, Tonbridge and Southborough UDCs, 1947–74; Chm., Tonbridge UDC, 1959–60. Governor, West Kent Coll., 1972–. Freeman of City of London, 1978. *Publications:* legal articles in various jls. *Recreations:* walking and talking.

CLAPHAM, Michael; MP (Lab) Barnsley West and Penistone, since 1992; *b* 15 May 1943; *s* of late Thomas Clapham and of Eva Clapham; *m* 1965, Yvonne Hallsworth; one *s* one *d*. *Educ:* Leeds Polytechnic (BSc); Leeds Univ. (PGCE); Bradford Univ. (MPhil). Miner, 1958–70; Lectr, 1975–77; Dep. Head, Yorks NUM Compensation Dept, 1977–83; Head of Industrial Relations, NUM, 1983–92. *Recreations:* reading, walking, gardening, squash. *Address:* (office) 18 Regent Street, Barnsley, Yorks S70 2HG. *T:* Barnsley (01226) 730692.

CLAPHAM, Sir Michael (John Sinclair), KBE 1973; Chairman: IMI Ltd, 1974–81; BPM Holdings Ltd, 1974–81; *b* 17 Jan. 1912; *s* of late Sir John Clapham, CBE and Lady Clapham, Cambridge; *m* 1935, Hon. Elisabeth Russell Rea (*d* 1994), *d* of 1st Baron Rea of Eskdale; two *s* one *d* (and one *s* decd). *Educ:* Marlborough Coll.; King's Coll., Cambridge (MA). Apprenticed as printer with University Press, Cambridge, 1933–35; Overseer and later Works Man., Percy Lund Humphries & Co. Ltd, Bradford, 1935–38; joined ICI Ltd as Man., Kynoch Press, 1938; seconded, in conseq. of developing a diffusion barrier, to Tube Alloys Project (atomic energy), 1941–45; Personnel Dir, ICI Metals Div., 1946; Midland Regional Man., ICI, 1951; Jt Man. Dir, ICI Metals Div., 1952; Chm. 1959; Dir, ICI, 1961–74, Dep. Chm. 1968–74; served as Overseas Dir; Dir, ICI of Austr. & NZ Ltd, 1961–74; Director: Imp. Metal Industries Ltd, 1962–70; Lloyds Bank Ltd, 1971–82 (Dep. Chm., 1974–80); Grindlay's Bank Ltd, 1975–84; Associated Communications Corp., 1982–88; Heytesbury (UK) Ltd, 1988–90. Mem., General Motors European Adv. Council, 1975–82. Dep. Pres., 1971–72, Pres., 1972–74, CBI. Member: IRC, 1969–71; Standing Adv. Cttee on Pay of Higher Civil Service, 1968–71; Review Body on Doctors' and Dentists' Remuneration, 1968–70; Birmingham Educn Cttee, 1949–56; W Mids Adv. Coun. for Techn., Commercial and Art Educn, and Regional Academic Bd, 1952; Life Governor, Birmingham Univ., 1955 (Mem. Coun., 1956–61); Member: Court, Univ. of London, 1969–85; Govt Youth Service Cttee (Albemarle Cttee), 1958; CNAA, 1964–77 (Chm., 1971–77); NEDC, 1971–76; Pres., Inst. of Printing, 1980–82. Hon. DSc Aston, 1973; Hon. LLD: CNAA, 1978; London, 1984. *Publications:* Printing, 1500–1730, in The History of Technology, Vol. III, 1957; Multinational Enterprises and Nation States, 1975; various articles on printing, personnel management and education. *Recreations:* sailing, cooking. *Address:* 26 Hill Street, W1X 7FU. *T:* 0171–499 1240. *Club:* Royal Yacht Squadron.

See also B. D. Till.

CLAPHAM, Peter Brian, PhD; CEng, FInstP; Director, National Physical Laboratory, since 1990; *b* 3 Nov. 1940; *s* of Wilfred Clapham and Una Frances (*née* Murray); *m* 1965, Jean Margaret (*née* Vigil); two *s*. *Educ:* Ashville Coll., Harrogate; University Coll. London (BSc, PhD). Research in optics and metrology, NPL, 1960–70; Sec., Adv. Cttee on Res. on Measurements and Standards, 1970–71; res. management and head of marketing, NPL, 1972–81; Res. and Technology Policy, DoI, 1981–82; Supt of Div. of Mech. and Optical Metrology, NPL, 1982–84; Dir 1985, Chief Exec. 1989, Nat. Weights and Measures Lab. Member: Presidential Council of Internat. Orgn of Legal Metrology, 1985–90; Chm., W European Legal Metrology Cooperation, 1989–90. Internat. Cttee of Weights and Measures, 1991–. *Publications:* numerous sci. contribs to learned jls. *Recreations:* peregrination, crafts. *Address:* c/o National Physical Laboratory, Teddington, Mddx TW11 0LW.

CLAPP, Captain Michael Cecil, CB 1982; FIMgt; MSI, MNI; RN retired; *b* 22 Feb. 1932; *s* of Brig. Cecil Douglas Clapp, CBE and Mary Elizabeth Emmeline Palmer Clapp; *m* 1975, Sarah Jane Alexander; one *s* two *d*. *Educ:* Chafyn Grove Sch., Salisbury; Marlborough College. Joined Royal Navy, 1950; HMS Norfolk, 1972; Directorate of Naval Plans, MoD, 1974; in Command, HMS Leander, 1977; Jt Maritime Op. Trng Staff, 1979; Commodore, Amphibious Warfare, Staff of Third Flotilla, 1980–83 (South Atlantic Campaign, 1982). Mem., Stock Exchange, 1987–. Governor: Kelly Coll., 1985–; St Michael Sch., Tavistock, 1985–. *Recreations:* sailing, shooting, fishing, skiing, genealogy, country life. *Address:* c/o Lloyds Bank, 234 High Street, Exeter, Devon EX4 3NL.

CLAPPISON, (William) James; MP (C) Hertsmere, since 1992; Parliamentary Under-Secretary of State, Department of the Environment, since 1995; *b* 14 Sept. 1956; *m* 1984, Helen Margherita Carter; one *s* two *d*. *Educ:* St Peter's Sch., York; Queen's Coll., Oxford (Schol.; PPE). Called to the Bar, Gray's Inn, 1981. Contested (C): Barnsley E, 1987; Bootle, May and Nov. 1990. *Recreations:* bridge, walking. *Address:* House of Commons, SW1A 0AA. *Clubs:* Carlton, United Oxford & Cambridge University.

CLARE, Prof. Anthony Ward, MD; FRCPsych; FRCPI; Clinical Professor of Psychiatry, Trinity College, Dublin, and Medical Director, St Patrick's Hospital, Dublin, since 1989; *b* 24 Dec. 1942; *s* of late Bernard Joseph Clare and Mary Agnes (*née* Dunne); *m* 1966, Jane Carmel Hogan; three *s* four *d*. *Educ:* Gonzaga Coll., Dublin; University Coll., Dublin. MB, BCh, BAO 1966, MD 1982; MPhil 1972; FRCPsych 1985 (MRCPsych 1973), FRCPI 1983 (MRCPI 1971). Auditor, Literary and Historical Soc., 1963–64. Internship, St Joseph's Hosp., Syracuse, New York, 1967; psychiatric training, St Patrick's Hosp., Dublin, 1967–69; Psychiatric Registrar, Maudsley Hosp., London, 1970–72, Sen.

Registrar, 1973–75; research worker, General Practice Research Unit, Inst. of Psychiatry, 1976–79, Sen. Lectr, 1980–82; Prof. and Head of Dept of Psychol Medicine, St Bartholomew's Hosp. Med. Coll., 1983–88. Radio series: In the Psychiatrist's Chair, 1982–; All in the Mind, 1988–; TV series: Motives, 1983. *Publications:* Psychiatry in Dissent, 1976, 2nd edn 1980; (ed with P. Williams) Psychosocial Disorders in General Practice, 1979; (with S. Thompson) Let's Talk About Me, 1981; (ed with R. Corney) Social Work and Primary Health Care, 1982; (ed with M. Lader) Psychiatry and General Practice, 1982; In the Psychiatrist's Chair, 1984, new edns 1992, 1995; Lovelaw, 1986; (with S. Milligan) Depression and How To Survive It, 1993. *Recreations:* tennis, broadcasting, theatre, family life. *Address:* 87 Coper's Cope Road, Beckenham, Kent BR3 1NR. *T:* 0181–650 1784; St Patrick's Hospital, PO Box No 136, James's Street, Dublin 8, Ireland; Delville, Lucan, Co. Dublin. *T:* Dublin 6798055. *Club:* Garrick.

CLARE, Herbert Mitchell N.; *see* Newton-Clare.

CLARE, James Paley S.; *see* Sabben-Clare.

CLARE, John Charles; Chief Executive, Dixons Group plc, since 1994; *b* 2 Aug. 1950; *s* of Sidney Charles and Joan Mildred Clare; *m* 1974, Anne Ross; two *s. Educ:* Edinburgh Univ. (BSc Hons Applied Maths). Sales and marketing roles in UK, Switzerland, Denmark, Sweden, Mars Ltd, 1972–82; Business Develt Dir and Marketing Dir, Racing Div., Ladbroke Gp plc, 1982–85; Dixons Group plc, 1985–: Marketing Dir 1985–86, Man. Dir 1986–88, Dixons Ltd; Gp Dir, 1988–92; Man. Dir, Dixons Stores Gp, 1988–92; Gp Man. Dir, 1992–94. *Recreations:* cricket, music, family, Tottenham Hotspur supporter. *Address:* Dixons House, Maylands Avenue, Hemel Hempstead, Herts HP2 7TG. *T:* Hemel Hempstead (01442) 353000.

CLARE, Pauline Ann; Chief Constable of Lancashire, since 1995; *b* 26 July 1947; *d* of Kathleen and Thomas Rostron; *m* 1983, Reginald Stuart Clare; two step *d. Educ:* St Mary's Secondary Modern Sch., Leyland, Lancs; Open Univ. (BA Hons). MIMgt. Lancashire Constabulary: Police Cadet, 1964; Constable to Inspector, Policewomen's Dept, Juvenile Liaison, 1966; Merseyside Police: Inspector Uniform Patrol and Computer Project Team, 1973; Chief Inspector, Uniform Patrol, Community Services Dept, 1983; Supt, Community Services Dept, Sub Divl and Dep. Divl Comd, Sefton, 1987; Chief Supt, Divl Comd, Sefton, 1991; Asst Chief Constable, Crime and Ops, 1992–94; Dep. Chief Constable, Cheshire Constabulary, 1994–95. Police Long Service and Good Conduct Medal, 1988. SSStJ 1985 (Chm., St John Ambulance Assoc., Southport). Hon. Fellow, Univ. of Central Lancashire, 1994. Lancashire Woman of the Year, 1993. *Recreations:* gardening, horse riding, tapestry, reading novels, entertaining at home. *Address:* Lancashire Police HQ, Hutton, Preston PR4 5SB. *Club:* Soroptimist International (Ormskirk).

CLARENDON, 7th Earl of, 2nd *cr* 1776; **George Frederick Laurence Hyde Villiers;** Chairman, 1985–93, and Managing Director, 1962–93, Seccombe Marshall and Campion plc; *b* 2 Feb. 1933; *o s* of Lord Hyde (*d* 1935) and Hon. Marion Féodorovna Louise Glyn, Lady Hyde (*d* 1970), *er d* of 4th Baron Wolverton; *S* grandfather, 1955; *m* 1974, Jane Diana, *d* of late E. W. Dawson; one *s* one *d.* Page of Honour to King George VI, 1948–49; Lieut RHG, 1951–53. *Heir: s* Lord Hyde, *qv. Address:* Soberton Mill, Swanmore, Hants SO3 2QF. *T:* Wickham (01329) 833118.

CLARFELT, Jack Gerald; Chairman, Heathcourt Properties Ltd, since 1987; *b* 7 Feb. 1914; *s* of Barnett Clarfelt and Rene (*née* Frankel); *m* 1948, Baba Fredman; one *s* one *d. Educ:* Grocers' Co. Sch.; Sorbonne. Qualified as Solicitor, 1937; Man. Dir, Home Killed Meat Assoc., 1940–43 and 1945–54; Queen's Royal Surreys, 1943–45; Man. Dir, Fatstock Marketing Corp., 1954–60; Chm., Smithfield & Zwanenberg Gp Ltd, 1960–75; Exec. Dep. Chm., 1975–79, Dir, 1979–83, FMC Ltd. Dir, S. and W. Berisford Ltd, 1973–75; Chm., Linhay Frizzell Insurance Brokers Ltd, 1984–88. Farming, Hampshire. Master, Worshipful Co. of Butchers, 1978. *Recreations:* golf, swimming. *Address:* Linhay Meads, Timsbury, Romsey, Hants SO51 0LA. *T:* Braishfield (01794) 68243. *Clubs:* City Livery, Farmers'.

See also R. E. Rhodes.

CLARIDGE, Prof. Michael Frederick; Professor of Entomology, University of Wales Cardiff (formerly College of Cardiff), since 1989; *b* 2 June 1934; *s* of Frederick William Claridge and Eva Alice (*née* Jeffrey); *m* 1967, Lindsey Clare Hellings; two *s* one *d. Educ:* Lawrence Sheriff Sch., Rugby; Keble Coll., Oxford (MA, DPhil). Lectr in Zoology 1959–74, Sen. Lectr in Zoology 1974–77, Univ. Coll., Cardiff; Reader in Entomology 1977–83, Prof. of Entomology, 1983–88, Head of Sch. of Biol., 1989–94, Univ. of Wales, Cardiff. President: Linnean Soc. of London, 1988–91; Systematics Assoc., 1991–94. *Publications:* chapters in: The Leafhoppers and Planthoppers, 1985; Organization of Communities – Past and Present, 1987; Prospects in Systematics, 1988; papers in Biol Jl of Linnean Soc., Ecological Entomology, Amer. Naturalist. *Recreations:* classical music, cricket, natural history. *Address:* School of Pure and Applied Biology, University of Wales Cardiff, Cardiff CF1 3TL. *T:* Cardiff (01222) 874147.

CLARK; *see* Chichester-Clark.

CLARK; *see* Stafford-Clark.

CLARK, family name of **Baron Clark of Kempston.**

CLARK OF KEMPSTON, Baron *cr* 1992 (Life Peer), of Kempston in the County of Bedfordshire; **William Gibson Clark,** Kt 1980; PC 1990; *b* 18 Oct. 1917; *m* 1944, Irene Dorothy Dawson Rands; three *s* one *d. Educ:* London. Mem., Chartered Association (formerly Association) of Certified Accountants, 1941. Served in Army, 1941–46 (UK and India), Major. Mem. Wandsworth Borough Council, 1949–53 (Vice-Chm. Finance Cttee). Contested (C) Northampton, 1955; MP (C): Nottingham South, 1959–66; East Surrey, 1970–74; Croydon South, 1974–92. Opposition Front Bench Spokesman on Economics, 1964–66, Chairman: Select Cttee on Tax Credits, 1973; Cons. Back bench Finance Cttee, 1979–92. Jt Deputy Chm., Conservative Party Organisation, 1975–77 (Jt Treasurer, 1974–75). Pres., City Gp for Smaller Cos, 1993–. Chm., Anglo-Austrian Soc., 1983–. Hon. Nat. Dir, Carrington £2 million Appeal, 1967–68. Freeman, City of London, 1987. Grand Gold Cross (Austria), 1989; Grand Decoration of Honour in Gold with Star (Austria), 1994. *Recreation:* gardening. *Address:* The Clock House, Box End, Bedford MK43 8RT. *T:* Bedford (01234) 852361; 3 Barton Street, SW1P 3NG. *T:* 0171–222 5759. *Clubs:* Carlton, Buck's.

CLARK, Rt. Rev. Alan Charles; RC Bishop of East Anglia, 1976–94; *b* 9 Aug. 1919; *s* of William Thomas Durham Clark and Ellen Mary Clark (*née* Compton). *Educ:* Westminster Cathedral Choir Sch.; Ven. English Coll., Rome, Italy. Priest, 1945; Curate, St Philip's, Arundel, 1945–46; postgrad. studies, Rome, 1946–48; Doctorate in Theol., Gregorian Univ., Rome, 1948; Tutor in Philosophy, English Coll., Rome, 1948–53, Vice-Rector, 1954–64; Parish Priest, St Mary's, Blackheath, SE3, 1965–69; Auxiliary Bishop of Northampton, 1969–76; Titular Bishop of Elmham, 1969–76. *Peritus* at Vatican Council, 1962–65; Jt Chm., The Anglican/Roman Catholic Internat. Commn, 1969–81 (Lambeth Cross); Chm., Dept for Mission and Unity, Bishops' Conf. of Eng. and Wales, 1984–94; Co-Moderator, Jt Working Group of RC Church and WCC, 1984–. Freeman, City of London, 1969. *Recreation:* music. *Address:* 19 Upgate, Poringland, Norwich NR14 7SH.

CLARK, Rt. Hon. Alan (Kenneth McKenzie), PC 1991; historian; *b* 13 April 1928; *s* of Baron Clark (Life Peer), OM, CH, KCB, CLit, FBA and late Elizabeth Martin; *m* 1958, (Caroline) Jane Beuttler; two *s. Educ:* Eton; Christ Church, Oxford (MA). Household Cavalry (Training Regt), 1946; RAuxAF, 1952–54. Barrister, Inner Temple, 1955. Mem., Inst. for Strategic Studies, 1963. MP (C) Plymouth, Sutton, Feb. 1974–1992. Parly Under Sec. of State, Dept of Employment, 1983–86; Minister for Trade, 1986–89; Minister of State, MoD, 1989–92. Chm., Internal Market Council of EEC Ministers, 1986–87. Mem., RUSI. *Publications:* The Donkeys, A History of the BEF in 1915, 1961; The Fall of Crete, 1963; Barbarossa, The Russo-German Conflict, 1941–45, 1965; Aces High: the war in the air over the Western Front 1914–18, 1973; (ed) A Good Innings: the private papers of Viscount Lee of Fareham, 1974; Diaries, 1993. *Address:* Saltwood Castle, Kent CT21 4QU. *T:* Hythe (01303) 267190. *Clubs:* Brooks's, Pratt's.

CLARK, Alan Richard; HM Diplomatic Service; Counsellor, Foreign and Commonwealth Office, since 1994; *b* 4 Sept. 1939; *s* of George Edward Clark and Norah Ivy Maria Clark (*née* Hope); *m* 1961, Ann Rosemary (*née* Hosford); one *s. Educ:* Chatham House Grammar Sch., Ramsgate. Foreign Office, 1958; HM Forces, 1960–62; FO 1962; served Tehran, 1964–66; Jedda, 1966–68; Second Sec. (Economic), later First Sec., Paris, 1969–71; FCO, 1972–76; Dep. Hd of Mission, Freetown, 1976–80; FCO, 1980–84; secondment (with rank of Counsellor) to Vickers Shipbuilding and Engineering Ltd, 1984–86; Counsellor and Head of Chancery, Bucharest, 1986–89; Consul-Gen., Montreal, 1990–93. *Recreations:* swimming, walking, reading. *Address:* c/o Foreign and Commonwealth Office, SW1A 2AH. *Club:* Commonwealth Trust.

CLARK, Albert William; His Honour Judge Clark; a Circuit Judge, since 1981; *b* 23 Sept. 1922; *s* of William Charles Clark and Cissy Dorothy Elizabeth Clark; *m* 1951, Frances Philippa, *d* of Dr Samuel Lavington Hart, Tientsin; one *s* one *d. Educ:* Christ's Coll., Finchley. War service, 1941–46, Royal Navy. Called to Bar, Middle Temple, 1949; Clerk of Arraigns, Central Criminal Court, 1951–56; Clerk to the Justices, E Devon, 1956–70; Metropolitan Magistrate, 1970–80; Acting Dep. Chm., Inner London QS, 1971; Dep. Circuit Judge, 1972–80. Mem., Central Council of Probation and After-Care Cttees, 1975–81. *Recreations:* fly-fishing, seafishing, walking, travel to remote places. *Address:* Pelham, 45 West Parade, Worthing, West Sussex BN11 5EF. *T:* Worthing (01903) 247472. *Club:* Royal Thames Yacht.

CLARK, Alistair Campbell; WS; Partner, Blackadder Reid Johnston (formerly Reid Johnston Bell & Henderson), Solicitors, Dundee, since 1961; *b* 4 March 1933; *s* of Peter Campbell Clark and Janet Mitchell Scott or Clark; *m* 1960, Evelyn M. Johnston; three *s. Educ:* St Andrews Univ. Admitted solicitor, 1957. WS 1991. Hon. Sheriff, Tayside Central and Fife, 1986–. Mem. Council, Law Soc. of Scotland, 1982–91 (Pres., 1989–90); Dean, Faculty of Procurators and Solicitors, Dundee, 1979–81 (Hon. Mem., 1991). Pres., Dovetail Enterprises. Founder Chm., Broughty Ferry Round Table; Founder Pres., Claverhouse Rotary Club, Dundee. *Recreations:* family, travel, erratic golf. *Address:* (office) 34 Reform Street, Dundee DD1 1RJ. *T:* Dundee (01382) 29222. *Clubs:* New (Edinburgh); Royal and Ancient (St Andrews); Panmure Angus Golf.

CLARK, Brian Robert, FRSL 1985; playwright; *b* 3 June 1932; *s* of Leonard and Selina Clark; *m* (marr. diss.); two *s*; *m* 1990, Cherry Potter. *Educ:* Merrywood Grammar Sch., Bristol; Redland Coll. of Educn, Bristol; Central Sch. of Speech and Drama, London; Nottingham Univ. BA Hons English. Teacher, 1955–61, and 1964–66; Staff Tutor in Drama, Univ. of Hull, 1966–70. Since 1971 has written some thirty television plays, incl. Whose Life Is It Anyway? and The Saturday Party; television film, (with Cherry Potter) House Games; also series: Telford's Change; Late Starter. Stage plays: Whose Life Is It Anyway? (SWET award for Best Play, 1977; filmed, 1982); Can You Hear Me At the Back?, 1978; Campions Interview; Post Mortem; Kipling, London and NY, 1985; The Petition, NY and Nat. Theatre, 1986; (with Kathy Levin) Hopping to Byzantium, Germany 1989, Sydney, Aust., 1990. Founded Amber Lane Press, publishing plays and books on the theatre, 1978. *Publications:* Group Theatre, 1971; Whose Life Is It Anyway?, 1978; Can You Hear Me At the Back?, 1979; Post Mortem, 1979; The Petition, 1986. *Address:* c/o Judy Daish Associates, 83 Eastbourne Mews, W2 6LQ. *T:* 0171–262 1101. *Club:* Garrick.

CLARK, Rt. Rev. Bruce Quinton; *see* Riverina, Bishop of.

CLARK, Charles Anthony, (Tony), CB 1994; Under Secretary, Higher Education, Department for Education and Employment (formerly Department of Education and Science, later Department for Education), since 1989; *b* 13 June 1940; *s* of late Stephen and Winifred Clark; *m* 1968, Penelope Margaret (*née* Brett); one *s* two *d. Educ:* King's Coll. Sch., Wimbledon; Pembroke Coll., Oxford (MA Nat. Sci.). Pressed Steel Co., 1961; Hilger & Watts Ltd, 1962–65; DES, subseq. DFE, 1965–; seconded to UGC, 1971–73; Under Sec., 1982–; Hd of Finance Br. and Prin. Finance Officer, 1987–89. *Recreations:* golf, gardening, travel. *Address:* Department for Education and Employment, Sanctuary Buildings, Great Smith Street, SW1P 3BT.

CLARK, Charles David Lawson; Legal Adviser: Publishers' Association, since 1984; Copyright Licensing Agency, since 1988 (Chairman, 1985–88); General Counsel, International Publishers Copyright Council, since 1990; Copyright Representative, Federation of European Publishers, since 1990; *b* 12 June 1933; *s* of Alec Fulton Charles Clark, CB, and of Mary Clark; *m* 1960, Fiona McKenzie Mill; one *s* three *d. Educ:* Edinburgh Acad.; Jesus Coll., Oxford (Exhibnr; MA). Called to the Bar, Inner Temple, 1960. Second Lieut 4th Regt RHA. Editor: Sweet and Maxwell, 1957–60; Penguin Books, 1960–66; Managing Director: Penguin Educn, 1966–72; Allen Lane the Penguin Press, 1967–69; Dir, LWT (Holdings) Ltd, 1982–84. Chairman: Bookrest, 1975–78; Book Marketing Council, 1979–81; Hutchinson Publishing Group, 1972–80 (Man. Dir, 1972); Chief Exec., Hutchinson Ltd, 1980–84. Member: Book Trade Working Party, 1970–72; Brit. Copyright Council, 1976–79 and 1984– (Treas. 1987–93); Council of Management, CLIP, 1990–94; Council of Management, MIND, the Nat. Assoc. of Mental Health, 1970–79 (Chm. MIND, 1976–79, Vice-Pres., 1980–). *Publications:* (ed) Publishing Agreements, 1980, 4th edn 1993; articles on publishing topics. *Recreations:* music, golf. *Address:* 19 Offley Road, SW9 0LR. *T:* 0171–735 1422. *Clubs:* Groucho, Le Beaujolais.

CLARK, Rt. Hon. Charles Joseph, (Joe); PC (Canada); United Nations Special Representative for Cyprus, since 1993; *b* 5 June 1939; *s* of Charles and Grace Clark; *m* 1973, Maureen McTeer (she retained her maiden name); one *d. Educ:* High River High Sch.; Univ. of Alta (BA History); Univ. of Alberta (MA Polit. Sci.). Journalist, Canadian Press, Calgary Herald, Edmonton Jl, High River Times, 1964–66; Prof. of Political Science, Univ. of Alberta, Edmonton, 1966–67; Exec. Asst to Hon. Robert L. Stanfield, Leader of HM's Loyal Opposition, 1967–70. MP (Progressive C) Rocky Mountain, later Yellowhead, Constituency, 1972–93; Leader of HM's Loyal Opposition, Canada, 1976–79; Prime Minister of Canada, 1979–80; Leader of HM's Loyal Opposition, 1980–83; Sec. of State for External Affairs, 1984–91; Minister for Constitutional Affairs,

1991–93. Pres., Queen's Privy Council for Canada, 1991–. Hon. LLD: New Brunswick, 1976; Calgary, 1984; Alberta, 1985. Alberta Award of Excellence, Alberta Univ., 1983. *Recreations:* riding, reading, walking, film going. *Address:* HQ UNFICYP, POB 1642, Nicosia, Cyprus.

CLARK, Christopher Harvey; QC 1989; a Recorder, since 1986; *b* 20 Dec. 1946; *s* of Harvey Frederick Beckford Clark and Winifred Julia Clark; *m* 1972, Gillian Elizabeth Ann Mullen; one *s* two *d. Educ:* Taunton's Grammar Sch., Southampton; The Queen's Coll., Oxford (BA 1968; MA 1987). Called to the Bar, Gray's Inn, 1969; Mem., Western Circuit, 1969–; Asst Recorder, 1982. Chancellor, dio. of Winchester, 1993–. *Recreations:* amateur dramatics, golf, cricket, gardening, youth club work, local community affairs, ski-ing, writing and producing pantomimes. *Address:* 3 Pump Court, Temple, EC4Y 7AJ. *T:* 0171–353 0711; 31 Southgate Street, Winchester, Hants SO23 9EE. *T:* Winchester (01962) 868161. *Club:* Hampshire (Winchester).

CLARK, David Beatson, CBE 1986; TD 1966; DL; Chairman, Rotherham District Health Authority, 1993–March 1996 (Member, 1985–96); *b* 5 May 1933; *s* of late Alec Wilson Clark, OBE, JP, DSc(Tech) and Phyllis Mary Clark; *m* 1959, Ann Morgan Mudford; two *s* one *d. Educ:* Wrekin College; Keele Univ. (BA Hons Physics and Econs). Beatson Clark: joined 1958; Managing Dir, 1971; Chm. and Managing Dir, 1979; Exec. Chm., 1984–88. Non-Executive Director: Royal Bank of Scotland, 1988–91; Yorkshire Electricity Gp, 1990–94 (Mem., Yorkshire Electricity Bd, 1980–90); Rotherham TEC, 1990–92. President: Rotherham Chamber of Commerce, 1975–76; Sheffield Br., BIM, 1983–86; Glass Manufacturers' Fedn, 1982–83; Mem. Council, Univ. of Sheffield, 1984–. Liveryman, Glass Sellers' Co., 1967; Freeman, Cutlers' Co. in Hallamshire, 1980. DL S Yorks, 1990; High Sheriff, S Yorks, 1992. Hon. Fellow, Sheffield City Polytechnic, 1988. *Address:* Sorrelstan, 154 Moorgate Road, Rotherham, South Yorks S60 3AZ. *T:* Rotherham (01709) 365539. *Club:* Army and Navy.

CLARK, David (George); MP (Lab) South Shields, since 1979; *b* 19 Oct. 1939; *s* of George and Janet Clark; *m* 1970, Christine Kirkby; one *d. Educ:* Manchester Univ. (BA(Econ), MSc); Sheffield Univ. (PhD 1978). Forester, 1956–57; Laboratory Asst in Textile Mill, 1957–59; Student Teacher, 1959–60; Student, 1960–63; Pres., Univ. of Manchester Union, 1963–64; Trainee Manager in USA, 1964; University Lecturer, 1965–70. Contested Manchester (Withington), Gen. Elec. 1966; MP (Lab) Colne Valley, 1970–Feb. 1974; contested Colne Valley, Oct. 1974; Opposition spokesman on Agriculture and Food, 1973–74, on Defence, 1980–81, on the Environment, 1981–86; opposition front bench spokesman on: environmental protection and develt, 1986–87; food, agriculture and rural affairs, 1987–92; defence, disarmament and arms control, 1992–. Pres., Open Spaces Soc., 1979–88. *Publications:* The Industrial Manager, 1966; Colne Valley: Radicalism to Socialism, 1981; Victor Grayson, Labour's Lost Leader, 1985; We Do Not Want The Earth, 1992; various articles on Management and Labour History. *Recreations:* fell-walking, ornithology, watching football, gardening. *Address:* House of Commons, SW1A 0AA.

CLARK, David John; Principal Establishment Officer and Head of Departmental Management Division, Department of Health, since 1994; *b* 20 Sept. 1947; *m* 1970, Caroline Russell; two *s* three *d. Educ:* Univ. of Kent at Canterbury (MA). Department of Health and Social Security, later Departments of Health and of Social Security: Asst Principal, 1969; Principal, 1973; Asst Sec., 1983; Under Sec., 1990; Head of Recruitment Studies Team, OPSS, Cabinet Office, 1994. *Address:* Departmental Management Division, Department of Health, Skipton House, 80 London Road, SE1 6LW.

CLARK, Denis; His Honour Judge Denis Clark; a Circuit Judge, since 1988; *b* 2 Aug. 1943; twin *s* of John and Mary Clark; *m* 1967, Frances Mary (*née* Corcoran); four *d. Educ:* St Anne's RC Primary, Rock Ferry, Birkenhead; St Anselm's Coll., Birkenhead; Sheffield Univ. LLB. Called to the Bar, Inner Temple, 1966; practised Northern Circuit, 1966–88; a Recorder, 1984–88. *Recreations:* medieval history, cricket, theatre. *Address:* c/o The Queen Elizabeth II Law Courts, Derby Square, Liverpool L2 1XA.

CLARK, Derek John, FCIS; Principal, DJC Services, since 1994; *b* 17 June 1929; *s* of Robert Clark and Florence Mary (*née* Wise); *m* 1949, Edna Doris Coome; one *s* one *d. Educ:* Selhurst Grammar Sch., Croydon; SE London Technical Coll. FCIS 1982 (ACIS 1961). National Service, RAF, 1948–49. Corp. of Trinity House, 1949–66; RICS, 1966–71; ICMA, 1971–82; Sec., IStructE, 1982–94. *Recreations:* athletics (until 1961), squash (until 1994). *Address:* 7 Elvington Green, Hayesford Park, Bromley, Kent BR2 9DE. *T:* 0181–460 9055.

CLARK, Desmond; *see* Clark, John Desmond.

CLARK, Lt-Gen. Findlay; *see* Clark, Lt-Gen. S. F.

CLARK, Sir Francis (Drake), 5th Bt *cr* 1886, of Melville Crescent, Edinburgh; *b* 16 July 1924; *yr s* of Sir Thomas Clark, 3rd Bt and Ellen Mercy (*d* 1987), *d* of late Francis Drake; *S* brother, 1991; *m* 1958, Mary (*d* 1994), *yr d* of late John Alban Andrews, MC, FRCS; one *s. Educ:* Edinburgh Acad. RN 1943–46. Dir, Clark Travel Service Ltd, London, 1948–80. *Recreations:* tennis, cricket, music, gardening. *Heir: s* Edward Drake Clark, *b* 27 April 1966. *Address:* Woodend Cottages, Burgh-next-Aylsham, Norfolk NR11 6TS.

CLARK, His Honour (Francis) Leo, QC 1972; a Circuit Judge, 1976–93; Designated Judge and Liaison Judge, Oxford Combined Court Centre, 1983–93; *b* 15 Dec. 1920; *s* of Sydney John Clark and Florence Lilian Clark; *m* 1st, 1957, Denise Jacqueline Rambaud; one *s*; 2nd, 1967, Dr Daphne Margaret Humphreys. *Educ:* Bablake Sch.; St Peter's Coll., Oxford (MA). Called to Bar, Lincoln's Inn, 1947. Dep. Chm., Oxford County QS, 1970; a Recorder of the Crown Court, 1972–76. Hon. Recorder, City of Oxford, 1989–. *Recreations:* music, reading, travel. *Address:* The Ivy House, Charlbury, Oxon OX7 3PX. *Club:* Union (Oxford).

CLARK, Frank, CBE 1991; General Manager, Lanarkshire Health Board, since 1985; *b* 17 Oct. 1946; *m*; two *d.* MHSM 1974; DipHSM 1974. Clerical Trainee, Bd of Mgt for Royal Cornhill and Associated Hosps, 1965–67; Higher Clerical Officer, Kingseat Hosp., 1967–69; Dep. Hosp. Sec., 1969–70, Hosp. Sec., 1970–71, Canniesburn and Schaw Hosps; Dep. Hosp. Sec., Glasgow Royal Infirmary and Sub-Gp, 1971–74; Administrator, Glasgow Royal Infirmary, 1974–77; Greater Glasgow Health Board Eastern District: Asst Dist Administrator, 1977–81; Dist Gen. Administrator, 1981–83; Hamilton and E Kilbride Unit, Lanarkshire Health Board: Dist Administrator, 1983–84; Dir of Admin. Services, June–Sept. 1984; Sec. to Bd, Lanarks Health Bd, 1984–85; Gen. Manager, Lothian Health Bd, May–Dec. 1990. Vis. Prof., Health Fac., Glasgow Caledonian Univ., 1993–. Chairman: W of Scotland Health Service Res. Network, 1990–; Scottish Health Bd Gen. Managers Gp, 1993–; Member: Chief Scientist's Health Service Res. Cttee, 1989–93; Scottish Health Service Adv. Council, 1990–93; Nat. Nursing Strategy Gp, 1990–93; Scottish Overseas Health Support Policy Bd, 1990–; Jt Wkg Gp on Purchasing, 1992–; Scottish Implementation Gp, Jun. Doctors' and Dentists' Hours of Work, 1992–; Scottish Council for Postgrad. Med. and Dental Educn, 1993–; Implementation Gp, Scottish Health Services Mgt Centre, 1993–; Strategy Gp, R&D Strategy for NHS in Scotland, 1994–. Mem. Bd, New Lanarkshire Ltd, 1992–. Mem. Editl Adv. Bd, Health Bulletin, 1993–. *Address:* Ash Lea, 5 Gullane Crescent, Westerwood Green, Cumbernauld G68 0HR.

CLARK, Gerald, CBE 1990; Inspector of Companies, Head of Companies Investigation Branches, Department of Trade and Industry, 1984–90; *b* 18 Sept. 1933; *s* of John George and Elizabeth Clark (*née* Shaw); *m* 1958, Elizabeth McDermott; one *s. Educ:* St Cuthbert's Grammar School, Newcastle upon Tyne. Chartered Secretary. National Health Service, Northumberland Exec. Council, 1949–55; National Coal Board 1955–60; Board of Trade, Official Receiver's Service, 1960–71; Companies Investigation Branch, 1971–79; Official Receiver, High Court of Justice, 1981–83; Principal Examiner, Companies Investigation Branch, 1983–84. Mem., Herts Area Cttee, Sanctuary Housing Assoc., 1990– (Chm., 1992–). *Recreations:* music, photography.

CLARK, Gerald Edmondson, CMG 1989; Secretary General, Uranium Institute, since 1994; *b* 26 Dec. 1935; *s* of Edward John Clark and Irene Elizabeth Ada Clark (*née* Edmondson); *m* 1967, Mary Rose Organ; two *d. Educ:* Johnston Grammar School, Durham; New College, Oxford. MA. HM Diplomatic Service, 1960–93: Foreign Office, 1960; Hong Kong, 1961; Peking, 1962–63; FO, 1964–68; Moscow, 1968–70; FCO, 1970–73; Head of Chancery, Lisbon, 1973–77; Asst Sec., Cabinet Office, 1977–79; seconded to Barclays Bank International, 1979–81; Commercial Counsellor, Peking, 1981–83; FCO, 1984–87; UK Perm. Rep to IAEA, UNIDO, and to UN in Vienna, 1987–92; Sen. DS, RCDS, 1993. Patron, New London Orchestra. *Recreations:* architecture, economics, the spread of scientific thinking. *Address:* c/o Uranium Institute, Bowater House, 68 Knightsbridge, SW1X 7LT. *T:* 0171–225 0303. *Clubs:* Athenæum, Commonwealth Trust.

CLARK, Prof. Gordon Leslie, PhD; Halford Mackinder Professor of Geography, University of Oxford, since 1995; Professorial Fellow, St Peter's College, Oxford, since 1995; *b* 10 Sept. 1950; *s* of Bryan Clark and Florence Lesley Clark (*née* Cowling); *m* 1972, Shirley Anne Spratling; one *s. Educ:* Monash Univ. (BEcon, MA); Univ. of Oxford (MA); McMaster Univ. (PhD 1978). Asst Prof., Harvard Univ., 1978–83; Associate Prof., Univ. of Chicago, 1983–85; Prof., Carnegie Mellon Univ., 1985–91; Monash University: Prof., 1989–95; Hd of Dept, 1990–93; Associate Dean, 1991–94; Actg Dean, 1993–94; Dir, Inst. of Ethics and Public Policy, 1991–95. Nat. Research Council Fellow, US Nat. Acad. of Sci., 1981–82; Fellow, Lincoln Land Inst., 1981–82. FASSA 1993. *Publications:* Interregional Migration, National Policy and Social Justice, 1983; (jtly) State Apparatus, 1984; Judges and the Cities, 1985; (jtly) Regional Dynamics, 1986; Unions and Communities Under Siege, 1989; Pensions and Corporate Restructuring in American Industry, 1993; (ed jtly) Multiculturalism, Difference and Postmodernism, 1993; (ed jtly) Management Ethics, 1995; (ed jtly) Asian Newly Industrialised Economies in the Global Economy, 1996. *Recreations:* walking, reading, holidays. *Address:* School of Geography, University of Oxford, Mansfield Road, Oxford OX1 3TB.

CLARK, Gregor Munro; Assistant Legal Secretary to the Lord Advocate and Scottish Parliamentary Counsel, since 1979; *b* 18 April 1946; *s* of Ian Munro Clark and Norah Isobel Joss; *m* 1974, Jane Maralyn Palmer; one *s* two *d. Educ:* Queen's Park Senior Secondary Sch., Glasgow; St Andrews Univ. (LLB Hons). Admitted Faculty of Advocates, 1972; entered Lord Advocate's Dept, 1974; Asst Parly Draftsman, then Dep. Parly Draftsman, 1974–79. *Recreations:* music, opera, Scandinavian languages and literature. *Address:* 64 Panton Street, Cambridge CB2 1HS. *T:* Cambridge (01223) 350201.

CLARK, Rt. Hon. Helen Elizabeth; PC 1990; MP (Lab) Mount Albert, New Zealand, since 1981; Leader of the Opposition, New Zealand, since 1993 (Deputy Leader, 1990–93); *b* 26 Feb. 1950; *d* of George and Margaret Clark; *m* 1981, Dr Peter Byard Davis. *Educ:* Epsom Girls' Grammar School; Auckland Univ. (BA 1971; MA Hons 1974). Junior Lectr in Political Studies, Auckland Univ., 1973–75; UGC Post Graduate Scholar, 1976; Lectr, Political Studies Dept, Auckland Univ., 1977–81. Minister: of Housing, of Conservation, 1987–89; of Health, of Labour, 1989–90; Dep. Prime Minister, 1989–90. *Recreations:* theatre, music, tennis, reading. *Address:* Parliament House, Wellington, New Zealand. *T:* (4) 4719799.

CLARK, Henry Maitland; journalist and feature writer, Avon Advertiser, since 1989; *b* 11 April 1929; *s* of Major H. F. Clark, Rockwood, Upperlands, Co. Londonderry; *m* 1972, Penelope Winifred Tindal (*d* 1994); one *s* two *d. Educ:* Shrewsbury Sch.; Trinity Coll., Dublin; Trinity Hall, Cambridge. Entered Colonial Service and appointed District Officer, Tanganyika, 1951; served in various Districts of Tanganyika, 1951–59; resigned from Colonial Service, 1959. Wine merchant, IDV Ltd and Cock Russell Vintners, 1972–76; Hd of Information, CoSIRA, 1977–89. MP (UU) Antrim North (UK Parliament), Oct. 1959–1970; Chm. Conservative Trade and Overseas Develt Sub-Cttee; Member: British Delegation to Council of Europe and WEU, 1962–65; Advisory Council Food Law Res. Centre, Univ. of Brussels; Exec. Cttee, Lepra (British Leprosy Relief Assoc.); Select Cttee on Overseas Aid and Develt, 1969–70; Grand Jury, Co. Londonderry, 1970. A Commonwealth Observer, Mauritius General Election, 1967. Vice-Pres., Dublin Univ. Boat Club. *Recreations:* rowing coach, sailing, shooting, golf, collecting old furniture. *Address:* Rockwood, Upperlands, Co. Derry, Northern Ireland BT46 5SB. *T:* Maghera (01648) 42237; Staddles, Hindon Lane, Tisbury, Wilts SP3 6PU. *T:* Tisbury (01747) 870330. *Clubs:* Kildare Street and University (Dublin); Royal Portrush Golf.
See also H. W. S. Clark.

CLARK, (Henry) Wallace (Stuart), MBE 1970; Vice-Lieutenant of County Londonderry, since 1993; Director, Wm Clark & Sons, Linen Manufacturers, since 1972, non-executive Director, since 1987; *b* 20 Nov. 1926; *s* of Major H. F. Clark, MBE, JP, RA, Rockwood, Upperlands, and Sybil Emily (*née* Stuart); *m* 1957, June Elisabeth Lester Deane; two *s. Educ:* Shrewsbury School. Lieut, RNVR, 1945–47 (bomb and mine disposal); Cattleman, Merchant Navy, 1947–48. District Comdt, Ulster Special Constabulary, 1955–70; Major, Ulster Defence Regt, 1970–81. Foyle's Lectr, USA tour, 1964. Led Church of Ireland St Columba commemorative curragh voyage, Derry to Iona, 1963; Dir and Skipper, Lord of the Isles Voyage, Galway to Stornaway in 16th century galley, 1991. Mem., Cttee of Management, RNLI, 1990–. DL 1962, High Sheriff 1969, Co. Londonderry. *Publications:* (jtly) North and East Coasts of Ireland, 1957; (jtly) South and West Coasts of Ireland, 1962, 2nd edn 1970; Guns in Ulster, 1967; Rathlin Disputed Island, 1972; Sailing Round Ireland, 1976; Linen on the Green, 1982; Lord of the Isles Voyage, 1993. *Recreation:* sailing to islands. *Address:* Gorteade Cottage, Upperlands, Co. Londonderry, N Ireland BT46 5SB. *T:* Maghera (01648) 42737. *Clubs:* Royal Cruising, Irish Cruising (Cdre 1962).
See also H. M. Clark.

CLARK, Ian Robertson, CBE 1979; Chairman: Clark & Associates Ltd; C & M (Hydraulics) Ltd; *b* 18 Jan. 1939; *s* of Alexander Clark and Annie Dundas Watson; *m* 1961, Jean Scott Waddell Lang; one *s* one *d. Educ:* Dalziel High Sch., Motherwell. FCCA, IPFA. Trained with Glasgow Chartered Accountant; served in local govt, 1962–76, this service culminating in the post of Chief Executive, Shetland Islands Council; full-time Mem., BNOC, from 1976 until privatisation in 1982; Jt Man. Dir, Britoil plc, 1982–85; Ventures Div., Costain Gp, subseq. Urban Enterprises Ltd, 1987–93. Member: Scottish Economic

Council, 1978–87; Glasgow Univ. Court, 1980–87. Hon. LLD Glasgow, 1979. *Publications:* Reservoir of Power, 1980; contribs to professional and religious periodicals. *Recreations:* theology, general reading, walking. *Address:* 16 Pan's Gardens, Camberley, Surrey GU15 1HY. *T:* Camberley (01276) 685728.

CLARK, James Leonard; Under Secretary, Establishment Personnel Division, Departments of Industry and Trade Common Services, 1980–83 (Under Secretary, Department of Trade, 1978–80); *b* 8 Jan. 1923; *s* of James Alfred and Grace Clark; *m* 1954, Joan Pauline Richards (*d* 1992). *Educ:* Mercers' School. Lieut (A), Fleet Air Arm, 1942–46. Clerical Officer, HM Treasury, 1939; Private Sec. to successive First Secs of State, 1964–67; Cabinet Office, 1969–71; Asst Sec., Price Commn, 1973–75; Dept of Industry, 1975–78. CBI, 1983–85; Hd of Administration, SIB, 1985–89. *Address:* 4 Westcott Way, Cheam, Surrey SM2 7JY. *T:* 0181–393 2622.

CLARK, James McAdam, CVO 1972; MC 1944; HM Diplomatic Service, retired; *b* 13 Sept. 1916; *er s* of late James Heriot Clark of Wester Coltfield, and late Ella Catherine McAdam; *m* 1946, Denise Thérèse (*d* 1994), *d* of late Dr Léon Dufournier, Paris; two *d.* *Educ:* Edinburgh Acad.; Edinburgh Univ. BSc (Hons) Tech. Chemistry, 1938. Asst Lectr, Edinburgh Univ., 1938–39. Served Royal Artillery, 1939–46 (MC), rank of Capt.; Royal Mil. Coll. of Science, 1945–46 (pac). Min. of Fuel and Power, 1947–48. Entered Foreign (now Diplomatic) Service, 1948; FO, 1948–50; Head of Chancery, Quito, 1950–53; FO, 1953–56; Head of Chancery, Lisbon, 1956–60; Counsellor, UK Rep. to and Alternate Gov. of Internat. Atomic Energy Agency, Vienna, 1960–64; Head of Scientific Relations Dept, FO, 1964–66; Counsellor on secondment to Min. of Technology, 1966–70; Consul-Gen., Paris, 1970–77. Officer Order of Christ of Portugal, 1957. *Publications:* a number of poems and articles. *Recreations:* golf, sailing, music, disputation. *Address:* Hill Lodge, Aldeburgh, Suffolk IP15 5DU. *Clubs:* Aldeburgh Yacht, Aldeburgh Golf.

CLARK, Rt. Hon. Joe; *see* Clark, Rt Hon. C. J.

CLARK, Sir John (Allen), Kt 1971; retired; Chief Executive Officer, The Plessey Company plc, 1962–89; Chairman, GEC-Plessey Telecommunications Holdings, 1988–89; *b* 14 Feb. 1926; *e s* of late Sir Allen Clark and Lady (Jocelyn) Clark, *d* of late Percy and Madeline Culverhouse; *m* 1952, Deirdre Kathleen (marr. diss. 1962), *d* of Samuel Herbert Waterhouse and Maeve Murphy Waterhouse; one *s* one *d*; *m* 1970, Olivia, *d* of H. Pratt and of late Mrs R. S. H. Shepard; twin *s* one *d. Educ:* Harrow; Cambridge. Served War of 1939–45; commnd RNVR (2nd Lieut). Received early industrial training with Metropolitan Vickers and Ford Motor Co.; spent over a year in USA, studying the electronics industry. Asst to Gen. Manager, Plessey International Ltd, 1949; Dir and Gen. Man., Plessey (Ireland) Ltd, and Wireless Telephone Co. Ltd, 1950; appointed to main board, The Plessey Co. Ltd, 1953; Gen. Man., Plessey Components Group, 1957; Dep. Chm., The Plessey Co. Ltd, 1967–70, Chm., 1970–89. Director: International Computers Ltd, 1968–79; Banque Nationale de Paris Ltd, 1976–89. Pres., Telecommunication Engineering and Manufacturing Assoc., 1964–66, 1971–73; Vice-President: Inst. of Works Managers; Engineering Employers' Fedn. Member: Nat. Defence Industries Council; Engineering Industries Council, 1975–89. CompIEE; FIM. Order of Henry the Navigator, Portugal, 1973. *Recreations:* horseriding, shooting. *Address:* Redenham Park, Redenham, near Andover, Hants SP11 9AQ. *Club:* Boodle's.
See also Michael W. Clark.

CLARK, Prof. John Benjamin; Professor of Neurochemistry, Institute of Neurology, University of London, since 1990; Hon. Consultant Neurochemist, National Hospital of Neurology and Neurosurgery, since 1990; *b* 30 Jan. 1941; *e s* of P. B. Clark and J. E. Clark (*née* Smith); *m* 1965, Joan Gibbons; one *s* one *d* (and one *s* decd). *Educ:* Southend High Sch. for Boys; University College London (BSc 1962; PhD 1964; DSc 1982). St Bartholomew's Hospital Medical College, University of London: Lectr, Sen. Lectr and Reader in Biochemistry, 1965–86; Prof. of Cell Biochemistry, 1986–90. MRC Travelling Fellow, Johnson Res. Foundn, Univ. of Pennyslvania, 1969–70; Vis. Prof., Dept of Biochem. and Molecular Biol., UCL, 1991–. *Publications:* numerous contribs to sci. jls on mitochondrial metabolism and brain development. *Recreations:* walking, fine wines, reading. *Address:* Miriam Marks Department of Neurochemistry, Institute of Neurology, Queen Square, WC1H 3BG. *T:* 0171–829 8722.

CLARK, Prof. J(ohn) Desmond, CBE 1960; PhD, ScD; FBA 1961; FSA 1952; FRSSAf 1959; Professor of Anthropology, University of California, Berkeley, USA, 1961–86, now Emeritus Professor; *b* London, 10 April 1916; *s* of late Thomas John Chown Clark and Catharine (*née* Wynne); naturalised American, 1993; *m* 1938, Betty Cable, *d* of late Henry Lea Baume and late Frances M. S. (*née* Brown); one *s* one *d. Educ:* Monkton Combe Sch.; Christ's Coll., Cambridge. PhD in Archaeology (Cambridge), 1950; ScD Cantab 1975. Dir, Rhodes-Livingstone Museum, Livingstone, N Rhodesia, 1938–61. Has conducted excavations in Southern, East and Equatorial Africa, the Sahara, Ethiopia, Syria, 1938–, India, 1980–82, China, 1990–. Military Service in East Africa, Abyssinia, The Somalilands and Madagascar, 1941–46. Founder Mem. and Sec., N Rhodesia Nat. Monuments Commn, 1948–61. Corr. Mem. Scientific Coun. for Africa South of the Sahara, 1956–64, etc. Lectures: Faculty Res. Berkeley, 1979; Raymond Dart, Johannesburg, 1979; Mortimer Wheeler, British Acad., 1981; John Mulvaney, ANU, 1991; Distinguished, Amer. Anthropol Assoc., 1992. Fellow, Amer. Acad. of Arts and Sciences, 1965; Mem., Nat. Acad. of Science, USA, 1993. Hon. DSc: Univ. of the Witwatersrand, 1985; Univ. of Cape Town, 1985. Huxley Medal, RAI, 1974; Gold Medal, Soc. of Antiquaries of London, 1985; Fellows Medal, Calif. Acad. of Scis, 1987; Gold Medal, Archaelogical Inst. of America, 1989. Comdr, Nat. Order of Senegal, 1968. *Publications:* The Prehistoric Cultures of the Horn of Africa, 1954; The Prehistory of Southern Africa, 1959; The Stone Age Cultures of Northern Rhodesia, 1960; Prehistoric Cultures of Northeast Angola and their Significance in Tropical Africa, 1963; (ed) Proc. 3rd Pan-African Congress on Prehistory, 1957; (comp.) Atlas of African Pre-history, 1967; (ed, with W. W. Bishop) Background to Evolution in Africa, 1967; Kalambo Falls Prehistoric Site, vol. I, 1969, vol. II, 1973; The Prehistory of Africa, 1970; (ed) Cambridge History of Africa, vol I, 1982; (ed with G. R. Sharma) Palaeoenvironment and Prehistory in the Middle Son Valley, India, 1983; (ed with Steven A. Brandt) From Hunters to Farmers: the causes and consequences of food production in Africa, 1984; (ed) Cultural Beginnings, 1991; 285 contribs to learned journals on prehistoric archaeology. *Recreations:* gardening, walking, photography. *Address:* 1941 Yosemite Road, Berkeley, CA 94707, USA. *T:* (510) 5254519. *Clubs:* Commonwealth Trust, United Oxford & Cambridge University.

CLARK, John Edward, OBE 1995; Secretary, National Association of Local Councils, since 1978; *b* 18 Oct. 1932; *s* of Albert Edward Clark and Edith (*née* Brown); *m* 1969, Judith Rosemary Lester; one *s* (one *d* decd). *Educ:* Royal Grammar Sch., Clitheroe; Keble Coll., Oxford (MA, BCL). Called to the Bar, Gray's Inn, 1957; practised at the Bar, 1957–61. Dep. Sec., National Assoc. of Local (formerly Parish) Councils, (part-time) 1959–61, (full-time) 1961–78. *Publications:* chapters on local govt, public health, and theatres, in Encyclopaedia of Court Forms, 2nd edn 1964 to 1975. *Recreations:* walking, indoor games, collecting detective fiction, fortifications.

CLARK, Sir John S.; *see* Stewart-Clark.

CLARK, Dr Jonathan Charles Douglas; Senior Research Fellow, All Souls College, Oxford, since 1995; *b* 28 Feb. 1951; *s* of Ronald James Clark and Dorothy Margaret Clark. *Educ:* Downing and Corpus Christi Colls, Cambridge (BA, MA, PhD). Research Fellow: Peterhouse, Cambridge, 1977–81; Leverhulme Trust, 1983; All Souls Coll., Oxford, 1986–95. Vis. Prof., Cttee on Social Thought, Univ. of Chicago, 1993. Gov., Pusey House, Oxford, 1991–. *Publications:* The Dynamics of Change, 1982; English Society 1688–1832, 1985; Revolution and Rebellion, 1986; (ed) The Memoirs and Speeches of James, 2nd Earl Waldegrave, 1988; (ed) Ideas and Politics in Modern Britain, 1990; The Language of Liberty 1660–1832, 1993; Samuel Johnson, 1994; articles in learned jls. *Recreations:* hunting, shooting, fishing. *Address:* All Souls College, Oxford OX1 4AL. *T:* Oxford (01865) 279379. *Club:* Beefsteak.

CLARK, Sir Jonathan (George), 5th Bt *cr* 1917, of Dunlambert, City of Belfast; Managing Director, Paragon Homes Ltd, since 1992; *b* 9 Oct. 1947; *o s* of Sir Colin Douglas Clark, 4th Bt and of Margaret Coleman Clark (*née* Spinks); *S* father, 1995; *m* 1971, Susan Joy, *d* of Brig. T. I. G. Gray; one *s* two *d. Educ:* Eton. Royal Green Jackets, 1966–78. Various appts within private health care industry, 1978–92. *Recreations:* horse trials, hunting. *Heir:* *s* Simon George Gray Clark, *b* 3 Oct. 1975. *Address:* Somerset House, Threapwood, Malpas, Cheshire SY14 7AW. *T:* Malpas (01948) 770205.

CLARK, Dame June; *see* Clark, Dame M. J.

CLARK, Keith; Senior Partner, Clifford Chance, solicitors, since 1993; *b* 25 Oct. 1944; *s* of Douglas William Clark and Evelyn Lucy (*née* Longlands); *m* 1974, Linda Sue Woodger; one *s* one *d. Educ:* Chichester High Sch. for Boys; St Catherine's Coll., Oxford (MA Jurisprudence; BCL). Joined Clifford Chance, 1971; Partner, 1976. *Publications:* (jtly) Syndicated Lending Practice Documentation, 1993; articles on banking and financial topics. *Recreations:* walking, ballet, theatre, novels. *Address:* (office) 200 Aldersgate Street, EC1A 4JJ. *T:* 0171–600 1000.

CLARK, Ven. Kenneth James, DSC 1944; Archdeacon of Swindon, 1982–92; *b* 31 May 1922; *er s* of Francis James Clark and Winifred Adelaide Clark (*née* Martin); *m* 1948, Elisabeth Mary Monica Helen Huggett; three *s* three *d. Educ:* Watford Grammar School; St Catherine's Coll., Oxford (MA); Cuddesdon Theological Coll. Midshipman RN, 1940; Lieutenant RN, 1942; served in submarines, 1942–46. Baptist Minister, Forest Row, Sussex, 1950–52; Curate of Brinkworth, 1952–53; Curate of Cricklade with Latton, 1953–56; Priest-in-Charge, then Vicar (1959), of Holy Cross, Inns Court, Bristol, 1956–61; Vicar: Westbury-on-Trym, 1961–72; St Mary Redcliffe, Bristol, 1972–82; Hon. Canon of Bristol Cathedral, 1974. Member, Gen. Synod of C of E, 1980–92. *Recreations:* music, travel, gardening. *Address:* 6 Saxon Road, Harnham, Salisbury, Wilts SP2 8JZ. *T:* Salisbury (01722) 421410.

CLARK, Leo; *see* Clark, F. L.

CLARK, Luther Johnson, (L. John Clark); Chief Executive and Managing Director, BET PLC, since 1991; *b* 27 Aug. 1941; *s* of E. T. Clark and Mary Opal Clark; *m* 1965, Judith Dooley; one *s* one *d. Educ:* Wharton Sch. of Finance & Commerce, Univ. of Pennsylavania (BS Econs/Finance 1963); Wharton Graduate Sch. of Finance & Commerce (MBA Marketing/Finance 1968). Captain, US Marine Corps, 1963–66. Singer Co.: joined 1968; Corp. Vice-Pres., 1978–81; Pres. and Chief Exec., Europe, Africa and Middle East, 1982–85; Exec. Vice-Pres., V. F. Corp., 1986–87; Chm. and Chief Exec., Coremark Internat. Inc., 1988–91. Non-executive Director: Rolls-Royce PLC, 1993–; Wharton School (Graduate Board), 1989–. *Address:* BET, Stratton House, Piccadilly, W1X 6AS. *T:* 0171–629 8886.

CLARK, Dr Lynda Margaret; QC (Scot.) 1989. *Educ:* St Andrews Univ. (LLB Hons); Edinburgh Univ. (PhD). Lectr, Univ. of Dundee, 1973–76; admitted Advocate, Scots Bar, 1977; called to the English Bar, Inner Temple, 1988. Contested (Lab) Fife North East, 1992. *Address:* Advocates' Library, Parliament Square, Edinburgh EH1 1RF. *T:* 0131–226 2881.

CLARK, Malcolm, CB 1990; Inspector General, Insolvency Service, Department of Trade and Industry, 1984–89, retired; *b* 13 Feb. 1931; *s* of late Percy Clark and Gladys Helena Clark; *m* 1956, Beryl Patricia Dale; two *s. Educ:* Wheelwright Grammar Sch., Dewsbury, Yorks. FCCA 1980. Department of Trade and Industry Insolvency Service: Examiner, 1953–62; Sen. Examiner, 1962–66; Asst Official Receiver, Rochester, 1966–70; Official Receiver, Lytham St Annes, 1970–79; Principal Inspector of Official Receivers, 1979–81; Dep. Inspector Gen., 1981–84. Member: Appeal Cttee, Chartered Assoc. of Certified Accountants, 1990–; Investigation Cttee, Insolvency Practitioners Assoc., 1992–. *Recreations:* theatre, gardening, reading. *Address:* Teak Cottage, 37 The Avenue, Poole, Dorset BH13 6LJ.

CLARK, Rev. Canon Malcolm Aiken; Dean, Collegiate Church of St Vincent since 1982, Dean of Edinburgh, 1983–85, Hon. Canon, since 1985; *b* 3 Oct. 1905; *s* of Hugh Aiken Clark, MB, CM, and Agnes Roberta Douglas Baxter; *m* 1936, Margherita Felicinna Columba Gannaway (*d* 1973); two *s* one *d. Educ:* Drax, Yorks; High School of Glasgow; Lichfield Theological College. Deacon 1934, priest 1935, Glasgow; Curate, St John's, Greenock; Rector, All Saints, Lockerbie, 1938–49, with All Saints, Langholm, 1939–42. Chaplain, RAFVR, 1942–46. Priest-in-charge, St Mary's, Dalkeith, 1949–56; Rector, Good Shepherd, Murrayfield, 1956–77; retired; warrant to officiate, dio. Edinburgh. Chaplain of St Vincent, Edinburgh, Order of St Lazarus of Jerusalem, 1977; Canon 1980, Dean 1982; also Canon of Cathedral Church of St Mary, Edinburgh and Dean, 1983. FSA (Scot.) 1979. *Address:* 12 St Vincent Street, Edinburgh EH3 6SH. *T:* 0131–557 3662.

CLARK, Dame (Margaret) June, DBE 1995; FRCN; Professor of Nursing, Middlesex University (formerly Polytechnic), since 1990; *b* 31 May 1941; *d* of Ernest Harold Hickery and Marion Louise Hickery (*née* Walters); *m* 1966, Roger Michael Geoffrey Clark; one *s* one *d. Educ:* Pontywaun Grammar Sch.; University College London (BA Hons Classics 1962); University College Hosp. (SRN 1965); Royal College of Nursing (RHV 1967); Univ. of Reading (MPhil 1972); PhD South Bank Polytechnic 1985. FRCN 1982. Nurse, 1965; health visitor, 1967; clinical nursing appts, combined with teaching and research while bringing up a family; resumed as health visitor, Berks, 1981; Senior Nurse (Research), 1983; Health Authority posts: Special Projects Co-ordinator, Lewisham and N Southwark, 1985–86; Dir, Community Nursing Services, W Lambeth, 1986–88; Chief Nursing Adviser, Harrow, 1988–90. Pres., RCN, 1990–94. Council of Europe Fellow, 1981. *Publications:* A Family Visitor, 1973; (with R. Hiller) Community Care, 1975; What Do Health Visitors Do?, 1981; (with S. Parsonage) Infant Feeding and Family Nutrition, 1981; (with J. Henderson) Community Health, 1983; (with M. Baly) District Nursing, 1981; contribs to nursing and med. jls. *Recreations:* travel, family caravan on South Wales coast. *Address:* c/o Royal College of Nursing, 20 Cavendish Square, W1M 0AB.

CLARK, Dr Michael; MP (C) Rochford, since 1983; *b* 8 Aug. 1935; *s* of late Mervyn Clark and of Sybilla Norma Clark (*née* Winscott); *m* 1958, Valerie Ethel, *d* of C. S. Harbord; one *s* one *d. Educ:* King Edward VI Grammar School, East Retford; King's College London (BSc (1st cl. Hons) Chemistry, 1956; FKC 1987); Univ. of Minnesota

(Fulbright Scholar, 1956–57); St John's College, Cambridge (PhD 1960). FRSC 1988. Research Scientist, later Factory Manager, ICI, 1960–66; Smith's Industries Ltd, 1966–69; PA International Management Consultants, 1969–73; Marketing Manager, St Regis Paper Co., 1973–78; Dir, Courtenay Stewart International, 1978–81; PA International Management Consultants, 1981–93. Treasurer, 1975–78, Chm., 1980–83, Cambs Cons. Assoc.; Cons. Eastern Area Exec., 1980–83; contested (C) Ilkeston, 1979. Member: Select Cttee for Energy, 1983–92 (Chm., 1989–92); Select Cttee on Trade and Industry, 1992–94; Council, Parly IT Cttee, 1984–90; Chairman: All Party Gp for the Chemical Industry, 1994– (Hon. Sec. 1985–90; Vice-Chm., 1990–94); Parly Gp for Energy Studies, 1992–; Bd, Parly Office of Sci. and Technol., 1993–; Hon. Secretary: Parly and Scientific Cttee, 1985–88; Parly Anglo-Nepalese Soc., 1985–90; Parly Anglo-Malaŵi Gp, 1987–; Parly Space Cttee, 1989–91; Cons. Backbench Energy Cttee, 1986–87 (Vice-Chm., 1987–90); Chairman: IPU, 1990–93 (Mem. Exec., 1987–); British–Russian Gp, 1994–; British–Venzuelan Gp, 1995–. Governor, Melbourn Village Coll., 1974–83 (Chm., 1977–80). *Publication:* The History of Rochford Hall, 1990. *Recreations:* history, DIY, gardening, golf. *Address:* c/o House of Commons, Westminster, SW1A 0AA; Rochford Hall, Rochford, Essex SS4 1NW. *T:* Southend-on-Sea (01702) 542042. *Club:* Rochford Conservative.

CLARK, Michael William, CBE 1977; DL; landowner; Deputy Chairman and Deputy Chief Executive, Plessey Co. plc, 1970–87; *b* 7 May 1927; *yr s* of late Sir Allen Clark and late Jocelyn Anina Maria Louise Clark (*née* Emerson Culverhouse); *m* 1st, 1955, Shirley (*née* MacPhadyen) (*d* 1974); two *s* one *d* (and one *d* decd); 2nd, 1985, Virginia, Marchioness Camden. *Educ:* Harrow. 1st Foot Guards, Subaltern, 1945–48. Plessey Co. plc, 1950–87: founded and built Electronics Div., 1951; Main Bd Dir, 1953; Dir, Corporate Planning, 1965, Man. Dir, Telecommunications Gp, 1967; Chief. Exec., Defence Electronics, 1970–87. Member: Electronics EDC, 1975–80; Council, Inst. of Dirs; Nat. Electronics Council; Ct of Univ. of Essex. President: Essex Br., SSAFA, 1988–; Essex Br., Grenadier Guards Assoc., 1988–. Comp. IEE, 1964; Comp. IERE, 1965. FIMgt (FBIM 1974). DL Essex, 1988, High Sheriff, 1991–92. *Recreations:* fishing, shooting, forestry. *Address:* Braxted Park, Witham, Essex CM8 3EN. *Clubs:* Boodle's, Pratt's.
See also Sir J. A. Clark.

CLARK, Oswald William Hugh, CBE 1978; Assistant Director-General, Greater London Council, 1973–79; *b* 26 Nov. 1917; *s* of late Rev. Hugh M. A. Clark and Mabel Bessie Clark (*née* Dance); *m* 1966, Diana Mary (*née* Hine); one *d*. *Educ:* Rutlish Sch., Merton; Univ. of London (BA; BD Hons); Univ. of Wales (LLM). Local Govt Official, LCC (later GLC), 1937–79. Served War, HM Forces, 1940–46: Major, 2nd Derbyshire Yeo., Eighth Army, Middle East, NW Europe. Member: Church Assembly (later General Synod), 1948–90; Standing and Legislative Cttees, 1950–90; Standing Orders Cttee (Chm.), 1950–90; Crown Appts Commn, 1987–90; Chm., House of Laity, 1979–85 (Vice-Chm., 1970–79); a Church Commissioner, 1958–88, Mem. Bd of Governors, 1966–68, 1969–73, 1977–88; Vice-Pres., Corp. of Church House, 1981–. Principal, Soc. of the Faith, 1987–92. Parish Clerk, 1992–, and Churchwarden, 1990–, St Andrew by the Wardrobe. Asst, Co. of Parish Clerks, 1992–. Life Fellow, Guild of Guide Lectrs, 1982. *Recreations:* London's history and development, commemorative and Goss china, heraldry. *Address:* 8 Courtlands Avenue, Hampton, Middlesex TW12 3NT. *T:* 0181–979 1081. *Clubs:* Cavalry and Guards, Pratt's.

CLARK, Air Vice-Marshal Paul Derek, CB 1993; CEng; FRAeS; Director of Military Support, Support Division, GEC–Marconi Avionics, since 1994; *b* 19 March 1939; *s* of John Hayes Clark and Kathleen Clark; *m* 1963, Mary Elizabeth Morgan; two *d*. *Educ:* Orange Hill Grammar Sch.; RAF Henlow Technical Coll. BA Open Univ., 1985. CEng 1970; FRAeS 1987. Commnd Engr Br., RAF, 1961; RAF Wittering, 1961–63, Topcliffe, 1963, Wittering, 1964–69, Cranwell, 1969–70; RAF Staff Coll., Bracknell, 1971; HQ Logistics Comd, USAF, 1972–74; HQ Strike Comd, 1974–76; Nat. Defence Coll., 1977; OC Engrg Wing, RAF Leuchars, 1977–79; HQ No 1 Gp, RAF Bawtry, 1980–81; Stn Comdr No 30 Maintenance Unit, RAF Sealand, 1981–83; RCDS, 1984; MoD, 1985–86; Directorate Electronics Radar Air, MoD (PE), 1986–87; Dir, European Helicopter 101 Project, MoD (PE), 1987–89; Comdt RAF Signals Engrg Estabt, 1990–91; AO, Engrg and Supply, HQ Strike Comd, 1991–93; retd, 1994. *Recreations:* theatre, art, high handicap golfing. *Club:* Royal Air Force.
See also Prof. T. J. H. Clark.

CLARK, Paul Nicholas Rowntree; His Honour Judge Paul Clark; a Circuit Judge, since 1985; *b* 17 Aug. 1940; *s* of late Henry Rowntree Clark and Gwendoline Victoria Clark; *m* 1967; two *s* one *d*. *Educ:* Bristol Grammar Sch.; New Coll., Oxford (Open Schol.; MA (Lit. Hum.)). Called to the Bar, Middle Temple, 1966 (Harmsworth Schol.), Bencher 1982; in practice on Midland and Oxford (formerly Oxford) Circuit, 1966–85; a Recorder, 1981–85. *Address:* 2 Harcourt Buildings, Temple, EC4Y 9DB. *T:* 0171–353 6961. *Club:* Garrick.

CLARK, Petula, (Sally Olwen); singer, actress; *b* 15 Nov. 1932; *d* of Leslie Clark; *m* 1961, Claude Wolff; one *s* two *d*. Own BBC radio series, Pet's Parlour, 1943; early British films include: Medal for the General, 1944; I Know Where I'm Going, 1945; Here Come the Huggetts, 1948; Dance Hall, 1950; White Corridors, 1951; The Card, 1951; Made in Heaven, 1952; The Runaway Bus, 1953; That Woman Opposite, 1957. Began career as singer in France, 1959. Top female vocalist, France, 1962; Bravos du Music Hall award for outstanding woman in show business, France, 1965; Grammy awards for records Downtown and I Know A Place. Numerous concert and television appearances in Europe and USA including her own BBC TV series. *Films:* Finian's Rainbow, 1968; Goodbye Mr Chips, 1969; Second to the Right and Straight on till Morning, 1982; *musicals:* The Sound of Music, Apollo Victoria, 1981; (also composer and creator) Someone Like You, Strand, 1990; Blood Brothers, NY, 1993, nat. tour, 1994–95. *Address:* c/o John Ashby, PO Box 288, Woking, Surrey GU22 0YN.

CLARK, Ramsey; lawyer in private practice, New York City, since 1969; *b* Dallas, Texas, 18 Dec. 1927; *s* of late Thomas Clark, and of Mary Ramsey; *m* 1949, Georgia Welch, Corpus Christi, Texas; one *s* one *d*. *Educ:* Public Schs, Dallas, Los Angeles, Washington; Univ. of Texas (BA); Univ. of Chicago (MA, JD). US Marine Corps, 1945–46. Engaged private practice of law, Dallas, 1951–61; Asst Attorney Gen., Dept of Justice, 1961–65; Dep. Attorney Gen., 1965–67, Attorney Gen., 1967–69. *Address:* 37 West 12th Street, New York, NY 10011–8502, USA.

CLARK, Richard David; Chief Executive, and Clerk to the Lieutenancy, Devon County Council, since 1989; *b* 2 Sept. 1934; *s* of David and Enid Clark; *m* 1958, Pamela Mary (*née* Burgess); two *d*. *Educ:* Keele Univ. (BA, DipEd); Univ. de Paris, Sorbonne. Teaching, Woodberry Down Comprehensive School, 1957–61; Education Admin., Herts CC, 1961–69; Asst Educn Officer, Lancs CC, 1969–71; Second Dep. County Educn Officer, Hants CC, 1972–76; Chief Educn Officer, Glos CC, 1976–83; County Educn Officer, Hants CC, 1983–88; Associate Clerk to Devon and Cornwall Police Authority, 1989–; Dir, Devon and Cornwall TEC, 1989–. Mem., Adv. Cttee on Supply and Educn of Teachers. Adviser to: Burnham Cttee, 1982–87; Educn Cttee, ACC, 1982–89, 1990–; Council of Local Educn Authorities, 1983–89. Fellow Commoner, Churchill Coll., Cambridge, 1983; Vis. Fellow, Southampton Univ., 1986–88; Hon. Fellow, Exeter Univ., 1992. FRSA 1977. *Recreations:* books, gardening. *Address:* Bickwell Brook, Bickwell Valley, Sidmouth, Devon EX10 8SQ. *T:* Sidmouth (01395) 514937. *Club:* Sidmouth.

CLARK, Sir Robert (Anthony), Kt 1976; DSC 1944; Chairman, since 1992, and Director, since 1991, Mirror Group plc (formerly Mirror Group Newspapers plc); Chairman, Rauscher Pierce & Clark, since 1992; *b* 6 Jan. 1924; *yr s* of John Clark and Gladys Clark (*née* Dyer); *m* 1949, Andolyn Marjorie Lewis; two *s* one *d*. *Educ:* Highgate Sch.; King's Coll., Cambridge. Served War, Royal Navy, 1942–46. Partner with Slaughter and May, Solicitors, 1953–61; Director: Alfred McAlpine plc (formerly Marchwiel plc), 1957–; Hill Samuel Bank Ltd, merchant bankers (formerly Philip Hill, Higginson, Erlangers Ltd, then Hill Samuel & Co. Ltd), 1961–91 (Chm., 1974–87); Bank of England, 1976–85; Eagle Star Holdings Ltd, 1976–87; BL, subseq. Rover Gp plc, 1977–88; Shell Transport and Trading Co., plc, 1982–94; SmithKline Beecham plc, 1987–95 (Vice-Chm.); Vodafone Group plc (formerly Racal Telecom PLC), 1988–; Chairman: Hill Samuel Gp plc, 1980–88 (Chief Exec., 1976–80); IMI plc, 1981–89; Marley plc, 1985–89; Deputy Chairman: TSB Gp, 1989–91 (Dir, 1987–91); Lowndes Lambert Group Hldgs plc, 1992–. Chairman: Industrial Development Adv. Bd, 1973–80; Review Body on Doctors' and Dentists' Remuneration, 1979–86; Council, Charing Cross and Westminster Med. Sch., 1982–; Dir, ENO, 1983–87. Hon. DSc Cranfield Inst. of Technol., 1982. *Recreations:* reading, music, collecting antiquarian books. *Address:* Munstead Wood, Godalming, Surrey GU7 1UN. *T:* Godalming (01483) 417867; Rauscher Pierce & Clark, 56 Green Street, W1Y 3RH. *T:* 0171–491 2434, *Fax:* 0171–491 9081. *Club:* Pratt's.

CLARK, Prof. Robert Bernard, DSc, PhD; FIBiol, FRSE; Professor of Zoology, University of Newcastle upon Tyne, 1966–89, now Emeritus; *b* 13 Oct. 1923; *s* of Joseph Lawrence Clark and Dorothy (*née* Halden); *m* 1st, 1956, Mary Eleanor (*née* Laurence) (marr. diss.); 2nd, 1970, Susan Diana (*née* Smith); one *s* one *d*. *Educ:* St Marylebone Grammar Sch.; Chelsea Polytechnic (BSc London 1944); University Coll., Exeter (BSc 1950); Univ. of Glasgow (PhD 1956); DSc London 1965. FIBiol 1966, FLS 1969, FRSE 1970. Asst Experimental Officer, DSIR Road Research Laboratory, 1944; Asst to Prof. of Zoology, Univ. of Glasgow, 1950; Asst Prof., Univ. of California (Berkeley), 1953; Lectr in Zoology, Univ. of Bristol, 1956; Head of Dept of Zoology and Dir of Dove Marine Laboratory, Univ. of Newcastle upon Tyne, 1966–77, Dir of Research Unit on Rehabilitation of Oiled Seabirds, 1967–76; Dir of NERC Research Unit on Rocky Shore Biology, 1981–87. Member: NERC, 1971–77 and 1983–86; Royal Commn on Environmental Pollution, 1979–83; Adv. Cttee on Pesticides, 1986–90; Mem. Council, Nature Conservancy, 1975. *Publications:* Neurosecretion (ed, jtly), 1962; Dynamics in Metazoan Evolution, 1964, corrected repr. 1967; Practical Course in Experimental Zoology, 1966; (jtly) Invertebrate Panorama, 1971; (jtly) Synopsis of Animal Classification, 1971; (ed, jtly) Essays in Hydrobiology, 1972; (ed) The Long-Term Effects of Oil Pollution on Marine Populations, Communities and Ecosystems, 1982; Marine Pollution, 1986, 3rd edn 1992; The Waters Around the British Isles: their conflicting uses, 1987; (ed jtly) Environmental Effects of North Sea Oil and Gas Development, 1987; Founder, 1968, and ed, Marine Pollution Bulletin; numerous papers in learned jls. *Recreations:* architecture, music, unambitious gardening, cooking. *Address:* Department of Marine Sciences, Ridley Building, University of Newcastle upon Tyne, Newcastle upon Tyne NE1 7RU. *T:* Newcastle upon Tyne 0191–222 6661; Highbury House, Highbury, Newcastle upon Tyne NE2 3LN. *T:* Newcastle upon Tyne 0191–281 4672.

CLARK, Rev. Canon Robert James Vodden; *b* 12 April 1907; *s* of Albert Arthur Clark and Bessie Vodden; *m* 1934, Ethel Dolina McGregor Alexander; one *d*. *Educ:* Dalry Normal Practising Episcopal Church Sch., Edinburgh; Church Army Coll.; Coates Hall Theol. Coll. Ordained, 1941. Men's Social Dept, Church Army, 1926; varied work in homes for men; special work in probation trng home under Home Office, 1934–39; St Paul and St George, Edinburgh, 1941–44; Rector, St Andrew's, Fort William, 1944–47; seconded to Scottish Educn Dept as Warden-Leader of Scottish Centre of Outdoor Trng, Glenmore Lodge, 1947–49; Curate i/c St David's, Edinburgh, 1949–54; Rector of Christ Church, Falkirk, 1954–69; Rector of St Leonards, Lasswade, 1969–79; Canon, Edinburgh, 1962; Dean of Edinburgh, 1967–76; Hon. Canon, Edinburgh, 1976; retd 1979. Mem., Royal Highland and Agric. Soc. *Recreations:* mountaineering, photography. *Address:* 15 North Street, St Andrews, Fife, Scotland KY16 9PW.

CLARK, Robert Joseph; Circuit Administrator, Western Circuit, Lord Chancellor's Department, since 1993; *b* 29 March 1942; *s* of late Edward Clark and Elsie Clark (*née* Bush); *m* 1970, Elke Agnes, *d* of late Hans Schmidt and Herma Schmidt; two *d*. *Educ:* state schools in London. Lord Chancellor's Department: Official Solicitor's Dept, 1960–70; Nat. Industrial Relns Court, 1970–74; HQ, 1974–77; Trng Centre, 1977–79; Chief Clerk, Court of Protection, 1979–83; S Eastern Circuit Office, 1983–88; Head: Civil Business Div., 1988–91; Judicial Appointments Div. II, 1991–93. *Recreations:* theatre, walking. *Address:* Western Circuit Office, Bridge House, Clifton Down, Bristol BS8 4BN. *T:* Bristol (0117) 974 3763.

CLARK, Prof. Robin Jon Hawes, FRS 1990; Sir William Ramsay Professor and Head of Department of Chemistry, University College London, since 1989; *b* 16 Feb. 1935; *s* of Reginald Hawes Clark, JP, BCom and Marjorie Alice Clark (*née* Thomas); *m* 1964, Beatrice Rawdin Brown, JP; one *s* one *d*. *Educ:* Christ's Coll., NZ; Canterbury University Coll., Univ. of NZ (BSc 1956; MSc (1st cl. hons) 1958); University Coll. London (British Titan Products Scholar and Fellow; PhD 1961); DSc London 1969. FRSC 1969. University College London: Asst Lectr in Chemistry, 1962; Lectr 1963–71; Reader 1972–81; Prof., 1982–89; Dean of Faculty of Science, 1988–89; Mem. Council, 1991–94; Fellow, 1993. Mem., Senate and Academic Council, Univ. of London, 1988–93. Visiting Professor: Columbia, 1965; Padua, 1967; Western Ontario, 1968; Texas A&M, 1978; Bern, 1979; Fribourg, 1979; Auckland, 1981; Odense, 1983; Sydney, 1985; Bordeaux, 1988; Pretoria, 1991; Lectures: Kresge-Hooker, Wayne State, 1965; John van Geuns, Amsterdam, 1979; Carman, SA Chemical Inst., 1994. Mem. Council, Royal Soc., 1993–94; Royal Society of Chemistry: Mem., Dalton Divl Council, 1985–88, Vice-Pres., 1988–90; Lectures: Tilden, 1983–84; Nyholm, 1989–90; Thomas Graham, 1991; Harry Hallam, 1993. Member: SRC Inorganic Chem. Panel, 1977–80; SERC Post-doctoral Fellowships Cttee, 1983; SERC Inorganic Chem. Sub-Cttee, 1993–94; Chairman: XI Internat. Conf. on Raman Spectroscopy, London, 1988; Steering Cttee, Internat. Confs on Raman Spectroscopy, 1990–92 (Mem., 1988–). Trustee, Ramsay Meml Fellowships Trust, 1993– (Chm. Adv. Council, 1989–). Mem., Academia Europaea, 1990. Hon. FRSNZ, 1989; FRSA 1992. *Publications:* The Chemistry of Titanium and Vanadium, 1968; (jtly) The Chemistry of Titanium, Zirconium and Hafnium, 1973; (jtly) The Chemistry of Vanadium, Niobium and Tantalum, 1973; (ed jtly) Advances in Spectroscopy, vols 1–24, 1975–95; (ed jtly) Raman Spectroscopy, 1988; (ed) monographs on Inorganic Chemistry, 1978–; some 350 contribs to learned jls, in fields of transition metal chem. and spectroscopy. *Recreations:* golf, tennis, swimming, ski-ing, long distance walking, travel, bridge, music, theatre, wine. *Address:* Christopher Ingold Laboratories, University College London, 20 Gordon Street, WC1H 0AJ; 3a Loom Lane, Radlett, Herts WD7 8AA. *T:* Radlett (01923) 857899. *Clubs:* Athenæum; Porters Park Golf (Radlett).

CLARK, Prof. Ronald George, FRCSE, FRCS; Professor of Surgery, since 1972, Pro-Vice-Chancellor, since 1988, University of Sheffield; Consultant Surgeon; Northern General Hospital, since 1966; Royal Hallamshire Hospital, since 1966; *b* 9 Aug. 1928; *s* of late George Clark and of Gladys Clark; *m* 1960, Tamar Welsh Harvie; two *d. Educ:* Aberdeen Acad.; Univ. of Aberdeen. MB, ChB; FRCSE 1960; FRCS 1980. House appts, Aberdeen Royal Infirmary, 1956–57; Registrar, Western Infirmary, Glasgow, 1958–60; Surgical Res. Fellow, Harvard, USA, 1960–61; Lectr in Surgery, Univ. of Glasgow, 1961–65; Sheffield University: Sen. Lectr in Surgery, 1966–72; Dean, Faculty of Medicine and Dentistry, 1982–85. Examiner, Universities of: Aberdeen, Glasgow, Edinburgh, Liverpool, Newcastle, Leicester, London, Southampton, Malta, Ibadan, Jos. Chm., European Soc. for Parenteral and Enteral Nutrition, 1982–; Council Mem., Nutrition Soc., 1982–85; Scientific Governor, British Nutrition Foundn, 1982–; Member: GMC, 1983–; GDC, 1990–; Assoc. of Surgeons of GB and Ireland, 1968–; Surgical Res. Soc., 1969–. Mem., Editorial Bd, Scottish Medical Jl, 1962–65; Editor-in-Chief, Clinical Nutrition, 1980–82. *Publications:* contribs to books and jls on surgical topics and metabolic aspects of acute disease. *Recreation:* golf. *Address:* Brookline, 2 Chesterwood Drive, Sheffield S10 5DU. *T:* Sheffield (0114) 266 3601. *Club:* Commonwealth Trust.

CLARK, Lt-Gen. (Samuel) Findlay, CBE 1945; CD 1950; MEIC; MCSEE; PEng; *b* 17 March 1909; *m* 1937, Leona Blanche Seagram. *Educ:* Univ. of Manitoba (BScEE); Univ. of Saskatchewan (BScME). Lieut, Royal Canadian Signals, 1933. Associate Prof. of Elec. and Mechan. Engrg (Capt.) at RMC Kingston, 1938. Overseas to UK, Aug. 1940 (Major); Comd 5th Canadian Armd Div. Sigs Regt (Lt-Col), 1941. GSO1 Can. Mil. HQ, London, 1942; Staff Course, Camberley, England (Col), 1942–43; CSO, HQ 2nd Canadian Corps until end of War (Brig. 1943). Dep. Chief of Gen. Staff, 1945; Imperial Defence Coll., 1948; Canadian Mil. Observer on Western Union Mil. Cttee; Maj.-Gen. 1949; Canadian Mil. Rep. NATO, London, 1949; Chm., Joint Staff, CALE, London, 1951; QMG of Canadian Army, 1951; GOC Central Comd, 1955; CGS, Sept. 1958–61. Chm., Nat. Capital Commission, 1961–67. Past Col Comdt, Royal Canadian Corps of Signals. FRCGS. Legion of Merit (USA), 1945; Comdr Order of Orange Nassau (Netherlands), 1945. OStJ 1975. *Address:* 301–1375 Newport Avenue, Victoria, BC V8S 5E8, Canada. *T:* (604) 5924338. *Club:* Union (Victoria).

CLARK, Sir Terence (Joseph), KBE 1990; CMG 1985; CVO 1978; HM Diplomatic Service, retired; *b* 19 June 1934; *s* of Joseph Clark and Mary Clark; *m* 1960, Lieselotte Rosa Marie Müller; two *s* one *d. Educ:* Thomas Parmiter's, London. RAF (attached to Sch. of Slavonic Studies, Cambridge), 1953–55; Pilot Officer, RAFVR, 1955. HM Foreign Service, 1955; ME Centre for Arab Studies, 1956–57; Bahrain, 1957–58; Amman, 1958–60; Casablanca, 1961–62; FO, 1962–65; Asst Polit. Agent, Dubai, 1965–68; Belgrade, 1969–71; Hd of Chancery, Muscat, 1972–73; Asst Hd of ME Dept, FCO, 1974–76; Counsellor (Press and Information), Bonn, 1976–79; Chargé d'Affaires, Tripoli, Feb.-March 1981; Counsellor, Belgrade, 1979–82. Dep. Leader, UK Delegn, Conf. on Security and Co-operation in Europe, Madrid, 1982–83; Hd of Information Dept, FCO, 1983–85; Ambassador to Iraq, 1985–89; Ambassador to Oman, 1990–94. Commander's Cross, Order of Merit of Fed. Republic of Germany, 1978. *Publications:* (jtly) The Saluqi: coursing hound of the East, 1995; articles on Salukis and coursing in magazines. *Recreations:* Salukis, tennis. *Address:* 29 Westleigh Avenue, SW15 6RQ. *Clubs:* Commonwealth Trust, Hurlingham.

CLARK, Thomas Alastair; Deputy Director, Bank of England, since 1994; *b* 27 Feb. 1949; *s* of Andrew Evans Clark and Freda (*née* Seal); *m* 1986, Shirley Anne Barker; one *s* one *d. Educ:* Stockport Grammar Sch.; Emmanuel Coll., Cambridge (MA Maths); London Sch. of Econs (MSc Econs). Bank of England, 1971–: PA to Dep. Governor, 1980–; UK Alternate Exec. Dir, IMF, 1983–; UK Alternate Dir, EIB, 1986–; Head: Financial Markets and Instns Div., 1987–; European Div., 1993–. *Recreations:* joinery, hill-walking. *Address:* Bank of England, Threadneedle Street, EC2R 8AH. *T:* 0171–601 4444.

CLARK, Sir Thomas (Edwin), Kt 1986; retired director; non-executive Deputy Chairman, Ceramco, since 1984; farming since 1986; *b* 6 Aug. 1916; *s* of Thomas Edwin and Margaret Clark; *m* 1st, 1938, Joan Mary Hodgson (marr. diss. 1954); one *s* two *d* (and one *d* decd); 2nd, 1954, Josephine Mary Buckley (*d* 1962); one *s* two *d*; 3rd, 1963, Patricia Mary France; two *s* one *d. Educ:* King's College, Auckland. General labourer, Amalgamated Brick and Pipe Co., 1932; Asst Factory Manager, 1937; Associate Director, 1939; Manager, R & D, 1938; Gen. Manager, 1942; Director and Jt Gen. Manager, 1946 (with brother M. M. Clark); Jt Man. Dir, 1954; company name changed to Ceramco, 1964; Man. Dir, 1972, retired 1984. Director: Geothermal Energy NZ (Dep. Chm.); Rinnai NZ; Morlynn, Australia; Southern Pacific Boatyard. Chm., West Auckland Hospice Trust. *Recreations:* motor racing, yachting, gardening. *Address:* Aotea Farms, South Kaipara Heads, RDI Helensville, New Zealand. *T:* (9) 4202854. *Clubs:* Auckland; Royal NZ Yacht Squadron, Titirangi Golf, Helensville Golf.

CLARK, Prof. Timothy John Hayes, FRCP; Consultant Physician to Royal Brompton National Heart and Lung Hospital (formerly Brompton Hospital), since 1970; Dean, and Professor of Pulmonary Medicine, National Heart and Lung Institute, since 1990; *b* 18 Oct. 1935; *s* of John and Kathleen Clark; *m* 1961, Elizabeth Ann Day; two *s* two *d. Educ:* Christ's Hospital; Guy's Hospital Medical Sch. BSc 1958; MB BS (Hons) 1961, MD 1967 London. FRCP 1973 (LRCP 1960, MRCP 1962); MRCS 1960. Fellow, Johns Hopkins Hosp., Baltimore USA, 1963; Registrar, Hammersmith Hosp., 1964; Lecturer and Sen. Lectr, Guy's Hospital Med. Sch., 1966; Consultant Physician, Guy's Hosp., 1968–90; Prof. of Thoracic Med., Guy's Hosp. Med. Sch., later UMDS, 1977–89; Dean: Guy's Hosp., 1984–89; UMDS, 1986–89; Pro-Vice-Chancellor for Medicine and Dentistry, Univ. of London, 1987–89. Mem., Council of Governors, UMDS, 1982–89, 1990–. Specialist Adviser to Social Services Cttee, 1981 and 1985. Special Trustee, Guy's Hosp., 1982–86. Pres., British Thoracic Soc., 1990–91; Vice-Chm., Nat. Asthma Campaign, 1993–. *Publications:* (jtly) Asthma, 1977, 3rd edn 1992; (ed) Small Airways in Health and Disease, 1979; (jtly) Topical Steroid Treatment of Asthma and Rhinitis, 1980; (ed) Clinical Investigation of Respiratory Disease, 1981; (jtly) Practical Management of Asthma, 1985; articles in British Medical Jl, Lancet, and other specialist scientific jls. *Recreation:* cricket. *Address:* 8 Lawrence Court, NW7 3QP. *T:* 0181–959 4411. *Club:* MCC.
See also Air Vice-Marshal P. D. Clark.

CLARK, Tony; *see* Clark, C. A.

CLARK, Wallace; *see* Clark, H. W. S.

CLARK, William P.; Chief Executive Officer, Clark Co., since 1958; Counsel, McCann Fitzgerald, Dublin, since 1990; Sinsheimer, Schiebelhut & Baggett, San Luis Obispo, since 1991; *b* 23 Oct. 1931; *s* of William and Bernice Clark; *m* 1955, Joan Brauner; three *s* two *d. Educ:* Stanford Univ., California; Loyola Law Sch., Los Angeles, California. Admitted to practice of law, California, 1958; Sen. Member, law firm, Clark, Cole & Fairfield, Oxnard, Calif, 1958–67. Served on Cabinet of California, Governor Ronald Reagan, first as Cabinet Secretary, later as Executive Secretary, 1967–69; Judge, Superior Court, State of California, County of San Luis Obispo, 1969–71; Associate Justice: California Court of Appeal, Second District, Los Angeles, 1971–73; California Supreme Court, San Francisco, 1973–81; Dep. Secretary, Dept of State, Washington, DC, 1981–82; Assistant to Pres. of USA for Nat. Security Affairs, 1982–83; Sec. of the Interior, 1983–85. Chm., Presidential Task Force on Nuclear Weapons Program Management, 1985; Member: Commn on Defense Management, 1985–86; Commn on Integrated Long-Term Strategy, 1987. *Publications:* judicial opinions in California Reports, 9 Cal. 3d through 29 Cal. 3d. *Recreations:* ranching, horseback riding, outdoor sports, flying. *Address:* (office) Clark Company, 1031 Pine Street, Paso Robles, CA 93446, USA. *Clubs:* Bohemia (San Francisco); California Cattleman's Association; Rancheros Visitadores (California).

CLARK-EDDINGTON, Paul; *see* Eddington.

CLARK HUTCHISON, Sir George Ian; *see* Hutchison.

CLARKE, Prof. Adrienne Elizabeth, AO 1991; PhD; FTS, FAA; Chairman, Commonwealth Scientific and Industrial Research Organisation, since 1991; Professor, Personal Chair in Botany, since 1985, and Director, Plant Cell Biology Research Centre, since 1982, University of Melbourne; *b* 6 Jan. 1938; *d* of A. L. Petty; *m* (marr. diss.); two *d* one *s. Educ:* Ruyton Grammar Sch.; Univ. of Melbourne (PhD). Melbourne University: Reader in Botany, 1981; Dep. Head, Sch. of Botany, 1992. Mem., Sci. Adv. Bd, Friedrich Meischer Inst., 1991. Director: Alcoa of Australia, 1993–; AMP Soc., 1994–. Foreign Associate, Nat. Acad. of Scis, USA; Comp., Inst. of Engrs, Australia. *Publications:* (ed with I. Wilson) Carbohydrate–Protein Recognition, 1988; (with B. A. Stone) Chemistry and Biology of Glucans, 1992; chapters in numerous books; contribs to learned jls. *Recreations:* swimming, bush walking. *Address:* Commonwealth Scientific and Industrial Research Organisation, PO Box 225, Dickson, ACT 2602, Australia. *T:* (6) 2766696.

CLARKE, Prof. Alan Douglas Benson, CBE 1974; Professor of Psychology, University of Hull, 1962–84, now Emeritus; *b* 21 March 1922; *s* of late Robert Benson Clarke and late Mary Lizars Clarke; *m* 1950, Prof. Ann Margaret (*née* Gravely); two *s. Educ:* Lancing Coll.; Univs of Reading and London. 1st cl. hons BA Reading 1948; PhD London 1950; FBPsS. Reading Univ., 1940–41 and 1946–48. Sen. Psychol., 1951–57 and Cons. Psychol., 1957–62, Manor Hosp., Epsom. Dean of Faculty of Science, 1966–68, and Pro-Vice-Chancellor 1968–71, Univ. of Hull. Vis. Prof., Univ. of Hertfordshire, 1992–. Rapporteur, WHO Expert Cttee on Organization of Services for Mentally Retarded, 1967; Mem. WHO Expert Adv. Panel on Mental Health, 1968–85; Chm., Trng Council for Teachers of Mentally Handicapped, 1969–74; Hon. Vice-Pres., Nat. Assoc. for Mental Health, 1970–; President: Internat. Assoc. for Sci. Study of Mental Deficiency, 1973–76 (Hon. Past-Pres., 1976–88; Hon. Life Pres., 1988–); BPsS, 1977–78. Member: Personal Social Services Council, 1973–77; DHSS/SSRC Organizing Gp Transmitted Deprivation, 1974–83 (Chm. 1978–83); Cons., OECD/NZ Conf. on Early Childhood Care and Educn, 1978; Chairman: Sec. of State's Adv. Cttee on Top Grade Clinical Psychologist Posts and Appts, NHS, 1981–82; Adv. Cttee, Thomas Coram Res. Unit, Univ. of London Inst. of Educn, 1981–. Lectures: Maudsley, RMPA, 1967; Stolz, Guy's Hosp., 1972; Tizard Meml, Assoc. for Child Psychol. and Psychiatry, 1983. Hon. Life Mem., Amer. Assoc. on Mental Deficiency, 1975 (Research award, 1977, with Ann M. Clarke). Hon. FRCPsych 1989. Hon. DSc Hull, 1986. (With Ann M. Clarke) Distinguished Achievement Award for Scientific Lit., Internat. Assoc. for Scientific Study of Mental Deficiency, 1982. Editor, Brit. Jl Psychol., 1973–79; Mem., Editorial Bds of other jls. *Publications* (with Ann M. Clarke): Mental Deficiency: the Changing Outlook, 1958, 4th edn 1985; Mental Retardation and Behavioural Research, 1973; Early Experience: myth and evidence, 1976; (with B. Tizard) Child Development and Social Policy: the life and work of Jack Tizard, 1983; (with P. Evans) Combating Mental Handicap, 1991; numerous in psychol and med. jls. *Address:* 109 Meadway, Barnet, Herts EN5 5JZ. *T:* 0181–441 9690.

CLARKE, Prof. Alan Maxwell, CMG 1995; FRACS; Director, Spinal Injuries Unit, Burwood Hospital, Christchurch, New Zealand, since 1992; *b* 12 Dec. 1932; *s* of John Maxwell Clarke and Daisy Martha Clarke; *m* 1956, Jane Malloch; three *s* one *d. Educ:* King's Coll., Auckland; Otago Univ., Dunedin (MB ChB 1956; ChM 1969). FRACS 1961. Otago University: Sen. Lectr in Surgery, 1964–69; Prof. of Surgery, 1970–85; Dean, Christchurch Sch. of Medicine, 1986–93. James IV Traveller in Surgery, 1970; Nuffield Travelling Fellow, 1993–94. Amer. Cancer Soc. Award, 1968 and 1976. *Publications:* Understanding Cancer, 1982; Cancer Consensus Manual, 1984; numerous papers in learned jls. *Recreations:* art, reading, flying light aeroplanes. *Address:* Spinal Injuries Unit, Burwood Hospital, Private Bag 4708, Christchurch, New Zealand. *T:* (3) 3836850, *Fax:* (3) 3836851.

CLARKE, Allen; *see* Clarke, C. A. A.

CLARKE, Hon. Sir Anthony (Peter), Kt 1993; **Hon. Mr Justice Clarke;** a Judge of the High Court of Justice, Queen's Bench Division, since 1993; Admiralty Judge, since 1993; *b* 13 May 1943; *s* of Harry Alston Clarke and Isobel Clarke; *m* 1968, Rosemary (*née* Adam); two *s* one *d. Educ:* Oakham Sch.; King's Coll., Cambridge (Econs Pt I, Law Pt II; MA). Called to the Bar, Middle Temple, 1965, Bencher, 1987; QC 1979; a Recorder, 1985–92. *Recreations:* golf, tennis, holidays. *Address:* Royal Courts of Justice, Strand, WC2A 2LL.

CLARKE, Arthur Charles, CBE 1989; *b* 16 Dec. 1917; *s* of Charles Wright Clarke and Nora Mary Willis; *m* 1953, Marilyn Mayfield (marr. diss. 1964). *Educ:* Huish's Grammar Sch., Taunton; King's Coll., London (BSc); FKC 1977; FRAS. HM Exchequer and Audit Dept, 1936–41. Served RAF, 1941–46. Instn of Electrical Engineers, 1949–50. Techn. Officer on first GCA radar, 1943; originated communications satellites, 1945. Chm., British Interplanetary Soc., 1946–47, 1950–53. Asst Ed., Science Abstracts, 1949–50. Since 1954 engaged on underwater exploration on Gt Barrier Reef of Australia and coast of Ceylon. Extensive lecturing, radio and TV in UK and US. Chancellor, Moratuwa Univ., Sri Lanka, 1979–; Vikram Sarabhai Prof., Physical Research Lab., Ahmedabad, 1980; Marconi Internat. Fellowship, 1982; Hon. Fellow, AIAA, 1976 (Aero-space Communications Award, 1974). Hon. DSc: Beaver Coll., Pa, 1971; Univ. of Moratuwa, Sri Lanka, 1979; Hon. DLitt Bath, 1988; Liverpool, 1995. Freeman of Minehead, 1992. Unesco, Kalinga Prize, 1961; Acad. of Astronautics, 1961; World Acad. of Art and Science, 1962; Stuart Ballantine Medal, Franklin Inst., 1963; Westinghouse-AAAS Science Writing Award, 1969; Nebula Award, Science Fiction Writers of America, 1972, 1974, 1979; John Campbell Award, 1974; Hugo Award, World Science Fiction Convention, 1974, 1980; Vidya Jyothi Medal (Presidential Science Award), 1986; Grand Master, SF Writers of America, 1986; Charles Lindbergh Award, 1987; Lord Perry Award, 1992. *Publications: non-fiction:* Interplanetary Flight, 1950; The Exploration of Space, 1951; The Young Traveller in Space, 1954 (publ. in USA as Going into Space); The Coast of Coral, 1956; The Making of a Moon, 1957; The Reefs of Taprobane, 1957; Voice Across the Sea, 1958; The Challenge of the Spaceship, 1960; The Challenge of the Sea, 1960; Profiles of the Future, 1962; Voices from the Sky, 1965; (with Mike Wilson): Boy Beneath the Sea, 1958; The First Five Fathoms, 1960; Indian Ocean Adventure, 1961; The Treasure of the Great Reef, 1964; Indian Ocean Treasure, 1964; (with R. A. Smith) The Exploration of the Moon, 1954; (with Editors of Life) Man and Space, 1964; (ed) The Coming of the Space Age, 1967; The Promise of Space, 1968; (with the astronauts) First on the Moon, 1970; Report on Planet Three, 1972; (with Chesley Bonestell) Beyond Jupiter, 1973; The

View from Serendip, 1977; (with Simon Welfare and John Fairley) Arthur C. Clarke's Mysterious World, 1980 (also TV series); (with Simon Welfare and John Fairley) Arthur C. Clarke's World of Strange Powers, 1984 (also TV series); Ascent to Orbit, 1984; 1984: Spring, 1984; (with Peter Hyams) The Odyssey File, 1985; (with editors of OMNI) Arthur C. Clarke's July 20, 2019, 1986; (with Simon Welfare and John Fairley) Arthur C. Clarke's Chronicles of the Strange and Mysterious, 1987; Astounding Days, 1988; How the World was One, 1992; (with Simon Welfare and John Fairley) Arthur C. Clarke's A–Z of Mysteries, 1993; By Space Possessed, 1993; The Snows of Olympus, 1994; The Colours of Infinity, 1995; *fiction:* Prelude to Space, 1951; The Sands of Mars, 1951; Islands in the Sky, 1952; Against the Fall of Night, 1953; Childhood's End, 1953; Expedition to Earth, 1953; Earthlight, 1955; Reach for Tomorrow, 1956; The City and the Stars, 1956; Tales from the White Hart, 1957; The Deep Range, 1957; The Other Side of the Sky, 1958; A Fall of Moondust, 1961; Tales of Ten Worlds, 1962; Dolphin Island, 1963; Glide Path, 1963; (with Stanley Kubrick) novel and screenplay, 2001: A Space Odyssey, 1968; The Lost Worlds of 2001, 1972; The Wind from the Sun, 1972; Rendezvous with Rama, 1973; Imperial Earth, 1975; The Fountains of Paradise, 1979; 2010: Space Odyssey II, 1982 (filmed 1984); The Songs of Distant Earth, 1986; 2061: Odyssey III, 1988; (with Gentry Lee) Cradle, 1988; Rama II, 1989; The Ghost from the Grand Banks, 1990; The Garden of Rama, 1991; (with Gregory Benford) Beyond the Fall of Night, 1991; The Hammer of God, 1993; (with G. Lee) Rama Revealed, 1993; *anthologies:* Across the Sea of Stars, 1959; From the Ocean, From the Stars, 1962; Prelude to Mars, 1965; The Nine Billion Names of God, 1967; Of Time and Stars, 1972; The Best of Arthur C. Clarke, 1973; Tales from Planet Earth, 1990; More than One Universe, 1991; papers in Electronic Engineering, Wireless World, Wireless Engineer, Aeroplane, Jl of British Interplanetary Soc., Astronautics, etc. *Recreations:* diving, table-tennis. *Address:* 25 Barnes Place, Colombo 7, Sri Lanka. *T:* Colombo 699757, 694255, *Fax:* Colombo 698730; c/o David Higham Associates, 5 Lower John Street, Golden Square, W1R 3PE. *Clubs:* British Sub-Aqua; Colombo Swimming, Otters.

CLARKE, Dr Arthur S.; Keeper, Department of Natural History, Royal Scottish Museum, 1980–83, retired; *b* 11 Feb. 1923; *yr s* of late Albert Clarke and Doris Clarke (*née* Elliott); *m* 1951, Joan, *er d* of Walter Andrassy; one *s* one *d. Educ:* Leeds Boys' Modern School; Aireborough Grammar School; Leeds Univ. (BSc 1948, PhD 1951). Pilot, RAF, 1943–46. Assistant Lecturer, Glasgow Univ., 1951; Asst Keeper, Royal Scottish Museum, 1954; Deputy Keeper, 1973. *Address:* Rose Cottage, Yarrow, Selkirk TD7 5LB.

CLARKE, Prof. Bryan Campbell, DPhil; FRS 1982; Foundation Professor of Genetics, 1971–93, Research Professor, since 1993, University of Nottingham; *b* 24 June 1932; *s* of Robert Campbell Clarke and Gladys Mary (*née* Carter); *m* 1960, Ann Gillian, *d* of late Prof. John Jewkes, CBE; one *s* one *d. Educ:* Fay Sch., Southborough, Mass, USA; Magdalen Coll. Sch., Oxford; Magdalen Coll., Oxford (MA, DPhil). FLS 1980. National Service, 1950–52 (Pilot Officer, RAF). Nature Conservancy Res. Student, Oxford Univ., 1956; Asst 1959, Lectr 1963, Reader 1969, Dept of Zoology, Univ. of Edinburgh. Res. Fellow, Stanford Univ., 1973; SRC Sen. Res. Fellow, 1976–81. Joint Founder, Population Genetics Gp, 1967; Pres., Section D (Biology), BAAS, 1989; Vice-President: Genetical Soc., 1981; Linnean Soc., 1985–87; Soc. for Study of Evolution, USA, 1990–91; Chairman: Terrestrial Life Sciences Cttee, NERC, 1984–87; Molecular Biology and Genetics Sub-Cttee, SERC, 1990–93; Biol Scis Sub-Cttee, HEFCE, 1992–. Mem. Council, Royal Soc., 1994–. Scientific expeditions to: Morocco, 1955; Polynesia, 1962, 1967, 1968, 1980, 1982, 1986, 1991, 1994. Lectures: Special, London Univ., 1973; Official Visitor, Australian Genetics Soc., 1979; Nelson, Rutgers Univ., 1980; R. A. Fisher, La Trobe Univ., 1986; Walton, Virginia Univ., 1988; Jinks, Birmingham Univ., 1991; Pilkington, Manchester Univ., 1993. Editor: Heredity, 1978–85; Proceedings of the Royal Society, Series B, 1989–93. *Publications:* Berber Village, 1959; contrib. scientific jls, mostly on ecological genetics and evolution. *Recreations:* sporadic painting and gardening; archaeology, computing. *Address:* Linden Cottage, School Lane, Colston Bassett, Nottingham NG12 3FD. *T:* Kinoulton (01949) 81243. *Club:* Royal Air Force.

CLARKE, Sir (Charles Mansfield) Tobias, 6th Bt *cr* 1831; *b* Santa Barbara, California, 8 Sept. 1939; *e s* of Sir Humphrey Orme Clarke, 5th Bt, and Elisabeth (*d* 1967), *d* of Dr William Albert Cook; *S* father, 1973; *m* 1971, Charlotte (marr. diss. 1979), *e d* of Roderick Walter; *m* 1984, Teresa L. A. de Chair, *d* of late Somerset de Chair; one *s* two *d. Educ:* Eton; Christ Church, Oxford (MA); Univ. of Paris; New York Univ. Graduate Business Sch. Bankers Trust Co., NY, 1963–80 (Vice-Pres., 1974–80). Associate Dir, Swiss Bank Corp., London, 1992–94. MSI 1993. Chm., Standing Council of the Baronetage, 1993–96 (Vice-Chm., 1990–92; Hon. Treas., 1980–92); Editor and originator, The Baronets Journal, 1987–; Chm., Baronets Trust, 1996 (Trustee, 1989–95). Lord of the Manor of Bibury. *Recreations:* accidental happenings, riding, gardening, photography, stimulating conversation; Pres., Bibury Cricket Club. *Heir: s* (Charles Somerset) Lawrence Clarke, *b* 12 March 1990. *Address:* South Lodge, 80 Campden Hill Road, W8 7AA. *T:* 0171–937 3932; The Church House, Bibury, Cirencester, Glos GL7 5NR. *T:* Cirencester (01285) 740225. *Clubs:* White's, Boodle's, Beefsteak, Pratt's; Pilgrims; Jockey (Paris); The Brook, Racquet & Tennis (New York).

CLARKE, (Christopher) Michael; Keeper, National Gallery of Scotland, since 1987; *b* 29 Aug. 1952; *s* of Patrick Reginald Clarke and Margaret Catherine Clarke (*née* Waugh); *m* 1978, Deborah Clare Cowling; two *s* one *d. Educ:* Felsted; Manchester Univ. (BA (Hons) History of Art). Art Asst, York City Art Gall., 1973–76; Res. Asst, British Mus., 1976–78; Asst Keeper in Charge of Prints, Whitworth Art Gall., Manchester Univ., 1978–84; Asst Keeper, Nat. Gall. of Scotland, 1984–87. Vis. Fellow, Yale Center for British Art, 1985. *Publications:* Pollaiuolo to Picasso: Old Master prints in the Whitworth Art Gallery, 1980; The Tempting Prospect: a social history of English watercolours, 1981; (co-ed with N. Penny) The Arrogant Connoisseur: Richard Payne Knight, 1982; The Draughtsman's Art: Master Drawings in the Whitworth Art Gallery, 1983; Lighting up the Landscape: French Impressionism and its origins, 1986; Corot and the Art of Landscape, 1991; Eyewitness Art: watercolour, 1993; articles, reviews, etc, in Apollo, Art Internat., Burlington Magazine, Museums Jl. *Recreations:* golf, travel. *Address:* 9A Summerside Street, Trinity, Edinburgh EH6 4NT.

CLARKE, Christopher Simon Courtenay Stephenson; QC 1984; a Recorder, since 1990; a Deputy High Court Judge, since 1993; *b* 14 March 1947; *s* of late Rev. John Stephenson Clarke and of Enid Courtenay Clarke; *m* 1974, Caroline Anne Fletcher; one *s* two *d. Educ:* Marlborough College; Gonville and Caius College, Cambridge (MA). Called to the Bar, Middle Temple, 1969, Bencher, 1991; Attorney of Supreme Court of Turks and Caicos Islands, 1975–. Councillor, Internat. Bar Assoc., 1988–90; Chm., Commercial Bar Assoc., 1993–. *Address:* 42 The Chase, SW4 0NH. *T:* 0171–622 0765; Brick Court Chambers, 15/19 Devereux Court, WC2R 3JJ. *T:* 0171–583 0777. *Clubs:* Brooks's, Hurlingham.

CLARKE, (Cyril Alfred) Allen, MA, DLitt; Headmaster, Holland Park Secondary School, 1957–71; *b* 21 Aug. 1910; *s* of late Frederick John Clarke; *m* 1934, Edna Gertrude Francis (decd); three *s. Educ:* Langley Sch., Norwich; Culham Coll. of Educn, Oxon; Birkbeck Coll., Univ. of London; King's Coll., Univ. of London. DLitt Knightsbridge Univ., Copenhagen, 1993. Entered London Teaching Service, 1933; Royal Artillery, 1940–46; Staff Officer (Major) in Educn Br. of Mil. Govt of Germany, 1945–46; Asst Master, Haberdashers' Aske's Hatcham Boys' Sch., 1946–51; Headmaster: Isledon Sec. Sch., 1951–55; Battersea Co. Sec. Sch., 1955–57. Hon. Gov., Langley Sch., 1994–. *Recreations:* photography, writing, reading, archaeology. *Address:* 16 Plasset Drive, Attleborough, Norfolk NR17 2NU. *T:* Attleborough (01953) 454518.

CLARKE, Prof. Sir Cyril (Astley), KBE 1974 (CBE 1969); FRS 1970; MD, ScD, FRCP, FRCOG; FIBiol; Emeritus Professor and Hon. Nuffield Research Fellow, Department of Genetics, and Hon. Research Fellow, Department of Geriatric Medicine, University of Liverpool (Professor of Medicine, 1965–72, Director, Nuffield Unit of Medical Genetics, 1963–72, and Nuffield Research Fellow, 1972–76); Consultant Physician, United Liverpool Hospitals (David Lewis Northern, 1946–58, Royal Infirmary since 1958) and to Broadgreen Hospital since 1946; *b* 22 Aug. 1907; *s* of Astley Vavasour Clarke, MD, JP, and Ethel Mary Clarke, *d* of H. Simpson Gee; *m* 1935, Frieda (Féo) Margaret Mary, *d* of Alexander John Campbell Hart and Isabella Margaret Hart; three *s. Educ:* Wyggeston Grammar Sch., Leicester; Oundle Sch.; Gonville and Caius Coll., Cambridge; Guy's Hosp. (Schol.). 2nd Class Hons, Natural Science Tripos Pt I; MD Cantab 1937; ScD Cantab 1963. FRCP 1949; FRCOG 1970; FRACP 1973; FRCPI 1973; FRSA 1973; FFCM 1974; FACP 1976; Fellow Ceylon Coll. of Physicians 1974; FRCPE 1975; FRCP(C) 1977; FLS 1981. House Phys., Demonstr in Physiology and Clin. Asst in Dermatology, Guy's Hosp., 1932–36. Life Insurance practice, Grocers' Hall, EC2, 1936–39. Served, 1939–46, as Med Specialist, RNVR: HM Hosp. Ship Amarapoora (Scapa Flow and N Africa), RNH Seaforth and RNH Sydney. After War, Med. Registrar, Queen Elizabeth Hosp., Birmingham. Visiting Prof. of Genetics, Seton Hall Sch. of Med., Jersey City, USA, 1963; Lectures: Lumleian, RCP, 1967; Ingleby, Univ. of Birmingham, 1968; Foundn, RCPath, 1971; Inaugural Faculty, Univ. of Leeds, 1972; P. B. Fernando Meml, Colombo, 1974; Marsden, Royal Free Hosp., 1976; Linacre, 1978; New Ireland, UCD, 1979; William Meredith Fletcher Shaw, RCOG, 1979; Harveian Oration, RCP, 1979; Sir Arthur Hall Meml, Sheffield, 1981; Ransom, Univ. of Nottingham, 1990. Examr in Med., Dundee Univ., 1965–69. Pres., RCP, 1972–77 (Censor, 1967–69, Sen. Censor, 1971–72, Dir, Med. Services Study Group, 1977–83, Dir, Med. Res. Unit, 1983–88); Pres. Liverpool Med. Instn, 1970–71; Chairman: British Heart Foundn Council, 1982–87; British Soc. for Res. on Ageing, 1987–92; Jt Cttee of Management, British Paediatric Surveillance Unit, 1990–; Member: MRC Working Party, 1966; Sub-Cttee of Dept of Health and Social Security on prevention of Rhesus hæmolytic disease, 1967–82 (Chm., 1973–82); Bd of Governors, United Liverpool Hosps, 1969; Assoc. of Hungarian Medical Socs, 1973; Res. Adv. Cttee Royal Hosp. and Home, Putney, 1988–94; President: Harveian Soc.; Royal Entomological Soc. of London, 1991–92; Governor and Councillor, Bedford Coll., 1974, Chm. of Council, 1975–85. Chm., Cockayne Trust Fund, Natural History Museum, 1974–. Hon. Fellow: Caius Coll., Cambridge, 1974; UMDS, 1992; British Blood Transfusion Soc., 1992; Leverhulme Emeritus Fellow, 1980. Hon. FRCPE 1981; Hon. FRCPath 1981; Hon. FRSM 1982; Hon. Mem., Liverpool Med. Inst., 1981. Hon. DSc: Edinburgh, 1971; Leicester, 1971; East Anglia, 1973; Birmingham, Liverpool and Sussex, 1974; Hull, 1977; Wales, 1978; London, 1980; Coll. of William and Mary, Williamsburg, USA, 1992. Gold Medal in Therapeutics, Worshipful Soc. of Apothecaries, 1970; James Spence Medal, Brit. Paediatric Assoc., 1973; Addingham Medal, Leeds, 1973; John Scott Medal and Award, Philadelphia, 1976; Fothergillian Medal, Med. Soc., 1977; Gairdner Award, 1977; Ballantyne Prize, RCPEd, 1979; (jtly) Albert and Mary Lasker Foundn Award, 1980; Linnean Medal for Zoology, 1981; Artois-Baillet Latour Health Prize, 1981; Gold Medal, RSM, 1986; Buchanan Medal, Royal Soc., 1990. *Publications:* Genetics for the Clinician, 1962; (ed) Selected Topics in Medical Genetics, 1969; Human Genetics and Medicine, 1970, 3rd edn 1987; (with R. B. McConnell) Prevention of Rhesus Hæmolytic Disease, 1972; (ed) Rhesus Hæmolytic Disease: selected papers and extracts, 1975; many contribs med. and scientific jls, particularly on prevention of Rhesus hæmolytic disease and on evolution of mimicry in swallowtail butterflies. *Recreations:* small boat sailing, breeding swallowtail butterflies. *Address:* 43 Caldy Road, West Kirby, Wirral, Merseyside L48 2HF. *T:* 0151–625 8811. *Clubs:* Athenæum; Oxford and Cambridge Sailing Society (Pres., 1975–77); West Kirby Sailing; United Hospitals Sailing (Pres., 1977–92).

CLARKE, David Clive; QC 1983; **His Honour Judge David Clarke;** a Circuit Judge, since 1993; *b* 16 July 1942; *s* of Philip George Clarke and José Margaret Clarke; *m* 1969, Alison Claire, *d* of Rt Rev. Percy James Brazier; two *s* (and one *s* decd). *Educ:* Winchester Coll.; Magdalene Coll., Cambridge. BA 1964, MA 1968. Called to the Bar, Inner Temple, 1965, Bencher, 1992. In practice, Northern Circuit, 1965–93 (Treas., 1988–92); a Recorder, 1981–93. *Recreations:* exploring canals, sailing, swimming. *Address:* Queen Elizabeth II Law Courts, Derby Square, Liverpool L2 1XA. *T:* 0151–473 7373. *Clubs:* Trearddur Bay Sailing (Anglesey); Oxton Cricket (Birkenhead).

CLARKE, David Stuart; Executive Chairman, Macquarie Bank Ltd, since 1985; Chairman, Brian McGuigan Wines Ltd, since 1991; *b* 3 Jan. 1942; *s* of Stuart Richardson Clarke and Ailsie Jean Talbot Clarke; *m* 1964, Margaret Maclean Partridge (marr. diss. 1994); two *s. Educ:* Knox Grammar Sch.; Sydney Univ. (BEcon Hons); Harvard Univ. (MBA). Director: Darling & Co. Ltd (now Schroder Australia Ltd), 1968–71; Babcock Aust. Holdings Ltd, 1972–81; Chairman: Accepting Houses Assoc. of Aust. (now Aust. Merchant Bankers Assoc.), 1974–76; Sceggs Darlinghurst Ltd, 1976–79; Hill Samuel Aust. Ltd, 1984–85 (Jt Man. Dir, 1971–77, Man. Dir, 1977–84); Barlile Corp. Ltd, 1986–93; Director: Hill Samuel & Co. Ltd (London), 1978–84; Hooker Corp. Ltd, 1984–86; Reil Corp. Ltd, 1986–87. Member: Lloyds of London, 1983–; Aust. Stock Exch. (Sydney) Ltd, 1987–; Fed. Govt Cttee under Financial Corporations Act, 1975–85; Exec. Cttee, Cttee for Econ. Develt of Australia, 1982–. Chairman: Australian Opera, 1986–95; Aust. Wool Realisation Commn, 1991–93. Member: Council, Royal Agricl Soc. of NSW, 1986– (Chm., Wine Cttee, 1990–); Harvard Bus. Sch. Alumni Council, 1986–89. Hon. Fed. Treas., Liberal Party of Aust., 1987–89. Member: Bd Trustees, Financial Markets Foundn for Children, 1989–; Sydney Adv. Bd, Salvation Army, 1990–; Corporate Citizens Cttee, Children's Leukaemia and Cancer Foundn, 1992; Chairman: Salvation Army Red Shield Appeal, 1990– (Cttee Mem., 1985–88; Dep. Chm., 1989–90); Menzies Res. Centre, 1994–. Co-Convener, Cook Soc., 1988–. Chm., NSW Rugby Union, 1989– (Treas., 1989). *Recreations:* opera, ski-ing, tennis, golf, bridge, philately, personal computers, ballet, wine. *Address:* 5 Keltie Bay, 15 Sutherland Crescent, Darling Point, NSW 2000, Australia. *T:* 3634966. *Clubs:* Australian, Harvard of Australia (Pres. 1977–79), Royal Sydney Golf, Elanora Country, Cabbage Tree (Sydney).

CLARKE, Prof. David William, DPhil; FEng, FIEE; Professor of Control Engineering, since 1992, and Head of Department of Engineering Science, since 1994, Oxford University; Fellow, New College, Oxford, since 1969; *b* 31 May 1943; *s* of Norman William Clarke and Laura (*née* Dewhurst); *m* 1967, Lynda Ann Weatherhead; two *s. Educ:* Balliol Coll., Oxford. MA, DPhil Oxon. FIEE 1984; FEng 1989. Oxford University: Astor Res. Fellow, New Coll., 1966–69; Lectr, 1969–86; Reader in Information Engrg, 1986–92. Sir Harold Hartley Silver Medal, Inst. of Measurement and Control, 1983. *Publications:* Advances in Model-Based Predictive Control, 1994; papers in learned jls.

Recreation: gardening. *Address:* New College, Oxford OX1 3BN. *T:* Oxford (01865) 279507.

CLARKE, Donald Roberts; Finance Director, 3i (formerly Investors in Industry) Group plc, 1988–91; *b* 14 May 1933; *s* of Harold Leslie Clarke and Mary Clarke; *m* 1959, Susan Charlotte Cotton; one *s* three *d*. *Educ:* Ealing Grammar Sch.; The Queen's Coll., Oxford (MA). Articled Peat Marwick Mitchell & Co., 1957–62; Accountant, The Collingwood Group, 1962–64; Industrial and Commercial Finance Corporation: Investigating Accountant, 1964; Controller, 1964–67; Br. Manager, 1967–68; Co. Sec., 1968–73; Investors in Industry Gp (formerly Finance for Industry): Sec./Treasurer, 1973–76; Asst Gen. Man., 1976–79; Gen. Man., Finance, 1979–88. Dir, Consumers' Assoc. Ltd, 1990–92. Member: UGC, 1982–85; Industrial, Commercial and Prof. Liaison Gp, National Adv. Body for Local Authority Higher Educn, 1983–85; Continuing Educn Standing Cttee, Nat. Adv. Body for Local Authority Higher Educn and UGC, 1985–89; Council, RHBNC, 1987–. *Publication:* (jtly) 3i: 50 years investing in industry, 1995. *Recreations:* music, gardening, photography. *Club:* United Oxford & Cambridge University.

CLARKE, Most Rev. Edwin Kent, DD; *b* 21 Jan. 1932. *Educ:* Bishop's Univ., Lennoxville (BA 1954, LST 1956); Union Seminary, NY (MRE 1960); Huron Coll., Ontario (DD). Deacon 1956, priest 1957, Ottawa. Curate of All Saints, Westboro, 1956–59; Director of Christian Education, Diocese of Ottawa, 1960–66; Rector of St Lambert, Montreal, 1966–73; Diocesan Sec., Diocese of Niagara, 1973–76; Archdeacon of Niagara, 1973–76; Bishop Suffragan of Niagara, 1976–79; Bishop of Edmonton, 1980; Archbishop of Edmonton and Metropolitan of Rupert's Land, 1986–87. *Address:* RR#3, Pembroke, Ontario K8A 6W4, Canada.

CLARKE, Edwin (Sisterson), MD, FRCP; Hon. Curator, Sherrington Room, University Laboratory of Physiology, Oxford University, since 1985; Director, Wellcome Institute for the History of Medicine, 1973–79, retired; *b* Felling-on-Tyne, 18 June 1919; *s* of Joseph and Nellie Clarke; *m* 1st, 1949, Margaret Elsie Morrison (marr. diss.); two *s*; 2nd, 1958, Beryl Eileen Brock (marr. diss.); one *d*; 3rd, 1982, Gaynor Crawford. *Educ:* Jarrow Central Sch.; Univ. of Durham Med. Sch. (MD); Univ. of Chicago Med. Sch. (MD). Neurological Specialist, RAMC, 1946–48; Nat. Hosp., Queen Square, 1950–51; Postgrad. Med. Sch. of London, 1951–58; Lectr in Neurology and Consultant Neurologist to Hammersmith Hosp., 1955–58; Asst Sec. to Wellcome Trust, 1958–60; Asst Prof., History of Medicine, Johns Hopkins Hosp. Med. Sch., 1960–62; Vis. Assoc. Prof., History of Medicine, Yale Univ. Med. Sch., 1962–63; Med. Historian to Wellcome Historical Med. Library and Museum, 1963–66; Sen. Lectr and Head of Sub-Dept of History of Medicine, University Coll. London, 1966–72, Reader, 1972–73. *Publications:* (jtly) The Human Brain and Spinal Cord, 1968; (ed) Modern Methods in the History of Medicine, 1971; (jtly) An Illustrated History of Brain Function, 1972; (trans.) Die historische Entwicklung der experimentellen Gehirn- und Rückenmarksphysiologie vor Flourens, by M. Neuburger, 1981; (jtly) Nineteenth Century Origins of Neuroscientific Concepts, 1987; articles in jls dealing with neurology and with history of medicine.

CLARKE, Sir Ellis (Emmanuel Innocent), TC 1969; GCMG 1972 (CMG 1960); Kt 1963 (but does not use the title within Republic of Trinidad and Tobago); President of Trinidad and Tobago, 1976–86 (Governor General and C-in-C, 1973–76); *b* 28 Dec. 1917; *o c* of late Cecil Clarke and of Mrs Elma Clarke; *m* 1952, Eyrmyntrude (*née* Hagley); one *s* one *d*. *Educ:* St Mary's Coll., Trinidad (Jerningham Gold Medal, 1936, and other prizes). London Univ. (LLB 1940); called to the Bar, Gray's Inn, 1940. Private practice at Bar of Trinidad and Tobago, 1941–54; Solicitor-Gen., Oct. 1954; Dep. Colonial Sec., Dec. 1956; Attorney-Gen., 1957–62; Actg Governor, 1960; Chief Justice designate, 1961; Trinidad and Tobago Perm. Rep. to UN, 1962–66; Ambassador: to United States, 1962–73; to Mexico, 1966–73; Rep. on Council of OAS, 1967–73. Chm. of Bd, British West Indian Airways, 1968–72. KStJ 1973. *Address:* Port of Spain, Trinidad. *Clubs:* Queen's Park Cricket (Port of Spain); Trinidad Turf, Arima Race (Trinidad); Tobago Golf (President, 1969–75).

CLARKE, Eric Lionel; MP (Lab) Midlothian, since 1992; *b* 9 April 1933; *s* of late Ernest and Annie Clarke; *m* 1955, June Hewat; two *s* one *d*. *Educ:* St Cuthbert's Holy Cross Acad.; W. M. Ramsey Tech. Coll.; Esk Valley Tech. Coll. Coalminer: Roslin Colliery, 1949–51; Lingerwood Colliery, 1951–69; Bilston Glen Colliery, 1969–77; Trade Union Official, 1977–89; Gen. Sec., NUM Scotland; redundant, unemployed, 1989–92. Mem., Midlothian CC and then Lothian Regl Council, 1962–78. An Opposition Whip, 1994–. *Recreations:* fly fishing, gardening, carpentry, football spectator. *Address:* 32 Mortonhall Park Crescent, Edinburgh EH17 8SY. *T:* 0131–664 8214; 0171–219 6373; (office) PO Box 11, 34 Buccleuch Street, Dalkeith EH22 1HL. *T:* 0131–654 1585, *Fax:* 0131–654 1586. *Clubs:* Mayfield Labour; Morris Working Men's; Danderhall Miners' Welfare.

CLARKE, Frederick, BSc; FBCS; Director, DS Information Systems, since 1991; *b* 8 Dec. 1928; *s* of George and Edna Clarke; *m* 1955, Doris Thompson (marr. diss. 1987); two *d*; *m* 1988, Dorothy Sugrue. *Educ:* King James I Grammar Sch., Bishop Auckland; King's Coll., Durham Univ. (BSc 1951). FBCS 1972. Served RAF, 1951–54. Schoolmaster, 1954–57; IBM, 1957–82 (final appts, Gen. Man. and Dir); Chm., Royal Ordnance plc (formerly Royal Ordnance Factories), 1982–85. Chm., Lingfield Park Racecourse, 1988–90; Dir, Leisure Investments, 1985–90. Mem., Reading Univ. Council, 1980–. Freeman, City of London, 1987. *Recreations:* golf, cricket, racing, reading. *Address:* Arran, Bute Avenue, Petersham, Richmond, Surrey TW10 7AX.

CLARKE, Geoffrey, RA 1976 (ARA 1970); ARCA; artist and sculptor; *b* 28 Nov. 1924; *s* of John Moulding Clarke and Janet Petts; two *s*. *Educ:* Royal College of Art (Hons). Exhibitions: Gimpel Fils Gallery, 1952, 1955; Redfern Gallery, 1965; Tranman Gallery, 1975, 1976, 1982; Yorkshire Sculpture Park, Chappel Gall., Colchester, and Friends Room, Royal Acad., 1994; touring exhibitions: Christchurch Mansions, Ipswich, 1994; Herbert Art Gall., Coventry, and Pallant House, Chichester, 1995. Works in public collections: Victoria and Albert Museum; Tate Gallery; Arts Council; Museum of Modern Art, NY; etc. Prizes for engraving: Triennial, 1951; London, 1953, Tokyo, 1957. Commissioned work includes: iron sculpture, Time Life Building, New Bond Street; cast aluminium relief sculpture, Castrol House, Marylebone Road; mosaics, Liverpool Univ. Physics Block and Basildon New Town; stained glass windows for Treasury, Lincoln Cathedral; bronze sculpture, Thorn Electric Building, Upper St Martin's Lane; relief sculpture on Canberra and Oriana; 3 stained glass windows, high altar, cross and candlesticks, the flying cross and crown of thorns, all in Coventry Cathedral; sculpture, Nottingham Civic Theatre; UKAEA Culham; Univs of Liverpool, Exeter, Cambridge, Oxford, Manchester, Lancaster, Loughborough and Warwick; screens in Royal Military Chapel, Birdcage Walk. Further work at Chichester, Newcastle, Manchester, Plymouth, Ipswich, Canterbury, Taunton, Winchester, St Paul, Minnesota, Lincoln, Nebraska, Newcastle Civic Centre, Wolverhampton, Leicester, Churchill Coll., Aldershot, Suffolk Police HQ, All Souls, W1, The Majlis, Abu Dhabi, York House, N1.

CLARKE, Graham Neil; Group Editor, IPC gardening titles, since 1993; Editor: Amateur Gardening, since 1986; Your Garden, since 1993; The Gardener, since 1993; *b* 23 July 1956; *s* of Henry Charles Owen Clarke, RVM and Doris May Clarke; *m* 1980, Denise Carole (*née* Anderson); two *d*. *Educ:* Rutherford Sch., N London; Wisley School of Horticulture (WisCertHort). Staff gardener, Buckingham Palace, 1975–76; Nurseryman, Hyde Park, 1976; Amateur Gardening: Sub-Editor, 1976–79; Chief Sub-Editor, 1979–81; Dep. Editor, 1981–86; Editor, Home Plus Magazine, 1984–85. FLS 1990; AIHort 1991. *Publications:* Step by Step Pruning, 1985; Autumn and Winter Colour in the Garden, 1986; Complete Book of Plant Propagation, 1990. *Recreations:* genealogy, philately, gardening. *Address:* c/o IPC Magazines Ltd, Westover House, West Quay Road, Poole, Dorset BH15 1JG. *T:* Poole (01202) 680586. *Club:* Royal Horticultural Society Garden (Surrey).

CLARKE, Guy Hamilton, CMG 1959; HM Ambassador to Nepal, 1962–63, retired; *b* 23 July 1910; 3rd *s* of late Dr and Mrs Charles H. Clarke, Leicester. *Educ:* Wyggeston Grammar Sch., Leicester; Trinity Hall, Cambridge. Probationer Vice-Consul, Levant Consular Service, Beirut, 1933; transf. to Ankara, 1936; Corfu, 1940; Adana, 1941; Baltimore, 1944; has since served at: Washington, Los Angeles (Consul 1945), Bangkok, Jedda, Kirkuk (Consul 1949), Bagdad, Kirkuk (Consul-Gen. 1951); Ambassador to the Republic of Liberia, 1957–60, and to the Republic of Guinea, 1959–60; Mem. United Kingdom Delegation to United Nations Gen. Assembly, New York, 1960; HM Consul-General, Damascus, Feb. 1961, and Chargé d'Affaires there, Oct. 1961–Jan. 1962. *Address:* 10 Fairlawn House, Christchurch Road, Winchester, Hants SO23 9SR.

CLARKE, Dr Helen, FSA, FRHistS; Director, Society of Antiquaries, 1990–94; *b* 25 Aug. 1939; *d* of George Parker and Helen (*née* Teare); *m* 1967, Giles Colin Scott Clarke; one *s*. *Educ:* Univ. of Birmingham (BA; PhD); Univ. of Lund, Sweden. FSA 1972; FRHistS 1990. Dir of Excavations, King's Lynn, 1963–67; Res. Fellow, Sch. of History, Birmingham Univ., 1965–67; Lecturer in Medieval Archaeology: Glasgow Univ., 1967–69; UCL, 1976–90. Visiting Professor in Medieval Archaeology: Lund Univ., Sweden, 1991; Århus Univ., Denmark, 1992; Kiel Univ., Germany, 1993. Editor and Translator: Royal Swedish Acad. of History and Antiquities, 1975–; Bd of National Antiquities, Sweden (also Consultant), 1990–; Consultant, English Heritage, 1987–. Member: Svenska Arkeologiska Samfundet, 1988; Vetenskapssocieten i Lund, 1988. Hon. Fil Dr Lund, 1991. *Publications:* Regional Archaeologies: East Anglia, 1971; Excavations in King's Lynn, 1963–1970, 1977; The Archaeology of Medieval England, 1984, 2nd edn 1986; Towns in the Viking Age, 1991, 2nd edn 1995. *Recreations:* attending opera, watching cricket, food, wine.

CLARKE, Henry Benwell; Joint Managing Director, People and Places International, since 1993; *b* 30 Jan. 1950; *yr s* of late Stephen Lampard Clarke and Elinor Wade Clarke (*née* Benwell); *m* 1973, Verena Angela Lodge; four *s* one *d*. *Educ:* St John's Sch., Leatherhead; South Bank Polytechnic (BSc Estate Management 1972); Imperial College London (MSc Management Science 1977; DIC 1977). ARICS 1973, FRICS 1986; ACIArb 1979. British Rail Property Board: S Region, 1972–78; NW Region, 1978–82; E Region, 1982–85; Regional Estate Surveyor and Manager, Midland Region, 1985–86; Chief Estate Surveyor, HQ, 1986–87; Nat. Develt Manager, 1987–88; Dep. Chief Exec., Crown Estate Comrs, 1988–92, Acting Chief Exec. and Accounting Officer, 1989. Mem., Gen. Council, British Property Fedn, 1989–92. Mem., Royal Armouries Partnership, 1991–. Member: Council, Christian Union for Estate Profession, 1983–88; Bd, Youth with a Mission (England), 1990–; advisor to various Christian trusts. MIMgt. *Recreations:* reading, walking, architecture, Church. *Address:* 42 Wordsworth Road, Harpenden, Herts AL5 4AF. *Club:* National.

CLARKE, Hilton Swift, CBE 1984; President, Atlantic International Bank Ltd, since 1987 (Director, 1969–86, Chairman, 1973–86); *b* 1 April 1909; *yr s* of Frederick Job Clarke; *m* 1st, 1934, Sibyl Muriel (*d* 1975), *d* of late C. J. C. Salter; one *s*; 2nd, 1984, Ann Elizabeth, *d* of late Leonard James Marchant. *Educ:* Highgate School. FCIB. Bank of England, 1927–67; Mem. UK Delegn, OEEC, Paris, 1948–49. Director: Charterhouse Group Ltd, 1967–82 (Chm. Charterhouse Japhet Ltd, 1971–73); United Dominions Trust Ltd, 1967–81; Guthrie Corp., 1967–79; Bank of Scotland Ltd (London Bd), 1967–79; Chairman: Astley & Pearce, 1981–86 (Dir, 1975–86); Exco International plc, 1981–84 (Dir, 1981–86). Freeman, City of London, 1973. Hon. FRCGP 1975. *Recreation:* gardening. *Address:* 4 Coverdale Avenue, Cooden, Bexhill, E Sussex TN39 4TY. *T:* Bexhill (01424) 845030. *Clubs:* Bankers', Sloane; Cooden Beach Golf.

CLARKE, James Samuel, MC 1943 and Bar 1944; Under-Secretary and Principal Assistant Solicitor, Inland Revenue, 1970–81, retired; Managing Director, Bishop and Clarke Ltd, since 1981; *b* 19 Jan. 1921; *s* of James Henry and Deborah Florence Clarke; *m* 1949, Ilse Cohen; two *d*. *Educ:* Reigate Grammar Sch.; St Catharine's Coll., Cambridge (MA). Army Service, 1941–45: Royal Irish Fusiliers; served 1st Bn N Africa and Italy; Major 1943. Called to Bar, Middle Temple, 1946. Entered Legal Service (Inland Rev.), 1953; Sen. Legal Asst, 1958; Asst Solicitor, 1965. *Recreation:* gardening. *Address:* Dormers, The Downs, Givons Grove, Leatherhead, Surrey KT22 8LH. *T:* Leatherhead (01372) 378254. *Clubs:* National Liberal, Royal Automobile.

CLARKE, Prof. John, FRS 1986; Professor of Physics, since 1973, and Luis W. Alvarez Memorial Chair for Experimental Physics, since 1994; University of California, Berkeley; *b* 10 Feb. 1942; *s* of Victor Patrick and Ethel May Clarke; *m* 1979, Grethe F. Pedersen; one *d*. *Educ:* Christ's Coll., Cambridge (BA, MA 1968); Darwin Coll., Cambridge (PhD 1968). Postdoctoral Scholar, 1968, Asst Prof., 1969, Associate Prof., 1971–73, Univ. of California, Berkeley. Alfred P. Sloan Foundn Fellow, 1970; Adolph C. and Mary Sprague Miller Inst. for Basic Research into Science Prof., 1975, 1994; John Simon Guggenheim Fellow, 1977; Vis. Fellow, Clare Hall, Cambridge, 1989. FAAAS 1982; Fellow, Amer. Phys. Soc., 1985. Charles Vernon Boys Prize, Inst. of Physics, 1977; Calif. Scientist of the Year, 1987; Fritz London Meml Award for Low Temperature Physics, 1987. *Publications:* numerous contribs to learned jls. *Address:* Department of Physics, University of California, Berkeley, CA 94720, USA. *T:* (510) 6423069.

CLARKE, Prof. John Frederick, FRS 1987; Professor of Theoretical Gas Dynamics, Cranfield Institute of Technology, 1972–91, Professor Emeritus, since 1992; *b* 1 May 1927; *s* of Frederick William Clarke and Clara Auguste Antonie (*née* Nauen); *m* 1953, Jean Ruth Gentle; two *d*. *Educ:* Warwick School; Queen Mary Coll., Univ. of London (BSc Eng 1st Cl. Hons, David Allan Low Prize, PhD; Hon. Fellow, 1993). FRAeS, FIMA. Qualified Service Pilot, RN, 1946–48; Aerodynamicist, English Electric Co., 1956–57; Lectr, Coll. of Aeronautics, 1958–65 (Vis. Associate Prof. and Fulbright Scholar, Stanford Univ., 1961–62); Reader, Cranfield Inst. of Technology, 1965–72. Vis. Prof. at univs in USA, Australia and Europe; Vis. Res. Fellow, Centre for Non-linear Studies, Univ. of Leeds, 1987–91; Benjamin Meaker Vis. Prof., Univ. of Bristol, 1988–89; first G. C. Steward Vis. Fellow, Gonville and Caius Coll., Cambridge, 1992. Member: NATO Collaborative Research Grants Panel, 1987–90; Esso Energy Award Cttee, 1988–93; Maths Cttee, SERC, 1990–91. Mem., Editl Bd, Qly Jl Mech. Appl. Math., 1982–. FRSA 1985. *Publications:* (with M. McChesney) The Dynamics of Real Gases, 1964; (with M. McChesney) Dynamics of Relaxing Gases, 1976; contribs to professional jls on gas dynamics and combustion theory. *Recreation:* Sunday painter. *Address:* Field House, Green Lane, Aspley Guise MK17 8EN. *T:* Milton Keynes (01908) 582234.

CLARKE, Prof. John Innes, DL; Chairman, North Durham (formerly Durham) District Health Authority, since 1990; *b* 7 Jan. 1929; *s* of late Bernard Griffith Clarke and Edith Louie (*née* Mott); *m* 1955, Dorothy Anne Watkinson; three *d*. *Educ:* Bournemouth Sch.; Univ. of Aberdeen (MA 1st cl., PhD); Univ. of Paris (French Govt scholar). FRGS 1963. RAF 1952–54 (Sword of Merit, 1953). Asst Lectr in Geog., Univ. of Aberdeen, 1954–55; Prof. of Geog., Univ. Coll. of Sierra Leone, 1963–65; University of Durham: Lectr in Geog., 1955–63; Reader in Geog., 1965–68; Prof. of Geog., 1968–90; Acting Principal, Trevelyan Coll., 1979–80; Pro-Vice-Chancellor and Sub-Warden, 1984–90. Visiting Professor: Univ. of Wisconsin, 1967–68; Cameroon, 1965, 1966, 1967; Clermont-Ferrand, 1974; Cairo, 1982; Shanghai, 1986. Acting Chm., Human Geog. Cttee, SSRC, 1975; RGS rep. on British Nat. Cttee for Geography, 1976–81, 1988–89; Chairman: IGU Commn on Population Geography, 1980–88; Higher Educn Support for Industry in the North, 1987–89; Cttee on Population and Environment, Internat. Union for Scientific Study of Population, 1990–95. Vice-President: Eugenics Soc., 1981–84; RGS, 1991–. DL Durham, 1990. FRSA 1990. Silver Medal, RSGS, 1947; Victoria Medal, RGS, 1991. *Publications:* Iranian City of Shiraz, 1963; (jtly) Africa and the Islands, 1964, 4th edn 1977; Population Geography, 1965, 2nd edn 1972; (with B. D. Clark) Kermanshah: an Iranian Provincial City, 1969; Population Geography and the Developing Countries, 1971; (jtly) People in Britain: a census atlas, 1980; *edited:* Sierra Leone in Maps, 1966, 2nd edn 1969; An Advanced Geography of Africa, 1975; Geography and Population: approaches and applications, 1984; *co-edited:* Field Studies in Libya, 1960; Populations of the Middle East and North Africa: a geographical approach, 1972; Human Geography in France and Britain, 1976; Régions Géographiques et Régions d'Aménagements, 1978; Change and Development in the Middle East, 1981; Redistribution of Population in Africa, 1982; Population and Development Projects in Africa, 1985; Population and Disaster, 1989; Mountain Population Pressure, 1990; Environment and Population Change, 1994; Population-Environment-Development Interactions, 1995; author of many learned articles. *Recreations:* travel, sports (now vicariously), countryside, family history. *Address:* Tower Cottage, The Avenue, Durham DH1 4EB. *T:* Durham (0191) 3848350.

CLARKE, (John) Neil; Chairman, British Coal, since 1991; *b* 7 Aug. 1934; *s* of late George Philip Clarke and Norah Marie Clarke (*née* Bailey); *m* 1958, Sonia Heather Beckett; three *s*. *Educ:* Rugby School; King's College London (LLB). FICA 1959. Partner, Rowley, Pemberton, Roberts & Co., 1960–69; Charter Consolidated, 1969–88: Dir, 1973; Exec. Dir, 1974; Man. Dir, 1979; Chief Exec., 1980; Dep. Chm. and Chief Exec., 1982–88; Chairman: Johnson Matthey, 1984–89; Molins, 1989–91 (Dir, 1987–91); Genchem Holdings, 1989–; Director: Anglo American Corp. of SA, 1976–90; Consolidated Gold Fields, 1982–89; Travis Perkins, 1990–; Porvair, 1994–. *Recreations:* music, tennis, golf. *Address:* High Willows, 18 Park Avenue, Farnborough Park, Orpington, Kent BR6 8LL. *T:* Farnborough, Kent (01689) 851651; (office) 0171–201 4100. *Clubs:* MCC; Royal West Norfolk Golf, Addington Golf.

CLARKE, Rear-Adm. John Patrick, LVO 1986; MBE 1978; Flag Officer Training and Recruiting, since 1994; *b* 12 Dec. 1944; *s* of Frank and Christine Clarke; *m* 1969, Ann Parham; one *s* two *d*. *Educ:* Epsom Coll.; BRNC. Commanding Officer, HM Ships: Finwhale, 1976; Oberon, 1977; Dreadnought, 1979–80; CO, Submarine CO's Qualifying Course, 1983–84; Exec. Officer, HM Yacht Britannia, 1985–86; Captain: Submarine Sea Training, 1986–89; Seventh Frigate Squadron, 1989–90; Asst Dir, Naval Staff Duties, 1990–92; Dir, Naval Welfare, 1992; Dir, Naval Management, Communications and Inf. Systems, 1993–94. *Recreations:* golf, bee keeping. *Address:* c/o Naval Secretary, Victory Building, HM Naval Base, Portsmouth PO1 3LS. *Clubs:* Lansdowne; Yeovil Golf.

CLARKE, Rt. Rev. John Robert; *see* Athabasca, Bishop of.

CLARKE, His Honour Sir Jonathan (Dennis), Kt 1981; a Circuit Judge, 1982–93; *b* 19 Jan. 1930; *e s* of late Dennis Robert Clarke, Master of Supreme Court, and of Caroline Alice (*née* Hill); *m* 1956, Susan Margaret Elizabeth (*née* Ashworth); one *s* three *d*. *Educ:* Kidstones Sch.; University Coll. London. Admitted Solicitor, 1956; partner in Townsends, solicitors, 1959–82; a Recorder of the Crown Court, 1972–82. Mem. Council, Law Soc., 1964–82, Pres., 1980–81; Sec., Nat. Cttee of Young Solicitors, 1962–64; Member: Matrimonial Causes Rule Cttee, 1967–78; Legal Studies Bd, CNAA, 1968–75; Judicial Studies Bd, 1979–82; Criminal Injuries Compensation Bd, 1993–. Governor, College of Law, 1970–90, Chm. of Governors, 1982. *Recreations:* sailing, skiing. *Address:* c/o Midland Bank, The Forum, Marlborough Road, Swindon, Wilts SN3 1QT. *Clubs:* Carlton, Farmers'; Royal Western Yacht.

CLARKE, Rt. Hon. Kenneth; PC 1984; QC 1980; MP (C) Rushcliffe Division of Nottinghamshire since 1970; Chancellor of the Exchequer, since 1993; *b* 2 July 1940; *e c* of Kenneth Clarke and Doris (*née* Smith), Nottingham; *m* 1964, Gillian Mary Edwards; one *s* one *d*. *Educ:* Nottingham High Sch.; Gonville and Caius Coll., Cambridge (BA, LLB). Chm., Cambridge Univ. Conservative Assoc., 1961; Pres., Cambridge Union, 1963; Chm., Fedn Conservative Students, 1963. Called to Bar, Gray's Inn 1963, Hon. Bencher, 1989; Mem., Midland Circuit. Research Sec., Birmingham Bow Group, 1965–66; contested Mansfield (Notts) in General Elections of 1964 and 1966. PPS to Solicitor General, 1971–72; an Asst Govt Whip, 1972–74 (Govt Whip for Europe, 1973–74); a Lord Comr, HM Treasury, 1974; Parly Sec., DoT, later Parly Under Sec. of State for Transport, 1979–82; Minister of State (Minister for Health), DHSS, 1982–85; entered Cabinet as Paymaster General and Minister for Employment, 1985–87; Chancellor of Duchy of Lancaster and Minister for Trade and Industry (with additl responsibility to co-ordinate Govt policy on Inner Cities), 1987–88; Secretary of State: for Health, 1988–90; for Educn and Science, 1990–92; for the Home Dept, 1992–93. Mem., Parly delegn to Council of Europe and WEU, 1973–74; Sec., Cons. Parly Health and Social Security Cttee, 1974; Opposition Spokesman on: Social Services, 1974–76; Industry, 1976–79. Hon. LLD: Nottingham, 1989; Huddersfield, 1993. *Publications:* New Hope for the Regions, 1969; pamphlets published by Bow Group, 1964–. *Recreations:* modern jazz music; watching Association Football and cricket, bird-watching. *Address:* House of Commons, SW1A 0AA. *Clubs:* Garrick; Nottinghamshire CC.

CLARKE, Dr Malcolm Alistair; Reader in Commercial Contract Law, Cambridge University, since 1993; Fellow, St John's College, Cambridge, since 1970; *b* 1 April 1943; *s* of Kenneth Alfred William Clarke and Marian Florence Clarke (*née* Rich); *m* 1968, Eva Olga Bergman; two *s*. *Educ:* Kingswood Sch., Bath; L'Ecole des Roches, Verneuil-sur-Avre, France; St John's Coll., Cambridge (LLB 1965; MA 1968; PHD 1973). Asst, Institut de Droit Comparé, Paris, 1965–66; Research Fellow, Fitzwilliam Coll., Cambridge, 1966–68; Lectr, Univ. of Singapore, 1968–70; Cambridge University: Asst Lectr in Law, 1970–75; Lectr, 1975–93; Dir of Studies, St John's Coll., Cambridge, 1972–92. Academic consultant, Allen & Overy, solicitors, 1990–. *Publications:* Aspects of the Hague Rules, 1976; (jtly) Shipbuilding Contracts, 1981, 2nd edn 1992; The International Carriage of Goods by Road: CMR, 1982, 2nd edn 1991; The Law of Insurance Contracts, 1989, 2nd edn 1994; (jtly) Contracts for the Carriage of Goods, 1993. *Recreations:* cycling, music, photography, more or less concurrently. *Address:* St John's College, Cambridge CB2 1TP. *T:* Cambridge (01223) 338600, *Fax:* (01223) 337720.

CLARKE, Prof. Malcolm Roy, FRS 1981; Senior Principal Scientific Officer, Marine Biological Association of the UK, 1978–87; *b* 24 Oct. 1930; *s* of Cecil Dutfield Clarke and Edith Ellen Woodward; *m* 1958, Dorothy Clara Knight; three *s* one *d*. *Educ:* eleven schools and finally Wallingford County Grammar Sch.; Hull Univ. BSc 1955, PhD 1958, DSc 1978. National Service, Private, RAMC, 1949–50. Teacher, 1951; Hull Univ., 1951–58; Whaling Inspector in Antarctic, 1955–56; Scientific Officer, later PSO, Nat. Inst. of Oceanography, 1958–71; led Oceanographic Expedns on RRS Discovery, RRS Challenger, RRS Frederick Russell and RV Sarsia; PSO, Marine Biol Assoc. of UK, 1972–78. Vis. Prof. in Zoology, Liverpool Univ., 1987–92. *Publications:* (ed jtly) Deep Oceans, 1971; Identification of Cephalopod Beaks, 1986; (ed jtly) Evolution, vol. 10, The Mollusca, 1986, vol. 11, Form and Function, 1987, vol. 12, Palaeontology and Neontology of the Cephalopoda, 1987; (ed jtly) Identification of "Larval" Cephalopods, 1987; papers on squids and whales in Jl of Marine Biol Assoc. etc, and a Discovery Report, 1980. *Recreations:* boating, painting. *Address:* Ancarva, Southdown, Millbrook, Torpoint, Cornwall PL10 1EZ. *T:* Plymouth (01752) 823054.

CLARKE, Marshal Butler C.; *see* Cholmondeley Clarke.

CLARKE, Prof. Martin Lowther; *b* 2 Oct. 1909; *s* of late Rev. William Kemp Lowther Clarke; *m* 1942, Emilie de Rontenay Moon (*d* 1991), *d* of late Dr R. O. Moon; two *s*. *Educ:* Haileybury Coll.; King's Coll., Cambridge. Asst, Dept of Humanity, Edinburgh Univ., 1933–34; Fellow of King's Coll., Cambridge, 1934–40; Asst Lecturer in Greek and Latin, University Coll., London, 1935–37. Foreign Office, 1940–45. Lecturer, 1946–47, and Reader, 1947–48, in Greek and Latin, University Coll., London; Prof. of Latin, University Coll. of North Wales, 1948–74, Vice-Principal, 1963–65, 1967–74. *Publications:* Richard Porson, 1937; Greek Studies in England, 1700 to 1830, 1945; Rhetoric at Rome, 1953; The Roman Mind, 1956; Classical Education in Britain, 1500–1900, 1959; George Grote, 1962; Bangor Cathedral, 1969; Higher Education in the Ancient World, 1971; Paley, 1974; The Noblest Roman, 1981. *Address:* 61 Ilges Lane, Cholsey, Wallingford OX10 9PA. *T:* Cholsey (01491) 651389.

CLARKE, Mary; Editor, Dancing Times, since 1963; *b* 23 Aug. 1923; *d* of Frederick Clarke and Ethel Kate (*née* Reynolds); unmarried. *Educ:* Mary Datchelor Girls' School. London Corresp., Dance Magazine, NY, 1943–55; London Editor, Dance News, NY, 1955–70; Asst Editor and Contributor, Ballet Annual, 1952–63; joined Dancing Times as Asst Editor, 1954. Dance critic, The Guardian, 1977–94, retired. Queen Elizabeth II Coronation Award, Royal Acad. of Dancing, 1990. Kt, Order of Dannebrog (Denmark), 1992. *Publications:* The Sadler's Wells Ballet: a history and an appreciation, 1955; Six Great Dancers, 1957; Dancers of Mercury: the story of Ballet Rambert, 1962; ed (with David Vaughan) Encyclopedia of Dance and Ballet, 1977; (with Clement Crisp): Ballet, an Illustrated History, 1973, 2nd edn 1992; Making a Ballet, 1974; Introducing Ballet, 1976; Design for Ballet, 1978; Ballet in Art, 1978; The History of Dance, 1981; Dancer, Men in Dance, 1984; Ballerina, 1987; contrib. Encycl. Britannica. *Address:* 54 Ripplevale Grove, N1 1HT. *T:* 0171–607 3422. *Club:* Gautier.

CLARKE, Matthew Gerard; QC (Scot) 1989; *s* of Thomas Clarke and Ann (*née* Duddy). *Educ:* Holy Cross High Sch., Hamilton; Univ. of Glasgow (MA; LLB). Solicitor, 1972. Lectr, Dept of Scots Law, Edinburgh Univ., 1972–78; admitted to Faculty of Advocates, 1978; Standing Junior Counsel to Scottish Home and Health Dept, 1983–89. Member: Consumer Credit Licensing Appeal Tribunal, 1976–; Estate Agents Tribunals, 1980–; Chm. (part-time), Industrial Tribunals, 1987–. Leader, UK Delegn, Council of the Bars and Laws Socs of EC, 1992– (Mem., 1989–92). *Publications:* (Scottish Editor) Sweet & Maxwell's Encyclopaedia of Consumer Law, 1980–; (contrib.) Corporate Law: the European dimension, 1991; (contrib.) Butterworth's EC Legal Systems, 1992. *Recreations:* opera, chamber music, the music of Schubert, travel. *Address:* 12 Strathearn Place, Edinburgh EH9 2AL. *T:* 0131–447 6074. *Club:* Scottish Arts (Edinburgh).

CLARKE, Michael; *see* Clarke, C. M.

CLARKE, Prof. Michael Gilbert; Professor and Head of School of Public Policy, University of Birmingham, since 1993; *b* 21 May 1944; *s* of Rev. Canon Reginald Gilbert Clarke and Marjorie Kathleen Clarke; *m* 1967, Angela Mary Cook; one *s* two *d*. *Educ:* Queen Elizabeth Grammar Sch., Wakefield; Sussex Univ. (BA 1966; MA 1967). Teaching Assistant, Essex Univ., 1967–69; Lectr and Dir of Studies in Politics, Edinburgh Univ., 1969–75; Asst Dir and Depute Dir, Policy Planning, Lothian Regl Council, 1975–81; Dir, LGTB, 1981–90; Chief Exec., Local Govt Mgt Bd, 1990–93. Chm., RIPA, 1990–92. Member: Gen. Synod of C of E, 1990–93; Council, Inst. for Citizenship Studies, 1992–. Vice-Chm. of Govs, St George's Sch., Harpenden. *Publications:* (ed) C. F. Strong, Modern Political Constitutions, 1975; Getting the Balance Right, 1990; Choices for Local Government: the 1990s and beyond, 1991; How Others See Us, 1995; Breaking Down the Barriers, 1995; contribs on public policy and management matters to various books and jls. *Recreations:* books, family, gardening. *Address:* Millington House, 15 Lansdowne Crescent, Worcester WR3 8JE. *T:* Worcester (01905) 617634. *Club:* Reform.

CLARKE, Maj.-Gen. Michael Hugo Friend; Immigration Appeals Adjudicator, since 1994; *b* 22 Sept. 1936; *s* of Patrick Joseph Clarke and Catherine Amy Clarke (*née* Friend); *m* 1962, Gerritje van der Horst; one *s* one *d*. *Educ:* Rutland House Sch.; Allhallows Sch. Called to the Bar, Lincoln's Inn, 1959; enlisted RASC, 1959; commissioned 2nd Lieut RASC, 1960; Captain, Army Legal Services, 1961; served BAOR, Singapore, Nairobi, Hong Kong, Cyprus, N Ireland; HQ Army Legal Aid, 1981; MoD, 1983; Army Legal Aid, BAOR, 1986; Army Legal Group UK, 1987; Brig., Legal HQ BAOR, 1989; Dir, Army Legal Services, 1992–94. Trustee, Inst. of Obs and Gyn., 1995. *Address:* c/o Lloyds Bank, Cox's and King's Branch, PO Box 1190, 7 Pall Mall, SW1Y 5NA. *Club:* Army Golf (Aldershot).

CLARKE, Neil; *see* Clarke, J. N.

CLARKE, Norman, OBE 1982; Secretary and Registrar, Institute of Mathematics and its Applications, from its foundation, 1964–87, now Emeritus; *b* 21 Oct. 1916; *o s* of late Joseph Clarke and of Ellen Clarke, Oldham; *m* 1940, Hilda May Watts; two *d*. *Educ:* Hulme Grammar Sch., Oldham; Univ. of Manchester (BSc). FInstP; FIMA, Hon. FIMA 1990. Pres., Manchester Univ. Union, 1938–39. External Ballistics Dept, Ordnance Bd, 1939–42; Armament Res. Estabt, Br. for Theoretical Res., 1942–45; Dep. Sec., Inst. Physics, 1945–65; Hon. Sec., Internat. Commn on Physics Educn, 1960–66. Southend-on-Sea County Borough Council: Mem., 1961–74; Alderman, 1964–74; Chm. of Watch Cttee, 1962–69 and of Public Protection Cttee, 1969–78; Vice-Chm., Essex Police Authority, 1969–85; Member: Essex CC, 1973–85; Southend-on-Sea Borough Council, 1974– (Mayor, 1975–76; Chm., Highways Cttee, 1980–84; Leader, 1984–87, 1990–93; Leader, Cons. Gp, 1984–93). *Publications:* papers on educn; editor and contributor: A Physics Anthology: (with S. C. Brown) International Education in Physics; Why Teach Physics; The Education of a Physicist; contributor: A Survey of the Teaching of Physics in Universities (Unesco); Metrication. *Recreations:* cricket, gastronomy, photography. *Address:* 106 Olive Avenue, Leigh-on-Sea, Essex SS9 3QE. *T:* Southend-on-Sea (01702) 558056. *Club:* MCC.

CLARKE, Prof. Patricia Hannah, DSc; FRS 1976; Emeritus Professor, University of London, since 1984; Hon. Research Fellow, Chemical and Biochemical Engineering Department, University College London, since 1984; *b* 29 July 1919; *d* of David Samuel Green and Daisy Lilian Amy Willoughby; *m* 1940, Michael Clarke; two *s*. *Educ:* Howells Sch., Llandaff; Girton Coll., Cambridge (BA). DSc London. Armament Res. Dept, 1940–44; Wellcome Res. Labs, 1944–47; National Collection of Type Cultures, 1951–53; Lectr, Dept of Biochemistry, UCL, 1953; Reader in Microbial Biochemistry, 1966, Prof. of Microbial Biochemistry 1974–84. Leverhulme Emer. Fellow, 1984–87; Hon. Professorial Fellow, UWIST, Univ. of Wales, 1984–90; Kan Tong-Po Prof., Chinese Univ. of Hong Kong, 1986. Chm., Inst. for Biotechnological Studies, 1986–87. Hon. Gen. Sec., Soc. for General Microbiology, 1965–70; Mem., CNAA, 1973–79. Lectures: Royal Soc. Leeuwenhoek, 1979; Marjory Stephenson, Soc. for Gen. Microbiology, 1981; A. J. Kluyver, Netherlands Soc. for Microbiology, 1981. A Vice-Pres., Royal Soc., 1981–82. Hon. DSc: Kent, 1984; CNAA, 1990. *Publications:* Genetics and Biochemistry of Pseudomonas (ed with M. H. Richmond), 1975; papers on genetics, biochemistry and enzyme evolution in Jl of Gen. Microbiol. and other jls. *Recreations:* walking, gardening, dress-making. *Address:* 7 Corinium Gate, Cirencester, Glos GL7 2PX.

CLARKE, Peter, CBE 1983; PhD, CChem, FRSC, FInstPet; Principal, Robert Gordon's Institute of Technology, Aberdeen, 1970–85, retired; Chairman, Scottish Vocational Education Council, 1985–91; *b* 18 March 1922; *er s* of Frederick John and Gladys May Clarke; *m* 1947, Ethel Jones; two *s*. *Educ:* Queen Elizabeth's Grammar Sch., Mansfield; University Coll., Nottingham (BSc). Industrial Chemist, 1942; Sen. Chemistry Master, Buxton Coll., 1947; Lectr, Huddersfield Technl Coll., 1949; British Enka Ltd, Liverpool, 1956; Sen. Lectr, Royal Coll. of Advanced Tech., Salford, 1962; Head of Dept of Chemistry and Biology, Nottingham Regional Coll. of Technology, 1963; Vice-Principal, Huddersfield Coll. of Technology, 1965–70. Member: SERC (formerly SRC), 1978–82; Council for Professions Supplementary to Medicine, 1977–85; Scottish Technical Educn Council, 1982–85; CNAA, 1982–87 (Chm., Cttee for Scotland, 1983). Chm., Assoc. of Principals of Colleges (Scotland), 1976–78; President: Assoc. of Principals of Colleges, 1980–81; Assoc. for Educnl and Trng Technol., 1993–. Chairman: Aberdeen Enterprise Trust, 1984–92; Industrial Trng Centre Aberdeen Ltd, 1989–; Trustee, Gordon Cook Foundn, 1989–. FRSA 1986. Burgess of Guild, City of Aberdeen, 1973. Hon. LLD Aberdeen, 1985; Hon. DEd CNAA, 1992. *Publications:* contribs to Jl of Chem. Soc., Chemistry and Industry. *Recreation:* gardening. *Address:* Dunaber, 12 Woodburn Place, Aberdeen AB1 8JR.

CLARKE, Major Sir Peter Cecil, KCVO 1992 (CVO 1969; LVO 1964); Chief Clerk, Duchy of Lancaster, 1969–92; Extra Equerry to HRH Princess Alexandra, the Hon. Mrs Angus Ogilvy; *b* 9 Aug. 1927; *s* of late Captain E. D. Clarke, CBE, MC, Binstead, Isle of Wight; *m* 1950, Rosemary Virginia Margaret Harmsworth, *d* of late T. C. Durham, Appomattox, Virginia, USA; one *s* two *d*. *Educ:* Eton; RMA, Sandhurst. 3rd The King's Own Hussars and 14th/20th King's Hussars, 1945–64; Adjt 3rd The King's Own Hussars, GSO2 2 Inf. Div., psc 1959. Seconded as Asst Private Secretary to HRH Princess Marina, Duchess of Kent, 1961–64; Comptroller, 1964–68; Comptroller to HRH Princess Alexandra, 1964–69. Mem. Court of Assts, Corp. of Sons of the Clergy, 1987–. JP Hants, 1971–81. *Recreations:* golf, fishing. *Address:* 6 Gordon Place, W8 4JD. *T:* 0171–937 0356. *Club:* Cavalry and Guards.

CLARKE, Prof. Peter Frederick, LittD; FBA 1989; Professor of Modern British History, Cambridge University, since 1991; Fellow of St John's College, Cambridge, since 1980; *b* 21 July 1942; *s* of late John William Clarke and of Winifred Clarke (*née* Hadfield); *m* 1st, 1969, Dillon Cheetham (marr. diss. 1990); two *d*; 2nd, 1991, Dr Maria Tippett, FRS(Can), Vancouver. *Educ:* Eastbourne Grammar Sch.; St John's Coll., Cambridge (BA 1963; MA 1967; PhD 1967; LittD 1989). FRHistS 1972. Asst Lectr and Lectr in History, 1966–78, Reader in Modern Hist., 1978–80, UCL; Cambridge University: Lectr in History, 1980–87; Tutor, St John's Coll., 1982–87; Sec., Faculty Bd of Hist., 1985–86; Reader in Modern History, 1987–91. Vis. Prof. of Modern British Hist., Harvard Univ., 1974; Vis. Fellow, Res. Sch. of Social Scis, ANU, 1983. Member: Council, RHistS, 1979–83; Adv. Council on Public Records, 1995–. Chm., S Cambs Area Party, SDP, 1981–82. Jt Review Ed., History, 1967–73; Chm., Editl Bd, Twentieth Century British History, 1988–. *Publications:* Lancashire and the New Liberalism, 1971, 2nd edn 1993; Liberals and Social Democrats, 1978, 3rd edn 1993; The Keynesian Revolution in the Making, 1988, 2nd edn 1990; A Question of Leadership: from Gladstone to Thatcher, 1991, 2nd edn 1992; articles in learned jls; contribs to TLS, London Rev. of Books, etc. *Recreations:* walking, cooking. *Address:* St John's College, Cambridge CB2 1TP. *T:* Cambridge (01223) 338726. *Club:* Royal Over-Seas League.

CLARKE, Peter James, CBE 1993; Secretary of the Forestry Commission, 1976–94, retired; *b* 16 Jan. 1934; *s* of Stanley Ernest Clarke and Elsie May (*née* Scales); *m* 1966, Roberta Anne, *y d* of Robert and Ada Browne; one *s* one *d*. *Educ:* Enfield Grammar Sch.; St John's Coll., Cambridge (MA). Exec. Officer, WO, 1952–62 (univ., 1957–60), Higher Exec. Officer, 1962; Sen. Exec. Officer, Forestry Commn, 1967, Principal 1972; Principal, Dept of Energy, 1975. *Recreations:* gardening, walking, travel. *Address:* 5 Murrayfield Gardens, Edinburgh EH12 6DG. *T:* 0131–337 3145.

CLARKE, Sir Robert (Cyril), Kt 1993; Chairman: Thames Water Plc, since 1994 (non-executive Director, since 1988); *b* 28 March 1929; *s* of Robert Henry Clarke and Rose Lilian (*née* Bratton); *m* 1952, Evelyn (Lynne) Mary, *d* of Cyrus Harper and Ann Ellen (*née* Jones); three *s* (incl. twin *s*) one *d*. *Educ:* Dulwich Coll.; Pembroke Coll., Oxford (MA Hist.; Hon. Fellow, 1993). Served Royal West Kent Regt, 1947–49. Joined Cadbury Bros, as trainee, 1952; Gen. Manager, John Forrest, 1954; Marketing Dir, Cadbury Confectionery, 1957; Man. Dir, 1962–69, Chm., 1969–71, Cadbury Cakes; Dir, Cadbury Schweppes Foods, 1969–71; Man. Dir, McVitie & Cadbury Cakes, 1971–74; Dir, 1974–95, Chm. and Man. Dir, 1984–95, United Biscuits UK Ltd; Man. Dir, UB Biscuits, 1977–84; Dir, 1984–95, Gp Chief Exec., 1986–90, Chm., 1990–95, United Biscuits (Holdings). Member: Council, Cake and Biscuit Alliance, 1965–83; Council, ISBA, 1977–84; Resources Cttee, Food and Drink Fedn, 1984–86; Bd of Dirs, Grocery Manufrs of America, 1991–95. Gov., World Economic Forum, 1990–. Special Trustee, Hosp. for Sick Children (Gt Ormond St), 1992–. FIGD, CIMgt. *Recreations:* reading, walking, renovating old buildings, planting trees. *Address:* Thames Water Plc, 14 Cavendish Place, W1M 9DJ.

CLARKE, Rev. Robert Sydney; Secretary and Director of Training, Hospital Chaplaincies Council, since 1994; Chaplain to HM the Queen, since 1987; *b* 31 Oct. 1935; *s* of George Sydney and Elizabeth Clarke. *Educ:* St Dunstan's College; King's Coll., Univ. of London (AKC 1964). Chaplain: New Cross Hospital, Wolverhampton, 1970–74; Herrison and West Dorset County Hosp., Dorchester, 1974–79; Westminster Hosp. and Westminster Medical School, Univ. of London, 1979–85; Winchester HA, 1985–94. Sen. Hon. Chaplain, Winchester and Eastleigh Health Care Trust, 1994–. *Recreations:* breeding and showing dogs, music, travel, DIY. *Address:* Church House, Westminster SW1P 3NZ. *T:* 0171–222 9011. *Club:* Kennel.

CLARKE, Robin Mitchell, MC 1944; JP; DL; Chairman, Gatwick Airport Consultative Committee, 1982–90; *b* 8 Jan. 1917; *e s* of Joseph and Mary Clarke; *m* 1946, Betty Mumford; twin *s* and *d*. *Educ:* Ruckholt Central Sch., Leyton. Middleton and St Bride's Wharf, Wapping, 1932–34; Town Clerk's Office, City of Westminster, 1935–40. War of 1939–45: 12th Regt, RHA (HAC) and 142 (Royal Devon Yeomanry) Fd Regt, RA; Major, 1944; served Sicily and Italy (wounded, despatches, MC). Town Clerk's Office, Westminster, 1946–48; Crawley Development Corporation, 1948–62; Manager, Crawley, Commn for the New Towns, 1962–78; Chief Exec., New Towns Commn, 1978–82. Vice-Pres., St Catherine's Hospice, Crawley, 1989– (Chm., 1983–89). Master, Worshipful Co. of Chartered Secs and Administrators, 1984–85. ACIS 1949; FCIS 1959 (Mem. Nat. Council, 1968–87; Pres., 1978). JP Crawley, 1971; DL West Sussex, 1982. FRSA 1980. *Address:* Mayford Cottage, 89 Golden Avenue, East Preston, W Sussex BN16 1QT. *T:* Rustington (01903) 771739. *Club:* Army and Navy.

CLARKE, Roger Eric; Under Secretary, Director of Shipping Policy, Department of Transport, since 1991; *b* 13 June 1939; *s* of Frederick Cuérel Clarke and late Hilda Josephine Clarke; *m* 1983, Elizabeth Jane, *d* of Gordon W. Pingstone and Anne Ellen Pingstone; one *d*. *Educ:* UCS, Hampstead; Corpus Christi Coll., Cambridge (MA). Various posts in civil aviation divs of Min. of Aviation, BoT and Depts of Trade and Transport, 1961–72 and 1980–85; Air Traffic Rights Advr to Govt of Fiji, 1972–74; Asst Sec., Insce and Overseas Trade Divs, Dept of Trade, 1975–80; Under Sec., Civil Aviation Policy Directorate, 1985–89, Public Transport Directorate, 1989–91. *Recreations:* family, friends, church, garden, walking, theatre, music, languages, travel. *Address:* Shipping Policy Directorate, Department of Transport, 2 Marsham Street, SW1P 3EB. *T:* 0171–276 5910. *Club:* Reform.

CLARKE, Roger Howard, PhD; Director, National Radiological Protection Board, since 1987; *b* 22 Aug. 1943; *s* of late Harold Pardoe and Laurie Gwyneth Clarke; *m* 1966, Sandra Ann (*née* Buckley); one *s* one *d*. *Educ:* King Edward VI Sch., Stourbridge; Univ. of Birmingham (BSc, MSc); Polytechnic of Central London (PhD). Res. Officer, Berkeley Nuclear Laboratories, CEGB, 1965–77; Hd of Nuclear Power Assessments, NRPB, 1978–83; Bd Sec., 1983–87. Deleg. to UN Sci. Cttee on the Effects of Atomic Radiation, 1979–; Chairman: OECD Nuclear Energy Agency Cttee on Radiation Protection and Public Health, 1987–92; Internat. Commn on Radiol Protection, 1993– (Mem., 1989–93); Mem., Gp of Experts, Article 31, Euratom, 1988–. Visiting Professor: Imperial Coll. of Science, Technol. and Medicine, 1993–; Univ. of Surrey, 1994–. Hon. FRCR 1994; Hon. FSRP 1995. *Publications:* Carcinogenesis and Radiation Risk (with W. V. Mayneord), 1975; numerous papers in sci. and technical literature. *Recreations:* gardening, theatre, travel. *Address:* Corner Cottage, Woolton Hill, Newbury, Berks RG15 9XJ. *T:* Highclere (01635) 253957.

CLARKE, Major Sir Rupert William John, 3rd Bt *cr* 1882; MBE 1943; late Irish Guards; Chairman: United Distillers Co., 1960–88; National Australia Bank Ltd (formerly National Bank of Australasia), 1986–92 (Director, since 1955); International Ranch Management Services Pty Ltd; P & O Australia Ltd, since 1983 (Director, since 1980); *b* 5 Nov. 1919; *s* of 2nd Bt and Elsie Florence (who *m* 2nd, 1928, 5th Marquess of Headfort), *d* of James Partridge Tucker, Devonshire; *S* father, 1926; *m* 1947, Kathleen, *d* of P. Grant Hay, Toorak, Victoria, Australia; two *s* one *d* (and one *s* decd). *Educ:* Eton; Magdalen Coll., Oxford (MA). Hon. Fellow, Trinity Coll., Melbourne, 1981. Served War of 1939–45 (despatches, MBE). Chm., Cadbury Schweppes Australia Ltd (formerly Schweppes (Australia)), 1955–89; Dir, Cadbury Schweppes, 1977–85; Chairman: Bank of South Pacific, 1986–92; First National Ltd, 1986–92; Director: Conzinc Riotinto of Australia, 1962–87; Custom Credit Corp.; Morganite Australia Pty (Chm., 1976–84); National Australia Gp (UK), 1990–92. Pres., Royal Humane Soc. of Australasia Inc., 1992–. Mem. Cttee, Vict. Amateur Turf Club (Chm., 1972–88); Councillor, Royal Agricl Soc. of Vic, 1965–. Hon. Consul General for Monaco, 1975– (Hon. Consul, 1961). Chevalier de la Légion d'Honneur, 1979; Ordre des Grimaldi (Monaco); Officer, Order of Leopold (Belgium), 1989. *Heir: s* Rupert Grant Alexander Clarke, LLB (Hons) [*b* 12 Dec. 1947; *m* 1978, Susannah, *d* of Sir Robert Law-Smith, *qv*; one *s* two *d*]. *Address:* Bolinda Vale, Clarkefield, Vic 3430, Australia; Richmond House, 56 Avoca Street, South Yarra, Vic 3141. *Fax:* (3) 6702629. *Clubs:* Cavalry and Guards, Lansdowne; Melbourne, Athenæum, Australian (Melbourne); Union (Sydney).

CLARKE, Samuel Laurence Harrison, CBE 1988; CEng, FIEE; Assistant Technical Director, GEC plc, 1981–91; Director: Sira Ltd, 1989–95; Filtronic Ltd, 1989–93; *b* 16 Dec. 1929; *s* of late Samuel Harrison Clarke, CBE; *m* 1952, Ruth Joan Godwin, *yr d* of Oscar and Muriel Godwin; one *s* three *d*. *Educ:* Westminster Sch.; Trinity Coll., Cambridge (BA). Technical Dir, GEC-Elliott Automation Ltd, 1970–74; Technical Dir (Automation), GEC-Marconi Electronics Ltd, 1974–81; Director, GEC Computers Ltd, 1971–83. Dep. Dir, 1983–87, Dir, 1987, Alvey Programme, DTI. *Publications:* various papers in learned and technical jls. *Recreations:* ski-ing, Scottish dancing, sailing, conservation. *Address:* Sarum End, Salisbury Road, Southwold, Suffolk IP18 6LG. *T:* Southwold (01502) 725116.

CLARKE, Stanley George, CBE 1975; Chief Inspector of the Prison Service, 1971–74; Member: Prisons Board, 1971–74; Parole Board, 1975–78; *b* Dunfermline, 5 May 1914; *s* of Stanley and Catherine Clarke; *m* 1940, Mary Preston Lewin; one *s* one *d*. *Educ:* Sutton High Sch., Plymouth (school colours: cricket, Rugby, soccer). Civil Service Clerk: Dartmoor Prison, 1931; Lowdham Grange Borstal, 1933; North Sea Camp, 1935; Borstal Housemaster: Portland, 1937; North Sea Camp, 1939. Served War, 1941–45 (despatches): Sqdn Ldr, RAF. Borstal Housemaster: Hollesley Bay Colony, 1945; Gaynes Hall, 1946. Dep. Governor, Manchester Prison, 1947; Governor: Norwich Prison, 1949; Nottingham Prison, 1952; Eastchurch Prison, 1955; Liverpool Prison, 1959. Asst Dir of Prisons, in charge of North Region, 1964; Asst Controller, Prison Dept, 1970. *Address:* 17 Grundy's Lane, Malvern Wells, Worcs WR14 4HS.

CLARKE, Mrs Stella Rosemary, JP; DL; Chairman of Council, Bristol University, since 1987 (Member, since 1982); Director, Fosters Rooms Ltd, since 1975; *b* 16 Feb. 1932; *d* of John Herbert and Molly Isabel Bruce King; *m* 1952, Charles Nigel Clarke; four *s* one *d*. *Educ:* Cheltenham Ladies' Coll.; Trinity Coll. Dublin. Long Ashton RDC: Councillor, Chm. Council, Housing and Public Health Cttees, 1955–73; Mem., Woodspring Dist Council, 1973–76; co-opted Mem., Somerset CC, Social Services and Children's Cttee, 1957–73. A Governor, BBC, 1974–81. Purchased and restored Theatre Royal, Bath, with husband, 1974–76. Chm., new initiatives in training and housing of the young and unemployed, 1982–. Member: Housing Corp., 1988–; Bristol Develt Corp., 1989–; Lord Chancellor's Lay Interviewers Panel for Judges, 1994. Vice Chm., Knightstone HA, 1989–. JP Bristol, 1968 (Chm., Bench, 1991–); DL Avon, 1986. *Recreations:* family and the variety of life. *Address:* Gatcombe Court, Flax Bourton, near Bristol BS19 1PX. *T:* Bristol (01275) 393141.

CLARKE, Stephen Patrick; His Honour Judge Stephen Clarke; a Circuit Judge, since 1995; *b* 23 March 1948; *s* of Leslie Clarke and Anne Mary Clarke; *m* 1974, Margaret Roberta Millar; two *s*. *Educ:* Rostrevor Coll., Adelaide, SA; Univ. of Hull (LLB Hons).

Called to the Bar, Inner Temple, 1971; practised as barrister on Wales and Chester Circuit, 1971–95; Circuit Junior, 1988–89; Asst Recorder, 1988–92; Recorder, 1992–95. Asst Parly Boundary Comr for Wales, 1994–95. *Recreations:* golf, watching cricket, theatre. *Address:* The Crown Court, The Castle, Chester CH1 2AN. *T:* Chester (01244) 317606. *Club:* Shrewsbury Golf.

CLARKE, Thomas, CBE 1980; JP; MP (Lab) Monklands West, since 1983 (Coatbridge and Airdrie, June 1982–1983); *b* 10 Jan. 1941; *s* of James Clarke and Mary (*née* Gordon). *Educ:* All Saints Primary Sch., Airdrie; Columba High Sch., Coatbridge; Scottish College of Commerce. Started working life as office boy with Glasgow Accountants' firm; Asst Director, Scottish Council for Educational Technology, before going to Parliament. Councillor: (former) Coatbridge Council, 1964; (reorganised) Monklands District Council, 1974; Provost of Monklands, 1975–77, 1977–80, 1980–82. Vice-President, Convention of Scottish Local Authorities, 1976–78, President, 1978–80. Opposition front bench spokesman on: Scottish Affairs, 1987; health and social security (personal social services), 1987–90; Scotland, 1992–93; overseas aid, 1993–94; disabled people's rights, 1994–95. Chm., PLP Foreign Affairs Cttee, 1983–86. Author and main sponsor, Disabled Persons (Consultation, Representation and Services) Act, 1986. Director, award winning amateur film, Give Us a Goal, 1972; former President, British Amateur Cinematographers' Central Council. JP County of Lanark, 1972. *Recreations:* films, reading, walking. *Address:* 37 Blairhill Street, Coatbridge, Lanarkshire ML5 1PG. *T:* Coatbridge (01236) 22550. *Clubs:* Coatbridge Municipal Golf, Easter Moffat Golf.

CLARKE, Sir Tobias; *see* Clarke, Sir C. M. T.

CLARKE, William Malpas, CBE 1976; Chairman, Central Banking Publications Ltd, since 1990; *b* 5 June 1922; *o s* of late Ernest and Florence Clarke; *m* 1st, 1946, Margaret Braithwaite; two *d*; 2nd, 1973, Faith Elizabeth Dawson. *Educ:* Audenshaw Grammar Sch.; Univ. of Manchester (BA Hons Econ). Served Royal Air Force, 1941–46; Flying Instructor, Canada, 1942–44; Flight-Lieut, 1945. Editorial Staff, Manchester Guardian, 1948–55; The Times, 1955–66: City Editor, 1957–62; Financial and Industrial Editor, 1962–66; Editor, The Banker, March-Sept. 1966, Consultant 1966–76. Dir, 1968–76, Dep. Chm. and Dir Gen., 1976–87, British Invisible Exports Council (formerly Cttee on Invisible Exports); Deputy Chairman: City Communications Centre, 1976–87; Trade Indemnity Co. Ltd, 1980–86; Chairman: Grindlays Bank (Jersey), 1981–92; ANZ Merchant Bank, 1987–91 (Dir, 1985–91); Transatlantic Capital (Biosciences) Ltd, 1989–92; Director: ANZ Grindlays Bank (formerly Grindlays Bank), 1966–85, 1987–92; Euromoney Ltd, 1969–84; Trade Indemnity plc, 1971–87; Swiss Reinsurance Co. (UK) plc, 1977–93; ANZ Holdings, 1985–87. Chm., Harold Wincott Financial Journalist Press Award Panel, 1971–92. Governor, The Hospitals for Sick Children, 1984–90; Chm., Great Ormond Street Wishing Well Redevelt Appeal Trust, 1985–94. Hon. DLitt London Guildhall Univ., 1992. *Publications:* The City's Invisible Earnings, 1958; The City in the World Economy, 1965; Private Enterprise in Developing Countries, 1966; (ed, as Director of Studies) Britain's Invisible Earnings, 1967; (with George Pulay) The World's Money, 1970; Inside the City, 1979, rev. edn 1983; How the City of London Works, 1986, 4th edn 1995; The Secret Life of Wilkie Collins, 1988; Planning for Europe: 1992, 1989; The Lost Fortune of the Tsars, 1994 (US and German edns, 1995). *Recreations:* books, theatre. *Address:* 37 Park Vista, Greenwich, SE10 9LZ. *T:* 0181–858 0979. *Club:* Reform.

CLARKE HALL, Denis; architect; President, Architectural Association, 1958–59; Chairman, Architects Registration Council of the UK, 1963–64; *b* 4 July 1910; *m* 1936, Mary Garfitt; one *s* two *d*. *Educ:* Bedales. Holds AA Dip. *Address:* Moorhouse, Iping, Midhurst, W Sussex GU29 0PJ.

CLARKSON, Ven. Alan Geoffrey; Archdeacon of Winchester since 1984; Vicar of Burley, Ringwood, since 1984; *b* 14 Feb. 1934; *s* of Instructor Captain Geoffrey Archibald Clarkson, OBE, RN and Essie Isabel Bruce Clarkson; *m* 1959, Monica Ruth (*née* Lightburne); two *s* one *d*. *Educ:* Sherborne School; Christ's Coll., Cambridge (BA 1957, MA 1961); Wycliffe Hall, Oxford. Nat. Service Commn, RA, 1952–54. Curate: Penn, Wolverhampton, 1959–60; St Oswald's, Oswestry, 1960–63; Wrington with Redhill, 1963–65; Vicar, Chewton Mendip with Emborough, 1965–74; Vicar of St John Baptist, Glastonbury with Godney, 1974–84; Priest in Charge: West Pennard, 1981–84; Meare, 1981–84; St Benedict, Glastonbury, 1982–84. Proctor in Convocation, 1970–75, 1990–95. Hon. Canon, Winchester Cathedral, 1984. *Recreations:* music, gardening, carpentry, wood-turning. *Address:* The Vicarage, Church Corner, Burley, Ringwood BH24 4AP. *T:* Burley (01425) 402303, *Fax:* Burley (01425) 403753.

CLARKSON, Prof. Brian Leonard, DSc; FEng 1986; Principal, University College of Swansea, 1982–94; Vice-Chancellor, University of Wales, 1987–89; *b* 28 July 1930; *s* of L. C. Clarkson; *m* 1953, Margaret Elaine Wilby; three *s* one *d*. *Educ:* Univ. of Leeds (BSc, PhD). FRAeS; Hon. FInst Acoustics. George Taylor Gold Medal, RAeS, 1963. Dynamics Engineer, de Havilland Aircraft Co., Hatfield, Herts, 1953–57; Southampton University: Sir Alan Cobham Research Fellow, Dept of Aeronautics, 1957–58; Lectr, Dept of Aeronautics and Astronautics, 1958–66; Prof. of Vibration Studies, 1966–82; Dir, Inst. of Sound and Vibration Res., 1967–78; Dean, Faculty of Engrg and Applied Science, 1978–80; Deputy Vice-Chancellor, 1980–82. Sen. Post Doctoral Research Fellow, Nat. Academy of Sciences, USA, 1970–71 (one year's leave of absence from Southampton). Chm., ACU, 1992– (Vice-Chm., 1990–92). Sec., Internat. Commn on Acoustics, 1975–81. Pres., Fedn of Acoustical Socs of Europe, 1982–84. Member: SERC, 1984–88; CNAA, 1988–91. Hon. DSc: Leeds, 1984; Southampton, 1987; Universiti Sains Malaysia, 1990. *Publications:* author of sections of three books: Technical Acoustics, vol. 3 (ed Richardson) 1959; Noise and Acoustic Fatigue in Aeronautics (ed Mead and Richards), 1967; Noise and Vibration (ed White and Walker), 1982; (ed) Stochastic Problems in Dynamics, 1977; technical papers on Jet Noise and its effect on Aircraft Structures, Jl of Royal Aeronautical Soc., etc. *Recreations:* walking, gardening, travelling, golf. *Address:* Highmead, 17 Southgate Road, Southgate, Swansea SA3 2BT.

CLARKSON, Derek Joshua; QC 1969; **His Honour Judge Clarkson;** a Circuit Judge, since 1977; Middlesex Liaison Judge, since 1985; *b* 10 Dec. 1929; *o s* of Albert and Winifred Charlotte Clarkson (*née* James); *m* 1960, Peternella Marie-Luise Ilse Canenbley; one *s* one *d*. *Educ:* Pudsey Grammar Sch.; King's Coll., Univ. of London. LLB (1st cl. Hons) 1950. Called to Bar, Inner Temple, 1951; Nat. Service, RAF, 1952–54 (Flt Lt). In practice as Barrister, 1954–77; Prosecuting Counsel to Post Office on North-Eastern Circuit, 1961–65; Prosecuting Counsel to Inland Revenue on North-Eastern Circuit, 1965–69; Recorder of Rotherham, 1967–71; Recorder of Huddersfield, 1971; a Recorder of the Crown Court, 1972–77. Mem., Gen. Council of the Bar, 1971–73. Inspector of companies for the Department of Trade, 1972–73, 1975–76. Pres., Middlesex Magistrates' Assoc., 1994–95. *Recreations:* theatre-going, walking, book collecting. *Address:* Millbank Court, 24 John Islip Street, Westminster, SW1P 4LG; 72A Cornwall Road, Harrogate HG1 2NE.

CLARKSON, Prof. Geoffrey Peniston Elliott, PhD; Chairman: Sealcorp Ltd, since 1990; Circle L Ltd, since 1990; *b* 30 May 1934; *s* of George Elliott Clarkson and Alice Helene (*née* Manneberg); *m* 1960, Eleanor M. (*née* Micenko); two *d*. *Educ:* Carnegie-Mellon Univ., Pittsburgh, Pa (BSc, MSc, PhD). Asst Prof., Sloan Sch. of Management, MIT, 1961–65, Associate Prof., 1965–67, Vis. Prof., 1975–77. Vis. Ford Foundn Fellow, Carnegie-Mellon Univ., 1965–66; Vis. Prof., LSE, 1966–67; Nat. Westminster Bank Prof. of Business Finance, Manchester Business Sch., Univ. of Manchester, 1967–77; Prof. of Business Admin, 1977–89, and Dean, Coll. of Business Admin, 1977–79, Northeastern Univ., Boston. Dir of and consultant to public and private manufng and financial services cos, 1969–; Chm., Polymerics Inc., 1983–89. MInstD 1973. *Publications:* Portfolio Selection: a simulation of trust investment, USA 1962 (Ford Dissertation Prize, 1961); The Theory of Consumer Demand: a critical appraisal, USA 1963; Managerial Economics, 1968; (with B. J. Elliott) Managing Money and Finance, 1969 (3rd edn 1982); Jihad, 1981. *Recreations:* fishing, sailing, reading.

CLARKSON, Gerald Dawson, CBE 1990; QFSM 1983; Chief Fire Officer and Chief Executive, London Fire and Civil Defence Authority, 1987–91, retired; Chairman: Dawson Usher International Ltd, since 1994; Vincent Sherman Associates Ltd, since 1993; *b* 4 June 1939; *s* of Alexander Dickie Clarkson and Agnes Tierney Price; *m* 1959, Rose Lilian Hodgson; one *s* one *d*. *Educ:* Westminster Technical Coll.; Polytechnic of Central London (BA Hons). FIMS, FIMgt, FRSH. Served Royal Engineers, 1960–61. Joined London Fire Bde, 1961; Dep. Chief Officer, 1983; Reg. Fire Comdr No 5, Greater London Region, 1987–91. Member: Central Fire Bdes Adv. Council, 1987–91; Fire Service Central Examinations Bd, 1987–; Ind. Mem., Kent Police Authy, 1995–; Adviser: Nat. Jt Council for Local Authorities Fire Bdes, 1987–91; Assoc. of Metropolitan Authorities, 1987–91; Chm., Fedn of British Fire Orgns, 1990–91; Dir, Nat. Fire Protection Assoc., USA, 1990–93; President: London Fire Brigade Widows' and Orphans' Friendly Soc., 1987–91; Commonwealth and Overseas Fire Service Assoc., 1990–. Freeman, City of London, 1985; Founder Master, Guild of Firefighters, 1988. OStJ 1989. Hon. FIFireE, 1989. *Recreations:* reading, golf, sailing, fishing. *Address:* Field Mill, Field Mill Lane, Egerton, Kent TN27 9AU. *Club:* East India.

CLARKSON, Patrick Robert James; QC 1991; *b* 1 Aug. 1949; *s* of Commander Robert Anthony Clarkson, LVO, RN and Sheelagh Clarissa Neale; *m* 1975, Bridget Cecilia Doyne; two *s* one *d*. *Educ:* Winchester. Called to the Bar, Lincoln's Inn, 1972. *Recreations:* cricket, motor racing, reading, country. *Address:* 1 Serjeants Inn, EC4Y 1NH. *T:* 0171–583 1355. *Club:* MCC.

CLARKSON, Dr Peter David; Executive Secretary, Scientific Committee on Antarctic Research, since 1989; *b* 19 June 1945; *s* of late Maurice Roland Clarkson and of Jessie Yoxall (*née* Baker); *m* 1974, Rita Margaret Skinner; one *d*. *Educ:* Epsom Coll.; Univ. of Durham (BSc 1967); Univ. of Birmingham (PhD 1977). FGS 1980. Geologist with British Antarctic Survey, 1967–89: wintered in Antarctica, Halley Bay, 1968 and 1969; Base Comdr, 1969; Antarctic field seasons in Shackleton Range (leader 3 times), 1968–78; in S Shetland Is, 1974–75; in Antarctic Peninsula, 1985–86 (leader). UK adviser to PROANTAR, Brazil, 1982. Grants Sec., Trans-Antarctic Assoc., 1993– (Hon. Sec., 1980–93). Polar Medal, 1976. *Publications:* articles on Antarctic geology. *Recreations:* walking, woodwork, photography, music, all matters Antarctic. *Address:* Scott Polar Research Institute, Lensfield Road, Cambridge CB2 1ER. *T:* Cambridge (01223) 362061; 35 King's Grove, Barton, Cambridge CB3 7AZ. *T:* Cambridge (01223) 263417. *Club:* Antarctic.

CLARRICOATS, Prof. Peter John Bell, FRS 1990; FEng; Professor of Electronic Engineering, Queen Mary and Westfield (formerly Queen Mary) College, University of London, since 1968, and Head of Department, since 1979; *b* 6 April 1932; *s* of John Clarricoats and Cecilia (*née* Bell); *m* 1st, 1955, Gillian (*née* Hall) (marr. diss. 1962); one *s* one *d*; 2nd, 1968, Phyllis Joan (*née* Lloyd); two *d* one step *s* one step *d*. *Educ:* Minchenden Grammar Sch.; Imperial College. BSc (Eng), PhD, DSc (Eng) 1968; FInstP 1964, FIEE 1967, FIEEE 1967, FCGI 1980, FEng 1983. Scientific Staff, GEC, 1953–58; Lectr, Queen's Univ. Belfast, 1959–62; Sheffield Univ., 1962–63; Prof. of Electronic Engineering, Univ. of Leeds, 1963–67. Mem., Governing Body, QMC, 1976–79, Dean of Engineering, 1977–80. Chm., British Nat. Cttee for Radio Sci., subseq. UK Panel for URSI, 1985–93; Vice-Pres., URSI, 1993–. Chairman: 1st Internat. Conf. on Antennas and Propagation, IEE, 1978; European Microwave Conf., 1979; Mil. Microwaves Conf., 1988. Distinguished Lectr, IEEE, 1987–88. Institution of Electrical Engineers: Vice-Pres., 1989–91; Mem. Council, 1964–67, 1977–80; Chm., Electronics Div., 1978–79; Hon. Fellow, 1993; awards: Premia, Electronics Section, 1960, 1961; Marconi, 1974; Coopers Hill Meml Prize, 1964; IEEE Cert. of Appreciation, 1989; European Microwave Prize, 1989; IEE Measurement Prize, 1989; J. J. Thomson Medal, IEE, 1989. Hon DSc Kent, 1993. Co-Editor, Electronics Letters (IEE Jl), 1964–. *Publications:* Microwave Ferrites, 1960; (with A.D. Olver) Corrugated Horns for Microwave Antennas, 1984; papers on antennas and waveguides. *Recreations:* music, photography, formerly squash and mountaineering. *Address:* 7 Falcon Close, Sawbridgeworth, Herts CM21 0AX. *T:* Bishop's Stortford (01279) 723561.

CLASPER, Michael, CBE 1995; Managing Director and Vice-President, Procter & Gamble Europe, since 1991; *b* 21 April 1953; *s* of Douglas and Hilda Clasper; *m* 1975, Susan Rosemary Shore; two *s* one *d*. *Educ:* Bede Sch., Sunderland; St John's Coll., Cambridge (1st cl. Hons Engineering). British Rail, 1974–78; joined Procter & Gamble 1978, Advertising Dir, 1985–88; Gen. Manager, Procter & Gamble Holland, 1988–91; Man. Dir, Procter & Gamble UK, July 1991. Chm., Soap and Detergent Industry Assoc., 1993–; Mem., Adv. Council on Business and the Envmt, 1993–. Member: Bd, The Newcastle Initiative, 1993–; Bd, Tyneside TEC, 1993–; Council, Newcastle Univ., 1993–. *Recreations:* swimming, cycling, ski-ing, tennis, golf. *Address:* Procter & Gamble Ltd, PO Box 1EE, Gosforth, Newcastle upon Tyne NE99 1EE. *T:* 0191–279 2000.

CLATWORTHY, Robert, RA 1973 (ARA 1968); sculptor; *b* 31 Jan. 1928; *s* of E. W. and G. Clatworthy; *m* 1954, Pamela Gordon (marr. diss.); two *s* one *d*. *Educ:* Dr Morgan's Grammar Sch., Bridgwater. Studied West of England Coll. of Art, Chelsea Sch. of Art, The Slade. Teacher, West of England Coll. of Art, 1967–71. Visiting Tutor, RCA, 1960–72; Mem., Fine Art Panel of Nat. Council for Diplomas in Art and Design, 1961–72; Governor, St Martin's Sch. of Art, 1970–71; Head of Dept of Fine Art, Central Sch. of Art and Design, 1971–75. Exhibited: Hanover Gall., 1954, 1956; Waddington Galls, 1965; Holland Park Open Air Sculpture, 1957; Battersea Park Open Air Sculpture, 1960, 1963; Tate Gallery, British Sculpture in the Sixties, 1965; British Sculptors 1972, Burlington House; Basil Jacobs Fine Art Ltd, 1972; Diploma Galls, Burlington Ho., 1977; Photographers Gall., 1980; Quinton Green Fine Art, London, 1986; British Sculpture 1950–65, New Art Centre, 1986; Chapman Gall., 1988, 1989; Keith Chapman, 1990; Austin Desmond Fine Art, 1991; Putney Bridge Gall., 1992. Work in Collections: Arts Council, Contemporary Art Soc., Tate Gallery, Victoria and Albert Museum, Greater London Council, Nat. Portrait Gall. (portrait of Dame Elisabeth Frink, 1985). Monumental Horse and Rider, Finsbury Avenue, London, 1984. *Address:* Moelfre, Cynghordy, Llandovery, Dyfed SA20 0UW. *T:* Llandovery (01550) 20201. *Club:* Chelsea Arts.

CLAUSEN, Alden Winship, (Tom); Chairman, Executive Committee, BankAmerica Corporation (Chairman and Chief Executive Officer, 1986–90); *b* 17 Feb. 1923; *s* of

Morton and Elsie Clausen; *m* 1950, Mary Margaret Crassweller; two *s*. *Educ:* Carthage Coll. (BA 1944); Univ. of Minnesota (LLB 1949); Grad. Harvard Advanced Management Program, 1966. Admitted to Minnesota Bar, 1949. Joined Bank of America, 1949: Vice-Pres., 1961–65; Sen. Vice-Pres., 1965–68; Exec. Vice-Pres., 1968–69; Vice-Chm. of Bd, 1969; Pres. and Chief Exec. Officer, 1970–81; Pres., The World Bank, 1981–86. President: Fed. Adv. Council, 1972; Internat. Monetary Conf., Amer. Bankers' Assoc., 1977. Former Director: US-USSR Trade and Econ. Council, 1974–81; Nat. Council for US-China Trade, 1974–81; Co-Chm., Japan-California Assoc., 1973–80. Hon. LLD: Carthage, 1970; Lewis and Clark, 1978; Gonzaga Univ., 1978; Univ. of Notre Dame, 1981; Hon. DPS Univ. Santa Clara, 1981. *Address:* c/o BankAmerica Corporation, PO Box 37000, San Francisco, CA 94137, USA.

CLAXTON, Maj.-Gen. Patrick Fisher, CB 1972; OBE 1946; General Manager, Regular Forces Employment Association, 1971–81; *b* 13 March 1915; *s* of late Rear-Adm. Ernest William Claxton and Kathleen O'Callaghan Claxton, formerly Fisher; *m* 1941, Jóna Gudrún Gunnarsdóttir (*d* 1980); two *d*. *Educ:* Sutton Valence Sch.; St John's Coll., Cambridge (BA). Served GHQ, India, 1943–45; Singapore, 1945–46; WO, 1946–48; British Element Trieste Force, 1949–51; HQ, BAOR, 1952–54; RASC Officers' Sch., 1955–56; Amphibious Warfare HQ and Persian Gulf, 1957–58; Col, WO, 1959–60; Brig., WO, 1961–62; DST, BAOR, 1963–65; CTO, BAOR, 1965–66; Comdt, Sch. of Transport, and ADC to the Queen, 1966–68; Transport Officer-in-Chief (Army), 1969–71, retired; Col. Comdt, RCT, 1972–80. Governor and Mem. Administrative Bd, Corps of Commissionaires, 1977–90. FCIT. *Publication:* The Regular Forces Employment Association 1885–1985, 1985. *Address:* The Lodge, Beacon Hill Park, Hindhead, Surrey GU26 6HU. *T:* Hindhead (01428) 604437. *Club:* MCC.

CLAY, Edward, CMG 1994; HM Diplomatic Service; High Commissioner to Uganda, since 1993; *b* 21 July 1945; *m* 1969, Anne Stroud; three *d*. FO, later FCO, 1968; Nairobi, 1970; Second, later First, Sec., Sofia, 1973; FCO, 1975; First Secretary: Budapest, 1979; FCO, 1982; Counsellor: Nicosia, 1985; FCO, 1989. *Address:* c/o Foreign and Commonwealth Office, SW1A 2AH.

CLAY, His Honour John Lionel, TD 1961; a Circuit Judge, 1977–88; *b* 31 Jan. 1918; *s* of Lionel Pilleau Clay and Mary Winifred Muriel Clay; *m* 1952, Elizabeth, *d* of Rev. Canon Maurice and Lady Phyllis Ponsonby; one *s* three *d*. *Educ:* Harrow Sch.; Corpus Christi Coll., Oxford (MA). Served War of 1939–45 (despatches): in 1st Bn Rifle Bde, N Africa (8th Army), Italy, 1941–44; Instr, Infantry Heavy Weapons Sch., 1944–45; 1st Bn Rifle Bde, Germany, 1945–46. London Rifle Bde Rangers (TA); Major (2nd i/c Bn) and 23 SAS (TA), 1948–60. Called to the Bar, Middle Temple, 1947; a Recorder of the Crown Court, 1975–77. Chm., Horserace Betting Levy Appeal Tribunal for England and Wales, 1974–77. Freeman of City of London, 1980; Liveryman, Gardeners' Co., 1980. *Recreations:* gardening, fishing. *Address:* Newtimber Place, Hassocks, Sussex BN6 9BU.

CLAY, John Martin; Deputy Chairman: Hambros plc, 1986–90 (Director, since 1970); Hambros Bank Ltd, 1972–84 (Director, 1961–84); *b* 20 Aug. 1927; *s* of late Sir Henry Clay and Gladys Priestman Clay; *m* 1952, Susan Jennifer, *d* of Lt-Gen. Sir Euan Miller, KCB, KBE, DSO, MC; four *s*. *Educ:* Eton; Magdalen Coll., Oxford. Chairman: Johnson & Firth Brown Ltd, 1973–93; Hambro Life Assurance Ltd, 1978–84. Dir, Bank of England, 1973–83. Mem., Commonwealth Develt Corp., 1970–88. FIMgt (FBIM 1971). *Recreation:* sailing. *Club:* Royal Thames Yacht.

CLAY, Prof. Dame Marie (Mildred), DBE 1987; FRSNZ 1994; Professor of Education, University of Auckland, New Zealand, 1975–91, now Emeritus, and Head of Department of Education, 1975–78 and 1986–88; *b* 3 Jan. 1926; *d* of Donald Leolin Irwin and Mildred Blanche Irwin (*née* Godier); *m* 1951, Warwick Victor Clay; one *s* one *d*. *Educ:* Wellington East Girls' College; Wellington Teachers' College; Univ. of New Zealand (MA Hons, DipEd); Univ. of Minnesota; Univ of Auckland (PhD). Teacher Training, 1943–45; Teacher of Retarded Children, 1945; Asst Psychologist, 1948–50; Fulbright Scholar, Univ. of Minnesota, 1950–51; Teacher, 1953–54; Psychologist, 1955–59; University of Auckland: Univ. Lectr, 1960–67; Sen. Lectr, 1968–72; Associate Prof., 1973–74. Distinguished Vis. Prof., Ohio State Univ., 1984–85; Vis. Fellow, Wolfson Coll., Oxford, 1987–88; George A. Miller Vis. Prof., Univ. of Illinois, 1991; Sen. Fulbright Fellow, Ohio State Univ., 1991; Vis. Prof, Univ. of London, 1991–93; President's Scholar, Texas Woman's Univ., 1994. Pres., Internat. Reading Assoc., 1992–93. FNZPsS 1978; Hon. FNZEI 1976. Hon. LHD Lesley Coll., Mass. Mackie Medal, ANZAAS, 1983. *Publications:* What Did I Write, 1975; Reading: the patterning of complex behaviour, 1972, 2nd edn 1979; The Early Detection of Reading Difficulties, 1972, 3rd edn 1985; Children of Parents Who Separate, 1978; Reading Begins at Home, 1979; Observing Young Readers, 1982; Round About Twelve, 1983; Writing Begins at Home, 1987; Quadruplets and Higher Multiple Births, 1989; Becoming Literate: the Construction of Inner Control, 1991.

CLAY, Sir Richard (Henry), 7th Bt *cr* 1841, of Fulwell Lodge, Middlesex; *b* 2 June 1940; *s* of Sir Henry Felix Clay, 6th Bt, and of Phyllis Mary, *yr d* of late R. H. Paramore, MD, FRCS; *S* father, 1985; *m* 1963, Alison Mary, *d* of Dr James Gordon Fife; three *s* two *d*. *Educ:* Eton. FCA 1966. *Recreation:* sailing. *Heir: s* Charles Richard Clay, *b* 18 Dec. 1965. *Address:* The Copse, Shiplate Road, Bleadon, Avon BS24 0NX. *Club:* Aldeburgh Yacht.

CLAY, Robert Alan; Chief Executive, Pallion Engineering Ltd, since 1992; *b* 2 Oct. 1946; *m* 1980, Uta Christa. *Educ:* Bedford Sch.; Gonville and Caius Coll., Cambridge. Busdriver, Tyne and Wear PTE, 1975–83. Branch Chm., GMBATU, 1977–83. MP (Lab) Sunderland North, 1983–92. Treas., 1983–86, Sec., 1986–87, Campaign Gp of Labour MPs. *Recreations:* walking, reading. *Address:* 12 Park Parade, Roker, Sunderland, Tyne and Wear SR6 9LU.

CLAYDON, Geoffrey Bernard, CB 1990; Member, Legal Directorate, Department of Transport, since 1990; *b* 14 Sept. 1930; *s* of Bernard Claydon and Edith Mary (*née* Lucas); unmarried. *Educ:* Leeds Modern; King Edward's, Birmingham; Birmingham Univ. (LLB). Articled at Pinsent & Co., Birmingham, 1950; admitted Solicitor, 1954. Legal Asst, 1959, Sen. Legal Asst, 1965, Treasury Solicitor's Dept; Asst Solicitor, DTI, 1973; Asst Treasury Solicitor, 1974; Principal Asst Treasury Solicitor and Legal Advr, Dept of Energy, 1980. Mem., Editorial Bd, Jl of Energy and Natural Resources Law, 1983–90. Sec., National Tramway Museum, 1958–84 (Vice-Chm., 1969–); Vice-Pres., Light Rail Transit Assoc. (formerly Light Railway Transport League), 1968– (Chm. of League, 1963–68); Vice-Pres., Tramway and Light Railway Soc., 1993– (Chm., 1967–93); Chm., Consultative Panel for Preservation of British Transport Relics, 1982–; Mem., Inst. of Transport Admin, 1972–. *Recreations:* rail transport, travel. *Address:* 23 Baron's Keep, W14 9AT. *T:* 0171–603 6400. *Club:* Royal Automobile.

CLAYMAN, David; Managing Director, Esso UK plc, since 1986; *b* 28 May 1934; *s* of Maurice and Nancy Clayman; *m* 1956, Patricia Moore; two *s*. *Educ:* Purley Grammar Sch.; University College London (BSc Chem. Engrg). Joined Esso Petroleum Co., 1956; Supply Manager, London, 1966–67, Esso Europe Inc., 1970–71; Marketing Div. Dir, 1971–79; Exec. Asst to Chm., Exxon Corp., 1979–80; Dir, Esso Petroleum Co., 1982, 1986–; Pres., Esso Africa Inc., 1983–85; Director: Esso Europe Inc., 1985; Esso Exploration and Production UK, 1986–; Esso Pension Trust, 1986–; Mainline Pipeline, 1986–. Vice-Pres., 1987–88, Pres., 1988–93, Dir, 1993–, UKPIA; Director: GCBS, 1986–87; Foundn for Management Educn, 1986–; Oil Industries Club, 1989–. *Address:* Esso House, Ermyn Way, Leatherhead, Surrey KT22 8UX. *T:* Leatherhead (01372) 223788. *Club:* Burhill Golf.

CLAYSON, Christopher William, CBE 1974 (OBE 1966); President, Royal College of Physicians of Edinburgh, 1966–70; retired; *b* 11 Sept. 1903; *s* of Christopher Clayson and Agnes Lilias Montgomerie Hunter; *m* 1st, 1933, Elsie Webster Breingan; 2nd, 1988, Anne Dorothy Miller or Middlemiss. *Educ:* George Heriot's Sch.; Edinburgh University. MB, ChB 1926; DPH 1929; MD (Gold Medal) Edinburgh 1936; FRCPE 1951; FRCP 1967. Physician: Southfield Hosp., Edinburgh, 1931–44; Edinburgh City Hosp., 1939–44; Lectr in Tuberculosis Dept, Univ. of Edinburgh, 1939–44; Med. Supt, Lochmaben Hosp., 1944–48; Consultant Phys. in Chest Medicine, Dumfries and Galloway, 1948–68; retd from clinical practice, 1968. Served on numerous Govt and Nat. Health Service cttees, 1948–; Chairman: Scottish Licensing Law Cttee, 1971–73; Scottish Council for Postgrad. Med. Educn, 1970–74. Mem., Scottish Soc. of Physicians; Mem., Thoracic Soc.; Hon. FACP 1968; Hon. FRACP 1969; Hon. FRCPGlas 1970; Hon. FRCGP 1971; Hon. FRCPE 1990. William Cullen Prize, RCPE, 1978. *Publications:* various papers on tuberculosis problem and on alcoholism in leading medical jls. *Recreations:* gardening, fishing. *Address:* Cockiesknowe, Lochmaben, Lockerbie, Dumfriesshire. *T:* Lochmaben (01387) 810231. *Clubs:* Caledonian; New (Edinburgh).

CLAYTON, Prof. Dame Barbara (Evelyn), (Dame Barbara Klyne), DBE 1988 (CBE 1983); MD, PhD; FRCP, FRCPath; Hon. Research Professor in Metabolism, Faculty of Medicine, University of Southampton, since 1987 (Professor of Chemical Pathology and Human Metabolism, 1979–87, and Dean of the Faculty of Medicine 1983–86); *b* 2 Sept. 1922; *m* 1949, William Klyne (*d* 1977); one *s* one *d*. *Educ:* Univ. of Edinburgh (MD, PhD). FRCP 1972; FRCPath 1971; FRCPE 1985. Consultant in Chem. Pathology, Hosp. for Sick Children, London, 1959–70; Prof. of Chem. Pathology, Inst. of Child Health, Univ. of London, 1970–78. Leverhulme Emeritus Fellow, 1988–90. Hon Consultant, 1979–92, Mem., 1983–87, Southampton and SW Hants HA. Member: Commonwealth Scholarship Commn, 1977–93; Royal Commn on Environmental Pollution, 1981–. Chm., Task Force on Nutrition, DoH, 1992–; Member: Standing Med. Adv. Cttee (DHSS), 1981–87; Cttee on Toxicity of Chemicals in Food, Consumer Products and the Environment, DoH (formerly DHSS), 1977–93; Systems Bd, MRC, 1974–77; British Nat. Cttees on Chemistry and Biochemistry, 1977–78; British Nat. Cttee on Problems of the Environment, 1988–89; Council, British Nutrition Foundn, 1987–; COMA Panel on Dietary Reference Values, 1987–91; WHO Expert Adv. Panel on Nutrition, 1989–; DoH Steering Gp on Undergrad. Med. and Dental Educn and Res., 1989–; Chairman: Adv. Cttee on Borderline Substances, 1971–83; MRC Adv. Gp on Lead and Neuropsychol Effects in Children, 1983–; Cttee on Med. Aspects of Contaminants in Air, Soil and Water, 1984–90; Standing Cttee on Postgrad. Med. and Dental (formerly Med.) Educn, 1988–; Med. and Scientific Panel, Leukaemia Res. Fund, 1989–; MRC Cttee on Toxic Hazards in the Workplace and the Environment, 1989–. Council, RCPath, 1982–(Pres., 1984–87); GMC, 1983–87. President: Assoc. of Clinical Biochemists, 1977, 1978; Soc. for Study of Inborn Errors of Metabolism, 1981–82; Biomedical Scis Sect., BAAS, 1989–90; British Dietetic Assoc., 1989–; Nat. Soc. for Clean Air and Envmtl Protection, 1995–. Member: Bd of Govs, Hosps for Sick Children, London, 1968–78; Scientific Adv. Cttee, Assoc. of Med. Res. Charities, 1990–. Lectures: Stanley Davidson, RCPE; Harben, RIPH&H; Hartley, Southampton Univ; Wilfred Fish Meml, GDC. Hon. Member: BPA, 1987; Soc. for Study of Inborn Errors of Metabolism, 1988; Assoc. of Clinical Biochemists, 1990; Corresponding Mem., Gesellschaft für Laboratoriumsmedizin, 1990. Hon. Fellow: British Dietetic Assoc., 1976; Faculty of Pathology, RCPI, 1986; Amer. Soc. of Clin. Pathologists, 1987. Hon. DSc: Edinburgh, 1985; Southampton, 1992. Jessie MacGregor Prize for Med. Sci., RCPE, 1985; Wellcome Prize, Assoc. of Clin. Biochemists, 1988. *Publications:* contrib. learned jls, incl. Jl Endocrinol., Arch. Dis. Childhood, and BMJ. *Recreations:* natural history, walking. *Address:* 16 Chetwynd Drive, Bassett, Southampton SO16 3HZ. *T:* Southampton (01703) 769937.

CLAYTON, Captain Sir David (Robert), 12th Bt *cr* 1732, of Marden; Shipmaster since 1970; *b* 12 Dec. 1936; *s* of Sir Arthur Harold Clayton, 11th Bt, DSC, and of Alexandra, Lady Clayton, *d* of late Sergei Andreevsky; *S* father, 1985; *m* 1971, Julia Louise, *d* of late Charles Henry Redfearn; two *s*. *Educ:* HMS Conway. Joined Merchant Service, 1953; promoted to first command as Captain, 1970. *Recreations:* shooting, sailing. *Heir: s* Robert Philip Clayton, *b* 8 July 1975. *Address:* Rock House, Kingswear, Dartmouth, Devon TQ6 0BX. *T:* Kingswear (01803) 752433. *Club:* Royal Dart Yacht (Kingswear).

CLAYTON, Prof. Frederick William; Professor of Classics, 1948–75, and Public Orator, 1965–73, University of Exeter; *b* 13 Dec. 1913; *s* of late William and Gertrude Clayton, Liverpool; *m* 1948, Friederike Luise Büttner-Wobst; two *s* two *d*. *Educ:* Liverpool Collegiate Sch.; King's Coll., Cambridge. Members' Essay Prizes (Latin and English), Porson Prize, Browne Medal, 1933; Craven Scholar in Classics, 1934; Chancellor's Medal for Classics, 1935; Fellow of King's Coll., 1937. Served War, Nov. 1940–Oct. 1946, Signals, Field Security, RAF Intelligence, India. *Publications:* The Cloven Pine, 1942; various articles. *Address:* Halwill, Clydesdale Road, Exeter, Devon EX4 4QX. *T:* Exeter (01392) 71810.

See also G. Clayton.

CLAYTON, Prof. George; Newton Chambers Professor of Applied Economics, University of Sheffield, 1967–83, Pro-Vice-Chancellor, 1978–82, now Emeritus Professor; *b* 15 July 1922; *s* of late William Clayton and late Gertrude Alison Clarke Clayton; *m* 1948, Rhiannon Jones, JP; two *s* two *d*. *Educ:* Liverpool Collegiate Sch.; King's Coll., Cambridge (Exhibnr). Served War of 1939–45: Pilot, RAF, 1941–45; Pilot, Fleet Air Arm, 1945. Univ. of Liverpool: Asst Lectr, 1947–50; Lectr, 1950–57; Sen. Lectr, 1957–60 and 1961–63; Sen. Simon Res. Fellow, Univ. of Manchester, 1960–61; Prof. and Head of Dept of Econs, UCW Aberystwyth, 1963–67; Luis Olariaga Lectr, Madrid Univ., 1959; Special Univ. Lectr, London, 1970; Page Fund Lectr, UC Cardiff, 1970. Member: Council, Royal Econ. Soc., 1965–68; (part-time) East Midland Gas Bd, 1967–70; Crowther Cttee on Consumer Credit, 1968–70; Scott Cttee on Property Bonds and Equity-linked Insce, 1970–72; Econs Cttee, SSRC, 1978–82 (Vice-Chm., 1979–82). Non-exec. Dir, Pioneer Mutual Assurance Co., 1976–90; Consultant, Eastern Caribbean Central Bank, 1987–. Chm., British, Canadian and Amer. Mission to British Honduras, 1966; Econ. Adviser: Govt of Tanzania, 1965–66; Govt of Gibraltar, 1974–82. Chm., Assoc. of Univ. Teachers of Economics, 1973–78. *Publications:* (contrib.) A New Prospect of Economics, ed G. L. S. Shackle, 1956; (contrib.) Banking in Western Europe, ed R. S. Sayers, 1959; Insurance Company Investment, 1965; Problems of Rail Transport in Rural Wales: Two Case Studies, 1967; Monetary Theory and Monetary Policy in the 1970s, 1971; British Insurance, 1971; articles in Econ. Jl, etc. *Recreations:* tennis, sailing, theatre, fell walking. *Address:* 108 Westbourne Road, Sheffield S10 2QT. *T:* Sheffield (0114) 2681833. *Clubs:* Hawks (Cambridge); Sheffield (Sheffield).

See also Prof. F. W. Clayton.

CLAYTON, John Pilkington, CVO 1986 (LVO 1975); MA, MB, BChir; Apothecary to HM Household at Windsor, 1965–86; Surgeon Apothecary to HM Queen Elizabeth the Queen Mother's Household at the Royal Lodge, Windsor, 1965–86; Senior Medical Officer, Eton College, 1965–86 (MO, 1962–65); *b* 13 Feb. 1921; *s* of late Brig.-Gen. Sir Gilbert Clayton, KCMG, KBE, CB, and Enid, *d* of late F. N. Thorowgood. *Educ:* Wellington Coll.; Gonville and Caius Coll., Cambridge; King's Coll. Hospital. RAFVR, 1947–49; Sqdn Ldr 1949. Senior Resident, Nottingham Children's Hosp., 1950. MO, Black and Decker Ltd, 1955–70; MO, 1953–62, SMO 1962–81, Royal Holloway Coll. *Address:* Knapp House, Market Lavington, near Devizes, Wilts SN10 4DP.

CLAYTON, Prof. Keith Martin, CBE 1984; Professor of Environmental Sciences, 1967–93, now Emeritus; *b* 25 Sept. 1928; *s* of Edgar Francis Clayton and Constance Annie (*née* Clark); *m* 1st, 1950 (marr. diss. 1976); three *s* one *d*; 2nd, 1976. *Educ:* Bedales Sch.; Univ. of Sheffield (MSc). PhD London. Demonstrator, Univ. of Nottingham, 1949–51. Served RE, 1951–53. Lectr, London Sch. of Economics, 1953–63; Reader in Geography, LSE, 1963–67; Univ. of E Anglia: Founding Dean, Sch. of Environmental Scis, 1967–71 and 1987–93; Pro-Vice-Chancellor, 1971–73; Dir, Centre of E Anglian Studies, 1974–81; Vis. Professor, State Univ. of New York at Binghamton, 1960–62. Chm., Adv. Cttee, Document Supply Centre, British Library, 1986–93; Member: NERC, 1970–73; UGC, 1973–84; Nat. Radiological Protection Bd, 1980–85; Nat. Adv. Bd for Local Authority Higher Educn, 1982–84; Cttee on Med. Aspects of Radiation in Environment, DHSS, 1985–; Ministerial Adv. Cttee on Envmt and Energy, MoD, 1990–; Broads Authy, 1994–. Vice-Chm., Broadland Housing Assoc., 1994–95. Councillor, Broadland DC, 1994–. Pres., IBG, 1984. Patron's Medal, RGS, 1989. *Publications:* Editor and publisher, Geo Abstracts, 1960–85. *Recreations:* gardening, work. *Address:* Well Close, Pound Lane, Thorpe, Norwich NR7 0UA. *T:* Norwich (01603) 33780.

CLAYTON, Lucie; *see* Kark, Evelyn F.

CLAYTON, Margaret Ann; Assistant Under-Secretary of State, Home Office (on leave of absence); *b* 7 May 1941; *d* of late Percy Thomas Clayton and of Kathleen Clayton (*née* Payne). *Educ:* Christ's Hospital, Hertford; Birkbeck Coll., London (BA, MSc). Entered Home Office, 1960; Executive Officer/Asst Principal, 1960–67; Asst Private Secretary to Home Secretary, 1967–68; Principal, 1968–75 (seconded to Cabinet Office, 1972–73); Asst Sec., 1975–82; Asst Under Sec. of State, 1983–: Resident Chm., CSSB, 1983; Dir of Services, Prison Service, 1986–90; Police Dept, 1990–93; Personnel Dept, 1994. *Recreations:* equitation, gardening, theatre. *Club:* Reform.

CLAYTON, Michael Aylwin; Editor of Horse and Hound, since 1973; Editor-in-Chief, IPC country titles, since 1994; *b* 20 Nov. 1934; *s* of late Aylwin Goff Clayton and Norah (*née* Banfield); *m* 1st, 1959, Mary L. B. Watson (marr. diss.); one *s* one *d*; 2nd, 1979, Barbara Jane Ryman (*née* Whitfield) (marr. diss. 1988); 3rd, 1988, Marilyn Crowhurst (*née* Orrin. *Educ:* Bournemouth Gammar School. National Service, RAF, 1954–56. Reporter: Lymington Times and New Milton Advertiser, 1951–54; Portsmouth Evening News, 1956–57; London Evening News, 1957–61; reporter/feature writer, New Zealand Herald, 1961; reporter, London Evening Standard, 1961, Dep. News Editor, 1962–64; News Editor, Southern Ind. Television, 1964–65; staff correspondent, BBC TV and radio (incl. Vietnam, Cambodia, India, Pakistan and Middle East), 1965–73; Presenter, Today, BBC Radio 4, 1973–75. Dir, IPC Magazines, 1994–. Chm., British Soc. of Magazine Editors, 1986. Mem., Press Complaints Commn, 1991–93. *Publications:* A Hunting We Will Go, 1967; (with Dick Tracey) Hickstead—the First Twelve Years, 1972; (ed) The Complete Book of Showjumping, 1975; (ed) Cross-Country Riding, 1977; The Hunter, 1980; The Golden Thread, 1984; Prince Charles: horseman, 1987; The Chase: a modern guide to foxhunting, 1987; Foxhunting in Paradise, 1993. *Recreations:* foxhunting, music. *Address:* King's Reach Tower, Stamford Street, SE1 9LS.

CLAYTON, Sir Robert (James), Kt 1980; CBE 1970 (OBE 1960); FEng, FInstP, FRAeS, FIEE, FIEEE; Technical Director, The General Electric Co. plc, 1968–83; GEC Director, 1978–83; *b* 30 Oct. 1915; *m* 1949, Joy Kathleen King; no *c*. *Educ:* Cambridge Univ. (Scholar, Christ's Coll.; MA; Hon. Fellow, 1983). GEC Research Labs, 1937; Manager, GEC Applied Electronics Labs, 1955; Dep. Dir, Hirst Research Centre, 1960; Man. Dir, GEC (Electronics), 1963; Man. Dir, GEC (Research), 1966. Member: Adv. Council for Applied R&D, 1976–80 (Chm. of Groups producing reports on Applications of Semiconductors, Computer Aided Design and Manufacture, and Inf. Technology); Adv. Council on R&D for Fuel and Power, 1976–83; NEB, 1978–80; Adv. Council, Science Mus., 1980–83, Trustee, 1984–90; British Library Bd, 1983–87; UGC, 1982–89; Monopolies and Mergers Commn, 1983–89; Chairman: Computer Systems and Electronics Requirements Bd, DoI, 1978–81; Open Technology Steering Gp, MSC, 1983–84; Policy Cttee, IT Skills Agency, 1985–88. Chm., Electronics Engrg Assoc., 1965; President: IEE, 1975–76 (Chm., Electronics Div., 1968–69); Inst. of Physics, 1982–84; Assoc. for Science Educn, 1983; IInfSc, 1985–86; Vice-President: Fellowship of Engineering, 1980–82; IERE, 1983–84. Vis. Prof., Electrical Engrg Dept, Imperial Coll. of Science and Technology, 1971–77; Lectures: IEE Faraday; CEI Graham Clarke; Christopher Hinton, Fellowship of Engineering. Hon. FIEE 1982. Hon. DSc: Aston, 1979; Salford, 1979; City, 1981; Oxon, 1988; Hon. DEng Bradford, 1985. *Publications:* The GEC Research Laboratories 1919–1984, 1989; (ed) A Scientist's War–the Diary of Sir Clifford Paterson, 1991; papers in Proc. IEE (premium awards). *Club:* United Oxford & Cambridge University.

CLAYTON, Prof. Robert Norman, FRS 1981; Professor, Departments of Chemistry and of the Geophysical Sciences, University of Chicago, since 1966; *b* 20 March 1930; *s* of Norman and Gwenda Clayton; *m* 1971, Cathleen Shelburne Clayton; one *d*. *Educ:* Queen's Univ., Canada (BSc, MSc); California Inst. of Technol. (PhD). Res. Fellow, Calif. Inst. of Technol., 1955–56; Asst Prof., Pennsylvania State Univ., 1956–58; University of Chicago: Asst Prof., 1958–62; Associate Prof., 1962–66. *Publications:* over 100 papers in geochemical journals. *Address:* 5201 South Cornell, Chicago, IL 60615, USA. *T:* (312)6432450.

CLAYTON, Stanley James; Town Clerk of the City of London 1974–82; *b* 10 Dec. 1919; *s* of late James John Clayton and late Florence Clayton; *m* 1955, Jean Winifred, *d* of late Frederick Etheridge; one *s* one *d*. *Educ:* Ensham Sch.; King's Coll., London (LLB). Served War of 1939–45, commnd RAF. Admitted Solicitor 1958. City of Westminster, 1938–52; Camberwell, 1952–60; Asst Solicitor, Holborn, 1960–63; Deputy Town Clerk: Greenwich, 1963–65; Islington, 1964–69; City of London, 1969–74. Comdr, Order of Dannebrog (Denmark); holds other foreign orders. *Address:* 27 Lakeside, Beckenham, Kent BR3 2LX. *Club:* Royal Air Force.

CLEALL, Charles; author; *b* 1 June 1927; *s* of Sydney Cleal and Dorothy (*née* Bound); *m* 1953, Mary, *yr d* of G. L. Turner, Archery Lodge, Ashford, Mddx; two *d*. *Educ:* Hampton Sch.; Univ. of London (BMus); Univ of Wales (MA); Jordanhill Coll. of Educn, Glasgow. ADCM, GTCL, FRCO(CHM), LRAM, HonTSC. Command Music Adviser, RN, 1946–48; Prof. of Singing and Voice Production, TCL, 1949–52; Conductor, Morley Coll. Orch., 1949–51; Choral Scholar, Westminster Abbey, 1949–52; Organist and Choirmaster, Wesley's Chapel, City Road, EC4, 1950–52; Conductor, Glasgow Choral Union, 1952–54; BBC Music Asst, Midland Region, 1954–55; Music Master, Glyn County Sch., Ewell, 1955–66; Conductor, Aldeburgh Festival Choir, 1957–60; Organist and Choirmaster: St Paul's, Portman Sq., W1, 1957–61; Holy Trinity, Guildford, 1961–65; Lectr in Music, Froebel Inst., 1967–68; Adviser in Music, London Borough of Harrow, 1968–72; Warden, Education Section, ISM, 1971–72; music specialist, N Div., HM Inspectorate of Schs in Scotland, 1972–87. Regd Teacher, Sch. of Sinus Tone, 1985–. Editor, Jl of Ernest George White Soc., 1983–88. Presented papers at: study-conf. of teachers of singing, The Maltings, Snape, 1976; Nat. Course on Develt of Young Children's Musical Skills, Univ. of Reading Sch. of Educn, 1979; annual conf., Scottish Fedn of Organists, 1980; Nat. Conf., Assoc. of Music Advisers in Scotland, 1987; Edinburgh Centre of ISM, 1993. Internat. Composition Prizeman of Cathedral of St John the Divine, NY; Limpus Fellowship Prizeman of RCO. *Publications:* Voice Production in Choral Technique, 1955, rev. edn 1970; The Selection and Training of Mixed Choirs in Churches, 1960; Sixty Songs from Sankey, 1960; (ed) John Merbecke's Music for the Congregation at Holy Communion, 1963; Music and Holiness, 1964; Plainsong for Pleasure, 1969; Authentic Chanting, 1969; Guide to Vanity Fair, 1982; Walking round the Church of St James the Great, Stonehaven, 1993. *Recreations:* watching sea-birds, reading, writing, walking. *Address:* 10 Carronhall, Stonehaven, Aberdeen AB3 2HF.

CLEARY, Denis Mackrow, CMG 1967; HM Diplomatic Service, retired; *b* 20 Dec. 1907; *s* of late Francis Esmonde Cleary and late Emmeline Marie Cleary (*née* Mackrow); *m* 1st, 1941, Barbara Wykeham-George (*d* 1960); 2nd, 1962, Mary Kent (*née* Dunlop), *widow* of Harold Kent; one step-*d*. *Educ:* St Ignatius Coll. and St Olave's Sch.; St John's Coll., Cambridge (Major Schol.). 1st Class Hons Pts I and II, Math. Tripos; BA 1930; MA 1934. Asst Principal, India Office, 1931; Principal, 1937; seconded to Min. of Home Security, 1940–44; Dep. Principal Officer to Regional Commissioner, Cambridge, March 1943–Sept. 1944; seconded to Foreign Office (German Section) as Asst Sec., 1946–49; transferred to CRO and posted to Delhi as Counsellor, 1949–51; Dep. High Commissioner, Wellington, 1955–58; Mem. of British Delegn to Law of the Sea Conf., Geneva, 1960; Dep. High Comr, Nicosia, 1962–64; Head of Atlantic Dept, Commonwealth Office, 1964–68 (Mem., Cttee for Exports to the Caribbean, 1965–67); retd 1968; re-employed in Internat. Div., DHSS, 1968–72; UK Delegate to Public Health Cttees, Council of Europe, 1968–72; Chm., Council of Europe Med. Fellowships Selection Cttee, 1972–74. *Recreations:* gardening, walking. *Address:* High Gate, Burwash, East Sussex TN19 7LA. *T:* Burwash (01435) 882712.

CLEARY, Jon Stephen; novelist; *b* 22 Nov. 1917; *s* of Matthew Cleary and Ida (*née* Brown); *m* 1946, Constantine Lucas; one *d* (and one *d* decd). *Educ:* Marist Brothers' Sch., Randwick, NSW. Variety of jobs, 1932–40; served with AIF, 1940–45; freelance writer, 1945–48; journalist with Australian News and Information Bureau: London, 1948–49; New York, 1949–51; subseq. full-time writer. Jt winner, Nat. Radio Play Contest, ABC, 1945; second prize, Sydney Morning Herald Novel Comp., 1946; Australian Lit. Soc. Gold Medal, 1950; regional winner, NY Herald Tribune World Short Story Contest, 1950. *Publications:* These Small Glories (short stories), 1946; You Can't See Round Corners, 1947 (2nd Prize, Novel Contest, Sydney Morning Herald); The Long Shadow, 1949; Just Let Me Be, 1950 (Crouch Gold Medal for best Australian novel); The Sundowners, 1952; The Climate of Courage, 1953; Justin Bayard, 1955; The Green Helmet, 1957; Back of Sunset, 1959; North from Thursday, 1960; The Country of Marriage, 1962; Forests of the Night, 1963; A Flight of Chariots, 1964; The Fall of an Eagle, 1964; The Pulse of Danger, 1966; The High Commissioner, 1967; The Long Pursuit, 1967; Season of Doubt, 1968; Remember Jack Hoxie, 1969; Helga's Web, 1970; Mask of the Andes, 1971; Man's Estate, 1972; Ransom, 1973; Peter's Pence (Edgar Award for best crime novel; Mystery Writers of America, Best Crime Novel), 1974; The Safe House, 1975; A Sound of Lightning, 1976; High Road to China, 1977; Vortex, 1977; The Beaufort Sisters, 1979; A Very Private War, 1980; The Golden Sabre, 1981; The Faraway Drums, 1981; Spearfield's Daughter, 1982; The Phoenix Tree, 1984; The City of Fading Light, 1985; Dragons at the Party, 1987; Now and Then, Amen, 1988; Babylon South, 1989; Murder Song, 1990; Pride's Harvest, 1991; Dark Summer, 1992; Bleak Spring, 1993; Autumn Maze, 1994. *Recreations:* tennis, reading. *Address:* c/o HarperCollins, 77–85 Fulham Palace Road, W6 8JB.

CLEASBY, Very Rev. Thomas Wood Ingram; Dean of Chester, 1978–86, Dean Emeritus, since 1986; *b* 27 March 1920; *s* of T. W. Cleasby, Oakdene, Sedbergh, Yorks, and Jessie Brown Cleasby; *m* 1st, 1956, Olga Elizabeth Vibert Douglas (*d* 1967); one *s* one *d* (and one *d* decd); 2nd, 1970, Monica, *e d* of Rt Rev. O. S. Tomkins; one *d*. *Educ:* Sedbergh Sch., Yorks; Magdalen Coll., Oxford; Cuddesdon Coll., Oxford. BA, MA (Hons Mod. History) 1947. Commissioned, 1st Bn Border Regt, 1940; served 1st Airborne Div., 1941–45, Actg Major. Ordained, Dio. Wakefield, 1949 (Huddersfield Parish Church). Domestic Chaplain to Archbishop of York, 1952–56; Anglican Chaplain to Univ. of Nottingham, 1956–63; Archdeacon of Chesterfield, 1963–78; Vicar of St Mary and All Saints, Chesterfield, 1963–70; Rector of Morton, Derby, 1970–78. *Recreations:* fell-walking, bird-watching, gardening, fishing, local history. *Address:* Low Barth, Dent, Cumbria LA10 5SZ. *T:* Dent (015396) 25476.

CLEAVE, Brian Elseley, CB 1995; Solicitor of Inland Revenue, since 1990; *b* 3 Sept. 1939; *s* of Walter Edward Cleave and Hilda Lillian Cleave (*née* Newman); *m* 1979, Celia Valentine Williams. *Educ:* Eastbourne Coll. (Duke of Devonshire's schol.); Exeter Univ. (LLB 1961); Kansas Univ.; Manchester Univ. Admitted Solicitor, 1966. Asst Solicitor, Wilkinson Howlett and Durham, 1966–67; Inland Revenue Solicitor's Office, 1967–: Asst Solicitor, 1978; Prin. Asst Solicitor, 1986. FRSA 1995. *Recreations:* theatre, travel, walking. *Address:* Solicitor's Office, Inland Revenue, Somerset House, WC2R 1LB. *T:* 0171–438 6645.

CLEAVER, Sir Anthony (Brian), Kt 1992; FBCS; Chairman, United Kingdom Atomic Energy Authority, since 1993; *b* 10 April 1938; *s* of late William Brian Cleaver and Dorothea Early Cleaver (*née* Peeks); *m* 1962, Mary Teresa Cotter; one *s* one *d*. *Educ:* Berkhamsted Sch.; Trinity Coll., Oxford (Schol.; MA; Hon. Fellow 1989). Joined IBM United Kingdom, 1962; IBM World Trade Corp., USA, 1973–74; Dir, DP Div., IBM UK, 1977; Vice-Pres. of Marketing, IBM Europe, Paris, 1981–82; Gen. Man., 1984, Chief Exec., 1986–91, Chm., 1990–94, IBM United Kingdom Holdings Ltd. Director: General Accident Fire & Life Assurance Corp., 1988–; Smith & Nephew PLC, 1993–; General Cable PLC, 1994– (Chm., 1995–). Dir, Nat. Computing Centre, 1976–80. Dir, ENO, 1988–; Member Board: UK Centre for Econ. and Environmental Develt, 1985– (Dep. Chm., 1992–); Business in the Community, 1985– (Chm., Business in the Envmt Target Team, 1988–; Mem., President's Cttee, 1988–91; Dep. Chm., 1991–); RIPA, 1985–89; Mem., Council, Assoc. for Business Sponsorship of the Arts, 1985– (Dir, 1991–). Chairman: Industrial Develt Adv. Bd, DTI, 1993–; TEC Ind. Assessors Cttees, 1994–; Member: Nat. Adv. Council for Educn and Trng Targets, 1993; Electronics EDC, NEDO, 1986–92; CBI, 1986– (Mem., President's Cttee, 1988–92); BOTB, 1988–91; Nat. Trng Task Force, 1989–92. Dir, American Chamber of Commerce, 1989–91. Member: HRH Duke of Edinburgh's Seventh Commonwealth Study Conf. Council, 1990–92; Council for Industry and Higher Educn, 1991–94; Carnegie Inquiry into Third

Age, 1991–93. Chm., Portsmouth Univ. Business Adv. Bd, 1992–; Member: Oxford Univ. Adv. Council on Continuing Educn, 1993–; President's Cttee, Oxford Univ. Appeal, 1988–; Appeal Chm., Trinity Coll., Oxford, 1989–; Member Council: Templeton Coll., Oxford, 1982–93; PSI, 1985–88; Chm. Govs, Birkbeck Coll., 1989–; Mem., Cttee of Chm. of Univ. Councils, 1992–. Hon. FCIM 1989 (Hon. Vice-Pres., 1991–; Pres., London Br., 1993–); FRSA 1987 (Chm., RSA Inquiry into Tomorrow's Co., 1993–). Mem. Council, WWF, 1988–92. Patron, Friends of the Classics, 1991–. Hon. LLD Nottingham, 1991. UN Envmt Program Global 500 Roll of Honour, 1989. *Recreations:* music, especially opera; sport, especially cricket, golf. *Address:* Rex House, 4–12 Regent Street, SW1Y 4PE. *T:* 0171–389 6553. *Clubs:* Reform, MCC.

CLEAVER, Air Vice-Marshal Peter (Charles), CB 1971; OBE 1945; *b* 6 July 1919; *s* of William Henry Cleaver, Warwick; *m* 1948, Jean, *d* of J. E. B. Fairclough, Ledbury; two *s*. *Educ:* Warwick Sch.; Coll. of Aeronautics (MSc). Staff Coll., Haifa, 1945; idc 1966. HM Asst Air Attaché, Bucharest, 1947–49; Coll. of Aeronautics, Cranfield, 1950–52; Structural Research, RAE Farnborough, 1952–55; Min. of Supply, 1955–57; HQ FEAF, 1957–60; Maintenance Comd, 1960–63; OC, Central Servicing Develt Estabt, 1963–64; Air Officer Engineering: HQ Flying Trg Comd, 1964–66; HQ FEAF, 1967–69; Air Support Command, 1969–72; retired 1972. Sec., Cranfield Inst. of Technology, 1973–78. Governor, Warwick Schs Foundn, 1978–85; Chm. Governors, Warwick Sch., 1980–85. CEng, FRAeS. *Recreation:* gardening. *Address:* Willow House, Watling Street, Little Brickhill, Milton Keynes MK17 9LS. *Club:* Royal Air Force.

CLEAVER, William Benjamin, CEng, FIMinE; JP; Deputy Director, South Wales Area, National Coal Board, 1969–85; *b* 15 Sept. 1921; *s* of David John Cleaver and Blodwen (*née* Miles); *m* 1943, Mary Watkin (*née* James); one *s* two *d*. *Educ:* Pentre (Rhondda) Grammar Sch.; University Coll. Cardiff (BSc Hons). National Coal Board: Manager: N Celynen Collieries, Gwent, 1947; Oakdale Colliery, Gwent, 1950; Production Manager (Group), S Wales, 1953; Area General Manager, No 2 S Wales Area, 1958. Sec., Contemporary Art Soc. for Wales, 1972–91; Member: Welsh Arts Council, 1977–83 (Vice-Chm., 1980–83); Arts Council of GB, 1980–83; Council, Nat. Museum of Wales, 1982–; Exec. Cttee, Council of Museums in Wales, 1983– (Chm., 1986–). Founder Pres., Cardiff Jun. Ch. of Commerce, 1953. Rugby Union Football: Cardiff RFC, 1940–50; Welsh Rugby International, 1947–50 (14 caps); British Lion to NZ and Aust., 1950; Barbarian Rugby Club, 1946; Founder Chm., Welsh Youth Rugby Union, 1949–57. JP Cardiff 1973. OstJ 1961. *Recreations:* theatre, fine arts. *Address:* 29 Lon-y-deri, Rhiwbina, Cardiff CF4 6JN. *T:* Cardiff (01222) 693242. *Clubs:* Savile; Cardiff and County (Cardiff).

CLEDWYN OF PENRHOS, Baron *cr* 1979 (Life Peer), of Holyhead in the Isle of Anglesey; **Cledwyn Hughes,** CH 1977; PC 1966; Leader of the Opposition, House of Lords, 1982–92 (Deputy Leader of the Opposition, 1981–82); *b* 14 Sept. 1916; *er s* of Rev. Henry David and Emily Hughes; *m* 1949, Jean Beatrice Hughes; one *s* one *d*. *Educ:* Holyhead Grammar Sch.; University Coll. of Wales, Aberystwyth (LLB; Hon. Fellow, 1986). Solicitor, 1940. Served RAFVR, 1940–45. Mem. Anglesey County Council, 1946–52. Contested (Lab) Anglesey, 1945 and 1950; MP (Lab) Anglesey, 1951–79; Opposition spokesman for Housing and Local Govt, 1959–64; Minister of State for Commonwealth Relations, 1964–66; Sec. of State for Wales, 1966–68; Min. of Agriculture, Fisheries and Food, 1968–70; Opposition spokesman on Agriculture, Fisheries and Food, 1970–72; Commissioner of the House of Commons, 1979; Chm., House of Lords Select Cttee on Agriculture and Food, 1980–83. Chairman: Welsh Parliamentary Party, 1953–54; Welsh Labour Group, 1955–56; Parly Labour Party, Oct. 1974–1979 (Vice-Chm., March–Oct. 1974); Welsh Cttee on Economic and Industrial Affairs, 1982–84. Member: Cttee of Public Accounts, 1957–64; Cttee of Privileges, 1974–79; Political Honours Cttee, 1992–. Jt Chm. TUC/Labour Party Liaison Cttee, 1974–79. Vice-Pres., Britain in Europe, 1975. Mem. Parly Delegn to Lebanon, 1957; represented British Govt at Kenya Republic Celebrations, 1964; led UK Delegn to The Gambia Independence celebrations, 1965; Mission to Rhodesia, July 1965; led UK Mission on Contingency Planning to Zambia, 1966; led Parliamentary Delegn to USSR, 1977; Prime Minister's Envoy to Southern Africa, Nov.–Dec. 1978. Director: Shell UK Ltd, 1980–84; Anglesey Aluminium Ltd, 1980–; Holyhead Towing Ltd, 1980–; a Regional Advr in Midland Bank, with special responsibilities for Wales, 1979–94. Member, County Councils' Assoc., 1980–; Chm., Welsh Theatre Co., 1981–85; President: Housing and Town Planning Council, 1980–92; Age Concern, Wales, 1980–85; Soc. of Welsh People Overseas, 1979–91; UCW, Aberystwyth, 1976–85; Assembly of Welsh Counties, 1990–. Pro-Chancellor, Univ. of Wales, 1985–94. Fellow: UCW, Aberystwyth, 1988; Trinity Coll., Carmarthen, 1993. Hon. Freedom of Beaumaris, 1972; Freeman, Borough of Anglesey, 1976. Hon. LLD: Wales, 1970; Sheffield, 1992. Alderman, Anglesey CC, 1973. *Publication:* Report on Conditions in St Helena, 1958. *Address:* Penmorfa, Trearddur, Holyhead, Gwynedd. *T:* Trearddur Bay (01407) 860544. *Club:* Travellers'.

CLEERE, Henry Forester, OBE 1992; FSA; Director, Council for British Archaeology, 1974–91; World Heritage Co-ordinator, International Council of Monuments and Sites, since 1991; *b* 2 Dec. 1926; *s* of late Christopher Henry John Cleere and Frances Eleanor (*née* King); *m* 1st, 1950, Dorothy Percy (marr. diss.); one *s* one *d*; 2nd, 1975, Pamela Joan Vertue; two *d*. *Educ:* Beckenham County Sch.; University Coll. London (BA Hons 1951; Fellow 1992); Univ. of London Inst. of Archaeology (PhD 1981). FSA 1967. Commissioned Royal Artillery, 1946–48. Successively, Production Editor, Asst Sec., Man. Editor, Dep. Sec., Iron and Steel Inst., 1952–71; Industrial Development Officer, UN Industrial Develt Org., Vienna, 1972–73. Archaeol Advr, GLC Historic Buildings Panel, 1979–84. Member: Exec. Cttee, ICOMOS, 1981–90; Duchy of Cornwall Archaeol Adv. Panel, 1983–90; Scientific Cttee, Centro Universitario Europeo per i Beni Culturali, 1985–95; NT Archaeol. Panel, 1990–94. President: Sussex Archaeol Soc., 1987–91; Europ. Forum of Heritage Assocs, 1991–93; Sec., Europ. Assoc. of Archaeologists, 1991–. MIFA 1982, Hon. MIFA 1991; FIMgt; FRSA 1991. Winston Churchill Fellow, 1979, Hon. Vis. Fellow, Univ. of York, 1988–; Vis. Res. Fellow, Univ. de Paris I (Sorbonne), 1989; UK Trust Sen. Fellow, Indian Nat. Trust for Art and Cultural Heritage, 1990. Hon. DLitt Sussex, 1993. Editor, Antiquity, 1992. *Publications:* Approaches to the Archaeological Heritage, 1984; (with D. W. Crossley) The Iron Industry of the Weald, 1985; Archaeological Heritage Management in the Modern World, 1988; papers in British and foreign jls on aspects of early ironmaking, Roman fleets, etc. *Recreations:* gardening, beekeeping, cookery. *Address:* Acres Rise, Lower Platts, Ticehurst, Wadhurst, East Sussex TN5 7DD. *T:* Ticehurst (01580) 200752; 11 rue Chapon, 75003 Paris, France. *T:* 42719719. *Club:* Athenæum.

CLEESE, John Marwood; writer and actor; *b* 27 Oct. 1939; *s* of Reginald and Muriel Cleese; *m* 1st, 1968, Connie Booth (marr. diss. 1978); one *d*; 2nd, 1981, Barbara Trentham (marr. diss. 1990); one *d*; 3rd, 1993, Alyce Faye Eichelberger. *Educ:* Clifton Sports Acad.; Downing College, Cambridge (MA). Founder and former Dir, Video Arts Ltd. Started making jokes professionally, 1963; started on British television, 1966; TV series have included: The Frost Report, At Last the 1948 Show, Monty Python's Flying Circus, Fawlty Towers. Films include: Interlude, The Magic Christian, And Now For Something Completely Different, Monty Python and the Holy Grail, Romance with a Double Bass, Life of Brian, Privates on Parade, The Meaning of Life, Yellowbeard, Silverado, Clockwise, A Fish Called Wanda, Erik the Viking, Splitting Heirs, Mary Shelley's Frankenstein, Rudyard Kipling's The Jungle Book, 1995. Hon. LLD St Andrews. *Publications:* (with Robin Skynner) Families and How to Survive Them, 1983; The Golden Skits of Wing Commander Muriel Volestrangler FRHS and Bar, 1984; The Complete Fawlty Towers, 1989; (with Robin Skynner) Life and How to Survive It, 1993. *Recreations:* gluttony, sloth. *Address:* c/o David Wilkinson, 115 Hazlebury Road, SW6 2LX.

CLEGG, Brian George Herbert; management consultant and company director; *b* 10 Dec. 1921; *s* of Frederic Bradbury Clegg and Gladys Butterworth; *m* 1st, 1949, Iris May Ludlow; one *s* one *d*; 2nd, 1976, Anne Elizabeth Robertson; one *s*. *Educ:* Manchester Grammar Sch.; Trinity Coll., Cambridge (Open Math. Schol., MA). FIS, FIM, CEng, FIGasE. Sci. Officer, Min. of Supply, 1942; Hon. Flt-Lt, RAFVR. Statistician, Liverpool Gas Co., 1946; Market and Operational Res. Man., Southern Gas Bd, 1957; Commercial Man., Southern Gas Bd, 1961; Dep. Dir of Marketing, Gas Council, 1968; Dir of Marketing, British Gas Corp., 1972; Chm., Northern Region of British Gas Corp., 1975–82, retired. Dir (nominee), Midland Montagu Ventures Ltd, 1984–92. *Publications:* numerous articles and papers on marketing and fuel matters. *Recreations:* swimming, ice-skating, electronic organ. *Address:* 30 The Pines, 40 The Avenue, Poole, Dorset BH13 6HJ.

CLEGG, Professor Edward John, MD, PhD; FIBiol; Regius Professor of Anatomy, University of Aberdeen, 1976–89; Professor of Biological Anthropology, University of Aberdeen, 1990–91, now Emeritus; *b* 29 Oct. 1925; *s* of Edward Clegg and Emily Armistead; *m* 1958, Sheila Douglas Walls; two *d* (and one *d* decd). *Educ:* High Storrs Grammar Sch., Sheffield; Univ. of Sheffield (MB, ChB Hons 1948, MD 1964). PhD Liverpool, 1957; FIBiol 1974. RAMC, 1948–50 and RAMC (TA), 1950–61; late Major, RAMC (RARO). Demonstr, Asst Lectr and Lectr in Anatomy, Univ. of Liverpool, 1952–63; Lectr, Sen. Lectr and Reader in Human Biology and Anatomy, Univ. of Sheffield, 1963–77. MO, British Kangchenjunga Expedn, 1955; Sci. Mem., Chogolungma Glacier Expedn, 1959; Leader, WHO/IBP Expedn, Simien Mountains, Ethiopia, 1967. Pres., Anat. Soc. of GB and Ire, 1988–89; Chm., Soc. for the Study of Human Biology, 1988–92. *Publications:* The Study of Man: an introduction to human biology, 1968 (2nd edn 1978); papers on anatomy, endocrinology and human biology. *Recreations:* mountaineering, fishing, sailing, music. *Address:* 22 Woodburn Avenue, Aberdeen AB1 8JQ; c/o School of Biomedical Sciences, Marischal College, Aberdeen AB9 1AS. *T:* Aberdeen (01224) 273081. *Clubs:* Alpine; Wayfarers (Liverpool).

CLEGG, Prof. Hugh Armstrong; Emeritus Professor of Industrial Relations, University of Warwick, since 1983; *b* 22 May 1920; *s* of late Rev. Herbert Hobson Clegg and of Mabel (*née* Duckering); *m* 1941, Mary Matilda (*née* Shaw); two *s* two *d*. *Educ:* Kingswood Sch., Bath; Magdalen Coll., Oxford. Served War, 1940–45; Official Fellow, Nuffield Coll., Oxford, 1949–66, Emeritus Fellow, 1966–; Prof. of Industrial Relns, Univ. of Warwick, 1967–79, Titular Prof. and Leverhulme Res. Fellow, 1979–83. Chm., Civil Service Arbitration Tribunal, 1968–71; Dir, Industrial Relations Res. Unit, SSRC, 1970–74; Member: Royal Commn on Trade Unions and Employers' Assocs, 1965–68; Cttee of Inquiry into Port Transport Industry, 1964–65; Ct of Inquiry into Seamen's Dispute, 1966–67; Nat. Board for Prices and Incomes, 1966–67; Ct of Inquiry into Local Authorities' Manual Workers' Pay Dispute, 1970; Council, ACAS, 1974–79; Chm., Standing Commn on Pay Comparability, 1979–80. Hon. DLitt Warwick, 1987. *Publications:* Labour Relations in London Transport, 1950; Industrial Democracy and Nationalisation, 1951; The Future of Nationalisation (with T. E. Chester), 1953; General Union, 1954; Wage Policy in the Health Service (with T. E. Chester), 1957; The Employers' Challenge (with R. Adams), 1957; A New Approach to Industrial Democracy, 1960; Trade Union Officers (with A. J. Killick and R. Adams), 1961; General Union in a Changing Society, 1964; A History of British Trade Unions: Vol. I (with A. Fox and A. F. Thompson), 1964, Vol. II, 1985, vol. III, 1994; The System of Industrial Relations in Great Britain, 1970, How to run an Incomes Policy and Why we made such a Mess of the Last One, 1971; Workplace and Union (with I. Boraston and M. Rimmer), 1975; Trade Unionism under Collective Bargaining, 1976; The Changing System of Industrial Relations in Great Britain, 1979. *Recreations:* walking, beer. *Address:* 7 John Nash Square, Regency Drive, Kenilworth, Warwicks CV8 1JE. *T:* Kenilworth (01926) 50794.

CLEGG, Philip Charles; His Honour Judge Clegg; a Circuit Judge, since 1987; *b* 17 Oct. 1942; *s* of Charles and Patricia Clegg; *m* 1965, Caroline Frances Peall; one *s* two *d*. *Educ:* Rossall; Bristol Univ. (LLB Hons). Called to the Bar, Middle Temple, 1966; in practice on Northern Circuit; Asst Recorder, 1980–83; a Recorder, 1983–87. *Recreations:* sailing, model engineering. *Address:* Hillside Cottage, The Hill, Polstead, near Colchester, Essex CO6 5AL.

CLEGG, Richard Ninian Barwick, QC 1979; a Recorder of the Crown Court, 1978–93; *b* 28 June 1938; *o s* of Sir Cuthbert Clegg, TD; *m* 1963, Katherine Veronica, *d* of A. A. H. Douglas; two *s* one *d*. *Educ:* Aysgarth; Charterhouse; Trinity Coll., Oxford (MA). Captain of Oxford Pentathlon Team, 1959. Called to Bar, Inner Temple, 1960, Bencher, 1985. Chm., NW section of Bow Group, 1964–66; Vice-Chm., Bow Group, 1965–66; Chm., Winston Circle, 1965–66; Pres., Heywood and Royton Conservative Assoc., 1965–68. *Publication:* (jtly) Bow Group pamphlet, Towards a New North West, 1964. *Recreations:* sport, music, travel. *Address:* The Old Rectory, Brereton, via Sandbach, Cheshire CW11 9RY. *T:* Holmes Chapel (01477) 32358; 61 Fleet Street, EC4Y 1JU. *T:* 0171–353 4363. *Club:* Lansdowne.

CLEGG, William; QC 1991; a Recorder, since 1992; *b* 5 Sept. 1949; *s* of Peter Hepworth Clegg and Sheila Clegg; *m* 1974, Wendy Doreen Chard; one *s* one *d*. *Educ:* St Thomas More High School; Bristol Univ. (LLB). Called to the Bar, Gray's Inn, 1972; in practice, SE Circuit. *Recreations:* squash, cricket. *Address:* 3 Hare Court, Temple, EC4Y 7DJ. *T:* 0171–353 7561. *Club:* Sudbury Racquet Centre.

CLEGG-HILL, family name of **Viscount Hill.**

CLEGHORN, Bruce Elliot; HM Diplomatic Service; Head of Non-Proliferation Department, Foreign and Commonwealth Office, since 1994; *b* 19 Nov. 1946; *s* of Ivan Robert Cleghorn and Margaret (*née* Kemplen); *m* 1976, Sally Ann Robinson; three *s*. *Educ:* Sutton Valence Sch., Kent; St John's Coll., Cambridge (BA Hons). Commonwealth Fellow, Panjab Univ., 1970–72; Jun. Res. Fellow, Inst. of Commonwealth Studies, Univ. of London, 1972–74; joined HM Diplomatic Service, 1974; Delegn to CSCE, 1974–75; FCO, 1975–76; First Secretary: Delegn to NATO, 1976–79; New Delhi, 1980–83; FCO, 1983–87; Counsellor, CSCE Delegn, Vienna, 1987–89; Dep. Hd, UK Delegn to negotiations on conventional arms control, Vienna, 1989–91; Dep. High Comr and Counsellor (Econ. and Commercial), Kuala Lumpur, 1992–94. *Publication:* (with V. N. Datta) A Nationalist Muslim and Indian Politics, 1974. *Recreations:* swimming, walking, studying British 20th century painters. *Address:* c/o Foreign and Commonwealth Office, King Charles Street, SW1A 2AH.

CLELAND, Dame Rachel, DBE 1980 (CBE 1966; MBE 1959); *b* Peppermint Grove, Jan. 1906; *d* of W. H. Evans, Perth, WA; *m* 1928, Sir Donald Cleland, *s* of E. D. Cleland; two *s*. *Educ:* Methodist Ladies' Coll., Perth, WA; Kindergarten Training Coll. Pres., Girl Guide Assoc., Papua and New Guinea, 1952–66; President: Red Cross, Papua and New Guinea, 1952–66; Branch of Aust. Pre-Sch. Assoc. (TPNG), 1952–66. *Publication:* Pathways to Independence: official and family life in Papua New Guinea 1951–1976, 1984, 2nd edn 1985. *Recreations:* music, theatre, reading. *Address:* 2/24 Richardson Avenue, Claremont, WA 6010, Australia. *Club:* Queen's (Sydney).

CLELAND, William Paton, FRCP, FRCS, FACS; Consulting Surgeon, National Heart and Chest Hospital; Consulting Thoracic Surgeon, King's College Hospital; Emeritus Consultant to the RN; late Adviser in Thoracic Surgery to the Department of Health and Social Security; *b* 30 May 1912; *o s* of late Sir John Cleland, CBE; *m* 1940, Norah, *d* of George E. Goodhart; two *s* one *d*. *Educ:* Scotch Coll., Adelaide; Univ. of Adelaide, S Australia. MB, BS (Adelaide). Resident appts, Royal Adelaide and Adelaide Children's Hosps, 1935–36; MRCP 1939; House Physician and Resident Surgical Officer, Brompton Chest Hosp., 1939–41. Served in EMS as Registrar and Surgeon, 1939–45. FRCS 1946. Consultant Thoracic Surg., King's Coll. Hosp., 1948; Surgeon, Brompton Chest Hospital, 1948; Sen. Lectr in Thoracic Surgery, Royal Postgrad. Med. Sch., 1949; Dir, Dept of Surgery, Cardio-Thoracic Inst., Brompton Hosp. Member: Assoc. Thoracic Surgeons of Gt Brit. and Ire.; Thoracic Soc.; British Cardiac Soc.; Amer. Coll. of Surgeons. Editor, Jl of Cardiovascular Surgery, 1978–83. Comdr, Order of Lion of Finland; Comdr, Order of Falcon of Iceland. *Publications:* (jt author) Medical and Surgical Cardiology, 1969; chapters on thoracic surgery in British Surgical Practice, Diseases of the Chest (Marshall and Perry), Short Practice of Surgery (Bailey and Love), and Operative Surgery (Rob and Rodney Smith); articles on pulmonary and cardiac surgery in medical literature. *Recreations:* fishing, gardening, beekeeping. *Address:* Green Meadows, Goodworth Clatford, Andover, Hants SP11 7HH. *T:* Andover (01264) 324327.

CLELLAND, David Gordon; MP (Lab) Tyne Bridge, since Dec. 1985; *b* 27 June 1943; *s* of Archibald and Ellen Clelland; *m* 1965, Maureen; two *d*. *Educ:* Kelvin Grove Boys' School, Gateshead; Gateshead and Hebburn Technical Colleges. Apprentice electrical fitter, 1959–64; electrical tester, 1964–81. Gateshead Borough Council: Councillor, 1972–86; Recreation Chm., 1976–84; Leader of Council, 1984–86. Nat. Sec., Assoc. of Councillors, 1981–85. Member: Home Affairs Select Cttee, 1986–88; Energy Select Cttee, 1989–90. Chairman: Backbench Envmt Cttee, 1990–; PLP Regl Govt Gp, 1992–93; Sec., Northern Gp of Lab MPs, 1990–. *Recreation:* golf, music, reading. *Address:* 19 Ravensworth Road, Dunston, Gateshead NE11 9AB. *T:* 0191–420 0300.

CLEMENS, Clive Carruthers, CMG 1983; MC 1946; HM Diplomatic Service, retired; High Commissioner in Lesotho, 1981–84; *b* 22 Jan. 1924; British; *s* of late M. B. Clemens, Imperial Bank of India, and late Margaret Jane (*née* Carruthers); *m* 1947, Philippa Jane Bailey; three *s*. *Educ:* Blundell's Sch.; St Catharine's Coll., Cambridge. War Service 1943–46: commissioned in Duke of Cornwall's Light Infantry; served in India and Burma, 1944–45. Entered HM Foreign Service and apptd to FO, 1947; Third Sec., Rangoon, 1948; Third (later Second) Sec., Lisbon, 1950; FO, 1953; First Sec., Budapest, 1954; Brussels, 1956; Seoul, 1959; FO, 1961; Strasbourg (UK Delegn to Council of Europe), 1964; Counsellor, Paris, 1967; Principal British Trade Comr, Vancouver, 1970–74; Dep. Consul-Gen., Johannesburg, 1974–78; Consul-Gen., Istanbul, 1978–81. *Recreations:* birdwatching, photography. *Address:* 9 Saxonhurst, Downton, Salisbury, Wilts SP5 3JN.

CLEMENT, David James; Chairman, HELM Corporation, since 1990; *b* 29 Sept. 1930; *s* of James and Constance Clement; *m* 1958, Margaret Stone; two *s* one *d*. *Educ:* Chipping Sodbury Grammar Sch.; Univ. of Bristol (BA). IPFA. Internal Audit Asst, City of Bristol, 1953–56; Accountancy/Audit Asst, 1956–60, Chief Accountancy Asst, 1960–65, City of Worcester; Dep. Chief Finance Officer, Runcorn Develt Corp., 1965–68; Chief Finance Officer, Antrim and Ballymena Develt Commn, 1968–72; Asst Sec., Dept of Finance, NI, 1972–75, Dep. Sec., 1975–80; Under Sec., DoE, NI, 1980–84. Financial consultant, 1985–90. *Recreations:* lawn tennis, Association football, contract bridge, philately.

CLEMENT, David Morris, CBE 1971; FCA, IPFA; Hon. FCGI; Chairman, Joint Mission Hospital Equipment Board Ltd, 1978–85; *b* 6 Feb. 1911; 2nd *s* of Charles William and Rosina Wannell Clement, Swansea; *m* 1938, Kathleen Mary (*d* 1991), *o d* of Ernest George Davies, ACA, Swansea; one *d*. *Educ:* Bishop Gore's Grammar Sch., Swansea. Mem. Inst. Chartered Accountants, 1933. A. Owen John & Co., Swansea, and Sissons Bersey Gain Vincent & Co., London, Chartered Accts, 1928–35; ICI Ltd, Lime Gp, 1935–40; Chloride Electrical Storage Co. Ltd, 1941–46; National Coal Board: Sec., North Western Div., 1946–49; Chief Acct, Northern and Durham Divs, 1950–55; Dep. Dir-Gen. of Finance, 1955–61; Dir-Gen. of Finance, 1961–69; Bd Mem., 1969–76; Chairman: NCB (Ancillaries) Ltd, 1973–79; Redwood-Corex Services Ltd, 1978–82. Chm., Public Corporations Finance Gp, 1975–76. Dep. Chm., Horizon Exploration Ltd, 1978–80. Underwriting Member of Lloyd's, 1978–. Member: Aircraft and Shipbuilding Industries Arbitration Tribunals, 1980–83; Council, CIPFA, 1975–76; Council, CGLI (Hon. Treas.), 1978–82. *Recreations:* golf, photography. *Address:* The Old Hall, Mulbarton, Norfolk NR14 8JS. *T:* Mulbarton (01508) 578655. *Clubs:* Directors'; Norfolk (Norwich).
See also D. J. Mellor.

CLEMENT, John; Chairman: Culpho Consultants, since 1991; Tuddenham Hall Foods, since 1991; Ransomes, since 1993 (Director, since 1991); National Car Auctions Ltd, since 1995; *b* 18 May 1932; *s* of Frederick and Alice Eleanor Clement; *m* 1956, Elisabeth Anne (*née* Emery); two *s* one *d*. *Educ:* Bishop's Stortford College. Howards Dairies, Westcliff on Sea, 1949–64; United Dairies London Ltd, 1964–69; Asst Managing Director, Rank Leisure Services Ltd, 1969–73; Chairman, Unigate Foods Div., 1973; Chief Executive, 1976–90, Chm., 1977–91, Unigate Group. Non-exec. Chm., The Littlewoods Organisation, 1982–90; Director: NV Verenigde Bedrijven Nutricia, 1981–92; Eagle Star Holdings plc, 1981–86; Eagle Star Insce Co., 1981–84; Anglo American Insce Co., 1991– (Chm., 1993–94); Kleinwort Second Endowment Trust plc, 1993–; Jarvis Hotels Ltd, 1994–. Mem., Securities and Investments Bd, 1986–89. Chm., King's Coll., Cambridge I-IV (Business Expansion Scheme), 1993–. CIMgt (FBIM 1977). *Recreations:* shooting, sailing, bridge, Rugby, tennis. *Address:* Tuddenham Hall, Tuddenham, Ipswich, Suffolk IP6 9DD. *T:* Ipswich (01473) 785217, *Fax:* (01473) 785405. *Clubs:* Farmers', London Welsh Rugby Football; Cumberland Lawn Tennis; Royal Harwich Yacht.
See also R. Clement.

CLEMENT, John Handel, CB 1980; Adviser to Gooding Group, since 1985; *b* 24 Nov. 1920; *s* of late William and Mary Hannah Clement; *m* 1946, Anita Jones; one *d* (and one *d* decd). *Educ:* Pontardawe Grammar Sch. RAF, 1940–46, Flt Lt (despatches). Welsh Board of Health: Clerical Officer, 1938; Exec. Officer, 1946; Higher Exec. Officer, 1948; Sen. Exec. Officer, 1956; Principal, Welsh Office, Min. of Housing and Local Govt, 1960, Asst Sec., 1966; Private Sec. to Sec. of State for Wales, 1966; Under-Sec., 1971–81, Dir of Industry Dept, 1976–81, Welsh Office. Sec., Council for Wales, 1955–59; Chm., Welsh Planning Bd, 1971–76. Member: Wales Tourist Bd, 1982–88; Midland Bank Adv. Council for Wales, 1985–94. Hon. MA Wales, 1982. *Recreations:* Welsh Rugby, fishing. *Address:* 6 St Brioc Road, Heath, Cardiff CF4 4HJ. *T:* Cardiff (01222) 624192.

CLÉMENT, René; Officier de la Légion d'Honneur; Grand Officier, Ordre National du Mérite; Commandeur des Arts et des Lettres; film director; *b* Bordeaux, 18 March 1913; *s* of Jean Maurice Clément and Marguérite Clément (*née* Bayle); *m* 1st, 1940, Bella Gurwich (decd); 2nd, 1987, Johanna Harwood. *Educ:* Ecole nationale supérieure des beaux-arts. *Films:* Soigne ton Gauche (short), 1936; *documentaries:* L'Arabie Interdite, 1937; La Grande Chartreuse, 1938; La Bièvre, 1939; Le Triage, 1940; Ceux du Rail, 1942; La Grande Pastorale, 1943; Chefs de Demain, 1944; *feature films:* La Bataille du Rail, 1946 (Cannes Fest. Prize); Le Père Tranquille, 1946; Les Maudits, 1947 (Cannes Fest. Prize); Au-delà des Grilles, 1948 (US Academy Award, British award); Le Chateau de Verre, 1950; Jeux Interdits, 1952 (US Academy Award, British award and Grand Internat. Prize Venice Biennale); Monsieur Ripois, 1954 (Cannes Fest. Prize); Gervaise, 1955 (Venice Internat. Prize); Barrage contre le Pacifique, 1958; Plein Soleil, 1959; Quelle Joie de Vivre, 1961; Le Jour et l'Heure, 1962; Les Félins, 1964; Paris, Brûle-t-il?, 1966 (Prix Europa); Le Passager de la Pluie, 1969; La Maison sous les Arbres, 1971; La Course du lièvre à travers les champs, 1971; The Baby Sitter, 1975. Founder Mem., Institut des hautes études cinématographiques; Mem., Institut de France. *Publication:* (with C. Audry) Bataille du rail, 1947. *Recreations:* antiques, painting, yachting. *Address:* 5 Avenue de St Roman, 98000 Monte Carlo, Monaco.

CLEMENT, Richard, (Dick); freelance writer, director and producer; *b* 5 Sept. 1937; *s* of Frederick and Alice Eleanor Clement; *m* 1st, Jennifer F. Sheppard (marr. diss. 1981); three *s* one *d*; 2nd, 1982, Nancy S. Campbell; one *d*. *Educ:* Bishop's Stortford Coll.; Westminster Sch., Conn, USA. Co-writer (with Ian La Frenais): *television:* The Likely Lads, 1964–66; Whatever Happened to the Likely Lads, 1972–73; Porridge, 1974–76; Thick as Thieves, 1974; Going Straight, 1978; Auf Wiedersehen, Pet, 1984; Freddie and Max, 1990; Full Stretch, 1993; *films:* The Jokers, 1967; Otley, 1968; Hannibal Brooks, 1968; Villain, 1971; Porridge, 1979; Water, 1984; Vice Versa, 1987; The Commitments, 1991; Director: *films:* Otley, 1968; A Severed Head, 1969; Porridge, 1979; Bullshot, 1983; Water, 1984; co-producer (with Ian La Frenais) Vice Versa, 1987; The Commitments, 1991 (jtly, Evening Standard Peter Sellers Award, 1992); *stage:* Billy, 1974; Anyone for Denis?, 1981. *Recreations:* work, tennis, dinner; supporting Essex at cricket and Los Angeles Dodgers at baseball. *Address:* 9700 Yoakum Drive, Beverly Hills, CA 90210, USA. *T:* (213)2764916.
See also John Clement.

CLEMENTI, David Cecil; Chief Executive, Kleinwort Benson Ltd, since 1994; *b* 25 Feb. 1949; *s* of Air Vice-Marshal Cresswell Montagu Clementi, CB, CBE and Susan (*née* Pelham); *m* 1972, Sarah Louise, (Sally), Cowley; one *s* one *d*. *Educ:* Winchester Coll.; Lincoln Coll., Oxford; Harvard Business Sch. (MBA 1975). With Arthur Andersen & Co., 1970–73; qualified as CA 1973; with Kleinwort Benson Ltd, 1975–: Dir, 1981–; Man. Dir, KB Securities, 1987–89; Head, Corporate Finance, 1989–94. *Recreation:* sailing. *Address:* Kleinwort Benson Ltd, 20 Fenchurch Street, EC3P 3DB. *T:* 0171–623 8000.

CLEMENTS, Alan William, CBE 1990; Chairman: David S. Smith (Holdings), since 1991; Cementone, since 1994; *b* 12 Dec. 1928; *s* of William and Kathleen Clements; *m* 1953, Pearl Dorling (*d* 1993); two *s* one *d*. *Educ:* Culford School, Bury St Edmunds; Magdalen College, Oxford (BA Hons). HM Inspector of Taxes, Inland Revenue, 1952–56; ICI: Asst Treasurer, 1966; Dep. Treasurer, 1971; Treasurer, 1976; Finance Director, 1979–90. Non-Exec. Director: Trafalgar House, 1980– (Chm., 1992–93); Cable & Wireless, 1985–91; Guinness Mahon Hldgs, 1988–92; Granada Gp, 1990–94; Mirror Gp Newspapers, 1991–; Brent Walker Gp, 1991–93. Lay Mem., Internat. Stock Exchange, 1984–88. *Publications:* articles on finance in jls. *Recreations:* golf, music, reading.

CLEMENTS, Andrew Joseph; Chief Music Critic, Guardian, since 1993; *b* 15 Sept. 1950; *s* of Joseph George Clements and Linda Helen Clements; *m* 1977, Kathryn Denise Coltman; two *d*. *Educ:* Crypt Sch., Gloucester; Emmanuel Coll., Cambridge (BA). Music Critic: New Statesman, 1977–88; Financial Times, 1979–93; Editor, Musical Times, 1987–88. Dir, Holst Foundn, 1992. *Recreation:* gardening. *Address:* c/o Guardian, 119 Farringdon Road, EC1R 3ER.

CLEMENTS, Judith M.; Chief Executive and National Director, National Association for Mental Health, since 1992; *b* 27 June 1953; *d* of Robert and Margaret Dunn; *m* 1975, Paul Clements (marr. diss. 1979). *Educ:* Birmingham Univ. (LLB Hons 1974); Brunel Univ. (MA Public and Social Admin 1979). Dip. Inst. Housing 1976. London Borough of Camden: Estate Manager, 1974–76; Sen. Estate Manager, 1976–79; Tenancy Services Officer, 1979–81; Business System Analyst, 1981–82; Asst Dir of Housing, 1982–87; Dep. Chief Housing Officer, Brighton BC, 1987–91; Hd of Management Practice, Local Govt Management Bd, 1991–92. *Recreations:* reading, especially crime fiction and feminist fiction, aerobic exercise, scuba diving. *Address:* (office) Granta House, 15–19 The Broadway, E15 4BQ. *T:* 0181–519 2122; 216 Hainault Road, Leytonstone, E11 1EP. *T:* 0181–558 0346.

CLEMENTS, Julia; *see* Seton, Lady, (Julia).

CLEMENTS, Richard Harry; author and journalist; Director, Citizens Income Trust, since 1993; *b* 11 Oct. 1928; *s* of Harry and Sonia Clements; *m* 1952, Bridget Mary MacDonald; two *s*. *Educ:* King Alfred Sch., Hampstead; Western High Sch., Washington, DC; Regent Street Polytechnic. Middlesex Independent, 1949; Leicester Mercury, 1951; Editor, Socialist Advance (Labour Party Youth paper), 1953; industrial staff, Daily Herald, 1954; joined Tribune, 1956, Editor, 1961–82; Political Adviser to the Leader of the Opposition, Rt Hon. Michael Foot, 1982–83; Exec. Officer to Leader of the Opposition, Rt Hon. Neil Kinnock, 1983–87. *Publication:* Glory without Power: a study of trade unions, 1959. *Recreation:* woodwork. *Address:* 68 Strafford Road, High Barnet, Herts EN5 4LR.

CLEMENTS, Prof. Ronald Ernest; Samuel Davidson Professor of Old Testament Studies, King's College, University of London, 1983–92, now Professor Emeritus; *b* 27 May 1929; *m* 1955, Valerie Winifred (*née* Suffield); two *d*. *Educ:* Buckhurst Hill County High Sch.; Spurgeon's Coll.; Christ's Coll., Cambridge; Univ. of Sheffield. MA, DD Cantab. Asst Lectr 1960–64, Lectr 1960–67, Univ. of Edinburgh; Lectr, Univ. of Cambridge, 1967–83. Hon. For. Sec., SOTS, 1973–83 (Pres., 1985–); Hon. Mem., OTWSA, 1979–. Hon. DLitt Acadia, Nova Scotia, 1982. *Publications:* God and Temple, 1965; Prophecy and Covenant, 1965; Old Testament Theology, 1978; Isaiah 1–39, 1979; A Century of Old Testament Study, 1976, 2nd edn 1983; Prayers of the Bible, 1986; Jeremiah, 1988; (ed) The World of Ancient Israel, 1989; Wisdom in Theology, 1993; contrib. Vetus Testamentum, Jl of Semitic Studies. *Recreations:* reading, travel, photography. *Address:* 8 Brookfield Road, Coton, Cambridge CB3 7PT.

CLEMINSON, Sir James (Arnold Stacey), KBE 1990; Kt 1982; MC 1945; DL; Deputy Chairman, J. H. Fenner plc, since 1993 (Director, since 1989); *b* 31 Aug. 1921; *s* of Arnold Russel Cleminson and Florence Stacey; *m* 1950, Helen Juliet Measor; one *s* two *d*. *Educ:* Rugby Sch. Served War, 1940–46, mainly in Parachute Regt. Reckitt & Colman, 1946–86: Chief Exec., 1973–80; Chm., 1977–86; Chairman: Jeyes Hygiene, 1986–89;

Riggs A P Bank, 1987–91 (Dir, 1985–); Director: Norwich Union, 1979–92 (Vice-Chm., 1981–92); United Biscuits, 1982–89; Eastern Counties Newspaper Gp, 1987–93; Riggs Nat. Bank of Washington, 1991–93; Member: Council, CBI, 1978– (Dep. Pres., 1983; Pres., 1984–86); London Cttee, Toronto Dominion Bank, 1982–90; NEDC, 1984–86. Jt Chm., Netherlands British Chamber of Commerce Council, 1978–84; Chairman: Food and Drink Industries Council, 1983–84; Nurses' Independent Pay Review Body, 1986–90; BOTB, 1986–90. Pres., Endeavour Trng, 1984–; Trustee, Airborne Forces Security Fund. Chm., Theatre Royal Norwich Trust, 1991–. Pro-Chancellor, Hull Univ., 1985–94. Hon. LLD Hull, 1985. DL Norfolk, 1983. *Recreations:* field sports, golf. *Address:* Loddon Hall, Hales, Norfolk NR14 6TB. *Clubs:* Boodle's; Norfolk (Norwich).

CLEMITS, John Henry, RIBA; Managing Director, PSA Projects Cardiff, 1990–92; *b* 16 Feb. 1934; *s* of late Cyril Thomas Clemits and Minnie Alberta Clemits; *m* 1958, Elizabeth Angela Moon; one *s* one *d. Educ:* Sutton High Sch.; Plymouth College of Art. ARIBA (Dist. in Thesis). National Service, RAF, 1959–61; Captain, RE (TA), 43 Wessex Div. and Royal Monmouthshire RE (Militia), 1964–69. Plymouth City Architects Dept, 1954–59; Watkins Gray & Partners, Architects, Bristol, 1961–63; SW RHB, 1963–65; Architect, MPBW, Bristol, 1965–69; Sen. Architect, MPBW, Regional HQ, Rheindahlen, Germany, 1969–71; Naval Base Planning Officer, MPBW, Portsmouth, 1971–73; Suptg Architect, PSA, Directorate of Bldg Develt, 1973–75; Suptg Planning Officer, PSA, Rheindahlen, 1975–79; Dir of Works (Army), PSA, Chessington, 1979–85; Dir for Wales, PSA, Central Office for Wales, DoE, 1985–90. Chairman: Cowbridge Choral Soc., 1988–90; Vale of Glamorgan Buildings Preservation Trust, 1994–; Mem. Cttee, Dewi Sant Housing Assoc., 1991–. *Recreations:* golf, music, DIY. *Address:* The Lodge, Hendrescythan, Creigiau, Cardiff CF4 8NN. *T:* Pentyrch (01222) 891786.

CLEMITSON, Ivor Malcolm; *b* 8 Dec. 1931; *s* of Daniel Malcolm Clemitson and Annie Ellen Clemitson; *m* 1960, Janet Alicia Meeke; one *s* one *d. Educ:* Harlington Primary Sch.; Luton Grammar Sch.; London Sch. of Economics (BScEcon); Bishops Theol College. Deacon 1958, Priest 1959. Curate: St Mary's (Bramall Lane), Sheffield, 1958–61; Christ Church, Luton, 1962–64; Industrial Chaplain, Dio. St Albans, 1964–69; Dir of Industrial Mission, Dio. Singapore, 1969–70; Research Officer, National Graphical Assoc., 1971–74. MP (Lab) Luton East, Feb. 1974–1979; contested (Lab) Luton South, 1983. *Publication:* (with George Rodgers) A Life to Live, 1981. *Recreations:* watching football, theatre, travel.

CLEMOES, Prof. Peter Alan Martin, PhD (Cantab); FRHistS; FSA; Elrington and Bosworth Professor of Anglo-Saxon, Cambridge University, 1969–82, Emeritus Professor since 1982; Official Fellow of Emmanuel College, Cambridge, 1962–69, Professorial Fellow 1969–82, Life Fellow since 1982; Fellow, Queen Mary and Westfield (formerly Queen Mary) College, London University, since 1975; *b* 20 Jan. 1920; *o s* of Victor Clemoes and Mary (*née* Paton); *m* 1956, Jean Elizabeth, *yr d* of Sidney Grew; two *s. Educ:* Brentwood Sch.; Queen Mary Coll., London; King's Coll., Cambridge. BA London (1st Cl. Hons English) 1950; Soley Student, King's Coll., Cambridge, 1951–53; Research Fellow, Reading Univ., 1954–55; PhD Cambridge 1956. Lectr in English, Reading Univ., 1955–61; Lectr in Anglo-Saxon, Cambridge Univ., 1961–69; Emmanuel College, Cambridge: Coll. Lectr in English, 1963–69 and Dir of Studies in English, 1963–65; Tutor, 1966–68; Asst Librarian, 1963–69. Hon. Sen. Res. Fellow, KCL, 1987–89. Mem., Council of Early English Text Soc., 1971–. Pres., Internat. Soc. of Anglo-Saxonists, 1983–85; Dir, Fontes Anglo-Saxonici (a register of written sources used by authors in Anglo-Saxon England), 1985–93. Founder and Chief Editor, Anglo-Saxon England, 1972–89. *Publications:* The Anglo-Saxons, Studies . . . presented to Bruce Dickins (ed and contrib.), 1959; General Editor of Early English Manuscripts in Facsimile (Copenhagen), 1963–74, and co-editor of vol. XIII, 1966, vol. XVIII, 1974; Rhythm and Cosmic Order in Old English Christian Literature (inaug. lecture), 1970; England before the Conquest: Studies . . . presented to Dorothy Whitelock (co-ed and contrib.), 1971; Interactions of Thought and Language in Old English Poetry, 1995; textual and critical writings, especially on the works of Ælfric and Old English poetry. *Festschrift:* Learning and Literature in Anglo-Saxon England: studies presented to Peter Clemoes on the occasion of his sixty-fifth birthday, ed Michael Lapidge and Helmut Gneuss, 1985. *Address:* 14 Church Street, Chesterton, Cambridge CB4 1DT. *T:* Cambridge (01223) 358655.

CLEOBURY, Nicholas Randall, MA; FRCO; conductor; *b* 23 June 1950; *s* of John and Brenda Cleobury; *m* 1978, Heather Kay; one *s* one *d. Educ:* King's Sch., Worcester; Worcester Coll., Oxford (MA Hons). Assistant Organist: Chichester Cathedral, 1971–72; Christ Church, Oxford, 1972–76; Chorus Master, Glyndebourne Opera, 1977–79; Asst Director, BBC Singers, 1977–79; Conductor: main BBC, provincial and London orchestras and opera houses, also in Australia, Austria, Belgium, Denmark, France, Germany, Holland, Italy, Norway, Spain, Sweden, Switzerland, USA; regular BBC, TV appearances. Principal Opera Conductor, Royal Academy of Music, 1981–88; Artistic Director: Aquarius, 1983–92; Cambridge Symphony Soloists, 1990–92; Britten Sinfonia, 1992–; Principal Guest Conductor, Gävle, Sweden, 1989–91. Music Dir, Broomhill Arts, 1990–94; Artistic Dir, Cambridge Fest., 1992. Hon. RAM 1985. *Recreations:* reading, food, wine, theatre, walking, cricket. *Address:* China Cottage, Church Lane, Petham, Canterbury CT4 5RD. *T:* Petham (01227) 700584, *Fax:* (01227) 700827. *Clubs:* Savage, MCC, Lord's Taverners.

See also S. J. Cleobury.

CLEOBURY, Stephen John, FRCM; FRCO; Fellow, Director of Music and Organist, King's College, Cambridge, since 1982; Organist, Cambridge University, since 1991; *b* 31 Dec. 1948; *s* of John Frank Cleobury and Brenda Julie (*née* Randall); *m* 1971, Penelope Jane (*née* Holloway); two *d. Educ:* King's Sch., Worcester; St John's Coll., Cambridge (MA, MusB). FRCO 1968; FRCM 1993. Organist, St Matthew's, Northampton, 1971–74; Sub-Organist, Westminster Abbey, 1974–78; Master of Music, Westminster Cathedral, 1979–82. President: IAO, 1985–87; Cathedral Organists' Assoc., 1988–90; RCO, 1990–92 (Hon. Sec., 1981–90); Mem. Council, RSCM, 1982–. Conductor, CUMS, 1983–. *Recreation:* reading. *Address:* King's College, Cambridge CB2 1ST. *T:* Cambridge (01223) 331224.

See also N. R. Cleobury.

CLERIDES, Glafcos John; President of Cyprus, since 1993; *b* Nicosia, 24 April 1919; *s* of Yiannis Clerides, CBE, QC and Elli Clerides; *m* 1946, Lilla Erulkar; one *d. Educ:* Pancyprium Gymnasium, Nicosia; King's Coll., London (LLB 1948). Served in RAF, 1939–45; shot down and taken prisoner, 1942–45 (mentioned in despatches). Called to the Bar, Gray's Inn, 1951; practised in Cyprus, 1951–60; Head, Greek Cypriot Delegn, Jt Constitutional Cttee, 1959–60; Minister of Justice, 1959–60; Mem. for Nicosia, House of Representatives, 1960–76, 1981–93; First Pres. of House, 1960–76; Leader, Greek Cypriot Delegn to London Conf., 1964; Rep. of Greek Cypriots to intercommunal talks, 1968–76; Actg Pres., July–Dec. 1974 (after Turkish invasion of Cyprus). Founder and Leader: Unified Party, 1969–76; Democratic Rally Party, 1976–93. Cert. of Honour and Life Mem., Cyprus Red Cross (Pres., 1961–63). Gold Medal, Order of the Holy Sepulchre, 1961. Grand Cross of the Redeemer (Greece), 1993. *Publication:* My Deposition, 4 vols. *Address:* Presidential Palace, Nicosia, Cyprus.

CLERK of Penicuik, Sir John Dutton, 10th Bt *cr* 1679; CBE 1966; VRD; FRSE 1977; JP; Lord-Lieutenant of Midlothian, 1972–92 (Vice-Lieutenant, 1965–72); Cdre RNR; retd; *b* 30 Jan. 1917; *s* of Sir George James Robert Clerk of Penicuik, 9th Bt, and Hon. Mabel Honor (*d* 1974), *y d* of late Col Hon. Charles Dutton and *sister* of 6th Baron Sherborne, DSO; *S* father, 1943; *m* 1944, Evelyn Elizabeth Robertson; two *s* two *d. Educ:* Stowe. Brig., 1973–89, Ensign, 1989–, Queen's Body Guard for Scotland, Royal Company of Archers. JP 1955, DL 1956, Midlothian. *Heir: s* Robert Maxwell Clerk, Younger of Penicuik [*b* 3 April 1945; *m* 1970, Felicity Faye, *yr d* of George Collins, Bampton, Oxford; two *s* one *d. Educ:* Winchester Coll.; London Univ. (BSc (Agric)). FRICS]. *Address:* Penicuik House, Penicuik, Midlothian EH26 9LA. *T:* Penicuik (01968) 674318. *Clubs:* Royal Over-Seas League; New (Edinburgh).

CLERKE, Sir John Edward Longueville, 12th Bt *cr* 1660; Captain Royal Wilts Yeomanry, RAC, TA; *b* 29 Oct. 1913; *er s* of Francis William Talbot Clerke (killed in action, 1916), *e s* of 11th Bt, and late Albinia Mary, *er d* of Edward Henry Evans-Lombe (who *m* 3rd, 1923, Air Chief Marshal Sir Edgar Rainey Ludlow-Hewitt, GCB, GBE, CMG, DSO, MC); *S* grandfather, 1930; *m* 1948, Mary (marr. diss. 1987), *d* of late Lt-Col I. R. Beviss Bond, OBE, MC; one *s* two *d. Heir: s* Francis Ludlow Longueville Clerke [*b* 25 Jan. 1953; *m* 1982, Vanessa Anne, *o d* of late Charles Cosman Citron and of Mrs Olga May Citron, Mouille Point, Cape Town; one *s* one *d*]. *Address:* 48 Savernake Avenue, Melksham, Wilts SN12 7HD. *T:* Melksham (01225) 703994.

CLEVELAND, Archdeacon of; *see* Hawthorn, Ven. C. J.

CLEVELAND, Harlan; Professor, 1980–88 and Dean, 1980–87, Hubert H. Humphrey Institute of Public Affairs, University of Minnesota, now Professor Emeritus; *b* 19 Jan. 1918; *s* of Stanley Matthews Cleveland and Marian Phelps (*née* Van Buren); *m* 1941, Lois W. Burton; one *s* two *d. Educ:* Phillips Acad., Andover, Mass; Princeton Univ.; Oxford Univ. Farm Security Admin., Dept of Agric., 1940–42; Bd of Econ. Warfare (subseq. Foreign Econ. Admin.), 1942–44; Exec. Dir Econ. Sect., 1944–45, Actg Vice-Pres., 1945–46, Allied Control Commn, Rome; Mem. US Delegn, UNRRA Council, London, 1945; Dept Chief of Mission, UNRRA Italian Mission, Rome, 1946–47; Dir, UNRRA China Office, Shanghai, 1947–48; Dir, China Program, Econ. Coop. Admin., Washington, 1948–49; Dept Asst Adminstr, 1949–51; Asst Dir for Europe, Mutual Security Agency, 1952–53; Exec. Editor, The Reporter, NYC, 1953–56, Publisher, 1955–56; Dean, Maxwell Sch. of Citizenship and Pub. Affairs, Syracuse Univ., 1956–61; Asst Sec. for Internat. Orgn Affairs, State Dept, 1961–65; US Ambassador to NATO, 1965–69; Pres., Univ. of Hawaii, 1969–74; Dir, Program in Internat. Affairs, Aspen Inst. for Humanistic Studies, 1974–80. Distinguished Vis. Tom Slick Prof. of World Peace, Univ. of Texas at Austin, 1979. Delegate, Democratic National Convention, 1960. Chm., Weather Modification Adv. Bd, US Dept of Commerce, 1977–78; Chm., Nat. Retiree Volunteer Coalition, 1989–92. Pres., World Acad. of Art and Sci., 1991–. Holds hon. degrees and foreign orders; US Medal of Freedom, 1946. Woodrow Wilson Award, Princeton Univ., 1968; Prix de Talloires, Groupe de Talloires, 1981. *Publications:* Next Step in Asia (jtly), 1949; (ed jtly) The Art of Overseasmanship, 1957; (jtly) The Overseas Americans, 1960; (ed) The Promise of World Tensions, 1961; (ed jtly) The Ethic of Power, 1962; (ed jtly) Ethics and Bigness, 1962; The Obligations of Power, 1966; NATO: the Transatlantic Bargain, 1970; The Future Executive, 1972; China Diary, 1976; The Third Try at World Order, 1977; (jtly) Humangrowth: an essay on growth, values and the quality of life, 1978; (ed) Energy Futures of Developing Countries, 1980; (ed jtly) Bioresources for Development, 1980; (ed) The Management of Sustainable Growth, 1981; The Knowledge Executive, 1985; The Global Commons, 1990; Birth of a New World, 1993. *Address:* Hubert H. Humphrey Institute of Public Affairs, HHH Center, 301 19th Avenue South, Minneapolis, MN 55455, USA. *T:* (612) 6245592, *Fax:* (612) 6253153. *Clubs:* Century (NY); International (Washington); Waikiki Yacht (Honolulu).

CLEVERDON, Julia Charity, (Mrs John Garnett); Chief Executive, Business in the Community, since 1992; *b* 19 April 1950; *d* of late Thomas Douglas James Cleverdon, BBC producer and of Elinor Nest Lewis; *m* 1st, 1973, Martin Christopher Ollard (marr. diss. 1978); 2nd, 1985, (William) John (Poulton Maxwell) Garnett, *qv*; two *d. Educ:* Newnham Coll., Cambridge (BA Hons History). Communication Adviser, British Leyland and Anglo-American Mining Corp., S Africa, 1972–75; Industrial Society: Head, Eastern and Public Services Dept, 1975–77; Head, Common Purpose Campaign, 1977–79; Dir, Communication and Publicity Div., 1979–81; founded Pepperell Dept for Inner Cities and Educn work, 1981–88; Man. Dir, Develt, BITC, 1988–92. *Publication:* Why Industry Matters, 1978. *Recreations:* children, gardening, collecting pink lustre. *Address:* 8 Stratton Street, W1X 5FD. *T:* 0171–629 1600; 8 Alwyne Road, Islington, N1 2HH.

CLEVERLEY FORD, Rev. Preb. Douglas William; Chaplain to The Queen, 1973–84; *b* 4 March 1914; *yr s* of late Arthur James and Mildred Ford; *m* 1939, Olga Mary (*d* 1993), *er d* of late Dr Thomas Bewley and Elizabeth Gilbart-Smith; no *c. Educ:* Great Yarmouth Grammar Sch.; Univ. of London. BD, MTh, ALCD (1st cl.). Deacon 1937, Priest 1938. London Coll. of Divinity: Tutor, 1937–39; Lectr, 1942–43 and 1952–58; Lectr, Church Army Trng Coll., 1953–60. Curate of Bridlington, Yorks, 1939–42; Vicar of Holy Trinity, Hampstead, 1942–55; Vicar of Holy Trinity with All Saints Church, South Kensington, 1955–74; Senior Chaplain to Archbishop of Canterbury, 1975–80; Hon. Dir, Coll. of Preachers, 1960–73; Rural Dean of Westminster, 1965–74; Prebendary of St Paul's Cathedral, 1968, now Prebendary Emeritus; Provincial Canon of York, 1969–; Lectr, Wey Inst. of Religious Studies, 1980–84; Tutor, Southwark Ordination Course, 1980–86. Six Preacher, Canterbury Cathedral, 1982–91. Chm., Queen Alexandra's House, Kensington Gore, 1966–74; Mem. Governing Body, Westminster City Sch. and United Westminster Schs, 1965–74; Hon. Life Governor: British and Foreign Bible Soc., 1948; Church's Ministry among the Jews, 1955. Queen's Jubilee Medal, 1977. *Publications:* An Expository Preacher's Notebook, 1960; The Christian Faith Explained, 1962; A Theological Preacher's Notebook, 1962; A Pastoral Preacher's Notebook, 1965; A Reading of St Luke's Gospel, 1967; Preaching at the Parish Communion, Vol. 1 1967, Vol. 2 1968, Vol. 3 1969; Preaching Today, 1969; Preaching through the Christian Year, 1971; Praying through the Christian Year, 1973; Have You Anything to Declare?, 1973; Preaching on the Special Occasions, 1974, Vol. 2 1981; Preaching at the Parish Communion (Series III), 1975; New Preaching from the Old Testament, 1976; New Preaching from the New Testament, 1977; The Ministry of the Word, 1979; Preaching through the Acts of the Apostles, 1979; More Preaching from the New Testament, 1982; More Preaching from the Old Testament, 1983; Preaching through the Psalms, 1984; Preaching through the Life of Christ, 1985; Preaching on Devotional Occasions, 1986; From Strength to Strength, 1987; Preaching the Risen Christ, 1988; Preaching on Great Themes, 1989; Preaching on the Holy Spirit, 1990; God's Masterpieces, 1991; Preaching the Incarnate Christ, 1992; Preaching on the Crucifixion, 1993; Preaching on the Historical Jesus, 1993; Preaching What We Believe, 1995; Preaching on the Sayings of Jesus, 1996; contrib. Churchman's Companion 1967, Expository Times. *Recreations:* gardening, music, languages. *Address:* Rostrevor, Lingfield, Surrey RH7 6BZ. *Club:* Athenæum.

CLEWS, Michael Arthur; Master of the Supreme Court Taxing Office, 1970–87; *b* Caudebec, France, 16 Sept. 1919; *s* of late Roland Trevor Clews and late Marjorie (*née*

Baily); *m* 1947, Kathleen Edith Hollingworth; one *s* two *d.* *Educ:* Epworth Coll., Rhyl; Clare Coll., Cambridge (MA). Served in Indian Army (Major, RA and V Force), 1940–46. Solicitor, 1953; Partner, W. H. House & Son, and Knocker & Foskett, Sevenoaks, 1957–70. Mem., Lord Chancellor's Adv. Cttee on Legal Aid, 1977–84. *Address:* Hameau de Coriolan 9, 83120 Plan de la Tour, Var, France.

CLIBBORN, Donovan Harold, CMG 1966; HM Diplomatic Service, retired; *b* 2 July 1917; *s* of Henry Joseph Fairley Clibborn and Isabel Sarah Jago; *m* 1st, 1940, Margaret Mercedes Edwige Nelson (*d* 1966); one *s* two *d*; 2nd, 1973, Victoria Ondiviela Garvi; one step *s* two step *d.* *Educ:* Ilford High Sch.; St Edmund Hall, Oxford (MA). Laming Travelling Fellow, Queen's Coll., Oxford, 1938–40. Entered Consular Service, 1939; Vice-Consul, Genoa, 1939–40. Army Service, 1940–45: Intelligence Corps and Royal Signals, Western Desert, Sicily, Italy, NW Europe (despatches); Major, 1944. Foreign Office, 1945–46; Consul, Los Angeles, 1946–48; Foreign Office, 1948–50; 1st Sec. (UK High Commn, India), Madras, 1950–52; 1st Sec. (Information), Rio de Janeiro, 1952–56; 1st Sec. (Commercial), Madrid, 1956–60; Consul (Commercial), Milan, 1960–62; Counsellor (Economic), Tehran, 1962–64; Counsellor, Rio de Janeiro, 1964–66; Consul-General, Barcelona, 1966–70; Ambassador, El Salvador, 1971–75. *Recreations:* reading, music, perpetrating light verse. *Address:* Paseo del Dr Moragas 188, Atico 1A, Barberá del Vallés, Prov. Barcelona 08210, Spain. *T:* (3) 7185377.
See also J. D. N. dalla R. Clibborn.

CLIBBORN, John Donovan Nelson dalla Rosa; HM Diplomatic Service; Counsellor, Washington, since 1993; *b* 24 Nov. 1941; *s* of Donovan Harold Clibborn, *qv*; *m* 1968, Juliet Elizabeth Pagden; one *s* two *d.* *Educ:* Downside Sch., Stratton-on-the-Fosse, Bath; Oriel Coll., Oxford (1st Cl. Hon. Mods and Lit.Hum. BA, MA). Joined HM Diplomatic Service, 1965; FCO, 1965–67; 3rd, subseq. 2nd Sec., Nicosia, 1967–69; FCO, 1970–72; 1st Secretary: Bonn, 1972–75; UK Mission to EC, Brussels, 1975–78; Jt Res. Centre, EEC, 1978–81; FCO, 1981–88; Counsellor, Washington, 1988–91; FCO, 1991–93. Member: Soc. for the Promotion of Roman Studies, 1963–; Soc. for the Promotion of Hellenic Studies, 1964–; Palestine Exploration Fund, 1965–. *Recreations:* classical literature, ancient history. *Address:* c/o Foreign and Commonwealth Office, SW1A 2AH. *Club:* Athenæum.

CLIBBORN, Rt. Rev. Stanley Eric Francis B.; *see* Booth-Clibborn.

CLIBURN, Van, (Harvey Lavan Cliburn Jr); pianist; *b* Shreveport, La, 12 July 1934; *o c* of Harvey Lavan Cliburn and late Rildia Bee (*née* O'Bryan). *Educ:* Kilgore High Sch., Texas; Juilliard Sch. of Music, New York. Made début in Houston, Texas, 1947; subsequently has toured extensively in United States and Europe. Awards include first International Tchaikovsky Piano Competition, Moscow, 1958, and every US prize, for pianistic ability. *Recreation:* swimming. *Address:* c/o Van Cliburn Foundation, 2525 Ridgmar Blvd, Suite 307, Fort Worth, TX 76116, USA.

CLIFFORD, family name of **Baron Clifford of Chudleigh.**

CLIFFORD OF CHUDLEIGH, 14th Baron *cr* 1672; **Thomas Hugh Clifford;** Count of The Holy Roman Empire; *b* 17 March 1948; *s* of 13th Baron Clifford of Chudleigh, OBE and of Hon. Katharine Vavasseur Fisher, 2nd *d* of 2nd Baron Fisher; *S* father, 1988; *m* 1st, 1980, (Muriel) Suzanne (marr. diss. 1993), *d* of Major Campbell Austin and Mrs Campbell Austin; two *s* one *d*; 2nd, 1994, Clarissa, *er d* of His Honour A. C. Goodall, *qv.* *Educ:* Downside Abbey. Commnd Coldstream Guards, 1967; stationed British Honduras, 1967–68; Instructor, Guards Depot, 1968–69; Northern Ireland; ADC to Chief of Defence Staff, 1972–73; served with Ace Mobile Force, 1973; Adjutant, Guards Depot, 1973–75. Royal Agricultural College, Cirencester, 1976–78. *Recreations:* shooting, fishing, tennis, croquet. *Heir: s* Hon. Alexander Thomas Hugh Clifford, *b* 24 Sept. 1985. *Address:* Ugbrooke Park, Chudleigh, South Devon TQ13 0AD. *T:* (office) Chudleigh (01626) 852179.

CLIFFORD, Clark McAdams; Special Counsel of the President of the United States, 1946–50; former Special Envoy of President Jimmy Carter; *b* 25 Dec. 1906; *s* of Frank Andrew Clifford and Georgia (*née* McAdams); *m* 1931, Margery Pepperell Kimball; three *d.* *Educ:* Washington Univ., St Louis (LLB). Served US Naval Reserve, 1944–46 (Naval Commendation Ribbon). Practised law in St Louis, 1928–43; specialised in trial cases, corporation and labour law; Senior Partner, Clifford & Miller, 1950–68; Secretary of Defense, USA, 1968–69; Sen. Partner, Clifford & Warnke, 1969–91. Medal of Freedom with Distinction, USA, 1969. *Recreation:* golf. *Address:* 815 Connecticut Avenue, Washington, DC 20006, USA.

CLIFFORD, Most Rev. Dermot; *see* Cashel and Emly, Archbishop of, (RC).

CLIFFORD, Rev. Paul Rowntree, MA; President, Selly Oak Colleges, Birmingham, 1965–79; *b* 21 Feb. 1913; *s* of Robert and Harriet Rowntree Clifford; *m* 1st, 1947, Marjory Jean Tait (*d* 1988); one *s* one *d*; 2nd, 1989, Dorothy Marion White, OBE. *Educ:* Mill Hill Sch.; Balliol Coll., Oxford; Mansfield and Regents Park Colls, Oxford. MA (Oxon) 1939. West Ham Central Mission, London: Asst Minister, 1938–43; Supt Minister, 1943–53; McMaster Univ., Hamilton, Canada: Asst Prof. of Homiletics and Pastoral Theology, 1953–59; Dean of Men and Chm. of Dept of Religion, 1959–64; Prof. of Religion, 1964–65. Hon. Treas., Internat. Assoc. for Mission Studies, 1974–88; Sec., Foundn for Study of Christianity and Society, 1980–90. *Publications:* The Mission of the Local Church, 1953; The Pastoral Calling, 1959; Now is the Time, 1970; Interpreting Human Experience, 1971; The Death of the Dinosaur, 1977; Politics and the Christian Vision, 1984; Government by the People?, 1986; An Ecumenical Pilgrimage, 1994; The Kingdom of God: fact or fiction?, 1995; articles in Jl of Religion, Metaphysical Review, Dialogue, Canadian Jl of Theology, Scottish Jl of Theology, Foundations, Religious Studies. *Recreations:* golf, gardening. *Address:* 12 Ravens Court, St John's Road, Eastbourne, Sussex BN20 7HY. *Club:* Reform (Chm., 1987–89).

CLIFFORD, Sir Roger (Joseph), 7th Bt *cr* 1887; *b* 5 June 1936; *s* of Sir Roger Charles Joseph Gerard Clifford, 6th Bt and Henrietta Millicent Kiver (*d* 1971); *S* father 1982; *m* 1968, Joanna Theresa, *d* of C. J. Ward, Christchurch, NZ; two *d.* *Educ:* Beaumont College, England. *Recreations:* golf, Rugby football. *Heir: b* Charles Joseph Clifford [*b* 5 June 1936; *m* 1983, Sally Green]. *Address:* 135 Totara Street, Christchurch 4, New Zealand. *T:* (3)485958. *Clubs:* Blenheim (Blenheim, NZ); Christchurch Golf.

CLIFFORD, Timothy Peter Plint, BA, AMA; Director, National Galleries of Scotland, since 1984; *b* 26 Jan. 1946; *s* of Derek Plint Clifford and late Anne (*née* Pierson); *m* 1968, Jane Olivia, *yr d* of Sir George Paterson, *qv*; one *d.* *Educ:* Sherborne, Dorset; Perugia Univ. (Dip. Italian); Courtauld Inst., Univ. of London (BA Hons, History of Art). Dip. Fine Art, Museums Assoc., 1972. Asst Keeper, Dept of Paintings, Manchester City Art Galleries, 1968–72, Acting Keeper, 1972; Asst Keeper, Dept of Ceramics, Victoria and Albert Mus., London, 1972–76; Asst Keeper, Dept of Prints and Drawings, British Mus., London, 1976–78; Dir, Manchester City Art Galls, 1978–84. Member: Manchester Diocesan Adv. Cttee for Care of Churches, 1978–84; NACF Cttee (Cheshire and Gtr Manchester Br.), 1978–84; North Western Museum and Art Gall. Service Jt Adv. Panel, 1978–84; Cttee, ICOM (UK), 1980–82; Chm., Internat. Cttee for Museums of Fine Art, ICOM, 1980–83 (Mem., Exec. Cttee, 1983–88); Member: Museums and Galleries Commn, 1983–88; British Council, 1987–92 (Fine Arts Adv. Cttee, 1988–92); Founder and Committee Member: Friends of Manchester City Art Galls, 1978–84; Patrons and Associates, Manchester City Art Galls, 1979–; Mem. Exec. Cttee, Scottish Museums Council, 1984–; Mem. Adv. Council, Friends of Courtauld Inst. Cttee Mem., Derby Internat. Porcelain Soc., 1983–86; Vice-President: Turner Soc., 1984–86, and 1989–; NADFAS, 1990–; Mem., Adv. Cttee, Come and See Scotland's Churches, 1989–90. Vice-Pres., Frigate Unicorn Preservation Soc., 1987–. Trustee, Lake Dist Art Gall. and Mus. Trust, 1989–. Mem., Accademia Italiana delle Arti Applicate, 1988–. FRSA; FSA(Scot) 1986. Freeman: Goldsmiths' Co., 1989; City of London, 1989. Cavaliere al Ordine della Repubblica Italiana, 1988. *Publications:* (with Derek Clifford) John Crome, 1968; (with Dr Ivan Hall) Heaton Hall, 1972; (with Dr T. Friedmann) The Man at Hyde Park Corner: sculpture by John Cheere, 1974; Vues Pittoresques de Luxembourg . . . par J. M. W. Turner, (Luxembourg) 1977; Ceramics of Derbyshire 1750–1975 (ed, H. G. Bradley), 1978; J. M. W. Turner, Acquerelli e incisioni, (Rome) 1980; Turner at Manchester, 1982; (with Ian Gow) The National Gallery of Scotland: an architectural and decorative history, 1988; (jtly) Raphael: the pursuit of perfection, 1994; (with Ian Gow) Duff House, 1995; contrib. Burlington Magazine, etc. *Recreations:* shooting, bird watching, entomology. *Address:* National Galleries of Scotland, The Mound, Edinburgh EH2 2EL. *Clubs:* Turf, Beefsteak; New (Edinburgh).

CLIFFORD, William Henry Morton, CB 1972; CBE 1966; Legal Consultant, Civil Service College, 1974–79, retired; *b* 30 July 1909; *s* of Henry Edward Clifford, FRIBA, Glasgow, and Margaret Alice, *d* of Dr William Gibson, Campbeltown, Argyll; *m* 1936, Katharine Winifred, *d* of Rev. H. W. Waterfield, Temple Grove, Eastbourne; one *s* two *d.* *Educ:* Tonbridge Sch.; Corpus Christi Coll., Cambridge. Admitted a solicitor, 1936. Entered Solicitor's Department, GPO, 1937. Served in Army, 1939–45: Major GS, Army Council Secretariat, WO, 1944–45. Transferred to Solicitor's Office, Min. of National Insurance, 1945; Assistant Solicitor, Min. of Pensions and Nat. Insurance (later Min. of Social Security), 1953; Solicitor, DHSS (formerly Min. of Social Security), 1968–74. *Recreations:* reading, listening to music (especially opera), genealogy, walking, sailing. *Address:* Woodbrook, 9 Lake Road, Tunbridge Wells, Kent TN4 8XT. *T:* Tunbridge Wells (01892) 521612.

CLIFT, Richard Dennis, CMG 1984; HM Diplomatic Service, retired; furniture restorer; *b* 18 May 1933; *s* of late Dennis Victor Clift and Helen Wilmot Clift (*née* Evans); *m* 1st, 1957, Barbara Mary Travis (marr. diss. 1982); three *d*; 2nd, 1982, Jane Rosamund Barker (*née* Homfray). *Educ:* St Edward's Sch., Oxford; Pembroke Coll., Cambridge. BA 1956. FO, 1956–57; Office of British Chargé d'Affaires, Peking, 1958–60; British Embassy, Berne, 1961–62; UK Delegn to NATO, Paris, 1962–64; FO, 1964–68; Head of Chancery, British High Commn, Kuala Lumpur, 1969–71; FCO, 1971–73; Counsellor (Commercial), Peking, 1974–76; Canadian Nat. Defence Coll., 1976–77; seconded to NI Office, 1977–79; Hd of Hong Kong Dept, FCO, 1979–84; High Comr in Freetown, 1984–86; Political Advr, Hong Kong Govt, 1987–89. Student, London Coll. of Furniture, 1989–91. *Recreations:* sailing, walking. *Address:* 18 Langwood Chase, Teddington, Middx TW11 9PH.

CLIFT, Prof. Roland, OBE 1994; FEng 1986; Professor of Environmental Strategy and Director, Centre for Environmental Strategy, University of Surrey, since 1992; *b* 19 Nov. 1942; *s* of Leslie William Clift and Ivy Florence Gertrude Clift (*née* Wheeler); *m* 1st, 1968, Rosena Valory (*née* Davison); one *d*; 2nd, 1979, Diana Helen (*née* Manning); two *s.* *Educ:* Trinity Coll., Cambridge (BA 1963; MA 1967); PhD McGill 1970. CEng, FIChem E. Technical Officer (Chem. Engr), ICI, 1964–67; Lectr, Asst Prof. and Associate Prof., McGill Univ., 1967–75; Lectr, Imperial Coll., London, 1975–76; Lectr, Univ. of Cambridge, 1976–81; Fellow, Trinity Coll., Cambridge, 1976–81 (Praelector, 1980–81); Prof. of Chem. Engrg, Univ. of Surrey, 1981–92. Vis. Prof., Univ. di Napoli, 1973–74; Director: ClifMar Associates, 1986–; Particle Consultants Ltd, 1988–. Chairman: Clean Technology Management Cttee, SERC, 1990–; Engrg Bd, AFRC, 1992–. Mem., Governing Body, Charterhouse Sch., 1982–91. Hon. Citizen of Augusta, Georgia, 1987. Editor in Chief, Powder Technology, 1987–. *Publications:* (jtly) Bubbles, Drops and Particles, 1978; (ed jtly) Fluidization, 1985; (jtly) Slurry Transport using Centrifugal Pumps, 1992. *Recreation:* music. *Address:* Centre for Environmental Strategy, University of Surrey, Guildford, Surrey GU2 5XH. *T:* Guildford (01483) 509271, *Fax:* Guildford (01483) 509394.

CLIFTON, Lord; Ivo Donald Stuart Bligh; *b* 17 April 1968; *s* and *heir* of 11th Earl of Darnley, *qv.* *Educ:* Marlborough Coll.; Edinburgh Univ. *Address:* Netherwood Manor, Tenbury Wells, Worcs WR15 8RT.

CLIFTON, Bishop of (RC), since 1974; **Rt. Rev. Mervyn Alban Newman Alexander,** DD; *b* London, 29 June 1925; *s* of William Paul Alexander and Grace Evelyn Alexander (*née* Newman). *Educ:* Bishop Wordsworth School, Salisbury; Prior Park College, Bath; Gregorian University, Rome (DD 1951). Curate at Pro-Cathedral, Clifton, Bristol, 1951–63; RC Chaplain, Bristol University, 1953–67; Parish Priest, Our Lady of Lourdes, Weston-super-Mare, 1967–72; Auxiliary Bishop of Clifton and Titular Bishop of Pinhel, 1972–74; Vicar Capitular of Clifton, 1974. *Address:* St Ambrose, Leigh Woods, Bristol BS8 3PW. *T:* Bristol (0117) 973 3072.

CLIFTON, Gerald Michael; His Honour Judge Clifton; a Circuit Judge, since 1992; *b* 3 July 1947; *s* of Frederick Maurice Clifton and Jane Clifton; *m* 1973, Rosemary Anne Vera Jackson; two *s.* *Educ:* Liverpool Coll.; Brasenose Coll., Oxford (Open Classical Schol., MA). Called to the Bar, Middle Temple, 1970; joined Northern Circuit, 1970; Asst Recorder, 1982; Recorder, 1988; Mem., Manx Bar, 1992. Life Gov., Liverpool Coll., 1992. *Recreations:* walking, philately, sailing, tennis. *Address:* c/o Circuit Administrator, Northern Circuit, 15 Quay Street, Manchester M60 9FD. *Clubs:* Bar Yacht; Heswall Lawn Tennis.

CLIFTON, Lt-Col Peter Thomas, CVO 1980; DSO 1945; DL; JP; Standard Bearer, HM Body Guard of Honourable Corps of Gentlemen at Arms, 1979–81; *b* 24 Jan. 1911; *s* of Lt-Col Percy Robert Clifton, CMG, DSO, TD, Clifton Hall, Nottingham; *m* 1st, 1934, Ursula (marr. diss. 1936), *d* of Sir Edward Hussey Packe; 2nd, 1948, Patricia Mary Adela, DStJ (who *m* 1935, Robert Cobbold, killed in action 1944), *d* of Major J. M. Gibson-Watt, Doldowlod, Radnorshire; two *d.* *Educ:* Eton; RMC Sandhurst. 2nd Lieut Grenadier Guards, 1931; served War of 1939–45: France, 1939–40; Italy, 1944–45; Lt-Col 1944; Palestine, 1945–47. Mem. HM Body Guard of Hon. Corps of Gentlemen at Arms, 1960–81 (Clerk of the Cheque and Adjutant, 1973–79). DL Notts 1954; JP Notts 1952–59, Hants 1964. *Address:* Dummer House, Basingstoke, Hants RG25 2AG. *T:* Dummer (01256) 397306. *Clubs:* Cavalry and Guards, White's; Royal Yacht Squadron.
See also Baron Gibson-Watt, Baron Wrottesley.

CLIFTON-BROWN, Geoffrey Robert; MP (C) Cirencester and Tewkesbury, since 1992; chartered surveyor and farmer; *b* 23 March 1953; *s* of Robert and Elizabeth Clifton-Brown; *m* 1979, Alexandra Peto-Shepherd; one *s* one *d.* *Educ:* Tormore Sch., Kent; Eton

Coll.; RAC, Cirencester. Chm., N Norfolk Cons. Assoc., 1986–91; Mem., Eastern Area Exec., 1986–91; Vice Chm., Norfolk Eur. Constituency Council, 1990–91. Mem., Envmt Select Cttee, 1992–; Secretary: Cons. Backbench Cttee on Eur. Affairs, 1992–; All Party Gp on Population and Develt. Vice Pres., Small Business Forum. Freeman, City of London, 1981; Liveryman, Farmers' Co., 1984. *Recreations:* fishing, all country pursuits. *Address:* House of Commons, SW1A 0AA. *T:* 0171–219 3000. *Clubs:* Carlton, Farmers'.

CLINCH, David John; Secretary, Open University, since 1981; *b* 14 Feb. 1937; *s* of Thomas Charles Clinch and Madge Isabel Clinch (*née* Saker); *m* 1963, Hilary Jacques; one *s* one *d. Educ:* Nautical Coll., Pangbourne; St Cuthbert's Soc., Univ. of Durham (BA); Indiana Univ. (MBA). National Service, Royal Navy (Sub-Lieut), Supply and Secretariat, 1955–57. Administrator, Univ. of Sussex, 1963–69; Deputy Secretary and Registrar, Open University, 1969–81; Registrar Counterpart, Allama Iqbal Open Univ., Pakistan, 1976–77. Member: Conf. of Univ. Administrators, 1973–; Conf. of Registrars and Secs, 1981– (Chm., 1990–91); British Fulbright Scholars Assoc., 1978–. Dir, Nat. Educnl Resources Information Service Trust, 1989–93; Trustee, Open Univ. Superannuation Scheme, 1989–. *Recreations:* music, natural history, reading, walking. *Address:* 39 Tudor Gardens, Stony Stratford, Milton Keynes MK11 1HX. *T:* Milton Keynes (01908) 562475.

CLINTON; *see* Fiennes-Clinton, family name of Earl of Lincoln.

CLINTON, 22nd Baron *cr* 1299 (title abeyant 1957–65); **Gerard Nevile Mark Fane Trefusis;** DL; landowner; *b* 7 Oct. 1934; *s* of Capt. Charles Fane (killed in action, 1940); assumed by deed poll, 1958, surname of Trefusis in addition to patronymic; *m* 1959, Nicola Harriette Purdon Coote; one *s* two *d. Educ:* Gordonstoun. Took seat in House of Lords, 1965. Mem., Prince of Wales's Councils, 1968–79. JP Bideford, 1963–83; DL Devon, 1977. *Recreations:* shooting, fishing, forestry. *Heir: s* Hon. Charles Patrick Rolle Fane Trefusis [*b* 21 March 1962; *m* 1992, Rosanna, *yr d* of John Izat; one *s*]. *Address:* Heanton Satchville, near Okehampton, North Devon EX20 3QE. *T:* Dolton (018054) 224. *Club:* Boodle's.

CLINTON, Alan; *see* Clinton, R. A.

CLINTON, Bill; *see* Clinton, W. J.

CLINTON, (Robert) Alan; Director, 1986–95, Managing Director, 1987–95, Picton House Group of Companies, property development cos; *b* 12 July 1931; *s* of John and Leah Clinton; *m* 1956, Valerie Joy Falconer. *Educ:* George Dixon Grammar Sch., Edgbaston, Birmingham. On leaving school, joined the Post Office, 1948; Member, North Western Postal Board, 1970; Asst Director (Personnel), London, 1975; Asst Director (Operations), London, 1976; Director of Eastern Postal Region, Colchester, 1978; Director of Postal Operations, London, 1979; Member Post Office Board, 1981–85: for Mails Network and Develt, 1981; for Mails Ops and Estates, 1982; for Corporate Services, 1984–85; Man. Dir, Counter Services, 1984–85. Mem. Mgt Cttee, Royal Assoc. in Aid of Deaf People, 1994. Pres., Clacton and NE Essex Arts and Literary Soc., 1992–; Mem. Cttee, St Osyth Historical Soc., 1995. FCIT 1982. Mem., Worshipful Company of Carmen, 1981; Freeman of City of London, 1979. *Recreations:* music, walking, sailing. *Address:* Summer Cottage, The Quay, St Osyth, Clacton-on-Sea, Essex CO16 8EW. *T:* St Osyth (01255) 820368. *Club:* City of London.

CLINTON, William Jefferson, (Bill), JD; President of the United States of America, since 1993; *b* 19 Aug. 1946; *s* of late Virginia Kelly; *m* 1975, Hillary Rodham; one *d. Educ:* Georgetown Univ. (BS 1968); University Coll., Oxford (Rhodes Schol.; Hon. Fellow, 1993; DCL by Diploma, 1994); Yale Univ. Law Sch. (JD 1973). Prof., Univ. of Arkansas Law Sch., 1974–76; Attorney Gen., Arkansas, 1977–79; with Wright, Lindsey & Jennings, law firm, 1981–83; Governor of Arkansas, 1979–81 and 1983–92. Chairman: Educn Commn of the States, 1986–87; Nat. Governors' Assoc., 1986–87 (Co-Chm., Task Force on Educn, 1990–91); Democratic Governors' Assoc., 1989–90 (Vice Chm., 1987–88); Democratic Leadership Council, 1990–91. Democrat. Hon. DCL Oxford, 1994. *Address:* The White House, Washington, DC 20500, USA.

CLINTON-DAVIS, family name of **Baron Clinton-Davis**.

CLINTON-DAVIS, Baron *cr* 1990 (Life Peer), of Hackney in the London Borough of Hackney; **Stanley Clinton Clinton-Davis;** consultant on European affairs and law, S. J. Berwin & Co., solicitors, since 1989; *b* 6 Dec. 1928; *s* of Sidney Davis; name changed to Clinton-Davis by deed poll, 1990; *m* 1954, Frances Jane Lucas; one *s* three *d. Educ:* Hackney Downs Sch.; Mercers' Sch.; King's Coll., London University. LLB 1950; admitted Solicitor 1953. Mem. Exec. Council, Nat. Assoc. of Labour Student Organisations, 1949–50. Councillor, London Borough of Hackney, 1959; Mayor of Hackney, 1968. Contested (Lab): Langstone Div. of Portsmouth, 1955; Yarmouth, 1959 and 1964. MP (Lab) Hackney Central, 1970–83; Parly Under-Sec. of State, Dept of Trade, 1974–79; Opposition spokesman on trade, prices and consumer protection, 1979–81, on foreign affairs, 1981–83; Opposition frontbench spokesman on transport, H of L, 1990–. Mem., Commn of EC, 1985–89. Chm., Adv. Cttee on Protection of the Sea, 1984–85, 1989–; Chair: Refugee Council, 1989–; Packaging Standards Council, 1992–. Pres., AMA, 1992–. Dep. Chair, Lab. Finance and Industry Gp, 1993–. Member: RIIA; Council and Exec. Cttee, Justice; UN Selection Cttee for Sasakawa, Envmt Project; formerly Mem., Bd of Deputies of British Jews; Parly Relations Sub-Cttee of the Law Soc. Mem. Council, British Maritime League, 1989–. Jt Pres., Soc. of Labour Lawyers, 1991–; President: UK Pilots Assoc. (Marine), 1991–; BALPA, 1994–; Vice-Pres., Chartered Instn of Envmtl Health Officers, 1991–. Pres., Hackney Br., Multiple Sclerosis Soc.; Vice-Pres., Hackney Assoc. for Disabled; Hon. Mem. Rotary Club, Hackney. Hon. Mem., 1979, and former Trustee, NUMAST (formerly Merchant Navy and Airline Officers' Assoc.); Hon. Fellow, QMW, 1993; FRSA 1992. Hon. Dr *hc* Polytechnical Inst., Bucharest, 1993. First Medal for Outstanding Services to Animal Welfare in Europe, Eurogroup for Animal Welfare, 1988. Grand Cross, Order of Leopold II, Belgium (for services to EC), 1990. *Recreations:* golf, Association football, reading biographical histories. *Address:* c/o S. J. Berwin & Co., 222 Gray's Inn Road, WC1X 8HB.

CLITHEROE, 2nd Baron *cr* 1955, of Downham; **Ralph John Assheton;** Bt 1945; FCIB; Chairman, Yorkshire Bank, since 1990; Vice Lord-Lieutenant of Lancashire, since 1995; *b* 3 Nov. 1929; *s* of 1st Baron Clitheroe, KCVO, PC, FSA, and Sylvia Benita Frances, Lady Clitheroe, FRICS, FLAS, (*d* 1991), *d* of 6th Baron Hotham; *S* father, 1984; *m* 1961, Juliet, *d* of Lt-Col Christopher Lionel Hanbury, MBE, TD; two *s* one *d. Educ:* Eton; Christ Church, Oxford (Scholar, MA). FCIB 1991. Served as 2nd Lieut Life Guards, 1948–49. Chairman: RTZ Chemicals Ltd, 1973–87; RTZ Borax Ltd, 1979–89; US Borax and Chemical Corp., 1979–89; RTZ Oil & Gas Ltd, 1983–88; Director: Borax Consolidated, 1960–89; RTZ Corp., 1968–89; First Interstate Bank of California, 1981–89; TR Natural Resources Investment Trust, 1982–87; American Mining Congress, 1982–89; Halliburton Co., Texas, 1987–. Mem., Council, Chemical Industries Assoc., 1984–88. FRSA 1991. Liveryman, Skinners' Co. DL Lancs, 1986. *Heir: s* Hon. Ralph Christopher Assheton, *b* 19 March 1962. *Address:* Downham Hall, Clitheroe, Lancs BB7 4DN. *Clubs:* Boodle's, Pratt's, Royal Automobile.

CLIVE, Viscount; Jonathan Nicholas William Herbert; *b* 5 Dec. 1979; *s* and *heir* of Earl of Powis, *qv*.

CLIVE, Eric McCredie; a Scottish Law Commissioner, since 1981; *b* 24 July 1938; *s* of Robert M. Clive and Mary L. D. Clive; *m* 1962, Kay M. McLeman; one *s* three *d. Educ:* Univs of Edinburgh (MA, LLB with dist.); Michigan (LLM); Virginia (SJD). Solicitor. Lecturer 1962–69, Sen. Lectr 1969–75, Reader 1975–77, Professor of Scots Law 1977–81, Univ. of Edinburgh. *Publications:* Law of Husband and Wife in Scotland, 1974, 3rd edn 1992; (jtly) Scots Law for Journalists, 1965, 5th edn 1988; articles and notes in legal jls. *Address:* 14 York Road, Edinburgh EH5 3EH. *T:* 0131–552 2875.

CLIVE, Nigel David, CMG 1967; OBE 1959; MC 1944; TD; HM Diplomatic Service, retired; *b* 13 July 1917; *s* of late Horace David and Hilda Mary Clive; *m* 1949, Maria Jeanne Tambakopoulou. *Educ:* Stowe; Christ Church, Oxford (Scholar). Commissioned 2nd Mddx Yeomanry, 1939; served in Middle East and Greece. Joined Foreign Office, 1946; served Athens, 1946–48; Jerusalem, 1948; FO, 1948–50; Baghdad, 1950–53; FO, 1953–58; Tunis, 1958–62; Algiers, 1962–63; FO, 1964–65; Head of Information Research Dept, FCO (formerly FO), 1966–69; Adviser to Secretary-General of OECD, 1970–80. *Publications:* A Greek Experience 1943–1948, 1985; (trans.) M. Koromila, In the Trail of Odysseus, 1994. *Recreations:* reading, travel. *Address:* Flat 2, 41 Lowndes Square, SW1X 9JL. *T:* 0171–235 1186. *Clubs:* Brooks's, Special Forces, MCC.

CLOAKE, John Cecil, CMG 1977; HM Diplomatic Service, retired; *b* 2 Dec. 1924; *s* of late Dr Cecil Stedman Cloake, Wimbledon, and Maude Osborne Newling; *m* 1956, Margaret Thomure Morris, Washington, DC, USA; one *s. Educ:* King's Coll. Sch., Wimbledon; Peterhouse, Cambridge. Served in Army, 1943–46 (Lieut RE). Foreign Office, 1948; 3rd Sec., Baghdad, 1949, and Saigon, 1951; 2nd Sec., 1952; FO, 1954; Private Sec. to Permanent Under-Sec., 1956, and to Parly Under-Sec., 1957; 1st Sec., 1957; Consul (Commercial), New York, 1958; 1st Sec., Moscow, 1962; FO, 1963; DSAO, 1965; Counsellor, 1966; Head of Accommodation Dept, 1967; Counsellor (Commercial), Tehran, 1968–72; Fellow, Centre for International Studies, LSE, 1972–73; Head of Trade Relations and Exports Dept, FCO, 1973–76; Ambassador to Bulgaria, 1976–80. Member: Council, British Inst. of Persian Studies, 1981–95 (Hon. Treas. 1982–90); Cttee of Honour for Bulgarian 1300th Anniv., 1981. Chairman: Richmond Soc. History Section, 1975–76, 1984–85; Richmond Local Hist. Soc., 1985–90 (Pres., 1990–); Richmond Museum Project, 1983–86; Mus. of Richmond, 1986–95. *Publications:* Templer: Tiger of Malaya, 1985; Richmond Past, 1991; Royal Bounty, 1992; Palaces and Parks of Richmond and Kew, Vol. 1, 1995; articles on local history. *Recreations:* gardening, painting, architecture, local history, genealogy. *Address:* 4 The Terrace, Richmond Hill, Richmond, Surrey TW10 6RN.

CLOGHER, Bishop of, since 1986; **Rt. Rev. Brian Desmond Anthony Hannon;** *b* 5 Oct. 1936; *s* of late Ven. Arthur Gordon Hannon and of Hilda Catherine Stewart-Moore Hannon (*née* Denny); *m* 1964, Maeve Geraldine Audley (*née* Butler); three *s. Educ:* Mourne Grange Prep. School, Co. Down; St Columba's Coll., Co. Dublin; Trinity Coll., Dublin (BA Hons 1959, 1st Class Divinity Testimonium 1961). Deacon 1961, priest 1962; Diocese of Derry: Curate-Assistant, All Saints, Clooney, Londonderry, 1961–64; Rector of Desertmartin, 1964–69; Rector of Christchurch, Londonderry, 1969–82; RD of Londonderry, 1977–82; Diocese of Clogher: Rector of St Macartin's Cathedral, Enniskillen, 1982–86; Canon of Cathedral Chapter, 1983; Dean of Clogher, 1985. President: CMS (Ireland), 1990–; Irish Council of Churches, 1992–94; Co-Chm., Irish Inter-Church Meeting, 1992–94; Mem., WCC Central Cttee, 1983–92. Chm. of Western (NI) Education and Library Bd, 1985–87 and 1989–91 (Vice-Chm., 1987–89 and 1991–93). Hon. MA TCD, 1962. *Publication:* (editor/author) Christ Church, Londonderry—1830 to 1980—Milestones, Ministers, Memories, 1980. *Recreations:* walking, music, travel, sport. *Address:* The See House, Fivemiletown, Co. Tyrone, Northern Ireland BT75 0QP. *T:* Fivemiletown (013655) 21265.

CLOGHER, Bishop of, (RC), since 1979; **Most Rev. Joseph Duffy,** DD; *b* 3 Feb. 1934; *s* of Edward Duffy and Brigid MacEntee. *Educ:* St Macartan's College, Monaghan; Maynooth College. MA, BD, HDipEd. Ordained priest, 1958; Teacher, 1960–72; Curate, 1972–79. *Publications:* Patrick in his own words, 1972; Lough Derg Guide, 1980; Monaghan Cathedral, 1992. *Recreations:* local history, travel. *Address:* Tigh an Easpaig, Monaghan, Ireland. *T:* (47) 81019, *Fax:* (47) 84773.

CLOKIE, Hilary Ann; *see* Nicolle, H. A.

CLOSE, Richard Charles, FCT; FCA; Managing Director for Finance, Post Office, since 1993; *b* 3 Sept. 1949; *s* of Richard Alwen Close and Marjorie Ann Close; *m* 1973, Elizabeth Janet Beatrice Brown; one *s* one *d. Educ:* Canford Sch., Wimborne, Dorset; Sidney Sussex Coll., Cambridge Univ. (MA). Qualified Inst. of Chartered Accountants, 1974. Arthur Young & Co., Chartered Accountants, 1971–74; Arthur Young, Milan, Italy, 1974–81; Regional Dir Internal Audit, Europe, ME and Africa, Sperry Corp., 1981–84; European Treasurer, Sperry Corp., 1984–86; Finance Dir, Unisys Ltd, 1986–87; Post Office: Corporate Finance Dir, 1987–89; Bd Mem. for Corporate Finance and Planning, 1989–93. *Publications:* contribs to financial jls. *Recreations:* tennis, fishing, walking. *Address:* Little Stanyard, 94 Potters Lane, Send, Woking, Surrey GU23 7AL. *T:* Woking (01483) 715138.

CLOSE, Roy Edwin, CBE 1973; Director General, British Institute of Management, 1976–85; *b* 11 March 1920; *s* of Bruce Edwin and Minnie Louise Close; *m* 1947, Olive Joan Forty; two *s. Educ:* Trinity County Sch., N London. Served Army, 1939–46; Para Regt and SAS, 1943–46 (Captain). Editorial Staff, The Times; Asst Editor, The Times Review of Industry, 1949–56; Executive, Booker McConnell GP; Dir, Bookers Sugar Estates, 1957–65; Directing Staff, Admin. Staff Coll., Henley, 1965; Industrial Adviser, NEDO, 1966–69; Industrial Dir, NEDO, 1969–73; MSc Univ. of Aston in Birmingham, 1973; Chm., Univ. of Aston Management Centre; Dean of Faculty of Management, 1973–76; Proprietor, Management Adv. Services, 1986–92. Director: Davies and Perfect, 1985–87; Flextech plc, 1985–87; Kepner Tregoe Ltd, 1986–89; Broad Street Group, 1986–91 (Chm., 1986–88). Chairman: Open Univ. Management Educn Sector Bd, 1984–87; Open Business Sch., 1984–87; Mem., Open Univ. Business Sch. Industrial and Professional Adv. Cttee, 1988–93 (Chm., 1988–90). Chm., Conservation Foundn, 1987– (Dir, 1986–). Mem. Council, Farm-Africa, 1987–92. CIMgt (FBIM 1979); FIIM (FIWM 1979); FRSA 1980. DUniv Open, 1987. *Publications:* various articles on industrial, economic subjects. *Recreations:* swimming, walking, reading, listening to music. *Address:* Cathedral Cottage, North Elmham, Dereham, Norfolk NR20 5JU. *Clubs:* Reform, Special Forces.

CLOTHIER, Sir Cecil (Montacute), KCB 1982; QC 1965; Chairman, Council on Tribunals, 1989–92; *b* 28 Aug. 1919; *s* of Hugh Montacute Clothier, Liverpool; *m* 1st, 1943, Mary Elizabeth (*d* 1984), *o d* of late Ernest Glover Bush; one *s* two *d*; 2nd, 1992, Diana Stevenson (*née* Durrant). *Educ:* Stonyhurst Coll.; Lincoln Coll., Oxford (BCL, MA; Hon. Fellow 1984). Served 1939–46, 51 (Highland) Div.; British Army Staff, Washington, DC; Hon. Lt-Col Royal Signals. Called to Bar, Inner Temple, 1950, Bencher, 1973.

Recorder of Blackpool, later of the Crown Court, 1965–78; Judge of Appeal, IoM, 1972–78. A Legal Assessor to Gen. Medical and Gen. Dental Councils, 1972–78; Mem., Royal Commn on NHS, 1976–78; Parly Comr for Admin, and Health Service Comr for England, Wales and Scotland, 1979–84; Chm., Police Complaints Authority, 1985–89; Mem., Sen. (formerly Top) Salaries Rev. Body, 1989–95; Vice-Pres., Interception of Communications Tribunal, 1986–; Chairman: Cttee on Ethics of Gene Therapy, 1990–92; Allitt Inquiry, 1993–94. Mem., Adv. Council, British Library, 1993–. John Snow Meml Lectr (Assoc. of Anaesthetists of GB and Ireland/Amer. Assoc. of Anaesthesiologists), 1981. Hon. Mem., Assoc. of Anaesthetists of GB and Ireland, 1987; Hon. FRPharmS 1990. Rock Carling Fellow, Nuffield Provincial Hosps Trust, 1987. Hon. LLD Hull, 1982. *Address:* 1 Temple Gardens, Temple, EC4Y 9BB.

CLOTHIER, Richard John; Chief Executive, Dalgety, since 1993; *b* 4 July 1945; *s* of J. Neil Clothier and Barbara Clothier; *m* 1972, Ingrid Hafner (*d* 1994); two *s*. *Educ:* Peterhouse, Zimbabwe; Univ. of Natal (BSc Agric.); Harvard (AMP). Milk Marketing Board, 1971–77; Dalgety Agriculture, 1977–88; Chief Exec., Pig Improvement Co., 1988–92. *Publication:* The Bundu Book, 1969. *Recreation:* yacht racing. *Address:* Dalgety, 100 George Street, W1H 5RH. *T:* 0171–486 0200. *Clubs:* Royal Thames Yacht, Royal Ocean Racing.

CLOUDSLEY-THOMPSON, Prof. John Leonard, MA, PhD (Cantab), DSc (London); FRES, FLS, FZS, CBiol, FWAAS; Professor of Zoology, Birkbeck College, University of London, 1972–86, now Emeritus (Reader 1971–72); *b* Murree, India, 23 May 1921; *s* of Dr Ashley George Gyton Thompson, MA, MD (Cantab), DPH, and Muriel Elaine (*née* Griffiths); *m* 1944, Jessie Anne Cloudsley, MCSP, DipBS, LCAD; three *s*. *Educ:* Marlborough Coll.; Pembroke Coll., Univ. of Cambridge. War of 1939–45: commissioned into 4th Queen's Own Hussars, 1941; transf. 4th Co. of Lond. Yeo. (Sharpshooters); N Africa, 1941–42 (severely wounded); Instructor (Capt.), Sandhurst, 1943; rejoined regt for D Day (escaped from Villers Bocage), Caen Offensive, etc, 1944 (Hon. rank of Capt. on resignation). Lectr in Zoology, King's Coll., Univ. of London, 1950–60; Prof. of Zoology, Univ. of Khartoum, and Keeper, Sudan Nat. Hist. Museum, 1960–71. Nat. Science Foundn Sen. Res. Fellow, Univ. of New Mexico, Albuquerque, USA, 1969; Visiting Professor: Univ. of Kuwait, 1978 and 1983; Univ. of Nigeria, Nsukka, 1981; Univ. of Qatar, 1986; Sultan Qaboos Univ., Muscat, 1988; Leverhulme Emeritus Fellow at UCL, 1987–89; Visiting Research Fellow: ANU, 1987; Desert Ecol. Res. Unit of Namibia, 1989. Hon. Consultant: Univ. of Malaya, 1969; Arabian Gulf Univ., Bahrain, 1986; Univ. of Kuwait, 1990; Indo-British Workshop on Biodiversity, 1993. Took part in: Cambridge Iceland Expedn, 1947; Expedn to Southern Tunisia, 1954; univ. expedns with his wife to various parts of Africa, 1960–73, incl. trans-Sahara crossing, 1967. Chairman: British Naturalists' Assoc., 1974–83 (Vice-Pres., 1985–); Biological Council, 1977–82 (Medal, 1985). President: British Arachnological Soc., 1982–85 (Vice-Pres., 1985–86); British Soc. for Chronobiology, 1985–87; Vice-President: Linnean Soc., 1975–76 and 1977–78; 1st World Congress of Herpetology, 1989. Hon. Member: Royal African Soc., 1969 (Medal, 1969); British Herpetological Soc., 1983 (Pres., 1991–March 96). Liveryman, Worshipful Co. of Skinners, 1952–. Silver Jubilee Gold Medal and Hon. DSc, Khartoum, 1981. Inst. of Biology K. S. S. Charter Award, 1981; J. H. Grundy Meml Medal, Royal Army Med. Coll., 1987; Foundn for Envmtl Conservation Prize, Geneva, 1989; Peter Scott Meml Award, British Naturalists' Assoc., 1993. Editor-in-Chief (formerly Editor) (assisted by wife), Jl of Arid Environments Vol. 1, 1978–; Editor: (with wife) Natural History of the Arabian Gulf (book series), 1981–82; Adaptations of Desert Organisms (book series), 1989–. *Publications:* Biology of Deserts (ed), 1954; Spiders, Scorpions, Centipedes and Mites, 1958 (2nd edn 1968); Animal Behaviour, 1960; Rhythmic Activity in Animal Physiology and Behaviour, 1961; Land Invertebrates (with John Sankey), 1961; Life in Deserts (with M. J. Chadwick), 1964; Desert Life, 1965; Animal Conflict and Adaptation, 1965; Animal Twilight: man and game in eastern Africa, 1967; Microecology, 1967; Zoology of Tropical Africa, 1969; The Temperature and Water Relations of Reptiles, 1971; Desert Life, 1974; Terrestrial Environments, 1975; Insects and History, 1976; Evolutionary Trends in the Mating of Arthropoda, 1976; (ed jtly) Environmental Physiology of Animals, 1976; Man and the Biology of Arid Zones, 1977; The Water and Temperature Relations of Woodlice, 1977; The Desert, 1977; Animal Migration, 1978; Why the Dinosaurs Became Extinct, 1978; Wildlife of the Desert, 1979; Biological Clocks: their functions in nature, 1980; Tooth and Claw: defensive strategies in the animal world, 1980; (ed) Sahara Desert, 1984; Guide to Woodlands, 1985; Evolution and Adaptation of Terrestrial Arthropods, 1988; Ecophysiology of Desert Arthropods and Reptiles, 1991; The Diversity of Desert Life, 1993; (novel) The Nile Quest, 1994; Predation and Defence Amongst Reptiles, 1994; contribs to Encyclopædia Britannica, Encyclopedia Americana; shorter monographs and eleven children's books; many scientific articles in learned jls, etc. *Recreations:* music (especially opera), photography, travel. *Address:* 10 Battishill Street, N1 1TE.

CLOUGH, Alan; *see* Clough, J. A.

CLOUGH, (Arthur) Gordon; broadcaster and writer, freelance since 1973; *b* 26 Aug. 1934; *s* of late James Stanley Gordon Clough and Annie Clough; *m* 1959, Carolyn Stafford (marr. diss. 1991; remarried 1994); one *s* three *d*. *Educ:* Bolton Sch., Bolton, Lancs; Magdalen Coll., Oxford (William Doncaster Schol.; BA Mod Langs, French and Russian). National Service, RN, 1953–55. BBC: Studio Man., 1958–60; Russian Service, 1960–68 (Prog. Organiser, 1963–68); Radio News Features, Sen. Duty Ed., 1968–73; 1973–: freelance presenter, World at One, PM, World this Weekend, Europhile; co-chm. and question setter, Round Britain Quiz, Round Europe Quiz and Transatlantic Quiz; presenter, Twentyfour Hours, BBC World Service. Writer/Reporter for many documentary progs for BBC Radio Four and World Service, notably: Let there be No More War, 1985; Revolution Without Shots, 1987; The Indissoluble Union, 1989 (Sony Award, Best Documentary Feature, Current Affairs, 1990); Whose shall be the Land?, 1990; Death of a Superpower, 1991; Ashes of Empire, 1991. Sony Award, Best Current Affairs Prog., World this Weekend,1984. *Publications:* translations from Russian: Years off my Life, General A. V. Gorbatov, (with Tony Cash), 1964; The Ordeal, V. Bykov, 1972; Hostages, G. Svirsky, 1976; The Yawning Heights, A. Zinoviev, 1979; The Radiant Future, A. Zinoviev, 1981; translations from French: The Elusive Revolution, Raymond Aron, 1971; The Art of the Surrealists, A. Alexandrian, 1972; (with Peter Sadecky) Octobriana, Progressive Political Pornography, 1972; occasional articles in The Listener, etc. *Recreations:* cooking, crossword puzzles, coarse chess. *Address:* 52 Ellerton Road, SW18 3NN. *T:* 0181–874 6514.

CLOUGH, (John) Alan, CBE 1972; MC 1945; Chairman, British Mohair Holdings plc (formerly British Mohair Spinners Ltd), 1980–84 (Deputy Chairman, 1970–80, Chief Executive, 1977–80, Joint Managing Director, 1980–83); *b* 20 March 1924; *s* of late John Clough and Yvonne (*née* Dollfus); *m* 1st, 1949, Margaret Joy Catton (marr. diss.); one *s* two *d*; 2nd, 1961, Mary Cowan Catherwood; one *s* one *d*. *Educ:* Marlborough Coll.; Leeds Univ. HM Forces, Queen's Bays, 1942–47, N Africa and Italy (Captain); TA Major, Yorkshire Hussars, 1947–55. Mayor, Co. of Merchants of Staple of England, 1969–70. Chairman: Wool Industries Res. Assoc., 1967–69; Wool Textile Delegn, 1969–72; Textile Res. Council, 1984–89; Member: Wool Textile EDC, 1967–72; Jt Textile Cttee, NEDO, 1972–74; President: Comitextil (Co-ordinating Cttee for Textile Industries in EEC), Brussels, 1975–77; British Textile Confedn, 1974–77; Textile Inst., 1979–81; Confedn of British Wool Textiles, 1982–84. Chm., Instant Muscle Ltd, 1989–94. CompTI 1975. Hon. DSc Bradford, 1987. *Recreations:* fishing, gardening, travel. *Address:* The Hays, Monks Eleigh, Suffolk IP7 7AE. *T:* Bildeston (01449) 740364. *Club:* Boodle's.

CLOUGH, Philip Gerard; Justice of Appeal, Hong Kong, 1986–92; *b* 11 March 1924; *s* of Gerard Duncombe Clough and Grace Margaret (*née* Phillips); *m* 1st, Mary Elizabeth Carter (marr. diss.); one *s*; 2nd, Margaret Joy Davies; one *s* one *d*. *Educ:* Dauntsey's Sch.; King's Coll., Cambridge (Exhibnr; MA). War service, Sub Lieut (A) RNVR, 1942–46. Called to the Bar, Inner Temple, 1949; Colonial Legal Service: Federal Counsel, Malaya, 1951–58; Chancery Bar, Lincoln's Inn, 1958–78; Legal Affairs Advr, Brunei, 1978–81; Dist Judge, Hong Kong, 1981–83; High Court Judge, Hong Kong, 1983–86. *Address:* Laurel House, Chapel Lane, Urchfont, Devizes, Wiltshire SN10 4QY. *T:* Devizes (01380) 840233, *Fax:* (01380) 840025. *Clubs:* Garrick; Hong Kong.

CLOUGH, Prunella; painter; *b* 1919; *d* of Eric Clough Taylor, poet and civil servant, and Thora Clough Taylor. *Educ:* privately; Chelsea Sch. of Art. Exhibited at Leger Gallery, 1947; Roland Browse & Delbanco, 1949; Leicester Galleries, 1953; Whitechapel Gallery, 1960; Grosvenor Gallery, 1964, 1968; Graves Art Gallery, Sheffield, 1972; New Art Centre, 1975, 1979; Serpentine Gallery, 1976; Warwick Arts Trust, 1982; Annely Juda Fine Art, 1989, 1993. City of London Midsummer Prize, 1977. *Address:* 19 Sherbrooke Road, SW6 7HX.

CLOUTMAN, Air Vice-Marshal Geoffrey William, CB 1980; FDSRCS; Director of Dental Services, Royal Air Force, 1977–80; *b* 1 April 1920; *s* of Rev. Walter Evans Cloutman and Dora Cloutman; *m* 1949, Sylvia Brown; three *d*. *Educ:* Cheltenham Grammar Sch.; Queen Mary Coll., and The London Hosp., Univ. of London. LDSRCS 1942, FDSRCS 1954. House Surg., London Hosp., 1942; joined RAFVR, 1942; War Service, UK and India; specialisation in preventive dentistry, 1948–55; dental hygiene trng; oral surgery appts, 1955–73: RAF Hosps, Fayid, Akrotiri, Aden, Wegberg, Wroughton, Uxbridge; Principal Dental Off., Strike Comd, 1973; QHDS, 1976–80. *Publications:* papers in Brit. Dental Jl and Dental Practitioner. *Recreations:* English church music, cricket, Rugby, Wells Cathedral (Sub-Deacon, 1984–), history of Wells Cathedral and Bishop's Palace. *Address:* Ivy Cottage, 27 Millers Gardens, Wells, Somerset BA5 2TN. *T:* Wells (01749) 679477.

CLOWES, A. W.; General Secretary, Ceramic and Allied Trades Union, 1980–95; *b* 17 Dec. 1931. Joined the Industry on leaving school; Asst Gen. Sec., Ceramic and Allied Trades Union, 1975–80.

CLUCAS, Sir Kenneth (Henry), KCB 1976 (CB 1969); Permanent Secretary, Department of Trade, 1979–82; Chairman, Nuffield Foundation Committee of Inquiry into Pharmacy, 1983–86; *b* 18 Nov. 1921; *o s* of late Rev. J. H. Clucas and Ethel Clucas (*née* Sim); *m* 1960, Barbara (*d* 1993), *e d* of Rear-Adm. R. P. Hunter, USN (Retd), Washington, DC; two *d*. *Educ:* Kingswood Sch.; Emmanuel Coll., Cambridge. Royal Signals, 1941–46 (despatches). Joined Min. of Labour as Asst Principal, 1948; 2nd Sec. (Labour), British Embassy, Cairo, 1950; Principal, HM Treasury, 1952; Min. of Labour, 1954; Private Sec. to Minister, 1960–62; Asst Sec., 1962; Under-Sec., 1966–68; Sec., Nat. Bd for Prices and Incomes, 1968–71; First Civil Service Comr, and Dep. Sec., CSD, 1971–73; Dep. Sec., DTI, 1974; Permanent Sec., Dept of Prices and Consumer Protection, 1974–79. Member: Council on Tribunals, 1983–89; Adv. Panel, Freedom of Information Campaign, 1984–; RIPA Wkg Gp on Politics and the Civil Service, 1985–86; Chairman: Cttee of Inquiry into Advertising Controls, 1986–87; Monitoring Cttee, ABI Code of Practice, 1989–93; FIMBRA, 1993– (Mem. Council, 1986–); Dep. Chm., CIBA Foundn Media Resource Steering Cttee, 1984–93; Chm., Lloyd's Wkg Pty on Consumer Guarantees, 1985; Lloyd's Members Ombudsman, 1988–94. Chm., Nat. Assoc. of Citizens' Advice Bureaux, 1984–89 (Vice Chm., 1983–84; Chm. Surrey and W Sussex Area Cttee, 1982–84); Mem. Management Cttee, Godalming CAB, 1982–85; Vice Pres., and Chm. of Trustees, Friends of CAB, 1991–95. FRSA. Hon. FRPharmS, 1989. *Recreations:* walking, theatre, opera, composing and solving puzzles. *Address:* Cariad, Knoll Road, Godalming, Surrey GU7 2EL. *T:* Godalming (01483) 416430.

CLUCKIE, Prof. Ian David, CEng, FIWEM; FICE; Professor of Water Resources, since 1988 and Chairman, Department of Civil Engineering, since 1991, University of Salford; Director, Telford Research Institute, since 1993; *b* Edinburgh, 20 July 1949; *s* of late William Cluckie and Doreen Cluckie (*née* Michael); *m* 1972, Linda Fox; one *s* one *d*. *Educ:* Penlan Sch., Swansea; Univ. of Surrey (BSc); Univ. of Birmingham (MSc, PhD). CEng, FIWEM 1983; FICE 1988; FRMetS 1979. Trainee Engr, W. S. Atkins, Swansea, 1966–72; Central Water Planning Unit, Reading, 1974–76; Lectr, Univ. of Birmingham, 1976–88. Acad. Dir, Salford Civil Engineering Ltd, 1989–. Natural Environment Research Council: Mem., AAPS Res. Grants and Trng Awards Cttee, 1988–91; Chm., AAPS Cttee, 1991–94; Mem., Terrestrial and Freshwater Scis, Marine Scis, Atmospheric Scis and Higher Educn Affairs Cttees, 1991–94. FRSA 1993. *Publications:* (with C. G. Collier) Hydrological Applications of Weather Radar, 1991; Stochastic Hydraulics, 1994; (with E. M. Wilson) Engineering Hydrology, 5th edn 1995; contribs to learned jls. *Recreations:* sailing, hill walking, gardening. *Address:* Yhelt Cottage, Waterswallows Road, Fairfield, Buxton, Derbys SK17 7EN. *T:* Buxton (01298) 71408.

CLUFF, John Gordon, (Algy); Chairman, since 1979, and Chief Executive, since 1971, Cluff Resources (formerly Cluff Oil); Chairman, The Spectator, since 1985 (Proprietor, 1981–85); *b* 19 April 1940; *s* of late Harold Cluff and of Freda Cluff, Waldeshare House, Waldeshare, Kent; *m* 1993, Blondel Hodge, Anguilla, WI; one *s*. *Educ:* Stowe Sch. 2/Lieut, Grenadier Guards, 1959; Captain, Guards Independent Parachute Co., 1963; served W Africa, Cyprus, Malaysia, retd 1964. Trustee, Anglo-Hong Kong Trust, 1989–. Gov., Commonwealth Inst., 1994–. *Address:* 58 St James's Street, SW1A 1LD; Clova House, Lumsden, West Aberdeenshire AB5 4YJ. *T:* Rhynie (014646) 331. *Clubs:* White's, Boodle's, Beefsteak, Pratt's; Royal St George's (Sandwich); Travellers' (Paris); Rand (Johannesburg).

CLUTTERBUCK, Vice-Adm. Sir David Granville, KBE 1968; CB 1965; *b* Gloucester, 25 Jan. 1913; *m* 1937, Rose Mere Vaile, Auckland, NZ; two *d*. Joined RN, 1929. Served War of 1939–45 (despatches twice): navigating officer of cruisers HMS Ajax, 1940–42, HMS Newfoundland, 1942–46 (present Japanese surrender at Tokyo). Subsequently commanded destroyers Sluys and Cadiz, 1952–53; Naval Attaché at British Embassy, Bonn; Capt. (D) of Third Training Squadron in HMS Zest, Londonderry, 1956–58; commanded cruiser HMS Blake, 1960–62; Chief of Staff to C-in-C Home Fleet and C-in-C Allied Forces Eastern Atlantic, 1963–66; Rear-Adm., 1963; Vice-Adm. 1966; Dep. Supreme Allied Comdr, Atlantic, 1966–68. *Address:* Burrard Cottage, Walhampton, Lymington, Hampshire SO41 5SA. *Clubs:* Army and Navy; Royal Lymington Yacht.

CLUTTERBUCK, Maj.-Gen. Richard Lewis, CB 1971; OBE 1958; writer, lecturer and broadcaster; *b* London, 22 Nov. 1917; *s* of late Col L. St J. R. Clutterbuck, OBE, late

RA, and late Mrs I. J. Clutterbuck; *m* 1948, Angela Muriel Barford; three *s*. *Educ:* Radley Coll.; Pembroke Coll., Cambridge. MA Cantab (Mech. Scis); PhD (Econ. and Pol.), London Univ., 1971. Commd in RE, 1937; War Service: France, 1940; Sudan and Ethiopia, 1941; Western Desert, 1941–43; Italy, 1944; subseq. service in: Germany, 1946 and 1951–53; Italy, 1946; Palestine, 1947; Malaya, 1956–58; Christmas Island (Nuclear Trials), 1958; USA, 1961–63; Singapore, 1966–68. Instructor, British Army Staff Coll., 1953–56; Instructor, US Army Staff Coll., 1961–63; idc 1965; Chief Engr, Far East Land Forces, 1966–68; Engr-in-Chief (Army), 1968–70; Chief Army Instructor, Royal Coll. of Defence Studies, 1971–72, retired. Col Comdt, RE, 1972–77. Sen. Lectr and Reader, Dept of Politics, Univ. of Exeter, 1972–83. FICE. *Publications:* Across the River (as Richard Jocelyn), 1957; The Long Long War, 1966; Protest and the Urban Guerrilla, 1973; Riot and Revolution in Singapore and Malaya, 1973; Living with Terrorism, 1975; Guerrillas and Terrorists, 1977; Britain in Agony, 1978, rev. edn 1980; Kidnap and Ransom, 1978; The Media and Political Violence, 1981, rev. edn 1983; Industrial Conflict and Democracy, 1984; Conflict and Violence in Singapore and Malaysia, 1985; The Future of Political Violence, 1986; Kidnap, Hijack and Extortion, 1987; Terrorism and Guerrilla Warfare, 1990; Terrorism, Drugs and Crime in Europe after 1992, 1990; International Crisis and Conflict, 1993; Terrorism in an Unstable World, 1994; Drugs, Crime and Corruption, 1995; contribs to British and US jls. *Address:* Department of Politics, University of Exeter, Exeter EX4 4RJ. *Clubs:* Commonwealth Trust, Army and Navy.

CLUTTON, Rafe Henry, CBE 1992; FRICS; Consultant to Cluttons, Chartered Surveyors, London, since 1992 (Partner, 1955–92); *b* 13 June 1929; *s* of late Robin John Clutton and Rosalie Muriel (*née* Birch); *m* 1954, Jill Olwyn Evans; four *s* one *d*. *Educ:* Tonbridge Sch., Kent. FRICS 1959. Director: Legal & General Group PLC (formerly Legal & General Assurance Soc. Ltd), 1972–93; Rodamco (UK) BV (formerly Haslemere Estates), 1990–. Member: Royal National Theatre Bd, 1976–93; Salvation Army London Adv. Bd, 1971–; Royal Commn for Exhibn of 1851, 1988–. Governor, Royal Foundn of Grey Coat Hosp., 1967– (Chm., 1981–). FRSA 1990. *Recreations:* grandchildren, books, admiring the view. *Address:* Fairfield, North Chailey, Sussex BN8 4DH. *T:* Newick (01825) 722431. *Club:* Royal Thames Yacht.

CLUTTON-BROCK, Prof. Timothy Hugh, PhD; ScD; FRS 1993; Professor of Animal Ecology, University of Cambridge, since 1994 (Reader, 1991–94); *b* 13 Aug. 1946; *s* of Hugh Alan Clutton-Brock and Eileen Mary Stableforth; *m* 1980, Dafila Kathleen Scott; one *s* one *d*. *Educ:* Rugby Sch.; Magdalene Coll., Cambridge (BA, MA, PhD, ScD). NERC res. fellowship, Animal Behaviour Res. Gp, Oxford, 1972; Lectr in Ethology, Univ. of Sussex, 1973; Cambridge University: Sen. Res. Fellow in Behavioural Ecology, King's Coll., 1976; SERC Advanced Fellow, Dept of Zoology, 1981; Royal Soc. Res. Fellow in Biology, 1983; Lectr in Zoology, 1987–91. Chm., IUCN Deer Specialist Gp, 1980–. Jt Editor, Princeton Monographs in Behavioral Ecology, 1982–. Scientific Medal, Zoological Soc. of London, 1984; Hart Merriam Award, Mammal Soc. of America, 1991. *Publications:* (ed) Primate Ecology, 1977; (ed) Readings in Sociobiology, 1978; Red Deer: the behaviour and ecology of two sexes, 1982; (ed) Rhum, Natural History of an Island, 1987; (ed) Reproductive Success, 1988; Red Deer in the Highlands, 1989; The Evolution of Parental Care, 1991; approx. 100 sci. papers on animal behaviour, ecology and evolution in Nature, Jl Animal Ecol., Evolution, Amer. Naturalist, Jl of Zoology, Animal Behaviour, Behaviour, Behavioral Ecol. and Sociobiol., Folia Primatologica and other jls. *Recreations:* bird watching, fish watching, fishing. *Address:* White Roses, Reach, Cambridgeshire CB5 0JQ; Department of Zoology, Downing Street, Cambridge CB2 3EJ. *T:* Cambridge (01223) 336600.

CLWYD, 3rd Baron *cr* 1919; **John Anthony Roberts;** Bt 1908; *b* 2 Jan. 1935; *s* of 2nd Baron Clwyd and Joan de Bois (*d* 1985); *d* of late Charles R. Murray; *S* father, 1987; *m* 1969, Geraldine, *yr d* of Charles Eugene Cannons, Sanderstead; three *s*. *Educ:* Harrow; Trinity College, Cambridge. Called to the Bar, Gray's Inn, 1970. *Heir:* *s* Hon. John Murray Roberts, *b* 27 Aug. 1971. *Address:* 24 Salisbury Avenue, Cheam, Sutton, Surrey SM1 2DJ.

CLWYD, Ann; journalist and broadcaster; MP (Lab) Cynon Valley, since May 1984; *b* 21 March 1937; *d* of Gwilym Henri Lewis and Elizabeth Ann Lewis; *m* 1963, Owen Dryhurst Roberts, TV director and producer. *Educ:* Halkyn Primary Sch.; Holywell Grammar Sch.; The Queen's Sch., Chester; University Coll., Bangor. Former: Student-teacher, Hope Sch., Flintshire; BBC Studio Manager; freelance reporter, producer; Welsh corresp., The Guardian and The Observer, 1964–79; Vice-Chm., Welsh Arts Council, 1975–79. Member: Welsh Hospital Board, 1970–74; Cardiff Community Health Council, 1975–79; Royal Commn on NHS, 1976–79; Working Party, report, Organisation of Out-Patient Care, for Welsh Hosp. Bd; Working Party, Bilingualism in the Hospital Service; Labour Party Study Gp., People and the Media; Arts Council of Gt Britain, 1975–80; Chm., Cardiff Anti-Racialism Cttee, 1978–80; Labour Party NEC, 1983–84. Chm., Labour back bench cttee on Health and Social Security, 1985–87; Vice-Chm., Labour back bench cttee on Defence, 1985–87; Opposition front bench spokesperson on women, 1987–88, on educn, 1987–88, on overseas develt and co-operation, 1989–92, on Wales, 1992, on Nat. Heritage, 1992–93, on employment, 1993–94, on foreign affairs, 1994–95; Mem., Shadow Cabinet, 1989–93. Member: NUJ; TGWU. Contested (Lab): Denbigh, 1970; Gloucester, Oct. 1974; Mem. (Lab) Mid and West Wales, European Parlt, 1979–84. *Address:* 6 Deans Court, Dean Street, Aberdare, Mid Glam CF44 7BN. *T:* Aberdare (01685) 871394.

CLYDE, Hon. Lord; James John Clyde; a Senator of the College of Justice in Scotland, since 1985; *b* 29 Jan. 1932; *s* of Rt Hon. Lord Clyde; *m* 1963, Ann Clunie Hoblyn; two *s*. *Educ:* Edinburgh Academy; Corpus Christi Coll., Oxford (BA); Edinburgh Univ. (LLB). Called to Scottish Bar, 1959; QC (Scot.) 1971; Advocate-Depute, 1973–74. Chancellor to Bishop of Argyll and the Isles, 1972–85; a Judge of the Courts of Appeal of Jersey and Guernsey, 1979–85. Chairman: Med. Appeal Tribunal, 1974–85; Cttee of Investigation for Scotland on Agricl Mktg, 1984–85; Scottish Valuation Adv. Council, 1987– (Mem., 1972–). Mem., UK Delegn to CCBE, 1978–84 (Leader, 1981–84). Hon. Pres., Scottish Young Lawyers' Assoc., 1988–; Vice-Pres., Royal Blind Asylum and Sch., 1987–; Assessor to Chancellor, 1989–, Vice-Chm., 1993–, Court of Edinburgh Univ. Dir, Edinburgh Acad., 1979–88; Trustee: St Mary's Music Sch., 1976–92; Nat. Library of Scotland, 1977–93; Chm. of Govs, St George's Sch. for Girls, 1989–; Gov., Napier Polytechnic, 1989–93. DUniv Heriot-Watt, 1991. *Publication:* (ed jtly) Armour on Valuation, 3rd edn, 1961, 5th edn, 1985. *Recreations:* music, gardening. *Address:* 9 Heriot Row, Edinburgh EH3 6HU. *T:* 0131–556 7114. *Club:* New (Edinburgh).

CLYDESMUIR, 2nd Baron *cr* 1948, of Braidwood; **Ronald John Bilsland Colville,** KT 1972; CB 1965; MBE 1944; TD; Lord High Commissioner to the General Assembly, Church of Scotland, 1971 and 1972; Lord-Lieutenant, Lanarkshire, 1963–92; a Captain, Royal Company of Archers, Queen's Body Guard for Scotland, 1985–88, Captain General since 1988; *b* 21 May 1917; *s* of 1st Baron Clydesmuir, PC, GCIE, TD, and Agnes Anne (*d* 1970), CI 1947, Kaisar-i-Hind Gold Medal; *S* father, 1954; *m* 1946, Joan Marguerita, *d* of Lt-Col E. B. Booth, DSO, Darver Castle, Co. Louth; two *s* two *d*. *Educ:* Charterhouse; Trinity Coll., Cambridge. Served in The Cameronians (Scottish Rifles), 1939–45 (MBE, despatches). Commanded 6/7th Bn The Cameronians, TA, 1953–56. Director: Colvilles Ltd, 1958–70; British Linen Bank (Governor, 1966–71); Bank of Scotland (Dep. Governor, 1971–72, Governor, 1972–81); Scottish Provident Instn, 1954–88; Scotbits Securities Ltd, 1960–78; The Scottish Western Investment Co., 1965–78; BSC Strip Mills Div., 1970–73; Caledonian Offshore Co. Ltd, 1971–87; Barclays Bank, 1972–82; Chm., North Sea Assets Ltd, 1972–87. President: Scottish Council (Development and Industry), 1978–86 (Chm., Exec. Cttee, 1966–78); Scottish Council of Physical Recreation, 1964–72; Scottish Br., National Playing Fields Assoc.; Chm., Council, Territorial, Auxiliary and Volunteer Reserve Assocs, 1969–73, Pres., 1974–81; Chm., Lanarkshire T&AFA, 1957–63, Pres. 1963–68; Pres., Lowland TA&VRA. Hon. Colonel: 6th/7th (Territorial) Bn, The Cameronians (Scottish Rifles), 1967–71; 52 Lowland Volunteers, T&AVR, 1970–75. Chm., Scottish Outward Bound Assoc. Trustee, MacRobert Trusts. DL Lanarkshire, 1955, Vice-Lieut, 1959–63. Hon. LLD Strathclyde, 1968; Hon. DSc Heriot-Watt, 1971. *Recreations:* shooting, fishing. *Heir:* *s* Hon. David Ronald Colville [*b* 8 April 1949; *m* 1978, Aline Frances, *er d* of Peter Merriam, Holton Lodge, Holton St Mary, Suffolk; one *s* two *d*]. *Address:* Langlees House, Biggar, Lanarkshire ML12 6NP. *T:* Biggar (01899) 20057. *Club:* New (Edinburgh).

See also Captain N. E. F. Dalrymple Hamilton.

COADY, Aubrey William Burleton, CMG 1959; Chairman, Electricity Commission of NSW, 1959–75 (Member, 1950–75); *b* Singleton, NSW, 15 June 1915; *s* of W. A. Coady, Belmont; *m* 1964, Phyllis K., *d* of late G. W. Mathews. *Educ:* Newcastle High Sch.; Sydney Univ. (BA, BEc). Under-Sec. and Comptroller of Accounts, NSW Treasury, 1955–59. *Address:* 42 Rickard Avenue, Mosman, NSW 2088, Australia.

COAKLEY, Prof. Sarah Anne; Professor of Christian Theology, Harvard University, since 1993; *b* 10 Sept. 1951; *d* of Frank Robert Furber, *qv* and Anne Wilson Furber; *m* 1975, Dr James Farwell Coakley; two *d*. *Educ:* Blackheath High Sch.; New Hall, Cambridge (MA, PhD); Harvard Divinity Sch. (ThM). Harkness Fellow, 1973–75; Univ. Lectr in Religious Studies, 1976–90, Sen. Lectr, 1990–91, Lancaster Univ.; Tutorial Fellow in Theology, Oriel Coll., and Univ. Lectr in Theology, Oxford, 1991–93. Select Preacher, Oxford Univ., 1991; Hulsean Lectr, Cambridge Univ., 1991–92; Henry Luce III Fellow, 1994–95. Consultant to C of E Doctrine Commn, 1982–84, Mem., 1984–92. *Publications:* Christ Without Absolutes: a study of the Christology of Ernst Troeltsch, 1988; (ed with David A. Pailin) The Making and Remaking of Christian Doctrine, 1993; contrib. to C of E reports and to theol. jls. *Recreations:* musical activities. *Address:* Harvard Divinity School, 45 Francis Avenue, Cambridge, MA 02138, USA.

COALES, Prof. John Flavell, CBE 1974 (OBE 1945); FRS 1970; FEng; Professor of Engineering, Cambridge University, 1965–74, now Emeritus; Fellow of Clare Hall, 1964–74, now Emeritus; *b* 14 Sept. 1907; *s* of John Dennis Coales and Marion Beatrice Coales (*née* Flavell); *m* 1936, Mary Dorothea Violet, *d* of Rev. Guthrie Henry Lewis Alison; two *s* two *d*. *Educ:* Berkhamsted Sch.; Sidney Sussex Coll., Cambridge (MA; ScD 1985). Admty Dept of Scientific Res., 1929–46; Res. Dir, Elliott Bros (London) Ltd, 1946; Engrg Dept, Cambridge Univ.: Asst Dir of Res., 1953; Lectr, 1956; Reader in Engrg, 1958; Prof., 1965. Part-time Mem., E Electricity Bd, 1967–73. Director: Tube Investments Technological Centre, 1955–60; TI R&D Bd, 1960–65; BSA Metal Components, 1967–73; BSA Gp Res. Bd (Dep. Chm.), 1967–73; Delta Materials Research Ltd, 1974–77. Mackay Vis. Prof. of Electrical Engrg, Univ. of Calif., Berkeley, 1963. Internat. Fedn of Automatic Control: MEC, 1957; Vice-Pres., 1961; Pres., 1963. Brit. Conf. on Automation and Computation: Gp B Vice-Chm., 1958; Chm., 1960. UK Automation Council: Chm. Res. and Develt Panel, 1960–63; Chm. For. Relations Panel, 1960–64; Vice-Chm., 1961–63; Chm., 1963–66. Instn of Electrical Engrs: Mem. Council, 1953–55, 1964–77; Chm., Measurement Section, 1953; Chm., Control and Automation Div., 1965, etc; Vice-Pres., 1966–71; Pres., 1971–72. Council of Engineering Institutions: Vice-Chm., 1974; Chm., 1975 (Mem. Council for Envtl Sci. and Engrg, 1973–76); Chm., Commonwealth Bd for Engrg Educn and Training, 1976–80; Pres., World Environment and Resources Council, 1973–74. Pres., Soc. of Instrument Technology, 1958. Member: Gen. Bd and Exec. Cttee of Nat. Physical Laboratory, 1959–64; Adv. Council, RMCS, 1963–73; Educn Adv. Cttee for RAF, 1967–76; Trng and Educn Adv. Cttee of RAF, 1976–79; Court of Cranfield Inst. of Technology, 1970–82; Governing Body, Nat. Inst. of Agric. Engrg, 1970–75; Envtl Design and Engrg Res. Cttee, DoE Bldg Res. Estab., 1973–76; British Council Sci. Adv. Cttee, 1973–75; Engrg and Bldgs Bd, ARC, 1973–77; British Library Adv. Council, 1975–81; Chm., IFAC Pubns Managing Bd, 1976–87. Governor: Hatfield Coll. of Technology, 1951–68; Hatfield Polytechnic, 1969–70 (Hon. Fellow, 1971–). FICE, FIEE (Pres., IEE, 1971–72; Hon. FIEE 1985), FIEEE, FInstP; Founder Fellow, Fellowship of Engineering, 1976 (Mem., Exec. Cttee and Chm., Activities Cttee, 1976–80); Hon. Mem., Inst. of Measurement and Control, 1971. For. Mem., Serbian Acad. of Scis, 1981. Hon. DSc City Univ., 1970; Hon. DTech Loughborough, 1977; Hon. DEng Sheffield, 1978. Harold Hartley Medal, 1971; Giorgio Quazza Medal, IFAC, 1981 (first recipient); Honda Prize, 1982. *Publications:* (ed) Automatic and Remote Control (Proc. First Congr. of Internat. Fedn of Automatic Control), 1961; original papers on radio direction finding, radar, information theory, magnetic amplifiers, automatic control, automation and technical education. *Recreations:* mountaineering, gardening. *Address:* 14 Chesterford House, Southacre Drive, Cambridge CB2 2TZ. *Clubs:* Athenæum, Alpine.

COASE, Prof. Ronald Harry, DSc; Professor Emeritus and Senior Fellow in Law and Economics, University of Chicago, since 1982; *b* 29 Dec. 1910; *s* of Henry Joseph Coase and Rosalie Elizabeth (*née* Giles); *m* 1937, Marian Ruth Hartung. *Educ:* Kilburn Grammar Sch.; LSE (BCom 1932; DSc Econ 1951). Assistant Lecturer: Dundee Sch. of Econs, 1932–34; Univ. of Liverpool, 1934–35; later Lectr, then Reader, LSE, 1935–40, 1946–51; War service: Hd of Statistical Div., Forestry Commn, 1940–41; Statistician, later Chief Statistician, Central Statistical Office, Offices of War Cabinet, 1941–46; Professor: Univ. of Buffalo, 1951–58; Univ. of Virginia, 1958–64; Clifford R. Musser Prof., Univ. of Chicago Law Sch., 1964–82. Fellow, Amer. Acad. of Arts and Scis, 1978; Dist. Fellow, Amer. Econ. Assoc., 1980; Membre Titulaire, European Acad., 1992; Corresp. Fellow, British Acad., 1985; Hon. Fellow, LSE. Hon. doctorates: Dr rer. pol. Cologne, 1988; DSocSc Yale, 1989; LLD Washington, St Louis, 1991; LLD Dundee, 1992. Nobel Prize for Economics, 1991. *Publications:* British Broadcasting: a study in monopoly, 1950; The Firm, the Market and the Law, 1988; Essays on Economics and Economists, 1994. *Address:* University of Chicago Law School, 1111 East 60th Street, Chicago, IL 60637, USA.

COATES, Sir Anthony Robert M.; *see* Milnes Coates.

COATES, David; HM Diplomatic Service; Head, Joint Assistance Unit, Central and Eastern Europe, Foreign and Commonwealth Office, since 1993; *b* 13 Nov. 1947; *s* of Matthew Coates and late Margaret Ann Davies Coates (*née* Ross); *m* 1974, Joanna Kay Weil; two *d*. *Educ:* Dame Allan's Boys' Sch., Newcastle; Univ. of Bristol (BA Hist.); Univ. of Hawaii; Joint Univ. Centre, Taiwan. FCO, 1974–77; language training, Hong Kong, 1977–78; First Sec., Peking, 1978–81; Iran Desk, FCO, 1981–83; Asst Head, S America Dept, 1983–86; First Sec., UKMIS, Geneva, 1986–89; Counsellor and Head, Political

Section, Peking, 1989–92. *Recreations:* ski-ing, theatre, hill-walking, leeks. *Address:* c/o Foreign and Commonwealth Office, SW1A 2AH.

COATES, Sir David (Charlton Frederick), 3rd Bt *cr* 1921, of Haypark, City of Belfast; *b* 16 Feb. 1948; *o s* of Sir Frederick Gregory Lindsay Coates, 2nd Bt and of Joan Nugent, *d* of Maj.-Gen. Sir Charlton Spinks, KBE, DSO; *S* father, 1994; *m* 1973, Christine Helen, *d* of Lewis F. Marshall; two *s*. *Educ:* Millfield. *Heir: s* James Gregory David Coates, *b* 12 March 1977. *Address:* 30 Hauxton Road, Little Shelford, Cambs CB2 5HJ.

COATES, David Randall; Chief Economic Adviser, Department of Trade and Industry, since 1990; *b* 22 March 1942. *Educ:* Leeds Grammar Sch.; Queen's Coll., Oxford; LSE. Res. Assistant, Univ. of Manchester and Manchester Business Sch., 1966–68; Economic Advr, Min. of Technology and DTI, 1968–74; Sen. Economic Advr, Dept of Trade and DTI, 1974–82; Asst Sec., DTI, 1982–89; Grade 3, DTI, 1989. *Recreations:* family, gardening, travel, music. *Address:* Department of Trade and Industry, Ashdown House, 123 Victoria Street, SW1E 6RB. *T:* 0171–215 6059.

COATES, Dudley James; Director of Regional Services (formerly of Regional Management), Ministry of Agriculture, Fisheries and Food, since 1989; *b* 15 Sept. 1946; *o s* of Edward Coates and late Margot Coates; *m* 1969, Dr Jean Walsingham; two *d*. *Educ:* Westcliff High School for Boys; Univ. of Sussex (BA (Hons)). Joined MAFF as Asst Principal, 1968; Second Sec., UK Delegn to the EC, Brussels, 1970–72; Principal, MAFF, 1973; Lectr, Civil Service Coll., 1978–81; Head of Animal Health Div. II, 1981–83, Head of Financial Management Team, 1983–87, MAFF; Dir Gen. of Corporate Services, Intervention Bd for Agricultural Produce, 1987–89. Methodist local preacher, 1970–; Member: Methodist Conf., 1988, 1989, 1993–; Ministries Bd, 1989–; Stationing Cttee, 1991–. *Publication:* (contrib.) Policies into Practice (ed David Lewis and Helen Wallace), 1984. *Recreations:* Christian activities, cycling, singing. *Address:* Ministry of Agriculture, Fisheries and Food, Nobel House, 17 Smith Square, SW1P 3JR. *T:* 0171–238 6717.

COATES, Prof. Geoffrey Edward, MA, DSc; Professor of Chemistry, University of Wyoming, 1968–79, now Emeritus; *b* 14 May 1917; *er s* of Prof. Joseph Edward Coates, OBE; *m* 1951, Winifred Jean Hobbs; one *s* one *d*. *Educ:* Clifton Coll.; Queen's Coll., Oxford. Research Chemist, Magnesium Metal Corp., 1940–45; Univ. of Bristol: Lecturer in Chemistry, 1945–53; Sub-Warden of Wills Hall, 1946–51; Prof. of Chemistry, Univ. of Durham, 1953–68. *Publications:* Organo-metallic Compounds (monograph), 1956, 3rd edn (2 vols), 1967–68; Principles of Organometallic Chemistry, 1968; papers in scientific journals. *Address:* 1801 Rainbow Avenue, Laramie, WY 82070–4318, USA. *Club:* Commonwealth Trust.

See also J. F. Coates.

COATES, James Richard, CB 1992; Under Secretary, Urban and Local Transport Directorate, Department of Transport, 1994; *b* 18 Oct. 1935; *s* of William Richard Coates and Doris Coral (*née* Richmond); *m* 1969, Helen Rosamund Rimington; one *s* one *d*. *Educ:* Nottingham High Sch.; Clare Coll., Cambridge (MA). Joined Ministry of Transport, 1959; Private Sec. to Permanent Sec., 1962–63; Principal, 1963; Private Sec. to Secretary of State for Local Govt and Regional Planning, 1969, and to Minister of Transport, 1970–71; Asst Sec., DoE, 1971; Under Secretary, 1977; Dir, London Reg., PSA, 1979–83; Department of Transport: Highways Policy and Prog. Directorate, 1983–85; Rlys Directorate, 1985–91; Urban and Gen. Directorate, 1991–93. *Recreations:* listening to music, looking at buildings, gardening. *Address:* 10 Alwyne Road, N1 2HH.

COATES, John Francis, OBE 1955; Deputy Director, Ship Design, Ministry of Defence, 1977–79, retired; *b* 30 March 1922; *s* of Joseph Edward Coates and Ada Maria Coates; *m* 1954, Jane Waymouth; two *s*. *Educ:* Clifton Coll.; Queen's Coll., Oxford (MA 1946). Entered RCNC, 1943; RCDS, 1971; Supt, Naval Construction Res. Estabt, Dunfermline, 1974. Dir, The Trireme Trust, 1985–. Hon. DSc Bath, 1989. *Publications:* (with J. S. Morrison) The Athenian Trireme, 1986; papers on naval architecture of ancient ships. *Recreation:* nautical research. *Address:* Sabinal, Lucklands Road, Bath BA1 4AU. *T:* Bath (01225) 423696.

See also Prof. G. E. Coates.

COATES, Prof. John Henry, FRS 1985; Sadleirian Professor of Pure Mathematics, since 1986, and Head of Department of Pure Mathematics and Mathematical Statistics, since 1991, Cambridge University; Professorial Fellow of Emmanuel College, Cambridge, since 1986; *b* 26 Jan. 1945; *s* of J. R. Coates and Beryl (*née* Lee); *m* 1966, Julie Turner; three *s*. *Educ:* Australian National Univ. (BSc); Trinity Coll., Cambridge (PhD). Assistant Prof., Harvard Univ., 1969–72; Associate Prof., Stanford Univ., 1972–74; Univ. Lectr, Cambridge, and Fellow, Emmanuel Coll., 1974–77; Prof., ANU, 1977–78; Prof. of Maths, Univ. de Paris, Orsay, 1978–86, Ecole Normale Supérieure, Paris, 1985–86. Pres., London Math. Soc., 1988–90; Vice-Pres., Internat. Mathematical Union, 1991–95; Mem. Council, Royal Soc., 1992–94. *Address:* Emmanuel College, Cambridge CB1 2EA; 104 Mawson Road, Cambridge CB1 2EA. *T:* Cambridge (01223) 60884.

COATES, Kenneth Howard, OBE 1993; CEng, FRAeS; Executive Chairman, Meggitt PLC, since 1984; *b* 13 May 1933; *s* of Cecil Howard Coates and late Frederica Margaret Coates (*née* Slaughter); *m* 1958, Jennefer Anne Holmes; one *s* two *d*. *Educ:* Royal High Sch.; Herriot-Watt Coll.; MIMechE, FIMI. Machinery Purchasing Agent, Ford Motor Co., 1961–69; Chief Exec., Marwin Holdings, 1969–73; Chief Exec., Kearney & Trecker Marwin, 1973–77; Man. Dir, Flight Refuelling, 1977–83. Hon. DTech Bournemouth, 1992. *Recreations:* golf, sailing. *Address:* Meggitt plc, Farrs House, Cowgrove, Wimborne, Dorset BH21 4EL. *T:* Wimborne (0202) 841141. *Clubs:* Poole Harbour Yacht; Ferndown Golf.

COATES, Kenneth Sidney; Member (Lab) European Parliament, Nottinghamshire North and Chesterfield, since 1994 (Nottingham, 1989–94); Special Professor in Adult Education, University of Nottingham, since 1990 (Reader, 1980–89); *b* 16 Sept. 1930; *s* of Eric Arthur Coates and Mary Coates; *m* 1969, Tamara Tura; three *s* three *d* (and one *d* decd). *Educ:* Nottingham Univ. (Mature State Scholar, 1956; BA 1st Cl. Hons Sociology, 1959). Coal miner, Notts Coalfield, 1948–56; student, 1956–60; Asst Tutor, Tutor, and Sen. Tutor in Adult Educn, Univ. of Nottingham, 1960–80. Chm., Human Rights Subcttee, Eur. Parlt, 1989–. Member: Bertrand Russell Peace Foundn, 1965–; Inst. of Workers' Control, 1968–; Jt Sec., European Nuclear Disarmament Liaison Cttee, 1981–89. *Publications:* (with A. J. Topham) Industrial Democracy in Great Britain, 1967, 3rd edn 1976; (with R. L. Silburn) Poverty, the Forgotten Englishmen, 1970, 4th edn 1983; (with A. J. Topham) The New Unionism, 1972, 2nd edn 1974; (with A. J. Topham) Trade Unions in Britain, 1980, 3rd edn 1988; Heresies, 1982; The Most Dangerous Decade, 1984; (with A. J. Topham) Trade Unions and Politics, 1986; Think Globally, Act Locally, 1988; (with A. J. Topham) The Making of the Transport and General Workers' Union, 1991. *Recreations:* walking, reading. *Address:* Bertrand Russell House, Gamble Street, Nottingham NG7 4ET. *T:* Nottingham (0115) 978 4504.

COATES, Michael Arthur, FCA; Chairman, Price Waterhouse, World Firm, 1982–88; *b* 12 May 1924; *yr s* of late Joseph Michael Smith Coates, OBE, Elmfield, Wylam, Northumberland, and late Lillian Warren Coates (*née* Murray); *m* 1st, 1952, Audrey Hampton Thorne (marr. diss. 1970); one *s* two *d*; 2nd, 1971, Sally Rogers (marr. diss. 1980). *Educ:* Uppingham Sch. Admitted Mem., Inst. of Chartered Accountants, 1951. Served RA, mainly in ME and Italy, 1942–47. Articled with Price Waterhouse & Co., Newcastle, 1942; returned to Price Waterhouse, 1947; transf. to London, 1954; Partner, Price Waterhouse & Co., 1959–82, Dep. Sen. Partner, 1974–75, Sen. Partner, 1975–82; Chm., Price Waterhouse Internat. Manpower Cttee, 1971–74; Mem., Policy Cttee, 1974–88. *Recreations:* diverse, including music, modern painting, antiques, gardens, reading, railways, photography. *Address:* 20 Wilton Crescent, SW1X 8SA. *T:* 0171–235 4423; Cantray House, Croy, Inverness-shire IV1 2PW. *T:* Croy (01667) 493204.

COATES, Reginald Charles, FEng 1978; Emeritus Professor of Civil Engineering, University of Nottingham, since 1983; *b* 28 June 1920; *s* of Wilfrid and Margaret Anne Coates; *m* 1942, Doris Sheila (*née* Sharrad) (*d* 1988); two *s* one *d*. *Educ:* New Mills Grammar Sch.; The Herbert Strutt Sch., Belper, Derbyshire; University Coll., Nottingham. Served War of 1939–45, Corps of Royal Engineers. Univ. of Nottingham: Lectr in Civil Engineering, 1946; Sen. Lectr, 1953; Prof. and Head of Dept of Civil Engrg, 1958–82; Dep. Vice-Chancellor, 1966–69; Prof. and Hd, Dept of Civil Engrg, Papua New Guinea Univ. of Technol., 1982–85. Member: Council, Instn of Civil Engineers, 1967–72 (Vice-Pres., 1975–78, Pres., 1978–79); Sheffield Regional Hosp. Bd, 1971–74; Notts AHA, 1974–75; Council, Construction Industry Research and Information Assoc., 1978–82; Adv. Cttee, Books for Overseas, British Council, 1974–82; Construction and Housing Res. Adv. Council, DoE, 1976–79. *Publications:* (with M. G. Coutie and F. K. Kong) Structural Analysis, 1972, 3rd edn 1987; occasional articles in technical press. *Recreations:* cooking and idling. *Address:* Dove House, Ashbourne, Derbys DE6 1FF.

COATS, Sir Alastair Francis Stuart, 4th Bt, *cr* 1905; *b* 18 Nov. 1921; *s* of Lieut-Col Sir James Stuart Coats, MC, 3rd Bt and Lady Amy Coats (*d* 1975), *er d* of 8th Duke of Richmond and Gordon; *S* father, 1966; *m* 1947, Lukyn, *d* of Capt. Charles Gordon; one *s* one *d*. *Educ:* Eton. Served War of 1939–45, Coldstream Guards (Capt.). *Heir: s* Alexander James Coats, *b* 6 July 1951. *Address:* Birchwood House, Durford Wood, Petersfield, Hants GU31 5AW. *T:* Liss (01730) 892254.

COATS, Sir William David, Kt 1985; DL; Chairman, Coats Patons PLC, 1981–86 (Deputy Chairman, 1979–81); Deputy Chairman, Clydesdale Bank, 1985–93 (Director, since 1962); *b* 25 July 1924; *s* of Thomas Heywood Coats and Olivia Violet Pitman; *m* 1950, Hon. Elizabeth Lilian Graham MacAndrew; two *s* one *d*. *Educ:* Eton Coll. Entered service of Coats Patons PLC, 1948: Director: The Central Agency Ltd (subsid. co.), 1953–55; Coats Patons PLC, 1960–86; Murray Caledonian Trust Co. Ltd, 1961–81; Weir Group Ltd, 1970–83; Murray Investment Trusts, 1986–92. Mem., S of Scotland Electricity Bd, 1972–81. Hon. LLD Strathclyde, 1977. DL Ayr and Arran, 1986. *Recreations:* shooting and golf. *Address:* The Cottage, Symington, Ayrshire KA1 5QG. *T:* Symington (01563) 830287. *Club:* Western (Glasgow).

COBB, Henry Nichols; Partner, Pei Cobb Freed and Partners, Architects, since 1960; *b* 8 April 1926; *s* of Charles Kane Cobb and Elsie Quincy Cobb; *m* 1953, Joan Stewart Spaulding; three *d*. *Educ:* Harvard College (AB 1947); Harvard Graduate Sch. of Design (MArch 1949). Architectural Div., Webb & Knapp, 1950–60; Pei Cobb Freed & Partners (formerly I. M. Pei & Partners), 1960–. Sch. of Architecture, Yale University: William Henry Bishop Vis. Prof., 1973, 1978; Charlotte Sheperd Davenport Vis. Prof., 1975; Graduate School of Design, Harvard: Studio Prof. and Chm., Dept of Architecture, 1980–85; Adjunct Prof. of Architecture and Urban Design, 1985–88; Vis. Lectr, 1988–. Hon. DFA Bowdoin Coll., 1985; Dr Technical Scis *hc*, Swiss Fed. Inst. of Technol., 1990. *Publications:* Where I Stand, 1980; Architecture and the University, 1985. *Address:* Pei Cobb Freed & Partners, 600 Madison Avenue, New York, NY 10022–1698, USA. *T:* (212) 7513122.

COBB, Henry Stephen, CBE 1991; FSA; FRHistS; Clerk of the Records, House of Lords, 1981–91; *b* 17 Nov. 1926; *y s* of Ernest Cobb and Violet Kate Cobb (*née* Sleath), Wallasey; *m* 1969, Eileen Margaret Downer. *Educ:* Birkenhead Sch.; London School of Economics (BA, MA); Liverpool Univ. (Dip. Archive Admin). Archivist, Church Missionary Soc., 1951–53; Asst Archivist, House of Lords, 1953–59, Asst Clerk of the Records, 1959–73, Dep. Clerk, 1973–81. Lecturer in Palaeography, School of Librarianship, North London Polytechnic, 1973–77. Pres., Soc. of Archivists, 1992– (Mem. Council, 1970–82; Chm., 1982–84); Mem. Council, British Records Assoc., 1978–81; Chm., London Record Soc., 1984–. Mem. Cttee of Management, Inst. of Historical Research, 1986–90. FSA 1967; FRHistS 1970. *Publications:* (ed) The Local Port Book of Southampton 1439–40, 1961; (ed with D. J. Johnson) Guide to the Parliament and the Glorious Revolution Exhibition, 1988; (ed) The Overseas Trade of London: Exchequer Customs Accounts 1480–1, 1990; contribs to Economic History Rev., Jl of Soc. of Archivists, Archives, etc. *Recreations:* music, historical research. *Address:* 1 Child's Way, Hampstead Garden Suburb, NW11 6XU. *T:* 0181–458 3688.

COBB, Richard Charles, CBE 1978; FBA 1967; Professor of Modern History, University of Oxford, 1973–84, Senior Research Fellow of Worcester College, Oxford, 1984–87; *b* 20 May 1917; *s* of Francis Hills Cobb, Sudan Civil Service, and Dora Cobb (*née* Swindale); *m* 1963, Margaret Tennant; three *s* one *d*. *Educ:* Shrewsbury Sch.; Merton Coll., Oxford (Hon. Fellow 1980). Postmastership in History, Merton, 1934. HM Forces, 1942–46. Research in Paris, 1946–55; Lectr in History, UCW Aberystwyth, 1955–61; Sen. Simon Res. Fellow, Manchester, 1960; Lectr, University of Leeds, 1962; Fellow and Tutor in Modern History, Balliol Coll., 1962–72, Hon. Fellow, 1977; Reader in French Revolutionary History, Oxford, 1969–72. Vis. Prof. in the History of Paris, Collège de France, 1971. Lectures: Ralegh, British Academy, 1974; Zaharoff, Oxford, 1976; Helmsley, Brandeis, 1981. DUniv Essex, 1981; Hon. LittD Leeds, 1988; Hon. DLitt Cambridge, 1989. Chevalier des Palmes Académiques, 1956; Officier de l'Ordre National du Mérite, 1977; Chevalier de la Légion d'Honneur, 1985. *Publications:* L'armée révolutionnaire à Lyon, 1952; Les armées révolutionnaires du Midi, 1955; Les armées révolutionnaires, vol. 1, 1961, vol. 2, 1963 (English trans., by Marianne Elliott, as The People's Armies: instrument of the Terror in the Departments, April 1793 to Floréal Year II, 1987); Terreur et Subsistances, 1965; A Second Identity: essays on France and French history, 1969; The Police and the People: French Popular Protest 1789–1820, 1970; Reactions to the French Revolution, 1972; Paris and its Provinces 1792–1802, 1975; A Sense of Place, 1975; Tour de France, 1976; Death in Paris 1795–1801, 1978 (Wolfson Prize, 1979); Streets of Paris, 1980; Promenades, 1980; French and Germans, Germans and French, 1983; People and Places, 1985; *autobiography:* Still Life: sketches from a Tunbridge Wells childhood, 1983 (J. R. Ackerley Prize); A Classical Education, 1985; Something to Hold Onto: autobiographical sketches, 1988. *Address:* Worcester College, Oxford OX1 2HB.

COBB, Timothy Humphry, MA; *b* 4 July 1909; *s* of Humphry Henry Cobb and Edith Muriel (*née* Stogdon); *m* 1952, Cecilia Mary Josephine, *d* of W. G. Chapman; two *s* one *d*. *Educ:* Harrow; Magdalene Coll., Cambridge. Asst Master, Middlesex Sch., Concord, Mass, USA, 1931–32; Bryanston Sch., Blandford, Dorset, 1932–47, Housemaster, Head of Classics, Estate Bursar; Headmaster of King's Coll., Budo, Kampala, Uganda, 1947–58;

formerly Sec., Uganda Headmasters' Association; Headmaster, Dover College, 1958–73. *Publication:* Certificate English Language Practice, 1958. *Recreations:* music, railways, producing vegetables. *Address:* Parkgate Farm, Framlingham, Woodbridge, Suffolk IP13 9JH. *T:* Badingham (01728) 638672. *Clubs:* MCC; Bluemantles Cricket (Tunbridge Wells and W Kent).

COBBAN, Sir James (Macdonald), Kt 1982; CBE 1971; TD; MA; DL; JP; Headmaster of Abingdon School, 1947–70; *b* 14 Sept. 1910; *s* of late A. M. Cobban, MIStructE, Scunthorpe, Lincs; *m* 1942, Lorna Mary (*d* 1961), *er d* of late G. S. W. Marlow, BSc, FRIC, barrister-at-law, Sydenham; four *d* (one *s* decd). *Educ:* Pocklington Sch.; Jesus Coll., Cambridge (Scholar); Univ. of Vienna. Classical Tripos, Part I, 1931, Part II, 1932; Sandys Student, 1932: Thirlwall Medallist and Gladstone Prizeman, 1935; MA, Cambridge; MA, Oxford (Pembroke Coll.). Asst Master, King Edward VI Sch., Southampton, 1933–36; Class. Sixth Form Master, Dulwich Coll., 1936–40, 1946–47. Intelligence Corps (TA), 1941; GSO3, Directorate of Mil. Intelligence, 1941; Intermediate War Course, Staff Coll., 1943; DAQMG, Combined Ops HQ, 1943; Staff Officer, CCG, 1944 (Lt-Col 1945). Rep. Diocese of Oxford on Gen. Synod, 1970–85 (Panel of Chairmen 1979–81); Vice-Pres., Dio. Synod, 1975–82; Chm., Abingdon Co. Bench, 1964–74; Member: Cttee GBA, 1972– (Dep. Chm., 1976–82; Hon. Life Mem., 1981); Direct Grant Schs Jt Cttee, 1966–80 (Chm., 1975–80); Cttee, GBGSA, 1976–81; Council, Ind. Schs Careers Orgn, 1972–80; Cttee, United Soc. Christian Lit., 1974–83; Thames Valley Police Authority, 1973–80; Vale of White Horse DC, 1973–76; Governor: Stowe Sch., 1970–83; Wellington Coll., 1970–81; Campion Sch., Athens, 1980–83; Sch. of St Helen and St Katharine, 1954–80, 1983–87 (Chm., 1958–67); Abingdon Coll. of Further Education, 1974–80; St Stephen's House, Oxford, 1982–85; Gloucester School of Ministry, 1984–86. JP Berks, 1950, Oxon, 1974; DL Berks, 1966, Oxon, 1974. *Publications:* Senate and Provinces, 78–49 BC, 1935; (in collaboration) Civis Romanus, 1936; Pax et Imperium, 1938; Church and School, 1963. *Address:* 10 Coverdale Court, Preston Road, Yeovil BA21 3AQ. *T:* Yeovil (01935) 77835.

COBBETT, David John, TD 1973; ERD 1962; railway and transportation management consultant; *b* 9 Dec. 1928; *m* 1952, Beatrix Jane Ogilvie Cockburn; three *s*. *Educ:* Royal Masonic Sch. FCIT. Gen. Railway admin. and managerial positions, 1949–67; Divl Movements Manager, Liverpool Street, 1967; Divl Manager, Norwich (British Railways Bd), 1968–70; Asst Managing Dir, Freightliners Ltd, 1970–73; Dep. Gen. Manager, British Railways Bd Scottish Region, 1973; Gen. Manager, British Railways Scottish Region, 1974–76; Chm., British Transport Ship Management, Scotland, 1974–76; Gen. Manager, BR Eastern Region, 1976–77; British Railways Board: Export Dir (Special Projects), 1977–78; Dir, Strategic Studies, 1978–83; Dir, Information Systems and Technology, 1983–85. Dir, Transmark, 1978. Chm., Railway Benevolent Instn, 1984– (Dep. Chm., 1981–84). Bt Col, Royal Corps of Transport (RARO), 1974. *Recreations:* military matters, historical reading, games. *Address:* Ballytruim, Newtonmore, Inverness-shire PH20 1DS. *T:* Newtonmore (01540) 673269. *Clubs:* Army and Navy; MCC.

COBBOLD; *see* Lytton Cobbold, family name of Baron Cobbold.

COBBOLD, 2nd Baron *cr* 1960, of Knebworth; **David Antony Fromanteel Lytton Cobbold,** DL; *b* 14 July 1937; *s* of 1st Baron Cobbold, KG, GCVO, PC, and of Lady Hermione Bulwer-Lytton, *er d* of 2nd Earl of Lytton, KG, GCSI, GCIE, PC; assumed by deed poll, 1960, additional surname of Lytton; *S* father, 1987; *m* 1961, Christine Elizabeth, 3rd *d* of Major Sir Dennis Frederic Bankes Stucley, 5th Bt; three *s* one *d*. *Educ:* Eton College; Trinity Coll., Cambridge (BA Hons Moral Sciences). Fellow, Assoc. of Corporate Treasurers. PO, RAF, 1955–57. NATO Flying Training Scheme, Canada 1956–57. Morgan Guaranty Trust Co., New York, 1961–62; Bank of London and South America Ltd, London, Zürich, Barcelona, 1962–72; Treasurer, Finance for Industry Ltd, 1974–79; Manager Treasury Div., BP Finance International, The British Petroleum Co. plc, 1979–87; Gen. Manager Financial Markets, TSB England & Wales plc, 1987–88; Dir, Hill Samuel Bank Ltd, and Head of TSB-Hill Samuel Treasury Div., 1988–89; Man. Dir, Gaiacorp Currency Managers, 1991–94 (Dir, 1989–94); Chm. and Man. Dir, Lytton Enterprises Ltd, Knebworth House, 1971 ; Director: 39 Production Co., 1988–; Close Brothers Gp, 1993–; Micell Ltd, 1993–; Forex Professionals Ltd, 1994–. Mem., Assoc. for Monetary Union in Europe, 1992–. Pres., Develt Cttee, 1991–, Mem., Bd of Govs, 1993–, Univ. of Hertfordshire (formerly Hatfield Poly.). Mem., Finance and Policy Cttee, HHA, 1973– (Hon. Treas., 1988–); Gov., Union of European HHAs, 1993–. Chm., Stevenage Community Trust, 1990–; Trustee, Pilgrim Trust, 1993–. Contested (L): Bishop Auckland, Oct. 1974; Hertfordshire, European Parly Election, 1979. DL Herts, 1993. *Recreation:* travel. *Heir: s* Hon. Henry Fromanteel Lytton Cobbold [*b* 12 May 1962; *m* 1987, Martha Frances, *d* of James Buford Boone, Jr; one *s* one *d*]. *Address:* Knebworth House, Knebworth, Herts SG3 6PY. *T:* Stevenage (01438) 812261, *Fax:* (01438) 811908.

COBBOLD, Rear-Adm. Richard Francis, CB 1994; Director, Royal United Services Institute for Defence Studies, since 1994; *b* 25 June 1942; *s* of Geoffrey Francis and Elizabeth Mary Cobbold; *m* 1975, Anne Marika Hjörne; one *s* one d. Educ.: Bryanston Sch.; BRNC Dartmouth. Early service, RN: HMS Kent; Staff of FO Naval Flying Training; HMS Juno; HMS Hermes; loan to RAN; RN Staff College 1973; Arctic Flight in comd, 1973–74; 820 Sqdn, Sen. Observer, 1974–75; MoD, 1975–77; HMS Mohawk in comd, 1977–79; MoD, 1979–83; RCDS 1984; HMS Brazen in comd, 1985–86; Dir of Defence Concepts, MoD, 1987–88; Captain 2nd Frigate Sqdn, 1989–90; ACDS Op. Requirements (Sea), 1991–94, and for Jt Systems, 1992–94. FRAeS 1994. *Recreations:* skiing, most sports, gardening, naval history. *Address:* Royal United Services Institute for Defence Studies, Whitehall, SW1A 2ET. *Club:* Naval and Military.

COBHAM, 11th Viscount *cr* 1718; **John William Leonard Lyttelton;** Bt 1618; Baron Cobham 1718; Lord Lyttelton, Baron of Frankley 1756 (renewed 1794); Baron Westcote (Ire.) 1776; *b* 5 June 1943; *e s* of 10th Viscount Cobham, KG, PC, GCMG, GCVO, TD, and Elizabeth Alison Viscountess Cobham (*d* 1986), *d* of J. R. Makeig-Jones, CBE; *S* father, 1977; *m* 1974, Penelope Ann (*see* Viscountess Cobham), *e d* of late Roy Cooper, Moss Farm, Ollerton, near Knutsford, Cheshire. *Educ:* Eton; Christ's College, New Zealand; Royal Agricultural College, Cirencester. *Recreations:* cricket, shooting. *Heir: b* Hon. Christopher Charles Lyttelton [*b* 23 Oct. 1947; *m* 1973, Tessa Mary, *d* of late Col A. G. J. Readman, DSO; one *s* one *d*]. *Address:* Hagley Hall, near Stourbridge, West Midlands DY9 9LG. *T:* Hagley (01562) 885823; 20 Kylestrome House, Cundy Street, Ebury Street, SW1Y 9JT. *T:* 0171–730 5756. *Club:* MCC.

COBHAM, Viscountess; Penelope Ann Lyttelton; *b* 2 Jan. 1954; *d* of Roy Cooper and Dorothy Henshall; *m* 1974, 11th Viscount Cobham, *qv*. *Educ:* St James's Sch., Malvern. Comr, Museum and Galls Commn, 1993–; Trustee, V&A, 1993–; Member: British Waterways Bd, 1993–95; LDDC, 1993–; BTA British Heritage Cttee, 1987–; Historic Royal Palaces Adv. Gp, 1990–; Arts and Heritage Adv. Cttee, 1988–; Exec. Council, HHA, 1985–; Chm., V&A Develt Cttee, 1995–. Pres., Heart of England Tourist Bd, 1990– (Vice-Chm., 1985–90). Chm., Heart of England Radio Ltd, 1993–; Dir, Heart of London Radio, 1994–. Guardian, Birmingham Assay Office, 1990–. Pres., governor and patron, numerous civic, charitable and educnl bodies. Freeman: City of London; Goldsmiths' Co. DL West Midlands, 1994–95. FRSA. *Address:* Hagley Hall, Stourbridge, West Midlands DY9 9LG. *T:* Hagley (01562) 882408; 20 Kylestrome House, Cundy Street, SW1W 9JT. *Club:* Birmingham Press (Hon. Mem.).

COBHAM, Sir Michael John, Kt 1995; CBE 1981; FRAeS; CIMgt; Chairman, Cobham plc (formerly Flight Refuelling (Holdings) Ltd, subseq. FR Group plc), since 1969 (Chief Executive, 1969–92); *b* 22 Feb. 1927; *s* of Sir Alan John Cobham, KBE, AFC, and Lady (Gladys) Cobham; *m* 1st, 1954, June Oakes (marr. diss. 1972); 2nd, 1973, Nadine Felicity, *e d* of William Abbott, Wimborne, Dorset; one *d*. *Educ:* Malvern; Trinity Coll., Cambridge (BA 1949, MA 1965). Served RN, 1945–47. Called to the Bar, Inner Temple, 1952; practised, 1952–55. Flight Refuelling Ltd: Dir, 1952; Man. Dir, 1964–77. Pres., 1976–77, Treasurer, 1980–84, SBAC; Mem. Council, Inst. of Dirs, 1976–. Life Vice-Pres., Air League, 1992 (Chm., 1990–92); Trustee, Fleet Air Arm Museum, 1987–. Hon. DEng Bournemouth, 1994. *Recreations:* ski-ing, sailing. *Address:* Cobham plc, Brook Road, Wimborne, Dorset BH21 2BJ. *Clubs:* Naval and Military; Royal Thames Yacht; Royal Southern Yacht (Hamble).

COCHRAN, William; PhD, MA; FRS 1962; Professor of Natural Philosophy, University of Edinburgh, 1975–87, now Emeritus; *b* 30 July 1922; *s* of James Cochran and Margaret Watson Cochran (*née* Baird); *m* 1953, Ingegerd Wall; one *s* two *d*. *Educ:* Boroughmuir Sch., Edinburgh; Edinburgh Univ. Asst Lectr, Edinburgh Univ., 1943–46; Demonstrator and Lectr, Univ. of Cambridge, 1948–62; Reader in Physics, Univ. of Cambridge, 1962–64. Fellow of Trinity Hall, Cambridge, 1951–64; University of Edinburgh: Prof. of Physics, 1964–75; Dean, Faculty of Science, 1978–81; Vice-Principal, 1984–87. Research fellowships abroad, 1950–51, 1958–59, 1970. Hon. Fellow, Trinity Hall, Cambridge, 1982. Hon. DSc: Heriot-Watt, 1992; Edinburgh, 1994. Guthrie medallist, Inst. Physics and Phys. Soc., 1966; Hughes medallist, Royal Soc., 1978; Potts medallist, Franklin Inst., 1985. *Publications:* Vol. III of The Crystalline State (with Prof. H. Lipson), 1954, new edn 1966; Dynamics of Atoms in Crystals, 1973. *Recreations:* Scots verse, family history. *Address:* Department of Physics, The University, The King's Buildings, Edinburgh EH9 3JZ; 3 Rustic Cottages, Colinton Road, Edinburgh EH13 0LD.

COCHRANE, family name of **Earl of Dundonald** and **Baron Cochrane of Cults.**

COCHRANE, Lord; Archie Iain Thomas Blair Cochrane; *b* 14 March 1991; *s* and *heir* of Earl of Dundonald, *qv*.

COCHRANE OF CULTS, 4th Baron *cr* 1919; **Ralph Henry Vere Cochrane;** DL; Chairman, Craigtoun Meadows Ltd; *b* 20 Sept. 1926; 2nd *s* of 2nd Baron Cochrane of Cults, DSO and Hon. Elin Douglas-Pennant (*d* 1934), *y d* of 2nd Baron Penrhyn; *S* brother, 1990; *m* 1956, Janet Mary Watson, *d* of late William Hunter Watson Cheyne, MB, MRCS, LRCP; two *s*. *Educ:* Eton; King's Coll., Cambridge (MA). Served RE, 1945–47 (Lt). Formerly: Vice-Chm., Cupar-Fife Savings Bank; Dir for Fife, Tayside Savings Bank. Underwriting Mem. of Lloyds, 1965–. Gen. Comr for Income Tax. Mem., Queen's Body Guard for Scotland (Royal Co. of Archers). DL Fife. *Heir: s* Hon. Thomas Hunter Vere Cochrane, LLB, ACII, *b* 7 Sept. 1957. *Address:* Cults, Cupar, Fife KY15 5RD. *Club:* New (Edinburgh).

COCHRANE, (Alexander John) Cameron, MBE 1987; MA; Principal, British International School, Cairo, 1992–95; *b* 19 July 1933; *s* of late Dr Alexander Younger Cochrane and of Jenny Johnstone Cochrane; *m* 1958, Rosemary Aline, *d* of late Robert Alexander Ogg and of Aline Mary Ogg; one *s* two *d*. *Educ:* The Edinburgh Academy; University Coll., Oxford. National Service in RA, 1952–54. Asst Master, St Edward's Sch., Oxford, 1957–66; Warden, Brathay Hall, Ambleside, Cumbria, 1966–70; Asst Dir of Educn, City of Edinburgh, 1970–74; Headmaster, Arnold Sch., Blackpool, 1974–79; Headmaster, Fettes Coll., Edinburgh, 1979–88; first Principal, Prince Willem-Alexander Coll., Holland, 1988–91. Member: Lancashire CC Educn Cttee, 1976–79; Council, Outward Bound Trust, 1979–88; Scottish Cttee, Duke of Edinburgh's Award, 1981–86; Chairman: Outward Bound Ullswater, 1979–84; Outward Bound Loch Eil, 1984–88; Lothian Fedn of Boys' Clubs, 1981–84 (Vice-Pres., 1986–). Commandant, XIII Commonwealth Games Village, Edinburgh, 1986. Governor: Aiglon Coll.; Pocklington Sch. *Recreations:* games, the countryside, photography, travel, family. *Address:* Fersit House, Roy Bridge, Inverness-shire PH31 4HE.

COCHRANE, Christopher Duncan; QC 1988; *b* 29 Aug. 1938; *s* of Harold Hubert and Joan Cochrane; *m* 1st, 1960, Caroline Beatrice Carey; two *d*; 2nd, 1970, Patricia Joan Godley; 3rd, 1984, Doreen Ann Suffolk; one step *d*. *Educ:* Ampleforth Coll.; Magdalen Coll., Oxford (Schol.; MA). Called to the Bar, Middle Temple, 1965; a Recorder, 1985. *Recreations:* travel, theatre, spectator sport, dining out. *Address:* 2 Gray's Inn Square, Gray's Inn, WC1R 5JH. *T:* 0171–242 4986.

COCHRANE, Sir (Henry) Marc (Sursock), 4th Bt *cr* 1903; *b* 23 Oct. 1946; *s* of Sir Desmond Oriel Alastair George Weston Cochrane, 3rd Bt, and of Yvonne Lady Cochrane (*née* Sursock); *S* father, 1979; *m* 1969, Hala (*née* Es-Said); two *s* one *d*. *Educ:* Eton; Trinity Coll., Dublin (BBS, MA). Director: Hambros Bank Ltd, 1979–85; GT Management PLC, 1986–. Hon. Consul General of Ireland in Beirut, 1979–84. Trustee, Chester Beatty Library and Gall. of Oriental Art, Dublin. *Recreations:* skiing, target shooting, electronics. *Heir: s* Alexander Desmond Cochrane, *b* 7 May 1973. *Address:* Woodbrook, Bray, Co. Wicklow, Ireland. *T:* (1) 2821421; Palais Sursock, PO Box 154, Beirut, Lebanon. *T:* (1) 331607.

COCKBURN, Prof. Forrester, MD; FRCPGlas; FRCPEd; Samson Gemmell Professor of Child Health, University of Glasgow, since 1977; *b* 13 Oct. 1934; *s* of Forrester Cockburn and Violet E. Bunce; *m* 1960, Alison Fisher Grieve; two *s*. *Educ:* Leith Acad.; Univ. of Edinburgh (MD). DCH Glasgow. FRCPE 1971; FRCPGlas 1978. Med. trng, Royal Infirmary of Edinburgh, Royal Hosp. for Sick Children, and Simpson Memorial Maternity Pavilion, Edinburgh, 1959–63; Huntingdon Hertford Foundn Res. Fellow, Boston Univ., Mass, 1963 65; Nuffield Sen. Res. Fellow, Univ. of Oxford, 1965–66; Wellcome Trust Sen. Med. Res. Fellow, Univ. of Edin. and Simpson Meml Maternity Pavilion, 1966–71; Sen. Lectr, Dept of Child Life and Health, Univ. of Edin., 1971–77. Chm., Wkg Gp on Weaning Diet, Cttee on Med. Aspects of Food Policy (Report, 1994). *Publications:* Neonatal Medicine, 1974; The Cultured Cell in Inherited Metabolic Disease, 1977; Inborn Errors of Metabolism in Humans, 1980; (with O. P. Gray) Children—A Handbook for Children's Doctors, 1984; (with J. H. Hutchison) Practical Paediatric Problems, 6th edn 1986; (with T. L. Turner and J. Douglas) Craig's Care of the Newly Born Infant, 8th edn 1988; Fetal and Neonatal Growth, 1988; (ed jtly and contrib.) Diseases of the Fetus and Newborn, 1989, 2nd edn 1995; contrib. Fetal and Neonatal Nutrition. *Recreation:* sailing. *Address:* University Department of Child Health, Royal Hospital for Sick Children, Yorkhill, Glasgow G3 8SJ. *T:* 0141–201 0000.

COCKBURN, Sir John (Elliot), 12th Bt of that Ilk, *cr* 1671; *b* 7 Dec. 1925; *s* of Lieut-Col Sir John Cockburn, 11th Bt of that Ilk, DSO and Isabel Hunter (*d* 1978), *y d* of late James McQueen, Crofts, Kirkcudbrightshire; *S* father, 1949; *m* 1949, Glory Patricia, *er d* of Nigel Tudway Mullings; three *s* two *d*. *Educ:* RNC Dartmouth; Royal Agricultural Coll., Cirencester. Served War of 1939–45, joined RAFVR, July 1944. *Recreation:* reading.

Heir: *s* Charles Christopher Cockburn [*b* 19 Nov. 1950; *m* 1985, Ruth, *d* of Samuel Bell; one *s* one *d* (twins)]. *Address:* 48 Frewin Road, SW18 3LP. *Club:* Naval and Military.

COCKBURN, William, CBE 1989; TD 1980; Chief Executive, The Post Office, since 1992; *b* 28 Feb. 1943. Entered Post Office, 1961; held various junior and middle management positions; Personal Assistant to Chm. of PO, 1971–73; Asst Dir of Finance and Planning, 1973–77; Dir, Central Finance Planning, 1977–78; Dir, Postal Finance, 1978–79; Dir, London Postal Region, 1979–82; apptd Mem., PO Board, 1981, Mem. for Finance, Counter Services and Planning, 1982–84; Mem. for Royal Mail Operations, 1984–86; Man. Dir, Royal Mail, 1986–92. Chm., Internat. Post Corp., 1994–; Non-executive Director: V. A. T. Watkins Holdings Ltd, 1985–93; Lex Service plc, 1993–; Member: Bd, BITC, 1990–; Council, Industrial Soc., 1992–. Col, RE Postal and Courier Service (V), 1986–91; Hon. Colonel: RE Postal and Courier Service, 1992–94; Royal Logistic Corps Postal and Courier Service, TA, 1994–. Gov., European Foundn for Quality Management, 1992. FCIT; FRSA; CIMgt 1993. Freeman, City of London. *Address:* The Post Office, 148 Old Street, EC1V 9HQ. *T:* 0171–250 2888.

COCKBURN-CAMPBELL, Sir Thomas; 6th Bt, *cr* 1821; *b* 8 Dec. 1918; *e s* of Sir Alexander Thomas Cockburn-Campbell, 5th Bt, and Maude Frances Lorenzo (*d* 1926), *o d* of Alfred Giles, Kent Town, Adelaide, SA; *S* father, 1935; *m* 1st, 1944, Josephine Zoi (marr. diss. 1981), *e d* of Harold Douglas Forward, Curjardine, WA; one *s;* 2nd, 1982, Janice Laraine (marr. diss. 1990), *y d* of William John Pascoe, Bundoora, Vic. *Educ:* Melbourne C of E Grammar Sch. *Heir:* *s* Alexander Thomas Cockburn-Campbell [*b* 16 March 1945; *m* 1969, Kerry Ann, *e d* of Sgt K. Johnson; one *s* one *d*]. *Address:* 14 Lincoln Street, York, WA 6302, Australia.

COCKCROFT, Dr Janet Rosemary, OBE 1975; Chairman, Bottoms Mill Co. Ltd, Todmorden, since 1980 (Director, since 1961, Deputy Chairman, 1974–80); *b* 26 July 1916; *er d* of late Major W. G. Mowat, MC, TD, JP, of Buchollie, Lybster, Caithness, Scotland, and late Mary Mowat; *m* 1942, Major Peter Worby Cockcroft (*d* 1980); two *s* one *d*. *Educ:* Glasgow Univ. MB, ChB 1938. Ho. Surg. and Ho. Phys., Glasgow Royal Infirmary, 1938–39; GP, 1939–43; Asst MOH, Co. of Caithness, 1943–46; MO, Maternity and Child Welfare, Halifax, 1950–53; Part-time MOH, WRCC, 1953–67; MO, Family Planning Assoc., 1947–75 (Halifax and Sowerby Bridge Clinics); MO, British Red Cross, Halifax, 1960–66; Chairman: N Midlands FPA Doctors' Gp, 1966–68; Halifax FPA Clinic, 1963–75. Mem., Food Additives and Contaminants Cttee, MAFF, 1972–81; Chm., Consumers' Cttees for England and Wales and for GB, MAFF, 1975–82; Vice-Pres., 1969–70, Pres., 1970–72, Nat. Council of Women of GB; Vice-Pres., Internat. Council of Women, 1973–76; UK Rep., UN Status of Women Commn, 1973–79 (Vice Chm., 1976; Chm., 1978–80); Member: BBC Northern Adv. Council, 1975–79; Gen. Adv. Council, BBC, 1980–87. Elder, United Reformed Church, 1973–. *Publication:* Not a Proper Doctor (autobiog.), 1986. *Recreations:* travel, reading. *Address:* Dalemore, Savile Park, Halifax, W Yorks HX1 3EA. *T:* Halifax (01422) 352621.

COCKCROFT, John Hoyle; writer and political and corporate adviser; various electronics consultancies and directorships, since 1977; *b* 6 July 1934; *s* of late Lionel Fielden Cockcroft and of Jenny Hoyle; *m* 1971, Tessa Fay Shepley; three *d*. *Educ:* Primary, Trearddur House; Oundle; St John's Coll., Cambridge (Sen. Maj. Scholar (History), 1953). MA Hons History and Econs 1958; Pres., Cambridge Union, 1958. Royal Artillery, 2nd Lieut, 1953–55. Feature writer, Financial Times, 1959–61; Economist, GKN, 1962–67 (re-acquisitions, 1962–65); seconded to Treasury, Public Enterprises Div., 1965–66; Econ. Leader-writer, Daily Telegraph, 1967–74. MP (C) Nantwich, Feb. 1974–1979; Mem. Select Cttee on Nationalised Industries, 1975–79; Company Secretaries Bill (Private Member's), 1978. Dir, BR (Eastern Region), 1984–89; Laurence Prust, stockbrokers, 1986–90; Consultant: and historian, GKN, 1971–76; Mail Users' Assoc., 1976–79; Inst. of Chartered Secretaries, 1977–79; Cray Electronics, 1982–84; Dowty, 1983–86; Wedgwood, 1983–84; Crystalate, 1983–86; Camden Associates, 1984–88; Cambridge Corp. Consultants, 1989–; Commed, 1990–93; Raitt Orr, 1992–; MAP Securities, 1992–. Advr and consultant, NEI History Archives, 1980–85. Member Council: European Movement, 1973–74, 1983–84; Conservative Gp for Europe, 1980–87; Mem., PITCOM, 1985–90. Treasurer, Cambridge Univ. Cons. Assoc., 1958. Columnist: and contributor, Microscope, 1982–85; electronic money transmission, Banking World, 1984–86; Westminster Watch, Electronics Times, 1985–90.Trustee, Sanderson Trust (Oundle), 1992–. *Publications:* (jtly) Reforming the Constitution, 1968; (jtly) Self-Help Reborn, 1969; Why England Sleeps, 1971; (jtly) An Internal History of Guest Keen and Nettlefolds, 1976; Microtechnology in Banking, 1984; Microelectronics (booklet), 1979 and 1982; leaders and leader page articles, reviews and interviews, Daily and Sunday Telegraphs, The European, The Scotsman, Jl of Contemp. British Hist., 1979–. *Recreations:* walking, reading, swimming, entertaining. *Address:* Mitchell's Farmhouse, Stapleford Tawney, Essex RM4 1SS. *T:* Stapleford (01708) 688254; 2 Philpot Lane, EC3M 8AQ. *T:* 0171–621 1770.

COCKCROFT, Sir Wilfred (Halliday), Kt 1983; Chairman, Educational Project Resources, since 1989; *b* 7 June 1923; *s* of Wilfred Cockcroft and Bessie Halliday; *m* 1st, 1949, Barbara Rhona Huggan; two *s;* 2nd, 1982, Vivien, *o d* of Mr and Mrs David Lloyd. *Educ:* Keighley Boys' Grammar Sch.; Balliol Coll., Oxford (Williams Exhibnr, 1941, Hon. Scholar, 1946). MA, DPhil Oxon; CMath; FIMA 1973; FRSA 1983. Technical Signals/Radar Officer, RAF, 1942–46. Asst Lectr, Univ. of Aberdeen, 1949, Lectr 1950; Lectr, Univ. of Southampton, 1957, Reader 1960; G. F. Grant Prof. of Pure Mathematics, Univ. of Hull, 1961; Vice-Chancellor, NUU, 1976–82; Chm. and Chief Exec., Secondary Exams Council, 1983–88. Vis. Lectr and Prof., Univs of Chicago, Stanford, State Univ. of NY, 1954, 1959, 1967. University Grants Committee: Mem., 1973–76; Mem., Math. Sciences Subcttee, 1967–72, Chm. 1973–76; Chm., Educn Subcttee, 1973–76; Mem., Management and Business Studies Subcttee, and Educnl Technology Subcttee, 1973–76. Science and Engineering Research Council (formerly Science Research Council): Mem., 1978–82; Mem., Maths Sub-Cttee, 1964–68 (Chm., 1969–73); Mem., Science Bd, 1969–73; Chm., Postgraduate Trng Cttee, 1979–82. Chairman: Nuffield Maths Project Consultative Cttee, 1963–71; Specialist Conf. on Maths in Commonwealth Schs, Trinidad, 1968. Cttee to review Rural Planning Policy, DoE, NI, 1977–78; Cttee to consider teaching of maths in schs in England and Wales, 1978–82; Standing Conference on Univ. Entrance, 1979–82; Nat. Foundn for Educnl Res., 1988–90; Royal Soc. Maths Curriculum Subcttee, 1991–94; Pres., British Accreditation Council for Ind. Further and Higher Educn, 1991–; Member: Computer Bd for Univs and Res. Councils, 1975–76; US/UK Educnl Commn, 1977–80; Educn Cttee, Royal Soc., 1990–94. Member, Council: London Mathematical Soc., 1973–76; IMA, 1974–77, 1982–85. Hon. Fellow, Humberside Higher Educn Coll., 1987; Hon. Mem., CGLI, 1987. Hon. DSc: Kent, 1983; Southampton, 1986; DUniv Open, 1984. *Publications:* Your Child and Mathematics, 1968; Complex Numbers, 1972. *Recreations:* mathematics textbook writing and editing, golf, swimming, sketching, bad piano playing. *Address:* The Old Rectory, Warmington, OX17 1BU. *T:* Farnborough (01295) 690531; (office) 126–128 Cromwell Road, SW7 4ET. *T:* 0171–373 7716. *Club:* Athenæum.

COCKELL, Michael Henry; a Deputy Chairman of Lloyd's, 1986; *b* 30 Aug. 1933; *s* of Charles and Elise Seaton; *m* 1961, Elizabeth Janet Meikle; one *s* three *d*. *Educ:* Harrow School. Underwriter for G. N. Rouse Syndicate 570, 1968–90; Chm., M. H. Cockell & Co., 1978; Senior Partner, M. H. Cockell & Partners, 1986. Dep. Chm., Lloyd's Non-Marine Assoc., 1982, Chm., 1983–; Mem. Council, Lloyd's, 1984–87, 1990–93 and 1995–. *Recreations:* all sport (especially cricket), ornithology, music (not loud pop), gardening, countryside. *Address:* Court Horeham, Cowbeech, Herstmonceaux, E Sussex BN27 4JN. *T:* Herstmonceaux (01323) 833171. *Clubs:* City of London, MCC; IZ.

COCKER, Victor; Chief Executive, Severn Trent Water, since 1995; *b* 30 Oct. 1940; *s* of Harold Nathan Cocker and Marjorie Cocker; *m* 1963, Jennifer Nicholls; two *d*. *Educ:* King Edward VII Sch., Sheffield; Nottingham Univ. (BA Econ Hons). NW Gas Board, 1962–68; West Midlands Gas, 1968–74; Severn Trent Water Authy, 1974–89; Man. Dir, Severn Trent Water Ltd, 1991–95. Chm., Forward Birmingham RNLI Lifeboat Campaign, 1994–. *Recreations:* hill walking, National Hunt, cinema, music. *Address:* Severn Trent Water, 2297 Coventry Road, Sheldon, Birmingham B26 3PU. *T:* 0121–722 4176.

COCKERAM, Eric (Paul); JP; *b* 4 July 1924; *er s* of Mr and Mrs J. W. Cockeram; *m* 1949, Frances Irving; two *s* two *d*. *Educ:* The Leys Sch., Cambridge. Served War, 1942–46: Captain The Gloucestershire Regt; "D Day" landings (wounded and later discharged). MP (C): Bebington, 1970–Feb. 1974; Ludlow, 1979–87. PPS: to Minister for Industry, 1970–72; to Minister for Posts and Telecommunications, 1972; to Chancellor of Exchequer, 1972–74. Mem., Select Cttee on Corporation Tax, 1971, on Industry and Trade, 1979–87; Mem., Public Accounts Cttee, 1983–87. Pres., Menswear Assoc. of Britain, 1964–65. Mem., Bd of Governors, United Liverpool Hosps, 1965–74; Chm., Liverpool NHS Exec. Council, 1970. Chairman: Watson Prickard Ltd, 1966–; Johnson Fry (Northern) Ltd, 1988–94; Director: TSB (NW), 1968–83; TSB (Wales & Border Counties), 1983–88; Liverpool Building Soc., 1975–82 (Vice-Chm., 1981–82); Midshires Building Soc., 1982–88; Muller Group (UK) Ltd, 1983–94. Member of Lloyd's. Liveryman, Worshipful Co. of Glovers, 1969–, Mem. Court, 1979–. Freeman: City of London; City of Springfield, Ill. JP, City of Liverpool, 1960. *Recreations:* bridge, golf, shooting, country walking. *Address:* Fairway Lodge, Caldy, Wirral, Cheshire L48 1NB. *T:* 0151–625 1100. *Club:* Carlton.

COCKERELL, Sir Christopher (Sydney), Kt 1969; CBE 1966; RDI 1987; FRS 1967; designer and inventor; *b* 4 June 1910; *s* of late Sir Sydney Cockerell; *m* 1937, Margaret Elinor Belsham; two *d*. *Educ:* Gresham's; Peterhouse, Cambridge (Hon. Fellow, 1974). Pupil, W. H. Allen & Sons, Bedford, 1931–33; Radio Research, Cambridge, 1933–35; airborne and navigational equipment research and development (36 patents), Marconi Wireless Telegraph Co. Ltd, 1935–51; inventor of and engaged on hovercraft since 1953 (56 patents); Consultant (hovercraft), Ministry of Supply, 1957–58; Consultant: Hovercraft Development Ltd, 1958–70 (Dir, 1959–66); British Hovercraft Corp., 1973–79; Chm., Ripplecraft Co. Ltd, 1950–79; Founder and Chm., Wavepower Ltd, 1974–82 (3 patents), Consultant, 1982–88. Foundn Pres., Internat. Air Cushion Engrg Soc., 1969–71 (Vice-Pres., 1971–); Pres., UK Hovercraft Soc., 1972–; Member, Min. of Technology's Adv. Cttee for Hovercraft, 1968–70. A Trustee of National Portrait Gallery, 1967–79. Hon. Fellow: Swedish Soc. of Aeronautics, 1963; Soc. of Engineers, 1966; Manchester Inst. of Sci. and Tech., 1967; Downing Coll., Cambridge, 1969. Hon. Mem., Southampton Chamber of Commerce, 1967. Hon. DSc: Leicester, 1967; Heriot-Watt, 1971; London, 1975; Hon. Dr RCA, 1968. Hon. Freeman, Borough of Ramsgate, 1971. Viva Shield, Worshipful Co. of Carmen, 1961; RAC Diamond Jubilee Trophy, 1962. Thulin Medal, Swedish Soc. of Aeronautics, 1963; Howard N. Potts Medal, Franklin Inst., 1965; Albert Medal, RSA, 1966; Churchill Medal, Soc. of Engineers, 1966; Royal Medal, Royal Soc., 1966; Mitchell Memorial Medal, Stoke-on-Trent Assoc. of Engineers, 1967; Columbus Prize, Genoa, 1968; John Scott Award, City of Philadelphia, 1968; Elmer A. Sperry Award, 1968; Gold Medal, Calais Chamber of Commerce, 1969; Bluebird Trophy, 1969; James Alfred Ewing Medal, ICE, 1977; James Watt Internat. Gold Medal, IMechE, 1983. *Recreations:* the visual arts, gardening, fishing. *Address:* 16 Prospect Place, Hythe, Hants SO4 6AU.

COCKERILL, Geoffrey Fairfax, CB 1980; Secretary, University Grants Committee, 1978–82; *b* 14 May 1922; *e s* of late Walter B. Cockerill and Mary W. Cockerill (*née* Buffery); *m* 1959, Janet Agnes Walters, JP, MA, *d* of late Archibald J. Walters, MBE, and Elsie Walters; two *s*. *Educ:* Humberstone Foundation Sch.; UC Nottingham. BA London 1947. Royal Artillery, 1941–45 (Captain). Min. of Labour, 1947; Min. of Educn, 1952; Private Sec. to last Minister of Educn and Secs of State for Educn and Science, 1963–65; Asst Sec., 1964; Sec., Public Schools Commn, 1966–68; Jt Sec., Schools Council for Curriculum and Examinations, 1970–72; Under-Sec., DES, 1972–77; Dep. Sec., 1978. Chairman: Anglo-Amer. Primary Educ. Project, 1970–72; Working Party on Nutritional Aspects of School Meals, 1973–75; Kingston-upon-Thames CAB, 1985–88; Member: Adv. Gp on London Health Services, 1980–81; RCN Commn on Nursing Educn, 1984–85; RCN Strategy Gp, 1985–87; UGC, Univ. of S Pacific, 1984–87; Vice-Pres., Experiment in Internat. Living, 1989–. Reviewed for Government: Central Bureau for Educational Visits and Exchanges, 1982; Youth Exchanges, 1983; Nat. Youth Bureau, 1983; Consultant to Cttee of Vice-Chancellors and Principals, 1984–85. Hon. Senior Research Fellow, KCL, 1982–86. *Recreations:* gardening, photography. *Address:* 29 Lovelace Road, Surbiton, Surrey KT6 6NS. *T:* 0181–399 0125. *Clubs:* Athenæum, National Liberal, Commonwealth Trust.

COCKERTON, Rev. Canon John Clifford Penn; Rector of Wheldrake with Thorganby, 1985–92 (Rector of Wheldrake, 1978–85); Canon of York (Prebend of Dunnington), 1987–92, Canon Emeritus 1992; *b* 27 June 1927; *s* of late William Penn Cockerton and Eleanor Cockerton; *m* 1974, Diana Margaret Smith (*d* 1987), *d* of Mr and Mrs W. Smith, Upper Poppleton, York. *Educ:* Wirral Grammar Sch.; Univ. of Liverpool; St Catherine's Society, Oxford; Wycliffe Hall, Oxford. Asst Master, Prenton Secondary Sch., 1949–51; Deacon 1954; Priest 1955; Asst Curate, St Helens Parish Church, 1954–58; Tutor 1958–60, Chaplain 1960–63, Cranmer Hall, Durham; Vice-Principal, St John's Coll., Durham, 1963–70; Principal, St John's College and Cranmer Hall, Durham, 1970–78. Examining Chaplain to Bishop of Durham, 1971–73; Proctor in Convocation, 1980–85. *Recreation:* music. *Address:* 50 Allerton Drive, Nether Poppleton, York YO2 6NW.

COCKETT, Frank Bernard, MS, FRCS; Consulting Surgeon to: St Thomas' Hospital; King Edward VII Hospital for Officers, London; *b* Rockhampton, Australia, 22 April 1916; *s* of late Rev. Charles Bernard Cockett, MA, DD; *m* 1945, Felicity Ann (*d* 1958), *d* of Col James Thackeray Fisher, DSO, Frieston, near Grantham, Lincs; one *s* two *d;* *m* 1960, Dorothea Anne Newman; twin *s*. *Educ:* Bedford Sch.; St Thomas's Hosp. Med. Sch. BSc (1st Cl. Hons), 1936; MRCS, LRCP 1939; MB, BS (London) 1940; FRCS Eng 1947; MS (London) 1953. Sqdn Ldr (Surgical Specialist) RAFVR, 1942–46; Surgical Registrar, St Thomas' Hosp., 1947–48; Resident Asst Surg., St Thomas' Hosp., 1948–50, Consultant, 1954–81; Senior Lecturer in Surgery, St Thomas's Hosp. Med. Sch., 1950–54; Consultant, King Edward VII Hosp. for Officers, 1974–81. Fellow Assoc. of Surgs of Gt Brit.; Mem. European Soc. of Cardiovascular Surgery; Pres., Vascular Surgical Soc. of GB and Ireland, 1980; Chm., Venous Forum, RSM, 1986–87. *Publications:* The Pathology and Surgery of the Veins of the Lower Limb, 1956, 2nd edn 1976; several contribs to

Operative Surgery (ed C. G. Rob and Rodney Smith), 1956; The War Diary of St Thomas' Hospital 1939–1945, 1991; various papers in medical and surgical journals. *Recreations:* sailing, tennis, squash, gardening, marine paintings. *Address:* 14 Essex Villas, Kensington, W8 7BN. *T:* 0171–937 9883. *Clubs:* Lansdowne, Little Ship; Royal Lymington Yacht.

COCKETT, Geoffrey Howard; consultant; Chief Scientific Officer, Ministry of Defence, and Deputy Director, Royal Armament Research and Development Establishment, 1983–86; *b* 18 March 1926; *s* of late William Cockett and Edith (*née* Dinham); *m* 1951, Elizabeth Bagshaw; two *d. Educ:* King Edward VI Sch., Southampton; Univ. of Southampton (BSc, Hons Maths, and Hons Physics). FInstP; CPhys. Royal Aircraft Establishment, 1948–52; Armament Research Estabt, Woolwich, 1952–62; RARDE, 1962–68; Supt of Physics Div., Chemical Defence Estabt, 1968–71; RARDE: Supt, Optics and Surveillance Systems Div., 1971–76; Head, Applied Physics Group, 1976–83. Chm., Sci. Recruitment Bds, CS Commn, 1985–94; Consultant, Directorate of Sci. (Land), MoD, 1986–. (Jtly) Gold Medal, Congrès des Materiaux Résistant à Chaud, Paris, 1951. *Publications:* official reports; scientific and technical papers in various learned jls. *Recreations:* the computer, photography, under gardening. *Address:* Royal Defence Research Agency, Fort Halstead, Sevenoaks, Kent TN14 7BP. *T:* Knockholt (0959) 32222. *Club:* Civil Service.

COCKFIELD, family name of **Baron Cockfield.**

COCKFIELD, Baron *cr* 1978 (Life Peer), of Dover in the County of Kent; **Francis Arthur Cockfield,** Kt 1973; PC 1982; a Vice-President, Commission of the European Communities, 1985–88; *b* 28 Sept. 1916; 2nd *s* of late Lieut C. F. Cockfield (killed on the Somme in Aug. 1916) and Louisa (*née* James); *m* Aileen Monica Mudie (*d* 1992), choreographer. *Educ:* Dover Grammar Sch.; London Sch. of Economics (LLB, BSc (Econ.)). Called to Bar, Inner Temple, 1942. Home Civil Service, Inland Revenue, 1938; Asst Sec. to Board of Inland Revenue, 1945; Commissioner of Inland Revenue, 1951–52; Dir of Statistics and Intelligence to Board of Inland Revenue, 1945–52; Boots Pure Drug Co. Ltd: Finance Dir, 1953–61; Man. Dir, and Chm. Exec. Management Cttee, 1961–67. Chm., Price Commn, 1973–77. Minister of State, HM Treasury, 1979–82; Sec. of State for Trade, 1982–83; Chancellor of the Duchy of Lancaster, 1983–84. Mem., NEDC, 1962–64, 1982–83; Advr on Taxation Policy to Chancellor of Exchequer, 1970–73. Mem., Court of Governors, Univ. of Nottingham, 1963–67. Pres., Royal Statistical Soc., 1968–69. Hon. Fellow, LSE, 1972. Hon. LLD Fordham Univ., NY, 1989; Sheffield, 1990; DUniv Surrey, 1989. Grand Cross, Order of Leopold II, Belgium, 1990. *Publication:* The European Union: creating the single market, 1994. *Address:* House of Lords, SW1A 0PW.

COCKIN, Rt. Rev. George Eyles Irwin; Assistant Bishop, Diocese of York, since 1969; *b* 15 Aug. 1908; *s* of late Charles Irwin Cockin, Solicitor, and Judith Cockin. *Educ:* Repton; Leeds University (BA); Lincoln Theological College. Tutor, St Paul's College, Awka, Nigeria, 1933–40; Supervisor, Anglican Schools, E Nigeria, 1940–52. Deacon, 1953, Priest, 1954; Curate, Kimberworth, Rotherham, 1953–55; Sen. Supervisor, Anglican Schools, E Nigeria, 1955–58; Canon, All Saints Cathedral, Onitsha, 1957; first Bishop of Owerri, 1959–69. Rector of Bainton, dio. York, 1969–78; Rural Dean of Harthill, 1973–78.

COCKING, Prof. Edward Charles Daniel, FRS 1983; Professor of Botany, University of Nottingham, since 1969; *b* 26 Sept. 1931; *y s* of late Charles Cocking and of Mary (*née* Murray); *m* 1960, Bernadette Keane; one *s* one *d. Educ:* Buckhurst Hill County High Sch., Essex; Univ. of Bristol (BSc, PhD, DSc). FIBiol. Civil Service Commission Research Fellow, 1956–59; Nottingham University: Lectr in Plant Physiology, 1959–66; Reader, 1966–69; Head of Dept of Botany, 1969. S. Yoshida Meml Lecture, Hangzhou Univ., China, 1987. Member: Lawes Agricl Trust Cttee, Rothamsted Experimental Stn, 1987–; Adv. Cttee on Forest Res., Forestry Commn, 1987–; Council, Royal Soc., 1986–88; AFRC, 1990–94 (Royal Soc. Assessor, 1988–90). Mem., Bd of Trustees, Royal Botanic Gardens, Kew, 1983–; Member, Governing Body: Glasshouse Crops Res. Inst., 1983–87; British Soc. Horticultural Res., 1987–89. Pres., Sect. K, BAAS, 1983. *Publications:* Introduction to the Principles of Plant Physiology (with W. Stiles, FRS), 3rd edn 1969; numerous scientific papers in botanical/genetics jls on plant genetic manipulations. *Recreations:* walking, travelling, especially by train, occasional chess. *Address:* Department of Life Science, University of Nottingham, University Park, Nottingham NG7 2RD. *T:* Nottingham (0115) 951 5151, ext. 8502; 30 Patterdale Road, Woodthorpe, Nottingham NG5 4LQ. *T:* Nottingham (0115) 926 2452.

COCKRAM, Sir John, Kt 1964; Director, 1952–79, General Manager, 1941–73, The Colne Valley Water Company; Director, 1970–86, Chairman, 1971–86, Rickmansworth Water Co. (formerly Rickmansworth and Uxbridge Valley Water Co.); *b* 10 July 1908; *s* of Alfred John and Beatrice Elizabeth Cockram; *m* 1937, Phyllis Eleanor (*d* 1994), *d* of Albert Henning; one *s* two *d. Educ:* St Aloysius Coll., Highgate. Chartered Accountant. Member: Herts CC, 1949–74 (Chm. 1961–65); Thames Conservancy, 1954–74; Exec. Cttee, British Waterworks Assoc., 1948–74 (Pres., 1957–58); Central Advisory Water Cttee, 1955–73; Thames Water Authy, 1973–76. Life Mem., Water Cos Assoc., 1985 (Mem., 1950–85; Chm., 1950–79; Dep. Pres., 1979–85). Life Governor, Haileybury. *Recreations:* fishing, gardening. *Address:* Rebels' Corner, The Common, Chorleywood, Hertfordshire WD3 5LT.

COCKROFT, Peter John; His Honour Judge Cockroft; a Circuit Judge, since 1993; *b* 24 Sept. 1947; *s* of Walter Philip Barron Cockroft and Nora (*née* Collett); *m* 1975, Maria Eugenia Coromina Perandones; one *s* two *d. Educ:* Queen Elizabeth I Grammar Sch., Darlington; Queens' Coll., Cambridge (BA, LLB). Called to the Bar, Middle Temple, 1970 (Astbury Scholar); practised NE Circuit; Asst Recorder, 1985–89; Recorder, 1989–93. *Recreations:* visiting Spain, gardening. *Address:* Brackenwell Cottage, North Rigton, N Yorks LS17 0DG. *T:* Harrogate (01423) 734585. *Clubs:* Yorkshire County Cricket; Yorkshire Rugby Football Union.

COCKS, family name of **Barons Cocks of Hartcliffe** and **Somers.**

COCKS OF HARTCLIFFE, Baron *cr* 1987 (Life Peer), of Chinnor in the County of Oxfordshire; **Michael Francis Lovell Cocks,** PC 1976; Vice-Chairman, Board of Governors, BBC, since 1993; *b* 19 Aug. 1929; *s* of late Dr H. F. Lovell Cocks; *m* 1st, 1954, Janet Macfarlane; two *s* two *d;* 2nd, 1979, Valerie Davis. *Educ:* Bristol University. Various posts in education from 1954; Lectr, Bristol Polytechnic, 1968. Contested (Lab): Bristol West, 1959; South Gloucestershire, 1964, 1966. MP (Lab) Bristol S, 1970–87. An Asst Govt Whip, 1974–76; Parly Sec. to the Treasury and Govt Chief Whip, 1976–79; Opposition Chief Whip, 1979–85. *Publication:* Labour and the Benn Factor, 1989. *Recreations:* swimming, listening to music, reading.

COCKS, Anna Gwenllian S.; *see* Somers Cocks.

COCKS, Rt. Rev. Francis William, CB 1959; *b* 5 Nov. 1913; *o s* of late Canon W. Cocks, OBE, St John's Vicarage, Felixstowe; *m* 1940, Irene May, (Barbara) (*d* 1989), 2nd *d* of H. Thompson, Bridlington; one *s* one *d. Educ:* Haileybury; St Catharine's Coll., Cambridge; Westcott House. Played Rugby Football for Cambridge Univ., Hampshire and Eastern Counties, 1935–38. Ordained, 1937. Chaplain RAFVR, 1939; Chaplain RAF, 1945; Asst Chaplain-in-Chief, 1950; Chaplain-in-Chief, and Archdeacon, Royal Air Force, 1959–65; Rector and Rural Dean of Wolverhampton, 1965–70; Bishop Suffragan of Shrewsbury, 1970–80. Hon. Chaplain to HM the Queen, 1959–65. Prebendary of S Botolph in Lincoln Cathedral, 1959; Canon Emeritus, 1965–70; Prebendary of Lichfield Cathedral, 1968–70; Select Preacher, Univ. of Cambridge, 1960; Hon. Canon of Lichfield Cathedral, 1970–. Dir, Mercia Television, 1980–81. Mem. of Council, Haileybury and Imperial Service Coll., 1949–87; Pres., Haileybury Soc., 1976–77. Fellow, Woodard Schools, 1970–83; Mem. Council: Denstone Sch., 1970–72; Shrewsbury Sch., 1971–80; Ellesmere Coll., 1971–80. Archbishops' Advr to HMC, 1975–80. President: Shropshire Horticultural Soc., 1979; Shropshire and W Midlands Agric. Soc., 1980; Buccaneers CC, 1965–89. *Recreations:* playing golf, watching TV, reading. *Address:* 41 Beatrice Avenue, Felixstowe, Suffolk IP11 9HB. *T:* Felixstowe (01394) 283574. *Clubs:* MCC, Royal Air Force; Hawks (Cambridge).

COCKS, Freda Mary, OBE 1972; JP; Deputy Leader, Birmingham City Council, 1982–86; *b* 30 July 1915; *d* of Frank and Mary Wood; *m* 1942, Donald Francis Melvin, *s* of Melvin J. Cocks; one *d* (and one *d* decd). *Educ:* St Peter's Sch., Harborne; Queen's Coll., Birmingham. Birmingham Council, 1957–78: Alderman, 1965–74; Lord Mayor of Birmingham, 1977–78; Dep. Chm., Housing Cttee, 1968–70, Chm. 1970–72. Founder Sec., Birmingham Sanatoria League of Friends, 1950–68; Founder, Birm. Hosps Broadcasting Assoc., 1952–78; Member: Little Bromwich Hosp. Management Cttee, 1953–68; West Birmingham Health Authority, 1981–92; Vice-Pres. and Mem., Nat. Careers Assoc., 1985–. Conservative Women's Central Council: Chm., 1968–71; Chm., Gen. Purposes Cttee, 1978; service on housing, finance, policies, and land cttees; Vice Pres., Edgbaston Conservative Assoc., 1992– (Pres., 1980–92). Member: Focus Housing Assoc.; Civic Housing Assoc.; Council Mem., Birmingham Rathbone Soc. Pres., Missions to Seamen, Birmingham, 1981–. JP Birmingham, 1968. Hon. Freeman: City of Birmingham, 1986; Du-Panne, Belgium, 1978. *Recreations:* hospitals and housing. *Address:* 49 Timber Mill Court, Serpentine Road, Harborne, Birmingham B17 9RD. *T:* 0121–427 9123.

COCKS, Dr Leonard Robert Morrison, (Dr Robin Cocks), TD 1979; Keeper of Palaeontology, Natural History Museum (formerly British Museum (Natural History)), since 1986; *b* 17 June 1938; *s* of late Ralph Morrison Cocks and of Lucille Mary Cocks (*née* Blackler); *m* 1963, Elaine Margaret Sturdy; one *s* two *d. Educ:* Felsted School; Hertford College, Oxford (BA, MA, DPhil, DSc). FGS. Commissioned Royal Artillery 1958; active service Malaya, 1958–59; DSIR Research Student, Oxford Univ., 1962–65; British Museum (Nat. Hist.), 1965–; Dep. Keeper of Palaeontology, 1980–86. Geologist, Royal Engineers, 1970–83. Pres., Paleontographical Soc., 1994–; Member: Council, Palaeontological Assoc., 1969–82, 1986–88 (Editor, 1971–82, Pres., 1986–88); Council, Geological Soc., 1982–89 (Sec., 1985–89; Coke Medal, 1995); NERC Geological Res. Grants Cttee, 1978–81, 1984. Comr, Internat. Commn on Zoological Nomenclature, 1982–. Vis. Fellow, Southampton Univ., 1988–96. *Publications:* The Evolving Earth, 1979; papers in sci. jls, on Ordovician-Silurian biostratigraphy and brachiopods, esp. from Britain, Canada, Norway, Sweden, China. *Recreations:* country pursuits. *Address:* Department of Palaeontology, Natural History Museum, Cromwell Road, SW7 5BD. *T:* 0171–938 8845.

COCKS, Robin; *see* Cocks, L. R. M.

COCKSHAW, Sir Alan, Kt 1992; FEng 1986; FICE; FIHT; Chairman, AMEC plc, since 1988 (Group Chief Executive, 1984–88); *b* 14 July 1937; *s* of John and Maud Cockshaw; *m* 1960, Brenda Payne; one *s* three *d. Educ:* Farnworth Grammar Sch.; Leeds Univ. (BSc). FIHT 1968; FICE 1985. Chief Executive: Fairclough Civil Engrg, 1978–85; Fairclough Parkinson-Mining, 1982–85; Fairclough Engrg, 1983–84; Non-exec. Dep. Chm., Norweb plc, 1992–. Chm., Oil and Gas Projects and Supplies Office, DTI, 1994–. *Recreations:* Rugby (both codes), cricket, walking, gardening. *Address:* AMEC plc, Sandiway House, Hartford, Northwich, Cheshire CW8 2YA. *T:* Sandiway (01606) 883885.

COCKSHUT, Gillian Elise, (Mrs A. O. J. Cockshut); *see* Avery, G. E.

CODD, Michael Henry, AC 1991; Director, Toogoolawa Consulting Pty Ltd, since 1993; Director, Menzies Foundation, since 1993; *b* 26 Dec. 1939; *s* of Ernest Applebee Codd and Nell Gregory (*née* Pavy). *Educ:* Univ. of Adelaide (BEc Hons). Statistician, 1962–69; joined Dept of Prime Minister, Australia, 1969; Under-Sec., Dept of Prime Minister and Cabinet, 1979–81; Sec., Dept of Employment and Ind. Relns, 1981–83; Chm., Industries Assistance Commn, 1983–85; Sec., Dept of Community Services, 1985–86; Head, Dept of Prime Minister and Cabinet and Sec. to Cabinet, 1986–91. Non-executive Director: Telstra (formerly AOTC), 1992–; Qantas, 1992–; IBM Australia, 1993–; ISSC Australia, 1994–; Consultant, Coopers and Lybrand, 1993–. *Address:* RMB 35A Monaro Highway, Williamsdale, NSW 2620, Australia. *T:* (6) 2350160.

CODD, Ronald Geoffrey, CEng; Managing Partner, InterChange Associates, since 1990; Director, Randolph Enterprise, since 1992; *b* 20 Aug. 1932; *s* of Thomas Reuben Codd and Betty Leyster Codd (*née* Sturt); *m* 1960, Christine Ellen Léone Robertson; one *s* two *d. Educ:* Cathedral Sch., Llandaff; The College, Llandovery. FBCS; FIMgt; CEng 1990. Dip. in Company Direction, 1989. Served RAF, Transport Comd, 1952–57. Rolls Royce, Aero-Engine Div., 1957–58; International Computers, 1958–61; Marconi Co., 1961–70; J. Bibby & Sons, Liverpool, 1970–74; Weir Gp, Glasgow, 1974–80; Brooke Bond Gp, 1981–86; Under Sec. and Dir., Information and Risks Management, ECGD, 1986–90. Advr to Bd, HM Customs and Excise, 1992–; Mem., Nat. Teleworking Adv. Council, 1991–. FInstD. Freeman, City of London, 1990; Liveryman, Co. of Inf. Technologists, 1990. *Publications:* contributor to business magazines. *Recreations:* competitive and leisure sailing, theatre, practical pastimes. *Address:* Chesterton House, Three Gates Lane, Haslemere, Surrey GU27 2LD. *Clubs:* City Livery; Royal Northern and Clyde Yacht.

CODRINGTON, John Ernest Fleetwood, CMG 1968; *b* 1919; *s* of late Stewart Codrington; *m* 1951, Margaret, *d* of late Sir Herbert Hall Hall, KCMG; three *d. Educ:* Haileybury; Trinity Coll., Cambridge. Served RNVR, 1940–42: HMS Enchantress, HMS Vanity; Royal Marines, 1942–46: 42 (RM) Commando; Colonial Administrative Service, 1946: Gold Coast (later Ghana), 1947–58; Nyasaland, 1958–64; Financial Sec., Bahamas, 1964–70; Bahamas Comr in London, 1970–73, acting High Comr, 1973–74; Financial Sec., Bermuda, 1974–77. Consultant, FCO, 1991–94. *Recreation:* sailing. *Address:* Chequers Close, Lymington, Hants SO41 8AH. *Clubs:* Army and Navy; Royal Lymington Yacht.

CODRINGTON, Sir Simon (Francis Bethell), 3rd Bt *cr* 1876; *b* 14 Aug. 1923; *s* of Sir Christopher William Gerald Henry Codrington, 2nd Bt, and Joan Mary Hague-Cook (*d* 1961); *S* father, 1979; *m* 1st, 1947, Joanne (marr. diss. 1959), *d* of J. W. Molineaux and *widow* of William Humphrey Austin Thompson; 2nd, 1959, Pamela Joy Halliday Wise (marr. diss. 1979); three *s*; 3rd, 1980, Sarah Gwynne Gaze (*née* Pennell) (marr. diss. 1987); 4th, 1989, Shirley Ann, *d* of Percival Davis. *Educ:* Eton. Late Coldstream Guards. *Heir: s* Christopher George Wayne Codrington [*b* 20 Feb. 1960; *m* 1991, Noelle, *d* of Dale Leverson; one *s*]. *Address:* Dodington, Chipping Sodbury, Bristol BS17 6SF. *T:* Chipping Sodbury (01454) 312354.

CODRINGTON, Sir William (Alexander), 8th Bt *cr* 1721; FNI; Director, World-Wide Shipping Agency Ltd, since 1994; Port Captain, Hong Kong, for Worldwide Shipping Agency, since 1979; *b* 5 July 1934; *e s* of Sir William Richard Codrington, 7th Bt, and Joan Kathleen Birellu, *e d* of Percy E. Nicholas, London, NW; *S* father, 1961. *Educ:* St Andrew Coll., S Africa; S African Naval Coll., General Botha. FNI 1976. Joined Merchant Navy, 1952; joined Union Castle Mail Steamship Co., 1960; Master Mariner's Certificate of Competency, 1961. Joined Worldwide Shipping 1976. Chm., HK Br., Nautical Inst., 1994–. Mem., Hon. Co. of Master Mariners. Pres., Tooting and Balham Sea Cadet Unit. *Recreations:* model engineering, sailing. *Heir: b* Giles Peter Codrington [*b* 28 Oct. 1943; *m* 1989, Shirley Linda Duke; two *s* one *d*]. *Address:* Flat A, 1st Floor, Seaview Gardens, 31 Cloudview Road, Hong Kong. *Club:* Foreign Correspondents (Hong Kong).

CODRON, Michael Victor, CBE 1989; theatrical producer; *b* 8 June 1930; *s* of I. A. Codron and Lily (*née* Morgenstern). *Educ:* St Paul's Sch.; Worcester Coll., Oxford (BA). Director: Aldwych Theatre; Hampstead Theatre; Theatres Mutual Insurance Co.; Bd mem., Royal Nat. Theatre; Co-owner, Vaudeville Theatre. Cameron Mackintosh Prof. of Contemporary Theatre, Oxford Univ., 1993. Productions include: Share My Lettuce, Breath of Spring, 1957; Dock Brief and What Shall We Tell Caroline?, The Birthday Party, Valmouth, 1958; Pieces of Eight, 1959; The Wrong Side of the Park, The Caretaker, 1960; Three, Stop It Whoever You Are, One Over the Eight, The Tenth Man, Big Soft Nellie, 1961; Two Stars for Comfort, Everything in the Garden, Rattle of a Simple Man, 1962; Next Time I'll sing to You, Private Lives (revival), The Lovers and the Dwarfs, Cockade, 1963; Poor Bitos, The Formation Dancers, Entertaining Mr Sloane, 1964; Loot, The Killing of Sister George, Ride a Cock Horse, 1965; Little Malcolm and his Struggle against the Eunuchs, The Anniversary, There's a Girl in my Soup, Big Bad Mouse, 1966; The Judge, The Flip Side, Wise Child, The Boy Friend (revival), 1967; Not Now Darling, The Real Inspector Hound, 1968; The Contractor, Slag, The Two of Us, The Philanthropist, 1970; The Foursome, Butley, A Voyage Round my Father, The Changing Room, 1971; Veterans, Time and Time Again, Crown Matrimonial, My Fat Friend, 1972; Collaborators, Savages, Habeas Corpus, Absurd Person Singular, 1973; Knuckle, Flowers, Golden Pathway Annual, The Norman Conquests, John Paul George Ringo . . . and Bert, 1974; A Family and A Fortune, Alphabetical Order, A Far Better Husband, Ashes, Absent Friends, Otherwise Engaged, Stripwell, 1975; Funny Peculiar, Treats, Donkey's Years, Confusions, Teeth 'n' Smiles, Yahoo, 1976; Dusa, Stas, Fish & Vi, Just Between Ourselves, Oh, Mr Porter, Breezeblock Park, The Bells of Hell, The Old Country, 1977; The Rear Column, Ten Times Table, The Unvarnished Truth, The Homecoming (revival), Alice's Boys, Night and Day, 1978; Joking Apart, Tishoo, Stage Struck, 1979; Dr Faustus, Make and Break, The Dresser, Taking Steps, Enjoy, 1980; Hinge and Bracket at the Globe, Rowan Atkinson in Revue, House Guest, Quartermaine's Terms, 1981; Season's Greetings, Noises Off, Funny Turns, The Real Thing, 1982; The Hard Shoulder, 1983; Benefactors, 1984; Why Me?, Jumpers, Who Plays Wins, Look, No Hans!, 1985; Made in Bangkok, Woman in Mind, 1986; Three Sisters, A View from the Bridge, 1987; Hapgood, Uncle Vanya, Re: Joyce, The Sneeze, Henceforward, 1988; The Cherry Orchard, 1989; Man of the Moment, Look Look, Hidden Laughter, Private Lives, 1990; What the Butler Saw, 70 Girls 70, The Revengers' Comedies, 1991; The Rise and Fall of Little Voice, 1992; Time of My Life, Jamais Vu, 1993; Kit and the Widow, Dead Funny, Arcadia, The Sisters Rosensweig, 1994; *film:* Clockwise, 1986. *Recreation:* collecting Caroline memorabilia. *Address:* Aldwych Theatre Offices, Aldwych, WC2B 4DF. *Club:* Garrick.

COE, Denis Walter; Joint Founder and Executive Chairman, British Youth Opera, since 1987; *b* 5 June 1929; *s* of James and Lily Coe, Whitley Bay, Northumberland; *m* 1953, Margaret Rae (marr. diss. 1979), *d* of William and Ida Chambers; three *s* one *d*; *m* 1979, Diana Rosemary, *d* of Maxwell and Flora Barr. *Educ:* Bede Trng Coll., Durham; London Sch. of Economics. Teacher's Certificate, 1952; BSc (Econ.) 1960; MSc (Econ.) 1966. National Service in RAF, 1947–50; Junior and Secondary Schoolmaster, 1952–59; Dep. Headmaster, Secondary Sch., 1959–61; Lectr in Govt, Manchester Coll. of Commerce, 1961–66. Contested (Lab) Macclesfield, 1964; MP (Lab) Middleton, Prestwich and Whitefield, 1966–70; Parly deleg. to Council of Europe and WEU, 1968–70. Dean of Students, NE London Polytechnic, 1970–74; Asst Dir, Middx Polytechnic, 1974–82; Dir of Cleveland Arts, 1986–89; Founder/Dir., Cleveland Music Fest., 1985–89. Member: Governing Council, Nat. Youth Theatre, 1968–; Planning Cttee, Arts Council, 1987–90. Vice-Pres., SKILL (formerly Nat. Bureau for Handicapped Students), 1983– (Chm., 1975–83). FRSA 1992; Hon. Fellow, South Bank Univ., 1993; Hon. GSM, 1993. *Recreations:* music, drama, walking.

COE, Sebastian Newbold, OBE 1990 (MBE 1982); MP (C) Falmouth and Camborne, since 1992; *b* 29 Sept. 1956; *s* of Peter and Angela Coe; *m* 1990, Nicola McIrvine; one *s* one *d*. *Educ:* Loughborough University (BSc Hons Economics and Social History). Won gold medal for running 1500m and silver medal for 800m at Moscow Olympics, 1980; gold medal for 1500m and silver medal for 800m at Los Angeles Olympics, 1984; European Champion for 800m, Stuttgart, 1986; set world records at 800m, 1000m and mile, 1981. Research Assistant, Loughborough Univ., 1981–84. Sports Council: Mem., 1983–89; Vice-Chm., 1986–89, Chm., Olympic Review Gp, 1984–85. Member: HEA, 1987–92; Olympic Cttee, Medical Commn, 1987–. Associate Mem., Académie des Sports, France; Mem., Athletes Commn, Internat. Olympic Cttee, Lausanne. Chm., Diadora (UK), 1987–. Hon. DTech Loughborough, 1985; Hon. DSc Hull, 1988. Principe de Asturias award (Spain), 1987. *Publications:* (with David Miller) Running Free, 1981; (with Peter Coe) Running for Fitness, 1983; The Olympians, 1984. *Recreations:* listening to recorded or preferably live jazz, theatre, reading, avoiding all strenuous activity away from the track. *Address:* c/o House of Commons, SW1A 0AA. *Clubs:* East India, Sportsman's.

COEN, Massimo (Aldo), Hon. CBE 1991; Cavaliere al Merito del Lavoro 1982; Grande Ufficiale nell'Ordine al Merito della Repubblica Italiana 1979; Hon. Life President, Italian Chamber of Commerce for Great Britain, 1994; President, Etrufin Reserco Ltd, since 1985; Chairman, Britalia Consultants Ltd, since 1993; Chief Adviser, International Affairs—Italy, Simmons & Simmons Solicitors, since 1993; *b* Bologna, 29 July 1918; *s* of Cavaliere Ragioniere Terzo Coen and Delia Coen Guetta; *m* 1946, Thelma Doreen Kelley (*d* 1993); one *s* three *d*. *Educ:* Liceo Marco Foscarini, Venice (dipl. 1937); Padua University; London School of Economics. Came to London from Venice because of racial laws, 1939; interned in Isle of Man, June-Dec. 1940; Netherland Shipping & Trading Cttee Ltd, Jan.-April 1941; Italian Section, BBC External Services, 1941–46 (Shift Leader and Senior Announcer Translator); Chairman and Managing Director: Granosa Trading Co. Ltd and subsidiaries (dealing in textiles), 1946–92; Florence (Arts & Crafts) Ltd, 1946–92; Thames Rugs & Tweed Fabrics Ltd, 1959–92. Dir, Business Develt–Italy, Levy Gee Chartered Accountants; Consultant, Cyril Leonard & Co., Surveyors and Real Estate Agents. Councillor, Italian Chamber of Commerce for GB, 1951–72, Vice-Pres., 1972–78, Pres., 1978–94; Chm., Club di Londra, 1985–. Many radio plays, talks and commentaries during the war years. Acted in Snowbound, 1947, Hotel Sahara, 1951. Cavaliere 1956, Ufficiale 1968, Commendatore 1972, nell'Ordine al Merito della Repubblica Italiana. *Recreations:* shooting, fishing; formerly golf, competition skiing and fencing. *Address:* 14 Acacia Road, St John's Wood, NW8 6AN. *T:* 0171–722 2459/4868, *Fax:* 0171–526 8595.

COETZEE, Prof. John M.; writer; Professor of General Literature, University of Cape Town, since 1983; *b* 9 Feb. 1940; one *d* (one *s* decd). Educ: Univ. of Cape Town (MA); Univ. of Texas (PhD). FRSL 1988. Assistant Professor of English, State University of New York at Buffalo, 1968–71; Lectr in English, Univ. of Cape Town, 1972–82. Butler Prof. of English, State Univ. of New York at Buffalo, 1984; Hinkley Prof. of English, Johns Hopkins Univ., 1986, 1989; Vis. Prof. of English, Harvard Univ., 1991. Hon. Fellow, MLA, 1989. Hon. DLitt: Strathclyde, 1985; State Univ. of New York, 1989. *Publications:* Dusklands, 1974; In the Heart of the Country, 1977 (CNA Literary Award, 1977; filmed as Dust, 1986); Waiting for the Barbarians, 1980 (CNA Literary Award, 1980; James Tait Black Prize, 1980; Geoffrey Faber Award, 1980); Life and Times of Michael K, 1983 (CNA Literary Award, 1983; Booker-McConnell Prize, 1983; Prix Femina Etranger, 1985); Foe, 1986 (Jerusalem Prize, 1987); (ed with André Brink) A Land Apart, 1986; White Writing, 1988; Age of Iron, 1990 (Sunday Express Award, 1990); Doubling the Point, 1992; The Master of Petersburg, 1994; essays in Comp. Lit., Jl of Mod. Lit., Linguistics, Mod. Lang. Notes, Pubns of MLA, etc. *Address:* PO Box 92, Rondebosch, Cape Province, 7700, South Africa.

COFFER, David Edwin, CBE 1973 (OBE 1963); General Secretary, The Royal British Legion, 1959–78; *b* 18 Sept. 1913; *s* of David Gilbertson Coffer and Florence Ellen Gard; *m* 1947, Edith Mary Moulton; three *d*. *Educ:* Colfe Grammar Sch. Member: Supplementary Benefits Appeal Tribunals, 1978–85; Central Advisory Cttee on War Pensions, 1976–87; Bromley, Croydon and Sutton War Pensions Cttee, 1953–87, Chm., 1976–87; Patron, SE County, Royal British Legion, 1978–. *Address:* 47 Malvern Road, Orpington, Kent BR6 9HA. *T:* Orpington (01689) 829007.

COFFEY, Ann; *see* Coffey, M. A.

COFFEY, Rev. David Roy; General Secretary, Baptist Union of Great Britain, since 1991; *b* 13 Nov. 1941; *s* of Arthur Coffey and Elsie Maud Willis; *m* 1966, Janet Anne Dunbar; one *s* one *d*. *Educ:* Spurgeon's Coll., London (BA). Ordained, 1967; Minister: Whetstone Baptist Church, Leicester, 1967–72; North Cheam Baptist Ch., London, 1972–80; Sen. Minister, Upton Vale Baptist Ch., Torquay, 1980–88; Sec. for Evangelism, BUGB, 1988–91. Pres., BUGB, 1986–87. *Publication:* Build that Bridge – a Study in Conflict and Reconciliation, 1986. *Recreations:* music, walking. *Address:* Baptist House, PO Box 44, 129 Broadway, Didcot, Oxon OX11 8RT. *T:* Didcot (01235) 512077.

COFFEY, (Margaret) Ann; MP (Lab) Stockport, since 1992; *b* 31 Aug. 1946; *d* of late John Brown, MBE, and of Marie Brown; *m* 1973 (marr. diss. 1989); one *d*. *Educ:* Poly. of South Bank (BSc); Manchester Univ. (MSc). Trainee Social Worker, Walsall Social Services Dept, 1971–72; Social Worker: Birmingham, 1972–73; Gwynedd, 1973–74; Wolverhampton, 1974–75; Stockport, 1977–82; Cheshire, 1982–88; Team Leader, Fostering, Oldham Social Services Dept, 1988–92. Mem. (Lab) Stockport MBC, 1984–92 (Leader, Labour Group, 1988–92). Contested (Lab) Cheadle, 1987. Mem., Trade and Industry Select Cttee, 1993–; Vice Chm., PLP Trade and Industry Cttee, 1993–. *Address:* House of Commons, SW1A 0AA.

COFFIN, Cyril Edwin, CBE 1984; Director General, Food Manufacturers' Federation, 1977–84; *b* 29 June 1919; *m* 1947, Joyce Mary Tobitt; one *s* one *d* (and one *d* decd). *Educ:* King's Coll. Sch., Wimbledon; King's Coll., Cambridge. War service, 1939–45, Captain RIASC; jssc 1950. Civil servant, 1946–77; Alternate UK Governor, Internat. Atomic Energy Agency, 1964; Under-Secretary: Min. of Technology, 1966, later DTI; Dept of Prices and Consumer Protection, 1974–77. FRSA 1979. *Publications:* Working with Whitehall, 1987; A Blackmore Vale Family, 1992; articles in various jls. *Recreations:* music, learning languages. *Address:* 54 Cambridge Avenue, New Malden, Surrey KT3 4LE. *T:* 0181–942 0763. *Clubs:* Athenæum; Union (Cambridge).

COGGAN, Baron *cr* 1980 (Life Peer), of Canterbury and of Sissinghurst in the County of Kent; **Rt. Rev. and Rt. Hon. (Frederick) Donald Coggan;** PC 1961; Royal Victorian Chain, 1980; MA; DD; *b* 9 Oct. 1909; *s* of late Cornish Arthur Coggan and late Fannie Sarah Coggan; *m* 1935, Jean Braithwaite Strain; two *d*. *Educ:* Merchant Taylors' School; St John's College, Cambridge; Wycliffe Hall, Oxford. Late Schol. of St John's Coll., Cambridge, 1st cl. Or. Lang. Trip. pt i, 1930; BA (1st cl. Or. Lang. Trip. pt ii) and Jeremie Sep. Prize, 1931, Naden Div. Student, 1931; Tyrwhitt Hebrew Schol. and Mason Prize, 1932; MA 1935. Asst Lectr in Semitic Languages and Literature, University of Manchester, 1931–34; Curate of St Mary Islington, 1934–37; Professor of New Testament, Wycliffe College, Toronto, 1937–44; Principal of the London College of Divinity, 1944–56; Bishop of Bradford, 1956–61; Archbishop of York, 1961–74; Archbishop of Canterbury, 1974–80. Chairman of the Liturgical Commission, 1960–64. President, Society for Old Testament Studies, 1967–68; first Life President, Church Army, 1981. Pro-Chancellor, York Univ., 1962–74, Hull Univ., 1968–74. Prelate, Order of St John of Jerusalem, 1967–90. Wycliffe Coll., Toronto: BD 1941, DD (*hc*) 1944; DD (Lambeth) 1957; Hon. DD: Cambridge, 1962; Leeds, 1958; Aberdeen, 1963; Tokyo, 1963; Saskatoon, 1963; Huron, 1963; Hull, 1963; Manchester, 1972; Moravian Theol Seminary, 1976; Virginia Theol Seminary, 1979. Hon. LLD Liverpool, 1972; HHD Westminster Choir Coll., Princeton, 1966; Hon. DLitt Lancaster, 1967; STD (*hc*) Gen. Theol Seminary, NY, 1967; Hon. DCL Kent, 1975; DUniv York, 1975; FKC, 1975. Hon. Freeman, City of Canterbury, 1976. *Publications:* A People's Heritage, 1944; The Ministry of the Word, 1945; The Glory of God, 1950; Stewards of Grace, 1958; Five Makers of the New Testament, 1962; Christian Priorities, 1963; The Prayers of the New Testament, 1967; Sinews of Faith, 1969; Word and World, 1971; Convictions, 1975; On Preaching, 1978; The Heart of the Christian Faith, 1978; The Name above All Names, 1981; Sure Foundation, 1981; Mission to the World, 1982; Paul—Portrait of a Revolutionary, 1984; The Sacrament of the Word, 1987; Cuthbert Bardsley: bishop, evangelist, pastor, 1989; God of Hope, 1991; Voice From the Cross, 1993; The Servant-Son, 1995; contributions to Theology, etc. *Recreations:* gardening, motoring, music. *Address:* 28 Lions Hall, St Swithun Street, Winchester SO23 9HW. *T:* Winchester (01962) 864289. *Club:* Athenæum.

COGGINS, Prof. John Richard, PhD; FRSE; Professor of Biochemistry, University of Glasgow, since 1986; *b* 15 Jan. 1944; *s* of Cecil Rex Coggins and Pamela Mary Coggins (*née* Burnet); *m* 1970, Lesley Frances Watson; one *s* one *d*. *Educ:* Bristol GS; Queen's Coll., Oxford (MA); Univ. of Ottawa (PhD). FRSE 1988. Research Fellow: Brookhaven Nat. Lab., USA, 1970–72; Cambridge Univ., 1972–74; Glasgow University: Lectr, 1974–78; Sen. Lectr, 1978–86. Chm., Biochem. and Biophys. Cttee, 1985–88, Mem., Biotechnol. Directorate Management Cttee, 1987–90, SERC; Member: Liby and Inf. Services Cttee, Scotland, 1982–88; Biotechnol. Jt Adv. Bd, 1989–94; Wkg Party on Biotechnol., NEDO, 1990–92; AFRC, 1991–94; Advr for Biochem., UFC, 1990–93.

Chm., Molecular Enzymol. Gp, Biochemical Soc., 1981–85. *Publications:* Multidomain Proteins: structure and evolution, 1986; contribs on enzymes and on plant and microbial biochem. to Biochem. Jl, Jl of Biol Chem., Jl Molecular Biol., etc. *Recreations:* sailing, travel, good food, reading. *Address:* Department of Biochemistry, University of Glasgow, Glasgow G12 8QQ. *T:* 0141–339 8855. *Club:* Clyde Cruising (Glasgow).

COGHILL, Sir Egerton James Nevill Tobias, (Sir Toby Coghill), 8th Bt *cr* 1778; *b* 26 March 1930; *s* of Sir Joscelyn Ambrose Cramer Coghill, 7th Bt and Elizabeth Gwendoline (*d* 1980), *d* of John B. Atkins; *S* father, 1983; *m* 1958, Gabriel Nancy, *d* of Major Dudley Claud Douglas Ryder; one *s* one *d. Educ:* Gordonstoun; Pembroke College, Cambridge. E-SU Walter Hines Page Scholar to USA. Architectural Asst with Sir Frederick Gibberd & Ptnrs, 1952–55; Industrial Developer, 1955–58; Admin. Manager, McKinsey and Co. Inc., 1959–61; Supply teacher, LCC, 1961–62; Housemaster, Aiglon Coll., Switzerland (Chm. Govs, 1991–), 1962–64; Headmaster, Aberlour House, 1964–89. Dir, Aiglon Coll., Switzerland (Chm. Govs, 1991–). Trustee, Scottish Dyslexia Trust, 1992–; Pres., Moray Soc. *Recreation:* country sports. *Heir: s* Patrick Kendal Farley Coghill, *b* 3 Nov. 1960. *Address:* Sourden, Rothes, Aberlour, Banffshire AB38 7AE. *Club:* Royal Ocean Racing.

COGHLAN, Terence Augustine; QC 1993; a Recorder, since 1989; *b* 17 Aug. 1945; *s* of late Austin Frances Coghlan and of Ruby Coghlan (*née* Comrie); *m* 1973, Angela Agatha Westmacott; one *s* two *d. Educ:* Downside; Perugia; New Coll., Oxford; Inns of Court. Called to the Bar, Inner Temple, 1968 (Scholar). Film extra, 1968; Dir, City of London Sinfonia, 1975–. *Recreations:* music, architecture, wine, windsurfing, hill-walking. *Address:* 1 Crown Office Row, Temple, EC4Y 7HH. *T:* 0171–797 7500. *Clubs:* Whitefriars, Les Six.

COGMAN, Very Rev. Frederick Walter; Dean of Guernsey, 1967–78; Rector of St Peter Port, Guernsey, 1976–78; *b* 4 March 1913; *s* of William Frederick Cogman and Mabel Cozens; *m* 1940, Rose Hélène Mauger; one *s* one *d. Educ:* Rutlish Sch., Merton; King's Coll., London. Asst Priest, Upton-cum-Chalvey, Slough, 1938–42; Chaplain and Housemaster, St George's Sch., Harpenden, 1942–48; Rector of St Martin, Guernsey, 1948–76. *Recreations:* music, painting.

COHAN, Robert Paul, CBE 1989; Founder Artistic Director, Contemporary Dance Trust; *b* 27 March 1925; *s* of Walter and Billie Cohan; British citizen, 1989. *Educ:* Martha Graham Sch., NYC. Joined Martha Graham Co., 1946; Partner, 1950; Co-Dir, Martha Graham Co., 1966; Artistic Dir, Contemporary Dance Trust Ltd, 1967; Artistic Dir and Principal Choreographer, 1969–87, Dir, 1987–89, London Contemporary Dance Theatre; Artistic Advr, Batsheva Co., Israel, 1980; Director: York Univ., Toronto Choreographic Summer Sch., 1977; Gulbenkian Choreographic Summer Sch., Univ. of Surrey, 1978, 1979, 1982; Banff Sch. of Fine Arts Choreographic Seminar, Canada, 1980; New Zealand Choreographic Seminar, 1982; Choreographic Seminar, Simon Frazer Univ., Vancouver, 1985; Internat. Dance Course for Professional Choreographers and Composers, Surrey Univ., 1985, 1989. With London Contemporary Dance Theatre toured Britain, E and W Europe, S America, N Africa and USA; major works created: Cell, 1969 (recorded for BBC TV, 1982); Stages, 1971; Waterless Method of Swimming Instruction, 1974 (recorded for BBC TV); Class, 1975; Stabat Mater, 1975 (recorded for BBC TV); Masque of Separation, 1975; Khamsin, 1976; Nympheas, 1976 (recorded for BBC TV, 1983); Forest, 1977 (recorded by BBC TV); Eos, 1978; Songs, Lamentations and Praises, 1979; Dances of Love and Death, 1981; Agora, 1984; A Mass for Man, 1985 (recorded for BBC TV); Ceremony, 1986; Interrogations, 1986; Video Life, 1986; Phantasmagoria, 1987; A Midsummer Night's Dream, 1993. Editor, Choreography and Dance. Hon. Fellow, York Univ., Toronto. Hon. DLitt Exeter, 1993; DUniv Middlesex, 1994. Evening Standard Award for most outstanding achievement in ballet, 1975; Soc. of West End Theatres Award for most outstanding achievement in ballet, 1978. *Publication:* The Dance Workshop, 1986. *Recreation:* dancing. *Address:* The Place, 17 Dukes Road, WC1H 9AB. *T:* 0171–387 0161.

COHEN; *see* Waley-Cohen.

COHEN, Prof. Bernard Woolf; Slade Professor, and Chair of Fine Art, University of London, since 1988; *b* 28 July 1933; *s* of Victor and Leah Cohen; *m* 1959, Jean Cohen; one *s* one *d. Educ:* Slade School of Fine Art, University Coll. London (Dip. Fine Art). Head of Painting, Wimbledon Sch. of Art, 1980–87. Vis. Prof., Univ. of New Mexico, USA, 1969–70. Fellow, UCL, 1992. First one man exhibn, Gimpel Fils Gall., 1958, again in 1960; other exhibitions: Molton Gall., 1962; Kasmin Gall., Bond Street, 1963, 1964, 1967; Waddington Gall., 1974, 1977, 1979, 1990; First New York exhibn, Betty Parsons Gall., 1967; major retrospective, Hayward Gall., 1972; print retrospective, Tate Gall., 1976; drawing retrospective, Ben Uri Gall., 1994; paintings, Tate Gall., 1995; represented GB at Venice Biennale, 1966. Work in collections of Tate Gall., Mus. of Modern Art, New York; Fogg Mus., Mass; Minneapolis Walker Art Centre; Carnegie Inst., Pittsburgh, and others. *Recreations:* painting, travel, food, wine, music. *Address:* Slade School of Fine Art, University College London, Gower Street, WC1E 6BT. *T:* 0171–387 7050.

COHEN, Betty; *see* Jackson, B.

COHEN, Sir Edward, Kt 1970; company director; Solicitor; Consultant, Corrs Chambers Westgarth, solicitors, Melbourne, Australia; *b* 9 Nov. 1912; *s* of Brig. Hon. H. E. Cohen; *m* 1939, Meryl D., *d* of D. G. Fink; one *s. Educ:* Scotch Coll., Melbourne (Exhibnr in Greek and Roman History); Ormond Coll., Univ. of Melbourne (LLB; Aust. Blue Athletics, Hockey). Served, 1940–45: AIF, 2/12 Fd Regt, 9th Div. Artillery, Captain 1942. Partner, Pavey, Wilson, Cohen & Carter, 1945–76; Director: Carlton and United Breweries, 1947–84 (Chm., 1967–84); Swan Brewery, 1947–57; Associated Pulp & Paper Mills Ltd, 1951–83 (Dep. Chm. 1981–83); Electrolytic Zinc Co., A'asia, 1951–84 (Chm., 1960–84); Glazebrooks Paints and Chemicals Ltd, 1951–61; Standard Mutual Bldg Soc., 1951–64; E. Z. Industries, 1956–84 (Chm., 1960–84, Pres., 1984–); Pelaco Ltd, 1959–68; Commercial Union Assurance, 1960–82 (Chm., 1964–82); Union Assce Soc. of Aust., 1960–75 (Local Advisor, 1951–60); Michaelis Bayley Ltd, 1964–80; Qld Brewery (later CUB Qld), 1968–84; Herald and Weekly Times Ltd, 1974–77 (Vice-Chm., 1976–77); Chairman: Derwent Metals, 1957–84; CUB Fibre Containers, 1963–84; Emu Bay Railway Co., 1967–84; Manufrs Bottle Co., Vic, 1967–84; Northern Aust. Breweries (CUB (N Qld)), 1967–84; Nat. Commercial Union, 1982–84. Past Member: Faculty of Law of Melbourne Univ.; Internat. Hse Council, Melbourne Univ.; Council of Legal Education and Bd of Examiners. Mem. Council Law Inst. of Victoria, 1959–68, Pres. 1965–66. Chairman: Pensions Cttee, Melbourne Legacy, 1961–84 (Mem., 1955–84); Royal Women's Hosp. 1968 Million Dollar Bldg Appeal; Eileen Patricia Goulding Meml Fund Appeal, 1983; Life Governor: Austin, Prince Henry's, Royal Children's, Royal Melbourne, Royal Women's Hosps; Corps of Commissionaires; Adult Deaf and Dumb Soc. of Victoria. Hon. Solicitor, Queens Fund, 1951–94. Twelfth Leonard Ball Orator, Victorian Foundn on Alcoholism and Drug Dependence, 1980. *Address:* 722 Orrong Road, Toorak, Victoria 3142, Australia; (office) 600 Bourke Street, Melbourne, Victoria 3000, Australia. *Clubs:* Naval and Military, Victoria Racing, Royal Automobile, Melbourne Cricket, Kooyong Lawn Tennis (Melbourne).

COHEN, George Cormack; Sheriff-Substitute of the Lothians and Peebles at Edinburgh, 1955–66; *b* 16 Dec. 1909; *s* of J. Cohen and Mary J. Cormack, Melfort House, Bearsden, Dunbartonshire; *m* 1939, Elizabeth, *d* of James H. Wallace, Malvern; one *s* one *d. Educ:* Kelvinside Academy, Glasgow; Glasgow Univ. MA 1930, LLB 1934. Admitted to Scottish Bar, 1935; Sheriff-Substitute of Caithness at Wick, 1944–51; of Ayr and Bute at Kilmarnock, 1951–55. *Recreations:* travel, gastronomy, philately, gardening. *Address:* 37B Lauder Road, Edinburgh EH9 1UE. *T:* 0131–668 1689.

COHEN, Prof. Gerald Allan, FBA 1985; Chichele Professor of Social and Political Theory and Fellow of All Souls, Oxford, since Jan. 1985; *b* 14 April 1941; *s* of Morrie Cohen and Bella Lipkin; *m* 1965, Margaret Florence Pearce; one *s* two *d. Educ:* Morris Winchevsky Jewish School, Montreal; Strathcona Academy, Montreal; Outremont High School, Montreal; McGill University (BA 1961); New College, Oxford (BPhil 1963). Lectr in Philosophy, University College London, 1963, Reader, 1978–84. Vis. Asst Prof. of Political Science, McGill Univ., 1965; Vis. Associate Prof. of Philosophy, Princeton Univ., 1975. *Publications:* Karl Marx's Theory of History: a defence, 1978; History, Labour and Freedom: themes from Marx, 1988; articles in anthologies, philosophical and social-scientific jls. *Recreations:* Guardian crosswords, the visual arts, the politics of India. *Address:* All Souls College, Oxford OX1 4AL. *T:* Oxford (01865) 279339.

COHEN, Harry; MP (Lab) Leyton, since 1983; accountant; *b* 10 Dec. 1949; *m* 1978, Ellen Hussain; one step *s* one step *d* and one foster *s.* Mem., Waltham Forest Borough Council, 1972–83 (formerly Chm., Planning Cttee and Sec., Labour Group). Mem., UNISON. *Address:* House of Commons, SW1A 0AA.

COHEN, Sir Ivor (Harold), Kt 1992; CBE 1985; TD 1968; Chairman, Remploy Ltd, 1987–93; *b* 28 April 1931; *s* of Jack Cohen and Anne (*née* Victor); *m* 1963, Betty Edith, *yr d* of Reginald George and Mabel Appleby; one *d. Educ:* Central Foundation Sch., EC2; University Coll. London (BA (Hons) Mod. Hist.; Fellow, 1987). Nat. Service, Royal Signals, 1952–54 (2nd Lieut); TA, Royal Signals, 1954–69 (Major 1964). Engrg industry, 1954–57; range of managerial posts, Mullard Ltd (subsid. of Philips (UK)), 1957–77; Dir, Philips Lighting, 1977–79; Man. Dir, Mullard Ltd, 1979–87; Dir, Philips Electronics (UK) Ltd, 1984–87. Non-Executive Director: AB Electronic Products Gp plc, 1987–93; Océ (UK) Ltd, 1988–; PA Holdings Ltd, 1989–; Redifon Holdings Ltd, 1989–94; Redifon Ltd, 1989–91; Magnetic Materials Gp plc, 1992; Electron Technologies Ltd, 1994–; Cons., Comet Gp plc, 1987–90; Advr, Apax & Co. Ventures (formerly Alan Patricof Associates), 1987–93; Mem., Adv. Cttee, Mitsubishi Electric (UK) Ltd, 1991–. Member: IT Adv. Panel, 1981–86; Teletext and Viewdata Steering Gp, DTI, 1981–86; Electronic Components EDC, NEDO, 1980–88; Electronics Ind. EDC, NEDO, 1982–86; Steering Cttee, Telecom. Infrastructure, DTI, 1987–88; Computing Software and Communications Requirements Bd, DTI, 1984–88; Steering Bd, Radiocommunications Agency, DTI, 1990–; Electronics Ind. Sector Gp, NEDO, 1988–92 (Chm., 1990–); Chairman: Electronic Applications Sector Gp, NEDO, 1988–90; Measurement Adv. Cttee, DTI, 1994–; Japan Electronics Business Assoc., 1991–; Member Council: Electronic Components Ind. Fedn, 1980–87; European Electronic Components Assoc., 1985–87; Dir, Radio Industries Council, 1980–87. Mem., Schs Examinations and Assessment Council, 1988–90; British Schools Technology: Mem. Council of Management, 1984–87, Trustee Dir, 1987–89; Mem., Management Adv. Gp IT Res. Inst., Brighton Poly., 1987–90. CompIEE 1988; Hon. Mem. CGLI, 1989; FInstD 1988; FRSA 1984; Hon. FEng 1992. Freeman, City of London, 1982; Liveryman: Sci. Instrument Makers' Co., 1982–; Co. of Information Technologists, 1992– (Freeman, 1990). Mem., Editl Bd, Nat. Electronics Review, 1987–90. *Publications:* articles on electronics policy and marketing and use of inf. technology in the technical press. *Recreations:* opera, reading, occasional sculpting, walking in towns. *Address:* 24 Selborne Road, Croydon, Surrey CR0 5JQ. *Club:* East India.

COHEN, Janet, (Mrs J. L. Cohen); Director, Charterhouse Bank Ltd, since 1988; a Governor, BBC, since 1994; *b* 4 July 1940; *d* of late George Edric Neel and of Mary Isabel Neel (*née* Budge); *m* 1971, James Lionel Cohen; two *s* one *d. Educ:* Newnham Coll., Cambridge (BA Hons Law 1962; Associate Fellow, 1988–91). Articled clerk, Frere Cholmeley, 1963–65; admitted solicitor, 1965; Consultant: ABT Associates, USA, 1965–67; John Laing Construction, 1968–69; Department of Trade and Industry: Principal, 1969–78; Asst Sec., 1978–82; Asst Dir, Charterhouse Bank Ltd, 1982–88. Chm., Café Pelican Ltd, 1984–90; Vice Chm., Yorks Building Soc., 1994– (Dir, 1991–94); Non-executive Director: BPP Hldgs, 1994–; John Waddington, 1994–. Mem., Schools Exam. and Assessment Council, 1990–93. *Publications:* as Janet Neel: Death's Bright Angel, 1988; Death on Site, 1989; Death of a Partner, 1991; Death among the Dons, 1993; as Janet Cohen: The Highest Bidder, 1992; Children of a Harsh Winter, 1994. *Recreation:* restaurants. *Address:* 50 Blenheim Terrace, NW8 0EG. *T:* 0171–625 7306/5809. *Club:* Reform.

COHEN, Laurence Jonathan, FBA 1973; Fellow and Praelector in Philosophy, 1957–90, Senior Tutor, 1985–90, Queen's College, Oxford, now Emeritus Fellow; British Academy Reader in Humanities, Oxford University, 1982–84; *b* 7 May 1923; *s* of Israel and Theresa Cohen; *m* 1953, Gillian Mary Slee; three *s* one *d. Educ:* St Paul's Sch., London; Balliol Coll., Oxford (MA 1947, DLitt 1982). Served War: Naval Intell. in UK and SEAC, 1942–45, and Lieut (Sp.) RNVR. Asst in Logic and Metaphysics, Edinburgh Univ., 1947–50; Lectr in Philosophy, St Andrews Univ. at Dundee, 1950–57; Commonwealth Fund Fellow in Logic at Princeton and Harvard Univs, 1952–53. Vis. Lectr, Hebrew Univ. of Jerusalem, 1952; Visiting Professor: Columbia Univ., 1967; Yale Univ., 1972; Northwestern Univ. Law Sch., 1988; Hon. Prof., Northwest Univ., Xian, China, 1987. Vis. Fellow, ANU, 1980. British Acad. Philosophical Lectr, 1975; Fry Lectr, Bristol Univ., 1976; Austin Lectr, UK Assoc. for Legal and Social Philos., 1982. Sec., Internat. Union of History and Philosophy of Science (Div. of Logic, Methodology and Philosophy of Science), 1975–83, Pres., 1987–91; Pres., British Soc. for Philosophy of Science, 1977–79; Chairman: British Nat. Cttee for Logic, Methodology and Philosophy of Science, 1987–91; Section K (Phil.), British Acad., 1994–; Sec.-Gen., ICSU, 1993–; Mem., Comité Directeur, Fédn Internat. des Socs de Philosophie, 1983–. Governor: Bartholomew Sch., Eynsham, 1989–93; Wood Green Sch., Witney, 1990–93. General Editor, Clarendon Library of Logic and Philosophy, 1973–. *Publications:* The Principles of World Citizenship, 1954; The Diversity of Meaning, 1962; The Implications of Induction, 1970; The Probable and the Provable, 1977; (ed jtly) Applications of Inductive Logic, 1980; (ed jtly) Logic, Methodology and Philosophy of Science, 1982; The Dialogue of Reason, 1986; An Introduction to the Philosophy of Induction and Probability, 1989; An Essay on Belief and Acceptance, 1992. *Recreations:* gardening; work for Council for Protection of Rural England. *Address:* Queen's College, Oxford OX1 4AW.

COHEN, Hon. Leonard Harold Lionel, OBE 1995; barrister-at-law; *b* 1 Jan. 1922; *s* of Rt Hon. Lord Cohen, PC (Life Peer), and Adelaide, Lady Cohen (*née* Spielmann); *m* 1949, Eleanor Lucy Quixano Henriques; two *s* one *d. Educ:* Eton Coll.; New Coll., Oxford (MA). War Service, Rifle Bde (wounded), Captain, 1941–45. Called to Bar, Lincoln's Inn, 1948, Bencher, 1989; practised at Chancery Bar, 1949–61. Chm., Secure Retirement PLC, 1987–92; Dir, M. Samuel & Co. Ltd (subseq. Hill Samuel & Co. Ltd), 1961–76. Dir-Gen., Accepting Houses Cttee, 1976–82; Chairman: United Services

Trustee, 1976–82; Council, Royal Free Hosp. Med. Sch., 1982–92; Community Trust for Berkshire, 1988–93; Pres., Jewish Colonization Assoc., 1976–92. Master of the Skinners' Co., 1971–72. Hon. Col, 39th (City of London) Signal Regt (V), 1973–78. High Sheriff of Berks, 1987–88. *Recreations:* shooting, golf, reading, opera. *Address:* Dovecote House, Swallowfield Park, Reading RG7 1TG. *T:* Reading (01734) 884775. *Club:* White's.

COHEN, Dr Louis; Executive Secretary, Institute of Physics, 1966–90, retired; *b* 14 Oct. 1925; *s* of late Harry Cohen and Fanny Cohen (*née* Abrahams); *m* 1948, Eve G. Marsh; one *s* two *d*. *Educ:* Manchester Central High Sch.; Manchester Univ.; Imperial Coll., London. BSc, PhD, FInstP. Research Physicist, Simon-Carves Ltd, 1953–63; Research Manager, Pyrotenax Ltd, 1963–66. Hon. Sec., Council of Science and Technology Insts, 1969–87; Treasurer, European Physical Soc., 1968–73; Corresp. Mem., Manchester Literary and Philosophical Soc., 1963. FRSA. *Publications:* papers and articles on physics and related subjects. *Recreations:* cooking, books, music, the theatre. *Address:* Flat 1, 21 Hamilton Road, W5 2EE. *T:* 0181–579 2227.

COHEN, Michael Antony; Chief Executive, The Guinness Trust, since 1987; *b* 18 April 1940; *s* of Gerald and Beatrice Cohen; *m* 1967, Jennifer Audrey Price; one *s* two *d*. *Educ:* Quarry Bank Grammar School, Liverpool; Univ. of Liverpool (BA Hons Econ.). FCA; MIH. Articled clerk, 1962–65; Accountant and Planning Manager, Bank of London & S America, 1965–72; posts in European and US banking, Lloyds Bank, 1972–78; Internat. Project Finance Manager, Lloyds Bank, 1978–82; Regional Dir, London and SE, Housing Corp., 1982–87. Mem. Council, London Borough of Barnet, 1972–78. Chairman: St Mungo Community Housing Assoc., 1991–; Barnet Housing Aid Centre, 1990–; Phoenix Cinema Trust Ltd. *Recreations:* walking, eating, France, theatre, finding time. *Address:* 6 Talbot Avenue, East Finchley, N2 0LS. *T:* 0181–883 9433.

COHEN, Lt-Col Mordaunt, TD 1954; DL; Regional Chairman of Industrial Tribunals, 1976–89 (Chairman, 1974–76); *b* 6 Aug. 1916; *s* of Israel Ellis Cohen and Sophie Cohen; *m* 1953, Her Honour Judge Myrella Cohen, *qv*; one *s* one *d*. *Educ:* Bede Collegiate Sch. for Boys, Sunderland. Admitted solicitor, 1938. Served War, RA, 1940–46: seconded RWAFF; despatches, Burma campaign; served TA, 1947–55: CO 463(M) HAA Regt, RA(TA), 1954–55. Alderman, Sunderland Co. Bor. Council, 1967–74; Chm., Sunderland Educn Cttee, 1970–72; Chm., NE Council of Educn Cttees, 1971; Councillor, Tyne and Wear CC, 1973–74; Dep. Chm., Northern Traffic Comrs, 1973–74. Chm., Mental Health Review Tribunal, 1967–76. Chm. of Governors, Sunderland Polytechnic, 1969–72; Mem. Court, Univ. of Newcastle upon Tyne, 1968–72. Pres., Sunderland Law Soc., 1970; Hon. Life Pres., Sunderland Hebrew Congregation, 1988; Mem., Bd of Deputies of British Jews (Chm., Provincial Cttee, 1985–91; Dir, Central Enquiry Desk, 1990–); former Mem., Chief Rabbinate Council; Vice Pres., AJEX, 1995– (Chm., 1993–95); Life Pres., Sunderland Br., AJEX, 1970; Trustee: Ajex Charitable Trust, 1978–; Colwyn Bay Synagogue Trust, 1978–. Chm. of Govs, Edgware Sch., 1991–. DL Tyne and Wear, 1986. *Recreations:* watching sport, playing bowls; communal service, promoting inter-faith understanding. *Address:* Flat 1, Peters Lodge, 2 Stonegrove, Edgware, Middlesex HA8 7TY.

COHEN, Myrella, QC 1970; **Her Honour Judge Myrella Cohen;** a Circuit Judge, since 1972; *b* 16 Dec. 1927; *d* of late Samuel and Sarah Cohen, Manchester; *m* 1953, Lt-Col Mordaunt Cohen, *qv*; one *s* one *d*. *Educ:* Manchester High Sch. for Girls; Colwyn Bay Grammar Sch.; Manchester Univ. (LLB 1948). Called to the Bar, Gray's Inn, 1950. Recorder of Hull, 1971; Dep. High Court Judge, Family Div. Mem., Parole Bd, 1983–86. Vice-Pres., N of England CRC, 1974–. Life Mem., Council, League of Jewish Women, 1991; Pres., 1968, 1988, Hon. Mem., 1989, Sunderland Soroptomists. Patron: Sunderland Council for the Disabled; Suzy Lamplugh Trust. FRSA 1993. Hon. LLD Sunderland, 1992. *Address:* c/o The Crown Court at Harrow, Hailsham Drive, Harrow, Middx HA1 4TJ. *Club:* Soroptimist Club of Great Britain.

COHEN, Lt-Col Nathan Leslie, OBE 1990; CPM 1956; TD 1949; JP; *b* 13 Jan. 1908; *s* of Reuben and Maud Cohen; unmarried. *Educ:* Stockton-on-Tees Grammar Sch.; Clifton Coll. In private practice as a Solicitor until 1939; called to the Bar, Lincoln's Inn, 1954. War Service, Aug. 1939–May 1945. Senior Legal Officer (Lt-Col), Military Govt, Carinthia, Austria, 1945–49; Pres. of Sessions Courts, Malaya, 1949–57; Justice of the Special Courts, Cyprus, 1958–59; Judge of HM Court of Sovereign Base Areas of Akrotiri and Dhekalia, Cyprus, 1960–61; Adjudicator under Immigration Appeals Act, 1970–71. Mem., Cleveland Co. Social Services Cttee 1978–80. Dist Hd, Forces Relief Soc., Stockton, 1975–; Vice-President: Northern Area, Royal British Legion; Cleveland British Red Cross Soc.; Patron, Durham and Cleveland Royal British Legion, 1985–; President: Stockton Physically Handicapped Club, 1990–; St John Ambulance Assoc., Stockton and Thornaby. SBStJ 1980. JP Stockton-on-Tees, 1967. Freedom, Stockton-on-Tees, 1991. Diamond Jubilee Medal (Johore), 1955; Royal Brit. Legion Gold Badge, 1979; British Red Cross Badge of Honour, 1981, Voluntary Medical Service Medal, 1982; Service Medal, Order of St John, 1993. *Recreations:* travelling, reading. *Address:* 35 Richmond Road, Stockton-on-Tees, Cleveland TS18 4DS. *T:* Stockton (01642) 674831. *Club:* Royal Over-Seas League.

COHEN, Prof. Philip, PhD; FRS 1984; FRSE 1984; Royal Society Research Professor, since 1984, and Director, Medical Research Council Protein Phosphorylation Unit, since 1990, University of Dundee; *b* 22 July 1945; *s* of Jacob Davis Cohen and Fanny (*née* Bragman); *m* 1969, Patricia Townsend Wade; one *s* one *d*. *Educ:* Hendon County Grammar Sch.; University Coll. London (BSc 1st Cl. Hons (Biochemistry Special), 1966; PhD Biochem., 1969; Fellow, 1993). SRC/NATO Postdoctoral Res. Fellow, Dept of Biochem., Univ. of Washington, Seattle, USA, 1969–71; Univ. of Dundee: Lectr in Biochem., 1971–78; Reader in Biochem., 1978–81; Prof. of Enzymology, 1981–84. Mem., Eur. Molecular Biology Orgn, 1982–; MAE 1990. Anniversary Prize, Fedn of Eur. Biochemical Socs, 1977; Colworth Medal, 1978, CIBA medal and prize, 1992, British Biochem. Soc.; Prix van Gysel, Belgian Royal Acads of Medicine, 1992; Dundee City of Discovery Roseball Award, 1993; Bruce Preller Prize, RSE, 1993. Man. Editor, Biochimica et Biophysica Acta, 1981–92. *Publications:* Control of Enzyme Activity, 1976, 2nd edn 1983; (ed series) Molecular Aspects of Cellular Regulation: vol. 1, 1980; vol. 2, 1982; vol. 3, 1984; vol. 4, 1985; vol. 5, 1988; vol. 6, 1991; over 300 original papers and revs in scientific jls. *Recreations:* chess, bridge, golf, natural history. *Address:* Inverbay II, Invergowrie, Dundee DD2 5DQ. *T:* Dundee (01382) 562328. *Club:* Downfield Golf.

COHEN, Dr Richard Henry Lionel, CB 1969; Chief Scientist, Department of Health and Social Security, 1972–73, retired; *b* 1 Feb. 1907; *y s* of Frank Lionel and Bertha Hendelah Cohen; *m* 1934, Margaret Clarkson Deas; one *s*. *Educ:* Clifton Coll.; King's Coll., Cambridge; St Bartholomew's Hospital. Miscellaneous hosp. appts, 1940–46; MRC, 1948–62; Dep. Chief Med. Off., MRC, 1957–62; Dept of Health and Social Security (formerly Min. of Health), 1962–73. *Address:* The End House South, Lady Margaret Road, Cambridge CB3 0BJ.

COHEN, Prof. Robert Donald, MD, FRCP; Professor of Medicine and Director, Academic Medical Unit, London Hospital Medical College, University of London, since 1981 (Professor of Metabolic Medicine, 1974–81); *b* 11 Oct. 1933; *s* of Dr Harry H. and Ruby Cohen; *m* 1961, Dr Barbara Joan Boucher; one *s* one *d*. *Educ:* Clifton Coll.; Trinity Coll., Cambridge. MA, MD (Cantab). Hon. Cons. Physician, London Hosp., 1967; Chm., Editorial Bd, Clinical Science and Molecular Medicine, 1973–74; Dir, Academic Unit of Metabolism and Endocrinology, London Hosp. Med. Coll., 1974; Chairman: Adv. Cttee on the Application of Computing Science to Medicine and the Nat. Health Service, 1976–77; DHSS Computer R&D Cttee, 1977–80; Jt Cttee on Higher Med. Trng, 1983–90 (Chm., Special Adv. Cttee on Gen. Internal Medicine, 1983–90); DHSS/MRC Monitoring Cttee on Magnetic Resonance Imaging, 1986–89; Review Body, British Diabetic Assoc., 1990–; Member: GMC, 1988–; Physiological Systems Bd, MRC, 1990–92; Physiological Medicine and Infections Bd, MRC, 1992–; Health Services and Public Health Bd, MRC, 1992–; Council, Imperial Cancer Res. Fund, 1989– (Vice-Chm., 1991–94; Chm., 1994–). Sen. Censor and Sen. Vice-Pres., RCP, 1991–93. *Publications:* Clinical and Biochemical Aspects of Lactic Acidosis (with H. F. Woods), 1976; (jtly) The Metabolic and Molecular Basis of Acquired Disease, 1990; papers in Clin. Sci. and Molecular Med., BMJ, Lancet, Biochemical Journal. *Address:* Medical Unit, The Royal London Hospital, Whitechapel Road, E1 1BB. *T:* 0171–377 7110, *Fax:* 0171–377 7636.

COHEN, Stanley; *b* 31 July 1927; *s* of Thomas and Teresa Cohen; *m* 1954, Brenda P. Rafferty; three *s* one *d*. *Educ:* St Patrick's and St Charles' Schools, Leeds. Served in Royal Navy, 1947–49. Employed in Clothing Industry, 1943–47 and 1949–51; Clerical Officer with British Railways, 1951–70. Mem. Leeds City Council, 1952–71; elected Alderman, 1968. Parly Candidate (Lab) Barkston Ash County Constituency, 1966; MP (Lab) Leeds South East, 1970–83. PPS to Minister of State, DES, 1976–79. Mem., Duke of Edinburgh's Commonwealth Study Conf. to Australia, 1968. *Recreations:* walking, camping, driving. *Address:* 9 Pendil Close, Whitkirk, Leeds LS15 0NE. *T:* Leeds (0113) 264 9568. *Clubs:* Crossgates Recreational; Irish Centre (Leeds).

COHEN, Prof. Stanley, PhD; Professor of Criminology, Hebrew University, Jerusalem, since 1981; *b* 23 Feb. 1942; *s* of Ray and Sie Cohen; *m* 1963, Ruth Kretzmer; two *d*. *Educ:* Univ. of Witwatersrand, Johannesburg (BA); LSE, Univ. of London (PhD). Psychiatric social worker, 1963–64; Lectr in Sociology: Enfield Coll., 1965–67; Univ. of Durham, 1967–72; Sen. Lectr in Sociol., Univ. of Essex, 1972–74, Prof. of Sociol., 1974–81. Vis. Centennial Prof., LSE, 1994–95. Sellin-Glueck Award, Amer. Soc. of Criminology, 1985. *Publications:* Images of Deviance, 1971; Folk Devils and Moral Panics, 1972; Psychological Survival, 1972; The Manufacture of News, 1973; Escape Attempts, 1976; Prison Secrets, 1978; Social Control and the State, 1984; Visions of Social Control: crime, punishment and classification, 1985; Against Criminology, 1988. *Address:* Institute of Criminology, Hebrew University, Mount Scopus, Jerusalem 91905, Israel.

COHEN, Prof. Stanley; Distinguished Professor, Department of Biochemistry, Vanderbilt University School of Medicine, since 1986; *b* 17 Nov. 1922; *s* of Louis Cohen and Fruma Feitel; *m* 1st, 1951, Olivia Larson; three *s*; 2nd, 1981, Jan Elizabeth Jordan. *Educ:* Brooklyn Coll., NY; Oberlin Coll., Ohio; Univ. of Michigan (BA, PhD). Teaching Fellow, Dept of Biochem., Univ. of Michigan, 1946–48; Instructor, Depts of Biochem. and Pediatrics, Univ. of Colorado Sch. of Medicine, 1948–52; Fellow, Amer. Cancer Soc., Dept of Radiology, Washington Univ., St Louis, 1952–53; Vanderbilt University School of Medicine, Nashville: Asst Prof. of Biochem., 1959–62; Associate Prof., 1962; Prof. 1967–86. Mem., Editl Bds of learned jls. Mem., Nat. Acad. of Science, and other sci. bodies. Hon. DSc Chicago, 1985. Nobel Prize for Physiology or Medicine, 1986 (jtly); other prizes and awards. *Publications:* papers in learned jls on cell biology, human developmental biology, embryology. *Address:* Department of Biochemistry, Vanderbilt University School of Medicine, 607 Light Hall, Nashville, TN 37232–0146, USA.

COHEN, Prof. Sydney, CBE 1978; FRS 1978; Professor of Chemical Pathology, Guy's Hospital Medical School, 1965–86, now Emeritus Professor, University of London; *b* Johannesburg, SA, 18 Sept. 1921; *s* of Morris and Pauline Cohen; *m* 1950, June Bernice Adler; one *s* one *d*. *Educ:* King Edward VIIth Sch., Johannesburg; Witwatersrand and London Univs. MD, PhD. Lectr, Dept of Physiology, Witwatersrand Univ., 1947–53; Scientific Staff, Nat. Inst. for Med. Research, London, 1954–60; Reader, Dept of Immunology, St Mary's Hosp. Med. Sch., 1960–65. Mem., MRC, 1974–76; Chm., Tropical Med. Research Bd, MRC, 1974–76; Chm., WHO Scientific Gp on Immunity to Malaria, 1976–81; Mem., WHO expert adv. panel on malaria, 1977–89; Mem. Council, Royal Soc., 1981–83; Royal Soc. Assessor, MRC, 1982–84. Nuffield Dominion Fellow in Medicine, 1954; Founder Fellow, RCPath, 1964; William Julius Mickle Fellow, Univ. of London, 1986. Hon. DSc Witwatersrand, 1987. *Publications:* papers on immunology and parasitic diseases in sci. jls. *Recreations:* golf, gardening, forestry. *Address:* 4 Frognal Rise, NW3 6RD. *T:* 0171–435 6507; Hafodfraith, Llangurig, Powys SY18 6QG. *Club:* Royal and Ancient (St Andrews).

COHN, Prof. Norman, MA; DLitt; FBA 1978; FRHistS; historian; Astor-Wolfson Professor, University of Sussex, 1973–80, now Professor Emeritus; *b* London, 12 Jan. 1915; *yr s* of late August Cohn, barrister-at-law, Middle Temple, and Daisy (*née* Reimer); *m* 1941, Vera, *d* of late Mark and Eva Broido, St Petersburg; one *s*. *Educ:* Gresham's Sch., Holt (Scholar); Christ Church, Oxford (Scholar). 1st Class Hons, Sch. of Medieval and Mod. Languages, 1936; DLitt Glasgow, 1957. Served War of 1939–45, Queen's Royal Regt and Intell. Corps. Lectr in French, Glasgow Univ., 1946–51; Professor of French: Magee Univ. Coll. (then associated with TCD), 1951–60; King's Coll., Durham Univ., 1960–63; changed career to become Dir, Columbus Centre, Sussex Univ. and Gen. Editor, Columbus Centre's Studies in the Dynamics of Persecution and Extermination, 1966–80; Professorial Fellow, Sussex Univ., 1966–73; advr on comparative study of genocide, Concordia Univ., Montreal, 1982–85; advr, Montreal Inst. for Genocide Studies, 1985–; Vis. Prof., KCL, 1986–89. Hugh Le May Fellow, Rhodes Univ., 1950; Fellow, Center for Advanced Study in the Behavioral Sciences, Stanford, Calif, 1966; Vis. Fellow, Center for Humanities, Wesleyan Univ., Conn, 1971; Fellow, Netherlands Inst. for Advanced Study, 1975–76; Canadian SSHRC Vis. Fellow, 1982, Canadian Commonwealth Vis. Fellow, 1983. Hon. LLD Concordia Univ., 1985. *Publications:* Gold Khan and other Siberian legends, 1946; The Pursuit of the Millennium: revolutionary millenarians and mystical anarchists of the middle ages, 1957, rev. edn 1993; Warrant for Genocide: the myth of the Jewish world-conspiracy and the Protocols of the Elders of Zion, 1967, rev. edn 1981 (Anisfield-Wolf Award in Race Relations, 1967); Europe's Inner Demons: an enquiry inspired by the great witch-hunt, 1975, rev. edn 1993; Cosmos, Chaos and the World to Come: the ancient roots of apocalyptic faith, 1993; contributor to various symposia, learned jls, and reviews. *Recreations:* walking, travel, looking at pictures, butterfly-watching. *Address:* Orchard Cottage, Wood End, Ardeley, Herts SG2 7AZ. *T:* Stevenage (01438) 869247. *Club:* Athenæum.

COHN, Prof. Paul Moritz, FRS 1980; Emeritus Professor of Mathematics, University of London, and Hon. Research Fellow in Mathematics, University College London, since 1989; *b* Hamburg, 8 Jan. 1924; *o c* of late James Cohn and late Julia Cohn (*née* Cohen); *m* 1958, Deirdre Sonia Sharon; two *d*. *Educ:* Trinity Coll., Cambridge. BA 1948, MA, PhD 1951. Chargé de Recherches, Univ. de Nancy, 1951–52; Lectr, Manchester Univ.,

1952–62; Reader, London Univ., at Queen Mary Coll., 1962–67; Prof. of Maths, London Univ. at Bedford Coll., 1967–84, at UCL, 1984–86; Astor Prof. of Maths, UCL, 1986–89. Visiting Professor: Yale Univ., 1961–62; Univ. of California (Berkeley), 1962; Univ. of Chicago, 1964; State Univ. of New York (Stony Brook), 1967; Rutgers Univ., 1967–68; Univ. of Paris, 1969; Tulane Univ., 1971; Indian Inst. of Technology, Delhi, 1971; Univ. of Alberta, 1972, 1986; Carleton Univ., Ottawa, 1973; Technion, Haifa, 1975; Iowa State Univ., 1978; Univ. of Bielefeld, 1979; Bar Ilan Univ., Ramat Gan, 1987; Univ. of Hamburg, 1992. Member: Mathematics Cttee, SRC, 1977–80; Council, Royal Soc., 1985–87; London Mathematical Society: Sec., 1965–67; Mem. Council, 1968–71, 1972–75, 1979–84; Pres., 1982–84; Editor, London Math. Soc. Monographs, 1968–77, 1980–93. Lester R. Ford Award (Mathematical Assoc. of America), 1972; Senior Berwick Prize, London Mathematical Soc., 1974. *Publications:* Lie Groups, 1957; Universal Algebra, 1965, 2nd edn 1981 (trans foreign langs); Free Rings and their Relations, 1971, 2nd edn 1985; Algebra, vol. I, 1974, 2nd edn 1982, vol. II, 1977, 2nd edn 1989, vol. III, 1990; Skewfield Constructions, 1977; Algebraic Numbers and Algebraic Functions, 1991; Elements of Linear Algebra, 1994; papers on algebra in various mathematical periodicals. *Recreations:* linguistics, etymology. *Address:* Department of Mathematics, University College London, Gower Street, WC1E 6BT. *T:* 0171–387 7050.

COID, Dr Donald Routledge; Chief Administrative Medical Officer and Director of Public Health, Tayside Health Board, since 1994; *b* 13 June 1953; *s* of Charles Routledge Coid and Marjory Macdonald Coid (*née* Keay); *m* 1985, Susan Kathleen Ramus (*née* Crocker); three *d. Educ:* Bromley Grammar Sch. for Boys; Harrow County Sch. for Boys; Univ. of Nottingham (BMedSci; BM, BS); LSHTM (MSc 1981). MRCP 1979; MFPHM 1989; FRACMA 1985; FAFPHM 1991. Hse Physician, Nottingham City Hosp., 1976; Hse Surgeon, Nottingham Gen. Hosp., 1977; Sen. Hse Officer, Brook Gen. Hosp., London, 1977–78; Res. Asst, Middlesex Hosp. Med. Sch., 1979; Field Med. Officer, Royal Flying Doctor Service, Australia, Eastern Goldfields Sect., 1979–80; MO, Community Health Services, WA, 1981–82; Regl Dir of Public Health, Eastern Goldfields, WA, 1982–85; Med. Supt, Kalgoorlie Reg. Hosp., WA, 1984–85; Fife Health Board: Cons. in Public Health, 1985–92; Asst Gen. Manager, 1992–93. *Publications:* on public health and related topics in learned jls. *Recreations:* golf, singing, cricket, piano. *Address:* Tayside Health Board, PO Box 75, Vernonholme, Riverside Drive, Dundee DD1 9NL; 90 Hepburn Gardens, St Andrews, Fife KY16 9LN. *T:* St Andrews (01334) 472710. *Clubs:* Royal & Ancient Golf, New Golf (St Andrews); St Michael's Golf (Leuchars).

COILEY, John Arthur, PhD; Keeper, National Railway Museum, York, 1974–92; *b* 29 March 1932; *o s* of Arthur George Coiley and Stella Coiley (*née* Chinnock); *m* 1956, Patricia Anne Coiley, BA, (*née* Dixon); two *s* one *d. Educ:* Beckenham and Penge Grammar Sch.; Selwyn Coll., Cambridge (BA, PhD Metallurgy). Scientific Officer, UKAEA, Harwell, 1957–60; Aeon Laboratories, Egham, 1960–65; Development Manager, Fulmer Research Laboratories, 1965–73; Asst Keeper, Science Museum, 1973–74. Mem. Bd, Internat. Assoc. of Transport Museums, 1977–91 (Pres., 1983–86; Vice-Pres., 1986–91). *Publication:* (jtly) Images of Steam, 1968, 2nd edn 1974. *Recreations:* photography, motoring. *Address:* 4 Beech Close, Farnham, Knaresborough, N Yorkshire HG5 9JJ. *T:* Boroughbridge (01423) 340497.

COKAYNE, family name of **Baron Cullen of Ashbourne.**

COKE, family name of **Earl of Leicester.**

COKE, Viscount; Thomas Edward Coke; *b* 6 July 1965; *er s* and *heir* of Earl of Leicester, *qv. Educ:* Eton; Univ. of Manchester (BA). Scots Guards, 1987–93. *Address:* Holkham, Wells-next-the-Sea, Norfolk NR23 1AB.

COKER, Paul, FCA; Managing Director, Ranks Hovis McDougall, 1992–93; *b* 27 July 1938; *s* of Leslie and Mabel Coker; *m* 1966, Delphine Rostron Baden; twin *s* one *d. Educ:* Merchant Taylors' Sch. Joined Ranks Hovis McDougall (Cerebos Group), 1964: Man. Dir, General Products, 1982–87; Planning Dir, 1987–89; Dep. Man. Dir, 1989–91; Finance Dir, 1991–92. *Recreations:* golf, cricket, gardening, theatre. *Address:* Courtlands, Nightingales Lane, Chalfont St Giles, Bucks HP8 4SL. *T:* Chalfont St Giles (01494) 762040.

COKER, Peter Godfrey, RA 1972 (ARA 1965); ARCA 1953; *b* 27 July 1926; *m* 1951, Vera Joyce Crook; one *s* decd. *Educ:* St Martin's Sch. of Art; Royal Coll. of Art (Royal Schol.). Brit. Inst. Schol., 1954. Arts Council Award to Artists, 1976. One-man Exhibitions: Zwemmer Gall., 1956, 1957, 1959, 1964, 1967; Magdalene Street Gall., Cambridge, 1968; Stone Gall., Newcastle, 1969; Thackeray Gall., London, 1970, 1972, 1974, 1975, 1976, 1978; Gallery 10, London, 1980, 1982, 1984, 1986, 1988; Flying Colours Gall., Edinburgh, 1990. Retrospective Exhibitions: Minories, Colchester, 1972; Victoria Gall., Bath, 1972; Morley Gall., London, 1973; Mappin Art Gall., Sheffield, 1973; Chelmsford and Essex Museum, 1978; Royal Acad., 1979; Fitzwilliam Mus., Cambridge, 1989 (working drawings and sketchbooks, 1955–88); Kendal, 1992, then tour to Carlisle, Royal Acad. and Ipswich (landscapes 1956–90). Represented in Group Exhibitions: Tate Gall., 1958; Jordan Gall., Toronto, 1958; John Moores, Liverpool, 1959, 1961; Northampton, 1960; Europaisches Forum, Alpbach, Austria, 1960; Neue Galerie, Linz, 1960; RCA, 1952–62; Painters in E Anglia, Arts Council, 1966; Bicentenary Exhibn, Royal Acad., 1768–1968, 1968; British Painting 1900–1960, Sheffield and Aberdeen, 1975–76; British Painting 1952–77, RA; Recent Chantrey Purchases, Tate Gall., 1981; Acquisitions since 1980, Tate Gall., 1982; The Forgotten Fifties, Sheffield and UK tour, 1984; Exhibition Road, RCA, 1988; The Kitchen Sink Painters, Mayor Gall., 1991; New Displays, Tate Gall., 1992. Works in permanent collections: Tate Gall.; British Museum; Scottish Nat. Gall. of Modern Art; Arts Council; Contemp. Art Soc., GB; Contemp. Art Soc., Wales; Chantrey Bequest; Nat. Portrait Gall.; V&A; Nat. Maritime Museum; Stedelijk Museum Ostend; Eastern Arts Assoc.; Rugby Library and Museum; Chelmsford and Essex Museum; Castle Museum, Norwich; Fitzwilliam Mus., Cambridge; Art Galls and Museums of Carlisle, Ipswich, Leicester, Rochdale, Doncaster; Art Galls of Bath (Victoria), Batley, Birmingham, Coventry (Herbert), Kendal (Abbot Hall), Kettering, Leeds City, Manchester City, Sheffield City, Southport (Atkinson), Salford; RCA; RA; Minories, Colchester; Beecroft Art Gall., Southend-on-Sea; Educn Cttees of Nottingham, Essex, Derbyshire, Lancs, ILEA; Liverpool Univ. *Publication:* Etching Techniques, 1976. *Address:* The Red House, Mistley, Manningtree, Essex CO11 1BX. *T:* Colchester (01206) 392179.

COKER, William John; QC 1994; *b* 19 July 1950; *s* of Edgar and Peggy Coker; *m* 1977, Ruth Elaine Pull; one *s* one *d. Educ:* Bedford Sch.; Manchester Univ. (LLB). Called to the Bar, Gray's Inn, 1973. *Recreations:* golf, fishing. *Address:* 9 Bedford Row, WC1R 4AZ. *T:* 0171–242 3555.

COLBERT, Claudette; Chevalier, Légion d'Honneur, 1988; stage and film actress; *b* Paris, 13 Sept. 1903; *d* of Georges Chauchoin and Jeanne Loew; *m* 1st, Norman Foster (marr. diss.); 2nd, Dr Joel J. Pressman (*d* 1968). Went to America, 1908. First appearances: New York Stage, 1923; London stage, 1928. Returned to Broadway stage, 1958–60. After success on Broadway, entered films, 1929. *Plays include:* Wild Westcotts, The Marionette Man, We've Got to Have Money, The Cat Came Back, Leah Kleschna, High Stakes, A Kiss in the Taxi, The Ghost Train, The Pearl of Great Price, The Barker, The Mulberry Bush, La Gringa, Within the Law, Fast Life, Tin Pan Alley, Dynamo, See Naples and Die, The Marriage-Go-Round, The Kingfisher, Talent for Murder, Aren't We All?. *Films include:* For the Love of Mike, The Lady Lies, Manslaughter, The Smiling Lieutenant, Sign of the Cross, Cleopatra, Private Worlds, Maid of Salem, It Happened One Night (Academy Award, 1934), The Gilded Lily, I Met Him in Paris, Bluebeard's Eighth Wife, Zaza, Midnight, Drums Along the Mohawk, Skylark, Remember the Day, Palm Beach Story, No Time for Love, So Proudly We Hail, Without Reservations, The Secret Heart, The Egg and I, Sleep My Love, Three Came Home, The Secret Fury, The Planter's Wife, Destiny, Versailles, Parrish, Since You Went Away (Academy Award nomination). *Film for television:* The Two Mrs Grenvilles, 1988 (Golden Globe award). Kennedy Center Honors Award, 1989. *Address:* Bellerive, St Peter, Barbados, West Indies.

COLCHESTER, Area Bishop of, since 1995; **Rt. Rev. Edward Holland;** *b* 28 June 1936; *s* of Reginald Dick Holland and Olive Holland (*née* Yeoman). *Educ:* New College School; Dauntsey's School; King's College London (AKC). National Service, Worcestershire Regt, 1955–57; worked for Importers, 1957–61; KCL, 1961–65. Deacon 1965, priest 1966, Rochester; Curate, Holy Trinity, Dartford, 1965–69; Curate, John Keble, Mill Hill, 1969–72; Precentor, Gibraltar Cathedral, and Missioner for Seamen, 1972–74; Chaplain at Naples, Italy, 1974–79; Vicar of S Mark's, Bromley, 1979–86; Suffragan Bishop of Gibraltar in Europe, 1986–95. *Recreations:* travel, being entertained and entertaining. *Address:* 1 Fitzwalter Road, Lexden, Colchester, Essex CO33 3SS. *T:* Colchester (01206) 576648. *Club:* National Liberal.

COLCHESTER, Archdeacon of; *see* Stroud, Ven. E. C. F.

COLCHESTER, Nicholas Benedick Sparrowe, OBE 1993; Editorial Director, Economist Intelligence Unit, since 1993; *b* 30 Dec. 1946; *s* of Rev. Halsey Sparrowe Colchester, CMG, OBE; *m* 1976, Laurence Lucie Antoinette Schloesing; two *s. Educ:* Dragon Sch.; Radley Coll.; Magdalen Coll., Oxford (BA). Joined Financial Times, 1968: New York Corresp., 1970–73; Bonn Corresp., 1974–77; For. Editor, 1981–86; joined The Economist, 1986, Dep. Editor, 1989–93. Non-exec. Dir, London Smaller Cos Investment Trust, 1994–; Mem., London Bd, Halifax Building Soc., 1993–. Chevalier de l'Ordre National du Mérite (France), 1988. *Publication:* Europe Relaunched (jtly), 1990. *Recreations:* music, theatre. *Address:* 37 Arundel Gardens, W11 2LW. *T:* 0171–221 2829. *Club:* Garrick.

COLCHESTER, Trevor Charles, CMG 1958; *b* London, 18 April 1909; *s* of Charles Colchester; *m* 1937, Nancy Joan Russell; one *d. Educ:* Corpus Christi Coll., Cambridge (MA). Colonial Service, 1931–64; in Kenya, Zanzibar, and Northern Rhodesia. Sec. to Cabinet, Kenya, 1954–57; Permanent Sec., Kenya, 1957–61. Sec., Commonwealth Assoc. of Architects, 1964–74; Consultant, Commonwealth Legal Education Assoc., 1974–84. Hon. FRIBA 1975. *Recreations:* conservation, gardening, fly-fishing, music. *Address:* Plomesgate, Aldeburgh, Suffolk IP15 5QB. *T:* Aldeburgh (01728) 452871.

COLCLOUGH, Ven. Michael John; personal assistant to the Bishop of London, since 1994; Priest-in-Charge, St Vedast-alias-Foster, since 1994; Deputy Priest in Ordinary to the Queen, since 1995; *b* 29 Dec. 1944; *s* of Joseph and Beryl Colclough; *m* 1983, Cynthia Flora Mary De Sousa; two *s. Educ:* Leeds Univ. (BA Hons English and Religious Studies); Cuddesdon Coll., Oxford. Ordained deacon, 1971, priest, 1972; Curate: St Werburgh, Burslem, 1971–75; St Mary, S Ruislip, 1975–79; Vicar, St Anselm, Hayes, 1979–86; Area Dean of Hillingdon, 1985–92; Team Rector, Uxbridge, 1986–92; Archdeacon of Northolt, 1992–94. *Recreations:* travel, walking in the English countryside, reading, people. *Address:* (office) London House, 8 Barton Street, Westminster, SW1P 3NE. *T:* 0171–222 8661, *Fax:* 0171–799 2629; (home) St Vedast's Rectory, 4 Foster Lane, EC2V 6HH.

COLDRICK, Albert Percival, OBE 1974; FCIT 1972; Chairman: National Health Service SE Thames Appeals Tribunal, 1974–89; Executive Committee, Industrial Participation Association, 1974–93; *b* 6 June 1913; *s* of Albert Percival and Florence Coldrick; *m* 1938, Esther Muriel Blades; three *s. Educ:* Britannia Bridge Elementary Sch., Wigan Mining and Technical College. Railway Controller, 1933–47; Transport Salaried Staffs' Assoc.: full-time Officer, 1948–62; Sen. Asst Sec., 1962–66; Asst Gen. Sec., 1967; Gen. Sec., 1968–73. Member: General Council, TUC, 1968–73; Industrial Tribunal, 1975–84. Member: Southern Gas Bd, 1970–73; Midlands and West Region Rlys Bd, 1975–77. Chm., Foundn for Industrial Understanding, 1979–93; Vice Chm., Nat. Exam. Bd for Supervisory Management, 1979–. Jt Editor, International Directory of the Trade Union Movement, 1977–. *Recreations:* reading, golf, walking, photography. *Address:* 10 Murray Avenue, Bromley, Kent BR1 3DQ. *T:* 0181–464 4089. *Club:* Royal Over-Seas League.

COLDSTREAM, Sir George (Phillips), KCB 1955 (CB 1949); KCVO 1968; QC 1960; *b* 20 Dec. 1907; *s* of late Francis Menzies Coldstream; *m* 1st, 1934, Mary Morna (marr. diss. 1948), *o d* of Major and Mrs A. D. Carmichael, Meigle, Perthshire; one *d* (and one *d* decd); 2nd, Sheila Hope, *widow* of Lt-Col J. H. H. Whitty, DSO, MC. *Educ:* Rugby; Oriel Coll., Oxford. Called to the Bar, Lincoln's Inn, 1930. Bencher, 1954; Asst to Parly Counsel to Treasury, 1934–39; Legal Asst, Lord Chancellor's Office, 1939–44; Dep. Clerk of the Crown, 1944–54; Clerk of the Crown in Chancery and Permanent Sec. to the Lord Chancellor, 1954–68. Member: British War Crimes Executive, 1944–46; Evershed Cttee on Supreme Court Practice and Procedure, 1947–53; British team, Anglo-Amer. Legal Exchanges, 1961–69; Royal Commn on Assizes and Quarter Sessions, 1967–70; Top Salaries Review Body, 1971–82. Sec., Party Leaders Conf. on Reform of House of Lords, Feb.–May 1948. Special Consultant, Amer. Inst. of Judicial Admin, NY, 1968–71. Part-time Chm., Industrial Tribunals, 1975–80. Chm., Council of Legal Educn, 1970–73. Pres., Old Rugbeian Soc., 1978–80. Hon. Mem., American Bar Assoc., 1969; Hon. Fellow, Amer. Coll. of Trial Lawyers, 1969. Hon. LLD Columbia Univ., 1966. *Address:* The Gate House, Seaford, East Sussex BN25 2AH. *T:* Seaford (01323) 892801. *Clubs:* Athenæum; Royal Cruising.

COLDSTREAM, Prof. John Nicolas, FSA; FBA 1977; Yates Professor of Classical Art and Archaeology, 1983–92, now Emeritus, Hon. Fellow, 1993, University College London; *b* 30 March 1927; *s* of Sir John Coldstream and Phyllis Mary Hambly; *m* 1970, Imogen Nicola Carr. *Educ:* Eton; King's College, Cambridge (Class. Tripos, BA 1951, MA 1956). FSA 1964. Nat. Service, Buffs and HLI (Egypt and Palestine), 1945–48. Asst Master, Shrewsbury Sch., 1952–56; Temp. Asst Keeper, Dept of Greek and Roman Antiquities, BM, 1956–57; Macmillan Student, British Sch. at Athens, 1957–60; Bedford College, London: Lectr, 1960–66; Reader, 1966–75; Prof. of Aegean Archaeology, 1975–83. Geddes-Harrower Vis. Prof. of Classical Archaeology, Univ. of Aberdeen, 1983; Vis. Prof., Australian Archaeol Inst., Athens, 1989; T. B. L. Webster Meml Vis. Prof., Stanford Univ., Calif, 1990; Vis. Prof., Univ. of Athens, 1992. Mem., 1966–, Chm., 1987–91, Managing Cttee, British Sch. at Athens. Chm., Nat. Organizing Cttee, XI Internat. Congress of Classical Archaeol., London, 1978. Member: European Acad. of Scis and Arts, Salzburg, 1991; Deutsches Archäologisches Inst., 1978; Corresponding Member: Nordrhein-Westfälische (formerly Rheinisch-Westfälische) Akademie der Wissenschaften,

1984; Acad. of Athens, 1993; Hon. Mem., Archaeol Inst. of America, 1994. Hon. Fellow, Archaiologikē Hetaireia Athenōn, 1987. Editor, Annual of the British School at Athens, 1968–73. *Publications:* Greek Geometric Pottery, 1968; (with G. L. Huxley) Kythera: Excavations and Studies, 1972; Knossos: The Sanctuary of Demeter, 1973; Geometric Greece, 1977; articles in British and foreign classical and archaeological journals. *Recreations:* music, travel. *Address:* 180 Ebury Street, SW1W 8UP.

COLDSTREAM, John Richard Francis; Literary Editor, The Daily Telegraph, since 1991; *b* 19 Dec. 1947; *s* of Gerald Coldstream and Marian Gatehouse; *m* 1977, Susan Elizabeth Pealing. *Educ:* Bradfield Coll.; Univ. of Nice; Univ. of Sussex. Evening Echo, Hemel Hempstead, 1971–74; joined Daily Telegraph, Peterborough column, 1974; Dep. Literary Editor, Daily Telegraph, 1984–91 and Sunday Telegraph, 1989–91. *Publication:* (ed) The Daily Telegraph Book of Contemporary Short Stories, 1995. *Recreations:* theatre; eating, France, when possible simultaneously. *Address:* The Daily Telegraph, 1 Canada Square, Canary Wharf, E14 5DT. *T:* 0171–538 5000. *Club:* Garrick.

COLDWELLS, Rev. Canon Alan Alfred; Canon of St George's Chapel, Windsor, since 1987; *b* 15 Jan. 1930; *yr s* of late Alfred Carpenter Coldwells and of Leila Philis Eugenie Coldwells (*née* Livings); *m* 1963, Mary Patricia, *d* of A. L. Hemsley; one *s* two *d*. *Educ:* Haileybury and ISC; University Coll., Oxford (MA); Wells Theological Coll. Deacon 1955, priest 1956; Curate, St Andrew's Parish, Rugby, 1955–62; Curate in charge, St George's, Rugby, 1956–62; Vicar of Sprowston and Rector of Beeston St Andrew, Norfolk, 1962–73; RD, Norwich North, 1970–72; Director, Samaritans, Norwich, 1970–72; Rector of Rugby, 1973–87; RD of Rugby, 1973–78; Hon. Canon, Coventry Cathedral, 1983. *Publications:* The Story of St Andrew's, Rugby, 1979; St George's Chapel, Windsor Castle, 1993. *Recreations:* art, painting, local history. *Address:* 6 The Cloisters, Windsor Castle, Berks SL4 1NJ. *T:* Windsor (01753) 866313.

COLE, family name of **Earl of Enniskillen.**

COLE, Sir (Alexander) Colin, KCB 1992; KCVO 1983 (CVO 1979; MVO 1977); TD 1972; FSA; Garter Principal King of Arms, 1978–92; *b* 16 May 1922; *er s* of Capt. Edward Harold Cole, and Blanche Ruby Lavinia (*née* Wallis) (both decd); *m* 1944, Valerie, *o d* of late Capt. Stanley Walter Card; four *s* three *d*. *Educ:* Dulwich; Pembroke Coll. Cambridge; Brasenose Coll., Oxford. BCL Oxon; MA Oxon. Served War of 1939–45, Capt. Coldstream Guards. Barrister-at-law (Inner Temple), 1949, Hon. Bencher, 1988. Fitzalan Pursuivant of Arms Extraordinary, 1953; Portcullis Pursuivant of Arms, 1957; Windsor Herald of Arms, 1966. HAC (TA), 1956; Major: Inf. Bn, 1961; 6th (Volunteer) Bn, Queen's Regt, 1971–73; Lt-Col RARO (Brevet, 1973); Hon. Col, 6/7 Bn, Queen's Regt, 1981–86. Mem. Court of Common Council of City of London (Castle Baynard Ward), 1964–; Sheriff, City of London, 1976–77. Freeman of City of London, Freeman and Liveryman, Scriveners', Basketmakers and Painter Stainers Companies of London. Fellow Heraldry Soc.; Hon. Heraldic Adviser, Monumental Brass Soc. Knight Principal, Imperial Soc. of Knights Bachelor, 1983–; Pres., Royal Soc. of St George, 1982–. FRSA 1979. OStJ. *Publications:* articles on heraldry and kindred subjects in their appropriate journals; illus. Visitations of London (1568) and Wiltshire (1623) (Harleian Soc.). *Recreations:* art, archæology, architecture, wine-bibbing. *Address:* Holly House, Burstow, Surrey RH6 9RG. *Clubs:* Cavalry and Guards, City Livery.

COLE, Prof. Boris Norman, BSc(Eng) (London), PhD (Birmingham), WhSch, CEng, FIMechE, FInstP; Professor of Mechanical Engineering, 1962–88, Head of Department of Mechanical Engineering, 1962–87, University of Leeds, now Professor Emeritus; *b* 8 Jan. 1924; *s* of James Edward Cole and Gertrude Cole; *m* 1945, Sibylle Duijts; two *s* one *d*. *Educ:* King Edward's Sch., Birmingham. Apprenticed to Messrs Belliss and Morcom Ltd, Engineers, Birmingham. Dept of Mech. Engrg, Univ. of Birmingham: Lectr, 1949–55; Sen. Lectr, 1955–58; Reader, 1958–62; Chm. of Faculty Bd of Applied Sciences, Birmingham Univ., 1955–57 and 1959–62. Dir, Univ. of Leeds Industrial Services Ltd. Member: Smethwick Co. Borough Educn Cttee, 1957–60; Engrg Materials Res. Requirements Bd, 1974–78, and various other govt cttees; Governor, Engrg Industries Training Bd, Leeds Training Centre, 1967–82. Prizewinner, IMechE, 1953 and 1962. *Publications:* numerous in fields of solid and fluid mechanics and in engineering education. *Recreations:* walking, music, social history of engineering. *Address:* 6 Wedgewood Grove, Leeds LS8 1EG. *T:* Leeds (0113) 266 4756.

COLE, (Claude Neville) David, CBE 1977; JP; Deputy Managing Director, International Thomson Organisation plc, 1985–86 (Joint Deputy Managing Director, 1980–84); Chairman, Thomson Foundation, since 1986; *b* 4 June 1928; 2nd *s* of late W. J. Cole and of Mrs M. J. Cole; *m* 1951, Alma Gwlithyn Williams (*d* 1990); one *s* one *d* (and one *s* decd); *m* 1992, Mary Agnes Rose Symonds. *Educ:* Royal Masonic School; Harvard Business Sch. Journalist: Merthyr Express; South Wales Echo; Daily Graphic (Manchester); Daily Sketch (London); Daily Recorder; Empire News (Cardiff); Editor, Western Mail, Cardiff, 1956–59; Managing Director: Western Mail and Echo Ltd, 1959–67 (now Chm.); Newcastle Chronicle and Journal Ltd, 1967–69; Thomson Regional Newspapers Ltd: Asst Man. Dir and Editorial Dir, 1969–72; Man. Dir and Chief Exec., 1972–82; Chm., 1980–82; Chm. and Chief Exec., Thomson Information Services, 1982–84. Chairman: Rainbird Publishing Gp, 1980–85; Hamish Hamilton, 1982–85; Thomson Books, 1980–85; Janes Publishing Co., 1981–86; Director: Thomson Organisation (Exec. Bd), 1973–80; Reuters Ltd, 1976–81; Press Assoc. (Chm. 1976–77, 1977–78); Welsh Nat. Opera Co. Ltd, 1960–71; Chairman: Celtic Press Ltd; Cole Cttee on Recruitment of Nurses in Wales, 1961–63; Working Party on Welsh Tourism, 1963–64; Barry Development Partnership, 1986–88; Civic Trust for Wales, 1986–; Director: Welsh Develt Agency, 1987–90; Celtic Trees plc. Member: Council, Newspaper Soc., 1974–86 (Pres., 1982); Press Council, 1976–80; PIRA Council, 1984–86; Trustee, Reuters Ltd, 1983–. Chairman: Univ. of Wales Investment Cttee; Univ. of Wales Press, 1992–; Member: Court of Governors of Univ. of Wales, 1962–; Council of Univ. of Wales, 1962–; Council of Welsh National Sch. of Medicine, 1964–67; Council, Univ. of Wales Coll., Cardiff, 1988–92; Governing Body of Cardiff Coll. of Music and Drama, 1963–67; Council of Cardiff New Theatre Trust, 1964–67; Welsh Nat. Theatre Cttee; Aberfan Disaster Fund, 1966–67; Welsh Hospitals Bd, 1962–67. Vice-Patron, Coun. for Wales, Brit. Empire and Commonwealth Games. Pres., Tenovus, 1963–. FIMgt. Hon. LLD Wales, 1989. OStJ. *Publications:* This and Other Worlds (poems), 1975; Meeting Places and other poems, 1977; Mount of Angels (poems), 1978; The New Wales, 1991. *Recreations:* two of the three R's. *Address:* Flatone, Gwentland, Marine Parade, Penarth, S Glam CF64 3BE. *T:* Penarth (01222) 703487. *Clubs:* East India, Devonshire, Sports and Public Schools; Cardiff and County (Cardiff).

COLE, Sir Colin; *see* Cole, Sir A. C.

COLE, David; *see* Cole, C. N. D.

COLE, Sir David (Lee), KCMG 1975 (CMG 1965); MC 1944; HM Diplomatic Service, retired; *b* 31 Aug. 1920; *s* of late Brig. D. H. Cole, CBE, LittD, and Charlotte Cole (*née* Wedgwood); *m* 1945, Dorothy (*née* Patton); one *s*. *Educ:* Cheltenham Coll.; Sidney Sussex Coll., Cambridge. MA (1st Cl. Hons History). Served Royal Inniskilling Fusiliers, 1940–45. Dominions Office, 1947; seconded to Foreign Office for service with UK Delegn to UN, New York, 1948–51; First Sec., Brit. High Commn, New Delhi, 1953–56; Private Sec. to Rt Hon. the Earl of Home (Sec. of State for Commonwealth Relations and Lord President of the Council), 1957–60; Head of Personnel Dept, CRO, 1961–63; British Dep. High Comr in Ghana, 1963–64; British High Comr in Malawi, 1964–67; Minister (Political), New Delhi, 1967–70; Asst Under-Sec. of State, FCO, 1970–73; Ambassador to Thailand, 1973–78. *Publications:* Thailand: Water Colour Impressions, 1977; Rough Road to Rome, 1983. *Recreation:* watercolour painting (exhibited RI, RBA). *Address:* 19 Burghley House, Somerset Road, Wimbledon, SW19 5JB.

COLE, Eileen Marie Lucy, CBE 1987; Chief Executive, Research International (Unilever Ltd), 1973–85 (in Rotterdam, 1973–77), retired 1985; *b* 22 April 1924; *d* of Arthur Walter Cole and Mary Agnes Boyd. *Educ:* grammar schs; Girton Coll., Cambridge (BA Hons Econ.). Joined Unilever as trainee, 1948; with associated cos and market res. div. of Unilever, 1948–60; Market Research Controller, Lever Bros Ltd, 1960–64; Research Bureau Ltd: Dir, 1964–67; Chm. and Man. Dir, 1967–72. Director: (non-exec.) Post Office, 1980–90; (part-time), LRT, 1984–88. Vice-Pres., 1979–, and Full Mem., UK Market Res. Soc. (Chm., 1977–79; Hon. Life Mem., 1985); Council Mem., Women in Management, 1971–; Mem., Careers Advisory Services: Cambridge Univ., 1968–75, 1979–83; Reading Univ., 1970–76, 1979–. FIMgt; Mem., Inst. of Dirs. Freeman: Marketors' Co., 1992; City of London, 1993. *Publications:* various in learned jls connected with market research. *Recreations:* gardening, cooking, reading, theatre. *Address:* Nicholas Farm, Lower Wield, Alresford, Hants SO24 9RX.

COLE, Frank; *see* Cole, (George) Francis.

COLE, George, OBE 1992; actor on stage, screen, radio and television; *b* 22 April 1925; *m* 1st, 1954, Eileen Moore (marr. diss. 1966); one *s* one *d*; 2nd, 1967, Penelope Morrell; one *s* one *d*. *Educ:* Surrey County Council Secondary Sch., Morden. Made first stage appearance in White Horse Inn, tour and London Coliseum, 1939; Cottage to Let, Birmingham, 1940; West End and on tour, 1940–41; subseq. West End plays included Goodnight Children, New, 1942; Mr Bolfry, Playhouse, 1943. Served in RAF, 1943–47. Returned to stage in Dr Angelus, Phoenix, 1947; The Anatomist, Westminster, 1948; Mr Gillie, Garrick, 1950; A Phoenix too Frequent and Thor with Angels, Lyric, Hammersmith, 1951; Misery Me, Duchess, 1955; Mr Bolfry, Aldwych, 1956; Brass Butterfly, Strand, 1958; The Bargain, St Martin's, 1961; The Sponge Room and Squat Betty, Royal Court, 1962; Meet Me on the Fence (tour), 1963; Hedda Gabler, St Martin's, 1964; A Public Mischief, St Martin's, 1965; Too True To Be Good, Strand, 1965; The Waiting Game, Arts, 1966; The Three Sisters, Royal Court, 1967; Doubtful Haunts, Hampstead, 1968; The Passionate Husband, 1969; The Philanthropist, Mayfair, 1971; Country Life, Hampstead, 1973; Déjà Revue, New London, 1974; Motive (tour), 1976; Banana Ridge, Savoy, 1976; The Case of the Oily Levantine, Guildford, 1977; Something Afoot, Hong Kong, 1978; Brimstone and Treacle, Open Space, 1979; Liberty Hall, Greenwich, 1980; The Pirates of Penzance, Drury Lane, 1982; A Month of Sundays, Duchess, 1986; A Piece of My Mind, Apollo, 1987; Peter Pan, Cambridge, 1987; The Breadwinner (tour), 1989; Natural Causes (tour), 1993; Theft (tour), 1995. *Films include:* Cottage to Let, 1941; Morning Departure, Laughter in Paradise, Scrooge, Top Secret, 1949–51; Will Any Gentleman?, The Intruder, 1952; Happy Ever After, Our Girl Friday, 1953; Belles of St Trinian's, 1954; Quentin Durward, 1955; The Weapon, It's a Wonderful World, The Green Man, 1956; Blue Murder at St Trinian's, Too Many Crooks, Don't Panic Chaps, The Bridal Path, 1957–59; The Pure Hell of St Trinian's, Cleopatra, Dr Syn, 1961–62; One Way Pendulum, Legend of Dick Turpin, 1964; Great St Trinian's Train Robbery, 1965; The Green Shoes, 1969; Vampire Lovers, 1970; Girl in the Dark, 1971; The Blue Bird, 1975; Minder on the Orient Express (TV film), 1985. TV Series include Life of Bliss (also radio), A Man of our Times, Don't Forget to Write, Minder (9 series), The Bounder (2 series), Blott on the Landscape, Comrade Dad, Life after Life, Single Voices, My Good Friend, An Independent Man. *Address:* c/o Joy Jameson, 2.19 The Plaza, 535 King's Road, SW10 0SZ.

COLE, George Francis, (Frank); Founder Director, Frank Cole (Consultancy) Ltd, since 1979; *b* 3 Nov. 1918; *m*; Gwendoline Mary Laver (decd); two *s* one *d*; Barbara Mary Booth (*née* Gornall). *Educ:* Manchester Grammar Sch. Dir and Gen. Manager, Clarkson Engineers Ltd, 1944–53; Gen. Man., Ariel Motors Ltd (BSA Group), 1953–55; Dir, then Man. Dir, Vono Ltd, 1955–67. Past Chairman: Grovewood Products Ltd; Portways Ltd; R. & W. H. Symington Holdings Ltd; National Exhibition Centre Ltd; Crane's Screw (Hldgs) Ltd; Stokes Bomford (Holdings) Ltd; Debenholt Ltd; Stokes Bomford (Foods) Ltd; James Cooke (Birmingham) Ltd; Franklin Medical Ltd; Aero Needles Gp plc; Needle Industries Gp Ltd; F. J. Neve & Co. Ltd; Wild Barnsley Engrg Gp Ltd; Past Director: Duport Ltd; Shipping Industrial Holdings Ltd; G. Clancey Ltd; Armstrong Equipment PLC (retd as Dep. Chm., 1989); William Mitchell (Sinkers) Ltd (Chm., 1982–89); Director: Alexander Stenhouse (formerly Reed Stenhouse) UK Ltd, 1981–91; Mitchell-Grieve Ltd, 1989–91. Pres., Birmingham Chamber of Commerce and Industry, 1968–69. Leader of Trade Missions to West Germany, Yugoslavia, Romania and Hungary. CIMgt; Life Governor, Birmingham Univ.; Liveryman of City of London. Radio and Television appearances. *Publications:* press articles on economics, exports, etc. *Recreations:* tennis (competes regularly in Nat. Veteran Championships of GB), oil painting, snooker, gardening. *Address:* Northcot, 128 Station Road, Balsall Common, Coventry, West Midlands CV7 7FF. *T:* Berkswell (01676) 532105.

COLE, Humphrey John Douglas; retired; Deputy Secretary and Chief Economic Adviser, Department of Transport, and Chief Economic Adviser, Department of the Environment, 1983–87; *b* 30 Jan. 1928; *s* of late G. D. H. Cole and Dame Margaret I. Cole, DBE; *m* 1955, Hilda Annette Robinson; two *s* one *d*. *Educ:* Winchester Coll.; Trinity Coll., Cambridge. Research, Oxford Inst. of Statistics, 1950–61; Head, Economic Indicators and Foreign Trade, OECD Statistics Div., 1961–66; Dept of Economic Affairs: Senior Economic Adviser (Regional), 1966–67; Asst Dir of Economics, 1967–69; Dir of Economics, Min. of Technology, 1969–70; Dir of Econs (Urban and Highways), DoE, 1970–72; Dir Gen., Econs and Resources, DoE, 1972–76; Chief Economic Advr, DoE and Dept of Transport, 1976–82. *Publications:* articles in Bulletin of Inst. of Statistics, 1950–61. *Recreation:* walking. *Address:* 3 The Mead, W13 8AZ. *T:* 0181–997 8285.

COLE, John Morrison; Political Editor, BBC, 1981–92; *b* 23 Nov. 1927; *s* of George Cole and Alice Jane Cole; *m* 1956, Margaret Isobel, *d* of Mr and Mrs John S. Williamson, Belfast; four *s*. *Educ:* Fortwilliam and Skegoneill Primary Schs, Belfast; Belfast Royal Acad.; London Univ. (BA External). Belfast Telegraph, 1945–56: successively reporter, industrial, municipal and political correspondent; The Guardian: reporter, 1956–57; Labour Correspondent, 1957–63; News Editor, 1963–69; Dep. Editor, 1969–75; The Observer: Asst Editor, 1975; Dep. Editor, 1976–81. DUniv Open, 1992; Hon. DSSc QUB, 1992; Hon. DLitt Ulster, 1992; Hon. LLD St Andrews, 1993. *Publications:* The Poor of the Earth, 1976; The Thatcher Years: a decade of revolution in British politics, 1987; As It Seemed To Me: political memoirs, 1995; contrib. to books on British and Irish politics. *Recreations:* reading, travel. *Address:* c/o BBC Office, House of Commons, Westminster, SW1A 0AA. *T:* 0171–219 4765. *Club:* Athenæum.

COLE, Prof. John Peter; Professor of Human and Regional Geography (formerly of Regional Geography), University of Nottingham, 1975–94, Emeritus since 1994; *b* Sydney, Australia, 9 Dec. 1928; *s* of Philip and Marjorie Cecelia Cole; *m* 1952, Isabel Jesús Cole (*née* Urrunaga); two *s*. *Educ:* Bromley Grammar Sch.; Univ. of Nottingham (State Schol., BA, MA, PhD, DLitt); Collegio Borromeo, Pavia Univ., Italy (British Council Schol.). Demonstrator, Univ. of Nottingham, 1951–52; Nat. Service with RN, Jt Services Sch. for Linguists, Russian Language Interpreter, 1952–54 (Lt Comdr RNR, retired); Oficina Nacional de Planeamiento y Urbanismo, Lima, Peru, 1954–55; Lectr in Geography, Univ. of Reading, 1955–56; Lectr in Geography, Univ. of Nottingham, 1956–69. Reader, 1969–75; Vis. Lectr or Prof., Univs of Washington, Columbia, Mexico, Valparaíso, Nanjing, Beijing. *Publications:* Geography of World Affairs, 1959, 6th edn 1983; (with F. C. German) Geography of the USSR, 1961, 2nd edn 1970; Italy, 1964; Latin America, 1965, 2nd edn 1975; (with C. A. M. King) Quantitative Geography, 1968; (with N. J. Beynon) New Ways in Geography, 1968, 2nd edn 1982; Situations in Human Geography, 1975; The Development Gap, 1981; Geography of the Soviet Union, 1984; China 1950–2000 Performance and Prospects, 1985; The Poverty of Marxism in Contemporary Geographical Applications and Research, 1986; Development and Underdevelopment, 1987; (with T. Buck) Modern Soviet Economic Performance, 1987; (with F. J. Cole) The Geography of the European Community, 1993; Geography of the World's Major Regions, 1995; contribs to learned jls, UK and overseas. *Recreations:* travel, languages, pen drawing and painting, gardening. *Address:* 10 Ranmore Close, Beeston, Nottingham NG9 3FR. *T:* Nottingham (0115) 925 0409.

COLE, Prof. Peter Geoffrey; journalist; Professor of Journalism, University of Central Lancashire, since 1993; *b* 16 Dec. 1945; *s* of Arthur and Elizabeth Cole; *m* 1982, Jane Ellison; two *s* one *d*. *Educ:* Tonbridge Sch.; Queens' Coll., Cambridge. Reporter, Evening News, 1968–72; Diary Editor, Evening Standard, 1976–78; News Editor, Deputy Editor, The Guardian, 1978–88; Editor, Sunday Correspondent, 1988–90; News Review Editor, The Sunday Times, 1990–93. *Publication:* Can You Positively Identify This Man? (with Peter Pringle), 1975. *Address:* Department of Journalism, University of Central Lancashire, Preston PR1 2HE. *Clubs:* Plymouth Argyle Supporters' (London Branch); Lancashire County Cricket.

COLE, Richard Raymond Buxton; His Honour Judge Richard Cole; a Circuit Judge, since 1984; *b* 11 June 1937; *s* of late Raymond Buxton Cole, DSO, TD, DL, and Edith Mary Cole; *m* 1962, Sheila Joy Rumbold; one *s* one *d*. *Educ:* Dragon School, St Edward's, Oxford. Admitted as Solicitor 1960; Partner in Cole & Cole Solicitors, Oxford, 1962–84; Recorder, 1976–84. Mem., Parole Bd, 1981–83. Pres., Berks, Bucks and Oxon Law Soc., 1981–82. Mem. Governing Body, Dragon Sch., 1975–92, Chm., 1986–92. Chm., Burford Parish Council, 1976–79, first Town Mayor, 1979. Master, Upholders' Co., 1992–93. Hon. Pres., Assoc. of Master Upholsterers, 1993–. *Recreations:* sport, gardening. *Clubs:* MCC; Frewen (Oxford).

COLE, Robert Templeman, CBE 1981; FEng 1982; DL; Chairman, Conder Group plc, 1979–87; *b* 14 Dec. 1918; *s* of Percival P. Cole and Amy Gladys Cole (*née* Templeman); *m* 1947, Elspeth Lawson; one *s* one *d*. *Educ:* Harrow; Cambridge Univ. (MA). FIStructE. Served RAF, 1940–46. Hampshire County Council, 1946–47; Founder Partner, Conder Engineering, 1947; Chairman: Conder Engineering Co. Ltd, 1950; Conder International Ltd, 1964. DL Hants 1988. Hon. DSc Southampton, 1980. *Recreations:* gliding, jogging, travel. *Address:* Dragons, 69 Chilbolton Avenue, Winchester, Hampshire SO22 5HJ. *T:* Winchester (01962) 854565.

COLE, Sir (Robert) William, Kt 1981; Director, Legal and General, Australia, since 1987; *b* 16 Sept. 1926; *s* of James Henry and Rita Sarah Cole; *m* 1956, Margaret Noleen Martin; one *s* one *d*. *Educ:* Univ. of Melbourne (BCom). Joined Australian Public Service, 1952; Res. Officer, Treasury, 1952–57; Technical Asst, IMF, Washington, 1957–59; various positions, Treasury, 1959–70; Dir, Bureau of Transport Econs, Dept of Shipping and Transport, 1970–72; First Asst Sec., Gen. Financial and Economic Policy Div., Treasury, 1972–76; Australian Statistician, 1976; Sec., Dept of Finance, 1977–78; Chm., Public Service Bd, 1978–83, Sec., Defence Dept, 1983–86. Hon. Treas., Winston Churchill Meml Trust. *Recreations:* reading, fishing, wine. *Address:* 1/106 Mugga Way, Red Hill, ACT 2603, Australia. *T:* Canberra 957089. *Club:* Commonwealth (Canberra).

COLE, Ven. Ronald Berkeley; Archdeacon Emeritus of Leicester; *b* 20 Oct. 1913; *s* of James William and Florence Caroline Cole; *m* 1943, Mabel Grace Chapman; one *s* one *d*. *Educ.* Bishop's Coll., Cheshunt. Registrar, London County Freehold and Leasehold Properties Ltd, 1934–40. Deacon, 1942; Priest, 1943; Curate, Braunstone, Leicester, 1942–48; Succentor, Leicester Cathedral, 1948–50; Vicar of St Philip, Leicester, 1950–73; Archdeacon of Loughborough, 1953–63, of Leicester, 1963–80; Residentiary Canon of Leicester Cathedral, 1977–80. Hon. Chaplain, 1949–53, Examining Chaplain, 1956–80, to Bishop of Leicester. RD of Repps, dio. Norwich, 1983–86. Hon. DLitt Geneva Theol. Coll., 1972. *Recreations:* gardening, motoring. *Address:* Harland Rise, 70 Cromer Road, Sheringham, Norfolk NR26 8RT.

COLE, Sir William; *see* Cole, Sir R. W.

COLE, William Charles, LVO 1966; DMus; FSA, FRAM, FRCM; FRCO; The Master of the Music at the Queen's Chapel of the Savoy, 1954–94, now Master of Music Emeritus; Member Council, Royal College of Organists, since 1960 (Hon. Treasurer, 1964–85; President, 1970–72); Member, Central Music Library Council (formerly Committee), since 1964 (Chairman, 1973–93); *b* 9 Oct. 1909; *s* of Frederick George Cole and Maria (*née* Fry), Camberwell, London; *m* 1st, Elizabeth Brown Caw (*d* 1942); three *d*; 2nd, Winifred Grace Mitchell (*d* 1991); one *s*. *Educ:* St Olave's Grammar Sch.; RAM. Organist and Choirmaster, Dorking Parish Church, 1930; Music Master, Dorking County Sch., 1931; served War of 1939–45, in Air Ministry; Hon. Musical Dir, Toynbee Hall, 1947–58; Prof. of Harmony and Composition, and Lectr in History of Music, Royal Academy of Music, 1945–62; Royal Academy of Dancing: Lectr, 1948–62; Chm., Music Cttee, 1961 68; Mem., Exec. Council, 1965–68, Mem., Grand Council, 1976–88; Conductor: People's Palace Choral Soc., 1947–63; Leith Hill Musical Festival, 1954–77; Sec., Associated Bd of Royal Schools of Music, 1962–74; Hon. Sec., Royal Philharmonic Soc., 1969–80. President: Surrey County Music Assoc., 1958–76; The London Assoc. of Organists, 1963–66. Member: Governing Cttee, Royal Choral Soc., 1972–92 (Chm., Music Cttee, 1975–78); Council, Musicians' Benevolent Fund, 1994– (Mem. Exec. Cttee, 1972–93). Mem. Education Cttee, Surrey CC, 1951–62. *Publications:* Rudiments of Music, 1951; chapter on Development of British Ballet Music, in The Ballet in Britain, 1962; The Form of Music, 1969; A catalogue of Netherlandish and North European roundels in Britain, 1993; articles in various musical jls and in various learned jls on stained glass. *Recreation:* stained glass. *Address:* Barnacre, Wood Road, Hindhead, Surrey GU26 6PX. *T:* Hindhead (01428) 734917. *Club:* Garrick.

COLE-HAMILTON, (Arthur) Richard, CBE 1993; BA; CA; FCIBS; Deputy Chairman, Stakis PLC, since 1994; Chief Executive, Clydesdale Bank PLC, 1987–92; *b* 8 May 1935; *s* of late John Cole-Hamilton, CBE; *m* 1963, Prudence Ann; one *s* two *d*. *Educ:* Ardrossan Academy; Loretto School; Cambridge Univ. (BA). Commissioned Argyll and Sutherland Highlanders, 1960–62. Brechin Cole-Hamilton & Co. (Chartered Accountants), 1962–67; Clydesdale Bank, 1967–92: Manager, Finance Corp. and Money Market, 1971; Asst Manager, Chief London Office, 1971; Supt of Branches, 1974; Head Office Manager, 1976; Asst Gen. Manager, 1978; Gen. Manager, 1979; Dep. Chief Gen. Manager, Feb. 1982; Chief Gen. Manager, July 1982; Dir, 1984–92. Chm., Cttee of Scottish Clearing Bankers, 1985–87, and 1991–92; Vice-Pres., Scottish Council for Develt and Industry, 1992–; Dir, Glasgow Chamber of Commerce, 1985–91; Pres., Ayrshire Chamber of Commerce and Industry, 1992–. Pres., Inst. of Bankers in Scotland, 1988–90. Mem. Council, Inst. of Chartered Accts of Scotland, 1981–85. Trustee: Nat. Galls of Scotland, 1986–; Princess Royal Trust for Carers, 1991–; Mem. Exec. Cttee, Erskine Hosp., 1976–. *Recreation:* golf. *Address:* Fairways, 26 Lady Margaret Drive, Troon, Ayrshire KA10 7AL. *T:* Troon (01292) 311338. *Clubs:* Western (Glasgow); Highland Brigade; Royal and Ancient Golf, Prestwick Golf.

COLEBROOK, Philip Victor Charles, CEng, MIChemE; retired 1984; Managing Director, Imperial Continental Gas Association, 1973–84 (Director, 1971; Director, CompAir Ltd, 1980–84); Director: Calor Group Ltd, 1969–84; Century Power & Light Ltd, 1980–84; Contibel SA (Belgium), 1978–84; *b* 8 March 1924; *s* of Frederick Charles Colebrook and Florence Margaret (*née* Cooper); *m* 1946, Dorothy Ursula Kemp; one *s* three *d*. *Educ:* Andover Grammar Sch.; Guildford Technical Coll.; Battersea Polytechnic, London. Served War of 1939–45, RNVR. Joined Pfizer as Works and Production Manager, 1952; Dir, 1956, Man. Dir, 1958–69, Pfizer Ltd; Chm. and Man. Dir, Pfizer Gp, 1961–69; Vice-Pres., Pfizer Internat., 1967–69; Man. Dir, Calor Gas Holding Co., 1969–80. Member: NHS Affairs Cttee, Assoc. of the British Pharmaceutical Industry, 1963–67; CBI Cttee on State Intervention in Private Business, 1975–78. Trustee and Mem. of Steering Cttee, Univ. of Kent at Canterbury, 1964–65. *Publication:* Going International, 1972. *Recreations:* sailing, ski-ing, golf. *Club:* Helford River Sailing.

COLEBY, Anthony Laurie; Non-executive Director: Halifax Building Society, since 1994; Anglo Irish Bank Corporation, since 1994; Italian International Bank, since 1994; *b* 27 April 1935; *s* of Dr Leslie James Moger Coleby and Laurie Coleby (*née* Shuttleworth); *m* 1966, Rosemary Melian Elisabeth, *d* of Sir Peter Garran, KCMG; one *s* two *d*. *Educ:* Winchester; Corpus Christi, Cambridge (BAEcon, MA). Bank of England: joined, 1961; Assistant Chief, Overseas Dept, 1969; Adviser, Overseas Dept, 1972; Dep. Chief Cashier, 1973; Asst Dir, 1980–86; Chief Monetary Advr to the Governor, 1986–90; Exec. Dir, 1990–94. Personal Asst to Managing Director, International Monetary Fund, 1964–67. *Recreations:* choral singing, railways and transport. *Address:* Halifax Building Society, Trinity Road, Halifax, W Yorks HX1 2RG. *Club:* Bankers'.

COLECLOUGH, Peter Cecil; Chairman, Howard Machinery Ltd, 1969–82 (Director, 1950–82); Director: National Westminster Bank (Chairman SE Region), 1976–86; NCR Ltd, 1971–87; *b* 5 March 1917; *s* of late Thomas James Coleclough and of Hilda Emma (*née* Ingram); *m* 1944, Pamela Beresford (*née* Rhodes); one *s* (and one *s* decd). *Educ:* Bradfield. Served War, Cheshire Yeomanry, 1939; commnd into Roy. Warwickshire Regt, 1940; served until 1946. Mem., FBI/CBI Council, 1962–72; Chm., E Region, CBI, 1971–72; Leader, OECD/BIAC Investment Gp to Ceylon, 1968 and 1969; Chm., Meat and Livestock Commn, 1971–74; Pres., Agricl Engrs Assoc., 1971–72; Pres., Royal Warrant Holders Assoc., 1971–72. Chm., Appeals and Management Cttee, S Essex Medical Educn and Research Trust, 1969–75. CIMgt (CBIM 1976); FRSA 1977. *Recreation:* fishing. *Address:* Longlands Hall, Stonham Aspal, Stowmarket, Suffolk IP14 6AR. *T:* Stowmarket (01449) 711242.

COLEGATE, Isabel Diana, (Mrs Michael Briggs); novelist; *b* 10 Sept. 1931; *d* of Sir Arthur Colegate, sometime MP, and Winifred Mary, *d* of Sir William Worsley, 3rd Bt; *m* 1953, Michael Briggs; two *s* one *d*. *Educ:* Runton Hill Sch., Norfolk. Worked as literary agent at Anthony Blond (London) Ltd, 1952–57. FRSL 1981. Hon. MA Bath, 1988. *Publications:* The Blackmailer, 1958; A Man of Power, 1960; The Great Occasion, 1962 (re-issued as Three Novels, 1983); Statues in a Garden, 1964; Orlando King, 1968; Orlando at the Brazen Threshold, 1971; Agatha, 1973 (re-issued as The Orlando Trilogy, 1984); News from the City of the Sun, 1979; The Shooting Party, 1980 (W. H. Smith Literary Award, 1980; filmed, 1985); A Glimpse of Sion's Glory, 1985; Deceits of Time, 1988; The Summer of the Royal Visit, 1991; Winter Journey, 1995. *Recreation:* walking the dog. *Address:* Midford Castle, Bath BA2 7BU.

COLEGATE, Raymond, CBE 1982; FCIT 1983; air transport consultant; Managing Director (Europe), Global Aviation Associates Ltd, since 1991; *b* 31 Aug. 1927; *s* of Ernest William and Violet Colegate; *m* 1961, Sally Healy; one *s* one *d*. *Educ:* County Sch. for Boys, Gravesend; LSE. BA London (Hons History). Joined BoT, 1949; seconded to Central Statistical Office, 1952–53; Asst Private Sec. to President, 1955–56; seconded to Treasury, 1957–59; seconded to EFTA Secretariat, Geneva and Brussels, 1960–64; CRE Dept, BoT, 1964–67; Aviation Dept, BoT/DTI, 1967–72; Civil Aviation Authority: Mem., 1974–90; Head, Economic Policy and Licensing Div., 1972–75; Head, Economic Dept, 1975–77; Gp Dir, Econ. Services, later Economic Regulation, 1977–89. Vice-Pres., CIT, 1988–91. *Publications:* articles. *Recreations:* music, travel, thinking. *Address:* 40 Lebanon Park, Twickenham TW1 3DG. *T:* 0181–892 8272.

COLEMAN, Prof. Alice Mary; Professor of Geography, King's College, London, since 1987; *b* 8 June 1923; *d* of Bertie Coleman and Elizabeth Mary (*née* White). *Educ:* Clarendon House Sch.; Furzedown Training Coll. (Cert. of Educn); Birkbeck Coll., Univ. of London (BA Hons 1st Cl.); King's Coll., Univ. of London (MA with Mark of Distinction). FKC 1980. Geography Teacher, Northfleet Central Sch. for Girls, 1943–48; Geography Dept, King's Coll., London: Asst Lectr, 1948; Lectr, 1951; Sen. Lectr, 1963; Reader, 1965. Vis. Prof. for Distinguished Women Social Scientists, Univ. of Western Ontario, 1976; BC/Mombusho Prof. of Geog., Hokkaido Univ. of Educn at Asahikawa, 1985. Initiated and directed Second Land Utilisation Survey of Britain, 1960–; Dir, Design Improvement Controlled Experiment, 1988–. Editor, The Graphologist. Gill Meml Award, RGS, 1963; The Times-Veuve Clicquot Award, 1974; Busk Award, RGS, 1987. *Publications:* The Planning Challenge of the Ottawa Area, 1969; Utopia on Trial, 1985; 120 land-use maps in eleven colours at the scale of 1:25,000; over 250 academic papers. *Recreations:* reading, graphology. *Address:* King's College, Strand, WC2R 2LS. *T:* 0171–873 2610.

COLEMAN, Arthur Percy; Deputy Director and Secretary to the Board of Trustees, British Museum (Natural History), 1976–82 (Museum Secretary, 1965–76); *b* 8 Feb. 1922; *s* of late Percy Coleman and Gladys May Coleman (*née* Fisher); *m* 1948, Peggy (*née* Coombs); two *d*. *Educ:* Wanstead Co. High Sch.; Bristol Univ. War Service in 1st King George V Own Gurkha Rifles, 1943–47; Min. of Public Building and Works, 1948–61; HM Treasury, 1961–64. *Recreations:* wild life, music. *Address:* Candleford, Hurst, Beaminster, Dorset DT8 3ES. *T:* Beaminster (01308) 862155.

COLEMAN, Bernard, CMG 1986; HM Diplomatic Service, retired; Ambassador to Paraguay, 1984–86; *b* 3 Sept. 1928; *s* of William Coleman and Ettie Coleman; *m* 1950, Sonia Dinah (*née* Walters); two *d*. *Educ:* Alsop High Sch., Liverpool. HM Forces (RAEC), 1946–48. Entered Foreign (later Diplomatic) Service, 1950; FO, 1950–53; Lima, 1953–56; Detroit, 1956–59; Second Secretary (Information): Montevideo, 1959–62; Caracas,

1962–64; First Sec. (Inf.), Caracas, 1964–66; FCO, 1967–69; First Sec. (Inf.), Ottawa, 1969–73; FCO, 1973–74; seconded to DTI, 1974–75; Consul-Gen., Bilbao, 1976–78; First Sec. (Commercial), Dublin, 1979–80; High Commissioner, Tonga, 1980–83. *Recreations:* golf, bowls, bridge, reading, walking, travel. *Address:* Apartado de Correos 517, 03730 Javea, Alicante, Spain.

COLEMAN, Prof. Dulcie Vivien, MD; FRCPath; Head of Department of Cytopathology and Cytogenetics, St Mary's Hospital, London, since 1972; Professor of Cell Pathology, St Mary's Hospital Medical School, since 1988; *b* 19 Oct. 1932; *d* of Dr Frank Stuart Coleman and Celia Coleman (*née* Walsman); *m* 1957, Jacob Benjamin Poznansky; three *s* one *d. Educ:* Bournemouth Sch. for Girls; Roedean Sch.; St Bartholomew's Hosp. Med. Sch. (MB, BS 1956; MD 1972). MRCPath 1980, FRCPath 1992. Hse Surgeon, Churchill Hosp., Oxford, 1956–57; Hse Physician, Plaistow Hosp., Essex, 1957–58; GP locums, 1959–64; Med. Asst (part-time), RPMS, 1967–70; Clin. Asst (part-time) (Cytopathol. and Cytogenetics), St Mary's Hosp., London, 1964–72; St Mary's Hospital Medical School: Sen. Lectr and Hon. Consultant in Cytopathol. and Cytogenetics, 1972–83; Reader in Cell Pathology, 1983–88. Member: Wkg Party on Safety of Chronic Villus sampling, MRC, 1987–90; Jt Wkg Party on Cytology Trng, DHSS, Inst. of Med. Lab. Scis and British Soc. for Clin. Cytol., 1988–90; Panel of Advrs, ACU, 1991–; Chairman: Wkg Party on Cervical Cancer Screening, Europe Against Cancer, 1990–; Wkg Party on Eur. Guidelines for Quality Assce in Cervical Screening (report pubd 1993); Cttee for Quality Assce, European Fedn of Cytology Socs, 1993–. Chm., Brit. Soc. for Clinical Cytology, 1989–92; Pres., Oncology section, RSM, 1988. Editor-in-Chief, Cytopathology, 1989–; Member, Editorial Board: Analytical Cellular Pathol.; Prenatal Diagnosis. Examr in Cytopathol. and Cytogenetics, Univs of London and Brunel, and RCPath. Hon. Member: Greek Cytology Soc.; CERDEC, France. Fellow, Internat. Acad. of Cytology. *Publications:* (with L. G. Koss) Advances in Clinical Cytology, Vol. 1 1981, Vol. 2 1984; (with D. M. D. Evans) Biopsy Pathology and Cytology of the Cervix, 1988; (with P. C. Chapman) Clinical Cytotechnology, 1989; numerous papers, chapters, reviews on human polyomaviruses, human papillomaviruses, and other virus cytopathol. and prenatal diagnosis, incl. new techniques for cytodiagnosis of malignant disease. *Recreations:* gardening, swimming, nature walks. *Address:* Flat 12, 24 Hyde Park Square, W2 2NN. *T:* 0171-262 0240.

COLEMAN, Isobel Mary; *see* Plumstead, I. M.

COLEMAN, John Ennis, CB 1990; Legal Adviser, Department of Education and Science, 1983–90, retired; *b* 12 Nov. 1930; *o s* of late Donald Stafford Coleman and Dorothy Jean Balieff (*née* Ennis); *m* 1958, Doreen Gwendoline Hellinger; one *s* one *d. Educ:* Dean Close Sch., Cheltenham; Dulwich Coll.; Worcester Coll., Oxford (MA). Solicitor (Hons), 1957. Legal Asst, Treasury Solicitor's Dept, 1958; Senior Legal Asst, 1964; Asst Solicitor, 1971; Under Sec. (Legal), Depts of Industry and Trade, 1980–83.

COLEMAN, Peter Anthony; Director of Organisation and Development, Labour Party, since 1993; *b* 10 Oct. 1945; *s* of William and Maggie Coleman; *m* 1966, Dorothy Edith Lawrence; two *d. Educ:* Avenue Primary Sch., Wellingborough; Park Road Junior Sch., Kettering; Kettering Sch. for Boys; Kettering Boot and Shoe Tech. Coll. Progress chaser: Holyoake Footwear, 1961–64; Wilson & Watsons, 1964–66; Labour Party: organiser: Peterborough, 1967–71; Nottingham, 1972–76; SE Derbys, 1976–78; Asst Regl Organiser, E Midland, 1978–83, Regl Organiser, 1983–93. Nat. Vice-Pres., Nat. Union of Labour Organisers, 1977–78. Mem. Exec. Cttee, Fabian Soc., 1994–95. *Publications:* (ed) Labour's Fundraising Guide, 1984; pamphlets on electoral law, Labour Party regeneration and polling-day systems. *Recreations:* theatre, travel, watching cricket and football. *Address:* 6 Raeburn Road, Sidcup, Kent DA15 8RB. *T:* 0181–859 1882. *Club:* Bromley Labour (Bromley).

COLEMAN, Rt. Rev. Peter Everard; *see* Crediton, Bishop Suffragan of.

COLEMAN, Prof. Robert George Gilbert; Professor of Comparative Philology, University of Cambridge, since 1985; Fellow of Emmanuel College, Cambridge, since 1960; *b* 2 Oct. 1929; *s* of Thomas Lichfield Danks and Sheila Carr Bush, adopted 1934 by George Gilbert Coleman and Rosina Emily Warner; *m* 1st, 1958, Dorothy Gabe (marr. diss.); one *s*; 2nd, 1992, Anne Thompson; one *s. Educ:* Rongotai and Wellington Colls, NZ; Victoria Univ. of Wellington (MA 1951); Emmanuel Coll., Cambridge (BA 1954; Burney Prize (shared), 1955; MA 1980). Lecturer: Dept of Humanity, Aberdeen Univ., 1955–60; Faculty of Classics, Cambridge Univ., 1960–85; Tutor, 1963–71, Librarian, 1980–85, Emmanuel Coll., Cambridge. *Publications:* (ed, with commentary) Vergil's Eclogues, 1977; essays and papers in classical and philological jls. *Recreations:* music, conversation, exploring strange towns. *Address:* 7 Linton Road, Balsham, Cambridge CB1 6HA.

COLEMAN, Robert John; Director General, Transport, European Commission, since 1991; *b* 8 Sept. 1943; *s* of Frederick and Kathleen Coleman; *m* 1966, Malinda Tigay Cutler; two *d. Educ:* Univ. of Oxford (MA); Univ. of Chicago (JD). Called to the Bar, Inner Temple, 1969. Lectr in Law, Univ. of Birmingham, 1967–70; Barrister at Law, 1970–73; European Commission: Administrator, subseq. principal administrator, 1974–82; Dep. Head of Div., safeguard measures and removal of non-tariff barriers, 1983; Head of Div., Intellectual Property and Unfair Competition, 1984–87; Dir, Public Procurement, 1987–90; Dir, Approximation of Laws, Freedom of Estabt, and Freedom to Provide Services, 1990–91. *Publications:* contribs and articles on legal and policy issues, concerning corporate accounting, employee participation, intellectual property and transport. *Recreations:* cycling, music. *Address:* 114 rue des Deux Tours, 1030 Brussels, Belgium. *T:* (2) 2183865.

COLEMAN, Ronald Frederick, CB 1991; DSc; CChem, FRSC; consultant in technology management, since 1992; Chief Engineer and Scientist, Department of Trade and Industry, 1987–92; *b* 10 Nov. 1931; *s* of late Frederick George Coleman and of Dorothy Alice Coleman (*née* Smith); *m* 1954, Maureen Mary Salt; one *s* one *d. Educ:* King Edward VI Sch., Birmingham; College of Technology, Birmingham (BSc, DSc). Chance Brothers Glassworks, Smethwick, 1949–54; UKAEA: Aldermaston, 1954–71; Harwell, 1972; Laboratory of the Government Chemist, 1973–77; National Physical Laboratory, 1977–81; Government Chemist, 1981–87. Dir, Beard Dore Ltd, 1994–. Visiting Professor: Kingston Polytechnic, 1981–91; Royal Holloway and Bedford New Coll., 1985–92. Pres., British Acad. of Forensic Sciences, 1982–83. Member: SERC, 1987–92; AFRC, 1987–92. Pres., Bioindustry Assoc., 1992–. Chm., Bd of Govs, Kingston Univ. (formerly Polytechnic), 1991–. DUniv Surrey, 1987; Hon. DSc: Poly. of Central London, 1989; Cranfield Inst. of Technology, 1992. *Publications:* various papers on analytical chemistry, nuclear chemistry and forensic science. *Recreations:* music, golf, gardening. *Address:* Lime Cottage, Thames Street, Sonning on Thames, Berks RG4 0UR. *T:* Reading (01734) 699837.

COLEMAN, Terry, (Terence Francis Frank); reporter and author; *b* 13 Feb. 1931; *s* of J. and D. I. B. Coleman; *m* 1st, 1954, Lesley Fox-Strangeways Vane (marr. diss.); two *d*; 2nd, 1981, Vivien Rosemary Lumsdaine Wallace; one *s* one *d. Educ:* 14 schs. LLB London. Formerly: Reporter, Poole Herald; Editor, Savoir Faire; Sub-editor, Sunday Mercury, and Birmingham Post; Reporter and then Arts Corresp., The Guardian, 1961–70, Chief Feature Writer, 1970–74; Special Writer with Daily Mail, 1974–76; The Guardian: Chief Feature Writer, 1976–79, writing mainly political interviews, inc. last seven British Prime Ministers; NY Correspondent, 1981; special corresp., 1982–89; Associate Editor, The Independent, 1989–91. Feature Writer of the Year, British Press Awards, 1982; Journalist of the Year, Granada Awards, 1987. *Publications:* The Railway Navvies, 1965 (Yorkshire Post prize for best first book of year); A Girl for the Afternoons, 1965; (with Lois Deacon) Providence and Mr Hardy, 1966; The Only True History: collected journalism, 1969; Passage to America, 1972; (ed) An Indiscretion in the Life of an Heiress (Hardy's first novel), 1976; The Liners, 1976; The Scented Brawl: collected journalism, 1978; Southern Cross, 1979; Thanksgiving, 1981; Movers and Shakers: collected interviews, 1987; Thatcher's Britain, 1987; Empire, 1993. *Recreations:* cricket, opera, circumnavigation. *Address:* c/o Peters, Fraser & Dunlop, The Chambers, Chelsea Harbour, SW10 0XF. *T:* 0171–720 2651. *Club:* MCC.

COLERAINE, 2nd Baron *cr* 1954, of Haltemprice; **James Martin Bonar Law;** *b* 8 Aug. 1931; *s* of 1st Baron Coleraine, PC, *y s* of Rt Hon. Andrew Bonar Law, and Mary Virginia (*d* 1978), *d* of A. F. Nellis, Rochester, NY; *S* father, 1980; *m* 1st, 1958, Emma Elizabeth Richards (marr. diss.); two *d*; 2nd, 1966, (Anne) Patricia (*d* 1993), *yr d* of Major-Gen. R. H. Farrant, CB; one *s* one *d* (and one *d* decd). *Educ:* Eton; Trinity College, Oxford. *Heir: s* Hon. James Peter Bonar Law, *b* 23 Feb. 1975. *Address:* 5 Kensington Park Gardens, W11 3HB.

See also Baron•Ironside.

COLERIDGE, family name of **Baron Coleridge.**

COLERIDGE, 5th Baron *cr* 1873, of Ottery St Mary; **William Duke Coleridge;** *b* 18 June 1937; *s* of 4th Baron Coleridge, KBE, and Cecilia Rosamund (*d* 1991), *d* of Adm. Sir William Wordsworth Fisher, GCB, GCVO; *S* father, 1984; *m* 1st, 1962, Everild Tania (marr. diss. 1977), *d* of Lt-Col Beauchamp Hambrough, OBE; one *s* two *d*; 2nd, 1977, Pamela, *d* of G. W. Baker, *qv*; two *d. Educ:* Eton; RMA Sandhurst. Commissioned into Coldstream Guards, 1958; served King's African Rifles, 1962–64; commanded Guards Parachute Company, 1970–72. *Heir:* Hon. James Duke Coleridge, *b* 5 June 1967. *Address:* The Chanters House, Ottery St Mary, Devon EX11 1DQ. *T:* Ottery St Mary (01404) 812417.

COLERIDGE, David Ean; Chairman of Lloyd's, 1991, 1992 (Deputy Chairman, 1985, 1988, 1989); *b* 7 June 1932; *s* of Guy Cecil Richard Coleridge, MC and Katherine Cicely Stewart Smith; *m* 1955, Susan Senior; three *s. Educ:* Eton. Glanvill Enthoven, 1950–57; R. W. Sturge & Co., 1957–95: Dir, 1966–95; Chm., A. L. Sturge (Holdings) Ltd (now Sturge Holdings PLC), 1978–. Chairman: Oxford Agency Hldgs Ltd, 1987–90; Ockam Hldgs, 1995–; Director: R. A. Edwards (Holdings) Ltd, 1985–90; Wise Speke Hldgs Ltd, 1987–94. Member: Cttee of Lloyd's Underwriting Agents Assoc., 1974–82 (Chm., 1981–82); Council and Cttee of Lloyd's, 1983–86, 1988–92. *Recreations:* golf, racing, gardening, family. *Address:* Spring Pond, Wispers, near Midhurst, W Sussex GU29 0QH. *T:* Midhurst (01730) 813277; 37 Egerton Terrace, SW3 2BU. *T:* 0171–581 1756. *Clubs:* City of London, Mark's.

See also N. D. Coleridge.

COLERIDGE, Geraldine Margaret, (Gill), (Mrs D. R. Leeming); Partner, Rogers Coleridge and White, Literary Agency, since 1988; *b* 26 May 1948; *d* of Antony Duke Coleridge and June Marian Caswell; *m* 1974, David Roger Leeming; two *s. Educ:* Queen Anne's School, Caversham; Marlborough Secretarial College, Oxford. BPC Partworks, Sidgwick & Jackson, Bedford Square Book Bang, to 1971; Publicity Manager, Chatto & Windus, 1971–72; Dir and Literary Agent, Anthony Sheil Associates, 1973–88. Pres., Assoc. of Authors' Agents, 1988–91. *Recreations:* entertaining, reading, music, sailing. *Address:* 113 Calabria Road, N5 1HS. *T:* 0171–226 5875.

COLERIDGE, Lady (Marguerite) Georgina; *b* 19 March 1916; *d* of 11th Marquess of Tweeddale; *m* 1941, Arthur Coleridge (*d* 1988), *yr s* of John Duke Coleridge; one *d. Educ:* home, abroad as a child. Freelance writer, Harpers Bazaar, etc., 1936–; joined National Magazine Co.: Circulation Dept, 1937; Advertisement Dept., 1938; joined Country Life, 1945; Editor of Homes and Gardens, 1949–63; Chm., Inst. of Journalists (London District), 1954, Fellow 1970; Chm., Women's Press Club, 1959 (Pres., 1965–67). Dir, Country Life Ltd, 1962–74; Dir, George Newnes Ltd, 1963–69; Publisher: Homes and Gardens; Woman's Journal, 1969–71; Ideal Home, 1970–71; Dir, Special Projects, IPC Women's Magazines, 1971–74; Consultant: IPC Women's Magazines, 1974–82; Public Relations Counsel Ltd, 1974–85 (Dir, 1978–85). Mem., Internat. Assoc. of Women and Home Page Journalists, 1968–74; Associate, Women in Public Relations, 1972–; Associate Mem., Ladies Jockeys Assoc. of GB, 1973–; Founder Mem., Media Soc. Ltd (Inst. of Journalists Foundn), 1973–76; Member: Information Cttee, Brit. Nutrition Foundn, 1975–79; Information Cttee, RCP, 1977–81; Vice-Pres., Greater London Fund for the Blind, 1981–; President: Dale Youth Club, N Kensington, 1978–; Friends of Moorfields, 1981–92. Freeman, Worshipful Co. of Stationers and Newspapermakers, 1973. *Publications:* Grand Smashional Pointers (book of cartoons), 1934; I Know What I Like (clichés), 1959; That's Racing, 1978; many features for various jls. *Recreations:* racing, writing, cooking; nothing highbrow. *Address:* 33 Peel Street, W8 7PA. *T:* 0171–727 7732.

COLERIDGE, Nicholas David; Managing Director, Condé Nast Publications, since 1992 (Editorial Director, 1989–91); *b* 4 March 1957; *s* of David Ean Coleridge, *qv*; *m* 1989, Georgia Metcalfe; two *s. Educ:* Eton; Trinity Coll., Cambridge. Associate Editor, Tatler, 1979–81; Columnist, Evening Standard, 1981–84; Features Editor, Harpers and Queen, 1985–86, Editor, 1986–89. Young Journalist of the Year, British Press Awards, 1983. *Publications:* Tunnel Vision, collected journalism, 1982; Around the World in 78 Days, 1984; Shooting Stars, 1984; The Fashion Conspiracy, 1988; How I Met My Wife and other stories, 1991; Paper Tigers, 1993. *Address:* 24 Chepstow Crescent, W11 3EB. *T:* 0171–221 4293. *Clubs:* Harry's Bar, Mark's, Thirty.

COLERIDGE, Paul James Duke; QC 1993; *b* 30 May 1949; *s* of James Bernard and Jane Evelina Coleridge; *m* 1973, Judith Elizabeth Rossiter; two *s* one *d. Educ:* Cranleigh Sch., Surrey; College of Law, London. Called to the Bar, Middle Temple, 1970; in practice at the Bar, 1970–85; Internat. Legal Advr to Baron Hans Heinrich Thyssen-Bornemisza, Switzerland, 1985–89; private practice, 1989–93. *Recreations:* Dorset, gardening, motor-bikes. *Address:* Queen Elizabeth Building, Temple, EC4Y 9BS. *T:* 0171–797 7837. *Clubs:* MCC; Lyons Gate Golf (Middlemarsh, Dorset).

COLES, Adrian Michael; Director-General: Building Societies Association, since 1993; Council of Mortgage Lenders, since 1993; *b* 19 April 1954; *s* of Kenneth Ernest Coles and Constance Mary (*née* Sykes); *m* 1981, Marion Alma Hoare; one *s* one *d. Educ:* Holly Lodge Grammar Sch., Smethwick; Univ. of Nottingham (BA Hons); Univ. of Sheffield (MA). Economist, Electricity Council, 1976–79; Building Societies Association: Economist, 1979–81; Head: Econs and Stats, 1981–86; External Relns, 1986–93. Chm., Thames Valley Housing Assoc., 1990–93. *Publications:* (with Mark Boleat) The Mortgage Market, 1987; numerous articles in housing and housing finance jls. *Recreations:* swimming, cycling, reading, family. *Address:* The Building Societies Association, 3 Savile Row, W1X 1AF. *T:* 0171–437 0655.

COLES, Sir (Arthur) John, KCMG 1989 (CMG 1984); HM Diplomatic Service; Permanent Under-Secretary of State and Head of the Diplomatic Service, since 1994; *b* 13 Nov. 1937; *s* of Arthur Strixton Coles and Doris Gwendoline Coles; *m* 1965, Anne Mary Sutherland Graham; two *s* one *d*. *Educ:* Magdalen Coll. Sch., Brackley; Magdalen Coll., Oxford (BA 1960). Served HM Forces, 1955–57. Joined HM Diplomatic Service, 1960; Middle Eastern Centre for Arabic Studies, Lebanon, 1960–62; Third Sec., Khartoum, 1962–64; FO (later FCO), 1964–68; Asst Political Agent, Trucial States (Dubai), 1968–71; FCO, 1971–75; Head of Chancery, Cairo, 1975–77; Counsellor (Developing Countries), UK Perm. Mission to EEC, 1977–80; Head of S Asian Dept, FCO, 1980–81; Private Sec. to Prime Minister, 1981–84; Ambassador to Jordan, 1984–88; High Commissioner to Australia, 1988–91; Dep. Under-Sec. of State, FCO, 1991–94. *Recreations:* walking, cricket, bird-watching, reading, music. *Address:* c/o Foreign and Commonwealth Office, King Charles Street, SW1A 2AH. *Club:* United Oxford & Cambridge University.

COLES, Bruce; *see* Coles, N. B. C.

COLES, Prof. Bryan Randell, DPhil; FRS 1991; FInstP; Professor of Solid State Physics, Imperial College, University of London, 1966–91, now Emeritus Professor (Pro-Rector, 1986–91); Dean of the Royal College of Science, 1984–86; *b* 9 June 1926; *s* of Charles Frederick Coles and Olive Irene Coles; *m* 1955, Merivan Robinson; two *s*. *Educ:* Canton High Sch., Cardiff; Univ. of Wales, Cardiff (BSc); Jesus Coll., Univ. of Oxford (DPhil). FInstP 1972. Lectr in Metal Physics, Imperial Coll., London, 1950; Res. Fellow, Carnegie Inst. of Technol., Pittsburgh, 1954–56. Vis. Prof., Univ. of Calif, San Diego, 1962 and 1969; Hill Vis. Prof., Univ. of Minnesota, 1983. Vice-Pres., Inst. of Physics, 1968–72; Mem. Physics Cttee, SRC, 1972–76 (Chm. 1973–76); Chm., Neutron Beam Cttee, SERC, 1985–88. Chm. Bd of Dirs, Taylor & Francis Ltd (Scientific Publishers), 1976–. *Publications:* Electronic Structures of Solids (with A. D. Caplin), 1976; papers on structure, electrical properties, superconductivity and magnetic properties of metals and alloys in Philosoph. Magazine, Advances in Physics, Jl of Physics. *Recreations:* music, natural history, theatre. *Address:* 61 Courtfield Gardens, SW5 0NQ. *T:* 0171–373 3539.

COLES, Rt. Rev. David John; *see* Christchurch, Bishop of.

COLES, Gerald James Kay; QC 1976; **His Honour Judge Gerald Coles;** a Circuit Judge, since 1985; *b* 6 May 1933; *o s* of James William Coles and Jane Elizabeth Coles; *m* 1958, Kathleen Yolande, *e d* of Alfred John Hobson, FRCS, and Kathleen Elizabeth Hobson; three *s*. *Educ:* Coatham Sch., Redcar; Brasenose Coll., Oxford; Harvard Law Sch., Harvard Univ. Meritorious Award, Hastings Schol., Queen's Coll., Oxford, 1949; Akroyd Open Schol. 1950; BA 1954, BCL 1955, Oxon; Westengard Schol., Harvard Law Sch., 1955; LLM 1956. Called to Bar, Middle Temple, 1957; practised at Bar, London and NE Circuit, 1957–85; Prosecuting Counsel to Inland Revenue, 1971–76; a Recorder, 1972–85; Designated Family Judge, York, 1990–; Resident Judge, Bradford Crown Court, 1992–. A Pres., Mental Health Review Tribunals, 1986–. Mem., Ethnic Minorities Adv. Cttee, Judicial Studies Bd, 1993–. *Recreations:* music, theatre, photography. *Address:* Redwood, Dean Lane, Hawksworth, Guiseley, Leeds, Yorks LS20 8NY.

COLES, Sir John; *see* Coles, Sir A. J.

COLES, John Morton, ScD, PhD; FBA 1978; Professor of European Prehistory, University of Cambridge, 1980–86; Fellow of Fitzwilliam College, since 1963, Honorary Fellow, 1987; *b* 25 March 1930; *s* of Edward John Langdon Coles and Alice Margaret (*née* Brown); *m* 1985, Bryony Jean Orme; two *s* two *d* of previous marr. *Educ:* Woodstock, Ontario; Univ. of Toronto (BA); Univ. of Cambridge (MA, ScD); Univ. of Edinburgh (PhD). Research Fellow, Univ. of Edinburgh, 1959–60; Asst Lectr, 1960–65, Lectr, 1965–76, Reader, 1976–80, Univ. of Cambridge. Fellow, McDonald Inst. for Archaeological Res., Univ. of Cambridge, 1992–; Hon. Prof., Univ. of Exeter, 1993–. President, Prehistoric Soc., 1978–82. Mem., Royal Commn on Ancient and Historical Monuments of Scotland, 1992–. MAE 1989; Hon. Mem., Inst. of Field Archaeologists, 1991. FSA 1963 (Vice-Pres., 1982–86). Grahame Clark Medal, British Acad., 1995. *Publications:* The Archaeology of Early Man (with E. Higgs), 1969; Field Archaeology in Britain, 1972; Archaeology by Experiment, 1973; (with A. Harding) The Bronze Age in Europe, 1979; Experimental Archaeology, 1979; (with B. Orme) Prehistory of the Somerset Levels, 1980; The Archaeology of Wetlands, 1984; (with B. J. Coles) Sweet Track to Glastonbury: the Somerset Levels in prehistory, 1986; (ed with A. Lawson) European Wetlands in Prehistory, 1987; Meare Village East, 1987; (with B. J. Coles) People of the Wetlands, 1989; Images of the Past, 1990; From the Waters of Oblivion, 1991; (with A. Goodall and S. Minnitt) Arthur Bulleid and the Glastonbury Lake Village 1892–1992, 1992; (with D. Hall) Fenland Survey, 1994; Rock Carvings of Uppland, 1994; (with S. Minnitt) Industrious and Fairly Civilised: the Glastonbury lake village, 1995; contrib. Proc. Prehist. Soc., Antiquaries Jl, Antiquity, Somerset Levels Papers, etc. *Recreations:* music, ancient art, wetlands, woodlands. *Address:* Fursdon Mill Cottage, Thorverton, Devon EX5 5JS. *T:* Exeter (01392) 860125.

COLES, Kenneth George, BE; FIEAust; CEng, FIMechE, FAIM; Chairman, Conveyor Co. of Australia Pty Ltd, 1957–91; *b* Melbourne, 30 June 1926; *s* of Sir Kenneth Coles; *m* 1st, 1950, Thalia Helen (marr. diss. 1980); one *s* two *d*; 2nd, 1985, Rowena Danziger. *Educ:* The King's Sch., Parramatta, NSW; Sydney Univ. (BE 1948). FIE(Aust) 1986; FIMechE 1969; FAIM 1959. Gained engrg experience in appliance manufacturing and automotive industries Nuffield Aust. Pty Ltd, Gen. Motors Holdens Pty Ltd and Frigidaire, before commencing own business manufacturing conveyors, 1955; Chm and Man. Dir, K. G. Coles & Co. Pty Ltd, 1955–76, Chm. 1976–95; Chm. and Man. Dir, K. G. C. Magnetic Tape Pty Ltd, 1973–80. Director: Australian Oil & Gas Corp. Ltd, 1969–89 (Dep. Chm., 1984–89); A. O. G. Minerals Ltd, 1969–87 (Dep. Chm., 1984–87); Coles Myer Ltd (formerly G. J. Coles & Coy Ltd), 1976–94; Electrical Equipment Ltd, 1976–84; Permanent Trustee Co. Ltd, 1978–94 (Vice Chm., 1990–91; Chm., 1991–94); Centre for Industrial Technol. Ltd, 1985–87; Chatham Investment Co. Ltd, 1987–94; NRMA Insurance Ltd, 1989–90; Stockland Trust Group, 1990–; Chairman: Innovation Council of NSW Ltd, 1984–89 (Dir, 1982–89); Nat. Engrg (now Metal and Engrg) Training Bd, 1989–. Metal Trades Industry Association: Gen. Councillor, NSW Br., 1976–94; Nat. Councillor, 1988–94; Mem. Bd, Sir William Tyrce Foundn, 1995–. Chm., Lizard Island Reef Res. Foundn, 1994– (Dir, 1992–). Member: Internat. Solar Energy Soc., 1957–; Science & Industry Forum, Australian Academy of Science, 1983–; Mem. and Employers' Rep., NSW Bd of Secondary Educn, 1987–90. Mem. Council, Nat. Roads and Motorists Assoc., NSW, 1986–90. Councillor and Mem. Bd of Governors, Ascham Sch., 1972–82; Employers' Rep., NSW Secondary Schs Bd, 1979–83. Fellow, Senate, Sydney Univ., 1983–. *Address:* 2/24 Rosemont Avenue, Woollahra, NSW 2025, Australia. *T:* and *Fax:* (2) 3286084. *Clubs:* Union, Australian, Sydney Rotary (Sydney); Royal Sydney Golf.

COLES, Norman, CB 1971; *b* 29 Dec. 1914; *s* of Fred and Emily Coles; *m* 1947, Una Valerie Tarrant; five *s*. *Educ:* Hanson High Sch., Bradford; Royal College of Science; City and Guilds Coll. Head, Armament Dept, RAE, 1959; Dir Gen. Equipment Research and Development, Min. of Aviation, 1962; Dep. Controller: of Aircraft (RAF), Min. of Technology, 1966–68; of Guided Weapons, Min. of Technology, 1968–69; Dep. Chief Adviser (Research and Studies), MoD, 1969–71; Dep. Controller, Establishments and Research, MoD, 1971–75. *Recreations:* carpentry, crossword puzzles. *Address:* Castle Gate, 27 Castle Hill, Banwell, Weston-super-Mare, Avon BS24 6NX. *T:* Banwell (01934) 822019.

COLES, (Norman) Bruce (Cameron); QC 1984; a Recorder, since 1986; *b* 28 Feb. 1937; *s* of Sir Norman Coles and of Dorothy Verna (*née* Deague); *m* 1961, Sally Fenella Freeman; one *s* three *d*. *Educ:* Melbourne Grammar Sch.; Univ. of Melbourne (LLB); Magdalen Coll., Oxford Univ. (BCL). 2nd Lieut, 6th Bn Royal Melbourne Regt, 1956–59. Associate to Sir Owen Dixon, Chief Justice of High Court of Australia, 1959–60; called to English Bar, Middle Temple, 1963, Bencher, 1991; admitted to Bar of Supreme Court of Victoria, 1964. Assistant Recorder, 1982. Chm., Bar Race Relations Cttee, 1994–. Mem. Council, Oxfam, 1985–. Chm. of Govs, Enstone Co. Primary Sch., 1993–. *Recreations:* mountaineering, cycling, theatre, music. *Address:* Fountain Court, Temple, EC4Y 9DH. *T:* 0171–583 3335. *Clubs:* Cyclist Touring (Surrey), Gentian Mountaineering.

COLEY, Dr Graham Douglas; Managing Director, Chemical and Biological Defence Establishment, Ministry of Defence, since 1995; *b* 16 Nov. 1946; *s* of late Douglas Leonard Coley and of Phyllis Adeline Coley (*née* Hughes); *m* 1972, Susan Elizabeth Thackery. *Educ:* Halesowen Grammar Sch.; Birmingham Univ. (BSc 1st Cl. Hons); Darwin Coll., Cambridge (PhD 1971). FIEE 1994. Midlands Res. Station, Gas Council, 1967–68; Atomic Weapons Research Establishment, Aldermaston, 1968–87: Supt, Explosives Technol. Br., 1982–85; Head, Chemical Technol. Div., 1985–87; Dir, Nuclear Resources, MoD PE, 1987–90; Dep. Head, Efficiency Unit, Prime Minister's Office, 1990–92; Asst Chief Scientific Advr (Projects), MoD, 1992–94. *Publications:* papers in technical jls and internat. conf. proc. *Recreations:* flyfishing, shooting, gardening (auriculas). *Address:* Chemical and Biological Defence Establishment, Porton Down, Salisbury, Wilts SP4 0JQ. *Club:* Flyfishers'.

COLFOX, Sir (William) John, 2nd Bt *cr* 1939; JP; DL; *b* 25 April 1924; *yr* and *o* surv. *s* of Sir (William) Philip Colfox, 1st Bt, MC, and Mary (Frances) Lady Colfox (*d* 1973); *S* father, 1966; *m* 1962, Frederica Loveday, *d* of Adm. Sir Victor Crutchley, VC, KCB, DSC; two *s* three *d*. *Educ:* Eton. Served in RNVR, 1942–46, leaving as Lieut. Qualified Land Agent, 1950. Chm., Land Settlement Assoc., 1980–81. Vice-Chm., TSW, 1981–92. JP Dorset, 1962, High Sheriff of Dorset, 1969, DL Dorset, 1977. *Heir: s* Philip John Colfox [*b* 27 Dec. 1962; *m* Julia, *yr d* of G. St G. Schomberg; twin *d*]. *Address:* Symondsbury House, Bridport, Dorset DT6 6HB. *T:* Bridport (01308) 22956.

COLGAN, Samuel Hezlett; His Honour Judge Colgan; a Circuit Judge, since 1990; *b* 10 June 1945; *s* of late Henry George Colgan and of Jane Swan Hezlett. *Educ:* Foyle College, Londonderry; Trinity College Dublin (MA, LLB). Called to the Bar, Middle Temple, 1969; a Recorder, SE Circuit, 1987. *Recreations:* travelling, the arts, reading, tennis. *Address:* Lord Chancellor's Department, SE Circuit, New Cavendish House, 18 Maltravers Street, WC2R 3EU.

COLGRAIN, 3rd Baron *cr* 1946, of Everlands; **David Colin Campbell;** *b* 24 April 1920; *s* of 2nd Baron Colgrain, MC, and of Margaret Emily (*d* 1989), *d* of late P. W. Carver; *S* father, 1973; *m* 1st, 1945, Veronica Margaret (marr. diss. 1964), *d* of late Lt-Col William Leckie Webster, RAMC; one *s* one *d*; 2nd, 1973, Mrs Sheila M. Hudson. *Educ:* Eton; Trinity Coll., Cambridge. Served War of 1939–45, 9th Lancers. Manager, Grindlays Bank Ltd, India and Pakistan, 1945–49; joined Antony Gibbs and Sons Ltd, 1949, Director, 1954–83, retired; Chm., Alexander and Berendt Ltd, 1967–. *Heir: s* Hon. Alastair Colin Leckie Campbell [*b* 16 Sept. 1951; *m* 1979, Annabel Rose, *yr d* of Hon. Robin Warrender, *qv*; two *s*]. *Address:* Bushes Farm, Weald, Sevenoaks, Kent TN14 6ND.

COLHOUN, Prof. John; Barker Professor of Cryptogamic Botany, University of Manchester, 1960–80, now Emeritus; Dean, Faculty of Science, 1974 and 1975; Pro-Vice-Chancellor, 1977–80; *b* 15 May 1913; *yr s* of late James and Rebecca Colhoun, Castlederg, Co. Tyrone; *m* 1949, Margaret, *e d* of late Prof. Gilbert Waterhouse, LittD, and Mary Elizabeth, *e d* of Sir Robert Woods; three *d*. *Educ:* Edwards Sch., Castlederg, Co. Tyrone; The Queen's Univ. of Belfast; Imperial Coll. of Science, London Univ. BSc, MAgr (Belfast), PhD, DSc (London), MSc (Manchester), DIC. Min. of Agriculture for Northern Ireland: Research Asst, 1939–46; Senior Scientific Officer, 1946–50; Principal Scientific Officer, 1951–60. The Queen's Univ., Belfast: Asst Lecturer in Agricultural Botany, 1940–42; Asst Lectr 1942–45, Jun. Lectr 1945–46, Lectr 1946–54, Reader 1954–60, in Mycology and Plant Pathology. Warden of Queen's Chambers, 1942–49. FLS 1955. FIBiol 1963. President: British Mycological Soc., 1963; The Queen's Univ. Assoc., 1960–61; The Queen's Univ. Club, London, 1983–85. Chm., Fedn of British Plant Pathologists, 1968; Hon. Mem., British Soc. for Plant Pathology, 1989. Jt Editor, Jl of Phytopathology (Phytopath. Zeitschrift), 1973–91. *Publications:* Diseases of the Flax Plant, 1947; Club Root Disease of Crucifers caused by *Plasmodiophora brassicae* Woron, 1958; numerous papers in Annals of Applied Biology, Annals of Botany, Trans Brit. Mycological Soc., Nature, Phytopath. Z. *Address:* 12 Southdown Crescent, Cheadle Hulme, Cheshire SK8 6EQ. *T:* 0161–485 2084. *Club:* Athenæum.

COLIN, Rt. Rev. Gerald Fitzmaurice, MA; an Assistant Bishop, Diocese of Lincoln, 1979–94; *b* 19 July 1913; *s* of Frederick Constant Colin and Jemima Fitzmaurice; *m* 1941, Iris Susan Stuart Weir; three *s* two *d*. *Educ:* Mountjoy Sch.; Trinity Coll., Dublin. MA (TCD) 1946. Deacon, 1936; Priest, 1937. St George's, Dublin, 1938; Chancellor's Vicar, St Patrick's Cathedral, Dublin, 1938; RAFVR, 1939–47; Vicar of Frodingham, Dio. of Lincoln, 1947–66; Bishop Suffragan of Grimsby, 1966–78. Canon of Lincoln Cathedral, 1960; Rural Dean of Manlake, 1960; Proctor in Convocation, 1960–65, 1966–70. *Recreation:* fishing. *Address:* 11 Upton Close, Norwich NR4 7PD. *T:* Norwich (01603) 51612.

COLL, Elizabeth Anne Loosemore E.; *see* Esteve-Coll.

COLL BLASINI, Néstor; Grand Cross, Libertador Simón Bolivar; Venezuelan Ambassador, retired 1991; *b* 10 June 1931; *s* of Guillermo Coll Nuñez and María de Lourdes Blasini de Coll; *m* 1952, Maritza Barrios de Coll; five *s* one *d*. *Educ:* Colegio La Salle, Caracas; Univ. Católica Andres Bello, Caracas. Entered Foreign Service, 1958, as Third Secretary, later Second Sec.; Head of Office that revised Reciprocal Commercial Treaty between Venezuela and USA; Economic Counsellor, Colombia; Minister Counsellor, Head of Cabinet of Min. of Foreign Affairs; Director of Frontiers, 1969; Ambassador of Venezuela in Panama, 1969–71; Asst Director General, Min. of For. Affairs, actg as Dir Gen. on several occasions, 1971–74; Ambassador of Venezuela: in Sweden and Finland, 1974–76; in Turkey, 1976–78; in Finland, 1978–79; in Italy, 1979–82; in UK, 1982–84; in Israel, 1984–91. Member: Sociedades Bolivarianas, Venezuela, Italy and Honduras; Academia Tiberina, Rome; Sociedad de Estudios Históricos Mirandinos, Venezuela. Grand Cross: Cavalieri di Gran Croce (Italy), Condor de los Andres (Bolivia), Libertador San Martin (Argentina), Yugoslav Flag (Yugoslavia), Polar Star (Sweden), and other decorations. *Publications:* La Opinion Publica en America Latina (Colombia), 1963; various articles in

Latin American newspapers. *Recreations:* reading, music, golf, ULM pilot, IP shooting. *Club:* Lagunita Country, Los Canales Country (Caracas).

COLLARD, Douglas Reginald, OBE 1976; HM Diplomatic Service, retired; Member: Council, Anglo-Arab Association, since 1990 (Director, 1976–90); Management Committee, Home for the Blind, Wanstead, Essex, since 1991; *b* 7 April 1916; *s* of late Hebert Carthew Collard and late Mary Ann (*née* Pugh); *m* 1947, Eleni Alkmini Kiortsi (marr. diss. 1969), Greece; two *s* three *d*. *Educ:* Wallasey Grammar Sch.; privately. Army Service, 1940–46 (despatches); UNRRA, Greece, 1946–47; Asst Commercial Adviser, British Econ. Mission to Greece, 1947; Consul, Patras, Greece, 1947–52; Beirut, 1952–54; 2nd Sec. (Commercial); Khartoum, 1954–56; Copenhagen, 1958–61; FCO, 1956–58 and 1967–69; 1st Sec. (Commercial): Tripoli, 1961–65; Lahore, 1965–67; Montevideo, 1969–71; 1st Sec., later Counsellor (Commercial), Algiers, 1971–73; Consul-Gen., Bilbao, 1973–76. Dir, Arab British Centre, 1981–90; Sec., Saudi British Soc., 1986–90. *Recreations:* reading, walking. *Address:* Flat 23, Westminster Court, 23 Cambridge Park, Wanstead, E11 2PU. *T:* 0181–530 8308.

COLLECOTT, Dr Peter Salmon; HM Diplomatic Service; Counsellor (European Union and Economic), Bonn, since 1994; *b* 8 Oct. 1950; *s* of George William Collecott and Nancy Alice Collecott (*née* Salmon); *m* 1982, Judith Patricia Pead. *Educ:* Chigwell Sch., Essex; St John's Coll., Cambridge (MA 1976; PhD 1976); MIT (Kennedy Schol. 1972). Royal Soc. Fellow, Max Planck Inst. for Physics and Astrophysics, Munich, 1976–77; joined HM Diplomatic Service, 1977: FCO, 1977–78; MECAS, Lebanon, later London, 1978–80; 1st Secretary: (Political), Khartoum, 1980–82; (Econ., Commercial, Agricl), Canberra, 1982–86; Head, Iran/Iraq Section, ME Dept, FCO, 1986–88; Asst Head, EC Dept (Ext.), FCO, 1988–89; Counsellor, Head of Chancery and Consul Gen., later Dep. Head of Mission, Jakarta, 1989–93. *Publications:* papers on theoretical physics in learned jls. *Recreations:* walking, reading. *Address:* c/o Foreign and Commonwealth Office, King Charles Street, SW1A 2AH. *Club:* United Oxford & Cambridge University.

COLLEE, Prof. John Gerald, CBE 1991; MD; FRCPath; FRCPE; Robert Irvine Professor of Bacteriology and Head of Department of Medical Microbiology (formerly Department of Bacteriology), University of Edinburgh, 1979–91, now Emeritus Professor; Chief Bacteriologist to Edinburgh Royal Infirmary and Consultant Bacteriologist, Lothian Health Board, 1979–91; Consultant Adviser in Microbiology to Scottish Home and Health Department, 1986–91; *b* 10 May 1929; *s* of John Gerald Collee and Mary Hay Wilson Kirsopp Cassels; *m* 1952, Isobel McNay Galbraith (marr. diss. 1995); two *s* one *d*; *m* 1995, Anne Ferguson. *Educ:* Bo'ness Acad.; Edinburgh Acad.; Edinburgh Univ. MB ChB, MD (Gold Medal). Ho. Phys., 1951–52. AMS (Captain RAMC), 1952–54. Lectr in Bacteriology, Edinburgh, 1955–63; WHO Vis. Prof. of Bacteriol., Baroda, 1963–64; Sen. Lectr, Edinburgh, and Hon. Cons. Bacteriologist, 1964–70; Reader in Bacteriol. 1970–74, Personal Prof. of Bacteriol. 1974–79, Edinburgh. Member: Scottish Health Service Planning Council Adv. Gp on Infection, 1981–90; Jt Cttee on Vaccination and Immunisation, 1982–95; Cttee on Safety of Medicines, 1987–89; Cttee on Vaccination and Immunisation Procedures, MRC, 1988–; Medicines Commn, 1992–. *Publications:* Applied Medical Microbiology, 1976, 2nd edn 1981; contrib. and ed several textbooks, incl. Mackie and McCartney's Practical Medical Microbiology, 1989; many sci. papers on aspects of infection, anaerobes of clin. importance, antimicrobial drugs and immunization. *Recreations:* woodwork, mechanics, fishing, music, painting. *Address:* 204 Newhaven Road, Edinburgh EH6 4QE. *T:* 0131–552 8810. *Club:* Scottish Arts (Edinburgh).

COLLENDER, Andrew Robert; QC 1991; a Recorder, since 1993; *b* 11 Aug. 1946; *s* of John and Kathleen Collender; *m* 1974, Titia Tybout; two *s*. *Educ:* Mt Pleasant Boys High Sch., Rhodesia; Univ. of Bristol (LLB Hons). Called to the Bar, Lincoln's Inn, 1969. *Recreations:* playing the violin, sailing, riding. *Address:* 2 Temple Gardens, Temple, EC4Y 9AY. *T:* 0171–583 6041.

COLLENETTE, Hon. David Michael; PC (Canada); MP (L) Don Valley East, since 1993; Minister of National Defence and Minister of Veterans' Affairs, Canada, since 1993; *b* 24 June 1946; *s* of David Henry and Sarah Margaret Collenette; *m* 1975, Penny Hossack; one *s*. *Educ:* Glendon Coll., York Univ. (BA Hons); postgrad. studies in legislative behaviour and urban studies, Carleton and York Univs. Admin. Officer, Marketing Div., Internat. Life Assurance Co., UK, 1970–72; Exec. Vice-Pres., Mandrake Management Consultants, Canada, 1987–93. MP (L) York East, 1974–79 and 1980–84; Sec.-Gen., Liberal Party of Canada, 1985–87 (Exec. Dir, Toronto, 1969–70, Ontario, 1972–74). *Recreations:* soccer, squash, theatre, classical music. *Address:* 121 East Block, House of Commons, Ottawa K1A 0A6, Canada. *T:* (613) 9963100. *Clubs:* National Liberal; University (Toronto).

COLLENS, Rupert; *see* Mackeson, Sir R. H.

COLLETT, Sir Christopher, GBE 1988; JP; Partner in Ernst & Young, Chartered Accountants, London, retired 1993; Lord Mayor of London, 1988–89; *b* 10 June 1931; 2nd *s* of Sir Henry Seymour Collett, 2nd Bt, and Lady (Ruth Mildred) Collett (*née* Hatch) (*d* 1994); *m* 1959, Christine Anne, *d* of Oswald Hardy Griffiths, Nunthorpe, Yorks; two *s* one *d*. *Educ:* Harrow; Emmanuel Coll., Cambridge. MA; FCA. Nat. Service, RA and Surrey Yeomanry; Captain TA (RA). Articled with Cassleton Elliott & Co., Chartered Accountants, 1954; qualified, 1958; Partner, Ghana 1960, London 1963; firm merged to become Josolyne Miles and Cassleton Elliott, Josolyne Layton Bennett & Co., Arthur Young, and then Ernst & Young. Mem., Court of Common Council (Broad Street Ward), City of London, 1973–79; Alderman, 1979–; Sheriff, City of London, 1985–86. Master, Worshipful Co. of Glovers, 1981; Hon. Liveryman, 1990, Asst, 1991, Third Warden, 1993, Haberdashers' Co.; Member: Guild of Freemen, 1983–; Worshipful Co. of Chartered Accts in Eng. and Wales, 1984– (Liveryman, 1984; Asst, 1986–93); City of London TAVR Cttee, 1980–92; Council Mem., Action Research for the Crippled Child, 1984–93. Governor: Haberdashers' Aske's Schs, Elstree, 1982–; Music Therapy Gp Ltd, 1986–; Bridewell Royal Hosp., 1987–; Hon. Treas., Lee House, Wimbledon. Pres., Broad Street Ward Club, 1979–. JP City of London, 1979. Hon. DSc City, 1988. KStJ 1988. Order of Merit (cl. II), State of Qatar, 1985; Orden del Merito Civil (cl. II), Spain, 1986; Commander, Order of Merit, Federal Republic of Germany, 1986; CON, 1st cl. (Nigeria), 1989. *Recreations:* gardening, fishing. *Address:* 13 Somerset House, Somerset Road, Wimbledon, SW19 5JA. *Club:* City Livery.

COLLETT, Sir Ian (Seymour), 3rd Bt *cr* 1934; *b* 5 Oct. 1953; *s* of David Seymour Collett (*d* 1962), and of Sheila Joan Collett (who *m* 1980, Sir James William Miskin, *qv*), *o d* of late Harold Scott; *S* grandfather, 1971; *m* 1982, Philippa, *o d* of James R. I. Hawkins, Preston St Mary, Suffolk; one *s* one *d*. *Educ:* Lancing College, Sussex. Notary Public, 1985. Mem., Law Society, 1979. *Recreations:* golf, fishing, cricket, shooting. *Heir: s* Anthony Seymour Collett, *b* 27 Feb. 1984. *Address:* The Red House, Ufford, Woodbridge, Suffolk IP13 6EL. *Clubs:* MCC; Aldeburgh Golf; Aldeburgh Yacht.

COLLEY, Maj.-Gen. (David) Bryan (Hall), CB 1988; CBE 1982 (OBE 1977; MBE 1968); FCIT; Director-General, Road Haulage Association, since 1988; *b* 5 June 1934; *s* of Lawson and Alice Colley; *m* 1957, Marie Thérèse (*née* Préfontaine); one *s* one *d*. *Educ:* King Edward's Sch., Birmingham; RMA, Sandhurst. Commissioned: RASC, 1954; RCT, 1965; regimental appts in Germany, Belgium, UK, Hong Kong and Singapore; Student, Staff Coll., Camberley, 1964; JSSC Latimer, 1970; CO Gurkha Transport Regt and 31 Regt, RCT, 1971–74; Staff HQ 1st (British) Corps, 1974–77; Comd Logistic Support Gp, 1977–80; Col AQ (Ops and Plans) and Dir Admin. Planning, MoD (Army), 1980–82; Comd Transport 1st (British) Corps, 1983–86; Dir Gen., Transport and Movts (Army), 1986–88, retired. Col Comdt, RCT, 1988–93; Col Comdt, Royal Logistic Corps, 1993–. Freeman, City of London, 1986; Hon. Liveryman, Worshipful Co. of Carmen, 1986. *Recreations:* travel, walking. *Address:* c/o Midland Bank, Redditch, Worcs B97 4EA. *Club:* Army and Navy.

COLLEY, Surg. Rear-Adm. Ian Harris, OBE 1963; Member, Committee of Management, Royal National Lifeboat Institution, since 1982; *b* 14 Oct. 1922; *s* of Aubrey James Colley and Violet Fulford Colley; *m* 1952, Joy Kathleen (*née* Goodacre). *Educ:* Hanley Castle Grammar Sch.; King's Coll., London and King's Coll. Hosp. MB, BS 1948; DPH; MFOM; FFCM. Royal Naval Medical Service, 1948–80: MO HMS Cardigan Bay and HMS Consort, 1949–52; service with Fleet Air Arm, 1955–78: as PMO HMS Centaur; MO i/c Air Med. Sch.; Pres., Central Air Med. Bd; Comd MO to Flag Officer, Naval Air Comd; Surg. Rear Adm. (Ships and Estabs), 1978–80, retired. QHP 1978–80. Consultant in Aviation Medicine; former Examr to Conjoint Bd, Royal College of Surgeons and Royal College of Physicians for DipAvMed. Vice-Pres., RNLI, 1989– (Chm., Med. and Survival Cttee, 1984–88). CStJ 1980. *Publications:* papers in field of aviation medicine. *Address:* c/o Royal Bank of Scotland, Inveraray, Argyll PA32 8TY.

COLLEY, Prof. Linda Jane, PhD, FRHistS; Richard M. Colgate Professor of History, since 1992, and Director, Lewis Walpole Library, since 1982, Yale University; *b* 13 Sept. 1949; *d* of Roy Colley and Marjorie (*née* Hughes); *m* 1982, David Nicholas Cannadine, *qv*; one *d* decd. *Educ:* Bristol Univ. (BA); Cambridge Univ. (MA, PhD). University of Cambridge: Eugenie Strong Research Fellow, Girton Coll., 1975–78; Fellow: Newnham Coll., 1978–79; Christ's Coll., 1979–81; Yale University: Asst Prof., History, 1982–85; Associate Prof., 1985–90; Prof., History, 1990–92. Vis. Prof., Birkbeck Coll., London Univ., 1995–. Journalist and work on TV. Anstey Lectr, Univ. of Kent, 1994; William Church Meml Lectr, Brown Univ., 1994; Dist Lectr in British Hist., Univ. of Texas at Austin, 1995. Mem., Women's Forum. FRHistS 1988. *Publications:* In Defiance of Oligarchy: The Tory Party 1714–60, 1982; Namier, 1989; Britons: forging the nation 1707–1837, 1992 (Wolfson Prize, 1993); Crown Pictorial: art and the British monarchy, 1990; numerous articles and reviews in UK and USA jls. *Recreations:* travel, looking at art. *Address:* Department of History, Yale University, New Haven, CT 06520, USA. *T:* (203) 7851080; c/o Curtis Brown, Haymarket House, 28–29 Haymarket, SW1Y 4SP. *Club:* Reform.

COLLIE, Alexander Conn, MBE 1979; JP; Chairman, Aberdeen Tourist Board, since 1984; Lord Provost of the City of Aberdeen, 1980–84; Member: Aberdeen District Council, 1975–95; Aberdeen Licensing Board, since 1984; *b* 1 July 1913; *s* of late Donald and Jane Collie; *m* 1942, Elizabeth Keith Macleod (*d* 1985); two *s*. *Educ:* Ferryhill Sch., Aberdeen; Ruthrieston Sch., Aberdeen. Member: Aberdeen Town Council, 1947–75; Aberdeen Harbour Board, 1947–74; North of Scotland Hydro-Electric Consultative Council, until Oct. 1980; Past Member: Scottish Sports Council; Scottish Bakers' Union Exec. Council. JP Aberdeen, 1956. OStJ 1981. *Address:* (home) 43 Brimmond Place, Aberdeen AB1 3EN. *T:* Aberdeen (01224) 874972.

COLLIER, family name of **Baron Monkswell.**

COLLIER, Andrew James, CB 1976; Deputy Secretary, Department of Health and Social Security, 1973–82; *b* 12 July 1923; *s* of Joseph Veasy Collier and Dorothy Murray; *m* 1950, Bridget, *d* of George and Edith Eberstadt, London; two *d*. *Educ:* Harrow; Christ Church, Oxford. Served Army, RHA, 1943–46. Entered HM Treasury, 1948; Private Sec. to: Sir Henry Wilson Smith, 1950; Sir Leslie Rowan, 1951; Chancellors of the Exchequer, 1956–59 (Rt Hon. Harold Macmillan, Rt Hon. Peter Thorneycroft, Rt Hon. Derick Heathcoat Amory); Asst Sec., 1961; Under-Sec., 1967; Under-Secretary: Civil Service Dept, 1968–71; DHSS, 1971–73. Mem., Special Hosps Service Authy, 1989–93. Consultant, 1983–. *Address:* 10 Lambourne Avenue, SW19 7DW. *T:* 0181–879 3560. *Club:* Athenæum.

COLLIER, Andrew John, CBE 1995; Chief Education Officer, Lancashire County Council, since 1980; *b* 29 Oct. 1939; *s* of Francis George Collier and Margaret Nancy (*née* Nockles); *m* 1964, Gillian Ann (*née* Churchill); two *d*. *Educ:* University College Sch.; St John's Coll., Cambridge (MA). Assistant Master, Winchester Coll., 1962–68; Hampshire County Educn Dept, 1968–71; Buckinghamshire County Educn Dept, 1971–77; Dep. Chief Educn Officer, Lancashire, 1977–80. Member: Open Univ. Vis. Cttee, 1982–88; Council for Accreditation of Teacher Educn, 1984–89; Nat. Training Task Force, 1989–92; Gen. Synod Bd of Educn, 1993–; Educn Cttee, Royal Soc., 1995–; Chm., County Educn Officers' Soc., 1987–88; Treasurer: Soc. of Educn Officers, 1987–92 (Pres., 1990); Schools Curriculum Award, 1987–92. Liveryman, Worshipful Company of Wheelwrights, 1972. Mem. Council, Univ. of Lancaster, 1981–86, 1988–94. Pres., Lancs Fedn of Young Farmers' Clubs, 1985–88. *Publications:* (contrib.) New Directions for County Government, 1989; articles in jls. *Recreations:* music, walking, gardening. *Clubs:* Athenæum; Leander (Henley-on-Thames).

COLLIER, John Gordon, FRS 1990; FEng; Chairman, Nuclear Electric plc, since 1990; *b* London, 22 Jan. 1935; *s* of John Collier and Edith Georgina (*née* de Ville); *m* 1956, Ellen Alice Mary Mitchell; one *s* one *d*. *Educ:* St Paul's Sch., Hammersmith; University Coll. London (BScEng). FIMechE, FIChemE, FINucE; FInstE. AERE, Harwell: apprenticeship in mech. and chem. engrg, 1951–56; SO, then SSO, Chem. Engrg Div., 1957–62; Sect. Hd, then Br. Hd, Exptl Engrg Br., Adv. Reactor Engrg Div., Atomic Energy of Canada Ltd (on leave of absence from UKAEA), 1962–64; SSO, then PSO, Chem. Engrg Div., AERE, Harwell, 1964–66; Hd, Engrg Div., Atomic Power Constructions Ltd, R&D Lab., Heston, 1966–70; UKAEA, Harwell: Hd of Engrg Scis Gp, later Engrg Scis Br., 1970–75; Hd of Chem. Engrg Div., 1975–77; Mem., Atomic Energy Technical Unit responsible to Dep. Chm., UKAEA, 1977–79; Hd, Atomic Energy Technical Unit, 1979–81; Dir of Technical Studies, UKAEA, Harwell, 1981–82; Dir, Safety and Reliability Directorate, UKAEA, Culcheth, 1982–83; Dir Gen., Generation Develt and Construction Div. of CEGB, Barnwood, Glos, 1983–86; Dep. Chm., 1986, Chm., 1987–90, UKAEA. Chm., Nationalised Industries Chairmen's Gp, 1990–92. Calvin Rice Lectr, ASME/AIChE Nat. Heat Transfer Conf., USA, 1993. Hon. Life Mem., ASME, 1993. Hon. DSc Cranfield, 1988; Hon. DEng Bristol, 1993. *Publications:* Convective Boiling and Condensation, 1972, 2nd edn 1981; (jtly) Introduction to Nuclear Power, 1987. *Recreations:* cricket, music. *Address:* Nuclear Electric plc, Barnett Way, Barnwood, Glos GL4 7RS.

COLLIER, Kenneth Gerald; Principal, College of the Venerable Bede, Durham, 1959–75; *b* 1910; *m* 1938, Gwendoline Halford; two *s*. *Educ:* Aldenham Sch.; St John's Coll., Cambridge. MA 1935; Diploma in Education (Oxon) 1945. Technical translation, Stockholm, 1931–32; Schoolmaster, 1933–41; Royal Ordnance Factories, 1941–44; Physics Master, Lancing Coll., 1944–49; Lectr, St Luke's Coll., Exeter, 1949–59. Editor,

Education for Teaching, 1953–58. Chm., Assoc. Teachers in Colls and Depts of Education, 1964–65. Vis. Prof. of Education, Temple Univ., Philadelphia, 1965, 1968. Consultant to Council for Educational Technology, 1971–80. British Council tours, 1976–79: India, Brazil and Portugal; lecture tours, USA, 1979, 1990; study tour, Kenya, 1988. Hon. Research Fellow, Univ. of East Anglia, 1978–81. FSRHE 1993. *Publications:* The Science of Humanity, 1950; The Social Purposes of Education, 1959; New Dimensions in Higher Education, 1968; (ed) Innovation in Higher Education, 1974; (ed) Values and Moral Development in Higher Education, 1974; (ed) Evaluating the New BEd, 1978; (ed) The Management of Peer-Group Learning, 1983; A New Teaching, A New Learning: a guide to theological education, 1989; articles in educational and other jls. *Recreations:* local history, music, the film. *Address:* 4 Robson Terrace, Shincliffe, Durham DH1 2NL. *T:* Durham (0191) 3841647.

COLLIER, Lesley Faye, CBE 1993; Ballet Mistress, Royal Ballet School, since 1995; Principal Dancer with the Royal Ballet, 1972–95; *b* 13 March 1947; *d* of Roy and Mavis Collier; twin *s*. *Educ:* The Royal Ballet School, White Lodge, Richmond. Joined Royal Ballet, 1965; has danced most principal roles in the Royal repertory. Evening Standard Ballet Award, 1987. *Address:* c/o Royal Ballet School, 155 Talgarth Road, W14 9DE.

COLLIER, Prof. Leslie Harold, MD, DSc; FRCP, FRCPath; Professor of Virology, University of London, 1966–86, now Emeritus; Consulting Pathologist, Royal London Hospital (formerly London Hospital), since 1987; *b* 9 Feb. 1921; *s* of late Maurice Leonard Collier and Ruth (*née* Phillips); *m* 1942, Adeline Barnett; one *s*. *Educ:* Brighton Coll.; UCH Med. Sch. MD London 1953; DSc London 1968; MRCP 1969; FRCPath 1975; FRCP 1980. House Phys., UCH, 1943; served RAMC, 1944–47; Asst Pathologist, St Helier Hosp., Carshalton, 1947; Lister Inst. of Preventive Medicine, 1948–78: Head, Dept of Virology, 1955–74; Dep. Dir, 1968–74; Dir, Vaccines and Sera Laboratories, 1974–78; Hon. Dir, MRC Trachoma Unit, 1957–73; Prof. of Virology and Sen. Lectr, Jt Dept of Virology, London Hosp. Med. Coll. and St Bartholomew's Hosp. Med. Coll., 1978–86; Hd, Dept of Virology, London Hosp. Med. Coll., 1982–86. Hon. Consultant in Virology, Tower Hamlets HA, 1978–86. Pres., Sect. of Pathology, RSM, 1986–88, Hon. Mem., 1994. Chibret Gold Medal, Ligue contre le Trachome, 1959; Luys Prize, Soc. de Médecine de Paris, 1963. *Publications:* (ed jtly) Topley and Wilson's Principles of Bacteriology, Virology and Immunity, 8th edn, 1990; (jtly) Human Virology, 1993; papers in med. and scientific jls. *Recreations:* various. *Address:* 8 Peto Place, Regent's Park, NW1 4DT. *T:* 0171–487 4848.

COLLIER, Prof. Paul, DPhil; Professor of Economics, since 1993 and Director, Centre for Study of African Economies, since 1991, Oxford University; Fellow, St Antony's College, Oxford, since 1986; *b* 23 April 1949; *s* of Charles and Doris Collier; partner, Christine Küchemann. *Educ:* King Edward VII Grammar Sch., Sheffield; Trinity Coll., Oxford (MA 1970); Nuffield Coll., Oxford (DPhil 1975). Oxford University: Fellow, Keble Coll. and Research Officer, Inst. of Econs and Stats, 1976–86; Univ. Lectr in Econs, 1986–89; Reader in Econs, 1989–92. Prof. Invité, Centre d'Études et de Recherches sur le Développement Internat., Univ. d'Auvergne, 1989–; Vis. Prof., Kennedy Sch. of Govt, Harvard, 1992–; Fellow, Centre for Economic Policy Res., 1993–; Associate, Tinbergen Inst., 1994–. Overseas Develt Council, Program Associates Gp, Washington, 1994–; Africa Panel, SSRC, NY, 1993–. Edgar Graham Prize, SOAS, 1988. *Publications:* Labour and Poverty in Kenya, 1986; Labour and Poverty in Rural Tanzania, 1986, 2nd edn 1991; Peasants and Governments, 1989; Controlled Open Economies, 1990, 2nd edn 1994. *Recreations:* cats, The Spectator. *Address:* Centre for Study of African Economies, St Cross Building, Manor Road, Oxford OX1 3UL. *Club:* Faculty (Harvard).

COLLIER, Peter Neville; QC 1992; a Recorder, since 1988; *b* 1 June 1948; *s* of late Arthur Neville Collier and of Joan Audrey Collier (*née* Brewer); *m* 1972, Susan Margaret Williamson; two *s*. *Educ:* Hymer's Coll., Hull; Selwyn Coll., Cambridge (MA). Called to the Bar, Inner Temple, 1970. Chancellor, dio. of Wakefield, 1992–. *Recreations:* walking, reading, music. *Address:* 32 Park Square, Leeds LS1 2PF. *T:* Leeds (0113) 243 6388.

COLLIER-WRIGHT, John Hurrell, CBE 1966; Member, British Transport Docks Board, 1974–77; *b* 1 April 1915; *s* of John Robert Collier Collier-Wright and Phyllis Hurrell Walters; *m* 1940, Pauline Beatrice Platts; three *s* (and one *s* decd). *Educ:* Bradfield Coll.; Queen's Coll., Oxford (MA). FCIT. Traffic Apprentice, LNER, 1936–39. Served War of 1939–45, RE, France, Iraq and Iran (Lt-Col; US Legion of Merit). East African Railways and Harbours, 1946–64; Chief Commercial Supt; joined British Transport Docks Bd, 1964; Chief Commercial Man., 1964–70; Asst Man. Dir, 1970–72; Dep. Man. Dir, 1972–77; Dir, British Transport Advertising, 1966–81. *Address:* 62 Marygate, York YO3 7BH. *Club:* Nairobi (Kenya).

COLLIGAN, John Clifford, CBE 1963 (OBE 1957); Director-General, Royal National Institute for the Blind, 1950–72; Secretary, British Wireless for the Blind Fund, 1950–84; Hon. Treasurer and Life Member, World Council for the Blind, since 1969 (British Representative, 1954–69); *b* 27 Oct. 1906; *s* of John and Florence Colligan, Wallasey, Cheshire; *m* 1st, 1934, Ethel May Allton (*d* 1948); one *s* one *d*; 2nd, 1949, Frances Bird (*d* 1988); 3rd, 1989, Beryl May Johns. *Educ:* Liscard High Sch., Wallasey. Dep. Sec., National Institute for the Blind, 1945–49. *Publications:* The Longest Journey, 1969; various articles on blind welfare. *Recreations:* watching cricket, walking, gardening. *Address:* 7 Grayburn Close, Back Lane, Chalfont St Giles, Bucks HP8 4NZ. *T:* High Wycombe (01494) 875193.

COLLIN, Maj.-Gen. Geoffrey de Egglesfield, CB 1975; MC 1944; DL; *b* 18 July 1921; *s* of late Charles de Egglesfield Collin and Catherine Mary Collin; *m* 1949, Angela Stella (*née* Young); one *s* three *d*. *Educ:* Wellington Coll., Berks. Served War of 1939–45: commissioned as 2nd Lt, RA, 1941; in India and Burma, 1942–45. Qualified as Army Pilot, 1946; attended Staff Coll., Camberley, 1951; Instructor at RMA, Sandhurst, 1954–56; served Kenya, 1956–58; JSSC, 1958; Instructor at Staff Coll., Camberley, 1960–62; comd 50 Missile Regt, RA, 1962–64; GSO 1 Sch. of Artillery, 1965; CRA, 4th Div., 1966–67; attended Imperial Defence College, London, 1968; Comdt, Royal School of Artillery, 1969–71; Maj.-Gen. RA, HQ BAOR, 1971–73; GOC North East District, York, 1973–76; retired 1976. Col Comdt, RA, 1976–83 (Rep. Col Comdt, 1982). Chairman: CS Selection Bd, 1981–91 (Mem., 1978); Retired Officer Selection Bd, 1979–. Hon. Dir, Great Yorks Show, 1976–87; Pres., Yorks Agricl Soc., 1988–89. DL N Yorks, 1977. *Recreations:* fishing, ornithology, music, keeping gun dog and garden under control. *Address:* c/o Lloyds Bank, 8 Cambridge Crescent, Harrogate HG1 1PQ. *Club:* Army and Navy.

COLLIN, Jack, MA, MD; FRCS; Clinical Reader in Surgery, University of Oxford, Consultant Surgeon, John Radcliffe Hospital, Oxford and Fellow of Trinity College, Oxford, since 1980; *b* 23 April 1945; *s* of John Collin and Amy Maud Collin; *m* 1971, Christine Frances Proud; three *s* one *d*. *Educ:* Univ. of Newcastle (MB BS, MD); Mayo Clinic, Minn. University of Newcastle: Demonstrator in Anatomy, 1969–70; Sen. Res. Associate, 1973–75; Registrar in Surgery, Royal Victoria Infirmary, Newcastle, 1971–80; Chm., Faculty of Clin. Medicine, Univ. of Oxford, 1990–92. Mayo Foundn Fellow, Mayo Clinic, Minn, 1977. Moynihan Fellow, Assoc. of Surgeons of GB and Ire., 1980; James IV Fellow, James IV Assoc. of Surgeons Inc., NY, 1993. Royal College of Surgeons: Arris and Gale Lectr, 1976; Jacksonian Prize, 1977; Hunterian Prof., 1988–89. Non-exec. Dir, Nuffield Orthopaedic Centre NHS Trust, 1990–93. Member: Internat. Soc. of Surgery, European Surgical Assoc. Jobst Prize, Vascular Surgical Soc. of GB and Ireland, 1990. *Publications:* papers on vascular surgery, intestinal myoelectrical activity and absorption, parenteral nutrition and pancreatic and intestinal transplantation. *Recreations:* gardening, walking. *Address:* Nuffield Department of Surgery, John Radcliffe Hospital, Oxford OX3 9DU. *T:* Oxford (01865) 221282, 221286.

COLLING, Rev. Canon James Oliver, MBE 1995; Rector of Warrington, since 1973; Canon Diocesan of Liverpool Cathedral, since 1976; Chaplain to The Queen, since 1990; *b* 3 Jan. 1930; *e s* of late Leonard Colling and Dorothy Colling (*née* Atherton); *m* 1957, Jean Wright; one *s* one *d* (one twin *s* decd). *Educ:* Leigh Grammar Sch.; Univ. of Manchester (BA 1950); Cuddesdon Coll., Oxford. Commissioned RAF, 1950–52 (Nat. Service). Deacon 1954; priest 1955; Asst Curate, Wigan Parish Church, 1954–59; Vicar of Padgate, 1959–71, Rector, 1971–73; Rural Dean of Warrington, 1970–82 and 1987–89, Area Dean, 1989–95. Chairman: Warrington CHC, 1974–82; Warrington Community Council, 1974–87; Vice-Chm., Warrington HA, 1982–89. Chairman: Warrington C of E Educnl Trust, 1973–; Warrington and Dist Soc. for the Deaf, 1974–93; Warrington Charities Trust, 1989–91; Mem., Cheshire Family Health Services Authority, 1990–94. Chairman: Governors, Sir Thomas Boteler High Sch., Warrington, 1988–; Boteler Educnl Trust, 1995. *Recreations:* looking at buildings and places, local history. *Address:* The Rectory, Warrington, Cheshire WA1 2TL. *T:* Warrington (01925) 35020.

COLLINGE, John Gregory; High Commissioner for New Zealand in the United Kingdom, since 1994, and concurrently High Commissioner in Nigeria and Ambassador to the Republic of Ireland; *b* 10 May 1939; *s* of Norman Gregory Collinge and Hilary Winifred Fendall; *m* 1st, 1965, Ngaire Jean Main; 2nd, 1984, Bronwyn Christine Waite; two *d*. *Educ:* Auckland Univ. (LLB); University Coll., Oxford (MLitt). Called to the Bar, 1963, and admitted Solicitor, 1963, High Court of NZ; called to the Bar, 1966, and admitted Solicitor, 1966, High Court of Australia. Sen. Lectr in Law, Melbourne Univ., 1967–70; Partner, law firm, Melbourne, Wellington and Auckland, 1969–94. Pres., NZ National Party, 1989–94. Chairman: Policy and Finance Cttee, Auckland Regl Authy, 1983–86; Commerce Commn, 1984–89; Alcohol Adv. Council of NZ, 1991–94; Nat. Civil Defence Energy Planning Cttee, 1992–94; Member: Auckland Electric Power Bd, 1977–80, 1992–93 (Chm., 1980–92); Electrical Develt Assoc. of NZ, 1990–91 (Pres., 1991–94); Council, Electricity Supply Assoc. of NZ, 1991–92. Chairman: New Zealand Pelagic Fisheries Ltd, 1975–81; United Distillers (NZ) Ltd, 1991 (Dir, 1986–91). Alternate Gov., EBRD, 1994–. Comr, Commonwealth War Graves Commn, 1994–; Gov., Commonwealth Foundn, 1994–; Mem. Bd of Govs, Commonwealth Inst., 1994–. Vice-Pres., Royal Over-Seas League, 1994–; Trustee, Waitangi Foundn, 1994–; Patron: Captain Cook Birthplace Trust, 1994–; Shakespeare Globe Trust, 1994–; British/NZ Trade Council, 1994–. Commemoration Medal, NZ, 1990. *Publications:* Restrictive Trade Practices and Monopolies in New Zealand, 1969, 2nd edn 1982; Tutorials in Contract, 1985, 4th edn 1989; The Law of Marketing in Australia and New Zealand, 1989, 2nd edn 1990. *Recreations:* New Zealand history, restoring colonial houses and colonial antiques, Rugby, cricket. *Address:* 43 Chelsea Square, SW3 6LH. *T:* 0171–352 5645. *Clubs:* East India; Vincent's (Oxford); Wellington (NZ).

COLLINGRIDGE, Jean Mary, (Mrs A. R. Collingridge); Chief Executive, Employment Division of the Manpower Services Commission, 1979–82, retired; Member, Civil Service Appeal Board, 1984–93; *b* 9 March 1923; *d* of Edgar and Elsie Bishop; *m* 1951, Albert Robert Collingridge (*d* 1994); one *d*. *Educ:* County High School, Loughton, Essex; University College London (BSc Econ); LSE (Social Science Course). Asst Personnel Officer, C. and J. Clark, 1945–49; Personnel Manager, Pet Foods Ltd, 1949–50; Ministry of Labour/Department of Employment: Personnel Management Adviser and Industrial Relations Officer, 1950–65; Regl Industrial Relations Officer/Sen. Manpower Adviser, 1965–71; Assistant Secretary, Office of Manpower Economics 1971–73, Pay Board 1973–74, Dept of Employment HQ 1974–76, Dep. Chief Exec., Employment Service Div. of Manpower Services Commn, 1976–79. Chm., Kent Area Manpower Bd, 1983–88. *Publication:* (jtly) Personnel Management in the Small Firm, 1953. *Recreation:* Open University courses. *Address:* 21 Burnham Wood, Fareham, Hants PO16 7UD. *T:* Fareham (01329) 313018.

COLLINGS, Juliet Jeanne d'Auvergne, *see* Campbell, J. J. d'A.

COLLINGWOOD, John Gildas, FEng, FIChemE; Director: Unilever Ltd, 1965–77; Unilever NV, 1965–77; Head of Research Division of Unilever Ltd, 1961–77; *b* 15 June 1917; *s* of Stanley Ernest Collingwood and Kathleen Muriel (*née* Smalley); *m* 1942, Pauline Winifred (*née* Jones); one *s* one *d*. *Educ:* Wycliffe Coll., Stonehouse, Glos; University Coll. London (BSc). English Charcoal, 1940–41; British Ropeway Engrg Co, 1941–44; De Havilland Engines, 1944–46; Olympia Oil and Cake Mills Ltd, 1946–49; British Oil and Cake Mills Ltd, 1949–51; Mem., UK Milling Group of Unilever Ltd, 1951–60; Dir, Advita Ltd, 1951–60; Dir, British Oil & Cake Mills Ltd, 1955–60. Instn of Chemical Engrs: Mem. Research Cttee, 1963–68; Mem. Council, 1964–67. Mem. Council of Univ. of Aston, 1971–83 (Chm., Academic Advisory Cttee, 1964–71); Mem., Research Cttee, CBI, 1970–71; Member: Council for Scientific Policy, 1971–72; Exec. Cttee, British Nutrition Foundn, 1978–82 (Council, 1970–85); Food Standards Cttee, 1972–80; Royal Commn on Environmental Pollution, 1973–79; Standing Commn on Energy and the Environment, 1978–81. A Gen. Sec., BAAS, 1978–83, 1986–88. Vice President: Nat. Children's Home, 1989– (Chm., F and GP Cttee, 1983–89); Wycliffe Coll., Stonehouse, Glos, 1989– (Mem. Council, 1967–; Chm. Council, 1985–89). Hon. DSc Aston, 1966; Fellow, University Coll. London, 1970. *Recreations:* sailing, music. *Address:* 54 Downs Road, Coulsdon, Surrey CR5 1AA. *T:* Downland (01737) 554817. *Club:* Athenæum.

COLLINS, Hon. Sir Andrew (David), Kt 1994; **Hon. Mr Justice Collins;** a Judge of the High Court of Justice, Queen's Bench Division, since 1994; *b* 19 July 1942, *s* of Rev. Canon Lewis John Collins, MA, and Diana (*née* Elliot); *m* 1970, Nicolette Anne Sandford-Saville; one *s* one *d*. *Educ:* Eton; King's Coll., Cambridge (BA, MA). Called to the Bar, Middle Temple, 1965, Bencher, 1992; QC 1985; a Recorder, 1986–94. *Address:* Royal Courts of Justice, Strand, WC2A 2LL.

COLLINS, Sir Arthur (James Robert), KCVO 1980; ERD 1989; *b* 10 July 1911; *s* of Col William Fellowes Collins, DSO, and Lady Evelyn Collins (*née* Innes Ker), OBE; *m* 1965, Elizabeth, *d* of Rear-Adm. Sir Arthur Bromley, Bt, and *widow* of 6th Baron Sudeley (*died* on war service, 1941). *Educ:* Eton; Christ Church, Oxford (MA). Admitted a Solicitor, 1935; Partner, Withers, 1937, Sen. Partner, 1962–81, now Consultant. Served with Royal Horse Guards, 1938–46; Adjt, 2nd Household Cavalry Regt, 1940–44 (despatches), Major 1943. *Address:* Kirkman Bank, Knaresborough, N Yorks HG5 9BT. *T:* Harrogate (01423) 863136; 38 Clarence Terrace, NW1 4RD. *T:* 0171–723 4198. *Clubs:* Turf, White's.

COLLINS, Arthur John, OBE 1973; HM Diplomatic Service, retired; Foreign and Commonwealth Office representative (protocol), since 1988; *b* 17 May 1931; *s* of Reginald and Margery Collins; *m* 1952, Enid Maureen, *d* of Charles and Sarah Stableford; one *s* one *d*. *Educ:* Purley Grammar Sch. Served RAF, 1949–51. Min. of Health, 1951–68 (Private Sec. to Perm. Sec., 1960–61, and to Parly Sec., 1962–63); transf. to HM Diplomatic Service, 1968; FCO, 1968–69; First Secretary and Head of Chancery: Dhaka, 1970–71; Brasilia, 1972–74; Asst Head of Latin America and Caribbean Depts, FCO, 1974–77; Counsellor, UK Del. to OECD, Paris, 1978–81; High Comr, Papua New Guinea, 1982–85; adviser on management, FCO, 1986–88; Consultant, EBRD, 1991; Assessor, VSO, 1993–. *Publications:* papers on early colonialism in New Guinea. *Recreations:* beekeeping, downland walking. *Address:* 60 Dean Court Road, Rottingdean, Sussex BN2 7DJ. *Club:* Commonwealth Trust.

COLLINS, Basil Eugene Sinclair, CBE 1983; Chairman, Nabisco Group, 1984–89; *b* 21 Dec. 1923; *s* of Albert Collins and Pauline Alicia (*née* Wright); *m* 1942, Doris Slott; two *d*. *Educ:* Great Yarmouth Grammar School. Sales Manager, L. Rose & Co. Ltd, 1945; Export Dir, Schweppes (Overseas) Ltd, 1958; Group Admin Dir, Schweppes Ltd, 1964, Chm. of Overseas Gp 1968; Chm. of Overseas Gp, Cadbury Schweppes Ltd, 1969, Dep. Man. Dir 1972, Man. Dir 1974, Dep. Chm. and Group Chief Exec., Cadbury Schweppes plc, 1980–83; Director: Thomas Cook Gp, 1980–85; British Airways Bd, 1982–88; Royal Mint, 1984–88. Royal College of Nursing: Chm., Finance and General Purposes Cttee, 1970–86; Hon. Treasurer, 1970–86; Vice-Pres., 1972, Life Vice-Pres., 1986. Fellow Inst. of Dirs, 1974, Council Mem., 1982–89; Managing Trustee, Inst. of Economic Affairs, 1987–91; Mem. Council, UEA, 1987–94. FZS 1975; CIMgt (FBIM 1976); Fellow, Amer. Chamber of Commerce, 1979, Dir 1984–89. FRSA 1984. Hon. Fellow, UEA, 1995. *Recreations:* music, languages, travel, English countryside. *Address:* Wyddial Parva, Buntingford, Herts SG9 0EL.

COLLINS, Gerard; *see* Collins, James G.

COLLINS, Henry Edward, CBE 1948; FEng 1976; Consulting Mining Engineer; *b* 4 Oct. 1903; *s* of James Collins; *m* 1934, Cecilia Harris (*d* 1975); no *c*. *Educ:* Rotherham Grammar Sch.; Univ. of Sheffield (MEng). Sen. Lectr in Mining, Univ. of Sheffield, 1935–38; Manager, Rossington Main Colliery, Doncaster, 1939–42; Agent, Markham Colliery, Doncaster, 1942–44; Chief Mining Agent, Doncaster Amalgamated Collieries Ltd, 1944–45; Dir Coal Production, CCG, 1945–47; British Chm., UK/US Coal Control Gp, Germany (later Combined Coal Control Gp), 1947–50; Production Dir, Durham Div., NCB, 1950–56; Dir-Gen. of Reconstruction, NCB, 1956–57; Board Mem. for Production, NCB, 1957–67; Consultant to NCB, 1967–69. Mem., Govtl Cttee on Coal Derivatives, 1959–60; Chairman: NCB Opencast Executive, 1961–67; NCB Brickworks Executive, 1962–67; Whittlesea Central Brick Co. Ltd, 1966–67; Field Research Steering Cttee, Min. of Power, 1964–67; Past Director: Omnia Concrete Sales Ltd; Bradley's (Concrete) Ltd; Powell Duffryn Technical Services Ltd; Inter-Continental Fuels Ltd. Member: Minister of Power's Adv. Council on Research and Develt, 1963–67; Min. of Power Nat. Jt Pneumoconiosis Cttee, 1964–67; Safety in Mines (Adv.) Bd; Mining Qualifications Bd, 1962–69. Pres., Inst. of Mining Engineers, 1962, Hon. Fellow, 1988. *Publications:* Mining Memories and Musings: the autobiography of a mining engineer, 1985; numerous papers on mining engineering subjects. *Address:* St Mary's Nursing Home, Ednaston, Brailsford, Derby DE6 3BA.

COLLINS, (James) Gerard; TD (FF) Limerick West, since 1967; Member, European Parliament, since 1994; *b* Abbeyfeale, Co. Limerick, 16 Oct. 1938; *s* of late James J. Collins, TD and Margaret Collins; *m* 1969, Hilary Tattan. *Educ:* University Coll., Dublin (BA). Teacher. Asst Gen. Sec., Fianna Fáil, 1965–67. Parly Sec. to Ministers for Industry and Commerce and for the Gaeltacht, 1969–70; Minister for Posts and Telegraphs, 1970–73; opposition front-bench spokesman on agriculture, 1973–75; spokesman on justice, 1975–77; Minister for Justice, 1977–81; Minister for Foreign Affairs, March-Dec. 1982; opposition front-bench spokesman on foreign affairs, 1983–87; Minister for Justice, 1987–89; Minister for Foreign Affairs, 1989–92. Mem., Consultative Assembly, Council of Europe, 1973–77; Chm., Parly Cttee on Secondary Legislation of European Communities, 1983–. Mem., Limerick CC, 1974–77. *Address:* The Hill, Abbeyfeale, Co. Limerick.

COLLINS, Prof. Jeffrey Hamilton, FRSE; FEng 1981; Specialist Advisor to Vice-Chancellor, Napier University, since 1994; *b* 22 April 1930; *s* of Ernest Frederick and Dora Gladys Collins; *m* 1956, Sally Parfitt; two *s*. *Educ:* London Univ. (BSc, MSc, DSc). FIEE, FInstP, FIEEE; CEng, CPhys. GEC Research Laboratories, London, 1951–56; Ferranti Ltd, Edinburgh, 1956–57; Univ. of Glasgow, 1957–66; Research Engr, Stanford Univ., Calif, 1966–68; Dir of Physical Electronics, Rockwell International, Calif, 1968–70; University of Edinburgh: Research Prof., 1970–73; Prof. of Industrial Electronics, 1973–77; Prof. of Electrical Engrg and Hd of Dept, 1977–84; Emeritus Prof., 1984; Chm., Parallel Computing Centre, 1991–94. Dir, Automation and Robotics Res. Inst., and Prof. of Electrical Engrg, Univ. of Texas at Arlington, 1987–90; Sen. Technical Specialist, Lothian Regl Council, 1991–93. Member: Electronics Res. Council, 1979; Computer Bd for Univs and Res. Councils, 1985–86; Information Systems Cttee, UFC, 1992–93; Jt Information Systems Cttee, HEFCs, 1993–94. Director: MESL, 1970–79; Racal-MESL, 1979–81; Advent Technology, 1981–86; Filtronics Components, 1981–85; Burr-Brown Ltd, 1985; River Bend Bank, Fort Worth, 1987–90. Member Honour Societies: Eta Kappa Nu; Tau Beta Pi; Upsilon Pi Epsilon; Phi Beta Delta. *Publications:* Computer-Aided Design of Surface Acoustic Wave Devices, 1976; 195 articles in learned soc. electrical engrg jls. *Recreations:* music, DIY, tennis. *Address:* 28 Muirfield Park, Gullane EH31 2DY.

COLLINS, Joan Henrietta; actress; *b* 23 May 1933; *er d* of Joseph Collins and Elsa (*née* Bessant); *m* 1st, 1954, Maxwell Reed (marr. diss. 1957; he *d* 1974); 2nd, 1963, (George) Anthony Newley, *qv* (marr. diss. 1970); one *s* one *d*; 3rd, 1972, Ronald S. Kass (marr. diss. 1983); one *d*; 4th, 1985, Peter Holm (marr. diss. 1987). *Educ:* Francis Holland Sch.; RADA. *Films include:* Lady Godiva Rides Again, I Believe in You, 1952; Our Girl Friday, The Square Ring, 1953; The Good Die Young, Turn the Key Softly, 1954; Land of the Pharaohs, The Virgin Queen, The Girl in the Red Velvet Swing, 1955; The Opposite Sex, 1956; The Wayward Bus, Island in the Sun, Sea Wife, 1957; The Bravados, 1958; Rally Round the Flag, Boys, 1959; Esther and the King, Seven Thieves, 1960; Road to Hong Kong, 1962; Warning Shot, The Subterfuge, 1967; Can Hieronymous Merkin Ever Forget Mercy Humppe and Find True Happiness?, Drive Hard Drive Fast, 1969; Up in the Cellar, The Executioner, 1970; Quest for Love, Revenge, 1971; Tales from the Crypt, Fear in the Night, 1972; Tales that witness Madness, 1973; Dark Places, Alfie Darling, 1974; The Call of the Wolf, I don't want to be born, 1975; The Devil within Her, 1976; Empire of the Ants, 1977; The Big Sleep, 1978; Sunburn, The Stud, 1979; The Bitch, 1980; The Nutcracker, 1984; The Cartier Affair, 1985; Decadence, 1994; In the Bleak Midwinter, 1995; *stage includes:* The Last of Mrs Cheyney, Cambridge Th., 1980; Private Lives, Aldwych, 1990, US tour and NY, 1992; *television includes:* serials: Dynasty, 1981–89; Sins, 1986; Monte Carlo, 1986; series: Tonight at 8.30, 1991; also appearances in plays and series. Awards: Best TV Actress, Golden Globe, 1982; Hollywood Woman's Press Club, 1982; Favourite TV Performer, People's Choice, 1985. *Publications:* Past Imperfect, 1978; The Joan Collins Beauty Book, 1980; Katy: a fight for life, 1982; Prime Time, 1988; Love and Desire and Hate, 1990; My Secrets, 1994; Too Damn Famous, 1995. *Address:* c/o Paul Keylock, 16 Bulbecks Walk, South Woodham Ferrers, Essex CM3 5ZN. *T:* South Woodham Ferrers (01245) 328367, *Fax:* (01245) 328625.

COLLINS, Sir John (Alexander), Kt 1993; Chief Executive, Vestey Group, since 1994; *b* 10 Dec. 1941; *s* of John Constantine Collins and Nancy Isobel Mitchell; *m* 1965, Susan Mary Hooper. *Educ:* Campbell Coll., Belfast; Reading Univ. Joined Shell International Chemicals, 1964; various appointments in Shell in Kenya, Nigeria, Columbia and UK, until 1989; Supply and Marketing Co-ordinator, and Dir, Shell Internat. Petroleum Co. Ltd, 1989–90; Chm. and Chief Exec., Shell UK, 1990–93. Director: BSkyB, 1994–; N. M. Rothschild & Sons, 1995–. Chm., Adv. Cttee on Business and Envmt, 1991–93; Mem., PM's Adv. Cttee for Queen's Awards for Export, Technological and Envmtl Achievement, 1992–. *Recreations:* opera, theatre, sailing, riding, golf, tennis, a love of the New Forest. *Address:* The Vestey Group, 16 St John's Lane, EC1M 4AF.

COLLINS, John Ernest Harley, MBE 1944; DSC 1945 and Bar 1945; DL; Chairman: Morgan Grenfell Holdings Ltd, 1974–79; Guardian Royal Exchange Assurance, 1974–88; *b* 24 April 1923; *o s* of late G. W. Collins, Taynton, Glos; *m* 1st, 1946, Gillian (*d* 1981), *e d* of 2nd Baron Bicester; one *s* one *d*; 2nd, 1986, Jennifer Faith, *widow* of Capt. A. J. A. Cubitt. *Educ:* King Edward's Sch., Birmingham; Birmingham Univ. Royal Navy, 1941–46. Morgan Grenfell & Co. Ltd, 1946, Dir 1957. Director: Royal Exchange Assce, 1957; Rank Hovis McDougall Ltd, 1965–91; Charter Consolidated Ltd, 1966–83; Hudson's Bay Co., 1957–74. Chm. United Services Trustee, 1968–76. DL Oxon, 1975; High Sheriff, Oxon, 1975. KStJ 1983. *Recreations:* shooting, stalking, fishing. *Address:* Chetwode Manor, Buckingham MK18 4BB. *T:* Finmere (01280) 848333. *Club:* White's.

COLLINS, (John) Martin, QC 1972; a Judge of the Courts of Appeal of Jersey and Guernsey, since 1984; *b* 24 Jan. 1929; *s* of John Lissant Collins and Marjorie Mary Collins; *m* 1957, Daphne Mary, *d* of George Martyn Swindells, Prestbury; two *s* one *d*. *Educ:* Uppingham Sch.; Manchester Univ. (LLB). Called to Bar, Gray's Inn, 1952, Bencher, 1981; called to the Bar of Gibraltar, 1990. Dep. Chm., Cumberland QS, 1969–72; a Recorder, 1972–88. Member: Senate of Inns of Court and Bar, 1981–84; Gen. Council of the Bar, 1991. Chm., Management Cttee, Gray's Inn, 1990. *Address:* 10 Essex Street, Outer Temple, WC2R 3AA; 19 avenue Messine, 75008 Paris, France; 12 Gray's Inn Square, WC1R 5JP. *T:* 0171–404 6299. *Club:* Carlton.

COLLINS, John Morris; a Recorder of the Crown Court, since 1980; *b* 25 June 1931; *s* of late Emmanuel Cohen, MBE, and Ruby Cohen; *m* 1968, Sheila Brummer; one *d*. *Educ:* Leeds Grammar Sch.; The Queen's Coll., Oxford (MA LitHum). Called to Bar, Middle Temple, 1956, Member of North Eastern Circuit; a Deputy Circuit Judge, 1970. Pres., Leeds Jewish Representative Council, 1986–89. *Publications:* Summary Justice, 1963; various articles in legal periodicals, etc. *Recreation:* walking. *Address:* (home) 14 Sandhill Oval, Leeds LS17 8EA. *T:* Leeds (0113) 268 6008; (professional) 9 Woodhouse Square, Leeds LS3 1AD. *T:* Leeds (0113) 245 1986, *Fax:* (0113) 244 8623.

COLLINS, Judith, (Mrs R. J. H. Collins); *see* McClure, J.

COLLINS, Kenneth Darlingston; Member (Lab) Strathclyde East, European Parliament, since 1979; *b* 12 Aug. 1939; *s* of Nicholas Collins and Ellen Williamson; *m* 1966, Georgina Frances Pollard; one *s* one *d*. *Educ:* St John's Grammar Sch.; Hamilton Acad.; Glasgow Univ. (BSc Hons); Strathclyde Univ. (MSc). FRSGS 1993. Left school, 1956; steelworks apprentice, 1956–59; univ., 1960–65; planning officer, 1965–66; WEA Tutor-Organiser, 1966–67; Lecturer: Glasgow Coll. of Bldg, 1967–69; Paisley Coll. of Technol., 1969–79. European Parliament: Dep. Leader, Labour Gp, 1979–84; Socialist spokesman on envmt, public health and consumer protection, 1984–89; Chm., Cttee on Envmt, Public Health and Consumer Protection, 1979–84 and 1989– (Vice Chm., 1984–87); Chm., Conf. of Cttee Chairmen, 1993–. Dir, Inst. for Eur. Envmt Policy, London; Eur. Advr, BECTU, AEEU and UNISON. Member: East Kilbride Town and Dist Council, 1973–79; Lanark CC, 1973–75; East Kilbride Develt Corp., 1976–79; Chm., NE Glasgow Children's Panel, 1974–76. Mem. Adv. Cttee, European Public Policy Inst., Univ. of Warwick, 1991–. Hon. Sen. Res. Fellow, Dept of Geography, Lancaster Univ., 1991–. Member: Socialist Internat. Envmt Cttee; Fabian Soc.; Amnesty Internat.; Labour Movement in Europe; Howard League; Scottish Educn and Action for Develt; Bd, Friends of the Earth (Scotland); Hon. Vice-President: Royal Envmtl Health Inst. of Scotland, 1983–; Internat. Fedn on Envmtl Health, 1987–; Inst. of Trading Standards Admin; Socialist Envmt and Resources Assoc.; Inst. of Environmental Health Officers; European Food Law Assoc.; European Consumer Safety Assoc.; Energy Action Scotland; Nat. Soc. for Clean Air; Town and Country Planning Assoc. Fellow, Industry and Parlt Trust, 1984–. *Publications:* contributed to European Parliament reports; various articles on European envmt policy. *Recreations:* Labour Party, music, boxer dogs, cycling. *Address:* 11 Stuarton Park, East Kilbride, Lanarkshire G74 4LA. *T:* East Kilbride (013552) 37282, *Fax:* (013552) 49670.

COLLINS, Lawrence Antony, LLD; FBA 1994; Partner, Herbert Smith, solicitors, since 1971; Fellow of Wolfson College, Cambridge, since 1975; *b* 7 May 1941; *s* of late Sol Collins and Phoebe (*née* Barnett); *m* 1982, Sara Shamni, psychotherapist; one *s* one *d*. *Educ:* City of London Sch.; Downing Coll., Cambridge (BA, George Long Prize, McNair Schol., 1963; LLB, Whewell Schol., 1964; LLD 1994); Columbia Univ. (LLM 1965). Mem. Inst de Droit Internat., 1989. Admitted solicitor, 1968. Vis. Prof., QMC, then QMW, 1982–. Member: Lord Chancellor's Wkg Party on Foreign Judgments, 1979–81; Bar and Law Soc. Jt Wkg Party on UK-US Judgments Convention, 1980–82; Law Commn Jt Wkg Party on Torts in Private Internat. Law, 1982–84. Hon. Sec., British Br., 1983–88, Chm., Cttee on Internat. Securities Regulations, 1988–, Internat. Law Assoc. Member: Editl Adv. Cttee, Law Qly Rev., 1988–; Bd of Eds, Internat. and Comparative Law Qly, 1988–; Editl Cttee, British Yearbook of Internat. Law, 1991–. *Publications:* European Community Law in the United Kingdom, 1975, 4th edn 1990; Civil Jurisdiction and Judgments Act 1982, 1983; Essays in International Litigation and the Conflict of Laws, 1994; (Gen. Ed.) Dicey & Morris, Conflict of Laws, 11th edn 1987, 12th edn 1993. *Address:* c/o Herbert Smith, Exchange House, Primrose Street, EC2A 2HS. *T:* 0171–374 8000.

COLLINS, Lesley Elizabeth; *see* Appleby, L. E.

COLLINS, Margaret Elizabeth, CBE 1983; RRC; Matron-in-Chief, Queen Alexandra's Royal Naval Nursing Service, 1980–83; *b* 13 Feb. 1927; *d* of James Henry Collins and Amy Collins. *Educ:* St Anne's Convent Grammar Sch., Southampton. RRC 1978 (ARRC 1965). Royal Victoria Hosp., Bournemouth, SRN 1949; West Middlesex Hosp., CMB Part 1; entered QARNNS as Nursing Sister, 1953; accepted for permanent service, 1958; Matron, 1972; Principal Matron, 1976. SSStJ 1978. QHNS, 1980–83. *Recreations:* gardening, theatre-going. *Address:* Lancastria, First Marine Avenue, Barton-on-Sea, Hants BH25 6DP. *T:* New Milton (01425) 612374.

COLLINS, Martin; *see* Collins, J. M.

COLLINS, Michael; aerospace consultant; Vice President, LTV Aerospace and Defense Company (formerly Vought Corporation), 1980–85; former NASA Astronaut; Command Module Pilot, Apollo 11 rocket flight to the Moon, July 1969; *b* Rome, Italy, 31 Oct.

1930; *s* of Maj.-Gen. and Mrs James L. Collins, Washington, DC, USA; *m* 1957, Patricia M. Finnegan, Boston, Mass; one *s* two *d*. *Educ:* St Albans Sch., Washington, DC (grad.). US Mil. Academy, West Point, NY (BSc); advanced through grades to Colonel; Harvard Business Sch. (AMP), 1974. Served as an experimental flight test officer, Air Force Flight Test Center, Edwards Air Force Base, Calif; he was one of the third group of astronauts named by NASA in Oct. 1963; served as backup pilot for Gemini 7 mission; as pilot with John Young on the 3–day 44–revolution Gemini 10 mission, launched 18 July 1966, he shared record-setting flight (successful rendezvous and docking with a separately launched Agena target vehicle; completed two periods of extravehicular activity); Command Module Pilot for Apollo flight, first lunar landing, in orbit 20 July 1969, when Neil Armstrong and Edwin Aldrin landed on the Moon. Asst Sec. of State for Public Affairs, US, 1970–71; Dir, Nat. Air and Space Museum, Smithsonian Institution, 1971–78; Under Sec., Smithsonian Inst., 1978–80. Maj. Gen. Air Force Reserve, retired. Member: Bd of Trustees, Nat. Geographic Soc.; Soc. of Experimental Test Pilots; Internat. Acad. of Astronautics of Internat. Astronautical Fedn; Washington Inst. of Foreign Affairs. FAIAA; Fellow, Amer. Astronautical Soc. Member, Order of Daedalians. Hon. degrees from: Stonehill Coll.; St Michael's Coll.; Northeastern Univ.; Southeastern Univ. Presidential Medal of Freedom, NASA; FAI Gold Space Medal; DSM (NASA); DSM (AF); Exceptional Service Medal (NASA); Astronaut Wings; DFC. *Publications:* Carrying the Fire (autobiog.), 1974; Flying to the Moon and Other Strange Places (for children), 1976; Liftoff, 1988; Mission to Mars, 1990. *Recreations:* fishing, handball. *Clubs:* Alfalfa, Alibi (Washington, DC).

COLLINS, Michael Brendan, OBE 1983 (MBE 1969); HM Diplomatic Service, retired; HM Consul-General, Istanbul, 1988–92; *b* 9 Sept. 1932; *s* of Daniel James Collins, GM and Mary Bridget Collins (*née* Kennedy); *m* 1959, Maria Elena Lozar. *Educ:* St Illtyd's College, Cardiff; University College London. HM Forces, 1953–55. FO 1956; Santiago, Chile, 1959; Consul, Santiago, Cuba, 1962; FO, 1964; Second, later First, Sec. (Admin.) and Consul, Prague, 1967; Dep. High Comr, Bathurst, The Gambia, 1970; Head of Chancery, Algiers, 1972; First Sec., FCO, 1975; Consul Commercial, Montreal, 1978; Consul for Atlantic Provinces of Canada, Halifax, 1981; Counsellor (Economic and Commercial), Brussels, 1983. *Recreations:* fishing, shooting, golf, walking, reading, music. *Address:* 1 Talbot Place, Blackheath, SE3 0TJ. *Club:* Army and Navy.

COLLINS, Michael Geoffrey; QC 1988; *b* 4 March 1948; *s* of late Francis Geoffrey Collins and Margaret Isabelle Collins; *m* 1985, Bonnie Gayle Bird. *Educ:* Peterhouse, Rhodesia (now Zimbabwe); Exeter Univ. (LLB). Called to the Bar, Gray's Inn, 1971. *Publication:* contributor, Private International Litigation, 1988. *Recreations:* golf, tennis, watercolours, amateur dramatics. *Address:* Essex Court Chambers, 24 Lincoln's Inn Fields, WC2A 3ED. *T:* 0171–813 8000.

COLLINS, Michael John; clarinettist; Professor, Royal College of Music, since 1983; *b* 27 Jan. 1962; *s* of Gwendoline Violet and Fred Allenby Collins. *Educ:* Royal Coll. of Music (ARCM, Clarinet and Piano with Hons). BBC Young Musician of the Year, 1978. Principal clarinet: London Sinfonietta, 1982–; Nash Ensemble, 1982–88; Philharmonia Orchestra, 1988–. Many solo recordings. Musicians' Co. Medal, 1980; competition winner: Leeds, 1980; Concert Artists' Guild, NY, 1982 (Amcon Award); Internat Rostrum of Young Performers, Unesco, 1985; Tagore Gold Medal, 1982. *Recreations:* walking, driving, wildlife. *Address:* 59 Harlington Road West, Feltham, Middx TW14 0JG. *T:* 0181–890 9326.

COLLINS, Neil Adam; City Editor, Daily Telegraph, since 1986; *s* of Clive and Joan Collins; *m* 1981, Vivien Goldsmith (marr. diss. 1994); one *d*. *Educ:* Uppingham School; Selwyn College, Cambridge (MA). City Editor: Evening Standard, 1979–84; Sunday Times, 1984–86. *Recreations:* walking, wine, fly fishing, opera. *Address:* Forest Cottage, Friston, near Eastbourne, East Sussex BN20 0UW. *T:* Eastbourne (01323) 422021; 0171–405 4536; (office) 0171–538 6900.

COLLINS, Nina; *see* Lowry, Noreen Margaret.

COLLINS, Paul Howard; His Honour Judge Collins; a Circuit Judge, since 1992; *b* 31 Jan. 1944; *s* of Michael and Madie Collins; *m* 1987, Susan Fallows; one step *s*. *Educ:* Orange Hill Grammar Sch.; St Catherine's Coll., Oxford (MA). Called to the Bar, Lincoln's Inn, 1966; a Recorder, 1989. *Recreations:* running, tennis, theatre. *Address:* Wandsworth County Court, 76/78 Upper Richmond Road, SW15 2SU. *T:* 081–870 2212. *Club:* Questors.

COLLINS, Pauline; actress (stage and television); *b* Exmouth, Devon, 3 Sept. 1940; *d* of William Henry Collins and Mary Honora Callanan; *m* John Alderton, *qv*; two *s* one *d*. *Educ:* Convent of the Sacred Heart, Hammersmith, London; Central Sch. of Speech and Drama. *Stage:* 1st appearance in A Gazelle in Park Lane, Theatre Royal, Windsor, 1962; 1st London appearance in Passion Flower Hotel, Prince of Wales, 1965; The Erpingham Camp, Royal Court, 1967; The Happy Apple, Hampstead, 1967, and Apollo, 1970; Importance of Being Earnest, Haymarket, 1968; The Night I chased the Women with an Eel, 1969; Come As You Are (3 parts), New, 1970; Judies, Comedy, 1974; Engaged, National Theatre, Old Vic, 1975; Confusions, Apollo, 1976; Rattle of a Simple Man, Savoy, 1980; Romantic Comedy, Apollo, 1983; Shirley Valentine, Vaudeville, 1988, NY, 1989 (Tony Award, Best Actress, 1989); Shades, Albery, 1992; *television,* 1962–: series: Upstairs Downstairs; No Honestly; P. G. Wodehouse; Thomas and Sarah; The Black Tower; Forever Green; plays: Long Distance Information, 1979; Knockback, 1984; *films:* Shirley Valentine, 1989 (Evening Standard Film Actress of the Year, 1989; BAFTA Best Actress Award, 1990); City of Joy, 1992. Dr *hc* Liverpool Poly., 1991. *Publication:* Letter to Louise, 1992. *Address:* c/o James Sharkey Associates, 15 Golden Square, W1R 3AG.

COLLINS, Peter G., RSA 1974 (ARSA 1966); painter in oil; lecturer, Duncan of Jordanstone College of Art, Dundee; *b* Inverness, 21 June 1935; *s* of E. G. Collins, FRCSE; *m* 1959, Myra Mackintosh (marr. diss. 1978); one *s* one *d*. *Educ:* Fettes Coll., Edinburgh; Edinburgh Coll. of Art. Studied in Italy, on Andrew Grant Major Travelling Scholarship, 1957–58. Work in permanent collections: Aberdeen Civic; Glasgow Civic; Scottish Arts Council. *Recreations:* music, art-historical research. *Address:* Royal Scottish Academy, The Mound, Edinburgh EH2 2EL; The Cottage, Hilltown of Ballindean, Inchture, Perthshire.

COLLINS, Air Vice-Marshal Peter Spencer, CB 1985; AFC 1961; Consultant, GEC-Marconi Research Centre, since 1989; *b* 19 March 1930; *s* of Frederick Wilbore Collins and Mary (*née* Spencer); *m* 1953, Sheila Mary (*née* Perks); three *s* one *d*. *Educ:* Royal Grammar Sch., High Wycombe; Univ. of Birmingham (BA (Hons) History). CIMgt (FBIM 1979). Joined RAF, 1951; flying tours incl. service on squadron nos: 63, 141, 41, AWDS, AFDS; RAF Handling Sqdn, nos 23 and 11; commanded: 111 Sqdn, 1970–72; RAF Gütersloh, 1974–76; staff tours include: Air Ministry, 1962–64; Strike Comd HQ, 1968–70 and 1972–74; Dir of Forward Policy (RAF), 1978–81; SASO, HQ 11 Gp, 1981–83; DG, Communications, Inf. Systems and Orgn (RAF), 1983–85; psc 1965, rcds 1977; retired 1985. Marconi Radar Systems: Dir, Business Develt, 1986–88; Consultant Dir, 1988–95. *Publications:* contribs to service jls and to Seaford House Papers, 1978. *Recreations:* golf, music, gardening. *Address:* Babylon, Boreham, Essex CM3 3EJ. *Club:* Royal Air Force.

COLLINS, Philip, LVO 1994; singer, drummer, songwriter, actor and record producer; Trustee, Prince's Trust, since 1983; patron of numerous charities; *b* 30 Jan. 1951; *s* of Greville and June Collins; *m* 1st, 1976 (marr. diss.); one *s* one *d*; 2nd, 1984, Jill Tavelman (marr. diss. 1995); one *d*. *Educ:* primary and secondary schs; Barbara Speake Stage Sch. Played parts in various television, film and stage productions, 1965–67; mem. of various rock groups, 1967–70; drummer, 1970–, lead singer, 1975–, Genesis; started writing songs, 1976; toured Japan, USA and Europe, 1978, 1987; first solo album, 1981; solo world tours, 1985, 1990; started producing records for other artists, 1981. *Albums* include: *with Genesis:* Nursury Crime, 1971; Foxtrot, 1972; Genesis Live, 1973; Selling England by the Pound, 1973; The Lamb Lies Down on Broadway, 1974; A Trick of the Tail, 1976; Genesis Rock Roots, 1976; Wind and Wuthering, 1977; Genesis Seconds Out, 1977; And Then There Were Three, 1978; Duke, 1980; Abacab, 1981; Three Sides Live, 1982; Genesis, 1983; Invisible Touch, 1986; We Can't Dance, 1991; *solo:* Face Value, 1981; Hello . . . I must be Going, 1982; No Jacket Required, 1985; But Seriously, 1989; Both Sides, 1993. *Films:* Buster (lead role), 1988; Frauds, 1993. Numerous awards, incl. Grammy (seven), Ivor Novello (six), Brit (four), Variety Club of GB (two), Silver Clef (two), and Elvis awards.

COLLINS, Prof. Philip Arthur William; Emeritus Professor of English, University of Leicester, since 1982; *b* 28 May 1923; *er s* of Arthur Henry and Winifred Nellie Collins; *m* 1st, 1952, Mildred Lowe (marr. diss. 1963); 2nd, 1965, Joyce Dickins; two *s* one *d*. *Educ:* Brentwood Sch.; Emmanuel Coll., Cambridge (Sen. Schol.). MA 1948. Served War (RAOC and Royal Norfolk Regt), 1942–45. Leicester: Staff Tutor in Adult Educn, 1947; Warden, Vaughan Coll., 1954; Sen. Lectr in English, 1962–64; Prof., 1964–82; Head, English Dept, 1971–76, 1981–82; Public Orator, 1975–78, 1980–82. Visiting Prof.: Univ. of California, Berkeley, 1967; Columbia, 1969; Victoria Univ., NZ, 1974. Sec., Leicester Theatre Trust Ltd, 1963–87; Member: Drama Panel, Arts Council of Gt Britain, 1970–75; National Theatre Bd, 1976–82; British American Drama Acad. Bd, 1983–; Pres., Dickens Fellowship, 1983–85; Chm. Trustees, Dickens House Museum, 1984–92; Chm., Tennyson Soc., 1984–. Many overseas lecture-tours; performances, talks and scripts for radio and television. *Publications:* James Boswell, 1956; (ed) English Christmas, 1956; Dickens and Crime, 1962; Dickens and Education, 1963; The Canker and the Rose (Shakespeare Quater-centenary celebration) perf. Mermaid Theatre, London, 1964; The Impress of the Moving Age, 1965; Thomas Cooper the Chartist, 1969; A Dickens Bibliography, 1970; Dickens's Bleak House, 1971; (ed) Dickens, the Critical Heritage, 1971; (ed) A Christmas Carol: the public reading version, 1971; Reading Aloud: a Victorian Métier, 1972; (ed) Dickens's Public Readings, 1975; Dickens's David Copperfield, 1977; (ed) Dickens: Interviews and Recollections, 1981; (ed) Thackeray: Interviews and Recollections, 1983; Trollope's London, 1983; (ed) Dickens: Sikes and Nancy and other Readings, 1983; Tennyson, Poet of Lincolnshire, 1984; (co-ed) The Annotated Dickens, 1986; contrib. to: Encyclopaedia Britannica, Listener, TLS, sundry learned journals. *Recreations:* theatre, music. *Address:* 26 Knighton Drive, Leicester LE2 3HB. *T:* Leicester (0116) 270 6026.

COLLINS, Stuart Verdun, CB 1970; retired; Chief Inspector of Audit, Department of the Environment (formerly Ministry of Housing and Local Government), 1968–76; *b* 24 Feb. 1916; *m* 1st, 1942, Helen Simpson (*d* 1968); two *d*; 2nd, 1970, Joan Mary Walmsley (widow); one *step s* two *step d*. *Educ:* Plymouth Coll. Entered Civil Service as Audit Assistant in the District Audit Service of the Ministry of Health, 1934; appointed District Auditor for the London Audit District, 1958. IPFA, FBCS. *Recreations:* golf, do-it-yourself, sailing. *Address:* Kemendine, Court Wood, Newton Ferrers, Devon PL8 1BW.

COLLINS, Terence Bernard; Chairman, 1984–87, Vice Chairman, 1976–84, Group Managing Director, 1975–86, Berger Jenson Nicholson; *b* 3 March 1927; *s* of George Bernard Collins and Helen Teresa Collins; *m* 1956, Barbara (*née* Lowday); two *s* two *d*. *Educ:* Marist Coll., Hull; Univ. of St Andrews (MA Hons). Trainee, Ideal Standard, 1951–52; Blundell Spence: Area Manager, 1953–55; Regl Manager, 1955–57; UK Sales Manager, 1957–59; Berger Jenson Nicholson: Sales Manager, 1959–62; Man. Dir, Caribbean, 1962–69; Overseas Regl Exec., 1969–70; Gp Dir UK, 1971–74. Chairman: Cranfield Conf. Services Ltd, 1987–93; Cranfield Ventures Ltd, 1990–93; CIT Hldgs Ltd, 1991–92 (Dir, 1989–93); Interact Ltd, 1994–; Director: A. G. Stanley Hldgs, 1977–87; Hoechst UK, 1979–87; Hoechst Australia Investments, 1980–87; Mayborn Gp PLC, 1986–91; Phoenix Develts Ltd, 1987–94; Aldehurst Consultants Ltd, 1987–94; Cranfield Precision Engineering Ltd, 1990–; Chm., Management Bd, Kingline Consultants Ltd, 1989–90. Mem., Duke of Edinburgh's Award Internat. Panel, 1978–86; Trustee, Atlas Econ. Foundn UK, 1986–93. Cranfield Institute of Technology: Mem. Court, 1977–; Mem. Council, 1981–93; Treasurer, 1991–92; Chm., Finance Cttee, 1991–92; University of Buckingham: Vice-Chm. Council, 1987–; Chm., F and GP Cttee, 1987–94. DUniv Buckingham, 1994. *Recreations:* golf, music, gardening. *Address:* Aldehurst, Church Walk, Aldeburgh, Suffolk IP15 5DX. *Clubs:* Directors; Aldeburgh Golf.

COLLINS, Brig. Thomas Frederick James, CBE 1945 (OBE 1944); JP; DL; *b* 9 April 1905; *s* of Capt. J. A. Collins and Emily (*née* Truscott); *m* 1942, Marjorie Morwenna (*d* 1992), *d* of Lt-Col T. Donnelly, DSO; one *d*. *Educ:* Haileybury; RMC, Sandhurst. Gazetted to Green Howards, 1924; Staff College, 1938. Served War of 1939–45 (despatches twice, OBE, CBE): France, 1940, NW Europe, 1944–45. Retired, with rank of Brig., 1948. Essex County Council: CC, 1960; Vice-Chm., 1967; Chm., 1968–71. JP 1968, DL 1969, Essex. Comdr, Order of Leopold II (Belgium), 1945. *Recreation:* shooting. *Address:* Ashdon Hall, Saffron Walden, Essex CB10 2HF. *T:* Ashdon (01799) 584232. *Club:* Army and Navy.

COLLINS, William Janson; Chairman, William Collins Sons & Co. (Holdings) Ltd, 1976–81; *b* 10 June 1929; *s* of late Sir William Alexander Roy Collins, CBE, and Lady Collins (Priscilla Marian, *d* of late S. J. Lloyd); *m* 1951, Lady Sara Elena Hely-Hutchinson, *d* of 7th Earl of Donoughmore; one *s* three *d*. *Educ:* Magdalen Coll., Oxford (BA). Joined William Collins Sons & Co. Ltd, 1952; Dir, then Man. Dir, 1967; Vice-Chm., 1971; Chm., 1976. *Recreations:* Royal tennis, shooting, fishing, tennis, golf. *Address:* House of Craigie, by Kilmarnock, Ayrshire KA1 5NA. *T:* Craigie (01563) 860246. *Club:* All England Lawn Tennis and Croquet.

COLLINSON, Prof. Patrick, CBE 1993; PhD; FBA 1982; FRHistS, FAHA; Regius Professor of Modern History, University of Cambridge, since 1988; Fellow of Trinity College, Cambridge, since 1988; *b* 10 Aug. 1929; *s* of William Cecil Collinson and Belle Hay (*née* Patrick); *m* 1960, Elizabeth Albinia Susan Selwyn; two *s* two *d*. *Educ:* King's Sch., Ely; Pembroke Coll., Cambridge (Exhibnr 1949, Foundn Scholar 1952; BA 1952, 1st Cl. Hons Hist. Tripos Pt II; Hadley Prize for Hist., 1952). PhD London, 1957; FRHistS 1967 (Mem. Council, 1977–81, Vice-Pres., 1983–87 and 1994–); FAHA 1974. University of London: Postgrad. Student, Royal Holloway Coll., 1952–54; Res. Fellow, Inst. of Hist. Res., 1954–55; Res. Asst, UCL, 1955–56; Lectr in Hist., Univ. of Khartoum, 1956–61; Asst Lectr in Eccles. Hist., King's Coll., Univ. of London, 1961–62, Lectr, 1962–69 (Fellow 1976); Professor of History: Univ. of Sydney, 1969–75; Univ. of Kent at

Canterbury, 1976–84; Prof. of Modern Hist., Sheffield Univ., 1984–88. Vis. Fellow, All Souls Coll., Oxford, 1981; Andrew W. Mellon Fellow, Huntington Library, California, 1984. Lectures: Ford's, in Eng. Hist., Univ. of Oxford, 1978–79; Birkbeck, Univ. of Cambridge, 1981; Stenton Meml, Univ. of Reading, 1985; Neale Meml, Univ. of Manchester, 1986; Anstey Meml, Univ. of Kent, 1986; Neale Meml, UCL, 1987; F. D. Maurice, KCL, 1990; Homer J. Crotty, Huntington Liby, 1990; Sir D. Owen Evans Meml, UCW Aberystwyth, 1992; A. H. Dodd Meml, UCNW Bangor, 1992; Raleigh, British Academy, 1993; S. T. Bindoff Meml, QMW, 1995. President: Ecclesiastical Hist. Soc., 1985–86; C of E Record Soc., 1991–. Mem. Council, British Acad., 1986–89. Mem., Academia Europaea, 1989; Corresp. Mem., Massachusetts Historical Soc., 1990. DUniv York, 1988; Hon. DLitt Kent at Canterbury, 1989; Hon. LittD TCD, 1992; Hon. LittD Sheffield, 1995. Chm., Adv. Editorial Bd, Jl of Ecclesiastical History, 1982–93. *Publications:* The Elizabethan Puritan Movement, 1967 (USA 1967; repr. 1982); Archbishop Grindal 1519–1583: the struggle for a Reformed Church, 1979 (USA 1979); The Religion of Protestants: the Church in English Society 1559–1625 (Ford Lectures, 1979), 1982; Godly People: essays on English Protestantism and Puritanism, 1983; English Puritanism, 1983; The Birthpangs of Protestant England: religious and cultural change in the 16th and 17th centuries, 1988; Elizabethan Essays, 1994; (jtly) A History of Canterbury Cathedral, 1995; articles and revs in Bull. Inst. Hist. Res., Eng. Hist. Rev., Jl of Eccles. Hist., Studies in Church Hist., TLS. *Recreations:* mountains, music, gardening. *Address:* 23 Hinton Avenue, Cambridge; The Winnats, Cannonfields, Hathersage, Sheffield S30 1AG; Trinity College, Cambridge CB2 1TQ; Faculty of History, West Road, Cambridge.

COLLISON, family name of **Baron Collison.**

COLLISON, Baron (Life Peer) *cr* 1964, of Cheshunt; **Harold Francis Collison,** CBE 1961; Chairman, Supplementary Benefits Commission, 1969–75; *b* 10 May 1909; *m* 1946, Ivy Kate Hanks. *Educ:* The Hay Currie LCC Sch.; Crypt Sch., Gloucester. Firstly, worked in a commercial office in London; farm worker in Glos, 1934–53. National Union of Agricultural Workers (later Nat. Union of Agricultural and Allied Workers): District Organiser in Gloucester and Worcs, 1944; Nat. Officer, 1946; General Secretary, 1953–69. Mem., TUC Gen. Coun., 1953–69, Chm., 1964–65; Chm., Social Insce and Industrial Welfare Cttee of TUC, 1957–69. President: Internat. Fedn of Plantation, Agricultural and Allied Workers, 1960–76; Assoc. of Agriculture, 1976–84; Member: Coun. on Tribunals, 1959–69; Nat. Insce Adv. Cttee, 1959–69; Governing Body of ILO, 1960–69; Pilkington Cttee on Broadcasting, 1960–62; Central Transport Consultative Cttee, 1962–70; Agric. Adv. Council, 1962–80; Adv. Cttee on Agricultural Educn, 1963; Royal Commn on Trades Unions and Employers' Assocs, 1965–68; Home-Grown Cereals Authority, 1965–78; former Member: Industrial Health Adv. Cttee; Economic Develt for Agriculture; Industrial Consultative Cttee, Approach to Europe; Overseas Labour Consultative Cttee; Agric. Productivity Cttee, British Productivity Council; Chairman: Land Settlement Assoc., 1977–79 (Vice-Chm., 1964–77); Agric. Apprenticeship Council, 1968–74; Mem., N Thames Gas Board (part-time), 1961–72. Mem., Governing Body, Brooklands Technical Coll., Weybridge, 1970–85 (Chm., 1977–85). *Recreations:* gardening, chess. *Address:* Honeywood, 163 Old Nazeing Road, Broxbourne, Herts EN10 6QT. *T:* Hoddesdon (01992) 463597.

COLLYEAR, Sir John (Gowen), Kt 1986; FEng 1979; Chairman, USM Texon Ltd (formerly United Machinery Group), 1987–95; *b* 19 Feb. 1927; *s* of John Robert Collyear and late Amy Elizabeth Collyear (*née* Gowen); *m* 1953, Catherine Barbara Newman; one *s* two *d.* *Educ:* Leeds Univ. (BSc). FIMechE (Hon. FIMechE 1995); FIM, FIEE; CIMgt. Graduate apprentice and Production Engr, Joseph Lucas Industries, 1951; Glacier Metal Company Ltd: Production Engr, 1953; Production Manager, 1956; Chief Production Engr, 1956; Factory Gen. Manager, 1959; Managing Director, 1969; Bearings Div. Man. Dir, Associated Engineering Ltd, 1972; Group Man. Dir, AE plc, 1975, Chm., 1981–86. Chairman: MK Electric Gp PLC, 1987–88; Fulmer Ltd, 1987–91; Dir, Hollis plc, 1987–88. Chm., Technology Requirements Bd, DTI, 1985–88. President: Motor Industry's Res. Assoc., 1987–; Inst. of Materials, 1992–94. FRSA 1987. *Publications:* Management Precepts, 1975; The Practice of First Level Management, 1976. *Recreations:* golf, bridge, piano music. *Address:* Walnut Tree House, Nether Westcote, Oxon OX7 6SD. *T:* Shipton-under-Wychwood (01993) 831247. *Club:* Athenæum.

COLMAN, Hon. Sir Anthony (David), Kt 1992; **Hon. Mr Justice Colman;** a Judge of the High Court of Justice, Queen's Bench Division, Commercial Court, since 1992; *b* 27 May 1938; *s* of late Solomon and Helen Colman; *m* 1964, Angela Glynn; two *d.* *Educ:* Harrogate Grammar Sch.; Trinity Hall, Cambridge (Aldis Schol.; Double First in Law Tripos; MA). FCIArb 1978. Called to the Bar, Gray's Inn, 1962, Master of the Bench, 1986; QC 1977; a Recorder, 1986–92. Mem., Bar Council, 1990–92 (Chm., Central and E European Sub-Cttee, 1991–92); Chairman: Commercial Bar Assoc., 1991–92 (Treasurer, 1989–91); Lloyd's Disciplinary Cttee for PCW and Minet, 1984; Mem., Cttee of Enquiry into Fidentia at Lloyd's, 1982–83. *Publications:* Mathew's Practice of the Commercial Court (1902), 2nd edn, 1967; The Practice and Procedure of the Commercial Court, 1983, 4th edn, 1995; (Gen. Editor and contrib.) Encylopedia of International Commercial Litigation, 1991. *Recreations:* cricket, tennis, music, gardening, the 17th Century, Sifnos, the River Chess. *Address:* Royal Courts of Justice, Strand, WC2A 2LL.

COLMAN, Anthony John; Leader of Council, London Borough of Merton, since 1991 (Councillor, since 1990); *b* 24 July 1943; *s* of late William Benjamin Colman and Beatrice (*née* Hudson); *m* Juliet Annabelle, *d* of Alec and June Owen; two *s*, and four *s* two *d* by prev. marriages. *Educ:* Paston Grammar Sch.; Magdalene Coll., Cambridge (MA); Univ. of E Africa, 1964–66; LSE, 1966. Unilever (United Africa Co.), 1964–69; Burton Group, 1969–90: Merchandise Manager, 1971–74, Buying and Merchandising Dir, 1974–76, Top Shop; Asst Man. Dir, Womenswear Sector, 1976–81; Director: Burton Menswear, 1976–81; Top Man, 1976–81; Dorothy Perkins, 1979–81; Dir, 1981–90. Director: GLE, 1990– (Chm., GLE Development Capital, 1990–); Aztec, 1990–; London First Centre Ltd, 1994–. Chairman: Low Pay Unit, 1990–; London Res. Centre, 1994–; Vice-Chm., ALA, 1991–95; Member: Price Commn, 1977–79; Exec., Labour Finance & Industry Gp, 1970–92; Labour Party Enquiry into Educn & Trng in Europe, 1991–93. Chm., Wimbledon Theatre Trust, 1991–; Dir, London Arts Bd, 1994–. Contested (Lab), SW Herts, 1979; Prospective Parly Cand. (Lab) Putney, 1995–. Industrial Fellow, Kingston Polytechnic, 1983–91. FRSA 1983. *Address:* 14 Lambourne Avenue, Wimbledon Village, SW19 7DW. *T:* 0181–879 0045. *Club:* Reform.

COLMAN, Sir Michael (Jeremiah), 3rd Bt *cr* 1907; Chairman, Reckitt and Colman plc, 1986–95; First Church Estates Commissioner, since 1993; *b* 7 July 1928; *s* of Sir Jeremiah Colman, 2nd Bt, and Edith Gwendolyn Tritton; *S* father, 1961; *m* 1955, Judith Jean Wallop, *d* of Vice-Adm. Sir Peveril William-Powlett, KCB, KCMG, CBE, DSO; two *s* three *d.* *Educ:* Eton. Director: Reckitt & Colman plc; Foreign and Colonial Ventures Advisors Ltd, 1988–. Member: Council of Royal Warrant Holders, 1977–, Pres., 1984–85; Trinity House Lighthouse Bd, 1985– (Younger Brother, 1994). Member: Council, Chemical Industries Assoc., 1982–84; Bd, UK Centre for Econ. and Environmental Develt, 1985–. Mem., Council, Scout Assoc., 1985–. Mem. Gen. Council and Mem. Finance Cttee, King Edward's Hosp. Fund for London, 1978–; Special Trustee, St Mary's Hosp., 1988–; Trustee: Royal Foundn of Grey Coat Hosp., 1989–; Allchurches Trust Ltd, 1994. Capt., Yorks Yeomanry, RARO, 1967. Mem. Ct, Skinners' Co., 1985– (Master, 1991–92). FRSA. Hon. LLD. *Recreations:* farming, shooting. *Heir:* *s* Jeremiah Michael Powlett Colman [*b* 23 Jan. 1958; *m* 1981, Susan Elizabeth, *yr d* of John Henry Britland, York; two *s* one *d*]. *Address:* Malshanger, Basingstoke, Hants RG23 7EY. *T:* Basingstoke (01256) 780241; 40 Chester Square, SW1W 9HT; Tarvie, Bridge of Cally, Blairgowrie, Perthshire PH10 7PJ. *Clubs:* Cavalry and Guards, Boodle's.

COLMAN, Timothy James Alan; Lord-Lieutenant of Norfolk, since 1978; *b* 19 Sept. 1929; 2nd but *o* surv. *s* of late Captain Geoffrey Russell Rees Colman and Lettice Elizabeth Evelyn Colman, Norwich; *m* 1951, Lady Mary Cecelia (Extra Lady in Waiting to Princess Alexandra), twin *d* of late Lt-Col Hon. Michael Claude Hamilton Bowes Lyon and Elizabeth Margaret, Glamis; two *s* three *d.* *Educ:* RNC, Dartmouth and Greenwich. Lieut RN, 1950, retd 1953. Chm., Eastern Counties Newspapers Group Ltd, 1969–; Director: Reckitt & Colman plc, 1978–89; Whitbread & Co. PLC, 1980–86; Anglia Television Group PLC, 1987–94; Trustee, Carnegie UK Trust (Chm., 1983–87). Pro-Chancellor, Univ. of E Anglia (Chm. Council, 1973–86); Chairman: Trustees, Norfolk and Norwich Festival, 1974–; Royal Norfolk Agricl Assoc., 1985– (Pres., 1982). Member: Countryside Commn, 1971–76; Water Space Amenity Commn, 1973–76; Adv. Cttee for England, Nature Conservancy Council, 1974–80; Eastern Regional Cttee, National Trust, 1967–71; Pres., Norfolk Naturalists Trust, 1962–78. Pres., E. Anglian TAVR, 1989–. JP 1958, DL 1968, High Sheriff 1970, Norfolk. Hon. DCL E Anglia, 1973. KStJ 1979. *Address:* Bixley Manor, Norwich, Norfolk NR14 8SJ. *T:* Norwich (01603) 625298. *Clubs:* Turf, Pratt's; Norfolk (Norwich); Royal Yacht Squadron.

COLNBROOK, Baron *cr* 1987 (Life Peer), of Waltham St Lawrence in the Royal County of Berkshire; **Humphrey Edward Gregory Atkins,** KCMG 1983; PC 1973; *b* 12 Aug. 1922; *s* of late Capt. E. D. Atkins, Nyeri, Kenya Colony; *m* 1944, Margaret, *d* of Sir Robert Spencer-Nairn, 1st Bt; one *s* three *d.* *Educ:* Wellington Coll. Special entry cadetship, RN, 1940; Lieut RN, 1943; resigned, 1948. MP (C): Merton and Morden, Surrey, 1955–70; Spelthorne, 1970–87. PPS to Civil Lord of the Admiralty, 1959–62; Hon.. Sec. Conservative Parly Defence Cttee, 1965–67; Opposition Whip, 1967–70; Treasurer of HM Household and Dep. Chief Whip, 1970–73; Parly Sec. to the Treasury and Govt Chief Whip, 1973–74; Opposition Chief Whip, 1974–79; Secretary of State for N Ireland, 1979–81; Lord Privy Seal, 1981–82. Chm., Select Cttee on Defence, 1984–87. Pres., Nat. Union of Conservative and Unionist Assocs, 1985–86; Chm., Assoc. of Conservative Peers, 1990–94. Mem., Press Complaints Commn, 1991–94. Vice-Chm., Management Cttee, Outward Bound Trust, 1966–70; Chm., Airey Neave Trust, 1984–90 (Pres., 1990–). *Address:* Tuckenhams, Waltham St Lawrence, Reading, Berks RG10 0JH. *Club:* Brooks's.

COLOMBO, Metropolitan Archbishop of, (RC), since 1977; **Most Rev. Nicholas Marcus Fernando;** *b* 6 Dec. 1932. *Educ:* St Aloysius' Seminary, Colombo; Universitas Propaganda Fide, Rome. BA (London); PhL (Rome); STD (Rome). Mem., Sacred Congregation for Evangelization of Peoples; Pres., Catholic Bishops' Conf. of Sri Lanka, 1989–. *Address:* Archbishop's House, Borella, Colombo 8, Sri Lanka. *T:* (1) 695471/2/3, *Fax:* (1) 692009.

COLOMBO, Emilio; Minister of Foreign Affairs, Italy, 1980–83 and 1992; *b* Potenza, Italy, 11 April 1920. *Educ:* Rome Univ. Deputy: Constituent Assembly, 1946–48; (Christian Democrat), Italian Parlt, 1948–94; Under-Secretary: of Agriculture, 1948–51; of Public Works, 1953–55; Minister: of Agriculture, 1955–58; of Foreign Trade, 1958–59; of Industry and Commerce, 1959–60, March-April 1960, July 1960–63; of the Treasury, 1963–70, Feb.–May 1972, 1974–76; Prime Minister, 1970–72; Minister of State for UN Affairs, 1972–73; Minister of Finance, 1973–74. European Parliament: Mem., 1976–80; Chm., Political Affairs Cttee, 1976–77; Pres., 1977–79. Formerly Vice-Pres., Italian Catholic Youth Assoc. Charlemagne Prize, 1979. *Address:* Via Aurelia 239, Rome, Italy.

COLQUHOUN, Andrew John, PhD; Secretary and Chief Executive, Institute of Chartered Accountants in England and Wales, since 1990; *b* 21 Sept. 1949; *s* of late Kenneth James Colquhoun, MC, and of Christine Mary Colquhoun (*née* Morris); *m* 1975, Patricia Beardall; one *s* one *d.* *Educ:* Tiffin Sch.; Nottingham Univ. (BSc 1st Cl. Hons 1971); Glasgow Univ. (PhD 1974); City Univ. Business Sch. (MBA Dist. 1987). Joined HM Diplomatic Service, 1974; Third Sec., FCO, 1974–75; Second Sec., MECAS, 1975–77; Second, later First, Sec., Damascus, 1977–79; First Sec., Tel Aviv, 1979–81; Principal, Cabinet Office, 1981–83; Planning Staff, FCO, 1983–84; Shandwick Consultants (on secondment to ICA), 1984–86; Dir of Educn and Trng, ICA, 1987–90. Sec., Consultative Cttee of Accountancy Bodies, 1990–. *Publications:* various articles on accountancy, educn and recruitment in nat., educnl and professional press. *Recreations:* boating, bird watching, country life, reading. *Address:* PO Box 433, Chartered Accountants' Hall, Moorgate Place, EC2P 2BJ. *Club:* Reform.

COLQUHOUN, Maj.-Gen. Sir Cyril (Harry), KCVO 1968 (CVO 1965); CB 1955; OBE 1945; late Royal Artillery; Secretary of the Central Chancery of the Orders of Knighthood, 1960–68; Extra Gentleman Usher to the Queen since 1968; *b* 1903; *s* of late Capt. Harry Colquhoun; *m* 1930, Stella Irene, *d* of late W. C. Rose, Kotagiri, India, and Cheam, Surrey; one *s.* *Educ:* RMA, Woolwich. Commnd RA, 1923; served War of 1939–45 (despatches, OBE); Palestine, 1946–48 (despatches); Comdr, 6th, 76th and 1st Field Regiments; CRA 61st Div., 1945; CRA 6th Airborne Div., 1947–48; CRA 1st Infantry Div., 1949–50; Comdt, Sch. of Artillery, 1951–53; GOC 50th (Northumbrian) Infantry Div. (TA), and Northumbrian District, 1954–56; GOC Troops, Malta, 1956–59; retired 1960. Col Commandant: Royal Artillery, 1962–69; Royal Malta Artillery, 1962–70. *Recreations:* gardening, shooting. *Address:* Longwalls, Shenington, Banbury, Oxon OX15 6NQ. *T:* Edge Hill (01295) 670246.

COLQUHOUN, Prof. David, FRS 1985; Professor of Pharmacology, since 1983, and Director, Wellcome Laboratory for Molecular Pharmacology, since 1993, University College London; *b* 19 July 1936; *s* of Gilbert Colquhoun and Kathleen Mary (*née* Chambers); *m* 1976, Margaret Ann Boultwood; one *s.* *Educ:* Birkenhead Sch.; Liverpool Technical Coll.; Leeds Univ. (BSc); Edinburgh Univ. (PhD). Lectr, Dept of Pharmacol., UCL, 1964–70; Vis. Asst, then Associate Prof., Dept of Pharmacol., Yale Univ. Med. Sch., 1970–72; Sen. Lectr, Dept of Pharmacol., Univ. of Southampton Med. Sch., 1972–75; Sen. Lectr, Dept of Pharmacol., St George's Hosp. Med. Sch., 1975–79; Reader, Dept of Pharmacol., UCL, 1979–83. Guest Prof., Max-Planck-Institut für Medizinische Forschung, Heidelberg, 1990–91. Krantz Lectr, Univ. of Maryland, 1987. Trustee, Sir Ronald Fisher Meml Cttee, 1975–. Alexander von Humboldt Prize, 1990. Member Editorial Board: Jl of Physiology, 1974–81; Series B, Proceedings of Royal Soc. *Publications:* Lectures on Biostatistics, 1971; articles in Jl of Physiology, British Jl of Pharmacology, Proc. of Royal Soc., etc. *Recreations:* walking, running, sailing, linear algebra. *Address:* Chiddingstone, Common Lane, Kings Langley, Herts WD4 8BL. *T:* Kings Langley (01923) 266154.

COLQUHOUN, Rev. Canon Frank, MA; Canon Residentiary of Norwich Cathedral, 1973–78, Canon Emeritus, since 1978; Vice-Dean, 1974–78; *b* 28 Oct. 1909; *s* of Rev.

R. W. Colquhoun; *m* 1st, 1934, Dora Gertrude Hearne Slater; one *s* one *d*; 2nd, 1973, Judy Kenney. *Educ:* Warwick Sch.; Durham Univ. LTh 1932, BA 1933, MA 1937, Durham. Deacon, 1933; Priest, 1934; Curate, St Faith, Maidstone, 1933–35; Curate, New Malden, Surrey, 1935–39; Vicar, St Michael and All Angels, Blackheath Park, SE3, 1939–46; Editorial Sec., Nat. Church League, 1946–52; Priest-in-Charge, Christ Church, Woburn Square, WC1, 1952–54; Vicar of Wallington, Surrey, 1954–61; Canon Residentiary of Southwark Cathedral, 1961–73; Principal, Southwark Ordination Course, 1966–72. Editor, The Churchman, 1946–53. *Publications:* The Living Church in the Parish (ed), 1952; Harringay Story, 1954; Your Child's Baptism, 1958; The Gospels, 1961; Total Christianity, 1962; The Catechism, 1963; Lent with Pilgrim's Progress, 1965; Christ's Ambassadors, 1965; (ed) Parish Prayers, 1967; (ed) Hard Questions, 1967; Preaching through the Christian Year, 1972; Strong Son of God, 1973; Preaching at the Parish Communion, 1974; Contemporary Parish Prayers, 1975; (ed) Moral Questions, 1977; Hymns that Live, 1980; Prayers that Live, 1981; New Parish Prayers, 1982; Family Prayers, 1984; Fourfold Portrait of Jesus, 1984; A Hymn Companion, 1985; Preaching on Favourite Hymns, 1986; (ed) Your Favourite Songs of Praise, 1987; Sing to the Lord, 1988; Prayers for Today, 1989; More Preaching on Favourite Hymns, 1990; God of our Fathers, 1990; Prayers for All, 1991; My God and King, 1993. *Recreations:* writing, listening to music. *Address:* 21 Buckholt Avenue, Bexhill-on-Sea, East Sussex TN40 2RS. *T:* Bexhill (01424) 221138.

COLQUHOUN OF LUSS, Captain Sir Ivar (Iain), 8th Bt *cr* 1786; JP; DL; Hon. Sheriff (formerly Hon. Sheriff Substitute); Chief of the Clan; Grenadier Guards; *b* 4 Jan. 1916; *s* of Sir Iain Colquhoun, 7th Bt, and Geraldine Bryde (Dinah) (*d* 1974), *d* of late F. J. Tennant; *S* father, 1948; *m* 1943, Kathleen, 2nd *d* of late W. A. Duncan and of Mrs Duncan, 53 Cadogan Square, SW1; one *s* one *d* (and one *s* decd). *Educ:* Eton. JP 1951, DL 1952, Dunbartonshire. *Heir: s* Malcolm Rory Colquhoun, Younger of Luss [*b* 20 Dec. 1947; *m* 1st, 1978, Susan Timmerman (marr. diss.); one *s*; 2nd, 1989, Katharine, *e d* of A. C. Mears; one *s* one *d*]. *Address:* Camstraddan, Luss, Dunbartonshire G83 8NX; 26A Thorney Crescent, SW11 3TT. *Clubs:* White's, Royal Ocean Racing.

See also Duke of Argyll.

COLQUHOUN, Ms Maureen Morfydd; political researcher and writer; Chief Executive, North West Government Relations, since 1994; *b* 12 Aug. 1928; *m* 1949, Keith Colquhoun (marr. diss. 1980); two *s* one *d*. Partner, 1975–, Ms Barbara Todd; extended family, two *d*. Mem. Labour Party, 1945–; Member: Shoreham UDC, 1965–74; Adur District Council, 1973–74; West Sussex CC, 1971–74; Hackney BC, 1982–90; Lakes Parish Council, 1994–. MP (Lab) Northampton North, Feb. 1974–1979. Information Officer, Gingerbread, 1980–82. Hon. Sec., All-Party Parly Gp on AIDS, 1987–88; Chm., Secretaries and Assistants' Council, H of C, 1992–93. Trustee and Hon. Treas., Albany Soc., 1980–90. Founder and Chm., Historic Ambleside Trust, 1992–. *Publications:* A Woman In the House, 1980; Inside the Westminster Parliament, 1992. *Recreations:* fell-walking, jazz, opera, theatre. *Address:* South Knoll, Rydal Road, Ambleside, Cumbria LA22 9AY.

COLSTON, Colin Charles; QC 1980; **His Honour Judge Colston;** a Circuit Judge, since 1983; Resident Judge, St Albans, since 1989; *b* 2 Oct. 1937; *yr s* of late Eric Colston, JP, and Catherine Colston; *m* 1963, Edith Helga, JP, *d* of late Med. Rat Dr Wilhelm and Frau Gisela Hille, St Oswald/Freistadt, Austria; two *s* one *d*. *Educ:* Rugby Sch.; The Gunnery, Washington, Conn, USA; Trinity Hall, Cambridge (MA). National Service, RN, 1956–58; commissioned, RNR, 1958–64. Called to the Bar, Gray's Inn, 1962; Midland and Oxford Circuit (formerly Midland Circuit); Recorder of Midland Circuit, 1968–69; Member, Senate of Inns of Court and Bar, 1977–80; Recorder of the Crown Court, 1978–83. Lay Judge, Court of Arches, Canterbury, 1992–. Mem., Criminal Cttee, Judicial Studies Bd, 1989–92. Chm., St Albans Diocesan Bd of Patronage, 1987–. *Address:* The Crown Court, Bricket Road, St Albans, Herts AL1 3HY.

COLSTON, Michael; Chairman: Colston Consultants Ltd, 1989–93; Quit Ltd, 1989–93; *b* 24 July 1932; *s* of Sir Charles Blampied Colston, CBE, MC, DCM, FCGI and Lady (Eliza Foster) Colston, MBE; *m* 1st, 1956, Jane Olivia Kilham Roberts (marr. diss.); three *d*; 2nd, 1977, Judith Angela Briggs. *Educ:* Ridley Coll., Canada; Stowe; Gonville and Caius Coll., Cambridge. Joined 17th/21st Lancers, 1952; later seconded to 1st Royal Tank Regt for service in Korea. Founder Dir, Charles Colston Group Ltd (formerly Colston Appliances Ltd) together with late Sir Charles Colston, 1955, Chm. and Man. Dir, 1969–89; Chm. and Man. Dir, Colston Domestic Appliances Ltd, 1969–79. Chairman: Tallent Engineering Ltd, 1969–89; Tallent Holdings plc, 1989–90; ITS Rubber Ltd, 1969–85; Dishwasher Council, 1970–75. Dir, Farming and Wildlife Adv. Gp, 1991–. Chm., Assoc. Manufrs of Domestic Electrical Appliances, 1976–79. Member Council: Inst. of Directors, 1977–93 (Pres., Thames Valley Br., 1983–93); CBI, 1984–90 (Chm., S Regl Council, 1986–88); British Electrotechnical Approvals Bd, 1976–79; SMMT, 1987–90. Trustee, Hawk and Owl Trust, 1991–. *Recreations:* fishing, shooting, tennis; founder Cambridge Univ. Water Ski Club. *Address:* C6 Albany, Piccadilly, W1V 9RF. *T:* 0171–734 2452.

COLT, Sir Edward (William Dutton), 10th Bt *cr* 1694; MB, FRCP, FACP; Associate Attending Physician, St Luke's-Roosevelt Hospital, New York; Associate Professor of Clinical Medicine (part-time), Columbia University, New York; *b* 22 Sept. 1936; *s* of Major John Rochfort Colt, North Staffs Regt (*d* 1944), and of Angela Miriam Phyllis (*née* Kyan; she *m* 1946, Capt. Robert Leslie Cock); *S* uncle, 1951; *m* 1st, 1966, Jane Caroline (marr. diss. 1972), *d* of James Histed Lewis, Geneva and Washington, DC; 2nd, 1979, Suzanne Nelson (*née* Knickerbocker); one *d* (one *s* decd). *Educ:* Stoke House, Seaford; Douai Sch.; University Coll., London. Lately: Medical Registrar, UCH; House Physician, Brompton Hosp. *Publications:* contribs, especially on sports medicine, particularly running, to British and American med. jls. *Recreations:* cycling, ski-ing, squash, tennis. *Heir:* none. *Address:* 12 E 88 Street, New York, NY 10128, USA.

COLTART, Simon Stewart; His Honour Judge Coltart; a Circuit Judge, since 1991; *b* 3 Sept. 1946; *s* of Gilbert McCallum Coltart and Mary Louise (*née* Kemp); *m* 1973, Sarah Victoria Birts; three *s*. *Educ:* Epsom Coll.; Leeds Univ. (LLB). Called to the Bar, Lincoln's Inn, 1969; a Recorder, 1987–91. Mem., Court of Assts, Grocers' Co., 1991–. *Recreations:* sailing, golf. *Address:* The Law Courts, Lewes, East Sussex BN2 3JH. *Club:* Rye Golf.

COLTHURST, Sir Richard La Touche, 9th Bt *cr* 1744; *b* 14 Aug. 1928; *er s* of Sir Richard St John Jefferyes Colthurst, 8th Bt, and Denys Maida Hanmer West (*d* 1966), *e d* of Augustus William West; *S* father, 1955; *m* 1953, Janet Georgina, *d* of L. A. Wilson-Wright, Coolcarrigan, Co. Kildare; three *s* one *d*. *Educ:* Harrow; Peterhouse, Cambridge (MA). Host and Organiser, Horse trials, Blarney Castle International 3 Day Event, 1992–. Liveryman of Worshipful Company of Grocers. Mem., Internat. Dendrology Soc. *Recreations:* forestry, cricket, tennis, swimming. *Heir: s* Charles St John Colthurst [*b* 21 May 1955; *m* 1987, Nora Mary, *d* of Mortimer Kelleher, Dooniskey, Lissarda, Co. Cork; one *s* three *d*. *Educ:* Eton; Magdalene Coll., Cambridge (MA); University Coll., Dublin]. *Address:* Blarney Castle, Co. Cork, Eire; Ardrum, Inniscarra, Co. Cork, Eire. *Club:* MCC.

COLTMAN, Anne Clare, (Mrs T. C. Coltman); *see* Riches, A. C.

COLTMAN, (Arthur) Leycester (Scott), CMG 1993; HM Diplomatic Service; Ambassador to Colombia, since 1994; *b* 24 May 1938; *s* of late Arthur Cranfield Coltman and Vera Vaid; *m* 1969, Maria Piedad Josefina Cantos Aberasturi; two *s* one *d*. *Educ:* Rugby School; Magdalene Coll., Cambridge. Foreign Office, 1961–62; Third Secretary, British Embassy, Copenhagen, 1963–64; Second Secretary, Cairo 1964–65, Madrid 1966–69; Manchester Business School, 1969–70; Foreign Office, 1970–74; Commercial Secretary, Brasilia, 1974–77; Foreign Office, 1977–79; Counsellor, Mexico City, 1979–83; Counsellor and Hd of Chancery, Brussels, 1983–87; Head: Mexico and Central America Dept; 1987–90; Latin America Dept, 1990; Ambassador to Cuba, 1991–94. *Recreations:* squash, chess, bridge, music. *Address:* c/o Foreign and Commonwealth Office, King Charles Street, SW1A 2AH.

COLTRANE, Robbie; actor and director; *b* Glasgow, 31 March 1950; partner, Rhona Irene Gemmell; one *s*. *Educ:* Trinity Coll., Glenalmond; Glasgow Sch. of Art (DA Drawing and Painting). *Television* includes: Laugh? I nearly paid my licence fee!, 1985; Hooray for Hollyrood, 1986; Tutti Frutti, 1986; The Miners' Strike, 1987; Mistero Buffo, 1990; Coltrane in a Cadillac, 1992; Cracker, 1993; Cracker II, 1994; numerous guest appearances on TV shows and series; *films* include: Absolute Beginners, 1985; Mona Lisa, 1985; Danny Champion of the World, 1988; Henry V, 1988; Nuns on the Run, 1989; The Pope Must Die, 1990; Oh, What a Night, 1991; Huck Finn, 1992; Goldeneye, 1995; *theatre:* has appeared and toured with Traverse Theatre Co. and Borderline Theatre Co., 1976–, incl. Mistero Buffo, 1990; Yr Obedient Servant, Lyric, 1987. Silver Rose Award, Montreux TV Fest., 1987; Evening Standard Peter Sellers Award, 1991; TV Best Actor Awards: BAFTA, 1993, 1994; Silver Nymph, Monte Carlo, 1994; BPG, 1994; RTS, 1994; FIPA (French Acad.), 1994; Cable Ace, 1994; Cannes TV Fest., 1994. *Publications:* Coltrane in a Cadillac, 1993; newspaper and magazine articles. *Recreations:* politics, drawing, vintage cars, reading, sailing, piano, fishing, arguing and drinking (together, usually), film, ships. *Address:* c/o CDA #17, 47 Courtfield Road, SW7 4DB. *T:* 0171–370 0708. *Clubs:* Groucho, Soho House, Chelsea Arts, Marzipan; Glasgow Arts.

COLVER, Hugh Bernard, CBE 1991; Director of Communications, Conservative Central Office, since 1995; *b* 22 Aug. 1945; *s* of Rev. Canon John Lawrence Colver and late Diana Irene (*née* Bartlett); *m* 1970, Gillian Ogilvie, *y d* of late Morris and Dorothy Graham, Christchurch, NZ; one *s* one *d*. *Educ:* King Edward VI Grammar Sch., Louth, Lincs. Reporter: Market Rasen Mail, 1961–63; Hereford Times and Hereford Evening News, 1963–67; Asst Editor, Helicopter World and Hovercraft World, 1967–68; Journalist, FT Surveys, Financial Times, 1968–71; freelance journalist, writer and PR consultant, 1971–75; Press Officer, MoD, 1975–78; PRO, RAE, 1978–79; Staff PRO to Flag Officer, Scotland and NI, 1979–81; Press Officer, Prime Minister's Office, 1981–82; Chief Press Officer, Dept of Employment, 1982–84; Dep. Dir of Information, Metropolitan Police, 1984–85; Ministry of Defence: Dep. Chief of PR, 1985–87; Chief of PR, 1987–92; Public Affairs Dir, British Aerospace Defence Ltd, 1992–95. FRSA. *Publication:* This is the Hovercraft, 1972. *Recreations:* rehabilitating houses, driving rapid cars, motor racing, walking, messing about in boats. *Address:* Conservative Central Office, 32 Smith Square, Westminster, SW1P 3HH. *Club:* Reform.

COLVILLE, family name of **Viscount Colville of Culross** and of **Baron Clydesmuir.**

COLVILLE OF CULROSS, 4th Viscount *cr* 1902; **John Mark Alexander Colville;** QC; 14th Baron (Scot.) *cr* 1604; 4th Baron (UK) *cr* 1885; **His Honour Judge The Viscount Colville of Culross;** a Circuit Judge, since 1993; *b* 19 July 1933; *e s* of 3rd Viscount and Kathleen Myrtle (*d* 1986), OBE 1961, *e d* of late Brig.-Gen. H. R. Gale, CMG, RE, Bardsey, Saanichton, Vancouver Island; *S* father, 1945; *m* 1st, 1958, Mary Elizabeth Webb-Bowen (marr. diss. 1973); four *s*; 2nd, 1974, Margaret Birgitta, Viscountess Davidson, LLB, JP, Barrister, *o d* of Maj.-Gen. C. H. Norton, CB, CBE, DSO; one *s*. *Educ:* Rugby (Scholar); New Coll., Oxford (Scholar) (MA). Lieut Grenadier Guards Reserve. Barrister-at-law, Lincoln's Inn, 1960 (Buchanan prizeman), Bencher, 1986; QC 1978; a Recorder, 1990–93. Minister of State, Home Office, 1972–74. Dir, Securities and Futures Authy (formerly Securities Assoc.), 1987–93. Chm., Norwich Information and Technology Centre, 1983–85; Director: Rediffusion Television Ltd, 1961–68; British Electric Traction Co. Ltd, 1968–72, 1974–84 (Dep. Chm., 1980–81); Mem., CBI Council, 1982–84. Chairman: Mental Health Act Commn, 1983–88; Alcohol Educn and Res. Council, 1984–90; Parole Bd, 1988–92; UK rep., UN Human Rights Commn, 1980–83; Mem., UN Working Gp on Disappeared Persons, 1980–84 (Chm., 1981–84); Special Rapporteur on Human Rights in Guatemala, 1983–86. Reports on Prevention of Terrorism Act and NI Emergency Powers Act, for HM Govt, 1986–93. Mem. Council, Univ. of E Anglia, 1968–72. Mem., Royal Company of Archers (Queen's Body Guard for Scotland). Governor, BUPA, 1990–93. *Heir: s* Master of Colville, *qv*. *Address:* House of Lords, SW1A 0PW.

See also Baron Carrington.

COLVILLE, Master of; Hon. Charles Mark Townshend Colville; *b* 5 Sept. 1959; *s* and *heir* of 4th Viscount Colville of Culross, *qv*. *Educ:* Rugby; Univ. of Durham. *Address:* Rookyards, Spexhall, near Halesworth, Suffolk.

COLVILLE, Lady Margaret, CVO 1994; an Extra Woman of the Bedchamber to HM Queen Elizabeth the Queen Mother, since 1990; *b* 20 July 1918; *d* of 4th Earl of Ellesmere; *m* 1948, Sir John Rupert Colville, CB, CVO (*d* 1987); two *s* one *d*. Served War of 1939–45 in ATS (Junior Subaltern). Lady in Waiting to the Princess Elizabeth, Duchess of Edinburgh, 1946–49. *Address:* The Close, Broughton, near Stockbridge, Hants SO20 8AA. *T:* Romsey (01794) 301331.

See also Duke of Sutherland.

COLVIN, Andrew James; Comptroller and City Solicitor, City of London, since 1989; *b* 28 April 1947; *s* of Gilbert Russell Colvin, OBE, MA, and Dr Beatrice Colvin, MRCS, LRCP, DPH; *m* 1971, Helen Mary Ryan; one *s* three *d*. *Educ:* qualified Solicitor, 1975. Articled to Borough Solicitor, subseq. Asst Town Clerk, London Borough of Ealing, 1971–82; Dep. Town Clerk and Borough Solicitor, Royal Borough of Kensington and Chelsea, 1982–89. Governor: St Gregory's RC Sch., 1989–93; Cardinal Wiseman RC Sch., 1992–. Freeman, City of London, 1989. *Recreations:* sailing, music, cycling. *Address:* Guildhall, EC2P 2EJ.

COLVIN, David, CBE 1991; Chief Adviser in Social Work, The Scottish Office, 1980–91; Scottish Secretary, British Association of Social Workers, since 1992; *b* 31 Jan. 1931; *s* of James Colvin and Mrs Crawford Colvin; *m* 1957, Elma Findlay, artist; two *s* three *d*. *Educ:* Whitehill Sch., Glasgow; Glasgow and Edinburgh Univs. Probation Officer, Glasgow City, 1955–60; Psychiatric Social Worker, Scottish Prison and Borstal Service, 1960–61; Sen. Psychiatric Social Worker, Crichton Royal Hosp., Child Psychiatric Unit, 1961–65; Director, Family Casework Unit, Paisley, 1965; Social Work Adviser, Social Work Services Gp, Scottish Educn Dept, 1966, and subseq.; Interim Dir of Social Work, Shetland Islands Council, 1991. At various times held office in Howard League for Penal Reform, Assoc. of Social Workers and Inst. for Study and Treatment of Delinquency. Sen. Associate Research Fellow, Brunel Univ., 1978. Chm., Dumfries Constituency Labour Party, 1963–65. Chairman: Scotland Cttee, Nat. Children's Homes, 1991–;

Marriage Council, Scotland, 1991–95. Governor, Nat. Inst. for Social Work, 1986–89; Mem., Exec. Cttee, Scottish Assoc. for Care and Rehabilitation of Offenders, 1992–94. Hon. Adviser, British Red Cross, 1982–90. Proprietor, Portobello Studios. Mem., Labour Party. *Recreations:* collector; swimming, climbing, social affairs. *Address:* The Studio, 53 Windsor Place, Edinburgh EH15 2AF. *Clubs:* Commonwealth Trust; Scottish Arts (Edinburgh).

COLVIN, David Hugh, CMG 1993; HM Diplomatic Service; Minister, Rome, since 1992; *b* 23 Jan. 1941; 3rd *s* of Major Leslie Hubert Boyd Colvin, MC, and Edna Mary (*née* Parrott); *m* 1971, (Diana) Caroline Carew, *y d* of Gordon MacPherson Lang Smith and Mildred (*née* Carew-Gibson); one *s* one *d*. *Educ:* Lincoln Sch.; Trinity Coll., Oxford (MA). Assistant Principal, Board of Trade, 1966. Joined HM Foreign (later Diplomatic) Service, 1967; Central Dept, FO, 1967; Second Secretary, Bangkok, 1968–71; European Integration Dept, FCO, 1971–75; First Sec., Paris, 1975–77; First Sec. (Press and Inf.), UK Permanent Representation to the European Community, 1977–82; Asst Sec., Cabinet Office, 1982–85; Counsellor and Hd of Chancery, Budapest, 1985–88; Hd, SE Asian Dept, FCO, 1988–91. *Recreations:* military history, squash, tennis, shooting. *Address:* c/o Foreign and Commonwealth Office, King Charles Street, SW1A 2AH. *Club:* Travellers'.

COLVIN, Sir Howard Montagu, Kt 1995; CVO 1983; CBE 1964; MA; FBA 1963; FRHistS; FSA, 1980; Fellow of St John's College, Oxford, 1948–87, now Emeritus (Tutor in History, 1948–78; Librarian, 1950–84); Reader in Architectural History, Oxford University, 1965–87; Member: Historic Buildings Council for England, 1970–84; Historic Buildings and Monuments Commission, 1984–85; Historic Buildings Advisory Committee, since 1984; Royal Commission on Ancient and Historical Monuments of Scotland, 1977–89; Royal Commission on Historical Manuscripts, 1981–88; Reviewing Committee on the Export of Works of Art, 1982–83; Royal Fine Art Commission, 1962–72; Royal Commission on Historical Monuments, England, 1963–76; President, Society of Architectural Historians of Great Britain, 1979–81; *b* 15 Oct. 1919; *s* of late Montagu Colvin; *m* 1943, Christina Edgeworth, *d* of late H. E. Butler, Prof. of Latin at University Coll., London; two *s*. *Educ:* Trent Coll.; University Coll., London (Fellow, 1974). Served in RAF, 1940–46 (despatches). Asst Lecturer, Dept of History, University Coll., London, 1946–48. Hon. FRIBA; Hon. FSA (Scot.) 1986. DUniv York, 1978. Wolfson Literary Award, 1978. *Publications:* The White Canons in England, 1951; A Biographical Dictionary of English Architects 1660–1840, 1954, 2nd edn as A Biographical Dictionary of British Architects 1600–1840, 1978, 3rd edn 1995; (General Editor and part author) The History of the King's Works, 6 Vols, 1963–82; A History of Deddington, 1963; Catalogue of Architectural Drawings in Worcester College Library, 1964; Architectural Drawings in the Library of Elton Hall (with Maurice Craig), 1964; (ed with John Harris) The Country Seat, 1970; Building Accounts of King Henry III, 1971; (introduction) The Queen Anne Churches, 1980; (ed with John Newman) Roger North, Of Architecture, 1981; Unbuilt Oxford, 1983; Calke Abbey, Derbyshire, 1985; The Canterbury Quadrangle, St John's College, Oxford, 1988; (with J. S. G. Simmons) All Souls: an Oxford college and its buildings, 1989; Architecture and the After-Life, 1991; articles on mediæval and architectural history in Archaeological Journal, Architectural Review, etc. *Recreation:* gardening. *Address:* 50 Plantation Road, Oxford OX2 6JE. *T:* Oxford (01865) 57460.

COLVIN, John Horace Ragnar, CMG 1968; HM Diplomatic Service, retired; Director, Robert Fraser and Partners; *b* Tokyo, 18 June 1922; *s* of late Adm. Sir Ragnar Colvin, KBE, CB and Lady Colvin; *m* 1st, 1948, Elizabeth Anne Manifold (marr. diss., 1963); one *s* one *d*; 2nd, 1967, Moranna Sibyl de Lerisson Cazenove; one *s* one *d*. *Educ:* RNC Dartmouth; University of London. Royal Navy, 1935–51. Joined HM Diplomatic Service, 1951; HM Embassies, Oslo, 1951–53 and Vienna, 1953–55; British High Commn, Kuala Lumpur, 1958–61; HM Consul-General, Hanoi, 1965–67; Ambassador to People's Republic of Mongolia, 1971–74; HM Embassy, Washington, 1977–80. Dir for Internat. Relations, Chase Manhattan Bank, 1980–86. Member: Research Council, Pacific Forum; Political Council, Asiaweek. *Publications:* Twice Around the World, 1991; Not Ordinary Men: the battle of Kohima re-assessed, 1994; Volcano Under Snow, 1995; contribs to British and US jls. *Address:* 12A Evelyn Mansions, Carlisle Place, SW1P 1NH. *Clubs:* Brooks's, Beefsteak.

COLVIN, Michael Keith Beale; MP (C) Romsey and Waterside, since 1983 (Bristol North West, 1979–83); *b* 27 Sept. 1932; *s* of late Captain Ivan Beale Colvin, RN, and Mrs Joy Colvin, OBE; *m* Hon. Nichola, *e d* of Baron Cayzer, *qv*; one *s* two *d*. *Educ:* Eton; RMA, Sandhurst; Royal Agricultural Coll., Cirencester. Served Grenadier Guards, 1950–57: Temp. Captain; served BAOR, Berlin, Suez campaign, Cyprus. J. Walter Thompson & Co. Ltd, 1958–63. Councillor: Andover RDC, 1965–72; Test Valley Bor. Council, 1972–74 (first Vice Chm.); Dep. Chm., Winchester Constituency Conservative Assoc., 1973–76; Mem. (part-time), Cons. Res. Dept, 1975–79. Member, Select Committee: on Employment, 1981–83; on Energy, 1990–92; on Defence, 1992–; Chairman: Conservative Aviation Cttee, 1982–83, 1987–92; Cttee of W Country Cons. MPs, 1982–83; Cons. Foreign and Commonwealth Affairs Cttee, 1992–; Vice-Chm., Conservative Smaller Businesses Cttee, 1980–83; Sec., Conservative Shipping and Shipbuilding Cttee, 1981–83; Parly Adviser to Play Board, 1983–86; PPS to Baroness Young, Dep. Foreign Sec., FCO, 1983–85, and to Richard Luce, Minister for Arts, 1983–87. Dir, Royal British Legion Trng Co., 1993–. President: Hampshire Young Farmers Clubs, 1973–74; Test Valley Br., CPRE, 1974–; Mem., Southern Sports Council, 1970–74; Vice-Chm., British Field Sports Soc., 1987–; Chm., Council for Country Sports, 1988–. Governor, Enham Village Centre. *Address:* Tangley House, near Andover, Hants SP11 0SH. *T:* Chute Standen (01264) 730215. *Clubs:* Kennel, Pratt's.

COLWYN, 3rd Baron, *cr* 1917; **Ian Anthony Hamilton-Smith,** CBE 1989; Bt 1912; Dental Surgeon since 1966; *b* 1 Jan. 1942; *s* of 2nd Baron Colwyn and Miriam Gwendoline, *d* of Victor Ferguson; *S* father 1966; *m* 1st, 1964, Sonia Jane (marr. diss. 1977), *d* of P. H. G. Morgan; one *s* one *d*; 2nd, 1977, Nicola Jeanne, *d* of Arthur Tyers, The Avenue, Sunbury-on-Thames; two *d*. *Educ:* Cheltenham Coll.; Univ. of London. BDS London 1966; LDS, RCS 1966. Director: Three B Consultants Ltd, 1978–94; Dental Protection Ltd, 1990– (Chm., 1995–); Medical Protection Soc.; Big City Radio Ltd, 1992–; Cortecs Internat. Ltd. President: Natural Medicines Soc., 1989–; Huntington's Disease Assoc., 1991–; Arterial Health Foundn, 1992–. Jt Pres., All Party Parly Gp for Alternative and Complementary Medicine, 1989–. Pres., Soc. for Advancement of Anaesthesia in Dentistry. Patron: Res. Council for Complementary Medicine; Blackie Foundn; Eastman Res. Fund. *Recreations:* riparian activities, music, dance band and orchestra, golf. *Heir:* *s* Hon. Craig Peter Hamilton-Smith, *b* 13 Oct. 1968. *Address:* (practice) 53 Wimpole Street, W1M 7DF. *T:* 0171–935 6809.

COLYER, John Stuart, QC 1976; **His Honour Judge Colyer;** a Circuit Judge, since 1991; *b* 25 April 1935; *s* of late Stanley Herbert Colyer, MBE, and Louisa (*née* Randle); *m* 1961, Emily Warner, *o d* of late Stanley Leland Dutrow and Mrs Dutrow, Blue Ridge Summit, Pa, USA; two *d*. *Educ:* Dudley Grammar Sch.; Shrewsbury; Worcester Coll., Oxford (Open History Scholarship; BA 1955, MA 1961). 2nd Lieut RA, 1954–55. Called to the Bar, Middle Temple, 1959 (Bencher, 1983); Instructor, Univ. of Pennsylvania, Philadelphia, 1959–60, Asst Prof., 1960–61; practised English bar, Midland and Oxford Circuit (formerly Oxford Circuit), 1961–91; a Recorder, 1986–91. Hon. Reader, 1985– and Mem. Council, 1985–91, Council of Legal Educn (Lectr (Law of Landlord and Tenant), 1970–89); Vice-Pres., Lawyers' Christian Fellowship, 1993– (Chm., 1981–89); Mem., Anglo-American Real Property Inst., 1980– (Treasurer, 1984). Blundell Meml Lectr, 1977, 1982, 1986. *Publications:* (ed jtly) Encyclopaedia of Forms and Precedents (Landlord and Tenant), vol. XI, 1965, vol. XII, 1966; A Modern View of the Law of Torts, 1966; Landlord and Tenant, in Halsbury's Laws of England, 4th edn, 1981, new edn, 1994; Gen. Ed., Megarry's The Rent Acts, 11th edn, 1988; articles in Conveyancer and other professional jls. *Recreations:* entertaining my family; opera; cultivation of cacti and of succulents (esp. Lithops); gardening generally; travel. *Address:* c/o Falcon Chambers, Falcon Court, EC4Y 1AA. *T:* 0171–353 2484, *Fax:* 0171–353 1261; c/o Law Courts, Barker Road, Maidstone ME16 5EW.

COLYER-FERGUSSON, Sir James Herbert Hamilton, 4th Bt, *cr* 1866; *b* 10 Jan. 1917; *s* of Max Christian Hamilton Colyer-Fergusson (*d* on active service, 1940) and Edith Jane (*d* 1936), singer, *d* of late William White Miller, Portage la Prairie, Manitoba; *S* grandfather, 1951. *Educ:* Harrow; Balliol Coll., Oxford. BA 1939; MA 1945. Formerly Capt., The Buffs; served War of 1939–45 (prisoner-of-war, 1940). Entered service of former Great Western Railway Traffic Dept, 1947, later Operating Dept of the Western Region of British Rlys. Personal Asst to Chm. of British Transport Commission, 1957; Passenger Officer in SE Division of Southern Region, BR, 1961; Parly and Public Correspondent, BRB, 1967; Deputy to Curator of Historical Relics, BRB, 1968. *Heir:* none. *Address:* 61 Onslow Square, SW7 3LS. *Club:* Naval and Military.

See also Sir Lingard Goulding, Bt, Viscount Monckton of Brenchley.

COLYTON, 1st Baron, *cr* 1956; **Henry Lennox d'Aubigné Hopkinson,** PC 1952; CMG 1944; *b* 3 Jan. 1902; *e s* of late Sir Henry Lennox Hopkinson, KCVO; *m* 1st, 1927, Alice Labouisse (*d* 1953), *d* of Henry Lane Eno, Bar Harbor, Maine, USA; one *s*; 2nd, 1956, Mrs Barbara Addams, *d* of late Stephen Barb, New York. *Educ:* Eton Coll.; Trinity Coll., Cambridge (BA History and Modern Languages Tripos). Entered Diplomatic Service, 1924; 3rd Sec., Washington, 1924; 2nd Sec., Foreign Office, 1929; Stockholm, 1931; Asst Private Sec. to Sec. of State for Foreign Affairs, 1932; Cairo, 1934; 1st Sec., 1936; Athens, 1938; War Cabinet Secretariat, 1939; Private Sec. to Permanent Under-Sec. for Foreign Affairs, 1940; Counsellor and Political Advr to Minister of State in the Middle East, 1941; Minister Plenipotentiary, Lisbon, 1943; Dep. Brit. High Comr in Italy, and Vice-Pres., Allied Control Commn, 1944–46. Resigned from Foreign Service to enter politics, 1946; Head of Conservative Parly Secretariat and Jt Dir, Conservative Research Dept, 1946–50; MP (C) Taunton Div. of Somerset, 1950–56; Sec. for Overseas Trade, 1951–52; Minister of State for Colonial Affairs, 1952–Dec. 1955; Mem., Consultative Assembly, Council of Europe, 1950–52; Delegate, General Assembly, United Nations, 1952–55; Chairman: Anglo-Egyptian Resettlement Board, 1957–60; Joint East and Central African Board, 1960–65; Tanganyika Concessions Ltd, 1965–72. Royal Humane Society's Award for saving life from drowning, 1919. OStJ 1959. Grand Cross, Order of Prince Henry the Navigator (Portugal), 1972; Dato, Order of the Stia Negara (Brunei), 1972; Grand Star, Order Paduka Stia Negara (Brunei), 1978; Commander, Order of the Zaire (Congo) 1971. *Heir:* *g s* Alisdair John Munro Hopkinson [*b* 7 May 1958; *m* 1980, Philippa J., *yr d* of Peter J. Bell; two *s* one *d*]. *Address:* Le Formentor, avenue Princesse Grace, Monte Carlo, Monaco. *T:* 309296. *Clubs:* Buck's, White's, Beefsteak.

COMBER, Ven. Anthony James; Archdeacon of Leeds, 1982–92, now Archdeacon Emeritus; *b* 20 April 1927; *s* of late Norman Mederson Comber and Nellie Comber. *Educ:* Leeds Grammar School; Leeds Univ. (MSc Mining); St Chad's Coll., Durham (DipTh); Munich Univ. Colliery underground official, 1951–53. Vicar: Oulton, 1960–69; Hunslet, 1969–77; Rector of Farnley, 1977–82. *Publication:* (contrib.) Today's Church and Today's World, 1977. *Recreations:* politics; walking in Bavaria. *Address:* 25 Chelwood Drive, Bradford BD15 7YD. *T:* Bradford (01274) 818232.

COMBERMERE, 5th Viscount, *cr* 1826; **Michael Wellington Stapleton-Cotton;** Bt 1677; Baron Combermere, 1814; Lecturer in Biblical and Religious Studies, University of London, Department of Extra-Mural Studies, 1972–94; Senior Lecturer, Centre for Extra-Mural Studies, Birkbeck College, 1988–94; *b* 8 Aug. 1929; *s* of 4th Viscount Combermere and Constance Marie Katherine (*d* 1968), *d* of Lt-Col Sir Francis Dudley W. Drummond, KBE; *S* father, 1969; *m* 1961, Pamela Elizabeth, *d* of Rev. R. G. Coulson; one *s* two *d*. *Educ:* Eton; King's Coll., Univ. of London. Palestine Police, 1947–48; Royal Canadian Mounted Police, 1948–50; Short-service commn as gen. duties Pilot, RAF, 1950–58, retd as Flt-Lt; Sales Rep., Teleflex Products Ltd, 1959–62; read Theology, KCL, 1962–67 (BD, MTh). Chm., World Congress of Faiths, 1983–88. *Heir:* *s* Hon. Thomas Robert Wellington Stapleton-Cotton, *b* 30 Aug. 1969. *Address:* Vanners, Bucklebury, Reading, Berks RG7 6RU. *T:* Woolhampton (01734) 713336. *Club:* Royal Automobile.

COMFORT, Alexander, PhD, DSc; physician; poet and novelist; Adjunct Professor, Neuropsychiatric Institute, University of California at Los Angeles, since 1980; Consultant, Ventura County Hospital (Medical Education), since 1981; *b* 10 Feb. 1920; *s* of late Alexander Charles and Daisy Elizabeth Comfort; *m* 1st, 1943, Ruth Muriel Harris (marr. diss. 1973); one *s*; 2nd, 1973, Jane Tristram Henderson (*d* 1991). *Educ:* Highgate Sch.; Trinity Coll., Cambridge (Robert Styring Scholar Classics, and Senior Scholar, Nat. Sciences); London Hospital (Scholar). 1st Cl. Nat. Sc. Tripos, Part I, 1940; 2nd Cl. Nat. Sc. Tripos, 1st Div. (Pathology), 1941; MRCS, LRCP 1944; MB, BCh Cantab 1944; MA Cantab 1945; DCH London 1945; PhD London 1949 (Biochemistry); DSc London 1963 (Gerontology). Refused military service in war of 1939–45. Lectr in Physiology, London Hospital Medical Coll., 1948–51; Hon. Research Associate, Dept of Zoology, 1951–73, and Dir of Research, Gerontology, 1966–73, UCL; Clin. Lectr, Dept Psychiatry, Stanford Univ., 1974–83; Prof., Dept of Pathol., Univ. of Calif Sch. of Med., Irvine, 1976–78; Consultant psychiatrist, Brentwood VA Hospital, LA, 1978–81. Pres., Brit. Soc. for Research on Ageing, 1967; Member: RSocMed.; Amer. Psychiatric Assoc. *Publications:* *fiction:* No Such Liberty, 1941; The Almond Tree, 1943; The Powerhouse, 1944; Letters from an Outpost (stories), 1947; On this side Nothing, 1948; A Giant's Strength, 1952; Come Out to Play, 1961; Tetrarch (trilogy), 1980; Imperial Patient, 1987; The Philosophers, 1989; *poetry:* France and Other Poems, 1942; A Wreath for the Living, 1943; Elegies, 1944; The Song of Lazarus (USA), 1945; The Signal to Engage, 1947; And All but He Departed, 1951; Haste to the Wedding, 1961; Poems, 1979; Mikrokosmos, 1994; *plays:* Into Egypt, 1942; Cities of the Plain (melodrama), 1943; Gengulphus, 1948; *songs:* Are You Sitting Comfortably?, 1962; *translation:* The Koka Shastra, 1964; *non-fiction:* The Silver River (travel), 1937; Art and Social Responsibility (essays), 1947; First Year Physiological Technique (textbook), 1948; The Novel and Our Time (criticism), 1948; Barbarism and Sexual Freedom (essays), 1948; Sexual Behaviour in Society (social psychology), 1950; The Pattern of the Future (broadcast lectures), 1950; Authority and Delinquency in the Modern State (social psychology), 1950; The Biology of Senescence (textbook), 1956, 2nd edn 1964, 3rd edn 1978; Darwin and the Naked Lady (essays), 1961; Sex and Society (social psychology), 1963; Ageing, the Biology of Senescence (textbook), 1964; The Process of Ageing (science), 1965; Nature and Human Nature (science), 1966; The Anxiety Makers (medical history), 1967; The Joy of Sex (counselling), 1973; More Joy (counselling), 1974; A Good Age, 1976; (ed) Sexual Consequences of Disability, 1978; I and That: notes on the Biology of Religion, 1979; (with Jane T. Comfort) The Facts of Love, 1979; A practice of Geriatric Psychiatry, 1979; What is a Doctor? (essays), 1980; Reality and Empathy, 1983; (with Jane T. Comfort) What about Alcohol? (textbook), 1983; The New Joy of Sex, 1991; Writings against Power and Death (essays), 1993. *Address:* 2 Fitzwarren House, Hornsey Lane, N6 5LX.

COMFORT, Anthony Francis; HM Diplomatic Service, retired; *b* Plymouth, 12 Oct. 1920; *s* of Francis Harold Comfort and Elsie Grace (*née* Martin); *m* 1948, Joy Margaret Midson; two *s* one *d. Educ:* Bristol Grammar Sch.; Oriel Coll., Oxford. Entered Foreign Service, 1947; 2nd Sec. (Commercial), Athens, 1948–51; Consul, Alexandria, 1951–53; 1st Sec. (Commercial), Amman, 1953–54; Foreign Office, 1954–57; seconded to Colonial Office, 1957–59; 1st Sec. (Commercial), Belgrade, 1959–60; 1st Sec. and Consul, Reykjavik, 1961–65; Inspector of Diplomatic Establishments, 1965–68, retired 1969. *Recreations:* walking, gardening, looking at churches. *Address:* Nymet Cottage, Trowbridge Road, Bradford on Avon, Wilts BA15 1EE. *T:* Bradford-on-Avon (01225) 866046.

COMINS, David; Rector, Glasgow Academy, since 1994; *b* 1 March 1948; *s* of Jack Comins and Marjorie Mabel (*née* Rowbotham); *m* 1972, Christine Anne Speak; one *s* two *d. Educ:* Scarborough Boys' High Sch.; Downing Coll., Cambridge (BA, MA, PGCE). Assistant Mathematics Teacher: Mill Hill Sch., 1971–75; Strathallan Sch., Perthshire, 1975–76; Glenalmond College, Perthshire: Asst Maths Teacher, 1976–80; Head of Maths, 1980–85; Dir of Studies, 1985–89; Dep. Head, Queen's Coll., Taunton, 1989–94. Churchill Fellow, 1981. *Recreations:* mountaineering, ballet, music, crosswords. *Address:* 11 Kirklee Terrace, Glasgow G12 0TH. *T:* 0141–357 1776. *Club:* Alpine.

COMMAGER, Henry Steele, MA Oxon; MA Cantab; Professor of American History, 1956–72, Simpson Lecturer, 1972–92, Amherst College; Professor of History, Columbia University, 1938–56; Hon. Professor, University of Santiago de Chile; *b* 25 Oct. 1902; *s* of James W. Commager and Anna Elizabeth Dan; *m* 1st, 1928, Evan Carroll; one *s* two *d*; 2nd, 1979, Mary Powlesland. *Educ:* Univ. of Chicago; Univ. of Copenhagen. AB, Univ. of Chicago, 1923; MA, 1924; PhD, 1928; Scholar Amer-Scand. Foundation, 1924–25; taught History, New York Univ., 1926–29; Prof. of History, 1929–38. Lectr on American History, Cambridge Univ., 1942–43; Hon. Fellow, Peterhouse; Pitt Prof. of Amer. Hist., Cambridge Univ., 1947–48; Lectr, Salzburg Seminar in Amer. Studies, 1951; Harold Vyvyan Harmsworth Prof. of American History, Oxford Univ., 1952; Gotesman Lectr, Upsala Univ., 1953; Special State Dept lectr to German Univs, 1954; Zuskind Prof., Brandeis Univ., 1954–55; Prof., Univ. of Copenhagen, 1956; Visiting Prof., Univ. of Aix-Provence, summer 1957; Lectr, Univ. of Jerusalem, summer 1958; Commonwealth Lectr, Univ. of London, 1964; Harris Lectr, Northwestern Univ., 1964; Visiting Prof., Harvard, Chicago, Calif, City Univ. NY, Nebraska, etc. Editor-in-Chief, The Rise of the American Nation, 50 vols; Consultant, Office War Information in Britain and USA; Mem. US Army War Hist. Commn; Mem. Historians Commn on Air Power; special citation US Army; Consultant US Army attached to SHAEF, 1945. Trustee; American Scandinavian Foundation; American Friends of Cambridge Univ. Member: Mass Historical Soc.; American Antiquarian Soc.; Colonial Soc. of Mass; Amer. Acad. of Arts and Letters (Gold Medal for History, 1972). Hon degrees: EdD Rhode I; LittD: Washington, Ohio Wesleyan, Pittsburgh, Marietta, Hampshire Coll., 1970; Adelphi Coll., 1974; NY State, 1985; Rutgers, 1988; DLitt: Cambridge, Franklin-Marshall, W Virginia, Michigan State; LHD: Brandeis, Puget Sound, Hartford, Alfred; LLD: Merrimack, Carleton; Dickinson Coll., 1967; Franklin Pierce Coll., 1968; Columbia Univ., 1969; Ohio State, 1970; Wilson Coll., 1970; W. C. Post Coll., 1974; Alassa Univ., 1974; DHL: Maryville Coll., 1970; Univ. of Mass, 1972. Pepper Medal for contrib. to social democracy, 1984; Jefferson Medal, Council for Advancement and Support of Educn, 1987; Gold Medal for Arts, Brandeis Univ., 1988. Knight of Order of Dannebrog (Denmark), 1957 (1st cl.). *Publications:* Theodore Parker, 1936; Growth of the American Republic, 1930, 2 vols 1939; sub-ed (with S. E. Morison) Documents of American History, 1934, 9th edn 1974; Heritage of America (with A. Nevins), 1939; America: Story of a Free People (with A. Nevins), 1943, new edn 1966; Majority Rule and Minority Rights, 1944; Story of the Second World War, 1945; ed Tocqueville, Democracy in America, 1947; ed America in Perspective, 1947; ed The St Nicholas Anthology, 1947; The American Mind, 1950; The Blue and the Gray, 2 vols 1950; Living Ideas in America, 1951; Robert E. Lee, 1951; Freedom, Loyalty, Dissent, 1954 (special award, Hillman Foundation); Europe and America since 1942 (with G. Bruun), 1954; Joseph Story, 1956; The Spirit of Seventy-Six, 2 vols (with R. B. Morris); Crusaders for Freedom; History: Nature and Purpose, 1965; Freedom and Order, 1966; Search for a Usable Past, 1967; Was America a Mistake?, 1968; The Commonwealth of Learning, 1968; The American Character, 1970; The Use and Abuse of History, 1972; Britain Through American Eyes, 1974; The Defeat of America, 1974; Essays on the Enlightenment, 1974; The Empire of Reason, 1978; Commager on Tocqueville, 1992; edited: Atlas of American Civil War; Winston Churchill, History of the English Speaking Peoples; Why the Confederacy Lost the Civil War; Major Documents of the Civil War; Theodore Parker, an Anthology; Immigration in American History; Lester Ward and the Welfare State; The Struggle for Racial Equality; Joseph Story, Selected Writings and Judicial Opinions; Winston Churchill, Marlborough, 1968; American Destiny, 12 vols. *Recreation:* music. *Address:* PO Box 2187, Amherst, MA 01004–2187, USA. *Clubs:* Lansdowne (London); Century (New York); St Botolph (Boston); (former Pres.) PEN (American Centre).

COMPSTON, Alastair; *see* Compston, D. A. S.

COMPSTON, Christopher Dean, MA; **His Honour Judge Compston;** a Circuit Judge, since 1986; *b* 5 May 1940; *s* of Vice Adm. Sir Peter Maxwell Compston, *qv*; *m* 1st, 1968, Bronwen Henniker Gotley (marr. diss. 1982); one *s* one *d* (and one *s* decd); 2nd, 1983, Caroline Philippa, *d* of Paul Odgers, *qv*; two *s* one *d. Educ:* Epsom Coll. (Prae Sum.); Magdalen Coll., Oxford (MA). Called to the Bar, Middle Temple, 1965; a Recorder, 1982–86. Mem. Senate, Inns of Court, 1983–86. *Publication:* Recovery from Divorce: a practical guide, 1993; (contrib.) Relational Justice, 1994. *Recreation:* the arts. *Address:* c/o Royal Courts of Justice, Strand, WC2A 2LL.

COMPSTON, Prof. (David) Alastair (Standish), FRCP; Professor of Neurology, University of Cambridge, since 1989; Fellow of Jesus College, Cambridge, since 1990; *b* 23 Jan. 1948; *s* of late Nigel Dean Compston and of Diana Mary Compston (*née* Standish); *m* 1973, Juliet Elizabeth, *d* of Sir Denys Lionel Page, FBA; one *d. Educ:* Rugby Sch.; Middlesex Hospital Med. Sch., London Univ. (MB BS (Hons); PhD). Jun. Hosp. appts, Nat. Hosp. for Nervous Diseases, 1972–82; Cons. Neurologist, University Hosp. of Wales, 1982–87; Prof. of Neurology, Univ. of Wales Coll. of Medicine, 1987–88. *Publications:* contribs to human and experimental demyelinating diseases, in learned jls. *Recreation:* being outside. *Address:* Pembroke House, Mill Lane, Linton, Cambridge CB1 6JY. *T:* Cambridge (01223) 893414.

COMPSTON, Vice-Adm. Sir Peter (Maxwell), KCB 1970 (CB 1967); *b* 12 Sept. 1915; *s* of Dr G. D. Compston; *m* 1st, 1939, Valerie Bocquet (marr. diss.); one *s* one *d*; 2nd, 1953, Angela Brickwood (*d* 1994). *Educ:* Epsom Coll. Royal Navy, 1937; specialised in flying duties. Served 1939–45, HMS Ark Royal, Anson, Vengeance; HMCS Warrior, 1946; HMS Theseus, 1948–50 (despatches); Directorate of RN Staff Coll., 1951–53; Capt. 1955; in comd HMS Orwell and Capt. 'D' Plymouth, 1955–57; Imperial Defence Coll., 1958; Naval Attaché, Paris, 1960–62; in comd HMS Victorious, 1962–64; Rear-Adm., Jan. 1965; Chief of British Naval Staff and Naval Attaché, Washington, 1965–67; Flag Officer Flotillas, Western Fleet, 1967–68; Dep. Supreme Allied Comdr, Atlantic, 1968–70, retired. Life Vice Pres., RNLI. *Recreations:* theatre, country life. *Address:* 10 Berehurst, Borovere Lane, Alton, Hants GU34 1PA. *Club:* Army and Navy.
See also C. D. Compston.

COMPSTON, Prof. William, PhD; FRS 1987; FAA; Professor in Isotope Geochemistry, Research School of Earth Sciences, Australian National University, since 1987; *b* 19 Feb. 1931; *s* of late J. A. Compston; *m* 1952, Elizabeth Blair; three *s* one *d. Educ:* Christian Brothers' Coll., Fremantle; Univ. of WA (BSc (Hons); PhD). Res. Fellow, CIT, 1956–58; Res. Fellow, Dept of Terrestrial Magnetism, Carnegie Inst. of Washington, 1958; Lectr, Univ. of WA, 1959–60; Fellow, then Sen. Fellow, 1961–74, Professorial Fellow, 1974–87, ANU. *Address:* Research School of Earth Sciences, Australian National University, Canberra, ACT 0200, Australia.

COMPTON, family name of **Marquess of Northampton.**

COMPTON, Earl; Daniel Bingham Compton; *b* 16 Jan. 1973; *s* and *heir* of Marquess of Northampton, *qv*. *Address:* Compton Wynyates, Tysoe, Warwicks CV35 0UD.

COMPTON, Denis Charles Scott, CBE 1958; professional cricketer, retired 1957; Sunday Express Cricket Correspondent, since 1950; BBC Television Cricket Commentator, since 1958; *b* 23 May 1918; *m* 1st; one *s*; 2nd; two *s*; 3rd, 1975, Christine Franklin Tobias; two *d. Educ:* Bell Lane Sch., Hendon. First played for Middlesex, 1936. First played for England *v* New Zealand, 1937; *v* Australia, 1938; *v* West Indies, 1939; *v* India, 1946; *v* S Africa, 1947. Played in 78 Test matches; made 123 centuries in first-class cricket. Association football: mem. of Arsenal XI; England XI, 1943; Editor, Denis Compton's Annual, 1950–57. *Publications:* Playing for England, 1948; Testing Time for England, 1948; In Sun and Shadow, 1952; End of an Innings, 1958, repr. 1988; Denis Compton's Test Diary, 1964; (jtly) Cricket and All That, 1978. *Recreation:* golf. *Address:* c/o Sunday Express, Ludgate House, 245 Blackfriars Road, SE1 9UX. *Clubs:* MCC, Middlesex CC (Pres., 1990–91); Wanderers (Johannesburg).

COMPTON, Rt. Hon. John George Melvin, PC 1983; Prime Minister of St Lucia, since 1982, and Minister for Finance, Planning and Development; *b* 1926; *m*; five *c. Educ:* London School of Economics. Called to the Bar, Gray's Inn; practice in St Lucia, 1951. Indep. Mem., Legislative Council, 1954; joined Labour Party, 1954; Dep. Leader, 1957–61; resigned, and formed Nat. Labour Movement, 1961 (later United Workers' Party; Leader, 1964); Chief Minister of St Lucia, 1964–67, Premier, 1967–79, Prime Minister, Feb.-July 1979, 1982–. *Address:* Office of the Prime Minister, Castries, St Lucia.

COMPTON, Michael Graeme, CBE 1987; Keeper of Museum Services, Tate Gallery, 1970–87, retired; *b* 29 Sept. 1927; *s* of Joseph Nield Compton, OBE, and Dorothy Margaret Townsend Compton; *m* 1952, Susan Paschal Benn; two *d. Educ:* Courtauld Institute, London (BA Hons History of Art). Asst to Director, Leeds City Art Gallery and Templenewsam, 1954–57; Keeper of Foreign Schools, Walker Art Gallery, Liverpool, 1957–59; Dir, Ferens Art Gall., Hull, 1960–65; Asst Keeper, Modern Collection, Tate Gall., 1965–70. Frederick R. Weisman Art Foundn Award, 1991. *Publications:* Optical and Kinetic Art, 1967; Pop Art, 1970; (jtly) Catalogue of Foreign Schools, Walker Art Gallery, 1963; Marcel Broodthaers, 1989; articles in art jls, exhibn catalogues. *Address:* Michaelmas Lodge, Rockfield Road, Oxted, Surrey RH8 0HB.

COMPTON, Robert Edward John; DL; Chairman: Time-Life International Ltd, 1979–90 (Chief Executive Officer, 1985–88); Time SARL, 1985–90; *b* 11 July 1922; *yr s* of late Major Edward Robert Francis Compton, JP, DL, and Sylvia Farquharson of Invercauld; *m* 1951, Ursula Jane Kenyon-Slaney; two *s. Educ:* Eton; Magdalen Coll., Oxford, 1940–41. Served War, Coldstream Guards, 1941–46 (4 medals, wounded); Mil. Asst to British Ambassador, Vienna (temp. Major), 1946. Studied fruit growing and horticulture (Diploma), 1946–48; with W. S. Crawford Ltd, Advertising Agency, 1951–54; Sen. Acct Exec., Crawfords Internat., 1954; joined Time International, 1954; advertising sales, 1954–58, UK Advtsg Dir, 1958–62; also Dir, Time-Life Internat. Ltd, 1958–79; New Projects Dir, Time-Life Internat. Europe, 1962–65; Public Affairs Dir, Europe, Time-Life Internat. Ltd, 1965. Chairman: Newby Hall Estate Co., 1964–69; CXL UK Ltd, 1971–73; Pres., Highline Finances Services, SA, and Dir, Highline Leasing Ltd, 1985–94; Bd Dir, Extel Corp., Chicago, 1973–80; Dir, Transtel Communications Ltd, Slough, 1974–83. National Trust: Vice-Chm., Yorks, 1970–85; Mem. Properties Cttee, 1970–85; Mem., Gardens Panel, 1970–85 and 1988–; Chm., Nat. Council for the Conservation of Plants and Gardens, 1988–94 (Pres., 1994–); Pres., Dales Centre, 1979–85; President: Ripon Tourist Assoc., 1977–; N of England Horticultural Soc., 1984–86; Northern Horticultural Soc., 1986–96; Yorks Agricl Soc., 1995–96. High Sheriff, 1978–79, DL 1981, N Yorks. VMH 1994. *Recreations:* gardening, shooting, golf, music. *Address:* Newby Hall, Ripon, Yorkshire HG4 5AE. *T:* Boroughbridge (01423) 322583; Flat 2, 17 Brompton Square, SW3 2AD. *Clubs:* White's; Swinley Forest (Ascot).
See also Captain A. A. C. Farquharson of Invercauld.

COMRIE, Rear-Adm. (Alexander) Peter, CB 1982; defence equipment consultant; Director, A. Comrie & Sons Ltd, since 1983; *b* 27 March 1924; *s* of Robert Duncan Comrie and Phyllis Dorothy Comrie; *m* 1945, Madeleine Irene (*née* Bullock) (*d* 1983); one *s* one *d. Educ:* Sutton Valence Sch., Kent; County Technical Coll., Wednesbury, Staffs, and in the Royal Navy. Joined Royal Navy, 1945; served in cruisers, frigates, minesweepers and RN air stations; RCDS 1973; Captain HMS Daedalus, 1974; Director of Weapons Coordination and Acceptance (Naval), 1975; Deputy Controller Aircraft, MoD, 1978–81; Dir-Gen. Aircraft (Navy), 1981–83, retired. Vice Pres., IEE, 1988–91 (Mem. Council, 1981–84); Member: IEE Electronics Divisional Bd, 1976–77; IEE Qualifications Bd, 1981–88; Chairman: IEE International (formerly Overseas) Bd, 1988–91; Executive Gp Cttee 3, Engrg Council, 1986–94. FIEE 1975; FRAeS 1978; Eur Ing 1987. *Recreations:* sailing, swimming, DIY. *Clubs:* Commonwealth Trust; Hayling Island Sailing.

COMYN, Hon. Sir James, Kt 1978; Judge of the High Court of Justice, Queen's Bench Division, 1979–85 (Family Division, 1978–79), resigned due to ill-health, Sept. 1985; *b* Co. Dublin, 8 March 1921; *o s* of late James Comyn, QC, Dublin and late Mary Comyn; *m* 1967, Anne (solicitor), *d* of late Philip Chaundler, MC, solicitor, Biggleswade, and late Mrs Chaundler; one *s* one *d. Educ:* Oratory Sch.; New Coll., Oxford (MA). Ex-Pres. of Oxford Union. With Irish Times (briefly), BBC and various war-time orgns, 1938–44. Inner Temple, 1942; called to Irish Bar, 1947, Hong Kong Bar, 1969; QC 1961. Recorder of Andover, 1964–71; Comr of Assize, Western Circuit, 1971; Hon. (life) Recorder of Andover, 1972; a Recorder of the Crown Court, 1972–77. Master of the Bench, Inner Temple, 1968; Mem. and Chm., Bar Council, 1973–74. Chairman: Court Line Enquiry,

1972–73; Solihull Hosp. Enquiry, 1974. Mem., Parole Bd, 1982–84, Vice-Chm. 1983–84. A Governor of the Oratory Sch., 1964–90; President: Oratory Sch. Assoc. (Sch. and Prep. Sch.), 1983–90; Oratory Sch. Soc. (old boys), 1984–. Owner of the "Clareville" herd of pedigree Aberdeen-Angus. *Publications:* Their Friends at Court, 1973; Irish at Law: a selection of famous and unusual cases, 1981; Lost Causes, 1982; Summing It Up (memoirs), 1991; Watching Brief (memoirs), 1993; Leave to Appeal (memoirs), 1995; various vols of light verse and books and articles on legal subjects. *Recreations:* cattle-breeding, farming, golf, planting trees. *Address:* Belvin, Tara, Co. Meath, Ireland. *Club:* Royal Dublin Society.

COMYNS, Jacqueline Roberta; a Metropolitan Stipendiary Magistrate, since 1982; a Recorder, since 1991; *b* 27 April 1943; *d* of late Jack and Belle Fisher; *m* 1963, Malcolm John Comyns, medical practitioner; one *s*. *Educ:* Hendon County Grammar Sch.; London Sch. of Econs and Pol. Science (LLB Hons 1964). Called to the Bar, Inner Temple, 1969. Practised on South Eastern Circuit. *Recreations:* theatre, travel, swimming, tennis. *Address:* Tower Bridge Magistrates' Court, Tooley Street, SE1 2JY. *T:* 0171–407 4232.

CONAN DOYLE, Air Comdt Dame Jean (Lena Annette), (Lady Bromet), DBE 1963 (OBE 1948); AE 1949; Director of the Women's Royal Air Force, 1963–66, retired; *b* 21 Dec. 1912; *d* of late Sir Arthur Conan Doyle and Lady Conan Doyle (*née* Jean Leckie); *m* 1965, Air Vice-Marshal Sir Geoffrey Bromet, KBE, CB, DSO, DL (*d* 1983). *Educ:* Granville House, Eastbourne. Joined No 46 (Co. of Sussex) ATS, RAF Company, Sept. 1938; commnd in WAAF, 1940; served in UK, 1939–45; commnd in RAF, 1949; Comd WRAF Admin Officer: BAFO, Germany, 1947–50; HQ Tech. Trng Comd, 1950–52 and 1962–63; Dep. Dir, 1952–54 and 1960–62; OC, RAF Hawkinge, 1956–59; Inspector of the WRAF, 1954–56 and 1959–60. Hon. ADC to the Queen, 1963–66. A Governor, Royal Star and Garter Home, 1968–82; Mem. Council, Officers' Pensions Soc., 1970–75, a Vice-Pres. 1981–88; Mem. Cttee, Not Forgotten Assoc., 1975–91, a Pres. 1981–91. Holder of USA copyright on her father's published works. *Recreation:* attempting to paint. *Address:* Flat 6, 72 Cadogan Square, SW1X 0EA. *Clubs:* Naval and Military, Royal Air Force.

CONANT, Sir John (Ernest Michael), 2nd Bt *cr* 1954; farmer and landowner, since 1949; *b* 24 April 1923; *s* of Sir Roger Conant, 1st Bt, CVO, and Daphne, Lady Conant, *d* of A. E. Learoyd; *S* father, 1973; *m* 1st, 1950, Periwinkle Elizabeth (*d* 1985), *d* of late Dudley Thorp, Kimbolton, Hunts; two *s* two *d* (and one *s* decd); 2nd, 1992, Mrs Clare Attwater, *yr d* of W. E. Madden. *Educ:* Eton; Corpus Christi Coll., Cambridge (BA Agric). Served in Grenadier Guards, 1942–45; at CCC Cambridge, 1946–49. Farming in Rutland, 1950–; High Sheriff of Rutland, 1960. *Recreations:* fishing, shooting, tennis. *Heir: s* Simon Edward Christopher Conant, *b* 13 Oct. 1958. *Address:* Periwinkle Cottage, Lyndon, Oakham, Rutland LE15 8TU. *T:* Manton (01572) 737275.

CONCANNON, Rt. Hon. John Dennis, (Rt. Hon. Don Concannon), PC 1978; *b* 16 May 1930; *m* 1953, Iris May Wilson; two *s* two *d*. *Educ:* Rossington Sec. Sch. Coldstream Guards, 1947–53; Mem. Nat. Union of Mineworkers, 1953–66; Branch Official, 1960–65. Mem., Mansfield Town Council, 1962–66. MP (Lab) Mansfield, 1966–87. Asst Govt Whip, 1968–70; Opposition Whip, 1970–74; Vice-Chamberlain, HM Household, 1974; Parly Under-Sec. of State, NI Office, 1974–76; Minister of State, NI Office, 1976–79; Opposition Spokesman for Defence, 1979–80, for NI, 1980–83. Mem., Commonwealth War Graves Commn, 1986–. *Recreations:* cricket, basket-ball. *Address:* 69 Skegby Lane, Mansfield, Notts NG19 6QS. *T:* Mansfield (01623) 27235.

CONDON, Denis David, OBE 1964; retired; Senior Representative at Lloyd's of London for Neilson McCarthy, Consultants, 1968–75; *b* 23 Oct. 1910; *s* of Capt. D. Condon and Mrs A. E. Condon; *m* 1933, Mary Marson; one *d*. *Educ:* Paston Grammar Sch., North Walsham, Norfolk. Journalist until 1939. War Service with Royal Artillery, UK and Burma (Major). Joined India Office, 1946; CRO, 1947; served India, Ceylon, Australia, Nigeria; Head of News Dept, CO, 1967–68. *Recreations:* fishing, bird-watching, gardening. *Address:* 3 Market Close, Brushford, Dulverton, Somerset TA22 9AG. *T:* Dulverton (01398) 23309. *Clubs:* Gymkhana (Delhi); Australasian Pioneers (Sydney).

CONDON, Sir Paul (Leslie), Kt 1994; QPM 1989; Commissioner, Metropolitan Police, since 1993; *m*; two *s* one *d*. *Educ:* St Peter's Coll., Oxford (Bramshill Scholar; MA). Joined Metropolitan Police, 1967; Inspector, 1975–78; Chief Inspector, 1978–81; Superintendent, Bethnal Green, 1981–82; Staff Officer to Comr as Superintendent, then as Chief Superintendent, 1982–84; Asst Chief Constable, Kent Constabulary, 1984–87; Dep. Asst Comr, 1987–88, Asst Comr, 1988–89, Metropolitan Police; Chief Constable, Kent Constabulary, 1989–92. CIMgt 1991; FRSA 1992. *Address:* New Scotland Yard, Broadway, SW1H 0BG.

CONGDON, David Leonard; MP (C) Croydon North East, since 1992; *b* 16 Oct. 1949; *s* of Archibald George Congdon and late Marjorie Congdon; *m* 1972, Teresa Winifred Hill; one *d*. *Educ:* Alleyn's Sch.; Thames Polytechnic (BSc Hons Econ.). Graduate Systems Analyst, ICL, 1970; Philips Electronics: Systems Analyst, 1973–85; Computer Consultant, 1985–92. London Borough of Croydon: Councillor, 1976–92; Vice-Chm., Educn Cttee, 1979–83; Chm., Social Services, 1983–86, 1990–91; Dep. Leader, 1986–92; Chm., Finance Sub-Cttee. Vice-Chm., local Cons. Assocs, 1979–82. Mem., Select Cttee on Health, 1992–. Governor, Croydon Coll., 1979–92. *Recreations:* tennis, badminton, reading political biographies, listening to music; lapsed Fulham fan. *Address:* House of Commons, SW1A 0AA. *T:* 0171–219 4188.

CONGDON, Timothy George; Managing Director, Lombard Street Research Ltd, since 1989; *b* 28 April 1951; *s* of D. G. Congdon and Olive Emma Congdon (*née* Good); *m* 1988, Dorianne Preston-Lowe; one *d*. *Educ:* Univ. of Oxford (BA 1st cl. Hons Mod. Hist. and Econs). MSI. On economics staff, The Times, 1973–76; Chief Economist, L. Messel & Co., 1976–86 (Partner, 1980–86); Chief London Economist, Shearson Lehman, 1986–88. Non-exec. Chm., SBW Insurance Research, 1994–; Econ. Advr, Gerrard & Nat., 1989–. Mem., Treasury Panel of Independent Forecasters, 1993–. Hon. Prof., Cardiff Business Sch., 1990–. FRSA 1991. *Publications:* Monetary Control in Britain, 1982; The Debt Threat, 1988; Reflections on Monetarism, 1992. *Recreations:* reading, walking, chess, opera. *Address:* Lombard Street Research Ltd, 33 Lombard Street, EC3V 9BQ. *T:* 0171–623 9981. *Clubs:* Carlton, Royal Automobile.

CONGLETON, 8th Baron *cr* 1841; **Christopher Patrick Parnell;** Bt 1766; *b* 11 March 1930; 3rd *s* of 6th Baron Congleton (*d* 1932) and Hon. Edith Mary Palmer Howard (MBE 1941) (she *m* 2nd, 1946, Flight Lieut A. E. R. Aldridge, who died 1950), *d* of late R. J. B. Howard and late Lady Strathcona and Mount Royal; *S* brother, 1967; *m* 1955, Anna Hedvig, *d* of G. A. Sommerfelt, Oslo, Norway; two *s* three *d*. *Educ:* Eton; New Coll., Oxford (MA). Mem., Salisbury and Wilton RDC, 1964–74; Vice-President: RDCA, 1973–74; Assoc. of District Councils, 1974–79. Chm., Salisbury and S Wilts Museum, 1972–77; Mem., Adv. Bd for Redundant Churches, 1981–87. President: Nat. Ski Fedn of GB, 1976–81; Ski Club of GB, 1991–; Mem., Eligibility Cttee, Internat. Ski Fedn, 1976–88. Trustee: Sandroyd Sch. Trust, 1975–92 (Chm., 1980–84); Wessex Med. Trust, 1984–90; Southampton Univ. Develt Trust, 1986–. Hon. LLD Southampton, 1990. *Recreations:* music, ski-ing, fishing. *Heir: s* Hon. John Patrick Christian Parnell [*b* 17 March 1959; *m* 1985, Marjorie-Anne, *o d* of John Hobdell, Cobham, Surrey; two *s* one *d*]. *Address:* Ebbesbourne Wake, Salisbury, Wilts SP5 5JW.

CONGO, Sonia, (Mrs C. W. Congo); *see* Lawson, S.

CONGREVE, Ambrose, CBE 1965; *b* London, 4 April 1907; *s* of Major John Congreve, DL, JP, and Helena Blanche Irene Ponsonby, *d* of 8th Earl of Bessborough; *m* 1935, Marjorie (*d* 1995), *d* of Dr Arthur Graham Glasgow, London, and Richmond, Virginia, and Margaret, *d* of John P. Branch, President of Virginia's Merchants National Bank. *Educ:* Eton; Trinity Coll., Cambridge. Employed by Unilever Ltd, in England and China, 1927–36; joined Humphreys & Glasgow Ltd, as Director, 1936; responsible for the company, 1939–83, in succession to Dr Glasgow who founded the firm in 1892. Served War of 1939–45: Air Intelligence for Plans and Bomber Command, then Min. of Supply. Hon. Fellow IChemE 1967. Veitch Meml Medal, RHS, 1987. *Recreation:* collection and large-scale outdoor cultivation in Ireland of plant species and hybrids from all over the world. *Address:* Mount Congreve, Waterford, Ireland. *T:* Waterford (51) 84103, *Fax:* (51) 84576; Warwick House, Stable Yard, St James's, SW1A 1BD. *T:* 0171–839 3301. *Club:* Beefsteak.

CONINGSBY, Thomas Arthur Charles; QC 1986; **His Honour Judge Coningsby;** a Circuit Judge, since 1992; Chancellor of the Diocese of York, since 1977, of the Diocese of Peterborough, since 1989; Vicar General of the Province of York, since 1980; *b* 21 April 1933; *s* of Francis Charles and Eilleen Rowena Coningsby; *m* 1959, Elaine Mary Coningsby; two *s* three *d*. *Educ:* Epsom; Queens' Coll., Cambridge (MA). Called to the Bar, Gray's Inn, 1957; Mem., Inner Temple, 1988. A Recorder, 1986–92; Head of Chambers, 3 Dr Johnson's Building, Temple, 1988–92. Member: Lord Chancellor's Matrimonial Causes Rule Cttee, 1986–89; Gen. Council of the Bar, 1988–90; Supreme Court Procedure Cttee, 1988–92; Chm., Family Law Bar Assoc., 1988–90 (Sec., 1986–88). Member, General Synod, 1970– (Member: Legal Adv. Commn, 1975–; Fees Adv. Commn, 1979–92). Mem. Governing Body, SPCK, 1990–92. *Recreation:* lawn tennis. *Address:* Leyfields, Chipstead, Surrey CR5 3SG. *T:* Downland (01737) 553304. *Club:* Athenæum.

CONLAN, Bernard; engineer; *b* 24 Oct. 1923; *m*; one *d*. *Educ:* Manchester Primary and Secondary Schs. Mem., AEU, 1940–, Officer, 1943–87. City Councillor, Manchester, 1954–66. Joined Labour Party, 1942; contested (Lab) High Peak, 1959. MP (Lab) Gateshead East, 1964–87. A Vice-Chm., Parly Lab. Party Trade Union Gp, 1974–. Member: House of Commons Expenditure Cttee (since inception), 1971–79; Trade and Industry Select Cttee, 1983–86; Select Cttee on Defence, 1979–83. *Address:* 33 Beccles Road, Sale, Cheshire M33 3RP. *T:* 0161–973 3991.

CONN, Edward, CBE 1979; FRCVS; Technical Consultant, Norbrook Laboratories Ltd, Newry, Northern Ireland, 1983–90, retired; *b* 25 March 1918; *s* of late Edward and Elizabeth Conn; *m* 1st, 1943, Kathleen Victoria Sandford (*d* 1974); three *d*; 2nd, 1975, Lilian Frances Miley. *Educ:* Coleraine Academical Instn; Royal (Dick) Veterinary Sch., Edinburgh Univ. Qual. Vet. Surgeon, 1940; Diploma; MRCVS 1940; FRCVS 1984. Gen. practice, Coleraine, 1940–43; Chief Vet. Officer, Hampshire Cattle Breeders, 1943–47; Dept of Agriculture, NI, 1947–83, Chief Vet. Officer, 1958–83. Pres., COBA, 1991–92. Governor, Coleraine Academical Instn, 1972–. *Recreations:* golf, walking; watching all sports, particularly Rugby and athletics. *Address:* Ardeena, 23 The Brae, Groomsport, Co. Down, BT19 2JQ. *Clubs:* Clandeboye Golf; Bangor Rugby and Athletic (Pres., 1972–73).

CONNARTY, Michael; MP (Lab) Falkirk East, since 1992; *b* 3 Sept. 1947; *m* 1969, Margaret Doran; one *s* one *d*. *Educ:* St Patrick's High Sch., Coatbridge; Stirling and Glasgow Univs (Srudent Pres., Stirling Univ., 1970–71); Jordanhill Coll. of Educn (BA; DCE). Teacher of children with special needs, 1976–92. Exec. Mem., Central region, EIS, 1978–84 (Pres., 1982–83). Rector, Stirling Univ., 1983–84. Mem. (Lab) Stirling DC, 1977–90 (Leader of Council, 1980–90); Chm., Lab. Party Scottish Local Govt Cttee, 1988–90. Mem., Lab. Party Socttish Exec., 1981, 1983–92. Contested (Lab) Stirling, 1983, 1987. Sec., PLP Sci. and Technol. Cttee, 1992–; Chm., Economy Industry Engrg Cttee, Scottish PLP Gp, 1994–; Co-ordinator, PLP Scottish Task Force, Skills and Trng, Youths and Students, 1994–; Treas., All-Party Gp on Chemical Industry. JP 1977–90. *Address:* House of Commons, SW1A 0AA; 81 Erskine Hill, Polmont, Falkirk FK2 0UH.

CONNELL, Charles Percy; Puisne Judge, Kenya Colony, 1951–64, retired; *b* 1 Oct. 1902; *s* of late C. R. Connell, Barrister-at-Law and late K. Adlard; *m* 1946, Mary O'Rourke. *Educ:* Charterhouse; New Coll., Oxford (Hons, Jurisprudence). Called to Bar, Lincoln's Inn, 1927. Joined Kenya Judicial Service, 1938 (Resident Magistrate). Served War of 1939–45 (8th Army Clasp and war medals); commissioned King's African Rifles, 1941; British Military Administration (Legal and Judicial), Eritrea and Tripolitania, 1942–46. Acting Puisne Judge, Kenya, 1950, retired 1964. *Recreations:* tennis, cricket and trout fishing. *Address:* c/o Isle of Man Bank, Bowring Road, Ramsey, Isle of Man.

CONNELL, Most Rev. Desmond; *see* Dublin, Archbishop of, and Primate of Ireland, (RC).

CONNELL, George Edward, OC 1987; PhD; FCIC; FRSC; President, University of Toronto, 1984–90; *b* 20 June 1930; *m* 1955, Sheila Horan; two *s* two *d*. *Educ:* Univ. of Toronto (BA, PhD Biochemistry). FCIC 1971; FRSC 1975. Post-doctoral Fellow, Div. of Applied Biol., National Res. Council, Ottawa, Ont, 1955–56; Fellow, National Science Foundn (US), Dept of Biochem., New York University Coll. of Medicine, 1956–57; University of Toronto: Asst Prof. of Biochem., 1957–62; Associate Prof. of Biochem., 1962–65; Prof. and Chm. Dept of Biochem., 1965–70; Associate Dean, Faculty of Med., 1972–74; Vice-Pres., Res. and Planning, 1974–77; Pres. and Vice-Chancellor, Univ. of Western Ontario, 1977–84. Prin. Advr, Commn of Enquiry on Blood System of Canada, 1993–. Chairman: Exec. Cttee, Internat. Congress of Biochem., 1979; Nat. Round Table on the Envmt and Economy, 1991–95; Technical Cttee 207 (Envmtl Management), ISO, 1993–; Task Force on Funding and Delivery of Med. Care in Ontario, 1995–; Vice-Chairman: Envmtl Assessment Bd, Ontario, 1990–93; Sustainable Cities Foundn, 1993–; Protein Engrg Nat. Centre of Excellence, 1994–; Member: MRC of Canada, 1966–70; Ont Council of Health, 1978–84; Bd of Dirs and Nat. Exec. Cttee, Canadian Arthritis and Rheumatism Soc., 1965–75; Bd of Dirs, Nat. Inst. of Nutrition, 1984–91; Bd of Res. Inst., Toronto Hosp., 1994–; Bd of Dirs, Southam Inc., 1985–93; Council, Ont Univs, 1977–90 (Chm., 1981–83); Bd of Governors, Upper Canada Coll., 1982–90; Bd of Trustees, Royal Ont Mus., 1984–90. Hon. LLD: Trent, 1984; Univ. of Western Ont, 1985; McGill, 1987; Hon. DSc Toronto, 1993. *Publications:* scientific papers in jls incl. Canadian Jl of Biochem., Biochemical Jl (UK), and Jl of Immunol. *Recreations:* skiing, tennis, wilderness canoe trips. *Address:* 240 Walmer Road, Toronto, Ont M5R 3R7, Canada. *Clubs:* Queen's, Badminton and Racquet (Toronto).

CONNELL, Prof. John Jeffrey, CBE 1985; PhD; FRSE; FIFST; Director, Torry Research Station, Aberdeen (Ministry of Agriculture, Fisheries and Food), 1979–87 (Assistant Director, 1969–79); Emeritus Professor, Aberdeen University, 1987; *b* 2 July 1927; *s* of John Edward Connell and Margaret Connell; *m* 1950, Margaret Parsons; one *s* two *d* (and one *d* decd). *Educ:* Burnage High Sch.; Univ. of Manchester (BSc 1947); Univ. of Edinburgh (PhD 1950). FIFST 1970; FRSE 1984. Torry Research Station: Scientific Officer, 1950; Sen. Sci. Officer, 1955; Principal Sci. Officer, 1961; Dep. Chief Sci. Officer, 1979; Officer i/c Humber Lab., Hull (Sen. Principal Sci. Officer), 1968–69. Res. Associate, 1969–79 and Hon. Res. Lectr, 1979–83, Aberdeen Univ. Mem., Fisheries Res. and Develt Bd, 1979–84. *Publications:* Control of Fish Quality, 1975, 4th edn 1995 (Spanish edn 1978); Trends in Fish Utilisation, 1982; scientific and technical papers related to use of fish as food. *Recreations:* music, hill walking. *Address:* 61 Burnieboozle Crescent, Aberdeen AB1 8NR. *T:* Aberdeen (01224) 315852.

CONNELL, John MacFarlane; Chairman, The Distillers Company plc, 1983–86; *b* 29 Dec. 1924; *s* of late John Maclean Connell and late Mollie Isobel MacFarlane; *m* 1949, Jean Matheson Sutherland Mackay, *d* of late Major George Sutherland Mackay and late Christine Bourne; two *s*. *Educ:* Stowe; Christ Church, Oxford. Joined Tanqueray, Gordon & Co. Ltd, 1946, Export Dir 1954, Man. Dir 1962–70; Dir, Distillers Co. Ltd, 1965, Mem., Management Cttee, 1971–86; Chm., United Glass Holdings plc, 1979–83. Chm., Gin Rectifiers and Distillers Assoc., 1968–71. Pres., Royal Warrant Holders Assoc., 1975. *Recreations:* golf, shooting, fishing. *Clubs:* East India; Royal and Ancient (St Andrews).

CONNELL, John Morris, OBE 1991; Chairman, Noise Abatement Society, since 1964; *b* 13 Sept. 1911; *s* of late James and Florence Connell; *m* 1939, Gertrude, *d* of late Judge Johann Adler, Vienna; three *d*. *Educ:* BeckenhamTechnical Sch.; Goldsmiths' Coll. MInstM 1935; MIPR 1965. Wholesale meat salesman, Smithfield Market, 1930–39; dir, own meat business, 1939–56; RN, 1941–46; company directorships, 1956–. Founded Noise Abatement Soc., 1959, Hon. Sec., 1959–64; Co-Founder, and Hon. Treasurer, Instn of Environmental Scis, 1970–; Co-Founder, Internat. Assoc. Against Noise, Zürich, 1960. *Publications:* articles and letters in the press. *Recreations:* gardening, reading newspapers. *Address:* Chalkhurst, Upper Austin Lodge Road, Eynsford, Kent DA4 0HT. *T:* Dartford (01322) 862789.

CONNELL, Hon. Sir Michael (Bryan), Kt 1991; **Hon. Mr Justice Connell;** a Judge of the High Court of Justice, Family Division, since 1991; *b* 6 Aug. 1939; *s* of Lorraine Connell and of late Joan Connell; *m* 1965, Anne Joan Pulham; three *s* one *d*. *Educ:* Harrow; Brasenose Coll., Oxford (MA Jurisprudence). Called to the Bar, Inner Temple, 1962, Bencher, 1988; QC 1981; a Recorder, 1980–91. Governor, Harrow Sch., 1983–. Mem., Jockey Club, 1988–. *Recreations:* steeplechasing, cricket, foxhunting. *Address:* Royal Courts of Justice, Strand, WC2A 2LL. *Club:* Buck's.
See also S. A. O'Sullivan.

CONNELL, Dame Ninette; *see* de Valois, Dame Ninette.

CONNELL, Dr Philip Henry, CBE 1986; Emeritus Physician, The Bethlem Royal Hospital and The Maudsley Hospital, 1986 (Physician, 1963–86); *b* 6 July 1921; *s* of George Henry Connell and Evelyn Hilda Sykes; *m* 1st, 1948, Marjorie Helen Gilham; two *s*; 2nd, 1973, Cecily Mary Harper. *Educ:* St Paul's Sch.; St Bartholomew's Hosp., London. MD, BS, MRCS, FRCP, FRCPsych, DPM (academic). St Stephen's Hosp., Fulham Road, 1951–53; Registrar and Sen. Registrar, The Bethlem Royal Hosp. and the Maudsley Hosp., 1953–57; Cons. Psychiatrist, Newcastle Gen. Hosp. and Physician i/c Child Psychiatry Unit, Newcastle Gen. Hosp. in assoc. with King's Coll., Durham Univ., and Assoc. Phys., Royal Victoria Infirm., 1957–63. Extensive nat. and internat. work on drug addiction and dependence (incl. work for WHO, Council of Europe and CENTO), and on maladjusted and psychiatrically ill children and adolescents. Mem. numerous adv. cttees and working parties, including: Standing Mental Health Adv. Cttee, DHSS (formerly Min. of Health), 1966–72 (Vice Chm., 1967–72); Standing Adv. Cttee on Drug Dependence (Wayne Cttee), 1966–71 (Mem., Hallucinogens Sub-Cttees on Cannabis, 1967–68, and on LSD and Amphetamines, 1968–70); Consultant Adviser (Addiction) to DHSS, 1965–71 and 1981–86; Pres., Soc. for Study of Addiction, 1972–75; Vice Pres., Internat. Council on Alcohol and Addictions, 1982– (Chm., Scientific and Prof. Adv. Bd, 1971–79, Mem., Bd of Management, 1984–88); Chairman: Inst. for Study of Drug Dependence, 1975–90; Adv. Council on Misuse of Drugs, 1982–88; Sec. of State for Transport's Hon. Med. Adv. Panel on Driving, Alcohol, Drug and Substance Misuse, 1988–; Member: Council, RMPA, 1962–67; Cttee of Management, Inst. of Psychiatry, 1968–74; Trethowan Cttee on Role of Psychologists in Health Service, 1968–72; Standing Mental Health Adv. Cttee, DHSS, 1966–71; GMC, 1979–91 (Preliminary Screener for Health, 1982–84, 1989–91; Dep. Screener, 1984–89); Vice-Pres., RCPsych, 1979–81 (Mem. Council, 1971–81; Chm., Child and Adolescent Specialist Section, 1971–74; observer on Council as Coll. appointee to GMC, 1979–91). Dent Meml Lectr, KCL and Soc. for Study of Addiction, 1985. Member of Bd of Governors: Bethlem Royal and Maudsley Hosps, 1966–73; Mowden Hall Sch., 1976–82. Hon. FRCPsych 1992. Mem., editorial bds, various jls. *Publications:* Amphetamine Psychosis (monograph), 1958; (ed jtly) Cannabis and Man, 1975; over 90 chapters in books, papers in sci. jls and proc. sci. confs. *Recreations:* theatre, bridge. *Address:* 25 Oxford Road, Putney, SW15 2LG. *T:* 0181–788 1416; 21 Wimpole Street, W1M 7AD. *T:* 0171–636 2220. *Club:* Athenæum.

CONNELL-SMITH, Prof. Gordon Edward, PhD; FRHistS; Professor of Contemporary History, University of Hull, 1973–85; *b* 23 Nov. 1917; 2nd *s* of George Frederick Smith and Margaret Smith (*née* Woolerton); surname changed to Connell-Smith by deed-poll, 1942; *m* 1954, Wendy Ann (*d* 1987), *o d* of John Bertram and Kathleen Tomlinson; one *s* one *d*. *Educ:* Richmond County Sch., Surrey; University Coll. of SW of England, Exeter (BA); Birkbeck Coll., London (PhD). FRHistS 1959. Served War, RA and Staff, 1940–46 (Staff Major). Julian Corbett Prize, Inst. of Historical Res., 1949; University of Hull: Staff Tutor/Lectr in Adult Educn and History Depts, 1952–63; Sen. Lectr, 1963–69; Reader in Contemp. Internat. History, 1969–73. Mem., Cttee of Management, Univ. of London Inst. of Latin Amer. Studies, 1973–85. Chm., Latin American Newsletters, Ltd, London, 1969–72. *Publications:* Forerunners of Drake, 1954; Pattern of the Post-War World, 1957; The Inter-American System, 1966 (Spanish edn 1971); (co-author) The Relevance of History, 1972; The United States and Latin America, 1974 (Spanish edn 1977); The Future of History, 1975; Latin American Relations with the World 1826–1976, 1976; contrib. to Bull. Inst. of Historical Res., Contemp. Rev., Econ. History Rev., Eng. Historical Rev., History, Internat. Affairs, Jl of Latin Amer. Studies, World Today, etc. *Recreations:* travel, sport. *Address:* 7 Braids Walk, Kirk Ella, Hull HU10 7PA. *T:* Hull (01482) 652624.

CONNER, Rt. Rev. David John; *see* Lynn, Bishop Suffragan of.

CONNERY, Sean, (Thomas Connery); actor; *b* 25 Aug. 1930; *s* of Joseph and Euphamia Connery; *m* 1st, 1962, Diane Cilento (marr. diss. 1974); one *s*; 2nd, 1975, Micheline Roquebrune; two step *s* one step *d*. Served Royal Navy. Has appeared in films: No Road Back, 1956; Action of the Tiger, 1957; Another Time, Another Place, 1957; Hell Drivers, 1958; Tarzan's Greatest Adventure, 1959; Darby O'Gill and the Little People, 1959; On the Fiddle, 1961; The Longest Day, 1962; The Frightened City, 1962; Woman of Straw, 1964; The Hill, 1965; A Fine Madness, 1966; Shalako, 1968; The Molly Maguires, 1968; The Red Tent (1st Russian co-production), 1969; The Anderson Tapes, 1970; The Offence, 1973; Zardoz, 1973; Ransom, 1974; Murder on the Orient Express, 1974; The Wind and the Lion, 1975; The Man Who Would Be King, 1975; Robin and Marian, 1976; The First Great Train Robbery, 1978; Cuba, 1978; Meteor, 1979; Outland, 1981; The Man with the Deadly Lens, 1982; Wrong is Right, 1982; Five Days One Summer, 1982; Highlander, 1986; The Name of the Rose, 1987 (BAFTA Award for Best Actor, 1988); The Untouchables, 1987 (Best Supporting Actor, Academy Awards, 1988; Golden Globe Award); The Presidio, 1989; Indiana Jones and the Last Crusade, 1989; Family Business, 1990; The Hunt for Red October, 1990; The Russia House, 1991; Highlander II–The Quickening, 1991; Medicine Man, 1992; Rising Sun, 1993; A Good Man in Africa, 1994; First Knight, 1995; Just Cause, 1995; *as James Bond:* Dr No, 1963; From Russia With Love, 1964; Goldfinger, 1965; Thunderball, 1965; You Only Live Twice, 1967; Diamonds are Forever, 1971; Never Say Never Again, 1983. FRSAMD 1984. Freedom of City of Edinburgh, 1991. Hon. DLitt: Heriot-Watt, 1981; St Andrews, 1988. BAFTA Life Time Achievement Award, 1990; Man of Culture Award, 1990; Scot of the Year Award, BBC Scotland, 1991; American Cinematique Award, 1992; Rudolph Valentino Award, 1992; Nat. Board of Review Award, 1994. Commander, Order of Arts and Literature (France), 1987; Légion d'Honneur. *Recreations:* golf, tennis, reading.

CONNING, David Michael, OBE 1994; FRCPath; FIBiol; Director-General, British Nutrition Foundation, 1985–94; *b* 27 Aug. 1932; *s* of Walter Henry Conning and Phyllis Elsie Conning (*née* Lovell); *m* 1st, 1956, Betty Sleightholme (marr. diss. 1991); three *s* one *d*; 2nd, 1991, Lesley Myra Yeomans (*née* Beresford). *Educ:* Dame Allan's Boys' Sch., Newcastle upon Tyne; Med. Sch., King's Coll., Univ. of Durham (MB, BS). FRCPath 1982; FIBiol 1984; FIFST 1988. RAMC, 1956–59. SMO Pathology, Middlesborough Gen. Hosp., 1959–61; Lectr in Pathology, Royal Victoria Infirmary, 1961–65; Hon. Consultant Pathologist, Newcastle and Dist Hosps, 1963–65; Dep. Dir. Central Toxicol. Lab., ICI plc, 1966–78; Dir, BIBRA, 1978–85. Chm., Brit. Toxicol Soc., 1981. Hon. Mem., European Toxicol Soc. (Pres., 1983–86). Hon. Prof. of Toxicology, Surrey Univ., 1977–86. *Publications:* Toxic Hazards in Foods, 1983; Experimental Toxicology, 1988, 2nd edn 1993; contrib. book chapters and articles in jls of toxicol. and nutrition. *Recreation:* mending things. *Address:* Blacksmith's Cottage, Totnor, Brockhampton, Hereford HR1 4TJ. *T:* Ross-on-Wye (01989) 740303. *Club:* Savage.

CONNOLLY, Edward Thomas; Regional Chairman of Industrial Tribunals, since 1988; *b* 5 Sept. 1935; *s* of Edward Connolly and Alice Joyce; *m* 1962, Dr Pamela Marie Hagan; one *s* one *d*. *Educ:* St Mary's Coll., Crosby; Prior Park Coll.; Liverpool Univ. (LLB). Qualified as solicitor, 1960. Asst Solicitor, Lancs CC, 1960–63; Asst Prosecuting Solicitor, Liverpool City Council, 1963–65; Dep. Chief Legal Officer, Skelmersdale Develt Corp., 1965–68; Asst Clerk of the Peace, Lancs CC, 1968–71; Dep. Circuit Administrator, Northern Circuit, 1971–76; Chm. of Industrial Tribunals, 1976–88. *Address:* (office) Alexander House, 14–22 The Parsonage, Manchester M3 2JA. *T:* 0161–833 0581. *Club:* Royal Automobile.

CONNOR, Bishop of, since 1995; **Rt Rev. James Edward Moore;** *b* 1933; *Educ:* Trinity Coll., Dublin (BA 1954; MA 1964). Ordained deacon, 1956, priest, 1957; Assistant Curate: Knock, 1956–60; St Comgall, Bangor, 1960–62; Priest-in-charge, Belvoir, 1962–68; Incumbent: Groomsport, 1968–75; Dundela, 1975–95; Archdeacon of Down, 1989–95. Canon, 1985–89, Treasurer, 1987–89, Down Cathedral.

CONNOR, Prof. James Michael, FRCPGlas, FRCPE; Burton Professor of Medical Genetics, Glasgow University, since 1987; *b* 18 June 1951; *s* of James Connor and Mona Connor (*née* Hall); *m* 1979, Dr Rachel Alyson Clare Brooks; two *d*. *Educ:* Liverpool Univ. (BSc (Hons); MB ChB (Hons); MD). MRCP 1977; FRCPGlas 1988; FRCPE 1990. Gen. med. professional trng in various Liverpool hosps, 1975–77; Resident in Internal Medicine, Johns Hopkins Hosp., Baltimore, 1977–78; Univ. Res. Fellow, Dept of Medicine, Liverpool Univ., 1978–81; Instr in Med. Genetics, John Hopkins Hosp., 1981–82; Cons. in Med. Genetics, 1982–84, Wellcome Trust Sen. Lectr in Med. Genetics, 1984–87, Duncan Guthrie Inst. of Med. Genetics, Glasgow. *Publications:* Essential Medical Genetics, 1984, 4th edn 1993; Prenatal Diagnosis in Obstetric Practice, 1989, 2nd edn 1995; Emery and Rimoin's Principles and Practice of Medical Genetics, 3rd edn, 1996; articles on pathophysiology and prevention of genetic disease. *Recreations:* windsurfing, farming, swimming. *Address:* East Collary, Waterside, by Fenwick, Ayrshire KA3 6JJ. *T:* Fenwick (01560) 600790. *Club:* Arlington Baths.

CONNOR, Jeremy George; Metropolitan Stipendiary Magistrate, since 1979; a Recorder, since 1986; *b* 14 Dec. 1938; *s* of Joseph Connor and Mabel Emmeline (*née* Adams), ARCA. *Educ:* Beaumont; University Coll., London (LLB; DRS). Called to the Bar, Middle Temple, 1961; S Eastern Circuit. Apptd to Treasury List, Central Criminal Court, 1973; a Chm., Inner London Youth Cts (formerly Juvenile Cts), 1980–; Chairman: Family Proceedings Court, 1991–94; Inner London and City Probation Cttee, 1989–; Mem. Exec. Cttee, Central Council of Probation for England and Wales, 1982–89. Referee, Mental Health Foundn, 1993–. Mem., Judicial Studies Bd, 1990–. Pres., British Acad. of Forensic Scis, 1989–90 (Chm., Exec. Council, 1983–86; Mem. Council, 1982–); Chm., Inst. for Study of Treatment of Delinquency, 1992–93. Trustee: Grubb Inst. of Social Studies, Stapleford Trust for Drug Treatment and Res. Freeman, City of London, 1980; Liveryman, Fanmakers' Co., 1981 (Mem., Livery Cttee, 1987–). *Publications:* chapter in Archbold, Criminal Pleading, Evidence and Practice, 38th and 39th edns. *Recreations:* travel, theatre, occasional broadcasting. *Address:* Bow Street Magistrates' Court, WC2E 7AS. *Clubs:* Garrick, Royal Society of Medicine.

CONNOR, Michael Henry; HM Diplomatic Service; Ambassador to El Salvador, 1991–95; *b* 5 Aug. 1942; *s* of late Henry Connor and Agnes Cecilia Connor (*née* Lindsey); *m* 1964, Valerie Jannita Cunningham; three *s*. *Educ:* St John's Coll., Portsmouth. Joined HM Diplomatic Service, 1964; FO, 1964–68; Attaché, Cairo, 1968–70; Commercial Officer, Vienna, 1970–73; Second Sec. (Commercial/Aid), Kathmandu, 1973–76; FCO, 1976–81; First Sec., 1979; Havana: First Sec. (Commercial) and Consul, 1981–82; First Sec. and Hd of Chancery, 1982–83; Hd of Chancery, Ottawa, 1983–88; First Sec., FCO, 1988–91. *Recreations:* swimming, photography, trekking, theatre. *Address:* c/o Foreign and Commonwealth Office, King Charles Street, SW1A 2AH.

CONNOR, Roger David; His Honour Judge Connor; a Circuit Judge, since 1991; *b* 8 June 1939; *s* of Thomas Bernard Connor and Susie Violet Connor (*née* Spittlehouse); *m* 1967, Sandra Home Holmes; two *s*. *Educ:* Merchant Taylors' School; Brunel College of Advanced Science and Technology; The College of Law. Solicitor; articled to J. R. Hodder, 1963–68; Asst Solicitor, 1968–70; Partner, Hodders, 1970–83; Metropolitan Stipendiary Magistrate, 1983–91; a Recorder, 1987–91. *Recreations:* music, golf, gardening. *Address:* Watford County Court, Cassiobury House, 11–19 Station Road, Watford, Herts WD1 1EZ. *Club:* Beaconsfield Golf.

CONNORS, James Scott, (Jimmy); tennis player; tennis commentator, CBS television; *b* 2 Sept. 1952; *s* of James Scott Connors and Gloria Thompson Connors; *m*; one *s*. *Educ:* Univ. of California at Los Angeles. Amateur tennis player, 1970–72, professional, 1972; major Championships won: Australia, 1974; Wimbledon, 1974, 1982; USA, 1974, 1976, 1978, 1982, 1983; South Africa, 1973, 1974; WCT, 1977, 1980; Grand Prix, 1978; played for USA, Davis Cup, 1976, 1981. BBC Overseas Sports Personality, 1982. *Address:* Pro Serv Inc., 888 17th Street NW, Washington, DC 2006, USA.

CONOLLY, Mrs Yvonne Cecile; Head of Inspection and Monitoring, London Borough of Islington, since 1995 (Senior Inspector for Primary Education, 1989–95); *b* 12 June 1939; *d* of Hugh Augustus and Blanche Foster; *m* 1965, Michael Patrick Conolly; one *d. Educ:* Westwood High Sch., Jamaica; Shortwood Coll., Jamaica (Teachers' CertEd); Polytechnic, N London (BEd Hons Primary Educn). Primary school teacher: Jamaica, 1960–63; London, 1963–68; Head Teacher, London, 1969–78; ILEA Inspector, Multi-ethnic Education, 1978–81; Inspector of Primary Schools, 1981–90, Dist Primary Inspector, 1988–90, ILEA. Member: Home Secretary's Adv. Council on Race Relations, 1977–86; IBA, 1982–86; Consumer Protection Adv. Cttee, 1974–75. Governor, former Centre for Information and Advice on Educnl Disadvantage, 1975–80; (first) Chm., Caribbean Teachers' Assoc., 1974–76. Registered Inspector, OFSTED, 1994–. *Publications:* (contrib.) Mango Spice, book of 44 Caribbean songs for schools, 1981; (contrib.) Against the Tide—Black Experience in the ILEA, 1990. *Recreations:* special interest in the activities of ethnic minority groups; travelling, conversing.

CONOLLY-CAREW, family name of **Baron Carew.**

CONQUEST, (George) Robert (Acworth), OBE 1955; writer; *b* 15 July 1917; *s* of late Robert Folger Westcott Conquest and Rosamund, *d* of H. A. Acworth, CIE; *m* 1st, 1942, Joan Watkins (marr. diss. 1948); two *s*; 2nd, 1948, Tatiana Mihailova (marr. diss. 1962); 3rd, 1964, Caroleen Macfarlane (marr. diss. 1978); 4th, 1979, Elizabeth, *d* of late Col Richard D. Neece, USAF. *Educ:* Winchester; Magdalen Coll., Oxford. MA Oxon 1972; DLitt 1975. Oxf. and Bucks LI, 1939–46; Foreign Service, 1946–56; Fellow, LSE, 1956–58; Vis. Poet, Univ. of Buffalo, 1959–60; Literary Editor, The Spectator, 1962–63; Fellow: Columbia Univ., 1964–65; Woodrow Wilson International Center, 1976–77; Hoover Instn, 1977–79 and 1981–; Distinguished Vis. Scholar, Heritage Foundn, 1980–81; Research Associate, Harvard Univ., 1982–83; Adjunct Fellow, Center for Strategic and Internat. Studies, 1983–. Jefferson Lecture in Humanities, 1993. FRSL 1972; Washington, Corresp. FBA 1994. *Publications:* Poems, 1955; A World of Difference, 1955; (ed) New Lines, 1956; Common Sense About Russia, 1960; Power and Policy in the USSR, 1961; Courage of Genius, 1962; Between Mars and Venus, 1962; (ed) New Lines II, 1963; (with Kingsley Amis) The Egyptologists, 1965; Russia after Khrushchev, 1965; The Great Terror, 1968; Arias from a Love Opera, 1969; The Nation Killers, 1970; Lenin, 1972; Kolyma, 1978; The Abomination of Moab, 1979; Present Danger, 1979; Forays, 1979; We and They, 1980; (with Jon Manchip White) What to do when the Russians Come, 1984; Inside Stalin's Secret Police, 1985; The Harvest of Sorrow, 1986; New and Collected Poems, 1988; Tyrants and Typewriters, 1989; Stalin and the Kirov Murder, 1989; The Great Terror Reassessed, 1990; Stalin: breaker of nations, 1991. *Address:* c/o Brown Shipley & Co., Founder's Court, Lothbury, EC2R 7HE; 52 Peter Coutts Circle, Stanford, CA 94305, USA. *Club:* Travellers'.

CONRAN, Elizabeth Margaret, OBE 1994; MA, FMA; Curator, The Bowes Museum, Barnard Castle, since 1979; *b* 5 May 1939; *d* of James Johnston and Elizabeth Russell Wilson; *m* 1970, George Loraine Conran (*d* 1986); one *d. Educ:* Falkirk High Sch.; Glasgow Univ. (MA). FMA 1969. Res. Asst, Dept of History of Fine Art, Glasgow Univ., 1959–60; Asst Curator, The Iveagh Bequest, Kenwood, 1960–63; Keeper of Paintings, City Art Galls, Manchester, 1963–74; Arts Adviser, Greater Manchester Council, 1974–79. FRSA 1987. *Publications:* exhibn catalogues; articles in art and museum jls. *Recreations:* gardens, ballet. *Address:* 31 Thorngate, Barnard Castle, Co. Durham DL12 8QB. *T:* Teesdale (01833) 631055.

CONRAN, Jasper Alexander Thirlby; Designer (clothing and theatre) and Managing Director, Jasper Conran Ltd, since 1978; *b* 12 Dec. 1959; *s* of Sir Terence Conran, *qv* and Shirley Conran, *qv. Educ:* Bryanston School, Dorset; Parsons School of Art and Design, New York. Costumes for: Anouilh's The Rehearsal, 1990 (Laurence Olivier Award, 1991); My Fair Lady, 1992; (also sets), Bintley's Tombeaux, Royal Opera House, 1993; Sleeping Beauty, Scottish Ballet, 1994. Fil d'Or (Internat. Linen Award), 1982 and 1983; British Fashion Council Designer of the Year Award, 1986–87; Fashion Group of America Award, 1987; British Collections Award, 1991. *Address:* 2 Munden Street, W14 0RH. *T:* 0171–603 6668.

CONRAN, Shirley Ida; writer; *b* 21 Sept. 1932; *d* of W. Thirlby Pearce and Ida Pearce; *m* 1955, Sir Terence Conran (marr. diss. 1962); two *s. Educ:* St Paul's Girls' Sch.; Southern College of Art, Portsmouth. Fabric Designer and Director of Conran Fabrics, 1956–62; Member, Selection Cttee, Design Centre, 1961–69. Journalist; (first) Woman's Editor, Observer Colour Magazine, 1964; Woman's Editor, Daily Mail, 1969; Life and Style Editor, Over 21, 1972–74. *Publications:* Superwoman, 1975, revd edn as Down with Superwoman, 1990; Superwoman Year Book, 1976; Superwoman in Action, 1977; (with E. Sidney) Futurewoman, 1979; Lace (novel), 1982; The Magic Garden, 1983; Lace 2 (novel), 1985; Savages (novel), 1987; The Amazing Umbrella Shop, 1990; Crimson (novel), 1991; Tiger Eyes (novel), 1994. *Recreations:* reading, swimming, Yoga.
See also J. A. T. Conran.

CONRAN, Sir Terence (Orby), Kt 1983; Chairman: The Conran Shop Ltd, since 1976; Terence Conran Ltd, since 1990; Conran Holdings Ltd, since 1993; C. D. Partnership, since 1993; Conran Restaurants Ltd, since 1994; *b* 4 Oct. 1931; *m*; two *s*; *m* 1963, Caroline Herbert; two *s* one *d. Educ:* Bryanston, Dorset. Chm., Conran Holdings Ltd, 1965–68; Jt Chm., Ryman Conran Ltd, 1968–71; Chairman: Habitat Group Ltd, 1971–88; RSCG Conran Design (formerly Conran Design Group/Conran Associates), 1971–92; Habitat France SA, 1973–88; Conran Stores Inc., 1977–88; J. Hepworth & Son Ltd, 1981–83 (Dir, 1979–83); Habitat Mothercare Ltd, 1982–88; Jasper Conran, 1982–; Heal & Sons Ltd, 1983–87; Richard Shops, 1983–87; Storehouse plc, 1986–90 (Chief Exec., 1986–88; non-exec. Dir, 1990); Butlers Wharf Ltd, 1984–90; Bibendum Restaurant Ltd, 1986–; Benchmark Ltd, 1989–; Blueprint Café Ltd, 1989–; Conran Shop Holdings Ltd, 1990–; Le Pont de La Tour Ltd, 1991–; Conran Shop SA, 1991–; The Butlers Wharf Chop-House Ltd, 1993–; Quaglino's Restaurant Ltd, 1991–; Mezzo Ltd, 1995–; Director: Conran Ink Ltd, 1969–; The Neal Street Restaurant, 1972–89; Conran Octopus, 1983–; BhS plc, 1986–88; Savacentre Ltd, 1986–88; Michelin House Investment Co. Ltd, 1989–; Vice-Pres., FNAC, 1985–89. Estabd Conran Foundn for Design Educn and Research, 1981–. Mem., Royal Commn on Environmental Pollution, 1973–76. Member: Council, RCA, 1978–81, 1986–; Adv. Council, V&A Mus., 1979–83; Trustee: V&A Museum, 1984–90; Internat. Design (formerly Design) Museum, 1989– (Chm., 1992–). Gov., Bryanston Sch. RSA Presidential Medal for Design Management to Conran Group; RSA Presidential Award for Design Management to Habitat Designs Ltd, 1975; SIAD Medal, 1981; Assoc. for Business Sponsorship of the Arts and Daily Telegraph Award to Habitat Mothercare, 1982; RSA Bicentenary Medal, 1982; President's Award, D&AD, 1989. Hon. FRIBA 1984. Commandeur de l'Ordre des Arts et des Lettres (France), 1991. *Publications:* The House Book, 1974; The Kitchen Book, 1977; The Bedroom & Bathroom Book, 1978; (with Caroline Conran) The Cook Book, 1980; The New House Book, 1985; Conran Directory of Design, 1985; Plants at Home, 1986; The Soft Furnishings Book, 1986; Terence Conran's France, 1987; Terence Conran's DIY by Design, 1989; Terence Conran's Garden DIY, 1990; Toys and Children's Furniture, 1992; Terence Conran's Kitchen Book, 1993; Terence Conran's DIY Book, 1994; The Essential House Book, 1994. *Recreations:* gardening, cooking. *Address:* 22 Shad Thames, SE1 2YU. *T:* 0171–378 1161, *Fax:* 0171–403 4309.
See also J. A. T. Conran.

CONROY, Harry; author; financial journalist; public relations consultant; General Secretary, National Union of Journalists, 1985–90; *b* Scotland, 6 April 1943; *s* of Michael Conroy and Sarah (*née* Mullan); *m* 1965, Margaret Craig (*née* Campbell); twin *s* one *d.* Trainee Lab. Technician, Southern Gen. Hosp., 1961–62; Night Messenger (copy boy), 1962–63, Jun. Features Sub-Editor, 1963–64, Scottish Daily Express; Daily Record: Reporter, 1964–66 and 1967–69; Financial Correspondent, 1969–85; Reporter, Scottish Daily Mail, 1966–67. Campaigns Dir, Scottish Constitutional Convention, 1990–92. Mem., ASTMS, 1961–62. National Union of Journalists: Mem., 1963–; Mem., Nat. Exec. Council, 1976–85; Vice-Pres., 1980–81; Pres., 1981–82. Associate Mem., GMBATU, 1984–85. *Recreations:* stamp and post-card collecting, supporting Glasgow Celtic FC. *Address:* 24 Eskdale Drive, Rutherglen, Glasgow G73 3JS.

CONS, Sir Derek, Kt 1990; Vice President, Court of Appeal, Supreme Court of Hong Kong, 1986–93; *b* 15 July 1928; *s* of Alfred Henry Cons and Elsie Margaret (*née* Neville); *m* 1952, Mary Roberta Upton Wilkes. *Educ:* Rutlish; Birmingham Univ. (LLB (Hons)). Called to Bar, Gray's Inn, 1953. RASC (2nd Lieut), 1946–48. Magistrate, Hong Kong, 1955–62, Principal Magistrate, 1962–66; District Judge, 1966–72; Judge of Supreme Court of Hong Kong, 1972–80, Justice of Appeal, 1980–86. *Recreations:* golf, skiing. *Address:* Mulberry Mews, Church Street, Fordingbridge, Hants SP6 1BE. *Club:* Bramshaw Golf (Hants).

CONSTABLE, (Charles) John, DBA; CIMgt; management educator and consultant; Chairman, Bright Tech Developments Ltd, since 1989; Director-General, British Institute of Management, 1985–86; *b* 20 Jan. 1936; *s* of Charles and Gladys Constable; *m* 1960, Elisabeth Mary Light; three *s* one *d. Educ:* Durham Sch.; St John's Coll., Cambridge (MA); Royal Sch. of Mines, Imperial Coll. London (BSc); Harvard Grad. Sch. of Bus. Admin. (DBA). NCB, 1959–60; Wallis & Linnel Ltd, 1960–63; Arthur Young & Co., 1963–64; Lectr and Sen. Lectr, Durham Univ. Business Sch., 1964–71; Prof. of Operations Management, Business Policy, 1971–82, Dir 1982–85, Cranfield Sch. of Management. Non-executive Director: IMS Ltd, 1984–91; Lloyds Abbey Life (formerly Abbey Life), 1987–. Member: Heavy Electrical EDC, NEDO, 1977–87; N Beds HA, 1987–90; Res. Grants Bd, ESRC, 1989–90. Chm. of Govs, Harpur Trust, 1995– (Governor, 1979–). *Publications:* (jtly) Group Assessment Programmes, 1966; (jtly) Operations Management Text and Cases, 1976; (jtly) Cases in Strategic Management, 1980; The Making of British Managers (BIM/CBI report), 1987. *Recreations:* golf, family. *Address:* 20 Kimbolton Road, Bedford MK40 2NR. *T:* Bedford (01234) 212576.

CONSTABLE, Sir Frederic S.; *see* Strickland-Constable.

CONSTANT, Antony; Group Management Development Executive, the Delta Group plc (formerly Delta Metal Co. Ltd), retired 1980 (Group Archivist, 1980–83); *b* 1916; *s* of Frederick Charles and Mary Theresa Constant; *m* 1947, Pamela Mary Pemberton (*d* 1989); one *s. Educ:* Dover Coll.; King's Coll., Cambridge. Asst master, Oundle Sch., 1939–45; Staff of Dir of Naval Intelligence, Admiralty, 1940–44; Educational Adviser to the Control Commission, Germany, 1945. Asst Master, and Asst House Master of School House, Rugby Sch., 1945–49; Rector of Royal Coll., Mauritius, 1949–53; Dir of Studies, RAF Coll., Cranwell, 1953–59; Educnl Advr, RAF Benevolent Fund, 1953–78; Advr to MoD on officer recruitment, and Chm. of Joint-Services Working Party, 1959–62; joined Delta Group of Companies, 1963, as Head of Group Training Dept. Mem. Bd for Postgraduate Studies, and Mem. Faculty Bd, Management Centre, Univ. of Aston, 1973–77. *Publications:* The Percy Lane Group 1932–52, 1982; articles on local history, ships and shipping. *Recreations:* genealogy, ornithology, ships, watching smoke. *Address:* Old Bonham's, Wardington, near Banbury, Oxon OX17 1SA.

CONSTANTINE, family name of **Baron Constantine of Stanmore.**

CONSTANTINE OF STANMORE, Baron *cr* 1981 (Life Peer), of Stanmore in Greater London; **Theodore Constantine;** Kt 1964; CBE 1956; AE 1945; DL; *b* 15 March 1910; *er s* of Leonard and Fanny Louise Constantine; *m* 1935, Sylvia Mary (*d* 1990), *y d* of Wallace Henry Legge-Pointing; one *s* one *d. Educ:* Acton Coll. Personal Asst to Chm. of public company, 1926–28; Executive in industry, 1928–38; Managing Dir of public company subsidiary, 1938–39. Served War of 1939–45, AAF (AEA 1945). Dir of Industrial Holding Company, 1956–59; Chm. of Public Companies, 1959–86. Organisational work for Conservative Party as Constituency Chm., Area Chm., Mem. Nat. Exec. Cttee, Policy Cttee, Nat. Advisory Cttee on Publicity. Chm., Nat. Union Cons. and Unionist Assocs, 1967–68, Pres. 1980. Trustee, Sir John Wolstenholme Charity; Master, Worshipful Co. of Coachmakers, 1975; Freeman of City of London, 1949. High Sheriff of Greater London, 1967; DL Greater London, 1967–85. *Recreations:* watching motor racing, reading, walking. *Address:* House of Lords, SW1A 0PW. *Club:* Carlton.

CONTI, Rt. Rev. Mario Joseph; *see* Aberdeen, Bishop of, (RC).

CONTI, Tom; actor, since 1960; director; *b* Scotland, 1942; *m* Kara Wilson; one *d.* London appearances include: Savages, Royal Court and Comedy, 1973; Other People, The Black and White Minstrels, Hampstead; The Devil's Disciple, RSC Aldwych, 1976; Whose Life is it Anyway?, Mermaid and Savoy, 1978, NY 1979 (SWET Award for Best Actor in a new play, Variety Club of GB Award for Best Stage Actor, 1978, Tony Award for Best Actor, 1979); They're Playing Our Song, Shaftesbury, 1980; Romantic Comedy, Apollo, 1983; An Italian Straw Hat, Shaftesbury, 1986; Otherwise Engaged (also directed), Theatre Royal, Windsor, 1990; The Ride Down Mount Morgan, Wyndham's, 1991; Present Laughter (also directed), Globe, 1993; *directed:* Last Licks, Broadway, 1979; Before the Party, Oxford Playhouse and Queen's, 1980; The Housekeeper, Apollo, 1982; Treats, Hampstead, 1989; *films include:* Galileo, Flame, 1974; Eclipse, 1975; Full Circle, The Duellists, 1977; The Wall, 1980; Merry Christmas, Mr Lawrence, 1983; Reuben, Reuben, 1983; American Dreamer, 1985; Miracles, 1985; Saving Grace, 1986; Heavenly Pursuits, 1987; Beyond Therapy, 1987; The Dumb Waiter (USA); White Roses; Shirley Valentine, 1989; Two Brothers Running; *television appearances include:* Madame Bovary, The Norman Conquests, Glittering Prizes, The Beate Klarsfeld Story, Fatal Dosage, The Quick and the Dead, Blade on the Feather. *Address:* c/o ICM, Oxford House, 76 Oxford Street, W1N 0AX.

CONTOGEORGIS, George; Member, Commission of the European Communities, 1981–85; *b* 21 Nov. 1912; *s* of Leonidas and Angeliki Contogeorgis; *m* 1949, Mary Lazopoulou. *Educ:* Athens Sch. (now University) of Economic and Commercial Sciences. Ministry of Trade, Greece: Administrator, 1937; Chief of Section, 1945; Dir, 1952; Dir Gen., 1964–67, resigned. Gen. Sec., Tourism, Govt of Nea Dimokratia, 1974; Dep. Minister of Co-ordination (Econs), 1974–77; Minister for EEC Affairs, 1977–81; Minister of Nat. Economy, 1989–90. MP, 1977–81. Grand Comdr, Order of the Phoenix (Greece),

1966; Grand Croix de l'Ordre de Leopold II (Belgium), 1984; Grand Comdr, Order of Lion (Finland), 1962; Comdr, OM (Germany, 1956, Italy, 1964 and France, 1977). *Publication:* Greece in Europe, 1985. *Address:* Rue Anagnostopoulou 26, Athens 10673, Greece. *T:* (1) 3616844.

CONWAY, Lord; William Francis Seymour; *b* 2 Nov. 1993; *o s* and *heir* of Earl of Yarmouth, *qv.*

CONWAY, Christopher John; Chief Executive, Digital Equipment Co. Ltd, since 1993; *b* 3 Nov. 1944; *s* of John Francis Conway and Monica Conway (*née* Hawksworth); *m* 1969, Gillian May Burrow; two *s* one *d. Educ:* Univ. of S Africa (BA Hons 1967). IBM (UK) Ltd, 1969–93: Dir, Southern Reg., 1989–92; Dir, Financial Services, 1992–93. *Recreations:* sailing, tennis, classical music. *Address:* Digital Equipment Co. Ltd, Worton Grange, Reading, Berks RG2 0TE. *T:* Reading (01734) 868711.

CONWAY, (David) Martin; President, Selly Oak Colleges, Birmingham, since 1986; *b* 22 Aug. 1935; *s* of Geoffrey S. and Dr Elsie Conway; *m* 1962, Ruth, *d* of Rev. Richard Daniel; one *s* two *d. Educ:* Sedbergh Sch.; Gonville and Caius Coll., Cambridge (BA, MA); and by friends and fellow Christians in many different cultures. Internat. Sec., SCM of GB and Ire., 1958–61; Study Sec., World Student Christian Fedn, Geneva, 1961–67; Sec. for Chaplaincies in Higher Educn, Gen. Synod of C of E, 1967–70; Publications Sec., WCC, 1970–74; Asst Gen. Sec. for Ecumenical Affairs, BCC, 1974–83; Dir, Oxford Inst. for Church and Society, and Tutor, Ripon Coll., Cuddesdon, Oxford, 1983–86. Simultaneous interpreter at assemblies and major world confs of WCC, 1961–; Consultant, Faith and Order Commn, WCC, 1971–82; Consultant, 1974–83, and Mem., 1986–91, C of E Bd for Mission and Unity. DLitt Lambeth, 1994. Editor: The Ecumenical Review, 1972–74; Christians Together, 1983–91; Oxford Papers on Contemporary Society, 1984–86. *Publications:* The Undivided Vision, 1966; (ed) University Chaplain?, 1969; The Christian Enterprise in Higher Education, 1971; Seeing Education Whole, 1971; Look Listen Care, 1983; That's When the Body Works, 1991; contribs to Student World, New Christian, Audenshaw Papers, Internat. Rev. of Mission, etc. *Recreations:* other people—family, friends, colleagues; travel, music. *Address:* President's House, Selly Oak Colleges, Birmingham B29 6LQ. *T:* 0121–472 4231.

CONWAY, Derek Leslie, TD 1990; MP (C) Shrewsbury and Atcham, since 1983; a Lord Commissioner of HM Treasury (Government Whip), since 1994; *b* 15 Feb. 1953; *s* of Leslie and Florence Conway; *m* 1980, Colette Elizabeth Mary (*née* Lamb); two *s* one *d. Educ:* Beacon Hill Boys' School. Borough Councillor and Dep. Leader of the Opposition, Gateshead Metropolitan Borough Council, 1974–78; Mem., Tyne and Wear Metropolitan County Council, 1977–83 (Leader, 1979–82); Member Board: Washington Develt Corp., 1979–83; North of England Develt Council, 1979–83; Newcastle Airport, 1980–83; Northern Arts, 1980–83. Principal Organiser, Action Research for the Crippled Child, 1974–83. PPS to Minister of State: Welsh Office, 1988–91; Dept of Employment, 1992–93; an Asst Govt Whip, 1993–94. Member, Select Committee: on Agric., 1987; on Transport, 1987–88; on Armed Forces Discipline, 1991. Chairman: British–Morocco Parly Gp, 1988–; British–Venezuelan Gp, 1987–93; Vice Chm., Cons. backbench Defence Cttee, 1991–; Mem. Exec. Cttee, IPU, 1986– (Vice-Chm., British Gp, 1992–93). Member, Conservative Party Committees: Nat. Exec. Cttee, 1971–81; Nat. Gen. Purposes Cttee, 1972–74; Nat. Local Govt Cttee, 1979–83; Nat. Vice-Chm., Young Conservatives, 1972–74. Mem. Exec. Cttee, British Venezuela Soc., 1987–93. Commnd RMA Sandhurst into Royal Regt of Fusiliers; Major, 5th Bn (TA) Light Infantry. *Recreation:* gardening. *Address:* House of Commons, SW1A 0AA. *T:* 0171–219 3000. *Club:* Beaconsfield (Shrewsbury).

CONWAY, Most Rev. Dominic Joseph; Bishop of Elphin (RC), 1971–94; *b* 1 Jan. 1918; *s* of Dominic Conway and Mary Hoare. *Educ:* Coll. of the Immaculate Conception, Sligo; Pontifical Irish Coll., Pontifical Lateran Univ., Pontifical Angelicum Univ., Gregorian Univ. (all in Rome); National Univ. of Ireland. BPh, STL, DEcclHist, Higher Diploma Educn. Missionary, Calabar Dio., Nigeria, 1943–48; Professor: All Hallows Coll., Dublin, 1948–49; Summerhill Coll., Sligo, 1949–51; Spiritual Dir, 1951–65, Rector, 1965–68, Irish Coll., Rome, Sec.-Gen., Superior Council of the Propagation of the Faith, Rome, 1968–70; Auxiliary Bishop of Elphin, 1970–71. *Address:* St Mary's, Sligo, Ireland. *T:* 62670.

CONWAY, Prof. Gordon Richard, FIBiol; Vice-Chancellor, University of Sussex, since 1992; *b* 6 July 1938, *s* of Cyril Conway and Thelma (*née* Goodwin); *m* 1965, Susan Mary, *d* of Harold Mumford and Ellen Martha (*née* Bingham); one *s* two *d. Educ:* Kingston Grammar Sch.; Kingston Polytechnic; University Coll. of North Wales, Bangor (BSc 1959). DipAgricSci, Cambridge, 1960; DTA University Coll. of West Indies, Trinidad, 1961; PhD Univ. of California, Davis, 1969; FIBiol 1978. Research Officer (Entomology), Agric. Res. Centre, State of Sabah, Malaysia, 1961–66; Statistician, Inst. Ecology, Univ. of California, Davis, 1966–69; Imperial College, London: Res. Fellow and Lectr, Dept of Zoology and Applied Entomology, 1970–76; Dir, 1977–80, Chm., 1980–86, Centre for Envtl Technol.; Reader in Environmental Management, Univ. of London, 1976–80; Prof. of Environmental Technol., 1980–88; Rep. for India, Nepal and Sri Lanka, Ford Foundn, 1989–92. Vis. Prof., Imperial Coll., 1989–. Director: Sustainable Agric. Prog., Internat. Inst. for Envt and Develt, 1986–88; BOC Foundn, 1994–. Mem., Royal Commn on Environmental Pollution, 1984–88. Chm. Bd, Inst. Develt Studies, 1992–; Member: Bd, Internat. Food Policy Res. Inst., Washington, 1994–; UK Round Table on Sustainable Develt, 1995–. *Publications:* Pest and Pathogen Control, 1984; (jtly) After the Green Revolution, 1990; (jtly) Unwelcome Harvest: agriculture and pollution, 1991; papers and reports on agricl ecology. *Recreations:* travel, music. *Address:* University of Sussex, Sussex House, Falmer, Brighton BN1 9RH.

CONWAY, Prof. John Horton, FRS 1981; John von Neumann Professor of Mathematics, Princeton University, USA. *Educ:* Gonville and Caius Coll., Cambridge. BA 1959; MA 1963; PhD 1964. Univ. Lectr in Pure Maths, Cambridge, to 1973; Reader in Pure Mathematics and Mathematical Statistics, 1973–83; Prof. of Maths, 1983; Fellow: Sidney Sussex Coll., Cambridge, 1964–70; Gonville and Caius Coll., Cambridge, 1970. Polya Prize, London Mathematical Soc., 1987. *Publications:* Regular Algebra and Finite Machines, 1971; On Numbers and Games, 1976; Atlas of Finite Groups, 1985. *Address:* Department of Mathematics, Princeton University, Fine Hall, Washington Road, Princeton, NJ 08544, USA.

CONWAY, Martin; *see* Conway, D. M.

CONWAY, Sari Elizabeth; Director of Education, City of Bradford Metropolitan Council, since 1991; *b* 3 March 1951; *d* of Gordon and Gladys Mary Wright; *m* 1973, Vincent Conway; three *s. Educ:* Leeds Polytechnic (Teaching Cert.); Leeds Univ. (Advanced Diploma in Guidance and Counselling; Postgrad. Cert. in Educn of Maladjusted Children); Nottingham Univ. (MPhil); Warwick Univ. (MEd). Teacher of Home Econs, Leeds LEA, 1973–75; Head of Girls' Studies, Nat. Children's Home, Leeds, 1975–77; Sen. Mistress, Disruptive Unit, and Head of Girls' Studies, Calderdale, 1977–79; part-time Adult Educn Tutor/Organiser, Youth Worker, and Lectr in Further Educn, Derbys, 1979–82; Educn Advr, Leics CC, 1982–88; Asst Dir of Community and Continuing Educn, South Tyneside MBC, 1988–91. *Publications:* Educational Perceptions of Unemployed Adolescents in an LEA, 1984; Women Senior Officers in the Statutory Youth Service, 1992. *Recreations:* travel, dressmaking, theatre, voluntary youth work. *Address:* (office) Education Directorate, Flockton House, Flockton Road, Bradford BD4 7RY; High Stones, 5 Malvern Brow, Chellow Dene, Bradford BD9 6AW.

CONWAY MORRIS, Dr Simon, FRS 1990; Reader in Evolutionary Palaeobiology, since 1991, and Fellow of St John's College, since 1987, Cambridge University; *b* 6 Nov. 1951; *s* of Richard Conway Morris and Barbara Louise Maxwell; *m* 1975, Zoë Helen James; two *s. Educ:* Univ. of Bristol (BSc Hons); Univ. of Cambridge (PhD). Research Fellow, St John's Coll., Cambridge, 1975–79; Lectr, Open Univ., 1979–83; Lectr in Palaeontology, Cambridge Univ., 1983–91. Gallagher Vis. Scientist, Univ. of Calgary, 1981; Nuffield Sci. Res. Fellowship, 1987–88; Merrill W. Haas Vis. Dist. Prof., Univ. of Kansas, 1988; Selby Fellow, Aust. Acad. of Scis, 1992. Chm., Internat. Trust for Zool Nomenclature, 1991–. Mem. Council, Systematics Assoc., 1981–85. Hon. DPhil Uppsala, 1993. Walcott Medal, Nat. Acad. of Scis, 1987; Charles Schuchert Award, Paleontol. Soc., 1989; George Gaylord Simpson Prize, Yale Univ., 1992. *Publications:* contribs to professional jls. *Recreations:* travel, wine, punting. *Address:* Department of Earth Sciences, Downing Street, Cambridge CB2 3EQ. *T:* Cambridge (01223) 333414.

CONYNGHAM, family name of **Marquess Conyngham.**

CONYNGHAM, 7th Marquess *cr* 1816; **Frederick William Henry Francis Conyngham;** Baron Conyngham, 1781; Viscount Conyngham, 1789; Earl Conyngham, Viscount Mount Charles, 1797; Earl of Mount Charles, Viscount Slane, 1816; Baron Minster (UK), 1821; late Captain Irish Guards; *b* 13 March 1924; *e s* of 6th Marquess Conyngham and Antoinette Winifred (*d* 1966), *er d* of late J. W. H. Thompson; *S* father, 1974; *m* 1st, 1950, Eileen Wren (marr. diss. 1970), *o d* of Capt. C. W. Newsam, Ashfield, Beauparc, Co. Meath; three *s*; 2nd, 1971, Mrs Elizabeth Anne Rudd; 3rd, 1980, Mrs D. G. A. Walker (*d* 1986); 4th, 1987, Annabelle Agnew. *Educ:* Eton. *Heir: s* Earl of Mount Charles, *qv. Address:* Myrtle Hill, Ramsey, Isle of Man. *Club:* Royal St George Yacht.

COOGAN, Ven. Robert Arthur William; Archdeacon of Hampstead, 1985–94, now Archdeacon Emeritus; *b* 11 July 1929; *s* of Ronald Dudley Coogan and Joyce Elizabeth Coogan (*née* Roberts). *Educ:* Univ. of Tasmania (BA); Univ. of Durham (DipTheol). Asst Curate, St Andrew, Plaistow, 1953–56; Rector of Bothwell, Tasmania, 1956–62; Vicar: North Woolwich, 1962–73; St Stephen, Hampstead, 1973–77; Priest in Charge, All Hallows, Gospel Oak, 1974–77; Vicar of St Stephen with All Hallows, Hampstead, 1977–85; Priest in Charge: Old St Pancras with St Matthew, 1976–80; St Martin with St Andrew, Gospel Oak, 1978–81; Area Dean, South Camden 1975–81, North Camden 1978–83; Prebendary of St Paul's Cathedral, 1982–85. Commissary for Bishop of Tasmania, 1968–88; Exam. Chaplain to Bishop of Edmonton, 1985–94. *Recreations:* reading, gardening, travel. *Address:* 30 Marchwood Gate, Marchwood, Chichester, W Sussex PO19 4HA. *T:* Chichester (01243) 528828. *Club:* Oriental.

COOK, Sir Alan (Hugh), Kt 1988; FRS 1969; Master of Selwyn College, Cambridge University, 1983–93; *b* 2 Dec. 1922; *s* of late Reginald Thomas Cook, OBE, and of Ethel Cook; *m* 1948, Isabell Weir Adamson; one *s* one *d. Educ:* Westcliff High Sch. for Boys; Corpus Christi Coll. Cambridge. MA, PhD, ScD. Admty Signal Estabt, 1943–46; Research Student, then Res. Asst, Dept of Geodesy and Geophysics, Cambridge, 1946–51; Metrology Div., Nat. Physical Laboratory, Teddington, 1952; Vis. Fellow, Jt Inst. for Laboratory Astrophysics, Boulder, Colorado, 1965–66; Supt, Standards (subseq. Quantum Metrology) Div., Nat. Physical Laboratory, 1966–69; Prof. of Geophysics, Univ. of Edinburgh, 1969–72; Cambridge University: Jacksonian Prof. of Natural Philosophy, 1972–90; Fellow, King's Coll., 1972–83; Head of Dept of Physics, 1979–84. Vis. Prof. and Green Schol., Univ. of Calif. at Los Angeles, Berkeley and San Diego, 1981–82; Vis. Fellow, Center of Theol Inquiry, Princeton, 1993. Mem. SERC, 1984–88. Chm., Press Syndicate, Cambridge Univ. Press, 1988–93. FInstP; FRSE 1970; Foreign Fellow, Acad. Naz. dei Lincei, 1971. Pres., RAS, 1977–79. Fellow, Explorers' Club, NY, 1980. C. V. Boys Prize, 1967, Charles Chree Medal and Prize, 1993, Inst. of Physics. *Publications:* Gravity and the Earth, 1969; Global Geophysics, 1970; Interference of Electromagnetic Waves, 1971; Physics of the Earth and Planets, 1973; Celestial Masers, 1977; Interiors of the Planets, 1980; The Motion of the Moon, 1988; Gravitational Experiments in the Laboratory, 1993; Observational Foundations of Physics, 1994; many contribs learned jls on gravity, artificial satellites, precise measurement, fundamental constants of physics and astronomy, history of science. *Recreations:* amateur theatre, travel, painting, gardening. *Address:* 8 Wootton Way, Cambridge CB3 9LX. *T:* Cambridge (01223) 356887.

COOK, Ann; *see* Christopher, A.

COOK, Maj.-Gen. Arthur Thompson, FRCP, FRCPE; Director of Army Medicine, 1977–81; *b* 21 Oct. 1923; *s* of Thomas and Mabel Elizabeth Cook; *m* 1960, Kathleen Lane; two *s* one *d. Educ:* China Inland Mission Sch., Chefoo, N China; City of London Sch.; St Thomas' Hosp., London (MB). FRCP 1955, FRCPE 1954. Joined RAMC, 1948. QHP, 1977–81. *Address:* The Old Cricketers, Cricket Hill, Yateley, Camberley, Surrey GU17 7BA. *T:* Yateley (01252) 879452.

COOK, Mrs Beryl Frances; painter; *b* 10 Sept. 1926; *d* of Adrian Lansley and Ella Farmer-Francis; *m* 1948, John Victor Cook; one *s. Educ:* Kendrick Girls' Sch., Reading, Berks. *Exhibitions:* Plymouth Arts Centre, 1975; Whitechapel Art Gallery, London, 1976; The Craft of Art, Walker Art Gallery, 1979; Musée de Cahors, 1981; Chelmsford Museum, 1982; Portal Gall., 1985, 1991; travelling, Plymouth, Stoke-on-Trent, Preston, Nottingham and Edinburgh, 1988–89; Drumcroon Arts Centre, Wigan, 1993. *Publications:* The Works, 1978; Private View, 1980; Seven Years and a Day (illustrations), 1980; One Man Show, 1981; Bertie and the Big Red Ball (illustrations), 1982; My Granny (illustrations), 1983; Beryl Cook's New York, 1985; Beryl Cook's London, 1988; Mr Norris Changes Trains (illustrations), 1990; Bouncers, 1991; The Loved One (illustrations), 1993. *Recreation:* reading. *Address:* Glanville House, 3 Athenæum Street, The Hoe, Plymouth PL1 2RQ.

COOK, Brian Francis, FSA; classical archaeologist; Keeper of Greek and Roman Antiquities, British Museum, 1976–93; *b* 13 Feb. 1933; *yr s* of late Harry Cook and Renia Cook; *m* 1962, Veronica Dewhirst. *Educ:* St Bede's Grammar Sch., Bradford; Univ. of Manchester (BA); Downing Coll. and St Edmund's House, Cambridge (MA); British Sch. at Athens. FSA 1971. NCO 16/5 Lancers, 1956–58. Dept of Greek and Roman Art, Metropolitan Museum of Art, New York: Curatorial Asst, 1960; Asst Curator, 1961; Associate Curator, 1965–69; Asst Keeper, Dept of Greek and Roman Antiquities, BM, 1969–76. Corr. Mem., German Archaeol. Inst., 1977. Hon. Member: Anglo-Hellenic League, 1981; Caryatids, 1992. *Publications:* Inscribed Hadra Vases in the Metropolitan Museum of Art, 1966; Greek and Roman Art in the British Museum, 1976; The Elgin Marbles, 1984; The Townley Marbles, 1985; Greek Inscriptions, 1987; (ed) The Rogozen Treasure, 1989; articles and revs on Greek, Etruscan and Roman antiquities in Brit. and foreign periodicals. *Recreations:* reading, gardening. *Address:* 4 Belmont Avenue, Barnet, Herts EN4 9LJ. *T:* 0181–440 6590.

COOK, Brian Hartley K.; *see* Kemball-Cook.

COOK, Charles Alfred George, MC 1945; GM 1945; FRCS; Consultant Ophthalmic Surgeon: Guy's Hospital, 1954–73; Moorfields Eye Hospital, 1956–73; Teacher of Ophthalmology, University of London (Guy's Hospital and Institute of Ophthalmology), 1955–73; *b* 20 Aug. 1913; *s* of late Charles F. Cook and Beatrice Grist; *m* 1939, Edna Constance Dobson; one *s* one *d*. *Educ:* St Edward's Sch., Oxford; Guy's Hospital. MRCS, LRCP 1939; DOMS (Eng.), 1946; FRCS 1950. Capt. and Major RAMC, 1939–45. Moorfields Eye Hospital: Clinical Asst, 1946–47; Ho. Surg., 1948–49; Sen. Resident Officer, 1950; Chief Clin. Asst, 1951–55. Sen. Registrar, Eye Dept, Guy's Hospital, 1951–55; Moorfields Research Fellow, Inst. of Ophthalmology, 1951–58; Ophthalmic Surg., West Middlesex Hospital, 1954–56. Mem., Court of Examrs, RCS; Examr for DOMS, RCP and RCS; Examr Brit. Orthoptic Board; Sec., Ophthalmological Soc. of UK, 1956–57. Member: Cttee of Management, Inst. of Ophthalmology, 1960–63 (Vice-Dean of Inst., 1959–62); Cttee of Management, London Refraction Hosp., 1983–; Council, Coll. of Opth. Opticians, 1979–83 (Hon. Fellow 1982); Bd of Governors, Faculty of Dispensing Opticians, 1980–84. Governor: Royal Nat. Coll. for Blind, 1967–; Moorfields Eye Hosp., 1962–65. Hon. DSc Aston, 1983. Renter Warden, Upper Warden, then Master, Worshipful Co. of Spectacle Makers, 1975–81. Freeman, City of London. *Publications:* (ed) S. Duke Elder, Embryology, vol. 3, 1963; (contrib.) Payling, Wright and Symers, Systematic Pathology, 1966; (jt) May and Worth, Diseases of the Eye, 1968; articles in Brit. Jl of Ophthalmology, Trans Ophthalmological Soc., Jl of Pathology and other Med. Jls. *Recreations:* swimming, reading; an interest in all outdoor recreations. *Address:* 13 Clarence Terrace, Regent's Park, NW1 4RD. *T:* 0171–723 5111. *Clubs:* Athenæum, Garrick.

COOK, Sir Christopher Wymondham Rayner Herbert, 5th Bt *cr* 1886; company director since 1979; Director, Diamond Guarantees Ltd, 1980–91; *b* 24 March 1938; *s* of Sir Francis Ferdinand Maurice Cook, 4th Bt and Joan Loraine, *d* of John Aloysius Ashton-Case; *S* father, 1978; *m* 1st, 1958, Mrs Malina Gunasekera (from whom he obtained a divorce, 1975); one *s* one *d*; 2nd, 1975, Mrs Margaret Miller, *d* of late John Murray; one *s* one *d*. *Educ:* King's School, Canterbury. *Recreations:* reading, philately, painting. *Heir: s* Richard Herbert Aster Maurice Cook, *b* 30 June 1959. *Address:* La Fontenelle, Ville au Roi, St Peter Port, Guernsey, CI GY1 1NZ.

COOK, David Somerville; solicitor; Senior Partner, Messrs Sheldon & Stewart, Solicitors, Belfast; Chairman, Police Authority for Northern Ireland, since 1994; Lord Mayor of Belfast, 1978–79; *b* 25 Jan. 1944; *s* of Francis John Granville Cook, *qv*; *m* 1972, Mary Fionnuala Ann Deeny; four *s* one *d*. *Educ:* Campbell Coll., Belfast; Pembroke Coll., Cambridge (MA). Alliance Party of Northern Ireland: Founder Member, 1970; Hon. Treasurer, 1972–75; Central Executive Cttee, 1970–78, 1980–85; Dep. Leader, 1980–84; Pres., 1992–. Chm., NI Voluntary Trust, 1979–. Mem., Belfast City Council, 1973–85; Mem. (Alliance) for Belfast S, NI Assembly, 1982–86; contested (Alliance): Belfast South, Feb. 1974, by-elections March 1982 and Jan. 1986, gen. election, 1987; N Ireland, European Parly elecn, 1984. Trustee: Ulster Museum, 1974–85; The Buttle Trust, 1991–; Vice Pres., NI Council on Alcohol, 1978–83; Member: NI Council, European Movement, 1980–84; Cttee, Charity Know How Fund, 1991–94; Exec. Cttee, Assoc. of Community Trusts and Foundns, 1992– (Chm., 1994–). Director: Ulster Actors' Co. Ltd, 1981–85; Crescent Arts Centre, Belfast, 1994–. Mem., Royal Naval Assoc. Gov., Brownlow Coll. (Integrated Secondary Sch.), 1994–. Obtained Orders of Mandamus and fines for contempt of court against Belfast City Council, following its unlawful protest against the Anglo-Irish Agreement, 1986, 1987. *Recreations:* clearing undergrowth, wine, marmalade making, observing politicians from a distance. *Address:* Banford House, Tullylish, Gilford, Co. Down BT63 6DL. *Clubs:* United Oxford & Cambridge University; Ulster Reform, Ulster Arts (Belfast).

COOK, Derek Edward, TD 1967; Deputy Chairman, 1987–92, and Group Managing Director, 1990–92, Pilkington plc (Director, 1984–92); *b* 7 Dec. 1931; 2nd *s* of late H. E. Cook and Mrs D. E. Cook (*née* Appleyard); *m* 1968, Prudence Carolyn Wilson; one *s* one *d*. *Educ:* Fyling Hall; Denstone Coll.; Corpus Christi Coll., Oxford (MA); Salford Univ.; Huddersfield Tech. Coll. FSS; CText, FTI. Commissioned Z Battery, BAOR, 1951; W Riding Artillery, 1952–68. Tootal Ltd, 1955–61; John Emsley Ltd, 1961–63; Man. Dir, A. & S. Henry & Co. Ltd (Bradford), 1963–70; Man. Dir, 1971–75, Chm., 1976–79, Fibreglass Pilkington Ltd, India; Chm. and Man. Dir, Hindusthan-Pilkington Glass Works Ltd, India, 1976–79; Director: R. H. Windsor Ltd, India, 1976–79; Killick Halco Ltd, India, 1977–79; Chm. and Man. Dir, Pilkington Cos, S Africa and Zimbabwe, 1979–84; Director: Pilkington Glass Ltd, 1982–85 (Chm., 1984–85); Pilkington Holdings Inc., 1984–89; Triplex Safety Glass Co. Ltd, 1984–85; Pilkington Floatglas AB, 1985–87; Flachglas AG, 1985–89. Chm., Pilkington Superannuation Scheme, 1987–; Director: Rowntree plc, 1987–88; Libby-Owens-Ford Co., USA, 1987–92; Charter Consolidated plc, 1988–; Powell Duffryn plc, 1989–; Leeds Permanent Building Soc., 1991–95; MFI (Furniture Group) plc, 1992–; Littlewoods Organisation plc, 1992–; Kwik Save Gp plc, 1993–; Minories Investment Trust plc, 1993–; Halifax Bldg Soc., 1995–; Hobart Pension Trustee Ltd, 1993–; Littlewoods Pension Trust Ltd, 1994–; Trustee, MFI Pension Plan, 1994–. Member: Council of Industry and Parlt Trust, 1987–92; Council, CBI, 1988–92; Council, Textile Inst., 1994–; Court, Univ. of Leeds, 1989–; Dir, Leeds Univ. Foundn Ltd, 1989–. Gov., Cathedral Sch., Bombay, 1974–79; Dir, Breach Candy Hosp. Trust, 1974–79. Mem., Cook Soc., 1985–. Holder of Royal Warrant of Appointment, 1984–85. FInstD; CIMgt; FRSA. Freeman, City of London; Liveryman, Glass Sellers' Co., 1991–. *Recreations:* sailing, general sporting and country life interests. *Address:* Windmill Farm, Wrigley Lane, Over Alderley, Macclesfield, Cheshire SK10 4SA. *T:* Prestbury (01625) 827985. *Clubs:* Oriental, Army and Navy, Cavalry and Guards, East India, Royal Thames, Royal Ocean Racing; Royal Yorkshire Yacht (Bridlington); Leander (Henley); St James's, Racquets (Manchester); Rand, Country (Johannesburg); Royal Bombay Yacht (Cdre, 1977–78).

COOK, Eric William; HM Diplomatic Service, retired; *b* 24 Feb. 1920; *s* of Ernest Gordon Cook and Jessie (*née* Hardy); *m* 1949, Pauline Elizabeth Lee; one *s*. *Educ:* various private estabts. RAF, 1940–46. GPO, 1947–49; FO (later FCO), 1949–80; Consul, Belgrade, 1961–64; Vice-Consul, Leopoldville, 1964–65; Consul, Cleveland, Ohio, 1967–69; also served at Rome, Moscow, Peking and Djakarta; Consul Gen., Adelaide, 1974–76; FCO, 1977–80. *Recreations:* music, writing and photography. *Address:* 11 St Ann's Court, Nizells Avenue, Hove, East Sussex BN3 1PR. *T:* Brighton (01273) 776100.

COOK, Francis; MP (Lab) Stockton North, since 1983; *b* 3 Nov. 1935; *s* of James Cook and Elizabeth May Cook; *m* 1959, Patricia, *d* of Thomas and Evelyn Lundrigan; one *s* three *d*. *Educ:* Corby School, Sunderland; De La Salle College, Manchester; Institute of Education, Leeds. Schoolmaster, 9½ years; Construction Project Manager with Capper-Neill International. *Recreations:* climbing, fell walking, singing, swimming. *Address:* 37 Windlestone Road, Billingham, Cleveland TS23 3JW. *T:* Stockton (01642) 370641.

COOK, Francis John Granville, MA Cantab; Headmaster of Campbell College, Belfast, 1954–71; *b* 28 Jan. 1913; *o s* of late W. G. Cook and Nora Braley; *m* 1942, Jocelyn McKay, *d* of late John Stewart, Westholm, Dunblane, Perthshire; one *s* two *d*. *Educ:* Wyggeston Sch.; Downing Coll., Cambridge. Historical Tripos, Law Tripos; Squire Scholar; Tancred Studentship, Lincoln's Inn. Asst Master, Rossall Sch., 1937; served War, 1940–46, with Royal Navy; Headmaster of Junior Sch., Rossall Sch., 1949–54. *Recreations:* gardening, books, people. *Address:* 49 Bryansford Village, Newcastle, Co. Down BT33 0PT. *T:* Newcastle (Co. Down) (013967) 25165.

See also D. S. Cook.

COOK, Frank Patrick, (Pat); Member, Commission for Local Administration in England and first Local Ombudsman for the North and North Midlands, 1974–85; *b* 28 March 1920; *o c* of Frank Cook, FRCS, FRCOG and Edith Harriet (*née* Reid); *m* 1st, 1945, Rosemary Eason (marr. diss. 1975); two *s* one *d*; 2nd, 1975, Margaret Rodgers, 2nd *d* of Dr J. W. Rodgers, PhD; one *s*. *Educ:* Rugby; Trinity Hall, Cambridge (Open Schol.); LSE (Personnel Management); ASC (Session 16). Royal Marines, 1939–46 (Major; despatches). Courtaulds Ltd, 1946–56; Nat. Coal Board, 1956–61; Venesta Ltd, 1961–64 (Dir, 1963); Principal, British Transport Staff Coll., 1964–69; First Chief Exec., English Tourist Board, 1970–74. Chm., Microtest Research Ltd, 1982–87; Dir and Sec., Mellory Ltd, 1993–. Indep. Mem., Council, FIMBRA, 1988–90; a Vice President: IPM, 1965–67; RCN, 1973–95; Member: Nat. Nursing Staff Cttee, 1967–72; Brighton and Lewes HMC, 1972–74; Ombudsman Adv. Bd, Internat. Bar Assoc., 1975–85; Exec. Cttee, Fawcett Soc., 1975–77; Council, Univ. of York, 1979–85; Merchant Taylors' Co. of York, 1981–; N Yorks FPC, 1985–87. Conducted inquiry into provision for health care in St Helens and Knowsley, 1990. Governor: Martin House Hospice for Children, 1984–86; Bootham and The Mount Quaker Schs, 1987–89. Chm., Cleeve Abbey Action Council of Management, 1988–91. Hon. LLD Hull, 1986. *Publications:* Shift Work, 1954; Ombudsman (autobiog.), 1981; articles on personnel management. *Address:* Mellory, Old Cleeve, near Minehead, Somerset TA24 6HS. *T:* Washford (01984) 640176.

COOK, George David, CEng, FIEE; Consultant, Quantel Ltd, 1985–93, retired; *b* 23 Sept. 1925; *s* of late John and Jean C. Cook; *m* 1954, Sylvia Ann Sampson; two *d*. *Educ:* Hendon College of Technology. BBC Planning and Installation Dept, 1947; Asst to Supt Engineer, Television Outside Broadcasts, 1955; Head of Engineering, Wales, 1963; Asst Chief Engr, Television, 1967; Chief Engr Transmitters, 1974; Asst Dir of Engrg, 1978; Dep. Dir of Engrg, 1984–85. *Recreations:* golf, theatre. *Address:* 26 Ridge Lane, Watford, Herts WD1 3TA. *T:* Watford (01923) 29638.

COOK, George Steveni L.; *see* Littlejohn Cook.

COOK, Gordon Charles, DSc, MD; FRCP; physician with special interest in tropical and infectious diseases; Senior Lecturer in Clinical Sciences, London School of Hygiene and Tropical Medicine, since 1976; *b* Wimbledon, 17 Feb. 1932; *e s* of late Charles Francis Cook and Kate Cook (*née* Grainger); *m* 1963, Elizabeth Jane, *d* of late Rev. Stephen Noel Agg-Large; one *s* three *d*. *Educ:* Wellingborough, Kingston-upon-Thames and Raynes Park Grammar Schs; Royal Free Hosp. Sch. of Medicine, London Univ. (BSc Physiol 1955; MB BS 1957; MD 1965; DSc 1976). MRCS; LRCP 1957, MRCP 1960, FRCP 1972; FRACP 1978; FLS 1989. Commissioned RAMC, seconded to Royal Nigerian Army, 1960–62. Hosp. appts, Royal Free, Hampstead Gen., Royal Northern, Brompton, St George's, 1958–63; Lectr, Royal Free Hosp Sch. of Medicine and Makerere Univ. Coll., Uganda, 1963–69; Prof. of Medicine and Cons. Physician, Univs of Zambia, 1969–74, Riyadh, 1974–75, Papua New Guinea, 1978–81; Sen. MO, MRC, 1975–76. Hon. Consultant Physician: Hosp. for Trop. Diseases and UCL Hosps, 1976–; St Luke's Hosp. for the Clergy, 1988–; Hon. Sen. Lectr in Medicine, UCL, 1981–; Hon. Lectr in Clinical Parasitology, St Bart's Hosp. Med. Coll., 1992–. Vis. Prof., Univs of Basrah, Mosul, Doha. Consultant, advr and mem., professional and learned bodies. Member: Assoc. of Physicians of GB and Ireland, 1973–; Council, Med. Writers Gp, Soc. of Authors, 1994–. Examiner for membership of RCP, 1977–84. Lectures: Ahmed Hafez Moussa Meml, 1994; Stanley Browne Meml, 1995. President: RSTM&H, 1993–95; Osler Club, London, 1993–95; Baconian Club of St Albans, 1995–; Vice-Pres., History of Medicine Sect., RSM, 1994–. Liveryman, Apothecaries' Co., 1981. Editor, Jl of Infection, 1995–; mem., editl bds, med. jls. Charlotte Brown Prize, and Cunning and Legg Awards, Royal Free Hosp. Sch. of Medicine, 1967–69; Frederick Murgatroyd Meml Prize, 1973. *Publications:* (ed) Acute Renal Failure, 1964; Tropical Gastroenterology, 1980; (jtly) 100 Clinical Problems in Tropical Medicine, 1987; Communicable and Tropical Diseases, 1988; Parasitic Disease in Clinical Practice, 1990; From the Greenwich Hulks to Old St Pancras: a history of tropical disease in London, 1992; (ed) Manson's Tropical Diseases, 20th edn, 1995; (ed) Gastroenterological Problems from the Tropics, 1995; (ed) Travel-associated disease, 1995; numerous research papers, chapters, reviews and editorials. *Recreations:* cricket, walking, listening to classical music, medical/scientific history. *Address:* 11 Old London Road, St Albans, Herts AL1 1QE. *T:* St Albans (01727) 869000; Department of Clinical Sciences, Hospital for Tropical Diseases, St Pancras Way, NW1 0PE. *T:* 0171–387 4411, *Fax:* 0171–388 7645. *Clubs:* Athenæum, MCC.

COOK, Harold James; a Metropolitan Stipendiary Magistrate, 1975–Dec. 1996; *b* 25 Jan. 1926; *s* of Harold Cook and Gwendoline Lydia (*née* List); *m* 1952, Mary Elizabeth (*née* Edwards); one *s*. *Educ:* The John Lyon Sch., Harrow; Edinburgh Univ. RN, 1943–47. Civil Service, 1947–52. Called to the Bar, Gray's Inn, 1952; Dep. Chief Clerk, Bow Street, and later Thames, Magistrates' Courts, 1952–54; Inner London QS, 1955; Dep. Clerk to Justices, Gore Div., Mddx, 1956–60; Clerk to Justices, Highgate Div., 1961, and also Barnet and South Mymms Divs, 1968. *Publications:* contrib. legal jls. *Address:* West London Magistrates' Court, Southcombe Street, W14 0RD.

COOK, Rt. Rev. Henry George; retired; *b* Walthamstow, London, England, 12 Oct. 1906; *s* of Henry G. Cook and Ada Mary Evans; *m* 1935, Opal May Thompson, Sarnia, Ont, *d* of Wesley Thompson and Charity Ellen Britney; two *s* one *d*. *Educ:* Ingersoll Collegiate Inst., Ont; Huron Coll. (LTh); Univ. of Western Ont, London, Canada (BA). Deacon, 1935, Priest, 1936; Missionary at Fort Simpson, 1935–43; Canon of Athabasca, 1940–43; Incumbent S Porcupine, Ont., 1943–44; Archdeacon of James Bay, 1945–48; Principal, Bp Horden Sch., Moose Factory, 1945–48; Mem., Gen Synod Exec., 1943–47; Supt of Indian Sch. Admin., 1948–62; Bishop Suffragan of the Arctic, 1963–66, of Athabasca, 1966–70 (the area of Mackenzie having been part first of one diocese and then of the other, constituted an Episcopal District, 1970); Bishop of Mackenzie, 1970–74. RCN(R) Chaplain, 1949–56. Hon. DD Huron Coll. and Univ. of Western Ont. 1946. *Recreations:* fishing, coin collecting, model carving. *Address:* 15 Plainfield Court, Stittsville, Ont K2S 1R4, Canada.

COOK, Cdre Henry Home; Vice-President, Chiltern Society, since 1994 (Chairman, 1988–93); Director of Public Relations, Scientific Exploration Society, 1984–88; *b* 24 Jan. 1918; *o s* of George Home Cook, Edinburgh; *m* 1943, Theffania, *yr d* of A. P. Saunders, Gerrards Cross; two *s* two *d*. *Educ:* St Lawrence Coll., Ramsgate; Pangbourne College. Entered RN as Paymaster Cadet, 1936; Comdr 1955; Captain 1963; Cdre 1970. Naval Sec. to Vice-Adm. Sir Guy Sayer, 1953–59; Sqdn Supply Officer, 1st S/m Sqdn, 1959; Comdr, RNC Greenwich, 1961; Naval Attaché, Ankara, 1964; Dir of Public Relations (RN), 1966; Defence Adviser to British High Comr, and Head of British Defence Liaison

Staff, Ottawa, 1970–72; retired, 1973. ADC to HM the Queen, 1971–72. A Gen. Comr of Income Tax, 1983–92. Dir, Ellerman City Liners Ltd, 1973–80. Pres., Anchorites, 1978; Vice-Pres., Inst. of Admin. Management, 1983–. FInstAM 1973 (Chm., 1982). DipCAM 1975. *Recreations:* fencing, swimming, sailing. *Address:* Ramblers Cottage, Layters Green, Chalfont St Peter, Bucks SL9 8TH. *T:* Gerrards Cross (01753) 883724. *Club:* Wig and Pen.

COOK, Rear-Adm. James William Dunbar, CB 1975; DL; Vice President, Surrey Branch of Soldiers', Sailors', and Airmen's Families Association; *b* 12 Dec. 1921; *s* of James Alexander Cook, Pluscarden, Morayshire; *m* 1949, Edith May Williams; one *s* two *d*. *Educ:* Bedford Sch.; HMS Worcester. CO, HM Ships Venus, Dido and Norfolk; Sen. British Naval Officer, S Africa, 1967–69 (as Cdre); Dir RN War College, 1969–71; Asst Chief of Naval Staff (Ops), 1973–75; retired from RN, 1975. Comdr 1957; Captain 1963; Rear-Adm. 1973; jssc 1958; sowc 1970. Pres., Age Concern (Haslemere), 1990–. DL Surrey, 1989. *Recreations:* golf, gardening. *Address:* Springways Cottage, Farnham Lane, Haslemere, Surrey GU27 1EY. *T:* Haslemere (01428) 643615. *Club:* Army and Navy.

COOK, John, FRCSEd; FRSE 1970; Consultant Surgeon, Eastern General Hospital, Edinburgh, 1964–87; *b* 9 May 1926; *s* of George Cook and Katherine Ferncroft (*née* Gauss); *m* 1953, Patricia Mary Bligh; one *s* four *d*. *Educ:* Fettes Coll., Edinburgh; Edinburgh Univ. (MB 1949, ChM 1963). FRCSEd 1954. Served Med. Br., RAF, 1950–52 (Flt Lieut). House Surgeon, Royal Infirmary, Edinburgh, 1949; Res. Asst, Radcliffe Infirm., Oxford, 1954–55; First Asst, Dept of Surg., Makerere University Coll., Uganda, 1955–64 (Reader in Surg., 1962–64). Royal Coll. of Surgeons of Edinburgh: Hon. Sec., 1969–72; Mem. Council, 1974–84. Representative Mem., GMC, 1982–86; Hon. Sec., Internat. Fedn of Surgical Colls, 1974–84. Hon. Fellow, Polish Assoc. of Surgeons, 1981. *Publications:* contrib. surgical jls. *Recreations:* music, fishing. *Address:* Medwel, Pleasant Row, Clehonger, Hereford HR2 9RE.

COOK, Dr John Barry; Principal, King George VI & Queen Elizabeth Foundation of St Catharine's at Cumberland Lodge, since 1995; *b* 9 May 1940; *er s* of Albert Edward and late Beatrice Irene Cook, Gloucester; *m* 1964, Vivien Margaret Roxana Lamb, *o d* of late Victor and Marjorie Lamb, St Albans; two *s* one *d*. *Educ:* Sir Thomas Rich's Sch., Gloucester; King's Coll., Univ. of London (BSc 1961, AKC 1961); Guy's Hosp. Med. Sch. (PhD 1965). Guy's Hospital Medical School: Biophysics research, 1961–64; Lectr in Physics, 1964–65; Haileybury College: Asst Master, 1965–72; Senior Science Master and Head of Physics Dept, 1967–72; Headmaster: Christ Coll., Brecon, 1973–82; Epsom Coll., 1982–92; Dir, Inner Cities Young People's Project, 1992–95. Church in Wales: Mem. Governing Body, 1976–83; Coll. of Episcopal Electors, 1980–83. Chairman: S Wales ISIS, 1978–82; Academic Policy Cttee, HMC, 1985–88. *Publications:* (jtly) Solid State Biophysics, 1969; Multiple Choice Questions in A-level Physics, 1969; Multiple Choice Questions in O-level Physics, 1970; papers in Nature, Molecular Physics, Internat. Jl of Radiation Biology, Jl of Scientific Instruments, Educn in Science, Conference and Trends in Education. *Recreations:* sports, photography, philately. *Address:* Cumberland Lodge, The Great Park, Windsor, Berks SL4 2HP. *T:* Egham (01784) 432316.

COOK, Joseph, CChem, FRSC; management consultant; *b* 7 April 1917; *y s* of Joseph Cook, MBE, JP, and Jane Cook (*née* Adams), Cumberland; *m* 1950, Betty, *d* of James and Elizabeth Barlow, Standish, Lancs; two *d*. *Educ:* Whitehaven Grammar Sch.; Univ. of Liverpool (BSc, DipEd). RAF, 1939–40. Posts in Ministries of Supply, Aviation, Technology and Defence 1941–59; Dir, ROF Burghfield, 1959–65; Gp Dir, Ammunition Factories, 1966; Dir Gen. (Prodn), ROF, 1966–74; Man. Dir, Millbank Tech. Services Ordnance Ltd, 1974–77 (on secondment from MoD). *Recreations:* gardening, golf. *Address:* Abbots-wood, Bramley Road, Pamber End, near Basingstoke, Hants RG26 5QP. *T:* Basingstoke (01256) 850304.

COOK, Michael John; His Honour Judge Michael Cook; a Circuit Judge, since 1986; *b* 20 June 1930; *s* of George Henry Cook and Nora Wilson Cook (*née* Mackman); *m* 1st, 1958, Anne Margaret Vaughan; three *s* one *d*; 2nd, 1974, Patricia Anne Sturdy; one *d*. *Educ:* Leeds Grammar Sch.; Worksop Coll.; Univ. of Leeds (LLB 2(1) Cl. Hons). Admitted Solicitor, 1953. National Service, commnd Royal Artillery, 1954. Willey Hargrave & Co., Solicitors, to 1957; Ward Bowie, Solicitors, 1957–86 (Senior Partner, 1965–86); a Recorder, 1980–86; Designated Child Care Judge, Guildford County Court. Past Hon. Sec. and Pres., London Solicitors' Litigation Assoc.; Member: Solicitors Disciplinary Tribunal, 1975–86; Law Society sub-cttees and working parties. Mem. Council, Royal Med. Foundn, 1990. Freeman, City of London, 1990. Gen. Editor, Butterworths Costs Service, 1991–; Consultant Editor, The Litigation Letter, 1986– (Editor, 1981–86). *Publications:* The Courts and You, 1976; The Taxation of Contentious Costs, 1979; The Taxation of Solicitors Costs, 1986; (contrib.) County Court Precedents and Pleadings, 1989; Cook on Costs, 1991, 2nd edn 1995; (contrib.) Cordery on Solicitors, 1995. *Recreations:* tennis, gardening, theatre, sitting on moving horses.

COOK, Pat; *see* Cook, F. P.

COOK, Prof. Paul Derek, MBE 1985; PhD; CEng; Chairman and Managing Director, Scientifica-Cook Ltd, since 1962; Professor of Environmental Science, Brunel University, since 1992; *b* 12 March 1934; *s* of James Walter Cook and Florence Jefferay; *m* 1954, Frances Ann James; four *d*. *Educ:* Queen Mary Coll., London (BSc Hons; PhD 1963; Sir John Johnson Scholar, 1959). CEng, MIEE 1963. Res. Scientist: MRC, 1960–62; Middlesex Hosp. Med. Sch., 1962–65. Prof. of Laser Physics, Brunel Univ., 1986–91. Scientific Adviser to: Minister for the Envmt and Countryside, DoE, 1990–92; British Gas, 1990–92; Laser Consultant, BAe, 1986–; former Consultant, W Midlands Police, 1991–92; Scientific Advr to Lady Olga Maitland, 1992–. Responsible for design and develt of numerous laser systems used in med. and mil. estabts throughout world, incl. ophthalmic LaserSpec; originator and inventor of Laser Guidance Systems for weapon alignment in each Tornado; major contrib. to Europe's first laser gyroscope in 1970s; invention of laser instrument that improves safety of motorists by detecting and correcting night myopia; estab. world's first Night Vision Clinic for treating night blindness disorders. Dep. Chm., Conserve, 1990–93; Founder/Pres., British Science and Technol. Trust, 1985–; UK Pres., Japanese Zen Nippon Airinkai, 1978–81. *Recreations:* breeding and rearing exotic Japanese carp, cultivating Japanese bonzai, inventing, experimenting with ideas. *Address:* Carlton House, 78 Bollo Bridge Road, W3 8AU; Chemistry Department, Brunel University, Uxbridge, Mddx UB8 3PH.

COOK, Dr Peter John; Director, British Geological Survey, since 1990; *b* 15 Oct. 1938; *s* of John and Rose Cook; *m* 1961, Norma Irene Walker; two *s*. *Educ:* Durham Univ. (BSc Hons, DSc); ANU (MSc); Univ. of Colorado (PhD). Geologist to Sen. Geologist, BMR, Canberra, 1961–76; Sen. Res. Fellow, ANU Res. Sch. of Earth Sci., 1976–82 (Vis. Fellow, 1982–90); Chief of Div./Chief Res. Scientist, BMR, 1982–90 (Prof., Univ. Louis Pasteur, Strasbourg, 1989). Adrian Fellow, Univ. of Leicester, 1992–. Chairman: Consortium for Ocean Geosci., 1980–82; Commonwealth/State Hydrogeol. Cttee, 1983–88; Member: Adv. Cttee, Aust. Nuclear Sci. and Tech. Orgn, 1984–90; Geolog. Adv. Panel, BM (Nat. Hist.), 1990–; Earth Scis Cttee, NERC, 1990–; Council, MIRO, 1991–; Chm., Ocean Sci. Resources Programme, IOC, 1984–. *Publications:* more than 100 contribs to books and learned jls, on phosphate deposits, marine mineral resources, coastal zone studies and palaeogeography. *Recreations:* ski-ing, hiking, travel, history. *Address:* British Geological Survey, Keyworth, Nottingham NG12 5GG. *T:* Nottingham (0115) 936 3226.

COOK, Reginald, FCA; Chairman, South Wales Electricity Board, 1977–81; Member, Electricity Council, 1977–81; *b* 29 Dec. 1918; *s* of Harold Cook and Gwendolyn Cook, Birmingham; *m* 1945, Constance Irene Holt, Norden, Lancs; one *s* one *d*. *Educ:* Rochdale High Sch.; Manchester Univ. (BA); Admin. Staff Coll. Served War, 1939–46; Staff Captain, RA. Local Govt Service with Corporations of Manchester, West Bromwich and York, 1946–52; Midlands Electricity Board: accountancy posts, 1952–59; Chief Accountant, 1959–69; Exec. Mem., 1964–69; Dep. Chm., S Wales Electricity Bd, 1969–77. CompIEE. Gold Medal, IMTA, 1949. *Recreations:* countryside activities, gardening, golf, bridge. *Address:* Heppleshaw, Itton, Chepstow, Gwent NP6 6BZ. *T:* Shirenewton (01291) 641265.

COOK, Brig. Richard Arthur, CBE 1961; *b* 26 May 1908; *m* 1940, Sheila Mary Ostell Prosser; two *s*. *Educ:* St Paul's; RMA, Woolwich. Commissioned, Royal Artillery, 1928. Posted to India, 1933. Served War of 1939–45 in India and Burma: Staff Coll., 1941; Regimental Comd, 1943; Joint Services Staff Coll., 1947; Col, 1948; Col Administrative Plans, GHQ, MELF, 1948–51; CRA (Brig.) 16th Airborne Div., 1954–56; NATO Defence Coll., 1957; BGS, Southern Command, 1958–61; retired from Army, 1961. *Address:* 3 Meadow Court, Whiteparish, Wilts SP5 2SE. *T:* Whiteparish (01794) 884409. *Club:* Army and Navy.

COOK, Robert Finlayson, (Robin F. Cook); MP (Lab) Livingston, since 1983 (Edinburgh Central, Feb. 1974–1983); *b* 28 Feb. 1946; *s* of late Peter Cook, headmaster and of Christina Cook (*née* Lynch); *m* 1969, Margaret K. Whitmore, medical consultant; two *s*. *Educ:* Aberdeen Grammar Sch.; Univ. of Edinburgh. MA Hons English Lit. Tutor-Organiser with WEA, 1970–74. Chm., Scottish Assoc. of Labour Student Organisations, 1966–67; Sec., Edinburgh City Labour Party, 1970–72; Mem., Edinburgh Corporation, 1971–74, Chm. Housing Cttee, 1973–74. An Opposition Treasury spokesman, 1980–83; opposition front bench spokesman on: European and community affairs, 1983–84; trade, 1986–87; health, 1987–92; trade and industry, 1992–94; foreign and commonwealth affairs, 1994–. Labour's Campaigns Co-ordinator, 1984–86. Mem., Tribune Group. *Recreations:* eating, reading, talking. *Address:* c/o House of Commons, SW1A 0AA. *T:* 0171–219 5120.

COOK, Maj.-Gen. Robert Francis Leonard, MSc, MPhil; CEng, FIEE; CPhys; Director General, Federation of the Electronics Industry (formerly Electronic Engineering Association), since 1993; *b* 18 June 1939; *s* of Lt-Col Frank Leonard Cook and Louise Alicia (*née* Davis); *m* 1961, Gillian Margaret Lowry; one *s* two *d*. *Educ:* Karachi Grammar Sch., Pakistan; St John's Coll., Southsea; University Coll. of Wales; Welbeck Coll.; RMA Sandhurst; RMCS; Staff Coll., Camberley; NATO Defence Coll., Rome. BSc 1962, MSc 1964, London; MPhil (Strategic Studies) Wales, 1989. Commnd Royal Signals, 1959; served Germany, Malaysia, UK, 1959–70; Directorate of Manning (Army), MoD, 1972; OC 7 Armd Bde, Signal Sqn, 1973; Project Management Staff, MoD (PE), 1975; Lt-Col DS, RMCS, 1976; CO 4 Armd Div. HQ and Signal Regt, 1978; Logistics Staff, HQ BAOR, 1981; Colonel, MoD Operational Requirements Staff, 1982; Brig., Comd 1 Signal Bde, 1 (BR) Corps, 1983; Sec., NATO Mil. Cttee, NATO HQ, Brussels, 1986. Signal Officer-in-Chief (Army), 1989–92, and DG Comd, Control, Communications and Information Systems (Army), 1990–92. Col. Comdt, RCS, 1993–. MInstD. Freeman, City of London, 1989; Liveryman: Engineers' Co., 1990; Information Technologists' Co., 1993. Hon. DTech De Montfort Univ., 1994. *Recreations:* mountain walking, winter and water sports, music, travel, wine. *Address:* c/o Lloyds Bank, 8 Market Place, Faringdon, Oxon SN7 7HN. *Club:* Army and Navy.

COOK, Prof. Robert Manuel, FBA 1976; Laurence Professor of Classical Archaeology, University of Cambridge, 1962–76; *b* 4 July 1909; *s* of Rev. Charles Robert and Mary Manuel Cook; *m* 1938, Kathleen (*d* 1979), *d* of James Frank and Ellen Hardman Porter. *Educ:* Marlborough Coll.; Cambridge Univ. Walston Student, Cambridge Univ., 1932; Asst Lectr in Classics, Manchester Univ., 1934; Lectr, 1938; Sub-warden, St Anselm's Hall, Manchester, 1936–38; Laurence Reader in Classical Archaeology, Cambridge Univ., 1945, Ord. Mem., German Archaeological Inst., 1953. Chm., Managing Cttee, British School at Athens, 1983–87. *Publications:* Corpus Vasorum Antiquorum, British Museum 8, 1954; Greek Painted Pottery, 1960, 3rd edn (trans. Greek), 1994; The Greeks till Alexander, 1962; (with Kathleen Cook) Southern Greece: an archaeological guide, 1968; Greek Art, 1972; Clazomenian Sarcophagi, 1981. *Address:* 15 Wilberforce Road, Cambridge CB3 0EQ. *T:* Cambridge (01223) 352863.

COOK, Robin; *see* Cook, Robert F.

COOK, Roger James; investigative journalist; presenter, The Cook Report, Central TV, since 1985; *b* 6 April 1943; *s* of Alfred and Linda Cook; *m* 1st, 1966, Madeline Koh (marr. diss. 1974); 2nd, 1982, Frances Knox; one *d*. *Educ:* Hurlstone Agricl Coll.; Sydney Univ. TV and radio reporter, ABC (Australia), 1960–66; TV and radio dir, Warnock Sandford Advertising (Aust.), 1966–68; reporter, BBC Radio 4, World at One, World This Weekend, PM, 1968–76; freelance documentary dir, 1968–72; creator and presenter, Checkpoint, Radio 4, 1973–85; presenter and reporter, Radio 4 documentary series: Time for Action; Real Evidence; investigative reporter, BBC TV: Nationwide; Newsnight, 1972–84. BPG Award, 1978; Radio Personality of the Year, 1979; Ross McWhirter Award for Bravery, 1980; Valiant for Truth Award, 1988, 1993; Radio and TV Industries Award, for best ITV prog., 1993. *Publication:* (with Tim Tate) What's Wrong With Your Rights?, 1988. *Recreations:* walking, music, motor sport. *Address:* c/o JRA Agencies Ltd, 46 Sutton Court Road, W4 4NL.

COOK, Timothy; Clerk to the Trustees, City Parochial Foundation, since 1986; *b* 25 April 1938; *s* of late Stephen Cook and of Kathleen (*née* Henwood); *m* 1967, Margaret Taylor; one *s* one *d*. *Educ:* Loughborough Grammar Sch.; Trinity Hall, Cambridge (BA); Brunel Univ. (MA). Called to the Bar, Middle Temple, 1961. Asst Lectr in Law, Sheffield Univ., 1960–61; Asst Warden, Norman House, 1962–64; Prison Welfare Officer, HM Prison, Blundeston, 1964–66; Dir, Alcoholics Recovery Project, 1966–74; Hd, Cambridge House and Talbot, 1975–77; Dir, Family Service Units, 1978–85. *Publications:* Vagrant Alcoholics, 1975; (ed jtly) The Drunkenness Offence, 1969; (ed) Vagrancy, 1979. *Recreations:* cinema, reading, theatre. *Address:* 26 Criffel Avenue, SW2 4AZ. *T:* 0181–674 3141.

COOK, William Birkett, MA; Master of Magdalen College School, Oxford, 1972–91; *b* 30 Aug. 1931; *e s* of late William James and Mildred Elizabeth Cook, Headington, Oxford; *m* 1958, Marianne Ruth, *yr d* of late A. E. Taylor, The Schools, Shrewsbury; one *s* one *d* (and one *d* decd). *Educ:* Dragon Sch.; Eton (King's Schol.); Trinity Coll., Cambridge (Schol.). National Service, 1950–51 (commnd in RA). Porson Prizeman, 1953; 1st cl. Classical Tripos Pt I, 1953, Pt II, 1954; Henry Arthur Thomas Student, 1954; MA Oxon by incorporation, 1972. Asst Master, Shrewsbury Sch., 1955–67, and Head of Classical Faculty, 1960–67; Headmaster of Durham Sch., 1967–72. Governor: Oxford High Sch.,

1979–; Bedford Modern Sch., 1992–. Administrator, Choir Schools' Assoc. Bursary Trust, 1987–92; Dir, Thomas Wall Trust, 1992–; Gov., Ewelme Exhibn Endowment, 1993–. *Recreations:* music, gardening, Scottish country dancing. *Address:* 2 Cannon's Field, Old Marston, Oxford OX3 0QR. *T:* Oxford (01865) 250882.

COOKE, family name of **Baron Cooke of Islandreagh**.

COOKE OF ISLANDREAGH, Baron *cr* 1992 (Life Peer), of Islandreagh in the County of Antrim; **Victor Alexander Cooke,** OBE 1981; DL; CEng, FIMechE; Chairman: Henry R. Ayton Ltd, Belfast, 1970–89; Springvale EPS (formerly Polyproducts) Ltd, since 1964; *b* 18 Oct. 1920; *s* of Norman Victor Cooke and Alice Harman Cooke (*née* Peavey); *m* 1951, Alison Sheila Casement; two *s* one *d*. *Educ:* Marlborough Coll., Wilts; Trinity Coll., Cambridge (MA). Engineer Officer, Royal Navy, 1940–46 (Lieut (E) RN). Henry R. Ayton Ltd, Belfast, 1946–89; Chairman: Belfast Savings Bank, 1963; Harland & Wolff Ltd, 1980–81 (Dir, 1970–87); Dir, NI Airports, 1970–85. Member: Senate, Parliament of N Ireland, 1960–68; N Ireland Economic Council, 1974–78; Commissioner, Belfast Harbour, 1968–79; Commissioner of Irish Lights, 1983– (Chm. of Comrs, 1990–92). DL Co. Antrim, 1970. *Recreations:* sailing, shooting. *Club:* Naval.

COOKE, Alexander Macdougall, DM; FRCP; Hon. Consulting Physician, United Oxford Hospitals, 1966; *b* 17 Oct. 1899; *s* of Arthur Clement Cooke, OBE and Isobel Gilles Macdougall; *m* Vera (*d* 1984), *d* of Charles Hermann Lea; one *s* three *d*. *Educ:* Merchant Taylors' School; Jesus College, Oxford; St Thomas's Hosp. (Mead Medal, 1923; Toller Prize). 1st Cl. Hons Nat. Sci. 1920; BM 1923; DM 1933; MRCP 1926, FRCP 1935. War Service, Royal Fusiliers, RFC and RAF, 1917–18. Resident Asst Physician, 1927–28, 1st Asst, Professorial Med. Unit, 1928–30 and Dep. Dir, 1930–32, St Thomas's Hosp.; Physician, Radcliffe Infirmary, 1932–66; May Reader in Medicine, 1933–47; Dir, Clinical Studies, Oxford Medical Sch., 1939–49; Fellow of Merton Coll., Oxford, 1942–66, Emeritus Fellow, 1966–. Lectures: Lumleian, RCP, 1955; Langdon-Brown, RCP, 1968; Litchfield, Oxford, 1964; Stopford Meml, Manchester, 1973. Royal College of Physicians: Examr, 1943–47 and 1952–62; Councillor, 1953–55; Censor, 1956–58; Sen. Censor, 1959–60; Oxford Univ. Rep., GMC, 1963–73. FRSocMed 1924, Hon. Fellow 1972 (Pres., Section of Medicine, 1960–62); Mem., Assoc. of Physicians, 1936 (Exec. Cttee, 1950–53), Hon. Mem., 1966; Hon. Mem., Royal Coll. of Radiologists. Sec. to Editors, 1937–50 and Editor, 1951–65, Quarterly Jl of Medicine. *Publications:* A History of the Royal College of Physicians of London, Vol. III, 1972; Sir E. Farquhar Buzzard, Bt, KCVO, 1975; The Cookes Tale, 1991; My Seventy Five Years of Medicine, 1994; articles and papers on medicine and med. hist. *Recreation:* inertia. Address: Grove Cottage, St Cross Road, Oxford OX1 3TX. *T:* Oxford (01865) 242419. *Club:* Athenæum.

COOKE, (Alfred) Alistair, KBE (Hon.) 1973; journalist and broadcaster; *b* 20 Nov. 1908; *s* of Samuel Cooke and Mary Elizabeth Byrne; *m* 1st, 1934, Ruth Emerson; one *s*; 2nd, 1946, Jane White Hawkes; one *d*. *Educ:* Blackpool Grammar Sch.; Jesus Coll., Cambridge (Scholar; Hon. Fellow, 1986); Yale Univ.; Harvard. Founded Cambridge University Mummers, 1928; First Class, English Tripos, 1929; Second Class, 1930. Editor, The Granta, 1931; Commonwealth Fund Fellow, 1932–34. BBC Film Critic, 1934–37; London Correspondent for NBC, 1936–37; Commentator on American Affairs for BBC, 1938–; Special Correspondent on American Affairs, The London Times, 1938–40; American Feature Writer, The Daily Herald, 1941–43; UN Correspondent of the Manchester Guardian (which changed name to Guardian, 1959), 1945–48; Chief Correspondent in US of The Guardian, 1948–72. Master of ceremonies: Ford Foundation's television programme, Omnibus, 1952–61; UN television programme, International Zone, 1961–67; Masterpiece Theatre, 1971–92. Wrote and narrated, America: a personal history of the United States, BBC TV, 1972–73 (Peabody Award for meritorious services to broadcasting, 1972; Writers' Guild of GB award for best documentary of 1972; Dimbleby Award, Soc. of Film and TV Arts, 1973; four Emmy awards of (US) Nat. Acad. of TV Arts and Sciences, 1973). Hon. LLD: Edinburgh, 1969; Manchester, 1973; Hon. LittD: St Andrews, 1975; Cantab, 1988. Peabody Award for internat. reporting, 1952 and 1983; Benjamin Franklin Medal, RSA, 1973; Howland Medal, Yale Univ., 1977. *Publications:* (ed) Garbo and the Night Watchmen, 1937, repr. 1972; Douglas Fairbanks: The Making of a Screen Character, 1940; A Generation on Trial: USA v Alger Hiss, 1950; Letters from America, 1951; Christmas Eve, 1952; A Commencement Address, 1954; (ed) The Vintage Mencken, 1955; Around the World in Fifty Years, 1966; Talk about America, 1968; Alistair Cooke's America, 1973; Six Men, 1977; The Americans: fifty letters from America on our life and times, 1979; (with Robert Cameron) Above London, 1980; Masterpieces, 1982; The Patient has the Floor, 1986; America Observed, 1988; Fun & Games with Alistair Cooke, 1994. *Recreations:* playing golf, watching tennis, music, biography. *Address:* 1150 Fifth Avenue, New York City, NY 10128, USA; Nassau Point, Cutchogue, Long Island, NY, USA. *Clubs:* Athenæum; Lotos, National Arts, Links (New York); San Francisco Golf.

COOKE, Rear-Adm. Anthony John, CB 1980; Private Secretary to Lord Mayor of London, 1981–92; *b* 21 Sept. 1927; *s* of Rear-Adm. John Ernest Cooke, CB and late Kathleen Mary Cooke; *m* 1st, 1951, Margaret Anne (marr. diss. 1994), *d* of late Frederick Charles Hynard; two *s* three *d*; 2nd, 1995, Patricia Sinclair, *d* of late William Sinclair Stewart and Margaret Jane Stewart; one step *s* two step *d*. *Educ:* St Edward's Sch., Oxford. Entered RN 1945; specialised in navigation, 1953; Army Staff Coll., 1958; Sqdn Navigating Officer, HMS Daring, Second Destroyer Sqdn, 1959–61; Staff Navigating Officer to Flag Officer, Sea Trng, 1961; Comdr 1961; Directorate of Naval Ops and Trade, 1961–63; i/c HMS Brighton, 1964–66; Directorate of Navigation and Tactical Control, 1966; Captain 1966; Captain of Dockyard and Queen's Harbourmaster, Singapore, 1967–69; Captain 1st Destroyer Sqdn, Far East, later Divnl Comdr 3rd Div. Western Fleet, i/c HMS Galatea, 1969–71; Dir, Royal Naval Staff Coll., 1971–73; Cdre Clyde i/c Clyde Submarine Base, 1973–75; Rear-Adm. 1976; Senior Naval Mem., Directing Staff, RCDS, 1975–78; Adm. Pres., RNC Greenwich, 1978–80, retd. Police Foundn, 1980–81. A Younger Brother, Trinity House, 1974. Freeman: City of London, 1979; Shipwrights' Co., 1980. OStJ 1990. *Address:* 4 Amherst Road, Ealing, W13 8ND. *T:* 0181–997 2620.

COOKE, Brian, JP; Circuit Administrator, South Eastern Circuit, 1989–95; *b* 16 Jan. 1935; *s* of Norman and Edith Cooke; *m* 1958, Edith Mary Palmer; two *s* one *d*. *Educ:* Manchester Grammar Sch.; University Coll. London (LLB). Served Royal Air Force, 1956–59. Called to Bar, Lincoln's Inn, 1959; Dept of Director of Public Prosecutions, 1960–68; Deputy Clerk of the Peace, Inner London Quarter Sessions, 1968–71; Dep. Circuit Administrator, North Eastern Circuit, 1971–81, Circuit Administrator 1981–82; Sec. of Commissions, 1982–88, Hd of Judicial Appointments Gp, 1987–88, Lord Chancellor's Dept. JP Mddx, 1985. *Recreations:* tennis, walking, theatre, music. *Address:* 12 The Pryors, East Heath Road, NW3 1BS. *Club:* Cumberland Lawn Tennis.

COOKE, Prof. Brian Ernest Dudley; Professor Emeritus, University of Wales, 1983; Professor of Oral Medicine and Oral Pathology, University of Wales, Dean of Welsh National School of Medicine Dental School and Consultant Dental Surgeon to University Hospital of Wales, 1962–82; *b* 12 Jan. 1920; *e s* of Charles Ernest Cooke and Margaret Beatrice Wood; *m* 1948, Marion Neill Orkney Hope; one *s* one *d*. *Educ:* Merchant Taylors' Sch.; London Univ. LDSRCS 1942; LRCP, MRCS 1949; FDSRCS 1952; MDSU London 1959; MRCPath 1965, FRCPath 1974. Served RNVR (Dental Br.), 1943–46. Nuffield Dental Fellow, 1950–52; Trav. Nuffield Fellow, Australia, 1964. Lectr 1952–57, Reader in Dental Med. 1958–62, Guy's Hosp. Dental School. Rep. Univ. of Wales on Gen. Dental Council, 1964–82; Mem. Bd of Faculty of Dental Surgery, RCS England, 1964–72 (Vice-Dean 1971–72); Chm., Dental Educn Adv. Council, GB, 1975–78 (Mem. 1962–82); Sec.-Gen., Assoc. for Dental Educn in Europe, 1982–84. Adviser in Dental Surgery to Welsh Hosp. Bd, 1962–74; Civilian Consultant in Dental Surgery to RN, 1967–. Hon. Adviser, Editorial Bd, British Jl of Dermatology, 1967–76. Mem., S Glamorgan AHA, 1974–76. Mem. Bd of Governors: United Cardiff Hosps, 1965–71; HMC (Cardiff) Univ. Hosp. of Wales, 1971–74. Vice-Provost, Welsh Nat. Sch. of Medicine, 1974–76. Examr in Dental Surgery and Oral Pathology, Liverpool, Manchester and London Univs; Examr for Primary Fellowship in Dental Surgery, RCS, 1967–73. Hon. Mem., Pierre Fauchard Acad., 1967. Charles Tomes Lectr, RCS, 1963; Guest Lectr, Students' Vis. Lectrs Trust Fund, Witwatersrand Univ., 1967; Vis. Prof., Univ. of Sydney Dental Sch., 1986–87. Pres., Section of Odontology, RSocMed, 1975 (Hon. Mem., 1990); Founder Pres., British Soc. for Oral Medicine, 1981. Hon. Coll. Fellow, Univ. of Wales Coll. of Medicine, 1990. Cartwright Prize and Medal, RCS, 1955; Chesterfield Prize and Medal, St John's Hosp. for Diseases of Skin, 1955. *Publications:* (jtly) Oral Histopathology, 1959, 2nd edn 1970; scientific contribs to medical and dental jls. *Recreations:* various. *Address:* 38 St Aidan Crescent, Heath, Cardiff CF4 4AU. *T:* Cardiff (01222) 693503.

COOKE, Sir Charles Fletcher F.; *see* Fletcher-Cooke.

COOKE, Colin Ivor; Chairman, Triplex Lloyd PLC, since 1991 (Director, since 1989); Non-Executive Chairman, Fenner PLC, since 1993; *b* 17 Dec. 1939; *m* 1983, Sheila Handley; four *s* one *d*. *Educ:* Cardiff High Sch.; Advanced Coll. of Technology, Newport (HND Metallurgy). GKN, 1956–63; Hepworth Ceramic, 1963–71; RTZ, 1971–72; Du-Port, 1972–80, Main Bd Dir, 1982–86; Non-Exec. Dir, Ash & Lacy, 1987–; Director: WDA, 1987–89; British Dredging, 1990–. Chm., Tipton City Challenge, 1993–. *Recreations:* golf, swimming, military history. *Address:* Triplex Lloyd, Quayside House, Sandwell Green, Rounds Green Road, Oldbury, W Midlands B69 2DH. *Clubs:* Wig and Pen; Royal Porthcawl Golf; Cardiff County.

COOKE, Cynthia Felicity Joan, CBE 1975; RRC 1969; Matron-in-Chief, Queen Alexandra's Royal Naval Nursing Service, 1973–76; *b* 11 June 1919; *d* of late Frank Alexander Cooke, MBE, DCM, and of Ethel May (*née* Buckle). *Educ:* Rosa Bassett Sch. for Girls; Victoria Hosp. for Children, Tite Street, Chelsea; RSCN, 1940; University Coll. Hosp., London, SRN, 1942; Univ. of London, Sister Tutor Diploma, 1949. Joined QARNNS, 1943; served in: Australia, 1944–45; Hong Kong, 1956–58; Malta, 1964–66. HMS: Collingwood, Gosling, Goldcrest; RN Hospitals: Chatham, Plymouth, Haslar. Principal Tutor, Royal Naval School of Nursing, 1967–70; Principal Matron, RN Hosp., Haslar, 1970–73. QHNS 1973–76. CStJ 1975. *Address:* The Banquet House, Kings Head Mews, The Pightle, Needham Market, Suffolk IP6 8AQ.

COOKE, David Charles; Partner, Pinsent & Co., solicitors, since 1969 (Senior Partner, 1986–94); *b* 22 March 1938; *s* of F. J. E. Cooke and Hilda Cooke. *Educ:* Bolton Sch.; Accrington Grammar Sch.; Manchester Univ. (LLB). Hall Brydon & Co., Manchester, 1961–64; King & Partridge, Madras, 1964–67; Asst Solicitor, 1967. Pinsent & Co., Birmingham *Recreations:* classical music, fell walking, theatre, reading. *Address:* Pinsent & Co., 3 Colmore Circus, Birmingham B4 6BH. *T:* 0121–200 1050. *Club:* Oriental.

COOKE, Col Sir David (William Perceval), 12th Bt *cr* 1661; freelance consultant/researcher; *b* 28 April 1935; *s* of Sir Charles Arthur John Cooke, 11th Bt, and Diana (*d* 1989), *o d* of late Maj.-Gen. Sir Edward Maxwell Perceval, KCB, DSO; *S* father, 1978; *m* 1959, Margaret Frances, *o d* of Herbert Skinner, Knutsford, Cheshire; three *d*. *Educ:* Wellington College; RMA Sandhurst; Open Univ. (BA). FCIT; FIMgt; Associate, Internat. Inst. of Risk and Safety Management. Commissioned 4/7 Royal Dragoon Guards, 1955; served BAOR, 1955–58; transferred to RASC, 1958; served: BAOR, 1958–60; France, 1960–62; Far East, 1962–65; UK. Transferred to RCT on formation, 1965, and served UK, 1965–76, and BAOR, 1976–80; AQMG, MoD, 1980–82; Comdr, Transport and Movements, HQ British Forces, Hong Kong, 1982–84; Comdr, Transport and Movts, NW Dist, Western Dist and Wales, 1984–87; Col, Movements 1 (Army), MoD, 1987–90. Operational service: Brunei, 1962; Malay Peninsula, 1964–65; N Ireland, 1971–72. Attended Staff Coll., Camberley, 1968 and Advanced Transport Course, 1973–74. Col 1984. Dir of Finance and Resources, Bradford City Technol. Coll., 1990–92. Silver Jubilee Medal, 1977. *Recreations:* fishing, ornithology, military history. *Heir: cousin* Edmund Harry Cooke-Yarborough [*b* 25 Dec. 1918; *m* 1952, Anthea Katharine, *er d* of J. A. Dixon; one *s* one *d*]. *Address:* c/o Midland Bank, Knutsford, Cheshire WA16 6BZ.

COOKE, George Venables, CBE 1978; *b* 8 Sept. 1918; *s* of William Geoffrey Cooke and Constance Eva (*née* Venables); *m* 1941, Doreen (*née* Cooke); one *s* two *d*. *Educ:* Sandbach Sch., Cheshire; Lincoln Coll., Oxford, 1936–39 and 1946. MA, DipEd (Oxon). Served Army, 1939–46 (Major). Teacher, Manchester Grammar Sch., 1947–51; Professional Asst (Educn), W Riding of Yorkshire CC, 1951–53; Asst Dir of Educn, Liverpool, 1953–58; Dep. Dir of Educn, Sheffield, 1958–64; Dir of Educn, Lindsey (Lincs) CC, 1965–74; County Educn Officer, Lincolnshire CC, 1974–78; Gen. Sec., Soc. of Education Officers, 1978–84. Chm., Secretary of State's Adv. Cttee on Handicapped Children, 1973–74; Vice-Chm., Nat. Cttee of Enquiry into Special Educn (Warnock Cttee), 1974–78; Member: Jt Adv. Cttee on Agricultural Educn (Hudson Cttee), 1971–74; Parole Bd, 1984–87. Pres., Soc. of Educn Officers, 1975–76; Chm., County Educn Officers' Soc., 1976–77. Chm., Lincs and Humberside Arts, 1987–92. Hon. LLD Hull, 1991. *Recreations:* golf, gardening. *Address:* White House, Grange Lane, Riseholme, Lincoln LN2 2LQ. *T:* Lincoln (01522) 522667. *Club:* Royal Over-Seas League.

COOKE, Gilbert Andrew, FCA; Chairman and Chief Executive, C. T. Bowring & Co. Ltd, 1982–88; Director, Marsh & McLennan Companies Inc., 1980–88; *b* 7 March 1923; *s* of Gilbert N. Cooke and Laurie Cooke; *m* 1949, Katherine Margaret Mary McGovern; one *s* one *d*. *Educ:* Bournemouth Sch. FCA 1950. Sen. Clerk, chartered accountants, 1950–54; Bowmaker Ltd: Chief Accountant, 1955; Dir, 1968; Man. Dir, 1968; Dep. Chm. and Chief Exec., 1972; C. T. Bowring & Co. Ltd: Dir, 1969; Gp Man. Dir, 1976–82. Chm., Bowring UK, 1984–88. Chm., Finance Houses Assoc., 1972–74. *Recreations:* music, reading. *Address:* Kilmarth, Onslow Road, Burwood Park, Walton-on-Thames, Surrey. *T:* Walton-on-Thames (01932) 240451.

COOKE, Sir Howard (Felix Hanlan), ON 1991; GCMG 1991; GCVO 1994; CD 1978; Governor-General of Jamaica, since 1991; *b* 13 Nov. 1915; *s* of David Brown Cooke and Mary Jane Minto; *m* 1939, Ivy Sylvia Lucille Tai; two *s* one *d*. Teacher, Mico Trng Coll., 1936–38; Headmaster, Belle Castle All-Age Sch., 1939–50; Teacher: Port Antonio Upper Sch., 1951; Montego Bay Boys' Sch., 1952–58; Br. Manager, Standard Life Insce Co., 1960–71; Unit Manager, Jamaica Mutual Life Assce Co., 1971–81; Br. Manager, Alico

Jamaica, 1982–91. Member: WI Federal Parlt, 1958–62; Senate, 1962–67; House of Representatives, 1967–80; Govt Minister, 1972–80. Sen. Elder, United Church of Jamaica and Grand Cayman; lay pastor and former Chm., Cornwall Council of Churches. Mem., Ancient and Accepted Order of Masons. Special Plaque for Distinguished Service, CPA, 1980. *Recreations:* cricket, football, gardening, reading. *Address:* (office) King's House, Hope Road, Kingston 6, Jamaica, WI. *T:* 9276143, 9276426.

COOKE, Jean Esme Oregon, RA 1972 (ARA 1965); (professional name Jean E. Cooke); Lecturer in Painting, Royal College of Art, 1964–74; *b* 18 Feb. 1927; *d* of Arthur Oregon Cooke, Grocer, and of Dorothy Emily Cooke (*née* Cranefield); *m* 1953, John Randall Bratby, RA (marr. diss., he *d* 1992); three *s* one *d*. *Educ:* Blackheath High Sch.; Central Sch. of Arts and Crafts, Camberwell; City and Guilds; Goldsmiths' Coll. Sch. of Art; Royal Coll. of Art. NDD in Sculpture, 1949. Pottery Workshop, 1950–53; Tutor, Summer Sch., Swiss Alps, 1992–94. Member: Council, Royal Acad., 1983–85 and 1992–94 (Sen. Hanger, 1993); Academic Bd, Blackheath Sch. of Art, 1986–; Governor: Central Sch. of Art and Design, 1984–; Tertiary Educn Bd, Greenwich, 1984–. Life Pres., Friends of Woodlands Art Gall., Blackheath, 1990. Purchase of self-portrait, 1969, and portrait of John Bratby (called Lilly, Lilly on the Brow), 1972, by Chantry Bequest; portraits: Dr Egon Wellesz and Dr Walter Oakshott for Lincoln Coll., Oxford; Mrs Bennett, Principal, for St Hilda's Coll., Oxford, 1976; Peter Carlisle, 1985–86; Clare Chalmers and Jane Lee, 1987–88; John Petty, 1989. Started Homage to Birling Gap (large painting), 1985. Television film: Portrait of John Bratby, BBC, 1978. *One-man shows:* Establishment Club, 1963; Leicester Gall., 1964; Bear Lane Gall., Oxford, 1965; Arun Art Centre, Arundel; Ashgate Gall., Farnham; Moyan Gall., Manchester; Bladon Gall., Hampshire, 1966; Lane Gall., Bradford, 1967; Gallery 66, Blackheath, 1967; Motley Gall., Lewisham, 1968; Phoenix, Suffolk, 1970; New Grafton Gall., 1971; Ansdell Gall., 1974; Woodlands Gall., Blackheath, 1976 and 1991; J. K. Taylor Gall., Cambridge, 1976; Garden Gall., Greenwich, 1983; Alpine Gall., 1986; Friends Room, RA, 1990; Bardolf Hall, Sussex, 1990, in aid of Birling Gap Safety Boat; Blackheath Concert Halls, 1990; Linton Court Gall., Settle, 1991; open studio for: Greenwich Festival, 1977–94; Blackheath High Sch. Art Fund, 1979; Bakehouse Gall., Blackheath, 1980; open studio in aid of: Royal Acad. Trust, 1982; Birling Gap Safety Boat, 1989. *Works exhibited:* annually, RA, 1956–; Furneaux Gall., 1968; Upper Grosvenor Gall., 1968; Ashgate Gall., 1973; Agnews, 1974; Gall. 10, Richmond Hill, 1974; Leonie Jonleigh Gall., 1976; Dulwich Coll. Picture Gall., 1976; British Painting 1952–77, Royal Acad., 1977; Business Art Galleries, 1978; New Ashgate Gall., 1979; Tate Gall., 1979; Grosvenor Street Gall., 1979, 1980; Norwich Gall., 1979, 1980; Imp. Coll. Gall., 1980; Patrick Seale Gall., Belgravia, 1981; WEA, 1987; Foss Gall. Gp, 1987, 1988, 1990; RCA, 1988; Hurlingham Gall., 1990; Patterson Gall., 1990, 1991, 1992, 1993, 1994; King Street Gall., 1992; Thompson's Gall., 1992; Sacker Galls, RA, 1993. *Publications:* Contemporary British Artists; The Artist, 1980; The Artist's Garden, 1989. *Recreations:* ungardening, talking, shouting, walking along the beach. *Address:* 7 Hardy Road, Blackheath, SE3 7NS. *T:* 0181–858 6288.

COOKE, Jeremy Lionel; QC 1990; *b* 28 April 1949; *s* of Eric Edwin Cooke and Margaret Lilian Cooke; *m* 1972, Barbara Helen Willey; one *s* two *d*. *Educ:* Whitgift Sch., Croydon; St Edmund Hall, Oxford (Open Exhibn, 1967; MA Jurisprudence, 1st cl. Hons 1970; Rugby blue, 1968, 1969). Admitted Solicitor, 1973; with Coward Chance, 1973–76; called to the Bar, Lincoln's Inn, 1976. Church Elder. *Address:* 7 King's Bench Walk, Temple, EC4Y 7AS. *T:* 0171–583 0404.

COOKE, John Arthur; Head of International Trade Policy Division, Department of Trade and Industry, since 1992; *b* 13 April 1943; *er s* of late Dr Arthur Hafford Cooke, MBE and Ilse Cooke (*née* Sachs); *m* 1970, Tania Frances, 2nd *d* of A. C. Crichton; one *s* two *d*. *Educ:* Dragon Sch.; Magdalen Coll. Sch., Oxford; Univ. of Heidelberg; King's Coll., Cambridge (Exhibnr, Sen. Scholar, BA History 1964, MA 1968); LSE. Mem., Cambridge Univ. expedition to Seistan, 1966. Asst Principal, Board of Trade, 1966; Second, later First, Sec., UK Delegn to European Communities, 1969–73; DTI, 1973–76; Office of UK Perm. Rep. to European Communities, 1976–77; Dept of Trade, 1977–80 (at Inst. Internat. d'Administration Publique, Paris, 1979); Asst Sec., Dept of Trade, 1980–84; seconded to Morgan Grenfell & Co. as Asst Dir, 1984–85; DTI, 1985–; Under Sec., Overseas Trade Div. 2, 1987–89; Head of Central Unit, 1989–92; Dir, Deregulation Unit, 1990–92. Dir (non-exec.), RTZ Pillar Ltd, 1990–93. Member: Bd, St Luke's Community Trust, 1983–93; Council, Marie Curie Meml Foundn, 1992–. *Recreations:* reading, travelling, looking at buildings. *Address:* c/o Department of Trade and Industry, Kingsgate House, 66–74 Victoria Street, SW1E 6SW. *T:* 0171–215 5000. *Clubs:* United Oxford & Cambridge University; Cambridge Union.

COOKE, Air Vice-Marshal John Nigel Carlyle, CB 1984; OBE 1954; Consultant Physician: Civil Aviation Authority, since 1985; King Edward VII Hospital, Midhurst, 1988–93; *b* 16 Jan. 1922; *s* of Air Marshal Sir Cyril Bertram Cooke, KCB, CBE and Phyllis Amelia Elizabeth Cooke; *m* 1958, Elizabeth Helena Murray Johnstone; two *s* one *d*. *Educ:* Felsted Sch.; St Mary's Hosp., Paddington (MD, BS(London)). FRCP, FRCPEd, MRCS, MFOM. House Physician, St Mary's, Paddington, 1945; RAF medical Br., 1945–85; Sen. Registrar, St George's, London, 1956–58; Consultant Physician, RAF, 1958–85; overseas service in Germany, Singapore, Aden; Prof. of Aviation Medicine, 1974–79; Dean of Air Force Medicine, 1979–83; Senior Consultant, RAF, 1983–85. UK Mem., Medical Adv. Bd, European Space Agency, 1978–84; Consultant to CAA, UK, 1972–; Consultant Advr to Sultan of Oman's Air Force, 1985–91. Chairman: Defence Med. Services Postgrad. Council, 1980–82; Ethics Cttee, RAF Inst. of Aviation Medicine, 1987–89; Pres., Assoc. of Aviation Med. Examiners, 1986–94. QHP 1979–85. *Publications:* articles on metabolic and aviation medicine subjects in numerous medical jls. *Recreations:* gliding, fly fishing. *Address:* 4 Lincoln Close, Stoke Mandeville, Bucks HP22 5YS. *Club:* Royal Air Force.

COOKE, Joseph; *see* Cooke, P. J. D.

COOKE, Kenneth; *see* Cooke, R. K.

COOKE, (Patrick) Joseph (Dominic), FIMC; Vice-Chairman, Daily Telegraph, since 1994 (Managing Director, 1987–94); *s* of Patrick Cooke and Mary (*née* Naughton); *m* 1960, Margaret Mary Brown; two *s* four *d*. *Educ:* St Joseph's Coll.; University Coll., Galway (BE). CEng, MICE, MIMechE; FIMC 1968; MIMgt; AIIRA. United Steel Cos, 1952–54; Workington Iron & Steel Co., 1954–61; Urwick, Orr and Partners Ltd, 1961–73: Sen. Partner, 1967; Principal Partner, 1970; founded Cooke Management Consultants Ltd, 1973; Non-Exec. Dir, EMAP plc, 1984–; Consultant, Daily Telegraph, 1985–87; Non-Executive Director: IFRA, 1990–; Hollinger, 1992–. Sandford Smith Award, Inst. Management Consultants, 1967. *Recreations:* golf, gardening. *Address:* The Telegraph plc, 1 Canada Square, Canary Wharf, E14 5DT. *T:* 0171–538 5000.

COOKE, Peter; *see* Cooke, W. P.

COOKE, Randle Henry, LVO 1971; Chairman, Randle Cooke and Associates, Recruitment Consultants, since 1992 (Managing Director, 1987–92); Fund-Raising Director, Royal Botanic Gardens, Kew, since 1995; *b* 26 April 1930; *o s* of late Col H. R. V. Cooke, Dalicote Hall, Bridgnorth, Salop and Mrs E. F. K. Cooke, Brodawel, Tremeirchion, N Wales; *m* 1961, Clare, *d* of C. J. M. Bennett, *qv*; one *s* one *d*. *Educ:* Heatherdown, Ascot; Eton College. 2nd Lieut, 8th King's Royal Irish Hussars, 1949; served Korea, 1950–53 with Regt and USAF (POW); ADC to GOC 7th Armoured Div., 1955; Regimental Adjt, 1957; Instructor, RMA Sandhurst, 1960; Sqdn Comdr, The Queen's Royal Irish Hussars, Malaya, Borneo and Germany, 1963; GSO3 (SD), HQ 1st Div., 1965. Equerry to the Duke of Edinburgh, 1968–71; Private Sec. to Lord Mayor of London, 1972–74. Dir, Personnel and Administration, Alginate Industries plc, 1974–78; Managing Director: ARA International Ltd, 1984–86; Mervyn Hughes International Ltd, 1986–87. Dep. Dir, Treasurers' Dept, Cons. Central Office, 1992–95. Freeman of City of London, 1971. *Recreations:* most things to do with water. *Address:* Coney Hill House, Great Missenden, Bucks HP16 9PE. *T:* Great Missenden (01494) 862147. *Club:* Cavalry and Guards.

COOKE, His Honour (Richard) Kenneth, OBE 1945; a Circuit Judge, 1980–92; *b* 17 March 1917; *s* of Richard and Beatrice Mary Cooke; *m* 1st, 1945, Gwendoline Mary Black (*d* 1985); no *c*; 2nd, 1986, E. A. Rowlands (*née* Bachmann). *Educ:* Sebright Sch., Wolverley; Birmingham Univ. Admitted Solicitor (Hons), 1939; Birmingham Law Soc. Prizeman. Sqdn Leader, RAFVR, 1939–45. Solicitor in private practice specialising in Magistrates' Courts, 1945–52; Clerk: to Prescot and St Helens Justices, 1952–57; to Rotherham County Borough and WR Justices, 1957–64; to Bradford City Justices, 1964–70; Metropolitan Stipendiary Magistrate, 1970–80; a Recorder of the Crown Court, 1972–80. Mem. Council, Magistrates' Assoc., 1973–89 (Chm. Legal Cttee; Hon. Sec. Inner London Branch, 1972–89; a Dep. Chm., 1981–82; Pres., SE London Br., 1985–89); Member: Lord Chancellor's Adv. Cttee on the Training of Magistrates, 1978–85; Adv. Bd, Crime Concern Trust, 1988–. Reader, Rochester Dio., 1970–. Hon. Mem., Justices' Clerks Soc., 1988. *Publications:* contribs to Criminal Law Review, Justice of the Peace and Local Govt Review, etc. *Recreations:* fishing, choral singing, sampling bin ends. *Address:* The Bridewell, 6 Liskeard Close, Chislehurst, Kent BR7 6RT. *T:* 0181–467 3908.

COOKE, Rt. Hon. Sir Robin (Brunskill), KBE 1986; Kt 1977; PC 1977; PhD; **Rt. Hon. Mr Justice Cooke;** President, Court of Appeal of New Zealand, since 1986 (Judge, 1976–86); *b* 9 May 1926; *s* of Hon. Philip Brunskill Cooke, MC (Judge of Supreme Court), and Valmai Digby Gore; *m* 1952, Phyllis Annette Miller; three *s*. *Educ:* Wanganui Collegiate Sch.; Victoria University Coll., Wellington (LLM); Clare Coll., Cambridge; Gonville and Caius Coll., Cambridge (MA, PhD). Trav. Scholarship in Law, NZ, 1950; Fellow, Gonville and Caius Coll., Cambridge, 1952 (Yorke Prize, 1954), Hon. Fellow, 1982. Called to the Bar, Inner Temple, 1954, Hon. Bencher 1985; practised at NZ Bar, 1955–72; QC 1964; Judge of Supreme Court, 1972; Pres., Court of Appeal of Western Samoa, 1982 and 1994, of Cook Is, 1981 and 1982. Administrator, NZ Govt, for periods in 1986, 1992 and 1993. Chm., Commn of Inquiry into Housing, 1970–71; Mem. Adv. Bd, Centre for Independence of Judges and Lawyers, 1989–; Commn Mem., Internat. Commn of Jurists, 1993–. Special Status Mem., Amer. Law Inst., 1993. Vis. Fellow, All Souls Coll., Oxford, 1990. Lectures: Sultan Azlan Shah Law, Malaysia, 1990; Peter Allan Meml, Hong Kong, 1994. Hon. LLD: Victoria Univ. of Wellington, 1989; Cambridge Univ., 1990; Hon. DCL Oxford, 1991. *Publications:* (ed) Portrait of a Profession (Centennial Book of NZ Law Society), 1969; (Editor in Chief), The Laws of New Zealand; articles in law reviews and papers at internat. law confs. *Recreations:* theatre, The Times crossword, watching cricket. *Address:* 4 Homewood Crescent, Karori, Wellington, New Zealand. *T:* (4) 4768059. *Clubs:* United Oxford & Cambridge University; Wellington, Wellington Golf (NZ).

COOKE, Roger Arnold; His Honour Judge Roger Cooke; a Circuit Judge, since 1989; *b* 30 Nov. 1939; *s* of late Stanley Gordon and of Frances Mabel Cooke; *m* 1970, Hilary Robertson; two *s* two *d*. *Educ:* Repton; Magdalen Coll., Oxford (BA 1961; MA 1966). Astbury Scholar, Middle Temple, 1962; called to the Bar, Middle Temple, 1962, *ad eund* Lincoln's Inn, 1967 (Bencher, 1994); in practice, Chancery Bar, 1963–89; Asst Recorder, 1982–87; Recorder, 1987–89. Sec., Chancery Bar Assoc., 1979–89; Mem., Bar Disciplinary Tribunal, 1988–89. Mem., Inst. of Conveyancers, 1983–; MRI. *Recreations:* gardening, photography, history, amateur dramatics, old buildings, food. *Address:* Mayor's & City of London Court, 32 Threadneedle Street, EC2R 8AY. *T:* 0171–374 2708. *Club:* Athenæum.

COOKE, Roger Malcolm; Managing Partner–Chief Financial Officer, Arthur Andersen, since 1993; *b* 12 March 1945; *s* of Sidney and Elsie Cooke; *m* 1968, Antoinette; one *s* one *d*. FCA, FTII. Qualified Chartered Accountant, 1968; Arthur Andersen & Co.: joined 1968, Tax Div.; Partner, 1976; Head, London Tax Div., 1979; area co-ordinator, tax practice, Europe, Middle East, Africa and India, 1989–93; Dep. Man. Partner, UK, and Area Co-Ordinator, Tax Europe, 1989–93. *Publication:* Establishing a Business in the United Kingdom, 1978. *Recreations:* playing tennis, travel, ski-ing, cricket, football, good food. *Address:* (office) 69 West Washington Street, Chicago, IL 60602, USA. *T:* (312) 5072249. *Club:* Mid-Town Tennis.

COOKE, Prof. Ronald Urwick, MSc, PhD, DSc; Vice-Chancellor, University of York, since 1993; *b* 1 Sept. 1941; *y s* of Ernest Cooke and Lillian (*née* Mount), Maidstone, Kent; *m* 1968, Barbara Anne, *d* of A. Baldwin; one *s* one *d*. *Educ:* Ashford Grammar Sch.; University College London, Univ. of London (BSc 1st Cl. Hons, MSc, PhD, DSc; Fellow, 1994); FGS. Lectr, UCL, 1961–75; Prof. of Geography, 1975–81, Dean of Science, 1978–80, and Vice-Principal, 1979–80, Bedford Coll., Univ. of London; Prof. and Hd of Dept of Geography, 1981–93, Dean of Arts, 1991–92, and Vice-Provost, 1991–93, UCL. Amer. Council of Learned Societies Fellow, UCLA, 1964–65 and 1973; Visiting Professor: UCLA, 1968; Univ. of Arizona, Tucson, 1970; Arizona State Univ., Tempe, 1988. Desert research in N and S America, N Africa and ME. Chm., Geomorphological Services Ltd, 1986–90. Mem., US-UK Fulbright Commn, 1995–. Chm., British Geomorphological Res. Group, 1979; Mem. Council: RGS, 1980–83 (Back Grant, 1977; Founder's Medal, 1994); Inst. of British Geographers, 1973–75 (Pres., 1991–92). Hon. Sec., York Archaeological Trust, 1994–; Trustee, Laurence Sterne Trust, 1994–. Fellow, RHBNC, 1993. *Publications:* (ed with J. H. Johnson) Trends in Geography, 1969; (with A. Warren) Geomorphology in Deserts, 1973; (with J. C. Doornkamp) Geomorphology in Environmental Management, 1974, 2nd edn 1990; (with R. W. Reeves) Arroyos and Environmental Change in the American Southwest, 1976; (contrib.) Geology, Geomorphology and Pedology of Bahrain, 1980; (contrib.) Urban Geomorphology in Drylands, 1982; Geomorphological Hazards in Los Angeles, 1984; (with A. Warren and A. S. Goudie) Desert Geomorphology, 1993; (with G. B. Gibbs) Crumbling Heritage?, 1993; contribs mainly on desert and applied geomorphology in prof. jls. *Address:* University of York, Heslington, York YO1 5DD. *T:* York (01904) 430000. *Club:* Athenæum.

COOKE, Roy, MA; JP; Director of Coventry School Foundation, 1977–92, retired; *b* Manchester, 6 May 1930; *s* of Reginald Herbert Cooke and Alice Cooke; *m* 1957, Claire Marion Medlicott Woodward, *d* of Lt-Col C. S. Woodward, CBE, JP, DL and Irene Anne Woodward, Glamorgan; three *s*. *Educ:* Manchester Grammar Sch. (schol.); Trinity Coll., Oxford (schol.; BA 1951; MA 1955; DipEd). Army service, 1951–54; commnd RAEC; Staff Officer in Germany (Captain, actg Major). Assistant Master: Gillingham

Grammar Sch., Kent, 1955–56; Woking Grammar Sch., Surrey, 1956–58; Manchester Grammar Sch., 1958–64; Head of For. Langs, Stockport Sch., 1964–68; Headmaster: Gravesend Sch. for Boys, 1968–74; King Henry VIII Sch., Coventry, 1974–77. JP Kent, 1972, W Midlands, 1976. *Recreations:* photography, gardening, fell-walking, music. *Address:* 10 Stivichall Croft, Coventry CV3 6GN. *Club:* East India.

COOKE, (William) Peter; Chairman, Price Waterhouse Regulatory Advisory Practice, since 1989; Deputy Chairman, Housing Corporation, since 1994 (Member of Board, since 1988); *b* 1 Feb. 1932; *s* of late Douglas Edgar Cooke, MC and Florence May (*née* Mills); *m* 1957, Maureen Elizabeth, *er d* of late Dr E. A. Haslam-Fox; two *s* two *d*. *Educ:* Royal Grammar Sch., High Wycombe; Kingswood Sch., Bath; Merton Coll., Oxford (MA). Entered Bank of England, 1955; Bank for Internat. Settlements, Basle, 1958–59; Personal Asst to Man. Dir, IMF, Washington, DC, 1961–65; Sec., City Panel on Takeovers and Mergers, 1968–69; First Dep. Chief Cashier, Bank of England, 1970–73; Adviser to Governors, 1973–76; Hd of Banking Supervision, 1976–85; Associate Dir, 1982–88. Chairman: City EEC Cttee, 1973–80; Group of Ten Cttee on Banking Regulations and Supervisory Practices at BIS, Basle, 1977–88. Director: Safra Republic Holdings SA, 1989–; FSA (UK), 1994–; Alexander & Alexander, NY, 1994–. Member: Nat. Cttee, English Churches Housing Group, 1977–94; British Invisibles Europe Cttee, 1988–; Council, RIIA, 1992–. Governor: Pangbourne Coll., 1982–; Kingswood Sch., 1991–. *Recreations:* music, golf, travel. *Address:* (office) Southwark Towers, 32 London Bridge Street, SE1 9SY; (home) Bow Wood Barn, Bottom House Farm Lane, Chalfont St Giles, Bucks HP8 4EE. *Clubs:* Reform; Denham Golf.

COOKE-PRIEST, Rear Adm. Colin Herbert Dickinson, CB 1993; National Director, The Trident Trust, since 1994; a Gentleman Usher to the Queen, since 1994; *b* 17 March 1939; *s* of Dr William Hereward Dickinson Priest and Harriet Lesley Josephine Priest (*née* Cooke); *m* 1965, Susan Mary Diana Hobler; two *s* two *d*. *Educ:* St Pirans, Maidenhead; Marlborough Coll.; BRNC, Dartmouth. Entered RN, 1957; Lieut, 1960; exchange service with RAN, 1968–70; commanded: HMS Plymouth, 1975–76; HMS Berwick, 1976; Airwarfare Directorate, Naval Staff, MoD, 1977–79; Naval Asst to C-in-C Fleet, 1979–81; Asst Dir, Naval Air Warfare, 1981–82; CO, HMS Boxer, 1983–85; Dir, Maritime Tactical Sch., 1985–87; CO, HMS Brilliant and Capt. Second Frigate Sqn, 1987–89; Dep. Asst Chief of Staff (Ops) to Supreme Allied Comdr Europe, 1989–90; Flag Officer, Naval Aviation, 1990–93. FRAeS 1992. Freeman, City of London, 1985; Hon. Liveryman, Coachmakers' and Coachharness Makers' Co., 1985. *Recreations:* tennis, cricket, golf. *Address:* Marleys, Heath Road, Petersfield, Hampshire GU31 4EJ. *Clubs:* Army and Navy, Royal Navy of 1765 and 1785.

COOKSEY, Sir David (James Scott), Kt 1993; Chief Executive, since 1981, and Chairman, since 1987, Advent Ltd; Chairman, Audit Commission for Local Government and the National Health Service in England and Wales, since 1986; a Director, Bank of England, since 1994; *b* 14 May 1940; *s* of Dr Frank S. Cooksey, CBE, and Muriel M. Cooksey; *m* 1973, Janet Clouston Bewley Wardell-Yerburgh (*née* Cathie, *widowed* 1970); one *s* one *d*, and one step *d*. *Educ:* Westminster Sch.; St Edmund Hall, Oxford Univ. (MA). Dir of Manufacturing, Formica International, 1969–71; Man. Dir, Intercobra Ltd, 1971–80; Director: Advent International Corp., 1985–90; Electra Risk Capital, 1981–90; Macro 4, 1982–88; Agricultural Genetics Co., 1983–; European Silicon Structures, 1985–; Maison Blanc Ltd, 1992–; SQL Systems International BV, 1992–; ISIS Innovation Ltd, 1993–; Bespak plc, 1993–. Member: Council, CBI, 1976–88; Scottish Economic Council, 1980–87; Vice Chancellors and Principals Adv. Cttee on Industry, 1984–87; Council, British Venture Capital Assoc., 1983–89 (Chm., 1983–84); Innovation Adv. Bd, DTI, 1988–93; Sci. and Industry Cttee, BAAS, 1988–; PPARC, 1994–. Mem., Pres's Cttee, Campaign for Oxford, 1988–. Mem. Council, Southampton Univ. *Publications:* papers in Philosophical Mag., Jl of Physics and Chemistry of Solids, Jl of Inst. of Metals. *Recreations:* sailing, property restoration, music, theatre. *Address:* 25 Buckingham Gate, SW1E 6LD. *T:* 0171–630 9811. *Clubs:* Boodle's, Royal Thames Yacht; Royal Yacht Squadron.

COOKSON, Dame Catherine (Ann), DBE 1993 (OBE 1985); author, since 1950; *b* 20 June 1906; *d* of Catherine Fawcett; *m* 1940, Thomas Cookson. Member: Society of Authors; Writers' and Authors' Guild. Paul Harris Fellow, Rotary International, Hexham, 1985. Catherine Cookson Foundation, Newcastle Univ., established 1985. Hon. MA Newcastle upon Tyne, 1983; Hon. DLitt Sunderland Polytechnic, 1991. Freeman of South Shields, 1978. *Publications:* Kate Hannigan, 1950; The Fifteen Streets, 1951 (staged 1987, London 1988); Colour Blind, 1953; Maggie Rowan, 1954; A Grand Man, 1954 (filmed as Jacqueline, 1956); The Lord and Mary Ann, 1956; Rooney, 1957 (filmed 1958); The Menagerie, 1958; The Devil and Mary Ann, 1958; Slinky Jane, 1959; Fanny McBride, 1959; Fenwick Houses, 1960; Love and Mary Ann, 1961; The Garment, 1962; Life and Mary Ann, 1962; The Blind Miller, 1963; Hannah Massey, 1964; Marriage and Mary Ann, 1964; The Long Corridor, 1965; Mary Ann's Angels, 1965; Matty Doolin, 1965; The Unbaited Trap, 1966; Katie Mulholland, 1967; Mary Ann and Bill, 1967; The Round Tower, 1968 (RSL Winifred Holtby Award for Best Regional Novel); Joe and the Gladiator, 1968; Our Kate (autobiog.), 1969; The Nice Bloke, 1969; The Glass Virgin, 1970; The Invitation, 1970; The Nipper, 1970; The Dwelling Place, 1971; Feathers in the Fire, 1971; Pure as the Lily, 1972; Blue Baccy, 1972; The Mallen Streak, 1973; The Mallen Girl, 1974; The Mallen Litter, 1974; Our John Willie, 1974; The Invisible Cord, 1975; The Gambling Man, 1975 (staged 1985); The Tide of Life, 1976; Mrs Flannagan's Trumpet, 1976; The Girl, 1977; Go Tell It To Mrs Golightly, 1977; The Cinder Path, 1978; The Man Who Cried, 1979; Tilly Trotter, 1980; Lanky Jones, 1980; Tilly Trotter Wed, 1981; Tilly Trotter Widowed, 1982; The Whip, 1983; Hamilton, 1983; The Black Velvet Gown, 1984; Goodbye Hamilton, 1984; A Dinner of Herbs, 1985; Harold, 1985; The Moth, 1986; Catherine Cookson Country (memoirs), 1986; Bill Bailey, 1986; The Parson's Daughter, 1987; Bill Bailey's Lot, 1987; The Cultured Handmaiden, 1988; Bill Bailey's Daughter, 1988; Let Me Make Myself Plain, 1988; The Harrogate Secret, 1989; The Black Candle, 1989; The Wingless Bird, 1990; The Gillyvors, 1990; My Beloved Son, 1991; The Rag Nymph, 1991; The House of Women, 1992; The Maltese Angel, 1992; The Year of the Virgins, 1993; *as Catherine Marchant:* Heritage of Folly, 1962; Fen Tiger, 1963; House of Men, 1964; Martha Mary Crawford, 1975; The Slow Awakening, 1976; The Iron Façade, 1977. *Recreations:* painting, gardening. *Address:* c/o Anthony Sheil Associates, 43 Doughty Street, WC1N 2LF. *Club:* PEN (English Centre).

COOKSON, Lt-Col Michael John Blencowe, OBE 1986; TD 1969; Vice Lord-Lieutenant of Northumberland, since 1987; land owner, agriculturist; *b* 13 Oct. 1927; *s* of late Col John Charles Blencowe Cookson, DSO, TD, DL; *m* 1957, Rosemary Elizabeth, *d* of David Aubrey Haggie; one *s* three *d*. *Educ:* Eton; Cirencester Agricl Coll., 1951–52. Served with: E African Forces, Kenya, 1947–48; Northumberland Hussars (TA), 1952–69; Queen's Own Yeomanry, 1969–72; Chm., Northumberland Hussars (TA) Regtl Assoc., 1977–87. Hon. Col, Northumberland Hussars Sqn QOY, 1988–92. Chm., Co. Cttee, Northumberland Assoc. Boys' Clubs, 1974–86 (Mem., 1964–73). Chm., Northumberland Queen's Silver Jubilee Appeal, 1978. High Sheriff, 1976, DL 1983, Northumberland. *Recreations:* hunting (Joint Master: Haydon Foxhounds, 1955–57; Morpeth Foxhounds, 1960–64, 1971–), gardening. *Address:* Meldon Park, Morpeth, Northumberland NE61 3SW. *T:* Hartburn (0167072) 661. *Club:* Northern Counties (Newcastle upon Tyne).

COOKSON, Prof. Richard Clive, MA, PhD; FRS 1968, FRSC; Research Professor of Chemistry in the University of Southampton, 1983–85, Emeritus Professor, since 1985 (Professor of Chemistry, 1957–83); *b* 27 Aug. 1922; *s* of late Clive Cookson; *m* 1948, Ellen Fawaz; two *s*. *Educ:* Harrow Sch.; Trinity Coll., Cambridge. BA 1944; MA, PhD Cantab 1947. Research Fellow, Harvard Univ., 1948; Research Div. of Glaxo Laboratories Ltd, 1949–51; Lectr, Birkbeck Coll., London Univ., 1951–57. *Publications:* papers, mainly in Jl Chem. Soc. *Address:* Northfield House, Coombe Bissett, Salisbury, Wilts SP5 4JZ.

COOLEY, Sir Alan (Sydenham), Kt 1976; CBE 1972; FIE; Secretary, Department of Productivity, 1977–80, retired 1981; *b* 17 Sept. 1920; *s* of Hector William Cooley and Ruby Ann Cooley; *m* 1949, Nancie Chisholm Young; four *d*. *Educ:* Geelong Grammar Sch.; Melbourne Univ. (BEngSc). Cadet Engr, Dept of Supply, 1940–43; Engrg Rep., London, 1951–52; Manager, Echuca Ball Bearing Factory, 1953–55; Supply Rep., Washington, 1956–57; Manager, Small Arms Factory, Lithgow, 1958–60; Dept of Supply: First Asst Sec. (Management Services and Planning), 1961–62; Controller-Gen. (Munitions Supply), 1962–66; Sec., 1966–71; Chm., Australian Public Service Bd, 1971–77. *Recreations:* golf, fishing. *Address:* PO Box 105, Milton, NSW 2538, Australia.

COOMBE, Gerald Hugh; His Honour Judge Gerald Coombe; a Circuit Judge, since 1986; *b* 16 Dec. 1925; *s* of William Stafford Coombe and Mabel Florence Coombe; *m* 1957, Zoë Margaret Richards; one *s* one *d*. *Educ:* Alleyn's School, Dulwich; Hele's School, Exeter; Exeter College, Oxford. MA 1950. RAF (Navigator), 1944–48; Solicitor, 1953; Partner, Whitehead Monckton & Co., Maidstone, 1956–86; HM Coroner, Maidstone, 1962–86; a Recorder, 1983–86. *Club:* Royal Air Force.

COOMBE, Michael Rew; His Honour Judge Coombe; a Circuit Judge, since 1985; *b* 17 June 1930; *s* of late John Rew Coombe and Phyllis Mary Coombe; *m* 1961, Elizabeth Anne Hull; two *s* one *d* (and one *s* decd). *Educ:* Berkhamsted; New Coll., Oxford. MA (Eng. Lang. and Lit.). Called to Bar, Middle Temple, 1957 (Harmsworth Scholar), Bencher 1984. 2nd Prosecuting Counsel to the Inland Revenue at Central Criminal Court and 5 Courts of London Sessions, 1971; 2nd Counsel to the Crown at Inner London Sessions, Sept. 1971; 1st Counsel to the Crown at Inner London Crown Court, 1974; 4th Junior Treasury Counsel at Central Criminal Court, 1974, 2nd Jun. Treasury Counsel, 1975, 1st Jun. Treasury Counsel, 1977; Recorder of the Crown Court, 1976–85; Sen. Prosecuting Counsel to the Crown, CCC, 1978–85. Freeman, City of London, 1986. *Recreations:* theatre, antiquity, art and architecture, printing. *Address:* Central Criminal Court, EC4M 7EH.

COOMBES, Keva Christopher; with R. M. Broudie & Co., solicitors; *b* 23 Dec. 1949; *s* of Arthur Edward Coombes and Beatrice Claire Coombes; *m* 1970, Kathy Gannon; two *s* one *d*. *Educ:* Chatham House Grammar Sch.; Univ. of East Anglia (BA). Admitted Solicitor, 1977; Consultant, David Phillips Harris & Whalley, 1986. Member: Liverpool CC, 1976–80, 1986–92 (Leader, 1987–90); Merseyside CC, 1981–86 (Leader, 1982–86). Contested (Lab) Hyndburn, 1987. *Address:* c/o R. M. Broudie & Co., 1–3 Sir Thomas Street, Liverpool L1 8BW. *T:* 0151–227 1429.

COOMBS, Anthony Michael Vincent; MP (C) Wyre Forest, since 1987; *b* 18 Nov. 1952; *s* of Clifford Keith Coombs and Celia Mary Gostling (*née* Vincent); *m* 1984, Andrea Caroline (*née* Pritchard); one *s*. *Educ:* Bilton Grange Sch.; Charterhouse; Worcester Coll., Oxford (MA). Birmingham City Council: Mem., 1978–; Deputy Chairman: Educn Cttee, 1982–84; Social Services Cttee, 1982–84; Cons. spokesman on educn, Birmingham MDC, 1984–86. PPS to Rt Hon. David Mellor, MP, 1989–92. Vice-Chairman: Cons. Back-Bench Educn Cttee, 1993– (Sec., 1987–93); Cons Parly Educn Cttee, 1993–; All Party Parly Sports Cttee, 1993–; Parly Human Rights Gp, 1993– (Sec., 1987–93); Parly Social Scis Gp, 1994–; Sec., Cons. Parly Finance Cttee, 1994–. Dir of several cos in Midlands, and Man. Dir, Grevayne Properties Ltd, 1972–. Pres., Wyre Forest "Solidarity" Campaign, 1987–; Mem., One Nation Gp. Vice-Chm., Friends of Cyprus, 1992–. Chm. of Governors, Perry Common Sch., Birmingham, 1978–; Governor: King Edward Foundn, 1982–88; Birmingham Coll. of Tourism, 1982–88. *Publications:* Reviving our Inner Cities, Bow Group Paper, 1986; numerous articles in newspapers and jls. *Recreations:* golf, tennis, occasional football, music, theatre, ballet. *Address:* Morningside, 35 Tilehouse Green Lane, Knowle, Solihull, W Midlands B93 9EZ; 47 Clarence Street, Kidderminster DY10 1RS. *T:* Kidderminster (01562) 752439.

COOMBS, Derek Michael; *b* 12 Aug. 1937; *m* 1986, Jennifer Lonsdale; two *s*, and one *s* one *d* by previous marriage. *Educ:* Rydal Prep. Sch.; Bromsgrove. Chm. and Man. Dir, S & U plc, 1976–; Dir, Metalrax Group plc, 1975–. Political journalist. MP (C) Yardley, 1970–Feb. 1974. Successfully introduced unsupported Private Member's Bill for relaxation of Earnings Rule, 1972, establishing parly record for a measure of its kind; author of Cons. rate scheme for Oct. 1974 Gen. Election; specialist on economic affairs. Lectured on foreign affairs at Cons. weekend confs. Active pro-European. Governor, Royal Hosp. and Home for Incurables. Named as one of top 100 in report, The British Entrepreneur 1988. *Publications:* numerous articles on home, economic and European affairs. *Recreations:* friends, reading, tennis, skiing. *Address:* Cheyne Row, SW3. *T:* 0171–352 6709.

COOMBS, Douglas Stafford, PhD; Controller, Books Division, British Council, 1980–83, retired; *b* 23 Aug. 1924; *s* of Alexander John Coombs and Rosina May (*née* Stafford); *m* 1950, Valerie Nyman; one *s* three *d*. *Educ:* Royal Liberty Sch., Romford; University College of Southampton; University College London (BA Hons, PhD). Served Royal Air Force, 1943–47. Lecturer in History, University College of the Gold Coast (subseq. Univ. of Ghana), 1952–60; British Council, 1960–: Nigeria, 1960–62; Overseas Student Centre, London, 1962–67; Bombay, 1967–73; Representative: Zambia, 1973–76; Yugoslavia, 1976–79; Visiting Fellow, Postgrad. School of Librarianship and Information Science, Univ. of Sheffield, 1979–80. Consultant, Byways and Bridleways Trust, 1984–; Chm., Wootton Rivers Village Soc., 1985–88. *Publications:* The Conduct of the Dutch, 1958; The Gold Coast, Britain and The Netherlands, 1963; Spreading the Word: the library work of the British Council, 1988; articles in historical jls. *Recreations:* travel, walking, watching cricket. *Address:* The Long House, Primrose Hill, Wootton Rivers, Marlborough, Wilts SN8 4NJ. *T:* Marlborough (01672) 810201.

COOMBS, Herbert Cole, MA, PhD; FAA; FAHA; FASSA; Visiting Fellow, Centre for Resource and Environmental Studies, Australian National University, since 1976; *b* 24 Feb. 1906; *s* of Francis Robert Henry and Rebecca Mary Coombs; *m* 1931, Mary Alice Ross; three *s* one *d*. *Educ:* Univ. of Western Australia, Perth, WA (MA); LSE (PhD). School teacher, Education Dept, WA, 1929; Asst Economist, Commonwealth Bank of Australia, 1935; Economist to Commonwealth Treasury, 1939; Mem., Commonwealth Bank Board, 1942; Dir of Rationing, 1942; Dir-Gen. of Post-War Reconstruction, 1943; Governor, Commonwealth Bank of Australia, 1949–60; Chm., Commonwealth Bank Board, 1951–60; Governor and Chm. of Board, Reserve Bank of Australia, 1960–68; Chancellor, ANU, 1968–76. Chairman: Australian Elizabethan Theatre Trust, 1954–68; Australian Council for Arts, 1968–74; Australian Council for Aboriginal Affairs, 1968–76; Royal Commn on Australian Govt Admin, 1974–76. Hon. LLD: Melbourne; ANU; Sydney; Hon. DLitt WA; Hon. DSc NSW; Hon. Fellow LSE, 1961. *Publications:* The Fragile Pattern, 1970; Other People's Money, 1971; Kulinma: Listening to Aboriginal

Australians, 1978; Trial Balance—issues in my working life, 1981; (jtly) A Certain Heritage: programs by and for Aborigines, 1983; Towards a National Aboriginal Conference, 1985; The Waitangi Treaty and Aborigines (Boyer Lect.), 1988; (jtly) Land of Promises—economic development and aborigines of the East Kimberly, 1989; The Return of Scarcity—Essays Economic and Ecological, 1989; Aborigines Made Visible – from Humbug to Politics (Myer Lect.), 1991; Aboriginal Autonomy, 1993. *Recreations:* walking, cooking, listening to music. *Address:* 119 Milson Road, Cremorne, NSW 2090, Australia.

COOMBS, Ven. Peter Bertram; Archdeacon of Reigate, 1988–95; *b* 30 Nov. 1928; *s* of Bertram Robert and Margaret Ann Coombs; *m* 1953, Catherine Ann (*née* Buckwell); one *s* one *d*. *Educ:* Reading Sch.; Bristol Univ. (MA 1960); Clifton Theological Coll. Curate, Christ Church, Beckenham, 1960–64; Rector, St Nicholas, Nottingham, 1964–68; Vicar, Christ Church, New Malden, 1968–75; Rural Dean of Kingston upon Thames, 1970–75; Archdeacon of Wandsworth, 1975–88. *Recreations:* walking, sketching. *Address:* 36 South Park, Sevenoaks, Kent TN13 1DU. *T:* Sevenoaks (01732) 457138.

COOMBS, Prof. Robert Royston Amos, ScD; FRS 1965; FRCPath 1969; Quick Professor in Immunology, University of Cambridge, 1966–88, now Emeritus; Fellow of Corpus Christi College, since 1962; *b* 9 Jan. 1921; *s* of Charles Royston Amos and Edris Owen Amos (formerly Coombs); *m* 1952, Anne Marion Blomfield; one *s* one *d*. *Educ:* Diocesan Coll., Cape Town; Edinburgh and Cambridge Univs. BSc, MRCVS Edinburgh 1943; PhD Cambridge 1947. Stringer Fellow, King's Coll., Cambridge, 1947–56; Asst Director of Research, Dept of Pathology, University of Cambridge, 1948; Reader in Immunology, University of Cambridge, 1963–66. Foreign Hon. Mem., Royal Belgium Acad. of Medicine, 1991. Hon. FRCP 1973; Hon. Fellow, Amer. Coll. of Allergists, 1979; Hon. FRSM 1992; Hon. Member: Amer. Assoc. of Immunologists, 1973–; British Blood Transfusion Soc., 1984–; British Soc. for Immunology, 1988–; British Soc. Allergy and Clin. Immunology, 1988–; Pathol. Soc. of GB and Ire., 1990–; British Soc. Haematology, 1993–. Hon. MD Linköping Univ. 1973; Hon. dr med. vet. Copenhagen, 1979; Hon. DSc: Guelph, 1981; Edinburgh, 1984. Landsteiner Award, Amer. Assoc. of Blood Banks, 1961; Gairdner Foundn Award, 1965; Henry Steele Gold Medal, RCVS, 1966; James Calvert Spence Medal, British Paediatric Assoc., 1967; Philip Levine Medal, Amer. Soc. Clin. Pathol, 1969; Oliver Meml Award, 1979; Clemens von Pirquet Medal, Austrian Soc. of Allergy and Immunology, 1988; British Soc. Haematology Medal, 1993. *Publications:* (with Anne M. Coombs and D. G. Ingram) Serology of Conglutination and its relation to disease, 1960; (ed with P. G. H. Gell) Clinical Aspects of Immunology, 1963, 3rd edn (also with P. J. Lachmann), 1975; numerous scientific papers on immunology. *Recreation:* retreat to the country. *Address:* 6 Selwyn Gardens, Cambridge CB3 9AX. *T:* Cambridge (01223) 352681.

COOMBS, Simon Christopher; MP (C) Swindon, since 1983; *b* 21 Feb. 1947; *s* of late Ian Peter Coombs and of Rachel Robins Coombs; *m* 1983, Kathryn Lee Coe Royce. *Educ:* Reading University (BA, MPhil); Wycliffe College. Marketing Executive, British Telecom and Post Office, Data and Telex, 1970–82; Marketing Manager, Telex Networks, British Telecom, 1982–83. Mem., Southern Electricity Consultative Council, 1981–84. Reading Borough Council: Mem., 1969–84; Chm., Transportation Cttee, 1976–83; Vice-Chm., Policy Cttee, 1976–83; Dep. Leader, 1976–81; Chief Whip, 1983. PPS to Minister of State for Industry and IT, 1984–85, to Parly Under-Sec. of State DoE, and Minister of State for the Environment, 1985, to Sec. of State for Scotland, 1993–. Member: Select Cttee on Employment, 1987–93; British-American Parly Gp, 1983–; CPA, 1983–; Chairman: Cable TV Gp, 1987– (Sec, 1986–87); British Malawi Parly Gp, 1989–93 (Sec., 1985–89); Pres., Parly Food and Health Forum, 1993– (Chm., 1989–93; Sec., 1985–89); Treasurer: Parly IT Cttee, 1987–; Anglo-Malta Gp, 1994–; Sec., Anglo-Tunisia Gp, 1994–. Vice-Chairman: Cons. Tourism Cttee, 1988–93 (acting Chm., 1993–); All Party Tourism Cttee, 1992–; All Party Manuf. Gp, 1993–; All Party Exports Gp, 1993–; Sec., Cons. Employment Cttee, 1991; Chm., Cons. Party, Wessex Area, 1980–83; Chm., Wessex Area Young Conservatives, 1973–76; Pres., Wilts Young Conservatives, 1984–; Vice Pres., N Wilts Disabled Drivers, 1985–. Member University Court: Univ. of Reading; Univ of Bath; Univ. of Berks; Univ. of Cranfield. *Recreations:* music, cricket, philately, reading. *Address:* House of Commons, SW1A 0AA. *T:* 0171–219 5049. *Clubs:* Swindon Conservative; Hampshire Cricket.

COONEY, Raymond George Alfred, (Ray Cooney); actor, author, director, theatrical producer; created Theatre of Comedy at Shaftesbury Theatre, and Little Theatre of Comedy at Ambassadors Theatre, 1983; purchased The Playhouse, London, 1992; *b* 30 May 1932; *s* of Gerard Cooney and Olive (*née* Clarke); *m* 1962, Linda Dixon; two *s*. *Educ:* Alleyn's Sch., Dulwich. First appeared in Song of Norway, Palace, 1946; toured in Wales, 1954–56; subseq. played in: Dry Rot and Simple Spymen, Whitehall; Mousetrap, Ambassador; Charlie Girl, Adelphi; Not Now Darling, Savoy (also film); Not Now Comrade (film); Run for your Wife, Guildford; Two into One, Leicester and Guildford; (and dir) It Runs in the Family, Playhouse, 1992. Productions (some jointly) include: Thark (revival); Doctor at Sea; The Queen's Highland Servant; My Giddy Aunt; Move Over Mrs Markham; The Mating Game; Lloyd George Knew My Father; That's No Lady-That's My Husband; Say Goodnight to Grandma; Two and Two Make Sex; At the End of the Day; Why Not Stay for Breakfast?; A Ghost on Tiptoe; My Son's Father; The Sacking of Norman Banks; The Bedwinner; The Little Hut; Springtime for Henry; Saint Joan; The Trials of Oscar Wilde; The Dame of Sark; Jack the Ripper; There Goes the Bride (and played leading role, Ambassadors, 1974); Ipi Tombi; What's a Nice Country Like US Doing In a State Like This?; Some of My Best Friends Are Husbands; Banana Ridge; Fire Angel; Elvis; Whose Life is it Anyway? (London and NY); Clouds; Chicago; Bodies; Beatlemania; Not Now Darling (revival); Hello Dolly (revival); Duet for One (London and NY); They're Playing Our Song; Children of a Lesser God; Run for your Wife; Aladdin; See How They Run; Pygmalion; Two Into One; Passion Play; Loot (revival); Intimate Exchanges; Wife Begins at Forty; An Italian Straw Hat (revival); It Runs in the Family; Out of Order. *Publications:* (with H. and M. Williams) Charlie Girl, 1965; *plays:* (with Tony Hilton) One for the Pot, 1961; Chase Me Comrade, 1964; (with Tony Hilton) Stand by your Bedouin, 1966; (with John Chapman) Not Now Darling, 1967; (with John Chapman) My Giddy Aunt, 1968; (with John Chapman) Move Over Mrs Markham, 1969; (with Gene Stone) Why Not Stay for Breakfast?, 1970; (with John Chapman) There Goes the Bride, 1973; Run for Your Wife, 1981; Two into One, 1983; Wife Begins at Forty, 1986; It Runs in the Family, 1989; Out of Order, 1990; Funny Money, 1994; One Good Turn, 1994. *Recreations:* tennis, swimming, golf. *Address:* The Playhouse, Northumberland Avenue, WC2N 5DE. *Club:* Dramatists'.

COOP, Sir Maurice (Fletcher); Kt 1973; Solicitor; *b* 11 Sept. 1907; *s* of George Harry and Ada Coop; *m* 1948, Elsie Hilda Brazier. *Educ:* Epworth Coll., Rhyl; Emmanuel Coll., Cambridge (BA). Admitted Solicitor of Supreme Court, 1932. Sec., Dunlop Rubber Co. Ltd, 1948–68; Dir, Dunlop Rubber Co. Ltd, 1966–70. Chm., Standing Adv. Cttee to Govt on Patents, 1972–74. *Recreations:* Association football, cricket. *Address:* 39 Hill Street, Berkeley Square, W1X 7FG. *T:* 0171-491 4549. *Club:* United Oxford & Cambridge University.

COOPER, family name of **Viscount Norwich.**

COOPER; *see* Ashley-Cooper, family name of Earl of Shaftesbury.

COOPER, Very Rev. Alan; *see* Cooper, Very Rev. W. H. A.

COOPER, Rev. Albert Samuel; Moderator, Free Church Federal Council, 1973–74; *b* 6 Nov. 1905; *s* of Samuel and Edith Cooper; *m* 1936, Emily (*d* 1983), *d* of Hugh and Emily Williams; one *s* one *d*. *Educ:* Birkenhead Inst.; London Univ. (external student; BA Hons Philosophy); Westminster Coll., Cambridge (DipTheol); Fitzwilliam House, Cambridge (BA Theol Tripos, MA). Ordained 1936. Pastoral charges: St Columba's Presbyterian Church, Grimsby, 1936–41; Blundellsands Presbyt. Ch., Liverpool, 1941–44; St Columba's Presbyt. Ch., Cambridge, 1944–60; St Columba's Presbyt. (later United Reformed) Ch., Leeds, 1960–72, retd 1972. Free Church Chaplain. Fulbourn Mental Hosp., Cambridgeshire, 1950–60. Moderator, Presbyt. Ch. of England, 1968–69. *Address:* 3 Abbeyfield House, 2 Gerald Road, Oxton, Birkenhead, Merseyside L43 2JX. *T:* 0151-651 1971.

COOPER, Andrew Ramsden, CBE 1965; FEng 1977; FIEE; Industrial Consultant, since 1966; Member for Operations and Personnel, Central Electricity Generating Board, 1957–66; *b* 1 Oct. 1902; *s* of Mary and William Cooper, Rotherham, Yorks; *m* 1922, Alice Robinson (marr. diss. 1982); one *s* two *d*; *m* 1982, Helen Louise Gordon. *Educ:* Rotherham Grammar Sch.; Sheffield Univ. CEng; SFInstE; Hon. Life FIEEE. Colliery Engineer, Yorks and Kent, 1918–28; Chief Electrical Engineer, Pearson & Dorman Long, 1928; Personal Asst to G. A. Mower, London, 1934; joined Central Electricity Board Operation Dept, NW England and N Wales, 1935; transf. to HQ, 1937; during War, evacuated to Surrey (formed Surrey Social Council for helping troops; introd. self-educn for isolated army units; granted rank of Capt.); Operation Engineeer, SE and E England, 1942; Chief Operation Engineer to Central Electricity Board, 1944; Controller, Merseyside and N Wales Div. (Central Electricity Authority), 1948–52; NW Div., 1952–54; N West, Merseyside and N Wales Reg., 1954–57; Mem. Ops and Personnel, CEGB, 1957–66. Inventor, ARCAID Deaf/Blind Conversation Machine; Pres. Electricity Industries Benevolent Assoc., 1964–65; Mem, GB-USSR Cttee, 1967–91. Faraday Lectr, 1952–53; Bernard Price Meml Lects, S African Inst. of Electr. Engrg, 1970. Pres., CIGRE, 1966–72. Mem., BBC Debating Soc., Manchester, 1952–55; Founder, Nasmyth Club, London and Manchester, 1936. Hon. Mem., Batti-Wallahs Assoc. Companion, EEIBA, 1994.Hon. MEng Liverpool Univ., 1954. Meritorious Service Award, Power Engrg Soc. of America, 1972; Willans Medal, IEE, 1952; Thornton Medal, AMEME, 1961; Donor, Power/Life Award, Power Engrg Soc., IEEE, 1970; Centennial Award and Plaque, IEEE, 1984. *Publications include:* Load Dispatching, with Special Reference to the British Grid System (a paper receiving John Hopkinson Award, 1948, and Willans Medal, 1952, IEE); The Human Approach to Management, 1989, 3rd edn 1994. *Recreations:* golf, art, music, writing, broadcasting, lecturing. *Address:* 32 Vanbrugh Court, 9 Eaton Gardens, Hove, E Sussex BN3 3TN. *T:* Brighton (01273) 724572. *Clubs:* Savile, Royal Over-Seas League, Energy Industries, 25, Dynamicables.

COOPER, Anthony; *see* Cooper, D. A.

COOPER, Beryl Phyllis, QC 1977; a Recorder of the Crown Court, since 1977; *b* 24 Nov. 1927; *o c* of late Charles Augustus Cooper and Phyllis Lillie (*née* Burrows). *Educ:* Surbiton High Sch. (Head Girl, 1945–46); Univ. of Birmingham (BCom 1950; Hon. Sec., Guild of Undergrads, 1949–50). Called to the Bar, Gray's Inn, 1960, Bencher, 1988; Dep. Circuit Judge, 1972–77; Dep. High Court Judge, 1980–. Hosp. Adminstr, Royal Free Hosp., 1951–57. Formerly: Councillor, St Pancras Metrop. Bor. Council; Mem., Homeopathic Hosp. Cttee; Mem., Bd of Visitors, Wandsworth Prison. Conservative Parly Candidate, Stepney, 1966; Founder Mem., Bow Gp (former Sec. and Council Mem.); Mem. Exec. Cttee, Soc. of Cons. Lawyers, 1981–87. Chm., Justice Report on Fraud Trials, 1985–86. Member: Cripps Cttee, Women and the Law; Home Office Cttee on Criminal Statistics (Perks Cttee); Housing Corp., 1976–79; Lambeth, Southwark and Lewisham AHA (Teaching), 1980–82; Criminal Injuries Compensation Bd, 1978–; Review Body for Nursing Staff, Midwives, Health Visitors, and Professions Allied to Medicine, 1983–90; Council of Justice, 1986–; Family Law Bar Assoc. Cttee, 1986–88. FRSA; FRHS. *Publications:* pamphlets for CPC, Justice, etc.; articles on social, legal, criminal and local govt matters. *Recreations:* travel, swimming, golf, gardening. *Address:* 231 Cromwell Tower, Barbican, EC2Y 8DD. *T:* 0171–588 1294; 9 Gough Square, EC4A 3DE. *T:* 0171–353 5371; 8d South Cliff Tower, Bolsover Road, Eastbourne, Sussex BN20 7JN. *T:* Eastbourne (01323) 32884. *Clubs:* English-Speaking Union; Caledonian (Edinburgh); Royal Eastbourne Golf.

COOPER, Prof. Cary Lynn; Professor of Organisational Psychology, University of Manchester, since 1975; *b* 28 April 1940; *s* of Harry and Caroline Cooper; *m* 1984, Rachel Faith Cooper; two *d*; one *s* one *d* from previous marr. *Educ:* Univ. of California (BS, MBA); Univ. of Leeds (PhD). FBPsS 1982. Lectr in Psychology, Univ. of Southampton, 1967–73. Advr to WHO and ILO, 1982–84. Member: Bd of Trustees, Amer. Inst. of Stress, 1984–; Adv. Council, Nat. Inst. of Clin. Applications of Behavioral Medicine, USA; Pres., British Acad. of Management, 1987–90. Vice Pres., Assoc. of Business Executives, 1994–. Myers Lectr, BPsS, 1986. FRSA 1990. Hon. Mem., Soc. of Psychosom. Res. Hon. MSc Manchester, 1979. Editor, Jl of Organizational Behavior, 1980–; Ed., Stress Medicine, 1992– (Associate Ed., 1987–92). *Publications:* T-Groups, 1971; Group Training for Individual and Organizational Development, 1973; Theories of Group Processes, 1975; Developing Social Skills in Managers, 1976; OD in the US and UK, 1977; Understanding Executive Stress, 1978; Advances in Experiential Social Processes, vol. 1, 1978, vol. 2, 1980; Stress at Work, 1978; Executives under Pressure, 1978; Behavioural Problems in Organizations, 1979; The Quality of Working Life in Western and Eastern Europe, 1979; Learning from Others in Groups, 1979; The Executive Gypsy, 1979; Current Concerns in Occupational Stress, 1980; Developing Managers for the 1980's, 1980; Combating Managerial Obsolescence, 1980; The Stress Check, 1980; White Collar and Professional Stress, 1981; Improving Interpersonal Relations, 1981; (jtly) Groups at Work, 1981; Executive Families Under Stress, 1981; (jtly) After Forty, 1981; Coping with Stress at Work, 1982; Psychology and Management, 1982; (jtly) Management Education, 1982; (jtly) Introducing Organization Behaviour, 1982; (jtly) High Pressure, 1982; Stress Research, 1983; (jtly) Human Behaviour in Organizations, 1983; (jtly) Stress and the Woman Manager, 1983; Public Faces, Private Lives, 1984; (jtly) Working Women, 1984; (jtly) Psychology for Managers, 1984; Psychosocial Stress and Cancer, 1984; (jtly) Women in Management, 1984; (jtly) The Change Makers, 1985; (jtly) Job Stress and Blue Collar Work, 1985; (jtly) International Review of Industrial and Organizational Psychology, annually 1986–; (jtly) Man and Accidents Offshore, 1986; (jtly) Stress and the Nurse Manager, 1986; (jtly) Pilots under Stress, 1986; (jtly) Psychosocial Factors at Work, 1987; (jtly) Retirement in Industrialized Societies, 1987; Living with Stress, 1988; Stress and Breast Cancer, 1988; (jtly) High Fliers, 1988; (jtly) Early Retirement, 1989; (jtly) Career Couples: contemporary lifestyles and how to manage them, 1989; (jtly) Understanding Stress: health care professionals, 1990; (jtly) Managing People at Work, 1990; Industrial and Organizational Psychology: critical writings, 1991; (jtly) Stress Survivors, 1991; (jtly) Cancer and Stress, 1991; (jtly) Work Psychology, 1991; (jtly) Stress and Accidents in the Offshore Oil and Gas Industry, 1991; Managing

Organizations in 1992, 1991; (jtly) On the Move: the psychology of change and transitions, 1991; Personality and Stress, 1991; (jtly) Mergers and Acquisitions: the human factor, 1992; (jtly) Shattering the Glass Ceiling: the woman manager, 1992; (jtly) Relax: dealing with stress, 1992; (jtly) Women's Career Development, 1992; (jtly) Total Quality and Human Resources, 1992; (jtly) Successful Stress Management, 1993; (jtly) Stress in the Dealing Room, 1993; (jtly) The Workplace Revolution, 1993; No Hassle: taking the stress out of work, 1994; (jtly) Business Elites, 1994; Handbook on Stress Medicine and Health, 1995; Trends in Organizational Behaviour, 1995; articles on social science and medicine, stress medicine. *Recreations:* reading 19th century Russian fiction, living in hope with Manchester City football, enjoying my four children. *Address:* 25 Lostock Hall Road, Poynton, Cheshire SK12 1DP. *T:* Poynton (01625) 871450. *Club:* St James's.

COOPER, David Antony; Metropolitan Stipendiary Magistrate, since 1991; *b* 12 June 1945; *s* of Rev. Stanley Francis Cooper and Jane Anne Cooper; *m* 1968, Françoise Armandine Henriette Fourré; three *s*. *Educ:* Sandown Grammar Sch., IoW; Exeter Univ. (LLB); College of Law. Articled to David Rule Pyott, Freshfields, London, 1966–69; admitted Solicitor, 1969; with Heppenstalls, Lymington, 1969–71; Solicitor and Partner in charge of criminal litigation, Ellison & Co., Colchester, 1971–91. *Recreation:* undisturbed reading. *Address:* Little Olivers, Colchester. *Club:* Law Society.

COOPER, Prof. David Edward; Professor of Philosophy, University of Durham, since 1986; *b* 1 Oct. 1942; *s* of late Edward Cooper and of Lilian Doris Cooper (*née* Turner); *m* 1st, 1971, Patricia Patterson; 2nd, 1980, Sheila Armstrong, *qv*. *Educ:* Highgate Sch.; St Edmund Hall, Oxford; Nuffield Coll., Oxford (MA, BPhil). Lectr in Philosophy, Pembroke and Jesus Colls, Oxford, 1966–69; Asst Prof. of Philosophy, Univ. of Miami, 1969–72; Lectr in Phil. of Educn, Univ. of London Inst. of Educn, 1972–74; Reader in Phil., Univ. of Surrey, 1974–85. Visiting Professor, Universities of: Khartoum, 1975; Minnesota, 1977; Capetown, 1979; Heidelberg and Tübingen, 1985; Trinity (Texas), 1986; Alberta, 1987; Vanderbilt, 1990; Malta, 1994; Vis. Sen. Res. Fellow, KCL, 1991–94. Fellow, Internat. Soc. for Intercultural Studies and Res., India, 1993–. Chairman: Phil. of Educn Soc., 1987–90; Friedrich Nietzsche Soc., 1991–94; President: Mind Assoc., 1991; Aristotelian Soc., 1993–94. Consultant, Born Free Foundn, 1991–. Patron, Earthkind, 1991–. Hon. Diploma, Univ. Nacional de Educación a Distancia, Madrid, 1992. *Publications:* Philosophy and the Nature of Language, 1973; Presupposition, 1974; Knowledge of Language, 1975; (ed). The Manson Murders, 1975; Illusions of Equality, 1980; Authenticity and Learning, 1983; Metaphor, 1986; (ed) Education, Values and Mind, 1986; Existentialism: a reconstruction, 1990; (ed jtly) The Environment in Question, 1992; (ed) Blackwell's Companion to Aesthetics, 1993; (ed jtly) Just Environments, 1995; World Philosophies: an historical introduction, 1995. *Recreations:* music, walking, wildlife. *Address:* Dept of Philosophy, University of Durham, 50 Old Elvet, Durham DH1 3HN. *T:* 0191–374 2541.

COOPER, (Derek) Anthony; General Secretary, Engineers and Managers Association, since 1991; *b* 11 Dec. 1943; *s* of Donald Cooper and Freda Cooper (*née* Sheridan); *m* 1967, June Iley; one *s* two *d*; one *s*. *Educ:* Whitehaven Grammar Sch.; Edinburgh Univ. (BSc Forestry and Wild Life Mgt). Forest Officer, Forestry Commn, 1967–76; Institution of Professionals, Managers and Specialists: Negotiations Officer, 1976–79; Asst Sec., 1979–82; Asst Gen. Sec., 1982–87; Dep. Gen. Sec., 1987–91. Chm., Aid Tspt Ltd, 1993–. Mem., Govt Energy Adv. Panel, 1993–. Trustee, Power Aid Logistics, 1993–. *Recreations:* reading, sailing, climbing. *Address:* 31 London Street, Chertsey, Surrey KT16 8AP.

COOPER, Derek Macdonald; author, broadcaster and journalist; *b* 25 May 1925; *s* of George Stephen Cooper and Jessie Margaret Macdonald; *m* 1953, Janet Marian Feaster; one *s* one *d*. *Educ:* Raynes Park Grammar Sch.; Portree High Sch.; University Coll., Cardiff; Wadham Coll., Oxford (MA Hons). Served RN, 1943–47. Joined Radio Malaya as producer, 1950, retired as Controller of Progs, 1960; Producer, Roving Report, ITN, 1960–61; has worked widely as presenter, interviewer and writer in both television and radio. Columnist: The Listener; Guardian; Observer magazine; Sunday Standard (House of Fraser Press Award, 1984); Homes & Gardens; Saga magazine; Woman's Journal; Scotland on Sunday. Founder Mem. and first Chm., 1985–88, Pres., 1988–, Guild of Food Writers. Glenfiddich Trophy as Wine and Food Writer, 1973, 1980; Broadcaster of the Year, 1984. *Publications:* The Bad Food Guide, 1967; Skye, 1970, 2nd edn 1977; The Beverage Report, 1970; The Gullibility Gap, 1974; Hebridean Connection, 1977; Guide to the Whiskies of Scotland, 1978; Road to the Isles, 1979 (Scottish Arts Council Award, 1980); (with Dione Pattullo) Enjoying Scotch, 1980; Wine With Food, 1982, 2nd edn 1986; (with Fay Godwin) The Whisky Roads of Scotland, 1982; The Century Companion to Whiskies, 1983; Skye Remembered, 1983, 2nd edn 1994; The World Of Cooking, 1983; The Road to Mingulay, 1985; The Gunge File, 1986; A Taste of Scotch, 1989; The Little Book of Malt Whiskies, 1992. *Address:* 4 St Helena Terrace, Richmond, Surrey TW9 1NR. *T:* 0181–940 7051; Seafield House, Portree, Isle of Skye IV51 9ES. *T:* Portree (01478) 612380.

COOPER, Wing Comdr Donald Arthur, CBE 1990; AFC 1961; Chief Inspector, Air Accidents Investigation Branch, Department of Transport, 1986–90; *b* 27 Sept. 1930; *s* of A. A. Cooper and E. B. Cooper (*née* Edmonds); *m* 1958, Belinda, 3rd *d* of Adm. Sir Charles Woodhouse, KCB and Lady Woodhouse; three *s*. *Educ:* Queen's Coll., British Guiana; RAF Coll., Cranwell. BA Open. ATPL (H) 1961, ATPL (A) 1972. FRAeS. Served on fighter and trng sqdns, 1952–56; Empire Test Pilot's Sch., 1957; RAE Farnborough, 1958–60; RAF sc 1961; Sqdn Comdr CFS Helicopter Wing, 1962–64; HQ FTC, 1964–66; Defence Operational Requirements Staff, MoD, 1966–70; joined Accidents Investigation Br., BoT, on retirement, 1970. *Recreations:* walking, ballroom dancing, amateur dramatics. *Address:* 7 Lynch Road, Farnham, Surrey GU9 8BZ.

COOPER, Rt Hon. Sir Frank, GCB 1979 (KCB 1974; CB 1970); CMG 1961; PC 1983; Chairman, High Integrity Systems Ltd, since 1986; Director: Babcock International Group, 1983–90; Morgan Crucible, 1983–94; N. M. Rothschild & Sons, since 1983; *b* 2 Dec. 1922; *s* of late V. H. Cooper, Fairfield, Manchester; *m* 1948, Peggie, *d* of F. J. Claxton; two *s* one *d*. *Educ:* Manchester Grammar Sch.; Pembroke Coll., Oxford (Hon. Fellow, 1976). War of 1939–45: Pilot, Royal Air Force, 1941–46. Asst Principal, Air Ministry, 1948; Private Secretary: to Parly Under-Sec. of State for Air, 1949–51; to Permanent Under-Sec. of State for Air, 1951–53; to Chief of Air Staff, 1953–55; Asst Sec., Head of the Air Staff, Secretariat, 1955–60; Dir of Accounts, Air Ministry, 1961–62; Asst Under-Sec. of State, Air Min., 1962–64, Min. of Defence, 1964–68; Dep. Under-Sec. of State, Min. of Defence, 1968–70; Dep. Sec., CSD, 1970–73; Permanent Under-Secretary of State: NI Office, 1973–76; MoD, 1976–82. Hon. Consultant, RUSI, 1982–. Chm., United Scientific Hldgs, 1985–89. Mem., Adv. Council on Public Records, 1989–92. Chm., Inst. of Contemp. British Hist., 1986–92. Member Council: KCL, 1981–89; Imperial Coll., 1983– (Chm., 1988–); Chm. Delegacy, King's Coll. Med. and Dental Sch., 1983–89; Chm., Liddell Hart Trustees, 1987–; Gov., Cranbrook Sch., 1982–92 (Chm., 1984–92). FKC 1987; FIC 1988. *Recreation:* walking. *Address:* 34 Camden Park Road, Chislehurst, Kent BR7 5HG. *Clubs:* Athenæum, Royal Air Force.

COOPER, Sir (Frederick Howard) Michael C.; *see* Craig-Cooper.

COOPER, Wing Comdr Geoffrey; free-lance writer; architect; Member: Gideons, since 1988; Pornography and Violence Research Trust (formerly Mary Whitehouse Educational and Research Trust), since 1985; *b* 18 Feb. 1907; *s* of Albert Cooper, Leicester, and Evelyn J. Bradnam, Hastings. *Educ:* Wyggeston Gram. Sch., Leicester; Royal Grammar School, Worcester. Accountancy, business management. Auxiliary Air Force, 1933; BOAC, 1939. Royal Air Force 1939–45, Pilot (mentioned in despatches). MP (Lab) for Middlesbrough West Div., 1945–51. Farming in Jersey, CI, 1951–61; founder and one of first directors, Jersey Farmers' Co-operative; Chm. Jersey Branch, RAFA. Architecture and land develt, Bahama Is, 1962–77; Pres., Estate Developers Ltd. Writing and social welfare voluntary work in S London, 1977–84; Captain, 56th London Boys' Brigade. *Publications:* Cæsar's Mistress (exposé of BBC and nationalisation); Christ Will Come Again, 1994; articles in England, Bahamas and USA on civil aviation, business management and government methods. *Recreations:* portrait and landscape painting, swimming. *Address:* PO Box N7117, Nassau, Bahamas; 91 Connor Court, Battersea Park, SW11 5HG. *Club:* Royal Air Force.

COOPER, George A.; marketing and business consultant; Chairman, Independent Television Publications Ltd, 1971–89; *b* 9 Oct. 1915; *s* of late Joseph Cooper; *m* 1944, Irene Burns; one *d*. Exec. with internat. publishing gp; served War of 1939–45, Royal Artillery (Captain); Exec., Hulton Press, 1949–55; Director: ABC Television Ltd, 1955–77; Thames Television Ltd, 1968 (Man. Dir, 1974–77); Independent Television News, 1976–77; Chm., Network Programme Cttee of Independent Television, 1975–77. FRTS 1987. *Recreations:* golf, walking. *Address:* 43 Rivermill, 151 Grosvenor Road, SW1V 3JN. *T:* 0171–821 9305. *Clubs:* Royal Automobile, Thirty.

COOPER, George Edward; Chairman, North Thames Gas Region (formerly North Thames Gas Board), 1970–78; Part-time Member, British Gas Corporation, 1973–78; *b* 25 Jan. 1915; *s* of H. E. Cooper and R. A. Jones, Wolverhampton; *m* 1941, Dorothy Anne Robinson (*d* 1993); one *s*. *Educ:* Wolverhampton Municipal Grammar Sch. Wolverhampton and Walsall Corp., 1933–40. Served War, 1940–45, with RA in Middle East (Bimbashi Sudan Defence Force), Captain. Qualified as Accountant, Inst. of Municipal Treasurers and Accountants (now Chartered Inst. of Public Accountants), 1947; Hemel Hempstead Development Corp., 1948–50; W Midlands Gas Bd (finally Dep. Chm.), 1950–70. IPFA (FIMTA 1965); CIGasE 1968. Officer OStJ 1976. *Recreations:* photography, geology, golf. *Club:* City Livery.

COOPER, Gen. Sir George (Leslie Conroy), GCB 1984 (KCB 1979); MC 1953; DL; Chief Royal Engineer, 1987–93; *b* 10 Aug. 1925; *s* of late Lt-Col G. C. Cooper and Mrs Y. V. Cooper, Bulmer Tye House, Sudbury; *m* 1957, Cynthia Mary Hume; one *s* one *d*. *Educ:* Downside Sch.; Trinity Coll., Cambridge. Commnd 1945; served with Bengal Sappers and Miners, 1945–48; Korea, 1952–53; psc 1956; jssc 1959; Instructor, RMA Sandhurst, 1959–62 and Staff Coll., Camberley, 1964; GSO1, 1st Div., 1964–66; CRE, 4th Div., 1966–68; MoD, 1968–69; Comdr, 19th Airportable Bde, 1969–71; Royal Coll. of Defence Studies, 1972; Dep. Dir Army Trng, 1973–74; GOC SW District, 1974–75; Dir, Army Staff Duties, 1976–79; GOC SE District, 1979–81; Adjt-Gen., 1981–84, retd. ADC General to the Queen, 1982–84. Mem., UK Bd of Management, and Dir of Management Develt, GEC, 1985–86. Colonel Commandant: RE, 1980–93; RPC, 1981–85; Col, Queen's Gurkha Engineers, 1981–91. Mem. Council, Nat. Army Mus., 1981–95. Chm., Knightstone Syndicate Management (formerly HGP Managing Agency), 1991–93 (Dir, 1990–91). Lay Rep., Senate and Bar Council Disciplinary Bodies, 1984–90. Chairman: Infantile Hypercalcæmia Foundn, 1980–95; Princess Alexandra's NHS Hosp. Trust, 1994–; Mem. Council, Action Research (formerly Nat. Fund for Res. into Crippling Diseases), 1982–. DL Essex, 1990. *Recreations:* shooting, gardening. *Address:* c/o Barclays Bank, 3–5 King Street, Reading, Berks RG1 2HD. *Clubs:* Army and Navy, MCC; Essex.

COOPER, Henry, OBE 1969; company director since 1972; *b* 3 May 1934; *s* of late Henry William Cooper and Lily Nutkins; *m* 1960, Albina Genepri; two *s*. *Educ:* Athelney Street Sch., Bellingham. Professional boxer, 1954–71. Presenter, Be Your Own Boss (series), Channel 4, 1983. KSG 1978. *Film:* Royal Flash, 1975. *Publications:* Henry Cooper: an autobiography, 1972; The Great Heavyweights, 1978; Henry Cooper's Book of Boxing, 1982; Henry Cooper's 100 Greatest Boxers, 1990. *Recreation:* golf. *Address:* 4 The Coach House, Dene Park, Shipbourne Road, Tonbridge TN11 9NS.

COOPER, Imogen; concert pianist; *b* 28 Aug. 1949; *d* of late Martin Du Pré Cooper, CBE; *m* 1982, John Alexander Batten. *Educ:* Paris Conservatoire, with Jacques Février and Yvonne Lefébure, 1961–67 (Premier Prix, 1967); privately in Vienna, with Alfred Brendel, 1970. Plays regularly with all major British orchestras; regular appearances at Proms, 1975–; first British pianist, and woman, to have appeared in South Bank Piano Series, 1975; British festivals include Bath, Cheltenham, Harrogate, Brighton and Edinburgh. Overseas engagements in Germany, Austria, Holland, France, Scandinavia, Spain, USA, Italy, NZ and Japan. Recordings include: Mozart's Concerti for Two and Three Pianos, with Alfred Brendel and Acad. of St Martin-in-the-Fields; Schubert's late works. Mozart Meml Prize, 1969. *Recreations:* architecture, reading, hill-walking. *Address:* c/o Van Walsum Management, 26 Wadham Road, SW15 2LR. *T:* 0181–874 6344, *Fax:* 0181–877 0077.

COOPER, Jilly, (Mrs Leo Cooper); author; *b* 21 Feb. 1937; *d* of Brig. W. B. Sallitt, OBE, and Mary Elaine Whincup; *m* 1961, Leo Cooper; one *s* one *d*. *Educ:* Godolphin Sch., Salisbury. Reporter, Middlesex Independent, Brentford, 1957–59; followed by numerous short-lived jobs as account executive, copy writer, publisher's reader, receptionist, puppy fat model, switchboard wrecker, and very temporary typist. Columnist: Sunday Times, 1969–82; Mail on Sunday, 1982–87. *Publications:* How to Stay Married, 1969; How to Survive from Nine to Five, 1970 (new edn as Work and Wedlock, 1978); Jolly Super, 1971; Men and Super Men, 1972; Jolly Super Too, 1973; Women and Super Women, 1974 (new edn as Super Men and Super Women, 1977); Jolly Superlative, 1975; Super Jilly, 1977; Class, 1979; The British in Love, 1980; (with Tom Hartman) Violets and Vinegar, 1980; Supercooper, 1980; Intelligent and Loyal, 1981; Jolly Marsupial, 1982; (with Imperial War Museum) Animals in War, 1983; The Common Years, 1984; Leo and Jilly Cooper on Cricket, 1985; (with Patrick Lichfield) Hot Foot to Zabrieskie Point, the Unipart Calendar Book, 1985; How to Survive Christmas, 1986; Leo and Jilly Cooper on Horse Mania, 1986; Turn Right at the Spotted Dog, 1987; Angels Rush In, 1990; *novels:* Emily, 1975; Bella, 1976; Harriet, 1976; Octavia, 1977; Prudence, 1978; Imogen, 1978; Riders, 1985 (televised, 1993); Rivals, 1988; Polo, 1991; The Man who made Husbands Jealous, 1993; Araminta's Wedding, 1993; *short stories:* Love and Other Heartaches, 1981; *for children:* Little Mabel, 1980; Little Mabel's Great Escape, 1981; Little Mabel Wins, 1982; Little Mabel Saves the Day, 1985. *Recreations:* merry-making, wild flowers, music, mongrels. *Address:* c/o Desmond Elliott, 38 Bury Street, St James's, SW1Y 6AU.

COOPER, Joan Davies, CB 1972; Hon. Research Fellow, University of Sussex, since 1979; *b* 12 Aug. 1914; *d* of late Valentine Holland Cooper and of Wynnefred Louisa Cooper; unmarried. *Educ:* Fairfield High Sch., Manchester; University of Manchester (BA). Asst Dir of Educn, Derbyshire CC, 1941; Children's Officer, E Sussex CC, 1948; Chief Inspector, Children's Dept, Home Office, 1965–71; Dir, Social Work Service,

DHSS, 1971–76; Nat. Inst. for Social Work, 1976–77. Mem., SSRC, 1973–76. Vice Pres., Nat. Children's Bureau, 1964–; Chairman: Parents for Children, 1979–87; NACRO Adv. Council on Juvenile Crime, 1982–87; Central Council for Educn and Trng in Social Work, 1984–86; E Sussex Care for the Carers, 1985–91 (Pres., 1991–). Chm., Internat. Conf. on Data Protection, 1987. Trustee, Homestart, 1981–89. Vice-Chm., Lewes Tertiary Coll., 1990–93. FRAI 1972. *Publications:* Patterns of Family Placement, 1978; Social Groupwork with Elderly Patients, 1981; Creation of the British Personal Social Services, 1962–74, 1983. *Recreation:* walking. *Address:* 44 Greyfriars Court, Court Road, Lewes, East Sussex BN7 2RF. *T:* Lewes (01273) 472604. *Club:* University Women's.

COOPER, Rev. Canon John Leslie; Assistant Curate, Holy Trinity, Sutton Coldfield, since 1993; *b* 16 Dec. 1933; *s* of Iris and Leslie Cooper; *m* 1959, Gillian Mary Dodds; two *s* one *d. Educ:* Tiffin School, Kingston, Surrey; Chichester Theological Coll. BD 1965, MPhil 1978, London Univ. (External Student). National Service, RA; commissioned, 1952–54. General Electric Co. management trainee, 1954–59; Chichester Theolog. Coll., 1959–62; Asst Curate, All Saints, Kings Heath, Birmingham, 1962–65; Asst Chaplain, HM Prison, Wandsworth, 1965–66; Chaplain: HM Borstal, Portland, Dorset, 1966–68; HM Prison, Bristol, 1968–72; Research Fellow, Queen's Coll., Birmingham, 1972–73; Priest-in-Charge 1973–81, Vicar 1981–82, St Paul's, Balsall Heath, Birmingham. Examining Chaplain to Bishop of Birmingham, 1981–82; Archdeacon of Aston, and Canon Residentiary, St Philip's Cathedral, Birmingham, 1982–90; Archdeacon of Coleshill, 1990–93. Hon. Canon, Birmingham Cathedral, 1993–. *Recreations:* music, reading, walking, travel, carpentry, photography. *Address:* 1 Trinity Hill, Sutton Coldfield, W Midlands B72 1SH. *T:* 0121–355 3352.

COOPER, Prof. John Philip, CBE 1983; DSc; FRS 1977; FIBiol; Emeritus Professor of Agricultural Botany, University of Wales, 1984; *b* Buxton, Derbyshire, 16 Dec. 1923; *o s* of Frank Edward and Nora Goodwin Cooper; *m* 1951, Christine Mary Palmer; one *s* three *d. Educ:* Stockport Grammar Sch.; Univ. of Reading (BSc 1945, PhD 1953, DSc 1964); FitzWilliam House, Cambridge (DipAgrSc 1946). Scientific Officer, Welsh Plant Breeding Station, 1946–50; Lectr, Univ. of Reading, 1950–54; Welsh Plant Breeding Station, University College of Wales, Aberystwyth: Plant Geneticist, 1950–59; Head, Dept of Develtl Genetics, 1959–75; Dir, and Prof. of Agricl Botany, 1975–83. Consultant, FAO Headquarters, Rome, 1956; Nuffield Royal Society Bursary, CSIRO, Canberra, 1962; Visiting Professor: Univ. of Kentucky, 1965; Univ. of Khartoum, 1975; Univ. of Reading, 1984–89; Hon. Fellow, AFRC Inst. for Grassland and Envmtl Res., 1992. Member: UK Seeds Exec., 1979–86; Internat. Bd for Plant Genetics Resources, 1981–86. *Publications:* (ed, with P. F. Wareing) Potential Crop Production, 1971; (ed) Photosynthesis and Productivity in Different Environments, 1975; various papers on crop physiology and genetics in sc. jls. *Recreations:* walking, field archaeology. *Address:* 31 West End, Minchinhampton, Glos GL6 9JA. *T:* Stroud (01453) 882533.

COOPER, Rear-Adm. John Spencer, OBE 1974; *b* 5 April 1933; *s* of Harold Spencer Cooper and Barbara (*née* Highet); *m* 1966, Jacqueline Street (*née* Taylor); two *d. Educ:* St Edward's Sch., Oxford; Clare Coll., Cambridge (MA 1959). Joined RN, 1951; served as Lieut on HM Ships Ceylon and Ark Royal; joined Submarines 1966, Polaris Systems Officer in HMS Renown; Comdr 1969, Captain 1976; Director, Trials, Chevaline programme, 1976–78; Special Proj., RN, Washington, 1978–80; Cdre 1981; Dir, Weapons (Stragetic Systems), 1981–83; Dir Gen., Strategic Weapon Systems, 1983–85; Chief Strategic Systems Exec., MoD, 1985–88. Operations Manager: Naval Command and Control Div., Ferranti International, 1988–90; Ferranti Naval Systems, 1990–93. *Recreation:* cruising in Eleonora. *Address:* 15c Hesketh Crescent, Torquay, Devon TQ1 2LJ. *T:* Torquay (01803) 201954.

COOPER, Joseph, OBE 1982; pianist and broadcaster; *b* 7 Oct. 1912; *s* of Wilfrid Needham and Elsie Goodacre Cooper; *m* 1st, 1947, Jean (*d* 1973), *d* of late Sir Louis Greig, KBE, CVO; no *c*; 2nd, 1975, Carol, *d* of Charles and Olive Borg. *Educ:* Clifton Coll. (music schol.); Keble Coll., Oxford (organ schol.). MA (Oxon), ARCM (solo piano). Studied piano under Egon Petri, 1937–39. Served War, in RA, 1939–46. Solo pianist debut, Wigmore Hall, 1947 (postponed, Oct. 1939, owing to War); concerto debut, Philharmonia Orchestra, 1950; BBC debut Promenade Concerts Royal Albert Hall, 1953. Since then has toured in: British Isles, Europe, Africa, India, Canada. Many solo piano records. Chm., BBC TV prog., Face The Music, 1966–84. Found a solution to riddle of Elgar's Enigma Variations, 1991. Hon. Chm., Barclaycard Composer of the Year Competition, 1983. Liveryman, Worshipful Co. of Musicians, 1963–; Member: Music Panel of Arts Council (and Chm. piano sub-cttee), 1966–71; Council, Musicians Benevolent Fund, 1987–90; Trustee, Countess of Munster Musical Trust, 1975–80. Governor, Clifton College. Ambrose Fleming award, Royal Television Soc., 1961; Music Trades Assoc. Record Award, 1976. *Publications:* Hidden Melodies, 1975; More Hidden Melodies, 1976; Still More Hidden Melodies, 1978; Facing the Music (autobiog.), 1979; Arrangement of Vaughan Williams Piano Concerto for 2 pianos (in collab. with composer). *Recreations:* jigsaws, church architecture. *Address:* Octagon Lodge, Ranmore, near Dorking, Surrey RH5 6SX. *T:* Guildford (01483) 282658. *Club:* Garrick.

COOPER, Kenneth Reginald, CB 1991; Chief Executive, The British Library, 1984–91; *b* 28 June 1931; *s* of Reginald and Louisa May Cooper; *m* 1955, Olga Ruth (*née* Harvey); two *s* two *d. Educ:* Queen Elizabeth's Grammar Sch., Barnet; New Coll., Oxford (MA). FIPM; FITD (Pres., 1981–83); FIInfSc (Pres., 1988–89). Various appointments, Min. of Labour, 1954–62; Principal, HM Treasury, 1962–65; Principal Private Secretary to Minister of Labour, 1966–67; Asst Sec. for Industrial Training, Min. of Labour, 1967–70; Chief Executive: Employment Services Agency, 1971–75; Training Services Agency, 1975–79; Dir Gen., Nat. Fedn of Building Trades Employers, 1979–84. Vis. Prof., Strathclyde Univ., 1987–91. Dep. Chm., CICI, 1988–92; Dir, Book Trust, 1988–93. CIMgt (CBIM 1989); FRSA, 1987. Hon. Fellow, Brighton Poly., 1991. *Recreations:* music, Rugby football.

COOPER, Prof. Leon N., PhD ; Thomas J. Watson, Sr, Professor of Science, Brown University, Providence, RI, since 1974; Director, Institute for Brain and Neural Systems; *b* NYC, 28 Feb. 1930; *s* of Irving Cooper and Anna Cooper (*née* Zola); *m* 1969, Kay Anne Allard; two *d. Educ:* Columbia Univ. (AB 1951, AM 1953, PhD 1954). Nat. Sci. Foundn post-doctoral Fellow, and Mem., Inst. for Advanced Study, 1954–55; Res. Associate, Univ. of Illinois, 1955–57; Asst Prof., Ohio State Univ., 1957–58; Associate Prof., Brown Univ., 1958–62, Prof., 1962–66, Henry Ledyard Goddard Prof., 1966–74. Consultant, various governmental agencies, industrial and educational organizations. Lectr, Summer Sch., Varenna, Italy, 1955; Visiting Professor: Brandeis Summer Inst., 1959; Bergen Internat. Sch. Physics, Norway, 1961; Scuola Internazionale di Fisica, Erice, Italy, 1965; Ecole Normale Supérieure, Centre Universitaire Internat., Paris, 1966; Cargèse Summer Sch., 1966; Radiation Lab., Univ. of Calif at Berkeley, 1969; Faculty of Scis, Quai St Bernard, Paris, 1970, 1971; Brookhaven Nat. Lab., 1972; Chair of Math. Models of Nervous System, Fondation de France, 1977–83; Mem., Conseil Supérieur de la Recherche, l'Université René Descartes, Paris, 1981–87. Alfred P. Sloan Foundn Res. Fellow, 1959–66; John Simon Guggenheim Meml Foundn Fellow, 1965–66. Co-Chm., Bd of Dirs, Nestor Inc. Fellow: Amer. Physical Soc.; Amer. Acad. of Arts and Sciences. Member: Amer. Philosoph. Soc.; National Acad. of Sciences; Sponsor Fedn of Amer. Scientists; Soc. for Neuroscience, Amer. Assoc. for Advancement of Science; Defense Science Bd. Mem. Bd of Govs, Internat. Neural Network Soc. (Jtly) Comstock Prize, Nat. Acad. of Scis, 1968; (jtly) Nobel Prize for Physics, 1972; Award of Excellence, Grad. Fac. Alumni, Columbia Univ., 1974; Descartes Medal, Acad. de Paris, Univ. René Descartes, 1977. Yrjö Reenpää Medal, Finnish Cultural Foundn, 1982; John Jay Award, 1985, Award for Distinguished Achievement, 1989, Columbia Univ. Hon. DSc: Columbia, 1973; Sussex, 1973; Illinois, 1974; Brown, 1974; Gustavus Adolphus Coll., 1975; Ohio State Univ., 1976; Univ. Pierre et Marie Curie, Paris, 1977. Public lectures, internat. confs, symposia. *Publications:* Introduction to the Meaning and Structure of Physics, 1968; (contrib.) The Physicist's Conception of Nature, 1973; contrib. The Many Body Problem, 1963; contrib. to numerous jls incl. Physics Rev., Amer. Jl Physics, Biological Cybernetics, Jl of Neurosci., Jl of Neurophysiol., Procs of the US Nat. Acad. of Scis. *Recreations:* music, theatre, skiing. *Address:* 49 Intervale Road, Providence, RI 02906, USA. *T:* (401) 4211181; Physics Department, Brown University, Providence, RI 02912, USA. *T:* (401) 8632172. *Clubs:* University, Faculty (Providence, RI).

COOPER, Sir Louis Jacques B.; *see* Blom-Cooper.

COOPER, Margaret Jean Drummond, OBE 1980; Chief Education Officer, General Nursing Council for England and Wales, 1974–82; *b* 24 March 1922; *d* of Canon Bernard R. Cooper and A. Jean Cooper (*née* Drackley). *Educ:* School of St Mary and St Anne, Abbots Bromley; Royal College of Nursing; Open Univ. (BA 1987). SRN, SCM, RNT. Nursing trng and early posts, Leicester Royal Infirmary, 1941–47; Midwifery trng, General Lying-in Hosp., SW1 and Coventry and Warwicks Hosp.; Nurse Tutor, Middlesex Hosp., 1953–55; Principal Tutor: General Hosp., Northampton, 1956–63; Addenbrooke's Hosp., Cambridge, 1963–68; Principal, Queen Elizabeth Sch. of Nursing, Birmingham, 1968–74. Chm., General Nursing Council for England and Wales, 1971–74 (Mem., 1965 and 1970). *Recreations:* birds, books, buildings. *Address:* 28 Lambert Cross, Saffron Walden, Essex CB10 2DP.

COOPER, Michael John; Director General, British Diabetic Association, since 1991; *b* 24 July 1937; *s* of Frederick Walton Cooper and Ivy Kathleen (*née* Harris); *m* 1961, Kathy Cockett; two *s* one *d. Educ:* King's Sch., Rochester; Univ. of Exeter (BA 1960); Oberlin Coll., Ohio; Internat. Management Develt Inst., Switzerland (MBA). RAF, 1955–57. Shell Internat. Petroleum Co. Ltd, 1961–69; Man. Dir, Panocean-Anco Ltd, 1970–82; Dir, Burmah Castrol PLC, 1982–91. Dir, E Sussex HA, 1992–. Vis. Prof., Univ. of Westminster, 1992–. *Recreations:* music, walking, cricket, tennis, travel. *Address:* Old Hall Cottage, High Hurstwood, Uckfield, E Sussex TN22 4AD. *T:* Uckfield (01825) 733268; Flat 5, 130 Belgrave Road, SW1V 2BL. *T:* 0171–834 3891. *Club:* Oriental.

COOPER, Nigel Cookson; Co-ordinator Wimbledon Tennis Championships, since 1988; *b* 7 May 1929; *s* of Richard and Violet Sarah Cooper; *m* 1972, Elizabeth Gillian Smith; two *s* one *d. Educ:* Leeds Training Coll., Leeds Univ. (LLB); State Univ. of Iowa, USA (MA). Teacher, primary and secondary schools, 1950–59; Lecturer: Trent Park Training Coll., 1959–61; Loughborough Training Coll., 1961–64; Provincial Supervisor (Schools and Community) for Nova Scotia, Canada, 1964–65; County Organiser of Schools for Norfolk, 1965–68; Asst Education Officer for Oldham, 1970–72; Asst Director of Educn for British Families Educn Service in Europe, 1972–78; Registrar, Kelvin Grove College of Advanced Education, Brisbane, Australia, 1978–82; Gen. Sec., BAAB, 1982–87. *Recreations:* playing the trumpet, squash, jogging. *Address:* 24 Southfields, East Molesey, Surrey KT8 0BP. *T:* 0181–398 6076.

COOPER, Sir Patrick Graham Astley, 6th Bt *cr* 1821; Director, Crendon Concrete Co. Ltd, Long Crendon, 1973–83; *b* 4 Aug. 1918; *s* of late Col C. G. A. Cooper, DSO, RA and I. M. M. A. Cooper, Abergeldie, Camberley, Surrey; *S* cousin, Sir Henry Lovick Cooper, 5th Bt, 1959; *m* 1942, Audrey Ann Jervoise, *d* of late Major D. P. J. Collas, Military Knight of Windsor; one *s* two *d. Educ:* Marlborough Coll. Qualified RICS, 1949; Sen. Asst Land Comr, Min. of Agric., Fisheries and Food, 1950–59. Joined Crendon Concrete Co. Ltd, 1959. Served 1939–40, Gunner, RA, 52 AA Bde TA (invalided out). *Recreations:* golf, tennis. *Heir: s* Alexander Paston Astley Cooper [*b* 1 Feb. 1943; *m* 1974, Minnie Margaret, *d* of Charles Harrison]. *Address:* White Cottage, 3 Townside, Haddenham, Aylesbury, Bucks HP17 8BG. *T:* Haddenham (01844) 292305.

COOPER, Peter James; QC 1993; a Recorder, since 1993; *b* 7 Oct. 1947; *s* of William James Cooper and Audrey (*née* Knight); *m* 1979, Jenifer Ann Redway; two *s. Educ:* Peter Symonds Sch., Winchester; Southampton Univ.; Council of Legal Educn. Called to the Bar, Gray's Inn, 1974; Asst Recorder, 1989–93. *Recreations:* golf, music. *Address:* 2 Harcourt Buildings, Temple, EC4Y 9DB. *T:* 0171–353 2112. *Club:* Midfearn Open Golfing Society (Ardgay, Ross-shire).

COOPER, Philip John, CB 1989; Comptroller-General of Patents, Designs and Trade Marks, Department of Trade and Industry, 1986–89; *b* 15 Sept. 1929; *s* of Charles Cooper and Mildred Annie Marlow; *m* 1st, 1953, Dorothy Joan Chapman (*d* 1982); two *d*; 2nd, 1986, Pamela Mary Pysden (*d* 1988); 3rd, 1993, Antoinette Erasmus. *Educ:* Deacon's Sch., Peterborough; University Coll., Leicester. BSc (Chem. 1st Cl. Hons). CChem, FRSC. Joined Dept (later Laboratory) of Govt Chemist, 1952; Nat. Service, 2nd Lt, R Signals, 1953–55; Dept of Scientific and Ind. Res., 1956–67; Principal, Min. of Technology, 1967; Prin. Private Sec. to Minister for Industrial Develt, 1972–73; Asst Sec., 1973–79, Under Sec., 1979–89, DoI and DTI; Dir, Warren Spring Lab., DTI, 1984–85. *Publications:* various papers on analytical and chemical matters. *Address:* 4b Downs Road, Epsom, Surrey KT18 5HE.

COOPER, Sir Richard (Powell), 5th Bt *cr* 1905, of Shenstone Court, Co. Stafford; *b* 13 April 1934; *s* of Sir Francis Ashmole Cooper, 4th Bt and of Dorothy Frances Hendrika, *d* of late Emile Deen; *S* father, 1987; *m* 1957, Angela Marjorie, *e d* of Eric Wilson, Norton-on-Tees; one *s* two *d. Educ:* Marlborough. Chm., Rare Breeds Survival Trust, 1978–80, 1990–92. *Recreation:* foxhunting. *Heir: s* Richard Adrian Cooper, *b* 21 Aug. 1960. *Address:* Lower Farm, Chedington, Beaminster, Dorset DT8 3JA. *T:* Corscombe (01935) 891463. *Clubs:* Buck's, Carlton.

COOPER, Robert Francis, MVO 1975; HM Diplomatic Service; Counsellor, Bonn, since 1993; *b* 28 Aug. 1947; *s* of Norman and Frances Cooper. *Educ:* Delamere Sch., Nairobi; Worcester Coll., Oxford (BA); Univ. of Pennsylvania (MA). Joined FCO 1970; Tokyo 1972; London 1977; seconded to Bank of England, 1982; UK Rep. to EC, 1984; Head of Management Review Staff, FCO, 1987; Head of Far Eastern Dept, FCO, 1987; Hd of Policy Planning Staff, FCO, 1989. *Recreations:* Shakespeare, bridge, bicycling. *Address:* Foreign and Commonwealth Office, SW1A 2AH.

COOPER, Robert George, CBE 1987; Chairman, Fair Employment Commission (formerly Agency) for Northern Ireland, since 1976; Member, Northern Ireland Standing Advisory Commission on Human Rights, since 1976; *b* 24 June 1936; *er s* of William Hugh Cooper and Annie (*née* Pollock); *m* 1974, Patricia, *yr d* of Gerald and Sheila Nichol, Belfast; one *s* one *d. Educ:* Foyle Coll., Londonderry; Queen's Univ., Belfast (LLB). Industrial Relations, International Computers Ltd, Belfast, 1958–63; Asst Sec., Engineering

Employers' Fedn, NI, 1963–67, Sec. 1967–72; Gen. Sec., Alliance Party of Northern Ireland, 1972–73. Member (Alliance): West Belfast, NI Assembly, 1973–75; West Belfast, NI Constitutional Convention, 1975–76; Minister, Manpower Services, NI, 1974. *Address:* Lynwood, 104 Bangor Road, Holywood, Co. Down, N Ireland. *T:* Holywood (0232) 422071.

COOPER, Dr Robin Hayes, FBA 1993; Reader in Cognitive Science, University of Edinburgh, since 1989; *b* 23 Dec. 1947; *s* of Dennis J. Cooper and Marjorie (*née* Wilding); *m* 1985, Elisabet B. Engdahl; two *d. Educ:* Corpus Christi Coll., Cambridge (MA); Univ. of Massachusetts at Amherst (PhD). Lektor, Universität Freiburg, 1969–71; Assistant Professor: Univ. of Texas at Austin, 1975–76; Univ. of Massachusetts at Amherst, 1976–77; Univ. of Wisconsin, Madison, 1977–81, Associate Prof., 1981–87; Docent, Lund Univ., 1984–87; Lectr, Univ. of Edinburgh, 1986–89. Mellon Fellow, Stanford Univ., 1980–81; Fellow, Center for Advanced Study in Behavioral Scis, Stanford, 1981–82; Guggenheim Fellow, Edinburgh and Stanford, 1986–87. *Publications:* Quantification and Syntactic Theory, 1983; (ed jtly) Situation Theory and its Applications, Vol 1, 1990; contribs to numerous books, contrib. Computational Intelligence, Ethnomusicology, Lang., Linguistics and Philosophy, Musique en Jeu, Nordic Jl Linguistics. *Recreations:* childcare, music. *Address:* Centre for Cognitive Science, University of Edinburgh, 2 Buccleuch Place, Edinburgh EH8 9LW. *T:* 0131–650 4407.

COOPER, Ronald Cecil Macleod, CB 1981; Deputy Secretary, Department of Transport, 1986–90; *b* 8 May 1931; *s* of Cecil Redvers Cooper and Norah Agnes Louise Cooper (*née* Macleod); *m* 1st, 1953, June Bicknell (marr. diss. 1967); 2nd, 1967, Christine Savage; one *s* two *d. Educ:* Royal Grammar Sch., Newcastle upon Tyne; St Edmund Hall, Oxford (MA). Asst Principal, Min. of Supply, 1954–59; Principal, Min. of Aviation, 1959–62; on loan to European Launcher Develt Org., Paris, 1962–67; Asst Sec., Min. of Technology, 1968–70, DTI, 1970–73; Under Sec., Dept of Trade, 1973–78; Sec., Price Commn, 1979; Dep. Sec. and Principal Estabt and Finance Officer, DTI, 1979–85. *Recreations:* music, reading.

COOPER, Hon. Russell; *see* Cooper, Hon. T. R.

COOPER, Sidney G.; *see* Grattan-Cooper.

COOPER, Sidney Pool; Head of Public Services, British Museum, 1973–76; *b* 29 March 1919; *s* of late Sidney Charles Henry Cooper and Emily Lilian Baptie; *m* 1940, Denise Marjorie Peverett; two *s* one *d. Educ:* Finchley County Sch.; Northern Polytechnic (BSc); University Coll. London (MSc). Laboratory of the Government Chemist, 1947; Asst Keeper, National Reference Library of Science and Invention, British Museum, 1963; Dep. Keeper, NRLSI, 1969. *Recreations:* gardening, golf. *Address:* 98 Kings Road, Berkhamsted, Herts HP4 3BP. *T:* Berkhamsted (01442) 864145.

COOPER, Maj.-Gen. Sir Simon (Christie), KCVO 1991; Master of HM's Household, since 1992; *b* 5 Feb. 1936; *s* of Maj.-Gen. Kenneth Christie Cooper, CB, DSO, OBE and Barbara Harding-Newman; *m* 1967, Juliet Elizabeth Palmer; one *s* one *d. Educ:* Winchester College; rcds, psc. Commissioned Life Guards, 1956; served Aden, London, BAOR, 1957–63; Captain-Adjt, Household Cavalry Regt, 1963–65; ADC to CDS Earl Mountbatten of Burma, 1965–66; Borneo, Malaya, 1966–67; Staff Coll., 1968; BAOR, 1969–75; CO Life Guards, 1974–76; GSO1, Staff Coll., 1976–78; OC Household Cavalry and Silver Stick in Waiting, 1978–81; Commander, RAC Centre, 1981–82; RCDS, 1983; Dir, RAC, 1984–87; Comdt, RMA, Sandhurst, 1987–89; GOC London Dist and Maj.-Gen. Commanding Household Div., 1989–91. Hon. Colonel: Westminster Dragoons, 1987–; Royal Yeomanry, 1987–. *Recreations:* cricket, skiing, sailing, shooting. *Club:* MCC.

COOPER, Prof. Susan, PhD; Professor of Experimental Physics, University of Oxford, since 1995; *b* USA, 1949. *Educ:* Colby Coll., USA (BA); Univ. of California at Berkeley (PhD). Guest Physicist, Deutsches Electronen Synchrotron, Germany, 1980–83; Research Associate, Stanford Linear Accelerator Center, USA, 1984–86; Asst Prof., MIT, 1987–89; Group leader, Max Planck Inst. of Physics, Munich, 1989. *Publications:* numerous papers in sci. jls. *Address:* Nuclear Physics Laboratory, Oxford University, Keble Road, Oxford OX1 3RH.

COOPER, (Theo) Russell; MLA (National Party) Crows Nest, Queensland, since 1992 (Roma, Queensland, 1983–92); *b* 4 Feb. 1941; *s* of Theo Beverley Cooper and Muriel Frances Cooper; *m* 1965, Penelope Anne Parkinson; one *s* three *d. Educ:* Surfers Paradise State Sch.; Correspondence Sch.; Toowoomba Prep. Sch.; King's Sch., Parramatta. Councillor, 1976–88, Dep. Chm., 1983–88, Bendemere Shire Council; Vice-Pres., Roma Electorate NP Council, 1982–84; Chm., Wallumbilla-Yuleba Branch, NP, 1974–84. Minister for: Corrective Services and Admin. Services, 1987–89; Police and Emergency Services, 1989; Premier of Qld, Sept.–Dec. 1989; Leader of the Opposition, 1989–91; Opposition spokesman for police and corrective services, 1992–. Vice-Pres., Maranoa Graziers Assoc., 1979–80 (Chm., Wallumbilla Br.); Pres., Roma and Dist Amateur Race Club, 1981–83. *Recreations:* golf, tennis (active), Rugby League, Rugby Union, cricket. *Address:* Donnabar, Wallumbilla, Qld 4428, Australia. *T:* (76) 234341; Allambie Park, Jondaryan, Qld 4403, Australia. *T:* (76) 927727. *Clubs:* Brisbane; Maranoa (Roma).

COOPER, Hon. Warren Ernest; MP (National Party) Otago, since 1975; Minister of Defence and Minister responsible for War Pensions, New Zealand, since 1990; also Minister of Civil Defence and of Internal Affairs, since 1993; *b* Dunedin, 21 Feb. 1933; *s* of William Cooper; *m* 1959, Lorraine Margaret, *d* of Angus T. Rees; three *s* two *d. Educ:* Musselburgh Sch.; King's High Sch., Dunedin. Formerly Minister of Tourism, Minister of Regional Develt, Minister in charge of Publicity and in charge of Govt Printing Office; Postmaster Gen., 1980; Minister of Broadcasting and Assoc. Minister of Finance, 1981; Minister of Foreign Affairs and Overseas Trade, 1981–84; Minister of Local Govt and of Radio and Television, 1990–93. Mem., Cabinet Cttees on Expenditure Control and Revenue, State Sector, Appts and Honours, Social and Family Policy, Treaty of Waitangi Issues, 1990–. Member Executive: S Island Publicity Assoc., 1971; NZ Municipal Assoc. Life Mem. and former Pres., Queenstown Jaycees. Mayor of Queenstown, 1968–71. JP Queenstown. *Address:* Parliament House, Wellington, New Zealand.

COOPER, William, (Harry Summerfield Hoff), FRSL; novelist; *b* 4 Aug. 1910; *m* 1951, Joyce Barbara Harris (*d* 1988); two *d. Educ:* Christ's Coll., Cambridge. Assistant Commissioner, Civil Service Commission, 1945–58; Personnel Consultant to: UKAEA, 1958–72; CEGB, 1958–72; Commn of European Communities, 1972–73; Asst Dir, Civil Service Selection Bd, 1973–75; Mem. Bd of Crown Agents, 1975–77; Personnel Advr, Millbank Technical Services, 1975–77. Adjunct Prof. of English Lit., Syracuse Univ., 1977–90. *Publications:* (as H. S. Hoff) Trina, 1934; Rhéa, 1935; Lisa, 1937; Three Marriages, 1946; (as William Cooper) Scenes from Provincial Life, 1950; The Struggles of Albert Woods, 1952; The Ever-Interesting Topic, 1953; Disquiet and Peace, 1956; Young People, 1958; C. P. Snow (British Council Bibliographical Series, Writers and Their Work, No 115) 1959; Prince Genji (a play), 1960; Scenes from Married Life, 1961; Memoirs of a New Man, 1966; You Want The Right Frame of Reference, 1971; Shall We Ever Know?, 1971; Love on the Coast, 1973; You're Not Alone, 1976; Scenes from Metropolitan Life, 1982; Scenes from Later Life, 1983; From Early Life (autobiog.), 1990; Immortality at any Price, 1991. *Address:* 22 Kenilworth Court, Lower Richmond Road, SW15 1EW. *T:* 0181–788 8326. *Club:* Savile.

COOPER, Sir William (Daniel Charles), 6th Bt *cr* 1863, of Woollahra; Company Director of The Garden Maintenance Service and G.M.S. Vehicles; *b* 5 March 1955; *s* of Sir Charles Eric Daniel Cooper, 5th Bt, and of Mary Elisabeth, *e d* of Captain J. Graham Clarke; *S* father, 1984; *m* 1988, Julia Nicholson. *Educ:* Northease Manor, Lewes, Sussex. *Heir: b* George John Cooper, *b* 28 June 1956.

COOPER, Maj.-Gen. William Frank, CBE 1971; MC 1945; consultant; *b* 30 May 1921; *s* of Allan Cooper, Officer of Indian State Railways, and Margaret Cooper; *m* 1945, Elisabeth Mary Finch; one *s* one *d. Educ:* Sherborne Sch.; RMA Woolwich. Commnd in RE, 1940; served N Africa and Italy (MC; despatches 1944); Malaya, 1956–58 (despatches); S Arabia, 1963–65 (OBE); Chief Engr FARELF, 1968–70; Dep. Dir Army Staff Duties, MoD, 1970–72; Dir, Mil. Assistance Office, 1972–73; DQMG, 1973–76, retd. Col Comdt, RE, 1978–83. Dir, Gin Rectifiers and Distillers Assoc. and Vodka Trade Assoc., 1976–90. *Recreations:* fishing, birdwatching, theatre, gardening. *Address:* c/o Lloyds Bank, 118 High Street, Hungerford, Berks RG17 0LY. *Club:* Army and Navy.

COOPER, Very Rev. (William Hugh) Alan; Priest-in-charge of Chrishall, 1981–88; *b* 2 June 1909; *s* of William and Ethel Cooper; *m* 1st, 1940, Barbara (*née* Bentall); one *s* two *d*; 2nd, 1980, Muriel Barnes. *Educ:* King's Coll. Sch., Wimbledon; Christ's Coll., Cambridge (MA); St John's Hall, London. ALCD. Curate of Lee, 1932–36; Holy Trinity, Cambridge, 1936–38; CMS Missionary and Diocesan Missioner of Dio. Lagos, 1938–41; Curate of Farnham, 1941–42; Rector of Ashtead, 1942–51; Vicar of St Andrew, Plymouth, 1951–62; Preb. of Exeter Cathedral, 1958–62; Provost of Bradford, 1962–77; Hon. Assistant to Bishop of Karachi, 1977–80. Hon. MA Bradford, 1978. *Address:* 4 Eastgate Gardens, Guildford, Surrey GU1 4AZ.

COORAY, (Bulathsinhalage) Anura (Siri); His Honour Judge Cooray; a Circuit Judge, since 1991; *b* 20 Jan. 1936; *s* of (Bulathsinhalage) Vincent Cooray, accountant, and Dolly Perera Manchanayake, Etul Kotte, Sri Lanka; *m* 1957, Manel Therese, *d* of late George Perera, planter, and late Myrtle Perera, Kandy, Sri Lanka; two *s* three *d. Educ:* Christian Coll., Kotte, Sri Lanka; London Univ. Called to the Bar, Lincoln's Inn, 1968. Served RAF, Cranwell and Locking, 1952–55 (RAF Boxing Assoc. Sigrist Trophy, 1953–54); served Royal Ceylon Air Force, 1955–60. Practised in Common Law Chambers at Middle Temple; later, Dep. Head of Chambers at No 1 Gray's Inn Sq.; Mem., South Eastern Circuit; Prosecuting Counsel for DPP and Met. Police Solicitors, 1969–82; a Metropolitan Stipendiary Magistrate, 1982–91; a Recorder, 1989–91. Mem., Cttee of Magistrates, 1989. *Recreations:* wine making (and tasting too!), gardening. *Address:* 1 Gray's Inn Square, WC1R 5AA; Kingsland, Etul Kotte, Kotte, Sri Lanka.

COOTE, Sir Christopher (John), 15th Bt *cr* 1621; Senior Baronetcy of Ireland in use; *b* 22 Sept. 1928; *s* of Rear-Adm. Sir John Ralph Coote, 14th Bt, CB, CBE, DSC, and of Noreen Una, *o d* of late Wilfred Tighe; *S* father, 1978; *m* 1952, Anne Georgiana, *d* of Lt-Col Donald Handford; one *s* one *d. Educ:* Winchester; Christ Church, Oxford (MA 1957). Coffee and tea merchant. *Heir: s* Nicholas Patrick Coote [*b* 28 July 1953; *m* 1980, Mona, *d* of late Moushegh Bedelian; one *s* one *d*].

COOTE, Prof. John Haven; Bowman Professor, since 1987, and Head of Department of Physiology, since 1984, Birmingham University; *b* 5 Jan. 1937; *m* 1976, Susan Hylton; one *s* two *d. Educ:* Royal Free Hosp. Sch. of Medicine (BSc (Hons) Physiol.; PhD London); DSc Birmingham 1980. CBiol, FIBiol 1988. Birmingham University: Prof. of Physiology, 1984–; Hd of Sch. of Basic Med. Scis, 1988–91. Vis. Scientist, Inst. de Medicina Experimental, Univ. of Caracas, Venezuela, 1971; Visiting Professor, Department of Physiology: Inst. of Gerontology, Tokyo, 1974–75; Inst. of Physiological Scis, Warsaw, 1977–78. Member: AAAS, 1989; NY Acad. of Scis, 1991. *Publications:* contribs to Jl of Physiol., Jl of the Autonomic Nervous System, Brain Res. *Recreation:* mountaineering. *Address:* Physiology Department, University of Birmingham, Birmingham B15 2TT.

COOTE, Rt. Rev. Roderic Norman, DD; *b* 13 April 1915; *s* of late Comdr B. T. Coote and late Grace Harriet (*née* Robinson); *m* 1964, Erica Lynette, *d* of late Rev. E. G. Shrubbs, MBE; one *s* two *d. Educ:* Woking County Sch.; Trinity Coll., Dublin. Curate Asst, St Bartholomew's, Dublin, 1938–41; Missionary Priest in the Diocese of Gambia and the Rio Pongas, 1942; Bishop of Gambia and the Rio Pongas, 1951–57; Suffragan Bishop of Fulham, 1957–66; Suffragan Bishop of Colchester, 1966–87; Archdeacon of Colchester, 1969–72. Member, General Synod of Church of England, 1969–72. *Recreations:* walking, piano (composer and broadcaster); Irish Champion 120 yds Hurdles. *Address:* 58 Broom Park, Teddington TW11 9RS.

COPE, David Robert, MA; Field Director, Zambia, Voluntary Service Overseas, since 1994; *b* 24 Oct. 1944; *yr s* of late Dr Cuthbert Cope, FRCP and Eileen Cope (*née* Putt); *m* 1966, Gillian Margaret Peck (marr. diss. 1994); one *s* two *d. Educ:* Winchester Coll. (Scholar); Clare Coll., Cambridge (Scholar). 1st Cl. Hons Hist. Tripos Part II, 1965; BA 1965; MA 1972. Asst Master, Eton Coll., 1965–67; Asst British Council Rep. (Cultural Attaché), Mexico City, 1968–70; Asst Master, Bryanston Sch., 1970–73; Headmaster: Dover College, 1973–81; British Sch. of Paris, 1981–86; Master of Marlborough Coll., 1986–93. Gov., Internat. Sch. of Lusaka. Councillor, Cathedral of the Holy Cross, Lusaka. FRSA. *Recreations:* music, running, tennis, travel. *Address:* Voluntary Service Overseas, PO Box 32965, Lusaka, Zambia. *T:* (1) 292041. *Clubs:* Athenæum; Lusaka.

COPE, David Robert; Executive Director, UK Centre for Economic and Environmental Development, since 1986; *b* 7 July 1946; *s* of Lawrence William and Ethel Anne Cope; *m* 1st, 1973, Sharon Marie Kelly (marr. diss. 1990); 2nd, 1992, Reiko Takashina. *Educ:* Fitzwilliam Coll., Cambridge Univ. (MA); London School of Economics (MScEcon, with dist.). Res. Officer, University Coll. London, 1969–70; Lectr, Nottingham Univ., 1970–81; Environment Team Leader, Internat. Energy Agency Coal Unit, 1981–86; Special Lectr in Energy and Environment Studies, Nottingham Univ., 1985–94; Vis. Lectr, Cambridge Univ., 1988–95. Member: Standing Cttee on the Envmt, ACOST, 1990–92; Climate Change Wkg Gp, 1993; Packaging Standards Council (formerly Packaging Council), 1992–; Envmtl Stats Adv. Cttee, DoE, 1994–. *Publications:* Energy Policy and Land Use Planning (with P. Hills and P. James), 1984; numerous papers on energy and environment topics. *Recreations:* hill walking, woodworking. *Address:* UK Centre for Economic and Environmental Development, Suite E, 3 King's Parade, Cambridge CB2 1SJ. *T:* Cambridge (01223) 367799, *Fax:* (01223) 367794.

COPE, Prof. F(rederick) Wolverson, DSc, CEng, FIMinE, FGS; Professor of Geology and Head of Geology Department, University of Keele, 1950–76, now Professor Emeritus; *b* 30 July 1909; *e s* of late Fred and Ida Mary Cope (*née* Chappells), Macclesfield; *m* 1st, 1935, Ethel May Hitchens, BSc (*d* 1961); one *s* two *d*; 2nd, 1962, Evelyn Mary Swales, BA, AKC, *d* of late John Frederick and Ada Mary Swales, Kingston-upon-Hull; one *d. Educ:* The King's Sch., Macclesfield; Univs of Manchester (DSc 1946) and London. Brocklehurst Scholar, 1928; John Dalton Prize, 1930; BSc with First Class Honours in Geology, 1931; MSc, Mark Stirrup Res. Scholar, Manchester, 1932. Demonstrator in

Geology, Bedford Coll., Univ. of London, 1933–34; Daniel Pidgeon Fund, Geol. Soc. of London, 1937; Prin. Geologist in Geological Survey of GB, 1934–50 (discoverer of Formby oilfield, 1937); Murchison Award of Geol. Soc. of London, 1948; Vis. Prof. of Geology, Univ. of Pisa, 1964. Sometime Examr, Univs of Bristol, Exeter, London, Manchester, Nottingham, Sheffield and Wales. FGS 1934 (Senior Fellow 1984); FIMinE 1968; CEng 1969. Chm., Essex Gp of Geologists' Assoc, 1980–; Life Mem., Geologists' Assoc., 1982 (Hon. Mem., 1994). *Publications:* The North Staffordshire Coalfields, in Coalfields of Great Britain (ed by late Sir Arthur Trueman), 1954; Geology Explained in the Peak District, 1976; various research publications mainly in the fields of stratigraphy and palaeontology. *Recreations:* hill walking, landscape sketching, servicing own cars, travel, geology, ornithology, Italy, reading and speaking Italian. *Address:* 6 Boley Drive, Clacton-on-Sea, Essex CO15 6LA. *T:* Clacton-on-Sea (01255) 421829.

COPE, Hon. James Francis, CMG 1978; Speaker of the Australian House of Representatives, 1973–75; *b* 26 Nov. 1907; *s* of G. E. Cope; *m* 1931, Myrtle Irene, *d* of S. J. Hurst; one *d*. *Educ:* Crown Street Public Sch., NSW. Hon. Treaurer, NSW Br., Aust. Glass Workers' Union; Delegate to Federal Council, 1953–55. MHR (Lab) for divs of: Cook, 1955; Watson, 1955–69; Sydney, 1969–75. *Recreations:* billiards, horse racing, cricket, football. *Address:* 1/38–40 Fontainebleau Street, Sans Souci, NSW 2219, Australia.

COPE, Rt. Hon. Sir John (Ambrose), Kt 1991; PC 1988; MP (C) Northavon, since 1983 (South Gloucestershire, Feb. 1974–1983); *b* 13 May 1937; *s* of George Cope, MC, FRIBA, Leicester; *m* 1969, Djemila Lovell Payne, *d* of Col P. V. L. Payne, Martinstown, Dorset and Mrs Tanetta Blackden; two *d*. *Educ:* Oakham Sch., Rutland. Chartered Accountant; Company Director. Commnd RA and RE, Nat Service and TA. Worked for Cons. party, Westminster, 1965–70; contested (C) Woolwich East, 1970; Special Asst to Sec. of State for Trade and Industry, 1972–74; a Govt Whip, 1979–87, and Lord Comr of HM Treasury, 1981–83; Treas. of HM Household and Dep. Chief Whip, 1983–87; Minister of State: Dept of Employment and Minister for Small Businesses, 1987–89; NI Office, 1989–90; Dep. Chm. and Jt Treas., Cons. Party, 1990–92; HM Paymaster Gen., 1992–94. Formerly Secretary: Cons. Parly Finance Cttee; Parly Gp for Concorde; Vice Chm., Cons. Parly Smaller Business Cttee, 1977–79 (Sec., 1975–77). Sen. Comr, Royal Hospital Chelsea, 1992–94. Pres., Inst. of Business Counsellors, 1988–90; Hon. Vice-Pres., National Chamber of Trade. Patron, Avon Riding for the Disabled. *Publications:* (with Bernard Weatherill) Acorns to Oaks (Policy for Small Business), 1967; (ed) A Funny Thing Happened, 1991; I'm sorry you were in when I called, 1992. *Recreation:* woodwork. *Address:* House of Commons, SW1A 0AA. *Clubs:* Carlton, Beefsteak; Tudor House (Chipping Sodbury), Chipping Sodbury Yacht.

COPE, Wendy Mary, FRSL; writer, freelance since 1986; *b* 21 July 1945; *d* of Fred Stanley Cope and Alice Mary (*née* Hand). *Educ:* Farringtons Sch.; St Hilda's Coll., Oxford (MA); Westminster College of Education, Oxford (DipEd). Teacher in London primary schs, 1967–81 and 1984–86; Arts editor, ILEA Contact, 1982–84; Television columnist, The Spectator, 1986–90. FRSL 1992. Cholmondeley Award for Poetry, 1987. *Publications:* Making Cocoa for Kingsley Amis (poems), 1986; Twiddling Your Thumbs (rhymes for children), 1988; (ed) Is That The New Moon?, 1989; The River Girl, 1991; Serious Concerns, 1992; (ed) The Orchard Book of Funny Poems, 1993. *Recreations:* music, swimming. *Address:* c/o Faber and Faber, 3 Queen Square, WC1N 3AU.

COPELAND, Dame Joyanne Winifred; *see* Bracewell, Hon. Dame J. W.

COPEMAN, Harold Arthur; Under-Secretary, HM Treasury, 1972–76; *b* 27 Jan. 1918; *s* of H. W. M. and G. E. Copeman; *m* 1948, Kathleen (Kay) Gadd (*d* 1992); one *s*. *Educ:* Manchester Grammar Sch.; The Queen's Coll., Oxford. BA, 1st Cl. Hons in PPE, 1939; MA. Served War, Army: Cheshire Regt, RA (Instructor in Gunnery) and Ordnance Board (Applied Ballistics Dept), 1940–45. HM Treasury, 1946–76. Consultant, Fiscal Affairs Dept, IMF, 1982. Vis. Fellow, Warwick Univ., 1976–84. *Publications:* (jtly) Health Care: priorities and management, 1980; The National Accounts: a short guide, 1981; Singing in Latin, 1990; The Pocket Singing in Latin, 1990. *Recreations:* music, Latin pronunciation, photography. *Address:* 22 Tawney Street, Oxford OX4 1NJ. *T:* Oxford (01865) 243830.

COPISAROW, Sir Alcon (Charles), Kt 1988; DSc; FInstP; CEng; FIEE; company chairman; a Chairman, General Commissioners for Income Tax, since 1975; *b* 25 June 1920; *o s* of late Dr Maurice Copisarow, Manchester; *m* 1953, Diana, *y d* of Ellis James Castello, MC, Bucklebury, Berks; two *s* two *d*. *Educ:* Manchester Central Grammar Sch.; University of Manchester; Imperial Coll. of Science and Technology; Sorbonne, Paris. Council of Europe Research Fellow. Served War, 1942–47; Lieut RN, 1943–47; British Admiralty Delegn, Washington, 1945. Home Civil Service, 1946–66; Office of Minister of Defence, 1947–54. Scientific Counsellor, British Embassy, Paris, 1954–60. Dir, Forest Products Research Laboratory, Dept of Scientific and Industrial Research, 1960–62; Chief Technical Officer, Nat. Economic Development Council, 1962–64; Chief Scientific Officer, Min. of Technology, 1964–66. Dir, McKinsey & Co. Inc., 1966–76; non-exec. Dir, British Leyland, 1976–77; Mem., BNOC, 1980–83; Dir, Touche Remnant Holdings, 1985–89. Special Advr, Ernst & Young, 1993–. Chairman: Commonwealth Forest Products Conf., Nairobi, 1962; CENTO Conf. on Investment in Science, Teheran, 1963; Member: Scientific Manpower Cttee, Advisory Council on Scientific Policy, 1963–64; Econ. Develt Cttees for Electronics Industry and for Heavy Electrical Industry; Trop. Prod. Adv. Cttee, 1965–66; Press Council, 1975–81; External Mem., Council of Lloyd's, 1982–90. Dep. Chm., Bd of Governors, English-Speaking Union, 1976–83; Chm., Youth Business Initiative, subseq. The Prince's Youth Business Trust, 1982–87. Dir, Windsor Fest., 1983–; Trustee, Duke of Edinburgh's Award, 1978–84; Member Council: Royal Jubilee Trusts, 1981–87; Zoological Soc., 1990–91. Patron, Société des Ingénieurs et des Scientifiques de France, 1992–. Governor, Benenden Sch., 1976–86. Freeman, City of London, 1981. Hon. FTCL. *Address:* 25 Launceston Place, W8 5RN. *Clubs:* Athenæum, Beefsteak, White's.

COPLAND, Rev. Canon Charles McAlester; *b* 5 April 1910; *s* of Canon Alexander Copland and of Violet Williamina Somerville McAlester; *m* 1946, Gwendoline Lorimer Williamson; two *d*. *Educ:* Forfar Academy; Denstone Coll.; Corpus Christi Coll., Cambridge (MA); Cuddesdon College. Reserve of Officers, 1933–38. Curate, Peterborough Parish Church, 1934–38; Mission Priest, Chanda, CP, India, 1938–53 (Head of Mission, 1942–53); Canon of Nagpur, 1952; Rector, St Mary's, Arbroath, 1953–59; Canon of Dundee, 1953; Provost of St John's Cathedral, Oban, 1959–79, also Dean of Diocese of Argyll and The Isles, 1977–79; Hon. Canon of Oban, 1979. *Publication:* Chanda: history of a mission, 1988. *Recreations:* formerly Rugby football, athletics; rifle shooting (shot for Cambridge, for Scotland 1932–84). *Address:* Fir Cottage, South Crieff Road, Comrie, Perthshire PH6 2HF. *T:* Comrie (01764) 670185.

COPLESTON, Ernest Reginald, CB 1954; Secretary, Committee of Enquiry into the Governance of the University of London, 1970–72; *b* 16 Nov. 1909; *s* of F. S. Copleston, former Chief Judge of Lower Burma; *m* Olivia Green. *Educ:* Marlborough Coll.; Balliol Coll., Oxford. Inland Revenue Dept, 1932; Treasury, 1942; Under-Sec., 1950; Dep. Sec., 1957–63, Sec., 1963–69, UGC; retired. *Address:* Arden, Bears Lane, Lavenham, Suffolk CO10 9RT. *T:* Lavenham (01787) 247470.

COPLESTONE-BOUGHEY, His Honour John Fenton; a Circuit Judge (formerly Judge of the County Courts), 1969–85; *b* 5 Feb. 1912; *o s* of late Comdr A. F. Coplestone-Boughey, RN; *m* 1944, Gilian Beatrice, *e d* of late H. A. Counsell, Appleby; one *s* one *d*. *Educ:* Shrewsbury School; Brasenose Coll., Oxford (Open Exhibitioner, Matthew Arnold Prizeman). Inner Temple, Entrance Scholar 1934, Barrister 1935. Legal Assistant, Min. of Health, 1937–40. Royal Artillery, 1940–46; Advanced Class, Military Coll. of Science, 1945. Chester Chronicle & Associated Newspapers, Ltd: Dir, 1947–56; Dep. Chm., 1956–65. Chairman, Nat. Insurance Tribunals (SW London), 1951–69; Referee, Nat. Service and Family Allowances Acts, 1957–69. Battersea etc Hospital Management Cttee: Member 1960–69, Chairman 1969–74; Mem., Wandsworth etc AHA, 1973–82. Chm., Chelsea Housing Improvement Soc., 1981–84. Governor, St Thomas' Hosp., 1971–74; Special Trustee, St George's Hospital, 1974–, Chm. of Trustees 1980–84. Mem. Council, Queen's Coll., London, 1976–, Vice-Chm. 1979–84, Chm. 1984–. *Publications:* contrib. to Halsbury's Laws of England. *Recreations:* walking, travel. *Address:* 82 Oakley Street, SW3 5NP. *T:* 0171–352 6287. *Club:* Athenæum.

COPLEY, John (Michael Harold); opera director; *b* 12 June, 1933; *s* of Ernest Harold Copley and Lilian Forbes. *Educ:* King Edward's, Five Ways, Birmingham; Sadler's Wells Ballet Sch.; Central Sch. of Arts and Crafts, London (Dip. with Hons in Theatre Design). Appeared as the apprentice in Britten's Peter Grimes for Covent Garden Opera Co, 1950; stage managed: both opera and ballet companies at Sadler's Wells, in Rosebery Avenue, 1953–57; also various musicals, plays, etc, in London's West End, incl. The World of Paul Slickey and My Fair Lady. Joined Covent Garden Opera Co.: Dep. Stage Manager, 1960; Asst Resident Producer, 1963; Associate Resident Producer, 1966; Resident Producer, 1972; Prin. Resident Producer, 1975–88. *Productions include: at Covent Garden:* Suor Angelica, 1965; Così fan Tutte, 1968, 1981; Orpheo ed Euridice, 1969; Le Nozze di Figaro, 1971, 1985; Don Giovanni, 1973; La Bohème, 1974, 1985; Faust, 1974; L'elisir d'amore, 1975, 1981, 1985; Benvenuto Cellini, 1976; Ariadne auf Naxos, 1976; Maria Stuarda; Royal Silver Jubilee Gala, 1977; Werther, 1979; La Traviata, Lucrezia Borgia, 1980; Alceste, 1981; Semele, 1982, 1988; Norma, 1987; L'elisir d'amore, 1992; *at London Coliseum (for Sadler's Wells, subseq. ENO):* Carmen, Il Seraglio, Il Trovatore, La Traviata, Mary Stuart; Rosenkavalier, La Belle Hélène, 1975; Werther, 1977; Manon, Aida, Julius Caesar, Les Mamelles de Tirésias, 1979; *Athens Festival:* Macbeth; *Netherlands Opera:* Lucia; *Opera National de Belge:* Lucia; *Wexford Festival:* La Clemenza di Tito; L'Infedelta delusa; *Dallas Civic Opera, Texas:* Lucia; Hansel and Gretel, 1991; *Chicago Lyric Opera:* Lucia; La Bohème, 1983; Orlando, 1986; Tancredi, 1989; The Barber of Seville, 1989; *Canadian Opera, Toronto:* Lucia; Falstaff; La Bohème, 1984; Adriana Lecouvreur, La Forza del Destino, 1987; *Greek Nat. Opera:* Madame Butterfly; Otello; *Australian Opera:* Fidelio, Nozze di Figaro, Rigoletto, Magic Flute, Jenufa, Ariadne auf Naxos, Madame Butterfly, Fra Diavolo, Macbeth, La Traviata, Manon Lescaut, Lucia di Lammermoor, Tosca, Manon; Adriana Lecouvreur, 1984; Peter Grimes, 1986; Carmen, 1987; La Forza del Destino, 1988; *Victoria State Opera:* Don Carlos, 1984; La Bohème, 1985; *WNO:* La Traviata, Falstaff, Peter Grimes, Tosca; Peter Grimes, 1983; *Opera North:* Les Mamelles de Tirésias, Madama Butterfly; *Scottish Opera:* Lucia, Ballo in Maschera, Dido and Aeneas; Acis and Galatea for English Opera Group in Stockholm, Paris, Aldeburgh Fest.; *New York City Opera:* Le Nozze di Figaro; Der Freischutz; Don Quichotte; *Santa Fé Opera:* Ariodanie, 1987; Così fan tutte, 1988; Der Rosenkavalier, La Traviata, 1989; La Bohème, 1990; Tosca, 1994; *Ottawa Festival:* Midsummer Night's Dream; Eugene Onegin, 1983; *Vancouver Opera:* Carmen; *San Francisco Opera:* Julius Caesar; The Midsummer Marriage, 1983; Don Giovanni, 1984; Orlando, 1985; Le Nozze di Figaro, Eugene Onegin, 1986; La Traviata, 1987; Idomeneo, 1989; Midsummer Night's Dream, 1992; Pique Dame, 1993; *San Diego Opera:* Eugene Onegin, 1985; Le Nozze di Figaro, 1986; Così fan tutte, 1991; *Staatsoper Munich:* Adriana Lecouvreur, 1984; *Teatro La Fenice, Venice:* Semele, 1991 and 1992; *Deutsche Oper, Berlin:* L'Elisir d'amore, 1988; *Metropolitan Opera, NY:* Julius Caesar, 1988; Semiramide, 1990; L'Elisir d'amore, 1991. Sang as soloist in Bach's St John Passion, Bremen, Germany, 1965; appeared as Ferdy in John Osborne's play, A Patriot for Me, at Royal Court Theatre, 1965. Co-directed (with Patrick Garland): Fanfare for Europe Gala, Covent Garden, 3 Jan. 1973; Fanfare for Elizabeth gala, Covent Garden, 21 April 1986. *Recreation:* cooking. *Address:* 9D Thistle Grove, SW10 9RR.

COPLEY, Peter Edward; His Honour Judge Copley; a Circuit Judge, since 1995; *b* 15 Feb. 1943; *s* of Edward Thomas Copley and Florence Hilda Copley; *m* 1st; one *s* one *d*; 2nd, 1986, Janice Patricia Webster; one *d*. *Educ:* College of Law. Qualified Solicitor, 1966. *Recreation:* sailing. *Address:* c/o Circuit Administrator, New Cavendish House, 18 Maltravers Street, WC2R 3EU. *Clubs:* Royal London Yacht, Island Sailing.

COPP, Darrell John Barkwell, OBE 1981; General Secretary, Institute of Biology, 1951–82; *b* 25 April 1922; *s* of J. J. H. Copp and L. A. Hoad; *m* 1944, Margaret Henderson; two *s* one *d*. *Educ:* Taunton's Sch., Southampton; Southampton Univ. (BSc). Scientific Officer, Admty Signals Estabt, 1942–45; Asst Sec., British Assoc. for Advancement of Science, 1947–51. Sec., Council for Nature, 1958–63; originator and co-ordinator of first National Nature Week, 1963. Hon. Treas., Parly and Scientific Cttee, 1980–83; Sec., European Community Biologists' Assoc., 1975–85. Trustee, Rye Art Gall., 1985–90. Hon. MTech Bradford, 1975; Hon. FIBiol 1984. *Publications:* reports and reviews in scientific jls. *Recreations:* walking, renovating farm buildings. *Address:* Underhill Farmhouse, Wittersham, Tenterden, Kent TN30 7EU. *T:* Wittersham (01797) 270633.

COPP, Prof. (Douglas) Harold, CC 1980 (OC 1971); MD, PhD; FRS 1971; FRSC; FRCP(C); Professor of Physiology, University of British Columbia, Canada, since 1950; *b* 16 Jan. 1915; *s* of Charles J. Copp and Edith M. O'Hara; *m* 1939, Winnifred A. Thompson; three *d*. *Educ:* Univ. of Toronto, Canada (BA, MD); Univ. of California, Berkeley, Calif (PhD); British Columbia College of Physicians and Surgeons (Lic.). Asst Prof. of Physiology, Calif, 1945–50. Co-ordinator, Health Scis, Univ. of British Columbia, 1976–77; Head of Dept of Physiology, Univ. of British Columbia, 1950–80. FRSC 1959 (Mem. Council, 1973–75, 1977–81; Vice-Pres., and Pres. Academy of Science, 1978–81); FRCP(C) 1974. Hon. LLD: Queen's Univ., Kingston, Ont, 1970; Univ. of Toronto, 1970; Hon. DSc: Univ. of Ottawa, 1973; Acadia Univ., 1975; Univ. of British Columbia, 1980. Inducted Canadian Medical Hall of Fame, 1994. Discovered calcitonin (ultimobranchial hormone) and stanniocalcin (corpuscles of Stannius). *Recreation:* gardening. *Address:* 4755 Belmont Avenue, Vancouver, British Columbia V6T 1A8, Canada. *T:* (604) 2243793.

COPPEN, Dr Alec James, MD, DSc; FRCP, FRCPsych; Director, Medical Research Council Neuropsychiatry Laboratory, and Emeritus Consultant Psychiatrist, West Park Hospital, Epsom, Surrey, 1974–89, retired; *b* 29 Jan. 1923; *y s* of late Herbert John Wardle Coppen and Marguerite Mary Annie Coppen; *m* 1952, Gunhild Margareta, *y d* of late Albert and Sigrid Andersson, Båstad, Sweden; one *s*. *Educ:* Dulwich Coll.; Univ. of Bristol (MB, ChB 1953; MD 1958; DSc 1978); Maudsley Hosp.; Univ. of London (DPM 1957); MRCP 1975, FRCP 1980, FRCPsych 1971 (Hon. FRCPsych 1995). Registrar, then Sen. Registrar, Maudsley Hosp., 1954–59; MRC Neuropsychiatry Research Unit,

1959–74, MRC External Staff, 1974–89; Consultant Psychiatrist: St Ebba's Hosp., 1959–64; West Park Hosp., 1964–89; Hon. Cons. Psychiatrist, St George's Hosp., 1965–70. Head of WHO designated Centre for Biological Psychiatry in UK, 1974–89; Consultant, WHO, 1977–89; Examiner, Royal Coll. of Psychiatry, 1973–77; Andrew Woods Vis. Prof., Univ. of Iowa, 1981; Lectr to learned socs and univs in Europe, N and S America, Asia and Africa. Mem. Council, RMPA (Chm., Research and Clinical Section), 1965–70; Chairman, Biolog. Psychiatry Section, World Psychiatric Assoc., 1972; President, British Assoc. of Psychopharmacology, 1975; Member: Internat. Coll. Neuropsychopharm., 1960– (Mem. Council, 1979; Pres., 1988–90); RSM, 1960–; British Pharmacol. Soc., 1977–; Special Health Auth., Bethlem Royal and Maudsley Hosp., 1982–87; Hon. Member: Mexican Soc. for Biolog. Psychiatry, 1973–; Mexican Inst. of Culture, 1974–; Swedish Psychiatric Assoc., 1977–; European Collegium Neuro-Psychipharmacolgicum, 1987–; Corresponding Member: Amer. Coll. of Neuropsychopharm., 1977–; Deutsche Gesellschaft für Psychiatrie und Nervenheilkunde; Distinguished Fellow, APA, 1981. Freeman, City of London, 1980; Soc. of Apothecaries: Yeoman, 1980; Liveryman 1985. Anna Monika Prize, 1969; European Prize for Psychopharmacology, 1991. *Publications:* (jtly) Recent Developments in Schizophrenia, 1967; (jtly) Recent Developments in Affective Disorders, 1968; (jtly) Psychopharmacology of Affective Disorders, 1979; contribs to text books; papers in Nature, Lancet, BMJ, etc (Current Contents Citation Classic, 1978, Biochemistry of the Affective Disorders). *Recreations:* golf, opera. *Address:* 5 Walnut Close, Epsom, Surrey KT18 5JL. *T:* Epsom (01372) 720800. *Clubs:* Athenæum, Royal Automobile.

COPPLESTONE, Frank Henry; Deputy Chairman, Westcountry Television Ltd, since 1991 (Director, since 1990); Managing Director, Southern Television Ltd, 1976–88; *b* 26 Feb. 1925; 2nd *s* of late Rev. Frank T. Copplestone; *m* 1st, 1950, Margaret Mary (*d* 1973), *d* of late Edward Walker; three *s*; 2nd, 1977, Penny Perrick (marr. diss. 1988); one step *s* one step *d*; 3rd, 1989, Fenella, *widow* of Prof. Gamini Salgado; one step *s* one step *d*. *Educ:* Truro Sch.; Nottingham Univ. (BA). Royal Horse Artillery, 1943–47. Pres., Univ. of Nottingham Union, 1952–53; Pres., Nat. Union of Students, 1954–56; Internat. Research Fellow, 1956–58; Regional Officer, Independent Television Authority, 1958–62; Head of Regional Services, ITA, 1962–63; Head of Programme Services, ITA, 1963–67; Controller, ITV Network Programme Secretariat, 1967–73; Dir, ITV Programme Planning Secretariat, 1973–75; Director: Independent Television News Ltd, 1977–81; Independent Television Publications Ltd, 1976–81. Dir, Trevithick Trust, 1992–94. Mem., Broadcasters' Audience Res. Bd, 1981. FRSA 1994. *Recreations:* sailing, reading, music. *Address:* Pen an Mor, 39 Esplanade, Fowey, Cornwall PL23 1HY. *T:* Fowey (01726) 832818. *Clubs:* Reform, Royal Over-Seas League; Royal Fowey Yacht, Fowey Gallants Sailing.

COPPOCK, Surgeon Rear-Adm. (D) David Arthur, CB 1990; Director, Defence Dental Services, 1988–90; *b* 19 April 1931; *s* of Oswald John Coppock and Ada Katherine Beaven; *m* 1st, 1956, Maria Averil Ferreira (*d* 1985); two *d*; 2nd, 1990, Sally Annette Arnold. *Educ:* Bishop Wordsworth School; Guy's Hosp. (BDS); George Washington Univ. (MSc). Entered RN 1955; HM Ships Eagle, 1956, Tamar, Hong Kong, 1959, Hermes, 1963, Rooke, Gibraltar, 1965; US Navy exchange, 1972; Dep. Dir, Naval Dental Services, 1980; Comd Dental Surgeon to C-in-C Naval Home Command, 1983; Dir, Naval Dental Services, 1983–88. QHDS, 1983–90. Mem., Assoc. of Professional Game Angling Instructors, 1991–. OStJ 1983. *Recreations:* fishing, tennis, golf. *Address:* Breamore Lodge, West Street, Hambledon, Hants PO7 4RW. *T:* Hambledon (01705) 632566. *Club:* Royal Society of Medicine.

COPPOCK, Prof. John Terence, (Terry), CBE 1987; FBA 1975; FRSE 1976; Secretary and Treasurer, Carnegie Trust for the Universities of Scotland, since 1986; *b* 2 June 1921; *s* of late Arthur Coppock and late Valerie Margaret Coppock (*née* Phillips); *m* 1953, Sheila Mary Burnett (*d* 1990); one *s* one *d*. *Educ:* Penarth County Sch.; Queens' Coll., Cambridge. MA (Cantab); PhD (London). Civil Servant: Lord Chancellor's Dept, Min. of Works, Board of Customs and Excise, 1938–47. Served War, Army (commissioned Welch Regt, 1941), 1939–46. Cambridge Univ., 1947–50. University Coll. London (Dept of Geography): successively, Asst Lecturer, Lecturer, Reader, 1950–65, Fellow, 1987; Ogilvie Prof. of Geography, Univ. of Edinburgh, 1965–86, Professor Emeritus, 1987–. Visiting Professor: Loughborough Univ., 1986–89; Birkbeck Coll., London, 1986–. Chm., British Acad./British Liby review panel on information needs in the humanities, 1990–92. Member: Scottish Sports Council, 1976–87; Ordnance Survey Rev. Cttee, 1978–79. FRSA 1980; FRSGS 1988. Ed., Internat. Jl of Geographical Information Systems, 1986–93. *Publications:* The Changing Use of Land in Britain (with R. H. Best), 1962; An Agricultural Atlas of England and Wales, 1964, 2nd edn 1976; Greater London (ed, with H. C. Prince), 1964; An Agricultural Geography of Great Britain, 1971; Recreation in the Countryside: a Spatial Analysis (with B. S. Duffield), 1975; Spatial Dimensions of Public Policy (ed, with W. R. D. Sewell), 1976; An Agricultural Atlas of Scotland, 1976; Second Homes: Curse or Blessing? (ed), 1977; Public Participation in Planning (ed, with W. R. D. Sewell), 1977; Land Use and Town and Country Planning (with L. F. Gebbett), 1978; Land Assessment in Scotland (ed, with M. F. Thomas), 1980; Agriculture in Developed Countries, 1984; Innovation in Water Management (with W. R. D. Sewell and A. Pitkethly), 1986; Geography, Planning and Policy Making (ed, with P. T. Kivell), 1986; numerous papers: mainly in geographical, but also historical, planning and agricultural periodicals, mainly on theme of rural land use in Great Britain. *Recreations:* listening to music, natural history. *Address:* 57 Braid Avenue, Edinburgh EH10 6EB. *T:* 0131–447 3443.

COPPOLA, Francis Ford; Artistic Director, Zoetrope Studios, since 1969; *b* 7 April 1939; *s* of late Carmine Coppola and of Italia Pennino; *m* 1963, Eleanor Neil; one *s* one *d* (and one *s* decd). *Educ:* Hofstra Univ. (BA); Univ. of Calif, LA (MFA). Films directed: Dementia 13, 1963; You're a Big Boy Now, 1967; Finian's Rainbow, 1968; The Rain People, 1969; The Godfather, 1972; The Conversation, 1974; The Godfather Part II, 1974; Apocalypse Now, 1979; One From the Heart, 1981; The Outsiders, 1983; Rumble Fish, 1983; The Cotton Club, 1984; Peggy Sue Got Married, 1987; Gardens of Stone, 1988; Tucker: The Man and his Dream, 1988; New York Stories (Life Without Zoe), 1989; The Godfather Part III, 1991; Bram Stoker's Dracula, 1993. Commandeur, Ordre des Arts et des Lettres, 1983. *Recreations:* reading, writing, scientific discovery. *Address:* Zoetrope Studios, 916 Kearny Street, San Francisco, CA 94133–5138, USA. *T:* (415) 7887500.

COPPS, Hon. Sheila Maureen; PC (Can.) 1993; Deputy Prime Minister of Canada and Minister of the Environment, since 1993; MP (L) Hamilton East, since 1984; *b* 27 Nov. 1952; *d* of Vic Copps and Geraldine (*née* Guthro); one *d*. *Educ:* Univ. of Western Ontario (BA Hons English and French); Univ. of Rouen; McMaster Univ. Journalist, 1974–77; MPP (L) Ontario, 1981–84; Official Opposition Critic for: Housing and Labour, 1984–87; Health and Welfare and Fitness and Amateur Sport, 1987–89; Envmt and Co-Critic for Social Policy, 1989–90; Industry, 1990–91; Dep. Leader of Opposition, 1991–93. *Publication:* Nobody's Baby, 1986. *Address:* Office of the Deputy Prime Minister, Room 509-S, Centre Block, House of Commons, Ottawa, Ont K1A 0A6, Canada. *T:* (819) 9971441, *Fax:* (819) 9533457.

CORBEN, Albert Edward; Assistant Under Secretary of State, Radio Regulatory Department, Home Office (and subsequently with Department of Trade and Industry), 1980–83, retired; *b* 25 Nov. 1923; *s* of Ebenezer Joseph James Corben and Frances Flora (*née* Orchard); *m* 1953, Doris Dodd; two *s*. *Educ:* Portsmouth Grammar Sch.; Sir John Cass Technical Inst. Served Royal Artillery, 1943–47. Entered Home Office, as Executive Officer, 1947; Higher Executive Officer, 1955–62; Sen. Executive Officer, 1962–66; Principal, 1966–72; Secretary to Advisory Council on Penal System, 1966–68; Sen. Principal, 1972–73; Asst Sec., 1973–80. *Recreations:* swimming, golf, walking. *Address:* The Gables, 30 Kingswood Road, Bromley, Kent BR2 0NF. *T:* 0181–460 4106.

CORBET, Dr Gordon Barclay; zoologist; *b* 4 March 1933; *s* of George and Mary Corbet; *m* 1959, Elizabeth Urquhart; one *s* one *d*. *Educ:* Morgan Acad., Dundee; Univ. of St Andrews. BSc, PhD. Asst Lectr in Biology, Sir John Cass Coll., London, 1958–59; British Museum (Natural History): Sen., later Principal, Scientific Officer, Dept of Zoology, 1960–71; Dep. Keeper of Zoology, 1971–76; Hd, Dept of Central Services, 1976–88. *Publications:* The Terrestrial Mammals of Western Europe, 1966; Finding and Identifying Mammals in Britain, 1975; The Handbook of British Mammals, 2nd edn (with H. N. Southern), 1977, 3rd edn (with S. Harris), 1991; The Mammals of the Palaearctic Region, 1978; The Mammals of Britain and Europe, 1980; A World List of Mammalian Species (with J. E. Hill), 1980, 3rd edn 1991; The Mammals of the Indomalayan Region (with J. E. Hill), 1992. *Recreations:* natural history. *Address:* Little Dumbarnie, Newburn, Upper Largo, Fife KY8 6JQ. *T:* Colinsburgh (01333) 340634.

CORBET, Lieut-Col Sir John (Vincent), 7th Bt, *cr* 1808; MBE 1946; DL; JP; RE (retired); *b* 27 Feb. 1911; *s* of Archer Henry Corbet (*d* 1950) and Anne Maria (*d* 1951), *d* of late German Buxton; *S* kinsman, Sir Gerald Vincent Corbet, 6th Bt, 1955; *m* 1st, 1937, Elfrida Isobel Francis; 2nd, 1948, Doreen Elizabeth Stewart (*d* 1964), *d* of Arthur William Gibbon Ritchie; 3rd, 1965, Annie Elizabeth Lorimer, MBE, MSc, Dunedin, NZ. *Educ:* Shrewsbury Sch.; RMA; Magdalene Coll., Cambridge. BA 1933, MA 1972. 2nd Lieut, RE, 1931; served North-West Frontier, India, 1935, and War of 1939–45 in India, Burma and Malaya (despatches, MBE); Lieut-Col, 1953; retd 1955. DL County of Salop, 1961; JP 1957; High Sheriff of Salop, 1966; CC Salop, 1963–81. OStJ; Mem., Church Assembly, later General Synod, 1960–75; former Chm., Board of Visitors, Stoke Heath Borstal. *Address:* Acton Reynald, near Shrewsbury, Salop SY4 4DS. *T:* Clive (01939) 220259. *Club:* Royal Thames Yacht.

CORBETT, family name of **Baron Rowallan.**

CORBETT, Rev. Canon Charles Eric. *Educ:* Jesus College, Oxford (BA 1939, MA 1943); Wycliffe Hall, Oxford. Deacon 1940, priest 1941, St Asaph; Curate of Gresford, 1940–44; CF, 1944–47; Curate of Eglwys-Rhos, 1947–49; Rector of Harpurhey, 1949–54; Vicar of St Catherine's, Wigan, 1954–61; Vicar of St Luke, Farnworth, 1961–71; Rural Dean of Farnworth, 1964–71; Archdeacon of Liverpool, 1971–79; Canon-Treasurer of Liverpool Cathedral, 1979–83. *Address:* 80 Latham Avenue, Helsby, Cheshire WA6 0EB. *T:* Helsby (019282) 724184.

CORBETT, Captain Hugh Askew, CBE 1968; DSO 1945; DSC 1943; RN; (Retired); *b* 25 June 1916; *s* of late Rev. F. St John Corbett, MA, FRSL, FRHistS and late Elsie L. V. Askew; *m* 1945, Patricia Nancy, *d* of late Thomas Patrick Spens, OBE, MC, LLD; three *s*. *Educ:* St Edmund's Sch., Canterbury. Joined Royal Navy, 1933; HMS Cæsar as Capt. (D), 8th Destroyer Sqdn, 1961–63; HMS Fearless, 1965–67 (Capt.). *Address:* Holly Cottage, 3 Clare Road, Cambridge CB3 9HN. *T:* Cambridge (01223) 357735.

CORBETT, Prof. John Patrick, MA; Professor of Philosophy, University of Bradford, 1972–76; *b* 5 March 1916; *s* of E. S. H. and K. F. Corbett; *m* 1st, 1940, Nina Angeloni; two *s*; 2nd, 1968, Jan Adams; two *d*. *Educ:* RNC, Dartmouth; Magdalen Coll., Oxford. Lieut, RA, 1940; POW in Germany, 1940–45. Fellow of Balliol, 1945–61; Prof. of Philosophy, Univ. of Sussex, 1961–72; Jowett Lectr in Philosophy. Council of Europe Fellow, 1957; Visiting Lectr, Yale Univ., 1958; NATO Fellow, 1960; Vis. Prof., Univ. of Toronto, 1968. *Publications:* Europe and the Social Order, 1959; Ideologies, 1965. *Address:* Kalokhorio, Limassol, Cyprus.

CORBETT, Michael McGregor; Hon. Mr Justice Corbett; Chief Justice of South Africa, since 1989; *b* 14 Sept. 1923; *s* of Alan Frederick Corbett and Johanna Sibella McGregor; *m* 1949, Margaret Murray Corbett (*née* Luscombe); two *s* two *d*. *Educ:* Rondebosch Boys' High Sch.; Univ. of Cape Town (BA, LLB); Trinity Hall, Cambridge (Elsie Ballot Scholarship, 1946; Law Tripos 1st cl. 1947; LLB 1st cl. 1948; Hon Fellow, 1992). Enlisted S African Tank Corps, 1942, commissioned 1943; active service, Egypt and Italy with Royal Natal Carbineers, 1943–44. Admitted Advocate, Cape Bar, 1948; QC 1961; Judge, Cape Provincial Div., Supreme Court, 1963; Judge of Appeal, 1974. Hon. Bencher, Lincoln's Inn, 1991. Hon. LLD: Cape Town, 1982; Orange Free State, 1990; Rhodes, 1990; Pretoria, 1993; Witwatersrand, 1994. *Publications:* (jtly) The Quantum of Damages in Bodily and Fatal Injury Cases, 1960, 3rd edn 1985; (jtly) The Law of Succession in South Africa, 1980. *Recreations:* tennis, walking. *Address:* 18 Ladies Mile Extension, Constantia, Cape 7800, South Africa. *Clubs:* City and Civil Service (Cape Town); Kelvin Grove (Newlands, Cape).

CORBETT, Maj.-Gen. Sir Robert (John Swan), KCVO 1994; CB 1991; Secretary to Dulverton Trust, since 1994; *b* 16 May 1940; *s* of Robert Hugh Swan Corbett and Pearl Patricia Elizabeth Corbett (*née* Cavan-Lambart); *m* 1966, Susan Margaret Anne O'Cock; three *s*. *Educ:* Woodcote House; Shrewsbury School; Army Staff Coll., 1973; US Armed Forces Staff Coll., 1980. Commissioned Irish Guards, 1959; served UK, Cyprus, Hong Kong, Falkland Is, Belize, BAOR; Brigade Major, HQ Household Div., 1980–81; CO, 1st Bn Irish Guards (4 Armoured Brigade, BAOR), 1981–84; Chief of Staff, British Forces Falkland Is, 1984–85; Comdr, 5th Airborne Brigade, 1985–87; Mem., RCDS, 1987; Dir, Defence Programme, MoD, 1987–89; GOC Berlin (British Sector) and British Comdt, Berlin, 1989–3 Oct. 1990 (German re-unification); attached HQ BAOR, 1990–91; GOC London Dist, and Maj. Gen. Comd Household Div., 1991–94. Mem. Adv. Bd, Deutsche Bank Berlin AG. Regtl Lt-Col, Irish Guards, 1988–91. Hon. Col, London Irish Rifles, 1993–. Liveryman, Vintners' Co., 1968. *Publication:* Berlin and the British Ally 1945–1990, 1993. *Recreations:* travel, reading, walking, English church architecture, building walls. *Address:* c/o RHQ Irish Guards, Wellington Barracks, SW1E 6HQ. *Clubs:* Pratt's, Cavalry and Guards, Buck's.

CORBETT, Robin; MP (Lab) Birmingham, Erdington, since 1983; communication and public affairs consultant; *b* 22 Dec. 1933; *s* of Thomas Corbett and Marguerite Adele Mainwaring; *m* 1970, Val Hudson; one *s* two *d*. *Educ:* Holly Lodge Grammar Sch., Smethwick. Newspaper and magazine journalist, 1950–69; Editoral Staff Develt Exec., IPC Magazines, 1969–72; Sen. Lab. Adviser, IPC Magazines, 1972–74. Mem. Nat. Union of Journalists Nat. Exec. Council, 1965–69. MP (Lab) Hemel Hempstead, Oct. 1974–1979; opposition front bench spokesman on home affairs, 1985–92, on broadcasting, the media and nat. heritage, 1992–94, on disabled people's rights, 1994–. Chairman: PLP Agric. Gp, 1977–78; PLP Home Affairs Cttee, 1984–86; Sec., PLP Civil Liberties Gp, 1974–79; Member: Expenditure Cttee, 1976–79; Commons Home Affairs Cttee, 1984–86; PLP

Campaign Unit, 1985–86; Vice Chm., All Party Animal Welfare Gp, 1976–79; Jt Sec., All Party Anzac Gp, 1985–; Jt Vice-Chm., All Party Motor Industry Gp, 1987–. Jt Vice-Chm., Friends of Cyprus, 1987–. Mem., Food and Agriculture Sub-Cttee, Labour Party Nat. Exec. Cttee, 1974–79; Chm., farm animal welfare co-ordinating exec., 1977–. Member, Council: RCVS, 1989–92; SCF, 1987–90; sponsor, Terrence Higgins Trust, 1987–. Fellow, Industry and Parlt Trust, 1979. *Publications:* (jtly) Can I Count on your Support?, 1986; On the Campaign Trail, 1987. *Recreations:* visiting North Wales; pottering. *Address:* House of Commons, SW1A 0AA. *Clubs:* Castle Vale Residents Association; Forget-Me-Not (Erdington).

CORBETT, Ronald Balfour, OBE 1978; comedian/character actor; *b* 4 Dec. 1930; *s* of William Balfour Corbett and Anne Elizabeth Corbett; *m* 1965, Anne Hart; two *d. Educ:* James Gillespie Sch., Edinburgh; Royal High Sch., Edinburgh. *Films:* Top of the Form; You're Only Young Once; Casino Royale, 1966; No Sex Please, We're British, 1974; *television:* Frost Report, 1966–67; Frost on Sunday, 1968–69; The Two Ronnies (12 in series), 1971–85; The Two Ronnies Christmas Special, 1982, 1987; Variety Specials, 1977; Sorry! (8 in series), 1981–; *theatre:* Twang (Lionel Bart musical), 1965; Cinderella, London Palladium, Christmas 1971–72; two seasons at London Palladium, 1978, 1983; The Dressmaker (Feydeau), 1990; Out of Order, UK and Australian tour, 1992–93. *Publications:* Small Man's Guide to Life; Armchair Golf, 1986. *Recreations:* golf, racing, soccer, cooking. *Clubs:* Annabel's; Addington Golf (Surrey); Wisley Golf; Gullane Golf (East Lothian); Hon. Company of Edinburgh Golfers (Muirfield).

CORBETT, Lt-Col Uvedale, CBE 1984; DSO 1944; DL; *b* 12 Sept. 1909; *s* of Major C. U. Corbett, Stableford, Bridgnorth, Shropshire; *m* 1st, 1935, Veronica Marian Whitehead (marr. diss., 1952); two *s* one *d*; 2nd, 1953, Mrs Patricia Jane Walker (*d* 1985); 3rd, 1987, Mrs Peggy Roberts. *Educ:* Wellington (Berks); RMA, Woolwich. Commissioned Royal Artillery, 1929; relinquished command 3rd Regt RHA 1945; retired. MP (C) Ludlow Div. of Shropshire, 1945–51. Chm., Sun Valley Poultry Ltd, 1961–83. DL Hereford and Worcester, 1983. *Address:* Shobdon Court, Leominster, Herefordshire HR6 9LZ. *T:* Leominster (01568) 708260. *Club:* Army and Navy.

CORBIN, Maurice Haig Alleyne; Justice of Appeal, Supreme Court, Trinidad and Tobago, 1972–81; *b* 26 May 1916; *s* of L. A. Corbin; *m* 1943, Helen Jocelyn Child; one *s* two *d*; *m* 1968, Jean Barcant. *Educ:* Harrison Coll., Barbados; Queen's Royal Coll., Trinidad. Solicitor, 1941; appointed Magistrate, Trinidad, 1945; called to the Bar, Middle Temple, 1949; Crown Counsel, 1953; Registrar, Supreme Court, 1954; Puisne Judge, Supreme Court, 1957–72. *Recreation:* tennis. *Address:* 77 Brook Road, Goodwood Park, Trinidad. *Club:* Queen's Park Cricket (Port of Spain, Trinidad).

CORBY, Sir (Frederick) Brian, Kt 1989; FIA; Chairman, Prudential Corporation plc, 1990–95; *b* 10 May 1929; *s* of Charles Walter and Millicent Corby; *m* 1952, Elizabeth Mairi McInnes; one *s* two *d. Educ:* Kimbolton Sch.; St John's Coll., Cambridge (MA). Joined Prudential Assce Co. Ltd, 1952; Dep. Gen. Manager, 1974; Gen. Manager, 1976–79; Gp Gen. Manager, Prudential Corp. Ltd, 1979–82; Dir, 1981–89, Chief Gen. Manager, 1982–85, Chm., 1985–89, Prudential Assce Co. Ltd; Chief Exec., Prudential Corp., 1982–90. Dir, 1982–90, Chm., 1985–90, Mercantile & General Reinsce Co. Chm., South Bank Bd, 1990–; a Dir, Bank of England, 1985–93. Vice-President, Inst. of Actuaries, 1979–82; Chm., Assoc. of British Insurers, 1985–87; Pres., CBI, 1990–92. Chancellor, Univ. of Hertfordshire, 1992–. Hon. DSc City, 1989; Hon. DLitt CNAA, 1991. *Publications:* contribs to Jl of Inst. of Actuaries. *Recreations:* reading, golf. *Address:* Fairings, Church End, Albury, Ware, Herts SG11 2JG.

CORBY, George Arthur; international meteorological consultant; *b* 14 Aug. 1917; *s* of Bertie John Corby and Agnes May (*née* Dale); *m* 1951, Gertrude Anne Nicoll; one *s* one *d. Educ:* St Marylebone Grammar Sch.; Univ. of London (BSc Special Maths 1st Cl.). Architect's Dept. LCC, 1936–42; entered Met. Office, 1942; Flt Lt, RAFVR, 1943; Sqdn Leader, Dep. Chief Met. Officer, ACSEA, 1945–46; Sen. Met. Off., Northolt Airport, 1947–53; research, 1953–73; Dep. Dir for Communications and Computing, 1973–76; Dir of Services and Dep. Dir Gen., 1976–78. Vice-Pres., Royal Meteorol Soc., 1975–77. *Publications:* official scientific pubns and res. papers on mountain airflow, dynamical meteorol., and numerical forecasting. *Recreations:* music, photography. *Address:* Kings Barn, High Street, Harwell, Oxon OX11 0EY. *T:* Abingdon (01235) 832883.

CORBYN, Jeremy Bernard; MP (Lab) Islington North, since 1983; *b* 26 May 1949; *s* of David Benjamin Corbyn. *Educ:* Adams Grammar Sch., Newport, Shropshire. NUPE Official, 1975–83; sponsored NUPE, then UNISON, MP. Mem., Haringey Borough Council, 1974– (Chm., Community Develt Cttee 1975–78, Public Works 1978–79, Planning Cttee 1980–81, 1982–83). Mem., Select Cttee on Social Security, 1990–; Chair: London Gp of Lab MPs, 1993– (Vice-Chair, 1985–93); Campaign for Non-alignment; Sec., Campaign Gp of Lab MPs, 1987. *Address:* (office) 129 Seven Sisters Road, N7 7QG. *T:* 0171–263 9450; House of Commons, SW1A 0AA. *T:* 0171–219 3545.

CORCORAN, Hon. (James) Desmond, AO 1982; Chairman, South Australia Greyhound Racing Board, 1983–95; Member, South Australia Totalisator Board, 1982–95; *b* 8 Nov. 1928; *s* of James and Catherine Corcoran; *m* 1957, Carmel Mary Campbell; four *s* four *d. Educ:* Tantanoola Public School. Enlisted Australian Regular Army, 1950; served Korea, Japan, Malaya and New Guinea (despatches twice); discharged, rank of Captain, 1962. Entered politics, contested and won House of Assembly seat of Millicen, SA Parliament, 1962, Member for Coles, 1975; MP (Lab) Hartley, 1977–82; held portfolios of Minister of Lands, Irrigation, Repatriation, Immigration and Tourism, in Labor Govt, 1965–68; Dep. Leader of Opposition, 1968–70; Dep. Premier, Minister of Works and Minister of Marine, 1970–77, additionally Minister of Environment, 1977–79; Premier, Treasurer, and Minister of Ethnic Affairs, of S Australia, Feb.–Sept. 1979. *Address:* 1 Aringa Court, Rostrevor, SA 5073, Australia.

CORDARA, Roderick Charles; QC 1994; *b* 26 March 1953; *s* of Carlo and Sylvia Cordara. *Educ:* City of London Sch.; Trinity Hall, Cambridge. Called to the Bar, Middle Temple, 1975. *Address:* Essex Court Chambers, 24 Lincoln's Inn Fields, WC2A 3ED. *Club:* United Oxford & Cambridge University.

CORDEROY, Rev. Graham Thomas; Minister, Hutton and Shenfield Union Church, since 1987; *b* 15 April 1931; *s* of Thomas and Gladys Corderoy; *m* 1957, Edna Marian Barnes; six *d. Educ:* Emanuel Sch., London; Manchester Univ. (BA Theology 1957). Ordained 1957; King's Lynn, 1957–62; commissioned RAF Chaplain, 1962; Principal Chaplain, Church of Scotland and Free Churches, and Hon. Chaplain to the Queen, 1984–87. Inst. of Alcohol Studies Bd, 1986–. *Recreations:* Rugby referee 1964–87; Gilbert and Sullivan buff. *Address:* San Michele, Friars Close, Shenfield, Essex CM15 8HX. *T:* Brentwood (01277) 211322. *Club:* Royal Air Force.

CORDINER, William Lawson, OBE 1995; HM Diplomatic Service, retired; High Commissioner, Kingdom of Tonga, and Consul for Pacific Islands under American sovereignty South of the Equator, 1990–94; *b* 9 March 1935; *s* of late Alexander Lamb Cordiner and Jessie Cordiner; *m* 1958, Anne Milton; one *s. Educ:* Peterhead Acad.; Boroughmuir, Edinburgh. Inland Revenue, 1952–60; E African Common Services Orgn, 1960–67; HM Diplomatic Service: London, 1967–68; Saigon, 1968–70; Addis Ababa, 1971–74; Kuwait, 1974–75; Baghdad, 1975–77; on secondment to Export Div., DHSS, 1977–79; Rhodesia Dept, FCO, 1979–80; Govt Rep., Antigua and Barbuda, and St Kitts Nevis, 1980–83; Consul for Pacific NW of USA, Seattle, 1983–87; Asst, Commonwealth Co-ordination Dept, FCO, 1988–90. British Delegn Sec., Commonwealth Heads of Govt Meeting, Kuala Lumpur, 1989. Hon. Citizen of Washington State, 1987; Hon. Ambassador of Goodwill, Washington State, 1987. *Recreations:* golf, gardening, oil painting, travel, music. *Address:* Les Mulots, 47120 Duras, France. *Clubs:* Commonwealth Trust; Château des Vigiers (Monestier, France).

CORDINGLEY, Maj-Gen. John Edward, OBE 1959; *b* 1 Sept. 1916; *s* of Air Vice-Marshal Sir John Cordingley, KCB, KCVO, CBE, and late Elizabeth Ruth Carpenter; *m* 1st, 1940, Ruth Pamela (marr. diss. 1961), *d* of late Major S. A. Boddam-Whetham; two *s*; 2nd, 1961, Audrey Helen Anne, *d* of late Maj-Gen. F. G. Beaumont-Nesbitt, CVO, CBE, MC; two step *d. Educ:* Sherborne; RMA, Woolwich. 2nd Lieut RA, 1936; served War of 1939–45, Europe and India. Brigade Comdr, 1961–62; Imperial Defence Coll., 1963; Dir of Work Study, Min. of Defence (Army), 1964–66; Dep. Dir, RA, 1967–68; Maj-Gen., RA, BAOR, 1968–71, retired. Controller, Royal Artillery Instn, 1975–82; Chm. Bd of Management, RA Charitable Fund, 1977–82. Col Comdt, RA, 1973–82. Bursar, Sherborne Sch., 1971–74; Chm., J. W. Carpenter Ltd, 1984–87. Fellow, Inst. of Work Study Practitioners, 1965; MIMgt (MBIM 1966); FInstD 1985. *Recreations:* golf and gardening. *Address:* Church Farm House, Rotherwick, Basingstoke, Hants RG27 9BG. *T:* Hook (0125676) 2734. *Clubs:* Army and Navy; Senior Golfers.

See also Maj.-Gen. P. A. J. Cordingley.

CORDINGLEY, Maj.-Gen. Patrick Anthony John, DSO 1991; General Officer Commanding Second Division, since 1995; *b* 6 Oct. 1944; *s* of Maj.-Gen. John Edward Cordingley, *qv* and Ruth Pamela St John Carpendale; *m* 1968, Melissa Crawley; two *d. Educ:* Sherborne School. Commissioned into 5th Royal Inniskilling Dragoon Guards, 1965; commanded, 1984–87; commanded 7th Armoured Brigade, 1988–91; served Libya, Cyprus, UK, BAOR, Gulf; Comdr, Combined Arms Trng Centre, 1991–92; GOC Eastern Dist, 1992–95. FRGS 1986. OStJ 1993. USA Bronze Star, 1991. *Publication:* Captain Oates: soldier and explorer, 1984, 3rd edn 1985. *Recreations:* riding, ski-ing, windsurfing. *Address:* c/o Lloyds Bank, Cox's & King's Branch, 7 Pall Mall, SW1Y 5NA. *Club:* Cavalry and Guards.

CORDINGLY, David Michael Bradley, DPhil; writer and exhibition organiser; *b* 5 Dec. 1938; *s* of late Rt Rev. Eric Cordingly, MBE, sometime Bishop of Thetford, and of Mary Mathews; *m* 1971, Shirley Elizabeth Robin; one *s* one *d. Educ:* Christ's Hosp., Horsham; Oriel Coll., Oxford; (MA); Univ. of Sussex (DPhil). Graphic designer, 1960–68; Exhibn designer at BM, 1968–71; Keeper of Art Gall., Royal Pavilion and Museums, Brighton, 1971–78; Asst Dir, Mus. of London, 1978–80; National Maritime Museum: Asst Keeper, 1980–82; Dep. Keeper, 1982–86; Keeper of Pictures, 1986–88; Head of Exhibns, 1988–93. Exhibns organised include: Looking at London, 1980; Sea Finland, 1986; Captain Cook, Brisbane Expo, 1988; Mutiny on the Bounty, 1989; Henry VIII at Greenwich, 1991; Pirates: Fact and Fiction, 1992. FRSA 1974. Order of the White Rose of Finland, 1986. *Publications:* Marine Painting in England, 1974; Painters of the Sea, 1979; (with W. Percival Prescott) The Art of the Van de Veldes, 1982; Nicholas Pocock, 1986; Captain James Cook, Navigator, 1988; Pirates: fact and fiction, 1992; articles in Apollo, Connoisseur and Burlington Magazine. *Recreations:* sailing, carpentry. *Address:* 2 Vine Place, Brighton, Sussex BN1 3HE. *Club:* Arts.

CORDLE, John Howard; *b* 11 Oct. 1912; *s* of late Ernest William Cordle; *m* 1st, 1938 (marr. diss., 1956); three *s* (and one *s* one *d* decd); 2nd, 1957 (marr. diss. 1971), *e d* of Col A. Maynard, OBE; one *s* three *d*; 3rd, 1976, Terttu, *y d* of Mikko Heikura, Finland; two *s. Educ:* City of London Sch. Served RAF (commissioned), 1940–45. Owner, Church of England Newspaper, 1960–71. Member: Archbishops of Canterbury and York Commission on Evangelism, 1945–46; Church Assembly, 1946–53; Oxford Churches Patronage Trust, 1947– (Chm., 1955–); Ecclesiastical Cttee of H of C, 1975–77; Hon. Treas., The World's Evangelical Alliance, 1949–53. Lay-Reader, Rochester, 1941–. Mem. of Lloyd's, 1952. Freeman of City of London, 1956, and Mem., Founders' Livery Co. (Master, 1990–91); Mem., Consultative Livery Cttee, City of London, 1991–92. Prospective Parly Cand. (C) NE Wolverhampton, 1949; contested (C) Wrekin Div., 1951; MP (C) Bournemouth E and Christchurch, Oct. 1959–1974, Bournemouth E, 1974–77; Chairman: West Africa Cttee, Conservative Commonwealth Council, 1962–77; Church and Parliament All-Party Gp, 1975–77; Sec., All Party Anglo-Libyan Gp, H of C, 1964–67. Member UK Delegation to: Council of Europe, Strasbourg, 1974–77 (Vice-Chm., Parly and Public Relations Cttee, 1976–77); WEU, Paris, 1974–77; Rapporteur, 1976–77, to Cttee on Social and Health Questions, on the institution of Internat. Medical Card. Primrose League: Chm., Finance Cttee, 1964–67; Hon. Treas., 1964–67; Chm., Gen. Purposes Cttee, 1967–68. Chm., Wessex Aid to Addicts Gp, 1985–; Pres. Salisbury District Speech-impaired Children Trust, 1988–. Governor, London Coll. of Divinity, 1947–52; Life Governor: St Mary's and St Paul's Coll., Cheltenham; Epsom Coll.; Mem. Court of University of Southampton, 1960–77. Gold Staff Officer, Coronation, 1953. Grand Band, Order of the Star of Africa (Liberia), 1964. *Recreations:* shooting, golf, gardening. *Address:* Malmesbury House, The Close, Salisbury, Wilts SP1 2EB. *Clubs:* Carlton, National (Trustee, 1946–), English-Speaking Union.

See also Viscount Cowdray.

CORDY, Timothy Soames; Director, Town and Country Planning Association, since 1995; *b* 17 May 1949; *s* of John Knutt Cordy and Margaret Winifred Cordy (*née* Sheward); *m* 1974, Dr Jill Margaret Tattersall; one *s* one *d. Educ:* Dragon Sch., Oxford; Sherborne Sch.; Durham Univ. (BA); Glasgow Univ. (MPhil). MRTPI 1976. Leicester City Council, 1974–85 (Asst City Planning Officer, 1980–85); Communauté Urbaine de Strasbourg, 1978–79; Asst Chief Exec., Bolton MBC, 1985–87; Chief Exec., RSNC, 1987–94. Director: UK 2000, 1987–; Volunteer Centre UK, 1989–. *Publications:* articles on housing renewal, local economic develt, biodiversity, sustainability. *Recreations:* music, France, food. *Address:* Town and Country Planning Association, 17 Carlton House Terrace, SW1Y 5AS. *T:* 0171–930 8903.

CORDY-SIMPSON, Maj.-Gen. Roderick Alexander, CB 1993; OBE 1984; General Officer Commanding 1st (UK) Armoured Division, since 1994; *b* 29 Feb. 1944; *s* of late Col John Roger Cordy-Simpson, CBE, MC and of Mrs Ursula Margaret Wadham; *m* 1974, Virginia Rosemary Lewis; one *s* one *d. Educ:* Radley College. Commissioned 1963, commanded, 1983–86, 13th/18th Royal Hussars (QMO); Comd 4th Armoured Brigade, 1988–90; COS, UN Bosnia Hercegovina, 1992–93; COS BAOR, 1993–94. *Recreations:* ski-ing, shooting, squash. *Address:* c/o Coutts & Co., 440 Strand, WC2R 0QS. *Club:* Cavalry and Guards.

COREN, Alan; writer and broadcaster; *b* 27 June 1938; *s* of Samuel and Martha Coren; *m* 1963, Anne Kasriel; one *s* one *d. Educ:* East Barnet Grammar Sch.; Wadham Coll., Oxford (Open scholar; MA); Yale; Univ. of California, Berkeley. Asst Editor, Punch, 1963–66, Literary Editor 1966–69, Dep. Editor 1969–77, Editor, 1978–87; Editor, The Listener,

1988–89. TV Critic, The Times, 1971–78; Columnist: Daily Mail, 1972–76; Mail on Sunday, 1984–92; The Times, 1988–; Sunday Express, 1992–; contributor to: Sunday Times, Atlantic Monthly, TLS, Observer, Tatler, London Review of Books. Commonwealth Fellowship, 1961–63. Rector, St Andrews Univ., 1973–76. Hon. DLitt Nottingham, 1993. *Publications:* The Dog It Was That Died, 1965; All Except the Bastard, 1969; The Sanity Inspector, 1974; The Bulletins of Idi Amin, 1974; Golfing For Cats, 1975; The Further Bulletins of Idi Amin, 1975; The Lady From Stalingrad Mansions, 1977; The Peanut Papers, 1977; The Rhinestone as Big as the Ritz, 1979; Tissues for Men, 1980; The Best of Alan Coren, 1980; The Cricklewood Diet, 1982; Present Laughter, 1982; (ed) The Penguin Book of Modern Humour, 1983; Bumf, 1984; Something For The Weekend, 1986; Bin Ends, 1987; Seems Like Old Times, 1989; More Like Old Times, 1990; A Year in Cricklewood, 1991; Toujours Cricklewood?, 1993; Sunday Best, 1993; (ed) Animal Passions, 1994; (ed) The Pick of Punch (annual), 1979–87; (ed) The Punch Book of Short Stories, Bk 1, 1979, Bk 2, 1980, Bk 3, 1981; The Arthur Books (for children), 1976–83. *TV series:* The Losers, 1978. *Recreations:* bridge, riding, broadcasting. *Address:* Robson Books, Bolsover House, Clipstone Street, W1P 7EB.

COREY, Prof. Elias James, PhD; Professor of Chemistry, Harvard University, since 1959; *b* 12 July 1928; *s* of Elias Corey and Tina Corey (*née* Hasham); *m* 1961, Claire Higham; two *s* one *d*. *Educ:* MIT (BS 1948; PhD 1951). University of Illinois, Urbana-Champaign: Instructor, 1951; Asst Prof., 1953–55; Prof. of Chemistry, 1955–59. Former Member: Bd of Dirs, physical sciences, Alfred P. Sloan Foundn; Sci. Adv. Bd, Robert A. Welch Foundn. Hon. DSc: Chicago, 1968; Hofstra, 1974; Oxford, 1982; Liège, 1985; Illinois, 1985; Hon. AM Harvard, 1959. Numerous awards, medals and prizes from univs and learned bodies in USA, Europe and Asia, incl. US Nat. Medal of Science, 1988 and Nobel Prize for Chemistry, 1990. *Publications:* numerous papers in learned jls on pure and synthetic chemistry, esp. on development of methods of organic synthesis, making possible mass production of medicinal and other products, based on natural materials. *Address:* Department of Chemistry, Harvard University, 12 Oxford Street, Cambridge, MA 02138, USA. *T:* (617) 4954033.

CORFIELD, Rt. Hon. Sir Frederick (Vernon), PC 1970; Kt 1972; QC 1972; a Recorder of the Crown Court, 1979–87; *b* 1 June 1915; *s* of late Brig. F. A. Corfield, DSO, OBE, IA, and M. G. Corfield (*née* Vernon); *m* 1945, Elizabeth Mary Ruth Taylor; no *c*. *Educ:* Cheltenham Coll. (Scholar); RMA, Woolwich. Royal Artillery, 1935; 8th Field Regt, RA, India, 1935–39; served War of 1939–45; Actg Captain and Adjutant, 23rd Field Regt, BEF, 3rd Div., 1939; 51st (Highland) Div., 1940 (despatches); prisoner of war, Germany, 1940–45. Called to Bar, Middle Temple, 1945; Bencher, 1980; JAG's Branch, WO, 1945–46; retired, 1946; farming, 1946–56. MP (C) South Glos, 1955–Feb. 1974; Jt Parly Sec., Min. of Housing and Local Govt, 1962–64; Minister of State, Board of Trade, June-Oct. 1970; Minister of Aviation Supply, 1970–71; Minister for Aerospace, DTI, 1971–72. Mem., British Waterways Bd, 1974–83 (Vice-Chm., 1980–83); Dir, Mid-Kent Water Co., 1975–91. Chm., London and Provincial Antique Dealers' Assoc., 1975–89. Pres., Council, Cheltenham Coll., 1985–88. *Publications:* Corfield on Compensation, 1959; A Guide to the Community Land Act, 1976; (with R. J. A. Carnworth) Compulsory Acquisition and Compensation, 1978. *Recreation:* gardening. *Address:* Wordings Orchard, Sheepscombe, near Stroud, Glos GL6 7RE. *Club:* Army and Navy.

CORFIELD, Sir Kenneth (George), Kt 1980; FEng; Chairman, 1979–85, and Managing Director, 1969–85, STC PLC (formerly Standard Telephones & Cables plc); Chairman, Tanks Consolidated Investments, 1990–; *b* 27 Jan. 1924; *s* of Stanley Corfield and Dorothy Elizabeth (*née* Mason); *m* 1960; one *d*. *Educ:* South Staffs Coll. of Advanced Technology. FEng 1979, FIMechE, CBIM. Management Develt, ICI Metals Div., 1946–50; Man. Dir, K. G. Corfield Ltd, 1950–60; Exec. Dir, Parkinson Cowan, 1960–66; Dep. Chm., STC Ltd, 1969–79; Sen. Officer, ITT Corp. (UK), 1974–84. Chairman: Standard Telephones and Cables (NI), 1974–85; Distributed Information Processing Ltd, 1987–; Vice-Pres., ITT Europe Inc., 1967–85; Director: Midland Bank Ltd, 1979–91; Britoil PLC, 1982–88; Octagon Investment Management, 1987–. Chairman: EDC for Ferrous Foundries Industry, 1975–78; British Engrg Council, 1981–85; Defence Spectrum Review, 1985–88; Radio Spectrum Review, 1990–; Mem., ACARD, 1981–84. President: TEMA, 1974–80; BAIE, 1975–79; Vice-Pres., Engineering Employers' Fedn, 1979–85; Member Council: CBI, 1971–85; Inst. of Dirs, 1981– (Pres. 1984–85); BIM, 1978– (Vice-Pres. 1978–83). Trustee, Science Museum, 1984–92 (Mem. Adv. Council, 1975–83). CompIEE 1974, Hon. FIEE 1985. Hon. Fellow: Sheffield Polytechnic, 1983; Wolverhampton Polytechnic, 1986. DUniv: Surrey, 1976; Open, 1985; Hon. DSc: City, 1981; Bath, 1982; Aston in Birmingham, 1985; Hon. DScEng London, 1982; Hon. DSc (Engrg) QUB, 1982; Hon. LLD Strathclyde, 1982; Hon. DTech Loughborough, 1983; Hon. DEngrg Bradford, 1984. Bicentennial Medal for design, RSA, 1985. *Publications:* Product Design, Report for NEDO, 1979; No Man An Island, 1982 (SIAD Award). *Recreations:* shooting, photography, music. *Address:* 8 John Street, WC1N 2ES. *Club:* Carlton.

CORK AND ORRERY, 14th Earl of, *cr* 1620; **John William Boyle,** DSC 1945; VRD 1952; Baron Boyle of Youghal 1616; Viscount Dungarvan 1620; Baron Boyle of Broghill 1621; Viscount Boyle of Kinalmeaky and Baron of Bandon Bridge 1621; Earl of Orrery 1660 (all Ire.); Baron Boyle of Marston (GB) 1711; *b* 12 May 1916; *yr s* of Hon. Reginald Courtenay Boyle, MBE, MC (*d* 1946), *ggs* of 8th Earl, and Violet (*d* 1974), *d* of Arthur Flower; *S* brother, 1995; *m* 1943, Mary Leslie, *o d* of Gen. Sir Robert Gordon-Finlayson, KCB, CMG, DSO; three *s*. *Educ:* Harrow; King's Coll., London (BSc). FICE. Served War 1939–45; Lt-Comdr RNVR, 1939–54 (despatches twice). *Recreations:* home, family, country life, reading. *Heir: s* Viscount Dungarvan, *qv*. *Address:* Nether Craigantaggart, Dunkeld, Perthshire PH8 0HQ. *T:* and *Fax:* Caputh (01738) 710239. *Club:* Lansdowne.

CORK, CLOYNE, AND ROSS, Bishop of, since 1988; **Rt. Rev. Robert Alexander Warke;** *b* 10 July 1930; *s* of Alexander and Annie Warke; *m* 1964, Eileen Charlotte Janet Minna Skillen; two *d*. *Educ:* Mountmellick National School; The King's Hospital; Trinity Coll., Dublin (BA 1952, BD 1960); Union Theol Seminary, New York (Dip. in Ecumenical Studies). Ordained, 1953; Curate: St Mark's, Newtownards, 1953–55; St Catherine's, Dublin, 1956–59; Rathfarnham, Dublin, 1959–64; Rector: Dunlavin, Hollywood and Ballymore-Eustace, 1964–67; Drumcondra, North Strand and St Barnabas, 1967–71; Zion, Dublin, 1971–88; Archdeacon of Dublin, 1980–88. *Publications:* St Nicholas Church and Parish, 1967; Light at Evening Time, 1986; The Passion according to St Matthew, 1990; Ripples in the Pool, 1993. *Recreations:* following sport, theatre, reading. *Address:* The Palace, Bishop Street, Cork, Ireland. *T:* Cork (21) 316114.

CORK, Richard Graham; Chief Art Critic, The Times, since 1991; *b* 25 March 1947; *s* of Hubert Henry Cork and Beatrice Hester Cork; *m* 1970, Vena Jackson; two *s* two *d*. *Educ:* Kingswood Sch., Bath; Trinity Hall, Cambridge (MA, PhD). Art critic, Evening Standard, 1969–77, 1980–83; Editor, Studio International, 1975–79; art critic, The Listener, 1984–90. Slade Prof. of Fine Art, Cambridge, 1989–90; Durning-Lawrence Lectr, UCL, 1987; Henry Moore Foundn Sen. Fellow, Courtauld Inst. of Art, 1992–95. Member: South Bank Bd Visual Art Advisory Panel; Fine Arts Advisory Cttee, British Council; Cttee, Contemp. Art Soc.; Chm., Visual Art Panel, Arts Council of England, 1995–. Trustee, Public Art Develt Trust. Organiser of many exhibns, incl. shows in Milan, Paris, Berlin and at Hayward Gall., Tate Gall. and RA. Frequent broadcaster on radio and television. John Llewelyn Rhys Meml Prize, 1976; Sir Banister Fletcher Award, 1986. *Publications:* Vorticism and Abstract Art in the First Machine Age, vol. I: Origins and Development, 1975, vol. II: Synthesis and Decline, 1976; The Social Role of Art, 1979; Art Beyond the Gallery in Early Twentieth Century England, 1985; David Bomberg, 1987; Architect's Choice, 1992; A Bitter Truth: avant-garde art and the Great War, 1994; contribs to arts magazines. *Recreations:* enjoying family, looking at art. *Address:* 24 Milman Road, NW6 6EG. *T:* 0181–960 2671.

CORK, Roger William; Partner, Moore Stephens, since 1994; *b* 31 March 1947; *s* of Sir Kenneth Cork, GBE and of Nina (*née* Lippold); *m* 1970, Barbara Anita Pauline, *d* of Reginald Harper; one *s* two *d*. *Educ:* St Martin's School, Northwood; Uppingham School. FCA, FICM, FIPA. Partner, W. H. Cork Gully subseq. Cork Gully, 1970–93; associated with Coopers & Lybrand, 1980–93. Chm. of Governors, St Dunstan's Coll. Educnl Foundn, 1991–. President: City of London Br., Inst. of Dirs, 1991– (Chm., 1987–91); Soc. of Young Freemen, 1994–; Vice Pres., Inst. of Credit Management, 1989– (Chm., 1985–87). City of London: Freeman, 1972; Alderman, Tower Ward, 1983–; Sheriff, 1992–93; Master, Bowyers' Co., 1990–92; Member Court: Chartered Accountants' Co.; World Traders' Co.; Member: Butchers' Co.; Envmntl Cleaners' Co. OStJ. Bintang Darjah Seri Padvka Makkota Brunei Yang Amat Mulia-Smb (Brunei); Order of Infante D. Henrique 3rd cl. (Portugal). *Recreations:* sailing, photography, DIY. *Address:* Rabbs, The Lee, Great Missenden, Bucks HP16 9NX. *T:* The Lee (01494) 837296. *Clubs:* City Livery, Tower Ward (Pres., 1984–), Billingsgate Ward (Master, 1980–81), Royal Yachting Association.

CORKERY, Michael; QC 1981; *b* 20 May 1926; *o s* of late Charles Timothy Corkery and of Nellie Marie Corkery; *m* 1967, Juliet Shore Foulkes, *o d* of late Harold Glyn Foulkes; one *s* one *d*. *Educ:* The King's Sch., Canterbury. Grenadier Guards, 1944; Commissioned in Welsh Guards, 1945; served until 1948. Called to Bar, Lincoln's Inn, 1949 (Bencher 1973, Master of the Library, 1991, Treasurer, 1992). Mem., South Eastern Circuit; 3rd Junior Prosecuting Counsel to the Crown at the Central Criminal Court, 1959; 1st Junior Prosecuting Counsel to the Crown, 1964; 5th Senior Prosecuting Counsel to the Crown, 1970; 3rd Sen. Prosecuting Counsel, 1971; 2nd Sen. Prosecuting Counsel, 1974; 1st Sen. Prosecuting Counsel, 1977–81. Mem., Hong Kong Bar Assoc., 1981–. *Recreations:* shooting, sailing, gardening, music. *Address:* 5 Paper Buildings, Temple, EC4Y 7HB. *Clubs:* Cavalry and Guards, Hurlingham; Guards' Polo; Itchenor Sailing.

CORLETT, Clive William, CB 1995; Deputy Chairman, Board of Inland Revenue, since 1994 (Under Secretary, 1985–92; Director General, 1992–94); *b* 14 June 1938; *s* of F. William and Hanna Corlett; *m* 1964, Margaret Catherine Jones; one *s*. *Educ:* Birkenhead Sch.; Brasenose Coll., Oxford (BA PPE). Merchant Navy, 1957. Joined Inland Revenue, 1960; seconded to: Civil Service Selection Bd, 1970; HM Treasury, 1972–74 (as Private Sec. to Chancellor of Exchequer) and 1979–81. *Address:* Board of Inland Revenue, Somerset House, Strand, WC2R 1LB.

CORLETT, Rev. Ewan Christian Brew, OBE 1985; MA, PhD; FEng 1978; Chairman, BCH Ltd (formerly Burness, Corlett & Partners Ltd), since 1954; *b* 11 Feb. 1923; *s* of Malcolm James John and Catherine Ann Corlett; *m* 1946, Edna Lilian Büggs; three *s*. *Educ:* King William's Coll., IOM; Oxford Univ. (MA Engrg Sci.); Durham Univ. (PhD Naval Architecture); Diocesan Training Inst., IOM. Dept of Director of Naval Construction, Admiralty, Bath, 1944–46; Tipton Engrg Co., Tipton, 1946–47; Aluminium Develt Assoc. Research Scholar, Durham Univ., 1947–50; Naval Architect, British Aluminium Co., 1950–53; Design Dir, Burness, Corlett & Partners Ltd, 1953–54, Man. Dir, 1954–88. Ordained deacon, 1991, priest, 1992; Asst Curate, Maughold Parish, IOM. Chm. Council, RINA, 1977–79, Vice-Pres., 1971–82, Hon. Vice-Pres., 1982. Home Office Assessor (Technical Inquiries), 1959–80; Assessor, Herald of Free Enterprise Inquiry, 1987. Hon. Naval Architect and Vice-Pres., SS Great Britain Project, 1970–. Mem. Board, Nat. Maritime Inst., 1978–82; Trustee, Nat. Maritime Museum, 1974–92. Mem. Court, Shipwrights' Co., 1976–, Prime Warden 1990. Hon. FRIN 1980; Hon. FNI 1992. *Publications:* The Iron Ship, 1976, revised edn 1990; The Revolution in Merchant Shipping 1950–1980, 1980; numerous papers to learned instns. *Recreations:* sailing, painting, astronomy. *Address:* Cottimans, Port-e-Vullen, Isle of Man IM7 1AP. *T:* Ramsey, IOM (01624) 814009. *Club:* Manx Sailing and Cruising.

CORLETT, Gerald Lingham; Chairman, Higsons Brewery plc, 1980–88; *b* 8 May 1925; *s* of Alfred Lingham Corlett and Nancy Eileen Bremner; *m* 1957, Helen Bromfield Williamson; three *s* one *d*. *Educ:* Rossall School; Aberdeen University (short war-time course). RA, 1943–47 (Lieut, Royal Indian Artillery). Higsons Brewery, 1947–88. Director: Westminster (Liverpool) Trust Co., 1960–; Midshires Building Soc. (Northern Bd), 1977–87; Radio City (Sound of Merseyside), 1982–88 (Chm., 1985–88); Boddington Gp, 1985–88; Watson Prickard, 1991– (Chm., 1991–). Member, Council: Brewers' Soc., 1964–88; Rossall Sch., 1956–. Mem., Brewers' Co., 1983–. *Recreation:* family. *Address:* Kirk House, 4 Abbey Road, West Kirby, Merseyside L48 7EW. *T:* 0151–625 5425. *Clubs:* Liverpool Racquet; West Kirby Sailing.

CORLEY, Sir Kenneth (Sholl Ferrand), Kt 1972; Chairman and Chief Executive, Joseph Lucas (Industries) Ltd, 1969–73; *b* 3 Nov. 1908; *s* of late S. W. Corley and late Mrs A. L. Corley; *m* 1937, Olwen Mary Yeoman; one *s* one *d*. *Educ:* St Bees, Cumberland. Joined Joseph Lucas Ltd, 1927; Director, 1948. Pres., Birmingham Chamber of Commerce, 1964. Governor, Royal Shakespeare Theatre; Life Governor, Birmingham Univ.; Pres., Soc. of Motor Mfrs and Traders, 1971. Chm. Governors, St Bees Sch., 1978–84. Chevalier, Légion d'Honneur, 1975. *Recreations:* fell-walking, bee-keeping, theatre. *Address:* 34 Dingle Lane, Solihull, West Midlands B91 3NG. *T:* 0121–705 1597; 4 Abbey Farm, St Bees, Cumbria CA27 0DY. *T:* Egremont (01946) 824667. *Club:* Royal Automobile.

CORLEY, His Honour Michael Early Ferrand; a Circuit Judge (formerly County Court Judge), 1967–82; *b* 11 Oct. 1909; *s* of late Ferrand Edward Corley, Christian College, Madras, and Elsie Maria Corley. *Educ:* Marlborough; Oriel Coll., Oxford. Called to Bar, 1934. War Service, RNVR, 1940–46. *Publication:* At The Gates—Tomorrow, 1983. *Address:* The Old Rectory, Rectory Road, Broome, Norfolk NR35 2HU.

CORLEY, Peter Maurice Sinclair; policy consultant; Under Secretary, Department of Trade and Industry, 1981–93; *b* 15 June 1933; *s* of Rev. James Maurice Corley, MLitt and Mrs Barbara Shearer Corley; *m* 1961, Dr Marjorie Constance Doddridge; two *d*. *Educ:* Marlborough Coll.; King's Coll., Cambridge (MA). Min. of Power, 1957–61; Min. of Transport, 1961–65; BoT, 1965–69; Commercial Sec., Brussels, 1969–71; Asst Sec., DTI, 1972–75; Dir Gen., Econ. Co-operation Office, Riyadh, 1976–78; Dept of Industry, 1978–81. *Recreation:* bookbinding. *Club:* United Oxford & Cambridge University.

CORLEY, Roger David, CBE 1993; Director, Clerical, Medical and General Life Assurance Society, since 1975 (Managing Director, 1982–95); *b* 13 April 1933; *s* of Thomas Arthur and Erica Trent Corley; *m* 1964, Brigitte (*née* Roeder), PhD, FRSA; three *s*. *Educ:* Hymers College, Hull; Univ. of Manchester (BSc). FIA 1960. Joined Clerical

Medical, 1956: Investment Manager, 1961–72; Actuary, 1972–80; Dep. Gen. Manager and Actuary, 1980–82. Director: Korea Asia Fund Ltd, 1990–; Nat. Westminster Life Assce Ltd, 1992–; Lands Improvement Gp Ltd, 1994–; City of Westminster Arts Council, 1994–. Pres., Inst. of Actuaries, 1988–90 (Mem. Council, 1976–94; Hon. Sec., 1980–82; Vice-Pres., 1985–88); Vice Pres., Internat. Actuarial Assoc., 1990– (Mem. Council, 1983–; Nat. Correspondent for England, 1984–90); Mem., Deutsche Gesellschaft für Versicherungsmathematik, 1975–. Master, Actuaries' Co., 1992–93 (Mem. Court, 1985–). FRSA 1990. *Recreations:* theatre, travel, music. *Address:* 15 St James's Square, SW1Y 4LQ. *Club:* Army and Navy.

CORLEY SMITH, Gerard Thomas, CMG 1952; HM Diplomatic Service, retired; *b* 30 July 1909; *s* of late Thomas and Nina Smith; *m* 1937, Joan Haggard (*d* 1984); one *s* three *d*. *Educ:* Bolton Sch.; Emmanuel Coll., Cambridge. Gen. Consular Service, 1931; has served in Paris, Oran, Detroit, La Paz, Milan, St Louis, New York, Brussels, and at various times in the Foreign Office. Became 1st Sec. and Consul, on appt as Labour Attaché to Embassy in Brussels 1945; Counsellor UK Deleg. to UNO at New York and UK Alternate Rep. on UN Economic and Social Council, 1949–52; Press Counsellor, Brit. Embassy, Paris, 1952–54; Labour Counsellor, Brit. Embassy, Madrid, 1954–59; British Ambassador: to Haiti, 1960–62; to Ecuador, 1962–67. Sec. Gen., Charles Darwin Foundn for the Galapagos Islands, 1972–82. Grand Officer, Order of Merit (Ecuador), 1980. *Recreations:* music, mountains, birds. *Address:* Greensted Hall, Chipping Ongar, Essex CM5 9LD. *T:* Ongar (01277) 362031.

CORMACK, Prof. Allan MacLeod; University Professor, Tufts University, 1980–95, now Emeritus; *b* 23 Feb. 1924; *s* of George Cormack and Amelia MacLeod; *m* 1950, Barbara Jeanne Seavey; one *s* two *d*. *Educ:* Univ. of Cape Town (BSc, MSc). Research Student, St John's Coll., Cambridge (Hon. Fellow, 1993). Lecturer, Univ. of Cape Town, 1950–56; Research Fellow, Harvard Univ., 1956–57; Tufts University: Asst Prof., 1957–60; Associate Prof., 1960–64; Prof. of Physics, 1964–80; Chairman, Physics Dept, 1968–76. Nelson Medical Lectr, Univ. of Calif, Davis, 1985; Watkins Vis. Prof., Wichita State Univ., 1986. Fellow, Amer. Physical Soc., 1964; Fellow, Amer. Acad. of Arts and Sciences, 1980; Mem., Nat. Acad. of Sciences, 1983; Hon. Member: Swedish Neuroradiological Soc., 1979; S African Inst. of Physics, 1985; Amer. Assoc. of Physicists in Medicine, 1988; Foreign Fellow, Royal Soc. of S Africa, 1983. Hon. DSc Tufts Univ., 1980. Ballou Medallist, Tufts Univ., 1978; (jtly) Nobel Prize for Physiology or Medicine, 1979; Medal of Merit, Univ. of Cape Town, 1980; Mike Hogg Medallist, Univ. of Texas, 1981; US Nat. Medal of Sci., 1990. *Publications:* articles on nuclear and particle physics, computed tomography, and related mathematics. *Address:* 18 Harrison Street, Winchester, MA 01890, USA. *T:* (617) 7290735.

CORMACK, Dr Douglas; Director, Environment, British Maritime Technology, since 1994; *b* 10 Jan. 1939; *s* of Douglas Cormack and Mary Hutton (*née* Bain); *m* 1966, Barbara Ann Jones; two *s*. *Educ:* Gourock High Sch.; Greenock High Sch.; Univ. of Glasgow (BSc 1961; PhD 1964). Res. Associate, Woods Hole Oceanographic Instn, Mass, USA, 1964–67; Warren Spring Laboratory: SSO, 1967–72; PSO, 1972–74; Sen. Principal and Hd, Oil Pollution Div., 1974–79; Scientific Advr, Marine Pollution Control Unit, Depts of Trade and Industry and Transport, 1979–86; Warren Spring Laboratory: Dep. Dir with responsibility for Envmtl Res. and Personnel, 1986–89; Dep. Dir and Business Manager, 1989–92; Chief Exec., 1992–94. Vice-Chm., Adv. Cttee on Protection of the Sea, 1992– (Chm., Scientific Sub-cttee, 1990–). Associate, Paragon Associates, Envmntl Consultants, 1994–. FRSA 1988. Editor, Jl of Oil and Chem. Pollution, 1985–91. *Publications:* Response to Oil and Chemical Pollution, 1983; numerous scientific papers and reports. *Recreations:* sailing, beagling, reading philosophy, history. *Address:* BMT Orlando House, 1 Waldegrave Road, Teddington TW12 8LZ. *T:* 0181–943 5544. *Club:* Civil Service.

CORMACK, John, CB 1982; Director, Parliamentary and Law, Institute of Chartered Accountants of Scotland, 1987–88 (Assistant Director, 1984–87); Fisheries Secretary, Department of Agriculture and Fisheries for Scotland, 1976–82; *b* 27 Aug. 1922; *yr s* of late Donald Cormack and Anne Hunter Cormack (*née* Gair); *m* 1947, Jessie Margaret Bain; one *s* one *d* (and one *d* decd). *Educ:* Royal High Sch., Edinburgh. Served RAPC, 1941–46; Captain and Command Cashier, CMF, 1946. Entered Department of Agriculture for Scotland, 1939: Principal, 1959; Private Sec. to Sec. of State for Scotland, 1967–69; Asst Sec., 1969; Under Sec., 1976. *Recreations:* golf, music. *Address:* 9/1 Murrayfield Road, Edinburgh EH12 6EW.

CORMACK, Sir Patrick (Thomas), Kt 1995; MP (C) Staffordshire South, since 1983 (Cannock, 1970–74; Staffordshire South West, 1974–83); *b* 18 May 1939; *s* of Thomas Charles and Kathleen Mary Cormack, Grimsby; *m* 1967, Kathleen Mary McDonald; two *s*. *Educ:* St James' Choir School and Havelock School, Grimsby; Univ. of Hull. Second Master, St James' Choir School, Grimsby, 1961–66; Company Education and Training Officer, Ross Group Ltd, Grimsby, 1966–67; Assistant Housemaster, Wrekin College, Shropshire, 1967–69; Head of History, Brewood Grammar School, Stafford, 1969–70. Vis. Lectr, Univ. of Texas, 1984. Dir, Historic House Hotels Ltd, 1981–89; Chm., Aitken Dott Ltd (The Scottish Gallery), 1983–89. Trustee, Historic Churches Preservation Trust, 1972–; Pres., Staffs Historic Buildings Trust, 1983–; Member: Historic Buildings Council, 1979–84; Faculty Jurisdiction Commn, 1979–84; Heritage in Danger (Vice-Chm., 1974–); Council for British Archaeology, 1979–; Royal Commn on Historical Manuscripts, 1981–; Council for Independent Educn (Chm., 1979–); Lord Chancellor's Adv. Cttee on Public Records, 1979–84; Council, Georgian Gp, 1985–; Council, Winston Churchill Meml Trust, 1983–93; Chm., William Morris Craft Fellowships, 1988–. Member: Select Cttee on Educn, Science and Arts, 1979–84; Chairman's Panel, H of C, 1983–; Chm., H of C Works of Art Cttee, 1987–; Member: All Party Heritage Cttee (Chm. 1979–); Cons. Party Arts and Heritage Cttee, 1979–84 (Chm.); Chm., Cons. Party Adv. Cttee on Arts and Heritage, 1988–. Chairman: British–Finnish Parly Gp, 1992–; British–Bosnian Parly Gp, 1992–; British–Croation Parly Gp, 1992–. Vis. Parly Fellow, St Antony's Coll., Oxford, 1994–95. Chm. Editorial Bd, Parliamentary Publications, 1983–. FSA 1978 (Vice Pres., 1994–). Rector's Warden, 1978–90, Parly Warden, 1990–92, St Margaret's Church, Westminster. Mem., Worshipful Co. of Glaziers, 1979–; Freeman, City of London, 1979. Hon. Citizen of Texas, 1985. *Publications:* Heritage in Danger, 1976; Right Turn, 1978; Westminster: Palace and Parliament, 1981; Castles of Britain, 1982; Wilberforce—the Nation's Conscience, 1983; Cathedrals of England, 1984. *Recreations:* fighting philistines, walking, visiting old churches, avoiding sitting on fences. *Address:* House of Commons, SW1A 0AA. *Clubs:* Athenæum, Brooks's.

CORMACK, Robert Linklater Burke, CMG 1988; HM Diplomatic Service, retired; *b* 29 Aug. 1935; *s* of late Frederick Eunson Cormack, CIE, and Elspeth Mary (*née* Linklater), Dounby, Orkney; *m* 1962, Eivor Dorotea Kumlin; one *s* two *d*. *Educ:* Trinity Coll., Glenalmond; Trinity Hall, Cambridge (BA Agric.). National Service, 2nd Lieut, The Black Watch, 1954–56. Dist Officer, Kenya (HMOCS), 1960–64; entered CRO (subseq. Diplomatic Service), 1964: Private Sec. to Minister of State, 1964–66; 1st Secretary: Saigon, 1966–68; Bombay, 1969–70; Delhi, 1970–72; FCO, 1972–77; Counsellor and Consul-Gen., Kinshasa, 1977–79; RCDS, 1980; Counsellor (Economic and Commercial), Stockholm, 1981–85; Hd of Information Technology Dept, FCO, 1985–87; Ambassador, Zaire and (non-resident) Rwanda and Burundi, 1987–91; Ambassador, Sweden, 1991–95. Comdr, Order of North Star (Sweden), 1983. *Address:* Westness, Rousay, Orkney KW17 2PT.

CORNBERG, Mrs Sol; *see* Gaskin, Catherine.

CORNELIUS, David Frederick, CPhys, FInstP; FIHT; transport and research consultant; *b* 7 May 1932; *s* of Frederick M. N. and Florence K. Cornelius; *m* 1956, Susan (*née* Austin); two *s* two *d*. *Educ:* Teignmouth Grammar Sch.; Exeter University Coll. (BSc (Hons) Physics). Royal Naval Scientific Service, 1953–58; UKAEA, 1958–64; Research Manager, Road Research Laboratory, 1964–72; Asst Director, Building Research Estabt, 1973–78; Head, Research, Transport and Special Programmes, 1978–80, Transport Science Policy Unit, 1980–82, Dept of Transport; Asst Dir, 1982–84, Dep. Dir, 1984–88, Actg Dir, 1988–89, Dir, 1989–91, Transport and Road Res. Lab. FRSA. *Publications:* scientific papers to nat. and internat. confs and in jls of various professional instns on range of topics in tribology, highway transportation and internat. collaboration in res. *Recreations:* swimming, cycling, youth work, antiques. *Address:* White Poplars, Webb Lane, Hayling Island, Hants PO11 9JE. *T:* Hayling Island (01705) 467212.

CORNELL, Jim Scott, FEng; FICE; FCIT; Managing Director, British Rail Infrastructure Services, since 1993; *b* 3 Aug. 1939; *s* of James William Cornell and Annie Cornell (*née* Scott); *m* 1962, Winifred Eileen Rayner; one *s* one *d*. *Educ:* Thirsk Grammar Sch.; Bradford Inst. of Technol. FICE 1983; FCIT 1986; FEng 1992. With British Rail, 1959–: jun. and middle mgt civil engrg posts, 1959–76; Divisional Civil Engineer: King's Cross, 1976–79; Newcastle, 1978–81; Asst Regl Civil Engr, York, 1981–83; Regl Civil Engr, Scotland, 1983–84; Dep. Gen. Manager, 1984–86, Gen. Manager, 1986–87, ScotRail; Dir, Civil Engrg, 1987–92; Man. Dir, Regl Railways, 1992–93. FIMgt 1987. *Recreations:* tennis, golf, gardening. *Address:* 105 Camberton Road, Leighton Buzzard, Beds LU7 7UW. *T:* Leighton Buzzard (01525) 851070.

CORNELL, Ward MacLaurin; retired; Deputy Minister, Ministry of Housing (formerly Ministry of Municipal Affairs and Housing), Province of Ontario, 1980–88; *b* London, Ont, 4 May 1924; *m* Georgina Saxon; three *s* two *d*. *Educ:* Pickering Coll.; Univ. of Western Ontario. Lectr in English and History, Pickering Coll., Ont, 1949–54; Vis. Lectr, Conestoga Coll.; Gen. Manager, Broadcast Div. (Radio), Free Press Printing Co., 1954–67; Pres., Creative Projects in Communications, 1967–72; Agent-Gen. for Ont. in UK, 1972–78; Gen. Manager, European Ops, Lenroc Internat. Ltd, 1978–80; Dep. Minister, Min. of Citizenship and Culture, Province of Ontario, 1980–82. *Recreations:* reading, tennis, travelling. *Address:* RR1, Uxbridge, Ontario L0C 1K0, Canada.

CORNER, Edred John Henry, CBE 1972; FRS 1955; FLS; Professor of Tropical Botany, University of Cambridge, 1966–73, now Emeritus; *b* 12 Jan. 1906; *s* of late Edred Moss Corner and Henrietta Corner (*née* Henderson); *m* 1953, Helga Dinesen Sondergoord; one *s* two *d* (by 1st *m*). *Educ:* Rugby Sch. Asst Dir, Gardens Dept, Straits Settlements, 1929–45; Principal Field Scientific Officer, Latin America, Unesco, 1947–48; Lecturer in Botany, Cambridge, 1949–59; Reader in Plant Taxonomy, 1959–65; Fellow, Sidney Sussex Coll., Cambridge, 1959–73. Member: American Mycological Soc.; Brit. Mycological Soc.; French Mycological Soc.; Fellow, American Assoc. for the Advancement of Science; Corr. Member: Botanical Soc. of America; Royal Netherlands Botanical Soc.; Hon. Member: Japanese Mycological Soc; Czechoslovak Scientific Soc. for Mycology; British Mycolog. Soc. Mem., Governing Body of Rugby Sch., 1959–75. Darwin Medal, Royal Soc., 1960; Patron's Medal, RGS, 1966; Gold Medal, Linnean Soc. of London, 1970; Victoria Medal of Honour, RHS, 1974; Allerton Award, Pacific Tropical Botanical Garden, Hawaii, 1981; Internat. Prize for Biology, Japan Acad., 1985. *Publications:* Wayside Trees of Malaya (2 vols), 1940, 3rd edn 1988; A Monograph of Clavaria and allied genera, 1950; Life of Plants, 1964; Natural History of Palms, 1966; Monograph of Cantharelloid Fungi, 1966; Boletus in Malaysia, 1972; Seeds of Dicotyledons, 2 vols, 1976; The Marquis: a tale of Syonan-to, 1981; Biographical Memoir of HM Hirohito, Emperor of Japan, 1990; Botanical Monkeys, 1992. *Address:* 91 Hinton Way, Great Shelford, Cambs CB2 5AH. *T:* Cambridge (01223) 842167.

CORNER, Frank Henry, CMG 1980; retired New Zealand Civil Servant and Diplomat; *b* 17 May 1920; *y s* of Charles William Corner, Napier, NZ, and Sybil Corner (*née* Smith); *m* 1943, Lynette Robinson; two *d*. *Educ:* Napier Boys' High Sch.; Victoria Univ. of Wellington. MA, 1st cl. History; James Macintosh and Post graduate Scholar. External Affairs Dept, NZ, and War Cabinet Secretariat, 1943; 1st Sec., NZ Embassy, Washington, 1948–51; Sen. Counsellor, NZ High Commn, London, 1952–58; Dep. Sec. NZ Dept of External Affairs, 1958–62; Perm. Rep. (Ambassador) to UN, 1962–67; Ambassador of NZ to USA, 1967–72; Permanent Head of Prime Minister's Dept, 1973–75; Secretary of Foreign Affairs, 1973–80; Administrator of Tokelau, 1976–85. Chm., NZ Defence Cttee of Enquiry, 1985–86. Mem., NZ Delegn to Commonwealth Prime Ministers' Meetings, 1944, 1946, 1951–57, 1973, 1975, 1977, 1979; Deleg. to UN Gen. Assembly, 1949–52, 1955, 1960–68, 1973, 1974; NZ Rep. to UN Trusteeship Council, 1962–66 (Pres., 1965–66; Chm., UN Vis. Mission to Micronesia, 1964); NZ Rep. on UN Security Coun., 1966; Adviser, NZ Delegn: Paris Peace Conf., 1946; Geneva Conf. on Korea, 1954; numerous other internat. confs as adviser or delegate. Mem., Bd of NZ-US Educnl Foundn, 1980–88; Patron, Assoc. of NZ Art Socs, 1973–88; Mem. Council, Victoria Univ. of Wellington, 1981–87. FRSA. *Recreations:* the arts, gardening, wine. *Address:* 26 Burnell Avenue, Wellington 1, New Zealand. *T:* (4) 4737022; 29 Kakariki Grove, Waikanae, New Zealand. *T:* (4) 2936235.

CORNER, Philip; Director General of Quality Assurance, Ministry of Defence Procurement Executive, 1975–84, retired; Chairman, Institute of Quality Assurance's Management Board (for qualification and registration scheme for lead assessors of quality assurance management system), 1984–92; *b* 7 Aug. 1924; *s* of late William Henry Corner and Dora (*née* Smailes); *m* 1948, Nora Pipes (*d* 1984); no *c*; *m* 1985, Paula Mason. *Educ:* Dame Allan's Boys' Sch., Newcastle upon Tyne; Bradford Technical Coll.; RNEC Manadon; Battersea Polytechnic. BScEng (London); CEng 1966; MIMechE 1952; MIEE 1957; Hon. FIQA 1985. Short Bros (Aeronautical Engrs), 1942–43; Air Br., RN, Sub-Lieut RNVR, 1944–46; LNER Co., 1946–47; Min. of Works, 1947–50; Min. of Supply, 1950; Ministry of Defence: Dir of Guided Weapons Prodn, 1968–72; Dir of Quality Assurance (Technical), 1972–75. Member: Metrology and Standards Requirements Bd, DoI, 1974–84; Adv. Council for Calibration and Measurement, DoI, 1975–84; BSI Quality Assurance Council, 1979–84; BSI Bd, 1980–84. *Recreations:* gardening, listening to music, building and flying radio controlled model aircraft. *Address:* 3 The Green, Dyke Road, Hove, E Sussex BN3 6TH.

CORNESS, Sir Colin (Ross), Kt 1986; Chairman: Nationwide Building Society, since 1991; Glaxo plc, since 1995; *b* 9 Oct. 1931; *s* of late Thomas Corness and Mary Evlyne Corness. *Educ:* Uppingham Sch.; Magdalene Coll., Cambridge (BA 1954, MA 1958); Graduate Sch. of Business Admin, Harvard, USA (Advanced Management Program Dip. 1970). Called to the Bar, Inner Temple, 1956. Dir, Taylor Woodrow Construction Ltd, 1961–64; Man. Dir, Redland Tiles Ltd, 1965–70; Redland PLC: Man. Dir, 1967–82; Chief Exec., 1977–91; Chm., 1977–95. Director: Chubb & Son PLC, 1974–84 (Dep.

Chm., 1984); W. H. Smith & Son (Holdings) PLC, 1980–87; Gordon Russell PLC, 1985–89; Courtaulds PLC, 1986–91; S. G. Warburg Gp, 1987–; Unitech, 1987–; Union Camp Corp., 1991–; Chubb Security, 1992–. A Dir, Bank of England, 1987–95. Chm., Building Centre, 1974–77; Pres., Nat. Council of Building Material Producers, 1985–87; Member: EDC for Building, 1980–84; Industrial Develt Adv. Bd, 1982–84. Mem., UK Adv. Bd, British-American Chamber of Commerce, 1987–91. *Recreations:* tennis, travel, music. *Address:* Glaxo plc, Lansdowne House, Berkeley Square, W1X 6BQ. *T:* 0171–493 4060. *Club:* Cavalry and Guards.

CORNFORD, Sir (Edward) Clifford, KCB 1977 (CB 1966); FEng 1980; Chief of Defence Procurement, Ministry of Defence, 1977–80; *b* 6 Feb. 1918; *s* of John Herbert Cornford; *m* 1945, Catherine Muir; three *s* three *d. Educ:* Kimbolton Sch.; Jesus Coll., Cambridge (BA). Joined RAE, 1938. Operational Research with RAF, 1939–45. Guided Weapons Res. at RAE, 1945–60; jssc 1951; Head of Guided Weapons Dept, RAE, 1956–61; Min. of Defence: Chm., Def. Res. Policy Staff, 1961–63; Asst Chief Scientific Adviser, 1963–64; Chief Scientist (Army), Mem. Army Board, Ministry of Defence, 1965–67; Chm. Programme Evaluation Group, MoD, 1967–Jan. 1968; Dep. Chief Adviser (Research and Studies), MoD, 1968–69; Controller of Guided Weapons and Electronics, Min. of Technology, later Min. of Aviation Supply and MoD (Procurement Executive), 1969–72; Ministry of Defence (PE): Controller (Policy), 1972–74; Dep. Chief Exec., 1974–75; Chief Exec. and Permanent Under Sec. of State, 1975–77. Mem., PO Board, 1981–87. FRAeS. *Publications:* on aeronautical subjects in jls of learned socs and technical publications. *Recreation:* travelling. *Address:* The Spinney, 7 Ash Grove, Liphook, Hants GU30 7HZ. *T:* Liphook (01428) 722780. *Club:* Athenæum.

CORNFORD, James Peters; Director, Paul Hamlyn Foundation, since 1994; *b* 1935; *s* of John Cornford and Rachel Peters; *m* 1960, Avery Amanda Goodfellow; one *s* three *d. Educ:* Winchester Coll.; Trinity Coll., Cambridge (MA). Fellow, Trinity Coll., Cambridge, 1960–64; Harkness Fellow, 1961–62; Univ. of Edinburgh: Lectr in Politics, 1964–68; Prof. of Politics, 1968–76; Dir, Outer Circle Policy Unit, 1976–80; Director: Nuffield Foundn, 1980–88; Inst. for Public Policy Res., 1989–94. Vis. Fellow, All Souls Coll., Oxford, 1975–76; Vis. Prof., Birkbeck Coll., Univ. of London, 1977–80. Mem., Cttee of Inquiry into Educn of Children from Ethnic Minority Gps (DES), 1981–85. Dir, Job Ownership Ltd, 1979–. Mem. Bd, Co-op. Develt Agency, 1987–90. Chairman of Council: RIPA, 1984–85; Campaign for Freedom of Information, 1984–. Chm. of Trustees, Southern African Advanced Educn Project, 1990–. Chm., The Political Quarterly, 1993– (Lit. Ed., 1976–93). *Publications:* contrib.: Cleavages, Ideologies and Party Systems, ed Allardt and Littunen, 1965; Ideas and Institutions of Victorian Britain, ed Robson, 1967; International Guide to Election Statistics, ed Meyriat and Rokkan, 1969; Government and Nationalism in Scotland, ed Wolfe, 1969; Mass Politics, ed Rokkan and Allardt, 1970; Philosophy, Politics and Society IV, ed Laslett, Runciman and Skinner, 1972; (ed) The Failure of the State, 1975; (ed) William Stubbs, The Constitutional History of England, 1979; contrib. to jls. *Address:* 9 Wallingford Avenue, W10 6QA. *T:* 0181–968 6109.

CORNFORTH, Sir John (Warcup), AC 1991; Kt 1977; CBE 1972; FRS 1953; DPhil; Royal Society Research Professor, University of Sussex, 1975–82, now Emeritus; *b* 7 Sept. 1917; *er s* of J. W. Cornforth, Sydney, Aust.; *m* 1941, Rita, *d* of W. C. Harradence; one *s* two *d. Educ:* Sydney High Sch.; Universities of Sydney and Oxford. BSc Sydney 1937; MSc Sydney, 1938; 1851 Exhibition Overseas Scholarship, 1939–42; DPhil Oxford, 1941; scientific staff of Med. Research Coun., 1946–62; Dir, Shell Research, Milstead Lab. of Chem. Enzymology, 1962–75. Assoc. Prof. in Molecular Sciences, Univ. of Warwick, 1965–71; Vis. Prof., Univ. of Sussex, 1971–75; Hon. Prof., Beijing Med. Univ., 1986–. Lectures: Pedler, Chem. Soc., 1968–69; Max Tishler, Harvard Univ., 1970; Robert Robinson, Chem. Soc., 1971–72; Sandin, Univ. of Alberta, 1977. For. Hon. Mem., Amer. Acad., 1973; Corresp. Mem., Aust. Acad., 1977; For. Associate, US Nat. Acad. of Scis, 1978; For. Mem., Royal Netherlands Acad. of Scis, 1978. Hon. Fellow, St Catherine's Coll., Oxford, 1976; Hon. DSc: ETH Zürich, 1975; Oxford, Warwick, Dublin, Liverpool, 1976; Aberdeen, Hull, Sussex, Sydney, 1977; Kent, 1995. Corday-Morgan Medal and Prize, Chem. Soc., 1953; (with G. J. Popjak) CIBA Medal, Biochem. Soc., 1965; Flintoff Medal, Chem. Soc., 1966; Stouffer Prize, 1967; Ernest Guenther Award, Amer. Chem. Soc., 1969; (with G. J. Popjak) Davy Medal, Royal Soc., 1968; Prix Roussel, 1972; (jtly) Nobel Prize for Chemistry, 1975; Royal Medal, Royal Soc., 1976; Copley Medal, Royal Soc., 1982. Has been deaf since boyhood. *Publications:* numerous papers on organic chemical and biochemical subjects. *Recreations:* lawn tennis, chess, gardening. *Address:* Saxon Down, Cuilfail, Lewes, East Sussex BN7 2BE.

CORNISH, Prof. Alan Richard Henry, PhD; CEng, FIChemE; Ramsay Memorial Professor of Chemical Engineering and Head of Department of Chemical and Biochemical Engineering, University College London, since 1990; *b* 14 March 1931; *s* of late Richard Heard Cornish and Evelyn Jennie Cornish (*née* Hatton); *m* 1957, Rita Ellen Wright; one *s* one *d. Educ:* Emanuel Sch.; Illinois Inst. of Technology (PhD). CEng, FIChemE, MIGasE, MInstE. Asst Lectr, Lectr, Sen. Lectr, Imperial Coll., London Univ., 1962–88; Prof. of Chemical Engineering, Univ. of Bradford, 1988–90. FRSA. *Publications:* contribs to professional jls. *Address:* 3 Merlin Close, Croydon, Surrey CR0 5UQ. *T:* 0181–681 5604. *Club:* Athenæum.

CORNISH, Francis; *see* Cornish, R. F.

CORNISH, Jack Bertram; HM Civil Service; Under-Secretary, Department of Health and Social Security, 1976–78; *b* 26 June 1918; *s* of Bertram George John Cornish and Nora Jarmy; *m* 1946, Mary Milton; three *d. Educ:* Price's Grammar Sch., Fareham; Cotham Grammar Sch., Bristol. Admiralty, 1937–61: London, Bath, Plymouth, Singapore; DHSS, 1961–78. Supply Ships in Singapore and Newfoundland, 1941 and 1942. *Recreations:* music, painting, gardening. *Address:* 13 Kingsley Road, Kingsbridge, South Devon TQ7 1EY. *T:* Kingsbridge (011548) 852585.

CORNISH, James Easton; Director and European Market Strategist, NatWest Securities (formerly County NatWest Securities), since 1990; *b* 5 Aug. 1939; *s* of Eric Easton Cornish and Ivie Hedworth (*née* McCulloch); *m* 1968, Ursula Pink; one *s. Educ:* Eton Coll.; Wadham Coll., Oxford (BA); Harvard. Joined FO, 1961; Bonn, 1963; British Mil. Govt, Berlin, 1965; FCO, 1968; Washington, 1973; Dep. Head of Planning Staff, FCO, 1977; Central Policy Rev. Staff, 1980; seconded to Phillips & Drew, 1982; resigned HM Diplomatic Service, 1985; Manager, Internat. Dept, Phillips & Drew, 1982–87; Asst Dir, subseq. Associate Dir, County Securities Ltd, 1987–. *Address:* c/o NatWest Securities, 135 Bishopsgate, EC2M 3XT.

CORNISH, (Robert) Francis, CMG 1994; LVO 1978; HM Diplomatic Service; Senior British Trade Commissioner, Hong Kong, since 1993; *b* 18 May 1942; *s* of Mr and Mrs C. D. Cornish; *m* 1964, Alison Jane Dundas; three *d. Educ:* Charterhouse; RMA Sandhurst. Commissioned 14th/20th King's Hussars, 1962–68; HM Diplomatic Service 1968; served Kuala Lumpur, Jakarta and FCO, 1969–76; First Sec., Bonn, 1976–80; Asst Private Sec. to HRH the Prince of Wales, 1980–83; High Comr, Brunei, 1983–86; Counsellor (Inf.), Washington, and Dir, British Inf. Service, NY, 1986–90; Head of News Dept, FCO, 1990–93. *Address:* c/o Foreign and Commonwealth Office, SW1A 2AH. *Club:* Cavalry and Guards.

CORNISH, Prof. William Rodolph, FBA 1984; Herchel Smith Professor of Intellectual Property Law, Cambridge University, since 1995 (Professor of Law, 1990–95); Fellow of Magdalene College, Cambridge, since 1990; *b* 9 Aug. 1937; *s* of Jack R. and Elizabeth E. Cornish, Adelaide, S Australia; *m* 1964, Lovedy E. Moule; one *s* two *d. Educ:* Univs of Adelaide (LLB) and Oxford (BCL). Lectr in Law, LSE, 1962–68; Reader in Law, Queen Mary Coll., London, 1969–70; Prof. of English Law, LSE, 1970–90. Ext. Acad. Mem., Max-Planck-Inst. for Patent, Copyright and Competition Law, Munich, 1989–. *Publications:* The Jury, 1968; (Jt Editor) Sutton and Shannon on Contracts, 1970; (jtly) Encyclopedia of United Kingdom and European Patent Law, 1977; Intellectual Property, 1981, 2nd edn 1989; Law and Society in England 1750–1950, 1989; articles etc in legal periodicals. *Address:* Magdalene College, Cambridge CB3 0AG.

CORNOCK, Maj.-Gen. Archibald Rae, CB 1975; OBE 1968; FIMgt; Chairman, London Electricity Consultative Council, 1980; *b* 4 May 1920; *s* of Matthew Cornock and Mrs Mary Munro MacRae; *m* 1951, Dorothy Margaret Cecilia; two *d. Educ:* Coatbridge. MBIM 1965. NW Frontier, 1940–42; Burma, 1942–43; transf. Royal Indian Navy, 1943; Burma (Arakan), 1944–46; Gordon Highlanders, 1947–50; transf. RAOC, 1950; psc 1954; GSO2 Intelligence, 1955–57; DAQMG Northern Army Gp, 1959–61; comd 16 Bn RAOC, 1961–64; SEATO Planning Staff, Bangkok, 1964; Defence Attaché, Budapest, 1965–67; Comdt 15 Base Ordnance Depot, 1967; DDOS Strategic Comd, 1968–70; Brig. Q (Maint.), MoD, 1970–72; Dir of Clothing Procurement, 1972; Dir of Army Quartering, 1973–75. Col Comdt, RAOC, 1976–80. Chm., Army Athletic Assoc., 1968–75; Mem. Council, Back Pain Assoc., 1979–. *Recreations:* sailing, opera, golf. *Clubs:* Royal Thames Yacht, Roehampton; Highland Brigade.

CORNOCK, Maj.-Gen. Charles Gordon, CB 1988; MBE 1974; Bursar, Cranleigh School, since 1990; *b* 25 April 1935; *s* of Gordon Wallace Cornock and Edith Mary (née Keeley); *m* 1963, Kay Smith; two *s. Educ:* King Alfred Sch., Plön, Germany; RMA, Sandhurst. Commnd RA, 1956; served, 1957–71: 33 Para Lt Regt; 1 RHA; RMA, Sandhurst; Staff Coll., Camberley; BMRA; Armed Forces Staff Coll., Norfolk, Va; Second in Comd, 1972–74 and CO 1974–76, 7 Para RHA; GSO1 DS Staff Coll., Camberley, 1977–78; Col GS HQ UKLF, 1979; CRA 3rd Armoured Div., 1980–81; RCDS, 1982; Dep. Comdt, Staff Coll., Camberley, 1983; Dir, RA, 1984–86; C of S and Head of UK Delegn, Live Oak, SHAPE, 1986–89. Col Comdt RA, 1986–94; Rep. Col Comdt, RA, 1991–92. Pres., RA Golfing Soc., 1989–; Vice-Pres., Combined Services and Army Hockey Assoc. FIMgt. *Recreations:* hockey, tennis, golf, skiing, water skiing. *Address:* Oranmore. Horseshoe Lane, Cranleigh, Surrey GU6 8QE. *Clubs:* West Hill Golf; La Moye Golf (Jersey); Senior Golfers' Soc.

CORNWALL, Archdeacon of; *see* Ravenscroft, Ven. R. L.

CORNWALL-LEGH, family name of **Baron Grey of Codnor.**

CORNWALLIS, family name of **Baron Cornwallis.**

CORNWALLIS, 3rd Baron *cr* 1927, of Linton, Kent; **Fiennes Neil Wykeham Cornwallis,** OBE 1963; DL; *b* 29 June 1921; *s* of 2nd Baron Cornwallis, KCVO, KBE, MC, and Cecily Etha Mary (*d* 1943), *d* of Sir James Walker, 3rd Bt; *S* father, 1982; *m* 1st, 1942, Judith Lacy Scott (marr. diss. 1948); one *s* (one *d* decd); 2nd, 1951, Agnes Jean Russell Landale; one *s* three *d. Educ:* Eton. Served War, Coldstream Guards, 1940–44. Pres., British Agricultural Contractors Assoc., 1952–54; Pres., Nat. Assoc. of Agricultural Contractors, 1957–63 and 1986–; Vice-Pres., Fedn of Agricl Co-operatives, 1984–86; Chm., Smaller Firms Council, CBI, 1978–81. Representative, Horticultural Co-operatives in the EEC, 1974–87. Chm., English Apples & Pears Ltd, 1990–94; Dir, Town & Country Building Soc.(formerly Planet, then Magnet & Planet, Bldg Soc.) 1967–92 (Chm., 1973–75; Dep. Chm., 1975–77; Chm., 1978–81 and 1991–92). Mem., Bd of Trustees, Chevening Estate, 1979–. Fellow, Inst. of Horticulture, 1986. Pro Grand Master, United Grand Lodge of England, 1982–91. DL Kent, 1976. *Recreations:* fishing, philately. *Heir: s* Hon. (Fiennes Wykeham) Jeremy Cornwallis [*b* 25 May 1946; *m* 1969, Sara Gray de Neufville, *d* of Lt-Col Nigel Stockwell, Benenden, Kent; one *s* two *d*]. *Address:* Ruck Farm, Horsmonden, Tonbridge, Kent TN12 8DT. *T:* Brenchley (01892) 722267; 25B Queen's Gate Mews, SW7 5QL. *T:* 0171–589 1167. *Clubs:* Brooks's, Pratt's.

CORNWELL, David John Moore, (John le Carré); writer; *b* 19 Oct. 1931; *s* of Ronald Thomas Archibald Cornwell and Olive (*née* Glassy); *m* 1954, Alison Ann Veronica Sharp (marr. diss. 1971); three *s*; *m* 1972, Valerie Jane Eustace; one *s. Educ:* Sherborne; Berne Univ.; Lincoln Coll., Oxford (1st cl. Modern Languages; Hon. Fellow 1984). Taught at Eton, 1956–58. Mem. of HM Foreign Service, 1960–64. Hon. Dr, Exeter, 1990. Cartier Diamond Dagger, CWA, 1988. *Publications:* Call for the Dead, 1961 (filmed as The Deadly Affair, 1967); A Murder of Quality, 1962; The Spy Who Came in from the Cold, 1963 (Somerset Maugham Award; Crime Writers' Assoc. Gold Dagger) (filmed); The Looking-Glass War, 1965 (filmed); A Small Town in Germany, 1968; The Naïve and Sentimental Lover, 1971; Tinker, Tailor, Soldier, Spy, 1974 (televised 1979); The Honourable Schoolboy, 1977 (James Tait Black Meml Prize; Crime Writers' Assoc. Gold Dagger); Smiley's People, 1980 (televised 1982); The Little Drummer Girl, 1983 (filmed 1985); A Perfect Spy, 1986 (televised 1987); The Russia House, 1989 (filmed 1991); The Secret Pilgrim, 1991; The Night Manager, 1993; Our Game, 1995. *Address:* David Higham Associates, 5–8 Lower John Street, Golden Square, W1R 4HA.

CORNWELL, Roger Eliot, FCA; Chairman, Louis Dreyfus & Co. Ltd, since 1982 (Director since 1978); *b* 5 Feb. 1922; *s* of Harold and Kathleen Cornwell. *Educ:* St Albans Sch.; Jesus Coll., Oxford (MA). FCA 1976. *Address:* 42 Brompton Square, SW3 2AF.

COROB, Sidney, CBE 1993; Chairman: Corob Consolidated Ltd, since 1984; Corob Holdings Ltd, since 1959; Corob Construction Co. Ltd, since 1952; *b* 2 May 1928; *s* of Wolf and Rachel Corob; *m* 1949, Elizabeth Springer; three *d. Educ:* Tree of Life Coll. Chief Exec., W. Corob & Son, 1951–59; Chairman: Western & Northern Investments Ltd, 1964–68; Corob Intercity Ltd, 1968–77; Mayfair & City Properties plc, 1984–87. Lloyds Underwriter, 1978–85. Chairman: British Technion Soc., 1984–; Internat. Centre for Enhancement of Learning Potential, 1991–. Vice-Chairman: CCJ, 1978–; Central Council for Jewish Social Services, 1989–. Hon. Treas., Westmount Housing Assoc., 1974–. Hon. DSc Technion, Israel Inst. of Engrg and Technology, 1986. *Recreations:* foreign travel, hiking, Bible studies, opera, reading. *Address:* 62 Grosvenor Street, W1X 9DA. *T:* 0171–499 4301. *Clubs:* Naval and Military, Lansdowne.

CORP, Maj.-Gen. Philip James Gladstone, CEng, FIMechE; Director-General Equipment Support (Army), since 1993; *b* 23 June 1942; *s* of Wilfred James Corp and Janet Maude Corp (*née* Gladstone); *m* 1st, 1965, Penelope Joan Smith (marr. diss. 1978); two *s*; 2nd, 1978, Dawn Phyllis Durrant (*née* Holder); one step *s* two step *d. Educ:* Warwick Sch.; Queen Elizabeth GS, Crediton; Pembroke Coll., Cambridge (MA Mech. Scis and Law). Commissioned REME from RMA Sandhurst, 1962; served ME, Germany, UK, to 1972; RMCS and Staff Coll., 1973–74; Op. Requirements, MoD, 1975–76; Comd 3

Field Workshop, 1977–78; REME Combat Develt, 1979–80; Dep. Project Manager, MoD (PE), 1981–83; Comd 7 Armd Workshop, BAOR, 1984–86; QMG Staff, MoD, 1987–89; Cmdt, REME Officers' Sch., 1990; Dir, Equipment Engrg, MoD, 1990–93. FRSA 1995. *Recreations:* music, board sailing, furniture restoration, idleness. *Address:* c/o National Westminster Bank, 59 Parade, Leamington Spa CV32 4BH.

CORREA, Charles Mark; Padma Shri, 1972; architect; *b* 1 Sept. 1930; *s* of Carlos M. Correa and Ana Florinda de Heredia; *m* 1961, Monika Sequeira; one *s* one *d*. *Educ:* Univ. of Michigan (BArch); MIT (MArch). Private practice, Bombay, 1958–; work includes: Mahatma Gandhi Memorial, Sabarmati Ashram; State Assembly for Madhya Pradesh; low cost housing projects in Delhi, Bombay, Ahmedabad and other cities in India; Jawahar Kala Kendra, Jaipur; Nat. Crafts Mus., and British Council HQ, Delhi; Chief Architect for planning of New Bombay. Jawaharlal Nehru Vis. Prof. and Fellow of Churchill Coll., Cambridge, 1985–86. Chm., Nat. Commn on Urbanisation, 1985–88. Founder Mem., Steering Cttee, Aga Khan Award for Architecture, 1977–86; Jury Mem., Pritzker Prize, 1993–. RIBA 1993; Member: French Acad., 1985; Internat. Acad. of Architects, Bulgaria, 1987; Finnish Assoc. of Architects, 1992; Amer. Acad. of Arts and Scis, 1993. Hon. Fellow, United Architects of Philippines. Hon. FAIA 1979. Hon. Dr Univ. of Michigan, 1980. Royal Gold Medal for Architecture, RIBA, 1984; Gold Medal, Indian Inst. of Architects, 1987; Gold Medal, IUA, 1990; Praemium Imperiale Prize, Japan Art Assoc., 1994. *Publication:* The New Landscape, 1984; *relevant publication:* S. Cantacuzino, Charles Correa, 1984. *Recreations:* tennis, model trains, chess. *Address:* 9 Mathew Road, Bombay 400004, India. *T:* (22) 3611858, (22) 3633307. *Clubs:* Bombay Gymkhana, United Services, Willingdon Sports, Bombay Sailing Association (Bombay); Bangalore (Bangalore).

CORRIE, John Alexander; Member (C) Worcestershire and South Warwickshire, European Parliament, since 1994; *b* 29 July 1935; *s* of John Corrie and Helen Brown; *m* 1965, Sandra Hardie; one *s* two *d*. *Educ:* Kirkcudbright Acad.; George Watson's Coll.; Lincoln Agric. Coll., NZ. Farmed in NZ, 1955–59, in Selkirk, 1959–65 and in Kirkcudbright, 1965–. Lectr for British Wool Marketing Bd and Agric. Trng Bd, 1966–74; Mem. Cttee, National Farmers Union, 1964–74 (Vice-Chm. Apprenticeship Council, 1971–74); Nuffield Scholar in Agriculture, 1972. District Officer, Rotary International, 1973–74 (Community service). Nat. Chm., Scottish Young Conservatives, 1964. Contested (C): North Lanark, 1964; Central Ayr, 1966; Cunninghame N, 1987; Argyll and Bute, 1992. MP (C): Bute and N Ayr, Feb. 1974–1983; Cunninghame N, 1983–87. Opposition spokesman on educn in Scotland, Oct. 1974–75; an Opposition Scottish Whip, 1975–76 (resigned over Devolution); PPS to Sec. of State for Scotland, 1979–81; Mem., Council of Europe and WEU, 1982–87. Treas., Scottish Cons. Back Bench Cttee, 1980, Chm. 1981–82; Leader, Cons. Gp on Scottish Affairs, 1982–84; Sec., Cons. Backbench Fish-farming Cttee, 1982–86. Mem. European Parlt, 1975–76 and 1977–79 (Mem. Cttees of Agriculture, Reg. Develt and Transport). Vice-President: EEC-Turkey Cttee, 1975–76; EEC Fisheries Cttee, 1977–79; EEC Mediterranean Agricl Cttee, 1977–79; Rapporteur for EEC Fisheries Policy, 1977–78. European Parliament: Mem., Regl and Local Authorities Cttee, Develt Cttee, ACP Cttee; Vice Chm., 1979 Back bench Cttee. Chm., Transport Users' Consultative Cttee for Scotland, 1989–; Mem., Central Transport Consultative Cttee, 1989– (Vice Chm., 1992–; Mem., Railways Industry Adv. Cttee, 1993–; Mem., Health Safety Cttee, 1993–). Member: Council, Scottish Landowners Fedn, 1990– (Vice Chm., SW Reg., 1992–); Judges Panel for Belted Galloway Soc., 1991–; Timber Growers UK (SW), 1991–; Dir, Ayr Agricl Soc., 1990–. Industry and Parlt Trust Fellowship with Conoco (UK) Ltd, 1986–87. *Publications:* (jtly) Towards a European Rural Policy, 1978; Towards a Community Forestry Policy, 1979; Fish Farming in Europe, 1979; The Importance of Forestry in the World Economy, 1980. *Recreations:* shooting, fishing, riding, tennis, golf, curling, bridge. *Address:* Kynaston Lodge, 5 King Stephen's Mount, Worcester WR2 5PL.

CORRIE, Rodney; *see* Corrie, W. R.

CORRIE, Thomas Graham Edgar; His Honour Judge Corrie; a Circuit Judge, since 1994; *b* 18 Dec. 1946; *s* of John Alexander Galloway Corrie, OBE, MC and Barbara Phyllis Corrie (*née* Turner); *m* 1971, Anna Catherina Logsdail; one *s* two *d*. *Educ:* Eton; Brasenose Coll., Oxford (BA). Called to the Bar, Gray's Inn, 1969; practised on Midland and Oxford Circuit, 1971–94; a Recorder, 1988–94. *Recreations:* gardening, swimming, canal boating. *Address:* 2 Harcourt Buildings, Temple, EC4Y 9DB. *T:* 0171–353 6961. *Club:* Frewen (Oxford).

CORRIE, W(allace) Rodney, CB 1977; *b* 25 Nov. 1919; *o c* of late Edward and Mary Ellen Corrie; *m* 1952, Helen Margaret (*née* Morice), *widow* of Flt-Lt A. H. E. Kahn; one *s* one *d*. *Educ:* Leigh Grammar School; Christ's Coll., Cambridge (BA 1941, MA 1944). Served Royal Signals, 1940–46 (despatches). Entered Civil Service, Min. of Town and Country Planning, 1947; Min. of Housing and Local Govt, 1951; Asst Secretary, 1961; Assistant Under-Secretary of State, DEA, 1969; Under-Secretary: Min. of Housing and Local Govt, 1969; Dept of the Environment, 1970; Chm., NW Econ. Planning Bd, 1969–80, and Regl Dir (NW), DoE, 1971–80, Dept of Transport, 1976–80. *Recreations:* exploring byways, catching up on things. *Address:* Brambledown, Chapel Lane, Hale Barns, Cheshire WA15 0AJ.

CORRIGAN, Prof. (Francis) Edward, PhD; FRS 1995; Professor of Mathematics, University of Durham, since 1992; *b* 10 Aug. 1946; *s* of late Anthony Corrigan and of Eileen Corrigan (*née* Ryan); *m* 1970, Jane Mary Halton; two *s* two *d*. *Educ:* St Bede's Coll., Manchester; Christ's Coll., Cambridge (MA, PhD). A. J. Wheeler Fellow, Durham, 1972–74; CERN Fellow, Geneva, 1974–76; Lectr, Sen. Lectr and Reader, Durham Univ., 1976–92. Joliot-Curie Fellow, ENS Paris, 1977–78; Vis. Associate, CIT, 1978–79; Vis. Fellow, Dept of Applied Maths and Theoretical Physics, Cambridge, 1983; Derman Christopherson Fellow, 1983–84. Life Mem., Clare Hall, Cambridge. *Publications:* articles on elementary particle theory and mathematical physics in learned jls. *Recreations:* playing and listening to music, squash, family camping. *Address:* University of Durham Mathematical Sciences, Science Laboratories, South Road, Durham DH1 3LE. *T:* Durham (0191) 374 2372.

CORRIGAN, Margaret Mary; Member, Radio Authority, since 1991; *d* of Joseph Hamilton and Mary Anna (*née* Monaghan); *m* 1979, Gerard Michael Corrigan; one *s* two *d*. *Educ:* Univ. of Strathclyde (BA Hons English). Trainee journalist with newspaper/magazine publishers D. C. Thomson, Dundee, 1977–78; Advertising Copywriter and Acct Exec., Austin Knight Advertising, Glasgow, 1978–81; Depute Dir of Public Relns, Cumbernauld Develt Corp., 1981–83. *Recreations:* swimming, music, theatre; member of Linlithgow Amateur Musical Productions.

CORRIGAN, Thomas Stephen; Chairman, Direct Mail Accreditation and Recognition Centre, since 1995; company director; *b* 2 July 1932; *s* of late Thomas Corrigan and Renée Victorine Chaborel; *m* 1963, Sally Margaret Everitt; two *d*. *Educ:* Beulah Hill; Chartered Accountant (Scottish Inst.). Nat. Service, Army, 1955–57. Chief Accountant, Lobitos Oilfields, 1957–62; Exec., Keyser Ullmann, 1962–64; Inveresk Group: Finance Dir, 1964; Man. Dir, 1971–74; Chm., 1974–83. Chairman: Havelock Europa, 1983–89; Rex Stewart Gp Ltd, 1987–90; dir of other cos. Pres., British Paper and Board Industry Fedn, 1975–77; Vice-Pres., European Confedn of Pulp, Paper and Board Industries, 1982–83; Mem., NEDC (Tripartite Sector Working Party on paper industry), 1976–77. Chm., POUNC, 1984–94. Master: Makers of Playing Cards Co., 1978–79; Stationers and Newspaper Makers' Co., 1990–91; Marketors' Co., 1995. FRSA. *Recreations:* golf, bridge, tennis, travel. *Address:* Woodend, The Chase, Kingswood, Surrey KT20 6HZ. *T:* Mogador (01737) 832709. *Clubs:* MCC, Royal Automobile, City Livery; Royal & Ancient Golf (St Andrews).

CORRIGAN-MAGUIRE, Mairead; Co-Founder, Community of the Peace People; Director, Peace People's Commitment to Active Non-Violence; *b* 27 Jan. 1944; *d* of Andrew and Margaret Corrigan; *m* 1981, Jackie Maguire; two *s* and three step *c*. *Educ:* St Vincent's Primary Sch., Falls Road, Belfast; Miss Gordon's Commercial Coll., Belfast. Secretarial qualification. Confidential Sec. to Managing Director, A. Guinness Son & Co. (Belfast) Ltd, Brewers, Belfast. Initiator of Peace Movement in Northern Ireland, Aug. 1976; Chm., Peace People Organisation, 1980–81. Hon. Dr of Law, Yale Univ., 1976; Nobel Prize for Peace (jtly), 1976; Carl-Von-Ossietzky Medaille for Courage, Berlin, 1976. *Address:* 224 Lisburn Road, Belfast 9, N Ireland. *T:* (business) (01232) 663465, *Fax:* (01232) 683947.

CORRIN, Prof. Bryan, MD; FRCPath; Professor of Thoracic Pathology, National Heart and Lung Institute, London University, since 1979; *b* 27 May 1933; *s* of George Henry Corrin and Eleanor (*née* Halliday); *m* 1957, Sheila Ann Carpenter; three *s* one *d*. *Educ:* King William's Coll., Isle of Man; St Mary's Hosp. Med. Sch., London Univ. (MB BS 1956; MD 1962). FRCPath 1977. Sen. House Officer, Birmingham Children's Hosp., 1957–58; Lectr in Pathology, Univ. of Manchester, 1958–64; Reader in Morbid Anatomy, St Thomas's Hosp. Med. Sch., London, 1964–79. Hon. Consultant Pathologist, Brompton Hosp., 1979–. *Publications:* The Lungs, 1990; (ed jtly) Clinical Atlas of Respiratory Disorders, 1990. *Recreation:* walking. *Address:* 14 Foxgrove Road, Beckenham, Kent BR3 2AT.

CORRIN, John William, CBE 1995; **His Honour Deemster Corrin;** HM's First Deemster, Clerk of the Rolls and Deputy Governor of the Isle of Man, since 1988; *b* 6 Jan. 1932; *s* of Evan Cain Corrin and Dorothy Mildred Corrin; *m* 1961, Dorothy Patricia, *d* of late J. S. Lace; one *d*. *Educ:* Murrays Road Primary Sch., Douglas; King William's Coll., IOM. Admitted to Manx Bar, 1954. Attorney Gen., IOM, 1974–80; Second Deemster, 1980–88. Chairman (all IOM): Criminal Injuries Compensation Tribunal, 1980–88; Licensing Appeal Court, 1980–88; Prevention of Fraud (Unit Trust) Tribunal, 1980–88; Income Tax Appeal Comrs, 1988–; Tynwald Ceremony Arrangements Cttee, 1988–. Chairman: Manx Blind Welfare Soc.; Manx Workshop for the Disabled; Hon. Mem., IOM Med. Soc.; President: IOM Br., Crossroads Care; Island Bridge Club; Lon Dhoo Male Voice Choir; IOM Br., SSAFA; Manx Asthma Assoc.; IOM Postgrad. Med. Centre; IOM Alcohol Adv. Council; Chm., Douglas Buxton Music Trust; Trustee: Manx Foundn for Physically Disabled; Manx Methodist Church. *Recreations:* music, gardening, bridge. *Address:* Carla Beck, 28 Devonshire Road, Douglas, Isle of Man. *T:* Douglas (01624) 621806. *Club:* Ellan Vannin (Douglas) (Past Pres.).

CORRY; *see* Lowry-Corry, family name of Earl of Belmore.

CORRY, Viscount; John Armar Galbraith Lowry-Corry; *b* 2 Nov. 1985; *s* and *heir* of Earl of Belmore, *qv*.

CORRY, Lt-Comdr Sir William (James), 4th Bt *cr* 1885, of Dunraven, Co. Antrim; RN retired; *b* 1 Aug. 1924; *s* of Sir James Perowne Ivo Myles Corry, 3rd Bt and Molly Irene, *d* of Major O. J. Bell; *S* father, 1987; *m* 1945, Pamela Diana Mary, *d* of late Lt-Col J. B. Lapsley, MC; four *s* two *d*. *Educ:* RNC Dartmouth. Joined RN, 1938; Lt-Comdr 1953; retired, 1977. *Recreation:* beagling. *Heir:* *s* James Michael Corry [*b* 3 Oct. 1946; *m* 1973, Sheridan Lorraine, *d* of A. P. Ashbourne; three *s*]. *Address:* East Hillerton House, Spreyton, Crediton, Devon EX17 5AD. *T:* Bow (01363) 82407.

CORSAR, Col Charles Herbert Kenneth, LVO 1989; OBE 1981; TD 1960; retired; Vice Lord Lieutenant, Lothian Region (District of Midlothian), since 1993; *b* 13 May 1926; *s* of Kenneth Charles Corsar and Winifred Paton (*née* Herdman); *m* 1953, Mary Drummond Buchanan Smith (*see* Hon. Dame Mary Corsar); two *s* two *d* (and one *d* decd). *Educ:* Merchiston Castle Sch.; King's Coll., Cambridge (MA). Farmer, 1953–89. Commnd Royal Scots TA, 1948; comd 8/9 Royal Scots, 1964–67; Edinburgh and Heriot-Watt Univs OTC, 1967–72; TA Col, 1972–75; Hon. ADC to the Queen, 1977–81; Chm., Lowland TAVRA, 1984–87; Hon. Col., 1/52 Lowland Vols, 1975–87. Zone Comr, Home Defence, E of Scotland, 1972–74. County Cllr, Midlothian, 1958–67. Vice-Pres., Boys' Brigade, 1970–91; Chairman: Scottish Standing Conf. of Voluntary Youth Orgns, 1973–78; Earl Haig Fund (Scotland), 1984–90; Mem., Scottish Sports Council, 1972–75; Secretary: Prince's Trust (Lothian & Borders), 1982–93; (for Scotland) Duke of Edinburgh's Award, 1966–87. JP Midlothian, 1964; DL Midlothian, 1975. *Recreations:* gardening, bee-keeping, shooting. *Address:* Burg Torloisk, Ulva Ferry, Isle of Mull, Argyll PA74 6NH. *T:* Ulva Ferry (01688) 500289; 11 Ainslie Place, Edinburgh EH3 6AS. *T:* 0131–225 6318. *Club:* New (Edinburgh).

CORSAR, Hon. Dame Mary (Drummond), DBE 1993; Chairman: TSB Foundation Scotland, since 1994 (Trustee, since 1993); Women's Royal Voluntary Service, 1988–93; *b* 8 July 1927; *o d* of Lord Balerno, CBE, TD, DL and Mary Kathleen Smith; *m* 1953, Col Charles Herbert Kenneth Corsar, *qv*; two *s* two *d* (and one *d* decd). *Educ:* Westbourne, Glasgow; St Denis, Edinburgh; Edinburgh Univ. (MA Hons). Dep. Chief Comr, Girl Guides, Scotland, 1972–77; Chm., Scotland WRVS, 1981–88. Member: Vis. Cttee, Glenochil Young Offenders Instn, 1976–94; Parole Bd for Scotland, 1982–89. Hon. Pres., Scottish Women's AAA, 1973–91. Member: Exec. Cttee, Trefoil Centre for Handicapped, 1975–; Convocation, Heriot Watt Univ., 1986–; Royal Anniversary Trust, 1990–93. Gov., Fettes Coll., 1984–. *Recreations:* hill walking, gardening, embroidery. *Address:* Burg, Torloisk, Isle of Mull, Argyll PA74 6NH. *T:* Ulva Ferry (01688) 500289; 11 Ainslie Place, Edinburgh EH3 6AS. *T:* 0131–225 6318. *Club:* New (Edinburgh) (Associate Mem.).

CORSTON, Jean Ann; MP (Lab) Bristol East, since 1992; *b* 5 May 1942; *d* of Charles Lawrence Parkin and late Eileen Ada Parkin; *m* 1st, 1961, Christopher John Davy Corston; one *s* one *d*; 2nd, 1985, Peter Brereton Townsend, *qv*. *Educ:* LSE (LLB 1989). Labour Party posts: Asst Regl Organiser, 1976, Regl Organiser, 1981, South West; Asst National Agent, London, 1985–86; sponsored as MP by TGWU. Called to the Bar, Inner Temple, 1991; Bristol chambers. Mem., Select Cttee on Agric., 1992–. Co-Chm., PLP Women's Gp, 1992–. *Recreations:* gardening, reading, walking. *Address:* House of Commons, SW1A 0AA. *T:* 0171–219 4575.

CORTAZZI, Sir (Henry Arthur) Hugh, GCMG 1984 (KCMG 1980; CMG 1969); HM Diplomatic Service, retired; Director: Foreign and Colonial Pacific Trust, since 1984; GT Japan Investment Trust plc, since 1984; Thornton Pacific (formerly Pacific) Investment Trust, since 1986; *b* 2 May 1924; *m* 1956, Elizabeth Esther Montagu; one *s* two *d*. *Educ:* Sedbergh Sch.; St Andrews and London Univs. Served in RAF, 1943–47; joined Foreign Office, 1949; Third Sec., Singapore, 1950–51; Third/Second Sec., Tokyo, 1951–54; FO, 1954–58; First Sec., Bonn, 1958–60; First Sec., later Head of Chancery, Tokyo, 1961–65;

FO, 1965–66; Counsellor (Commercial), Tokyo, 1966–70; Royal Coll. of Defence Studies, 1971–72; Minister (Commercial), Washington, 1972–75; Dep. Under-Sec. of State, FCO, 1975–80; Ambassador to Japan, 1980–84. Dir, Hill Samuel & Co., later Hill Samuel Bank, 1984–91. Senior Adviser: NEC Corp., Japan, 1992–; Dai-ichi Kangyo Bank, Japan, 1992–; Bank of Kyoto, 1992–; Wilde Sapte, solicitors, 1992–; PIFC, 1993. Mem., ESRC, 1984–89. Pres., Asiatic Soc. of Japan, 1982–83; Chm., Japan Soc. of London, 1985–. Mem., Council and Court, Sussex Univ., 1985–92. Hon. Fellow, Robinson Coll., Cambridge, 1988. Hon. Dr Stirling, 1988. Grand Cordon, Order of the Sacred Treasure (Japan), 1995. *Publications:* trans. from Japanese, Genji Keita: The Ogre and other stories of the Japanese Salarymen, 1972; The Guardian God of Golf and other humorous stories, 1972, reprinted as The Lucky One, 1980; (ed) Mary Crawford Fraser, A Diplomat's Wife in Japan: sketches at the turn of the century, 1982; Isles of Gold: antique maps of Japan, 1983; Higashi No Shimaguni, Nishi No Shimaguni (collection of articles and speeches in Japanese), 1984; Dr Willis in Japan, 1985; (ed) Mitford's Japan, 1985; Victorians in Japan: in and around the Treaty Ports, 1987; for Japanese students of English: Thoughts from a Sussex Garden (essays), 1984; Second Thoughts (essays), 1986; Japanese Encounter, 1987; Zoku, Higashi no Shimaguni, Nishi no Shimaguni, 1987; (ed with George Webb) Kipling's Japan, 1988; The Japanese Achievement: a short history of Japan and Japanese culture, 1990; (ed) A British Artist in Meiji Japan, by Sir Alfred East, 1991; (ed) Building Japan 1868–1876, by Richard Henry Brunton, 1991; (ed with Gordon Daniels) Britain and Japan 1859–1991, 1991; Themes and Personalities, 1991; Modern Japan: a concise survey, 1993; (ed with Terry Bennett) Caught in Time: Japan, 1995; articles on Japanese themes in English and Japanese pubns. *Recreations:* Japanese studies, the arts including antiques. *Address:* Ballsocks, Vines Cross, Heathfield, E Sussex TN21 9ET. *Club:* Royal Air Force.

CORVEDALE, Viscount; Benedict Alexander Stanley Baldwin; *b* 28 Dec. 1973; *s* and *heir* of 4th Earl Baldwin of Bewdley, *qv*. Reading music at Newcastle Univ.

CORY, (Charles) Raymond, CBE 1982; Chairman: John Cory & Sons Ltd, 1965–91 (Director 1948–91); Milford Haven Port Authority (formerly Conservancy Board), 1982–94; *b* 20 Oct. 1922; *s* of Charles and Ethel Cory; *m* 1st, 1946, Vivienne Mary Roberts (*d* 1988), Kelowna, BC, Canada; three *d*; 2nd, 1989, Betty, *widow* of Lt-Col Roy Horley. *Educ:* Harrow; Christ Church, Oxford. Served RNVR, Ord. Seaman to Lieut, 1942–46; Russian and N Atlantic convoys and Normandy landings (C-in-C's Commendation June 1944). Vice-Chm., A. B. Electronics Products Group PLC, 1979–92. Dir and Mem. Executive, Baltic and Internat. Maritime Conf., Copenhagen, 1957–67; Mem., Lloyd's Register of Shipping, 1963–67. Chairman: Barry Pilotage Authority, 1963–74 (Mem. 1953); Port Talbot Pilotage Authority, 1970–74; SE Wales Pilotage Authority, 1974–80; Welsh Council Mission to Seamen, 1984–95; Vice-Chm., BTDB, 1969–79 (Mem., 1966–79; Chm., S Wales Local Bd, 1966); Pres., Cardiff Chamber of Commerce, 1959–60. Chm., S Glamorgan HA, 1974–84. Church in Wales: Member: Governing Body, 1957–60; Rep. Body, 1960– (Dep. Chm., 1985–95; Treasurer, 1988–); Finance Cttee, 1960–88 (Vice-Chm. 1971, Chm. 1975–88); Dep. Chm., Finance and Resources Cttee, 1988–95. RNLI: Chm. Cardiff Br., 1950–73; Mem. Cttee of Management, 1954–; Vice-Pres. 1969–; Dep. Chm., 1985–93; Mem., Exec. Cttee, 1970–93. Chm., Council, Univ. of Wales Coll. of Medicine, 1988– (Mem., 1984–). *Publication:* A Century of Family Shipowning, 1954. *Recreations:* skiing, sailing, gardening. *Address:* The Coach House, Llanblethian, Cowbridge, South Glamorgan CF7 7JF. *T:* Cowbridge (01446) 772251. *Club:* Cardiff and County.

CORY, Sir (Clinton Charles) Donald, 5th Bt *cr* 1919, of Coryton, Whitchurch, Glamorgan; *b* 13 Sept. 1937; *s* of Sir Clinton James Donald Cory, 4th Bt and of Mary, *o d* of Dr Arthur Douglas Hunt; *S* father, 1991. *Educ:* Brighton Coll.; abroad. *Recreations:* collecting Greek and Roman antiquities, student of classical studies. *Heir: uncle* Philip Cecil Donald Cory, *b* 20 Feb. 1913. *Address:* 18 Cloisters Road, Letchworth, Herts SG6 3JS. *T:* Letchworth (01462) 677206.

CORY, John; Vice Lord-Lieutenant of South Glamorgan, since 1990; Director, John Cory & Sons Ltd, 1949–91; *b* 30 June 1928; *s* of John and Cecil Cory; *m* 1965, Sarah Christine, *d* of John Meade, JP, DL; two *d*. *Educ:* Eton; Trinity College, Cambridge. Chm., Cardiff RDC, 1971–72. Member, Governing Body, 1957–74, Representative Body, 1960–, Church in Wales. Pres., Nat. Light Horse Breeding Soc., 1977–78. Joint Master, Glamorgan Hounds, 1962–67. High Sheriff, 1959, JP 1961, DL 1968, Glamorgan. KStJ. *Address:* The Grange, St Brides-super-Ely, Cardiff CF5 6XA. *T:* Peterston-super-Ely (01446) 760211. *Clubs:* MCC; Cardiff and County (Cardiff).

CORY, Raymond; *see* Cory, C. R.

CORY-WRIGHT, Sir Richard (Michael), 4th Bt *cr* 1903; *b* 17 Jan. 1944; *s* of Capt. A. J. J. Cory-Wright (killed in action, 1944), and Susan Esterel (*d* 1993; she *m* 2nd, 1949, Lt-Col J. E. Gurney, DSO, MC), *d* of Robert Elwes; *S* grandfather, 1969; *m* 1976, Veronica (marr. diss. 1994), *o d* of James Bolton; three *s*. *Educ:* Eton; Birmingham Univ. *Heir: s* Roland Anthony Cory-Wright, *b* 11 March 1979. *Address:* 21 Trenchard Close, Wallingford, Oxon OX10 9BB.

COSGRAVE, Liam, SC; *b* April 1920; *s* of late William T. Cosgrave; *m* 1952, Vera Osborne; two *s* one *d*. *Educ:* Synge Street Christian Brothers; Castlenock College, Dublin; King's Inns. Served in Army during Emergency. Barrister-at-Law, 1943; Senior Counsel, 1958. Member, Dail Eireann, 1943–81; Chairman Public Accounts Committee, 1945; Parliamentary Secretary to Taoiseach and Minister for Industry and Commerce, 1948–51; Minister for External Affairs, 1954–57; Leader, Fine Gael Party, 1965–77; Taoiseach (Head of Govt of Ireland), 1973–77; Minister for Defence, 1976. Leader first delegation from Ireland to the UN Assembly, 1956. Hon. LLD: Duquesne Univ., Pittsburg, Pa, and St John's Univ., Brooklyn, 1956; de Paul Univ., Chicago, 1958; NUI, 1974; Dublin Univ., 1974. Knight Grand Cross of Pius IX, 1956. *Address:* Beechpark, Templeogue, Co. Dublin.

COSGRAVE, Patrick John, PhD; writer; *b* 28 Sept. 1941; *s* of Patrick John Cosgrave and Margaret FitzGerald; *m* 1st, 1965, Ruth Dudley Edwards (marr. diss.); 2nd, 1974, Norma Alicia Green (marr. diss.); one *d*; 3rd, 1981, Shirley Ward. *Educ:* St Vincent's Sch., Dublin; University Coll., NUI, Dublin (BA, MA); Univ. of Cambridge (PhD). London Editor, Radio Telefis Eireann, 1968–69; Conservative Research Dept, 1969–71; Political Editor, The Spectator, 1971–75; Features Editor, Telegraph Magazine, 1974–76. Special Adviser to Rt Hon. Mrs Margaret Thatcher, 1975–79. Managing Editor, Quartet Crime (Quartet Books), 1979–81. *Publications:* The Public Poetry of Robert Lowell, 1970; Churchill at War: Alone, 1974; Cheyney's Law (novel), 1977; Margaret Thatcher: a Tory and her party, 1978, 2nd edn as Margaret Thatcher: Prime Minister, 1979; The Three Colonels (novel), 1979; R. A. Butler: an English Life, 1981; Adventure of State (novel), 1984; Thatcher: the First Term, 1985; Carrington: a life and a policy, 1985; The Lives of Enoch Powell, 1989; The Strange Death of Socialist Britain, 1992; contribs to Proc. of Royal Irish Academy, Irish Historical Studies, Encounter, Policy Rev., New Law Jl, The Times, Daily Telegraph, Sunday Telegraph, The Independent, Sunday Tribune. *Recreations:* thriller fiction, cooking, roses, cricket. *T:* 0171–627 0306.

COSGROVE, Hazel Josephine, (Mrs J. A. Cosgrove); *see* Aronson, H. J.

COSSERAT, Kay, RDI 1986; Director, Cosserat Design Ltd, since 1976; Part-time Lecturer, Royal College of Art, since 1990, and Chelsea School of Art, since 1985; *b* 24 Oct. 1947; *d* of Robert and Elizabeth Macklam; *m* 1972, Christopher Graham Peloquin Cosserat; two *s*. *Educ:* Cleveland Sch., Eaglescliffe; Goldsmiths' Sch. of Art (Dip AD 1st cl. Hons); Royal Coll. of Art (MA Textiles 1972); Sanderson Travel Scholarship, 1972. Formed Cosserat Design Partnership, 1974; Founder Mem., London Designer Collections, 1974; currently producing textile and garment designs on a consultancy basis. Mem., Fashion and Textile Bd, CNAA, 1978. Vis. Prof., London Inst., 1992–; Part-time Lecturer: St Martins Sch. of Art, 1972–80; RCA, 1976–79; External Assessor: Central Sch. of Art, 1982–85; Trent Poly., 1983–85; Liverpool Poly., 1985–87; Huddersfield Poly., 1985–88; QUB, 1990–92; Univ. of Ulster, 1990–93; Winchester Sch. of Art, 1991–93. *Recreations:* gardening, ski-ing, collecting '30s pottery. *Address:* The Manor, Sherington, Bucks MK16 9NB.

COSSHAM, Christopher Hugh, CB 1989; Senior Assistant Director of Public Prosecutions (Northern Ireland), 1973–89; *b* 12 April 1929; *s* of Lorimer and Gwendolin Cossham; *m* 1958, Joanna Howard Smith; one *s* one *d*. *Educ:* Monkton Combe Sch.; Bristol Univ. Called to Bar, Gray's Inn, 1958. Board of Trade, 1958–62; Director of Public Prosecutions Dept, 1962–73. Dep. Metropolitan Stipendiary Magistrate, 1978–86. Mem., Wkg Party on handling of complaints against police, 1974. *Recreations:* cycling, listening to music, writing humorous verse. *Address:* Valhalla, 1 The Grange, High Street, Portishead, Avon BS20 9QL. *T:* Portishead (0117) 984 5237. *Clubs:* Civil Service, Northern Law.

COSSONS, Sir Neil, Kt 1994; OBE 1982; Director, Science Museum, since 1986; *b* 15 Jan. 1939; *s* of Arthur Cossons and Evelyn (*née* Bettle); *m* 1965, Veronica Edwards; two *s* one *d*. *Educ:* Henry Mellish Sch., Nottingham; Univ. of Liverpool (MA). FSA 1968; FMA 1970; FRSA 1988. Curator of Technology, Bristol City Museum, 1964; Dep. Dir, City of Liverpool Museums, 1969; Dir, Ironbridge Gorge Museum Trust, 1971; Dir, Nat. Maritime Museum, 1983–86. Comr, Historic Buildings and Monuments Commn for England (English Heritage), 1989– (Mem., Ancient Monuments Adv. Cttee, 1984–); Member: Curatorium Internat. Committee for the Conservation of the Industrial Heritage, 1973–78; BBC General Adv. Council, 1987–90; NEDO Tourism and Leisure Industries Sector Gp (formerly Leisure Industries EDC), 1987–90; Council, RCA, 1989–; Design Council, 1990–94; Comité Scientifique, Conservatoire Nat. des Arts et Métiers, 1991–. President: Assoc. for Industrial Archaeology, 1977–80; Assoc. of Independent Museums, 1983– (Chm., 1978–83); Museums Assoc., 1981–82; Mem. Council: Newcomen Soc. for Study of Hist. of Engrg and Technol., 1992– (Mem., 1963–); Council, FMI, 1993–. Trustee, Civic Trust, 1987–93. Gov., Imperial Coll. of Sci., Technology and Medicine, 1989–93. Hon. Prof., Univ. of Birmingham, 1994–. Hon. Fellow, RCA, 1987; Comp IEE, 1991. Hon. DSocSc Birmingham, 1979; DUniv Open, 1984; Hon. LittD Liverpool, 1989; Hon. DLitt: Bradford, 1991; Nottingham Trent, 1994; Hon. DSc Leicester, 1995. Norton Medlicott Medal, Historical Assoc., 1991; President's Medal, Royal Acad. of Engrg, 1993. *Publications:* (with R. A. Buchanan) Industrial Archaeology of the Bristol Region, 1968; (with K. Hudson) Industrial Archaeologists' Guide, 1969, 2nd edn 1971; Industrial Archaeology, 1975, 3rd edn 1993; (ed) Transactions of the First International Congress on the Conservation of Industrial Monuments, 1975; (ed) Rees's Manufacturing Industry, 1975; (with H. Sowden) Ironbridge—Landscape of Industry, 1977; (with B. S. Trinder) The Iron Bridge—Symbol of the Industrial Revolution, 1979, 2nd edn (Japanese) 1989; (ed) Management of Change in Museums, 1985; (ed) Making of the Modern World, 1992; numerous papers, articles and reviews. *Recreations:* travel, industrial archaeology. *Address:* Science Museum, SW7 2DD; The Old Rectory, Rushbury, Shropshire SY6 7EB. *T:* Longville (01694) 771603. *Club:* Athenæum.

COSTA-LOBO, António; Ambassador of Portugal to the Court of St James's, since 1995; *b* 22 May 1932; *s* of Gumersindo da Costa Lobo and Maria Magdalena Teixeira Leal da Costa Lobo; *m* 1980, Maria Catarina de Locher Machado. *Educ:* Univ. of Coimbra, Portugal (Law degree). Joined Ministry of Foreign Affairs, Portugal, 1956: served Havana, 1961–63; The Hague, 1964–66; Consul-Gen., San Francisco, 1966–70; Perm. Mission to UN, NY, 1973–77; Council of Europe, 1980–82; Ambassador to China, 1982–85; Perm. Mission, Geneva, 1985–90; Ambassador to Russia, 1990–93. Grã-Cruz da Ordem do Infante Dom Henrique (Portugal), 1985. *Publication:* As Operações de Paz das Nações Unidas, 1969. *Recreations:* reading, riding, ski-ing. *Address:* 12 Belgrave Square, SW1X 8PP. *T:* 0171–235 5331. *Clubs:* Travellers', Queen's; Grémio Literário (Lisbon).

COSTAIN, Noel Leslie, OBE 1964; Director of Works, University of Sheffield, 1964–78; *b* 11 Jan. 1914; *s* of George Wesley Costain and Minnie Grace Pinson; *m* 1945, Marie José Elizabeth (*née* Bishton); two *d*. *Educ:* King Edward's Sch., Five Ways, Birmingham; Univ. of Birmingham (BSc). CEng, MICE, FINucE. Engineer with Sir R. MacAlpine & Sons, 1937–38; Epsom and Ewell BC, 1939; Air Min., Directorate-Gen. of Works; Section Officer, Orkneys and Shetlands, 1940–43; Prin. Works Officer, Sierra Leone, 1944–46; Superintending Engr, Air Ministry, 1946–51; RAF Airfield Construction Br.: Cmdg 5352 Wing, Germany, and OC, RAF Church Lawford, 1951–54; Superintending Engr, Works Area, Bristol, 1954–58; Chief Engr, MEAF, 1958–60; Chief Resident Engr, BMEWS, Fylingdales, 1960–63. Vice-Chm., Yorkshire Univs Air Squadron Cttee. Mem. Council, Instn of Nuclear Engineers, 1965; Vice-Pres., 1969; President, 1972–76. *Recreations:* travel, gardening. *Address:* Villa Marie José, Avenida 3 no 59, Urbanisation Hacienda Las Chapas, Marbella, Málaga, Spain.

See also R. M. Bateman.

COSTAIN, Peter John, FCA; Group Chief Executive, Costain Group Plc, since 1980; Director: Pearl Group, since 1989; London Life Ltd, since 1994; AMP UK plc, since 1994; *b* 2 April 1938; *s* of Sir Albert Costain; *m* 1963, Victoria M. Pope; three *s*. *Educ:* Charterhouse. Peat Marwick Mitchell & Co., 1956–63; Richard Costain Ltd, 1963–65; Costain Australia Ltd, 1965–: Board Member, 1967; Managing Director, 1971; Chief Executive, 1973. Mem., London Adv. Bd, Westpac Banking Corp., 1981–86. Mem. Bd, CITB, 1989–93. FAIB. *Recreations:* sailing, skiing, golf. *Address:* 111 Westminster Bridge Road, SE1 7UE. *Clubs:* Royal Thames Yacht; Athenæum (Melbourne); Rye Golf, Royal St George's Golf.

COSTANZI, Edwin J. B.; *see* Borg-Costanzi.

COSTELLO, Declan; Hon. Mr Justice Costello; President, High Court of the Republic of Ireland, since 1995; *b* 1 Aug. 1926; *s* of John A. Costello and Ida (*née* O'Malley); *m* 1953, Joan Fitzsimms; three *s* two *d*. *Educ:* Xavier Sch., Dublin; University Coll., Dublin. King's Inns, Dublin; Called to the Bar, 1948; Inner Bar, 1965. TD (FG): Dublin NW, 1951–69; Dublin SW, 1973–77; Attorney-Gen., 1973–77; Judge of the High Court, 1977–95. Mem., Consultative Assembly, Council of Europe, 1957–63. Chairman: Nat. Youth Policy Cttee, Ireland, 1983; Cttee on Fund-raising for Charitable Purposes, Ireland, 1989. *Recreations:* tennis, reading, film-going. *Address:* 8 Clonskeagh Road, Dublin 6, Republic of Ireland. *T:* Dublin (1) 2697963. *Clubs:* St Stephen's Green (Dublin); Fitzwilliam Lawn Tennis (Dublin).

COSTELLO, Gordon John; Chief Accountant of the Bank of England, 1975–78; *b* 29 March 1921; *s* of late Ernest James Costello and Hilda May Costello; *m* 1946, Joan Lilian Moore; two *s* one *d.* *Educ:* Varndean Sch. Served War, 1939–45 (RA). Bank of England, 1946; worked in various Departments; Asst Chief Accountant, 1964; Asst Sec., 1965; Dep. Sec., 1968; Dep. Chief Cashier, 1970. *Recreations:* music, travel, walking, tennis. *Address:* 26 Peacock Lane, Brighton, Sussex BN1 6WA. *T:* Brighton (01273) 552344.

COSTELOE, Prof. Michael Peter, PhD; Professor of Hispanic and Latin American Studies, since 1981, and Dean of Arts, since 1993, University of Bristol; *b* 12 March 1939; *s* of late John Myles Costeloe and of Etheleen Winifred Costeloe, Bishop Auckland; *m* 1962, Eleanor, *d*, of late William and Margaret Bonney; one *d.* *Educ:* King James I Grammar Sch., Bishop Auckland; Univ. of Durham (BA 1961); Univ. of Newcastle (DipEd 1962; PhD 1965). University of Bristol: Asst Lectr and Lectr in Latin American Studies, 1965–76; Reader, 1976–81. Vis. Prof., Univ. of Texas, 1967. *Publications:* Church Wealth in Mexico, 1967; (ed and trans.) Alienation of Church Wealth in Mexico, by J. Bazant, 1971; (with C. Steele) Independent Mexico, 1973; La primera república federal de Mexico, 1975; Mexico State Papers, 1976; Response to Revolution: Imperial Spain and the Spanish American Revolutions, 1986; The Central Republic in Mexico 1835–1846, 1993. *Recreations:* Anthony Trollope, golf. *Address:* Department of Hispanic Studies, University of Bristol, 15 Woodland Road, Bristol BS8 1TE. *T:* Bristol (0117) 930 3403. *Club:* Henbury Golf.

COTES, Peter, (Sydney Arthur Boulting); author, lecturer, play producer, stage, film and television director; *e s* of Arthur Boulting and Rose Bennett; *m* 1st, 1938, Myfanwy Jones (marr. diss.); 2nd, 1948, Joan Miller (*d* 1988). *Educ:* Taplow; Italia Conti and privately. Was for some years an actor; made theatrical debut, Portsmouth Hippodrome, in the arms of Vesta Tilley. Formed own independent play-producing co. with Hon. James Smith, 1949, presented Rocket to the Moon, St Martin's Theatre, and subsequently produced, in association with Arts Council of Great Britain, notable seasons in Manchester and at Embassy, Swiss Cottage and Lyric Theatres, Hammersmith. Founded: New Lindsey, 1946; New Boltons, 1951. West-End Productions include: Pick Up Girl, 1946; The Animal Kingdom, 1947; The Master Builder, 1948; Miss Julie, 1949; Come Back, Little Sheba, 1951; The Father, 1951; The Biggest Thief in Town, 1951; The Mousetrap, 1952; The Man, 1952; A Pin to see the Peepshow, Broadway, 1953; Happy Holiday, 1954; Book of the Month, 1955; Hot Summer Night, 1958; Epitaph for George Dillon (Holland), 1959; The Rope Dancers, 1959; Girl on the Highway, 1960; A Loss of Roses, 1962; The Odd Ones, 1963; Hidden Stranger, Broadway, 1963; What Goes Up. . .!, 1963; So Wise, So Young, 1964; Paint Myself Black, 1965; The Impossible Years, 1966; Staring at the Sun, 1968; Janie Jackson, 1968; The Old Ladies, 1969; Look, No Hands!, 1971. Films: The Right Person; Two Letters; Jane Clegg; Waterfront; The Young and the Guilty; has prod. and adapted numerous plays for BBC Television and ITV; was Sen. Drama Dir, AR-TV, 1955–58; producing stage plays and films, 1959–60; Supervising Producer of Drama Channel 7, Melbourne, 1961; produced and adapted plays for Anglia TV, 1964; produced first TV series of P. G. Wodehouse short stories, on BBC; wrote George Robey centenary TV Tribute, BBC Omnibus series, 1969; wrote and dir. in One Pair of Eyes series, BBC TV, 1970; has written, adapted and narrated many productions for radio incl. Back into the Light, The Prime Minister of Mirth, Mervyn Peake, Portrait of an Actor; collaborated 1980–81 on: The Song is Ended, Who Were You With Last Night, Who's Your Lady Friend, The Black Sheep of the Family (BBC); scripted and presented: Old Stagers, 1979–87; This Fabulous Genius (BBC), 1980; Wee Georgie Wood (BBC), 1980. FRSA; Member: Theatrical Managers' Assoc.; Medico-Legal Soc.; Our Society; Guild of Drama Adjudicators. Kt of Mark Twain, 1980. *Publications:* No Star Nonsense, 1949; The Little Fellow, 1951; A Handbook of Amateur Theatre, 1957; George Robey, 1972; The Trial of Elvira Barney, 1976; Circus, 1976; Origin of a Thriller, 1977; JP (The Man Called Mitch), 1978; Misfit Midget, 1979; Portrait of an Actor, 1980; (jtly) The Barbirollis: a musical marriage, 1983; Dickie: the story of Dickie Henderson, 1988; Thinking Aloud (autobiog.), 1993; contrib. to The Field, Spectator, Queen, Guardian, etc. *Address:* 7 Hill Lawn Court, Chipping Norton, Oxon OX7 5NF. *Recreations:* book collecting, writing letters, criminology. *Clubs:* Savage, Our Society.

COTILL, John Atrill T.; *see* Templeton-Cotill.

COTRAN, Eugene, LLD; **His Honour Judge Cotran;** a Circuit Judge, since 1992; *b* Jerusalem, Palestine, 6 Aug. 1938; *s* of Michael Cotran and Hassiba (*née* Khoury); *m* 1963, Christiane Avierino; three *s* one *d.* *Educ:* Victoria Coll., Alexandria, Egypt; Univ. of Leeds (LLB, LLM 1958); Trinity Hall, Univ. of Cambridge (Dip. Internat. Law 1959); LLD London, 1971. FCIArb. Called to the Bar, Lincoln's Inn, 1959. Res. Officer in African Law, SOAS, Univ. of London, 1960–63, Lectr, 1963–77; practised at the Bar, 1963–92; Law Comr, Kenya, 1967–68; High Court Judge, Kenya, 1977–82; a Recorder, 1989–92. Vis. Prof. of Law and Chm., Centre for Islamic and ME Law, SOAS, 1987–. Internat. Arbitrator, Internat. Court of Arbitration, Paris and London, 1985–92. *Publications:* Restatement of African Law, Kenya: Vol. I, Marriage and Divorce, Vol. II, Succession, 1968; Casebook on Kenya Customary Law, 1987; Butterworth's Immigration Law Service, 1991; articles in internat. law jls and African law jls. *Recreations:* horse-racing, swimming, bridge. *Address:* 16 Hart Grove, Ealing, W5 3NB. *T:* 0181–992 0432.

COTRUBAS, Ileana, (Mme Manfred Ramin); opera singer, retired 1990; *b* Rumania; *d* of Vasile and Maria Cotrubas; *m* 1972, Manfred Ramin. *Educ:* Conservatorul Ciprian Porumbescu, Bucharest. Opera and concert engagements all over Europe, N America and Japan. Formerly permanent guest at Royal Opera House, Covent Garden; Member, Vienna State Opera (Hon. Mem., 1991); also frequently sang in Scala, Milan, Munich, Berlin, Paris, Chicago, NY Metropolitan Opera. Main operatic roles: Susanna, Pamina, Gilda, Traviata, Manon, Tatyana, Mimi, Melisande, Amina, Elisabetta, Nedda, Marguerite. Has made numerous recordings. Kammersängerin, Austria, 1981; Grand Officer, Sant Iago da Espada (Portugal), 1990.

COTTAM, Harold; Chairman: Haden MacLellan Holdings, since 1992; Anglo United, since 1993; *b* 12 Oct. 1938; *s* of Frank and Elizabeth Cottam; *m* 1962, Lyn Minton; two *d.* *Educ:* Bedford School. FCA. Smith Kline UK, 1964–66; Simon Engineering Group, 1966–68; Ernst & Whinney, subseq. Ernst & Young, 1968–92; UK Man. Partner, 1987–92; Chairman: Ernst & Young Case Services (Internat.), 1992–93; Ernst & Young Pan-European Consulting Gp, 1992–93. Dir, Allied Colloids Gp, 1992–. *Recreations:* piano, opera, tennis. *Address:* (office) Haleworth House, Tite Hill, Egham, Surrey TW20 0LT.

COTTELL, Michael Norman Tizard, OBE 1988; FEng 1990; FICE, FIHT; Executive Consultant, Travers Morgan, since 1991; President, Institution of Civil Engineers, 1992–93; *b* 25 July 1931; *s* of Norman James Cottell and Eileen Clare Cottell (*née* Tizard); *m* 1957, Joan Florence Dolton; two *s.* *Educ:* Peter Symonds Sch., Winchester; University Coll., Southampton. CEng; FIHT 1954; MICE 1958, FICE 1976; MIM 1972; MASCE 1990. Trainee Civil Engr, Hants CC, 1949–51; Nat. Service, RE, Malaya and Suez, 1951–53, 1956; Engineering Assistant: Glos CC, 1954–57; Northants CC, 1957–58; Resident Engr, Oxford Western Bypass, 1958–61; Project Engr, M4 Motorway, Glos, 1961–67; Asst County Surveyor, Suffolk CC, 1967–73; Dep. County Surveyor, E Sussex CC, 1973–76; County Surveyor: Northants CC, 1976–84; Kent CC, 1984–91. Lt-Col, RE & Transport Staff Corps (TA), 1992–. *Recreations:* sailing, swimming, walking, theatre, jazz, travel, viewing historic buildings, as a spectator keen on most sports. *Address:* Salcey Lawn, Harrow Court, Stockbury, Kent ME9 7UQ. *Clubs:* Athenæum, Royal Automobile.

COTTENHAM, 8th Earl of, *cr* 1850; **Kenelm Charles Everard Digby Pepys;** Bt 1784 and 1801; Baron Cottenham, 1836; Viscount Crowhurst, 1850; *b* 27 Nov. 1948; *s* of 7th Earl of Cottenham and Lady Angela Isabel Nellie Nevill, *d* of 4th Marquess of Abergavenny; *S* father, 1968; *m* 1975, Sarah, *d* of Captain S. Lombard-Hobson, CVO, OBE, RN; two *s* one *d.* *Educ:* Eton. *Heir:* *s* Viscount Crowhurst, *qv.*

See also Baron McGowan.

COTTER, Lt-Col Sir Delaval James Alfred, 6th Bt, *cr* 1763; DSO 1944; late 13th/18th Royal Hussars; *b* 29 April 1911; *s* of 5th Bt and Ethel Lucy (*d* 1956), *d* of Alfred Wheeler; *S* father, 1924; *m* 1st, 1943, Roma (marr. diss., 1949), *widow* of Sqdn Ldr K. A. K. MacEwen and *o d* of late Adrian Rome, Dalswinton Lodge, Salisbury, SR; two *d*; 2nd, 1952, Mrs Eveline Mary Paterson (*d* 1991), *widow* of Lieut-Col J. F. Paterson, OBE, and *d* of late E. J. Mardon, ICS (retired). *Educ:* Malvern Coll; RMC, Sandhurst. Served War of 1939–45 (DSO); retired, 1959. JP Wilts, 1962–63. *Heir:* *n* Patrick Laurence Delaval Cotter [*b* 21 Nov. 1941; *m* 1967, Janet, *d* of George Potter, Barnstaple; one *s* two *d*]. *Address:* Green Lines, Iwerne Courtney, Blandford Forum, Dorset DT11 8QR.

COTTERELL, Geoffrey; author; *b* 24 Nov. 1919; *yr s* of late Graham Cotterell and Millicent (*née* Crews). *Educ:* Bishops Stortford College. Served War of 1939–45, Royal Artillery, 1940–46. *Publications:* Then a Soldier, 1944; This is the Way, 1947; Randle in Springtime, 1949; Strait and Narrow, 1950; Westward the Sun, 1952 (repr. 1973); The Strange Enchantment, 1956 (repr. 1973); Tea at Shadow Creek, 1958; Tiara Tahiti, 1960 (filmed 1962, screenplay with Ivan Foxwell); Go, said the bird, 1966; Bowers of Innocence, 1970; Amsterdam, the life of a city, 1972. *Recreation:* golf. *Address:* 2 Fulbourne House, Blackwater Road, Eastbourne, Sussex BN20 7DN. *Clubs:* Royal Automobile; Cooden Beach Golf.

COTTERELL, Sir John (Henry Geers), 6th Bt *cr* 1805; Chairman: Radio Wyvern, since 1981; Herefordshire Community Health NHS Trust, since 1991; *b* 8 May 1935; *s* of Sir Richard Charles Geers Cotterell, 5th Bt, CBE, and Lady Lettice Cotterell (*d* 1973), *d* of 7th Earl Beauchamp; *S* father, 1978; *m* 1959, Vanda Alexandra Clare, *d* of Major Philip Alexander Clement Bridgewater; three *s* one *d.* *Educ:* Eton; RMA Sandhurst. Officer, Royal Horse Guards, 1955–61. Vice-Chm. Hereford and Worcs CC, 1973–77, Chm., 1977–81. Pres., Nat. Fedn of Young Farmers Clubs, 1986–91 (Dep. Pres., 1979–86); Mem., Jockey Club, 1990–. Chairman: Hereford Mappa Mundi Trust, 1990–; Rural Voice, 1991–92. *Recreations:* cricket, shooting. *Heir:* *s* Henry Richard Geers Cotterell [*b* 22 Aug. 1961; *m* 1986, Carolyn, *er d* of John Beckwith-Smith, Maybanks Manor, Rudgwick, Sussex; one *d*]. *Address:* Garnons, near Hereford HR4 7JU. *T:* Bridge Sollars (0198122) 232. *Club:* White's.

COTTERILL, Kenneth William, CMG 1976; Chairman, Commercial and Political Risk Consultants Ltd, since 1986 (Deputy Chairman, 1981–86); *b* 5 June 1921; *s* of William and Ada May Cotterill; *m* 1948, Janet Hilda Cox; one *d.* *Educ:* Sutton County Sch.; London School of Economics, BSc (Econ). Served War in Royal Navy, 1941–46. After the war, joined ECGD; Principal, 1956; Asst Sec., 1966; Under Sec., 1970; Dep. Head of Dept, 1976–81. Dir, Tarmac Internat., 1981–86; Consultant: NEI International, 1981–87; Barclays Bank, 1981–87. *Recreations:* reading, walking, gardening. *Address:* 15 Minster Drive, Croydon CR0 5UP. *T:* 0181–681 6700.

COTTESLOE, 5th Baron (UK) *cr* 1874; **Comdr John Tapling Fremantle;** Bt 1821; Baron of Austrian Empire 1816; RN (retired); JP; Lord-Lieutenant of Buckinghamshire, since 1984; *b* 22 Jan. 1927; *s* of 4th Baron Cottesloe, GBE and his 1st wife, Lady Elizabeth Harris (*d* 1983), *o d* of 5th Earl of Malmesbury; *S* father, 1994; *m* 1958, Elizabeth Ann, *e d* of late Lt-Col H. S. Barker, DSO; one *s* two *d.* *Educ:* Summer Fields, Hastings; Eton College. Joined RN, 1945; CO HMS Palliser, 1959–61; retired at own request, 1966. Governor, Stowe School, 1983–89. Radcliffe Trustee, 1983–. Vice President: RASE, 1991–; British Assoc. for Shooting and Conservation, 1975–; Hospital Saving Assoc., 1979–; Bucks County Agricl Assoc., 1988–; Pres. Bucks Br., CLA, 1983–. High Sheriff, 1969–70, JP, 1984, Bucks. KStJ 1984. DUniv Buckingham, 1993. *Recreations:* shooting, stalking, crosswords. *Heir:* *s* Hon. Thomas Francis Henry Fremantle, *b* 17 March 1966. *Address:* The Old House, Swanbourne, Milton Keynes, Bucks MK17 0SH. *T:* (home) Mursley (0129672) 0263; (office) Mursley (0129672) 0256. *Clubs:* Travellers'; Royal Naval and Royal Albert Yacht (Portsmouth).

COTTHAM, George William; Chairman and Managing Director: Yorkshire Rider Ltd, since 1986; Rider Holdings Ltd, since 1988; Rider York Ltd, since 1990; *b* 11 July 1944; *s* of George William and Elizabeth Cottham; *m* 1967, Joan Thomas; two *d.* *Educ:* Univ. of London; Polytechnic of Liverpool; Liverpool Coll. of Commerce. BSc 1st Cl. Hons, LLB 2nd Cl. Hons. FCIT. Various posts, Liverpool City Transport, 1960–74; District Transport Manager, St Helens, 1974–77; Transport General Manager, Newport, 1977–80; Gen. Manager, Cleveland Transit, 1980–83; Dir Gen., W Yorks PTE, 1983–86. *Recreations:* family, home, garden, music, photography. *Address:* Brow Lee, 118 Huddersfield Road, Brighouse, West Yorkshire HD6 3RH. *T:* Brighouse (01484) 713019.

COTTON; *see* Stapleton-Cotton, family name of Viscount Combermere.

COTTON, Bernard Edward, CBE 1976; Chairman, South Yorkshire Residuary Body, 1985–89; *b* 8 Oct. 1920; *s* of Hugh Harry Cotton and Alice Cotton; *m* 1944, Stephanie Anne, *d* of Rev. A. E. and Mrs Furnival; three *s.* *Educ:* Sheffield City Grammar Sch.; Sheffield Univ. Served Army, 1939–45, latterly as Lieut, Worcs Yeomanry (53rd Airlanding Light Regt RA). Joined Round Oak Steelworks, Brierley Hill, 1949, Sales Man., 1954–57; Gen. Man., Samuel Osborn (Canada) Ltd, Montreal, 1957–63; Samuel Osborn & Co. Ltd: Sales Dir, 1963–69; Man. Dir, 1969; Chm. and Chief Exec., 1969–78; Pres., 1978–80. Dir, Renold Ltd, 1979–84; Dep. Chm., Baker Perkins plc, 1983–86. Chairman: Yorks and Humberside Reg. Econ. Planning Council, 1970–79; Health Service Supply Council, 1980–85; Mem., BR Eastern Bd, 1977–85; Pres., Yorks and Humberside Devclt Assoc., 1973–84. Chm., BIM Working Party on Employee Participation, 1975. Pro Chancellor, Sheffield Univ., 1982–87. Master, Cutlers' Co. in Hallamshire, 1979–80. Hon. Fellow, Sheffield City Poly., 1980. CIMgt. Hon. LLD Sheffield, 1988. *Recreations:* gardening and other quiet pursuits. *Address:* Stubbin House, Carsick Hill Road, Sheffield S10 3LU. *T:* Sheffield (0114) 230 3082. *Club:* Sheffield (Sheffield).

COTTON, Christopher P.; *see* Powell-Cotton.

COTTON, Diana Rosemary, (Mrs R. B. Allan); QC 1983; *b* 30 Nov. 1941; *d* of Arthur Frank Edward and Muriel Cotton; *m* 1966, Richard Bellerby Allan; two *s* one *d.* *Educ:* Berkhamsted School for Girls; Lady Margaret Hall, Oxford (MA). Joined Middle Temple, 1961; called to Bar, 1964; Bencher, 1990; Member, Midland and Oxford Circuit; a

Recorder of the Crown Court, 1982. Mem., Criminal Injuries Compensation Bd, 1989–. *Recreation:* her family and other animals. *Address:* Devereux Chambers, Devereux Court, Temple, WC2R 3JJ. *T:* 0171–353 7534. *Club:* Western (Glasgow).

COTTON, His Honour John Anthony; a Circuit Judge, 1973–93; *b* 6 March 1926; *s* of Frederick Thomas Hooley Cotton and Catherine Mary Cotton; *m* 1960, Johanna Aritia van Lookeren Campagne; three *s* two *d. Educ:* Stonyhurst Coll.; Lincoln Coll., Oxford. Called to the Bar, Middle Temple, 1949; Dep. Chm., W Riding of Yorks QS, 1967–71; Recorder of Halifax, 1971; a Recorder and Hon. Recorder of Halifax, 1972–73. *Recreation:* golf. *Address:* Myrtle Garth, Rossett Beck Close, Harrogate HG2 9NU.

COTTON, Sir John Richard, KCMG 1969 (CMG 1959); OBE 1947 (MBE 1944); retired from HM Diplomatic Service, 1969; Adjudicator, Immigration Appeals, 1970–81; *b* 22 Jan. 1909; *s* of late J. J. Cotton, ICS, and late Gigia Ricciardi Arlotta; *m* 1937, Mary Bridget Connors, Stradbally, County Waterford, Ireland; three *s. Educ:* Wellington Coll.; RMC, Sandhurst. Commissioned 1929; 8th King George's Own Light Cavalry (IA), 1930–34; transferred to Indian Political Service, 1934; served in: Aden, Abyssinia (Attaché HM Legation, 1935), Persian Gulf, Rajputana, Hyderabad, Kathiawar, Baroda, New Delhi (Dep. Sec. Political Dept). Transferred to HM Foreign Service, 1947; served in Karachi (First Sec.), 1947–48, Foreign Office, 1949–51, Madrid (Commercial Counsellor, HM Embassy), 1951–54; Consul-Gen., Brazzaville, 1954–55, Leopoldville, 1955–57; Counsellor (Commercial), HM Embassy, Brussels, 1957–62. Consul-Gen., São Paulo, Brazil, 1962–65; Ambassador to Kinshasa, Congo Republic (now Zaire), and to Burundi, 1965–69. *Recreation:* golf. *Address:* Lansing House, Hartley Wintney, Hants RG27 8RY. *T:* Hartley Wintney (01252) 842681.

COTTON, Hon. Sir Robert (Carrington), KCMG 1978; AO 1993; Chairman of Directors, Kleinwort Benson Australian Income Fund Inc., since 1986; *b* 29 Nov. 1915; *s* of H. L. Carrington Cotton; *m* 1937, Eve Elizabeth Macdougall; one *s* two *d. Educ:* St Peter's Coll., Adelaide, SA. FCPA 1977. State President of Liberal Party (NSW), 1956–59; Federal Vice-Pres., 1960–61; elected to Senate, 1965; Minister for Civil Aviation, 1969–72; Shadow Minister for Manufacturing Industry (in Opposition), 1972–75; Minister for Industry and Commerce, 1975–77; Australian Consul-Gen. in NY, 1978–81; Ambassador to USA, 1982–85. Chm. (acting), Allders International Pty Ltd, Australia. Sen. Advr, Hill & Knowlton Inc., 1988–93. Mem. Bd, Reserve Bank of Australia, 1982–83. Chairman: Australian Nat. Gall. Foundn, 1991–94; Australian Photonics Co-operative Res. Centre, 1992–. *Recreations:* swimming, writing, photography. *Address:* 47/2 Spruson Street, Neutral Bay, NSW 2089, Australia. *T:* (2) 9545066. *Clubs:* The Brook (NY); Australian (Sydney); Commonwealth (Canberra, ACT).

COTTON, William Frederick, (Bill Cotton), CBE 1989 (OBE 1976); Chairman, Noel Gay Television, since 1988; Director, Noel Gay Organisation, since 1988; Deputy Chairman, Meridian Broadcasting, since 1992; Director, Alba plc, since 1988; *b* 23 April 1928; *s* of late William Edward (Billy) Cotton and Mabel Hope; *m* 1st, 1950, Bernadine Maud (*née* Sinclair) (*d* 1964); three *d*; 2nd, 1965, Ann Corfield (*née* Bucknall) (marr. diss. 1989); one step *d*; 3rd, 1990, Kathryn Mary (*née* Ralphes). *Educ:* Ardingly College. Jt Man. Dir, Michael Reine Music Co., 1952–56; BBC-TV: Producer, Light Entertainment Dept, 1956–62; Asst Head of Light Entertainment, 1962–67; Head of Variety, 1967–70; Head of Light Entertainment Gp, 1970–77; Controller, BBC 1, 1977–81; Dep. Man. Dir, 1981–82; Dir of Programmes, Television, and Dir of Develt, BBC, 1982; Chm., BBC Enterprises, 1982–86 and 1987–88 (Vice Chm., 1986–87); Man. Dir, Television, BBC, 1984–88. Vice-Pres., Marie Curie Foundn, 1990–. FRTS 1983 (Vice-Pres., 1984–92; Pres., 1992–95). *Recreation:* golf. *Address:* 14 Beauchamp Road, East Molesey, Surrey KT8 0PA. *Club:* Royal & Ancient Golf (St Andrews).

COTTRELL, Sir Alan (Howard), Kt 1971; FRS 1955; FEng; Master of Jesus College, Cambridge, 1974–86 (Hon. Fellow 1986); Vice-Chancellor, University of Cambridge, 1977–79; *b* 17 July 1919; *s* of Albert and Elizabeth Cottrell; *m* 1944, Jean Elizabeth Harber; one *s. Educ:* Moseley Grammar Sch.; University of Birmingham. BSc 1939; PhD 1942; ScD(Cantab) 1976. Lectr in Metallurgy, University of Birmingham, 1943–49; Prof. of Physical Metallurgy, University of Birmingham, 1949–55; Deputy Head of Metallurgy Division, Atomic Energy Research Establishment, Harwell, Berks, 1955–58; Goldsmiths' Prof. of Metallurgy, Cambridge Univ., 1958–65; Fellow of Christ's Coll., Cambridge, 1958–70, Hon. Fellow, 1970; Dep. Chief Scientific Adviser (Studies), Min. of Defence, 1965–67, Chief Adviser, 1967; Dep. Chief Scientific Advr to HM Govt, 1968–71, Chief Scientific Advr, 1971–74. Part-time Mem., UKAEA, 1962–65, 1983–87; Member: Adv. Council on Scientific Policy, 1963–64; Central Adv. Council for Science and Technology, 1967–; Exec. Cttee, British Council, 1974–87; Adv. Council, Science Policy Foundn, 1976–; Security Commn, 1981–92. Dir, Fisons plc, 1979–90. A Vice-Pres., Royal Society, 1964, 1976, 1977. Foreign Hon. Mem., American Academy of Arts and Sciences, 1960; Foreign Associate: Nat. Acad. of Sciences, USA, 1972; Nat. Acad. of Engrg, USA, 1976; Mem., Academia Europaea, 1991–; Hon. Member: Amer. Soc. for Metals, 1972 (Fellow, 1974); Metals Soc., 1977 (Hon. FIM, 1989); Japan Inst. of Metals, 1981. FIC 1991; FEng 1979; Fellow, Royal Swedish Acad. of Scis; Hon. Fellow, Internat. Congress on Fracture, 1985–. Hon. DSc: Columbia Univ., 1965; Newcastle Univ., 1967; Liverpool Univ., 1969; Manchester, 1970; Warwick, 1971; Sussex, 1972; Bath, 1973; Strathclyde, 1975; Cranfield, 1975; Aston, 1975; Oxford, 1979; Birmingham, 1983; DUniv Essex, 1982; Hon. DEng Tech. Univ. of Nova Scotia, 1984. Rosenhain Medallist of the Inst. of Metals; Hughes Medal, 1961, Rumford Medal, 1974, Royal Society; Inst. of Metals (Platinum) Medal, 1965; Réaumur Medal, Société Française de Métallurgie, 1964; James Alfred Ewing Medal, ICE, 1967; Holweck Medal, Société Française de Physique, 1969; Albert Sauveur Achievement Award, Amer. Soc. for Metals, 1969; James Douglas Gold Medal, Amer. Inst. of Mining, Metallurgy and Petroleum Engrs, 1974; Harvey Science Prize, Technion Israel Inst., 1974; Acta Metallurgica Gold Medal, 1976; Guthrie Medal and Prize, Inst. of Physics, 1977; Gold Medal, Amer. Soc. for Metals, 1980; Brinell Medal, Royal Swedish Acad. of Engrg Sciences, 1980; Kelvin Medal, ICE, 1986; Hollomon Award, Acta Metallurgica, 1991. *Publications:* Theoretical Structural Metallurgy, 1948, 2nd edn 1955; Dislocations and Plastic Flow in Crystals, 1953; The Mechanical Properties of Matter, 1964; Theory of Crystal Dislocations, 1964; An Introduction to Metallurgy, 1967; Portrait of Nature, 1975; Environmental Economics, 1978; How Safe is Nuclear Energy?, 1981; Introduction to the Modern Theory of Metals, 1988; scientific papers to various learned journals. *Recreation:* music. *Address:* 40 Maids Causeway, Cambridge CB5 8DD. *T:* Cambridge (01223) 63806.

COTTRELL, Bryce Arthur Murray; Fellow and Funding Director, Corpus Christi College, Oxford, 1990–92; *b* 16 Sept. 1931; *s* of late Brig. A. F. B. Cottrell, DSO, OBE and Mrs M. B. Cottrell (*née* Nicoll); *m* 1955, Jeane Dolores Monk; two *s* two *d. Educ:* Charterhouse; Corpus Christi Coll., Oxford (MA). Joined Phillips & Drew, 1955; Partner, 1963; Sen. Partner, 1983; Chm., 1985–88. Dir, Long Term Capital Portfolio (Gp) Ltd, 1994–. *Recreations:* sport, railways. *Address:* Portreeves House, East Street, Tonbridge TN9 1HP. *T:* Tonbridge (01732) 773277. *Club:* City of London.

COTTRELL, Richard John; Director: Balkan Broadcasting, Bulgaria, since 1993; Boyana Developments (Bulgaria), since 1994; Chairman, RCA International, since 1991; *b* 11 July 1943; *s* of John Cottrell and Winifred (*née* Barter); *m* 1st, 1965, Dinah Louise (*née* David) (marr. diss. 1986); two *d*; 2nd, 1987, Tracy Katherine (née Wade); one *d. Educ:* Court Fields Sch., Wellington, Somerset. Journalist: Wellington Weekly News, 1958; South Devon Jl, 1960; Topic (internat. news weekly), 1962; Evening Argus, Brighton, 1963; Lincolnshire Standard, 1964; Evening Post, Bristol, 1965; TWW, subseq. HTV, 1967–79. Contested (C) Bristol, European Parly elecn, 1989. MEP (C) Bristol, 1979–89; Sec., backbench cttee, European Dem. Gp, 1979; Member: Transport Cttee, 1979–83; External Econ. Relns Cttee, 1979–82; Information Cttee, 1981–84; ACP-EEC Convention, 1981–84; Agriculture Cttee, 1982–86; Rules Cttee, 1982–89; Environment Cttee, 1983–89; Budget Cttee, 1983–86; Energy Cttee, 1986–88; deleg. to China, 1987. European Vice-Pres., Assoc. of District Councils; Vice-President: Nat. Council on Inland Transport; Railway Develt Soc. *Publications:* Energy, the Burning Question for Europe (jtly), 1981; (ed and contrib.) Transport for Europe, 1982; Blood on their Hands: the killing of Ann Chapman, 1987; The Sacred Cow, 1987; contribs to Encounter, Contemporary Review. *Recreations:* travel, reading, transport studies, appreciation of real ale. *Address:* Dean House, Bower Ashton, Bristol. *T:* Bristol (0117) 966 3404.

COTTS, Sir Richard Crichton Mitchell, 4th Bt *cr* 1921, of Coldharbour Wood, Rogate, Sussex; *b* 26 July 1946; *er s* of Sir Robert Crichton Mitchell Cotts, 3rd Bt and Barbara Mary Winifrede (*d* 1982), *o d* of Captain H. J. A. Throckmorton, RN; *S* father, 1995. *Educ:* Oratory Sch. *Heir: b* Hamish William Anthony Mitchell Cotts, *b* 15 Sept. 1951.

COUCHMAN, James Randall; MP (C) Gillingham, since 1983; *b* 11 Feb. 1942; *s* of Stanley Randall Couchman and Alison Margaret Couchman; *m* 1967, Barbara Jean (*née* Heilbrun); one *s* one *d. Educ:* Cranleigh School; King's College, Newcastle upon Tyne; Univ. of Durham. Oil industry, 1964–70; Public House Manager, family company, 1970–74; Gen. Manager, family licensed trade co., 1974–80, Director, 1980–. Councillor, London Borough of Bexley, 1974–82 (Chm., Social Services, 1975–78, 1980–82). Chm., Bexley HA, 1981–83. Member: Assoc. of Metropolitan Authorities Social Services Cttee, 1975–80; Central Council for Educn and Training of Social Workers, 1976–80; Governor, Nat. Inst. for Social Workers, 1976–80. PPS to Minister of State for Social Security, 1984–86, to Minister of Health, 1986–88, to Chancellor of Duchy of Lancaster, 1988–89, to Sec. of State for Social Security, 1989–90. Member: Social Services Select Cttee, 1983–85; Select Cttee on Health, 1990–92; Public Accounts Cttee, 1992–. Fellow, Industry and Parlt Trust, 1987. Mem., Vintners' Co. *Recreations:* travel, reading, listening to music, politics. *Address:* c/o House of Commons, SW1A 0AA.

COUCHMAN, Martin; Deputy Chief Executive, British Hospitality Association, since 1993; *b* 28 Sept. 1947; *s* of late Frederick Alfred James Couchman and of Pamela Mary Couchman (*née* Argent); *m* 1983, Carolyn Mary Constance Roberts; three *s* one *d. Educ:* Sutton Valence Sch.; Exeter Coll., Oxford (BA Jurisprudence). Building Industry, 1970–77; National Economic Development Office, 1977–92: Industrial Advr, 1977–84; Hd of Administration, 1984–87; on secondment as UK Dir of European Year of the Environment, 1987–88; Sec., NEDC, 1988–92. FRSA 1988. *Recreations:* Anglo-Saxon history, armchair archaeology, amateur dramatics. *Address:* The Old Rectory, Halstead, Kent TN14 7HG. *T:* Knockholt (01959) 532253.

COULL, Prof. Alexander, PhD; DSc; FRSE; FICE, FIStructE; Regius Professor of Civil Engineering, University of Glasgow, 1977–92; *b* 20 June 1931; *s* of William Coull and Jane Ritchie (*née* Reid); *m* 1962, Frances Bruce Moir; one *s* two *d. Educ:* Peterhead Acad.; Univ. of Aberdeen (BScEng, PhD; DSc 1983). FRSE 1971; FICE 1972, FIStructE 1973; Res. Asst, MIT, USA, 1955; Struct. Engr, English Electric Co. Ltd, 1955–57; Lectr in Engrg, Univ. of Aberdeen, 1957–62; Lectr in Civil Engrg, Univ. of Southampton, 1962–66; Prof. of Struct. Engrg, Univ. of Strathclyde, 1966–76. Chm., Clyde Estuary Amenity Council, 1981–86. *Publications:* Tall Buildings, 1967; Fundamentals of Structural Theory, 1972; (with B. Stafford Smith) Tall Building Structures: Planning Analysis and Design, 1991; author or co-author of 130 res. papers in scientific jls. *Recreations:* golf, hill walking, ski-ing. *Address:* 11 Blackwood Road, Milngavie, Glasgow G62 7LB. *T:* 0141–956 1655. *Club:* Buchanan Castle Golf (Drymen).

COULL, Maj.-Gen. John Taylor, CB 1992; FRCS; FRCSE; Medico-Legal Adviser, Army Medical Directorate, Ministry of Defence, since 1992; *b* 4 March 1934; *s* of late John Sandeman Coull and Ethel Marjory (*née* Taylor); *m* 1958, Mildred Macfarlane; three *s. Educ:* Robert Gordon's College; Aberdeen Univ. Med. Sch. MB ChB. House appts, Aberdeen Royal Infirmary, 1958–60; Commissioned RAMC, 1960; Surgeon: Colchester Mil. Hosp., 1960–63; Queen Alexandra Mil. Hosp., 1963; Sen. Registrar, Edinburgh East Gen. Hosp., 1963–65; Royal Herbert Hosp., 1965–67; Sen. Registrar, Birmingham Accident Hosp., 1967; Consultant Surgeon, BMH Singapore, 1967–70; Lectr, Dept of Orthopaedics, Univ. of Edinburgh, 1970–71; Consultant Orthopaedic Surgeon, BAOR, 1971–77; Consultant Adviser in Orthop. Surgery and Sen. Consultant, Queen Elizabeth Mil. Hosp., 1977–86; Consulting Surgeon, HQ BAOR, 1986–88; Dir of Army Surgery, 1988–92. Hon. Col 202 (Midland) Gen. Hosp. RAMC (V), 1992–; Col Comdt, RAMC, 1994–. QHS 1988–92. GSM N Ireland, 1976; Mitchiner Medal, RCS, 1980. OStJ. *Publications:* chapters in: Field Pocket Surgery, 1981; R. Smith's The Hand, 1985; Trauma, 1989; articles in learned jls. *Recreations:* home maintenance, carpentry, gardening, travel. *Address:* Royal Army Medical College, Millbank, SW1P 4RJ. *Club:* Royal Society of Medicine.

COULSFIELD, Hon. Lord; John Taylor Cameron; a Senator of the College of Justice in Scotland, since 1987; a Judge of the Employment Appeal Tribunal, since 1992; *b* 24 April 1934; *s* of late John Reid Cameron, MA, formerly Director of Education, Dundee; *m* 1964, Bridget Deirdre Sloan; no *c. Educ:* Fettes Coll.; Corpus Christi Coll., Oxford; Edinburgh Univ. BA (Oxon), LLB (Edinburgh). Admitted to Faculty of Advocates, 1960. Lecturer in Public Law, Edinburgh Univ., 1960–64. QC (Scot.) 1973; Keeper of the Advocates' Library, 1977–87; an Advocate-Depute, 1977–79. Judge, Courts of Appeal of Jersey and Guernsey, 1986–87. Chm., Medical Appeal Tribunals, 1985–87. Editor, Scottish Law and Practice Qly, 1995–. *Publications:* articles in legal jls.

COULSHED, Dame (Mary) Frances, DBE 1953 (CBE 1949); TD 1951; Brigadier, Women's Royal Army Corps, retired; *b* 10 Nov. 1904; *d* of Wilfred and Maud Coulshed. *Educ:* Parkfields Cedars, Derby; Convent of the Sacred Heart, Kensington. Served War of 1939–45 (despatches); North-West Europe, 1944–45, with General Headquarters Anti-Aircraft Troops and at Headquarters Lines of Communications; Deputy Dir, Anti-Aircraft Command, 1946–50; Dep. Dir, War Office, July-Dec. 1950; Director, WRAC, 1951–54. ADC to the King, 1951, to the Queen, 1952–54. Order of Leopold I of Belgium with palm, Croix de Guerre with palm, 1946. *Address:* 49–51 Holton, West Heath Road, NW3.

COULSON, Mrs Ann Margaret; General Manager, Age Concern, Solihull, 1991–94; *b* 11 March 1935; *d* of Sidney Herbert Wood and Ada (*née* Mills); *m* 1958, Peter James Coulson; two *s* one *d. Educ:* The Grammar Sch., Chippenham, Wilts; UCL (BScEcon); Univ. of Manchester (DSA); Wolverhampton Technical Teachers' Coll. (CertEd). Hosp. Admin, 1956–62; Lectr in Econs and Management, Bromsgrove Coll. of Further Educn, 1968–76; Asst Dir, North Worcestershire Coll., 1976–80; Service Planning and Develt

Co-ordinator, 1980–83, Regl Planning Administrator, 1983–88, Dir of Planning, 1988–91, W Midlands RHA. City of Birmingham Dist Council, 1973–79; special interest in Social Services. Mem., IBA, 1976–81. FIMgt. *Recreations:* cooking, music, theatre. *Address:* Rowans, Leamington Hastings, near Rugby, Warwicks CV23 8DY. *T:* Marton (01926) 633264.

COULSON, His Honour (James) Michael; a Circuit Judge, Midland and Oxford Circuit, 1983–90; *b* 23 Nov. 1927; *s* of William Coulson, Wold Newton Hall, Driffield, E Yorks; *m* 1st, 1955, Dilys Adair Jones (marr. diss.; she *d* 1994); one *s*; 2nd, 1977, Barbara Elizabeth Islay, *d* of Dr Roland Moncrieff Chambers; one *s* one *d*. *Educ:* Fulneck Sch., Yorks; Merton Coll., Oxford; Royal Agricultural Coll., Cirencester. Served E Riding Yeomanry (Wenlocks Horse); Queen's Own Yorks Yeomanry (Major). Called to Bar, Middle Temple, 1951; Mem. North Eastern Circuit; Asst Recorder of Sheffield, 1965–71; Dep. Chm., NR of Yorks QS, 1968–71; a Chm. of Industrial Tribunals, 1968–83; a Recorder of the Crown Court, 1981–83. Dep. Chm., Northern Agricl Land Tribunal, 1967–73. Former Mem., Tadcaster RDC. MP (C) Kingston-upon-Hull North, 1959–64; PPS to Solicitor Gen., 1962–64; Mem., Executive Cttee, Conservative Commonwealth Council. Sometime Sec., Bramham Moor and York and Ainsty Point to Point Race Meetings. *Recreations:* hunting, reading, travel. *Address:* The Tithe Barn, Wymondham, Melton Mowbray, Leics LE14 2AS. *Club:* Cavalry and Guards.

COULSON, Sir John Eltringham, KCMG 1957 (CMG 1946); President, Hampshire Branch, British Red Cross Society, 1972–79; Secretary-General of EFTA, 1965–72, retired; *b* 13 Sept. 1909; *er s* of H. J. Coulson, Bickley, Kent; *m* 1944, Mavis Ninette Beazley; two *s*. *Educ:* Rugby; Corpus Christi Coll., Cambridge (Hon. Fellow 1975). Entered Diplomatic Service in 1932. Served in Bucharest, Min. of Econ. Warfare, War Cabinet Office, Foreign Office and Paris. Sometime Dep. UK representative to UN, New York; Asst Under-Sec., Foreign Office, 1952–55; Minister British Embassy, Washington, 1955–57; Asst to Paymaster-Gen., 1957–60; Ambassador to Sweden, 1960–63; Dep. Under-Sec. of State, Foreign Office, 1963–65; Chief of Administration of HM Diplomatic Service, Jan.-Sept. 1965. Director: Atlas Copco (GB), 1972–80; Sheerness Steel Co., 1972–84. Knight Grand Cross, Order of the North Star, Sweden, 1982. *Recreations:* fishing, golf. *Address:* The Old Mill, Selborne, Hants GU34 3LG. *Club:* Brooks's.

COULSON, Michael; *see* Coulson, J. M.

COULTASS, (George Thomas) Clive; historian; Keeper of Audio-Visual Records, Imperial War Museum, 1983–91; *b* 5 July 1931; *m* 1962, Norma Morris. *Educ:* Tadcaster Grammar Sch.; Univ. of Sheffield (BA Hons). Teacher in various London schools, 1955–62; Lectr/Sen. Lectr in History, James Graham Coll., Leeds, 1962–69; Imperial War Museum: Keeper of Film Programming, 1969–70; Keeper, Dept of Film, 1970–83. Vice-Pres., Internat. Assoc. for Audio-Visual Media in Hist. Res. and Educn, 1978–85. Organiser: various film historical confs, 1973–90; exhibn on British film and World War II, 1982. *Publications:* Images for Battle, 1989; sections in: The Historian and Film, 1976; Britain and the Cinema in the Second World War, 1988; articles in various historical jls. *Recreations:* travel, music, including opera, reading. *Address:* 39 Fairfield Grove, SE7 8UA.

COULTHARD, Air Vice-Marshal Colin Weal, CB 1975; AFC 1953 (Bar 1958); retired; *b* 27 Feb. 1921; *s* of late George Robert Coulthard and Cicely Eva Coulthard (*née* Minns); *m* 1st, 1941, Norah Ellen Creighton (marr. diss.); one *s* two *d*; 2nd, 1957, Eileen Pamela (*née* Barber); one *s*. *Educ:* Watford Grammar Sch.; De Havilland Aeronautical Tech. Sch. Commissioned RAF, 1941; Fighter Pilot, 1942–45 (despatches, 1945); HQ Fighter Comd, 1948–49; RAF Staff Coll., 1950; OC 266 Sqn, Wunstorf, 1952–54, DFLS, CFE, 1955; OC Flying, 233(F) OCU, 1956–57; OC AFDS, CFE, 1957–59; HQ Fighter Comd, 1959–60; Stn Cdr, Gutersloh, 1961–64; MoD, 1964–66; SOA, AHQ Malta, 1966–67; DOR 1(RAF), MoD, 1967–69; Air Attaché, Washington, DC, 1970–72; Mil. Dep. to Head of Defence Sales, MoD, 1973–75. Governor, Truro Sch., 1981–91. Hon. FRAeS 1975. *Recreations:* walking, shooting, motor sport. *Address:* Fiddlers, Old Truro Road, Goonhavern, Truro TR4 9NN. *T:* Truro (01872) 540312. *Club:* Royal Air Force.

COULTON, Very Rev. Nicholas Guy; Provost of St Nicholas' Cathedral, Newcastle-upon-Tyne, since 1990; *b* 14 June 1940; *s* of Nicholas Guy Coulton and Audrey Florence Furneaux Coulton (*née* Luscombe); *m* 1978, Edith Mary Gainford; one *s* two *d*. *Educ:* Blundell's School, Tiverton; Cuddesdon Coll., Oxford. BD London 1972. Admitted Solicitor, 1962; Asst Solicitor, Burges, Salmon & Co., Bristol, 1962–65. Ordination training, 1965–67; Curate of Pershore Abbey with Birlingham, Wick and Pinvin, 1967–71; Domestic Chaplain to Bishop of St Albans, 1971–75; Vicar of St Paul's, Bedford, 1975–90; part-time Industrial Chaplain, 1976–89. Proctor in Convocation, 1985–90; Hon. Canon of St Alban's Cathedral, 1989–90. Chm., NE CCJ, 1991–. *Publication:* Twelve Years of Prayer, 1989. *Recreations:* gardening, reading, listening to music, historical exploration, rearing children. *Address:* The Cathedral Vicarage, 26 Mitchell Avenue, West Jesmond, Newcastle-upon-Tyne NE2 3LA. *T:* 0191–232 1939.

COUNSELL, Hazel Rosemary; Her Honour Judge Hazel Counsell; a Circuit Judge, 1978–April 1996; *b* 7 Jan. 1931; *d* of late Arthur Henry Counsell and Elsie Winifred Counsell; *m* 1980, Peter Fallon, *qv*. *Educ:* Clifton High Sch.; Switzerland; Univ. of Bristol (LLB). Called to the Bar, Gray's Inn, 1956; Western Circuit, 1956–; a Recorder of the Crown Court, 1976–77. Legal Dept, Min. of Labour, 1959–62. Mem. of Council, Univ. of Bristol, 1992–. *Recreations:* reading, swimming, travel, gardening. *Address*: The Law Courts, Small Street, Bristol BS1 1DA.

COUPER, Prof. Alastair Dougal, FNI; FRICS; FCIT; Professor of Maritime Studies, University of Wales College of Cardiff (formerly University of Wales Institute of Science and Technology), since 1970; *b* 4 June 1931; *s* of Daniel Alexander Couper and Davina Couper (*née* Rilley); *m* 1958, Norma Milton; two *s* two *d*. *Educ:* Robert Gordon's School of Navigation (Master Mariner); Univ. of Aberdeen (MA, DipEd); Australian National Univ. (PhD). FCIT 1974; FNI 1979; FRICS 1986. Cadet and Navigating Officer, Merchant Navy, 1947–57; student, Univ. of Aberdeen, 1958–62, postgraduate teaching course, 1962–63; Research Schol., Sch. of Pacific Studies, ANU, Canberra, 1963–66; Lectr, Univ. of Durham, 1967–70. Prof., World Maritime Univ. (UN), Malmö, Sweden, 1987–89 (on secondment). UN Consultant, 1972–; Chm., Maritime Bd, CNAA, 1978–85; Assessor, Chartered Inst. of Transport, 1976–85; Founder Mem., Council, British Maritime League, 1982–85; Mem. Exec. Bd, Law of the Sea Inst., USA, 1989–95. Trustee, Nat. Maritime Mus., 1992–. Editor (and Founder), Journal of Maritime Policy and Management, 1973–84. *Publications:* Geography of Sea Transport, 1971; The Law of the Sea, 1978; (ed) Times Atlas of the Oceans, 1983; contrib. Pacific, in World Atlas of Agriculture, 1969; Pacific in Transition (ed Brookfield), 1973; New Cargo Handling Techniques: implications for port employment and skills, 1986; (ed) Development and Social Change in the Pacific, 1988; (ed) The Shipping Revolution, 1992; several UN Reports, UNCTAD, ILO, IMO; articles in jls; conf. papers. *Recreations:* hill walking, sailing, archaeology, Pacific history. *Address:* University of Wales College of Cardiff, Cardiff CF1 3YP. *T:* Cardiff (01222) 874000.

COUPER, Heather Anita, FRAS; science broadcaster and author, since 1983; Director, Pioneer TV Productions, since 1988; *b* 2 June 1949; *o d* of George Couper Elder Couper and late Anita Couper (*née* Taylor). *Educ:* St Mary's Grammar Sch., Northwood, Mddx; Univ. of Leicester (BSc Hons Astronomy and Physics); Univ. of Oxford. FRAS 1970. Management trainee, Peter Robinson Ltd, 1967–69; Res. Asst, Cambridge Observatories, 1969–70; Lectr, Greenwich Planetarium, Old Royal Observ., 1977–83. Gresham Prof. of Astronomy, 1993–. Mem., Millennium Commn, 1994–. President: Brit. Astron. Assoc., 1984–86; Jun. Astron. Soc., 1987–89. Presenter on television: Heavens Above, 1981; Spacewatch, 1983; The Planets, 1985; The Stars, 1988; The Neptune Encounter, 1989; A Close Encounter of the Second Kind, 1992; ET—Please Phone Earth, 1992; Space Shuttle Discovery, 1993; Electric Skies, 1994; Presenter on radio: Science Now, 1983; Cosmic Pursuits, 1985; Seeing Stars, 1991–; ET on Trial, 1993; also appearances and interviews on wide variety of television and radio progs. Astronomy columnist, The Independent. Hon. DLitt Loughborough, 1991; Hon. DSc Hertfordshire, 1994. *Publications:* Exploring Space, 1980; (jtly) Heavens Above, 1981; Journey into Space, 1984; (jtly) Starfinder, 1984; (jtly) The Halley's Comet Pop-Up Book, 1985; (jtly) The Universe: a 3-dimensional study, 1985; Space Scientist series, 1985–87: Comets and Meteors; The Planets; The Stars; jointly: The Sun; The Moon; Galaxies and Quasars; Satellites and Spaceprobes; Telescopes and Observatories; *with Nigel Henbest:* Space Frontiers, 1978; The Restless Universe, 1982; Physics, 1983; Astronomy, 1983; The Planets, 1985; The Stars, 1988; The Space Atlas, 1992; Guide to the Galaxy, 1994; How the Universe Works, 1994; numerous articles in nat. newspapers and magazines. *Recreations:* travel, the English countryside, classical music; wine, food and winemaking. *Address:* Pioneer Productions, Pinewood Studios, Pinewood Road, Iver Heath, Bucks SL0 0NH.

COUPER, Sir (Robert) Nicholas (Oliver), 6th Bt *cr* 1841; *b* 9 Oct. 1945; *s* of Sir George Robert Cecil Couper, 5th Bt, and Margaret Grace (*d* 1984), *d* of late Robert George Dashwood Thomas; *S* father, 1975; *m* 1972, Curzon MacKean (marr. diss. 1986); one *s* one *d*; *m* 1991, Katrina Frances, *d* of Sir Michael Walker, *qv*. *Educ:* Eton; RMA, Sandhurst. Major, Blues and Royals; retired, 1975. Now working as a property consultant. *Heir: s* James George Couper, *b* 27 Oct. 1977. *Address:* 79 Devonshire Road, W4 2HU.

COUPLAND, Prof. Rex Ernest; Professor of Human Morphology, 1967–89, and Dean of Medicine, 1981–87, University of Nottingham; Hon. Consultant, Trent Regional Hospital Board, 1970–89; *b* 30 Jan. 1924; *s* of late Ernest Coupland, company dir and Doris Coupland; *m* 1947, Lucy Eileen Sargent; one *s* one *d*. *Educ:* Mirfield Grammar Sch.; University of Leeds. MB, ChB with honours, 1947; MD with distinction, 1952; PhD 1954; DSc 1970. House appointments, Leeds General Infirmary, 1947; Demonstrator and Lecturer in Anatomy, University of Leeds, 1948, 1950–58; Asst Prof. of Anatomy, University of Minnesota, USA, 1955–56; Prof. of Anatomy, Queen's Coll., Dundee, University of St Andrews, 1958–67. Medical Officer, RAF, 1948–50. FRSE 1960. Member: Biological Research Board of MRC, 1964–70; Med. Adv. Bd, Crippling Diseases Foundn, 1971–75; CMO's Academic Forum, 1984–89; Chm., MRC Non-Ionizing Radiations Cttee, 1970–89; Derbyshire AHA, 1978–81; Trent RHA, 1981–88; Chm., Nottingham Div., BMA, 1978–79; GMC, 1982–88; Med. sub-cttee, UGC, 1984–89. President: Anat. Soc. GB and Ireland, 1976–78; British Assoc. of Clinical Anat., 1977–82. Wood Jones Medal for contrib. to clinical anatomy, RCS, 1984. *Publications:* The Natural History of the Chromaffin Cell, 1965; (ed jtly) Chromaffin, Enterochromaffin and Related Cells, 1976; (ed jtly) Peripheral Neuroendocrine Interaction, 1978; papers in jls of anatomy, physiology, endocrinology, pathology and pharmacology on endocrine and nervous systems and in jls of radiology on NMR imaging; *chapters on:* Anatomy of the Human Kidney, in Renal Disease (ed Black), 1962, 1968, 1973; The Chromaffin System, in Catecholamines (ed Blaschko and Muscholl), 1973; The Blood Supply of the Adrenal Gland, in Handbook of Physiology, 1974; The Adrenal Medulla, in The Cell in Medical Science (ed Beck and Lloyd), 1976; Endocrine System, in Textbook of Human Anatomy (ed W. J. Hamilton), 1976; *contribs to:* Hormones and Evolution, Vol. I, ed Barrington, 1979; Biogenic Amines in Development, ed Parvez and Parvez, 1980; Hormones in Human Tissues, Vol. I, ed Fotherby and Pal, 1981; Asst Editor, Gray's Anatomy (ed Davies), 1967. *Recreations:* shooting, gardening, watercolour painting. *Address:* Foxhollow, Quaker Lane, Farnsfield, Newark, Notts NG22 8EE. *T:* Mansfield (01623) 882028.

COURAGE, Maj.-Gen. Walter James, CB 1994; MBE 1979; Director-General, Territorial Army, since 1995; *b* 25 Sept. 1940; *s* of late Walter Henry Phipps and of Nancy Mary Courage (*née* Reeves, who *m* 3rd, John Frederick Gardner), and step *s* of late Lt-Col Nigel Anthony Courage, MC; *m* 1964, Lavinia Patricia, *d* of late John Emerson Crawhall Wood; one *s* one *d*. *Educ:* Abingdon Sch.; RMA, Sandhurst. Commnd 5th Royal Inniskilling Dragoon Guards, 1961; served BAOR, Libya and Canada, 1961–81; commanded Regt, 1982–84; Div. Col Staff Coll., 1985; Comdr 4th Armoured Bde, 1985–88; Chief of Staff, UN Force in Cyprus, 1988–90; Chief Joint Services Liaison Officer, BAOR, Bonn, 1990–95. FIMgt. *Recreations:* shooting, cricket, ski-ing, polo, fine art. *Address:* c/o Lloyds Bank, Cox's and King's Branch, 7 Pall Mall, SW1Y 5NH. *Clubs:* Cavalry and Guards, MCC; I Zingari.

COURCY; *see* de Courcy.

COURT, Hon. Sir Charles (Walter Michael), AK 1982; KCMG 1979; Kt 1972; OBE 1946; MLA (Liberal Party) for Nedlands, 1953–82; Premier of Western Australia, 1974–82; also Treasurer, and Minister co-ordinating Economic and Regional Development, 1974–82; *b* Crawley, Sussex, 29 Sept. 1911; *s* of late W. J. Court, Perth; *m* 1936, Rita M., *d* of L. R. Steffanoni; five *s*. *Educ:* Leederville and Rosalie State Schs; Perth Boys' Sch. Chartered Accountant, 1933; Foundn Partner, Hendry, Rae & Court, 1938–70. Served AIF, 1940–46, Lt-Col. State Registrar, Inst. Chartered Accountants in Aust. (WA Br.), 1946–52, Mem. State Council, 1952–55. Dep. Leader, 1957–59, 1971–72, and Leader, 1972–74, of Opposition, WA; Minister, Western Australia: for Industrial Development and the NW, 1959–71; for Railways, 1959–67; for Transport, 1965–66. Chm., Adv. Cttee under WA Prices Control Act, 1948–52; President: WA Band Assoc., 1954–59; Order of Australia Assoc., 1987–89. Warden, WA State War Meml, 1991–92. Chm. Adv. Council, Asia Res. Council, Murdoch Univ. Patron, WA Div., PGA. Hon. Colonel: WA Univ. Regt, 1969–75; SAS Regt, 1976–80. Paul Harris Fellow, 1982, Sapphire Pin, 1991, Rotary. FCA; FCIS; FASA. Hon. FAIM 1980. Freeman: City of Nedlands, 1982; Shire of West Kimberley, WA, 1983. Hon. LLD Univ. of WA, 1969; Hon. DTech WA Inst. of Technol., 1982; Hon. Dr Murdoch Univ., 1995. Manufacturers' Export Council Award, 1969; James Kirby Award, Inst. of Production Engrs, 1971; Australian Chartered Accountant of the Year, 1983. Life Member: Musicians Union, 1953; ASA, 1979; Returned Services League, 1981; Inst. of Chartered Accountants in Australia, 1982. Order of the Sacred Treasure, 1st cl. (Japan), 1983; Kt Comdr, Order of Merit (Italian Republic), 1991; Order of Brilliant Star with Grand Cordon (Taiwan), 1991. *Publications:* many professional papers on accountancy, and papers on economic and resource development. *Recreations:* music and other cultural and sporting interests. *Address:* 46 Waratah Avenue, Nedlands, WA 6009, Australia. *Clubs:* Weld, Western Australia, Commercial Travellers Association (Perth); Nedlands Rotary, Lions.

COURT, Hon. Richard Fairfax; MLA (L) Nedlands, since 1982; Premier of Western Australia, Treasurer and Minister for Public Sector Management and for Federal Affairs, since 1993; Minister for Tourism, since 1994; *b* 27 Sept. 1947; *s* of Hon. Sir Charles Court, *qv*; *m* 1989, Joanne, *d* of B. Moffat; one *s* one *d* by previous marriage. *Educ:* Univ. of Western Australia (BCom). Man. Dir, Court Marine Pty, 1974–82. Shadow Minister for Small Business, 1986; Dep. Leader, Parly Lib. Party, 1987–90; Shadow Minister for: Resources, Develt, Mines, Fuel and Energy, NW and Goldfields, 1990–91; Resource and Industrial Develt, Mines and Aboriginal Affairs, 1991–92; Public Sector Management, also Leader of the Opposition and Shadow Treas., 1992–93. *Address:* (office) 19th Floor, 197 St George's Terrace, Perth, WA 6000, Australia.

COURTAULD, Rev. (Augustine) Christopher (Caradoc); Vicar of St Paul's, Knightsbridge, since 1978; *b* 12 Sept. 1934; *s* of late Augustine Courtauld and of Lady Butler of Saffron Walden; *m* 1978, Dr Elizabeth Ann Molland, MD, FRCPath, *d* of late Rev. Preb. John W. G. Molland; two *d*. *Educ:* Trinity College, Cambridge (BA 1958, MA 1961); Westcott House, Cambridge. Deacon 1960, priest 1961, Manchester; Curate of Oldham, 1960–63; Chaplain: Trinity College, Cambridge, 1963–68; The London Hospital, 1968–78. Area Dean, Westminster (St Margaret), 1992–. *Recreation:* sailing. *Address:* St Paul's Vicarage, 32 Wilton Place, SW1X 8SH.

COURTENAY, family name of **Earl of Devon.**

COURTENAY, Lord; Hugh Rupert Courtenay; DL; landowner, farmer; *b* 5 May 1942; *o s* of 17th Earl of Devon, *qv*; *m* 1967, Dianna Frances, *er d* of J. G. Watherston, Jedburgh, Roxburghshire; one *s* three *d*. *Educ:* Winchester; Magdalene Coll., Cambridge (BA). ARICS. Captain, Wessex Yeomanry, retd. Chm., Devon Br., CLA, 1987–89. DL Devon, 1991. *Recreations:* riding, hunting, shooting. *Heir: s* Hon. Charles Peregrine Courtenay, *b* 14 Aug. 1975. *Address:* Powderham Castle, near Exeter, Devon EX6 8JQ. *T:* Starcross (01626) 890370.

COURTENAY, Thomas Daniel, (Tom Courtenay); actor; *b* 25 Feb. 1937; *s* of late Thomas Henry Courtenay and Annie Eliza Quest; *m* 1st, 1973, Cheryl Kennedy (marr. diss. 1982); 2nd, 1988, Isabel Crossley. *Educ:* Kingston High Sch., Hull; University Coll., London (Fellow 1994). RADA, 1958–60; started acting professionally, 1960; Old Vic, 1960–61: Konstantin Treplieff, Poins, Feste and Puck; Billy Liar, Cambridge Theatre, June 1961–Feb. 1962 and on tour; Andorra, National Theatre (guest), 1964; The Cherry Orchard, and Macbeth, Chichester, 1966; joined 69 Theatre Co., Manchester, 1966: Charley's Aunt, 1966; Romeo, Playboy of the Western World, 1967; Hamlet (Edinburgh Festival), 1968; She Stoops to Conquer, (transferred to Garrick), 1969; Peer Gynt, 1970; Charley's Aunt, Apollo, 1971; Time and Time Again, Comedy, 1972 (Variety Club of GB Stage Actor Award, 1972); The Norman Conquests, Globe, 1974; The Fool, Royal Court, 1975; Prince of Homburg, The Rivals, Manchester (opening prods of The Royal Exchange), 1976; Otherwise Engaged, NY, 1977; Clouds, Duke of York's, 1978; Crime and Punishment, Manchester, 1978; The Dresser, Manchester and Queen's, 1980 (Drama Critics Award and New Standard Award for best actor, 1980), NY 1981; The Misanthrope, Manchester and Round House, 1981; Andy Capp, Manchester and Aldwych, 1982; Jumpers, Manchester, 1984; Rookery Nook, Shaftesbury, 1986; The Hypochondriac, Lyric, Hammersmith, 1987; Dealing with Clair, Richmond, 1988; The Miser, Manchester, 1991; Moscow Stations (one-man show), Traverse Theatre, Edinburgh, 1993, 1994, Garrick, 1994 (Evening Standard and Critics Circle Award); Poison Pen, Manchester, 1993; Uncle Vanya, NY, 1995. Began acting in films, 1962. *Films:* The Loneliness of the Long Distance Runner; Private Potter; Billy Liar; King and Country (Volpi Cup, 1964); Operation Crossbow; King Rat; Dr Zhivago; The Night of the Generals; The Day the Fish Came Out; A Dandy in Aspic; Otley; One Day in the Life of Ivan Denisovitch; Catch Me a Spy; The Dresser (Golden Globe Award); The Last Butterfly; Let Him Have It; Redemption; *television* includes Old Curiosity Shop (film), 1995. Best Actor Award, Prague Festival, 1968; TV Drama Award (for Oswald in Ghosts), 1968. *Recreations:* listening to music (mainly classical, romantic and jazz); watching sport (and occasionally taking part in it, in a light-hearted manner), the countryside, playing the flute. *Address:* Putney. *Club:* Garrick.

COURTNEY, Prof. Edward, MA; Gildersleeve Professor of Classics, University of Virginia, since 1993; *b* 22 March 1932; *s* of George and Kathleen Courtney; *m* 1962, Brenda Virginia Meek; two *s*. *Educ:* Royal Belfast Academical Instn; Trinity Coll., Dublin (BA); BA (by incorporation) 1955, MA 1957, Oxford. University studentship, Dublin, 1954–55; Research Lectr, Christ Church, Oxford, 1955–59; Lectr in Classics, 1959, Reader in Classics, 1970, Prof. of Latin, 1977, King's Coll., London; Prof. of Classics, 1982–93, Leonard Ely Prof. of Humanistic Studies, 1986–93, Stanford Univ. *Publications:* (ed) Valerius Flaccus, Argonautica (Leipzig), 1970; (ed jtly) Juvenal, Satires 1, 3, 10, 1977; (ed jtly) Ovid, Fasti (Leipzig), 1978, 3rd edn 1988; A Commentary on the Satires of Juvenal, 1980; (ed) Juvenal, The Satires, a text, 1984; (ed) Statius, Silvae, 1990; The Poems of Petronius, 1991; The Fragmentary Roman Poets, 1993; many articles and reviews. *Recreation:* chess (schoolboy champion of Ireland, 1950). *Address:* 1500 West Pines Drive, Charlottesville, VA 22901, USA.

COURTNEY, Roger Graham, CPhys, FInstP; Chief Executive, Building Research Establishment, Department of the Environment, since 1990; *b* 11 July 1946; *s* of late Ronald Samuel Courtney and of Marjorie Dixon Courtney; *m* 1973, Rosemary Madeleine Westlake; four *d*. *Educ:* Roan School for Boys, SE3; Trinity Coll., Cambridge (MA); Univ. of Bristol (MSc); Brunel Univ. (MTech(OR)). CPhys 1991, FInstP 1991; MCIOB 1993; FCIBSE 1993. Building Research Station (later, Building Research Establishment), 1969–77: res. on bldg and urban services and energy conservation; Sci. Officer, 1969–72; Sen. Sci. Officer, 1972–75; PSO, 1975–81; Inner Cities Directorate, DoE, 1977–78; Sci. and Technology Secretariat, Cabinet Office, 1978–84 (Sec. to ACARD and IT Adv. Panel); SPSO, 1981–83; DCSO, 1983–86; Technical Dir, Energy Efficiency Office, Dept of Energy, 1984–86; Dep. Dir, 1986–88, Dir, 1988–90, BRE. *Publications:* papers in sci. and professional jls. *Address:* Building Research Establishment, Garston, Watford WD2 7JR. *T:* Watford (01923) 894040.

COURTNEY, William Reid; Regional Chairman of Industrial Tribunals, Scotland, since 1991; *b* 22 Nov. 1927; *s* of Samuel Courtney and Louisa Reid or Courtney; *m* 1951, Jean Ursula Page; one *s* two *d*. *Educ:* Allan Glens Sch., Glasgow; Glasgow Univ. (LLB). Solicitor, Supreme Courts. Failed professional cricketer, fell back on Law; Edinburgh solicitor, 1952–77; Chm., Industrial Tribunals, Scotland, 1978–91. *Recreations:* sea, hills. *Address:* 30 Millig Street, Helensburgh, Dunbartonshire G84 9PN. *T:* Helensburgh (01436) 76900. *Clubs:* Royal Northern & Clyde Yacht, Clyde Corinthian Yacht, Clyde Cruising, Old Gaffers.

COURTOWN, 9th Earl of, *cr* 1762; **James Patrick Montagu Burgoyne Winthrop Stopford;** Baron Courtown (Ire.), 1758; Viscount Stopford, 1762; Baron Saltersford (GB), 1796; a Lord in Waiting (Government Whip), since 1995; *b* 19 March 1954; *s* of 8th Earl of Courtown, OBE, TD, DL, and of Patricia, 3rd *d* of Harry S. Winthrop, Auckland, NZ; *S* father, 1975; *m* 1985, Elisabeth, *yr d* of I. R. Dunnett, Broad Campden, Glos; one *s* one *d*. *Educ:* Eton College; Berkshire Coll. of Agriculture; RAC, Cirencester. ARICS 1989. *Heir: s* Viscount Stopford, *qv*. *Address:* House of Lords, SW1A 0PW.

COUSE, Philip Edward, FCA; Partner, Coopers & Lybrand, 1966–91; Director: Birmingham Heartlands (formerly East Birmingham) Hospital NHS Trust, since 1991; William King Ltd, since 1993; Part-time Commissioner, Friendly Societies Commission, since 1992; *b* 24 March 1936; *s* of Oliver and Marion Couse; *m* 1st (marr. diss. 1973); two *s* one *d*; 2nd, Carol Ann Johannessen Pruitt; one step *d*. *Educ:* Uppingham Sch.; Hackley Sch., USA. Qualified as Chartered Accountant, 1961. Birmingham Chartered Accountants' Students Society: Sec., 1958–59; Chm., 1967–69; Pres., 1977–78; Birmingham and West Midlands Soc. of Chartered Accountants: Mem. Cttee, 1974–92, Pres., 1982–83; Institute of Chartered Accountants: Mem. Council, 1978–92; Chm. of various cttees; Pres., 1989–90; Chartered Accountants' Dining Club: Mem. Cttee, 1981–92; Treas., 1985–89; Pres., 1989–91. Dir, Hillstone Sch. Trust, Malvern, 1971–86; Chairman: Edgbaston C of E Coll. for Girls, 1982–88; Birmingham Rep. Theatre Foundn, 1991–; Dir, Birmingham Rep. Th., 1991–; Chm., Birmingham Dio. Bd of Finance, 1992–, and Mem. of various cttees; Mem., Council of Management, and Treas., Ironbridge Heritage Foundn, 1991–; Trustee, Birmingham Eye Foundn, 1981– (Treas., 1981–91). Liveryman, Co. of Chartered Accountants in England and Wales, 1977– (Mem., Court, 1987–90). *Recreations:* music, horse racing, woodwork, theatre going. *Address:* 15 Chad Road, Edgbaston, Birmingham B15 3ER. *Clubs:* Royal Automobile; Birmingham (Birmingham).

COUSINS, Brian Harry, CBE 1981; Principal Establishment and Finance Officer, Lord Chancellor's Department, 1989–93; *b* 18 July 1933; *s* of late William and Ethel Margaret Cousins; *m* 1957, Margaret (*née* Spark); two *s*. *Educ:* Devonport High School. Served RAF, pilot, 1952–54. Joined Ministry of Defence, 1954; Private Sec. to Permanent Secretary, 1962–65; Private Sec. Parliamentary Secretary, 1971–72; ndc 1972; Civil Sec., British Forces Germany, 1973–76; Asst Under Sec. of State, MoD, 1981–85, 1986–89; Chm., CSSB, 1985–86. *Recreations:* tennis, music, gardening.

COUSINS, Air Marshal David, CB 1991; AFC 1980; Air Member for Personnel, and Air Officer Commanding-in-Chief, Personnel and Training Command, since 1995; *b* 20 Jan. 1942; *s* of late Peter and Irene Cousins; *m* 1966, Mary Edith McMurray, *e d* of late Rev. A. W. S. Holmes; two *s* one *d*. *Educ:* St Edward's Sch., Malta; Prince Rupert's Sch., Wilhelmshaven; RAF College; Open Univ. (BA 1992). 92 Sqn (Lightnings), 1965–68; ADC to CAS, 1968–70; 15 Sqn (Buccaneers), 1970–73; Air Plans, HQ RAF Germany, 1973; RAF Staff Coll., 1974; Staff Officer to ACAS (OR), 1975–77; OC 16 Sqn (Buccaneers), 1977–80; Central Trials and Tactics Orgn, 1980; PSO to CAS, 1981–83; OC RAF Laarbruch, 1983–85; RCDS 1986; Dir, Air Offensive, MoD, 1987–89; Dir Gen. Aircraft 2, MoD (PE), 1989–91; AOC and Comdt, RAF Coll., Cranwell, 1992–94; AOC No 38 Gp, and SASO Strike Comd, 1994–95. ADC to the Queen, 1984–85. *Recreations:* squash, dinghy sailing, horology. *Address:* Personnel and Training Command, RAF Innsworth, Glos GL3 1EZ. *Club:* Royal Air Force.

COUSINS, James Mackay; MP (Lab) Newcastle upon Tyne Central, since 1987; *b* 23 Feb. 1944; *m*; two *s* (one step *s* one step *d*). *Educ:* New Coll., Oxford (Schol.); London School of Economics. Contract Researcher, and Lectr in steel, shipbuilding and inner city job markets for trade unions, Commn on Industrial Relns and Depts of Employment and the Environment. Member: Wallsend Borough Council, 1969–73; Tyne and Wear County Council, 1973–86 (Dep. Leader, 1981–86). Founder, North Low Pay Unit. Member: CND; MSF. *Address:* (office) First Floor, 21 Portland Terrace, Newcastle upon Tyne NE2 1QQ; House of Commons, SW1A 0AA.

COUSINS, John Peter; Chairman, Crown Asset Management Ltd, Hong Kong, since 1994; *b* 31 Oct. 1931; *s* of Rt Hon. Frank Cousins, PC; *m* 1976, Pauline Cousins (*née* Hubbard); three *d*. *Educ:* Doncaster Central Sch. Motor engineering apprentice, 1947–52; RAF Engineering, 1952–55; BOAC cabin crew and clerical work, 1955–63; Full Time Official, TGWU, 1963–75, Nat. Sec., 1966–75; Dir of Manpower and Industrial Relations, NEDO, 1975–79; Dir of Personnel, Plessey Telecommunications and Office Systems Ltd, 1979–81; Dir of Personnel and Industrial Relns, John Brown PLC, 1981–83; Gen. Sec., Clearing Bank Union, 1983–86; Head of Personnel, Scottish Daily Record & Sunday Mail (1986) Ltd, 1987; Personnel Dir, Maxwell Pergamon Publishing Corp., 1988–89; Sen. Consultant, Contract 2000, 1989–90; Man. Dir, Cousins Financial Services Ltd (Gibraltar), 1990. Mem., Transport and Local Govt Cttees, TUC; UK Deleg., ILO; International Transport Workers Federation: Member: Aviation Sect.; Local Govt Cttee; Chemical Cttee; Civil Aviation Cttee; Mem. Industrial Training Bds. Member: Countryside Commn, 1972–84; New Towns Commn, 1975–79; Sandford Cttee to review National Parks in England and Wales, 1972–73; Council, RSPB, 1982; Bd of Trustees, Royal Botanic Gardens, Kew, 1983–88. Chm., British Council of Productivity Assocs, 1977–82. Travelling Fellow, Kingston Reg. Management Centre, 1977. FIMgt. *Recreation:* music. *Address:* 76 Tia Wai New Village, Shatin, New Territories, Hong Kong.

COUSINS, Philip, CB 1982; Deputy Comptroller and Auditor General, National Audit Office (formerly Secretary, Exchequer and Audit Department), 1979–84; *b* 28 Feb. 1923; *s* of Herbert and Ella Cousins; *m* 1948, Ruby Laura Morris; two *d*. *Educ:* Royal Liberty School, Romford. Served in Royal Air Force, 1943–47. Joined Treasury, 1949; Under Secretary, 1974–79. *Address:* 102 Philbeach Gardens, SW5 9ET. *T:* 0171–373 6164.

COUSTEAU, Jacques-Yves; Commandeur, Légion d'Honneur; Croix de Guerre with Palm; Officier du Mérite Maritime; Chevalier du Mérite Agricole; Officier des Arts et des Lettres; Member of Académie Française, 1989; marine explorer; *b* 11 June 1910; *s* of Daniel and Elizabeth Cousteau; *m* 1937, Simone Melchior (*d* 1990); one *s* (and one *s* decd); *m* 1992, Francine Triplet. *Educ:* Stanislas, Paris; Navy Academy, Brest. Lt de vaisseau, War of 1939–45. Inventor with Emile Gagnan, 1943, of the Aqualung, a portable breathing device for divers; with André Laban, perfected first underwater camera equipment for television transmission, 1951; with Jean Mollard, produced the diving saucer, 1959; development with Lucien Malavard and Bertrand Charrier of Turbosail (wind-propulsion system for ships), 1985. Established Undersea Research Group, 1946; Founder and President: Campagne Océanographiques Françaises, 1950; Centre d'Etudes Marines Avancées, 1952; since 1951 has made oceanographic expdns on his ship Calypso, and film records of his undersea expdns; promoted Conshelf saturation dive programme, 1962–65; Founder, Cousteau Soc., 1973. Dir, Musée Océanographique, Monaco, 1957–88; Gen. Sec., Internat. Commn for Scientific Exploration of the Mediterranean Sea, 1966; Chm., Council on Rights of Future Generations, 1993–. Fellow, BAFTA, 1975; For. Assoc. Mem., Nat. Acad. Scis, USA, 1968; Corresp. Mem., Hellenic Inst. of Marine Archaeology, 1975; Hon. Mem., Indian Acad. of Scis, 1978. Hon. DSc: California, 1970; Brandeis, 1970; Rensselaer Polytechnic Inst., 1979; Harvard, 1979; Ghent, 1983; Dr *hc* Univ. Autónoma de Guadalajara, 1989. Gold Medal, RGS, 1963; Pott's Medal, Franklin Inst., 1970; Gold Medal, Nat. Geographic Soc., and Gold Medal Grand Prix d'Océanographie Albert Ier, 1971; Grande Médaille d'Or, Soc. d'encouragement au Progrès, 1973; Award of New England Aquarium, 1973; Prix de la couronne d'or, 1973; Polena della Bravura, 1974; Gold Medal "Sciences" (Arts, Sciences, Lettres), 1974; Manley Bendall Prize, Marine Acad., 1976; Special Cervia prize, 1976; Internat. Pahlavi Environment Prize, 1977; (with Sir Peter Scott) UN Internat. Envmtl Prize, 1977; Jean Sainteny Prize, 1980; Kiwanis Internat. Europe Prize, 1980; Lindbergh Award, 1982; Neptune Award, Amer. Oceanic Orgn, 1982; Bruno H. Schubert Foundn Award, 1983;

US Presidential Medal of Freedom, 1985; Founder's Award, Internat. Council of Nat. Acad. of Arts and Scis, 1987; Centennial Award, Nat. Geographic Soc., 1988; inducted into Diving Equipment Manufrs Assoc. Hall of Fame, 1989 (Reaching Out Award, 1989). *Films:* The Silent World (Grand Prix, Gold Palm, Cannes 1956; Oscar, 1957); The Golden Fish (Oscar, best short film, 1959); World without Sun (Oscar, 1965); Voyage to the Edge of the World, 1975; Cries from the Deep, 1982; St Lawrence: stairway to the sea, 1982; Jacques Cousteau: the first seventy-five years, 1985; Riders of the Wind, 1986; Island of Peace, 1988; Outrage at Valdez, 1990; Lilliput in Antarctica, 1990; *TV film series:* The Undersea World of Jacques Cousteau, 1968–76 (numerous Emmy awards); Oasis in Space, 1977; The Cousteau Odyssey, 1977–82; Cousteau/Amazon, 1982–85; Cousteau/Mississippi, 1985; Cousteau/Rediscovery of the World, 1985–. *Publications:* Par 18 mètres de fond, 1946; La Plongée en Scaphandre, 1950; (with Frederic Dumas) The Silent World, 1953 (New York and London), first published in English, then in 21 other languages; (ed with James Dugan) Captain Cousteau's Underwater Treasury, 1959 (London); The Living Sea, 1963 (London); World Without Sun, 1965 (film awarded Oscar, 1966); (with P. Cousteau) The Shark, 1970; with P. Diolé: Life and Death in a Coral Sea, 1971; Diving for Sunken Treasure, 1971; The Whale: mighty monarch of the sea, 1972; Octopus and Squid, 1973; Galapagos, Titicaca, the Blue Holes: three adventures, 1973; The Ocean World of Jacques Cousteau (21 vol. encyclopedia), 1973; Diving Companions, 1974; Dolphins, 1975; Jacques Cousteau: the ocean world, 1979; The Cousteau Almanac, 1981; Jacques Cousteau's Calypso, 1983; (with Mose Richards) Jacques Cousteau's Amazon Journey, 1984; Jacques Cousteau: Whales, 1988; articles in National Geographical Magazine, 1952–66. *Address:* The Cousteau Society Inc., 870 Greenbrier Circle, Suite 402, Chesapeake, VA 23320–2641, USA.

COUTTS; *see* Money-Coutts.

COUTTS, Gordon; *see* Coutts, T. G.

COUTTS, Herbert, FSAScot; FMA; City Curator, City of Edinburgh Museums and Art Galleries, since 1973; *b* 9 March 1944; *s* of late Herbert and Agnes Coutts, Dundee; *m* 1970, Angela Elizabeth Mason Smith; one *s* three *d. Educ:* Morgan Acad., Dundee. FSAScot 1965; AMA 1970, FMA 1976. Asst Keeper of Antiquities and Bygones, Dundee City Museums, 1965–68, Keeper, 1968–71; Supt, Edinburgh City Museums, 1971–73. Vice Pres., Museums Assts Gp, 1967–70; Member: Bd, Scottish Museums Council, 1971–74, and 1986–88; Govt Cttee on Future of Scotland's National Museums and Galleries, 1979–80 (report publd 1981); Council, Museums Assoc., 1977–78, 1987–88; Council, Soc. of Antiquaries of Scotland, 1981–82; Museums Advr, COSLA Arts and Recreation Cttee, 1985–90. Member: Paxton House Trust, 1988–; E Lothian Community Develt Trust, 1989–. Building Projects: City of Edinburgh Art Centre (opened 1980); Museum of Childhood Extension (opened 1986); People's Story Museum (opened 1989); City of Edinburgh Art Centre Extension (opened 1992). Exhibitions at City of Edinburgh Art Centre: The Emperor's Warriors, 1985; Gold of the Pharaohs, 1988; Gold of Peru, 1990; Golden Warriors of the Ukrainian Steppes, 1993. Contested (Lab) Angus South, 1970. SBStJ 1977. *Publications:* Ancient Monuments of Tayside, 1970; Tayside Before History, 1971; Edinburgh: an illustrated history, 1975; Huntly House, 1980; Lady Stair's House, 1980; (ed) Gold of the Pharaohs, 1988; (ed) Dinosaurs Alive, 1990; (ed) Gold of Peru, 1990; (ed) Golden Warriors of the Ukrainian Steppes, 1993; exhibn catalogues; contrib. Museums Jl and archaeol jls. *Recreations:* relaxing with family, gardening, going to the opera, writing, reading, walking. *Address:* Kirkhill House, Queen's Road, Dunbar, East Lothian EH42 1LN. *T:* Dunbar (01368) 63113.

COUTTS, Ian Dewar, CBE 1982; in practice as chartered accountant, since 1950; Member, Forestry Commission, 1984–93; Director, Eastern Electricity plc, since 1990 (Member, Eastern Electricity Board, 1982–90); *b* 15 May 1927; *s* of David Dewar Coutts and Dorothy Helen Coutts; *m* 1st, 1950, Sheila Margaret Cargill (marr. diss. 1983); one *s* two *d*; 2nd 1983, Hilary Ballard; one *s* one *d. Educ:* Ipswich Sch.; Culford Sch. Chartered Accountant, 1949. Served 1st Essex Regt, 1946–48. Norfolk County Councillor, 1970–89; Leader, Norfolk CC, 1973–79. Chm., ACC Finance Cttee, 1977–83; Mem., Consultative Council on Local Govt Finance, 1977–83. Mem., Local Govt Audit Commn, 1983–90. Chm., S Norfolk Conservative Assoc., 1970–73; Parly Cand., Norwich S, 1979. Mem., Council, Univ. of East Anglia, 1974–86. *Recreation:* sailing. *Address:* Old Rectory, Little Ellingham, Attleborough, Norfolk NR17 1JN.

COUTTS, Prof. John Archibald; Professor of Jurisprudence in the University of Bristol, 1950–75, now Emeritus; Pro-Vice Chancellor, 1971–74; *b* 29 Dec. 1909; *e s* of Archibald and Katherine Jane Coutts; *m* 1940, Katherine Margaret Alldis; two *s. Educ:* Merchant Taylors', Crosby; Downing Coll., Cambridge (MA, LLB). Barrister Gray's Inn, 1933; lectured in Law: University Coll., Hull, 1934–35; King's Coll., London, 1935–36; Queen's Univ., Belfast, 1936–37; Trinity Coll., Dublin, 1937–50; Prof. of Laws, University of Dublin, 1944–50. Fellow, Trinity College, Dublin, 1944–50. Visiting Professor: Osgoode Hall Law Sch., Toronto, 1962–63; Univ. of Toronto, 1970–71, 1975–76. *Publications:* The Accused (ed); contributions to legal journals. *Address:* 22 Hurle Crescent, Clifton, Bristol BS8 2SZ. *T:* Bristol (0117) 973 6984.

COUTTS, T(homas) Gordon, QC (Scotland) 1973; *b* 5 July 1933; *s* of Thomas Coutts and Evelyn Gordon Coutts; *m* 1959, Winifred Katherine Scott, MLitt; one *s* one *d. Educ:* Aberdeen Grammar Sch.; Aberdeen Univ. (MA, LLB). Admitted Faculty of Advocates, 1959; Standing Junior Counsel to Dept Agric. (Scot.), 1965–73. Temporary Judge, Court of Session, Scotland, 1991–. Part-time Chairman: Industrial Tribunals, 1972–; Medical Appeal Tribunal, 1984–; VAT Tribunal, 1990–; Mem., Panel of Arbitrators, 1995. FCIArb 1994. *Recreations:* travel, golf, stamp collecting. *Address:* 6 Heriot Row, Edinburgh EH3 6HU. *Club:* New (Edinburgh).

COUTURE, Most Rev. Maurice; *see* Quebec, Archbishop of, (RC).

COUVE DE MURVILLE, Maurice; Commandeur de la Légion d'Honneur; Ambassadeur de France; Member of Senate, for Paris, since 1986; *b* 24 Jan. 1907; *m* 1932, Jacqueline Schweisguth; three *d. Educ:* Paris Univ. Inspecteur des finances, 1930; directeur des finances extérieures, 1940; membre du Comité français de la libération nationale (Alger), 1943; représentant de la France, Conseil consultatif pour l'Italie, 1944; Ambassador in Rome, 1945; directeur général des affaires politiques, Ministère des Affaires Etrangères, 1945–50; Ambassador in Egypt, 1950–54; French Permanent Rep., NATO, Sept. 1954–Jan. 1955; Ambassador in the US, 1955–56; Ambassador of France to the Federal Republic of Germany, 1956–58; Ministre des Affaires Etrangères, 1958–68, de l'Economie et des Finances, June–July 1968; Prime Minister of France, 1968–69; Deputy, French Nat. Assembly, Paris 8ème Arrondissement, 1973–86. *Publications:* Une Politique étrangère 1958–69, 1973; Le Monde en face, 1989. *Address:* 44 rue du Bac, 75007 Paris, France.

COUVE DE MURVILLE, Most Rev. Maurice Noël Léon; *see* Birmingham, Archbishop of, (RC).

COUZENS, Sir Kenneth (Edward), KCB 1979 (CB 1976); Chairman, Crédit Lyonnais Capital Markets, since 1991 (Director, since 1989); *b* 29 May 1925; *s* of Albert Couzens and May Couzens (*née* Biddlecombe); *m* 1947, Muriel Eileen Fey; one *s* one *d. Educ:* Portsmouth Grammar Sch.; Caius Coll., Cambridge. Inland Revenue, 1949–51; Treasury, 1951–68, and 1970–82; Civil Service Dept, 1968–70. Private Sec. to Financial Sec., Treasury, 1952–55, and to Chief Sec., 1962–63; Asst Sec., 1963–69; Under-Secretary: CSD, 1969–70; Treasury, 1970–73; Dep. Sec., Incomes Policy and Public Finance, 1973–77; Second Perm. Sec. (Overseas Finance), 1977–82; Perm. Under-Sec. of State, Dept of Energy, 1983–85. Dep. Chm., NCB, subseq. British Coal, 1985–88; Chm., Coal Products, 1988–92 (Dir, 1986–92). Chm., Monetary Cttee, European Community, 1982; Member: UK Adv. Bd, Nat. Econ. Res. Assocs, 1986–; Local Govt Commn, 1993–. *Address:* Coverts Edge, Woodsway, Oxshott, Surrey KT22 0ND. *T:* Oxshott (01372) 843207. *Club:* Reform.

COVACEVICH, Sir (Anthony) Thomas, Kt 1978; DFC 1943; Senior Partner, MacDonnells, Solicitors and Notaries Public, Cairns, Queensland, Australia, 1963–92 (Partner, 1939); *b* 1 March 1915; *s* of Prosper and Ellen Covacevich; *m* 1944, Gladys Rose (*née* Bryant); one *s* one *d. Educ:* Townsville and Brisbane Grammar Schools. Admitted Solicitor, Supreme Court of Queensland, 1938. Formerly Director of five publicly listed Australian companies, including Foxwood Ltd, a timber company (Chm.). *Recreation:* fishing. *Address:* 17 Temora Close, Edge Hill, Cairns, Queensland, Australia. *T:* (70) 300600; Box 5046, Cairns Mail Centre, Queensland 4870, Australia. *Clubs:* North Queensland (Townsville, Qld); Cairns Game Fishing (Cairns, Qld).

COVEN, Major Edwina Olwyn, CBE 1988; JP; DL; HM Lieutenant, City of London, since 1981; Director, Crockfords Plc, since 1993; *b* 23 Oct. 1921; *d* of Sir Samuel Instone, DL, and Lady (Alice) Instone; *m* 1951, Frank Coven, *qv. Educ:* Queen's Coll., London; St Winifred's, Ramsgate; Lycée Victor Duruy, Paris; Marlborough Gate Secretarial Coll., London (1st Cl. Business Diploma). Volunteered for Mil. Service, Private ATS; commnd ATS (subseq. WRAC); Army Interpreter (French); served UK and overseas, incl. staff appts, Plans and Policy Div., Western Union Defence Org. and NATO, Directorate Manpower Planning, WO, 1942–56. 1959–: Children's Writer, Fleetway Publications; Gen. Features Writer, National Magazine Co.; Reporter, BBC Woman's Hour; performer and adviser, children's and teenage progs, ITV. Mem. Adv. Council, Radio London (BBC), 1978–81. Dir, 1985–93, Dep. Chm., 1990–93, TV-am. Chm., Davbro Chemists, 1967–71; stores consultant on promotion and fashion, 1960–77; Mem., Women's Adv. Cttee (Clothing and Footwear Sub-Cttee), BSI, 1971–73. JP Inner London, North Westminster, 1965–72 (Dep. Chm., 1971–72); JP City of London Commn, 1969–88 (Dep. Chm., 1971–88); Greater London: DL 1987, Rep. DL Hammersmith and Fulham, 1989–94; Mem., Central Council Probation and After-Care Cttee, 1971; Chm., City of London Probation and After-Care Cttee, 1971–77; Chm, City of London Police Cttee, 1984–87 (Dep. Chm., 1983–84); Mem., Police Cttee, AMA, 1985–. Mem., Jt Cttee of Management, London Court of Internat. Arbitration 1983–89. Dowgate Ward, City of London: Court of Common Council, 1972–; elected Alderman, 1973 and 1974; Deputy, 1975–. Chief Commoner, City of London, 1987–88. Freedom, City of London, 1967; Mem., Guild of Freemen, City of London, 1971; Freeman, Loriners' Co., 1967; Liveryman, Spectacle Makers' Co., 1972; Hon. Liveryman, Lightmongers' Co., 1990. Member: Council, WRAC Assoc., 1973–90 (Vice Pres., 1984–88; Vice-Chm., 1985–89; Chm., 1989–90); TAVRA, City of London, 1979–86; Associated Speakers, 1975–; London Home Safety Council, 1980–84; Vice Chm., Cities of London and Westminster Home Safety Council, 1984–89; Vice President: Nat. Org. for Women's Management Educn, 1983–90; FANY, 1989–; Operation Raleigh, 1989–95; Chm., Cttee for Celebration of 800th Year of Mayoralty, Corp. of London, 1988–90. Member: Court, Sussex Univ., 1994–; Bd of Governors, City of London Sch., 1972–77; Chm., Bd of Governors, City of London Sch. for Girls, 1978–81; Mem., Royal Soc. of St George, 1972–; Chm., Vintry and Dowgate Wards Club, 1977. FRSA 1988. Hon. Captain of Police, Salt Lake City, 1986; Order of Wissam Alouite (Morocco), 1987. OStJ 1987. *Publication:* Tales of Oaktree Kitchen, 1959 (2nd edn 1960; adapted for ITV children's educnl series). *Recreations:* looking after much-loved husband and homemaking generally; lawn tennis; watching a variety of spectator sports. *Address:* 23 Tavistock, Devonshire Place, Eastbourne, Sussex BN21 4AG. *Clubs:* Queen's, Hurlingham; Devonshire (Eastbourne).

COVEN, Frank; London and European Director, The Nine Television Network of Australia, since 1974; *b* 26 April 1910; *s* of Isaac L. Coven and Raie Coven; *m* 1951, Edwina Coven (*née* Instone), *qv. Educ:* The Perse, Cambridge; France and Germany. Studied film prodn, UFA and EFA Studios, Berlin. TA (Ranks), 1938; War Service, 1939–45 (commnd 1941). Film admin and prodn, Gaumont British Studies, 1932; Studio Manager, Gainsborough Pictures, 1935; TV prodn, BBC/Daily Mail, 1937–38; Jt Dep. Organiser, Daily Mail Ideal Home Exhibition (radio, television, special features), 1945; Manager, Public Relations, Associated Newspapers, 1949; interviews, Wimbledon tennis commentaries, children's series "Write it Yourself" BBC TV, 1949–54 (subseq. ITV); TV Adviser, Bd of Associated Newspapers, 1953, Associated Rediffusion, 1954; London Rep., Television Corporation Ltd, Sydney, and Herald-Sun Pty, Melbourne, 1954; Dir, Compagnie Belge Transmarine SA and Imperial Stevedoring Co. SA, 1959; Head of Publicity and Promotions, Associated Newspapers, 1961; 1962: Dir, Associated Newspapers Gp; Dir, Bouverie Investments Ltd; Managing Director: Northcliffe Developments Ltd; Frank Coven Enterprises Ltd, presenting (with John Roberts) plays in London, incl. The Professor, How's the World Treating You? and, with London Traverse Theatre Co., works by Saul Bellow and others, 1964–69; Gen. Man., United Racecourses Ltd (Epsom, Sandown Park, Kempton Park), 1970, Man. Dir 1970, Vice-Chm. 1972. Mem., Variety Club of GB. Mem., Royal Soc. of St George, 1972. *Publications:* various Daily Mail Guides to Television Development in UK. *Recreations:* lawn tennis, swimming, study of varied media (current affairs). *Address:* 23 Tavistock, Devonshire Place, Eastbourne, Sussex BN21 4AG. *Clubs:* Saints and Sinners; Hurlingham, Queen's; Devonshire (Eastbourne).

COVENEY, Prof. James; Professor of French, University of Bath, 1969–85, now Professor Emeritus; *b* 4 April 1920; *s* of James and Mary Coveney; *m* 1955, Patricia Yvonne Townsend; two *s. Educ:* St Ignatius Coll., Stamford Hill, London; Univ. of Reading (BA, 1st Cl. hons French, 1950); Univ. of Strasbourg (Dr Univ. 1953). Served War of 1939–45: enlisted in ranks of The Welch Regt, 1940; commnd in Queen's Own Royal West Kent Regt, 1941; served subsequently as Pilot in RAF; Flt-Lt, 1945. Univ. of Strasbourg: French Govt Research Scholar, 1950–51; Lecteur d'anglais, 1951–53. Lectr in French, Univ. of Hull, 1953–58; Asst Dir of Exams (Mod. Langs), Civil Service Commn, 1958–59; UN Secretariat, New York, 1959–61; NATO Secretariat, 1961–64; University of Bath: Head of Mod. Langs Gp, 1964–68; Head of Sch. of Mod. Langs, 1969–77 and 1980–83. Visiting Professor: Ecole Nat. d'Administration, Paris, 1974–85; Univ. of Buckingham, 1974–86; Bethlehem Univ., 1985. Consultant, Univ. of Macau, 1988. Member: British-French Mixed Cultural Commn, 1973–79; Cttee of Management, British Inst. in Paris, 1975–79; Council, Fédération Britannique de l'Alliance Française, 1976–81; Exec. Cttee, Council for the Advancement of Arab-British Understanding, 1987–. Trustee, Friends of Birzeit Univ., 1991–. Corresp. Mem., Académie des Sciences, Agriculture, Arts et Belles Lettres, Aix-en-Provence, 1975. Chevalier de l'Ordre des Palmes Académiques, 1978. Officier de l'Ordre National du Mérite, 1986. *Publications:* La Légende de l'Empereur Constant, 1955; (with S. Moore) Glossary of French and English Management Terms,

1972; (with J. Grosjean) Le français pour l'ingénieur, 1974; (with C. Degens) Glossary of German and English Management Terms, 1977; (with J. Amey) Glossary of Spanish and English Management Terms, 1978; (with S. Kempa) Guide to French Institutions, 1978; (with J. Amey) English-Portuguese Business Dictionary, 1982; (with W. R. Ghali, S. Moore, H. G. Tabri) Dictionary of Management Terms in English-French-Arabic, 1990; (with S. Moore) Harrap's French Business Management Terms, 1993; (with D. Head) Harrap's German Business Management Terms, 1993; (with Hajime Takamizawa) Harrap's Japanese Business Management Terms, 1995; articles in British, French and American periodicals. *Address:* 40 Westfield Close, Bath BA2 2EB. *T:* Bath (01225) 316670. *Club:* Travellers'.

COVENEY, Michael William; theatre critic, The Observer, since 1990; *b* 24 July 1948; *s* of William Coveney and Violet Amy Coveney (*née* Perry); *m* 1977, Susan Monica Hyman; one *s*. *Educ:* St Ignatius College, London; Worcester College, Oxford. Editor, Plays and Players, 1975–78; theatre critic, Financial Times, 1981–89. *Publications:* The Citz, 1990; Maggie Smith, 1992; The Aisle is Full of Noises, 1994. *Recreations:* music, tennis, travel. *Address:* c/o The Observer, 119 Farringdon Road, EC1 3ER.

COVENTRY, family name of **Earl of Coventry.**

COVENTRY, 11th Earl of, *cr* 1697; **George William Coventry;** Viscount Deerhurst, 1697; *b* 25 Jan. 1934; *o s* of 10th Earl and Hon. Nesta Donne Philipps, *e d* of 1st Baron Kylsant; *S* father, 1940; *m* 1st, 1955, Marie Farquhar-Medart (marr. diss. 1963); one *s*; 2nd, 1969, Ann (marr. diss. 1975), *d* of F. W. J. Cripps, Bickley, Kent; 3rd, 1980, Valerie Anne Birch (marr. diss. 1988); 4th, 1992, Rachel Wynne, *d* of J. Mason. *Educ:* Eton; RMA, Sandhurst. *Heir: s* Viscount Deerhurst, *qv*. *Address:* Earls Croome Court, Earls Croome, Worcester WR8 9DE.
See also Earl of Harrowby.

COVENTRY, Bishop of, since 1985; **Rt. Rev. Simon Barrington-Ward;** Prelate of the Most Distinguished Order of St Michael and St George, since 1989; *b* 27 May 1930; *s* of Robert McGowan Barrington-Ward and Margaret Adele Barrington-Ward; *m* 1963, Jean Caverhill Taylor; two *d*. *Educ:* Eton; Magdalene Coll., Cambridge (MA; Hon. Fellow, 1987). Lektor, Free Univ., Berlin, 1953–54; Westcott House, Cambridge, 1954–56; Chaplain, Magdalene Coll., Cambridge, 1956–60; Asst Lectr in Religious Studies, Univ. of Ibadan, 1960–63; Fellow and Dean of Chapel, Magdalene Coll., Cambridge, 1963–69; Principal, Crowther Hall, Selly Oak Colls, Birmingham, 1969–74; Gen. Sec., CMS, 1975–85; Hon. Canon of Derby Cathedral, 1975–85; a Chaplain to the Queen, 1984–85. Chairman: Partnership for World Mission, 1986–; Internat. Affairs Cttee, Bd for Social Responsibility of Gen. Synod, 1987–. Pres., St John's Coll., Nottingham, 1987. FRAI. Hon. DD Wycliffe Coll., Toronto, 1984. *Publications:* contributor to: Christianity in Independent Africa (ed Fasholé Luke and others), 1978; Today's Anglican Worship (ed C. Buchanan), 1980; Renewal—An Emerging Pattern, by Graham Pulkingham and others, 1980; A New Dictionary of Christian Theology (ed Alan Richardson and John Bowden), 1983; Love Will Out (anthology of news letters), 1988; Christianity Today, 1988; The World's Religions, 1988; The Weight of Glory (ed D. W. Hardy and P. H. Sedgwick), 1991; Why God?, 1993; CMS Newsletter, 1975–85. *Address:* Bishop's House, Davenport Road, Coventry, W Midlands CV5 6PW.

COVENTRY, Archdeacon of; *see* Russell, Ven. H. I. L.

COVENTRY, Provost of; *see* Petty, Very Rev. J. F.

COVENTRY, Rev. John Seton, SJ; Master, St Edmund's House, Cambridge, 1976–85; *b* 21 Jan. 1915; *yr s* of late Seton and Annie Coventry, Barton-on-Sea, Hants. *Educ:* Stonyhurst; Campion Hall, Oxford. MA Oxon 1945. Entered Society of Jesus, 1932; ordained, 1947; Prefect of Studies, Beaumont, 1950; Rector, Beaumont, 1956–58; Provincial, English Province of Soc. of Jesus, 1958–64; Lectr in Theology, Heythrop Coll., 1965–76. *Publications:* Morals and Independence, 1946; The Breaking of Bread, 1950; Faith Seeks Understanding, 1951; The Life Story of the Mass, 1959; The Theology of Faith, 1968; Christian Truth, 1975; Faith in Jesus Christ, 1980; Reconciling, 1985; Our God Reigns, 1995. *Address:* 114 Mount Street, W1Y 6AH. *T:* 0171–493 7811.

COVILLE, Air Vice-Marshal Christopher Charles Cotton, CB 1995; Assistant Chief of Defence Staff, Operational Requirements (Air), since 1994; *b* 2 June 1945; *s* of Henry and Anna Coville; *m* 1967, Irene Johnson; one *s* two *d*. *Educ:* De La Salle Grammar Sch., Liverpool; RAF Coll., Cranwell. BA Open. Lightning Pilot and Instructor, 1969–73; Phantom Pilot and Instructor, 1973–78; Central Tactics and Trials Orgn, 1978–80; Personal Staff Officer to UK Mil. Rep., Brussels, 1981–83; OC Ops Wing, RAF Stanley, 1983; OC 111 Fighter Sqn, 1983–85; Gp Capt. Air, HQ 11 Fighter Group, 1985–86; OC RAF Coningsby, 1986–88; RCDS 1989; Air Cdre Flying Training, HQ RAF Support Command, 1990–92; AO Trng and AOC Trng Gp, 1992–94; Chief Exec., Trng Gp Defence Agency, Apr.–Sept. 1994. FIPD (FITD 1993); FRAeS 1994. *Recreations:* RAF Microlight Association (Pres.), mountaineering, shooting. *Address:* c/o Lloyds Bank, PO Box 1190, 7 Pall Mall, SW1Y 5NA. *Club:* Royal Air Force.

COVINGTON, Nicholas; Director, Office of Manpower Economics, 1986–89; *b* 9 June 1929; *s* of late Cyril Tim Covington and Margaret Joan (*née* Bray); *m* 1st, 1953, Patricia Sillitoe (marr. diss.); one *s* two *d*; 2nd, 1983, Kathleen Hegarty. *Educ:* Cranleigh Sch.; Oriel Coll., Oxford (BA). RAF, 1947–49. Metal Box Co. Ltd, 1952–57; Gen. Manager and Dir, Garnier & Co. Ltd, 1957–66; entered Min. of Labour, 1966; Asst Sec., 1971; Industrial Relns Div., Dept of Employment, 1976–86. *Recreations:* history, walking. *Address:* Dovecote House, Lower Slaughter, near Cheltenham, Glos GL54 2HY.

COWAN, Brig. Alan; *see* Cowan, Brig. J. A. C.

COWAN, Prof. Charles Donald, (Jeremy), CBE 1988; MA Cantab, PhD London; FRAS; Chairman of Convocation, University of London, 1990–94; *b* London, 18 Nov. 1923; *s* of W. C. Cowan and Minnie Ethel (*née* Farrow); *m* 1st, 1945, Mary Evelyn (marr. diss. 1960), *d* of Otto Vetter, Perth, WA; two *d*; 2nd, 1962, Daphne Eleanor, *d* of Walter Rishworth Whittam, Rangoon. *Educ:* Kilburn Grammar Sch.; Peterhouse, Cambridge. Served Royal Navy, 1941–45. Lecturer in History, Raffles Coll., Singapore, 1947–48, and University of Malaya, 1948–50; School of Oriental and African Studies, University of London: Lectr in the History of South-East Asia, 1950–60; Prof., 1961–80, Prof. of Oriental History, 1980–89; Dir, 1976–89; Pro-Vice-Chancellor, 1985–86, Dep. Vice-Chancellor, 1988–90, London Univ. Visiting Prof. of Southeast Asian Hist., Cornell Univ., 1960–61. Chm., Cttee for SEAsian Studies, British Acad., 1990–. Governor: James Allen's Girls School, 1977–89; Alleyn's Coll. of God's Gift, Dulwich, 1980–; Richmond Coll., 1988–92. *Publications:* Nineteenth Century Malaya, 1961; (ed) The Economic Development of South-East Asia, 1964; (ed) The Economic Development of China and Japan, 1964; (with P. L. Burns) Sir Frank Swettenham's Malayan Journals, 1975; (with O. L. Wolters) Southeast Asian History and Historiography, 1976. *Address:* University of London, Senate House, WC1E 7HU. *T:* 0171–636 8000.

COWAN, Brig. Colin Hunter, CBE 1984; Chief Executive, Cumbernauld Development Corporation, 1970–85; *b* 16 Oct. 1920; *s* of late Lt-Col S. Hunter Cowan, DSO and Mrs Jean Hunter Cowan; *m* 1st, 1949, Elizabeth Williamson, MD (*d* 1985); one *s* one *d* (and one *s* decd); 2nd, 1988, Mrs Jen Burnett, *widow* of A. H. Burnett. *Educ:* Wellington Coll.; RMA Woolwich; Trinity Coll., Cambridge (MA). MICE. Comd Engineer Regt, 1960–63; Defence Adviser, UK Mission to the UN, 1964–66; Brigadier Engineer Plans, MoD (Army), 1968–70. DL Dunbartonshire, 1973–88. *Recreations:* music, photography. *Address:* 12B Greenhill Gardens, Edinburgh EH10 4BW. *T:* 0131–447 9768. *Club:* New (Edinburgh).

COWAN, Maj.-Gen. George Osborne, OBE 1986; QHP 1993; FRCP, FRCPE; Commandant and Post-Graduate Dean, Royal Army Medical College, since 1993; *b* 5 Sept. 1939; *s* of late John Jardine Cowan and Marion Ramsay Cowan (*née* Corrie); *m* 1981, Beatrice Mary Hill, MA, MPhil, *d* of Leonard Charles Hill, OBE, DSC, FRGS and Joyce (*née* Snelus). *Educ:* Merchiston Castle Sch., Edinburgh; Univ. of St Andrews (MB ChB 1963). MRCPE 1967, FRCPE 1978; DTM&H 1968; MRCP 1967, FRCP 1983. Commissioned RAMC, 1963; served Australia, Hong Kong, Malaysia, Singapore, Nepal, The Gambia, Germany and NI; Consultant Physician in Army Hosps, 1973–; Prof. of Mil. Medicine, RAMC, 1987–92; Dir of Army Medicine, 1992–93. Hon. Associate Physician, Hosp. for Tropical Diseases, 1988–. Cohen Lectr, Univ. of Liverpool, 1991. Examr in Trop. Med. to Univ. of Liverpool and RCP. Pres., RSTM&H, 1995– (Vice-Pres., 1993–95). OStJ 1994. *Publications:* (ed) Atlas of Medical Helminthology and Protozoology, 3rd edn, 1991; (with B. J. Heap) Clinical Tropical Medicine, 1993; (with N. R. H. Burgess) Atlas of Medical Entomology, 1993. *Recreations;* golf, music, medical history. *Address:* Royal Army Medical College, Millbank, SW1P 4RJ. *T:* 0171–414 8200. *Club:* Royal & Ancient Golf (St Andrews).

COWAN, Brig. (James) Alan (Comrie), CBE 1992 (MBE 1956); Secretary, Government Hospitality Fund, 1980–93; *b* 20 Sept. 1923; *s* of late Alexander Comrie Cowan and Helen May Isobel (*née* Finlayson); *m* 1948, Jennifer Evelyn Bland; two *s* one *d*. *Educ:* Rugby Sch., Warwicks. Commnd Rifle Bde, 1942; served War, Italy and Egypt, 1942–46; served Army, 1947–60: OU Trng Corps, BAOR, Army Staff Coll., WO, Kenya and Malaya; DS, Army Staff Coll., 1961–63; CO 1 Royal Leicesters, later 4 Royal Anglian, UK, Aden and Malta, 1964–66; GSO1 17 Div., Malaysia, 1966–67; Col GS MoD, 1967–69; Comd 8 Inf. Bde, NI, 1970–71; DAG HQ UKLF, 1972–75; entered Civil Service and joined NI Office, with responsibility for industrial, economic and social affairs, 1975; Principal, 1975–78; Asst Sec., 1978–80. *Recreations:* current affairs, music, theatre, the countryside. *Address:* c/o C. Hoare & Co., 37 Fleet Street, EC4P 4DQ. *Clubs:* Army and Navy, MCC.

COWAN, James Robertson, CBE 1983 (OBE 1974); CEng, FIMinE; Chairman, NCB Coal Products, 1985–88; *b* 12 Sept. 1919; *s* of John and Jean Cowan; *m* 1945, Harriet Good Forrest; two *d*. *Educ:* Dalziel High Sch., Motherwell; Glasgow Univ. (BSc 1st Cl. Hons). CEng, FIMinE 1971. National Coal Board: Dir, Scottish Area, 1970–80; Bd Mem., 1977–85; Mem. for Industrial Relns, 1980–85; Dep. Chm., 1982–85. Chm., Scottish Brick Corp., 1980–88 (Dir, 1974–88); Dep. Chm., British Investment Trust (Dir, 1978–). Vis. Prof., Strathclyde Univ., 1978. CIMgt. *Recreation:* golf. *Address:* 31 Muirfield Park, Gullane, Scotland EH31 2DY. *T:* Gullane (01620) 843398. *Club:* Caledonian.

COWAN, Jeremy; *see* Cowan, C. D.

COWAN, Lionel David, (Nick Cowan); personnel management consultant; *b* 18 Dec. 1929; *m* 1953, Pamela Ida, *e d* of Hubert and Winifred Williams, Totton, Hants; one *s* two *d*. *Educ:* Surbiton County Grammar Sch.; King's Coll., London (BA Hons Spanish); Univ. of Salamanca. FIMgt (FBIM 1972); FIPD (CIPM 1979; AMIPM 1965). Served Royal Navy, 1945–61: Fleet Air Arm Aircrew (Lieut), 1953; Sen. Instr, RAN, 1958–60. Training Officer, Shoe and Allied Trades Res. Assoc., 1961–62; Perkins Engines Gp, 1962–72 (Dir of Personnel and Industrial Relns 1970–72); Dir of Personnel, Philips Electronic and Associated Industries, 1972–78; Gp Personnel Dir, Unigate Ltd, 1978–79; Dir and Sec., Fedn of London Clearing Bank Employers, 1980–87; Personnel Dir, TSB England & Wales, 1987–89. Chm., W Lambeth HA, 1982–86; Member: Editorial Panel, Personnel Management, 1967–91; BIM Adv. Bd on Industrial Relations, 1970–75; Employment Relns Cttee, IPM, 1971–81; Council, Independent Res. and Assessment Centre, 1975–89; Engrg Industry Trng Bd, 1976–79; Employment Appeal Tribunal, 1976–; Editorial Panel, Industrial Relns Law Reports, 1977–; Employment Policy Cttee, CBI, 1978–89; Civil Service Arbitration Tribunal, 1979–; CBI Council, 1980–87; Central Arbitration Cttee, 1984–; Youth Training Bd, 1984–85; Equal Opportunities Commn, 1988–91; NEDO Enquiry, Industrial Relns Trng for Managers, 1976, Supply and Demand for Skilled Manpower, 1977. Vice-Pres. (Employee Relations), IPM, 1977–79. Director, Oxford Univ. Business Summer Sch., 1980. Lecturer and writer on personnel management and industrial relations. *Publications:* Personnel Management and Banking, 1984; The Clearing Banks and the Trade Unions, 1984; numerous articles, papers and other pubns on various aspects of personnel management and industrial relations. *Recreations:* things Spanish, music and opera, bridge. *Address:* 15 Somerville Road, Cobham, Surrey KT11 2QT. *T:* Oxshott (01372) 843441. *Club:* Naval and Military.

COWAN, Lt-Gen. Samuel, CBE 1988 (OBE 1983); Inspector General Training, Ministry of Defence, since 1995; *b* 9 Oct. 1941; *s* of late Samuel Cowan and Rachel Cowan; *m* 1971, Anne Gretton; one *s* one *d*. *Educ:* Lisburn Technical Coll.; Open Univ. (BA). Commissioned Royal Signals, 1963; CO 2 Armd Div. HQ and Signal Regt, 1980–82; Comdr Communications and Comdr 1 Signal Brigade, 1 (BR) Corps, 1985–87; Director of Public Relations (Army), 1987–88; Comdt, RMCS, 1989–91; ACDS OR (Land), 1991–94. Dep. Col Comdt, Adjutant General's Corps, 1993–; Colonel Comdt, Brigade of Gurkhas, 1994–. *Recreations:* sport, trekking in Nepal. *Address:* c/o RHQ Royal Signals, 56 Regency Street, SW1P 4AD. *T:* 0171–414 8422. *Club:* Army and Navy.

COWAN, William Graham, MBE 1943; Chairman, J. H. Carruthers & Co. Ltd, since 1981 (Managing Director, 1981–84); *b* 29 April 1919; *s* of William Cowan, WS, Edinburgh, and Dorothy Isobel Horsbrugh; *m* 1st, 1960, Karen Wendell Hansen (marr. diss. 1991), Crestwood, NY; two *s* one *d*; 2nd, 1994, Ann, *d* of Col Noel Carrington Smith and *widow* of G. L. B. Mundell. *Educ:* Edinburgh Academy; Cambridge Univ. (MA). CEng, FIMechE, FCSD, FSA(Scot), FRSA. Served 1940–46, Royal Engrs and Gen. Staff, Africa, Italy (Lt-Col). Asst Man. Dir, North British Locomotive Co. Ltd, 1947–50; Man. Dir, J. H. Carruthers and Co. Ltd, 1950–79. Dir, Glasgow Sch. of Art, 1979–82. Mem. Exec. Cttee, Scottish Council (Develt and Industry), 1972–74; Pres., Scottish Engrg Employers' Assoc., 1972. Member: Design Council, 1974–78 (Chm., Scottish Cttee, 1976–78); Council, Nat. Trust for Scotland, 1984–89; Dir, Scottish Transport Group, 1977–80. *Address:* The Old Inn, Fowlis Wester, Perthshire PH7 3NL. *T:* Madderty (01764) 683319. *Club:* New (Edinburgh).

COWAN, Dr William Maxwell, FRS 1982; Vice President and Chief Scientific Officer, Howard Hughes Medical Insitute, since 1988; *b* 27 Sept. 1931; *s* of Adam Cowan and Jessie Sloan Cowan (*née* Maxwell); *m* 1956, Margaret Sherlock; two *s* one *d*. *Educ:* Univ. of the Witwatersrand, S Africa (BSc Hons); Hertford Coll., Oxford Univ. (MA, DPhil, BM, BCh). University Lecturer in Anatomy, Oxford, 1958–66; Fellow of Pembroke

Coll., Oxford, 1958–66 (Hon. Fellow, 1986); Associate Prof., Univ. of Wisconsin, 1966–68; Washington University, St Louis: Professor and Head of Dept of Anatomy, Sch. of Medicine, 1968–80; Director, Div. of Biological Sciences, 1975–80; Salk Institute for Biological Studies: non-resident Fellow, 1977–80; Professor, 1980–86; Vice Pres. and Dir, Develt Neurobiol., 1980–86; Provost and Exec. Vice-Chancellor, Washington Univ., St Louis, 1986–87. Mem., Amer. Philosophical Soc., 1987. Fellow, Amer. Acad. of Arts and Scis, 1975; For. Mem., Norwegian Acad. of Scis, 1980; Foreign Associate: US National Academy of Sciences, 1981; Royal Soc. of S Africa, 1986. Hon. Fellow, Pembroke Coll., Oxford, 1986. *Publications:* The Use of Axonal Transport for Studies of Neuronal Connectivity, 1975; Aspects of Cellular Neurobiology, 1978; Studies in Developmental Neurobiology, 1981; Annual Reviews of Neuroscience, Vol. 1 1978, Vols 2–18, 1979–94. *Recreations:* photography, reading, travel. *Address:* Howard Hughes Medical Institute, 4000 Jones Bridge Road, Chevy Chase, MD 20815, USA. *T:* (301) 2158803.

COWARD, David John, CMG 1965; OBE 1962; Registrar General, Kenya, 1955–82; *b* 21 March 1917; *s* of late Robert J. Coward, Exmouth, Devon; *m* 1954, Joan, *d* of late Reginald Frank, Doncaster; three *d. Educ:* Exmouth Grammar Sch. and Law Society's Sch. of Law. FCIS 1961; ACIArb 1984. Admitted a solicitor, 1938. Joined RN as a rating at outbreak of war, 1939; commissioned, 1941; demobilized as Lieut-Comdr (S) RNVR, 1947. ADC to Governor of Trinidad, 1947. Joined Colonial Legal Service, 1948, Asst Registrar Gen., Kenya; Dep. Registrar Gen., 1952; Registrar Gen., Official Receiver and Public Trustee, 1955–82. Acted as Permanent Sec. for Justice and Constitutional Affairs, 1963–64. Served in Kenya Police Reserve, 1949–63, latterly as Senior Superintendent i/c Nairobi Area. Chm., Working Party on future of Company Secretarial Profession in Kenya; Mem. Accountants' Registration Bd, 1978–82; Trustee, Nat. Museums of Kenya, 1979–82. Chm., Storrington Br., Royal British Legion, 1993–. Liveryman, Chartered Secretaries' and Administrators' Co., 1985–. Silver Medal, Internat. Olympic Cttee, 1981. *Recreations:* golf, genealogy. *Address:* North Perretts, Spinney Lane, West Chiltington, W Sussex RH20 2NX. *T:* Storrington (01903) 742521. *Clubs:* Naval; Nairobi and Limuru Country (Kenya).

COWARD, Vice Adm. Sir John (Francis), KCB 1990; DSO 1982; Lieutenant Governor and Commander-in-Chief of Guernsey, Channel Islands, since 1994; *b* 11 Oct. 1937; *s* of Reginald John Coward and Isabelle (*née* Foreman); *m* 1963, Diana (*née* Taylor); two *s. Educ:* Downside; RNC, Dartmouth. Served submarines, 1959–76, i/c HMS Oracle and HMS Valiant; Naval Asst to First Sea Lord, 1978–80; i/c HMS Brilliant, 1980–82; S Atlantic, 1982; Dir, Naval Operational Requirements, 1984; Flag Officer: Sea Trng, 1987–88; Flotilla One, 1988–89; Submarines, and Comdr Submarines Eastern Atlantic, 1989–91; Comdt, RCDS, 1992–94. Rear Adm. 1987; Vice Adm. 1989; retd 1994. Younger Brother, Trinity Hse. *Recreations:* sailing, gardening, golf. *Clubs:* Royal Navy of 1765 and 1785, Sloane; Royal Naval Sailing Association; Royal Yacht Squadron.

COWARD, John Stephen, QC 1984; barrister-at-law; a Recorder of the Crown Court, since 1980; *b* 15 Nov. 1937; *s* of Frank and Kathleen Coward; *m* 1967, Ann Lesley Pye; four *d. Educ:* King James Grammar Sch., Almondbury, Huddersfield; University Coll. London (LLB). Lecturer in Law and Constitutional History, University Coll. London and Police Staff Coll., 1962–64; called to the Bar, Inner Temple, 1964; in practice on Midland and Oxford Circuit, 1964–. *Recreation:* trying to grow calceolarias and a decent row of peas. *Address:* The Grange, Scaldwell, Northampton NN6 9JP. *T:* Northampton (01604) 880255. *Club:*Scaldwell (Scaldwell, Northants).

COWARD, Richard Edgar; retired; Director for Library Planning, OCLC Inc., 1980–81; *b* 1927; *s* of Edgar Frank Coward and Jean (*née* McIntyre); *m* 1949, Audrey Scott Lintern; one *s* two *d. Educ:* Richmond Grammar Sch., Surrey. FLA. Dir Gen., Bibliographic Servs Div., British Library, 1975–79. Member: Adv. Cttee on BBC Archives, 1976–79; Library Adv. Council (England), 1976–. *Address:* Gaios, Paxos, Greece; 12 Marylebone Mews, W1M 7LF. *T.* 0171–486 7316.

COWBURN, Norman; Chairman, Britannia Building Society, 1987–90 (Managing Director, 1970–84; Deputy Chairman, 1986–87); *b* 5 Jan. 1920; *s* of Harold and Edith Cowburn; *m* 1945, Edna Margaret Heatley; two *s* one *d. Educ:* Queen Elizabeth's Grammar Sch., Blackburn. FCIS, FBS. Burnley Building Soc., 1936. Served War, 1940–46. Burnley Building Soc., 1946; Leek and Westbourne Building Soc., 1954 (re-named Britannia Building Soc., Dec. 1975). *Recreations:* golf, gardening. *Address:* Greywoods, Birchall, Leek, Staffs. *T:* Leek (01538) 383214.

COWDEROY, Brenda; General Secretary, Girls' Friendly Society, 1978–85; *b* 27 June 1925; *o c* of late Frederick Cowderoy and of Evelyn Cowderoy (*née* Land). *Educ:* Surbiton High Sch.; St Hugh's Coll., Oxford (MA). Called to Bar, Gray's Inn, 1949. John Lewis Partnership: Asst Legal Adviser, 1954–56; Head of Legal Dept, 1956–70; Nat. Gen. Sec., YWCA, 1971–77. *Recreations:* gardens, golf. *Address:* 26 Rossetti Road, Birchington, Kent CT7 9ER. *Club:* Commonwealth Trust.

COWDRAY, 4th Viscount, *cr* 1917; **Michael Orlando Weetman Pearson;** Bt 1894; Baron 1910; *b* 17 June 1944; *s* of 3rd Viscount Cowdray and of his 1st wife, Lady Anne Pamela Bridgeman, *d* of 5th Earl of Bradford; *S* father, 1995; *m* 1st, 1977, Ellen (marr. diss. 1984), *d* of Hermann Erhardt; 2nd, 1987, Marina Rose, *d* of John H. Cordle, *qv*, and of Mrs H. J. Ross Skinner; one *s* three *d. Educ:* Gordonstoun. *Recreations:* classic motor rallies, pistol shooting. *Heir: s* Hon. Peregrine John Dickinson Pearson, *b* 27 Oct. 1994. *Club:* White's.

COWDREY, Sir Colin; *see* Cowdrey, Sir M. C.

COWDREY, Rev. Herbert Edward John, FBA 1991; Emeritus Fellow, St Edmund Hall, Oxford, since 1994 (Senior Research Fellow in Modern History, 1987–94); *b* 29 Nov. 1926; *s* of Herbert and Winifred Cowdrey; *m* 1959, Judith Watson Davis; one *s* two *d. Educ:* Queen Mary's Sch., Basingstoke; Trinity Coll., Oxford (BA Modern Hist. and Theology, 1951; MA); St Stephen's House, Oxford. Nat. service, RN, 1945–47. Deacon, 1952; priest, 1953; Tutor and Chaplain, St Stephen's House, Oxford, 1952–56; Fellow and Tutor in Modern History, St Edmund Hall, Oxford, 1956–87. *Publications:* The Cluniacs and the Gregorian Reform, 1970; The Epistolae vagantes of Pope Gregory VII, 1972; Two Studies in Cluniac History, 1978; The Age of Abbot Desiderius, 1983; Popes, Monks and Crusaders, 1984; articles and reviews in learned jls. *Recreations:* travel, listening to music, gardening. *Address:* 30 Oxford Road, Old Marston, Oxford OX3 0PQ. *T:* Oxford (01865) 243360.

COWDREY, Sir (Michael) Colin, Kt 1992; CBE 1972; Chairman, International Cricket Council, 1989–93; Consultant: Barclays Bank PLC; BZW; *b* 24 Dec. 1932; *s* of Ernest Arthur Cowdrey and Kathleen Mary Cowdrey (*née* Taylor), BEM; *m* 1956, Penelope Susan Cowdrey (*née* Chiesman) (marr. diss. 1985); three *s* one *d*; *m* 1985, Lady Herries of Terregles, *qv. Educ:* Homefield, Sutton, Surrey; Tonbridge; Brasenose Coll., Oxford. Cricket: 5 years Tonbridge Sch. XI (Capt., 1949–50); Public Schs (Lord's) (Capt. 1950); (3 years) Oxford XI (Capt. 1954); Kent Cap, 1951 (Captain, 1957–71); 117 appearances for England, 1954–75; Capt. 23 times; 11 Overseas Tours; 107 centuries in first class cricket, of which 22 were Test centuries; on retirement in 1975, held record for most runs and most catches in Test Matches. Runner-up Amateur Rackets Title, Queen's Club, 1953 and Doubles, 1965. Chm., Internat. Cricket Conf., 1986–87. Mem. Council, Winston Churchill Meml Trust, 1969–88. Mem. Council, Britain Australia Soc. Master, Skinners' Co., 1985; Freeman, City of London, 1962. *Publications:* Cricket Today, 1961; Time for Reflection, 1962; Tackle Cricket This Way, 1969; The Incomparable Game, 1970; MCC: the Autobiography of a Cricketer, 1976. *Recreation:* golf. *Address:* Angmering Park, Littlehampton, W Sussex BN16 4EX. *T:* Patching (01903) 871423. *Clubs:* MCC (Mem. Cttee; Pres., 1986–87), Boodle's; Royal & Ancient Golf.

COWE, (Robert George) Collin; Fellow and Senior Bursar, Magdalen College, Oxford, 1970–80; *b* 24 Sept. 1917; *s* of Peter and Annie Cowe, Berwick-upon-Tweed; *m* 1943, Gladys May, *d* of William Greenwood Wright and Jessie Wright, Bingley, Yorks; one *d. Educ:* The Duke's Sch., Alnwick; The Grammar Sch., Berwick-upon-Tweed; Edinburgh Univ. MA (Hons Classics) 1939; MA Oxon, 1970. Served Royal Regiment of Artillery, Field Branch, 1939–46; Major, RA, 1944–46; Instructor in Gunnery, Sch. of Artillery, UK, and CMF, 1943–46. National Coal Board, 1947–70; Private Sec. to Chm., 1947–49; Principal Private Sec. to Chm., 1949–52; Sec., East Midlands Div., 1952–55; Staff Dir, North-Eastern Div., 1955–58; Dep.-Sec. to NCB, 1958–59; Sec., 1960–67; Man. Dir, Associated Heat Services Ltd (associate co. of NCB), 1967–69. Mem., Advisory Council, BBC Radio Oxford, 1985–88. *Recreation:* listening to overseas broadcasts, especially BBC World Service. *Address:* Brookside Cottage, Brook End, Chadlington, Oxford OX7 3NF. *T:* Chadlington (01608) 676025.

COWELL, John Richard; Secretary, Royal Horticultural Society, 1975–88; *b* 30 April 1933; *er s* of late Frank Richard Cowell, CMG, PhD, and Lilian Margaret (*née* Palin); *m* 1972, Josephine Suzanne Elizabeth, *d* of I.A.F. Craig, Nun Monkton, Yorks; two *s* one *d. Educ:* Westminster Sch.; Trinity Coll., Cambridge (MA). Secretariat: London Chamber of Commerce, 1957–58; Royal Horticultural Soc., 1958–88. Mem. Council, London Children's Flower Soc., 1988–. *Recreations:* gardening, fishing. *Address:* The Old House, Boreham Street, near Hailsham, E Sussex BN27 4SF. *T:* Herstmonceux (01323) 832128. *Club:* Athenæum.

COWELL, Prof. Raymond; Vice-Chancellor, The Nottingham Trent University, since 1992 (Director and Chief Executive, Nottingham Polytechnic (formerly Trent Polytechnic Nottingham), 1988–92); *b* 3 Sept. 1937; *s* of Cecil Cowell and Susan Cowell (*née* Green); *m* 1963, Sheila (*née* Bolton); one *s* one *d. Educ:* St Aidan's Grammar Sch., Sunderland; Bristol Univ. (BA, PhD); Cambridge Univ. (PGCE). Head of English, Nottingham Coll. of Educn, 1970–73; Dean of Humanities 1974–81, Dep. Rector 1981–87, Sunderland Polytechnic. Member: CNAA, 1974–77 and 1981–85; Unit for Develt of Adult and Continuing Educn, 1986–90; British Council Cttee for Internat. Co-op. in Higher Educn, 1990–; Bd, Greater Nottingham TEC, 1990–93; Directing Gp, Prog. on Instnl Management in Higher Educn, OECD, 1990–; Council, NCVQ, 1991–; Bd, Higher Educn Business Enterprise, 1993–; Policy Liaison Gp, Open Learning Foundn, 1993–. Chairman: Staff and Educnl Develt Assoc., 1993–; CVCP working gp on vocational higher educn, 1993–; Management Bd and Members Adv. Gp, Univs Staff Develt Unit, 1993–. Mem. Bd, Nottingham City Challenge, 1992–93. *Publications:* Twelve Modern Dramatists, 1967; W. B. Yeats, 1969; (ed) Richard II, 1969; Critics on Yeats, 1971; Critics on Wordsworth, 1973; The Critical Enterprise, 1975; articles and reviews on higher education. *Recreations:* books, music, theatre. *T:* Nottingham (0115) 941 8418. *Club:* Athenæum.

COWEN, Rt. Hon. Sir Zelman, AK 1977; GCMG 1977 (CMG 1968); GCVO 1980; Kt 1976; PC 1981; QC; Provost of Oriel College, Oxford, 1982–90; Pro-Vice-Chancellor, University of Oxford, 1988–90; Director, John Fairfax Holdings Ltd, since 1992 (Chairman, 1992–94); *b* 7 Oct. 1919; *s* of late Bernard and of Sara Cowen; *m* 1945, Anna Wittner; three *s* one *d. Educ:* Scotch Coll., Melbourne; Univ. of Melbourne; New and Oriel Colls, Oxford. BA 1939, LLB 1941, LLM 1942, Melbourne; BCL, MA 1947, DCL 1968, Oxford. Lieut, RANVR, 1941–45. Called to Bar, Gray's Inn, 1947; Hon. Bencher, 1978; called to Vic (Aust.) Bar, 1951, Queensland Bar, 1971; QC 1972. Victorian Rhodes Schol., 1941; Vinerian Schol., Oxford Univ., 1947. Fellow and Tutor, Oriel Coll., Oxford, 1947–50, Hon. Fellow 1977; Prof. of Public Law and Dean of Faculty of Law, Univ. of Melbourne, 1951–66; Dominion Liaison Officer to Colonial Office (UK), 1951–66; Prof. Emer., Univ. of Melbourne, 1967; Vice-Chancellor and Professor, Univ. of New England, Armidale, NSW, 1967–70; Vice-Chancellor, Qld Univ., 1970–77; Governor-General of Australia, 1977–82. Visiting Professor: Univ. of Chicago, 1949; Harvard Law Sch. and Fletcher Sch. of Law and Diplomacy, 1953–54 and 1963–64; Univ. of Utah, 1954; Univ. of Illinois, 1957–58; Washington Univ., St Louis, 1959; Tagore Law Prof., Univ. of Calcutta, 1975; Menzies Schol. in Res., Univ. of Va, 1983; Lee Kuan Yew Dist. Vis. Fellow, Singapore, 1986; Dist. Vis. Prof., Victoria Univ. of Technol., 1994–. Broadcaster on radio and TV on nat. and internat. affairs; Mem. and Chm., Victorian State Adv. Cttee of Australian Broadcasting Commn (at various times during 1950's and 1960's); Mem., Chief Justice's Law Reform Cttee, 1951–66; President: Asthma Foundn of Victoria, 1963–66; Adult Educn Assoc. of Australia, 1968–70; Aust. Inst. of Urban Studies, 1973–77; Mem., Law Reform Commn, Australia, 1976–77; Chairman: Aust. Vice-Chancellors' Cttee, 1977; Aust. Studies Centre Cttee, London, 1982–90; Nat Council, Australian Opera, 1983–; Press Council, 1983–88; Trustees, Visnews Ltd, 1986–91; Victoria League for Commonwealth Friendship, 1987–89. Mem., Club of Rome, 1974–77. National President: Order of Australia Assoc. Ltd, 1992–95; Australia–Britain Soc., 1993–. Academic Governor, Bd of Governors, Hebrew Univ. of Jerusalem, 1969–77, 1982–; Mem., Academic Bd of Govrs, Tel Aviv Univ., 1983–; Weizmann Inst., 1988–. Trustee: Van Leer Inst. of Jerusalem, 1985– (Chm. Trustees, 1988–); Winston Churchill Meml Trust, 1987–89; Sir Robert Menzies Meml Trust, 1987–; Dir, Sir Robert Menzies Meml Foundn Ltd, 1990–. For. Hon. Mem., Amer. Acad. of Arts and Scis, 1965. FRSA 1971; Hon. FASSA 1977; Hon. FACE 1978; Hon. FRAIA 1978; Hon. FTS 1979; Hon. FRACP 1979; Hon. FAHA 1980; Hon. FASA 1980; Hon. FRACMA 1981; Hon. FRACOG 1981; Hon. FCA 1981; Hon. FACRM 1982; Hon. Fellow: New Coll. Oxford 1978; University House, ANU, 1978; ANZAAS 1983; TCD, 1985; St John's Coll., Univ. of Qld, 1985; Australian Council of Educnl Admin, 1991. Hon. Law Prof., Griffith Univ., Qld, 1992. Hon. LLD: Hong Kong, 1967; Queensland, 1972; Melbourne, 1973; Western Australia, 1981; Turin, 1981; ANU, 1985; Tasmania, 1990; Hon. DLitt: New England, 1979; Sydney, 1980; James Cook Univ. of N Qld, 1982; Oxford, 1983; Hon. DHL: Hebrew Union Coll., Cincinnati, 1980; Redlands Univ., Calif., 1986; DUniv: Newcastle, 1980; Griffith, 1981; Hon. DPhil: Hebrew Univ. of Jerusalem, 1982; Tel Aviv, 1985. KStJ (A) 1977. Kt Grand Cross, Order of Merit (Italy), 1990. *Publications:* (ed jtly) Dicey's Conflict of Laws, 1949; Australia and the United States: Some Legal Comparisons, 1954; (with P. B. Carter) Essays on the Law of Evidence, 1956; American-Australian Private International Law, 1957; Federal Jurisdiction in Australia, 1959; (with D. M. da Costa) Matrimonial Causes Jurisdiction, 1961; Sir John Latham and other papers, 1965; British Commonwealth of Nations in a Changing World, 1964; Isaac Isaacs, 1967; The Private Man, 1969; Individual Liberty and the Law, 1977; The Virginia Lectures, 1984; Reflections on Medicine, Biotechnology, and the Law, 1986; A Touch of Healing, 1986; articles and chapters in legal works in UK, US, Canada, Germany, Australia. *Recreations:* swimming, music, performing and visual arts. *Address:* Commonwealth Offices, 4 Treasury Place, East Melbourne, Vic 3002, Australia. *Clubs:* United Oxford & Cambridge University; Queensland (Brisbane); Pioneer (Sydney).

COWEY, Prof. Alan, PhD; FRS 1988; Professor of Physiological Psychology, and Professorial Fellow of Lincoln College, University of Oxford, since 1981; Director, Oxford Research Centre in Brain and Behaviour, since 1991; *b* 28 April 1935; *s* of Harry and Mary Cowey; *m* 1959, Patricia Leckonby; three *d. Educ:* Bede Grammar Sch., Sunderland; Emmanuel Coll., Cambridge (MA, PhD). Rockefeller Foundn Fellow, Center for Brain Research, Univ. of Rochester, New York, 1961–62; Univ. Demonstrator in Experimental Psychology, Cambridge, 1962–67; Fellow and Coll. Tutor, Emmanuel Coll., Cambridge, 1964–67; Vis. Sen. Fulbright Fellow, Psychology Dept, Harvard Univ., 1967; Sen. Res. Officer, Inst. of Experimental Psychology, Univ. of Oxford, 1967–68; Nuffield Sen. Res. Fellow, Lincoln Coll., Oxford, 1968–81; Henry Head Res. Fellow of Royal Society, 1968–73; Reader in Physiolog. Psychology, Oxford Univ., 1973–81. Member: MRC Neurosciences Grants Cttee, 1974–77 (Chm., 1979–81); MRC Neurosciences Board, 1979–83 (Chm., 1981–83); Mem. Council, MRC, 1981–85. President: European Brain and Behaviour Soc., 1986–88; Experimental Psychology Soc., 1990–92. Spearman Medal, British Psychological Soc., 1967. *Publications:* numerous articles in psychological and physiological jls. *Recreations:* squash, swimming, reading. *Address:* Department of Experimental Psychology, South Parks Road, Oxford OX1 3UD. *T:* Oxford (01865) 271351.

COWEY, Brig. Bernard Turing Vionnée, DSO 1945; OBE 1976; DL; *b* 20 Nov. 1911; *s* of late Lt-Col R. V. Cowey, DSO, RAMC and late Mrs B. A. Cowey (*née* Blancke); *m* 1947, Margaret Heath Dean (*née* Godwin) (*d* 1994). *Educ:* Wellington; RMC Sandhurst. Commnd The Welch Regt, 1931; served War of 1939–45: N Africa, 1939–41 (despatches 1941); psc 1941; India, 1942–43; Burma, 1944–45; CO 2 York and Lancs, 1944; CO 2 Welch, 1945–47; Co. Comdr RMA Sandhurst, 1947–49; Chief Instructor, Staff Coll., Quetta, 1952–53; CO 1 Welch, 1953–56; Comd (Brig.) 9 Indep. Armd Bde Gp TA, 1956 and 148 Inf. Bde Gp TA, 1956–58; Inspector of Intelligence, 1961–63; retd 1963. Sec., Notts T&AFA, 1965–67; TAVR Council (formerly TA Council): Dep. Sec., 1967–72; Sec., 1973–75. Regional Organiser, Army Benevolent Fund, 1975–91; Regional Sec., British Field Sports Soc., 1976–83. DL Notts, 1973. *Recreations:* Rugby football (played for Wales, Barbarians and Army, 1934–35; Chm., Army Rugby Union Referees Soc., 1963–73); Arab horses (Hon. Show Dir, Arab Horse Show, 1968–81). *Address:* East Leake Hall, near Loughborough, Leics LE12 6LQ. *T:* East Leake (01509) 854009. *Clubs:* Army and Navy, British Sportsman's.

COWGILL, Bryan; television producer; *b* 27 May 1927; *m* 1966, Jennifer E. Baker; two *s. Educ:* Clitheroe Grammar School. Marine, subseq. Lieut, 3rd Royal Marine Commando Bde, SE Asia, 1943–47. Copy boy, then reporter, then feature writer with Lancashire Evening Post and Preston Guardian Group, 1942–50; edited local newspaper, Clitheroe, 1950–55; joined BBC TV as Outside Broadcasts prodn asst, 1955; produced Sportsview and Grandstand, 1957–63; Head of BBC Sport, 1963; founder, Match of the Day, 1964, Sportsnight, 1968; coined phrase 'action replay' for slow motion video, first introd. in BBC World Cup coverage, 1966; Head of TV Outside Broadcasts Group, 1972; Controller, BBC1, 1974–77; Dir, News and Current Affairs, BBC, 1977; Man. Dir, Thames Television, 1977–85; Dep. Chm., Mirror Gp Newspapers, 1986–87; Man. Dir, Championship Television, 1989–90. Chairman: Euston Films, 1977–85; Cosgrove Hall Productions, 1977–85; Thames Television Internat., 1982–85; WTN (formerly UPITN), 1983–85; Thames Cable and Satellite Services, 1984–85. FRTS 1984. *Recreation:* golf. *Address:* Nethergill Barn, Bolton-by-Bowland, Clitheroe, Lancs BB7 4NW.

COWIE, Hon. Lord; William Lorn Kerr Cowie; a Senator of the College of Justice in Scotland, 1977–94; *b* 1 June 1926; *s* of late Charles Rennie Cowie, MBE and Norah Slimmon Kerr; *m* 1958, Camilla Henrietta Grizel Hoyle; two *s* two *d. Educ:* Fettes Coll.; Clare Coll., Cambridge; Glasgow Univ. Sub-Lieut RNVR, 1944–47; Cambridge, 1947–49; Glasgow Univ., 1949–51; Mem., Faculty of Advocates, 1952; QC (Scotland) 1967. *Address:* 20 Blacket Place, Edinburgh EH9 1RL. *T:* 0131–667 8238. *Clubs:* New (Edinburgh); Royal Scottish Automobile (Glasgow).

COWIE, Mervyn Hugh, CBE 1960; ED 1954; FCA; *b* 13 April 1909; *s* of Capt. Herbert Hugh Cowie, JP; *m* 1st, 1934, Erica Mary Beaty (*d* 1956); two *s* one *d*; 2nd, 1957, Valori Hare Duke; one *s* one *d. Educ:* Brighton; Brasenose Coll., Oxford. Hon. Game Warden, 1932–; Mem. Nairobi District Council, 1932–36; KAR, Reserve of Officers, 1932–38 (3rd and 5th Battalions); Kenya Regt, 1939; served War of 1939–45; Abyssinia, Middle East, Madagascar (retd Lieut-Col). MLC Kenya, 1951–60; Dir of Manpower, Mau-Mau Emergency, 1953–56. Founder and Dir, Royal National Parks of Kenya, 1946–66. Vice-Pres. E African Tourist Travel Assoc., 1950–65; Mem. Nat. Parks Commn, Internat. Union for Conservation of Nature, 1959–66; Hon. Trustee, Uganda Nat. Parks, 1950–; Vice-Pres., Fauna Preservation Soc., London; Hon. Vice-Chm., East African Wild Life Soc.; Financial Dir, African Med. and Res. Foundn (Flying Doctor Services), 1972–79. TV and Radio (BBC Natural History Section). Editor, Royal Nat. Parks of Kenya Annual Reports, 1946–65. Lectures (tours USA and Britain). Gold Medal, San Diego Zool Soc., 1972. Order of the Golden Ark, Netherlands, 1975. *Publications:* Fly Vulture, 1961; I Walk with Lions (USA), 1964; African Lion, 1965. Contributor to International Journals and Conferences. *Recreation:* wild life conservation. *Address:* Kikenni, Walnut Tree Farm, Benhall, Saxmundham, Suffolk IP17 1JB. *T:* Saxmundham (01728) 603397. *Clubs:* Shikar; Explorer's (New York); Muthaiga Country (Nairobi).

COWIE, Sir Thomas, (Sir Tom), Kt 1992; OBE 1982; Life President, T. Cowie, subseq. Cowie Group, motor vehicle distribution and finance, since 1993 (Chairman, 1948–93); *b* 9 Sept. 1922; *s* of late Thomas Stephenson Knowles Cowie and Florence Cowie; *m* 1st, 1948, Lillas Roberts Hunnam (marr. diss.; she *d* 1994); one *s* four *d*; 2nd, 1975, Diana Carole Wentworth Kenyon; three *d* and one step *s* one step *d. Educ:* Bede Grammar School, Sunderland. *Publication:* The Tom Cowie Story, 1988. *Recreations:* game shooting, walking, music. *Address:* Broadwood Hall, Lanchester, Co. Durham DH7 0TD. *T:* Lanchester (01207) 520464.

COWIE, William Lorn Kerr; *see* Cowie, Hon. Lord.

COWLEY, 7th Earl *cr* 1857; **Garret Graham Wellesley;** Baron Cowley, 1828; Viscount Dangan, 1857; Investment Partner, Thos R. Miller & Son (Bermuda), Isle of Man, since 1990; *b* 30 July 1934; 3rd *s* of 4th Earl Cowley (*d* 1962) and of Mary (Elsie May), Countess Cowley; *S* nephew, 1975; *m* Paige Deming, Reno, Nevada; one *s* five *d*, and one *s* one *d* of former marriage. *Educ:* Univ. of S California (BSc Finance 1957); Harvard Univ. (MBA 1962). Investment Research Analyst: Wells Fargo Bank, San Francisco, 1962–64; Dodge & Cox, San Francisco, 1964–66; Asst Head, Investment Research Dept, Wells Fargo Bank, 1966–67; Vice-Pres., Investment Counsel, Thorndike, Doran, Paine & Lewis, Los Angeles, 1967–69; Sen. Vice-Pres., Exec. Cttee Mem., Securities, Real Estate and Company Acquisition Advisor, Shareholders Capital Corp., Los Angeles, 1969–74; Vice-Pres., and Sen. Investment Manager, Trust Dept, Bank of America, San Francisco, 1974–78; Gp Vice-Pres. and Dir, Internat Investment Management Service, Bank of America NT & SA, 1980–85; Director: Bank of America Internat., London, 1978–85; BankAmerica Trust Co. (Hong Kong), 1980–85; Bank of America Banking & Trust Co. (Gibraltar), 1981–85; Bank of America Trust Co. (Jersey), 1982–85; Bank of America Banking & Trust Co. (Nassau), 1982–85; Bank of America Banking & Trust Co. (Cayman), 1982–85; indep. financial advr and co. dir, 1985–90. Served US Army Counter Intelligence Corps, primarily in France, 1957–60. Member: Assoc. of Conservative Peers, 1981–; Parly Arts and Heritage Gp, 1981–, Defence Gp, 1982–, and Anglo-Amer. Gp, 1987–, H of L. *Heir: s* Viscount Dangan, *qv. Address:* PO Box 221, Douglas, Isle of Man; Château du Tignet, 06530 Peymeinade, France. *Clubs:* Brooks's; Harvard (San Francisco).

COWLEY, Prof. Alan Herbert, FRS 1988; Robert A. Welch Professor of Chemistry, University of Texas at Austin, since 1991; *b* 29 Jan. 1934; *s* of late Herbert Cowley and of Dora Cowley; *m* 1975, Deborah Elaine Cole; two *s* three *d. Educ:* Univ. of Manchester (BSc, MSc; Dalton Chem. Schol., 1956–58; PhD 1958). Technical Officer, ICI, 1960–61; University of Texas at Austin: Asst Prof. of Chemistry, 1962–67; Associate Prof., 1967–70; Prof., 1970–84; George W. Watt Centennial Prof., 1984–88; Richard J. V. Johnson Regents Prof. of Chemistry, 1989–91; Sir Edward Frankland Prof. of Inorganic Chem., Imperial Coll., London, 1988–89. Deutsche Akademische Austauschdienst Fellow, 1973; Guggenheim Fellow, 1976–77; Lectures: Jeremy I. Musher Meml, Hebrew Univ., Jerusalem, 1979; Mobay, Univ. of New Hampshire, 1985; Karcher, Univ. of Oklahoma, 1985; Reilly, Univ. of Notre Dame, 1987; Fischel, Vanderbilt Univ., 1991; Baxter, Northern Illinois Univ., 1992; Vis. Prof., Univ. of Western Ont., 1987. Member: Chem. Soc., subseq. RSC, 1961 (Award for Main-Gp Element Chem., 1980; Centenary Medal and Lectureship, 1986); Amer. Chem. Soc., 1962 (Southwest Regl Award, 1986). Stiefvater Meml Award and Lectureship, Univ. of Nebraska, 1987; Chemical Pioneer Award, Amer. Inst. of Chemists, 1994. Mem. Bd of Trustees, Gordon Res. Confs, 1989– (Vice-Chm., 1993–94). Member, Editorial Board: Inorganic Chemistry, 1979–83; Chemical Reviews, 1984–88; Polyhedron, 1984–; Jl of Amer. Chem. Soc., 1986–91; Jl of Organometallic Chemistry, 1987–; Organometallics, 1988–91; Mem. Bd, Inorganic Syntheses, 1983– (Ed.-in-Chief, vol. 31). *Publications:* over 300 pubns in learned jls. *Recreations:* squash, sailing, music. *Address:* Department of Chemistry and Biochemistry, University of Texas at Austin, Austin, TX 78712, USA. *Clubs:* Athenæum; Headliners (Austin).

COWLEY, Maj.-Gen. John Cain, CB 1971; DL; Paymaster-in-Chief and Inspector of Army Pay Services, Ministry of Defence, 1967–72, retired; with de Zoete and Bevan, Stockbrokers, 1972–79; *b* 17 July 1918; *er s* of late Philip Richard and Eleanor Cowley, Ballaquane, Peel, Isle of Man; *m* 1948, Eileen Rosemary, CBE 1982, *d* of late George Percival Stewart, Aigburth, Liverpool; three *s. Educ:* Douglas School, Isle of Man. War of 1939–45: commissioned, RAPC, 1940; served: Palestine, Western Desert, Italy, France, Belgium, Holland, Germany. Dep. Asst Adj.-Gen., Middle East, 1949–51; GSOI, with Permanent Under Sec., War Office, 1952–54; West African Frontier Force, 1956–59; Dep. Paymaster-in-Chief: War Office, 1960–63; BAOR, 1963–65; Chief Paymaster, Eastern Command, 1965–67. Capt. 1946, Maj. 1953, Lt-Col 1955, Col. 1960, Brig. 1963, Maj.-Gen. 1967; psc, 1948; jssc, 1955; Administrative Staff Coll., 1960. Col Comdt, RAPC, 1974–79. Chm., W Sussex, Duke of Edinburgh's Award Scheme, 1986–95; Vice-Pres., W Sussex Scouts, 1992–. Vice-Pres., St Catherine's Hospice, 1981–; Governor, St Michaels, Burton Park, 1982–88 (Chm. of Govs, 1986–88). High Sheriff, W Sussex, 1984–85; DL W Sussex, 1986. *Recreations:* shooting, fishing, ornithology. *Address:* The Old Post Office, Nuthurst, Horsham, West Sussex RH13 6LH. *T:* Lower Beeding (01403) 891266. *Club:* Army and Navy.

COWLEY, Dr John Maxwell, FRS 1979; FAA; Galvin Professor of Physics, Arizona State University, USA, since 1970 (Regents' Professor, 1988–94, Emeritus, since 1994); *b* 18 Feb. 1923; *s* of Alfred E. and Doris R. Cowley; *m* 1951, Roberta J. (*née* Beckett); two *d. Educ:* Univ. of Adelaide (BSc 1942, MSc 1945, DSc 1957); MIT (PhD 1949). FAA 1961. Res. Officer, CSIRO, Australia, 1945–62; Prof. of Physics, Univ. of Melbourne, 1962–70. International Union of Crystallography: Mem. Exec. Cttee, 1963–69; Chm., Commn on Electron Diffraction, 1987–93; Ewald Prize, 1987. *Publications:* Diffraction Physics, 1975; approx. 300 articles in learned jls. *Recreations:* painting, music. *Address:* 2625 E Southern Avenue C-90, Tempe, AZ 85282–7670, USA. *T:* (602) 8313123.

COWLEY, Kenneth Edward, AO 1988; Chief Executive, since 1980, and Chairman, since 1992, News Ltd; Executive Chairman, Ansett Transport Industries, since 1992; *b* 17 Nov. 1934; *s* of Edward Clegg Cowley and Patricia Bertha (*née* Curran); *m* 1958, Maureen Yvonne Manahan; one *s* one *d.* Sen. Exec., The Australian, 1964–; Director: News Ltd, 1976–; Internat. Bd, News Corp., 1980–; Chairman: Pacific Magazines and Printing Ltd, 1991–; R. M. Williams Holdings Ltd, 1994–. Director: Australian Associated Press Inf. Services Pty Ltd, 1983–; Qld Press Ltd, 1987–; Independent Newspapers Ltd (NZ), 1990–. Councillor, Royal Agricl Soc. of NSW, 1979–. Trustee, Art Gall. of NSW, 1986–; Chm., Australian Stockman's Hall of Fame & Outback Heritage Centre, 1976–. *Address:* 2 Holt Street, Surry Hills, NSW 2010, Australia. *T:* (2) 2883209. *Clubs:* Union, Royal Sydney Yacht Squadron (Sydney).

COWLEY, Kenneth Martin, CMG 1963; OBE 1956; *b* 15 May 1912; *s* of late Robert Martin Cowley, OBE, and late Mabel Priscilla Cowley (*née* Lee); *m* 1948, Barbara (*née* Tannahill); one *s* (and one step *s*). *Educ:* Merchant Taylors' Sch., Crosby; Exeter Coll., Oxford (MA). District Officer, Kenya, 1935–44; Asst Sec., 1944–46; District Comr, 1946–49; Actg Native Courts Officer, 1949–53; Sec. for African Affairs, 1953–56; Provincial Commissioner, Southern Province, Kenya, 1956–63 (despatches, 1957); Sec., Kenya Regional Boundaries and Constituencies Commns, 1962; Sen. Administrative Manager, Express Transport Co. Ltd, Kenya, 1963–70. Sec., Overseas Service Pensioners' Assoc., 1971–79. *Recreation:* natural history. *Address:* Oakview Cottage, Cricket Green, Hartley Wintney, Hants RG27 8PZ. *T:* Hartley Wintney (01252) 844210. *Club:* Nairobi (Kenya).

COWLEY, Prof. Roger Arthur, FRS 1978; FRSE 1972; Dr Lee's Professor of Experimental Philosophy, and Fellow of Wadham College, since 1988, Chairman of Physics, since 1993, University of Oxford; *b* 24 Feb. 1939; *s* of Cecil A. Cowley and Mildred S. Cowley; *m* 1964, Sheila J. Wells; one *s* one *d. Educ:* Brentwood Sch., Essex; Cambridge Univ. (MA, PhD). Fellow, Trinity Hall, Cambridge, 1962–64; Research Officer, Atomic Energy of Canada Ltd, 1964–70; Prof. of Physics, Edinburgh Univ., 1970–88. Max Born Medal, 1973; Holweck Medal and Prize, 1990. *Publication:* Structural Phase Transitions, 1981. *Address:* Oxford Physics Clarendon Laboratory, Parks Road, Oxford OX1 3PU. *T:* Oxford (01865) 272224; Tredinnock, Harcourt Hill, Oxford OX2 9AS. *T:* Oxford (01865) 247570.

COWLEY, Prof. Stanley William Herbert, PhD; CPhys; FRAS; FBIS; Professor of Physics, since 1988, and Head, Space and Atmospheric Physics Group, since 1990, Blackett Laboratory, Imperial College, University of London; *b* 11 April 1947; *s* of late Herbert William Leslie Cowley and of Annie Jenny Cowley (*née* Clark); *m* 1970, Lynn Doreen Moore; two *s* one *d. Educ:* Imperial Coll., Univ. of London (BSc, ARCS, PhD, DIC). FBIS 1975; MInstP 1975; FRAS 1986; CPhys 1989. Imperial College, University of

London: SERC Advanced Fellow, 1977–82; Lectr, 1982–85; Reader, 1985–88. Mem., Particle Physics and Astronomy Res. Council, 1994–. Chapman Medal, RAS, 1991. *Publications:* contrib. numerous papers in solar system plasma physics in learned jls. *Recreation:* walking the dog. *Address:* Blackett Laboratory, Imperial College, SW7 2BZ. *T:* 0171–594 7773.

COWLING, Gareth; *see* Cowling, T. G.

COWLING, James Roy; HM Diplomatic Service; High Commissioner to Lesotho, since 1992; *b* 9 Feb. 1940; *m* 1st, 1962, Monique Lassimonillas; 2nd, 1983, Janet Bell Barnshaw. Second Sec., Karachi, 1964; FCO, 1968; First Sec., Buenos Aires, 1972, Copenhagen, 1975; FCO, 1977; on loan to ODA, 1980; First Sec., Nairobi, 1983; First Sec., subseq. Counsellor, FCO, 1987. *Address:* c/o Foreign and Commonwealth Office, SW1A 2AH.

COWLING, Maurice John; Fellow of Peterhouse, Cambridge, 1963–93, now Emeritus; *b* 6 Sept. 1926; *s* of Reginald Frederick Cowling and May (*née* Roberts). *Educ:* Battersea Grammar Sch.; Jesus Coll., Cambridge (Historical Tripos, Pt I 1948, Pt II 1949). Served British and Indian Armies (Captain Queen's Royal Regt), 1944–48. Fellow, Jesus Coll., Cambridge, 1950–53; Res. Fellow, Univ. of Reading, 1953–54; FO, 1954; Mem. Editorial Staff: The Times, 1955–56; Daily Express, 1957–58; Fellow, Jesus Coll., Cambridge, 1961–63; Lectr in History, then Reader in Modern English History, Univ. of Cambridge, 1961–88. Olin Vis. Prof. of Religion, Columbia Univ., 1989. Literary Editor, The Spectator, 1970–71. Founder Mem. and Mem. Exec. Cttee, Salisbury Gp, 1978–. Contested (C) Bassetlaw, 1959; Mem., Cambs and Isle of Ely CC, 1966–70. *Publications:* The Nature and Limits of Political Science, 1963; Mill and Liberalism, 1963, 2nd edn 1989; Disraeli, Gladstone and Revolution, 1967; The Impact of Labour, 1971; The Impact of Hitler, 1975; (ed) Conservative Essays, 1978; Religion and Public Doctrine in Modern England, Vol. i 1980, Vol. ii 1985. *Address:* Peterhouse, Cambridge CB2 1RD.

COWLING, Peter John; Director, Royal Society of Arts, since 1994; *b* 11 Nov. 1944; *s* of Harold Cowling and Irene (*née* Phillips); *m* 1979, Sara Fox; two *d*. *Educ:* Bletchley Grammar Sch.; Britannia Royal Naval Coll. Joined RN 1963; commanded: HMS Naiad, 1979; HMS York and 3rd Destroyer Sqdn, 1988; Sen. Naval Officer, Middle East, 1991; Dir, Naval Ops, MoD, 1992; retired 1994. Queen's Gold Medal, 1967. *Recreations:* sailing, tennis, gardening. *Address:* Royal Society of Arts, 8 John Adam Street, WC2N 6EZ. *T:* 0171–930 5115. *Club:* Lansdowne.

COWLING, (Thomas) Gareth; Stipendiary Magistrate for Hampshire, since 1989; *b* 12 Nov. 1944; *s* of late Clifford Cowling and of Beryl Elizabeth Cowling (*née* Thomas); *m* 1970, Jill Ann Stephens; one *s* one *d*. *Educ:* Eastbourne Coll.; College of Law. Articled to Clifford Cowling, of Clifford Cowling & Co., Hampshire, 1964; admitted Solicitor of Supreme Court, 1969; Solicitor, Solicitor's Dept, New Scotland Yard, 1969–72; called to Bar, Middle Temple, 1972; private practice at Bar, London and Winchester, Western Circuit, 1972–88; Metropolitan Stipendiary Magistrate, 1988–89. *Recreations:* family life, eating and drinking with friends, trying to play tennis and badminton, opera. *Address:* c/o The Law Courts, Winston Churchill Avenue, Portsmouth, Hants PO1 2DQ. *Clubs:* Hampshire (Winchester); Bourne (Farnham).

COWPERTHWAITE, David Jarvis; Under-Secretary, Scottish Home and Health Department, 1974–81, retired; *b* 14 Sept. 1921; *s* of J. J. Cowperthwaite and Mrs J. W. B. Cowperthwaite (*née* Jarvis); *m* 1944, Patricia Stockdale (*d* 1993); two *d*. *Educ:* Edinburgh Academy; Exeter Coll., Oxford (MA). Nigerian Admin. Service, 1942–48; joined Home Civil Service (Scottish Home Dept), 1948. *Recreations:* cricket, golf. *Address:* 69 Northumberland Street, Edinburgh EH3 6JG. *T:* 0131–557 0215.
See also Sir J. J. Cowperthwaite.

COWPERTHWAITE, Sir John James, KBE 1968 (OBE 1960); CMG 1964; International Adviser to Jardine Fleming & Co. Ltd, Hong Kong, 1972–81; Financial Secretary, Hong Kong, 1961–71; *b* 25 April 1915; *s* of late John James Cowperthwaite and Jessie Wemyss Barron Jarvis Cowperthwaite; *m* 1941, Sheila Mary, *d* of Alexander Thomson, Aberdeen; one *s*. *Educ:* Merchiston Castle Sch.; St Andrews Univ; Christ's Coll., Cambridge. Entered Colonial Administrative Service, Hong Kong, 1941; seconded to Sierra Leone, 1942–45. *Address:* 25 South Street, St Andrews, Fife KY16 9QS. *T:* St Andrews (01334) 74759. *Clubs:* Royal Hong Kong Jockey, Royal Hong Kong Golf; Royal and Ancient.

COWTAN, Maj.-Gen. Frank Willoughby John, CBE 1970 (MBE 1947); MC 1942 and Bar, 1945; *b* 10 Feb. 1920; *s* of late Air Vice-Marshal F. C. Cowtan, CB, CBE, KHS and late Mrs N. A. Cowtan (*née* Kennedy); *m* 1949, Rose Isabel Cope; one *s* one *d*. *Educ:* Wellington Coll.; RMA Woolwich. 2nd Lieut Royal Engineers, 1939; served War of 1939–45, BEF, N Africa, Italy, NW Europe (Captain); Palestine, Kenya, Middle East, 1945–50 (Major); psc 1951; Middle East, UK, BAOR, 1952–58; Liaison Officer to US Corps of Engrs, USA, 1958–60 (Bt Lt-Col); CO 131 Parachute Engr Regt, 1960–62; CO Victory Coll., RMA Sandhurst, 1962–65 (Lt-Col); Comd 11 Engr Bde, BAOR, 1965–67 (Brig.); ndc (Canada) 1967–68; Dir of Quartering (Army), 1968–70; Dep. QMG, MoD(AD), 1970–71; Comdt, RMCS, 1971–75, retired. Hon. Col, 131 Indep. Commando Sqn, RE, 1975–80; Col Comdt RE, 1977–82. Dep. Dir, CLA Game Fair, 1978–86. *Recreations:* golf, shooting, wildfowling, sailing, travel, languages. *Address:* Rectory Cottage, Coleshill, Swindon, SN6 7PR. *Club:* Army and Navy.

COX; *see* Roxbee Cox, family name of Baron Kings Norton.

COX, family name of **Baroness Cox.**

COX, Baroness *cr* 1982 (Life Peer), of Queensbury in Greater London; **Caroline Anne Cox;** a Deputy Speaker, House of Lords, since 1986; Director, Nursing Education Research Unit, Chelsea College, University of London, 1977–84; *b* 6 July 1937; *d* of Robert John McNeill Love, MS, FRCS and Dorothy Ida Borland; *m* 1959, Dr Murray Cox, FRCPsych; two *s* one *d*. *Educ:* Channing School. BSc (Sociology, 1st Cl. Hons) 1967, MSc (Economics) 1969, London Univ.; FRCN 1985. SRN, London Hosp., 1958; Staff Nurse, Edgware Gen. Hosp., 1960; Research Associate, Univ. of Newcastle upon Tyne, 1967–68. Department of Sociology, Polytechnic of North London: Lecturer, Senior Lectr, Principal Lectr, 1969–74; Head of Department, 1974–77. Vis. Prof., Faculty of Health and Social Work, Anglia Poly. Univ., Essex, 1990–. Dir, Centre for Policy Studies, 1983–85. A Baroness in Waiting, April–Aug. 1985. Chancellor, Bournemouth Univ., 1992–. Chairman: Academic Council for Peace and Freedom, 1984–; Jagiellonian Trust, 1984–93; Parental Alliance for Choice in Education, 1985–; Health Studies Cttee, CNAA, 1987–93; Mem., Council and Management Cttee, Freedom Assoc., 1985–. Mem. Council of Management, St Christopher's Hospice, 1986–; Vice Pres., RCN, 1990–. Pres., IAPS, 1991–. Trustee, Medical Emergency Relief Internat.; Patron: Medical Aid for Poland Fund; Assoc. for a Free Russia. Co-editor, Internat. Jl of Nursing Studies. Hon. PhD Polish Univ. in London. Commander's Cross, Order of Merit (Poland), 1990. *Publications:* (ed jtly) A Sociology of Medical Practice, 1975; (jtly) Rape of Reason: The Corruption of the Polytechnic of North London, 1975; (jtly) The Right to Learn, 1982; Sociology: A Guide for Nurses, Midwives and Health Visitors, 1983; (jtly) The Insolence of Office, 1989; (jtly) Choosing a State School: how to find the best education for your child, 1989; Trajectories of Despair: misdiagnosis and maltreatment of Soviet orphans, 1991; (with John Eibner) Ethnic Cleansing in Progress: war in Nagorno Karabakh, 1993. *Recreations:* campanology, squash, hill walking. *Address:* The White House, Wyke Hall, Gillingham, Dorset SP8 5NS. *T:* Gillingham (017476) 3436; 1 Arnellan House, 144–146 Slough Lane, Kingsbury, NW9 8XJ. *T:* 0181–204 2321. *Clubs:* Commonwealth Trust, Royal Over-Seas League.

COX, Sir Alan (George), Kt 1994; CBE 1988; FCA; Chief Executive, ASW Holdings PLC, since 1987; *b* 23 Aug. 1936; *s* of late George Henry Cox and Florence Ivy Cox. *Educ:* Oldbury Grammar Sch. FCA 1959; ACMA 1961. Chm. and Chief Exec., GKN Rolled and Bright Steel Ltd, 1978–80; Corporate Management Dir, GKN, PLC, 1980–81; Chm. and Chief Exec., Allied Steel and Wire Ltd, 1981–87; Dir, Morgan Crucible Co. plc, 1995–. Member: Bd, Cardiff Bay Develt Corp., 1989–; School Teachers Review Body, 1991–. *Recreations:* cookery, opera, walking. *Address:* PO Box 207, St Mellons, Cardiff CF3 0YJ. *Club:* Cardiff and County.

COX, Alan Seaforth; Clerk to the Grocers' Company, 1965–81; Secretary, Grocers' Trust Company Ltd, 1968–81; *b* 15 Oct. 1915; *m* 1st, 1944, Jean Heriot-Maitland (marr. diss. 1952); one *s*; 2nd, 1954, Mary Thornton (*d* 1990); three *s* one *d*. Served War: London Scottish and Gold Coast Regt, 1939–45; Staff Officer, WO, 1945–46. Farming and banking, Argentine (Patagonia), 1947–52; joined Grocers' Co., 1954. Sec., Governing Body of Oundle Sch., 1965–81. Hon. Mem. Ct, Grocers' Co., 1981–. *Recreations:* bridge, cribbage, dining and wining. *Address:* The Mount, Winchelsea, East Sussex TN36 4EG. *T:* Rye (01797) 226543.

COX, Alister Stransom, MA; Headmaster, Royal Grammar School, Newcastle upon Tyne, 1972–94; *b* 21 May 1934; *s* of Rev. Roland L. Cox and F. Ruth Cox; *m* 1960, Janet (*née* Williams); one *s* two *d*. *Educ:* Kingswood School, Bath; New College, Oxford (Scholar). Hon. Mods (1st Class); Lit. Hum. BA 1957, MA 1961. Sixth Form Master, Clifton Coll., 1957–63; Head of Classics, Wellington Coll., 1963–69; Dep. Head, Arnold Sch., Blackpool, 1969–72. Vis. Lectr in Greek, Bristol Univ., 1968. Founder Mem., Sinfonia Chorus, Northern Sinfonia of England, 1973–94 (Mem., Management Cttee, 1980–85). FRSA 1982. *Publications:* Lucretius on Matter and Man, 1967; Didactic Poetry, in Greek and Latin Literature (ed Higginbotham), 1969; articles in Greece and Rome, Times Educnl Supp. and educnl jls. *Recreations:* music, especially singing; walking in the Lake District and living (partly) in France. *Address:* 3 Lower Gale, Ambleside, Cumbria LA22 0BD. *T:* Ambleside (015394) 32634.

COX, Anthony; *see* Cox, J. A.

COX, Anthony Robert, PhD, CEng; Counsellor, Science and Technology, British Embassy, Tokyo, since 1993; *b* 30 Nov. 1938; *s* of Robert George Cox and Gladys Cox; *m* 1963, Constance Jean Hammond; one *s* two *d*. *Educ:* Brockley County School; Imperial College, London. BScEng (Metallurgy). ARSM, MIM. RARDE, 1960–69; Exchange Scientist, US Naval Research Lab., Washington DC, 1969–71; Dep. Materials Supt, RARDE, 1971–75; Asst Dir, Armour and Materials, Military Vehicle Engineering Estab., 1975–80; MoD Central Staffs Defence Science, 1980–83; Counsellor, Science and Technol., Washington DC, 1983–87; Superintendent, Radiation Sci. and Acoustics, NPL, 1988–92. *Publications:* papers on refractory metals, structure and strengthening mechanism on high strength steel, fractography, explosive effects, archaeological artefacts corrosion, composites, space, robotics, science policy, metrology. *Recreations:* sailing, squash, skiing, foreign travel. *Address:* British Embassy, 1 Ichiban-cho, Chiyoda-ku, Tokyo 102, Japan.

COX, Prof. Archibald; Carl M. Loeb University Professor, Harvard University, 1976–84, now Emeritus; Visiting Professor of Law, Boston University, since 1984; *b* 17 May 1912; *s* of Archibald Cox and Frances Bruen (*née* Perkins); *m* 1937, Phyllis Ames; one *s* two *d*. *Educ:* St Paul's Sch., Concord; Harvard Univ. AB 1934, LLB 1937. Admitted to Mass Bar, 1937. Gen. practice with Ropes, Gray, Best, Coolidge & Rugg, 1938–41; Office of Solicitor-Gen., US Dept of Justice, 1941–43; Assoc. Solicitor, Dept of Labor, 1943–45; Lectr on Law, Harvard, 1945–46, Prof. of Law, 1946–61; Solicitor-Gen., US Dept of Justice, 1961–65; Williston Prof. of Law, Harvard Law Sch., 1965–76. Pitt Prof., Univ. of Cambridge, 1974–75. Co-Chm., Constrn Industry Stablizn Commn, 1951–52; Chm., Wage Stablzn Bd, 1952; Mem. Bd Overseers, Harvard, 1962–65. Special Watergate Prosecutor, 1973. Hon. LLD: Loyola, 1964; Cincinnati, 1967; Rutgers, Amherst, Denver, 1974; Harvard, 1975; Michigan, 1976; Wheaton, 1977; Northeastern, 1978; Clark, 1980; Notre Dame, 1983; Hon. LHD: Hahnemann Med. Coll., 1980; Univ. of Mass, 1981; Illinois, 1985. *Publications:* Cases on Labor Law, 9th edn 1981; (jtly) Law and National Labor Policy, 1960; Civil Rights, the Constitution and the Courts, 1967; The Warren Court, 1968; The Role of the Supreme Court in American Government, 1976; Freedom of Expression, 1981; The Court and the Constitution, 1987; miscellaneous articles. *Address:* PO Box 393, Wayland, MA 01778, USA; (office) Harvard Law School, Cambridge, MA 02138, USA. *T:* (617) 4953133. *Clubs:* Somerset (Boston, Mass); Century Association (New York).
See also A. Cox, Jr.

COX, Archibald, Jr; Chairman, Sextant Group Inc., since 1993; *b* 13 July 1940; *s* of Archibald Cox, *qv*; *m* 1977, Jean Inge; two *s* one *d*. *Educ:* Harvard Coll. (ABEcon 1962); Harvard Business Sch. (MBA 1964). Associate 1964–70, Vice Pres. 1971–72, Man. Dir, 1973–88, Morgan Stanley & Co. Incorp.; Man. Dir and Head of London Office, Morgan Stanley Internat., 1977–88; Pres. and Chief Exec. Officer, First Boston Corp., 1990–93. Member: Securities and Investments Board, 1986–88; Bd, Securities Industry Assoc., 1990–93. *Recreations:* cycling, sailing. *Address:* 998 Fifth Avenue, New York, NY 10028–0126, USA. *Clubs:* Links (New York); New York Yacht.

COX, Arthur George Ernest S.; *see* Stewart Cox.

COX, Brian; *see* Cox, Charles B.

COX, Brian Dennis; actor, director, teacher and writer; *b* 1 June 1946; *s* of Charles Mcardle Campbell Cox and Mary Ann Gillerline (*née* Mccann); *m* 1968, Caroline Burt (marr. diss. 1987); one *s* one *d*. *Educ:* LAMDA. *Stage appearances:* début, Dundee Rep., 1961; Royal Lyceum, Edinburgh, 1965–66; Birmingham Rep., 1966–68; As You Like It, Birmingham and Vaudeville (London début), 1967; title rôle, Peer Gynt, Birmingham, 1967; When We Dead Awaken, Edinburgh Fest., 1968; In Celebration, Royal Court, 1969; The Wild Duck, Edinburgh Festival, 1969; The Big Romance, Royal Court, 1970; Don't Start Without Me, Garrick, 1971; Mirandolina, Brighton, 1971; Getting On, Queen's, 1971; The Creditors, Open Space, 1972; Hedda Gabler, Royal Court, 1972; Playhouse, Nottingham: Love's Labour's Lost, title rôle, Brand, What The Butler Saw, The Three Musketeers, 1972; Cromwell, Royal Court, 1973; Royal Exchange, Manchester: Arms and the Man, 1974; The Cocktail Party, 1975; Pilgrims Progress, Prospect Th., 1975; Emigres, Nat. Theatre Co., Young Vic, 1976; Olivier Theatre: Tamburlaine The Great, 1976; Julius Caesar, 1977; The Changeling, Riverside Studios, 1978; National Theatre: title rôle, Herod, The Putney Debates, 1978; On Top, Royal Court, 1979; Macbeth, Cambridge Th. and tour of India, 1980; Summer Party, Crucible, 1980; Have You Anything to Declare?, Manchester then Round House, 1981; title role,

Danton's Death, Nat. Theatre Co., Olivier, 1982; Strange Interlude, Duke of York, 1984 (Drama Mag. Best Actor Award, 1985), Nederlander, NY, 1985; Rat in the Skull, Royal Court, 1984 (Drama Mag. and Olivier Best Actor Awards, 1985) and NY, 1985; Fashion, The Danton Affair, Misalliance, Penny for a Song, 1986, The Taming of the Shrew, Titus Andronicus (title rôle), 1987, The Three Sisters, 1989, RSC, and Titus Andronicus on tour, Madrid, Paris, Copenhagen, 1988 (Olivier Award, Best Actor in a Revival, and Drama Mag. Best Actor Award for RSC 1988 season); Frankie and Johnny in the Clare-de-Lune, Comedy, 1989; Richard III, and title rôle, King Lear, National and world tour, 1990–91; The Master Builder, Edinburgh, 1993, Riverside, 1994; *films:* Nicholas and Alexandra, 1971; In Celebration, 1975; Manhunter, 1986; Shoot for the Sun, 1986; Hidden Agenda, 1990; Braveheart, 1994; The Cutter, 1994; Rob Roy, 1995; *TV appearances:* Churchill's People: The Wallace, 1972; The Master of Ballantrae, 1975; Henry II, in The Devil's Crown, 1978; Thérèse Raquin, 1979; Dalhousie's Luck, Bothwell, 1980; Bach, 1981; Pope John Paul II, 1984; Florence Nightingale, 1985; Beryl Markham: a shadow in the sun, 1988; Secret Weapon, 1990; Acting in Tragedy (BBC Masterclass), 1990; The Lost Language of Cranes, The Cloning of Joanna May, 1992; The Big Battalions, 1992; The Negotiator, 1994; Witness for Hitler, 1995; Blow Your Mind See A Play, 1995; *directed:* Edinburgh Festival: The Man with a Flower in his Mouth, The Stronger, 1973; Orange Tree, Richmond: I Love My Love, 1982; Mrs Warren's Profession, 1989; The Crucible, Moscow Art Theatre, London and Edinburgh, 1988–89; The Philanderer, Hampstead Th. Club, 1991 (world première of complete version). Internat. Theatre Inst. Award, 1990. *Publications:* Salem to Moscow: an actor's Odyssey, 1991; The Lear Diaries, 1992. *Recreation:* keeping fit. *Address:* c/o Conway van Gelder, 18–21 Jermyn Street, SW1Y 6HP. *T:* 0171–287 0077. *Club:* Savile.

COX, Brian (Robert) Escott, QC 1974; a Recorder of the Crown Court, since 1972; *b* 30 Sept. 1932; *yr s* of late George Robert Escott Cox; *m* 1st, 1956; one *s* two *d*; 2nd, 1969, Noelle Gilormini; one *s* one *d*. *Educ:* Rugby Sch.; Oriel Coll., Oxford (BA, MA). Called to Bar, Lincoln's Inn, 1954, Bencher, 1985. Midland and Oxford Circuit. *Recreations:* listening to and playing jazz. *Address:* 1 King's Bench Walk, Temple, EC4Y 7DB. *T:* 0171–353 8436.

COX, Prof. (Charles) Brian, CBE 1990; John Edward Taylor Professor of English Literature, University of Manchester, 1976–93, now Emeritus; *b* 5 Sept. 1928; *s* of late Hedley E. Cox and Rose Thompson; *m* 1954, Jean Willmer; one *s* two *d*. *Educ:* Wintringham Sec. Sch.; Pembroke Coll., Cambridge (MA, MLitt). Lectr, Univ. of Hull, 1954–66; Manchester University: Prof. of English Lit., 1966–76; Dean, Faculty of Arts, 1984–86; Pro-Vice-Chancellor, 1987–91. Vis. Associate Prof., Univ. of Calif, Berkeley, 1964–65; Brown Fellow, Univ. of the South, Sewanee, Tennessee, 1980; Lord Northcliffe Lectr, UCL, 1991; Visiting Professor: KCL, 1994–; Sheffield Hallam Univ., 1994–. Pres., Nat. Council for Educnl Standards, 1984–89 (Chm., 1979–84); Mem., Kingman Cttee, 1987–88; Chm., Nat. Curriculum English Working Gp, 1988–89. Chairman: NW Arts Bd, 1994–; Arvon Foundn, 1994–. Co-editor: Critical Qly, 1959–; Black Papers on Education, 1969–77. FRSL 1993. Hon. Fellow, Westminster Coll., Oxford, 1994. *Publications:* The Free Spirit, 1963; (ed with A. E. Dyson) Modern Poetry, 1963; (ed with A. E. Dyson) Practical Criticism of Poetry, 1965; Joseph Conrad: the modern imagination, 1974; Every Common Sight (poems), 1981; Two-Headed Monster (poems), 1985; Cox on Cox: an English curriculum for the 1990s, 1991; The Great Betrayal (autobiog.), 1992; Collected Poems, 1993; The Battle for the English Curriculum, 1995. *Recreations:* Manchester United, walking. *Address:* 20 Park Gates Drive, Cheadle Hulme, Stockport SK8 7DF. *T:* 0161–485 2162. *Club:* Lansdowne.

COX, Prof. Christopher Barry, PhD, DSc; Professor, Division of Life Sciences, and Assistant Principal, King's College London, since 1989; *b* 29 July 1931; *s* of Herbert Ernest Cox and May Cox; *m* 1961, Sheila (*née* Morgan); two *s* one *d*. *Educ:* St Paul's Sch., Kensington; Balliol Coll., Oxford (MA); St John's Coll., Cambridge (PhD); DSc London. Asst Lectr in Zoology, King's Coll. London, 1956–59; Harkness Fellow of Commonwealth Fund, at Mus. of Comparative Zoology, Harvard, 1959–60; King's College London: Lectr in Zoology, 1956–66; Sen. Lectr, 1966–69; Reader, 1970–76; Prof., 1976–; Head: Dept of Zoology, 1982–85; Dept of Biology, 1985–88; Fulbright Schol., Stanford Univ., Calif, 1988–89. Mem. Council, Palaeontological Assoc., 1967–69, 1974; Vice-Pres., 1969–81. Editor, Palaeontology, 1975–79. Palaeontological collecting expedns to Central Africa, 1963; Argentina, 1967; N Brasil, 1972; Qld, Aust., 1978. *Publications:* Prehistoric Animals, 1969; (with P. D. Moore) Biogeography—an ecological and evolutionary approach, 1973, 5th edn 1993; (jtly) The Prehistoric World, 1975; (jtly) Illustrated Encyclopedia of Dinosaurs and Prehistoric Animals, 1988; (jtly) Atlas of The Living World, 1989; research papers on vertebrate palaeontology and historical biogeography, in Phil. Trans. Royal Soc., Proc. Zool. Soc., Nature, Bull. Brit. Mus. (Nat. Hist.), Jl Biogeog., etc. *Recreations:* gardening, theatre. *Address:* Forge Cottage, Blacksmith Close, Ashtead, Surrey KT21 2BD. *T:* Ashtead (01372) 273167.

COX, Prof. Sir David (Roxbee), Kt 1985; PhD; FRS 1973; Warden of Nuffield College, Oxford, 1988–94, Hon. Fellow, 1994; *b* 15 July 1924; *s* of S. R. Cox, Handsworth, Birmingham; *m* 1948, Joyce (*née* Drummond), Keighley, Yorks; three *s* one *d*. *Educ:* Handsworth Grammar Sch., Birmingham; St John's Coll., Cambridge (MA). PhD Leeds, 1949. Posts at Royal Aircraft Establishment, 1944–46; Wool Industries Research Assoc., 1946–50; Statistical Laboratory, Cambridge, 1950–55; Visiting Prof., University of N Carolina, 1955–56; Reader in Statistics, Birkbeck College, 1956–60, Professor of Statistics, 1961–66; Prof. of Statistics, 1966–88 and Head of Dept of Maths, 1970–74, Imperial Coll. of Sci. and Technology. SERC Sen. Res. Fellow, 1983–88. President: Bernoulli Soc., 1979–81; Royal Statistical Soc., 1980–82; Pres., ISI, 1995–. For. Mem., Royal Danish Acad. of Scis and Letters, 1983; For. Hon. Mem., Amer. Acad. of Arts and Sciences, 1974; For. Associate, Nat. Acad. of Scis, USA, 1988. FIC 1994. Hon. FIA 1991. Hon. DSc: Reading, 1982; Bradford, 1982; Helsinki, 1986; Heriot-Watt, 1987; Limburg's Univ. Centrum, 1988; Queen's Univ., Kingston, Ont, 1989; Waterloo, 1991; Neuchâtel, 1992; Padua, 1994; Minnesota, 1994; Dundee, 1994; Toronto, 1994. Weldon Meml Prize, Univ. of Oxford, 1984; Kettering Medal, General Motors Cancer Foundn, 1990; (jtly) Max Planck Forschungspreis, 1993. Editor of Biometrika, 1966–91. *Publications:* Statistical Methods in the Textile Industry, 1949 (jt author); Planning of Experiments, 1958; (jtly) Queues, 1961; Renewal Theory, 1962; (jtly) Theory of Stochastic Processes, 1965; (jtly) Statistical Analysis of Series of Events, 1966; Analysis of Binary Data, 1970, 2nd edn 1989; (jtly) Theoretical Statistics, 1974; (jtly) Problems and Solutions in Theoretical Statistics, 1978; (jtly) Point Processes, 1980; (jtly) Applied Statistics, 1981; (jtly) Analysis of Survival Data, 1984; (jtly) Asymptotic Methods, 1989; Inference and Asymptotics, 1994; papers in Jl of Royal Statistical Society, Biometrika, etc. *Address:* Nuffield College, Oxford OX1 1NF.

COX, Dennis George; Under-Secretary (Industrial Relations), Department of Employment, 1971–74; a Deputy Chairman, Central Arbitration Committee, 1977–84; *b* 23 Feb. 1914; *s* of George and Amelia Cox; *m* 1938, Victoria Barraclough; one *s* (and one *s* decd). *Educ:* University College Sch.; Queens' Coll., Cambridge. Royal Navy, 1942–45; served with Netherlands and Norwegian navies, Lieut RNVR. Entered Min. of Labour, 1936; Asst Sec. 1966; Regional Controller, SW Region. *Recreations:* gardening, fishing. *Address:* 22 Ashley Court, Morpeth Terrace, SW1P 1EN; Church Cottage, Laughton, Lewes, East Sussex BN8 6AH. *T:* Ripe (01323) 811382. *Club:* Army and Navy.

COX, Sir (Ernest) Gordon, KBE 1964; TD; DSc; FRS 1954; FRSC; FInstP; FIBiol; Secretary of the Agricultural Research Council, 1960–71; *b* 24 April 1906; *s* of Ernest Henry Cox (*d* 1987) and Rosina Ring; *m* 1st, 1929, Lucie Grace Baker (*d* 1962); one *s* one *d*; 2nd, 1968, Prof. Mary Rosaleen Truter, DSc, *d* of Dr D. N. Jackman. *Educ:* City of Bath Boys' Sch.; University of Bristol. Research Asst, Davy-Faraday Laboratory, Royal Institution, 1927; Chemistry Dept, Univ. of Birmingham, 1929–41 (Reader in Chemical Crystallography, 1940); Prof. of Inorganic and Structural Chemistry, University of Leeds, 1945–60; commissioned in Territorial Army, 1936; special scientific duties, War Office, 1942–44; attached to HQ staff of 21 Army Group, France and Germany, as Technical Staff Officer, Grade I, 1944–45. Vice-Pres., Institute of Physics, 1950–53; Mem. Agric. Research Council, 1957–60. Hon. DSc: Newcastle, 1964; Birmingham, 1964; Bath, 1973; East Anglia, 1973; Hon. LLD Bristol, 1969; Hon. ARCVS, 1972. *Publications:* numerous scientific papers in jls of various learned societies, chiefly on the crystal structures of chemical compounds. *Recreations:* music, gardening, natural history. *Address:* 117 Hampstead Way, NW11 7JN. *T:* 0181–455 2618. *Clubs:* Athenæum, English-Speaking Union, Lansdowne.

See also K. G. Cox, P. A. Cox.

COX, Sir Geoffrey (Sandford), Kt 1966; CBE 1959 (MBE 1945); *b* 7 April 1910; *s* of Sandford Cox, Wellington, NZ, and Mary Cox (*née* MacGregor); *m* 1935, Cecily Barbara Talbot Turner (*d* 1993); two *s* two *d*. *Educ:* Southland High Sch., New Zealand; Otago Univ., New Zealand (MA); Rhodes Scholar, 1932–35; Oriel Coll., Oxford (BA). Reporter, Foreign and War Corresp. News Chronicle, 1935–37, Daily Express, 1937–40. Enlisted New Zealand Army, 1940; commissioned, Dec. 1940; served in 2 New Zealand Div., Greece, Crete, Libya, Italy; Major, Chief Intelligence Officer, Gen. Freyberg's staff (despatches twice). First Sec. and Chargé d'Affaires, NZ Legation, Washington, 1943; NZ Rep., first UNRRA Conf., 1943; Political Corresp., News Chronicle, 1945; Asst Editor, News Chronicle 1954. Regular Contributor, BBC radio and TV, 1945–56; Editor and Chief Exec., Independent Television News, 1956–68; founded News at Ten, 1967; Dep. Chm., Yorkshire Television, 1968–71; Chm., Tyne Tees Television, 1971–74; Chm., LBC Radio, 1978–81; independent Dir, The Observer, 1981–89. TV Producers' Guild Award Winner, 1962; Fellow, Royal TV Soc. (Silver Medal, 1963; Gold Medal, 1978); Fellow, British Kinematograph and TV Soc. *Publications:* Defence of Madrid, 1937; The Red Army Moves, 1941; The Road to Trieste, 1946; The Race for Trieste, 1977; See It Happen, 1983; A Tale of Two Battles, 1987; Countdown to War, 1988. *Recreations:* fishing, tracing Roman roads. *Club:* Garrick.

COX, George Edwin; Chief Executive, Unisys Ltd, since 1995; *b* 28 May 1940; *s* of George Herbert Cox and Beatrice Mary Cox; *m* 1963, Gillian Mary Mannings (separated 1987); two *s*; partner, Lorna Janet Peach; one *d*. *Educ:* Quintin Sch.; Queen Mary Coll., Univ. of London (BScAeEng). FIMC. Engineer, BAC, 1962–64; Molins Machine Co.: Systems Designer, 1964–67; Manufacturing Admin Manager, 1967–69; Management Consultant, Urwick Orr & Partners, 1969–73; Dir, UK Ops, Diebold Gp, 1973–77; Man. Dir, Butler Cox, 1977–92; Chm., 1992–94, Chief Exec., 1993–94, P-E International. Advr, Bd of Inland Revenue, 1995–. Vis. Prof., Royal Holloway, Univ. of London, 1995–. Pres., Management Consultancies Assoc., 1991. Mem., Information Technologists Co., 1992–. CIMgt. *Publications:* contribs to various jls. *Recreations:* theatre, rowing (Chief Coach, Univ. of London Boat Club, 1976–78, Chm. of Selectors, GB Men's Rowing, 1978–80), gliding, history of aviation. *Address:* Merlins, Manor Lane, Gerrards Cross, Bucks SL9 7NJ. *T:* Gerrards Cross (01753) 891289. *Club:* Leander.

COX, Sir (George) Trenchard; *see* Cox, Sir Trenchard.

COX, Sir Gordon; *see* Cox, Sir E. G.

COX, Graham Loudon; QC (Scot.) 1993; Sheriff Principal of South Strathclyde, Dumfries and Galloway, since 1993; *b* 22 Dec. 1933; *s* of Rev. Thomas Loudon Cox and Leonainie Violet Rose (*née* Watson); *m* 1st, 1959, June Mary Constance Gunner (marr. diss. 1975); three *d*; 2nd, 1977, Jean Nelson. *Educ:* Hamilton Acad.; Grove Acad.; Univ. of Edinburgh (MA 1954; LLB 1956). Commnd RASC, 1957; transferred to Directorate Army Legal Services, 1956–61. Called to Scottish Bar, 1962; Advocate Depute, 1967; Sheriff, Tayside Central and Fife, at Dundee, 1968–93. *Recreations:* golf, ski-ing, gardening, *ie* labouring in vain. *Address:* Sheriff Principal's Chambers, Sheriff Court, Airdrie ML6 6EE; Crail House, Crail, Fife KY10 3SJ. *T:* Crail (01333) 450270. *Clubs:* Royal & Ancient Golf (St Andrews); Western (Glasgow).

COX, Major Horace B. T.; *see* Trevor Cox.

COX, His Honour (James) Anthony; a Circuit Judge, 1976–94; *b* 21 April 1924; *s* of Herbert Sidney Cox and Gwendoline Margaret Cox; *m* 1950, Doris Margaret Fretwell; three *s* one *d*. *Educ:* Cotham Sch., Bristol; Bristol Univ. LLB Hons 1948. War Service, Royal Marines, 1943–46. Called to Bar, Gray's Inn, 1949; a Recorder of the Crown Court, 1972–76. Pres., Anchor Soc., 1985–86. *Recreations:* cricket, sailing, golf, the arts. *Address:* Haldonhay, Lower Court Road, Newton Ferrers, Plymouth, Devon PL8 1DE. *Clubs:* MCC; Royal Western Yacht (Plymouth); Yealm Yacht; Bigbury Golf.

COX, John; Production Director, Royal Opera House, Covent Garden, 1988–94; *b* 12 March 1935; *s* of Leonard John Cox and Ethel M. (*née* McGill). *Educ:* Queen Elizabeth's Hosp., Bristol; St Edmund Hall, Oxford (MA; Hon. Fellow, 1991). Vis. Fellow, European Humanities Res. Centre, Oxford, 1995. Freelance director of plays, opera, revue and musicals in Britain and abroad, incl. La Scala, Milan, and Metropolitan Opera, New York, Vienna, Stockholm, Brussels, Amsterdam, Florence, Sydney, Monte Carlo, Cologne, Frankfurt, Munich, Salzburg, Spoleto, Wexford, Santa Fe, Houston, San Francisco, Washington, Dallas, Madrid, Chicago, Lisbon, 1959–; Dir of Prodn, Glyndebourne Festival Opera, 1971–81; Gen. Adminr, 1981–85, Artistic Dir, 1985–86, Scottish Opera. A Board Mem., Greenwich Theatre. Productions include: *opera:* Glyndebourne: Richard Strauss cycle, Rake's Progress, The Magic Flute, La Cenerentola; ENO: Così Fan Tutte, Patience; Scottish Opera: L'Egisto, Manon Lescaut, Marriage of Figaro, Lulu; Royal Opera: Manon, Die Fledermaus, Guillaume Tell, Capriccio, Die Meistersinger, Il Viaggio a Reims, Die Frau ohne Schatten, Tosca, Eugene Onegin. *Address:* 7 West Grove, SE10 8QT. *T:* 0181–692 2450.

COX, John Colin Leslie, CBE 1994; Chief Executive, London First Centre, since 1995; *b* 23 Oct. 1933; *s* of late Dr Leslie Reginald Cox, OBE, FRS, and Hilda Cecilia Cox; *m* 1983, Avril Joyce Butt; one *s* one *d*. *Educ:* University College Sch., London; Queens' Coll., Cambridge (BA). National Service, 2nd Lieut, 2nd 10th Princess Mary's Own Gurkha Rifles, 1956–58 (GSM Malaya 1958). Joined Shell Group, 1958: Executive positions in Shell Ghana, 1962–65, and in Shell Gp in London, 1966–77; Shell Chemicals UK: Personnel Dir, 1978–81; Dir, Business Develt, and chm. of subsid. cos, 1981–86; Dir Gen., CIA, 1987–95. Member: Armed Forces Pay Review Body, 1993–; Steering Bd, Lab. of the Govt Chemist, 1992–; Adv. Council, European Movement, 1995. Mem.,

Caux Round Table, 1991–. FRSA 1989. *Recreations:* sailing, antiques, country pursuits, photography. *Address:* London First Centre, 1 Hobhouse Court, Suffolk Street, SW1Y 4HH. *T:* 0171–925 2000. *Clubs:* Army and Navy, Hurlingham; Leander (Henley on Thames); Royal Solent Yacht (IoW).

COX, Vice-Adm. Sir John (Michael Holland), KCB 1982; Director, Sound Alive, since 1988; Flag Officer Naval Air Command, 1982–83; *b* Peking, China, 27 Oct. 1928; *s* of late Thomas Cox, MBE, and of Daisy Anne Cox; *m* 1962, Anne Garden Farquharson Seth-Smith; one *s* one *d*. *Educ:* Hilton Coll., Natal, SA. Joined BRNC, 1946; ADC to C-in-C Allied Forces, N Europe, 1952–53; ADC to Governor of Victoria, 1955; commanded HM Ships: Dilston, 1957 (despatches); Stubbington, 1958; sc Camberley, 1960; Cadet Trng Officer, BRNC Dartmouth, 1962; CSO, London Div., RNR, 1963; commanded HMS: Surprise, 1964; Naiad, 1965; Comdr, Sea Trng, Staff of Flag Officer Sea Trng, 1967; Naval Attaché, Bonn, 1969; comd HMS Norfolk, 1972; Dir, Naval Ops and Trade, 1973–75; Comdr, Standing Naval Force Atlantic, 1976–77; COS to C-in-C, Naval Home Command, 1977–79; Flag Officer Third Flotilla and Comdr Anti-Submarine Group Two, 1979–82. Dir, Spastics Soc., 1984–88. *Recreation:* gardening. *Club:* Lansdowne.

COX, Ven. John Stuart; Archdeacon of Sudbury, since 1995; *b* 13 Sept. 1940; *s* of Arthur F. W. Cox and Clarice M. Cox; *m* Mary Diane Cox; one *s* one *d*. *Educ:* Fitzwilliam House, Cambridge (MA); Linacre Coll., and Wycliffe Hall, Oxford (BA); Birmingham Univ. (DPS). Ordained deacon, 1968, priest, 1969; Assistant Curate: St Mary's, Prescot, 1968–71; St George, Newtown, Birmingham, 1971–73; Rector, St George, Newtown, Birmingham, 1973–78; Selection Sec., ACCM, 1978–83 (Sen. Selection Sec., 1979–83); Canon Residentiary, Southwark Cathedral, 1983–91; Diocesan Dir of Ordinands and Dir of Post-Ordination Training, Southwark, 1983–91; Vicar, Holy Trinity Church in the Ecumenical Parish of Roehampton, 1991–95. *Publications:* (contrib.) Religion and Medicine, Vol. 1, 1970; (contrib.) Say One for Me, 1992. *Recreations:* music, reading, theatre, golf, wine-making. *Address:* 84 Southgate Street, Bury St Edmunds, Suffolk IP33 2BJ.

COX, Dr Keith Gordon, FRS 1988; Reader in Petrology, Department of Earth Sciences, Oxford University, since 1990; Fellow of Jesus College, Oxford, since 1973; *b* 25 April 1933; *s* of Sir (Ernest) Gordon Cox, *qv*; *m* 1960, Gillian Mary Palmer; two *s* one *d*. *Educ:* Leeds Grammar Sch.; Queen's Coll., Oxford (MA); Leeds Univ. (PhD). Lectr in Geology, Univ. of Edinburgh, 1962–71; Lectr, Dept of Earth Scis, Oxford Univ., 1972–90. Editor: Earth & Planetary Science Letters, 1981–85; Jl of Petrology, 1981–83. *Publications:* (with J. D. Bell and R. J. Pankhurst) The Interpretation of Igneous Rocks, 1979; scientific papers, mainly in field of basalt petrology. *Recreation:* water colours. *Address:* 59 Bagley Wood Road, Kennington, Oxford OX1 5LY. *T:* Oxford (01865) 735590.

See also P. A. Cox.

COX, Laura Mary, (Mrs David Cox); QC 1994; a Recorder, since 1995; *b* 8 Nov. 1951; *d* of John Arthur Bryant and Mary Eileen Bryant (*née* Clarke); *m* 1970, David Cox; three *s*. *Educ:* Queen Mary Coll., Univ. of London (LLB 1973; LLM 1975). Called to the Bar, Inner Temple, 1975; in practice at the Bar, 1976–. *Recreations:* music, theatre, cinema, watching football, cooking, novels, walking, arguing with sons! *Address:* Cloisters, 1 Pump Court, Temple, EC4Y 7AA. *T:* 0171–583 0303.

COX, Nigel John; HM Diplomatic Service; Counsellor, Peking, since 1992; *b* 23 April 1954; *s* of Basil Cox, DFC and Anne (*née* Webber); *m* 1992, Olivia Jane Paget. *Educ:* The High Sch., Dublin; Trinity Coll., Dublin (BA, LLB); Ecole Nat. d'Administration, Paris. FCO 1975; Chinese lang trng, Cambridge and Hong Kong, 1976–78; Second Sec., Peking, 1978; Second, later First, Sec., FCO, 1981; Asst Political Advr, Hong Kong, 1984; First Sec., Paris, 1985; Assistant Head: Western European Dept, FCO, 1990; Hong Kong Dept, FCO, 1991. *Recreation:* sinological claptrap. *Address:* c/o Foreign and Commonwealth Office, SW1A 2AH. *Club:* Travellers'.

COX, Norman Ernest, CMG 1973; MA; HM Diplomatic Service, retired; *b* 28 Aug. 1921; *s* of late Ernest William Cox and late Daisy Beatrice (*née* Edmonds); *m* 1945, Maruja Margarita (*née* Cruz); one *s* one *d*. *Educ:* Lycée Français de Madrid; King's Coll., London (BA (Hons) 1956). Tax Officer, Inland Revenue, 1938–41; Army, Intell. Corps, 1941–45: Gibraltar, 1942–45; Attaché, Madrid, 1945–47; FO, 1947–50; 2nd Sec., Sofia, 1950–52; 2nd Sec., Montevideo, 1952–54; FO, 1954–57; Dep. Regional Information Officer for SE Asia, Singapore, 1957–60; FO, 1960–62: Laos Conf., Geneva, 1961; Sec. to UK Conf. Delegn to ECSC, Luxemburg, 1962–63; 1st Sec. (Commercial), Madrid, 1963–66; Counsellor (Information), Mexico, Regional Information Officer for Central American Republics, PRO to Duke of Edinburgh for 1968 Olympics, 1966–68; Counsellor (Commercial), Moscow, 1969–72; Inst. of Latin American Studies, London Univ., 1972–73; Diplomatic Service Inspector, 1973–74; Ambassador to: Ecuador, 1974–77; Mexico, 1977–81. Vice-Pres., British Mexican Soc., 1985– (Chm., 1982–84). Order of Aztec Eagle, 1994. *Publication:* (jtly) Politics in Mexico, 1985. *Recreations:* swimming, walking, travelling, archaeology, history, linguistics, comparative religion. *Club:* Royal Automobile.

COX, Oliver Jasper, CBE 1982; RIBA; Partner, Jean & Oliver Cox, since 1989; *b* 20 April 1920; *s* of William Edward and Elsie Gertrude Cox; *m* 1953, Jean; one *s* two *d*. *Educ:* Mill Hill Sch.; Architectural Association School of Architecture (AADip Hons). DistTP. Architects Dept, Herts CC, New Schools Division, 1948–49; Architects Dept, LCC Housing Division, 1950–59; Dep. Chief Architect, and Leader, Research and Development Gp, Min. of Housing and Local Govt, 1960–64; Partner, Shankland/Cox Partnership, 1965–85. *Recreations:* painting, drawing and screen printing. *Address:* 22 Grove Terrace, NW5 1PL. *T:* 0171–485 6929.

See also P. W. Cox.

COX, Patricia Ann, CB 1989; Under Secretary, Scottish Home and Health Department, 1985–88, retired; *b* 25 May 1931; *d* of Sir (Ernest) Gordon Cox, *qv*. *Educ:* Leeds Girls' High Sch.; Newnham Coll., Cambridge (MA). Asst Principal, Dept of Health for Scotland, 1953; Principal: SHHD, 1959–62; HM Treasury, 1962–65; SHHD, 1965–67; Asst Sec., 1967–76, Under Sec., 1976–85, Scottish Educn Dept. *Publication:* Sandal Ash (novel for children), 1950. *Recreations:* opera, archaeology, needlework, walking. *Address:* 2 Gloucester Place, Edinburgh EH3 6EF. *T:* 0131–225 6370.

See also K. G. Cox.

COX, Patricia Anne, (Mrs Roger Cox); *see* Edwards, P. A.

COX, Paul William; freelance artist and illustrator, since 1982; *b* 31 July 1957; *s* of Oliver Jasper Cox, *qv*; *m* 1987, Julia Claire Nichol; one *s* one *d*. *Educ:* Port Regis and Stanbridge Earls School; Camberwell Sch. of Art and Crafts (BA Hons); Royal Coll. of Art (MA). Contributor to: The Times, Daily Telegraph, Independent, Spectator, Punch, Sunday Times, Observer, New Yorker, Vanity Fair; founder contributor to Blueprint, 1984; designed PO stamps for 600th Lord Mayor's Show, 1989; exhibns of watercolour drawings: Workshop Gallery, 1984; Illustrators' Gallery, 1985; Chris Beetles Gallery, 1989, 1993. Vis Lectr in Illustration, Camberwell Sch. of Art and Crafts, 1982–90. *Publications:* illustrated books: Experiences of an Irish RM, 1984; The Common Years, 1984; A Varied Life, 1984; The Outing, 1985; The Character of Cricket, 1986; Romantic Gardens, 1988; Evacuee, 1988; Rebuilding the Globe, 1989; Dear Boy, 1989; Leave it to Psmith, 1989; Three Men in a Boat, 1989; The Cricket Match, 1991; Honourable Estates, 1992; The Darling Buds of May, 1992; The Russian Tea Room, 1993; The Wind in the Willows, 1993; Rumpole, 1994; Look out London, 1995. *Address:* The Old Rectory, Tilney All Saints, King's Lynn, Norfolk PE34 4SJ. *Fax:* King's Lynn (01553) 827392. *Club:* Chelsea Arts.

COX, Peter Arthur, BSc Eng; FEng, FICE; FCGI; FIC; consulting engineer; *b* 30 Oct. 1922; *m* 1944, Rosemary; one *s* two *d*. *Educ:* Westcliff High Sch., Essex; City and Guilds Coll., Imperial Coll., London (FIC 1991). Commissioned, Royal Engineers, 1942 (despatches). Lewis & Duvivier, 1947; Rendel Palmer & Tritton, 1952; Peter Lind & Co. Ltd, 1954; Sir Bruce White Wolfe Barry & Partners, 1955; Rendel Palmer & Tritton Ltd, Consulting Engineers, 1956, Partner, 1966, Sen. Partner, 1978–85, Chm., 1985–88. Chm., Ceemaid Ltd, 1984–85. Member: Dover Harbour Bd, 1983–89; Nat. Maritime Inst. Ltd, 1983–85; British Maritime Technology Ltd, 1986–93. Institution of Civil Engineers: Pres., 1980–81; Mem., Infrastructure Policy (formerly Planning) Gp, 1981–92 (Chm. 1981–84); Chm., Legal Affairs Cttee, 1988–92; Member: Smeatonian Soc. of Civil Engrs, 1980–; British Acad. of Experts, 1991–. Mem., Commonwealth Scholarship Commn, 1982–88. Pres., Old Centralians, 1989–90. Governor, Westminster Coll., Wandsworth, 1990–92. *Publications:* papers to Instn of Civil Engrs on Leith Harbour and Belfast Dry Dock; many papers to conferences. *Recreations:* walking, gardening. *Address:* 18 Ranmore Avenue, Croydon, Surrey CR0 5QA. *Club:* East India.

COX, Peter Denzil John H.; *see* Hippisley-Cox, P. D. J.

COX, Peter Frederick; Head of Libraries, BBC, since 1993; *b* 1 Dec. 1945; *s* of George William and Edna May Cox; *m* 1968, Gillian Mary Stevens; two *d*. *Educ:* Bedford Sch.; University Coll. London (BA). ALA 1968. Chartered Librarian, 1968; Sen. Asst County Librarian, Herts, 1979–88; City of Westminster: City Librarian, 1989–92; Asst Dir (Leisure and Libraries), 1992–93. Member: Library and Information Services Council for England and Wales, 1992–; Cttee of report of Cttee on Public Library Objectives, 1992. FRSA 1991. *Publications:* professional articles and symposia papers. *Recreations:* sailing, gardening. *Address:* 94 Downlands, Stevenage, Herts SG2 7BJ. *T:* Stevenage (01438) 359698.

COX, Peter Richmond, CB 1971; Deputy Government Actuary, 1963–74; *b* 3 Sept. 1914; *s* of Richard R. Cox, Civil Servant, and Nellie (*née* Richmond); *m* 1971, Faith Blake Schenk. *Educ:* King's Coll. Sch., Wimbledon. Entered Government Actuary's Dept, 1933. Qualified as Fellow, Institute of Actuaries, 1939. Joint Hon. Sec., Institute of Actuaries, 1962–64 (Vice-Pres., 1966–68). Pres., Eugenics Soc., 1970–72. Chm., CS Insurance Soc., 1973–78. Silver Medal, Inst. of Actuaries, 1975. *Publications:* Demography, 1950 (5 edns); (with R. H. Storr-Best) Surplus in British Life Assurance, 1962; (ed jtly) Population and Pollution, 1972; Resources and Population, 1973; Population and the New Biology, 1974; Equalities and Inequalities in Education, 1975; various papers on actuarial and demographic subjects. *Recreations:* music, painting, gardening. *Address:* The Level House, Mayfield, East Sussex TN20 6BW. *T:* Mayfield (01435) 872217. *Club:* Actuaries.

COX, Philip (Joseph), DSC 1943; QC 1967; a Recorder, and Honorary Recorder of Northampton, since 1972; *b* 28 Sept. 1922; *s* of Joseph Parriss Cox, Rugby; *m* 1951, Margaret Jocelyn Cox, *d* of R. C. H. Cox, Purley, Surrey; one *s* one *d*. *Educ:* Rugby Sch; Queens' Coll., Cambridge. RNVR, 1942–46 (Lieut). Called to Bar, Gray's Inn, 1949; Bencher, 1972 (Vice-Treas., 1990; Treas., 1991); practised at Bar, Birmingham, 1949–67. Mem. County Court Rules Cttee, 1962–68; Dep. Chm., Northants QS, 1963–71; Dep. Chm., Warwicks QS, 1966–71; Leader, Midland and Oxford Circuit, 1975–79; Mem. Senate, Inns of Court and Bar, 1974–80. Legal Assessor to Disciplinary Cttee, RCVS, 1969–; Chm., Cttee of Enquiry into London Smallpox Outbreak, 1973; Chairman: Code of Practice Appeal Bd, Prescription Medicines Code of Practice Authy, 1993–; Code of Practice Cttee, Assoc. of British Pharmaceut. Industries, 1978–92; Code of Practice Cttee, Internat. Fedn of Pharmaceut. Manufacturers Assocs, 1985–; Gen. Optical Council, 1985–88; Code of Practice Cttee, Nat. Office of Animal Health, 1987–92. Pres., Mental Health Review Tribunals, 1984–95. Pres., Edgbaston Liberal Assoc., 1974–86. *Recreations:* sailing, golf, gardening, reading. *Address:* 9 Sir Harry's Road, Edgbaston, Birmingham B15 2UY. *T:* 0121–440 0278. *Clubs:* Naval; Royal Cruising, Bar Yacht.

COX, Richard Charles, MBE 1961; HM Diplomatic Service, retired; *b* 27 May 1920; *s* of Charles Victor Cox and Marjorie Eleanor Cox (*née* Fox); *m* 1941, Constance (*née* Goddard); one *s*. *Educ:* Gravesend Grammar Sch.; BA Open Univ., 1985. Served War of 1939–45, RAF; released with rank of Sqdn Leader, 1946. Entered Colonial Office, 1937; Dominions Office, 1946; High Commn, Colombo, 1949–52; Second Sec., Calcutta, 1953–54; CRO, 1954–56; First Sec., Bombay, 1956–59; CRO, 1960–63; First Sec., Valletta, 1964–68; FCO, 1968–72; NI Office, 1972–74; Dep. Sec. Gen., Cento, 1975–77. *Recreations:* swimming, gardening, watching Rugby football. *Address:* 31 Lotfield Street, Orwell, near Royston, Herts SG8 5QT. *T:* Cambridge (01223) 207969.

COX, Roger Charles; His Honour Judge Roger Cox; a Circuit Judge, since 1988; *b* 18 April 1941; *s* of late Reginald William Cox and of Hilda Cox; *m* 1970, Patricia Anne Edwards, *qv*. *Educ:* Cheltenham Grammar Sch.; Birmingham Univ. (LLB, LLM). Called to the Bar, Gray's Inn, 1965. Asst Lectr, Faculty of Law, Bristol Univ., 1964–66; Lord Justice Holker Sen. Schol., Gray's Inn, 1966; a Recorder, 1986. *Recreations:* travel, music, theatre, reading. *Address:* Southwark Crown Court, 1 English Grounds, Battlebridge Lane, SE1 2HU. *T:* 0171–403 4141.

COX, Stephen James; Director General, Commonwealth Institute, since 1991; *b* 5 Dec. 1946; *s* of late Harold James West Cox and of Norah Cox (*née* Wilkinson); *m* 1969, Pauline Victoria Greenwood; one *s* one *d*. *Educ:* Queen Elizabeth Grammar Sch., Blackburn; Atlantic Coll.; Birmingham Univ. (BA Hons Geography 1969); Leeds Univ. (Postgrad. Dip. ESL 1970); Sussex Univ. (MA Educn 1977). VSO, Bolivia, 1965–66. British Council: Warsaw, 1970; Western Europe Dept, London, 1973; Accra, 1977; Staff Training Dept, 1981; Chm., British Council Whitley Council, Trade Union Side, 1981–84; Educn Attaché, Washington DC, 1984–85; Asst Sec., Royal Society, 1985–91. Member: Jt Commonwealth Socs Council, 1992–; Court, RCA, 1993–. FRGS (Mem., Sci. and Public Affairs Cttee, 1993–); FRSA. Hon. Mem., ESU, 1994–. Mem., Editl Bd, Round Table, 1994–. *Recreations:* cricket, travel, visiting galleries. *Address:* Commonwealth Institute, Kensington High Street, W8 6NQ. *T:* 0171–603 4535, *Fax:* 0171–602 7374. *Clubs:* Royal Over-Seas League, Geographical; Middlesex County Cricket.

COX, Thomas Michael; MP (Lab) Tooting, since 1983 (Wandsworth Central, 1970–74; Wandsworth Tooting, 1974–83); *b* London, 1930. *Educ:* state schools; London Sch. of Economics. Electrical worker. Former Mem., Fulham Borough Council; contested (Lab) GLC elections, 1967; contested (Lab) Stroud, 1966. An Asst Govt Whip, 1974–77; a Lord Commr of the Treasury, 1977–79. Member: ETU; Co-operative Party. *Address:* House of Commons, SW1A 0AA.

COX, Prof. Timothy Martin, MD; FRCP; Professor of Medicine, since 1989 and Fellow of Sidney Sussex College, since 1990, University of Cambridge; *b* 10 May 1948; *s* of William Neville Cox and Joan Desirée Cox (*née* Ward); *m* 1975, Susan Ruth Mason; three *s* one *d*. *Educ:* Oundle Sch.; London Hosp. Med. Coll., Univ. of London (Price Entrance Scholar; MB 1971, MSc 1978, MD 1979); MA Cantab 1990, MD Cantab 1991. FRCP 1984. Junior posts, Med. Unit, Royal London Hosp., 1971; Dept of Morbid Anatomy, Bernard Baron Inst., Hammersmith and United Oxford Hosps, 1972–77; Royal Postgraduate Medical School, London University: MRC Training Fellow, Cell Biology Unit, 1977–79; Wellcome Sen. Clinical Fellow and Sen. Lectr, Dept of Medicine, 1979–87; Sen. Lectr, Depts of Haematology and Medicine, 1987–89. Vis. Scientist, Dept of Biology, MIT, 1983–84. Lectures: A. J. MacFazean, Univ. of Hong Kong, 1990; Schorstein Meml, London Hosp. Med Coll., 1994. External examiner in Medicine: Univ. of Hong Kong, 1990; Univ. of London, 1993–. Mem., Assoc. of Physicians of GB and Ire., 1984– (Mem., Exec. Cttee, 1995–). *Publications:* contrib. chapters to Oxford Textbook of Medicine; contribs to sci. and med. jls. *Recreations:* natural history, piano. *Address:* Department of Medicine, University of Cambridge School of Clinical Medicine, Hills Road, Cambridge CB2 2QQ. *T:* Cambridge (01223) 336864.

COX, Sir Trenchard, Kt 1961; CBE 1954; MA; FRSA (Vice-President 1964–68); FMA; FSA; Director and Secretary, Victoria and Albert Museum, 1956–66; *b* 31 July 1905; *s* of late William Pallett Cox and Marion Beverley; *m* 1935, Mary Désirée (*d* 1973), *d* of late Sir Hugh Anderson, Master of Gonville and Caius Coll., Cambridge. *Educ:* Eton; King's Coll., Cambridge. Worked as volunteer at the National Gallery and Brit. Museum (Dept of Prints and Drawings), 1929–32; spent a semester at the University of Berlin in the Dept of Arts, 1930; Asst to the Keeper, Wallace Collection, 1932–39; seconded for war-time duties, to Home Office, 1940–44; Dir of Birmingham Museum and Art Gallery, 1944–55. Member: Ancient Monuments Board for England, 1959–69; Standing Commn on Museums and Galleries, 1967–77. People's Warden, St Martin-in-the Fields, 1968–79. Hon. DLitt Birmingham, 1956. Hon. Fellow, Royal Acad., 1981. Chevalier, Légion d'Honneur, 1967. *Publications:* The National Gallery, a Room-to-Room Guide, 1930; Jehan Foucquet, Native of Tours, 1931; part editor of the Catalogue to the Exhibition of French Art at Burlington House, Jan.–March 1932; The Renaissance in Europe, 1933; A General Guide to the Wallace Collection, 1933; A Short Illustrated History of the Wallace Collection and its Founders, 1936; David Cox, 1947; Peter Bruegel, 1951; Pictures: a Handbook for Curators, 1956. *Recreations:* reading, travelling. *Address:* 33 Queen's Gate Gardens, SW7 5RR. *T:* 0171–584 0231. *Club:* Athenæum.

COX, William Trevor; *see* Trevor, William.

COXETER, Harold Scott Macdonald, FRS 1950; PhD Cambridge, 1931; Professor of Mathematics, University of Toronto, 1948–80, now Emeritus Professor; *b* 9 Feb. 1907; *s* of Harold Samuel Coxeter and Lucy (*née* Gee); *m* 1936, Hendrina Johanna Brouwer, The Hague; one *s* one *d*. *Educ:* King Alfred Sch., London; St George's Sch., Harpenden; Trinity Coll., Cambridge. Entrance Scholar, Trinity Coll., 1926; Smith's Prize, 1931. Fellow Trinity Coll., Cambridge, 1931–36; Rockefeller Foundation Fellow, Princeton, 1932–33; Procter Fellow, Princeton, 1934–35; Asst Prof., 1936–43, Associate Prof., 1943–48, University of Toronto. Visiting Professor: Notre Dame, 1947; Columbia Univ., 1949; Dartmouth Coll., 1964; Univ. of Amsterdam, 1966; Univ. of Edinburgh, 1967; Univ. of E Anglia, 1968; ANU, 1970; Univ. of Sussex, 1972; Univ. of Warwick and Univ. of Utrecht, 1976; Calif. Inst. of Technology, 1977; Univ. of Bologna, 1978. Editor Canadian Jl of Mathematics, 1948–57. President: Canadian Mathematical Congress, 1965–67; Internat. Mathematical Congress, 1974. Foreign Mem., Koninklijke Nederlandse Akademie van Wetenschappen, 1975; Hon. Member: Mathematische Gesellschaft, Hamburg, 1977; Wiskundig Genootschap, Amsterdam, 1978; London Mathematical Soc., 1978. Hon. LLD: Alberta, 1957; Trent, 1973; Toronto, 1979; Hon. DMath Waterloo, 1969; Hon. DSc: Acadia, 1971; Carleton, 1984; McMaster, 1988; Hon. Dr rer. nat. Giessen, 1984. *Publications:* Non-Euclidean Geometry, 1942, 6th edn 1994; Regular Polytopes, 1948, 3rd edn 1973; The Real Projective Plane, 1949, 3rd edn 1992; (with W. O. J. Moser) Generators and Relations, 1st edn, 1957, 4th edn, 1980; Introduction to Geometry, 1961 and 1969; Projective Geometry, 1964, 2nd edn, revd 1987; (with S. L. Greitzer) Geometry Revisited, 1967; Twelve Geometric Essays, 1968; Regular Complex Polytopes, 1974, 2nd edn 1990; (with W. W. Rouse Ball) Mathematical Recreations and Essays, 11th edn 1939, 13th edn 1987; (with R. W. Frucht and D. L. Powers) Zero-symmetric Graphs, 1981; Kaleidoscopes, 1994; various mathematical papers. *Recreation:* music. *Address:* 67 Roxborough Drive, Toronto M4W 1X2, Canada.

COXWELL-ROGERS, Col Richard Annesley; Vice Lord-Lieutenant of Gloucestershire, since 1993; *b* 26 April 1932; *s* of Maj.-Gen. Norman Annesley Coxwell-Rogers, CB, CBE, DSO (*d* 1985) and Diana Coxwell-Rogers (*née* Coston); *m* 1965, Martha Felicity Hurrell; two *s*. *Educ:* Eton Coll.; RMA Sandhurst. Commissioned 15th/19th Hussars, 1952; served Germany, UK, Malaya, Cyprus; Comd 15th/19th Hussars, 1973–75; Col, 15th/19th Hussars, 1988–92. Area Appeals Organiser, CRC, 1982–93. DL Glos 1990; High Sheriff of Glos, 1994. *Recreations:* country sports. *Address:* Close Farm House, Coberley, Cheltenham, Glos GL53 9QZ. *T:* Cheltenham (01242) 870519. *Club:* Cavalry and Guards.

COYLE, Eurfron Gwynne, (Mrs Michael Coyle); *see* Jones, E. G.

COYNE, James Elliott; Canadian banker and financial consultant; *b* Winnipeg, 17 July 1910; *s* of James Bowes Coyne and Edna Margaret Coyne (*née* Elliott); *m* 1957, Meribeth Stobie; one *s* one *d*. *Educ:* University of Manitoba (BA); University of Oxford (BCL). RCAF (Flying Officer), 1942–44. Admitted to the Bar, Manitoba, 1934; solicitor and barrister in Manitoba, 1934–38; Financial Attaché, Canadian Embassy, Washington, DC, 1941; Mem. War-time Prices and Trade Board, Ottawa, 1942 (Dep.-Chm.). Bank of Canada, Ottawa: Asst to the Governors, 1944–49; Deputy-Governor, 1950–54; Governor, 1955–61. *Address:* 16 Ruskin Row, Winnipeg, Manitoba R3M 2R7, Canada.

COZENS, Robert William, CBE 1989; QPM 1981; Director, Police Requirements for Science and Technology, Home Office, 1985–88, retired; *b* 10 Nov. 1927; *s* of Sydney Robert and Rose Elizabeth Cozens; *m* 1952, Jean Dorothy Banfield; one *s* one *d*. *Educ:* Stoke C of E Sch., Guildford. Constable to Chief Superintendent, Surrey Constabulary, 1954–72; Asst Dir, Command Courses, Police Staff Coll., Bramshill, 1972–74; Asst Chief Constable, S Yorks Police, 1974–78; seconded to Federal Judicial Police in Mexico for advisory duties, 1975; Dep. Chief Constable, Lincs Police, 1978–81; Chief Constable, W Mercia Constabulary (Hereford, Worcester and Shropshire), 1981–85. *Recreations:* tennis, making friends.

CRABB, Most Rev. Frederick Hugh Wright, BD, DD; *b* Luppitt, Devon, 24 April 1915; *s* of William Samuel and Florence Mary Crabb; *m* 1946, Alice Margery Coombs; two *s* two *d*. *Educ:* Luppitt Parochial Sch.; Univ. of London (St John's Hall, Highbury, London). BD Lond. (1st Cl. Hons); ALCD (1st Cl. Hons). Asst Curate, St James', West Teignmouth, Devon, 1939–41; Asst Priest, St Andrew's, Plymouth, 1941–42; Missionary at Akot, S Sudan, 1942–44; Principal, Bishop Gwynne Divinity Sch., S Sudan, 1944–51; Vice Principal, London Coll. of Divinity, 1951–57; Principal, Coll. of Emmanuel and St Chad, Saskatoon, Sask., 1957–67; Assoc. Priest, Christ Church, Calgary, Alberta, 1967–69; Rector, St Stephen's Church, Calgary, 1969–75; Bishop of Athabasca, 1975–83; Metropolitan of Rupert's Land, 1977–82; Hon. Asst, St Cyprian, Calgary, and Dir, Anglican Sch. of Lay Ministry, 1983–87. Hon. Chaplain, Calgary Div., RCMP Veterans' Assoc., 1985–. Mem. Governing Council, Athabasca Univ., 1982–85. Hon. DD: Wycliffe Coll., Toronto, 1960; St Andrew's Coll., Saskatoon, 1967; Coll. of Emmanuel and St Chad, Saskatoon, 1979. *Publication:* (jtly) Rupert's Land: A Cultural Tapestry, 1988. *Recreations:* gardening, mountain hiking. *Address:* 3483 Chippendale Drive NW, Calgary, Alberta T2L 0W7, Canada.

CRABB, Tony William; media consultant, since 1992; *b* 27 June 1933; *s* of William Harold Crabb and Ellen Emily Crabb; *m* 1957, Brenda Margaret (*née* Sullman); one *s* one *d*. *Educ:* Chiswick Grammar School; London School of Economics (BScEcon); Intelligence Corps Russian Interpreters Course, 1952–54. BBC, 1957–88; seconded as news adviser to Govt of Libya, 1968–69; Managing Editor: BBC TV News, 1979–82; BBC Breakfast Time, 1982–84; Controller, Corporate News Services, BBC, 1984–87; Special Asst, News and Current Affairs, BBC, 1987–88; Dep. Dir of Broadcasting, Radio TV Hong Kong, 1988–92. *Address:* 38 The Avenue, Sunbury-on-Thames, Middx TW16 5ES.

CRABBE, Kenneth Herbert Martineau, TD; *b* 4 Nov. 1916; *m* 1st, 1940, Rowena Leete (*d* 1981); one *s*; 2nd, 1982, Belinda V. Fitzherbert (*née* Batt); three step *s* one step *d*. *Educ:* Stowe Sch. Commnd TA, 1937; psc; Major. Member, Stock Exchange, London, 1937–; Mem. Council, The Stock Exchange, 1963–78 (Dep. Chm., 1970–73). *Recreations:* golf, fishing, shooting, painting. *Address:* Spandrels, Walliswood, Dorking, Surrey RH5 5RJ. *T:* Okewood Hill (01306) 627275. *Clubs:* Boodle's; West Sussex Golf.

CRABBE, Mrs Pauline, (Mrs Joseph Benjamin), OBE 1969; JP; National Vice-Chairman, Brook Advisory Centres, 1980–86; *b* 1 April 1914; *y d* of Cyril and Edith Henriques, Kingston, Jamaica; *m* 1st, 1936, Geoffrey Henebery (marr. diss. 1948); one *d*; 2nd, 1949, Neville Crabbe (marr. diss. 1960); one *s*; 3rd, 1969, Joseph Benjamin; three step *s*. *Educ:* Highgate Convent; London Academy of Music and Drama; London Univ. (extra-mural course in Psychology). Actress and broadcaster, 1945–53; secretarial work with British Actors' Equity and WEA, 1953–56; then with Old People's Welfare and London Council of Social Service, 1956–57; Welfare Sec. and Dep. Gen. Sec. to Nat. Council for Unmarried Mother and her Child, 1957–69; Conciliation Officer for Race Relations Bd, 1969–71; Sec., 1971–76, Sen. Counsellor, 1976–80, London Brook Adv. Centres. Founder Mem., Haverstock Housing Trust for Fatherless Families, 1966; Mem. Bd, Housing Corp., 1968–75; Member: Community Relations Commn, 1972–77; Standing Adv. Council on Race Relations, 1977–; Parole Bd, 1978–82. Hon. Fellow, Manchester Polytechnic, 1979. Radio and TV broadcaster and panellist. JP London, 1967. FRSA 1972. *Publications:* articles and book reviews in social work jls. *Recreations:* entertaining, walking, indoor gardening, the theatre and the arts. *Address:* 88 Osprey House, Sillwood Place, Brighton, Sussex BN1 2NF. *Club:* Magistrates' Association.

CRABBE, Reginald James Williams, FIA, FSS; President for Life, Provident Life Association Ltd (Chairman, 1967–82, and President, 1982–86, Provident Life Association of London Ltd); Chairman: United Standard Insurance Co. Ltd, 1967–79; Vigilant Assurance Co. Ltd, 1970–79; *b* 22 June 1909; *e s* of late Harry James and Annie Martha Crabbe; *m* 1948, Phyllis Maud Smith; two *d*. *Educ:* Chigwell Sch., Essex. Entered National Mutual Life Assurance Soc., 1926; FIA 1933; joined Provident Life as Asst Actuary, 1935; Man. Dir, 1956–74; Dir, 1956–86; Dep. Chm., 1971–85, Chm., 1975–77, Cope & Timmins Holdings. Chm., Life Offices' Assoc., 1965, 1966. *Publication:* (with C. A. Poyser, MA, FIA) Pension and Widows' and Orphans' Funds, 1953. *Recreations:* reading, gardening, music, art.

CRABBIE, Christopher Donald, CMG 1995; HM Diplomatic Service; Ambassador to Algeria, since 1994; *b* 17 Jan. 1946; *s* of late William George Crabbie and of Jane (*née* Coe). *Educ:* Rugby Sch.; Newcastle Univ.; Liverpool Univ.; Corpus Christi Coll., Oxford. Second Sec., FCO, 1973; First Secretary: Nairobi, 1975; Washington, 1979; FCO, 1983; Counsellor and Hd of European Communities Div., HM Treasury, 1985; Counsellor, FCO, 1987; Dep. UK Perm. Rep., OECD, Paris, 1990; Counsellor, British Embassy, Paris, 1990–94. *Recreations:* ski-ing, flying, sailing, gardening. *Address:* c/o Foreign and Commonwealth Office, SW1A 2AH. *Club:* New (Edinburgh).

CRABBIE, Mrs (Margaret) Veronica, CBE 1977; *b* 26 Nov. 1910; *d* of late Sir Christopher Nicholson Johnston (Lord Sands, Senator of the College of Justice, Scotland), and Lady Sands; *m* 1938, John Patrick Crabbie; two *s* one *d*. *Educ:* St Denis Sch., Edinburgh; Queen Margaret's Sch., Escrick, York. Chairman: Edinburgh Home for Mothers and Infants, 1951–66; Walpole Housing Assoc., 1969–72; Scottish Council for the Unmarried Mother and her Child, 1966–72; WRVS, Scotland, 1972–77. *Recreation:* curling. *Club:* New (Edinburgh).

CRABTREE, Maj-Gen. Derek Thomas, CB 1983; *b* 21 Jan. 1930; *s* of late William Edward Crabtree and of Winifred Hilda Burton; *m* 1960, Daphne Christine Mason; one *s* one *d*. *Educ:* St Brendan's Coll., Bristol. Commissioned, 1953; Regimental Service: 13th/18th Royal Hussars (QMO), 1953–56; Royal Berkshire Regt, 1956–59; Technical Staff Course, RMCS, 1960–62; sc Camberley, 1964; BM 11 Inf. Bde, BAOR, 1965–67; CO 1st Bn Duke of Edinburgh's Royal Regt, UK and Berlin, 1970–72; Col GS, MGO Secretariat, MoD, 1974–76; Dep. Comdr and Chief of Staff Headquarters British Forces Hong Kong, 1976–79; Dep. Comdt RMCS, 1979–80; Dir Gen. of Weapons (Army), MoD, 1980–84. Sen. Mil. Advr, Short Bros, 1984–86; Gen. Manager, Regular Forces Employment Assoc., 1987–94. Col, Duke of Edinburgh's Royal Regt, 1982–87, 1988–89. Gov., Lucas-Tooth Gymnasium, 1989–; Co-optative Trustee: Soldiers', Widows' & Widowers' Fund, 1990–; Single Soldiers' Dependents' Fund, 1990–. *Recreations:* golf, tennis, ski-ing, sailing, gardening, beekeeping. *Address:* 53 High Street, Shrivenham, Swindon SN6 8AW. *Club:* Army and Navy.

CRABTREE, Jonathan; His Honour Judge Crabtree; a Circuit Judge, since 1986; *b* 17 April 1934; *s* of Charles H. Crabtree and Elsie M. Crabtree; *m* 1st, 1957, Caroline Ruth Keigwin (*née* Oliver) (marr. diss. 1976); one *s* three *d* (and one *s* decd); 2nd, 1980, Wendy Elizabeth Hudson (*née* Ward). *Educ:* Bootham; St John's Coll., Cambridge (MA, LLM). Called to Bar, Gray's Inn, 1958. A Recorder, 1974–86. *Recreations:* cricket, cooking, history, archaeology. *Address:* c/o Crown Court, Sheffield S1 2EA. *T:* Sheffield (0114) 275 5866.

CRABTREE, Prof. Lewis Frederick, PhD, FRAeS; FAIAA; Sir George White Professor of Aeronautical Engineering, University of Bristol, 1973–85, now Emeritus; *b* 16 Nov. 1924; *m* 1955, Averil Joan Escott; one *s* one *d*. *Educ:* Univ. of Leeds; Imperial Coll. of Science and Technology; Cornell Univ., USA. BSc (Mech. Eng) Leeds, 1945; DIC (Aeronautics), 1947; PhD (Aero Eng), Cornell, 1952. Air Engr Officer, RNVR, 1945–46. Grad. apprentice, Saunders-Roe Ltd, E Cowes, IoW, 1947–50; ECA Fellowship, Grad. Sch. of Aero. Engrg, Cornell Univ., 1950–52; Aerodynamics Dept, RAE, Farnborough, 1953–73; Head of: Hypersonics and High temperature Gasdynamics Div., 1961–66; Low Speed Aerodynamics Div., 1966–70; Propulsion Aerodynamics and Noise Div., 1970–73.

Visiting Prof., Cornell Univ., 1957. First Chm., Aerospace Technol. Bd, DSAC, 1980–83. Chairman: Brecknock Wildlife Trust, 1988–91; Welsh Wildlife Trusts Ltd, 1994–. Lectures to RAeS: Lanchester Meml, 1977; Handley Page, 1979; Barnwell, 1981. Pres., RAeS, 1978–79 (Usborne Meml Prize, 1955). *Publications:* Elements of Hypersonic Aerodynamics, 1965; contributor to: Incompressible Aerodynamics, 1960; Laminar Boundary Layers, 1963; Engineering Structures, 1983; articles chiefly in Jl RAeS, Aeron. Quart., Jl Aeron. Sci., Jahrbuch der WGLR, and Reports and Memos of ARC. *Address:* Dan-y-Coity, Talybont-on-Usk, Brecon LD3 7YN. *T:* Talybont-on-Usk (01874) 676216.

CRABTREE, Simon; *see* Wharton, Michael B.

CRACKNELL, Malcolm Thomas; His Honour Judge Cracknell; a Circuit Judge, since 1989; *b* 12 Dec. 1943; *s* of late Percy Thomas Cracknell and of Doris Louise Cracknell; *m* 1st, 1968, Ann Carrington (*née* Gooding) (marr. diss. 1980); one *s* one *d*; 2nd, 1988, Felicity Anne Davies; two *s* one *d*. *Educ:* Royal Liberty Sch., Romford; Hull Univ. (LLB); King's Coll., London (LLM). Called to Bar, Middle Temple, 1969. Lectr in Law, Univ. of Hull, 1968–74; Barrister, NE Circuit, 1970–89; a Recorder, 1988. *Recreations:* golf, gardening, walking, cricket, reading. *Address:* Garden House, High Street, Boston Spa, West Yorkshire LS23 6DR. *T:* Boston Spa (01937) 842085.

CRACKNELL, (William) Martin; Chief Executive, Glenrothes Development Corporation, 1976–93; *b* 24 June 1929; *s* of John Sidney Cracknell and Sybil Marian (*née* Wood); *m* 1962, Gillian Goatcher; two *s* two *d*. *Educ:* St Edward's School, Oxford; RMA Sandhurst. Regular Army Officer, Royal Green Jackets, 1949–69; British Printing Industries Fedn, 1969–76. Mem. Exec., Scottish Council (Develt and Industry), 1984–90; Chm., Scottish Cttee, German Chamber of Industry and Commerce in UK, 1987–92. Director: Glenrothes Enterprise Trust, 1983–89; New Enterprise Develt, 1987–90. Cross of Order of Merit (Germany), 1992. *Address:* West End Cottage, Frenchie, Fife KY7 7EZ. *T:* Falkland (01337) 857849. *Club:* Royal Green Jackets.

CRACROFT, Air Vice-Marshal Peter Dicken, CB 1954; AFC 1932; *b* 29 Nov. 1907; *s* of Lt-Col H. Cracroft, Bath; *m* 1932, Margaret Eliza Sugden Patchett; two *s*. *Educ:* Monkton Combe Sch., Bath. Commissioned RAF 1927; Fleet Air Arm, 1928–31; Central Flying Sch. Instructors' Course, 1931; Flying Instructor, Leuchars, 1931–35; Adjt HMS Courageous, 1936–37; Chief Flying Instructor, Oxford Univ. Air Sqdn, 1937–39; RAF Stn Mount Batten, 1939–40; Air Staff, Coastal Command, 1940–41; OC RAF Station, Chivenor, 1941–43; SASO 19 Gp (later 17 Gp), 1933–44; OC 111 Op. Trg Unit, Bahamas, 1944–45; SASO HQ Air Comd, SE Asia, Mil. Gov. Penang, 1945; AOC Bombay, 1945–46; SASO, HQ 19 Gp, 1946–48; RAF Dir and CO, Jt Anti-Submarine Sch., Londonderry, 1948–50; Sen. Air Liaison Officer, S Africa, 1950–52; AOC 66 Gp, Edinburgh, 1952–53; Senior Air Staff Officer, Headquarters Coastal Command, 1953–55; AOC Scotland and 18 Group, 1955–58; retired from RAF, Dec. 1958. *Recreations:* tennis, fishing, shooting. *Address:* Alderney House, Burton Bradstock, Bridport, Dorset DT6 4NQ. *T:* Burton Bradstock (01308) 897270. *Club:* Royal Air Force.

CRACROFT-ELEY, Bridget Katharine; Lord-Lieutenant of Lincolnshire, since 1995; *b* 29 Oct. 1933; *d* of Weston Cracroft-Amcotts and Rhona (*née* Clifton-Brown); *m* 1959, Robert Peel Charles Cracroft-Eley; one *s* one *d*. *Educ:* Lincoln Girls' High Sch.; Crofton Grange Sch., Buntingford, Herts. Voluntary and charity work, incl. WRVS, Girl Guides, Lincs Old Churches Trust and RNIB Looking Glass Appeal, 1970–95. Parish Councillor, Hackthorn and Cold Hanworth, 1980–. Gov., Hackthorn C of E Primary Sch., 1988–. High Sheriff, Lincs, 1989. *Recreations:* upholstery, gardening. *Address:* Hackthorn Hall, Lincoln LN2 3PQ. *T:* Market Rasen (01673) 860212.

CRADDOCK, (William) Aleck, LVO 1981; Director, Harrods Ltd, 1964–88 (Managing Director, 1980–84, Chairman, 1981–86, Deputy Chairman, 1987–88); Director, Cartier Ltd, since 1986; *b* Nov. 1924; *m* 1947, Olive May Brown; one *s* one *d*. *Educ:* City of London School. Joined Druce and Craddock, Craddock and Tomkins Ltd (family firm), Meat and Provision Merchants, Marylebone, London, 1946; joined Harrods Ltd as Asst to Food Manager, 1954; Member of the Board, 1964; Director and General Manager, 1970; Asst Managing Director, 1975; a Director of House of Fraser, 1980–91. Vice Chm., Drapers' Cottage Homes, 1987–94 (Pres., Appeal, 1985–86); Pres., Twenty Club, 1988. Mem. Court of Assts, Worshipful Company of Cooks, 1993– (Liveryman, 1972). Cavaliere Ufficiale (Fourth Cl.), Order Al Merito Della Repubblica Italiana, 1980. *Recreations:* fell walking, watercolour painting. *Address:* 17 Tretawn Park, Mill Hill, NW7 4PS. *Clubs:* Arts; Guards' Polo (Life Mem.).

CRADOCK, John Anthony, CB 1980; MBE 1952; Deputy Secretary, Ministry of Defence, 1981–82; *b* 19 Oct. 1921; *o s* of John Cradock and Nan Cradock (*née* Kelly); *m* 1948, Eileen (*née* Bell); one *s* one *d*. *Educ:* St Brendan's College, Bristol; Bristol Univ. (BA 1946). Military service, 1941–46 (Captain Royal Signals); Malayan Civil Service, 1946–57; War Office, 1957–67; MoD, 1967–75; Under Sec., N Ireland Office, 1975–77; MoD, 1977–82. *Address:* c/o Lloyds Bank, Morpeth, Northumberland NE61 1AN.

CRADOCK, Rt. Hon. Sir Percy, GCMG 1983 (KCMG 1980; CMG 1968); PC 1993; the Prime Minister's Foreign Policy Adviser, 1984–92; *b* 26 Oct. 1923; *m* 1953, Birthe Marie Dyrlund. *Educ:* St John's Coll., Cambridge (Hon. Fellow, 1982). Served Foreign Office, 1954–57; First Sec., Kuala Lumpur, 1957–61, Hong Kong, 1961, Peking, 1962; Foreign Office, 1963–66; Counsellor and Head of Chancery, Peking, 1966–68; Chargé d'Affaires, Peking, 1968–69; Head of Planning Staff, FCO, 1969–71; Under-Sec., Cabinet Office, 1971–75; Ambassador to German Democratic Republic, 1976–78; Leader, UK Delegn to Comprehensive Test Ban Discussions at Geneva, 1977–78; Ambassador to People's Republic of China, 1978–83; Leader of UK team in negotiations over Hong Kong, 1983; Dep. Under Sec. of State, FCO, supervising Hong Kong negotiations, 1984. *Publication:* Experiences of China, 1994. *Club:* Reform.

CRADOCK-HARTOPP, Sir J. E.; *see* Hartopp.

CRAFT, Prof. Alan William, MD; FRCP; Professor of Paediatric Oncology, since 1991, and of Child Health, since 1993, University of Newcastle upon Tyne; *b* 6 July 1946; *s* of William and Yvonne Craft; *m* 1st, 1968, Dorothy Noble (decd); one *s*; 2nd, 1992, Anne Nicholson. *Educ:* Rutherford Grammar Sch., Newcastle upon Tyne; Univ. of Newcastle upon Tyne (MB, BS; MD). FRCP 1982. House Officer, Royal Victoria Infirmary, Newcastle upon Tyne, 1969–70; Sen. House Officer, then Registrar and Sen. Registrar, Newcastle Hosps, 1970–77; MRC Trng Fellow, Royal Marsden Hosp., 1976–77; Consultant Paediatrician: N Tyneside Hosp., 1977–86; Royal Victoria Infirmary, 1977–. Chm., European Osteosarcoma Intergroup, 1994–; Sec., Internat. Paediatric Oncology Soc., 1993–. *Publications:* papers on childhood cancer and other childhood disorders in BMJ, Lancet, Archives of Disease in Childhood, etc. *Recreations:* marathon running, orienteering. *Address:* 2 Ruthven Court, Adderstone Crescent, Newcastle upon Tyne NE2 2HH. *T:* 0191–281 6718.

CRAFT, Prof. Ian Logan, FRCS; FRCOG; Director, London Gynaecology and Fertility Centre, since 1990; *b* 11 July 1937; *s* of Reginald Thomas Craft and Lois Mary (*née* Logan); *m* 1959, Jacqueline Rivers Symmons; two *s*. *Educ:* Owens Sch., London; Westminster Med. Sch., Univ. of London (MB, BS). FRCS 1966; MRCOG 1970, FRCOG 1986. Sen. Registrar, Westminster Hosp. Teaching Gp (Westminster Hosp. and Kingston Hosp.), 1970–72; Sen. Lectr and Consultant, Inst. of Obstetrics and Gynaecology, Queen Charlotte's Hosp., London, 1972–76; Prof. of Obstetrics and Gynaecology, Royal Free Hosp., London, 1976–82; Dir of Gynaecology, Cromwell Hosp., 1982–85; Dir of Fertility and Obstetric Studies, Humana Hosp. Wellington, 1985–90. FRSocMed. *Publications:* contrib. BMJ, Lancet and other medical jls. *Recreations:* art, music, ornithology, sports of most types. *Address:* 5 Devonshire Mews North, W1N 1FR; London Gynaecology and Fertility Centre, Cozens House, 112A Harley Street, W1N 1AF. *T:* 0171–224 0707.

CRAFT, Prof. Maurice, PhD, DLitt; Co-ordinator for Research in Education, University of Greenwich, since 1994; *b* 4 May 1932; *er s* of Jack and Polly Craft, London; *m* 1957, Alma, *y d* of Elio and Dinah Sampson, Dublin; two *d*. *Educ:* LCC Elem. Sch. and Colfe's Grammar Sch., SE13; LSE, Univ. of London (BSc Econ); Sch. of Education, Trinity Coll., Univ. of Dublin (HDipEd); Inst. of Education, Univ. of London (AcadDipEd); Dept of Sociology, Univ. of Liverpool (PhD 1972); Univ. of Nottingham (DLitt 1990). 2/Lt RAOC (Nat. Service), 1953–55. Asst Master, Catford Secondary Sch., SE6, 1956–60; Princ. Lectr and Head of Dept of Sociology, Edge Hill Coll. of Education, Ormskirk, Lancs, 1960–67; Sen. Lectr in Education, i/c Advanced Courses, Univ. of Exeter, 1967–73; Sub-Dean, Faculty of Educn, 1969–73; Prof. of Education, and Chairman, Centre for the Study of Urban Education, La Trobe Univ., Melbourne, 1973–75; Goldsmiths' Prof. of Education, Inst. of Educn, Univ. of London, and Head of Dept of Advanced Studies in Education, Goldsmiths' Coll., 1976–80; Univ. of Nottingham: Prof. of Educn, and Hd, Div. of Advanced Studies, 1980–89; Dean, Faculty of Educn, 1981–83; Chm., Sch. of Educn, 1983–85, 1988–89; Pro-Vice-Chancellor, 1983–87; Foundn Dean of Humanities and Social Science, Hong Kong Univ. of Science and Technol., 1989–92; Sen. Consultant to Dir, Open Learning Inst. of Hong Kong, 1992–94. Adviser: Devon CC, 1970–72; Aust. Federal Poverty Commn, 1974–75; State Coll., Vict., Aust., 1974–75; Assoc. of Commonwealth Univs, 1976, 1979; CNAA, 1978–89; Centre for Advice and Inf. on Educn Disadvantage (Chm., Teacher Educn Working Gp, 1979–80); Schools Council, 1979; CRE (Chm., Teacher Educn Adv. Gp, 1980–84); H of C Home Affairs Cttee, 1981; Swann Cttee, 1982–84; Leverhulme Trust, 1982–; Council for Educn and Trng in Youth and Community Work (Chm., In-service Wkg Gp, 1983); UNESCO, 1985; QUB, 1986; Univ. of Kuwait, 1988; Hong Kong Council for Academic Accreditation, 1991; Hong Kong Educn Commn, 1991; City Polytechnic of Hong Kong, 1992; Hong Kong Baptist Univ., 1994. Mem., UK Delegn to EEC Colloquium on Ethnic Min. Educn, Brussels, 1979, 1982; UK delegate to: Council of Europe Seminars on Intercultural Trng of Teachers, Lisbon, 1981, Rome, 1982, Strasbourg, 1983; UNESCO Colloquium on Educnl Disadvantage, Thessalonika, 1984. Member: Council of Validating Univs, 1982–89 (Vice-Chm., 1987–89); E Midlands Reg. Consultative Gp on Teacher Educn, 1980–84 (Chm., 1980–84); Exec. Cttee, Univs Council for Educn of Teachers, 1984–88 (Chm., Standing Cttee on Validation, 1984–87); Cttee of Vice-Chancellors and Principals, 1986–88 (Cttee on Validation, 1986–88); Hong Kong Govt Bd of Inquiry in Educn, 1992; Hong Kong Govt Adv. Cttee on Teacher Educn and Qualifications, 1993. Mem. Management Cttee, Sociology of Educn Abstracts, 1965–; Member, Editorial Board: Jl of Multilingual and Multicultural Develt, 1979–; Multicultural Educn Abstracts, 1981–; Internat. Studies in Sociology of Educn, 1991–. FRSA 1989. *Publications:* (ed jtly) Linking Home and School, 1967 (3rd edn, 1980); (ed jtly) Guidance and Counselling in British Schools, 1969 (2nd edn, 1974); (ed) Family, Class and Education: a Reader, 1970; Urban Education—a Dublin case study, 1974; School Welfare Provision in Australia, 1977; (ed) Teaching in a Multicultural Society: the Task for Teacher Education, 1981; (jtly) Training Teachers of Ethnic Minority Community Languages, 1983; (ed jtly) Change in Teacher Education, 1984; (ed) Education and Cultural Pluralism, 1984; The Democratisation of Education, 1985; Teacher Education in a Multicultural Society, 1986, (ed jtly) Ethnic Relations and Schooling, 1995; contrib. to numerous books and to the following jls: Educnl Research, Internat. Review of Educn, Educnl Review, Social and Econ. Admin., Cambridge Jl of Educn, Educn for Teaching, British Jl of In-Service Educn, Internat. Social Work, Aust. Jl of Social Work, Aust. Educnl Researcher, THES, Higher Educn Jl, New Society, Education, Administration, New Era, Studies. *Recreations:* music, walking. *Address:* Faculty of Education, University of Greenwich, Avery Hill Road, Eltham, SE9 2HB. *T:* 0181–331 9688. *Club:* Royal Over-Seas League.

CRAFTS, Prof. Nicholas Francis Robert, FBA 1992; Professor of Economic History, University of Warwick, since 1988; *b* 9 March 1949; *s* of Alfred Hedley Crafts and Flora Geraldine Mary Crafts; *m* 1969, Barbara Daynes; one *s* two *d*. *Educ:* Brunts Grammar Sch., Mansfield; Trinity Coll., Cambridge (BA Econs 1st cl., 1970). Lectr in Econ. Hist., Exeter Univ., 1971–72; Lectr in Econs, Warwick Univ., 1972–77; Fellow in Econs, University Coll., Oxford, 1977–86; Prof. of Econ. Hist., Leeds Univ., 1987–88. Vis. Asst Prof. of Econs, Univ. of Calif., Berkeley, 1974–76; Vis. Prof. of Econs, Stanford Univ., 1982–83. *Publications:* British Economic Growth during the Industrial Revolution, 1985; contrib. to Economic Jl, Jl of Economic Hist., Economic Policy, Population Studies, etc. *Recreations:* betting on horses, drinking beer. *Address:* Department of Economics, University of Warwick, Coventry CV4 7AL. *T:* Coventry (01203) 523510.

CRAGG, Rt. Rev. (Albert) Kenneth, DPhil; *b* 8 March 1913; *yr s* of Albert and Emily Cragg; *m* 1940, Theodora Melita (*d* 1989), *yr d* of John Wesley Arnold; three *s* (one *d* decd). *Educ:* Blackpool Grammar Sch.; Jesus Coll., Oxford; Tyndale Hall, Bristol. BA Oxon 2nd Cl. Hons Mod. Hist., 1934; MA Oxon 1938; DPhil 1950. Ellerton Theol. Essay Prize, Oxford, 1937; Green Moral Philos. Prize, Oxford, 1947. Deacon, 1936; Priest, 1937; Curate, Higher Tranmere Parish Church, Birkenhead, 1936–39; Chaplain, All Saints', Beirut, Lebanon, 1939–47; Warden, St Justin's House, Beirut, 1942–47; Asst Prof. of Philos., Amer. University of Beirut, 1942–47; Rector of Longworth, Berks, 1947–51; Sheriff's Chap., Berks, 1948; Prof. of Arabic and Islamics, Hartford Seminary, Conn, USA, 1951–56; Rockefeller Travelling Schol., 1954; Res. Canon, St George's Collegiate Church, Jerusalem, 1956–61; Fellow, St Augustine's Coll., Canterbury, 1959–60, Sub-Warden, 1960–61, Warden, 1961–67; Examng Chaplain to Archbishop of Canterbury, 1961–67; Hon. Canon of Canterbury, 1961–80; Asst Bishop to Archbishop in Jerusalem, 1970–74; Reader in Religious Studies, Sussex Univ., and Asst Bishop, dio. of Chichester, 1973–78; Vicar of Helme, W Yorks, and Asst Bishop, dio. Wakefield, 1978–81; Asst Bishop, dio. Oxford, 1982–. Select Preacher: Cambridge, 1961; Dublin, 1962; Oxford, 1974. Proctor in Convocation, Canterbury, 1965–68; Visiting Prof., Union Theological Seminary, New York, 1965–66; Lectr, Faculty of Divinity, Cambridge, 1966; Jordan Lectr, Sch. of Oriental and African Studies, University of London, 1967; Vis. Prof., University of Ibadan, Nigeria, 1968; Bye-Fellow, Gonville and Caius Coll., Cambridge, 1968–74; Vis. Prof., Virginia Theol Seminary, 1984, 1985. Hon. DD Leeds, 1993. Editor, The Muslim World Quarterly, 1952–60. *Publications:* The Call of the Minaret, 1956, 2nd edn 1986; Sandals at the Mosque, 1959; The Dome and the Rock, 1964; Counsels in Contemporary Islam, 1965; Christianity in World Perspective, 1968; The Privilege of Man, 1968; The House of Islam, 1969; Alive to God, 1970; The Event of the Qur'ān, 1971; The Mind of the Qur'ān, 1973; The Wisdom of the Sufis, 1976; The Christian and Other Religion, 1977; Islam from Within, 1979; This Year in Jerusalem, 1982; Muhammad and the Christian, 1983; The Pen and the Faith, 1985; Jesus and the Muslim, 1985; The Christ and the Faiths, 1986; Readings in the Qur'ān, 1988; What Decided Christianity, 1989; The Arab Christian, 1991; Troubled by Truth, 1992; To Meet and to Greet, 1992; Faith and Life Negotiate (autobiog.), 1994; translated: City of Wrong, 1959; The Theology of Unity, 1965; A Passage to France, 1976; The Hallowed Valley, 1977; contributor: Journal of World History, 1957; Religion in the Middle East, 1969. *Address:* 3 Goring Lodge, White House Road, Oxford OX1 4QE.

CRAGG, Anthony Douglas, RA 1994; sculptor; Professor and Co-Director, Düsseldorf Kunstakademie, since 1988; *b* 9 April 1949; *m* 1990, Tatjana (*née* Verhasselt); one *s* one *d*, and two *s* by former *m*. *Educ:* Wimbledon Sch. of Art; Royal Coll. of Art. *One-man exhibitions include:* Lisson Gall., 1979, 1980, 1985, 1991, 1992; Whitechapel Art Gall., 1981; Kanrasha Gall., Tokyo, 1982, 1984, 1989, 1990; Konrad Fischer, Düsseldorf, 1982, 1986, 1989, 1990; Marian Goodman, NY, 1982, 1983, 1986, 1987, 1989; Palais des Beaux-Arts, Brussels, 1985; Brooklyn Mus. of Art, NY, 1986; Venice Biennale, 1986, 1988; Hayward Gall., 1987; Tate Gall., Liverpool, 1988; Tate Gall., 1989; Stedelijik Van Abbemus., Eindhoven, 1989, 1991; Corcoran Gall. of Art, Washington, 1991; Wiener Secession, 1991; IVAM, Valencia, 1992; *group exhibitions:* Documenta 7, Documenta 8, 1987, Kassel; Mus. van Hedendaagse Kunst, Ghent, 1980; Bienal de São Paulo, 1983; Tate Gall., 1983, 1985; Sydney Biennale, 1984, 1990; Hayward Gall., 1985, 1990; and many others throughout Europe, US, Japan and Australia. Turner Prize, 1988. Chevalier des Arts et des Lettres (France), 1992. *Address:* Adolf Vorwerk Strasse 24, 5600 Wüppertal 2, Germany.

CRAGG, Anthony John; Assistant Secretary General for Defence Planning and Policy, NATO, since 1993; *b* 16 May 1943; *s* of Leslie Cragg and late Gwendolen Cragg (*née* Pevler); *m* 1971, Jeanette Ann Rix; two *d*. *Educ:* Hastings Grammar School; Lincoln College, Oxford (Open Schol.; BA). Ministry of Defence, 1966–: Asst Private Sec. to Sec. of State for Defence, 1974; UK Delegn to NATO, 1977; Asst Sec., 1979; Chief Officer, Sovereign Base Areas, Cyprus, 1983–85; RCDS 1988; Asst Under Sec. of State, 1990; Dir Gen. of Mgt Audit, MoD, 1991–93; Chm., Defence Organisation Planning Team, 1991–92. *Recreations:* the performing arts, reading. *Address:* c/o NATO Headquarters, B1110 Brussels, Belgium.

CRAGG, James Birkett; Emeritus Professor of Environmental Science, University of Calgary, Alberta; *b* 8 Nov. 1910; *s* of late A. W. Cragg, N Shields; *m* 1937, Mary Catherine Macnaughtan (marr. diss. 1968); four *s* (and one *s* one *d* decd); *m* Jean Moore. *Educ:* private sch.; Tynemouth High Sch.; Durham Univ. BSc King's Coll., University of Durham, 1933; DThPT, 1934; MSc, 1937; DSc Newcastle, 1965. Demonstrator, Physiology Dept, Manchester Univ., 1935; Asst Lecturer, and later Lecturer, in Zoology, University Coll. of North Wales, 1937; seconded to Agricultural Research Council, 1942; Scientific Officer, ARC Unit of Insect Physiology, 1944; Reader in Zoology, Durham Colls, in University of Durham, 1946; Prof. of Zoology, University of Durham, 1950–61; Dir, Merlewood Research Station (Nature Conservancy, NERC), Grange-over-Sands, Lancs, 1961–66; Dir, Environmental Sciences Centre, and Prof. of Biology, 1966–72, Killam Meml Prof., 1966–76, Vice-Pres. (Academic), 1970–72, Univ. of Calgary, Alberta. Pres., British Ecol. Soc., 1960–61; Former Chairman: Commn for Ecology; Internat. Union for Conservation of Nature; Convenor, Internat. Biological Programme PT Cttee; Mem., Internat. Biological Programme Cttees; Consultant, Ford Foundation, 1965. Commonwealth Prestige Fellow (New Zealand), 1964. Jubilee medal, 1977. Hon. FIBiol 1981. *Publications:* papers in scientific periodicals; formerly Editor, Advances in Ecological Research. *Recreation:* books. *Address:* 2112 Uralta Road, Calgary, Alberta T2N 4B4, Canada. *Club:* Athenæum.

CRAGG, Rt. Rev. Kenneth; *see* Cragg, Rt. Rev. A. K.

CRAGG, Dr Martin Robert; Chief Executive and Secretary, Institution of Highways and Transportation, since 1990; *b* 8 June 1941; *s* of Robert Brooks Cragg and Hilda Cragg (*née* Bateman); *m* 1966, Pamela Watts; one *s* two *d*. *Educ:* Dixie Grammar Sch., Market Bosworth; Sheffield Univ. (BSc Hons Chem.; PhD Fuel Technol. 1966); London Business Sch. (Sloan Fellow). Industrial Advr, NEDO, 1979–88; Dir, then Dir-Gen. and Chief Exec., Business Equipt and Information Technol. Assoc., 1988–89, then Sen. Exec., Electronic and Business Equipt Assoc., 1989–90. *Recreations:* golf, bridge, fly fishing. *Address:* 10 Woodside Road, New Malden, Surrey KT3 3AH. *T:* 0181–942 8008.

CRAGGS, Prof. James Wilkinson, BSc, PhD; Professor of Engineering Mathematics, University of Southampton, 1967–81; *b* 3 Feb. 1920; *s* of Thomas Gibson Craggs and Margaret (*née* Wilkinson); *m* 1946, Mary Baker; two *s* one *d*. *Educ:* Bede Collegiate Sch., Sunderland; University of Manchester. BSc 1941, PhD 1948, Manchester; PhD Cambridge, 1953. Junior Lectr, Royal Military Coll. of Science, 1941–45; Asst Lectr, University of Manchester, 1947–49; Lecturer, Queen's Coll., Dundee, 1951–52; King's Coll., Newcastle upon Tyne: Lectr, 1952–56; Senior Lecturer, 1956–60; Reader in Mathematics, 1960–61; Prof. of Mathematics, University of Leeds, 1961–63; Prof. of Applied Mathematics, Melbourne Univ., 1963–67. *Publications:* contrib. learned journals regarding the mechanics of solids and fluids. *Recreation:* Methodist lay preacher. *Address:* 23 Redhill, Bassett, Southampton SO1 7BR.

CRAGGS, Prof. John Drummond, MSc, PhD, FInstP; retired; Professor of Electronic Engineering, University of Liverpool, 1955–82; *b* 17 May 1915; *s* of Thomas Lawson Craggs and Elsie Aidrienne Roberts; *m* 1941, Dorothy Ellen Margaret Garfitt; two *d*. *Educ:* Huddersfield Coll.; University of London. Research Student, King's Coll., London Univ., 1937–38; Metropolitan-Vickers High Voltage Research Laboratory, Manchester, 1938–48; University of California, Radiation Laboratory, 1944–45; apptd Sen. Lectr, 1948, and, later, Reader, Dept of Electrical Engineering, University of Liverpool. A Pro-Vice-Chancellor, Liverpool Univ., 1969–72. Hon. DSc NUI, 1986. *Publications:* Counting Tubes, 1950 (with S. C. Curran); Electrical Breakdown of Gases, 1953; High Voltage Laboratory Technique, 1954 (with J. M. Meek); Electrical Breakdown of Gases (with J. M. Meek), 1978; papers in various professional jls. *Address:* Stone Cottage, Newton-cum-Larton, West Kirby, Wirral, Merseyside L48 1PG. *T:* 0151–625 5055.

CRAGGS, Madeleine Jennifer; Secretary, Imperial Cancer Research Fund, since 1991; *b* 28 Dec. 1945; *d* of René Beaumont-Craggs and Muriel (*née* Robinson). *Educ:* Couvent des Ursulines, Brussels; Alexandra Grammar Sch., Singapore; WRAC Coll., Camberley. MIMgt. Commnd WRAC, 1965; served in UK and Germany, incl. staff appts, MoD and HQ BAOR; Maj., 1970; WRAC Advr, 16th Signal Regt, 1973–75; Battery Comdr, Royal Sch. Artillery, 1975–77; SO2(A), HQ York Dist, 1977–79; Chief Instructor, WRAC Trng Centre, 1979–81; Detachment Comdr, Manning and Records Office, Chester, 1981–82; SO2 (Manpower & Planning), WRAC Directorate, MoD, 1982–84; Develt Dir, St Bartholomew's Hosp. Med. Coll., 1984–90. *Recreations:* good wine, good food, good company. *Address:* Felstead Wharf, 38 Ferry Street, E14 3DT.

CRAIB, Douglas Duncan Simpson, CBE 1974; FRAgS 1971; farmer, 1937–83; Member, Potato Marketing Board of Great Britain, 1968–83; *b* 5 April 1914; *s* of Peter Barton Salsbury Simpson and Helen Duncan; changed name by deed poll, 1930; *m* 1939, Moyra Louise Booth; one *s* one *d*. *Educ:* Aberdeen Grammar Sch.; Dundee High School. Commerce, 1934. Captain, 7th Bn Seaforth Highlanders, 1939–42. Dir, NALCO Ltd, Aberdeen, 1956–68. Chm., Elec. Cons. Council, N Scotland Area, 1971–79; Mem., N of Scotland Hydro-Elec. Bd, 1971–79. Dir, Royal Highland and Agric. Soc. of Scotland, 1961–74 (Chm., 1967–69; Hon. Sec. and Hon. Treas., 1970–74; Hon. Vice-Pres., 1978–79, 1987–88); Member: Highland Agric. Exec. Cttee, 1958–72 (Chm., 1970–72); Scottish Agric. Consultative Panel, 1963–87; Scottish Council of Technical Educn, 1973–85 (Assessor, 1981–85); President: Moray Area, NFU, 1945; Moray Farmers' Club, 1950; Governor: N of Scotland Coll. of Agriculture, 1970–84; Rowett Res. Inst., Aberdeen, 1973–86; Trustee, The MacRobert Trusts, Scotland, 1970–84. DL Moray, 1974–90. *Address:* The Old School, Mosstodloch, Fochabers, Morayshire IV32 7LE. *T:* Fochabers (01343) 820733. *Clubs:* Farmers'; Elgin (Elgin, Morayshire).

CRAIG, family name of **Viscount Craigavon** and of **Baron Craig of Radley.**

CRAIG OF RADLEY, Baron *cr* 1991 (Life Peer), of Helhoughton in the County of Norfolk; **Marshal of the Royal Air Force David Brownrigg Craig,** GCB 1984 (KCB 1981; CB 1978); OBE 1967; Chief of the Defence Staff, 1988–91; *b* 17 Sept. 1929; *s* of Major Francis Brownrigg Craig and Mrs Olive Craig; *m* 1955, Elisabeth June Derenburg; one *s* one *d*. *Educ:* Radley Coll.; Lincoln Coll., Oxford (MA; Hon. Fellow 1984). FRAeS 1986. Commnd in RAF, 1951; OC RAF Cranwell, 1968–70; ADC to the Queen, 1969–71; Dir, Plans and Ops, HQ Far East Comd, 1970–71; OC RAF Akrotiri, 1972–73; ACAS (Ops), MoD, 1975–78; AOC No 1 Group, RAF Strike Command, 1978–80; Vice-Chief of Air Staff, 1980–82; AOC-in-C, RAF Strike Command and C-in-C, UK Air Forces, 1982–85; CAS, 1985–88. Air ADC to the Queen, 1985–88. Dir, M. L. Holdings plc, 1991–92. Hon. DSc Cranfield, 1988. *Recreations:* fishing, shooting, golf. *Address:* House of Lords, SW1A 0PW. *Club:* Royal Air Force.

CRAIG, Sir (Albert) James (Macqueen), GCMG 1984 (KCMG 1981; CMG 1975); HM Diplomatic Service, retired; President, Middle East Association, since 1993 (Director General, 1985–93); Lecturer at Pembroke College, University of Oxford, since 1985; *b* 13 July 1924; *s* of James Craig and Florence Morris; *m* 1952, Margaret Hutchinson; three *s* one *d*. *Educ:* Liverpool Institute High Sch.; Univ. of Oxford. Queen's Coll., Oxford (Exhibr), 1942; 1st cl. Hon. Mods Classics, 1943 (Hon. Schol.); Army, 1943–44; 1st cl. Oriental Studies (Arabic and Persian), 1947; Sen. Demy, Magdalen Coll., 1947–48; student, Cairo Univ., 1950–51. Lectr in Arabic, Durham Univ., 1948–55; seconded to FO, 1955 as Principal Instructor at Middle East Centre for Arab Studies, Lebanon; joined Foreign Service substantively, 1956; served: FO, 1958–61; HM Political Agent, Trucial States, 1961–64; 1st Sec., Beirut, 1964–67; Counsellor and Head of Chancery, Jedda, 1967–70; Supernumerary Fellow, St Antony's Coll., Oxford, 1970–71; Head of Near East and N Africa Dept, FCO, 1971–75; Dep. High Comr, Kuala Lumpur, 1975–76; Ambassador to: Syria, 1976–79; Saudi Arabia, 1979–84. Vis. Prof. in Arabic, Univ. of Oxford, 1985–91. Director: Saudi-British Bank, 1985–94; Hong Kong Egyptian Bank, 1987–94; Special Adviser, Hong Kong Bank Gp, 1985–92; Chm., Roxby Engineering Internat., 1988–. Pres., British Soc. for ME Studies, 1987–94; Vice-Chm., Middle East Internat., 1990–. Sen. Associate Mem., St Antony's Coll., Oxford, 1989. Hon. Fellow, Middle East Centre, Durham Univ., 1987–. OStJ 1985; Mem. Council, Order of St John, 1985–90. *Address:* c/o 33 Bury Street, SW1Y 6AX. *T:* 0171–839 2137. *Club:* Travellers'.

CRAIG, Surgeon Rear-Admiral Alexander, QHP 1992; Medical Director General (Naval), since 1994; *b* 22 Nov. 1943; *s* of Rev. Dr Albert Craig and Agnes Nicol (*née* Wards); *m* 1968, Kate Margaret Elliott; one *s* two *d*. *Educ:* George Watson's Boys' Coll., Edinburgh; Edinburgh Univ. (MB ChB 1967). Royal Infirmary, Edinburgh, 1968; Regimental MO, 45 Commando, RM, 1969–72; Jt Services Families Clinic, Malta, 1972–74; OC Med. Sqn, CDO LOG Regt, 1974–78; MoD, 1978–80, NDC 1981; UK Support Unit, Naples, 1981–83; CSO to Surgeon Cdre (NMT), 1983–86; PMO, HMS Sultan, 1986–87; CSO to SRA (OMS), 1987–89; MO i/c, Inst. of Naval Medicine, 1989–90; Dir, Med. Organisation, MoD, 1990–93; Surg. Rear-Adm. Support Med. Services, 1993–94. *Recreation:* travel. *Address:* Victory Building, HM Naval Base, Portsmouth PO1 3LS.

CRAIG, Mrs Barbara Denise, MA Oxon; Principal of Somerville College, Oxford, 1967–80, Honorary Fellow, 1980; *b* 22 Oct. 1915; *o d* of John Alexander Chapman and Janie Denize (*née* Callaway); *m* 1942, Wilson James Craig, CBE (*d* 1989); no *c*. *Educ:* Haberdashers' Aske's Girls' Sch., Acton; Somerville Coll., Oxford. Craven Fellow, 1938; Goldsmiths' Sen. Student, 1938; Woolley Fellow in Archæology of Somerville Coll., 1954–56. Temp. Asst Principal, Mins of Supply and Labour, 1939–40; Asst to Prof. of Greek, Aberdeen Univ., 1940–42; Temp. Asst Principal, Min. of Home Security, 1942; Temp. Principal, Min. of Production, 1943–45. Unofficial work as wife of British Council officer in Brazil, Iraq, Spain, Pakistan, 1946–65; from 1956, archæological work on finds from British excavations at Mycenae. *Recreations:* bird-watching (Mem. Brit. Ornithologists' Union); walking. *Address:* The Wynd, Gayle, Hawes, North Yorkshire DL8 3SD. *T:* Wensleydale (01969) 667289.

CRAIG, Charles (James); opera singer (tenor); *b* 3 Dec. 1919; *s* of James and Rosina Craig; *m* 1946, Dorothy Wilson; one *s* one *d*. *Educ:* in London. Protégé of Sir Thomas Beecham; Principal Tenor with Carl Rosa Opera Co., 1953–56; joined Sadler's Wells Opera Co., 1956. Has appeared regularly at internat. opera houses, incl. Covent Garden, Milan, Rome, Vienna, Paris, Berlin, Buenos Aires, etc; repertoire of 48 operas, incl. Otello, Aida, Turandot, Norma, Andrea Chenier, Die Walküre, Götterdämmerung, Lohengrin, etc. Concerts, TV and radio, and records. International Opera Medal Award, 1962. *Recreations:* motoring, cooking. *Address:* Whitfield Cottage, Whitfield, Brackley, Northants NN13 5TE.

CRAIG, Christopher John Sinclair, CB 1991; DSC 1982; RN retired; *b* 18 May 1941; *s* of Richard Michael Craig and Barbara Mary Craig; *m* 1973, Daphne Joan Underwood; two *s*. *Educ:* Portchester Sch., Bournemouth. Joined RN as officer cadet, 1959; qualified as Naval helicopter pilot, 1963; operational flying and sea service (Far East), 1963–70; in comd HMS Monkton, 1970–72, naval air sqdns 705 and 826, 1973–76; Asst Sec. to Chiefs of Staff, 1978–80; in command: HMS Alacrity, 1980–82 (incl. Falklands War); HMS Avenger and Fourth Frigate Sqdn, 1986–87; RNAS Portland/HMS Osprey, 1987–89; HMS Drake, 1989–90; RN Forces Afloat, Gulf War, 1991; COS to Flag Officer, Naval Aviation, 1991–94. United States Bronze Star, 1991. *Recreations:* walking, reading, golf, horse-racing. *Address:* National Westminster Bank, 48 Blue Boar Row, Salisbury, Wilts SP1 1DF.

CRAIG, Prof. David Parker, AO 1985; FRS 1968; FAA 1969; FRSC; University Fellow and Emeritus Professor, Australian National University, since 1985; *b* 23 Dec. 1919; *s* of Andrew Hunter Craig, Manchester and Sydney, and Mary Jane (*née* Parker); *m* 1948, Veronica, *d* of Cyril Bryden-Brown, Market Harborough and Sydney; three *s* one *d*. *Educ:* Sydney Church of England Grammar Sch.; University of Sydney; University Coll., London. MSc (Sydney) 1941, PhD (London) 1950, DSc (London) 1956. Commonwealth Science Scholar, 1940. War Service: Capt., Australian Imperial Force, 1941–44. Lectr in Chemistry, University of Sydney, 1944–46; Turner and Newall Research Fellow,

1946–49, and Lectr in Chemistry, University Coll., London, 1949–52; Prof. of Physical Chemistry, Univ. of Sydney, 1952–56; Prof. of Chemistry, University Coll., London, 1956–67; Prof. of Chemistry, 1967–85, Dean, Research Sch. of Chemistry, 1970–73 and 1977–81, ANU. Vis. Prof., UCL, 1968–; Firth Vis. Prof., Univ. of Sheffield, 1973; Vis. Prof., University Coll., Cardiff, 1975–89. Part-time Mem., CSIRO Exec., 1980–85. Chm., Adv. Cttee, Aust. Nat. Botanic Gdns, 1986–89. Pres., Australian Acad. of Sci., 1990–94. Fellow of University Coll., London, 1964–. Hon. FRSC 1987. Hon. Dr Chem Bologna, 1985; Hon. DSc Sydney, 1985. *Publications:* books and original papers on chemistry in scientific periodicals. *Address:* 199 Dryandra Street, O'Connor, ACT 2601, Australia. *Club:* Athenæum.

CRAIG, Douglas, OBE 1965; freelance opera producer, adjudicator and lecturer; *b* 26 May 1916; *m* 1955, Dorothy Dixon; two *d. Educ:* Latymer Upper Sch.; St Catharine's Coll., Cambridge (MA). FRCM, FRSA. Winchester Prize, Cambridge, 1938. Intell. Corps, 1940–46, Major 1944. Baritone, Sadler's Wells Opera and elsewhere, 1946–; Artistic Dir, Opera for All, 1949–65; Stage Dir, Glyndebourne, 1952–55; Asst Gen. Man., Glyndebourne, 1955–59; Producer, Royal Coll. of Music, 1958–; Freelance Opera Producer, 1959–; Dep. Dir, London Opera Centre, 1965–66; Administrator, Welsh Nat. Opera, 1966–70; Dir, Sadler's Wells Theatre, 1970–78; Dir, Opera and Drama Sch., RCM, 1976–80. Master Teacher in Residence, Adelaide Coll. of the Arts, 1981; taught in Adelaide, Canberra, Melbourne, Sydney and Hong Kong, 1984 (specialist tour award from British Council); prodns for S Australia Coll. of Advanced Educn and for NSW State Conservatorium of Music, master classes and lectures, Australia, 1985; Nat. Adjudicator, Australian Singing Competition, 1985. Pres., Council of Friends of Sadler's Wells, 1987–; Vice Pres., Sussex Opera and Ballet Soc., 1974–. Mem. Exec. and Editor, Music Jl of ISM, 1979–84. *Publication:* (ed) Delius: Koanga (opera), 1975. *Recreation:* travel. *Address:* 43 Park Road, Radlett, Herts WD7 8EG. *T:* Radlett (01923) 857240. *Club:* Garrick.

CRAIG, Edward Anthony, (works also under name of Edward Carrick), FRSA; writer and lecturer, designer for film and theatre; independent film art director; *b* 3 Jan. 1905; *s* of late Edward Gordon Craig, CH; *m* 1960, Mary, *d* of late Lieut-Col H. A. Timewell, OBE. Studied art, the theatre and photography in Italy, 1917–26; has discovered numerous documents of great value to the history of the theatre; Art Dir to the Welsh Pearson Film Co., 1928–29; Art Dir for Associated Talking Pictures, 1932–36; Supervising Art Dir, Criterion Film, 1937–39; established AAT Film Sch., 1937; Art Dir to the Crown Film Unit (Ministry of Information), 1939–46; Executive Art Dir, Independent Producers (Rank), 1947–49; wood-engravings, oil paintings, and scene designs exhibited at: the St George's Gallery, 1927 and 1928; at the Redfern Gallery, 1929, 1931, 1938; The Grubb Group, 1928–38; also in the principal Galleries of Canada and North America; designer of scenes and costumes for numerous London productions and at Stratford-upon-Avon, 1949. *Official Purchasers:* the British Museum; Victoria and Albert Museum; Metropolitan Museum, New York; Yale Univ., USA; The University, Austin, Texas. *Publications:* Designing for Moving Pictures, 1941; Meet the Common People, 1942; Art and Design in British Films, 1948; Designing for Films, 1949; Gordon Craig, The Story of his Life, 1968, Polish trans., 1977, Amer. edn 1985; (in Italian) Fabrizio Carini Motta, 1972; William Nicolson's An Alphabet, 1978; Robinson Crusoe and Gordon Craig, 1979; William Nicolson's An Almanac, 1980; (ed) Gordon Craig: the last eight years, by Ellen Gordon Craig, 1983; Baroque Theatre Construction, 1982. *Illustrations:* The Georgics of Virgil, 1931, etc; books of verse by John Keats, Edith Sitwell, Edmund Blunden, W. H. Davies, etc. *Recreations:* books and music. *Address:* Southcourt Cottage, Long Crendon, Aylesbury, Bucks HP18 9AQ.

CRAIG, Dr Edward John, FBA 1993; Reader in Modern Philosophy, University of Cambridge, since 1992; Fellow, Churchill College, Cambridge, since 1966; *b* 26 March 1942; *s* of Charles William Craig and Annie (*née* Taylor); *m* 1st, 1973, Isabel Nina Barnard (marr. diss. 1986); two *d;* 2nd, 1987, Gillian Helen Elizabeth Edwards. *Educ:* Charterhouse, Trinity Coll., Cambridge (MA 1966; PhD 1970). Cricket for Cambridge Univ. and Lancs CCC, 1961–63; Asst Lectr and Univ. Lectr in Philosophy, Cambridge, 1966–92. Visiting University appointments: Melbourne, 1974; Hamburg, 1977–78; Heidelberg, 1981. Chief Ed., Routledge Encyclopedia of Philosophy, 1991–; Editor, Ratio, 1988–92. *Publications:* David Hume: eine Einführung in seine Philosophie, 1979; The Mind of God and the Works of Man, 1987; Knowledge and the State of Nature, 1990; Pragmatische Untersuchungen zum Wissensbegriff, 1993. *Recreations:* music, golf. *Address:* Churchill College, Cambridge CB3 0DS. *T:* Cambridge (01223) 336000.

CRAIG, George Charles Graham; Under Secretary, Welsh Office, since 1986; *b* 8 May 1946; *s* of late George Craig and of E. S. Craig (*née* Milne); *m* 1968, (Ethne) Marian, *er d* of late H. H. A. Gallagher and of E. F. Gallagher; two *s* one *d. Educ:* Brockley County Grammar Sch.; Nottingham Univ. (BA). Asst Principal, Min. of Transport, 1967; Welsh Office: Private Sec. to Minister of State, 1970–72; Principal, 1972; PPS to Sec. of State for Wales, 1978–80; Asst Sec., 1980; Under Sec., 1986. *Address:* Welsh Office, Cathays Park, Cardiff CF1 3NQ. *T:* Cardiff (01222) 825111.

CRAIG, Sir James; *see* Craig, Sir A. J. M.

CRAIG, Dr (James) Oscar (Max Clark), FRCS, FRCP, FRCSI, FRCR; Consultant Radiologist since 1963, and Hon. Senior Clinical Lecturer, since 1987, St Mary's Hospital, London; President, Royal College of Radiologists, 1989–92; *b* 7 May 1927; *s* of James Oscar Max Clark Craig and Olivia Craig; *m* 1950, Louise Burleigh; four *d. Educ:* Royal College of Surgeons in Ireland. LRCP&SI 1950; FRCSI 1956; DMRD 1959; FRCR (FFR 1962); FRCS 1982; MRCP 1989, FRCP 1993; FRCGP 1991. Asst GP, 1950–51; Ho. Surg., St Helier Hosp., Carshalton, 1951–52; Gen. practice, Sutton, 1952–54. Surg., RAF, 1954–56. Sen. Ho. Officer, Surgery, Hammersmith Hosp., 1956–57; Registrar and Sen. Registrar, Dept of Radiology, St Mary's Hosp., London, 1957–63; Lectr in Radiology, London Univ., 1963–87; Dir of Clinical Studies, 1969–75, Dir of Post Grad. Studies, 1979–81, St Mary's Hosp. Med. Sch. Hon. Mem., Radiological Soc. of N America, 1993. Hon. FFR RCSI 1985. *Publications:* numerous papers and chapters in books on clinical radiology, phlebography, lymangiography, gastro-intestinal radiology, medico-legal medicine and the develt of digital radiology. *Recreation:* country-walking. *Address:* The White House, 18 Sandy Lane, Cheam, Surrey SM2 7NR. *T:* 0181–642 2696. *Clubs:* Royal Society of Medicine, MCC.

CRAIG, John Egwin, OBE 1990; FCA 1961; Chairman: Powerscreen International PLC, since 1989; Jupiter European Investment Trust PLC, since 1990; Belfast International Airport Holdings Ltd, since 1994; Government Director, International Fund for Ireland, since 1989; *b* 16 Aug. 1932; *s* of late Thomas Joseph Alexander Craig, CIE, and Mabel Frances (*née* Quinnell); *m* 1959, Patricia Costa Lopes; three *s. Educ:* Charterhouse. Cooper Bros (later Coopers & Lybrands), 1958–61; Council of Stock Exchange, 1961–64; N. M. Rothschild & Sons, 1964–91, Dir, 1970–91; Man. Dir, N. M. Rothschild, 1981–89; Dir, Standard Chartered, 1989–94. Dir, Jupiter Tyndall Gp, 1991– (Vice Chm., 1991–94). Member: Exec. Council, BBA, 1981–89 (Chm., 1987–89); Deposit Protection Bd, 1986–89. Mem. Council, LPO, 1983–87. FRSA 1988. *Address:* Saxonbury House, Frant, near Tunbridge Wells, Kent TN3 9HJ. *Club:* Brooks's.

CRAIG, John Frazer, CB 1994; Deputy Secretary (Head of Economic and Industrial Affairs), Welsh Office, since 1990; *b* 8 Nov. 1943; *s* of late John Frazer Craig and Margaret Jane Gibson Craig; *m* 1st, 1963, Ann Bardo (marr. diss. 1972); two *s* one *d;* 2nd, 1973, Janet Elizabeth. *Educ:* Robert Richardson Grammar Sch., Sunderland. Customs and Excise, 1961–69; Nat. Bd for Prices and Incomes, 1969–70; Welsh Office, 1970–: Private Sec. to Perm. Sec., 1972–74; Private Sec. to Sec. of State for Wales, 1980–82; Asst Sec., 1982–85, Under Sec. (Dir), 1985–87, Industry Dept; Under Sec. (Principal Finance Officer), Welsh Office, 1987–90. *Address:* c/o Welsh Office, Cathays Park, Cardiff CF1 3NQ. *T:* Cardiff (01222) 825111.

CRAIG, Rev. Maxwell Davidson; General Secretary, Action of Churches Together in Scotland, since 1990; Chaplain to The Queen in Scotland, since 1986; *b* 25 Dec. 1931; *s* of Dr William Craig and Alice M. Craig (*née* Semple); *m* 1957, Janet Margaret Macgregor; one *s* three *d. Educ:* Oriel Coll., Oxford (MA (Hons) Lit.Hum.); Edinburgh Univ. (BD); Princeton Theol Seminary, NJ (ThM). 2nd Lieut, 1st Bn Argyll and Sutherland Highlanders, 1954–56. Ministry of Labour: Asst Principal, 1957–61; Pvte Sec. to Parly Sec., 1959–61. Fulbright Schol., Princeton, 1964; ordained minister, Grahamston Parish Church, Falkirk, 1966; Minister, Wellington Church, Glasgow, 1973–89; Minister, St Columba's Parish Church, Aberdeen, 1989–90. Convener of the Church and Nation Cttee, Church of Scotland, 1984–88. Chairman: Falkirk Children's Panel, 1970–72; Hillhead Housing Assoc., 1977–89. *Publication:* Stella: the story of Stella J. Reekie, 1984. *Recreations:* hill-walking, reading. *Address:* Scottish Churches' House, Dunblane, Perthshire FK15 0AJ. *T:* Dunblane (01786) 823588.

CRAIG, Norman; Assistant Under-Secretary of State, Ministry of Defence, 1972–79; *b* 15 May 1920; *s* of George Craig, OBE; *m* 1st, 1946, Judith Margaret Newling (marr. diss. 1957); one *s;* 2nd, 1960, Jane Hudson; two *s* one *d. Educ:* Penarth County Sch.; Cardiff Univ. Army Service, Royal Sussex Regt, 1940–47. Board of Trade, 1948; Min. of Supply (later Aviation), 1953; Private Sec. to Minister, 1959–60; Min. of Technology, 1964; Sec. to Cttee of Inquiry into Aircraft Industry, 1964–65; course at IDC, 1968; MoD, 1971. Lord Chancellor's Department: official, 1979–85; consultant, 1986–87; lay observer, 1990. *Publication:* The Broken Plume, 1982. *Address:* 51 Hayes Lane, Beckenham, Kent BR3 2RE. *T:* 0181–650 7916.

CRAIG, Oscar; *see* Craig, J. O. M. C.

CRAIG, Paul Philip; Reader in Law, since 1990, and Fellow of Worcester College, since 1976, University of Oxford; *b* 27 Sept. 1951; *s* of Maurice and Beatrice Craig; *m* 1991, Dr Anita Cooper. *Educ:* Worcester Coll., Oxford (MA, BCL). Vis. Prof. in Univs of Virginia, Cornell, Connecticut, York (Osgoode Hall) Canada, Indiana, Queensland. *Publications:* Administrative Law, 1983, 3rd edn 1994; Public Law and Democracy in the United Kingdom and the United States of America, 1990; Text, Cases and Materials on Community Law, 1995; articles in jls. *Recreations:* riding, ski-ing, theatre, acting, ballet. *Address:* Worcester College, Oxford OX1 2HB. *T:* Oxford (01865) 278358.

CRAIG, Maj.-Gen. Robert Peter, MD; FRCS; Consultant in Accident and Emergency Medicine, Wansbeck General Hospital, Ashington, since 1994; *b* 24 June 1940; *s* of late Dr Robert Theodore Gilpin Craig, TD, MB BS, MRCGP and Jessie Craig (*née* McKinstry); *m* 1971, Jean Toft, MA; one *s* two *d. Educ:* George Watson's Boys' Coll.; Durham Univ. Med. Sch. (MB BS 1964); MD Newcastle upon Tyne 1987; FRCS 1972; FFAEM 1994. Commissioned RA (TA) 1958; RAMC 1963; Royal Victoria Infirmary, Newcastle, 1964–65; RMO 1/2 Gurkha Rifles, 1966–68; Queen Alexandra Mil. Hosp.; Birmingham Accident Hosp.; Dept of Surgery, Univ. of Newcastle upon Tyne; BMH Rinteln; Guy's Hosp., 1974–78; Consultant Surgeon: BMH Hong Kong, 1979–81; Queen Elizabeth Mil. Hosp., 1981–86; Sen. Lectr in Mil. Surgery, Royal Army Med. Coll., 1981–86; BMH Rinteln, 1986–89, CO, 1987–89; Comd Med., 4th Armoured Div., 1989–90; Comd Surgeon, HQ BAOR, 1990–92; Dir of Army Surgery, 1992–93; Comdr Medical, UKLF, 1993–94. QHS 1992–94. GSM Oman 1973, NI 1979. Montefiore Meml Medal, 1979; Leishman Meml Medal, 1987. OStJ 1993. *Publications:* contribs to surgical jls. *Recreations:* golf, squash, bridge, travel. *Address:* c/o Drummonds Branch, Royal Bank of Scotland, 49 Charing Cross, SW1A 2DX. *Clubs:* Royal Society of Medicine; Northumberland Golf, Wildernesse (Sevenoaks).

CRAIG, Rt. Hon. William, PC (N Ire.) 1963; solicitor and company director; *b* 2 Dec. 1924; *s* of late John Craig and Mary Kathleen Craig (*née* Lamont); *m* 1960, Doris Hilgendorff; two *s. Educ:* Dungannon Royal Sch.; Larne Grammar Sch.; Queen's Univ., Belfast. Served War of 1939–45, Royal Air Force, 1943–46. Qualified as solicitor, 1952. MP (U) Larne Div. of Antrim, NI Parliament, 1960–73; Mem. (Vanguard Unionist Progressive), N Antrim, NI Assembly, 1973–75; Mem. (UUC), E Belfast, NI Constitutional Convention, 1975–76; MP (UU) Belfast East, Feb. 1974–79. Chief Whip, Parliament of Northern Ireland, 1962–63; Minister of Home Affairs, 1963–64, and 1966–68; Minister of Health and Local Government, 1964; Minister of Development, 1965–66. Founder: Ulster Vanguard, 1972 (Leader, 1972–77); Vanguard Unionist Party, 1973 (Leader, 1973–77). Member: Council of Europe, 1976–79; WEU, 1976–79. *Recreations:* travel, motoring, shooting.

CRAIG-COOPER, Sir (Frederick Howard) Michael, Kt 1991; CBE 1982; TD 1968 (3 bars); DL; Director: Craig-Lloyd, since 1968; Tichborne Enterprises Ltd, since 1993; National Bank of Kuwait (International) plc, since 1993; Whichford International Ltd, since 1994; Ely Place Holdings Ltd, since 1994; Craigmyle & Co. Ltd, since 1995; *b* 28 Jan. 1936; *s* of late Frederick William Valentine Craig-Cooper and of Elizabeth Oliver-Thompson Craig-Cooper (*née* Macdonald) (she *m* 1970, Col J. H. Carroll-Leahy, MC (decd)); *m* 1968, Elizabeth Snagge, MVO; one *s. Educ:* Horris Hill; Stowe; College of Law. Solicitor, 1961. National Service, RA, 1954–56; TA, 1956–88; Comdr, Naval Gunfire Liaison Unit, 29 Commando Regt, RA, 1972–75; Mem., Greater London TAVRA (Chm., Employers Support Cttee, 1987–90). Jaques & Co., 1956–61; Allen & Overy, 1962–64; Inco, 1964–85; Dir, Paul Ray Internat., 1984 (merged with Carre Orban & Partners, 1989). Royal Borough of Kensington & Chelsea: Councillor, 1968–74; Chief Whip, 1971–74; Chm. Finance Cttee, 1972–74; Alderman, 1974–78; Mem. Investment Panel, 1973–. Contested (C) Houghton-le-Spring, 1966, 1970; Chm., Cons. Nat. Property Adv. Cttee, 1986–93 (Mem., 1993–); Pres., Kensington and Chelsea (formerly Chelsea), Cons. Assoc., 1983– (Chm., 1974–77). Trustee: Copper Develt Trust Fund, 1974–85; Order of Malta Homes Trust, 1980–; Orders of St John Trust, 1988–. Mem. Council, Mining Assoc., 1977–82; Chm. Appeal Cttee, CIMA, 1994–. Freeman, City of London, 1964; Liveryman, Drapers' Co., 1970– (Mem. Court of Assistants, 1987–). DL Greater London, 1986–; Rep. DL Kensington & Chelsea, 1987–. FCIArb 1992. KStJ 1990 (Chm., Council for London, 1990–94; Mem., Chapter-Gen., 1993–). Officer, SMO Malta, 1986. *Publications:* (with Philippe De Backer) Management Audit: how to create an effective management team, 1993; (jtly) Maw on Corporate Governance, 1994. *Recreation:* admiring wife's gardening. *Address:* c/o Whichford International Ltd, Whichford House, Parkway Court, Oxford Business Park, Cowley, Oxford OX4 2JY. *Clubs:* Beefsteak, Pratt's, White's.

CRAIG-McFEELY, Comdt Elizabeth Sarah Ann, CB 1982; Director, Women's Royal Naval Service, 1979–82; *b* 28 April 1927; *d* of late Lt-Col Cecil Michael Craig McFeely, DSO, OBE, MC, and late Nancy Sarah (*née* Mann, later Roberts). *Educ:* St Rose's Convent, Stroud, Glos; Anstey College of Physical Educn, Birmingham. DipPhysEducn London. Taught PE at St Angela's Ursuline Convent Sch., 1948–52; joined WRNS, 1952; Third Officer, 1953; served in various Royal Naval, Royal Marines and Royal Naval Reserve Estabts, 1952–67; in charge, WRNS, Far Eastern Fleet, 1967–69; various appts, MoD (Navy), 1969–74; HMS Centurion, 1974–76; Supt WRNS, 1977. Naval member, NAAFI Bd of Management, 1977–79; Hon. ADC to the Queen, 1979–82; retired 1982. *Recreations:* gardening and country pursuits. *Address:* Moonrakers, Mockbeggar Lane, Biddenden, Kent TN27 8ES. *T:* Biddenden (01580) 291325.

CRAIGAVON, 3rd Viscount *cr* 1927, of Stormont, Co. Down; **Janric Fraser Craig;** Bt 1918; *b* 9 June 1944; *s* of 2nd Viscount Craigavon; *S* father, 1974. *Educ:* Eton; London Univ. (BA, BSc). FCA. *Heir:* none.

CRAIGEN, Desmond Seaward; Director: Prudential Corporation plc, 1982–89; Pioneer Concrete (Holdings) Ltd, 1982–89; *b* 31 July 1916; *s* of late John Craigen and Ann Amelia Craigen (*née* Brebner); *m* 1961, Elena Ines (*née* Oldham Florez) (*d* 1995); one *s* one *d*. *Educ:* Holloway Sch.; King's Coll., London (BA Hons). Prudential Assurance Co. Ltd, 1934–81; India, 1950–57; attached O&M Div., Treasury, 1957–58; Dep. General Manager, 1968–69; General Manager, 1969–78; Chief General Manager, 1979–81; Chm., Vanbrugh Life Assurance Co. Ltd, 1982–87. Served War of 1939–45: 53rd Reconnaisance Regt RAC (Major; despatches). *Recreations:* music, reading. *Address:* 44 Crondace Road, SW6 4BT.

CRAIGEN, James Mark, JP; Director and Secretary, Scottish Federation of Housing Associations, 1988–90; freelance writer; *b* 2 Aug. 1938; *e s* of James Craigen, MA and Isabel Craigen; *m* 1971, Sheena Millar. *Educ:* Shawlands Academy, Glasgow; Strathclyde University. MLitt, Heriot-Watt, 1974. CIMgt. Compositor, 1954–61. Industrial Relations Asst, Scottish Gas Bd, 1963–64; Head of Organisation and Social Services at Scottish TUC, 1964–68; Asst Sec., and Industrial Liaison Officer, Scottish Business Educn Council, 1968–74. Glasgow City Councillor, 1965–68, Magistrate, 1966–68. Member: Scottish Ambulance Service Bd, 1966–71; Race Relations Bd, Scottish Conciliation Cttee, 1967–70; Police Adv. Bd for Scotland, 1970–74; ITC Viewer Consultative Council for Scotland, 1990–93; S Scotland Electricity Consumers' Cttee, 1994–. Contested Ayr constituency, 1970. MP (Lab and Co-op) Glasgow Maryhill, Feb. 1974–1987 (retired on grounds of experience, not age). PPS to Rt Hon. William Ross, MBE, MP, Sec. of State for Scotland, 1974–76; Opposition Spokesman on Scottish Affairs, 1983–85. Member: Select Cttee on Employment, 1979–83 (Chm., 1982–83); Select Cttee on Scottish Affairs, 1987; Chairman: Co-op. Party Parly Group, 1978–79; Scottish Group, Labour MPs, 1978–79; PLP Employment Gp, 1981–83. Mem., UK Delegn to Council of Europe Assembly, 1976–80. Trustee, Industry and Parliament Trust, 1983–88 (Fellow, 1978–79). Mem., Bd of Trustees, Nat. Museums of Scotland, 1985–91. Hon. Vice-Pres., Building Societies Assoc., 1985–88. Hon. Lectr, Strathclyde Univ., 1980–85; Fellow, Inst. of Advanced Studies in Humanities, Edinburgh Univ., 1990–91. JP: Glasgow, 1966; Edinburgh, 1975. *Publications:* (contrib.) Forward! Labour Politics in Scotland 1888–1988, 1989; contribs to Co-operative News. *Address:* 38 Downie Grove, Edinburgh EH12 7AX.

CRAIGMYLE, 3rd Baron, *cr* 1929, of Craigmyle; **Thomas Donald Mackay Shaw;** Chairman, Craigmyle & Co. Ltd; *b* 17 Nov. 1923; *s* of 2nd Baron and Lady Margaret Cargill Mackay (*d* 1958), *e d* of 1st Earl of Inchcape; *S* father, 1944; *m* 1955, Anthea Esther Christine, *y d* of late E. C. Rich; three *s* three *d*. *Educ:* Eton; Trinity Coll., Oxford (MA). Served RNVR, 1943–46. FRSA. Kt Grand Cross of Obedience, SMO Malta, and Pres., British Assoc., 1989–95 (Hospitaller, 1962–73; Sec.-Gen., 1979–83; Vice-Pres., 1983–89). KStJ 1989. *Publication:* (ed with J. Gould) Your Death Warrant?, 1971. *Recreation:* home baking. *Heir:* *s* Hon. Thomas Columba Shaw [*b* 19 Oct. 1960; *m* 1987, Alice, second *d* of David Floyd; three *s*]. *Address:* 18 The Boltons, SW10 9SY; Scottas, Knoydart, Inverness-shire PH41 4PL. *Clubs:* Caledonian; Royal Thames Yacht; Bengal (Calcutta).
See also W. B. Dean.

CRAIK, Duncan Robert Steele, CB 1979; OBE 1971; Auditor-General for Australia, 1973–81; *b* 17 Feb. 1916; *s* of Henry Steele Craik and Lilian Kate Ellis; *m* 1943, Audrey Mavis Ion; four *d*. *Educ:* Univ. of Sydney (BEc). FASA 1973–87; FAIM 1975–86; FRAIPA 1983. Commonwealth Bank, 1933–40; Taxation Br., 1940–60; Treasury: Asst Sec., 1960–66; First Asst Sec., 1966–69; Dep. Sec., 1969–73. Part-time Mem., Admin. Appeals Tribunal, 1981–86. Mem. Council, ANU, 1981–83. *Recreation:* gardening. *Address:* 78 Grayson Street, Hackett, ACT 2602, Australia.

CRAIK, Roger George, QC (Scot.) 1981; Sheriff of Lothian and Borders, since 1984; *b* 22 Nov. 1940; *s* of George and Frances Craik; *m* 1964, Helen Sinclair Sutherland; one *s* one *d*. *Educ:* Lockerbie Academy; Breadalbane Academy, Aberfeldy; George Watson's Boys' Coll.; Edinburgh Univ. (MA 1960, LLB 1962). Qualified as solicitor, 1962; worked for Orr Dignam & Co., Solicitors, Pakistan, 1963–65; called to Scottish Bar, 1966. Standing junior counsel to Min. of Defence (Army), 1974–80; Advocate Depute, 1980–83. Mem., Sheriff Court Rules Council, 1990–. *Publications:* The Advocates' Library 1689–1989, 1989; James Boswell: The Scottish Perspective, 1994. *Recreations:* Scottish antiquities, modern jazz. *Address:* Sheriff Court House, Chambers Street, Edinburgh EH1 1LB.

CRAM, Prof. Donald James; University Professor Emeritus, University of California, Los Angeles, since 1990; *b* 22 April 1919; *s* of William Moffet and Joanna Shelley Cram; *m* 1969, Jane L. Maxwell. *Educ:* Rollins Coll., Fla (BS); Univ. of Nebraska (MS); Harvard Univ. (PhD). Chemist, Merck & Co., 1942–45; University of California, LA, 1947–90: Instr, ACS Fellow, 1947–48; Asst Prof., 1948–51; Associate Prof., 1951–56; Prof. of Chemistry, 1956; S. Winstein Prof. of Chemistry, 1985–95; Univ. Prof., 1988–90. Guggenheim Fellow, 1955. Centenary Lectr, London, 1976. Chemical Consultant: Upjohn Co., 1952–88; Union Carbide Corp., 1961–82; Eastman Kodak, 1982–91; Technicon Co., 1984–91; Istituto Guido Donegani, Milan, 1988–91. MACS 1945; MRSC 1955; MNAS 1961; Mem., Amer. Acad. of Arts and Scis, 1967; Sigma Xi, Phi Beta Kappa (Hon.). Hon. FRSC 1989. Hon. Dr: Uppsala, 1977; Rollins, 1988; Hon. DSc: S California, 1983; Nebraska, 1989; Western Ontario, 1990; Sheffield, 1991. Nobel Laureate, Chemistry, 1987. ACS Awards: Creative Work in Org. Chem., 1965; Arthur C. Cope, for Dist Achievement, 1974; Roger Adams, in Org. Chem., 1985; Willard Gibbs Medal 1985; Richard Tolman Medal 1985; Calif. Scientist of the Year, 1974; Armand Hammer Award, Nat. Acad. of Scis, 1992. Fields of interest in org. chem.: molecular complexation, stereochemistry, carbanions, carbonium ions, organosulfur chemistry, paracyclophanes, mold metabolites. *Publications:* (jtly) Organic Chemistry, 1959, 4th edn (jtly), 1980 (trans. into 12 langs); Carbanions, 1965; (jtly) Elements of Organic Chemistry, 1967; (jtly) Essence of Organic Chemistry, 1978; From Design to Discovery, 1990; (jtly) Container Molecules and Their Guests, 1994; numerous articles in ACS Jl, Jl Org. Chem., Chemical Communications, Angewandte Chemie, Tetrahedron. *Recreations:* surfing, ski-ing, tennis, guitar, reading. *Address:* 72935 Carriage Tr, Palm Desert, CA 92260, USA. *Clubs:* Ironwood Country; San Onofre Surfing, Surfers' Medical Association (California).

CRAMOND, Ronald Duncan, CBE 1987; Chairman, Strathclyde Greenbelt Company, since 1992; *b* 22 March 1927; *s* of Adam and Margaret Cramond; *m* 1954, Constance MacGregor (*d* 1985); one *s* one *d*. *Educ:* George Heriot's Sch.; Edinburgh Univ. (MA). Sen. Medallist History 1949. FBIM; FSAScot 1978. Commnd Royal Scots, 1950. Entered War Office, 1951; Private Sec. to Parly Under-Sec. of State, Scottish Office, 1956; Principal, Dept of Health for Scotland, 1957; Mactaggart Fellow (Applied Econs), Glasgow Univ., 1962; Haldane Medallist in Public Admin, 1964; Asst Sec., Scottish Develt Dept, 1966, Under Sec., 1973; Under Sec., Dept of Agric. and Fisheries for Scotland, 1977; Dep. Chm., Highlands and Islands Develt Bd, 1983–88. Dir, Cairngorm Chairlift Co., 1988–90. Chm., Scottish Museums Council, 1990–93; Member: Scottish Museums Adv. Bd, 1984–85; Scottish Tourist Board, 1985–88; CCS, 1988–92; Trustee: Nat. Museums of Scotland, 1985–; Scottish Civic Trust, 1988–; Vice-Pres., Architectural Heritage Soc. of Scotland, 1988–93. *Publication:* Housing Policy in Scotland, 1966. *Recreations:* golf, hill walking, testing a plastic hip. *Address:* c/o Strathclyde Greenbelt Company, 61 Holland Street, Glasgow G2 4NJ. *Club:* Scottish Arts (Edinburgh).

CRAMOND, Dr William Alexander, AO 1994; OBE 1960; FRSE; Professor of Clinical Psychiatry, Flinders University, South Australia, 1983–92, Emeritus Professor of Psychiatry, 1993; *b* 2 Oct. 1920; *er s* of William James Cramond, MBE and of May Battisby, Aberdeen; *m* 1949, Bertine J. C. Mackintosh, MB, ChB, FRANZCP, Dornoch; one *s* one *d*. *Educ:* Robert Gordon's Coll., Aberdeen; Aberdeen Univ. MB, ChB, MD, FRCPsych, FRANZCP, FRACP, DPM. Physician Supt, Woodilee Mental Hosp., Glasgow, 1955–61; Dir of Mental Health, S Australia, 1961–65; Prof. of Mental Health, Univ. of Adelaide, 1963–71; Principal Medical Officer in Mental Health, Scottish Home and Health Dept, 1971–72; Dean of Faculty of Medicine and Prof. of Mental Health, Univ. of Leicester, 1972–75; Principal and Vice-Chancellor, Stirling Univ., 1975–80; Dir of Mental Health Services, NSW, 1980–83; Clinical Dir, Cleland House, Glenside Hosp., SA, 1983–85; Chm., Bd of Dirs, SA Mental Health Services, 1993–95. Hon. Prof., Clinical Psychiatry, Sydney, 1980–83. DUniv Stirling, 1984. *Publications:* papers on psychosomatic medicine and on care of dying in Brit. Jl Psychiat., Lancet, BMJ. *Recreations:* reading, theatre. *Address:* 28 Tynte Street, North Adelaide, SA 5006, Australia. *Club:* Adelaide (Adelaide).

CRAMP, Prof. Rosemary Jean, CBE 1987; Professor of Archaeology, University of Durham, 1971–90, now Emeritus; *b* 6 May 1929; *er d* of Robert Kingston and Vera Cramp, Cranoe Grange, Leics. *Educ:* Market Harborough Grammar Sch.; St Anne's Coll., Oxford (MA, BLitt). Lectr, St Anne's Coll., Oxford, 1950–55; Lectr, Durham Univ., 1955, Sen. Lectr, 1966. Vis. Fellow, All Souls Coll., Oxford, 1992. Commissioner: Royal Commn on Ancient and Historical Monuments of Scotland, 1975–; Historic Bldgs and Monuments Commn, 1984–89 (Mem., Adv. Cttee (Archaeology), 1984–89). Trustee, BM, 1978–. Member: Adv. Bd for Redundant Churches, 1984–; Validation Panel, Museums' Trng Inst., 1993–; Reviewing Cttee on Export of Works of Art, 1994–. President: Council for British Archaeology, 1989–92 (Hon. Vice-Pres., 1992–); Cumberland and Westmorland Antiquarian and Archaeol Soc., 1984–87; Vice-Pres., Royal Archaeol Inst., 1992–. Gen. Editor, Corpus of Anglo-Saxon Stone Sculpture, 1974–. *Publications:* Corpus of Anglo-Saxon Stone Sculpture, vol. I, Durham and Northumberland, 1984, vol. 2, (with R. N. Bailey) Cumberland and Westmorland, 1986; contribs in the field of Early Monasticism, Early Medieval Sculpture and Northern Archaeology. *Address:* 5 Leazes Place, Durham DH1 1RE.

CRAMPIN, Peter; QC 1993; a Recorder, since 1995; *b* 7 July 1946; *s* of John Hames Crampin and Gwendoline Edith (*née* Richardson); *m* 1975, Frida Yvonne Schoemann; one *s*. *Educ:* St Albans Sch.; University Coll., Oxford (Open Exhibnr; MA). Admitted Solicitor, 1973; called to the Bar, Middle Temple, 1976; in practice at Chancery Bar, 1978–; an Asst Recorder, 1990–95; 2nd Jun. Counsel to Attorney General in Charity Matters, 1988–93. *Address:* 11 New Square, Lincoln's Inn, WC2A 3QB. *T:* 0171–831 0081.

CRAMPTON, (Arthur Edward) Seán, MC 1943; GM(mil.) 1944; TD 1946; PPRBS (FRBS 1965; ARBS 1952); sculptor; *b* 15 March 1918; *e s* of late Joshua Crampton, architect, and Ethel Mary (*née* Dyas); *m* 3rd, 1959, Patricia, *e d* of late L. J. Cardew Wood; one *s* one *d*; three *d* by former marriages. *Educ:* St Joseph de Cluny, Stafford; Vittoria Jun. Sch. of Art, Birmingham; Birmingham Central Coll. of Art; London; Paris. Served TA, London Irish Rifles, Western Desert, Sicily, Italy, 1938–46. Prof. de Sculpture, Anglo-French Art Centre, 1946–50; served on juries for Thomas More and Winston Churchill meml statues. Member, Art Workers Guild, 1971 (Master, 1978); Pres., RBS, 1966–71. Mem., Accademia Italia, 1981. Governor: Camberwell Sch. of Arts and Crafts, 1970–88 (Chm., 1983–88); London Inst., 1986–88. FRSA 1973. *Exhibitions: general:* RA and RI Galls; *one-man:* fourteen exhibns in London, 1948–82. *Major heroic size works:* Persephone, Crowmallie, Aberdeen; Horseman (RBS Silver Medal, 1965); Simon de Montfort, County Hall, Leics; Three Judges, Churchill Coll., Cambridge; Three Kings, Knochallachie, Aberdeen; Cascade, Duke of Westminster, Eaton, Chester; Two Geese, Goose Green, Altrincham (Civic Trust Award, 1984); Bird Flight, St John's Coll., Cambridge; *works in churches:* St Mary and Child, Midhurst; Our Lady, St Michael and Crucifix, Wolverhampton; Crucifix, Church of Child Jesus, Birmingham; Risen Christ and sanctuary furniture, St Vincent's Convent, Mill Hill; Our Lady and Child, Convent of Sisters of Mercy, Brentwood; Crucifix, St Cedd's, Goodmayes; Our Lady, St Mary's Coll., Wallasey; Cross Motif, St Thomas More, Manor House; Risen Christ, St Albans, Derby; Stations of the Cross, St Edmunds, Calne (RBS Medal, 1986), etc. *Publication:* Humans, Beasts, Birds (with Hicks and Anderson), 1981. *Recreations:* gardening, painting, cooking. *Address:* Rookery Farmhouse, Calne, Wilts SN11 0LH. *T:* Calne (01249) 814068. *Clubs:* Athenæum, Chelsea Arts.

CRAMPTON, Peter Duncan; Member (Lab) Humberside, European Parliament, since 1989; *b* 10 June 1932; *s* of Edmund Crampton and Louisa Crampton (*née* Thurman); *m* 1955, Councillor Margaret Eva McMillan; two *s*. *Educ:* Blackpool Grammar School; Nottingham Univ. (BA Hons Geography); Birmingham Univ. (MA African Studies); Hull Univ. (Dip. W European Studies); London Univ. (PGCE). Casual work, mainly as farm worker, 1954–55; Statistician, Plessey Co., 1955–56; Geography Teacher, Coventry, 1957–61; Educn Officer, Uganda, 1961–64; Lectr i/c Geography, Technical Coll., Birmingham, 1964–70; Lectr in Geography, Hull Coll. of Educn, then Humberside Coll. of HE, 1970–85; part-time work as lectr, writer, parly assistant, 1985–89. Chairman: European Nuclear Disarmament Campaign, 1984–86; Internat. Cttee, CND, 1988–. First Vice-Pres., Political Affairs Cttee, 1989–, For. Affairs Cttee, 1989–94, European Parlt. *Publications:* (contrib.) Voices for One World, 1988; articles in jls on population geography in Africa, electoral behaviour and nuclear disarmament. *Recreations:* travel, hill walking, music. *Address:* 135 Westbourne Avenue, Hull HU5 3HU. *T:* Hull (01482) 449337.

CRAMPTON SMITH, Alex; *see* Smith, Alexander C.

CRAN, James Douglas; MP (C) Beverley, since 1987; *b* 28 Jan. 1944; *s* of James Cran and Jane McDonald Cran, Aberdeenshire; *m* 1973, Penelope Barbara Wilson; one *d*. *Educ:*

Ruthrieston Sch., Aberdeen; Aberdeen Coll. of Commerce; King's Coll., Univ. of Aberdeen (MA Hons). Researcher, Cons. Res. Dept, 1970–71; Sec., 1971–73, Chief. Exec., 1973–79, Nat. Assoc. of Pension Funds; Northern Dir, 1979–84, West Midlands Dir, 1984–87, CBI. Councillor (C), London Borough of Sutton, 1974–79 (Chm., Health and Housing Cttee). Mem., Select Cttee on Trade and Industry, 1987–92, on NI, 1994–; Vice Chairman: Cons. Backbench NI Cttee, 1992–; All-Party Anglo-Mongolian Gp, 1993–; Order of St John All-Party Gp, 1994–; Secretary: Cons. Backbench Cttee on Constitutional Affairs, 1989–91, on European Affairs, 1989–91; All-Party Anglo-Malta Gp, 1992–94; Co-Founder, Parly Gp on Occupational Pensions, 1992. Fellow: Armed Forces Parly Scheme, attached to RM, 1992; Parlt and Industry Trust, 1994. Parly consultant, Lincoln Nat. (UK) plc. Treas., European Res. Gp, 1994. Vice-Pres., Beverley Combined Div., St John Ambulance. Council Mem., Pension Trustees Forum, 1992–. Member of Court: Univ. of Birmingham, 1984–87; Univ. of Hull, 1987–. Dux Medallion, City of Aberdeen, 1959; Daily Mirror Nat. Speaking Trophy, 1969. OStJ. *Recreations:* travelling, reading biographies, autobiographies and history. *Address:* House of Commons, SW1A 0AA. *T:* 0171–219 3000.

CRAN, Mark Dyson Gordon; QC 1988; *b* 18 May 1948; *s* of William Broadbent Gordon Cran and Diana Rosemary Cran (*née* Mallinson); *m* 1983, Prudence Elizabeth Binning (marr. diss.). *Educ:* Gordonstoun; Millfield; Bristol Univ. (LLB). Called to the Bar, Gray's Inn, 1973. *Recreations:* country sports, convivial disputation, wine and food, books, theatre. *Address:* Brick Court Chambers, 15/19 Devereux Court, WC2R 3JJ. *T:* 0171–583 0777.

CRANBORNE, Viscount; Robert Michael James Cecil; PC 1994; DL; Lord Privy Seal and Leader of the House of Lords, since 1994; *b* 30 Sept. 1946; *s* and *heir* of 6th Marquess of Salisbury, *qv*; *m* 1970, Hannah Ann, *er d* of Lt-Col William Joseph Stirling of Keir; two *s* three *d*. *Educ:* Eton; Oxford. MP (C) Dorset South, 1979–87. Summoned to the Upper House of Parliament, 1992, as Baron Cecil, of Essendon in the County of Rutland; Parly Under-Sec. of State for Defence, MoD, 1992–94. DL Dorset, 1987. *Heir:* *s* Hon. Robert Edward William Cecil, *b* 18 Dec. 1970. *Address:* Manor House, Cranborne, Wimborne, Dorset BH21 5PP.

CRANBROOK, 5th Earl of, *cr* 1892; **Gathorne Gathorne-Hardy;** Viscount Cranbrook, 1878; Baron Medway, 1892; DL; Chairman, English Nature, since 1991; *b* 20 June 1933; *er s* of 4th Earl of Cranbrook, CBE, and of the Dowager Countess of Cranbrook (Fidelity, OBE 1972, *o d* of late Hugh E. Seebohm); *S* father, 1978; *m* 1967, Caroline, *o d* of Col Ralph G. E. Jarvis, Doddington Hall, Lincoln; two *s* one *d*. *Educ:* Eton; Corpus Christi Coll., Cambridge (MA); University of Birmingham (PhD). Asst, Sarawak Museum, 1956–58; Fellow, Yayasan Siswa Lokantara (Indonesia), 1960–61; Sen. Lectr in Zoology, Univ. of Malaya, 1961–70. Editor of Ibis, 1973–80. Bd Mem., Anglian Water Authy, 1987–89; non-exec. Dir, Anglian Water, 1989–. Member: Royal Commn on Environmental Pollution, 1981–92; NERC, 1982–88; Foundn for Eur. Envmtl Policy, 1987– (Chm., 1990–); Broads Authy, 1988–; Harwich Haven Authy, 1989–; NCC, 1990–91; Environment Sub-cttee, H of L Select Cttee on European Communities, 1979–85, 1987–90 (Chm., 1980–83 and 1987–90); Suffolk Coastal DC, 1974–83; Pres., Suffolk Wildlife Trust (formerly Suffolk Trust for Nature Conservation), 1979–. Trustee, BM (Natural History), 1982–86. Skinner and Freeman of the City of London. DL Suffolk, 1984. FLS; FZS; FRGS; FIBiol; MBOU. Hon. DSc Aberdeen, 1989. OStJ. *Publications:* Mammals of Borneo, 1965, 2nd edn 1977; Mammals of Malaya, 1969, 2nd edn 1978; (with D. R. Wells) Birds of the Malay Peninsula, 1976; Riches of the Wild: mammals of South East Asia, 1987, 2nd edn 1991; (ed) Key Environments: Malaysia, 1988; (with D. S. Edwards) Belalong: a rain forest, 1994. *Heir:* *s* Lord Medway, *qv*. *Address:* c/o House of Lords, SW1A 0PW. *Fax:* (home) Saxmundham (01728) 663339.

CRANE, Prof. (Francis) Roger; Professor of Law, Queen Mary College, University of London, 1965–78, now Emeritus; *b* 19 Dec. 1910; *m* 1938, Jean Berenice Hadfield (*d* 1986); two *s* one *d*. *Educ:* Highgate Sch.; University Coll., London. LLB 1933; Solicitor, 1934, Clifford's Inn Prize. Lecturer in Law; King's Coll. and private practice, 1935–38; Lecturer in Law, University of Manchester, 1938–46; Prof. of Law, University of Nottingham, 1946–52; Prof. of English Law, King's Coll., London, 1952–65; Dean of the Faculty of Law, QMC, London, 1965–76. University of London: Mem. Senate, 1969–71, 1973–78; Chm. Academic Council, 1975–78; Mem. Court, 1975–78. Visiting Professor: Tulane Univ., 1960; University of Khartoum, 1963; Dean of the Faculty of Law and Visiting Prof., University of Canterbury (New Zealand), 1964; Vis. Professor: Univ. of Melbourne, 1972; Monash Univ., 1972; Univ. of Sydney, 1980. Served War of 1939–45: Royal Corps of Signals, Major, 1944. Pres., Soc. of Public Teachers of Law, 1975–76. FKC 1976; Fellow QMW (Fellow QMC 1980). *Publications:* (jointly) A Century of Family Law, 1957; articles and notes in legal periodicals. *Address:* 25 Winston Drive, Isham, Kettering, Northants NN14 1HS. *T:* Burton Latimer (01536) 723938.

See also P. F. Crane.

CRANE, Geoffrey David; Head of Freight Directorate, Department of Transport, 1989–90; *b* 13 Oct. 1934; *s* of late Frederick David Crane and Marion Doris Crane; *m* 1962, Gillian Margaret, *d* of late Harry Thomas Austin; one *d*. *Educ:* City of London Sch. (John Carpenter Schol.); Trinity Hall, Cambridge (Schol., MA). Served RAF, 1956–58, Flying Officer. Assistant Principal, Min. of Works, 1958; Asst Private Sec. to Minister of Works, 1961–62; Principal, 1962; Secretary, Historic Buildings Council for Scotland and Ancient Monuments Bd for Scotland, 1962–66; Private Sec. to Minister of Public Building and Works, 1968–69; Asst Sec., Machinery of Govt Div., CSD, 1970–72; Dep. Dir, Central Unit on Environmental Pollution, DoE, 1972–76; Personnel Management and Trng, 1976–78, Under Sec. and Dir of Res. Ops, 1978–80, Dir, Personnel Management and Trng, 1981–85, Regl Dir, Eastern Region, 1985–89, DoE and Dept of Transport. *Recreations:* music, industrial archaeology, mathematics. *Address:* 6 The Paddock, Datchet, Berks SL3 9DL. *Clubs:* Royal Air Force, Civil Service.

CRANE, Sir James (William Donald), Kt 1980; CBE 1977; HM Chief Inspector of Constabulary, 1979–82; *b* 1 Jan. 1921; *s* of late William James Crane and Ivy Winifred Crane; *m* 1942, Patricia Elizabeth Hodge; one *s* one *d*. *Educ:* Hampshire schs. Served RE, RA, Royal Hampshire Regt, 1939–46. Joined Metrop. Police, 1946; Comdr and Dep. Asst Comr, Fraud Squad and Commercial Br., 1970–76; Inspector of Constabulary, 1976–79. Member: Parole Bd, 1983–85; Fraud Trials Cttee, 1984–85. Mem. Council, Univ. of Wales Coll. of Cardiff, 1988–. *Recreations:* gardening, walking, reading. *Address:* Home Office, 50 Queen Anne's Gate, SW1H 9AT. *Club:* Commonwealth Trust.

CRANE, Peter Francis; His Honour Judge Crane; a Circuit Judge, since 1987; Resident Judge, Peterborough Crown and County Court, since 1992; *b* 14 Jan. 1940; *s* of Prof. Francis Roger Crane, *qv*, and late Jean Berenice Crane (*née* Hadfield); *m* 1967, Elizabeth Mary Pittman; four *d*. *Educ:* Nottingham High Sch.; Highgate Sch.; Gonville and Caius Coll., Cambridge (MA, LLM); Tulane Univ., New Orleans (LLM). Called to the Bar, Gray's Inn, 1964 (Barstow Scholar, 1963); in practice on Midland and Oxford Circuit, 1965–87; Recorder, 1982–87. Mem., Senate of Inns of Court and the Bar, 1983–86 (Member: Professional Conduct Cttee, 1984–86; Bar Cttee, 1985–86). Mem., Judicial Studies Bd, 1993– (Mem., Criminal Cttee, 1993–). Chairman: Kettering Constituency Liberal Assoc., 1981–84; Pytchley Parish Council, 1985–86. *Publication:* (co-ed) Phipson on Evidence, 14th edn, 1990. *Recreations:* walking, gardening, reading, wine. *Address:* The Glebe House, Pytchley, Northants NN14 1EW. *T:* Kettering (01536) 790322.

CRANE, Roger; *see* Crane, F. R.

CRANFIELD, Rev. Prof. Charles Ernest Burland, FBA 1982; Emeritus Professor of Theology, University of Durham, since 1980; *b* 13 Sept. 1915; *s* of Charles Ernest Cranfield and Beatrice Mary Cranfield (*née* Tubbs); *m* 1953, Ruth Elizabeth Gertrude, *d* of Rev. T. Bole; two *d*. *Educ:* Mill Hill Sch.; Jesus Coll., Cambridge; Wesley House, Cambridge. MA Cantab. Research in Basel, cut short before it properly began by outbreak of war. Probationer in Methodist Church, 1939; ordained 1941; Minister, Shoeburyness; Chaplain to the Forces, 1942–46; from end of hostilities worked with German prisoners-of-war and was first staff chaplain to POW Directorate, War Office; Minister, Cleethorpes, 1946–50; admitted to Presbyterian Church of England (now United Reformed Church) as a minister, 1954. Lecturer in Theology, Durham Univ., 1950–62; Sen. Lectr, 1962–66; Reader, 1966–78; Prof. of Theology (personal), 1978–80. Joint general editor, new series of International Critical Commentary, 1966–. Hon. DD Aberdeen, 1980. Burkitt Medal for Biblical Studies, 1989. *Publications:* The First Epistle of Peter, 1950, 4th imp. 1958; The Gospel according to Saint Mark, 1959, supplemented and somewhat revised over the years, 10th imp. 1989; I and II Peter and Jude, 1960; A Ransom for Many, 1963; The Service of God, 1965; A Commentary on Romans 12–13, 1965; A Critical and Exegetical Commentary on the Epistle to the Romans, vol. 1 1975, 7th (corrected) imp. 1990, vol. 2 1979, 5th (corrected) imp. 1989; Romans: a shorter commentary, 1985, 4th imp. 1991; If God Be For Us: a collection of sermons, 1985; The Bible and Christian Life: a collection of essays, 1985; The Apostles' Creed: a faith to live by, 1993; contribs to composite works and to various theological periodicals. *Address:* 30 Western Hill, Durham City DH1 4RL. *T:* Durham (0191) 3843096.

CRANLEY, Viscount; Rupert Charles William Bullard Onslow; *b* 16 June 1967; *s* and *heir* of 7th Earl of Onslow, *qv*. *Educ:* Eton; Western Kentucky Univ., USA. *Recreations:* photography, riding, shooting.

CRANMER, Philip; Secretary, Associated Board of the Royal Schools of Music, 1974–83; *b* 1 April 1918; *s* of Arthur Cranmer and Lilian Phillips; *m* 1939, Ruth Loasby; one *s* three *d*. *Educ:* Wellington; Christ Church, Oxford (BMus, MA). Asst Music Master, Wellington Coll. 1938–40; served RA, 1940–46; Major, Education Officer, Guards Div., 1946; Dir of Music, King Edward's Sch., Birmingham, 1946; Staff Accompanist, Midland Region, BBC, 1948; Lectr in Music, Birmingham Univ., 1950; Hamilton Harty Prof. of Music, Queen's Univ., Belfast, 1954–70; Prof. of Music, Univ. of Manchester, 1970–74. Pres., Incorporated Soc. of Musicians, 1971; Chm., Musicians' Benevolent Fund, 1980–87. FRCO 1947; Hon. RAM 1967; FRNCM 1974; FRCM 1976. Hon. DMus QUB, 1985. Chevalier de l'Ordre de Léopold II, 1947; Croix de Guerre Belge, 1947. *Publications:* The Technique of Accompaniment, 1970; Sight-reading for Young Pianists, 1979; How to Follow a Score, 1982; Two Sonatinas for piano duet, 1981 and 1985. *Address:* Quince Cottage, Underhill Lane, Clayton, Hassocks, W Sussex BN6 9PJ.

CRANSTON, Prof. William Ian; Professor of Medicine, United Medical and Dental Schools of Guy's and St Thomas' Hospitals (formerly St Thomas's Hospital Medical School), 1964–93, now Emeritus; *b* 11 Sept. 1928; *s* of Thomas and Margaret Cranston; *m* Pamela Isabel Pearson; four *s*. *Educ:* High Sch. for Boys, Glasgow; Aberdeen Grammar Sch.; Boys' High Sch., Oswestry; University of Aberdeen, FRCP London 1965 (MRCP 1952); MB, ChB (Hons), 1949; MD Aberdeen 1957; MA Oxon. 1962. Royal Infirmary, Aberdeen: House Physician, 1949–50; Medical Registrar, 1952–53; Asst in Medical Unit, St Mary's Hospital, Paddington, 1953–56; 1st Asst in Dept of Regius Prof. of Med., Radcliffe Inf., Oxford, 1961–64. Mem., Med. Res. Soc. *Recreations:* reading, gardening, painting. *Address:* 31 Berrylands, Surbiton, Surrey KT5 8JT.

CRANWORTH, 3rd Baron, *cr* 1899; **Philip Bertram Gurdon;** Lieutenant, Royal Wiltshire Yeomanry; *b* 24 May 1940; *s* of Hon. Robin Gurdon (killed in action, 1942) and Hon. Yoskyl Pearson (she *m* 2nd, 1944, as his 2nd wife, Lieut-Col. Alistair Gibb, and 3rd, 1962, as his 2nd wife, 1st Baron McCorquodale of Newton, PC, KCVO; she *d* 1979), *d* of 2nd Viscount Cowdray; *S* grandfather, 1964; *m* 1968, Frances Henrietta Montagu Douglas Scott, *d* of late Lord William Scott and of Lady William Scott, Beechwood, Melrose; two *s* one *d*. *Educ:* Eton; Magdalene Coll., Cambridge. *Heir:* *s* Hon. Sacha William Robin Gurdon, *b* 12 Aug. 1970. *Address:* Grundisburgh Hall, Woodbridge, Suffolk IP13 6TW.

See also Marquess of Huntly.

CRASTON, Rev. Canon (Richard) Colin; Rector of St Paul with Emmanuel, Bolton, 1986–93, retired (Vicar, 1954); Hon. Canon, Manchester Cathedral, since 1968; Area Dean of Bolton, 1972–92; Chaplain to the Queen, 1985–92; *b* 31 Dec. 1922; *s* of Albert Edward Craston and Ethel Craston; *m* 1st, 1948, Ruth Taggart (*d* 1992); one *s* one *d*; 2nd, 1993, Rev. Brenda H. Fullalove. *Educ:* Preston Grammar Sch.; Univ. of Bristol (BA Hons); Univ. of London (BD Hons); Tyndale Hall, Bristol. Served War, RN, 1941–46. Ordained 1951; Curate, St Nicholas, Durham, 1951–54. Chm., House of Clergy, Dio. of Manchester, 1982–94; Member: Gen. Synod, 1970–95 (Mem., Standing Cttee, 1975–95; Chm., Business Sub-Cttee, 1991–95); ACC, 1981– (Mem., Standing Cttee, 1981–, Vice-Chm., 1986–90; Chm., 1990–); Crown Appts Commn, 1982–92. DD Lambeth, 1992. *Publications:* Biblical Headship and the Ordination of Women, 1986; (ed) Open to the Spirit—Essays on Renewal, 1987; (contrib.) Authority in the Anglican Communion, 1987; (jtly) Anglicanism and the Universal Church, 1990; (ed) By Word and Deed, 1992; contrib. Anvil. *Recreation:* football and cricket spectating. *Address:* 12 Lever Park Avenue, Horwich, Bolton BL6 7LE. *T:* Horwich (01204) 699972, *Fax:* (01204) 690813. *Club:* Union Jack.

CRATHORNE, 2nd Baron *cr* 1959; **Charles James Dugdale;** Bt 1945; DL; consultant and lecturer in Fine Art; director of hotel cos; *b* 12 Sept. 1939; *s* of 1st Baron Crathorne, PC, TD, and Nancy, OBE (*d* 1969), *d* of Sir Charles Tennant, 1st Bt; *S* father, 1977; *m* 1970, Sylvia Mary, *yr d* of Brig. Arthur Herbert Montgomery, OBE, TD; one *s* two *d*. *Educ:* Eton College; Trinity Coll., Cambridge. MA Cantab (Fine Arts). Impressionist and Modern Painting Dept, Sotheby & Co., 1963–66; Assistant to the President, Parke-Bernet, New York, 1966–69; James Dugdale & Associates, London, Independent Fine Art Consultancy Service, 1969–77; James Crathorne & Associates, 1977–; Dir, Woodhouse Securities, 1989–. Member: Yorks Regl Cttee, NT, 1978–84 and 1988–94; Council, RSA, 1982–88; Exec. Cttee, Georgian Gp, 1985– (Chm., 1990–); Cons. Adv. Gp on Arts and Heritage, 1988–; Dep. Chm., Jt Cttee, Nat. Amenity Socs, 1993–; President: Cleveland Assoc., NT, 1982–; Yarm Civic Soc., 1987–; Hambledon Dist, CPRE, 1988–; Cleveland Family History Soc., 1988–; Cleveland Sea Cadets, 1988–; Vice Pres., Cleveland Wildlife Trust, 1990–; Patron, Cleveland Community Foundn, 1990–. Member: Works of Art Sub-Cttee, H of L, 1983–; Editorial Bd, House Magazine, 1983–; Hon. Sec., All-Party Parly Arts and Heritage Gp, 1981–. Trustee: Captain Cook Trust, 1978– (Chm., 1993–); Georgian Theatre Royal, Richmond, Yorks, 1970–; Christian Inheritance, 1989–; Nat. Heritage Meml Fund, 1992–; Patron, Attingham Trust for Study of the British

Country House, 1991–. Church Warden, All Saints, Crathorne, 1977–. Annual lecture tours to America, 1970–; lecture series, Metropolitan Mus., NY, 1981; Australian Bicentennial Lecture Tour, 1988. Mem. Ct, Univ. of Leeds, 1985–; Gov., Queen Margaret's Sch. York Ltd, 1986–. FRSA 1972. DL Cleveland, 1983. *Exhibitions:* Photographs, Middlesbrough Art Gall., 1980; Royal Photographic Soc., Bath, 1992–. *Publications:* Edouard Vuillard, 1967; (co-author) Tennant's Stalk, 1973; (co-author) A Present from Crathorne, 1989; Cliveden: the place and the people, 1995; contribs to Apollo and The Connoisseur. *Recreations:* photography, travel, collecting, shooting, fishing, music. *Heir: s* Hon. Thomas Arthur John Dugdale, *b* 30 Sept. 1977. *Address:* Crathorne House, Yarm, Cleveland TS15 0AT. *T:* Stokesley (01642) 700431, (office) 0171–730 5420; House of Lords, SW1A 0PW. *T:* 0171–219 5224.

CRAUFURD, Sir Robert (James), 9th Bt *cr* 1781; *b* 18 March 1937; *s* of Sir James Gregan Craufurd, 8th Bt and of Ruth Marjorie, *d* of Frederic Corder; *S* father, 1970; *m* 1st, 1964, Catherine Penelope (marr. diss.), *yr d* of late Captain Horatio Westmacott, Torquay; three *d*; 2nd, 1987, Georgina Anne, *d* of late John D. Russell, Lymington. *Educ:* Harrow; University College, Oxford. Elected Member of the London Stock Exchange, 1969. Associated with Greig, Middleton & Co. *Address:* 7 Waldemar Avenue, SW6 5LB.

CRAVEN, family name of **Earl of Craven.**

CRAVEN, 9th Earl of, *cr* 1801; **Benjamin Robert Joseph Craven;** Baron Craven, 1665; Viscount Uffington, 1801; *b* 13 June 1989; *s* of 8th Earl and of Teresa Maria Bernadette Craven; *S* father, 1990. *Heir: cousin* Rupert José Evelyn Craven, Lt-Comdr RN [*b* 22 March 1926; *m* 1955, Margaret Campbell (*d* 1985), *d* of Alexander Smith, MBE].

CRAVEN, Archdeacon of; *see* Grundy, Ven. M. L.

CRAVEN, John Anthony; Chairman, Morgan Grenfell Group PLC, since 1989 (Chief Executive, 1987–89); Member, Board of Managing Directors, Deutsche Bank AG, Frankfurt, since 1990; *b* 23 Oct. 1940; *s* of William Herbert Craven and Hilda Lucy Craven; *m* 1st, 1961, Gillian Margaret (*née* Murray); one *s* one *d*; 2nd, 1970, Jane Frances (*née* Stiles-Allen); three *s*. *Educ:* Michaelhouse, S Africa; Jesus Coll., Cambridge (BA Hons Law); Queen's Univ., Kingston, Ont. Clarkson Gordon & Co., Toronto, Chartered Accountants, 1961–64; Wood Gundy, Investment Bankers, 1964–67; S. G. Warburg & Co., 1967–73, Dir 1969–73; Gp Chief Exec., White Weld & Co. Ltd, 1973–78; Vice Chm., S. G. Warburg & Co., 1979; Founder and Chm., Phoenix Securities Ltd, 1981–89; Dir, Mercury Securities Ltd, 1979. Non-exec. Chm., Tootal Group PLC, 1985–91; Director: New Rothmans, subseq. Rothmans Internat., plc, 1993–; Rothmans Internat. NV, 1993–. Mem., Conseil d'Administration, Société Générale de Surveillance, Switzerland, 1989–; Dir, SIB, 1990–93. Member: Ontario Inst. of Chartered Accts; Canadian Inst. of Chartered Accountants. *Recreations:* hunting, shooting, skiing. *Address:* Morgan Grenfell Group, 23 Great Winchester Street, EC2P 2AX. *Clubs:* City; Links (New York).

CRAVEN, Air Marshal Sir Robert Edward, KBE 1970 (OBE 1954); CB 1966; DFC 1940; *b* 16 Jan. 1916; *s* of Gerald Craven, Port Elizabeth, S Africa, and Edith Craven, York; *m* 1940, Joan Peters (*d* 1991); one *s* one *d*. *Educ:* Scarborough Coll. MN, 1932–37; Pilot Officer, RAF, 1937; 201, 210, 228 Sqdns, 1937–41; RAF Staff Coll., 1942; Staff Appts: Coastal Command, 1942 (despatches thrice); Directing Staff, RAF Staff Coll., 1944; HQ, Mediterranean and Middle East, Cairo, 1945; CO Eastleigh, Kenya, 1946; RN Staff Coll., 1948; Directing Staff, Joint Services Staff Coll., 1949; Standing Group, NATO Washington, 1951; RAF St Eval, 1954; Directing Staff, RAF Staff Coll., 1957; Group Capt. 1957; CO RAF Lyneham, 1959; Director, Personal Services, RAF, 1961; Air Cdre 1961; Air Officer Admin., Transport Comd, 1964; Air Vice-Marshal, 1965; SASO, Flying Training Comd, 1967–68, Training Comd, 1968–69; Commander, Maritime Air Forces, 1969–72, retired. Order of Menelik (Ethiopia), 1955. *Recreations:* water fowl breeding, antique furniture restoration and reproduction. *Address:* Letcombe House, Letcombe Regis, Oxon OX12 9LD. *Club:* Royal Air Force.

CRAWFORD, 29th Earl of, *cr* 1398, **AND BALCARRES,** 12th Earl of, *cr* 1651; **Robert Alexander Lindsay,** PC 1972; Lord Lindsay of Crawford, before 1143; Lord Lindsay of Balcarres, 1633; Lord Balniel, 1651; Baron Wigan (UK), 1826; Baron Balniel (Life Peer), 1974; Premier Earl of Scotland; Head of House of Lindsay; DL; Lord Chamberlain to the Queen Mother, since 1992; *b* 5 March 1927; *er s* of 28th Earl of Crawford and 11th of Balcarres, KT, GBE, and Mary (*d* 1994), 3rd *d* of late Lord Richard Cavendish, PC, CB, CMG; *S* father, 1975; *m* 1949, Ruth Beatrice, *d* of Leo Meyer-Bechtler, Zürich; two *s* two *d*. *Educ:* Eton; Trinity College, Cambridge. Served with Grenadier Guards, 1945–49. MP (C) Hertford, 1955–74, Welwyn and Hatfield, Feb.-Sept. 1974; Parliamentary Private Secretary: to Financial Secretary of Treasury, 1955–57; to Minister of Housing and Local Government, 1957–60; Opposition front-bench spokesman on health and social security, 1967–70; Minister of State for Defence, 1970–72; Minister of State for Foreign and Commonwealth Affairs, 1972–74. First Crown Estate Comr, 1980–85. Chairman: Lombard North Central Bank, 1976–80; Abela Hldgs (UK), 1983–95; Director: Nat. Westminster Bank, 1975–88; Scottish American Investment Co., 1978–88; a Vice-Chm., Sun Alliance & London Insurance Gp, 1975–91. President, Rural District Councils Assoc., 1959–65; Chairman: National Association for Mental Health, 1963–70; Historic Buildings Council for Scotland, 1976–83; Royal Commn on Ancient and Historical Monuments of Scotland, 1985–95; Bd of Trustees, Nat. Library of Scotland, 1990–. DL Fife. *Heir: s* Lord Balniel, *qv*. *Address:* House of Lords, SW1A 0PW.

CRAWFORD, Prof. Andrew Charles, FRS 1990; Professor of Neurophysiology, Cambridge University, since 1992; Fellow of Trinity College, Cambridge, since 1974; *b* 12 Jan. 1949; *s* of Charles and Vera Crawford; *m* 1974, Catherine Jones; one *s* one *d*. *Educ:* King Edward VI Camp Hill Sch., Birmingham; Downing Coll., Cambridge (BA 1970); Emmanuel Coll., Cambridge (MA, PhD 1974). Cambridge University: Research Fellow, Emmanuel Coll., 1972; Univ. Demonstrator, 1974; Lectr, 1977; Reader in Sensory Physiology, 1987. *Publications:* contribs on physiology of hearing, in learned jls. *Address:* Physiological Laboratory, Downing Street, Cambridge CB2 3EG. *T:* Cambridge (01223) 333879.

CRAWFORD, Douglas; *see* Crawford, G. D.

CRAWFORD, Prof. Sir Frederick (William), Kt 1986; FEng 1985; Vice-Chancellor, Aston University, since 1980; *b* 28 July 1931; *s* of William and Victoria Maud Crawford; *m* 1963, Béatrice M. J. Hutter, LèsL, MA, PhD, Paris; one *d* (one *s* decd). *Educ:* George Dixon Grammar Sch., Birmingham; Univ. of London (BSc Eng (1st cl. hons), MSc, DSc); Univ. of Liverpool (DipEd, PhD, DEng). Pres., Guild of Undergraduates, 1955–56; Mem. Court, 1955–62 and 1981–; Treas., NUS, 1957–59; Winner, NUS-Observer Fifth Nat. Student Debating Tourn., 1958. ACT Birmingham 1952; FIEE 1965; FIEEE 1972; FInstP 1964; FAPS 1965; FIMA 1978; CIMgt (CBIM 1986). Research Trainee, J. Lucas Ltd, 1948–52; Scientist, NCB Mining Res. Estabt, 1956–57; Sen. Lectr in Elec. Engrg, CAT Birmingham, 1958–59; Stanford University, California, 1959–82: Res. Associate, W. W. Hansen Labs of Physics, 1959–64; Institute for Plasma Research: Prof. (Research), 1964–67; Associate Prof., 1967–69; Prof., 1969–82; Consulting Prof., 1983–84; Chm., 1974–80; Dir, Centre for Interdisciplinary Res. and Associate Dean of Graduate Studies, 1973–77. Vis. Scientist, French Atomic Energy Commn, and Cons. to Comp. Française Thomson-Houston, 1961–62; Visiting Professor: Japan, 1969; Univ. of Paris, 1971; Australia, 1972; Mathematical Inst., Oxford Univ., also Vis. Fellow, St Catherine's Coll., Oxford, 1977–78. Union Radio-Scientifique Internationale: Member: US Nat. Cttee, 1975–81; UK Nat. Cttee, 1980–84; Commn H (Waves in Plasmas); US Chm., 1975–78; Internat. Chm., 1978–81; UK Rep., 1982–84; Chm. Internat. Sci. Cttee, Internat. Conf. on Phenomena in Ionised Gases, 1979–81; University Space Research Association: Member: Council, 1973–81 (Chm. 1977–78); Bd of Trustees, 1975–81 (Chm. 1976–77); Mem. numerous cttees on Space Shuttle, NASA, 1972–80. Dir, Sigma Xi, 1976–78; Mem. Council, Amer. Assoc. of Univ. Profs, 1980–82; Vice-Chm., CVCP, 1993–; Vice-Pres., Parly and Scientific Cttee, 1992– (Vice-Chm., 1989–92). Mem., Council, IEE, 1985–88, 1989–92 and 1993–. Director: Aston Technical Management and Planning Services, 1980–; Birmingham Technology Ltd, 1982–; West Midlands Technology Transfer Centre, 1985–93; Legal & General Gp plc, 1988–; Bowater plc, 1989–; PowerGen plc, 1990–. Member: US-UK Educnl Commn, 1981–84; British-North American Cttee, 1987–; Franco-British Council, 1987–; Vice-President: Birmingham Civic Soc., 1990– (Chm., 1983–88). Freeman, City of London, 1986; Liveryman, Co. of Information Technologists, 1993; Sen. Warden, Co. of Engineers, 1994–95. High Sheriff, W Midlands, 1995. Hon. FIL, 1987. *Publications:* numerous papers on plasma physics in sci. books and jls. *Address:* Vice-Chancellor's Office, Aston University, Birmingham B4 7ET. *T:* 0121–359 3611. *Club:* Athenæum.

CRAWFORD, (George) Douglas; Editor, Business and Finance, since 1993; journalist, The Herald (formerly Glasgow Herald), since 1989; *b* 1 Nov. 1939; *s* of Robert and Helen Crawford; *m* 1964, Joan Burnie; one *s* one *d*. *Educ:* Glasgow Academy; St Catharine's Coll., Cambridge (MA). Features Editor, Business, 1961–63; Industrial Corresp., Glasgow Herald, 1963–66; Editor, Scotland Magazine, 1966–70; Dir, Polecon Gp of Cos, 1970–89. MP (SNP) Perth and East Perthshire, Oct. 1974–1979; contested (SNP) Perth and Kinross, 1983. *Recreations:* hill-walking, swimming, playing piano and clavichord, watching cricket. *Address:* 43b 1 William Street, Edinburgh EH3 7LW.

CRAWFORD, Iain; Director, Veterinary Field and Investigation Services (formerly Veterinary Field Service), Ministry of Agriculture, Fisheries and Food, since 1988; *b* 8 April 1938; *s* of James and Agnes Crawford, Baillieston,, Glasgow; *m* 1962, Janette Mary Allan; two *s* one *d*. *Educ:* Coatbridge High Sch., Lanarks; Glasgow Univ. (BVMS). MRCVS 1961. Entered private vet. practice, 1961; joined MAFF as a Vet. Officer, 1968; Dep. Regl Vet. Officer, Bristol, 1981; Vet. Head of Sect. (Regl Vet. Officer), 1983; Asst Chief Vet. Officer, 1986. *Recreations:* sailing, walking. *Address:* 14 Camilla Close, Great Bookham, Leatherhead, Surrey KT23 4BU.

CRAWFORD, Maj.-Gen. (Ian) Patrick, GM 1964; FFCM, FFOM; Commandant and Postgraduate Dean, Royal Army Medical College, Millbank, 1989–93; *b* 11 Oct. 1933; *s* of Donald Patrick and Florence Ireland Crawford; *m* 1956, Juliet Treharne James; two *s* one *d*. *Educ:* Chatham House, Ramsgate; St Thomas' Hosp., London. MRCS, LRCP; FFCM 1982; FFOM 1987; DPH, DIH, DTM&H. House Surgeon, Casualty and Orthopaedics and House Physician, Royal Sussex County Hosp., 1959–60; Nat. Service, RAMC, 1960–63; on active service, Borneo, 1962–64; commnd 1963; Regimental MO, 20 Regt RA and 1st/7th Gurkha Rifles, Malaya and Borneo, 1963–68; Staff Officer: Army Health Home Counties Dist, 1968; HQ Singapore Dist, 1968–70; Instructor, Sch. of Army Health, 1970–71; MoD, 1971–72; Exchange Officer, Australia, 1972–75; MoD, 1975–78; HQ 1 BR Corps, 1978–81; Parkes Prof. of Preventive Medicine, Royal Army Med. Coll., 1981–84; Defence Med. Services Directorate, 1984–86; Comdr, Saudi Arabian Nat. Guard Med. Team, 1986–88; Defence Med. Services Directorate, 1988–89. QHP 1991–93. Specialist in Preventive Medicine, Singapore, Australia, PNG, BAOR, Saudi Arabia and UK; Consultant Advr, Saudi Arabia Nat. Guard, Jeddah, 1986–88. Hon. Lectr, Dept of Occupational Med., Queensland Univ., 1973–75. FRSM 1981. OStJ 1992. *Publications:* papers and pubns on military preventive medicine. *Recreations:* golf, computing, travel, bridge. *Address:* Mill Cottage, Mill Lane, Cocking, near Midhurst, W Sussex GU29 0HJ. *T:* Midhurst (01730) 817685. *Club:* Goodwood Golf.

CRAWFORD, Prof. James Richard, DPhil; barrister; Whewell Professor of International Law, University of Cambridge, and Fellow of Jesus College, Cambridge, since 1992; *b* 14 Nov. 1948; *s* of James Allen and Josephine Margaret Crawford; *m* 1st, 1971, Marisa Luigina (marr. diss. 1991); two *d*; 2nd, 1992, Patricia Hyndman; two *d*. *Educ:* Adelaide Univ. (LLB Hons; BA 1971); Oxford Univ. (DPhil 1977). Called to the Bar, High Court of Australia, 1979. University of Adelaide: Lectr, 1974; Sen. Lectr, 1977; Reader, 1982; Prof. of Law, 1983; Challis Prof. of Internat. Law, 1986–92, Dean, Faculty of Law, 1990–92, Univ. of Sydney. Comr, Australian Law Reform Commn, 1982–90; Mem., UN Internat. Law Commn, 1992–. *Publications:* The Creation of States in International Law, 1979; Australian Courts of Law, 1982, 2nd edn 1988; (ed) The Rights of Peoples, 1988. *Recreations:* cricket, reading. *Address:* Jesus College, Cambridge CB5 8BL.

CRAWFORD, John Michael; Director of Education (formerly Chief Education Officer), Birmingham, 1977–88; *b* 6 Dec. 1938; *s* of James and Emily Crawford; *m* 1962, Geraldine Kay Weaver; two *d*. *Educ:* Ipswich Sch.; University Coll., London (BA); Fitzwilliam House, Cambridge. Asst Master, Merchant Taylor's, Crosby, 1961–63; Admin. Asst, E Suffolk CC, 1963–66; Sen. Admin. Asst, Lancs CC, 1966–68; Asst Educn Officer, W Riding CC, 1968–73; Dep. Educn Officer, Birmingham, 1973–77. *Address:* July Green, Snuff Mill Walk, Bewdley, Worcs DY12 2HG. *T:* Bewdley (01299) 400174.

CRAWFORD, Lionel Vivian, FRS 1988; Principal Scientist, Imperial Cancer Research Fund Tumour Virus Group, Department of Pathology, Cambridge University, 1988–94; *b* 30 April 1932; *s* of John Mitchell Crawford and Fanny May Crawford (*née* Barnett); *m* 1957, Elizabeth Minnie (*née* Green); one *d*. *Educ:* Rendcomb College, Cirencester; Emmanuel College, Cambridge (BA, MA, PhD). Virus Lab., Berkeley, Calif., 1958–59; Calif. Inst. of Technology, 1959–60; Inst. of Virology, Glasgow, 1960–68; Molecular Virology Lab., Imperial Cancer Res. Fund, 1968–88. Member: Soc. for Gen. Microbiology; EMBO. FRSE 1970. *Publications:* numerous scientific articles. *Recreation:* restoring old houses.

CRAWFORD, Michael, OBE 1987; actor since 1955; *b* 19 Jan. 1942. *Educ:* St Michael's Coll., Bexley; Oakfield Sch., Dulwich. In orig. prodn of Britten's Noyes Fludde and of Let's Make an Opera; *stage appearances include:* Come Blow Your Horn, Prince of Wales, 1961; Travelling Light, 1965; The Anniversary, 1966; No Sex Please, We're British, Strand, 1971; Billy, Drury Lane, 1974; Same Time, Next Year, Prince of Wales, 1976; Flowers for Algernon, Queen's, 1979; Barnum, Palladium, 1981, 1983, Victoria Palace, 1985–86; The Phantom of the Opera, Her Majesty's, 1986, NY, 1988 (Tony Award, Best Actor in a Musical), Los Angeles, 1989. *Films include:* Soap Box Derby; Blow Your Own Trumpet; Two Left Feet; The War Lover; Two Living, One Dead; The Knack, 1964; A Funny Thing Happened on the Way to the Forum, 1965; The Jokers, How I Won the War, 1966; Hello Dolly, 1968; The Games, 1969; Hello and Goodbye, 1970; Alice in Wonderland, 1972; The Condorman, 1980. Numerous radio broadcasts and TV appearances; *TV series include:* Some Mothers Do 'Ave 'Em; Chalk and Cheese. *Address:* c/o ICM Ltd, Oxford House, 76 Oxford Street, W1R 1RB. *T:* 0171–636 6565.

CRAWFORD, Prof. Michael Hewson, FBA 1980; Professor of Ancient History, University College London, since 1986; *b* 7 Dec. 1939; *s* of late Brian Hewson Crawford and Margarethe Bettina (*née* Nagel). *Educ:* St Paul's School; Oriel College, Oxford (BA, MA). Scholar, British School at Rome, 1962–64; Jane Eliza Procter Visiting Fellow, Princeton Univ., 1964–65; Cambridge University: Research Fellow, 1964–69, Fellow, 1969–86, Christ's Coll.; Lectr, 1969–86. Visiting Professor: Univ. of Pavia, 1983, 1992; Ecole Normale Supérieure, Paris, 1984; Univ. of Padua, 1986; Sorbonne, Paris, 1989; San Marino, 1989; Milan, 1990; L'Aquila, 1990. Joint Director: Excavations of Fregellae, 1980–86; Valpolcevera Project, 1987–93; Velleia Project, 1994–. Chm., JACT, 1992– (Chm., Ancient History Cttee, 1978–84); Vice-Pres., Roman Soc., 1981–. Membro Straniero, Istituto Lombardo, 1990. Editor: Papers of the British Sch. at Rome, 1975–79; Jl of Roman Studies, 1980–84. *Publications:* Roman Republican Coin Hoards, 1969; Roman Republican Coinage, 1974; The Roman Republic, 1978; La Moneta in Grecia e a Roma, 1981; (with D. Whitehead) Archaic and Classical Greece, 1982; Sources for Ancient History, 1983; Coinage and Money under the Roman Republic, 1985; (with M. Beard) Rome in the Late Republic, 1985; L'impero romano e la struttura economica e sociale delle province, 1986; (with A. M. Burnett) The Coinage of the Roman World in the Late Republic, 1987; (with C. Ligota and J. B. Trapp) Medals and Coins from Budé to Mommsen, 1990; (ed) Antonio Agustín between Renaissance and Counter-reform, 1993; (ed) Roman Statutes, 1994; contribs to Annales, Economic History Rev., Jl of Roman Studies, etc. *Address:* University College, Gower Street, WC1E 6BT.

CRAWFORD, Maj.-Gen. Patrick; *see* Crawford, I. P.

CRAWFORD, Peter John, QC 1976; **His Honour Judge Peter Crawford;** a Senior Circuit Judge, since 1992 (a Circuit Judge, 1988–92); *b* 23 June 1930; *s* of William Gordon Robertson and Doris Victoria Robertson (*née* Mann, subseq. Crawford); *m* 1st, 1955, Jocelyn Lavender; two *s* two *d*; 2nd, 1979, Ann Allen Travis. *Educ:* Berkhamsted Sch.; Brasenose Coll., Oxford (MA). Called to Bar, Lincoln's Inn, 1953; Bencher, 1984; a Recorder, 1974–88; Recorder of Birmingham, 1992–. Pres., Trent Region, Mental Health Review Tribunal, 1986–; Vice Chm., Appeal Cttee, ICA, 1987–88; Member: Council of Justice, 1986–88; Parole Bd, 1992–. Mem., Paddington Borough Council, 1962–65; Chm., W London Family Service Unit, 1972–79; Mem., Family Service Units Nat. Council, 1975–81. *Recreation:* gardening. *Address:* Queen Elizabeth II Law Courts, Newton Street, Birmingham B4 7NA. *Clubs:* Garrick, Royal Over-Seas League.

CRAWFORD, Robert Gammie, CBE 1990; Chairman, Highlands and Islands Airports Ltd, 1986–93; *b* 20 March 1924; *s* of William and Janet Beveridge Crawford; *m* 1947, Rita Veiss; one *d*. *Educ:* Robert Gordon's Coll., Aberdeen. Solicitor of the Supreme Court, England. Navigator, RAF, 1942–47. Practised as Solicitor, 1950–73, Partner, Ince and Co. (Internat. Shipping Lawyers); Director: UK Freight Demurrage and Defence Assoc. Ltd, 1976– (Chm., 1987–90); UK Mutual Steamship Assurance Assoc. Ltd, 1980–94 (Chm., 1983–90); Sturge Aviation Syndicates Management Ltd, 1994–; L. R. Integrity Management Ltd, 1994–; Chm., UK Mutual War Risk Assoc. Ltd, 1982– (Dir, 1980–). Mem., Lloyd's, 1975. Member: Bd, CAA, 1984–93; Bd, Lloyd's Register of Shipping, 1982–94; Bd, PLA, 1985–92 (Vice Chm., 1986–92). Freeman: City of London, 1988; Co. of Watermen and Lightermen, 1988. *Recreations:* shooting, golf, reading, conversation. *Address:* 9 London House, Avenue Road, NW8 7PX. *T:* 0171–483 2754; West Mains of Auchenhove, Lumphanan, Aberdeenshire AB31 4QT. *T:* Lumphanan (013398) 83667. *Club:* Royal Northern and University (Aberdeen).

CRAWFORD, (Robert) Norman, CBE 1973; Chairman, R. N. Crawford & Co., Business Advisors, since 1968; Director, William Clark & Sons, 1983–88 (Chief Executive, 1983–87); *b* 14 June 1923; *s* of Wm Crawford and Annie Catherine (*née* Rexter); *m* 1948, Jean Marie Patricia (*née* Carson); one *s* five *d*. *Educ:* Foyle Coll., Londonderry; Queen's Univ., Belfast (BComSc). FCA. Sec./Accountant, John McNeill Ltd, 1948–60; Dep. Man. Dir, McNeill Group Ltd, 1960–66, Man. Dir 1966–68; Chm., N Ireland Transport Holding Co., 1968–75; Divisional Hd, NI Develt Agency, 1976–82. Pres., N Ireland Chamber of Commerce and Industry, 1966–67; Chairman: N Ireland Regional Bd, BIM, 1966–69; Nature Reserves Cttee, 1967–85; NI Outward Bound Assoc., 1969–76 (Pres., 1983–92); Open Door Housing Assoc., 1979–84; Retirement Assoc. of NI, 1982–83; Mem., CEED, 1985–92. Member Senate, Queen's University, Belfast, 1968–93 (Pres., Queen's Univ. Assoc., 1982–83); Pres., Foyle Coll. Old Boys' Assoc., 1981–82. Chm., NI Wildlife Campaign, 1986–88. FRSA. *Address:* 23 Corberry Mews, Dumfries DG2 7AX. *T:* Dumfries (01387) 261236. *Club:* Ulster Reform (Belfast).

CRAWFORD, Sir (Robert) Stewart, GCMG 1973 (KCMG 1966; CMG 1951); CVO 1955; HM Diplomatic Service, retired; *b* 27 Aug. 1913; *s* of late Sir William Crawford, KBE; *m* 1938, Mary Katharine (*d* 1992), *d* of late Eric Corbett, Gorse Hill, Witley, Surrey; three *s* one *d* (and one *s* decd). *Educ:* Gresham's Sch., Holt; Oriel Coll., Oxford. Home Civil Service (Air Ministry), 1936; Private Sec. to Chief of Air Staff, 1940–46; Asst Sec., Control Office for Germany and Austria, 1946; Foreign Office, 1947; Counsellor, British Embassy, Oslo, 1954–56; Counsellor, later Minister, British Embassy, Baghdad, 1957–59; Dep. UK Delegate to OEEC Paris, 1959–60; Asst Under Sec., Foreign Office, 1961–65; Political Resident, Persian Gulf, 1966–70; Dep. Under-Sec. of State, FCO, 1970–73. Chm., Cttee on Broadcasting Coverage, 1973–74; Mem., BBC Gen. Adv. Council, 1976–84; Chm., Broadcasters' Audience Res. Bd, 1980–88. *Recreations:* opera, bookbinding. *Address:* 19 Adam Court, Bell Street, Henley-on-Thames, Oxon RG9 2BJ. *T:* Henley (01491) 574702. *Clubs:* United Oxford & Cambridge University; Phyllis Court (Henley-on-Thames).

CRAWFORD, Robert William Kenneth; Director-General, Imperial War Museum, since 1995 (Deputy Director-General, 1982–95); *b* 3 July 1945; *s* of late Hugh Merrall Crawford, FCA, and Mary Crawford (*née* Percival); *m* 1975, Vivienne Sylvia Polakowski; one *d* one *s*. *Educ:* Culford Sch.; Pembroke Coll., Oxford (Cleobury Schol.; BA). Joined Imperial War Museum as Research Asst, 1968: Head of Research and Information Office, 1971–89; Keeper, Dept of Photographs, 1975–83; Asst Director, 1979–82. *Address:* c/o Imperial War Museum, Lambeth Road, SE1 6HZ. *T:* 0171–416 5206.

CRAWFORD, Vice-Adm. Sir William (Godfrey), KBE 1961; CB 1958; DSC 1941; *b* 14 Sept. 1907; *s* of late H. E. V. Crawford, Wyld Court, Axminster, and late Mrs M. E. Crawford; *m* 1939, Mary Felicity Rosa, *d* of late Sir Philip Williams, 2nd Bt; three *s* one *d*. *Educ:* RN Coll., Dartmouth. Lieut RN, 1929; specialised in gunnery, 1932; Lieut-Comdr, 1937; Gunnery Officer, HMS Rodney, 1940–42; Comdr Dec. 1941; Exec. Officer, HMS Venerable, 1944–46; Capt. 1947; in comd HMS Pelican and 2nd Frigate Flotilla, Med., 1948–49; Dep.-Dir RN Staff Coll., 1950–52; in comd HMS Devonshire, 1952–53; in comd RN Coll., Dartmouth, 1953–56; Rear-Adm. 1956; Imperial Defence Coll., 1956–58; Flag Officer, Sea Training, 1958–60; Vice-Adm. 1959; Comdr British Navy Staff and Naval Attaché Washington, 1960–62; retired list, 1963. Dir, Overseas Offices, BTA, 1964–72. *Recreations:* sailing, fishing. *Address:* Broadlands, Whitchurch Canonicorum, Bridport, Dorset DT6 6RJ. *T:* Chideock (01297) 489591. *Club:* Cruising.

CRAWFORD, William Hamilton Raymund, QC 1980; **His Honour Judge Crawford;** a Circuit Judge, since 1986; *b* 10 Nov. 1936; *s* of late Col Mervyn Crawford, DSO, DL, JP, and Martha Hamilton Crawford; *m* 1965, Marilyn Jean Colville; one *s* two *d*. *Educ:* West Downs, Winchester; Winchester Coll.; Emmanuel Coll., Cambridge (BA). Called to the Bar, Inner Temple, 1964; Dep. Chm., Agricultural Land Tribunal, 1978; a Recorder, 1979–86. *Recreations:* hill farming, fishing, shooting (shot for GB in Kolapore Match, and for Scotland in Elcho and Twenty Matches on several occasions; mem., Scottish Rifle Team, Commonwealth Games, Jamaica, 1966). *Address:* c/o The Crown Court, Newcastle-upon-Tyne. *Clubs:* Naval and Military; Northern Counties (Newcastle).

CRAWLEY, Mrs Christine Mary; Member (Lab) Birmingham East, European Parliament, since 1984; Deputy Leader, European Parliamentary Labour Party, since 1994; *b* 9 Jan. 1950; *m*; three *c* (incl. twins). *Educ:* Notre Dame Catholic Secondary Girls' School, Plymouth; Digby Stuart Training College, Roehampton. Formerly teacher; S Oxfordshire District Council; contested (Lab) Staffordshire SE, gen. election, 1983. Chair, Women's Rights Cttee, EP, 1989–94. *Address:* c/o Birmingham District Labour Party, 16 Bristol Street, Birmingham B5 7AF.

CRAWLEY, Most Rev. David Perry; *see* Kootenay, Archbishop of.

CRAWLEY, Frederick William, FCIB; Chairman: Alliance & Leicester Building Society, 1991–94 (Director, since 1988; Deputy Chairman, 1990–91); Girobank PLC, 1992–94 (Director, since 1990; Deputy Chairman, 1990–92); *b* 10 June 1926; *s* of William Clement Crawley and Elsie Florence Crawley; *m* 1951, Ruth Eva Jungman; two *d*. Joined Lloyds Bank, 1942; Chief Accountant, 1969–72; Asst Chief Gen. Man., 1977–78; Dep. Chief Gen. Man., 1978–82; Chief Exec., Lloyds Bank, Calif, 1982–83; Dep. Chief Gen. Man., 1983–84, Chief Gen. Man., 1984–85, Dep. Chief Exec., 1985–87, Lloyds Bank plc. Chairman: Black Horse Agencies Ltd, 1985–88; Betta Stores, 1990–92; Legal & General Recovery Investment Trust, 1994–; Director: Black Horse Life Assce Co., 1977–82; Lloyds Bank Unit Trust Managers, 1977–82; Lloyds Leasing, 1977–82; Lloyds Development Capital, 1981–82; Lloyds Bank International, 1982–83; Internat. Commodies Clearing House Hldgs, 1984–87; Lloyds Bank, 1984–88; Lloyds Bank Export Finance, 1985–87; Lloyds Bowmaker Finance, 1985–87; FS Assurance, 1988–90; Barratt Developments, 1988–; Lloyds Development Capital, 1988–92; Aeroclub Ltd, 1987–. RAF Benevolent Fund: Hon. Treas., 1988–, and Dep. Chm., 1988–, RAF Benevolent Fund Enterprises (formerly Internat. Air Tattoo); Dir, Battle of Britain Appeal, 1988–91. FCIB (FIB 1971); CIMgt. *Recreations:* aviation, shooting, photography. *Address:* 4 The Hexagon, Fitzroy Park, N6 6HR. *T:* 0181–341 2279.

CRAWLEY, John Cecil, CBE 1972 (MBE 1944); Chairman of Trustees of Visnews, 1976–86; *b* 1909; *s* of John and Kathleen Crawley; *m* 1933, Constance Mary Griffiths; two *d*. *Educ:* William Ellis Sch. War Service, Army, 1939–45. Journalism: Reynolds, 1927; Central News Agency, 1928; National Press Agency, 1929; Press Secretaries, 1933; BBC: Sub-Editor, 1945; Foreign Correspondent, New York, 1959–63; Foreign News Editor, 1963–67; Editor of News and Current Affairs, 1967–71; Chief Asst to Dir-Gen., BBC, 1971–75. *Recreations:* walking, bird-watching. *Address:* 157 Clarence Gate Gardens, NW1 6AP. *T:* 0171–723 6876.

CRAWLEY, John Maurice, CB 1992; Under Secretary (Principal Finance Officer), Inland Revenue, 1979–93; *b* 27 Sept. 1933; *s* of late Charles William and Kathleen Elizabeth Crawley; *m* 1978, Jane Meadows Rendel; three *s*. *Educ:* Rugby Sch.; New Coll., Oxford (MA). Assistant Principal, Inland Revenue, 1959; Principal, 1963; Asst Secretary, 1969; Under Sec., 1979; seconded to Cabinet Office (Central Policy Review Staff), 1973–76 and 1979–81. *Recreations:* music, walking.

CRAWLEY-BOEVEY, Sir Thomas (Michael Blake), 8th Bt *cr* 1784; *b* 29 Sept. 1928; *er s* of Sir Launcelot Valentine Hyde Crawley-Boevey, 7th Bt, and Elizabeth Goodeth (*d* 1976), *d* of Herbert d'Auvergne Innes, late Indian Police; *S* father, 1968; *m* 1957, Laura Coelingh (*d* 1979); two *s*. *Educ:* Wellington Coll.; St John's Coll., Cambridge (BA 1952, MA 1956). 2nd Lieut, Durham Light Infantry, 1948. With Shipping Agents, 1952–61; with Consumers' Association, 1961–82; Editor: Money Which?, 1968–76; Which?, 1976–82; Editor-in-Chief, Which? magazines, 1980–82. Mem. Council, Insce Ombudsman Bureau, 1985–. *Publications:* Buying, Selling and Owning Shares, 1987; Finance Your Future, 1989. *Heir: er s* Thomas Hyde Crawley-Boevey, *b* 26 June 1958. *Address:* Trebanau, Cilycwm, Llandovery, Dyfed SA20 0HP. *T:* Llandovery (01550) 20496. *Clubs:* Gower and Swansea Bay Windsurfing, Grafham Water Sailing.

CRAWSHAW, 4th Baron, *cr* 1892; **William Michael Clifton Brooks;** Bt *cr* 1891; DL; *b* 25 March 1933; *s* of 3rd Baron and Sheila (*d* 1964), *o d* of late Lieut-Col P. R. Clifton, CMG, DSO; *S* father, 1946. *Educ:* Eton; Christ Church, Oxford. Jt Master, Oxford Univ. Drag Hounds, 1952–53. Treasurer, Loughborough Div. Conservative Assoc., 1954–58; County Commissioner, Leics Boy Scouts, 1958–. Pres., Leics Assoc. of the Disabled; Chm., Quorn Hunt Cttee, 1971–. Lord of the Manor of Long Whatton. Patron of the Living of Shepshed. DL Leics, 1992. *Heir: b* Hon. David Gerald Brooks [*b* 14 Sept. 1934; *m* 1970, Belinda Mary, *d* of George Burgess, Melbourne, and of Mrs J. P. Allen, Coleman's Hatch, Sussex; four *d*. *Educ:* Eton; Royal Agricultural College, Cirencester]. *Address:* Whatton, Loughborough, Leics LE12 5BG. *TA:* Kegworth. *Clubs:* Boodle's, MCC.

CRAWSHAY, Elisabeth Mary Boyd, (Lady Crawshay), CBE 1986; JP, DL; Chairman, Local Government Boundary Commission, Wales, 1981–94; Deputy Chief Commissioner, St John's Ambulance Brigade, Wales, 1979–84; *b* 2 July 1927; *d* of Lt-Col Guy Franklin Reynolds, late 9th Lancers, and Katherine Isobel (*née* Macdonell); *m* 1950, Col Sir William (Robert) Crawshay, *qv*. *Educ:* Convent of Sacred Heart, Roehampton; St Anne's Coll., Oxford (MA). Mem., Mental Health Act Commn, 1983–88. DL Gwent 1978; JP Abergavenny, 1972, Chm., Juvenile Bench, 1980–, Mem., Borstal Board of Visitors, 1975–84. DJStJ 1970. *Address:* Llanfair Court, Abergavenny, Gwent NP7 9BB.

CRAWSHAY, Col Sir William (Robert), Kt 1972; DSO 1945; ERD; TD; Vice Lord-Lieutenant of Gwent, since 1979; *b* 27 May 1920; *o s* of late Captain J. W. L. Crawshay, MC, Caversham Park, Oxon, and late Hon. Mrs. George Egerton, Brussels; *m* 1950, Elisabeth Mary Boyd Reynolds (*see* Lady Crawshay). *Educ:* Eton. Served Royal Welch Fus.(SR), 1939–46; SOE 1944 (DSO, despatches twice); TA, 1947–62, Parachute Regt, Welch Regt, SW Brigade. ADC to HM the Queen, 1966–71. Hon. Colonel: 3rd RRW (V) Bn, 1970–82; Cardiff Univ. OTC, 1977–85. Mem., Arts Council of GB, 1962–74; Chairman: Welsh Arts Council, 1968–74; Council, University Coll. of Cardiff, 1966–87; Member: Council and Court, Univ. of Wales, 1967; Welsh Council, 1966–69, 1970–; Council and Court, Nat. Museum of Wales, 1966–92 (Pres., 1977–82). Vice-Pres., Royal British Legion, 1989– (Pres., Wales Area, 1974–88). Mem., Crafts Adv. Council, 1974–78. Hon. LLD, Univ. of Wales, 1975. DL Glamorgan, 1964, Monmouthshire, 1970, Gwent, 1974. Chevalier, Légion d'honneur, 1956; Croix de Guerre (France) with Palms twice, 1944, 1945. KStJ (formerly KJStJ) 1969. *Address:* Llanfair Court, Abergavenny, Gwent NP7 9BB. *Clubs:* White's; Cardiff and County (Cardiff).

CRAXTON, Antony, CVO 1977 (MVO 1968); freelance television consultant; *b* 23 April 1918; 2nd *s* of late Harold Craxton, OBE, and Essie Craxton; *m* 1944, Anne Sybil Cropper (marr. diss. 1978); one *s* one *d*. *Educ:* St George's Chapel Choir Sch., Windsor; Royal Acad. of Music; Gordonstoun Sch., Scotland. Joined BBC Radio, 1941; Home and Overseas Announcer, 1942–45; joined TV Service as Outside Broadcast Producer, 1951; resp. for coverage of all major Royal occasions, 1953–77, Jubilee Day being 200th broadcast involving the Queen and Royal Family; retd, 1979. Helped pioneer presentation of internat. cricket, rugby and golf in early 50s; covered over 100 orchestral concert relays from many parts of country, 1953–71. Chief Royal Occasions: Queen's 1st Christmas Television Broadcast and Prince Philip's 1st major TV appearance, Round the World in 40 Minutes, 1957; Princess Margaret's Wedding, 1960; Duke of Kent's Wedding, 1961; Princess Alexandra's Wedding, 1963; State Funeral of Sir Winston Churchill, 1965; Investiture of Prince Charles as Prince of Wales, 1969; Lying in State of Duke of Windsor, 1972; Queen's Silver Wedding Celebrations, 1972; Princess Anne's Wedding, 1973; Funeral of Duke of Gloucester, 1974; Funeral of Field-Marshal Montgomery, 1976; Queen's Silver Jubilee Day Celebrations, 1977; 10 State visits abroad and 19 visits by Foreign Heads of State to Britain, 1954–76. News Chronicle Readers' Award for Prince Philip's Round the World Documentary, 1957; Guild of TV Producers' Award for Princess Alexandra's Wedding, 1963; French TV Internat. Award for Investiture of Prince Charles, 1970; BAFTA Award for Jubilee Day (1977), 1978. Silver Jubilee Medal, 1977. *Recreations:* golf, cricket, classical music. *Club:* MCC.

CRAXTON, John Leith, RA 1993; artist; *b* 3 Oct. 1922; *s* of late Harold Craxton, OBE, LRAM and Essie Craxton. *Educ:* various private schs incl. Betteshanger, Kent; Westminster and Central Schs of Art; Goldsmiths' Coll. (with Lucian Freud). First solo exhibn, Leicester Galls, 1944; with Lucian Freud, worked in Scilly Is, then Greece, 1945–47, and held joint exhibn, London Gall., 1947; designed sets and costumes for Daphnis and Chloë, Royal Ballet, 1951, Apollo, 1966; Cotteral Meml Tapestry for Stirling Univ., 1971–74. Principal solo exhibitions include: St George's Gall., London, 1945; Galerie Gasser, Zürich, 1946; British Council, Athens, 1946, 1949, 1985; Mayor Gall., London, 1950; Leicester Galls, London, 1951, 1954, 1956, 1961, 1966; Crane Gall., Manchester, 1955; Whitechapel Art Gall., 1967; Hamet Gall., London, 1971; Christopher Hull Gall., London, 1982, 1985, 1987, 1993; Chrysostomos Gall., Hania, 1985. Work in public collections includes: Tate Gall.; V&A; BM; Gall. of Modern Art, Edinburgh; Nat. Mus. of Wales; Arts Council; British Council; Govt Picture Collection; Nat. Gall., Melbourne; Metropolitan Mus., NY; work in many private collections. HM Consular Correspondent, Hania, Crete. *Relevant publication:* Illustrated Monograph 1941–1948, by Geoffrey Grigson. *Recreations:* music, museums, motorbikes, archaeology, seafood, cooking. *Address:* c/o Christopher Hull Gallery, 17 Motcomb Street, SW1X 8LB; 14 Kidderpore Avenue, NW3 7SU.

See also A. Craxton.

CRAY, Rev. Graham Alan; Principal, Ridley Hall Theological College, since 1992; *b* 21 April 1947; *s* of Alan Cray and late Doris Mary Kathleen Cray; *m* 1973, Jacqueline Webster; two *d*. *Educ:* Leeds Univ. (BA 1968); St John's Coll., Nottingham. Ordained: deacon, 1971; priest, 1972; Asst Curate, St Mark, Gillingham, 1971–75; N Area Co-ordinator, Youth Dept, CPAS, 1975–78; Asst Curate, 1978–82, Vicar, 1982–92, St Michael-le-Belfrey, York. *Recreations:* listening to rock music, following sport, reading theology. *Address:* The Principal's Lodge, Ridley Hall, Cambridge CB3 9HG. *T:* Cambridge (01223) 358665.

CREAGH, Maj.-Gen. Sir Kilner Rupert B.; *see* Brazier-Creagh.

CREAMER, Brian; Consulting Physician, St Thomas' Hospital, London, 1991 (Physician, 1959–91); Senior Lecturer in Medicine, United Medical and Dental Schools (St Thomas's), 1959–91; Hon. Consultant in Gastroenterology to the Army, 1970–90; *b* 12 April 1926; *s* of late L. G. Creamer and Mrs Creamer, Epsom; *m* 1953, Margaret Holden Rees; two *s* one *d*. *Educ:* Christ's Hosp.; St Thomas' Hosp. MB, BS Hons London, 1948; MD London, 1952; FRCP 1966 (MRCP 1950); Research Asst, Mayo Clinic, Rochester, USA, 1955–56; Dean: St Thomas's Hosp. Med. Sch., 1979–84; UMDS of Guy's and St Thomas's Hosps, 1984–86. Vis. Prof., Shiraz Univ., Iran, 1977–78. Sir Arthur Hurst Memorial Lectr, 1968; Watson Smith Lectr, RCP, 1971. Member: SE Thames RHA, 1982–85; Medway DHA, 1987–89; W Lambeth DHA, 1989–90. Member: British Soc. of Gastroenterology; Assoc. of Physicians of GB and NI; Exec. Subcttee, Univ. Hosps Assoc., 1981–86. Chm. Council, Trinity Hospice, 1987–92. Member: Collegiate Council, Univ. of London, 1980–86; Senate, Univ. of London, 1981–86; Council of Almoners, Christ's Hosp., 1986–. *Publications:* (ed) Modern Trends in Gastroenterology, vol. 4, 1970; (ed) The Small Intestine, 1974; contributions to med. jls. *Recreations:* grappling with drawing and painting, listening to music. *Address:* Vine House, Highfields, East Horsley KT24 5AA. *T:* East Horsley (01483) 283320. *Club:* Royal Over-Seas League.

CREAN, Hon. Frank; *b* Hamilton, Vic, 28 Feb. 1916; *s* of J. Crean; *m* 1946, Mary, *d* of late A. E. Findlay; three *s*. *Educ:* Hamilton High Sch.; Melbourne High Sch.; Melbourne Univ. BA Hons; BCom. DPA; FCPA. Income Tax Assessor, 1934–45. MLA: for Albert Park, Vic, 1945–47; for Prahran, 1949–51; MHR for Melbourne Ports, 1951–77; Mem. Exec., Federal Parly Labour Party, 1956–72, Dep. Leader, 1975–76; Mem., Jt Parly Cttee on Public Accounts, 1952–55; Treasurer, Commonwealth of Australia, 1972–74; Minister for Overseas Trade, 1974–75, also Deputy Prime Minister, 1975. Chm., Council of Adult Educn, 1947–74. Pres., Vict. Br., Aust. Inst. Internat. Affairs, 1983–86; Chm., Vict. Br., Freedom from Hunger Campaign, 1979. *Publication:* (with W. J. Byrt) Government and Politics in Australia, 1972, 2nd edn 1982. *Address:* 31/27 Queens Road, Melbourne, Vic 3004, Australia.

CREASY, Leonard Richard, CB 1972; OBE 1961; CEng, FICE, FIStructE; civil engineer in private practice with son, since 1974; *b* 20 Dec. 1912; *s* of William and Ellen Creasy; *m* 1937, Irene Howard; one *s* one *d*. *Educ:* Wimbledon Technical Coll. BSc(Eng) London. Served War, RE, E Africa, 1944–46. Service in Industry, 1928–34; HM Office of Works, Asst Engr, 1935; Min. of Works, Suptg Engr, 1959; MPBW: Dir, Civil Engrg, 1966; Dir, Central Services, 1968; Dir of Civil Engrg Develt, Dept of the Environment, 1970–73. Concerned with Inquiries into disasters at Aberfan, Ronan Point and Brent, and with design of Radio and Radar Towers, London Heathrow and Birmingham; Plant House, Royal Botanical Gardens, Edinburgh; Wind Tunnels, Bedford RAE; and other structures. Bronze Medal, Reinforced Concrete Assoc.; Manby and Telford Premiums, Instn Civil Engrs; Pres., Instn Struct. Engrs, 1973 (Bronze Medal and Certif. of Merit of the Instn). *Publications:* Pre-stressed Concrete Cylindrical Tanks, 1961; James Forrest Lecture, 1968; many other papers on civil and structural engrg projects and engrg economics. *Recreations:* music, opera, languages. *Address:* 5 The Oaks, Epsom, Surrey KT18 5HH. *T:* Epsom (01372) 722361.

CREDITON, Bishop Suffragan of, 1984–April 1996; **Rt. Rev. Peter Everard Coleman;** *b* 28 Aug. 1928; *s* of Geoffrey Everard Coleman and Lilian Coleman; *m* 1960, HSH Princess Elisabeth-Donata Reuss; two *s* two *d*. *Educ:* Haileybury; King's Coll., London Univ. (LLB, AKC); Bristol Univ. (MLitt). Mil. Service, RHG and RA, 1947–49. Called to the bar, Middle Temple, 1965. Ordained, Bristol, 1955; Chaplain and Lectr, King's Coll., London, 1960–66; Vicar of St Paul's, Clifton, and Chaplain, Bristol Univ., 1966–71; Canon Residentiary and Dir of Training, Bristol, 1971–81; Archdeacon of Worcester, 1981–84. Clerical Member, Court of Arches, 1980–91; Mem. General Synod, 1974–81, 1990–. Provost, Western Div., Woodard Corp., 1992– (Fellow, 1985–). OStJ 1993. Jt Editor, Theology, 1982–91. *Publications:* Experiments with Prayer, 1961; A Christian Approach to Television, 1968; Christian Attitudes to Homosexuality, 1980; Gay Christians—a moral dilemma, 1989; The Ordination of Women to the Priesthood, 1990. *Recreations:* film making, fishing. *Address:* 10 The Close, Exeter EX1 1EZ. *Club:* Commonwealth Trust.

CREE, Brig. Gerald Hilary, CBE 1946; DSO 1945; Colonel, The Prince of Wales's Own Regiment of Yorkshire, 1960–70; *b* 23 June 1905; *s* of late Maj.-Gen. Gerald Cree; *m* 1945, Joan Agnes, *d* of late Lt-Col W. R. Eden, RA; one *d*. *Educ:* Kelly Coll.; RMC Sandhurst. Commissioned, The West Yorks Regt, 1924; King's African Rifles, 1931–36; comd 2nd Bn West Yorks Regt, 1942–44; 1st Bn 1946–48; Comdr 25 (East African) Infantry Bde, 1944–45 and Brig. 1953. Served Palestine, East Africa, Abyssinia, Western Desert, Iraq, Burma, 1938–45. Commander 127 (East Lancs) Infantry Brigade (TA), 1953–56; Col, The West Yorks Regt, 1956–57, Col, PWO Regt of Yorkshire, 1960–70, retd. *Address:* Laurels, Sharpham Drive, Totnes, Devon TQ9 5HE. *T:* Totnes (01803) 862902.

CREEK, Malcolm Lars, LVO 1980; OBE 1985; HM Diplomatic Service, retired; Consul-General, Auckland, 1988–90; *b* 2 April 1931; *s* of Edgar Creek and Lily Creek (*née* Robertshaw); *m* 1st, 1953, Moira Pattison (marr. diss. 1970); one *s* one *d*; 2nd, 1970, Gillian Bell; one *s* two *d*. *Educ:* Belle Vue School, Bradford. BA Hons London. National Service, 1950–52. Foreign Office, 1953; served Mogadishu, Harar, Mexico City, Abidjan, Chile; First Sec., San José, 1968; Havana, 1971; FCO, 1974; Head of Chancery, Tunis, 1978; Lima, 1981; High Comr, Vanuatu, 1985. *Recreations:* reading, family history, cricket. *Address:* 17 Bertram Drive North, Meols, Wirral, Merseyside L47 0LN. *T:* 0151–632 5520.

CREESE, Nigel Arthur Holloway, AM 1988; Executive Officer, Association of Heads of Independent Schools of Australia, since 1989 (Chairman, 1985–87); *b* 4 June 1927; *s* of late H. R. Creese; *m* 1951, Valdai (*née* Walters); two *s* two *d*. *Educ:* Blundell's Sch.; Brasenose Coll., Oxford. Assistant Master: Bromsgrove Sch., 1952–55; Rugby Sch., 1955–63; Headmaster: Christ's Coll., Christchurch, NZ, 1963–70; Melbourne Grammar Sch., 1970–87. *Recreations:* Nordic ski-ing, tennis. *Address:* 75 Charles Street, Kew, Vic 3101, Australia. *Club:* Melbourne (Melbourne).

CREIGHTMORE, Peter Beauchamp; Master of Supreme Court, Queen's Bench Division, since 1975; *b* 15 Jan. 1928; *s* of late Maximilian Louis Creightmore, MRCS, LRCP and Mary Arnell Beauchamp; *m* 1957, June Patricia, *d* of Harold William Hedley, Captain Suez Canal Co. (Pilote Majeur), and Gwendoline Pugh; one *s* one *d*. *Educ:* Geelong Grammar Sch. (H. H. Whittingham Student, 1945); Worcester Coll., Oxford (MA). O/Sig, RNVR, 1952, commnd 1955. Called to Bar, Inner Temple, 1954; Oxford, later Oxford and Midland, Circuit. *Recreation:* music. *Address:* Royal Courts of Justice, Strand, WC2A 2LL.

CREIGHTON, Alan Joseph, CEng, FRINA; RCNC; Chief Underwater Systems Executive, Ministry of Defence, 1989–91, retired; *b* 21 Nov. 1936; *s* of Joseph Kenneth and Iris Mary Creighton; *m* 1959, Judith Bayford; two *d*. *Educ:* Gillingham County Grammar School; Royal Naval College, Greenwich. Joined Admiralty, 1953; Cadetship to Royal Corps of Naval Constructors, 1957; pass out, RNC Greenwich, 1961; RCDS 1980; secondment to industry, 1981; resumed MoD (PE) career, 1984; Dir Gen., Surface Ships, 1986–89. *Recreations:* music, dinghy sailing, cabinet making. *Address:* Home Farm Cottage, West Littleton, Marshfield SN14 8JE. *T:* Bath (01225) 891021.

CREIGHTON, Harold Digby Fitzgerald; *b* 11 Sept. 1927; *s* of late Rev. Digby Robert Creighton and Amy Frances Rohde; *m* 1964, Harriett Mary Falconer Wallace, *d* of late A. L. P. F. Wallace of Candacraig (Mem., Queen's Body Guard for Scotland); four *d*. *Educ:* Haileybury. Consolidated Tin Smelters, Penang, 1950–52; Dir, machine tool companies, London, 1952–63; Chm., Scottish Machine Tool Corp. Ltd, Glasgow, 1963–68. Chm., 1967–75, Editor, 1973–75, The Spectator. *Address:* 5 Upper Brook Street, W1Y 1PA. *Clubs:* Beefsteak, Brooks's.

See also Baron Fairhaven.

CREMONA, Hon. John Joseph; Judge, 1965–92, Vice-President, 1986–92, European Court of Human Rights; Judge, 1985–92, Vice-President, 1987–92, European Tribunal in matters of State immunity; Emeritus Professor, University of Malta, since 1965; Chief Justice of Malta and President of the Constitutional Court, Court of Appeal and Court of Criminal Appeal, 1971–81; *b* 6 Jan. 1918; *s* of late Dr Antonio Cremona, KM, MD and Anne (*née* Camilleri); *m* 1949, Marchioness Beatrice Barbaro of St George; one *s* two *d*. *Educ:* Malta Univ. (BA 1936, LLD *cum laude* 1942); Rome Univ. (DLitt 1939); London Univ. (BA 1st Cl. Hons 1946, PhD in Laws 1951). DrJur Trieste, 1972. Crown Counsel, 1947; Lectr in Constitutional Law, Malta Univ., 1947–65, Prof. of Criminal Law, 1959–65; Attorney-Gen., 1957–64; Vice-Pres., Constitutional Court and Court of Appeal, 1965–71; sometime Actg Governor General and Actg Pres., Republic of Malta. Chm., UN Cttee on Elimination of Racial Discrimination (CERD), 1986–88 (Mem., 1984–88). Chairman: Human Rights Section, World Assoc. of Lawyers; Planning Council, Foundn for Internat. Studies, Malta Univ.; Vice-Pres., Internat. Inst. of Studies, Documentation and Info. for the Protection of Envt, Italy; Member: Cttee of Experts of Human Rights and Cttee on State Immunity, Council of Europe, Strasbourg; Scientific Council, Revue des Droits de l'Homme, Paris; Scientific Council Centro Internazionale per Protezione dei Diritti dell' Uomo, Pesaro, Italy; Editorial Adv. Board: Checklist of Human Rights Documents, NY; Rivista Internazionale dei diritti dell'vomo, Milan; delegate and rapporteur, internat. confs. FRHistS; Fellow *ex titulo*, Internat. Acad. of Legal Medicine and Social Medicine; Hon. Fellow, LSE; Hon. Mem., Real Acad. de Jurisprudencia y Legislacion, Madrid. KStJ 1984 (Chm., St John Council, Malta, 1983–). KSG 1972. Kt, Sovereign Military Order of Malta, 1966; Companion, Order of Merit (Malta), 1994. Kt Comdr, 1968, Grand Officier, 1989, Order of Merit (Italy); Kt Comdr, 1971, Grand Cross of Merit, 1981, Constantinian Order of St George; Chevalier de la Légion d'Honneur (France), 1990. *Publications:* The Treatment of Young Offenders in Malta, 1956; The Malta Constitution of 1835, 1959; The Doctrine of Entrapment in Theft, 1959; The Legal Consequences of a Conviction, 1962; The Constitutional Development of Malta, 1963; From the Declaration of Rights to Independence, 1965; Human Rights Documentation in Malta, 1966; Selected Papers 1946–1989, 1990; The Maltese Constitution and Constitutional History, 1994; articles in French, German, Italian, Portuguese and American law jls. *Recreation:* gardening. *Address:* Villa Barbaro, Main Street, Attard, Malta. *T:* 440818.

CRESPIN, Régine; Officier de la Légion d'Honneur, 1981 (Chevalier, 1969); Commandeur de l'Ordre National du Mérite, 1987 (Chevalier, 1965); Commandeur des Arts et des Lettres, 1974; soprano singer; Professor of Singing, Conservatoire National Supérieur de Musique de Paris, since 1976; *b* Marseille, 23 Feb.; *d* of Henri Crespin and Marguerite (*née* Meirone); *m* 1962, Lou Bruder, French novelist, critic, poet, translator. *Educ:* Nîmes; Conservatoire National, Paris (Baccalauréat). Worked at the Opera, Paris,

1951–, in all the famous opera houses of Europe and all over the world, giving concerts, recitals, etc.; *Operas include:* Otello, Tosca, Il Trovatore, Le Nozze di Figaro, Ballo in Maschera, Der Rosenkavalier, Tannhäuser, Lohengrin, Die Walküre, Parsifal, Les Troyens, Dialogues of the Carmelites, Tales of Hoffmann, Iphigenie auf Tauris, Carmen, Le Medium. *Publication:* La vie et l'amour d'une femme (autobiog.), 1982. *Recreations:* sea, sun, sleep, books, theatre; and my dog! *Address:* 3 Avenue Frochot, 75009 Paris, France.

CRESSON, Edith; Commandeur du Mérite Agricole, 1983; Member, European Commission, since 1995; Mayor of Chatellerault, Vienne, since 1983; *b* 27 Jan. 1934; *née* Campion; *m* Jacques Cresson; two *d*. *Educ:* Diplômée de l'Ecole des Hautes Etudes Commerciales; Dr en démographie (doctoral thesis: the life of women in a rural district of Guémené-Penfao, Loire-Atlantique). Mem., Convention des Institutions Républicaines (responsible for agricl problems), 1966; Dir of Studies, Bureau des Etudes Economiques privés (dealing especially with industrial investment, particularly in Canada); National Secretary, Parti Socialiste (in charge of youth organisation), 1974; Mem. Directing Cttee, Parti Socialiste; contested (for Parti Socialiste) Châtellerault, 1975; Mem., Eur. Parlt, 1979–81 (Mem., Cttee on Agriculture); Minister: of Agriculture, France, 1981–83; of For. Trade and Tourism, 1983–84; for Industrial Redeployment and Foreign Trade, 1984–86; for European Affairs, 1988–90; Pres.-Dir Gen., Schneider Industries Services Internat., 1990–91; Prime Minister of France, 1991–92; Pres. Dir Gen., Services Industries Strategies Internat. et Envmt, 1993–95. Pres., Assoc. Démocratique des Français à l'Etranger, 1986–91. Mayor of Thure, Vienne, 1977; Member, Conseil Général of Vienne, 1978–. *Publication:* Avec le soleil, 1976. *Address:* 200 Rue de la Loi, 1049 Brussels, Belgium; La Mairie, 86108 Chatellerault cedex, France.

CRESSWELL, Rev. Amos Samuel; Chairman, Plymouth and Exeter District of the Methodist Church, 1976–91; President of the Methodist Conference, 1983–84; *b* Walsall Wood, 21 April 1926; *s* of Amos and Jane Cresswell; *m* 1956, Evelyn Rosemary Marchbanks; two *s* one *d*. *Educ:* Queen Mary's Grammar School, Walsall; University College, Durham Univ.; Wesley House, and Fitzwilliam Coll., Cambridge; Theological Seminary, Bethel bei Bielefeld, Westphalia. BA (Dunelm), Classics, 1947; BA (Cantab), Theology, 1952, MA (Cantab) 1956. Teacher of English and Latin, High School for Boys, Colchester, 1947–49; Methodist Minister, Clitheroe Circuit, 1949–50; Asst Tutor in New Testament, Richmond Coll., London, 1953–56; Minister in Darlaston (Slater St), 1956–61; Tutor in New Testament, Cliff Coll., Derbyshire, 1961–66; Minister in Bramhall Circuit (Cheadle Hulme), 1966–73; Superintendent Minister, Welwyn Garden City, 1973–76. Pres., Devonshire Assoc., 1985–86. Editor, Advance (religious weekly, formerly Joyful News), 1961–63; (with Evelyn Cresswell), Founder, Vigo Press, 1991. *Publications:* The Story of Cliff (a history of Cliff College), 1965, 2nd edn 1983; The Story They Told (a short study of the Passion Narratives in the Gospels), 1966, 2nd edn 1992; Life Power and Hope—a study of the Holy Spirit, 1972; Lord! I've had enough! (a collection of sermons), 1991. *Recreations:* compulsive watching of sport (especially West Bromwich Albion); collecting Roman Imperial coins; reading about American Civil War; listening to music and to Shakespeare; involvement in local radio. *Address:* 85 Sandringham Drive, Paignton, Devon TQ3 1HH. *T:* Paignton (01803) 665776.

CRESSWELL, Helen, (Mrs Brian Rowe); freelance author and television scriptwriter; *b* July 1934; *d* of Annie Edna Clarke and Joseph Edward Cresswell; *m* 1962, Brian Rowe; two *d*. *Educ:* Nottingham Girls' High Sch.; King's College London (BA English Hons). *Television series:* Lizzie Dripping, 1973–75; Jumbo Spencer, 1976; The Bagthorpe Saga, 1980; The Secret World of Polly Flint, 1985; Moondial, 1988; The Return of the Psammead, 1993; The Watchers, 1994; The Famous Five, 1995; The Demon Headmaster, 1995; *adaptation:* Five Children and It, 1990; numerous TV plays. *Publications:* Sonya-by-the-Shire, 1961; Jumbo Spencer, 1963; The White Sea Horse, 1964; Pietro and the Mule, 1965; Jumbo Back to Nature, 1965; Where the Wind Blows, 1966; Jumbo Afloat, 1966; The Piemakers, 1967; A Tide for the Captain, 1967; The Signposters, 1968; The Sea Piper, 1968; The Barge Children, 1968; The Night-watchman, 1969; A Game of Catch, 1969; A Gift from Winklesea, 1969; The Outlanders, 1970; The Wilkses, 1970; The Bird Fancier, 1971; At the Stroke of Midnight, 1971; The Beachcombers, 1972; Lizzie Dripping, 1972; The Bongleweed, 1972; Lizzie Dripping Again, 1974; Butterfly Chase, 1975; The Winter of the Birds, 1975; My Aunt Polly, 1979; My Aunt Polly By the Sea, 1980; Dear Shrink, 1982; The Secret World of Polly Flint, 1982; Ellie and the Hagwitch, 1984; The Bagthorpe Saga: Pt 1, Ordinary Jack, 1977; Pt 2, Absolute Zero, 1978; Pt 3, Bagthorpes Unlimited, 1978; Pt 4, Bagthorpes *v* The World, 1979; Pt 5, Bagthorpes Abroad, 1984; Pt 6, Bagthorpes Haunted, 1985; Pt 7, Bagthorpes Liberated, 1988; Pt 8, The Bagthorpe Triangle, 1992; Moondial, 1987; Time Out, 1987; Rosie and the Boredom Eater, 1989; Whatever Happened in Winklesea?, 1989; Meet Posy Bates, 1990; Posy Bates Again, 1991; Lizzie Dripping and the Witch, 1991; The Return of the Psammead, 1992; Posy Bates and the Bag Lady, 1992; The Watchers, 1993; (ed) Puffin Book of Funny Stories, 1993; Classic Fairy Tales, 1993; Polly Thumb, 1994; Stonestruck, 1995; Bagthorpes Besieged, 1995; Mystery at Winklesea, 1995; Giant, 1995; Birdspell, 1995. *Recreations:* watercolour painting, collecting books, antiques and coincidences, sundial watching. *Address:* Old Church Farm, Eakring, Newark, Notts NG22 0DA. *T:* Mansfield (01623) 870401.

CRESSWELL, Hon. Sir Peter (John), Kt 1991; **Hon. Mr Justice Cresswell;** a Judge of the High Court of Justice, Queen's Bench Division, since 1991; *b* 24 April 1944; *s* of Jack Joseph and Madeleine Cresswell; *m* 1972, Caroline Ward; one *s* (and one *s* decd). *Educ:* St John's Sch., Leatherhead; Queens' Coll., Cambridge (MA, LLM). Called to the Bar, Gray's Inn, 1966 (Malcolm Hilbery Award), Bencher, 1989; QC 1983; a Recorder, 1986–91; Nominated Commercial List Judge, 1991– (Judge in Charge, 1993–94). Mem., Senate of Inns of Court and Bar, 1981–84, 1985–86; Chm., Common Law and Commercial Bar Assoc., 1985–87; Mem., 1987–88, Vice Chm., 1989, Chm., 1990, Gen. Council of the Bar. Mem., Council and Exec. Cttee, Cystic Fibrosis Res. Trust, 1983–. Hon. Mem., Canadian Bar Assoc., 1990. *Publication:* Encyclopaedia of Banking Law, 1982, and subseq. service issues. *Recreations:* fly-fishing, river management, the Outer Hebrides. *Address:* Royal Courts of Justice, Strand, WC2A 2LL. *Club:* Flyfishers'.

CRESWELL, Jack Norman; Deputy Chairman of Lloyd's, 1972, 1974; *b* 20 April 1913; *s* of late Sydney and Dora Creswell; *m* 1938, Jean (Lilian Jane) Maxwell; two *s*. *Educ:* Highgate School. Served War, 1942–46, 2nd Household Cavalry Regt; Captain and Adjt, The Life Guards, 1945–46. Member of Lloyd's, 1946: Mem. Cttee, 1969–72, 1974; Mem. Cttee Lloyd's Underwriters Non-Marine Assoc., 1968–74, Chm. 1973. *Recreations:* photography, family croquet. *Address:* Lullington Court, near Polegate, E Sussex BN26 5QY. *T:* Alfriston (01323) 870548. *Club:* Devonshire (Eastbourne).

CRETNEY, Stephen Michael, DCL; FBA 1985; Fellow of All Souls College, Oxford, since 1993; *b* 25 Feb. 1936; *yr s* of late Fred and Winifred M. V. Cretney; *m* 1973, Rev. Antonia Lois Vanrenen, *o d* of late Lt-Comdr A. G. G. Vanrenen, RN; two *s*. *Educ:* Cheadle Hulme Sch.; Magdalen Coll., Oxford (Demy in Mod. Hist.; 1st Cl. Hons Jurisprudence, 1959; DCL, 1985). Nat. Service, 1954–56. Solicitor. Partner, Macfarlanes, London, 1964; Lecturer: Kenya Sch. of Law, Nairobi, 1966; Southampton Univ., 1968; Fellow and Tutor, Exeter Coll., Oxford, 1969–78; a Law Comr, 1978–83; Prof. of Law, 1984–93, and Dean, Faculty of Law, 1984–88, Univ. of Bristol. Pt-time Chm. of Social Security and other Appeal Tribunals, 1985–. Member: Departmental Cttee on Prison Disciplinary System, 1984–85; Family and Civil Cttee, Judicial Studies Bd, 1985–90; Lord Chancellor's Adv. Cttee on Legal Educn, 1987–88. Chm., Cttee of Heads of Univ. Law Schs, 1986–88. Hon. QC 1992. *Publications:* Theobald on Wills, (ed jtly) 13th edn 1970; Principles of Family Law, 1974, 6th edn (ed jtly) 1996; Family Law (Teach Yourself series), 1982; The Enduring Power of Attorney, 1986, 3rd edn 1991; Elements of Family Law, 1987, 2nd edn 1992; (jtly) Simple Quarrels, 1994; articles and notes in legal jls. *Recreations:* cooking, taking snapshots. *Address:* 15 Canynge Square, Clifton, Bristol BS8 3LA. *T:* Bristol (0117) 973 2983; All Souls College, Oxford OX1 4AL. *T:* Oxford (01865) 279379. *Club:* United Oxford & Cambridge University.

CREW, Air Vice-Marshal Edward Dixon, CB 1973; DSO 1944 and Bar 1950; DFC 1941 and Bar 1942; FRAeS 1972; Planning Inspectorate, Department of the Environment, 1973–87; *b* 24 Dec. 1917; *er s* of F. D. Crew, MB, MRCS, LRCP; *m* 1945, Virginia Martin; one *s*. *Educ:* Felsted Sch.; Downing Coll., Cambridge (MA). Commissioned RAFVR, 1939; served War of 1939–45: night fighter sqdns; 604 sqdn, 85 Sqdn; Comd 96 Sqdn; permanent commission, 1945. Malayan Emergency, Comd No 45 Sqdn, 1948–50; on exchange, RCAF, 1952–54; CFE, 1954–56; Comd RAF Brüggen, Germany, 1959–62; Comdr, Air Forces Borneo, 1965–66; AOC Central Reconnaissance Estabt, 1968; Dep. Controller, Nat. Air Traffic Services, 1969–72; various Air Staff jobs at Air Min. and MoD; retd 1973. Mem., Cotswold DC, 1991–95. *Recreation:* golf. *Address:* National Westminster Bank, 10 Benet Street, Cambridge. *Club:* Royal Air Force.

CREWE, Albert V., PhD; Professor, Department of Physics and the Enrico Fermi Institute, since 1963 (Assistant Professor, 1956–59; Associate Professor, 1959–63; William E. Wrather Distinguished Service Professor, 1977), Dean of Physical Sciences Division, 1971–81, University of Chicago; *b* 18 Feb. 1927; *m* 1949, Doreen Patricia Blunsdon; one *s* three *d*. *Educ:* Univ. of Liverpool (BS, PhD). Asst Lectr, 1950–52, Lectr, 1952–55, Univ. of Liverpool; Div. Dir, Particle Accelerator Division, Argonne National Laboratory, 1958–61; Dir, Argonne National Laboratory, 1961–67. Pres., Orchid One Corp., 1987–90. Member: Nat. Acad. of Sciences; Amer. Acad. of Arts and Sciences. Hon. FRMS 1984. Named Outstanding New Citizen by Citizenship Council of Chicago, 1962; received Immigrant's Service League's Annual Award for Outstanding Achievement in the Field of Science, 1962; Illinois Sesquicentennial Award, 1968; Industrial Research Award, 1970; Distinguished Service Award, Electron Microscope Soc. of America, 1976; Albert A. Michelson Award, Franklin Inst., 1977; Ernst Abbe Award, NY Microscope Soc., 1979; Duddell Medal, Inst. of Physics, 1980. *Publications:* Research USA (with J. J. Katz), 1964; contribs to: Proc. Royal Soc.; Proc. Phys. Soc.; Physical Review; Science; Physics Today; Jl of Applied Physics; Reviews of Scientific Instruments; Optik; Ultramicroscopy, etc. *Address:* 63 Old Creek Road, Palos Park, IL, USA. *T:* (708) 4488738. *Clubs:* Quadrangle, Wayfarers' (Chicago).

CREWE, Prof. Ivor Martin; Professor of Government, since 1982, and Pro-Vice-Chancellor (Academic), since 1992, University of Essex; *b* 15 Dec. 1945; *s* of Francis and Lilly Crewe; *m* 1968, Jill Barbara (*née* Gadian); two *s* one *d*. *Educ:* Manchester Grammar Sch.; Exeter Coll., Oxford (MA); London School of Economics (MScEcon). Assistant Lecturer, Univ. of Lancaster, 1967–69; Junior Research Fellow, Nuffield Coll., Oxford, 1969–71; Lectr, Dept of Govt, Univ. of Essex, 1971–74; Dir SSRC Data Archive, 1974–82. Co-Dir, Feb. 1974, Oct. 1974, 1979 British Election Studies; elections analyst for: BBC TV, 1982–89; The Times, 1990–92; Channel 4, 1991–; The Guardian and The Observer, 1993–. Editor, 1977–82, Co-editor, 1984–92, British Journal of Political Science. *Publications:* (with A. H. Halsey) Social Survey of the Civil Service (HMSO), 1969; ed, British Political Sociology Yearbook, vol. 1 1974, vol. 2 1975; (with Bo Sarlvik) Decade of Dealignment, 1983; (with Anthony Fox) British Parliamentary Constituencies, 1984; (ed jtly) Electoral Change in Western Democracies, 1985; (ed jtly) Political Communications: the general election campaign of 1983, 1987; (with Anthony Fox and Neil Day) The British Electorate 1963–87, 1991; (with Anthony King) SDP: the birth, life and death of the British Social Democratic Party, 1995; articles in various academic jls on public opinion and elections in Britain. *Recreations:* opera, walking. *Address:* 141 Maldon Road, Colchester, Essex CO3 3BJ. *T:* Colchester (01206) 760745.

CREWE, Quentin Hugh; writer and journalist; *b* 14 Nov. 1926; *s* of Major Hugh Crewe and Lady Annabel Crewe; *m* 1st, 1956, Martha Sharp; one *s* one *d*; 2nd, 1961, Angela Huth; one *d* (one *s* decd); 3rd, 1970, Susan Cavendish (*see* S. A. Crewe) (marr. diss.); one *s* one *d*. *Educ:* Eton; Trinity Coll., Cambridge. Joined Evening Standard, 1953; subseq. worked for Queen, Vogue, Daily Mail, Sunday Mirror; freelance, 1970–, contrib. to Times, Sunday Times, Sunday Telegraph, and Spectator. *Publications:* A Curse of Blossom, 1960; Frontiers of Privilege, 1961; Great Chefs of France, 1978; Pocket Book of Food, 1980; In Search of the Sahara, 1983; The Last Maharaja, 1985; Touch the Happy Isles, 1987; In the Realms of Gold, 1989; Well, I Forget the Rest (autobiog.), 1991; Foods from France, 1993; Crewe House, the Royal Embassy of the Kingdom of Saudi Arabia, 1995. *Recreation:* travel. *Address:* 9 Bliss Mill, Chipping Norton, Oxon OX7 5JR. *T:* Chipping Norton (01608) 642176, *Fax:* (01608) 642178.

CREWE, Susan Anne; Editor, House and Garden, since 1994; *b* 31 Aug. 1949; *d* of late Richard Cavendish and Pamela Cavendish; *m* 1st, 1970, Quentin Crewe, *qv* (marr. diss.); one *s* one *d*; 2nd, 1984, C. N. J. Ryan, *qv* (marr. diss.). *Educ:* St Mary's Sch., Wantage; Cheshire Coll. of Agriculture. Harpers & Queen magazine, 1986–92: shopping editor, 1987; consultant editor, 1990; social editor, 1991–92; subseq. freelance writer, broadcaster, journalist; contribs to The Times, Daily Telegraph, Daily Mail, Evening Standard and Literary Review. *Recreations:* gardening, sea-swimming, music. *Address:* Ladysyke House, Haverthwaite, Ulverston, Cumbria LA12 8PQ. *Club:* Academy.

See also Baron Cavendish of Furness.

CRIBB, Air Cdre Peter Henry, CBE 1957; DSO 1942, and Bar, 1944; DFC 1941; JP; retired 1983; *b* 28 Sept. 1918; *s* of late Charles B. Cribb and Mrs Ethel Cribb; *m* 1949, Vivienne Janet, *yr d* of late Col S. T. J. Perry, MC, TD, DL, Oxton, Birkenhead, Ches; three *s*. *Educ:* Bradford Grammar Sch.; Prince Henry's Sch., Otley. Flt Cadet, RAF Coll., 1936–38; Flying duties in Bomber Comd, 1938–45 (Comd No. 582 Sqdn, RAF Little Staughton); Comdg RAF Salbani, RAF Peshawar, India and Staff No. 1 Indian Gp, 1945–47; OC 203 Sqdn, 1947, and HQ Staff, 1950, Coastal Comd; RAF Staff Coll., Bracknell, 1951; Asst Dir Tech. Intell., Air Min., 1951–53; Gp Capt. Plans and Policy, HQ Bomber Comd, 1953–57; 2nd TAF, Germany (OC Oldenburg, Ahlhorn and Gutersloh), 1957–60; Air Min., Dep. Dir Air Staff Briefing, 1959–61, Dir, 1961–62; SASO, Air Forces, Middle East, 1962–63; IDC, 1964; Deputy to Asst Chief of Defence Staff (Joint Warfare), MoD 1965–66; retired, 1966. Administrative Manager, Goldsworthy Mining Ltd, 1966–68. Associate Fellow, Australian Inst. of Management, 1969; Past State Pres., Ryder-Cheshire Foundn of WA, Inc.; Past Pres., Pathfinder Assoc. of WA. Foundn Chm. Council, Univ. of Third Age (Univ. of Western Australia) Inc., 1986–88. Patron (RAF), UK Combined Services Fedn, WA, 1990–. JP Western Australia, 1968. *Recreations:* mainly cerebral. *Address:* Peniston, 66 Sherington Road, Greenwood, WA 6024, Australia.

CRICHTON, family name of **Earl of Erne.**

CRICHTON, Viscount; John Henry Michael Ninian Crichton; *b* 19 June 1971; *s* and *heir* of Earl of Erne, *qv. Educ:* Sunningdale Prep. Sch.; Shiplake Coll.; L'Institut de Touraine, Tours. *Address:* Flat 4, 40 Harcourt Terrace, SW10 9JR.

CRICHTON, Sir Andrew Maitland-Makgill-, Kt 1963; Director, P&OSN Co., 1957–81; Vice-Chairman, Port of London Authority, 1967–76 (Member, 1964–67); *b* 28 Dec. 1910; *s* of late Lt-Col D. M.-M.-Crichton, Queen's Own Cameron Highldrs, and Phyllis (*née* Cuthbert); *m* 1948, Isabel, *d* of Andrew McGill, Sydney, NSW. *Educ:* Wellington Coll. Joined Gray, Dawes & Co., 1929; transf. India to Mackinnon Mackenzie & Co. (Agents of BI Co. and for P & O on Indian Continent and in parts of Far East), 1931. Joined IA, 1940; DDM (Shipping), Col, at GHQ India, 1944. Mackinnon Mackenzie, Calcutta, 1945–48; P&O Co., UK (Gen. Manager, 1951); Chm., Overseas Containers Ltd, 1965–73; former Director: Standard Chartered Group; Inchcape Insurance Hldgs Ltd; London Tin Corp.; Dir, Butler's Warehousing & Distrib. Ltd. Chairman: Nat. Assoc. Port Employers, 1958–65; EDC for GPO, 1965–70; Vice-Chm., British Transport Docks Bd, 1963–68; Member: Baltic Exchange; Nat. Freight Corp., 1969–73; Court of The Chartered Bank; Police Council for GB (Arbitrator), 1969–79; Industrial Arbitration Bd. FRSA; FCIT (a past Vice-Pres.). *Recreations:* golf, music. Freeman, Co. of Watermen and Lightermen. *Address:* 55 Hans Place, Knightsbridge, SW1X 0LA. *T:* 0171–584 1209. *Clubs:* City of London, Caledonian.

See also Maj.-Gen. Edward Maitland-Makgill-Crichton.

CRICHTON, Charles Ainslie; film director; *b* 6 Aug. 1910; *s* of John Douglas Crichton and Hester Wingate Ainslie; *m* 1st, 1936, Vera Pearl Harman-Mills; two *s*; 2nd, 1962, Nadine Haze. *Educ:* Oundle; Univ. of Oxford (BA History). Pictures, 1944–88, include: Painted Boats, Hue and Cry, Against the Wind, Dance Hall, Lavender Hill Mob (Dirs' Guild Awards Nomination, 1953), Hunted, Titfield Thunderbolt, The Love Lottery, Divided Heart, Man in the Sky, Battle of the Sexes, The Third Secret, He Who Rides a Tiger, A Fish Called Wanda (Directors' Guild Awards Nomination, 1989; Oscar Nomination, 1989; BAFTA Award, 1989; Evening Standard Award, 1989). Television: Danger Man, The Avengers, Strange Report, Black Beauty, Space 1999, Dick Turpin, Smuggler; Video Arts shorts. *Recreations:* fishing, photography. *Address:* 1 Southwell Gardens, SW7 4SB.

CRICHTON, David George, LVO 1968; British Consul-General, Nice, 1970–74; *b* 31 July 1914; *e s* of late Col Hon. Sir George Crichton, GCVO; *m* 1st, 1941, Joan Fenella (*d* 1992), *d* of late Col D. W. Cleaver, DSO; one *s* one *d*; 2nd, 1994, Betty, *widow* of Andrew Hughes-Onslow. *Educ:* Eton. Worked as journalist, Reading and Manchester, and on Daily Telegraph, Paris and London, 1933–39; served War of 1939–45 in Derbyshire Yeomanry (despatches); Major 1944; entered Foreign Service, 1946; served in Belgrade, Singapore, Alexandria, Miami, La Paz and Santiago. *Address:* 29B Thorney Crescent, Morgan's Walk, SW11 3TT. *T:* 0171–738 9694. *Club:* Boodle's.

See also R. J. V. Crichton.

CRICHTON, Maj.-Gen. Edward Maitland-Makgill-, OBE 1948 (MBE 1945); GOC 51st Highland Division, 1966–68, retired; *b* 23 Nov. 1916; *s* of late Lt-Col D. E. Maitland-Makgill-Crichton, Queen's Own Cameron Highlanders and Phyllis (*née* Cuthbert); *m* 1951, Sheila Margaret Hibbins, Bexhill-on-Sea; three *s*. *Educ:* Bedford Sch.; RMC Sandhurst. 2nd Lieut Queen's Own Cameron Highlanders, 1937; Adjt 5th Bn Cameron Highlanders, 1939; served with 5th Cameron Highlanders and 51 (Highland) Div., N Africa, Sicily, Normandy, NW Europe, 1940–45; GSO 1, HQ British Commonwealth Occupation Force, Japan, 1946–47; Mobilisation Br., WO 1948–50; 1st Bn Cameron Highlanders, Tripoli and Canal Zone, 1950–52; Jt Services Staff Coll., 1953; GSO 1, 3rd Inf. Div. (UK Strategic Reserve), Canal Zone, Egypt, UK and Suez, 1953–57; with 1st Bn Cameron Highlanders, Aden, 1957; comd 1st Liverpool Scottish, 1958–61; Comdr 152 (Highland) Inf. Bde, 1962–64; Dep. Dir Army Staff Duties, MoD, 1965–66. *Recreations:* shooting, golf, gardening, fishing. *Address:* 211 Braid Road, Edinburgh EH10 6HT. *T:* 0131–447 5662.

See also Sir Andrew Maitland-Makgill-Crichton.

CRICHTON, Nicholas; Metropolitan Stipendiary Magistrate, since 1987; a Recorder, since 1995; *b* 23 Oct. 1943; s of Charles Ainslie Crichton and Vera Pearl McCallum; *m* 1973, Ann Valerie (*née* Jackson); two *s*. *Educ:* Haileybury & ISC; Queen's Univ., Belfast (LLB, 2nd Cl. Hons). Schoolmaster, Pembroke House Sch., Gilgil, Kenya, 1963; cowhand, Montana, USA, 1966; articled to late T. J. Burrows, Currey & Co., SW1, 1968–70; Assistant Solicitor: Currey & Co., 1970–71; Nicholls Christie & Crocker, 1972–74; Partner, Nicholls Christie & Crocker, 1974–86. An Asst Recorder, 1991–95. *Recreations:* cricket (playing, coaching and watching), golf, watching rugby, gardening, walking, reading, bird watching, photography. *Address:* c/o Inner London Family Proceedings Court, 185 Marylebone Road, NW1 5QG. *Clubs:* Middlesex CC; Old Haileyburian RFC; Flackwell Heath Golf.

CRICHTON, Col Richard John Vesey, CVO 1986; MC 1940; *b* 2 Nov. 1916; *s* of late Col Hon. Sir George Crichton, GCVO, and Lady Mary Crichton; *m* 1948, Yvonne Avril Catherine, *d* of late Dr and Mrs H. E. Worthington; three *s*. *Educ:* Eton; RMC, Sandhurst. Commissioned 2/Lieut Coldstream Guards, 1936; served World War II: Belgium, 1940, Italy, 1943–44 (twice wounded, MC, despatches); Commanded: 1st Bn Coldstream Guards, 1954–57; Coldstream Guards, 1958–61, retired 1961. Comptroller, Union Jack Services Clubs, 1964–66; Member, HM Body Guard, Hon. Corps of Gentlemen at Arms, 1966–86; Clerk of the Cheque and Adjutant, 1979–81; Lieutenant, 1981–86. Mem., Hants CC and Police Authority, 1964–67. *Publication:* The Coldstream Guards 1946–1970, 1972. *Address:* Derwent House, Hartley Wintney, Hampshire RG27 8RE. *Club:* Cavalry and Guards.

See also D. G. Crichton.

CRICHTON-BROWN, Sir Robert, KCMG 1980; Kt 1972; CBE 1970; TD; Executive Chairman, Rothmans International plc, 1985–88; *b* Melbourne, 23 Aug. 1919; *s* of late L. Crichton-Brown, Sydney; *m* 1941, Norah Isabelle, *d* of late A. E. Turnbull; one *s* one *d*. *Educ:* Sydney Grammar Sch. Served War, 1939–45, BEF; Major, Royal Artillery and Gen. Staff, France, Iceland, India, Burma (despatches twice). Chairman: Lumley Corp. Ltd (formerly Edward Lumley Ltd), 1974–89 (Man. Dir, 1952–82); Lumley Life Ltd, 1961–87 (Dir, 1961–89); Lumley Gen. Insce Ltd, 1974–88 (Dir, 1952–88); NEI Pacific Ltd, 1961–85; Rothmans of Pall Mall (Australia) Ltd, 1981–85 (Dir, 1971–85 and 1987–88); Commercial Banking Co. of Sydney Ltd, 1976–82 (Dir, 1970–82); Commercial & General Acceptance Ltd, 1977–82; Westham Dredging Co. Pty Ltd, 1975–85; Vice Chairman: Nat. Australia Bank Ltd, 1982–85; Custom Credit Corp., 1982–85; Director: Daily Mail and General Trust Ltd (UK), 1979–95; Edward Lumley Hldgs, 1989–. Fed. Pres., Inst. of Dirs in Aust., 1967–80 (Chm., NSW Branch, 1965–80; Councillor, 1980–89; Hon. Life Mem.). Mem. Federal Exec. and Federal Hon. Treas., Liberal Party of Australia, 1973–85. Pres., Med. Foundn, Sydney Univ., 1962–87; Dir, Royal Prince Alfred Hosp., 1970–84; Hon. Life Governor, Aust. Postgraduate Fedn in Medicine; Member: Cttee, RACP, 1973–85; Adv. Bd, Girl Guides Assoc. of Australia, 1973–85; Adv. Bd, Salvation Army, 1973–85; Internat. Forum and Panel, Duke of Edinburgh's Award, 1979–84 (Nat. Co-ordinator, Duke of Edinburgh's Award Scheme in Aust., 1979–84); Council, Imperial Soc. of Knights Bachelor (Vice-Chm., Pacific Reg.); Nat. Councillor, Scout Assoc. of Aust., 1980–85; Mem. Council, Maritime Trust (formerly Cutty Sark Maritime Trust), 1987–; Gov., Cutty Sark Soc., 1987–89. Underwriting Mem. of Lloyd's, 1946–. Hon. Fellow, Sydney Univ., 1987. Mem., Australia's winning Admiral's Cup Team (Balandra), UK, 1967; winner, Sydney-Hobart Yacht Race (Pacha), 1970. *Clubs:* White's, Royal Cruising; Royal Yacht Squadron; Australian, Union (Sydney); Cruising Yacht Club of Australia, Royal Sydney Yacht Squadron, Royal Prince Alfred Yacht.

CRICHTON-MILLER, Donald, TD; MA; *b* 1906; *s* of late Hugh Crichton-Miller, MA, MD, FRCP; *m* 1931, Monica, *d* of late B. A. Glanvill, JP, Bromley, Kent; two *s* one *d*. *Educ:* Fettes Coll., Edinburgh; Pembroke Coll., Cambridge (Exhibitioner). Played Rugby Football for Cambridge and Scotland; Asst Master: Monmouth Sch., 1929–31; Bryanston Sch., 1931–34; Stowe Sch., 1934–36; Head Master: Taunton Sch., Somerset, 1936–45; Fettes Coll., 1945–58; Stowe Sch., 1958–63. Carried out education surveys in Pakistan, 1951, and Malta, 1956. *Recreations:* governing schools and managing properties. *Address:* Glencorse, Compton, Newbury, Berks RG16 0RE. *T:* Compton (01635) 578384.

CRICHTON-STUART, family name of **Marquess of Bute.**

CRICK, Alan John Pitts, OBE 1956; *b* 14 May 1913; *er s* of Owen John Pitts Crick and Margaret Crick (*née* Daw), late of Minehead, Somerset; *m* 1941, Norah (*née* Atkins) (*d* 1984); two *d*. *Educ:* Latymer Upper Sch.; King's Coll., London Univ. (MA); Heidelberg Univ. (Dr.phil). Vice-Consul, British Consulate-Gen., Free City of Danzig, 1938–39. Served War, Army, 1939–46: Egypt and Libya, 1941–43, HQ Eighth Army; NW Europe, 1944–46 (despatches); Major, GSO2, Intell., SHAEF; HQ 21 Army Group and HQ BAOR. Min. of Defence Jt Intell. Bureau, 1946–63; jssc, 1948; British Jt Services Mission, Washington, 1953–56; Asst Dir, Jt Intell. Bureau, 1957–63; idc, 1960; Counsellor, British Embassy, Washington, 1963–65; Asst Sec., Cabinet Office, 1965–68; Def. Intell. Staff, MoD, 1968–73; Director of Economic Intelligence, MoD, 1970–73. Adviser to Commercial Union Assurance Co., 1973–78. *Recreations:* travel, antiquarian interests, books. *Address:* 16 Church Square, Rye, East Sussex TN31 7HE. *T:* Rye (01797) 222050. *Club:* Naval and Military.

See also R. P. Crick.

CRICK, Prof. Bernard, BSc (Econ.), PhD (London); writer; Literary Editor, Political Quarterly, since 1993; Emeritus Professor, University of London; *b* 16 Dec. 1929; *s* of Harry Edgar and Florence Clara Crick. *Educ:* Whitgift Sch.; University Coll., London. Research student, LSE, 1950–52; Teaching Fellow, Harvard, 1952–54; Asst Prof., McGill, 1954–55; Vis. Fellow, Berkeley, 1955–56; Asst Lectr, later Lectr, later Sen. Lectr, LSE, 1957–65; Prof. of Political Theory and Institutions, Sheffield Univ., 1965–71; Prof. of Politics, Birkbeck Coll., Univ of London, 1971–84. Joint Editor, Political Quarterly, 1966–80; Chm., Political Qly Publishing Co., 1980–93. Joint Sec., Study of Parlt Gp, 1964–68; Jt Chm., British S African Conf., 1991–. Hon. Pres., Politics Assoc., 1970–76; Hon. Mem., Hansard Soc., 1993 (Mem. Council, 1962–93). Hon. Fellow, Univ. of Edinburgh, 1986. FRSA 1992. Hon. DSc Belfast, 1986; Hon. DLitt: Sheffield, 1990; E London Poly., 1990. *Publications:* The American Science of Politics, 1958; In Defence of Politics, 1962, 4th edn 1992 (trans. German, Japanese, Spanish, Italian); The Reform of Parliament, 1964, 2nd edn 1968; (ed) Essays on Reform, 1967; (ed with W. A. Robson) Protest and Discontent, 1970; (ed) Machiavelli: The Discourses, 1971; Political Theory and Practice, 1972; (ed with W. A. Robson) Taxation Policy, 1973; Basic Forms of Government, 1973; Crime, Rape and Gin, 1975; (ed with Alex Porter) Political Education and Political Literacy, 1978; George Orwell: a Life, 1980, 3rd edn 1992; (ed) Unemployment, 1981; (ed) Clarendon edn, Orwell's Nineteen Eighty-Four, 1984; (ed with Audrey Coppard) Orwell Observed, 1984; Socialism, 1987; Essays on Politics and Literature, 1989; Political Thoughts and Polemics, 1990; (ed) National Identities, 1991. *Recreations:* polemicising, lecturing, theatre, hill-walking, bee-keeping. *Address:* 8A Bellevue Terrace, Edinburgh EH7 4DT. *T:* 0131–557 2517. *Clubs:* Savile; Scottish Arts (Edinburgh).

CRICK, Francis Harry Compton, OM 1991; FRS 1959; BSc London, PhD Cantab; J. W. Kieckhefer Distinguished Professor, since 1977, President, since 1994, The Salk Institute for Biological Studies; Adjunct Professor of Psychology, University of California, San Diego; *b* 8 June 1916; *e s* of late Harry Crick and late Annie Elizabeth (*née* Wilkins); *m* 1st, 1940, Ruth Doreen Dodd (divorced, 1947); one *s*; 2nd, 1949, Odile Speed; two *d*. *Educ:* Mill Hill Sch.; University Coll., London; Caius Coll., Cambridge (Hon. Fellow, 1976). Scientist in Admiralty, 1940–47; Strangeways Laboratory, Cambridge, 1947–49; MRC Lab. of Molecular Biology, Cambridge, 1949–77; Brooklyn Polytechnic, NY, USA, 1953–54. Vis. Lectr Rockefeller Inst., NY, USA, 1959; Vis. Prof., Chemistry Dept, Harvard, 1959; Fellow, Churchill Coll., Cambridge, 1960–61; Vis. Biophysics Prof., Harvard, 1962; Non-resident Fellow, Salk Inst. for Biological Studies, San Diego, 1962–73; Ferkauf Foundn Visiting Prof., Salk Inst., 1976–77; Fellow, UCL, 1962; For. Hon. Mem., Amer. Acad. of Arts and Sciences, 1962; Hon. Mem., Amer. Soc. Biological Chem., 1963; Hon. MRIA, 1964; Hon. Fellow: Churchill Coll., Cambridge, 1965; Caius Coll., Cambridge, 1976; FAAAS 1966; Hon. FRSE, 1966; Fellow, INSA, 1982; Hon. Fellow, Indian Acad. of Scis, 1985; For. Associate, US Nat. Acad. of Sciences, 1969; Mem., German Acad. of Science, Leopoldina, 1969; For. Mem., American Philos. Soc., Philadelphia, 1972; Hon. Mem., Hellenic Biochem. and Biophys. Soc., 1974. Associate For. Mem., French Acad. of Scis, 1978. 60 named lectures, 1959–94. Warren Triennial Prize, Boston, USA (with J. D. Watson), 1959; Lasker Award (jointly), 1960; Prix Charles Léopold Mayer, French Académies des Sciences, 1961; Research Corp. Award (with J. D. Watson), 1961; Gairdner Foundation Award, Toronto, 1962; Nobel Prize for Medicine (jointly), 1962; Royal Medal, Royal Soc., 1972; Copley Medal, Royal Soc., 1975; Michelson-Morley Award, Cleveland, 1981; Benjamin P. Cheney Medal, Spokane, Washington, 1986; Golden Plate Award, Phoenix, 1987; Albert Medal, RSA, 1987; Wright Prize VIII, Harvey Mudd Coll., Calif., 1988; Joseph Priestly Award, Dickinson Coll., Pennsylvania, 1988. *Publications:* Of Molecules and Men, 1966; Life Itself, 1981; What Mad Pursuit: a personal view of scientific discovery, 1988; The Astonishing Hypothesis: The scientific search for the soul, 1994; papers and articles on molecular and cell biology and on neurobiology in scientific journals. *Address:* The Salk Institute for Biological Studies, PO Box 85800, San Diego, CA 92186–5800, USA; 1792 Colgate Circle, La Jolla, CA 92037, USA.

CRICK, R(onald) Pitts, FRCS, FRCOphth; Honorary Ophthalmic Surgeon, King's College Hospital, since 1982 (Ophthalmic Surgeon, 1950–82); Recognised Teacher in the Faculty of Medicine, University of London, 1960–82, Emeritus Lecturer, King's College Hospital Medical School, 1982; Visiting Research Fellow, University of Sussex, since 1976; *b* 5 Feb. 1917; *yr s* of Owen J. Pitts Crick and Margaret Daw, Minehead, Som; *m* 1941, Jocelyn Mary Grenfell Robins, *yr d* of Leonard A. C. Robins and Geraldine Grenfell, Hendon; four *s* one *d*. *Educ:* Latymer Upper Sch., London; King's Coll. and (Science Schol.) King's Coll. Hosp. Med. Sch., Univ. of London. MRCS, LRCP 1939; DOMS 1946; FRCS 1950; FRCOphth 1988. Surgeon, MN, 1939–40; Surg. Lieut,

RNVR, 1940–46. Ophthalmic Registrar, King's Coll. Hosp., 1946–48; Surgical First Asst, Royal Eye Hosp., 1947–50; Ophth. Surg., Epsom County Hosp., 1948–49; Ophth. Registrar, Belgrave Hosp. for Children, 1948–50; Ophth. Surg., Sevenoaks Hosp., 1948–50; Sen. Ophthalmic Surg., Royal Eye Hosp., 1950–69; Ophthalmic Surg., Belgrave Hosp. for Children, 1950–66. Chm., Ophthalmic Post-Grad. Trng, SE Thames RHA, 1972–82. Examr to RCS for Diploma in Ophthalmology, 1961–68. Hon. Ophth. Surg., Royal London Soc. for the Blind, 1954–57. FRSocMed, Vice-Pres. Ophthalmological Section, 1964, and Mem. Council Ophthalmolog. Section, 1953–54 and 1956–58. Member: Oxford Ophthalmolog. Congress; Southern Ophthalmolog. Soc. (Vice-Pres., 1969; Pres., 1970); Chm., Internat. Glaucoma Assoc., 1975–; Charter Member: Internat. Glaucoma Congress, USA, 1977–; Internat. Assoc. of Ocular Surgeons, 1981. Alim Meml Lectr, Ophthalmolog. Soc. of Bangladesh, Dhaka, 1991. Sir Stewart Duke-Elder Glaucoma Award, Internat. Glaucoma Congress, 1985; Lederle Medal for Ophthalmology, Amer. Soc. of Contemp. Ophthalmol., 1985. *Publications:* All About Glaucoma, 1981; A Textbook of Clinical Ophthalmology, 1986; Cardiovascular Affections, Arteriosclerosis and Hypertension (Section in Systemic Ophthalmology, ed A. Sorsby), 1950 and 1958; Computerised Monitoring of Glaucoma (Section in Glaucoma, ed J. G. Bellows), 1979; Diagnosis of Primary Open Angle Glaucoma (in Glaucoma, ed J. E. Cairns), 1986; medical and ophthalmic contribs to Brit. Jl Ophthalmology, BMJ, Lancet, Eye, etc. *Recreations:* walking, motoring, sailing. *Address:* Ophthalmic Department, King's College Hospital, Denmark Hill, SE5 9RS. *T* and *Fax:* 0171–737 3265; Sandbanks House, 2 Panorama Road, Sandbanks, Poole, Dorset BH13 7RD. *T* and *Fax:* Canford Cliffs (01202) 707560. *Clubs:* Royal Automobile; Royal Motor Yacht.

See also A. J. P. Crick.

CRICKHOWELL, Baron *cr* 1987 (Life Peer), of Pont Esgob in the Black Mountains and County of Powys; **Roger Nicholas Edwards,** PC 1979; Chairman, National Rivers Authority, 1989–April 1996 (Chairman, Advisory Committee, 1988–89); Director: HTV Group, since 1987; Associated British Ports Holdings, since 1988; Anglesey Mining, since 1988 (Vice-Chairman); *b* 25 Feb. 1934; *s* of late (H. C.) Ralph Edwards, CBE, FSA, and Marjorie Ingham Brooke; *m* 1963, Ankaret Healing; one *s* two *d*. *Educ:* Westminster Sch.; Trinity Coll., Cambridge, 1954–57; read History: BA 1957, MA, 1968. Member of Lloyds, 1965–. MP (C) Pembroke, 1970–87. Sec. of State for Wales, 1979–87. Opposition spokesman on Welsh affairs, 1975–79. Pres., Univ. of Wales Coll. of Cardiff, 1988– (Hon. Fellow, UC, Cardiff, 1985). Dir, WNO, 1988–92. President: Contemporary Art Society for Wales, 1988–93; SE Arts Assoc., 1988–94; Mem., Cttee, AA, 1988–. *Publications:* articles and reviews in The Connoisseur and other jls. *Recreations:* fishing, gardening, collecting watercolours and drawings. *Address:* Pont Esgob Mill, Fforest Coal Pit, near Abergavenny, Gwent NP7 7LS; 4 Henning Street, SW11 3DR. *Clubs:* Brooks's; Cardiff and County.

CRICKMAY, John Rackstrow, FRICS; Chairman, Percy Bilton PLC, 1984–89 (Director, 1980–89); *b* 16 May 1914; *s* of Edward John Crickmay and Constance May Bowyer; *m* 1939, Margaret Hilda Rainer (decd); one *s*. *Educ:* Brighton Coll. Legal & General Assurance Society: Surveyor, 1936–46; Chief Estates Surveyor, 1946–74. Artist Rifles, 1936; Royal Regt of Artillery, 1939–46: served in Far East, 1940–45 (POW, 1942–45); TEM 1946. Cons. to property interests, 1974–; Dir, Ecclesiastical Insce Office, 1980–84. President: British Chapter Real Property Fedn, 1966; Chartered Auctioneers & Estate Agents Inst., 1968; Mem. Council, RICS, 1972–85, Hon. Treas., 1980–85. Gov., Royal Star & Garter, Richmond, 1975–90; Dep. Chm., Christ's Hosp., 1984–89, Almoner, 1977–89. Master, Ironmongers' Co., 1976–77. Hon. Fellow, Coll. of Estate Management, Reading, 1988. Medal of Internat. Real Estate Fedn, 1974; Silver Jubilee Medal, 1977. *Recreations:* cricket, golf. *Address:* Old Walls, Rectory Lane, Pulborough, West Sussex RH20 2AF. *T:* Pulborough (01798) 872336. *Clubs:* Oriental, MCC; West Sussex Golf.

CRIGHTON, Prof. David George, FRS 1993; Professor of Applied Mathematics, since 1986, and Head of Department of Applied Mathematics and Theoretical Physics, since 1991, University of Cambridge; Fellow of St John's College, Cambridge, since 1986; *b* 15 Nov. 1942; *s* of George Wolfe Johnston Crighton and Violet Grace Crighton (*née* Garrison); *m* 1st, 1969, Mary Christine West (marr. diss. 1985); one *s* one *d*; 2nd, 1986, Johanna Veronica Hol. *Educ:* St John's College, Cambridge (BA 1964; MA 1980; ScD 1993); Imperial College London (PhD 1969). Research Asst, Imperial College London, 1967–74; Prof. of Applied Mathematics, Univ. of Leeds, 1974–85. *Publications:* papers on fluid mechanics and wave theory in jls, conf. procs. *Recreations:* music, opera. *Address:* The Laurels, 58 Girton Road, Girton, Cambridge CB3 0LN. *T:* Cambridge (01223) 277100.

CRIGMAN, David Ian; QC 1989; *b* 16 Aug. 1945; *s* of late Jack Crigman and of Sylvia Crigman; *m* 1980, Judith Ann Penny; one *s*. *Educ:* King Edward's Sch., Birmingham; Univ. of Leeds (LLB Hons). Called to the Bar, Gray's Inn, 1969; a Recorder, 1985. *Recreations:* tennis, ski-ing, writing, travel. *Address:* 1 Fountain Court, Steelhouse Lane, Birmingham B4 6DR. *T:* 0121–236 5721.

CRILL, Sir Peter (Leslie), KBE 1995 (CBE 1980); Kt 1987; FCIArb; Bailiff of Jersey, and President of the Court of Appeal of Jersey, 1986–95; Judge, Court of Appeal of Jersey and Guernsey, since 1986; *b* 1 Feb. 1925; *s* of S. G. Crill, Connetable of St Clement, 1916–58, and Olive Le Gros; *m* 1953, A. F. R. Dodd, MB, *d* of E. A. Dodd, JP, Dromara, NI; three *d*. *Educ:* Victoria Coll., Jersey; Exeter Coll., Oxford (King Charles I Scholar; MA; Hon. Fellow, 1991). Called to the Bar, Middle Temple, 1949; called to the Jersey Bar, 1949. In private practice in Jersey, 1949–62. States of Jersey Deputy for St Clement, 1951–58; States of Jersey Senator, 1960–62; Solicitor General, Jersey, 1962–69; Attorney General, Jersey, 1969–75. Dep. Bailiff, 1975–86. Mem. Council, University of Buckingham. Pres., La Société Jersiaise, 1980–85. CStJ 1994. *Recreations:* music, books, horses, boats, pottering about. *Address:* Beechfield House, Trinity, Jersey, Channel Islands. *T:* Jersey (01534) 20270. *Clubs:* United Oxford & Cambridge University; United, Victoria (Jersey); Royal Yacht Squadron, Royal CI Yacht, St Helier Yacht.

CRIPPIN, Harry Trevor, FCIS; Chief Executive and Town Clerk, Cardiff City Council, 1979–88; *b* 14 May 1929; *s* of Harry and Mary Elizabeth Crippin; *m* 1959, Hilda Green, JP; one *s* one *d*. *Educ:* Leigh Grammar Sch., Lancs. DMA; FBIM; FCIS 1975. Asst Town Clerk, Manchester, 1970–74; City Sec., Cardiff CC, 1974–79. OStJ 1986. *Address:* 23 Greenwood Road, Llandaff, Cardiff CF5 2QD. *T:* Cardiff (01222) 564103.

CRIPPS, family name of **Baron Parmoor.**

CRIPPS, Anthony L.; *see* Cripps, M. A. L.

CRIPPS, Sir (Cyril) Humphrey, Kt 1989; DL; MA; CChem, FRSC; Managing Director, Pianoforte Supplies Ltd, Roade, Northampton, since 1960, Chairman since 1979; Founder Member, Cripps Foundation, Chairman since 1979; Chairman: Velcro Industries NV, since 1973; Air BVI, 1971–86; *b* 2 Oct. 1915; *o s* of Sir Cyril Thomas Cripps, MBE, and Lady (Amy) Cripps; *m* 1942, Dorothea Casson, *o d* of late Reginald Percy Cook, architect; two *s* (and one *s* one *d* decd). *Educ:* Northampton Grammar Sch. (schol.); St John's Coll., Cambridge (Nat. Sci. Prelim. Cl. 1, Tripos Pts I and II, Cl. 2; BA, MA). FCS 1935; FRIC 1977; FRSC 1979. Founder of private businesses in UK, Australia, Canada and Brit. Virgin Islands. Member, Northamptonshire CC, 1963–74 (Leader of Independents, to 1974; formerly Vice-Chm., Educn and Planning Cttees); Mem., (new) Northants CC, 1973–81; Board Mem., Northampton Develt Corp., 1968–85. Life Mem., Ct, Univ. of Nottingham, 1953; Governor: Northampton Grammar Sch., 1963–74; Northampton Sch. for Boys, 1977–81; (Vice-Chm., 1970–81, 1986–88, Chm., 1988–, Foundn Trust); Northampton High Sch. for Girls, 1966–92 (Chm., 1972–84); Foundn Governor, Bilton Grange Prep. Sch., 1957–80. Trustee, Cripps Postgrad. Med. Centre, Northampton Gen. Hosp., 1969–; Member of Trusts: Peterborough Cath., 1975–; All Saints Church, Northampton, 1975–; Trustee, Univ. of Nottingham Develt Trust, 1990–. Hon. Fellow: Cambridge Univ.: St John's, 1966; Magdalene, 1971; Selwyn, 1971; Queens', 1979; Cripps Hall, Nottingham Univ., 1959; Hon. DSc Nottingham, 1975; Hon. LLD Cantab 1976; Pres., Johnian Soc., 1966. Liveryman, Worshipful Co. of Wheelwrights, 1957, Mem. Court 1970, Master 1982; Liveryman, Worshipful Co. of Tallow Chandlers, 1983; Freeman, City of London (by redemption), 1957. High Sheriff, Northants, 1985–86; DL Northants, 1986. *Recreations:* travel, photography, natural history—entomology (espec. Rhopalocera), philately. *Address:* Bull's Head Farm, Stoke Goldington, Newport Pagnell, Bucks MK16 8LP. *T:* Stoke Goldington (01908) 551223.

CRIPPS, (Matthew) Anthony Leonard, CBE 1971; DSO 1943; TD 1947; QC 1958; a Recorder, 1972–85 (Recorder of Nottingham, 1961–71); Deputy Senior Judge, British Sovereign Base Areas, Cyprus, 1978–90; *b* 30 Dec. 1913; *s* of late Major Hon. L. H. Cripps; *heir-pres.* to 4th Baron Parmoor, *qv*; *m* 1941, Dorothea Margaret (*d* 1992) (Surrey CC 1965–67), *d* of G. Johnson Scott, Ashby-de-la-Zouch; three *s*. *Educ:* Eton; Christ Church, Oxford; Combined Army and RAF Staff Coll., Haifa, 1944–45. Royal Leicestershire Regt, TA, 1933. Served War of 1939–45: Norway, Sweden, Finland, Iceland, N Africa, Italy, Egypt, 1939–44 (Capt. to Lt-Col); Staff Officer, Palestine and Syria, 1944–46. Barrister-at-law, Middle Temple, 1938 (Bencher 1965; Treasurer, 1983), Inner Temple, 1961, Hong Kong, 1974 and Singapore, 1987. Hon. Judge of Court of Arches, 1969–80. Comr for Local Govt Petitions, 1978–84. Chairman: Disciplinary Cttees, Milk Marketing Bd, 1956–90, Potato and Egg Marketing Bds, 1956–67; Isle of Man Govt Commn on Agricultural Marketing, 1961–62; Home Sec's Adv. Cttee on Service Candidates, 1966–94 (Dep. Chm., 1965); Nat. Panel, Approved Coal Merchants Scheme, 1972–89; Legal Adv. Cttee, RSPCA, 1978–90; Univ. of London Appeals Cttee, 1980–90. Member: Agricultural Wages Bd, 1964–67; Northumberland Cttee of Inquiry into Foot and Mouth Disease, 1968–69; Cttee of Inquiry, Export of Live Animals for Slaughter, 1973–74. Pres., Coal Trade Benevolent Assoc., 1983. Mem., Ct of Assts, Fuellers' Co., 1985– (Master, 1990). *Publications:* Agriculture Act 1947, 1947; Agriculture Holdings Act, 1948, 1948; (ed) 9th edn, Cripps on Compulsory Purchase: Powers, Procedure and Compensation, 1950; Spice of Life, 1992; legal articles, especially on agricultural matters, for Law Jl and Encyclopaedia Britannica. *Recreations:* family life, writing, forestry. *Address:* Woodhurst, McCrae's Walk, Wargrave, Berks RG10 8LN. *T:* Wargrave (0173440) 3449. *Clubs:* Brooks's; Phyllis Court (Henley-on-Thames).

CRISP, Prof. Arthur Hamilton, MD, DSc; FRCP, FRCPE, FRCPsych; Professor of Psychiatry, University of London at St George's Hospital Medical School, since 1967, and Dean, Faculty of Medicine, University of London, 1976–80; *b* 17 June 1930; *s* of John and Elizabeth Crisp; *m* 1958, Irene Clare (*née* Reid); three *s*. *Educ:* Watford Grammar Sch.; Univ. of London (MD; DSc). FRCP 1973, FRCPE 1972, FRCPsych 1971. Previously Lectr, then Sen. Lectr in Psych., Middlesex Hosp. Med. Sch., London. Chairman: Educn Cttee, GMC, 1982–88; Adv. Cttee on Med. Educn, EEC, 1983–85. *Publications:* (jtly) Sleep, Nutrition and Mood, 1976; Anorexia Nervosa: Let Me Be, 1980; (jtly) Anorexia Nervosa and the Wish to Change, 1990; approx. 300 articles in learned jls. *Recreations:* golf, study of the River Wandle. *Address:* 113 Copse Hill, Wimbledon, SW20 0NT. *T:* 0181–946 0976. *Clubs:* Athenæum; Royal Wimbledon Golf, Aldeburgh Golf.

CRISP, Clement Andrew; contributor, since 1956, and Dance Critic, since 1970, Financial Times; *b* 21 Sept. 1931; *s* of Charles Evelyn Gifford Crisp and Bertha Dorothy (*née* Dean). *Educ:* Oxted Sch.; Bordeaux Univ.; Keble Coll., Oxford Univ. (BA). Critic and dance writer to various jls, 1956–; Ballet Critic, The Spectator, 1966–70. Lectr, Librarian and Archivist to Royal Acad. of Dancing, 1963–85, Archivist, 1985–. Associate Prof., Univ. of Notre Dame (London Faculty), 1987–. Queen Elizabeth II Coronation Award, Royal Acad. of Dancing, 1992. Knight, Order of Dannebrog (Demark), 1992. *Publications include:* (with Peter Brinson) Ballet for All, 1971, rev. edn 1980; with Mary Clarke: Ballet: an illustrated history, 1973, rev. edn 1992; Making a Ballet, 1974; Ballet in Art, 1976; Design for Ballet, 1978; Introducing Ballet, 1978; Ballet-goer's Guide, 1981; History of Dance, 1981; How to Enjoy Ballet, 1983, 2nd edn 1987; Dancer, 1984; Ballerina, 1987; London Contemporary Dance, 1989. *Recreations:* avoiding noise, gardening, despair about dancing. *Address:* 82 Marsham Court, Marsham Street, SW1P 4LA.

CRISP, (Edmund) Nigel (Ramsay); Chief Executive, Oxford Radcliffe Hospital NHS Trust, since 1993; *b* 14 Jan. 1952; *s* of Edmund Theodore Crisp and Dorothy Shephard Crisp (*née* Ramsay); *m* 1976, Siân Elaine Jenkins; one *s* one *d*. *Educ:* Uppingham Sch.; St John's Coll., Cambridge (BA Hons 1973; MA 1976). Dep. Dir, Halewood Community Council, 1973; Production Manager, Trebor, 1978; Dir, Cambs Community Council, 1981; Unit Gen. Manager, E Berks HA, 1986; Chief Exec., Heatherwood and Wexham Park Hosps, 1988. *Recreation:* the countryside. *Address:* John Radcliffe Hospital, Headley Way, Oxford OX3 9DU. *T:* Oxford (01865) 221610. *Club:* Tutts Clump Tennis.

CRISP, Sir (John) Peter, 4th Bt *cr* 1913; *b* 19 May 1925; *o s* of Sir John Wilson Crisp, 3rd Bt, and Marjorie (*d* 1977), *d* of F. R. Shriver; *S* father, 1950; *m* 1954, Judith Mary, *d* of late H. E. Gillett; three *s* one *d*. *Educ:* Westminster. *Heir: s* John Charles Crisp [*b* 10 Dec. 1955; *m* 1992, Mary Jo, *er d* of Dr and Mrs D. MacAuley]. *Address:* Crabtree Cottage, Drungewick Lane, Loxwood, Billingshurst, West Sussex RH14 0RP. *T:* Loxwood (01403) 752374.

CRISP, Nigel; *see* Crisp, E. N. R.

CRITCHETT, Sir Ian (George Lorraine), 3rd Bt *cr* 1908; BA Cantab; HM Diplomatic Service, retired; Counsellor, Foreign and Commonwealth Office, 1977–80; *b* 9 Dec. 1920; *s* of Sir Montague Critchett, 2nd Bt, and Innes (*d* 1982), 3rd *d* of late Col F. G. A. Wiehe, The Durham Light Infantry; *S* father, 1941; *m* 1st, 1948, Paulette Mary Lorraine (*d* 1962), *e d* of late Col H. B. Humfrey; 2nd, 1964, Jocelyn Daphne Margret, *e d* of late Comdr C. M. Hall; one *s* one *d*. *Educ:* Harrow; Clare Coll., Cambridge. RAFVR, 1942–46. Joined Foreign Office, 1948; 3rd Sec. (Commercial), at Vienna, 1950–51; 2nd Sec. (Commercial) at Bucharest, 1951–53; 2nd Sec. at Cairo, 1956; First Sec., FO, 1962. *Heir: s* Charles George Montague Critchett, *b* 2 April 1965. *Address:* Uplands Lodge, Pains Hill, Limpsfield, Oxted, Surrey RH8 0RF. *Clubs:* Travellers', MCC.

CRITCHLEY, Sir Julian (Michael Gordon), Kt 1995; MP (C) Aldershot, since 1974 (Aldershot and North Hants, 1970–74); writer, broadcaster and journalist; *b* 8 Dec. 1930; *s* of Dr Macdonald Critchley, *qv*; *m* 1955, Paula Joan Baron (divorced 1965); two *d*; *m* 1965, Mrs Heather Goodrick; one *s* one *d*. *Educ:* Shrewsbury; Sorbonne; Pembroke Coll., Oxford (MA). MP (C) Rochester and Chatham, 1959–64; contested Rochester and Chatham, 1966. Mem., Armed Forces Select Cttee, 1975–79; Vice-Chairman: Cons.

Party Broadcasting Cttee, 1975; Cons. Party Defence Cttee, 1979–87; Chm., Cons. Party Media Cttee, 1976–81; Mem., One Nation Gp of Cons. MPs. Delegate to WEU and Council of Europe, 1973–79; Chm., WEU Defence Cttee, 1975–79; Deleg. to N Atlantic Assembly, 1979–83. Chm., Bow Gp, 1966–67; Pres., Atlantic Assoc. of Young Political Leaders, 1968–70. Steward, British Boxing Bd of Control, 1987–. *Publications:* (with O. Pick) Collective Security, 1974; Warning and Response, 1978; The North Atlantic Alliance and the Soviet Union in the 1980s, 1982; (jtly) Nuclear Weapons in Europe, 1984; Westminster Blues, 1985; (ed) Britain: a view from Westminster, 1986; Heseltine: the unauthorised biography, 1987, rev. edn 1994; Palace of Varieties: an insider's view of Westminster, 1989; Hung Parliament, 1991; Floating Voter, 1992; Some of Us, 1992; Borderlands: Shropshire and the Welsh Marches, 1993; A Bag of Boiled Sweets (autobiog.), 1994; various Bow Group and CPC pamphlets. *Recreations:* watching boxing, the country, reading military history, looking at churches, collecting early Staffordshire. *Address:* 19 Broad Street, Ludlow SY8 1NG. *T:* Ludlow (01584) 877084.

CRITCHLEY, Macdonald, CBE 1962; MB, ChB 1st Class Hons (Bristol), MD; FRCP; Consulting Neurologist; *b* 2 Feb. 1900; *s* of Arthur Frank and Rosina Matilda Critchley; *m* 1st, Edna Auldeth Morris (decd); two *s*; 2nd, Eileen Hargreaves. *Educ:* Christian Brothers Coll.; Univ. of Bristol (Lady Haberfield Scholarship in Medicine, Markham Skerritt Prize for Original Research). MD 1925. Goulstonian Lectr, RCP, 1930; Hunterian Prof., RCS, 1935; Royal Coll. of Physicians: Bradshaw Lectr, 1942; Croonian Lectr, 1945; Harveian Orator, 1966; Pres., World Fedn of Neurology, 1965–73; Hon. Consulting Neurologist, King's Coll. Hosp.; Hon. Consulting Physician, National Hosp., Queen Square; formerly Dean, Inst. of Neurology; Neurological Physician, Royal Masonic Hosp.; formerly Neurologist to Royal Hosp. and Home for Incurables, Putney. Consulting Neurologist to Royal Navy, 1939–77; Long Fox Lectr, Univ. of Bristol, 1935; William Withering Lectr, Univ. of Birmingham, 1946; Tisdall Lectr, Univ. of Manitoba, 1951; Semon Lectr, Univ. of London, 1951; Sherrington Lectr, Univ. of Wisconsin; Orator, Medical Soc. of London, 1955. Pres. Harveian Soc., 1947. Hunterian Orator, 1957; Doyne Memorial Lectr, 1961; Wartenberg Lectr, 1961; Victor Horsley Memorial Lectr, 1963; Honyman Gillespie Lectr, 1963; Schorstein Lectr, 1964; Hughlings Jackson Lectr and Medallist, RSM, 1964; Gowers Lectr and Medallist, 1965; Veraguth Gold Medallist, Bern, 1968; Sam T. Orton Award for work on Dyslexia, 1974; Arthur Hall Memorial Lectr, 1969; Rickman Godlee Lectr, 1970; Cavendish Lectr, 1976; Vis. Prof., Winston-Salem, NC, 1983. Pres. Assoc. of British Neurologists, 1962–64; Second Vice-Pres., RCP, 1964; Mem., GMC, 1957–73; Founder-Pres., Migraine Trust. Hon. FACP; MD Zürich *hc*; DenM (Aix-Marseille) *hc*; MD Madrid *hc*; Hon. Fellow: Faculty of History and Philosophy of Medicine and Pharmacy; Pan-African Assoc. of Neurological Scis; Hon. Mem., RSM; Hon. Corresp. Mem. Académie de Médecine de France, Norwegian Academy of Science and Letters, Royal Academy of Medicine, Barcelona, and Neurological Socs of France, Switzerland, Holland, Turkey, Uruguay, US, Canada, Australia, Brazil, Argentine, Germany, Chile, Spain, Roumania, Norway, Czechoslovakia, Greece, Italy, Bulgaria, Hungary, Peru, Poland and Sweden. Visiting Prof., Univs of: Istanbul, 1949; California, 1950 and 1964; Hawaii, 1966. Master, Worshipful Soc. of Apothecaries, 1956–57. Served European War, 1917–18; Surgeon Captain RNVR, 1939–46. *Publications:* Mirror Writing; Neurology of Old Age; Observations on Pain; Language of Gesture; Shipwreck-survivors; Sir William Gowers; The Parietal Lobes; The Black Hole; Developmental Dyslexia; Aphasiology; The Dyslexic Child; Silent Language; (ed jtly) Music and the Brain, 1976; (jtly) Dyslexia defined, 1978; The Divine Banquet of the Brain, 1979; The Citadel of the Senses, 1986; The Ventricle of Memory, 1990; various articles on nervous diseases. *Address:* Hughlings House, Mill Lane, Nether Stowey, Bridgwater, Somerset TA5 1NL.

See also Sir J. M. G. Critchley.

CRITCHLEY, Philip, CB 1990; Director of Network Management and Maintenance, Department of Transport, 1990–91; *b* 31 Jan. 1931; *s* of Henry Stephen and Edith Adela Critchley; *m* 1962, Stella Ann Barnes; two *s* one *d*. *Educ:* Manchester Grammar Sch.; Balliol Coll., Oxford (MA, 2nd Classical Mods and Greats). National Service, Intelligence Corps, 1953–55. Joined Min. of Housing and Local Govt (now Dept of Environment), 1955: Principal, 1960; Asst Sec., 1969; Under Sec., 1980; Dir of Waste Disposal, 1983; Dir of Contracts, Highways Administration and Maintenance, Dept of Transport, 1985–90. FRSA 1990. *Recreations:* philosophy, writing poetry. *Address:* Redstone House, Maidstone Road, Ashford, Kent TN25 4NP. *T:* Ashford (01233) 621037. *Clubs:* Blackheath Harriers; Oxford Union Society.

CRITCHLEY, Tom; international business adviser, since 1990; Senior Partner, Tom Critchley Associates, since 1990; Managing Director: Bio. Flo, since 1991; Eurosep, Poland, since 1992; *b* 17 Aug. 1928; *s* of late Leonard and Jessie Critchley; *m* 1951, Margaret Bland; one *s*. *Educ:* Sheffield College of Technology. Davy-Ashmore Group, 1951–66; Cammell Laird and Upper Clyde Groups, 1966–69; J. C. B. Group, 1969–70; EMI Group, 1970–80; Head, Investment Casting Mission to Canada; UN Adviser to Tanzanian Govt; Adviser to UN High Commn for Refugees; Chm., MATC Ltd; Senior Partner, internat. consultancy practice, 1980–85; Under Sec., DHSS, subseq. Dept of Health, and NHS Management Bd Mem., 1986–90; Head, healthcare missions to Japan, Philippines, Indonesia, USSR and Poland, 1989–90; UK Chm., Anglo-Soviet Healthcare Gp, 1989–91. Chairman: UK Trade Assoc., 1990–92; European Timeshare Fedn, 1991–92; Mem. Board, Nat. Inst. of Govt Purchasing, USA, 1977–78; Sen. UK Deleg., Internat. Fedn of Purchasing & Materials Management, 1980–85; Dir, Internat. Management Inst., Paris, 1980–88; Faculty Mem., Management Centre Europe, Brussels, 1980–85; Mem., Business in the Community, 1989–92. Inst. of Purchasing & Supply: Fellow, 1967; Chm. Council, 1974–75; Pres., 1977–78; Chm., Ext. Affairs, 1978–82; Mem., Internat. Council, 1979–82. *Recreations:* competitive sports, live theatre, North American history. *Address:* 3 Lincoln Close, Stoke Mandeville, Bucks HP22 5YS. *T:* Aylesbury (01296) 612511, *Fax:* (01296) 614203.

CROAN, Thomas Malcolm; Sheriff of North Strathclyde, since 1983; *b* 7 Aug. 1932; *s* of John Croan and Amelia Sydney; *m* 1959, Joan Kilpatrick Law; one *s* three *d*. *Educ:* St Joseph's Coll., Dumfries; Edinburgh University. MA 1953; LLB 1955. Admitted to Faculty of Advocates, 1956; Standing Junior Counsel, to Scottish Develt Dept, 1964–65 and (for highways work) 1967–69; Advocate Depute, 1965–66; Sheriff of Grampian, Highland and Islands (formerly Aberdeen, Kincardine and Banff), 1969–83. *Recreations:* sailing, reading. *Address:* Overdale, 113 Bentinck Drive, Troon KA10 6JB.

CROCKATT, Lieut Comdr (Douglas) Allan, OBE 1981 (MBE 1971); RD 1978; RNR retired; Vice Lord-Lieutenant of West Yorkshire, 1985–92; *b* 31 Jan. 1923; *s* of late Douglas Crockatt, JP, LLD and Ella Crockatt (*née* Lethem); *m* 1946, Helen Townley Tatton (*d* 1985), *d* of late Capt. T. A. Tatton, MC; one *d*. *Educ:* Bootham School, York; Trinity Hall, Cambridge; Dept of Navigation, Southampton Univ. RNVR 1942–46, Western Approaches and N Russia; RNVSR 1946–64; RNR active list, 1964–82. Director: Johnson Group Cleaners, 1961–84 (Dep. Chm., 1976–84); Johnson Group Inc. (USA) (formerly Apparelmaster Inc.), 1975–84 (Dep. Chm., 1981–84); local Dir, Martins and Barclays Banks W Yorks Bd, 1964–84. Mem., Multiple Shops' Fedn Council, 1972–77. Life Vice-Pres., W Yorks Branch Magistrates' Assoc., 1980 (Hon. Sec., 1958–72; Chm., 1975–77; Pres., 1977–79); Mem. Council, Magistrates' Assoc., 1959–80 (Chm., Training Cttee, 1974–80); Member: Lord Chancellor's Adv. Cttee for training of Magistrates, 1964–79; Lord Chancellor's Magistrates' Courts Rule Cttee, 1979–81. CC, W Riding of Yorks, 1953–58; JP 1956, DL 1971, West (formerly WR) Yorks. Freeman, City of London, 1958; Liveryman, Dyers' Co., 1958. Hon. LLD Leeds, 1990. *Recreations:* cricket, sailing, fishing. *Address:* Paddock House, Sicklinghall, Wetherby, W Yorks LS22 4BJ. *T:* Wetherby (01937) 582844. *Club:* Army and Navy.

CROCKER, John Fraser; His Honour Judge Crocker; a Circuit Judge, since 1995; *b* 27 May 1943; *o s* of late Noel John Fraser Crocker and Marjorie Jean Crocker (*née* Heaton); *m* 1969, Janet Butteriss; one *s* twin *d*. *Educ:* The Leys, Cambridge; Christ's Coll., Cambridge (MA). Admitted Solicitor, 1969; called to the Bar, Inner Temple, 1973; a Recorder, 1991–95. *Recreations:* reading thrillers, avoiding gardening. *Address:* Esher, Surrey. *T:* 0181–224 2392.

CROCKER, His Honour Peter Vernon; a Circuit Judge, 1974–91; *b* 29 June 1926; *s* of Walter Angus Crocker and Fanny Victoria Crocker (*née* Dempster); *m* 1950, Nancy Kathleen Sargent. *Educ:* Oundle; Corpus Christi Coll., Cambridge (BA). Called to Bar, Inner Temple, 1949. *Recreations:* gardening, tennis, swimming.

CROCKER, Sir Walter (Russell), KBE 1978 (CBE 1955); Australian diplomat, retired 1970; Lieutenant-Governor of South Australia, 1973–82; *b* 25 March 1902; *e s* of late Robert Crocker and Alma Bray, Parnaroo, SA; *m* 1951, Claire (marr. diss. 1968), *y d* of F. J. Ward, Headmaster of Prince Alfred Coll., Adelaide, and *widow* of Dr John Gooden, Physicist; two *s*. *Educ:* University of Adelaide; Balliol Coll., Oxford; Stanford University, USA. Entered Colonial Administrative Service (Nigeria), 1930; transf. to League of Nations, 1934, and to ILO (Asst to Dir-Gen). Served War, 1940–45 (Lt-Col, Croix de Guerre avec palme, Ordre royal du Lion, Belgium). Farming at Parnaroo, 1946; UN Secretariat (Chief of Africa Sect.), 1946–49; Prof. of Internat. Relations, Aust. Nat. Univ., 1949–52; Actg Vice-Chancellor, 1951; High Commissioner for Australia to India, 1952–55; Ambassador of Australia to Indonesia, 1955–57; High Comr to Canada, 1957–58; High Comr for Australia to India and Ambassador to Nepal, 1958–62; Amb. of Australia to the Netherlands and Belgium, 1962–65; Ambassador to Ethiopia and High Commissioner to Kenya and Uganda, 1965–67; Ambassador to Italy, 1967–70. Hon. Colonel, Royal South Australia Regt, 1977–. L'Ordre royal du Lion (Belgium), 1945; Cavaliere di Gr. Croce dell'Ordine al Merito (Italy), 1970; Order of Malta (Grand' Uffiziale del Merito Melitense), 1975. *Publications:* The Japanese Population Problem, 1931; Nigeria, 1936; On Governing Colonies, 1946; Self-Government for the Colonies, 1949; Can the United Nations Succeed?, 1951; The Race Question as a factor in International Relations, 1955; Nehru, 1965; Australian Ambassador, 1971; Memoirs, 1981; Sir Thomas Playford, 1983. *Recreations:* gardening, walking, music; previously skiing, tennis. *Address:* 624 Seaview Road, Grange, SA 5022, Australia. *Club:* Adelaide.

CROCKETT, Andrew Duncan; General Manager, Bank for International Settlements, since 1994; *b* 23 March 1943; *s* of Dr Andrew Stuart Crockett and Sheilah Crockett (*née* Stewart); *m* 1966, Marjorie Frances Hlavacek; two *s* one *d*. *Educ:* Queens' College, Cambridge (MA Econ.); Yale Univ. (MA). Bank of England, 1966–72; International Monetary Fund, 1972–89; Exec. Dir, Bank of England, 1989–93. *Publications:* Money: theory, policy, institutions, 1973; International Money: issues and analysis, 1977; contribs to professional jls. *Recreations:* reading, golf, tennis. *Address:* Bank for International Settlements, Centralbahnplatz 2, 4002 Basle, Switzerland.

CROFT, family name of **Baron Croft.**

CROFT, 2nd Baron *cr* 1940, of Bournemouth; **Michael Henry Glendower Page Croft;** Bt 1924; *b* 20 Aug. 1916; *s* of 1st Baron Croft, PC, CMG, and Hon. Nancy Beatrice Borwick (*d* 1949), *y d* of 1st Baron Borwick; *S* father, 1947; *m* 1948, Lady Antoinette Fredericka Conyngham (*d* 1959), *o d* of 6th Marquess Conyngham; one *s* one *d*. *Educ:* Eton; Trinity Hall, Cambridge (BA). Served War of 1939–45, Capt. RASC. Called to the Bar, Inner Temple, 1952. Director: Henry Page & Co. Ltd, 1946–57; Ware Properties Ltd, 1958–65; Hereford and Worcester, Building Preservation Trust Ltd, 1986–. Underwriting Mem., Lloyd's, 1971–. Member Executive Cttee: Contemporary Arts Soc., 1960–68 and 1970–81 (Hon. Sec., 1971–76, Hon. Treasurer, 1976–80, Vice-Chm., 1980–81); British Museum Soc., 1969–76. Hon. Keeper of Contemporary Art, Fitzwilliam Museum, Cambridge, 1984. FRSA. OStJ. *Heir:* *s* Hon. Bernard William Henry Page Croft [*b* 28 Aug 1949. *Educ:* Stowe; Univ. of Wales, Cardiff. BScEcon]. *Address:* Croft Castle, near Leominster, Herefordshire HR6 9PW; 19 Queen's Gate Gardens, SW7 5LZ. *Club:* Athenæum.

CROFT, David Legh, QC 1982; **His Honour Judge Croft;** a Circuit Judge, since 1987; *b* 14 Aug. 1937; *s* of late Alan Croft and of Doreen Mary Berry (*née* Mitchell); *m* 1963, Susan Mary (*née* Bagnall); two *s*. *Educ:* Haileybury and ISC; Nottingham Univ. (LLB). Called to the Bar, Middle Temple, 1960; called to the Hong Kong Bar, 1984; a Recorder, 1985–87. *Recreations:* patience and reflection at leisure.

CROFT, (Ivor) John, CBE 1982; painter; Head of Home Office Research and Planning Unit, 1981–83 (Head, Home Office Research Unit, 1972–81); *b* 6 Jan. 1923; *s* of Oswald Croft and Doris (*née* Phillips). *Educ:* Westminster Sch.; Christ Church, Oxford (Hinchcliffe Scholar in Mod. Hist.; MA); Inst. of Education, Univ. of London (MA); LSE. Temp. jun. admin. officer, FO, 1942–45; asst teacher, LCC, 1949–51; Inspector, Home Office Children's Dept, 1952–66; Sen. Research Officer, Home Office Research Unit, 1966–72. Member: Criminological Scientific Council, Council of Europe, 1978–83, Chm., 1981–83; Conservative Study Gp on Crime, 1983–87; Kensington Crime Prevention Panel, 1984–87; Tribunal under I of M Interception of Communications Act, 1989–94. Governor, ILEA Secondary Schs, 1959–68. Mem. Exec. Cttee, English Assoc., 1966–77 (Hon. Treas. 1972–75); Chairman: Pembridge Assoc., 1985–87; Cttee, Peel Heritage Trust, 1991–93 (Mem., 1989–93). Group shows, 1958, 1963, 1967, 1968, 1969, 1973, 1992, 1993; one-man shows, 1970, 1971. *Publications:* booklets and pamphlets, and various studies of crime, criminological research and the administration of justice. *Address:* 15 Circus Mews, Bath BA1 2PW. *Club:* Reform.

CROFT, Col Noel Andrew Cotton, DSO 1945; OBE 1970; MA Oxon; Essex Regiment; retired; *b* 30 Nov. 1906; *s* of late Rev. Canon R. W. Croft, MA; *m* 1952, Rosalind, 2nd *d* of late Comdr A. H. de Kantzow, DSO, RN; three *d*. *Educ:* Lancing Coll.; Stowe Sch.; Christ Church, Oxford; Sch. of Technology, Manchester. Cotton Trade, 1929–32; Mem. British Trans-Greenland Expedition, 1933–34; ADC to Maharajah of Cooch Behar, India, 1934–35; Second-in-Command, Oxford Univ. Arctic Expedition to North-East Land, 1935–36; Ethnological Exped. to Swedish Lapland, 1938; Sec. to Dir of Fitzwilliam Museum, Cambridge, 1937–39. Served War of 1939–45, Capt. 1939; WO Mission to Finno-Russian War, 1939–40; Bde Intelligence Officer Independent Companies, Norwegian Campaign, 1940; Combined Ops, 1940–41; Major, 1941; Asst Mil. Attaché, Stockholm, 1941–42; sea or parachute ops in Tunisia, Corsica, Italy, France, and Denmark, 1943–45; Lieut-Col 1945; Asst Dir Scientific Research, War Office, 1945–49; WO

Observer on Canadian Arctic "Exercise Musk-Ox", 1945–46, and on NW Frontier Trials, India, 1946–47; attached Canadian Army, 1947–48; GSO1, War Office, 1949–51; Liaison Officer HQ Continental Army, USA, 1952–54; comd The Infantry Junior Leaders Bn, 1954–57; Col 1957; Comdt Army Apprentices Sch., Harrogate, 1957–60; Comdt, Metropolitan Police Cadet Corps, 1960–71. Vice-Pres., Women's Transport Service (FANY), 1987– (Chm., 1972–87). Corresp. Fellow, Arctic Inst. of North America; Mem., Reindeer Council of UK, 1949–89 (Chm., 1962–82). Polar Medal (clasp Arctic, 1935–36), 1942; Back Award, RGS, 1946 and 1947. *Publications:* (with A. R. Glen) Under the Pole Star, 1937; Polar Exploration, 1939, 2nd edn 1947; A Talent for Adventure (autobiog.), 1991. *Recreations:* mountaineering, ski-ing, sailing, photography. *Address:* River House, Strand-on-the-Green, W4 3PD. *T:* 0181–994 6359. *Clubs:* Alpine, Special Forces, Geographical.

CROFT, Sir Owen (Glendower), 14th Bt *cr* 1671; grazier; *b* 26 April 1932; *s* of Sir Bernard Hugh Denman Croft, 13th Bt, and of Helen Margaret (*née* Weaver); *S* father, 1984; *m* 1959, Sally Patricia, *d* of Dr T. M. Mansfield, Brisbane; one *s* two *d*. *Educ:* Armidale School, NSW. Mem., State Council of Advice to Rural Lands Protection Bds of NSW; Member: NSW Feral Animal Control Council; NSW Footrot Strategic Plan Steering Cttee; NSW Non-Indigenous Species Adv. Cttee; Chm., Armidale Dist Adv. Cttee to NSW Nat. Parks and Wildlife Service. *Recreations:* tennis; National Trust activities. *Heir: s* Thomas Jasper Croft [*b* 3 Nov. 1962; *m* 1989, Catherine Fiona, *d* of Graham William White]. *Address:* Salisbury Court, Uralla, NSW 2358, Australia. *T:* (67) 784624.

CROFT, Roy Henry Francis, CB 1983; Member, Monopolies and Mergers Commission, since 1995; *b* 4 March 1936; *s* of late William Henry Croft and Dorothy Croft; *m* 1961, Patricia Ainley; one *s* two *d*. *Educ:* Isleworth Grammar Sch.; Christ's Coll., Cambridge (MA). BoT, 1959; Treasury, 1961–62; DEA, 1964–67; Private Sec. to Pres. Bd of Trade, 1968–70; Cabinet Office, 1970–72; Civil Aviation Div., Dept of Trade, 1973–76; Finance and Economic Appraisal Div., DoI, 1976–79; Posts and Telecommunications Div., DoI, 1979–80; Dep. Sec. DTI, 1980–85; Exec. Dir and Chief Operating Officer, SIB, 1985–93.

CROFT, Stanley Edward, TD 1951; life insurance consultant; formerly HM Diplomatic Service; *b* 18 Oct. 1917; *s* of Edward John and Alice Lucy Croft; *m* 1950, Joan Mary Kaye; four *s* two *d*. *Educ:* Portsmouth Grammar School. TA, 1939; served War of 1939–45, RA, Middle East, Aden, Italy, Germany. Min. of Labour, 1935; Admty, 1937–39 and 1946–47; transf. to Diplomatic Service, 1947; Vice-Consul, Barcelona, 1950; 2nd Sec., Lahore, 1951; Washington, 1955; Madrid, 1956; 1st Sec., FO, 1960; Consul, Geneva, 1961; FO and CRO, 1965–70; Consul-Gen., Madrid, 1970; Counsellor and Consul-Gen., Luanda, 1974–77. Sen. Associate, Abbey Life Assurance Co., 1977–90. *Recreations:* swimming, tennis, camping, fishing, carpentry.

CROFT, Sir Thomas (Stephen Hutton), 6th Bt *cr* 1918, of Cowling Hall, Yorkshire; Principal, Thomas Croft, Architect, since 1988; *b* 12 June 1959; *o s* of Major Sir John Croft, 5th Bt and of Lucy Elizabeth, *d* of late Major William Dallas Loney Jupp, OBE; *S* father, 1990. *Educ:* King's Sch., Canterbury; University Coll., London (BSc); Royal Coll. of Art, London (MA). Architect, Richard Meier & Partners, Architects, New York, 1985–86; Project Architect, Rick Mather, Architects, London, 1986–88. *Heir: uncle* Cyril Bernard Croft, *b* 6 June 1918. *Address:* 53 Leinster Square, W2 4PU.

CROFTON, family name of **Baron Crofton.**

CROFTON, 7th Baron *cr* 1797 (Ire.); **Guy Patrick Gilbert Crofton;** Bt 1758; Lieutenant Colonel, 9/12 Royal Lancers (Prince of Wales's); Defence Attaché, Berne, since 1995; *b* 17 June 1951; *s* of 5th Baron Crofton and of Ann Pamela, *d* of Gp Capt. Charles Herbert Tighe, OBE, DFC; *S* brother, 1989; *m* 1985, Gillian, *o d* of Harry Godfrey Mitchell Bass, *qv*; twin *s*. *Educ:* Theresianistische Akademie, Vienna; Midhurst GS. Commissioned 9/12 Royal Lancers, 1971. *Recreations:* shooting, ski-ing. *Heir: er* twin *s* Hon. Edward Harry Piers Crofton, *b* 23 Jan. 1988. *Address:* c/o British Embassy, Thunstrasse 50, 3005 Berne, Switzerland. *Club:* Cavalry and Guards.

CROFTON, Denis Hayes, OBE 1948 (MBE 1943); retired Home and Indian Civil Servant; Member, Panel of Inspectors, Department of the Environment, 1969–79; President, Tunbridge Wells and District Branch, Civil Service Retirement Fellowship, since 1985 (Chairman, 1972–85); *b* 14 Dec. 1908; *s* of late Richard Hayes Crofton, Colonial Civil Service and Mabel Annie Crofton (*née* Smith); *m* 1933, Alison Carr, *d* of late Andrew McClure and Ethel McClure; three *s* one *d*. *Educ:* Tonbridge Sch.; Corpus Christi Coll., Oxford (Class. Mods, Lit. Hum., MA). Indian Civil Service, 1932; served in Bihar; subdivisional Magistrate, Giridih, 1934, Jamshedpur, 1935; Under-Sec. to Govt of Bihar, Polit. and Appt Depts, 1936; Under-Sec. to Govt of India, Dept of Labour, 1939; Private Sec. to Indian Mem., Eastern Gp Supply Council, 1941; Dist Mag. and Collector, Shahabad, Bihar, 1942; Sec. to Gov. of Bihar, 1944; apptd to Home Civil Service, 1947; Principal, Min. of Fuel and Power, Petroleum Div. 1948; Asst Sec., Petroleum Div. and Chm., OEEC Oil Cttee, Paris, 1950–53; Asst Sec., Monopolies and Restrictive Practices Commn, 1953; Asst Sec., Min. of Fuel and Power, Electricity Div., 1956; Petroleum Div., 1961; Accountant General and Under-Secretary for Finance, 1962–68. *Publications:* The Children of Edmonstown Park: memoirs of an Irish family, 1981; Andrew Hayes leaves the King's County: some footnotes on a diaspora, 1990; Souvenirs of a Competition Wallah: letters and sketches from India 1932–1947, 1994; edited: The Surgery at Aberffrwd: some encounters of a colliery doctor, 1982; A GP's Progress to the Black Country, 1984 (both by Francis Maylett Smith). *Recreations:* reading, gardening. *Address:* 26 Vauxhall Gardens, Tonbridge, Kent TN11 0LZ. *T:* Tonbridge (01732) 353465. *Club:* Commonwealth Trust.

CROFTON, (Sir) Hugh Dennis, (8th Bt *cr* 1801, of Mohill); *S* nephew, 1987, but does not use the title. *Heir: b* Major Edward Morgan Crofton.

CROFTON, Sir John (Wenman), Kt 1977; retired; Professor of Respiratory Diseases and Tuberculosis, University of Edinburgh, 1952–77; *b* 1912; *s* of Dr W. M. Crofton; *m* 1945, Eileen Chris Mercer, MBE 1984; two *s* three *d*. *Educ:* Tonbridge; Sidney Sussex Coll., Cambridge; St Thomas's Hosp. Medical qualification, 1936; War of 1939–45, RAMC; France, Middle East, Germany. Lecturer in Medicine, Postgraduate Medical Sch. of London, 1947–51, Senior Lecturer, 1951; Part-time Tuberculosis Unit, Medical Research Council, Brompton Hosp., 1947–50; Dean of Faculty of Medicine, 1964–66, and Vice-Principal, 1969–70, Univ. of Edinburgh. Vice-Pres., 1972–73, Pres., 1973–76, RCPE. Hon. Mem., Acads of Medicine of Argentina, Catalonia and Singapore. Hon. FRCPE; Hon. FRCPI; Hon. FRACP; Hon. FACP; Hon. FFCM. Weber-Parkes Prize, RCP, 1966; City of Edinburgh Medal for Sci. and Soc., 1995. *Publications:* (jtly) Respiratory Diseases, 1969, 3rd edn 1981; (jtly) Clinical Tuberculosis, 1992; Housing and Health in Scotland, 1993; contributor to BMJ, Lancet, Thorax, etc. *Recreations:* conversation, family life, mountains. *Address:* 13 Spylaw Bank Road, Edinburgh EH13 0JW. *T:* 0131–441 3730. *Club:* University Staff (Edinburgh).

CROFTON, Sir Malby (Sturges), 5th Bt *cr* 1838 (orig. *cr* 1661); Partner, Messrs Fenn & Crosthwaite; Member of the London Stock Exchange, 1957–75; *b* 11 Jan. 1923; *s* of Sir Malby Richard Henry Crofton, 4th Bt, DSO and Bar, and Katharine Beatrix Pollard; *S* father, 1962. *Educ:* Eton (King's Scholar); Trinity Coll., Cambridge (scholar). Served with Life Guards, 1942–46, in Middle East and Italy. Member: Kensington Borough Council, 1962, Leader, 1968–77, Mayor, Kensington and Chelsea, 1978; GLC, 1970–73; ILEA, 1970–73; Ealing N, GLC, 1977–81; Leader, GLC Scrutiny Cttee, 1977–78. Vice-Chm., NW Thames RHA, 1980–85. Hon.Treasurer, Marie Curie Meml Foundn; Dir, St Edward's Housing Assoc.; Chm., Kensington and Chelsea, Age Concern, 1987–. Pres., Ealing N Cons. Assoc. Freeman, Royal Bor. of Kensington and Chelsea, 1983. Hon. Fellow, Chelsea Coll. *Recreations:* tennis, swimming, motoring, planting trees, farming. *Heir: kinsman* Henry Edward Melville Crofton [*b* 15 Aug. 1931; *m* 1955, Brigid, twin *d* of Gerald K. Riddle; two *s* one *d*]. *Address:* 12 Caithness Road, W14 0JB; Longford House, Co. Sligo, Eire. *Clubs:* Cavalry and Guards, Hurlingham.

CROFTS, Roger Stanley; Chief Executive, Scottish Natural Heritage, since 1991; *b* 17 Jan. 1944; *s* of Stanley Crofts and Violet May Crofts (*née* Dawson); *m* 1971, Jill Watt; one *s* one *d*. *Educ:* Hinckley Grammar Sch.; Liverpool Univ. (BA); Leicester Univ. (PGCE); Aberdeen Univ. (MLitt). Res. Asst to Prof. K. Walton, Aberdeen Univ., 1966–72; British Geomorphocological Res. Gp, UCL, 1972–74; Central Res. Unit, Scottish Office, 1974–84; Scottish Office: Head of Highlands and Tourism, 1984–88; Head of Rural Affairs, 1988–91. Vis. Prof. of Geography, Royal Holloway, Univ. of London, 1992–. Member: Council, NT for Scotland; Council, Scottish Wildlife Trust; Hon. Pres., Scottish Assoc. of Geography Teachers. *Publications:* contribs to books on marginal regions, geomorph. mapping, second homes, field studies; numerous articles. *Recreations:* designing gardens, choral singing, flower photography, cooking, hill walking. *Address:* 19 Manor Place, Edinburgh EH3 7DX. *T:* 0131–225 1177.

CROHAM, Baron *cr* 1978 (Life Peer), of the London Borough of Croydon; **Douglas Albert Vivian Allen,** GCB 1973 (KCB 1967; CB 1963); Chairman, Guinness Peat Group, 1983–87; Head of the Home Civil Service and Permanent Secretary, Civil Service Department, 1974–77; *b* 15 Dec. 1917; *s* of late Albert Allen; *m* 1941, Sybil Eileen Allegro (*d* 1994), *d* of late John Marco Allegro; two *s* one *d*. *Educ:* Wallington County Grammar Sch.; London School of Economics. BSc (Econ.) First Class Hons, 1938. Entered Board of Trade, 1939; Royal Artillery, 1940–45; Cabinet Office, 1947; Treasury, 1948–58; Under-Secretary, Ministry of Health, 1958–60; Under-Secretary, Treasury, 1960–62, Third Secretary, 1962–64; Dept of Economic Affairs: Dep. Under-Sec. of State, 1964–66; Second Permanent Under-Sec. of State, May-Oct. 1966; Permanent Under-Sec. of State, 1966–68; Permanent Sec., HM Treasury, 1968–74. Director: Pilkington plc (formerly Pilkington Bros), 1978–92; Guinness Mahon & Co., 1989–92; Dep. Chm., 1978–82, Chm., 1982–85, BNOC; Chm., Trinity Insurance, 1988–92. An Industrial Adviser to the Governor, Bank of England, 1978–83. President: Inst. for Fiscal Studies, 1979–92; British Inst. of Energy Economies, 1985–94. A Trustee, Anglo-German Foundn, 1977– (Chm., 1982–). CIMgt; FRSA 1975. Hon. Fellow, LSE, 1969; Hon. DSc (Social Sciences) Southampton, 1977. *Recreation:* woodwork. *Address:* 9 Manor Way, South Croydon, Surrey CR2 7BT. *T:* 0181–688 0496. *Club:* Reform.

CROLL, Prof. James George Arthur, FEng 1990; Chadwick Professor of Civil Engineering, and Head of Department of Civil Engineering, University College London, since 1992; *b* 16 Oct. 1943; *s* of late Keith Waghorn Croll and Jean Croll; *m* 1966, Elisabeth Joan (*née* Spracketts); one *s* one *d*. *Educ:* Palmerston North Boys' High Sch., NZ; Univ. of Canterbury, NZ (BE 1st cl. Hons, PhD). FIStructE, FIMA, CEng. Asst Engineer, Min. of Works, NZ, 1962–67; University College London: Res. Fellow, 1967–70; Lectr, 1970–81; Reader in Structural Engrg, 1981–85; Prof. of Structural Engrg, 1985–92. Vis. Fellow, Princeton, 1979; Visiting Professor: Fed. Univ. of Rio de Janeiro, 1973, 1981, 1984; Univ. of Hong Kong, 1985. *Publications:* Elements of Structural Stability, 1972; Force Systems and Equilibrium, 1974. *Recreations:* singing, piano, painting, drawing, sailing, ski-ing, travel. *Address:* 36 Bisham Gardens, Highgate, N6 6DD. *T:* 0181–348 4753. *Clubs:* Natural Science (UCL); Hayling Island Sailing.

CROLL, (Mary) Louise, CBE 1995; HM Diplomatic Service, retired; Ambassador to Costa Rica, 1992–95; *b* 10 Sept. 1935. Joined FO, subseq. FCO, 1953; Bahrain, 1957; Addis Ababa, 1959; UK Mission, NY, 1961; FO, 1964; S America floater, 1967; Bilbao, 1969; Lusaka, 1972; First Sec., Madrid, 1979, FCO, 1984; Consul, Florence, 1988.

CROLY, Brig. Henry Gray, CBE 1958; JP; *b* 7 June 1910; *s* of late Lt-Col W. Croly, DSO, late RAMC, Ardvarna, Tralee; *m* 1939, Marjorie Rosanne, *er d* of late Major J. S. Knyvett, late R Warwickshire Regt, Clifford Manor Road, Guildford; two *s* two *d*. *Educ:* Sherborne Sch.; RMA Woolwich; BA Open Univ., 1993. 2nd Lieut RA, 1930; served in India: Mohmand Ops, 1935; Waziristan, 1936–37 (despatches); served War of 1939–45, mostly India and Burma; GSO1, British Mil. Mission to France, 1946–47; 2nd-in-Comd 26 Medium Regt RA, 1947–48; jssc 1949; GSO1, WO, 1950–51; Col GS, SHAPE, 1952; OC 26 Field Regt Suez Canal Zone, 1953–55; Dep. Sec., Chiefs of Staff Cttee, 1955–58; UK Nat. Mil. Rep. to SHAPE, 1959–61; retd 1962. Sec., Health Visitor Trng Council and Council for Trng in Social Work, 1963–66; Asst Sec. of Commns, Lord Chancellor's Office, 1966–74; Sec., Wolfenden Cttee on Voluntary Orgns, 1974–78. JP Surrey, 1968. *Recreations:* golf, reading. *Address:* 20 Middle Bourne Lane, Farnham, Surrey GU10 3NH. *T:* Farnham (01252) 714851. *Clubs:* Army and Navy, MCC; Hankley Common Golf.

CROMARTIE, 5th Earl of, *cr* 1861; **John Ruaridh Grant Mackenzie;** Viscount Tarbat, Baron Castlehaven, Baron MacLeod, 1861; Chief of the Clan Mackenzie; MIExpE; explosives engineer; *b* 12 June 1948; *s* of 4th Earl of Cromartie, MC, TD and of Olga, *d* of late Stuart Laurance; *S* father, 1989; *m* 1973, Helen, *d* of John Murray; (one *s* decd); *m* 1985, Janet Clare, *d* of Christopher J. Harley; two *s*. *Educ:* Rannoch School, Perthshire; Strathclyde University. Mem. Council, IExpE. *Publications:* Selected Climbs in Skye, 1982; articles in Classic Rock Climbs and Cold Climbs. *Recreations:* mountaineering, art, astronomy, geology. *Heir: s* Viscount Tarbat, *qv*. *Address:* Castle Leod, Strathpeffer, Ross-shire IV14 9AA. *Clubs:* Army and Navy; Scottish Mountaineering.

CROMBIE, Alistair Cameron, MA, BSc, PhD; FBA 1990; Fellow, 1969–83, garden master, 1971–81, Trinity College, Oxford (Hon. Fellow, 1994); Lecturer in History of Science, University of Oxford, 1953–83; *b* 4 Nov. 1915; 2nd *s* of William David Crombie and Janet Wilmina (*née* Macdonald); *m* 1943, Nancy Hey (*d* 1993); three *s* one *d* (and one *s* decd). *Educ:* Geelong Grammar Sch.; Trinity Coll., Melbourne Univ.; Jesus Coll., Cambridge. Zoological Lab., Cambridge, 1941–46; Lectr in History and Philosophy of Science, University Coll., London, 1946–53, nominated Reader, resigned; All Soul's Coll., Oxford, 1954–69. Kennedy Prof. in the Renaissance, 1982, Prof. of History of Science and Medicine, 1983–85, Smith Coll., Mass. Visiting Professor: Technische Hochschule, Aachen, 1948; Univ. of Washington, 1953–54; Princeton Univ., 1959–60; Australian Univs (guest of Vice-Chancellors' Cttee), 1963; Tokyo Univ. (guest of Japan Soc. for Promotion of Sci.), 1976; All-India Inst. of Med. Scis, and guest of Indian Nat. Sci. Acad., 1976; Virginia Mil. Inst., 1977; Williams Coll., Mass. (Bernhard Vis. Prof.), 1984; Prof. d'Histoire des Sciences, Sorbonne (Univ. of Paris I), 1982–83; Directeur Associé, Ecole des Hautes Etudes, Paris, 1989. Conseil Scientifique, Dépt d'Hist. et Philosophie de la Médecine, Univ. of Paris XII, 1981–85. Mem. Council, Science

Museum, London, 1962–66; Mem., British Nat. Cttee for History of Science, 1963–69. Editor: Brit. Jl Philos. Sci., 1949–54; Hist. Sci., 1961–; Dir, Oxford Univ. Symp. Hist. Sci., 1961; Pres., Brit. Soc. Hist. Sci., 1964–66; Pres., Internat. Acad. Hist. Sci., 1968–71; Member: Internat. Acad. Hist. Med.; Academia Leopoldina (Pontifical Acad. of Scis); FRHistS. Hon. DLitt Durham, 1979; Dr *hc* Université de Paris X, 1993. Galileo Prize, Domus Galileana, 1969; Alexander von Humboldt Res. Award, 1994. *Publications:* Augustine to Galileo, 1952, 4th edn 1979; Robert Grosseteste and the Origins of Experimental Science, 1953, 3rd edn 1971; Scientific Change, 1963; The Mechanistic Hypothesis and the Scientific Study of Vision, 1967; The Rational Arts of Living, 1987; Science Optics and Music in Medieval and Early Modern Thought, 1990; Science, Art and Nature in Medieval and Modern Thought, 1995; Styles of Scientific Thinking in the European Tradition, 1994; contrib. Annals of Sci., Brit. Jl Hist. Sci., EHR, Isis, Jl Animal Ecol., Physis, Proc. Royal Soc. Lond., Rev. de Synthèse, TLS, Dict. Sci. Biogr., Encyc. Brit., New Cambridge Modern Hist., etc. *Recreations:* literature, travel, landscape gardening. *Address:* Orchardlea, Boars Hill, Oxford OX1 5DF. *T:* Oxford (01865) 735692. *Club:* Brooks's.

CROMBIE, Prof. Leslie, FRS 1973; CChem, FRSC; Sir Jesse Boot Professor of Organic Chemistry, University of Nottingham, 1969–88, now Emeritus (Dean of Science, 1980–83); *b* 10 June 1923; *s* of Walter Leslie Crombie and Gladys May Crombie (*née* Clarkson); *m* 1953 Winifred Mary Lovell Wood; two *s* two *d*. *Educ:* Portsmouth Municipal Coll.; King's Coll., London. PhD, DSc, FKC 1978. Admiralty Chemical Lab., Portsmouth Naval Dockyard, 1941–46. Lectr, Imperial Coll., London, SW7, 1950–58; Reader in Organic Chemistry, King's Coll., London Univ., 1958–63, Fellow, 1978; Prof. of Organic Chemistry, University Coll. (Univ. of Wales), Cardiff, 1963–69. Pres., British Association, Section B, 1978; Chm., Phytochemical Soc. of Europe, 1986–88 (Vice-Chm., 1984–86, 1988–90). Member: British Libraries Chemical Inf. Review Panel, 1976–77; UGC Physical Scis Sub-Cttee, 1978–85; Royal Society: Govt Grants Cttee, 1976–77 (Chm., 1978–79); Sect. Cttee 3, 1977–78 (Chm., 1978–80); Chemical Educn Cttee, 1981–82 (Chm., 1983–87); Educn Cttee, 1983–85 (Chm., 1986–91); Travelling Expenses Cttee, 1984–86; Council, 1984–86; Higher Educn Study Gp, 1991–93; Science Research Council: Chem. Cttee, 1970–75; Enzyme Cttee, 1973–75; Chemical Society: Council, 1962–64 and 1972–80; Library Cttee, 1959–63; Primary Jls Cttee, 1964–69; Reports and Reviews Cttee, 1964–69 (Chm., 1969–73); Pub. Services Bd, 1969–77; Perkin Div. Council, 1971–85 (Pres., 1976–79); Presidents' Cttee, 1972–74; Tertiary Pub. Cttee, 1974–76; Exec. Cttee, 1976–79; Div. and Annual Congress Cttee, 1976–79; UKCIS Bd, 1972–77; Royal Inst. of Chemistry: Jt Cttee for HNC and HND quals, 1962–84; Council, 1975–78; Exams and Institns Cttee, 1976–78; Quals and Admissions Cttee, 1976–78; Royal Society of Chemistry: Council, 1980–81; Jls Bd, 1981–85; Quals and Exams Bd, 1983–86; Chm., Perkin Jls Editorial Bd, 1981–85; Pedler Lectr, 1982; Robert Robinson Lectr, 1993; Flintoff Medal, 1984. Lectures, Chemical Society: Tilden, 1970; Simonsen, 1975; Hugo Müller, 1977. Natural Products Chemistry award, RIC, 1980; Phytochem. Soc. of Europe medal, 1990. Hon. Fellow, Portsmouth Univ. (formerly Polytechnic), 1983. Trustee, Uppingham Sch., 1994–. *Publications:* (ed) Recent Advances in the Chemistry of Insect Control, Vol. II, 1990; Royal Soc. report on GCSE (Chm.); over 380 original papers in learned chemical jls, especially those of RSC, London. *Recreation:* gardening. *Address:* 153 Hillside Road, Bramcote, Beeston, Nottingham NG9 3BD. *T:* (0115) 925 9412. *Club:* Athenæum.

CROMER, 4th Earl of, *cr* 1901; **Evelyn Rowland Esmond Baring;** Baron Cromer, 1892; Viscount Cromer, 1899; Viscount Errington, 1901; Director: Inchcape Pacific Ltd, 1985–94; Managing Director, Inchcape Special Markets Ltd, 1990–94; *b* 3 June 1946; *e s* of 3rd Earl of Cromer, KG, GCMG, MBE, PC and of Hon. Esmé Harmsworth, CVO, *d* of 2nd Viscount Rothermere; *S* father, 1991; *m* 1971, Plern Isarangkun Na Ayudhya (marr. diss. 1993); 2nd, 1993, Shelly Hu Cheng-Yu, *e d* of Hu Guoquin, Shanghai; one *s*. *Educ:* Eton. Deputy Chairman: The Motor Transport Co. of Guangdong & Hong Kong Ltd (China), 1979–94; Land-Ocean Inchcape Container Transport Co. Ltd (China), 1985–94; Managing Director: Inchcape (China) Ltd, 1979–94; Inchcape Vietnam Ltd, 1987–94; Director: Cluff Oil (Hong Kong) Ltd; Cluff Oil China Ltd; Dodwell Travel Ltd (Hong Kong), 1988–94; China & Eastern Investments Ltd (Hong Kong), 1980–83; Khmer Agencies Co. Ltd (Cambodia), 1990–94; Inchcape Saigon Motors Corporation (Vietnam), 1988–94; New Asia Inchcape Business Systems Ltd (China), 1989–94; Jardine Fleming China Region Fund Inc. (USA); China & Eastern Investments Ltd; Lazard Vietnam Fund Ltd (Guernsey). Chm., Lloyd George Standard Chartered China Fund Ltd (Hong Kong). Mem. St John's Council (Hong Kong), 1980–85. *Recreations:* mountain climbing, deep sea diving. *Heir: s* Viscount Errington, *qv*. *Address:* GPO Box 36, Hong Kong. *T:* (office) (852) 8424600; House of Lords, SW1A 0PW. *Clubs:* White's, Oriental; Siam Society; Hong Kong, China (Hong Kong).

CROMPTON, Dan, QPM 1990; Chief Constable, Nottinghamshire Constabulary, since 1990; *b* 15 Feb. 1941; *s* of Arthur and Elizabeth Crompton; *m* 1962, Olive Ramsden; one *s*. *Educ:* Didsbury Technical Sch., Manchester. Manchester City Police, 1960–68; Manchester and Salford Police, 1968–74; Greater Manchester Police, 1974–87; Nottinghamshire Constabulary, 1987–. *Recreations:* reading, popular classics, gardening, cricket, Rugby. *Address:* Police HQ, Sherwood Lodge, Arnold, Nottingham NG5 8PP. *T:* Nottingham (0115) 967 0999.

CROMPTON, Prof. Gareth, FRCP, FFCM; Professor of Public Health Medicine, University of Wales College of Medicine, since 1989; Chief Administrative Medical Officer and Director of Public Health Medicine, South Glamorgan Health Authority, since 1989; *b* 9 Jan. 1937; *s* of late Edward Crompton, Drefach-Felindre, Dyfed; *m* 1965; one *d*. *Educ:* Llandysul Grammar Sch.; Welsh Nat. Sch. of Medicine. MB, BCh Wales, 1960; DObstRCOG 1962; DPH Wales, 1964; FFCM 1976; FRCP 1986 (MRCP 1980). County Med. Officer, County Welfare Officer and Principal Sch. Med. Officer, Anglesey CC, 1966–73; Area Med. Officer, Gwynedd Health Authority, 1974–77; CMO, Welsh Office, 1978–89. Specialty Advr, Health Service Comr for England and Wales, 1974–77; Advr in Wales, Faculty of Community Medicine, 1974–77. Chm., Anglesey Disablement Adv. Cttee, 1969–77; Sec., Fluoridation Study Gp, Soc. of Med. Officers of Health, 1969–73; Mem., Welsh Hosp. Bd, 1970–74. Member: GMC, 1981–83 and 1987–89; Bd, PHLS, 1990–; Exec. Bd, FPHM, 1990–. Med. Fellow, Council of Europe, 1971. QHP 1984–87. *Publications:* papers on the effects of fluoridated water supplies on dental caries, and the epidemiology and management of chronic sickness and disablement. *Recreations:* bowls, golf, watching Rugby, reading contemporary Welsh verse. *Address:* Temple of Peace and Health, Cathays Park, Cardiff CF1 3NW. *T:* Cardiff (01222) 231021.

CROMPTON, Ian William; His Honour Judge Crompton; a Circuit Judge, since 1994; *b* 28 June 1936; *s* of Thomas and Hilda Crompton; *m* 1962, Audrey (*née* Hopewell); two *s*. *Educ:* Manchester Grammar School; Victoria University of Manchester. LLB. Asst Solicitor, County Magistrates' Court, Strangeways, Manchester, 1961–62; Asst Solicitor, O'Collier, Littler & Kilbeg, 1962–65, Partner, 1965–72; Clerk to the Justices: County Magistrates' Court, Strangeways, 1972–74; Eccles Magistrates' Court, 1974–83; Stipendiary Magistrate for S Yorks, 1983–94; a Recorder, 1989–94. *Recreations:* ballroom and Latin American dancing, golf. *Club:* Hallamshire Golf (Sheffield).

CROMPTON, Kenneth Charles; Agent-General for Victoria, since 1993; *b* 19 July 1948; *s* of late Charles Frederic Crompton and of Margaret Joan Crompton; *m* 1971, Elizabeth Anne Meek; one *s* two *d*. Educ: Melbourne Univ. (LLB). Solicitor, Morris Komesaroff, Aarons & Co., 1971–75; Seton Williams & Smyth, 1975–79; Gen. Manager, Legal and Technical Services, Victorian Chamber of Manufactures, 1979–87; Dir, Industrial Relations, 1987–88, Chief Exec. (Vic.), 1988–92, Aust. Chamber of Manufactures; Chief Exec., Corporate Counsel Pty, 1992–. *Recreations:* wind surfing, tennis, photography, walking. *Address:* Victoria House, Melbourne Place, Strand, WC2B 4LG. *T:* 0171–836 2656. *Clubs:* Royal Over-Seas League; Athenæum (Melbourne); Royal Automobile (Vic.); Melbourne Cricket.

CROMWELL, 7th Baron *cr* 1375 (called out of abeyance, 1923); **Godfrey John Bewicke-Copley;** *b* 4 March 1960; *s* of 6th Baron Cromwell and of Vivian, *y d* of late Hugh de Lisle Penfold, Isle of Man; *S* father, 1982; *m* 1990, Elizabeth, *d* of John Hawksley. *Heir: b* Hon. Thomas David Bewicke-Copley, *b* 6 Aug. 1964. *Address:* House of Lords, SW1A 0PW.

CRONIN, Vincent Archibald Patrick; author; *b* 24 May 1924; *s* of late Archibald Joseph Cronin, MD, MRCP, DPH and of Agnes Mary Gibson, MB, ChB; *m* 1949, Chantal, *d* of Comte Jean de Rolland; two *s* three *d*. *Educ:* Ampleforth; Harvard; Trinity Coll., Oxford. Rifle Bde, 1943–45. *Publications:* The Golden Honeycomb, 1954; The Wise Man from the West, 1955; The Last Migration, 1957; A Pearl to India, 1959; The Letter after Z, 1960; Louis XIV, 1964; Four Women in Pursuit of an Ideal, 1965; The Florentine Renaissance, 1967; The Flowering of the Renaissance, 1970; Napoleon, 1971; Louis and Antoinette, 1974; trans., Giscard d'Estaing, Towards a New Democracy, 1977; Catherine, Empress of all the Russias, 1978; The View from Planet Earth, 1981; Paris on the Eve, 1989; Paris: City of Light 1919–1939, 1995. *Address:* Manoir de Brion, Dragey Par, 50530 Sartilly, France.

CROOK, family name of **Baron Crook.**

CROOK, 2nd Baron *cr* 1947, of Carshalton, Surrey; **Douglas Edwin Crook,** CEng, MICE; *b* 19 Nov. 1926; *s* of 1st Baron Crook and Ida Gertrude (*d* 1985), *d* of Joseph Haddon; *S* father, 1989; *m* 1954, Ellenor, *d* of late Robert Rouse; one *s* one *d*. *Educ:* Whitgift School, Croydon; Imperial Coll., London (BSc Eng, DIC, ACGI). *Heir: s* Hon. Robert Douglas Edwin Crook, BSc, MBA [*b* 19 May 1955; *m* 1981, Suzanne Jane Robinson, BA, LLB; two *s*]. *Address:* Ridge Hill Barn, Etchinghill, Folkestone, Kent CT18 8BP.

CROOK, Arthur Charles William; Consultant to Times Newspapers, since 1974; Editor, The Times Literary Supplement, 1959–74; *b* 16 Feb. 1912; *m* 1948, Sarita Mary Vivien Bushell (marr. diss.); one *s* two *d*. Editorial staff of The Times; Asst Editor, The Times Literary Supplement, 1951–59. Pres. and Chm., Royal Literary Fund, 1984–90. *Recreation:* theatre. *Address:* 70 Regent's Park Road, NW1 7SX. *T:* 0171–722 8446. *Club:* Garrick.

CROOK, Colin, FEng; Chairman, Corporate Technology Committee, Citicorp, since 1990; *b* 1 June 1942; *s* of Richard and Ruth Crook; *m* 1965, Dorothy Jean Taylor; two *d*. *Educ:* Harris Coll., Preston; Liverpool Polytechnic (ACT Hons; Dip. Elec. Engrg). FEng 1981 (CEng 1977). MIEE 1976; MIERE 1976; MIEEE 1976; MACM 1977. Electronics Engr, Canadian Marconi, 1962–64; Computer Designer, The Plessey Co., 1964–68; Systems Engr, Eli Lilly Co., 1968–69; sen. appts, Motorola Semiconductor Div., Switzerland and USA, 1969–79; sen. appts, The Rank Organisation, 1979–83, including: Man. Dir, RPI, 1979–81; Man. Dir, Zynar, CEO Nestar Systems, USA, 1981–83; Mem. of Bd, British Telecom, and Man. Dir, BT Enterprises, 1983–84; Sen. Vice Pres., Data General Corp., 1984–89. *Publications:* articles and learned papers on electronics and computers. *Recreations:* photography, walking, reading, wine, sailing. *Address:* The Old School House, Harvest Hill, Hedsor, Bourne End, Bucks SL8 5JJ. *T:* Bourne End (016285) 27479.

CROOK, Frances Rachel; Director, Howard League for Penal Reform, since 1986; *b* 18 Dec. 1952; *d* of Sheila Sibson-Turnbull and Maurice Crook; one *d*. *Educ:* Camden School; Liverpool University (BA Hons History). Historical Researcher, Liverpool, 1977–78; Teacher, 1978–79; Campaign Co-ordinator, Amnesty International, 1980–85. Councillor (Lab) Barnet, 1982–90. *Recreation:* demonstrations. *Address:* The Howard League, 708 Holloway Road, N19 3NL. *T:* 0171–281 7722.

CROOK, Maj.-Gen. James Cooper, MD, FRCPath; late RAMC, retired 1981; Civilian Medical Practitioner, Army Blood Supply Depot, Aldershot, 1982–88; *b* 19 March 1923; *s* of late Francis William Crook and late Mary Catherine Perry, *d* of late Sir Edwin Cooper Perry, GCVO, MD, Superintendent of Guy's Hospital and Vice-Chancellor of London Univ.; *m* 1950, Ruth, *d* of late W. A. Bellamy of Santa Cruz, Tenerife; one *s* two *d*. *Educ:* Worksop Coll.; Guy's Hosp. Med. Sch., Univ. of London. MB BS 1946, MD 1953; DTM&H 1952; FRCPath 1968. Guy's and Pembury Hosps, 1946; Commnd RAMC 1946; served Egypt and N Africa, 1946–49; Pathologist, Queen Alexandra's Mil. Hosp., 1950; David Bruce Laboratories, 1953; med. liaison officer to MRC Radiobiology Unit, AERE, Harwell, 1954; Asst Dir of Pathology, Middle East, 1957; Cons. in Pathology, 1958; RAMC Specialist, Chem. Defence Estab., Porton, 1960; Asst Dir of Pathology, Eastern Comd, 1963; ADGMS, 1966; Comd Cons. in Pathology, BAOR, 1969; Prof. of Pathology, Royal Army Med. Coll., 1974; Dir of Army Pathology and Consulting Pathologist to the Army, 1976–81; Hon. Physician to HM The Queen, 1978–81. Hon. Col, 380 Blood Supply Unit RAMC, TAVR, 1982–86. *Publications:* articles in Jl of Clinical Path., Nature, Med. Sci. and the Law, Jl of RAMC, British Jl of Radiology. *Recreations:* gardening, beekeeping. *Address:* Egloshayle, Fore Street, Kingsand, Torpoint, Cornwall PL10 1NB. *T:* Plymouth (01752) 823666.

CROOK, Prof. John Anthony, MA; Professor of Ancient History, University of Cambridge, 1979–84; Fellow of St John's College, Cambridge, since 1951; *b* 5 Nov. 1921; *s* of Herbert Crook and Hilda Naomi (*née* Flower). *Educ:* St Mary's C of E Sch., Balham; Dulwich Coll.; St John's Coll., Cambridge 1939–41 and 1945–47 (John Stewart of Rannoch Scholar); BA 1947, Craven Student, 1947; Research Student of Balliol Coll., Oxford, 1947–48; MA (Cantab) 1949. Served War, Private and Corporal, 9th Royal Fusiliers, 1941–43 (PoW Stalag VIIIB, 1943–45); Sgt, RAEC, 1945. Univ. Asst Lectr in Classics, Reading Univ., 1948, Lectr, 1949–51; St John's Coll., Cambridge: Tutor, 1956–64; President, 1971–75; Univ. Asst Lectr in Classics, Cambridge Univ., 1953, Lectr, 1955–71, Reader in Roman History and Law, 1971–79, and Brereton Reader, 1974–79. FBA 1970–80. Dr jur *hc* Freiburg, 1995. *Publications:* Consilium Principis, 1955; Law and Life of Rome, 1967; Legal Advocacy in the Roman World, 1995. *Address:* St John's College, Cambridge CB2 1TP. *T:* Cambridge (01223) 338621.

CROOK, Prof. Joseph Mordaunt, FBA 1988; Professor of Architectural History, University of London at Royal Holloway and Bedford New College (formerly at Bedford College), since 1981; *b* 27 Feb. 1937; *e s* of late Austin Mordaunt Crook and late Irene Woolfenden; *m* 1st, 1964, Margaret, *o d* of late James Mulholland; 2nd, 1975, Susan, *o d* of late F. H. Mayor. *Educ:* Wimbledon Coll.; Brasenose Coll., Oxford. BA (1st cl. Mod. Hist.) 1958; DPhil 1961, MA 1962, Oxon; FSA 1972. Research Fellow: Inst. of Historical

Res., 1961–62; Bedford Coll., London, 1962–63; Warburg Inst., London, 1970–71; Asst Lectr, Univ. of Leicester, 1963–65; Lectr, Bedford Coll., London, 1965–75, Reader in Architectural Hist., 1975–81; Dir, Victorian Studies Centre, RHBNC, 1990–. Slade Prof. of Fine Art, Oxford Univ., 1979–80; Vis. Fellow: Brasenose Coll., Oxford, 1979–80; Humanities Res. Centre, ANU, Canberra, 1985; Waynflete Lectr and Vis. Fellow, Magdalen Coll., Oxford, 1984–85; Vis. Fellow, Gonville and Caius Coll., Cambridge, 1986; Humanities Fellow, Princeton Univ., 1990. Public Orator, Univ. of London, 1988–90. Member: Exec. Cttee, Soc. Architect. Historians of Gt Britain, 1964–77 (Pres., 1980–84); RIBA Drawings Cttee, 1969–75; Exec. Cttee, Georgian Gp, 1970–77; Exec. Cttee, Victorian Soc., 1970–77, Council, 1978–88; Historic Buildings Council for England, 1974–80; Council, Soc. of Antiquaries, 1980–82; Adv. Council, Paul Mellon Centre for Studies in British Art, 1985–90; Gen. Cttee, Incorp. Church Building Soc., 1987–; Council, British Acad., 1989–92; Adv. Bd for Redundant Churches, 1991–; Westminster Abbey Architectural Adv. Panel, 1993–. Freeman, 1979, Liveryman, 1984, Worshipful Co. of Goldsmiths. Editor, Architectural History, 1967–75. *Publications:* The Greek Revival, 1968; Victorian Architecture: A Visual Anthology, 1971; The British Museum, 1972, 2nd edn 1973; The Greek Revival: Neo-Classical Attitudes in British Architecture 1760–1870, 1972, 2nd edn 1995; The Reform Club, 1973; (jtly) The History of the King's Works, Vol. VI, 1782–1851, 1973 (Hitchcock Medallion, 1974), Vol. V, 1660–1782, 1976; William Burges and the High Victorian Dream, 1981; (jtly) Axel Haig and The Victorian Vision of the Middle Ages, 1984; The Dilemma of Style: architectural ideas from the picturesque to the post-modern, 1987, 2nd edn 1989; John Carter and the Mind of the Gothic Revival, 1995; *edited:* Eastlake, A History of the Gothic Revival, 1970, rev. edn, 1978; Emmet, Six Essays, 1972; Kerr, The Gentleman's House, 1972; The Strange Genius of William Burges, 1981; Clark, The Gothic Revival, 1995; *contrib. to:* Concerning Architecture, 1967; The Country Seat, 1970; The Age of Neo-Classicism, 1972; The Building of Early America, 1976; Seven Victorian Architects, 1976; The Ruskin Polygon, 1982; In Search of Modern Architecture, 1983; Rediscovering Hellenism, 1989; The University of London and the World of Learning 1836–1986, 1990; Brooks's: a social history, 1991; London: World City 1800–1840, 1992; Scottish Country Houses, 1995; The Question of Style in Philosophy and the Arts, 1995; numerous articles in Architect. History, Architect. Review, Country Life, History Today, Jl Royal Soc. Arts, RIBA Jl, Antiquaries Jl, TLS, Architect Design, etc. *Recreation:* strolling. *Address:* 55 Gloucester Avenue, NW1 7BA. *T:* 0171–485 8280. *Clubs:* Athenæum, Brooks's.

CROOK, Kenneth Roy, CMG 1978; HM Diplomatic Service, retired; Ambassador to Afghanistan, 1976–79; *b* 30 July 1920; *s* of Alexander Crook, Prescot, Lancs, and Margaret Kay Crook; *m* 1943, Freda Joan Vidler; two *d*. *Educ:* Prescot Grammar Sch., Lancs; Skerry's Coll., Liverpool. Appointed to: Board of Trade, 1937; Min. of War Transport, 1939. Royal Navy, 1941–46. Board of Trade, 1946–49; Commonwealth Relations Office, 1949; Second Sec., Canberra, 1951–54; First Sec., Madras, 1956–59; Deputy High Commissioner: Peshawar, W Pakistan, 1962–64; Dacca, E Pakistan, 1964–67; Counsellor, FCO, 1967; Head of Information Research Dept, FCO, 1969–71; Governor, Cayman Is, 1971–74; Canadian Nat. Defence Coll., 1974–75; Head of Science and Technology Dept, FCO, 1975–76. *Recreations:* walking, gardening, music appreciation. *Address:* 16 Burntwood Road, Sevenoaks, Kent TN13 1PT. *T:* Sevenoaks (01732) 452774.

CROOK, Brig. Paul Edwin, CBE 1965 (OBE 1946); DSO 1957; *b* 19 April 1915; *s* of late Herbert Crook and Christine Crook, Lyme Regis; *m* 1st, 1944, Joan (marr. diss. 1967), *d* of late William Lewis; one *d*; 2nd, 1967, Betty, *d* of late John William Wyles. *Educ:* Uppingham Sch.; Emmanuel Coll., Cambridge. BA 1936, MA 1956. Commnd into QORWK Regt, 1935; served: India and Palestine, 1937–39; War of 1939–45, Africa, NW Europe, Burma; Chief Civil Affairs Officer (Col), Netherlands East Indies, 1946; comd 3rd Bn The Parachute Regt, 1954–57; Suez Ops, 1956; comd Army Airborne Trng and Develt Centre, 1959–62; Comdr and Chief of Staff, Jamaica Defence Force, 1962–65; Security Ops Advisor to High Comr for Aden and S Arabia, 1965–67; Comdr, Rhine Area, 1969–70. Col, 1959; Brig., 1963; retired 1971. ADC to The Queen, 1965. Hon. Col, 16 Lincoln Co. Parachute Regt (VR), 1974–79; Dep. Hon. Col, The Parachute Regt (TAVR): 15th (Scottish) Bn, 1979–83; 4th Bn, 1984–85. Chm., Lincs County Scouts, 1975–88; Pres., British Assoc. of Paragliding Clubs. Bronze Star (US), 1945. *Publication:* Came the Dawn, 1989. *Recreations:* cricket, golf, jazz. *Address:* The Longhouse, Diptford, Totnes, Devon TQ9 7LY. *T:* Gara Bridge (01548) 821609. *Clubs:* Naval and Military, MCC; Jamaica (W Indies).

CROOKENDEN, Maj.-Gen. George Wayet Derek; DL; Emeritus Fellow, Peterhouse, Cambridge, since 1989; *b* 11 Dec. 1920; *o s* of late Lt-Col John Crookenden and Iris Margherita Gay; *m* 1948, Elizabeth Mary Angela Bourke; one *s* one *d*. *Educ:* Winchester Coll.; Christ Church, Oxford. Commnd Royal Artillery, 1941. GSO1, SHAPE, 1961–62; CO, 19 Field Regt, RA, 1962–64; Comdr, 7 Artillery Bde, 1964–67; Exercise Controller, CICC (West), 1969–71; Chief, British Commanders-in-Chief Liaison Mission, 1971–72; C of S, Contingencies Planning, SHAPE, 1972–75. Col Comdt, RA, 1977–82. Fellow and Sen. Bursar, Peterhouse, Cambridge, 1975–88. DL Cambs, 1984. *Address:* c/o Lloyds Bank, 95–97 Regent Street, Cambridge CB2 1BQ. *Club:* Army and Navy.

CROOKENDEN, Lt-Gen. Sir Napier, KCB 1970 (CB 1966); DSO 1945; OBE 1954; DL; Lieutenant, HM Tower of London, 1975–81; *b* 31 Aug. 1915; 2nd *s* of late Col Arthur Crookenden, CBE, DSO; *m* 1948, Patricia Nassau, *d* of 2nd Baron Kindersley, CBE, MC, and of Nancy Farnsworth, *d* of Dr Geoffrey Boyd; two *s* two *d*. *Educ:* Wellington Coll.; RMC, Sandhurst. Commissioned, Cheshire Regt, 1935; Bde Major, 6th Airlanding Bde, 1943–44; CO, 9th Bn, The Parachute Regt, 1944–46; GSO1 (Plans) to Dir of Ops, Malaya, 1952–54; Comdr, 16th Parachute Bde, 1960–61; idc 1962; Dir, Land/Air Warfare MoD (Army Dept), 1964–66; Commandant, RMCS, Shrivenham, 1967–69; GOC-in-C, Western Comd, 1969–72. Col, The Cheshire Regt, 1969–71; Col Comdt, The Prince of Wales Div., 1971–74. Director: SE Regional Bd, Lloyds Bank Ltd, 1973–86; Flextech Ltd, 1978–86. A Trustee, Imperial War Museum, 1973–83. Chm., SS&AFA, 1974–85; a Vice-Pres., RUSI, 1978–85. DL Kent, 1979. *Publications:* Dropzone Normandy, 1976; Airborne at War, 1978; Battle of the Bulge 1944, 1980. *Club:* Army and Navy.

CROOKS, Air Marshal David Manson, CB 1985; OBE 1969; FRAeS; Chief of Defence Staff, New Zealand Armed Forces, 1986–87, retired; aviation and defence industry consultant, since 1988; *b* 8 Dec. 1931; *s* of James and Gladys Meta Crooks; *m* 1954, Barbara Naismith McDougall; four *d*. *Educ:* Rangiora, NZ. Joined RNZAF, 1951; Head, NZ Defence Liaison Staff, Singapore, 1967–70; Commanding Officer: RNZAF Base: Ohakea, 1971–72; Wigram, 1973–74; RCDS, UK, 1974–75; AOC RNZAF Ops Gp, 1978–80; DCAS, 1980–83; CAS, RNZAF, 1983–86. Chairman: Friends of RNZAF Museum, 1988–; Patriotic Fund Bd, 1992–; Defence Cttee, NZRSA, 1992– (Mem. Dom. Exec. Cttee, 1992–); Member: Bd, RNZAF Museum Trust, 1988–; Public Adv. Cttee on Arms Control, 1991–; President: Air Cadet League of NZ, 1989–; RNZAF Assoc., 1992–. *Recreations:* tramping, gardening, reading, sailing. *Address:* 13 Burrows Avenue, Karori, Wellington 5, New Zealand. *T:* (4) 4764588. *Club:* Wellington (Wellington, NZ).

CROOM-JOHNSON, Rt. Hon. Sir David Powell, Kt 1971; DSC 1944; VRD 1953; PC 1984; a Lord Justice of Appeal, 1984–89; *b* 28 Nov. 1914; 3rd *s* of late Hon. Sir Reginald Powell Croom-Johnson, sometime a Judge of the High Court, and late Lady (Ruby) Croom-Johnson; *m* 1940, Barbara Douglas (*d* 1994), *y d* of late Erskine Douglas Warren, Toronto; one *d*. *Educ:* The Hall, Hampstead; Stowe Sch.; Trinity Hall, Cambridge (MA; Hon. Fellow, 1985). RNVR (London Div.) 1936–53; served with Royal Navy, 1939–46. Called to Bar, Gray's Inn, 1938, Master of the Bench, 1964, Treasurer, 1981; Western Circuit. QC 1958; Recorder of Winchester, 1962–71; Judge of Courts of Appeal, Jersey and Guernsey, 1966–71; Judge of High Court of Justice, Queen's Bench Div., 1971–84. Member: Gen. Council of the Bar, 1958–62; Senate of Inns of Court, 1966–70. Conducted Home Office Inquiry concerning amalg. of Lancs Police Areas, 1967–68; Vice-Chm., Home Office Cttee on Mentally Abnormal Offenders, 1972–75; Chm., Crown Agents Tribunal, 1978–82. Mem., Council, Oakdene Sch., 1956–79; Chm., Knightsbridge Assoc., 1965–71. *Recreations:* books, music. *Address:* 59 Coleherne Court, Old Brompton Road, SW5 0EF. *Club:* Garrick.

CROOME, (John) Lewis, CMG 1957; *b* 10 June 1907; *s* of John and Caroline Croome; *m* 1st, 1931, Honoria Renée Minturn (*née* Scott; as Honor Croome, Editorial Staff of The Economist) (*d* 1960); four *s* one *d* (and one *s* decd); 2nd, 1961, Pamela Siola, *o d* of Lt-Col Tyrrel Hawker, Hurstbourne Priors, Hants; one *s*. *Educ:* Henry Thornton Sch., Clapham; London Sch. of Economics. Imperial Economic Cttee, 1931–39; Ministry of Food, 1939–48; Deputy (later Head), British Food Mission, Ottawa, 1942–46; HM Treasury (Central Economic Planning Staff), 1948–51; Min. of Food, 1951–54; UK Delegation to OEEC, Paris, 1954–57; Ministry of Agriculture, Fisheries and Food, 1957–58; Chief Overseas Relations Officer, UKAEA, 1958–72, retired. *Recreations:* painting, reading. *Address:* 8 The Holdens, Bosham, West Sussex PO18 8LN. *T:* Bosham (01243) 572292.

CROPPER, Hilary Mary; Chief Executive, FI Group, since 1985; *b* 9 Jan. 1941; *d* of Arnold Trueman and Madeline Emily Trueman (*née* Sutton); *m* 1963, Peter John Cropper; one *s* two *d*. *Educ:* Univ. of Salford (BSc Hons Maths). Sen. management positions, ICL, 1970–85; Non-exec. Dir, TSB, 1987–90; Non-exec. Member: POB, 1990–; BOTB, 1992–. Mem. Council, Inst. of Dirs, 1991–. Freeman, City of London, 1987. CIMgt, FBCS, FRSA. *Address:* FI Group, Campus 300, Maylands Avenue, Hemel Hempstead, Herts HP2 7EZ. *T:* Hemel Hempstead (01442) 233339; Woodlands, Pink Road, Parslows Hillock, Princes Risborough, Bucks HP27 0RJ. *T:* High Wycombe (01494) 488227.

CROPPER, James Anthony, FCA; Chairman, James Cropper PLC, since 1971; Lord-Lieutenant of Cumbria, since 1994 (Vice Lord-Lieutenant, 1991–94); *b* 22 Dec. 1938; *s* of Anthony Charles Cropper and Philippa Mary Gloria (*née* Clutterbuck); *m* 1967, Susan Rosemary (*née* Davis); one *s* one *d* (and one *s* decd). *Educ:* Eton; Magdalene Coll., Cambridge (BA). FCA 1966. James Cropper, 1966–, Dir, 1967–; Dir, East Lancashire Paper Group, 1982–84. Member: Lancs River Authority, 1968–74; NW Water Authority, 1973–80, 1983–89; Dir, NW Water Group, 1989–90. Dir, Cumbria Rural Enterprise Agency, 1986–; Mem., NW Business Leadership Team, 1991–. Pres., British Paper and Bd Fedn, 1988–90. Chm., Frieda Scott Charitable Trust, 1981–94; Trustee, Abbot Hall Art Gall. and Mus., 1992– (Chm. Govs, 1983–88). Member (Indep.): S Westmorland RDC, 1967–74; S Lakeland DC, 1974–77. High Sheriff of Westmorland, 1971; DL Cumbria, 1985. *Recreations:* shooting, wind-surfing. *Address:* Tolson Hall, Kendal, Cumbria LA9 5SE. *T:* Kendal (01539) 722011. *Club:* Brooks's.

CROPPER, Peter John, CBE 1988; *b* 18 June 1927; *s* of late Walter Cecil Cropper and Kathleen Cropper; *m* 1965, Rosemary Winning; one *s*. *Educ:* Hitchin Grammar Sch.; Gonville and Caius Coll., Cambridge (MA). Served Royal Artillery, 1945–48. Conservative Research Dept, 1951–53, 1975–79, Dir, 1982–84; investment analyst, Mem. of London Stock Exchange, 1953–75; Special Adviser: to Chief Sec. to the Treasury, 1979–82; to Chancellor of the Exchequer, 1984–88. *Address:* 77 Hadlow Road, Tonbridge, Kent TN9 1QB. *Club:* Reform.

CROSBIE, Hon. John Carnell; PC (Canada) 1979; Counsel, Halley, Hunt, Barristers and Solicitors, St John's; *b* 30 Jan. 1931; *s* of Chesley Arthur Crosbie and Jessie Carnell; *m* 1952, Jane Furneaux; two *s* one *d*. *Educ:* Bishop Field Coll., St John's, Nfld; St Andrew's Coll., Aurora, Ont.; Queen's Univ., Kingston, Ont. (Pol. Sc. and Econs); Dalhousie Univ., Halifax, NS (Law); LSE, London, Eng. Joined Newfoundland Law Soc. and Newfoundland Bar; entered law practice, St John's, 1957; Mem. City Council, St John's, 1965; Dep. Mayor, 1966; Minister of Municipal Affairs and Housing, Province of Newfoundland, (Lib. Admin), July 1966; MHA, Prov. of Newfoundland, Sept. 1966; Minister of Health, 1967; resigned from Govt, 1968; re-elected Member for St John's West (Progressive Conservative), Provincial election, 1971; Minister of Finance, Pres. of Treasury Bd and Minister of Econ. Develt, 1972–74; Minister of Fisheries, Min. for Intergovtl Affairs and Govt House Leader, 1974–75; Minister of Mines and Energy and Minister for Intergovtl Affairs, 1975–76; resigned from Newfoundland Govt, Sept. 1976; elected to House of Commons, Oct. 1976; MP (PC) St John's West, Newfoundland, 1976–93; Chm. of Progressive Conservative Caucus Cttee on Energy, 1977; PC parly critic for Industry, Trade and Commerce, 1977–79; Minister of Finance, 1979–80; Party Finance Critic, 1980; Party External Affairs Critic, 1981–83; Minister of Justice and Attorney General, 1984–86; Minister of Transport, 1986–88; Minister for International Trade, 1988–91; Minister for Fisheries and Oceans and for Atlantic Canada Opportunities Agency, 1991–93. Chancellor, Meml Univ. of Newfoundland, 1994–. *Address:* PO Box 23119, St John's, Newfoundland, A1B 4J9, Canada.

CROSBIE, William, BA; RSA 1973; RGI 1977; artist; *b* Hankow, China, 31 Jan. 1915; *s* of Archibald Shearer Crosbie, marine engineer, and Mary Edgar, both Scottish; *m* 1st, 1944, M. G. McPhail (decd); one *d* (and one *d* decd); 2nd, 1975, Margaret Anne Roger. *Educ:* Chinese Tutor; Renfrew primary sch.; Glasgow Academy; Glasgow Sch. of Art, Glasgow Univ. (4 yrs under Forrester Wilson). Haldane Travelling Schol., 1935, for 3 yr period of study in British Schs in Athens, Rome and Paris (Beaux Arts); studied history and theory of techniques, in Beaux Arts and Sorbonne, and finally took a post-grad. qualif. in these (continues to acquire craftsmanship); passed into studio of Fernand Leger, Paris, and remained until war declared. Served War of 1939–45: ambulance service, WVS driving pool, and at sea. Has exhibited, on average, every two yrs, 1946–; principally one-man exhibns: Glasgow, Edinburgh, London, etc; also in USA, Brussels, Hamburg, etc. *Works in:* Kelvingrove Galls, Glasgow; Scottish provincial galls; Edinburgh City Arts Centre (mural), 1980; Scottish Gall. of Modern Art, 1980; Nat. Portrait Gall. of Scotland, 1994; Sydney State Gall., Australia; Wellington, NZ; Royal collection, UK, etc; also in many private collections. *Recreation:* sailing. *Address:* Rushes House, 10 Winchester Road, Petersfield, Hants GU32 3BY. *Clubs:* Glasgow Art; Royal Northern and Clyde Yacht (Rhu).

CROSFIELD, Rev. Canon (George) Philip (Chorley), OBE 1990; Provost of St Mary's Cathedral, Edinburgh, 1970–90, retired, Hon. Canon, 1991; *b* 9 Sept. 1924; *s* of James Chorley Crosfield and Marjorie Louise Crosfield; *m* 1956, Susan Mary Jullion (*née* Martin); one *s* two *d*. *Educ:* George Watson's Coll., Edinburgh; Selwyn Coll., Cambridge (BA 1950; MA 1955). Royal Artillery, 1942–46 (Captain). Priest, 1952; Asst Curate: St David's, Pilton, Edinburgh, 1951–53; St Andrew's, St Andrews, 1953–55; Rector, St Cuthbert's, Hawick, 1955–60; Chaplain, Gordonstoun School, 1960–68; Canon and Vice Provost, St

Mary's Cathedral, Edinburgh, 1968–70. *Recreations:* walking, reading, carpentry. *Address:* 21 Biggar Road, Silverburn, Penicuik EH26 9LQ. *T:* Penicuik (01968) 676607.

CROSLAND, Susan Barnes; writer; *b* Baltimore, Maryland; *y c* of Susan Owens and Mark Skinner Watson; *m* 1st, Patrick Skene Catling (marr. diss.); two *d*; 2nd, Rt Hon. (Charles) Anthony (Raven) Crosland, PC, MP (*d* 1977). Journalism: Sunday Express, 1960–64; freelance, 1964–; profile-writer and columnist, Sunday Times and various jls. Trustee, Nat. Portrait Gallery, 1978–92. *Publications:* Behind the Image, 1974; Tony Crosland, 1982; Looking Out, Looking In, 1987; *novels:* Ruling Passions, 1989; Dangerous Games, 1991; The Magnates, 1994. *Recreation:* freedom. *Address:* 16 Stanford Court, 45 Cornwall Gardens, SW7 4AB. *Club:* Academy.

CROSS, family name of **Viscount Cross.**

CROSS, 3rd Viscount, *cr* 1886; **Assheton Henry Cross;** late Lieut Scots Guards; *b* 7 May 1920; *e s* of 2nd Viscount and Maud Evelyn (who *m* 2nd, 1944, Guy Hope Coldwell (*d* 1948), Stoke Lodge, Ludlow, Salop; she *d* 1976), *d* of late Maj.-Gen. Inigo Jones, CVO, CB, Kelston Park, Bath; *S* father, 1932; *m* 1952, Patricia Mary (marr. diss., 1957; she *m* 1960, Comdr G. H. H. Culme-Seymour), *e d* of E. P. Hewetson, JP, The Craig, Windermere, Westmorland; two *d*; *m* 1972, Mrs Victoria Webb (marr. diss. 1977); *m* 1983, Mrs Patricia J. Rossiter (marr. diss. 1987). *Educ:* Shrewsbury; Magdalene Coll., Cambridge. *Heir:* none. *Club:* Cavalry and Guards.

CROSS, Alexander Galbraith, MA, MD, FRCS; Ophthalmic Surgeon; lately Dean of the Medical School, St Mary's Hospital; Civilian Consultant in Ophthalmology, RN, 1946–76; Consultant Surgeon, Moorfields Eye Hospital, 1947–73; Consultant Ophthalmic Surgeon, St Mary's Hospital, 1946–73; Consultant Ophthalmic Surgeon, Royal National Throat, Nose, and Ear Hospital, 1954–73; Ophthalmic Surgeon, St Dunstan's, 1946–84; Hon. Consultant Ophthalmologist, Royal National Institute for the Blind, 1968–82; *b* 29 March 1908; *er s* of late Walter Galbraith Cross and Mary Stewart Cross, Wimbledon; *m* 1939, Eileen Longman, twin *d* of late Dr H. B. Corry, Liss, Hants; one *d*. *Educ:* King's Coll. Sch.; Gonville and Caius Coll., Cambridge; St Mary's Hosp., London (University Scholar). Meadows Prize, 1932, Broadbent and Agnes Cope Prizes, 1933, Cheadle Gold Medallist, 1933, St Mary's Hospital. House Phys. and House Surg., St Mary's, 1933–35; House Surg. and Sen. Res. Officer, Moorfields Eye Hosp., 1937–39; Ophthalmic Surgeon: West Middlesex Hosp., 1938–48; Tite Street Children's Hosp., 1939–48; Princess Beatrice Hosp., 1939–47; Royal Masonic Hosp., 1961–71. Wing Comdr, RAFVR, 1941–46 and Adviser in Ophthalmology, South-East Asia Air Forces. Examiner in Fellowship and in Diploma of Ophthalmology for RCS and in Ophthalmology for Univ. of Bristol; Recognised Teacher of Ophthalmology, University of London. Co-opted Mem. Council RCS, 1963–68. Mem. Bd of Governors: St Mary's Hosp., 1951–60; Moorfields Eye Hosp., 1962–65 and 1968–75. Mem. Paddington Group Hosp. Management Cttee, 1952–60. Pres. Ophthalmological Soc. of UK, 1975–77 (Sec. 1949–51; Vice-Pres., 1963–66); Member: RSocMed (Sec., Ophthalmic Section, 1951; Vice-Pres., 1960; Hon. Mem. 1979); BMA (Sec., Ophthalmic Section, 1948; Vice-Pres., 1957). Chm., Ophthalmic Gp Cttee, 1963–75; Mem. Council, Faculty of Ophthalmologists, 1963–72, Vice-Pres. 1964, Pres. 1968–71; Dean, Inst. of Ophthalmology, 1967–75 (Deputy Dean, 1966–67); Mem., Orthoptists Bd, 1970, Vice-Chm. 1971, Chm. 1972–75. *Publications:* 12th Edn, May and Worth's Diseases of the Eye; articles in British Jl of Ophthalmology, the Lancet, and other med. jls, dealing with ophthalmology. *Recreations:* gardening, lawn tennis, golf, squash racquets. *Address:* 4A Cottenham Park Road, Wimbledon, SW20 0RZ. *T:* 0181–946 3491.

CROSS, Alistair Robert Sinclair B.; *see* Bassett Cross.

CROSS, Prof. Anthony Glenn, FBA 1989; Professor of Slavonic Studies, since 1985, and Fellow of Fitzwilliam College, since 1986, Cambridge University; *b* 21 Oct. 1936; *s* of Walter Sidney Cross and Ada Cross; *m* 1960, Margaret (*née* Elson); two *d*. *Educ:* High Pavement Sch., Nottingham; Trinity Hall, Cambridge (BA 1960, MA 1964, PhD 1966); Harvard Univ. (AM 1961); LittD East Anglia 1981. Frank Knox Fellow, Harvard Univ., 1960–61; Univ. of East Anglia: Lectr in Russian, 1964–69; Sen. Lectr in Russian, 1969–72; Reader, 1972–81; Roberts Prof. of Russian, Univ. of Leeds, 1981–85. Vis. Fellow: Univ. of Illinois, 1969–70; All Souls Coll., Oxford, 1977–78. Pres., British Univs Assoc. of Slavists, 1982–84; Chm., British Academic Cttee for Liaison with Soviet Archives, 1983–. Reviews Editor, Jl of European Studies, 1971–; Editor, Study Group on Eighteenth-Century Russia Newsletter, 1973–. *Publications:* N. M. Karamzin, 1971; Russia Under Western Eyes 1517–1825, 1971; (ed) Russian Literature in the Age of Catherine the Great, 1976; Anglo-Russian Relations in the Eighteenth Century, 1977; (ed) Great Britain and Russia in the Eighteenth Century, 1979; By the Banks of the Thames, 1980; (ed) Russia and the West in the Eighteenth Century, 1981; The Tale of the Russian Daughter and her Suffocated Lover, 1982; (ed jtly) Eighteenth Century Russian Literature, Culture and Thought: a bibliography, 1984; The Russian Theme in English Literature, 1985; (ed jtly) Russia and the World of the Eighteenth Century, 1988; (ed) An English Lady at the Court of Catherine the Great, 1989; Anglophilia on the Throne: the British and the Russians in the age of Catherine II, 1992; (ed) Engraved in the Memory: James Walker, Engraver to Catherine the Great and his Russian anecdotes, 1993; Anglo-Russica: aspects of Anglo-Russian cultural relations in the Eighteenth and early Nineteenth centuries, 1993; (ed jtly) Literature, lives and legality in Catherine's Russia, 1994. *Recreations:* book collecting, cricket watching. *Address:* Department of Slavonic Studies, University of Cambridge, Sidgwick Avenue, Cambridge CB3 9DA. *T:* Cambridge (01223) 335007.

CROSS, Beverley; playwright; *b* 13 April 1931; *s* of George Cross, theatrical manager, and Eileen Williams, actress; *m* 1975, Maggie Smith (*see* Dame Maggie Smith). *Educ:* Nautical Coll., Pangbourne; Balliol Coll., Oxford. Mem. Shakespeare Memorial Theatre Company, 1954–56; then began writing plays. One More River, Duke of York's, 1959; Strip the Willow, Arts, Cambridge, 1960 (Arts Council Drama Award for both, 1960); The Singing Dolphin, Oxford, 1960; The Three Cavaliers, Birmingham Rep., 1960; Belle, or The Ballad of Dr Crippen, Strand, 1961; Boeing-Boeing, Apollo, 1962; Wanted On Voyage, Marlowe, Canterbury, 1962; Half A Sixpence, Cambridge, London, 1963; Jorrocks, New, London, 1966; The Owl on the Battlements, Nottingham, 1971; Catherine Howard, York, 1972; The Great Society, Mermaid, 1974; Hans Andersen, Palladium, 1974; Happy Birthday, Apollo, 1979; Haworth, Birmingham Rep., 1981; The Scarlet Pimpernel, Chichester, Her Majesty's, 1985; Miranda, Chichester Fest., 1987. *Libretti:* The Mines of Sulphur, Sadler's Wells, 1965; All the King's Men, 1969; Victory, Covent Garden, 1970; The Rising of the Moon, Glyndebourne, 1970; A Capital Transfer, British Council, London, 1981. *Screen plays of:* Jason and the Argonauts, 1962; The Long Ships, 1963; Genghis Khan, 1965; Half A Sixpence, 1966; (with Carlo Lizzani) Mussolini: Ultimo Atto, 1973; Sinbad and the Eye of the Tiger, 1977; The Clash of the Titans, 1981. *Television plays:* The Nightwalkers, 1960; The Dark Pits of War, 1960; Catherine Howard, 1969; March on, Boys!, 1975; A Bill of Mortality, 1975. *Directed:* Boeing-Boeing, Sydney, 1964; The Platinum Cat, Wyndham's, 1965. *Publications:* Mars in Capricorn, 1955; The Nightwalkers, 1956; Plays For Children, 1960. *Address:* c/o Write on Cue, 15 New Row, WC2N 4LA. *T:* 0171–379 4915.

CROSS, Clifford Thomas, CB 1977; Commissioner, Customs and Excise, 1970–79; *b* 1 April 1920; *o s* of late Arthur and Helena Cross; *m* 1942, Ida Adelaide Barker; one *s* two *d*. *Educ:* Latymer Upper Sch., Hammersmith; Univ. of London (LLB). Joined Inland Revenue, 1939; Customs and Excise, 1946; Asst Sec. 1959; Comr 1970. *Recreations:* gardening, crosswords, watching television, etc. *Address:* Longacre, 101 Histon Road, Cottenham, Cambs CB4 4UQ. *T:* Cottenham (01954) 250757.

CROSS, Dr Dolores Evelyn; President, Chicago State University, since 1990; *b* 29 Aug. 1938; *d* of Ozie Johnson Tucker and Charles Tucker; *m* 1956, Thomas Edwin Cross; one *s* one *d*. *Educ:* Seton Hall Univ. (BS 1963); Hofstra Univ. (MS 1968); Univ. of Michigan (PhD 1971). Teaching posts, NY and Michigan, 1961–71; Asst Prof. in Educn, Northwestern Univ., 1971–74; Associate Prof. in Educn, Claremont Graduate Sch., 1974–78; Vice-Chancellor for student affairs and special programs, City Univ., NY, and Prof. in Educn, Brooklyn Coll., 1978–81; Pres., NY State Higher Educn Services Corp., 1981–88; Associate Provost and Associate Vice-Pres. for Academic Affairs, Univ. of Minnesota, 1988–90. Hon. LLD: Marymount Manhattan, 1984; Skidmore Coll., 1988. NAACP Muriel Silverberg Award, NY, 1987; John Jay Award, NYC Commn of Indep. Colls and Univs, 1989. *Publications:* Influence of Individual Difference on Theories of Instruction, 1974; Teaching in a Multi-Cultural Society, 1977. *Recreations:* jogging, marathon running. *Address:* Chicago State University, 95th Street at King Drive Avenue, Chicago, IL 60628, USA. *T:* (312) 9952400.

CROSS, Prof. George Alan Martin, FRS 1984; André and Bella Meyer Professor of Molecular Parasitology, Rockefeller University, New York, since 1982; *b* 27 Sept. 1942; *s* of George Bernard and Beatrice Mary Cross; *m* 1986, Nadia Nogueira; one *d*. *Educ:* Cheadle Hulme Sch.; Downing Coll., Univ. of Cambridge (BA, PhD). ICI Postdoctoral Fellow, Biochemistry, Cambridge, 1967–69; Research Fellow, Fitzwilliam Coll., Cambridge, 1967–70; Scientist, MRC Biochemical Parasitology Unit, Molteno Inst., Cambridge, 1969–77; Head, Dept of Immunochemistry, Wellcome Research Laboratories, 1977–82. Fleming Lectr, Soc. for General Microbiology, 1978. Chalmers Medal, Royal Soc. for Tropical Medicine and Hygiene, 1983; (jtly) Paul Ehrlich and Ludwig Darmstaedter Prize, 1984. *Publications:* in journals of parasitology, biochemistry, microbiology and molecular biology. *Recreations:* sailing, tennis, building projects, observing people. *Address:* Rockefeller University, 1230 York Avenue, New York, NY 10021, USA. *T:* (212) 3277571.

CROSS, Gillian Clare, DPhil; author; *b* 1945; *d* of James Eric Arnold and Joan Emma (*née* Manton); *m* 1967, Martin Francis Cross; two *s* two *d*. *Educ:* North London Collegiate Sch. for Girls; Somerville Coll., Oxford (MA); Univ. of Sussex (DPhil). Mem., Soc. of Authors. Mem., Octavian Droobers. *Publications:* The Runaway, 1979; The Iron Way, 1979; Revolt at Ratcliffe's Rags, 1980; Save Our School, 1981; A Whisper of Lace, 1981; The Dark Behind the Curtain, 1982; The Demon Headmaster, 1982; Born of the Sun, 1983; The Mintyglo Kid, 1983; On the Edge, 1984; The Prime Minister's Brain, 1985; Chartbreak, 1986 (USA as Chartbreaker, 1987); Swimathon, 1986; Roscoe's Leap, 1987; A Map of Nowhere, 1988; Rescuing Gloria, 1989; Wolf, 1990 (Carnegie Medal, LA, 1990); The Monster from Underground, 1990; Twin and Super-Twin, 1990; Gobbo The Great, 1991; Rent-A-Genius, 1991; The Great Elephant Chase, 1992 (Smarties Book Prize and Whitbread Children's Novel Award, 1992); Beware Olga!, 1993; Furry Maccaloo, 1993; The Tree House, 1993; Hunky Parker is Watching You, 1994; What will Emily Do?, 1994; New World, 1994; The Crazy Shoe Shuffle, 1995; Posh Watson, 1995. *Recreations:* playing the piano, orienteering. *Address:* The Gate House, 39 Main Street, Wolston, Coventry CV8 3HH. *T:* Coventry (01203) 542516.

CROSS, Hannah Margaret, (Mrs E. G. Wright); barrister-at-law; *b* 25 April 1908; *o d* of late F. J. K. Cross and Eleanor Mary Cross (*née* Phillimore); *m* 1936, Edmund Gordon Wright, Barrister-at-Law (*d* 1971); one *s* one *d*. *Educ:* Downe House Sch.; St Hilda's Coll., Oxford. BA 1929. Called to Bar, Lincoln's Inn, 1931; first woman Mem. of Gen. Council of Bar, 1938–45; Civil Defence, 1939–45. *Address:* The Quay House, Sidlesham, near Chichester, West Sussex PO20 7LX. *T:* Sidlesham (01243) 641258.

CROSS, James Richard, (Jasper), CMG 1971; Under-Secretary, Principal Establishment Officer, Department of Energy, 1978–80; *b* 29 Sept. 1921; *s* of J. P. Cross and Dinah Cross (*née* Hodgins); *m* 1945, Barbara Dagg; one *d*. *Educ:* King's Hosp., Dublin; Trin. Coll., Dublin. Scholar, First Cl. Moderatorship Economics and Polit. Science. RE (Lieut). Asst Principal, Bd of Trade, 1947; Private Sec. to Parly Sec., 1947–49; Principal, 1950; Trade Commissioner: New Delhi, 1953–56; Halifax, 1957–60; Winnipeg, 1960–62; Asst Sec., 1962; Sen. Trade Comr, Kuala Lumpur, 1962–66; Bd of Trade, 1966–67; Under Sec., 1968; Sen. British Trade Comr, Montreal, 1968–70 (kidnapped by terrorists and held for 59 days, Oct.–Dec. 1970); Under-Sec., Export Planning and Devel Div., DTI, 1971–73; Sec., British Overseas Trade Bd, 1972; Coal Div., DTI, later Dept of Energy, 1973–78. *Recreations:* theatre, bridge, the New Forest. *Address:* The Small House, Queen Katherine Road, Lymington, Hants SO41 3RY.

CROSS, Air Chief Marshal Sir Kenneth (Brian Boyd), KCB 1959 (CB 1954); CBE 1945; DSO 1943; DFC 1940; *b* 4 Oct. 1911; *s* of Pembroke H. C. Cross and Mrs Jean Cross; *m* 1945, Brenda Megan (*d* 1991), *d* of Wing-Comdr F. J. B. Powell; two *s* one *d*. *Educ:* Kingswood Sch., Bath. Pilot Officer, RAF, 1930; Flying Badge, 1931; 25 Fighter Sqdn, 1931; Flying Officer, 1932; Flying Instructor, No 5 FTS Sealand and Cambridge Univ. Air Sqdn, 1934; Flt Lt 1935; Sqdn Ldr 1938; commanded No 46 Fighter Sqdn UK, Norway, 1939–40; Wing Comdr 1940; posted Middle East, 1941; Actg Group Capt. 1941; Actg Air Commodore, 1943; Director Overseas Operations, Air Ministry, 1944; Imperial Defence Coll., 1946; reverted Group Capt., 1946; Group Capt. Operations HQ BAFO Germany, 1947; OC Eastern Sector Fighter Command, 1949; Dir of Weapons, Air Ministry, 1952; subs. Air Cdre, 1953; Dir of Ops, Air Defence, 1954–Dec. 1955; Air Vice-Marshal, 1956; AOC No 3 (Bomber) Group, 1956–59; Air Marshal, 1961; AOC-in-C, Bomber Comd, 1959–63; AOC-in-C, Transport Comd, 1963–66; Air Chief Marshal, 1967; retd, 1967. Director: Suffolk Branch, 1968, London Branch, 1974, British Red Cross Soc. Norwegian War Cross, 1941; USA Legion of Merit, 1944; French Legion of Honour, 1944; French Croix de Guerre, 1944; Dutch Order of Orange Nassau, 1945. *Recreations:* Rugby football and golf (colours RAF). *Address:* 12 Callow Street, Chelsea, SW3 6BE. *Club:* Royal Air Force.

CROSS, Dame Margaret Natalie; *see* Smith, Dame Maggie.

CROSS, Prof. Robert Craigie, CBE 1972; MA Glasgow, MA Oxford; FRSE; Regius Professor of Logic, 1953–78, Vice-Principal, 1974–77, University of Aberdeen; *b* 24 April 1911; *s* of Matthew Cross and Margaret Dickson; *m* 1943, Peggy Catherine Elizabeth Vernon; two *d*. *Educ:* Glasgow Univ.; Queen's Coll., Oxford. MA 1st Cl. Hons Classics, Glasgow, 1932; 1st Cl. Hons Classical Mods, Oxford, 1934; 1st Cl. Lit. Hum., Oxford, 1936. Fellow and Tutor in Philsophy, Jesus Coll., Oxford, 1938; served War, 1941–45, Navy and Admiralty; Senior Tutor, Jesus Coll., Oxford, 1948–53. Trustee, Scottish Hospital Endowments Research Trust, 1968–80; Mem., University Grants Cttee, 1965–74; Mem., North Eastern Regional Hospital Bd, 1958–65. *Publications:* (with A. D. Woozley) Plato's Republic: A Philosophical Commentary, 1964; contributions to learned jls. *Address:* Heatherlands, Ancrum, Roxburghshire TD8 6XA. *T:* Ancrum (01835) 830282.

CROSSE, Gordon; composer; *b* 1 Dec. 1937; *s* of Percy and Marie Crosse; *m* 1965, Elizabeth Bunch. *Educ:* Cheadle Hulme Sch.; St Edmund Hall, Oxford; Accad. di S Cecilia, Rome. Music Fellow, Essex Univ., 1969–74; Composer in residence, King's Coll., Cambridge, 1974–76; Vis. Lectr, Univ. of Calif at Santa Barbara, 1977–78. Hon. RAM, 1980. *Operas:* Purgatory, 1966; The Grace of Todd, 1967; The Story of Vasco, 1970; Potter Thompson, 1973; *ballets:* Playground, 1979; Wildboy, 1981; *other compositions:* Concerto da Camera, 1962; Meet My Folks, 1963; "Symphonies", 1964; Second Violin Concerto, 1970; Memories of Morning: Night, 1972; Ariadne, 1973; Symphony 2, 1975; Wildboy (clarinet concerto), Play Ground, 1977; Dreamsongs, 1978; Cello Concerto, 1979; String Quartet, 1980; Dreamcanon (chorus), 1981; Trio for piano, violin and cello, 1986; Trumpet Concerto, 1986; Sea Psalms, 1990; much other orchestral, vocal and chamber music. *Address:* Brant's Cottage, Blackheath, Wenhaston, Halesworth, Suffolk IP19 9EX.

CROSSETT, Robert Nelson, (Tom), DPhil; Secretary General, National Society for Clean Air and Environmental Protection, since 1992; *b* 27 May 1938; *s* of Robert Crossett and Mary Nelson; *m* 1966, Susan Marjorie Legg; two *s*. *Educ:* British School, Hamburg; Campbell College, Belfast; Queen's Univ., Belfast (BSc, BAgr); Lincoln College, Oxford (DPhil); Univ. of East Anglia. FIFST 1986. Group Leader Environmental Studies, Aust. Atomic Energy Commn, 1966; Sen. Sci. Officer, ARC Letcombe Lab., 1969; Develt Officer (Crops), Scottish Agricl. Develt Council, 1972; PSO, Dept of Agric. and Fisheries for Scotland, 1975; Ministry of Agriculture, Fisheries and Food: Sci. Liaison Officer (Horticulture and Soils), 1978; Head, Food Sci. Div., 1984; Chief Scientist (Fisheries and Food), 1985–89; Head of Envmtl Policy, 1989–90, Envmt Dir, 1990–91, National Power. Member: NERC, 1985–89; AFRC, 1985–89; UK Delgn, Tripartite Meetings on Food and Drugs, 1985–88; Cttee on Med. Aspects of Food Policy, 1985–89; Adv. Gp to Sec. of State for Envmt on Eco-Management and Audit, 1994–; UK Round Table on Sustainable Develt, 1995–. *Publications:* papers in plant physiology, marine biology, food science and envmtl management. *Recreations:* walking, gardening, orienteering, boats. *Address:* National Society for Clean Air and Environmental Protection, 136 North Street, Brighton BN1 1RG.

CROSSLAND, Anthony, FRCO; Organist and Master of the Choristers, Wells Cathedral, since 1971; *b* 4 Aug. 1931; *s* of Ernest Thomas and Frances Elizabeth Crossland; *m* 1960, Barbara Helen Pullar-Strecker; one *s* two *d*. *Educ:* Christ Church, Oxford. MA, BMus (Oxon), FRCO (CHM), ARCM. Asst Organist: Christ Church Cathedral, Oxford, 1957–61; Wells Cathedral, 1961–71. Conductor: Wells Cathedral Oratorio Soc., 1966–; Wells Sinfonietta, 1985–; Organs Advr to dio. of Bath and Wells, 1971–. Pres., Cathedral Organists' Assoc., 1983–85. DMus Lambeth, 1994. *Recreations:* reading, photography. *Address:* 15 Vicars' Close, Wells, Somerset BA5 2UJ. *T:* Wells (Somerset) (01749) 673526.

CROSSLAND, Sir Bernard, Kt 1990; CBE 1980; MSc (London); PhD (Bristol); DSc (Nottingham); FRS 1979; FEng 1979; MRIA; FIMechE; FIEI; Emeritus Professor, The Queen's University, Belfast, since 1984 (Professor and Head of Department of Mechanical and Industrial Engineering, 1959–82, Research Professor, 1982–84; Dean, 1964–67; Pro-Vice-Chancellor, 1978–82); *b* 20 Oct. 1923; *s* of R. F. Crossland and K. M. Rudduck; *m* 1946, Audrey Elliott Birks; two *d*. *Educ:* Simon Langton's, Canterbury. Apprentice, Rolls Royce Ltd, 1940–41; Nottingham Univ., 1941–43; Technical Asst, Rolls Royce, 1943–45; Asst Lectr, Lectr and then Senior Lectr in Mechanical Engineering, Univ. of Bristol, 1946–59. Member: AFRC, 1981–87; Engrg Council, 1983–88; Chairman: Bd for Engineers' Registration, 1983–86; Youth Careers Guidance Cttee, N Ireland, 1975–79, 1979–81; NI Manpower Council, 1981–86; Adv. Bd for Postgrad. Awards, NI Dept of Educn, 1982–; Member: NI Training Council, 1964–76, 1977–81; NI Economic Council, 1981–85; NI Industrial Develt Bd, 1982–87. Dir, Gilbert Associates (Europe) Ltd, 1991–94. Assessor, King's Cross Fire Investigation, 1988; Chm., Public Hearing into Bilsthorpe Colliery Accident, 1994. Mem. Council and a Vice-Pres., Royal Soc., 1984–86; Mem. Council, Fellowship of Engrg, 1985–88; Pres., Section 6, British Assoc., 1987; Institution of Mechanical Engineers: Chm., Engineering Sciences Div., 1980–84; Vice-Pres., 1983–84; Dep. Pres., 1984–86; Pres., 1986–87; Past Pres., 1987–91; Leonardo da Vinci Lectr, 1970; George Stephenson Lectr, 1989; George Stephenson and Thomas Hawksley Medals. Richard Weck Lectr, Welding Inst., 1992; Seamus Timoney Lectr, NUI, 1993. Trustee, Mackie Foundn, 1983–94. Freeman, City of London, 1987; Liveryman, Worshipful Co. of Engrs, 1988. Hon. MASME 1987; Hon. FWeldI 1990; Hon. FIEI 1993. Hon. Fellow, Luton, 1994. Hon. DSc: NUI, 1984; Dublin, 1985; Edinburgh, 1987; QUB 1988; Aston, 1988; Cranfield Inst. of Technology, 1989; Hon. DEng: Bristol, 1992; Limerick, 1993; Liverpool, 1993. Kelvin Medal, ICE, 1992. *Publications:* An Introduction to the Mechanics of Machines, 1964; Explosive Welding and its Application, 1982; various papers on fatigue of metals and effect of very high fluid pressures on properties of materials; strength of thick-walled vessels, explosive welding, friction welding, design and history of engineering. *Recreation:* walking. *Address:* The Queen's University, Belfast BT7 1NN. *T:* Belfast (01232) 247303; 16 Malone Court, Belfast BT9 6PA. *T:* Belfast (01232) 667495. *Club:* Athenæum.

CROSSLAND, Sir Leonard, Kt 1969; farmer since 1974; Chairman: Eaton Ltd (UK), 1972–88; Ford Motor Co. Ltd, 1968–72; Energy Research and Development Ltd (formerly Sedgeminster Technical Developments Ltd), since 1974; *b* 2 March 1914; *s* of Joseph and Frances Crossland; *m* 1st, 1941, Rhona Marjorie Griffin; two *d*; 2nd, 1963, Joan Brewer. *Educ:* Penistone Grammar Sch. Purchase Dept, Ford Motor Co. Ltd, 1937–39. Royal Army Service Corps, 1939–45 (despatches twice). Ford Motor Co. Ltd. Purchase Dept. 1945–54; Chief Buyer, Tractor and Implement Dept, 1954–57; Chief Buyer, Car and Truck Dept, 1957–59; Asst Purchase Manager, 1959–60; Purchase Manager, 1960–62; Exec. Dir, Supply and Services, 1962–66; Dir, Manufacturing Staff and Services, 1966; Asst Man. Dir, 1966–67; Man. Dir, 1967; Dep. Chm., 1967; Chm., Autolite Motor Products Ltd; Director: Henry Ford & Son Ltd, Cork; Eaton Corp. (US), 1974–81. Farmer. *Recreations:* shooting, fishing, golf. *Address:* Abbotts Hall, Great Wigborough, Colchester, Essex CO5 7RZ. *T:* Peldon (01206) 735456. *Clubs:* City Livery, Royal Automobile, British Racing Drivers'; American.

CROSSLAND, Prof. Ronald Arthur, FSA 1982; Professor of Greek, University of Sheffield, 1958–82, now Emeritus (Dean, Faculty of Arts, 1973–75); *b* 31 Aug. 1920; *s* of late Ralph Crossland, BSc, and late Ethel Crossland (*née* Scattergood). *Educ:* Stanley Road Elementary Sch., Nottingham; Nottingham High Sch.; King's Coll., Cambridge. Major Scholar in Classics, King's Coll., Cambridge, 1939–41 and 1945–46. National Service in Royal Artillery, 1941–45. Henry Fellow, Berkeley Coll., Yale Univ., 1946–47; Instructor in Classics, Yale Univ., 1947–48; Senior Student of Treasury Cttee for Studentships in Foreign Languages and Cultures (for research in Hittite Philology and Linguistics), 1948–51; Hon. Lectr in Ancient History, University of Birmingham, 1950–51; Lecturer in Ancient History, King's Coll., University of Durham, Newcastle upon Tyne, 1951–58. Harris Fellow of King's Coll., Cambridge, 1952–56. Vis. Prof., Univ. Texas, 1962; Collitz Vis. Prof., Univ. Michigan, 1967; Vis. Fellow, Victoria Univ. of Wellington, NZ, 1979. Pres., South Shields Archaeological and Historical Soc., 1976–77. *Publications:* Bronze Age Migrations in the Aegean (with A. Birchall), 1973; Teaching Classical Studies, 1976; chapters on: Immigrants from the North, in Cambridge Ancient History, rev. edn, 1967; Linguistic Problems of the Balkan Area, in Cambridge Ancient History, rev. edn, 1982; Early Greek Migrations, in Civilization of the Ancient Mediterranean (ed M. Grant), 1987; articles in Trans Philological Soc., Archivum Linguisticum, Studia Balcanica, Past and Present, Antiquity. *Recreations:* music, travel, pastime with good company. *Address:* 59 Sherlock Close, Cambridge CB3 0HP. *T:* Cambridge (01223) 358085; (enquiries) Sheffield (0114) 276 8555.

CROSSLEY, family name of **Baron Somerleyton.**

CROSSLEY, Geoffrey Allan, CMG 1974; HM Diplomatic Service, retired; Director, External Relations, Continuing Education, European Institute of Business Administration, INSEAD, Fontainebleau, 1980–84; *b* 11 Nov. 1920; *s* of Thomas Crossley and Winifred Mary Crossley (*née* Ellis); *m* 1945, Aline Louise Farcy; two *s* one *d*. *Educ:* Penistone; abroad; Gonville and Caius Coll., Cambridge (Scholar). Served War of 1939–45: Min. of Supply, 1941–; Foreign Office, 1942–; in Algeria and France. Foreign Service, 1945–: Second Sec., Paris, 1945–48; FO, 1948–49; Alternate UK Deleg. on UN Balkans Commn, Greece, 1949–52; Dep. Regional Inf. Officer with Commissioner-Gen. for SE Asia, Singapore, 1952–55; FO, 1955–57; Consulate-Gen., Frankfurt, for Saar Transition from France to Germany, 1957–59; Political Office, NE Command, Cyprus (later in charge), 1959–61; Head of Chancery, Berne, 1961–65; on secondment to Min. of Overseas Development, as Head of W and N African Dept, 1965–67; Dep. High Comr, Lusaka, 1967–69; Counsellor, Oslo, 1969–73; Ambassador to Colombia, 1973–77; Envoy to the Holy See, 1978–80. Founder Mem., Cambridge Soc. Mem., French Inst. of Internat. Relations. *Recreations:* various. *Address:* 22 Rue Emeriau, 75015 Paris, France.

CROSSLEY, Harry; DL; Chief Executive, Derbyshire County Council, 1974–79, retired; *b* 2 Sept. 1918; *s* of late Percy Crossley and Nellie McMinnies Crossley, Burnley, Lancs; *m* 1949, Pamela, *e d* of late Ald. E. A. C. Woodcock, Kettering, Northants; two *s*. *Educ:* Burnley Grammar Sch. Solicitor. LAM RTPI. War service, RA, attached Indian Army (Major), 1939–46. Private practice and local govt service as solicitor; Derbyshire CC: Dep. Clerk of Peace and of CC, 1960–69; Clerk of Peace and of CC, 1969–74. Clerk to Derbyshire Lieutenancy, 1969–79; Sec., Lord Chancellor's Adv. Cttee for Derbyshire, 1969–79. Clerk, Peak Park Planning Bd, 1969–74. DL Derbyshire, 1978. *Publications:* articles for legal and local govt jls. *Recreations:* golf, tennis, gardening. *Address:* Alpine, Bracken Lane, Holloway, Matlock DE4 5AS. *T:* Dethick (01629) 534382.

CROSSLEY, Sir Nicholas John, 4th Bt *cr* 1909, of Glenfield, Dunham Massey, Co. Chester; *b* 10 Dec. 1962; *s* of Sir Christopher John Crossley, 3rd Bt and of Carolyne Louise, *d* of late L. Grey Sykes; *S* father, 1989. *Heir: b* Julian Charles Crossley, *b* 11 Dec. 1964. *Address:* 155 South Plymouth Boulevard, Los Angeles, CA 90004, USA.

CROSSLEY, Paul Christopher Richard, CBE 1993; concert pianist; Artistic Director, London Sinfonietta, 1988–94; *b* 17 May 1944; *s* of late Frank Crossley and Myra Crossley (*née* Barrowcliffe). *Educ:* Silcoates Sch., Wakefield; Mansfield Coll., Oxford (BA, MA). International concert pianist; recitals and concerts with all major orchestras; numerous recordings and films for TV. *Recreations:* Mah-Jongg, reading. *Address:* c/o Van Walsum Management, 26 Wadham Road, SW15 2LR. *T:* 0181–874 6344.

CROSSLEY, Maj.-Gen. Ralph John, CB 1987; CBE 1981; Chairman, Salisbury Healthcare NHS Trust, since 1994 (Chairman, Salisbury Health Authority, 1990–93); *b* 11 Oct. 1933; *s* of Edward Crossley and Eva Mary Crossley (*née* Farnworth); *m* 1957, Marion Hilary Crossley (*née* Bacon); one *s* one *d*. *Educ:* Quainton Sch., Harrow; Felsted School. Commnd 1952 (Nat. Service); Air Observation Post Pilots course, 1953; Regimental Duty: Canal Zone,1954–56; BAOR, 1956–59; Instructor in Gunnery, Larkhill, 1959–63; Technical Staff Course, 1963–65; Regtl Duty, BAOR, 1965–67, 1969–71; Weapons Staff, UK, 1967–69; Gen. Staff, UK, 1971–72; Instructor, RMCS, 1972–74; CO, 94 Locating Regt, 1974–77; Project Manager, 155 Systems, 1977–81; Dep. Comdt, RMCS, 1981–84; Dir Gen. of Weapons (Army), 1984–86; retired 1986. Defence Advr, Avon Rubber, 1987–; Dir, Select Industries plc, 1991–. *Recreations:* golf, walking, gardening. *Address:* c/o Odstock Hospital, Salisbury, Wilts.

CROSSLEY-HOLLAND, Kevin John William; author; *b* 7 Feb. 1941; *s* of Prof. Peter Charles Crossley-Holland and Joan Mary Crossley-Holland (*née* Cowper), MBE; *m* 1st, 1963, Caroline Fendall, *er d* of Prof. L. M. Thompson; two *s*; 2nd, 1972, Ruth, *er d* of John Marris; 3rd, 1982, Gillian Paula, *er d* of Peter Cook; two *d*. *Educ:* Bryanston Sch.; St Edmund Hall, Oxford (MA Hons). Editor, Macmillan & Co., 1962–69; Gregory Fellow in Poetry, Univ. of Leeds, 1969–71; Talks Producer, BBC, 1972; Editl Dir, Victor Gollancz, 1972–77; Lectr in English: Tufts-in-London Program, 1967–78; Regensburg Univ., 1978–80; Arts Council Fellow in Writing, Winchester Sch. of Art, 1983 and 1984; Vis. Prof. of English and Fulbright Scholar in Residence, St Olaf Coll., Minnesota, 1987–90; Prof. and Endowed Chair in Humanities and Fine Arts, Univ. of St Thomas, Minnesota, 1991–95; Vis Lectr for British Council in Germany, Iceland, India, Yugoslavia. Editl Consultant, Boydell & Brewer, 1983–90. Chm., Literature Panel, Eastern Arts Assoc., 1986–89; Trustee, Wingfield Coll., 1989– (Chm., Friends, 1989–91). Dir, Minnesota Composers Forum, 1993–. Contribs to radio (incl. drama), TV (incl. educl series), and musical works. *Publications: poetry:* The Rain-Giver, 1972; The Dream-House, 1976; Time's Oriel, 1983; Waterslain, 1986; The Painting-Room, 1988; New and Selected Poems, 1991; *for children:* Havelok the Dane, 1964; King Horn, 1965; The Green Children, 1966 (Arts Council Award); The Callow Pit Coffer, 1968; (with Jill Paton Walsh) Wordhoard, 1969; Storm and Other Old English Riddles, 1970; The Pedlar of Swaffham, 1971; The Sea Stranger, 1973; The Fire-Brother, 1974; Green Blades Rising, 1975; The Earth-Father, 1976; The Wildman, 1976; The Dead Moon, 1982; Beowulf, 1982; (with Gwyn Thomas) The Mabinogion, 1984; Axe-Age, Wolf-Age, 1985; Storm, 1985 (Carnegie Medal); (with Susanne Lugert) The Fox and the Cat, 1985; British Folk Tales, 1987; Wulf, 1988; (with Gwyn Thomas) The Quest for Olwen, 1988; Piper and Pooka, 1988; Small Tooth Dog, 1988; Boo!, 1988; Dathera Dad, 1989; (with Ian Penney) Under the Sun and Over the Moon, 1989; Sleeping Nanna, 1989; Sea Tongue, 1991; Tales from Europe, 1991; Long Tom and The Dead Hand, 1992; (with Gwyn Thomas) Taliesin, 1992; The Labours of Herakles, 1993; Norse Myths, 1993; The Green Children, 1994; The Dark Horseman, 1995; *travel:* Pieces of Land, 1972; *mythology:* The Norse Myths, 1980; *history:* (with Andrew Rafferty) The Stones Remain, 1989; *translations from Old English:* (with Bruce Mitchell) The Battle of Maldon, 1965; (with Bruce Mitchell) Beowulf, 1968; The Exeter Book Riddles, 1978; The Illustrated Beowulf, 1987; The Anglo-Saxon Elegies, 1988; *edited:* Running to Paradise, 1967; Winter's Tales for Children 3, 1967; Winter's Tales 14, 1968; (with Patricia Beer) New Poetry 2, 1976; The Faber Book of Northern Legends, 1977; The Faber Book of Northern Folk-Tales, 1980; The Anglo-Saxon World, 1982; The Riddle Book, 1982; Folk-Tales of the British Isles, 1985; The Oxford Book of Travel Verse, 1986; Northern Lights, 1987; Medieval Lovers, 1988; Medieval Gardens, 1990; Peter Grimes by George Crabbe, 1990; *operas:* (with Nicola LeFanu): The Green Children, 1990; The Wildman, 1995. *Recreations:* opera, wine, walks, archaeological sites. *Address:* The Old Vicarage, Walsham-le-Willows, Bury St Edmunds, Suffolk IP31 3BZ; c/o Rogers, Coleridge and White, 20 Powis Mews, W11 1JT.

CROSTHWAIT, Timothy Leland, CMG 1964; MBE 1944; HM Diplomatic Service, retired; *b* 5 Aug. 1915; *s* of Lt-Col L. G. Crosthwait, Survey of India; *m* 1959, Anne Marjorie, *d* of Col T. M. M. Penney. *Educ:* Wellington Coll.; Peterhouse, Cambridge (MA). Appointed to Indian Civil Service, 1937; Asst Private Sec. to Viceroy, 1942–44; Air Min., 1948–55; Commonwealth Relations Office, 1955; British Deputy High Commissioner in Ceylon, 1957–61; Asst Sec., CRO, 1961–63; British High Commissioner, Zanzibar, 1963–64; British Deputy High Commissioner, Malta, 1965–66; British High Commissioner, Guyana, 1966–67; Ambassador, Malagasy Republic, 1970–75. *Address:* 39 Eaton Terrace, SW1W 8TP. *T:* 0171–730 9553. *Club:* United Oxford & Cambridge University.

CROUCH, Colin John, DPhil; Professor of Comparative Social Institutions, European University Institute, Florence, since 1995; Fellow and Tutor in Politics, Trinity College, Oxford, since 1985 (on leave of absence); *b* 1 March 1944; *s* of Charles and Doris Crouch; *m* 1970, Joan Ann Freedman; two *s*. *Educ:* Latymer Upper Sch.; London School of Economics (BASoc; Pres., Students Union, 1968; Hobhouse Prize, 1969); Nuffield Coll., Oxford (MA, DPhil). Lectr 1969–70 and 1973–79, Sen. Lectr 1979–80, Reader 1980–85, in Sociology, London Sch. of Economics and Political Science; Lectr in Sociology, Univ. of Bath, 1972–73; Jun. Proctor, Univ. of Oxford, 1990–91. Mem., Exec. Cttee, Fabian Soc., 1969–78 (Chm., 1976); Dir, Andrew Shonfield Soc., 1989–. Mem., Standing Cttee, Court of Govs, LSE, 1980–84. Curator, Bodleian Library, 1991–95; Delegate, OUP, 1992–. Joint Editor, The Political Quarterly, 1985–95. Political Studies Assoc. Book Prize, 1993. *Publications:* The Student Revolt, 1970; (ed jtly) Stress and Contradiction in Modern Capitalism, 1975; (ed) British Political Sociology Year Book, vol. III, 1977; Class Conflict and the Industrial Relations Crisis, 1977; (ed jtly) The Resurgence of Class Conflict in Western Europe since 1968, 2 vols, 1978; (ed) State and Economy in Contemporary Capitalism, 1979; The Politics of Industrial Relations, 1979, 2nd edn 1982; Trade Unions: the logic of collective action, 1982; (ed jtly) International Yearbook of Organizational Democracy, vol. I, 1983; (ed jtly) The New Centralism: Britain out of step in Europe?, 1989; (ed jtly) European Industrial Relations: the challenge of flexibility, 1990; (ed jtly) Corporatism and Accountability: organised interests in British public life, 1990; (ed jtly) The Politics of 1992: beyond the single European market, 1990; (ed jtly) Towards Greater Europe?, 1992; Industrial Relations and European State Traditions, 1993; (ed jtly) Ethics and Markets: co-operation and competition in capitalist economies, 1993; (ed jtly) Reinventing Collective Action: the global and the local, 1995; numerous articles on industrial relns, politics and social structure in Britain and Western Europe. *Recreations:* playing violin, music, gardening, watching and refereeing football matches. *Address:* European University Institute, Badia Fiesolana, via dei Roccettini, S. Domenico da Fiesole (FI), Italy. *T:* (55) 4685236.

CROUCH, Sir David (Lance), Kt 1987; DL; Chairman, David Crouch & Co. Ltd, 1964–89; *b* 23 June 1919; *s* of late Stanley Crouch and Rosalind Kate Crouch (*née* Croom); *m* 1947, Margaret Maplesden, *d* of Major Sydney Maplesden Noakes, DSO and Norah Parkyns Maplesden Noakes (*née* Buckland), Shorne, Kent; one *s* one *d*. *Educ:* University Coll. Sch. Served in City of London Yeomanry (TA), 1938–39; served War of 1939–45, Royal Artillery: Major 1943; attached RAF Staff (GSO2), 1944–45. Joined British Nylon Spinners Ltd, 1946; ICI Ltd, 1950; Dir of Publicity, Internat. Wool Secretariat, 1962–64. Formed own co., David Crouch & Co. Ltd, as international marketing and public relations consultants; Director: Pfizer Ltd, 1969–88; Burson Marsteller Ltd, 1972–83; Kingsway Public Relations (Hldgs) Ltd, 1985–89; Westminster Communications Gp Ltd, 1989–. Contested (C) West Leeds, 1959. MP (C) Canterbury, 1966–87. Chairman: British-Egyptian Parly Gp, 1972–87; British-Algerian Gp, 1980–87; All-Party Gp for the Chemical Industry, 1970–85; All-Party Gp for Energy Studies, 1980–85; British Gp, Inter-Parly Union, 1985–87; Vice-Chm., Cons. Middle East Council, 1980–87; Member: Select Cttee for Nationalized Industries, 1966–74; Public Accounts Cttee, 1974–79; Speaker's Panel, 1982–87; Select Cttee for Social Services, 1983–84; Adv. Cttee on the Arts to Mr Speaker, 1970–87 (Chm., 1983–87). Life Pres., Theatres Trust, 1992 (Trustee, 1977–92; Dep. Chm., 1979–87; Chm., 1987–92); Chm., Channel Theatre Co., 1984–87. Member: SE Thames RHA, 1970–85; MRC, 1984–87; Soc. of Chemical Industry; Council, Univ. of Kent, 1971–95; Council, RSA, 1974–78 (Fellow, 1971). Pres., Kent Soc., 1987–94; Gov., Kent Inst. of Art and Design, 1988–93; Chm., Kent Wishing Well Appeal, 1988–89. DL Kent, 1992. Hon. DCL Kent, 1987. *Publication:* A Canterbury Tale, 1987. *Recreations:* painting, golf. *Address:* The Oast House, Fisher Street, Badlesmere, Faversham, Kent ME13 0LB. *Clubs:* Athenæum, MCC; Kent and Canterbury (Canterbury); Royal St George's Golf.

CROW, (Hilary) Stephen, CB 1995; FRTPI, FRICS; FRGS; Chief Planning Inspector and Chief Executive, Planning Inspectorate, executive agency in Department of the Environment and Welsh Office, 1992–94; *b* 2 Sept. 1934; *s* of late Aubrey Everard Crow and Ivy Marion (*née* Warltier); *m* 1958, Margaret Anderson; two *s* one *d*. *Educ:* Leek High Sch.; William Ellis Sch.; St Catharine's Coll., Cambridge (MA). FRGS 1963; FRTPI 1986; FRICS 1992. Planning Asst, various grades, with Lancashire CC and Southport CBC, 1957–72; Divl Planning Officer, 1972–74, Prin. Asst County Planning Officer, 1974–76, Herts CC; joined Planning Inspectorate, 1976: Prin. Inspector for Wales, 1982–85; Asst Chief Inspector, 1985–88; Dep. Chief Inspector, then Chief Inspector, 1988. C of E Lay Reader, 1979–. *Recreations:* music, reading, garden. *Address:* The Pines, Lyncombe Vale Road, Bath BA2 4LS.

CROW, Dr Timothy John, FRCP, FRCPsych; MRC External Scientific Staff Member, University Department of Psychiatry, Warneford Hospital, Oxford, and Scientific Director designate, Prince of Wales Centre for Research into Schizophrenia and Depression, since 1994; *b* 7 June 1938; *s* of late Percy Arthur Crow and of Barbara Bonner Davies; *m* 1966, Julie Carol Carter; one *s* one *d*. *Educ:* Shrewsbury Sch.; London Hosp. Med. Coll. MB BS, PhD, DPM. Maudsley Hosp., 1966; University of Aberdeen: Lectr in Physiology, 1966–70; Lectr in Mental Health, 1970–72; Sen. Lectr in Psychiatry, Univ. of Manchester, 1972–73; Head, Div. of Psychiatry, Clinical Res. Centre, Northwick Park Hosp., 1974–94. Part-time Mem., Sci. Staff, Div. Neurophysiology and Neuropharmacology, Nat. Inst. for Med. Res., 1974–83; Dep. Dir, Clinical Res. Centre, 1984–89. Member: MRC Neuroscis Projects Grants Cttee, 1978–80; Neuroscis Bd, 1986–90; Chm., Biol. Psych. Gp, RCPsych, 1983–88 (Sec., 1980–83). Andrew W. Woods Vis. Prof., Univ. of Iowa, 1980; Lectures: St George's Hosp., 1980; St Louis, 1981; Univ. of Minnesota, 1981; Univ. of Ohio, 1986; RSocMed, 1988; Roche, RCPsych, Dublin, 1988; Stockholm, 1988; Maudsley, RCPsych, 1989; APA Internat. Scholars, 1990; Univ. of Oregon, 1991. A. P. Noyes Award, 1988; US Nat. Alliance Lieber Award, 1989; Res. Prize, World Fedn of Socs of Biol Psychiatry, 1991. Editor: Disorders of Neurohumoural Transmission, 1982; Recurrent and Chronic Psychoses, 1987. *Publications:* papers on brain reward mechanisms, learning and schizophrenia in sci. and med. jls. *Recreations:* sciolistic archaeology, anthropology. *Address:* 16 Northwick Circle, Kenton, Middx HA3 0EJ. *T:* 0181–907 6124. *Club:* Royal Society of Medicine.

CROWDEN, James Gee Pascoe, JP; FRICS, FCIArb; Senior Partner, Grounds & Co., 1974–88, consultant, 1988–91; Lord-Lieutenant and Custos Rotulorum of Cambridgeshire, since 1992; *b* 14 Nov. 1927; *yr s* of late Lt-Col R. J. C. Crowden, MC, and Nina Mary (*née* Gee), Peterborough; *m* 1955, Kathleen Mary (*d* 1989), *widow* of Captain F. A. Grounds and *d* of late Mr and Mrs J. W. Loughlin, Upwell; one *s* decd. *Educ:* Bedford Sch.; Pembroke Coll., Cambridge (MA; Hon. Fellow, 1993). Chartered surveyor; FRICS 1959; FCIArb 1977. Commissioned Royal Lincs Regt, 1947. Rowed in Oxford and Cambridge Boat Race, 1951 and 1952 (Pres., 1952); Captain, Great Britain VIII, European Championships, Macon, 1951 (Gold Medallists); also rowed in 1950 European Championships and 1952 Olympics; coached 20 Cambridge crews, 1953–75; Steward, Henley Royal Regatta, 1959– (Mem., Cttee of Management, 1964–92); Mem. Council, Amateur Rowing Assoc., 1957–77; Mem. of Court and Freeman, Co. of Watermen and Lightermen of the River Thames (Master, 1991–92). Vice-Pres., British Olympic Assoc., 1988–; Chairman: Cambridgeshire Olympic Appeal, 1984, 1988 and 1992; Appeal Exec. Cttee, Peterborough Cathedral, 1979–80; Member: Ely Diocesan Pastoral Cttee, 1969–89; Ely Cathedral Fabric Cttee, 1986–90. Chm., Order of St Etheldreda, 1992–. Former Pres. Agricl Valuers' Assocs for Cambs, Herts, Beds and Bucks, Lincs, Norfolk, and Wisbech. President: Cambs TAVR and Cadet Cttee, 1992–; Cambs Scouts, 1992–. Patron: Cambs RBL, 1992–; Cambs Red Cross, 1992–; Duke of Endinburgh's Award County Cttee, 1992–; Vice-Pres., E Anglian TAVRA, 1992–. Governor: March Grammar Sch., 1960–70 (Chm., 1967–70); King's Sch., Peterborough, 1980–90; St Hugh's Sch., Woodhall Spa, 1981–92. JP Wisbech, 1969; DL 1971, Vice Lord-Lieut 1985, Cambridgeshire; High Sheriff, Cambridgeshire and Isle of Ely, 1970. FRSA 1990. KStJ 1992. *Recreations:* rowing, shooting. *Address:* 19 North Brink, Wisbech, Cambridgeshire PE13 1JR. *T:* Wisbech (01945) 583320. *Clubs:* East India, Devonshire, Sports and Public Schools, Sette of Odd Volumes; Hawks', University Pitt, Cambridge County (Cambridge); Leander (Henley-on-Thames).

CROWDER, F(rederick) Petre, QC 1964; a Recorder (formerly Recorder of Colchester), 1967–91; Barrister-at-Law; *b* 18 July 1919; *s* of late Sir John Ellenborough Crowder; *m* 1948, Hon. Patricia Stourton, *d* of 25th Baron Mowbray, MC (also 26th Baron Segrave and 22nd Baron Stourton); two *s*. *Educ:* Eton; Christ Church, Oxford. Served War of 1939–45; joined Coldstream Guards, 1939, and served in North Africa, Italy, Burma; attained rank of major. Called to the Bar, Inner Temple, 1948 (Master of the Bench, 1971; Reader, 1990; Treasurer, 1991). South Eastern Circuit; North London Sessions. Recorder of Gravesend, 1960–67; Herts QS: Dep. Chm., 1959–63; Chm., 1963–71. Contested (C) North Tottenham, by-elec. 1945; MP (C) Ruislip-Northwood, 1950–74, Hillingdon, Ruislip-Northwood, 1974–79; PPS to Solicitor-Gen., 1952–54; PPS to Attorney General, 1954–62. *Address:* 2 Harcourt Buildings, Temple, EC4Y 9DB. *T:* 0171–353 2112; 8 Quarrendon Street, SW6 3SU. *T:* 0171–731 6342. *Clubs:* Carlton, Pratt's, Turf.

CROWDER, Ven. Norman Harry; Archdeacon of Portsmouth, 1985–93, now Archdeacon Emeritus; *b* 20 Oct. 1926; *s* of Laurence Smethurst Crowder and Frances Annie (*née* Hicks); *m* 1971, Pauleen Florence Alison (*née* Styles); one *s*. *Educ:* Nottingham High School; St John's Coll., Cambridge (MA); Westcott House, Cambridge. Curate, St Mary's, Radcliffe-on-Trent, 1952–55; Residential Chaplain to Bishop of Portsmouth, 1955–59; Asst Chaplain, Canford School, 1959–64, Chaplain 1964–72; Vicar, St John's, Oakfield, Ryde, IoW, 1972–75; Dir of Religious Educn, Portsmouth Dio., and Res. Canon of Portsmouth Cathedral, 1975–85. *Recreations:* water colour, travel. *Address:* 37 Rectory Road, Salisbury SP2 7SD. *T:* Salisbury (01722) 320052. Club: MCC.

CROWDY, Maj.-Gen. Joseph Porter, CB 1984; Commandant and Postgraduate Dean, Royal Army Medical College, 1981–84, retired; Hon. Consultant on nutrition to Army, 1985–88; *b* 19 Nov. 1923; *s* of late Lt-Col Charles R. Crowdy and Kate Crowdy (*née* Porter); *m* 1948, Beryl Elisabeth Sapsford; four *d*. *Educ:* Gresham's Sch.; Edinburgh Univ. MB, ChB 1947, DTM&H 1956, DPH 1957, DIH 1957; FFCM 1974; MFOM 1981; FRIPHH 1982. House Surgeon, Norfolk and Norwich Hosp., 1947–48; joined RAMC, 1949; North Africa, 1952–55; Singapore, 1960–62; Head of Applied Physiology, Army Personnel Res. Estabt, 1963–73; Prof. of Army Health, Royal Army Med. Coll., 1973–76; SMO, Land Forces Cyprus, 1976–78; Dir, Army Preventive Medicine, 1978–81. Col Comdt, RAMC, 1985–88. QHP 1981–84. Editor, RAMC Jl, 1978–83. *Publications:* articles in medical jls, on smoking and health, nutrition, physical fitness and obesity. *Recreation:* antique furniture restoration. *Address:* Pepperdon Mine, Lustleigh, Newton Abbot, Devon TQ13 9SN. *T:* Lustleigh (01647) 277419.

CROWE, Brian Lee, CMG 1985; Director General for External Relations, Council of the European Union, since 1994; *b* 5 Jan. 1938; *s* of Eric Crowe and Virginia Crowe; *m* 1969, Virginia Willis; two *s*. *Educ:* Sherborne; Magdalen Coll., Oxford (1st Cl. Hons PPE). Joined FO, 1961; served: Moscow, 1962–64; London, 1965–67; Aden, 1967; Washington, 1968–73; Bonn, 1973–76; Counsellor and Hd of Policy Planning Staff, FCO, 1976–78; Hd of Chancery, UK Perm. Representation to EEC, Brussels, 1979–81; Counsellor and Hd of EEC Dept (External), FCO, 1982–84; Minister, Commercial, Washington, 1985–89; Ambassador to Austria, 1989–92; Economic Dir (Dep. Under-Sec. of State), FCO, 1992–94. *Recreations:* winter sports, tennis, riding, swimming. *Address:* Secretariat of the Council, Rue de la Loi 170, B-1048 Brussels, Belgium.

CROWE, Gerald Patrick, QC 1973; **His Honour Judge Crowe;** a Circuit Judge, since 1980; *b* 3 April 1930; *y s* of Patrick Crowe and Ethel Maud Crowe (*née* Tooth); *m* 1954, Catherine Mary, *d* of Joseph and Rose Murphy, Newry, N Ireland. *Educ:* St Francis Xavier's Coll.; Liverpool Univ. (LLB). Called to Bar, Gray's Inn, 1952; practised Northern Circuit. A Recorder of the Crown Court, 1976–80. Mem., Lord Chancellor's Adv. Cttee on Legal Aid, 1984–91. *Recreations:* golf, fishing. *Address:* The Spinney, Long Hey Road, Caldy, Cheshire L48 1LY. *T:* 0151–625 8848; Goldsmith Building, Temple, EC4Y 7BL.

CROWE, Dr Michael John, DM; FRCP, FRCPsych; Consultant Psychiatrist, Bethlem Royal and Maudsley Hospital, London, since 1978; *b* 16 Oct. 1937; *s* of Robert James Crowe and Olive (*née* Kingston-Jones); *m* 1968, Diane Jordan; one *s* one *d*. *Educ:* St Paul's Sch., London; Exeter Coll., Oxford (MA, BM 1963); London Hosp. Med. Coll. MPhil London, 1970; DM Oxon, 1977. MRCP 1967; MRCPsych 1973; FRCPsych 1984; FRCP 1992. House Officer: London Hosp., 1964; Chelmsford and Essex Hosp., 1964; Senior House Officer: Addenbrooke's Hosp., 1965–66; London Hosp., 1966–67; Maudsley Hospital: Registrar, 1967–69; Sen. Registrar, Res. Worker and Lectr, 1970–74; Sen. Lectr, Inst. of Psychiatry, 1974–77 (Course Leader, Couple Therapy Dip. Course, 1989–). Vis. Fellow, Univ. of Vermont, USA, 1969. Lectr on behavioural and couple therapy, USA, Trinidad, Denmark, Italy, etc. Founder Mem., Inst. of Family Therapy, London, 1976–. Chm., Assoc. of Sexual and Marital Therapists, 1986–88. Gaskell Gold Medal, RCPsych, 1972. *Publications:* (with J. Ridley) Therapy with Couples, 1990; papers in med. and psychol. jls on behaviour therapy, couple therapy and sexual dysfunctions. *Recreations:* music (performing and listening), poetry, literature, languages, walking. *Address:* 66 Palace View, Shirley, Croydon CR0 8QN. *T:* 0181–777 4823; 21 Wimpole Street, W1M 7AD. *T:* 0171–637 0146.

CROWE, Rev. Philip Anthony; Rector, Overton, Penley and Erbistock, since 1995; *b* 16 Aug. 1936; *s* of late Frederick Francis Crowe and of Hilda Crowe; *m* 1963, Freda

Maureen Gill; two *s* one *d*. *Educ:* Repton School; Selwyn Coll., Cambridge; Ridley Hall, Cambridge. National service, RA, 1955–57. Tutor in NT Greek and Mission, Oak Hill, 1962–65; Curate at Christchurch, Cockfosters, 1962–65; Editor, Church of England Newspaper, 1967–70; Sec., Bursary Scheme for Overseas Students, 1967–70; Senior Staff Member, St Martin-in-the Bull Ring, Birmingham, 1970–76; Rector of Breadsall, Derby, 1977–88; Derby Diocesan Missioner, 1977–83; Tutor in Ethics, St John's Coll., Nottingham, 1986–88; Principal, Salisbury and Wells Theol Coll., 1988–94. Hon. Canon, Salisbury Cathedral, 1991–. Mem., Gen. Synod, C of E, 1992–95. *Publications:* (contrib.) Mission in the Modern World, Church and Sacraments, 1977; Pastoral Reorganisation, 1978; Christian Baptism, 1980; The Use and Abuse of Alcohol, 1980; A Whisper will be Heard, 1994. *Recreations:* gardening, music, squash, walking, caravanning. *Address:* 4 Sundorne, Overton-on-Dee, Wrexham LL13 0EB. *T:* Wrexham (01978) 710229.

CROWE, Dame Sylvia, DBE 1973 (CBE 1967); landscape architect in private practice since 1945; *b* 1901; *d* of Eyre Crowe; unmarried. *Educ:* Berkhamsted; Swanley Hort. Coll. Designed gardens, 1927–39. Served FANY and ATS, 1939–45. Since 1945, private practice as landscape architect has included: work as consultant to: Harlow and Basildon New Town Corporations; Wimbleball and Rutland Water reservoirs; Central Electricity Generating Board, for Trawsfynydd and Wylfa Nuclear Power Stations; Forestry Commission; reclamation of land after 1952 floods and design of public gardens at Mablethorpe and Sutton on Sea; gardens for Oxford Univ., various Colls and Commonwealth Inst., London; design of Commonwealth Gardens, Canberra, Australia. Sec., Internat. Federation Landscape Architecture, 1948–59; Vice-Pres., 1964; Pres., Inst. Landscape Architects, 1957–59; Corresp. Mem., Amer. Soc. of Landscape Architects, 1960; Hon. Fellow, Aust. Inst. of Landscape Architects, 1978. Chm., Tree Council, 1974–76. Hon. FRIBA, 1969; Hon. FRTPI, 1970. Hon. DLitt: Newcastle, 1975; Heriot-Watt, 1976; Hon. LLD Sussex, 1978. VMH 1990. *Publications:* Tomorrow's Landscape, 1956; Garden Design, 1958, 3rd edn 1994; The Landscape of Power, 1958; Landscape of Roads, 1960; Forestry in the Landscape, 1966; The Landscapes of Forests and Woodlands, 1979; Patterns of Landscape, 1986. *Recreations:* walking and gardening. *Address:* 59 Ladbroke Grove, W11 3AT. *T:* 0171–727 7794.

CROWE, William James, Jr, DDSM, DSM; Ambassador of the United States of America to the Court of St James's, since 1994; *b* Kentucky, 2 Jan. 1925; *s* of William James Crowe and Eula (*née* Russell); *m* 1954, Shirley Mary Grenell; two *s* one *d*. *Educ:* US Naval Acad. (BS 1946); Stanford Univ. (MA 1956); Princeton (PhD 1965). Commnd Ensign, USN, 1946; Comdr, ME Force, Bahrain, 1976–77; Dep. Chief of Naval Ops, Navy Dept, Washington, 1977–80; C-in-C Allied Forces, S Europe, 1980–83; C-in-C Pacific, 1983–85; Chm., Jt Chiefs of Staff, 1985–89; retd 1989 in rank of Adm. Prof. of Geopolitics, Oklahoma Univ., 1989–94. Chm., Foreign Intelligence Adv. Bd, Washington, 1993–94. Director of several public cos. Numerous US and foreign decorations. *Publications:* (jtly) The Line of Fire, 1993; Reducing Nuclear Danger: the road away from the brink, 1993; articles on military and foreign policy. *Address:* Embassy of the United States of America, 24 Grosvenor Square, W1A 2LH. *T:* 0171–499 9000.

CROWFOOT, Maj.-Gen. Anthony Bernard, CB 1991; CBE 1982 (MBE 1974); General Officer Commanding North West District, 1989–91, retired; *b* 12 Aug. 1936; *s* of Thomas Bernard Crowfoot and Gladys Dorothy Crowfoot; *m* 1960, Bridget Sarah Bunting; three *s* one *d*. *Educ:* King Edward VII Sch., Norfolk; Royal Military Academy, Sandhurst, psc. Commissioned 1956; 1 E Yorks 1PWO: BAOR, UK, Aden, Gibraltar, 1956–60; Instructor, School of Infantry, 1960–62; 1PWO: BAOR, UK, Aden, 1962–66; Army Staff Coll. 1967; Brigade Major, HQ 5 Inf. Bde, 1968–69; Coy Comd 1PWO, Cyprus, 1970–71; DAAG, MoD, 1971–73; CO 1PWO: UK, BAOR, N Ireland, 1973–76; Instructor, Army Staff College, 1976–77; Col GS, MoD, 1977–80; Comd 39 Inf. Bde, N Ireland, 1980–82; Student, US Army War Coll., 1982–83; Dep. Comdr/COS, HQ British Forces Hong Kong, 1983–86; Dir Gen. Army Manning and Recruiting, MoD, 1986–89. Col, PWO Regt of York, 1986–. *Recreations:* sailing, philately, golf. *Club:* Army and Navy.

CROWHURST, Viscount; Mark John Henry Pepys; *b* 11 Oct. 1983; *s* and *heir* of 8th Earl of Cottenham, *qv*.

CROWLEY, Rear-Adm. George Clement, CB 1968; DSC 1942, and Bar 1944; Official Fellow and Domestic Bursar of Corpus Christi College, Oxford University, 1969–75; *b* 9 June 1916; *s* of Charles Edmund Lucas Crowley and Beatrice Cicely Crowley; *m* 1948, Una Margaret Jelf (*d* 1991); two *s*. *Educ:* Pangbourne Coll. Cadet, HMS Frobisher, 1933; served in China and New Zealand, 1934–39; served War of 1939–45, destroyers; comdg HMS Walpole, 1943–45; comdg HMS Tenacious, 1945–46 (despatches); RN Staff Course, 1947; Staff appts, 1948–53; Exec. Off., HMS Newfoundland, 1953–55; Drafting Comdr, Chatham, 1955–57; Asst Dir Plans, 1957–59; Capt. (D) 7th Destroyer Sqdn, 1959–61; CO New Entry, Trng Estab. HMS Raleigh, 1961–63; Capt. of Fleet to Flag Off. C-in-C Far East Fleet, 1963–64; Staff of Jt Exercise Unison, 1964–65; Staff of Defence Operational Analysis Estab., W Byfleet, 1965–66; Director-General, Naval Personal Services, 1966–68. Capt. 1957; Rear-Adm. 1966. *Recreations:* fishing, tennis, gardening. *Address:* Windrush, Shroton, Blandford, Dorset.

CROWLEY, Rt. Rev. John; *see* Middlesbrough, Bishop of (RC).

CROWLEY, John Desmond, QC 1982; a Recorder of the Crown Court, since 1980; *b* 25 June 1938; *s* of John Joseph Crowley and late Anne Marie (*née* Fallon); *m* 1977, Sarah Maria, *er d* of Christopher Gage Jacobs and Joan Zara (*née* Atkinson); two *d*. *Educ:* St Edmund's College, Ware; Christ's College, Cambridge (BA 1961, LLB 1962). National Service, 2/Lieut 6th Royal Tank Regt, 1957–58. Called to the Bar, Inner Temple, 1962, Bencher, 1989. Mem., Criminal Injuries Compensation Bd, 1985–. *Recreations:* tennis, the turf, wine. *Address:* 2 Crown Office Row, Temple, EC4Y 7HJ. *T:* 0171–797 8100.

CROWLEY, Niall, FCA; Chairman: Cahill May Roberts Group, since 1989; Allied Irish Banks Ltd Group, 1977–89; *b* 18 Sept. 1926; *s* of Vincent Crowley and Eileen (*née* Gunning); *m* 1953, Una Hegarty; five *s* one *d*. *Educ:* Xavier Sch.; Castleknock Coll. FCA 1955. Entered father's accounting firm, Stokes Kennedy Crowley & Co., as articled clerk, 1944: qualified, 1949; Partner, 1950, subseq. Managing Partner; Consultant to the firm, which also represents KPMG (formerly Peat Marwick Mitchell & Co.) in Ireland, 1977–84. Director: Irish Life Assurance Co. Ltd, 1964–84 (Chm., 1974–83); Alliance & Leicester Building Soc., 1990– (Dep. Chm., 1991–); Girobank, 1990–; J. Rothschild International Assurance, 1992–. President: Inst. of Chartered Accountants in Ireland, 1971–72; Dublin Chamber of Commerce, 1983–84; Irish Bankers Fedn, 1985–87; Inst. of Bankers, 1987–88. Chairman: Financial Services Industry Assoc., 1984–88; British-Irish Assoc., 1994–. Mem. Exec. Bd, Anglo-Irish Encounter Gp, 1983–. Member, Company of Goldsmiths of Dublin, 1973–. Hon. LLD NUI, 1982; Hon. DPhil Pontifical Univ., Maynooth, 1988. *Recreations:* bridge, golf. *Address:* (office) 46 Upper Mount Street, Dublin 2. *T:* Dublin 6762464; (home) 18 Whitebeam Road, Clonskeagh, Dublin 14, Ireland. *T:* Dublin 2694642. *Clubs:* Stephens Green; Portmarnock Golf; Milltown Golf; Fitzwilliam Lawn Tennis (Dublin).

CROWLEY-MILLING, Air Marshal Sir Denis, KCB 1973; CBE 1963; DSO 1943; DFC 1941, Bar 1942; Registrar and Secretary, Order of the Bath, 1985–90 (Gentleman Usher of the Scarlet Rod, 1979–85); *b* 22 March 1919; *s* of T. W. and G. M. Crowley-Milling (*née* Chinnery); *m* 1943, Lorna Jean Jeboult (*née* Stuttard); two *d* (one *s* decd). *Educ:* Malvern Coll., Worcs. Rolls Royce apprentice and RAF Volunteer Reserve, 1937–39; Fighters and Fighter Bombers, Nos 615, 242, 610 and 181 Sqdns, 1939–44; Air Ministry Operational Requirements, 1945–47; OC No 6 Sqdn, Middle East, 1947–50; Personal Staff Officer C-in-C Fighter Comd, 1950–52; Wing Comdr Flying, RAF Odiham, 1952–54; Directing Staff, RAF Staff Coll., Bracknell, 1954–57; Flying Coll., RAF Manby, 1957–58; Plans Staff Fighter Comd, 1958–59; Group Capt. Operations Central Fighter Establishment, 1959–62; Station Comdr, RAF Leconfield, 1962–64; AOC RAF Hong Kong, 1964–66; Dir Operational Requirements, MoD (Air), 1966–67; Comdr, RAF Staff and Principal Air Attaché, Washington, 1967–70; AOC No 38 Gp, RAF Odiham, 1970–72; AOC 46 Gp RAF Upavon, 1973; UK Rep., Perm. Mil. Deputies Gp, Cento, 1974–75. Controller, RAF Benevolent Fund, 1975–81, Mem. Council, 1981–; Mem. Council, Malvern Coll., 1972–90. Pres., Malverian Soc., 1993–. Chm., Douglas Bader Foundn, 1988–. Master, GAPAN, 1992–93. *Recreations:* golf and shooting. *Address:* c/o Barclays Bank, 46 Park Lane, W1A 4EE. *Club:* Royal Air Force.
See also M. C. Crowley-Milling.

CROWLEY-MILLING, Michael Crowley, CMG 1982; CEng, FIEE; consultant on computer control systems; *b* 7 May 1917; *s* of Thomas William Crowley-Milling and Gillian May (*née* Chinnery); *m* 1958, Gee Dickson. *Educ:* Radley Coll.; St John's Coll., Cambridge (MA 1943). CEng, FIEE 1956. R&D on radar systems, Metropolitan-Vickers Electrical Co. Ltd, Manchester, 1938–46; design and develt of electron linear accelerators for physics, medical and irradiation purposes, 1946–63; contrib. to construction of electron synchrotron, Daresbury Nuclear Physics Lab., Warrington, 1963–71; CERN, Geneva: resp. for control system for Super Proton Synchrotron (SPS), 1971–75; SPS Div. Leader, 1977–78; Dir, Accelerator Prog., 1979–80; Consultant, 1982–83; Consultant to: SLAC, Stanford Univ., Calif., 1984–85; Los Alamos Nat. Lab., New Mexico, 1986–94; SSC Lab., Dallas, 1991–93; Dir, Crowley Consultants, 1984–. Crompton Premium, IEE, 1959; Glazebrook Medal, Inst. of Physics, 1980. Captain LMBC, 1938. Patents for improvements in radar systems and particle accelerators, 1940–60. *Publications:* (ed) Accelerator Control Systems, 1986; (ed) Accelerator and Large Experimental Control Systems, 1990, 1994; John Bertram Adams, Engineer Extraordinary, 1993; articles and chapters in books on particle accelerators and computer control systems. *Recreations:* vintage cars, sailing. *Address:* Apt 15, Les Ruches II, 1264–St Cergue, Switzerland. *Clubs:* Vintage Sports Car; Llanbedr & Pensarn Yacht.
See also Sir Denis Crowley-Milling.

CROWSON, Richard Borman, CMG 1986; HM Diplomatic Service, retired; High Commissioner in Mauritius, 1985–89, and concurrently Ambassador (non-resident) to Federal Islamic Republic of the Comoros, 1986–89; *b* 23 July 1929; *s* of late Clarence Borman Crowson and Cecilia May Crowson (*née* Ramsden); *m* 1st, 1960, Sylvia Cavalier (marr. diss. 1974); one *s* one *d*; 2nd, 1983, Judith Elaine Turner. *Educ:* Downing Coll., Cambridge (MA). FCIS. HMOCS, Uganda, 1955–62; Foreign Office, 1962–63; First Sec. (Commercial), Tokyo, 1963–68; Dep. High Commissioner, Barbados, 1968–70; FCO, 1970–75; Counsellor (Commercial and Aid), Jakarta, 1975–77; Counsellor for Hong Kong Affairs, Washington, 1977–82; Counsellor and Head of Chancery, Berne, 1983–85. *Recreations:* music, drama, travel. *Address:* 67 Crofton Road, Orpington, Kent BR6 8HU. *T:* Orpington (01689) 891320. *Club:* Commonwealth Trust.

CROWTHER, Prof. Derek, PhD; FRCP, FRCR; Professor and Director, Cancer Research Campaign Department of Medical Oncology, Christie Hospital and Manchester University, since 1974; *s* of Robinson Westgarth Crowther and Gladys Hannah Crowther; *m* 1959, Margaret Frances Dickinson; two *d* (one *s* decd). *Educ:* City of London Sch.; Clare Coll., Cambridge (Foundn Scholar; MB, BChir, MA 1963); Royal Postgraduate Medical Sch., Hammersmith (PhD 1968); Royal Marsden Hosp. MSc Manchester, 1977. FRCP 1976; FRCR 1993. Sen. Lectr and Dep. Dir of Med. Oncology, St Bartholomew's Hosp., 1972–74. Prizes in medicine, paediatrics, and pathology, St Bartholomew's Hosp.; Gold Medal in Obstetrics and Gynaeocology, Univ. of Cambridge, 1963. *Publications:* edited: Manual of Cancer Chemotherapy, 1978 (trans. several langs); Interferons, 1991; more than 200 publications in the field of anti-cancer therapy. *Recreations:* gardening, travel, camping, cosmology, oriental and modern art. *Address:* 52 Barlow Moor Road, Didsbury, Manchester M20 2TR. *T:* 0161–434 6685.

CROWTHER, Eric (John Ronald), OBE 1977; Metropolitan Magistrate, 1968–89; a Recorder of the Crown Court, since 1983; *b* 4 Aug. 1924; *s* of Stephen Charles Crowther, company secretary, and Olive Beatrix Crowther (*née* Selby); *m* 1959, Elke Auguste Ottilie Winkelmann; one *s* one *d*. *Educ:* University College Sch., Hampstead. Royal Navy, 1943–47 (Medit. Area of Ops). Awarded Tancred Studentship in Common Law, 1948; Called to Bar, Lincoln's Inn, 1951; winner of Inns of Court Contest in Advocacy, 1951; Lectr and Student Counsellor, British Council, 1951–81; Lecturer: on Elocution and Advocacy for Council of Legal Educn, 1955–91 (Dir of Studies, Post-Final Gps, 1975–77); on Evidence to RN, 1968–89. Joined Inner Temple *ad eundem*, 1960. Practised at Criminal Bar, 1951–68. Chairman: Inner London Magistrates' Assoc. Trng Sub-Cttee, 1981–89; Prisoners' Wives Service, 1982–85. Mem. Council, British Council, 1985– (lectures world-wide); Mem., Bd of Academic Studies, St Catherine's, Cumberland Lodge, 1977–82; Director of Studies: Cromwell Sch. of English, 1973–91; Oxford Study Centre, 1992–94. Trustee, Professional and Academic Regional Visits Organisation, 1977–89. Mem. Cttee, RADA, 1979–84. Hon. Officer, Internat. Students' Hse, 1981–. Editor, Commonwealth Judicial Jl, 1973–77. *Publications:* Advocacy for the Advocate, 1984; Last in the List, 1988; Look What's on the Bench!, 1992. *Recreations:* travel, transport, the theatre, debating, student welfare, Scottish dancing. *Club:* International Students' House.

CROWTHER, (Joseph) Stanley; *b* 30 May 1925; *s* of Cyril Joseph Crowther and Florence Mildred (*née* Beckett); *m* 1948, Margaret Royston; two *s*. *Educ:* Rotherham Grammar Sch.; Rotherham Coll. of Technology. Royal Signals, 1943–47. Journalist: Rotherham Advertiser, 1941–43 and 1947–50; Yorkshire Evening Post, 1950–51; freelance, 1951–. Mem., Rotherham Borough Council, 1958–59, 1961–76; Mayor of Rotherham, 1971–72, 1975–76; Chm., Yorkshire and Humberside Develt Assoc., 1972–76. MP (Lab) Rotherham, June 1976–1992. Vice-Pres., Town and Country Planning Assoc. *Recreations:* walking, singing, listening to jazz. *Address:* 15 Clifton Crescent South, Rotherham S65 2AR. *T:* Rotherham (01709) 364559. *Clubs:* Central Labour, Eastwood View Working Men's (Rotherham).

CROWTHER, Dr Richard Anthony, FRS 1993; Member of Scientific Staff, Medical Research Council Laboratory of Molecular Biology, Cambridge, since 1969; Fellow of Peterhouse, Cambridge, since 1981; *b* 26 July 1942; *s* of Albert Crowther and Joyce Edith Crowther (*née* Anthony); *m* 1964, Susan Elizabeth Hope; two *s*. *Educ:* Manchester Grammar Sch.; Jesus Coll., Cambridge (BA); PhD Cantab. Res. Fellow, Edinburgh Univ., 1968. *Publications:* research papers and reviews in sci. jls. *Recreations:* walking, bird watching.

Address: MRC Laboratory of Molecular Biology, Hills Road, Cambridge CB2 2QH. *T:* Cambridge (01223) 402410.

CROWTHER, Thomas Rowland; QC 1981; **His Honour Judge Crowther;** a Circuit Judge since 1985; *b* 11 Sept. 1937; *s* of Kenneth Vincent Crowther, MB, BCh, and late Winifred Anita Crowther, MPS; *m* 1969, Gillian Jane (*née* Prince); one *s* one *d*. *Educ:* Newport High Sch.: Keble Coll., Oxford (MA). President, Oxford Univ. Liberal Club, 1957; Editor, Oxford Guardian, 1957. Called to the Bar, Inner Temple, 1961; Junior and Wine Steward, Wales and Chester Circuit, 1974. A Recorder, 1980–85. Contested (L) General Elections: Oswestry, 1964 and 1966; Hereford, 1970. Founder Mem., Gwent Area Broadcasting, 1981. *Recreation:* garden. *Address:* Lansor, Llandegfedd, Caerleon, Gwent NP6 1LS. *T:* Tredunnock (01633) 450224. *Clubs:* Cardiff and County; Newport Golf.

CROWTHER, William Ronald Hilton; QC 1980; a Recorder, since 1984; *b* 7 May 1941; *s* of Ronald Crowther and Ann Bourne Crowther; *m* 1964, Valerie Meredith (*née* Richards); one *s*. *Educ:* Oundle Sch.; Univ. of Oxford (BA Jurisprudence). Called to the Bar, Inner Temple, 1963, Bencher, 1985. *Recreations:* bird-watching and all aspects of natural history.

CROXFORD, Ian Lionel; QC 1993; *b* 23 July 1953; *s* of Peter Patrick Croxford and Mary Helen Croxford (*née* Richardson); *m* 1976, Sandra McCord; one *s* one *d*. *Educ:* Westcliff High Sch. for Boys; Univ. of Leicester (LLB 1st Cl. Hons). Called to the Bar, Gray's Inn, 1976 (Bacon Schol.); Lincoln's Inn, *ad eundem*, 1977. *Recreation:* watching sport. *Address:* 2/3 Gray's Inn Square, Gray's Inn, WC1R 5JH. *T:* 0171–242 4986.

CROXON, Raymond Patrick Austen, QC 1983; *b* 31 July 1928; *s* of late Randolph Croxon, bandmaster, Salvation Army, and Rose Harvey, Home League Sec., Salvation Army; *m* 1952, Monica Howard (marr. diss. 1992); two *s* two *d*. *Educ:* Strand College; King's College London. LLB. Served in RAMC, 1946–49. Called to the Bar, Gray's Inn, 1960. *Recreations:* travel, walking, swimming, reading, music, theatre, modern Greek language. *Address:* 8 King's Bench Walk, Temple EC4Y 7DU. *T:* 0171–797 8888, *Fax:* 0171–797 8880. *Club:* Savage.

CROXTON-SMITH, Claude; Chartered Accountant in public practice, Bristol, 1946–83, retired; President, Institute of Chartered Accountants in England and Wales, 1970–71; *b* 24 Aug. 1901; *m* 1928, Joan Norah Bloss Watling (*d* 1989); two *d*. *Educ:* Dulwich Coll.; Gonville and Caius Coll., Cambridge. The Sales Staff, Anglo American Oil Co. Ltd, 1924–31; Articled Clerk, Inst. of Chartered Accountants in England and Wales, 1932–36; Chartered Accountant, 1936–39. Served War of 1939–45, RAOC (Major). *Recreations:* walking, reading. *Address:* New Cote Rest Home, Cote House Lane, Westbury-on-Trym, Bristol BS9 3UW. *T:* Bristol (0117) 962 8341.

CROYDON, Area Bishop of; Rt. Rev. Wilfred Denniston Wood; appointed Bishop Suffragan of Croydon, 1985; *b* Barbados, WI, 15 June 1936; *s* of Wilfred Coward and Elsie Elmira Wood; *m* 1966, Ina Eileen, *d* of L. E. Smith, CBE, Barbadian MP; three *s* two *d*. *Educ:* Combermere Sch. and Codrington Coll., Barbados. Lambeth Dip. in Theol., 1962. Ordained deacon, St Michael's Cath., Barbados, 1961; ordained priest, St Paul's Cath., London, 1962. Curate of St Stephen with St Thomas, Shepherd's Bush, 1962–66, Hon. Curate, 1966–74; Bishop of London's Officer in Race Relations, 1966–74; Vicar of St Laurence, Catford, 1974–82; RD of East Lewisham, 1977–82; Archdeacon of Southwark, 1982–85; Hon. Canon of Southwark Cathedral, 1977–85. Mem., General Synod, 1987–. Chairman: Martin Luther King Meml Trust; Cttee on Black Anglican Concerns, 1986–91. Member: Royal Commn on Criminal Procedure, 1978–80; Archbishop of Canterbury's Commn on Urban Priority Areas, 1983–85; Housing Corp. Bd, 1986–. Non-exec. Dir, Mayday Healthcare NHS Trust, 1993–. JP Inner London, 1971–85. Hon. DD Gen. Theol Seminary, NY, 1986. *Publications:* (contrib.) The Committed Church, 1966; (with John Downing) Vicious Circle, 1968; Keep the Faith, Baby!, 1994. *Recreations:* reading, cricket; armchair follower of most sports. *Address:* 53 Stanhope Road, Croydon CR0 5NS. *T:* 0181–686 1822; (office) St Matthew's House, 100 George Street, Croydon CR0 1PE. *T:* 0181–681 5496, *Fax:* 0181–686 2074.

CROYDON, Archdeacon of; *see* Davies, Ven. V. A.

CROYDON, Rear-Adm. John Edward Kenneth, JP; DL; CEng, FIEE; *b* 25 Feb. 1929; *s* of late Kenneth P. Croydon and Elizabeth V. Croydon; *m* 1953, Brenda Joyce Buss, MA; one *s* two *d*. *Educ:* King Edward's Sch., Birmingham; Selwyn Coll., Cambridge (MA). BA London; CEng, FIEE 1975; jssc 1969. RN Special Entry Cadet (L), 1947; HMS Verulam and HMS Undine, 1954–55; Royal Naval Coll., Dartmouth, 1959–61; HMS Devonshire, 1961–64; HMS London, 1970–72; MoD, 1972–74; Captain Weapon Trials, 1974–77; Dir, Underwater Weapon Projects (Naval), 1978–80; Dir Gen. Weapons (Naval), 1981–83; Dep. Controller, Warships Equipment, MoD (Navy), 1983–84, retd. Rear Cdre (Dinghies), Royal Naval Sailing Assoc., 1980. Gov., Milton Abbey Sch., 1985–. County Comr for Scouts, Dorset, 1986–93. JP Weymouth, 1985; DL Dorset, 1993. *Recreations:* sailing, music, walking. *Clubs:* Royal Naval Sailing Association; Weymouth Sailing.

CROZIER, Brian Rossiter; writer and consultant on international affairs; Contributing Editor, National Review, New York, since 1982; Co-founder Institute for the Study of Conflict, 1970, and Director, 1970–79; *b* 4 Aug. 1918; *s* of R. H. Crozier and Elsa (*née* McGillivray); *m* 1940, Mary Lillian Samuel (*d* 1993); one *s* three *d*. *Educ:* Lycée, Montpellier; Peterborough Coll., Harrow; Trinity Coll. of Music, London. Music and art critic, London, 1936–39; reporter-sub-editor, Stoke-on-Trent, Stockport, London, 1940–41; aeronautical inspection, 1941–43; sub-editor: Reuters, 1943–44; News Chronicle, 1944–48; and writer, Sydney Morning Herald, 1948–51; corresp., Reuters-AAP, 1951–52; features editor, Straits Times, 1952–53; leader writer, corresp. and editor, Foreign Report, Economist, 1954–64; commentator, BBC English, French and Spanish overseas services, 1954–66; Chm., Forum World Features, 1965–74; Columnist: Now!, 1979–81; The Times, 1982–83; Freedom Today (formerly The Free Nation), 1982–89. Adjunct Scholar, Heritage Foundn, Washington, 1984–. *Publications:* The Rebels, 1960; The Morning After, 1963; Neo-Colonialism, 1964; South-East Asia in Turmoil, 1965 (3rd edn 1968); The Struggle for the Third World, 1966; Franco, 1967; The Masters of Power, 1969; The Future of Communist Power (in USA: Since Stalin), 1970; De Gaulle, vol. 1 1973, vol. 2 1974; A Theory of Conflict, 1974; The Man Who Lost China (Chiang Kai-shek), 1976; Strategy of Survival, 1978; The Minimum State, 1979; Franco: crepúsculo de un hombre (Spanish orig.), 1980; The Price of Peace, 1980, new edn 1983; (jtly) Socialism Explained, 1984; (jtly) This War Called Peace, 1984; (as John Rossiter) The Andropov Deception (novel), 1984 (pubd under own name, NY, 1986); Socialism: dream and reality, 1987; (ed) The Grenada Documents, 1987; The Gorbachev Phenomenon, 1990; Communism: why prolong its death-throes?, 1990; Free Agent, 1993; The KGB Lawsuits, 1995; contrib. to jls in many countries. *Recreations:* piano, taping stereo. *Address:* Flat AA, 1 Carlisle Place, SW1P 1NP. *T:* 0171–931 8046. *Club:* Royal Automobile.

CROZIER, Julian Smyth, CB 1995; Chief Executive, Training and Employment Agency, Northern Ireland, since 1990; *b* 19 Sept. 1935; *m* 1961, Rose Mary Maurna; two *s* one *d*. *Educ:* Campbell Coll., Belfast; Queens' Coll., Cambridge (BA). HMOCS, N Rhodesia, 1958–64; N Ireland Civil Service, 1965–95: served in Dept of Agriculture, Office of Comr for Complaints (Ombudsman), Depts of Health and Social Services, Finance and Personnel, Economic Develt. *Recreations:* hobby farming, country pursuits, golf, fishing, sailing, reading. *Address:* Training and Employment Agency, Clarendon House, Adelaide Street, Belfast BT2 8DJ. *T:* Belfast (01232) 541662. *Clubs:* Commonwealth Trust; Royal Co. Down Golf.

CRUDDAS, Rear-Adm. Thomas Rennison, CB 1974; CEng, FIMechE; engineering consultant; *b* 6 Feb. 1921; *s* of late Thomas Hepple Wheatley Cruddas, MBE, and Lily (*née* Rennison); *m* 1943, Angela Elizabeth Astbury; one *s* one *d*. *Educ:* Queen Elizabeth Grammar Sch., Darlington; RN Engineering College, Keyham. Joined RN 1938; RNEC, 1939–42; served War, 1939–45: in Mediterranean and E Indies, in HM Ships Unicorn and Valiant; HMS Cardigan Bay, 1948–50; specialised aeronautical engrg, 1950; RNAY Donibristle, 1951–53; Comdr, 1953; HMS Ark Royal, 1953–55; RNAY Fleetlands, 1956–58; Admiralty, 1958–61; Staff of Flag Officer Aircraft Carriers, 1961–63; Captain, 1963; Asst Dir Ship Prodn, 1964–66; service with USN, Washington, DC, as Programme Manager UK Phantom Aircraft, 1967–69; Comd Engr Officer, Staff FONAC, 1970–72; Rear-Adm. Engineering, Naval Air Comd, 1972; Dep. Controller Aircraft B, MoD (PE), 1973–76, retired. Dir, Pressure Vessels Quality Assurance Bd, 1977–86. *Recreation:* country living. *Address:* Beeches Close, Bishop's Waltham, Hants SO3 1FZ. *T:* Bishop's Waltham (01489) 892335.

CRUFT, John Herbert; Hon. Treasurer, Royal Society of Musicians, 1976–87; *b* 4 Jan. 1914; *er s* of late Eugene and Winifred Cruft; *m* 1938, Mary Margaret Miriam, *e d* of late Rev. Pat and Miriam McCormick; two *s*. *Educ:* Westminster Abbey Choir Sch.; Westminster Sch.; Royal College of Music (K. F. Boult Conducting Scholar). Oboist in BBC Television, London Philharmonic and Suisse Romande Orchestras, 1936–40. Served with Royal Corps of Signals, 1940–46. London Symphony Orchestra: Oboist, 1946–49; Sec., 1949–59. British Council: Dir of Music Dept, 1959–61; Dir of Drama and Music Dept, 1961–65; Music Dir, Arts Council of GB, 1965–79; a Dir, National Jazz Centre, 1982–87. Member: Council, RCM, 1983–90, Life Gov., 1990; Council for Dance Educn and Trng, 1990–92. Trustee: Loan Fund for Musical Instruments, 1980–; Electro-Acoustic Music Trust, 1980–88; Governor: London Festival Ballet Trust Ltd, 1980–84; Contemporary Dance Trust Ltd, 1982–88. FRCM, Hon. RAM. *Publication:* The Royal College of Music: a Centenary Record 1883–1983 (with late H. C. Colles), 1982. *Address:* 11 Broadhinton Road, Clapham, SW4 0LU. *T:* 0171–720 2330.

CRUICKSHANK, Alistair Ronald; Under Secretary (Agricultural Imports, Plant Protection and Emergencies), Ministry of Agriculture, Fisheries and Food, since 1995; *b* 2 Oct. 1944; *s* of late Francis John Cruickshank and of Kate Cameron Cruickshank (*née* Brittain); *m* 1967, Sandra Mary Noble; three *d*. *Educ:* Aberdeen Grammar School; Aberdeen University (MA). Joined MAFF as Assistant Principal, 1966; Principal, 1970; Head, successively, of Eggs and Poultry Br. and Milk Br.; Asst Secretary, 1978; Head, successively, of Marketing Policy and Potatoes, Meat Hygiene, and Milk Divs; Under Sec. (Animal Health), 1986; Principal Finance Officer, 1989–94. *Recreations:* church activities, gardening, looking at old buildings. *Address:* c/o Ministry of Agriculture, Fisheries and Food, 10 Whitehall Place, SW1A 2HH.

CRUICKSHANK, Donald Gordon; Director General of Telecommunications, since 1993; *b* 17 Sept. 1942; *s* of Donald Campbell Cruickshank and Margaret Buchan Cruickshank (*née* Morrison); *m* 1964, Elizabeth Buchan Taylor; one *s* one *d*. *Educ:* Univ. of Aberdeen (MA); Inst. of Chartered Accountants of Scotland (CA); Manchester Business School (MBA). McKinsey & Co., 1972–77; Times Newspapers, 1977–80; Pearson, 1980–84; Man. Dir, Virgin Group, 1984–89. Non-exec. Dir, Christian Salvesen, 1994–. Chm., Wandsworth HA, 1986–89; Chief Exec., NHS in Scotland, 1989–93. *Recreations:* sport, golf, opera. *Address:* Office of Telecommunications, 50 Ludgate Hill, EC4M 7JJ.

CRUICKSHANK, Prof. Durward William John, PhD, ScD; FRS 1979; CChem, FRSC; Professor of Chemistry (Theoretical Chemistry), 1967–83, now Emeritus, and Hon. Professorial Research Fellow, since 1983, University of Manchester Institute of Science and Technology; *b* 7 March 1924; *s* of William Durward Cruickshank, MB, ChB, and Margaret Ombler Meek, MA, MRCS, LRCP; *m* 1953, Marjorie Alice Travis (*d* 1983), MA, PhD; one *s* one *d*. *Educ:* St Lawrence Coll., Ramsgate; Loughborough Coll. (DLC 1944; BScEng 1st Cl. Hons London, 1944); Cambridge Univ. (Wrangler, Math. Tripos, 1949; Dist. Pt III Math. Tripos, 1950; BA 1949, MA 1954, ScD 1961). PhD Leeds, 1952; CChem, FRIC 1971. Engrg Asst, WO and Admiralty (Naval Opl Res.), 1944–46; Leeds University: Res. Asst, Chemistry Dept, 1946–47; Lectr, 1950–57; Reader in Math. Chemistry, 1957–62; Fellow, St John's Coll., Cambridge, 1953–56; Joseph Black Prof. of Chem. (Theor. Chem.), Glasgow Univ., 1962–67; Dep. Principal, UMIST, 1971–72. Hon. Vis. Prof. of Physics, York Univ., 1985–88. Treasurer, 1966–72, and Gen. Sec., 1970–72, Internat. Union of Crystallography. Companion of UMIST, 1992. 1977 Chemical Soc. Award for Struct. Chem., 1978; (first) Dorothy Hodgkin Prize, British Crystallographic Assoc., 1991. *Publications:* (ed jtly) P. P. Ewald and his Dynamical Theory of X-ray Diffraction, 1992; (ed jtly) Time-resolved Macromolecular Crystallography, 1992; scientific papers on crystallography, molecular structure determination and theoretical chemistry in Acta Cryst., Proc. Royal Soc., and Jl Chem. Soc. *Recreations:* golf, genealogy. *Address:* 105 Moss Lane, Alderley Edge, Cheshire SK9 7HW. *T:* Alderley Edge (01625) 582656; Chemistry Department, University of Manchester Institute of Science and Technology, Manchester M60 1QD. *T:* 0161–236 3311.

CRUICKSHANK, Prof. Eric Kennedy, OBE 1961; MD; FRCP, FRCPGlas; Dean of Postgraduate Medicine, University of Glasgow, 1972–80; retired; *b* 29 Dec. 1914; *s* of John Cruickshank, CBE, and Jessie (*née* Allan); *m* 1st, 1951, Ann Burch; two *s* two *d*; 2nd, 1969, Josephine Williams. *Educ:* Aberdeen Grammar Sch.; Univ. of Aberdeen (MB, ChB Hons, 1937; MD Hons and gold medal, 1948). Fellow, Harvard and Massachusetts Gen. Hosp., USA, 1938–39; Lectr, then Sen. Lectr, Dept of Medicine, Univ. of Aberdeen, 1939–50; Hon. Consultant in Medicine, NHS, 1948–50; First Dean, Medical Faculty, and Prof. of Medicine, Univ. of West Indies, Kingston, Jamaica, 1950–72. Served War of 1939–45: Captain RAMC, Medical Specialist, Changi Prisoner of War Camp, Singapore (despatches twice). WHO Consultant in Medical Educn, 1959–, Nutrition, 1955–; Member: GMC, 1972–80; Inter-Univ. Council, 1972–84; Greater Glasgow Health Bd, 1972–80. Hon. FACP 1969. *Publications:* on nutrition, neurology, medical educn. *Recreations:* tennis, golf, gardening, ornithology. *Address:* Parsonage House, Oare, Wilts SN8 4JA.

CRUICKSHANK, Flight-Lieut John Alexander, VC 1944; ED 1947; late RAF; with Grindlay's Bank Ltd, London, 1952–76; retired; Administrator, Northern Division, North West Securities Ltd, 1977–85; *b* 20 May 1920; *s* of James C. Cruickshank, Aberdeen, and Alice Bow, Macduff, Banffshire; *m* 1955, Marion R. Beverley (*d* 1985), Toronto, Canada. *Educ:* Aberdeen Grammar Sch.; Daniel Stewart's Coll., Edinburgh. Entered Commercial Bank of Scotland, 1938; returned to banking, 1946. Mem. of Territorial Army and called for service, Aug. 1939, in RA; transferred to RAF 1941 and commissioned in 1942; all

RAF service was with Coastal Command. ADC to Lord High Commissioner to the Gen. Assembly of the Church of Scotland, 1946–48. *Clubs:* Royal Northern and University (Aberdeen); Merchants of Edinburgh Golf.

CRUM, Douglas Vernon E.; *see* Erskine Crum.

CRUMP, Maurice, CBE 1959; *b* 13 Jan. 1908; *s* of William Hamilton Crump and Jean Morris Alan Crump (*née* Esplen); *m* 1946, Mary Arden (*d* 1995), *d* of Austin Stead, Montreal, PQ, Canada. *Educ:* Harrow; Oxford. Called to Bar, Inner Temple, 1931, practised Western Circuit. RAF Reserve, 1929–35; recommissioned RAF Volunteer Reserve, 1940; served War of 1939–45, as pilot, 1940–45; Capt. in Command on North Atlantic Return Ferry, 1944–45. In Dept of Dir of Public Prosecutions, 1945; Asst Dir, 1951–58, Deputy Dir, 1958–66. *Recreations:* flying, travelling. *Address:* No 2, 46 Elm Park Road, SW3 6AX. *T:* 0171–351 2126.

CRUMP, Rt. Rev. William Henry Howes; *b* London, Ontario, Canada, 13 March 1903; *m* 1st, 1932, Betty Margaret Dean Thomas; one *s* one *d*; 2nd, 1964. *Educ:* London, Ontario; University of Western Ontario; Huron College; Trinity College, Toronto. Ordained Deacon, 1926; Curate, Wawanesa, Manitoba, 1926; Priest, 1927. Rector: Glenboro, Manitoba, 1927; Holland, Manitoba, 1931; Boissevain, Manitoba, 1933; St Aidan's, Winnipeg, 1933–44; Christ Church, Calgary, 1944–60; Canon of St Paul, Diocese of Calgary, 1949; Bishop of Saskatchewan, 1960–71.

CRUMP, William Maurice Esplen; *see* Crump, Maurice.

CRUMPTON, Michael Joseph, CBE 1992; PhD; FRS 1979; Director, Imperial Cancer Research Technology Ltd, since 1989 (Chief Operating Officer, 1993–94); Director of Research (Laboratories), Imperial Cancer Research Fund Laboratories, London, 1991–93, retired (Deputy Director of Research, 1979–91); *b* 7 June 1929; *s* of Charles E. and Edith Crumpton; *m* 1960, Janet Elizabeth Dean; one *s* two *d*. *Educ:* Poole Grammar Sch., Poole; University Coll., Southampton; Lister Inst. of Preventive Medicine, London. BSc, PhD, London. National Service, RAMC, 1953–55. Member, scientific staff, Microbiological Research Estabt, Porton, Wilts, 1955–60; Visiting Scientist Fellowship, Nat. Insts of Health, Bethesda, Maryland, USA, 1959–60; Research Fellow, Dept of Immunology, St Mary's Hosp. Med. Sch., London, 1960–66; Mem., scientific staff, Nat. Inst. for Med. Research, Mill Hill, 1966–79, Head of Biochemistry Div., 1976–79. Visiting Fellow, John Curtin Sch. of Med. Research, ANU, Canberra, 1973–74. Member: EMBO, 1982–; WHO Steering Cttee for Encapsulated Bacteria, 1984–91 (Chm., 1988–91); Cell Board, MRC, 1979–83; Scientific Adv. Cttee, Lister Inst., 1986–91; Sloan Cttee, General Motors Res. Foundn, 1986–88 (Chm., 1988); MRC AIDS Directed Prog. Steering Cttee, 1987–91; Scientific Cttee, Swiss Inst. for Experimental Cancer Res., 1989–; DTI/SERC Biotech. Jt Adv. Bd, 1989–93. Member Council: Royal Instn, 1986–90 (Mem., Davy Faraday Lab. Cttee, 1985–90, Chm. of Cttee, 1988–90); MRC, 1986–90; Royal Soc., 1990–92; Mem. Sci. Council, Celltech Ltd, 1980–90; Chairman: Sci. Adv. Bd, Biomed. Res. Centre, Univ. of British Columbia, Vancouver, 1987–91; DoH/HSE Adv. Cttee on Dangerous Pathogens, 1991–94; Mem. Sci. Adv. Bd, Ciba Foundn, 1990–94. Non-Exec. Dir, Amersham Internat., 1990–. Member Council: Inst. of Cancer Res., 1994– (Mem., Governing Body); Imperial Coll. of Sci., Technol. and Medicine, 1994–; Mem. Governing Body, BPMF, 1987–; Gov., Strangeways Res. Lab., 1993–. Mem. Editorial Board: Biochemical Jl, 1966–73 (Dep. Chm., 1969–72); Eur. Jl of Immunology, 1972–86; Immunochemistry, 1975–79; Immunogenetics, 1979–85; Biochemistry Internat., 1980–86; Molecular Biol. and Medicine, 1983–86; Human Immunology, 1985–; Regional Editor, Molecular Immunology, 1982–86. Biochem. Soc. Vis. Lectr, Australia, 1983. Sen. Treas., Royal Soc. Club, 1988–89. *Publications:* contribs to learned scientific jls. *Recreations:* gardening, reading. *Address:* 33 Homefield Road, Radlett, Herts WD7 8PX. *T:* Radlett (01923) 854675.

CRUTCHLEY, Brooke, CBE 1954; Printer of the University of Cambridge, 1946–74; Fellow of Trinity Hall, 1951–73, Emeritus Fellow, 1977 (Vice-Master, 1966–70); Honorary Fellow of St Edmund's College (formerly St Edmund's House), Cambridge, since 1980; *b* 31 July 1907; *yr s* of late Ernest Tristram Crutchley, CB, CMG, CBE, and Anna, *d* of James Dunne; *m* 1936, Diana, *d* of late Lt-Col Arthur Egerton Cotton, DSO, and Beryl Marie (who *m* 2nd, John Lee Booker); two *s* one *d*. *Educ:* Shrewsbury; Trinity Hall, Cambridge. Editorial Staff of Yorkshire Post, 1929–30; Asst Univ. Printer at Cambridge, 1930–45; Secretary's Dept of the Admiralty, 1941–45. Pres., Inst. of Printing, 1972–74. Hon. Col, Commonwealth of Kentucky, 1974. Bicentenary Medal, RSA, 1977. *Publication:* To be a printer, (autobiog.), 1980. *Address:* 39 High Street, Great Shelford, Cambridge CB2 5EH. *T:* Cambridge (01223) 845168. *Club:* Double Crown.

CRUTCHLOW, John Adrian; Director of Finance, Metropolitan Police, since 1986; *b* 30 March 1946; *s* of James William Crutchlow and Elsie Nellie Crutchlow (*née* King); *m* 1971, Valerie Elizabeth Farage. *Educ:* Finchley County Grammar Sch.; HNC (with dist.) in Business Studies; BA Open; postgraduate Dip. Management Studies. Paymaster General's Office, 1962–65; Metropolitan Police Civil Staff, 1965–; Principal, 1974–81; Dep. Dir of Finance, 1981–84; Dep. Estabt Officer, 1984–86; Asst Sec., 1986–92; Asst Under-Sec. of State, 1992–; Dep. to Receiver, Metropolitan Police Dist, 1994–. Pres., New Scotland Yard Civil Staff Assoc., 1994–. FIMgt. *Recreations:* reading, gardening, renovating old houses. *Address:* New Scotland Yard, Broadway, SW1H 0BG. *T:* 0171–230 8995.

CRUTHERS, Sir James (Winter), Kt 1980; company director; Vice-Chairman and Executive Vice-President, News America Publishing Inc., 1984–90 (Director, since 1983); Vice-Chairman, News America Holdings Inc., 1984–90 (Director, since 1984); *b* 20 Dec. 1924; *s* of James William and Kate Cruthers; *m* 1950, Alwyn Sheila Della; one *s* one *d*. *Educ:* Claremont Central State Sch.; Perth Technical College. Started as junior in Perth Daily News, 1939; war service, AIF and RAAF (Pilot), 1942; Journalist, Perth Daily News, 1946; Editor, Weekly Publications, West Australian Newspapers Ltd, 1953; TVW Enterprises Ltd: General Manager, 1958; Managing Director, 1969; Dep. Chm., 1974; Chm., 1976–81; Chm., Australian Film Commn, 1982–83. Director: News Corp. Ltd, 1981–92; Satellite Television plc, 1984–90 (Chm., 1985–88). Western Australian Citizen Of The Year, Industry and Commerce, 1980. *Recreations:* golf, jogging. *Address:* 8 Bird Street, Mosman Park, WA 6012, Australia. *Clubs:* Weld (Perth); Lake Karrinyup Country (Perth).

CRUTTWELL, Mrs Geraldine; *see* McEwan, Geraldine.

CRUTTWELL, Hugh (Percival); Principal of Royal Academy of Dramatic Art, 1966–84, retired; *b* 31 Oct. 1918; *s* of Clement Chadwick Cruttwell and Grace Fanny (*née* Robin); *m* 1953, Geraldine McEwan, *qv*; one *s* one *d*. *Educ:* King's Sch., Bruton; Hertford Coll., Oxford. *Address:* 8 Ranelagh Avenue, Barnes, SW13 0BY.

CRWYS-WILLIAMS, Air Vice-Marshal David Owen, CB 1990; Managing Director: Services Sound and Vision Corporation, since 1994 (Deputy Managing Director, 1993–94); SSVC Services Ltd; Columbia Communications Europe, since 1993; Teleport London International, since 1994; *b* 24 Dec. 1940; *s* of Gareth Crwys-Williams and Frances Ellen Crwys-Williams (*née* Strange); *m* 1st, 1964, Jennifer Jean (*née* Pearce) (marr. diss. 1971); one *s* one *d*; 2nd, 1973, Irene Thompson (Suzie) (*née* Whan); one *s* two *d*. *Educ:* Oakham Sch.; RAF Coll., Cranwell. Commnd as pilot, RAF, 1961; served No 30 Sqn, Kenya, 1962–64, No 47 Sqn, Abingdon, 1964–66; ADC to C-in-C RAF Trng Comd, 1966–68; OC 46 Sqn, 1969; RAF Masirah, 1972; Army Staff Coll., 1973; Personal Staff Officer to C-in-C NEAF, 1974–75; OC No 230 Sqn, 1976–77; Air Sec. Dept, MoD, 1977–78; Dep. Dir Air Plans, MoD, 1979–82; OC RAF Shawbury, 1983–84; RCDS 1985; Dir of Air Support and Dir of Air Staff Duties, MoD, 1986–88; Comdr, British Forces Falkland Is, 1988–89; Dir Gen., RAF Personal Services, MoD, 1989–92. Gp Captain 1979; Air Cdre 1985; Air Vice-Marshal 1988. FIPM 1991; FIMgt 1993. *Recreations:* furniture restoration, walking, building, fishing. *Address:* c/o Barclays Bank, PO Box 41, Abingdon, Oxon OX14 1GU. *Club:* Royal Air Force.

CRYSTAL, Prof. David, OBE 1995; author, lecturer, broadcaster on language and linguistics, and reference books editor; Hon. Professorial Fellow, University of Wales, Bangor (formerly University College of North Wales), since 1985; *b* 6 July 1941; *s* of Samuel Cyril Crystal and Mary Agnes Morris; *m* 1st, 1964, Molly Irene Stack (*d* 1976); one *s* two *d* (and one *s* decd); 2nd, 1976, Hilary Frances Norman; one *s*. *Educ:* St Mary's Coll., Liverpool; University Coll. London (BA 1962); London Univ. (PhD 1966). Res. Asst, UCL, 1962–63; Asst Lectr, UCNW, 1963–65; University of Reading: Lectr, 1965–69; Reader, 1969–75; Prof., 1975–85. Vis. Prof., Bowling Green State Univ., 1969. Dir, Ucheldre Centre, Holyhead, 1991–. Sec., Linguistics Assoc. of GB, 1965–70. Mem., Academic Bd, Coll. of Speech Therapists, 1972–79; Hon. Pres., Soc. of Indexers, 1992–; Chm., Nat. Literacy Assoc., 1995–. Editor: Language Res. in Progress, 1966–70; Jl of Child Language, 1973–85; The Language Library, 1978–; Applied Language Studies, 1980–84; Child Language Teaching and Therapy, 1985–; Linguistics Abstracts, 1985–; Blackwells Applied Language Studies, 1986–; Consultant Editor, English Today, 1985–94; Adv. Editor, Penguin Linguistics, 1968–75; Associate Editor, Jl of Linguistics, 1970–73; Co-Editor, Studies in Language Disability, 1974–. Regular BBC broadcasts on English language and linguistics. FCST 1983; FRSA 1983. *Publications:* Systems of prosodic and paralinguistic features in English (with R. Quirk), 1964; Linguistics, language and religion, 1965; (ed jtly) Proceedings, Modern approaches to language teaching at university level, 1967; What is linguistics?, 1968, 5th edn 1985; Prosodic systems and intonation in English, 1969; (with D. Davy) Investigating English style, 1969; (ed with W. Bolton) The English language, vol. 2, 1969; Linguistics, 1971, 2nd edn 1985; Basic linguistics, 1973; Language acquisition, 1973; The English tone of voice, 1975; (with D. Davy) Advanced conversational English, 1975; (with J. Bevington) Skylarks, 1975; (jtly) The grammatical analysis of language disability, 1976, 2nd edn 1989; Child language, learning and linguistics, 1976, 2nd edn 1987; Working with LARSP, 1979; Introduction to language pathology, 1980, 3rd edn 1993; A first dictionary of linguistics and phonetics, 1980, 3rd edn 1991; (ed) Eric Partridge: in his own words, 1980; Clinical linguistics, 1981; Directions in applied linguistics, 1981; Profiling linguistic disability, 1982, 2nd edn 1992; (ed) Linguistic controversies, 1982; Who cares about English usage?, 1984; Language handicap in children, 1984; Linguistic encounters with language handicap, 1984; Listen to your child, 1986; (ed with W. Bolton) The English language, 1987; Cambridge Encyclopaedia of Language, 1987; Rediscover grammar, 1988; The English Language, 1988; Pilgrimage, 1988; (with J. C. Davies) Convent, 1989; (ed) Cambridge Encyclopedia, 1990, 2nd edn 1994; Language A to Z, 1991; Making Sense of English Usage, 1991; Nineties Knowledge, 1992; Introducing Linguistics, 1992; An Encyclopedic Dictionary of Language and Languages, 1992; (ed) Cambridge Concise Encyclopedia, 1992, 2nd edn 1995; (ed) Cambridge Paperback Encyclopedia, 1993, 2nd edn 1995; (ed) Cambridge Factfinder, 1993, 2nd edn 1995; (ed) Cambridge Biographical Encyclopedia, 1994; Cambridge Encyclopedia of the English Language, 1995; (with J. L. Foster) Databank series: Heat, Light, Sound, Roads, Railways, Canals, Manors, Castles, Money, Monasteries, Parliament, Newspapers, 1979, The Romans, The Greeks, The Ancient Egyptians, 1981; Air, Food, Volcanoes, 1982; Deserts, Dinosaurs and Electricity, 1983; Motorcycles, Computers, Horses and Ponies, Normans, Vikings, Anglo-Saxons, Celts, 1984; The Stone Age, Fishing, 1985; (with J. L. Foster) Datasearch series: Air and Breathing, Heating and Cooling, Light and Seeing, Sound and Hearing, 1991; contributions to: The Library of Modern Knowledge, 1978; A Dictionary of Modern Thought, 1978, 2nd edn 1987; Reader's Digest Great Illustrated Dictionary, 1984; Reader's Digest Book of Facts, 1985; A Comprehensive Grammar of the English Language, 1985; and to numerous volumes on language, style, prosody, communication, religion, handicap, teaching and reading; symposia and proceedings of learned socs; articles and reviews in jls on linguistics, English language, speech pathology and education. *Recreations:* cinema, music, bibliophily, development of the arts. *Address:* Akaroa, Gors Avenue, Holyhead, Anglesey, Gwynedd LL65 1PB. *T:* Holyhead (01407) 762764, *Fax:* Holyhead (01407) 769728.

CRYSTAL, Michael; QC 1984; Honorary Senior Visiting Fellow, Centre for Commercial Law Studies, Queen Mary and Westfield College (formerly Queen Mary College), University of London, since 1987; *b* 5 March 1948; *s* of Dr Samuel Cyril Crystal, OBE, and Rachel Ettel Crystal; *m* 1972, Susan Felicia Sniderman; one *s* one *d*. *Educ:* Leeds Grammar Sch.; Queen Mary Coll., Univ. of London (LLB Hons); Magdalen Coll., Oxford (BCL). Called to the Bar, Middle Temple, 1970, Bencher, 1993; called to the Bar *ad eundem*, Gray's Inn, 1989; Lecturer in Law, Pembroke Coll., Oxford, 1971–76. DTI Inspector into County NatWest Ltd and County NatWest Securities Ltd, 1988–89, and into National Westminster Bank plc, 1992. Mem., Insolvency Rules Adv. Cttee, 1993–. Gov., RSC, 1988–. *Publications:* various legal text books. *Recreations:* travel, music, theatre. *Address:* 27 Rosslyn Hill, NW3 5UJ. *T:* 0171–435 7290; 3/4 South Square, Gray's Inn, WC1R 5HP. *T:* 0171–696 9900. *Clubs:* Royal Automobile, MCC.

CUBBON, Sir Brian (Crossland), GCB 1984 (KCB 1977, CB 1974); Permanent Under Secretary of State, Home Office, 1979–88; Member, Press Complaints Commission, since 1995; *b* 9 April 1928; *m* 1956, Elizabeth Lorin Richardson; three *s* one *d*. *Educ:* Bury Grammar Sch.; Trinity Coll., Cambridge. Entered Home Office, 1951; Cabinet Office, 1961–63, 1971–75; Private Sec. to Home Sec., 1968–69; Permanent Under-Sec. of State, Northern Ireland Office, 1976–79. *T:* (01892) 832534. *Clubs:* United Oxford & Cambridge University, Beefsteak.

CUBBON, Maj.-Gen. John Hamilton, CB 1962; CBE 1958 (OBE 1940); DL; *b* 15 March 1911; *s* of Joseph Cubbon; *m* 1951, Amelia Margaret Yates; two *s* one *d*. *Educ:* St Bees Sch.; RMC Sandhurst. 2nd Lieut Ches Regt, 1931; Commanded: 1st Bn The Parachute Regt, 1946–49; 1st Bn The Ches Regt, 1951–54; 18th Infantry Bde, Malaya, 1956–57. Maj.-Gen. 1960; GOC SW Dist, 1960–63; GOC Land Forces, Middle East Command, 1963–65. DL Devon, 1969. *Recreation:* sailing. *Address:* Highfield, Harpford, Sidmouth, Devon EX10 0NJ.

CUBIE, George; Clerk of the Overseas Office, House of Commons, since 1991; *b* 30 Aug. 1943; *s* of Dr Alexander Cubie and of late Elsie B. C. Thorburn; *m* 1966, Kathleen S. Mullan; one *s*. *Educ:* Dollar Acad.; Edinburgh Univ. (MA Hons). Clerk in H of C, 1966; Clerk of Financial Cttees, H of C, 1987–89; Sec. to Public Accounts Commn, 1987–89; Clerk of Select Cttees, H of C, 1989–91. *Recreation:* walking. *Address:* 97 Ember Lane, Esher, Surrey KT10 8EQ. *T:* 0181–398 1232.

CUBITT, family name of **Baron Ashcombe.**

CUBITT, Sir Hugh (Guy), Kt 1983; CBE 1977; FRICS; JP; DL; Chairman, Rea Brothers Group PLC, since 1995; Director, PSIT PLC (formerly Property Security Investment Trust PLC), since 1962; *b* 2 July 1928; *s* of late Col Hon. (Charles) Guy Cubitt, CBE, DSO, TD, and Rosamond Mary Edith, *d* of Sir Montagu Cholmeley, 4th Bt; *m* 1958, Linda Ishbel, *d* of late Hon. Angus Campbell, CBE; one *s* two *d*. *Educ:* RNC Dartmouth and Greenwich. Lieut RN, 1949; served in Korea, 1949–51; Flag Lieut to Adm., BJSM Washington, 1952 and to C-in-C Nore, 1953; retd 1953. Qual. Chartered Auctioneer and Estate Agent, 1958; Chartered Surveyor (FRICS) 1970. Partner: Rogers Chapman & Thomas, 1958–67; Cubitt & West, 1962–79. Regl Dir, 1970–77, Dir, 1977–90, Mem., UK Adv. Bd, 1990–91, National Westminster Bank; Chairman: Lombard North Central PLC, 1980–91; The Housing Corp., 1980–90. Comr, and Chm., London Adv. Cttee, English Heritage, 1988–94. Mem. Westminster City Council, 1963–78; Leader of Council, 1972–76; Alderman, 1974–78; Lord Mayor and Dep. High Steward of Westminster, 1977–78. Pres., London Chamber of Commerce, 1988–91. Chairman: Anchor Gp of Housing Assocs, 1991–; Housing Assocs' Charitable Trust, 1991–; Gov., Peabody Trust, 1991–; Chairman of Governors: West Heath Sch., 1978–91; Cranleigh Sch., 1981–95; Dir and Mem. Governing Body, RAM, 1978–. Hon. Steward, Westminster Abbey, 1978. Mem., Bd of Green Cloth Verge of Palaces, 1980–. FRSA; Hon. FRAM 1985. JP Surrey, 1964; Chairman: Dorking PSD, 1991–93; SE Surrey PSD, 1993–95. High Sheriff of Surrey, 1983–84; DL Greater London, 1978. *Recreations:* country sports, travel, photography. *Address:* Chapel House, Westhumble, Dorking, Surrey RH5 6AY. *T:* Dorking (01306) 882994. *Club:* Boodle's.

CUCKNEY, Baron *cr* 1995 (Life Peer), of Millbank in the City of Westminster; **John Graham Cuckney;** Kt 1978; Chairman, The Orion Publishing Group Ltd, since 1994; Vice Chairman, Glaxo Holdings plc, since 1993 (Director, since 1990); Director, Brixton Estate plc, since 1985; *b* 12 July 1925; *s* of late Air Vice-Marshal E. J. Cuckney, CB, CBE, DSC and Lilian (*née* Williams); *m* 2nd, 1960, Muriel, *d* of late Walter Scott Boyd. *Educ:* Shrewsbury; St Andrews Univ. (MA). War Service, Royal Northumberland Fusiliers, King's African Rifles, followed by attachment to War Office (Civil Asst, Gen. Staff), until 1957; subseq. appts with various industrial and financial cos including: Chairman: Brooke Bond Gp, 1981–84 (Dir, 1979–84); Thomas Cook Gp, 1978–87; John Brown, 1983–86 (Dir, 1981–86; Dep. Chm., 1982–83); Westland Gp, 1985–89; Royal Insce Hldgs plc, 1985–94 (Dir, 1979–89; Dep. Chm., 1983–85); Investors in Industry Gp, subseq. 3i Gp, 1987–92 (Dir, 1986–92); Dep. Chm., TI Gp, 1985–90; Director: Lazard Brothers, 1964–70 and 1988–90; Midland Bank, 1978–88. Public appointments include: Chm., Mersey Docks and Harbour Board, 1970–72; Chief Executive (Second Perm. Sec.), Property Services Agency, DoE, 1972–74; Chm., International Military Services Ltd (an MoD company), 1974–85; Sen. Crown Agent and Chm. of Crown Agents, for Oversea Governments and Administrations, 1974–78. Independent Mem., Railway Policy Review Cttee, 1966–67; special Mem., Hops Marketing Bd, 1971–72; Chairman: EDC for Building, 1976–80; Port of London Authority, 1977–79; Internat. Maritime Bureau, Internat. Chamber of Commerce, 1981–85; NEDC Working Party on European Public Purchasing, 1991–; Member: Docklands Joint Cttee, 1977–79; Council, British Exec. Service Overseas, 1981–84; Council, Foundn for Science and Technology, 1987–90; Dir, SBAC, 1986–89. Vice Pres., Liverpool Sch. of Tropical Med., 1985–93. Governor, Centre for Internat. Briefing, Farnham Castle, 1974–84; Chm., Understanding Industry Trust, 1988–91; Controller, ROH Land Develt Trust, 1993–; Trustee, RAF Mus., 1987–. Freeman, City of London, 1977. Elder Brother of Trinity House, 1980. Hon. DSc Bath, 1991; Hon. LLD St Andrews, 1993. *Address:* The Orion Publishing Group Ltd, Orion House, 5 Upper St Martin's Lane, WC2H 9EA. *T:* 0171–240 3444. *Club:* Athenæum.

CUDLIPP, family name of **Baron Cudlipp.**

CUDLIPP, Baron *cr* 1974 (Life Peer), of Aldingbourne, W Sussex; **Hugh Cudlipp,** Kt 1973; OBE 1945; Chairman: International Publishing Corporation Ltd, 1968–73 (Deputy Chairman, 1964–68); International Publishing Corporation Newspaper Division, 1970–73; Deputy Chairman (editorial), Reed International Board, 1970–73; Director, Associated Television Ltd, 1956–73; *b* 28 Aug. 1913; *s* of William Cudlipp, Cardiff; *m* 2nd, 1945, Eileen Ascroft (*d* 1962); 3rd, 1963, Jodi, *d* of late John L. Hyland, Palm Beach, Fla, and Mrs D. W. Jones, Southport. *Educ:* Howard Gardens Sch., Cardiff. Provincial newspapers in Cardiff and Manchester, 1927–32; Features Ed., Sunday Chronicle, London, 1932–35; Features Ed., Daily Mirror, 1935–37; Ed., Sunday Pictorial, 1937–40. Military Service, 1940–46; CO, British Army Newspaper Unit, CMF, 1943–46. Ed., Sunday Pictorial, 1946–49; Managing Ed., Sunday Express, 1950–52; Editorial Dir, Daily Mirror and Sunday Pictorial, 1952–63; Joint Managing Dir, Daily Mirror and Sunday Pictorial, 1959–63; Chm., Odhams Press Ltd, 1961–63; Chm., Daily Mirror Newspapers Ltd, 1963–68. Mem., Royal Commn on Standards of Conduct in Public Life, 1974–76. Exec. Founder Chm., Chichester Festivities, 1975–80; Mem. Bd, Productions Co., Chichester Fest. Th., 1980–87; Vice-Pres., Chichester Fest. Th. Trust, 1987–. *Publications:* Publish and be Damned, 1955; At Your Peril, 1962; Walking on the Water, 1976; The Prerogative of the Harlot, 1980. *Recreation:* music. *Address:* 14 Tollhouse Close, Avenue de Chartres, Chichester, West Sussex PO19 1SF. *Clubs:* Garrick; Chichester City.

CUDLIPP, Michael John; Secretary, The History of Advertising Trust, since 1994 (Governor, 1984–86; Hon. Secretary and Administrator, 1986–94); *b* 24 April 1934; *o s* of late Percy Cudlipp and Mrs Gwendoline May Cudlipp; *m* 1st, 1957, Margaret Susannah Rees (marr. diss. 1975); one *d*; 2nd, 1985, Jane Gale; two *d*. *Educ:* Tonbridge Sch., Kent. Trainee reporter, feature writer, gossip columnist, sub-editor, South Wales Echo, Cardiff, 1953–57; Sub-editor, Evening Chronicle, Manchester (various freelance jobs on daily and Sunday newspapers in Manchester), 1957–58; News Editor and Asst Editor (News), Sunday Times, 1958–67; Asst Editor (Night), Jt Man. Editor and sen. Dep. Editor, The Times, 1967–73; Chief Editor, London Broadcasting Co., 1973–74; Consultant on Public Relations to NI Office (temp. Civil Servant with rank of Under-Sec.), 1974–75; Dir of Information, Nat. Enterprise Bd, 1975–78; Director: External and Internal Communications, Internat. Thomson Orgn, 1979–85; The Georgian Gp, 1992–94. Mem., Consumer and Advertising Studies Course Adv. Cttee, Univ. of East London, 1992–. US State Dept Leader Grant (to study race relations in the US), 1962. *Recreations:* wooden boats, conservation, Welsh rugby football. *Address:* Stepping Hill House, 25 Ballygate, Beccles, Suffolk NR34 9ND.

CUDLIPP, Reginald; writer specialising on Japan; Director, Anglo-Japanese Economic Institute, London, 1961–86, retired; *b* Cardiff, 11 Dec. 1910; *s* of William and Mrs B. A. Cudlipp, Cardiff; *m* 1945, Rachel Joyce Braham. *Educ:* Cardiff Technical Coll. Began journalistic career on Penarth News, Glamorgan; Sub-Ed., Western Mail, Cardiff; joined News of the World Sub-Editorial Staff, 1938; served War, 1940–46; rejoined News of the World and became Special Correspondent in USA, 1946–47; Features Ed., 1948–50, Dep. Ed., 1950–53, Ed., 1953–59; Dir, News of the World Ltd, 1955–60. Extensive industrial tours and on-the-spot economic study of Japan regularly, 1962–86. Completed 60 years in active journalism, 1926–86. Life Mem., NUJ, 1929. Editor, Japan (quarterly review and monthly survey), and special publications on the Japanese scene, 1961–86. Lecturer and writer on Japan's past, present and future; also first-hand research on developing nations and economic co-operation, especially in Africa and Asia; invited to Japan, 1989, to brief businessmen on the Japan/EEC partnership after 1992. Order of the Sacred Treasure, Japan, 1982. *Publications:* numerous contribs to newspapers and periodicals, on Japan and Anglo-Japanese affairs. *Recreations:* music, travel, and reading, writing and talking about Japan. *Address:* 42 Martlets Court, Queen Street, Arundel, West Sussex BN18 9NZ.

CUDMORE, Harold; yachtsman; *b* 21 April 1944; *s* of Harold Cudmore, LLD and late Sheila Coleman; *m* 1993, Lauren E. Dagge. Skipper, White Crusader, British challenger, America's Cup, 1986; Manager and sailor, British Admiral's Cup winning team, 1989; Adviser and Coach, America 3, America's Cup winning team, 1992. Winner of many world championships, internat. match-racing regattas and major events. *Recreations:* other sports, walking, travelling, socialising. *Address:* 6 Castle Road, Cowes, Isle of Wight PO31 7QY. *T:* Cowes (01983) 291376, *Fax:* (01983) 291771. *Clubs:* Royal Thames Yacht, Royal Ocean Racing; Royal Cork Yacht, Island Sailing, Royal Corinthian Yacht, Ocean Cruising, Irish Cruising, Fort Worth Boat.

CUENOD, Hugues; Swiss tenor, retired; *b* 26 June 1902; *s* of Frank Cuenod and Gabrielle de Meuron. *Educ:* Swiss schools and colleges; Conservatoire Basel; Vienna; with Mme Singer-Burian. First concert, Paris, 1928; gave many performances of classical and light music, incl. musical comedy, in Europe and USA; numerous concerts with Clara Haskil and Nadia Boulanger; taught at Conservatoire de Genève, 1940–46; after returning to Paris, concentrated on sacred and classical music; sang in all major opera houses, incl. Glyndebourne (début 1954) and NY Metropolitan (début 1987); latterly specialised in French songs; many master classes. Hon. Citizen of Boston, 1972. Händel and Haydn Soc. Medal, Boston, 1972; Fidelis Medal, Geneva, 1987. Commandeur de l'Ordre des Arts et des Lettres (France), 1976. *Relevant publications:* Hugues Cuenod: un diable de musicien, by Jerôme Spycket, 1978. *Address:* 21 Place du Marché, 1800 Vevey, Switzerland; Château de Lully sur Morges, Switzerland.

CUEVAS-CANCINO, Francisco, GCVO (Hon.) 1985; Mexican Ambassador to Austria, 1986–90, and Permanent Mexican Representative to UNIDO and IAEA; *b* 7 May 1921; *s* of José Luis Cuevas and Sofía Cancino; *m* 1946, Ana Hilditch; two *s* one *d*; *m* Cristina Flores de Cuevas. *Educ:* Free School of Law, Mexico (lawyer, 1943); McGill Univ., Montreal (MCL 1946). Entered Mexican Foreign Service, as Vice-Consul, 1946, reaching rank of Ambassador by own merit; Permanent Representative to UN, 1965–70; Mexican Rep. to UNESCO, 1971–75, and Mem. Exec. Council during first four years; Perm. Rep. to UN, 1978–79; Ambassador: to Brazil, 1979–80; to Belgium, 1980–83; to UK and to Republic of Ireland, 1983–85. Chm., Group of 77, Vienna, 1988. Order of the Liberator, 1970, Order Andrés Bello, 1971, (Venezuela); Medal of Mexican For. Service (25 years), 1972; Order Cruzeiro do Sur (Brazil), 1980; Great Cross of Order of the Crown (Belgium), 1983. *Publications:* La nullité des actes juridiques, 1947; La doctrina de Suárez en el derecho natural (award, Madrid), 1952; Roosevelt y la buena vecindad, 1955; Del Congreso de Panamá a la Conferencia de Caracas, 1955, re-ed 1979; Tratado sobre la organización internacional, 1962; (ed) Porvenir de México by Luis G. Cuevas, 1961; (ed) Pacto de Familia (vol. forms part of Hist. Archives of Mexican Diplomatic Service, 2nd series), 1963; (ed) Foro Internacional, 1961–62; contrib. to book of essays in homage to Hans Morgenthau, 1978; several works and articles on Bolivarian theatre, and on Simón Bolívar (The Liberator), incl.: Visión Surrealista del Libertador, (Bogotá) 1980; Homenaje a Bolívar en el Sesquicentenario de su Muerte, (Bogotá) 1980. *Address:* Secretariat for Foreign Affairs, Ricardo Flores Magón, 1 Tlatelolco, 06995 México DF, México.

CULHAM, Michael John, CB 1992; Assistant Under Secretary of State (Civilian Management (Administrators)), Ministry of Defence, 1987–92, retired; *b* 24 June 1933; *s* of Cecil and Constance Culham; *m* 1963, Christine Mary Daish; one *s* two *d*. *Educ:* Reading Sch.; Lincoln Coll., Oxford (MA). National Service, Queen's Own Royal West Kent Regt, RAEC, 1952–54. Exec. Officer, WO, 1957–61; Asst Principal, Air Min., 1962; Private Sec. to Under-Sec. of State for Air, 1962–64; Principal, MoD, 1964–72; Jt Services Staff Coll., 1969; 1st Sec. (Defence), UK Delegn to NATO, Brussels, 1972–74; Asst Sec., MoD, 1974–82; Asst Under-Sec. of State (Adjt-Gen.), MoD, 1982–87. Member: Royal Patriotic Fund Corp., 1983–87; Adv. Council, RMCS, Shrivenham, 1983–87. Commissioner: Duke of York's Royal Mil. Sch., 1982–87; Queen Victoria Sch., 1982–87; Welbeck Coll., 1985–87; Royal Hosp. Chelsea, 1985–88. Chm., Defence Sports and Recreation (formerly MoD Recreation) Assoc., 1985–92; Vice President: CS RFU, 1992–; Farnham Town Boys' FC, 1987– (Chm., 1983–85). Trustee, Nat. Army Mus., 1985–88. *Recreations:* music, sailing, walking, watching cricket. *Address:* 39 Waverley Lane, Farnham, Surrey GU9 8BH. *Clubs:* Civil Service; Surrey County Cricket.

CULHANE, Prof. John Leonard, FRS 1985; Professor of Physics, since 1981, Director, Mullard Space Science Laboratory, since 1983, and Head of Department of Space and Climate Physics, since 1993, University College London; *b* 14 Oct. 1937; *s* of late John Thomas Culhane and Mary Agnes Culhane; *m* 1961, Mary Brigid, *d* of James Smith; two *s*. *Educ:* Clongowes Wood College, Co. Kildare; University College Dublin (BSc Phys 1959; MSc Phys 1960); UCL (PhD Phys 1966). Physics Department, University College London: Res. Asst, 1963; Lectr, 1967; Reader, 1976; Prof., 1981. Sen. Scientist, Lockheed Palo Alto Res. Lab., 1969–70. Chairman: SERC/BNSC Space Sci. Prog. Bd, 1989–92 (Vice-Pres., and UK Deleg., ESA Sci. Prog. Cttee, 1990–94); Royal Soc. Space Res. Cttee, 1990–93; COSPAR Commn E, 1994–; Member: Council, RAS, 1975–78; Space Sci. Adv. Cttee, ESA, 1985–89 (Chm., Astrophysics Working Group, 1985–89); SERC/BNSC Earth Obs. Prog. Bd, 1986–88; SERC Astron. Plan. Sci. Bd, 1989–92; Adv. Panel, ESA Space Sci. Dept, 1995–. Mem. Council, Surrey Univ., 1985–90. Member: IAU; Amer. Astronomical Soc.; Amer. Geophys. Union; IEEE Professional Group on Nuclear Sci. *Publications:* X-ray Astronomy (with P. W. Sanford), 1981; over 240 papers on solar and cosmic X-ray astronomy, X-ray instrumentation and plasma spectroscopy. *Recreations:* music, racing cars. *Address:* 24 Warnham Road, Horsham, West Sussex RH12 2QU. *T:* (lab.) Guildford (01483) 274111.

CULLEN, Hon. Lord; (William) Douglas Cullen; a Senator of the College of Justice in Scotland, and Lord of Session, since 1986; *b* 18 Nov. 1935; *s* of late Sheriff K. D. Cullen and Mrs G. M. Cullen; *m* 1961, Rosamond Mary Downer; two *s* two *d*. *Educ:* Dundee High Sch.; St Andrews Univ. (MA); Edinburgh Univ. (LLB). FRSE 1993. Called to the Scottish Bar, 1960. Standing Jun. Counsel to HM Customs and Excise, 1970–73; QC (Scot.) 1973; Advocate-depute, 1978–81. Chairman: Medical Appeal Tribunal, 1977–86; Court of Inquiry into the Piper Alpha disaster, 1988–90; Member: Scottish Valuation Adv. Council, 1980–86; Royal Commn on Ancient and Historical Monuments of Scotland, 1987–. Chairman: Council, Cockburn Assoc. (Edinburgh Civic Trust), 1984–86; Govs, St Margaret's Sch., Edinburgh, 1994–. Hon. LLD Aberdeen, 1992; DUniv Heriot-Watt, 1995. OTC Meritorious Achievement Citation, 1993; Alick Buchanan-Smith Meml Award, 1994. *Publications:* The Faculty Digest Supplement 1951–60, 1965; non-legal booklets on buildings in Edinburgh. *Recreations:* gardening, natural history. *Address:* The Court of Session, Parliament House, Edinburgh EH1 1RQ. *T:* 0131–225 2595. *Club:* New (Edinburgh).

CULLEN OF ASHBOURNE, 2nd Baron *cr* 1920; **Charles Borlase Marsham Cokayne,** MBE 1945; a Lord in Waiting (Government Whip), 1979–82; Major, Royal Signals; *b* 6 Oct. 1912; *e s* of 1st Baron and Grace Margaret (*d* 1971), *d* of Rev. Hon. John Marsham; *S* father, 1932; *m* 1942, Valerie Catherine Mary (marr. diss. 1947), *o d* of late W. H. Collbran; one *d*; *m* 1948, Patricia Mary, *er d* of late Col S. Clulow-Gray and late Mrs Clulow-Gray, formerly of Clare Priory, Suffolk. *Educ:* Eton. Served War of 1939–45 (MBE). Amateur Tennis Champion, 1947, 1952. One of HM Lieutenants, City of London, 1976–. Former Chm., Osteopathic Educnl Foundn; President: Fedn of Ophthalmic & Dispensing Opticians (formerly Fedn of Optical Corporate Bodies), 1983–; Gen. Council and Register of Osteopaths, 1987–89. Dep. Chm. of Cttees, 1982–91. *Heir:* *b* Hon. Edmund Willoughby Marsham Cokayne [*b* 18 May 1916; *m* 1943, Janet Manson, *d* of late William Douglas Watson and of Mrs Lauritson, Calgary]. *Address:* 75 Cadogan Gardens, SW3 2RB. *T:* 0171–589 1981. *Clubs:* MCC; Swinley Forest Golf.

CULLEN, Prof. Alexander Lamb, OBE 1960; DSc(Eng); FRS 1977; FEng 1977, FIEE, FIEEE, FInstP, FCGI; Emeritus Professor, University of London; Hon. Research Fellow, Department of Electronic and Electrical Engineering, University College London, since 1984 (SERC Senior Research Fellow, 1980–84); *b* 30 April 1920; *s* of Richard and Jessie Cullen, Lincoln; *m* 1940, Margaret, *er d* of late Alexander Lamb, OBE; two *s* one *d*. *Educ:* Lincoln Sch.; City and Guilds Coll., London. Staff of Radio Dept, RAE Farnborough, working on development of radar, 1940–46; Lectr in Electrical Engineering, University Coll., London, 1946–55 (title of Reader conferred 1955); Prof. of Electrical Engineering, University of Sheffield, 1955–67; Pender Prof. of Electrical Engineering, University College London, 1967–80. Hon. Prof., Northwestern Polytechnical Univ., Xian, China, 1981. Mem., IBA, 1982–89. Instn of Electrical Engineers: Kelvin premium, 1952; Extra premium, 1953 (with Prof. H. M. Barlow and Dr A. E. Karbowiak); Radio Sect. premium, 1954; Ambrose Fleming premium, 1956 (with J. C. Parr), 1975 (with Dr J. R. Forrest), 1988 (with S. P. Yeo); Duddell premium, 1957 (with Dr H. A. French); Electronics and Communications Sect. premium, 1959; Electronics Letters premium, 1985; Faraday Medal, 1984. Microwave Career Award, IEEE, 1989. Chm., Brit. Nat. Cttee, URSI, 1981–85; Vice-Pres., Internat. URSI, 1981–87, Pres., 1987–90; Mem. Council, Royal Soc., 1984–86. Clifford Paterson Lecture, Royal Soc., 1984; Clerk Maxwell Lecture, IERE, 1986. Hon. FIERE 1987; Hon. Fellow, UCL, 1993. Hon. DSc: Chinese Univ. of Hong Kong, 1981; Kent, 1986. Hon. DEng Sheffield, 1985. Royal Medal, Royal Soc., 1984. *Publications:* Microwave Measurements (jointly with Prof. H. M. Barlow), 1950; a number of papers on electromagnetic waves and microwave measurement techniques in IEE proceedings and elsewhere. *Recreations:* music and reading. *Address:* Department of Electronic and Electrical Engineering, University College London, Torrington Place, WC1E 7JE.

CULLEN, Douglas; *see* Cullen, Hon. Lord.

CULLEN, Sir (Edward) John, Kt 1991; PhD; FEng 1987; Chairman, Health and Safety Commission, 1983–93; *b* 19 Oct. 1926; *s* of William Henry Pearson Cullen and Ellen Emma Cullen; *m* 1954, Betty Davall Hopkins; two *s* two *d*. *Educ:* Cambridge Univ. (MA 1952, PhD 1956); Univ. of Texas (MS 1953). UKAEA, 1956–58; ICI, 1958–67; Rohm and Haas Co., 1967–83: Eur. Dir for Engrg and Regulatory Affairs, 1981–83; Dep. Chm., Rohm and Haas (UK) Ltd, 1981–83. Chm., British Nat. Cttee for Internat. Engrg Affairs, 1990–; Member: Engrg Council, 1990–; Council, Royal Acad. of Engrg, 1981–92. Pres., IChemE, 1988–89. MInstD 1978; FRSA 1988. Liveryman, Engineers' Co., 1989–. Hon. DSc Exeter, 1993. *Publications:* articles on gas absorption, in Trans Faraday Soc., Trans IChemE, Chem. Engrg Science; numerous articles on health and safety. *Recreations:* reading (detective stories), photography, swimming, gardening. *Address:* 14 Gloucester Walk, W8 5JH. *T:* 0171–937 0709. *Club:* Institute of Directors.

CULLEN, Sir John; *see* Cullen, Sir E. J.

CULLEN, Raymond; Chairman, The Calico Printers' Association Ltd and subsidiaries, 1964–68; *b* 27 May 1913; *s* of late John Norman Cullen and Bertha (*née* Dearden); *m* 1940, Doris (*d* 1984), *d* of A. W. Paskin; two *d*. *Educ:* King's Sch., Macclesfield; St Catharine's Coll., Cambridge (Scholar, MA). Joined The Calico Printers' Assoc. Ltd Commn Printing, 1934; transf. overseas, 1938; service in India and China. Dir, W. A. Beardsell & Co. (Private) Ltd, Madras, 1946 (Chm. and Man. Dir, 1949–55); Chm. and Man. Dir, Mettur Industries Ltd, 1949–55; Chm. and Man. Dir, Marshall Fabrics Ltd, 1955–62; Director: Calico Printers' Assoc. Ltd, 1962–68; Barclays Bank Ltd Manchester Local Bd, 1965–69. Member: Textile Coun., 1967–69; Coun., Inst. of Directors, 1967–69; NW Economic Planning Coun., 1968–69; Governor, Manchester Grammar Sch., 1968–83. *Recreations:* fishing, golf (Pres., Cheshire Union of Golf Clubs, 1977–78). *Address:* Cranford, Ladybrook Road, Bramhall, Cheshire SK7 3NB. *T:* 0161–485 3204.

CULLEN, Terence Lindsay Graham, QC 1978; *b* 29 Oct. 1930; *s* of late Eric Graham Cullen and Jean Morrison Hunter (*née* Bennett); *m* 1958, Muriel Elisabeth Rolfe; three *s*. *Educ:* RNC, Dartmouth. RN, 1948–55; Prestige Group Ltd, 1955–61. Called to the Bar: Lincoln's Inn, 1961 (Bencher, 1986); Singapore, 1978; Malaysia, 1980; Hong Kong, 1986; Bermuda, 1990. *Recreation:* the Turf. *Address:* 13 Old Square, Lincoln's Inn, WC2A 3UA. *T:* 0171–404 4800; 54 Canonbury Park North, N1 2JT.

CULLIMORE, Charles Augustine Kaye, CMG 1993; HM Diplomatic Service, retired; High Commissioner to Uganda, 1989–93; *b* 2 Oct. 1933; *s* of Charles Cullimore and Constance Alicia Kaye Cullimore (*née* Grimshaw); *m* 1956, Val Elizabeth Margot (*née* Willemsen); one *s* one *d*. *Educ:* Portora Royal Sch., Enniskillen; Trinity Coll., Oxford (MA). N Ireland Short Service Commn, 1955–57. HMOCS, Tanganyika, 1958–61; ICI Ltd, 1961–71; joined HM Diplomatic Service, 1971; FCO, 1971–73; Bonn, 1973–77; FCO, 1977–79; Counsellor, New Delhi, 1979–82; Dep. High Comr, Canberra, 1982–86; FCO, 1986–89. *Recreations:* theatre, walking, tennis. *Address:* Deacon House, Bidborough, Kent TN3 0UP. *Clubs:* Commonwealth Trust; Commonwealth (Canberra).

CULLIMORE, Colin Stuart, CBE 1978; Chairman, NAAFI, since 1993 (non-executive Director, since 1984); *b* 13 July 1931; *s* of Reginald Victor Cullimore and May Maria Cullimore; *m* 1952, Kathleen Anyta Lamming; one *s*. *Educ:* Westminster Sch.; Grenoble Univ.; National Coll. of Food Technol. Commnd Royal Scots Fusiliers, 1951; seconded Parachute Regt; transf. when perm. officer cadre formed; Major 1956; 10th Bn Parachute Regt TA, 1960. Gen. Man., Payne & Son (Butchers) Ltd, 1960; Asst Gen. Man., J. H. Dewhurst Ltd, 1965, Gen. Man. 1969, Man. Dir, 1976–90; Dir of External Affairs, Vestey Gp, 1990–92; Dir, Airborne Initiative Holdings Ltd, 1991–93. Trustee, Western United Gp Pension Scheme, 1986–. Chairman: Retail Consortium Food Cttee, 1973–74; Multiple Shops Fedn, 1977–78; Vice-Chairman: Multiple Food Retailers Assoc., 1972–74; Governors, Coll. for Distributive Trades, 1976–79, 1984–88; Retail Consortium, 1985–89; Pres., British Retailers Assoc., 1984–89 (Vice Pres., 1978–84); Dep. Chm., Meat Promotion Exec., 1975–78; Vice Pres., Bd of Admin, CECD (European Retailers), 1986–88 (Mem., 1981–85). Member: EDC for Distrib. Trades, 1972–80; Council and Management Cttee, Inst. of Meat (Vice-Chm., 1981–83); Cttee of Commerce and Distribn, EEC, 1984–93; Council, Industry & Parlt Trust, 1987–93. Vice Pres., Royal Smithfield Club, 1991– (Mem. Council, 1993–95). Gov., Court of London Inst., 1984–87 and 1989–90; Exec. Trustee, Airborne Assault Normandy Trust, 1983–; Chm., Reserve Forces Ulysses Trust, 1992–; Member: Regtl Council, Parachute Regt, 1991–; Lincoln Diocese Trust and Bd of Finances, 1993– (Chm. Resources Cttee, 1994–). Liveryman, Butchers' Co. (Mem. Court, 1992–). FInstD, 1979; CIMgt (CBIM 1984); FRSA 1987. Gold Medal: Inst. of Meat, 1956; Butchers' Co., 1956. OStJ 1988. *Address:* Wyberton Park, Wyberton, Boston, Lincs PE21 7AF. *T:* Boston (01205) 311423. *Clubs:* Naval and Military, Farmers', Institute of Directors.

CULLINAN, Edward Horder, CBE 1987; RA 1991 (ARA 1989); Senior Partner, Edward Cullinan Architects, since 1965; *b* 17 July 1931; *s* of Dr Edward Cullinan and Joy (*née* Horder); *m* 1961, Rosalind Yeates; one *s* two *d*. *Educ:* Ampleforth Coll.; Cambridge Univ. (Anderson and Webb Schol., 1951; BA); Univ. of California at Berkeley (George VI Meml Fellow, 1956). AADip; RIBA. With Denys Lasdun, 1958–65. Bannister Fletcher Prof., UCL, 1978–79; Graham Willis Prof., Univ. of Sheffield, 1985–87; George Simpson Prof., Univ. of Edinburgh, 1987–. Designed and built: Horder House, Hampshire, 1959–60; Marvin House, Calif, 1959–60; Minster Lovell Mill, 1969–72; Parish Ch. of St Mary, Barnes, 1978–84; Lambeth Community Care Centre, 1979–84; RMC Internat. HQ, 1985–90; Fountains Abbey visitor centre and landscape, 1987–92; all have received awards and been published internationally. FRSA. *Publications:* Edward Cullinan, Architects, 1984; contribs to many architectural jls. *Recreations:* horticulture, surfing, skiing, Sahara travel, building, history, geography. *Address:* The Wharf, Baldwin Terrace, N1 7RU. *T:* 0171–704 1975.

CULLINGFORD, Eric Coome Maynard, CMG 1963; *b* 15 March 1910; *s* of Francis James and Lilian Mabel Cullingford; *m* 1938, Friedel Fuchs; two *s* one *d*. *Educ:* City of London Sch.; St Catharine's Coll., Cambridge (Exhibitioner). Entered Ministry of Labour as Third Class Officer, 1932; Principal, 1942. Served with Manpower Div. of CCG, 1946–50. Asst Sec., Min. of Labour, 1954. Labour Attaché, Bonn, 1961–65, 1968–72. Regional Controller, Eastern and Southern Region, Dept of Employment and Productivity, 1966–68; retired 1973. *Publications:* Trade Unions in West Germany, 1976; Pirates of Shearwater Island, 1983. *Address:* Combermere, Flat 1, 25 Avenue Road, Malvern, Worcs WR14 3AY.

CULLINGWORTH, Prof. (John) Barry; Senior Research Fellow, Department of Land Economy, University of Cambridge, since 1994; Emeritus Professor of Urban Affairs and Public Policy, University of Delaware, since 1994; *b* 11 Sept. 1929; *s* of Sidney C. and Winifred E. Cullingworth; *m* 1951, Betty Violet (*née* Turner); one *s* two *d*. *Educ:* High Pavement Sch., Nottingham; Trinity Coll. of Music, London; London Sch. of Economics. Research Asst, Asst Lectr and Lectr, Univ. of Manchester, 1955–60; Lectr, Univ. of Durham, 1960–63; Sen. Lectr and Reader, Univ. of Glasgow, 1963–66; Dir, Centre for Urban and Regional Studies, Univ. of Birmingham, 1966–72. Dir, Planning Exchange, Scotland, 1972–75; Official Historian, Cabinet Office, 1975–77. Chm., Dept of Urban and Regional Planning, 1977–80, Res. Prof., Centre for Urban and Community Studies, 1980–82, Prof. of Planning, 1982–83, Univ. of Toronto; Unidel Prof. of Urban Affairs and Public Policy, Univ. of Delaware, 1983–94. Vis. Prof., Univ. of Strathclyde, 1980–86. Vice-Chm., Scottish Housing Adv. Cttee; Chairman: Cttee on Community Facilities in Expanding Towns (Report, The Needs of New Communities, 1967); Cttee on Unfit Housing in Scotland (Report, Scotland's Older Houses, 1967); Cttee on Allocation of Council Houses (Report, Council Housing: Purposes, Procedures and Practices, 1968); Adv. Cttee on Rent Rebates and Rent Allowances, 1973–77. Mem., Ont. Council of Health, 1979–83; Vice-Pres., Housing Centre Trust, 1972–. FRSA 1974; Hon. MRTPI. *Publications:* Housing Needs and Planning Policy, 1960; Housing in Transition, 1963; Town and Country Planning in England and Wales, 1964; English Housing Trends, 1965; Housing and Local Government, 1966; Scottish Housing in 1965, 1967; A Profile of Glasgow Housing, 1968; (with V. Karn) Ownership and Management of Housing in New Towns, 1968; Housing and Labour Mobility, (Paris) 1969; Town and Country Planning in Britain, 1972, 11th edn (with V. Nadin) 1994; Problems of an Urban Society (3 vols), 1973; Environmental Planning—Reconstruction and Land Use Planning, 1975; Essays on Housing Policy, 1979; New Towns Policy, 1980; Canadian Housing Policy Research, 1980; Land Values, Compensation and Betterment, 1981; Rent Control, 1983; Canadian Planning and Public Participation, 1984; Urban and Regional Planning in Canada, 1987; Energy, Land and Public Policy, 1990; The Political Culture of Planning, 1993. *Address:* 25 The Woodlands, Linton, Cambs CB1 6UG. *T:* Linton (01223) 890129.

CULLIS, Prof. Charles Fowler; Professor of Physical Chemistry, City University, 1967–84, now Emeritus (Head, Chemistry Department, 1973–84; Pro-Vice-Chancellor, 1980–84; Saddlers' Research Professor, 1984–87; Leverhulme Emeritus Research Fellow, 1987–89); *b* 31 Aug. 1922; 2nd *s* of late Prof. C. G. Cullis, Prof. of Mining Geology, Univ. of London, and Mrs W. J. Cullis (*née* Fowler); *m* 1958, Marjorie Elizabeth, *er d* of late Sir Austin Anderson and of Lady Anderson; two *s* two *d*. *Educ:* Stowe Sch. (Open Schol.); Trinity Coll., Oxford. BA 1944, BSc 1st Cl. Hons Chem. 1945, DPhil 1948, MA 1948, DSc 1960; FRSC (FRIC 1958); FRSA. ICI Research Fellow in Chem., Oxford, 1947–50; Lectr in Phys. Chem., Imperial Coll., London, 1950–59; Sen. Lectr in Chem. Engrg and Chem. Tech., Imperial Coll., 1959–64; Reader in Combustion Chemistry, Univ. of London, 1964–66. Vis. Prof., College of Chem., Univ. of California, Berkeley, 1966; Vis. Scientist, CSIRO, Sydney, 1970. Mem. Council, Chem. Soc., 1969–72, 1975–78; Hon. Sec., Brit. Sect. of Combustion Inst., 1969–74; Mem., Rockets Sub-cttee, 1968–73, and of Combustion Sub-cttee, 1969–72, Aeronautical Research Council; Member: Navy Dept Fuels and Lubricants Adv. Cttee (Fire and Explosion Hazards Working Gp), 1967–83; Safety in Mines Research Adv. Bd, 1973–88 (Chm., 1980–88); Chem. Cttee, Defence Sci. Adv. Council, 1979–82; Chem. Bd, 1982–87, Phys. Sci. Cttee, 1987–89, CNAA. Scientific Editor, Internat. Union of Pure and Applied Chem., 1976–78. Non-exec. Dir, City Technology Ltd, 1977–91. Mem., Mid Sussex DC, 1986–. Mem. Council, Sussex Univ., 1993–; Governor, City of London Polytechnic, 1982–84. Trustee, Sino-British Fellowship Trust, 1992–. Freeman, City of London, 1983; Liveryman, Bakers' Co., 1983. Joseph Priestley Award, 1974, Combustion Chem. Medal and Award, 1978, Chem. Soc. *Publications:* The Combustion of Organic Polymers (jtly with M. M. Hirschler), 1981; numerous sci. papers in Proc. Royal Soc., Trans Faraday Soc., Jl Chem. Soc., etc, mainly concerned with chemistry of combustion reactions. *Recreations:* music, travel. *Address:* Quinces, Courtmead Road, Cuckfield, W Sussex RH17 5LP. *T:* Haywards Heath (01444) 453513. *Club:* Athenæum.

See also M. F. Cullis.

CULLIS, Michael Fowler, CVO 1955; HM Diplomatic Service, retired; Director, UK Committee, European Cultural Foundation, Amsterdam, 1983–92; *b* 22 Oct. 1914; *s* of late Emeritus Prof. Charles Gilbert Cullis, Imperial Coll. of Science and Technology, London Univ., and late Winifred Jefford Cullis (*née* Fowler); *m* Catherine Robertson, Arbroath, Scotland; no *c*. *Educ:* Wellington Coll. (scholar); Brasenose Coll., Oxford (Hulme Open Scholar). MA, classics. Law (Lincoln's Inn), and journalism, 1938–39. Military Intelligence, Gibraltar, 1939–40; served Min. of Economic Warfare (London, Spain and Portugal), 1940–44; joined FO as head of Austrian Section, 1945; Political Adviser on Austrian Treaty negotiations (London, Moscow, Vienna, Paris, New York),

1947–50; Special Asst, Schuman Plan, 1950; First Sec., British Embassy, Oslo, 1951–55; Regional (Information) Counsellor for the five Nordic countries, British Embassy, Copenhagen, 1955–58; Dep. Gov. of Malta, 1959–61; Sen. Research Associate, Atlantic Institute, Paris, 1962–65; writing, lecturing, etc, at various European centres, 1965–66; Dir, Arms Control and Disarmament Res., FO, then FCO, 1967–74; Advr on relations with non-govtl bodies, FCO, 1974–79; consultant for acad. and institutional fund-raising, and European parly affairs, 1980–82; Historical Advr to Royal Mint, 1986. Unsuccessful candidate (C), European Elections, 1979. Vice-President: Inst. of Linguists, 1984–89; Internat. Eisteddfod 1984–. FRSA. Chevalier (1st cl.) Order of Dannebrog, 1957. *Publications:* (contrib.) The Price of Victory, 1983; (contrib.) Festschrift for Gerald Stourzh, 1990; articles and broadcasts, mainly on international affairs. *Recreation:* writing newspaper obituaries of friends. *Address:* Peel House, Buntingford, Herts SG9 9AE. *T:* Buntingford (01763) 272209. *Club:* Athenæum.
See also C. F. Cullis.

CULME-SEYMOUR, Comdr Sir Michael; *see* Seymour.

CULSHAW, John Douglas; Assistant Chief Scientific Adviser (Capabilities), Ministry of Defence, 1985–87; *b* 22 Oct. 1927; *s* of Alfred Henry Douglas Culshaw and Dorothy Yeats Culshaw (*née* Hogarth); *m* 1951, Hazel Speirs Alexander; one *s* one *d*. *Educ:* Alderman Smith Grammar Sch., Washington, Co. Durham; University Coll., Nottingham. BSc London 1949; MSc Nottingham 1950. Joined Weapons Dept, Royal Aircraft Estabt, Min. of Supply, Farnborough, 1950; OC (Scientific) 6 Joint Services Trials Unit RAF (UK), 1956; OC (Sci.) 16 JSTU RA Weapons Research Estabt, Salisbury, S Australia, 1961; Co-ordinating Research and Development Authority Technical Project Officer, RAE, 1964; Supt Mine Warfare Br., Royal Armament R&D Estabt, MoD, Sevenoaks, 1967; Director, Scientific Adv. Br., Home Office, 1970; Dept of Chief Scientific Adviser (Army), 1972; Head of Mathematics and Assessment Dept, RARDE, MoD, Sevenoaks, 1974; Head of Defence Science II, MoD, 1975; RCDS 1976; Dep. Dir, Scientific and Technical Intelligence, 1977; Dir, Defence Operational Analysis Estabt and Asst Chief Scientific Advr (Studies), MoD, 1979–84. *Recreations:* war games, wine-making, folk-song collecting, bee-keeping, historical research. *Club:* Civil Service.

CULSHAW, Robert Nicholas, MVO 1979; HM Diplomatic Service; Minister-Counsellor (Trade Policy), Washington, since 1995; *b* 22 Dec. 1952; *s* of Ivan Culshaw and Edith Marjorie Jose Barnard; *m* 1977, Elaine Ritchie Clegg; one *s*. *Educ:* University Coll. Sch., Hampstead; King's Coll., Cambridge (BA 1st Cl. Hons Classics 1974; Major Univ. Scholarship for Classics, 1974; MA 1977). FCO, 1974–75; MECAS, Lebanon and Jordan, 1975–77; 3rd Sec., Muscat, 1977–79; 2nd Sec., Khartoum, 1979–80; 1st Sec., Rome, 1980–84; FCO, 1984–88; Head of Chancery, 1988–90, Dep. Hd of Mission and Consul-Gen., 1991–93, Athens; FCO Spokesman and Hd of News Dept, 1993–95. *Recreations:* ski-ing, singing, poetry. *Address:* c/o Foreign and Commonwealth Office, King Charles Street, SW1A 2AH.

CULVER, John Howard; HM Diplomatic Service; Ambassador to Nicaragua, since 1992; *b* 17 July 1947; *m* 1973, Margaret Ann Davis; two *s* one *d*. BoT, 1967; entered FO, 1968; Moscow, 1974; La Paz, 1977; FCO, 1980; First Sec. (Commercial), Rome, 1983; Head of Chancery, Dhaka, 1987; FCO, 1990. *Address:* c/o Foreign and Commonwealth Office, SW1A 2AH.

CULYER, Prof. Anthony John; Professor of Economics, since 1979, Head of the Department of Economics and Related Studies, since 1986, and Deputy Vice-Chancellor, since 1994, University of York; status-only Professor, University of Toronto, since 1989; *b* 1 July 1942; *s* of late Thomas Reginald Culyer and Betty Ely (*née* Headland); *m* 1966, Sieglinde Birgit; one *s* one *d*. *Educ:* King's Sch., Worcester; Exeter Univ. (BA Hons); Univ. of California at Los Angeles. Tutor and Asst Lectr, Exeter Univ., 1965–69; Lectr, Sen. Lectr and Reader, Univ. of York, 1969–79; Deputy Director, Inst. of Social and Economic Research, Univ. of York, 1971–82. Sen. Research Associate, Ontario Economic Council, 1976, Vis. Professorial Lectr, Queen's Univ., Kingston, 1976; William Evans Vis. Professor, Otago Univ., 1979; Vis. Fellow, Australian National Univ., 1979; Visiting Professor: Trent Univ., 1985–86; Inst. für Med. Informatik und Systemforschung, Munich, 1990–91; Toronto Univ., 1991. Lectures: Woodward, Univ. of BC, 1986; Perey, McMaster Univ., and Chaplain, Trent Univ., Canada, 1990; Francis Fraser, BPMF, 1994. Member: Standing Cttee, Conf. of Heads of Univ. Depts of Econs, 1988–; Coll. Cttee, King's Fund Coll., London, 1989–92; Adv. Cttee for Centre for Health and Society, UCL, 1992–; Rev. Adv. Cttee on London SHAs, 1992–93; Adv. Cttee, Canadian Inst. for Advanced Res., 1992–; Future Health Care Options Wkg Pty, IHSM, 1992–93; British Council Health Adv. Cttee, 1995–. Chm., York Dist, RSCM, 1984–. Mem., 1982–90, Non-Exec. Mem., 1990–92, Northallerton HA; Non-Exec. Mem., N Yorks HA, 1994–; Member: Yorks RHA R&D Cttee, 1992–94; Northern and Yorks Regl R&D Adv. Cttee, 1995–; Central R&D Cttee, NHS, 1991–; NHS Standing Gp on Health Technol., 1992–; Chair: Methodology Panel, NHS Standing Gp on Health Technol., 1993–; NHS Task Force on Supporting R&D in NHS, 1994. Pres., Econs Section, BAAS, 1994. Co-Editor, Jl of Health Econs, 1982–; Mem., Editl Policy Cttee and Editl Bd, Office of Health Econs, 1990–; Member, Editorial Board: Econ. Rev., 1983–; Med. Law Internat., 1992–; Mem. Managing Cttee, Jl of Med. Ethics, 1994–. *Publications:* The Economics of Social Policy, 1973; (ed with M. H. Cooper) Health Economics, 1973; (ed) Economic Policies and Social Goals, 1974; Need and the National Health Service, 1976; (with J. Wiseman and A. Walker) Annotated Bibliography of Health Economics, 1977; (ed with V. Halberstadt) Human Resources and Public Finance, 1977; Measuring Health: Lessons for Ontario, 1978; (ed with K. G. Wright) Economic Aspects of Health Services, 1978; The Political Economy of Social Policy, 1980; (ed) Health Indicators, 1983; (ed with B. Horisberger) Economic and Medical Evaluation of Health Care Technologies, 1983; Economics, 1985; (ed with G. Terny) Public Finance and Social Policy, 1985; (ed with B. Jonsson) Public and Private Health Services: complementarities and conflicts, 1986; (jtly) The International Bibliography of Health Economics: a comprehensive annotated guide to English language sources since 1914, 1986; Canadian Health Care Expenditures: myth and reality, past and future, 1988; (ed) Standards for the Socio-economic Evaluation of Health Care Products and Services, 1990; (ed jtly) Competition in Health Care: reforming the NHS, 1990; (ed) The Economics of Health, 1991; (ed jtly) Some Recent Developments in Health Economics, 1992; (ed jtly) Swedish Health Care: the best in the world?, 1993; articles in Oxford Econ. Papers, Economica, Scottish Jl of Political Economy, Public Finance, Jl of Public Economics, Kyklos, Qly Jl of Economics, Jl Royal Statistical Soc., Jl of Health Economics, and others. *Recreation:* church music. *Address:* The Laurels, Barmby Moor, York YO4 5EJ. *T:* Pocklington (01759) 302639.

CUMANI, Luca Matteo; racehorse trainer; *b* 7 April 1949; *s* of Sergio Cumani and Elena Cardini Cumani; *m* 1979, Sara Doon Plunket; one *s* one *d*. *Educ:* Milan. Riding career: 85 winners in Italy, France and UK; champion amateur, Italy, 1972; won Moët and Chandon on Meissen, 1972; Prix Paul Noël de la Houtre on Harland, 1970, 1972, 1973; Asst to Sergio Cumani and to H. R. A. Cecil, 1974–75; first held licence, 1976; numerous major races won, incl. St Leger (Commanche Run), 1984; Derby and Irish Sweeps Derby, 1988 (Kahyasi); Breeders Cup Mile, 1994 (Barathea). *Address:* Bedford House Stables, Bury Road, Newmarket, Suffolk CB8 7BX. *T:* Newmarket (01638) 665432.

CUMBERLEGE, family name of **Baroness Cumberlege**.

CUMBERLEGE, Baroness *cr* 1990 (Life Peer), of Newick in the County of East Sussex; **Julia Frances Cumberlege,** CBE 1985; Parliamentary Under-Secretary of State, Department of Health, since 1992; *b* 27 Jan. 1943; *d* of Dr L. U. Camm and late M. G. G. Camm; *m* 1961, Patrick Francis Howard Cumberlege; three *s*. *Educ:* Convent of the Sacred Heart, Tunbridge Wells. Mem., East Sussex AHA, 1977–81; Chairman: Brighton HA, 1981–88; SW Thames RHA, 1988–92; Mem. Council, NAHA, 1982–88 (Vice-Chm., 1984–87; Chm., 1987–88). Member: Lewes DC, 1966–79 (Leader, 1977–78); East Sussex CC, 1974–85 (Chm., Social Services Cttee, 1979–82). Chairman: Review of Community Nursing for England, 1985 (report, Neighbourhood Nursing—a focus for care, 1986); Expert Maternity Gp, 1993 (report, Changing Childbirth, 1993). Member: Social Security Adv. Cttee, 1980–82; DHSS Expert Adv. Gp on AIDS, 1987–89; Council, UK Central Council for Nursing, Midwifery and Health Visiting, 1989–92; NHS Policy Bd, 1989–. Lay Mem., 1977–83, Mem. Appts Commn, 1984–90, Press Council. Vice President: Age Concern, Brighton, 1984–; RCN, 1989–. Trustee, Princess Royal Trust for Carers, 1992–93. Mem. Council, Brighton Poly, 1987–89; Governor: Chailey Comprehensive Sch., 1972–86; Ringmer Comprehensive Sch., 1979–85; Newick Primary Sch., 1977–85; Chailey Heritage Sch. and Hosp., 1982–88. Founder: Newick Playgp; Newick Youth Club. FRSA 1989. DL 1986, Vice Lord-Lieut, 1992, E Sussex; JP East Sussex, 1973–85. DUniv: Surrey, 1990; Brighton, 1994. *Recreations:* bicycling, other people's gardens. *Address:* Vuggles Farm, Newick, Lewes, Sussex BN8 4RU. *T:* Barcombe (01273) 400453, *Fax:* (01273) 401084. *Club:* Royal Society of Medicine.

CUMING, Frederick George Rees, RA 1974 (ARA 1969); ARCA 1954; NDD 1948; NEAC 1960; painter; *b* 16 Feb. 1930; *m* Audrey Lee Cuming; one *s* one *d*. *Educ:* University School, Bexley Heath; Sidcup Art School; Royal College of Art; travelling schol., Italy. Exhbns in Redfern, Walker, New Grafton, Thackeray, Fieldborne Galleries; Group shows at NEAC, RA, Schools' Exhbn, John Moores London Group; One Man exhbns at Thackeray Gall., galls in Chichester, Lewes, Eastbourne, Guildford, Durham, Chester, Folkstone, Canterbury, New York; works in collections: Dept. of Envt; Treasury; Chantrey Bequest; RA; Kendal Mus.; Scunthorpe Mus.; Bradford; Carlisle; Nat. Mus. of Wales; Brighton and Hove Mus.; Maidstone Mus.; Towner Gall., Eastbourne; Monte Carlo Mus.; St John's Coll., Oxford; Worcester Coll., Oxford; Faringdon Trust, Oxon; works in galls in Canada, France, Germany, Greece, Holland. *Address:* The Gables, Wittersham Road, Iden, near Rye, E Sussex TN31 7WY. *T:* Iden (01797) 280322.

CUMMING; *see* Gordon Cumming and Gordon-Cumming.

CUMMING, Valerie Lynn, FMA; Deputy Director, Museum of London, since 1988; *b* 11 Oct. 1946; *d* of John Gunson Carter and Edna Ruth Carter (*née* Willis); *m* 1972, John Lawrence Cumming. *Educ:* Abbey Sch., Reading; Univ. of Leicester (BA); Courtauld Inst. of Art (Courtauld Cert. in History of Dress). Admin. trainee, Univ. of Surrey, 1968–69; Asst, Chertsey Mus., 1971–73; Res. Asst, 1973–75, Sen. Asst Keeper, 1975–78, Mus. of London; Curator, Court Dress Collection, Kensington Palace, 1978–81; Asst Dir, Mus. of London, 1981–88. Trustee, Olive Matthews Collection, Chertsey Mus., Surrey, 1983–. Curatorial advr, Chartered Insurance Inst., 1991–. *Publications:* Exploring Costume History 1500–1900, 1981; Gloves, 1982; (contrib.) Tradescant's Rarities, 1983; A Visual History of Costume: the Seventeenth Century, 1984; (with Aileen Ribeiro) The Visual History of Costume, 1989; Royal Dress, 1989; (contrib.) The Late King's Goods, 1989; (contrib.) London – World City 1800–1840, 1992. *Recreations:* gardening, watching cricket. *Address:* Museum of London, London Wall, EC2Y 5HN. *T:* 0171–600 3699.

CUMMING-BRUCE, Rt. Hon. Sir (James) Roualeyn Hovell-Thurlow-, PC 1977; Kt 1964; MA; a Lord Justice of Appeal, 1977–85; *b* 9 March 1912; *s* of 6th Baron Thurlow and Grace Catherine, *d* of Rev. Henry Trotter; *m* 1955, Lady (Anne) Sarah Alethea Marjorie Savile (*d* 1991), *d* of 6th Earl of Mexborough; two *s* one *d*. *Educ:* Shrewsbury; Magdalene Coll., Cambridge (Hon. Fellow, 1977). Barrister, Middle Temple, 1937 (Harmsworth Scholar); Master of the Bench, 1959; Treasurer, 1975. Served War of 1939–45 (Lt-Col RA). Chancellor of Diocese of Ripon, 1954–57; Recorder of Doncaster, 1957–58; Recorder of York, 1958–61; Junior Counsel to the Treasury (Common Law), 1959–64; Judge of the High Court, Family Div. (formerly Probate, Divorce and Admiralty Div.), 1964–77; Judge of the Restrictive Practices Court, 1968; Presiding Judge, North Eastern Circuit, 1971–74. *Address:* 1 Mulberry Walk, Chelsea, SW3 6DZ. *T:* 0171–352 5754. *Clubs:* Pratt's, United Oxford & Cambridge University.
See also Sir A. J. Gore-Booth, Bt, Baron Thurlow.

CUMMINGS, Constance, CBE 1974; actress; *b* Seattle, USA; *d* of Kate Cummings and Dallas Vernon Halverstadt; *m* 1933, Benn Wolfe Levy, MBE (*d* 1973); one *s* one *d*. *Educ:* St Nicholas Girls Sch., Seattle, Washington, USA. Began stage work, 1932; since then has appeared in radio, television, films and theatre; joined National Theatre Co., 1971. Member: Arts Council, 1965–71; Council, English Stage Co., 1978–; Chm., Young People's Theatre Panel, 1966–70. *Plays include:* Goodbye, Mr Chips, 1938; The Taming of the Shrew, 1938; The Good Natured Man, 1939; St Joan, 1939; Romeo and Juliet, 1939; The Petrified Forest, 1942; Return to Tyassi, 1952; Lysistrata, 1957; The Rape of the Belt, 1957; JB, 1961; Who's Afraid of Virginia Woolf?, 1964; Justice is a Woman, 1966; Fallen Angels, 1967; A Delicate Balance, 1969; Hamlet, 1969; Children, 1974; Stripwell, 1975; All Over, 1976; Wings, 1978 (televised, USA, 1982); Hay Fever, 1980; The Chalk Garden, NY, 1982; Mrs Warren's Profession, Vienna, 1982; Eve, 1984; The Glass Menagerie, USA, then London, 1985; Crown Matrimonial, 1988; Tête à Tête, USA, 1989; *National Theatre:* Coriolanus, Amphitryon 38, 1971; A Long Day's Journey into Night, 1972; The Cherry Orchard, The Bacchae, 1973; The Circle, 1974–75. Fanny Kemble at Home, one woman show, 1986; has appeared Albert Hall, performing with orchestra Peter and the Wolf and Honegger's Jeanne d'Arc au Bûcher. *Recreations:* anthropology and music. *Address:* 68 Old Church Street, SW3 6EP. *T:* 0171–352 0437.

CUMMINGS, John Scott; MP (Lab) Easington, since 1987; *b* 6 July 1943; *s* of George Scott Cummings and Mary (*née* Cain); unmarried. *Educ:* Murton Council Infants, Jun. and Sen. Schs; Easington Technical Coll. Colliery apprentice electrician, 1958–63, colliery electrician, 1963–87. Vice-Chm., Coalfields Community Campaign, 1985–87; Member: Northumbrian Water Authority, 1977–83; Aycliffe and Peterlee Develt Corp., 1980–87; Easington RDC, 1970–73; Easington DC, 1973–87 (Chm., 1975–76; Leader, 1979–87). Mem., Council of Europe, 1992–. *Recreations:* Jack Russell terriers, walking, travel. *Address:* 18 Grasmere Terrace, Murton, Seaham, Co. Durham SR7 9NU. *T:* 0191–526 1142; House of Commons, SW1A 0AA. *Clubs:* Murton Victoria, Democratic, Ex-Servicesman's (Murton); Peterlee Labour; Thornley Catholic.

CUMMINS, Frank; Examinations Liaison Officer, Sandwell Local Education Authority, 1987–89; Headmaster, Thomas Telford High School, Sandwell, West Midlands, 1973–87; *b* 20 Jan. 1924; *s* of Archibald Ernest and Ruth Elizabeth Cummins; *m* 1st, 1943, Joyce Swale (marr. diss.); three *s*; 2nd, 1973, Brenda Valerie Swift. *Educ:* Whitgift Middle Sch.,

Croydon; London School of Economics and Institute of Education, London Univ. Served Royal Signals, 1943–46. Assistant Teacher, Shireland Boys' Sch., Smethwick, 1949; Dep. Headmaster, 1956, Headmaster, 1961, Sandwell Boys' Sch., Smethwick. W Midlands Examinations Board: Chm., Exams Cttee, 1983–86 (Vice-Chm., 1980–83); Vice-Chm., Council, 1986–89; Chm., Bd, 1989–92; Mem. Jt Management Cttee, 1985–94, Governing Council, 1993–94, Midland Examining Gp for GCSE (Chm. Appeals Cttee, 1991–94). Chairman, Community Relations Councils: Warley, 1969, Sandwell, 1974; part-time Commissioner for Racial Equality, 1977–82; Chm., Schools Council Steering Group on Educn in a Multi-Cultural Soc., 1981–83. *Recreations:* cooking, camping, walking, theatre, City of Birmingham Symphony Orchestra. *Address:* 21 Green Street, Smethwick, Warley, West Midlands B67 7EB. *T:* 0121–558 8484.

CUMMINS, Gus, RA 1992; artist; *b* 28 Jan. 1943; *s* of Harold George Cummins and Honor Cecilia (*née* Bird); *m* 1968, Angela Braven; two *s* one *d. Educ:* Sutton and Wimbledon Schs of Art; RCA (NDD, MA). Part-time teacher at art schs and colls, 1969–; currently at: Chelsea, Hastings, Wimbledon, City and Guilds and RA schs. Exhibns, mainly in UK, 1980–; 5 solo exhibns, 1991–. Henry Moore Prize, London Gp, 1982; Spirit of London 2nd Prize, 1983; Daler-Rowney Prize, RA, 1987; Hunting Gp 1st Prize, Mall Gall., 1990; House & Garden Prize and Blackstone Award, RA Summer Show, 1992. *Recreations:* music, poetry, literature, swimming, cycling, pubs, snooker. *Address:* Harpsichord House, Cobourg Place, Hastings, Sussex TN34 3HY. *T:* Hastings (01424) 426429.

CUNDY, Rt. Rev. Ian Patrick Martyn; *see* Lewes, Bishop Suffragan of.

CUNEO, Terence Tenison, CVO 1994; OBE 1987; portrait and figure painter, ceremonial, military and engineering subjects; *b* 1 Nov. 1907; *s* of Cyrus Cuneo and Nell Marion Tenison; *m* 1934, Catherine Mayfield Monro (*d* 1979), *yr d* of Major E. G. Monro, CBE; one *d. Educ:* Sutton Valence Sch.; Chelsea and Slade. Served War of 1939–45: RE, and as War Artist; special propaganda paintings for Min. of Information, Political Intelligence Dept of FO, and War Artists Advisory Cttee; representative of Illustrated London News, France, 1940. Royal Glasgow Inst. of Fine Arts; Pres. of Industrial Painters Group; Exhibitor, RA, RP, ROI Paris Salon (Hon. Mention, 1957). Has painted extensively in North Africa, South Africa, Rhodesia, Canada, USA, Ethiopia, Far East and Antarctica; one-man exhibition, Underground Activities in Occupied Europe, 1941; one-man exhibitions: RWS Galleries, London, 1954 and 1958; Sladmore Gall., 1971, 1972, 1974; Mall Galls, 1988. Best known works include: Meml Paintings of El Alamein and The Royal Engineers, King George VI at The Royal Artillery Mess, Woolwich, King George VI and Queen Elizabeth at The Middle Temple Banquet, 1950; Meml Painting of The Rifle Brigade, 1951; Visit to Lloyd's of Queen Elizabeth II with the Duke of Edinburgh to lay Foundation Stone of Lloyd's New Building, 1952; Queen's Coronation Luncheon, Guildhall, The Duke of Edinburgh at Cambridge, 1953; Portraits of Viscount Allendale, KG, as Canopy Bearer to Her Majesty, 1954; Coronation of Queen Elizabeth II in Westminster Abbey (presented to the Queen by HM's Lieuts of Counties), 1955; Queen's State Visit to Denmark, Engineering Mural in Science Museum, 1957; Queen Elizabeth II at RCOG, 1960; Queen Elizabeth II at Guildhall Banquet after Indian Tour, 1961; Equestrian Portrait of HM the Queen as Col-in-Chief, Grenadier Guards, 1963; Garter Ceremony, 1964; Commonwealth Prime Ministers' Banquet, Guildhall, 1969; first official portraits of Rt Hon. Edward Heath, 1971, of Field Marshal Viscount Montgomery of Alamein, 1972; HM the Queen as Patron of Kennel Club, 1975; King Hussein of Jordan, 1980; Col H. Jones, VC, 1984; 40th Anniversary of D-Day, 1984. Set of stamps commemorating: the 150th anniv. of GWR; the Channel Tunnel, 1994. *Publications:* (autobiog.) The Mouse and his Master, 1977; The Railway Painting of Terence Cuneo, 1984; articles in The Studio, The Artist; *relevant publication:* Terence Cuneo, Railway Painter of the Century, by Narisa Chakra, 1990. *Recreations:* writing, sketching, travel, riding. *T:* 0181–398 1986.

CUNINGHAME, Sir John Christopher Foggo M.; *see* Montgomery Cuninghame.

CUNINGHAME, Sir William Henry F.; *see* Fairlie-Cuninghame.

CUNLIFFE, family name of **Baron Cunliffe.**

CUNLIFFE, 3rd Baron *cr* 1914, of Headley; **Roger Cunliffe,** RIBA; MIMgt; consulting architect; *b* 12 Jan. 1932; *s* of 2nd Baron and Joan Catherine Lubbock (*d* 1980); *S* father, 1963; *m* 1957, Clemency Ann Hoare; two *s* one *d. Educ:* Eton; Trinity Coll., Cambridge (MA); Architectural Association (AA Dipl.); Open Univ. With various architectural firms in UK and USA, 1957–65; Associate, Robert Matthew, Johnson-Marshall & Partners, 1966–69; Dir, Architectural Assoc., 1969–71; Partner, SCP, 1973–78; own practice as architectural, planning and management consultant, 1977–; Dir, Exhibition Consultants Ltd, 1981–; Member: Urban Motorways Cttee, 1969–72; Council, British Consultants Bureau, 1986–90. Member: Council, Lancing Coll., 1967–85; Delegacy, Goldsmiths' Coll., 1972–78; Bd, Coll. of Estate Management, 1992–. Chm., Suffolk Craft Soc., 1994–. Mem. Ct, Goldsmiths' Co., 1986– (Third Warden, 1995). *Publications:* (with Leonard Manasseh) Office Buildings, 1962; contrib. various professional jls. *Recreations:* photography, taxonomy, planting trees. *Heir: s* Hon. Henry Cunliffe, *b* 9 March 1962. *Address:* The Broadhurst, Brandeston, Woodbridge, Suffolk IP13 7AG.

CUNLIFFE, Prof. Barrington Windsor, CBE 1994; FBA 1979; FSA; Professor of European Archaeology, Oxford University, and Fellow of Keble College, since 1972; *b* 10 Dec. 1939. *Educ:* Portsmouth; St John's Coll., Cambridge (MA, PhD, LittD). Lecturer, Univ. of Bristol, 1963–66; Prof. of Archæology, Univ. of Southampton, 1966–72. O'Donnell Lectr in Celtic Studies, Oxford Univ., 1983–84. Member: Ancient Monuments Bd for England, 1976–84; Historic Bldgs and Monuments Commn for England, 1987–92 (Mem., Ancient Monuments Adv. Cttee, 1984–); President: Council for British Archaeology, 1976–79; Soc. of Antiquaries, 1991– (Vice-Pres., 1982–86). Gov., Mus. of London, 1995–. Hon. DLitt Sussex, 1983; Hon. DSc Bath, 1984. *Publications:* Fishbourne, a Roman Palace and its Garden, 1971; Roman Bath Discovered, 1971, rev. edn 1984; The Cradle of England, 1972; The Making of the English, 1973; The Regni, 1973; Iron Age Communities in Britain, 1974; Rome and the Barbarians, 1975; Hengistbury Head, 1978; Rome and her Empire, 1978; The Celtic World, 1979; Danebury: the anatomy of an Iron Age hillfort, 1984; The City of Bath, 1986; Greeks, Romans and Barbarians, 1988; Wessex before AD 1000, 1991; (ed) The Oxford Illustrated Prehistory of Europe, 1994; contribs to several major excavation reports and articles to Soc. of Antiquaries, and in other learned jls. *Recreation:* mild self-indulgence. *Address:* Institute of Archaeology, 36 Beaumont Street, Oxford OX1 2PG.

CUNLIFFE, His Honour Christopher Joseph; a Circuit Judge (formerly County Court Judge), 1966–82; *b* 28 Feb. 1916; *s* of Lt-Col E. N. Cunliffe, OBE, RAMC, Buckingham Crescent, Manchester, and Harriet Cunliffe (*née* Clegg); *m* 1942, Margaret Hamer Barber; two *d. Educ:* Rugby Sch.; Trinity Hall, Cambridge. BA 1937. Called to the Bar, Lincoln's Inn, 1938. Legal Cadet, Br. North Borneo Civil Service. 1939–40. Served RAFVR, 1941–46; Intelligence, Judge Advocate General's Branch. Practised on Northern Circuit, 1946; Dep. Coroner, City of Liverpool, 1953; Chairman: National Insurance Tribunal, Bootle, 1956–; Mental Health Review Tribunal for SW Lancs and W Ches, 1961–. *Recreations:* golf, gardening. *Address:* Field House, Compton, W Sussex PO18 9HE. *T:* Compton (01705) 631270.

CUNLIFFE, Sir David Ellis, 9th Bt *cr* 1759; business development manager; *b* 29 Oct. 1957; *s* of Sir Cyril Henley Cunliffe, 8th Bt and of Eileen Lady Cunliffe, *d* of Frederick William and Nora Anne Parkins; *S* father, 1969; *m* 1983, Linda Carol, *d* of John Sidney and Ella Mary Batchelor; three *d. Educ:* St Albans Grammar School. *Heir: b* Andrew Mark Cunliffe [*b* 17 April 1959; *m* 1980, Janice Elizabeth, *d* of Ronald William Kyle; one *s* three *d*]. *Address:* Sunnyside, Burnthouse Lane, Needham, near Harleston, Norfolk IP20 9LN.

CUNLIFFE, Lawrence Francis; MP (Lab) Leigh, since 1979; *b* 25 March 1929; *m* 1950, Winifred (marr. diss. 1985), *d* of William Haslem; three *s* two *d. Educ:* St Edmund's RC Sch., Worsley, Manchester. Engr, NCB, 1949–79. Member, Farnworth Borough Council, 1960–74, Bolton MDC, 1974–79; contested (Lab) Rochdale, Oct. 1972 and Feb. 1974. An Opposition Whip, 1985–87. JP 1967–79. *Address:* House of Commons, SW1A 0AA.

CUNLIFFE, Peter Whalley, CBE 1980; Chairman: Pharmaceuticals Division, Imperial Chemical Industries PLC, 1976–87; British Pharma Group, 1987–90; *b* 29 Oct. 1926; *s* of Fred Cunliffe and Lillie Whalley; *m* 1951, Alice Thérèse Emma Brunel; one *d. Educ:* Queen Elizabeth's Grammar Sch., Blackburn; Trinity Hall, Cambridge (Scholar; BA 1st Class Hons, 1948). Joined ICI Ltd, Pharmaceuticals Div., 1950; Services Dir, 1968; Overseas Dir, 1970; Dep. Chm., 1971. Pres., Assoc. of British Pharmaceutical Industry, 1981–83; Member: Council, Internat. Fedn of Pharmaceutical Manufrs Assoc., 1979–87 (Vice Pres., 1982–84, Pres. 1984–86); Exec. Cttee, European Fedn of Pharmaceutical Industries Assocs, 1982–85. *Recreations:* reading, walking. *Address:* 10 Sandringham Court, Alderley Road, Wilmslow, Cheshire SK9 1PW.

CUNLIFFE, Stella Vivian, MBE 1993; consultant statistician; *b* 12 Jan. 1917; *d* of Percy Cunliffe and Edith Blanche Wellwood Cunliffe. *Educ:* privately, then Parsons Mead, Ashtead; London School of Economics (BScEcon). Danish Bacon Co, 1939–44; Voluntary Relief Work in Europe, 1945–47; Arthur Guinness Son and Co. Ltd, 1947–70; Head of Research Unit, Home Office, 1970–72; Dir of Statistics, Home Office, 1972–77. Statistical Adviser to Cttee of Enquiry into Engineering Profession, 1978–80. Pres., Royal Statistical Soc., 1975–77. *Recreations:* work with youth organisations; gardening; prison after-care. *Address:* 69 Harriotts Lane, Ashtead, Surrey KT21 2QE. *T:* Ashtead (01372) 272343.

CUNLIFFE-LISTER, family name of **Baroness Masham of Ilton** and **Earl of Swinton.**

CUNLIFFE-OWEN, Sir Hugo Dudley, 3rd Bt *cr* 1920, of Bray; *b* 16 May 1966; *s* of Sir Dudley Herbert Cunliffe-Owen, 2nd Bt, and of Jean, *o d* of late Surg.-Comdr A. N. Forsyth, RN; *S* father, 1983. *Heir:* none.

CUNNANE, Most Rev. Joseph; Archbishop of Tuam, (RC), 1969–87, retired; *b* 5 Oct. 1913; *s* of William and Margaret Cunnane, Knock, Co. Mayo. *Educ:* St Jarlath's Coll., Tuam; St Patrick's Coll., Maynooth. BA 1st Hons, Ancient Classics, 1935; DD 1941; Higher Dip. Educn 1941. Priest, 1939. Prof. of Irish, St Jarlath's Coll., 1941–57; Curate, Balla, Co. Mayo, 1957–67; Curate, Clifden, Co. Galway, 1967–69. Cross of Chaplain Conventual, SMO Malta, 1970. *Publications:* Vatican II on Priests, 1967; contribs to Irish Ecclesiastical Record, Furrow, Doctrine and Life, Studies in Pastoral Liturgy, etc. *Address:* St Jarlath's Presbytery, Knock, Co. Mayo, Ireland.

CUNNINGHAM, Alexander Alan; Executive Vice President, General Motors, 1984–86, retired; *b* Bulgaria, 7 Jan. 1926; naturalised citizen, US; *m* 1976, Mary Helen; one *s* three *d* of former marr. *Educ:* General Motors Inst., Michigan. BSc (Industrial Engrg) 1951. Served War of 1939–45, navigation electronics radar specialist, RAF. General Motors: Jun. Process Engr, Frigidaire Div., 1951; Asst to Frigidaire Man., NY, Gen. Motors Overseas Ops, 1952; Prodn Planning Technician for Adam Opel AG, Germany, 1953; Exec. Asst to Man. Dir, GM Ltd, London, 1956; Master Mechanic, Gen. Motors do Brasil, 1957, Works Man. 1958; Works Man., Gen. Motors Argentina SA, 1962; Man. Dir, Gen. Motors do Brasil, 1963; Man., Adam Opel's Bochum plant, 1964; Asst Gen. Manufrg Man., Adam Opel AG, 1966, Gen. Manufrg Man. 1969; Man. Dir, Adam Opel AG, 1970; Gen. Dir, European Organisations, Gen. Motors Overseas Corp., 1974–76; Vice Pres., Group Exec. Overseas, 1978; Group Exec., Body Assembly, 1980. Exec. Vice-Pres., N American Cars, 1982. Trustee, Detroit SO, 1983–. *Address:* 70–671 Orville Circle, Rancho Mirage, CA 92270, USA. *T:* (619)3288671; (summer) 16472 Malden Circle, Huntington Beach, CA 92649, USA. *Clubs:* Thunderbird Country, Mission Hills Country (Rancho Mirage); Center (Orange County).

CUNNINGHAM, Sir Charles (Craik), GCB 1974 (KCB 1961; CB 1946); KBE 1952; CVO 1941; *b* Dundee, 7 May 1906; *s* of late Richard Yule Cunningham, Abergeldie, Kirriemuir, and Isabella Craik; *m* 1934, Edith Louisa Webster (*d* 1990); two *d. Educ:* Harris Acad., Dundee; University of St Andrews. Entered Scottish Office, 1929; Private Sec. to Parliamentary Under Sec. of State for Scotland, 1933–34; Private Sec. to Sec. of State for Scotland, 1935–39; Asst Sec., Scottish Home Dept, 1939–41; Principal Asst Sec., 1941–42; Dep. Sec., 1942–47; Sec., 1948–57; Permanent Under-Sec. of State, Home Office, 1957–66; Dep. Chm., UKAEA, 1966–71; Chm., Radiochemical Centre Ltd, 1971–74. Dir, Securicor Ltd, 1971–81. Chm., Uganda Resettlement Bd, 1972–73. Mem., Nat. Radiological Protection Bd, 1971–74. Hon. LLD St Andrews, 1960. *Address:* 25 Regent Terrace, Edinburgh EH7 5BS. *T:* 0131–556 9614. *Clubs:* Reform; New (Edinburgh).

CUNNINGHAM, George, BA, BSc; Chief Executive, Library Association, 1984–92; *b* 10 June 1931; *s* of Harry Jackson Cunningham and Christina Cunningham, Dunfermline; *m* 1957, Mavis Walton; one *s* one *d. Educ:* Univs of Manchester and London. Nat. Service in Royal Artillery (2nd Lieut), 1954–56; on staff of Commonwealth Relations Office, 1956–63; 2nd Sec., British High Commn, Ottawa, 1958–60; Commonwealth Officer of Labour Party, 1963–66; Min. of Overseas Development, 1966–69. MP South West Islington, 1970–74, Islington South and Finsbury, 1974–83 (Lab, 1970–81, Ind, 1981–82, SDP, 1982–83). Opposition front bench spokesman (Lab) on home affairs, 1979–81. Contested (SDP) Islington South and Finsbury, 1983, 1987. Mem., Parlt of European Community, 1978–79. *Publications:* (Fabian pamphlet) Rhodesia, the Last Chance, 1966; (ed) Britain and the World in the Seventies, 1970; The Management of Aid Agencies, 1974; Careers in Politics, 1984. *Address:* 28 Manor Gardens, Hampton, Middlesex TW12 2TU. *T:* 0181–979 6221.

CUNNINGHAM, Lt-Gen. Sir Hugh (Patrick), KBE 1975 (OBE 1966); *b* 4 Nov. 1921; *s* of late Sir Charles Banks Cunningham, CSI; *m* 1955, Jill (*d* 1992), *d* of J. S. Jeffrey, East Knoyle; two *s* two *d. Educ:* Charterhouse. 2nd Lieut, RE, 1942; served War of 1939–45, India, New Guinea, Burma; Greece, 1950–51; Egypt, 1951–53; Instructor, Sch. of Infantry, 1955–57, RMA Sandhurst, 1957–60; Camerons, 1960–61; CRE 3 Div., Cyprus and Aden, 1963–66; comd 11 Engr Bde, BAOR, 1967–69; comd Mons OCS, 1969–70; Nat. Defence Coll., Canada, 1970–71; GOC SW District, 1971–74; ACGS (OR), 1974–75; DCDS (OR), 1976–78, retired. Lieutenant of Tower of London, 1983–86. Col, Queen's Gurkha Engineers (formerly Gurkha Engrs), 1976–81; Col Comdt, RE, 1976–81; Col, Bristol Univ. OTC, 1977–87. Director: Fairey Holdings Ltd, 1978–86; Fairey

Engineering, 1981–86; MEL, 1982–89; TREND Communications Ltd, 1984–86, 1990–93; Chairman: LL Consultants Ltd, 1984–89; TREND Group, 1986–90. Pres., Old Carthusian Soc., 1982–87. Master, Glass Sellers' Co., 1981. Chm. of Governors, Port Regis School, 1982–94; Gov., Suttons Hosp. in Charterhouse, 1984–. *Recreations:* bird-watching, opera, tennis. *Address:* Brickyard Farm, East Knoyle, Salisbury, Wilts SP3 6BP. *T:* East Knoyle (01747) 830281; 607 Duncan House, Dolphin Square, SW1V 3LX. *T:* 0171–821 7960. *Clubs:* Army and Navy, MCC.

CUNNINGHAM, James Dolan; MP (Lab) Coventry South East, since 1992; *b* Coatbridge, 4 Feb. 1941; *s* of Adam and Elizabeth Cunningham; *m* 1985, Marion Douglas; one *s* one *d* and one step *s* one step *d*. *Educ:* St Columbia High Sch., Coatbridge. Trade Union Diplomas in Industrial Law and Social Sciences. Engineer, 1964–88. Mem. (Lab) Coventry CC, 1972–92 (Leader, 1988–92; formerly Dep. Leader, Chief Whip, Chm. and Vice Chm. of Cttees). Mem., MSF. *Address:* House of Commons, SW1A 0AA.

CUNNINGHAM, Group Captain John, CBE 1963 (OBE 1951); DSO 1941; (Bars 1942, 1944); DFC 1941 (Bar); AE 1941; DL; Executive Director, British Aerospace, Hatfield, 1978–80; *b* 27 July 1917; *s* of late A. G. Cunningham and of E. M. Cunningham. *Educ:* Whitgift. Apprenticed to De Havilland Aircraft Co., Hatfield, 1935–38; employed, 1938–Aug. 1939, with De Havillands, Light Aircraft Development and Test Flying. Called up Aug. 1939; joined AAF, 1935; commanded 604 Sqdn, 1941–42; Staff job, 1942–43; commanded 85 Sqdn, 1943–44 (DSO and two bars, DFC and bar); Group Capt. Night Operations HQ 11 Group, 1944. Chief Test Pilot, de Havilland Aircraft Co., 1946–77; Exec. Dir, Hawker Siddeley Aviation, 1963–77. International Record Flight, 16 Oct. 1957: London to Khartoum direct; distance 3,064 statute miles in 5 hrs 51 mins, by Comet 3; average speed 523 statute mph. Derry and Richards Memorial Medal, GAPAN, 1965; Segrave Trophy, 1979; Air League Founders' Medal, 1979. DL: Middx, 1948; Greater London, 1965. Russian Order of Patriotic War 1st cl., 1944; USA Silver Star, 1945. *Address:* Canley, Kinsbourne Green, Harpenden, Herts AL5 3PE.

CUNNINGHAM, John, DM, FRCP; Physician to the Royal Household, since 1993; Consultant Physician, Royal London (formerly London) Hospital, since 1982; Physician, King Edward VII's Hospital for Officers, since 1993; *b* 27 June 1949; *s* of Daniel John Chapman Cunningham and Judith (*née* Hill); *m* 1970, Deborah Alison Yeates; three *s*. *Educ:* Magdalen Coll. Sch., Oxford; Trinity Hall, Cambridge (BA 1970); St John's Coll., Oxford (BM, BCh 1973; DM 1988). FRCP 1988. Junior appointments, 1973–77: Radcliffe Infirmary, Oxford; Whittington Hosp., London; Brompton Hosp., London; Central Middx Hosp., London; Lectr in Medicine, London Hosp. Med. Coll., 1977–80; Res. Fellow, Washington Univ. Sch. of Medicine, St Louis, USA, 1980–82; Sub-Dean for Med. Student Admissions, London Hosp. Med. Coll., 1990–. Special Trustee, Royal London Hosp., 1985–. Jan Brod Meml Lecture, Prague, 1993, and other invited lectures. *Publications:* contrib. chapters in books, reviews and numerous articles in scientific jls. *Recreations:* music, sport, walking. *Address:* 3 King Henry's Road, NW3 3QP. *T:* 0171–722 3883.

CUNNINGHAM, Rt Hon. John A., (Jack); PC 1993; DL; PhD; MP (Lab) Copeland, since 1983 (Whitehaven, Cumbria, 1970–83); *b* 4 Aug. 1939; *s* of Andrew Cunningham; *m* 1964, Maureen; one *s* two *d*. *Educ:* Jarrow Grammar Sch.; Bede Coll., Durham Univ. Hons Chemistry, 1962; PhD Chemistry, 1966. Formerly: Research Fellow in Chemistry, Durham Univ.; School Teacher; Trades Union Officer. PPS to Rt Hon. James Callaghan, 1972–76; Parly Under-Sec. of State, Dept of Energy, 1976–79; opposition spokesman on industry, 1979–83; elected to Shadow Cabinet, 1983; spokesman on the environment, 1983–89; Shadow Leader, H of C, 1989–92; opposition front bench spokesman on foreign and Commonwealth affairs, 1992–94; on trade and industry, 1994–. DL Cumbria, 1991. *Recreations:* fell walking, fly-fishing, gardening, classical and folk music, reading, listening to other people's opinions. *Address:* House of Commons, SW1A 0AA.

CUNNINGHAM, Merce; Artistic Director, Merce Cunningham Dance Company, since 1953; *b* 16 April 1919; *s* of Clifford D. Cunningham. *Educ:* Cornish Coll., Seattle, Washington. Martha Graham Dance Co., 1939–45; 1st solo concert, NY, 1944; choreographed: The Seasons, for Ballet Society (later NY City Ballet), 1947; Un Jour ou deux, for Ballet of Paris Opéra, 1973; more than 100 works for own company; other works revived for NY City Ballet, American Ballet Theatre, Rambert Dance Co. (formerly Ballet Rambert), Théâtre du Silence, France, Ohio Ballet, Boston Ballet, Pacific Northwest Ballet. Hon. Mem., Amer. Acad. and Inst. of Arts and Letters, 1984. DLitt Univ. of Illinois, 1972. Samuel H. Scripps American Dance Festival Award for lifetime contribs to dance, 1982; Award of Honor for Arts and Culture, NY, 1983; MacArthur Award, 1985; Kennedy Center Honors, 1985; Laurence Olivier Award, 1985; Meadows Award for excellence in the arts, Meadows Sch. of Arts, Southern Methodist Univ., Dallas, 1987; Nat. Medal of Arts, USA, 1990; Digital Dance Premier Award, 1990. Comdr, Order of Arts and Letters, France, 1982; Chevalier de la Légion d'Honneur, 1989. *Publications:* Changes: notes on choreography (ed Frances Starr), 1968; Le Danseur et la danse: entretiens avec Jacqueline Lesschaeve, 1980, English edn The Dancer and the Dance, 1985; articles in 7 Arts, trans/formation, TriQuarterly. *Address:* 55 Bethune Street, New York, NY 10014, USA. *T:* 212 255 8240.

CUNNINGHAM, Robert Kerr, CMG 1983; PhD; FIBiol; FRSC; Chief Natural Resources Adviser, Overseas Development Administration, 1976–83, and Head of Natural Resources Department, 1980–83, retired; *b* 7 June 1923; *s* of John Simpson Cunningham and Agnes Stewart Cunningham; *m* 1947, Jean Sinclair (*née* Brown); one *s* one *d*. *Educ:* Bathgate Acad., Scotland; Edinburgh Univ. (BSc); London Univ. (PhD). FRIC 1964. Served War, RAF, 1942–46. Science Teacher, W Lothian County Educn Cttee, 1947–50; Science Lectr and Chemist, Govt of Bahamas, 1950–55; Colonial Res. Fellowship, Rothamsted Experimental Stn, 1955–56; Res. Off., W African Cocoa Res. Inst., Gold Coast and Ghana, 1956–60; Principal Scientific Off., Rothamsted Experimtl Stn, 1960–64; Prof. of Chemistry and Soil Science, Univ. of WI, Trinidad, 1964–67; Adviser on Res. and Nat. Resources, Min. of Overseas Develt, 1967–76. *Publications:* many scientific papers dealing mainly with soil chem. and plant nutrition in jls; several reports on organisation of R&D in developing countries; (co-author) reports on Brit. and internat. aid in natural resources field. *Recreations:* walking, reading, golf. *Address:* 19 Coleridge Court, Milton Road, Harpenden, Herts AL5 5LD. *T:* Harpenden (01582) 460203. *Club:* Royal Air Force.

CUNNINGHAM, Roseanna; MP (SNP) Perth and Kinross, since May 1995; *b* 27 July 1951; *d* of Hugh and Catherine Cunningham. *Educ:* Univ. of Western Australia (BA Hons Politics 1975); Edinburgh Univ. (LLB 1982); Aberdeen Univ. (Dip. Legal Practice 1983). SNP Research Asst, 1977–79; Solicitor, 1983–90; admitted Faculty of Advocates, 1990; in practice, 1990–95. *Recreations:* music, reading, stirring up trouble. *Address:* 14/367 Argyle Street, Glasgow G2 8LT. *T:* 0141–221 5651.

CUNNINGHAM, Thomas Anthony, (Tony); Member (Lab) Cumbria and Lancashire North, European Parliament, since 1994; *b* 16 Sept. 1952; *s* of late Daniel Cunningham and of Bessie Cunningham; *m* 1985, Anne Gilmore; one *d*, and one step *s* one step *d*. *Educ:* Workington GS; Liverpool Univ. (BA Hons). Mem., Allerdale DC, then BC, 1987– (Leader, 1992–); Mayor of Workington, 1990–91. *Address:* 17 Carlton Road, Workington, Cumbria CA14 4BX. *T:* Workington (01900) 605799.

CUNNINGHAM-JARDINE, Ronald Charles; Lord-Lieutenant, Dumfries and Galloway Region, districts of Nithsdale, Annandale and Eskdale, since 1991 (Vice Lord-Lieutenant, 1988–91); *b* 19 Sept. 1931; *s* of Charles Frederick Cunningham and Dorothy Agnes Jessie Jardine; *m* 1959, Constance Mary Teresa Inglis; one *s* one *d*. *Educ:* Ludgrove; Eton College; RMA Sandhurst. Royal Scots Greys, 1950–58; Edinburgh Agricultural College, 1959–60; farming, 1960–. *Recreations:* all country sports. *Address:* Fourmerkland, Lockerbie, Dumfriesshire DG11 1EH. *T:* Lochmaben (01387) 810226. *Clubs:* White's; Muthaiga (Kenya).

CUNYNGHAME, Sir Andrew (David Francis), 12th Bt *cr* 1702; FCA; *b* 25 Dec. 1942; *s* of Sir (Henry) David St Leger Brooke Selwyn Cunynghame, 11th Bt, and of Hon. Pamela Margaret Stanley (*d* 1991), *d* of 5th Lord Stanley of Alderley; *S* father, 1978; *m* 1st, 1972, Harriet Ann, *d* of C. T. Dupont, Montreal; two *d*; 2nd, 1989, Isabella King, *d* of late Edward Everett Watts, Jr and of Isabella Hardy Watts. *Educ:* Eton. *Heir: b* John Philip Henry Michael Selwyn Cunynghame [*b* 9 Sept. 1944; *m* 1981, Marjatta, *d* of Martti Markus; one *s* one *d*]. *Address:* 12 Vicarage Gardens, W8 4AH. *Club:* Brooks's.

CUOMO, Mario Matthew; lawyer; Democrat; *b* 15 June 1932; *s* of Andrea and late Immaculata Cuomo; *m* 1954, Matilda M. Raffa; two *s* three *d*. *Educ:* St John's Coll., NY (Latin Amer. Studies, English, Philosophy; BA 1953); St John's Univ. (LLB 1956). Admitted to NY Bar, 1956, US Supreme Court, 1960; Asst to Judge A. P. Burke, NY State Court of Appeals, 1956–58; joined Corner, Weisbrod, Froeb & Charles (later Corner, Finn, Cuomo & Charles), 1958, Partner, 1963–75; Prof., St John's Univ. Law Sch., 1963–73; Sec. of State for NY, 1975–78 (Chm., NY Urban & Rural Affairs, Adv. Council on Disabled; 1st NY Ombudsman); Lt-Governor, NY, 1979–82; Governor, NY State, 1983–95. *Publications:* The Forest Hills Controversy: a report and comment, 1972; Forest Hills Diary: the crisis of low income housing, 1974; Diaries of Mario M. Cuomo: the campaign for Governor, 1984; (ed jtly) Lincoln on Democracy, 1990; More than Words: the speeches of Mario Cuomo, 1993; New York Idea: an experiment in democracy, 1994; articles in legal jls.

CUPITT, Rev. Don; Fellow of Emmanuel College, since 1965 (Dean, 1966–91) and University Lecturer in Divinity, Cambridge, since 1973; *b* 22 May 1934; *s* of late Robert and of Norah Cupitt; *m* 1963, Susan Marianne (*née* Day); one *s* two *d*. *Educ:* Charterhouse; Trinity Hall, Cambridge; Westcott House, Cambridge. Curate, St Philip's Church, Salford, 1959–62; Vice-Principal, Westcott House, Cambridge, 1962–65. Hon. DLitt Bristol, 1985. *Publications:* Christ and the Hiddenness of God, 1971; Crisis of Moral Authority, 1972; The Leap of Reason, 1976; The Worlds of Science and Religion, 1976; (with Peter Armstrong) Who Was Jesus?, 1977; Jesus and the Gospel of God, 1979; The Nature of Man, 1979; The Debate about Christ, 1979; Explorations in Theology, 1979; Taking Leave of God, 1980; The World to Come, 1982; The Sea of Faith, 1984 (TV series, 1984); Only Human, 1985; Life Lines, 1986; The Long-Legged Fly, 1987; The New Christian Ethics, 1988; Radicals and the Future of the Church, 1989; Creation Out of Nothing, 1990; What is a Story?, 1991; The Time Being, 1992; Rethinking Religion, 1992; After All, 1994; The Last Philosophy, 1995. *Address:* Emmanuel College, Cambridge CB2 3AP. *T:* Cambridge (01223) 334200.

CURDS, Prof. Colin Robert, DSc, PhD; CBiol, FIBiol; Keeper of Zoology, Natural History Museum, since 1991; *b* 16 Sept. 1937; *s* of Robert Redvers Curds and Daisy Violet Curds (*née* Howsam); *m* 1961, Pauline (Polly) Armitage; one *s* one *d*. *Educ:* East Ham Grammar Sch.; Univ. of London (BSc 1960; PhD 1963; DSc 1978). FIBiol 1979, CBiol 1982. Jun. Res. Fellow, Water Pollution Res. Lab., 1963–65; Min. of Technology, 1965–71; British Museum (Natural History), 1971–: Dep. Keeper of Zoology, 1976–89; Acting Keeper of Zoology, 1989–91. Visiting Lecturer: Chelsea Coll., 1965–73; Aston Univ., 1967–75; Surrey Univ., 1971–85; Vis. Prof., Mexico Univ., 1989–. Former mem., biol. and microbiol. cttees, 1972–; Member: Publications Policy Cttee, Inst. Biol., 1979–85; Council of Management, Project Urquhart, 1991–. Gov., Powell-Cotton Mus., 1992–. *Publications:* (ed jtly) Ecological Aspects of Used-water Treatment Processes, vol. 1, 1979, vols 2 and 3, 1983; British and other freshwater ciliated protozoa, Pt 1, 1982, Pt 2 (jtly), 1983; Protozoa in the Water Industry, 1992; contribs to professional jls. *Recreations:* family life, furniture design, cabinet-making, France, cats, snorkelling, genealogy. *Address:* Department of Zoology, Natural History Museum, Cromwell Road, SW7 5BD. *T:* 0171–938 8985.

CURE, (George) Nigel C.; *see* Capel Cure.

CURE, Kenneth Graham, OBE 1984; Executive Councilman, Amalgamated Engineering Union, 1979–89, retired; Member, Labour Party National Executive, 1981–89; *b* 22 Feb. 1924; *s* of Herbert and Doris Edith Cure; *m* 1949, Kathleen (*née* Taylor); two *s* one *d*. *Educ:* King Edward VI Grammar School, Birmingham. Apprentice, BSA; trained as Universal Miller and draughtsman; served War of 1939–45, RN (Atlantic convoys and combined ops). Joined AEU, 1952; Founder Sec., Castle Vale Birmingham Branch, 1970; held numerous offices in Branch and District; former Mem., W Midlands Regional Labour Party Exec.; former Chm., Disputes Cttee, Lab. Party NEC; former Mem., Gen. Purposes Cttee, TUC. Former Director: Co-operative Press Ltd; Prince's Trust Educn and Training. Member: Panel, Central Arbitration Cttee; ACAS. Chair, East Birmingham Coll. Corp. (formerly Govs), 1973–; Chm., Birmingham Metropolitan Inst. of Technology, 1992–; Governor, Fircroft Coll., 1981–94. FRSA. Hon. MSc CNAA, 1986. *Recreation:* reading.

CURIE, Eve, (Mrs Henry R. Labouisse), writer and journalist; *b* Paris, 6 Dec. 1904; *d* of late Marie and Pierre Curie; *m* 1954, Henry Richardson Labouisse (*d* 1987). *Educ:* by governesses, generally Polish; Sévigné College; Bachelor of Science and Bachelor of Philosophy. Accompanied her mother in her tour of the US 1921; devoted several years to the study of the piano and gave her first concert in 1925 in Paris; later she took up musical criticism and under a pseudonym acted for several years as musical critic of the weekly journal Candide; after the death of her mother in 1934 she collected and classified all the papers, manuscripts, and personal documents left by Mme Curie and went to Poland in 1935 to obtain material as to Mme Curie's youth; wrote Mme Curie's biography; went to America again in 1939 and has gone several times since on lecture tours; was a co-ordinator of the women's war activities at the Ministry of Information in Paris at the beginning of the war, until she went on a lecture tour in the USA; came back to Paris 2 May 1940; after the French capitulation went to live in London for six months, then to America for her third lecture tour; Vichy Govt deprived her of French citizenship in April 1941; in 1942, travelled, as a war correspondent to the battlefronts of Libya, Russia, Burma, China; enlisted in the Fighting French corps, Volontaires Françaises, 1943, as a private; received basic training in England; 2nd Lieut 1943; 1st Lieut 1944. Co-publisher of Paris-Presse, an evening paper in Paris, 1944–49. Special Adviser to the Sec. Gen. of NATO, Paris, Aug. 1952–Nov. 1954. *Publications:* Madame Curie (in US), 1937 (trans. into 32 langs); Journey Among Warriors, 1943. *Recreation:* swimming. *Address:* 1 Sutton Place South, New York, NY 10022, USA.

CURLE, James Leonard; Member and Managing Director, Civil Aviation Authority, 1984–87; *b* 14 Nov. 1925; *s* of Leonard and Mary Curle; *m* 1952, Gloria Madaleine Roch; one *s* one *d*. *Educ:* St Joseph's Academy, Blackheath; SE London Technical College; Borough Polytechnic. CEng, MIEE. Royal Signals, 1944–49; joined Telecommunications Div., MTCA, 1957; Dir Telecommunications, ATS, 1976–79; Dir Gen. Telecommunications, NATS, 1979–84. *Address:* 6 Nightingale Lane, Bickley, Kent BR1 2QH. *T:* 0181–460 8023.

CURLE, Sir John (Noel Ormiston), KCVO 1975 (CVO 1956); CMG 1966; HM Diplomatic Service, retired; *b* 12 Dec. 1915; *s* of Major W. S. N. Curle, MC, Melrose, Scotland; *m* 1st, 1940, Diana Deane; one *s* one *d*; 2nd, 1948, Pauline, *widow* of Capt. David Roberts; two step *d* (one step *s* decd). *Educ:* Marlborough; New Coll., Oxford. 1st Class Hons, MA, Laming Travelling Fellow of Queen's Coll. Diplomatic Service, 1939; Irish Guards, 1939; War Cabinet Secretariat, 1941–44. Has served in Lisbon, Ottawa, Brussels, Stockholm (Counsellor), Athens (Counsellor); Boston (Consul-Gen., 1962–66); Ambassador to: Liberia, 1967–70 and Guinea, 1968–70; the Philippines, 1970–72; Vice Marshal of Diplomatic Corps, 1972–75; retired 1975; Dir of Protocol, Hong Kong, 1976–85; Advr for coronation of the King of Swaziland, 1986. Liveryman, Masons Company. *Recreations:* skiing (represented Oxford *v* Cambridge, and British Univs *v* Swiss Univs). *Address:* Appletree House, near Aston-le-Walls, Daventry, Northants NN11 6UG. *T:* Chipping Warden (0129586) 211. *Clubs:* Cavalry and Guards, Beefsteak; Hong Kong.

CURNOW, Rt Rev. Andrew William; Assistant Bishop, Diocese of Melbourne, since 1994; *b* 26 Feb. 1950; *s* of Thomas William Curnow and Esma Jean Curnow (*née* Cook); *m* 1978, Jan Christina Jenkins; two *s* one *d*. *Educ:* Univ. of Melbourne (BComm); Melbourne Coll. of Divinity (BD); Presbyterian Sch. of Christian Educn, Richmond, VA, USA, (MA). Asst Curate, St Alban's, West Coburg, 1973–75; Rector, Parish of Milloo, 1975–79; on leave, USA, dios New York and Virginia, 1979–80; Rector of Elmore, 1980–83; Dir, Council for Christian Educn in Schools, Prov. of Victoria, 1983–89; Vicar of St George's, Malvern, 1989–94; Archdeacon of Kew, 1991–94. *Recreations:* reading, theatre, travel. *Address:* St Paul's Cathedral, 209 Flinders Lane, Melbourne, Vic 3000, Australia. *T:* (3) 96534220; 66 Baroda Street, Ascot Vale, Vic 3032, Australia. *T:* (3) 93704147. *Club:* Melbourne (Melbourne).

CURNOW, (Elizabeth) Ann (Marguerite); QC 1985; a Recorder of the Crown Court, since 1980; *b* 5 June 1935; *d* of Cecil Curnow and Doris Curnow (*née* Behr); *m* 1981, (William) Neil Denison, *qv*. *Educ:* St Hilda's Sch., Whitby, Yorks; King's Coll., London (LLB). Called to the Bar, Gray's Inn, 1957, Bencher, 1985. Treasury Counsel, Mddx Crown Court, 1972–77; Central Criminal Court: Jun. Treasury Counsel, 1977–81; Sen. Prosecuting Counsel to the Crown, 1981–85. Mem., Parole Bd, 1992–94. *Recreations:* Burmese cats, listening to music, tapestry, gardening. *Address:* 6 King's Bench Walk, Temple, EC4Y 7DR. *T:* 0171–583 0410, *Fax:* 0171–353 8791.

CURRALL, Alexander, CB 1970; CMG 1965; Managing Director, Post Office, 1972–77; *b* 30 Jan. 1917; *s* of late R. T. Currall, Edinburgh; *m* 1940, Madeleine Crombie Saunders; one *s*. *Educ:* George Watson's Coll., Edinburgh; Edinburgh Univ. Min. of Supply, 1939–40; Royal Artillery and Indian Artillery, 1940–46. Successively in Min. of Supply, Min. of Materials and Board of Trade, concerned mainly with internat. economic negotiations, excepting the period 1950–54, when responsible for public trading in non-ferrous metals, and 1954–55, when holding a Commonwealth Fellowship for travel and study in USA. Seconded to Foreign Office as Dep. Consul-Gen., New York, 1960–62; Minister (Commercial), British High Commn, Ottawa, 1962–66; Under-Secretary: Board of Trade, 1966–67; DEA, 1967–68; Dir, Dept for Nat. Savings, 1968–72. Director: Renold, 1977–84; National Counties Building Soc., 1977–87 (Chm., 1984–86); Applied Photophysics Ltd, 1980–86 (Chm., 1981–86); Photophysics Research Ltd, 1980–86 (Chm., 1981–86); Grantham House Ltd, 1980–86 (Chm., 1981–86); The Pryors Ltd, 1983–87. Manager, Royal Instn, 1972–75, 1977–80, 1981–84. *Address:* Fairlawn, Buckden, Skipton, North Yorkshire BD23 5JA. *Club:* Caledonian.

CURRAN, Edmund Russell; Editor, Belfast Telegraph, since 1993; *b* 29 Sept. 1944; *s* of William John Curran and Elizabeth (*née* Russell); *m* 1st, 1968, Romaine Carmichael (marr. diss. 1991); two *s* two *d*; 2nd, 1994, Pauline Hall. *Educ:* Royal Sch., Dungannon; Queen's Univ., Belfast (BSc, DipEd). Dep. Editor, Belfast Telegraph, 1974–88; Editor, Sunday Life (NI), 1988–92; Actg Editor, Wales on Sunday, 1991. Newspaper Focus UK Regl Newspaper Editor of Year, 1991. *Recreations:* tennis, golf, reading newspapers. *Address:* Belfast Telegraph, 124/144 Royal Avenue, Belfast BT1 1EB. *T:* Belfast (01232) 264400. *Clubs:* Belfast Boat, Belvoir Park Golf (Belfast).

CURRAN, Leo Gabriel Columbanus, CEng, FIMechE, FIMarE; Chairman, Paleagle Ltd; *b* 23 Nov. 1930; *s* of B. L. Curran and R. Fanning; *m* 1957, Margaret Hickey; one *s* two *d*. *Educ:* St Malachy's Coll., Belfast; Dublin Coll. of Higher Technol. CEng 1974, FIMechE 1969; FIMarE 1974; MIProdE 1970. Managing Director: British Silverware Ltd, 1970–71; Delta Electrical (South African Delta Metal Electrical Pty) Ltd, 1971–73; Gen. Man. and Dir, Harland & Wolff Ltd, 1973–76; Man. Dir, Plessey Hydraulics International Ltd, 1976–79; Bd Mem. for Enginebuilding and Gen. Engrg, British Shipbuilders, 1979–80; Dir, Mica & Micanite (Ireland) Ltd, 1987–. *Recreations:* music, walking. *Address:* Paleagle Ltd, Camac House, John F. Kennedy Park, Bluebell, Dublin 12, Ireland. *T:* Dublin 500777. *Club:* Institute of Directors.

CURRAN, Patrick David; QC 1995; a Recorder, since 1992; *b* 2 March 1948; *s* of late David Alban Curran and of Noreen Mary Curran; *m* 1976, Anne, *d* of Prof. M. S. John Pathy; two *s* two *d*. *Educ:* Ratcliffe; Queen's Coll., Oxford (MA). Called to the Bar, Gray's Inn, 1972; Asst Recorder, 1988–92; admitted to Bar of Ireland, 1993. Asst Comr, Parly Boundary Commn for Wales, 1994–. Editor, Personal Injuries and Quantum Reports, 1992–. *Publications:* Personal Injury Pleadings, 1994; (contrib.) Criminal Law and Forensic Psychiatry, 1995; Injuries at Work, 1996; contrib. Criminal Law Rev., Personal Injuries and Quantum Reports. *Recreations:* theatre, reading, walking. *Address:* 30 Park Place, Cardiff CF2 6BH. *T:* Cardiff (01222) 398421; Farrar's Building, Temple, EC4 7BD.

CURRAN, Prof. Robert Crowe, MD; FRSE 1962; Leith Professor of Pathology, Birmingham University, 1966–86, now Emeritus; Hon. Consultant Pathologist, Birmingham Central Health District, 1966–86; *b* 28 July 1921; *s* of John Curran and Sarah Crowe, Netherton, Wishaw, Lanarkshire; *m* 1947, Margaret Marion Park; one *s* one *d*. *Educ:* Glasgow Univ. MB, ChB 1943, MD 1956; FRCPath 1967; FRCP 1969; Hon. FFPath, RCPI, 1983. RAMC, 1945–47. Lectr in Pathology, Glasgow Univ., 1950–55. Sen. Lectr and Cons. Pathologist, Sheffield Univ., 1955–58; Prof. of Pathology, St Thomas's Hospital Medical Sch., 1958–66. Registrar, Royal Coll. of Pathologists, 1968–73, Vice-Pres., 1977–80, Pres., 1981–84; Mem., GMC, 1979–86; Hon. Sec., Conf. of Med. Royal Colls and their Faculties in UK, 1982–86. *Publications:* Colour Atlas of Histopathology, 1966, 3rd edn 1985; The Pathological Basis of Medicine, 1972; Gross Pathology—a Colour Atlas, 1974; Tumours: Structure and Diagnosis, 1991; scientific papers on lymphoid tissue, disorders of connective tissue, etc. *Recreations:* golf, music. *Address:* 34A Carpenter Road, Edgbaston, Birmingham B15 2JH.
See also Sir S. C. Curran.

CURRAN, Sir Samuel (Crowe), Kt 1970; FRS 1953; FRSE 1947; FEng 1983; Principal and Vice-Chancellor, University of Strathclyde, 1964–80, Fellow, since 1990; *b* 23 May 1912; *s* of John Curran, Kinghorn, Fife, and Sarah Owen Crowe, Ballymena, Ulster; *m* 1940, Joan Elizabeth, *yr d* of Charles William Strothers and Margaret Beatrice (*née* Millington); three *s* one *d*. *Educ:* Glasgow Univ. (MA, BSc; PhD 1937; DSc 1950); St John's Coll., Cambridge (PhD Cantab, 1941; Hon. Fellow, 1971). Cavendish Laboratory, 1937–39; RAE, 1939–40; Min. of Aircraft Production and Min. of Supply, 1940–44; Manhattan Project (Min. of Supply), Univ. of California, 1944–45 (Invention of Scintillation Counter, 1944). Natural Philosophy, Glasgow Univ. 1945–55 (Invention of Proportional Counter, 1948); UK Atomic Energy Authority, 1955–58; Chief Scientist, AWRE, Aldermaston, Berks, 1958–59; Principal, Royal Coll. of Science and Technology, Glasgow, 1959–64. Vis. Prof. in Energy Studies, Univ. of Glasgow, 1980–88. Pres., Scottish Soc. for the Mentally Handicapped, 1954–. Member: Council for Scientific and Industrial Research, 1962–65; Science Research Council, 1965–68; Adv. Council on Technology, 1965–70; Chairman: Adv. Cttee on Med. Research, 1962–75; Adv. Bd on Relations with Univs, 1966–70; Electricity Supply Res. Council, 1978–80 (Dep. Chm., 1980–82); Dep. Chm., Electricity Council, 1977–79; Chief Scientific Adviser to the Sec. of State for Scotland, 1967–77; Member: Oil Develt Council for Scotland, 1973–78; Adv. Cttee on Safety of Nuclear Installations, 1977–80; Radioactive Waste Management Adv. Cttee, 1978–81; Adv. Council of A Power for Good (APG), 1978–; UK Nat. Commn for Unesco, and Educn Adv. Cttee, 1978–; Standing Commn on Scottish Economy, 1987–. Director: Scottish Television, 1964–82; Hall Thermotank Ltd, 1969–76; Cetec Systems Ltd, 1965–77; Internat. Res. & Develt Co. Ltd, 1970–78; Gen. Steels Div., BSC, 1970–73; Nuclear Structures (Protection) Ltd, 1981–. Hon. Pres., Scottish Polish Cultural Assoc., 1972–; President: St Andrews' Soc., Glasgow, 1982–88; Inst. of Envmtl Safety, 1992. FRCPS (Hon.) 1964; FIEE (Hon.) 1989. Hon. LLD: Glasgow, 1968; Aberdeen, 1971; Hon. ScD Lodz, 1973; Hon. DSc Strathclyde, 1980; Hon. DEng Nova Scotia, 1982. Freeman: Motherwell and Wishaw, 1966; City of Glasgow, 1980. DL Glasgow, 1969. St Mungo Prize, 1976. Comdr, St Olav (Norway), 1966; Comdr, Order Polish People's Republic, 1976. *Publications:* (with J. D. Craggs) Counting Tubes, 1949; Luminescence and the Scintillation Counter, 1953; Alpha, Beta and Gamma Ray Spectroscopy, 1964; (jt) Energy Resources and the Environment, 1976; (with J. S. Curran) Energy and Human Needs, 1979; Issues in Science and Education, 1988; papers on nuclear researches and education in Proc. Royal Society. *Recreations:* horology, golf. *Address:* 93 Kelvin Court, Glasgow G12 0AH. *T:* 0141–334 8329.
See also R. C. Curran.

CURRAN, Terence Dominic; Deputy High Commissioner, Bombay, since 1993; *b* 14 June 1940; *m* 1969, Penelope Ford; two *s* one *d*. Diplomatic Service Admin, 1966; Peking, 1968; FCO, 1969; Dakar, 1970; Asst Trade Comr, then Consul, Edmonton, 1973; First Secretary: FCO, 1978; Pretoria, 1980; FCO, 1984; Counsellor: Singapore, 1987; FCO, 1990. *Address:* c/o Foreign and Commonwealth Office, SW1A 2AH.

CURREY, Rear-Adm. Edmund Neville Vincent, CB 1960; DSO 1944; DSC 1941; *b* 1 Oct. 1906; *s* of Dr and Mrs E. F. N. Currey, Lismore, Co. Waterford, Ireland; *m* 1941, Rosemary Knight (*d* 1992); one *d*. *Educ:* Royal Naval Colls, Osborne and Dartmouth. Joined RNC Osborne 1920; served in submarines and destroyers as junior officer; served War of 1939–45; commanded HM ships Wrestler, Escapade and Musketeer; Comdr, 1942; Capt., 1949; subsequently served with British Naval Mission to Greece; Naval Asst to Adm. Commanding Reserves; in command of HMS Bermuda; Naval Asst to Second Sea Lord; Rear-Adm., 1958; Chief of Staff to C-in-C, Portsmouth, 1958–61, retired. Polish Gold Cross of Merit, with swords, 1943. *Recreation:* golf. *Address:* 75 Great Pulteney Street, Garden Flat, Bath, Avon BA2 4DL. *T:* Bath (01225) 463743.

CURREY, Prof. Harry Lloyd Fairbridge, FRCP; Arthritis and Rheumatism Council Professor of Rheumatology, University of London, 1983–87, now Emeritus Professor of Rheumatology; Director, Bone and Joint Unit, London Hospital Medical College, 1976–87; Consulting Rheumatologist, London Hospital, since 1988; *b* 5 June 1925; *s* of late Ronald Fairbridge Currey and of Dorothy (*née* White); *m* 1st, 1950, Chrystal Komlosy (decd); one *s* two *d*; 2nd, 1973, Jacqueline Harris. *Educ:* Cordwalles, S Africa; Michaelhouse, Natal; Univ. of Cape Town (MB, ChB 1950, MMed 1960). FRCP 1971 (MRCP 1962). Intern, Groote Schuur Hosp., and House Officer, City Hosp. and Peninsular Maternity Hosps, Cape Town, 1951–53; gen. practice, Port Elizabeth, 1953–58; Med. Registrar, Groote Schuur Hosp., Cape Town, 1959–61; Intern, Hammersmith Hosp., London, 1962; Registrar, Dept of Rheumatology, London Hosp., 1963–65; London Hosp. Med. College: Sen. Lectr, 1965–70; Reader in Rheumatol., 1970–74; Prof of Rheumatol., 1974–83; Res. Fellow, Southwestern Med. Sch., Dallas, Texas, 1966. Philip Ellman Lectr, RCP, 1977. Pres., Heberden Soc., 1980–81; Heberden Round presented 1972. Editor, Annals of the Rheumatic Diseases, 1983–88. *Publications:* Mason and Currey's Clinical Rheumatology, 1970, 4th edn 1986; Essentials of Rheumatology, 1983, 2nd edn 1988; (with S. A. Hull) Rheumatology for GPs, 1987; articles on rheumatol topics in learned jls. *Recreations:* gardening, music, golf, fell-walking, inland waterways. *Address:* The Heights, Galloway Road, Bishop's Stortford, Herts CM23 2HS. *T:* Bishop's Stortford (01279) 654717.

CURRIE, Austin; *see* Currie, J. A.

CURRIE, Brian Murdoch; Deputy President, Institute of Chartered Accountants in England and Wales, 1995–June 1996 (Vice-President, 1994–95); *b* 20 Dec. 1934; *s* of William Murdoch Currie and Dorothy (*née* Holloway), *m* 1961, Patricia Maria, *d* of Capt. Frederick Eaton-Farr; three *s* one *d*. *Educ:* Blundell's Sch. (Scholar); Oriel Coll., Oxford (Open Scholar; MA). ACA 1963, FCA 1973; MIMC 1968, FIMC 1990. Commnd RTR, 1957–59; Arthur Andersen Chartered Accountants, 1959–90: Partner, 1970–90; Dep. Man. Partner, 1975; Man. Partner, London, 1977–82; Chm., Partnership Council, 1983–85. Dist Auditor, 1982–87. Dept of Trade Inspector, Fourth City and other cos, 1978; Mem., Foster Cttee of Inquiry into Road Haulage Licensing, 1977. Member: Management Bd, HMSO, 1972–74; Restrictive Practices Court, 1979–; (occasional) Takeover Panel, 1989–; GDC (Crown nominee), 1994–. Institute of Chartered Accountants in England and Wales: Mem. Council, 1988–; Chm., Practice Regulation, 1993; Chm., Chartered Accountants Jt Ethics Cttee, 1994–. Trustee, Oriel Coll. Develt Trust, 1980–94. *Publications:* official public reports; papers and articles in professional and technical pubns. *Recreations:* natural history, Exmoor, church (lay assisting). *Address:* Westbrook House, Bampton, Tiverton, Devon EX16 9HU. *T:* Bampton (01398) 331418. *Clubs:* Athenæum, Reform.

CURRIE, Dr Christopher Richard John, FRHistS, FSA; General Editor, Victoria History of the Counties of England, since 1994; *b* 3 March 1948; *s* of George Samson Currie, MC and Norah Currie (*née* Kennedy); *m* 1981, Katherine Ruth Gommon; one *s* one *d*. *Educ:* Winchester; Balliol Coll., Oxford (MA 1976, DPhil 1976). FRHistS 1979; FSA 1984. Victoria County History: Asst Editor, Staffs, 1972–78; Dep. Editor, 1978–94.

Hon. Editor, Vernacular Architecture, 1980–82. *Publications:* (ed with C. P. Lewis) English County Histories: a guide, 1994; articles in Victoria County Hist. and learned jls. *Recreation:* sleep. *Address:* 14 Keston Road, N17 6PN. *T:* 0181–801 2185.

CURRIE, Prof. David Anthony; Professor of Economics, since 1988, and Deputy Principal, since 1992, London Business School; *b* 9 Dec. 1946; *s* of Kennedy Moir Currie and Marjorie Currie (*née* Thompson); *m* 1st, 1975, Shaziye Gazioglu Currie (marr. diss. 1992); two *s*; 2nd, 1995, Angela Mary Piers Dumas. *Educ:* Battersea Grammar Sch.; Univ. of Manchester (BSc 1st cl. Maths); Univ. of Birmingham (MSocSci Econs); PhD Econs London. Economist: Hoare Govett, 1971–72; Economic Models, 1972; Lectr, Reader and Prof. of Economics, Queen Mary College, Univ. of London, 1972–88; London Business School: Res. Dean, 1989–92; Gov., 1989–; Dir, Centre for Econ. Forecasting, 1988–95. Res. Fellow, Centre for Economic Policy Research, 1983–. Houblon-Norman Res. Fellow, Bank of England, 1985–86; Vis. Scholar, IMF, 1987. Member: ABRC, 1992–93; Retail Price Index Adv. Cttee, 1992–; Treasury's Panel of Independent Forecasters, 1992–. Director: Internat. Schs of Business Mgt, 1992–; Joseph Rowntree Reform Trust (Investments) Ltd, 1989; Joseph Rowntree Reform Trust (Properties) Ltd, 1991. Trustee, Joseph Rowntree Reform Trust, 1991. *Publications:* Advances in Monetary Economics, 1985; (with Charles Goodhart and David Llewellyn) The Operation and Regulation of Financial Markets, 1986; (with David Vines) Macroeconomic Interactions Between North and South, 1988; (with Paul Levine) Rules, Reputation and Macroeconomic Policy Co-ordination, 1993; articles in jls. *Recreations:* music, literature, swimming. *Address:* London Business School, Sussex Place, NW1 4SA. *T:* 0171–262 5050. *Club:* Reform.

CURRIE, Sir Donald Scott, 7th Bt *cr* 1847; Chief of Maintenance, National Park Service, Department of the Interior, 1976; *b* 16 Jan. 1930; *s* of George Donald Currie (*d* 1980) (*g g s* of 1st Bt) and of Janet K., *d* of late James Scott; *S* cousin, 1987; *m* 1st, 1948, Charlotte (marr. diss. 1951), *d* of Charles Johnstone; one *s* twin *d*; 2nd, 1952, Barbara Lee, *d* of A. P. Garnier; one *s* two *d*. Rancher and farmer, 1949–75. *Heir: s* Donald Mark Currie [*b* 1949; *m*; one *s*]. *Clubs:* American Legion (Colorado, USA); National Rifle Association (USA); North American Hunting.

CURRIE, Edwina; MP (C) Derbyshire South, since 1983; *b* 13 Oct. 1946; *m* 1972, Raymond F. Currie, BA, FCA; two *d*. *Educ:* Liverpool Inst. for Girls; St Anne's Coll., Oxford (MA 1972); London Sch. of Econs and Pol Science (MSc 1972). Teaching and lecturing posts in econs, econ. history and business studies, 1972–81. Birmingham City Council: Mem., 1975–86; Chm., Social Services Cttee, 1979–80; Chm., Housing Cttee, 1982–83. Chm., Central Birmingham HA, 1981–83; Mem., Birmingham AHA, 1975–82. PPS to Sec. of State for Educn and Science, 1985–86; Parly Under-Sec. of State (Health), DHSS, later Dept of Health, 1986–88. Mem., Parly Select Cttee on Social Services, 1983–86. Member: European Standing Cttee, 1991–93; European Movement; Cons. Gp on Europe. Contested (C) Bedfordshire and Milton Keynes, Eur. Parly elecns, 1994. Columnist, Today, 1990–91; regular contributor to nat. newspapers and magazines. Speaker of the Year, Assoc. of Speakers' Clubs, 1990. *Publications:* Financing our Cities (Bow Group pamphlet), 1976; Life Lines, 1989; What Women Want, 1990; (jtly) Three-Line Quips, 1992; A Parliamentary Affair (novel), 1994. *Recreations:* family, domestic arts, writing. *Address:* House of Commons, SW1A 0AA. *T:* 0171–219 3611. *Club:* Swadlincote Conservative (Derbyshire).

CURRIE, Heriot Whitson; QC (Scot) 1992; *b* 23 June 1952; *s* of Heriot Clunas Currie and Evelyn Whitson; *m* 1975, Susan Carolyn Hodge; three *d*. *Educ:* Edinburgh Academy; Wadham Coll., Oxford (MA); Edinburgh Univ. (LLB). Admitted to Faculty of Advocates, 1979; practice as Advocate, 1979–; called to the Bar, Gray's Inn, 1991. *Recreations:* chamber music, cinema, golf, foreign languages. *Address:* 16 Greenhill Gardens, Edinburgh EH10 4BW. *T:* 0131–447 4366. *Club:* New (Edinburgh).

CURRIE, James McGill; Deputy Head of European Communities Delegation to United States of America, since 1993; *b* 17 Nov. 1941; *s* of late David Currie and of Mary (*née* Smith); *m* 1968, Evelyn Barbara MacIntyre; one *s* one *d*. *Educ:* St Joseph's High Sch., Kilmarnock; Blairs Coll., Aberdeen; Royal Scots Coll., Valladolid; Univ. of Glasgow (MA). Asst Principal, Scottish Home and Health Dept, 1968–72; Principal, Scottish Educn Dept, 1972–75; Secretary, Management Gp, Scottish Office, 1975–77; Scottish Development Dept: Principal, 1977–79; Asst Sec., 1979–81; Asst Sec., Scottish Economic Planning Dept, 1981–82; Counsellor, UK Perm. Representation to EEC, 1982–87; Dir of Regional Policy, EEC, 1987–89; Chef de Cabinet to Leon Brittan, EEC, 1989–92. *Recreations:* tennis, guitar, good food. *Address:* EC Delegation, 2300 M Street NW, Washington, DC 20037, USA.

CURRIE, (Joseph) Austin; Teachta Dala (TD) (FG) for Dublin West, Dail Eireann (Irish Parliament), since 1989; Minister of State, Departments of Health, Education and Justice, since 1994; *b* 11 Oct. 1939; *s* of John Currie and Mary (*née* O'Donnell); *m* 1968, Anne Ita Lynch; two *s* three *d*. *Educ:* Edendork Sch.; St Patrick's Academy, Dungannon; Queen's Univ., Belfast (BA). MP (Nat) Tyrone, Parlt of N Ireland, 1964–72; Mem. (SDLP), Fermanagh and S Tyrone, NI Assembly, 1973–75, NI Constitutional Convention, 1975–76, NI Assembly, 1982–86; Minister of Housing, Planning and Local Govt, 1974. Contested (FG) Presidency of Ireland, 1990. Mem., Anglo-Irish Parly tier; frontbench spokesperson: on communications, 1991–93; on equality and law reform, 1993–94. Only person to have been elected to both Irish Parlts. Mem., Forum for Peace and Reconciliation. Advr to Eur. Commn, 1984–. Res. Fellow, Faculty of Economic and Social Studies, TCD, 1977–78. *Recreations:* Gaelic football, golf, snooker, reading. *Address:* Dungannon, Co. Tyrone, N Ireland; Ballyowen Lane, Lucan, Co. Dublin, Ireland.

CURRIE, Sir Neil (Smith), Kt 1982; CBE 1977; Chairman, Coal & Allied Industries Ltd, since 1988 (Director, since 1987); *b* 20 Aug. 1926; *s* of Sir George Currie; *m* 1951, Geraldine Evelyn; two *s* two *d*. *Educ:* Wesley Coll., Perth, W Australia; Univ. of Western Australia (BA). Department of External Affairs, 1948–59; Dept of Trade and Industry, 1959–71; Secretary: Dept of Supply, 1971–74; Dept of Manufacturing Industry, 1974–76; Dept of Industry and Commerce, 1976–82; Australian Ambassador to Japan, 1982–86. Dep. Chm., Westpac Banking Corp., 1991–92 (Dir, 1987–92). Chm., Australia Japan Foundn, 1989– (Mem., 1986–). *Recreations:* golf, tennis. *Address:* c/o Coal and Allied Industries Ltd, 1 York Street, Sydney, NSW 2000, Australia.

CURRIE, Rev. Piers William Edward, MC 1945; Assistant Priest, St Mary in the Marsh, Norwich, since 1990; Hon. Priest Vicar, Norwich Cathedral, since 1993; *b* 26 Feb. 1913; *e c* of late P. A. and Mrs Currie; *m* 1956, Ella Rosaleen, *y c* of late Rev. W. and Mrs Bennett-Hughes; no *c*. *Educ:* Rugby Sch.; Brasenose Coll., Oxford (MA). Solicitor, admitted Dec. 1939. Served War, 1940–45, in 4th Regt RHA. Sen. Legal Asst, Nat. Coal Bd, 1946–53; Asst Sec., 1953–55; Sec., W Midlands Divisional Bd, 1955–60; Sec. and Legal Adviser, 1960–62; Dep. Sec., NCB, 1962–67; Legal Adviser, Land Commission, 1967–71; Deputy Master, Court of Protection, 1971–77. Ordained deacon, 1980; priest, 1981; Hon. Curate of Holt with Edgefield, 1980–82; permanent permission to officiate, dio. Norwich, 1982; Priest in charge of Baconsthorpe and Hempstead by Holt, dio. Norwich, 1983–85; Staff mem., Glaven Assoc. of Parishes, 1986–90. *Recreations:* gardening, natural history. *Address:* 48 The Close, Norwich NR1 4EG.

CURRIE, Prof. Ronald Ian, CBE 1977; FIBiol; FRSE; Professorial Fellow, Grant Institute of Geology, University of Edinburgh, 1988–90; *b* 10 Oct. 1928; *s* of Ronald Wavell Currie and Elizabeth Currie; *m* 1956, Cecilia, *d* of William and Lilian de Garis; one *s* one *d*. *Educ:* The Univ., Glasgow (BSc 1st Cl. Hons Zool., 1949); Univ. of Copenhagen. FIBiol 1967; FRSE 1969. Joined Royal Naval Scientific Service, 1949; seconded to National Inst. of Oceanography; Head of Biol. Dept, 1962–66; Dir and Sec., Scottish Marine Biological Assoc., 1966–87 (Hon. Mem., 1989). Hon. Prof., Heriot-Watt Univ., 1979–. William Scoresby Expedn, S Africa, 1950; Discovery Expedn, Antarctica, 1951; res. voyages, N Atlantic, 1955–64; Chm., Biol. Planning Cttee, Internat. Indian Ocean Expedn, 1960; Indian Ocean Expedn, 1963 and 1964. Secretary: Internat. Assoc. for Biol Oceanography, 1964–66 (Pres., 1966–70); Scientific Cttee on Oceanic Res., Internat. Council of Scient. Unions, 1972–78. Chm., NERC Adv. Cttee on Internat. Ocean. Affairs, 1981–87; Member: Scottish Cttee, Nature Conservancy Council; Council, N British Hotels Trust; Royal Nat. Mission to Deep Sea Fishermen; Chm., Kilmore Community Council, 1977–86; Hon. Sec., Challenger Soc., 1956–88; Hon. Mem., Challenger Soc. for Marine Sci., 1989. *Publications:* (with T. J. Hart) The Benguela Current (Discovery Report), 1960; scientific papers on organic prodn in the sea and fertility of the ocean. *Recreations:* cooking, gardening, local history. *Address:* Tigh-nan-Eala, Kilmore, by Oban, Argyll PA34 4XT. *T:* Kilmore (01631) 770248.

CURRY, Dr Alan Stewart; retired; Controller, Forensic Science Service, Home Office, 1976–82; *b* 31 Oct. 1925; *s* of late Richard C. Curry and of Margaret Curry; *m* 1973, J. Venise Hewitt; one *s* (by previous marriage). *Educ:* Arnold Sch., Blackpool; Trinity Coll., Cambridge (Scholar; MA; PhD 1952). CChem, FRSC, FRCPath. Served War of 1939–45 with RAF. Joined Home Office Forensic Science Service, 1952; served in NE Region, 1952–64; Dir, Nottingham Forensic Sci. Lab., 1964–66; Dir, Home Office Central Research Estabt, Aldermaston, 1966–76. Pres., Internat. Assoc. of Forensic Toxicologists, 1969–75; UN Consultant in Narcotics, 1972–91; Hon. Consultant in Forensic Toxicology to RAF, 1973–91; Consultant in Toxicology to British Airways, 1982–91. Fellow, Indian Acad. of Forensic Scis; Mem., Amer. Acad. of Forensic Scis; Hon. Mem., Belg. Pharmaceutical Soc. Hon. DSc Ghent, 1985. Stas Gold Medal, Gesellschaft für Toxicologische und Forensische Chemie, 1983. *Publications:* Poison Detection in Human Organs, 1962, 4th edn 1988; (ed) Methods in Forensic Science, vols 3 and 4, 1964–65; Advances in Forensic and Clinical Toxicology, 1973; (ed) Analytical Methods in Human Toxicology, Part 1 1985, Part 2 1986; (ed, with wife) The Biochemistry of Women: Clinical Concepts; Methods for Clinical Investigation, 1974; over 100 papers in med. and sci. and police jls. *Recreations:* sailing, amateur radio. *T:* Reading (01734) 581481. *Club:* Athenæum.

CURRY, David Maurice; MP (C) Skipton and Ripon, since 1987; Minister of State, Department of the Environment, since 1993; *b* 13 June 1944; *s* of Thomas Harold Curry and Florence Joan (*née* Tyerman); *m* 1971, Anne Helene Maud Roullet; one *s* two *d*. *Educ:* Ripon Grammar Sch.; Corpus Christi Coll., Oxford (MA Hons); Kennedy Sch. of Govt, Harvard (Kennedy Scholar, 1966–67). Reporter, Newcastle Jl, 1967–70; Financial Times: Trade Editor, Internat. Cos Editor, Brussels Corresp., Paris Corresp., and European News Editor, 1970–79. Sec., Anglo-American Press Assoc. of Paris, 1978; Founder, Paris Conservative Assoc., 1977. MEP (C) Essex NE, 1979–89; Chm., Agriculture Cttee, 1982–84; Vice-Chm., Budgets Cttee, 1984–85; spokesman on budgetary matters for European Democratic Gp, 1985–89; Gen. Rapporteur for EEC's 1987 budget. Parly Sec., 1989–92, Minister of State, 1992–93, MAFF. *Publication:* The Food War: the EEC, the US and the battle for world food markets, 1982. *Recreations:* digging, windsurfing, bee-keeping. *Address:* Newland End, Arkesden, Essex CB11 4HF. *T:* Saffron Walden (01799) 550368.

CURRY, Dr Gordon Barrett; Reader, Department of Geology and Applied Geology, University of Glasgow, since 1992 (Royal Society University Research Fellow, 1984–92); *b* 27 June 1954; *s* of Robert and Violet Curry; *m* 1983, Gillian. *Educ:* Masonic Sch., Dublin; Trinity Coll., Dublin (BA Mod.); Imperial Coll. London (PhD, DIC). FGS. Research Asst to Sir Alwyn Williams, Univ. of Glasgow, 1980–84. President's Award, Geolog. Soc., 1985; Clough Award, Edinburgh Geolog. Soc., 1985–86; Wollaston Fund, Geolog. Soc., 1989. *Publications:* (jtly) British Brachiopods, 1979; (ed) Allochthonous Terranes, 1991; (jtly) Molecules through Time: fossil molecules and biochemical systematics, 1991; Biology of Living Brachiopods, 1992; numerous contribs to learned jls. *Recreations:* music, swimming, cricket, travel. *Address:* Department of Geology and Applied Geology, University of Glasgow, Lilybank Gardens, Glasgow G12 8QQ. *T:* 0141–330 5444.

CURRY, John Arthur Hugh; Chairman, ACAL, since 1986; *b* 7 June 1938; *s* of Alfred Robert and Mercia Beatrice Curry; *m* 1962, Anne Rosemary Lewis; three *s* one *d*. *Educ:* King's College School, Wimbledon; St Edmund Hall, Oxford (MA); Harvard Univ. Graduate College (MBA). FCA. Arthur Andersen, 1962–64; Man. Dir, Unitech, 1966–86 (non-exec. Dir, 1986–). Non-exec. Dir, Dixons, 1993–. *Publication:* Partners for Profit, 1966. *Recreations:* tennis, Rugby. *Clubs:* All England Lawn Tennis and Croquet (Chm., 1989–, Mem. Cttee, 1979–); International Lawn Tennis.

CURRY, (Thomas) Peter (Ellison), QC 1966, 1973; *s* of Maj. F. R. P. Curry; *m* 1950, Pamela Joyce, *d* of late Group Capt. A. J. Holmes, AFC, JP; two *s* two *d*. *Educ:* Tonbridge; Oriel Coll., Oxford. BA 1948; MA 1951. Served War of 1939–45; enlisted 1939; commnd, 1941; 17th Indian Div., India and Burma, 1941–45. War Office, 1946. Called to Bar, Middle Temple, 1953, Bencher, 1979. QC 1966. Solicitor, 1968; partner in Freshfields, Solicitors, 1968–70; returned to Bar; re-appointed QC 1973. Pres., Aircraft and Shipbuilding Industries Arbitration Tribunal, 1978–80. Chm., Chancery Bar Assoc., 1980–85; Dep. Chm., Barristers' Benevolent Assoc., 1989–91 (Hon. Treas., 1964–71, 1984–89). Rep. Army, Oxford and Sussex at Squash Racquets (described as fastest mover in squash, 1947; triple blue, Oxford; twice cross country winner); World Student Games (5000 m), 1947; British Steeplechase champion 1948, Olympic Games, 1948. Served on AAA Cttee of Inquiry, 1967. Holder of French certificate as capitaine-mécanicien for mechanically propelled boats. *Publications:* (ed jtly) Palmer's Company Law, 1959; (ed jtly) Crew on Meetings, 1966, 1975. *Recreations:* gardening, the Turf. *Address:* Hurlands, Dunsfold, Surrey GU8 4NT. *T:* Dunsfold (01483) 200356. *Club:* Army and Navy.

CURTEIS, Ian Bayley; television playwright; *b* 1 May 1935; *m* 1st, 1964, Mrs Joan Macdonald (marr. diss.); two *s*; 2nd, 1985, Joanna Trollope, *qv*; two step *d*. *Educ:* Iver Council Sch.; Slough Grammar Sch.; Slough Trading Estate; London Univ. Director and actor in theatres all over Great Britain, and BBC-tv script reader, 1956–63; BBC and ATV staff director (drama), directing plays by John Betjeman, John Hopkins, William Trevor and others, 1963–67. Chm., Cttee on Censorship, Writers' Guild of GB, 1981–85. *Television plays:* Beethoven, Sir Alexander Fleming (BBC's entry at 1973 Prague Fest.), Mr Rolls and Mr Royce, Long Voyage out of War (trilogy), The Folly, The Haunting, Second Time Round, A Distinct Chill, The Portland Millions, Philby, Burgess and

Maclean (British entry 1978 Monte Carlo Fest., BAFTA nomination), Hess, The Atom Spies, Churchill and the Generals (BAFTA nomination; Grand Prize, Best Programme of 1980, NY Internat. Film and TV Fest.), Suez 1956 (BAFTA nomination), Miss Morison's Ghosts (British entry 1982 Monte Carlo Fest.), The Mitford Girls, BB and Joe (trilogy), Lost Empires (adapted from J. B. Priestley), The Trials of Lady Sackville, Eureka (1st Euroserial simultaneously shown in UK, West Germany, Austria, Switzerland, Italy and France), The Nightmare Years, Cecil Rhodes, The Zimmerman Telegram, The Choir (dramatisation of Joanna Trollope novel); also originated and wrote numerous popular television drama series; *film screenplays:* Andre Malraux's La Condition humaine, 1982; Graham Greene's The Man Within, 1983; Tom Paine (for Sir Richard Attenborough), 1983; *play:* A Personal Affair, Globe, 1982. *Publications: plays:* Long Voyage out of War (trilogy), 1971; Churchill and the Generals, 1979; Suez 1956, 1980; The Falklands Play, 1987. *Recreation:* dissidence. *Address:* c/o Coutts & Co., Campbell's Office, 440 Strand, WC2R 0QS. *Clubs:* Beefsteak, Garrick.

CURTEIS, Joanna, (Mrs I. B. Curteis); see Trollope, J.

CURTIS, Prof. Adam Sebastian Genevieve, PhD; Professor of Cell Biology, University of Glasgow, since 1967; *b* 3 Jan. 1934; *s* of Herbert Lewis Curtis and Nora Patricia Curtis (*née* Stevens); *m* 1958, Ann Park; two *d. Educ:* Aldenham Sch.; King's Coll., Cambridge (BA 1955; MA); Univ. of Edinburgh (PhD 1957). University College London: Hon. Research Asst, 1957–62; Lectr in Zool., 1962–67; University of Glasgow: Head, Molecular and Cellular Biol. Planning Unit, 1991–94; Head, Molecular and Cellular Biol. Div., 1994–. Cuvier Medal, Zool Soc. of France, 1972. *Publications:* The Cell Surface, 1967; (with J. M. Lackie) Measuring Cell Adhesion, 1991; numerous articles in scientific jls; also articles on scuba diving. *Recreations:* scuba diving, underwater photography, gardening. *Address:* 2 Kirklee Circus, Glasgow G12 0TW. *T:* 0141–339 2152. *Club:* Lansdowne.

CURTIS, Sir Barry (John), Kt 1992; Mayor of Manukau, New Zealand, since 1983; *b* 27 Feb. 1939; *s* of John Dixon Cory Curtis and Vera Gladys Curtis (*née* Johnson); *m* 1961, Miriam Ann Brooke (marr. diss. 1991); three *d. Educ:* Otahuhu College; Univ. of Auckland (Dip. TP). ARICS, MNZIS, MNZPI, MPMI. Town Planner, Chartered and Registered Surveyor. Manukau City Councillor, 1968–83; Member: Auckland Regl Authy, 1971–84 (Chm., Regl Planning Cttee, 1977–83); Prime Minister's Safer Communities Council, 1990–; Chairman: Hillary Commn Task Force on Recreation, 1988; Jean Batten Meml Trust, 1989; Manukau Healthy City Cttee, 1989–93; Manukau Safer Community Council, 1990–93; Auckland Mayors' Forum, 1990–. Past Pres., NZ Sister Cities Cttee. A Dir, XIVth Commonwealth Games Ltd, 1989– (Mem. Exec. Bd, 1989–90). Patron, Auckland Hockey Assoc. Seiuli (High Chief Matai title) conferred by HE Malietoa Tanumafili II, Western Samoa, 1993. *Recreations:* jogging, surfing, gardening, follower of Rugby, hockey, cricket, tennis, yachting. *Address:* 42 The Parade, Bucklands Beach, City of Manukau, Auckland Region, New Zealand. *T:* (9) 5348153. *Clubs:* Pakuranga Combined Bowling (Foundn Chm.), Pakuranga Men's Bowling (Foundn Pres.).

CURTIS, Prof. Charles David; Professor of Geochemistry, since 1988, and Research Dean, Faculty of Science and Engineering, since 1994, University of Manchester (Head of Department of Geology, 1989–92); *b* 11 Nov. 1939; *s* of Charles Frederick Curtis and Kate Margaret Curtis (*née* Jackson); *m* 1963, Dr Diana Joy Saxty; two *d. Educ:* Imperial College London; Univ. of Sheffield (BSc, PhD). University of Sheffield: Lectr, Sen. Lectr, Reader, 1965–83; Personal Chair in Geochem., 1983–88. Vis. Prof., Dept of Geology and Geophys., UCLA, 1970–71; Res. Associate, British Petroleum Res. Centre, 1987–88. Member: Council, NERC, 1990–93; Radioactive Waste Mgt Adv. Cttee, 1994–. Pres., Geological Soc., 1992–94. Murchison Medal, Geological Soc., 1987. *Publications:* numerous articles in learned jls. *Recreations:* mountaineering, gardening, photography. *Address:* Department of Geology, The University, Oxford Road, Manchester M13 9PL. *T:* 0161–275 3803.

CURTIS, Colin Hinton Thomson, CVO 1970; ISO 1970; retired; Chairman, Metropolitan Public Abattoir Board, 1971–81; Member, Queensland Meat Industry Authority, 1972–78; *b* 25 June 1920; *s* of A. Curtis, Brisbane; *m* 1943, Anne Catherine Drevesen; one *s. Educ:* Brisbane Grammar School. RANR Overseas Service, 1940–45. Sec. and Investigation Officer to Chm., Sugar Cane Prices Board, 1948–49; Asst Sec. to Central Sugar Cane Prices Board, 1949; Sec. to Premier of Queensland, 1950–64; Mem., Qld Trade Missions to SE Asia, 1963 and 1964; Asst Under-Sec., Premier's Dept, 1961–64; Assoc. Dir and Dir of Industrial Development, 1964–66; Under-Sec., Premier's Dept and Clerk of Exec. Council, 1966–70; State Dir, Royal Visit, 1970; Agent-General for Queensland in London, 1970–71. *Recreations:* squash, yachting, swimming. *Address:* 57 Daru Avenue, Runaway Bay, Gold Coast, Qld, Australia. *Clubs:* RSL Memorial, Rugby League (Queensland).

CURTIS, Prof. David Roderick, AC 1992; FRACP 1987; FRS 1974; FAA 1965; Emeritus Professor, and University Fellow, Australian National University, since 1993; *b* 3 June 1927; *s* of E. D. and E. V. Curtis; *m* 1951, Lauri Sewell; one *s* one *d. Educ:* Univ. of Melbourne; Australian National Univ. MB, BS Melbourne 1950, PhD ANU 1957. John Curtin School of Medical Research, Australian National University: Department of Physiology: Research Scholar, 1954–56; Research Fellow, 1956–57; Fellow, 1957–59; Sen. Fellow, 1959–62; Professorial Fellow, 1962–66; Prof. of Pharmacology, 1966–68; Prof. of Neuropharmacology, 1968–73; Prof. and Foundn Head, Dept of Pharmacology, 1973–88; Chm., Div. of Physiol Sciences, 1988–89; Howard Florey Prof. of Med. Res., and Dir of the Sch., 1989–92. President: Aust. Acad. of Sci, 1986–90 (Burnet Medal, 1983); Australian Physiol and Pharmacol Soc., 1992–95; Chairman: Res. Adv. Bd, Nat. Multiple Sclerosis Soc., Australia, 1978–83, 1993–; Inaugural Australia Prize Cttee, 1989–90. *Publications:* papers in fields of neurophysiology, neuropharmacology in Jl Physiology, Jl Neurophysiol., Brain Research, Exper. Brain Research, etc. *Recreations:* tennis, wombling. *Address:* 7 Patey Street, Campbell, Canberra, ACT 2601, Australia. *T:* Canberra (6) 2485664; John Curtin School of Medical Research, Australian National University, GPO Box 334, ACT 2601, Australia. *T* and *Fax:* Canberra (6) 2492757.

CURTIS, Sir (Edward) Leo, Kt 1965; Lord Mayor of Melbourne, Australia, 1963–64 and 1964–65; *b* London, 13 Jan. 1907. Joined Melbourne City Council, Dec. 1955; retired March 1975. Past President of Retail Traders Association of Victoria. *Address:* 4 Armadale Street, Armadale, Vic 3143, Australia. *Clubs:* Athenæum, Kelvin (Melbourne); various sporting.

CURTIS, Most Rev. Ernest Edwin, CBE 1976; Hon. Assistant Bishop of Portsmouth, since 1976; *b* 24 Dec. 1906, *s* of Ernest John and Zoe Curtis; *m* 1938, Dorothy Anne Hill (*d* 1965); one *s* one *d*; *m* 1970, Evelyn Mary Josling. *Educ:* Sherborne; Foster's Sch.; Royal College of Science, London. BSc (hons Chem.) London, 1927; ARCSc 1927; Dipl. Educn, London, 1928. Asst Master, Lindisfarne Coll., Westcliff, 1928–31; Wells Theol Coll., 1932–33; Asst Curate, Holy Trinity, Waltham Cross, 1933–36; Chaplain i/c parishes Rose Hill and Bambous, and Principal, St Paul's Theol Coll., Mauritius, 1937–44; Missions to Seamen Chaplain, Port Louis, 1944; Priest i/c St Wilfrid, Portsmouth, 1945–47; Vicar, All Saints, Portsmouth, and Chaplain, Royal Portsmouth Hospital, 1947–55; Priest i/c St Agatha, Portsmouth, 1954–55; Vicar, St John Baptist, Locks Heath, 1955–66; Warden of Readers, Dio. Portsmouth, 1956–66; Rural Dean of Alverstoke, 1964–66; Bishop of Mauritius and Seychelles, 1966–72, of Mauritius, 1973–76; Archbishop of the Indian Ocean, 1973–76; Priest-in-charge of St Mary and St Rhadagunde, Whitwell, 1976–82. *Recreations:* walking, hill-climbing, piano. *Address:* 5 Elizabeth Gardens, Havenstreet, Ryde, Isle of Wight PO33 4DU. *T:* Isle of Wight (01983) 883049.

CURTIS, Frank; *see* Curtis, R. F.

CURTIS, Very Rev. Frank; *see* Curtis, Very Rev. W. F.

CURTIS, Genevra Fiona Penelope Victoria, (Mrs J. W. O. Curtis); *see* Caws, G. F. P. V.

CURTIS, James William Ockford; QC 1993; a Recorder, since 1991; *b* 2 Sept. 1946; *s* of Eric William Curtis, MC, TD and Margaret Joan Curtis (*née* Blunt); *m* 1985, Genevra Fiona Penelope Victoria Caws, *qv*; one *d. Educ:* Bedford Sch.; Worcester Coll., Oxford (MA Jurisp). Called to the Bar, Inner Temple, 1970. *Recreations:* farming, field sports, ski-ing, classics. *Address:* 6 King's Bench Walk, Temple, EC4Y 7DR. *T:* 0171–583 0410.

CURTIS, Most Rev. John Barry; *see* Calgary, Archbishop of.

CURTIS, John Edward, PhD; FSA; Keeper of Western Asiatic Antiquities, British Museum, since 1989; *b* 23 June 1946; *yr s* of late Arthur Norman Curtis and of Laura Letitia Ladd (*née* Thomas); *m* 1977, Vesta Sarkhosh; one *s* one *d. Educ:* Collyer's Grammar Sch., Horsham; Univ. of Bristol (BA); Inst. of Archaeology, Univ. of London (Postgrad. Diploma in Western Asiatic Archaeology; PhD 1979). FSA 1984. Fellow, British Sch. of Archaeology in Iraq, 1969–71; Res. Asst, Dept of Western Asiatic Antiquities, British Museum, 1971–74, Asst Keeper, 1974–89. Hon. Sec., British Assoc. for Near Eastern Archaeol., 1987–; Hon. Sec. and Trustee, Vladimir G. Lukonin Meml Fund, 1987–; Member: Governing Council, 1980–, Exec. Cttee, 1982–, British Sch. of Archaeol. in Iraq; Governing Council, British Inst. of Persian Studies, 1991–; Exec. Cttee, Soc. for Arabian Studies, 1992–. *Publications:* (ed) Fifty Years of Mesopotamian Discovery, 1982; Nush-i Jan III: the Small Finds, 1984; (ed) Bronzeworking Centres of Western Asia *c* 1000–539 BC, 1988; Excavations at Qasrij Cliff and Khirbet Qasrij, 1989; Ancient Persia, 1989; (ed) Early Mesopotamia and Iran: Contact and Conflict 3500–1600 BC, 1993; (ed with J. E. Reade) Art and Empire: treasures from Assyria in the British Museum, 1995; (ed) Later Mesopotamia and Iran: tribes and empires 1600–539 BC, 1995; articles in learned jls. *Recreations:* collecting, local history, geneaology. *Address:* 13 St Mary's Road, NW11 9UE. *T:* 0181–458 3117; 1 Francis Cottage, Sandy Hill Road, Saundersfoot, Dyfed SA69 9HW.

CURTIS, John Henry, CB 1981; FAIM, FTS; Chairman, Nortel Australia Pty Ltd, 1989–92, retired; *b* 20 March 1920; *s* of K. H. and E. M. Curtis; *m* 1943, Patricia Foote; one *s* one *d. Educ:* Ipswich Grammar Sch.; Queensland Univ. (BE Hons 1950, BSc 1951, BA 1957). FIEAust 1981; FAIM 1970; FTS 1979. Dir of Posts and Telegraphs, Qld, 1971–73; Dep. Dir Gen., Postmaster-Gen.'s Dept, 1973–75; Man. Dir, Australian Telecommunications Commn, 1975–81; Chairman: D. Richardson & Sons, later Richardson Pacific, 1982–90; A. W. A. Nortel, 1986–89. Comr, Overseas Telecommunications Commn (Australia), 1974–87. Pres., Victorian Div., Aust. Inst. of Management, 1979–81; Dir, Cttee for Econ. Develt of Aust., 1981–93 (Hon. Life Mem., 1993). Mem., Bd of Management, Defence Aerospace, 1984–86. Gov., Internat. Council for Computer Communication, 1982–94. Hon. Life Mem., IREE, 1982. *Address:* 101 Kadumba Street, Yeronga, Qld 4104, Australia. *T:* (7) 8922743.

CURTIS, Sir Leo; *see* Curtis, Sir E. L.

CURTIS, Michael Howard; Executive Aide to HH The Aga Khan, 1959–86; Director, Aga Khan Health and Education Services, Geneva, 1985–92; Chairman, Nation Printers and Publishers, Nairobi, Kenya, 1972–77; Director, Nation Newspapers, 1959–94 (Managing Director and Chief Executive, 1959, retired); *b* 28 Feb. 1920; *e s* of late Howard and Doris May Curtis; *m* 1st, 1947, Barbara Winifred Gough; two *s* two *d*; 2nd, 1961, Marian Joan Williams (*d* 1984); two step *s. Educ:* St Lawrence Coll.; Sidney Sussex Coll., Cambridge (MA). Eastern Daily Press, Norwich, 1945; News Chronicle: Leader Writer, 1946; Dep. Editor, 1952; Editor, 1954–57; Dir, News Chronicle Ltd, 1954–57; Personal Aide to HH The Aga Khan, 1957–59. *Address:* La Vieille Maison, Villemétrie, 60300 Senlis, France. *Clubs:* Garrick, Travellers'; Muthaiga (Nairobi).

CURTIS, His Honour Philip; a Circuit Judge (formerly a Judge of County Courts), 1969–80; *b* 29 April 1908; *s* of James William and Emma Curtis; *m* 1937, Marjorie Lillian Sharp; two *s* one *d. Educ:* St Mary's RC, Denton, Lancs; Manchester Grammar; Brasenose Coll., Oxford. Called to the Bar, Gray's Inn, 1944. *Address:* Mottram Hall Farm, Mottram St Andrew, Macclesfield, Cheshire SK10 4QT. *T:* Prestbury (01625) 829509.

CURTIS, Hon. Sir Richard Herbert, Kt 1992; **Hon. Mr Justice Curtis;** a Judge of the High Court of Justice, Queen's Bench Division, since 1992; Presiding Judge, Wales and Chester Circuit, since 1994. *Educ:* Oxford Univ. (MA). Called to Bar, Inner Temple, 1958, Bencher, 1985; QC 1977; a Recorder, 1974–89; Recorder of Birmingham, 1989–92; Hon. Recorder, City of Hereford, 1981; Sen. Circuit Judge, Oxford and Midland Circuit, 1989–92. *Address:* c/o Royal Courts of Justice, Strand, WC2A 2LL.

CURTIS, Prof. (Robert) Frank, CBE 1985; PhD, DSc; Chairman, Norfolk Mental Health Care NHS Trust, since 1994; Professor, University of East Anglia, 1977–88, now Hon. Professor; *b* 8 Oct. 1926; *s* of late William John Curtis, Somerset, and Ethel Irene Curtis, Bath; *m* 1954, Sheila Rose, *y d* of Bruce Rose, Huddersfield, two *s* one *d. Educ:* City of Bath Sch.; Univ. of Bristol (BSc 1949, PhD 1952, DSc 1972). FRIC 1966; FIFST 1977. Johns Hopkins University: W. H. Grafflin Fellow, 1952; Instr in Chemistry, 1953; Technical Officer, ICI Ltd, Manchester, 1954–56; Res. Fellow, Univ. of WI, 1956–57; Lectr in Chem., University Coll., Swansea, 1957–62, Sen. Lectr, 1962–69; Reader, Univ. of Wales, 1969–70; Head, Chem. Div., 1970–77, Dir, 1977–85, ARC Food Res. Inst.; Dir, AFRC Inst. of Food Res., Reading, 1985–88. Chm., Food Adv. Cttee, MAFF, 1983–88 (Chm., Food Standards Cttee, 1979–83); Mem. Management Bd, AFRC, 1987–88. Mem., Norwich HA, 1989–93 (Vice-Chm., 1993–94); Mem. Council, RVC, 1991–. Hon. ScD UEA, 1988. *Publications:* res. papers on chemistry and food science in jls of learned socs. *Address:* Manor Barn, Colton, Norwich NR9 5BZ. *T:* Norwich (01603) 880379.

CURTIS, Stephen Russell; Chief Executive, Driver and Vehicle Licensing Agency, since 1990; *b* 27 Feb. 1948; *s* of Barry Russell and Joyce Muriel (*née* Smith); *m* 1972, Gillian Mary Pitkin; three *s* one *d. Educ:* Forest Sch., E17; Exeter Univ. (BA Econs and Stats). Asst Statistician, Business Stats Office, 1970–72; DTI, 1972–78, Statistician, Export Stats, 1975–78; Statistician, 1978–83, Chief Statistician, 1983–85, Business Stats Office; Registrar of Companies, 1985–90, and Chief Exec., 1988–90, Companies House. *Recreations:* travel, photography, walking. *Address:* c/o Driver and Vehicle Licensing Agency, Swansea SA6 7JL. *Club:* Civil Service.

CURTIS, Very Rev. (Wilfred) Frank; Provost of Sheffield, 1974–88, Provost Emeritus since 1988; *b* 24 Feb. 1923; *s* of W. A. Curtis, MC and Mrs M. Curtis (*née* Burbidge); *m* 1951, Muriel (*née* Dover); two *s* two *d*. *Educ:* Foster's Sch., Sherborne; Bishop Wordsworth's Sch., Salisbury; King's Coll., London (AKC). Served in RA, 1942–47; Major 1946. London Univ., 1947–52; Curate of High Wycombe, 1952–55; staff of Church Missionary Soc., 1955–74: Area Sec., Devon and Cornwall, 1955–65; Adviser in Rural Work, 1957–65; SW Regional Sec., 1962–65; Home Sec., 1965–74; Vice-Pres., 1977–. Rural Dean of Okehampton, 1989–92. Mem., General Synod, 1977–85. Chm., Community Action Panel (S Yorks Police), 1983–86; Mem., Sheffield Council Voluntary Service, 1978–88; Chm., Radio Sheffield Religious Adv. Panel, 1985–88. Chaplain to Master Cutler, 1976, 1978, 1982, 1984; Hon. Fellow, Sheffield City Polytechnic, subseq. Sheffield Hallam Univ., 1980. Hon. Canon, 1982–93, and Bishop's Commissary, 1983–93, Maseno North Diocese, Kenya; Bishop's Commissary, Nambale, Kenya, 1988–93. *Recreations:* walking, photography, nature study. *Address:* Ashplant's Fingle Cottage, Drewsteignton, Exeter, Devon EX6 6QX. *T:* Drewsteignton (01647) 281253.

CURTIS, Sir William (Peter), 7th Bt *cr* 1802; *b* 9 April 1935; *s* of Sir Peter Curtis, 6th Bt, and of Joan Margaret, *d* of late Reginald Nicholson; *S* father, 1976. *Educ:* Winchester College; Trinity College, Oxford (MA); Royal Agricultural College, Cirencester. *Heir: cousin* Major Edward Philip Curtis, 16th/5th The Queen's Royal Lancers (retd) [*b* 25 June 1940; *m* 1978, Catherine, *d* of H. J. Armstrong, Christchurch, NZ; two *s* two *d*. *Educ:* Bradfield; RMA Sandhurst]. *Address:* Oak Lodge, Bank Street, Bishop's Waltham, Hants SO3 1AN.

CURTIS-RALEIGH, Dr Jean Margaret Macdonald; Consultant Psychiatrist, Queen Mary's University Hospital, Roehampton, since 1979; *b* 12 July 1933; *d* of late Dr Harry Hubert Steadman and Janet Gilchrist Steadman (*née* Macdonald); *m* 1964, His Honour Judge Nigel Hugh Curtis-Raleigh (*d* 1986); five *s*. *Educ:* Convent of the Sacred Heart, Epsom, Surrey; Sutton High Sch. for Girls; Guy's Hospital Med. Sch. (MB BS); MRCPsych; DPM. Psychiatric trng, Maudsley and Bethlem Royal Hosps, 1963–66. Mem., Broadcasting Standards Council, 1988–95. *Recreations:* opera, gardening, walking. *Address:* c/o Hoare's Bank, 37 Fleet Street, EC4P 4DQ.
See also J. H. Steadman.

CURTISS, Air Marshal Sir John (Bagot), KCB 1981 (CB 1979); KBE 1982; FRAeS; Military and Policy Advisor, Memorial Fund for Disaster Relief, since 1990; *b* 6 Dec. 1924; *s* of Major E. F. B. Curtiss, RFC; *m* 1946, Peggy Drughorn Bowie; three *s* one *d*. *Educ:* Radley Coll.; Wanganui Collegiate Sch., NZ; Worcester Coll., Oxford. Served War: Oxford Univ. Air Sqdn, 1942–43; Bomber Comd, 578 and 158 sqdns, 1944–45; Transport Comd, 51 and 59 sqdn, 1945–49; Training Comd, 1950–53; Fighter Comd, 29 and 5 sqdns, 1953–64; Dir, RAF Staff Coll., 1967–69; Stn Comdr RAF Bruggen, RAFG, 1970–72; Gp Capt Ops, HQ Strike Comd, 1972–74; SASO, HQ 11 Gp, 1974–75; Dir-Gen. Organisation, RAF, 1975–77; Comdt, RAF Staff Coll., 1977–80; Air Comdr, Falklands Operations, 1982; AOC No 18 Gp, 1980–83, retd. Dir and Chief Exec., SBAC, 1984–89; Sec., Defence Inds Council, 1985–89. Finance Dir, Dinghy Ltd, 1991. Member, Executive Committee: Air League, 1982–; Forces Help Soc., 1984–86; Pres., Aircrew Assoc., 1987–. Trustee, Buskaid. Chm., Governors, Canford Sch., 1990–95. CIMgt (CBIM 1981). FRAeS 1984. *Recreations:* sailing, reading, bicycling. *Address:* 21 Carlisle Mansions, Carlisle Place, SW1P 1EZ. *Clubs:* MCC, Royal Air Force, Pilgrims; Colonels (Pres. and Founder Mem.); Keyhaven Yacht.

CURWEN, Sir Christopher (Keith), KCMG 1986 (CMG 1982); HM Diplomatic Service, retired; *b* 9 April 1929; *s* of late Rev. R. M. Curwen and Mrs M. E. Curwen; *m* 1st, 1956, Noom Tai (marr. diss. 1977); one *s* two *d*; 2nd, 1977, Helen Anne Stirling; one *s* one *d*. *Educ:* Sherborne Sch.; Sidney Sussex Coll., Cambridge (BA). Served HM Forces, 4th Queen's Own Hussars, 1948–49 (despatches). Joined FO, 1952; Bangkok, 1954; Vientiane, 1956; FO, 1958; Bangkok, 1961; Kuala Lumpur, 1963; FO, 1965; Washington, 1968; FCO, 1971; Geneva, 1977; FCO, 1980–88; Dep. Sec., Cabinet Office, 1989–91. Mem., Security Commn, 1991–. *Recreations:* books, gardening, motoring.

CURZON; *see* Roper-Curzon, family name of Baron Teynham.

CURZON, family name of **Earl Howe** and **Viscount Scarsdale.**

CURZON, Viscount; Thomas Edward Penn Curzon; *b* 22 Oct. 1994; *s* and *heir* of Earl Howe, *qv*.

CURZON, Leonard Henry, CB 1956; *b* 4 Jan. 1912; *s* of late Frederick Henry Curzon; *m* 1935, Greta, *e d* of late Willem and Anny van Praag; one *s*. *Educ:* Sir Walter St John's Sch.; Jesus Coll., Cambridge (Scholar, BA, LLB). Civil Servant, 1934–72: Import Duties Adv. Cttee; Air Ministry, Ministries of Aircraft Production, Supply, Aviation and Defence. IDC 1947. *Address:* Southease, Derringstone Hill, Barham, Kent CT4 6QD. *T:* Canterbury (01227) 831449.

CUSACK, Henry Vernon, CMG 1955; CBE 1947; HM Overseas Civil Service (retired); Deputy Director General of the Overseas Audit Service, 1946–55; *b* 26 June 1895; 2nd *s* of late Edward Cusack, Bray, Co. Wicklow, and of Constance Louisa Vernon, *e d* of late Col Vernon, DL, JP, Clontarf Castle, Dublin; unmarried. *Educ:* Aravon Sch., Ireland. Served European War, 1914–19 (General Service and Victory medals), France, Belgium and North Russia, as Captain, RASC, attached RGA; entered Colonial Audit Service, 1920; Asst Auditor: Sierra Leone, 1920–22, Nigeria, 1922–28; Sen. Asst Auditor, Nyasaland, 1928–33; Asst Director, Central Office, Colonial Audit Dept London, 1933–37; Auditor, Gold Coast, 1937–46; a Governor of the King's Hospital Sch., Dublin (Chm., 1964–69). FRGS. Coronation Medal, 1953. *Address:* Our Lady's Manor, Bulloch Castle, Dalkey, Co. Dublin. *Clubs:* Naval and Military; Royal St George Yacht (Dun Laoghaire, Co. Dublin).

CUSDIN, Sidney Edward Thomas, OBE 1946; DSc (Hong Kong); FRIBA, AADip; *b* 28 July 1908; *s* of Sidney Herbert Cusdin, London; *m* 1936, Eva Eileen (Peggy), *d* of F. P. Dorizzi, London; no *c*. *Educ:* Municipal School of Arts and Crafts, Southend-on-Sea, Essex; Architectural Assoc., London. AA Holloway Scholarship, 1927; Fifth Year Travelling Studentship, 1929; joined staff of Stanley Hall & Easton and Robertson: British Pavilions at Brussels Internat. Exhibition and Johannesburg Exhibition; elected Member of AA Council, 1937, and worked on RIBA Cttees. Served War of 1939–45, RAF, on staff of HQ, No. 26 Group (despatches twice, OBE). Re-joined firm of Easton & Robertson, 1946; firm later known as Easton & Robertson, Cusdin, Preston and Smith, until 1965 when this partnership was dissolved; Sen. Partner, Cusdin, Burden and Howitt, until 1976. Pres. AA, 1950–51; Mem. Council RIBA, 1950–51. Awarded Henry Saxon Snell Prize and Theakston Bequest, 1950; Principal works: London: Development of the Hosp. for Sick Children, Great Ormond Street, British Postgraduate Medical Fedn, and London Univ., Inst. of Child Health; Medical Coll. of St Bartholomew's Hosp., New Hostel and Labs; Middlesex Hosp. Medical Sch.; New Sch. Buildings and Astor Coll.; National Inst. for Medical Research Develt, Mill Hill; Cambridge: Dept of Engineering, New Workshops and Laboratories; Univ. Chemistry Laboratories; United Cambridge Hosps, Addenbrooke's Hosp., Hills Rd, New Develt; MRC, extension of Lab. of Molecular Biology; Harlow: Princess Alexandra Hosp.; Belfast: Queen's Univ. of Belfast, Inst. of Clin. Science; Royal Victoria Hosp. Develt; Royal Belfast Hosp. for Sick Children, alterations and additions; Malaya: plans for Develt of Univ. of Malaya; Hong Kong; plans for develt of Univ. of Hong Kong; Cons. Architect for: Queen Elizabeth Hosp., Hong Kong (awarded RIBA Bronze Medal); Faculty of Medicine, Univ. of Riyad, Saudi Arabia. Chm., British Consultants Bureau, 1972–74. Gov., Brendoncare Foundn, 1987–94 (Dir, 1992; Vice Patron, 1993). Hon. Freeman, Apothecaries' Soc., 1981. *Publications:* (with James Crooks) Suggestions and Demonstration Plans for Hospitals for Sick Children, 1947. *Recreations:* theatre, travel, fishing; spending time in believing that "WS" was Shakespeare. *Address:* 34 Ringshall, Little Gaddesden, near Berkhamsted, Herts HP4 1ND. *T:* Little Gaddesden (01442) 843364. *Clubs:* Savile, Royal Air Force, The Sette of Odd Volumes.

CUSENS, Prof. Anthony Ralph, OBE 1989; PhD; FRSE; FEng 1988; FICE, FIStructE; Professor of Civil Engineering, University of Leeds, 1979–92, now Emeritus (Dean, Faculty of Engineering, 1989–91); *b* 24 Sept. 1927; *s* of James Cusens and May Edith (*née* Thomas); *m* 1953, Pauline Shirin German; three *d*. *Educ:* St John's Coll., Southsea; University Coll. London (BSc Eng; PhD 1955). FICE 1966; FIStructE 1972; FAmSCE 1972; MConsE 1995. FRSE 1974. Res. Engr, British Cast Concrete Fedn, 1952–54; Sen. Lectr, RMCS, Shrivenham, 1954–56; Sen. Lectr, Univ. of Khartoum, Sudan, 1956–60; Prof. of Structl Engrg, Asian Inst. of Technol., Bangkok, 1960–65; Prof. of Civil Engineering: Univ. of St Andrews, 1965–67; Univ. of Dundee, 1967–78. Visitor, Transport and Road Res. Lab., 1982–88; President: Concrete Soc., 1983–84; IStructE, 1991–92; Chairman: Jt Bd of Moderators of ICE, IStructE and CIBSE, 1986–89; UK Certifying Authy for Reinforcing Steels, 1994–. Consultant, Brian Clancy Partnership, 1993–. Hon. DSc Aston, 1993. *Publications:* (jtly) Bridge Deck Analysis, 1975; Finite Strip Method in Bridge Engineering, 1978; res. papers on concrete technol. and structures. *Recreations:* golf, gardening. *Address:* Old Hall Cottage, Bramham, West Yorks LS23 6QR. *Clubs:* East India; Pannal Golf (Harrogate).

CUSHING, David Henry, DPhil; FRS 1977; Deputy Director, Fisheries Research, England and Wales, 1974–80; *b* 14 March 1920; *s* of W. E. W. Cushing and Isobel (*née* Batchelder); *m* 1943, Diana R. C. Antona-Traversi; one *d*. *Educ:* Duke's Sch., Alnwick; Newcastle upon Tyne Royal Grammar Sch.; Balliol Coll., Oxford (MA, DPhil). RA, 1940–45; 1st Bn, Royal Fusiliers, 1945–46. Fisheries Lab., 1946–80. Rosenstiel Gold Medal for Oceanographic Science, Rosenstiel Inst. for Marine and Atmospheric Scis, Miami, 1980; Albert Medal for Oceanography, Institut Océanographique, Paris, 1984; Award for Excellence, Amer. Fisheries Soc., 1986; Ecology Inst. Prize, 1993. *Publications:* The Arctic Cod, 1966; Fisheries Biology, 1968 (USA); Detection of Fish, 1973; Fisheries Resources and their Management, 1974; Marine Ecology and Fisheries, 1975; Science and the Fisheries, 1977; Climate and Fisheries, 1982; The Provident Sea, 1988. *Address:* 198 Yarmouth Road, Lowestoft, Suffolk NR32 4AB. *T:* Lowestoft (01502) 565569.

CUSHING, Penny; District Judge, Principal Registry, Family Division, since 1994; *b* 10 April 1950; *d* of George Norman Cushing and Doris Cushing; *m* 1995, Michael, (Mik), Norman. *Educ:* Birkenhead High Sch. (GPDST); University Coll., London (LLB Hons 1971). Admitted solicitor, 1974; Solicitor: London Bor. of Harrow, 1974–75; Camden Community Law Centre, 1975–80; Trng Officer, Law Centres Fedn, 1980–83; Partner, Cushing & Kelly, subseq. Clinton Davis Cushing & Kelly, solicitors, 1983–90. Mem., Mental Health Act Commn, 1991–94. *Recreations:* walking my dog Jim, British Rail timetable. *Address:* Principal Registry, Family Division, Somerset House, Strand, WC2R 1LP.

CUSHING, Selwyn John, CMG 1994; FCA; Chairman, Electricity Corporation of New Zealand, since 1993; *b* 1 Sept. 1936; *s* of Cyril John Cushing and Henrietta Marjory Belle Cushing; *m* 1964, Kaye Dorothy Anderson; two *s*. *Educ:* Hastings High Sch.; Univ. of NZ. FCA 1957; ACIS 1958; CMA 1959. Partner, Esam Cushing & Co., sharebrokers, Hastings, 1960–86; Exec. Dir, Brierley Investments Ltd, 1986–93; Dep. Chm., Air New Zealand, 1988–; Chm., Carter Holt Harvey Ltd, 1991–93. *Recreations:* cricket, music. *Address:* 1 Beatson Road, Hastings, New Zealand. *T:* (6) 8786160. *Clubs:* Wellington; Auckland; Dunedin.

CUST, family name of **Baron Brownlow.**

CUSTANCE, Michael Magnus Vere, CB 1959; *b* 3 Jan. 1916; *e s* of late Mrs Arthur Long (Marjorie Bowen, novelist); *m*; one *s* one *d*. *Educ:* St Paul's (schol.); The Queen's Coll., Oxford (open hist. schol., BA Hons, 1st cl., Mod. Hist., 1937). Asst Principal, Board of Trade, 1938; Ministry of Shipping, 1939; Royal Air Force, 1941–45; Principal, Ministry of War Transport, 1943; Asst Sec., Min. of Transport, 1948; Under-Sec., Min. of Transport and Civil Aviation, 1956; Dep. Sec., Min. of Transport and Civil Aviation, 1958; in Ministry of Aviation, 1959–63; in Ministry of Transport, 1963–66; in Min. of Social Security, later DHSS, 1966–75; Chief Advr to Supplementary Benefits Commn, 1968–75. IDC (1952 Course). *Address:* 7 Claremont Way, Midhurst, West Sussex GU29 9QM.

CUSTIS, Patrick James, CBE 1981; FCA, FCMA, FCIS; director of companies; *b* 19 March 1921; *er s* of late Alfred and Amy Custis; *m* 1954, Rita, *yr d* of late Percy and Annie Rayner; one *s*. *Educ:* The High Sch., Dublin. JDipMA. FCA 1951; FCMA 1950; FCIS 1945. Served articles with Josolyne Miles & Co., Chartered Accountants, Cheapside, London, 1945–51; Asst to Gen. Man., Rio Tinto Co. Ltd, London, 1952–54; Gp Chief Accountant and Dir of subsid. cos, Glynwed Ltd, W Midlands, 1955–66; Guest Keen & Nettlefolds Ltd, W Midlands, 1967–81 (Dir of Finance, 1974–81); various sen. appts prior to 1974. Mem., Midlands and N Wales Reg. Bd (formerly Birmingham and W Midlands Reg. Bd), Lloyds Bank plc, 1979–91; Director: New Court Property Fund Managers Ltd, 1978–91; Associated Heat Services plc, 1981–90; Wolseley plc, 1982–90; Birmingham Technology Ltd, 1983–93; Wyko Group PLC, 1985–94; Chairman: MCD Gp plc, 1983–86; Leigh Interests plc, 1993– (Dep. Chm., 1982–93). Member: HM Prisons Bd, Home Office, 1980–85; Bi-Centenary Adv. Bd, Birmingham Gen. Hosp., 1978–90. Co-opted Mem. Council, Inst. of Chartered Accountants in England and Wales, 1979–85; Liveryman, Worshipful Co. of Chartered Accountants in England and Wales; Pres., Wolverhampton Soc. of Chartered Accountants, 1985–86. FRSA 1987. *Recreations:* walking, gardening, reading. *Address:* West Barn, Westmancote, near Tewkesbury, Glos GL20 7ES. *T:* Bredon (01684) 72865. *Clubs:* Royal Over-Seas League, Lansdowne.
See also R. A. Custis.

CUSTIS, Ronald Alfred; Director General, Energy Industries Council, 1981–92; *b* 28 Feb. 1931; *yr s* of late Alfred and Amy Custis, Dublin; *m* 1st, 1957, Enid Rowe (*d* 1984); one *s* one *d*; 2nd, 1986, Valerie Mackett (*née* Holbrook). *Educ:* The High Sch., Dublin. Joined HM Treasury, 1947; DES, 1964; Min. of Technology, 1964–70: Private Sec. to Permanent Under Sec., 1964–66; Principal, 1967; Sec. to Cttee of Inquiry into the Brain Drain, 1967–68; Min. of Aviation Supply, later MoD (Procurement Exec.), 1970–74: Private Sec. to Sec. of State for Defence, 1971–73; Asst Sec., 1973; Dept of Energy, 1974–81: Private Sec. to successive Secs of State for Energy, 1974–75; Under Sec., 1978; Dir Gen., Offshore Supplies Office, 1980–81. *Recreations:* reading, walking, listening to music, gardening. *Address:* 1 The Coaches, Fields Road, Chedworth, Glos GL54 4NQ.

T: Cirencester (01285) 720479.
See also P. J. Custis.

CUTHBERT, Prof. Alan William, PhD; FRS 1982; Sheild Professor of Pharmacology, University of Cambridge, since 1979; Master of Fitzwilliam College, Cambridge, since 1990; *b* 7 May 1932; *s* of late Thomas William Cuthbert and Florence Mary (*née* Griffin); *m* 1957, Harriet Jane Webster; two *s*. *Educ:* Leicester Coll. of Technol.; St Andrews Univ. (BSc); London Univ. (BPharm, PhD). MA Cantab. Instructor Lieut, RN, 1953–56. Res. Fellow, then Asst Lectr, Dept of Pharmacology, Sch. of Pharmacy, Univ. of London, 1959–63; Demonstrator in Pharmacol., 1963–66, Lectr, 1966–73, and Reader, 1973–79, Dept of Pharmacol., Univ. of Cambridge; Fellow of Jesus Coll., Cambridge, 1968–90 (Hon. Fellow, 1991). Chm. Editorial Bd, British Jl of Pharmacology, 1974–82. Member: AFRC, 1988–90; Council, Royal Soc., 1986–88; Council, Zool Soc. of London, 1988–91. Hon. DSc De Montfort, 1993; Hon. LLD Dundee, 1994. Pereira Medal in Materia Medica, Pharmaceutical Soc. of GB, 1953; Sir James Irvine Medal in Chemistry, St Andrews Univ., 1955. *Publications:* scientific papers in pharmacol and physiol jls. *Recreations:* travel, painting, growing orchids, Duodecimos. *Address:* Master's Lodge, Fitzwilliam College, Cambridge CB3 2DG. *T:* Cambridge (01223) 332000.

CUTHBERT, Lady, (Betty Wake), CBE 1946 (OBE 1943); OStJ 1944; *b* 1904; *d* of Guy Shorrock and Emma Wake; *m* 1928, Vice-Adm. Sir John Cuthbert, KBE, CB (*d* 1987); no *c*. Joined Auxiliary Fire Service, London, as driver, 1938; Fire Staff, Home Office, 1941; Chief Woman Fire Officer, National Fire Service, 1941–46. Nat. Chm., Girls' Venture Corps, 1946–67 (Pres. 1967). Mem., Hampshire CC, 1967–74. *Address:* Ibthorpe Manor Farm, Hurstbourne Tarrant, Andover, Hants.

CUTHBERT, Ian Holm; *see* Holm, Ian.

CUTLER, Sir (Arthur) Roden, VC 1941; AK 1981; KCMG 1965; KCVO 1970; CBE 1957; Governor of New South Wales, 1966–81; company director; Chairman, State Bank of New South Wales, 1981–86; *b* 24 May 1916; *s* of Arthur William Cutler and Ruby Daphne (*née* Pope); *m* 1st, 1946, Helen Gray Annetta (*née* Morris), AC 1980 (*d* 1990); four *s*; 2nd, 1993, Joan Edith (*née* Goodwin). *Educ:* Sydney High Sch.; University of Sydney (BEc). Public Trust Office (NSW), 1935–42; War of 1939–45 (VC). State Secretary, RSS & AILA (NSW), 1942–43; Mem., Aliens Classification and Adv. Cttee to advise Commonwealth Govt, 1942–43; Asst Dep. Dir, Security Service, NSW, 1943; Asst Comr Repatriation, 1943–46; High Comr for Australia to New Zealand, 1946–52; High Comr for Australia to Ceylon, 1952–55; HM's Australian Minister to Egypt, 1955–56; Secretary General, SEATO Conference, 1957; Chief of Protocol, Dept of External Affairs, Canberra, 1957–58; State President of RSL, formerly RSSAILA (ACT), 1958; Australian High Comr to Pakistan, 1959–61; Australian Representative to Independence of Somali Republic, 1960; Australian Consul-General, New York, 1961–65; Ambassador to the Netherlands, 1965. Delegate to UN General Assembly, and Australian Rep., Fifth Cttee, 1962–63–64. Chairman: Occidental Life Assurance Co. of Australia, 1987–90; Ansett Express (formerly Air New South Wales), 1981–92; First Australia Fund, 1985–; First Australia Prime Income Fund, 1986–; First Australia Prime Income Investment Co., 1986–; Rothmans Foundn, 1987–; First Commonwealth Fund, 1992–; Director: Rothmans Hldgs Ltd (formerly Rothmans of Pall Mall), 1981–93; Permanent Trustee Co., 1981–92; Rothsay Property Investments Ltd, 1991–. Dep. Pres., VC and GC Assoc., 1991–. Hon. Col, Royal New South Wales Regt, 1966–85; Hon. Col, Sydney Univ. Regt, 1966–85; Hon. Air Cdre RAAF. Hon. LLD, Univ. of Sydney; Hon. DSc: Univ. of New South Wales; Univ. of Newcastle; Hon. DLitt: Univ. of New England; Univ. of Wollongong. KStJ 1965. *Recreations:* swimming, shooting, yachting. *Address:* 22 Ginahgulla Road, Bellevue Hill, NSW 2023, Australia. *T:* (2)3261233. *Clubs:* Australian, Union (Sydney); Royal Sydney Yacht Squadron, Royal Prince Alfred Yacht (Sydney), Royal Sydney Golf.

CUTLER, Hon. Sir Charles (Benjamin), KBE 1973; ED 1960; Director, 1976–90, Chairman, 1978–90, Sun Alliance (Australia); *b* Forbes, NSW, 20 April 1918; *s* of George Hamilton Cutler and Elizabeth Cutler; *m* 1943, Dorothy Pascoe (OBE 1976); three *s* one *d*. *Educ:* rural and high schs, Orange, NSW. MLA for Orange, NSW, 1947; Leader of Country Party (NSW), 1959; Dep. Premier and Minister for Educn, 1965; Dep. Premier, 1972–76, Minister for Local Govt, 1972–76, and Minister for Tourism, 1975–76, NSW. Chm., United World Colls (Aust.) Trust, 1977. Hon. DLitt Newcastle Univ., NSW, 1968. *Recreation:* golf. *Address:* 52 Kite Street, Orange, NSW 2800, Australia. *T:* (63)626418. *Clubs:* Royal Automobile, Imperial Service, Union (Sydney); Orange Golf.

CUTLER, Sir Horace (Walter), Kt 1979; OBE 1963; DL; Member of Greater London Council for Harrow West, 1964–86; Chairman, Branch Retirement Homes PLC, since 1985; *b* London, N16, 28 July 1912; *s* of Albert Benjamin and Mary Ann Cutler; *m* 1957, Christiane, *d* of Dr Klaus Muthesius; one *s* three *d* (and one *s* of previous marriage). *Educ:* Harrow Grammar Sch.; Hereford. Served War of 1939–45: RNVR, 1941–46, Lieut. Harrow Borough Council: elected 1952; Chm. Planning Cttee, 1954; Chm. Housing Cttee, 1955–58; Dep. Mayor, 1958; Alderman, 1959; Mayor, 1959–60; Leader of Council, 1961–65; Chm., Gen. Purposes Cttee, 1962–65; Middlesex CC: elected, 1955; Vice-Chm., Estates and Housing Cttee, 1957; Chm. Planning Cttee, 1961–65; Dep. Leader of CC, 1962; Leader, 1963–65; Greater London Council: Dep. Leader of Opposition, 1964–67 and 1973–74; Dep. Leader, 1967–73; Leader of Opposition, 1974–77 and 1981–82; Leader, 1977–81; Chm. Housing Cttee, 1967–70; Policy and Resources Cttee, 1970–73. Chm., Central Milton Keynes Shopping Management Co. Ltd, 1976–89; Member. Milton Keynes New City Develt Corp, 1967–86; Central Housing Adv. Cttee, Min. of Housing and Local Govt, 1967–74; Nat. Housing and Town Planning Exec Cttee, 1967–74 (Vice-Chm., London Region, 1968); Dir, S Bank Theatre Bd; Mem., Nat. Theatre Bd, 1975–82; Trustee, Nat. Theatre, 1976–83. Contested (C) Willesden East, 1970; Pres., Harrow West Conservative Assoc., 1964– (Chm., 1961–64). Freeman of Harrow, and City of London. DL Greater London, 1981. FRSA. OStJ. *Publication:* The Cutler Files, 1982. *Recreations:* golf, ski-ing, classical music, travel. *Address:* Hawkswood, Hawkswood Lane, Gerrards Cross, Bucks SL9 7BN. *T:* Fulmer (01753) 663182. *Clubs:* Constitutional, United & Cecil.

CUTLER, Ivor; humorist, poet, illustrator, playwright, singer and composer, since 1957; *b* 1923; *s* of Jack and Polly Cutler; two *s*. *Educ:* Shawlands Academy. *Radio and television:* Monday Night at Home, Radio 4, 1959–63; John Peel, Radio 1, 1969–; 14 radio plays, Radio 3, 1979–88; Prince Ivor (opera), Radio 3, 1983; King Cutler I to VI (with Phyllis King), Radio 3, 1990–; Magical Mystery Tour, TV, 1967; Ivor Cutler has 15, 1990, Cutler the Lax, 1991, Radio 4 (radio archive selections); A Stuggy Pren (series), Radio 3, 1994; *stage:* Establishment Club (cabaret), 1961–62; An Evening of British Rubbish, Comedy Th., 1963. Cartoonist, Private Eye and Observer, 1962–63. Pye Radio Award for humour, 1980. *Gramophone records:* Ivor Cutler of Y'hup, 1959; Get Away from the Wall, 1961; Who Tore Your Trousers?, 1961; Ludo, 1967; Dandruff, 1974; Velvet Donkey, 1975; Jammy Smears, 1976; Life in a Scotch Sitting Room, vol. 2, 1978, reissued 1987; Privilege, 1983; Women of the World (single), 1983; Prince Ivor, 1986; Gruts, 1986. Poetry cartoons, Scotland on Sunday mag., 1992–93. *Publications: stories:* Cockadoodle don't, 1967; (illustr. Martin Honeysett): Gruts, 1961, repr. 1986; Life in a Scotch Sitting Room, vol. 2, 1984; Fremsley, 1987; Glasgow Dreamer, 1990; *children's books:* (illustr. Helen Oxenbury): Meal One, 1971; Balooky Klujypop, 1974; The Animal House, 1977; (illustr. Alfreda Benge): Herbert the Chicken, 1984; Herbert the Elephant, 1984; (illustr. M. Honeysett) One and a Quarter, 1987; (illustr. Patrick Benson) Herbert: Five Stories, 1988; (illustr. Jill Barton) Grape Zoo, 1990; (illustr. Claudio Muñoz) Doris the Hen, 1992; (illustr. Claudio Muñoz) The New Dress, 1995; *poetry:* Many Flies Have Feathers, 1973; A Flat Man, 1977; Private Habits, 1981; Large et Puffy, 1984; Fresh Carpet, 1986; A Nice Wee Present from Scotland, 1988; (illustr. M. Honeysett) Fly Sandwich and other Menu, 1992; Is that your flap, Jack?, 1992; (photogr. Katrina Lithgow) A Stuggy Pren, 1994; Stupid Poems, 1995; *philosphy:* (illustr. Martin Honeysett) Befriend a Bacterium, 1992. *Recreation:* alleviating boredom (unsuccessfully). *Address:* c/o BBC, Broadcasting House, W1A 1AA.

CUTLER, Robin; *see* Cutler, T. R.

CUTLER, Sir Roden; *see* Cutler, Sir A. R.

CUTLER, Timothy Robert, (Robin), CBE 1995; Director-General and Deputy Chairman, Forestry Commission, since 1990; *b* 24 July 1934; *s* of Frank Raymond Cutler and Jeannie Evelyn Cutler (*née* Badenoch); *m* 1958, Ishbel Primrose; one *s* one *d*. *Educ:* Banff Academy; Aberdeen Univ. (BSc Forestry 1956). National Service, Royal Engineers, 1956–58. Colonial Forest Service, Kenya, 1958–64; New Zealand Forest Service: joined 1964; Dir of Forest Management, 1978; Dep. Dir-Gen., 1986; Chief Exec., Min. of Forestry, 1988–90. Hon. DSc Aberdeen, 1992. *Recreations:* tennis, golf, gardening, stamps. *Address:* Forestry Commission, 231 Corstorphine Road, Edinburgh EH12 7AT. *T:* 0131–334 0303. *Club:* Commonwealth Trust.

CUTT, Rev. Canon Samuel Robert; Canon Residentiary, 1979–93, and Treasurer, 1985–93, Wells Cathedral (Chancellor, 1979–85); *b* 28 Nov. 1925; *er s* of Robert Bush Cutt and Lilian Elizabeth Cutt (*née* Saint); *m* 1972, Margaret Eva (*d* 1975), *yr d* of Norman and Eva McIntyre. *Educ:* Skegness Grammar Sch.; Selwyn Coll., Cambridge; Cuddesdon Coll., Oxford. BA Cantab 1950, MA 1954. Deacon 1953, Priest 1954. Asst Curate, St Aidan, West Hartlepool, 1953–56; Tutor for King's Coll. London at St Boniface Coll., Warminster, 1956–59; Sub-Warden for KCL at St Boniface Coll., 1959–65; Lectr and Tutor of Chichester Theol Coll., 1965–71; Priest Vicar of Chichester Cath., 1966–71; Minor Canon, 1971–79, and Succentor, 1974–79, St Paul's Cathedral, and Warden, Coll. of Minor Canons, 1974–79, part-time Lectr, Theological Dept, KCL, 1973–79; Priest in Ordinary to the Queen, 1975–79; Dio. Dir of Ordinands, Bath and Wells, 1979–86, Examining Chaplain to Bishop of Bath and Wells, 1980–93; Warden, Community of St Denys, Warminster, 1987–91. OStJ 1981. *Recreations:* walking, music, biographical studies, heraldry, cooking. *Address:* 9 Eastfield Grove, Eastfield, Peterborough PE1 4BB. *T:* Peterborough (01733) 345197.

CUTTER, Prof. Elizabeth Graham, PhD, DSc; FRSE; FLS; George Harrison Professor of Botany, University of Manchester, 1979–89, now Emeritus; *b* 9 Aug. 1929; *d* of Roy Carnegie Cutter and Alexandra (*née* Graham). *Educ:* Rothesay House Sch., Edinburgh; Univ. of St Andrews (BSc, DSc); Univ. of Manchester (PhD). Asst Lecturer in Botany, 1955–57, Lectr in Botany, 1957–64, Univ. of Manchester; Associate Professor of Botany, 1964–68, Professor of Botany, 1968–72, Univ. of California, Davis; Sen. Lectr in Cryptogamic Botany, 1972–74, Reader in Cryptogamic Botany, 1974–79, Univ. of Manchester. *Publications:* Trends in Plant Morphogenesis (principal editor), 1966; Plant Anatomy: Experiment and Interpretation, pt 1, Cells and Tissues, 1969, 2nd edn 1978; pt 2, Organs, 1971. *Recreations:* photography, fishing. *Address:* Barnyard Butts, Bakers Road, Gattonside, Melrose, Roxburghshire TD6 9NA. *T:* Melrose (01896) 822139.

CUTTS, Rt. Rev. Richard Stanley; Assistant Bishop, diocese of Lincoln, and Assistant Curate (NSM) in the Uffington Group, since 1992 (in the South Lafford Group, 1990–92); *b* 17 Sept. 1919; *s* of Edward Stanley and Gabrielle Cutts; *m* 1960, Irene Adela Sack; one *s* three *d*. *Educ:* Felsted School, Essex. Asst Curate, SS Peter and Paul, Godalming, 1951–56; Director of St Cyprian's Mission, Etalaneni and Priest-in-Charge Nkandhla Chapelry, Zululand, 1957–63; Director, Kambula Mission District, 1963–65; Rector, St Mary's, Kuruman and Director, Kuruman Mission District, 1965–71; Archdeacon of Kuruman, 1969–71; Dean of Salisbury, Rhodesia, 1971–75; Bishop in Argentina and Eastern South America, 1975; name of dio. changed to Argentina and Uruguay 1986, to Argentina 1988; retired 1989. *Address:* 37 King Street, West Deeping, Lincs PE6 9HP.

D

d'ABO, Jennifer Mary Victoria; Chairman: Moyses Stevens Investments, since 1990; Moyses Stevens Ltd, since 1989; Roffey Brothers Ltd, since 1988; *b* 14 Aug. 1945; *d* of Michael Hammond-Maude and Rosamond Hammond-Maude (*née* Patrick); *m* 1st, David Morgan-Jones; one *d*; 2nd, Peter Cadbury, *qv*; one *s*; 3rd, Robin d'Abo (marr. diss. 1987). *Educ:* Hatherop Castle, Glos. Chm., Ryman Ltd, 1981–87; Director: Burlingtons Furnishing Co., 1977–80; Jean Sorelle, toiletry manufacturing co., 1980–83; Stormgard plc, 1985–87; London Docklands Develt Corp., 1985–88; Channel Four Television, 1986–87; (non.-exec.) Pentos plc, 1987–88; Mem., Industrial Develt Bd for NI, 1992–94. Mem., Doctors' and Dentists' Remuneration Review Body, 1989–92. Imperial Cancer Research Fund: Mem. Council, 1994–; Pres., Nat. Events Cttee, 1993–. Trustee, BM (Natural History), 1988–. *Address:* 13 Wilton Crescent, SW1X 8RN; 7 Green Street, W1Y 3RF.

d'ABREU, Francis Arthur, ERD 1954; Consultant Surgeon, 1946–69, now retired, Westminster Hospital; Surgeon, 1950–69, now Emeritus, Hospital of St John and St Elizabeth; *b* 1 Oct. 1904; *s* of Dr John Francis d'Abreu and Teresa d'Abreu; *m* 1945, Margaret Ann Bowes-Lyon; one *s* one *d* (and one *d* decd). *Educ:* Stonyhurst Coll.; Birmingham Univ. MB, ChB Birmingham 1929; MRCS, LRCP 1929; FRCS, 1932; ChM Birmingham 1935. House Surgeon, Gen. Hosp., Birmingham, 1929; Res. Surgical Officer, Gen. and Queen's Hosps, Birmingham, 1930–34; Surg. Registrar, St Bartholomew's Hosp., London, and Westminster Hosp., 1934–39. Formerly: Examiner to Soc. of Apothecaries; Examiner to Univs of Cambridge and London; Mem., Ct of Examiners, RCS. Mem. Bd of Management, Inst. of Sports Medicine. Lieut RAMC (Supp. Reserve), 1939. Served War of 1939–45: Major, RAMC, 1939, Lt-Col 1942–45. Kt of Magistral Grace, Sov. and Mil. Order of Malta; Kt Comdr, Order of St Gregory (Holy See), 1977. *Publications:* contrib. to various medical jls. *Recreation:* gardening. *Address:* 36 Cumberland Terrace, Regent's Park, NW1 4HP.

DACCA; *see* Dhaka.

DACIE, Prof. Sir John (Vivian), Kt 1976; FRS 1967; MD, FRCP; Professor of Haematology, Royal Post-graduate Medical School of London, University of London, 1957–77, now Emeritus; *b* 20 July 1912; British; *s* of John Charles and Lilian Maud Dacie, Putney; *m* 1938, Margaret Kathleen Victoria Thynne; three *s* two *d*. *Educ:* King's Coll. Sch., Wimbledon; King's Coll., London: King's Coll. Hospital, London. MB, BS London 1935; MD 1952; MRCP 1936; FRCP 1956; Hon. FRSM 1984; MD (Hon.): Uppsala, 1961; Marseille, 1977; FRCPath (Pres., 1973–75); Pres., RSM, 1977. Various medical appointments, King's Coll. Hospital, Postgraduate Medical Sch. and Manchester Royal Infirmary, 1936–39. Pathologist, EMS, 1939–42; Major, then Lieut-Col, RAMC, 1943–46. Senior Lecturer in Clinical Pathology, then Reader in Haematology, Postgraduate Medical Sch., 1946–56. Chm., Med. and Scientific Adv. Panel, Leukaemia Research Fund, 1975–85. *Publications:* Practical Haematology, 1950, 2nd edn, 1956, 8th edn (jointly), 1995; Haemolytic Anaemias, 1954: 2nd edn, Part I, 1960, Part II, 1962, Parts III and IV, 1967, 3rd edn, Part I, 1985, Part II, 1988, Part III, 1992; various papers on anaemia in medical journals. *Recreations:* music, entomology, gardening. *Address:* 10 Alan Road, Wimbledon, SW19 7PT. *T:* 0181–946 6086.

DACOMBE, William John Armstrong; Chairman: Brown Shipley Holdings, since 1991; Campbell Lutyens Hudson & Co., since 1994; *b* 21 Sept. 1934; *s* of late John Christian Dacombe and of Eileen Elizabeth Dacombe; *m* 1962, Margaretta Joanna (*née* Barrington); two *d*. *Educ:* Felsted School; Corpus Christi College, Oxford (MA). Kleinwort Benson, 1961–65; N. M. Rothschild & Sons, 1965–73 (Dir, 1970–73); Dir, 1973–84, Asst Chief Exec., 1979–82, Williams & Glyn's Bank; Group Exec. Dir, Royal Bank of Scotland Group, 1982–84; Chief Exec. Dir, Rea Brothers Group, 1984–88; Director: W. A. Tyzack, 1987–89; Campbell Lutyens Hudson & Co., 1988–91. Mem., Export Guarantees Adv. Council, 1982–86 (Dep. Chm., 1985–86). FRSA. *Recreations:* art, historic buildings, reading. *Address:* Mullion Cottage, Well Lane, SW14 7AJ. *T:* 0181–876 4336. *Clubs:* Brooks's, Bankers.

da COSTA, Harvey Lloyd, CMG 1962; **Hon. Mr Justice da Costa;** Judge of Appeal, Court of Appeal for Bermuda, since 1982; *b* 8 Dec. 1914; *s* of John Charles and Martha da Costa. *Educ:* Calabar High Sch., Jamaica; St Edmund Hall (Sen. Exhibnr; Rhodes Schol.), Oxford. BA (Hons) London; MA, BLitt Oxon; Practised at Chancery Bar, 1950–52; Crown Counsel, Jamaica, 1952–54; Sen. Crown Counsel, Jamaica, 1954–56; Asst Attorney-Gen., Jamaica, 1956–59; QC Jamaica 1959; Attorney-Gen. of West Indies, 1959–62; practised Private Bar, Jamaica, 1962–77; Puisne Judge 1978–80, Chief Justice, 1980–81, Bahamas Supreme Court; Judge of Appeal, Court of Appeal for Bahamas, 1982–85. Mem., Anguilla, British Virgin Is and Seychelles Commns. Hon. LLD Univ. of W Indies, 1990. *Recreation:* swimming. *Address:* c/o Court of Appeal, Hamilton HM12, Bermuda.

da COSTA, Sergio Corrêa, GCVO; Brazilian diplomat, retired; *b* 19 Feb. 1919; *s* of Dr I. A. da Costa and Lavinia Corrêa da Costa; *m* 1943, Zazi Aranha; one *s* two *d*. *Educ:* Law Sch., Univ. of Brazil; post grad. UCLA; Brazilian War Coll. Career diplomat; Sec. of Embassy, Buenos Ayres, then Washington, 1944–48; Acting Deleg., Council of OAS, Wash., 1946–48; Inter-American Econ. and Social Coun., Washington, 1946–48; Dep. Head, Economic Dept, Min. of Ext. Relations, 1952; Actg Pres., Braz. Nat. Techn. Assistance Commn, 1955–58; Minister-Counsellor, Rome, 1959–62; Permanent Rep. to FAO, Rome, 1960; Mem., Financial Cttee of FAO, 1962–63; Ambassador to Canada, 1962–65; Asst Sec.-Gen. for Internat. Organizations at Min. Ext. Relations, 1966; Sec.-Gen., Min. of Ext. Relations, 1967–68; Acting Minister for External Relations, 1967–68; Ambassador to UK, 1968–75; Permanent Rep. to UN in NY, 1975–83; Ambassador to USA, 1983–86. Member: Brazilian Acad. of Letters; Brazilian Hist. and Geographical Inst.; Brazilian Soc. of Internat. Law; American Soc. of Internat. Law. Grand Officer: Military Order of Aeronautical Merit, Brazil, 1967; Order of Naval Merit, Brazil, 1967; Grand Cross of Victorian Order (Hon. GCVO), Gt Britain, 1968; also numerous Grand Crosses, etc, of Orders, from other countries, 1957–. *Publications:* (mostly in Brazil): As 4 Coroas de Pedro I, 1941; Pedro I e Metternich, 1942; Diplomacia Brasileira na Questao de Leticia, 1943; A Diplomacia do Marechal, 1945; Every Inch a King—A biography of Pedro I, Emperor of Brazil, 1950 (NY 1964, London 1972). *Recreations:* reading, writing, boating. *Address:* 8/10 rue Guynemer, 75006 Paris, France. *Clubs:* White's, Travellers' (London); Rideau, Country (Ottawa); Circolo della Caccia (Rome).

DACRE, Baroness (27th in line), *cr* 1321; **Rachel Leila Douglas-Home;** *b* 24 Oct. 1929; *er* surv. *d* of 4th Viscount Hampden, CMG (*d* 1965) (whose Barony of Dacre was called out of abeyance in her favour, 1970) and of Leila Emily, *o d* of late Lt-Col Frank Evelyn Seely; *m* 1951, Hon. William Douglas-Home (*d* 1992), author and playwright; one *s* three *d*. *Heir: s* Hon. James Thomas Archibald Douglas-Home [*b* 16 May 1952; *m* 1979, Christine (*née* Stephenson); one *d*]. *Address:* Derry House, Kilmeston, near Alresford, Hants SO24 0NR.

DACRE OF GLANTON, Baron *cr* 1979 (Life Peer), of Glanton in the County of Northumberland; **Hugh Redwald Trevor-Roper;** Master of Peterhouse, Cambridge, 1980–87 (Hon. Fellow, 1987); *b* 15 January 1914; *er s* of late Dr B. W. E. Trevor-Roper, Glanton and Alnwick, Northumberland; *m* 1954, Lady Alexandra Howard-Johnston, *e d* of late Field-Marshal Earl Haig, KT, GCB, OM. *Educ:* Charterhouse; Christ Church, Oxford. Research Fellow Merton Coll., 1937–39 (Hon. Fellow, 1980). Student of Christ Church, Oxford, 1946–57; Censor 1947–52; Hon. Student, 1979; Regius Prof. of Modern Hist., and Fellow of Oriel Coll., Oxford Univ., 1957–80 (Hon. Fellow, 1980). Dir, Times Newspapers Ltd, 1974–88. Chevalier, Legion of Honour, 1975. *Publications:* Archbishop Laud, 1940; The Last Days of Hitler, 1947; The Gentry, 1540–1640, 1953; (ed) Hitler's Table Talk, 1953; (ed with J. A. W. Bennett) The Poems of Richard Corbett, 1955; Historical Essays, 1957; (ed) Hitler's War Directives, 1939–45, 1964; (ed) Essays in British History Presented to Sir Keith Feiling, 1964; The Rise of Christian Europe, 1965; Religion, The Reformation and Social Change, 1967; (ed) The Age of Expansion, 1968; The Philby Affair, 1968; The European Witch-Craze of the 16th and 17th Centuries, 1970; The Plunder of the Arts in the Seventeenth Century, 1970; Princes and Artists, 1976; A Hidden Life, 1976; (ed) The Goebbels Diaries, 1978; Renaissance Essays, 1985; Catholics, Anglicans and Puritans, 1987; From Counter-Reformation to Glorious Revolution, 1992. *Address:* The Old Rectory, Didcot, Oxon OX11 7EB. *Clubs:* Beefsteak, United Oxford & Cambridge University.

See also Earl Haig, P. D. Trevor-Roper.

DACRE, Paul Michael; Editor, Daily Mail, since 1992; *b* 14 Nov. 1948; *s* of Joan and Peter Dacre; *m* 1973, Kathleen Thomson; two *s*. *Educ:* University College Sch.; Leeds Univ. (Hons English). Reporter, feature writer, Associate Features Editor, Daily Express, 1970–76; Washington and NY corresp., Daily Express, 1976–79; Daily Mail: NY Bureau Chief, 1980; News Editor, 1981–85; Asst Editor (News and Foreign), 1986; Exec. Editor (Features), 1987; Associate Editor, 1989–91; Editor, Evening Standard, 1991–92. Dir, Associated Newspaper Holdings, 1991–. *Address:* Daily Mail, Northcliffe House, 2 Derry Street, W8 5TT. *T:* 0171–938 6000.

da CUNHA, His Honour John Wilfrid, JP; a Circuit Judge (formerly Judge of County Courts), 1970–92; *b* 6 Sept. 1922; 2nd *s* of Frank C. da Cunha, MD, DPH, and Lucy (*née* Finnerty); *m* 1953, Janet, MB, ChB, *d* of Louis Savatard, (Hon.) MSc, LSA, and Judith Savatard, MB, BS; one *s* four *d*. *Educ:* Stonyhurst Coll., Lancs; St John's Coll., Cambridge. MA Cantab 1954. Served 1942–47: 23rd Hussars (RAC); wounded Normandy, 1944; Judge Advocate Gen. (War Crimes); Hon. Major. Called to Bar, Middle Temple, 1948; Northern Circuit. Chm., Local Appeal Tribunal, Min. of Social Security (Wigan), 1964–69. Asst Recorder, Oldham County Borough QS, 1966–70; Chm., Industrial Tribunals, 1966–70; Dep. Chm., Lancs County QS, 1968–71. Comr, NI (Emergency Provisions) Act, 1973; Member: Appeals Tribunal; Parole Bd, 1976–78; Criminal Injuries Compensation Bd, 1992–. Pres., Bristol Medico-Legal Soc., 1989–91. Governor, Mount Carmel Sch., Alderley Edge, 1962–78. JP Lancs 1968. *Recreations:* gardening, pottering.

DADZIE, Kenneth Kweku Sinaman; High Commissioner for Ghana in London, since 1994; *b* 10 Sept. 1930; *s* of Kwesi Sinaman Dadzie and Sarah Eyaah. *Educ:* Achimoto Coll., Ghana; Queens' Coll., Cambridge (Econs Tripos) (Hon. Fellow, 1991). Various posts in Ghana CS, 1952–56; Ghana Foreign Service, 1957–64; Chargé d'Affaires, Paris, 1957–58; Dep. Perm. Rep., UN, NY, 1960–64; various posts in Foreign Service alternating with posts on secondment to UN Secretariat, 1964–75; Ambassador to Switzerland and concurrently to Austria, and Perm. Rep. to UN in Geneva, 1975–78; UN Dir-Gen. for Develt and Internat. Econ. Co-operation, 1978–82; High Comr, London (with rank of Sec. of State), 1982–86; Sec.-Gen., UNCTAD, 1986–94. Member Council: ODI, 1995–; VSO, 1995–. Order of the Volta (Ghana), 1978. *Publications:* contribs to learned jls and compilations on internat. develt policy and on UN. *Address:* Ghana High Commission, 104 Highgate Hill, N6 5HE. *T:* 0181–342 8686. *Clubs:* United Oxford & Cambridge University, Travellers'.

D'AETH, Prof. Richard, PhD; President, Hughes Hall, Cambridge, 1978–84; *b* 3 June 1912; *e s* of Walter D'Aeth and Marion Turnbull; *m* 1943, Pamela Straker; two *d*. *Educ:* Bedford Sch.; Emmanuel Coll., Cambridge (Scholar; 1st Cl. Hons Nat. Sci., PhD); Harvard Univ. (Commonwealth Fellow; AM). Served War, RAF, 1941–46 (Wing Comdr). Master, Gresham's Sch., 1938–40; HM Inspector of Schs, 1946–52; Prof. of Education: University Coll. of West Indies, 1952–58; Univ. of Exeter, 1958–77. Mem., Internat. Assoc. for Advancement of Educnl Res. (Pres., Warsaw, 1969); sometime mem.

cttees of Schools Council, BBC, Schs Broadcasting Council, RCN and NSPCC. *Publications:* Education and Development in the Third World, 1975; articles in jls. *Address:* Barton House, Rydon Acres, Stoke Gabriel, Totnes, Devon TQ9 6QJ.

DAFFERN, Paul George; Executive Director, Finance, AEA Technology, since 1991; *b* 5 May 1953; *s* of late George Thomas Daffern and Kathleen Esther Daffern; *m* 1984, Hilary Margaret Jenkins; one *s* one *d*. *Educ:* Foxford School, Coventry. Unbrako Ltd, 1969–73; Massey-Ferguson UK, 1973–75; Chrysler UK, 1975–77; Lucas Service UK, 1978–79; National Freight Co., 1980–88; Autoglass, 1988–91. *Recreations:* golf, ski-ing. *Address:* 329 Harwell, Oxfordshire OX11 0RA. *T:* Rowstock (01235) 432899.

DAFIS, Cynog Glyndwr; MP (Plaid Cymru) Ceredigion and Pembroke North, since 1992; *b* 1 April 1938; *s* of Annie and George Davies; *m* 1963, Llinos Iorwerth Jones; two *s* one *d*. *Educ:* Aberaeron County Secondary Sch.; Neath Boys' Grammar Sch.; UCW Aberystwyth (BA Hons English, MEd). Teacher of English: Coll. of Further Educn, Pontardawe, 1960–62; Newcastle Emlyn Secondary Modern Sch., 1962–80; Aberaeron Comprehensive Sch., 1980–84; Dyffryn Teifi Comprehensive Sch., Llandysul, 1984–91; Research Officer, Dept of Adult Continuing Educn, UC Swansea, 1991–92. Contested (Plaid Cymru) Ceredigion and Pembroke North, 1983 and 1987. *Publications:* pamphlets and booklet (in Welsh) on bilingualism and Welsh politics. *Recreations:* walking, jogging, reading, listening to music. *Address:* Crugyreryr Uchaf, Talgarreg, Llandysul, Dyfed SA44 4HB. *T:* Pontshaen (0154555) 632.

DAHL, Mildred; *see* Gordon, M.

DAHL, Robert Henry, TD 1950; MA Oxford; Head Master of Wrekin College, 1952–71; *b* 21 April 1910; *y s* of Murdoch Cameron Dahl, London, and Lilian May Edgcumbe; *m* 1936, Lois Helen Allanby; three *s*. *Educ:* Sedbergh Sch.; Exeter Coll., Oxford. Asst Master (Modern Langs) at Merchant Taylors' Sch., 1934–38. Asst Master and Housemaster at Harrow Sch., 1938–52. Served War of 1939–45: Intelligence Corps, Middle East, 1941–43; Major, 1943; Political Intelligence Dept of Foreign Office, 1943–46. FRSA 1969. *Publication:* Joint Editor, Selections from Albert Schweitzer, 1953. *Recreations:* golf, music, painting. *Address:* 72 Eastgate Street, Bury St Edmunds, Suffolk IP33 1YR.

DAHRENDORF, Baron *cr* 1993 (Life Peer), of Clare Market in the City of Westminster; **Ralf Dahrendorf,** KBE 1982; PhD, DrPhil; FBA 1977; Warden of St Antony's College, Oxford, since 1987; *b* Hamburg, 1 May 1929; adopted British nationality, 1988; *s* of Gustav Dahrendorf and Lina Dahrendorf (*née* Witt); *m* 1980, Ellen Joan (*née* Krug). *Educ:* several schools, including Heinrich-Hertz Oberschule, Hamburg; studies in philosophy and classical philology, Hamburg, 1947–52; DrPhil 1952; postgrad. studies at London Sch. of Economics, 1952–54; Leverhulme Research Schol., 1953–54; PhD 1956. Habilitation, and University Lecturer, Saarbrücken, 1957; Fellow at Center for Advanced Study in the Behavioural Sciences, Palo Alto, USA, 1957–58; Prof. of Sociology, Hamburg, 1958–60; Vis. Prof. Columbia Univ., 1960; Prof. of Sociology, Tübingen, 1960–64; Vice-Chm., Founding Cttee of Univ. of Konstanz, 1964–66; Prof. of Sociology, Konstanz, 1966–69; Parly Sec. of State, Foreign Office, W Germany, 1969–70; Mem., EEC, Brussels, 1970–74; Dir, 1974–84, Governor, 1986–, LSE; Prof. of Social Sci., Konstanz Univ., 1984–87. Member: Hansard Soc. Commn on Electoral Reform, 1975–76; Royal Commn on Legal Services, 1976–79; Cttee to Review Functioning of Financial Instns, 1977–80. Trustee, Ford Foundn, 1976–88. Chm. Bd, Friedrich Naumann Stiftung, 1982–88; Non-Exec. Dir, Glaxo Holdings PLC, 1984–92. Vis. Prof. at several Europ. and N American univs. Reith Lecturer, 1974; Jephcott Lectr, RSocMed, 1983. Hon. Fellow: LSE; Imperial Coll. Hon. MRIA 1974; Fellow, St Antony's Coll., Oxford, 1976. Foreign Hon. Member: Amer. Acad. of Arts and Sciences, 1975–; Nat. Acad. of Sciences, USA, 1977; Amer. Philosophical Soc., 1977; FRSA 1977; Hon. FRCS 1982. Hon. DLitt: Reading, 1973; Dublin, 1975; Hon. LLD: Manchester, 1973; Wagner Coll., NY, 1977, York, Ontario, 1979; Columbia, NY, 1989; Hon. DHL: Kalamazoo Coll., 1974; Johns Hopkins, 1982; Hon. DSc: Ulster, 1973; Bath, 1977; Queen's Univ. Belfast, 1984; Birmingham, 1991; DUniv: Open, 1974; Maryland, 1978; Surrey, 1978; Hon. Dr Univ. Catholique de Louvain, 1977; Hon. Dr sc.pol. Bologna, 1991. Journal Fund Award for Learned Publication, 1966. Grand Croix de l'Ordre du Mérite du Sénégal, 1971; Grosses Bundesverdienstkreuz mit Stern und Schulterband (Federal Republic of Germany), 1974; Grand Croix de l'Ordre du Mérite du Luxembourg, 1974; Grosses goldenes Ehrenzeichen am Bande für Verdienste um die Republik Österreich (Austria), 1975; Grand Croix de l'Ordre de Léopold II (Belgium), 1975; Comdr's Cross, Order of Civil Merit (Spain), 1990. *Publications include:* Marx in Perspective, 1953; Industrie- und Betriebssoziologie, 1956 (trans. Italian, Spanish, Dutch, Japanese, Chinese); Soziale Klassen und Klassenkonflikt, 1957 (Class and Class Conflict, 1959; also trans. French, Italian, Spanish, Finnish, Japanese); Homo Sociologicus, 1959 (trans. English, Italian, Portuguese, Finnish); Die angewandte Aufklärung, 1963; Gesellschaft und Demokratie in Deutschland, 1965 (Society and Democracy in Germany, 1966; also trans. Italian); Pfade aus Utopia, 1967 (Uscire dall'Utopia, 1971); Essays in the Theory of Society, 1968; Konflikt und Freiheit, 1972; Plädoyer für die Europäische Union, 1973; The New Liberty, 1975 (trans. German, Italian, Urdu, Arabic, Japanese, Korean); Life Chances, 1979 (trans. German, Japanese, Italian); On Britain, 1982; Die Chancen der Krise, 1983; Reisen nach innen und aussen, 1984; Law and Order, 1985; The Modern Social Conflict, 1988; Reflections on the Revolution in Europe, 1990; LSE: a history of the London School of Economics and Political Science 1895–1995, 1995. *Address:* St Antony's College, Oxford OX2 6JF. *Clubs:* PEN, Reform, Garrick, United Oxford & Cambridge University.

DAICHES, David, CBE 1991; MA Edinburgh; MA, DPhil Oxon; PhD Cantab; FRSL; FRSE; Director, Institute for Advanced Studies in the Humanities, Edinburgh University, 1980–86; Professor of English, University of Sussex, 1961–77, and Dean of the School of English Studies, 1961–68; now Emeritus Professor; *b* 2 Sept. 1912; *s* of late Rabbi Dr Salis Daiches and Flora Daiches (*née* Levin); *m* 1st, 1937, Isobel J. Mackay (*d* 1977); one *s* two *d*; 2nd, 1978, Hazel Neville (*née* Newman) (*d* 1986). *Educ:* George Watson's Coll., Edinburgh; Edinburgh Univ. (Vans Dunlop Schol., Elliot Prize); Balliol Coll., Oxford (Elton Exhibnr). Asst in English, Edinburgh Univ., 1935–36; Andrew Bradley Fellow, Balliol Coll., Oxford, 1936–37; Asst Prof. of English, Univ. of Chicago, 1939–43; Second Sec., British Embassy, Washington, 1944–46; Prof. of English, Cornell Univ., USA, 1946–51; University Lecturer in English at Cambridge, 1951–61; Fellow of Jesus Coll., Cambridge, 1957–62. Visiting Prof. of Criticism, Indiana Univ., USA, 1956–57; Hill Foundation Visiting Prof., Univ. of Minnesota, Spring 1966. Lectures: Elliston, Univ. of Cincinnati, 1960; Whidden, McMaster Univ., Canada, 1964; Ewing, Univ. of Calif, 1967; Carpenter Meml, Ohio Wesleyan Univ., 1969; Alexander, Univ. of Toronto, 1980; Gifford, Univ. of Edinburgh, 1983. Hon. Prof., Stirling Univ., 1980; Sen. Mellon Fellow, Nat. Humanities Center, USA, 1987–88. Fellow, Centre for the Humanities, Wesleyan Univ., Middletown, Conn, 1970. Hon. Fellow, Sunderland Polytechnic, 1977. Hon. LittD, Brown Univ; Docteur *hc* Sorbonne; Hon. DLitt: Edinburgh, 1976; Sussex, 1978; Glasgow, 1987; Guelph, 1990; DUniv Stirling, 1980; Dott. *in honorem* Bologna, 1989. Lifetime Achievement Award, 18th Century Scottish Studies Soc., 1988; Fletcher of Saltoun Award for Services to Scotland, 1988. *Publications:* The Place of Meaning in Poetry, 1935; New Literary Values, 1936; Literature and Society, 1938; The Novel and the Modern World, 1939 (new edn, 1960); Poetry and the Modern World, 1940; The King James Bible: A Study of its Sources and Development, 1941; Virginia Woolf, 1942; Robert Louis Stevenson, 1947; A Study of Literature, 1948; Robert Burns, 1950 (new edn 1966); Willa Cather: A Critical Introduction, 1951; Critical Approaches to Literature, 1956; Two Worlds (autobiog.), 1956; Literary Essays, 1956; John Milton, 1957; The Present Age, 1958; A Critical History of English Literature, 1960; George Eliot's Middlemarch, 1963; The Paradox of Scottish Culture, 1964; (ed) The Idea of a New University, 1964; English Literature (Princeton Studies in Humanistic Scholarship), 1965; More Literary Essays, 1968; Some Late Victorian Attitudes, 1969; Scotch Whisky, 1969; Sir Walter Scott and his World, 1971; A Third World (autobiog.), 1971; (ed) The Penguin Companion to Literature: Britain and the Commonwealth, 1971; Robert Burns and his World, 1971; (ed with A. Thorlby) Literature and Western Civilization, vol. I, 1972, vols II and V, 1973, vols III and IV, 1975; vol. VI, 1976; Charles Edward Stuart: the life and times of Bonnie Prince Charlie, 1973; Robert Louis Stevenson and his World, 1973; Was, 1975; Moses, 1975; James Boswell and his World, 1976; Scotland and the Union, 1977; Glasgow, 1977; Edinburgh, 1978; (with John Flower) Literary Landscapes of the British Isles: a narrative atlas, 1979; (ed) Selected Writings and Speeches of Fletcher of Saltoun, 1979; (ed) Selected Poems of Robert Burns, 1979; (ed) A Companion to Scottish Culture, 1981; Literature and Gentility in Scotland, 1982; Robert Fergusson, 1982; Milton's Paradise Lost, 1983; God and the Poets, 1984; Edinburgh, A Travellers' Companion, 1986; A Wee Dram, 1990; A Weekly Scotsman and Other Poems, 1994; Gen. Editor, Studies in English Literature, 1961–85. *Recreations:* talking, music. *Address:* 22 Belgrave Crescent, Edinburgh EH4 3AL.

See also L. H. Daiches.

DAICHES, Lionel Henry, QC (Scot) 1956; *b* 8 March 1911; *s* of late Rev. Dr. Salis Daiches, Edinburgh, and Mrs Flora Daiches; *m* 1947, Dorothy Estelle Bernstein (marr. diss. 1973); two *s*. *Educ:* George Watson's Coll., Edinburgh; Edinburgh Univ. (MA, LLB). Pres., Edinburgh Univ. Diagnostic Soc., 1931; Convener of Debates, Edinburgh Univ. Union, 1933; Editor, The Student, 1933. Served 1940–46 in N Stafford Regt and Major, JAG Branch in N Africa and Italy, including Anzio Beach-head. Admitted Scots Bar, 1946. Standing Junior Counsel to Board of Control, Scotland, 1950–56; Sheriff-Substitute of Lanarkshire at Glasgow, 1962–67. Fellow, Internat. Acad. of Trial Lawyers, 1976. Contested (L) Edinburgh South, 1950. *Publication:* Russians at Law, 1960. *Recreations:* walking and talking. *Address:* 10 Heriot Row, Edinburgh EH3 6HU. *T:* 0131–556 4144. *Clubs:* New, Scottish Arts (Edinburgh).

See also D. Daiches.

DAIN, Rt. Rev. Arthur John, OBE 1979; *b* 13 Oct. 1912; *s* of Herbert John Dain and Elizabeth Dain; *m* 1st, 1939, Edith Jane Stewart, MA, *d* of Dr Alexander Stewart, DD; four *d*; 2nd, 1986, Hester A. Quirk, BSc. *Educ:* Wolverhampton Gram. Sch.; Ridley Coll., Cambridge. Missionary in India, 1935–40; 10th Gurkha Rifles, 1940–41; Royal Indian Navy, 1941–47; Gen. Sec., Bible and Medical Missionary Fellowship, formerly Zenana Bible and Medical Mission, 1947–59; Overseas Sec., British Evangelical Alliance, 1950–59; Federal Sec., CMS of Australia, 1959–65; Hon. Canon of St Andrew's Cathedral, 1963; Asst Bishop, Diocese of Sydney, 1965–82; Sen. Asst Bishop and Chief Executive Officer, 1980–82. *Publications:* Mission Fields To-day, 1956; Missionary Candidates, 1959. *Recreation:* sport. *Address:* 14 Kipling Court, Winnals Park, Haywards Heath, West Sussex RH16 1EX.

DAIN, David John Michael, CMG 1991; HM Diplomatic Service; Under Secretary, Foreign and Commonwealth Office, since 1994; *b* 30 Oct. 1940; *s* of late John Gordon Dain and of Joan (*née* Connop); *m* 1969, Susan Kathleen Moss; one *s* four *d*. *Educ:* Merchant Taylors' Sch.; St John's Coll., Oxford (MA Lit.Hum.). Entered HM Diplomatic Service, 1963; Third, later Second Sec., Tehran and Kabul, 1964–68; seconded to Cabinet Office, 1969–72; First Sec., Bonn, 1972–75; FCO, 1975–78; Head of Chancery, Athens, 1978–81; Counsellor and Dep. High Comr, Nicosia, 1981–85; Head of Western European Dept, FCO, 1985–89; on attachment to CSSB, 1989–90; High Comr, Cyprus, 1990–94. FIL 1986. Royal Order of Merit, Norway, 1988. *Recreations:* tennis, bridge, flying, golf, walking, natural history. *Address:* c/o Foreign and Commonwealth Office, SW1A 2AH. *Clubs:* United Oxford & Cambridge University; Oxford Union Society.

DAINTITH, Prof. Terence Charles; Professor of Law, University of London, since 1988; Dean, University of London School of Advanced Study, since 1994; *b* 8 May 1942; *s* of Edward Terence and Irene May Daintith; *m* 1965, Christine Anne Bulport; one *s* one *d*. *Educ:* Wimbledon Coll.; St Edmund Hall, Oxford (BA Jurisp., MA); Univ. of Nancy (Leverhulme European Schol.). Called to the Bar, Lincoln's Inn, 1966. Associate in Law, Univ. of California, Berkeley, 1963–64; Lectr in Constitutional and Admin. Law, Univ. of Edinburgh, 1964–72; University of Dundee: Prof. and Head of Dept of Public Law, 1972–83 (leave of absence, 1981–83); Dir, Centre for Petroleum and Mineral Law Studies, 1977–83; European University Institute, Florence: Prof. of Law, 1981–87; Head, Law Dept, 1982, 1986–87; External Prof., 1988–; Dir, Inst. of Advanced Legal Studies, Univ. of London, 1988–95; Dean, Univ. of London Insts of Advanced Study, 1991–94. Mem., Acad. Europaea, 1989– (Chm., Law Cttee, 1993–). Editor, Jl Energy and Natural Resources Law, 1983–92. *Publications:* The Economic Law of the United Kingdom, 1974; (with G. Willoughby) United Kingdom Oil and Gas Law, 1977, 2nd edn 1984; (with L. Hancher) European Energy Strategy: the legal framework, 1986, French edn 1987; (with S. Williams) The Legal Integration of Energy Markets, 1987; Law as an Instrument of Economic Policy, 1988; (with G. R. Baldwin) Harmonisation and Hazard, 1992; Implementing EC Law in the United Kingdom, 1995; contribs to UK and foreign law jls. *Recreations:* cycling, carpentry. *Address:* School of Advanced Study, Senate House, Malet Street, WC1E 7HU. *T:* 0171–636 8000. *Club:* Athenæum.

DAINTON, family name of **Baron Dainton.**

DAINTON, Baron *cr* 1986 (Life Peer), of Hallam Moors in South Yorkshire; **Frederick Sydney Dainton;** Kt 1971; FRS 1957; MA, BSc Oxon, PhD, ScD Cantab; Chancellor, Sheffield University, since 1978; *b* 11 Nov. 1914; *y s* of late George Whalley and Mary Jane Dainton; *m* 1942, Barbara Hazlitt, JP, PhD, *o d* of late Dr W. B. Wright, Manchester; one *s* two *d*. *Educ:* Central Secondary Sch., Sheffield; St John's Coll., Oxford; Sidney Sussex Coll., Cambridge. Open Exhibitioner, 1933; Casberd Prizeman, 1934, Casberd Scholar, 1935, Hon. Fellow 1968, St John's Coll., Oxford; Goldsmiths' Co. Exhibitioner, 1935, 1st class Hons Chemistry, 1937, University of Oxford; Research Student, 1937, Goldsmiths' Co. Senior Student, 1939, University Demonstrator in Chemistry, 1944, H. O. Jones Lecturer in Physical Chemistry, 1946, University of Cambridge. Fellow, 1945, Praelector, 1946, Hon. Fellow 1961, St Catharine's Coll., Cambridge. Prof. of Physical Chemistry, University of Leeds, 1950–65; Vice-Chancellor, Nottingham Univ., 1965–70; Dr Lee's Prof. of Chemistry, Oxford University, 1970–73; Chm., UGC, 1973–78. Vis. Prof., Univ. Toronto, 1949; Tilden Lectr, 1950, Faraday Lectr, 1973, Chem. Soc.; Peter C. Reilly Lectr, Univ. of Notre Dame, Ind., USA, 1952; Arthur D. Little Visiting Prof., MIT, 1959. Lectures: Lady Masson, Melbourne, 1959; George Fisher Baker, Cornell Univ., 1961; Boomer, Univ. of Alberta, 1962; Rede, Cambridge, 1981; Crookshank, RCR, 1981; Stamp, London Univ., 1983; Convocation, Newcastle Univ., 1986; Boyle,

RSA, 1987; Dainton, British Liby, 1987; Gray Hartley, Manchester Univ., 1987; John Snow, Assoc. of Anaesthetists, 1987; Lee Kuan Yew, Singapore Univ., 1989. Chm., Cttee on Swing away from Science (report published as Enquiry into the Flow of Candidates in Science and Technology into Higher Education, Cmnd 3541, 1968). Chairman: Assoc. for Radiation Research, 1964–66; Nat. Libraries Cttee, 1968–69; Adv. Cttee on Sci. and Tech. Information, 1966–70; Adv. Bd for Res. Councils, 1972–73; British Cttee, Harkness Fellowship, 1977–81 (Mem., 1973–); British Library Bd, 1978–85; Nat. Radiological Protection Bd, 1978–85. President: Faraday Soc., 1965–67; Chemical Soc., 1972–73 (Hon. Fellow, 1983–); Assoc. for Science Education, 1967; Library Assoc., 1977; BAAS, 1980; Soc. of Designer Craftsmen, 1985–; Arthritis and Rheumatism Council for Res., 1988–. Member: Council for Scientific Policy, 1965–79 (Chm. 1969–72); Central Advisory Council for Science and Technology, 1967–70; Council, Foundn for Science and Technol., 1987–94; Crafts Council, 1984–88; Museums and Galleries Commn, 1985–92; Trustee: Natural Hist. Museum, 1974–84; Wolfson Foundn, 1978–88; Patron, English Place Name Soc. Chairman: Edward Boyle Meml Trust, 1982–; Council, Royal Post-grad. Med. Sch., 1979–90 (Pres., 1990–). Prime Warden, Goldsmiths' Co., 1982–83. Foreign Member: Swedish Acad. of Sci., 1968; Amer. Acad. of Arts and Scis, 1972; Acad. of Scis, Göttingen, 1975; Acad. Mediterranae della Scienze, 1982; Amer. Philos. Soc., 1991. Privelegeiate, St Hilda's Coll., Oxford; Hon. Fellow: Goldsmiths' Coll., London, 1985; Queen Mary Coll., London, 1985; Birkbeck Coll., London, 1986; RPMS, 1990; Hon. FRCP 1979; Hon. FRSC 1983; Hon. FRCR 1984; Hon. FLA 1986. Hon. ScD: Łódź, 1966; Dublin, 1968; Hon. DSc: Bath Univ. of Technology, 1970; Loughborough Univ. of Technology, 1970; Heriot-Watt, 1970; Warwick, 1970; Strathclyde, 1971; Exeter, 1971; QUB, 1971; Manchester, 1972; E Anglia, 1972; Leeds, 1973; McMaster, 1975; Uppsala, 1977; Liverpool, Salford, 1979; Kent, 1981; Hon. LLD: Nottingham, 1970; Aberdeen, 1972; Sheffield, Cambridge, 1979; London, 1984; Lancaster, 1989; Hon. DCL Oxford, 1988; Hon. DLitt CNAA, 1991. Sylvanus Thompson Medal, BIR, 1958; Davy Medal, Royal Soc., 1969; Faraday Medal, RSC, 1974; Crookshank Medal, RCR, 1981; 1300 Years Bulgaria Medal, 1982; Curie Medal, Poland, 1983; John Snow Medal, Coll. Anaesthetists, 1987; Firth Medal, Forensic Science Soc., 1993. Kt Comdr, Order of Merit (Poland), 1985. *Publications:* Chain Reactions, 1956; (ed and contrib.) Photochemistry and Reaction Kinetics, 1967; Choosing a British University, 1981; (contrib.) The Parliament of Science, 1981; Universities and the National Health Service, 1983; papers on physico-chemical subjects in scientific jls. *Recreation:* walking. *Address:* 36 Charlbury Road, Oxford OX2 6UX. *T:* Oxford (01865) 510868. *Club:* Athenæum.

DAINTY, Prof. (John) Christopher, PhD; Pilkington Professor of Applied Optics, Imperial College of Science and Technology, University of London, since 1984; *b* 22 Jan. 1947; *s* of Jack Dainty and Mary Elizabeth (*née* Elbeck); *m* 1978, Janice Hancock; one *s* one *d*. *Educ:* George Heriot's, Edinburgh; City of Norwich Sch.; Polytechnic of Central London (Diploma); Imperial Coll. of Science and Technol. (MSc; PhD 1972). Lectr, Queen Elizabeth Coll., Univ. of London, 1974–78; Associate Prof., Inst. of Optics, Univ. of Rochester, NY, USA, 1978–83. Sen. Res. Fellow, SERC, 1987–92. Pres., Internat. Commn for Optics, 1990–93. Internat. Commn of Optics Prize, 1984; Thomas Young Medal and Prize, Inst. of Physics, 1993. *Publications:* (with R. Shaw) Image Science, 1974; (ed) Laser Speckle and Related Phenomena, 1975, 2nd edn 1984; (ed. with M. Nieto-Vesperinas) Scattering in Volumes and Surfaces, 1989; scientific papers. *Address:* Blackett Laboratory, Imperial College of Science and Technology, SW7 2AZ. *T:* 0171–594 7712.

DAKERS, Lionel Frederick, CBE 1983; DMus; FRCO; Director, Royal School of Church Music, 1972–89 (Special Commissioner, 1958–72); Examiner to the Associated Board of the Royal Schools of Music, 1958–94; Director, Hymns Ancient and Modern, since 1976; *b* Rochester, Kent, 24 Feb. 1924; *o s* of late Lewis and Ethel Dakers; *m* 1951, Mary Elisabeth, *d* of Rev. Claude Williams; four *d*. *Educ:* Rochester Cathedral Choir Sch. Studied with H. A. Bennett, Organist of Rochester Cathedral, 1933–40, with Sir Edward Bairstow, Organist of York Minster, 1943–45, and at Royal Academy of Music, 1947–51. Organist of All Saints', Frindsbury, Rochester, 1939–42. Served in Royal Army Educational Corps, 1943–47. Cairo Cathedral, 1945–47; Finchley Parish Church, 1948–50; Asst Organist, St George's Chapel, Windsor Castle, 1950–54; Asst Music Master, Eton Coll., 1952–54; Organist of Ripon Cathedral, 1954–57; Conductor Ripon Choral Soc. and Harrogate String Orchestra, 1954–57; Hon. Conductor, Exeter Diocesan Choral Association, 1957–72; Lectr in Music, St Luke's Coll., Exeter, 1958–70; Organist and Master of the Choristers, Exeter Cathedral, 1957–72; Conductor: Exeter Musical Soc., 1957–72; Exeter Chamber Orchestra, 1959–65. President: Incorporated Assoc. of Organists, 1972–75; London Assoc. of Organists, 1976–78; ISM, 1990–91; Vice-President: Fedn of Cathedral Old Choristers' Assocs, 1980–; Herbert Howells Soc., 1987–; Church Music Soc., 1990–; Mem. Council, Royal Coll. of Organists, 1967– (Pres., 1976–78); Sec., Cathedral Organists' Assoc., 1972–88. Chairman: Organs Adv. Cttee of Council for Care of Churches of C of E, 1974–; Nat. Learn the Organ Year, 1989–90; Friends of the Musicians' Chapel, 1988–; Salisbury Diocesan Adv. Cttee, 1990–; Nat. Organ Teachers' Encouragment Scheme, 1990–92. Member: Archbishops' Commn in Church Music, 1988–92; Salisbury Diocesan Liturgical Adv. Cttee, 1992–. Lay Canon, Salisbury Cathedral, 1993–. Gov., Godolphin Sch., 1990–94. Trustee, Ouseley Trust, 1990–. Hon. Mem., US Assoc. of Anglican Musicians, 1978; Hon. Life Mem., Methodist Church Music Soc., 1990. ARCO, 1944; FRCO, 1945; ADCM, 1952; BMus Dunelm, 1951; ARAM 1955; FRAM, 1962; FRSCM 1969; FRCM 1980. Fellow, St Michael's Coll., Tenbury, 1973. Hon. Fellow, Westminster Choir Coll., USA, 1975. Hon. DMus: Lambeth, 1979; Exeter, 1990. Compositions: church music, etc. *Publications:* Church Music at the Crossroads, 1970; A Handbook of Parish Music, 1976; Making Church Music Work, 1978; (ed) Music and the Alternative Service Book, 1980; (ed) The Choristers Companion, 1980; (ed) The Psalms—their use and performance today, 1980; The Church Musician as Conductor, 1982; Church Music in a Changing World, 1984; Choosing and Using Hymns, 1985; (ed) New Church Anthem Book, 1992; The Church Anthem Handbook, 1994. *Recreations:* book collecting, gardening, continental food, travel. *Address:* 6 Harcourt Terrace, Salisbury, Wilts SP2 7SA. *T:* Salisbury (01722) 324880. *Clubs:* Athenæum; St Wilfrid's (NY) (Hon. mem.).

DAKIN, Dorothy Danvers, OBE 1982; JP; Assistant Chaplain, HM Prison and Remand Centre, Pucklechurch, 1984–87; *b* 22 Oct. 1919; *d* of Edwin Lionel Dakin, chartered civil engr and Mary Danvers Dakin (*née* Walker), artist. *Educ:* Sherborne Sch. for Girls; Newnham Coll., Cambridge. MA Geography. 2nd Officer WRNS (Educn), 1943–50; Housemistress, Wycombe Abbey Sch., 1950–60; Headmistress, The Red Maids' School, Bristol, 1961–81; Chm., ISIS Assoc., 1982–84. President: West of England Br., Assoc. of Headmistresses, 1969–71; Assoc. of Headmistresses of Girls' Boarding Schs, 1971–73; Girls' Schs Assoc. (Independent), 1973–75; Chm. Council, ISIS, 1975–81. Licensed Reader, C of E, 1982–. FRSA 1988. JP Bristol, 1974. *Recreations:* fencing, painting, travel, embroidery. *Address:* 41 Park Grove, Henleaze, Bristol BS9 4LF.

DALAI LAMA; *see* Tenzin Gyatso.

DALAL, Maneck Ardeshir Sohrab; Director: Tata Ltd, SW1, since 1977 (Managing Director, 1977–88; Vice-Chairman, 1989–94); Tata Industries, Bombay, since 1979; *b* 24 Dec. 1918; *s* of Ardeshir Dalal, OBE and Amy Dalal; *m* 1947, Kathleen Gertrude Richardson; three *d*. *Educ:* Trinity Hall, Cambridge (MA). Cambridge Univ. Captain, tennis and squash rackets. Called to the Bar, Middle Temple, 1945. Manager: Air-India New Delhi, 1946–48; Air-India London, 1948–53; Regional Traffic Manager, 1953–59; Regional Director, 1959–77; Minister for Tourism and Civil Aviation, High Commn for India, 1973–77. President: Indian Chamber of Commerce in Great Britain, 1959–62; Indian Management Assoc. of UK, 1960–63; UK Pres., World Conf. on Religions and Peace, UK and Ireland Gp, 1985–; Vice-Pres., Friends of Vellore, 1979–; Chairman: Foreign Airlines Assoc. of UK, 1965–67; Indian YMCA in London, 1972–; Bharatiya Vidhya Bhavan in London (Indian Cultural Inst. of Gt Britain), 1975–; Northbrook Soc., 1985– (Mem. Cttee, 1975–); Indian Women's Educn Assoc., 1985– (Mem. Cttee, 1975–); Vice-Chm., Fest. of India in GB, 1980–81; Member: Sub-Cttee on Transport, Industrial Trng Bd of GB, 1975–77; Assembly, British Council of Churches, 1984–87; Internat. Bd, United World Colls, 1985–; Bd Govs, Nat. Inst. for Social Work, 1986–; Chm. Central Council, Royal Over-Seas League, 1986–89 (Dep. Chm. Central Council, 1982–86; Mem., 1974–; Vice-Pres., 1989–). Patron, Internat. Centre for Child Studies, 1984–. FCIT 1975; FIMgt. *Recreations:* reading, walking. *Address:* Tall Trees, Marlborough Road, Hampton, Mddx TW12 3RX. *T:* 0181–979 2065. *Clubs:* Hurlingham, Royal Over-Seas League, MCC; Hawks (Cambridge).

DALBY, Ven. John Mark Meredith; Archdeacon of Rochdale, since 1991; *b* 3 Jan. 1938; *s* of William and Sheila Mary Dalby (*née* Arkell). *Educ:* King George V Sch., Southport; Exeter Coll., Oxford, (MA 1965); Ripon Hall, Oxford; Univ. of Nottingham (PhD 1977). Ordained deacon 1963, priest 1964; Curate: Hambleden, Bucks, 1963–68; Fawley, Fingest, Medmenham and Turville, Bucks, 1965–68; Vicar of St Peter, Spring Hill, Birmingham, 1968–75; Rural Dean of Birmingham City, 1973–75; Sec., Cttee for Theol Educn, and Selection Sec., ACCM, 1975–80; Hon. Curate of All Hallows, Tottenham, 1975–80; Vicar of St Mark, Worsley, 1980–84; Team Rector of Worsley, 1984–91; Rural Dean of Eccles, 1987–91. Examining Chaplain to the Bp of Manchester, 1980–. Member: Gen. Synod of C of E, 1985–; Liturgical Commn, 1986–. *Publications:* Open Communion in the Church of England, 1959; The Gospel and the Priest, 1975; Tottenham Church and Parish, 1979; The Cocker Connection, 1989; Open Baptism, 1989. *Recreations:* travel, family history, philately, liturgy. *Address:* 21 Belmont Way, Rochdale OL12 6HR. *T:* Rochdale (01706) 48640. *Club:* Commonwealth Trust.

DALBY, Dr (Terry) David (Pereira); Reader in West African Languages, School of Oriental and African Studies, University of London, 1967–83, now Emeritus; Directeur, Observatoire linguistique, since 1987; *b* 7 Jan. 1933; *s* of Ernest Edwin Dalby and Rose Cecilia Dalby; *m* 1st, 1957, Winifred Brand; two *d*; 2nd, 1982, Catherine Jansens; one *s*. *Educ:* Cardiff High Sch.; Queen Mary Coll., London (BA 1954, PhD 1961; Hon. Life Mem., Queen Mary Coll. Union Soc., 1954). Served to Lieut, Intell. Corps, 1954–56. United Africa Co. Ltd, London and W Africa, 1957–60; Lectr in Mod. Languages, University Coll. of Sierra Leone, 1961–62; Lectr in W African Langs, SOAS, Univ. of London, 1962–67. Hanns Wolff Vis. Prof., Indiana Univ., 1969. Chm., Centre for Afr. Studies, Univ. of London, 1971–74; Dir, Internat. African Inst., 1974–80; Chairman: Internat. Conf. on Manding Studies, 1972, and Drought in Africa Conf., 1973; UK Standing Cttee on Univ. Studies of Africa, 1978–82 (Dep. Chm., 1975–78). Vice-Pres., Unesco Meeting on Cultural Specificity in Africa, Accra, 1980. Member: Governing Body, SOAS, 1969–70; Council, African Studies Assoc. of UK, 1970–73; Cttee of Management, British Inst. in Paris, 1975–82; Conseil Internat. de Recherche et d'Etude en Linguistique Fondamentale et Appliquée, 1980– (Président, 1984); Centre Internat. de Recherche sur le Bilinguisme, Laval Univ., Que, 1981–; Eur. Council on African Studies, 1985–; Centre Internat. des Industries de la Langue, Univ. Paris X, 1993–; Comité Français des Etudes Africaines, 1993–. Hon. Mem., SOAS, 1983. Editor, African Language Review, 1962–72; Co-editor, Africa, 1976–80. *Publications:* Lexicon of the Mediaeval German Hunt, 1965; Black through White: patterns of communication in Africa and the New World, 1970; (ed) Language and History in Africa, 1970; (ed jtly) Drought in Africa, 1st vol. 1973, 2nd vol. 1978; Language Map of Africa and the adjacent islands, 1977; Clavier international de Niamey, 1984; (jtly) Les langues et l'espace du français, 1985; Afrique et la lettre, 1986; (jtly) Thesaurus of African Languages, 1987; (ed) World Language Register, 1993–; articles in linguistic and other jls. *Recreations:* cartography, local history. *Address:* Cressenville, 27440 Ecouis, France. *T:* 32493560.

DALE, Barry Gordon, FCA; Group Chief Executive, Littlewoods Organisation Plc, 1993–95 (Group Finance Director, 1988–92; Group Chief Executive designate, 1992–93); *b* 31 July 1938; *s* of Francis and Catherine Dale; *m* 1963, Margaret (*née* Fairbrother); one *s* one *d*. *Educ:* Queen Elizabeth Grammar Sch., Blackburn. Coopers Lybrand, Montreal, 1960–62; Pilkington Brothers Glass, St Helens, 1962–65; ICI, 1965–85: Mond Div., Cheshire, 1966–68; Head Office, 1968–72; Dep. Chief Acct, Mond Div., 1972–78; Finance Dir, ICI Latin America (Wilmington, USA), 1978–80; Chief Acct, Organics Div., Manchester, 1980–84; Bd Mem. for Finance, LRT, 1985–88. Director: Ellis & Everard, 1978–81; Magadi Soda Co. (Kenya), 1980–82; London Buses Ltd, 1985–88; London Underground Ltd, 1985–88; LRT Bus Engineering Ltd, 1985–88; Chairman: London Transport Trustee Co., 1985–88; London Transport Pension Fund Trustees, 1985–88; Datanetworks, 1987–88. *Recreations:* golf, fell walking, other sports. *Address:* c/o The Littlewoods Organisation Plc, 100 Old Hall Street, Liverpool L70 1AB. *T:* 0151–235 2181. *Clubs:* Tatton (Knutsford); West Surrey Golf, Knutsford Golf.

DALE, David Kenneth Hay, CBE 1976; Governor, Montserrat, West Indies, 1980–85, retired 1988; *b* 27 Jan. 1927; *s* of Kenneth Hay Dale and Francesca Sussana Hoffman; *m* 1956, Hanna Szydlowska; one *s*. *Educ:* Dorchester Grammar Sch. Joined Queen's Royal Regt, 1944; 2/Lieut 8th Punjab Regt, 1945; Lieut 4 Bn (PWO) 8th Punjab Regt, 1946; Lieut Royal Regt of Artillery, 1948, Captain 1955: served Kenya and Malaya (despatches); Dist Officer, Kenya, 1960, Dist Comr, 1962; Admin Officer Cl. B, subseq. Cl. A, Anglo-French Condominium, New Hebrides, W Pacific, 1965–73; Perm. Sec., Min. of Aviation, Communications and Works, Seychelles, 1973–75; Dep. Governor, Seychelles, 1975; Sec. to Cabinet, Republic of Seychelles, 1976; FCO, 1977–80. Clerk, Shipwrights' Co., 1986–87. Pres., Somerton Frome Constit. Cons. Assoc., 1994– (Vice-Chm., Finance, 1990–94). *Recreations:* birdwatching, walking, colonial and military history. *Address:* Chatley Cottage, Batcombe, near Shepton Mallet, Somerset BA4 6AF. *T:* Upton Noble (0174985) 449. *Club:* East India.

DALE, Jim; actor, singer, composer, lyricist; *b* 15 Aug. 1935; *m*; three *s* one *d*. *Educ:* Kettering Grammar School. Music Hall comedian, 1951; singing, compèring, directing, 1951–61; films, 1965–, include: Lock Up Your Daughters, The Winter's Tale, The Biggest Dog in the World, National Health, Adolf Hitler—My Part in his Downfall, Joseph Andrews, Pete's Dragon, Bloodshy, The Spaceman and King Arthur, Scandalous, Carry on Columbus. Joined Frank Dunlop's Pop Theatre for Edinburgh Festival, 1967–68; National Theatre, 1969–71: main roles in National Health, Love's Labour's Lost, Merchant of Venice, Good-natured Man, Captain of Kopenick; also appeared at Young Vic in Taming of the Shrew, Scapino (title rôle and wrote music); title rôle in musical The Card, 1973; Compère of Sunday Night at the London Palladium, 1973–74; Scapino (title rôle),

Broadway, 1974–75 (Drama Critics' and Outer Circle Awards for best actor; Tony award nomination for best actor); Privates on Parade, Long Wharf Theatre, New Haven, Conn., 1979; Barnum, Broadway, 1980 (Tony award for best actor in a musical, Drama Desk Award); A Day in the Death of Joe Egg, NY, 1985 (Tony nomination for best actor; Outer Circle Award for best actor); Me and My Girl, NY, 1987–88; Privates on Parade, NY, 1989; television includes: host of Ringling Brothers Barnum and Bailey Circus (TV special), 1985; Adventures of Huckleberry Finn, 1985. Composed film music for: The Winter's Tale, Shaliko, Twinky, Georgy Girl (nominated for Academy Award), Joseph Andrews. *Address:* c/o Gottlieb, Schiff, Bomser & Sendroff, PC, 555 5th Avenue, New York, NYC 10017, USA. *T:* (212) 9221880.

DALE, Robert Alan; business consultant; Director, Business Development, Lucas Industries plc, 1992–93; *b* 31 Oct. 1938; *s* of Horace and Alice Dale; *m* 1963, Sheila Mary Dursley; one *s* one *d*. *Educ:* West Bromwich Grammar Sch.; Birmingham Univ. (BA Hons). Joined Lucas Industries as graduate apprentice, 1960; first management appt, 1965; first Bd appt, 1971; Dir, Lucas CAV, 1972–77; Dir and Gen. Man., Lucas Batteries, 1978–81; joined Exec. Cttee of Lucas (Joseph Lucas Ltd), 1980; Managing Director: Lucas World Service, 1981–85; Lucas Electrical, 1985–87; Lucas Automotive, 1987–92; Dir, Lucas Industries, 1987–93. *Recreations:* sport, photography, travel.

DALE, Sir William (Leonard), KCMG 1965 (CMG 1951); International legal consultant; Director of Studies, Government Legal Advisers Course, since 1976; *b* 17 June 1906; *e s* of late Rev. William Dale, Rector of Preston, Yorks; *m* 1966, Mrs Gloria Spellman Finn, Washington, DC; one *d*. *Educ:* Hymers Coll., Hull; London (LLB); Barrister, Gray's Inn, 1931. Asst Legal Adviser, Colonial and Dominions Offices, 1935; Min. of Supply, 1940–45; Dep. Legal Adviser, Colonial and Commonwealth Relations Offices, 1945; Legal Adviser, United Kingdom of Libya, 1951–53; Legal Adviser: Min. of Educn, 1954–61; CRO, subseq. CO, 1961–66. Special Asst to the Law Officers, 1967–68; Gen. Counsel, UNRWA, Beirut, 1968–73. Hon. LLD Hull, 1978. *Publications:* Law of the Parish Church, 1932, 6th edn 1989; Legislative Drafting: a new approach, 1977; The Modern Commonwealth, 1983; (ed) Anglo-French Statutory Drafting, 1987; Preparation and Accessibility of the Written Law in France, 1993; Time Past Time Present (autobiog.), 1994; contributions to journals. *Recreation:* music (except Wagner). *Address:* 20 Old Buildings, Lincoln's Inn, WC2A 3UP. *T:* 0171–242 9365. *Club:* Travellers'.

DALES, Richard Nigel, CMG 1993; HM Diplomatic Service; High Commissioner, Zimbabwe, since 1992; *b* 26 Aug. 1942; *s* of late Kenneth Richard Frank Dales and of Olwen Mary (*née* Preedy); *m* 1966, Elizabeth Margaret Martin; one *s* one *d*. *Educ:* Chigwell Sch.; St Catharine's Coll., Cambridge (BA 1964). Entered FO, 1964; Third Sec., Yaoundé, Cameroon, 1965–67; FCO, 1968–70; Second Sec., later First Sec., Copenhagen, 1970–73; FCO, 1973; Asst Private Sec. to Foreign and Commonwealth Sec., 1974–77; First Sec., Head of Chancery and Consul, Sofia, Bulgaria, 1977–81; FCO, 1981; Counsellor and Head of Chancery, Copenhagen, 1982–86; Dep. High Comr, Harare, 1986–89; Head of Southern Africa, later Central and Southern Africa, Dept, FCO, 1989–91; Resident Chm. (FCO), CSSB, 1991–92. *Recreations:* music, walking. *Address:* c/o Foreign and Commonwealth Office, King Charles Street, SW1A 2AH. *Club:* United Oxford & Cambridge University.

DALEY, Judith Mary Philomena; Her Honour Judge Daley; a Circuit Judge, since 1994; *b* 12 Aug. 1948; *d* of James Patrick Daley and Mary Elizabeth Daley (*née* Rawcliffe), BA. *Educ:* Seafield Convent Grammar Sch., Crosby; King's Coll. London (LLB Hons). Called to the Bar, Gray's Inn, 1970; Asst Recorder, 1984; Recorder, 1989–94 (Northern Circuit). *Recreations:* swimming, travel, collecting antiques. *Address:* Warrington Combined Court Centre, Legh Street, Warrington, Cheshire WA1 1UR. *T:* Warrington (01925) 572192. *Club:* Liverpool Racquet.

DALGARNO, Prof. Alexander, PhD; FRS 1972; Phillips Professor of Astronomy, since 1977, Chairman of Department of Astronomy, 1971–76, Associate Director of Centre for Astrophysics, 1973–80, Harvard University; Member of Smithsonian Astrophysical Observatory, since 1967; *b* 5 Jan. 1928; *s* of William Dalgarno; *m* 1st, 1957, Barbara Kane (marr. diss. 1972); two *s* two *d*; 2nd, 1972, Emily Izsák (marr. diss. 1987). *Educ:* Southgate Grammar Sch.; University Coll., London (Fellow 1976). BSc Maths, 1st Cl. Hons London, 1947; PhD Theoretical Physics London, 1951; AM Harvard, 1967. The Queen's University of Belfast: Lectr in Applied Maths, 1952; Reader in Maths, 1956; Dir of Computing Lab, 1960; Prof. of Quantum Mechanics, 1961; Prof. of Mathematical Physics, 1966–67; Prof. of Astronomy, Harvard Univ., 1967–77; Acting Dir, Harvard Coll. Observatory, 1971–73. Chief Scientist, Geophysics Corp. of America, 1962–63. Spiers Meml Lectr, Faraday Div., RSC, 1992. Editor, Astrophysical Journal Letters, 1973–. Fellow: Amer. Acad. of Arts and Sciences, 1968; Amer. Geophysical Union, 1972; Amer. Physical Soc., 1980; Mem., Internat. Acad. Astronautics, 1972; Hon. MRIA 1988. FUMIST 1992. Hon. DSc QUB, 1980. Prize of Internat. Acad. of Quantum Molecular Sci., 1969; Hodgkins Medal, Smithsonian Instn, 1977; Davisson-Germer Prize, Amer. Physical Soc., 1980; Gold Medal, Royal Astronomical Soc., 1986; Meggers Prize, Optical Soc. of America, 1986; Fleming Medal, Amer. Geophys. Union, 1995. *Publications:* numerous papers in scientific journals. *Recreations:* squash, books. *Address:* c/o Harvard-Smithsonian Center for Astrophysics, 60 Garden Street, Cambridge, MA 02138, USA.

DALGETY, Ramsay Robertson; QC (Scot.) 1986; **Hon. Mr Justice Dalgety;** a Judge of the Supreme Court, Tonga, since 1991; *b* 2 July 1945; *s* of James Robertson Dalgety and Georgia Dalgety (*née* Whyte); *m* 1971, Mary Margaret Bernard; one *s* one *d*. *Educ:* High School of Dundee; Univ. of St Andrews (LLB Hons). Advocate, 1972; Temp. Sheriff, 1987–91. Dep. Traffic Comr for Scotland, 1988–93. Councillor, City of Edinburgh, 1974–80. Director/Chairman: Archer Transport Ltd and Archer Transport (London) Ltd, 1982–85; Venture Shipping Ltd, 1983–85. Director: Scottish Opera Ltd, 1980–90; Scottish Opera Theatre Trust Ltd, 1987–90; Chm., Opera Singers Pension Fund, 1990– (Dep. Chm., 1989–90; Trustee, 1983–); Dep. Chm., Edinburgh Hibernian Shareholders Assoc., 1990–92. *Recreations:* golf, boating, opera, travel, cricket, football. *Address:* Supreme Court, PO Box 11, Nuku'alofa, Kingdom of Tonga, South Pacific. *T:* 23599, *Fax:* 23098; Apartment–N, 116 Queensferry Road, Edinburgh EH4 2BT. *T:* 0131–332 1417. *Clubs:* Surrey County Cricket; Nuku'alofa (Tonga).

DALGLISH, Captain James Stephen, CVO 1955; CBE 1963; *b* 1 Oct. 1913; *e s* of late Rear-Adm. Robin Dalglish, CB; *m* 1939, Evelyn Mary, *e d* of late Rev. A. Ll. Meyricke, Vicar of Aislaby, near Whitby; one *s* one *d*. *Educ:* RN Coll., Dartmouth. Commanded HMS Aisne, 1952–53; HM Yacht Britannia, 1954, HMS Woodbridge Haven and Inshore Flotilla, 1958–59; HMS Excellent, 1959–61; HMS Bulwark, 1961–63; jssc 1950; idc 1957; retired from RN, 1963. Welfare Officer, Metropolitan Police, 1963–73. *Publication:* Life Story of a Fish (autobiog.), 1992. *Recreations:* gardening, painting. *Address:* Park Hill, Aislaby, Whitby, North Yorks YO21 1SW. *T:* Whitby (01947) 810213.

DALHOUSIE, 16th Earl of, *cr* 1633; **Simon Ramsay,** KT 1971; GCVO 1979; GBE 1957; MC 1944; LLD; Baron Ramsay, 1619; Lord Ramsay, 1633; Baron Ramsay (UK), 1875; Lord Chamberlain to the Queen Mother, 1965–92; Lord-Lieutenant of Angus, 1967–89; Chancellor, Dundee University, 1977–92; *b* 17 Oct. 1914; 2nd *s* of 14th Earl (*d* 1928) and Lady Mary Adelaide Heathcote Drummond Willoughby (*d* 1960), *d* of 1st Earl of Ancaster; *S* brother, 1950; *m* 1940, Margaret Elizabeth, *d* of late Brig.-Gen. Archibald and Hon. Mrs Stirling of Keir; three *s* two *d*. *Educ:* Eton; Christ Church, Oxford. Served TA, Black Watch, 1936–39; embodied, 1939. MP (C) for County of Angus, 1945–50; Conservative Whip, 1946–48 (resigned). Governor-General, Fedn of Rhodesia and Nyasaland, 1957–63. Hon. LLD: Dalhousie, 1952; Dundee, 1967. *Heir:* *s* Lord Ramsay, *qv*. *Address:* Brechin Castle, Brechin, Angus DD9 6SH. *T:* Brechin (013562) 2176; 199 Cranmer Court, Sloane Avenue, SW3 3HG. *T:* 0171–589 8938. *Club:* White's.

See also Sir J. C. L. Keswick, Earl of Scarbrough.

DALITZ, Prof. Richard Henry, FRS 1960; Professor Emeritus, Oxford University, and Emeritus Fellow of All Souls, since 1990; *b* 28 Feb. 1925; *s* of Frederick W. and Hazel B. Dalitz, Melbourne, Australia; *m* 1946, Valda (*née* Suiter) of Melbourne, Australia; one *s* three *d*. *Educ:* Scotch Coll., Melbourne; Univ. of Melbourne; Trinity Coll., Univ. of Cambridge, PhD Cantab, 1950. Lecturer in Mathematical Physics, Univ. of Birmingham, 1949–55; Research appointments in various Univs, USA, 1953–55; Reader in Mathematical Physics, Univ. of Birmingham, 1955–56; Prof. of Physics, Univ. of Chicago, 1956–66; Royal Soc. Res. Prof., Oxford Univ., 1963–90; Fellow of All Souls Coll., Oxford, 1964–90. Mem. Council, Royal Soc., 1979–81. Corresp. Mem., Australian Acad. of Science, 1978; Foreign Member: Polish Acad. of Sci., 1980; Nat. Acad. of India, 1990; For. Assoc., US Nat. Acad. Scis, 1991. Maxwell Medal and Prize, Institute of Physics and the Physical Soc., 1966; Bakerian Lectr and Jaffe Prize, 1969, Hughes Medal, 1975, Royal Medal, 1982, Royal Soc.; J. Robert Oppenheimer Meml Prize, Univ. of Miami, 1980; Harrie Massey Prize, Inst. of Physics and Aust. Inst. of Physics, 1990. *Publications:* Strange Particles and Strong Interactions, 1962 (India); Nuclear Interactions of the Hyperons, 1965 (India); (ed jtly) High Energy Physics, 1965 (New York); (jtly) Nuclear Energy Today and Tomorrow, 1971; numerous papers on theoretical physics in various British and American scientific jls. *Recreations:* mountain walking, travelling, biographical research, study of the Sorbian (Wendish) people, especially their language and emigration. *Address:* 1 Keble Road, Oxford OX1 3NP. *T:* Oxford (01865) 273966; All Souls College, Oxford.

DALKEITH, Earl of; Richard Walter John Montagu Douglas Scott, DL; *b* 14 Feb. 1954; *s* and *heir* of 9th Duke of Buccleuch, *qv*; *m* 1981, Lady Elizabeth Kerr, *d* of Marquess of Lothian, *qv*; two *s* two *d*. *Educ:* Eton; Christ Church, Oxford. Dir, Border Television, 1989–90. Member: Nature Conservancy Council, 1989–91; Nature Conservancy Council for Scotland, 1991–92; Scottish Natural Heritage, 1992– (Chm., SW Reg., 1992–95); IBA, 1990; ITC, 1991–; Millennium Fund Commn, 1994–. Dist Councillor, Nithsdale, 1984–90. DL Nithsdale and Annandale and Eskdale, 1987. *Heir:* *s* Lord Eskdaill, *qv*. *Address:* Dabton, Thornhill, Dumfriesshire. *T:* Thornhill (01848) 330467; 24 Lansdowne Road, W11 3LL. *T:* 0171–727 6573.

DALLEY, Christopher Mervyn, CMG 1971; MA Cantab; CEng; Director: London and Scottish Marine Oil Co. Ltd, 1979–84; *b* 26 Dec. 1913; *er s* of late Christopher Dalley; *m* 1947, Elizabeth Alice, *yr d* of late Lt-Gen. Sir James Gammell, KCB, DSO, MC; one *s* three *d*. *Educ:* Epsom Coll., Surrey; Queens' Coll., Cambridge. Served in RN, 1939–45. Joined British Petroleum Co., 1946; joined Oil Operating Companies in Iran, 1954: Asst Gen. Managing Dir, 1958; joined Iraq Petroleum Co. and associated companies, 1962, Man. Dir, 1963, Chm., 1970–73; Chm., Oil Exploration Holdings Ltd, 1973–79; Dir, Viking Resources Trust, 1973–84. Pres., Inst. of Petroleum, 1970; Mem. Council, World Petroleum Congress, 1970. Mem., Governing Body, Royal Medical Foundn (Epsom Coll.), 1970–94. *Address:* Mead House, Woodham Walter, near Maldon, Essex CM9 6RD. *T:* Chelmsford (01245) 222404. *Club:* Athenæum.

DALMENY, Lord; Harry Ronald Neil Primrose; *b* 20 Nov. 1967; *s* and *heir* of 7th Earl of Rosebery, *qv*; *m* 1994, Caroline, *e d* of Ronald Daglish and Mrs William Wyatt-Lowe. *Educ:* Dragon Sch., Oxford, Eton Coll.; Trinity Coll., Cambridge (BA Hons). *Address:* Dalmeny House, South Queensferry, West Lothian EH30 9TQ. *T:* 0131–331 1784. *Clubs:* Beefsteak; University Pitt (Cambridge); St Moritz Tobaggan.

DALRYMPLE, family name of **Earl of Stair.**

DALRYMPLE, Viscount; John David James Dalrymple; *b* 4 Sept. 1961; *s* and *heir* of 13th Earl of Stair, *qv*.

DALRYMPLE, Sir Hew (Fleetwood) Hamilton-, 10th Bt, *cr* 1697; KCVO 1985 (CVO 1974); JP; late Major, Grenadier Guards; Lord-Lieutenant of East Lothian, since 1987 (Vice-Lieutenant, 1973–87); *b* 9 April 1926; *er s* of Sir Hew (Clifford) Hamilton-Dalrymple, 9th Bt, JP; *S* father, 1959; *m* 1954, Lady Anne-Louise Mary Keppel, *d* of 9th Earl of Albemarle, MC, and of (Diana Cicely) Countess of Albemarle, *qv*; four *s*. *Educ:* Ampleforth. Commnd, Grenadier Guards, 1944; Staff Coll., Camberley, 1957; DAAG HQ 3rd Div., 1958–60; Regimental Adjt, Grenadier Guards, 1960–62; retd 1962. Adjt, 1964–85, Pres. of Council, 1988–, and Captain, Queen's Body Guard for Scotland (Royal Company of Archers). Vice-Chm., Scottish & Newcastle Breweries, 1983–86 (Dir, 1967–86); Chm., Scottish American Investment Co., 1967–91 (Dir, 1967–93). DL 1964, JP 1987, East Lothian. *Heir:* *e s* Hew Richard Hamilton-Dalrymple [*b* 3 Sept. 1955; *m* 1987, Jane Elizabeth, *yr d* of Lt-Col John Morris; one *s* two *d*. *Educ:* Ampleforth; Corpus Christi Coll., Oxford (MA); Clare Hall, Cambridge (MPhil); Birkbeck Coll., London (MSc). ODI Fellow, Swaziland, 1982–84]. *Address:* Leuchie, North Berwick, East Lothian EH39 5NT. *T:* North Berwick (01620) 892903. *Club:* Cavalry and Guards.

DALRYMPLE-HAMILTON of Bargany, Captain North Edward Frederick, CVO 1961; MBE 1953; DSC 1943; JP; DL; Royal Navy; *b* 17 Feb. 1922; *s* of Admiral Sir Frederick Dalrymple-Hamilton of Bargany, KCB; *m* 1st, 1949, Hon. Mary Colville (*d* 1981), *d* of 1st Baron Clydesmuir, PC, GCIE, TD, two *s*; 2nd, 1983, Antoinette, *widow* of Major Rowland Beech, MC. *Educ:* Eton. Entered Royal Navy, 1940; Comdr 1954; Captain 1960. Comdg Officer HMS Scarborough, 1958; Executive Officer, HM Yacht Britannia, 1959; Captain (F) 17th Frigate Squadron, 1963; Dir of Naval Signals, 1965; Dir, Weapons Equipment Surface, 1967; retd, 1970. Lieut, Royal Company of Archers, Queen's Body Guard for Scotland. DL 1973, JP 1980, Ayrshire. *Address:* Lovestone House, Bargany, Girvan, Ayrshire KA26 9RF. *T:* Old Dailly (01465) 871227. *Clubs:* Pratt's, MCC; New (Edinburgh).

DALRYMPLE-HAY, Sir James Brian, 6th Bt, *cr* 1798; estate agent, retired; *b* 19 Jan. 1928; *e s* of Lt-Col Brian George Rowland Dalrymple-Hay (*d* on active service, 1943) and Beatrice (*d* 1935), *d* of A. W. Inglis; *S* cousin, 1952; *m* 1958, Helen Sylvia, *d* of late Stephen Herbert Card and of Molly M. Card; three *d*. *Educ:* Hillsbrow Preparatory Sch., Redhill; Blundell's Sch., Tiverton, Devon. Royal Marine, 1946–47; Lieut Royal Marine Commando, 1947–49. Estate Agent and Surveyor's Pupil, 1949; Principal, 1955–67; Partner, Whiteheads PLC, Estate Agents, 1967, Dir, 1983–85; Principal, Dalrymple-Hay Overseas, 1985–87. *Heir:* *b* John Hugh Dalrymple-Hay [*b* 16 Dec. 1929; *m* 1962, Jennifer, *d* of late Brig. Robert Johnson, CBE; one *s*]. *Address:* The Red House, Church Street, Warnham, near Horsham, W Sussex RH12 3QW.

DALRYMPLE-WHITE, Sir Henry Arthur Dalrymple, 2nd Bt, *cr* 1926; DFC 1941 and Bar 1942; *b* 5 Nov. 1917; *o s* of Lt-Col Sir Godfrey Dalrymple-White, 1st Bt, and late

Hon. Catherine Mary Cary, *d* of 12th Viscount Falkland; *S* father 1954; *m* 1948, Mary (marr. diss. 1956), *o d* of Capt. Robert H. C. Thomas; one *s*. *Educ:* Eton; Magdalene Coll., Cambridge; London Univ. Formerly Wing Commander RAFVR. Served War of 1939–45. *Heir: s* Jan Hew Dalrymple-White, *b* 26 Nov. 1950. *Address:* c/o Aero Club of East Africa, PO Box 40813, Nairobi, Kenya.

DALSAGER, Poul Christian; Member, Commission of the European Communities, 1981–84; *b* 5 March 1929; *m* 1951, Betty Jørgensen; two *s*. *Educ:* grammar sch. Bank employee, 1945–64; Mem. (Social Democrat), Danish Parliament, 1964–81; Chm., Market Cttee of Parlt, 1971–73; Chm., Social-Democratic Gp in Parlt, 1978–79; Minister for: Agriculture and Fisheries, 1975–77 and 1979–81; Agriculture, 1977–78. Mem. and Vice Pres., European Parlt, 1973 and 1974. Delegate to UN Gen. Assembly, 1969–71. Mayor, Hjørring, 1990– (Dep. Mayor, 1986–90). *Address:* Gram Mikkelsensvej 12, 9800 Hjørring, Denmark.

DALTON, Sir Alan (Nugent Goring), Kt 1977; CBE 1969; DL; Chairman: Devon and Cornwall Development Company, 1988–91; British Railways (Western) Board, 1978–92; *b* 26 Nov. 1923; *s* of Harold Goring Dalton and Phyllis Marguerite (*née* Ash). *Educ:* Shendish Prep. Sch., King's Langley; King Edward VI Sch., Southampton. Man. Dir, English Clays, Lovering Pochin & Co. Ltd, 1961–84; Dep. Chm., 1968–84, Chm., 1984–89, English China Clays PLC. Member: Sun Alliance & London Assurance Group Bd, 1976–89; Western (formerly SW) Adv. Bd, Nat. Westminster Bank PLC, 1977–91; Director, Westland plc (formerly Westland Aircraft), 1980–85. CIMgt; FRSA. DL Cornwall, 1982. *Recreations:* sailing, painting, reading.

DALTON, Alfred Hyam, CB 1976; Deputy Chairman, Board of Inland Revenue, 1973–82 (Commissioner of Inland Revenue, 1970–82); *b* 29 March 1922; *m* 1946, Elizabeth Stalker (*d* 1992); three *d*. *Educ:* Merchant Taylors' Sch., Northwood; Aberdeen Univ. Served War, REME, 1942–45 (despatches). Entered Inland Revenue, 1947; Asst Sec., 1958; Sec. to Board, 1969. *Address:* 10 Courtmead Close, Burbage Road, SE24 9HW. *T:* 0171–733 5395.

DALTON, Vice-Adm. Sir Geoffrey (Thomas James Oliver), KCB 1986; President, Royal British Legion, since 1993; Secretary-General of Mencap, 1987–90; *b* 14 April 1931; *s* of late Jack Rowland Thomas Dalton and Margaret Kathleen Dalton; *m* 1957, Jane Hamilton (*née* Baynes); four *s*. *Educ:* Parkfield, Sussex; Reigate Grammar Sch.; RNC Dartmouth. Midshipman 1950; served in HM Ships Illustrious, Loch Alvie, Cockade, Virago, Flag Lieut to C-in-C The Nore, and HMS Maryton (in comd), 1950–61; served HMS Murray, RN Staff Course and HMS Dido, 1961–66; served HMS Relentless (in Comd), RN Sch. of PT, HMS Nubian (in Comd), Staff of Flag Officers Second in Comd Far East Fleet and Second Flotilla, 1966–72; Asst Dir of Naval Plans, 1972–74; RCDS, 1975; Captain RN Presentation Team, 1976–77; in Comd HMS Jupiter, 1977–79 and HMS Dryad, 1979–81; Asst Chief of Naval Staff (Policy), 1981–84; Dep. SACLANT, 1984–87. Commander, 1966; Captain, 1972; Rear-Adm. 1981; Vice-Adm. 1984. Vice Chm., Regular Forces Employment Assoc., 1993–. Gov., QMW, 1992–. Mem. Ct of Assts, Drapers' Co., 1989–. FIMgt (FBIM 1987). *Recreations:* tennis, fishing, gardening, walking. *Address:* Farm Cottage, Catherington, Portsmouth, Hants PO8 0TD. *Club:* Royal Over-Seas League.

DALTON, Prof. Howard, FRS 1993; Professor of Biological Sciences, Warwick University, since 1983; *b* 8 Feb. 1944; *s* of Leslie Alfred and Florence Dalton; *m* 1971, Kira Rozdestvensky; three *s* one *d*. *Educ:* Queen Elizabeth Coll., London Univ. (BSc); Univ. of Sussex (DPhil). Univs of London, 1962–65, and Sussex, 1965–68; Postdoctoral Fellow: Purdue Univ., Indiana, 1968–70; Sussex Univ., 1970–73; posts at Warwick Univ., 1973–. *Publications:* contribs to learned scientific jls. *Recreations:* Real tennis, Japanese gardening. *Address:* Groves Mill, Shakers Lane, Long Itchington, Warwickshire CV23 8QB. *T:* Marton (01926) 632746. *Club:* Leamington Tennis Court.

DALTON, Irwin, CBE 1986; Executive Vice-Chairman, 1985–88, and Chief Executive (Operations), 1986–88, National Bus Company; *b* 25 July 1932; *s* of Harry Farr Dalton and Bessie Dalton; *m* 1954, Marie Davies; two *d*. *Educ:* Cockburn High Sch., Leeds. FCA 1973; FCIT 1978. Accountancy profession, 1947–62; Asst Company Sec., 1962–67, Company Sec., 1968–70, West Riding Automobile, Wakefield; Company Sec., Crosville Motor Services, 1971–74; Dir and Gen. Manager, Ribble Motor Services, 1974–76; National Bus Company: Regional Dir, 1977–81; Mem. for Personnel Services, 1981–83; Exec. Bd Mem., 1983–84. Dir, Leyland Bus Gp, 1987–88. A Vice-Pres., Bus and Coach Council, 1983–87, Pres., 1987–88. *Recreations:* golf, other sporting activities. *Address:* Westview, 1 Birling Park Avenue, Birling Road, Tunbridge Wells, Kent TN2 5LQ. *T:* Tunbridge Wells (01892) 533459. *Club:* Tunbridge Wells Golf.

DALTON, Maurice Leonard, LVO 1986 (MVO 1981); HM Diplomatic Service; Assistant Marshal of the Diplomatic Corps and Assistant Head of Protocol Department, Foreign and Commonwealth Office, since 1992; *b* 18 May 1944; *s* of late Albert William Dalton and of Mildred Eliza (*née* Wraight); *m* 1982, Cathy Lee Parker. *Educ:* Hillside Sch., Folkestone. Joined FO, 1965; Enugu and Lagos, 1967–68; FCO, 1968–70; Attaché, Ankara, 1970–72; Third Secretary: E Berlin, 1973–74; Abu Dhabi, 1974–76; Second Sec., FCO, 1977–79; Second, later First Sec., Oslo, 1979–83; First Secretary: Kuala Lumpur, 1983–86; Peking, 1986; FCO, 1987–92. Royal Norwegian Order: of St Olav, 1981; of Merit, 1994. *Recreations:* cross-country ski-ing, sailing. *Address:* c/o Foreign and Commonwealth Office, King Charles Street, SW1A 2AH. *T:* 0171–210 6389.

DALTON, Peter Gerald Fox, CMG 1958; *b* 12 Dec. 1914; *s* of late Sir Robert (William) Dalton, CMG; *m* 1944, Josephine Anne Helyar; one *s* one *d*. *Educ:* Uppingham Sch.; Oriel Coll., Oxford. HM Embassy, Peking 1937–39; HM Consulate-Gen., Hankow, 1939–41; HM Embassy, Chungking, 1941–42; Foreign Office, 1942–46; HM Legation, Bangkok, 1946; HM Embassy, Montevideo, 1947–50; Foreign Office, 1950–53; Political Adviser, Hong Kong, 1953–56; Foreign Office, 1957–60; HM Embassy, Warsaw, 1960–63; HM Consul-General: Los Angeles, 1964–65; San Francisco, 1965–67; Minister, HM Embassy, Moscow, 1967–69; retd from HM Diplomatic Service, 1969. *Address:* North Lodge, North Street, Mayfield, Sussex TN20 6AN. *T:* Mayfield (01435) 873421.

DALTON, Richard John; HM Diplomatic Service; Consul General, Jerusalem, since 1993; *b* 10 Oct, 1948; *s* of Maj.-Gen. John Cecil D'Arcy Dalton, CB, CBE and Pamela Frances (*née* Segrave); *m* 1972, Elisabeth Mary Keays; two *s* two *d* (and one *s* decd). *Educ:* Winchester Coll.; Magdalene Coll., Cambridge (BA). Joined HM Diplomatic Service, 1970: FCO, 1971; MECAS, 1971–73; 3rd Sec., Amman, 1973–75; 2nd, later 1st, Sec., Mission to UN, NY, 1975–79; FCO, 1979–83; Dep. Head of Mission, Muscat, 1983–87; Dep. Head, Southern African Dept, FCO, 1987–88; Head, Tropical Foods Div. and Ext. Relns and Trade Div., MAFF, 1988–91; Vis. Fellow, RIIA, 1991–92; Head, CSCE Unit, FCO, 1992–93. *Publication:* Peace in the Gulf: a long term view, 1992. *Recreation:* land and woodland management. *Address:* c/o Foreign and Commonwealth Office, King Charles Street, SW1A 2AH; Hauxwell Hall, Leyburn, N Yorks DL8 5LR.

DALY, His Eminence Cardinal Cahal Brendan; *see* Armagh, Archbishop of, (RC).

DALY, Hon. Francis Lenton; His Honour Judge Daly; Judge of District Courts, Queensland, Australia, since 1989; *b* 23 June 1938; *s* of late Sydney Richard Daly and Lilian May Daly (*née* Lindholm); *m* 1964, Joyce Brenda (*née* Nicholls). *Educ:* Forest School; London School of Economics (LLB). Called to Bar, Gray's Inn, 1961 (Lord Justice Holker Exhibn). English Bar, 1961–66; Legal Secretary, Lord Chancellor's Office, 1966; Bermudian Bar, 1966–72; Asst Judge Advocate General to the Forces, UK, 1972–78; Principal Magistrate, Malaita, Solomon Islands, 1978; Attorney General, 1979, Chief Justice, 1980–84, Solomon Islands; Chief Justice, Nauru, 1983; admitted, Qld Bar, 1984. *Publications:* contribs to International and Comparative Law Qly, Commonwealth Judicial Jl. *Recreations:* yachting, rowing, reading. *Address:* Judges' Chambers, Court House, Cairns, Qld 4870, Australia. *T:* (70) 523408. *Club:* Cairns Yacht.
See also O. L. Aikin.

DALY, James, CVO 1994; HM Diplomatic Service; High Commissioner, Vanuatu, since 1995; *b* 8 Sept. 1940; *s* of late Maurice Daly and Christina Daly; *m* 1990, Dorothy Lillian Powell; two *s*. *Educ:* St Thomas More, Chelsea; University College London (BSc Hons Econ). Served RM, 1958–67. Joined Foreign Office, 1968: Third Secretary: Accra, 1971–73; Moscow, 1973–76; Second Sec., Karachi, 1976–78; First Secretary: FCO, 1978–79; Sofia, 1979–86; Consul-Gen., Paris, 1986–92; Counsellor and Consul-Gen., Moscow, 1992–95. *Recreations:* reading, music, walking. *Address:* c/o Foreign and Commonwealth Office, King Charles Street, SW1A 2AH. *Club:* Lansdowne.

DALY, Lawrence; General Secretary, National Union of Mineworkers, 1968–84, retired; *b* 20 Oct. 1924; *s* of James Daly and late Janet Taylor; *m* 1948, Renée M. Baxter; four *s* one *d*. *Educ:* primary and secondary schools. Glencraig Colliery (underground), 1939; Workmen's Safety Inspector, there, 1954–64. Part-time NUM lodge official, Glencraig, 1946; Chm., Scottish NUM Youth Committee, 1949; elected to Scottish Area NUM Exec. Cttee, 1962; Gen. Sec., Scottish NUM, 1964; National Exec., NUM, 1965. Mem., TUC General Council, 1971–81. TUC Gold Badge, 1981. *Publications:* (pamphlets): A Young Miner Sees Russia, 1946; The Miners and the Nation, 1968. *Recreations:* literature, politics, folk-song. *Address:* Glencraig, 45 Hempstead Lane, Potten End, Berkhamsted, Herts HP4 2RZ.

DALY, Margaret Elizabeth; *b* 26 Jan. 1938; *d* of Robert and Elizabeth Bell; *m* 1964, Kenneth Anthony Edward Daly; one *d*. *Educ:* Methodist Coll., Belfast. Departmental Head, Phoenix Assurance Co., 1956–60; Trade Union Official, Guild of Insurance Officials, later Union of Insurance Staffs, and subseq. merged with ASTMS, 1960–71; Consultant, Cons. Party, 1976–79; Nat. Dir of Cons. Trade Unionists, 1979–84. MEP (C) Somerset and Dorset W, 1984–94; Contested (C) Somerset and N Devon, Eur. Parly elecns, 1994; Mem., Develt Cttee, Eur. Parlt, 1984–94 (Vice Chm., 1987–89; Cons. spokesman, 1989–94); Vice-Pres., Jt EEC/African Caribbean Pacific Lomé Assembly, 1988–94. *Recreations:* swimming, music, travel. *Address:* The Old School House, Aisholt, Bridgwater, Somerset TA5 1AR.

DALY, Michael de Burgh, MA, MD, ScD Cambridge; FRCP; Emeritus Professor of Physiology in the University of London, since 1984; Visiting Scientist, Department of Physiology, Royal Free Hospital School of Medicine, London, since 1984; *b* 7 May 1922; *s* of late Dr Ivan de Burgh Daly, CBE, FRS; *m* 1948, Beryl Esmé, *y d* of late Wing Commander A. J. Nightingale; two *s*. *Educ:* Loretto Sch., Edinburgh; Gonville and Caius Coll., Cambridge; St Bartholomew's Hospital. Nat. Science Tripos. Part I, 1943, Part II, 1944, Physiology with Pharmacology. House-physician, St Bartholomew's Hospital, 1947; Asst Lecturer, 1948–50, and Lecturer, 1950–54, in Physiology, University Coll., London. Rockefeller Foundation Travelling Fellowship in Medicine, 1952–53; Locke Research Fellow of Royal Soc., 1955–58; St Bartholomew's Hospital Medical College: Prof. of Physiology, 1958–84; Governor, 1975–; Treas., 1983–84. Vis. Prof. of Physiology, Univ. of NSW, 1966; Vis. Lectr, Swedish Univs, 1959–60; G. L. Brown Lectr, Physiological Soc., 1985–86. Member: Personnel Res. Ethical Cttee, MoD (Navy) (formerly Adv. Panel for Underwater Personnel Res., MoD), 1975– (Chm., 1990–); MRC/RN Personnel Res. Cttee, Underwater Physiology Sub-Cttee, 1975–94; Res. Funds Cttee, British Heart Foundn, 1982–85; Chm., Armed Services Consultant Approval Bd in Applied Physiology/Aviation Medicine, MoD, 1989–. Chm., Editorial Bd of Monographs of Physiological Soc., 1981–87; Co-Editor of Journal of Physiology, 1956–63, 1984–89. FRSM 1959. Member: Soc. of Experimental Biol., 1965–; Physiological Soc., 1951–86 (Hon. Mem., 1986); Osler Med. Club, 1974–87; European Underwater Biomed. Soc., 1971–; Undersea Med. Soc. Inc., 1971–88. Schafer Prize in Physiology, University Coll., London, 1953; Thruston Medal, Gonville and Caius Coll., 1957; Sir Lionel Whitby Medal, Cambridge Univ., 1963; Gold Medal (jtly), BMA, 1972. *Publications:* contributor to: Lippold and Winton, Human Physiology; Starling, Principles of Human Physiology; Emslie-Smith, Paterson, Scratcherd and Read, Textbook of Physiology; papers on the integrative control of respiration and the cardiovascular system in Journal of Physiology; contrib. to film on William Harvey and the Circulation of the Blood. *Recreation:* model engineering. *Address:* 7 Hall Drive, Sydenham, SE26 6XL. *T:* 0181–778 8773.

DALY, Michael Francis, CMG 1989; HM Diplomatic Service, retired; *b* 7 April 1931; *s* of late William Thomas Daly and Hilda Frances Daly; *m* 1st, 1963, Sally Malcolm Angwin (*d* 1966); one *d*; 2nd, 1971, Juliet Mary Siragusa (*née* Arning); one step-*d*. *Educ:* Downside; Gonville and Caius Coll., Cambridge (Scholar; BA Hons). Mil. Service, 1952–54: 2nd Lieut, Intell. Corps. E. D. Sassoon Banking Co., London, 1954; Transreef Industrial & Investment Co., Johannesburg, 1955–66; General Electric Co., London, 1966; HM Diplomatic Service: 1st Sec., FCO, 1967; 1st Sec. (Commercial), Rio de Janeiro, 1969; 1st Sec. (Inf.) and Head of Chancery, Dublin, 1973; Asst, Cultural Relations Dept, FCO, 1976; Counsellor, Consul-Gen. and Head of Chancery, Brasilia, 1977–78; Ambassador to Ivory Coast, Upper Volta and Niger, 1978–83; Head of West African Dept, FCO, and Ambassador (non-resident) to Chad, 1983–86; Ambassador: to Costa Rica and (non-resident) to Nicaragua, 1986–89; to Bolivia, 1989–91. Chm., Anglo-Central American Soc., 1991–; Sec., Margaret Mee Amazon Trust, 1993–. *Recreations:* sailing, theatre, golf. *Address:* 45 Priory Road, Kew, Surrey TW9 3DQ. *T:* 0181–940 1272. *Clubs:* Canning; Johannesburg Country (S Africa); Andino, La Paz Golf (Bolivia).

DALY, Lt-Gen. Sir Thomas (Joseph), KBE 1967 (CBE 1953; OBE 1944); CB 1965; DSO 1945, Chief of the General Staff, Australia, 1966–71; *b* 19 March 1913; *s* of late Lt-Col T. J. Daly, DSO, VD, Melbourne; *m* 1946, Heather, *d* of late James Fitzgerald, Melbourne; three *d*. *Educ:* St Patrick's Coll., Sale; Xavier Coll., Kew, Vic; RMC, Duntroon (Sword of Honour). 3rd LH, 1934; attached for training 16/5 Lancers, India, 1938; Adj, 2/10 Aust. Inf. Bn, 1939; Bde Major, 18 Inf. Bde, 1940; GSO2 6 Aust. Div., 1941; GSO1 5 Aust. Div., 1942; Instructor, Staff Sch. (Aust.), 1944; CO 2/10 Inf. Bn, AIF, 1944; Instr, Staff Coll., Camberley, UK, 1946; Joint Services Staff Coll., Latimer, 1948; Dir of Mil. Art, RMC Duntroon, 1949; Dir of Infantry, AHQ, 1951; Comd 28 Brit. Commonwealth Inf. Bde, Korea, 1952; Dir, Ops and Plans, AHQ, 1953; IDC, London, 1956; GOC Northern Command, Australia, 1957–60; Adjt Gen., 1961–63; GOC, Eastern Command, Australia, 1963–66. Col Comdt, Royal Australian Regt, and Pacific Is Regt, 1971–75. Director: Jennings Industries Ltd, 1974–85; Fruehauf Australia Ltd, 1974–88; Associated Merchant Bank (Singapore), 1975–77. Mem., Nat. Council,

Australian Red Cross, 1972–75; Chm., Council, Australian Nat. War Memorial, 1974–82 (Mem., 1966–74); Councillor, Royal Agricl Soc. of NSW, 1972–85. Legion of Merit (US), 1953. *Recreations:* golf, watching football, cricket. *Address:* 16 Victoria Road, Bellevue Hill, NSW 2023, Australia. *Clubs:* Australian (Sydney); Ski Club of Australia (Thredbo, NSW); Royal Sydney Golf.

DALYELL, Kathleen Mary Agnes; National Trust for Scotland Administrator at The Binns, since 1972; Member, Royal Fine Art Commission for Scotland, since 1992; *b* 17 Nov. 1937; *o d* of Rt. Hon. Lord Wheatley and Agnes (Nancy) Lady Wheatley (*née* Nichol); *m* 1963, Tam Dalyell, *qv*; one *s* one *d*. *Educ:* Convent of the Sacred Heart, Aberdeen; Edinburgh Univ. (MA Hons History 1960); Craiglochart Teacher Trng Coll., Edinburgh. Teacher of History: St Augustine's Secondary Sch., Glasgow, 1961–62; James Gillespie's High Sch. for Girls, Edinburgh, 1962–63. Member: Historic Buildings Council for Scotland, 1975–87; Lady Provost of Edinburgh's Delegn to China, 1987; Nat. Cttee of Architectural Heritage Soc. for Scotland, 1983–89 (Vice-Chm., 1986–89); Ancient Monuments Bd for Scotland, 1989–. Chm., Bo'ness Heritage Trust, 1988–93; Dir, Heritage Educn Trust, 1987–; Trustee, Paxton Trust, 1988–92. *Publication:* House of The Binns, 1973. *Recreations:* reading, travel, chess, hill walking. *Address:* The Binns, Blackness, Linlithgow, Scotland EH49 7NA. *T:* Philipstoun (0150683) 4255).

DALYELL, Tam; MP (Lab) Linlithgow, since 1983 (West Lothian, 1962–83); *b* 9 Aug. 1932; *s* of late Gordon and Eleanor Dalyell; *m* 1963, Kathleen Dalyell, *qv*; one *s* one *d*. *Educ:* Eton; King's Coll., Cambridge; Moray House Teachers' Training Coll., Edinburgh. Trooper, Royal Scots Greys, 1950–52; Teacher, Bo'ness High Sch., 1956–60. Contested (Lab) Roxburgh, Selkirk, and Peebles, 1959. Dep.-Director of Studies on British India ship-school, Dunera, 1961–62. Member Public Accounts Cttee, House of Commons, 1962–66; Secretary, Labour Party Standing Conference on the Sciences, 1962–64; PPS to Rt Hon. Richard Crossman, Minister of Housing, Leader of H of C, Sec. of State for the Social Services, 1964–70; Opposition spokesman on science, 1980–82; Chairman: PLP Education Cttee, 1964–65; PLP Sports Group, 1964–74; PLP Foreign Affairs Gp, 1974–75; Vice-Chairman: PLP Defence and Foreign Affairs Gps, 1972–74; Scottish Labour Group of MPs, 1973–75; Parly Lab. Party, Nov. 1974–; Sub-Cttee on Public Accounts; Mem., Labour Party NEC, 1986–87. Member: European Parlt, 1975–79; European Parlt Budget Cttee, 1976–79; European Parlt Energy Cttee, 1979; Member: House of Commons Select Cttee on Science and Technology, 1967–69; Liaison Cttee between Cabinet and Parly Labour Party, 1974–76; Council, National Trust for Scotland. Mem. Scottish Council for Devlt and Industry Trade Delegn to China, Nov. 1971. Political columnist, New Scientist, 1967–. Hon. DSc Edinburgh, 1994. *Publications:* The Case of Ship-Schools, 1960; Ship-School Dunera, 1963; Devolution: the end of Britain?, 1977; One Man's Falklands, 1982; A Science Policy for Britain, 1983; Thatcher's Torpedo, 1983; Misrule, 1987; Dick Crossman: a portrait, 1989. *Recreations:* tennis, swimming. *Address:* The Binns, Linlithgow, Scotland EH49 7NA. *T:* Philipstoun (0150683) 4255.

DALZELL PAYNE, Henry Salusbury Legh, (Harry), CBE 1973; *b* 1929; *m* 1963, Serena Helen (marr. diss. 1980), *d* of Col Clifford White Gourlay, MC, TD; two *d*. *Educ:* Cheltenham; RMA Sandhurst; Staff Coll.; RCDS. Commissioned, 7th Hussars, 1949; served Queen's Own Hussars, 1957–66; seconded to Sultan of Muscat's Armed Forces, 1959–60; commanded: 3rd Dragoon Guards, 1967–69; 6th Armoured Bde, 1974–75; 3rd Armoured Div., 1979– 80 ; resigned, 1981. *Recreations:* travel, the turf, fine wines. *Clubs:* Cavalry and Guards, Turf, White's.

DALZIEL, Geoffrey Albert; British Commissioner, Leader of Salvation Army activities in Great Britain, 1974–80; *b* 10 Dec. 1912; *s* of Alexander William and Olive Mary Dalziel; *m* 1937, Ruth Edith Fairbank; two *s* one *d*. *Educ:* Harrow Elementary Sch. Commissioned Salvation Army Officer, 1934; Corps Officer in Gt Britain, to 1946; on Internat. Trng Coll. Staff, 1946–51; Divisional Youth Sec., 1951–59; Trng Coll. Principal, Melbourne, Aust., 1959–64; Chief Side Officer, Internat. Trng Coll., London, 1964–66; Chief Secretary: Sydney, Aust., 1966–68; Toronto, Canada, 1968–70; Territorial Comdr, Kenya, Uganda and Tanzania, E Africa, 1970–74. *Recreations:* walking, gardening, reading.

DALZIEL, Ian Martin; chairman and director of companies; *b* 21 June 1947; *s* of late John Calvin Dalziel and of Elizabeth Roy Dalziel, *e d* of Rev. Ian Bain, FRSE and Mrs Christian Stuart Fisher Bain, Gairloch; *m* 1972, Nadia Maria Iacovazzi; four *s*. *Educ:* Daniel Stewart's Coll., Edinburgh; St John's Coll., Cambridge (BA Hons 1968; LLB Hons 1969; MA 1972); Université Libre de Bruxelles (Weiner Anspach Foundation Scholarship, 1970); London Business Sch. Mullens & Co., 1970–72; Manufacturers Hanover Ltd, 1972–83. Mem., Richmond upon Thames Council, 1978–79. Mem. (C) Lothian, European Parlt, 1979–84. Chairman: Continental Assets Trust plc, 1989–; Cymbolic Sciences International Inc., 1992–; Venturi SA, 1992–94; CFC Daum SA, 1995–; Director: Adam & Co. Gp plc, 1983–92; Independent Insurance Co., 1989–91; Lepercq-Amcur Fund NV, 1989–; Gen. Man., Devin SA, 1992–; Consultant, Primwest Hldg NV, 1992–. *Recreations:* golf, shooting, tennis, ski-ing. *Address:* 13 Chemin des Meunières, 1222 Vésenaz, Switzerland. *T:* (22) 7525233; (business) 7 cours de Rive, 1204 Geneva, Switzerland. *T:* (22) 3104522, *Fax:* (22) 3104525. *Clubs:* Brooks's; New (Edinburgh); Royal and Ancient Golf (St Andrews).

DALZIEL, Malcolm Stuart, CBE 1984; international funding consultant, since 1991; Associate Consultant, since 1988, and Director, since 1990, Consultants in Economic Regeneration in Europe Services; *b* 18 Sept. 1936; *s* of late Robert Henderson Dalziel and Susan Aileen (*née* Robertson); *m* 1961, Elizabeth Anne Harvey; one *s* two *d*. *Educ:* Banbury Grammar Sch.; St Catherine's Coll., Oxford (BA 1960, MA 1965). National Service, 2nd Lieut Northamptonshire Regt, 1955–57. The British Council, 1960–87. Asst Educn Officer, Lahore, Pakistan, 1961–63; Regional Dir, Penang, Malaya, 1963–67; Regional Rep., Lahore, 1967–70; Rep., Sudan, 1970–74; Dir, Management Services Dept, and Dep. Controller, Estabs Div., 1975–79; Rep., Egypt, and Counsellor (Cultural) British Embassy, Cairo, 1979–83; Controller, Higher Educn Div., British Council and Sec., IUPC, 1983–87. Affiliate, Internat., Develt Centre, Queen Elizabeth House, Oxford Univ., 1988–. Dep. Chm., Council for Educn in the Commonwealth, 1990– (Mem. Exec. Cttee, 1986–); Mem. Court, Univ. of Essex, 1986–88. Vice-Pres., Northants CCC, 1990–. *Recreations:* theatre, ballet, walking, Rugby. *Address:* 368 Woodstock Road, Oxford OX2 8AE. *T:* Oxford (01865) 58969. *Club:* United Oxford & Cambridge University.

DAMER; *see* Dawson-Damer, family name of Earl of Portarlington.

DAMERELL, Derek Vivian; Governor, 1974–88, and Deputy Chairman, 1984–88, BUPA (Chief Executive, 1974–84); *b* 4 Aug. 1921; *s* of William James Damerell (Lt-Col), MBE and Zoe Damerell; *m* 1942, Margaret Isabel Porritt, *d* of Prof. B. D. Porritt; three *s* three *d*. *Educ:* ISC; Edinburgh Univ.; Harvard Business Sch. Parent Bd, BPB Industries, 1953–64; Regional Dir, Internat. Wool Secretariat, 1965–73. Dir, Murrayfield plc, 1982–87. Governor, Nuffield Nursing Homes Trust, 1974–80; Founder, Independ. Hosp. Gp (Chm., 1975–80); Internat. Fedn of Voluntary Health Service Funds: Mem. Council, 1976–; Dep. Pres., 1980–81, Pres., 1981–84; Mem. Bd of Governors, Assoc. Internat. de la Mutualité, 1974–83. *Recreations:* sailing (jt founder, BCYC, 1947); travel. *Address:* Chevry-sous-le-Bignon, 45210 Ferrières, France. *T:* 38909363. *Clubs:* various yacht.

DAMMERS, Very Rev. Alfred Hounsell, (Horace); Dean of Bristol, 1973–87; *b* 10 July 1921; *s* of late B. F. H. Dammers, MA, JP; *m* 1947, Brenda Muriel, *d* of late Clifford Stead; two *s* two *d*. *Educ:* Malvern Coll. (Schol.); Pembroke Coll., Cambridge (Schol., MA); Westcott House, Cambridge. Served RA (Surrey and Sussex Yeo.), 1941–44. Asst Curate, Adlington, Lancs, 1948; Asst Curate, S Bartholomew's, Edgbaston, Birmingham, and Lectr at Queen's Coll., Birmingham, 1950; Chaplain and Lectr at S John's Coll., Palayamkottai, S India, 1953; Vicar of Holy Trinity, Millhouses, Sheffield, and Examining Chaplain to Bishop of Sheffield, 1957; Select Preacher at Univ. of Cambridge, 1963; Select Preacher at Univ. of Oxford, 1975, 1989; Chairman, Friends of Reunion, 1965; Canon Residentiary and Director of Studies, Coventry Cathedral, 1965. Founder, The Life Style Movement, 1972. Companion, Community of the Cross of Nails, 1975. *Publications:* Great Venture, 1958; Ye Shall Receive Power, 1958; All in Each Place, 1962; God is Light, God is Love, 1963; AD 1980, 1966; Lifestyle: a parable of sharing, 1982; A Christian Life-style, 1986; Lord Make Us One, 1988. *Recreations:* travel (home and abroad); walking, candle making. *Address:* 4 Bradley Avenue, Shirehampton, Bristol BS11 9SL.

DANCE, Brian David, MA; Headmaster, St Dunstan's College, Catford, 1973–93; *b* 22 Nov. 1929; *s* of late L. H. Dance and late Mrs M. G. Swain (*née* Shrivelle); *m* 1955, Chloe Elizabeth, *o d* of late J. F. A. Baker, CB, FEng; two *s* two *d*. *Educ:* Kingston Grammar Sch.; Wadham Coll., Oxford. BA 1952, MA 1956. Asst Master, Kingston Grammar Sch., 1953–59; Sen. History Master: Faversham Grammar Sch., 1959–62; Westminster City Sch., 1962–65; Headmaster: Cirencester Grammar Sch., 1965–66; Luton Sixth Form Coll., 1966–73. Member: Cambridge Local Examination Syndicate, 1968–73; Headmasters' Assoc. Council, 1968–76 (Exec. Cttee, 1972–76, Hon. Legal Sec. 1975–76); Chm., London Area, SHA, 1984–85. Chm., Lewisham Environment Trust, 1987–88. *Publications:* articles in: Times Educnl Supp.; Headmasters' Assoc. 'Review'. *Recreations:* watching most ball games (especially cricket and Rugby football), music, philately, theatre. *Address:* 59 Albyfield, Bickley, Bromley, Kent BR1 2HY. *T:* 0181–467 9458.

DANCEY, Roger Michael, MA; Headmaster, City of London School, since 1995; *b* 24 Nov. 1945; *s* of Michael and Rosalind Dancey; *m* 1988, Elizabeth Jane Shadbolt; one step *s* one step *d*. *Educ:* Lancing Coll.; Exeter Univ. (MA). Careers Master, Whitgift Sch., 1972–76; Head of Sixth Form, Greenshaw High Sch., 1976–81; Sen. Master, Royal Grammar Sch., Worcester, 1982–86; Headmaster, King Edward VI Camp Hill Sch. for Boys, 1986–95. *Recreations:* cricket, golf, theatre, cinema. *Address:* City of London School, Queen Victoria Street, EC4V 3AL.

d'ANCONA, John Edward William, CB 1994; Director General, Offshore Supplies Office, Department of Trade and Industry (formerly of Energy), 1981–94; *b* 28 May 1935; *o s* of late Adolph and late Margaret d'Ancona; *m* 1958, Mary Helen, *o d* of late Sqdn-Ldr R. T. Hunter and late Mrs Hunter; three *s*. *Educ:* St Edward's Coll., Malta; St Cuthbert's Grammar Sch., Newcastle upon Tyne. BA (Hons) Mod. History, DipEd (Durham). Teacher, 1959–61; Civil Service, 1961–94: Asst Principal, Dept of Educn and Science, 1961; Private Sec. to Minister of State, DES, 1964–65; Principal: DES, 1965–67; Min. of Technology and DTI, 1967–74; Asst Sec., DoE, 1974; Under Sec., DoE OSO, 1981. *Recreations:* cricket, philately, wine-bibbing. *Address:* c/o Department of Trade and Industry, 1 Victoria Street, SW1H 0ET.

DANCY, Prof. John Christopher, MA; Professor of Education, University of Exeter, 1978–84, now Emeritus; *b* 13 Nov. 1920; *e s* of late Dr J. H. Dancy and Dr N. Dancy; *m* 1944, Angela Bryant; two *s* one *d*. *Educ:* Winchester (Scholar); New Coll., Oxford (Scholar, MA). 1st Class, Classical Hon. Mods., 1940; Craven Scholar, 1946; Gaisford Greek Prose Prize, 1947; Hertford Scholar, 1947; Arnold Historical Essay Prize, 1949. Served in Rifle Brigade, 1941–46; Capt. GSO(3)I, 30 Corps, 1945; Major, GSO(2)I, 1 Airborne Corps, 1945–46. Lecturer in Classics, Wadham Coll., 1946–48; Asst Master, Winchester Coll., 1948–53; Headmaster of Lancing Coll., 1953–61; Master, Marlborough Coll., 1961–72; Principal, St Luke's Coll. of Educn, Exeter, 1972–78. Dir, St Luke's Coll. Foundn, 1978–86. Member, Public Schools' Commission, 1966–68. Chm., Higher Educn Foundn, 1981–86. Chm., British Accreditation Council for Independent Further and Higher Educn, 1984–93. *Publications:* Commentary on 1 Maccabees, 1954; The Public Schools and the Future, 1963; Commentary on Shorter Books of Apocrypha, 1972. *Address:* Wharf House, Mousehole, Penzance, Cornwall TR19 6RX. *T:* Penzance (01736) 731137.

DANGAN, Viscount; Garret Graham Wellesley, (Jr); Manager, Ing (London) Derivatives Ltd, since 1991; *b* 30 March 1965; *s* and *heir* of 7th Earl Cowley, *qv*; *m* 1990, Claire Lorraine, *d* of P. W. Brighton, Stow Bridge, Norfolk; one *s*. *Educ:* Franklin Coll., Switzerland (Associate of Arts degree). Traded Options, Hoare Govett, 1985–88. *Heir: s* Hon. Henry Arthur Peter Wellesley; *b* 3 Dec. 1991. *Address:* c/o Grasmere, Stow Bridge, King's Lynn, Norfolk PE34 3PH.

DANIEL, Gerald Ernest, IPFA, FCA, IRRV; County Treasurer, Nottinghamshire County Council, 1974–84; *b* 7 Dec. 1919; *s* of Ernest and Beata May Daniel; *m* 1942, Ecila Roslyn Dillow; one *s* one *d*. *Educ:* Huish's Grammar Sch., Taunton. Served War, 1939–46, Somerset LI. Various appts in Borough Treasurers' Depts at Taunton, Scunthorpe and Bexhill, 1935–50; Cost and machine accountant, subseq. Chief Accountant, City Treasury, Bristol, 1950–60; Dep. Borough Treasurer, Reading, 1960–64; Borough Treasurer, West Bromwich, 1965–68; City Treasurer, Nottingham, 1968–74. Public Sector Advr, Pannell Kerr Forster, Chartered Accountants, 1984–93. Sec., 1971–76, Chm., 1976–81, Officers Side, Jt Negotiating Cttee for Chief Officers in Local Govt. Dir, Horizon Travel, 1975–85. Treasurer: E Midlands Airport, 1968–84; E Midlands Arts Assoc., 1969–84. President. Nottingham Soc. of Chartered Accountants, 1976; Assoc. of Public Service Finance Officers, 1978; Soc. of County Treasurers, 1979; Chartered Inst. of Public Finance and Accountancy, 1983–84 (Mem. Council, 1971–85; Vice-Pres., 1982). FMAAT (Mem. Council, 1981–83). FRSA. *Recreations:* gardening, music. *Address:* Brookvale, Star Lane, Blackboys, Uckfield, East Sussex TN22 5LD. *T:* Framfield (01825) 890712.

DANIEL, Sir Goronwy Hopkin, KCVO 1969; CB 1962; DPhil Oxon; HM Lieutenant for Dyfed, 1978–89; *b* Ystradgynlais, 21 March 1914; *s* of David Daniel; *m* 1940, Lady Valerie, *d* of 2nd Earl Lloyd George; one *s* two *d*. *Educ:* Pontardawe Secondary Sch.; Amman Valley County Sch.; University College of Wales, Aberystwyth; Jesus Coll., Oxford (Hon. Fellow, 1979). Fellow of University of Wales; Meyricke Scholar, Jesus Coll.; Oxford Institute of Statistics, 1937–40; Lecturer, Dept of Economics, Bristol Univ., 1940–41; Clerk, House of Commons, 1941–43; Ministry of Town and Country Planning, 1943–47; Ministry of Fuel and Power, Chief Statistician, 1947–55; Under-Sec., Coal Div., 1955–62, Gen. Div., 1962–64; Permanent Under-Sec. of State, Welsh Office, 1964–69; Principal, Aberystwyth UC, 1969–79; Vice-Chancellor, Univ. of Wales, 1977–79; Chm., Welsh Fourth Channel Authority, 1981–86. Pres., West Wales Assoc. for the Arts, 1971–85; Member: Welsh Language Council, 1974–78; Gen. Adv. Council, BBC, 1974–79; Adv. Council on Energy Conservation, 1977–79; SSRC, 1980–83; Dep. Chm., Prince of Wales' Cttee, 1980–86. Dir, Bank of Wales, 1972–90 (Dep. Chm., 1985–90). Chairman: Home-Grown Timber Adv. Cttee, 1974–81; Cttee on Water Charges in

Wales, 1974–75; Welsh Congregational Meml Coll., 1985–90; Working Gp on Powers and Functions of Univ. of Wales, 1988–89. Hon Mem., Gorsedd of Bards, 1966. Hon. LLD, Univ. of Wales, 1980. Hon. Freeman, City of London, 1982. *Publications:* papers in statistical, fuel and power, and other journals. *Recreations:* country pursuits, sailing. *Address:* Cae Ffynnon, 67 St Michaels Road, Cardiff CF5 2AN. *T:* Cardiff (01222) 553150. *Club:* Travellers'.

DANIEL, Gruffydd Huw Morgan; His Honour Judge Daniel; DL; a Circuit Judge, since 1986; Deputy Senior Judge, Sovereign Base Area, Cyprus, since 1995; *b* 16 April 1939; *s* of Prof. John Edward Daniel, MA, and Catherine Megan Daniel; *m* 1968, Phyllis Margaret (*née* Bermingham); one *d. Educ:* Ampleforth; University College of Wales (LLB); Inns of Court School of Law. Commissioned 2nd Lieut First Bn Royal Welch Fusiliers, 1959; Captain 6/7 Bn Royal Welch Fusiliers (TA), 1965; served MELF, Cyprus. Called to the Bar, Gray's Inn, 1967; Wales and Chester Circuit (Circuit Junior, 1975); Recorder, 1980–86; Asst Liaison Judge, 1983–87, Liaison Judge, 1988–, Gwynedd. Asst Parly Boundary Comr for Wales, 1981–82, 1985–86. Pres., Caerns Br., SSAFA, 1995. DL Gwynedd, 1993. *Recreations:* gardening, shooting, fishing, sailing. *Address:* (residence) Rhiwgoch, Halfway Bridge, Bangor, Gwynedd LL57 3AX. *Clubs:* Reform; Royal Anglesey Yacht, Bristol Channel Yacht.

DANIEL, Jack; *see* Daniel R. J.

DANIEL, John, MA; Headmaster, Royal Grammar School, Guildford, 1977–92; *b* 7 March 1932; *s* of John Daniel and Mary (*née* Young); *m* 1956, Heather Joy Retey; two *d. Educ:* Truro Sch.; New Coll., Oxford (Hons Modern Langs 1955). Thomas Hedley & Son, 1955–57; Linton Lodge Hotel, Oxford, 1957–59; Hartford Motors, Oxford, 1959–62; Royal Grammar Sch., Worcester, 1963–65; Malvern Coll., 1965–72; Royal Grammar School, Guildford: Dep. Headmaster, 1972–75; Acting Headmaster, 1975–77. Chm. of Govs, Tormead Sch., Guildford, 1981–. Asst Dir, Gap Activity Projects Ltd, 1994–. Chm., Guildford Symphony Orch., 1995–. *Recreations:* watching Rugby football, playing the piano and double bass. *Address:* 1 Orchard Road, Shalford, Guildford, Surrey GU4 8ER. *T:* Guildford (01483) 36033.

DANIEL, Sir John (Sagar), Kt 1994; DSc; Vice-Chancellor, Open University, since 1990; *b* 31 May 1942; *s* of John Edward Daniel and Winifred (*née* Sagar); *m* 1966, Kristin Anne Swanson; one *s* two *d. Educ:* Oxford Univ. (BA Metallurgy, MA); Univ. of Paris (DSc Metallurgy); Thorneloe Univ., Ont (Associate). Asst Prof., then Associate Prof., Ecole Polytechnique, Montreal, 1969–73; Dir, Etudes Télé-Univ., Univ. of Quebec, 1973–77; Vice Pres., Learning Services, Athabasca Univ., Alberta, 1979–80; Vice-Rector, Academic Affairs, Concordia Univ., Montreal, 1980–84; Pres., Laurentian Univ., Sudbury, Ont., 1984–90. Member: Higher Educn Quality Council, 1992–94; Council of Foundn, Internat. Baccalaureate, 1992–. Trustee, Carnegie Foundn for Advancement of Teaching, 1993–. Hon. Fellow, St Edmund Hall, Oxford, 1990. Hon. DLitt Deakin, Aust., 1985; Hon. DSc: Royal Mil. Coll., St Jean, Canada, 1988; Open Univ., Sri Lanka, 1994; Hon. DEd CNAA, 1992; Hon. LLD Univ. of Waterloo, Canada, 1993. Officier, Ordre des Palmes Académiques (France), 1991 (Chevalier, 1987). *Publications:* Learning at a Distance: a world perspective, 1982; numerous articles to professional pubns. *Address:* The Open University, Walton Hall, Milton Keynes MK7 6AA. *T:* Milton Keynes (01908) 653214.

DANIEL, Prof. Peter Maxwell, MA, MB, BCh Cambridge; MA, DM Oxon; DSc London; FRCP; FRCS; FRCPath (Founder Fellow); FRCPsych (Founder Fellow); FLS; FInstBiol; Senior Research Fellow, Department of Applied Physiology and Surgical Science, Hunterian Institute, Royal College of Surgeons, since 1976; Visiting Senior Research Fellow, St Thomas's Hospital Medical School, since 1981; Emeritus Professor, lately Professor of Neuropathology, University of London, at the Institute of Psychiatry, Maudsley Hospital, 1957–76; Emeritus Physician, Bethlem Royal and Maudsley Hospitals, since 1977; *b* 14 Nov. 1910; *s* of Peter Daniel, FRCS, surgeon to Charing Cross Hospital, and Beatrice Laetitia Daniel; *m* 1st, Sarah Shelford; two *s* three *d*; 2nd, F. Dawn Bosanquet; one *s*; 3rd, Marion F. Bosanquet. *Educ:* Westminster Sch.; St John's Coll., Cambridge; New Coll., Oxford. Hon. Consultant Pathologist, Radcliffe Infirmary, 1948–56; Senior Research Officer, University of Oxford, 1949–56; Hon. Consultant in Neuropathology to the Army at Home, 1952–77; Hon. Consultant Neuropathologist, Bethlem Royal and Maudsley Hosps, 1956–76. Emeritus Fellow, Leverhulme Trust, 1978–80; Hon. Librarian, RCPath, 1981–; Mem., Library Cttee, Linnean Soc., 1987–. John Hunter Medal and Triennial Prize, 1946–48, and Erasmus Wilson Lectr, 1964, RCS. Editorial Board of: Jl of Physiology, 1958–65; Jl of Neurology, Neurosurgery and Psychiatry, 1953–64; Journal of Neuroendocrinology, 1966–77; Brain, 1974–76; Qly Jl Exp. Physiol., 1980–84. President: British Neuropathological Society, 1963–64; Neurological Section, RSM, 1970–71; Harveian Soc. London, 1966 (Trustee, 1971–; Hon. Mem., 1985); Section of Hist. of Med., RSM, 1979–82; Osler Club, 1979–82; Mem. Council: Royal Microscopical Soc., 1968–72; Neonatal Soc., 1959–61; Assoc. of British Neurologists, 1966–69 (Hon. Mem., 1985); Med. Soc. of London, 1981– (Hon. Librarian, 1984–; Pres., 1987–88). Hon. Mem., Physiological Soc., 1981. Member: Bd of Govs, Bethlem Royal and Maudsley Hosps, 1966–75; Council, Charing Cross Hosp. Medical Sch., 1972–85. Chm., Academic Bd, Inst. of Psychiatry, 1966–70; Vice-Chm., Central Academic Council, British Postgrad. Med. Fedn, 1975–76; Mem., Bd of Studies in Physiology, Univ. of London, 1981–. Life Mem., Anatomical Soc. of GB. Liveryman, Soc. of Apothecaries, 1952–. *Publications:* (jointly) Studies of the Renal Circulation, 1947; The Hypothalamus and Pituitary Gland, 1975; papers in various medical and scientific journals. *Recreations:* books, medical history. *Address:* 5 Seaforth Place, Buckingham Gate, SW1E 6AB. *T:* 0171–834 3087. *Clubs:* Athenæum, Garrick, Green Room.

DANIEL, (Reginald) Jack, OBE 1958; FEng, FRINA, FIMarE; RCNC; *b* 27 Feb. 1920; *o s* of Reginald Daniel and Florence Emily (*née* Woods); *m* 1st, Joyce Earnshaw (marr. diss.); two *s*; 2nd, 1977, Elizabeth, *o d* of George Mitchell, Long Ashton, Som. *Educ:* Royal Naval Engineering Coll., Keyham; Royal Naval Coll., Greenwich. Grad., 1942; subseq. engaged in submarine design. Served War of 1939–45; Staff of C-in-C's Far East Fleet and Pacific Fleet, 1943–45. Atomic Bomb Tests, Bikini, 1946; Admty, Whitehall, 1947–49; Admty, Bath, Aircraft Carrier Design, 1949–52; Guided Missile Cruiser design, 1952–56; Nuclear and Polaris Submarine design, 1956–65; IDC, 1966; Materials, R&D, 1967–68; Head of Forward Design, 1968–70; Director, Submarine Design and Production, 1970–74; Dir-Gen. Ships and Head of RCNC, MoD, 1974–79; British Shipbuilders: Bd Mem., 1979; Man. Dir, for Warshipbuilding, 1980–83; Dir (Training, Educn, Safety), 1981–85; Dir of Technology (Warships), British Shipbuilders, 1983–84; Dir, British Shipbuilders Australia Pty, 1983–86. Dep. Chm., Internationale Schiff Studien GmbH Hamburg, 1984–88; Man. Dir, Warship Design Services Ltd, 1984–87; VSEL Canadian Project Dir, 1987–91; Director: VSEL Australia Pty, 1986–91; VSEL Defence Systems Canada Inc., 1987–91; Chm., VSEL-CAP, 1987–91. Vice Pres., RINA, 1982. Liveryman, Worshipful Co. of Shipwrights, 1980. Hon. Res. Fellow, UCL, 1974; Founder Fellow, Fellowship of Engineering, 1976. *Publications:* Warship Design, New Concepts and New Technology, Parsons Meml Lecture, 1976; papers for RINA, etc. *Recreations:* gardening, motoring, music. *Address:* Meadowland, Cleveland Walk, Bath BA2 6JU.

DANIEL, William Wentworth; independent social scientist; Director, Policy Studies Institute, 1986–93; *b* 19 Nov. 1938; *s* of late George Taylor Daniel and Margaret Elizabeth Daniel; *m* 1st, 1961, Lynda Mary Coles Garrett (marr. diss.); one *s* two *d*; 2nd, 1990, Eileen Mary Reid (*née* Loudfoot). *Educ:* Shebbear Coll., Devon; Victoria Univ. of Manchester (BA Hons); Univ. of Manchester Inst. of Science and Technology (MSc Tech). Directing Staff, Ashorne Hill Management Coll., 1963–65; Sen. Res. Officer, Research Services Ltd, 1965–67; Senior Research Fellow: Bath Univ., 1967–69; PSI (formerly PEP), 1969–81; Dep. Dir, PSI, 1981–86. Member: ESRC, 1992–; Eur. Foundn for Improvement of Living and Wkg Conditions, Dublin, 1992–. *Publications:* Racial Discrimination in England, 1968; Whatever Happened to the Workers in Woolwich?, 1972; The Right to Manage?, 1972; A National Survey of the Unemployed, 1974; Sandwich Courses in Higher Education, 1975; Pay Determination in Manufacturing Industry, 1976; Where Are They Now?: a follow-up survey of the unemployed, 1977; The Impact of Employment Protection Laws, 1978; Maternity Rights: the experience of women, 1980; Maternity Rights: the experience of employers, 1981; Workplace Industrial Relations in Britain, 1983; Workplace Industrial Relations and Technical Change, 1987; The Unemployed Flow, 1989; (with Terence Hogarth) Britain's New Industrial Gypsies, 1989. *Recreations:* golf, lawn tennis. *Address:* Flat 2, 64 Queensway, W2 3RL. *T:* 0171–229 6317; Chyvarton, Higher Upton, Bude, N Cornwall EX23 0LY. *Clubs:* Reform; Bude & N Cornwall Golf, David Lloyd Slazenger Racquet (Heston).

DANIELL, Brig. Averell John, CBE 1955 (MBE 1939); DSO 1945; *b* 19 June 1903; *s* of late Lt-Col Oswald James Daniell, QO Royal West Kent Regt, and late May Frances Drummond Daniell (*née* Adams); *m* 1934, Phyllis Kathleen Rhona Grove-Annesley; two *s* one *d. Educ:* Wellington Coll.; RM Acad., Woolwich. Commissioned, Royal Field Artillery, 1923; Captain, RA, 1936; Major, 1940; Lt-Col, 1943. Served War of 1939–45; Middle East, Iraq, Burma. Col, 1948; Brig., 1952; retired, 1955. Administrative Officer, Staff Coll., Camberley, 1955–61. Colonel Commandant, Royal Artillery, 1956–66. *Address:* Oak Lodge, 21 Hillside Street, Hythe, Kent CT21 5EJ. *T:* Hythe (01303) 266494.

DANIELL, Sir Peter (Averell), Kt 1971; TD 1950; DL; Senior Government Broker, 1963–73; *b* 8 Dec. 1909; *s* of R. H. A. Daniell and Kathleen Daniell (*née* Monsell); *m* 1935, Leonie M. Harrison; two *s* one *d. Educ:* Eton Coll.; Trinity Coll., Oxford (MA). Joined Mullens & Co., 1932, Partner, 1945; retd 1973. Served KRRC, 1939–45, Middle East and Italy. Master, Drapers' Co., 1980–81. DL Surrey 1976. *Recreations:* shooting, fishing, golf. *Address:* Glebe House, Buckland, Betchworth, Surrey RH3 7BL. *T:* Betchworth (01737) 842320. *Clubs:* Brooks's, Alpine.

DANIELL, Ralph Allen, CBE 1965 (OBE 1958); HM Diplomatic Service, retired; *b* 26 Jan. 1915; 2nd *s* of late Reginald Allen Daniell; *m* 1943, Diana Lesley (*née* Tyndale); one *s* three *d. Educ:* Lancing Coll.; University Coll., Oxford. Appointed to Board of Trade, 1937. Joined HM Forces, 1942; served with Royal Tank Regt in North Africa and Italian campaigns, 1943–45. Appointed to HM Foreign Service as First Sec., 1946; Mexico City, 1946; Rome, 1949; Foreign Office, 1951; Helsinki, 1953; Counsellor, 1958; Washington, 1958; New York, 1959; Cairo, 1962; Wellington, 1967; Consul-Gen., Chicago, 1972–74. *Address:* 1A Collins Lane, Ringwood, Hants BH24 1LD. *T:* Ringwood (01425) 473662.

DANIELS, George, MBE 1982; FSA, FBHI; author, watch maker, horological consultant; *b* 19 Aug. 1926; *s* of George Daniels and Beatrice (*née* Cadou); *m* 1964, Juliet Anne (*née* Marryat); one *d. Educ:* elementary. 2nd Bn E Yorks Regt, 1944–47. Started professional horology, 1947; restoration of historical watches, 1956–; hand watch making to own designs, 1969–. President: British Horological Inst., 1980 (Fellow, 1951); British Clock and Watchmakers' Benevolent Soc., 1980; Chm., Horological Industries Cttee, 1985–. Worshipful Co. of Clockmakers: Liveryman, 1968; Warden, 1977; Master, 1980; Tompion Gold Medal, 1981; Asst Hon. Surveyor. Freeman, Goldsmiths' Co., 1979; FSA 1976. Hon. DSc City, 1994. Arts, Sciences and Learning Award, City Corporation, London, 1974; Victor Kullberg Medal, Stockholm Watch Guild, 1977; Gold Medal, British Horol Inst., 1981; Gold Badge and Hon. Fellow, Amer. Watchmakers Inst., 1985; Hon. FCGI 1986; City and Guilds Gold Medal for Craftsmanship, 1991. *Publications:* Watches (jtly), 1965 (3rd edn 1978); English and American Watches, 1967; The Art of Breguet, 1975 (3rd edn 1985); (jtly) Clocks and Watches of the Worshipful Company of Clockmakers, 1975; Sir David Salomons Collection, 1978; Watchmaking, 1981 (2nd edn 1985). *Recreations:* vintage cars, fast motorcycles, opera, Scotch whisky. *Address:* 34 New Bond Street, W1A 2AA.

DANIELS, Harold Albert; *b* 8 June 1915; *s* of Albert Pollikett Daniels and Eleanor Sarah Maud Daniels (*née* Flahey); *m* 1946, Frances Victoria Jerdan; one *s* decd. *Educ:* Mercers' Sch.; Christ's Coll., Cambridge. BA 1937; Wren Prize 1938; MA 1940. Asst Principal, Post Office, 1938; Admiralty, 1942; Post Office, 1945; Principal, 1946; Asst Sec., 1950; Under-Sec., 1961; Min. of Posts and Telecommunications, 1969. Asst Under Sec. of State, Home Office, 1974–76. *Address:* Lyle Court Cottage, Bradbourne Road, Sevenoaks, Kent TN13 3PZ. *T:* Sevenoaks (01732) 454039.

DANIELS, Prof. Henry Ellis, FRS 1980; Professor of Mathematical Statistics, University of Birmingham, 1957–78, now Emeritus Professor; Senior Research Associate, Statistical Laboratory, University of Cambridge, 1978–81; *b* 2 Oct. 1912; *s* of Morris and Hannah Daniels; *m* 1950, Barbara Edith Pickering; one *s* one *d. Educ:* Sciennes Sch., Edinburgh; George Heriot's Sch., Edinburgh; Edinburgh Univ.; Clare Coll., Cambridge (Hon. Fellow, 1992). MA Edinburgh 1933, BA Cantab 1935, PhD Edinburgh 1943, ScD Cantab 1981. Statistician, Wool Industries Research Assoc., 1935–47; Ministry of Aircraft Production, 1942–45; Lecturer in Mathematics, University of Cambridge, 1947–57; Fellow, King's Coll. Cambridge, 1975–76. Pres., Royal Statistical Soc., 1974–75; Fellow Inst. of Mathematical Statistics; elected Mem., 1956, Hon. Mem., 1993, Internat. Statistical Inst. Freeman, Clockmakers' Co., 1981, Liveryman 1984. Guy Medal (Silver) 1957, (Gold) 1984, Royal Statistical Society. *Publications:* papers in Journal of the Royal Statistical Society, Annals of Mathematical Statistics, Biometrika, etc. *Recreations:* playing the English concertina, repairing watches. *Address:* 12 Kimberley Road, Cambridge CB4 1HH. *T:* Cambridge (01223) 313402.

DANILOVA, Alexandra; lecturer, teacher and choreographer, actress; *b* Pskoff, Russia, 20 Nov. 1906; *d* of Dionis Daniloff and Claudia Gotovzeffa; *m* 1st, 1931, Giuseppe Massera (*d* 1936); 2nd, 1941, Kazimir Kokic (marr. annulled, 1949). *Educ:* Theatrical Sch., Petrograd. Maryinski Theatre, Leningrad, 1923–24; Diaghileff Company, 1925–29; Waltzes from Vienna, 1931; Colonel de Basil Company, 1933–37; Prima Ballerina, Ballet Russe de Monte Carlo, 1938–58. Teacher (on Faculty) of School of American Ballet. Guest artist Royal Festival Hall, London, 1955; Ballerina in Oh Captain (Musical), New York, 1958. With own Company has toured West Indies, Japan, Philippines, USA, Canada and S Africa. Capezio Award (for outstanding services to Art of the Dance), 1958; Guest Choreographer Metropolitan Opera House, Guest Teacher and Choreographer, Germany (Krefeld Festival of Dance) and Amsterdam, 1959–60; Choreographed Coppelia for La Scala di Milano, 1961; Lecture performances throughout US; Guest Choreographer, Washington Ballet, 1962–64. Choreographed Coppelia (with George Balanchine), NY City Ballet, 1975. Screen acting debut in film, The Turning Point, 1977. Kennedy Center

Honors Award, 1989; Handel Medal, New York City, 1989. *Recreations:* needlework, ping-pong, gardening. *Address:* Carnegie House, 100 West 57th Street, New York, NY 10019, USA.

DANINOS, Pierre; French author; *b* Paris, 26 May 1913; *m* 1st, 1942, Jane Marrain; one *s* two *d*; 2nd, 1968, Marie-Pierre Dourneau. *Educ:* Lycée Janson de Sailly, Paris. Began to write for newspapers, 1931; reporter for French press in England, USA, etc. Liaison agent with British Army, Dunkirk, 1940. Published first book in Rio de Janeiro, 1940; returned to France, 1941, from South America, Chronicler for Le Figaro. *Publications:* Les Carnets du Bon Dieu (Prix Interallié 1947); L'Eternel Second, 1949; Sonia les autres et moi (Prix Courteline, 1952) (English trans., Life with Sonia, 1958); Les Carnets du Major Thompson, 1954 (English trans., Major Thompson Lives in France, 1955); Le Secret du Major Thompson, 1956 (English trans., Major Thompson and I, 1957); Vacances à Tous Prix, 1958; Un certain Monsieur Blot, 1960 (English trans., 1961); Le Jacassin, 1962; Snobissimo, 1964; Le 36ème dessous, 1966; Le Major Tricolore, 1968; Ludovic Morateur, 1970; Le Pyjama, 1972; Les Touristocrates, 1974; Made in France, 1977; La Composition d'Histoire, 1979; Le Veuf Joyeux, 1981; La Galerie des Glaces, 1983; La France dans tous ses états, 1985; Profession: écrivain (autobiog.), 1988; Candidement Vôtre, 1992. *Recreations:* tennis, ski-ing, collecting British hobbies. *Address:* 15 rue Chauveau, 92200 Neuilly, France.

DANKERT, Pieter; Kt of Order of Netherlands Lion; Commander, Order of Orange Nassau; State Secretary for European Affairs, Netherlands, since 1989; *b* Jan. 1934; *m* 1962, Paulette Puig; one *s* two *d*. *Educ:* Amsterdam Free Univ. Mem. (Partij van de Arbeid) Tweede Kamer, Netherlands; formerly: Internat. Sec., Partij van de Arbeid; Mem., NATO Assembly, WEU Assembly and Assembly of Council of Europe, 1971–77; Mem., European Parlt, 1977–89 (Pres., 1982–84). *Address:* Hoogstraat 1, 1135 BZ Edam, Netherlands.

DANKS, Sir Alan (John), KBE 1970; Chairman, New Zealand University Grants Committee, 1966–77; *b* 9 June 1914; *s* of T. E. Danks; *m* 1943, Loma Beryl Hall (*née* Drabble). *Educ:* West Christchurch High Sch.; Canterbury Coll. (MA). Teaching profession, 1931–43; Economics Dept, Univ. of Canterbury (formerly Canterbury University Coll.), 1943–66; Prof., 1962; Pro-Vice Chancellor, 1964. Chm., Information Authy, 1982–88. Hon. LLD Canterbury, 1973. *Address:* 116 Upland Road, Wellington 5, New Zealand.

DANKWORTH, Mrs C. D.; *see* Laine, Cleo.

DANKWORTH, John Philip William, CBE 1974; FRAM 1973; musician; *b* 20 Sept. 1927; British; *m* 1958, Cleo Laine, *qv*; one *s* one *d*. *Educ:* Monoux Grammar Sch. Studied Royal Academy of Music, 1944–46. ARAM 1969. Closely involved with post-war development of British jazz, 1947–60; formed large jazz orchestra, 1953. Pops Music Dir, LSO, 1985–90; Principal Guest Pops Conductor, San Francisco Orch., 1987–89. Composed works for combined jazz and symphonic musicians including: Improvisations (with Matyas Seiber, 1959); Escapade (commissioned by Northern Sinfonia Orch., 1967); Tom Sawyer's Saturday, for narrator and orchestra (commissioned by Farnham Festival), 1967; String Quartet, 1971; Piano Concerto (commissioned by Westminster Festival, 1972); Grace Abounding (for RPO), 1980; The Diamond and the Goose (for City of Birmingham Choir and Orch.), 1981; Reconciliation (commnd for Silver Jubilee of Coventry Cathedral), 1987. Many important film scores (1964–) including: Saturday Night and Sunday Morning, Darling, The Servant, Morgan, Accident; other works include: Palabras, 1970; dialogue and songs for Colette, Comedy, 1980. Numerous record albums, incl. Echoes of Harlem, Misty, Symphonic Fusions. Variety Club of GB Show Business Personality Award (with Cleo Laine), 1977. Hon. MA Open Univ., 1975; Hon. DMus. Berklee Sch. of Music, 1982; York, 1993. *Recreations:* driving, household maintenance. *Address:* Deke Arlon, D. & J. Arlon Enterprises Ltd, Pinewood Studios, Pinewood Road, Iver, Bucks SL0 0NH. *T:* Iver (01753) 650808.

DANN, Mrs Jill; *b* 10 Sept. 1929; *d* of Harold Norman Cartwright and Marjorie Alice Thornton; *m* 1952, Anthony John Dann; two *s* two *d* (and one *s* decd). *Educ:* Solihull High Sch. for Girls, Malvern Hall; Birmingham Univ. (LLB); St Hilda's Coll., Oxford (BCL). Called to the Bar, Inner Temple, 1952. Mayoress of Chippenham, 1964–65. Church Commissioner, 1968–93; Member: General Synod of Church of England, 1965–, and of its Standing Cttee, 1971–90 (Vice-Chm. House of Laity, 1985–90); Crown Appointments Commn, 1977–87; Chairman: House of Laity, Bristol Diocesan Synod, 1982–88; C of E Evangelical Council, 1985–89; Trustee, Church Urban Fund, 1987–. Vice Chm., Trinity Coll., Bristol; Pres. of Fellows, Cheltenham and Gloucester Coll. of Higher Educn. Dir, Wiltshire Radio, 1981–88. Pres., Inner Wheel, 1978–79. *Recreations:* reading, enjoying being a grandmother. *Address:* The Riverbank, Reybridge, Lacock, Wilts SN15 2PF. *T:* Lacock (01249) 730205.

DANN, Most Rev. Robert William; *b* 28 Sept. 1914; *s* of James and Ruth Dann; *m* 1949, Yvonne (*née* Newnham); one *s* two *d*. *Educ:* Trinity Coll., Univ. of Melbourne. BA Hons Melbourne 1946. Deacon, 1945; Priest, 1946. Dir of Youth and Religious Education, Dio. Melbourne, 1946; Incumbent: St Matthew's, Cheltenham, 1951; St George's, Malvern, 1956; St John's, Footscray, 1961; Archdeacon of Essendon, 1961; Dir of Evangelism and Extension, Dio. Melbourne, 1963; Bishop Coadjutor, Dio. Melbourne, 1969–77; Archbishop of Melbourne and Metropolitan of Province of Victoria, 1977–83. *Address:* 1 Myrtle Road, Canterbury, Vic 3126, Australia.

DANNATT, Prof. (James) Trevor, MA; RA 1983 (ARA 1977); FRIBA; Senior Partner, Trevor Dannatt & Partners, Architects; Professor of Architecture: Manchester University, 1975–86; Royal Academy, 1988; *b* 15 Jan. 1920; *s* of George Herbert and Jane Ellen Dannatt; *m* 1953, Joan Howell Davies (marr. diss. 1991); one *s* one *d*; *m* 1994, Dr Ann Crawshaw (*née* Critchley). *Educ:* Colfes Sch.; Sch. of Architecture, Regent Street Polytechnic (Dip. Arch.). Professional experience in office of Jane B. Drew and E. Maxwell Fry, 1943–48; Architects Dept, LCC (Royal Festival Hall Gp), 1948–52; commenced private practice, 1952. Vis. Prof., Washington Univ., St Louis, 1976 and 1987. Assessor for national and international architectural competitions, Civic Trust; Member: Cathedrals Adv. Commn, 1986–91; Historic Bldgs Adv. Cttee, English Heritage, 1988–91; Fabric Cttees of Cathedrals: Lichfield, 1985–; Portsmouth, 1990–; St Paul's, 1991–. Founder Mem., and Chm., South Bank Gp, 1993–. Trustee, Documents of the Modern Movement, 1991–. Editor, Architects' Year Book, 1945–62. Architectural work includes private houses, housing, school buildings (for LCC, Bootham, St Paul's, Colfe's), university buildings (residences, Leicester, Hull; Trinity Hall Combination Room, Cambridge; Vaughan Coll. and Jewry Wall Mus., Leicester; develt plan and extensive works for Univ. of Greenwich, formerly Thames Polytechnic, 1980–), welfare buildings (for London boroughs, Lambeth, Southwark, Greenwich), conservation and restoration, interiors for private, corporate and public clients; Architects for British Embassy and Diplomatic Staff housing, Riyadh, 1985; Consultant Architects, Royal Botanic Gardens, Kew, 1989; Victoria Gate visitors' reception and facilities building, 1992. Won internat. competition for conference complex in Riyadh, Saudi Arabia, completed 1974. Hon. FAIA, 1988. *Publications:* Modern Architecture in Britain, 1959; Trevor Dannatt: Buildings and Interiors 1951–72, 1972; (Editorial Adviser, and foreword) Buildings and Ideas 1933–83 from the Studio of Leslie Martin, 1983; contribs to Architectural Rev., Architects' Jl, and various foreign journals. *Recreations:* the arts, including architecture. *Address:* 115 Crawford Street, W1H 1AG. *T:* 0171–486 6844. *Clubs:* Travellers', Arts.

DANSON, Hon. Barnett Jerome, PC (Canada); consultant, since 1984; company director; *s* of Joseph B. Danson and Saidie W. Danson, Toronto; *m* 1943, Isobel, *d* of Robert John Bull, London, England; four *s*. *Educ:* Toronto public and high schs. Served War: enlisted Queen's Own Rifles as Rifleman, 1939; commnd, 1943; wounded in France, 1944; retd 1945, Lieut. Manager, Jos. B. Danson & Sons Ltd, Toronto, 1945–50; Sales Man., Maple Leaf Plastics Ltd, 1950–53; Principal (Pres.), Danson Corp. Ltd, Scarborough, 1953–74; Chairman: CSPG Consultants, 1980–84; de Havilland Aircraft of Canada Ltd, 1981–84; Canadian Consul General, Boston, Mass, 1984–86. Active in Liberal Party, 1946–: MP (L) for York North, 1968–79; Parly Sec. to Prime Minister Trudeau, 1970–72; Minister of State for Urban Affairs, 1974–76; Minister of Nat. Defence, Canada, 1976–79; former Mem., Standing Cttee on Finance, Trade and Econ. Affairs, and Ext. Affairs and National Defence. Chm., GSW Thermoplastics Co.; Dir, Algoma Central Railway Ltd. Dir Emeritus, Canadian Council of Native Business; Director: Atlantic Council of Canada; Canadian Inst. of Strategic Studies; Canadian Centre for Global Security; Canadian Exec. Services Orgn, Toronto. Chm. Bd, No Price Too High Foundn; former Pres. and first Chm. Bd, Soc. of Plastics Engineers Inc. Dir, Canadian Council of Christians and Jews. Hon. Dir, Empire Club, Canada. Former Hon. Lt-Col, Queen's Own Rifles of Canada. Dr of Laws (*hc*) Royal Military Coll. of Canada, 1993. Officer, Order of Merit (France), 1994. *Recreations:* fishing, reading, music. *Address:* 1132 Bay Street, Apt 1501, Toronto, Ontario M5S 2Z4, Canada.

DANTZIC, Roy Matthew, CA; Director, Smith New Court Corporate Finance, since 1995; *b* 4 July 1944; *s* of David and Renee Dantzic; *m* 1969, Diane Clapham; one *s* one *d*. *Educ:* Brighton Coll., Sussex. CA 1968. Coopers & Lybrand, 1962–69; Kleinwort, Benson Ltd, 1970–72; Drayton Corporation Ltd, 1972–74; Samuel Montagu & Co. Ltd, 1974–80 (Exec. Dir, 1975); Mem. for Finance, BNOC, subseq. Finance Dir, Britoil plc, 1980–84; Dir, Pallas SA, 1984–85; Dir, Wood Mackenzie & Co., 1985–89; Finance Dir, Stanhope Properties, 1989–95; Chm., Premier Portfolio Ltd, 1985–95; non-executive Director: Moor Park (1958) Ltd, 1980–90; Saxon Oil plc, 1984–85. Pt-time Mem., CEGB, 1984–87; Pt-time Dir, BNFL, 1987–91. Governor, Brighton Coll., 1990–. *Recreations:* theatre, playing golf, watching cricket. *Address:* 12 Bedford Road, Moor Park, Northwood, Mddx HA6 2AZ. *Clubs:* MCC; Moor Park Golf.

DARBY, Dr Francis John, TD 1964; MRCGP; MFOM; *b* 24 Feb. 1920; *o s* of Col John Francis Darby, CBE, late Royal Signals, and Georgina Alice (*née* Dean); *m* 1969, Pamela Lisbeth, *o d* of Sydney Hill, Sutton Coldfield; one *s* by former *m*. *Educ:* Nottingham High Sch.; Edinburgh Acad.; Edinburgh Univ. (MB ChB 1950). MRCGP 1970; DIH 1963; DMJ 1965; MFOM RCP 1982; DPhilMed 1994. Commissioned, Royal Signals, 1939–46: N Africa (despatches), Italy and Egypt, 1942–46. Hospital and general practice, 1950–64; Department of Health and Social Security, 1964–82: Dep. Chief Medical Advr, 1978–80; Chief Medical Advr (Social Security), 1980–82; CMO and Consultant Physician, Cayman Is, 1983–85. Mem. BMA, 1950. Freeman, City of London, 1979; Liveryman, Soc. of Apothecaries of London, 1982 (Fellow, Faculty of History and Philosophy of Medicine, 1991). QHP, 1980–84. *Recreations:* sailing, swimming. *Address:* Ruardean, Captains Row, Lymington, Hants SO41 9RP. *T:* Lymington (01590) 677119. *Clubs:* Army and Navy; Royal Signals Yacht; Royal Lymington Yacht.

DARBY, John Oliver Robertson; Chairman, ABB Transportation (Holdings) Ltd (formerly BREL Group Ltd), 1989–94; *b* 5 Jan. 1930; *s* of Ralph Darby and Margaret Darby (*née* Robertson); *m* 1955, Valerie Leyland Cole; three *s*. *Educ:* Charterhouse. FCA 1953. Pilot Officer, RAF, 1953–55; Arthur Young, Chartered Accts, 1955–87: Partner, 1959; Chm., 1974–87. Chairman: Nat. Home Loans Hldgs PLC, 1985–92; Property Lending Bank (formerly Property Lending Trust) PLC, 1987–92; Ultramar, 1988–91; Dir, British Rail Engineering Ltd, 1986–89. *Recreations:* racing, golf. *Address:* The Tithe Barn, Headley, Bordon, Hants GU35 8PW. *Clubs:* Garrick, Royal Thames Yacht; Royal & Ancient Golf (St Andrews); Liphook Golf.

DARBY, Dr Michael Douglas, FRES, FRGS; Surveyor General, Carroll Art Collection, 1990–94; *b* 2 Sept. 1944; *s* of Arthur Douglas Darby and Ilene Doris Darby (*née* Eatwell); *m* 1977, Elisabeth Susan Done; two *s*. *Educ:* Rugby School; Reading Univ. (PhD). FRES 1977; FRGS 1984; AMA 1990. Asst to Barbara Jones, 1963; Victoria and Albert Museum: Textiles Dept, 1964–72; Prints and Drawings Dept, 1973–76; Exhibitions Officer, 1977–83; Dep. Dir, 1983–87; Hd of Publications, Exhibitions and Design, 1988–89. Member: Crafts Council, 1984–88; IoW Adv. Cttee, English Heritage, 1986–; Council, Royal Entomol Soc., 1988–90; Council, National Trust, 1989–93. FRSA 1989. *Publications:* Marble Halls, 1973; Early Railway Prints, 1974, 2nd edn 1979; British Art in the Victoria and Albert Museum, 1983; John Pollard Seddon, 1983; The Islamic Perspective, 1983; articles in art, architectural and entomological periodicals. *Recreations:* beetles, books. *Address:* The Old Malthouse, Sutton Mandeville, near Salisbury, Wilts SP3 5ND. *T:* Fovant (01722) 714295.

DARBY, Sir Peter (Howard), Kt 1985; CBE 1973; QFSM 1970; HM Chief Inspector of Fire Services, 1981–86; *b* 8 July 1924; *s* of William Cyril Darby and Beatrice Colin; *m* 1948, Ellen Josephine Glynn; one *s* one *d*. *Educ:* City of Birmingham Coll. of Advanced Technology. Fire Brigades: Dep. Ch. Officer, Suffolk and Ipswich FB, 1963; Chief Officer, Nottingham FB, 1966; Chief Officer, Lancashire FB, 1967; County Fire Officer, Greater Manchester FB, 1974; Regional Fire Comdr (No 10) NW Region, 1974–76; Regional Fire Adviser (No 5) Greater London Region, 1977; Chief Officer of the London Fire Brigade, 1977–80. Pres., Chief and Asst Chief Fire Officers' Assoc., 1975–76; Mem. Adv. Council, Central Fire Brigades, 1977; Principal Adviser to Sec. of State on Fire Service matters, 1981–86; Chm., Fire Services Central Examinations Bd, 1985. Chm., Certifire Ltd, 1987–; non-exec. Dir, Argus Alarms Ltd, 1987–. Foundation Gov., St James's Catholic High (formerly Secondary Modern) Sch., Barnet, 1985– (Chm. Governors, 1987–). Freeman, City of London; Liveryman, Worshipful Co. of Basketmakers. CStJ 1983. *Recreations:* fell-walking, golf, fishing, sailing. *Address:* 10 Moor Lane, Rickmansworth, Herts WD3 1LG. *Clubs:* City Livery, KSC.

D'ARCY, Most Rev. Eric; *see* Hobart (Australia), Archbishop of, (RC).

DARCY DE KNAYTH, Baroness (18th in line), *cr* 1332; **Davina Marcia Ingrams** (*née* **Herbert);** *b* 10 July 1938; *d* of late Squadron Leader Viscount Clive (*d* on active service, 1943), and of Vida, *o d* of late Captain James Harold Cuthbert, DSO, Scots Guards (she *m* 2nd, 1945, Brig. Derek Schreiber, MVO (*d* 1972)); *S* to father's Barony, 1943; *m* 1960, Rupert George Ingrams (*d* 1964), *s* of late Leonard Ingrams and of Mrs Ingrams; one *s* two *d*. *Heir: s* Hon. Caspar David Ingrams, *b* 5 Jan. 1962. *Address:* Camley Corner, Stubbings, Maidenhead, Berks SL6 6QW.

D'ARCY HART, Philip Montagu; *see* Hart, P. M. D'A.

DARELL, Brig. Sir Jeffrey (Lionel), 8th Bt, *cr* 1795; MC 1945; *b* 2 Oct. 1919; *s* of late Lt-Col Guy Marsland Darell, MC (3rd *s* of 5th Bt); *S* cousin, 1959; *m* 1953, Bridget Mary, *e d* of Maj.-Gen. Sir Allan Adair, 6th Bt, GCVO, CB, DSO, MC; one *s* two *d*. *Educ:* Eton; RMC, Sandhurst. Commissioned Coldstream Guards, July 1939; served War of 1939–45: Coats Mission, 1940–41 (to guard Royal Family in case of invasion); ADC to GOC-in-C, Southern Comd, 1942; Bde Major, Guards Bde, 1953–55; Officer Comdg 1st Bn Coldstream Guards, 1957–59; GSO1, PS12, War Office, 1959; College Comdr RMA Sandhurst, 1961–64; Comdg Coldstream Guards, 1964–65; Comdr, 56 Inf. Brigade (TA), 1965–67; Vice-Pres., Regular Commns Bd, 1968–70; Comdt, Mons OCS, 1970–72; MoD, 1972–74; retd 1974. ADC to HM the Queen, 1973–74. Trustee and Mem., London Law Trust, 1981–. High Sheriff, Norfolk, 1985. *Recreations:* normal. *Heir: s* Guy Jeffrey Adair Darell [*b* 8 June 1961; *m* 1988, Justine Samantha, *d* of Mr Justice T. Reynolds, Quambi Place, Sydney, Australia; one *s* two *d*]. *Address:* Denton Lodge, Harleston, Norfolk IP20 0AD. *T:* Homersfield (01986) 788206. *Clubs:* Army and Navy, MCC.

DARESBURY, 3rd Baron *cr* 1927, of Walton, Co. Chester; **Edward Gilbert Greenall;** Bt 1876; *b* 27 Nov. 1928; *s* of 2nd Baron Daresbury and Josephine (*d* 1958), *y d* of Brig.-Gen. Sir Joseph Laycock, KCMG, DSO; *S* father, 1990; *m* 1st, 1952, Margaret Ada (marr. diss. 1986), *y d* of late C. J. Crawford; three *s* one *d*; 2nd, 1986, Mary Patricia, *d* of late Lewis Parkinson. *Educ:* Eton. Chm., Randall & Vautier Ltd; formerly Chm., Grunhalle Lager Internat. *Heir: s* Hon. Peter Gilbert Greenall, *qv*. *Address:* Crossbow House, Trinity, Jersey, CI. *T:* Jersey (01534) 863316.

DARGIE, Sir William Alexander, Kt 1970; CBE 1969 (OBE 1960); FRSA 1951; artist; portrait, figure and landscape painter; Chairman, Commonwealth Art Advisory Board, Prime Minister's Department, 1969–73 (Member, 1953–73); *b* 4 June 1912; *s* of Andrew and Adelaide Dargie; *m* 1937, Kathleen, *d* of late G. H. Howitt; one *s* one *d*. Official War Artist (Capt.) with AIF in Middle East, Burma, New Guinea, India, 1941–46. Dir, National Gallery of Victoria Art Schs, 1946–53. Member: Interim Council of Nat. Gallery Canberra, 1968–72; Nat. Capital Planning Cttee, Canberra, 1970–73; Aboriginal Arts Adv. Cttee, 1970–72; Trustee: Native Cultural Reserve, Port Moresby, Papua-New Guinea, 1970–73; Museum of Papua-New Guinea, 1970–73; Mem. Council, Nat. Museum, Victoria, 1978–83; Chm., Bd of Trustees, McClelland Gall., 1981–87. MA *hc* Footscray Inst. of Technol., 1986. Archibald Prize for portraiture, 1941, 1942, 1945, 1946, 1947, 1950, 1952, 1956; Woodward Award, 1940; McPhillimy Award, 1940; McKay Prize, 1941. Painted portrait of The Queen for Commonwealth of Aust., 1954; the Duke of Gloucester, 1947; the Duke of Edinburgh for City of Melbourne, 1956. Portraits of Sir Macfarlane Burnet, Sir William Ashton, Sir Lionel Lindsay, acquired for Commonwealth Nat. Collection. Rep. in public and private collections in Aust., NZ, England and USA. One-man exhibition, Leger Galls, London, 1958. Exhibits with RA and Royal Soc. of Portrait Painters. *Publication:* On Painting a Portrait, 1956. *Recreations:* books, chess, tennis. *Address:* 19 Irilbarra Road, Canterbury, Victoria 3126, Australia. *T:* (3) 8363396. *Clubs:* Melbourne, Melbourne Savage (Melbourne).

DARK, Sir Anthony Michael B.; *see* Beaumont-Dark.

DARKE, Geoffrey James, RIBA; Principal, Geoffrey Darke Associates, Architects and Planners, since 1987; *b* 1 Sept. 1929; *s* of late Harry James Darke and Edith Anne (*née* Rose); *m* 1959, Jean Yvonne Rose, ARCM; one *s* two *d*. *Educ:* Prince Henry's Grammar Sch., Evesham, Worcs; Birmingham School of Architecture (DipArch); ARIBA 1956. National Service, Malaya, commnd RE, 1954–56. Asst Architect, Stevenage Development Corp., 1952–58; private practice, 1958–61; Partner, Darbourne and Darke, Architects and Landscape Planners, 1961–87. Work has included many large commissions, particularly public buildings. Success in national and internat. competitions, in Stuttgart, 1977, Hanover, 1979 and 1980, and in Bolzano, Italy, 1980; numerous medals and awards for architectural work; co-recipient of Fritz Schumacher Award, Hamburg, 1978, for services to architecture and townplanning. Mem. Council, RIBA, 1977–83; Chm., RIBA Competitions Cttee, 1979–84; has served on many professional committees; Mem., Access Cttee for England, 1992–. Mem., Aldeburgh Festival Snape Maltings Foundn, 1979–. FRSA 1981. *Recreation:* music. *Address:* Neptune House, 43 King Street, Aldeburgh, Suffolk IP15 5BY. *Club:* Reform.

DARKE, Marjorie Sheila; writer, since 1962; *b* 25 Jan. 1929; *d* of Christopher Darke and Sarah Ann (*née* Palin); *m* 1952; two *s* one *d*. *Educ:* Worcester Grammar Sch. for Girls; Leicester Coll. of Art and Technol.; Central Sch. of Art, London. Worked in textile studio of John Lewis Partnership, 1950–54. *Publications:* Ride the Iron Horse, 1973; The Star Trap, 1974; A Question of Courage, 1975; The First of Midnight, 1977; A Long Way to Go, 1978; Comeback, 1981; Tom Post's Private Eye, 1982; Messages and Other Shivery Tales, 1984; A Rose from Blighty, 1990; *for young children:* Mike's Bike, 1974; What Can I Do, 1975; Kipper's Turn, 1976; The Big Brass Band, 1976; My Uncle Charlie, 1977; Carnival Day, 1979; Kipper Skips, 1979; Imp, 1985; The Rainbow Sandwich, 1989; Night Windows, 1990; Emma's Monster, 1992. *Recreations:* reading, music, sewing, country walks, jogging. *Address:* c/o Rogers, Coleridge & White Ltd, Literary Agency, 20 Powis Mews, W11 1JN. *Clubs:* Society of Authors; International PEN.

DARLEY, Gillian Mary, (Mrs Michael Horowitz); architectural writer, lecturer and photographer; Director, Landscape Foundation, since 1994; *b* 28 Nov. 1947; *d* of Lt Col Robert Darley, MC and Caroline (*née* Swanston Ward); *m* 1986, Michael Horowitz, *qv*; one *d* (one *s* decd). *Educ:* Courtauld Inst. of Art, London Univ. (BA Hons 1969); Birkbeck Coll., London (MSc Politics and Admin 1986). Journalist and radio and TV broadcaster; contributor to daily and Sunday newspapers, magazines and professional press, 1975–; Architectural correspondent, Observer, 1991–93. Joint Partner, Edifice, architectural photographic liby, 1987–. Vice-Chm., SPAB, 1991–93, 1994– (Mem., Main Cttee, 1982–). External Assessor, Sch. of Three Dimensional Design, Kingston Univ., 1992–95. *Publications:* Villages of Vision, 1975; The National Trust Book of the Farm, 1981; Built in Britain, 1984; (with P. Lewis) Dictionary of Ornament, 1986; Octavia Hill: a life, 1990; (contrib.) Name of the Room, 1993; (with A. Saint) The Chronicles of London, 1994. *Recreations:* gardening in a small space, Jack Russell.

DARLING; *see* Stormonth Darling and Stormonth-Darling.

DARLING, family name of **Baron Darling.**

DARLING, 2nd Baron, *cr* 1924, of Langham; **Robert Charles Henry Darling;** DL; Major retired, Somerset Light Infantry; *b* 15 May 1919; *s* of late Major Hon. John Clive Darling, DSO; *S* grandfather, 1936; *m* 1942, Bridget Rosemary Whishaw, *d* of Rev. F. C. Dickson; one *s* two *d*. *Educ:* Wellington Coll.; RMC Sandhurst. Retired, 1955. Sec., later Chief Executive, Royal Bath and West and Southern Counties Soc., 1961–79, Pres., 1989. DL Somerset 1972, Avon 1974. *Recreations:* fishing, gardening. *Heir: s* Hon. Robert Julian Henry Darling, FRICS [*b* 29 April 1944; *m* 1970, Janet, *yr d* of Mrs D. M. E. Mallinson, Richmond, Yorks; two *s* one *d*]. *Address:* Puckpits, Limpley Stoke, Bath, Avon BA3 6JH. *T:* Limpley Stoke (01225) 722146.

DARLING, Alistair Maclean; MP (Lab) Edinburgh Central, since 1987; advocate; *b* 28 Nov. 1953; *m* 1986, Margaret McQueen Vaughan; one *s* one *d*. *Educ:* Aberdeen Univ. Admitted to Faculty of Advocates, 1984. Member: Lothian Regl Council, 1982–87 (Chm., Transport Cttee, 1986–87); Lothian and Borders Police Bd, 1982–86. Mem., Apex. Gov., Napier Coll., Edinburgh, 1982–87. *Address:* House of Commons, SW1A 0AA.

DARLING, Sir Clifford, GCVO 1994; Kt 1977; Govenor-General, Bahamas, 1992–94; *b* Acklins Island, 6 Feb. 1922; *s* of Charles and Aremelia Darling; *m* Igrid Smith. *Educ:* Acklins Public Sch.; several public schs in Nassau. Became taxi-driver (Gen. Sec. Bahamas Taxicab Union for 8 yrs, Pres. for 10 yrs). An early Mem., Progressive Liberal Party; MHA for Englerston; Senator, 1964–67; Dep. Speaker, House of Assembly, 1967–69; Minister of State, Oct. 1969; Minister of Labour and Welfare, Dec. 1971; Minister of Labour and Nat. Insurance, 1974–77; Speaker, House of Assembly, 1977–92. Past Chm., Tourist Advisory Bd; instrumental in introd. of a comprehensive Nat. Insce Scheme in the Bahamas, Oct. 1974. Member: Masonic Lodge; Elks Lodge; Acklins, Crooked Is and Long Cays Assoc. *Address:* PO Box N-1050, Nassau, Bahamas.

DARLING, Rt. Rev. Edward Flewett; *see* Limerick and Killaloe, Bishop of.

DARLING, Gerald Ralph Auchinleck, RD 1967; QC 1967; DL; MA; Lieutenant-Commander, retired; Judge, Admiralty Court of the Cinque Ports, since 1979; *b* 8 Dec. 1921; *er s* of late Lieut-Col R. R. A. Darling and Moira (*née* Moriarty); *m* 1954, Susan Ann, *d* of late Brig. J. M. Hobbs, OBE, MC; one *s* one *d*. *Educ:* Harrow Sch. (Reginald Pole Schol.); Hertford Coll., Oxford (Baring Schol., Kitchener Schol.; MA 1948). Served with RNVR, 1940–46: Fleet Fighter Pilot with 807 Seafire Sqdn in HM Ships Furious, Indomitable, Battler and Hunter; Test Pilot, Eastern Fleet and Chief Test Pilot, British Pacific Fleet in HMS Unicorn; RNR until 1967. Called to Bar, Middle Temple, 1950 (Harmsworth Law Schol.), Bencher, 1972, Treasurer, 1991; Barrister, Northern Ireland, 1957, Hon. Bencher, 1992; QC Hong Kong 1968. Member: Panel of Lloyd's Arbitrators in Salvage Cases, 1967–78, Appeal Arbitrator, 1978–91; Panel of Wreck Commissioners, 1967–. Trustee, Royal Naval Museum, 1985–90. DL Co. Tyrone, 1990; High Sheriff, Co. Tyrone, 1993. Freeman of City of London, 1968. Lloyd's Silver Medal, 1991. *Publications:* (contrib.) 3rd edn Halsbury's Laws of England (Admiralty and Ship Collisions), 1952; (contrib.) International Commercial and Maritime Arbitration, 1988; (with Christopher Smith) LOF90 and the New Salvage Convention, 1991. *Recreations:* fly fishing, shooting. *Address:* Crevenagh House, Omagh, Northern Ireland BT79 0EH; Queen Elizabeth Building, Temple, EC4Y 9BS. *T:* 0171–353 9153. *Clubs:* Naval and Military; Tyrone County (Omagh).

DARLING, Sir James Ralph, Kt 1968; CMG 1958; OBE 1953; MA Oxon; Hon. DCL, Hon. LLD; FACE; Headmaster, Geelong Church of England Grammar School, Corio, Victoria, Australia, 1930–61; *b* 18 June 1899; *s* of late Augustine Major Darling and Jane Baird Nimmo; *m* 1935, Margaret Dunlop, *er d* of late John Dewar Campbell; one *s* three *d*. *Educ:* Repton Sch.; Oriel Coll., Oxford (Hon. Fellow, 1986). 2nd Lieut Royal Field Artillery, 1918–19, France and Germany; Asst Master Merchant Taylors' Sch., Crosby, Liverpool, 1921–24; Asst Master Charterhouse Sch., Godalming, 1924–29; in charge of Public Schs Empire Tour to NZ, 1929; Hon. Sec. Headmasters' Conference of Australia, 1931–45, Chm., 1946–48; Member: Melbourne Univ. Council, 1933–71 (Hon. MA Melbourne); Commonwealth Univs Commission, 1942–51; Commonwealth Immigration Advisory Council, 1952–68; Australian Broadcasting Control Board, 1955–61. President: Australian Coll. of Educn, 1959–63 (Hon. Fellow 1970); Australian Road Safety Council, 1961–70; Chairman: Australian Expert Gp on Road Safety, 1970–71; Australian Frontier Commission, 1962–71 (President, 1971–73); Australian Broadcasting Commission, 1961–67; Commonwealth Immigration Publicity Council, 1962–71; Pres., Elizabethan Trust, 1970–82. Mem. Council, Marcus Oldham Farm Management (formerly Agricl) Coll., 1961–91; Chm. (Victoria), United World Colls, 1972–91. Hon. DCL Oxon, 1948; Hon. LLD Melbourne, 1973; Hon. DLitt Deakin, 1989. *Publications:* The Education of a Civilized Man, 1962; Timbertop (with E. H. Montgomery), 1967; Richly Rewarding, 1978; Reflections for the Age, 1991. *Address:* 3 Myamyn Street, Armadale, Victoria 3143, Australia. *T:* (3) 8226262. *Clubs:* Australian (Sydney); Melbourne (Melbourne).

DARLING, Gen. Sir Kenneth (Thomas), GBE 1969 (CBE 1957); KCB 1963 (CB 1957); DSO 1945; Commander-in-Chief, Allied Forces, Northern Europe, 1967–69, retired; *b* 17 Sept. 1909; *s* of late G. K. Darling, CIE; *m* 1941, Pamela Beatrice Rose Denison-Pender (*d* 1990). *Educ:* Eton; Royal Military College, Sandhurst. Commissioned 7th Royal Fusiliers, 1929; jssc 1946; idc 1953. Served NW Europe, 1944–45: Comd 5th Parachute Bde, 1946; Comd Airborne Forces Depot, 1948; Comd 16th Parachute Bde, 1950; Brig. A/q 1st (Br) Corps, 1954; Chief of Staff 1st (Br) Corps, 1955; Chief of Staff 2nd Corps, 1956. Dep. Dir of Staff Duties (D), WO, 1957–58; GOC Cyprus District and Dir of Ops, 1958–60; Dir of Infantry, 1960–62; GOC 1st (Br) Corps, 1962–63; GOC-in-C, Southern Command, 1964–66. Colonel: The Royal Fusiliers (City of London Regt), 1963–68; The Royal Regt of Fusiliers, 1968–74; Col Comdt, The Parachute Regt, 1965–67. ADC Gen., 1968–69. *Recreation:* riding. *Address:* Vicarage Farmhouse, Chesterton, Bicester, Oxon OX6 8UQ. *T:* Bicester (01869) 252092. *Club:* Army and Navy.

DARLING, Susan; Policy and Planning, Aboriginal and Torres Strait Islander Commission; *b* 5 May 1942; *d* of Eric Francis Justice Darling and Monica Darling (*née* Grant). *Educ:* Nonsuch County Grammar Sch. for Girls, Cheam; King's Coll., London (BA Hons). Joined BoT as Asst Principal, 1963; transf. to FCO, 1965; Nairobi, 1967–69; Second, later First Sec., Econ. and Social Affairs, UK Mission to UN, 1969–73; FCO, 1973–74; resigned, 1974; reinstated, 1975; FCO, 1975–78; Dep. High Comr and Head of Chancery, Suva, 1981–84; FCO, 1984–87; Consul-Gen., Perth, WA, 1987–88; resigned FCO, 1988; Dept of Chief Minister, NT, Australia, 1989–90; Indo-China Co-ordinator, Quaker Service Australia, 1991–93. *Recreations:* travel, draught horses. *Address:* Box 547, Derby, West Kimberley, WA 6728, Australia.

DARLING, William Martindale, CBE 1988 (OBE 1972); FRPharmS; Managing Director, J. M. & W. Darling Ltd, since 1957; Chairman, South of Tyne (formerly South Tyneside) Health Authority, since 1974; *b* 7 May 1934; *s* of William Darling, MPS and Muriel Darling; *m* 1958, Ann Edith Allen; two *s*. *Educ:* Mortimer Road Primary Sch.; Newcastle Royal Grammar Sch.; Sunderland Polytechnic Sch. of Pharmacy. MPS 1956. Member: Medicines Commn, 1971–79; Health Educn Council, 1971–78; Pharmacy Bd, CNAA, 1972–78; Cttee on Safety of Medicines, 1979–86; Cttee on Review of Medicines, 1986–; Health Services Supply Council, 1978–84 (Chm. and Vice-Chm.); GMC, 1994–; Chairman: Standing Pharmaceutical Adv. Cttee, 1974–; Nat. Pharmaceutical Supplies Gp, 1984–; Head, UK Pharm. Delegn to EEC, 1972–; Pres., Pharm. Gp, EEC, 1985–86; Mem., Comité Consultatif pour formation des pharmaciens, 1988–; Mem. Council, NAHA, 1974–90 (Chm., 1980–82; Hon. Treasurer, 1988–89); first Chm., Nat. Assoc. of Health Authorities and Trusts, 1990–93; Mem. Council, Pharmaceutical, later Royal Pharmaceutical Soc., 1962– (Vice-Pres., 1969–71; Pres., 1971–73; Treas., 1992–95); Pres. designate, Internat. Hosp. Fedn. Chm. Bd of Govs, Univ. of Sunderland (formerly Sunderland Poly.) (Gov., 1989–; Hon. Fellow, 1990). Hon. Life Mem., South Shields and Westoe Club, 1990. Pharm. Soc. Gold Medal, 1985. *Recreations:* horse racing, sunbathing, eating good food, growing prize flowers and vegetables. *Address:* Hartside, 6 Whitburn Road, Cleadon, near Sunderland SR6 7QL. *T:* 0191–536 2089.

DARLINGTON, Rear-Adm. Sir Charles (Roy), KBE 1965; BSc; Director of the Naval Education Service and Head of Instructor Branch, Royal Navy, Oct. 1960–Oct. 1965, retired; on staff of Haileybury, 1965–75; *b* 2 March 1910; *o s* of C. A. Darlington, Newcastle under Lyme, Staffs; *m* 1935, Nora Dennison Wright, Maulds Meaburn, Westmorland; one *s* one *d*. *Educ:* Orme Sch., Newcastle under Lyme; Manchester Univ. (BSc). Double First in Maths 1931; Sen. Maths Master, William Hulme's Gram. Sch., 1937–40. Entered Royal Navy, 1941 (Instructor Lieut); served in: HM Ships Valiant and Malaya during War, and later in HM Ships Duke of York, Implacable, Vanguard and Tyne. On Staff of C-in-C Home Fleet, 1954–55, as Fleet Meteorological Officer; for various periods in Admty, HMS Excellent and HMS Collingwood. Rear-Adm. 1960. *Recreations:* cricket, hill-walking, mathematics and trying to avoid ignorance of the arts, and particularly of history.

DARLINGTON, Joyce, (Mrs Anthony Darlington); *see* Blow, Joyce.

DARLINGTON, Stephen Mark, FRCO; Organist and Official Student in Music, Christ Church, Oxford, since 1985; *b* 21 Sept. 1952; *s* of John Oliver Darlington and Bernice Constance Elizabeth (*née* Murphy); *m* 1975, Moira Ellen (*née* Hill); three *d*. *Educ:* King's Sch., Worcester; Christ Church, Oxford (Organ Schol.; MA). Asst Organist, Canterbury Cathedral, 1974–78; Master of the Music, St Albans Abbey, 1978–85. Artistic Dir, Internat. Organ Fest., 1979–85. *Recreations:* travel, walking, punting, Italian food. *Address:* Christ Church, Oxford OX1 1DP. *T:* Oxford (01865) 276195.

DARNLEY, 11th Earl of, *cr* 1725; **Adam Ivo Stuart Bligh;** Baron Clifton of Leighton Bromswold, 1608; Baron Clifton of Rathmore, 1721; Viscount Darnley, 1723; *b* 8 Nov. 1941; *s* of 9th Earl of Darnley and of Rosemary, *d* of late Edmund Basil Potter; *S* half-brother, 1980; *m* 1965, Susan Elaine, JP, *y d* of late Sir Donald Anderson; one *s* one *d*. *Educ:* Harrow; Christ Church, Oxford. Dir, City of Birmingham Touring Opera, 1990–. Governor, Cobham Hall Sch., 1981–. *Heir:* *s* Lord Clifton, *qv*. *Address:* Netherwood Manor, Tenbury Wells, Worcs WR15 8RT. *Clubs:* Brooks's, MCC.

DARNLEY-THOMAS, Mrs John; *see* Hunter, Rita.

DART, Dr Edward Charles; Research Director, ZENECA (formerly ICI) Seeds, since 1986; *b* 8 March 1941; *s* of Arthur and late Alice Dart; *m* 1964, Jean Ellen Long; one *s* two *d*. *Educ:* Univ. of Manchester Inst. of Science and Technol. (BSc 1962; PhD 1965); Univ. of Calif, LA; Univ. of Calif, Berkeley. Imperial Chemical Industries: Sen. Res. Scientist, Petrochemical and Polymer Lab. (and Lectr in Org. Chem., Univ. of Liverpool), 1968–71; Sen. Res. Scientist, Corporate Lab., 1971–73; Jt Gp Head, Bioscience Gp, 1973–75; Gp Head, Bioscience, 1975–78; Jt Lab. Manager, Corporate Lab. Policy Gp, 1981–83; Head, Corporate Bioscience and Colloids Lab., 1983–85; Associate Res. Dir, Plant Protection Div., 1985–86. Science and Engineering Research Council: Mem., Biotechnol. Directorate, 1981–84, Chm., 1984–89; Member: Molecular Biology Sub Cttee, 1980–82; Science Bd, 1985–88. Member: BBSRC, 1994– (Chm., Technol. Interaction Bd, 1994–); BBSRC/Science Mus. Consensus Conf. Steering Cttee, 1994. Chm., Biotechnol. Jt Adv. Bd, 1992–; Member: Adv. Cttee on Genetic Manipulation, 1984–; Biotechnol. Jt Adv. Bd, 1992–; DTI/MAFF Agro Food Quality Link Cttee, 1991–; John Innes Council, 1986–94; MAFF/AFRC Arable Crops Sectoral Gp, 1991–93. Pres., Berks and Oxfordshire Assoc. for Science Educn, 1989–92. *Publications:* review articles in scientific books; papers in chemical and bioscience jls. *Recreations:* travel, books, music, occasional golf, gardening. *Address:* Jealott's Hill Research Station, Bracknell, Berks RG12 6EY. *T:* Bracknell (01344) 414392.

DART, Geoffrey Stanley; Head of Regional Development Division, Department of Trade and Industry, since 1995; *b* 2 Oct. 1952; *s* of Wilfred Stanley Dart and Irene Jean Dart; *m* 1974, Rosemary Penelope Hinton; one *s* one *d*. *Educ:* Torquay Boys' Grammar Sch.; St Peter's Coll., Oxford (BA and MA Mod. Hist.). Researcher, Electricity Council, 1974–77; Department of Energy: Energy Policy, Offshore Supplies, Oil Policy, Gas, Asst Private Sec. to Sec. of State, to 1984; Cabinet Secretariat, 1984–85; Principal Private Sec. to Sec. of State for Energy, 1985–87; Asst Sec., Electricity Div., 1987–89; Offshore Safety Div., 1989–91; Estabt and Finance Div., 1991–92; Competitiveness Div., DTI, 1992–94; Under Sec., 1994–; Dir, Deregulation Unit, 1994. Director: European Investment Bank; Laing Engineering. *Recreations:* gardening, reading, music, films. *Address:* Department of Trade and Industry, 1 Victoria Street, SW1H 0ET. *T:* 0171–215 2510.

DARTMOUTH, 9th Earl of, *cr* 1711; **Gerald Humphry Legge;** Baron Dartmouth, 1682; Viscount Lewisham, 1711; *b* 26 April 1924; *s* of 8th Earl of Dartmouth, CVO, DSO; *S* father, 1962; *m* 1948, Raine (marr. diss. 1976), *d* of late Alexander McCorquodale; three *s* one *d*; *m* 1980, Mrs G. M. Seguin. *Educ:* Eton. Served War, 1943–45, Coldstream Guards, Italy (despatches). FCA 1951. Dir, Rea Brothers Group PLC, Bankers, 1958–89. Chairman: Royal Choral Soc., 1970–92; Anglo-Brazilian Soc., 1975–94. Hon. LLD Dartmouth Coll., USA, 1969. Grand Officer, Order of the Southern Cross (Brazil), 1994. *Heir:* *s* Viscount Lewisham, *qv*. *Address:* The Manor House, Chipperfield, King's Langley, Herts WD4 9BN. *Clubs:* Buck's (Pres., 1994–), Boodle's.

See also Baron Herschell.

DARVALL, Sir (Charles) Roger, Kt 1971; CBE 1965; former company director; *b* 11 Aug. 1906; *s* of late C. S. Darvall; *m* 1931, Dorothea M., *d* of late A. C. Vautier; two *d*. *Educ:* Burnie, Tasmania. FASA. Gen. Manager, Australia & New Zealand Bank Ltd, Melbourne, 1961–67; former Director: Broken Hill Pty; Rothmans of Pall Mall Aust.; H. C. Sleigh Ltd; Australia New Guinea Corp.; Electrolux Pty; L. M. Ericsson Pty; Munich Re-Insurance Co. of Aust; Australian Eagle Insurance Co. Comr, State Electricity Commn of Vic, 1969–79. *Recreations:* motoring, gardening, outdoors. *Address:* 22 Barton Street, Mont Albert, Vic 3127, Australia. *Club:* Athenæum (Melbourne).

DARVALL, Sir Roger; *see* Darvall, Sir C. R.

DARWALL SMITH, Simon Crompton; His Honour Judge Simon Darwall Smith; a Circuit Judge, since 1992; *b* 13 April 1946; *s* of Randle Darwall Smith and late Barbara Darwall Smith (*née* Crompton); *m* 1968, Susan Patricia Moss (*see* Susan Darwall Smith); two *d*. *Educ:* Charterhouse. Called to the Bar, Gray's Inn, 1968; in practice on Western Circuit, 1968–92; a Recorder, 1986–92. *Recreations:* opera, travel, ballet, theatre, concerts. *Address:* The Law Courts, Small Street, Bristol BS1 2HL. *Club:* Army and Navy.

DARWALL SMITH, Susan Patricia; Her Honour Judge Darwall Smith; a Circuit Judge, since 1992; *b* 27 Oct. 1946; *d* of late George Kenneth Moss, JP and of Jean Margaret Moss (*née* Johnston); *m* 1968, Simon Crompton Darwall Smith, *qv*; two *d*. *Educ:* Howell's Sch., Denbigh. Called to the Bar, Gray's Inn, 1968; in practice on Western Circuit, 1968–92; a Recorder, 1986–92. Mem., Family Proceedings Rules Cttee, 1995–. Gov., Red Maids' Sch., Bristol, 1990–; Mem. Council, St Christopher's Sch., Burnham-on-Sea, 1990–. *Recreations:* travel, opera, ballet, theatre, gardening. *Address:* The Law Courts, Small Street, Bristol BS1 2HL. *Club:* Army and Navy.

DARWEN, 3rd Baron *cr* 1946, of Heys-in-Bowland; **Roger Michael Davies;** *b* 28 June 1938; *s* of 2nd Baron Darwen and of Kathleen Dora, *d* of George Sharples Walker; *S* father, 1988; *m* 1961, Gillian Irene, *d* of Eric G. Hardy, Bristol; two *s* three *d*. *Educ:* Bootham School, York. *Heir:* *s* Hon. Paul Davies, *b* 1962. *Address:* Labourer's Rest, Green Street, Pleshey, Chelmsford CM3 1HT.

DARWENT, Rt. Rev. Frederick Charles; JP; Bishop of Aberdeen and Orkney, 1978–92; *b* Liverpool, 20 April 1927; *y s* of Samuel Darwent and Edith Emily Darwent (*née* Malcolm); *m* 1st, 1949, Edna Lilian (*d* 1981), *o c* of David Waugh and Lily Elizabeth Waugh (*née* McIndoe); twin *d*; 2nd, 1983, Roma Evelyn, *er d* of John Michie and Evelyn Michie (*née* Stephen). *Educ:* Warbreck Sch., Liverpool; Ormskirk Grammar Sch., Lancs; Wells Theological Coll., Somerset. Followed a Banking career, 1943–61 (War service in Far East with Royal Inniskilling Fusiliers, 1945–48). Deacon 1963; priest 1964, Diocese of Liverpool; Curate of Pemberton, Wigan, 1963–65 (in charge of St Francis, Kitt Green, 1964–65); Rector of: Strichen, 1965–71; New Pitsligo, 1965–78; Fraserburgh, 1971–78; Canon of St Andrew's Cathedral, Aberdeen, 1971; Dean of Aberdeen and Orkney, 1973–78. JP Aberdeen City, 1988. Hon. LTh, St Mark's Inst. of Theology, 1974. *Recreations:* amateur stage (acting and production), music (especially jazz), calligraphy. *Address:* 107 Osborne Place, Aberdeen AB2 4DD. *T:* Aberdeen (01224) 646497. *Clubs:* Rotary International; Club of Deir (Aberdeens).

DARWIN, Kenneth; retired civil servant; *b* 24 Sept. 1921; *s* of late Robert Lawrence and Elizabeth Darwin (*née* Swain), Ripon, Yorks. *Educ:* Elementary Sch.; Ripon Grammar Sch.; University Coll., Durham; Oflag VIIB (1943–45). BA 1947, MA 1948. Served 2nd Bn Lancs Fus., N Africa, (Captain) POW, 1942–46; TA Captain (Intelligence Corps), 1949–54. Asst Keeper, Public Record Office (NI), 1948; Dep. Keeper of Records of N Ireland, 1955–70; Vis. Lectr in Archives, UC Dublin, 1967–71; Fellow Commoner, Churchill Coll., Cambridge, 1970; Asst Sec., Min. of Commerce (NI), 1970–74; Sen. Asst Sec., Dept of Finance (NI) and Dept of Civil Service (NI), 1974–77; Dep. Sec., Dept of Finance (NI), 1977–81. Member: Irish MSS Commn, Dublin, 1955–70; Adv. Bd for New History of Ireland, Royal Irish Acad., 1968–; Trustee: Ulster Historical Foundn, 1956–87; Ulster Museum, 1982–88 (Vice-Chm., 1984–86); Lyric Th., Belfast, 1966–69. Ed., Familia: Ulster Genealogical Rev., 1985–93. *Publications:* articles on archives, history and genealogy, in jls and Nat. Trust guides. *Recreations:* travel, piano playing, walking, gardening. *Address:* 18 Seymour Road, Bangor, Co. Down BT19 1BL. *T:* Bangor (01247) 460718. *Clubs:* Commonwealth Trust; Royal British Legion (Bangor, Co. Down).

DASGUPTA, Prof. Partha Sarathi, PhD; FBA 1989; Frank Ramsey Professor of Economics, Cambridge University, since 1994 (Professor of Economics, 1985–94), and Fellow of St John's College, Cambridge, since 1985; *b* 17 Nov. 1942; *s* of late Prof. Amiya Dasgupta and of Shanti Dasgupta, Santiniketan, India; *m* 1968, Carol Margaret, *d* of Prof. James Meade, *qv*; one *s* two *d*. *Educ:* Univ. of Delhi (BSc Hons 1962); Univ. of Cambridge (BA 1965, PhD 1968; Stevenson Prize, 1967). Res. Fellow, Trinity Hall, Cambridge, 1968–71, Supernumerary Fellow, 1971–74; Lectr, 1971–75, Reader, 1975–78, Prof. of Econs, 1978–84, LSE (Hon. Fellow, 1994); Prof. of Econs and Philosophy, Stanford Univ., 1989–92. Sen. Res. Fellow, Inst. for Policy Reform, 1992–94. Visiting Professor: Stanford Univ., 1974–75 and 1983–84; Delhi Univ., 1978; Harvard Univ., 1987; Princeton Univ., 1988. Res. Advr, WIDER (UN Univ., 1989–94). Mem., Expert Panel on Environmtl Health, WHO, 1975–85. Chm., Beijer Internat. Inst. of Ecological Econs, Stockholm, 1991–; Mem. Science Cttee, Santa Fe Inst., 1992–. For. Hon. Mem., Amer. Acad. of Arts and Scis, 1991; For. Mem., Royal Swedish Acad. of Scis, 1991. Fellow, Econometric Soc., 1975. *Publications:* (with S. Marglin and A. K. Sen) Guidelines for Project Evaluation, 1972; (with G. Heal) Economic Theory and Exhaustible Resources, 1979; The Control of Resources, 1982; (with K. Binmore) Economic Organizations as Games, 1986; (with K. Binmore) The Economics of Bargaining, 1987; (with P. Stoneham) Economic Policy and Technological Performance, 1987, An Inquiry into Well-Being and Destitution, 1993; articles on develt planning, optimum population, taxation and trade, welfare and justice, nat. resources, game theory, indust. org. and technical progress, poverty and unemployment, in Econ. Jl, Econometrica, Rev. of Econ. Stud., etc. *Address:* 1 Dean Drive, Holbrook Road, Cambridge CB1 4SW. *T:* Cambridge (01223) 212179.

DASHWOOD, Prof. Arthur Alan; Professor of European Law, and Fellow, Sidney Sussex College, University of Cambridge, since 1995; *b* 18 Oct. 1941; *s* of late Alan Stanley Dashwood and of Dorothy Mary Dashwood (*née* Childe); *m* 1971, Julie Rosalind Pashley. *Educ:* Michaelhouse, Natal, SA; Rhodes Univ., Grahamstown, SA (BA Hons 1962); Oriel Coll., Oxford (MA). Called to the Bar, Inner Temple, 1969. Asst Lectr, Dept of Civil Law, Univ. of Glasgow, 1966–67; Lecturer: Dept of Law, UCW, Aberystwyth, 1968–73; Centre of European Governmental Studies, Univ. of Edinburgh, 1973–75; Reader, Univ. of Sussex, 1975–78; Legal Sec. to Advocate General, Court of Justice of ECs, 1978–80; Prof. of Law, Univ. of Leicester, 1980–87; Dir, Legal Service, Council of EU, 1987–94. Editor, European Law Rev., 1975–91. *Publications:* The Substantive Law of the EEC, 1980, 3rd edn (with D. Wyatt) as Wyatt and Dashwood's European Community Law, 1993; contrib. to legal jls. *Recreation:* salmon and trout fishing. *Address:* Sidney Sussex College, Cambridge CB2 3HU. *T:* Cambridge (01223) 338874; 2 Harcourt Buildings, Temple, EC4Y 9DB. *T:* 0171–583 9020; The White House, The Square, Shearsby, near Lutterworth, Leics LE17 6PJ.

DASHWOOD, Sir Francis (John Vernon Hereward), 11th Bt, *cr* 1707; (Premier Baronet of Great Britain); *b* 7 Aug. 1925; *s* of Sir John Lindsay Dashwood, 10th Bt, CVO, and Helen Moira Eaton (*d* 1989); *S* father, 1966; *m* 1st, 1957, Victoria Ann Elizabeth Gwynne de Rutzen (*d* 1976); one *s* three *d*; 2nd, 1977, Marcella (*née* Scarafia), formerly wife of Giuseppe Sportoletti Baduel and *widow* of Jack Frye, CBE; one step *s* (from wife's first *m*). *Educ:* Eton; Christ Church, Oxford (BA 1948, MA 1953); Henry Fellow, Harvard Business Sch., USA. Foreign Office, 1944–45. Aluminum Company of Canada Ltd, 1950–51; EMI Ltd, 1951–53. Member of Buckinghamshire County Council, 1950–51; Member Lloyd's, 1956. Contested (C) West Bromwich, 1955, Gloucester, 1957. High Sheriff Bucks, 1976. SBStJ. *Publications:* The Dashwoods of West Wycombe, 1987; The Great Lloyd's Robbery, 1992. *Heir:* *s* Edward John Francis Dashwood [*b* 25 Sept. 1964; *m* 1989, Lucinda, *d* of G. H. F. Miesegaes; two *s* one *d*]. *Address:* West Wycombe Park, Buckinghamshire HP14 3AJ. *T:* High Wycombe (01494) 523720. *Clubs:* White's, Portland.

DASHWOOD, Sir Richard (James), 9th Bt *cr* 1684, of Kirtlington Park; TD 1987; Partner, Harris Allday Lea & Brooks, stockbrokers; *b* 14 Feb. 1950; *s* of Sir Henry George Massy Dashwood, 8th Bt, and Susan Mary (*d* 1985), *er d* of late Major V. R. Montgomerie-Charrington, Hunsdon House, Herts; *S* father, 1972; *m* 1984, Kathryn Ann (marr. diss. 1993), *er d* of Frank Mahon, Eastbury, Berks; one *s*. *Educ:* Maidwell Hall Preparatory Sch.; Eton College. Commissioned 14th/20th King's Hussars, 1969, later King's Royal Hussars; T&AVR, 1973– (Major 1992). *Heir:* *s* Frederick George Mahon Dashwood, *b* 29 Jan. 1988. *Address:* Ledwell Cottage, Sandford St Martin, Oxfordshire OX7 7AN. *T:* Great Tew (01608) 683267.

da SILVA, John Burke, CMG 1969; HM Diplomatic Service, retired; Adviser, Commercial Union Assurance Co., 1973–84; *b* 30 Aug. 1918; *o s* of late John Christian da Silva and

Gabrielle Guittard; *m* 1st, 1940, Janice (decd), *d* of Roy Mayor, Shrewsbury, Bermuda; one *d*; 2nd, 1963, Jennifer, *yr d* of late Capt. the Hon. T. T. Parker, DSC, RN, Greatham Moor, Hants; one *s* two *d*. *Educ:* Stowe Sch.; Trinity Coll., Cambridge (MA). Commnd Intell. Corps 1940, served with 1st Airborne Div., N Africa and Italy, GS02 SHAEF, France and Germany (despatches); Control Commn Germany and Austria. Joined Foreign Service, 1948; served Rome, Hamburg, Bahrain, Aden, Washington, FCO; retired 1973. Chm., Governors, Virginia Water Junior Sch., 1973–83; a Vice-Pres., Royal Soc. for Asian Affairs, 1983–86; Mem. Council, Oriental Ceramic Soc., 1977–80, 1984–87 (Hon. Treas., 1992–94). *Publications:* contributor: Oriental Art, Trans OCS, Asian Affairs, etc. *Recreation:* Oriental Art. *Address:* Copse Close, Virginia Water, Surrey GU25 4PH. *T:* Wentworth (01344) 842342. *Club:* Travellers'.

DATE, William Adrian, CBE 1973; *b* 1 July 1908; *er s* of James C. Date; *m* 1st, 1933, Dorothy MacGregor Grant (*d* 1979); two *d*; 2nd, 1981, Rhoda Elaine Minors (*d* 1989). *Educ:* Queen's Royal Coll., Trinidad; Grenada Boys' Secondary Sch.; Lodge Sch., Barbados; Middle Temple, London. Magistrate and District Govt Officer, St Lucia, 1933–39; Crown Attorney, St Vincent, 1939–44; Legal Draughtsman, Jamaica, 1944–47; Chief Secretary, Windward Islands, 1947–50; Puisne Judge of the Supreme Court of the Windward and Leeward Islands, 1950–56; Puisne Judge of Supreme Court, British Guiana, 1956–64, retd. Dir, Grenada Co-op. Bank, 1976–. *Recreation:* bridge. *Address:* PO Box 133, St George's, Grenada, West Indies.

DATTA, Dr Naomi, FRS 1985; Professor Emeritus, London University; *b* 17 Sept. 1922; *d* of Alexander and Ellen Henrietta Goddard; *m* 1943, S. P. Datta; two *d* one *s*. *Educ:* St Mary's Sch., Wantage; University Coll. London; W London Hosp. Med. Sch. MB BS (external); MD London. Junior medical posts, 1946–47; Bacteriologist in PHLS, 1947–57; Lectr, later Prof. of Microbial Genetics, RPMS, London Univ., 1957–84; retired 1984. *Publications:* papers on the genetics and epidemiology of antibiotic resistance in bacteria. *Recreations:* gardening, cooking, travelling. *Address:* 9 Duke's Avenue, W4 2AA. *T:* 0181-995 7562.

DAUBE, Prof. David, MA, DCL, PhD, Dr jur; FBA 1957; Director of the Robbins Hebraic and Roman Law Collections and Professor-in-Residence at the School of Law, University of California, Berkeley, 1970–81, Emeritus Professor of Law, since 1981; Emeritus Regius Professor, Oxford University, since 1970; Member, Academic Board, Institute of Jewish Studies, London, since 1953; *b* Freiburg, 8 Feb. 1909; 2nd *s* of Jakob Daube; *m* 1st, 1936 (marr. diss., 1964); three *s*; 2nd, 1986, Helen Smelser (*née* Margolis). *Educ:* Berthold-gymnasium, Freiburg; Universities of Freiburg, Göttingen and Cambridge. Fellow of Caius Coll., 1938–46, Hon. Fellow, 1974; Lecturer in Law, Cambridge, 1946–51; Professor of Jurisprudence at Aberdeen, 1951–55; Regius Prof. of Civil Law, Oxford Univ., and Fellow of All Souls Coll., 1955–70, Emeritus Fellow, 1980. Senior Fellow, Yale Univ., 1962; Delitzsch Lecturer, Münster, 1962; Gifford Lecturer, Edinburgh, for 1962 and 1963 (lectures delivered, 1963–64); Olaus Petri Lecturer, Uppsala, 1963; Ford Prof. of Political Science, Univ. of California, Berkeley, 1964; Riddell Lectr, Newcastle, 1965; Gray Lectr, Cambridge, 1966; Pope John Lectr, Catholic Univ. of America, Washington, 1966; Lionel Cohen Lectr, Jerusalem, 1970; inaug. Frosty Gerard Lectr, UC Irvine, 1981; G. Hitchings Terriberry Lectr, Tulane Univ., 1982; inaug. Gerald Goldfarb Meml Lectr, Univ. of Judaism, Los Angeles, 1991. Vis. Prof. of History, 1966–78, Hon. Prof., 1980, Univ. of Constance. President: Société d'Histoire des Droits de l'Antiquité, 1957–58; Classical Assoc. of GB, 1976–77; Jewish Law Assoc., 1983–85; Founder-Pres., B'nai B'rith Oxford, 1961. Corresp. Mem., Akad. Wiss., Göttingen, 1964, Bayer. Akad. Wiss., Munich, 1966; Hon. Mem. Royal Irish Acad., 1970; Fellow: Amer. Acad. of Arts and Sciences, 1971; World Acad. of Art and Sci., 1975; Amer. Acad. for Jewish Research, 1979; Amer. Soc. for Legal History, 1983; Hon. Fellow, Oxford Centre for Postgraduate Hebrew Studies, 1973. Hon. LLD: Edinburgh 1960; Leicester 1964; Cambridge 1981; Aberdeen, 1990; Dr *hc* Paris 1963; Hon. DHL: Hebrew Union Coll., 1971; Graduate Theol Union, Berkeley, 1988; Dr jur *hc* Munich, 1972; Dr phil *hc* Göttingen, 1987. *Publications:* Studies in Biblical Law, 1947; The New Testament and Rabbinic Judaism, 1956; Forms of Roman Legislation, 1956; The Exodus Pattern in the Bible, 1963; The Sudden in the Scriptures, 1964; Collaboration with Tyranny in Rabbinic Law, 1965; He that Cometh, 1966; Roman Law, 1969; Civil Disobedience in Antiquity, 1972; Ancient Hebrew Fables, 1973; Wine in the Bible, 1975; Medical and Genetic Ethics, 1976; Duty of Procreation, 1977; Typologie im Werk des Flavius Josephus, 1977; Ancient Jewish Law, 1981; Geburt der Detektivgeschichte, 1983; Das Alte Testament im Neuen, 1984; Sons and Strangers, 1984; (with C. Carmichael) Witnesses in Bible and Talmud, 1986; Appeasement or Resistance and other essays on New Testament Judaism, 1987; (ed) Studies in memory of F. de Zulueta, 1959; (with W. D. Davies) Studies in honour of C. H. Dodd, 1956, and articles; *Festschriften:* Daube Noster, 1974; Studies in Jewish Legal History in Honour of D.D., 1974; Donum Gentilicium, 1978; Berkeley and Oxford Symposium in Honour of D.D., 1993. *Address:* School of Law, University of California, Berkeley, CA 94720, USA.

DAUBENY DE MOLEYNS, family name of **Baron Ventry.**

DAULTANA, Mumtaz Mohammad Khan; Ambassador of Pakistan to the Court of St James's, 1972–78; *b* 23 Feb. 1916; *o s* of Nawab Ahmadyar Daultana; *m* 1943, Almas Jehan; one *s* one *d*. *Educ:* St Anthony's Sch., Lahore; Government Coll., Lahore (BA (Hons)); Corpus Christi Coll., Oxford (MA); Called to Bar, Middle Temple, 1940; 1st cl. 1st position in Bar exam. Mem., All India Muslim League, 1942–; unopposed election as Mem. Punjab Legislative Assembly, 1943; Gen. Sec., Punjab Muslim League, 1944; Sec., All India Muslim League Central Cttee of Action, 1945; Elected Member: Punjab Assembly, 1946; Constituent Assembly of India, 1947; Constituent Assembly, Pakistan, 1947; Finance Minister, Punjab, 1947–48; Pres., Punjab Muslim League, 1948–50; Chief Minister of Punjab, 1951–53; Finance Minister, West Pakistan, 1955–56; Defence Minister, Pakistan, 1957; Pres., Pakistan Muslim League, 1967–72. Elected Member: Nat. Assembly of Pakistan, 1970; Constitution Cttee of Nat. Assembly, 1972. *Publications:* Agrarian Report of Pakistan Muslim League, 1950; Thoughts on Pakistan's Foreign Policy, 1956; Kashmir in Present Day Context, 1965. *Recreations:* music, squash. *Address:* 8 Durand Road, Lahore, Pakistan. *T:* (42) 302459, (21) 532387. *Clubs:* United Oxford & Cambridge University; Gymkhana (Lahore).

DAUNCEY, Brig. Michael Donald Keen, DSO 1945; DL; *b* 11 May 1920; *o s* of late Thomas Gough Dauncey and Alice Dauncey (*née* Keen); *m* 1945, Marjorie Kathleen, *d* of H. W. Neep, FCA; one *s* two *d*. *Educ:* King Edward's School, Birmingham; Inter. Exam., Inst. of Chartered Accountants. Commissioned, 22nd (Cheshire) Regt, 1941; seconded to Glider Pilot Regt, 1943; Arnhem, 1944 (wounded three times; taken prisoner, later escaped); MA to GOC-in-C, Greece, 1946–47; seconded to Para. Regt, 1948–49; Staff Coll., 1950; Instructor, RMA, 1957–58; CO, 1st Bn 22nd (Cheshire) Regt, 1963–66, BAOR and UN peace keeping force, Cyprus; DS plans, JSSC, 1966–68; Comdt, Jungle Warfare Sch., 1968–69; Comdt, Support Weapons Wing, Sch. of Infantry, 1969–72; Defence and Military Attaché, Madrid, 1973–75; retired 1976. Col, 22nd (Cheshire) Regt, 1978–85; Hon. Col, 1st Cadet Bn, Glos Regt (ACF), 1981–90. Pres., Glider Pilot Regtl Assoc., 1994–. DL Glos 1983. *Recreations:* rough shooting, travelling, tennis; also under-gardener. *Address:* Uley Lodge, Uley, near Dursley, Glos GL11 5SN. *T:* Dursley (01453) 860216. *Club:* Army and Navy.

DAUNT, Maj.-Gen. Brian, CB 1956; CBE 1953; DSO 1943; late RA; *b* 16 March 1900; *s* of Dr William Daunt, Parade House, Hastings; *m* 1938, Millicent Margaret, *d* of Capt. A. S. Balfour, Allermuir House, Colinton, Edinburgh; two *d* (one *s* decd). *Educ:* Tonbridge; RMA, Woolwich. Commissioned RA, 1920; served NW Frontier, India, 1929–30; War of 1939–45; France, 1940, as 2 i/c Regt; CO Anti-Tank Regt, 1941; Italy, as CO 142 Field Regt, RA, Royal Devon Yeo., 1943 (DSO); CRA: 1st Armoured Div., 1944; 46 Div., 1944; 10 Indian Div., 1946; Italy, 1945 (despatches). Has had various Brigadier's appts. Commandant Coast Artillery Sch. and Inspector Coast Artillery, 1950–53; General Officer Commanding Troops, Malta, 1953–Nov. 1956; retired, 1957; Controller, Home Dept, British Red Cross Society, 1957–66. Col Comdt RA, 1960–65. CStJ 1966. *Recreations:* gardening, music, drama. *Address:* 10 Church Lane, Wallingford, Oxon OX10 0DX. *T:* Wallingford (01491) 38111. *Club:* Army and Navy.

DAUNT, Patrick Eldon; Head of Bureau for Action in favour of Disabled People, EEC, 1982–87, retired; international consultant on education and disability; *b* 19 Feb. 1925; *s* of Dr Francis Eldon Daunt and Winifred Doggett Daunt (*née* Wells); *m* 1958, Jean Patricia, *d* of Lt-Col Percy Wentworth Hargreaves and of Joan (*née* Holford); three *s* one *d*. *Educ:* Rugby Sch.; Wadham Coll., Oxford. BA, 1st Cl. Hons Lit. Hum., 1949, MA 1954, Oxon. Housemaster, Christ's Hosp., 1959; Headmaster, Thomas Bennett Comprehensive Sch., Crawley, 1965. Chm., Campaign for Comprehensive Educn, 1971–73; Principal Administrator, EEC, 1974–82. Vis. Fellow, London Inst. of Educn, 1988–94. Chm., ASBAH, 1990–. UNESCO consultant, special educn in Romania, 1992. Ravenswood Foundn Internat. Award, 1992. *Publications:* Comprehensive Values, 1975; Meeting Disability, a European Response, 1991; (ed) Teacher Education for Special Needs in Europe, 1995. *Recreations:* books, botany. *Address:* 4 Bourn Bridge Road, Little Abington, Cambridge CB1 6BJ. *T:* Cambridge (01223) 891485. *Club:* United Oxford & Cambridge University.

DAUNT, Sir Timothy Lewis Achilles, KCMG 1989 (CMG 1982); HM Diplomatic Service, retired; *b* 11 Oct. 1935; *s* of L. H. G. Daunt and Margery (*née* Lewis Jones); *m* 1962, Patricia Susan Knight; one *s* two *d*. *Educ:* Sherborne; St Catharine's Coll., Cambridge. 8th KRI Hussars, 1954–56. Entered Foreign Office, 1959; Ankara, 1960; FO, 1964; Nicosia, 1967; Private Sec. to Permanent Under-Sec. of State, FCO, 1970; Bank of England, 1972; UK Mission, NY, 1973; Counsellor, OECD, Paris, 1975; Head of South European Dept, FCO, 1978–81; Associate at Centre d'études et de recherches internationales, Paris, 1982; Minister and Dep. UK Perm. Rep. to NATO, Brussels, 1982–85; Asst Under-Sec. of State (Defence), FCO, 1985–86; Ambassador to Turkey, 1986–92; Dep. Under-Sec. of State (Defence), FCO, 1992–95. *Address:* c/o Messrs C. Hoare & Co., 37 Fleet Street, EC4P 4DQ.

DAUSSET, Prof. Jean Baptiste Gabriel Joachim; Grand Croix de la Légion d'Honneur; Professeur de Médecine Expérimentale au Collège de France, 1977–87; *b* 19 Oct. 1916; *s* of Henri Dausset and Elizabeth Brullard; *m* 1962, Rose Mayoral; one *s* one *d*. *Educ:* Lycée Michelet, Paris; Faculty of Medicine, University of Paris. Associate Professor, 1958–68, Professor of Immunohaematology, 1968–77, University of Paris. Institut Nationale de la Santé et de la Recherche Médicale: Director of Research Unit on Immunogenetics of Human Transplantation, 1968–84; Centre National de la Recherche Scientifique: Co-Director, Oncology and Immuno-haematology Laboratory, 1968–84. Gairdner Foundn Prize, 1977; Koch Foundn Prize, 1978; Wolf Foundn Prize, 1978; Nobel Prize for Physiology or Medicine, 1980. *Publications:* Immuno-hématologie biologique et clinique, 1956; (with F. T. Rapaport) Human Transplantation, 1968; (with G. Snell and S. Nathanson) Histocompatibility, 1976; (with M. Fougereau) Immunology 1980, 1980; (with M. Pla) HLA, 1985. *Recreation:* plastic art. *Address:* 9 rue de Villersexel, 75007 Paris, France. *T:* 42221882.

DAVAN WETTON, Hilary John; Director of Music, Tonbridge School, since 1993; conductor; *b* 23 Dec. 1943; *s* of late Eric Davan Wetton, CBE and (Kathleen) Valerie Davan Wetton (*née* Edwards); *m* 1st, 1964, Elizabeth Jane Tayler; three *d*; 2nd, 1989, Alison Mary Moncrieff Kelly; one *s*. *Educ:* Westminster Sch.; Royal Coll. of Music (ARCM); Brasenose Coll., Oxford (BA, MA, DipEd). Director of Music: St Alban's Sch., 1965–67; Cranleigh Sch., 1967–74; Stantonbury Music Centre, 1974–78; St Paul's Girls' Sch., 1978–93. Conductor: Guildford Choral Soc., 1968–; Milton Keynes City Orch., 1974–; Holst Singers, 1978–91; City of London Choir, 1989–; Wren Orch., 1990–; Scottish Schools Orch., 1984–95; Edinburgh Youth Orch., 1994–; guest conducting and recording with Philharmonia, LPO, Royal Phil. Orch., BBC Concert Orch., Ulster Orch., orchestras in Bulgaria, Iceland, USA, Australia. Presenter, Classic FM Masterclass. Hon. MA Open, 1984; Hon. DMus De Montfort, 1994. Diapason d'Or for Holst recording, 1994. *Publications:* contrib. musical jls and Guardian. *Recreation:* tennis. *Address:* Hartlake Roundels, Hartlake Road, Golden Green, Kent TN11 0BL. *Clubs:* Garrick, Royal Society of Arts, Pepys Society.

DAVENPORT, (Arthur) Nigel; President, British Actors' Equity Association, 1986–92; *b* 23 May 1928; *s* of Arthur Henry Davenport and Katherine Lucy (*née* Meiklejohn); *m* 1st, 1951, Helena White (*d* 1978); one *s* one *d*; 2nd, 1972, Maria Aitken, *qv* (marr. diss.); one *s*. *Educ:* Cheltenham Coll.; Trinity Coll., Oxford (MA). Entered acting profession, 1951; for first ten years worked almost exclusively in theatre; original mem. English Stage Co. at Royal Court Th., 1956; A Taste of Honey, on Broadway, 1960; mainly television and films, 1961–; starred or co-starred in over 30 cinema films, incl. A High Wind in Jamaica, 1964; Man for All Seasons, 1966; Play Dirty, Royal Hunt of the Sun, Virgin Soldiers, 1969; A Last Valley, 1970; Living Free, Mary, Queen of Scots, 1972; Phase IV, 1973; The Island of Dr Moreau, 1977; Night Hawks, Chariots of Fire, 1980; Greystoke, 1982; *television:* South Riding; George III in The Prince Regent; Howard's Way, 1987–88, 1990; Trainer, 1991. Toured England: King Lear (title rôle), 1986; The Old Country, 1989; Sleuth, 1990; The Constant Wife, 1994–95; Brideshead Revisited, 1995. Murder is Easy, Duke of York's, 1993. Mem. Council, British Actors' Equity, 1976; Vice Pres., 1978–82, 1985–86. *Recreations:* gardening, travel.

DAVENPORT, Brian John; QC 1980; *b* 17 March 1936; *s* of R. C. Davenport, FRCS, and Mrs H. E. Davenport; *m* 1969, Erica Tickell, *yr d* of Prof. E. N. Willmer, *qv*; two *s* one *d*. *Educ:* Bryanston Sch.; Worcester Coll., Oxford (MA). 2 Lieut RE, 1955–56. Called to the Bar, Gray's Inn, 1960 (Atkin Scholar); Bencher, 1983. Junior Counsel: to Export Credit Guarantees Dept, 1971–74; to Dept of Employment, 1972–74; (Common Law), to Bd of Inland Revenue, 1974–80; (Common Law), to the Crown, 1978–80; a Law Comr, 1981–88. Mem., Gen. Council of the Bar, 1969–73. Mem. Cttee of Management, Barristers Benevolent Assoc., 1963–78, Jt Hon. Sec. 1978–87. *Publications:* (ed jtly with F. M. B. Reynolds) 13th and 14th edns of Bowstead on Agency. *Address:* 43 Downshire Hill, NW3 1NU. *T:* 0171–435 3332; c/o Norton Rose, Kempson House, Camomile Street, EC3A 7AN. *T:* 0171–583 2434.

DAVENPORT, Major (retd) David John Cecil, CBE 1989; DL; Member, Rural Development Commission, 1982–90 (Deputy Chairman, April–Oct. 1988); *b* 28 Oct.

1934; *s* of late Major John Lewes Davenport, DL, JP, and Louise Aline Davenport; *m* 1st, 1959, Jennifer Burness (marr. diss. 1969); two *d*; 2nd, 1971, Lindy Jane Baker; one *s*. *Educ:* Eton College; Royal Military Academy, Sandhurst. Commnd into Grenadier Guards, 1954, retired 1967. RAC, Cirencester, 1968–69. Chairman, Leominster District Council, 1975–76. Chm., CoSIRA, 1982–88. Chm., Regional Adv. Cttee of the Forestry Commn (SW), 1974–87; Pres., Royal Forestry Soc., 1991–93. DL, 1974, High Sheriff, 1989–90, Hereford and Worcester. *Address:* Mansel Lacy House, Hereford HR4 7HQ. *T:* Bridge Sollars (0198122) 224. *Clubs:* Boodle's, MCC.

DAVENPORT, Maurice Hopwood, FCIB; Director, First National Finance Corporation plc, 1985–95; *b* 19 March 1925; *s* of Richard and Elizabeth Davenport; *m* 1954, Sheila Timms; one *s* two *d*. *Educ:* Rivington and Blackrod Grammar Sch. FIB 1982. Served RN, 1943–46. Joined Williams Deacon's Bank, 1940; Sec., 1960; Asst Gen. Man., 1969; Dir, 1978–85, Man. Dir, 1982–85, Williams & Glyn's Bank; Dir, Royal Bank of Scotland Gp and Royal Bank of Scotland, 1982–85. *Recreations:* walking, gardening, reading. *Address:* Pines, Dormans Park, East Grinstead, West Sussex RH19 2LX. *T:* Dormans Park (01342) 870439.

DAVENPORT, Nigel; *see* Davenport, A. N.

DAVENPORT, Walter Arthur B.; *see* Bromley-Davenport.

DAVENPORT-HANDLEY, Sir David (John), Kt 1980; OBE 1962; JP; DL; Chairman, Clipsham Quarry Co., since 1947; *b* 2 Sept. 1919; *s* of John Davenport-Handley, JP; *m* 1943, Leslie Mary Goldsmith; one *s* one *d*. *Educ:* RNC Dartmouth. RN retd 1947. Chm., Rutland and Stamford Conservative Assoc., 1952–65; Treasurer, East Midlands Area Conservative Assoc., 1965–71, Chm. 1971–77; Vice-Chm., Nat. Union of Conservative & Unionist Assocs, 1977–79, Chm., 1979–80. Member: Consumers' Cttees for GB and for England and Wales, 1956–65; Parole Bd, 1981–84. Chm., Rutland Historic Churches Preservation Trust, 1987–. President: E Midlands Area Cons. Assoc., 1987–94; Nat. Union of Cons. and Unionist Assocs, 1990–91. Governor, Swinton Conservative Coll., 1973–77; Chairman: Board of Visitors, Ashwell Prison, 1955–73; Governors, Casterton Community Coll., 1960–78; Trustee, Oakham Sch., 1970–86. JP 1948, High Sheriff 1954, DL 1962, Vice-Lieutenant 1972, Rutland; Chm., Rutland Petty Sessional Div., 1957–84; DL Leicestershire 1974. *Recreations:* gardening, music, travel. *Address:* Clipsham Hall, Oakham, Rutland, Leics LE15 7SE. *T:* Castle Bytham (01780) 410204. *Club:* English-Speaking Union.

DAVENTRY, 3rd Viscount *cr* 1943; **Francis Humphrey Maurice FitzRoy Newdegate;** Lord-Lieutenant of Warwickshire, since 1990; *b* 17 Dec. 1921; *s* of Comdr Hon. John Maurice FitzRoy Newdegate, RN (*y s* of 1st Viscountess; he assumed by Royal Licence, 1936, additional surname and arms of Newdegate and *d* 1976) and Lucia Charlotte Susan, OBE (*d* 1982), *d* of Sir Francis Alexander Newdigate Newdegate, GCMG; *S* uncle, 1986; *m* 1959, Hon. Rosemary, *e d* of 1st Baron Norrie, GCMG, GCVO, CB, DSO, MC; two *s* one *d*. *Educ:* Eton. Served War of 1939–45 with Coldstream Guards, N Africa and Italy; Captain 1943. ADC to Viceroy of India, 1946–48. JP 1960, DL 1970, High Sheriff 1970, Vice-Lieut, 1974–90, Warwickshire. KStJ 1991. *Heir:* *s* Hon. James Edward FitzRoy Newdegate [*b* 27 July 1960; *m* 1994, Georgia, *d* of John Lodge, Cirencester]. *Address:* Temple House, Arbury, Nuneaton, Warwickshire CV10 7PT. *T:* Nuneaton (01203) 383514. *Club:* Boodle's.

DAVEY, David Garnet, OBE 1949; MSc, PhD; Research Director of Pharmaceuticals Division, Imperial Chemical Industries Ltd, 1969–75; *b* 8 Aug. 1912; *y s* of I. W. Davey, Caerphilly, Glamorgan; *m* 1938, Elizabeth Gale; one *s* two *d*. *Educ:* University Coll., Cardiff (1st cl. Hons Zoology; MSc 1935); Gonville and Caius Coll., Cambridge (PhD 1938); Harvard Univ. Med. Sch. (Research Fellow). Inst. of Animal Pathology, Univ. of Cambridge, 1938; Lectr, University Coll., Cardiff, 1939–40; Min. of Supply (Radar), 1941; joined ICI 1942; Biological Research Manager, Pharmaceuticals Div., 1957–69. Pres., European Soc. for Study of Drug Toxicity, 1964–69; Member: MRC, 1971–75; Cttee on Review of Medicines, 1975–81; Sub-cttee on Toxicity, Clinical Trials, and Therapeutic Efficacy, Cttee on Safety of Medicines, 1976–81. Chalmers Gold Medal, Royal Soc. Tropical Medicine and Hygiene, 1947; Therapeutics Gold Medal, Apothecaries Soc., 1947. *Publications:* contribs to Annals Trop. Med.; Trans Royal Soc. Tropical Medicine and Hygiene; British Med. Bulletin; Proc. European Soc. for Study of Drug Toxicity, etc. *Recreation:* gardening. *Address:* Aragon Lodge, Star Lane, Morcombelake, Dorset DT6 6DN. *T:* Chideock (01297) 489458.

DAVEY, David Herbert P.; *see* Penry-Davey.

DAVEY, Francis, MA; Headmaster of Merchant Taylors' School, 1974–82; *b* 23 March 1932; *er s* of Wilfred Henry Davey, BSc and Olive (*née* Geeson); *m* 1960, Margaret Filby Lake, MA Oxon, AMA, *o d* of Harold Lake, DMus Oxon, FRCO; one *s* one *d*. *Educ:* Plymouth Coll.; New Coll., Oxford (Hon. Exhibr); Corpus Christi Coll., Cambridge (Schoolmaster Fellow Commoner). 1st cl. Class. Hon. Mods 1953, 2nd cl. Lit. Hum. 1955, BA 1955, MA 1958. RAF, 1950–51; Classical Upper Sixth Form Master, Dulwich Coll., 1955–60; Head of Classics Dept, Warwick Sch., 1960–66; Headmaster, Dr Morgan's Grammar Sch., Bridgwater, 1966–73. *Publications:* articles in Enciclopedia dello Spettacolo and Classical Review. *Recreations:* Rugby, swimming, gardening, travel. *Address:* Crossings Cottage, Dousland, Yelverton, S Devon PL20 6LU. *T:* Yelverton (01822) 853928. *Clubs:* East India, Devonshire, Sports and Public Schools; Union (Oxford).

DAVEY, Geoffrey Wallace, a Recorder of the Crown Court, since 1974; *b* 16 Oct. 1924; *s* of late Hector F. T. Davey and Alice M. Davey; *m* 1964, Joyce Irving Steel (*d* 1995); two *s* one *d*. *Educ:* Queen Elizabeth Grammar Sch., Faversham; Wadham Coll., Oxford (MA). Called to Bar, Lincoln's Inn, 1954; admitted Ghana Bar, 1957; resumed practice NE Circuit, 1970. Chm., Med. Appeal Tribunal, 1982–; Dep. Chm., Agricl Land Tribunal, 1982–. FCIArb (ACIArb 1992). *Recreations:* golf, cooking, carpentry. *Address:* 22 Mill Hill Lane, Northallerton, N Yorkshire DL6 1DN. *T:* Northallerton (01609) 775943; 19 Baker Street, Middlesbrough, Cleveland TS1 2LF. *T:* Middlesbrough (01642) 217037–8; 5 King's Bench Walk, Temple, EC4Y 7DN.

DAVEY, Idris Wyn; Under-Secretary, Welsh Office, 1972–77; Deputy Chairman, Local Government Boundary Commission for Wales, 1979–89; *b* 8 July 1917; *m* 1943, Lilian Lloyd-Bowen; two *d*. Admiralty, 1940–47; Welsh Bd of Health: Asst Principal, 1948; Principal, 1951; Sec. Local Govt Commn for Wales, 1959–62; Welsh Office: Asst Sec. (in Min. of Housing and Local Govt), 1962; Establishment Officer, 1966–72; Under-Sec., 1972; seconded as Sec. and Mem., Local Govt Staff Commn for Wales and NHS Staff Commn for Wales, 1972–73. Mem., Sports Council for Wales, 1978–88. *Recreations:* University of the Third Age, watching Rugby football, gardening. *Address:* 4A Southgate Road, Southgate, Swansea SA3 2BT. *T:* Bishopston (01792) 234320.

DAVEY, Jocelyn; *see* Raphael, Chaim.

DAVEY, John Trevor, FCA; Director 1968–91, and Deputy Chairman 1988–91, Thames Television PLC; *b* 20 March 1923; *s* of Clarence Reginald Davey and Ivy Ellender Davey (*née* Lippiatt); *m* 1962, Margaret June Cobby; two *d*. *Educ:* Richmond (Surrey) County Secondary Sch. Binder Hamlyn & Co., Chartered Accountants, 1939–55 (during which time served under Articles); Gp Accountant, British Lion Films Ltd, 1955–58; Co. Sec. and Financial Controller, Pulsometer Engrg Co. Ltd, 1958–61; British Electric Traction Co., later BET PLC, 1961–88: Chm. and/or Man. Dir, various subsids, and Main Bd Dir, 1978–88. *Address:* 20 Mulberry Hill, Shenfield, Brentwood, Essex CM15 8JS.

DAVEY, Jon Colin; Director of Cable and Satellite, Independent Television Commission, since 1991; *b* 16 June 1938; *s* of late Frederick John Davey and Dorothy Mary Davey; *m* 1962, Ann Patricia Streames; two *s* one *d*. *Educ:* Raynes Park Grammar Sch. Joined Home Office, 1957; served in Civil Defence, Immigration, Criminal Policy, Prison and Criminal Justice Depts; Asst Sec., Broadcasting Dept, 1981–85; Dir-Gen., Cable Authy, 1985–90. Asst Sec., Franks Cttee on Sect. 2 of Official Secrets Act, 1971–72; Secretary: Williams Cttee on Obscenity and Film Censorship, 1977–79; Hunt Inquiry into Cable Expansion and Broadcasting Policy, 1982. Vice-Chm., Media Policy Cttee, Council of Europe, 1983–84; Mem., British Screen Adv. Council, 1990–. Hon. Fellow, Soc. of Cable Television Engrs, 1994. *Recreations:* lawnmaking, Bach, English countryside. *Address:* Independent Television Commission, 33 Foley Street, W1P 7LB. *T:* 0171–306 7799, *Fax:* 0171–306 7866.

DAVEY, Julian; International Advisor, Anglia Polytechnic University, since 1994; *b* 24 July 1946; *s* of Frederick Victor Davey and Dorothy Davey (*née* Stokes); *m* 1971, Prof. Katherine O'Donovan; one *d*. *Educ:* Kingston Grammar Sch.; Selwyn Coll., Cambridge; Inst. of Education, London Univ. (MA 1973). British Council: Ethiopia, 1969–72; E Asia Dept, 1973–75; Mgt Accountant, 1975–78; Malaysia, 1978–81; Dep. Controller, Finance, 1981–85; Dir, Hong Kong, 1985–90; Regl Dir, Asia-Pacific, 1992–94. *Recreations:* ski-mountaineering, boat-building, performing arts, arboriculture. *Address:* Potts Gill, Caldbeck, Cumbria CA7 8LB. *T:* Caldbeck (016974) 78499. *Clubs:* Commonwealth Trust; Hong Kong (Hong Kong).

DAVEY, Keith Alfred Thomas, CB 1973; Solicitor and Legal Adviser, Department of the Environment, 1970–82; *b* 1920; *s* of W. D. F. Davey; *m* 1949, Kathleen Elsie, *d* of Rev. F. J. Brabyn; one *s* one *d*. *Educ:* Cambridge and County High Sch.; Fitzwilliam House, Cambridge (MA). Served War of 1939–45, Middle East (Captain). Called to the Bar, Middle Temple, 1947. Principal Asst Solicitor, DHSS, 1968–70. *Recreations:* looking at churches, reading history, keeping cats and dogs. *Address:* 165 Shelford Road, Trumpington, Cambridge CB2 2ND. *Clubs:* Athenæum, Sette of Odd Volumes.

DAVEY, Peter Gordon, CBE 1986; Managing Director, Oxford Intelligent Machines Ltd, since 1990; *b* 6 Aug. 1935; *s* of late Lt-Col Frank Davey, Royal Signals and H. Jean Davey (*née* Robley); *m* 1961; two *s* two *d*. *Educ:* Winchester Coll.; Gonville and Caius Coll., Cambridge (Mech. Scis Tripos, pt 2 Electrical; MA 1961). MIEE; MBCS 1967. Engineer: GEC Applied Electronics Labs, Stanmore, 1958–61; Lawrence Radiation Lab, Berkeley, Calif, 1961–64; Guest Researcher, Heidelberg Univ., 1964–65; Oxford University: Project Engr, Nuclear Physics Lab., 1966–79; Co-ordinator, Indust. Robotics Research Prog., SERC, 1979–84; Head of Inter-active Computing Facility, Rutherford Lab, SRC, 1978–80; of Robot Welding Project, Engrg Sci. Lab., 1979–84; Sen. Res. Fellow, St Cross Coll., 1981–89. Tech. Dir, Electro Pneumatic Equipment Ltd, Letchworth, 1968–; Man. Dir, Meta Machines Ltd, 1984–87 (Dir, 1984–91). Ed., Open University Press Industrial Robotics Series, 1982–. Hon. Prof., UCW, Aberystwyth, 1988–. Hon. DSc Hull, 1987. *Publications:* (with W. F. Clocksin) A Tutorial Introduction to Industrial Robotics: artificial intelligence skills, 1982; (contrib.) Robot Vision, 1982; contribs to learned jls on robotics and image analysis systems. *Recreations:* buildings restoration, squash, sailing. *Address:* 22 Park Town, Oxford OX2 6SH.

DAVEY, Peter John; Editor, Architectural Review, since 1981; *b* 28 Feb. 1940; *s* of John Davey and Mary (*née* Roberts); *m* 1968, Carolyn Pulford; two *s*. *Educ:* Oundle Sch.; Edinburgh University (BArch). RIBA. News and Features Editor, 1974, Man. Editor, 1978, Architects' Journal; Managing Editor, Architectural Review, 1980. Mem. Council, RIBA, 1990–93 (Vice Pres. and Hon. Librarian, 1991–93). Kt 1st Cl., Order of White Rose (Finland), 1991. *Publications:* Architects' Journal Legal Handbook (ed), 1973; Arts and Crafts Architecture, 1980, 2nd edn 1995; numerous articles in architectural jls. *Recreations:* pursuit of edible fungi, fishing, cooking. *Address:* 44 Hungerford Road, N7 9LP. *Club:* Athenæum.

DAVEY, Dr Ronald William; Physician to the Queen, since 1986; *b* 25 Oct. 1943; *s* of Frederick George Davey and Cissy Beatrice Davey (*née* Lawday); *m* 1st, 1966; one *s* one *d*; 2nd, 1991, Priscilla Anne Kennedy. *Educ:* Trinity School of John Whitgift; King's College London; King's College Hosp. (MB BS; FFHom; AKC). Gen. med. practice, 1970–77; Private homoeopathic medical practice, 1978–; research into electro-stimulation and drug addiction, 1978–79; Hon. Med. Res. Dir, Blackie Foundn Trust, 1980–; Hon. Res. Fellow, Nat. Heart and Lung Inst., Univ. of London, 1990– (Blackie Res. Fellow, 1988–90); former Consultant to Res. Council for Complementary Medicine (Vice-Chm., 1986–87). *Publications:* medical papers. *Recreations:* riding, ski-ing, music, writing. *Address:* 1 Upper Wimpole Street, W1M 7TD. *T:* 0171–580 5489. *Club:* Royal Society of Medicine.

DAVEY, Roy Charles; Headmaster, King's School, Bruton, 1957–72; *b* 25 June 1915; *s* of William Arthur Davey and Georgina (*née* Allison); *m* 1940, Kathleen Joyce Sumner; two *d*. *Educ:* Christ's Hospital; Brasenose Coll., Oxford (Open Scholar). Asst Master, Weymouth Coll., 1937–40. War Service, Royal Artillery, 1940–46. Senior Master, 1946–49, Warden, 1949–57, The Village Coll., Impington. FRSA. *Recreations:* poetry, botany, gardening, games. *Address:* Fir Trees, Buckland Newton, Dorchester, Dorset DT2 7BY. *T:* Buckland Newton (01300) 345262. *Club:* East India, Devonshire, Sports and Public Schools.

DAVEY, Prof. William, CBE 1978; PhD; FRSC; President, Portsmouth Polytechnic, 1969–82; Honorary Professor, University of Westminster (formerly Polytechnic of Central London), since 1979; *b* Chesterfield, Derbyshire, 15 June 1917; *m* 1941, Eunice Battye; two *s*. *Educ:* University Coll., Nottingham; Technical Coll., Huddersfield. BSc, PhD (London, external). Chemist: ICI Scottish Dyes, 1940; Boots, 1941; Shell, 1942–44. Lectr and Sen. Lectr in Organic Chemistry, Acton Techn. Coll., 1944–53; Head of Dept of Chemistry and Biology, The Polytechnic, Regent Street, London, W1, 1953–59; Principal, Coll. of Technology, Portsmouth, 1960–69. FRSA, FRSC, CIMgt. DUniv Portsmouth, 1993. *Publications:* Industrial Chemistry, 1961; numerous original papers in: Jl Chem. Soc., Inst. Petroleum, Jl Applied Chem. *Recreations:* motoring, foreign travel. *Address:* 67 Ferndale, Waterlooville, Portsmouth PO7 7PH. *T:* Waterlooville (01705) 263014.

DAVID, family name of **Baroness David.**

DAVID, Baroness *cr* 1978 (Life Peer), of Romsey in the City of Cambridge; **Nora Ratcliff David;** JP; *b* 23 Sept. 1913; *d* of George Blockley Blakesley, JP, and Annie Edith Blakesley; *m* 1935, Richard William David, CBE (*d* 1993); two *s* two *d*. *Educ:* Ashby-de-la-Zouch Girls' Grammar School; St Felix, Southwold; Newnham Coll., Cambridge (MA; Hon. Fellow 1986). Mem. Bd, Peterborough Develt Corp., 1976–78. A Baroness-in-

Waiting (Government Whip), 1978–79; Opposition Whip, 1979–82; Dep. Chief Opposition Whip, 1982–87; opposition spokesman on education. Pres., Inst. for Study and Treatment of Delinquency, 1987–. Member: Cambridge City Council, 1964–67, 1968–74; Cambs County Council, 1974–78. Fellow, Anglia Poly. Univ (formerly Higher Educn Coll.), 1989. JP Cambridge City, 1965–. *Recreations:* swimming, theatre, travel. *Address:* 50 Highsett, Cambridge CB2 1NZ. *T:* Cambridge (01223) 350376; Cove, New Polzeath, Cornwall PL27 6UF. *T:* Trebetherick (01208) 863310.

DAVID, Sir (Jean) Marc, Kt 1986; CBE 1982; QC (Mauritius) 1969; Barrister, in private practice since 1964; Hon. Professor of Law, University of Mauritius, since 1990; *b* 22 Sept. 1925; *s* of late Joseph Claudius David and Marie Lucresia David (*née* Henrisson); *m* 1948, Mary Doreen Mahoney; three *s* three *d. Educ:* Royal Coll., Port Louis; Royal Coll., Curepipe, Mauritius (Laureate (classical side) of English Scholarship, 1945); LSE (LLB Hons). Called to the Bar, Middle Temple, 1949. Barrister in private practice, 1950–54; Dist Magistrate, then Crown Law Officer (Crown Counsel, Sen. Crown Counsel and Actg AAG), 1954–64. Chm., Mauritius Bar Assoc., 1968, 1979. Chairman: various arbitration tribunals, commns of enquiry and cttees apptd by govt, 1958–; Electoral Supervisory and Boundaries Commns, 1973–82 (Mem., 1968–73); Mem., Panel of Conciliators and Arbitrators, Internat. Centre for Settlement of Investment Disputes, 1969–. Visitor, Univ. of Mauritius, 1980–81. *Recreations:* reading, listening to music, horse racing. *Address:* (home) Villa da Mar, Trou-aux-Biches, Triolet, Mauritius. *T:* 2615070; (chambers) 11 Jules Koenig Street, Port-Louis, Mauritius. *T:* 2088938. *Clubs:* City (Port Louis); Turf, Racing (Mauritius).

DAVID, Robert Allan; Head of International and Tourism Division, Department of Employment, 1989–91; *b* 27 April 1937; *s* of George David and Mabel Edith David; *m* 1961, Brenda Marshall; three *d. Educ:* Cathays High Sch., Cardiff. BoT, 1955–71; Dept of Employment, 1971–91. *Recreations:* badminton, tennis, gardening. *Address:* The Briars, Ninehams Road, Tatsfield, Westerham, Kent TN16 2AN. *T:* Tatsfield (01959) 577357.

DAVID, Sir Robert Daniel George, (Sir Robin), Kt 1995; QC 1968; DL; **His Honour Judge David;** a Circuit Judge (formerly Chairman, Cheshire Quarter Sessions), since 1968; *b* 30 April 1922; *s* of late Alexander Charles Robert David and late Edrica Doris Pole David (*née* Evans); *m* 1944, Edith Mary David (*née* Marsh); two *d. Educ:* Christ Coll., Brecon; Ellesmere Coll., Salop. War Service, 1943–47, Captain, Royal Artillery. Called to Bar, Gray's Inn, 1949; joined Wales and Chester Circuit, 1949. Dep. Chairman, Cheshire QS, 1961; Dep. Chairman, Agricultural Land Tribunal (Wales), 1965–68; Commissioner of Assize, 1970; Mem., Parole Bd for England and Wales, 1971–74. DL Cheshire 1972. *Publication:* The Magistrate in the Crown Court, 1982. *Address:* (home) Hallowsgate House, Kelsall, Cheshire CW6 0QA. *T:* Kelsall (01829) 51456; (chambers) 4 Paper Buildings, Temple, EC4Y 7EX. *T:* 0171–353 8408, 0171–353 0196; (chambers) 40 King Street, Chester CH1 2AH. *T:* Chester (01244) 323886.

DAVID, Timothy James; HM Diplomatic Service; Counsellor, Middle East Department, Foreign and Commonwealth Office, since 1995; *b* 3 June 1947; *s* of Herman Francis David and Mavis Jean David (*née* Evans). *Educ:* Stonyhurst Coll.; New Coll., Oxford (BA Hons 1969; MA Hons 1978); Univ. of Rhodesia (Grad. Cert. in Educn 1972); Univ. of London. Volunteer Teacher, Southern Rhodesia, 1965–66; Headmaster, St Peter's Community Secondary Sch., Salisbury (now Harare, Zimbabwe), 1970–71; British Council, 1973; Educn Dir, Help the Aged, 1974; FCO by open competition, 1974; 2nd, later 1st, Sec., Dar es Salaam, 1977–80; Commonwealth Co-ordination Dept, 1980–82; Sec. to UK Delegn to Commonwealth Heads of Govt Meeting, Melbourne, 1981; UKMIS to UN, NY, 1982; Central and Southern Africa Dept, ODA, 1983–84; UKMIS to UN, Geneva, 1985–88; Head of Internat. and Planning Section and Dep. Head, Aid Policy Dept, 1988–89; Counsellor and Head, Narcotics Control and Aids Dept, 1989–91; Ambassador to Fiji and High Comr to Nauru and Tuvalu, 1992–95, and to Kiribati, 1994–95. UK Dir, Tuvalu Trust Fund, 1992–95. Mem. Council, Univ. of S Pacific, 1993–95. Patron, SCF (Fiji), 1993–95. *Recreations:* friends, reading, music, tennis, squash, walking. *Address:* c/o Foreign and Commonwealth Office, SW1A 2AH. *Clubs:* Commonwealth Trust; All England Lawn Tennis and Croquet; Fiji.

DAVID, Tudor, OBE 1984; freelance journalist and publisher; Executive Editor, Oil and Gas Finance and Accounting (formerly Journal of Oil and Gas Accountancy), since 1986; Publisher, Langham Publishing, since 1985; *b* 25 April 1921; *s* of Thomas and Blodwen David; *m*1st, 1943, Nancy Ramsay (*d* 1984); one *s* one *d*; 2nd, 1987, Margaret Dix. *Educ:* Barry Grammar Sch.; Univ. of Manchester (BA Hons); Univ. of Oxford. Technical Officer, RAF, 1942–47; Extra-mural Lectr, Univ. of Newcastle upon Tyne, 1947–49; Careers Officer, 1950–55; Asst Editor, Education, 1955–65; Editor, The Teacher, 1965–69; Managing Editor, Education, 1969–86. Mem., Welsh Acad., 1969–. FCP 1980. *Publications:* (ed) Scunthorpe and its Families, 1954; Defence and Disarmament, 1959; Church and School, 1963; (jtly) Perspectives in Geographical Education, 1973; (jtly) Education, the wasted years 1973–86, 1988. *Recreations:* Wales, the Isle of Dogs, opera. *Address:* 21 Pointers Close, Isle of Dogs, E14 3AP. *T:* 0171–987 8631. *Club:* London Welsh.

DAVID, Wayne; Member (Lab) European Parliament, South Wales Central, since 1994 (South Wales, 1989–94); *b* 1 July 1957; *s* of D. Haydn David and Edna A. David; *m* 1991, Catherine Thomas. *Educ:* Cynffig Comprehensive Sch.; University Coll., Cardiff (BA Hons History; PGCE); University Coll., Swansea. History teacher, Brynteg Comprehensive Sch., Bridgend, 1983–85; Mid Glam Tutor Organiser, S Wales Dist, WEA, 1985–89. Treas., 1989–91, Leader, 1994–, European Parly Labour Party (formerly British Labour Gp); 1st Vice-Pres., Regl Policy and Planning Cttee, Eur. Parlt, 1992–; Sec., Tribune Gp of MEPs, 1992–94. Mem., Labour Party NEC, 1994–. Vice President: ACC, 1995–; Assoc. of Dist Councils, 1995–. Vice-Pres., City of Cardiff Br., UNA, 1989–; Mem., Cefn Cribwr Community Council, 1985–91. *Publications:* (contrib.) Oxford Companion to the Literature of Wales, 1986; two pamphlets; contrib. Llafur—Jl of Welsh Labour History. *Recreations:* music, reading. *Address:* Tŷ Cathway, Bryn Rhedyn, (off The Rise), Tonteg, Pontypridd, Mid Glam CF38 1UY. *T:* Pontypridd (01443) 217810.

DAVID-WEILL, Michel Alexandre; Senior Partner, Lazard Frères & Co., New York, since 1977; Deputy Chairman, Lazard Brothers & Co., London, since 1991 (Chairman, 1990–91); Partner, Lazard Frères et Cie, Paris, since 1965; *b* 23 Nov. 1932; *s* of Berthe Haardt and Pierre David-Weill; *m* 1956, Hélène Lehideux; four *d. Educ:* Institut de Sciences Politiques, Paris; Lycée Francais de New York. Brown Brothers Harriman, 1954–55; Lehman Brothers, NY, 1955–56; Lazard Frères & Co., NY, 1956–, Partner, 1961–; Lazard Brothers & Co., London, Dir, 1965–; Chm., Lazard Partners, 1984–. Dir, French Amer. Foundn, NY; Member Council: Musée de la Légion d'Honneur, Paris; Cité Internat. des Arts, Paris; Mem., Acad. des Beaux-Arts; Trustee: MMA, NY; Pierpont Morgan Liby, NY; Solomon R. Guggenheim Mus. and Foundn, NY; Pres., Conseil Artistique de la Réunion des Musées Nationaux, Paris. Gov., NY Hosp. Officier, Legion of Honour (France), 1990. *Address:* Lazard Frères & Co., One Rockefeller Plaza, New York, NY 10020, USA. *T:* (212) 6326000. *Clubs:* Knickerbocker, Brook (NY); Creek (Locust Valley).

DAVIDSON, family name of **Viscount Davidson.**

DAVIDSON, 2nd Viscount *cr* 1937, of Little Gaddesden; **John Andrew Davidson;** Captain of the Yeomen of the Guard (Deputy Government Chief Whip), 1986–91; *b* 22 Dec. 1928; *er s* of 1st Viscount Davidson, PC, GCVO, CH, CB, and Frances Joan, Viscountess Davidson (Baroness Northchurch), DBE (*d* 1985), *y d* of 1st Baron Dickinson, PC, KBE; *S* father, 1970; *m* 1st, 1956, Margaret Birgitta Norton (marr. diss. 1974); four *d* (including twin *d*); 2nd, 1975, Mrs Pamela Dobb (*née* Vergette). *Educ:* Westminster School; Pembroke College, Cambridge (BA). Served in The Black Watch and 5th Bn KAR, 1947–49. A Lord in Waiting (Govt Whip), 1985–86. Director: Strutt & Parker (Farms) Ltd, 1960–75; Lord Rayleigh's Farms Inc., 1960–75; Member of Council: CLA, 1965–75; RASE, 1973; Chm., Management Committee, Royal Eastern Counties Hospital, 1966–72; Mem., East Anglia Economic Planning Council, 1971–75. *Recreation:* music. *Heir: b* Hon. Malcolm William Mackenzie Davidson [*b* 28 Aug. 1934; *m* 1970, Mrs Evelyn Ann Carew Perfect, *yr d* of William Blackmore Storey; one *s* one *d*]. *Address:* House of Lords, SW1A 0PW.

See also Baron Rayleigh.

DAVIDSON, Hon. Lord; Charles Kemp Davidson, FRSE 1985; a Senator of the College of Justice in Scotland, since 1983; Chairman, Scottish Law Commission, since 1988; *b* Edinburgh, 13 April 1929; *s* of Rev. Donald Davidson, DD, Edinburgh; *m* 1960, Mary (OBE 1994), *d* of Charles Mactaggart, Campbeltown, Argyll; one *s* two *d. Educ:* Fettes Coll., Edinburgh; Brasenose Coll., Oxford; Edinburgh Univ. Admitted to Faculty of Advocates, 1956; QC (Scot.) 1969; Vice-Dean, 1977–79; Dean, 1979–83; Keeper, Advocates' Library, 1972–76. Procurator to Gen. Assembly of Church of Scotland, 1972–83. Dep. Chm., Boundary Commn for Scotland, 1985–. *Address:* 22 Dublin Street, Edinburgh EH1 3PP. *T:* 0131–556 2168.

DAVIDSON, Alan Eaton, CMG 1975; author; HM Diplomatic Service, retired; Managing Director, Prospect Books Ltd, since 1982; *b* 30 March 1924; *s* of William John Davidson and Constance (*née* Eaton); *m* 1951, Jane Macatee; three *d. Educ:* Leeds Grammar Sch.; Queen's Coll., Oxford. 1st class hons Class. Mods. and Greats. Served in RNVR (Ordinary Seaman, later Lieut) in Mediterranean, N Atlantic and Pacific, 1943–46. Member of HM Foreign Service, 1948; served at: Washington, 1950–53; The Hague, 1953–55; FO, 1955–59; First Secretary, British Property Commission, and later Head of Chancery, British Embassy, Cairo, 1959–61; Head of Chancery and Consul, Tunis, 1962–64; FO, 1964; Counsellor, 1965; Head, Central Dept, FO, 1966–68; Head of Chancery, UK Delegn to NATO, Brussels, 1968–71; seconded, as Vis. Fellow, Centre for Contemporary European Studies, Univ. of Sussex, 1971–72; Head of Defence Dept, FCO, 1972–73; Ambassador to Vientiane, 1973–75. *Publications:* Seafish of Tunisia and the Central Mediterranean, 1963; Snakes and Scorpions Found in the Land of Tunisia, 1964; Mediterranean Seafood, 1972; The Role of the Uncommitted European Countries in East-West Relations, 1972; Fish and Fish Dishes of Laos, 1975; Seafood of South East Asia, 1976; (with Jane Davidson) Dumas on Food, 1978; North Atlantic Seafood, 1979; (with Jennifer Davidson) Traditional Recipes of Laos, 1981; On Fasting and Feasting (annotated anthology), 1988; A Kipper with My Tea, 1988; (with Charlotte Knox) Seafood, 1989; (with Charlotte Knox) Fruit, 1991. *Address:* 45 Lamont Road, World's End, SW10 0HU. *T:* 0171–352 4209.

DAVIDSON, Alfred Edward; international lawyer; Vice-President and General Counsel, Technical Studies, 1957–70, and 1973–91; *b* New York, 11 Nov. 1911; *s* of Maurice Philip Davidson and Blanche Reinheimer; *m* 1934, Claire H. Dreyfuss (*d* 1981); two *s. Educ:* Harvard Univ. (AB); Columbia Law Sch. (LLB). Advocate, Bar of New York, 1936; of Dist of Columbia, 1972; Asst to Gen. Counsel, US Dept of Labour, Wash., 1938–40; review section, Solicitor's Office, 1940–41; Legis. Counsel, Office of Emergency Management, in Exec. Office of President, 1941–43; Asst Gen. Counsel, Lend-Lease Admin. (later Foreign Economic Admin.), 1943–45; Gen. Counsel, 1945–; Gen. Counsel, UNRRA, Nov. 1945; Counsel, Preparatory Commn for Internat. Refugee Org., 1947; Dir, European Headqrs of UNICEF, 1947–51; Advisor, Office of Sec.-Gen. of UN, 1951–52; Gen. Counsel, UN Korean Reconstr. Agency, 1952–54; Exec. Asst to Chm., Bd of Rio Tinto of Canada, 1955–58; European Representative, Internat. Finance Corp., 1970–72; Counsel to Wilmer, Cutler & Pickering, Attorneys at Law, 1972–75. Dir, Channel Tunnel Study Gp, 1960–70; Hon. Chm., Democratic Party Abroad, 1989. Co-Founder, Assoc. for Promotion of Humor in Internat. Affairs; Co-Chm., Bipartisan Cttees on Medicare Overseas and Absentee Voting; Hon. Chm., Common Cause Overseas. *Publications:* contribs. various periodicals and newspapers. *Recreations:* tennis, bridge, chess, reading. *Address:* 5 rue de la Manutention, 75116 Paris, France. *Clubs:* Lansdowne (London); Standard Athletic (France).

DAVIDSON, Arthur; QC 1978; *b* 7 Nov. 1928. *Educ:* Liverpool Coll.; King George V Sch., Southport; Trinity Coll., Cambridge. Served in Merchant Navy. Barrister, Middle Temple, 1953. Trinity Coll., Cambridge, 1959–62; Editor of the Granta. Legal Director: Associated Newspapers Hldgs, 1987–90; Mirror Gp, 1991–93. MP (Lab) Accrington, 1966–83; PPS to Solicitor-General, 1968–70; Chm., Home Affairs Gp, Parly Labour Party, 1971–74; Parly Sec., Law Officers' Dept, 1974–79; Opposition spokesman on Defence (Army), 1980–81, on legal affairs, 1981–83, Shadow Attorney-General, 1982–83; Member: Home Affairs Select Cttee, 1980–83; Armed Forces Bill Select Cttee, 1981–83. Contested (Lab): Blackpool S, 1955; Preston N, 1959; Hyndburn, 1983. Member: Council, Consumers' Association, 1970–74; Exec. Cttee, Soc. of Labour Lawyers, 1981–; Nat. Exec., Fabian Soc.; Council, Nat. Youth Jazz Orchestra; Chm., House of Commons Jazz Club, 1973–83. *Recreations:* lawn tennis, ski-ing, theatre, listening to good jazz and playing bad jazz; formerly Member Cambridge Univ. athletics team. *Address:* 1 Pump Court, Temple, EC4Y 7AA. *Clubs:* James Street Men's Working (Oswaldtwistle); Free Gardeners (Rishton); King Street, Marlborough Working Men's (Accrington).

DAVIDSON, Basil Risbridger, MC 1945; author and historian; *b* 9 Nov. 1914; *s* of Thomas and Jessie Davidson; *m* 1943, Marion Ruth Young; three *s.* Served War of 1939–45 (despatches twice, MC, US Bronze Star, Jugoslav Zasluge za Narod); British Army, 1940–45 (Balkans, N Africa, Italy); Temp. Lt-Col demobilised as Hon. Major. Editorial staff of The Economist, 1938–39; The Star (diplomatic correspondent, 1939); The Times (Paris correspondent, 1945–47; chief foreign leader-writer, 1947–49); New Statesman (special correspondent, 1950–54); Daily Herald (special correspondent, 1954–57); Daily Mirror (leader-writer, 1959–62). Vis. Prof., Univ. of Ghana, 1964; Vis. Prof., 1965, Regents' Lectr, 1971, Univ. of California; Montagu Burton Vis. Prof. of Internat. Relations, Edinburgh Univ., 1972; Sen. Simon Res. Fellow, Univ. of Manchester, 1975–76; Hon. Res. Fellow, Univ. of Birmingham, 1978–; Agnelli Vis. Prof., Univ. of Turin, 1990. A Vice-Pres., Anti-Apartheid Movement, 1969–. Author/presenter, Africa (8-part TV documentary series), 1984. Associate Mem., Acad. des Scis d'Outre-Mer, Paris, 1973. Freeman of City of Genoa, 1945. DLitt *hc:* Ibadan, 1975; Dar es Salaam, 1985; DUniv: Open, 1980; Edinburgh, 1981. Haile Selassie African Research Award, 1970; Medalha Amílcar Cabral, 1976. *Publications: novels:* Highway Forty, 1949; Golden Horn, 1952; The Rapids, 1955; Lindy, 1958; The Andrassy Affair, 1966; *non-fiction:* Partisan Picture, 1946; Germany: From Potsdam to Partition, 1950; Report on Southern Africa,

1952; Daybreak in China, 1953; The New West Africa (ed.), 1953; The African Awakening, 1955; Turkestan Alive, 1957; Old Africa Rediscovered, 1959; Black Mother, 1961, rev. edn 1980; The African Past, 1964; Which Way Africa?, 1964; The Growth of African Civilisation: West Africa AD 1000–1800, 1965; Africa: History of a Continent, 1966; A History of East and Central Africa to the late 19th Century, 1967; Africa in History: Themes and Outlines, 1968; The Liberation of Guiné, 1969; The Africans, An Entry to Cultural History, 1969; Discovering our African Heritage, 1971; In the Eye of the Storm: Angola's People, 1972; Black Star, 1974; Can Africa Survive?, 1975; Discovering Africa's Past, 1978 (Children's Rights Workshop Award, 1978); Africa in Modern History, 1978; Crossroads in Africa, 1980; Special Operations Europe, 1980; The People's Cause, 1980; No Fist is Big Enough, 1981; Modern Africa, 1982; The Story of Africa, 1984; The Fortunate Isles, 1989; African Civilisation Revisited, 1991; The Black Man's Burden: Africa and the curse of the nation-state, 1992; The Search for Africa (essays), 1994. *Address:* Old Cider Mill, North Wootton, Somerset BA4 4HA.

DAVIDSON, Brian, CBE 1965; *b* 14 Sept. 1909; *o s* of late Edward Fitzwilliam Davidson and late Esther Davidson (*née* Schofield); *m* 1935, Priscilla Margaret (*d* 1981), *d* of late Arthur Farquhar and Florence Chilver; one *s* one *d* (and one *s* decd). *Educ:* Winchester Coll. (Scholar); New Coll., Oxford (Scholar). Gaisford Prize for Greek Verse; 1st class Honour Mods.; 2nd class LitHum; President, Oxford Union Society; President OU Conservative Assoc.; BA 1932. Cholmeley Student Lincoln's Inn; Barrister-at-Law, 1933; Law Society Sheffield Prize; Solicitor, 1939; Air Ministry and Ministry of Aircraft Production, 1940. With Bristol Aeroplane Co., 1943–68: Business Manager, 1946; Director, 1950–68; Director, Bristol Siddeley Engines Ltd, 1959–68. Solicitor with Gas Council, later British Gas Corp., 1969–75. Member: Monopolies Commission, 1954–68; Gloucestershire CC (and Chairman Rating Valuation Appeals Cttee), 1953–60; Cttee Wine Society, 1966–83. *Recreations:* fox-hunting, sailing (represented Oxford Univ.), Scottish country dancing, bridge. *Address:* Sands Court, Dodington, Avon BS17 6SE. *T:* Chipping Sodbury (01454) 313077.

See also N. R. Davidson.

DAVIDSON, Charles Kemp; *see* Davidson, Hon. Lord.

DAVIDSON, Charles Peter Morton; Metropolitan Stipendiary Magistrate, since 1984; a Recorder, since 1991; *b* 29 July 1938; *s* of late William Philip Morton Davidson, MD, and Muriel Maud Davidson (*née* Alderson); *m* 1966, Pamela Louise Campbell-Rose. *Educ:* Harrow; Trinity Coll., Dublin (MA, LLB). Called to the Bar, Inner Temple, 1963; employed by Legal and General Assurance Soc., 1963–65; in practice at Bar, 1966–84. Chairman, London Rent Assessment Panel, 1973–84; part-time Immigration Appeals Adjudicator, 1976–84; a Chairman: Inner London Juvenile Courts, 1985–88; Family Court, 1991–. Contested (C) North Battersea, 1966 General Election; Councillor, London Boroughs: of Wandsworth, 1964–68, of Merton, 1968–71. *Recreations:* music, gardening. *Address:* c/o Camberwell Green Magistrates' Court, 15 D'Eynsford Road, SE5 7UP. *Club:* Hurlingham.

DAVIDSON, Edward Alan; QC 1994; *b* 12 July 1943; *o s* of late Alan T. Davidson and of H. Muriel Davidson, Sheffield; *m* 1973, Hilary Jill, *er d* of late Major N. S. Fairman, MBE; two *s*. *Educ:* King's Sch., Canterbury; Gonville and Caius Coll., Cambridge (schol., Tapp Postgrad. Schol.; MA, LLB). Called to the Bar, Gray's Inn, 1966 (Atkin and Birkenhead Schol.). *Recreations:* tennis, bridge, gardening. *Address:* 4 Stone Buildings, Lincoln's Inn, WC2A 3XT. *T:* 0171–242 5524, *Fax:* 0171–831 7907.

DAVIDSON, Francis, CBE 1961; Finance Officer, Singapore High Commission, London, 1961–71; *b* 23 Nov. 1905; *s* of James Davidson and Margaret Mackenzie; *m* 1937, Marial Mackenzie, MA; one *s* one *d*. *Educ:* Millbank Public Sch., Nairn; Nairn Academy. Commercial Bank of Scotland Ltd, 1923–29; Bank of British West Africa Ltd, 1929–41; Colonial Service (Treasury), 1941–61; retired from Colonial Service, Nov. 1961, as Accountant-General of Federation of Nigeria. *Recreation:* philately. *Address:* Woolton, Nairn, Scotland. *T:* Nairn (01667) 52187. *Club:* Royal Over-Seas League.

DAVIDSON, Ian Graham; MP (Lab) Glasgow, Govan, since 1992; *b* 8 Sept. 1950; *s* of Graham Davidson and Elizabeth Crowe; *m* 1978, Morag Mackinnon; one *s* one *d*. *Educ:* Jedburgh Grammar Sch.; Galashiels Acad.; Edinburgh Univ. (MA Hons); Jordanhill Coll. (Teacher Cert.). Chm., Nat. Orgn of Labour Students, 1973–74; Pres., Jordanhill Coll. Students' Assoc., 1975–76; PA/Researcher, Janey Buchan, MEP, 1978–85; Community Service Volunteers, 1985–92. Councillor, Strathclyde Region, 1978–92 (Chm., Educn Cttees, 1986–92). *Recreations:* running, swimming, family. *Address:* House of Commons, SW1A 0AA.

DAVIDSON, Ian Thomas Rollo, QC 1977; **His Honour Judge Ian Davidson;** a Circuit Judge, since 1984; *b* 3 Aug. 1925; *s* of late Robert Davidson and Margaret Davidson; *m* 1954, Gyöngyi (marr. diss. 1982), *d* of Prof. Cs. Anghi; one *s* one *d*; *m* 1984, Barbara Ann Watts; one *s*. *Educ:* Fettes Coll.; Corpus Christi Coll., Oxford (Schol.). MA, Lit. Hum. Royal Armoured Corps, 1943–47, Lieut Derbs Yeomanry. Called to Bar, Gray's Inn, 1955. Asst Lectr, University Coll., London, 1959–60; Deputy Recorder, Nottingham, 1971; a Recorder of the Crown Court, 1974. *Recreations:* music, golf, photography. *Address:* c/o Crown Court, Canal Street, Nottingham NG1 7EJ.

DAVIDSON, Ivor Macaulay; Chairman, D. O. Sanbiet Ltd, since 1980; *b* 27 Jan. 1924; *s* of late James Macaulay and Violet Alice Davidson; *m* 1948, Winifred Lowes; four *s* one *d*. *Educ:* Bellahouston Sch.; Univ. of Glasgow. Royal Aircraft Establishment, 1943; Power Jets (R&D) Ltd, 1944; attached RAF, 1945; National Gas Turbine Establishment, 1946: Dep. Dir, 1964; Dir, 1970–74; Dir-Gen. Engines, Procurement Exec., MoD, 1974–79. *Publications:* numerous, scientific and technical. *Recreations:* music, gardening.

DAVIDSON, James Alfred, OBE 1971; retired RN and Diplomatic Service; *b* 22 March 1922; *s* of Lt-Comdr A. D. Davidson and Mrs (Elizabeth) Davidson; *m* 1955, Daphne (*née* While); two *d*, and two step *s*. *Educ:* Christ's Hospital; RN Coll., Dartmouth. Royal Navy, 1939–60 (war Service Atlantic, Mediterranean and Far East); commanded HM Ships Calder and Welfare; Comdr 1955; retd 1960. Holds Master Mariner's Cert. of Service. Called to the Bar, Middle Temple, 1960. Joined CRO (later FCO) 1960; served Port of Spain, Phnom Penh (periods as Chargé d'Affaires 1970 and 1971); Dacca (Chargé d'Affaires, later Dep. High Comr, 1972–73); Vis. Scholar, Univ. of Kent, 1973–74; British High Comr, Brunei, 1974–78; participated, Sept. 1978, in finalisation of Brunei Independence Treaty; Governor, British Virgin Islands, 1978–81. Vis. Fellow, LSE Centre for Internat. Studies, 1982–84. Legal Mem. and Pres., Mental Health Review Tribunal, 1982–95; a Chm., Pensions Appeals Tribunals, 1984–95. *Publications:* Brunei Coinage, 1977; Indo-China: Signposts in the Storm, 1979. *Address:* Little Frankfield, Seal Chart, near Sevenoaks, Kent TN15 0HA. *T:* Sevenoaks (01732) 761600. *Club:* Army and Navy.

DAVIDSON, James Duncan Gordon, OBE 1984; MVO 1947; Hon. Director, Flower of Scotland Campaign, since 1992; Chief Executive, Royal Highland and Agricultural Society of Scotland, 1970–91; *b* 10 Jan. 1927; *s* of Alastair Gordon Davidson and M. Valentine B. Davidson (*née* Osborne); *m* 1st, 1955, Catherine Ann Jamieson; one *s* two *d*; 2nd, 1973, Janet Stafford; one *s*. *Educ:* RN Coll., Dartmouth; Downing Coll., Cambridge. Active List, RN, 1944–55. Subseq. farming, and political work; contested (L) West Aberdeenshire, 1964; MP (L) West Aberdeenshire, 1966–70. FRAgS; MIEx. *Recreations:* family, walking, ski-ing, fishing, music. *Address:* Coire Cas, Newtonmore, Inverness-shire PH20 1AR. *T:* Newtonmore (01540) 673322.

DAVIDSON, James Patton, CBE 1980; *b* 23 March 1928; *s* of Richard Davidson and Elizabeth Ferguson Carnichan; *m* 1st, 1953, Jean Stevenson Ferguson Anderson (marr. diss. 1981); two *s*; 2nd, 1981, Esmé Evelyn Ancill. *Educ:* Rutherglen Acad.; Glasgow Univ. (BL). Mil. service, commissioned RASC, 1948–50. Clyde Navigation Trust, 1950; Asst Gen. Manager, 1958. Clyde Port Authority: Gen. Manager, 1966; Managing Dir, 1974; Dep. Chm. and Man. Dir, 1976; Chm., 1980–83. Chairman: Ardrossan Harbour Co. Ltd, 1976–83; Clydeport Stevedoring Services Ltd, 1977–83; Clyde Container Services Ltd, 1968–83; S. & H. McCall Transport (Glasgow) Ltd, 1972–83; Rhu Marina Ltd, 1976–80; Scotway Haulage Ltd, 1976–81; R. & J. Strang Ltd, 1976–81; Nat. Assoc. of Port Employers, 1974–79; British Ports Assoc., 1980–83 (Dep. Chm., 1978–80); Port Employers' & Registered Dock Workers' Pension Fund Trustee Ltd, 1978–83; Pilotage Commn, 1983–91 (Mem., 1979–83); UK Dir, 1976–83 and Mem., Exec. Cttee, 1977–83, Hon. Mem., 1983, Internat. Assoc. of Ports and Harbours. Dir, Iron Trades Insurance Gp, 1981–94; Chm., Foods & Feeds (UK), 1982–83. FCIT, CIMgt; FRSA. *Recreations:* golf, bridge, travel, reading, sailing. *Clubs:* Oriental; Nautico (Altea).

DAVIDSON, Prof. John Frank, FRS 1974; FEng; Shell Professor of Chemical Engineering, University of Cambridge, 1978–93 (Professor of Chemical Engineering, 1975–78); Vice-Master, Trinity College, Cambridge, 1992–Feb. 1996; *b* 7 Feb. 1926; *s* of John and Katie Davidson; *m* 1948, Susanne Hedwig Ostberg; one *s* one *d*. *Educ:* Heaton Grammar Sch., Newcastle upon Tyne; Trinity Coll., Cambridge. MA, PhD, ScD; FEng, FIChemE, MIMechE. 1st cl. Mech. Scis Tripos, Cantab, 1946, BA 1947. Engrg work at Rolls Royce, Derby, 1947–50; Cambridge Univ.: Research Fellow, Trinity Coll., 1949; research, 1950–52; Univ. Demonstrator, 1952; Univ. Lectr, 1954; Steward of Trinity Coll., 1957–64; Reader in Chem. Engrg, Univ. of Cambridge, 1964–75. Visiting Professor: Univ. of Delaware, 1960; Univ. of Sydney, 1967. Member: Flixborough Ct of Inquiry, 1974–75; Adv. Cttee on Safety of Nuclear Installations, HSC, 1977–87. Pres., IChemE, 1970–71; Vice Pres. and Mem. Council, Royal Soc., 1988. Founder FEng, 1976. For. Associate, Nat. Acad. of Engrg, US, 1976; For. Fellow, Indian National Science Acad., 1990. Dr *hc* Institut Nat. Polytech. de Toulouse, 1979; Hon. DSc Aston, 1989. Leverhulme Medal, Royal Soc., 1984; Messel Medal, Soc. of Chemical Industry, 1986. *Publications:* (with D. Harrison): Fluidised Particles, 1963; Fluidization, 1971; 2nd edn (with R. Clift and D. Harrison), 1985; (with D. L. Keairns) Fluidization (Conference Procs), 1978. *Recreations:* hill walking, gardening, mending bicycles and other domestic artefacts. *Address:* 5 Luard Close, Cambridge CB2 2PL. *T:* Cambridge (01223) 246104.

DAVIDSON, John Roderick; Director of Administration, since 1991, Clerk of the Council, since 1994, University of London; *b* 29 Jan. 1937; *yr s* of late Alexander Ross Davidson and Jessie Maud (*née* Oakley). *Educ:* Portsmouth Northern Grammar Sch.; Univ. of Manchester (BA). Advr to students, Chelsea Sch. of Art, 1966–68; Asst Sch. Sec., RPMS, 1968–74; Imperial College of Science, Technology and Medicine: Asst Sec., 1974–77; Personnel Sec., 1977–85; Admin. Sec., 1985–89; London University: Clerk of Senate, 1989–94; Mem., Exams and Assessment Council, 1991–. Director: London E Anglian Gp, 1990–; Superannuation Arrangements of Univ. of London Trustee Co., 1993–. Gov., Charterhouse Sch., 1994–. *Recreations:* theatre, opera, genealogy. *Address:* Senate House, University of London, Malet Street, WC1E 7HU. *T:* 0171–636 8000; 10 Lansdowne, Carlton Drive, SW15 2BY. *T:* 0181–789 0021.

DAVIDSON, Keith; *see* Davidson, W. K.

DAVIDSON, Neil Forbes; QC (Scot.) 1993; *b* 13 Sept. 1950; *s* of John and Flora Davidson; *m* 1980, Regina Anne Sprissler, Philadelphia. *Educ:* Univs of Stirling (BA), Bradford (MSc), Edinburgh (LLB, LLM). Admitted Faculty of Advocates, 1979; Standing Jun. Counsel to Registrar Gen., 1982, to Depts of Health and Social Security, 1988; called to the Bar, Inner Temple, 1990. Commissioner, Scottish Council for Internat. Arbitration, 1990–; Dir, City Disputes Panel, 1993–. Legal Assessor, Clan Davidson Assoc., 1990–. *Publications:* (jtly) Judicial Review in Scotland, 1986; (contrib.) ADR in Scotland, 1995. *Address:* Parliament House, Parliament Square, Edinburgh EH1 1RF. *T:* 0131–226 5071; 2 Moray Place, Edinburgh EH3 6DS. *T:* 0131–225 6177; Inchdowrie House, Clova, Angus DD8 4QS.

DAVIDSON, Nicholas Ranking; QC 1993; *b* 2 March 1951; *s* of Brian Davidson, *qv* and of late Priscilla Margaret (*née* Chilver); *m* 1978, Gillian Frances Watts; two *d*. *Educ:* Winchester (Schol.); Trinity Coll., Cambridge (Exhibnr; BA). Called to the Bar, Inner Temple, 1974 (Treas's Prize, Hughes Parry Prize and Inner Temple Scholarship, 1974). *Recreations:* bridge, music, ski-ing. *Address:* 4 Paper Buildings, Temple, EC4Y 7EX. *T:* 0171–353 3366.

DAVIDSON, Very Rev. Prof. Robert, FRSE; Professor of Old Testament Language and Literature, University of Glasgow, since 1972; Principal, Trinity College, Glasgow, since 1982; *b* 30 March 1927; *s* of George Braid Davidson and Gertrude May Ward; *m* 1952, Elizabeth May Robertson; four *s* three *d*. *Educ:* Univ. of St Andrews (MA 1st Cl Hons Classics, 1949; BD, Distinction in Old Testament, 1952). FRSE 1989. Asst Lectr, then Lectr in Biblical Studies, Univ. of Aberdeen, 1953–60; Lectr in Hebrew and Old Testament, Univ. of St Andrews, 1960–66; Lectr in Old Testament Studies, Univ. of Edinburgh, 1966–69, Sen. Lectr, 1969–72. Edward Cadbury Lectr, Birmingham Univ., 1988–89. Moderator, Gen. Assembly, Church of Scotland, 1990–91. Hon. DD: Aberdeen, 1985; Glasgow, 1993. *Publications:* The Bible Speaks, 1959; The Old Testament, 1964; (with A. R. C. Leaney) Biblical Criticism (Vol. 3 of Pelican Guide to Modern Theology), 1970; Genesis 1–11 (Cambridge Bible Commentary), 1973; Genesis 12–50 (Cambridge Bible Commentary), 1979; The Bible in Religious Education, 1979; The Courage to Doubt, 1983; Jeremiah 1–20 (Daily Study Bible), 1983; Jeremiah II, Lamentations (Daily Study Bible), 1986; Ecclesiastes and Song of Songs (Daily Study Bible), 1986; Wisdom and Worship, 1990; A Beginner's Guide to the Old Testament, 1992; articles in Vetus Testamentum, Annual Swedish Theol Inst., Expository Times, Scottish Jl of Theol., Epworth Review and The Furrow. *Recreations:* music, gardening. *Address:* 30 Dumgoyne Drive, Bearsden, Glasgow G61 3AP. *T:* 0141–942 1810.

DAVIDSON, Sir Robert (James), Kt 1989; Chairman, Devonport Management Ltd, since 1994; Director, BICC plc, since 1991 (non-executive, since 1994); *b* 21 July 1928; *m* 1953, Barbara Elsie Eagles; two *s* two *d*. *Educ:* Royal Tech. Coll., Glasgow (DRC 1949); Imperial Coll., London (DIC 1953). FEng 1984; FIMechE. Joined English Electric Co. as grad. apprentice, 1949; Develt Engr, 1951–52; Design Engr, Hydro Electric Project, 1953–55; Project Manager, Priest Rapids Hydro-Electric Power Stn, USA, 1956–61; Manufg Manager, then Gen. Manager, Netherton Works, 1962–69; English Electric taken over by GEC, 1969; Manager, Outside Construction Dept, 1969–72, Manufg Dir, 1972–74, Man. Dir, 1974–88, GEC Turbine Generators Ltd; Dir, GEC plc, 1985–91; Man. Dir, GEC Power Systems Ltd, 1988–89; Vice-Chm. and Chief Exec. Officer, GEC Alsthom NV, 1989–91; Chm. and Man. Dir, GEC ALSTHOM Ltd,

1989–91; Dir, GEC ALSTHOM SA, 1989–91; Chairman: NNC, 1988–91; Balfour Beatty Ltd, 1991–94. Mem., British Coal Corp., 1993–. Hon. DSc Strathclyde, 1991. *Recreations:* walking, gardening, listening to music. *Address:* BICC plc, Devonshire House, Mayfair Place, W1X 5FH.

DAVIDSON, Air Vice-Marshal Rev. Sinclair Melville, CBE 1968; Priest-in-charge, Holy Trinity, High Hurstwood, 1982–88; *b* 1 Nov. 1922; *s* of late James Stewart Davidson and Ann Sinclair Davidson (*née* Cowan); *m* 1944, Jean Irene, *d* of late Edward Albert Flay; one *s* (and one *s* decd). *Educ:* Bousfield Sch., Kensington; RAF Cranwell; RAF Techn. College; Chichester Theol College. CEng, FRAeS, FIEE. War service with 209, 220 and 53 Sqdns RAF, 1941–45 (despatches); Staff RAF Coastal and Fighter Comds, 1946–53; Air Staff, Egypt, Iraq and Cyprus, 1954–55; psa 1956; Air Staff, Air Min., 1957–60; jssc 1960; Dirg Staff, RAF Staff Coll., Bracknell, 1961–63; Asst Comdt, RAF Locking, 1963–64; Chm. Jt Signal Bd (Middle East), 1965; Chief Signal Officer and Comd Electrical Engr, Near East Air Force, 1966–67; idc 1968; Dir of Signals (Air), MoD, 1969–71; AO Wales and Stn Comdr, RAF St Athan, 1972–74; Asst Chief of Defence Staff (Signals), 1974–77. Sec., IERE, 1977–82. Deacon 1981, priest 1982. *Address:* Trinity Cottage, High Hurstwood, E Sussex TN22 4AA. *T:* Buxted (01825) 732151. *Club:* Royal Air Force.

DAVIDSON, Dr (William) Keith, CBE 1982; FRCGP; JP; Chairman, Scottish Health Service Planning Council, 1984–90; *b* 20 Nov. 1926; *s* of James Fisher Keith Davidson and Martha Anderson Davidson (*née* Milloy); *m* 1952, Dr Mary Waddell Aitken Davidson (*née* Jamieson); one *s* one *d*. *Educ:* Coatbridge Secondary Sch.; Glasgow Univ. DPA 1967; FRCGP 1980. MO 1st Bn Royal Scots Fusiliers, 1950; 2nd Command (Major) 14 Field Ambulance, 1950–51; MO i/c Holland, 1952. Gen. Medical Practitioner, 1953–90. Chairman: Glasgow Local Medical Cttee, 1971–75; Glasgow Area Medical Cttee, 1975–79; Scottish Gen. Medical Services Cttee, 1972–75; Dep. Chm., Gen. Medical Services Cttee (UK), 1975–79; Member: Scottish Medical Practices Cttee, 1968–80; Scottish Council on Crime, 1972–75; GMC, 1983–94; Scottish Health Service Policy Bd, 1985–88; Greater Glasgow Health Bd, 1989–93. British Medical Association: Mem. Council, 1972–81; Fellow, 1975; Chm., Scottish Council, 1978–81; Vice-Pres., 1983–. Hon. Pres., Glasgow Eastern Med. Soc., 1984–85; Pres., Scottish Midland and Western Med. Soc., 1985–86; FRSocMed 1986. Vice-Chm., Chryston High Sch. Bd, 1990–. Mem., Bonnetmaker Craft. Elder, Church of Scotland, 1956–; Session Clerk, 1983–. JP Glasgow, 1962. SBStJ 1976. *Recreations:* gardening, caravanning. *Address:* Dunvegan, Stepps, Glasgow G33 6DE. *T:* 0141–779 2103. *Club:* Royal Scottish Automobile (Glasgow).

DAVIE, Alan, CBE 1972; RWA 1991; HRSA 1977; painter, poet, musician, silversmith and jeweller; *b* 28 Sept. 1920. *Educ:* Edinburgh Coll. of Art. DA. Gregory Fellowship, Leeds Univ., 1956–59. Teaching, Central Sch. of Arts and Crafts, London, 1953–56 and 1959–60, and Emily Carr Coll. of Art, Vancouver, 1982. *One-man exhibitions:* Gimpel Fils Galleries in London, Zürich and New York, 1946–; Edinburgh Fest., 1972; Brussels, Paris, Athens and London, 1977; London, Florida, Stuttgart, Zürich, Amsterdam, St Andrews and Edinburgh, 1978; Florida, Edinburgh Fest., Belgium, Sydney and Perth, Australia, 1979; New York, Australia, Colchester and Philadelphia, 1980; London, Frankfurt, NY and Toronto, 1981; Toronto, Edinburgh, Basle, Harrogate, Hong Kong, Paris (Foire Internat. d'Art Contemporain) and Vancouver, 1982; Amsterdam, FIAC Paris, Basel, Madrid, Glasgow and London, 1983; New York, Frankfurt, Cologne, Edinburgh, Windsor, Hertford and Bath, 1984; London (Art Fair, Olympia), Edinburgh and Bonn, 1985; London, Arizona and NY, 1986; Gal. Carre and FIAC, Paris, London, Edinburgh, 1987; Paintings 1956–88, touring Scotland, Helsingborg, 1988; Edinburgh (Scottish Art Gall., and Nat. Gall. of Modern Art), and galleries and museums in Scotland and Sweden, 1989; Madrid, Paris, Helsingford, New York, 1990; Bath, Cracow, Penzance, Copenhagen, 1991; Edinburgh, Vienna, and British Council Travelling Exhibn, 1992; Brighton, Hastings, Ramsgate, Newcastle upon Tyne, Nottingham, Stirling, 1993; Porto, Lisbon, 1994; *retrospective exhibitions:* Sheffield and Lincoln, 1965; Texas, Montreal and Oakland, 1970; Edinburgh, 1972; Germany, 1973; Edinburgh, and Glasgow, 1992; S America, 1993; Barbican, NY and Ireland, 1993; Chicago, 1994. Work represented in exhibitions: 4th Internat. Art Exhibn, Japan; Pittsburgh Internat.; Documenta II & III, Kassel, Germany; British Painting 1700–1960, Moscow; Salon de Mai, Paris; Peggy Guggenheim Collection; ROSC Dublin; Peter Styvesant Collection; British Painting and Sculpture 1960–1970, Washington; III Bienal de Arte Coltejer, Colombia; Hannover, 1973; British Paintings, 1974; Hayward Gall., 1974; Paris, 1975; Lausanne, 1975; 25 years of British Art, RA, 1977; South America, 1977; Kassell, 1977; Sydney, 1979; Works on paper, Gimpel Fils, 1989; SW Arts Touring Exhibn, 1989; Glasgow and Edinburgh, and Royal W of England Acad., 1992. Works in Public Collections: Tate Gall., Gulbenkian Foundn London, Belfast, Bristol, Durham, Edinburgh, Hull, Leeds, Manchester, Newcastle, Wakefield; Boston, Buffalo, Dallas, Detroit, Yale New Haven, Phoenix, Pittsburgh, Rhode Island, San Francisco; Ottawa, Adelaide, Sydney, Auckland, São Paulo, Tel Aviv, Venice, Vienna, Baden-Baden, Bochum, Munich, Amsterdam, Eindhoven, The Hague, Rotterdam, Oslo, Basle, Stockholm, Gothenburg, St Paul de Vence and Paris. Created mural, Tarot Sculpture Gdn, Garavicchio, Tuscany, 1987. First public recital of music, Gimpel Fils Gall., 1971; music and lecture tour, Sydney, Melbourne, Canberra, 1979. Vis. Prof., Brighton Univ., 1993–. Hon. DLitt Heriot-Watt, 1994. Prize for Best Foreign Painter, VII Bienal de São Paulo, 1963; Saltire Award, 1977. *Publication:* Magic Reader: eighteen original lithographs, 1992; *relevant publications:* Alan Davie (ed Alan Bowness), 1967; Alan Davie, by D. Hall and M. Tucker, 1992; Alan Davie: the quest for the miraculous (ed Michael Tucker), 1993. *Address:* Gamels Studio, Rush Green, Hertford SG13 7SB.

DAVIE, Sir Antony Francis F.; *see* Ferguson Davie.

DAVIE, Prof. Donald Alfred, FBA 1987; Andrew W. Mellon Professor of Humanities, Vanderbilt University, 1978–88; *b* 17 July 1922; *s* of George Clarke Davie and Alice (*née* Sugden); *m* 1945, Doreen John; two *s* one *d*. *Educ:* Barnsley Holgate Gram. Sch.; St Catharine's Coll., Cambridge (Hon. Fellow, 1973). BA 1947; PhD 1951. Served with Royal Navy, 1941–46 (Sub-Lieut RNVR). Lecturer in Dublin Univ., 1950–57; Fellow of Trinity Coll., Dublin, 1954–57, Hon. Fellow, 1978; Visiting Prof., University of Calif., 1957–58; Lecturer, Cambridge Univ., 1958–64; Fellow of Gonville and Caius Coll., Cambridge, 1959–64; George Elliston Lecturer, University of Cincinnati, 1963; Prof. of Literature, University of Essex, 1964–68, and Pro-Vice-Chancellor, 1965–68; Prof. of English, 1968–74, Olive H. Palmer Prof. in Humanities, 1974–78, Stanford Univ. Clark Lectr, Trinity Coll., Cambridge, 1976. Hon. DLitt Univ. of Southern California, 1978. Fellow, Amer. Acad. of Arts and Scis, 1973. *Publications: poetry:* Brides of Reason, 1955; A Winter Talent, 1957; The Forests of Lithuania, 1959; A Sequence for Francis Parkman, 1961; Events and Wisdoms, 1964; Essex Poems, 1969; Six Epistles to Eva Hesse, 1970; Collected Poems, 1972; The Shires, 1975; In the Stopping Train, 1977; Three for Water-Music, 1981; Collected Poems 1971–1983, 1983; To Scorch or Freeze, 1989; Collected Poems, 1990; *criticism and literary history:* Purity of Diction in English Verse, 1952; Articulate Energy, 1957, 2nd edn 1976; The Heyday of Sir Walter Scott, 1961; Ezra Pound: Poet as Sculptor, 1965; Introduction to The Necklace by Charles Tomlinson, 1955; Thomas Hardy and British Poetry, 1972; Pound, 1976; The Poet in the Imaginary Museum: essays of two decades, 1978; A Gathered Church: the literature of the English dissenting interest 1700–1930, 1978; Trying to Explain (essays), 1980; Dissentient Voice, 1982; Czeslaw Milosz and the Insufficiency of Lyric, 1986; Under Briggflatts, 1989; Slavic Excursions, 1990; The Eighteenth-Century Hymn in England, 1994; *anthologies:* The Late Augustans, 1958; (with Angela Livingstone) Modern Judgements: Pasternak, 1969; Augustan Lyric, 1974; The New Oxford Book of Christian Verse, 1981. *Recreations:* verse-translation; literary politics; travel. *Address:* 4 High Street, Silverton, Exeter EX5 4JB. *Club:* Savile.

DAVIE, Rex; *see* Davie, S. R.

DAVIE, Prof. Ronald, PhD; FBPsS; CPsychol; consulting psychologist; Visiting Professor, Oxford Brookes University (formerly Oxford Polytechnic), since 1991; *b* 25 Nov. 1929; *s* of late Thomas Edgar Davie and Gladys (*née* Powell); *m* 1957, Kathleen, *d* of William Wilkinson, Westhoughton, Lancs; one *s* one *d*. *Educ:* King Edward VI Grammar Sch., Aston, Birmingham; Univ. of Reading (BA 1954); Univ. of Manchester (PGCE and Dip. Deaf Educn 1955); Univ. of Birmingham (Dip. Educnl Psych. 1961); Univ. of London (PhD 1970). FBPsS 1973. Teacher, schs for normal and handicapped children, 1955–60; Co. Educnl Psychologist, IoW, 1961–64; Nat. Children's Bureau, London: Sen. Res. Officer, 1964; Dep. Dir, 1968; Dir of Res., 1972; Prof. of Educnl Psychology, Dept of Educn, UC Cardiff, 1974–81; Dir, Nat. Children's Bureau, 1982–90. Vis. Fellow, Inst. of Educn, Univ. of London, 1985–93; Hon. Res. Fellow, UCL, 1991–. Co-Dir, Nat. Child Develt Study, 1968–77; Scientific Adviser: Local Authority Social Services Res. Liaison Gp. DHSS, 1975–77; Mental Handicap in Wales Res. Unit, 1977–79; Mental Handicap Res. Liaison Gp, DHSS, 1977–81; Prof. Advr, All Party Parly Gp for Children, 1983–91; Consultant, Whitefield Sch., 1994– (Chm., Academic Bd, 1991–94); Hon. Consultant: Play Board, 1984–87; 1981 Educn Act Res. Dissemination Project, 1986–89. President: Links Assoc., 1977–90; Child Develt Soc., 1990–91; Nat. Assoc. for Special Educnl Needs, 1992–94; Vice-Pres., British Assoc. for Early Childhood Educn, 1984–, Young Minds, 1991–; Chairman: Trng and Educn. Cttee, Nat. Assoc. Mental Health, 1969–72; Assoc. for Child Psychol. and Psychiatry, 1972–73 (Hon. Sec. 1965–70); Standing Conf. of Professional Assocs in S Wales Concerned with Children, 1974–84; Working Party, Children Appearing Before Juvenile Courts, Children's Reg. Planning Cttee for Wales, 1975–77; Develt Psychol. Section, Brit. Psychol. Soc., 1975–77 (Treas. 1973–75); Wales Standing Conf. for Internat. Year of the Child, 1978–79; Steering Cttee, Child Health and Educn Study, 1979–84; Adv. Bd, Whitefield Library, 1983–; Task Gp on Special Educnl Needs, 1989, Steering Gp on Severe Learning Difficulties, 1991, Nat. Curriculum Council; Policy Sub-Cttee, Nat. Assoc. for Special Educnl Needs. Member: Council of Management, Nat. Assoc. Mental Health, 1969–77; Working Party, Children at Risk, DHSS, 1970–72; Educn and Employment Cttee, Nat. Deaf Children's Soc., 1972–78; Management Cttee, Craig y Parc Sch., 1974–76; Cttee, Welsh Br., Assoc. for Child Psychol. and Psychiatry, 1975–80; Bd of Assessors, Therapeutic Educn, 1975–82; Council, British Psychol. Soc., 1977–80; Experimental Panel on Children in Care, SSRC, 1978–79; NCSE Internat. Conf. Prog. Cttee, 1982–85; Council, Child Accident Prevention Trust, 1982–88; Evaluation Panel, Royal Jubilee Trusts, 1982–94; Steering Cttee on Special Educn Needs Res., DES, 1983–86; Bd of Trustees, Stress Syndrome Foundn, 1983–85; Adv. Bd, Ravenswood Village, 1984–91; Bd of Governors, Elizabeth Garrett Anderson Sch. 1985–88; Council, Caldecott Community, 1985–; Research Cttee, Froebel Inst., 1987–88; Nat. Curriculum Council, 1988–90; BBC/IBA Central Appeals Adv. Cttee, 1989–93. Patron, Action for Special Educnl Needs. Hon. Mem., BPA, 1985. FRSA 1991. Hon. DEd CNAA. Member Editorial Board: Internat. Jl of Adolescence and Youth, 1986–; Children and Society, 1987–90. *Publications:* (co-author) 11,000 Seven-Year Olds, 1966; Directory of Voluntary Organisations concerned with Children, 1969; Living with Handicap, 1970; From Birth to Seven, 1972; Child Sexual Abuse: the way forward after Cleveland, 1989; Listening to Children in Education, 1995; chapters in books and papers in sci. and other jls on special educn, psychol., child care and health. *Recreations:* photography, antiques. *Address:* 3 Grange Grove, Canonbury, N1 2NP. *T:* 0171–226 3761.

DAVIE, (Stephen) Rex, CB 1993; Principal Establishment and Finance Officer (Under Secretary), Cabinet Office, 1989–93; *b* 11 June 1933; *s* of late Sydney and Dorothy Davie; *m* 1955, Christine Stockwell; one *s* one *d*. *Educ:* Ilfracombe Grammar Sch. Executive Officer, Inland Revenue, 1951. National Service, RAF, 1952–54. Office of Minister for Science, 1962; NEDO, 1967; CSD, 1970; Asst Sec. 1979; Cabinet Office, 1983; Sen. Sec., Security Commn, 1979–89. Mem. Council, Inst. of Cancer Res., 1993– (Vice Chm., 1995–). *Recreations:* reading, gardening, travel. *Address:* 2 Linnet Close, Basingstoke, Hants RG22 5PD. *Club:* Civil Service.

DAVIES; *see* Llewelyn-Davies.

DAVIES; *see* Prys-Davies.

DAVIES, family name of **Barons Darwen** and **Davies.**

DAVIES, 3rd Baron, *cr* 1932, of Llandinam; **David Davies,** MA; CEng, MICE, MBA; Chairman, Welsh National Opera Company, since 1975; *b* 2 Oct. 1940; *s* of 2nd Baron and Ruth Eldrydd (*d* 1966), 3rd *d* of Major W. M. Dugdale, CB, DSO; *S* father (killed in action), 1944; *m* 1972, Beryl, *d* of W. J. Oliver; two *s* two *d*. *Educ:* Eton; King's Coll., Cambridge. *Heir: s* Hon. David Daniel Davies, *b* 23 Oct. 1975. *Address:* Plas Dinam, Llandinam, Powys SY17 5DQ.

DAVIES, Adele, (Mrs R. O. Davies); *see* Biss, A.

DAVIES, Air Marshal Sir Alan (Cyril), KCB 1979 (CB 1974); CBE 1967; Co-ordinator of Anglo-American Relations, Ministry of Defence, since 1984; *b* 31 March 1924; *s* of Richard Davies, Maidstone; *m* Julia Elizabeth Ghislaine Russell; two *s* (and one *s* decd). Enlisted RAF, 1941; commnd 1943; comd Joint Anti-Submarine School Flight, 1952–54; comd Air Sea Warfare Development Unit, 1958–59; comd No 201 Sqdn, 1959–61; Air Warfare Coll., 1962; Dep. Dir, Operational Requirements, MoD, 1964–66; comd RAF Stradishall, Suffolk, 1967–68; idc 1969; Dir of Air Plans, MoD, 1969–72; ACAS (Policy), MoD, 1972–74; Dep. COS (Ops and Intell.), HQ Allied Air Forces Central Europe, 1974–77; Dep. C-in-C, RAF Strike Command, 1977; Dir, Internat. Mil. Staff, NATO, Brussels, 1978–81; Hd, Support Area Economy Review Team, RAF, 1981–83. Pres., Corps of Commissionaires, 1992 (Chm., 1989–92). *Address:* 10 Crispin Close, Caversham, Berks RG4 7JS. *Club:* Royal Air Force.

DAVIES, Albert John; Chief Agricultural Officer, Agricultural Development and Advisory Service, Ministry of Agriculture, Fisheries and Food, 1971–79; *b* 21 Jan. 1919; *s* of David Daniel Davies and Annie Hilda Davies; *m* 1944, Winnifred Ivy Caroline Emberton; one *s* one *d*. *Educ:* Amman Valley Grammar Sch.; UCW Aberystwyth. BSc Hons Agric. 1940. FIBiol. Adv. Staff, UCW Aberystwyth, 1940–41; Asst Techn. Adviser, Montgomeryshire War Agricultural Cttee, 1941–44; Farm Supt, Welsh Plant Breeding Stn, 1944–47; Nat. Agricultural Adv. Service: Crop Husbandry Adviser Wales, 1947–51; Grassland Husbandry Adviser Wales, 1951–57 and E Mids, 1957–59; Dep. Dir Wales, 1959–64; Regional Dir SW Region, 1964; Chief Farm Management Adviser, London Headquarters, 1964–67; Sen. Agric. Adviser, 1967–68; Dep. Dir, 1968–71. *Publications:* articles in learned jls and agric. press. *Recreations:* golf, Rugby, gardening. *Address:* Cefncoed, 38A Ewell Downs Road, Ewell, Surrey KT17 3BW. *T:* 0181–393 0069. *Clubs:* Farmers'; Epsom Golf.

DAVIES, (Albert) Meredith, CBE 1982; Principal, Trinity College of Music, 1979–88; Guest Conductor, Royal Opera House, Covent Garden, and Sadler's Wells, 1960–72; also BBC; *b* 30 July 1922; 2nd *s* of Reverend E. A. Davies; *m* 1949, Betty Hazel, *d* of late Dr Kenneth Bates; three *s* one *d*. *Educ:* Royal College of Music; Stationers' Company's Sch.; Keble Coll., Oxford; Accademia di S. Cecilia, Rome. Junior Exhibitioner, RCM, 1930; Organist to Hurstpierpoint Coll., Sussex, 1939; elected Organ Scholar, Keble Coll., 1940. Served War of 1939–45, RA, 1942–45. Conductor St Albans Bach Choir, 1947; Organist and Master of the Choristers, Cathedral Church of St Alban, 1947–49; Musical Dir, St Albans Sch., 1948–49; Organist and Choirmaster, Hereford Cathedral, and Conductor, Three Choirs' Festival (Hereford), 1949–56; Organist and Supernumerary Fellow of New Coll., Oxford, 1956; Associate Conductor, City of Birmingham Symphony Orchestra, 1957–59; Dep. Musical Dir, 1959–60; Conductor, City of Birmingham Choir, 1957–64; Musical Dir, English Opera Group, 1963–65; Musical Dir, Vancouver Symphony Orchestra, 1964–71; Chief Conductor, BBC Trng Orchestra, 1969–72; Music Dir, Royal Choral Soc., 1972–85; Conductor, Leeds Phil. Soc., 1975–84. Pres., ISM, 1985–86. Chm., Delius Trust, 1991–. *Address:* 40 Monmouth Street, Bridgwater, Somerset TA6 5EJ.

DAVIES, Sir (Alfred William) Michael, Kt 1973; a Judge of the High Court of Justice, Queen's Bench Division, 1973–91; *b* 29 July 1921; *er s* of Alfred Edward Davies, Stourbridge; *m* 1947, Margaret, *y d* of Robert Ernest Jackson, Sheffield; one *s* three *d*. *Educ:* King Edward's Sch., Birmingham; University of Birmingham (LLB). Called to Bar, Lincoln's Inn, 1948, Bencher 1972, Treasurer 1991; QC 1964; Dep. Chm. Northants QS, 1962–71; Recorder of: Grantham, 1963–65; Derby, 1965–71; Crown Court, 1972–73. Leader of Midland Circuit, 1968–71, Jt Leader of Midland and Oxford Circuit, 1971–73. Chm. Mental Health Review Tribunal, for Birmingham Area, 1965–71; Comr of Assize (Birmingham), 1970; Chancellor, Dio. of Derby, 1971–73; Mem., Gen. Council of the Bar, 1968–72. Chm., Hospital Complaints Procedure Cttee, 1971–73. Conducted Visitor's Inquiry, UC, Swansea, 1992–93. *Publications:* articles and stories. *Recreations:* golf and the theatre. *Address:* c/o Child & Co., 1 Fleet Street, EC4Y 1BD. *T:* (mobile) (0374) 275154. *Club:* Garrick.

DAVIES, Very Rev. Alun Radcliffe; Dean of Llandaff, 1977–93; *b* 6 May 1923; *s* of Rev. Rhys Davies and Jane Davies; *m* 1952, Winifred Margaret Pullen; two *s* one *d*. *Educ:* Cowbridge Grammar Sch.; University Coll., Cardiff (BA 1945; Fellow, 1983); Keble Coll., Oxford (BA 1947, MA 1951); St Michael's Coll., Llandaff. Curate of Roath, 1948–49; Lecturer, St Michael's Coll., Llandaff, 1949–53; Domestic Chaplain to Archbishop of Wales, 1952–57, to Bishop of Llandaff, 1957–59; Chaplain RNR, 1953–60; Vicar of Ystrad Mynach, 1959–75; Chancellor of Llandaff Cathedral, 1969–71; Archdeacon of Llandaff, 1971–77; Residentiary Canon of Llandaff Cathedral, 1975–77. Chaplain, Lieutenancy of S Glam, 1994–. *Address:* 15 Sinclair Drive, Penylan, Cardiff CF3 7AH. *T:* Cardiff (01222) 456149.

DAVIES, Sir Alun Talfan, Kt 1976; QC 1961; MA; LLB; *b* Gorseinon, 22 July 1913; *s* of late Rev. W. Talfan Davies, Presbyterian Minister, Gorseinon; *m* 1942, Eiluned Christopher, *d* of late Humphrey R. Williams, Stanmore, Middx; one *s* three *d*. *Educ:* Gowerton Gram. Sch.; Aberystwyth Univ. Coll. of Wales (LLB), Hon. Professorial Fellow, 1971; Gonville and Caius Coll., Cambridge (MA, LLB). Called to the Bar, Gray's Inn, 1939, Bencher, 1969. Contested (Ind.) University of Wales (by-elec.), 1943; contested (L): Carmarthen Div., 1959 and 1964; Denbigh, 1966. Mem. Court of University of Wales and of Courts and Councils of Aberystwyth and Swansea University Colls. Recorder: of Merthyr Tydfil, 1963–68; of Swansea, 1968–69; of Cardiff, 1969–71; of the Crown Court, 1972–85; Hon. Recorder of Cardiff, 1972–86; Dep. Chm., Cardiganshire QS, 1963–71; Judge of the Courts of Appeal, Jersey and Guernsey, 1969–84. Member: Commn on the Constitution, 1969–73; Criminal Injuries Compensation Bd, 1977–85. President: Court of Nat. Eisteddfod of Wales, 1977–80; Court, Welsh Nat. Opera, 1978–80; Welsh Centre of Internat. Affairs, 1985–89; Wales Internat., 1991–. Dir, Cardiff World Trade Centre Ltd, 1985–. Chm., Bank of Wales, 1991– (Dep. Chm., Commercial Bank of Wales, 1973–91; Dir, 1971–); Dir, HTV Ltd, 1967–83 (Vice-Chm., and Chm. Welsh Bd, 1978–83); Vice-Chm., HTV (Group) Ltd, 1978–83. Chm. Trustees, Aberfan Fund (formerly Aberfan Disaster Fund), 1969–88. Hon. Fellow: Trinity Coll., Carmarthen, 1994; UCW, Aberystwyth, 1994. Hon. LLD Wales: Aberystwyth, 1973. *Address:* 10 Park Road, Penarth, South Glam CF6 2BD. *T:* Penarth (01222) 701341. *Club:* Cardiff and County (Cardiff).

DAVIES, Prof. Alwyn George, FRS 1989; Professor of Chemistry, University College London, 1969–91, now Emeritus; *b* 13 May 1926; *s* of John Lewis and Victoria May Davies; *m* 1956, Margaret Drake; one *s* one *d*. *Educ:* Hamond's Grammar Sch., Swaffham; University College London (BSc, PhD, DSc; Fellow 1991). CChem, FRSC. Lectr, Battersea Polytechnic, 1949; Lectr, 1953, Reader, 1964, UCL. Ingold Lectr, RSC, 1992–93. Medal for Organic Reaction Mechanism, RSC, 1989; Humboldt Prize, Freiburg Univ., 1994. *Publications:* Organic Peroxides, 1959; scientific papers on physical organic chemistry and organometallic chemistry in learned jls. *Address:* Chemistry Department, University College London, 20 Gordon Street, WC1H 0AJ. *T:* 0171–387 7050.

DAVIES, Andrew Owen Evan; Senior Partner, Lee Bolton & Lee, since 1987; Registrar and Legal Adviser of the Diocese of Canterbury, since 1982; *b* 1936; *s* of late Ninian Rhys Davies and Gweneth Elizabeth Davies; *m* 1963, G. Margaret Stephens; one *s* two *d*. *Educ:* Shrewsbury Sch. Solicitor, Notary Public. National Service, Royal Fusiliers, 1954–56. Law studies and articles, 1956–62; admitted Solicitor, 1962; Partner, Evan Davies & Co., 1964–80; Evan Davies & Co. amalgamated with Lee Bolton & Lee, 1980; Partner, Lee Bolton & Lee, 1980–83, Dep. Sen. Partner, 1983–87. *Recreations:* country pursuits, golf, reading, family. *Address:* 1 The Sanctuary, Westminster, SW1P 3JT. *T:* 0171–222 5381. *Club:* Boodle's.

DAVIES, Andrew Wynford; writer; *b* Rhiwbina, Cardiff, 20 Sept 1936; *e s* of Wynford and Hilda Davies; *m* 1960, Diana Lennox Huntley; one *s* one *d*. *Educ:* Whitchurch Grammar Sch., Cardiff; University College London. Teacher: St Clement Danes Grammar Sch., 1958–61; Woodberry Down Comprehensive Sch., 1961–63; Lecturer: Coventry Coll. of Educn, 1963–71; Univ. of Warwick, 1971–87. Guardian Children's Fiction Award, 1979; Boston Globe Horn Award, 1979; BPG Award, 1980, 1990; Pye Colour TV Award, best children's writer, 1981; writer's awards: RTS, 1986–87; BAFTA, 1989, 1993; Writers' Guild, 1991, 1992; Primetime Emmy, 1991. *Television includes:* To Serve Them All My Days, 1979; A Very Peculiar Practice, 1986–87; Mother Love, 1989; House of Cards, 1990; Filipina Dreamers, 1991; The Old Devils, Anglo-Saxon Attitudes, A Very Polish Practice, 1992; Anna Lee, Harnessing Peacocks, To Play the King, 1993; Middlemarch, A Few Short Journeys of the Heart, 1994; Game On, Pride and Prejudice, 1995; *stage plays:* Rose, 1981; Prin, 1990. *Publications: for children:* The Fantastic Feats of Dr Boox, 1972; Conrad's War, 1978; Marmalade and Rufus, 1980; Marmalade Atkins in Space, 1981; Educating Marmalade, 1982; Danger Marmalade at Work, 1983; Marmalade Hits the Big Time, 1984; Alfonso Bonzo, 1987; Marmalade on the Ball, 1995; (with Diana Davies): Poonam's Pets, 1990; Ras in Charge, 1994; *fiction:* A Very Peculiar Practice, 1986; The New Frontier, 1987; Getting Hurt, 1989; Dirty Faxes, 1990; B. Monkey, 1992. *Recreations:* tennis, food, alcohol. *Address:* c/o Lemon, Unna & Durbridge, 24 Pottery Lane, W11 4LZ.

DAVIES, (Angie) Michael; Chairman: Perkins Foods (formerly John Perkins Meats), since 1987; Calor Group, since 1989 (Director, since 1987); National Express Group, since 1992; Simon Engineering, since 1993; *b* 23 June 1934; *s* of Angelo Henry and Clarice Mildred Davies; *m* 1962, Jane Priscilla, *d* of Oliver Martin and Kathleen White; one *d* (one *s* decd). *Educ:* Shrewsbury Schools; Queens' College, Cambridge. Director: Ross Group, 1964–82; Fenchurch Insurance Holdings, 1969–76; Brown Brothers Corp., 1976–81; Imperial Group, 1972–82; Chairman: Imperial Foods, 1979–82; Tozer Kemsley & Millbourn (Holdings) plc, 1982–86; Bredero Properties, 1986–94; Worth Investment Trust, 1987–95; Wiltshier, 1988–; Dep. Chm., TI Gp, 1990–93 (Dir, 1984–93); GPA Gp, 1993–; Director: Littlewoods Organisation, 1982–88; Avdel (formerly Newman Industries), 1983–; British Airways, 1983–; TV-am, 1983–89; Broadwell Land, 1984–90; James Wilkes, 1987–88; Blue Arrow, later Manpower, 1987–92; Worcester Gp, 1991–92; Falcon Agencies, 1994–. *Address:* Little Woolpit, Ewhurst, Cranleigh, Surrey GU6 7NP. *T:* Cranleigh (01483) 277344.

DAVIES, Prof. Anna Elbina, (A. Morpurgo Davies), FBA 1985; Professor of Comparative Philology, Oxford University, since 1971; Fellow of Somerville College, Oxford, since 1971; *b* Milan, 21 June 1937; *d* of Augusto Morpurgo and Maria (*née* Castelnuovo); *m* 1962, J. K. Davies, *qv* (marr. diss. 1978). *Educ:* Liceo-Ginnasio Giulio Cesare, Rome; Univ. of Rome. Dott.lett. Rome, 1959; Libera docente, Rome, 1963; MA Oxford, 1964. Asst in Classical Philology, Univ. of Rome, 1959–61; Junior Research Fellow, Center for Hellenic Studies, Harvard Univ., 1961–62; Univ. Lectr in Classical Philology, Oxford, 1964–71; Fellow of St Hilda's Coll., Oxford, 1966–71, Hon. Fellow, 1972–. Visiting Professor: Univ. of Pennsylvania, 1971; Yale Univ., 1977; Collitz Prof. of Ling. Soc. of America, Univ. of South Florida, 1975; Webster Vis. Prof., Stanford Univ., 1988. Lectures: Semple, Univ. of Cincinnati, 1983; Jackson, Harvard Univ., 1990. Pres., Philological Soc., 1976–80, Hon. Vice-Pres., 1980–. FSA 1974; Foreign Mem., Amer. Philosophical Soc., 1991; Foreign Hon. Mem., Amer. Acad. of Arts and Sciences, 1986; Corresponding Member: Österreichische Akademie der Wissenschaften, Vienna, 1988; Inst. de France (Acad. des inscriptions et belles-lettres), 1992; Mem., Academia Europaea, 1989; Hon. Mem., Linguistic Soc. of America, 1993. Hon. DLitt St Andrews, 1981. *Publications:* (as A. Morpurgo) Mycenaeae Graecitatis Lexicon, 1963; articles and reviews on comparative and classical philology in Italian, German, British and American jls. *Address:* Somerville College, Oxford OX2 6HD. *T:* Oxford (01865) 270600.

DAVIES, Ven. Anthony; *see* Davies, Ven. V. A.

DAVIES, Rear-Adm. Anthony, CB 1964; CVO 1972; Royal Navy, retired; *b* 13 June 1912; *s* of late James Arthur and Margaret Davies; *m* 1940, Lilian Hilda Margaret (*d* 1980), *d* of late Admiral Sir Harold Martin Burrough, GCB, KBE, DSO, and Lady (Nellie Wills) Burrough; two *s* two *d*. *Educ:* Royal Naval College, Dartmouth; Open Univ. (BA 1983). Midshipman, HMS Danae, 1930–32; Sub-Lieut, HMS Despatch, 1934; Lieut, HMS Duncan, 1935–37; Gunnery course, 1938; HMS Repulse, 1939; HMS Cossack 1940–41; Lieut-Comdr, HMS Indefatigable, 1943–45; Comdr, HMS Triumph, 1950; HMS Excellent, 1951–54; Capt., HMS Pelican, 1954–55; Dep. Dir, RN Staff Coll., 1956–57; Far East Fleet Staff, 1957–59; Dep. Dir, Naval Intelligence, 1959–62; Rear-Adm., 1963; Head of British Defence Liaison Staff, Canberra, Australia, 1963–65. Warden, St George's House, Windsor Castle, 1966–72. *Address:* Witts Piece, 11A South Street, Aldbourne, Marlborough, Wilts SN8 2DW. *T:* Marlborough (01672) 40418.

DAVIES, (Anthony) Roger; Metropolitan Stipendiary Magistrate, since 1985; Chairman: London Youth Court (formerly London Juvenile Courts), since 1986; Family Courts, since 1989; a Recorder, since 1993; *b* 1 Sept. 1940; *er s* of late R. George Davies and Megan Davies, Penarth, Glam; *m* 1967, Clare, *e d* of Comdr W. A. Walters, RN; twin *s* one *d*. *Educ:* Bridgend; King's Coll., London. LLB (Hons); AKC. Called to the Bar, Gray's Inn, 1965 (Lord Justice Holker Sen. Schol.). Practised at Bar, London and SE Circuit, 1965–85. *Recreations:* reading (history, biography), music (especially opera), travel, family life. *Address:* c/o Horseferry Road Magistrates' Court, SW1P 2AX. *Club:* Travellers'.

DAVIES, Prof. Arthur; Reardon-Smith Professor of Geography, University of Exeter, 1948–71; Deputy Vice-Chancellor, University of Exeter, 1969–71; Dean of the Faculty of Social Studies, 1961–64; *b* 13 March 1906; *s* of Richard Davies, Headmaster, and Jessie Starr Davies, Headmistress; *m* 1933, Lilian Margaret Morris; one *d*. *Educ:* Cyfarthfa Castle Sch.; University Coll. of Wales, Aberystwyth, 1st cl. Hons in Geography and Anthropology, 1927; MSc Wales 1930; Fellow, University of Wales, 1929–30, Asst Lecturer in Geography, Manchester Univ., 1930–33; Lecturer in Geography, Leeds Univ., 1933–40. Served War of 1939–45, RA 1940–45, Normandy (despatches twice, Major); Mem., High Mil. Tribunal of Hamburg, 1945. Hon. FRGS 1982. *Publications:* Yugoslav Studies, Leplay Soc., London, 1932; Polish Studies, Leplay Soc., London, 1933; numerous papers in learned jls on Great Age of Discovery, Columbus, Drake (resolving California/San Francisco problem), John Lloyd's discovery of America in 1477, etc. *Recreations:* gardening and architecture. *Address:* Morlais, Winslade Park, Clyst St Mary, Devon EX5 1DA. *T:* Topsham (01392) 3296.

DAVIES, Dr Arthur Gordon; Managing Director, Medical & Electrical Instrumentation Co. Ltd, 1965–90; *b* 6 Nov. 1917; *s* of Louis Bernard Davies and Elizabeth Davies; *m* 1945, Joan (*née* Thompson); two *d*. *Educ:* Westminster Hosp. (MB, BS 1943). LRCP, MRCS 1943. Called to the Bar, Lincoln's Inn, 1955. Served War, RAMC (Captain). Coroner to the Royal Household, 1959–83; Coroner, Inner South London, 1959–87. *Recreations:* chess, bridge, photography, electronics.

DAVIES, Brian; *see* Davies, E. B.

DAVIES, Brian Meredith; *see* Davies, J. B. M.

DAVIES, Brigid Catherine Brennan; *see* Gardner, B. C. B.

DAVIES, Bryan; MP (Lab) Oldham Central and Royton, since 1992; *b* 9 Nov. 1939; *s* of George William and Beryl Davies; *m* 1963, Monica Rosemary Mildred Shearing; two *s* one *d*. *Educ:* Redditch High Sch.; University Coll., London; Inst. of Education; London Sch. of Economics. BA Hons History London, Certif. Educn, BScEcons London. Teacher, Latymer Sch., 1962–65; Lectr, Middlesex Polytechnic at Enfield, 1965–74. Sec., Parly Labour Party, 1979–92. Contested (Lab): Norfolk Central, 1966; Newport W, 1983. MP (Lab) Enfield North, Feb. 1974–1979; an Asst Govt Whip, 1979; front bench spokesman on Higher Educn, 1993–. Member: Select Cttee on Public Expenditure, 1975–79; Select Cttee on Overseas Devel, 1975–79; Select Cttee on Nat. Heritage, 1992–93. Mem., MRC, 1977–79. *Recreations:* sport, literature. *Address:* 28 Churchfields, Broxbourne, Herts EN10 7JS. *T:* Hoddesdon (01992) 466427.

DAVIES, Bryn, CBE 1987 (MBE 1978); DL; Member, General Council, Wales Trades Union Congress, 1974–91 (Vice-Chairman, 1983–84, Chairman, 1984–85); *b* 22 Jan. 1932; *s* of Gomer and Ann Davies; *m* 1st, 1956, Esme Irene Gould (*d* 1988); two *s*; 2nd, 1991, Katherine Lewis. *Educ:* Cwmlai School, Tonyrefail. Served HM Forces (RAMC), 1949–51; Forestry Commn, 1951–56; South Wales and Hereford Organiser, Nat. Union of Agricultural and Allied Workers, subseq. TGWU (following merger),1956–91. Chm., Mid Glamorgan AHA, 1978–94; Member: Welsh Council, 1965–81; Development Commn, 1975–81; Nat. Cttee (Wales), Forestry Commn, 1978–; Nat. Water Council, 1982–85; Council, British Heart Foundn, 1986–. DL Mid Glamorgan, 1992. *Publication:* Better Pensions for All, 1993. *Recreations:* cricket and Rugby football. *Address:* 3 Lias Cottages, Porthcawl, Mid Glamorgan CF36 3AD. *T:* Bridgend (01656) 785851. *Clubs:* Tonyrefail Rugby (Pres., 1985–88); Bridgend Rugby Football; St Mary's Golf (Chm., 1989–).

DAVIES, Byron, CEng, FICE; Chief Executive: South Glamorgan County Council, 1992–April 1996; Cardiff County Council, from April 1996; *b* 23 April 1947; *s* of Cecil and Elizabeth Gwendoline Davies; *m* 1972, Sarah Kay Lott; one *s* one *d*. *Educ:* Swansea Univ. (BSc Hons); Univ. of Glamorgan (MPhil). CEng 1976; FICE 1992. Work in private sector orgns, 1968–72; with Swansea CC and Devon CC, 1972–77; South Glamorgan County Council, 1977–April 1996: various sen. civil engrg, property develt and gen. mgt posts; Dir, Property Services, 1990–92. Dir, Cardiff-Wales Airport, 1992–. Clerk to Lieutenancy of S Glam, 1992–; Sec. to Lord Chancellor's Adv. Cttee for S Glam, 1992–. Ex-Officio Mem., Court, Univ. of Wales, Cardiff, 1992–. FIMgt 1992. *Publications:* contrib. on engrg and mgt to professional jls. *Recreations:* walking, sport, cinema, photography. *Address:* 11 Heol Denys, Lisvane, Cardiff, S Glam CF4 5RU. *T:* Cardiff (01222) 750530.

DAVIES, Caleb William, CMG 1962; FFPHM; MRCS; LRCP; DPH; retired; Regional Specialist in Community Medicine, 1974–82 (Acting Regional Medical Officer, 1977–78, 1979–80), South Western Regional Health Authority; *b* 27 Aug. 1916; *s* of Caleb Davies, KIH, MB, ChB, and Emily (*née* Platt); *m* 1939, Joan Heath; three *s* one *d*. *Educ:* Kingswood Sch., Bath; University Coll. and University Coll. Hosp. Med. Sch., London; Edinburgh Univ.; London Sch. of Hygiene and Tropical Med. Kenya: MO, 1941; MOH, Mombasa, 1946; Tanganyika: Sen. MO, 1950; Asst Dir of Med. Services, 1952; Uganda: Dep. Dir of Medical Services, 1958; Permanent Sec. and Chief Medical Officer, Ministry of Health, 1960; retired 1963; South-Western Regional Hosp. Bd: Asst SMO, 1963–66; Principal Asst SMO, 1966–74. *Recreations:* swimming, photography. *Address:* 76 Westwood Green, Cookham, Maidenhead, Berks SL6 9DE. *T:* Maidenhead (01628) 527980.

DAVIES, Christopher Evelyn K.; *see* Kevill-Davies.

DAVIES, Christopher Graham; MP (Lib Dem) Littleborough and Saddleworth, since July 1995; *b* 7 July 1954; *s* of Caryl St John Davies and Margaret (*née* McLeod); *m* 1979, Carol Hancox; one *d*. *Educ:* Cheadle Hulme Sch.; Gonville and Caius Coll., Cambridge (BA 1975); Univ. of Kent (MA 1977). Member: Liverpool City Council, 1980–84 (Chm., Housing Cttee, 1982–83); Oldham MBC, 1994–. Manager: Public Affairs Div., Extel, 1983–85; Northern PR, Liverpool, 1985–87; Dir, Abercromby Consultancy Ltd, 1988–91; marketing and communications consultant, 1991–95; Communications Manager, MTL Trust Holdings, 1993–95. Contested (Lib Dem) Littleborough and Saddleworth, 1987, 1992. *Recreations:* fell running. *Address:* House of Commons, SW1A 0AA; 4 Higher Kinders, Greenfield, Oldham OL3 7BU. *T:* 0161–628 4778.

DAVIES, (Claude) Nigel (Byam); *b* 2 Sept. 1920; unmarried. *Educ:* Eton. Studied at Aix en Provence University, 1937, and at Potsdam, 1938. PhD London (archaeology). Entered Sandhurst, 1939, and later commissioned Grenadier Guards. Served Middle East, Italy and Balkans, 1942–46. Formerly Managing Dir of Windolite Ltd from 1947. MP (C) Epping Div. of Essex, 1950–51. *Publications:* Los Señoríos Independientes del Imperio Azteca, 1968; Los Mexicas: Primeras Pasos Hacia el Imperio, 1973; The Aztecs, 1973; The Toltecs, 1977; Voyagers to the New World: fact and fantasy, 1979; The Toltec Heritage, 1980; Human Sacrifice, 1981; The Ancient Kingdoms of Mexico, 1983; The Rampant God, 1984; The Aztec Empire, 1987. *Recreation:* travel. *Address:* Sonora 75, Colonia Chapultepec, Tijuana, Baja California, Mexico. *T:* (66) 861036. *Club:* Carlton.

DAVIES, Colin; architectural journalist; Lecturer, University of North London, since 1992; *b* 24 March 1948; *s* of John and Hazel Davies; *m* 1st, 1973, Diana Lamont (marr. diss.); one *s*; 2nd, 1992, Susan Wallington. *Educ:* King Henry VIII Sch., Coventry; Oxford Polytechnic; Architectural Assoc.; University College London (MSc). AADip, RIBA. Asst Editor, Building Magazine, 1975–77; Associate Partner, Derek Stow and Partners, 1977–81; freelance journalist, 1981–88; Editor, Architects' Jl, 1989–90. Lectr, Bartlett, Canterbury and Brighton Schs of Architecture, 1983–91. *Publications:* High Tech Architecture, 1988; Century Tower, 1992; Hopkins, 1993; contribs to arch. jls. *Recreation:* choral singing. *Address:* 148 Muswell Hill Road, N10 3JE.

DAVIES, Colin Godfrey, CEng, FIEE; Director General, Projects and Engineering, National Air Traffic Services, since 1991; *b* 9 Nov. 1934; *s* of Thomas William Godfrey Davies and Kathleen Mabel Davies; *m* 1966, Enid Beryl Packham; two *s*. *Educ:* King's Sch., Bruton; Loughborough Univ. (BSc Hons). FIEE 1986. RAF Flying Officer (Aircrew), 1952–54. Cable and Wireless, 1955–90: Radio Technician, 1955–59; student, 1960–64; Special Projects Engr, Engr-in-Chief's Dept, 1964–68; Project Manager, 1968–75; Manager Transmission, Omantel, 1975–76; Manager Engrg, Fintel, 1976–77; Chief Engr Long Distance Services, Emirtel, 1978–79; Manager Internat. Services, 1980–82, Gen. Manager, 1983–87, Qatar; Dir of Corporate Technology and of two associated cos, 1987–90; Dep. Dir, Communications, NATS, 1990–91. *Recreations:* sport (badminton, sailing, ski-ing), motor cycling, gardening, photography. *Address:* Ibex House, Church Lane, Worplesdon, Guildford, Surrey GU3 3RU. *T:* Guildford (01483) 233214. *Club:* Exiles (Twickenham).

DAVIES, Cynog Glyndwr; *see* Dafis, C. G.

DAVIES, Cyril James, CBE 1987; DL; Chief Executive, City of Newcastle upon Tyne, 1980–86; *b* 24 Aug. 1923; *s* of James and Frances Davies; *m* 1948, Elizabeth Leggett; two *s* two *d*. *Educ:* Heaton Grammar Sch. CIPFA. Served RN, Fleet Air Arm, 1942–46. Entered City Treasurer's Dept, Newcastle upon Tyne, 1940: Dep. City Treas., 1964; City Treas., 1969; Treas., Tyne and Wear Co., 1973–80. Mem., Council, Univ. of Newcastle upon Tyne, 1982–; Director: Theatre Royal Trust, 1986–; Tyne Theatre Trust, 1986–. DL Tyne and Wear, 1989. *Recreations:* theatre, walking, music. *Address:* 36 Lindisfarne Close, Jesmond, Newcastle upon Tyne NE2 2HT. *T:* Newcastle upon Tyne (0191) 2815870. *Club:* Naval.

DAVIES, Dr David; Director: Elmhirst Trust, since 1987; Open College of the Arts, since 1989 (Administrative Director, 1988–89); *b* 11 Aug. 1939; *s* of Trefor Alun and Kathleen Elsie Davies; *m* 1968, Joanna Rachel, *d* of David Brian Peace, *qv*; one *s* three *d*. *Educ:* Nottingham High Sch.; Peterhouse, Cambridge. MA, PhD. Res. Scientist, Dept of Geophysics, Cambridge, 1961–69; Leader, Seismic Discrimination Gp, MIT Lincoln Laboratory, 1970–73; Editor of Nature, 1973–79; Dir, Dartington N Devon Trust, 1980–87. Rapporteur, Seismic Study Gp of Stockholm Internat. Peace Res. Inst. (SIPRI), 1968–73; Chm., British Seismic Verification Res. Project, 1987–91. Member: Warnock Cttee on artificial human fertilisation, 1982–84; BMA Working Party on Surrogacy, 1988–89. Chm., Ivanhoe Trust, 1986–. Member Council: Internat. Disaster Inst., 1979; Beaford Arts Centre, 1980–87; Voluntary Arts Network, 1992–; Trustee, Bristol Exploratory, 1983–90; Yorks Organiser, Open Coll. of the Arts, 1987–89. Musical Dir, Blackheath Opera Workshop, 1977–79; Conductor, Exmoor Chamber Orchestra, 1980–87. Hon. Lectr, Bretton Hall Coll., 1987–. Hon. Fellow: Univ. of Leicester, 1988; Univ. of Leeds, 1989. *Publications:* Seismic Methods for Monitoring Underground Explosions, 1968; numerous scientific papers. *Recreations:* orchestral and choral conducting. *Address:* The Manor House, 24 Huddersfield Road, West Bretton, Wakefield, Yorks WF4 4JY.

DAVIES, Air Vice-Marshal David Brian Arthur Llewellyn, FRCGP; Principal Medical Officer, Headquarters RAF Support Command, 1989–91; *b* 4 Feb. 1932; *s* of Graham and Iris Davies; *m* 1958, Jean Mary Goate; two *s*. *Educ:* University Coll. London (BSc); University Coll. Hosp. (MB BS). MFCM, MFOM; DipAvMed. Sen. MO, various RAF units, incl. Brize Norton, Scampton, Gütersloh and HQ AFCENT, 1958–80; Dep. Dir, Medical Personnel, MoD, 1980–82; OC RAF Hosp., Wegberg, 1982–85; Comdt, Central Med. Estabt, 1985–87; Dep. PMO, Strike Command, 1987–88. QHP, 1989–91. *Recreations:* travel, music, theatre, gardening. *Address:* 28 Boyne Hill Road, Maidenhead, Berks SL6 4HG. *Club:* Royal Air Force.

DAVIES, David Cyril, BA, LLB; Headmaster, Crown Woods School, 1971–84; *b* 7 Oct. 1925; *s* of D. T. E. Davies and Mrs G. V. Davies, JP; *m* 1952, Joan Rogers, BSc; one *s* one *d*. *Educ:* Lewis Sch., Pengam; UCW Aberystwyth. Asst Master, Ebbw Vale Gram. Sch., 1951–55; Head, Lower Sch., Netteswell Bilateral Sch., 1955–58; Sen. Master and Dep. Headmaster, Peckham Manor Sch., 1958–64; Headmaster: Greenway Comprehensive Sch., 1964–67; Woodberry Down Sch., 1967–71. Pres., Inverliever Lodge Trust, 1971–84. *Recreations:* reading, Rugby and roughing it. *Address:* 9 Plaxtol Close, Bromley, Kent BR1 3AU. *T:* 0181–464 4187.

DAVIES, Sir David (Evan Naunton), Kt 1994; CBE 1986; PhD, DSc; FRS 1984; FEng 1979; Chief Scientific Adviser, Ministry of Defence, since 1993; *b* 28 Oct. 1935; *s* of David Evan Davies and Sarah (*née* Samuel); *m* 1st, 1962, Enid Patilla (*d* 1990); two *s*; 2nd, 1992, Jennifer E. Rayner. *Educ:* Univ. of Birmingham (MSc 1958; PhD 1960; DSc 1968). FIEE 1969; FIERE 1975. Lectr and Sen. Lectr in Elec. Engrg, Univ. of Birmingham, 1961–67 (also Hon. SPSO, RRE, Malvern, 1966–67); Asst Dir of Elec. Res., BR Bd, Derby, 1967–71; Vis. Industrial Prof. of Elec. Engrg, Loughborough Univ. of Technol., 1969–71; University College London: Prof. of Elec. Engrg, 1971–88; Pender Prof. and Hd of Dept of Electronic and Electrical Engrg, 1985–88; Vice-Provost, 1986–88; Vice-Chancellor, Loughborough Univ. of Technology, 1988–93. Director: Gaydon Technology (Rover Group), 1986–88; Loughborough Consultants, 1988–93; Inst. Consumer Ergonomics, 1988–93. Member: SERC, 1985–89; IT Adv. Bd, DTI, 1988–91; EPSRC, 1994–; Chm., Defence Scientific Adv. Council, 1992–93. Hon DSc: Birmingham, Loughborough, South Bank, 1994. Rank Prize for Optoelectronics, 1984; Callendar Medal, Inst. of Measurement & Control, 1984; Faraday Medal, IEE, 1987. *Publications:* technical papers and articles on radar, antennae and aspects of fibre optics. *Address:* Ministry of Defence, Main Building, Whitehall, SW1A 2HB. *T:* 0171–218 6588.

DAVIES, (David) Garfield; General Secretary, Union of Shop, Distributive and Allied Workers, since 1986; *b* 24 June 1935; *s* of David John Davies and Lizzie Ann Davies; *m* 1960, Marian (*née* Jones); four *d*. *Educ:* Heolgam Secondary Modern School; Bridgend Tech. Coll. (part time). Served RAF, 1956–58. Junior operative, Electrical Apprentice and Electrician, British Steel Corp., Port Talbot, 1950–69; Area Organiser, USDAW, Ipswich, 1969–73; Dep. Divl Officer, USDAW, London/Ipswich, 1973–78; Nat. Officer, USDAW, Manchester, 1978–85. Mem., TUC Gen. Council, 1986–; Chm., TUC Internat. Cttee, 1992–. Mem., Employment Appeal Tribunal, 1991–. JP 1972–79. *Recreations:* most sport, badminton, squash, swimming, jogging; formerly soccer, cricket, Rugby. *Address:* USDAW, Oakley, 188 Wilmslow Road, Fallowfield, Manchester M14 6LJ. *T:* 0161–224 2804; 64 Dairyground Road, Bramhall, Stockport, Cheshire SK7 2QW. *T:* 0161–439 9548.

DAVIES, Sir David (Henry), Kt 1973; first Chairman, Welsh Development Agency, 1976–79; General Secretary, Iron and Steel Trades Confederation, 1967–75; *b* 2 Dec. 1909; British; *m* 1934, Elsie May Battrick; one *s* one *d* (and one *d* decd). *Educ:* Ebbw Vale, Mon. Organiser, 1950, Asst. Gen. Sec., 1953–66, Iron and Steel Trades Confederation. Chm., Jt Adv. Cttee on Safety and Health in the Iron and Steel Industry, 1965–67; Vice-Chm., Nat. Dock Labour Bd, 1966–68; Hon. Treas. WEA, 1962–69 (Mem. Central Coun. and Central Exec. Cttee, 1954–69); Hon. Treas., British Labour Party, 1965–67 (Chm., 1963; Mem. Nat. Exec., 1954–67); Hon. Sec., Brit. Sect., Internat. Metalworkers Federation, 1960–; Member: Ebbw Vale UDC, 1945–50; Royal Institute of International Affairs, 1954–; Iron and Steel Operatives Course Adv. Cttee, City and Guilds of London Institute Dept of Technology, 1954–68; Iron and Steel Industry Trng Bd, 1964–; Constructional Materials Gp, Economic Development Cttee for the Building and Civil Engrg Industries, 1965–68; Iron and Steel Adv. Cttee, 1967–; English Industrial Estates Corporation, 1971–; Vice-Pres., European Coal and Steel Community Consultative Cttee, 1975– (Pres., 1973–74). Governor: Ruskin Coll., Oxford, 1954–68; Iron and Steel Industry Management Trng Coll., Ashorne Hill, Leamington Spa, 1966–. Mem. TUC Gen. Coun., 1967–75. *Address:* 82 New House Park, St Albans, Herts AL1 1UP. *T:* St Albans (01727) 56513.

DAVIES, Sir (David Herbert) Mervyn, Kt 1982; MC 1944; TD 1946; a Judge of the High Court of Justice, Chancery Division, 1982–93; *b* 17 Jan. 1918; *s* of Herbert Bowen Davies and Esther Davies, Llangunnor, Carms; *m* 1951, Zita Yollanne Angelique Blanche Antoinette, 2nd *d* of Rev. E. A. Phillips, Bale, Norfolk. *Educ:* Swansea Gram. Sch. Travers Smith Scholar, Daniel Reardon Prize. Solicitor, 1939. 18th Bn Welch Regt and 2nd London Irish Rifles, Africa, Italy and Austria, 1939–45. Called to Bar, Lincoln's Inn, 1947; Bencher, 1974; QC 1967; a Circuit Judge, 1978–82. Mem., Bar Council, 1972; Mem., Senate of Inns of Court, 1975. *Address:* The White House, Great Snoring, Norfolk NR21 0AH. *T:* Walsingham (01328) 820575.

DAVIES, (David) Hywel, MA, PhD; FEng 1988; FIEE; consultant; Deputy Director-General for Science, Research and Development, EEC, Brussels, 1982–86; *b* 28 March 1929; *s* of John and Maggie Davies; *m* 1961, Valerie Elizabeth Nott; one *s* two *d*. *Educ:* Cardiff High Sch.; Christ's Coll., Cambridge. Radar Research Estabt, 1956; Head of Airborne Radar Group, RRE, 1970; Head of Weapons Dept, Admty Surface Weapons Estabt, 1972; Asst Chief Scientific Advr (Projects), MoD, 1976–79; Dir, RARDE, MoD, 1979–80; Dep. Controller, Res. Programmes, MoD, 1980–82. Man. Dir, Topexpress Ltd, 1988–89. *Publications:* papers on electronics, radar and remote sensing, in Proc. IEE, etc. *Recreations:* Europe, computing, knots. *Address:* 52 Brittains Lane, Sevenoaks, Kent TN13 2JP. *T:* Sevenoaks (01732) 456359.

DAVIES, David John; Chairman, since 1990, Chief Executive, since 1994, Johnson Matthey plc; Chairman, Sketchley PLC, since 1990; *b* 1 April 1940; *s* of late Stanley Kenneth Davies, CBE and Stephanie Davies; *m* 1st, 1967, Deborah Frances Loeb (marr. diss.); one *s*; 2nd, 1985, Linda Wong Lin-Tye; one *s* one *d*. *Educ:* Winchester Coll., Winchester; New Coll., Oxford (MA); Harvard Business Sch. (Advanced Management Program). Chase Manhattan Bank, 1963–67; Hill Samuel Group, 1967–73: Dir, Hill Samuel Inc., New York, 1970–73; Dir, Hill Samuel Ltd, London, 1973; Finance Dir, 1973–83, and Vice-Chm., 1977–83, MEPC; Man. Dir, The Hongkong Land Co. Ltd, 1983–86; Dir, 1986–88, Chief Exec. and Exec. Vice Chm., 1987–88, Hill Samuel Gp; Jt Chm., Hill Samuel & Co., 1987–88. Chairman: Wire Ropes Ltd, Wicklow, 1979–; Mandarin Oriental Hotel Group, 1983–86; Dairy Farm Ltd, 1983–86; Imry Merchant Developers (formerly Imry Internat.), 1987–89; Imry Holdings, 1992–; Dep. Chm., Charter Consolidated, 1988–89; Director: Jardine Matheson Group, 1983–86; Hong Kong Electric Co., 1983–85; American Barrick Resources Corp., Toronto, 1986–94; Delaware North Cos Inc., Buffalo, NY, 1986–; Singapore Land Ltd, 1986–90; Fitzwilton PLC, Dublin, 1987–90; Asia Securities, Hong Kong, 1987–89; Hardwicke Ltd, Dublin, 1987–; TSB Group, 1987–89; First Pacific Co., Hong Kong, 1988–91; Irish Life Assce, 1991–; The Wharf (Holdings), Hong Kong, 1992–; Prince of Wales Business Leaders Forum (formerly Internat. BITC), 1991–; Glyndebourne Productions Ltd, 1990–; Adv. Cttee on Business and the Envmt, 1993–; Prince of Wales Business and the Envmt Prog., 1993–. Mem. Council, Ireland Fund of GB, 1988–; Trustee, Anglo-Hong Kong Trust, 1989–. Mem. Adv. Cttee for Fund Raising, Ashmolean Mus., 1991–. Mem., Cook Soc. Trustee, Monteverdi Trust, 1991–. *Recreations:* farming, ski-ing, tennis, travel, opera. *Address:* 23 Robinson Road, Apartment 25D, Hong Kong; 41 Kensington Square, W8 5HP. *Clubs:* Turf, Beefsteak, Garrick; Cardiff and County (Cardiff); Kildare Street and University (Dublin); Hong Kong, China (Hong Kong); Knickerbocker (New York).

DAVIES, Rt. Hon. (David John) Denzil; PC 1978; MP (Lab) Llanelli since 1970; *b* 9 Oct. 1938; *s* of G. Davies, Conwil Elfed, Carmarthen; *m* 1963, Mary Ann Finlay (marr. diss. 1988), Illinois; one *s* one *d*. *Educ:* Queen Elizabeth Grammar Sch., Carmarthen; Pembroke Coll., Oxford. Bacon Scholar, Gray's Inn, 1961; BA (1st cl. Law) 1962; Martin Wronker Prize (Law), 1962. Teaching Fellow, Univ. of Chicago, 1963; Lectr in Law, Leeds Univ., 1964; called to Bar, Gray's Inn, 1964. Member: Select Cttee on Corporation Tax, 1971; Jt Select Cttee (Commons and Lords) on Delegated Legislation, 1972; Public Accounts Cttee, 1974–; PPS to the Secretary of State for Wales, 1974–76; Minister of State, HM Treasury, 1975–79; Opposition spokesman on Treasury matters, 1979–81, on foreign affairs, 1981–82, on defence, 1982–83; chief opposition spokesman: on Welsh affairs, 1983; on defence and disarmament, 1983–88. *Address:* House of Commons, SW1A 0AA.

DAVIES, David Levric, CB 1982; OBE 1962; Under Secretary (Legal), Treasury Solicitor's Office, 1977–82; *b* 11 May 1925; *s* of Benjamin and Elizabeth Davies; *m* 1955, Beryl Justine Hammond. *Educ:* Llanrwst Grammar Sch.; University Coll. of Wales, Aberystwyth (LLB Hons). Called to the Bar, Middle Temple, 1949. Served War, 1943–46: Sub-Lt RNVR. Crown Counsel, Aden, 1950–55; Tanganyika: Asst to Law Officers, 1956–58; Parly Draftsman, 1958–61; Solicitor-Gen., 1961–64; Home Civil Service, 1964–82: seconded to Jamaica as Sen. Parly Draftsman, 1965–69, and to Seychelles as Attorney-Gen., 1970–72; Sen. Legal Asst, Treasury Solicitor's Office, 1972–73; Asst Treasury Solicitor, 1973–77. *Recreations:* gardening, loafing, reading. *Address:* Greystones, Breach Lane, Shaftesbury, Dorset SP7 8LF. *T:* Shaftesbury (01747) 851224.

DAVIES, Prof. David Roy, OBE 1995; PhD; Professor of Applied Genetics, University of East Anglia, 1968–94, now Professor Emeritus (Dean of School of Biological Sciences, 1985–91); Deputy Director, John Innes Institute, 1978–94; *b* 10 June 1932; *s* of late J. O. Davies and A. E. Davies; *m* 1957, Winifred Frances Davies, JP, BA (*née* Wills); two *s* two *d*. *Educ:* Llandyssul and Grove Park, Wrexham Grammar Schs; Univ. of Wales. BSc, PhD. UK Atomic Energy Authority, 1956–62 and 1963–68; US Atomic Energy Commn, 1962–63. Editor, Heredity, 1975–82. *Publications:* edited: The Plant Genome, 1980; Temperate Legumes, 1983; Peas: genetics, molecular biology and biotechnology, 1993; papers on radiobiology and plant genetics in scientific jls. *Address:* 57 Church Lane, Eaton, Norwich NR4 6NY. *T:* Norwich (01603) 51049.

DAVIES, David Theodore Alban; His Honour Judge David Davies; a Circuit Judge, since 1994; *b* 8 June 1940; *s* of late John Rhys Davies, Archdeacon of Merioneth, and Mabel Aeronwy Davies; *m* 1966, Janet Mary, *er d* of late Frank and Barbara Welburn, Cheadle Hulme, Cheshire; one *s* one *d*. *Educ:* Rossall School (Scholar); Magdalen College, Oxford (Exhibnr, 2nd cl. Mods 1960, 1st cl. Lit Hum, 1962, BA 1962; Eldon Law Schol., 1963; MA 1967). Called to the Bar, Gray's Inn, 1964 (Entrance Schol., Arden Atkin and Mould Prize, Lord Justice Holker Sen. Schol.). Practised SE Circuit, 1965–83; Registrar, then a Dist Judge, Family Div., High Court, 1983–94; a Recorder, 1989–94. Sec., Family Law Bar Assoc., 1976–80, Treasurer, 1980–83; Member: Senate Law Reform Cttee, 1979–83; Civil and Family Cttee, 1988–, Main Bd, 1991–93, Judicial Studies Bd. *Publication:* (ed jtly) Jackson's Matrimonial Finance and Taxation, 2nd edn 1975, 5th edn 1992. *Recreations:* reading, walking, history. *Address:* Chester County Court, Centurion House, 77 Northgate Street, Chester CH1 2HQ.

DAVIES, Rt. Hon. Denzil; *see* Davies, Rt. Hon. David J. D.

DAVIES, Dickie; television sports presenter, since 1964; *s* of Owen John Davies and Ellen Davies; *m* 1962, Elisabeth Ann Hastings Mann; twin *s*. *Educ:* William Ellis Sch., Highgate; Oldershaw Grammar Sch., Wallasey, Cheshire. Purser, Cunard Line, 1953–60; Television Announcer, Southern TV, 1960–63; World of Sport Presenter, 1964–85, Presenter: ITV Sport, 1985–89; Sportsmasters, 1988–92; The World of Golf, 1990. *Recreations:* golf, horse-riding, carriage driving.

DAVIES, Donald, CBE 1978 (OBE 1973); consultant; *b* 13 Feb. 1924; *s* of late Wilfred Lawson Davies and Alwyne Davies; *m* 1948, Mabel (*née* Hellyar); two *d*. *Educ:* Ebbw Vale Grammar Sch.; UC Cardiff (BSc). CEng, FIMinE. Nationl Coal Board: Colliery Man., 1951–55; Gp Man., 1955–58; Dep. Prodn Man., 1958–60; Prodn Man., 1960–61; Area Gen. Man., 1961–67; Area Dir, 1967–73; Bd Mem., 1973–84; Chairman: Nat. Fuel Distributors, 1973–89; Southern Depot Co., 1973–89; NCB (Ancillaries), 1979–89; Horizon Exploration, 1981–89. FRSA, FBIM. *Recreations:* golf, walking. *Address:* Wendy Cottage, Dukes Wood Avenue, Gerrards Cross, Bucks SL9 7LA. *T:* Gerrards Cross (01753) 85083.

DAVIES, Donald Watts, CBE 1983; FRS 1987; Consultant, Data Security, since 1984; *b* 7 June 1924; *s* of John and Hilda Davies; *m* 1955, Diane Lucy (*née* Burton); two *s* one *d*. *Educ:* Portsmouth Boys' Southern Secondary Sch.; Imperial Coll. of Science and Technology. ARCS, BSc (Physics, 1st cl. hons), 1943, ARCS, BSc (Maths, 1st cl. hons), 1947. Wartime research, 1943–46; Nat. Physical Laboratory, 1947–84: pioneer of digital computing, 1947–50; pioneer of packet switching (data communication), 1965–70; Supt of Computer Science Div., 1966–78; Individual Merit DCSO, 1978–84. Consultant to financial insts for data security, 1976–. Vis. Prof. RHBNC, London Univ., 1987–. Commonwealth Fund Fellow, 1954–55. Dist. Fellow, BCS, 1975. Hon. DSc Salford, 1989. Sir John Lubbock Prize in Maths, 1946; John Player Award, BCS, 1975; John von Neumann Award, J. v. Neumann Soc., Budapest, 1985. *Publications:* Digital Techniques, 1963; Communication Networks for Computers, 1973; Computer Networks and their Protocols, 1979; Security for Computer Networks, 1984, 2nd edn 1989; papers in learned jls. *Recreations:* mathematical games and puzzles, cipher machines of World War II, travel.

DAVIES, Douglas; *see* Davies, Percy D.

DAVIES, Ednyfed Hudson, BA (Wales); MA (Oxon); barrister; *b* 4 Dec. 1929; *s* of Rev. E. Curig Davies and Enid Curig (*née* Hughes); *m* 1972, Amanda Barker-Mill, *d* of Peter Barker-Mill and Elsa Barker-Mill; two *d*. *Educ:* Friars Sch., Bangor; Dynevor Grammar Sch., Swansea; University College of Swansea; Balliol Coll., Oxford. Called to the Bar, Gray's Inn, 1975. Lecturer in Dept of Extra-Mural Studies, University of Wales, Aberystwyth, 1957–61; Lecturer in Political Thought, Welsh Coll. of Advanced Technology, Cardiff, 1961–66. MP: (Lab) Conway, 1966–70; Caerphilly, 1979–83 (Lab, 1979–81, SDP, 1981–83); Mem., H of C Select Cttee on Energy, 1980–83; Sec., H of C All-Party Tourism Cttee, 1979–83. Contested (SDP) Basingstoke, 1983. Part-time TV and Radio Commentator and Interviewer on Current Affairs, 1962–66; on full-time contract to BBC presenting Welsh-language feature programmes on overseas countries, 1970–76; Chm., Wales Tourist Board, 1976–78. Chm., Lincs FM plc, 1991–; Dep. Chm., Ocean Sound Radio, 1989–94 (Dir, 1986–); Dir, Southern Radio, 1989–. Director: New Forest Butterfly Farm, 1984–94; New Forest Industrial Assoc. Ltd, 1989–. Trustee, 1986–, Chm., 1994–, New Forest Ninth Centenary Trust. *Address:* 2 King's Bench Walk, Temple, EC4Y 7DE. *Club:* Cardiff and County (Cardiff).

DAVIES, Prof. (Edward) Brian, DPhil; FRS 1995; Professor of Mathematics, King's College London, since 1981; *b* 13 June 1944; *s* of Arthur Granville Davies and Mary Davies (*née* Scudamore); *m* 1968, Jane Christine Phillips; one *s* one *d*. *Educ:* Jesus Coll., Oxford (BA 1965; MA); Brasenose Coll., Oxford (DPhil Maths 1968). Tutorial Fellow, St John's Coll., Oxford, 1970–81; Univ. Lectr, Oxford Univ., 1973–81; Head, Dept of Maths, KCL, 1990–93. Editor, Qly Jl of Mathematics, 1973–81; Founding Editor, London Mathematical Soc. Student Text Series, 1983–90. *Publications:* Quantum Theory of Open Systems, 1976; One-Parameter Semigroups, 1980; Heat Kernels and Spectral Theory, 1989; Spectral Theory and Differential Operators, 1995. *Recreations:* family, scientific reading. *Address:* Department of Mathematics, King's College, Strand, WC2R 2LS.

DAVIES, (Edward) Hunter; author, broadcaster, publisher; *b* Renfrew, Scotland, 7 Jan. 1936; *s* of late John Hunter Davies and Marion (*née* Brechin); *m* 1960, Margaret Forster, *qv*; one *s* two *d*. *Educ:* Creighton Sch., Carlisle; Carlisle Grammar Sch.; University Coll., Durham. BA 1957, DipEd 1958; Editor of Palatinate. Reporter: Manchester Evening Chronicle, 1958–59; Sunday Graphic, London, 1959–60; Sunday Times, 1960–84: Atticus, 1965–67; Chief Feature Writer, 1967; Editor, Look pages, 1970; Editor, Scene pages, 1975; Editor, Sunday Times Magazine, 1975–77; Columnist: Punch, 1979–89; Stamp News, 1981–86; London Evening Standard, 1987; The Independent, 1989–; Presenter, Bookshelf, Radio 4, 1983–86. Mem., British Library Consultative Gp on Newspapers, 1987–89; Dir, Edinburgh Book Festival Bd, 1990–. *Television:* The Playground (play), 1967; The Living Wall, 1974; George Stephenson, 1975; A Walk in the Lakes, 1979. *Publications: fiction:* Here We Go, Round the Mulberry Bush, 1965 (filmed, 1968); The Rise and Fall of Jake Sullivan, 1970; (ed) I Knew Daisy Smuten, 1970; A Very Loving Couple, 1971; Body Charge, 1972; Flossie Teacake's Fur Coat, 1982; Flossie Teacake—Again!, 1983; Flossie Teacake Strikes Back, 1984; Come on Ossie!, 1985; Ossie Goes Supersonic, 1986; Ossie the Millionaire, 1987; Saturday Night, 1989; S.T.A.R.S (12 books in Penguin series), 1989–90; Snotty Bumstead, 1991; Striker, 1992; Snotty Bumstead and the Rent-a-Mum, 1993; Snotty the Hostage, 1995; *non-fiction:* The Other Half, 1966; (ed) The New London Spy, 1966; The Beatles, 1968, 2nd edn 1985; The Glory Game, 1972, 3rd edn 1990; A Walk Along the Wall, 1974, 2nd edn 1984; George Stephenson, 1975; The Creighton Report, 1976; (ed) Sunday Times Book of Jubilee Year, 1977; A Walk Around the Lakes, 1979; William Wordsworth, 1980; The British Book of Lists, 1980; The Grades, 1981; Father's Day, 1981 (television series, 1983); Beaver Book of Lists, 1981; A Walk Along the Tracks, 1982; England!, 1982; (with Frank Herrmann) Great Britain: a celebration, 1982; A Walk Round London Parks, 1983; The Joy of Stamps, 1983; London at its Best, 1984; (also publisher) The Good Guide to the Lakes, 1984, 4th edn 1993; The Grand Tour, 1986; The Good Quiz Book to the Lakes, 1987; Back in the USSR, 1987; Beatrix Potter's Lakeland, 1988; My Life in Football, 1990; In Search of Columbus, 1991; Teller of Tales: in search of Robert Louis Stevenson, 1994; Hunting People: thirty years of interviews with the famous, 1994; Wainwright: the biography, 1995. *Recreations:* stamps, Lakeland books, Beatles memorabilia, swimming. *Address:* 11 Boscastle Road, NW5 1EE. *T:* 0171–485 3785; Grasmoor House, Loweswater, Cumbria CA13 0RU.

DAVIES, Emrys Thomas, CMG 1988; HM Diplomatic Service, retired; Secretary General, Tripartite Commission for Restitution of Monetary Gold, Brussels, since 1995; *b* 8 Oct. 1934; *s* of Evan William Davies and Dinah Davies (*née* Jones); *m* 1960, Angela Audrey, *er d* of late Paul Robert Buchan May, ICS and of Esme May; one *s* two *d*. *Educ:* Parmiters Foundation Sch. RAF, 1953–55. Sch. of Slavonic Studies, Cambridge Univ., 1954; Sch. of Oriental and African Studies, London Univ., 1955–56. Served Peking, 1956–59; FO, 1959–60; Bahrain, 1960–62; FO, 1962–63; Asst Political Adviser to Hong Kong Govt, 1963–68; First Sec., British High Commn, Ottawa, 1968–71; FCO, 1972–76; Commercial Counsellor, Peking, 1976–78 (Chargé, 1976 and 1978); Oxford Univ. Business Summer Sch., 1977; NATO Defense Coll., Rome, 1979; Dep. High Comr, Ottawa, 1979–82; Overseas Inspector, FCO, 1982–84; Dep. UK Perm. Rep. to OECD, and Counsellor (Econ. and Financial) to UK Delegn, Paris, 1984–87; Ambassador to Hanoi, 1987–90; High Comr, Barbados, Grenada, St Lucia, Dominica, Antigua and Barbuda, St Vincent and the Grenadines, and St Kitts and Nevis, 1990–94. Head, UK Delegn to EC Monitoring Mission to former Yugoslavia, 1995. Mem., Cambridge Soc. *Address:* Taringa, 1 Bloomfield Park, Bath BA2 2BY. *Club:* Commonwealth Trust.

DAVIES, Dr Ernest Arthur, JP; management consultant and lecturer, retired 1987; *b* 25 Oct. 1926; *s* of Daniel Davies and Ada (*née* Smith), Nuneaton; *m* 1st, 1956, Margaret Stephen Tait Gatt (marr. diss. 1967), *d* of H. Gatt, Gamesley, near Glossop; no *c*; 2nd, 1972, Patricia (marr. diss. 1980), *d* of S. Bates, Radford, Coventry; no *c*. *Educ:* Coventry Jun. Techn. Coll.; Westminster Trng Coll., London; St Salvator's Coll., University of St Andrews; St John's Coll., Cambridge. PhD Cantab 1959; MInstP 1959, CPhys 1986. RAF Aircraft Apprentice, 1942–43 (discharged on med. grounds). Westminster Trng Coll., 1946–48; Teacher, Foxford Sch., Coventry, 1948–50; University of St Andrews, 1950–54 (1st cl. hons Physics, Neil Arnott Prize, Carnegie Schol.); subseq. research in superconductivity, Royal Society Mond Lab., Cambridge; AEI Research Scientist, 1957–63; Lectr in Physics, Faculty of Technology, University of Manchester, 1963–66; Management Selection Consultant, MSL, 1970–81; Lectr in Business Studies, Hammersmith and West London Coll., 1981–87. MP (Lab) Stretford, 1966–70; Parliamentary Private Secretary to: PMG (Mr Edward Short), Nov.-Dec. 1967; Foreign Secretary (Mr George Brown), Jan.-Mar. 1968; Foreign and Commonwealth Sec. (Mr Michael Stewart), 1968–69; Jt Parly Sec., Min. of Technology, 1969–70. Co-Vice-Chm.,

Parly Labour Party's Defence and Services Group; Mem., Select Cttee on Science and Technology, 1966–67, 1967–68, 1968–69; Parly Deleg. to 24th Gen. Assembly of UN (UK Rep. on 4th Cttee). Councillor: Borough of Stretford, 1961–67; Borough of Southwark, 1974–82. JP Lancs, 1962, Inner London, 1972. *Publications:* contribs to Proc. Royal Society, Jl of Physics and Chem. of Solids. *Recreations:* reading, walking. *Address:* 43 Frensham Drive, Nuneaton, Warwickshire CV10 9QH.

DAVIES, Prof. Eurfil Rhys, CBE 1990; FRCR, FRCPE; FFR (RCSI); FDSRCS; Professor of Clinical Radiology (formerly Radiodiagnosis), University of Bristol, 1981–93; *b* 18 April 1929; *s* of late Daniel Haydn Davies and Mary Davies; *m* 1962, Zoë Doreen Chamberlain; three *s.* *Educ:* Rhondda Grammar Sch.; Llandovery Coll.; Clare Coll., Cambridge (MB, BChir 1953; MA); St Mary's Hosp., London. FRCR (FFR 1964); FRCPE 1971; FFR (RCSI) 1978; FDSRCS 1989. Served RAMC, 1954–56. Sen. Registrar, St Mary's Hosp., 1963–66; Consultant Radiologist, United Bristol Hosps, 1966–81; Clinical Lectr, 1972–81, Hd, Clinical Sch., 1992–93, Univ. of Bristol. Vis. Sen. Lectr, Lagos Univ., 1971; Mayne Vis. Prof., Queensland Univ., 1982. Civilian Cons. Advr to RN, 1989–. Mem., Bristol and Weston DHA, 1983–86. Member: Admin of Radio Active Substances Adv. Cttee, DHSS, 1978–83; Clin. Standards Adv. Cttee, 1991–93; GMC, 1989–93; Ionising Radiation Adv. Cttee, HSC, 1995–. Royal Coll. of Radiologists: Sen. Examr, 1973–74; Mem., Fellowship Bd, 1974–76; Registrar, 1976–81; Chm., Examining Bd, 1981–84; Warden of the Fellowship, 1984–86; Pres., 1986–89; Chairman: Nuclear Medicine Cttee, 1972–78; Examng Bd, 1982–84; Knox Lectr, 1990. Pres., Nuclear Medicine Soc., 1974–76; Chm., Inter Collegiate Standing Cttee for Nuclear Medicine, 1982–84 (Sec., 1980–82). Hon. Fellow, Faculty of Radiologists, RCSI, 1978. *Publications:* (contrib.) Textbook of Radiology, ed Sutton, 1969, 5th edn 1990; (contrib.) Textbook of Urology, ed J. P. Blandy, 1974; (jtly) Radioisotopes in Radiodiagnosis, 1976; (contrib.) Radiological Atlas of Biliary and Pancreatic Disease, 1978; Textbook of Radiology by British Authors, 1984; (ed with W. E. G. Thomas) Nuclear Medicine for Surgeons, 1988; papers in Clin. Radiology, British Jl of Radiology, Lancet. *Recreations:* theatre, walking, wine. *Address:* 19 Hyland Grove, Bristol BS9 3NR.

DAVIES, Frank John, CBE 1993; Chairman: Health and Safety Commission, since 1993; Nuffield Orthopaedic Centre NHS Trust, since 1990; Chairman, Bardon Group plc, since 1994; *b* 24 Sept. 1931; *s* of late Lt-Col F. H. Davies and Veronica Josephine Davies; *m* 1956, Sheila Margaret Bailey; three *s.* *Educ:* Monmouth Sch.; UMIST. BPB Industries plc, 1953–63; RTZ Piller Ltd, 1964–67; Alcan Aluminium (UK) Ltd, 1967–83: Div. Man. Dir, 1971–83; Dir, 1977–83; Dir, Alcan Booth, 1982; Gp Chief Exec., Rockware Gp, 1983–93. Chairman: Dartington Crystal, 1989–94; ACI Europe Ltd, 1991–93; BTR Nylex, 1991–94; Director: Ian Proctor M. Masts, 1974–83; Ardagh plc, 1985–; Saltire (formerly Cannon St Investments), 1993–. Mem., Oxfordshire HA, 1981–90. President: Glass Manufrs Fedn, 1985, 1986; Fédn Européene de Verre d'Emballage, 1987–88; Member: Council, CPIU, Brussels, 1984–86; Council, Aluminium Fedn, 1980–82; Council, CBI, 1985–93; Council, Industry Council for Packaging and the Envmt, 1986–93; Packaging Standards Council, 1992–93; Vice-Pres., Inst. of Packaging. Trustee, British Occupnl Health Res. Foundn. CIMgt (CBIM 1986); FRSA. Freeman, City of London; Liveryman: Basketmakers' Co., Glass-Sellers' Co. OStJ 1977 (Vice-Pres., Council, Oxfordshire, 1973–); Vice-Chm., St John Ambulance, Oxford, 1973–. *Recreations:* NHS, gardening, theatre, travel. *Address:* Health and Safety Commission, Rose Court, 2 Southwark Bridge, SE1 9HS. *T:* 0171–717 6610, *Fax:* 0171–717 6644; Stonewalls, Castle Street, Deddington, Banbury, Oxon OX15 0TE. *Clubs:* Carlton, Royal Automobile.

DAVIES, Col (Frederic) Nicolas (John); Chief Clerk, Duchy of Lancaster, since 1992; *b* 11 May 1939; *s* of late Rev. William John Davies and Winifred Mary Davies (*née* Lewis); *m* 1970, Caroline Tweedie; one step *s* one step *d*; one *s* one *d* by previous *m.* *Educ:* King's Coll., Taunton; RMA Sandhurst. FIMgt. Nat. Service, Queen's Royal Regt, 1957; commnd Royal Regt of Artillery, 1959; served in UK, Cyprus, Hong Kong and Germany; COS, Catterick Garrison, N Yorks, 1982–85; Defence and Military Attaché, Hungary, 1986–91; retd 1992. Mem., Surrey Council for Order of St John, 1995–. Gov., St Ives Sch., Haslemere, 1995–. Hon. Mem., Order of Vitéz (Hungary). *Recreations:* carriage driving, shooting, gardening. *Address:* Duchy of Lancaster Office, Lancaster Place, Strand, WC2E 7ED. *T:* 0171–836 8277. *Club:* Army and Navy.

DAVIES, Gareth, CBE 1992; FCA; Group Chief Executive since 1984, Chairman since 1987, Glynwed International plc; *b* 13 Feb. 1930; *s* of Lewis and Margaret Ann Davies; *m* 1953, Joan Patricia Prosser; one *s.* *Educ:* King Edward's Grammar School, Aston, Birmingham. Joined Glynwed Group, 1957; Computer Manager, 1964; Financial Dir, 1969; Man. Dir, 1981. Non-Executive Director: Midlands Electricity Plc (formerly Midlands Electricity Bd), 1989–; W Midlands Devlt Agency Ltd, 1994–; Midlands Indep. Newspapers Ltd, 1994–; Lloyds Chemists plc, 1995–. *Recreations:* music, gardening. *Address:* 4 Beechgate, Roman Road, Little Aston Park, Sutton Coldfield, West Midlands B74 3AR. *T:* 0121–353 4780.

DAVIES, Gareth Lewis; His Honour Judge Gareth Davies; a Circuit Judge, since 1990; *b* 8 Sept. 1936; *s* of David Edward Davies and Glynwen Davies; *m* 1962; two *s* two *d.* *Educ:* Brecon County Grammar Sch.; Univ. of Wales (LLB). National Service, RAF, 1954–56. Articled 1959, qualified Solicitor, 1962; Partner, Ottaways', Solicitors, St Albans, 1965–90; a Recorder, 1987. *Recreations:* sailing instructor, ski-ing, cycling. *Address:* Bronllys Castle, Bronllys, Brecon, Powys LD3 0HL. *T:* Brecon (01874) 711930.

DAVIES, Garfield; *see* Davies, D. G.

DAVIES, Gavyn, OBE 1979; Partner, since 1988, Chief International Economist and Head of European Investment Research, since 1993, Goldman Sachs; *b* 27 Nov. 1950; *s* of W. J. F. Davies and M. G. Davies; *m* 1989, Susan Jane Nye; one *d.* *Educ:* St John's Coll., Cambridge (BA); Balliol Coll., Oxford. Economic Advr, Policy Unit, 10 Downing Street, 1974–79; Economist, Phillips and Drew, 1979–81; Chief UK Economist, Simon & Coates, 1981–86; Goldman Sachs: Chief UK Economist, 1986–93; Hd of Investment Res. (London), 1991–93. Vis. Prof. of Economics, LSE, 1988–. Principal Econs Commentator, The Independent, 1991–. Mem., HM Treasury's Indep. Forecasting Panel, 1993–. *Recreation:* Southampton FC. *Address:* Peterborough Court, 133 Fleet Street, EC4A 2BB. *T:* 0171–774 1161.

DAVIES, George Raymond, (Gerry), OBE 1977; FLA; Director, The Booksellers Association of Great Britain and Ireland, 1964–66 and 1970–81 (Hon. Life Member, 1981); *b* 3 Oct. 1916; *s* of George John Davies and Eva Florence Davies; *m* 1945, Sylvia Newling; one *s* one *d.* *Educ:* East Ham Grammar Sch. FLA 1948. Local govt service, 1934–40; land reclamation, 1940–45; estate under-bailiff, 1945–46; W Suffolk and Cambridge Public Libraries, 1947–54 (Dep. City Librarian, 1953); Gen. Sec., Booksellers Assoc., 1955–64; Man. Dir, Bowker Publishing Co. Ltd, 1966–67; Editor, Publishers Inf. Card Services Ltd, 1968–69; Jt Dep. Editor, The Bookseller, 1969–70. Founder-Mem., Internat. Community of Booksellers Assocs, 1956 (Mem. Council, 1972–78); Mem. Council, Internat. Booksellers Fedn, 1978–85 (Pres. 1978–81; Editor, Booksellers International, 1982–88; Hon. Life Mem., 1989); Chm., BA Service House Ltd, 1977–82; Patron, Book Trade Benevolent Soc., 1989– (Chm., 1974–86; Pres., 1986–89). *Publications:* (ed jtly) Books are Different, 1966; A Mortal Craft, 1980; One Hundred Years: the history of the Booksellers Association, 1995; (contrib.) The Book of Westminster, 1964; (contrib.) Books and Their Prices, 1967; contrib. to Logos, Library Rev., Library World, Year's Work in Librarianship, Canadian Bookseller, American Bookseller, Australian Bookseller and Publisher, Publishers Weekly, and The Bookseller. *Recreations:* estate management, writing words and music. *Address:* Crotchets, Rotherfield Lane, Mayfield, East Sussex TN20 6AS. *T:* Mayfield (01435) 872356. *Club:* Savile.

DAVIES, George William; Managing Director, George Davies Partnership plc, since 1989; *b* 29 Oct. 1941; *s* of George and Mary Davies; *m* 1st, 1964, Anne; three *d*; 2nd, 1985, Liz; two *d*; 3rd, 1992, Fiona; two *s.* *Educ:* Netherton Moss Primary Sch.; Bootle Grammar Sch.; Birmingham Univ. Littlewoods, 1967–72; School Care (own business), 1972–75; Pippa Dee (subsid. of Rosgill Hldgs)—Party Plan/Lingerie, 1975–81; J. Hepworth & Son plc (responsible for launch of Next), 1981; Jt Gp Man. Dir, J. Hepworth & Son, 1984; Chief Exec., 1985–88, Chm., 1987–88, Next (name changed from J. Hepworth & Son). Sen. Fellow, RCA, 1988. FRSA. Hon. DBA Liverpool Polytechnic, 1989. Guardian Young Businessman of the Year, 1985; Wood Mackenzie Retailer of the Year, 1987; Marketing Personality of the Year, 1988. *Publication:* What Next? (autobiog.), 1989. *Recreations:* tennis, squash, golf. *Address:* (office) Magna House, Magna Park, Lutterworth, Leicester LE17 4XN. *Clubs:* Formby Golf; Liverpool Ramblers; Blackwell Golf.

DAVIES, Geraint Talfan; Controller, BBC Wales, since 1990; *b* 30 Dec. 1943; *s* of late Aneirin Talfan Davies, OBE and Mary Anne (*née* Evans); *m* 1967, Elizabeth Shân Vaughan (*née* Yorath); three *s.* *Educ:* Cardiff High Sch.; Jesus Coll., Oxford (MA). Western Mail, Cardiff, 1966–71; The Journal, Newcastle upon Tyne, 1971–73; The Times, 1973; Asst Editor, Western Mail, Cardiff, 1974–78; HTV Wales: Head, News and Current Affairs, 1978–82; Asst Controller of Progs, 1982–87; Dir of Progs, Tyne Tees TV, 1987–90. Chairman: Newydd Housing Assoc., 1975–78; Inst. Welsh Affairs, 1992–. Mem., Prince of Wales' Cttee, 1993–; Trustee: Tenovus Cancer Appeal, 1984–87; British Bone Marrow Donor Appeal, 1987–. Mem., Management Cttee, Northern Sinfonia, 1989–90; Director: Northern Stage Co., 1989–90; Newcastle Initiative, 1989–90. Gov., Welsh Coll. of Music and Drama, 1993–. *Recreations:* theatre, music, architecture. *Address:* BBC Wales, Broadcasting House, Llandaff, Cardiff CF5 2YQ; 15 The Parade, Whitchurch, Cardiff CF4 2EF. *T:* Cardiff (01222) 626571. *Club:* Cardiff and County.

DAVIES, Glyn; *see* Davies, Thomas G.

DAVIES, Prof. Glyn Arthur Owen, CEng, FRAeS; Professor of Aeronautical Structures, Imperial College of Science, Technology and Medicine, London, since 1985 (Head of Department of Aeronautics, 1982–89); *b* 11 Feb. 1933; *s* of Arthur and Florence Davies; *m* 1959, Helen Rosemary (*née* Boot); two *d.* *Educ:* Liverpool Inst., Univ. of Liverpool (BEng); Cranfield Inst. of Technology (DCAe); PhD Sydney, 1966. Res. Asst, MIT, 1956; Advanced Project Engr, Brit. Aerospace, 1957–59; Lectr, Sen. Lectr, Dept of Aeronautics, Univ. of Sydney, 1959–66; Lectr, Sen. Lectr, Dept of Aeronautics, Imperial Coll. of Sci. and Technol., 1966–72. Consultant to: ARC, 1975–81; MoD, 1980–; Nat. Agency for Finite Element Methods and Standards, 1983–; SERC, 1986–90 (Supercomputing, 1991–93); The Computer Bd, 1989–91; ABRC (Supercomputing), 1991–94; UFC (IT), 1991–93; DTI (Aviation), 1991–. FRAeS 1987. *Publications:* Virtual Work in Structural Analysis, 1982; Mathematical Methods in Engineering, 1984; Finite Element Primer, 1986; Background to Benchmarks, 1993. *Recreations:* photography, theatre, music. *Address:* Hedsor School House, Bourne End, Bucks SL8 5DP.

DAVIES, Prof. Graeme John, FEng 1988; Principal and Vice-Chancellor, University of Glasgow, since 1995; *b* 7 April 1937; *s* of Harry John Davies and Gladys Edna Davies (*née* Pratt); *m* 1959, Florence Isabelle Martin; one *s* one *d.* *Educ:* Mount Albert Grammar School, Auckland, NZ; Univ. of Auckland (BE, PhD); St Catharine's College, Cambridge (MA, ScD). FIM, FIMechE; FRSNZ 1993. Junior Lectr, Univ. of Auckland, 1960–62; University of Cambridge: TI Research Fellow, 1962–64; Univ. Demonstrator in Metallurgy, 1964–66; Lectr, 1966–77; Fellow of St Catharine's Coll., 1967–77 (Hon. Fellow 1989); Prof. of Metallurgy, Univ. of Sheffield, 1978–86; Vice Chancellor, Univ. of Liverpool, 1986–91; Chief Executive: UFC, 1991–93; PCFC, 1992–93; HEFCE, 1992–95. Visiting Professor: Brazil, 1976–77; Israel, 1978; Argentina, 1980; China, 1981; Hon. Prof., Zhejiang Univ., China, 1985. Mem., ACOST, 1991–93. Mem., Merseyside Enterprise Forum, 1986–90. Guardian, Sheffield Assay Office, 1983–86; Member Council: Inst. Metals, 1981–86; Sheffield Metallurgical and Engineering Assoc., 1978–86 (Pres., 1984–85); ACU, 1987–91. Trustee: Bluecoat Soc. of Arts, 1986–91; Museums and Galls on Merseyside, 1987–92. Gov., Shrewsbury Sch., 1989–. FRSA 1989; CIMgt (CBIM 1991). Freeman, City of London, 1987; Liveryman, Co. of Ironmongers, 1989 (Mem., Court, 1992–). DL Merseyside, 1989–92. Hon. LLD Liverpool, 1991. Rosenhain Medal, Inst. of Metals, 1982. *Publications:* Solidification and Casting, 1973; Texture and Properties of Materials, 1976; Solidificacao e Fundicao das Metais e Suas Ligas, 1978; Hot Working and Forming Processes, 1980; Superplasticity, 1981; Essential Metallurgy for Engineers, 1985; papers to learned jls. *Recreations:* cricket, birdwatching, golf. *Address:* The Principal's Lodging, The University, Glasgow G12 8QQ. *Club:* Athenæum.

DAVIES, Prof. Graham Michael; Professor of Psychology, University of Leicester, since 1989; *b* 19 Feb. 1943; *s* of Harold Cecil Davies and Mona Florence Daisy Wisbey; *m* 1st, 1966, Heather Jane Neale; one *s* one *d*; 2nd, 1987, Noelle Robertson; one *d.* *Educ:* Bodmin Grammar Sch.; Univ. of Hull (BA, PhD, DSc). CPsychol, FBPsS. Lectr in Psychology, 1967–77, Sen. Lectr, 1977–87, Univ. of Aberdeen; Prof. of Psychology, NE London Poly., 1987–89. Editor, Applied Cognitive Psychology. *Publications:* Perceiving and Remembering Faces, 1981; Identification Evidence: a psychological evaluation, 1982; Memory in Context, 1988; Memory in Everyday life, 1993; Psychology, Law and Criminal Justice: international developments in research and practice, 1995. *Recreations:* reading, walking. *Address:* Department of Psychology, University of Leicester, University Road, Leicester LE1 7RH. *T:* Leicester (0116) 252 2178.

DAVIES, (Gwilym) E(dnyfed) Hudson; *see* Davies, Ednyfed H.

DAVIES, Rev. Gwynne Henton; Principal, Regent's Park College, Oxford, 1958–72, Emeritus since 1973; *b* 19 Feb. 1906; *m* 1935, Annie Bronwen (*née* Williams), BA Wales; two *d.* *Educ:* Perse Sch., Cambridge; University College of South Wales, Cardiff (BD, MA); St Catherine's and Regent's Park Colls, Oxford Univ. (MLitt, MA); Marburg/Lahn, Germany. Minister West End Baptist Church, London, W6, 1935–38; Tutor Bristol Baptist Coll., 1938–51; special Lecturer in Hebrew, University of Bristol, 1948–51; (First) Prof. of Old Testament Studies, Faculty of Theology, Durham Univ., 1951–58, Dean of Faculty, 1956; Select Preacher to the Universities of Cambridge and Oxford. OT Editor, The Teachers' Commentary (revised 7th edn), 1955. Secretary, Society for Old Testament Study, 1946–62 (President, 1966). Vice-Pres., Baptist Union of GB and Ireland, 1970–71, Pres., 1971–72. OT Lecture, Pantyfedwen Foundn, 1975; Distinguished Visiting Professor: Meredith Coll., USA, 1978, 1979; William Jewell Coll., 1982, 1983. Vice Pres., Pembrokeshire History Soc., 1985–. Hon. Moderator, 1991–, Penuel Baptist Ch., Manorbier. Hon. DD: Glasgow, 1958; Stetson, 1965. *Publications:* (with A. B. Davies) The

Story in Scripture, 1960; Exodus, 1967; Who's Who in the Bible, 1970; Deuteronomy, in Peake's Commentary on the Bible, rev. edn, 1962; 20 articles in The Interpreter's Bible Dictionary, 1962; The Ark in the Psalms, in Promise and Fulfilment (ed F. F. Bruce), 1963; essay in R. Goldman's Breakthrough, 1968; Genesis, in The Broadman Bible Commentary, 1969; Gerhard von Rad, in O.T. Theology in Contemporary Discussion (ed R. Laurin). *Address:* 50 Whitlow, Saundersfoot, Dyfed SA64 9AE. *T:* Saundersfoot (01834) 813750.

DAVIES, Handel, CB 1962; MSc; FEng; Hon. FRAeS; FAIAA; aeronautical engineering consultant; *m* 1942, Mary Graham Harris. *Educ:* Aberdare Grammar Sch.; University of Wales. FRAeS 1948, Hon. FRAeS 1982. Royal Aircraft Establishment and Ministry of Aircraft Production, 1936–47; Head of Aerodynamics Flight Division, RAE, 1948–52. Chief Superintendent, Aeroplane and Armament Experimental Establishment, Boscombe Down, 1952–55; Scientific Adviser to Air Ministry, 1955–56; Director-General, Scientific Research (Air), Ministry of Supply, 1957–59; Dep. Director, RAE, Farnborough, 1959–63. Dep. Controller of Aircraft, (R&D), Ministry of Aviation, 1963–67, Ministry of Technology, 1967–69. Tech. Dir, British Aircraft Corp., 1969–77. Pres., RAeS, 1977–78. Chm., Standing Conf. on Schools Sci. and Technology, 1978–82. Fellow, University Coll., Cardiff, 1981. Gold Medal, RAeS, 1974. Wilbur and Orville Wright Meml Lectr, 1979. *Publications:* papers in Reports and Memoranda of Aeronautical Research Council and in Journal of Royal Aeronautical Society. *Recreation:* sailing. *Address:* Keel Cottage, Woodham Road, Horsell, Woking, Surrey GU21 4DL. *T:* Woking (01483) 714192. *Club:* Royal Air Force Yacht (Hamble).

DAVIES, Harry, JP; DL; Member, Greater Manchester County Council, 1973–86 (Chairman, May 1984–85); *b* 5 March 1915; *s* of Herbert Jacob Davies and Mary Elizabeth Johnson; *m* 1941, Elsie Gore; three *d. Educ:* Bedford Methodist Primary School; Leigh Grammar School; Padgate Teacher Training College. 6th Royal Tank Regt, 1941–46. Dep. Head, Westleigh C of E School, 1958; Headmaster, Bedford Methodist School, 1964–77. Mem., Leigh Borough Council, 1959; Mayor, Borough of Leigh, 1971–72. JP Leigh, 1969; DL Greater Manchester, 1987. Silver Jubilee Medal, 1977. *Recreations:* gardening, bread baking, wine making. *Address:* 45 Edale Road, Leigh WN7 2BD. *T:* Leigh (01942) 672583.

DAVIES, Howard John; Deputy Governor, Bank of England, since 1995; *b* 12 Feb. 1951; *s* of late Leslie Powell Davies and of Marjorie Davies; *m* 1984, Prudence Mary Keely; two *s. Educ:* Manchester Grammar Sch.; Memorial Univ., Newfoundland; Merton Coll., Oxford (MA History and Mod. Langs); Stanford Graduate Sch. of Business, USA (MS Management Science). Foreign Office, 1973–74; Private Sec. to HM Ambassador, Paris, 1974–76; HM Treasury, 1976–82; McKinsey & Co. Inc., 1982–87 (Special Adviser to Chancellor of the Exchequer, 1985–86); Controller, Audit Commn, 1987–92; Dir Gen., CBI, 1992–95. Dir, GKN plc, 1990–95; Mem., NatWest Internat. Adv. Bd, 1992–95. Director: BOTB, 1992–; BITC, 1992–95. Pres., Age Concern England, 1994–. Sen. Academic Fellow, De Montfort Univ. (formerly Leicester Polytechnic), 1988 (Gov., 1988–95). Hon. DLitt Leicester Poly., 1991. *Recreations:* cricket, children. *Address:* c/o Bank of England, EC2R 8AH. *Clubs:* Barnes Common Cricket; Manchester City Supporters.

DAVIES, Rt. Rev. Howell Haydn; Vicar of St Jude's Parish, Wolverhampton, 1987–93; *b* 18 Sept. 1927; *s* of Ivor Thomas Davies and Sarah Gladys Davies (*née* Thomas); *m* 1958, Jean Wylam (*née* King); three *s* three *d. Educ:* Birmingham. DipArch (Birm.) 1954; ARIBA 1955. Corporal Clerk (Gen. Duties) RAF, Mediterranean and Middle East, 1945–48. Assistant Architect, 1952–56. Deacon 1959, priest 1960; Curate, St Peter's Parish, Hereford, 1959–61; Missionary of Bible Churchmen's Missionary Soc. in Kenya, 1961–79; Archdeacon of Maseno North, 1971–74; Provost of Nairobi, 1974–79; Vicar of Woking, 1979–81; Bishop of Karamoja, Uganda, 1981–87. Buildings designed and completed in Kenya: Church Trng Centre, Kapsabet; Teachers' Coll. Chapel, Mosoriot; St Andrew's Parish Centre, Kapenguria; Cathedral Church of the Good Shepherd, Nakuru; three-storey admin block, bookshop and staff housing for Maseno N Dio., Kakamega; various church and mission staff housing in Kenya and Uganda. *Recreations:* walking, reading, d-i-y, building design. *Address:* 3 Gilberts Wood, Ewyas Harold, Hereford HR2 0JL. *T:* Golden Valley (01981) 240984.

DAVIES, Hugh Llewelyn, CMG 1994; HM Diplomatic Service; British Senior Representative, Sino-British Joint Liaison Group, Hong Kong (with personal rank of Ambassador), since 1993; *b* 8 Nov. 1941; *s* of Vincent Davies (formerly ICS), OBE, and late Rose (*née* Temple); *m* 1968, Virginia Ann Lucius; one *d* one *s. Educ:* Rugby School; Churchill College, Cambridge (Hons History degree). Joined Diplomatic Service, 1965; Chinese Language Studies, Hong Kong, 1966–68; Second Sec., Office of British Chargé d'Affaires, Peking, 1969–71; Far Eastern Dept, FCO, 1971–74; First Sec. (Econ.), Bonn, 1974–77; Head of Chancery, Singapore, 1977–79; Asst Head, Far Eastern Dept, FCO, 1979–82; on secondment, Barclays Bank International, 1982–83; Commercial Counsellor, Peking, 1984–87; Dep. British Permanent Rep., OECD, Paris, 1987–90; Hd, Far Eastern Dept, FCO, 1990–93; Sen. British Trade Comr, Hong Kong, June–Sept. 1993. *Recreations:* watersports, sketching, tennis, gardens, walking. *Address:* c/o Foreign and Commonwealth Office, SW1A 2AH.

See also J. M. Davies.

DAVIES, Humphrey; *see* Davies, Morgan Wynn Humphrey.

DAVIES, Hunter; *see* Davies, E. H.

DAVIES, Huw Humphreys; Group Director of Television, HTV, since 1989; *b* 4 Aug. 1940; *s* of William Davies and Harriet Jane Davies (*née* Humphreys); *m* 1966, Elizabeth Shân Harries; two *d. Educ:* Llangynog Primary School; Llandovery College; Pembroke College, Oxford. MA (LitHum) 1964. Director/Producer: Television Wales and West, 1964; HTV 1968; HTV Cymru/Wales: Asst Controller of Programmes, 1978; Controller of Programmes, 1979–81; Dir of Programmes, 1981–87; Chief Exec., 1987–91. Produced and directed many programmes and series in English and Welsh; latterly numerous plays and drama-documentaries. Chm., Regional Controllers, ITV, 1987–88. Mem., Gorsedd of Bards; Governor, Welsh Coll. of Music and Drama. *Recreations:* reading, swimming. *Address:* 27 Victoria Road, Penarth, S Glamorgan CF64 2HY. *T:* Penarth (01222) 712293.

DAVIES, Hywel; *see* Davies, D. H.

DAVIES, Lt-Col Hywel William; Chief Executive, Royal Highland and Agricultural Society of Scotland, since 1991; *b* 28 June 1945; *s* of late William Lewis Davies, JP and Barbara Beatrice Eleanor Davies, JP, MFH, Pantyderi, Boncath, Pembs; *m* 1969, Patricia, *d* of Lt-Col E. B. Thornhill, *qv*; one *s* one *d. Educ:* Harrow; Magdalene Coll., Cambridge (MA). Commnd RHG (The Blues, later Blues & Royals), 1965; Staff Coll., 1977; Operational Requirements, MoD, 1978–80; Defence Intelligence, MoD, 1982–84; CO, Blues & Royals, 1985–87; with Pilkington Optronics, 1988–89; Director: G. D. Golding & Son Ltd, 1988–; Challenger Consultancy Ltd, 1987–91 (Sen. Consultant, 1989–91); Scottish Assoc. of Agriculture, 1991–; Scottish Agricl & Rural Develt Centre Ltd, 1992–. *Recreations:* equestrian pursuits (represented UK at Four-in-Hand Carriage Driving, 1984–87), shooting, fishing, gardening. *Address:* Peatland, Gatehead, Ayrshire KA2 9AN. *T:* Kilmarnock (01563) 851020. *Clubs:* Farmers'; Coaching.

DAVIES, Ian Hewitt, TD; **His Honour Judge Ian Davies;** a Circuit Judge, since 1986; *b* 13 May 1931; *s* of late Rev. J. R. Davies; *m* 1962, Molly Cecilia Vaughan Vaughan. *Educ:* Kingswood Sch.; St John's Coll., Cambridge (MA). Nat. Service, commnd KOYLI; served with 3rd Bn Parachute Regt, 1950–51; TA, 1952–71 (Lt-Col). Called to the Bar, Inner Temple, 1958. *Address:* c/o Croydon Combined Court Centre, Croydon CR9 5AB. *Clubs:* Boodle's, Royal Automobile, MCC, Hurlingham.

DAVIES, Ian Leonard, CB 1983; MA; CEng, FIEE; Director, Admiralty Underwater Weapons Establishment, 1975–84; *b* 2 June 1924; *s* of late H. Leonard Davies and Mrs J. D. Davies; *m* 1951, Hilary Dawson, *d* of late Rear-Adm. Sir Oswald Henry Dawson, KBE; two *s* two *d. Educ:* Barry County Sch.; St John's Coll., Cambridge. Mechanical Sciences Tripos, 1944, and Mathematical Tripos Pt 2, 1949. Telecommunications Research Estabt, 1944; Blind Landing Experimental Unit, 1946. TRE (later the Royal Radar Establishment), 1949–69; Imperial Defence Coll., 1970; Asst Chief Scientific Adviser (Projects), MoD, 1971–72; Dep. Controller Electronics, 1973, Dep. Controller Air Systems (D), 1973–75, MoD(PE). Mem. Council, IEE, 1974–77 (Chm., Electronics Div. Bd, 1975–76). *Publications:* papers on information theory, radar, and lasers. *Recreations:* music, walking. *Address:* 37 Bowleaze Coveway, Preston, Weymouth, Dorset DT3 6PL. *T:* Weymouth (01305) 832206. *Club:* Athenæum.

DAVIES, Rev. Jacob Arthur Christian; Assistant Director-General, Regional Representative for Africa, FAO, 1982; *b* 24 May 1925; *s* of Jacob S. Davies and Christiana; *m* Sylvia Onikeh Cole; two *s* two *d. Educ:* Univ. of Reading (BSc 1950); Selwyn Coll., Cambridge; Imperial Coll. of Tropical Agriculture. Permanent Secretary, Min. of Agriculture and Natural Resources, Sierra Leone, 1961–63; Chief Agriculturist, 1962–67; Project Co-manager, UNDP, FAO, 1967–69; Chm., Public Service Commn, 1969–71; Ambassador to USA, 1971–72; High Comr for Sierra Leone in London, 1972–74; Non-resident Ambassador to Denmark, Sweden and Norway, 1972–74; Dep. Dir, Agricl Ops Div., 1974–76, Dir, Personnel Div., 1976–82, FAO. *Recreations:* philately, sports. *Address:* 50 Kissy Road, Freetown, Sierra Leone.

DAVIES, Jacqueline; Her Honour Judge Jacqueline Davies; a Circuit Judge, since 1993; *b* 21 May 1948; one *d. Educ:* Manchester High Sch. for Girls; Univ. of Leeds (LLB Hons). Called to the Bar, Middle Temple, 1975; a Recorder, 1991–93. *Address:* The Crown Court, Lowgate, Kingston upon Hull HU1 2EX.

DAVIES, (James) Brian Meredith, MD, DPH, FFCM; Director of Social Services, City of Liverpool, 1971–81; *b* 27 Jan. 1920; *s* of late Dr G. Meredith Davies and Caroline Meredith Davies; *m* 1944, Charlotte (*née* Pillar); three *s. Educ:* Bedford Sch.; Medical Sch., St Mary's Hosp., London Univ. MB, BS (London) 1943 MD (London) 1948, DPH 1948, MFCM 1972, FFCM 1974. Various hosp. appts. Served War, RAMC, Captain, 1944–47. Asst MOH, Lancashire CC, 1948–50; Dep. MOH, City of Oxford, 1950–53; Clin. Asst (infectious Diseases), United Oxford Hosps, 1950–53; Dep. MOH, 1953–69, Dir of Personal Health and Social Services, 1969–71, City of Liverpool; pt-time Lectr in Public Health, 1953–71, and Hon. Lectr in Preventive Paediatrics, 1964–85, Liverpool Univ. Chm., Liverpool div., BMA, 1958–59; Council of Europe Fellowship, to study Elderly: in Finland, Sweden, Norway and Denmark, 1964 (report awarded special prize); Mem. Public Health Laboratory Service Bd, 1966–71. Teaching Gp of Soc. of Community Med. (Sec. of Gp, 1958–72, Pres. Gp, 1972–73). Member: Personal Social Services Council, 1978–80; Mental Health Review Tribunal, Mersey Area, 1982–. Governor, Occupational Therapy Coll., Huyton, Liverpool, 1969–85; Dir of MERIT (Merseyside Industrial Therapy Services Ltd), 1970–75; Mem. Council, Queen's Inst. of District Nursing, 1971–78; Assoc. of Dirs of Social Services: Chm., NW Br., 1971–73; Mem. Exec. Council, 1973–78; Pres. 1976–77; Mem. Exec. Cttee of Central Council for the Disabled, 1972–76; Adviser to Social Services Cttee of Assoc. of Metropolitan Authorities, 1974–81; Member: RCP Cttee on Rheumatism and Rehabilitation, 1974–83; DES Cttee of Enquiry into Special Educn for Disabled Children, 1975–78; Exec. Cttee, Liverpool Personal Services Soc., 1973–81; Adv. Panel Inf. Service, Disabled Living Foundn, 1979–81; UK Steering Cttee, Internat. Year for the Disabled, 1979–80; Jt Cttee on Mobility of Blind and Partially Sighted People, 1980–81; Exec. Cttee, N Regional Assoc. for the Blind, 1980–81. Vice Pres., MIND Appeal, 1978–79. Christopher Kershaw Meml Lectr, London, 1984. Pres., Merseyside Ski Club, 1970–77. Mem. Council, Prospect Hall Coll., 1973–77; Chm., Bd of Governors, William Rathbone Staff Coll., Liverpool, 1961–75. *Publications:* Community Health and Social Services, 1965, 5th edn 1991; Community Health, Preventive Medicine and Social Services, 1966, 6th edn 1993; (contrib.) Going Home (a Guide for helping the patient on leaving hospital), 1981; The Disabled Child and Adult, 1982; (contrib.) Rehabilitation: a practical guide to the management of physical disability in adults, 1988; numerous papers on Public Health, Physically and Mentally Handicapped and various social services, in scientific and other jls. *Recreations:* skiing, golf, fishing, gardening, music. *Address:* Tree Tops, Church Road, Thornton Hough, Wirral, Merseyside. *T:* 0151–336 3435. *Clubs:* Royal Over-Seas League; Bromborough Golf.

DAVIES, Janet Mary H.; *see* Hewlett-Davies.

DAVIES, Dame Jean; *see* Lancaster, Dame J.

DAVIES, John; *see* Davies, L. J.

DAVIES, John Alun Emlyn; retired 1977; *b* 4 May 1909; *s* of Robert Emlyn and Mary Davies; *m* 1941, Elizabeth Boshier; three *s. Educ:* Ruabon Grammar Sch.; Trinity Coll., Cambridge (Scholar). BA 1st cl. Pts I and II, History Tripos, MA 1984. Called to Bar, Lincoln's Inn, 1936. Served War of 1939–45: DAA&QMG 2nd Parachute Bde, 1943; DAAG 1st Airborne Div., 1944. Joined BoT, 1946; Asst Solicitor, 1963; Principal Asst Solicitor, DTI, 1968–72; Asst Solicitor, Law Commn, 1972–74; part-time Asst, Law Commn, 1974–77. Asst Sec. to Jenkins Cttee on Company Law, 1959–62. *Recreations:* gardening, walking. *Address:* 29 Crescent Road, Sidcup, Kent DA15 7HN. *T:* 0181–300 1421.

DAVIES, Prof. John Brian, FEng 1988; FIEE; FIEEE; Professor of Electrical Engineering, University College London, since 1985; *b* 2 May 1932; *s* of John Kendrick Davies and Agnes Ada Davies; *m* 1956, Shirley June (*née* Abrahart); one *s* two *d. Educ:* Jesus Coll., Cambridge (MA); Univ. of London (MSc, PhD, DSc Eng). Research Engineer, Mullard Res. Labs, Redhill, 1955–63; Lectr, Dept of Electrical Engineering, Univ. of Sheffield, 1963; Sen. Lectr 1967, Reader 1970–85, Dean of Engrg, 1989–91, University College London. Vis. Scientist, Nat. Bureau of Standards, Boulder, Colo, 1971–72; Visitor, Univ. of Oxford, 1983; Vis. Prof., Univ. of Colorado, 1988–89. *Publications:* Electromagnetic Theory, vol. 2, 1972; (contrib.) Numerical Techniques for Microwave and Millimeter Wave Passive Structures, 1989. *Recreations:* fell walking, music, ski-ing. *Address:* 14 Gaveston Drive, Berkhamsted, Herts HP4 1JE. *T:* Berkhamsted (01442) 864954.

DAVIES, Rt. Rev. John Dudley; Bishop Suffragan of Shrewsbury, 1987–94; *b* 12 Aug. 1927; *s* of Charles Edward Steedman Davies and Minnie Paton Davies; *m* 1956, Shirley Dorothy Gough; one *s* two *d*. *Educ:* Trinity Coll., Cambridge (BA 1951, MA 1963); Lincoln Theol Coll. Deacon 1953, priest 1954, dio. Ripon; Curate: Halton, Leeds, 1953–56; Yeoville, Johannesburg, 1959; Priest-in-Charge, Evander, dio. Johannesburg, 1957–61; Rector and Dir of Missions, Empangeni, dio. Zululand and Swaziland, 1961–63; Anglican Chaplain, Univ. of Witwatersrand and Johannesburg Coll. of Educn, 1963–70; Chm., Div. of Christian Educn, S African Council of Churches, 1964–70; Mem. Exec., Univ. Christian Movement of Southern Africa, 1966–67; Sec. for Chaplaincies of Higher Educn, C of E Bd of Educn, 1970–74; Vicar of Keele and Chaplain, Univ. of Keele, 1974–76; Principal, Coll. of Ascension, Selly Oak, 1976–81; Preb. of Sandiacre, Lichfield Cathedral, 1976–87; Diocesan Missioner, St Asaph, 1982–87; Canon Res. and Hellins Lectr, St Asaph, 1982–85; Vicar/Rector, Llanrhaeadr-ym-Mochnant, Llanarmon-Mynydd-Mawr, Pennant, Hirnant and Llangynog, 1985–87. *Publications:* Free to Be, 1970; Beginning Now, 1971; Good News in Galatians, 1975; Creed and Conflict, 1979; The Faith Abroad, 1983; (with John J. Vincent) Mark at Work, 1986; World on Loan, 1992; contribs to jls. *Address:* Angorfa, 3 Canal Terrace, Canalside, Froncysyllte, near Llangollen, Clwyd LL20 7RB. *T:* Chirk (01691) 773517.

DAVIES, John Duncan, OBE 1984; DSc, PhD; Director, Polytechnic of Wales, 1978–92; *b* 19 March 1929; *s* of Ioan and Gertrude Davies; *m* 1949, Barbara, *d* of Ivor and Alice Morgan; three *d*. *Educ:* Pontardawe School; Treforest School of Mines. BSc, MSc, PhD, DSc, Univ. of London. Junior Engineer, Consulting Engineers, 1949; Site Engineer, Cleveland Bridge Co., 1950–54; Royal Engineers, 1952–53; Design Engineer, Local Authority, 1955–56; Asst Lectr, Manchester Univ., 1957–58; University College, Swansea: Lecturer, 1959; Senior Lecturer, 1965; Reader, 1968; Professor of Civil Engineering, 1971–76; Dean, 1974–76; Principal, West Glamorgan Inst. of Higher Education, 1976–77. Member: Open University Delegacy, 1978–83; OU Cttee, 1987–90; Manpower Services Cttee (Wales), 1980–83; Wales Adv. Bd for Public Sector Higher Educn, 1982–83, 1986–89; Council, CNAA, 1985–93; Chm., Coleg Powys Corp. Hon. DTech. *Publications:* contribs to Structural Mechanics. *Address:* Beech House, Dehewydd Lane, Llantwit Fardre, Mid Glam.

DAVIES, Rev. Canon John Howard; Director of Theological and Religious Studies, University of Southampton, since 1981; *b* 19 Feb. 1929; *s* of Jabez Howard and Sarah Violet Davies; *m* 1956, Ina Mary (*d* 1985), *d* of Stanley William and Olive Mary Bubb; three *s* (and one *s* decd). *Educ:* Southall Grammar Sch.; St John's Coll., Cambridge (MA); Westcott House, Cambridge; Univ. of Nottingham (BD); FRCO 1952. Ordained deacon, 1955, priest 1956. Succentor of Derby Cathedral, 1955; Chaplain of Westcott House, 1958; Lectr in Theology, Univ. of Southampton, 1963, Sen. Lectr 1974. Canon Theologian of Winchester, 1981–91. *Publication:* A Letter to Hebrews, 1967. *Recreations:* music, architecture, the countryside. *Address:* 13 Glen Eyre Road, Southampton SO2 3GA. *T:* Southampton (01703) 679359.

DAVIES, John Howard Gay; Editorial Director, Thomson Regional Newspapers Ltd, 1972–82; *b* 17 Jan. 1923; *er s* of late Edgar and Beatrice (Gay) Davies, Nicholaston, Gower; *m* 1st, 1948, Eira Morgan (marr. dissolved, 1953); 2nd, 1955, Betty Walmsley; one *s*. *Educ:* Bromsgrove Sch.; Wadham Coll., Oxford (Exhibnr; MA). Welsh Guards, 1942–46 (despatches). Western Mail, 1950–52; Daily Telegraph, 1952–55; Deputy Editor, Western Mail, 1955–58; an Assistant Editor, Sunday Times, 1958–62; Exec. Assistant to Editorial Director, Thomson Newspapers Ltd, 1962–64; Editor, Western Mail, 1964, 1965. *Address:* 46 Coalecroft Road, SW15 6LP.

DAVIES, John Irfon; MBE (mil.) 1963; Under Secretary, Welsh Office, 1985–90, retired; Chairman, Health Promotion Authority for Wales, since 1992; *b* 8 June 1930; *s* of Thomas M. Davies and late Mary M. Davies (*née* Harris); *m* 1950, Jean Marion Anderson; one *d*. *Educ:* Stanley School; Croydon Polytechnic. psc, awc; Specialist Navigator course. Joined RAF, 1948, commissioned 1950; Chief Navigation Instructor, Cranwell, 1967; OC Flying, Muharraq, 1967–69; MoD, 1970–72; Cabinet Office, 1972–74; Principal, Welsh Office, 1974, Asst Sec., 1978. Mem., GMC, 1990–. *Recreations:* golf, piano, fishing, books. *Address:* Friston, 15 Windsor Road, Radyr, Cardiff CF4 8BQ. *T:* Cardiff (01222) 842617. *Clubs:* Royal Air Force; Cardiff and County; Radyr Golf.

DAVIES, Prof. John Kenyon, MA, DPhil; FSA; FBA 1985; Rathbone Professor of Ancient History and Classical Archaeology, University of Liverpool, since 1977; *b* 19 Sept. 1937; *s* of Harold Edward Davies and Clarice Theresa (*née* Woodburn); *m* 1st, 1962, Anna Elbina Morpurgo (*see* Anna Elbina Davies) (marr. diss. 1978); 2nd, 1978, Nicola Jane, *d* of Dr and Mrs R. M. S. Perrin; one *s* one *d*. *Educ:* Manchester Grammar Sch.; Wadham Coll., Oxford (BA 1959; MA 1962; DPhil 1966). FSA 1986. Harmsworth Sen. Scholar, Merton Coll., Oxford, 1960–61 and 1962–63; Jun. Fellow, Center for Hellenic Studies, Washington, DC, 1961–62; Dyson Jun. Res. Fellow, Balliol Coll., Oxford, 1963–65; Lectr in Ancient History, Univ. of St Andrews, 1965–68; Fellow and Tutor in Ancient History, Oriel Coll., Oxford, 1968–77; Pro-Vice-Chancellor, Univ. of Liverpool, 1986–90. Vis. Lectr, Univ. of Pennsylvania, 1971. Chairman: St Patrick's Isle (IOM) Archaeological Trust Ltd, 1982–86; NW Archaeol Trust, 1982–91. FRSA. Editor: Jl of Hellenic Studies, 1972–77; Archaeol Reports, 1972–74. *Publications:* Athenian Propertied Families 600–300 BC, 1971; Democracy and Classical Greece, 1978, 2nd edn 1993 (Spanish trans. 1981, German and Italian trans. 1983); Wealth and the Power of Wealth in Classical Athens, 1981; (ed with L. Foxhall) The Trojan War: its historicity and context, 1984; articles and reviews in learned jls. *Recreation:* choral singing. *Address:* 20 North Road, Grassendale Park, Liverpool L19 0LR. *T:* 0151–427 2126.

DAVIES, John Michael; Clerk Assistant, since 1991, and Principal Finance Officer, since 1994, House of Lords; *b* 2 Aug. 1940; *s* of Vincent Ellis Davies and late Rose Trench (*née* Temple); *m* 1971, Amanda Mary Atkinson, JP; two *s* one *d*. *Educ:* The King's Sch., Canterbury; Peterhouse, Cambridge. Joined Parliament Office, House of Lords, 1964; seconded to Civil Service Dept as Private Sec. to Leader of House of Lords and Govt Chief Whip, 1971–74; Establishment Officer and Sec. to Chm. of Cttees, 1974–83; Principal Clerk, Overseas and European Office, H of L, 1983–85; Principal Clerk, Private Bill and Overseas Offices and Examiner of Petitions for Private Bills, H of L, 1985–88; Reading Clerk, 1988–90, and Clerk of Public Bills, 1988–94, H of L. Secretary: Soc. of Clerks-at-the-Table in Commonwealth Parlts, and Jt Editor, The Table, 1967–83; Statute Law Cttee, 1974–83. *Address:* 26 Northchurch Terrace, N1 4EG.
See also H. L. Davies.

DAVIES, (John) Quentin; MP (C) Stamford and Spalding, since 1987; *b* 29 May 1944; *e s* of Dr Michael Ivor Davies and Thelma Davies (*née* Butler), Oxford; *m* 1983, Chantal, *e d* of Lt-Col R. L. C. Tamplin, 17/21 Lancers, Military Kt of Windsor, and Claudine Tamplin (*née* Pleis); two *s*. *Educ:* Dragon Sch.; Leighton Park (exhibnr); Gonville and Caius Coll., Cambridge (Open Scholar; BA Hist. Tripos 1st cl. Hons 1966); Harvard Univ. (Frank Know Fellow, 1966–67). HM Diplomatic Service, 1967; 3rd Sec., FCO, 1967–69; 2nd Sec., Moscow, 1969–72; 1st Sec., FCO, 1973–74. Morgan Grenfell & Co.: Manager, later Asst Dir, 1974–78; Rep. in France, later Dir-Gen. and Pres., Morgan Grenfell France SA, 1978–81; Director, 1981–87; Consultant, 1987–93. Dir, Dewe Rogerson International, 1987–; Advr, NatWest Securities, 1993–; Parly Advr, Chartered Inst. of Taxation, 1993–. Contested (C) Birmingham, Ladywood, Aug. 1977. Parliamentary Private Secretary: to Minister of State for Educn, 1988–90; to Minister of State, Home Office, 1990–91. Mem., Treasury Select Cttee, 1992–; Vice-Chairman: Cons. back bench Deregulation Cttee, 1994–; Anglo-German Parly Gp, 1993–; Secretary: Cons. back bench Finance Cttee, 1991–; Cons. back bench Trade and Industry Cttee, 1991–. Chm., City in Europe Cttee, 1975. Liveryman, Goldsmiths' Co. Freeman, City of London. *Recreations:* reading, walking, riding, ski-ing, travel, playing bad tennis, looking at art and architecture. *Address:* House of Commons, SW1A 0AA. *Clubs:* Brooks's, Beefsteak, Travellers'; Constitutional (Spalding); South Lincolnshire Conservative (Bourne).

DAVIES, J(ohn) R(obert) L.; *see* Lloyd Davies.

DAVIES, John Thomas, FCIB; Director, since 1990, a Deputy Chairman, since 1995, Lloyd Bank plc; *b* 9 Feb. 1933; *s* of Joseph Robert and Dorothy Mary Davies; *m* 1957, Margaret Ann Johnson; two *s* three *d*. *Educ:* King Edward's Grammar Sch., Camp Hill, Birmingham. FCIB. Joined Lloyds Bank, 1949; served RAF, 1951–53; Lloyds Bank: Manager of branches, 1963–78; Gen. Management, 1978–89; Dir, Internat. Banking Div., 1989–91; Asst Chief Exec., 1991–92; Dep. Chief Exec., 1992–94. Director: Nat. Bank of NZ, 1989–90 and 1995–; Lloyds Abbey Life, 1995–; Cheltenham & Gloucester Building Society, 1995–. *Recreations:* gardening, walking, reading. *Address:* Lloyds Bank Plc, 71 Lombard Street, EC3P 3BS.

DAVIES, Jonathan, MBE 1995; Rugby League footballer; *b* 24 Oct. 1962; *s* of Len and Diana Davies; *m* 1984, Karen Hopkins; three *c*. *Educ:* Gwendraeth Grammar Sch. Rugby Union footballer to 1989; played for Neath and Llanelli; 27 Wales caps, 4 as Captain; transferred to Rugby League, 1989; with Widnes, 1989–93, Warrington, 1993–; with N Queensland Cowboys, Australian Rugby League, 1995–. Player of the Year Award, 1991, 1994; Stones Bitter Man of Steel, 1994. *Publication:* Jonathan (autobiog.), 1989. *Recreations:* golf, football. *Address:* Warrington Rugby League Football Club, Wilderspool, Fletcher Street, Warrington WA4 6PY.

DAVIES, His Honour Joseph Marie, QC 1962; a Circuit Judge (formerly Judge of County Courts), 1971–91; *b* 13 Jan. 1916; *s* of Joseph and Mary Davies, St Helen's; *m* 1948, Eileen Mary (*née* Dromgoole); two *s* two *d*. *Educ:* Stonyhurst Coll.; Liverpool Univ. Called to Bar, Gray's Inn, Nov. 1938; practice in Liverpool. Recorder of Birmingham, 1970–71; Cumberland Co. QS: Dep. Chm., 1956–63, 1970–71; Chm., 1963–70. Served War of 1939–45; The King's Regt, Nov. 1939–Dec. 1941; RIASC and Staff Allied Land Forces, SE Asia, 1942–46. *Address:* 4 Elm Grove, Eccleston Park, Prescot, Lancs. *T:* 0151–426 5415. *Clubs:* Athenæum (Liverpool); Cumberland County.

DAVIES, Prof. Julian Edmund, PhD; FRS 1994; Professor and Head of Department of Microbiology and Immunology, University of British Columbia, since 1992; *b* 9 Jan. 1932; *s* of Norman Alfred Davies and Lilian Constance (*née* Clarke); *m* 1957, Dorothy Jean Olney; two *s* one *d*. *Educ:* Univ. of Nottingham (BSc Hons Chem., Maths and Phys.; PhD 1956). Lectr in Chem., Univ. of Manchester, 1959–62; Associate in Bacteriol., Harvard Univ., 1962–67; University of Wisconsin: Associate Prof. of Biochem., 1967–70; Prof., 1970–80; Biogen: Res. Dir, 1980–83; Pres., 1983–85; Prof., Inst. Pasteur, Paris, 1986–91; Dir, West-East Center, Univ. of BC, 1993–. Mem., Orion Soc., 1994–. Hoechst-Roussel Award, Amer. Soc. for Microbiol., 1986; Thom Award, Soc. for Industrial Microbiol., 1993. *Publications:* Elementary Biochemistry, 1980; Milestones in Biotechnology, 1992. *Recreations:* cycling, ski-ing, squash, wine. *Address:* 4428 West 6th Avenue, Vancouver, BC V6R 1Z3, Canada. *T:* (604) 2228235. *Club:* University of British Columbia Squash.

DAVIES, Karl; *see* Davies, R. K.

DAVIES, Prof. Kay Elizabeth, CBE 1995; DPhil; Professor of Genetics, and Fellow of Keble College, Oxford University, since 1995; *b* 1 April 1951; *d* of Harry Partridge and Florence Partridge (*née* Farmer); *m* 1973, Stephen Graham Davies; one *s*. *Educ:* Stourbridge Girl's High Sch.; Somerville Coll., Oxford (BA, MA; DPhil; Hon. Fellow, 1995). MRCPath 1990. Guy Newton Jun. Res. Fellow, Wolfson Coll., Oxford, 1976–78; Royal Soc. European Post-doctoral Fellow, Service de Biochimie, Centre d'Etudes, Gif-sur-Yvette, France, 1978–80; St Mary's Hospital Medical School: Cystic Fibrosis Res. Fellow, 1980–82; MRC Sen. Res. Fellow, 1982–84; Nuffield Department of Clinical Medicine, John Radcliffe Hospital, Oxford: MRC Sen. Res. Fellow, 1984–86; MRC Ext. Staff, 1986–92; Univ. Res. Lectr, 1990; MRC Ext. Staff, Inst. of Molecular Medicine, Oxford, 1989–95; Fellow of Green Coll., Oxford, 1990–95; MRC Res. Dir, MRC Clin. Scis Centre, Hammersmith Hosp., 1992–94. Editor (with S. Tilghman), Genome Analysis Reviews, 1990–. Bristol-Myers Prof., USA, 1986; 7th Annual Colleen Giblin Dist. Lectr, Columbia Univ., 1992; Dist. Lectr, Mayo Clinic, USA, 1994. Hon. FRCP 1994. Hon. DSc Victoria, Canada, 1990. *Publications:* (with A. P. Read) Molecular Analysis of Inherited Diseases, 1988, rev. edn 1992; (ed) Human Genetics Diseases: a practical approach, 1988, rev. edn 1993; (ed) Genome Analysis: a practical approach, 1988; (ed) The Fragile X Syndrome, 1989; (ed) Application of Molecular Genetics to the Diagnosis of Inherited Diseases, 1989; numerous reviews and contribs to learned jls. *Recreations:* sport, music. *Address:* Genetics Laboratory, University of Oxford, Oxford OX1 3QU. *T:* Oxford (01865) 275314.

DAVIES, Keith Laurence M.; *see* Maitland Davies.

DAVIES, Sir Lancelot Richard B.; *see* Bell Davies.

DAVIES, Leighton; *see* Davies, R. L.

DAVIES, His Honour (Lewis) John, QC 1967; a Circuit Judge (Official Referee), 1984–93; *b* 15 April 1921; *s* of William Davies, JP, and Esther Davies; *m* 1956, Janet Mary Morris; one *s* two *d*. *Educ:* Pontardawe Grammar Sch.; University College of Wales, Aberystwyth; Trinity Hall (Common Law Prizeman, 1943; Scholar, 1943–44), Cambridge. LLB Wales 1942 (1st cl.); BA Cantab (1st cl.); LLB Cantab (1st cl.). Asst Principal, HM Treasury, 1945–46; Senior Law Lecturer, Leeds Univ., 1946–48; Administrative Asst, British Petroleum, 1949–52. Called to the Bar, Middle Temple, 1948, Bencher, 1973; a Recorder, 1974–84. Mem., Bar Council, 1969–71; Mem., Senate, 1976–78. Mem., Council of Legal Educn, 1976–79. Inspector, DoT, 1977. Mem., Gorsedd, 1986–. *Recreations:* gardening, golf. *Address:* Old Manor Cottage, 24 Park Road, Teddington, Mddx TW11 0AQ. *T:* 0181–977 3975. *Club:* Travellers'.

DAVIES, Lewis Mervyn, CMG 1966; CBE 1984 (OBE 1962); HM Overseas Civil Service, retired; *b* 5 Dec. 1922; *s* of late Rev. Canon L. C. Davies; *m* 1st, 1950, Ione Podger (*d* 1973); one *s*; 2nd, 1975, Mona A. Birley; two step *s*. *Educ:* St Edward's Sch., Oxford. Served with Fleet Air Arm, 1941–46: Lieut A, RNVR. District Commissioner, Gold Coast, 1948; Western Pacific: Senior Asst Secretary, 1956–62; Financial Secretary, 1962–65; Chief Secretary, 1965–70; Deputy Governor, Bahamas, 1970–73; Secretary for Security, Hong Kong, 1973–82; Secretary (Gen. Duties), Hong Kong, 1983–85. Lay

Canon, Cathedral Church of St Barnabas, Honiara, Solomon Islands, 1965–70. Commandeur de l'Ordre National du Mérite, 1966. *Address:* Apartado 123, Felanitx, Mallorca 07200, Spain. *T:* (71) 842152. *Clubs:* Oriental; Vall D'or Golf (Mallorca); Royal Hong Kong Yacht.

DAVIES, Linda Hillary; Her Honour Judge Linda Davies; a Circuit Judge, since 1992; *b* 31 May 1945; *d* of Lt-Col Robert Blowers and Doris Rhoda (*née* Hillary); *m* 1966, Michael Llewelyn Lifton Davies; two *d. Educ:* Folkestone Grammar Sch. for Girls; King's Coll., London (LLB Hons). Called to the Bar, Gray's Inn, 1969. Financial Assistant, Shell Mex BP, 1966–68; Legal Assistant, AA, 1968–70; full-time, later part-time tutor, Council of Legal Educn, 1970–72; Barrister, 1972–92; a Recorder, 1990–92, Western Circuit. Part-time Chm., Ind. Tribunals, 1986–92.

DAVIES, Ven. Lorys Martin; Archdeacon of Bolton, since 1992; *b* 14 June 1936; *s* of Evan Tudor Davies and Eigen Morfydd Davies; *m* 1960, Barbara Ethel (*née* Walkley); two *s. Educ:* Whitland Grammar Sch.; St David's Coll., Lampeter, Univ. of Wales (BA Hons); Philips Hist. Schol.; Organ Exhibnr. Wells Theol Coll. ALCM 1952. Ordained: deacon, 1959; priest, 1960; Curate, St Mary's, Tenby, 1959–61; Asst Chaplain, Brentwood Sch., 1962–66; Chaplain and Head of Dept, Solihull Sch., 1966–68; Vicar, St Mary's, Moseley, 1968–81; Residentiary Canon, Birmingham Cathedral, 1981–92; Diocesan Dir of Ordinands, Birmingham, 1982–90. Chm., House of Clergy, Birmingham Diocesan Synod, 1990–91. JP Birmingham, 1978–92. *Recreations:* sport, theatre, music, reading. *Address:* 45 Rudgwick Drive, Brandlesholme, Bury, Lancs BL8 1YA. *T:* 0161–761 6117.

DAVIES, Marcus John A.; *see* Anwyl-Davies.

DAVIES, Meredith; *see* Davies, Albert Meredith.

DAVIES, Hon. Sir Mervyn; *see* Davies, Hon. Sir D. H. M.

DAVIES, Hon. Sir Michael; *see* Davies, Hon. Sir A. W. M.

DAVIES, Michael; *see* Davies, A. M.

DAVIES, Prof. (Morgan Wynn) Humphrey, DSc; CEng, FIEE; FCGI; Professor of Electrical Engineering, Queen Mary College, University of London, 1956–79, now Emeritus (Fellow of the College, 1984); *b* 26 Dec. 1911; *s* of late Richard Humphrey Davies, CB; *m* 1944, Gwendolen Enid, *d* of late Canon Douglas Edward Morton, Camborne, Cornwall; one *s. Educ:* Westminster Sch.; University College of N Wales, Bangor (MSc (MIT) 1940); Charlottenburg Technische Hochschule, Berlin. Grad. Apprentice with Metropolitan-Vickers, 1933; Lecturer in Electrical Engineering, University of Wales, 1935–42; Commonwealth Fellow, Mass Inst. of Technol., 1938–39; Education Officer to Instn of Electrical Engineers, 1944–47; Lecturer, 1947, and University Reader, 1952, in Electrical Engineering, Imperial Coll., University of London, 1947–56; Dean of Engrg, Univ. of London, 1976–79. Member: Council, IEE, 1948–51, 1958–61 (Chm., Science and Gen. Div. 1964–65). Council, City & Guilds of London Inst., 1952–62; Engineering Adv. Cttee, BBC, 1965–71; Computer Bd for Univs and Res. Councils, 1968–71; Council, University Coll. of N Wales, Bangor, 1976– (Chm., Finance and GP Cttee, 1981–); Chm., Bd of Univ. of London Computer Centre, 1968–79. Gov., Howell's Sch., Denbigh, 1987–96; Chm., Educn Cttee, 1991–96. Hon. LLM London, 1977; Hon. DSc Wales, 1985. *Publications:* Power System Analysis (with J. R. Mortlock), 1952; papers in Proc. of Instn of Electrical Engineers. *Recreation:* travel. *Address:* Church Bank, Beaumaris, Anglesey LL58 8AB. *Club:* Athenæum.

DAVIES, Neil; *see* Davies, W. M. N.

DAVIES, Dr Nicholas Barry, FRS 1994; Reader in Behavioural Ecology, University of Cambridge, since 1992, and Fellow of Pembroke College, Cambridge, since 1979; *b* 23 May 1952; *s* of Anthony Barry Davies and Joyce Margaret Davies (*née* Parrington); *m* 1979, Jan Parr; two *d. Educ:* Merchant Taylors' Sch., Crosby; Pembroke Coll., Cambridge (BA 1973, MA 1977); Edward Grey Inst., Oxford Univ. (DPhil 1976). Demonstrator, Dept of Zoology (Edward Grey Inst. of Field Ornithology), Oxford Univ., 1976–79, and Jun. Res. Fellow, Wolfson Coll., Oxford, 1977–79; Demonstrator and Lectr in Zoology, Univ. of Cambridge, 1979–92. Scientific Medal, Zoolog. Soc., 1987. *Publications:* (ed with J. R. Krebs) Behavioural Ecology, 1978, 3rd edn 1991; (with J. R. Krebs) An Introduction to Behavioural Ecology, 1981, 3rd edn 1993; Dunnock Behaviour and Social Evolution, 1992; contribs to learned jls. *Recreations:* bird watching, cricket. *Address:* Department of Zoology, Downing Street, Cambridge CB2 3EJ. *T:* Cambridge (01223) 336600.

DAVIES, Nicola Velfor; QC 1992; *b* 13 March 1953. *Educ:* Bridgend Girls' Grammar School; Birmingham Univ. (LLB). Called to the Bar, Gray's Inn, 1976. *Address:* 3 Serjeants Inn, EC4Y 1BQ. *T:* 0171–353 5537.

DAVIES, Col Nicolas; *see* Davies, F. N. J.

DAVIES, Nigel; *see* Davies, Claude N. B.

DAVIES, Rev. Noel Anthony; General Secretary, Cytun, Churches Together in Wales, since 1990; *b* 26 Dec. 1942; *s* of late Rev. Ronald Anthony Davies and of Anne Davies; *m* 1968, Patricia Barter. *Educ:* UCNW, Bangor (BSc Chem. and Biochem.); Mansfield College, Oxford (BA Theol.). Ordained, 1968; Minister, Bryn Seion Welsh Congregational Church, Glanaman, 1968; Gen. Sec., Council of Churches for Wales and Commn of Covenanted Churches in Wales, 1977. Chm., Union of Welsh Independents (Congregational) Council, 1990–93; Moderator, Churches' Commn on Mission, CCBI, 1991–. *Publications:* articles in ecumenical jls and Welsh language items. *Recreations:* classical music and hi-fi, gardening, West Highland White terriers, oriental cookery. *Address:* First Floor, 21 St Helens Road, Swansea SA1 4AP. *T:* (office) Swansea (01792) 460876.

DAVIES, (Norah) Olwen, MA; Headmistress, St Swithun's School, Winchester, 1973–86; *b* 21 March 1926; *d* of late Rev. and Mrs E. A. Davies. *Educ:* Tregaron County Sch.; Walthamstow Hall, Sevenoaks; Edinburgh Univ. (MA). DipEd Oxon. Staff of Girls' Remand Home, Essex, 1948–50; Russell Hill Sch., Purley, 1950–53; Woodford House, NZ, 1953–57 (Dep. Headmistress); Westonbirt Sch., 1957–65; Headmistress, St Mary's Hall, Brighton, 1965–73. Pres., Girls' Schools Association, 1981–82. Governor: Tormead Sch., Guildford; Godolphin Sch., Salisbury; Lord Mayor Treloar Coll., Alton. *Address:* 28 Arle Gardens, Alresford, Hants SO24 9BA.

DAVIES, Col Norman Thomas, MBE 1970; JP; Registrar, General Dental Council, since 1981; *b* 2 May 1933; *s* of late Edward Ernest Davies and of Elsie Davies (*née* Scott); *m* 1961, Penelope Mary, *e d* of Peter Graeme Agnew, *qv*; one *s* one *d. Educ:* Holywell; RMA, Sandhurst; Open Univ. (BA 1979). Commnd RA, 1954; Regtl and Staff Appts, Malaya, Germany and UK, 1954–64; ptsc 1966; psc 1967; Mil. Asst to C of S Northern Army Gp, 1968–69; Commanded C Bty RHA and 2IC 3RHA, 1970–72; GSOI (DS), Staff Coll., Camberley, and Canadian Land Forces Comd and Staff Coll., 1972–74; Commanded 4 Field Regt, RA, 1975–77; Mil. Dir of Studies, RMCS, Shrivenham, 1977–80. Mem., EEC Adv. Cttee on the Training of Dental Practitioners, 1983–. Hon. Mem., BDA, 1990. JP Hants, 1984. *Recreations:* Rugby football, fly fishing, gardening, wine. *Address:* Lowfields Cottage, London Road, Hartley Wintney, Hants RG27 8HY. *T:* Hartley Wintney (01252) 843303. *Club:* Royal Society of Medicine.

DAVIES, Olwen; *see* Davies, N. O.

DAVIES, Sir Oswald, Kt 1984; CBE 1973; DCM 1944; Director, AMEC plc (holding company of Fairclough Construction Group and William Press Group), since 1982 (Chairman, 1982–84); *b* 23 June 1920; *s* of George Warham Davies and Margaret (*née* Hinton); *m* 1942, Joyce Eaton; one *s* one *d. Educ:* Central Schs, Sale; Manchester Coll. of Technology. FIHT, FCIOB, FFB; CBIM; FRGS; FRSA. Served War of 1939–45: Sapper, bomb disposal squad, RE, Europe and ME, from 1940 (DCM (ME) 1944); returned to Europe, where involved with his unit in clearance of waterways, port, docks and bridge reconstruction. Dir, 1948–, Jt Man. Dir, 1951, Chm., 1965–83, Fairclough Construction Group plc (formerly Leonard Fairclough Ltd). *Recreations:* gardening, sport. *Address:* (office) AMEC plc, Sandiway House, Northwich, Cheshire CW8 2YA. *T:* Northwich (01606) 883885.

DAVIES, Patrick Taylor, CMG 1978; OBE 1967; HM Overseas Civil Service, retired; *b* 10 Aug. 1927; *s* of Andrew Taylor Davies and Olive Kathleen Mary Davies; *m* 1959, Marjorie Eileen (*née* Wilkinson); two *d. Educ:* Shrewsbury Sch.; St John's Coll., Cambridge (MA); Trinity Coll., Oxford. Lieut, RA, Nigeria, 1945–48. Colonial Admin. Service, Nigeria, 1952; Permanent Sec., Kano State, 1970; Chief Inspector, Area Courts, Kano State, 1972–79. *Address:* Rose Cottage, Childs Ercall, Salop TF9 2DB. *T:* Childs Ercall (01952) 840255.

DAVIES, Paul; General Manager, St John's, Smith Square, since 1985; *b* 28 Dec. 1955; *s* of Thomas Rees Davies and Eirlys Davies. *Educ:* Gowerton Boys' Grammar Sch.; University Coll. London (BA Hons English). Asst, Camden Fest. and Shaw Theatre, 1978–79; Wigmore Hall: Concert Asst, 1979–84; Dep. Manager, 1984–85. *Recreations:* music, opera, theatre, reading, swimming. *Address:* 227 Portnall Road, W9 3BL.

DAVIES, (Percy) Douglas, CB 1981; *b* 17 Sept. 1921; *s* of late Mr and Mrs Thomas Davies; *m* 1947, Renée Margaret Billings; one *s* one *d. Educ:* Liverpool Collegiate School; Open Univ. (BA 1989). Clerical Officer, Ministry of Transport, 1938; served Royal Armoured Corps, 1941–46; Chief Executive Officer, Min. of Transport, 1963; Asst Secretary, 1966; Principal Establishment Officer, Under Secretary, Property Services Agency, Dept of the Environment, 1972–81. Chm., Council of Management, London Hostels Assoc., 1983–. *Recreations:* gardening, making things work. *Address:* 3 Court Avenue, Old Coulsdon, Surrey CR5 1HG. *T:* Downland (01737) 553391.

DAVIES, Peter Douglas Royston, CMG 1994; HM Diplomatic Service; Consul-General, Toronto, and Director-General of Trade and Investment in Canada, since 1991; *b* 29 Nov. 1936; *e s* of Douglas and Edna Davies; *m* 1967, Elizabeth Mary Lovett Williams; one *s* two *d. Educ:* Brockenhurst County High Sch.; LSE (BSc(Econ)). Joined HM Diplomatic Service, 1964; FO, 1964–66; Second Sec., Nicosia, 1966–67; FO, 1967–68; First Sec., Budapest, 1968–71; FCO, 1971–74; Consul (Commercial), Rio de Janeiro, 1974–78; Counsellor (Commercial): The Hague, 1978–82; Kuala Lumpur, 1982–83; Dep. High Comr, Kuala Lumpur, 1983–85; RCDS 1986; Head of Arms Control and Disarmament Dept, FCO, 1987–91. *Recreations:* tennis, ski-ing, biography. *Address:* c/o Foreign and Commonwealth Office, SW1A 2AH.

DAVIES, Sir Peter Maxwell, Kt 1987; CBE 1981; composer and conductor; *b* 8 Sept. 1934; *s* of Thomas and Hilda Davies. *Educ:* Leigh Grammar Sch.; Manchester Univ. (MusB (Hons) 1956); Royal Manchester Coll. of Music. FRNCM 1978. Studied with Goffredo Petrassi in Rome (schol. 1957); Harkness Fellow, Grad. Music Sch., Princetown Univ., NJ, 1962. Dir of Music, Cirencester Grammar Sch., 1959–62; lecture tours in Europe, Australia, NZ, USA, Canada and Brazil; Visiting Composer, Adelaide Univ., 1966; Founder and Co-Dir, with Harrison Birtwistle, of Pierrot Players, 1967–70; Prof. of Composition, Royal Northern Coll. of Music, 1975–80; Founder and Artistic Director: The Fires of London, 1971–87; St Magnus Fest., Orkney Is, 1977–86 (Pres., 1986–); Artistic Dir, Dartington Hall Summer Sch. of Music, 1979–84; Associate Conductor/Composer: Scottish Chamber Orch., 1985–94 (Composer Laureate, 1994–); BBC Philharmonic Orch., 1992–; RPO, 1992–. Retrospective Festival, South Bank Centre, 1990. President: Schs Music Assoc., 1983–; Composers' Guild of GB, 1986–; Nat. Fedn of Music Socs, 1989–; Cheltenham Arts Fests, 1994–. Series for Schools Broadcasts, BBC Television. Hon. Member: RAM, 1978; Guildhall Sch. of Music and Drama, 1981; Royal Philharmonic Soc., 1987; Hon. DMus: Edinburgh, 1979; Manchester, 1983; Bristol, 1984; Open Univ., 1986; Glasgow, 1994; Hon. DL Aberdeen, 1981; Hon. DLitt Warwick, 1986. Cobbett Medal, for services to chamber music, 1989; (first) Award, Assoc. of British Orchs, 1991; Gulliver Award, 1992. Officier de l'Ordre des Arts et des Lettres (France), 1988. *Major compositions include: orchestral:* First Fantasia on an In Nomine of John Taverner, 1962, Second Fantasia, 1964; St Thomas Wake, 1968; Worldes Blis, 1969; Symphony No 1, 1976; Symphony No 2, 1980; Sinfonia Concertante, 1982; Symphony No 3, 1985; An Orkney Wedding, with Sunrise, 1985; Violin Concerto, 1985; Concerto for trumpet and orch., 1988; Symphony No 4, 1989; Ojai Festival Overture, 1991; A Spell for Green Corn: The MacDonald Dances, 1993; Symphony No 5, 1994; Cross Lane Fair, 1994; The Beltane Fire, 1995; Strathclyde Concertos: No 1, 1987; No 2, 1988; No 3, for horn, trumpet and orch., 1989; No 4, for clarinet and orch., 1990; No 5 for violin, viola and string orch., 1991; No 6, for flute and orch., 1991; No 7, for double bass and orch., 1992; No 8, for bassoon and orch., 1993; No 9, for woodwind and strings, 1994; *instrumental:* Sonata for trumpet and piano, 1955; Piano Sonata, 1981; Brass Quintet, 1981; *for ensemble:* Alma redemptoris mater, 1957; Antechrist, 1967; Missa super L'Homme Armé, 1968; Ave Maris Stella, 1975; A Mirror of Whitening Light, 1977; Image, Reflection, Shadow, 1982; *opera:* Taverner, 1970; The Martyrdom of Saint Magnus, 1976; The Two Fiddlers, 1978; The Lighthouse, 1979; Cinderella, 1979; Resurrection, 1987; *music theatre:* Eight Songs for a Mad King, 1969; Vesalii Icones, 1969; Miss Donnithorne's Maggot, 1974; Le Jongleur de Notre Dame, 1978; The No 11 Bus, 1984; The Great Bank Robbery, 1989; *ballet:* Salome, 1978; Caroline Mathilde, 1990; *for accompanied voices:* Five Motets, 1959; O Magnum Mysterim, 1960; Revelation and Fall, 1965; From Stone to Thorn, 1971; Black Pentecost, 1979; Solstice of Light, 1979; Into the Labyrinth, 1983; The Turn of the Tide, 1992. *Address:* c/o Mrs Judy Arnold, 50 Hogarth Road, SW5 0PU.

DAVIES, Maj.-Gen. Peter Ronald, CB 1992; Director General, Royal Society for the Prevention of Cruelty to Animals, since 1991; *b* 10 May 1938; *e s* of Lt-Col Charles Henry Davies and Joyce Davies (*née* Moore); *m* 1960, Rosemary Julia, *er d* of late David Felice of Douglas, IoM; one *s* one *d. Educ:* Llandovery College; Welbeck College; RMA Sandhurst; student: RMCS 1969; Staff Coll., 1970; RCDS, 1984. Commissioned Royal Corps of Signals, 1958; service in BAOR, Berlin, Borneo, Cyprus and UK, 1958–68; OC Artillery Bde Sig. Sqn, 1971–72; Bde Maj., 20 Armd Bde, 1973–75; Directing Staff, Staff Coll., Camberley, 1975–76; CO 1 Armd Div. Signal Regt, 1976–79; Col GS SD, HQ UKLF, 1979–82; Brigade Comdr, 12 Armd Brigade, 1982–84; Dep. Comdt and Dir of Studies, Staff College, Camberley, 1985–86; Comdr Communications, BAOR, 1987–90; GOC Wales, 1990–91. Mem., Internat. Strategic Planning and Adv. Bd, Andrew Corp., USA, 1991–92. Executive Director: WSPA, 1992–; Eurogroup for Animal Welfare, 1992–;

Chm., Freedom Food Ltd, 1994–. Colonel, King's Regt, 1986–94; Chm., Regtl Council and King's and Manchester Regts' Assoc., 1986–94; Col Comdt, RCS, 1990–. Mem., Exec. Cttee, Lord Roberts Workshops and Forces Help Soc., 1994–. Gov., Welbeck Coll., 1980–81; Trustee, Llandovery Coll., 1992–. CIMgt 1994; FIPD; FITD 1991; FZS 1994. *Recreations:* music, wine, Welsh nostalgia, constant motion. *Address:* c/o RSPCA Headquarters, Causeway, Horsham, Sussex RH12 1HG. *Clubs:* Buck's, Army and Navy, Fadeaways.

DAVIES, Ven. Philip Bertram; Archdeacon of St Albans, since 1987; *b* 13 July 1933; *s* of Rev. Bertram Davies and Nancy Jonsson Davies (*née* Nicol); *m* 1963, (Elizabeth) Jane, *d* of late Ven. John Farquhar Richardson; two *s* one *d* (and one *d* decd). *Educ:* Lancing College. Travancore Tea Estates Ltd, 1954–58; Lewis's Ltd, 1959–61. Cuddesdon Theological College, 1961–63. Curate, St John the Baptist, Atherton, 1963–66; Vicar, St Mary Magdalene, Winton, Eccles, 1966–71; Rector, St Philip with St Stephen, Salford, 1971–76; Vicar, Christ Church, Radlett, 1976–87; RD of Aldenham, 1979–87. *Recreations:* gardening, fishing. *Address:* 6 Sopwell Lane, St Albans, Herts AL1 1RR. *T:* St Albans (01727) 857973, *Fax:* (01727) 844469.

DAVIES, Philip John; Parliamentary Counsel, since 1994; *b* 19 Sept. 1954; *s* of Glynn Davies and Mary (*née* Adams); *m* 1981, Jacqueline Sara Boutcher; one *d*. *Educ:* St Julian's High Sch., Newport, Gwent; Hertford Coll., Oxford (MA, BCL). Called to the Bar, Middle Temple, 1981; Lectr in Law, Univ. of Manchester, 1977–82; Asst and Sen. Asst Parly Counsel, 1982–90; Dep. Parly Counsel, 1990–94 (seconded to Law Commn, 1992–94). *Publications:* articles and notes in Law Qly Rev., Modern Law Rev. and other legal jls. *Recreations:* family, Welsh terrier. *Address:* Office of the Parliamentary Counsel, 36 Whitehall, SW1A 2AY. *T:* 0171–210 6630.

DAVIES, Maj.-Gen. Philip Middleton, OBE 1975; *b* 27 Oct. 1932; *s* of Mrs C. H. Allen (*née* Tickler); *m* 1956, Mona Wallace; two *d*. *Educ:* Charterhouse; RMA, Sandhurst. Commnd Royal Scots, 1953; served Korea, Canal Zone, Cyprus, Suez, Berlin, Libya 1st Bn Royal Scots, 1953–63; Staff Coll., 1963; National Defence Coll., 1971; commanded: 1st Bn Royal Scots, 1973–76; 19 Bde/7 Fd Force, 1977–79; RCDS, 1980; Comd Land Forces, Cyprus, 1981–83; GOC NW Dist, 1983–86; retired. *Recreations:* fishing, gardening. *Club:* Ebury Court.

DAVIES, Quentin; *see* Davies, J. Q.

DAVIES, Rees; *see* Davies, Robert R.

DAVIES, Rhys Everson, QC 1981; **His Honour Judge Rhys Davies;** a Circuit Judge, since 1990; Hon. Recorder of Manchester, since 1990; *b* 13 Jan. 1941; *s* of late Evan Davies and Nancy Caroline Davies; *m* 1963, Katharine Anne Yeates; one *s* one *d*. *Educ:* Cowbridge Grammar School; Neath Grammar School; Victoria University of Manchester. LLB (Hons). Called to the Bar, Gray's Inn, 1964, Bencher, 1993. On Northern Circuit, 1964–90; a Recorder, 1980–90. Mem. Court and Council, Univ. of Manchester, 1993–. *Recreations:* music, conversation. *Address:* Crown Court, Crown Square, Manchester M3 3FL. *T:* 0161–954 1800.

DAVIES, Richard Llewellyn; QC 1994; *b* 7 April 1948; *s* of Richard Henry Davies and Margaret Davies; *m* 1979, Elizabeth Ann Johnston; one *s* one *d*. *Educ:* St Julian's High Sch., Newport, Gwent; Univ. of Liverpool (LLB Hons). Called to the Bar, Inner Temple, 1973. *Recreations:* music, wine, reading, cycling. *Address:* 39 Essex Street, WC2R 3AT.

DAVIES, Robert David, CB 1982; CVO 1977; RD 1963; JP; Director, Office of the Premier, Department of the Premier and Cabinet, Western Australia, 1983 and Clerk of Executive Council, 1975–83, retired; *b* 17 Aug. 1927; *s* of late William Harold Davies and of Elsie Davies; *m* 1948, Muriel Patricia Cuff; one *s* one *d*. *Educ:* Fremantle Boys High Sch.; Perth Technical Coll. Senior AASA. Defence Service, 1945–47; Asst Commissioner, State Taxation Dept, 1973; Under Sec., Premier's Dept, WA, 1975. Comdr, RANR, 1972. JP 1970. *Recreations:* fishing, sailing. *Address:* 68 Beazley Road, Leeming, WA 6149, Australia. *T:* (9) 3324041.

DAVIES, Rt. Rev. Robert Edward, CBE 1981; MA, ThD; *b* Birkenhead, England, 30 July 1913; *s* of late R. A. Davies, Canberra; *m* 1953, Helen M., *d* of H. M. Boucher; two *d*. *Educ:* Cessnock High School; Queensland University; St John's Theological College, Morpeth, NSW. Assistant Priest, Christ Church Cathedral, Newcastle, NSW, 1937–41. War of 1939–45: Toc H Army Chaplain, 1941–42; Chaplain, Royal Australian Air Force, Middle East and Mediterranean, 1942–46. Vice-Warden, St John's College, University of Queensland, Brisbane, 1946–48; Archdeacon of Canberra and Rector of Canberra, 1949–53; Archdeacon of Wagga Wagga, NSW, 1953–60; Assistant Bishop of Newcastle and Warden of St John's Theological College, Morpeth, NSW, 1960–63; Bishop of Tasmania, 1963–81. *Recreations:* golf, tennis. *Address:* 12 Elboden Street, Hobart, Tasmania 7000, Australia. *Clubs:* Tasmanian, Naval Military and Air Force of Tas. (Tas.).

DAVIES, Robert Henry, MBE 1962; DFC 1943; HM Diplomatic Service, retired; *b* 17 Aug. 1921; *s* of John and Lena Davies; *m* 1st, 1945, Marion Ainsworth (marr. diss. 1973); one *s* one *d*; 2nd, 1973, Maryse Deuson. *Educ:* John Bright County Sch., Llandudno. RAF, 1940–46; flew with S African Air Force, N Africa, 1942–43. Joined Min. of Food, 1946; transf. to CRO, 1954; served in India, 1954–57 and Canada, 1959–62; HM Diplomatic Service, 1965; served in Brussels, 1967–70; Consul-Gen. and Counsellor (Admin), Moscow, 1973–75; FCO, 1975–76; Counsellor, Paris, 1976–81. *Recreations:* golf, birdwatching, reading. *Address:* 16 Beechcroft Drive, Guildford, Surrey GU2 5SA. *Club:* Bramley Golf.

DAVIES, (Robert) Karl; Chief Executive, Plaid Cymru, since 1993; *b* 26 July 1963; *s* of R. Keith Davies and Dilys Catherine Davies (*née* Hughes). *Educ:* Ysgol Glan Clywd, St Asaph; University Coll. of Wales, Aberystwyth (BA). Editor, Tafod Y Ddraig, 1983–84; Chm., Welsh Lang. Soc., 1984–85; Res. Dir, Plaid Cymru, 1985–89; BBC Wales: Producer, Radio, 1989–90; Parly Editor, 1990–93. Mem. Council, UCW, Aberystwyth, 1988–91. *Publication:* Beth am Gynnau Tân?, 1985. *Recreations:* travel, cinema, gossip, Italy. *Address:* Plaid Cymru, 51 Cathedral Road, Cardiff CF1 9HD. *T:* Cardiff (01222) 231944/343859. *Clubs:* London Welsh; Cameo, Ifor Bach (Cardiff).

DAVIES, (Robert) Leighton; QC 1994; a Recorder, since 1994; *b* 7 Sept. 1949; *s* of Robert Brinley Davies and Elizabeth Nesta Davies (*née* Jones); *m* 1979, Linda Fox; two *s* one *d*. *Educ:* Rhondda Co. Grammar Sch., Porth, Rhondda; Corpus Christi Coll., Oxford (MA, BCL; boxing blue, 1971–72); Inns of Court Sch. of Law. Called to the Bar, Gray's Inn, 1975; practising on Wales and Chester Circuit, 1975–; Asst Recorder, 1990–94. *Recreations:* fly-fishing, gardening, military history. *Address:* 9 Park Place, Cardiff CF1 3DP. *T:* Cardiff (01222) 382731; Bryn Corun, Glyncoli Road, Treorchy, Mid-Glamorgan CF42 6SB. *T:* Treorchy (01443) 774559. *Club:* Vincent's (Oxford).

DAVIES, Prof. (Robert) Rees, CBE 1995; DPhil; FBA 1987; Professor of History, since 1976, and British Academy Wolfson Research Professor in the Humanities, since 1993, University (formerly University College) of Wales, Aberystwyth; *b* 6 Aug. 1938; *s* of William Edward Davies and Sarah Margaret Williams; *m* 1966, Carys Lloyd Wynne; one *s* one *d*. *Educ:* University College London (BA); Merton Coll., Oxford (DPhil). FRHistS 1968. Asst Lectr, UC, Swansea, 1961–63; Lectr, UCL, 1963–76; Vice-Principal, UCW, Aberystwyth, 1988–91. Wiles Lectr, QUB, 1988; James Ford Special Lectr, Univ. of Oxford, 1988; Vis. Fellow, Magdalen Coll., Oxford, 1992; Special History Lectr, Univ. of Newcastle upon Tyne, 1994. Chm., Nat. Curriculum History Cttee for Wales, 1989–91; Mem., Res. Gp, HEFCW, 1993–. Convenor, History at Univs Defence Gp, 1991–92. Member: Ancient Monuments Bd for Wales, 1977– (Dep. Chm., 1993–); Council, Nat. Museum of Wales, 1987–90; Council, Historical Assoc., 1991–93; President: RHistS, 1992– (Mem. Council, 1979–82; Vice Pres., 1987–91); Assoc. of History Teachers of Wales, 1994–; Chm., British Nat. Cttee, Internat. Congress of Historical Scis, 1993–. Mem., Welsh Acad., 1990. Hon. Fellow, UC of Swansea, 1993. Wolfson Literary Award for History, 1987; Norton Medlicott Medal, Historical Assoc., 1994. Asst Editor and Review Editor, History, 1963–73. *Publications:* Lordship and Society in the March of Wales 1282–1400, 1978; (ed) Welsh Society and Nationhood, 1984; Conquest, Co-existence and Change: Wales 1063–1415, 1987; (ed) The British Isles 1100–1500, 1988; Domination and Conquest: the experience of Ireland, Scotland and Wales 1100–1300, 1990; numerous contribs to learned jls. *Recreations:* walking, music. *Address:* Maeshyfryd, Ffordd Llanbadarn, Aberystwyth, Dyfed SY23 1HB. *T:* Aberystwyth (01970) 617113.

DAVIES, Prof. Rodney Deane, CBE 1995; DSc, PhD; FRS 1992; CPhys, FInstP; FRAS; Professor of Radio Astronomy, University of Manchester, since 1976; Director, Nuffield Radio Astronomy Laboratories, Jodrell Bank, since 1988; *b* 8 Jan. 1930; *s* of Holbin James Davies and Rena Irene (*née* March), Mallala, S Australia; *m* 1953, Valda Beth Treasure; one *s* two *d* (and one *s* decd). *Educ:* Adelaide High Sch.; Univ. of Adelaide (BSc Hons, MSc); Univ. of Manchester (PhD, DSc). Research Officer, Radiophysics Div., CSIRO, Sydney, 1951–53; Univ. of Manchester: Asst Lectr, 1953–56; Lectr, 1956–67; Reader, 1967–76. Visiting Astronomer, Radiophysics Div., CSIRO, Australia, 1963. Member: Internat. Astronomical Union, 1958; Org. Cttee and Working Gps of various Commns; Bd and various panels and cttees of Astronomy Space and Radio Bd and Science Bd of Science Research Council; British Nat. Cttee for Astronomy, 1974–77. Royal Astronomical Society: Mem. Council, 1972–75 and 1978–; Sec., 1978–86; Vice-Pres., 1973–75 and 1986–87; Pres., 1987–89. *Publications:* Radio Studies of the Universe (with H. P. Palmer), 1959; Radio Astronomy Today (with H. P. Palmer and M. I. Large), 1963; The Crab Nebula (co-ed with F. G. Smith), 1971; numerous contribs to Monthly Notices of RAS and internat. jls on the galactic and extragalactic magnetic fields, structure and dynamics of the Galaxy and nearby external galaxies, use of radio spectral lines, the early Universe and studies of the Cosmic Microwave Background. *Recreations:* gardening, fell-walking. *Address:* University of Manchester, Nuffield Radio Astronomy Laboratories, Jodrell Bank, Macclesfield, Cheshire SK11 9DL. *T:* Lower Withington (01477) 71321.

DAVIES, Roger; *see* Davies, A. R.

DAVIES, Roger Oliver; Chairman, Going Places, since 1994; Director, Airtours PLC, since 1994; Member, Monopolies and Mergers Commission, since 1989; *b* 4 Jan. 1945; *s* of Griffith William Davies and Dorothy Anne Davies; *m* 1973, Adele Biss, *qv*; one *s*. *Educ:* Reading Sch.; Devonport High Sch.; London School of Economics (BScEcon). Marketing Dir, 1972, Man. Dir, 1977, Thomson Holidays; Man. Dir, 1982, Chm., 1984–90, Thomson Travel Gp. Commandeur de la République (Tunisia), 1987. *Recreations:* walking, ski-ing, reading.

DAVIES, Ronald; MP (Lab) Caerphilly, since 1983; *b* 6 Aug. 1946; *s* of late Ronald Davies; *m* 1981, Christina Elizabeth Rees; one *d*. *Educ:* Bassaleg Grammar Sch.; Portsmouth Polytechnic; Univ. Coll. of Wales, Cardiff. Schoolteacher, 1968–70; WEA Tutor/Organiser, 1970–74; Further Educn Adviser, Mid-Glamorgan LEA, 1974–83. Opposition Whip, 1985–87; Opposition spokesman on agriculture and rural affairs, 1987–92, front bench spokesman on food, agriculture and rural affairs, 1992–, on Wales, 1992–. Councillor, Rhymney Valley DC (formerly Bedwas and Machen UDC), 1969–84 (Vice-Chm.). *Address:* House of Commons, SW1A 0AA. *T:* 0171–219 3000.

DAVIES, Rt. Rev. Roy Thomas; *see* Llandaff, Bishop of.

DAVIES, Ryland; opera singer; tenor; *b* 9 Feb. 1943; *s* of Gethin and Joan Davies; *m* 1st, 1966, Anne Elizabeth Howells (marr. diss. 1981), *qv*; 2nd, 1983, Deborah Rees; one *d*. *Educ:* Royal Manchester College of Music (Fellow, 1971) (studied with Frederic R. Cox, OBE). Voice teacher, RNCM, 1987–94. Début as Almaviva in The Barber of Seville, WNO, 1964; Glyndebourne Fest. Chorus, 1964–66; has since sung with Royal Opera, Sadler's Wells Opera, WNO, Scottish Opera, at Glyndebourne, and in Brussels, Chicago, NY, San Francisco, Paris, Salzburg, Buenos Aires, Hong Kong and Stuttgart; solo rôles include: Belmonte in Il Seraglio, Fenton in Falstaff, Ferrando in Così Fan Tutte, Flamand in Capriccio; Tamino in The Magic Flute; Essex in Britten's Gloriana; Hylas in The Trojans; Don Ottavio in Don Giovanni; Cassio in Otello; Ernesto in Don Pasquale; Lysander in A Midsummer Night's Dream; title rôle in Werther; Prince in L'Amour des Trois Oranges; Nemorino in L'Elisir d'amore; Alfredo in La Traviata, Pelléas in Pelléas et Melisande, Berlin and Hamburg; Eneas in Esclarmonde, Royal Opera; Jack in The Midsummer Marriage, San Francisco. Many concerts at home with all major British orchestras, and abroad with such orchestras as: Boston Symphony, Cleveland Symphony, Chicago Symphony, Philadelphia, San Francisco, Los Angeles, Bavarian Radio and Vienna Symphony. Principal oratorio rôles include: Bach, B minor Mass; Beethoven: Mass in C; Berlioz, narrator in L'Enfance du Christ; Elgar, St John, in The Kingdom; Handel: Acis, in Acis and Galatea; title rôle, Judas Macoabeus; Messiah; Jonathan, in Saul; Haydn: Nelson Mass; The Seasons; Mendelssohn: Obidiah, in Elijah; Hymn of Praise; Rossini, Messe Solenelle; Schubert, Lazarus; Tippett, Child of Our Time. Has sung in all major religious works including: Missa Solemnis, Verdi's Requiem, Dream of Gerontius, St Matthew Passion, The Creation. Many recordings incl. Il Seraglio, The Trojans, Saul, Così Fan Tutte, Thérèse, Monteverdi Madrigals, Idomeneo, Haydn's The Seasons, Messiah, L'Oracolo (Leone), Judas Maccabaeus, Il Matrimonio Segreto (Cimarosa), L'Amore dei Tre Re (Montemezzi), La Navarraise (Massenet), Lucia di Lammermoor (Donizetti). John Christie Award, 1965. *Recreations:* antiques, art, cinema, sport.

DAVIES, Sam; *see* Davies, Stanley Mason.

DAVIES, Siobhan; *see* Davies, Susan.

DAVIES, Stanley Mason, (Sam Davies), CMG 1971; Director, Alliance International Health Care Fund (formerly Trust), since 1986 (Consultant, 1984–86); *b* 7 Feb. 1919; *s* of late Charles Davies, MBE and Constance Evelyn Davies; *m* 1943, Diana Joan (*née* Lowe); three *d*. *Educ:* Bootle Grammar School. War Service, UK and W Europe, 1939–46; Royal Army Dental Corps, 1939–41 (Sgt); Corps of Royal Engineers, 1941–46 (Staff Captain). Clerical Officer, Min. of Labour, 1936; Exec. Officer, Inland Revenue, 1938; Higher Exec. Officer, Min. of Pensions, 1946–53; Min. of Health, 1953–68; Asst Sec., DHSS, 1968–75; Under Sec., Industries and Exports Div., DHSS, 1975–76. Consultant: Monsanto Health Care, 1977–85; Sterling Winthrop Drug, 1977–86. Mem., NY Acad. of Scis. FSAScot. Croix de Guerre (France), 1944. *Recreations:* reading, archæology, philately.

Address: 31 Leverstock Green Road, Hemel Hempstead, Herts HP2 4HH. *T:* Hemel Hempstead (01442) 254312. *Club:* Savile.

DAVIES, Susan, (Siobhan Davies), MBE 1995; freelance choreographer; Director, Siobhan Davies Dance Company, since 1988; *b* 18 Sept. 1950; *d* of Grahame Henry Wyatt Davies and Tempé Mary Davies (*née* Wallich); lives with David John Buckland; one *s* one *d*. *Educ:* too many schools, ending with Queensgate School for Girls; Hammersmith College of Art and Building. With London Contemporary Dance Theatre, 1967–87: first choreography, 1970; Associate Choreographer, 1971; Associate Dir, 1983. Formed Siobhan Davies and Dancers, 1980; Jt Dir, with Ian Spink, Second Stride, 1981–86; Associate Choreographer, Rambert Dance Co., 1989–93. Arts Award, Fulbright Commn, 1987, to travel and study in America; Digital Dance Award, 1988, 1989, 1990, 1992; Laurence Olivier Award for Outstanding Achievement in Dance, 1993. *Recreation:* imagining having more time than I do.

DAVIES, Susan Elizabeth, (Mrs John Davies), OBE 1988; Founder and Director, Photographers' Gallery, 1971–91; freelance consultant; *b* 14 April 1933; *d* of Stanworth Wills Adey and Joan Mary Margaret Adey (*née* Charlesworth); *m* 1954, John Ross Twiston Davies; two *d* (and one *d* decd). *Educ:* Nightingale Bamford Sch., NY; Eothen Sch., Caterham. Municipal Journal, 1952–54; local and voluntary work, 1960–67; Artists Placement Group, 1967–68; ICA, 1968–71. Hon. FRPS (President's Medal, 1982). Photokina Award, 1986; National Artist Karel Plicka Medal, Czechoslovakia, 1989. *Recreations:* jazz live and recorded, reading, walking, sleeping. *Address:* Walnut Tree Cottage, 53 Britwell Road, Burnham, Bucks SL1 8DH. *T:* Burnham (016286) 04811. *Club:* Chelsea Arts.

DAVIES, (Thomas) Glyn, CBE 1966; *b* 16 Aug. 1905; *s* of Thomas Davies, Gwaelod-y-Garth, Cardiff; *m* 1935, Margaret Berry; one *d*. *Educ:* Pontypridd Grammar Sch.; Univ. of Wales, Cardiff (MA). Asst Master, Howard Gardens High Sch., Cardiff, 1927–37; Warden, Educational Settlement, Pontypridd, 1937–43; Director of Education: Montgomeryshire, 1943–58; Denbighshire, 1958–70, retd. Mem. ITA, later IBA, 1970–75. Mem., Court and Council, UC Bangor. Fellow, UC Cardiff, 1981. *Recreations:* travel, music. *Address:* 42 Park Avenue, Wrexham, Clwyd LL12 7AH. *T:* Wrexham (01978) 352697.

DAVIES, Trevor Arthur L.; *see* Lloyd Davies.

DAVIES, Ven. (Vincent) Anthony; Archdeacon of Croydon, since 1994; *b* 15 Sept. 1946; *s* of Vincent Davies and Maud Mary Cecilia Davies (*née* Hackett); unmarried. *Educ:* Brasted Place Theol Coll.; St Michael and All Angels Theol Coll., Llandaff. Curate: St James, Owton Manor, dio. Durham, 1973–76; St Faith, Wandsworth, dio. Southwark, 1976–78; Parish Priest: St Faith, Wandsworth, 1978–81; St John, Walworth, 1981–94; RD of Southwark and Newington, 1988–93. *Recreations:* walking, swimming, country pubs, all things Italian. *Address:* 246 Pampisford Road, South Croydon, Surrey CR2 6DD. *T:* 0181–688 2943; (office) St Matthew's House, 100 George Street, Croydon CR0 5NS. *T:* 0181–681 5496.

DAVIES, Vivian; *see* Davies, W. V.

DAVIES, Walter, OBE 1966; Secretary-General and Chief Executive of The British Chamber of Commerce for Italy 1961–86, retired; *b* 7 Dec. 1920; *s* of late William Davies and late Frances Poole; *m* 1947, Alda, *d* of Tiso Lucchetta, Padua; two *d*. *Educ:* St Margaret's Higher Grade Sch., Liverpool; Liverpool Coll. of Commerce. Served War: RA, 1940–41; Scots Guards, 1942–47. Commendatore dell'Ordine al Merito della Repubblica Italiana, 1967. *Recreations:* good food, good company, fishing, motoring. *Address:* Via G. Dezza 27, 20144 Milan, Italy. *T:* (2) 4694391.

DAVIES, Prof. Wendy Elizabeth, FSA; FRHistS; FBA 1992; Professor of History, since 1985, and Dean of Social and Historical Sciences, since 1994, University College London; *b* 28 Aug. 1942; *d* of Douglas Charles Davies and Lucy (*née* Evans). *Educ:* University Coll. London (BA, PhD). Temporary Lectr 1970, Res. Fellow 1971, Lectr 1972, Univ. of Birmingham; University College, London: Lectr 1977; Reader 1981; Hd, Dept of Hist., 1987–92; Dean of Arts, 1991–94. Mem., Ancient Monuments Board for Wales, 1994. Gov., Mus. of London, 1995–. *Publications:* An Early Welsh Microcosm, 1978; The Llandaff Charters, 1979; Wales in the Early Middle Ages, 1982; (ed with P. Fouracre) Settlement of Disputes in Early Medieval Europe, 1986; Small Worlds: the village community in early medieval Brittany, 1988; Patterns of Power, 1990; (with G. Astill) The East Brittany Survey, Field Work and Field Data, 1994; (ed with P. Fouracre) Property and Power, 1995; papers in Eng. Historical Rev., Past and Present, Francia, Bull. of Bd of Celtic Studies, Etudes Celtiques, Hist. and Anthropology, etc. *Recreations:* walking, gardening, early music. *Address:* Department of History, University College London, Gower Street, WC1E 6BT. *T:* 0171–391 1348.

DAVIES, William Llewellyn M.; *see* Monro Davies.

DAVIES, (William Michael) Neil; Member, Inner London Education Authority, 1980–86 (Chairman, 1982–83); *b* 5 Feb. 1931; *s* of William Henry Davies and Hilda Mary (*née* Fielding); *m* 1955, Myra Blanch Clair Smalley (marr. diss. 1981); two *s* one *d*; *m* 1983, Elizabeth Ann Virgin, textile artist, lecturer and author. *Educ:* Neath Technical Coll.; Fircroft Coll.; Birmingham Univ. Probation Officer, Birmingham, Monmouthshire and Somerset, 1962–76; Principal Child Care Adviser, Lambeth Bor. Council, 1976–82. Member: Taunton Bor. Council, 1968–74; London Bor. of Bexley, 1978–82. Greater London Council: Mem. for Woolwich W, 1980–86; Vice-Chm., Public Services and Fire Bde Cttee, 1980–86; Chm., Thames Barrier Sub Cttee, Edn Cttee, and London Youth Cttee, 1980–86; Vice-Chm., Greater London Trng Bd, and Sports Sub Cttee, 1980–86; Mem., Staff Cttee, Arts and Recreation Cttee, Transport Cttee, and Entertainments Licensing Cttee, 1980–86. Member, National Joint Councils: Fire Bde, 1980–86; Probation Service, 1980–86; Local Authority Bldg Trades, 1980–86. Member: Thames Water Authority, 1980–84; NEC National Assoc. of Maternal and Child Welfare, 1980–86. Contested (Lab.) Ripon, 1979. Founder: Avalon Athletic League, 1966; Westwood Athletic League, 1967. Alcalde, San Antonio, Texas, 1985. *Recreations:* sport (athletics coach), music, cooking, walking, crafts. *Address:* 1 Wingrad House, Jubilee Street, E1 3BJ. *T:* 0171–790 1093. *Clubs:* London Welsh Association, Rugby.

DAVIES, Rev. Dr William Rhys; Principal of Cliff College, Sheffield, 1983–94; Moderator of the Free Church Federal Council, 1991–92; *b* Blackpool, 31 May 1932; *m* 1955, Barbara; one *s* one *d*. *Educ:* Junior, Central Selective and Grammar schools, Blackpool; Hartley Victoria Methodist Coll., Manchester; Univ. of Manchester. BD London 1955; MA 1959, PhD 1965, Manchester. Junior Rating and Valuation Officer (Clerical), Blackpool Corp., 1950–51. Methodist Circuit Minister: Middleton, Manchester, 1955–60; Fleetwood, 1960–65; Stockton-on-Tees, 1965–66; Sen. Lectr in Religious Studies, Padgate Coll. of Higher Education, and Methodist Minister without pastoral charge on Warrington Circuit, 1966–79; Superintendent Minister, Bradford Methodist Mission, 1979–83. Pres., Methodist Conf., 1987–88. Methodist Committees: Chm., Cttee for Relations with People of Other Faiths, 1988–; Member: Cliff Coll. Gen. Cttee, 1974–77 and 1981–94; Faith and Order Cttee, 1975–82; Doctrinal Cttee, 1979–82; Divl Bd for Social Responsibility, 1982–85; Home Mission Bd, 1983–94. Mem. Council, Garden Tomb (Jerusalem) Assoc., 1992–. Co-Editor, Dunamis (renewal magazine for Methodists), 1972–. *Publications:* (with Ross Peart) The Charismatic Movement and Methodism, 1973; Spirit Baptism and Spiritual Gifts in Early Methodism, (USA) 1974; Gathered into One (Archbishop of Canterbury's Lent Book), 1975; (with Ross Peart) What about the Charismatic Movement?, 1980; Rocking the Boat, 1986; (contrib.) A Dictionary of Christian Spirituality, 1983; contribs to jls. *Recreations:* reading, sport (soccer). *Address:* 25 Grange Avenue, Thornton Cleveleys, Lancs FY5 4PA. *T:* Cleveleys (01253) 864678.

DAVIES, (William) Vivian, FSA 1980; Keeper of Egyptian Antiquities, British Museum, since 1988; *b* 14 Oct. 1947; *s* of Walter Percival Davies and Gwenllian Davies (*née* Evans); *m* 1970, Janet Olwen May Foat (marr. diss. 1994); one *s* one *d*. *Educ:* Llanelli Grammar Sch.; Jesus Coll., Oxford (BA, MA). Randall-MacIver Student in Archaeology, Queen's Coll., Oxford, 1973–74; Asst Keeper, 1974–81, Dep. Keeper, 1981–88, Dept of Egyptian Antiquities, BM. Vis. Prof. of Egyptology, Univ. of Heidelberg, 1984–85. Hon. Librarian, 1975–85, Gen. Ed. of Pubns, 1990–, Egypt Exploration Soc.; Chm., Sudan Archaeol Res. Soc., 1991–; Member: Governing Council, British Inst. in Eastern Africa, 1989–; German Archaeol Inst., 1992–. Reviews Editor, Jl of Egyptian Archaeology, 1975–85. *Publications:* A Royal Statue Reattributed, 1981; (with T. G. H. James) Egyptian Sculpture, 1983; The statuette of Queen Tetisheri: a reconsideration, 1984; (with A. el-Khouli, A. B. Lloyd, A. J. Spencer) Saqqara Tombs, I: The Mastabas of Mereri and Wernu, 1984; (ed with J. Assmann and G. Burkard) Problems and Priorities in Egyptian Archaeology, 1987; Egyptian Hieroglyphs, 1987; Catalogue of Egyptian Antiquities in the British Museum, VII: Tools and Weapons—1: Axes, 1987; (ed) Egypt and Africa: Nubia from prehistory to Islam, 1991; (ed with R. Walker) Biological Anthropology and the Study of Ancient Egypt, 1993; (ed with L. Schofield) Egypt, the Aegean and the Levant: interconnections in the second millenium BC, 1995; contribs to : Egypt's Golden Age: the art of living in the New Kingdom, 1982; Excavating in Egypt: The Egypt Exploration Society 1882–1982, 1982; Tanis: l'or des pharaons, 1987; reviews and articles in learned jls. *Recreations:* art, chess, music, real ale. *Address:* Department of Egyptian Antiquities, British Museum, WC1B 3DG. *T:* 0171–323 8306.

DAVIES-SCOURFIELD, Brig. Edward Grismond Beaumont, CBE 1966 (MBE 1951); MC 1945; DL; General Secretary, National Association of Boys Clubs, 1973–82; *b* 2 Aug. 1918; 4th *s* of H. G. Davies-Scourfield and Helen (*née* Newton); *m* 1945, Diana Lilias (*née* Davidson); one *s* one *d*. *Educ:* Winchester Coll.; RMC Sandhurst. Commnd into KRRC, 1938; served War of 1939–45 (despatches 1945); psc; commanded: 3rd Green Jackets (Rifle Bde), 1960–62; Green Jackets Bde, 1962–64; British Jt Services Trng Team (Ghana), 1964–66; British Troops Cyprus and Dhekelia Area, 1966–69; Salisbury Plain Area, 1970–73; retd 1973. DL Hants, 1984. *Publications:* In presence of my foes: travels and travails of a POW, 1991. *Recreations:* country pursuits. *Address:* Old Rectory Cottage, Medstead, Alton, Hants GU34 5LX. *T:* Alton (01420) 562133. *Clubs:* Army and Navy, Mounted Infantry.

DAVIGNON, Viscount Etienne; Ambassador of HM the King of the Belgians; Chairman: Société Générale de Belgique, since 1989 (Executive Director, 1984–89); Sibeka, since 1985; Union Minière; Royal Institute for International Relations, since 1987; Foundation P. H. Spaak, since 1983; *b* Budapest, 4 Oct. 1932; *m* 1959, Françoise de Cumont; one *s* two *d*. *Educ:* University of Louvain (LLD). Diplomat; Head of Office of Minister for Foreign Affairs, Belgium, 1963; Political Director, Ministry for Foreign Affairs, Belgium, 1969; Chm., Gov. Board, Internat. Energy Agency, 1974. Mem., 1977–84 (with responsibility for internal mkt, customs, union and industl affairs), and Vice-Pres., 1981–84 (with responsibility for industry, energy and research policies), EEC. Director: Solvay SA, 1985–; Alcatel SA, 1987–; ICL, 1991–; Cie de Suez, 1989 ; Petrofina, 1990–; Générale de Banque, 1987–; Associate, Kissinger Associates, 1985 . *Recreations:* tennis, golf, skiing. *Address:* 12 Avenue des Fleurs, 1150 Brussels, Belgium.

DAVIS; *see* Clinton-Davis.

DAVIS; *see* Lovell-Davis.

DAVIS, Alan Roger M.; *see* Maryon Davis.

DAVIS, Andrew Frank, CBE 1992; conductor; Musical Director, Glyndebourne Festival Opera, since 1988; Chief Conductor, BBC Symphony Orchestra, since 1989; *b* 2 Feb. 1944; *m* 1989, Gianna Rolandi; one *s*. *Educ:* Watford Grammar Sch.; King's Coll., Cambridge (MA, BMus); Accademia di S Cecilia, Rome. Assistant Conductor, BBC Scottish Symphony Orchestra, 1970–72; Asst Conductor, New Philharmonia Orchestra, 1973–77; Artistic Dir and Chief Conductor, Toronto Symphony, 1975–88, now Conductor Laureate. Principal Guest Conductor, Royal Liverpool Philharmonic Orchestra, 1974–77. Has conducted major US orchestras: New York, Boston, Chicago, Cleveland and LA. Particularly noted for interpretations of Strauss operas; conducts at: La Scala, Milan; Metropolitan Opera, NY; Glyndebourne; Royal Opera House, Covent Gdn. Toronto Symphony Orchestra tours: US Centres, China, Japan, 1978; Europe, 1983, 1986, incl. London, Helsinki, Bonn, Paris and Edinburgh Fest.; BBC SO tours: Far East, 1990; Europe, 1992; Japan, 1993. Many commercial recordings include: complete Dvorak Symphonies, Philharmonia Orch.; Mendelssohn Symphonies, Bavarian Radio Symphony; Borodin Cycle, Holst's The Planets and Handel's Messiah, Toronto Symphony; Tippett's The Mask of Time, BBC SO and Chorus (Record of the Year, Gramophone Awards, 1987); The British Line (British Orchestral Series), BBC SO. *Recreation:* the study of mediaeval stained glass. *Address:* c/o Harold Holt Ltd, 31 Sinclair Road, W14 0NS.

DAVIS, Anthony Ronald William James; media consultant, since 1990; *b* 26 July 1931; *e s* of Donald William Davis, Barnes and Mary Josephine Davis (*née* Nolan-Byrne), Templeogue Mill, Co. Dublin; *m* 1960, Yolande Mary June, *o d* of Patrick Leonard, retd civil engr; one *s* two *d* (and one *d* decd). *Educ:* Hamlet of Ratcliffe and Oratory; Regent Street Polytechnic. Joint Services School for Linguists on Russian course as National Serviceman (Army), 1953–55; Architectural Asst, Housing Dept, Mddx County Architect's Dept, 1956–58; Sub-Editor, The Builder, 1959; Editor: Official Architecture and Planning, 1964–70; Building, 1970–74; Director, Building, 1972–77; Editor-in-Chief, New World Publishers Ltd, 1978–83; Editl Dir, New World Publishers Ltd, Middle East Construction and Saudi Arabian Construction, 1983–86; Editor, World Property, 1986–90. Member Board: Architecture and Planning Publications Ltd, 1966; Building (Publishers) Ltd, 1972. Mem. Council, Modular Soc., 1970–71. JP Berkshire, 1973–81. *Publications:* contribs to various, architectural and technical. *Recreations:* collecting porcelain, music and dreaming. *Address:* 5 Stukeley Park, Chestnut Grove, Great Stukeley, Huntingdon, Cambs PE17 5AQ. *T:* Huntingdon (01480) 458175. *Club:* Architecture.

DAVIS, (Arthur) John, RD 1967; FCIB; Vice-Chairman, Lloyds Bank, 1984–91 (Chief General Manager, 1978–84); *b* 28 July 1924; *s* of Alan Wilfrid Davis and Emily Davis; *m* 1950, Jean Elizabeth Edna Hobbs; one *s* one *d* (and one *d* decd). *Educ:* grammar schs. FCIB (FIB 1969). Served War, RN, 1942–46. Entered Lloyds Bank, 1941; Jt Gen. Manager, 1973; Asst Chief Gen. Man., 1973; Dep. Chief Gen. Man., 1976. Pres.,

Chartered Inst. of Bankers, 1985–87. *Recreations:* gardening, music, country pursuits. *Address:* Little Barley End, Aldbury, Tring, Herts HP23 5RZ. *T:* Aldbury Common (0144285) 321. *Clubs:* Naval, Overseas Bankers.

DAVIS, Dr Brian Elliott; Chief Executive, Nationwide Building Society, since 1994; *b* 22 Sept. 1944; *s* of William and Bessie Davis; *m* 1972, Elizabeth Rose; one *s* two *d*. *Educ:* St John's Coll., Southsea; Sussex Univ. (BSc); Sheffield Univ. (PhD). With Esso Petroleum Co., 1969–86; joined Nationwide Building Soc., 1986; Gen. Manager (Technology), 1987; Resource Dir, 1989; Ops Dir, 1992. FRSA 1990; CIMgt 1994. *Recreations:* squash, amateur dramatics, computing. *Address:* Nationwide Building Society, Pipers Way, Swindon SN38 1NW. *T:* Swindon (01793) 513513.

DAVIS, Brian Michael; Chairman and Chief Executive, Mobil Oil Company Ltd, 1990–92; *b* 28 May 1937; *s* of Frederick Thomas Davis and Irene Florence (*née* Burgess); *m* 1962, Patricia Ann Wilkinson; three *s*. *Educ:* London Univ., LSE (BSc Econs). FCMA. Joined Mobil Oil Co. Ltd, 1958: various positions in accounting and finance systems, marketing, planning and supply in UK, Europe and USA, 1958–77; Gen. Manager, Mobil Kenya Gp, 1977–79; Strategic/Marketing Planning, Mobil South Inc./Mobil Europe Inc., 1979–84; Pres., Mobil Oil Portuguesa, 1984–86; Area Exec., Mobil Europe, 1986–87; Pres., Mobil Oil Italiana, 1987–90. *Recreations:* golf, tennis, music, theatre.

DAVIS, Most Rev. Brian Newton; *see* New Zealand, Primate and Archbishop of.

DAVIS, Maj.-Gen. Brian William, CB 1985; CBE 1980 (OBE 1974); Head of Public Affairs, Royal Ordnance plc, 1987–94 (Director, Product Support Group, 1985–87); *b* 28 Aug. 1930; *s* of late Edward William Davis, MBE, and Louise Jane Davis (*née* Webber); *m* 1954, Margaret Isobel Jenkins; one *s* one *d*. *Educ:* Weston-super-Mare Grammar Sch.; Mons OCS, Aldershot. Commissioned Royal Artillery, 1949; Regtl Duty, 1949–56 and 1960–61, UK/BAOR; Instr-in-Gunnery, 1956–59; Staff Coll. Camberley, 1962; DAA and QMG HQ 7 Armd Bde BAOR, 1963–66; GSO2 SD UN Force, Cyprus, 1966; Regtl Duty, 1967–69; Lt-Col 1969, Directing Staff, Staff Coll. Camberley, 1969–71; CO 32 Lt Regt RA BAOR/England/N Ireland, 1971–74; Col AQ Ops HQ BAOR, 1975; Brig. 1975; CRA 3 Div., 1976–77; RCDS 1978; Chief of Staff N Ireland, 1979–80; Chief of Comdrs-in-Chief Mission to Soviet Forces in Germany, 1981–82; Maj. Gen., 1982; C of S, Logistic Exec. (Army), 1982–83; DGLP (A) (formerly VQMG), MoD, 1983–85, retired. Col Comdt RA, 1987–93. Mem., HAC, 1987–. *Recreations:* Rugby (President, RARFC, 1975–78; Dep. Pres., Army Rugby Union, 1984–89), cricket, fishing, ornithology. *Clubs:* Army and Navy, Special Forces, Commonwealth Trust, British Sportsman's, MCC; Somerset County Cricket; Piscatorial Society.

DAVIS, Carl; composer; Principal Guest Conductor, Munich Symphony Orchestra, since 1990; *b* 28 Oct. 1936; *s* of Isadore and Sara Davis; *m* 1971, Jean Boht; two *d*. *Educ:* New England Conservatory of Music; Bard Coll. (BA). Associate Conductor, London Philharmonic Orchestra, 1987–88; Principal Conductor, Bournemouth Pops, 1984–87; *major TV credits:* The Snow Goose, 1971; World at War (Emmy Award), 1972; The Naked Civil Servant, 1975; Marie Curie, 1977; Our Mutual Friend, 1978; Prince Regent, The Old Curiosity Shop, 1979; Hollywood, Oppenheimer, The Sailor's Return, Fair Stood the Wind for France, 1980; The Commanding Sea, Private Schulz, 1981; The Last Night of the Poms, Home Sweet Home, La Ronde, 1982; The Unknown Chaplin, The Tale of Beatrix Potter, The Far Pavilions, 1983; The Day the Universe Changed, 1985; Hotel du Lac, 1986; The Accountant (BAFTA Award), The Pied Piper, 1989; Flight Terminal, Secret Life of Ian Fleming, 1990; The Black Velvet Gown, Buried Mirror, Yellow Wallpaper, The Last of the Romantics, Ashenden, Separate But Equal, 1991; The Royal Collection, A Very Polish Practice, A Sense of History, Fame in the 20th Century, 1992; A Year in Provence, Genghis Cohen, Thatcher: the Downing Street Years, 1993; Red Eagle, Hope in the Year 2, 1994; *scores:* for RSC and National Theatre; *musicals:* The Projector, 1971; Pilgrim, 1975; Cranford, 1976; Alice in Wonderland, 1978; The Wind in the Willows, 1985; Kip's War, 1987; *opera:* Peace, 1978; *TV operas:* The Arrangement, 1967; Orpheus in the Underground, 1976; *West End:* Forty Years On, 1969; Habeas Corpus, 1973; *films:* The French Lieutenant's Woman (BAFTA Original Film Score Award), 1981; Champions, 1984; King David, 1985; Girl in a Swing, Scandal, The Rainbow, 1988; Frankenstein Unbound, Fragments of Isabella, 1989; Crucifer of Blood, Raft of the Medusa, 1991; The Voyage, 1992; The Trial, 1993; *silent films:* Napoleon, 1980; The Crowd, 1981; Flesh and the Devil, Show People, How to Make Movies, 1982; Broken Blossoms, The Wind, The Musketeers of Pig Alley, An Unseen Enemy, 1983; Thief of Baghdad, 1984; The Big Parade, Greed, 1985; The General, Ben Hur, 1987; Mysterious Lady, Intolerance, City Lights (re-creation of Chaplin score), 1988; Safety Last, Kid Brother, 1989; The Immigrant, 1991; IT, The Four Horsemen of the Apocalypse, 1992; Wings; The Gold Rush (re-creation of Chaplin score), 1993; *ballets:* Dances of Love and Death, 1981; Fire and Ice (ice ballet for Torvill and Dean), 1986; The Portrait of Dorian Gray (for SWRB), 1987; A Simple Man (based on L. S. Lowry, for Northern Ballet Theatre), 1987; Liaisons Amoureuses, 1988; Lipizzaner (Northern Ballet Theatre), 1988; A Christmas Carol (Northern Ballet Theatre), 1992; Savoy Suite (English Nat. Ballet), 1993; *orchestral compositions:* Lines on London (symphony), 1984 (commnd by Capital Radio); Clarinet Concerto, 1984; Fantasy for flute, 1985 (commnd by Acad. of St Martin's-in-the-Fields); Glenlivit Firework Music, 1987; Beginners Please!, 1987; (with Paul McCartney) Paul McCartney's Liverpool Oratorio, 1991. Has made numerous recordings. Mem. BAFTA, 1979–. First winner, BAFTA Award for Original TV Music, 1981. Chevalier de L'Ordre des Arts et des Lettres, 1983. *Publications:* sheet music of television themes. *Recreations:* reading, gardening, playing chamber music, cooking. *Address:* c/o Paul Wing, 35 Priory Road, N8. *T:* 081–348 6604, *Fax:* 081–340 8434.

DAVIS, Sir Charles (Sigmund), Kt 1965; CB 1960; Counsel to the Speaker (European Legislation), (formerly Second Counsel), House of Commons, 1974–83; *b* London, 22 Jan. 1909; *y s* of late Maurice Davis (*b* Melbourne, Australia) and Alfreda Regina Davis; *m* 1940, Pamela Mary, *er d* of late J. K. B. Dawson, OBE, and Phyllis Dawson; two *d*. *Educ:* Trinity Coll., Cambridge. Double 1st Cl. Hons, Law Tripos; Sen. Schol., Exhibitioner and Prizeman of Trinity, 1927–30; MA 1934. Called to the Bar, Inner Temple (Studentship and Certif. of Honour), 1930, and in Sydney, Australia, 1931; practised as barrister in London, 1931–34; entered Legal Branch, Ministry of Health, 1934; held legal posts in various public offices, 1938–46 (Corporal, Home Guard, 1940–45); Asst Solicitor, Min. of Agric. and Fisheries, 1946–55; Prin. Asst Solicitor, MAFF, 1955–57; Legal Adviser and Solicitor, MAFF, and Forestry Commission, 1957–74, retired. Vice-Pres., Cancer Relief Macmillan Fund (formerly Nat. Soc. for Cancer Relief), 1989– (Chm. Council, 1983–85; Trustee, 1985–89). *Recreations:* music (LRAM, ARCM) and much else. *Address:* 9 Beech Court, 33b Arterberry Road, SW20 8AG.

DAVIS, Mrs Chloë Marion, OBE 1975; Chairman, Consumer Affairs Group of National Organisations, 1973–79; Member: Council on Tribunals, 1970–79; Consumer Standards Advisory Committee of British Standards Institution, 1965–78 (Chairman 1970–73); *b* Dartmouth, Devon, 15 Feb. 1909; *d* of Richard Henry Pound and Mary Jane Chapman; *m* 1928, Edward Thomas Davis (*d* 1983), printer and sometime writer; one *s*. *Educ:* limited formal, USA and England. Various part-time voluntary social and public services from 1929; Birth Control Internat. Information Centre, 1931–38; voluntary activity in bombing etc emergencies, also cookery and domestic broadcasting during War of 1939–45; information service for Kreis Resident Officers, Control Commn for Germany, Berlin, 1946–48; regional Citizens Advice Bureaux office, London Council of Social Service, 1949–55; Sen. Information Officer to Nat. Citizens Advice Bureaux Council, 1956–69. Member: Nat. House-Building Council, 1973–76; Consumer Consultative Cttee, EEC, 1973–76; Exec. Cttee, Housewife's Trust, 1970–77. *Recreations:* reading present history in the morning in newspapers and past history in books in the evening; gardening, walking, talking with friends. *Address:* Auberville Cottage, 246 Dover Road, Walmer, Kent CT14 7NP. *T:* Deal (01304) 374038.

DAVIS, Sir Colin (Rex), Kt 1980; CBE 1965; Principal Conductor, London Symphony Orchestra, since 1995; *b* 25 Sept. 1927; *s* of Reginald George and Lillian Davis; *m* 1949, April Cantelo (marr. diss., 1964); one *s* one *d*; *m* 1964, Ashraf Naini; three *s* two *d*. *Educ:* Christ's Hospital; Royal College of Music. Orchestral Conductor, Freelance wilderness, 1949–57; Asst Conductor, BBC Scottish Orchestra, 1957–59. Conductor, Sadler's Wells, 1959, Principal Conductor, 1960–65, Musical Director, 1961–65; Chief Conductor, BBC Symphony Orchestra, 1967–71, Chief Guest Conductor, 1971–75; Musical Dir, Royal Opera House, Covent Garden, 1971–86; Chief Conductor, Bavarian Radio Symphony Orch., 1983–92; Principal Guest Conductor: Boston SO, 1972–84; LSO, 1974–95; Hon. Conductor, Dresden Staatskapelle, 1990. Conducted at: Metropolitan Opera House, New York, 1969, 1970, 1972; Bayreuth Fest., 1977; Vienna State Opera, 1986; Bavarian State Opera, 1994. Sibelius Medal, Finland Sibelius Soc., 1977; Grosse Schallplattenpreis, 1978; Shakespeare Prize, Hamburg, 1984; Gold Medal, Royal Philharmonic Soc., 1995. Commendatore of Republic of Italy, 1976; Chevalier, Légion d'Honneur (France), 1982; Commander's Cross, Order of Merit (FRG), 1987; Commandeur, l'Ordre des Arts et des Lettres (France), 1990. *Recreations:* reading, cooking, gardening. *Address:* c/o Alison Glaister, 39 Huntingdon Street, N1 1BP. *Club:* Athenæum.

DAVIS, Crispin Henry Lamert; Chief Executive Officer, Aegis Plc, since 1994; *b* 19 March 1949; *s* of Walter Patrick Davis and Jane (*née* Lamert); *m* 1970, Anne Richardson; three *d*. *Educ:* Charterhouse; Oriel Coll., Oxford (MA Mod. Hist.). Joined Procter & Gamble, 1970: Man. Dir, Procter & Gamble Germany, 1981–84; Vice-Pres., Food Div., Procter & Gamble USA, 1984–90; European Man. Dir, 1990–92, Gp Man. Dir, 1992–94, United Distillers. *Recreations:* sport: tennis, squash, golf, ski-ing; gardening, collecting antique furniture. *Address:* Hills End, Titlarks Hill, Sunningdale, Berks SL5 0JD. *T:* Bracknell (01344) 291233. *Clubs:* MCC; Wentworth.
See also N. A. L. Davis.

DAVIS, David; *see* Davis, William Eric.

DAVIS, David Michael; MP (C) Boothferry, since 1987; Minister of State, Foreign and Commonwealth Office, since 1994; *b* 23 Dec. 1948; *s* of Ronald and Elizabeth Davis; *m* 1973, Doreen Margery Cook; one *s* two *d*. *Educ:* Warwick Univ. (BSc); London Business Sch. (MSc); Harvard (AMP). Joined Tate & Lyle, 1974; Financial Dir, Manbré & Garton, 1977; Man. Dir, Tate & Lyle Transport, 1980; Pres., Zymaize, 1982; Strategic Planning Dir, Tate & Lyle plc, 1984–87; Dir, 1987–89. PPS to Parly Under-Sec. of State, DTI, 1989–90; an Asst Govt Whip, 1990–93; Parly Sec., Office of Public Service and Science, Cabinet Office, 1993–94. Mem., Financial Policy Cttee, CBI, 1977–79; Exec. Mem., Industrial Soc., 1985–87. Chm., Fedn of Cons. Students, 1973–74. *Recreations:* writing, flying, mountaineering. *Address:* House of Commons, SW1A 0AA.

DAVIS, Derek Alan, CEng; Director, World Energy Council Commission, 1990–93; *b* 5 Oct. 1929; *s* of Irene Davis (*née* Longstaff) and Sydney George Davis; *m* 1954, Ann Margery Willett; three *s*. *Educ:* private schools; Battersea Polytechnic; London University. BScEng (First Hons) 1950; MIMechE; CBIM. De Havilland Engine Co Ltd: post-graduate apprentice, 1950–52; develt engineer, Gas Turbine Div., 1952–53, Rocket Div., 1953–56; Central Electricity Generating Board: Research Labs, 1956–60; Manager, Mech. and Civil Engineering, 1960–65; Group Head Fuel, 1965, System Econ. Engineer, 1970, System Planning Engineer, 1973–75, Planning Dept; Dir, Resource Planning, later Dir Production, NE Region, 1975–81; Dir Corporate Strategy Dept, 1981–84; Mem., 1984–90. Member: SERC, 1989–94; Meteorology Cttee, MoD, 1986–; ACORD, Dept of Energy, 1990–92. *Publications:* articles in tech. and engineering jls. *Recreations:* playing, now watching, sport; gardening, DIY, reading.

DAVIS, Derek Richard; Director General, British National Space Centre, since 1993; *b* 3 May 1945; *s* of Stanley Lewis Davis, OBE and Rita Beatrice Rachel (*née* Rosenheim); *m* 1987, Diana Levinson; one *s* one *d*. *Educ:* Clifton Coll., Bristol; Balliol Coll., Oxford (BA 1967). Asst Principal, BoT, 1967; Pvte Sec. to Perm. Sec., DTI, 1971–72; Principal, 1972; Asst Sec., Dept of Energy, 1977; Secretary: Energy Commn, 1977–79; NEDC Energy Task Force, 1981; seconded to NCB, 1982–83; Under Sec., Gas Div., 1985–87, Oil and Gas Div., 1987–93, Dept of Energy, subseq. DTI. *Address:* British National Space Centre, Bridge Place, 88/89 Eccleston Square, SW1V 1PT. *T:* 0171–215 0877.

DAVIS, Hon. Sir (Dermot) Renn, Kt 1981; OBE 1971; **Hon. Mr Justice Davis;** Chief Justice, Supreme Court of the Falkland Islands, since 1987; Judge, Supreme Court of the British Antarctic Territory, since 1988; Judge, Court of Appeal: for Gibraltar, since 1989; of St Helena, since 1991; for the British Indian Ocean Territory, since 1991; *b* 20 Nov. 1928; *s* of Captain Eric R. Davis, OBE and Norah A. Davis (*née* Bingham); *m* 1984, Mary, *widow* of William James Pearce and *d* of late Brig. T. F. K. Howard, DSO, RA. *Educ:* Prince of Wales Sch., Nairobi; Wadham Coll., Oxford (BA Hons). Called to the Bar, Inner Temple, 1953; Daly and Figgis, Advocates, Nairobi, 1953–56; Attorney-General's Chambers, Kenya, 1956–62; Attorney-General, British Solomon Islands Protectorate, and Legal Advr, Western Pacific High Commn, 1962–73; British Judge, New Hebrides Condominium, 1973–76; Chief Justice, Solomon Islands, 1976–80 and Chief Justice, Tuvalu, 1978–80; Chief Justice, Gibraltar, 1980–86. *Recreations:* music, walking. *Address:* The Supreme Court, Stanley, Falkland Islands; c/o Barclays Bank, 30 High Street, Hungerford, Berks RG17 0NQ. *Clubs:* United Oxford & Cambridge University; Muthaiga Country (Nairobi); Royal Gibraltar Yacht.

DAVIS, Sir (Ernest) Howard, Kt 1978; CMG 1969; OBE 1960; Deputy Governor, Gibraltar, 1971–78; *b* 22 April 1918; *m* 1948, Marie Davis (*née* Bellotti); two *s*. *Educ:* Christian Brothers Schs, Gibraltar and Blackpool; London Univ. (BA 1st cl. hons). Gen. Clerical Staff, Gibraltar, 1936–46; Asst Sec. and Clerk of Councils, 1946–54; seconded Colonial Office, 1954–55; Chief Asst Sec., Estabt Officer and Public Relations Officer (responsible for opening Radio Gibraltar), Gibraltar, 1955–62; Director of Labour and Social Security, 1962–65; Financial and Development Secretary, 1965–71; Acting Governor, various periods, 1971–77. Chairman, Committee of Enquiry: PWD, 1980–81; Electricity Dept, 1982; Chm., Gibraltar Broadcasting Corp., 1982–83. Pres., Calpe Rowing Club, 1985–92. *Recreations:* cricket, gardening, bridge. *Address:* Flat 6, Mount Pleasant, South Barrack Road, Gibraltar. *T:* 70358.

DAVIS, Godfrey Rupert Carless, CBE 1981; FSA; Secretary, Royal Commission on Historical Manuscripts, 1972–81; *b* 22 April 1917; *s* of late Prof. Henry William Carless

Davis and Rosa Jennie Davis (*née* Lindup); *m* 1942, Dorothie Elizabeth Mary Loveband (*d* 1994); one *s* two *d*. *Educ:* Highgate Sch.; Balliol Coll., Oxford (MA, DPhil). Rome Scholar in Ancient History, 1938. Army Service, 1939–46, Devon Regt and Intell. Corps, Captain 1942. Dept of MSS, British Museum: Asst Keeper, 1947; Dep. Keeper, 1961–72. FRHistS 1954 (Treas. 1967–74); FSA 1974. *Publications:* Medieval Cartularies of Great Britain, 1958; Magna Carta, 1963; contrib. British Museum Cat. Add. MSS 1926–1950 (6 vols); learned jls.

DAVIS, Rear-Adm. Graham Noel, CB 1993; software development consultant, since 1993; *b* 24 Dec. 1937; *s* of Edward Davis and Ruth (*née* Bullen); *m* 1964, Mary Jenkins; one *s* one *d*. *Educ:* Eltham Coll.; London Univ. (BSc Hons Physics). FIMgt 1984. Joined RN 1963: Comdr, 1973; Capt., 1981; Dean, RNC, Greenwich, 1981–83; rcds 1983; Dir, various depts, MoD, 1984–90; Rear-Adm., 1991; Dir-Gen., Fleet Support for Ops and Plans, 1991–93. *Recreations:* Net surfing, cooking, exploring UK and European canals by boat, gardening by choice, D-I-Y by necessity. *Address:* Lynchetts, Lewes Road, Ringmer, Lewes, E Sussex BN8 5ET. *T:* Lewes (01273) 812907.

DAVIS, Rt. Hon. Helen Elizabeth; *see* Clark, Rt. Hon. H. E.

DAVIS, Sir Howard; *see* Davis, Sir E. H.

DAVIS, Ivor John Guest, CB 1983; Director, Common Law Institute of Intellectual Property, 1986–91; *b* 11 Dec. 1925; *s* of Thomas Henry Davis and Dorothy Annie Davis; *m* 1954, Mary Eleanor Thompson; one *s* one *d*. *Educ:* Devonport High Sch.; HM Dockyard Sch., Devonport. BSc London (ext.). Apprentice, HM Dockyard, Devonport, 1941–45, Draughtsman, 1946–47; Patent Office, Dept of Trade: Asst Examr, 1947; Asst Comptroller, 1973; Comptroller Gen., Patents, Designs and Trade Marks, 1978. Pres., Administrative Council, European Patent Office, 1981–85. Mem. Adv. Panel, Centre d'études de la propriété industrielle, Strasbourg, 1979–85. Mem. Council, Inst. of Intellectual Property, 1991–. Mem., Editorial Adv. Bd, World Patent Information Journal, 1979–85. *Recreations:* music, gardening. *Address:* 5 Birch Close, Eynsford, Dartford DA4 0EX.

DAVIS, James Gresham, CBE 1988; MA; FCIT; FICS; Chairman: Simpler Trade Procedures Board, since 1987; International Maritime Industries Forum, since 1981; DFDS Ltd, since 1984 (Director, 1975); Bromley Shipping plc, since 1989; Trinitas Marine Services, since 1993; *b* 20 July 1928; *s* of Col Robert Davis, OBE, JP and Josephine Davis (*née* Edwards); *m* 1973, Adriana Johanna Verhoef, Utrecht, Holland; three *d*. *Educ:* Bradfield Coll.; Clare Coll., Cambridge (MA). FCIT 1969. Served RN, 1946–49. P&OSN Co., 1952–72: Calcutta, 1953; Kobe, Japan, 1954–56; Hong Kong, 1956–57; Director: P&O Lines, 1967–72; Kleinwort Benson Ltd, 1973–88; Pearl Cruises of Scandinavia Inc., 1982–86; Rodskog Shipbrokers (Hong Kong) Ltd, 1983–88; Associated British Ports Holdings plc, 1983–; Transport Develt Gp plc, 1984–92; Global Ocean Carriers Ltd, 1988–; Sedgwick Marine & Cargo Ltd, 1988–; Sedgwick Gp Develt Ltd, 1992–; Hempel Ltd, 1992–; Chm., TIP Europe, 1990–93 (Dir, 1987). Mem. Adv. Board: J. Lauritzen A/S, Copenhagen, 1981–85; DFDS A/S, Copenhagen, 1981–85; Adviser, Tjaereborg (UK) Ltd, 1985–87. Mem. (part-time), British Transport Docks Bd, 1981–83; Dir, British Internat. Freight Assoc., 1989–; Chm., Danish-UK Chamber of Commerce, 1992–. Chairman: Friends of the World Maritime Univ., 1985–; Marine Soc., 1987–93; Anglian Bd, BR, 1988–92; Mem. Council, Missions to Seamen, 1981–. President: World Ship Soc., 1969, 1971, 1984–86; CIT, 1981–82; Inst. of Freight Forwarders, 1984–86; National Waterways Transport Assoc., 1986–91; Inst. of Supervisory Management, 1989–93; Internat. Cttee, Bureau Veritas, 1989–; Inst. of Chartered Shipbrokers, 1990–92 (Vice-Pres., 1988–90); Harwich Lifeboat, RNLI, 1984–; Vice-President: British Maritime League, 1984–88; Inst. of Export, 1991–; Member: Baltic Exchange, 1973; Greenwich Forum, 1981; Guild of World Traders, 1991. Trustee, Nat. Maritime Mus., 1993–. Gov., World Maritime Univ., 1992–. FRSA 1986. Hon. FNI 1985; Hon. FInstFF 1986. Liveryman and Mem., Court of Assts, Worshipful Co. of Shipwrights; Freeman, City of London, 1986. Younger Brother, Trinity House, 1989. *Recreations:* golf, family, ships. *Address:* 115 Woodsford Square, W14 8DT. *T:* 0171–602 0675; Summer Lawn, Dovercourt, Essex, CO12 4EF. *T:* Harwich (01255) 502981. *Clubs:* Brooks's, Hurlingham, Golfers; Fanlingerers; Harwich & Dovercourt Golf, Royal Calcutta Golf; Holland Park Lawn Tennis.

DAVIS, John; *see* Davis, A. J.

DAVIS, Prof. John Allen, MD, FRCP; Professor of Paediatrics, and Fellow of Peterhouse, University of Cambridge, 1979–88, now Professor Emeritus and Fellow Emeritus; *b* 6 Aug. 1923; *s* of Major H. E. Davis, MC, and Mrs M. W. Davis; *m* 1957, Madeleine Elizabeth Vinicombe Ashlin (author with D. Wallbridge of Boundary and Space: introduction to the work of D. W. Winnicott, 1981) (*d* 1991); three *s* two *d*. *Educ:* Blundells Sch., Tiverton (Scholar); St Mary's Hosp. Med. Sch. (Scholar; MB, BS 1946; London Univ. Gold Medal); MSc Manchester 1967; MA Cantab 1979, MD 1988. FRCP 1967. Army Service, BAOR, 1947–49. House Physician: St Mary's Hosp., 1947; Gt Ormond St Hosp. for Sick Children, 1950; Registrar/Sen. Registrar, St Mary's Paediatric Unit and Home Care Scheme, 1951–57; Sen. Asst Resident, Children's Med. Centre, Boston, Mass, and Harvard Teaching Fellow, 1953; Nuffield Res. Fellowship, Oxford, 1958–59; Sen. Lectr, Inst. of Child Health, and Reader, Hammersmith Hosp., 1960–67; Prof. of Paediatrics and Child Health, Victoria Univ. of Manchester, 1967–79. Second Vice Pres., RCP, 1986; Member: Assoc. of Physicians; Société française de pédiatrie; Hon. Member: BPA (former Chm., Academic Bd); Hungarian Acad. Paediatrics; Neonatal Soc.; Pres., Eur. Soc. for Pediatric Research, 1984–85; Patron: Soc. for Reproductive and Infant Psychology, 1981–; Child Psychotherapy Trust, 1987–; Arts for Health, 1989–; Squiggle Foundn, 1993–. Greenwood Lectr, Univ. of Exeter, 1981; Teale Lectr, RCP, 1990. Dawson Williams Prize, BMA, 1986; James Spence Medal, BPA, 1991; Hunterian Medal, Hunterian Soc., 1995. *Publications:* Scientific Foundations of Paediatrics (ed and contrib.), 1974 (2nd edn 1981); Place of Birth, 1978; (ed jtly) Parent-Baby Attachment in Premature Infants, 1984; papers in various medical and scientific jls. *Recreations:* collecting and painting watercolours, gardening, reading, music. *Address:* Four Mile House, 1 Cambridge Road, Great Shelford, Cambridge CB2 5JE.

DAVIS, John Darelan R.; *see* Russell-Davis, J. D.

DAVIS, Sir John (Gilbert), 3rd Bt *cr* 1946; consultant to pulp and paper industry; *b* 17 Aug. 1936; *s* of Sir Gilbert Davis, 2nd Bt, and of Kathleen, *d* of Sidney Deacon Ford; *S* father, 1973; *m* 1960, Elizabeth Margaret, *d* of Robert Smith Turnbull; one *s* two *d*. *Educ:* Oundle School; Britannia RNC, Dartmouth. RN, 1955–56. Joined Spicers Ltd, 1956; emigrated to Montreal, Canada, 1957; joined Inter City Papers and progressed through the company until becoming Pres., 1967; transf. to parent co, Abitibi-Price Inc., 1976 and held several exec. positions before retiring as Exec. Vice-Pres., 1989. *Recreations:* sports, golf, tennis, squash; music, reading. *Heir:* *s* Richard Charles Davis, *b* 11 April 1970. *Address:* 5 York Ridge Road, Willowdale, Ont M2P 1R8, Canada. *T:* 222–4916. *Clubs:* Donalda, Toronto (Toronto); Rosedale Golf.

DAVIS, John Horsley Russell, PhD; FBA 1988; Warden of All Souls College, Oxford, since 1995; *b* 9 Sept. 1938; *s* of William Russell Davis and Jean (*née* Horsley); *m* 1981, Dymphna Gerarda Hermans; three *s*. *Educ:* University Coll., Oxford (BA); Univ. of London (PhD). University of Kent, 1966–90: progressively, Lectr, Sen. Lectr, Reader, Social Anthropology; Prof., 1982–90; Prof. of Social Anthropology, and Fellow of All Souls College, Univ. of Oxford, 1990–95. Chm., European Assoc. of Social Anthropologists, 1993–94. *Publications:* Land and Family in Pisticci, 1973; People of the Mediterranean, 1977; Libyan Politics: tribe and revolution, 1987; Exchange, 1992. *Recreations:* gardens, music. *Address:* All Souls College, Oxford OX1 4AL.

DAVIS, John Michael N.; *see* Newsom Davis.

DAVIS, Leslie Harold Newsom, CMG 1957; *b* 6 April 1909; *s* of Harold Newsom Davis and Aileen Newsom Davis (*née* Gush); *m* 1950, Judith Anne, *d* of L. G. Corney, CMG; one *s* two *d*. *Educ:* Marlborough; Trinity Coll., Cambridge. Apptd to Malayan Civil Service, 1932; Private Sec. to Governor and High Comr, 1938–40; attached to 22nd Ind. Inf. Bde as Liaison Officer, Dec. 1941; interned by Japanese in Singapore, 1942–45; District Officer, Seremban, 1946–47; British Resident, Brunei, 1948; Asst Adviser, Muar, 1948–50; Sec. to Mem. for Education, Fed. of Malaya, 1951–52. Mem. for Industrial and Social Relations, 1952–53; Sec. for Defence and Internal Security, Singapore, 1953–55; Permanent Sec., Min. of Communications and Works, Singapore, 1955–57; Special Rep., Rubber Growers' Assoc. in Malaya, 1958–63. *Recreation:* golf. *Address:* Berrywood, Heyshott, near Midhurst, West Sussex GU29 0DH. *Club:* United Oxford & Cambridge University.

DAVIS, Madeline; Regional Nursing Officer, Oxford Regional Health Authority, 1973–83; retired; *b* 12 March 1925; *d* of late James William Henry Davis, JP, and Mrs Edith Maude Davis; *m* 1977, Comdr William Milburn Gibson, RN (*d* 1991). *Educ:* Haberdashers' Aske's Hatcham Girls' Sch.; Guy's Hosp. (SRN); British Hosp. for Mothers and Babies, Woolwich; Bristol Maternity Hosp. (SCM). Ward Sister, then Dep. Night Supt, Guy's Hosp., 1949–53; Asst Matron, Guy's Hosp., 1953–57; Admin. Sister then Dep. Matron, St Charles' Hosp., London, 1957–61; Asst Nursing Officer, 1962–68, Chief Regional Nursing Officer, 1968–73, Oxford Regional Hosp. Bd. Formerly Mem., Central Midwives Board. *Recreations:* village community work, theatre, golf. *Address:* Cherry Holt, Middle Street, Islip, Oxon OX5 2SF. *Clubs:* New Cavendish; North Oxford Golf.

DAVIS, Prof. Mark Herbert Ainsworth; Director, Head of Research and Product Development, Mitsubishi Finance International plc, since 1995; *b* 1 May 1945; *s* of Christopher A. Davis and Frances E. Davis (*née* Marsden); *m* 1988, Jessica I. C. Smith. *Educ:* Oundle Sch.; Clare College, Cambridge (BA 1966, MA 1970, ScD 1983); Univ. of California (PhD 1971). FSS 1985; FIMS 1994. Research Asst, Electronics Res. Lab., Univ. of California, Berkeley, 1969–71; Lectr, 1971–79, Reader, 1979–84, Prof. of System Theory, 1984–94, Imperial College, London. Visiting appointments: Polish Acad. of Sciences, 1973; Harvard, 1974; MIT, 1978; Washington Univ., St Louis, 1979; ETH Zurich, 1984; Oslo Univ., 1991. Editor, Stochastics and Stochastics Reports, 1979–94; Founding Co-Editor, Mathematical Finance, 1991–93. *Publications:* Linear Estimation and Stochastic Control, 1977, Russian edn 1984; (with R. B. Vinter) Stochastic Modelling and Control, 1985; Markov Models and Optimization, 1993; jl articles on stochastic analysis, control theory, maths of finance. *Recreation:* classical music (violin and viola). *Address:* 11 Chartfield Avenue, SW15 6DT. *T:* 0181–789 7677.

DAVIS, Dr Michael; Hon. Director General, Commission of European Communities, Brussels, since 1989; *b* 9 June 1923; *s* of William James Davis and Rosaline Sarah (*née* May); *m* 1951, Helena Hobbs Campbell, *e d* of Roland and Catherine Campbell, Toronto. *Educ:* UC Exeter (BSc); Bristol Univ. (PhD). CEng, FIMM; CPhys, FInstP. Radar Officer, Flagship, 4th Cruiser Sqdn, British Pacific Fleet, Lieut (Sp. Br.) RNVR, 1943–46 (despatches). Res. Fellow, Canadian Atomic Energy Project, Toronto Univ., 1949–51; Sen. Sci. Officer, Services Electronics Res. Lab., 1951–55; UKAEA: Commercial Dir and Techn. Adviser, 1956–73; Dir of Nuclear Energy, Other Primary Sources and Electricity, EEC, 1973–81; Dir for Energy Saving, Alternative Sources of Energy, Electricity and Heat, EEC, 1981–88. Chm., OECD Cttee on World Uranium Resources, 1969–73; Dir, NATO Advanced Study Inst., 1971; advised NZ Govt on Atomic Energy, 1967. McLaughlin Meml Lectr, Instn of Engineers of Ireland, 1977. *Publications:* (ed jtly) Uranium Prospecting Handbook, 1972; papers in various sci. jls. *Recreation:* sculpture. *Club:* United Oxford & Cambridge University.

DAVIS, Michael McFarland; Director for Wales, Property Services Agency, Department of the Environment, 1972–77; *b* 1 Feb. 1919; 2nd *s* of Harold McFarland and Gladys Mary Davis; *m* 1942, Aline Seton Butler; three *d*. *Educ:* Haberdashers' Aske's, Hampstead. Entered Air Ministry, 1936. Served War, RAF, 1940–45 (PoW, 1942–45). Private Sec. to Chiefs and Vice-Chiefs of Air Staff, 1945–49, and to Under-Secretary of State for Air, 1952–54; Harvard Univ. Internat. Seminar, 1956; Student, IDC, 1965; Command Sec., FEAF, 1966–69; on loan to Cabinet Office (Central Unit on Environmental Pollution), 1970; transf. to Dept of Environment, 1971. Delegate to UN Conf. on Human Environment, Stockholm, 1972. Hon. Archivist: Sidmouth Mus., 1991–; Sid Vale Assoc., 1991–. *Recreations:* doing up old things, music, croquet, wine. *Address:* 18 Roselands, Sidmouth, Devon EX10 8PB. *T:* Sidmouth (01395) 577123. *Club:* Sidmouth Croquet.

DAVIS, Miles Garth H.; *see* Hunt-Davis.

DAVIS, Nathanael Vining; Chairman, 1947–86, and Chief Executive Officer, 1947–79, Alcan Aluminium Limited; *b* 26 June 1915; *s* of Rhea Reineman Davis and Edward Kirk Davis; *m* 1941, Lois Howard Thompson; one *s* one *d*. *Educ:* Harvard Coll.; London Sch. of Economics. With Alcan group since 1939 with exception of 3 years on active duty with US Navy. Director: Bank of Montreal, 1961–86; Canada Life Assurance Co., Toronto, 1961–86. *Address:* Box 309, Osterville, MA 02655, USA. *Clubs:* Mount Royal (Montreal); University (New York).

DAVIS, Nigel Anthony Lamert; QC 1992; *b* 10 March 1951; *s* of Walter Patrick Carless Davis and Jane (*née* Lamert); *m* 1977, Sheila Ann Gillies Nickel (marr. diss. 1992); three *d*. *Educ:* Charterhouse; University Coll., Oxford (BA 1975; MA 1983). Called to the Bar, Lincoln's Inn, 1975 (Hardwicke Schol., Kennedy Schol.). Jun. Counsel to Crown (Chancery), 1985–92. *Address:* 7 Stone Buildings, Lincoln's Inn, WC2A 3SZ. *T:* 0171–405 3886. *Clubs:* Riverside, MCC; Vincent's (Oxford).

DAVIS, Peter Anthony; Director General, National Lottery, since 1993; *b* 10 Oct. 1941; *s* of Stanley H. S. Davis and Betty H. Davis (*née* Back); *m* 1971, Vanessa C. E. Beale; two *s*. *Educ:* Winchester Coll.; Lincoln Coll., Oxford (MA Law). CA 1967. With Price Waterhouse, 1963–80, Gen. Audit Partner, 1974–80; Exec. Dep. Chm., Harris Queensway PLC, 1980–87; Sturge Holdings PLC: Gp Finance Dir, 1988–93; Dep. Chm., 1991–93; Abbey National PLC: non-exec. Dir, 1982–94; Dep. Chm., 1988–94; Chm., Audit Cttee, 1988–93, and Scottish Adv. Bd, 1989–92. Non-executive Director: Horne Bros, 1984–87; Symphony Gp, 1984–87; Avis Europe, 1987–89; Provident Financial, 1994–; Proned Holdings, 1992–94. Institute of Chartered Accountants in England and Wales: Council Mem., 1989–; Chm., Bd for Chartered Accountants in Business, 1991–94; Mem., Senate,

1989–. MInstD 1993. *Recreations:* fishing, tennis, football, theatre. *Address:* 29 Arthur Road, SW19 7DN. *Club:* Hurlingham.

DAVIS, Peter John; Group Chief Executive, Prudential Corporation plc, since 1995; Director, Boots Co. PLC, since 1991; *b* 23 Dec. 1941; *s* of John Stephen Davis and Adriaantje de Baat; *m* 1968, Susan Hillman; two *s* one *d*. *Educ:* Shrewsbury Sch.; Grad. Inst. of Marketing (Drexler Travelling Schol., 1961). Management trainee and sales, Ditchburn Orgn, 1959–65; marketing and sales posts, General Foods Ltd, Banbury, 1965–72; Fitch Lovell Ltd, 1973–76: Marketing Dir, Key Markets; Man. Dir, Key Markets and David Greig; joined J. Sainsbury, 1976; Marketing Dir, 1977; Asst Man. Dir, 1979; Dep. Chief Exec., 1986, Chief Exec., 1986–92, Chm., 1990–94, Reed Internat.; Chief Exec., 1993, Chm., 1993–94, Reed Elsevier. Chairman: Adult Literacy and Basic Skills Unit, 1989–; Nat. Adv. Council for Educn and Training Targets, 1993–; Dep. Chm., BITC, 1991–. Vice Pres., Chartered Inst. of Marketing, 1991–. Trustee: Royal Opera House, 1994–; V&A Mus., 1994–. Governor: Duncombe Sch., Hertford, 1976–; Queenswood Sch., 1993–. FRSA. *Recreations:* sailing, reading, opera, wine. *Address:* Prudential Corporation plc, 142 Holborn Bars, EC1N 2NH. *T:* 0171–548 3143. *Club:* Trearddur Bay Sailing (Cdre, 1982–84).

DAVIS, Hon. Sir Renn; *see* Davis, Hon. Sir D. R.

DAVIS, Air Vice-Marshal Robert Leslie, CB 1984; RAF, retired 1983; *b* 22 March 1930; *s* of Sidney and Florence Davis; *m* 1956, Diana, *d* of Edward William Bryant; one *s* one *d*. *Educ:* Wolsingham Grammar Sch., Co. Durham; Bede Sch. Collegiate, Sunderland, Co. Durham; RAF Coll., Cranwell. Commnd, 1952; served fighter units, exchange posting, USAF, Staff Coll., OR and Ops appts, MoD, DS Staff Coll., 1953–69; comd No 19 Sqdn, 1970–72; Dep. Dir Ops Air Defence, MoD, 1972–75; comd RAF Leuchars, 1975–77; Comdr RAF Staff, and Air Attaché, British Defence Staff, Washington, DC, 1977–80; Comdr, British Forces Cyprus, and Administrator, Sovereign Base Areas, Cyprus, 1980–83, retired. Man. Dir, Bodenseewerk Geratetechnik/British Aerospace GmbH, 1983–86, retd. *Recreations:* golf, antiques, music. *Address:* High Garth Farm, Witton-le-Wear, Bishop Auckland, Co. Durham DL14 0BL.

DAVIS, Sir Rupert C. H.; *see* Hart-Davis.

DAVIS, Prof. Stanley Stewart, CChem, FRSC; Lord Trent Professor of Pharmacy, Nottingham University, since 1975; *b* 17 Dec. 1942; *s* of William Stanley and Joan Davis; *m* 1984, Lisbeth Illum; three *s*. *Educ:* Warwick Sch.; London Univ. (BPharm, PhD, DSc). FRPharmS. Lecturer, London Univ., 1976–80; Sen. Lectr, Aston Univ., 1970–75. Fulbright Scholar, Univ. of Kansas, 1978–79; various periods as visiting scientist to pharmaceutical industry. Chairman: Danbiosyst (UK) Ltd; Pharmaceutical Profiles Ltd. Mem., Medicines Commn, 1994–. *Publications:* (co-ed) Radionuclide Imaging in Drug Research, 1982; (co-ed) Microspheres and Drug Therapy, 1984; (co-ed) Site Specific Drug Delivery, 1986; (co-ed) Polymers in Controlled Drug Delivery, 1988; (co-ed) Drug Delivery to the Gastrointestinal Tract, 1989; (co-ed) Pharmaceutical Application of Cell and Tissue Culture to Drug Transport, 1991; ed jtly over 500 research pubns in various scientific jls. *Recreations:* tennis, ski-ing. *Address:* 19 Cavendish Crescent North, The Park, Nottingham NG7 1BA. *T:* Nottingham (0115) 948 1866; University of Nottingham, University Park, Nottingham NG7 2RD. *T:* Nottingham (0115) 951 5121.

DAVIS, Steve, MBE 1988; snooker player; *b* 22 Aug. 1957; *s* of Harry George Davis and Jean Catherine Davis; *m* 1990, Judy Greig; two *s*. *Educ:* Alexander McLeod Primary School and Abbey Wood School, London. Became professional snooker player, 1978; has won numerous championships in UK and abroad; major titles include: UK Professional Champion, 1980, 1981, 1984, 1985, 1986, 1987; Masters Champion, 1981, 1982, 1988; International Champion, 1981, 1983, 1984, 1987, 1988, 1989; World Professional Champion, 1981, 1983, 1984, 1987, 1988, 1989. BBC Sports Personality of the Year, 1988. Mem. Bd, World Professional Billiards and Snooker Assoc., 1993–. *Publications:* Steve Davis, World Champion, 1981; Frame and Fortune, 1982; Successful Snooker, 1982; How to be Really Interesting, 1988. *Recreations:* chess, keep fit, listening to records (jazz/soul), Tom Sharpe books. *Address:* 10 Western Road, Romford, Essex RM1 3JT. *T:* Romford (01708) 730480. *Club:* Matchroom (Romford).

DAVIS, Terence Anthony Gordon, (Terry Davis); MP (Lab) Birmingham, Hodge Hill, since 1983 (Birmingham, Stechford, 1979–83); *b* 5 Jan. 1938; *s* of Gordon Davis and Gladys (*née* Avery), Stourbridge, West Midlands; *m* 1963, Anne, *d* of F. B. Cooper, Newton-le-Willows, Lancs; one *s* one *d*. *Educ:* King Edward VI Grammar Sch., Stourbridge, Worcestershire; University Coll. London (LLB); Univ. of Michigan, USA (MBA). Company Executive, 1962–71. Motor Industry Manager, 1974–79. Joined Labour Party, 1965; contested (Lab): Bromsgrove, 1970, Feb. and Oct. 1974; Birmingham, Stechford, March 1977. MP (Lab) Bromsgrove, May 1971–Feb. 1974; Opposition Whip, 1979–80; opposition spokesman: on the health service and social services, 1980–83; on Treasury and economic affairs, 1983–86; on industry, 1986–87. Member: Public Accounts Cttee, 1987–94; Adv. Council on Public Records, 1989–94; British delegn to Council of Europe Assembly and WEU Assembly, 1992–. Mem., MSF. Member, Yeovil Rural District Council, 1967–68. *Address:* 5 Hodge Hill Court, Bromford Road, Hodge Hill, Birmingham B36 8AN.

DAVIS, Hon. Sir Thomas (Robert Alexander Harries), KBE 1981; Pa Tu Te Rangi Ariki 1979; Prime Minister, Cook Islands, 1978–87; *b* 11 June 1917; *s* of Sidney Thomes Davis and Mary Anne Harries; *m* 1940, Myra Lydia Henderson; three *s*; *m* 1979, Pa Tepaeru Ariki. *Educ:* King's Coll., Auckland, NZ; Otago Univ. Med. Sch. (MB, ChB 1945); Sch. of Tropical Medicine, Sydney Univ., Australia (DTM&H 1950); Harvard Sch. of Public Health (Master of Public Health 1952). FRSTM&H 1949. MO and Surg. Specialist, Cook Islands Med. Service, 1945–48; Chief MO, Cook Is Med. Service, 1948–52; Res. Staff, Dept of Nutrition, Harvard Sch. of Public Health, 1952–55; Chief, Dept of Environmental Medicine, Arctic Aero-medical Lab., Fairbanks, Alaska, 1955–56; Res. Physician and Dir, Div. of Environmtl Med., Army Medical Res. Lab., Fort Knox, Ky, 1956–61; Dir of Res., US Army Res. Inst. of Environmtl Med., Natick, 1961–63; Res. Exec., Arthur D. Little, Inc., 1963–71. Involved in biol aspects of space prog., first for Army, later for NASA, 1957–71. Formed Democratic Party, Cook Islands, 1971; private med. practice, Cook Islands, 1974–78. Mem., RSocMed, 1960; twice Pres., Med. and Dental Assoc., Cook Islands; President: Liby and Mus. Soc., 1991–92; Cook Islands Voyaging Soc. Sailed Polynesian voyaging canoe—Rarotonga, Tahiti, Moovea, Huahine, Raiatea, Bora-Bora, Rarotonga. Silver Jubilee Medal, 1977; Order of Merit, Fed. Republic of Germany, 1978. *Publications:* Doctor to the Islands, 1954; Makutu, 1956; Island Boy, 1992; Vaka, 1992; over 80 scientific and other pubns. *Recreations:* deep sea fishing, yacht racing, agriculture/planting, amateur radio. *Address:* Aremango, Rarotonga, Cook Islands. *Clubs:* Harvard (Boston, Mass); Wellington (NZ); Avatiu Sports (patron), Ivans (Pres. 1990), Rarotonga Yacht (patron); Avatiu Cricket (patron).

DAVIS, William; author, publisher, and broadcaster; Editor and Publisher of High Life, since 1973; Chairman: Premier Magazines, since 1992; Allied Leisure, since 1993; Director, Thomas Cook, since 1988; *b* 6 March 1933; *m* 1967, Sylvette Jouclas. *Educ:* City of London Coll. On staff of Financial Times, 1954–59; Editor, Investor's Guide, 1959–60; City Editor, Evening Standard, 1960–65 (with one year's break as City Editor, Sunday Express); Financial Editor, The Guardian, 1965–68; Editor, Punch, 1968–77; Editor-in-Chief, Financial Weekly, 1977–80. Presenter, Money Programme, BBC TV, 1967–69. Chairman: Headway Publications, 1977–90; BTA, 1990–93; English Tourist Bd, 1990–93; Director: Fleet Publishing International, Morgan-Grampian, and Fleet Holdings, 1977–80; British Invisibles, 1990–93. Mem., Develt Council, Royal Nat. Theatre, 1990–92. Knight, Order of Merit of Italian Republic. *Publications:* Three Years Hard Labour: the road to devaluation, 1968; Merger Mania, 1970; Money Talks, 1972; Have Expenses, Will Travel, 1975; It's No Sin to be Rich, 1976; (ed) The Best of Everything, 1980; Money in the 1980s, 1981; The Rich: a study of the species, 1982; Fantasy: a practical guide to escapism, 1984; The Corporate Infighter's Handbook, 1984; (ed) The World's Best Business Hotels, 1985; The Supersalesman's Handbook, 1986; The Innovators, 1987; Children of the Rich, 1989. *Recreations:* drinking wine, travelling, playing tennis, thinking about retirement. *Address:* Premier Magazines, Berger House, 36/38 Berkeley Square, W1X 5DA. *T:* 0171–495 8788. *Club:* Garrick.

DAVIS, William Eric, (professionally known as **David Davis),** MBE 1969; MA Oxon; LRAM, ARCM; *b* 27 June 1908; *s* of William John and Florence Kate Rachel Davis; *m* 1935, Barbara de Riemer (*d* 1982); one *s* two *d*. *Educ:* Bishop's Stortford Coll.; The Queen's Coll., Oxford (MA). Schoolmaster, 1931–35; joined BBC as mem. of Children's Hour, 1935. Served with RNVR Acting Temp. Lieut, 1942–46. BBC, 1946–70; Head of Children's Hour, BBC, 1953–61; Head of Children's Programmes (Sound), BBC, 1961–64; Producer, Drama Dept, 1964–70, retired. *Publications:* various songs, etc. including: Lullaby, 1943; Fabulous Beasts, 1948; Little Grey Rabbit Song Book, 1952; *poetry:* A Single Star, 1973; various speech recordings, including: Black Beauty; Just So Stories; The Wind in the Willows (complete text), 1986. *Recreations:* children, cats, growing roses. *Address:* 18 Mount Avenue, W5 2RG. *T:* 0181–997 8156. *Club:* Garrick.

DAVIS, Hon. William Grenville, PC (Can.) 1982; CC (Canada) 1986; QC (Can.); barrister and solicitor; Counsel to Tory Tory DesLauriers & Binnington, Toronto; Member of the Provincial Parliament, Ontario, 1959–85; Premier of Ontario, Canada, and President of the Council, Ontario, 1971–85; Leader, Progressive Conservative Party, 1971–85; *b* Brampton, Ont., 30 July 1929; *s* of Albert Grenville Davis and Vera M. Davis (*née* Hewetson); *m* 1st, 1953, Helen MacPhee (*d* 1962), *d* of Neil MacPhee, Windsor, Ontario; 2nd, 1963, Kathleen Louise, *d* of Dr R. P. Mackay, California; two *s* three *d*. *Educ:* Brampton High Sch.; University Coll., Univ. of Toronto (BA); Osgoode Hall Law Sch. (grad. 1955). Called to Bar of Ontario, 1955; practised gen. law, Brampton, 1955–59. Elected Mem. (C) Provincial Parlt (MPP) for Peel Riding, 1959, 1963, Peel North Riding, 1967, 1971, Brampton Riding, 1975, 1977, 1981. Minister of Educn, 1962–71; also Minister of Univ. Affairs, 1964–71; Special Envoy on Acid Rain, apptd by Prime Minister of Canada, 1985–86. Director: Ford Motor Co. of Canada; Inter-City Products Corp.; Magna Internat. Inc.; NIKE Canada; Power Corp. of Canada; Seagram Co.; Canadian Imperial Bank of Commerce; Honeywell Ltd; Bramalea Inc. (Chm. of Bd, 1987–); St Lawrence Cement; Hemlo Gold Mines Inc.; Algoma Steel Inc.; Corel Corp.; First American Title Insurance Co.; Fleet Aerospace Corp.; Olympia & York Cos USA. Holds hon. doctorates in Law from eight Ontario Univs: Waterloo Lutheran, W Ontario, Toronto, McMaster, Queen's, Windsor; Hon. Graduate: Albert Einstein Coll. of Med.; Yeshiva Univ. of NY; NUI; Ottawa; Tel Aviv. Amer. Transit Assoc. Man of the Year, 1973. A Freemason. *Publications:* Education in Ontario, 1965; The Government of Ontario and the Universities of the Province (Frank Gerstein Lectures, York Univ.), 1966; Building an Educated Society 1816–1966, 1966; Education for New Times, 1967. *Address:* 61 Main Street South, Brampton, Ontario L6Y 1M9, Canada; Tory Tory DesLauriers & Binnington, Suite 3000, Aetna Tower, PO Box 270, Toronto-Dominion Centre, Toronto, Ont M5K IN2, Canada. *Clubs:* Kiwanis, Shriners, Masons, Albany (Ont.).

DAVIS, William Herbert, BSc; CEng, FIMechE; former executive with BL and Land Rover Ltd, retired 1983; *b* 27 July 1919; *s* of William and Dora Davis; *m* 1945, Barbara Mary Joan (*née* Sommerfield); one *d*. *Educ:* Waverley Grammar Sch.; Univ. of Aston in Birmingham (BSc). Austin Motor Co.: Engr Apprentice, 1935–39; Mech. Engr and Section Leader, Works Engrs, 1946–51; Supt Engr, 1951; Asst Production Manager, 1954; Production Manager, 1956; Dir and Gen. Works Manager, 1958. British Motor Corp. Ltd: Dir of Production, 1960; Dep. Managing Dir (Manufacture and Supply), 1961; Dep. Managing Dir, British Leyland (Austin-Morris Ltd), 1968; Chairman and Chief Executive, Triumph Motor Co. Ltd, 1969; Managing Dir, Rover Triumph BLUK Ltd, 1972; Dir (Manufacture), British Leyland Motor Corporation, 1973; Dir, Military Contracts and Govt Affairs, Leyland Cars, 1976–81; Consultant, BL and Land Rover Ltd, 1981–83; Dir, Land Rover Santana (Spain), 1976–83. FIIM, SME(USA). Silver Jubilee Medal, 1977. *Recreations:* motoring, photography; interests in amateur boxing. *Address:* Goulds, Staverton, Totnes, S Devon TQ9 6AH. *T:* Staverton (01803) 762568.

DAVIS-GOFF, Sir Robert William; *see* Goff.

DAVIS-RICE, Peter; Director of Nursing and Personnel, North Western Regional Health Authority, 1990–94; *b* 1 Feb. 1930; *s* of Alfred Davis-Rice and Doris Eva (*née* Bates); *m* 1993, Joan Margaret Walton; one *s* two *d* by previous marriage. *Educ:* Riley High Sch., Hull; Royal Coll. of Nursing, Edinburgh; Harefield Hosp., Mddx; City Hosp., York. SRN; British Tuberculosis Assoc. Cert.; MIMgt; NAdmin(Hosp)Cert. Staff Nurse, Charge Nurse, St Luke's Hosp., Huddersfield, 1954–57; Theatre Supt, Hull Royal Infirmary, 1957–62; Asst Matron (Theatres), Walton Hosp., Liverpool, 1962–66; Matron, Billinge Hosp., Wigan, 1966–69; Chief Nursing Officer, Oldham and District HMC, 1969–73; Regl Nursing Officer, 1973–90, Asst Gen. Manager (Personnel Services), 1985–90, N Western RHA. Nursing Officer, Greater Manchester Br., BRCS, 1990–. Mem., Management Cttee, Manchester CAB, 1995–. *Publications:* contrib. Nursing Times. *Recreations:* walking, music. *Address:* 17 Storthbank, Simmondley, Glossop, Derbys SK13 9UX. *T:* Glossop (01457) 856224.

DAVISON, family name of **Baron Broughshane.**

DAVISON, Ian Frederic Hay, FCA; Chairman, The National Mortgage Bank plc, since 1992; non-executive Chairman: Storehouse plc, since 1990; McDonnell Information Systems Group plc, since 1993; *b* 30 June 1931; *s* of late Eric Hay Davison, FCA, and Inez Davison; *m* 1955, Maureen Patricia Blacker; one *s* two *d*. *Educ:* Dulwich Coll.; LSE (BScEcon); Univ. of Mich. ACA 1956, FCA 1966. Managing Partner, Arthur Andersen & Co., Chartered Accountants, 1966–82; Dep. Chm. and Chief Exec., Lloyd's of London, 1983–86; Chm., CL-Alexanders Laing & Cruickshank Hldgs, later Crédit Lyonnais Capital Markets, 1988–91; Director: Midland Bank, 1986–88; Newspaper Publishing, 1986–94 (non-exec. Chm., 1993–94). Chloride plc, 1988–; Cadbury-Schweppes plc, 1990–; CIBA plc, 1991–. Mem. Council, ICA, 1975–; Chm., Accounting Standards Cttee, 1982–84. Indep. Mem., NEDC for Bldg Industry, 1971–77; Member: Price Commn, 1977–79; Audit Commn, 1983–85; Chairman: EDC for Food and Drink Manufg Industry, 1981–83; Securities Review Cttee, Hong Kong, 1987–88. Dept of Trade Inspector, London Capital Securities, 1975–77; Inspector, Grays Building Soc.,

1978–79. Trustee, V&A Museum, 1984–93; Dir and Trustee, Royal Opera House, 1984–86; Chm., Monteverdi Trust, 1979–84. Pres., Nat. Council for One-Parent Families, 1991–. Council Mem., Nat. Trust, 1992–94. Governor, LSE, 1982– (Mem., Standing Cttee; Chm., Finance Panel). Councillor and Alderman, London Bor. of Greenwich, 1961–73. *Publication:* A View of the Room: Lloyd's change and disclosure, 1987. *Recreations:* opera, theatre, music, ski-ing, gardening under supervision, bell-ringing. *Address:* 40 Earlham Street, WC2H 8LN. *Clubs:* Athenæum, MCC.

DAVISON, (John) Stanley, OBE 1981; Secretary General, World Federation of Scientific Workers, since 1987; *b* 26 Sept. 1922; *s* of George Davison and Rosie Davison (*née* Segger); *m* 1959, Margaret Smith; two *s* one *d*. *Educ:* Timothy Hackworth Sch., Shildon, Co. Durham; Shildon Senior Boys' Sch.; St Helens Tech. Coll. RAF, 1941–46. Civil Servant (Technical), 1946–52; Regional Organiser, 1953–60, Dep. Gen. Sec., 1960–68, Assoc. of Scientific Workers; Dep. Gen. Sec., ASTMS, 1968–87. Member: Engineering Council, 1986–; Heavy Electrical NEDO, 1976–87; Exec. Council, CSEU, 1981–88; Exec. Council, Internat. Metalworkers' Fedn, 1986–87; All Party Energy Cttee, 1982–88; Chm., Trade Union Side, GEC NJC, 1965–87; Governor, Aston CAT, 1955–60; Mem. Council, Brunel Univ., 1989–. *Recreations:* science policy, amateur dramatics, bridge, caravanning. *Address:* 27 Barnfield Avenue, Shirley, Croydon CR0 8SF. *T:* 0181–654 7092. *Clubs:* Players' Theatre; Addington Theatre Group; Caravan.

DAVISON, Rt. Hon. Sir Ronald (Keith), GBE 1978; CMG 1975; PC 1978; Chief Justice of New Zealand, 1978–89; *b* 16 Nov. 1920; *s* of Joseph James Davison and Florence May Davison; *m* 1948, Jacqueline May Carr; one *s* one *d* (and one *s* decd). *Educ:* Auckland Univ. (LLB). Admitted as barrister and solicitor, 1948; QC (NZ) 1963. Chairman: Environmental Council, 1969–74; Legal Aid Bd, 1969–78; Member: Council, Auckland Dist Law Soc., 1960–65 (Pres., 1965–66); Council, NZ Law Soc., 1963–66; Auckland Electric Power Bd (13 yrs); Aircrew Indust. Tribunal, 1970–78. Chm., Montana Wines Ltd, 1971–78; Dir, NZ Insurance Co. Ltd, 1975–78. *Recreations:* golf, fishing, bowls. *Address:* 1 Lichfield Road, Parnell, Auckland, New Zealand. *Clubs:* Wellington; Northern (Auckland, NZ).

DAVISON, Stanley; *see* Davison, J. S.

DAVSON, Sir Geoffrey Leo Simon, 2nd Bt; *see* Glyn, Sir Anthony, 2nd Bt.

DAWBARN, Sir Simon (Yelverton), KCVO 1980; CMG 1976; HM Diplomatic Service, retired; *b* 16 Sept. 1923; *s* of Frederic Dawbarn and Maud Louise Mansell; *m* 1948, Shelby Montgomery Parker; one *s* two *d*. *Educ:* Oundle Sch.; Corpus Christi Coll., Cambridge. Served in HM Forces (Reconnaissance Corps), 1942–45. Reckitt & Colman (Overseas), 1948–49. Joined Foreign Service, 1949. Foreign Office, 1949–53; Brussels, 1953; Prague, 1955; Tehran, 1957; seconded to HM Treasury, 1959; Foreign Office, 1961; Algiers, 1965; Athens, 1968; FCO, 1971–75. Head of W African Dept and concurrently non-resident Ambassador to Chad, 1973–75; Consul-General, Montreal, 1975–78; Ambassador to Morocco, 1978–82. *Address:* 44 Canonbury Park North, N1 2JT. *T:* 0171–226 0659.

DAWE, Donovan Arthur; Principal Keeper, Guildhall Library, London, 1967–73, retired; *b* 21 Jan. 1915; *s* of late Alfred Ernest and Sarah Jane Dawe, Wallington, Surrey; *m* 1946, Peggy Marjory Challen; two *d*. *Educ:* Sutton Grammar Sch. Associate, Library Assoc., 1938. Entered Guildhall Library as junior assistant, 1931. Served with Royal West African Frontier Force in Africa and India, 1941–46. Freeman of City of London and Merchant Taylors' Company, 1953. FRHistS 1954. *Publications:* Skilbecks: drysalters 1650–1950, 1950; 11 Ironmonger Lane: the story of a site in the City of London, 1952; The City of London: a select book list, 1972; Organists of the City of London 1666–1850, 1983; contribs professional literature, Connoisseur, Musical Times, Genealogists' Magazine, etc. *Recreations:* the countryside, local history, musicology. *Address:* 46 Green Lane, Purley, Surrey CR8 3PJ. *T:* 0181–660 4218.

DAWE, Roger James, CB 1988; OBE 1970; Director General for Further and Higher Education and Youth Training, Department for Education and Employment, since 1995; *b* 26 Feb. 1941; *s* of Harry James and Edith Mary Dawe; *m* 1965, Ruth Day Jolliffe; one *s* one *d*. *Educ:* Hardyes Sch., Dorchester; Fitzwilliam House, Cambridge. BA Cantab. Entered Min. of Labour, 1962; Dept of Economic Affairs, 1964–65; Private Sec. to Prime Minister, 1966–70; Principal, Dept of Employment, 1970; Private Sec. to Secretary of State for Employment, 1972–74; Asst Sec., Dept of Employment, 1974–81; Under Sec., MSC, 1981; Chief Exec., Trng Div., MSC, 1982–84; Dep Sec., Dept of Employment, 1985–87; Dir Gen., MSC, then Training Commn, subseq. Training Agency, 1988–90; Dir Gen., Training Enterprise and Educn Directorate, 1990–92, Dep. Sec., Further and Higher Educn, 1992–95, Dept of Employment. *Recreations:* tennis, Plymouth Argyle supporter, music, theatre. *Address:* c/o Department for Education and Employment, Sanctuary Buildings, Great Smith Street, SW1P 3BT.

DAWES, Prof. Edwin Alfred, CBiol, FIBiol; CChem, FRSC; Reckitt Professor of Biochemistry, University of Hull, 1963–90, now Emeritus; *b* 6 July 1925; *s* of late Harold Dawes and Maude Dawes (*née* Barker); *m* 1950, Amy Rogerson; two *s*. *Educ:* Goole Grammar Sch.; Univ. of Leeds. BSc, PhD, DSc. Asst Lectr, later Lectr, in Biochemistry, Univ. of Leeds, 1947–50; Lectr, later Sen. Lectr, Univ. of Glasgow, 1951–63; Hull University: Head of Biochemistry Dept, 1963–86; Dean of Science, 1968–70; Pro-Vice-Chancellor, 1977–80; Dir, Biomed. Res. Unit, 1981–92. Visiting Lecturer: Meml Univ., Newfoundland, Dalhousie Univ., 1959; Univ. of Brazil, 1960, 1972; Univ. of S California, 1962; Univ. of Rabat, 1967; Univ. of Göttingen, 1972; Osmania Univ., Hyderabad, 1986; Univ. of Massachusetts, Amherst, 1989; Univ. of Padua, 1991; Lectures: Biochemical Soc., Australia and NZ, 1975; Amer. Medical Alumni, Univ. of St Andrews, 1980–81; Biodegradable Plastics Soc., Japan, 1991. Editor, Biochemical Jl, 1958–65; Editor-in-Chief, Jl of Gen. Microbiol., 1976–81; Man. Editor, Fedn of European Microbiol Socs, and Editor-in-Chief, FEMS Microbiology Letters, 1982–90. Dep. Chm., 1987–, Chm., Scientific Adv. Cttee, 1978–, Yorks Cancer Res. Campaign; Member: Scientific Adv. Cttee, Whyte-Watson-Turner Cancer Res. Trust, 1984–91; Adv. Gp for Cancer Res., Sheffield Univ., 1991–. President: Hull Lit. Philosophical Soc., 1976–77; British Ring of Internat. Brotherhood of Magicians, 1972–73; Hon. Pres., Scottish Conjurers' Assoc.; Hon. Vice-President: Magic Circle (Official Historian, 1987–; Mem., 1959–); Scottish Assoc. Magical Socs, 1992. Governor, Pocklington Sch., 1965–74; Member, Court: Leeds Univ., 1974–; Bradford Univ., 1985–. Mem., Hall of Fame and H. A. Smith Literary Award, Soc. Amer. Magicians, 1984; Literary Fellowship and Hon. Life Mem., Acad. Magical Arts, USA, 1985; Hon. Mem. Bd, Houdini Historical Center, Wisconsin, 1990–. Hon DSc Hull, 1992. Maskelyne Literary Award, 1988. *Publications:* Quantitative Problems in Biochemistry, 1956, 6th edn 1980; (jtly) Biochemistry of Bacterial Growth, 1968, 3rd edn 1982; The Great Illusionists, 1979; Isaac Fawkes: fame and fable, 1979; The Biochemist in a Microbial Wonderland, 1982; Vonetta, 1982; The Barrister in the Circle, 1983; (ed) Environmental Regulation of Microbial Metabolism, 1985; (ed) Enterobacterial Surface Antigens, 1985; Microbial Energetics, 1985; (jtly) The Book of Magic, 1986, re-issued as Making Magic, 1992; The Wizard Exposed, 1987; (ed) Continuous Culture in Biotechnology and Environment Conservation, 1988; (contrib.) Philip Larkin: the man and his work, 1989; Henri Robin: expositor of science and magic, 1990; (ed) Molecular Biology of Membrane-Bound Complexes in Photosynthetic Bacteria, 1990; (ed) Novel Biodegradable Microbial Polymers, 1990; The Magic of Britain, 1994; numerous papers in scientific jls. *Recreations:* conjuring, book-collecting. *Address:* Dane Hill, 393 Beverley Road, Anlaby, N Humberside HU10 7BQ. *T:* Hull (01482) 657998.

DAWES, Prof. Geoffrey Sharman, CBE 1981; FRS 1971; Director of Charing Cross Medical Research Centre, 1984–89; *b* 21 Jan. 1918; *s* of Rev. W. Dawes, Thurlaston Grange, Derbyshire; *m* 1941, Margaret Monk; two *s* two *d*. *Educ:* Repton Sch.; New Coll., Oxford. BA 1939; BSc 1940; BM, BCh 1943; DM 1947. Rockefeller Travelling Fellowship, 1946; Fellow, Worcester Coll., Oxford, 1946–85, Emeritus Fellow, 1985; University Demonstrator in Pharmacology, Oxford, 1947; Foulerton Research Fellow, Royal Society, 1948; Dir, Nuffield Inst. for Medical Research, Oxford, 1948–85. Mem., MRC, 1978–82; Chm., Physiological Systems and Disorders Bd, MRC, 1978–80. Chm., Lister Inst. for Preventive Medicine, 1988–. Governor of Repton, 1959–88, Chm., 1971–85. A Vice-Pres., Royal Society, 1976, 1977. FRCOG, FRCP; Hon. FACOG. Max Weinstein Award, 1963; Gairdner Foundation Award, 1966; Maternité Award of European Assoc. Perinatal Medicine, 1976; Virginia Apgar Award, Amer. Acad. of Pediatrics, 1980; Osler Meml Medal, Oxford Univ., 1990. *Publications:* Foetal and Neonatal Physiology, 1968; various publications in physiological, pharmacological and obstetric journals. *Recreation:* fishing. *Address:* 8 Belbroughton Road, Oxford OX2 6UZ. *T:* Oxford (01865) 58131.

DAWES, Rt. Rev. Peter Spencer; Bishop of Derby, 1988–95; *b* 1928; *s* of Jason Spencer Dawes and Janet Dawes; *m* 1954, Ethel Marrin; two *s* two *d*. *Educ:* Bickley Hall School; Aldenham School; Hatfield Coll., Durham (BA); Tyndale Hall, Bristol. Assistant Curate: St Andrew's, Whitehall Park, 1954–57; St Ebbe's, Oxford, 1957–60; Tutor, Clifton Theological Coll., 1960–65; Vicar, Good Shepherd, Romford, 1965–80; Archdeacon of West Ham, 1980–88. Examining Chaplain to Bishop of Chelmsford, 1970–95. Member, General Synod, 1970–95. *Address:* 45 Arundell, Ely, Cambs CB6 1BQ.

DAWICK, Viscount; Alexander Douglas Derrick Haig; farmer; *b* 30 June 1961; *s* and *heir* of 2nd Earl Haig, *qv*. *Educ:* Stowe School; Royal Agricl Coll., Cirencester. *Address:* Third Farm, Melrose, Roxburgh TD6 9DR. *Club:* New (Edinburgh).

DAWKINS, Dr (Clinton) Richard; Reader in Zoology, University of Oxford, since 1989 (Lecturer, 1970–89); Fellow, New College, Oxford, since 1970; *b* 26 March 1941; *s* of Clinton John Dawkins and Jean Mary Vyvyan (*née* Ladner); *m*; one *d*. *Educ:* Oundle Sch.; Balliol Coll., Oxford (MA, DPhil, DSc). Asst Prof. of Zoology, Univ. of California, Berkeley, 1967–69. Gifford Lectr, Glasgow Univ., 1988; Sidgwick Meml Lectr, Newnham Coll., Cambridge, 1988; Kovler Vis. Fellow, Univ. of Chicago, 1990; Nelson Lectr, Univ. of California, Davis, 1990; Royal Instn Christmas Lects for Young People, 1991. Presenter, BBC TV Horizon progs, 1985, 1986. Editor: Animal Behaviour, 1974–78; Oxford Surveys in Evolutionary Biology, 1983–86. Hon. Fellow, Regent's Coll., London, 1988. Hon. DLitt St Andrews, 1995. Silver Medal, Zool Soc., 1989; Michael Faraday Award, Royal Soc., 1990; Nakayama Prize, Nakayama Foundn for Human Scis, 1994. *Publications:* The Selfish Gene, 1976, 2nd edn 1989; The Extended Phenotype, 1982; The Blind Watchmaker, 1986 (RSL Prize 1987; LA Times Lit. Prize 1987); River Out of Eden, 1995. *Recreation:* the Apple Macintosh. *Address:* New College, Oxford OX1 3BN. *T:* Oxford (01865) 271280.

DAWKINS, Douglas Alfred; Associate Director, Bank of England, 1985–87; *b* 17 Sept. 1927; *s* of Arthur Dawkins and Edith Annie Dawkins; *m* 1953, Diana Pauline (*née* Ormes); one *s* one *d*. *Educ:* Edmonton County Secondary Sch.; University Coll. London (Rosa Morison Scholar; BA Hons). Entered Bank of England, 1950; Bank for Internat. Settlements, 1953–54; Adviser to Governors, Bank of Libya, 1964–65; Asst Chief of Overseas Dept, 1970; First Dep. Chief of Exchange Control, 1972; Chief of Exchange Control, 1979; Asst Dir, 1980. *Address:* c/o Bank of England, Threadneedle Street, EC2R 8AH.

DAWKINS, Hon. John Sydney; economist, consultant, company director; Australian special investment representative, since 1994; *b* 2 March 1947; *s* of Dr A. L. Dawkins and M. Dawkins (*née* Lee Steere); *m* 1987, Maggie Maruff; one *d*, one step *s*, and one *s* one *d* by previous marr. *Educ:* Roseworthy Agricl Coll., SA (RDA); Univ. of WA (BEc). MHR, Tangney, 1974–75; Press Officer, WA Trades and Labor Council, 1976–77; MP (ALP) Fremantle, WA, 1977–94; Shadow Minister for Educn, 1980–83; Minister: for Finance and assisting Prime Minister for Public Service Matters, 1983–84; for Trade and assisting Prime Minister for Youth Affairs, 1984–87; for Employment, Educn and Trng, 1987–91; Treasurer of Australia, 1991–93. *Address:* PO Box 7400, Cloisters, Perth, WA 6850, Australia.

DAWKINS, Richard; *see* Dawkins, C. R.

DAWKINS, Simon John Robert, MA; Headmaster, Merchant Taylors' School, Crosby, since 1986; *b* 9 July 1945; *s* of Col William John Dawkins, TD and Mary Doreen Dawkins (*née* King); *m* 1968, Janet Mary Stevens; one *s* one *d*. *Educ:* Solihull Sch.; Univ. of Nottingham (BA); Queens' Coll., Cambridge (PGCE); Birkbeck Coll. London (MA distn). Head of Economics: Eltham Coll., 1968–71; Dulwich Coll., 1971–86 (Housemaster, 1979–86). *Recreations:* physical exercise, tennis, golf, reading. *Address:* Brackenwood, St George's Road, Hightown, Liverpool L38 3RT. *T:* 0151–929 3546. *Clubs:* East India; Hightown (Lancs); Formby Golf, St Enodoc Golf.

DAWNAY, family name of **Viscount Downe.**

DAWOOD, Nessim Joseph; Arabist and Middle East Consultant, Managing Director, The Arabic Advertising and Publishing Co. Ltd, London, since 1958; Director, Contemporary Translations Ltd, London, since 1962; *b* Baghdad, 27 Aug. 1927; 4th *s* of late Yousef Dawood, merchant, and Muzli (*née* Tweg); *m* 1949, Juliet, 2nd *d* of late M. and N. Abraham, Baghdad and New York; three *s*. *Educ:* The American Sch. and Shamash Sch., Baghdad; Iraq State Scholar in England, UC Exeter, 1945–49; Univ. of London, BA (Hons). FIL 1959. Dir, Bradbury Wilkinson (Graphics) Ltd, 1975–86. Has written and spoken radio and film commentaries. *Publications:* The Muqaddimah of Ibn Khaldun, 1967 (US, 1969); Penguin Classics: The Thousand and One Nights, 1954; The Koran, 1956, 40th edn 1995, parallel Arabic/English edn, 1990; Aladdin and Other Tales, 1957; Tales from The Thousand and One Nights, 1973, 20th edn 1995; Arabian Nights (illus. children's edn), 1978; Puffin Classics: Aladdin & Other Tales, 1989; Sindbad the Sailor & other Tales, 1989; contribs to specialised and technical English-Arabic dictionaries; translated numerous technical publications into Arabic; occasional book reviews. *Recreation:* going to the theatre. *Address:* 1 Hyde Park Gate, SW7 5XE. *T:* 0171–584 7000. *Club:* Hurlingham.

DAWS, Dame Joyce (Margaretta), DBE 1975; FRCS, FRACS; Surgeon, Queen Victoria Memorial Hospital, Melbourne, Victoria, Australia, 1958–85; Thoracic Surgeon, Prince Henry's Hospital, Melbourne, since 1975; President, Victorian Branch Council, Australian Medical Association, 1976; *b* 21 July 1925; *d* of Frederick William Daws and

Daisy Ethel Daws. *Educ:* Royal School for Naval and Marine Officers' Daughters, St Margaret's, Mddx; St Paul's Girls' Sch., Hammersmith; Royal Free Hosp., London. MB, BS (London) 1949; FRCS 1952, FRACS. Ho. Surg., Royal Free Hosp.; SHMO, Manchester Royal Infirmary; Hon. Surg., Queen Victoria Meml Hosp., Melb., 1958; Asst Thoracic Surg., Prince Henry's Hosp., Melb., 1967–75. Pres., Bd of Management, After-Care Hosp., Melbourne, 1980–85; Chairman: Victorian Nursing Council, 1983–89; Academic and Professional Panel, Victoria, for Churchill Fellowship Awards, 1984; Jt Adv. Cttee on Pets in Society, 1984; Internat. Protea Assoc., 1987–. Hon. Sec., Victorian Br., AMA, 1974. *Recreations:* opera, ballet, theatre, desert travel, protea grower. *Address:* 26 Edwin Street, Heidelberg West, Victoria 3081, Australia. *T:* (3) 4572579. *Clubs:* Lyceum, Soroptimist International (Melbourne).

DAWSON, Hon. Lord; Thomas Cordner Dawson; a Senator of the College of Justice in Scotland, since 1995; *b* 14 Nov. 1948; *s* of Thomas Dawson and Flora Chisholm (*née* Dunwoodie); *m* 1975, Jennifer Richmond Crombie; two *s*. *Educ:* Royal High Sch. of Edinburgh; Edinburgh Univ. (LLB Hons). Advocate, 1973; QC (Scot.) 1986. Lectr, Univ. of Dundee, 1971–74; Advocate Depute, 1983–87; Solicitor-Gen. for Scotland, 1992–95. Member: Supreme Court Legal Aid Cttee, 1980–83; Criminal Injuries Compensation Bd, 1988–92. *Recreations:* golf, cricket, reading, crosswords. *Address:* 19 Craiglea Drive, Edinburgh EH10 5PB. *T:* 0131–447 4427. *Club:* Caledonian (Edinburgh).

DAWSON, Sir Anthony (Michael), KCVO 1993; MD, FRCP; Physician to the Royal Household, 1974–82, to the Queen, 1982–93, and Head of HM Medical Household, 1989–93; Physician, King Edward VII Hospital for Officers, since 1968; Consulting Physician, St Bartholomew's Hospital, since 1986 (Physician, 1965–86); *b* 8 May 1928; *s* of Leslie Joseph Dawson and Mabel Jayes; *m* 1956, Barbara Anne Baron Forsyth, *d* of late Thomas Forsyth, MB, ChB; two *d*. *Educ:* Wyggeston Sch., Leicester; Charing Cross Hosp. Med. Sch. MB, BS 1951, MD 1959, London; MRCP 1954, FRCP 1964. Jun. appts, Charing Cross Hosp., Brompton Hosp., Royal Postgrad. Med. Sch., Central Middlesex Hosp., 1951–57; MRC and US Public Health Res. Fellow, Harvard Med. Sch. at Massachusetts Gen. Hosp., 1957–59; Lectr and Sen. Lectr in Medicine, Royal Free Hosp. Med. Sch., 1959–65; formerly Physician, King Edward VII Convalescent Home for Officers, Osborne. Hon. Sec., Assoc. of Physicians of Gt Britain and Ireland, 1973–78, Treasurer 1978–83. Examnr, London and Oxford, MRCP; Censor, RCP, 1977–78, Treasurer, 1985–91; Treasurer, St Bartholomew's Hosp. Med. Coll., 1976–79, Vice-Pres., 1979–84; Vice-Chm., 1978–83, Dep. Chm., 1983–93, Bd of Management, King Edward's Hosp. Fund for London. Chm. Council, BHF, 1993–; Vice-Chm., Exec. Cttee, Royal Med. Benevolent Fund, 1993–; Treas., British Digestive Foundn, 1992–; Trustee, Distressed Gentlefolk's Aid Assoc., 1994–; Special Trustee, St Bartholomew's and St Mark's Hosps, 1994–. *Publications:* contrib. med. books and jls. *Recreations:* music, gardening. *Address:* Flat 1, 11 Adamson Road, NW3 3HX. *Club:* Garrick.
See also J. L. Dawson.

DAWSON, (Archibald) Keith; Headmaster, Haberdashers' Aske's School, Elstree, 1987–Aug. 1996; *b* 12 Jan. 1937; *s* of Wilfred Joseph and Alice Marjorie Dawson; *m* 1961, Marjorie Blakeson; two *d*. *Educ:* Nunthorpe Grammar School for Boys, York; The Queen's College, Oxford. MA, Dip Ed distinction. Ilford County High School for Boys, 1961–63; Haberdasher's Aske's Sch., 1963–71 (Head of History, 1965–71); Headmaster, John Mason Sch., Abingdon, 1971–79; Principal, Scarborough Sixth Form Coll., 1979–84; Principal, King James's College of Henley, 1984–87. FIMgt (FBIM 1984). *Publications:* Society and Industry in 19th Century England (with Peter Wall), 1968; The Industrial Revolution, 1971. *Recreations:* theatre, music, cricket, hill walking. *Address:* Haberdashers' Aske's School, Elstree, Borehamwood, Herts WD6 3AF. *T:* 0181–207 4323.

DAWSON, Hon. Sir Daryl (Michael), AC 1988; KBE 1982; CB 1980; **Hon. Justice Dawson;** Justice of the High Court of Australia, since 1982; *b* 12 Dec. 1933; *s* of Claude Charles Dawson and Elizabeth May Dawson; *m* 1971, Mary Louise Thomas. *Educ:* Canberra High Sch.; Ormond Coll., Univ. of Melbourne (LLB Hons); LLM Yale. Sterling Fellow, Yale Univ., 1955–56. QC 1971; Solicitor-General for Victoria, 1974–82. Mem. Council, Univ. of Melbourne, 1976–86; Chm. Council, Ormond Coll., Univ. of Melbourne, 1991–92. Chm., Australian Motor Sport Appeal Court, 1986–88 (Mem., 1970–86). *Recreation:* squash. *Address:* High Court of Australia, Canberra, ACT 2600, Australia. *Clubs:* Melbourne, Savage, RACV, Beefsteaks (Melbourne).

DAWSON, (Edward) John; Chairman, Walsingham Community Homes Ltd, since 1991 (Director, since 1990); *b* 14 Oct. 1935; *s* of late Edward Dawson and Kathleen Dawson (*née* Naughton); *m* 1963, Ann Prudence (*née* Hicks); two *s* one *d*. *Educ:* St Joseph's Coll., Blackpool; London Graduate Sch. of Business Studies (Sloan Fellow, 1969–70); Manchester Coll., Univ. of Oxford (BA Hons PPE 1994). FCIB. Entered Lloyds Bank, 1952; served RAF, 1954–56; General Manager, Lloyds Bank and Exec. Dir, Lloyds Bank International, 1982–84; Asst Chief Gen. Manager, 1985, Dir, UK Retail Banking, 1985–88, Asst Chief Exec., 1989–90, Dir, 1989–91, Lloyd's Bank; Chairman: Lloyds Bowmaker Finance, 1988–90 (Dir, 1985–90); Black Horse Agencies, 1988–89 (Dir, 1985–89). *Recreations:* golf, cricket, choral singing. *Address:* c/o Lloyds Bank, Westminster House, 4 Dean Stanley Street, SW1P 3HU. *Clubs:* MCC; Sandy Lodge Golf.

DAWSON, Sir (Hugh) Michael (Trevor), 4th Bt *cr* 1920, of Edgewarebury; *b* 28 March 1956; *s* of Sir (Hugh Halliday) Trevor Dawson, 3rd Bt; *S* father, 1983. *Heir:* *b* Nicholas Antony Trevor Dawson, *b* 17 Aug. 1957.

DAWSON, Ian David; Assistant Under-Secretary of State (Policy), Ministry of Defence, 1991–93; *b* 24 Nov. 1934; *s* of Harry Newton Dawson and Margaret (*née* Aspinall); *m* 1955, Barbara (*née* Mather); two *s* one *d*. *Educ:* Hutton Grammar Sch.; Fitzwilliam House, Cambridge (MA). Directorate of Military Survey, 1958–71; Principal, MoD, 1971; Private Sec. to CAS, 1975–77; Asst Sec., Naval Staff, 1977–80; Sec., AWRE, 1980–83; RCDS, 1984; Dir, Defence and Security Agency, WEU, Paris, 1986–88; Asst Under-Sec. of State (Resources), MoD, 1988–90; Fellow, Center for Internat. Affairs, Harvard, 1990–91. *Recreations:* music, mountaineering, travel. *Address:* The Dawn, Dawn Road, Looe, Cornwall PL13 2DS.

DAWSON, James Gordon, CBE 1981; FEng, FIMechE, FSAE; Consultant; *b* 3 Feb. 1916; *s* of James Dawson and Helen Mitchell (*née* Tawse); *m* 1941, Doris Irene (*née* Rowe) (*d* 1982); one *s* one *d*. *Educ:* Aberdeen Grammar Sch.; Aberdeen Univ. (BScEng Hons Mech. Eng, BScEng Hons Elect. Eng). Develt Test Engr, Rolls Royce Ltd, Derby, 1942; Chief Engr, Shell Research Ltd, 1946; Technical Dir, Perkins Engines Ltd, 1955; Dir, Dowty Group Ltd, 1966; Man. Dir, Zenith Carburetter Co. Ltd, 1969, Chm., 1977–81. Pres., IMechE, 1979–80; FIMechE 1957; Hon. FIMechE 1986. *Publications:* technical papers publd in UK and abroad. *Recreation:* golf. *Address:* Mildmay House, Apethorpe, Peterborough PE8 5DP. *T:* Kingscliffe (01780) 470348. *Club:* Caledonian.

DAWSON, John; *see* Dawson, E. J.

DAWSON, Prof. John Alan; Professor of Marketing, University of Edinburgh, since 1990; *b* 19 Aug. 1944; *s* of Alan and Gladys Dawson; *m* 1967, Jocelyn M. P. Barker; one *s* one *d*. *Educ:* University College London (BSc, MPhil); University of Nottingham (PhD). Lectr, Univ. of Nottingham, 1967–71; Lectr, 1971, Sen. Lectr, 1974, Reader, 1981–83, Univ. of Wales, Lampeter; Fraser of Allander Prof. of Distributive Studies, and Dir, Inst. for Retail Studies, Univ. of Stirling, 1983–90. Vis. Lectr, Univ. of Western Australia, 1973; Vis. Res. Fellow, ANU, 1978; Visiting Professor: Florida State Univ., 1982; Chuo Univ., 1986. Chm., Nat. Museums of Scotland Trading Co., 1992–. Member: Distributive Trades EDC, 1984–87; Board, Cumbernauld Develt Corp., 1987–. Hon. Sec., Inst. of British Geographers, 1985–88. *Publications:* Evaluating the Human Environment, 1973; Man and His World, 1975; Computing for Geographers, 1976; Small Scale Retailing in UK, 1979; Marketing Environment, 1979; Retail Geography, 1980; Commercial Distribution in Europe, 1982; Teach Yourself Geography, 1983; Shopping Centre Development, 1983; Computer Programming for Geographers, 1985; Shopping Centres Policies and Prospects, 1985; Evolution of European Retailing, 1989; Competition and Markets, 1991; Retail Environments in Developing Countries, 1991; Distribution Statistics, 1992; articles in geographical, management and marketing jls. *Recreations:* sport, travel. *Address:* Department of Business Studies, University of Edinburgh, Edinburgh EH8 9JY. *T:* 0131–650 3830.

DAWSON, John Anthony Lawrence, FICE, FIHT; Director, Group Public Affairs, Automobile Association, since 1995; *b* 6 Feb. 1950; *m* 1980, Frances Anne Elizabeth Whelan; two *d*. *Educ:* Mill Hill Sch.; Southampton Univ. British Rail Engineering Scholar, 1968–72; Depts of Envt and Transport, 1972–81; Overseas Transport Consultant, 1981–85; Dir (Transport), London Regl Office, Dept of Transport, 1985–88; Chief Road Engineer, Scottish Develt Dept, 1988; Dir of Roads and Chief Road Engr, Scottish Office, 1989–95. *Recreations:* touring, hard rock. *Address:* Automobile Association, Norfolk House, Priestley Road, Basingstoke, Hants RG24 9NY. *Club:* Royal Scottish Automobile (Glasgow).

DAWSON, John Leonard, CVO 1992; MB, MS; FRCS; Surgeon: King's College Hospital, since 1964; Bromley Hospital, since 1967; King Edward VII Hospital for Officers, since 1975; Dean of the Faculty of Clinical Medicine, King's College School of Medicine and Dentistry, since 1988; *b* 30 Sept. 1932; *s* of Leslie Joseph Dawson and Mabel Annie Jayes; *m* 1958, Rosemary Brundle; two *s* one *d*. *Educ:* Wyggeston Boys' Grammar Sch., Leicester; King's College Hosp., Univ. of London. MB, BS 1955, MS 1964; FRCS 1958. Served RAMC, 1958–60. Surgeon to Royal Household, 1975–83; Surgeon to the Queen, 1983–90, Serjeant Surgeon, 1990–91. Nuffield Scholarship, Harvard Univ., 1963–64; Sir Arthur Sims Travelling Prof., Australasia, 1981. Examiner in Surgery: Univs. of London, 1966–, and Cambridge, 1980–; Soc. of Apothecaries; Primary FRCS, 1974–80; Mem. Ct of Examrs, RCS, 1981–. Mem. Council, Med. Protection Soc., 1979–88. Vice-Chm., British Jl of Surgery, 1981–89. *Publications:* contribs to surgical text-books and jls on abdominal surgery. *Recreations:* theatre, skiing, gardening, reading. *Address:* 107 Burbage Road, Dulwich, SE21 7AF. *T:* 0171–733 3668.
See also Sir A. M. Dawson.

DAWSON, (Joseph) Peter; Co-ordinator for Europe, Education International, since 1993; *b* 18 March 1940; *s* of Joseph Glyn and Winifred Olwen Dawson; *m* 1964, Yvonne Anne Charlton Smith; one *s* one *d*. *Educ:* Bishop Gore Grammar Sch., Swansea; University College of Swansea (BSc, DipEd). Assistant Master, Chiswick Grammar Sch., 1962; Field Officer, 1965, Sen. Field Officer, 1966, NUT; Asst Sec., 1969, Negotiating Sec., 1974, ATTI; Negotiating Sec., 1976, Gen. Sec., 1979–89, Asst Sec. (Pensions and Memship Services) and Internat. Rep., 1989–93, NATFHE. Gen. Sec., ETUCE, 1991–93 (Mem. Exec. Bd, 1984–93; Chm., Higher Educn Working Gp, 1989–93). Vice-Pres., 1962–64, Sen. Treasurer, 1965–68, National Union of Students. Member: Teachers' Panel, Teachers' Superannuation Working Party, 1969–93 (Chm., 1979–93); Eur. Cttee, World Confedn of Organisations of Teaching Profession, 1983–93. Hon. FCP 1984. *Recreations:* football, cricket, theatre. *Address:* Education International, 155 boulevard Emile Jacqmain, 1210 Brussels, Belgium. *T:* (2) 2240611. *Club:* Surrey County Cricket.

DAWSON, Keith; *see* Dawson, A. K.

DAWSON, Sir Michael; *see* Dawson, Sir H. M. T.

DAWSON, Peter; *see* Dawson, J. P.

DAWSON, Ven. Peter; Archdeacon of Norfolk, 1977–93, now Emeritus; *b* 31 March 1929; *s* of late Leonard Smith and Cicely Alice Dawson; *m* 1955, Kathleen Mary Sansome; one *s* three *d*. *Educ:* Manchester Grammar School; Keble Coll., Oxford (MA); Ridley Hall, Cambridge. Nat. service, Army, 1947–49; University, 1949–52; Theological College, 1952–54. Asst Curate, St Lawrence, Morden, Dio. Southwark, 1954–59; Vicar of Barston, Warwicks, Dio. Birmingham, 1959–63; Rector of St Clement, Higher Openshaw, Dio. Manchester, 1963–68; Rector of Morden, Dio. Southwark, 1968–77, and Rural Dean of Merton, 1975–77. *Recreations:* gardening, politics, the rural community, historical studies. *Address:* Elm Cottage, The Drift, Tostock, Bury St Edmunds IP30 9PD. *T:* Beyton (01359) 270005.

DAWSON, Rev. Peter, OBE 1986; OFSTED Registered Inspector of Schools, since 1993; *b* 19 May 1933; *s* of Richard Dawson and Henrietta Kate Dawson (*née* Trueman); *m* 1957, Shirley Margaret Pentland Johnson; two *d*. *Educ:* Beckenham Technical Sch.; Beckenham Grammar Sch.; London School of Economics (BScEcon); Westminster Coll. (Postgrad. CertEd). Schoolmaster Fellow Commoner, Keble Coll., Oxford, 1969, and Corpus Christi Coll., Cambridge, 1979. Asst Master, Roan Grammar School for Boys, London, 1957–62; Head of Upper School, Sedgehill Sch., London, 1962–67; Second Master, Gateacre Comprehensive Sch., Liverpool, 1967–70; Headmaster, Eltham Green Sch., London, 1970–80; Gen. Sec., Professional Assoc. of Teachers, 1980–92. Methodist Minister, ordained 1985; Asst Minister, Queen's Hall Methodist Mission, Derby, 1984–87; Minister, Spondon Methodist Ch., Derby, 1989–90; Free Church Minister, Church on Oakwood, Derby, 1990–94. Member: Burnham Cttee, 1981–87; Council of Managerial and Professional Staffs, 1989–92 (Pres.); Econ. and Social Cttee, EC, 1990–94; Employment Appeal Tribunal, 1992–. *Publications:* Making a Comprehensive Work, 1981; Teachers and Teaching, 1984. *Recreations:* reading, golf, grandparenthood. *Address:* 72 The Ridings, Ockbrook, Derby DE72 3SF. *T:* Derby (01332) 672669. *Club:* Horsley Lodge (Derby).

DAWSON, Air Vice-Marshal Reginald Thomas, CBE 1987; Director of Legal Services, Royal Air Force, 1989–92, retired; *b* 6 Aug. 1930; *s* of Herbert James and Lilian Ethel Dawson; *m* 1963, Geraldine Sandra Peters; one *s* one *d*. *Educ:* Hastings Grammar Sch.; Skinners' Sch., Tunbridge Wells. Qualified as solicitor, 1953. Nat. service, RAF, as pilot, 1953–55; in private practice as solicitor, 1955–57; RAF Reserve, 1955–57; rejoined RAF, 1957; Flt Lt, later Sqn Ldr, RAF Legal Branch, 1957–68; Wing Comdr, 1968; Dep. Dir of Legal Services, NEAF, 1968–71; UK Legal Officer, Australian, NZ and UK Force, Singapore, 1971–74; Gp Captain, 1974; Dep. Dir of Legal Services, RAF Germany, 1974–78; Legal Services 1, RAF, 1978–82, Dep. Dir, 1982–89; Air Cdre, 1982; Air Vice-Marshal, 1989. *Recreations:* game shooting, sailing, walking, gardening, reading. *Address:* The Minstrels, Netherfield Hill, Battle, E Sussex TN33 0LH. *T:* Battle (01424) 772186. *Club:* Royal Air Force.

DAWSON, Rex Malcolm Chaplin, FRS 1981; PhD, DSc; Deputy Director and Head of Biochemistry Department, Institute of Animal Physiology, Babraham, Cambridge, 1969–84, retired (Deputy Chief Scientific Officer, 1969–84); *b* 3 June 1924; *s* of late James Dawson and Ethel Mary Dawson (*née* Chaplin); *m* 1946, Emily Elizabeth Hodder; one *s* one *d*. *Educ:* Hinckley Grammar Sch.; University Coll., London (BSc 1946, DSc 1960); Univ. of Wales (PhD 1951). MRC Fellowship followed by Beit Meml Fellowship, Neuropsychiatric Res. Centre, Whitchurch Hosp., Cardiff, 1947–52; Betty Brookes Fellow, Dept of Biochemistry, Univ. of Oxford, 1952–55. Vis. Res. Fellow, Harvard Univ., 1959; Vis. Prof., Northwestern Univ., Chicago, 1974. International Lipid Prize, Amer. Oil Chemists' Assoc., 1981. *Publications:* Metabolism and Physiological Significance of Lipids, 1964; Data for Biochemical Research, 1959, 3rd edn 1986; Form and Function of Phospholipids, 1973; numerous papers on structure, turnover and role of phospholipids in cell membranes in various scientific jls. *Recreations:* mercantile marine history, sailing, gardening. *Address:* Kirn House, Holt Road, Langham, Norfolk NR25 7BX. *T:* Binham (01328) 830396.

DAWSON, Prof. Sandra June Noble; KPMG Peat Marwick Professor of Management Studies and Director, Judge Institute of Management Studies, University of Cambridge, since 1995; *b* 4 June 1946; *d* of Wilfred Denyer and Joy (*née* Noble); *m* 1969, Henry R. C. Dawson; one *s* two *d*. *Educ:* Dr Challoner's Grammar Sch., Amersham; Univ. of Keele (BA 1st Cl. Hons Hist. and Sociol. 1968). Research Officer, Govt Social Survey, 1968–69; Imperial College of Science, Technology and Medicine: Res. Officer, Lectr, then Sen. Lectr, Industrial Sociol. Unit, Dept of Social and Econ. Studies, 1969–90; Prof. of Organisational Behaviour, Mgt Sch., 1990–95. Non-Exec. Dir, Riverside HA, 1990–92; Chm., Riverside Mental Health Trust, 1992–95. *Publications:* Analysing Organisations, 1986, 2nd edn 1990; Safety at Work: the limits of self regulation, 1988; Managing in the NHS, 1995; contribs to mgt learned jls. *Recreations:* music, walking, family. *Address:* Judge Institute of Management Studies, Trumpington Street, Cambridge CB2 1AG. *T:* Cambridge (01223) 337051.

DAWSON, Stephen Eric; a Metropolitan Stipendiary Magistrate, since 1994; *b* 16 Feb. 1952; *s* of Leslie Eric Dawson and Margaret Kathleen Dawson; *m* 1977, Sandra Mary Bate; two *d*. *Educ:* St Joseph's Acad., Blackheath; Coll. of Law. Admitted Solicitor, 1977. Articled and subseq. Partner, Victor Lissack, solicitors, 1978–82; Partner, Reynolds Dawson, 1982–94. Treas. and Mem. Council, British Acad. of Forensic Scis, 1985–; Treas. and Mem. Cttee, London Criminal Courts Solicitors' Assoc., 1987–94; Mem., Criminal Law Cttee, Law Soc., 1993–. *Publication:* Profitable Legal Aid, 1991. *Recreations:* occasional gardening, gentle jogging. *Address:* c/o Principal Chief Clerk's Office, Secretariat Department, 65 Romney Street, SW1P 3RD.

DAWSON, Thomas Cordner; *see* Dawson, Hon. Lord.

DAWSON, William John Richard Geoffrey Patrick, CMG 1980; OBE 1967; HM Diplomatic Service, retired; *b* 21 Sept. 1926; *m* 1956, June Eaton Dangerfield; one *s* one *d*. Served HM Forces, 1942–45; joined FO, 1951; served in British Middle East Office, Tehran, Lomé, Dar es Salaam, 1952–72; FCO, 1972–73; Nairobi, 1973–77; Counsellor, FCO, 1977–86.

DAWSON-DAMER, family name of **Earl of Portarlington.**

DAWSON-MORAY, Edward Bruce, CMG 1969; *b* 30 June 1909; *s* of late Alwyn Bruce Dawson-Moray and late Ada (*née* Burlton); *m* 1st, 1933, Ursula Frances (*née* Woodbridge) (marr. diss.); one *s* one *d*; 2nd, Beryl Barber. *Educ:* Cranbrook Sch.; University of London (BA Hons). Housemaster, Chillon Coll., Switzerland, 1938–42. British Legation, Berne, 1942; 3rd Secretary, 1944; 3rd Secretary and Vice-Consul, Rome, 1947–48; Consul: Leopoldville, 1948–50; Detroit, 1950–51; 1st Secretary and Consul, Rangoon, 1952–54; Information Officer and Consul, Naples, 1954–56; Foreign Office, 1956–60; Consul, Casablanca, 1960–63; Chief Establishment Officer, Diplomatic Wireless Service, 1963–69; Civil Service Dept, 1969–74; retired. Dir, Pre-retirement Training, CSD, 1975–82. Senior Editor, Foreign Office List, 1957–60. *Recreations:* literature, photography, opera, travel. *Address:* 2 Pennypiece, Cleeve Road, Goring-on-Thames, Reading, Berks RG8 9BY. *T:* Goring-on-Thames (01491) 873314.

DAWTRY, Sir Alan, Kt 1974; CBE 1968 (MBE (mil.) 1945); TD 1948; Chief Executive (formerly Town Clerk), Westminster City Council, 1956–77; Chairman: Sperry Rand Ltd, 1977–86; Sperry Rand (Ireland) Ltd, 1977–86; President, London Rent Assessment Panel, 1979–86; *b* 8 April 1915; *s* of Melancthon and Kate Nicholas Dawtry, Sheffield; unmarried. *Educ:* King Edward VII Sch., Sheffield; Sheffield Univ. (LLB). Served War of 1939–45: commissioned RA; campaigns France, N Africa, Italy (MBE, despatches twice); released with rank of Lt-Col. Admitted Solicitor, 1938; Asst Solicitor, Sheffield, 1938–48; Deputy Town Clerk, Bolton, 1948–52; Deputy Town Clerk, Leicester, 1952–54; Town Clerk, Wolverhampton, 1954–56; Hon. Sec., London Boroughs Assoc., 1965–78. Member: Metrication Bd, 1969–74; Clean Air Council, 1960–75; Council of Management, Architectural Heritage Fund, 1977–89; CBI Council, 1982–86. Pres., Soc. of Local Authority Chief Execs, 1975–76. Vice-Chm., Dolphin Square Trust, 1985–. FIMgt (FBIM 1975); FRSA 1978. Foreign Orders: The Star (Afghanistan); Golden Honour (Austria); Leopold II (Belgium); Rio Branco (Brazil); Merit (Chile); Legion of Honour (France); Merit (W Germany); the Phœnix (Greece); Merit (Italy); Homayoun (Iran); The Rising Sun (Japan); the Star (Jordan); African Redemption (Liberia); Oaken Crown (Luxembourg); Loyalty (Malaysia); the Right Hand (Nepal); Orange-Nassau (Netherlands); the Two Niles (Sudan); the Crown (Thailand), Zaire (Zaire). *Address:* 901 Grenville House, Dolphin Square, SW1V 3LR. *T:* 0171–798 8100.

DAY, Prof. Alan Charles Lynn; Professor of Economics, London School of Economics, University of London, 1964–83, now Professor Emeritus; *b* 25 Oct. 1924; *s* of late Henry Charles Day, MBE, and of Ruth Day; *m* 1962, Diana Hope Bocking (*d* 1980); no *c*; *m* 1982, Dr Shirley E. Jones. *Educ:* Chesterfield Grammar Sch.; Queens' Coll., Cambridge. Asst Lecturer, then Lecturer, LSE, 1949–54; Economic Adviser, HM Treas., 1954–56; Reader in Economics, London Univ., 1956–64. Ed., National Inst. Econ. Review, 1960–62; Econ. Correspondent, The Observer, intermittently, 1957–81. Economic Adviser on Civil Aviation, BoT, later Dept of Trade and Industry, 1968–72; Economic Adviser, Civil Aviation Authority, 1972–78. Member: Council, Consumers' Assoc., 1963–82; Board, British Airports Authority, 1965–68; SE Region Econ. Planning Council, 1966–69; Home Office Cttee on the London Taxicab Trade, 1967–70; Layfield Cttee on Local Govt Finance, 1974–76; Air Transport Users' Cttee, CAA, 1978–79; Home Office Adv. Panel on Satellite Broadcasting Standards, 1982. British Acad. Leverhulme Vis. Prof., Graduate Inst. for International Studies, Geneva, 1971. Governor, LSE, 1971–76, 1977–79, Pro-Director, 1979–83; Hon. Fellow, 1988. *Publications:* The Future of Sterling, 1954; Outline of Monetary Economics, 1956; The Economics of Money, 1959; (with S. T. Beza) Wealth and Income, 1960. *Address:* Chart Place, Chart Sutton, Maidstone, Kent ME17 3RE. *T:* Maidstone (01622) 842236; 13 Gower Mews Mansions, WC1E 6HP. *T:* 0171–631 3928.

DAY, Bernard Maurice, CB 1987; Panel Chairman, Civil Service Selection Board, since 1988; *b* 7 May 1928; *s* of M. J. Day and Mrs M. H. Day; *m* 1956, Ruth Elizabeth Stansfield; two *s* one *d*. *Educ:* Bancroft's Sch.; London School of Economics (BScEcon). Army service, commnd RA, 1946–48. British Electric Traction Fedn, 1950–51; Asst Principal, Air Ministry, 1951; Private Sec. to Air Mem. for Supply and Organisation, 1954–56; Principal, 1956; Cabinet Secretariat, 1959–61; Asst Sec., 1965; Sec., Meteorological Office, 1965–69; Estabt Officer, Cabinet Office, 1969–72; Head of Air Staff Secretariat, MoD, 1972–74; Asst Under Sec. of State, MoD, 1974; Civilian Staff Management, 1974–76; Operational Requirements, 1976–80; Programmes and Budget, 1980–82; Supply and Orgn, Air, 1982–84; Resident Chm., CSSB, 1984–85; Asst Under-Sec. of State (Fleet Support), MoD, 1985–88. Chairman: MoD Branch, First Div. Assoc., 1983–84; MoD Liaison Cttee with CS Benevolent Fund, 1975–84. *Recreations:* swimming, gardening, Parochial Church Council, Elmbridge Mental Health Association. *Address:* 2 Farmleigh Grove, Walton-on-Thames, Surrey KT12 5BU. *T:* Walton-on-Thames (01932) 227416. *Club:* Commonwealth Trust.

DAY, Prof. Christopher, DPhil; Professor, School of Education, University of Nottingham, since 1993; *b* 3 May 1943; *s* of Walter Day and Patricia Jane Day; *m* 1984, Alison Jane Stewart; two *s*. *Educ:* St Luke's Coll., Exeter (Cert Ed 1964); Univ. of Sussex (MA 1976; DPhil 1979). LRAM 1966. School teacher, 1964–68; Lectr, 1968–71; LEA Advr, London Borough of Barking and Dagenham, 1972–76; Associate Prof., Univ. of Calgary, Alberta, 1979–81; Lectr, Sen. Lectr and Reader, Univ. of Nottingham, 1981–93. Hon. PhD Linköping, Sweden, 1993. FRSA 1972. Editor, Developing Teachers and Schools series, 1991–94. *Publications: jointly:* Managing Primary Schools, 1985; Appraisal and Professional Development in Primary Schools, 1987; Reconceptualising School-Based Curriculum Development, 1990; Managing Primary Schools in the 1990s, 1990; Leadership and Curriculum in Primary Schools, 1993; *edited jointly:* Staff Development in Secondary Schools, 1986; Partnership in Educational Management, 1988; Insights into Teachers' Thinking and Practice, 1990; Managing the Professional Development of Teachers, 1991; Research on Teacher Thinking, 1993. *Recreations:* hockey, tennis, reading. *Address:* School of Education, University of Nottingham, University Park, Nottingham NG7 2RD. *T:* Nottingham (0115) 951 4423.

DAY, David Vivian; Principal, St John's College, University of Durham, since 1993; *b* 11 Aug. 1936; *s* of Frederick Vivian Day and Enid Blodwen (*née* Evans); *m* 1959, Lorna Rosemary Taylor; two *s* one *d*. *Educ:* The Grammar Sch., Tottenham; QMC, Univ. of London (BA Classics); Univ. of Nottingham (MEd, MTheol). Classics Master, Southgate County Sch., 1958–64; Head of Religious Education: Southgate Sch., 1964–66; Bilborough Sch., 1966–73; Sen. Lectr in Theol., Bishop Lonsdale Coll., Derby, 1973–79; Sen. Lectr in Educn, Univ. of Durham, 1979–93. *Publications:* This Jesus, 1980, 2nd edn 1981; Jeremiah: speaking for God in a time of crisis, 1987; Teenage Beliefs, 1991; (ed jtly) The Contours of Christian Education, 1992. *Recreations:* playing squash, watching Rugby and soccer. *Address:* St John's College, Durham DH1 3RJ. *T:* Durham (0191) 3743561.

DAY, Sir Derek (Malcolm), KCMG 1984 (CMG 1973); HM Diplomatic Service, retired; High Commissioner to Canada, 1984–87; *b* 29 Nov. 1927; *s* of late Mr and Mrs Alan W. Day; *m* 1955, Sheila Nott; three *s* one *d*. *Educ:* Hurstpierpoint Coll.; St Catharine's Coll., Cambridge. Royal Artillery, 1946–48. Entered HM Foreign Service, Sept. 1951; Third Sec., British Embassy, Tel Aviv, 1953–56; Private Sec. to HM Ambassador, Rome, 1956–59; Second, then First Sec., FO, 1959–62; First Sec., British Embassy, Washington, 1962–66; First Sec., FO, 1966–67; Asst Private Sec. to Sec. of State for Foreign Affairs, 1967–68; Head of Personnel Operations Dept, FCO, 1969–72; Counsellor, British High Commn, Nicosia, 1972–75; Ambassador to Ethiopia, 1975–78; Asst Under-Sec. of State, 1979, Dep. Under-Sec. of State, 1980, and Chief Clerk, 1982–84, FCO. Dir, Monenco Ltd (Canada), 1988–92, Chm., Crystal Palace Sports and Leisure Ltd, 1992–. Mem., Commonwealth War Graves Commn, 1987–92; Vice-Chm. of Council, British Red Cross, 1988–94. Chm. Governors, Hurstpierpoint Coll., 1987–; Gov., Bethany Sch., 1987–. *Address:* Etchinghill, Goudhurst, Kent TN17 1JP. *Club:* United Oxford & Cambridge University.

DAY, Douglas Henry; QC 1989; a Recorder, since 1987; *b* 11 Oct. 1943; *s* of James Henry Day and Nancy Day; *m* 1970, Elizabeth Margaret (*née* Jarman); two *s* one *d*. *Educ:* Bec Sch.; Selwyn Coll., Cambridge (MA). Called to the Bar, Lincoln's Inn, 1967. Asst Parly Boundary Comr, 1994–. *Address:* Farrar's Building, Temple, EC4Y 7BD. *T:* 0171–583 9241. *Club:* Bec Old Boys Rugby.

DAY, Sir Graham; *see* Day, Sir J. G.

DAY, John King, TD; MA, BSc; Principal, Elizabeth College, Guernsey, CI, 1958–71; *b* Ipoh, Perak, FMS, 27 Oct. 1909; *s* of Harold Duncan Day, Mining Engineer, and Muriel Edith Day; *m* 1935, Mary Elizabeth Stinton, *er d* of late Tom Stinton, Headmaster of the High Sch., Newcastle-under-Lyme; three *s*. *Educ:* Stamford Sch.; Magdalen Coll., Oxford. Demy 1928–32. Honour School of Natural Science (Chemistry) Class 2. Assistant Master, Kendal Sch., Westmorland, 1932; Asst Master and Housemaster, Gresham's Sch., 1933–57. Served Royal Norfolk Regt (7th Bn) and Military College of Science, 1939–45. *Recreations:* walking, fishing and sketching. *Address:* 1 Pearson's Road, Holt, Norfolk NR25 6EJ. *T:* Holt (01263) 713435.

See also N. E. Day.

DAY, Air Vice-Marshal John Romney, OBE 1985; Air Officer Commanding No 1 Group, since 1994; *b* 15 July 1947; *er s* of John George Day and Daphne Myrtle Kelly; *m* 1969, Jane Richards; two *s*. *Educ:* King's Sch., Canterbury; Imperial Coll., Univ. of London (BSc Aer. Eng.). No 72 Sqn, 1970–73; Flying Instructor, RAF Linton-on-Ouse, 1973–76; OC Oxford Univ. Air Sqn, 1976–79; RAF Staff Coll., 1981, PSO to Air Mem. for Personnel, 1982–83; OC No 72 Sqn, 1983–85; OC RAF Odiham, 1987–89; RCDS, 1990; Dir, Air Force Plans and Progs, MoD, 1991–94. *Address:* c/o Lloyds Bank, Ashford, Kent. *Club:* Royal Air Force.

DAY, Sir (Judson) Graham, Kt 1989; Chairman, PowerGen, 1990–93 (Director, 1990–93); *b* 3 May 1933; *s* of Frank Charles Day and Edythe Grace (*née* Baker); *m* 1958, Leda Ann (*née* Creighton); one *s* two *d*. *Educ:* Queen Elizabeth High Sch., Halifax, NS; Dalhousie Univ., Halifax, NS (LLB). Private practice of Law, Windsor, Nova Scotia, 1956–64; Canadian Pacific Ltd, Montreal and Toronto, 1964–71; Chief Exec., Cammell Laird Shipbuilders Ltd, Birkenhead, Eng., 1971–75; Dep. Chm., Organising Cttee for British Shipbuilders and Dep. Chm. and Chief Exec. designate, British Shipbuilders, 1975–76; Prof. of Business Admin and Dir, Canadian Marine Transportation Centre, Dalhousie Univ., NS, 1977–81; Vice-Pres., Shipyards & Marine Develt, Dome Petroleum Ltd, 1981–83; Chm. and Chief Exec., British Shipbuilders, 1983–86; Chief Exec., 1986–88, Chm., 1986–91, BL, subseq. The Rover Gp Hldgs. Chm., Cadbury Schweppes, 1989–93 (Dir, 1988–93); Dep. Chm., MAI plc, 1989–93 (Dir, 1988–93); Director: The Laird Gp plc, 1985–; British Aerospace, 1986– (Chairman, 1991–92); Crownx Inc. (Canada), 1989–; Bank of Nova Scotia (Canada), 1989–; NOVA Corp. of Alberta, 1990–. Pres., ISBA, 1991–. Member: Nova Scotia Barristers' Soc.; Law Soc. of Upper Canada; Canadian Bar Assoc. Freeman, City of London. ARINA. Hon. Fellow, Univ. of Wales

Coll. of Cardiff, 1990. Hon. doctorates: Dalhousie; City; CNAA; Cranfield; Aston; Warwick; Humberside. *Recreation:* reading. *Address:* 18 Avon Street, Hantsport, NS B0P 1P0, Canada.

DAY, Lance Reginald; Keeper, Science Museum Library, 1976–87; *b* 2 Nov. 1927; *s* of late Reginald and of Eileen Day; *m* 1959, Mary Ann Sheahan; one *s* two *d.* *Educ:* Sherrardswood Sch., Welwyn Garden City; Alleyne's Grammar Sch., Stevenage; Northern Polytechnic and University Coll., London (MSc). Res. Asst, Science Museum Library, 1951–64, Asst Keeper 1964–70; Asst Keeper, Science Museum, Dept of Chemistry, 1970–74; Keeper, Science Museum, Dept of Communications and Electrical Engrg, 1974–76. Sec., Nat. Railway Museum Cttee, 1973–75; Newcomen Society: Hon. Sec., 1973–82; Hon. Ed., 1990–. *Publications:* (contrib.) Encyclopaedia of the History of Technology, 1990; (ed jtly and contrib.) Biographical Dictionary of Technology, 1995; reviews and articles. *Recreation:* music. *Address:* 12 Rhinefield Close, Brockenhurst, Hants SO42 7SU. *T:* Lymington (01590) 622079.

DAY, Lucienne, RDI 1962; in freelance practice, since 1948; Consultant, with Robin Day, to John Lewis Partnership, 1962–87; *b* 1917; *d* of Felix Conradi and Dulcie Lilian Duncan-Smith; *m* 1942, Robin Day, *qv*; one *d.* *Educ:* Convent Notre Dame de Sion, Worthing; Croydon School of Art; Royal Coll. of Art. ARCA 1940; FSIAD 1955; Mem. Faculty of Royal Designers for Industry, 1962 (Master, 1987–89). Teacher, Beckenham Sch. of Art, 1942–47; began designing full-time, dress fabrics and later furnishing fabrics, carpets, wallpapers, table-linen, 1947 for Edinburgh Weavers, Heal's Fabrics, Cavendish Textiles, Tomkinsons, Wilton Royal, Thos Somerset etc, and firms in Scandinavia, USA and Germany; also china decoration for Rosenthal China, Selb, Bavaria, 1956–68; work for Barbican Art Centre, 1979; currently designing and making silk wall-hangings (silk mosaics). Retrospective exhibitions: Whitworth Art Gall., Manchester, and RCA, 1993; Aberdeen, 1994. Work in permanent collections: V&A; Trondheim Museum, Norway; Cranbrook Museum, Michigan, USA; Art Inst. of Chicago; Röhsska Mus., Gothenberg, Sweden (silk mosaics); Musée des Arts Décoratifs, Montreal. Member: Rosenthal Studio-line Jury, 1960–68; Cttee, Duke of Edinburgh's Prize for Elegant Design, 1960–63; Council, RCA, 1962–67; RSA Design Bursaries Juries. Hon. DDes Southampton, 1995. First Award, Amer. Inst. of Decorators, 1950; Gold Medal, 9th Triennale di Milano, 1951; Gran Premio, 10th Triennale di Milano, 1954; Design Council Awards, 1957, 1960, 1968. *Recreations:* plant collecting in Mediterranean regions, gardening. *Address:* 49 Cheyne Walk, Chelsea, SW3 5LP. *T:* 0171–352 1455.

DAY, Sir Michael (John), Kt 1992; OBE 1981; Chairman, Commission for Racial Equality, 1988–93; *b* 4 Sept. 1933; *s* of Albert Day and Ellen Florence (*née* Itter); *m* 1960, June Marjorie, *d* of late Dr John William and Edith Mackay; one *s* one *d.* *Educ:* University College Sch., Hampstead; Selwyn Coll., Cambridge (MA); London School of Economics (Cert. Social Work and Social Admin). Probation Officer, Surrey, 1960–64; Sen. Probation Officer, W Sussex, 1964–67; Asst Prin. Probation Officer, 1967–68, Chief Probation Officer, 1968–76, Surrey; Chief Probation Officer, W Midlands, 1976–88. Chm., Chief Probation Officers' Conf., 1974–77; First Chm., Assoc. Chief Officers of Probation, 1982–84. *Publications:* contribs to professional jls and others. *Recreations:* family, books, music, gardening, the countryside. *Address:* Thornhill, Oldbury, Bridgnorth, Shropshire WV16 5EQ.

DAY, Prof. Nicholas Edward, PhD; Professor of Public Health, since 1989, and Fellow of Hughes Hall, since 1992, University of Cambridge; *b* 24 Sept. 1939; *s* of John King Day, *qv*; *m* 1961, Jocelyn Deanne Broughton; one *s* one *d.* *Educ:* Magdalen Coll., Oxford (BA Maths); Aberdeen Univ. (PhD Med. Stats). Res. Fellow, Aberdeen Univ., 1962–66; Fellow, ANU, 1966–69; Statistician, 1969–78, Head, Unit of Biostats and Field Studies, 1979–86, Internat. Agency for Res. on Cancer, Lyon; Cancer Expert, Nat. Cancer Inst., USA, 1978–79; Dir, 1986–89, Hon. Dir, 1989–, MRC Biostats Unit; Fellow, Churchill Coll., Cambridge, 1986–92. *Publications:* Statistical Methods in Cancer Research, vol. 1 1980, vol. 2 1988; Screening for Cancer of the Uterine Cervix, 1986; Screening for Breast Cancer, 1988; over 200 articles in scientific jls. *Recreations:* sea fishing, fruit growing. *Address:* Porch House, Haddenham, Ely, Cambs CB6 3TJ. *T:* Ely (01353) 740472.

DAY, Prof. Peter, DPhil; FRS 1986; Director of the Royal Institution, and of the Davy Faraday Research Laboratory, since 1991, and Fullerian Professor of Chemistry, since 1994; Visiting Professor, University College London, since 1991; *b* 20 Aug. 1938; *s* of Edgar Day and Ethel Hilda Day (*née* Russell); *m* 1964, Frances Mary Elizabeth Anderson; one *s* one *d.* *Educ:* Maidstone Grammar School; Wadham College, Oxford (BA 1961; MA, DPhil 1965; Hon. Fellow, 1991). Cyanamid European Research Institute, Geneva, 1962; Jun. Res. Fellow, 1963–65, Official Fellow, 1965–91, St John's College, Oxford; Departmental Demonstrator, 1965–67, Lectr in Inorganic Chemistry, 1967–89, *ad hominem* Prof. of Solid State Chemistry, 1989–91, Oxford Univ. Dir, Inst. Laue-Langevin, Grenoble, 1988–91 (on secondment); Resident Prof. of Chemistry, Royal Instn, 1991–94. Prof. Associé, Univ. de Paris-Sud, 1975; Guest Prof., Univ. of Copenhagen, 1978; Vis. Fellow, ANU, 1980; Senior Research Fellow, SRC, 1977–82. Du Pont Lectr, Indiana Univ., 1988; Royal Soc. Blackett Meml Lectr, 1994. Science and Engineering Research Council: Member: Neutron Beam Res. Cttee, 1983–88; Chemistry Cttee, 1985–88; Molecular Electronics Cttee, 1987—88; Nat. Cttee on Superconductivity, 1987–88; Materials Commn, 1988–90; COPUS, 1991–. Mem., Sci. and Engrg Council, British Council, 1991–; Council Member: Inst. for Molecular Scis, Okazaki, Japan, 1991–95; Parly and Scientific Cttee, 1992–. Royal Society of Chemistry: Vice-Pres., Dalton Div., 1986–88; Corday-Morgan Medal, 1971; Solid State Chem. Award, 1986. Gov., Birkbeck Coll., London, 1993–. Mem., Academia Europaea, 1992. Hon. Foreign Mem., Indian Soc. of Materials Res., 1994. Hon. Fellow, Indian Acad. of Sci., 1995. Hon. DSc Newcastle, 1994. *Publications:* Physical Methods in Advanced Inorganic Chemistry (ed with H. A. O. Hill), 1968; Electronic States of Inorganic Compounds, 1974; Emission and Scattering Techniques, 1980; Electronic Structure and Magnetism of Inorganic Compounds, vols 1–7, 1972–82; (ed with A. K. Cheetham) Solid State Chemistry, vol. 1 1987, vol. 2 1992; papers in Jl Chem. Soc.; Inorg. Chem. *Recreation:* driving slowly through rural France. *Address:* 21 Albemarle Street, W1X 4BS. *T:* 0171–409 2992.

DAY, Peter Rodney, PhD; Director, Center for Agricultural Molecular Biology, Rutgers University, New Jersey, since 1987; *b* 27 Dec. 1928; *s* of Roland Percy Day and Florence Kate (*née* Dixon); *m* 1950, Lois Elizabeth Rhodes; two *s* one *d.* *Educ:* Birkbeck Coll., Univ. of London (BSc, PhD). John Innes Institute, 1946–63; Associate Prof. of Botany, Ohio State Univ., 1963–64; Chief, Dept of Genetics, Connecticut Agricl Experiment Station, 1964–79; Dir, Plant Breeding Inst., Cambridge, 1979–87. Sec., Internat. Genetics Fedn, 1984–93. Special Prof. of Botany, Nottingham Univ., 1982–88. Commonwealth Fund Fellow, 1954; John Simon Guggenheim Meml Fellow, 1973. *Publications:* Fungal Genetics (with J. R. S. Fincham), 1963, 4th edn 1979; Genetics of Host-Parasite Interaction, 1974; contrib. Genetical Research, Genetics, Heredity, Nature, Proc. Nat. Acad. Sci., Phytopathology, etc. *Recreation:* Scottish country dancing. *Address:* Center for Agricultural Molecular Biology, Rutgers, State University of New Jersey, NJ 08903, USA. *T:* (908) 9328165.

DAY, Sir Robin, Kt 1981; television and radio journalist; *b* 24 Oct. 1923; *s* of late William and Florence Day; *m* 1965, Katherine Ainslie (marr. diss. 1986); two *s.* *Educ:* Bembridge Sch.; St Edmund Hall, Oxford (Hon. Fellow, 1989). Military service, 1943–47; commd RA, 1944. Oxford, 1947–51: Union debating tour of American universities, 1949; President, Oxford Union, 1950; BA Hons (Jurisprudence), 1951; MA. Middle Temple: Blackstone Entrance Scholar, 1951; Harmsworth Law Scholar, 1952–53; called to Bar, 1952; Hon. Bencher, 1990. British Information Services, Washington, 1953–54; BBC Talks Producer (radio), 1955; Newscaster and Parliamentary Correspondent, Independent Television News, 1955–59; columnist in News Chronicle, 1959; ITV programmes, 1955–59: Roving Report (ITN); Tell the People (ITN); Under Fire (Granada); since 1959 BBC TV programmes including: Panorama, Gallery, People to Watch, Daytime, 24 Hours, Midweek, To-night, Sunday Debate, Talk-in, Newsday, Question Time; The Elder Statesmen, 1992; The Parliament Programme (ITN), 1992. BBC radio programmes: It's Your Line, 1970–76; Election Call, 1974, 1979, 1983, 1987; The World at One, 1979–87. Chm., Hansard Soc., 1981–83. Mem., Phillimore Cttee on Law of Contempt, 1971–74. Contested (L) Hereford, 1959. Hon. LLD: Exeter, 1986; Keele, 1988; DU Essex, 1988. Guild of TV Producers' Merit Award, Personality of the Year, 1957; Richard Dimbleby Award for factual television, 1974; Broadcasting Press Guild Award, for Question Time, 1980; RTS Judges' Award for 30 yrs TV journalism, 1985. *Publications:* Television: A Personal Report, 1961; The Case for Televising Parliament, 1963; Day by Day, 1975; Grand Inquisitor—memoirs, 1989; . . . But With Respect—memorable interviews, 1993. *Recreations:* reading, talking, walking. *Clubs:* Garrick, Royal Automobile.

DAY, Robin, OBE 1983; RDI 1959; FCSD (FSIAD 1948); design consultant and freelance designer; *b* 25 May 1915; *s* of Arthur Day and Mary Shersby; *m* 1942, Lucienne Conradi (*see* Lucienne Day); one *d.* *Educ:* Royal Coll. of Art (ARCA). National scholarship to RCA, 1935–39; teacher and lectr for several yrs; Design Consultant: Hille International, 1948–; John Lewis Partnership, 1962–87. Commissions include: seating for many major concert halls, theatres, stadia, etc.; interior design of Super VC10 and other aircraft. Mem., juries for many national and internat. indust. design competitions. Many awards for design work, including: 6 Design Centre awards; Gold Medal, Triennale di Milano, 1951, and Silver Medal, 1954; Designs Medal, SIAD, 1957. *Recreations:* mountaineering, ski touring, hill-walking. *Address:* 49 Cheyne Walk, Chelsea, SW3 5LP. *T:* 0171–352 1455. *Clubs:* Alpine, Alpine Ski, Climbers'.

DAY, Simon James; farmer; *b* 22 Jan. 1935; *s* of late John Adam Day and Kathleen Day (*née* Hebditch); *m* 1959, Hilary Maureen Greenslade Gomm; two *s* (and one *s* decd). *Educ:* Bedales Sch.; S Devon Tech. Coll.; Emmanuel Coll., Cambridge (MA Hist.). Nat. Service, RN, 1954–56. Devon County Council: Councillor, Modbury Div., 1964–74, Salcombe Div., 1974–; Whip, 1981–89; Dep. Leader, 1989, Leader, 1991–93. Non-Exec. Dir, SW Water, 1989–; Regl Dir, Portman Building Soc., 1989–91; Director: Plymouth Sound Radio, 1966–80; Plymouth Develt Corp., 1993–; Chm., West of England Newspapers Gp, 1981–86. Underwriting Mem. of Lloyds, 1974–. Mem., Exec. Council, ACC, 1981–85, 1990– (Chm., Police Cttee, 1991; Dep. Leader, 1992; Vice Chm., 1993–; Leader Cons. Gp, 1993–); Chm., Devon and Cornwall Police Authy, 1990–93; Member: Police Adv. Bd, Home Office, 1989–; Police Negotiating Bd, 1989–; Chairman: Devon Sea Fisheries Cttee, 1986–; Assoc. of Sea Fisheries Cttees, England and Wales, 1993– (Vice-Chm., 1991–93); Mem., Govt Salmon Adv. Cttee, 1987–90; Chm., Devon and Cornwall Develt Bureau, 1989–91; Vice Chairman: Nat. Parks Cttee for England and Wales, 1981–83; Local Govt Finance Cttee, 1983–85; Member: Consultative Council, Local Govt Finance, 1983–85; Standing Conf. of Local and Regl Authies, Council of Europe, 1990–; Cttee of Regions, EU, 1994–; Chm., Cons. Nat. Local Govt Adv. Cttee, 1994–. Pres., S Devon Herd Book Soc., 1986. Chm. Govs, Bicton Coll. of Agric., 1983–. Mem. Court, Exeter Univ., 1964–. Contested (C): Carmarthen, 1966, bye-election 1966; N Cornwall, 1970. Hereditary Freeman, City of Norwich. *Recreations:* shooting, sailing, fishing. *Address:* Keaton House, near Ivybridge, Devon PL21 0LB. *T:* Plymouth (01752) 691212. *Clubs:* Buck's, Royal Thames Yacht; Royal Yacht Squadron.

DAY, Stephen Nicholas; Stipendiary Magistrate, Middlesex, since 1991; *b* 17 Aug. 1947; *s* of late Robert Weatherston Day and of Margaret Diana (*née* McKenzie); *m* 1973, Shama (*née* Tak); one *s* one *d.* *Educ:* St Mary's Coll., Southampton; King Edward VI Sch., Southampton; Brasenose Coll., Oxford (MA). Called to the Bar, Middle Temple, 1972. Sen. Court Clerk, Nottingham, 1973–77; Justices Clerk, Abingdon, Didcot and Wantage, 1977–91. *Address:* c/o The Court House, The Hyde, Hendon, NW9 7BY. *T:* 0181–441 9042.

DAY, Stephen Peter, CMG 1989; HM Diplomatic Service, retired; consultant, Middle East affairs; *b* 19 Jan. 1938; *s* of Frank William and Mary Elizabeth Day; *m* 1965, Angela Doreen (*née* Waudby); one *s* two *d.* *Educ:* Bancroft's School; Corpus Christi Coll., Cambridge. MA. Entered HMOCS as Political Officer, Western Aden Protectorate, 1961, transf. to FO, 1965; Senior Political Officer, South Arabian Federation, 1964–67; FO, 1967–70; First Sec., Office of C-in-C, Far East, Singapore, 1970–71; First Sec. (Press), UK Mission to UN, NY, 1971–75; FCO, 1976–77; Counsellor, Beirut, 1977–78; Consul-Gen., Edmonton, 1979–81; Ambassador to Qatar, 1981–84; Head of ME Dept, FCO, 1984–87; attached to Household of the Prince of Wales, 1986; Ambassador to Tunisia, 1987–92; Sen. British Trade Comr, Hong Kong, 1992–93; Dir, Council for Advancement of Arab-British Understanding, 1993–94. Adviser: Internat. Maghreb Merchant Bank, 1995–; All-Party Parly Gp on Kuwait, 1995–. Member: Maghreb Adv. Gp, BOTB, 1995–; Exec. Cttee, Soc. for Arabian Studies, 1995–. Chairman: British-Tunisian Soc., 1993–; Palestine Exploration Fund, 1995–. *Publication:* At Home in Carthage, 1991. *Recreations:* walking, family. *Address:* Oakfield Cottage, 92 West End Lane, Esher, Surrey KT10 8LF. *T:* and *Fax:* Esher (01372) 464138. *Clubs:* Athenæum; Hong Kong.

DAY, Stephen Richard; MP (C) Cheadle, since 1987; *b* 30 Oct. 1948; *s* of Francis and Anne Day; *m* 1982, Frances (*née* Booth); one *s* by former marriage. *Educ:* Otley Secondary Modern Sch.; Park Lane Coll., Leeds; Leeds Polytechnic. MIEx 1972. Sales Clerk, William Sinclair & Sons, stationary manufrs, Otley, W Yorks, 1965–70, Asst Sales Manager (working in Home and Export Depts), 1970–77; Sales Representative: Larkfield Printing Co. Ltd (part of Hunting Group), Brighouse, W Yorks, 1977–80; A. H. Leach & Co. (part of Hunting Gp), photographic processing lab., Brighouse, 1980–84; Sales Executive: PPL Chromacopy, photographic labs, Leeds and Manchester, 1984–86; Chromogene, photographic lab., Leeds, 1986–87. Vice-President: Stockport Chamber of Commerce, 1987–; Stockport and Dist Heart Foundn, 1985–. Chm., Yorks Area Cons. Political Centre, 1983–86; Vice-Chm., NW Leeds Constituency, 1983–86. Town Councillor, Otley, 1975–76 and 1979–83; City Councillor, Leeds, 1975–80. Contested (C) Bradford West, 1983. Mem., Select Cttee on Social Security, 1990–; Co-Chm., Parly Adv. Council for Transport Safety, 1989–; Vice-Chm., All-Party Non-Profit-Making Clubs Gp. Co-Chm., West Coast Main Line Gp. Sponsor, Private Member's Bill to introduce compulsory wearing of rear car seat belts by children, 1988. Hon. Mem., Bramhall and Woodford Rotary Club. *Publications:* pamphlets on Otley and on rate reform. *Recreations:* movies, music, history (particularly Roman). *Clubs:* Cheadle Hulme Conservative (Cheadle Hulme); Royal Wharfedale (Otley).

DAY-LEWIS, Daniel; actor; *s* of Cecil Day-Lewis, CBE and Jill Angela Henriette Balcon. *Educ:* Bedales; Bristol Old Vic Theatre Sch. *Stage:* The Recruiting Officer, Troilus and Cressida, Funny Peculiar, Old King Cole, A Midsummer Night's Dream, Class Enemy, Edward II, Oh! What a Lovely War, Look Back in Anger, Dracula, Another Country, Romeo and Juliet, The Futurists, Hamlet; *films:* Gandhi, 1981; The Saga of HMS Bounty, 1983; My Beautiful Laundrette, 1985; A Room With a View, 1985; Nanou, 1985; The Unbearable Lightness of Being, 1986; Stars and Bars, 1987; My Left Foot, 1988 (Oscar best actor and numerous other awards); Ever Smile New Jersey, 1988; Last of the Mohicans, 1991 (Variety Club best actor); Age of Innocence, 1992; In the Name of the Father, 1993; principal roles in TV. *Address:* c/o Julian Belfrage Associates, 68 St James's Street, SW1A 1PH.

DAY-LEWIS, Séan; journalist and author; *b* 3 Aug. 1931; *s* of Cecil Day-Lewis, CBE, CLit and Mary Day-Lewis; *m* 1960, Anna Mott; one *s* one *d.* *Educ:* Allhallows Sch., Rousdon, Devon. National Service, RAF, 1949–51. Bridport News, 1952–53; Southern Times, Weymouth, 1953–54; Herts Advertiser, St Albans, 1954–56; Express and Star, Wolverhampton, 1956–60; The Daily Telegraph, 1960–86, TV and Radio Editor, 1970–86; TV Editor, London Daily News, 1987. Arts Editor, Socialist Commentary, 1966–71; Founder-Chm., 1975, Chm., 1990–92, BPG; Vice Pres., Bulleid Soc., 1970; Member, BAFTA, 1976. *Publications:* Bulleid: last giant of steam, 1964; C. Day-Lewis: an English literary life, 1980; (ed) One Day in the Life of Television, 1989; TV Heaven: a review of British television from the 1930s to the 1990s, 1992. *Recreations:* being in Devon, listening to J. S. Bach and others, failing at ball games, giving in to temptation. *Address:* 52 Masbro Road, W14 0LT. *T:* 0171–602 3221; Restorick Row, Rosemary Lane, Colyton, Devon EX13 6LW. *T:* Colyton (01297) 553039.

DAYKIN, Christopher David, CB 1993; FIA; Government Actuary, since 1989; *b* 18 July 1948; *s* of John Francis Daykin and Mona Daykin; *m* 1977, Kathryn Ruth (*née* Tingey); two *s* one *d.* *Educ:* Merchant Taylors' Sch., Northwood; Pembroke Coll., Cambridge (BA 1970, MA 1973). FIA 1973. Government Actuary's Department, 1970; VSO, Brunei, 1971; Govt Actuary's Dept, 1972–78; Principal (Health and Social Services), HM Treasury, 1978–80; Govt Actuary's Dept, 1980–, Principal Actuary, 1982–84, Directing Actuary (Social Security), 1985–89. Mem., Council, Inst. of Actuaries, 1985–91 (Hon. Sec., 1988–90; Vice Pres., 1993–94; Pres., 1994–); Chairman: Perm. Cttee for Statistical, Actuarial and Financial Studies, ISSA, 1992–; Educn Cttee, Groupe Consultatif des Assocs d'Actuaires des Pays des Communautés Européennes, 1992– Mem. Pensions Observatory, EC Commn, 1992–. Treasurer, Emmanuel Church, Northwood, 1982–87; Chm., VSO Harrow and Hillingdon, 1976–91. *Publications:* Practical Risk Theory, 1993; articles and papers on pensions, demography, consumer credit, social security and insurance. *Recreations:* travel, photography, languages. *Address:* Government Actuary's Department, 22 Kingsway, WC2B 6LE. *T:* 0171–242 6828.

DEACON, Keith Vivian; Under Secretary, since 1988, and Director of Quality Development, since 1993, Inland Revenue; *b* 19 Nov. 1935; *s* of Vivian and Louisa Deacon; *m* 1960, Brenda Chater; one *s* one *d.* *Educ:* Sutton County Grammar School; Bristol Univ. (BA Hons English Lang. and Litt.). Entered Inland Revenue as Inspector of Taxes, 1962; Regional Controller, 1985; Dir, Technical Div. I until Head Office reorganisation, 1988; Dir, Insce and Specialist Div., 1988–91; Dir of Operations, 1991–93. Part time work for Civil Service Selection Board: Observer, 1969–72; Chairman, 1985–87. FRSA 1992. *Recreations:* reading, photography, music, gardening. *Address:* Board of Inland Revenue, New Wing, Somerset House, WC2R 1LB.

DEACON ELLIOTT, Air Vice-Marshal Robert, CB 1967; OBE 1954; DFC 1941; AE 1944 (2 mentions); *b* 20 Nov. 1914; *m* 1948, Grace Joan Willes, Leamington Spa; two *s* one *d.* *Educ:* Northampton. 72 Fighter Sqdn (Dunkirk and Battle of Britain), 1939–41; HQ Fighter Comd, 1942–43; 84 Group 2 ATAF, 1944–46; Air Ministry (OR 5), 1946–48; OC Flying Wing and OC 26 APC in Cyprus, 1948–51; HQ Fighter Comd, Head of Admin. Plans, 1951–54; Army Staff Coll., on Directing Staff, 1954–56; CO, RAF Leconfield, 1956–57; CO, RAF Driffield, 1957–58; Air University USAF, Maxwell AFB, USA, 1958–61; Commandant, Officer and Aircrew Selection Centre, 1962–65; AOC, RAF Gibraltar, 1965–66; AOC, RAF Malta, and Dep. C-in-C (Air), Allied Forces Mediterranean, 1966–68, retd; Bursar, Civil Service Coll., 1969–79. *Recreations:* shooting, photography. *Address:* Thor House, Old Roar Road, St Leonards-on-Sea, E Sussex TN37 7HH. *T:* Hastings (01424) 752699. *Club:* Royal Air Force.

DEAKIN, Sir (Frederick) William (Dampier); *see* Deakin, Sir William.

DEAKIN, Michael; writer, documentary and film maker; Director, Griffin Productions Ltd, since 1985; *b* 21 Feb. 1939; *s* of Sir William Deakin, *qv*, and Margaret Hodson (*née* Beatson-Bell). *Educ:* Bryanston; Univ. d'Aix-Marseille; Emmanuel Coll., Cambridge (MA Hons). Founding Partner, Editions Alecto, Fine Art Publishers, 1960–64; Producer, BBC Radio Current Affairs Dept, 1964–68; Producer, then Editor, Yorkshire Television Documentary Unit, 1968–81. Documentary film productions include: Out of the Shadow into the Sun—The Eiger; Struggle for China; The Children on the Hill; Whicker's World—Way Out West; The Japanese Experience; The Good, the Bad and the Indifferent; Johnny Go Home (British Academy Award, 1976); David Frost's Global Village; The Frost Interview—The Shah; Rampton—The Secret Hospital; Painting With Light (co-prodn with BBC); Act of Betrayal, 1987 (TV film); Not a Penny More, Not a Penny Less, 1990 (TV mini series); Secret Weapon, 1990 (film); The Supergun, 1994 (film); Good King Wenceslas, 1994 (film); also many others. Founding Mem., TV-am Breakfast Television Consortium, 1980; Consultant, TV-am, 1984–87 (Dir of Programmes, 1982–84; Bd Mem., 1984–85). *Publications:* Restif de la Bretonne—Les Nuits de Paris (critical edn and trans. with Nicholas Deakin), 1968; Gaetano Donizetti—a biography, 1968; (for children) Tom Grattan's War, 1970, 2nd edn 1971; The Children on the Hill, 1972, 9th edn 1982; (with John Willis) Johnny Go Home, 1976; (with Antony Thomas) The Arab Experience, 1975, 2nd edn 1976; Flame in the Desert, 1976; (with David Frost) I Could Have Kicked Myself, 1982, 2nd US edn 1983; (with David Frost) Who Wants to be a Millionaire, 1983; (with David Frost) If You'll Believe That You'll Believe Anything . . ., 1986. *Recreations:* travel, music, books, pictures, dalmatians, motorcycling. *Address:* 6 Glenhurst Avenue, NW5 1PS; La Marsaulaie, Saint Mathurin, 49250 Beaufort-en-Vallée, France. *Clubs:* British Academy of Film and Television Arts, Hat.
See also N. D. Deakin.

DEAKIN, Prof. Nicholas Dampier; Professor of Social Policy and Administration, since 1980, Dean, Faculty of Commerce and Social Science, 1986–89, University of Birmingham; *b* 5 June 1936; *s* of Sir (Frederick) William Deakin, *qv* and Margaret Ogilvy Hodson; *m* 1st, 1961, Rose Albinia Donaldson (marr. diss. 1988), *d* of Baron Donaldson of Kingsbridge, *qv*; one *s* two *d*; 2nd, 1988, Lucy Moira, *d* of Jack and Moira Gaster. *Educ:* Westminster Sch.; Christ Church Coll., Oxford (BA (1st cl. Hons) 1959, MA 1963); DPhil Sussex 1972. Asst Principal, Home Office, 1959–63, Private Sec. to Minister of State, 1962–63; Asst Dir, Nuffield Foundn Survey of Race Relations in Britain, 1963–68; Res. Fellow, subseq. Lectr, Univ. of Sussex, 1968–72; Head of Social Studies, subseq. Head of Central Policy Unit, GLC, 1972–80. Scientific Advr, DHSS, later Dept of Health, 1986–91. Vice-Chm., Social Affairs Cttee, ESRC, 1984–86. Chair, Social Policy Assoc., 1989–92; Member: Exec. Cttee, NCVO, 1988–90; Council, RIPA, 1984–88; Governing Council, Family Policy Studies Centre, 1987–. *Publications:* (ed and trans.) Memoirs of the Comte de Gramont, 1965; Colour and the British Electorate 1964, 1965; Colour, Citizenship and British Society, 1969; (with Clare Ungerson) Leaving London, 1977; (jtly) Government and Urban Poverty, 1983; (ed) Policy Change in Government, 1986; The Politics of Welfare, 1987, 2nd edn 1994; (ed jtly) Consuming Public Services, 1990; (jtly) The Enterprise Culture and the Inner Cities, 1992; (ed jtly) The Costs of Welfare, 1993; contribs to other vols and learned jls. *Recreations:* reading fiction, music. *Address:* Department of Social Policy and Social Work, University of Birmingham, PO Box 363, Birmingham B15 2TT; 55 Estria Road, Birmingham B15 2LG. *T:* 0121–440 6251. *Club:* British Academy of Film and Television Arts.
See also M. Deakin.

DEAKIN, Sir William, Kt 1975; DSO 1943; MA; Warden of St Antony's College, Oxford, 1950–68, retired; Hon. Fellow, 1969; *b* 3 July 1913; *e s* of Albert Witney Deakin, Aldbury, Tring, Herts; *m* 1st, 1935, Margaret Ogilvy (marr. diss. 1940), *d* of late Sir Nicholas Beatson Bell, KCSI, KCIE; two *s*; 2nd, 1943, Livia Stela, *d* of Liviu Nasta, Bucharest. *Educ:* Westminster Sch.; Christ Church, Oxford (Hon. Student, 1979). 1st Class, Modern History, 1934; Amy Mary Preston Read Scholar, 1935. Fellow and Tutor, Wadham Coll., Oxford, 1936–49; Research Fellow, 1949; Hon. Fellow, 1961. Served War of 1939–45; with Queen's Own Oxfordshire Hussars, 1939–41; seconded to Special Operations, War Office, 1941; led first British Military Mission to Tito, May 1943. First Secretary, HM Embassy, Belgrade, 1945–46. Hon. FBA, 1980. Russian Order of Valour, 1944; Chevalier de la Légion d'Honneur, 1953; Grosse Verdienstkreuz, 1958; Yugoslav Partisan Star (1st Class), 1969. *Publications:* The Brutal Friendship, 1962; (with G. R. Storry) The Case of Richard Sorge, 1964; The Embattled Mountain, 1971. *Address:* 83330 Le Castellet Village, Var, France. *Clubs:* White's, Brooks's.
See also M. Deakin, N. D. Deakin.

DEAKINS, Eric Petro; international public affairs consultant; *b* 7 Oct. 1932; *er s* of late Edward Deakins and Gladys Deakins; *m* 1990, Sandra Weaver; one *s* one *d.* *Educ:* Tottenham Grammar Sch.; London Sch. of Economics. BA (Hons) in History, 1953. Executive with FMC (Meat) Ltd, 1956; General Manager, Pigs Div., FMC (Meat) Ltd, 1969. Contested (Lab): Finchley, 1959; Chigwell, 1966; Walthamstow, 1967. MP (Lab): Walthamstow W, 1970–74; Walthamstow, 1974–87. Parly Under-Sec. of State, Dept of Trade, 1974–76, DHSS, 1976–79. *Publications:* A Faith to Fight For, 1964; You and your MP, 1987; What Future for Labour?, 1988. *Recreations:* writing, cinema, squash, football. *Address:* 36 Murray Mews, NW1 9RJ.

DEAL, Hon. Timothy Edward; Minister and Deputy Chief of Mission, Embassy of the United States of America in London, since 1992; *b* 17 Sept. 1940; *s* of Edward Deal and Loretta (*née* Fuemuller); *m* 1964, Jill Brady; two *s.* *Educ:* Univ. of California at Berkeley (AB Pol Sci.). First Lieut, US Army, 1963–65. Joined Foreign Service, US Dept of State, 1965; served Teguugalpa, Honduras, Warsaw, Poland, and Washington, 1965–76; Sen. Staff Mem., Nat. Security Council, 1976–79 and 1980–81; Special Asst to Asst Sec. of State for European Affairs, 1979–80; Counsellor for Econ. Affairs, London, 1981–85; Dep. US Rep., OECD, Paris, 1985–88; Dir, Office of Eastern European Affairs, Washington, 1988–89; Special Asst to President and Sen. Dir for Internat. Econ. Affairs, Nat. Security Council, 1989–92. Presidential Awards for: Meritorious Service, 1991; Distinguished Service, 1993. *Recreations:* theatre, cinema, horse racing. *Address:* American Embassy, 24 Grosvenor Square, W1A 1AE. *T:* 0171–408 8124.

DEALTRY, Prof. (Thomas) Richard; Professor of Strategic Management, International Management Centres, Buckingham, since 1989; Regional Director, Diverco Ltd, since 1985; *b* 24 Nov. 1936; *s* of George Raymond Dealtry and Edith (*née* Gardner); *m* 1962, Pauline (*née* Sedgwick) (marr. diss. 1982); one *s* one *d.* *Educ:* Cranfield Inst. of Advanced Technol.; MBA. CEng, MIMechE; MInstM; FIMCB. National Service Commn, 1959–61: Temp. Captain 1960. Divl Exec., Tube Investments Ltd, 1967–71; Sen. Exec., Guest, Keen & Nettlefold Gp Corporate Staff, 1971–74; Dir, Simpson-Lawrence Ltd, and Man. Dir, BUKO BV, Holland, 1974–77; Under Sec./Industrial Adviser, Scottish Econ. Planning Dept, 1977–78; Director, Gulf Regional Planning, Gulf Org. for Industrial Consulting, 1978–82; Man. Dir, RBA Management Services Ltd, London and Kuwait, 1982–85. *Recreations:* golf, squash. *Address:* 43 Hunstanton Avenue, Harborne, Birmingham B17 8SX.

DEAN, family name of **Baron Dean of Beswick.**

DEAN OF BESWICK, Baron *cr* 1983 (Life Peer), of West Leeds in the County of West Yorkshire; **Joseph Jabez Dean;** *b* 1922. Engineer; formerly Shop Steward, AUEW. Formerly Leader, Manchester City Council. MP (Lab) Leeds West, Feb. 1974–1983; PPS to Minister of State, CSD, 1974–77; an Asst Govt Whip, 1978–79; Labour Party Pairing Whip, 1982–83, 1985–; Labour Party front bench spokesman on housing, building, sport and energy. Contested (Lab) Leeds West, 1983. *Address:* House of Lords, SW1A 0PW.

DEAN OF HARPTREE, Baron *cr* 1993 (Life Peer), of Wedmore in the County of Somerset; **Arthur Paul Dean,** Kt 1985; PC 1991; company director; *b* 14 Sept. 1924; *s* of Arthur Percival Dean and Jessie Margaret Dean (*née* Gaunt); *m* 1st, 1957, Doris Ellen Webb (*d* 1979); 2nd, 1980, Peggy Parker. *Educ:* Ellesmere Coll., Shropshire; Exeter Coll., Oxford (MA, BLitt). Former President Oxford Univ. Conservative Assoc. and Oxford Carlton Club. Served War of 1939–45, Capt. Welsh Guards; ADC to Comdr 1 Corps BAOR. Farmer, 1950–56. Resident Tutor, Swinton Conservative Coll., 1957; Conservative Research Dept, 1957–64, Assistant Director from 1962. MP (C) Somerset North, 1964–83, Woodspring, Avon, 1983–92. A Front Bench Spokesman on Health and Social Security, 1969–70; Parly Under-Sec. of State, DHSS, 1970–74; Dep. Chm. of Ways and Means and Dep. Speaker, 1982–92. Member: Exec. Cttee, CPA, UK Branch, 1975–92; House of Commons Services Select Cttee, 1979–82; House of Commons Chairman's Panel, 1979–82; Chm., Conservative Health and Social Security Cttee, 1979–82. Mem., Exec. Cttee, Assoc. of Conservative Peers, 1995–. Formerly, Member Governing Body of Church in Wales. *Publications:* contributions to political pamphlets. *Recreation:* fishing. *Address:* Archer's Wyck, Knightcott, Banwell, Weston-super-Mare, Avon BS24 6HS. *Club:* United Oxford & Cambridge University.

DEAN OF THORNTON-LE-FYLDE, Baroness *cr* 1993 (Life Peer), of Eccles in the Metropolitan County of Greater Manchester; **Brenda Dean;** Chairman, Independent Committee for Supervision of Standards of Telephone Information Services, since 1993 (Member, since 1991); *b* 29 April 1943; *d* of Hugh Dean and Lillian Dean; *m* 1988, Keith Desmond McDowall, *qv.* *Educ:* St Andrews Junior Sch., Eccles; Stretford High Sch. for Girls. Admin. Sec., SOGAT, 1959–72; SOGAT Manchester Branch: Asst Sec., 1972–76; Sec., 1976–83; Mem., Nat. Executive Council, 1977–83; Pres., 1983–85, Gen.-Sec., 1985–91, SOGAT '82; Dep. Gen. Sec., Graphical, Paper and Media Union, 1991–92. Dir, Inveresk plc, 1994–. Co-Chm., Women's Nat. Commn, 1985–87; Member: Printing and Publishing Trng Bd, 1974–82; Supplementary Benefits Commn, 1976–80; Price Commn, 1977–79; Occupational Pensions Bd, 1983–87; Gen. Adv. Council, BBC, 1984–88; TUC

Gen. Council, 1985–92; NEDC, 1989–92; Employment Appeal Tribunal, 1991–; Armed Forces Pay Review Body, 1993–; Broadcasting Complaints Commn, 1993–94; Press Complaints Commn, 1993–. Mem. Council, ABSA, 1990–. Member: Council, City Univ., 1991–; Bar Council of Legal Educn, 1992–; Gov., Ditchley Foundn, 1992–. FRSA 1992. Hon. Fellow, Lancs Poly., 1991. Hon. MA Salford, 1986; Hon. DCL City, 1993. *Recreations:* sailing, reading, relaxing, thinking! *Address:* House of Lords, SW1P 0PW. *Club:* Reform.

DEAN, Anne, (Mrs Stafford Dean); *see* Howells, Anne.

DEAN, (Cecil) Roy; HM Diplomatic Service, retired; writer and broadcaster; *b* 18 Feb. 1927; *s* of Arthur Dean and Flora Dean (*née* Clare); *m* 1954, Heather Sturtridge; three *s*. *Educ:* Watford Grammar Sch.; London Coll. of Printing and Graphic Arts (diploma); Coll. for Distributive Trades (MIPR). Served RAF, 1945–48, India and Pakistan; Central Office of Information, 1948–58; Second, later First Sec., Colombo, 1958–62; Vancouver, 1962–64; Lagos, 1964–68; FCO, 1968–71; Consul, Houston, 1971, Acting Consul-Gen., 1972–73; FCO, 1973–76; Dir, Arms Control and Disarmament Res. Unit, 1976–83; Dep. High Comr, Accra, 1983–86, Acting High Comr, 1986. Mem., UN Sec.-General's expert group on disarmament instns, 1980–81. Trustee, Urbanaid, 1987–. Editor: Insight, 1964–68; Arms Control and Disarmament, 1979–83; author and presenter, The Poetry of Popular Song (BBC Radio Four series), 1989–91. Press Officer: Bromley Chamber Music Soc.; Bromley Art Soc.; Bromley Arts Council; Bromley Nat. Trust Centre; Bromley Town Twinning Assoc.; Drawing Room Singers. *Compositions:* A Century of Song, 1995. *Publications:* Peace and Disarmament, 1982; chapter in Ethics and Nuclear Deterrence, 1982; (contrib.) Christmas Crackers, 1982; (contrib.) More Christmas Crackers, 1990; numerous research papers; contribs to learned jls. *Recreations:* crosswords (Times national champion, 1970 and 1979), humour, light verse, song-writing, book collecting. *Address:* 14 Blyth Road, Bromley, Kent BR1 3RX. *T:* 0181–402 0743. *Club:* Bromley Labour.

DEAN, His Honour (Charles) Raymond, QC 1963; a Circuit Judge (formerly Judge of County Courts), 1971–88; Senior Circuit Judge, 1985–88; *b* 28 March 1923; *s* of late Joseph Irvin Gledhill Dean and late Lilian Dean (*née* Waddington); *m* 1948, Pearl Doreen (*née* Buncall); one *s* one *d*. *Educ:* Hipperholme Grammar Sch.; The Queen's Coll., Oxford (1941–42 and 1945–47). RAF Flying Duties, 1942–45 (Flt Lieut). BA (Jurisprudence) 1947, MA 1948; called to Bar, Lincoln's Inn, 1948; Deputy Chairman, West Riding QS, 1961–65; Recorder: of Rotherham, 1962–65; of Newcastle upon Tyne, 1965–70; of Kingston-upon-Hull, 1970–71. *Recreations:* fishing, motoring, reading, Rugby Union (now non-playing), golf. *Address:* Inner Court, 3 Hudson Mews, Boston Spa, West Yorks LS23 6AD. *T:* Boston Spa (01937) 844155. *Club:* Leeds.

DEAN, Christopher Colin, MBE 1981; professional ice skater; *b* 27 July 1958; *s* of Colin Gordon Dean and Mavis (*née* Pearson) and step *s* of Mary Betty (*née* Chambers); *m* 1st, 1991, Isabelle Duchesnay (marr. diss. 1993); 2nd, 1994, Jill Trenary. *Educ:* Calverton Manor Sch., Nottingham; Sir John Sherbrooke Sch., Nottingham; Col Frank Seely Sch., Nottingham. Ice dancer, with Jayne Torvill, *qv*: British Champions, 1978, 1979, 1980, 1981, 1982, 1983, 1994; European Champions, 1981, 1982, 1984, 1994; World Champions, 1981, 1982, 1983, 1984; Olympic Champions, 1984; Olympic Bronze Medallists, 1994. Hon. MA Nottingham Trent, 1993. *Recreations:* motor racing, films, dance. *Address:* c/o 59 Goodwin Avenue, Swalecliffe, Kent CT5 2RA. *T:* Canterbury (01227) 793721. *Club:* Groucho.

DEAN, His Honour Joseph (Jolyon); a Circuit Judge, South Eastern Circuit, 1975–87; *b* 26 April 1921; *s* of late Basil Dean, CBE; *m* 1962, Hon. Jenefer Mills, *yr d* of late 5th Baron Hillingdon, MC, TD; one *s* two *d*. *Educ:* Elstree Sch.; Harrow Sch.; Merton Coll., Oxford (MA Classics and Law). 51st (Highland) Div., RA, 1942–45. Called to the Bar, Middle Temple, 1947; Bencher 1972. *Publication:* Hatred, Ridicule or Contempt, 1953 (paperback edns 1955 and 1964). *Recreation:* domestic maintenance. *Address:* The Hall, West Brabourne, Ashford, Kent TN25 5LZ.
See also Winton Dean.

DEAN, Katharine Mary Hope, (Mrs Robert Dean); *see* Mortimer, K. M. H.

DEAN, Michael; QC 1981; **His Honour Judge Dean;** a Circuit Judge, since 1991; *b* 2 Feb. 1938; *s* of late Henry Ross Dean and Dorothea Alicia Dean; *m* 1967, Diane Ruth Griffiths. *Educ:* Altrincham Co. Grammar Sch.; Univ. of Nottingham. Lectr in Law, Univ. of Manchester, 1959–62; called to the Bar, Gray's Inn, 1962; Northern Circuit, Manchester, 1962–65; Lectr in Law, LSE, 1965–67; practice at the Bar, London, 1968–; an Asst Recorder, 1986–89; a Recorder, 1989–91. *Publications:* articles in various legal periodicals. *Recreations:* conversation, music, theatre, sailing. *Address:* 7 King's Bench Walk, Temple, EC4. *T:* 0171–383 0404.

DEAN, Dr Paul, CB 1981; writer and adviser; Director, National Physical Laboratory, 1977–90 (Deputy Director, 1974–76); *b* 23 Jan. 1933; *s* of late Sydney and Rachel Dean; *m* 1961, Sheila Valerie Gamse; one *s* one *d*. *Educ:* Hackney Downs Grammar Sch.; Queen Mary Coll., Univ. of London (Fellow, 1984). BSc (1st cl. Hons Physics), PhD; CPhys; FInstP, FIMA, CMath. National Physical Laboratory: Sen. Sci. Officer, Math. Div., 1957; Principal Sci. Officer, 1963; Sen. Principal Sci. Officer (Individual Merit), 1967; Head of Central Computer Unit, 1967; Supt, Div. of Quantum Metrology, 1969; Under-Sec., DoI (Head of Space and Air Res. and R&D Contractors Divs), 1976–77; initiated testing lab. accreditation in UK, leading to NAMAS, 1985. Part-time Head, Res. Estabts Management Div., DoI, 1979–82; Exec. Dep. Chm., Council of Res. Estabts, 1979–82. Mem., Internat. Cttee of Weights and Measures, 1985–90; Pres., Comité Consultatif pour les Etalons de Mesure des Rayonnements Ionisants, 1987–90; Founder Pres., British Measurement and Testing Assoc., 1990–95; First Chm., EUROMET, 1988–90. *Publications:* papers and articles in learned, professional and popular jls. *Recreations:* mathematics, computing, astronomy, chess, music, bridge. *Address:* Surrey and Dorset.

DEAN, Peter Henry, CBE 1993; free-lance business consultant, since 1985; *b* 24 July 1939; *s* of late Alan Walduck Dean and Gertrude (*née* Bürger); *m* 1965, Linda Louise Keating; one *d*. *Educ:* Rugby Sch.; London Univ. (LLB). Admitted Solicitor, 1962. Joined Rio Tinto-Zinc Corp., 1966; Sec., 1972–74; Dir, 1974–85. Director: Associated British Ports Holdings, 1982– (Mem., British Transport Docks Bd, 1980–82); Liberty Life Assce Co., 1986–95; Seeboard, 1993–. Dep. Chm., Monopolies and Mergers Commn, 1990– (Mem., 1982–). Chm., Council of Management, Highgate Counselling Centre, 1991– (Mem., 1985–); Chm., English Baroque Choir, 1985–89. *Recreations:* choral singing, skiing. *Address:* 52 Lanchester Road, Highgate, N6 4TA. *T:* 0181–883 5417, *Fax:* 0181–365 2398.

DEAN, Raymond; *see* Dean, C. R.

DEAN, Roy; *see* Dean, C. R.

DEAN, Winton (Basil), FBA 1975; author and musical scholar; *b* Birkenhead, 18 March 1916; *e s* of late Basil Dean, CBE, and Esther, *d* of A. H. Van Gruisen; *m* 1939, Hon. Thalia Mary Shaw, 2nd *d* of 2nd Baron Craigmyle; one *s* one adopted *d* (and two *d* decd). *Educ:* Harrow; King's Coll., Cambridge (MA). Translated libretto of Weber's opera Abu Hassan (Arts Theatre, Cambridge) 1938. Served War of 1939–45: in Admiralty (Naval Intelligence Div.), 1944–45. Member: Music Panel, Arts Council, 1957–60, Cttee of Handel Opera Society (London), 1955–60; Council, Royal Musical Assoc., 1965– (Vice-Pres., 1970–). Ernest Bloch Prof. of Music, 1965–66, Regent's Lectr, 1977, Universiy of California (Berkeley); Matthew Vassar Lectr, Vassar Coll., Poughkeepsie, NY, 1979. Member: Management Cttee, Halle Handel Soc., 1979– (Vice-Pres., 1991–); Kuratorium, Göttingen Handel Fest., 1981–; Corresp. Mem., Amer. Musicological Soc., 1989–. Ed, with Sarah Fuller, Handel's opera Julius Caesar (Barber Inst. of Fine Arts, Birmingham), performed 1977. Hon. RAM 1971. *Publications:* The Frogs of Aristophanes (trans. of choruses to music by Walter Leigh), 1937; Bizet (Master Musicians), 1948 (3rd rev. edn, 1975); Carmen, 1949; Introduction to the Music of Bizet, 1950; Franck, 1950; Hambledon *v* Feathercombe, the Story of a Village Cricket Match, 1951; Handel's Dramatic Oratorios and Masques, 1959; Shakespeare and Opera (Shakespeare in Music), 1964; Georges Bizet, His Life and Work, 1965; Handel and the Opera Seria, 1969; Beethoven and Opera (in The Beethoven Companion), 1971; ed, Handel, Three Ornamented Arias, 1976; (ed) E. J. Dent, The Rise of Romantic Opera, 1976; The New Grove Handel, 1982; (with J. M. Knapp) Handel's Operas 1704–1726, 1987, 2nd edn 1995; Essays on Opera, 1990; contributed to Grove's Dictionary of Music and Musicians (5th and 6th edns), New Oxford History of Music and to musical periodicals and learned journals. *Recreations:* cricket, shooting, salmon fishing, naval history. *Address:* Hambledon Hurst, Godalming, Surrey GU8 4HF. *T:* Wormley (01428) 682644.
See also J. J. Dean.

DEANE, family name of **Baron Muskerry.**

DEANE, Prof. Basil; Professor of Music, University of Birmingham, 1987–92, retired; *b* 27 May 1928; *s* of Canon Richard A. Deane and Lorna Deane; *m* 1955, Norma Greig (*d* 1991); two *s*. *Educ:* Armagh Royal School; The Queen's Univ., Belfast (BA, BMus). PhD Glasgow. FRNCM 1978. Lecturer in Music, Glasgow Univ., 1953–59; Senior Lectr, Melbourne Univ., 1959–65; Lectr, Nottingham Univ., 1966–68; Prof., Sheffield Univ., 1968–74; Prof., Manchester Univ., 1975–80; Music Dir, Arts Council, 1980–83; Dir, Hongkong Acad. for Performing Arts, 1983–87. Member of Arts Council, 1977–79 (Chairman, Music Advisory Panel, 1977–79); Chairman of Music Board, Council for Nat. Academic Awards, 1978–80. *Publications:* Albert Roussel, 1962; Cherubini, 1965; Hoddinott, 1979; contribs to periodicals. *Address:* 48 Beacon Street, Lichfield, Staffs WS13 7AJ.

DEANE, Derek; Artistic Director, English National Ballet, since 1993; *b* 18 June 1953; *s* of William Gordon Shepherd and Margaret Shepherd; adopted Deane as stage name. *Educ:* Royal Ballet School. With Royal Ballet Co., 1972–89; Asst Dir, Rome Opera, 1990–92. *Recreations:* theatre, all performing arts, travelling, tennis. *Address:* English National Ballet, Markova House, 39 Jay Mews, SW7 2ES. *T:* 0171–581 1245.

DEANE, Prof. Phyllis Mary, FBA 1980; Professor of Economic History, University of Cambridge, 1981–83, now Emeritus; Fellow of Newnham College, 1961–83, Honorary Fellow, 1983; *b* 13 Oct. 1918; *d* of John Edward Deane and Elizabeth Jane Brooks; single. *Educ:* Chatham County Sch.; Hutcheson's Girls' Grammar Sch., Glasgow; Univ. of Glasgow. MA Hons Econ. Science Glasgow 1940; MA Cantab; FRHistS. Carnegie Research Scholar, 1940–41; Research Officer, Nat. Inst. of Econ. and Social Research, 1941–45; Colonial Research Officer, 1946–48; Research Officer: HM Colonial Office, 1948–49; Cambridge University: Dept of Applied Econs, 1950–61; Lectr, Faculty of Econs and Politics, 1961–71; Reader in Economic History, 1971–81. Vis. Prof., Univ. of Pittsburgh, 1969. Editor, Economic Jl, 1968–75. Pres., Royal Economic Soc., 1980–82. Hon. DLitt Glasgow, 1989. *Publications:* (with Julian Huxley) The Future of the Colonies, 1945; The Measurement of Colonial National Incomes, 1948; Colonial Social Accounting, 1953; (with W. A. Cole) British Economic Growth 1688–1959, 1962; The First Industrial Revolution, 1965; The Evolution of Economic Ideas, 1978; The State and the Economic System, 1989; papers and reviews in econ. jls. *Recreations:* walking, gardening. *Address:* 4 Stukeley Close, Cambridge CB3 9LT.

DEANE, Hon. Sir William (Patrick), AC 1988; KBE 1982; Justice of the High Court of Australia (desig. Hon. Justice Deane), 1982–Feb. 1996; Governor General of Australia, from Feb. 1996; *b* 4 Jan. 1931. Called to the Bar of NSW, 1957; QC 1966; Judge, Supreme Court of NSW, 1977, and Judge, Fed. Court of Australia, 1977–82; Pres., Trade Practices Tribunal, 1977–82. *Address:* (until Feb. 1996) High Court of Australia, Canberra, ACT 2600, Australia; (from Feb. 1996) Government House, Canberra, ACT 2600, Australia.

DEANE-DRUMMOND, Maj.-Gen. Anthony John, CB 1970; DSO 1960; MC 1942 and Bar, 1945; *b* 23 June 1917; *s* of late Col J. D. Deane-Drummond, DSO, OBE, MC; *m* 1944, Mary Evangeline Boyd; four *d*. *Educ:* Marlborough Coll.; RMA, Woolwich. Commissioned Royal Signals, 1937. War Service in Europe and N Africa; POW, Italy, 1941 (escaped, 1942); Staff Coll., 1945; Bde Major, 3rd Parachute Bde, 1946–47; Instructor, Sandhurst, 1949–51 and Staff Coll., 1952–55; CO, 22 Special Air Service Regt, 1957–60; Bde Comdr, 44 Parachute Bde, 1961–63; Asst Comdt, RMA, Sandhurst, 1963–66; GOC 3rd Division, 1966–68; ACDS (Operations), 1968–70, retired 1971. Col Comdt, Royal Corps of Signals, 1966–71. Director: Paper and Paper Products Industry Trng Bd, 1971–79; Wood Burning Centre, 1980–83. British Gliding Champion, 1957; Pilot, British Gliding Team, 1958, 1960, 1963, 1965. *Publications:* Return Ticket, 1951; Riot Control, 1975; Arrows of Fortune (autobiog.), 1991. *Recreations:* carpentry and carving, antique furniture restoration, shooting. *Address:* c/o Royal Bank of Scotland, 67 Lombard Street, EC3P 3DL.

DEAR, Geoffrey James, QPM 1982; DL; HM Inspector of Constabulary, since 1990; *b* 20 Sept. 1937; *er s* of Cecil William Dear and Violet Mildred (*née* Mackney); *m* 1958, Judith Ann Stocker; one *s* two *d*. *Educ:* Fletton Grammar Sch., Hunts; University Coll., London (LLB). Joined Peterborough Combined Police after cadet service, 1956; Mid-Anglia (now Cambridgeshire) Constab., 1965; Bramshill Scholarship, UCL, 1965–68 (Fellow, 1990); Asst Chief Constable (Ops), Notts (City and County), 1972–80; seconded as Dir of Comd Training, Bramshill, 1975–77; Metropolitan Police: Dep. Asst Comr, 1980–81; Asst Comr, 1981–85 (Personnel and Trng, 1981–84; Ops, 1984–85); Chief Constable, W Midlands Police, 1985–90. Member: Govt Adv. Cttee on Alcoholism, 1975–78; Council, RUSI, 1982–89 (Mem. Cttee, 1976–94). Lecture tour of Eastern USA univs, 1978; visited Memphis, Tenn, USA to advise on reorganisation of Police Dept, 1979. Vice Chm., London and SE Reg., Sports Council, 1984–85. Vice President: Warwickshire CCC, 1985–; W Midlands and Hereford & Worcester Grenadier Guards Assocs, 1992–. Hon. Fellow, Univ. of Central England in Birmingham, 1991. FRSA 1990. DL W Midlands, 1985. OStJ 1990. Queen's Commendation for Brave Conduct, 1979. *Publications:* (contrib.) The Police and the Community, 1975; articles in Police Jl and other pubns. *Recreations:* field sports, Rugby football (Pres., Met. Police RFC, 1983–85), fell-walking, reading, gardening, music. *Address:* Home Office, Block A,

Government Buildings, Whittington Road, Worcester WR5 2PA. *T:* Worcester (01905) 359564. *Club:* East India.

DEARING, Sir Ronald (Ernest), (Sir Ron), Kt 1984; CB 1979; Chairman: School Curriculum and Assessment Authority, since 1993; Camelot Group plc, since 1993; *b* 27 July 1930; *s* of late E. H. A. Dearing and of M. T. Dearing (*née* Hoyle); *m* 1954, Margaret Patricia Riley; two *d.* *Educ:* Doncaster Grammar Sch.; Hull Univ. (BScEcon); London Business Sch. (Sloan Fellow). Min. of Labour and Nat. Service, 1946–49; Min. of Power, 1949–62; HM Treasury, 1962–64; Min. of Power, Min. of Technology, DTI, 1965–72; Regional Dir, N Region, DTI, 1972–74, and Under-Sec., DTI later Dept of Industry, 1972–76; Dep. Sec. on nationalised industry matters, Dept of Industry, 1976–80; Dep. Chm., 1980–81, Chm., 1981–87, Post Office Corp.; Chm., Co. Durham Develt Co., 1987–90. Director (non-executive): Whitbread Co. plc, 1987–90; Prudential plc, 1987–91; IMI plc, 1988–95; British Coal, 1988–91; Erisson Ltd, 1988–93; English Estates, 1988–90; Chm., Northern Devel Co., 1990–94. Chairman: NICG, 1983–84; Accounting Standards Review Cttee, CCAB, 1987–88; Financial Reporting Council, 1990–93. Mem. Council, Industrial Soc., 1985–. CIMgt (CBIM 1981; Mem. Council, 1985–88; Vice-Chm., 1986; Gold Medal, 1994). Chairman: CNAA, 1987–88; PCFC, 1988–93; UFC, 1991–93; HEFCE, 1992–93. Mem. Governing Council, London Business Sch., 1985–89, Fellow, 1988; Mem. Council, Durham Univ., 1988–91; Chm., London Educn Business Partnership, 1989–92. Chm., Northern Sinfonia Appeals Cttee, 1993–94. Pres., Inst. of Direct Mkting, 1994–. Chancellor, Nottingham Univ., 1993–. Freeman, City of London, 1982. Hon. FEng 1992; Hon. FTCL 1993; Hon. Fellow, Inst. of Educn, 1995. Hon. Fellow, Sunderland Poly., 1991. Hon. DSc Hull, 1986; Hon. DTech CNAA, 1991; Hon. DCL: Durham, 1992; Northumbia, 1993; Hon. LLD Nottingham, 1993; Dr *hc* Humberside, 1993. *Recreations:* gardening, postal history. *Address:* c/o School Curriculum and Assessment Authority, 45 Notting Hill Gate, W11 3JB.

DEARNALEY, Dr Geoffrey, FRS 1993; Institute Scientist and Program Manager, Southwest Research Institute, since 1993; *b* 22 June 1930; *s* of Eric and Dora Dearnaley; *m* 1957, Jean Rosalind Beer; two *s.* *Educ:* Univ. of Cambridge (MA 1955; PhD 1956). Research Fellow, Pembroke Coll., Cambridge, 1955–58; joined AERE, Harwell, Nuclear Physics Division, 1958: Individual Merit Promotion, 1975; Chief Scientist, Surface Technologies, 1991–93. Vis. Prof. in Physics, Sussex Univ., 1972–. *Publications:* Semiconductor Counters for Nuclear Radiations, 1963; Ion Implantation, 1973; numerous articles on interaction of energetic ion beams with materials. *Recreations:* travel, walking, the life and work of William Blake. *Address:* Southwest Research Institute, 6220 Culebra Road, PO Drawer 28510, San Antonio, TX 78228–0510, USA. *T:* (210) 5225579.

DEARNLEY, Christopher Hugh, LVO 1990; MA (Oxon), DMus, FRCO; Organist and Director of Music, St Paul's Cathedral, 1968–90; *b* 11 Feb. 1930; 3rd *s* of Rev. Charles Dearnley; *m* 1957, Bridget (*née* Wateridge); three *s* one *d.* *Educ:* Cranleigh Sch., Surrey; Worcester Coll., Oxford. Organ Scholar, Worcester Coll., Oxford, 1948–52. Asst Organist, Salisbury Cathedral, and Music Master, the Cathedral Sch., Salisbury, 1954–57; Organist and Master of the Choristers, Salisbury Cathedral, 1957–67; Acting Dir of Music, Christ Church, St Laurence, Sydney, 1990–91; Organist *locum tenens,* St David's Cathedral, Hobart, 1991; Dir of Music, Trinity Coll., Univ. of Melbourne, 1992–93; Organist and Master of Choristers, St George's Cathedral, Perth, 1993–94. Pres., Incorporated Assoc. of Organists, 1968–70; Chairman: Friends of Cathedral Music, 1971–90 (Vice-Pres., 1990–); Harwich Festival, 1982–89 (Pres., 1989–); Percy Whitlock Trust, 1982–89 (Pres., 1989–). Dir, English Hymnal Co., 1970–. Patron: Nat. Accordian Orgn, 1989–; Organ Historical Trust of Australia, 1990–; Hon. Gov., Corp. of Sons of the Clergy, 1989–. *Publications:* The Treasury of English Church Music, Vol. III, 1965; English Church Music 1650–1750, 1970. *Recreations:* sketching, gardening, bush walking. *Address:* PO Box 102, Wilberforce, NSW 2756, Australia. *T:* (45) 750453.

DEAVE, John James; barrister-at-law; a Recorder of the Crown Court, since 1980; *b* 1 April 1928; *s* of Charles John Deave and Gertrude Debrit Deave; *m* 1958, Gillian Mary, *d* of Adm. Sir Manley Power, KCB, CBE, DSO; one *s* one *d.* *Educ:* Charterhouse; Pembroke Coll., Oxford (MA). Served RA, 2nd Lieut, 1946–48; Pembroke Coll., 1948–51; called to the Bar, Gray's Inn, 1952; in practice at Nottingham, 1957–. *Recreations:* history, gardening. *Address:* (chambers) 1 High Pavement, Nottingham NG1 1HF. *T:* Nottingham (0115) 941 8218. *Club:* Nottinghamshire United Services.

DeBAKEY, Prof. Michael Ellis, MD, MS; Chancellor, Baylor College of Medicine, since 1979 (Professor of Surgery, since 1948, Chairman of Department of Surgery, 1948–93, President, 1969–79, Chief Executive Officer, 1968–69, Baylor University College of Medicine; Vice-President for Medical Affairs, Baylor University, 1968–69); Surgeon-in-Chief, Ben Taub General Hospital, Houston, Texas, 1963–93; Director: First National Heart and Blood Vessel Research and Demonstration Center, 1976–84; DeBakey Heart Center, Baylor College of Medicine, since 1985; President, DeBakey Medical Foundation, since 1961; Consultant in Surgery to various Hospitals etc., in Texas, and to Walter Reed Army Hospital, Washington, DC; *b* 7 Sept. 1908; *s* of Shaker Morris and Raheeja Zorba DeBakey; *m* 1st, 1936, Diana Cooper (*d* 1972); four *s*; 2nd, 1975, Katrin Fehlhaber; one *d.* *Educ:* Tulane Univ., New Orleans, La, USA (Distinguished Alumnus of Year, 1974). Residency in New Orleans, Strasbourg, and Heidelberg, 1933–36; Instructor, Dept of Surgery, Tulane Univ., 1937–40; Asst Prof. of Surgery, 1940–46; Associate Prof. of Surgery, 1946–48. Colonel Army of US (Reserve). In Office of Surgeon-General, 1942–46, latterly Director Surgical Consultant Div. (US Army Legion of Merit, 1945). Chairman, President's Commission on Heart Disease, Cancer and Stroke, 1964; US Chm., Task for Mechanical Circulatory Assistance, Jt US-USSR Cttee, 1974; Dir, Cardiovascular Res. and Trng Center, Methodist Hosp. (Houston), 1968–75; Adv. Council, Nat. Heart, Lung, Blood Inst., 1982–86; has served on governmental and university cttees, etc., concerned with public health, research and medical education. Mem. Adv. Editorial Bds: Ann. Surg., 1970–; Coeur, 1969–; Biomedical Materials and Artificial Organs, 1971–; Editor, Jl of Vascular Surgery, 1984–88. Member and Hon. Member of medical societies, including: Inst. of Medicine, Nat. Acad. of Sciences (Sen. Mem., 1981); American Assoc. for Thoracic Surgery (Pres. 1959); International Cardiovascular Society (Pres. 1959); BMA (Hon. Foreign Corresp. Member 1966); Royal Society Med., London; Acad. of Medical Sciences, USSR; US—China Physicians Friendship Assoc., 1974; Assoc. Internat. Vasc. Surgeons (Pres., 1983); Southern Surgical Assoc. (Pres., 1989–90); Assoc. Française de Chirurgie, 1991; Acad. of Athens, 1992; Royal Coll. of Physicians and Surgeons of USA (Hon. Dist. Fellow, 1992); Amer. Inst. Med. and Biol Engrng (Founding Fellow, 1993). Hon. FRCS 1974. Has received numerous awards from American and foreign medical institutions, and also honorary doctorates; Hektoen Gold Medal, Amer. Med. Assoc., 1954, 1970; Presidential Medal of Freedom with Distinction, 1969; Meritorious Civilian Service Medal, 1970; USSR Acad. of Science 50th Anniversary Jubilee Medal, 1973; Nat. Medal of Science, 1987; Markowitz Award, Acad. of Surgical Res., 1989; Assoc. of Amer. Med. Colls. Award, 1988; Crile Award, Internat. Platform Assoc., 1988; Thomas Alva Edison Foundn Award, 1988; Scripps Clinic and Res. Foundn Inaugural Award, 1988; first Michael DeBakey Medal, American Soc of Mech. Engrs, 1989; Gibbon Award, Amer. Soc. for Extracorporeal Tech., 1992; Jacobs Award, Amer. Task Force for Lebanon, 1992; Maxwell Finland Award, Nat. Foundn for Infectious Diseases, 1992; Ellis Island Medal of Honor, Nat. Ethics Coalition of Orgns, 1993; Lifetime Achievement Award, Amer. Heart Assoc., 1994. Merit Order of the Republic, 1st class (Egypt), 1980; The Independence of Jordan Medal, 1st class, 1980; Sovereign Order of the Knights of the Hospital of St John (Denmark), 1980; Commander's Cross, Order of Merit (Germany), 1992; Order of Independence 1st cl. medal (UAE), 1992. *Publications:* The Blood Bank and the Technique and Therapeutics of Transfusions, 1942; (with B. M. Cohen) Buerger's Disease, 1962; A Surgeon's Diary of a Visit to China, 1974; The Living Heart, 1977; The Living Heart Diet, 1984; The Living Heart Brand Name Shopper's Guide, 1992; The Living Heart Guide to Eating Out, 1993; contributions to standard textbooks of medicine and surgery, and many symposia; Editor, Year Book of General Surgery, etc; numerous articles in medical journals. *Recreations:* literature, music. *Address:* Baylor College of Medicine, One Baylor Plaza, Houston, TX 77030, USA. *T:* (713) 7979353. *Clubs:* Cosmos, University Federal (Washington, DC); River Oaks Country (Houston, Texas).

de BASTO, Gerald Arthur; Judge of the High Court of Hong Kong, 1982–89; *b* London, 31 Dec. 1924; *s* of Bernard de Basto and Lucie Marie, *d* of Raoul Melchior Pattard, Paris; *m* 1961, Diana, *d* of Dr Frederick Osborne Busby Wilkinson; two *s.* *Educ:* Riverview Coll., Sydney, Australia; Univ. of Sydney (LLB). Called to the Bar: Supreme Court of New South Wales and High Court of Australia, 1952; Lincoln's Inn, 1955; admitted to the Hong Kong Bar, 1957; Chairman, Hong Kong Bar, 1968–70, 1973; QC 1968; Judge of the District Court of Hong Kong, 1973–82; Pres., Deportation Tribunal, 1986–89. *Recreations:* antiques, travel, reading. *Address:* Canterbury Lodge, 21 Canterbury Drive, Bishopscourt, 7700, South Africa. *T:* (21) 7625626. *Clubs:* Boodle's; Hong Kong, Royal Hong Kong Jockey (Hong Kong).

de BELLAIGUE, Sir Geoffrey, KCVO 1986 (CVO 1976; LVO 1968); FSA; FBA 1992; Director of the Royal Collection, 1988–March 1996; Surveyor of the Queen's Works of Art, 1972–March 1996; *b* 12 March 1931; *s* of Vicomte Pierre de Bellaigue and Marie-Antoinette Ladd; *m* 1971, Sheila, MVO, 2nd *d* of late Rt Rev. J. K. Russell; two *d.* *Educ:* Wellington Coll.; Trinity Coll., Cambridge (BA 1954, MA 1959); Ecole du Louvre. With J. Henry Schroeder & Co., 1954–59; with the National Trust, Waddesdon Manor, 1960–63 (Keeper of the Collection, 1962–63); Dep. Surveyor, the Queen's Work's of Art, 1963–72. Mem., Exec. Cttee, Nat. Art Collections Fund, 1977–. Hon. Pres., French Porcelain Soc., 1985–. Officier de l'Ordre des Arts et des Lettres (France), 1987. *Publications:* The James A. de Rothschild Collection at Waddesdon Manor: furniture, clocks and gilt bronzes, 1974; (jtly) Buckingham Palace, 1986; Sèvres Porcelain in the Collection of HM the Queen, Vol. I, 1986; (with S. Eriksen) Sèvres Porcelain, 1987; articles in art historical jls and exhibn catalogues, principally for The Queen's Gallery. *Address:* Store Tower, Windsor Castle, Windsor, Berks SL4 1NJ.

DE BENEDETTI, Carlo; Cavaliere del Lavoro, Italy, 1983; Chairman 1983, Chief Executive 1978, Olivetti SpA; Vice-Chairman/Chief Executive: Compagnie Industriali Riunite, 1976; Compagnia Finanziaria De Benedetti, 1985; Chairman: Cerus, 1986; Sogefi, 1981; Vice-Chairman, Cofir, 1987; *b* 14 Nov. 1934; *m*; three *s.* *Educ:* Turin Polytechnic (degree in electrotech. engrg). Chm./Chief Exec., Gilardini, 1972–76; Chief Exec., Fiat, 1976. Director: Pirelli SpA; Editoriale Valeo; GIM; l'Espresso SpA; Member: Exec. Cttee, Confindustria; Internat. Council, J. P. Morgan, NY, 1980; European Adv. Cttee, NY Stock Exchange, 1985; Internat. Adv. Council, Allianz, Germany, 1989. Dir, Center for Strategic and Internat. Studies, Washington, 1978; Member: Bd of Trustees, Solomon R. Guggenheim Foundn, NY, 1984; Roundtable of European Industrialists, Brussels. Foreign Mem., Royal Swedish Acad. of Engrg Scis, Stockholm, 1987. *Publications:* lectures and articles in business jls. *Address:* Olivetti SpA, Via Jervis 77, 10015 Ivrea, Italy. *T:* (125) 522011.

DEBENHAM, Sir Gilbert Ridley, 3rd Bt, *cr* 1931; *b* 28 June 1906; 2nd *s* of Sir Ernest Ridley Debenham, 1st Bt, JP; *S* brother, Sir Piers Debenham, 2nd Bt, 1964; *m* 1935, Violet Mary (*d* 1994), *e d* of late His Honour Judge (George Herbert) Higgins; two *s* one *d* (and one *s* decd). *Educ:* Eton; Trinity Coll., Cambridge (BA 1928; BChir 1935). DPM 1946; MRCPsych 1971. *Heir: g s* Thomas Adam Debenham, *b* 28 Feb. 1971. *Address:* Tonerspuddle Farm, Dorchester, Dorset.

DEBENHAM TAYLOR, John, CMG 1967; OBE 1959; TD 1967; HM Diplomatic Service, retired; *b* 25 April 1920; *s* of John Francis Taylor and Harriett Beatrice (*née* Williams); *m* 1966, Gillian May James; one *d.* *Educ:* Aldenham School. Eastern Counties Farmers Assoc. Ltd, Ipswich and Great Yarmouth, 1936–39. Commd in RA (TA), Feb. 1939; served War of 1939–46 in Finland, Middle East, UK and SE Asia (despatches, 1946). Foreign Office, 1946; Control Commn for Germany, 1947–49; 2nd Sec., Bangkok, 1950; Actg Consul, Songkhla, 1951–52; Vice-Consul, Hanoi, 1952–53; FO, 1953–54; 1st Sec., Bangkok, 1954–56; FO, 1956–58; Singapore, 1958–59; FO, 1960–64; Counsellor, 1964; Counsellor: Kuala Lumpur, 1964–66; FCO (formerly FO), 1966–69; Washington, 1969–72; Paris, 1972–73; FCO, 1973–77. *Recreations:* walking, reading, history. *Address:* The East Wing, Gunton Hall, Norfolk NR11 7HJ. *T:* Cromer (01263) 768301. *Club:* Naval and Military.

de BERNIÈRE-SMART, Major Reginald Piers Alexander; Director, The Shaftesbury Homes and Arethusa, 1988–89, retired (General Secretary, 1971–88); general duties, Chichester Division, SSAFA/FHS, since 1995 (caseworker, 1990–94); *b* 3 March 1924; *s* of Kenneth de Bernière-Smart and Audrey (*née* Brown); *m* 1951, Jean Ashton Smithells; one *s* two *d.* *Educ:* Bowden House, Seaford; Bradfield Coll. Commnd The Queen's Bays (2nd Dragoon Guards), 1943; Italian Campaign, 1944–45 (despatches); Staff, RAC OCTU and Mons OCS, 1948–49; GSO 3 7th Armd Bde, 1951, Adjt, The Queen's Bays, 1952–54; Adjt, RAC Centre, Bovington, 1956–58; retired from 1st The Queen's Dragoon Guards, 1959. Exec. Sec., British Diabetic Assoc., 1960–65; joined Shaftesbury Homes and Arethusa exec. staff, 1966. Dir, Wad (West Wittering) Management Co., 1992–94. Chm., Management Cttee, Bradfield Club, Peckham, 1990–92 (Mem. Council, 1992–). Member: IAM, 1959–; NCVCCO, 1971–89. West Wittering PCC, 1991–. Life Governor, ICRF, 1990. *Recreations:* open air activities, photography, steam and model railways, theatre, poetry, militaria. *Address:* 9 The Wad, West Wittering, Chichester, W Sussex PO20 8AH. *T:* Birdham (01243) 511072. *Clubs:* Victoria League for Commonwealth Friendship; West Wittering Sailing.

de BLANK, Justin Robert; Chairman and Managing Director, Justin de Blank Provisions Ltd, since 1968; Chairman, de Blank Restaurants, since 1986; Managing Director, Justin de Blank Foods Ltd, 1993; *b* 25 Feb. 1927; *s* of William de Blank and Agnes Frances de Blank (*née* Crossley); *m* 1st, 1972, Mary Jacqueline Christina du Bois Godet (Molly); 2nd, 1977, Melanie Alexandra Margaret Irwin; three *d.* *Educ:* Grenham House School, Birchington-on-Sea; Marlborough College; Corpus Christi College, Cambridge (BA); Royal Acad. Sch. of Architecture. Unilever, 1953–58; J. Walter Thompson, London and Paris, 1958–66; Conran Design Group, 1967; formed own company, 1968. Director: Kitchen Range Foods Ltd, 1976–; Millers Damsels Ltd, 1989–. *Recreations:* gardening, golf, food and wine. *Address:* 42 Elizabeth Street, SW1W 9NZ. *T:* 0171–730 2607;

Breck's Farmhouse, Thornage, Holt, Norfolk NR25 7JJ. *T:* Holt (01263) 713276. *Clubs:* Annabel's; Royal West Norfolk Golf.

de BOER, Anthony Peter, CBE 1982; Vice-Chairman, Royal Automobile Club, 1985–90, retired (Member, Committee, 1984–90); *b* 22 June 1918; *s* of Goffe de Boer and Irene Kathleen (*née* Grist); *m* 1942, Pamela Agnes Norah Bullock; one *s*. *Educ:* Westminster School. Served War of 1939–45: RE (AA), 1939–40; Indian Army, 6th Gurkha Rifles, 1940–43; RIASC, 1944–46; Major 1944. Joined Royal Dutch/Shell Gp, 1937: served in China, Sudan, Ethiopia, Egypt, Palestine, 1946–58; Area Co-ordinator, Africa and Middle East, 1959–63; Chm., Shell Trinidad, 1963–64; Man. Dir, Marketing, Shell Mex & BP, 1964–67; Deputy Chairman: Wm Cory & Son, 1968–71; Associated Heat Services Ltd, 1969–76; Chairman: Anvil Petroleum plc (formerly Attock Oil Co.), 1974–85; Tomatin Distillers plc, 1978–85; Steel Brothers Hldgs, 1980–87 (Dir, 1971–87); Channel Tunnel Develts (1981), 1981–84; British Road Fedn, 1972–87 (Vice-Pres., 1987–); Director: Nat. Bus Co., 1969–83; Tarmac plc, 1971–83; British Transport Advertising, 1973–83; Internat. Road Fedn, 1974–87; Chloride Gp, 1976–85; Burmah Oil plc, 1978–85; Mem. Policy Cttee, Price Waterhouse, 1979–86. Mem., Bd, British Travel Assoc., 1965–67. Chm., Keep Britain Tidy Gp, 1969–79 (Vice-Pres., 1979–). Mem. Council, CBI, 1980–83; Mem. Court, Sussex Univ., 1991– (Mem. Council, 1969–91); Chm., Indep. Schools Careers Org., 1973–88 (Vice-Pres., 1988–); Pres., Fuel Luncheon Club, 1967–69; Dir, Brighton and Hove Albion Football Club, 1969–72. Freeman, City of London; Liveryman, Coach Makers' and Coach Harness Makers' Co. FIMgt (FBIM 1970; Mem. Council 1974). *Recreations:* racing, theatre, gardening. *Address:* Southmead, South Avenue, Hurstpierpoint, Hassocks, W Sussex BN6 9QB. *T:* Brighton (01273) 833068. *Clubs:* Royal Automobile, Garrick.

de BONO, Dr Edward Francis Charles Publius; Lecturer in Medicine, Department of Medicine, University of Cambridge, 1976–83; Director of The Cognitive Research Trust, Cambridge, since 1971; Secretary-General, Supranational Independent Thinking Organisation (SITO), since 1983; *b* 19 May 1933; *s* of late Prof. Joseph de Bono, CBE and of Josephine de Bono; *m* 1971, Josephine Hall-White; two *s*. *Educ:* St Edward's Coll., Malta; Royal Univ. of Malta; Christ Church, Oxford (Rhodes Scholar). BSc, MD Malta; DPhil Oxon; PhD Cantab. Research Asst, Dept of Regius Prof. of Medicine, Univ. of Oxford, 1958–60; Jun. Lectr in Med., Oxford, 1960–61; Asst Dir of Res., Dept of Investigative Medicine, Cambridge Univ., 1963–76. Research Associate: also Hon. Registrar, St Thomas' Hosp. Med. Sch., Univ. of London; Harvard Med. Sch., and Hon. Consultant, Boston City Hosp., 1965–66. TV series: The Greatest Thinkers, 1981; de Bono's Thinking Course, 1982. *Publications:* The Use of Lateral Thinking, 1967; The Five-Day Course in Thinking, 1968; The Mechanism of Mind, 1969; Lateral Thinking: a textbook of creativity, 1970; The Dog Exercising Machine, 1970; Technology Today, 1971; Practical Thinking, 1971; Lateral Thinking for Management, 1971; Beyond Yes and No, 1972; Children Solve Problems, 1972; Eureka!: an illustrated history of inventions from the wheel to the computer, 1974; Teaching Thinking, 1976; The Greatest Thinkers, 1976; Wordpower, 1977; The Happiness Purpose, 1977; The Case of the Disappearing Elephant, 1977; Opportunities: a handbook of business opportunity search, 1978; Future Positive, 1979; Atlas of Management Thinking, 1981; de Bono's Thinking Course, 1982; Tactics: the art and science of success, 1984; Conflicts: a better way to resolve them, 1985; Six Thinking Hats, 1985; Masterthinker's Handbook, 1985; Letters to Thinkers, 1987; I am Right, You are Wrong, 1990; Positive Revolution for Brazil, 1990; Handbook for a Positive Revolution, 1990; Six Action Shoes, 1992; Sur/Petition, 1992; Serious Creativity, 1992; Teach your child to think, 1992; Water Logic, 1993; contribs to Nature, Lancet, Clinical Science, Amer. Jl of Physiology, etc. *Recreations:* travel, toys, thinking. *Address:* L2 Albany, Piccadilly, W1V 9RR. *Club:* Athenæum.

de BOTTON, Gilbert; Chairman, Global Asset Management Ltd, since 1983; *b* 16 Feb. 1935; *s* of Jacques and Yolande de Botton; *m* 1st, 1962, Jacqueline (*née* Burgauer) (marr. diss. 1988); one *s* one *d*; 2nd, 1990, Hon. Mrs Janet Green, *d* of Baron Wolfson, *qv*. *Educ:* Victoria College, Alexandria, Egypt; Hebrew Univ., Jerusalem (BA Econ 1955); Columbia Univ. (MA 1957). Ufitec SA Union Financière, Zürich, 1960–68; Managing Director, Rothschild Bank AG, Zürich, 1968–82. Trustee, Tate Gallery, 1985–92. *Address:* 1 Eaton Close, SW1W 8JX. *T:* 0171–730 9305; (office) 0171–493 9990. *Club:* Carlton.

DEBRÉ, Jean Louis; Minister of the Interior, France, since 1995; *b* Toulouse, 30 Sept. 1944; *s* of Michel Jean-Pierre Debré, *qv*; *m* 1971, Anne-Marie Engel; two *s* one *d*. *Educ:* Lycée Janson-de-Sailly; Institut d'Etudes Politiques, Paris; Faculté de Droit, Paris (DenD); Ecole Nationale de la Magistrature. Asst, Faculté de Droit, Paris, 1972–75; Technical Counsellor, then Chargé de Mission, office of Jacques Chirac, as Minister of Agric., 1973–74, Minister of the Interior, 1974 and Prime Minister, 1974–76; Dep. Public Prosecutor, High Court of Evry, 1976–78; Magistrate, Central Admin, Ministry of Justice, 1978; Chef de Cabinet to Minister of the Budget, 1978; Examng Magistrate, High Court of Paris, 1979. Deputy (RPR) for Eure, 1986–; Vice-Pres., RPR Gp in Nat. Assembly, 1990–. Councillor, Evreux, 1989–. *Publications:* Les Idées constitutionnelles du Général de Gaulle, 1974; La Constitution de la Ve République, 1974; Le Pouvoir politique, 1977; Le Gaulisme, 1978; La Justice au XIXe, 1981; Les Républiques des Avocats, 1984; Le Curieux, 1986. *Recreations:* horse-riding, tennis. *Address:* Ministère de l'Interieur, place Beauvau, 75800 Paris, France.

DEBRÉ, Michel Jean-Pierre; Membre de l'Académie française, 1988; Deputy from La Réunion, French National Assembly, 1963–86 (re-elected 1967, 1968, 1973, 1978, 1981, 1982) and since 1988; *b* 15 Jan. 1912; *s* of late Prof. Robert Debré and Dr Jeanne Debré (*née* Debat-Ponsan); *m* 1936, Anne-Marie Lemaresquier; four *s*. *Educ:* Lycée Louis-le-Grand; Faculté de Droit de Paris (LLD); Ecole Libre des Sciences Politiques; Cavalry Sch., Saumur. Auditeur, Conseil d'Etat, 1934; French Army, 1939–40; Résistance clandestine, 1941–44; Commissaire de la République, Angers region, 1944–45; Saar Economic Mission, 1947; Secretary-General for German and Austrian Affairs, 1948. Senator from Indre et Loire, 1948, re-elected 1955; Minister of Justice, 1958–59; Prime Minister, 1959–62; Minister of Economic Affairs and Finances, 1966–68; Minister for Foreign Affairs, 1968–69; Minister for National Defence, 1969–73. Member, European Parliament, 1979–80. Mem. from Amboise, Conseil Général of Indre-et-Loire, 1951–70, 1976–82 and 1988; Mayor of Amboise, 1966–89. Member, Rassemblement pour la République. Officer Légion d'Honneur, Croix de Guerre, Rosette of Résistance, Free French Medal, Medal of Escaped Prisoners. *Publications:* La Mort de l'Etat Républicain, 1947; La République et son Pouvoir, 1950; La République et ses Problèmes, 1952; Ces Princes qui nous Gouvernent, 1957; Au Service de la Nation, 1963; Jeunesse, quelle France te faut-il?, 1965; (with Jean-Louis Debré) Le gaullisme, 1967; Une certaine idée de la France, 1972; Combat pour les Elections, 1973; Une Politique pour la Réunion, 1974; Ami ou Ennemi du Peuple, 1975; Français, choisissons l'espoir, 1979; Lettre ouverte aux Français sur la reconquête de la France, 1980; Peut-on lutter contre le chômage?, 1982; Trois Républiques pour une France (mémoires): vol. I, Combattre, 1984; vol. II, Agir, 1988; vol. III, Gouverner, 1988; vol. IV, Gouverner autrement, 1993; vol. V, Combattre toujours, 1994; Entretiens avec le Général de Gaulle, 1993; as de Jacquier (with M. Emmanuel Monick): Refaire la France, 1944; Demain la Paix, 1945. *Recreation:* equitation. *Address:* 20 rue Jacob, 75006 Paris, France.

DEBREU, Prof. Gerard; Professor of Economics, 1962–91, Professor of Mathematics, 1975–91, and University Professor, 1985–91, now Emeritus, University of California, Berkeley; *b* 4 July 1921; *s* of Camille Debreu and Fernande (*née* Decharne); *m* 1945, Françoise Bled; two *d*. *Educ:* Ecole Normale Supérieure, Paris; Agrégé de l'Université, Paris, 1946. DSc Univ. de Paris, 1956. Research Associate: Centre National de la Recherche Scientifique, Paris, 1946–48; Cowles Commn for Research in Economics, Univ. of Chicago, 1950–55; Associate Prof. of Economics, Cowles Foundn for Research in Economics, Yale Univ., 1955–61. Fellow, Amer. Acad. of Arts and Sciences, 1970; President: Econometric Soc., 1971; American-Economic Assoc., 1990. Member: Nat. Acad. of Sciences, USA, 1977; Amer. Philos. Soc., 1984; Dist. Fellow, Amer. Economic Assoc., 1982; For. Associate, French Acad. of Scis, 1984. Hon. degrees: Bonn, 1977; Lausanne, 1980; Northwestern, 1981; Toulouse, 1983; Yale, 1987; Université de Bordeaux I, 1988. Nobel Prize in Economic Sciences, 1983. Officier de la Légion d'Honneur, 1993 (Chevalier, 1976); Comdr de l'Ordre National du Mérite, 1984. *Publications:* Theory of Value: an axiomatic analysis of economic equilibrium, 1959, 2nd edn 1971 (trans. into French, Spanish, German and Japanese); Mathematical Economics: twenty papers, 1983; contribs to Econometrica, Procs of Nat. Acad. of Sciences, Review of Economic Studies, Economie Appliquée, Procs of Amer. Math. Soc., Internat. Economic Review, Review of Economic Studies, La Décision, Jl of Mathematical Economics, Amer. Economic Review. *Address:* Department of Economics, 787 Evans Hall, University of California, Berkeley, CA 94720, USA. *T:* (510) 6427284.

de BROKE; *see* Willoughby de Broke.

de BRUYNE, Dr Norman Adrian, FRS 1967; FEng 1976; Chairman, Techne Inc., 1973–88 (President, 1967–73); *b* 8 Nov. 1904; *s* of Pieter Adriaan de Bruyne and Maud de Bruyne (*née* Mattock); *m* 1940, Elma Lilian Marsh; one *s* one *d*. *Educ:* Lancing Coll.; Trinity Coll., Cambridge. MA 1930, PhD 1930. Fellow of Trinity Coll., Cambridge, 1928–44. Managing Director: Aero Research Ltd, 1934–48; Ciba (ARL) Ltd, 1948–60; Techne (Cambridge) Ltd, 1964–67. Dir, Eastern Electricity Bd, 1962–67. Awarded Simms Gold Medal, RAeS, 1937. FInstP 1944; FRAeS 1955; *Recreation:* inventing. *Address:* 3700 Brunswick Pike, Princeton, NJ 08540, USA. *T:* (609) 4529275.

DE BUTTS, Brig. Frederick Manus, CMG 1967; OBE 1961 (MBE 1943); DL; *b* 17 April 1916; *s* of late Brig. F. C. De Butts, CB, DSO, MC, and K. P. M. O'Donnell; *m* 1944, Evelyn Cecilia, *d* of Sir Walter Halsey, 2nd Bt; one *s* one *d*. *Educ:* Wellington Coll.; Oriel Coll., Oxford. Commissioned into Somerset LI, 1937. Served War of 1939–45, in Middle East, Italy, France and Germany (despatches, 1941, 1944). Staff Coll., 1944; Malaya (despatches, 1950); Joint Services Staff Coll., 1954; Bt Lieut-Colonel, 1957; Commanded 3rd Bn Aden Protectorate Levies, 1958–60; Bde Colonel, Light Infantry, 1961–64; Comdr, Trucial Oman Scouts, 1964–67; HQ Home Counties District, Shorncliffe, Kent, 1967–68; Defence Attaché, Cairo, 1968–71; retired 1971; employed on contract as COS (Brig.), MoD, United Arab Emirates, 1971–73; Hon. Brig. 1973. Mem., Dacorum DC, 1976–83. Hon. Dir, Herts Soc., 1981–91. County Chm., 1973–76, County Comr, 1976–81, Vice-Pres., 1981–89, Pres., 1989–, Herts Scouts; Vice-Pres., Herts Girl Guides, 1981–; Governor, Abbot's Hill School, 1971–92 (Chm., 1975–84). DL Herts 1975. *Publication:* Now the Dust has Settled: memories of war and peace 1939–1994, 1995. *Recreations:* tennis, hill-walking, ski-ing. *Address:* Church Cottage, Hoggeston, Buckingham, Bucks MK18 3LL. *T:* Winslow (01296) 713811.

DEBY, John Bedford; QC 1980; a Recorder of the Crown Court, since 1977; *b* 19 Dec. 1931; *s* of Reginald Bedford Deby and Irene (*née* Slater). *Educ:* Winchester Coll.; Trinity Coll., Cambridge (MA). Called to the Bar, Inner Temple, 1954, Bencher, 1986. *Address:* 11 Britannia Road, Fulham, SW6 2HJ. *T:* 0171–736 4976.

de CARDI, Beatrice Eileen, OBE 1973; retired 1973, but continuing archæological research in Lower Gulf countries; *b* 5 June 1914; *d* of Edwin Count de Cardi and Christine Berbette Wurrflein. *Educ:* St Paul's Girls' Sch.; University Coll. London (BA). Secretary (later Asst), London Museum, 1936–44; Personal Asst to Representative of Allied Supplies Exec. of War Cabinet in China, 1944–45; Asst UK Trade Comr: Delhi, 1946; Karachi, 1947; Lahore, 1948–49; Asst Sec. (title changed to Sec.), Council for British Archæology, 1949–73. Archæological research: in Kalat, Pakistan Baluchistan, 1948; in Afghanistan, 1949; directed excavations: in Kalat, 1957; at Bampur, Persian Baluchistan, 1966; survey in Ras al-Khaimah (then Trucial States), 1968; Middle East lecture tour for British Council, 1970; survey with RGS's Musandam Expedn (Northern Oman), 1971–72; directed archæological research projects: in Qatar, 1973–74; in Central Oman, 1974–76, 1978; survey in Ras al-Khaimah, 1977, 1982, 1992. Winston Churchill Meml Trust Fellowship for work in Oman, 1973. FSA 1950 (Vice-Pres., 1976–80; Dir, 1980–83). Al-Qasimi Medal (UAE), 1989 (for services to Ras al-Khaimah); Burton Meml Medal, RAS, 1993. *Publications:* Excavations at Bampur, a third millennium settlement in Persian Baluchistan, 1966 (Vol. 51, Pt 3, Anthropological Papers of the American Museum of Natural History), 1970; Archaeological Surveys in Baluchistan 1948 and 1957 (Inst. of Archaeology, Occasional Paper No 8), 1983; contribs to Antiquity, Iran, Pakistan Archæology, East and West, Jl of Oman Studies, Oriens Antiquus, Proc. Seminar for Arabian Studies. *Recreations:* archæological fieldwork, travel, cooking. *Address:* 1a Douro Place, Victoria Road, W8 5PH. *T:* 0171–937 9740.

de CARMOY, Hervé Pierre, Comte de Carmoy; Chairman and Chief Executive, Banque Industrielle et Mobilière Privée, since 1992; *b* 4 Jan. 1937; *s* of Guy de Carmoy and Marie de Gourcuff; *m* Roseline de Rohan Chabot; two *c*. *Educ:* Institut d'Etudes Politiques, Paris; Cornell Univ. Gen. Man., Western Europe, Chase Manhattan Bank, 1963–78; Chm., Exec. Bd, Midland Bank, Paris, 1978–79; Gen. Man., Europe, Midland Bank, London, 1979–84; Chief Exec., Internat. Midland Bank, London, 1984–86; Dir and Chief Exec., Global Banking Sector, Midland Bank, 1986–88; Chief Exec. Officer, Société Générale de Belgique, 1988–91; Chm. and Chief Exec., Union Minière, 1989–91. Chairman: Cimenteries Belges Réunies, 1989–; Gechem, 1989–; Parvalind Gérance, 1991–; Vice Chm., Générale de Banque, 1989–. Commandeur de la Légion d'Honneur (Côte d'Ivoire), 1978; Chevalier de l'Ordre du Mérite (France), 1987; Chevalier de la Légion d'Honneur (France), 1992. *Publications:* Third World Debt, 1987; Stratégie Bancaire: le refus de la dérive, 1988. *Recreations:* tennis, music. *Address:* 10 rue Guynemer, 75006 Paris, France; Banque Industrielle et Mobilière Privée, 39 rue d'Anjou, 75008 Paris. *Club:* Travellers' (Paris).

de CHAMBRUN, Comtesse; Raine; *b* 9 Sept. 1929; *d* of late Alexander George McCorquodale and of Dame Barbara Cartland, *qv*; *m* 1st, 1948, Earl of Dartmouth (marr. diss. 1976), *qv*; three *s* one *d*; 2nd, 1976, 8th Earl Spencer, LVO; 3rd, 1993, Comte Jean-François de Chambrun. Westminster City Councillor, 1954–65 (served on various cttees); Member: for Lewisham West, LCC, 1958–65 (served on Town Planning, Parks, Staff Appeals Cttees); for Richmond upon Thames, GLC, 1967–73; GLC Gen. Purposes Cttee, 1971–73; Chm., GLC Historic Buildings Bd, 1968–71; Mem., Environmental Planning Cttee, 1967–71; Chm., Covent Garden Develt Cttee, 1971–72; Chm., Govt working party on Human Habitat in connection with UN Conf. on Environment, Stockholm (June 1972), 1971–72 (report: How Do You Want to Live?); Chm., UK Exec., European

Architectural Heritage Year, 1975. British Tourist Authority: Member: Infrastructure Cttee, 1972–86; Board, 1982–93; Chairman: Spas Cttee, 1982–83; Accommodation Cttee (formerly Hotels and Restaurants Cttee), 1983–93; Develt Cttee, 1986–93; Commended Hotels Panel, 1986–90; Cttee, Britain Welcomes Japan, 1990–93; Come to Britain Awards, 1990–93; Member: English Tourist Bd, 1971–75; Adv. Council, V&A Museum, 1980–83; Cttee of Honour, Business Sponsorship of the Arts, 1980–; Tourism Deptl Adv. Cttee, Surrey Univ.; Commn de Tourisme Prestige, Nice. Mem. Jury, improvement of Promenade des Anglais, Nice. Formerly LCC Voluntary Care Cttee Worker, Wandsworth and Vauxhall. Hon. Dr Laws, Dartmouth Coll., USA. *Publications:* What Is Our Heritage?, 1975; The Spencers on Spas (with photographs by Earl Spencer), 1983; Japan and the East (with photographs by Earl Spencer), 1986. *Address:* 24 Farm Street, W1X 7RE. *T:* 0171–495 4525, *Fax:* 0171–495 4524; Château de Garibondy, Chemin de Garibondy, 06110 Le Cannet, France.

de CHASSIRON, Charles Richard Lucien; HM Diplomatic Service; Ambassador to Estonia, since 1994; *b* 27 April 1948; *s* of Hugo and Deane de Chassiron; *m* 1974, Britt-Marie Medhammar; one *s* one *d.* *Educ:* Jesus Coll., Univ. of Cambridge (BA Hons 1969, MA 1973); Univ. of Harvard (MPA 1971). Joined Diplomatic Service, 1971; service in: Stockholm, 1972–75; Maputo, 1975–78; Mem., UK Delegn at Lancaster House Conf. on Rhodesia, 1979; FCO, 1980–82; service in Brasilia, 1982–85; Asst Hd, later Hd, S America Dept, FCO, 1985–89; Counsellor (Comm./Econ.), Rome, 1989–94. *Recreations:* art history, walking, tennis. *Address:* c/o Foreign and Commonwealth Office, SW1A 2AH.

DECIES, 7th Baron *cr* 1812 (Ire.); **Marcus Hugh Tristram de la Poer Beresford;** *b* 5 Aug. 1948; *o s* of 6th Baron Decies and of his 2nd wife, Diana, *d* of Wing Comdr George Turner-Cain and *widow* of Major David Galsworthy; *S* father, 1992; *m* 1st, 1970, Sarah Jane Gunnell (marr. diss. 1974); 2nd, 1981, Edel Jeannette, *d* of late Vincent Hendron; two *s* one *d.* *Educ:* St Columba's Coll.; Dublin Univ. (MLitt). *Heir:* *s* Hon. Robert Marcus Duncan de la Poer Beresford, *b* 14 July 1988.

DE CLERCQ, Willy; MP; Member (L) European Parliament, 1979–81, and since 1989; Minister of State, Belgium, since 1985; *b* 8 July 1927; *s* of Frans De Clercq; *m* 1953, Fernande Fazzi; three *c.* *Educ:* Ghent Univ. (Dr in Law 1950); Univ. of Syracuse, USA (MA SocSci 1951). Called to Belgian Bar, 1951; Municipal Councillor, Ghent, 1952–79; Dep. Sec.-Gen., Belgian Liberal Party, 1957; MP Ghent-Eeklo, 1958–85; Dep. State Sec., Min. of Budget, 1960; Leader, Parly Gp of Belgian Liberal Party, 1965; Dep. Prime Minister, 1966–68; created Flemish Liberal Party (PVV) (Chm., 1972–73 and 1977–81); Dep. Prime Minister, 1973; Minister of Finance, 1974–77 (Chm., Interim Cttee, IMF; Mem., Bd of Governors, EIB; Governor, World Bank); Dep. Prime Minister and Minister of Finance and Foreign Trade, 1981–85; Mem., Commn of European Communities, 1985–88; Chm., External Econ. Relations Cttee, Eur. Parlt, 1989–. Pres., European Liberal Democrat and Reform Party (formerly Fedn of Europ. Liberal Democratic and Reform Parties), 1981–85 and 1991–. Comdr, Order of Leopold; Grand Cross, Order of Leopold II; holds numerous foreign decorations. *Address:* (office) Belliardstraat 97–113, 1047 Brussels, Belgium. *T:* (2) 2845149; (home) Cyriel Buyssestraat 12, 9000 Ghent, Belgium. *T:* (9) 2211813.

de CLIFFORD, 27th Baron *cr* 1299; **John Edward Southwell Russell;** *b* 8 June 1928; *s* of 26th Baron de Clifford, OBE, TD, and Dorothy Evelyn (*d* 1987), *d* of late Ferdinand Richard Holmes Meyrick, MD; *S* father, 1982; *m* 1959, Bridget Jennifer, *yr d* of Duncan Robertson, Llangollen, Denbighshire. *Educ:* Eton. *Heir:* *b* Hon. William Southwell Russell [*b* 26 Feb. 1930; *m* 1961, Jean Brodie, *d* of Neil Brodie Henderson; one *s* two *d*]. *Address:* Riggledown, Pennymoor, Tiverton, Devon EX16 8LR. *Club:* Naval and Military.

de COURCY, family name of **Baron Kingsale.**

de COURCY, Kenneth Hugh; (Duc de Grantmesnil); Chancellor, Order of the Three Orders, since 1977; Chairman, Kilbrittain Newspapers, since 1987; *b* 6 Nov. 1909; 2nd *s* of late Stephen de Courcy of Co. Galway and Hollinwood Mission (*s* of 8th Duc de Grantmesnil), and late Minnie de Courcy (*née* Schafer), *d* of late Frederick and Sophia Schafer-Andres, Schloss Kyburgh, Kirn am Nahe; *m* 1950, Rosemary Catherine (marr. diss. 1973), *o d* of late Comdr H. L. S. Baker, OBE, RN (retired), Co. Roscommon, Eire; two *s* two *d.* *Educ:* King's College Sch. and by travelling abroad. 2nd Lieut, 3rd City of London Regt (Royal Fusiliers) TA (Regular Army Candidate), 1927. 2nd Lieut Coldstream Guards (Supplementary Reserve), 1930; Lieut and resigned, 1931; Hon. Secretary to late Sir Reginald Mitchell-Banks' unofficial cttee on Conservative policy, 1933; 1934, formed with late Earl of Mansfield, late Viscount Clive, late Lord Phillimore, and late Sir Victor Raikes, KBE, Imperial Policy Group and was Hon. Secretary 1934–39; travelled as Group's chief observer of Foreign Affairs in Europe and America, 1935–39; special visit of enquiry to Mussolini, Doctor Beneš, Dr Schuschnigg, 1936; to King Boris of Bulgaria, etc., 1938; to Italy and King Boris, 1939–40; FCO released 45 secret reports from 1936–40 to PRO, 1972; adviser on War Intelligence to United Steel Companies Ltd, 1944–45. Formerly published monthly serial memoranda on Foreign Affairs and Strategy, (1938–); Proprietor of: Intelligence Digest, 1938–76; The Weekly Review, 1951–76; Director, Ringrone Newspapers Ltd, 1966–68. Editor: Bankers Digest, 1969–72; Special Office Brief, 1973–.Trustee, Marquis de Verneuil Trust, 1971–. Hon. Citizen of New Orleans, La, USA, 1950; Hon. Life Mem., Mark Twain Soc., 1977; Companion of Western Europe, 1979. Gave collection of historic documents to Hoover Instn, Stanford Univ., 1983. *Publications:* Review of World Affairs (23 vols since 1938); Mayerling, 1983; Secret Reports of Prime Minister Chamberlain 1938–40, 1984; The Carolingian Crown of France, 1984; The Great Marshal Philippe Pétain, 1995; various articles on Strategy and Foreign Affairs. *Recreation:* climbing. *Address:* Yeomans Cottage, Longborough, Moreton-in-Marsh, Glos GL56 0QG. *Fax:* Moreton-in-Marsh (01608) 650540; (office) 37 Upper Mount Street, Dublin 2, Ireland. *T:* Dublin 760705, *Fax:* 766560.

de COURCY-IRELAND, Patrick Gault, CVO 1980; HM Diplomatic Service, retired; Director of Marketing, Alireza Group of Companies, since 1987; Director, Rezayat Europe Ltd, since 1988; *b* 19 Aug. 1933; *e s* of late Lawrence Kilmaine de Courcy-Ireland and Elizabeth Pentland Gault; *m* 1957, Margaret Gallop; one *s* three *d.* *Educ:* St Paul's Sch.; Jesus Coll., Cambridge (MA). HM Forces (2nd Lieut), 1952–54. Joined Foreign Service, 1957; Student, ME Centre for Arab Studies, 1957–59; Third, later Second Sec., Baghdad, 1959–62; Private Sec. to HM Ambassador, Washington, 1963; Consul (Commercial), New York, 1963–67; UN (Polit.) Dept, 1967–69; Asst Head of Amer. Dept, 1969–71; First Sec. and Hd of Chancery, Kuwait, 1971–73; Asst Hd of SW Pacific Dept, 1973–76; Hd of Trng Dept and Dir, Diplomatic Serv. Language Centre, FCO, 1976–80; Consul-Gen., Casablanca, 1980–84; Consul-Gen., Jerusalem, 1984–87. Chm., British Sch. of Archaeology in Jerusalem, 1990–; Member: Exec. Cttee, Palestine Exploration Fund, 1991–; Council, Soc. for Moroccan Studies, 1992–. MInstPet 1992. Great Comdr, Order of KHS, 1985. *Recreations:* book collecting, opera. *Address:* 49 Napier Court, Ranelagh Gardens, SW6 3UU. *T:* 0171–736 0622; 9 Rosewin Row, Truro TR1 1HG.

de COURCY LING, John, CBE 1990; HM Diplomatic Service, 1959–78; politician, since 1978; *b* 14 Oct. 1933; *s* of Arthur Norman Ling, Warwick, and Veronica de Courcy, Painestown, Co. Kildare; *m* 1959, Jennifer Haynes; one *s* three *d.* *Educ:* King Edward's Sch., Edgbaston; Clare Coll., Cambridge. 2nd Lieut, Royal Ulster Rifles, 1956; Lieut on active service, Cyprus, 1957–58. FO, 1959; a private sec. to Lord Harlech, 1960–61, to Joseph Godber, 1961–63; 2nd Sec., Santiago, 1963–66; 1st Sec., Nairobi, 1966–69; Chargé d'Affaires, Chad, 1973; Counsellor, HM Embassy, Paris, 1974–77; left FO, 1978. Farmed at: Bellehatch Park, Henley-on-Thames, 1977–85; Old Chalford, Chipping Norton, 1985–93. MEP (C) Midlands Central, 1979–89; Conservative Chief Whip, 1979–83; Vice-Chm., Develt Aid Cttee, 1984–87; Chm., EEC Delegn to Israel, 1979–82; Mem., Catholic Bishops' Cttee on Europe, 1986–. Mem., Exec. Cttee of Nat. Union of Conservative Assocs, 1979–83. Mem., Council of Lloyds, 1986–88. Chm., Chipping Norton Gleeson Partnership, 1990–. Mem. Council, RIIA, 1990–93. Pres., Henley Agricl Assoc., 1980–81. Trustee, Maison Française, Oxford, 1992–. *Publications:* (with T. R. McK. Sewell) Famine and Surplus, 1985; Tales of Imperial Decline, 1993; contribs to The Tablet and various political papers. *Recreations:* sailing, skiing, opera, bridge. *Address:* Coutts & Co., 440 Strand, WC2 0QS. *Clubs:* Beefsteak; Leander (Henley-on-Thames); Royal Leamington Spa Conservative; Chipping Norton Golf.
See also Sir Alan Wigan, Bt.

DeCRANE, Alfred Charles, jun.; Chairman of the Board, since 1987 and Chief Executive Officer, since 1993, Texaco Inc.; *b* 11 June 1931; *s* of Alfred Charles DeCrane and Verona (Marquard) DeCrane; *m* 1954, Joan Hoffman; one *s* five *d.* *Educ:* Notre Dame Univ. (BA); Georgetown Univ. (LLB). Texaco Inc.: Attorney, Houston and NY, 1959–65; Asst to Vice-Chm., 1965–67; Asst to Chm., 1967–68; Gen. Manager, 1968–70, Vice-Pres., 1970–76, Producing Dept, E Hemisphere; Sen. Vice-Pres., General Counsel, 1976–78; Board Dir, 1977–; Exec. Vice-Pres., 1978–83; Pres., 1983. *Address:* Texaco Inc., 2000 Westchester Avenue, White Plains, NY 10650, USA. *T:* (914) 2534000.

de DENEY, Sir Geoffrey Ivor, KCVO 1992 (CVO 1986); Clerk of the Privy Council, 1984–92; *b* 8 Oct. 1931; *s* of late Thomas Douglas and Violet Ivy de Deney; *m* 1959, Diana Elizabeth Winrow; two *s.* *Educ:* William Ellis Sch.; St Edmund Hall, Oxford (MA, BCL); Univ. of Michigan. Home Office: joined, 1956; Asst Principal, 1956–61 (Private Sec. to Parly Under Sec. of State, 1959–61); Principal, 1961–69; Sec. to Graham Hall Cttee on maintenance limits in magistrates' courts; Sec. to Brodrick Cttee on Death Certification and Coroners; Private Sec. to Sec. of State, 1968; Asst Sec., 1969–1978; seconded to Cabinet Office, 1975; Asst Under Sec. of State, 1978–84; Community Programmes and Equal Opportunities Dept, 1978–80; General Dept (and Registrar of the Baronetage), 1980–84. *Recreations:* books, walking. *Address:* 17 Ladbroke Terrace, W11 3PG.

de DUVE, Prof. Christian René Marie Joseph, Grand Cross Order of Leopold II 1975; Professor of Biochemistry, Catholic University of Louvain, 1951–85, now Emeritus; Founding Member and Past President, International Institute of Cellular and Molecular Pathology, Brussels; Andrew W. Mellon Professor at Rockefeller University, New York, 1962–88, now Emeritus; *b* England, 2 Oct. 1917; *s* of Alphonse de Duve and Madeleine Pungs; *m* 1943, Janine Herman; two *s* two *d.* *Educ:* Jesuit Coll., Antwerp; Catholic Univ. of Louvain; Med. Nobel Inst., Stockholm; Washington Univ., St Louis. MD 1941, MSc 1946, Agrégé de l'Enseignement Supérieur 1945, Louvain. Lectr, Med. Faculty, Catholic Univ. of Louvain, 1947–51. Vis. Prof. at various univs. Mem. editorial and other bds and cttees; mem. or hon. mem. various learned socs, incl. For. Assoc. Nat. Acad. of Scis (US) 1975, and For. Mem of Royal Soc., 1988. Holds hon. degrees. Awards incl. Nobel Prize in Physiol. or Med., 1974. *Publications:* A Guided Tour of the Living Cell, 1985; Blueprint for a Cell, 1991; Vital Dust, 1995; numerous scientific. *Recreations:* tennis, ski-ing, bridge. *Address:* Le Pré St Jean, 239 rue de Weert, 1390 Nethen (Grez-Doiceau), Belgium. *T:* (10) 866628; 80 Central Park West, New York, NY 10023, USA. *T:* (212) 7248048.

DEECH, Ruth Lynn; Principal, St Anne's College, Oxford, since 1991; Chairman, Human Fertilisation and Embryology Authority, since 1994; *b* 29 April 1943; *d* of Josef Fraenkel and Dora (*née* Rosenfeld); *m* 1967, Dr John Stewart Deech; one *d.* *Educ:* Christ's Hosp., Hertford; St Anne's Coll., Oxford (BA 1st Cl. 1965; MA 1969); Brandeis Univ., USA (MA 1966). Called to the Bar, Inner Temple, 1967. Legal Asst, Law Commn, 1966–67; Asst Prof., Faculty of Law, Univ. of Windsor, Canada, 1968–70; Oxford University: Fellow and Tutor in Law, 1970–91, Vice-Principal, 1988–91, St Anne's Coll.; CUF Lectr in Law, 1971–91; Sen. Proctor, 1985–86; Mem., Hebdomadal Council, 1986–94; Chm., Jt Undergrad. Admissions Cttee, 1993–. Mem., Cttee of Inquiry into Equal Opportunities on Bar Vocational Course, 1993–94. Non-exec. Dir, Oxon HA, 1993–94. Mem., Exec. Council, Internat. Soc. on Family Law, 1988–. Vis. Prof., Osgoode Hall Law Sch., York Univ., Canada, 1978. Governor: Carmel Coll., 1980–90; Oxford Centre for Hebrew and Jewish Studies, 1994–. Trustee, Jewish Continuity, 1994–. *Publications:* articles on family law and property law. *Recreations:* after-dinner speaking, music, entertaining. *Address:* St Anne's College, Oxford OX2 6HS. *T:* Oxford (01865) 274800.

DEEDES, family name of **Baron Deedes.**

DEEDES, Baron *cr* 1986 (Life Peer), of Aldington in the County of Kent; **William Francis Deedes,** MC 1944; PC 1962; DL; Editor, The Daily Telegraph, 1974–86; *b* 1 June 1913; *s* of (Herbert) William Deedes; *m* 1942, Evelyn Hilary Branfoot; one *s* three *d* (and one *s* decd). *Educ:* Harrow. Journalist with Morning Post, 1931–37; war correspondent on Abyssinia, 1935. Served war of 1939–45, Queen's Westminsters (12 KRRC). MP (C) Ashford Div. of Kent, 1950–Sept. 1974; Parliamentary Sec., Ministry of Housing and Local Government, Oct. 1954–Dec. 1955; Parliamentary Under-Sec., Home Dept., 1955–57; Minister without Portfolio, 1962–64. DL, Kent, 1962. Hon. DCL Kent, 1988. *Address:* New Hayters, Aldington, Kent. *T:* Aldington (01233) 720269. *Club:* Carlton.
See also Baron Latymer.

DEEDES, Maj.-Gen. Charles Julius, CB 1968; OBE 1953; MC 1944; *b* 18 Oct. 1913; *s* of General Sir Charles Deedes, KCB, CMG, DSO; *m* 1939, Beatrice Murgatroyd, Brockfield Hall, York; three *s.* *Educ:* Oratory Sch.; Royal Military Coll., Sandhurst. Served War of 1939–45 (despatches); Asst Military Secretary, GHQ Middle East, 1945; Officer Comdg Glider Pilot Regt, 1948; GSO1 War Office, 1950; Officer Comdg 1st Bn KOYLI, 1954 (despatches); Colonel General Staff, War Office, 1956; Comd 146 Infantry Brigade (TA), 1958; Deputy Director, MoD, 1962; C of S, HQ Eastern Comd, 1965; C of S, HQ Southern Comd, 1968. Colonel of the KOYLI, 1966–68. Dep. Colonel, The Light Infantry (Yorks), 1968–72. Military Cross (Norway), 1940. *Recreations:* riding, tennis. *Address:* Lea Close, Brandsby, York YO6 4RW. *T:* Brandsby (01347) 888239.

DEELEY, Michael; film producer; *b* 6 Aug. 1932; *s* of John Hamilton-Deeley and Anne Deeley; *m* 1955, Teresa Harrison; one *s* two *d*; *m* 1970, Ruth Stone-Spencer. *Educ:* Stowe. Entered film industry as film editor, 1952; Distributor, MCA TV, 1958–60; independent producer, 1961–63; Gen. Man., Woodfall Films, 1964–67; indep. prod., 1967–72; Man. Director: British Lion Films Ltd, 1973–76; EMI Films Ltd, 1976–77; Pres., EMI Films Inc., 1977–79; Chief Exec. Officer, Consolidated Television Inc., 1984–90. Dep. Chm., British Screen Adv. Council, 1985–. Member: Prime Minister's Film Industry Working

Party, 1975–76; Film Industry Interim Action Cttee, 1977–84. *Films* include: Robbery; The Italian Job; The Knack; Murphy's War; Conduct Unbecoming; The Man who fell to Earth; The Deer Hunter (Academy Award, Best Picture Producer, 1978); Convoy; Blade Runner; many TV films and series. *Address:* PO Box 397, Osterville, MA 02655–0397, USA. *Clubs:* Garrick; New York Yacht.

DEER, Prof. William Alexander, MSc Manchester, PhD Cantab; FRS 1962; FGS; Emeritus Professor of Mineralogy and Petrology, Cambridge University; Hon. Fellow of Trinity Hall, Cambridge, 1978; *b* 26 Oct. 1910; *s* of William Deer; *m* 1939, Margaret Marjorie (*d* 1971), *d* of William Kidd; two *s* one *d*; *m* 1973, Rita Tagg. *Educ:* Manchester Central High Sch.; Manchester Univ.; St John's Coll., Cambridge. Graduate Research Scholar, 1932, Beyer Fellow, 1933, Manchester Univ.; Strathcona Studentship, St John's Coll., Cambridge, 1934; Petrologist on British East Greenland Expedition, 1935–36; 1851 Exhibition Senior Studentship, 1938; Fellow, St John's Coll., Cambridge, 1939; served War of 1939–45, RE, 1940–45. Murchison Fund Geological Soc. of London, 1945 (Murchison Medal, 1974); Junior Bursar, St John's Coll., 1946; Leader NE Baffin Land Expedition, 1948; Bruce Medal, Royal Society of Edinburgh, 1948; Tutor, St John's Coll., 1949; Prof. of Geology, Manchester Univ., 1950–61; Fellow of St John's Coll., Cambridge, 1961–66, Hon. Fellow, 1969; Prof. of Mineralogy and Petrology, 1961–78, Vice-Chancellor, 1971–73, Cambridge Univ.; Master of Trinity Hall, Cambridge, 1966–75. Percival Lecturer, Univ. of Manchester, 1953; Joint Leader East Greenland Geological Expedition, 1953; Leader British East Greenland Expedition, 1966. Trustee, British Museum (Natural History), 1967–75. President: Mineralogical Soc., 1967–70; Geological Soc., 1970–72; Member: NERC, 1968–71; Marshall Aid Commemoration Commn, 1973–79. Hon. DSc Aberdeen, 1983. *Publications:* (jtly) Rock-forming Minerals, 5 vols, 1962–63, 2nd edn 1978– (vol. IIA 1978, vol. IA 1982, vol. IB 1986, Introduction 1992); Introduction to Rock-forming Minerals, 1966, 2nd edn 1992; papers in Petrology and Mineralogy. *Recreations:* walking, bassoon playing. *Address:* 12 Barrington House, Southacre Drive, Cambridge CB2 2TY.

DEERHURST, Viscount; Edward George William Omar Coventry; *b* 24 Sept. 1957; *s* and *heir* of 11th Earl of Coventry, *qv*.

de FARIA, Antonio Leite, Hon. GCVO 1973; Grand Cross of Christ (Portugal), 1949; Portuguese Ambassador to the Court of St James's, 1968–73; retired; *b* 23 March 1904; *s* of Dr Antonio B. Leite de Faria and Dona Lucia P. de Sequeira Braga Leite de Faria; *m* 1926, Dona Herminia Cantilo de Faria; two *s*. *Educ:* Lisbon University (Faculty of Law). Attaché to Min. of Foreign Affairs, 1926; Sec. to Portuguese Delegn, League of Nations, 1929–30; 2nd Sec., Rio de Janeiro, 1931, Paris, 1933, Brussels, 1934; 1st Sec., London, 1936; Counsellor, London, 1939; Minister to Exiled Allied Govts, London, 1944; Minister to The Hague, 1945; Dir Gen., Political Affairs, and Acting Sec. Gen., Min. of Foreign Affairs, 1947; Ambassador: Rio de Janeiro, 1950; NATO, 1958; Paris, 1959; Rome (Holy See), 1961; London, 1968. Holds many foreign decorations. *Address:* Rua da Horta Seca 11, 1200 Lisboa, Portugal. *T:* (1) 3422538; Casa do Bom Retiro, S Pedro de Azurem, Guimarães, Portugal. *T:* (53) 416418.

de FERRANTI, Sebastian Basil Joseph Ziani; Chairman, Ferranti plc, 1963–82 (Managing Director, 1958–75; Director 1954); Director, GEC plc, since 1982; *b* 5 Oct. 1927; *er s* of Sir Vincent de Ferranti, MC, and late Dorothy H. C. Wilson; *m* 1st, 1953, Mona Helen, *d* of T. E. Cunningham; one *s* two *d*; 2nd, 1983, Naomi Angela Rae. *Educ:* Ampleforth. 4th/7th Dragoon Guards, 1947–49. Brown Boveri, Switzerland, and Alsthom, France, 1949–50. Director: British Airways Helicopters, 1982–84; Nat. Nuclear Corp., 1984–88. President: Electrical Research Assoc., 1968–69; BEAMA, 1969–70; Centre for Educn in Science, Educn and Technology, Manchester and region, 1972–82. Chm., Internat. Electrical Assoc., 1970–72. Member: Nat. Defence Industries Council, 1969–77; Council, IEE, 1970–73. Trustee, Tate Gallery, 1971–78; Chm., Civic Trust for the North-West, 1978–83; Comr, Royal Commn for Exhibn of 1851, 1984–. Vice-Pres., RSA, 1980–84. Chm., Hallé Concerts Soc., 1988–. Mem. Bd of Govs, RNCM, 1988–. Chm. assessors, architect for Manchester City Art Gall extn, 1995–. Lectures: Granada, Guildhall, 1966; Royal Instn, 1969; Louis Blériot, Paris, 1970; Faraday, 1970–71. High Sheriff of Cheshire, 1988–89. Hon. Fellow, Univ. of Manchester Inst. of Science and Technology. Hon. DSc: Salford Univ., 1967; Cranfield Inst. of Technology, 1973. *Address:* Henbury Hall, Macclesfield, Cheshire SK11 9PJ. *Clubs:* Cavalry and Guards, Pratt's.

de FONBLANQUE, John Robert, CMG 1993; HM Diplomatic Service; Assistant Under-Secretary of State, Foreign and Commonwealth Office, since 1994; *b* 20 Dec. 1943; *s* of late Maj.-Gen. E. B. de Fonblanque, CB, CBE, DSO and of Elizabeth de Fonblanque; *m* 1984, Margaret Prest; one *s*. *Educ:* Ampleforth; King's College, Cambridge (MA); London School of Economics (MSc). FCO, 1968; Second Sec., Jakarta, 1969; Second, later First Sec., UK Representation to European Community, Brussels, 1972; Principal, HM Treasury, 1977; FCO, 1980; Asst Sec., Cabinet Office, 1983; Head of Chancery, New Delhi, 1986; Counsellor (Pol and Instnl), UK Repn to EC, Brussels, 1988; Vis. Fellow, RIIA, 1993. Mem., PPARC, 1994–. *Recreation:* mountain walking. *Address:* c/o Foreign and Commonwealth Office, SW1A 2AH.

de FRANCIA, Prof. Peter Laurent; Professor, School of Painting, Royal College of Art, London, 1973–86; *b* 25 Jan. 1921; *s* of Fernand de Francia and Alice Groom. *Educ:* Academy of Brussels; Slade Sch., Univ. of London. Canadian Exhibition Commn, Ottawa, 1951; American Museum, Central Park West, NY, 1952–53; BBC, Television, 1953–55; Teacher, St Martin's Sch., London, 1955–63; Tutor, Royal College of Art, 1963–69; Principal, Dept of Fine Art, Goldsmiths Coll., 1969–72. Work represented in public collections: Tate Gall.; V&A Mus.; Mus. of Modern Art, NY; Arts Council of GB; British Mus.; Graves Art Gall., Sheffield; Mus. of Modern Art, Prague. *Publications:* Fernand Léger, 1969; Léger, 1983; Untitled, 1990. *Address:* 44 Surrey Square, SE17 2JX. *T:* 0171–703 8361.

DE FREYNE, 7th Baron *cr* 1851; Feudal Baron of Coolavin; **Francis Arthur John French;** Knight of Malta; *b* 3 Sept. 1927; *s* of 6th Baron and Victoria (*d* 1974), *d* of Sir J. Arnott, 2nd Bt; *S* father 1935; *m* 1st, 1954 (marr. diss. 1978); two *s* one *d*; 2nd, 1978, Sheelin Deirdre, *widow* of William Walker Stevenson and *y d* of late Lt-Col H. K. O'Kelly, DSO. *Educ:* Ladycross, Glenstal. *Heir:* *s* Hon. Fulke Charles Arthur John French [*b* 21 April 1957; *m* 1986, Julia Mary, *o d* of Dr James H. Wellard; two *s*].

de GENNES, Prof. Pierre-Gilles, PhD; Professor of Solid State Physics, Collège de France, since 1971; *b* 24 Oct. 1932; *s* of Robert de Gennes and Yvonne de Gennes (*née* Morin-Pons). *Educ:* Ecole Normale Supérieure, Paris. Prof., Univ. Orsay, 1961–71; Dir, Ecole de Physique et Chimie, 1976–. Nobel Prize in Physics, 1991. *Publications:* Superconductivity of Metals and Alloys, 1966; The Physics of Liquid Crystals, 1974; Scaling Concepts in Polymer Physics, 1979. *Recreations:* ski, kayak, windsurfing. *Address:* 10 rue Vauquelin, Paris 75005, France. *T:* 40 79 45 00.

de GREY, family name of **Baron Walsingham.**

de GRUCHY, Nigel Ronald Anthony; General Secretary, National Association of Schoolmasters Union of Women Teachers, since 1990; *b* 28 Jan. 1943; *s* of Robert Philip de Gruchy and Dorothy Louise de Gruchy (*née* Cullinane); *m* 1970, Judith Ann Berglund, USA; one *s*. *Educ:* De La Salle Coll., Jersey; Univ. of Reading (BA Hons (Econs and Philosophy) 1965); PGCE London Univ. 1969; Cert. Pratique de Langue Française, Paris Univ., 1968; Cert. de Française Parlé et du Diplôme de Langue Française, L'Alliance Française, 1968. TEFL, Berlitz Schs, Santander, 1965–66, Versailles, 1966–67; student of French/Tutor in English, Paris, 1967–68; Head of Econs Dept, St Joseph's Acad., ILEA, 1968–78; Asst Sec., 1978–82, Dep. Gen. Sec., 1982–89, NAS UWT. Sec., London Assoc., 1975–78, Mem., Nat. Exec., 1975–78, NAS UWT. Member: Gen. Council, TUC, 1989–; Exec., The Educn Internat., 1993–. *Publications:* contribs to Career Teacher. *Recreations:* golf, cricket, football, literature, music, opera, France, Spain. *Address:* (office) 5 King Street, Covent Garden, WC2E 8HN. *T:* 0171–379 9499.

DEHAENE, Jean-Luc; Prime Minister of Belgium, since 1992; *b* Montpellier, 7 Aug. 1940; *s* of late Albert Dehaene and of Andrée Verstraete; *m* 1965, Celie Verbeke; four *c*. *Educ:* Univ. of Namur; Univ. of Kul. Comr, Flemish Assoc. of Catholic Scouts, 1963–67; Christian Social Party (CVP): Nat. Vice Pres., CVP Youth, 1967–71; Mem., Nat. Cttee; Councillor: for Public Works, 1972–73; for Public Health, 1973–74; then Leader of Cabinet for Econ. Affairs, 1974–77; Leader of Cabinet for Flemish Affairs, 1977–78; Pres., CVP, Bruxelles-Hal-Vivorde, 1977–81; Leader of Cabinet, 1979–81; Leader of Cabinet for Instnl Reforms, 1981; co-opted Senator, 1982–87; Deputy, 1987–; Minister of Social Affairs and Instnl Reforms, 1981–88; Dep. Prime Minister and Minister of Communications and Instnl Reforms, 1988–92. *Address:* Office of the Prime Minister, 16 Rue de la Loi, 1000 Brussels, Belgium. *T:* (2) 5010211; Berkendallaan 52, 1800 Vilvoorde, Belgium.

de HAMEL, Christopher Francis Rivers, DPhil; FSA; FRHistS; Director, Western and Oriental Manuscripts, Sotheby's, since 1982; *b* 20 Nov. 1950; *s* of Dr Francis Alexander de Hamel and Joan Littledale de Hamel (*née* Pollock); *m* 1st, 1978 (marr. diss. 1989); two *s*; 2nd, 1993, Mette Tang Simpson (*née* Svendsen). *Educ:* Otago Univ., NZ (BA Hons); Oxford Univ. (DPhil). FSA 1981; FRHistS 1986. Sotheby's: Cataloguer of medieval manuscripts, 1975; Asst Dir, 1977. Hon. LittD St John's, Minn, 1994. *Publications* include: Glossed Books of the Bible and the Origins of the Paris Booktrade, 1984; A History of Illuminated Manuscripts, 1986, 2nd edn 1994; (with M. Manion and V. Vines) Medieval and Renaissance Manuscripts in New Zealand Collections, 1989; Syon Abbey, The Library of the Bridgettine Nuns and their Peregrinations after the Reformation, 1991; Scribes and Illuminators, 1992; all of Sotheby's medieval manuscript catalogues, 1975–. *Address:* Sotheby's, 34/35 New Bond Street, W1A 2AA. *T:* 0171–408 5330, *Fax:* 0171–408 5960. *Clubs:* Grolier (New York); Association Internationale de Bibliophilie (Paris).

de HAVILLAND, Olivia Mary; actress; *b* Tokyo, Japan, 1 July 1916; *d* of Walter Augustus de Havilland and Lilian Augusta (*née* Ruse) (parents British subjects); *m* 1st, 1946, Marcus Aurelius Goodrich (marr. diss., 1953); one *s*; 2nd, 1955, Pierre Paul Galante (marr. diss. 1979); one *d*. *Educ:* in California; won scholarship to Mills Coll., but career prevented acceptance. Played Hermia in Max Reinhardt's stage production of Midsummer Night's Dream, 1934. *Legitimate theatre* (USA): Juliet in Romeo and Juliet, 1951; Candida, 1951 and 1952; A Gift of Time, 1962. Began film career 1935, Midsummer Night's Dream. Nominated for Academy Award, 1939, 1941, 1946, 1948, 1949; Acad. Award, 1946, 1949; New York Critics' Award, 1948, 1949; San Francisco Critics' Award, 1948, 1949; Hollywood Foreign Press Assoc. Golden Globe Award, 1949, 1986; Women's National Press Club Award for 1950; Belgian Prix Femina, 1957; British Films and Filming Award, 1967; Filmex Tribute, 1978; Amer. Acad. of Achievement Award, 1978. *Important films:* The Adventures of Robin Hood, 1938; Gone With the Wind, 1939; Hold Back the Dawn, 1941; Princess O'Rourke, 1943; To Each His Own, 1946; The Dark Mirror, 1946; The Snake Pit, 1948; The Heiress, 1949; My Cousin Rachel, 1952; Not as a Stranger, 1955; The Ambassador's Daughter, 1956; Proud Rebel, 1957; The Light in the Piazza, 1961; Lady in a Cage, 1963; Hush . . . Hush, Sweet Charlotte, 1965; The Adventurers, 1969; Pope Joan, 1971; Airport '77, 1976; The Swarm, 1978. *Television includes:* Noon Wine, 1966; The Screaming Woman, 1971; Roots, The Next Generations, 1979; 3 ABC Cable-TV Cultural Documentaries, 1981; Murder is Easy, 1982; Charles & Diana, a Royal Romance, 1982; North and South, Book II, 1986; Anastasia, 1986; The Woman He Loved, 1988. US Lecture tours, 1971, 1972, 1973, 1974, 1975, 1976, 1978, 1979, 1980. Pres. of Jury, Cannes Film Festival, 1965. Took part in narration of France's BiCentennial Gift to US, Son et Lumière, A Salute to George Washington, Mount Vernon, 19 May 1976; read excerpts from Thomas Jefferson at BiCentennial Service, American Cathedral in Paris, 4 July 1976. Hon. DHL Amer. Univ. of Paris, 1994. Amer. Legion Humanitarian Medal, 1967; Freedoms Foundn Exemplar American Award, 1981. *Publications:* Every Frenchman Has One, 1962; (contrib.) Mother and Child, 1975. *Address:* BP 156–16, 75764 Paris, Cedex 16, France.

DEHENNIN, Baron Herman; Hon. Grand Marshal of Belgian Royal Court; Belgian Ambassador to the Court of St James's, 1991–94; *b* 20 July 1929; created Baron, 1990; *s* of Alexander Dehennin and Flora Brehmen; *m* 1954, Margareta-Maria Donvil; two *s*. *Educ:* Catholic Univ. of Leuven. Dr in Law 1951. Lieut, Royal Belgian Artillery, 1951–53; entered Belgian Diplomatic Service, 1954; served The Hague, New Delhi, Madrid, the Congo; Ambassador to Rwanda, 1966–70; Economic Minister, Washington, 1970–74; Dir-Gen., Foreign Econ. Relations, Brussels, 1974–77; Ambassador to Japan, 1978–81; Grand Marshal, Belgian Royal Court, 1981–85; Ambassador to USA, 1985–91. Grand Cross, Order of Leopold, 1985; Grand Cross, Order of the Crown, 1983; foreign Orders: France, Greece, Japan, Luxembourg, Mexico, Portugal, Rwanda, Zaire. *Recreations:* jogging, hiking, tennis, fishing, hunting, reading (history, philosophy). *Address:* Vogelzanglaan 175, 1160 Brussels, Belgium. *Clubs:* Prince Albert, University Foundation, Warande, Order of the Prince (Brussels); Royal Golf of Belgium.

DEHMELT, Prof. Hans Georg; Professor of Physics, University of Washington, Seattle, since 1961; *b* 9 Sept. 1922; *s* of Georg Karl Dehmelt and Asta Ella Dehmelt (*née* Klemmt); US Citizen, 1961; *m* 1st; one *s*; 2nd, 1989, Diana Elaine Dundore. *Educ:* Graues Kloster, Berlin; Technische Hochschule, Breslau; Univ. of Göttingen (Dr rer. nat. 1950). Res. Fellow, Inst. Kopfermann, Göttingen, 1950–52; Res. Associate, Duke Univ., USA, 1952–55; Vis. Asst Prof., 1955, Associate Prof., 1957, Univ. of Washington. Consultant, Varian Associates, Palo Alto, Calif, 1956–70. Member: Amer. Acad. of Arts and Scis; Nat. Acad. of Scis; Fellow, Amer. Phys Soc.; FAAAS. Numerous awards and hon. degrees; Nobel Prize for Physics (jtly), 1989. Leader of group which first saw with own eyes individual atom at rest in free space, 1979, reported 1980. *Publications:* papers on electron and atomic physics, esp. subatomic particles, charged atoms, anti-matter particles, proposed cosmonium world-atom hypothesis of big bang. *Address:* 1600 43rd Avenue East, Seattle, Washington, DC 98112, USA.

DEHN, Conrad Francis, QC 1968; Barrister; a Recorder of the Crown Court, since 1974; a Deputy High Court Judge, since 1988; *b* London, 24 Nov. 1926; *o s* of late C. G. Dehn, Solicitor and Cynthia Dehn (*née* Fuller) painter, as Francyn; *m* 1st, 1954, Sheila (*née* Magan) (marr. diss.); two *s* one *d*; 2nd, 1978, Marilyn, *d* of late Peter Collyer and of

Constance Collyer. *Educ:* Charterhouse (Sen. Exhibr); Christ Church, Oxford (Holford Schol.). Served RA, Best Cadet Mons Basic OCTU, 1946, 2nd Lieut 1947. 1st cl. hons PPE Oxon. 1950, MA 1952; Holt Schol., Gray's Inn, 1951; Pres., Inns of Court Students Union, 1951–52. WEA Tutor, 1951–55. Called to Bar, Gray's Inn, 1952; Bencher, 1977; Chm., Management Cttee, 1987; Vice-Treas., 1995. Head, Fountain Court Chambers, 1984–89. Chairman: Bar Council Working Party on Liability for Defective Products, 1975–77; Planning Cttee, Senate of Inns of Court and Bar, 1980–83; London Univ. Disciplinary Appeals Cttee, 1986–; Adv. Cttee, Gen. Comrs of Income Tax, Gray's Inn, 1994–. Dir, Bar Mutual Indemnity Fund Ltd, 1988–. Mem., Foster Cttee of Inquiry into Operators' Licensing, Dept of Transport, 1978. Member: Council of Legal Educn, 1981–86; London Legal Aid Cttee, 1965–92 (Vice-Chm., 1987–92); Hon. Advr, S London Psychotherapy Centre, 1982–; Hon. Legal Advr, Age Concern Greater London, 1987–. Mem. Governing Body, United Westminster Schs, 1953–57. *Publication:* contrib. to Ideas, 1954. *Recreations:* theatre, living in France, walking. *Address:* Fountain Court, Temple, EC4Y 9DH. *T:* 0171–583 3335. *Club:* Reform.

de HOGHTON, Sir (Richard) Bernard (Cuthbert), 14th Bt *cr* 1611; KM; DL; *b* 26 Jan. 1945; 3rd *s* of Sir Cuthbert de Hoghton, 12th Bt, and of Philomena, *d* of late Herbert Simmons; *S* half-brother, 1978; *m* 1974, Rosanna Stella Virginia (*née* Buratti); one *s* one *d*. *Educ:* Ampleforth College, York; McGill Univ., Montreal (BA Hons); Birmingham Univ. (MA); PhD (USA). Turner & Newall Ltd, 1967–70; international fund management, Vickers Da Costa & Co. Ltd, 1970–77; international institutional brokerage, de Zoete & Bevan & Co., 1977–86 (Partner, 1984–86); Dir, BZW Ltd (Europe), 1986–89; Asst Dir, Brown Shipley, 1989–94; Teather & Greenwood, 1994–. Historic house and estate management, 1978–. DL Lancs, 1988. Constantinian Order of S George (Naples), 1984; Kt SMO, Malta, 1980. *Recreations:* tennis, shooting, travelling. *Heir: s* Thomas James Daniel Adam de Hoghton, *b* 11 April 1980. *Address:* Hoghton Tower, Hoghton, Preston, Lancs PR5 0SH. *T:* (office) 0171–256 6131.

DEHQANI-TAFTI, Rt. Rev. Hassan Barnaba; Hon. Assistant Bishop of Winchester, since 1990 (Assistant Bishop, 1982–90); *b* 14 May 1920; *s* of Muhammad Dehqani-Tafti and Sakinneh; *m* 1952, Margaret Isabel Thompson; three *d* (one *s* decd). *Educ:* Stuart Memorial Coll., Isfahan, Iran; Tehran Univ.; Ridley Hall, Cambridge. Iran Imperial Army, 1943–45; layman in Diocese of Iran, 1945–47; theological coll., 1947–49; Deacon, Isfahan, 1949; Priest, Shiraz, 1950; Pastor: St Luke's Church, Isfahan, 1950–60; St Paul's Church, Tehran, 1960–61; Bishop in Iran, 1961–90, Vicar-Gen., 1990–91; Pres.-Bishop, Episcopal Church in Jerusalem and Middle East, 1976–86; Episcopal Canon, St George's Cathedral, Jerusalem, 1976–90; Commissary to Bishop in Iran, 1991–. Chm., Friends of the Diocese of Iran, 1991–. Hon. DD, Virginia Theolog. Seminary, USA, 1981. *Publications:* many books in Persian; in English: Design of my World, 1959; The Hard Awakening, 1981. *Recreations:* Persian poetry (primarily mystical); painting in water colours; walking.

DEISENHOFER, Prof. Johann, PhD; Regental Professor and Professor in Biochemistry, University of Texas Southwestern Medical Center at Dallas, since 1988; Investigator, Howard Hughes Medical Institute, since 1988; *b* 30 Sept. 1943; *s* of Johann and Thekla Deisenhofer; *m* 1989, Kirsten Fischer-Lindahl, PhD. *Educ:* Technische Universität München (Physics Diploma 1971; PhD 1974). Max-Planck-Institut für Biochemie: graduate student, 1971–74; Postdoctoral Fellow, 1974–76; Staff Scientist, 1976–88. (Jtly) Biological Physics Prize, Amer. Physical Soc., 1986; (jtly) Otto Bayer Preis, 1988; (jtly) Nobel Prize in Chemistry, 1988. *Publications:* contribs to Acta Crystallographica, Biochemistry, Jl of Molecular Biology, Nature, Methods in Enzymology, etc. *Recreations:* ski ing, swimming, classical music. *Address:* University of Texas Southwestern Medical Center, 5323 Harry Hines Boulevard, Dallas, TX 75235–9050, USA. *T.* (214) 6485089.

de JONGH, Nicholas Raymond; Theatre Critic, Evening Standard, since 1991; *b* London, 2 March 1947; *s* of Louis de Jongh and late Vivian (*née* Creditor). *Educ:* Hall Sch., Hampstead; St Paul's Sch.; University Coll. London (BA Hons, MPhil). Secker & Warburg, 1967; Scriptwriter, BBC External Services, 1968; The Guardian: Reporter, 1968; Theatre Reviewer, 1969; Dep. Theatre Critic, 1970–91; Arts Reporter, 1973–78; Arts Corresp., 1978–90; Theatre Critic, Mail on Sunday, 1983. Chm., Drama Section, Critics' Circle, 1984–86. *Publications:* (ed) Bedside Guardian, 1989, 1990; Not in Front of the Audience, 1992. *Recreations:* fantasising, riding hobby-horses. *Address:* Evening Standard, Northcliffe House, 2 Derry Street, W8 5EE. *Club:* Groucho.

DEJOUANY, Guy Georges André; Commandeur, Légion d'Honneur; Chairman and Managing Director: Compagnie Générale des Eaux, since 1976; Société Générale Entreprises, since 1988; Compagnie des Eaux et de l'Ozone, since 1970; *b* 15 Dec. 1920; *s* of André Dejouany and Jeanne (*née* Imbard); *m* 1958, Véronique Honoré (decd); two *s* one *d*. *Educ:* Ecole Polytechnique, Paris; Ponts et Chaussées, Paris. Civil Engineer: Metz, 1945–49; Paris, 1949–50; joined Compagnie Générale des Eaux, 1950: Manager, 1961–65; Dep. Man. Dir, 1965–72; Man. Dir, 1972–73; Dir, 1973–. Chairman: Soc. Monégasques des Eaux, 1971–; Anjou Internat., 1981–; Director: Cie de St Gobain; Alcatel Alsthom; Cie UAP; Soc. Générale; Canal Plus; Havas; Electrafina; Pétrofina; Cie Luxembourgeoise Multi Média; Cies Réunies Electrobel-Tractionel-Tractebel; Cie Générale de Chauffe. *Recreation:* tennis. *Address:* (office) 52 rue d'Anjou, 75008 Paris, France; 7 avenue Vion Whitcomb, 75016 Paris, France.

de KLERK, Frederik Willem; Deputy President of South Africa, since 1994 (State President, 1989–94); *b* 18 March 1936, *s* of J. de Klerk; *m* 1959, Marike Willemse; two *s* one *d*. *Educ:* Monument High School, Krugersdorp; Potchefstroom Univ. Law practice, 1961–72; MP (Nat. Party) Vereeniging, 1972–89; Information Officer, Transvaal, Nat. Party, 1975; Minister: of Posts and Telecommunications and Social Welfare and Pensions, 1978; of Posts and Telecommunications and of Sport and Recreation, 1978–79; of Mines, Energy and Environmental Planning, 1979–80; of Mineral and Energy Affairs, 1980–82; of Internal Affairs, 1982–85; of Nat. Educn and Planning, 1984–89; Leader, Nat. Party, 1989 (Transvaal Leader, 1982–89); Chm., Council of Ministers, 1985–89. Hon. LLD: Potchefstroom Univ., 1990; Bar-Ilan Univ., Tel Aviv; Hon. DPhil: Stellenbosch Univ., 1990; Nat. Chengchi Univ., Taipei, Taiwan. Nobel Peace Prize (with N. R. Mandela), 1993. *Address:* Private Bag X 999, Cape Town 8000, South Africa.

de LA BARRE de NANTEUIL, Luc; Commandeur de l'Ordre National du Mérite; Officier de la Légion d'Honneur; Ambassadeur de France; Chairman, Les Echos Group, since 1991; *b* 21 Sept. 1925; *m* 1st, Philippa MacDonald; one *s*; 2nd, 1973, Hedwige Frerejean de Chavagneux; one *s* one *d*. *Educ:* school in Poitiers; BA, LLB Lyon and Paris; Dip. d'Etudes Supérieures (Econ); Graduate, Ecole Nat. d'Admin, 1949. French Ministry of Foreign Affairs: Economic Affairs Dept, 1950–51; Secrétariat Général, 1951–52; Pacts Service, 1952–53; Econ. Affairs Dept, 1954–59; First Sec., London, 1959–64; Asst Dir, Afr. and ME Affairs Dept, 1964–70; Hd of Econ. Co-operation Service, Directorate of Econ. Affairs, 1970–76; Ambassador to the Netherlands, 1976–77; French Permanent Representative: to EEC, Brussels, 1977–82 and 1985–86; to Security Council and to UN, New York, 1981–84; Diplomatic Adviser, 1986; Ambassador to UK, 1986–91. *Publication:* David (Jacques Louis), 1985. *Address:* Les Echos, 46 rue la Boetie, Paris 75008, France. *T:* 49536565.

De la BÈRE, Sir Cameron, 2nd Bt *cr* 1953; jeweller, Geneva; *b* 12 Feb. 1933; *s* of Sir Rupert De la Bère, 1st Bt, KCVO, and Marguerite (*d* 1969), *e d* of late Sir John Humphery; *S* father, 1978; *m* 1964, Clairemonde, *o d* of late Casimir Kaufmann, Geneva; one *d*. *Educ:* Tonbridge, and on the Continent. Translator's cert. in Russian. British Army Intelligence Corps, 1951–53. Company director of Continental Express Ltd (subsid. of Hay's Wharf), 1958–64. Engaged in promotion of luxury retail jewellery stores, Switzerland and France, 1965–. Liveryman, Skinners' Co. *Recreations:* riding, swimming, history. *Heir: b* Adrian De la Bère, *b* 17 Sept. 1939. *Address:* 1 Avenue Theodore Flournoy, 1207 Geneva, Switzerland. *T:* (22) 7860015. *Clubs:* Hurlingham, Société Litéraire (Geneva).

de la BILLIÈRE, Gen. Sir Peter (Edgar de la Cour), KCB 1988; KBE 1991 (CBE 1983); DSO 1976; MC 1959 and Bar 1966; DL; Middle East Adviser to Ministry of Defence, 1991–92, retired; non-executive Director, Robert Fleming Holdings, since 1992; *b* 29 April 1934; *s* of Surgeon Lieut Comdr Claude Dennis Delacour de Labillière (killed in action, HMS Fiji, 1941) and of Frances Christine Wright Lawley; *m* 1965, Bridget Constance Muriel Goode; one *s* two *d*. *Educ:* Harrow School; Staff College; RCDS. Joined KSLI 1952; commissioned DLI; served Japan, Korea, Malaya (despatches 1958), Jordan, Borneo, Egypt, Aden, Gulf States, Sudan, Oman, Falkland Is; CO 22 SAS Regt, 1972–74; GSO1 (DS) Staff Coll., 1974–77; Comd British Army Training Team, Sudan, 1977–78; Dir SAS and Comd, SAS Group, 1978–83; Comd, British Forces Falkland Is and Mil. Comr, 1984–85; GOC Wales, 1985–87; GOC SE Dist, and Perm. Peace Time Comdr, Jt Forces Operations Staff, 1987–90; Comdr British Forces, ME, 1990–91. Col Comdt, Light Div., 1986–89. Mem. Council, RUSI, 1975–77. Mem. Bd, Farm Africa, 1992–. Chm., Jt Services Hang Gliding, 1986–89; Cdre, Army Sailing Assoc., 1989–91. President: SAS Assoc., 1991; ACF, 1992–. Comr, Duke of York's Mil. Sch., 1988–90. Trustee, Imperial War Mus., 1992. Freeman, City of London, 1991; Hon. Freeman, Fishmongers' Co., 1991. Stowaway Mem., Southampton Master Mariners Assoc., 1992. DL Hereford and Worcester, 1993. Hon. DSc Cranfield Inst. of Technol., 1992; Hon. DCL Durham, 1993. Order of Bahrain, 1st Cl., 1991; Chief Comdr, Legion of Merit (USA), 1992; Meritorious Service Cross, (Canada), 1992; Order of Abdul Aziz, 2nd Cl. (Saudi Arabia), 1992; Kuwait Decoration, 1st Cl., 1992; Qatar Sash of Merit, 1992. *Publications:* Storm Command: a personal story, 1992; (autobiog.) Looking for Trouble, 1994. *Recreations:* family, squash, down market apiculture, tennis, farming, sailing. *Clubs:* Farmers', Army and Navy, Special Forces.

DELACOUR, Jean-Paul; Officer of Legion of Honour; Knight of National Order of Merit; Inspector General of Finance; Vice-Chairman and Chief Operating Officer, Société Générale, Paris; *b* 7 Nov. 1930; *s* of Henri Delacour and Denise Brochet; *m* 1958, Claude Laurence; four *s* one *d*. *Educ:* Inst. of Political Studies, Paris (Dipl.); ENA (Nat. Sch. of Administration). Inspector of Finance, 1955–61; Dep. Dir, Crédit National, 1961–68; Dir, 1969, Dep. Gen. Manager, 1974, Bd Mem. and Man. Dir, 1986, Société Générale; Chm. and Chief Exec. Officer, Soc. Gén. Alsacienne de Banque, 1978–82; Chm., Sogebail, 1985–; senior functions in internat. banking and financial insts. Chm., Bd of Catholic Inst. Paris, 1984–. *Address:* Société Générale, 29 boulevard Haussmann, 75009 Paris, France. *T:* 40982000.

DELACOURT-SMITH OF ALTERYN, Baroness *cr* 1974 (Life Peer), of Alteryn, Gwent; **Margaret Delacourt-Smith;** *b* 1916; *d* of Frederick James Hando; *m* 1st, 1939, Charles Smith (subsequently Lord Delacourt-Smith, PC) (*d* 1972); one *s* two *d*; 2nd, 1978, Professor Charles Blackton. *Educ:* Newport High School for Girls; St Anne's College, Oxford (MA). *Address:* House of Lords, SW1A 0PW.

DELAFONS, John, CB 1982; Visiting Professor, Department of Land Management and Development, University of Reading, since 1993; *b* 14 Sept. 1930; *m* 1957, Sheila Egerton; four *d*. *Educ:* Ardingly; St Peter's College, Oxford. 1st cl. Hons English. Asst Principal, Min. of Housing and Local Govt, 1953; Harkness Fellowship, Harvard, 1959–60; Principal, 1959–66; Principal Private Sec. to Minister, 1965–66; Department of the Environment: Assistant Sec., 1966–72; Under Sec., 1972–77; Under Sec., Cabinet Office, 1977–79; Dep. Sec., DoE, 1979–90, retd. Bd Mem., English Industrial Estates Corp. 1984–85. Leverhulme and Nuffield Fellowship, 1989–90; Res. Associate, Inst. of Urban and Regl Develt, Univ. of California, 1990; Associate, Dept of Land Economy, Univ. of Cambridge, 1990–93. Associate Consultant, DNLA Planning and Develt Consultants, 1992–; Consultant, Denton Hall, 1993–94. Chm., RIPA, 1981–83, Vice Pres., 1985–92; Mem. Council, TCPA, 1992–. *Publications:* Land-Use Controls in the United States, 1962, revd edn 1969; Development Impact Fees, 1990; Aesthetic Control, 1991. *Address:* 34 Castlebar Road, W5 2DD.

de la LANNE-MIRRLEES, Robin Ian Evelyn Stuart; *see* Mirrlees.

de la MADRID HURTADO, Miguel; President of Mexico, 1982–88; Director General, Fondo de Cultura Económica, since 1990; *b* 12 Dec. 1934; *m* 1959, Paloma Cordero de la Madrid; four *s* one *d*. *Educ:* Nat. Autonomous Univ., Mexico (Law degree with hon. mention for thesis; with master); Harvard Univ. (MPA). Legal Dept, Nat. Bank of Foreign Trade, 1953–57; Asst Gen. Man., Bank of Mexico, 1960–64; Asst Dir Gen., Credit Mexican, Min. of Treasury, 1965–70; Dir of Finance, Pemex, 1970–72; Gen. Dir, Credit, 1972–75, Under Sec., 1975–79, Min. of Treasury; Minister, Nat. Planning and Budget, Govt of Mexico, 1979–81. *Publications:* economic and legal essays. *Address:* (office) Parras #46, Barrio Sta Catarina, Deleg. Coyoacán, 04010, México DF. *T:* 6584459.

de la MARE, Prof. Albinia Catherine, OBE 1993; FBA 1987; Professor of Palaeography, King's College, London, since 1989; *b* 2 June 1932; *d* of Richard Herbert Ingpen de la Mare and Amy Catherine Donaldson. *Educ:* Queen's Coll., Harley St., W1; Lady Margaret Hall, Oxford (MA); Warburg Inst., London (PhD). FRHistS; FSA. Dept of Western MSS, Bodleian Liby, 1962–88, Asst Librarian, 1964–88. Susette Taylor Fellow, 1964, Hon. Res. Fellow, 1979, Hon. Fellow, 1989, Lady Margaret Hall, Oxford; Guest Scholar, J. Paul Getty Museum, Malibu, 1992. Mem., Comité Internat. de Paléographie Latine, 1986–. *Publications:* Catalogue of the Italian manuscripts of Major J. R. Abbey (with J. J. G. Alexander), 1969; Catalogue of the Lyell Manuscripts, Bodleian Library, Oxford, 1971; The Handwriting of Italian Humanists, 1973; New Research on Humanistic Scribes in Florence, in Miniatura Fiorentina del Rinascimento, ed A. Garzelli, 1985; articles in learned periodicals, etc. *Recreations:* music, gardening, travel. *Address:* Tithe Barn House, High Street, Cumnor, Oxford OX2 9PE. *T:* Oxford (01865) 863916.

de la MARTINEZ, Odaline, (Odaline de la Caridad Martinez); Cuban conductor and composer; *b* 31 Oct. 1949; *d* of Julian J. Martinez and Odaline M. Martinez. *Educ:* schs and univ. in USA; Royal Acad. of Music, London; Surrey Univ. Jt Founder, Lontano (chamber ensemble), 1976; first woman to conduct an entire Promenade Concert programme, Royal Albert Hall, 1984; Dir, European Women's Orchestra, 1990–. Founder Mem., Women in Music, 1985. *Compositions include:* First String Quartet; *opera:* Sister Aimée: an American Legend, 1984. *Publication:* Mendelssohn's Sister. *Address:* c/o Kantor Concert Management, 67 Teignmouth Road, NW2 4EA.

DELAMERE, 5th Baron *cr* 1821; **Hugh George Cholmondeley;** *b* 18 Jan. 1934; *s* of 4th Baron Delamere, and Phyllis Anne (*d* 1978), *e d* of late Lord George Scott, OBE; *S* father, 1979; *m* 1964, Mrs Ann Willoughby Tinne, *o d* of late Sir Patrick Renison, GCMG and Lady Renison, Mayfield, Sussex; one *s*. *Educ:* Eton; Magdalene Coll., Cambridge. MA Agric. *Heir: s* Hon. Thomas Patrick Gilbert Cholmondeley, *b* 19 June 1968. *Address:* Soysambu, Elmenteita, Kenya.

de la MORENA, Felipe; Ambassador of Spain; Chairman, British Hispanic Foundation, Madrid; *b* 22 Oct. 1927; *s* of Felipe de la Morena and Luisa Calvet; *m* 1958, María Teresa Casado Bach; two *s* two *d*. *Educ:* Univ. Complutense de Madrid; Univs of Grenoble and Oxford; Diplomatic Sch., Madrid. Entered diplomatic service 1957; served Beirut, Berne, Washington and Min. of Foreign Affairs, Madrid; Dir, Technical Office, later Dir-Gen., Territorial Planning, Min. of Develt Planning, 1974–76; Minister Counsellor, Lisbon, 1976; Ambassador to People's Republic of China, 1978; Dir-Gen., Foreign Policy for Latin America, 1982; Ambassador to Syria and Cyprus (residence Damascus), 1983; Ambassador to Tunisia, 1987, to UK, 1990–93. Orders: Alfonso X el Sabio, 1965; Mérito Civil, 1973; Isabel la Católica, 1970; Carlos III, 1980; Gran Cruz del Mérito Naval, 1992; holds foreign decorations. *Recreation:* golf. *Clubs:* Travellers; Puerta de Hierro, Real Automóvil de España (Madrid).

DELANEY, Francis James Joseph, (Frank); writer and broadcaster, since 1972; *b* 24 Oct. 1942; 5th *s* of Edward Delaney and Elizabeth Josephine O'Sullivan; *m* 1st, 1966, Eilish (*née* Kelliher) (marr. diss. 1978); three *s*; 2nd, 1988, Susan Jane Collier. *Educ:* Abbey Schools, Tipperary, Ireland; Rosse Coll., Dublin. Bank of Ireland, 1961–72; journalism, 1972–: includes: broadcasting news with RTE, Dublin; current affairs with BBC Northern Ireland, BBC Radio Four, London, and BBC Television. Chm., NBL, 1984–86. *Publications:* James Joyce's Odyssey, 1981; Betjeman Country, 1983; The Celts, 1986; A Walk in the Dark Ages, 1988; My Dark Rosaleen (fiction), 1989; The Sins of the Mothers (fiction), 1992; Telling the Pictures (fiction), 1993; A Walk to the Western Isles, 1993; A Stranger in their Midst (fiction), 1995; sundry criticisms and introductions. *Recreations:* reading, conversation, walking. *Address:* 45A Old Town, SW4 0JL. *Clubs:* Athenæum, Chelsea Arts.

DELANEY, Shelagh; playwright; *b* Salford, Lancs, 1939; one *d*. *Educ:* Broughton Secondary Sch. *Plays:* A Taste of Honey, Theatre Royal, Stratford, 1958 and 1959, Wyndhams, 1959, New York, 1960 and 1961, off-Broadway revival, trans. to Broadway, 1981 (Charles Henry Foyle New Play Award, Arts Council Bursary, New York Drama Critics' Award); The Lion in Love, Royal Court 1960, New York 1962. *Films:* A Taste of Honey, 1961 (British Film Academy Award, Robert Flaherty Award); The White Bus, 1966; Charlie Bubbles, 1968 (Writers Guild Award for best original film writing); Dance with a Stranger, 1985 (Prix Film Jeunesse-Etranger, Cannes, 1985). *TV plays:* St Martin's Summer, LWT, 1974; Find Me First, BBC TV, 1979; *TV series:* The House that Jack Built, BBC TV, 1977 (stage adaptation, NY, 1979). *Radio plays:* So Does the Nightingale, BBC, 1980; Don't Worry About Matilda, 1983. FRSL 1985. *Publications:* A Taste of Honey, 1959 (London and New York); The Lion in Love, 1961 (London and New York); Sweetly Sings the Donkey, 1963 (New York), 1964 (London). *Address:* c/o Tessa Sayle, 11 Jubilee Place, SW3 3TE.

DELANO, Juan Carlos; Director, Icare; *b* Santiago, 14 June 1941; *m* Maria Paz Valenzuela; three *s* one *d*. *Educ:* St George's Coll., Catholic Univ., Chile; OCD, Belgium. Private enterprise: Distribuidora Audicol SA, Commercial Magara Ltd; Pres., Trading Assoc. of Chile, Dir, Chamber of Commerce of Santiago, 1979–83; Pres., Chilean Nat. Chamber of Commerce and Advr to Confedn of Trade and Industry, 1983–85; Minister of Economy, Promotion and Reconstruction, 1985–87; Ambassador to UK, 1987–90. *Address:* Cruz del Sur No 133, Of. 1003, Santiago, Chile. *Clubs:* Union, Polo.

De-la-NOY, Michael; author; *b* 3 April 1934; *yr s* of late Eric De-la-Noy Walker and of Kathleen Harvard (*née* Johnson). *Educ:* Bedford Sch. Commnd RAC; served in Egypt, 1952–54. Member, editorial staff: Bedfordshire Times, 1954–57; Brighton & Hove Herald, 1958–60; Editor, Richard Thomas & Baldwin, 1961–62; Religious Editor, Prism Pubns, 1962–65; Editor, Pergamon Press, 1966–67; Press Officer to Archbp of Canterbury and Asst Information Officer, Church Inf. Office, 1967–70; Dir, Albany Trust and Sec., Sexual Law Reform Soc., 1970–71; Editor, Open Univ., 1975–77. Member: House of Laity, Church Assembly, 1965–67; Steering Cttee on Liturgical Revision, 1965–67. *Publications:* Before the Storm (poems), 1958; A Child's Life of Christ, 1964; Young Once Only: a study of boys on probation, 1965; The Fields of Praise: an anthology of religious poetry, 1968; A Day in the Life of God, 1971; Elgar: the man, 1983; (ed) The Journals of Denton Welch, 1984; Denton Welch: the making of a writer, 1984; The Honours System, 1985, rev. edn 1992; Acting as Friends: the story of the Samaritans, 1987; (ed) Fragments of a Life Story: the collected short writings of Denton Welch, 1987; Eddy: the life of Edward Sackville-West, 1988; Michael Ramsey: a portrait, 1990; Windsor Castle: past and present, 1990; Exploring Oxford, 1991; The Church of England: a portrait, 1993; The Queen Behind the Throne, 1994; The King who never was: the story of Frederick, Prince of Wales, 1995; contrib. DNB. *Recreation:* going for very short walks. *Address:* c/o Scott Ferris Associates, Box 317, 15 Gledhow Gardens, SW5 0AY. *T:* 0171–373 2762. *Club:* Wig and Pen.

de LAROSIÈRE de CHAMPFEU, Jacques (Martin Henri Marie); Officer, Legion of Honour, 1988; Chevalier, National Order of Merit, 1970; Inspector General of Finance, since 1981; President, European Bank for Reconstruction and Development, since 1993; Chairman, Committee of Group of Ten, since 1990; *b* 12 Nov. 1929; *s* of Robert de Larosière and Hugayte de Champfeu; *m* 1960, France du Bos; one *s* one *d*. *Educ:* Institut d'Etudes Politiques, Paris (L ès L, licencié en droit); Nat. Sch. of Administration, Paris. Inspecteur des Finances, 1958; appointments at: Inspectorate-General of Finance, 1961; External Finance Office, 1963; Treasury 1965; Asst Dir, Treasury, 1967; Dep. Dir then Head of Dept, Min. of Economics and Finance, 1971; Principal Private Sec. to Minister of Economics and Finance, 1974; Dir, Treasury, 1974–78; Dir Gen., IMF, 1978–87; Gov., Bank of France, 1987–93. Director: Renault, 1971–74; Banque Nat. de Paris, 1973–78; Air France and French Railways, 1974–78; Société nat. industrielle aérospatiale, 1976–78. Director appointed by Treasury, General Council, Bank of France, 1974–78; Auditor: Crédit national, 1974–78; Comptoir des entrepreneurs, 1973–75; Crédit foncier de France, 1975–78. Vice Pres., Caisse nat. des télécommunications, 1974–78. Chairman: OECD Econ. and Develt Review Cttee, 1967–71; Deputies Group of Ten, 1976–78. Mem., Acad. of Moral and Pol Scis, 1993; Hon. Mem., Société des Cincinnatti de France. *Address:* European Bank for Reconstruction and Development, 1 Exchange Square, 175 Bishopsgate, EC2.

de la RUE, Sir Andrew (George Ilay), 4th Bt *cr* 1898, of Cadogan Square; company director; farmer; *b* 3 Feb. 1946; *s* of Sir Eric Vincent de la Rue, 3rd Bt and Cecilia (*d* 1963), *d* of late Maj. Walter Waring; *S* father, 1989; *m* 1984, Tessa Ann, *er d* of David Dobson; two *s*. *Educ:* Millfield. With Lloyd's (Insurance), 1966; Dir, Private Company, 1976–. *Recreations:* shooting, coursing, tennis. *Heir: s* Edward Walter de la Rue, *b* 25 Nov. 1986. *Address:* Stragglethorpe Grange, Brant Broughton, Lincolnshire LN5 0QZ. *T:* Newark (01636) 626505; 27 Kersley Street, SW11 4PR. *T:* 0171–585 1254.

de LASTIC, Most Rev. Alen; *see* Delhi, Archbishop of, (RC).

de la TOUR, Frances; actress; *b* 30 July 1944; *d* of Charles de la Tour and Moyra (*née* Fessas); one *s* one *d*. *Educ:* Lycée français de Londres; Drama Centre, London. Royal Shakespeare Company, 1965–71: rôles include Audrey in As You Like It, 1967; Hoyden in The Relapse, 1969; Helena in A Midsummer Night's Dream (Peter Brooks's production), 1971 (also USA tour); Belinda in The Man of Mode, 1971; Violet in Small Craft Warnings, Comedy, 1973 (Best Supporting Actress, Plays and Players Award); Ruth Jones in The Banana Box, Apollo, 1973; Isabella in The White Devil, Old Vic, 1976; appearances at Hampstead Theatre, and Half Moon Theatre incl. title rôle in Hamlet, 1979; Stephanie in Duet for One (written by Tom Kempinski), Bush Theatre and Duke of York's, 1980 (Best New Play, and Best Perf. by Actress, Drama Awards, Best Perf. by Actress in New Play, SWET Award, Best Actress, New Standard Award); Jean in Skirmishes, Hampstead, 1982 (also television, 1982); Sonya in Uncle Vanya, Haymarket, 1982; Josie in A Moon for the Misbegotten, Riverside, 1983 (SWET Best Actress award); title rôle in St Joan, Nat. Theatre, 1984; Dance of Death, Riverside, 1985; Sonya and Masha in Chekhov's Women, Lyric, 1985; Brighton Beach Memoirs, NT, 1986; Lillian, Lyric, 1986, Fortune, 1987; Façades, Lyric, Hammersmith, 1988; Regan in King Lear, Old Vic, 1989; Arkadina, Ranyevskaya and Olga Knipper in Chekhov's Women, Moscow Art Theatre, 1990; Miss Belzer in When She Danced, Globe, 1991 (Olivier Award); Witch in The Pope and the Witch, Comedy, 1992; Yoko Sitsuki in Greasepaint, Lyric, Hammersmith, 1993; Leonie in Les Parents Terribles, NT, 1994; Three Tall Women, Wyndham's, 1994. *Films:* include Our Miss Fred, 1972; To the Devil a Daughter, 1976; Rising Damp, 1979 (Best Actress, New Standard British Film Award, 1980). *Television:* Crimes of Passion, 1973; Play for Today (twice), 1973–75; Rising Damp (series), 1974, 1976; Cottage to Let, 1976; Flickers, 1980; Murder with Mirrors, 1984; Duet for One, 1985; A Kind of Living, 1987; Bejewelled, 1990; Silver Lining, Downwardly Mobile, 1993. *Address:* c/o Penny Wesson, Marmont Management, 308 Regent Street, W1R 5AL. *T:* 0171–637 3183.

DE LA WARR, 11th Earl *cr* 1761; **William Herbrand Sackville;** Baron De La Warr, 1299 and 1572; Viscount Cantelupe 1761; Baron Buckhurst 1864; Stockbroker, Credit Lyonnais Laing (formerly CL-Alexanders Laing and Cruickshank, later Laing & Cruickshank) since 1980; dairy farmer; *b* 10 April 1948; *s* of 10th Earl De La Warr and of Anne Rachel, *d* of Geoffrey Devas, MC; *S* father, 1988; *m* 1978, Anne, Countess of Hopetoun, *e d* of Arthur Leveson; two *s* and two step *s*. *Educ:* Eton. *Heir: s* Lord Buckhurst, *qv*. *Address:* Buckhurst Park, Withyham, Sussex TN7 4BL; 14 Bourne Street, SW1. *Clubs:* White's, Turf.

See also Hon. T. G. Sackville.

DELBRIDGE, Richard; Group Finance Director, HSBC Holdings plc, since 1993; *b* 21 May 1942; *s* of late Tom Delbridge and of Vera Kate Delbridge (*née* Lancashire); *m* 1966, Diana Genevra Rose Bowers-Broadbent; one *s* two *d*. *Educ:* Copleston Sch., Ipswich; LSE (BSc Econ); Univ. of California at Berkeley (MBA). FCA. Arthur Andersen & Co., 1963–66 and 1968–76, Partner 1974–76; Morgan Guaranty Trust Co., NY: Vice-Pres., 1976–79; Sen. Vice-Pres. and Comptroller of Morgan Guaranty Trust Co. and J. P. Morgan Inc., 1979–85; Asst Gen. Manager, 1985–87 and Gen. Manager, 1987–89, London offices; Dir, Group Finance, Midland Bank, 1990–92. Mem. Bd, Securities Assoc. 1988–89. *Recreations:* hill walking, books. *Address:* 48 Downshire Hill, NW3 1NX.

DELHI, Archbishop of, (RC), since 1991; **Most Rev. Alen de Lastic;** *b* 24 Sept. 1929. Ordained priest, 1958; Auxiliary Bishop of Calcutta, 1979–84; Bishop of Lucknow, 1984–90. *Address:* Archbishop's House, Ashok Place, New Delhi 110001, India. *T:* 343593, 343457, *Fax:* 3746575.

DELIGHT, Ven. John David; Archdeacon of Stoke, 1982–90, Archdeacon Emeritus, 1990; *b* 24 Aug. 1925. *Educ:* Christ's Hospital, Horsham; Liverpool Univ.; Oak Hill Theolog. Coll.; Open Univ. (BA). RNVR (Fleet Air Arm), 1943–46. Curate: Tooting Graveney, 1952–55; Wallington, 1955–58; Travelling Sec., Inter-Varsity Fellowship, 1958–61; Vicar, St Christopher's, Leicester, 1961–69; Chaplain, Leicester Prison, 1965–67; Rector of Aldridge, 1969–82; RD, Walsall, 1981–82; Prebendary of Lichfield Cathedral, 1980–82; volunteer associate of Crosslinks (formerly BCMS) and CMS, to develop theol educn by extension in dio. of Machakos, Kenya, 1990–94; retired 1994 and licensed to officiate, dio. of Lichfield. Hon. Canon, All Souls Cathedral, Machakos. *Publication:* (contrib.) Families, Facts and Frictions, 1976. *Recreations:* walking, music, gardening, reading. *Club:* Christ's Hospital.

DE L'ISLE, 2nd Viscount *cr* 1956; **Philip John Algernon Sidney,** MBE 1977; Baron De L'Isle and Dudley 1835; Bt 1806; Bt 1818; *b* 21 April 1945; *s* of 1st Viscount De L'Isle, VC, KG, GCMG, GCVO, PC and Hon. Jacqueline Vereker (*d* 1962), *o d* of Field-Marshal 6th Viscount Gort, VC, GCB, CBE, DSO, MVO, MC; *S* father, 1991; *m* 1980, Isobel Tresyllian, *y d* of Sir Edmund Compton, GCB, KBE; one *s* one *d*. *Educ:* Tabley House; Mons OCS; RMA Sandhurst. Commnd Grenadier Guards, 1966. Served BAOR, UKLF, NI, Belize and Sudan at Regtl Duty; GSO3 Ops/SD HQ 3 Inf. Bde, 1974–76; retired 1979. Landowner, 1979–. Mem., H of L Adv. Panel on Works of Art, 1994–. Chm., Kent County Cttee, CLA, 1983–85. Hon. Col, 5th (V) Bn, Princess of Wales's Royal Regt, 1992–. Freeman, City of London; Liveryman, Goldsmiths' Co. *Heir: s* Hon. Philip William Edmund Sidney, *b* 2 April 1985. *Address:* Penshurst Place, Penshurst, Tonbridge, Kent TN11 8DG. *T:* Penshurst (01892) 870307. *Clubs:* White's, Pratt's.

de LISLE, Everard John Robert March Phillipps; stockbroker; Vice Lord-Lieutenant of Leicestershire, since 1990; *b* 8 June 1930; *s* of late Maj. J. A. F. M. P. de Lisle, DL and Elizabeth Muriel de Lisle; *m* 1959, Hon. Mary Rose, *d* of 1st Viscount Ingleby, PC; two *s* one *d*. *Educ:* Eton; RMA Sandhurst. Commnd RHG, 1950; Captain, 1954; Major, 1960; retired 1962. Mem., London Stock Exchange, 1965–. High Sheriff, 1974–75, DL 1980, Leics. *Recreations:* shooting, country pursuits. *Address:* Stockerston Hall, Oakham, Leics LE15 9JD; 11 Buckingham Court, Kensington Park Road, W11 3BP. *Clubs:* MCC; Leicestershire.

DELL, David Michael, CB 1986; Chief Executive, British Overseas Trade Board, 1987–91, retired; *b* 30 April 1931; *s* of late Montague Roger Dell and Aimée Gabrielle Dell; unmarried. *Educ:* Rugby Sch.; Balliol Coll., Oxford (MA). 2nd Lieut Royal Signals, Egypt and Cyprus, 1954–55. Admiralty, 1955; MoD, 1960; Min. of Technol., 1965; DTI, 1970; DoI, 1974, Under Sec., 1976; Regl Dir, Yorks and Humberside, DTI, 1976–78; DTI, 1979; Dep. Sec., 1983–91; Dir, Industrial Develt Unit, 1984–85; Dir, EIB, 1984–87. Dir, Nesbit Evans Gp, 1991–93. Chm., Christ Church Bentinck Sch., 1979–92. Comp., BITC, 1992. *Recreations:* committees, dining out. *Clubs:* Royal Automobile, St Stephen's Constitutional; Leeds (Leeds).

DELL, Rt. Hon. Edmund, PC 1970; *b* 15 Aug. 1921; *s* of late Reuben and Frances Dell; *m* 1963, Susanne Gottschalk. *Educ:* Elementary schls; Owen's Sch., London; Queen's Coll., Oxford (Open Schol.). 1st Cl. Hons Mod. Hist., BA and MA 1947. War Service,

1941–45, Lieut RA (Anti-tank). Lecturer in Modern History, Queen's Coll., Oxford, 1947–49; Executive in Imperial Chemical Industries Ltd, 1949–63. Mem., Manchester City Council, 1953–60. Contested (Lab) Middleton and Prestwich, 1955. Pres., Manchester and Salford Trades Council, 1958–61. Simon Research Fellow, Manchester Univ., 1963–64. MP (Lab) Birkenhead, 1964–79; Parly Sec., Min. of Technology, 1966–67; Jt Parly Under-Sec. of State, Dept of Economic Affairs, 1967–68; Minister of State: Board of Trade, 1968–69; Dept of Employment and Productivity, 1969–70; Paymaster General, 1974–76; Sec. of State for Trade, 1976–78. Chm., Public Accts Cttee, 1973–74 (Acting Chm., 1972–73). Mem., Cttee of Three apptd by European Council to review procedures of EEC, 1978–79. Chm. and Chief Exec., Guinness Peat Gp, 1979–82; Founder Chm., Channel Four TV Co., 1980–87; Dir, Shell Transport and Trading Co. plc, 1979–92. Pres., London Chamber of Commerce and Industry, 1991–92 (Dep. Chm., 1988–90; Chm., 1990–91; Chm., Commercial Educn Trust, 1989–92). Chairman: Hansard Soc. Commn on Financing of Politics, 1980–81; Public Finance Foundn, 1984–91; Working Party on Internat. Business Taxation, Inst. for Fiscal Studies, 1982; Wkg Pty on Company Political Donations (apptd by Hansard Soc. and Constitutional Reform Centre), 1985; Canada–UK Dalhousie Colloquium, 1987; Prison Reform Trust, 1988–93; Wkg Pty on 1992: Ownership, Productivity and Investment, 1988–89. Dep. Chm., Governing Body, Imperial Coll. of Science, Technology and Medicine, 1988–91. Boys' Chess Champion of London, 1936. Hon. Fellow, Fitzwilliam Coll., Cambridge, 1986. *Publications:* (ed with J. E. C. Hill) The Good Old Cause, 1949; Brazil: The Dilemma of Reform (Fabian Pamphlet), 1964; Political Responsibility and Industry, 1973; (with B. Biesheuvel and R. Marjolin) Report on European Institutions, 1979; The Politics of Economic Interdependence, 1987; A Hard Pounding: politics and economic crisis 1974–76, 1991; Britain and the Origins of the European Monetary System, in Contemporary European History Vol. 3, Pt 1, 1994; The Schumann Plan and the British Abdication of Leadership in Europe, 1995; articles in learned journals. *Recreation:* listening to music. *Address:* 4 Reynolds Close, NW11 7EA.

DELL, Dame Miriam (Patricia), ONZ 1993; DBE 1980 (CBE 1975); JP (NZ); Hon. President, International Council of Women, 1986–88 (President, 1979–86; Vice-President, 1976–79); *b* 14 June 1924; *d* of Gerald Wilfred Matthews and Ruby Miriam Crawford; *m* 1946, Richard Kenneth Dell; four *d*. *Educ:* Epsom Girls Grammar Sch.; Univ. of Auckland (BA); Auckland Teachers' Coll. (Teachers' Cert. (Secondary Sch.)). Teaching, 1945–47, 1957–58 and 1961–71. Nat. Pres., Nat. Council of Women, 1970–74 (Vice-Pres., 1967–70); Chm., Cttee on Women, NZ, 1974–81; Chm., Envmt and Conservation Orgns of NZ, 1989–; Chm., 1993 Suffrage Centennial Year Trust, 1991–. Member: Nat. Develt Council, 1969–74; Cttee of Inquiry into Equal Pay, 1971–72; Nat. Commn for UNESCO, 1974–83; Social Security Appeal Authority, 1974–; Project Develt Bd, Mus. of NZ, 1988–92; Nat. Convener, Internat. Women's Year, 1975; Co-ordinator, Internat. Council of Women Develt Prog., 1988–91; Sec., Inter-Church Council on Public Affairs, 1986–89 (Chm., 1982–86); Convener, Public Affairs Unit, Anglican Church of NZ, 1988–92. JP NZ 1975. Jubilee Medal, 1977; NZ Commemoration Medal, 1990; NZ Suffrage Centennial Medal, 1993. *Publications:* Role of Women in National Development, 1970; numerous articles in popular and house magazines, on role and status of women. *Recreations:* gardening, reading, handcrafts, beachcombing. *Address:* 98 Waerenga Road, Otaki, New Zealand. *T:* Otaki (6) 3647267; (office) PO Box 12–117, Wellington, New Zealand. *T:* (4) 4737623.

DELL, Ven. Robert Sydney; Archdeacon of Derby, 1973–92, now Archdeacon Emeritus; Canon Residentiary of Derby Cathedral, 1981–92, now Canon Emeritus; *b* 20 May 1922; *s* of Sydney Edward Dell and Lilian Constance Palmer; *m* 1953, Doreen Molly Layton; one *s* one *d*. *Educ:* Harrow County Sch.; Emmanuel Coll., Cambridge (MA); Ridley Hall. Curate of: Islington, 1948; Holy Trinity, Cambridge, 1950; Asst Chaplain, Wrekin Coll., 1953; Vicar of Mildenhall, Suffolk, 1955; Vice-Principal of Ridley Hall, Cambridge, 1957; Vicar of Chesterton, Cambridge, 1966 (Dir, Cambridge Samaritans, 1966–69). Mem., Archbishops' Commn on Intercommunion, 1965–67; Proctor in Convocation and Mem. Gen. Synod of C of E, 1970–85. Vis. Fellow, St George's House, Windsor Castle, 1981. Hon. Fellow, Univ. of Derby, 1994. *Publications:* Atlas of Christian History, 1960; contributor to: Charles Simeon, 1759–1836: essays written in commemoration of his bi-centenary, 1959; Jl of Ecclesiastical History. *Recreations:* reading, walking, travelling. *Address:* 7 Moss Drive, Haslingfield, Cambs CB3 7JB. *T:* (01223) 872194.

DELLAL, Jack; Chairman, Allied Commercial Holdings Ltd; *b* 2 Oct. 1923; *s* of Sulman and Charlotte Dellal; *m* 1952, Zehava Helmer; one *s* five *d* (and one *d* decd). *Educ:* Heaton Moor Coll., Manchester. Chm., Dalton, Barton & Co. Ltd, 1962–72; Dep. Chm., Keyser Ullman Ltd, 1972–74; Chm., Highland Electronics Group Ltd, 1971–76; Director: Anglo African Finance PLC, 1983–; General Tire & Rubber (SA) Ltd, 1983–87; Williams, Hunt South Africa Ltd, 1983–87. Vice-Pres., Anglo-Polish Conservative Society, 1970–. Officer, Order of Polonia Restituta, 1970. Freeman Citizen of Glasgow, 1971. *Recreations:* lawn tennis, squash, music, art. *Clubs:* Royal Thames Yacht, Queen's, Hurlingham.

DELLOW, Sir John (Albert), Kt 1990; CBE 1985 (OBE 1979); DL; Deputy Commissioner, Metropolitan Police, 1987–91; *b* 5 June 1931; *s* of Albert Reginald and Lily Dellow; *m* 1952, Heather Josephine Rowe; one *s* one *d*. *Educ:* William Ellis Sch., Highgate; Royal Grammar Sch., High Wycombe. Joined City of London Police, 1951; seconded Manchester City Police, 1966; Superintendent, Kent County Constabulary, 1966, Chief Supt, 1968; jssc 1969; Asst Chief Constable, Kent Co. Constabulary, 1969; Metropolitan Police: Deputy Assistant Commissioner: Traffic Planning, 1973; Personnel, 1975; No 2 Area, 1978; 'A' Dept Operations, 1979; Inspectorate, 1980; Assistant Commissioner: 'B' Dept, 1982; Crime, 1984; Asst Comr (Specialist Ops), 1985–87. Pres., ACPO, 1989–90 (Vice-Pres., 1988–89). Trustee, Metropolitan Museum Trust; Former Chairman: Metropolitan Police History Soc.; Metropolitan Police Climbing, Canoe, Rowing and Heavy Boat Sections; Cdre, Metropolitan Police Sailing Club. Member Council: London Dist, Order of St John of Jerusalem, 1988–; RUSI, 1991–95. DL Greater London, 1991. *Publications:* contrib. RUSI Defence Studies series and other jls. *Recreations:* walking, history, listening to wireless.

DELMAS, Jacques Pierre Michel C.; *see* Chaban-Delmas.

DELORS, Jacques Lucien Jean; President, Commission of the European Economic Community, 1985–95; *b* 20 July 1925; *s* of Louis and Jeanne Delors; *m* 1948, Marie Lephaille; one *s* one *d*. *Educ:* Paris Univ. Joined Banque de France, 1945; in office of Chief of Securities Dept, 1950–62, and in Sect. for the Plan and Investments, Conseil Economique et Social, 1959–61; Chief of Social Affairs, Gen. Commissariat of Plan Monnet, 1962–69; Gen. Sec., Interministerial Cttee for Professional Educn, 1969–73; Mem., Gen. Council, Banque de France, 1973–79, and Dir, on leave of absence, 1973. Special Advr on Social Affairs to Prime Minister, 1969–72. Socialist Party Spokesman on internat. econ. matters, 1976–81; Minister of the Economy and Finance, 1981–83; Minister of Economy, Finance and Budget, 1983–84. Mem., European Parlt, 1979–81 (Pres., Econ. and Financial Cttee, 1979–81). Mayor of Clichy, 1983–84. Associate Prof., Univ. of Paris-Dauphine, 1973–79. Dir, Work and Society Res. Centre, 1975–79. Founder, Club Echange et Projets, 1974. *Publications:* Les indicateurs sociaux, 1971; Changer, 1975; (jtly) En sortir ou pas, 1985; La France par L'Europe, 1988 (Our Europe: the community and national development, 1992); Le Nouveau Concert Européen, 1992; L'unité d'un homme, 1994; essays, articles and UN reports on French Plan. *Address:* c/o 200 Rue de la Loi, 1049 Brussels, Belgium.

de los ANGELES, Victoria; Cross of Lazo de Dama of Order of Isabel the Catholic, Spain; Condecoracíon Banda de la Orden Civil de Alfonso X (El Sabio), Spain; Opera and Concert-Artiste (singing in original languages), Lyric-Soprano, since 1944; *b* Barcelona, Spain, 1 Nov. 1923; *m* 1948, Enrique Magriñá (decd); two *s*. *Educ:* Escoles Milà i Fontanals de la Generalitat de Catalunya, Barcelona; Conservatorium of Barcelona; University of Barcelona. Studied until 1944 at Conservatorium, Barcelona; first public concert, in Barcelona, 1944; début at Gran Teatro del Liceo de Barcelona, in Marriage of Figaro, 1945; concert and opera tours in Spain and Portugal, 1945–49; winner of first prize at Concours International of Geneva, 1947; first appearances at Paris Opéra, Stockholm Royal Opera, Copenhagen Royal Opera, and début at the Scala, Milan, also South-American and Scandinavian concert tours, 1949; first appearance at Covent Garden, and Carnegie Hall Début, 1950; first United States concert tour, and Metropolitan Opera of New York season, first appearances at La Monnaie, Brussels, Holland and Edinburgh Festivals, 1951; first appearances at Teatro Colón, Buenos Aires, and Teatro Municipal, Rio de Janeiro, 1952. Since 1952 has appeared at the most important opera theatres and concert halls of Europe, North, South and Central America and Canada; first tour in S Africa, 1953; first tour in Australia and New Zealand, 1956; first appearance, Vienna State Opera, 1957; opening Festival, Bayreuth, with Tannhäuser, 1961; first tour in Japan and Far East, 1964. Gold Medal, Barcelona, 1958; Silver Medal, province of Barcelona, 1959; Premio Nacional de Música, Spain; Medal Premio Roma, 1969, and various French, Italian, Dutch and American awards; Gold Disc for 5 million copies sold, UK; Hon. Dr Univ. of Barcelona. *Address:* Avenida de Pedralbes 57, 08034 Barcelona, Spain.

DELVE, Sir Frederick (William), Kt 1962; CBE 1942; Chief Officer, London Fire Brigade, 1948–62, retired; Hon. President, Securicor plc, since 1985 (Director and Vice-Chairman, 1962–82, Vice-President, 1982–85); *b* 28 Oct. 1902; *s* of Frederick John Delve, Master Tailor, Brighton; *m* 1924, Ethel Lillian Morden (*d* 1980); no *c*. *Educ:* Brighton. Royal Navy, 1918–23; Fire Service since 1923; Chief Officer, Croydon Fire Brigade, 1934–41; Dep. Inspector-in-Chief of NFS, 1941–43; Chief Regional Fire Officer, No 5 London Region, National Fire Service, 1943–48. Pres., Institution of Fire Engineers, 1941–42; King's Police and Fire Services Medal, 1940. *Address:* 53 Ashley Court, Grand Avenue, Hove, East Sussex BN3 2NL. *T:* Brighton (01273) 774605.

DELVIN, Lord; title borne by eldest son of Earl of Westmeath, *qv*; not at present used.

DELVIN, Dr David George; television and radio broadcaster, writer and doctor; *b* 28 Jan. 1939; *s* of William Delvin, Ayrshire and Elizabeth Falvey, Kerry; *m* 1st, Kathleen Sears, SRN, SCM; two *s* one *d*; 2nd, Christine Webber. *Educ:* St Dunstan's Coll.; King's Coll., Univ. of London; King's Coll. Hosp. (MB, BS 1962; psychol medicine, forensic medicine and public health prizes, 1962). LRCP, MRCS 1962; MRCGP 1974; DObstRCOG 1965; DCH 1966; DipVen, Soc. of Apothecaries, 1977; FPA Cert. 1972; FPA Instructing Cert. 1974. Dir, Hosp. Medicine Film Unit, 1968–69. Vice-Chm., Med. Journalists' Assoc., 1982–87; General Medical Council: Elected Mem., 1979–94; Member: Health Cttee 1980–86; Professional Conduct Cttee, 1987–94; Standards & Ethics Cttee, 1992–94. Member: Educn Cttee, Back Pain Assoc., 1983–87; Faculty of Family Planning, RCOG, 1993–. Medical Consultant: FPA, 1981–90; Nat. Assoc. of Family Planning Doctors, 1990–93; Med. Advisor to various BBC and ITV progs, 1974–. Med. Editor, General Practitioner, 1972–90; Chm., Editorial Boards of Medeconomics, Monthly Index of Med. Specialities, and MIMS Magazine, 1988–91; Dr Jekyll Columnist in World Medicine, 1973–82; Mem. Editorial Adv. Bd, British Jl of Family Planning, 1994–. Cert. of Special Merit, Med. Journalists' Assoc., 1974 and (jtly) 1975. American Medical Writers' Assoc. Best Book Award, 1976; Consumer Columnist of the Year Award, 1986. Médaille de la Ville de Paris (échelon argent), 1983. *Publications:* The Good Sex Guide, and other books, articles, TV and radio scripts, short stories, humorous pieces, medical films and videos; papers on hypertension and contraception in BMJ etc. *Recreations:* athletics, opera, orienteering, scuba-diving, hang-gliding (retired hurt). *Address:* c/o Coutts, 2 Harley Street, W1A 1EE. *Club:* Royal Society of Medicine.

DEMARCO, Prof. Richard, OBE 1985; RSW, SSA; Professor of European Cultural Studies, Kingston University, since 1993; Trustee, Kingston Demarco European Cultural Foundation, since 1993; *b* 9 July 1930; *s* of Carmine Demarco and Elizabeth (*née* Fusco); *m* 1957, Anne Muckle. *Educ:* Holy Cross Academy, Edinburgh; Edinburgh College of Art. National Service, KOSB and RAEC, 1954–56. Art Master, Duns Scotus Academy, Edinburgh, 1956–67; Co-Founder, Traverse Theatre Club; Vice-Chm. and Director, Traverse Art Gall., 1963–67; Dir, Richard Demarco Gall., Melville Crescent, Edinburgh, 1966–92, appointed by co-founders John Martin, Andrew Elliott and James Walker; introduced contemporary visual arts into official Edinburgh Festival programme with Edinburgh Open 100 Exhibn, 1967; introduced work of 330 internat. artists to UK, mainly through Edinburgh Fest. exhibns, from Canada, 1968, W Germany, 1970, Romania, 1971, Poland, 1972 and 1979, France, 1973, Austria, 1973, Yugoslavia, 1975, Aust. and NZ, 1984, Netherlands, 1990; incl. Joseph Beuys, 1970, Gunther Uecker, 1991, and Tadeusz Kantor's Cricot Theatre, with prodns of The Water Hen, 1972, Lovelies and Dowdies, 1973, The Dead Class, 1976. Has presented, 1969–, annual programmes of theatre, music and dance prodns, incl. the Freehold Company's Antigone, 1970; Dublin Project Company's On Baille Strand, 1977; Mladen Materio's Obala Theatre from Sarajevo, 1988 and 1989, Teatro Settimo from Turin, and Grupa Chwilowa from Lublin, 1991; Yvette Bozsik Theatre from Budapest, 1993. Prod Macbeth for Edinburgh Fest., on Inchcolm Is, 1988 and 1989. Director: Sean Connery's Scottish Internat. Educn Trust, 1972–74; Edinburgh Arts annual summer sch. and expedns, 1972–92; Artistic Advr, Eur. Youth Parlt, 1992–. Has directed annual exhib. prog. with Special Unit, HM Prison, Barlinnie, with partic. reference to sculpture of James Boyle, 1974–80; directed Edinburgh Fest. Internat. Confs, Towards the Housing of Art in the 21st Century, 1983, Art and the Human Environment, 1984 (also at Dublin Fest.). Was subject of film, Walkabout Edinburgh, dir. by Edward McConnell, 1970; acted in feature films: Long Shot, 1978; That Sinking Feeling, 1980; subject of TV film, The Demarco Dimension, 1987. Has broadcast regularly on television and radio, 1966–; has lectured in over 150 univs, art colls, schools, art galls; as water-colour painter and printmaker is represented in over 1600 public and private collections, incl. Nat. Gall. of Modern Art of Scotland, V&A Museum, Scottish Arts Council. Contributing Editor, Studio International, 1982–. SSA 1964; RWSScot 1966. Mem. AICA, 1992. Hon. FRIAS 1991. Hon. DFA Atlanta Coll. of Art, 1993. Gold Order of Merit, Polish People's Republic, 1976; Order of the Cavaliere della Repùbblica d'Italia, 1987; Chevalier de l'Ordre des Arts et des Lettres, France, 1991. *Publications:* The Artist as Explorer, 1978; The Road to Meikle Seggie, 1978; A Life in Pictures, 1994. *Recreations:* exploring: the small and secret spaces in townscape; cathedrals, abbeys, parish churches; coastlines and islands and The Road to Meikle Seggie. *Address:* Kingston University, Millenium House, 21 Eden Street, Kingston-upon-Thames, Surrey KT1 1BL. *Club:* Scottish Arts (Hon. Mem.) (Edinburgh).

de MARÉ, Eric, RIBA; writer and photographer; *b* 10 Sept. 1910; *s* of Bror and Ingrid de Maré; *m* 1st, 1936, Vanessa Burrage (*d* 1972); 2nd, 1974, Enid Verity. *Educ:* St Paul's Sch., London; Architectural Assoc., London (Dip.). RIBA 1934. Asst in several arch. practices, 1933–36; in private practice, 1936–40. War Service, survived, with spell in Home Guard designing frondy camouflage. Editor, Architects' Jl, 1942–46; freelance writer and photographer, mostly on architectural, topographical and photographic subjects, 1946–. Has travelled extensively in British Isles, Europe and USA in search of freelance fodder; much lecturing. Hon. Treasurer, Social Credit Party, 1938–46. Hon. Mem., Glos Architectural Assoc., 1986. Photography exhibitions: Architectural Assoc., 1990; Glasgow Sch. of Architecture, 1991. *Publications:* Britain Rebuilt, 1942; The Canals of England, 1950, 2nd edn 1952, repr. 1987; Scandinavia, 1952; Time on the Thames, 1952; The Bridges of Britain, 1954, 3rd edn 1989; Gunnar Asplund, 1955; Penguin Photography, 1957, 7th edn 1980; London's Riverside: past, present and future, 1958; (with Sir James Richards) The Functional Tradition in Early Industrial Buildings, 1958; Photography and Architecture, 1961; Swedish Cross Cut: the story of the Göta Canal, 1964; London's River: the story of a city, 1964, 2nd edn 1975 (Runner-up for 1964 Carnegie Award); The City of Westminster: heart of London, 1968; London 1851: the year of the Great Exhibition, 1972; The Nautical Style, 1973; The London Doré Saw: a Victorian evocation, 1973; Wren's London, 1975; Architectural Photography, 1975; The Victorian Wood Block Illustrators, 1980 (Yorkshire Post Award for best book on art, 1980); A Matter of Life or Debt, 1983, 4th edn 1986; contrib. Arch. Rev., TLS, Illustrated London News, etc.; *relevant publication:* Eric de Maré, Builder with Light, 1990 (Architectural Association monograph of selected photographs, with text by Andrew Higgott and bibliography). *Recreations:* talking to friends, reading history, philosophizing, looking at trees, preaching Douglas Social Credit and the Age of Leisure. *Address:* Dynevor House, New Street, Painswick, Glos GL6 6UN. *T:* Stroud (01452) 812543.

de MAULEY, 6th Baron, *cr* 1838; **Gerald John Ponsonby;** *b* 19 Dec. 1921; *er s* of 5th Baron de Mauley and Elgiva Margaret (*d* 1987), *d* of late Hon. Cospatrick Dundas and Lady Cordeaux; *S* father, 1962; *m* 1954, Helen Alice, *d* of late Hon. Charles W. S. Douglas and *widow* of Lieut-Col B. L. L. Abdy Collins, OBE, MC, RE. *Educ:* Eton; Christ Church, Oxford (MA). Served War of 1939–45, France; Lieut Leics Yeo., Captain RA. Called to Bar, Middle Temple, 1949. *Heir: b* Col Hon. Thomas Maurice Ponsonby, TD, late Royal Glos Hussars [*b* 2 Aug. 1930; *m* 1956, Maxine Henrietta, *d* of W. D. K. Thellusson; two *s*]. *Address:* Langford House, Little Faringdon, Lechlade, Glos GL7 3QN.

DEMERITTE, Richard Clifford; Auditor-General, Commonwealth of the Bahamas, 1980–84 and since 1988; *b* 27 Feb. 1939; *s* of R. H. Demeritte and late Miriam Demeritte (*née* Whitfield); *m* 1966, Ruth Smith; one *s* two *d*. *Educ:* Bahamas Sch. of Commerce; Metropolitan Coll., London; Century Univ., USA. Treasury Department, Bahamas: Asst Accountant, 1967; Accountant, 1969–71; Asst Treasurer, Jan.–Dec. 1972; Dep. Treasurer, 1973–79; High Comr, London, 1984–88; Amb. to EEC, 1986–88, and to Belgium, France, FRG, 1987–88. Fellow: Inst. of Admin. Accountants, London, 1969; Corp. of Accountants and Auditors, Bahamas, 1971 (Pres., 1973–84; Hon. Fellow, 1983); Assoc. of Internat. Accountants, 1976 (Pres./Chm. Council, 1985–); Mem., Bahamas Inst. of Chartered Accountants, 1991; Certified Gen. Accountant, Canada, 1982; FIMgt (FBIM 1985); FRSA 1988. Hon. Life Pres.: YMCA (Grand Bahama); Toastmasters Internat. (Grand Bahama). *Recreations:* chess, golf, billiards, weightlifting. *Address:* (office) PO Box N-3027, Nassau, Bahamas; (home) Rurick, Cable Beach, PO Box CB 11001, Nassau, Bahamas.

DEMEURE de LESPAUL, Edouard Henri; Officer, Order of Leopold II; General Manager, Marketing, Petrofina SA, since 1993; *b* 6 Jan. 1928; *s* of Charles Demeure de Lespaul and Adrienne Demeure de Lespaul (*née* Escoyez); *m* 1953, Myriam van Cutsem; two *d*. *Educ:* Univ. of Louvain (Mining Engineering); ENSP 1952 (Petroleum Engineering). Petrofina: Exploration and Production Dept, Brussels, 1952–53; Manager, Drilling Activities, Congo, 1955–56; Man. Dir, Egypt, 1956–61; Manager, Exploration and Production, Brussels, 1961–63; Chm. and Man. Dir, Finaneste NV, Belgium, 1963–89; Man. Dir and Chief Exec., Petrofina UK, later Fina plc, 1989–92. Military Medal, war voluntary. *Recreations:* swimming, history reading, mountain walking. *Address:* Petrofina SA, Rue de l'Industrie 52, 1040 Brussels, Belgium.

de MILLE, Peter Noël; His Honour Judge de Mille; a Circuit Judge, Midland and Oxford Circuit, since 1992; *b* 11 Nov. 1944; *s* of late Noël James de Mille and of Ailsa Christine (*née* Ogilvie); *m* 1977, Angela Mary Cooper; one *d*. *Educ:* Fettes Coll.; Trinity Coll., Dublin (BA, LLB). Called to the Bar, Inner Temple, 1968; a Recorder, 1987–92. *Recreations:* sailing, music, theatre. *Address:* 5 Fountain Court, Steelhouse Lane, Birmingham B4 6DR. *T:* 0121–236 5771. *Club:* Aldeburgh Yacht.

DE MOLEYNS; *see* Daubeny de Moleyns, family name of Baron Ventry.

de MOLLER, June Frances; Managing Director, Carlton Communications, since 1993; *b* 25 June 1947; *m* 1967 (marr. diss. 1980). *Educ:* Roedean; Hastings Coll.; Sorbonne Univ., Paris. Exec. Dir, Carlton Communications, 1983–93. Non-Executive Director: Anglian Water, 1992–; Riverside Mental Health Unit, 1992–. *Recreations:* reading, riding, tennis, Rare Breed Society. *Address:* Carlton Communications, 15 St George Street, Hanover Square, W1R 9DE.

de MONTEBELLO, (Guy) Philippe (Lannes); Director, Metropolitan Museum of Art, since 1978; *b* 16 May 1936; *s* of Roger Lannes de Montebello and Germaine (*née* Croisset); *m* 1961, Edith Bradford Myles; two *s* one *d*. *Educ:* Harvard Coll. (BA *magna cum laude*); New York Univ., Inst. of Fine Arts (MA). Curatorial Asst, European Paintings, Metropolitan Mus. of Art, 1963; Asst Curator, Associate Curator, MMA, until 1969; Director, Museum of Fine Arts, Houston, Texas, 1969–74; Vice-Director: for Curatorial Affairs, MMA, Jan. 1974–June 1974; for Curatorial and Educnl Affairs, 1974–77; Actg Dir, MMA, 1977–78. Gallatin Fellow, New York Univ., 1981; Hon. LLD: Lafayette Coll., East Pa, 1979; Bard Coll., Annandale-on-Hudson, NY, 1981; Hon. DFA Iona Coll., New Rochelle, NY, 1982. Alumni Achievement Award, New York Univ., 1978. *Publication:* Peter Paul Rubens, 1968. *Address:* 1150 Fifth Avenue, New York, New York 10028, USA. *T:* (212) 2894475. *Club:* Knickerbocker (New York).

de MONTMORENCY, Sir Arnold (Geoffroy), 19th Bt *cr* 1631; Chairman, Contemporary Review Co. Ltd, 1962, and Literary Editor 1960–90; *b* 27 July 1908; *s* of Prof. James Edward Geoffrey de Montmorency (*d* 1934) and Caroline Maud Saumarez (*d* 1973), *d* of Maj.-Gen. James de Havilland; *S* cousin, 1979; *m* 1949, Nettie Hay Anderson (marr. annulled 1953, remarried 1972), *d* of late William Anderson and Janet Hay, Morayshire; no *c*. *Educ:* Westminster School (Triplett Exhibn); Peterhouse, Cambridge. BA 1930, LLM 1931, MA 1934. Harmsworth Law Scholar. Called to the Bar, 1932. Served War, RASC and staff in ME, Italy and Yugoslavia, 1940–45. Contested (L) Cambridge, 1959, Cirencester and Tewkesbury, 1964. Chm. (pt-time), Industrial Tribunals, 1975–81. Member, RIIA; Pres., Friends of Peterhouse. *Publication:* Integration of Employment Legislation, 1984. *Heir:* none. *Club:* National Liberal.

DEMPSEY, Andrew; *see* Dempsey, J. A.

DEMPSEY, Dr Anthony Michael; Headmaster, Tiffin School, since 1988; *b* 12 June 1944; *s* of Michael and Bertha Laura Dempsey; *m* 1970, Sandra Lynn Atkins; one *s*. *Educ:* Tiffin Sch.; Bristol Univ. (BSc, PhD). Chemistry Teacher, King's College Sch., 1969–73; Heathland School, Hounslow: Head of Sci., 1973–75; Head, Maths and Sci. Faculty, 1975–79; Feltham Community School: Dep. Head, 1979–82; Sen. Dep. Head, 1982–88. *Publications:* Visual Chemistry, 1983; Science Master Pack, 1985; contrib. to Nuffield Chemistry books; papers in carbohydrate res. *Recreations:* walking, travel, sport, church, industrial archaeology. *Address:* Tiffin School, Queen Elizabeth Road, Kingston, Surrey KT2 6RL; 63 Gilpin Crescent, Twickenham TW2 7BP. *T:* 0181–898 2860.

DEMPSEY, (James) Andrew; Associate Curator, Hayward Gallery, South Bank Centre, since 1994 (Assistant Director responsible for the Gallery, 1987–94); *b* 17 Nov. 1942; *s* of James Dempsey, Glasgow; *m* 1966, Grace, *d* of Dr Ian MacPhail, Dumbarton; one *s* one *d*. *Educ:* Ampleforth Coll.; Glasgow Univ. Whistler Research Asst, Fine Art Dept, Univ. of Glasgow, 1963–65; exhibn work for art dept of Arts Council, 1966–71; Keeper, Dept of Public Relations, V&A, 1971–75; Asst Dir of Exhibitions, Arts Council of GB, 1975–87. *Address:* Royal Festival Hall, South Bank, SE1 8XX.

DEMPSEY, Michael Bernard, RDI 1994; Chairman and Creative Director, CDT Design Ltd, since 1993; *b* 25 July 1944; *s* of John Patrick Dempsey and Britannia May (*née* Thompson); *m* 1st, 1967, Sonja Green (marr. diss. 1988); two *s* one *d*; 2nd, 1989, Charlotte Antonia Richardson; two *d*. *Educ:* St Vincent RC Primary Sch., Dagenham; Bishop Ward RC Secondary Mod. Sch., Dagenham. Asst designer, Cheveron Studio, 1963–64; in-house designer, Bryan Colmer Artist Agent, 1964–65; freelance designer, 1965–66; Designer, Cato Peters O'Brien, 1966–68; Art Director: William Heinemann Publishers, 1968–74; William Collins Publishers, 1974–79; Founder Partner, Carroll & Dempsey Ltd, 1979–85; Partner, Carroll, Dempsey Thirkell Ltd, later CDT Design Ltd, 1985–. *Publications:* Bubbles: early advertising art from A. & F. Pears, 1978; The Magical Paintings of Justin Todd, 1978; Pipe Dreams: early advertising art from the Imperial Tobacco Company, 1982. *Recreations:* art history, photography, film, theatre, opera. *Address:* 114 De Beauvoir Road, N1 4DJ. *T:* 0171–241 1361.

DEMPSTER, John William Scott, CB 1994; Deputy Secretary, Department of Transport, since 1990; *b* 10 May 1938; *m* 1965, Ailsa Newman (marr. diss. 1972). *Educ:* Plymouth Coll.; Oriel Coll., Oxford (MA(PPE)). HM Inspector of Taxes, Inland Revenue, 1961–65; Ministry of Transport: Asst Principal, 1965–67; Principal, 1967–73; Asst Sec., Property Services Agency, 1973–76; Principal Private Sec. to Sec. of State for the Environment, 1976–77; Asst Sec., Dept of Transport, 1977–80; Principal Estabt and Finance Officer, Lord Chancellor's Dept, 1980–84; Department of Transport: Head of Marine Directorate, 1984–89; Principal Establishment Officer, 1989–90; Principal Establishment and Finance Officer, 1990–91; Dir Gen. of Highways, 1991–. *Recreations:* mountaineering, sailing, bridge, Munro collecting. *Address:* 2 Marsham Street, SW1P 3EB. *Clubs:* Alpine, Fell and Rock; Royal Southampton Yacht.

DEMPSTER, Nigel Richard Patton; Editorial Executive, Mail Newspapers Plc (formerly Associated Newspapers), since 1973; Editor: Mail Diary, since 1973; Mail on Sunday Diary, since 1986; *b* 1 Nov. 1941; *s* of Eric R. P. Dempster and Angela Grace Dempster (*née* Stephens); *m* 1st, 1971, Emma de Bendern (marr. diss. 1974), *d* of Count John de Bendern and Lady Patricia Douglas, *d* of 11th Marquess of Queensberry; 2nd, 1977, Lady Camilla Godolphin Osborne, *o c* of 11th Duke of Leeds and Audrey (who *m* 1955, Sir David Lawrence, Bt, *qv*); one *d*. *Educ:* Sherborne. Broker, Lloyd's of London, 1958–59; Stock Exchange, 1959–60; PR account exec., Earl of Kimberley Associates, 1960–63; journalist, Daily Express, 1963–71; columnist, Daily Mail, 1971–. London correspondent, Status magazine, USA, 1965–66; contributor to Queen magazine, 1966–70; columnist ('Grovel'), Private Eye magazine, 1969–85. Broadcaster with ABC (USA) and CBC (Canada), 1976–, and with TV-am, 1983–92; resident panellist, Headliners, Thames TV, 1987–89. *Publications:* HRH The Princess Margaret—A Life Unfulfilled (biog.), 1981; Heiress: the story of Christina Onassis, 1989; Nigel Dempster's Address Book, 1990; (with Peter Evans) Behind Palace Doors, 1993. *Recreations:* photography, squash, running marathons, bicycling. *Address:* c/o Daily Mail, Northcliffe House, Derry Street, W8 5TT. *Clubs:* Royal Automobile; Chappaquiddick Beach (Mass, USA).

de NAVARRO, Michael Antony; QC 1990; a Recorder, since 1990; *b* 1 May 1944; *s* of A. J. M. (Toty) de Navarro and Dorothy M. de Navarro; *m* 1975, Jill Margaret Walker; one *s* two *d*. *Educ:* Downside School; Trinity College, Cambridge (BA Hons). Called to the Bar, Inner Temple, 1968; pupil of Hon. Mr Justice Cazalet and Hon. Mr Justice Turner; Mem., Western Circuit. *Recreations:* opera, cricket, gardening, cooking. *Address:* 2 Temple Gardens, Temple, EC4Y 9AY. *T:* 0171–583 6041.

DENBIGH, 12th Earl of, *cr* 1622, **AND DESMOND,** 11th Earl of, *cr* 1622; **Alexander Stephen Rudolph Feilding;** Baron Feilding 1620; Viscount Feilding 1620; Viscount Callan 1622; Baron St Liz 1663; *b* 4 Nov. 1970; *o s* of 11th Earl of Denbigh and of Caroline Judith Vivienne, *o d* of Lt-Col Geoffrey Cooke; *S* father, 1995. *Heir: great uncle* Hon. Hugh Richard Feilding [*b* 15 July 1920; *m* 1944, Sheila Katharine Bolton; one *s*].

DENBIGH, Prof. Kenneth George, FRS 1965; MA Cantab, DSc Leeds; Principal of Queen Elizabeth College, University of London, 1966–77; Professor Emeritus in the University of London, 1977; Visiting Research Fellow, King's College, London, since 1985; *b* 30 May 1911; *s* of late G. J. Denbigh, MSc, Harrogate; *m* 1935, Kathleen Enoch; two *s*. *Educ:* Queen Elizabeth Grammar Sch., Wakefield; Leeds University. Imperial Chemical Industries, 1934–38, 1945–48; Lecturer, Southampton Univ., 1938–41; Ministry of Supply (Explosives), 1941–45; Lecturer, Cambridge Univ., Chemical Engineering Dept, 1948–55; Professor: of Chemical Technology, Edinburgh, 1955–60, of Chemical Engineering Science, London Univ., 1960–61; Courtauld's Prof., Imperial Coll., 1961–66. Dir, Council for Science and Society, 1977–83. Fellow, Imperial Coll., 1976; FKC, 1985. Hon. DèsSc Toulouse, 1960; Hon. DUniv. Essex, 1967. *Publications:* The Thermodynamics of the Steady State, 1951; The Principles of Chemical Equilibrium, 1955; Science, Industry and Social Policy, 1963; Chemical Reactor Theory, 1965; An Inventive Universe, 1975; Three Concepts of Time, 1981; (with J. S. Denbigh) Entropy in Relation to Incomplete Knowledge, 1985; various scientific papers. *Address:* 19 Sheridan Road, Merton Park, SW19 3HW.

DENBY, Patrick Morris Coventry, CMG 1982; Assistant Director-General (Treasurer and Financial Comptroller), International Labour Office, Geneva, 1976–81; *b* 28 Sept. 1920; *s* of Robert Coventry Denby and Phyllis Denby (*née* Dacre); *m* 1950, Margaret Joy, *d* of Lt-Col C. L. Boyle; one *d* (and two *d* decd). *Educ:* Bradford Grammar Sch.; Corpus Christi Coll., Oxford (Open Scholar) (Honour Mods, Cl. II, MA). War service with Intelligence Corps, as Temp. Lieut RNVR, and with Foreign Office, 1941–46. Unilever Ltd, UK and Australia: management trainee and product manager, 1946–51; joined International Labour Office, 1951: Professional Officer, 1951; Chief of Budget and Control Div., 1959; Chief of Finance and General Services Dept, Treasurer and Financial Comptroller, 1970; Chm., Investments Cttee; Mem., UN Pension Board, 1971–75; Chm., WIPO Appeal Bd, 1985–91. *Recreations:* skiing, mountain walking, tennis. *Address:*

7 Framers Court, Ellis Way, Lane End, High Wycombe, Bucks HP14 3LL. *Club:* Stoke Poges Lawn Tennis.

DENCH, Dame Judith Olivia, (Dame Judi Dench), DBE 1988 (OBE 1970); actress (theatre, films and television); *b* 9 Dec. 1934; *d* of Reginald Arthur Dench and Eleanora Olave Dench (*née* Jones); *m* 1971, Michael Williams, *qv*; one *d*. *Educ:* The Mount Sch., York; Central Sch. of Speech and Drama. *Theatre:* Old Vic seasons, 1957–61: parts incl.: Ophelia in Hamlet; Katherine in Henry V; Cecily in The Importance of Being Earnest; Juliet in Romeo and Juliet; also 1957–61: two Edinburgh Festivals; Paris-Belgium-Yugoslavia tour; America-Canada tour; Venice (all with Old Vic Co.). Subseq. appearances incl.: Royal Shakespeare Co., 1961–62: Anya in The Cherry Orchard; Titania in A Midsummer Night's Dream; Dorcas Bellboys in A Penny for a Song; Isabella in Measure for Measure; Nottingham Playhouse tour of W Africa, 1963; Oxford Playhouse, 1964–65: Irina in The Three Sisters; Doll Common in The Alchemist; Nottingham Playhouse, 1965: Saint Joan; The Astrakhan Coat (world première); Amanda in Private Lives; Variety London Critics' Best Actress of the Year Award for perf. as Lika in The Promise, Fortune, 1967; Sally Bowles in Cabaret, Palace, 1968; Associate Mem., RSC, 1969–; London Assurance, Aldwych, 1970, and New, 1972; Major Barbara, Aldwych, 1970; Bianca in Women Beware Women, Viola in Twelfth Night, doubling Hermione and Perdita in The Winter's Tale, Portia in The Merchant of Venice, the Duchess in The Duchess of Malfi, Beatrice in Much Ado About Nothing, Lady Macbeth in Macbeth, Adriana in The Comedy of Errors, Regan in King Lear, Imogen in Cymbeline; The Wolf, Oxford and London, 1973; The Good Companions, Her Majesty's, 1974; The Gay Lord Quex, Albery, 1975; Too True to be Good, Aldwych, 1975, Globe, 1976; Pillars of the Community, The Comedy of Errors, Aldwych, 1977; The Way of the World, 1978; Juno and the Paycock, Aldwych, 1980 (Best Actress award, SWET, Evening Standard, Variety Club, and Plays and Players); The Importance of Being Earnest, A Kind of Alaska, Nat. Theatre, 1982; Pack of Lies, Lyric, 1983 (SWET award); Mother Courage, Barbican, 1984; Waste, Barbican and Lyric, 1985; Mr and Mrs Nobody, Garrick, 1986; Antony and Cleopatra (Best Actress award, SWET, Evening Standard), Entertaining Strangers, Nat. Theatre, 1987; Hamlet, Royal Nat. Theatre, and Dubrovnik Theatre Fest., 1989; The Cherry Orchard, Aldwych, 1989; The Plough and the Stars, Young Vic, 1991; The Sea, Nat. Theatre, 1991; Coriolanus, Chichester, 1992; The Gift of the Gorgon, Barbican, 1992, transf. Wyndham's, 1993; The Seagull, RNT, 1994; Absolute Hell, RNT, 1995; Director, for Renaissance Theatre Co.: Much Ado About Nothing, 1988; Look Back in Anger, 1989; Director: The Boys from Syracuse, Regent's Park, 1991; Romeo and Juliet, Regent's Park, 1993. Recital tour of W Africa, 1969; RSC tours: Japan and Australia, 1970; Japan, 1972. *Films:* He Who Rides a Tiger; A Study in Terror; Four in the Morning (Brit. Film Acad. Award for Most Promising Newcomer, 1965); A Midsummer Night's Dream; The Third Secret; Dead Cert; Saigon: Year of the Cat; Wetherby; A Room with a View; 84 Charing Cross Road; A Handful of Dust; Henry V, 1990; Goldeneye, 1995. *Television* appearances include, 1957–: Talking to a Stranger (Best Actress of Year award, Guild of Television Dirs, 1967); Major Barbara; Hilda Lessways; Langrishe, Go Down; Macbeth; Comedy of Errors; On Giant's Shoulders; A Village Wooing; Love in a Cold Climate; Saigon; A Fine Romance (BAFTA Award, 1985); The Cherry Orchard; Going Gently; Mr and Mrs Edgehill (Best Actress, Amer. Cable Award, 1988); The Browning Version; Make or Break; Ghosts; Behaving Badly; Absolute Hell; Can You Hear Me Thinking?; As Time Goes By. Mem. Bd, Royal Nat. Theatre, 1988–. Awards incl. British and foreign, for theatre, films and TV, incl. BAFTA awards: for best television actress, 1981; for best supporting actress (A Room with a View), 1987, and (A Handful of Dust), 1988. Hon. DLitt: Warwick, 1978; Birmingham, 1989; Loughborough, 1991; London, 1994; DUniv: York, 1983; Open, 1992. *Recreations:* sewing, drawing, catching up with letters.

DENEUVE, Catherine; French film actress; *b* 22 Oct. 1943; *d* of Maurice Dorléac and Renée (*née* Deneuve); one *s* by Roger Vadim; *m* 1967, David Bailey, *qv* (marr. diss.); one *d* by Marcel Mastroianni. *Educ:* Lycée La Fontaine, Paris. Pres.-Dir Gen., Films de la Citrouille, 1971–79. Chm. Jury, Cannes Film Fest., 1994. *Films include:* Les petits chats, 1959; Les portes claquent, 1960; Le vice et la vertu, 1962; Les parapluies de Cherbourg, 1963; La Constanza della Ragione, 1964; Repulsion, 1964; Liebes Karusell, 1965; Belle de jour, 1967; Folies d'avril, 1969; Un flic, 1972; Le sauvage, 1975; Âmes perdues, 1976; Hustle, 1976; A nous deux, 1978; Le dernier métro, 1980 (César for best actress, 1981); Le choc, 1982; The Hunger, 1982; Le bon plaisir, 1984; Let's Hope It's A Girl, 1987; Drôle d'Endroit pour une Rencontre (Strange Place to Meet), 1989; Indochine, 1992; Ma Saison préférée, 1994; The Convent, 1995. *Address:* c/o Artmedia, 10 avenue George-V, 75008 Paris, France.

DENHAM, 2nd Baron, *cr* 1937, of Weston Underwood; **Bertram Stanley Mitford Bowyer,** KBE 1991; PC 1981; 10th Bt, *cr* 1660, of Denham; 2nd Bt, *cr* 1933 of Weston Underwood; Captain of the Gentlemen at Arms (Government Chief Whip in the House of Lords), 1979–91; *b* 3 Oct. 1927; *s* of 1st Baron and Hon. Daphne Freeman-Mitford, 4th *d* of 1st Baron Redesdale; *S* father 1948; *m* 1956, Jean, *o d* of Kenneth McCorquodale, Fambridge Hall, White Notley, Essex; three *s* one *d*. *Educ:* Eton; King's Coll., Cambridge. Mem. Westminster CC, 1959–61. A Lord-in-Waiting to the Queen, 1961–64 and 1970–71; Opposition Jun. Whip, 1964–70; Captain of the Yeomen of the Guard, 1971–74; Opposition Dep. Chief Whip, 1974–78; Opposition Chief Whip, 1978–79. Countryside Comr, 1993–. Dep. Pres., British Field Sports Soc., 1992–. *Publications:* The Man who Lost his Shadow, 1979; Two Thyrdes, 1983; Foxhunt, 1988. *Recreations:* field sports. *Heir:* *s* Hon. Richard Grenville George Bowyer [*b* 8 Feb. 1959; *m* 1988, Eleanor, *o d* of A. Sharpe]. *Address:* The Laundry Cottage, Weston Underwood, Olney, Bucks MK46 5JZ. *T:* Bedford (01234) 711535. *Clubs:* White's, Pratt's, Buck's, Beefsteak.

DENHAM, Ernest William; Deputy Keeper of Public Records, Public Record Office, 1978–82; *b* 16 Sept. 1922; *s* of William and Beatrice Denham; *m* 1957, Penelope Agatha Gregory; one *s* one *d*. *Educ:* City of London Sch.; Merton Coll., Oxford (Postmaster). MA 1948. Naval Intell., UK and SEAC, 1942–45. Asst Sec., Plant Protection Ltd, 1947–49; Asst Keeper 1949, Principal Asst Keeper 1967, Records Admin. Officer 1973, Public Record Office; Lectr in Palaeography and Diplomatic, UCL, 1957–73. *Recreation:* armchair criticism. *Address:* 4 The Ridge, Green Lane, Northwood, Mddx HA6 1AE. *T:* Northwood (01923) 827382.

DENHAM, John Yorke; MP (Lab) Southampton, Itchen, since 1992; *b* 15 July 1953; *s* of Albert Edward Denham and Beryl Frances Ada Denham; *m* 1979, Ruth Eleanore Dixon; one *s* one *d*. *Educ:* Woodroffe Comprehensive Sch., Lyme Regis; Univ. of Southampton (BSc Hons Chemistry; Pres., Students' Union, 1976–77). Advr, Energy Advice Service, Durham, 1977; Transport Campaigner, Friends of the Earth, 1977–79; Head, Youth Affairs, British Youth Council, 1979–82; Publications Sec., Clause IV Publications, 1982–84; Campaigns Officer, War on Want, 1984–88; Consultant to develt NGOs, 1988–92. Member (Lab): Hants CC, 1981–89; Southampton CC, 1989–93 (Chm., Housing Cttee, 1990–92). Contested (Lab) Southampton, Itchen, 1983, 1987. *Recreations:* cricket, gardening, walking, family, cooking. *Address:* House of Commons, SW1A 0AA; 145 Avenue Road, Southampton SO2 1BD.

DENHAM, Maurice, OBE 1992; actor since 1934; *b* 23 Dec. 1909; *s* of Norman Denham and Winifred Lillico; *m* 1936, Margaret Dunn (*d* 1971); two *s* one *d*. *Educ:* Tonbridge Sch. Hull Repertory Theatre, 1934–36; theatre, radio and television, 1936–39. Served War of 1939–45: Buffs, 1939–43; Royal Artillery, 1943–45; despatches, 1946. Theatre, films, radio and television, 1946–. *Radio includes:* ITMA, 1939–40; Much Binding in the Marsh, 1946; Winston, 6 series, 1986–93; Tale of Two Cities, 1988; The Sitter, 1990; Forsyte Chronicles, 1990; Six P. G. Wodehouse stories, 1995. *Theatre includes:* The Andersonville Trial, Mermaid, 1960; Macbeth, King John, Old Vic, 1961; The Apple Cart, Mermaid, 1970; Uncle Vanya, Hampstead, 1979; Incident at Tulse Hill, Hampstead, 1981. *Films include:* The Purple Plain, 1954; Doctor at Sea, 1955; Day of the Jackal, 1972; 84 Charing Cross Road, 1986. *Television includes:* Talking to a Stranger, 1968; All Passion Spent, 1986; Klaus Barbie, 1987; Behaving Badly, 1988; Inspector Morse, 1991; La Nonna, 1991; You Rang M'Lord, 1992; Lovejoy, 1992; Memento Mori, 1992; Sherlock Holmes, 1992; Peak Practice, 1993–; Bed, 1994. *Recreations:* conducting gramophone records, golf. *Clubs:* Garrick, Green Room; Stage Golfing.

DENHAM, Pamela Anne, PhD; Regional Director, Government Office for the North East, since 1994; *b* 1 May 1943; *d* of late Matthew Gray Dobson and Jane (*née* Carter); *m* 1965, Paul Denham (marr. diss. 1980); partner, Brian Murray (*d* 1993). *Educ:* Central Newcastle High Sch.; King's Coll., Univ. of London (BSc 1964; PhD 1969). Asst Principal, Ministry of Technol., 1967–72; Department of Trade and Industry: Principal, 1972–79; Asst Sec., 1979–85; Under Sec., 1985–89; Under Sec., Cabinet Office (Office of Minister for CS), 1989–90; Regl Dir, DTI NE, 1990–94. Non-exec. Dir, Mono Pumps and Saunders Valve, 1982–85. Member: Governing Body, Sunderland Univ., 1993; Local Governing Body, Central Newcastle High Sch., 1992–. FRSA. Hon. LLD Sunderland, 1994. *Publications:* papers in scientific jls. *Recreations:* travel, reading, ski-ing, cooking. *Address:* Government Office for the North East, Stanegate House, 2 Groat Market, Newcastle upon Tyne NE1 1YN. *T:* 0191–235 7201.

DENHAM, Lt-Col Seymour Vivian G.; *see* Gilbart-Denham.

DENHOLM, Allan; *see* Denholm, J. A.

DENHOLM, Sir Ian; *see* Denholm, Sir J. F.

DENHOLM, (James) Allan, CBE 1992; Chairman, East Kilbride Development Corporation, 1983–94 (Member, 1979–94); Director, William Grant & Sons Ltd, since 1975 (Secretary, since 1966); President, Institute of Chartered Accountants of Scotland, 1992–93; *b* 27 Sept. 1936; *s* of James Denholm and Florence Lily Keith (*née* Kennedy); *m* 1964, Elizabeth Avril McLachlan, CA; one *s* one *d*. *Educ:* Hutchesons' Boys' Sch., Glasgow. CA. Apprentice with McFarlane Hutton & Patrick, 1954–60; Chief Accountant, A. & W. Smith & Co. Ltd, 1960–66. Councillor, Eastwood DC, 1962–64. Mem., Council, Inst. of Chartered Accountants, Scotland, 1978–83 (Sen. Vice-Pres., 1991–92). Director: Scottish Cremation Soc. Ltd, 1980–; Scottish Mutual Assurance Soc., 1987– (Dep. Chm., 1992–); Abbey National, 1992–. Trustee, Scottish Cot Death Trust, 1985–. Elder, New Kilpatrick Parish Church, Bearsden, 1971–. FRSA 1992. *Recreations:* golf, shooting. *Address:* William Grant & Sons Ltd, Phoenix Crescent, Strathclyde Business Park, Motherwell ML4 3AN. *T:* Motherwell (01698) 843843; Greencroft, 19 Colquhoun Drive, Bearsden, Glasgow G61 4NQ. *T:* 0141–942 1773. *Club:* Royal Scottish Automobile (Glasgow).

DENHOLM, Sir John Ferguson, (Sir Ian), Kt 1989; CBE 1974; JP; DL; Chairman, J. & J. Denholm Ltd, since 1974; *b* 8 May 1927; *s* of Sir William Lang Denholm, TD; *m* 1952, Elizabeth Murray Stephen; two *s* two *d*. *Educ:* St Mary's Sch., Melrose; Loretto Sch., Musselburgh. Joined J. & J. Denholm Ltd, 1944. Chm., Murray Investment Trusts, 1985–93; Deputy Chairman: P&O, 1980–85 (Dir, 1974–85); Murray Johnstone Ltd, 1985–93; Director: Fleming Mercantile Investment Trust, 1985–94; Murray Trusts, 1973–93; Member: London Bd, Bank of Scotland, 1988–91; West of Scotland Bd, Bank of Scotland, 1991–95. Member: Nat. Ports Council, 1974–77; Scottish Transport Gp, 1975–82. President: Chamber of Shipping of the UK, 1973–74; Gen. Council of British Shipping, 1988–89; Baltic and Internat. Maritime Council, 1991–93. Hon. Norwegian Consul in Glasgow, 1975–. DL, 1980, JP, 1984, Renfrewshire. *Recreation:* fishing. *Clubs:* Western (Glasgow); Royal Thames Yacht, Royal Northern and Clyde Yacht.

DENINGTON, family name of **Baroness Denington.**

DENINGTON, Baroness *cr* 1978 (Life Peer), of Stevenage in the County of Hertfordshire; **Evelyn Joyce Denington,** DBE 1974 (CBE 1966); Chairman, Stevenage Development Corporation, 1966–80 (Member, 1950–80); Chairman, Greater London Council, 1975–76; *b* 9 Aug. 1907; *d* of Phillip Charles Bursill and Edith Rowena Bursill; *m* 1935, Cecil Dallas Denington. *Educ:* Blackheath High Sch.; Bedford Coll., London. Journalism, 1927–31; Teacher, 1933–50; Gen. Sec., Nat. Assoc. of Labour Teachers, 1938–47; Member: St Pancras Borough Council, 1945–59; LCC, 1946–65 (Chm. New and Expanding Towns Cttee, 1960–65); GLC, 1964–77 (Chm. Housing Cttee, 1964–67; Dep. Leader (Lab), Opposition, 1967–73; Chm., Transport Cttee, 1973–75); Central Housing Adv. Cttee, 1955–73 (Chm. Sub-Cttee prod. report Our Older Homes); SE Economic Planning Council, 1966–79; Chm., New Towns Assoc., 1973–75. Member: Sutton Dwellings Housing Trust, 1976–82; North British Housing Assoc., 1976–88; Sutton (Hastoe) Housing Assoc. Ltd, 1981–88. Freeman, City of London. Hon. FRIBA; Hon. MRTPI. *Address:* Flat 3, 29 Brunswick Square, Hove BN3 1EJ.

DENISON, family name of **Baron Londesborough.**

DENISON, Ann, (Mrs W. N. Denison); *see* Curnow, E. A. M.

DENISON, Dulcie Winifred Catherine, (Dulcie Gray), CBE 1983; actress, playwright, authoress; *b* 20 Nov. 1920; *d* of late Arnold Savage Bailey, CBE, and of Kate Edith (*née* Clulow Gray); *m* 1939, Michael Denison, *qv*. *Educ:* England and Malaya. In Repertory in Aberdeen, 1st part Sorrel in Hay Fever, 1939; Repertory in Edinburgh, Glasgow and Harrogate, 1940; BBC Serial, Front Line Family, 1941; Shakespeare, Regents Park; Alexandra in The Little Foxes, Piccadilly; Midsummer Night's Dream, Westminster, 1942; Brighton Rock, Garrick; Landslide, Westminster, 1943; Lady from Edinburgh, Playhouse, 1945; Dear Ruth, St James's; Wind is 90, Apollo, 1946; on tour in Fools Rush In, 1946; Rain on the Just, Aldwych, 1948; Queen Elizabeth Slept Here, Strand, 1949; The Four-poster, Ambassadors, 1950 (tour of S Africa, 1954–55); See You Later (Revue), Watergate, 1951; Dragon's Mouth, Winter Garden, 1952; Sweet Peril, St James's, 1952; We Must Kill Toni, Westminster; The Diary of a Nobody, Arts, 1954; Alice Through the Looking Glass, Chelsea Palace, 1955, Ashcroft Theatre, Croydon, 1972; appeared in own play, Love Affair, Lyric Hammersmith, 1956; South Sea Bubble, Cape Town, 1956; Tea and Sympathy, Melbourne and Sydney, 1956; South Sea Bubble, Johannesburg, 1957; Double Cross, Duchess, 1958; Let Them Eat Cake, Cambridge, 1959; Candida, Piccadilly and Wyndham's, 1960; Heartbreak House, Wyndham's, 1961; A Marriage Has Been Arranged, and A Village Wooing (Hong Kong); Shakespeare Recital (Berlin Festival); Royal Gambit for opening of Ashcroft Theatre, Croydon, 1962; Where Angels Fear to Tread, Arts and St Martin's, 1963; An Ideal Husband, Strand, 1965; On Approval, St

Martin's, 1966; Happy Family, St Martin's, 1967; Number 10, Strand, 1967; Out of the Question, St Martin's, 1968; Three, Fortune, 1970; The Wild Duck, Criterion, 1970; Clandestine Marriage (tour), 1971; Ghosts, York; Hay Fever (tour), 1972; Dragon Variation (tour), 1973; At the End of the Day, Savoy, 1973; The Sack Race, Ambassadors, 1974; The Pay Off, Comedy, 1974, Westminster, 1975; Time and the Conways (tour), 1976; Ladies in Retirement (tour), 1976; Façade, QEH, 1976; The Cabinet Minister (tour), 1977; A Murder is Announced, Vaudeville, 1977; Bedroom Farce, Prince of Wales, 1979; The Cherry Orchard, Exeter, 1980; Lloyd George Knew my Father (tour), 1980; The Kingfisher, Windsor, 1980, Worthing and on tour, 1981; Relatively Speaking (Dinner Theatre Tour, Near and Far East), 1981; A Coat of Varnish, Haymarket, 1982; Cavell, Chichester Fest., 1982; School for Scandal, Haymarket, transf. to Duke of York's, and British Council 50th Anniversary European Tour, 1983; There Goes the Bride (Dinner Theatre tour, Near and Far East), 1985; The Living Room, Royalty, 1987; The Chalk Garden, Windsor and tour, 1989; The Best of Friends (tour) 1990, 1991; The Importance of Being Earnest (tour), 1991; Tartuffe, Playhouse, 1991–92; Bedroom Farce (tour), 1992; An Ideal Husband, Globe, 1992, tour, 1993; Pygmalion, and The Schoolmistress, Chichester Fest., 1994; The Importance of Being Earnest, Leatherhead. *Films include:* They were Sisters, 1944; Wanted for Murder, 1945; A Man about the House, 1946; Mine Own Executioner, 1947; My Brother Jonathan, 1947; The Glass Mountain, 1948; The Franchise Affair, 1951; Angels One Five, 1952; There was a Young Lady, 1953; A Man Could Get Killed, 1965; The Black Crow, 1994. Has appeared in television plays and radio serials; *television series:* Howard's Way, 1985–90. Fellow, Linnean Soc., 1984. FRSA. Queen's Silver Jubilee Medal, 1977. *Publications: play:* Love Affair; *books:* Murder on the Stairs; Murder in Melbourne; Baby Face; Epitaph for a Dead Actor; Murder on a Saturday; Murder in Mind; The Devil Wore Scarlet; No Quarter for a Star; The Murder of Love; Died in the Red; The Actor and His World (with Michael Denison); Murder on Honeymoon; For Richer, For Richer; Deadly Lampshade; Understudy to Murder; Dead Give Away; Ride on a Tiger; Stage-Door Fright; Death in Denims; Butterflies on my Mind (TES Senior Information Book Prize, 1978); Dark Calypso; The Glanville Women; Anna Starr; Mirror Image; Looking Forward, Looking Back (autobiog.). *Recreations:* swimming, butterflies. *Address:* Shardeloes, Amersham, Bucks HP7 0RL; c/o Barry Burnett plc, 42 Grafton House, 2 Golden Square, W1. *Club:* Lansdowne.

DENISON, John Law, CBE 1960 (MBE (mil.) 1945); FRCM; Hon. RAM; Hon. GSM; Director, South Bank Concert Halls (formerly General Manager, Royal Festival Hall), 1965–76; Chairman, Arts Educational Schools, 1977–91; *b* 21 Jan. 1911; *s* of late Rev. H. B. W. and Alice Dorothy Denison; *m* 1st, 1936, Annie Claudia Russell Brown (marriage dissolved, 1946); 2nd, 1947, Evelyn Mary Donald (*née* Moir) (*d* 1958), *d* of John and Mary Scott Moir, Edinburgh; one *d*; 3rd, 1960, Audrey Grace Burnaby (*née* Bowles) (*d* 1970); 4th, 1972, Françoise Charlotte Henriette Mitchell (*née* Garrigues) (*d* 1985). *Educ:* Brighton Coll.; Royal Coll. of Music. Played horn in BBC Symphony, London Philharmonic, City of Birmingham, and other orchestras, 1934–39. Served War of 1939–45; gazetted Somerset Light Inf., 1940; DAA and QMG 214 Inf. Bde and various staff appts, 1941–45 (despatches). Asst Dir, Music Dept, British Council, 1946–48; Music Dir, Arts Council of Great Britain, 1948–65. Chairman: Cultural Programme, London Celebrations Cttee, Queen's Silver Jubilee, 1976–78; Royal Concert Cttee, St Cecilia Fest., 1976–88; Hon. Treasurer, Royal Philharmonic Soc., 1977–89 (Hon. Mem., 1989); Member: Council, RCM, 1975–90; Council, Musicians Benevolent Fund, 1992– (Exec. Cttee, 1984–92); Trustee, Prince Consort Foundn, 1990–. FRSA. Comdr, Order of Lion (Finland), 1976; Chevalier de l'Ordre des Arts et des Lettres (France), 1988. *Publications:* articles for various musical publications. *Address:* 9 Hays Park, near Shaftesbury, Dorset SP7 9TR. *Clubs:* Garrick, Army and Navy.

DENISON, (John) Michael (Terence Wellesley), CBE 1983; actor; *b* 1 Nov. 1915; *s* of Gilbert Dixon Denison and Marie Louise (*née* Bain); *m* 1939, Dulcie Gray (*see* D. W. C. Denison). *Educ:* Harrow; Magdalen Coll., Oxford (BA). Dramatic Sch., 1937–38; Westminster Theatre, 1938; Aberdeen Repertory, 1939. First film, 1940. Served War of 1939–45, Royal Signals and Intelligence Corps, 1940–46. Has appeared in following plays (in London, unless stated): Ever Since Paradise, 1946; Rain on the Just, 1948; Queen Elizabeth Slept Here, 1949; The Four-poster, 1950; Dragon's Mouth, 1952; Sweet Peril, 1952; The Bad Samaritan, 1953; Alice Through the Looking Glass, 1953, 1955 and 1972; We Must Kill Toni, 1954; tour of S Africa, 1954–55; All's Well That Ends Well, Twelfth Night, Merry Wives of Windsor, Titus Andronicus, Stratford-on-Avon, 1955; prod. and acted in Love Affair, 1956; A Village Wooing and Fanny's First Play (Edinburgh and Berlin festivals), 1956; Meet Me By Moonlight, 1957; Let Them Eat Cake, 1959; Candida, 1960; Heartbreak House, 1961; My Fair Lady (Melbourne); A Village Wooing (Hong Kong); Shakespeare Recital (Berlin Festival), 1962; Where Angels Fear to Tread, 1963; Hostile Witness, 1964; An Ideal Husband, 1965; On Approval, 1966; Happy Family; Number 10, 1967; Out of the Question, 1968; Three, 1970; The Wild Duck, 1970; Clandestine Marriage (tour), 1971; The Tempest, 1972; Twelfth Night, 1972, 1978, 1985; The Dragon Variation (tour), 1973; At the End of the Day, 1973; The Sack Race, 1974; Peter Pan, 1974; The Black Mikado, 1975; The First Mrs Fraser (tour), 1976; The Earl and the Pussycat (tour), 1976; Robert and Elizabeth (tour), 1976; The Cabinet Minister (tour), 1977; The Lady's Not For Burning, Ivanov, 1978; Bedroom Farce, 1979; The Kingfisher (tour), 1980–81; Venus Observed (Windsor), 1980; Relatively Speaking (Far and Near East tour), 1981; A Coat of Varnish, Captain Brassbound's Conversion, 1982; School for Scandal, 1982, 1983; See How They Run, 1984; There Goes the Bride (Near and Far East tour), 1985; Ring Round the Moon, 1985 and 1988; The Apple Cart, 1986; Court in the Act, 1986, 1987; You Never Can Tell, 1987; The Chalk Garden (tour), 1989; Dear Charles (tour), 1990; The Best of Friends (tour), 1990, 1991; The Importance of Being Earnest (tour), 1991; Bedroom Farce (tour), 1992; An Ideal Husband, 1992 (Chichester Fest., 1994); The Schoolmistress, Pygmalion, Chichester, 1994. *Films include:* My Brother Jonathan, 1947; The Glass Mountain, 1948; Landfall, 1949; The Franchise Affair, 1950; Angels One Five, The Importance of Being Earnest, 1951; The Truth About Women, 1957; Shadowlands, 1994. Many television appearances including title role Boyd, QC, 1956–61 and 1963. Director: Allied Theatre Productions, 1966–75; Play Company of London, 1970–74; New Shakespeare Company, 1971–. On Council British Actors Equity Assoc., 1949–76 (Vice-Pres. 1952, 1961–63, 1973); Mem. Drama Panel, Arts Council, 1975–78. FRSA. *Publications:* (with Dulcie Gray) The Actor and His World, 1964; memoirs: vol. 1, Overture and Beginners, 1973, vol. 2, Double Act, 1985; DNB articles on Sir Noël Coward and Sir Peter Daubeny, 1983, Peter Bridge, 1987, Glen Byam Shaw, 1994. *Recreations:* golf (Pres., Stage Golf Soc., 1991), painting, watching cricket, gardening, motoring. *Address:* Shardeloes, Amersham, Bucks HP7 0RL. *Clubs:* Richmond Golf (Richmond); MCC, Middlesex County Cricket.

DENISON, Michael; *see* Denison, J. M. T. W.

DENISON, (William) Neil; QC 1980; **His Honour Judge Denison;** a Circuit Judge, since 1985; Common Serjeant in the City of London, since 1993; *b* 10 March 1929; *s* of William George Denison and Jean Brodie; *m*; three *s*; *m* 1981, Elizabeth Ann Marguerite Curnow, *qv*. *Educ:* Queen Mary's Sch., Walsall; Univ. of Birmingham (LLB); Hertford Coll., Univ. of Oxford (BCL). Called to the Bar, Lincoln's Inn, 1952, Bencher, 1993. A Recorder of the Crown Court, 1979–85. Liveryman, Wax Chandlers' Co., 1988. *Recreations:* walking, reading rubbish. *Club:* Garrick.

DENISON-PENDER, family name of **Baron Pender.**

DENISON-SMITH, Lt-Gen. Sir Anthony (Arthur), KBE 1995 (MBE 1973); General Officer Commanding Fourth Division, since 1995; *b* 24 Jan. 1942; *s* of late George Denison-Smith and Dorothy Gwendolin Phillips; *m* 1966, Julia Henrietta Scott; three *s*. *Educ:* Harrow; RMA, Sandhurst. Commissioned Grenadier Guards, 1962; Staff Coll., 1974; Brigade Major, 7th Armoured Brigade, 1977–79; Directing Staff, Staff Coll., 1979–81; CO 2nd Bn Grenadier Guards, 1981–83; Chief of Staff, 4th Armoured Div., 1983–85; Comdr, 22nd Armoured Brigade, 1985–87; Chief of Staff, 1 (BR) Corps, 1987–89; Dir Gen. Trng and Doctrine (Army), 1990–91; Comdr, 4th Armoured Div., 1991–93; Comdr, 1st (UK) Armoured Div., 1993–94; GOC Southern Dist, 1994–95. Col, Princess of Wales's Royal Regt (Queen's and Royal Hampshires), 1992–. *Recreations:* cricket, fishing, Hawkwoods. *Address:* c/o RHQ Grenadier Guards, Birdcage Walk, Wellington Barracks, SW1A 6HQ. *Clubs:* Cavalry and Guards, MCC.

DENMAN, family name of **Baron Denman.**

DENMAN, 5th Baron *cr* 1834; **Charles Spencer Denman,** CBE 1976; MC 1942; TD; Bt 1945; *b* 7 July 1916; *e s* of Hon. Sir Richard Douglas Denman, 1st Bt; *S* father, 1957 and to barony of cousin, 1971; *m* 1943, Sheila Anne (*d* 1987), *d* of late Lt-Col Algernon Bingham Anstruther Stewart, DSO, Seaforth Highlanders, of Ornockenoch, Gatehouse of Fleet; three *s* one *d*. *Educ:* Shrewsbury. Served War of 1939–45 with Duke of Cornwall's Light Infantry (TA), India, Middle East, Western Desert and Dodecanese Islands; Major, 1943. Contested (C) Leeds Central, 1945. Director: Close Brothers Group Plc; British Water & Wastewater Ltd; Albaraka Internat. Bank Ltd; Arab-British Centre Ltd; New Zealand Holdings (UK) Ltd; formerly Chairman: Marine and General Mutual Life Assurance Soc.; Tennant Guaranty Ltd; Gold Fields Mahd adh Dhahab Ltd; Arundell House Plc; formerly Director: C. Tennant Sons & Co. Ltd; Consolidated Gold Fields Plc; British Bank of the Middle East. Saudi British Bank; British Arabian Corp.; Fletcher Challenge Corp.; MGM Life Assurance Soc. Member: Cttee for ME Trade, 1963– (Chm., 1971–75); Advisory Council of Export Credits Guarantee Department, 1963–68; British National Export Council, 1965; Cttee on Invisible Exports, 1965–67; British Invisible Exports Council; Guild of World Traders in London; Res. Inst. for Study of Conflict and Terrorism; UK/Saudi Jt Cultural Cttee; Lord Kitchener Nat. Meml Fund. President: RSAA, 1984–; NZ–UK Chamber of Commerce and Industry; Vice Pres., ME Assoc.; Chairman: Arab British Chamber Charitable Foundn; Saudi-British Soc.; formerly Chm., Governors of Windlesham House Sch. *Heir: s* Hon. Richard Thomas Stewart Denman [*b* 4 Oct. 1946; *m* 1984, (Lesley) Jane, *d* of John Stevens; three *d*]. *Address:* House of Lords, SW1A 0PW. *Club:* Brooks's.

DENMAN, Prof. Donald Robert; Professor of Land Economy, 1968–78 and Head of Department of Land Economy, 1962–78, Cambridge University, now Professor Emeritus; Fellow of Pembroke College, Cambridge, 1962–78, now Emeritus; *b* 7 April 1911; 2nd *s* of Robert Martyn Denman and Letitia Kate Denman, Finchley; *m* 1941, Jessica Hope, 2nd *d* of Richard H. Prior, Chichester; two *s*. *Educ:* Christ's Coll., Finchley. BSc 1938; MSc 1940; PhD 1945; MA 1948; Hon. DSc 1979; FRICS 1949; Dep. Exec. Off., Cumberland War Agricultural Exec. Cttee, 1939–46; University Lectr, Cambridge Univ., 1948–68. Land Management Cttee of Agricultural Improvement Coun., 1953–60; Member: Church Assembly, 1957–69; Standing Cttee of Istituto de Diritto Agrario Internazionale e Comparato, Florence, 1960–; Nat. Commn of Unesco, 1972–74; Advisor to Min. of Co-operation and Rural Affairs, Iran, 1968–75; Mem., Commn on Ecology, IUCN, 1987. Mem. Council, University Coll. at Buckingham, 1973–81. Chm., Commonwealth Human Ecology Council, 1984–88; Mem., Land Decade Educnl Council, 1981–. Patron, Small Farmers' Assoc. Hon. Fellow, Ghana Instn of Surveyors, 1970; Fellow, Royal Swedish Acad. of Forestry and Agriculture, 1971. Gold Medal, RICS, 1972. Distinguished Order of Homayoun of the Imperial Court of Persia, 1974. *Publications:* Tenant Right Valuation: In History and Modern Practice, 1942; Tenant Right Valuation and Current Legislation, 1948; Estate Capital: The Contribution of Landownership to Agricultural Finance, 1957; Origins of Ownership: A Brief History of Landownership and Tenure, 1958; Bibliography of Rural Land Economy and Landownership 1900–1957 (*et al*), 1958; Farm Rents: A Comparison of Current and Past Farm Rents in England and Wales, 1959; (ed and contrib.) Landownership and Resources, 1960; (ed and contrib.) Contemporary Problems of Landownership, 1963; Land in the Market, 1964; (jtly) Commons and Village Greens: A Study in Land Use, Conservation and Management, 1967; (ed and contrib.) Land and People, 1967; Rural Land Systems, 1968; Land Use and the Constitution of Property, 1969; Land Use: An Introduction to Proprietary Land Use Analysis, 1971; Human Environment: the surveyor's response, 1972; The King's Vista (Persian Land reform), 1973; Prospects of Co-operative Planning (Warburton Lecture), 1973; Land Economy: an education and a career (British Assoc. lecture), 1975; The Place of Property, 1978; Land in a Free Society, 1980; The Fountain Principle, 1982; Markets under the Sea?, 1984; Survival and Responsibility, 1987; After Government Failure?, 1987; (jtly) Planning Fails the Inner Cities, 1987; A Half and Half Affair: the chronicles of a hybrid don, 1993; numerous monographs, articles and papers in academic and professional jls and nat. press in Britain and abroad. *Recreation:* travel. *Address:* Pembroke College, Cambridge CB2 1RF; 12 Chaucer Road, Cambridge CB2 2EB. *T:* Cambridge (01223) 357725. *Clubs:* Carlton, Farmers'.

DENMAN, Sir George Roy; *see* Denman, Sir Roy.

DENMAN, Sir Roy, KCB 1977 (CB 1972); CMG 1968; consultant in international trade; *b* 12 June 1924; *s* of Albert Edward and Gertrude Ann Denman; *m* 1966, Moya Lade; one *s* one *d*. *Educ:* Harrow Gram. Sch.; St John's Coll., Cambridge. War Service 1943–46; Major, Royal Signals. Joined BoT, 1948; Asst Private Sec. to successive Presidents, 1950–52; 1st Sec., British Embassy, Bonn, 1957–60; UK Delegn, Geneva, 1960–61; Counsellor, Geneva, 1965–67; Under-Sec., 1967–70, BoT; Deputy Secretary: DTI, 1970–74; Dept of Trade, 1974–75; Second Permanent Sec., Cabinet Office, 1975–77; Dir-Gen. for External Affairs, EEC Commn, 1977–82; Head, Commn of Eur. Communities Delegn in Washington, 1982–89; Business Fellow, John F. Kennedy Sch. of Govt, Harvard, 1989–90. Mem. negotiating delegn with European Communities, 1970–72. Mem., British Overseas Trade Bd, 1972–75. *Address:* c/o Coutts & Co., 2 Lower Sloane Street, SW1W 8BJ. *Club:* United Oxford & Cambridge University.

DENMAN, Sylvia Elaine, CBE 1994; Deputy Director of Education, Inner London Education Authority, 1989–90; *b* Barbados; *d* of late Alexander Yarde and Euleen Yarde (*née* Alleyne), Barbados; *m* Hugh Frederick Denman (marr. diss.); one *d*. *Educ:* Queen's College, Barbados; LSE (LLM); called to the Bar, Lincoln's Inn, 1962. Lectr then Sen. Lectr, Oxford Polytechnic, 1965–76; Sen. Lectr and Tutor, Norman Manley Law Sch., Univ. of West Indies, Jamaica, 1977–82; Fulbright Fellow, New York Univ. Sch. of Law, 1982–83; Prin. Equal Opportunities Officer, ILEA, 1983–86; Pro Asst Dir, Polytechnic of South Bank, 1986–89. Member: Oxford Cttee for Racial Integration, 1965–76; Oxford, Bucks and Berks Conciliation Cttee, Race Relations Bd, 1965–70; London Rent

Assessment Panel, 1968–76 and 1984–; Race Relations Bd, 1970–76; Equal Opportunities Commission, 1975–76; Lord Chancellor's Adv. Cttee on Legal Aid, 1975–76; Criminal Justice Consultative Council, 1991–; Council, NACRO, 1994–; Camden and Islington (formerly Bloomsbury and Islington) HA, 1992–. Trustee: Runnymede Trust, 1985–91; Windsor Fellowship, 1994–. Governor, Haverstock Sch., 1989–94. FRSA. *Recreations:* music, theatre, wandering about in the Caribbean.

DENNAY, Charles William, CEng, FIEE; FIEIE; Consultant, Quantel Ltd, since 1993; *b* 13 May 1935; *s* of Charles Dennay and Elsie May Smith; *m* 1955, Shirley Patricia Johnston; one *s*. *Educ:* Humberston Foundation Sch.; Borough Polytechnic. DipEE; MIERE. Scientific Asst (Govt), 1953; Technician, BBC, 1956; Transmitter Engineer, 1958; Asst Lectr/Lectr, 1961; Head of Ops Transmitters, 1973; Head of Engrg Transmitter Ops, 1976; Asst Chief Engineer, Transmitters, 1978; Chief Engineer, External Broadcasting, 1979; Controller, Ops and Engineering Radio, 1984; Asst Dir of Engineering, 1985; Dir of Engineering, 1987; Man. Dir, Resources Engrg and Services, 1993, retd. Pres., IEIE, 1994– (Vice-Pres., 1990–94); a Vice-Pres., RTS, 1989–94. FRSA 1993. *Recreations:* photography, music, civil aviation. *Address:* Junipers, 111 Winchester Street, Overton, Basingstoke, Hants RG25 3HZ. *T:* Basingstoke (01256) 770183.

DENNE, Christopher James Alured, CMG 1991; HM Diplomatic Service; Deputy Head of Mission, Athens, since 1993; *b* 20 Aug. 1945; *s* of Lt Comdr John Richard Alured Denne, DSC, RN (retd) and Alison Patricia Denne; *m* 1968, Sarah Longman; two *s* one *d*. *Educ:* Wellington Coll.; Southampton Univ. (BSc Soc. Sci. 1967). Entered Diplomatic Service, 1967; New Delhi, 1969–72; Second Sec., FCO, 1972–74; First Sec. (Information), Lagos, 1974–77; FCO, 1977; resigned, 1978; BBC External Services, 1979–80; reinstated FCO, 1983; First Sec. and Dep. Permanent Rep., UK Mission to UN, Vienna, 1985–89; Head of Consular Dept, FCO, 1989–92. *Recreations:* photography, Dartmoor. *Address:* c/o Foreign and Commonwealth Office, SW1A 2AH.

DENNER, Dr William Howard Butler; Chief Scientist (Food), Ministry of Agriculture, Fisheries and Food, since 1992; *b* 14 May 1944; *s* of William Ormonde Ralph Denner and late Violet Evelyn Arscott; *m* 1966, Gwenda Williams; two *d*. *Educ:* Cyfarthfa Castle Grammar School, Merthyr Tydfil; UCW Cardiff (BSc, PhD Biochem.). Research Associate: Miami Univ., 1968; Cardiff Univ., 1969; Ministry of Agriculture, Fisheries and Food, 1972–: Secretary: Food Additives and Contaminants Cttee, 1974–84; Cttee on Toxicity of Chemicals in Food, Consumer Products and the Environment, 1978–84; Mem., Jt FAO/WHO Expert Cttee on Food Additives, 1978–85; Head of Food Composition and Information Unit, 1984; Chm., Codex Cttee on Fats and Oils, 1987–92; Assessor, Adv. Cttees on Novel Foods and Processes and on Genetic Modification, 1985–92; Head of Food Sci. Div. II, 1989. Lectr and Judge, E Anglia Fedn of Photographic Alliance of GB, 1978–88; Judge, Essex Internat. Salon of Photography, 1987–88. One-man exhibn of photographs, Half Moon Gallery, 1974; individual photographs in internat. exhibns, newspapers, jls and books. AFIAP 1972. *Publications:* papers on food safety in learned jls. *Recreations:* photography, golf. *Address:* Ministry of Agriculture, Fisheries and Food, Nobel House, 17 Smith Square, SW1P 3JR. *T:* 0171–238 6192.

DENNING, Baron (Life Peer) *cr* 1957, of Whitchurch; **Alfred Thompson Denning,** PC 1948; Kt 1944; DL; Master of the Rolls, 1962–82; Hon. Fellow: Magdalen College, Oxford, 1948; Nuffield College, Oxford, 1982; Hon. LLD: Ottawa, 1955; Glasgow, 1959; Southampton, 1959; London, 1960; Cambridge, 1963; Leeds, 1964; McGill, 1967; Dallas, 1969; Dalhousie, 1970; Wales, 1973; Exeter, 1976; Columbia, 1976; Tilburg (Netherlands), 1977; W Ontario, 1979; British Columbia, 1979; Sussex, 1980; Buckingham, 1983; Nottingham, 1984; Hon. DCL Oxford, 1965; *b* 23 Jan. 1899; *s* of Charles and Clara Denning, *m* 1st, 1932, Mary Harvey (*d* 1941); one *s*; 2nd, 1945, Joan (*d* 1992), *d* of J. V. Elliott Taylor, and *widow* of J. M. B. Stuart, CIE. *Educ:* Andover Grammar Sch.; Magdalen Coll., Oxford (Demy). 1st Class Mathematical Moderations; 1st Class Mathematical Final School; 1st Class Final Sch. of Jurisprudence; Eldon Scholar, 1921; Prize Student Inns of Court; called to the Bar, 1923; KC 1938; Judge of the High Court of Justice, 1944; a Lord Justice of Appeal, 1948–57; a Lord of Appeal in Ordinary, 1957–62. Chancellor of Diocese of London, 1942–44; and of Southwark, 1937–44; Recorder of Plymouth, 1944; Bencher of Lincoln's Inn, 1944; Nominated Judge for War Pensions Appeals, 1945–48; Chm. Cttee on Procedure in Matrimonial Causes, 1946–47; Chm., Royal Commission on Historical MSS, 1962–82. Held inquiry into circumstances of resignation of Mr J. D. Profumo, Sec. of State for War, 1963. Chairman: Cttee on Legal Education for Students from Africa, 1960; British Institute of International and Comparative Law, 1959–86. Pres., Birkbeck Coll., 1952–83; Treas., Lincoln's Inn, 1964. Hon. Bencher: Middle Temple, 1972; Gray's Inn, 1979; Inner Temple, 1982. Dimbleby Lectr, BBC TV, 1980. Hon. FBA 1979. Served in RE 1917–19 (BEF France). DL Hants, 1978. *Publications:* Joint Editor of Smith's Leading Cases, 1929; of Bullen and Leake's Precedents, 1935; Freedom under the Law, (Hamlyn Lectures), 1949; The Changing Law, 1953; The Road to Justice, 1955; The Discipline of Law, 1979; The Due Process of Law, 1980; The Family Story, 1981; What Next in the Law, 1982; The Closing Chapter, 1983; Landmarks in the Law, 1984; Leaves from my Library, 1986. *Address:* The Lawn, Whitchurch, Hants RG28 7AS. *T:* Whitchurch (01256) 892144.

DENNINGTON, Dudley, FEng; FICE; FIStructE; FHKIE; Partner, 1972–92, Senior Partner, 1989–92, Bullen & Partners; *b* 21 April 1927; *s* of John Dennington and Beryl Dennington (*née* Hagon); *m* 1951, Margaret Patricia Stewart; two *d*. *Educ:* Clifton Coll., Bristol; Imperial Coll., London Univ. (BSc). National Service, 2nd Lieut, RE, 1947–49; Sandford Fawcett and Partners, Consulting Engineers, 1949–51; D. & C. Wm Press, Contractors, 1951–52; AMICE 1953; Manager, Design Office, George Wimpey & Co., 1952–65; GLC 1965–72: Asst Chief Engineer, Construction, 1965–67; Chief Engineer, Construction, 1967–70; Traffic Comr and Dir of Development, 1970–72. Mem., Bd for Engineers' Registration, Engrg Council, 1983–85. Vis. Prof., King's Coll., London Univ., 1978–81. FICE 1966 (Mem. Council, 1975–78 and 1981–84; Vice-Pres., 1990–92); FHKIE 1982; FCGI 1984; FEng 1985. *Recreations:* mathematics, painting. *Address:* 25 Corkran Road, Surbiton, Surrey KT6 6PL. *T:* 0181–399 2977. *Club:* Reform.

DENNIS, Maj.-Gen. Alastair Wesley, CB 1985; OBE 1973; *b* 30 Aug. 1931; *s* of late Ralph Dennis and of Helen (*née* Henderson); *m* 1957, Susan Lindy Elgar; one *s* two *d*. *Educ:* Malvern Coll.; RMA, Sandhurst. Commanded 16th/5th The Queen's Royal Lancers, 1971–74; Col GS, Cabinet Office, 1974–75; Comd 20 Armoured Bde, 1976–77; Dep. Comdt, Staff Coll., 1978–80; Director of Defence Policy (B), MoD, Whitehall, 1980–82; Dir, Military Assistance Overseas, MoD, 1982–85. Sec., Imperial Cancer Res. Fund, 1985–91; Chm., Assoc. of Med. Res. Charities, 1987–91. Mem., Malvern Coll. Council, 1988–92. Col, 16th/5th The Queen's Royal Lancers, 1990–93, The Queen's Royal Lancers, 1993–. *Recreations:* fishing, golf, gardening. *Address:* c/o Barclays Bank, 2 Market Place, Wallingford, Oxon.

DENNIS, Rt. Rev. John; *see* St Edmundsbury and Ipswich, Bishop of.

DENNIS, Maxwell Lewis, CMG 1971; Chairman, South Australia Totalizator Agency Board, 1973–79; *b* 19 April 1909; *s* of Frank Leonard and Ethel Jane Dennis; *m* 1935, Bernice Abell Symons; one *d* (one *s* decd). *Educ:* Gladstone High Sch., South Australia. FCPA 1990. Entered South Australian Public Service, 1924, Public Service Commissioner, 1965; Chm., Public Service Bd, 1968–73; Life Governor, Royal Soc. for the Blind. *Address:* 31 Hill Street, Victor Harbor, SA 5211, Australia.

DENNISON, Brig. Malcolm Gray; Lord-Lieutenant of Orkney, since 1990; *b* 19 March 1924; *s* of John Reid Dennison of Shapinsay and Margaret Gray of Roeberry. *Educ:* Lincoln Sch.; Edinburgh Univ. RAF, 1942–52: Bomber Comd, 1944–45; Sen. Intell. Officer, 219 and 205 Groups, 1946–47; MECAS, 1947–48; HQ Middle East Air Force, 1948–51; retired 1952. Bahrain Petroleum Co., 1953–55; Sultan's Armed Forces, Intelligence, 1955–83. Sultan's Commendation, 1970; DSM (Oman), 1972; Order of Oman (Military), 1974. *Recreation:* book collecting. *Address:* Roeberry House, St Margaret's Hope, Orkney KW17 2TW. *T:* St Margaret's Hope (01856) 831228. *Clubs:* Royal Air Force, Special Forces, Royal Over-Seas League.

DENNISON, Stanley Richard, CBE 1990; PhD; FRSC; Group Chief Executive, ECC Group (formerly English China Clays) plc, 1988–90; *b* 28 May 1930; *s* of Arthur and Ellen Dennison; *m* 1955, Margaret Janet Morrison; two *s* two *d*. *Educ:* Latymer's Sch., Edmonton; University Coll. London (BSc, PhD). CBIM 1988. Chemist, Min. of Supply, 1954; English China Clays: Res. Chemist, 1956; Res. Man., 1970; Res. Dir, Clay Div., 1980; Man. Dir, Clay Div., 1984; Dir, English China Clays PLC, 1984. Dir, Devon and Cornwall TEC, 1990–91. Chm., Cornwall and Is of Scilly DHA, 1994–. *Publications:* on industrial minerals, their technology and application in paper, in a number of pubns. *Recreations:* music, walking. *Address:* Lower Colvreath Farm, Roche, St Austell, Cornwall PL26 8LR.

DENNISS, Gordon Kenneth, CBE 1979; Consultant Chartered Surveyor, Eastman & Denniss, Surveyors, 1983–88 (Senior Partner, 1945–83); Senior Partner, G. K. Denniss Farms, since 1990; *b* 29 April 1915; *e s* of late Harold W. Denniss; *m* 1939, Violet Fiedler, Montreal; one *s* two *d*. *Educ:* Dulwich Coll.; Coll. of Estate Management. FRICS. Articled to uncle, Hugh F. Thoburn, Chartered Surveyor, Kent, developing building estates, 1935, professional asst 1938; Eastman & Denniss: Junior Partner, 1943; sole principal, 1945. Crown Estate Comr, 1965–71. Farming 2500 acres in E Sussex and Kent. Pres., Ashurst CC, Kent, 1989–. *Recreations:* farming, cricket, political economy, golf. *Address:* Evans Leap, Withyham, Hartfield, E Sussex TN7 4DA. *T:* Hartfield (01892) 770720; 4 Winterhaldenweg, 79856 Hinterzarten, Black Forest, Germany. *Clubs:* Farmers', MCC; Surrey County Cricket; Tunbridge Wells Golf.

DENNISTON, Rev. Robin Alastair; Oxford Publisher and Senior Deputy Secretary to the Delegates, Oxford University Press, 1984–88 (Academic and General Publisher, 1980–84); *b* 25 Dec. 1926; *s* of late Alexander Guthrie Denniston, CMG, CBE, head of Govt code and cipher school, and late Dorothy Mary Gilliat; *m* 1st, 1950, Anne Alice Kyffin Evans (*d* 1985), *y d* of late Dr Geoffrey Evans, MD, FRCP, consulting Physician at St Bartholomew's Hosp., and late Hon. E. M. K. Evans; one *s* two *d*; 2nd, 1987, Dr Rosa Susan Penelope Beddington, *yr d* of Roy Julian Beddington, artist, and late Anna Dorothy Beddington. *Educ:* Westminster Sch. (King's Schol.; Captain of School, 1945); Christ Church, Oxford (Classical Schol.; 2nd cl. Hons Lit. Hum.). MSc Edinburgh 1992. National Service: commnd into Airborne Artillery, 1948. Editor at Collins, 1950–59; Man. Dir, Faith Press, 1959–60; Editor, Prism, 1959–61; Promotion Man., Hodder & Stoughton Ltd, 1960–64, Editorial Dir, 1966, Man. Dir, 1968–72; Dir, Mathew Hodder Ltd (and subsid. cos), 1968–72; Dep. Chm., George Weidenfeld & Nicolson (and subsid. cos), 1973–75; Non-exec. Chm., A. R. Mowbray & Co., 1974–88; Dir, Thomson Publications Ltd, 1975–77; also Chm. of Michael Joseph Ltd, Thomas Nelson & Sons (and subsid. cos), George Rainbird Ltd, 1975–77 and Sphere Books, 1975–76; Academic Publisher, OUP, 1978; non-exec. Dir, W. W. Norton, 1989–. Student of Christ Church, 1978–88. Ordained Deacon, 1978, Priest, 1979; Hon. Curate: Clifton-on-Teme, 1978; New with South Hinksey, 1985; Non-Stipendiary Minister: Great with Little Tew, 1987–90; West Fife Team Ministry, 1990–93. A Church Comr, 1989–90. *Publications:* The Young Musicians, 1956; Partly Living, 1967; (ed) Part Time Priests?, 1960; (co-ed) Anatomy of Scotland, 1992; articles in Intelligence and Nat. Security. *Recreations:* forestry, music. *Address:* 112 Randolph Avenue, W9 1PQ. *Club:* Lansdowne.

DENNY, Sir Anthony Coningham de Waltham, 8th Bt, *cr* 1782, of Tralee Castle, Co. Kerry, Ireland; designer; Partner in Verity and Beverley, Architects and Designers (offices in London, Tetbury and Lisbon), since 1959; *b* 22 April 1925; *s* of Rev. Sir Henry Lyttleton Lyster Denny, 7th Bt, and Joan Lucy Dorothy, *er d* of Major William A. C. Denny, OBE; *S* father 1953; *m* 1949, Anne Catherine, *e d* of S. Beverley, FRIBA; two *s* one adopted *d*. *Educ:* Clayesmore Sch. Served War of 1939–45: Middle East, RAF (Aircrew), 1943–47. Anglo-French Art Centre, 1947–50; Mural Painter and Theatrical Designer, 1950–54. Trustee, Waltham Abbey. Hereditary Freeman of City of Cork. FRSA; MCSD. *Recreations:* architecture and painting. *Heir:* *s* Piers Anthony de Waltham Denny [*b* 14 March 1954; *m* 1987, Ella Jane, *o d* of Peter P. Huhne; two *d*]. *Address:* The Priest's House, Muchelney, Langport, Somerset TA10 0DQ. *T:* Langport (01458) 252621.

See also B. L. Denny.

DENNY, Barry Lyttelton, LVO 1979; HM Diplomatic Service, retired; *b* 6 June 1928; *s* of Rev. Sir Henry Lyttelton Lyster Denny, 7th Bt, and Joan Lucy Dorothy, *er d* of Major William A. C. Denny, OBE; *m* 1st, 1951 (marr. diss. 1968); one *s* one *d*; 2nd, 1969, Anne Rosemary Jordon, *o d* of late Col James F. White, MC; one *d*. *Educ:* Clayesmore Sch.; RMA, Sandhurst. Indian Army Cadet, 1946–47; commnd RA, 1949; retd from HM Forces as Captain (Temp. Major), 1960. Joined Foreign Office, 1962; First Sec., Nicosia, 1964; FO, later FCO, 1966; Kaduna, 1969; FCO, 1972; Vientiane, 1973; FCO, 1975; Kuwait, 1977; Counsellor, Oslo, 1980; seconded to MoD, 1984–89. Comdr, Order of St Olav (Norway), 1981. *Recreations:* polo, collecting, photography.

See also Sir A. C. de W. Denny.

DENNY, Sir Charles Alistair Maurice, 4th Bt *cr* 1913, of Dumbarton, co. Dunbarton; *b* 7 Oct. 1950; *e s* of Sir Alistair Maurice Archibald Denny, 3rd Bt and of Elizabeth Hunt, *y d* of Major Sir Guy Lloyd, 1st Bt, DSO; *S* father, 1995; *m* 1981, Belinda, *yr d* of J. P. McDonald; one *s* one *d*. *Educ:* Wellington Coll.; Edinburgh Univ. *Heir:* *s* Patrick Charles Alistair Denny, *b* 2 Jan. 1985.

DENNY, Margaret Bertha Alice, (Mrs E. L. Denny), OBE 1946; DL; Under Secretary, Ministry of Transport and Civil Aviation, 1957–58; *b* 30 Sept. 1907; *o d* of late Edward Albert Churchard and late Margaret Catherine (*née* Arnold) and step-*d* of late William Ray Lenanton, JP; *m* 1957, Edward Leslie Denny, JP, formerly Chm., William Denny Bros, Shipbuilders, Dumbarton. *Educ:* Dover County Sch.; Bedford Coll. for Women, London Univ. (BA Hons PhD). Entered Civil Service as Principal Ministry of Shipping, 1940; Asst Sec., 1946. Gov., Bedford Coll., University of London. Member: Scottish Adv. Coun. for Civil Aviation, 1958–67; Western Regional Hospital Board, Scotland, 1960–74; Scottish Cttee, Council of Industrial Design, 1961–71; Gen. Advisory Council, BBC, 1962–66; Gen. Nursing Council, Scotland, 1962–78; Board of Management, State Hosp., Carstairs, 1966–76; Vice-Chm., Argyll and Clyde Health Bd, 1974–77. National Trust for Scotland: Mem. Council, 1973–; Mem. Exec. Cttee, 1974–; Vice-Pres., 1981–91; Vice-Pres. Emeritus, 1991. County Comr, Girl Guides, Dunbartonshire, 1958–68. DL

Dunbartonshire, 1973. Officer, Order of Orange Nassau, 1947. *Address:* Gartochraggan Cottage, Gartocharn, by Alexandria, Dunbartonshire G83 8NE. *T:* Gartocharn (01389) 830272.

DENNY, Rev. Norwyn Ephraim; retired Methodist minister; President of the Methodist Conference, 1982–83; *b* 23 Oct. 1924; *s* of Percy Edward James Denny and Dorothy Ann Denny (*née* Stringer); *m* 1950, Ellen Amelia Shaw; three *d. Educ:* City of Norwich School; Wesley College, Bristol. BD (Hons), London Univ. Ordained Methodist Minister, 1951; Methodist Minister in Jamaica, 1950–54; Minister in Peterborough, 1955–61; Member of Notting Hill Group (Ecumenical) Ministry, 1961–75; Chm., Liverpool Dist Methodist Church, 1975–86; Supt, Lowestoft and E Suffolk Methodist Church, 1986–91. *Publications:* (with D. Mason and G. Ainger) News from Notting Hill, 1967; Caring, 1976; Worship, 1995. *Recreations:* gardening, astronomy, association football. *Address:* 5 Red Hill, Lodge Park, Redditch, Worcs B98 7JE. *T:* Redditch (01527) 522426.

DENNY, Ronald Maurice; Director, Electrocomponents, since 1984; *b* 11 Jan. 1927; *s* of Maurice Denny and Ada (*née* Bradley); *m* 1952, Dorothy Hamilton; one *s* two *d. Educ:* Gosport County Sch. CEng, FIEE. BBC Engineering, 1943; served Royal Navy, 1946–49; BBC Engr (TV), 1949–55; ATV Ltd, 1955, Gen. Man., ATV, 1967; Rediffusion Ltd, 1970; Chief Exec., 1979–85, Chm., 1985–89, Rediffusion PLC; Director: (non-exec.) Thames Television, 1981–89; BET, 1983–89. Mem. of Trust, Philharmonia Orch., 1983–93. Hon. Mem., RCM, 1984–. FRSA 1985. *Recreations:* music, sport. *Address:* 19 Nichols Green, W5 2QU. *T:* 0181–998 3765. *Clubs:* Athenæum, Arts.

DENNY, William Eric, CBE 1984; QC 1975; a Recorder of the Crown Court, since 1974; *b* 2 Nov. 1927; *s* of William John Denny and Elsie Denny; *m* 1960, Daphne Rose Southern-Reddin; one *s* two *d. Educ:* Ormskirk Grammar Sch.; Liverpool Univ. (Pres., Guild of Undergraduates, 1952–53; LLB). Served RAF, 1946–48. Called to the Bar, Gray's Inn, 1953, Bencher, 1985. Lectured at LSE, 1953–58. Chm., Home Secretary's Adv. Bd on Restricted Patients, 1980–85 (Mem., 1979). *Recreations:* music, sailing, gardening. *Address:* 1 Hare Court, Temple, EC4Y 7BE.

DENNYS, Nicholas Charles Jonathan; QC 1991; *b* 14 July 1951; *m* 1977, Frances Winifred Markham; four *d. Educ:* Eton; Brasenose Coll., Oxford (BA 1973). Admitted Middle Temple, 1973; called to the Bar, 1975. *Recreations:* windsurfing, golf, music. *Address:* The Old Rectory, Arborfield, Berks RG2 9HZ. *T:* Reading (01734) 761003.

DENT, Sir John, Kt 1986; CBE 1976 (OBE 1968); Chairman, Civil Aviation Authority, 1982–86; *b* 5 Oct. 1923; *s* of Harry F. Dent; *m* 1954, Pamela Ann, *d* of Frederick G. Bailey; one *s. Educ:* King's Coll., London Univ. BSc(Eng), FEng, FRAeS, FIMechE, FIEE, CBIM. Admty Gunnery Estabs at Teddington and Portland, 1944–45; Chief Engr, Guided Weapons, Short Bros & Harland Ltd, Belfast, 1955–60; Chief Engr, Armaments Div., Armstrong Whitworth Aircraft, Coventry, 1961–63; Dir and Chief Engr, Hawker Siddeley Dynamics Ltd, Coventry, 1963–67; Director: Engrg Gp, Dunlop Ltd, Coventry, 1968–76; Dunlop Holdings Ltd, 1970–82; Industrie Pirelli SpA, 1978–81; Dunlop AG, 1979–82; Pirelli Gen. plc, 1980–92; Pirelli Ltd, 1985–92; Man. Dir, Dunlop Ltd, 1978–82. President: Coventry and District Engrg Employers' Assoc., 1971 and 1972; Engrg Employers' Fedn, 1974–76 (1st Dep. Pres., 1972–74); Inst. of Travel Managers, 1986–94; Internat. Fedn of Airworthiness, 1987–89; Chm., Nationalized Industries' Chairman's Group, 1984–85. Member: Engineering Industries Council, 1975–76; Review Bd for Government Contracts, 1976–82; Royal Dockyards Policy Bd, 1976–82; NCB, 1980–82. *Recreations:* gardening, fishing, cabinet-making. *Address:* Helidon Grange, Helidon, near Daventry, Northants NN11 6LG.

DENT, Maj.-Gen. Jonathan Hugh Baillie, CB 1984; OBE 1974; Director General, Fighting Vehicles and Engineer Equipment, Ministry of Defence, 1981–85; *b* 19 July 1930; *s* of Joseph Alan Guthrie Dent and Hilda Ina Dent; *m* 1957, Anne Veronica Inglis; one *s* three *d. Educ:* Winchester College. Commissioned, Queen's Bays, 1949; regtl and instructional employment in BAOR, UK, Jordan, Libya, 1949–61; Adjt 1958; Adjt Shropshire Yeomanry, 1959–60; Staff trng, RMCS, 1962–63; Staff Coll. Camberley, 1964; Sqdn Comd, Queen's Dragoon Guards, N Ireland and Borneo, 1965–66; MoD (Operational Requirements), 1967–69; Second in Comd, Queen's Dragoon Guards, 1970; Ministry of Defence: MGO Secretariat, 1971–74; Project Manager Chieftain, 1974–76; RCDS 1977; Defence R&D Attaché, British Embassy, Washington, 1978–80. *Recreations:* fishing, bird watching, walking, shooting, classical music.

DENT, Sir Robin (John), KCVO 1992; a Managing Director, Baring Brothers & Co. Ltd, 1967–86; Director, Barings plc, 1985–89; *b* 25 June 1929; *s* of late Rear-Adm. John Dent, CB, OBE; *m* 1952, Hon. Ann Camilla Denison-Pender, *d* of 2nd Baron Pender, CBE; two *d. Educ:* Marlborough. Bank of England, 1949–51; joined M. Samuel & Co. Ltd, 1951: Director, 1963–65; Dir, Hill Samuel & Co. Ltd, 1965–67; Dir (London Board), Commercial Banking Co. of Sydney Ltd, 1964–82. Chm., Mase Westpac Ltd, 1989–93. Member, London Adv. Cttee, Hong Kong & Shanghai Banking Corp., 1974–81; Dir, TR City of London Trust PLC, 1977–. Mem., Deposit Protection Bd, 1982–85; Dep. Chm., Export Guarantees Adv. Council, 1983–85; Chm., Executive Cttee, British Bankers' Assoc., 1984–85; Comr, Public Works Loan Bd, 1987– (Chm., 1990–). Member of Council: Cancer Research Campaign, 1967–; King Edward's Hosp. Fund for London, 1974– (Treas., 1974–92); Special Trustee, St Thomas' Hosp., 1988–; Chm., Florence Nightingale Mus. Trust, 1993–. *Address:* 44 Smith Street, SW3 4EP. *T:* 0171–352 1234. *Club:* White's.

DENT, Ronald Henry; Chairman, Cape Industries Ltd, 1962–79; *b* 9 Feb. 1913; *s* of late Henry Francis Dent, MA, and Emma Bradley; *m* 1939, Olive May, *d* of late George Wilby, FCA; one *s* one *d. Educ:* Portsmouth Grammar Sch. Chartered accountant, 1936. Served War, 1939–45: UK, France, India; War Office, 1942–45. Joined Cape Industries, 1947; Man. Dir, 1957–71. Cancer Research Campaign: Mem. Council, 1965–, Vice-Chm. 1975–83; Chm., Finance Cttee, 1969–75; Chm., Exec. Cttee, 1975–83. Dep. Chm., Finance Cttee, Union Internationale contre le Cancer, Geneva, 1978–90; Dir, Internat. Cancer Foundn, 1978–90. British Inst. of Management: Fellow 1965; Mem. Council, 1968–77; Mem., Bd of Fellows, 1971–77; Chm. Finance Cttee, and Vice-Chm. of Inst., 1972–76. Mem. Council, UK S Africa Trade Assoc., 1969–80. FRSA. *Recreations:* golf, gardening. *Address:* Badgers Copse, Birtley Green, Bramley, Surrey GU5 0LE. *T:* Guildford (01483) 893649. *Club:* St George's Hill Golf.

DENTON, family name of **Baroness Denton of Wakefield**.

DENTON OF WAKEFIELD, Baroness *cr* 1991 (Life Peer), of Wakefield in the County of West Yorkshire; **Jean Denton,** CBE 1990; Parliamentary Under-Secretary of State, Northern Ireland Office, since 1994 (spokesman on the economy, agriculture and women's issues, House of Lords); *b* 29 Dec. 1935; *d* of late Charles J. Moss and Kathleen Moss (*née* Tuke). *Educ:* Rothwell Grammar Sch.; LSE (BScEcon). Procter & Gamble, 1959–61; EIU, 1961–64; IPC, 1964–66; Hotel and Catering Dept, Univ. of Surrey, 1966–69; racing/rally driver, 1969–72; Marketing Director: Huxford Gp, 1972–78; Heron Motor Gp, 1978–80; Man. Dir, Herondrive, 1980–85; External Affairs Dir, Austin Rover, 1985–86; Dep. Chm., Black Country Develt Corp., 1987–91. Director: Ordnance Survey, 1985–88; British Nuclear Fuels, 1987–92; Burson-Marsteller, 1987–92; London & Edinburgh Insce Group, 1989–92; Triplex Lloyd, 1990–92; Think Green, 1989–92. Baroness in Waiting (Govt Whip), 1991–92; Parliamentary Under-Secretary of State: DTI, 1992–93; DoE, 1993–94. Pres., Forum UK, 1992– (Chm., 1989–92); Chairman: Marketing Gp of GB, 1987, 1988; Women on the Move against Cancer, 1979–92 (Pres., 1992–); Member: Board, UK 2000, 1986–88; Engrg Council, 1986–91; Teachers' Pay Review, 1989, 1990 and 1991; NHS Policy Bd, 1990–91. Mem. Adv. Bd, Royal Acad., 1986–87; Mem. Council, RSA, 1991; Governor, LSE, 1982–91; Trustee, Brooklands Museum, 1987–89. *Recreation:* talking shop. *Address:* House of Lords, SW1A 0PW. *Fax:* 0171–735 2642. *Club:* British Women Racing Drivers.

DENTON, Dame Catherine Margaret Mary; *see* Scott, Dame M.

DENTON, Charles; Head of Drama, BBC Television, since 1993; *b* 20 Dec. 1937; *s* of Alan Charles Denton and Mary Frances Royle; *m* 1961, Eleanor Mary Player; one *s* two *d. Educ:* Reading Sch.; Bristol Univ. BA History (Hons). Deckhand, 1960; advertising trainee, 1961–63; BBC TV, 1963–68; freelance television producer with Granada, ATV and Yorkshire TV, 1969–70; Dir, Tempest Films Ltd, 1969–71; Man. Dir, Black Lion Films, 1979–81; ATV: Head of Documentaries, 1974–77; Controller of Programmes, 1977–81; Dir of Progs, Central Indep. TV, 1981–84; Dir, Central Indep. Television plc, 1981–87; Chief Exec., Zenith Prodns, 1984–93; Chairman: Zenith North Ltd, 1988–93; Action Time Ltd, 1988–93; Producers Alliance for Cinema and TV, 1991–93. Governor, BFI, 1992–. FRSA 1988; FRTS 1988. *Recreations:* walking, music. *Address:* The Garden House, Norman Court, West Tytherley, near Salisbury, Wilts SP5 1NL.

DENTON, Sir Eric (James), Kt 1987; CBE 1974; FRS 1964; ScD; Director, Laboratory of Marine Biological Association, Plymouth, 1974–87; Member, Royal Commission on Environmental Pollution, 1973–76; *b* 30 Sept. 1923; *s* of George Denton and Mary Anne (*née* Ogden); *m* 1946, Nancy Emily, *d* of Charles and Emily Jane Wright; two *s* one *d. Educ:* Doncaster Grammar Sch.; St John's Coll., Cambridge. Biophysics Research Unit, University Coll., London, 1946–48; Lectr in Physiology, University of Aberdeen, 1948–56; Physiologist, Marine Biological Assoc. Laboratory, Plymouth, 1956–74; Royal Soc. Res. Professor, Univ. of Bristol, 1964–74, Hon. Professor, 1975. Fellow, University Coll., London, 1965. Hon. Sec., Physiological Soc., 1963–69. Hon. DSc: Exeter, 1976; Göteborg, 1978. Royal Medal, Royal Soc., 1987; Frink Medal, Zool Soc. of London, 1987; International Prize for Biology, Japan Soc. for the Promotion of Science, 1989. *Publications:* Scientific papers in Jl of Marine Biological Assoc., etc. *Recreation:* gardening. *Address:* Fairfield House, St Germans, Saltash, Cornwall PL12 5LS. *T:* St Germans (Cornwall) (01503) 30204; The Laboratory, Citadel Hill, Plymouth PL1 2PB. *T:* Plymouth (01752) 222772.

DENTON, Prof. John Douglas, PhD; FEng 1993; Professor of Turbomachinery Aerodynamics, Cambridge University, since 1991; Fellow of Trinity Hall, Cambridge, since 1977; *b* 1 Dec. 1939; *s* of Donald and Mary Denton; *m* 1966, Maureen Hunt; three *d. Educ:* Trinity Hall, Cambridge (BA, PhD); Univ. of British Columbia (MASc). MIMechE, CEng. Lectr, Univ. of East Africa, 1967–69; Res. Officer, later Section Head, CEGB, 1969–77; Lectr, Dept of Engrg, Cambridge, 1977–91. *Recreations:* travel, mountain walking, bee-keeping. *Address:* 16 Green End, Comberton, Cambridge CB3 7DY.

DENTON, John Grant, OBE 1977; General Secretary, Anglican Church of Australia, 1969–94 (part time until 1977); *b* 16 July 1929; *s* of Ernest Bengrey Denton and Gladys Leonard Stevenson; *m* 1956, Shirley Joan Wise; two *s* two *d. Educ:* Camberwell C of E Grammar School, Melbourne. Personnel and Industrial Relations Dept, Mobil Oil (Aust.), 1950–54; Administrative Sec., Dio. of Central Tanganyika, as CMS missionary, 1954–64; Dir of Information, Dio. of Sydney, 1964–69; Registrar, Dio. of Sydney, 1969–77 (part time). Mem., ACC, 1976–84 (Chm., 1980–84); Chm., Aust. Churches' Cttee for Seventh Assembly of WCC, Canberra, 1991. *Recreation:* model railway. *Address:* 1/50 Scenic Circle, Budgewoi, NSW 2262, Australia.

DENTON, Dame Margaret; *see* Scott, Dame M.

DENTON-THOMPSON, Aubrey Gordon, OBE 1958; MC 1942; *b* 6 June 1920; *s* of late M. A. B. Denton-Thompson; *m* 1944, Ruth Cecily Isaac (*d* 1959); two *s* (one *d* decd); *m* 1961, Barbara Mary Wells. *Educ:* Malvern Coll. Served in RA 1940–44; seconded to Basutoland Administration, 1944; apptd to HM Colonial Service, 1945; transferred to Tanganyika as Asst District Officer, 1947; seconded to Colonial Office, 1948–50, District Officer; seconded to Secretariat, Dar es Salaam, as Asst Sec., 1950; Colonial Sec., Falkland Islands, 1955–60; Dep. Permanent Sec., Ministry of Agriculture, Tanganyika, 1960–62; retired from Tanganyika Civil Service, 1963. Man. Dir, Tanganyika Sisal Marketing Assoc. Ltd, 1966–68 (Sec. 1963); Sen. Agricl Advr, UNDP, 1968–78, and FAO Country Rep.: Korea, 1970–73, Indonesia, 1973–76, Turkey, 1976–78; Sen. Advr to Director General, FAO, Rome, July–Dec. 1978; retd Jan. 1979. Chm., New Forest Conservative Assoc., 1985–88 (Dep. Chm., 1983–85). *Address:* Octave Cottage, Ramley Road, Pennington, Lymington, Hants SO41 8GZ. *T:* Lymington (01590) 676626.

DENYER, Roderick Lawrence; QC 1990; a Recorder, since 1990; *b* 1 March 1948; *s* of Oliver James Denyer and Olive Mabel Jones; *m* 1973, Pauline (*née* Vann); two *d. Educ:* Grove Park Grammar School for Boys, Wrexham; London School of Economics (LLM). Called to the Bar, Inner Temple, 1970; Lectr in Law, Bristol Univ., 1971–73; in practice at Bar, 1973–. Vis. Fellow, UWE, 1994–. Mem., Bar Council, 1992–. *Publications:* Children and Personal Injury Litigation, 1993; various, in legal jls. *Recreations:* cricket, 19th Century history, theatre, restaurants. *Address:* St John's Chambers, Small Street, Bristol BS1 1DW.

DENZA, Mrs Eileen, CMG 1984; Second Counsel to Chairman of Committees and Counsel to European Communities Committee, House of Lords, since 1987; *b* 23 July 1937; *d* of Alexander L. Young and Mrs Young; *m* 1966, John Denza; two *s* one *d. Educ:* Aberdeen Univ. (MA); Somerville Coll., Oxford (MA); Harvard Univ. (LLM). Called to the Bar, Lincoln's Inn, 1963. Asst Lectr in Law, Bristol Univ., 1961–63; Asst Legal Adviser, FCO (formerly FO), 1963–74; Legal Counsellor, FCO, 1974–80; Counsellor (Legal Adviser), Office of UK Perm. Rep. to European Communities, 1980–83; Legal Counsellor, FCO, 1983–86. Pupillage and practice at the Bar, 1986–87. Part-time Lectr, UCL, 1989–. Member: EC Law Section of Adv. Bd, British Inst. of Internat. and Comparative Law, 1988–; Adv. Bd, Inst. of European Public Law, 1992–. *Publications:* Diplomatic Law, 1976; contribs to: Satow's Guide to Diplomatic Practice, 5th edn; Essays in Air Law; Lee's Consular Law and Practice, 2nd edn; Institutional Dynamics of European Integration; articles in British Yearbook of Internat. Law, Revue du Marché Commun, International and Comparative Law Quarterly, Statute Law Review. *Recreation:* music making.

DEOL, Prof. Malkiat Singh, PhD, DSc; Professor of Genetics, University College London, 1981–93, now Emeritus; *b* 1 May 1928; *s* of Santa Singh and Dilip Kaur; *m* 1955, Johanna Stolze; *m* 1990, Luise del Torto. *Educ:* Delhi Univ. (MSc); Univ. of London (PhD, DSc). Res. Assistant, UCL, 1954–55; Res. Fellow, Sloane-Kettering Inst., NY, 1955–56; Res. Associate, Columbia Univ., NY, 1956–57; Scientific Staff, MRC, 1957–69;

Reader in Genetics, UCL, 1969–81. *Publications:* pubns on genetics of hearing, pigmentation and mosaicism. *Recreations:* reading, walking. *Address:* c/o Department of Genetics and Biometry, University College London, Gower Street, WC1E 6BT. *T:* 0171–387 7050.

de OLLOQUI, Dr José Juan; Ambassador of Mexico to the Court of St James's, 1979–82 and 1993–95; *b* 5 Nov. 1931; *m*; three *s* one *d*. *Educ:* Autonomous Univ. of Mexico (LLB 1956, LLD 1979); Univ. of George Washington, Washington, DC (MEc 1970). Official, Bank of Mexico, 1951–91; Head of Dept of Banking, Currency and Investment, Min. of Finance, 1958–66; Exec. Dir, Interamerican Develt Bank, 1966–71 and also Dep. Dir General for Credit, Min. of Finance, 1966–70; Rep. of Mexico to Exec. Permanent Council of Interamerican Econ. and Social Commn, 1970–71; Chm., Nat. Securities Commn, 1970; Ambassador of Mexico to USA and concurrently Ambassador to Govt of Barbados, 1971–76; Under Sec. of State for Foreign Affairs, 1976–79; Ambassador (non-resident) to Ireland, 1980–82; Pres. and Chief Exec. Officer, Serfin Financial Gp, Mexico, 1982–91; Gen. Dir, Inst. of Fund for Mexican Workers' Housing, 1991–93. Chm., Euro-Latinamerican Bank, 1982–84; Chm. of Bd, Carnet Credit Co. (Mastercard), 1983–90; Mem. Bd of Govs, Central Bank, 1985. Prof. of History of Economic Thought, Faculty of Law, Nat. Autonomous Univ. of Mexico, 1964 (by open competition), Life Prof., 1966 (Mem. Bd of Trustees, 1983–); Prof. of Internat. Law Research, Sch. of Post-Graduate and PhD Candidates, 1983–; Prof., Nat. Autonomous Univ. of Mexico and Universidad Iberoamericana, on Mexico's Econ. Problems, Econ. Theory and History of Econ. Thought. Pres., Mexico's Nat. Assoc. of Banks, 1984–85; Mem., Bd of several credit instns and official bodies in Mexico, and has represented Mexico, Interamerican Develt Bank and Permanent Council of the Interamerican Econ. and Social Commn at various internat. confs. Pres. and Founder, Miner's Assoc. of Zacatecas, Zac. and Parral, Chihuahua, Mexico, 1963–71. A Vice-Pres., World Food Council. Member: Mexican Lawyer's Bar; Acad. of Political Sciences; Nat. Coll. of Economists; Mexican Acad. of Internat. Law. Dr *hc* in Human Letters St Mary's Coll. 1975. Holds numerous foreign decorations and awards. *Publications:* Mexico fuera de Mexico, 1980, 2nd edn 1988; Financiamiento Externo y Desarrollo en América Latina, 1984; Consideraciones Sobre Dos Gestiones; Servicio Exterior y Banca, 1986; Implicationes Jurídicas de la Apertura Comercial, 1991; Temas Selectos de Banca y Política Exterior Mexicana (1983–90), 1991; several books, articles and bibliographical reviews on legal and econ. matters. *Address:* Francisco Sosa 78, Coyoacán, 04000 Mexico DF, Mexico.

DEPARDIEU, Gérard; actor; *b* 27 Dec. 1948; *m* 1970, Elisabeth Guignot; one *s* one *d*. *Educ:* Ecole d'art dramatique de Jean Laurent Cochet. Pres., Cannes Film Fest. Jury, 1992. Fellow BFI, 1989. Chevalier, Ordre Nat. du Mérite (France), 1985. *Stage:* Les Garçons de la Bande, Th. Edouard VII, 1968; Une fille dans ma soupe, 1970, Galapagos, 1971, Th. de la Madeleine; Saved, Th. Nat. de Chaillot, 1972; Home, 1972, Isme, Isaac, 1973, La Chevauchée sur le Lac de Constance, 1974, Espace Pierre Cardin; Les Gens deraisonnables sont en voie de disparition, Nanterre, 1977; Tartuffe, Strasbourg, 1983; Lily Passion (musical), Zénith, 1986. *Films:* Le Tueur, 1971; L'affaire Dominici, Un peu de soleil dans l'eau froide, Au rendez-vous de la mort joyeuse, La Scoumoune, Deux hommes dans la ville, Le viager, 1972; Rude journée pour la reine, Stavisky, Les Gaspards, Les Valseuses, 1973; Vincent, François, Paul et les autres, Pas si méchant que ça, 1974; 1900, La dernière femme, Sept morts sur ordonnance, Maîtresse, 1975; Barocco, René la Canne, Baxter, Vera Baxter, 1976; Dites-lui que je l'aime, Le Camion, La nuit tous les chats sont gris, Préparez vos mouchoirs, Rêve de singe, 1977; Le Sucre, Les chiens, Le Grand embouteillage, 1978; Buffet froid, Rosy la bourrasque, Loulou, Mon oncle d'Amérique, 1979; Le dernier métro (Caesar best actor award, 1980), Inspecteur la Bavure, Je vous aime, 1980; Le Choix des armes, La Femme d'à côté, La Chèvre, Le Retour de Martin Guerre, Danton, 1981; Le Grand frère, La Lune dans le caniveau, 1982; Les Compères, Fort Saganne, 1983; Tartuffe (also dir), Rive droite, rive gauche, Police, 1984; Une femme ou deux, Tenue de soirée, Jean de Florette, 1985; Les Fugitifs, Sous le soleil de Satan, 1986; Camille Claudel, 1987; Drôle d'endroit pour une rencontre, Deux, Trop belle pour toi, I Want to go Home, 1988; Cyrano de Bergerac, 1989 (Best Actor, Cannes, 1990; Caesar and de Donatello best actor awards, 1991); Green Card (Golden Globe award, 1991), Uranus, Merci la vie, 1990; Mon Père ce héros, 1492: Colombus, Tous les matins du monde, 1991; Hélas pour moi, Germinal, 1992; Une pure formalité, Le Colonel Chabert, 1993; La Machine, Elisa, Les Cents et une nuits, Les anges gardiens, 1994; has also appeared on TV. *Publication:* Lettres volées, 1988. *Address:* c/o Artmédia, 10 avenue George V, 75008 Paris, France.

de PAULA, (Frederic) Clive, CBE 1970; TD 1950 and Clasp 1951; FCA, JDipMA; Chairman: de Paula plc, since 1984; Dennys Sanders & Greene Ltd, since 1987; *b* 17 Nov. 1916; 2nd *s* of late F. R. M. de Paula, CBE, FCA, and Agnes Smithson de Paula (*née* Clark) (American Medal of Freedom, 1947). *Educ:* Rugby Sch.; Spain and France. ACA 1940; JDipMA 1966. 2nd Lieut, TA, 1939; Liaison Officer, Free French Forces in London and French Equatorial Africa, 1940; Specially employed Middle East and E Africa, 1941; SOE Madagascar, 1942; comd special unit with 11th E African Div., Ceylon and Burma, 1943; Finance Div., Control Commn, Germany, 1945; demobilised as Major, 1946; Captain 21st Special Air Service Regt (Artists) TA, 1947–56. Articled to de Paula, Turner, Lake & Co., chartered accountants, London, 1934–39; joined Robson, Morrow & Co., management consultants, 1946; Partner, 1951; seconded to DEA then to Min. of Technology as an Industrial Adviser, 1967; Co-ordinator of Industrial Advisers to Govt, 1969; returned as Sen. Partner, Robson, Morrow & Co., 1970–71; Man. Dir, Agricultural Mortgage Corp. Ltd, 1971–81; Dir, 1972–83, Dep. Chm., 1978–80, Chm., 1980–83, Tecalemit plc; Non-Exec. Dir, Green's Economiser Group plc, 1972–83; Dep. Chm., C. & J. Clark Ltd, 1985–86. Mem., EDC for Agric., 1972–81. Member: ICAEW, 1940–; Inst. of Cost & Works Accountants, 1947–72; British Computer Soc., 1964–74 (Mem. Council, 1965–68); Management Consultants Assoc., 1964–72 (Mem. Council, 1970–71); BIM, 1970–84 (Mem. Council, 1971–76; CIMgt 1970). Gen. Comr of Income Tax, Winslow Div., Bucks, 1965–82. Vice Pres., Schoolmistresses and Governesses Benevolent Instn, 1982– (Hon. Treas., 1947–81); Chm., Internat. Wine and Food Soc., 1980–83. *Publications:* Accounts for Management, 1954; (ed) P. Tovey, Balance Sheets: how to read and understand them, 4th edn, 1954; (ed) F.R.M. de Paula, The Principles of Auditing, 12th edn 1957 (trans. Sinhalese, 1967), (with F.A. Attwood) 15th edn as Auditing: Principles and Practice, 1976, (with F. A. Attwood and N. D. Stein) 17th edn as de Paula's Auditing, 1986; Management Accounting in Practice, 1959 (trans. Japanese, 1960); (ed with A. G Russell) A.C. Smith, Internal Control and Audit, 2nd edn, 1968; (with A. W. Willsmore) The Techniques of Business Control, 1973; (with F. A. Attwood) Auditing Standards, 1978. *Address:* c/o National Westminster Bank, 13 Bridge Road, East Molesey, Surrey KT8 9EZ.

de PEYER, David Charles; Director General, Cancer Research Campaign, since 1984; *b* 25 April 1934; *s* of late Charles de Peyer, CMG and Flora (*née* Collins); *m* 1959, Ann Harbord. *Educ:* Rendcomb Coll., Cirencester; Magdalen Coll., Oxford (BA PPE). Asst Principal, Min. of Health, 1960; Sec., Royal Commn on NHS, 1976–79; Under Sec., DHSS, 1979–84. *Address:* Cancer Research Campaign, 6–10 Cambridge Terrace, Regent's Park, NW1 4JL.

de PEYER, Gervase; solo clarinettist; conductor; Founder and Conductor, The Melos Sinfonia; Founder Member, The Melos Ensemble of London; Founder, Melos Sinfonia of Washington, 1992; Director, London Symphony Wind Ensemble; Associate Conductor, Haydn Orchestra of London; solo clarinettist, Chamber Music Society of Lincoln Center, New York, since 1969; Resident Conductor, Victoria International Festival, BC, Canada; Co-founder and Artistic Director, Innisfree Music Festival, Pa, USA; *b* London, 11 April 1926; *m* 1980, Katia Perret Aubry. *Educ:* King Alfred's, London; Bedales; Royal College of Music. Served HM Forces, 1945 and 1946. Principal Clarinet, London Symphony Orchestra, 1955–72. ARCM; FRCM 1992; Hon. ARAM. Gold Medallist, Worshipful Co. of Musicians, 1948; Charles Gros Grand Prix du Disque, 1961, 1962; Plaque of Honour for recording, Acad. of Arts and Sciences of America, 1962. Most recorded solo clarinettist in world. *Recreations:* travel, cooking, kite-flying, sport, theatre. *Address:* Porto Vecchio #109, 1250 S Washington Street, Alexandria, VA 22314, USA. *T:* (703) 7390824.

de PIRO, His Honour Alan C. H., QC 1965; FCIArb 1978; a Circuit Judge, 1983–91; *e s* of late J. W. de Piro and Louise Bell Irvine; *m* 1947, Mary Elliot (deceased); two *s*; *m* 1964, Mona Addington (Baroness and Bohemian); one step *s* one step *d*. *Educ:* Repton; Trinity Hall, Cambridge (Sen. Scholar). MA 1947 (1st cl. Hons Nat. Sci. and Law). Royal Artillery, 1940–45 (Capt.); West Africa. Called to Bar, Middle Temple, 1947; Inner Temple, 1962; Bencher, Middle Temple, 1971, Reader, 1988; in practice at the Bar, London and Midlands, 1947–83; Deputy Chairman: Beds QS, 1966–71; Warwicks QS, 1967–71; a Recorder of the Crown Court, 1972–83. Inspector, Canvey Island (Liquid Natural Gas) Public Local Inquiry, 1981–82. Member: Gen. Council of the Bar, 1961–65, 1966–70, 1971–73; Senate of the Inns of Court and the Bar, 1976–81; Council Internat. Bar Assoc., 1967–86 (Chm., Human Rights Cttee, 1979–82); Editorial Advisory Cttee, Law Guardian, 1965–73; Law Panel British Council, 1967–74. Vice-Pres., L'Union Internat. des Avocats, 1968–73, Co-Pres., 1969. Legal Assessor, Disciplinary Cttee, RCVS, 1970–83. *Recreations:* conversation, gardening, inland waterways. *Address:* The Toll House, Bascote Locks, near Leamington, Warwicks CV33 0DT; 23 Birmingham Road, Stoneleigh, Warwicks CV8 3DD. *Club:* Hawks (Cambridge).

de PURY, David; Chairman, Brown Boveri Ltd, since 1992; Co-Chairman, ABB Asea Brown Boveri Group, since 1992; *b* 4 Dec. 1943; *s* of Jean Jacques de Pury and Marguerite de Pury (*née* Miescher); *m* 1991, Maria Eugenia Echeverria. *Educ:* Geneva Univ. (law degree). Attorney; Mem., Geneva Bar. Swiss Diplomatic Service, 1970–91: served in Washington, Mission to EC in Brussels, The Hague and Berne; Ambassador Plenipotentiary and Delegate of Swiss Govt for Trade Agreements, 1986–91; Chm., OECD Trade Cttee, 1989–91; Gov. for Switzerland, Inter-American Develt Bank, 1987–88; Director: Ciba-Geigy, 1992–; Zurich Insce, 1991–; Nestlé, 1993–; UNOTEC, 1992–; CS (Credit Suisse) Hldg., 1992–. Member: European Adv. Bd, Bankers' Trust, 1992–; Eur. Roundtable of Industrialists, 1994–. *Publications:* numerous articles in Swiss and internat. papers and jls. *Recreations:* ski-ing, tennis, music. *Address:* c/o ABB, PO Box 8131, 8050 Zurich, Switzerland. *T:* (1) 3183401, *Fax:* (1) 3183411.

DERAMORE, 6th Baron *cr* 1885; **Richard Arthur de Yarburgh-Bateson,** Bt 1818; Chartered Architect, retired; *b* 9 April 1911; *s* of 4th Baron Deramore and of Muriel Katherine (*née* Duncombe); *S* brother, 1964; *m* 1948, Janet Mary, *d* of John Ware, BA Cantab, MD Edin., Askham-in-Furness, Lancs; one *d*. *Educ:* Harrow; St John's Coll., Cambridge. AA Diploma, 1935; MA Cantab 1936; ARIBA 1936. Associate, A. W. Kenyon, FRIBA, 1936–39. Served as Navigator, RAFVR, 1940–45: 14 Sqdn, RAF, 1942–44 and 1945. County Architect's Dept, Herts, 1949–52; in private practice, London, Buckinghamshire and Yorkshire, 1952–81. Member: Council, Queen Mary Sch., Duncombe Park, Helmsley, 1977–85; Management Cttee, Purey Cust Nursing Home, York, 1976–84; Governor: Heslington Sch., York, 1965–88; Tudor Hall Sch., Banbury, 1966–75. Fellow, Woodard Schs (Northern Div.) Ltd, 1978–84. *Publications:* freelance articles and short stories. *Recreations:* cycling, water-colour painting. *Heir:* none. *Address:* Heslington House, Aislaby, Pickering, North Yorks YO18 8PE. *Clubs:* Royal Air Force, Royal Automobile.

DE RAMSEY, 4th Baron *cr* 1887, of Ramsey Abbey, Huntingdon; **John Ailwyn Fellowes;** DL; Chairman, Environment Agency, since 1995; *b* 27 Feb. 1942; *s* of 3rd Baron De Ramsey, KBE and Lilah Helen Suzanne (*d* 1987), *d* of Frank Labouchere; *S* father, 1993; m 1st, 1973, Phyllida Mary Forsyth; one *s*; 2nd, 1984, Alison Mary Birkmyre; one *s* two *d*. *Educ:* Winchester Coll.; Writtle Inst. of Agriculture. Dir, Cambridge Water Co., 1976–94 (Chm., 1985–91). Crown Estate Comr, 1994–. President: CLA, 1991–93; Assoc. of Drainage Authorities, 1993–94. FRAgS 1993. DL Cambs, 1993. *Recreations:* golf, fishing, fine arts. *Heir: s* Freddie John Fellowes, *b* 31 May 1978. *Address:* Abbots Ripton Hall, Huntingdon PE17 2PQ. *T:* Abbots Ripton (01487) 773555. *Club:* Boodle's.

DERBY, 19th Earl of, *cr* 1485; **Edward Richard William Stanley;** Bt 1627; Baron Stanley 1832; Baron Stanley of Preston 1886; merchant banker with Robert Fleming Holdings Ltd, since 1987; *b* 10 Oct. 1962; *er s* of Hon. Hugh Henry Montagu Stanley (*d* 1971), *g s* of 17th Earl, and of Mary Rose Stanley (*née* Birch); *S* uncle, 1994. *Educ:* Ludgrove; Eton Coll.; RAC Cirencester. Commnd Grenadier Guards, 1982, resigned 1985. Director: Culverin Holdings Ltd, 1989–; Culverin Consortium Ltd, 1989–94; Fleming Private Fund Management Ltd, 1991–; Fleming Private Asset Management Ltd, 1992–; Monlostan Nominees Ltd, 1992–; Fleming Private Nominees Ltd, 1992–; Embankment Properties Ltd, 1994–; Embankment Properties (Management) Ltd, 1994–; Embankment Properties (Trading) Ltd, 1994–; The Haydock Park Racecourse Co. Ltd, 1994–; Knowsley Salads Ltd, 1995–. Aintree Trustee, 1995–. Pres., Liverpool Chamber of Commerce and Industry, 1995–. *Recreations:* shooting, ski-ing, food and wine. *Heir: b* Hon. Peter Hugh Charles Stanley [*b* 4 March 1961; *m* 1990, Hon. Frances Caroline Burke Roche, *o d* of 5th Baron Fermoy; one *s* one *d*]. *Address:* Knowsley, Prescot, Merseyside L34 4AF. *T:* and *Fax:* 0151–489 6148. *Clubs:* White's, Turf, Jockey Club Rooms.

DERBY, Bishop of, since 1995; **Rt Rev. Jonathan Sansbury Bailey;** *b* 24 Feb. 1940; *s* of late Walter Eric and of Audrey Sansbury Bailey; *m* 1965, Rev. Susan Mary Bennett-Jones; three *s*. *Educ:* Quarry Bank High School, Liverpool; Trinity College, Cambridge (MA). Assistant Curate: Sutton, St Helens, Lancs, 1965–68; St Paul, Warrington, 1968–71; Warden, Marrick Priory, 1971–76; Vicar of Wetherby, Yorks, 1976–82; Archdeacon of Southend and Bishop's Officer for Industry and Commerce, dio. of Chelmsford, 1982–92; Suffragan Bishop of Dunwich, 1992–95. *Recreations:* theatre, music, beekeeping, carpentry. *Address:* (home) The Bishop's House, 6 King Street, Duffield, Belper, Derbyshire DE56 4EU; (office) Bishop's Office, Derby Church House, Full Street, Derby DE1 3DR. *T:* Derby (01332) 346744, *Fax:* (01332) 295810.

DERBY, Provost of; *see* Lewers, Very Rev. B. H.

DERBY, Archdeacon of; *see* Gatford, Ven. I.

DERBYSHIRE, Sir Andrew (George), Kt 1986; FRIBA; Chairman, Robert Matthew, Johnson-Marshall & Partners & RMJM Ltd, 1983–89; President, RMJM Group, since 1989; *b* 7 Oct. 1923; *s* of late Samuel Reginald Derbyshire and late Helen Louise Puleston Derbyshire (*née* Clarke); *m*, Lily Rhodes (*née* Binns), *widow* of late Norman Rhodes; three *s* one *d*. *Educ:* Chesterfield Grammar Sch.; Queens' Coll., Cambridge; Architectural Assoc. MA (Cantab), AA Dip. (Hons). Admty Signals Estabt and Bldg Research Station, 1943–46. Farmer & Dark, 1951–53 (Marchwood and Belvedere power stations); West Riding County Architect's Dept, 1953–55 (bldgs for educn and social welfare). Asst City Architect, Sheffield, 1955–61; responsible for central area redevelt. Mem. Research Team, RIBA Survey of Architects' Offices, 1960–62. Since 1961, as Mem. RM, J-M & Partners, later RMJM Ltd, responsible for: develt of Univ. of York, Central Lancs New Town, NE Lancs Impact Study, Univ. of Cambridge, West Cambridge Develt and New Cavendish Laboratory, Preston Market and Guildhall, London Docklands Study, Hillingdon Civic Centre, Cabtrack and Minitram feasibility studies, Suez Master Plan Study; Castle Peak Power Stations, and Harbour Reclamation and Urban Growth Study, Hong Kong. Member: RIBA Council, 1950–72, 1975–81 (Senior Vice-Pres., 1980); NJCC, 1961–65; Bldg Industry Communications Res. Cttee, 1964–66 (Chm. Steering Cttee); DoE Planning and Transport Res. Adv. Council, 1971–76; Standing Commn on Energy and the Environment, 1978–. Pt-time Mem., CEGB, 1973–84; Board Member: Property Services Agency, 1975–79; London Docklands Develt Corp., 1984–88; Construction Industry Sector Group, NEDC, 1988–92; Mem., Construction Industry Council, 1990–94. Hoffman Wood Prof. of Architecture, Univ. of Leeds, 1978–80; External Prof., Dept of Civil Engineering, Univ. of Leeds, 1981–85; Gresham Prof. of Rhetoric, Gresham Coll., 1990–92; Hon. Fellow, Inst. of Advanced Architectural Studies, Univ. of York, 1994; Hon. FIStructE 1992. FRSA 1981 (Chm., Art for Architecture Project, 1995–). DUniv York, 1972. *Publication:* (jtly) The Architect and his Office, 1962. *Recreation:* his family. *Address:* 4 Sunnyfield, Hatfield, Herts AL9 5DX. *T:* Hatfield (01707) 265903; 83 Paul Street, EC2A 4NQ. *T:* 0171–251 5588.

DERHAM, Sir Peter (John), Kt 1980; FAIM; FPIA; FInstD; Chairman: Circadian Technologies Ltd (formerly Circadian Pharmaceuticals Ltd), since 1984; Multistack International, since 1993; Greenchip Development Capital Ltd, since 1993; *b* 21 Aug. 1925; *s* of John and Mary Derham; *m* 1950, Averil C. Wigan; two *s* one *d*. *Educ:* Melbourne Church of England Grammar School; Univ. of Melbourne (BSc 1958); Harvard Univ. (Advanced Management Programme). Served RAAF and RAN, 1944–46. Joined Moulded Products (Australasia) Ltd (later Nylex Corp.), 1943; Dir, 1953–82, Sales Dir, 1960, Gen. Manager, 1967, Man. Dir, 1972–80. Chairman: Internat. Pacific Corp. Ltd, later Rothschild Australia Ltd, 1981–85; Australia New Zealand Foundn, 1978–83; Australian Canned Fruits Corp., 1981–89; Robert Bryce & Co. Ltd, 1982–91; Davy McKee Pacific Pty, 1984–90; Leasing Corp. Ltd, 1987–93; Deputy Chairman: Prime Computer of Australia Ltd, 1986–92; Australian Mutual Provident Society State Board of Advice, 1990–91 (Dir, Victoria Br. Bd, 1974–90); Director: Lucas Industries Aust., 1981–84; Station 3XY Pty, 1980–87; Radio 3XY Pty, 1980–87; Perpetual Trustees Victoria Ltd, 1992–93; Perpetual Trustees Australia Ltd, 1993–; Advance Australia Foundn, 1983–; Jt Chm., Advance Australia America Cup Challenge Ltd, 1981–83; Councillor Enterprise Australia, 1975–82 (Dep. Chm., 1975–78). Chairman: Nat. Training Council, 1971–80; Adv. Bd, CSIRO, 1981–86; Australian Tourist Commn, 1981–85; Member: Manufg Industries Adv. Council, 1971–74; Victorian Econ. Develt Corp., 1981–82. Federal Pres., Inst. of Directors in Australia, 1980–82 (Mem., 1975–89, Chm., 1975–82, Victorian Council; Life Mem., 1986) Councillor: Yooralla Soc. of Victoria, 1972–79 (Chm. Workshops Cttee, 1972–81); Aust. Industries Develt Assoc., 1975–80; State Councillor, Industrial Design Council, 1967–73, Federal Councillor, 1970–73; Mem. Council, Inst. of Public Affairs, 1971–; Life Mem., Plastics Inst. of Australia Inc. (Victorian Pres., 1964–66; Nat. Pres., 1971–72); Mem. Board of Advisors, Inst. of Cultural Affairs, 1971–81. Member: Rotary Club of Melbourne (Mem., Bd of Dirs, 1974–75, 1975–76); Victorian State Cttee, Child Accident Prevention Foundn of Australia; Appeal Cttee, Royal Victorian Eye and Ear Hosp.; Bd of Management, Alfred Hosp., 1980–93 (Pres., 1990–92), Amalgamated Alfred, Caulfield and Royal Southern Meml Hosp., 1987–93; St John Ambulance, 1988– (Chm., State Council, 1991–); Chm., Caulfield Hosp. Cttee, 1984–87 (Dir, 1981–87; Vice Pres., 1989). President: Alcohol and Drug Foundn (formerly Victorian Foundn on Alcoholism and Drug Dependence), 1986–91 (Appeal Chm., 1981–86); Victorian Soc. for Prevention of Child Abuse and Neglect, 1987–; Dep Chm., Australian Assoc. for Support of Educn, 1983–87; Mem., Melbourne C of E Grammar Sch. Council, 1974–75, 1977–80; Pres., Old Melburnians, 1974–75; Governor, Ian Clunies Ross Meml Foundn, 1979–; Chairman: Trade & Industry Cttee, Victoria's 150th Anniv. Celebration; Police Toy Fund for Underprivileged Children; Pres., Somers Area, Boy Scout Assoc. of Australia, 1985–90; Vict. Trustee, Australian Koala Foundn Inc., 1986–92; Trustee, H & L Hecht Trust, 1990–; Life Governor, Assoc. for the Blind. CStJ (OStJ 1991). *Recreations:* golf, sailing, tennis, gardening, viticulture. *Address:* 2A Ashley Grove, Malvern, Vic 3144, Australia. *T:* (3) 98220770. *Clubs:* Australian, Melbourne (Melbourne); Royal Melbourne Golf, Flinders Golf, Royal South Yarra Lawn Tennis, Melbourne Cricket.

DERMOTT, William, CB 1984; Under Secretary, Head of Agricultural Science Service, Agricultural Development and Advisory Service, Ministry of Agriculture, Fisheries and Food, 1976–84, retired; *b* 27 March 1924; *s* of William and Mary Dermott; *m* 1946, Winifred Joan Tinney; one *s* one *d*. *Educ:* Univ. of Durham. BSc, MSc. Agricl Chemist, Univ. of Durham and Wye Coll., Univ. of London, 1943–46; Soil Scientist, Min. of Agriculture, at Wye, Bangor and Wolverhampton, 1947–70; Sen. Sci. Specialist, and Dep. Chief Sci. Specialist, MAFF, 1971–76; Actg Dir Gen., ADAS, 1983–84. Pres., British Soc. of Soil Science, 1981–82. *Publications:* papers on various aspects of agricultural chemistry in scientific journals. *Recreations:* gardening, the countryside. *Address:* 22 Chequers Park, Wye, Ashford, Kent TN25 5BB. *T:* Wye (01233) 812694.

de ROS, 28th Baron *cr* 1264 (Premier Barony of England); **Peter Trevor Maxwell;** *b* 23 Dec. 1958; *s* of Comdr John David Maxwell, RN, and late Georgiana Angela Maxwell, 27th Baroness de Ros; *S* mother, 1983; *m* 1987, Siân Ross; one *s* one *d*. *Educ:* Headfort School, Kells, Co. Meath; Stowe School, Bucks; Down High School, Co. Down. Upholstered furniture maker. *Recreations:* gardening, travel and sailing. *Heir:* *s* Hon. Finbar James Maxwell, *b* 14 Nov. 1988.

de ROTHSCHILD; *see* Rothschild.

DERRETT, Prof. (John) Duncan (Martin), MA, PhD, DCL, LLD, DD; Professor of Oriental Laws in the University of London, 1965–82, now Emeritus; Curator, Blockley Southcottian Collection, since 1991; *b* 30 Aug. 1922; *s* of John West Derrett and Fay Frances Ethel Kate (*née* Martin); *m* 1950, Margaret Esmé Griffiths; four *s* one *d*. *Educ:* Emanuel Sch., London; Jesus Coll., Oxford; Sch. of Oriental and Afr. Studies, London; Inns of Court School of Law. MA 1947, DCL 1966 (Oxon); PhD 1949, LLD 1971, DD 1983 (London). Called to the Bar, Gray's Inn, 1953. Lectr in Hindu Law, SOAS, 1949; Reader in Oriental Laws, 1956, Prof. of Oriental Laws, 1965, Univ. of London; Tagore Prof. of Law, Univ. of Calcutta, 1953 (lectures delivered, 1955); Vis. Professor: Univ. of Chicago, 1963; Univ. of Michigan, 1970; Wilde Lectr in Natural and Compar. Religion, Univ. of Oxford, 1978–81; Japan Soc. Prom. Sci. Fellow and Vis. Prof., Oriental Inst., Univ. of Tokyo, 1982. Fellow, Indian Law Inst., Delhi, 1988. Mem., Editorial Bd, Zeitschrift für vergleichende Rechtswissenschaft, 1954–85, subseq. of Kannada Studies, Bharata Manisha, Kerala Law Times. Mem. Selection Cttee, Fac. of Law, Univs of Dacca and Rajshahi, 1978–. Mem., Stud. Novi Test. Soc., 1971. Barcelona Prize in Comparative Law, 1954; N. C. Sen-Gupta Gold Medal, Asiatic Soc. (Calcutta), 1977. *Publications:* The Hoysalas, 1957; Hindu Law Past and Present, 1957; Introduction to Modern Hindu Law, 1963; Religion, Law and the State in India, 1968; Critique of Modern Hindu Law, 1970; Law in the New Testament, 1970; Jesus's Audience, 1973; Dharmaśāstra and Juridical Literature, 1973; History of Indian Law (Dharmaśāstra), 1973; Henry Swinburne (?1551–1624) Civil Lawyer of York, 1973; Bhāruci's Commentary on the Manusmrti, 1975; Essays in Classical and Modern Hindu Law, vols I-IV, 1976–79; Studies in the New Testament, vols I-VI, 1977–96; The Death of a Marriage Law, 1978; Beiträge zu Indischem Rechtsdenken, 1979; The Anastasis: the Resurrection of Jesus as an Historical Event, 1982; A Textbook for Novices: Jayarakshita's Perspicuous Commentary on the 'Compendium of Conduct', 1983; The Making of Mark, 1985; New Resolutions of Old Conundrums: a fresh insight into Luke's Gospel, 1986; The Ascetic Discourse: an explanation of the Sermon on the Mount, 1989; The Victim: the Johannine passion narrative reexamined, 1993; The Sermon on the Mount, 1994; Prophecy in the Cotswolds 1804–1947, 1994; Two Masters: the Buddha and Jesus, instructors in ethics, 1995; trans. R. Lingat, Classical Law of India, 1973; (ed) Studies in the Laws of Succession in Nigeria, 1965; (ed) Introduction to Legal Systems, 1968; (ed) (with W. D. O'Flaherty) The Concept of Duty in South Asia, 1978; (ed) A Second Blockley Miscellany, 1994; collab. with Yale Edn, Works of St Thomas More, Société Jean Bodin, Brussels, Max Planck Inst., Hamburg, Fritz Thyssen Stiftung, Cologne, Institut für Soziologie, Heidelberg, Aufstieg und Niedergang der Römischen Welt, Tübingen, and Sekai Kyusei Kyo, Atami; *Festschriften:* Indology and Law, 1982; Novum Testamentum, 24, 1982, fasc. 3 and foll. *Recreations:* listening to music, gardening, clocks. *Address:* Half Way House, High Street, Blockley, Moreton-in-Marsh, Glos GL56 9EX. *T:* Blockley (01386) 700828.

DERRICK, Patricia, (Mrs Donald Derrick); *see* Lamburn, P.

DERRIDA, Jacques; writer; *b* 15 July 1930; *s* of Aimé Derrida and Georgette Safar; *m* 1957, Marguérite Aucouturier; two *s*. *Educ:* Ecole Normale Supérieure, Paris. Taught at Sorbonne, 1960–64; at Ecole Normale Supérieure, 1965–84. Hon. DLitt Cambridge, 1992. *Publications:* La voix et le phénomène, 1967; De la grammatologie, 1967; L'écriture et la différence, 1967; Marges, 1972; La dissémination, 1972; Glas, 1974; La vérité en peinture, 1979; La carte postale, 1980; Positions, 1981; Spurs: Nietzsche's styles, 1981; Archaeology of the Frivolous, 1987; Psyché, 1987; De l'esprit, 1987; Mémoires: pour Paul De Man, 1988; Du droit à la philosophie, 1990; Mémoires d'aveugle, 1990; Le problème de la genèse dans la philosophie de Husserl, 1990; L'autre cap, 1991; Donner le temps, 1991; Qu'est-ce que la poésie?, 1991; Reader, 1991; Acts of Literature, 1992; Cinders, 1992; Spectres de Marx, 1993; Aporias, 1994. *Address:* Ecole des Hautes Etudes en Sciences Sociales, 54 boulevard Raspail, 75006 Paris, France.

DERRY, Bishop of, (RC), since 1994; **Most Rev. Séamus Hegarty;** *b* 26 Jan. 1940; *s* of James Hegarty and Mary O'Donnell. *Educ:* Kilcar National School; St Eunan's Coll., Letterkenny; St Patrick's Coll., Maynooth; University Coll., Dublin. Priest, 1966; post-grad. studies, University Coll., Dublin, 1966–67; Dean of Studies 1967–71, President 1971–82, Holy Cross College, Falcarragh; Bishop of Raphoe, 1982–94. *Publication:* contribs to works on school administration and student assessment. *Recreations:* bridge, fishing. *Address:* St Eugene's Cathedral, Derry BT48 9AP. *T:* Londonderry (01504) 262302.

DERRY AND RAPHOE, Bishop of, since 1980; **Rt. Rev. James Mehaffey;** *b* 29 March 1931; *s* of John and Sarah Mehaffey; *m* 1956, Thelma P. L. Jackson; two *s* one *d*. *Educ:* Trinity College, Dublin (MA, BD); Queen's University, Belfast (PhD). Curate Assistant: St Patrick's, Belfast, 1954–56; St John's, Deptford, London, 1956–58; Minor Canon, Down Cathedral, 1958–60; Bishop's Curate, St Christopher's, Belfast, 1960–62; Incumbent: Kilkeel, Diocese of Dromore, 1962–66; Cregagh, Diocese of Down, 1966–80. *Address:* The See House, 112 Culmore Road, Londonderry BT48 8JF. *T:* Londonderry (01504) 351206.

DERRY, Thomas Kingston, OBE 1976; Kt, Order of St Olav, Norway, 1981; MA, DPhil Oxon; *b* 5 March 1905; *y s* of late Rev. W. T. Derry, Wesleyan Minister; *m* 1930, Gudny (*d* 1989), *e d* of late Hjalmar Wesenberg, Commander of Order of Vasa, Oslo, Norway. *Educ:* Kingswood Sch., Bath; Queen's Coll., Oxford (Bible Clerk and Taberdar). 1st Class, Classical Moderations, 1925; 1st Class, Final Sch. of Modern History, 1927; Senior George Webb Medley Scholar, 1927; Gladstone Prizeman, 1928; Sixth Form Master and Chief History Master, Repton Sch., 1929–37; Headmaster, Mill Hill School, 1938–40; Political Intelligence Dept of Foreign Office, 1941–45; Asst Master, St Marylebone Grammar Sch., 1945–65; Visiting Prof., Wheaton Coll., Mass, 1961–62. *Publications:* (with T. L. Jarman) The European World, 1950, rev. and extended edn 1975; The Campaign in Norway (official military history), 1952; A Short History of Norway, 1957; (with T. I. Williams) A Short History of Technology, 1960; The United Kingdom Today, 1961; A Short Economic History of Britain, 1965; (with E. J. Knapton) Europe 1815–1914, 1965; Europe 1914 to the Present, 1966; (with T. L. Jarman and M. G. Blakeway) The Making of Britain, 3 vols, 1956–69; A History of Modern Norway, 1814–1972, 1973; A History of Scandinavia, 1979; (with T. L. Jarman) Modern Britain, 1979; A History of St Edmund's Church, Oslo, 1884–1994, 1994. *Address:* Nils Lauritssons vei 27, 0854 Oslo 8, Norway. *T:* (2) 22231432.

DERVAIRD, Hon Lord; John Murray; Dickson Minto Professor of Company Law (formerly of Company and Commercial Law), since 1990 and Dean, Faculty of Law, since 1994, Edinburgh University; a Senator of the College of Justice in Scotland, 1988–89; *b* 8 July 1935; *o s* of J. H. Murray, farmer, Stranraer; *m* 1960, Bridget Jane, *d* of Sir William Godfrey, 7th Bt, and of Lady Godfrey; three *s*. *Educ:* Stranraer schs; Edinburgh Academy; Corpus Christi Coll., Oxford (BA 1st cl. Lit. Hum., 1959); Edinburgh Univ. (LLB 1962). FCIArb 1991. Advocate, 1962; QC (Scot.) 1974. Mem., Scottish Law Commn, 1979–88. Chairman: Scottish Lawyers' European Gp, 1975–78; Scottish Council of Law Reporting, 1978–88; Scottish Cttee on Law of Arbitration, 1986–; Scottish Council for Arbitration, 1989–; Member: City Disputes Panel, 1994–; Panel of Arbitrators, Internat. Centre for Investment Disputes, 1995–; Vice-President: Agricultural Law Assoc., 1985–91 (Chm., 1979–85); Comité Européen de Droit Rural, 1989–91, 1995–. Hon. Pres., Advocates' Business Law Group, 1988–. Dir and Chm., Scottish Ensemble Ltd, 1988–. Corresp. Mem., ICC Cttee on Business Law, Paris, 1994–. Trustee, David Hume Inst, 1994–. Grand Chaplain, Von Poser Soc. of Scotland. *Publications:* contributed to: Festschrift für Dr Pikalo, 1979; Mélanges offert à Jean Megret, 1985; Encyclopedia of Scots Law, 1987, 1992; Scottish Legal Tradition, 1991; Corporate Law – the European Dimension, 1991; European Company Law, 1992; International Handbook on Commercial Arbitration, 1995; articles in legal and ornithological jls. *Recreations:* farming, gardening, birdwatching, music, curling, field sports. *Address:* 4 Moray Place, Edinburgh EH3 6DS. *T:* 0131–225 1881, *Fax:* 0131–220 0644; Auchenmalg House, Auchenmalg, Glenluce, Wigtownshire DG8 0JS. *T:* Auchenmalg (01581) 500205; Wood of Dervaird Farm, Glenluce DG8 9JT. *T:* Glenluce (01581) 300222. *Clubs:* New, Puffin's (Edinburgh); Aberlady Curlers.

DERWENT, 5th Baron *cr* 1881; **Robin Evelyn Leo Vanden-Bempde-Johnstone,** LVO 1957; Bt 1795; DL; Managing Director, Hutchison Whampoa (Europe) Ltd, since 1985; Director: Cliff Resources PLC, since 1989; F&C (Pacific) Investment Trust Ltd, since 1989; Scarborough Building Society, since 1991; *b* 30 Oct. 1930; *s* of 4th Baron Derwent, CBE and Marie-Louise (*d* 1985), *d* of Albert Picard, Paris; *S* father, 1986; *m* 1957, Sybille, *d* of late Vicomte de Simard de Pitray and Madame Jeanine Hennessy; one *s* three *d*. *Educ:* Winchester College; Clare Coll., Cambridge (Scholar, MA 1953). 2nd Lieut 1949, 60th Rifles; Lieut 1950, Queen Victoria's Rifles (TA). HM Diplomatic Service, 1954–69; served FO, Paris, Mexico City, Washington. Director, NM Rothschild & Sons, Merchant Bankers, 1969–85. Chm., London & Provincial Antique Dealers' Assoc., 1989–95. DL N Yorks, 1991. Chevalier de la Légion d'Honneur (France), 1957; Officier de l'Ordre National du Mérite (France), 1978. *Recreations:* shooting, fishing. *Heir:* *s* Hon. Francis Patrick Harcourt Vanden-Bempde-Johnstone [*b* 23 Sept. 1965; *m* 1990, Cressida, *o d* of Christopher John Bourke, *qv*]. *Address:* Hackness Hall, Hackness, Scarborough YO13 0BL; 30 Kelso Place, W8 5QG. *Club:* Boodle's.

DERWENT, Henry Clifford Sydney; Director, National Roads Policy (formerly Under Secretary, Highways Policy and Resources), Department of Transport, since 1992; *b* 19 Nov. 1951; *s* of late Clifford Sydney Derwent and of Joan Kathleen (*née* Craft); *m* 1988, Rosemary Patricia Jesse Meaker; three *d*. *Educ:* Berkhamsted Sch.; Worcester Coll., Oxford. Department of the Environment, 1974–86; planning policy; PSA; London housing; commercial property; Rayner scrutiny; seconded to Midland Bank; inner cities; Department of Transport, 1986–: private office; local finance; vehicle licensing; central finance; highways. *Recreations:* flute, trombone, riding, watercolours. *Address:* c/o Department of Transport, 2 Marsham Street, SW1P 3EB. *T:* 0171–276 5710.

DERX, Donald John, CB 1975; non-executive Director, Glaxo Holdings plc, since 1991; *b* 25 June 1928; *s* of John Derx and Violet Ivy Stroud; *m* 1956, Luisa Donzelli; two *s* two *d*. *Educ:* Tiffin Boys' Sch., Kingston-on-Thames; St Edmund Hall, Oxford (BA). Asst Principal, BoT, 1951; seconded to Cabinet Office, 1954–55; Principal, Colonial Office, 1957; Asst Sec., Industrial Policy Gp, DEA, 1965; Dir, Treasury Centre for Admin. Studies, 1968; Head of London Centre, Civil Service Coll., 1970; Under Sec., 1971–72, Dep. Sec., 1972–84, Dept of Employment; Dir, Policy Studies Inst., 1985–86; with Glaxo Holdings plc, 1986–.

DESAI, family name of **Baron Desai**.

DESAI, Baron *cr* 1991 (Life Peer), of St Clement Danes in the City of Westminster; **Meghnad Jagdishchandra Desai,** PhD; Professor of Economics, since 1983, and Director, Centre for the Study of Global Governance, since 1992, London School of Economics and Political Science; *b* 10 July 1940; *s* of late Jagdishchandra and of Mandakini Desai; *m* 1970, Gail Graham Wilson; one *s* two *d*. *Educ:* Univ. of Bombay (BA Hons, MA); Univ. of Pennsylvania (PhD 1964). Associate Specialist, Dept of Agricultural Econs, Univ. of Calif, Berkeley, 1963–65; London School of Economics: Lectr, 1965–77, Sen. Lectr, 1977–80, Reader, 1980–83, Dept. of Econs; Head, Develt Studies Inst., 1990–95. Pres., Assoc. of Univ. Teachers in Econs, 1987–90; Mem. Council, REconS, 1988. Chm., Islington South and Finsbury Constituency Labour Pty, 1986–. Hon. DSc Kingston, 1992; Hon. DSc (Econ) E London, 1994; DUniv Middlesex, 1993. *Publications:* Marxian Economic Theory, 1974; Applied Econometrics, 1976; Marxian Economics, 1979; Testing Monetarism, 1981; (Asst Editor to Prof. Dharma Kumar) The Cambridge Economic History of India 1757–1970, 1983; (ed jtly) Agrarian Power and Agricultural Productivity in South Asia, 1984; (ed) Lenin on Economics, 1987; Macroeconomics and Monetary Theory: selected essays, vol. 1, 1995; Poverty, Famine and Economic Development: selected essays, vol. 2, 1995; (ed jtly) Global Governance, 1995; (ed) On Inequality, 1995; contrib. Econometrica, Econ. Jl, Rev. of Econ. Studies, Economica, Econ. Hist. Rev. *Address:* London School of Economics and Political Science, Houghton Street, Aldwych, WC2A 2AE.

DESAI, Anita, FRSL; novelist; *b* 24 June 1937; *d* of Toni Nimé and D. N. Mazumbar; *m* 1958, Ashvin Desai; two *s* two *d*. *Educ:* Queen Mary's Sch., Delhi; Miranda House, Univ. of Delhi (BA Hons). FRSL 1963. First story published 1946; novelist and book reviewer (freelance), 1963–. Helen Cam Vis. Fellow, 1986–87, Hon. Fellow, 1988, Girton Coll., Univ. of Cambridge; Elizabeth Drew Prof., Smith Coll., USA, 1987–88; Purington Prof. of English, Mount Holyoke Coll., USA, 1988–92; Prof. of Writing, MIT, 1993–; Ashby Fellow, 1989, Hon. Fellow, 1991, Clare Hall, Univ. of Cambridge. Hon. Mem., Amer. Acad. of Arts and Letters, 1993. Padma Sri, 1990. *Publications:* Cry, The Peacock, 1963; Voices in the City, 1965; Bye-Bye Blackbird, 1971; Where Shall We Go This Summer?, 1973; Fire on the Mountain, 1978 (Winifred Holtby Award, RSL, 1978); Games at Twilight, 1979; Clear Light of Day, 1980; The Village by the Sea, 1983 (Guardian Prize for Children's Fiction, 1983; filmed, 1992); In Custody, 1984 (screenplay, filmed 1994); Baumgartner's Bombay, 1988 (Hadassah Prize, Hadassah Magazine, NY, 1989); Journey to Ithaca, 1995. *Address:* c/o Deborah Rogers Ltd, 20 Powis Mews, W11 1JN.

DE ST JORRE, Danielle Marie-Madeleine J.; *see* Jorre De St Jorre.

de STE. CROIX, Geoffrey Ernest Maurice, DLitt; FBA 1972; Fellow and Tutor in Ancient History, New College, Oxford, 1953–77, Emeritus Fellow, 1977, Hon. Fellow, 1985; *b* 8 Feb. 1910; *s* of Ernest Henry de Ste Croix and Florence Annie (*née* Macgowan); *m* 1st, 1932, Lucile (marr. diss. 1959); one *d* (decd); 2nd, 1959, Margaret Knight; two *s*. *Educ:* Clifton Coll. (to 1925); University Coll. London (1946–50) (Fellow, 1987). BA 1st cl. Hons History, London, 1949; MA Oxon, 1953; DLitt Oxon, 1978. Solicitor, 1931. Served War, RAF, 1940–46. Asst Lectr in Ancient Economic History, London Sch. of Economics, and Part-time Lectr in Ancient History, Birkbeck Coll., London, 1950–53. Vis. Prof., Univ. of Amsterdam, 1978. Lectures include: J. H. Gray, Cambridge Univ., 1972–73; Gregynog, UCW, Aberystwyth, 1986; Townsend, Cornell Univ., 1988; has given many other lectures in Europe and N America. *Publications:* The Origins of the Peloponnesian War, 1972; The Class Struggle in the Ancient Greek World, from the Archaic Age to the Arab Conquests, 1981 (Isaac Deutscher Meml Prize, 1982; Spanish edn 1988; Greek edn 1995); contributions to: Studies in the History of Accounting, 1956; The Crucible of Christianity, 1969; Studies in Ancient Society, 1974; Debits, Credits, Finance and Profits, 1974; articles and reviews in various learned jls. *Recreation:* listening to music. *Address:* Evenlode, Stonesfield Lane, Charlbury, Oxford OX7 3ER. *T:* Charlbury (01608) 810453.

de SAUMAREZ, 7th Baron *cr* 1831; **Eric Douglas Saumarez;** Bt 1801; farmer; *b* 13 Aug. 1956; *s* of 6th Baron de Saumarez and Joan Beryl, (Julia), *d* of late Douglas Raymond Charlton; *S* father, 1991; *m* 1st, 1982, Christine Elizabeth (marr. diss. 1990), *yr d* of B. N. Halliday; two *d*; 2nd, 1991, Susan M. Hearn. *Educ:* Milton Abbey; Nottingham Univ.; RAC, Cirencester. *Recreations:* flying, shooting, ski-ing, fishing. *Heir:* *twin b* Hon. Victor Thomas Saumarez, *b* 13 Aug. 1956. *Address:* Shrubland Park, Coddenham, Ipswich, Suffolk IP6 9QQ.

de SAVARY, Peter John; international entrepreneur; *b* 11 July 1944; *m* 1986, (Lucille) Lana Paton; three *d* (and two *d* by a former marriage). *Educ:* Charterhouse. Activities in the energy, property, finance, maritime and leisure fields. Chm., Victory Syndicate, 1983 British Challenge for America's Cup. Chm., Carnegie Club. Tourism Personality of the Year, English Tourist Bd, 1988. *Recreations:* sailing, riding, carriage driving. *Address:* Littlecote House, Hungerford, Berks; Skibo Castle, Dornoch, Sutherland. *Clubs:* St James's, Royal Automobile, Royal Thames Yacht; Royal Burnham Yacht, Royal Torbay Yacht, Royal Corinthian Yacht, Port Pendennis Yacht (Cdre).

DESCH, Stephen Conway; QC 1980; a Recorder of the Crown Court, since 1979; *b* 17 Nov. 1939; *o s* of Harold Ernest Desch and Gwendolen Lucy Desch; *m* 1973, Julia Beatrice Little; two *d*. *Educ:* Dauntsey's Sch.; Magdalen Coll., Oxford (BCL, MA); Northwestern Univ., Chicago. Called to the Bar, Gray's Inn, 1962, Bencher, 1990; joined Midland Circuit, 1964. Lectr in Law, Magdalen Coll., Oxford, 1963–65. *Publication:* Legal Notes to H. E. Desch: Structural Surveying, 1970, 2nd edn (with Stephen Mika), 1988. *Recreations:* country pursuits, farming, mountain walking. *Address:* 2 Crown Office Row, Temple, EC4Y 7HJ. *T:* 0171–353 9337.

de SILGUY, Count Yves-Thibault; Member, European Commission, since 1995; *b* Rennes, 22 July 1948; *s* of Raymond de Silguy and Claude de Pompery; *m* 1976, Jacqueline de Montillet de Grenaud; one *s* one *d*. *Educ:* Collège Saint-Martin; Univ. of Rennes (Law and Econ Scis); Sch. of Public Service, Institut d'Etudes Politiques, Paris (Dip.); Ecole Nationale d'Administration. Sec. for Foreign Affairs to Dir for Econ. and Financial Affairs, 1976–80; Advr, then Dep. Staff Dir for Vice-Pres. Ortoli, Comr for Econ. and Monetary Affairs, 1981–84; Advr i/c Econ. Affairs, EC in Washington, 1985–86; Tech. Advr to Prime Minister i/c European Affairs and Internat. Econ. and Financial Affairs, 1986–88; Manager, Internat. Business Div. and Gp Internat. Business Dir, Usinor Sacilor, 1988–93; Sec. Gen., Interministerial Cttee for European Econ. Co-operation and Advr for European Affairs to Prime Minister, 1993–95. Gen. Deleg. of French Steel Fedn, 1993–95; Chm. Bd, Professional Center for Steel Stats, 1993–95; Chm., Finance Cttee, Eurofer, 1993–95. Chevalier du Mérite Agricole (France), 1985; Officier des Arts et des Lettres (France), 1994. *Recreations:* tennis, yachting, hunting. *Address:* European Commission, 200 Rue de la Loi, 1049 Brussels, Belgium. *Club:* Polo (Paris).

de SILVA, Desmond (George Lorenz); QC 1984; *b* 13 Dec. 1939; *s* of Edmund Frederick Lorenz de Silva, MBE, retired Ambassador, and Esme Gregg de Silva; *m* 1987, HRH Princess Katarina of Yugoslavia, *d* of HRH Prince Tomislav of Yugoslavia and Princess Margarita of Baden; one *d*. *Educ:* Dulwich College Prep Sch.; Trinity College, Ceylon. Served with 3rd Carabiniers (3rd Dragoon Guards). Called to the Bar: Middle Temple, 1964; Sierra Leone, 1968; The Gambia, 1981; Gibraltar, 1992. Vice-Chm., Westminster Community Relations Council, 1980–82; Councilman, City of London, 1980–; Main Session Chm., First Internat. Conf. on Human Value, 1981. Member: Home Affairs Standing Cttee, Bow Gp, 1982; Editl Adv. Bd, Crossbow, 1984; Crime and Juvenile Delinquency Study Gp, Centre for Policy Studies, 1983–. Member: Governing Council, Manorial Soc. of GB, 1982–; Nat. Cttee for 900th anniv. of Domesday. Liveryman, Fletchers' Co. Vice-Pres., St John Ambulance London (Prince of Wales's) Dist., 1984–; KStJ 1994. *Publication:* (ed) English Law and Ethnic Minority Customs, 1986. *Recreations:* politics, shooting, travel. *Address:* 2 Paper Buildings, Temple, EC4Y 7ET; 28 Sydney Street, SW3 6PP; Villa Taprobane, Taprobane Island, off Weligama, Sri Lanka. *Clubs:* Carlton, City Livery; Orient (Colombo).

de SILVA, Harendra (Aneurin Domingo); QC 1995; a Recorder, since 1991; *b* 29 Sept. 1945; *s* of Annesley de Silva and Maharani of Porbandar; *m* 1972, Indira Raj; one *s* one *d*. *Educ:* Doon Sch., Dehra Dun, India; Millfield Sch.; Queens' Coll., Cambridge (MA, LLM). Called to the Bar, Middle Temple, 1970. *Recreations:* golf, bridge. *Address:* 2 Paper Buildings, Temple, EC4Y 7ET. *T:* 0171–936 2611. *Clubs:* Roehampton; Ooty (Ootacamund, S India).

DESIO, Prof. Ardito, Dr rer. nat; FRGS; Professor of Geology (and Past Director of Institute of Geology), at the University of Milan, and of Applied Geology, at the Engineering School of Milan, 1931–72, now Emeritus; *b* Palmanova, Friouli, 18 April 1897; *s* of Antonio Desio and Caterina Zorzella; *m* 1932, Aurelia Bevilacqua; one *s* one *d*. *Educ:* Udine and Florence. Grad. Univ. of Florence in Nat. Sciences, 1920. Asst, University of Florence, 1922, and of Pavia, 1923, also Univ. and Engineering Sch., Milan, 1924–25 to 1930–31; Lectr in Geology, Phys. Geography, University of Milan, 1929–30 and in Palaeontology there until 1935. Volunteer, 1st World War, 1915, Lieut, Alpine Troops, 1916–17, POW, 1917–18; Captain, 1924–53; Major, 1954. Geol Consultant, Edison Co. and Public Power Corp. of Greece, 1948–79. Pres., Italian Geological Cttee, 1966–73. Dir., Rivista Italiana di Paleontologia e Stratigrafia, 1942–; Past Dir., Geologia Tecnica. Past Pres., Ital. Geolog. Soc.; Mem. (Hon. Pres.) Ital. Assoc. of Geologists; Past Pres., Ital. Order of Geologists; Mem., Ital. Order of Journalists; Hon. Member: Ital. Paleont. Soc.; Gesellschaft für Erdkunde zu Berlin, 1941; Italian Geog. Soc., 1955; Faculty of Sciences University of Chile, 1964; Geological Soc. of London, 1964; Indian Paleont. Soc.; Soc. Ital. Progresso delle Scienze, 1978; Ist. per il Medio ed Estremo Oriente, 1979; Assoc. Mineraria Subalpina, 1985; Corresp. Member: Soc. Géol. Belgique, 1952; Explorer Club, USA, 1987; Life Mem., Geog. Soc., USA, 1955; Member: Institut d'Egypte, 1936; Accademia Naz. Lincei, 1948; Inst. Lombardo Accad. Scienze Lettere, 1949. In 1938 discovered first deposits of natural oil and gas in subsoil of Libya and Mg-K salt deposit in Marada Oasis; led expedition to K2 (8611 m, 2nd highest peak in the World; reached for 1st time on 31 July 1954), and 18 expeditions in Africa (Libya, Ethiopia) and Asia (Iran, Afghanistan, Pakistan, Nepal, Burma, Philippines, Tibet); in summer 1987 organised expedition which re-measured height of two highest mts in the world, Mt Everest and K2; in summer 1988 expedition visited the northern slope of Karakorum as far as the Kun Lun mountain range; in summers 1989 and 1990 organised a permanent scientific lab. (a glass and aluminium pyramid) in Nepal below the top of Everest at 5050m; also organised every year until 1993 a dozen ambient expeditions in the Himalaya and Karakorum, concerning geodesy, geophysics, geology, ethnography, physiology, and medicine of high altitude. Santoro Prize, 1931; Royal Prize, 1934, Royal Acad. Lincei; Gold Medal of the Republic of Pakistan, 1954; Gold Medal of the Sciences, Letters and Arts, of Italy, 1956; Patrons medal of Royal Geog. Soc. of London, 1957; USA Antarctic Service Medal, 1974; Gold Lyon of Lion's Club, Udine, 1976; Paul Harris Award, Internat. Rotary Club, 1986; Gold Medal of Ital. Geol. Soc., 1988; Gold Medal of Rotary Club, 1988. Kt Grand Cross, Order of Merit, Italy, 1955. *Publications:* about 440, among them: Le Isole Italiane dell'Egeo, 1931; La spedizione geografica Italiana al Karakoram 1929, 1936; scientific reports of his expedn to Libyan Sahara, 7 vols, 1938–42; Le vie della sete, 1950; Geologia applicata all'ingegneria, 1949, 3rd edn 1973–89; Ascent of K2, 1956 (11 languages, 15 editions); Geology of the Baltoro Basin (Karakorum), 1970; Results of half-a-century investigation on the glaciers of the Ortler-Cevedale, 1973; La Geologia dell'Italia, 1973; Geology of Central Badakhshan (NE Afghanistan), 1975; Geology of the Upper Shaksgam Valley, Sinkiang, China, 1980; L'Antartide, 1985; Sulle Vie della Sete, dei Ghiacci e dell'Oro, 1987; Which is the highest mountain in the world?, 1988; Geographic features of the Karakorum, 1991; some 250 articles in newspapers and magazines of different countries. *Recreation:* alpinist. *Address:* Viale Maino 14, 20129 Milano, Italy. *T:* 76003845;

(office) Dipart. Scienze della Terra dell 'Univ., via Mangiagalli 34, 20133 Milano. *T:* 236981221. *Clubs:* Italian Alpine; Touring (Italy); Hon. Member: Alpine; Internat. Rotary; Panatlon; Himalayan; Excursionista Carioca (Brazil); Alpin Français.

DESLONGCHAMPS, Prof. Pierre, OC 1989; PhD; FRS 1983; FRSC 1974; FCIC; Professor of Organic Chemistry, Université de Sherbrooke, Canada, since 1972; *b* 8 May 1938; *s* of Rodolphe Deslongchamps and Madeleine Magnan; *m* 1st, 1960, Micheline Renaud (marr. diss. 1975); two *c*; 2nd, 1976, Shirley E. Thomas (marr. diss. 1983); 3rd, 1987, Marie-Marthe Leroux. *Educ:* Univ. de Montréal (BSc Chem., 1959); Univ. of New Brunswick (PhD Chem., 1964). FCIC 1980; FAAAS 1988. Post-doctoral Student with Dr R.B. Woodward, Harvard Univ., USA, 1965; Asst Prof., Univ. de Montréal, 1966; Asst Prof. 1967, Associate Prof. 1968, Univ. de Sherbrooke. A.P. Sloan Fellow, 1970–72; E. W. R. Steacie Fellow, 1971–74. Member: New Swiss Chemical Soc.; Amer. Chem. Soc.; Assoc. of Harvard Chemists; Ordre des Chemistes du Québec; Assoc. Canadienne-Française pour l'Avancement des Sciences; Assoc. for Advancement of Science in Canada; Canadian Cttee of Scientists and Scholars; Soc. Française de Chimie. Dr *hc:* Univ. Pierre et Marie Curie, Paris, 1983; Bishop's Univ., Univ. de Montréal, and Univ. Laval, 1984; New Brunswick Univ., 1985. Scientific Prize of Québec, 1971; E. W. R. Steacie Prize (Nat. Scis), NRCC, 1974; Médaille Vincent, ACFAS, 1975; Merck, Sharp and Dohme Lectures Award, CIC, 1976; Canada Council Izaak Walton Killam Meml Scholarship, 1976–77; John Simon Guggenheim Meml Foundn Fellow, 1979; Medáille Pariseau, ACFAS, 1979; Marie-Victorin Médaille, Province of Que., 1987; Alfred Bader Award in Organic Chemistry, Canadian Soc. of Chemistry, 1991; Canada Gold Medal for Science and Engrng, NSERCC, 1993; Lemieux Award, Canadian Soc. for Chemistry, 1994. Holder of 9 patents. *Publications:* Stereoelectronic Effects in Organic Chemistry, 1983; over 150 contribs on organic chemistry in Tetrahedron, Jl Amer. Chem. Soc., Canadian Jl of Chem., Pure Applied Chem., Synth. Commun., Nouv. Jl Chim., Heterocycles, Jl Molecular Struct., Interface, Aldrichimica Acta, and Bull. Soc. Chim., France. *Recreations:* fishing, hockey, reading. *Address:* Department of Chemistry, Faculty of Sciences, Université de Sherbrooke, Sherbrooke, PQ J1K 2R1, Canada. *T:* (819) 8217002, *Fax:* (819) 8217910; RR 1, 11 McFarland Road, North Hatley, PQ J0B 2C0. *T:* (819) 8424238.

DESPRÉS, Robert; President, DRM Holdings Inc., since 1987; *b* 27 Sept. 1924; *s* of Adrien Després and Augustine Marmen; *m* 1949, Marguerite Cantin; two *s* two *d*. *Educ:* Académie de Québec (BA 1943); Laval Univ. (MCom 1947); (postgrad. studies) Western Univ. Comptroller, Québec Power Co., 1947–63; Reg. Manager, Administration & Trust Co., 1963–65; Dep. Minister, Québec Dept of Revenue, 1965–69; Pres. and Gen. Man., Québec Health Insurance Bd, 1969–73; Pres., Université du Québec, 1973–78; Pres. and Chief Exec. Officer, National Cablevision Ltd, 1978–80, and Netcom Inc., 1978–89; Chm. of the Bd, Atomic Energy of Canada Ltd, 1978–86. Mem. Board of Directors: Norcen Energy Resources Ltd; Camdev Corporation; Camdev Properties Inc.; Sidbec-Dosco Inc.; Canada Malting Co. Ltd; Sidbec Corp.; UniMedia; Wajax Ltd; Réseau de télévision Quatre Saisons Inc.; South Shore Industries Ltd; CFCF Inc.; Greyvest Inc.; PMG Financial Inc.; GDL Inc.; Greyvest Capital Inc.; Alliance Forest Products Inc.; Genivar Inc.; Nat. Optics Inst.; Canadian Certified General Accountants' Res. Foundn; Council for Canadian Unity; la Soc. du Musée du Séminaire de Québec; Inst de cardiologie de Québec. *Publications:* contrib. Commerce, and Soc. of Management Accountants Revue. *Recreations:* golf, reading. *Address:* 890 rue Dessane, Québec, Québec G1S 3J8, Canada. *T:* (418) 6872100. *Clubs:* Rideau, Cercle Universitaire; Lorette Golf.

de SWIET, Eleanor Jane, (Mrs Michael de Swiet), MA; Headteacher, The Henrietta Barnett School, since 1989; *b* 18 Aug. 1942; *d* of Richard and Joan Hawkins; *m* 1964, Dr Michael de Swiet; two *s* one *d*. *Educ:* Girton Coll., Cambridge (MA Classics); Inst. of Education (PGCE). Francis Holland Sch., 1965–67; St Paul's Girls' Sch., 1967–70; break from teaching to have children and to travel to US for a year; Head of Careers, Queen's Coll., London, 1975–84; Head of Classics, Head of 4th and 5th years, City of London Sch., 1984–89. Treas., Assoc. of Maintained Girls' Schs. Pres., JACT, 1995–. Member: The Ramblers; National Trust; Friends of Covent Garden. *Recreations:* walking, reading, Yorkshire, travelling. *Address:* 60 Hornsey Lane, N6 5LU. *T:* 0171–272 3195.

de THIER, Baron Jacques; Grand Officer, Order of Léopold II; Commander, Order of Léopold and Order of the Crown, Belgium; Civic Cross (1914–18); Grand Cross of Royal Victorian Order (Hon. GCVO); Director, Compagnie Financière et de Gestion pour l'Etranger (Cometra), Brussels, 1966–73; Counsellor, Cometra Oil Company, 1974–86; *b* Heusy, Belgium, 15 Sept. 1900; created Baron, 1975; *m* 1946, Mariette Negroponte (*d* 1973); three step *s*. *Educ:* University of Liège. Doctor of Laws (University of Liège), 1922; Mem. Bar (Liège and Verviers), 1923–29. Attached to Prime Minister's Cabinet, Brussels, 1929–32; entered Diplomatic Service, 1930; Attaché, Belgian Legation, Berlin, 1933; Chargé d'Affaires in Athens, 1935, Teheran, 1936; First Sec., Berlin, 1937–38; First Sec., then Counsellor, Washington, 1938–44; Chargé d'Affaires, Madrid, 1944–46; Asst to Dir-Gen., Polit. Dept, Min. of Foreign Affairs, Brussels, 1947, then Asst Head of Belgian Mission in Berlin; Consul-Gen. for Belgium, NY, 1948–55; Pres., Soc. of Foreign Consuls in New York, 1954; Belgian Ambassador: to Mexico, 1955–58; in Ottawa, 1958–61; Mem. Belgian Delegns to Gen. Assemblies of UN, 1956, 1957, 1959 and 1960; Belg. Rep. to Security Council, Sept. 1960; Belgian Ambassador to Court of St James's, 1961–65, and concurrently Belgian Perm. Rep. to Council of WEU, 1961–65. Hon. Chairman: Soc. Belgo-Allemande; Belgian Nat. Cttee, United World Colls. Holds foreign decorations. *Publications:* Un diplomate au vingtième siècle, 1991; articles in La Revue Générale, Brussels: Dans l'Iran d'autrefois, 1979; Souvenirs d'un diplomate belge, Washington, 1938–44, 1981; Pourquoi l'Espagne de Franco n'a pas livré Degrelle, 1983. *Recreation:* golf. *Address:* 38 avenue des Klauwaerts, 1050 Brussels, Belgium. *Clubs:* Anglo-Belgian; Cercle Royal Gaulois, Cercle du Parc, Royal Golf de Belgique (Brussels).

de TRAFFORD, Sir Dermot Humphrey, 6th Bt *cr* 1841; VRD 1963; Director, 1977–90, Chairman, 1982–90, Low & Bonar plc (Deputy Chairman, 1980–82); Chairman: GHP Group Ltd, 1965–77 (Managing Director, 1961); Calor Gas Holding, 1974–88; *b* 19 Jan. 1925; *s* of Sir Rudolph de Trafford, 5th Bt, OBE and June Lady Audley (*née* Chaplin), MBE (*d* 1977); *S* father, 1983; *m* 1st, 1946, Patricia Mary Beeley (marr. diss. 1973); three *s* six *d*; 2nd, 1973, Mrs Xandra Caradini Walter. *Educ:* Harrow Sch.; Christ Church, Oxford (MA). Trained as Management Consultant, Orr & Boss and Partners Ltd, 1949–52; Director: Monks Investment Trust; Imperial Continental Gas Assoc., 1963–87 (Dep. Chm., 1972–87); Petrofina SA, 1971–87. Chm. Council, Inst. of Dirs, 1990–93. *Recreations:* golf, travel. *Heir: s* John Humphrey de Trafford [*b* 12 Sept. 1950; *m* 1975, Anne, *d* of J. Faure de Pebeyre; one *s* one *d*]. *Address:* The Old Vicarage, Appleshaw, Andover, Hants SP11 9BH. *T:* Andover (01264) 772357. *Clubs:* White's, Royal Ocean Racing; Berkshire Golf; Island Sailing.

DEUCHAR, Patrick Lindsay; Chief Executive, Royal Albert Hall, since 1989; *b* 27 March 1949; *s* of David and Marian Deuchar; *m* Gwyneth Miles (marr. diss.); one *s* one *d*; partner, Liz Robertson; one *d*. *Educ:* Christ's Hospital; Lackham Coll. of Agriculture. Farming, 1967–72; IPC Business Press, 1972–74; PR Manager, RASE, 1974–77; PR Manager, Earls Court and Olympia, 1977–80; European Dir, World Championship Tennis, 1981–89. Chm., Sparks Charity, 1992; Member: Nat. Fundraising Cttee, Muscular Dystrophy Group, 1989–92; Nat. Music Day Cttee, 1993–; London Visitor Council, 1994–; Royal Concert Cttee, 1994–. Trustee: Albert Meml Trust, 1994–; Cardiff Bay Opera House, 1994–. Barker, Variety Club of GB, 1992; Mem., Inst. of Dirs. FRSA 1992. *Recreations:* music, theatre, art, cooking, wines, family life. *Address:* Royal Albert Hall, Kensington Gore, SW7 2AP. *T:* 0171–589 3203.

DEUKMEJIAN, George; lawyer; Partner, Sidley & Austin, since 1991; Republican; *b* 6 June 1928; *s* of C. George Deukmejian and Alice (*née* Gairdan); *m* 1957, Gloria M. Saatjian; one *s* two *d*. *Educ:* Watervliet Sch., NY; Siena College (BA 1949); St John's Univ., NY (JD 1952). Admitted to NY State Bar, 1952, Californian Bar, 1956, US Supreme Court Bar, 1970. US Army, 1953–55. Law practice, Calif., 1955; Partner, Riedman, Dalessi, Deukmejian & Woods; Mem., Calif. Assembly, 1963–67; Mem., Calif. Senate (minority leader), 1967–79; Attorney Gen., Calif., 1979–83; Governor, California, 1983–91. *Address:* Sidley & Austin, 555 W 5th Street, 40th Floor, Los Angeles, CA 90013-1010, USA.

DEUTSCH, André, CBE 1989; President, André Deutsch Ltd, 1989–91 (Chairman and Managing Director, 1951–84; Joint Chairman and Joint Managing Director, 1984–87; Joint Chairman, 1987–89); Director, Libra, Budapest, since 1991; *b* 15 Nov. 1917; *s* of late Bruno Deutsch and Maria Deutsch (*née* Havas); unmarried. *Educ:* Budapest; Vienna; Zurich. First job in publishing, with Nicholson & Watson, 1942; started publishing independently under imprint of Allan Wingate (Publishers) Ltd, 1945; started André Deutsch Limited, in 1951. Founded: African Universities Press, Lagos, Nigeria, 1962; East Africa Publishing House, Nairobi, Kenya, 1964. *Recreations:* travel preferably by train, ski-ing, publishing, talking. *Address:* 5 Selwood Terrace, SW7 3QN. *Clubs:* Garrick, Groucho.

DEVA, Niranjan Joseph Aditya, (Nirj), DL; MP (C) Brentford and Isleworth, since 1992; *b* Colombo, 11 May 1948; *s* of late Thakur Dr Kingsley de Silva Deva Aditya and of Zita Virginia Deva; *m* Indra Lavinia, *d* of Romy Govindia; one step *s*. *Educ:* St Joseph's Coll., Colombo; Loughborough Univ. of Technol. (BTech Hons Aero. Eng.). Company dir and adviser. Pol. Officer, 1979, Chm., 1981, Bow Gp. Organiser, Conf. on Overseas Develt and Brandt Report, 1979. Member: Governing Council, Royal Commonwealth Soc., 1979–83; Nat. Consumer Council, 1982–88; Dept of Employment Adv. Cttee, 1988–91; Chairman: DTI/NCC Cttee on De-regulation of European Air Transport, 1985–86; One Nation Forum Political Cttee, 1986–91. Contested (C) Hammersmith, 1987. Mem., Select Cttee on Parly Admin (Ombudsman), 1992–, on Educn, 1995–; Vice-Chm., Cons. back bench Aviation Cttee, 1994– (Jt Sec., 1992); Member: Asylum Bill Cttee, 1992; Deregulation Bill Cttee, 1994–; European Standing Cttee B, 1992–; All-Party Manufacturing Gp, 1993–; Hon. Sec., All-Party Uganda Gp, 1994–. Editor, Crossbow, 1983–85. DL Greater London, 1986. *Recreations:* riding, reading, tennis. *Address:* House of Commons, SW1A 0AA. *Clubs:* Carlton; Hounslow Conservative.

de VALOIS, Dame Ninette, OM 1992; CH 1982; DBE 1951 (CBE 1947); Founder and Director of the Royal Ballet, 1931–63 (formerly the Sadler's Wells Ballet, Royal Opera House, Covent Garden, and the Sadler's Wells Theatre Ballet, Sadler's Wells Theatre); Founder of The Royal Ballet School (formerly The Sadler's Wells School of Ballet); *b* Baltiboys, Blessington, Co. Wicklow, 6 June 1898; 2nd *d* of Lieut-Col T. R. A. Stannus, DSO, Carlingford; *m* 1935, Dr A. B. Connell. Prima ballerina the Royal Opera Season Covent Garden (International), May to July 1919 and again in 1928. Première danseuse British National Opera Company, 1918; Mem., The Diaghileff Russian Ballet, 1923–26; choreographic dir to the Old Vic, the Festival Theatre, Cambridge, and The Abbey Theatre, Dublin, 1926–30; Founder of The National Sch. of Ballet, Turkey, 1947. Principal choreographic works: Job, The Rake's Progress, Checkmate, and Don Quixote. Hon. MusDoc London, 1947; Hon. DLitt: Reading, 1951; Oxford, 1955; New Univ. of Ulster, 1979; Hon. DMus: Sheffield, 1955; Durham, 1982; Hon. MusD Trinity Coll., Dublin, 1957; Hon. DFA Smith Coll., Mass, USA, 1957; Hon. LLD: Aberdeen, 1958; Sussex, 1975; FRAD 1963. Chevalier of the Legion of Honour, 1950. Gold Albert Medal, RSA, 1964; (jtly) Erasmus Prize Foundn Award (first woman to receive it), 1974; Irish Community Award, 1980. *Publications:* Invitation to the Ballet, 1937; Come Dance with Me, 1957; Step By Step, 1977. *Address:* c/o Royal Ballet School, 153 Talgarth Road, W14.

DEVANEY, John Francis, CEng, FIEE, FIMechE; Managing Director, since 1992, and Chief Executive, since 1993, Eastern Group (formerly Eastern Electricity) plc, since 1993; *b* 25 June 1946; *s* of George Devaney and late Alice Ann Devaney; *m* 1969, Joan Mary Hargreaves; one *s* one *d*. *Educ:* St Mary's Coll., Blackburn; Sheffield Univ. (BEng). FIMechE. Perkins Engines, 1968–89: manufacturing positions, Peterborough, 1968–76; Project Manager, Ohio, 1976–77; Director posts, UK, 1977–82; President, 1983–88; Group Vice-Pres., European Components Group, Peterborough, 1988 and Enterprises Group, Toronto, 1988–89; Chm. and Chief Exec. Officer and Group Vice-Pres., Kelsey-Hayes Corp., Michigan, 1989–92. Non-executive Director: Midland Bank, 1994–; Penske Transportation Inc., USA. Pres., Electricity Assoc., 1994–95. *Recreations:* ski-ing, golf, tennis, scuba diving. *Address:* Eastern Group, Wherstead Park, PO Box 40, Wherstead, Ipswich, Suffolk IP9 2AQ. *Clubs:* Reform; Bloomfield Hills (Detroit).

DEVAUX, John Edward; His Honour Judge Devaux; a Circuit Judge, since 1993; *b* 25 March 1947; *s* of Henry Edward Devaux and Anne Elizabeth Devaux; *m* 1979, Fiona O'Conor; two *d*. *Educ:* Beaumont Coll.; Bristol Univ. (LLB). Called to the Bar, Lincoln's Inn, 1970; a Recorder, 1989–93. *Address:* Ipswich Crown Court, The Courthouse, Civic Drive, Ipswich, Suffolk IP1 2DX. *T:* Ipswich (01473) 213841.

DEVENPORT, Rt. Rev. Eric Nash; Auxiliary Bishop in the diocese of Europe, and Archdeacon of Italy and Chaplain of St Mark's, Florence, since 1992; *b* 3 May 1926; *s* of Joseph and Emma Devenport; *m* 1954, Jean Margaret Richardson; two *d*. *Educ:* Kelham Theological Coll. BA (Open Univ.). Curate, St Mark, Leicester, 1951–54; St Matthew, Barrow-in-Furness, 1954–56; Succentor, Leicester Cathedral, 1956–59; Vicar of Shepshed, 1959–64; Oadby, 1964–73; Proctor in Convocation, 1964–80; Hon. Canon of Leicester Cathedral, 1973–80; Leader of Mission, Diocese of Leicester, 1973–80; Bishop Suffragan of Dunwich, 1980–92, retd. Chairman: Diocesan Communication Officers Cttee, 1986–92; C of E Hospital Chaplaincies Council, 1986–91; Jt Hosp. Chaplaincies Cttee, 1988–91; E Anglian Ministerial Trng Course, 1990–92. Chaplain, Worshipful Company of Framework Knitters, 1964–80; Area Chaplain, Actors' Church Union, 1980–92. Chm., Local Radio Adv. Council for Radio Suffolk, 1990–92. *Publication:* Preaching at the Parish Communion: ASB Gospels-Sundays: Year One, Vol. 2, 1989. *Recreation:* theatre. *Address:* St Mark's Church, Via Maggio 16/18, 50125 Florence, Italy. *T:* 55294764. *Club:* Commonwealth Trust.

de VERE, Anthony Charles Mayle, CMG 1986; HM Diplomatic Service, retired; Foreign and Commonwealth Office, 1986–93; *b* 23 Jan. 1930; *m* 1st, 1959, Geraldine Gertrude Bolton (*d* 1980); 2nd, 1986, Rosemary Edith Austin. *Educ:* St John's College, Cambridge. Served Army, Malaya, 1950–52; joined Colonial Service (later HMOCS), 1953, Provincial Admin, Tanganyika; Kibondo, 1953–56; in charge Kondoa–Irangi Develt Scheme, 1957–59; Res. Magistrate, Singida, 1959; Dist Comr, Tunduru, 1960–61, Kigoma, 1961–62; Head of local govt, Western Region, 1962–63, retired 1963; joined

FO, later FCO, 1963; First Sec., Lusaka, 1967–70, NY, 1972–74; Counsellor, Washington, 1982–86. *Recreations:* riding, most things rural, sculpture, music, books. *Address:* Haddiscoe Hall, Norfolk NR14 6PE. *Club:* Athenæum.

DEVEREAU, (George) Michael; Chief Executive (formerly Director General), Central Office of Information, since 1989; Head of Government Information Service, since 1990; *b* 10 Nov. 1937; *s* of George Alfred Devereau and Elspeth Mary Duff Devereau; *m* 1961, Sarah Poupart; four *s*. *Educ:* King William's Coll., Isle of Man; University Coll. London. Asst Ed., Architects' Jl, 1962; Information Officer, MPBW, BRE and DoE, 1967–75; Chief Information Officer: Price Commn, 1975; DoE, 1978; Dept of Transport, 1982; Gp Dir, 1985, Dep. Dir Gen., 1987, COI. *Publication:* Architects Working Details, 1964. *Recreations:* house restoration, travel. *Address:* Central Office of Information, Hercules House, Hercules Road, SE1 7DU.

DEVERELL, Sir Colville (Montgomery), GBE 1963 (OBE 1946); KCMG 1957 (CMG 1955); CVO 1953; retired from Government Service, Nov. 1962; Secretary-General, International Planned Parenthood Federation, 1964–69; *b* 21 Feb. 1907; *s* of George Robert Deverell and Maude (*née* Cooke); *m* 1935, Margaret Wynne, *d* of D. A. Wynne Willson; three *s*. *Educ:* Portora Sch., Enniskillen, Ulster; Trinity Coll., Dublin (LLB); Trinity Coll., Cambridge. District Officer, Kenya, 1931; Clerk to Exec. and Legislative Councils, 1938–39; Civil Affairs Branch, E Africa Comd, 1941–46, serving Italian Somaliland, British Somaliland, Ethiopia; Mem. Lord de la Warr's Delegation, Ethiopia, 1944; seconded War Office in connection Italian Peace Treaty, 1946. Sec., Development and Reconstruction Authority, Kenya, 1946; acted as Financial Sec. and Chief Native Comr, 1949; Administrative Secretary, Kenya, 1949; Colonial Sec., Jamaica, 1952–55; Governor and Comdr-in-Chief, Windward Islands, 1955–59; Governor and Comdr-in-Chief, Mauritius, 1959–62. Chm. UN(FP) Mission to India, 1965; Mem., UN Mission on Need for World Population Inst., 1970; Chairman: UN Family Planning Evaluation Mission to Ceylon, 1971; UN Family Planning Assoc. Feasability Mission, Al Azhar Univ., Cairo, 1972. Constitutional Adviser: Seychelles, 1966; British Virgin Islands, 1973. LLD *jure dignitatis*, Dublin, 1964. *Recreations:* cricket, tennis, squash, golf and fishing.

DEVERELL, Maj.-Gen. John Freegard, OBE 1986; Commandant, Royal Military Academy Sandhurst, since 1995; *b* 27 April 1945; *s* of Harold James Frank Deverell and Joan Beatrice Deverell (*née* Carter); *m* 1973, Jane Ellen Solomon; one *s* one *d*. *Educ:* King Edward's Sch., Bath; RMA Sandhurst. Commnd Somerset and Cornwall LI, 1966; RN Staff Coll., Greenwich, 1977; Comd 3rd Bn LI, 1984–86; Mil. Dir of Studies, RMCS, Shrivenham, 1988; Higher Command and Staff Course, Camberley, 1988; Comdr 1st Infantry Bde (UK Mobile Force), 1988–90; NDC, India, 1991; Dir, Army Recruiting, 1992–93; Dir Gen., Army Manning and Recruiting, 1993–95. *Recreations:* cricket, horses. *Address:* Royal Military Academy Sandhurst, Camberley, Surrey GU15 4PQ. *Clubs:* Cavalry and Guards; Free Foresters, I Zingari.

DEVEREUX, family name of **Viscount Hereford.**

DEVEREUX, Alan Robert, CBE 1980; DL; Founder Director, Quality Scotland Foundation, since 1991; Director: Scottish Mutual Assurance Society, since 1975; Gleneagles Group, since 1990; *b* 18 April 1933; *s* of Donald Charles and Doris Devereux; *m* 1st, 1959, Gloria Alma Hair (*d* 1985); one *s*; 2nd, 1987, Elizabeth Tormey Docherty. *Educ:* Colchester School; Clacton County High School; Mid-Essex Technical Coll. CEng, MIEE, CIMgt. Marconi's Wireless Telegraph Co., 1950–56; Halex Div. of British Xylonite Co., 1956–58; Spa Div., Sanitas Trust, 1958–65; Gen. Man., Dobar Engineering, 1965–67; Norcros Ltd, 1967–69; Gp Man. Dir 1969–78, Dep. Chm. 1978–80, Scotcros Ltd; Dir-Gen., Scotcros Europe SA, 1976–79. Director: Walter Alexander PLC, 1980–90; Hambros Scotland Ltd, 1984–, Scottish Advisor, Hambros Bank, 1984–90. Chm., Scottish Ambulance Service NHS Trust, 1994–. Dep. Chm. 1975–77, Chm. 1977–79, CBI Scotland; CBI: Council Mem., 1972–; Mem. President's Adv. Cttee, 1979; UK Regional Chm., 1979; Mem., F and GP Cttee, 1982–84. Chairman: Small Industries Council for Rural Areas of Scotland, 1975–77; Scottish Tourist Bd, 1980–90; Member: Scottish Development Agency, 1977–82; BTA, 1980–90. Chm., Police Dependants' Trust, Scotland. Scottish Free Enterprise Award, 1978. DL Renfrewshire, 1985. *Recreations:* reading, work, Glasgow City Mission. *Address:* South Fell, 24 Kirkhouse Road, Blanefield, Stirlingshire G63 9BX. *T:* Blanefield (01360) 770464. *Club:* East India, Devonshire, Sports and Public Schools.

de VERE WHITE, Hon. Mrs; *see* Glendinning, Hon. Victoria.

de VESCI, 7th Viscount *cr* 1766; **Thomas Eustace Vesey;** Bt 1698; Baron Knapton, 1750; *b* 8 Oct. 1955; *s* of 6th Viscount de Vesci and Susan Anne (*d* 1986), *d* of late Ronald (Owen Lloyd) Armstrong-Jones, MBE, QC, DL, and of the Countess of Rosse; *S* father, 1983; *m* 1987, Sita-Maria, *o c* of late Baron de Breffny; two *s* one *d*. *Educ:* Eton and Oxford. Assistant Trainer to M. V. O'Brien, 1978–80; Bloodstock Agent in Los Angeles, Calif, 1980–83; returned to family home on death of father to continue bloodstock business, also stud farm, forestry and farming. *Address:* 14 Rumbold Road, SW6 2JA.

See also Earl of Snowdon.

DEVESI, Sir Baddeley, GCMG 1980; GCVO 1982; Minister for Health and Medical Sciences, Solomon Islands, 1992; *b* 16 Oct. 1941; *s* of Mostyn Tagabasoe Norua and Laisa Otu; *m* 1969, June Marie Barley; four *s* two *d* (and one *d* decd). *Educ:* St Stephen's Sch., Auckland, NZ; Ardmore Teachers' Coll., Auckland, NZ. MLC and Mem. Exec. Council, 1967–69. Headmaster, St Nicholas Sch., Honiara, 1968; Educn Officer and Lectr, 1970–72; Dist. Officer, 1973; District Comr and Clerk to Malaita Council, 1974; Permanent Secretary, 1976; Governor-Gen. of the Solomon Islands, 1978–88; Minister for For. Affairs and Trade Relations, 1989–90; Minister for Home Affairs and Dep. Prime Minister, 1990–92. Dep. Chm., Solomon Islands Broadcasting Corp., 1976. Chancellor, Univ. of S Pacific, 1980–83. Captain, Solomon Islands team, 2nd South Pacific Games, 1969. Comr, Boy Scouts Assoc., 1968. Hon. DU Univ. of the South Pacific, 1981. KStJ 1984. *Recreations:* reading, swimming, lawn tennis, cricket, snooker.

de VIGIER, William Alphonse, Hon. CBE 1978; formerly: Chairman (also founder), Acrow plc; Chairman: Acrow Corp. of America; Acrow Canada; Acrow Botswana; *b* 22 Jan. 1912; *m* 1939, Betty Kendall; two *d*. *Educ:* La Chataigneraie, Coppet, Switzerland. Board Member: Acrow Peru SA; Acrow Zimbabwe. Mem., British Airways Bd, 1973–78; Vigierhof AG, Switzerland. Knight of Star of the North (Sweden); Grand Commander, Order of Star of Africa. *Recreations:* tennis, skiing, swimming. *Address:* Sommerhaus, Solothurn 4504, Switzerland; Tinkers Lodge, Marsh Lane, Mill Hill, NW7. *Clubs:* East India; Metropolitan (New York).

DE VILLE, Sir Harold Godfrey, (Sir Oscar), Kt 1990; CBE 1979; Chairman, Meyer International plc, 1987–91 (Deputy Chairman, 1985–87; Director, 1984–91); *b* Derbyshire, 11 April 1925; *s* of Harold De Ville and Anne De Ville (*née* Godfrey); *m* 1947, Pamela Fay Ellis; one *s*. *Educ:* Burton-on-Trent Grammar Sch.; Trinity Coll., Cambridge (MA). Served RNVR, 1943–46. With Ford Motor Co. Ltd, 1949–65; BICC, 1965–84: Dir, 1971–84; Exec. Vice-Chm., 1978–80; Exec. Dep. Chm., 1980–84; Chm., BICC Pension Funds, 1973–84. Director: Balfour Beatty Ltd, 1971–78; Phillips Cables Ltd, Canada, 1982–84; Metal Manufacturers Ltd, Australia, 1983–84; Scottish Cables Ltd, S Africa, 1983–84. Mem., BRB, 1985–91. Chairman: Iron and Steel EDC, 1984–86; Govt Review of vocational qualifications, 1985–86; NCVQ, 1986–90; Nat. Jt Council for Engrg Construction Industry, 1985–87. Member: Commn on Industrial Relations, 1971–74; Central Arbitration Cttee, 1976–77; Council: Inst. of Manpower Studies, 1971–91; ACAS, 1976–91; Industrial Soc., 1976–85; BIM, 1982–86 (Mem., Bd of Companions, 1981–91); Confederation of British Industry: Member: Employment Policy Cttee, 1971–78; Council, 1977–85; Finance Cttee, 1984–85; Chm., Working Parties on Employee Participation, 1975–78, on Pay Determination, 1976–78. Mem. Council, Reading Univ., 1985–91. *Recreations:* genealogy, fell-walking. *Address:* Bexton Cottage, 18 Pound Lane, Sonning on Thames, Berks RG4 0XE.

de VILLIERS, 3rd Baron, *cr* 1910; **Arthur Percy de Villiers;** retired; *b* 17 Dec. 1911; *s* of 2nd Baron and Adelheid, *d* of H. C. Koch, Pietermaritzburg, Natal; *S* father 1934; *m* 1939, Lovett (marr. diss. 1958), *d* of Dr A. D. MacKinnon, Williams Lake, BC; one *s* two *d*. *Educ:* Magdalen Coll., Oxford. Barrister, Inner Temple, 1938. Farming in New Zealand. Admitted as a barrister to the Auckland Surpreme Court, 1949. *Recreations:* gardening, golf. *Heir:* *s* Hon. Alexander Charles de Villiers, *b* 29 Dec. 1940. *Address:* PO Box 66, Kumeu, Auckland 1250, NZ. *T:* (9) 4118173. *Club:* Royal Commonwealth Society (Auckland).

de VILLIERS, Dawid Jacobus, DPhil; Minister for the Environment, South Africa, since 1994; *b* 10 July 1940; *m* 1964, Suzaan Mangold; one *s* three *d*. *Educ:* Univ. of Stellenbosch (BA Hons Philosophy; BTh, DPhil); Rand Afrikaans Univ. (MA Phil., 1972). Abe Bailey Scholar, 1963–64; Markotter Scholar, 1964. Part-time Lectr in Philosophy, Univ. of Western Cape, 1963–64; Minister of Dutch Reformed Church, Wellington, Cape, 1967–69; Lectr in Philosophy, 1969–72, and Pres. Convocation, 1973–, Rand Afrikaans Univ.; MP for Johannesburg W, 1972–79, for Piketberg, 1981–; Chm., Nat. Party's Foreign Affairs Cttee in Parlt; Ambassador of S Africa to London, 1979–80; Minister: of Trade and Industry (formerly Industries, Commerce and Tourism), SA, 1980–86; of Budget and Welfare, 1986–88; for Admin and Privatisation, 1988–90; for Public Enterprises, 1989–94; for Mineral and Energy Affairs, 1990–91; Leader, Houses of Parliament, 1989–92. Leader, Nat. Party, Cape Province, 1990–. National Party Delegn Leader, Constitutional Conf., Convention for a Democratic S Africa, 1992. Visited: USA on US Leaders Exchange Prog., 1974; UK as guest of Brit. Govt, 1975; Israel as guest of Israeli Govt, 1977. Represented S Africa in internat. Rugby in S Africa, UK, Ireland, Australia, NZ, France and the Argentine, 1962–70 (Captain, 1965–70). State President's Award for Sport, 1968 and 1970; S African Sportsman of the Year, 1968; Jaycee's Outstanding Young Man of the Year Award, 1971; State President's Decoration for Meritorious Service, Gold, 1988. *Recreations:* sports, reading. *Address:* Private Bag X9079, Cape Town, 8000, South Africa.

DEVINE, Hon. (Donald) Grant; MLA for Estevan, since 1982; Premier of Saskatchewan, 1982–91; founded Grant Devine Management Inc., 1992; *b* Regina, 5 July 1944; *m* 1966, (Adeline) Chantal Guillaume; two *s* three *d*. *Educ:* Saskatchewan Univ. (BScA 1967); Alberta Univ. (MSc 1969; MBA 1970); Ohio State Univ. (PhD 1976). Farming, 1962–; marketing specialist, Fed. Govt, Ottawa, 1970–72; Graduate Assistant, Ohio State Univ., 1972–76; Prof. of Agricl Econs, Saskatchewan Univ., 1976–79. Leader, Progressive Cons. Party of Saskatchewan, 1979–92; Leader, Official Opposition, Saskatchewan, 1991–92; Minister of Agriculture, 1985–91. Re-elected MLA for Estevan, 1986 and 1991. Advisor: Food Prices Rev. Bd and Provincial Govts; Sask. Consumers' Assoc. Member: Amer. Econ. Assoc.; Amer. Marketing Assoc.; Amer. Assoc. for Consumer Res.; Canadian Agricl Econs Soc.; Consumers' Assoc. of Canada. *Publications:* contribs to professional jls on retail food pricing and market performance. *Recreations:* golf, ski-ing, baseball. *Address:* Progressive Conservative Caucus Office, Room 265, Legislative Building, 2405 Legislative Drive, Regina, Sask S4S 0B3, Canada.

DEVINE, Rt. Rev. Joseph; *see* Motherwell, Bishop of, (RC).

DEVINE, Prof. Thomas Martin, PhD, DLitt; FBA 1994; FRSE; FRHistS; Professor of Scottish History, since 1988, Director of Research Centre in Scottish History, since 1993, and Deputy Principal, since 1994, University of Strathclyde; *b* 30 July 1945; *s* of Michael Gerard Devine and Norah Martin; *m* 1971; Catherine Mary Lynas; two *s* three *d*. *Educ:* Strathclyde Univ. (BA; PhD 1972; DLitt 1992). FRHistS 1980; FRSE 1992. University of Strathclyde: Lectr in History, 1969–78; Sen. Lectr in History, 1978–83; Reader in Scottish History, 1983–88; Dean, Faculty of Arts and Social Studies, 1993–94. Adjunct Prof. in History, Univ. of Guelph, Canada, 1989–. Chm., Econ. and Social History Soc. of Scotland, 1984–88; Convenor of Council, Scottish Catholic Historical Assoc., 1990–95. Gov., St Andrews Coll. of Educn, 1990–. *Publications:* The Tobacco Lords, 1975, 2nd edn 1990; Ireland and Scotland 1600–1850, 1983; Farm Servants and Labour in Lowland Scotland, 1984; A Scottish Farm in Virginia 1767–77, 1984; People and Society in Scotland, 1988; The Great Highland Famine, 1988; Improvement and Enlightment, 1989; Conflict and Stability in Scottish Society 1700–1850, 1990; Irish Immigrants and Scottish Society in 18th and 19th Centuries, 1991; Scottish Emigration and Scottish Society, 1992; The Transformation of Rural Scotland 1660–1815, 1994; Clanship to Crofters' War, 1994; Scottish Elites, 1994; Glasgow, vol. I, 1995; The Scottish Past, 1995. *Recreations:* walking, foreign travel, music, soccer. *Address:* Department of History, University of Strathclyde, Glasgow G1 1XQ. *T:* 0141–552 4400.

de VIRION, Tadeusz; Cross of Valour, Cross of the Home Army, Warsaw Uprising Cross, 1944; Polish Ambassador to the Court of St James's, 1990–93; *b* 28 March 1926; *s* of Jerzy de Virion (killed in Auschwitz, 1941); *m* 1985, Jayanti Hazra; two *d*. *Educ:* Univ. of Warsaw (LLM). Barrister, 1950–, specialising in criminal law; Judge of Tribunal of State, elected by Polish Parlt, 1989, 1990, 1993–. Cross of Knights of Malta, 1980; Golden Insignia of Barrister's Merit, 1988; Comdr's Cross, Order of Polonia Restituta; Grand Officier, Order of Pro Merito Melitensi. *Recreations:* Jayanti, books. *Address:* ul. Zakopiańska 17, 03 934 Warsaw, Poland. *T:* (2) 6178880. *Clubs:* Polish Hearth, Travellers', Special Forces.

DEVITT, Lt-Col Sir Thomas Gordon, 2nd Bt, *cr* 1916; Partner of Devitt & Moore, Shipbrokers; *b* 27 Dec. 1902; *e s* of Arthur Devitt (*d* 1921) *e s* of 1st Bt and Florence Emmeline (*d* 1951), *e d* of late William Forbes Gordon, Manar, NSW; *S* grandfather, 1923; *m* 1st, 1930, Joan Mary (who obtained a divorce, 1936), 2nd *d* of late Charles Reginald Freemantle, Hayes Barton, Pyrford, Surrey; 2nd, 1937, Lydia Mary (marr. diss. 1953; she *d* 1995), *o d* of late Edward Milligen Beloe, King's Lynn, Norfolk; two *d*; 3rd, 1953, Janet Lilian, *o d* of late Col H. S. Ellis, CBE, MC; one *s* one *d*. *Educ:* Sherborne; Corpus Christi Coll., Cambridge. 1939–45 War as Lt-Col, Seaforth Highlanders and OC Raiding Support Regt. Royal Order of Phœnix of Greece with swords. Chm. Macers Ltd, 1961–70. Chairman: Board of Governors, The Devitt and Moore Nautical Coll., Pangbourne, 1948–61; Nat. Service for Seafarers, 1948–77. Governor, Sherborne Sch., 1967–75. *Recreations:* shooting, fishing. *Heir:* *s* James Hugh Thomas Devitt [*b* 18 Sept. 1956; *m* 1985, Susan Carol, *d* of Dr Michael Duffus; two *s* one *d*]. *Address:* 49 Lexden Road, Colchester, Essex CO3 3PY. *T:* Colchester (01206) 577958. *Club:* MCC.

DEVLIN, Alexander, OBE 1977; JP; Member, Glenrothes New Town Development Corporation, 1958–78; *b* 22 Dec. 1927; *s* of Thomas Devlin and Jean Gibson; *m* 1949, Annie Scott Gordon. *Educ:* Cowdenbeath St Columba's High Sch.; National Council of Labour Colls (Local Govt and Public Speaking). Member: Fife CC, 1956–74; Fife Regional Council, 1974–78; Chm., Fife Educn Cttee, 1963–78; Vice-Chm., Educn Cttee of Convention of Scottish Local Authorities, 1974–78. Member: Dunning Cttee on Scottish System for Assessment of Pupils after 4 years Secondary Educn, 1974–77; Scottish Sports Council, 1964–74; Manpower Services Commn, 1978–79. Mem. Bd, Glenrothes Coll., 1992–. JP Fife, 1963. *Address:* 40 Falcon Drive, Glenrothes, Fife KY7 5HP. *T:* Glenrothes (01592) 759883.

DEVLIN, (Josephine) Bernadette; *see* McAliskey, J. B.

DEVLIN, His Honour Keith Michael, PhD; a Circuit Judge, 1984–95; *b* 21 Oct. 1933; *e s* of Francis Michael Devlin and Norah Devlin (*née* Gregory); *m* 1958, Pamela Gwendoline Phillips; two *s* one *d. Educ:* Price's Sch., Fareham; Eaton Hall OCS; King's Coll., London Univ. (LLB 1960, MPhil 1968, PhD 1976). Commnd RAOC, 1953. Called to the Bar, Gray's Inn, 1964; Dep. Chief Clerk, Metropolitan Magistrates' Courts Service, 1964–66; various appts as Dep. Metropolitan Stipendiary Magistrate, 1975–79; a Recorder, 1983–84; Liaison Judge, Bedfordshire, 1990–93; Resident Judge, Luton Crown Court, 1991–93. Brunel University: Lectr in Law, 1966–71; Reader in Law, 1971–84; Associate Prof. of Law, 1984–; Mem., Court, 1985–88. Fellow, Netherlands Inst. for Advanced Study in the Humanities and Social Sciences, Wassenaar, 1975–76. Chm., Mental Health Review Tribunals, 1991–93. Mem., Consumer Protection Adv. Cttee, 1976–81. MRI (Member: Finance Cttee, 1988–; Council, 1994–). Magistrates' Association: Mem., 1974–89, Vice-Chm., 1984–89, Legal Cttee; co-opted Mem. Council, 1980–88; a Vice-Pres., Bucks Br., 1993–. Mem. Court, Luton Univ., 1994–. JP Inner London (Juvenile Court Panel), 1968–84 (Chm., 1973–84). Liveryman, Feltmakers' Co. (Mem., Ct of Assts, 1991–). FRSA 1989. Jt Founder and Editor, Anglo-Amer. Law Rev., 1972–84. *Publications:* Sentencing Offenders in Magistrates' Courts, 1970; (with Eric Stockdale) Sentencing, 1987; articles in legal jls. *Recreations:* watching cricket, fly-fishing, Roman Britain. *Clubs:* Athenæum, MCC; Hampshire County Cricket.

DEVLIN, Stuart Leslie, AO 1988; CMG 1980; goldsmith, silversmith and designer in London since 1965; Goldsmith and Jeweller by appointment to HM The Queen, 1982; *b* 9 Oct. 1931; *m* 1986, Carole Hedley-Saunders. *Educ:* Gordon Inst. of Technology, Geelong; Royal Melbourne Inst. of Technology; Royal Coll. of Art. DesRCA (Silversmith), DesRCA (Industrial Design/Engrg). Art Teacher, Vic. Educn Dept, 1950–58; Royal Coll. of Art, 1958–60; Harkness Fellow, NY, 1960–62; Lectr, Prahran Techn. Coll., Melbourne, 1962; one-man shows of sculpture, NY and Sydney, 1961–64; Inspr Art in Techn. Schs, Vic. Educn Dept, 1964–65; exhibns of silver and gold in numerous cities USA, Australia, Bermuda, Middle East and UK, 1965–. Executed many commns in gold and silver: designed coins for Australia, Singapore, Cayman Is, Gibraltar, IoM, Burundi, Botswana, Ethiopia and Bhutan; designed and made: cutlery for State Visit to Paris, 1972; Duke of Edinburgh trophy for World Driving Championship, 1973; silver to commemorate opening of Sydney Opera House, 1973; Grand National Trophy, 1975, 1976; Australian Bravery Awards, 1975; Regalia for the Order of Australia, 1975–76; Queen's Silver Jubilee Medal, 1977; Centrepiece for RE to commemorate their work in NI, 1984; Bas-relief portrait of Princess of Wales for Wedgwood, 1986; full set of Defence Awards for Australia, 1989; Whitbread Employee Volunteering Award, 1990; portraits of HM the Queen Mother, HRH the Princess of Wales, HRH the Princess Royal, HRH the Princess Margaret, 1991; British Athletics Fedn Badge and Chain of Office, 1992. Developed strategy for use of champagne diamonds in jewellery for Argyle Diamond Mines, 1987. Freeman, City of London, 1966; Liveryman, 1972, Mem. Ct of Assts, 1986, Prime Warden, May 1996–97, Goldsmiths' Co. *Recreations:* work, computer graphics, tennis, windsurfing. *Address:* Southbourne Court, Copsale, Sussex RH13 7DJ. *T:* Southwater (01403) 733000.

DEVLIN, Tim; Founder, Tim Devlin Enterprises, public relations consultancy, 1989; *b* 28 July 1944; 3rd *s* of Rt Hon. Lord Devlin, PC, FBA, and of Madeleine, *yr d* of Sir Bernard Oppenheimer, 1st Bt; *m* 1967, Angela Denise, *d* of Mr A. J. G. and late Mrs Laramy; two *s* two *d. Educ:* Winchester Coll.; University Coll., Oxford (Hons degree, History). Feature Writer, Aberdeen Press & Journal, 1966; Reporter, Scotsman, 1967; Educn Reporter, Evening Echo, Watford, 1968–69; Reporter, later News Editor, The Times Educnl Supplement, 1969–71; Reporter, The Times, 1971–73, Educn Corresp., 1973–77; Nat. Dir, ISIS, 1977–84; Public Relations Dir, Inst. of Dirs, 1984–86; Assoc. Dir, Charles Barker Traverse-Healy, 1986–89. *Publications:* (with Mary Warnock) What Must We Teach?, 1977; Good Communications Guide, 1980; Independent Schools—The Facts, 1981; Choosing Your Independent School, 1984; (with Brian Knight) Public Relations and Marketing for Schools, 1990; (with Hywel Williams) Old School Ties, 1992. *Recreations:* writing, art, tennis, children. *T:* Staplehurst (01580) 893176.

DEVLIN, Timothy Robert; MP (C) Stockton South, since 1987; *b* 13 June 1959; *e s* of H. Brendan Devlin, FRCS and Anne Elizabeth Devlin, MB BCh; *m* 1st, 1986 (marr. diss. 1989); 2nd, 1991, Carol-Anne Aitken. *Educ:* Dulwich Coll.; LSE; City Univ. Called to the Bar, Lincoln's Inn, 1985 (Hardwick and Thomas More Scholar). Mem., Cons. Research Dept, 1981; former Chm., LSE Conservatives; Sec., 1985, Chm., 1986, Islington North Cons. Assoc. PPS to Attorney Gen., 1992–94. Mem., Select Cttee on Scottish Affairs, 1995–; former Chm., Parly Panel on Charity Law; Vice-Chm., All-Party Japan Parly Gp; Sec., All-Party Nepal Gp; Treas., All-Party Tibet Gp; Chm., Northern Gp of Cons. MPs, 1992–; Dep. Chm., Foreign Affairs Forum, 1990–92; Member: Stockton on Tees Cons. Assoc.; Soc. of Cons. Lawyers; Franco-British Parly Group, 1987–; RIIA; All-Party Clubs Group; Yarm Civic Soc.; Yarm-Vernouillet twinning Assoc.; NT; Friends of the RA; Rare Breeds Survival Trust; Scotch Malt Whisky Soc. Trustee, NSPCC, 1993–; Gov., Yarm Sch., 1988–. *Recreations:* hill-walking, opera, ski-ing. *Address:* 2 Russell Street, Stockton-on-Tees, Cleveland TS18 1NS. *T:* Stockton-on-Tees (01642) 605035.

DEVON, 17th Earl of, *cr* 1553; **Charles Christopher Courtenay,** Bt 1644; RARO Lieutenant (W/Captain) Coldstream Guards; *b* 13 July 1916; *o surv. s* of 16th Earl and Marguerite (*d* 1950), *d* of late John Silva; *S* father, 1935; *m* 1939, Venetia, Countess of Cottenham, *d* of Captain J. V. Taylor; one *s* one *d. Educ:* Winchester; RMC, Sandhurst. Served war of 1939–45 (despatches). *Recreations:* shooting and fishing. *Heir: s* Lord Courtenay, *qv. Address:* Stables House, Powderham, Exeter EX6 8JQ. *T:* Starcross (01626) 890253.

DEVONPORT, 3rd Viscount *cr* 1917, of Wittington, Bucks; **Terence Kearley;** Bt 1908; Baron 1910; architect and landowner; Chairman, Millhouse Developments Ltd, since 1989; *b* 29 Aug. 1944; *s* of 2nd Viscount Devonport and of Sheila Isabel, *e d* of Lt-Col C. Hope Murray; *S* father, 1973; *m* 1968, Elizabeth Rosemary, *d* of late John G. Hopton (marr. diss. 1979); two *d. Educ:* Aiglon Coll., Switzerland; Selwyn Coll., Cambridge (BA, DipArch, MA); Newcastle Univ. (MPhil). Architect: Davis Brody, New York City, 1967–68; London Borough of Lambeth, 1971–72; Barnett Winskell, Newcastle-upon-Tyne, 1972–75; landscape architect, Ralph Erskine, Newcastle, 1977–78; in private practice, 1979–84 (RIBA, ALI); Forestry Manager, 1973–; farmer, 1978–. Member: Lloyds, 1976–; Internat. Dendrology Soc., 1978–; N Adv. Cttee, TGEW, 1978–; N Adv. Cttee, CLA, 1980–85; Nat. Land Use and Envmt Cttee, TGUK, 1984–87. Vice President: Arboricultural Assoc., 1987–; Forestry Commn Reference Panel, 1987–. Man. Dir, Tweedswood Enterprises, 1979–, and dir various other cos, 1984–. MInstD. Order of Mark Twain (USA), 1977. *Recreations:* nature, travel and good food; interests: trees, the arts, country sports. *Heir: cousin* Chester Dagley Hugh Kearley [*b* 29 April 1932; *m* 1974, Josefa Mesquida]. *Address:* Ray Demesne, Kirkwhelpington, Newcastle upon Tyne NE19 2RG. *Clubs:* Royal Automobile, Beefsteak, Farmers', MCC; Northern Counties (Newcastle upon Tyne).

DEVONS, Prof. Samuel; FRS 1955; Professor of Physics, Columbia University, New York, 1960–85, now Emeritus (Chairman, Dept of Physics, 1963–67); Director, History of Physics Laboratory, Barnard College, Columbia University, 1970–85; *b* 1914; *s* of Rev. David I. Devons and E. Edleston; *m* 1938, Celia Ruth Toubkin; four *d. Educ:* Trinity Coll., Cambridge. BA 1935; MA, PhD 1939. Exhibition of 1851 Senior Student, 1939. Scientific Officer, Senior Scientific Officer, Air Ministry, MAP, and Ministry of Supply, 1939–45. Lecturer in Physics, Cambridge Univ., Fellow and Dir of Studies, Trinity Coll., Cambridge, 1946–49; Prof. of Physics, Imperial Coll. of Science, 1950–55; Langworthy Prof. of Physics and Dir of Physical Laboratories, Univ. of Manchester, 1955–60. Royal Soc. Leverhulme Vis. Prof., Andhra Univ., India, 1967–68; Balfour Vis. Prof., History of Science, Weizmann Inst., Rehovot, Israel, 1973; Racah Vis. Prof. of Physics, Hebrew Univ., Jerusalem, 1973–74. Rutherford Meml Lectr, Royal Soc., Australia, 1989. Rutherford Medal and Prize, Inst. of Physics, 1970. *Publications:* Excited States of Nuclei, 1949; (ed) Biology and Physical Sciences, 1969; (ed) High Energy Physics and Nuclear Structure, 1970; contributions to Proc. Royal Society, Proc. Phys. Soc., etc. *Recreations:* plastic arts, travel. *Address:* Nevis Laboratory, Columbia University, PO Box 137, Irvington-on-Hudson, NY 10533, USA. *T:* (914) 5918100, *Fax:* (914) 5918120.

DEVONSHIRE, 11th Duke of, *cr* 1694; **Andrew Robert Buxton Cavendish,** PC 1964; MC; Baron Cavendish, 1605; Earl of Devonshire, 1618; Marquess of Hartington, 1694; Earl of Burlington, 1831; Baron Cavendish (UK) 1831; Vice-Lord-Lieutenant of the County of Derby, 1957–87; Chancellor of Manchester University, 1965–86; *b* 2 Jan. 1920; *o surv. s* of 10th Duke of Devonshire, KG, and Lady Mary Cecil, GCVO, CBE (*d* 1988), *d* of 4th Marquess of Salisbury, KG, GCVO; *S* father, 1950; *m* 1941, Hon. Deborah Vivian Freeman-Mitford, *d* of 2nd Baron Redesdale; one *s* two *d. Educ:* Eton; Trinity Coll., Cambridge. Served War of 1939–45, Coldstream Guards (MC). Contested (C) Chesterfield Div. of Derbyshire, 1945 and 1950. Parliamentary Under-Sec. of State for Commonwealth Relations, Oct. 1960–Sept. 1962; Minister of State, Commonwealth Relations Office, Sept. 1962–Oct. 1964 and for Colonial Affairs, 1963–Oct. 1964. Steward of the Jockey Club, 1966–69. Mem., Horserace Totalisator Board, 1977–86; a Trustee, Nat. Gallery, 1960–68; President: The Royal Hosp. and Home, Putney, 1954–91; Derbyshire Boy Scouts Assoc.; Lawn Tennis Assoc., 1955–61; RNIB, 1979–85; Nat Assoc. for Deaf Children, 1978–; Building Societies Assoc., 1954–61; Vice-Pres., London Library, 1993–; Chairman: Grand Council, British Empire Cancer Campaign, 1956–81; Throughbred Breeders' Assoc., 1978–81; Patron, Polite Soc., 1991–. Mayor of Buxton, 1952–54. Hon. Col, Manchester and Salford Univs OTC, 1981–85. Hon. LLD: Manchester; Sheffield; Liverpool; Hon. Dr Law, Memorial Univ. of Newfoundland. *Publication:* Park Top: a romance of the Turf, 1976. *Heir: s* Marquess of Hartington, *qv. Address:* Chatsworth, Bakewell, Derbyshire DE45 1PP. *T:* Baslow (01246) 582204; 4 Chesterfield Street, W1. *T:* 0171–499 5803. *Clubs:* Brooks's, Jockey, White's.

See also Lady E. G. A. Cavendish, Lady E. Tennant.

DEVONSHIRE, Michael Norman, TD 1969; **His Honour Judge Devonshire;** a Circuit Judge, since 1991; *b* 23 May 1930; *s* of late Norman George Devonshire and late Edith Devonshire (*née* Skinner); *m* 1962, Jessie Margaret Roberts. *Educ:* King's Sch., Canterbury. Military Service, 2nd Lt, RA, served Korea, 1953–55; 4/5 Bn Queen's Own Royal West Kent Regt TA and 8 Bn Queen's Regt TA, 1955–69; retired in rank of Major, 1969. Admitted Solicitor, 1953; Partner, Doyle Devonshire Co., 1957–79; Master of the Supreme Court, Taxing Office, 1979–91; a Recorder, 1987–91. Pres., London Solicitors' Litigation Assoc., 1974–76; Mem., Law Soc. Family Law and Contentious Remuneration Cttees, 1969–79. Mem., Recreation and Conservation Cttee, Southern Water Authy, 1984–89. Mem., Council, Royal Yachting Assoc., 1978–92 and 1993– (Trustee, Seamanship Foundn, 1981–85; Chm. SE Region, 1993–); Chm., Internat. Regs Cttee, IYRU, 1994– (Vice Chm., 1991–94). *Publications:* (with M. J. Cook and W. H. Elliott) The Taxation of Contentious Costs, 1979; (consultant ed) Greenslade on Costs, 1991. *Recreation:* sailing. *Address:* The Law Courts, Altyre Road, Croydon, Surrey CR9 5AB. *Club:* Royal Thames Yacht.

DEW, Leslie Robert; Member, Bermuda Insurance Advisory Committee, 1979–93; President and Managing Director, Britamco Ltd, 1977–84; President, Insco Ltd, Bermuda (Gulf Oil Corporation Insurance Subsidiaries), 1980–84 (Executive Vice President-Underwriter, 1977–80); Chairman, 1971–77 and formerly Non-Marine Underwriter, Roy J. M. Merrett Syndicates; *b* 11 April 1914; *er s* of Robert Thomas Dew, RHA and Ellen Dora Frampton; *m* 1st, 1939, Vera Doreen Wills (marr. diss. 1956); 2nd, 1956, Patricia Landsberg (*née* Hyde); one *s. Educ:* privately. Underwriting Member of Lloyd's, 1950–; Mem. Cttee of Lloyd's, 1969–72, 1974–77; Dep. Chm. of Lloyd's, 1971, 1975, 1977; Mem. Cttee, Lloyd's Non-Marine Assoc., 1957–77 (Dep. Chm. 1963 and 1965, Chm. 1966); Chm., Lloyd's Common Market Working Gp, 1971–77; Dep. Chm., British Insurers' European Cttee, 1972–77. Binney Award for Civilian Bravery, 1975. *Recreations:* music, reading. *Club:* Metropolitan (NY).

DEW, Prof. Ronald Beresford; Professor Emeritus, University of Manchester Institute of Science and Technology, since 1980; *b* 19 May 1916; *s* of Edwyn Dew-Jones, FCA, and Jean Robertson Dew-Jones, BA, (*née* McInnes); *m* 1940, Sheila Mary Smith, BA; one *s* one *d. Educ:* Sedbergh; Manchester Univ. (LLB); Cambridge Univ. (MA). Barrister-at-Law, Middle Temple, 1965. Lieut, RNVR, 1940–45. Asst Managing Dir, P-E Consulting Gp, 1952–62. Visiting Prof. of Industrial Administration, Manchester Univ., 1960–63; Head of Dept of Management Sciences, Univ. of Manchester Inst. of Science and Technology, 1963–70 and 1974–77; Prof. of Industrial Administration, Manchester Univ., 1963–67; Prof. of Management Sciences, 1967–80. Mem. Council, Internat. Univ. Contact for Management Educn, 1966–71; Dir, Centre for Business Research, 1965–69; Dir, European Assoc. of Management Training Centres, 1966–71; Dep. Chm., Manchester Polytechnic, 1970–72; Co-Chm., Conf. of Univ. Management Schools (CUMS), 1970–73. Member: Council of BIM, 1971–76 (Bd of NW Region, 1966–80); Council of Manchester Business School, 1967–76; Court of Manchester Univ., 1978–80; Trustee, European Foundation for Management Develt, 1975–77. CIMgt; FCA. *Recreations:* archaeology, ornithology, bee-keeping, travel. *Address:* University of Manchester Institute of Science and Technology, Department of Management Sciences, Sackville Street, Manchester M60 1QD. *T:* 0161–236 3311.

de WAAL, Sir Constant Hendrik, (Sir Henry), KCB 1989 (CB 1977); QC 1988; First Parliamentary Counsel, 1987–91; *b* 1 May 1931; *s* of late Hendrik de Waal and Elizabeth von Ephrussi; *m* 1964, Julia Jessel; two *s*. *Educ:* Tonbridge Sch. (scholar); Pembroke Coll., Cambridge (scholar; Hon. Fellow, 1992). 1st cl. Law Tripos, 1st cl. LLM. Called to the Bar, Lincoln's Inn, 1953, Bencher 1989; Buchanan Prize, Cassel Scholar. Fellow of Pembroke Coll., Cambridge, and Univ. Asst Lectr in Law, 1958–60. Entered Parliamentary Counsel Office, 1960; with Law Commission, 1969–71; Parly Counsel, 1971–81; Second Parly Counsel, 1981–86. *Recreation:* remaining (so far as possible) unaware of current events. *Address:* 62 Sussex Street, SW1V 4RG.

See also Rev. V. A. de Waal.

de WAAL, Rt. Rev. Hugo Ferdinand; *see* Thetford, Bishop Suffragan of.

de WAAL, Rev. Victor Alexander; Chaplain, Society of the Sacred Cross, Tymawr, since 1990; *b* 2 Feb. 1929; *s* of late Hendrik de Waal and Elizabeth von Ephrussi; *m* 1960, Esther Aline Lowndes Moir, PhD; four *s*. *Educ:* Tonbridge School; Pembroke Coll., Cambridge (MA); Ely Theological College. With Phs van Ommeren (London) Ltd, 1949–50; Asst Curate, St Mary the Virgin, Isleworth, 1952–56; Chaplain, Ely Theological Coll., 1956–59; Chaplain and Succentor, King's Coll., Cambridge, 1959–63; Chaplain, Univ. of Nottingham, 1963–69; Chancellor of Lincoln Cathedral, 1969–76; Dean of Canterbury, 1976–86. Hon. DD Nottingham, 1983. *Publications:* What is the Church?, 1969; The Politics of Reconciliation: Zimbabwe's first decade, 1990; contrib.: Theology and Modern Education, 1965; Stages of Experience, 1965; The Committed Church, 1966; Liturgy Reshaped, 1982; Liturgie et Espace Liturgique, 1987; Vie Ecclesiale—communauté et communautés, 1989; Beyond Death, 1993. *Address:* The Cwm, Rowlestone, Pontrilas, Hereford HR2 0DP. *T:* Golden Valley (01981) 240391.

See also Sir C. H. de Waal.

DEWAR, family name of **Baron Forteviot.**

DEWAR, David Alexander; an Assistant Auditor General, National Audit Office, 1984–94; *b* 28 Oct. 1934; *s* of James and Isabella Dewar; *m* 1959, Rosalind Mary Ellen Greenwood; one *s* one *d*. *Educ:* Leith Academy, Edinburgh. Entered Exchequer and Audit Dept, 1953; Chief Auditor, 1966; Deputy Director of Audit, 1973; Director of Audit, 1977; Dep. Sec. of Dept, 1981. *Recreations:* gardening, golf. *Address:* Magnolia Cottage, Grantley Avenue, Wonersh Park, Wonersh, Guildford, Surrey GU5 0QN. *T:* Guildford (01483) 898475.

DEWAR, Donald Campbell; MP (Lab) Glasgow, Garscadden, since April 1978; consultant with Ross Harper & Murphy, Glasgow; *b* 21 Aug. 1937; *s* of Dr Alasdair Dewar, Glasgow; *m* 1964, Alison McNair (marr. diss. 1973); one *s* one *d*. *Educ:* Glasgow Acad.; Glasgow Univ. (MA, LLB). MP (Lab) South Aberdeen, 1966–70; PPS to Pres. of Bd of Trade, 1967; Chm., Select Cttee on Scottish Affairs, 1979–81; front bench spokesman on Scottish Affairs, 1981–92, on Social Security, 1992–; Mem., Shadow Cabinet, 1984–. *Address:* 23 Cleveden Road, Glasgow G12 0PQ.

DEWAR, George Duncan Hamilton; chartered accountant; Partner, Peat, Marwick, Mitchell & Co., Glasgow, 1949–81; *b* 11 Sept. 1916; *s* of George Readman Dewar and Elizabeth Garrioch Sinclair Hamilton; *m* 1940, Elizabeth Lawson Potts Lawrie; one *s* one *d*. *Educ:* High Sch. of Glasgow. Mem. Inst. Chartered Accountants of Scotland (admitted, 1940; Mem. Coun., 1960–65; Vice-Pres., 1969–70; Pres., 1970–71). Mem., Scottish Tourist Bd, 1977–80. *Recreation:* golf. *Address:* Flat 28, Muirfield Court, 20 Muirend Road, Glasgow G44 3QP. *T:* 0141–637 5683. *Club:* Western (Glasgow).

DEWAR, Ian Stewart; JP; Member, South Glamorgan County Council, 1985–93 (Vice-Chairman, 1990–91; Finance Chairman, 1992–93); *b* 29 Jan. 1929; *er s* of late William Stewart Dewar and of Eileen Dewar (*née* Godfrey); *m* 1968, Nora Stephanie House; one *s* one *d*. *Educ:* Penarth County Sch.; UC Cardiff; Jesus Coll., Oxford (MA). RAF, 1947–49. Asst Archivist, Glamorgan County Council, 1952–53. Entered Min. of Labour, 1953; Asst Private Sec. to Minister, 1956–58; Principal, Min. of Labour and Civil Service Commn, 1958–65; Asst Sec., Min. of Labour, Dept of Employment and Commn on Industrial Relations, 1965–70; Asst Sec., 1970–73, and Under-Sec., 1973–83, Welsh Office. Member, Governing Body: Univ. of Wales, 1985–93; Nat. Mus. of Wales, 1985–93; Chm., Museum Schs Service Cttee, 1989–93. JP S Glam, 1985. *Address:* 59 Stanwell Road, Penarth, South Glamorgan CF64 3LR. *T:* Cardiff (01222) 703255.

DEWAR, Prof. Michael James Steuart, FRS 1960; MA, DPhil Oxon; Robert A. Welch Professor of Chemistry, University of Texas, 1963–90; Graduate Research Professor, University of Florida, since 1990; *b* 24 Sept. 1918; *s* of Francis D. Dewar, ICS, and Nan B. Keith; *m* 1944, Mary Williamson (*d* 1994); two *s*. *Educ:* Winchester Coll. (First Scholar); Balliol Coll., Oxford (Brackenbury, Frazer and Gibbs Scholar; Hon. Fellow, 1974). ICI Fellow in Chemistry, Oxford, 1945; Courtaulds Ltd, Fundamental Research Laboratory, 1945–51; Reilly Lecturer at Notre Dame Univ., USA, 1951; Prof. of Chemistry and Head of Dept of Chemistry at Queen Mary Coll., University of London, 1951–59 (Hon. Fellow, 1993); Prof. of Chemistry, University of Chicago, 1959–63. Visiting Professor: Yale Univ., USA, 1957; Arthur D. Little, MIT, 1966; Maurice S. Kharasch, Univ. of Chicago, 1971; Firth, Sheffield, 1972; Dist. Bicentennial, Univ. of Utah, 1976; Pahlavi, Iran, 1977. Hon. Sec. Chemical Soc., 1957–59. Lectures: Tilden, Chem. Soc., 1954; Falk-Plaut, Columbia Univ., 1963; Daines Memorial, Univ. of Kansas, 1963; Glidden Company, Western Reserve Univ., 1964; Marchon Visiting, Univ. of Newcastle upon Tyne, 1966; Glidden Company, Kent State Univ., 1967; Gnehm, Eidg. Tech. Hochschule, Zurich, 1968; Barton, Univ. of Oklahoma, 1969; (first) Kahlbaum, Univ. of Basel, 1970; (first) Benjamin Rush, Univ. of Pennsylvania, 1971; Venable, Univ. of N Carolina, 1971; Foster, State Univ. of NY at Buffalo, 1973, Robinson, Chem. Soc., 1974; Sprague, Univ. of Wisconsin, 1974; Bircher, Vanderbilt Univ., 1976; Faraday, Northern Illinois Univ., 1977; Priestley, Pennsylvania State Univ., 1980; J. Clarence Karcher, Univ. of Oklahoma, 1984; Res. Scholar Lectr, Drew Univ., 1984; (first) Charles O. A. Coulson, Univ. of Georgia, 1988. Fellow, Amer. Acad. of Arts and Sciences, 1966; Mem., Nat. Acad. of Sciences, 1983. Harrison Howe Award of Amer. Chem. Soc., 1961; (first) G. W. Wheland Meml Medal, Univ. of Chicago, 1976; Evans Award, Ohio State Univ., 1977; South West Regional Award, Amer. Chem. Soc., 1978; Davy Medal, Royal Soc., 1982; James Flack Norris Award, Amer. Chem. Soc., 1984; William H. Nichols Award, Amer. Chem. Soc., 1986; Auburn Kosolapoff Award, Amer. Chem. Soc., 1988; Tetrahedron Prize, 1989; World Assoc. of Theoretical Organic Chemistry Medal, 1989; Chemical Pioneer Award, Amer. Inst. of Chemists, 1990; Award for Computers in Chemistry, Amer. Chem. Soc., 1994. *Publications:* The Electronic Theory of Organic Chemistry, 1949; Hyperconjugation, 1962; Introduction to Modern Chemistry, 1965; The Molecular Orbital Theory of Organic Chemistry, 1969; Computer Compilation of Molecular Weights and Percentage Compositions, 1970; The PMO Theory of Organic Chemistry, 1975; papers in scientific journals. *Address:* 10520 Northwest 36th Lane, Gainesville, FL 32606-5075, USA. *T:* (904) 3322050, *Fax:* (904) 3322055.

DEWAR, Robert James, CMG 1969; CBE 1964; World Bank, retired 1984; *b* 13 Jan. 1923; *s* of late Dr Robert Scott Dewar, MA, MB, ChB, and Mrs Roubaix Dewar, Dumbreck, Glasgow; *m* 1947, Christina Marianne, *d* of late Olof August Ljungberger, Stockholm, Sweden; two *s* one *d*. *Educ:* High Sch. of Glasgow; Edinburgh Univ. (BSc, Forestry); Wadham Coll., Oxford. Asst Conservator of Forests, Colonial Forest Service, Nigeria and Nyasaland, 1944–55; Dep. Chief Conservator of Forests, Nyasaland, 1955–61; Chief Conservator of Forests, Dir of Forestry and Game, Nyasaland (now Malawi), 1961–64; Mem. Nyasaland Legislative Council, 1960. Permanent Secretary, Malawi: Min. of Natural Resources, 1964–67 and 1968–69; Min. of Economic Affairs, 1967–68; retd from Malawi CS, 1969; World Bank: Sen. Agriculturalist, 1969–74; Chief of Agricl Div., Regl Mission for Eastern Africa, 1974–84. Mem. Nat. Development Council, Malawi, 1966–69. Vice-Chm. of Trustees, Zimbabwe Trust, 1993–. *Recreations:* gardening, golf, angling. *Address:* Hawkshaw, Comrie Road, Crieff, Perthshire PH7 4BJ. *T:* Crieff (01764) 654830. *Clubs:* Commonwealth Trust, New Cavendish.

See also R. S. Dewar.

DEWAR, Robert Scott; HM Diplomatic Service; Deputy High Commissioner, Harare, since 1992; *b* 10 June 1949; *s* of Robert James Dewar and Christina Marianne Dewar (*née* Ljungberger); *m* 1979, Jennifer Mary Ward; one *d*. *Educ:* Springvale, Southern Rhodesia; Loretto; Brasenose Coll., Oxford. VSO, Port Sudan, 1971–72; Scottish Office, 1972–73; FCO, 1973; served Colombo and FCO, to 1981, Asst Sec. Gen. to Lancaster House Conf. on Southern Rhodesia, 1979; Head of Chancery, Luanda, 1981–84; FCO, 1984–88; Dep. Head of Mission, Dakar, 1988–92. *Recreations:* sport, esp. fly fishing. *Address:* c/o Foreign and Commonwealth Office, SW1A 2AH.

DEWAR, His Honour Thomas; a Circuit Judge (formerly Judge of the County Court), 1962–84; Joint President, Council of Circuit Judges, 1980 (Vice-President, 1979); *b* 5 Jan. 1909; *s* of James Stewart Dewar and Katherine Rose Dewar; *m* 1950, Katherine Muriel Johnson; one *s* decd. *Educ:* Penarth Intermediate School; Cardiff Technical Coll.; Sch. of Pharmacy, University of London; Birkbeck Coll., University of London. Pharmaceutical Chemist, 1931; BPharm 1931, PhD 1934, BSc (Botany, 1st cl. hons) 1936, London. Called to Bar, Middle Temple, 1939; Blackstone Pupillage Prize, 1939. Admin. staff of Pharmaceutical Soc., 1936–40; Sec., Middx Pharmaceutical Cttee, 1940–41; Asst Dir, Min. of Supply, 1943; Sec., Wellcome Foundation, 1943–45. Mem. of Western Circuit, 1945–62; Judge of the County Court (circuit 59, Cornwall and Plymouth), 1962–65, (circuit 38, Edmonton, etc), 1965–66 (circuit 41, Clerkenwell), 1966–71; Circuit Judge, SE circuit, 1972–84. Presided over inquiry into X-ray accident at Plymouth Hosp., 1962. Mem. Executive Council, Internat. Law Assoc., 1974–89. Governor, Birkbeck Coll., 1944–46 and 1971–82. *Publications:* Textbook of Forensic Pharmacy, 1946 and four subsequent editions; scientific papers in Quarterly Jl of Pharmacy and Pharmacology. *Recreations:* horticulture, travel. *Address:* 1 Garden Court, Temple, EC4Y 9BJ. *T:* 0171–353 3326. *Club:* Royal Over-Seas League.

de WARDENER, Prof. Hugh Edward, CBE 1982 (MBE (mil.) 1946); MD, FRCP; Professor of Medicine, University of London, Charing Cross Hospital, 1960–81, now Emeritus; Honorary Consultant Physician to the Army, 1975–80; *b* 8 Oct. 1915; *s* of Edouard de Wardener and Becky (*née* Pearce); *m* 1st, 1939, Janet Lavinia Bellis Simon (marr. diss. 1947); one *s*; 2nd, 1947, Diana Rosamund Crawshay (marr. diss. 1954); 3rd, 1954, Jill Mary Foxworthy (marr. diss. 1969); one *d*; 4th, 1969, Josephine Margaret Storey, MBE; two *s*. *Educ:* Malvern Coll. St Thomas's Hosp., 1933–39; RAMC, 1939–45; St Thomas's Hosp., 1945–60, Registrar, Senior Lecturer, Reader. MRCP 1946, MD 1949, FRCP 1958. Hon. MD, Univ. Pierre et Marie Curie, Paris, 1980. President: Internat. Soc. of Nephrology, 1969–72; Renal Assoc., 1973–76; Mem. Council, Imp. Cancer Res. Fund, 1981–88. *Publications:* The Kidney: An Outline of Normal and Abnormal Structure and Function, 1958, 5th edn 1986; papers in various scientific journals. *Recreations:* normal and scything. *Address:* 9 Dungarvan Avenue, Putney, SW15 5QU. *T:* 0181–878 3130.

DEWBERRY, David Albert; HM Diplomatic Service; First Secretary, Foreign and Commonwealth Office, since 1991; *b* 27 Sept. 1941; *s* of Albert Dewberry and Grace Dewberry (*née* Tarsey); *m* 1974, Catherine Mary (*née* Stabback); three *s* one *d*. *Educ:* Cray Valley Sch., Foots Cray, Kent. Joined CRO, 1958; Karachi, 1963; Kingston, 1966; Warsaw, 1970; Brussels, 1971; Second Sec. (Aid), Dhaka, 1972; FCO, 1974; Consul: Mexico City, 1977; Buenos Aires, 1980; FCO, 1982; Dep. High Comr, Dar es Salaam, 1987. *Recreations:* reading, walking. *Address:* Foreign and Commonwealth Office, SW1A 2AH.

DEWDNEY, Duncan Alexander Cox, CBE 1968; Director, The Coverdale Organisation, since 1973; *b* 22 Oct. 1911; *o s* of late Claude Felix Dewdney and Annie Ross Cox; *m* 1935, Ann (*d* 1993), *d* of Walter Riley and Emily Sterratt; two *d*. *Educ:* Bromgrove Sch., Worcs; University of Birmingham (BSc Hons, Cadman Medallist). Served War of 1939–45; RAF, 1940–45 (Wing Comdr); Air Staff appts, Head RE8 Min. of Home Security (R&D Dept). British Petroleum Co., 1932–36; International Assoc. (Pet. Ind.) Ltd, 1936–40; Research Man., Esso Development Co., 1945–51; joined Esso Petroleum Co., 1951; Dir, 1957; Man. Dir, 1963–67; Vice-Chm., 1968. Seconded to NBPI as Jt Dep. Chm., 1965–66, part-time Mem. Bd, 1967–69. Exec. Dir, Rio Tinto Zinc Corporation, 1968–72; Chairman: Irish Refining Co. Ltd, 1958–65; Anglesey Aluminium, 1968–71; RTZ Britain, 1969–72; RTZ Development Enterprises, 1970–72; Dep. Chm., Manpower Services Commn, 1974–77; Dir, Esso Chemicals SA, 1964. Chairman: National Economic Develt Cttee for the Mechanical Engrg Industry, 1964–68; Welsh Industrial Develt Bd, 1972–75; Underwater Training Centre, 1977–79. Legion of Merit, 1945. *Address:* Salters, Harestock, Winchester, Hants SO22 5JP. *T:* Winchester (01962) 52034. *Club:* Travellers'.

DEWE, Roderick Gorrie; Chairman, Dewe Rogerson Group Ltd, since 1969; *b* 17 Oct. 1935; *s* of Douglas Percy Dewe and Rosanna Clements Gorrie; *m* 1964, Carol Anne Beach Thomas; one *s* one *d*. *Educ:* abroad and University Coll., Oxford (BA Hons). FIPR. Treasury, Fedn of Rhodesia and Nyasaland Govt, 1957–58; Angel Court Consultants, 1960–68; founded Dewe Rogerson, 1969, Chm., 1969–95. *Recreations:* golf, travel. *Address:* 55 Duncan Terrace, N1 8AG; Old Southhill Station House, near Biggleswade, Beds SG18 9LP. *T:* Hitchin (01462) 811274. *Club:* City of London.

DEWE MATHEWS, Marina Sarah, (Mrs John Dewe Mathews); *see* Warner, M. S.

de WET, Dr Carel; South African Ambassador to the Court of St James's, 1964–67 and 1972–77; Director of companies; farmer; *b* Memel, OFS, S Africa, 25 May 1924; *g s* of Gen. Christian de Wet; *m* 1949, Catharina Elizabeth (Rina) Maas, BA; one *s* three *d*. *Educ:* Vrede High Sch., OFS; Pretoria Univ. (BSc); University of Witwatersrand (MB, BCh). Served at Nat. Hosp., Bloemfontein; subseq. practised medicine at Boksburg, Transvaal, at Winburg, OFS, and, from 1948, at Vanderbijlpark, Transvaal. Mayor of Vanderbijlpark, 1950–53; MP (Nat. Party) for Vanderbijlpark, 1953–64, for Johannesburg West, 1967–72; Mem. various Parly and Nat. Party Cttees, 1953–64; Minister of Mines and Health, Govt of S Africa, 1967–72. *Recreations:* game farming, golf, rugby, cricket, hunting, deep sea fishing. *Address:* PO Box 70292, Bryanston, 2021, South Africa. *T:* (office) 8861446; (home) 7066202, *Fax:* 8861496. *Clubs:* Royal Automobile, East India, Institute of Directors, MCC, Les Ambassadeurs, Eccentric, Wentworth; Here XVII (Cape Town); Constantia (Pretoria); New, Rand Park Golf, Country (Johannesburg); Maccauvlei Country (Vereeniging), Emfuleni Golf (Vanderbijlpark).

DEWEY, Sir Anthony Hugh, 3rd Bt, *cr* 1917; JP; *b* 31 July 1921; *s* of late Major Hugh Grahame Dewey, MC (*e s* of 2nd Bt), and Marjorie Florence Isobell (who *m* 2nd, 1940, Sir Robert Bell, KCSI; she *d* 1988), *d* of Lieut-Col Alexander Hugh Dobbs; *S* grandfather, 1948; *m* 1949, Sylvia, *d* of late Dr J. R. MacMahon, Branksome Manor, Bournemouth; two *s* three *d*. JP Somerset, 1961. *Heir: s* Rupert Grahame Dewey [*b* 29 March 1953; *m* 1978, Suzanne Rosemary, *d* of late Andrew Lusk, Perthshire; two *s* one *d*]. *Address:* Rag, Galhampton, Yeovil, Som BA22 7AJ. *T:* North Cadbury (01963) 40213. *Club:* Army and Navy.

DEWEY, Prof. John Frederick, FRS 1985; FGS; Professor of Geology and Fellow of University College, University of Oxford, since 1986; *b* 22 May 1937; *s* of John Edward and Florence Nellie Mary Dewey; *m* 1961, Frances Mary Blackhurst, MA, DSc; one *s* one *d*. *Educ:* Bancroft's School; Queen Mary Coll. and Imperial Coll., Univ. of London (BSc, PhD, DIC); MA 1965, ScD 1988, Cantab. CGeol 1990. Lecturer: Univ. of Manchester, 1960–64; Univ. of Cambridge, 1964–70; Prof., State Univ. of New York at Albany, 1970–82; Prof. of Geology, Durham Univ., 1982–86. Mem., Academia Europaea, 1990. Numerous honours and awards, UK and overseas, incl. Penrose Medal, Geol Soc. of America, 1992; Arthur Holmes Medal, Europ. Union of Geoscis, 1993. *Publications:* contribs to Geol Soc. of America Bulletin, Geol Soc. London Jl, Jl Geophysical Res. and other learned jls. *Recreations:* skiing, cricket, water colour painting, English music 1850–1950, model railways. *Address:* University College, Oxford OX1 4BH.

DEWHURST, Prof. Sir (Christopher) John, Kt 1977; FRCOG, FRCSE; Professor of Obstetrics and Gynaecology, University of London, at Queen Charlotte's Hospital for Women, 1967–85, now Professor Emeritus; *b* 2 July 1920; *s* of John and Agnes Dewhurst; *m* 1952, Hazel Mary Atkin; two *s* one *d*. *Educ:* St Joseph's Coll., Dumfries; Manchester Univ. MB, ChB. Surg. Lieut, RNVR, 1943–46. Sen. Registrar, St Mary's Hosp., Manchester, 1948–51; Lectr, Sen. Lectr and Reader, Sheffield Univ., 1951–67. Pres., RCOG, 1975–78. Hon. FACOG 1976; Hon. FRCSI 1977; Hon. FCOG (SA) 1978; Hon. FRACOG 1985. Hon. DSc Sheffield, 1977; Hon. MD Uruguay, 1980. *Publications:* A Student's Guide to Obstetrics and Gynaecology, 1960, 2nd edn 1965; The Gynaecological Disorders of Infants and Children, 1963; (jtly) The Intersexual Disorders, 1969; (ed) Integrated Obstetrics and Gynaecology for Postgraduates, 1972, 3rd edn 1981; (jtly) A General Practice of Obstetrics and Gynaecology, 1977, 2nd edn 1984; Practical Paediatric and Adolescent Gynaecology, 1980; Royal Confinements, 1980; Female Puberty and its Abnormalities, 1984. *Recreations:* cricket, gardening, music. *Address:* 21 Jack's Lane, Harefield, Middlesex UB9 6HE. *T:* Harefield (01895) 825403.

de WILDE, (Alan) Robin; QC 1993; *b* 12 July 1945; *s* of late Capt. Ronald Cedric de Wilde and of Dorothea Elizabeth Mary (*née* Fenningworth); *m* 1977, Patricia Teresa Bearcroft; three *s*. *Educ:* Dean Close Sch.; RAF Coll., Cranwell; Inns of Court Sch. of Law. Called to the Bar, Inner Temple, 1971. *Address:* 199 Strand, WC2R 1DR. *T:* 0171–379 9779, *Fax:* 0171–379 9481.

de WINTER, Carl; Secretary General, Federation of British Artists, 1978–84; *b* 18 June 1934; *s* of Alfred de Winter; *m* 1958, Lyndall Bradshaw; one *s* one *d*. *Educ:* Pangbourne. Purser, Orient Line, 1951–60. Art Exhibitions Bureau: PA to Man. Dir, 1961–66; Director, 1967–84; Royal Soc. of Portrait Painters: Asst Sec., 1962–78; Sec., 1978–84; Royal Soc. of Miniature Painters, Sculptors and Gravers: Asst Sec., 1964–67; Sec., 1968–84; Hon. Mem., 1984; Royal Soc. of Marine Artists: Asst Sec., 1964–70; Sec., 1971–78; Royal Soc. of British Artists: Asst Keeper, 1969–73; Keeper, 1974–84; Royal Inst. of Oil Painters: Sec., 1973–84; Royal Inst. of Painters in Watercolours: Sec., 1979–84; National Soc. of Painters, Sculptors and Printmakers: Sec., 1973–84; New English Art Club: Sec., 1973–84; United Soc. of Artists: Sec., 1975–81. *Address:* Holbrook Park House, Holbrook, near Horsham, W Sussex RH12 5PW.

de WINTON, Michael Geoffrey, CBE 1960 (OBE 1952); MC 1944; Assistant Legal Secretary to the Law Officers, 1972–80; *b* 17 Oct. 1916; *s* of John Jeffreys de Winton and Ida de Winton; *m* 1948, Ursula Mary, *d* of E. E. Lightwood, MB; two *s* one *d*. *Educ:* Monmouth School. Admitted Solicitor, 1939. War service, 1939–46: commnd S Wales Borderers, 1940; Company Comdr 2nd Punjab Regt, Indian Army, in India, Middle East and Burma, 1942–45 (despatches twice). Administrative officer, Nigeria, 1946–48; Crown Counsel, 1948–53; called to the Bar, Gray's Inn, 1953; Principal legal draftsman, W Nigeria, 1954; Solicitor General and Permanent Sec. to Min. of Justice, W Nigeria, 1957–61; retired from HM Overseas CS and re-admitted solicitor, 1961; Asst Legal Adviser, Colonial Office, 1961–66, CRO 1967, FCO 1968; Asst Solicitor, Law Officers Dept (Internat. and Commonwealth affairs), 1969; Under Secretary, 1974; retired, 1980. Legal consultant to overseas govts and internat. organizations; Principal Legal Adviser, British Indian Ocean Territory, 1982–83. *Recreations:* music, art. *Address:* Stable Cottage, Church Walk, Stalbridge, Dorset DT10 2LR. *T:* Stalbridge (01963) 62834.

DE WOLF, Vice-Adm. Harry George, CBE 1946; DSO 1944; DSC 1944; *b* 26 June 1903; *s* of late Henry George De Wolf, Bedford, NS; *m* 1931, Gwendolen Fowle, *d* of Thomas St George Gilbert, Somerset, Bermuda; one *s* (one *d* decd). Served War of 1939–45. Asst Chief of Naval Staff, Canada, 1944–47; Sen. Canadian Naval Officer Afloat, 1947–48; Flag Officer, Pacific Coast, 1948–50; Vice-Chief of Naval Staff, 1950–52; Chm. of Canadian Joint Staff, Washington, 1953–55; Chief of Naval Staff, Canada, 1956–60, retired. Hon. DSc (M): Royal Military College of Canada, 1966; Royal Roads Mil. Coll., 1980. *Address:* Apt 1006, 200 Rideau Terrace, Ottawa, Ont K1M 0Z3, Canada.

DEWS, Peter; Theatre and TV Director; *b* 26 Sept. 1929; *er s* of John Dews and Edna (Bloomfield); *m* 1960, Ann Rhodes. *Educ:* Queen Elizabeth Grammar Sch., Wakefield; University Coll., Oxford (MA). Asst Master, Holgate and District Grammar Sch., Barnsley, 1952–53; BBC Midland Region Drama Producer (Radio and TV), 1953–63; Dir, Ravinia Shakespeare Festival, Chicago, 1963–64; Artistic Director: Birmingham Repertory Theatre, 1966–72; Chichester Fest. Theatre, 1978–80. Directed: TV: An Age of Kings, 1960 (SFTA Award 1960); The Spread of the Eagle, 1963; Theatre: As You Like It, Vaudeville, 1967; Hadrian VII, Mermaid, 1968, Haymarket and NY, 1969 (Tony Award 1969), Edmonton, 1987; Antony and Cleopatra, Chichester, 1969; Vivat Vivat Regina, Chichester, 1970, Piccadilly and NY, 1972; The Alchemist, Chichester, 1970; Crown Matrimonial, Haymarket, 1972, NY 1973; The Director of the Opera, Chichester, 1973; The Waltz of the Toreadors, Haymarket, 1974; King John, Stratford, Ont, 1974; The Pleasure of His Company, Toronto, 1974; Coriolanus, Tel Aviv, 1975; Othello, Chichester, 1975; Equus, Vancouver, 1975; Number Thirteen Rue de l'Amour, Phœnix, 1976; The Circle, Chichester, transf. to Haymarket, 1976; The Pleasure of His Company, Phœnix, 1976; Man and Superman, Don Juan in Hell, When We Are Married, Ottawa, 1977; Julius Caesar, Chichester, 1977; A Sleep of Prisoners, Chichester Cathedral, 1978; Julius Caesar, A Sleep of Prisoners, Hong Kong Festival, 1979; The Devil's Disciple, The Importance of Being Earnest, Chichester, 1979; Terra Nova, Much Ado About Nothing, Chichester, 1980; Plenty, Toronto, 1981; The Taming of the Shrew, The Comedy of Errors, Stratford, Ont, 1981; Cards on the Table, Vaudeville, 1981; 56 Duncan Terrace, Edmonton, A Midsummer Night's Dream, Plymouth, and Terra Nova, Durban, 1982; Pierewaaien, Arnhem, 1983; Time and the Conways, Chichester, 1983; On The Razzle, Durban, 1983; Romeo and Juliet, Stratford, Ont, and Measure for Measure, Tel Aviv, 1984; Waiting for Godot, and Galileo, Scottish Theatre Co., 1985; King Lear, tour, 1986; An Inspector Calls, Clwyd and Westminster, 1987, tour, 1988; She Stoops to Conquer, tour, 1987. Hon. DLitt: Bradford, 1988; De Paul Univ., Chicago, 1990. *Address:* c/o Larry Dalzell Associates Ltd, Suite 12, 17 Broad Court, WC2B 5QN.

DEXTER, Edward Ralph; Managing Director, Ted Dexter & Associates, since 1978; *b* 15 May 1935; *m* 1959, Susan Georgina Longfield; one *s* one *d*. *Educ:* Radley College; Jesus College, Cambridge (Captain of cricket). Served 11th Hussars, 1956–57 (Malaya Campaign Medal 1955). Cricketer, 1958–68; Captain of Sussex, 1960–65; Captain of England, 1962–65; freelance journalist, 1965–88; sports promotion consultant, 1978–. Chm., England (Cricket) Cttee, TCCB, 1989–93. Contested (C) Cardiff, 1965. *Publications:* Ted Dexter's Cricket Book, 1963; Ted Dexter Declares, 1966; (jtly) Test Kill, 1976; Deadly Putter, 1979; From Bradman to Boycott, 1981; My Golf, 1982. *Recreations:* golf, reading, motor cycling. *Address:* 20A Woodville Gardens, Ealing, W5 2LQ. *T:* 0181–998 6863. *Clubs:* MCC; Sunningdale Golf, Royal and Ancient Golf.

DEXTER, Harold; Organist; Professor, Guildhall School of Music and Drama (Head of General Musicianship Department, 1962–85); Organist, St Botolph's, Aldgate; *b* 7 Oct. 1920; *s* of F. H. and E. Dexter; *m* 1942, Faith Grainger; one *d*. *Educ:* Wyggeston Grammar Sch., Leicester; Corpus Christi Coll., Cambridge, 1939–41 and 1946. ARCO 1938; College Organ Scholar, 1939; John Stewart of Rannoch Scholar, 1940; FRCO 1940; ARCM 1941. BA, MusB 1942; MA 1946; RCO Choirmaster's Diploma; John Brook Prize, 1946; ADCM, 1948. Royal Navy and RNVR, 1941–46. Organist, Louth Parish Church and Music-Master, King Edward VI Grammar Sch., Louth, 1947–49; Organist, Holy Trinity, Leamington Spa, 1949–56; Music Master, Bablake Sch., Coventry, 1952–56; Master of the Music, Southwark Cathedral, 1956–68. FGSM 1962, FRSCM 1964 (Hon. diplomas). *Address:* 29 Allington Court, Outwood Common Road, Billericay, Essex CM11 2JB. *T:* Billericay (01277) 652042.

DEXTER, Prof. Thomas Michael, FRS 1991; Professor of Haematology and Head of Department of Experimental Haematology, since 1982, Deputy Director, since 1994; Paterson Institute for Cancer Research; *b* 15 May 1945; *s* of Thomas Richard Dexter and Agnes Gertrude Deplege; *m* 1966, Frances Ann Sutton (marr. diss. 1978); one *s* one *d* (twins); one *s* one *d* by Dr Elaine Spooncer. *Educ:* Salford Univ. (BSc 1st class Hons 1970; DSc 1982); Manchester Univ. (PhD 1973). MRCPath 1987. Lady Tata Meml Scholar, 1970–73; Res. Scientist, Paterson Inst., 1973; Life Fellow, Cancer Res. Campaign, Manchester, 1978; Personal Chair, Univ. of Manchester, 1985; Gibb Res. Fellow, CRC, 1992–. Visiting Fellow: Sloan Kettering Inst., NY, 1976–77; Weizmann Inst., Israel, 1980. Lectures: Annual, Leukaemia Res. Fund, 1987; Michael Williams, RSM, 1990; Maximov, Leningrad, 1990; Medawar, RPMS, 1994. Member: MRC, 1993– (Chm., Molecular and Cellular Medicine Bd, 1994–); Scientific Cttee, Leukaemia Res. Fund, 1983–86; Scientific Grants Cttee, CRC, 1987–93; Scientific Adv. Bd, Biomedical Res. Center, BC, 1987–91; Scientific Adv. Bd, Wellcome/CRC Inst., Cambridge, 1992–; AFRC Grants Cttee, 1992–94. Pres., Internat. Soc. for Exptl Hematology, 1988. Mem. editl bd of 12 scientific jls. Hon. MRCP 1995. *Publications:* author of 260 articles in scientific jls; editor of four books. *Recreations:* folk singing, gardening, poetry, dominoes. *Address:* Cancer Research Campaign Laboratory of Experimental Haematology, Paterson Institute for Cancer Research, Christie Hospital, Withington, Manchester M20 9BX. *T:* 0161–446 3235.

de YARBURGH-BATESON, family name of **Baron Deramore.**

DEYERMOND, Prof. Alan David, DLitt; FSA; FBA 1988; Professor of Spanish, Queen Mary and Westfield College, London (formerly Westfield College), since 1969; *b* 24 Feb. 1932; *s* of late Henry Deyermond and Margaret Deyermond (*née* Lawson); *m* 1957, Ann Marie Bracken; one *d*. *Educ:* Quarry Bank High Sch., Liverpool; Victoria Coll., Jersey; Pembroke Coll., Oxford (MA; BLitt 1957; DLitt 1985). FSA 1987. Westfield College, London: Asst Lectr, 1955; Lectr, 1958; Reader, 1966; Senior Tutor, 1967–72; Dean, Faculty of Arts, 1972–74, 1981–84; Head of Dept of Spanish, 1983–89; Vice-Principal, 1986–89. Visiting Professor, Universities of: Wisconsin, 1972; California LA, 1977; Princeton, 1978–81; Victoria, 1983; N Arizona, 1986; Johns Hopkins, 1987; Nacional Autónoma de México, 1992. President: Internat. Courtly Literature Soc., 1977–83, Hon. Life Pres., 1983; Asociación Internacional de Hispanistas, 1992–95 (Vice-Pres., 1983–89). Corresponding Fellow: Medieval Acad. of America; Real Acad. de Buenas Letras de Barcelona; Mem., Hispanic Soc. of America; Hon. Fellow, Asociación Hispánica de Literatura Medieval. Hon. LHD Georgetown, 1995. Premio Internacional Elio Antonio de Nebrija, 1994. *Publications:* The Petrarchan Sources of La Celestina, 1961, 2nd edn 1975; Epic Poetry and the Clergy, 1969; A Literary History of Spain: The Middle Ages, 1971; Apollonius of Tyre, 1973; Lazarillo de Tormes: a critical guide, 1975; Historia y crítica de la literatura española: Edad Media, 1980, supplement, 1991; El Cantar de Mio Cid y la épica medieval española, 1987; La literatura perdida de la Edad Media castellana: catálogo y estudio, vol. 1, 1995; contribs to Bulletin of Hispanic Studies etc. *Recreations:* dog-walking, psephology, vegetarian cookery. *Address:* 20 Lancaster Road, St Albans, Herts AL1 4ET. *T:* St Albans (01727) 855383.

d'EYNCOURT, Sir Mark Gervais T.; *see* Tennyson-d'Eyncourt.

DHAKA, Archbishop of, (RC), since 1978; **Most Rev. Michael Rozario,** STL; *b* Solepore, Dhaka, Bangladesh, 18 Jan. 1926; *s* of Urban Rozario. *Educ:* Little Flower Seminary, Dhaka, Bangladesh; St Albert's Seminary, Ranchi, India. Jagannath Coll., Dhaka, Bangladesh, 1948–50; Univ. of Notre Dame, USA, 1951–53; Urbano Univ., Rome, 1953–57. Ordained priest, 1956; Bishop of Dinajpur, 1968. Pres., Catholic Bishops' Conf. of Bangladesh. *Address:* Archbishop's House, PO Box 3, Dhaka 1000, Bangladesh.

DHENIN, Air Marshal Sir Geoffrey (Howard), KBE 1975; AFC 1953 and Bar, 1957; GM 1943; MA, MD, DPH; FFCM 1975; FRAeS 1971; Director-General, Medical Services (RAF), 1974–78; *b* 2 April 1918; *s* of Louis Richard Dhenin and Lucy Ellen Dagg; *m* 1946, Claude Andree Evelyn Rabut; one *s* two *d* (and one *s* decd). *Educ:* Hereford Cathedral Sch.; St John's Coll., Cambridge; Guy's Hosp., London. Joined RAF; various sqdn and other med. appts, Bomber Comd, 2nd TAF, 1943–45 (despatches 1945); pilot trng, 1945–46; various med. officer pilot appts, 1946–58; Staff Coll., Bracknell, 1958–59; comd Princess Mary's RAF Hosp. Akrotiri, Cyprus, 1960–63; comd RAF Hosp. Ely, 1963–66; PMO Air Support Comd, 1966–68; Dir of Health and Research, RAF, 1968–70; Dep. DGMS, RAF, 1970–71; PMO Strike Comd, 1971–73. Fellow, Internat. Acad. of Aerospace Medicine, 1972. CStJ 1974. QHP 1970–78. Adviser to Saudi Arabian Nat. Guard, 1978–79. *Publication:* (ed) Textbook of Aviation Medicine, 1978. *Recreations:* golf, ski-ing, sub-aqua. *Address:* Ruxbury Lodge, St Ann's Hill, Chertsey, Surrey KT16 9NL. *T:* Chertsey (01932) 563624. *Clubs:* Royal Air Force, Wentworth.

DHRANGADHARA, Maharaja Sriraj of Halvad-, His Highness Jhaladhipati Maharana Sriraj Meghrajji III, KCIE 1947; 45th Ruler, Head of Jhalla–Makhvan Clan; MP for Jhalavad (Gujarat State), 1967–70; *b* 3 March 1923; *s* of HH Maharaja Sriraj Ghanashyamsinhji Bava, GCIE, KCSI, late Ruler, and HH Maharani Srirajni

Anandkunvarba Saheba, Rajmata Maij; *S* father 1942, assumed government 1943 on termination of political minority; *m* 1943, Princess Brijrajkunvarba Saheba, *d* of HH the Maharaja of Marwar-Jodhpur, GCSI, GCIE, KCVO; three *s*. *Educ:* Dhrangadhara Rajmahal Shala (Palace Sch.) which was moved to UK to become Millfield Sch., Som., 1935; Heath Mount Sch.; Haileybury Coll.; St Joseph's Academy, Dehra Dun; Sivaji Military Sch., Poona; acquired administrative experience at Baroda, then at Dhrangadhra; Christ Church, Oxford, 1952–58 (Mem. High Table and Senior Common Room); Philosophy course; Ruskin Sch. of Drawing; Diploma in Social Anthropology (distinction), 1955; research in Indian Sociology, 1956–58 (BLitt Oxon.). FRAS, FRAI; Associate, Royal Historical Soc. As ruler, pursued active policy of social, agrarian and labour reforms, promulgated compulsory free primary educn, fundamental rights and local self-government; liquidated the State's debts; accepted attachment of Lakhtar, Sayla, Chuda and Muli States and the transfer of British suzerainty over them to the Dhrangadhara Darbar, 1943; Mem., Standing Cttee, Chamber of Princes, 1945–47; proposed Confedn of Saurashtra, 1945, carried it in Saurashtra States-General meeting (also Chm.), 1946; first state in W India to accept participation in Constituent Assembly of India; signed Instrument of Accession to India, 1947; also Covenant for Saurashtra; Uparajpramukh, Actg Rajpramukh and C-in-C of State Forces of United State of Saurashtra, 1948–52; proclaimed Indian constitution, 1949; Promoter and Intendant General, Consultation of Rulers of Indian States in Concord for India, 1967. Mem. Gujarat Legislative Assembly (from Dhrangadhra), Feb.–March 1967, resigned. Life Member: Indian Council of World Affairs, 1967; Indian Parly Gp, 1967; CPA, 1967; Linguistic Soc. of India; Numismatic Soc. of India; Heraldry Soc.; WWF. Perm. Pres., Srirajman (Educ.) Foundn; Pres., Rajkumar Coll., Rajkot, 1966–; Mem., Ind. Cttee, United World Colls. Patron, Bhandarkar Oriental Res. Inst. *Heir: s* Maharajkumar Shri Sodhsalji, Yuvaraj Saheb of Halvad–Dhrangadhara, *b* 22 March 1944. *Address:* Ajitnivas Palace, Dhrangadhara-Nagar, Jhalavad, Gujarat 363310, India; Dhrangadhara Bhavan, Chatuvsringi Road, Pune 41106, India; India Lodge, 108 Malcha Marg, Chanakyapuri Diplomatic Enclave, New Delhi 110021, India.

DIAMAND, Peter, Hon. CBE 1972; Artistic Adviser, Orchestre de Paris, since 1976; *b* 1913; *m* 1st, 1948, Maria Curcio, pianist (marr. diss. 1971); 2nd, Sylvia Rosenberg, violinist (marr. diss. 1979); one *s*. *Educ:* Schiller-Realgymnasium, Berlin; Berlin Univ. Studied Law and Journalism. Left Germany, 1933; became Private Sec. to Artur Schnabel, pianist. Personal Asst to Dir of Netherlands Opera, Amsterdam, 1946, subsequently Artistic Adviser until 1965; Gen. Manager of Holland Festival, 1948–65; Dir, Edinburgh Internat. Festival, 1965–78; Artistic Advr, Teatro alla Scala, Milan, 1977–78; Dir and Gen. Manager, RPO, 1978–81. Mem. Board of Netherlands Chamber Orchestra, 1955–77. Hon. LLD Edinburgh, 1972. Knight, Order of Oranje Nassau, Holland, 1959; Grosses Ehrenzeichen fuer Verdienste, Austria, 1964; Medal of Merit, Czechoslovakia, 1966; Commander Italian Republic, 1973; Officier, Ordre des Arts et des Lettres, France, 1985. *Address:* 28 Eton Court, Eton Avenue, NW3 3HJ. *T:* 0171-586 1203.

DIAMOND, family name of **Baron Diamond.**

DIAMOND, Baron *cr* 1970 (Life Peer), of the City of Gloucester; **John Diamond,** PC 1965; FCA; Chairman: Royal Commission on Distribution of Income and Wealth, 1974–79; Industry and Parliament Trust, 1976–82; Trustee, Social Democratic Party, 1981–82, Leader of SDP in House of Lords, 1982–88; *b* Leeds, 30 April 1907; *s* of Henrietta and Rev. S. Diamond, Leeds; *m*; two *s* two *d*. *Educ:* Leeds Grammar Sch. Qualified as Chartered Accountant, 1931, and commenced practice as John Diamond & Co. MP (Lab) Blackley Div. of Manchester, 1945–51, Gloucester, 1957–70; Chief Secretary to the Treasury, 1964–70 (in the Cabinet, 1968–70); formerly PPS to Minister of Works; Deputy Chm. of Cttees, House of Lords, 1974. Chm., Prime Minister's Adv. Cttee on Business Appts of Crown Servants, 1975–88. Chm. of Finance Cttee, Gen. Nursing Council, 1947–53; Dir of Sadler's Wells Trust Ltd, 1957–64; Hon. Treas., Fabian Soc., 1950–64. Hon. LLD Leeds, 1978. *Publications:* Socialism the British Way (jtly), 1948; Public Expenditure in Practice, 1975. *Recreations:* music, gardening, reading the classics. *Address:* Aynhoe, Doggetts Wood Lane, Chalfont St Giles, Bucks HP8 4TH.

DIAMOND, Anthony Edward John; QC 1974; **His Honour Judge Diamond;** a Circuit Judge, since 1990; *b* 4 Sept. 1929; *s* of late Arthur Sigismund Diamond, former Master of the Supreme Court, and of Gladys Elkah Diamond (*née* Mocatta); m 1965, Joan Margaret Gee; two *d*. *Educ:* Rugby; Corpus Christi Coll., Cambridge (MA). Served RA, 1947–49. Called to the Bar, Gray's Inn, 1953 (Bencher, 1985); practised at Bar as a specialist in commercial law, 1958–90; Head of Chambers at 4 Essex Court, EC4, 1984–90; Dep. High Court Judge, 1982–90; a Recorder, 1985–90; Judge i/c of Central London County Court Business List, 1994. Chm., Banking Act Appeals, 1980; Mem., indep. review body under colliery review procedure, 1985. *Publications:* papers on maritime law. *Recreation:* the visual arts. *Address:* 1 Cannon Place, NW3 1EH. *T:* 0171–435 6154. *Club:* Athenæum.

DIAMOND, Prof. Aubrey Lionel; Professor of Law, University of Notre Dame, and Co-Director, London Law Centre, since 1987; Emeritus Professor of Law, University of London; solicitor; *b* 28 Dec. 1923; *s* of Alfred and Millie Diamond, London; *m* 1955, Dr Eva M. Bobasch; one *s* one *d*. *Educ:* elementary schs; Central Foundation Sch., London; London Sch. of Economics (LLB, LLM; Hon. Fellow, 1984). Clerical Officer, LCC, 1941–48. Served RAF, 1943–47. Admitted a solicitor, 1951. Sen. Lectr, Law Society's Sch. of Law, 1955–57; Asst Lectr, Lectr and Reader, Law Dept, LSE, 1957–66; Prof. of Law, Queen Mary Coll., Univ. of London, 1966–71; Law Comr, 1971–76; Prof. of Law and Dir, Inst. of Advanced Legal Studies, Univ. of London, 1976–86, now Emeritus; Fellow, QMW, 1989 (Fellow, QMC, 1984). Partner in Lawford & Co., Solicitors, 1959–71 (consultant, 1986–). Part-time Chm. of Industrial Tribunals, 1984–90; Dep. Chm., Data Protection Tribunal, 1985–; Consultant, DTI, 1986–88. Member: Central London Valuation Court, 1956–73; Consumer Advisory Council, BSI, 1961–63; Council, Consumers' Assoc., 1963–71 (Vice-Pres., 1981–84); Consumer Council, 1963–66, 1967–71; Cttee on the Age of Majority, 1965–67; Council, Law Society, 1976–92. Chairman: Social Sciences and the Law Cttee, SSRC, 1977–80; Hamlyn Trust, 1977–88; Advertising Adv. Cttee, IBA, 1980–88. President: Nat. Fedn of Consumer Groups, 1977–81 (Chm., 1963–67); British Insurance Law Assoc., 1988–90; Vice-Pres., Inst. of Trading Standards Administration, 1975–. Visiting Professor: University Coll. Dar es Salaam, Univ. of E Africa, 1966–67; Law Sch., Stanford Univ., 1971; Melbourne Univ., 1977; Univ. of Virginia, 1982; Tulane Univ., 1984; Vis. teacher, LSE, 1984–93. Hon. QC 1992. Hon. MRCP 1990. Hon. DCL City, 1992. *Publications:* The Consumer, Society and the Law (with Sir Gordon Borrie), 1963 (4th edn, 1981); Introduction to Hire-Purchase Law, 1967 (2nd edn. 1971); (ed) Instalment Credit, 1970; (co-ed) Sutton and Shannon on Contracts (7th edn) 1970; Commercial and Consumer Credit: an introduction, 1982; A Review of Security Interests in Property, 1989; articles and notes in legal and medical jls and symposia. *Address:* University of Notre Dame, London Law Centre, 7 Albemarle Street, W1X 4NB. *T:* 0171–493 9002. *Club:* Reform.

DIAMOND, Prof. Derek Robin; Professor of Geography with special reference to Urban and Regional Planning, London School of Economics and Political Science, since 1982; *b* 18 May 1933; *s* of John Diamond (Baron Diamond, *qv*) and Sadie Diamond; *m* 1957, Esme Grace Passmore; one *s* one *d*. *Educ:* Oxford Univ. (MA); Northwestern Univ., Illinois (MSc). Lecturer: in Geography, 1957–65, in Town and Regional Planning, 1965–68, Glasgow Univ.; Reader in Geography, London School of Economics, 1968–82. Pres., IBG, 1994–95. Hon. MRTPI, 1989. Hon. Prof. of Human Geography, Inst. of Geography, Beijing, 1990. Editor: Progress in Planning, 1973–; Geoforum, 1974–93. *Publications:* Regional Policy Evaluation, 1983; Infrastructure and Industrial Costs in British Industry, 1989; Evaluating the Effectiveness of Land Use Planning, 1992. *Recreation:* philately. *Address:* 9 Ashley Drive, Walton-on-Thames, Surrey KT12 1JL. *T:* Walton-on-Thames (01923) 223280. *Club:* Geographical.

DIAMOND, (Peter) Michael, MA, FMA; Director, Birmingham City Museums and Art Gallery, since 1980; *b* 5 Aug. 1942; *s* of late William Howard and Dorothy Gladys Diamond; *m* 1968, Anne Marie; one *s* one *d*. *Educ:* Bristol Grammar Sch.; Queens' Coll., Cambridge (BA Fine Art 1964, MA 1966). Dip. of Museums Assoc. 1968, FMA 1980. Sheffield City Art Galleries: Art Asst, 1965; Keeper, Mappin Art Gall., 1967; Dep. Dir, 1969; City Arts and Museums Officer, Bradford, 1976. Chairman: Gp of Dirs of Museums, 1985–89; Public Art Commns Agency, 1987–88. Member, Executive Committee: Yorks Arts Assoc., 1977–80; Yorks Sculpture Park, 1978– (Chm., 1978–82); Pres., Yorks Fedn of Museums, 1978–80; Member: Crafts Council, 1980–84; Council, Museums Assoc., 1987–90; Board, Museums Training Inst., 1990–93. Mem. Council, Aston Univ., 1983–92. FRSA 1990. Hon. DSc Aston, 1993. *Publications:* numerous exhibition catalogues incl. Victorian Paintings, 1968; Art and Industry in Sheffield 1850–75, 1975; (contrib.) Manual of Curatorship, 1984 and 1992; articles in Museums Jl. *Address:* Birmingham City Museums and Art Gallery, Chamberlain Square, Birmingham B3 3DH.

DIBBEN, Michael Alan Charles; HM Diplomatic Service; Foreign and Commonwealth Office, since 1995; *b* 19 Sept. 1943; *s* of Lt-Col Alan Frank Dibben and Eileen Beatrice Dibben (*née* Donoghue). *Educ:* Dulwich College. With Ottoman Bank, London, 1961–64; CRO 1964; Min. of Overseas Develt, 1965; Protocol Dept, FCO, 1966; served Montreal, Nassau, Stuttgart, Port of Spain, Douala; First Sec., 1981; Nuclear Energy Dept, FCO, 1981–83; Munich and Hamburg, 1983–87; Inf. Dept, FCO, 1987–90; Ambassador to Paraguay, 1991–95. Mem., Horners' Co. *Recreations:* reading, walking, golf, classical music. *Address:* c/o Foreign and Commonwealth Office, King Charles Street, SW1A 2AH. *Clubs:* National Liberal, City Livery.

DIBDIN, Michael; crime writer; *b* 21 March 1947; *s* of Frederick John Dibdin and Peigi (*née* Taylor); *m* 1st, 1971, Benita Mitbrodt (marr. diss. 1986); one *d*; 2nd, 1987, Sybil Sheringham (marr. diss. 1995); one *d*. *Educ:* Univ of Sussex (BA English Lit.); Univ. of Alberta (MA). Gold Dagger, CWA, 1988; Grand Prix de Littérature Policière (France), 1994. *Publications:* The Last Sherlock Holmes Story, 1978; A Rich Full Death, 1986; Ratking, 1988; The Tryst, 1989; Vendetta, 1990; Dirty Tricks, 1991; Cabal, 1992; The Dying of the Light, 1993; (ed) The Picador Book of Crime Writing, 1993; Dead Lagoon, 1994; Dark Spectre, 1995. *Recreations:* music, travel. *Address:* c/o Pat Kavanagh, Peters Fraser & Dunlop, 503/4 The Chambers, Chelsea Harbour, SW10 0XF. *T:* 0171–344 1000.

DIBELA, Sir Kingsford, GCMG 1983 (CMG 1978); Governor-General of Papua New Guinea, 1983–89; *b* 16 March 1932; *s* of Norman Dibela and Edna Dalauna; *m* 1952, Winifred Tomolarina; two *s* four *d*. *Educ:* St Paul's Primary Sch., Dogura. Qualified as primary school teacher; teacher, 1949–63. Pres., Weraura Local Govt Council, 1963–77; MP, PNG, 1975–82; Speaker of Nat. Parlt, 1977–80. *Recreations:* golf, cricket. *Address:* c/o Government House, PO Box 79, Port Moresby, Papua New Guinea. *T:* 214466 (BH). *Club:* Port Moresby Golf.

DICE, Brian Charles; Chief Executive, British Waterways Board, since 1986; *b* 2 Sept. 1936; *s* of late Frederic Charles Dice; *m* 1965, Gwendoline Tazeena Harrison; two *d*. *Educ:* Clare College, Cambridge; Middle Temple. Cadbury Schweppes, 1960–86, Director, 1979; Managing Director, Schweppes, 1983. *Address:* Stratton Wood, Beaconsfield, Bucks HP9 1HS.

DICK, Air Vice-Marshal (Alan) David, CB 1978; CBE 1968; AFC 1957; FRAeS 1975; *b* 7 Jan. 1924; *s* of late Brig. Alan MacDonald Dick, CBE, IMS(Retd), and Muriel Angela Dick; *m* 1951, Ann Napier Jeffcoat, *d* of late Col A. C. Jeffcoat, CB, CMG, DSO; two *s* two *d*. *Educ:* Fettes; Aitchison Coll., Lahore; King's Coll., Cambridge. MA. Joined RAF, 1942; SE Asia Command, 1943–45; Fighter Comd, 1945–46. Central Flying Sch., 1950–53; Empire Test Pilots Sch., 1953; Test Pilot, A&AEE, 1954–57; Fighter Comd, 1957–60; RAF Staff Coll., 1960 63; OC 207 Sqdn, Bomber Comd, 1963–64; Supt of Flying, A&AEE, 1964–68; Strike Comd, 1968–69; IDC 1970; MoD Air Staff, 1971–74; Comdt, A&AEE, 1974–75; Dep. Controller Aircraft/C, MoD(PE), 1975–78. Sec., British Assoc. of Occupational Therapists, 1979–84. *Recreations:* photography, walking, bird watching. *Club:* Royal Air Force.

DICK, Gavin Colquhoun; Vice-Chairman, Mobile Radio Training Trust, since 1990; *b* 6 Sept. 1928; *s* of late John Dick and Catherine MacAuslan Henderson; *m* 1952, Elizabeth Frances, *e d* of late Jonathan Hutchinson; two *d*. *Educ:* Hamilton Academy; Glasgow Univ. (MA 1950); Balliol Coll., Oxford (Snell Exhibnr, 1949, MA 1957); SOAS (Cert. in Turkish, 1986). National Service, 3rd RTR (Lieut), 1952–54. Asst Principal, BoT, 1954, Principal, 1958; UK Trade Comr, Wellington, NZ, 1961–64; Asst Sec., 1967; Jt Sec., Review Cttee on Overseas Representation, 1968–69; Under-Sec., 1975–84, Dept of Industry, 1981–84. Consultant: Office of Telecommunications, 1984–87; DTI Radiocommunications Div., 1987–89. Bd Mem., English Industrial Estates Corp., 1982–84. Governor, Coll. of Air Training (Hamble), 1975–80. Hon. Pres., Anglo–Turkish Assoc. of Academics and Professionals, 1995. *Recreation:* words. *Address:* Fell Cottage, Bayley's Hill, Sevenoaks, Kent TN14 6HS. *T:* Sevenoaks (01732) 453704. *Club:* United Oxford & Cambridge University.

DICK, Prof. George (Williamson Auchinvole), MD (Edinburgh), DSc (Edinburgh), FRCPE, FRCP, FRCPath, MPH (Johns Hopkins); FIBMS; Emeritus Professor of Pathology, University of London; *b* 14 Aug. 1914; *s* of Rev. David Auchinvole Dick and Blanche Hay Spence; *m* 1941, Brenda Marian Cook; two *s* two *d*. *Educ:* Royal High Sch., Edinburgh; Univ. of Edinburgh; The Johns Hopkins Univ., Baltimore, Md, USA. BSc 1939 (1st Cl. Hons Path.); Vans Dunlop Scholar; Buchanan Medal; MD (Gold Medal) 1949. Asst Pathologist, Royal Infirmary, Edinburgh, 1939–40; Pathologist, RAMC, 1940–46; OC Medical Div. (Lt-Col) (EA Comd), 1945; Pathologist, Colonial Med. Res. Service, 1946–51; Rockefeller Foundn Fellow (Internat. Health Div.), Rockefeller Inst., New York and Johns Hopkins Univ., 1947–48; Res. Fellow, Sch. of Hygiene and Public Health, Johns Hopkins Univ., Baltimore, Md, 1949–50; Scientific Staff, MRC, 1951–54; Prof. of Microbiology, QUB, 1955–65; Dir, Bland-Sutton Inst. and Sch. of Pathology, Middlesex Hosp. Med. Sch., Univ. of London, 1966–73; Bland-Sutton Prof. of Pathology, Univ. of London, 1966–73; Asst Dir, BPMF, and Postgraduate Dean, SW Thames RHA, 1973–81; Prof. of Pathology, Univ. of London, and Hon. Lectr and Hon. Consultant, Inst. of Child Health, 1973–81. Examnr, Med. Schools in UK, Dublin, Nairobi, Kampala, Riyadh, Jeddah; Assessor, HNC and CMS, S London Coll. Pres., Inst. of Med. Laboratory Technology, 1966–76; Member: Mid Downs Health Authority, W Sussex, 1981–84; Jt

Bd of Clinical Nursing Studies, 1982–85; Chm., DHSS/Regl Librarians Jt Wking Party. Pres., Rowhook Med. Soc., 1975–. Treasurer, RCPath, 1973–78; Member: RSM; BMA; Internat. Epidemiol. Soc.; Path. Soc. GB and Ireland; Soc. of Scholars, Johns Hopkins Univ., 1979; Alpha Chapter, Delta Omega Hon. Soc., USA, 1981. Hon. FLA. Freeman, City of London, 1981; Liveryman, Worshipful Co. of Apothecaries, 1981. Singapore Gold Medal, Edinburgh Univ., 1952 and 1958; Laurence Biedl Prize for Rehabilitation, 1958; Sims Woodhead Medal, 1976; Outstanding Alumnus in Public Health award, Johns Hopkins Univ., 1986; Hero of Public Health, Johns Hopkins Univ. Sch. of Hygiene and Public Health, 1992. *Publications:* Immunisation, 1978, re-issued as Practical Immunisation, 1986; Immunology of Infectious Diseases, 1979; Health on Holiday and other Travels, 1982; papers on yellow fever, Uganda S, Zika and other arbor viruses, Mengovirus, Marburgvirus, poliomyelitis; hepatitis (MHV); EHA (rabies) virus; smallpox, poliomyelitis, whooping cough and combined vaccines; vaccine reactions, immunisation policies, subacute sclerosing panencephalitis; multiple sclerosis, travel, etc. *Address:* Waterland, Rowhook, Horsham RH12 3PX. *T:* Slinfold (01403) 790549.

DICK, Iain Charles M.; *see* Mackay-Dick, I. C.

DICK, James Brownlee, CB 1977; MA, BSc, FInstP, FCIBS, FIOB; consultant; *b* 19 July 1919; *s* of James Brownlee Dick and Matilda Forrest; *m* 1944, Audrey Moira Shinn; two *s*. *Educ:* Wishaw High Sch.; Glasgow Univ. Royal Naval Scientific Service, 1940. Building Research Station, later Building Research Establishment: Physics Div., 1947; Head of User Requirements Div., 1960; Head of Production Div., 1963; Asst Dir, 1964; Dep. Dir, 1969; Dir, 1969–79. Pres., Internat. Council for Building Res., 1974–77. *Publications:* papers in professional and scientific journals. *Address:* 10 Stanier Rise, Berkhamsted, Herts HP4 1SD. *T:* Berkhamsted (01442) 862580.

DICK, John Kenneth, CBE 1972; FCA, FRSA; Director, N. M. Rothschild & Sons Ltd, 1978–90; *b* 5 April 1913; *s* of late John Dick and Beatrice May Dick (*née* Chitty); *m* 1942, Pamela Madge, 3rd *d* of late Maurice Salmon and Katie Salmon (*née* Joseph); two *s* (and one *s* decd). *Educ:* Sedbergh. Qual. with Mann Judd & Co., Chartered Accountants, 1936; Partner, Mann Judd & Co., 1947; Mitchell Cotts Group Ltd: Jt Man. Dir, 1957; Sole Man. Dir, 1959–78; Dep. Chm., 1964; Chm., 1966–78; Chm., Hume Holdings Ltd, 1975–80. Mem., Commonwealth Develt Corp., 1967–80; Gov., City of London Soc.; Member: British Nat. Export Cttee, 1968–71; Covent Gdn Mkt Authority, 1976–82; Chm., Cttee for Middle East Trade, 1968–71; Pres., Middle East Assoc., 1976–81 (a Vice-Pres., 1970–76). *Recreation:* golf. *Address:* Overbye, Church Street, Cobham, Surrey KT11 3EG. *T:* (office) Cobham (Surrey) (01932) 867770; (home) (01932) 864393. *Club:* Caledonian.

DICK, Kay; writer; *b* 29 July 1915; *o d* of Mrs Kate Frances Dick. *Educ:* Geneva, Switzerland; Lycée Français de Londres, S Kensington. Worked in publishing and bookselling; edited (as Edward Lane) 13 issues of magazine, The Windmill. *Publications: fiction:* By the Lake, 1949; Young Man, 1951; An Affair of Love, 1953; Solitaire, 1958; Sunday, 1962; They, 1977 (South-East Arts Literature Prize, 1977); The Shelf, 1984; *non-fiction:* Pierrot, 1960; Ivy and Stevie, 1971; Friends and Friendship, 1974; *edited:* London's Hour: as seen through the eyes of the fire-fighters, 1942; Late Joys at the Players Theatre, 1943; The Mandrake Root, 1946, At Close of Eve, 1947, The Uncertain Element, 1950 (three vols of strange stories); Bizarre and Arabesque (anthology from Edgar Allan Poe), 1967; Writers at Work, 1972. *Recreations:* friends, gardening, walking the dog. *Address:* Flat 5, 9 Arundel Terrace, Brighton, East Sussex BN2 1GA. *T:* Brighton (01273) 697243.

DICK, Air Vice-Marshal Ronald, CB 1988; writer and lecturer in air power history; Head of British Defence Staff, Washington, and Defence Attaché, 1984–88, retired; *b* Newcastle upon Tyne, 18 Oct. 1931; *s* of Arthur John Craig Dick and Lilian Dick; *m* 1955, Pauline Lomax; one *s* one *d*. *Educ:* Beckenham and Penge County Grammar Sch.; RAF Coll., Cranwell. Commnd 1952; served, 1953–69: No 64 Fighter Sqdn; Flying Instr, No 5 FTS; Central Flying Sch. Examg Wing and Type Sqdn; Flt Comdr, 3615th Pilot Trng Sqdn, USAF, and No IX Bomber Sqdn; Trng (Operational) 2a (RAF), MoD; RAF Staff Coll., Bracknell; Ops B2 (RAF), MoD; Jt Services Staff Coll.; OC No IX Bomber Sqdn, RAF Akrotiri, 1970–72; Staff, RCDS, 1972–74; PSO to Dep. SACEUR, SHAPE, 1974–77; OC RAF Honington, 1978–80; Air Attaché, Washington, DC, 1980–83; Dir of Organization and Estabts, 1983–84, of Organization and Quartering, 1984, RAF. Internat. Fellow, Nat. Air and Space Mus., Smithsonian Instn, 1988–91; Vis. Prof. in Air Power History, USAF Air Univ., Ala, 1992–94. Mem., Bd of Trustees, Amer. Airpower Heritage Foundn, 1987–94. Consulting Editor, Air & Space Smithsonian Magazine, 1990–. FRAeS 1987. Wright Jubilee Aerobatic Trophy Winner, 1956. *Recreations:* wild life conservation, bird watching, private flying, military history, opera. *Address:* Cherrywood, 3011 Jenny Lane, Woodbridge, VA 22192, USA. *Club:* Royal Air Force.

DICK-LAUDER, Sir Piers Robert; *see* Lauder.

DICKEN, Air Vice-Marshal Michael John Charles Worwood, CB 1990; Private Secretary to Lord Mayor of London, since 1992; Air Officer Administration and Air Officer Commanding Support Group, RAF Support Command, 1989–92; *b* 13 July 1935; *s* of late Air Cdre Charles Worwood Dicken, CBE and Olive Eva Dicken (*née* Eustice); *m* 1962, Jennifer Ann Dore; two *d* (one *s* decd). *Educ:* Sherborne; St Peter's Hall, Oxford; RAF College, Cranwell. Commissioned 1958; served Cyprus, Borneo and UK to 1970; RAF Staff College, 1971; Asst Defence Advr, Canberra, 1972–74; RAF Uxbridge, 1975–76; NDC, 1976; RAF Coningsby, 1977–79; Staff Coll. Directing Staff and Dir, Comd and Staff Training, 1980–82; OC RAF Hereford, 1982–83; HQ 1 Gp, 1984–85; Dir of Personnel Management (Airmen), 1986–88. Hon. Freeman, Chartered Secretaries' and Administrators' Co., 1989; Liveryman, Scriveners' Co., 1991–. *Recreations:* golf, gliding, light aircraft, field sports. *Club:* Royal Air Force.

DICKENS, Prof. Arthur Geoffrey, CMG 1974; FBA 1966; Director, Institute of Historical Research and Professor of History in the University of London, 1967–77, now Emeritus Professor; *b* 6 July 1910; *er s* of Arthur James Dickens and Gertrude Helen Dickens (*née* Grasby), both of Hull, Yorks; *m* 1936, Molly (*d* 1978), *er d* of Walter Bygott; two *s*. *Educ:* Hymers Coll., Hull; Magdalen Coll., Oxford. Demy, 1929–32, Senior Demy, 1932–33, of Magdalen Coll.; BA with 1st Class Hons in Mod. Hist., 1932; MA 1936; DLit London, 1965. Fellow and Tutor of Keble Coll., Oxford, 1933–49, Hon. Fellow, 1971; Oxford Univ. Lecturer in Sixteenth Century English History, 1939–49. Served in RA, 1940–45; demobilised as Staff Capt. G. F. Grant Prof. of History, Univ. of Hull, 1949–62; Dep. Principal and Dean of Faculty of Arts, 1950–53; Pro-Vice-Chancellor, 1959–62; Prof. of History, King's Coll., Univ. of London, 1962–67; FKC, 1977. Mem. Senate and Academic Council, Univ. of London, 1974–77. Pres., Ecclesiastical History Soc., 1966–68. Member: Advisory Council on Public Records, 1968–76; Adv. Council on Export of Works of Art, 1968–76; Records Cttee, Essex CC, 1965–71; History of Medicine Adv. Panel, Wellcome Trust, 1974–79; Steering Cttee, Business History Unit, LSE, 1978–85. Chm., Victoria History of the Counties of England, 1967–68. Sec., 1967–73, Chm. and Gen. Sec., 1973–79, British Nat. Cttee of Historical Sciences; Foreign Sec., British Acad., 1969–79 (Vice-Pres., 1971–72); Vice-Pres., British Record Soc., 1978–80; Hon. Vice-President: RHistS, 1977– (Vice-Pres., 1969–73); Historical Assoc., 1977– (Pres., Central London Branch, 1982–); Sec., Anglo-German Group of Historians, 1969–76; Pres., German History Soc., 1979–89. Editor, Bulletin of the Inst. of Historical Research, 1967–77. Visiting Prof., Univ. of Rochester, NY, 1953–54; Birkbeck Lectr, Trinity Coll., Cambridge, 1969–70. Fellow, 1954, Vis. Prof., 1972, Folger Library, Washington, DC; Strassberg Vis. Prof., Univ. of Western Australia, 1981; Lectures: James Ford Special, Univ. of Oxford, 1974; Neale, UCL, 1977; Bithell, Inst. of Germanic Studies, 1978; Stenton, Reading, 1980. Hon. Professorial Fellow, Univ. of Wales, Aberystwyth, 1979–. Governor, Highgate Sch., 1976–86. FRHistS 1947; FSA 1962. Medlicott Medal, Historical Assoc., 1985 (first recipient). Hon. DLitt: Kent, 1976; Hull, 1977; Leicester, 1978; Sheffield, 1978; Hon. LittD Liverpool, 1977. Comdr's Cross, Order of Merit, Fed. Repub. of Germany, 1980. *Publications:* Lübeck Diary, 1947; The Register of Butley Priory, 1951; The East Riding of Yorkshire, 1954; Lollards and Protestants, 1959; Thomas Cromwell, 1959; Tudor Treatises, 1960; Clifford Letters, 1962; The English Reformation, 1964, 2nd edn 1989; Reformation and Society in 16th Century Europe, 1966; Martin Luther and the Reformation, 1967; (ed jtly) The Reformation in England to the Accession of Elizabeth I, 1967; The Counter-Reformation, 1968; The Age of Humanism and Reformation, 1972, UK edn 1977; The German Nation and Martin Luther, 1974; (ed and contrib.) The Courts of Europe, 1977; Reformation Studies, 1982; (with J. M. Tonkin) The Reformation in Historical Thought, 1985; Late Monasticism and the Reformation, 1994; (jtly) Erasmus the Reformer, 1994; (Gen. Editor) Documents of Modern History Series, 1966–; (Gen. Editor) A New History of England Series, 1975–; about 60 articles in: English Historical Review, Church Quarterly Review, Yorkshire Archæological Jl, Cambridge Antiquarian Jl, Bodleian Library Record, Archiv für Reformationsgeschichte, Britain and the Netherlands, Victoria County History, York, Trans Royal Hist. Soc., Jl of Ecclesiastical History, Archæological Jl, Encycl. Britannica, Chambers's Encycl., etc; *Festschrift:* Reformation Principle and Practice: essays in honour of A. G. Dickens, ed P. N. Brooks, 1980. *Recreations:* travel, 20th Century British art. *Address:* 401 Carole House, Oldfield Estate, Fitzroy Road, NW1 8UA.

DICKENS, James McCulloch York, OBE 1991; Chief Personnel Officer, Agricultural and Food Research Council, 1983–91; *b* 4 April 1931; *e s* of A. Y. Dickens and I. Dickens (*née* McCulloch); *m* 1st, 1955, M. J. Grieve (marr. diss. 1965); 2nd, 1969, Mrs Carolyn Casey. *Educ:* Shawlands Academy, Glasgow; Newbattle Abbey Coll., Dalkeith, Midlothian; Ruskin Coll. and St Catherine's Coll., Oxford. Administrative Asst, National Coal Board, 1956–58; Industrial Relations Officer, National Coal Board, 1958–65; Management Consultant, 1965–66; MP (Lab) West Lewisham, 1966–70; Asst Dir of Manpower, Nat. Freight Corp., 1970–76; National Water Council: Asst Dir (Ind. Rel.), Manpower Services Div., 1976–80; Dir of Manpower, 1980–82; Dir of Manpower and Trng, 1982–83. Trustee, Citizens Income Trust, 1995. *Recreations:* music, theatre, the countryside. *Address:* 64 Woodbastwick Road, Sydenham, SE26 5LH. *T:* 0181–778 7446.

DICKENSON, Sir Aubrey Fiennes T.; *see* Trotman-Dickenson.

DICKENSON, Lt-Col Charles Royal, CMG 1965; Postmaster-General of Rhodesia, 1964–68, retired; *b* 17 June 1907; *e s* of Charles Roland and Gertrude Dickenson; *m* 1950, Hendrika Jacoba Margaretha Schippers; two *d*. *Educ:* Shaftesbury Grammar Sch., Dorset. Entered British Post Office as Engineering Apprentice, 1923; British Post Office HQ, 1932–39. Served War in Royal Signals, 1939–45, attaining rank of Lieut-Col. BPO NW Regional HQ as Asst Controller of Telecommunications, 1945–47; BPO HQ, London, 1947–50; loaned to S Rhodesia Govt, 1950–54; Controller of Telecommunications. Ministry of Posts, Federation of Rhodesia and Nyasaland, 1954–57; Regional Controller for N Rhodesia, Fedn of Rhodesia and Nyasaland, 1957–61; Dep. Postmaster-Gen., Rhodesia and Nyasaland, 1961–62; Postmaster-Gen., Rhodesia and Nyasaland, 1962–63. Hon. Mem., S Africa Inst. of Electronic and Radio Engineers (Hon. M(SA) IERE), 1966. ICD, OLM, Rhodesia, 1979. *Recreations:* growing orchids, photography. *Address:* 4600 Gatlin Oaks Lane, Orlando, FL 32806, USA.

DICKENSON, Joseph Frank, PhD, CEng, FIMechE; Director, North Staffordshire Polytechnic, 1969–86, retired; *b* 26 Nov. 1924; *s* of late Frank Brand Dickenson and late Maud Dickenson (*née* Beharrell); *m* 1948, Sheila May Kingston; two *s* one *d*. *Educ:* College of Technology, Hull. BSc (1st Cl. Hons) Engrg, PhD (both London). Engrg apprenticeship and Jun. Engr's posts, 1939–52; Lectr and Sen. Lectr, Hull Coll. of Technology, 1952–59; Head of Dept of Mechanical Engrg and later Vice-Principal, Lanchester Coll. of Technology, 1960–64; Principal, Leeds Coll. of Technology, 1964–69. *Recreation:* motor cars. *Address:* 5 Byron Walk Mews, Harrogate HG2 0LQ. *T:* Harrogate (01423) 525899.

DICKIE, Brian James; Artistic Counsellor, Opéra de Nice, since 1994; *b* 23 July 1941; *s* of late Robert Kelso Dickie, OBE and Harriet Elizabeth (*née* Riddell); *m* 1st, 1968, Victoria Teresa Sheldon (*née* Price); two *s* one *d*; 2nd, 1989, Nancy Gustafson. *Educ:* Haileybury; Trinity Coll., Dublin. Admin. Asst, Glyndebourne Opera, 1962–66; Administrator, Glyndebourne Touring Opera, 1967–81; Glyndebourne Festival Opera: Opera Manager, 1970–81; Gen. Administrator, 1981–89. Artistic Dir, Wexford Fest., 1967–73; Artistic Advr, Théâtre Musical de Paris, 1981–87; Gen. Dir, Canadian Opera Co., 1989–93. Mem. Bd, Opera America, 1991–. Chm., London Choral Soc., 1978–85; Vice-Chm., TNC, 1980–85 (Chm., TNC Opera Cttee, 1976–85); Vice-Pres., Theatrical Management Assoc., 1983–85. *Address:* 9 rue de la Terrasse, 06300 Nice, France; 405 Edgemere Way North, Naples, FL 33999, USA. *T:* (813) 4342682. *Club:* Garrick.

DICKINS, Basil Gordon, CBE 1952 (OBE 1945); BSc, ARCS, DIC, PhD; Deputy Controller of Guided Weapons, Ministry of Technology, 1966–68; *b* 1 July 1908; *s* of late Basil Dickins; *m* 1st, 1935, Molly Aileen (*d* 1969), *d* of late H. Walters Reburn; 2nd, 1971, Edith, *widow* of Warren Parkinson. *Educ:* Royal Coll. of Science, London. Royal Aircraft Establishment, 1932; Air Min., 1936, later Min. of Aircraft Production; Head of Operational Research Section, HQ Bomber Command, 1941; Asst Scientific Adviser, Air Ministry, 1945; Dir of Tech. Personnel Administration, Min. of Supply, 1948; Dep. Scientific Adviser to Air Ministry, 1952; Dir of Guided Weapons Research and Development, Min. of Supply, 1956; Dir-Gen. of Atomic Weapons, Min. of Supply, 1959; Dir-Gen. of Guided Weapons, Ministry of Aviation, 1962. *Publications:* papers in Proc. Royal Society and Reports and Memoranda of Aeronautical Research Council. *Address:* 5 Batisse de la Mielle, Route de la Haule, St Brelade, Jersey.

DICKINS, Mark Frederick Hakon S.; *see* Scrase-Dickins.

DICKINSON, family name of **Baron Dickinson.**

DICKINSON, 2nd Baron *cr* 1930, of Painswick; **Richard Clavering Hyett Dickinson;** *b* 2 March 1926; *s* of late Hon. Richard Sebastian Willoughby Dickinson, DSO (*o s* of 1st Baron) and of May Southey, *d* of late Charles Lovemore, Melsetter, Cape Province, S Africa; *S* grandfather, 1943; *m* 1st, 1957, Margaret Ann (marr. diss. 1980), *e d* of late Brig. G. R. McMeekan, CB, DSO, OBE; two *s*; 2nd, 1980, Rita Doreen Moir. *Heir: s* Hon. Martin Hyett Dickinson [*b* 30 Jan. 1961; *m* 1995, Caroline, *d* of Nigel Edwards]. *Address:* Painswick House, Painswick, Glos GL6 6TH. *T:* Painswick (01452) 813646.

See also Very Rev. H. G. Dickinson, Hon. P. M. de B. Dickinson.

DICKINSON, Anne; *see* Dickinson, V. A.

DICKINSON, Basil Philip Harriman; Under Secretary, Department of the Environment (formerly Ministry of Transport), 1959–74; *b* 10 Sept. 1916; *yr s* of F. H. and I. F. Dickinson; *m* 1941, Beryl Farrow; three *s* one *d*. *Educ:* Cheltenham Coll.; Oriel Coll., Oxford. *Address:* c/o Child & Co., 1 Fleet Street, EC4Y 1BD.

DICKINSON, Sir Ben; *see* Dickinson, Sir S. B.

DICKINSON, Brian Henry Baron; Under Secretary, Food Safety Group, Ministry of Agriculture, Fisheries and Food, since 1989; *b* 2 May 1940; *s* of Alan Edgar Frederic Dickinson and Ethel Mary Dickinson (*née* McWilliam); *m* 1971, Sheila Minto Lloyd. *Educ:* Leighton Park School, Reading; Balliol College, Oxford (BA). Ministry of Agriculture, Fisheries and Food, 1964; Dept of Prices and Consumer Protection, 1975; MAFF, 1978; Under Sec., 1984; Principal Finance Officer, 1986. *Recreation:* bird-watching. *Address:* Ministry of Agriculture, Fisheries and Food, Ergon House, 17 Smith Square, SW1P 3JR. *T:* 0171–238 6429.

DICKINSON, Prof. Christopher John, DM, FRCP; ARCO; Professor of Medicine and Chairman, Department of Medicine, St Bartholomew's Hospital Medical College, 1975–92, now Professor Emeritus; *b* 1 Feb. 1927; *s* of Reginald Ernest Dickinson and Margaret Dickinson (*née* Petty); *m* 1953, Elizabeth Patricia Farrell; two *s* two *d*. *Educ:* Berkhamsted School; Oxford University (MA, MSc, DM); University College Hospital Medical College. FRCP 1968. Junior med. posts, UCH, 1953–54; RAMC (Junior Med. Specialist), 1955–56; Registrar and Research Fellow, Middlesex Hosp., 1957–60; Rockefeller Travelling Fellow, Cleveland Clinic, USA, 1960–61; Lectr, then Sen. Lectr and Consultant, UCH and Med. Sch., 1961–75. R. Samuel McLoughlin Vis. Prof., McMaster Univ., Canada, 1970; King Edward Fund Vis. Fellow, NZ, 1972. Sec., European Soc. for Clinical Investigation, 1969–72; Censor, 1978–80, Senior Censor and Vice-Pres., 1982–83, Croonian Lectr, 1986, RCP; Chairman: Med. Research Soc., 1983–87; Assoc. of Professors of Medicine, 1983–87; Mem., MRC, 1986–90. ARCO 1987. *Publications:* Electrophysiological Technique, 1950; Clinical Pathology Data, 1951, 2nd edn 1957; (jtly) Clinical Physiology, 1959, 5th edn 1984; Neurogenic Hypertension, 1965; A Computer Model of Human Respiration, 1977; (jtly) Software for Educational Computing, 1980; Neurogenic Hypertension, 1991; papers on hypertension and respiratory physiology. *Recreations:* theatre, opera, playing the organ. *Address:* Wolfson Institute of Preventive Medicine, Charterhouse Square, EC1M 6BQ. *T:* 0171–982 6219; Griffin Cottage, 57 Belsize Lane, NW3 5AU. *T:* 0171–431 1845. *Club:* Garrick.

DICKINSON, Sir Harold (Herbert), Kt 1975; Director: Development Finance Corporation Ltd, 1979; Australian Fixed Trusts Ltd, 1979; Chairman, AFT Property Co. Ltd, 1980; *b* 27 Feb. 1917; *s* of late William James Dickinson and Barwon Venus Clarke; *m* 1946, Elsie May Smith; two *d*. *Educ:* Singleton Public Sch.; Tamworth High Sch.; Univ. of Sydney (LLB, 1st Cl. Hons). Barrister-at-Law. Served War, 2nd AIF HQ 22 Inf. Bde, 1940–45 (despatches); Japanese POW (Sgt). Dept of Lands, NSW, 1933–40; NSW Public Service Bd, 1946–60: Sec. and Sen. Inspector, 1949–60; Chief Exec. Officer, Prince Henry Hosp., 1960–63; NSW Public Service Bd: Mem., 1963–70; Dep. Chm., 1970–71; Chm., 1971–79. Hon. Mem., NSW Univs Bd, 1967–71; Hon. Dir, Prince Henry, Prince of Wales, Eastern Suburbs Teaching Hosps, 1965–75, Chm. of Dirs, 1975; Governor, NSW Coll. of Law, 1972–77. *Publications:* contribs to administration jls. *Recreation:* sailing. *Address:* 649 Old South Head Road, Rose Bay North, NSW 2030, Australia. *T:* 3717475. *Clubs:* Union, Rotary (Sydney).

DICKINSON, Prof. Harry Thomas, DLitt; FRHistS; Richard Lodge Professor of British History, University of Edinburgh, since 1980; *b* 9 March 1939; *s* of Joseph Dickinson and Elizabeth Stearman Dickinson (*née* Warriner); *m* 1961, Jennifer Elizabeth Galtry; one *s* one *d*. *Educ:* Gateshead Grammar Sch.; Durham Univ. (BA 1960, DipEd 1961, MA 1963); Newcastle Univ. (PhD 1968); DLitt Edinburgh 1986. History Master, Washington Grammar Sch., 1961–64; Earl Grey Fellow, Newcastle Univ., 1964–66; Asst Lectr, Lectr and Reader, Edinburgh Univ., 1966–80. Fulbright Award, 1973; Huntington Library Fellowship, 1973; Folger Shakespeare Library Sen. Fellowship, 1973; Winston Churchill Meml Trust Travelling Fellowship, 1980; Leverhulme Award, 1986–87; William Andrews Clark Library Fellow, 1987. Vis. Prof., Nanjing Univ., 1980, 1983, Concurrent Prof. of Hist., 1987–; Anstey Meml Lectr, Kent Univ., 1989; Vis. Lectr to USA, Japan, France, Czechoslovakia and Germany; Scottish Universities Summer School: Dean, 1979–85; Assoc. Dean of Arts (Postgrad. Studies), 1992–. Acad. Sponsor, Scotland's Cultural Heritage, 1984–91; Mem., Marshall Aid Commemoration Commn, 1986–; Specialist Advr, CNAA, 1987–93 (Mem., Cttee on Humanities, 1990–93), Auditor, Quality Assurance Gp, Higher Educn Quality Council, 1992–; Mem., Hist. Panel, UFC Res. Assessment Exercise, 1992. Mem., Council, HA, 1982– (Chm. of Publications, 1991–); Vice-Pres., RHistS, 1991–95 (Mem., Council, 1986–90). Editor, History, 1993–; Mem. Editl Bds, Nineteenth Century Short Title Catalogue and Nineteenth Century Microfiche Series. *Publications:* (ed) The Correspondence of Sir James Clavering, 1967; Bolingbroke, 1970; Walpole and the Whig Supremacy, 1973; (ed) Politics and Literature in the Eighteenth Century, 1974; Liberty and Property, 1977; (ed) The Political Works of Thomas Spence, 1982; British Radicalism and the French Revolution 1789–1815, 1985; Caricatures and the Constitution 1760–1832, 1986; (ed) Britain and the French Revolution 1789–1815, 1989; The Politics of the People in Eighteenth Century Britain, 1995; pamphlets, essays, articles and reviews. *Recreations:* films, watching sports. *Address:* 44 Viewforth Terrace, Edinburgh EH10 4LJ. *T:* 0131–229 1379.

DICKINSON, Very Rev. Hugh Geoffrey; Dean of Salisbury, since 1986; *b* 17 Nov. 1929; *s* of late Hon. Richard Sebastian Willoughby Dickinson, DSO (*o s* of 1st Baron Dickinson) and of May Southey, *d* of late Charles Lovemore; *m* 1963, Jean Marjorie Storey; one *s* one *d*. *Educ:* Westminster School (KS); Trinity Coll., Oxford (MA, DipTh); Cuddesdon Theol Coll. Deacon 1956, priest 1957; Curate of Melksham, Wilts, 1956–58; Chaplain: Trinity Coll., Cambridge, 1958–63; Winchester College, 1963–67; Bishop's Adviser for Adult Education, Diocese of Coventry, 1969–77; Vicar of St Michael's, St Albans, 1977–86. *Recreations:* woodturning, fishing, gardening. *Address:* The Deanery, 7 The Close, Salisbury, Wilts SP1 2EF.

See also Hon. P. M. de B. Dickinson.

DICKINSON, Prof. Hugh Gordon; Sherardian Professor of Botany, Oxford, since 1991; *b* 5 Aug. 1944; *s* of Reginald Gordon Dickinson and Jean Hartley Dickinson; *m* 1980, Alana Gillian Fairbrother; one *s* one *d*. *Educ:* St Lawrence Coll., Ramsgate; Univ. of Birmingham (BSc, PhD, DSc). Postdoctoral Fellow, UCL, 1969–72; University of Reading: Lectr, 1972–79; Reader, 1979–85; Prof. of Plant Cell Genetics, 1985–91. *Publications:* (ed with C. W. Evans) Controlling Events in Meiosis, 1984; (ed with P. Goodhew) Proceedings of IXth European Congress for Electron Microscopy, 1988; (ed jtly) Post-Translational Modification in Plants, 1992; contribs to internat. sci. jls, magazines and newspapers. *Recreations:* owning and restoring Lancia cars of the '50s and '60s, rock music 1955–75, Mozart operas. *Address:* Magdalen College, Oxford OX1 4AU.

DICKINSON, John Lawrence, (Bob), CBE 1973; DL; FCA; Chairman: SKF Steel Ltd, 1974–82; Bofors Cos (UK), 1974–83; General Manager, SKF Holding Co. (Holland), 1975–83; *b* 16 Nov. 1913; *s* of Tom Dickinson and Jennie Louise Dickinson; *m* 1937, Bettine Mary Jenkins; two *d*. *Educ:* Taunton Sch. Qual. as Chartered Accountant, 1937; Chief Accountant, Lucas Industries, 1937–44; SKF (UK) Ltd: Finance Dir and Sec., 1944–62; Sales Dir, 1962–66; Man. Dir, 1967–75, retired. Chairman: Sheffield Twist Drill & Steel Co. Ltd, 1978–81 (Dep. Chm., 1974–78); Weyroc Ltd (subsid. of Swedish Match Co.), 1975–82; British Rail (Eastern) Bd, 1970–81; Mem., National Enterprise Bd, 1975–79; Chm., NEDO Industrial Engines Sector Working Party, 1976–79; Mem. Gen. Council, also Finance and Gen. Purposes Cttee, CBI, until 1977; first Chm., Eastern Regional Council. Dep. Chm., Cranfield Inst., retd 1983. Hon. Life Vice-Pres., Luton and District Chamber of Commerce and Industry. High Sheriff, Bedfordshire, 1972–73, DL Beds 1976–. Gold Medal, Royal Patriots Soc. (Sweden), 1975. *Recreations:* gardening, National Hunt racing. *Address:* Arkle House, Upton End, Shillington, Hitchin, Herts SG5 3PG. *T:* Hitchin (01462) 711554.

DICKINSON, Patric Laurence; Richmond Herald of Arms, since 1989; *b* 24 Nov. 1950; *s* of John Laurence Dickinson and April Katherine, *d* of Robert Forgan, MC, MD, sometime MP. *Educ:* Marling Sch.; Exeter Coll., Oxford (Stapeldon Schol.; MA). Pres., Oxford Union Soc., 1972. Called to the Bar, Middle Temple, 1979. Res. Asst, College of Arms, 1968–78; Rouge Dragon Pursuivant, 1978–89. Hon. Treasurer: English Genealogical Congress, 1975–91; Bar Theatrical Soc., 1978–; Hon. Sec. and Registrar, British Record Soc., 1979–; Vice-Pres., Assoc. of Genealogists and Record Agents, 1988–. *Recreation:* savouring the delights of middle age. *Address:* College of Arms, Queen Victoria Street, EC4V 4BT. *T:* 0171–236 9612. *Club:* Brooks's.

DICKINSON, Prof. Peter, DMus; composer, pianist; Professor of Music, Goldsmiths College, London University, since 1991; *b* 15 Nov. 1934; *s* of late Frank Dickinson, FBOA(Hons), FAAO, DOS, FRSH, contact lens specialist, and of Muriel Porter; *m* 1964, Bridget Jane Tomkinson, *d* of late Lt-Comdr E. P. Tomkinson, DSO, RN; two *s*. *Educ:* The Leys Sch.; Queens' Coll., Cambridge (organ schol., Stewart of Rannoch schol.; MA); Juilliard Sch. of Music, New York (Rotary Foundn Fellow). DMus London 1992; LRAM, ARCM; FRCO. Teaching and freelance work in New York, 1958–61, London and Birmingham, 1962–74; first Prof. of Music, Keele Univ., 1974–84, subseq. Prof. Emeritus; founded Centre for American Music, Keele Univ. Concerts, broadcasts and records as pianist, mostly with sister Meriel Dickinson, mezzo soprano, incl. French, American and British works, some specially commissioned, 1960–. Member: Bd, Trinity Coll. of Music, 1984–; Royal Soc. of Musicians, 1985–. FRSA 1981. Hon. FTCL 1992. *Publications: compositions include: orchestral:* Monologue for Strings, 1959; Five Diversions, 1969; Transformations, 1970; Organ Concerto, 1971; Piano Concerto, 1984; Violin Concerto, 1986; Jigsaws, 1988; Merseyside Echoes, 1988; *chamber:* String Quartet No 1, 1958; Juilliard Dances, 1959; Fanfares and Elegies, 1967; Translations, 1971; String Quartet No 2, 1975; American Trio, 1985; London Rags, 1986; Sonatas for piano and tape playback, 1987; Auden Studies, 1988; Swansongs, 1992; works for solo organ, piano, clavichord, recorder, flute, violin, guitar and baryton; *vocal:* Four Auden Songs, 1956; A Dylan Thomas Cycle, 1959; Elegy, 1966; Five Poems of Alan Porter, 1968; Extravaganzas, 1969; An E. E. Cummings Cycle, 1970; Winter Afternoons (Emily Dickinson), 1970; Three Comic Songs (Auden), 1972; Surrealist Landscape (Lord Berners), 1973; Lust (St Augustine), 1974; A Memory of David Munrow, 1977; Reminiscences (Byron), 1979; The Unicorns (John Heath Stubbs), 1982; Stevie's Tunes (Stevie Smith), 1984; Larkin's Jazz (Philip Larkin), 1989; Summoned by Mother (Betjeman), 1991; *choral:* Martin of Tours (Thomas Blackburn), 1966; The Dry Heart (Alan Porter), 1967; Outcry, 1969; Late Afternoon in November, 1975; A Mass of the Apocalypse, 1984; Tiananmen 1989 (Dickinson), 1990; *ballet:* Vitalitas, 1959; *musical drama:* The Judas Tree (Thomas Blackburn), 1965; various church music, music for children and for films; (ed) Twenty British Composers, 1975; (ed) Songs and Piano Music by Lord Berners, 1982; The Music of Lennox Berkeley, 1989; contrib. to The New Grove, and various books and periodicals. *Recreation:* book collecting. *Address:* Goldsmiths College, University of London, New Cross, SE14 6NW. *Club:* United Oxford & Cambridge University.

DICKINSON, Hon. Peter Malcolm de Brissac; author; *b* 16 Dec. 1927; *s* of late Hon. Richard Sebastian Willoughby Dickinson and of May Southey (Nancy) Lovemore; *m* 1st, 1953, Mary Rose Barnard (*d* 1988), two *d* two *s*; 2nd, 1992, Robin McKinley. *Educ:* Eton; King's Coll., Cambridge (BA). Asst Editor, Punch, 1952–69. Chm., Management Cttee, Soc. of Authors, 1978–80. *Publications: children's books:* The Weathermonger, 1968; Heartsease, 1969; The Devil's Children, 1970 (trilogy republished 1975 as The Changes); Emma Tupper's Diary, 1970; The Dancing Bear, 1972; The Gift, 1973; The Iron Lion, 1973; Chance, Luck and Destiny, 1975; The Blue Hawk, 1976 (Guardian Award); Annerton Pit, 1977; Hepzibah, 1978; Tulku, 1979 (Whitbread Prize; Carnegie Medal); The Flight of Dragons, 1979; City of Gold, 1980 (Carnegie Medal); The Seventh Raven, 1981; Healer, 1983; Giant Cold, 1984; (ed) Hundreds and Hundreds, 1984; A Box of Nothing, 1985; Mole Hole, 1987; Merlin Dreams, 1988; Eva, 1988; AK, 1990 (Whitbread Children's Award); A Bone from a Dry Sea, 1992; Time and the Clockmice etcetera, 1993; Shadow of a Hero, 1994; *TV series,* Mandog (Mandog, by Lois Lamplugh, 1972, is based on this series); *novels:* Skin Deep, 1968; A Pride of Heroes, 1969; The Seals, 1970; Sleep and His Brother, 1971; The Lizard in the Cup, 1972; The Green Gene, 1973; The Poison Oracle, 1974; The Lively Dead, 1975; King and Joker, 1976; Walking Dead, 1977; One Foot in the Grave, 1979; A Summer in the Twenties, 1981; The Last House-party, 1982; Hindsight, 1983; Death of a Unicorn, 1984; Tefuga, 1986; Perfect Gallows, 1988; Skeleton-in-Waiting, 1989; Play Dead, 1991; The Yellow Room Conspiracy, 1994. *Recreation:* manual labour. *Address:* Bramdean Lodge, near Alresford, Hants SO24 0JN.

See also Baron Dickinson, Very Rev. H. G. Dickinson.

DICKINSON, Robert Henry; Senior Partner, Dickinson Dees, since 1987; Chairman, Northern Rock Building Society, since 1992; *b* 12 May 1934; *s* of Robert Joicey Dickinson and Alice Penelope Dickinson (*née* Barnett); *m* 1963, Kyra Irina Boissevain; one *s* two *d*. *Educ:* Christ Church, Oxford (MA). Admitted solicitor (Hons), 1960; Partner, Dickinson Dees, 1963–87. Chairman: Northern Investors PLC, 1984–; Grainger Trust PLC, 1992–; Director: Reg Vardy PLC, 1988–; Yorkshire Tyne Tees TV PLC, 1992–. *Recreations:* shooting, fishing. *Address:* Styford Hall, Stocksfield, Northumberland NE43 7TX; Cross House, Westgate Road, Newcastle upon Tyne NE99 1SB. *T:* 0191–261 1911, *Fax:* 0191–261 5855. *Clubs:* Boodle's, Pratt's; Northern Counties (Newcastle).

DICKINSON, Sally Jane; Secretary, Magistrates' Association, since 1994; *b* 12 Sept. 1955; *d* of Colin James Rayner Godden and Margaret Godden (*née* Cowin); *m* 1987, James Anthony Dickinson. *Educ:* Chatham Grammar Sch. for Girls; Bristol Univ. (BA Theol); Bristol Poly. (BA Law). Clerical Officer, Inland Revenue Collection, 1978–81; Exec. Officer, Law Soc. (Legal Aid), 1981–85; Regl Dir, Apex Charitable Trust, 1985–92; Cttee Sec., Magistrates' Assoc., 1992–93. *Recreations:* walking, cycling, sleeping, dogs. *Address:* 3 Ingleborough Street, SW9 0DL. *T:* 0171–733 2524. *Club:* New Cavendish.

DICKINSON, Sir Samuel Benson, (Sir Ben Dickinson), Kt 1980; Chairman, Burmine Pty Ltd, 1985–88; Mining Advisor to South Australian Government, 1975–84; Chairman, South Australian Government Uranium Enrichment Committee, 1979–84; *b* 1 Feb. 1912; *s* of Sydney Rushbrook Dickinson and Margaret Dickinson (*née* Clemes); *m* 1960, Dorothy Joan Weidenhofer; three *s* one *d*. *Educ:* Haileybury College, Melbourne; Univ. of

Melbourne. MSc. N Australia Aerial Geological and Geophysical Survey, 1935–36; geologist: Electrolytic Zinc, Mt Lyell, Mt Isa, mining cos, 1937–41; S Australian Geological Survey, 1941–42. Dir of Mines, Govt Geologist, Sec. to Minister of Mines, Dep. Controller, Mineral Production, Chm. Radium Hill Mines, 1943–56; Director: Rio Tinto Mining Co. of Australia, 1956–60; Sir Frank Duval's Gp of Cos, 1960–62; Chief Technical Adviser, Pechiney Australia, 1962–65; Project Manager, Clutha Development Ltd and Daniel K. Ludwig Cos Australia, 1965–75. *Publications:* technical reports for Australian Dept of Mines, Inst. of Mining and Metallurgy and mining jls and bulletins. *Recreations:* golf, bowls. *Address:* 21 Tiers Road, Woodside, SA 5244, Australia. *T:* (8) 3696089. *Clubs:* Athenæum (Melbourne); American National (Sydney).

DICKINSON, (Vivienne) Anne, (Mrs Basil Phillips); Director: Leedex Public Relations, since 1993; The Birkdale Group plc, since 1991; *b* 27 Sept. 1931; *d* of F. Oswald Edward Dickinson and M. Ida Ismay Dickinson; *m* 1st, 1951, John Kerr Large (marr. diss.); one *s* decd; 2nd, 1979, David Hermas Phillips (*d* 1989); 3rd, 1993, Basil B. Phillips, OBE. *Educ:* Nottingham Girls' High School. Account Executive, W. S. Crawford, 1960–64; Promotions Editor: Good Housekeeping, 1964–65; Harpers Bazaar, 1965–67; Dir in charge of Promotions, Nat. Magazine Co., 1967–68; Dir, Benson PR (later Kingsway), 1968–69; Chm. and Chief Exec., Kingsway Rowland, 1969–89; Chairman: The Rowland Co., 1989–90; Graduate Appointments Ltd, 1993–94. Vice-Chm., PR Consultants' Assoc., 1989– (Chm., Professional Practices Cttee, 1989–). Chm., Family Welfare Assoc., 1990–. FIPR 1985; CIMgt (CBIM 1986). PR Professional of the Year, PR Week, 1988–89. *Recreations:* friends, food, horses. *Address:* 26 Bedford Gardens, W8 7EH; 2 St Mary's House, Church Square, Rye TN31 7HF.

DICKINSON, William Michael, MBE 1960; Managing Director, Africa Research Ltd, 1966–90; *b* 13 Jan. 1930; *s* of late Comdr W. H. Dickinson, RN, and Ruth Sandeman Betts; *m* 1971, Enid Joy Bowers; one *s* two *d*. *Educ:* St Edward's Sch., Oxford. Army Service, 1948–51; 2/Lieut, Oxford and Bucks LI, Sept. 1948; seconded Somaliland Scouts; Lieut 1950; Colonial Service Devonshire Course, 1951–52; Somaliland Protectorate: Admin. Officer, 1952; Dist Officer, 1953–54; Asst Sec. (Political), 1955–56; seconded to British Liaison Orgn, Ethiopia, as Sen. Asst Liaison Officer, 1957–59; Brit. Liaison Officer in charge, 1959; transf. N Rhodesia as Dist Officer, 1960; Dist Comr, 1961; seconded to FO as HM Consul-Gen., Hargeisa, 1961–63; Principal, External Affairs Section, Office of Prime Minister, N Rhodesia, during 1964; Sen. Principal, Min. of Foreign Affairs, Govt of Zambia, 1964–65. *Address:* Durfold Manor, Blisland, Bodmin, Cornwall PL30 4JL. *T:* Bodmin (01208) 850560.

DICKS, Terence Patrick, (Terry); MP (C) Hayes and Harlington, since 1983; *b* 17 March 1937; *s* of Frank and Winifred Dicks; *m*; one *s* two *d*. *Educ:* London Sch. of Econs and Pol Science (BScEcon); Oxford Univ. (DipEcon). Clerk: Imperial Tobacco Co. Ltd, 1952–59; Min. of Labour, 1959–66; Admin. Officer, GLC, 1971–86. Contested (C) Bristol South, 1979. Mem., Select Cttee on Transport, 1986–92. Member: Council of Europe, 1993–; WEU, 1993–. *Address:* House of Commons, SW1A 0AA.

DICKSON, Arthur Richard Franklin, CBE 1974; QC (Belize), 1979; Commissioner for Law Revision, Belize, 1978; *b* 13 Jan. 1913; *m* 1949, Joanna Maria Margaretha van Baardwyk; four *s*. *Educ:* Rusea's Secondary Sch. and Cornwall Coll., Jamaica. Called to the Bar, Lincoln's Inn, 1938. Judicial Service. HM Overseas Judiciary: Jamaica, 1941; Magistrate, Turks and Caicos Islands, 1944–47; Asst to Attorney-Gen., and Legal Draftsman, Barbados, 1947–49; Magistrate, British Guiana, 1949–52; Nigeria, 1952–62: Magistrate, 1952–54; Chief Magistrate, 1954–56; Chief Registrar, High Court, Lagos, 1956–58; Judge of the High Court, Lagos, 1958–62; retired. Temp. appointment, Solicitors Dept, GPO London, 1962–63; served Northern Rhodesia (latterly Zambia), 1964–67; Judge of the High Court, Uganda, 1967–71; Deputy Chm., Middlesex QS, July–Aug., 1971; Chief Justice, Belize, 1973–74; Judge of the Supreme Court, Anguilla (part-time), 1972–76; part-time Chm., Industrial Tribunals, 1972–85. *Publications:* Revised Ordinances (1909–1941) Turks and Caicos Islands, 1944; (ed) Revised Laws of Belize, 1980. *Recreations:* gardening, walking, swimming. *Address:* 14 Meadow Lane, Lindfield, Haywards Heath, West Sussex RH16 2RJ. *T:* Lindfield (01444) 484450.

DICKSON, Rt. Hon. Brian, CC 1991; PC (Can) 1984; Chief Justice of Canada, 1984–90; *b* 25 May 1916; *s* of Thomas and Sarah Elizabeth Dickson (*née* Gibson); *m* 1943, Barbara Melville, *d* of Henry E. Sellers; three *s* one *d*. *Educ:* Regina Collegiate Institute; University of Manitoba; Manitoba Law School. LLB 1938 (Gold Medal). Served with Royal Canadian Artillery, 1940–45 (wounded, despatches); Hon. Col, 30th Field Regt, Royal Canadian Artillery, retd. Called to the Bar of Manitoba, 1940; practised law with Aikins, MacAulay & Co., 1945–63; Lectr, Manitoba Law Sch., 1948–54; QC (Can) 1953; Court of Queen's Bench, Manitoba, 1963; Manitoba Court of Appeal, 1967; Supreme Court of Canada, 1973; Life Bencher, Law Soc. of Manitoba; Chm., Board of Governors, Univ. of Manitoba, 1971–73; Chancellor of Diocese of Rupert's Land, 1960–71. Hon. Pres., Conf. of Defense Assoc.; Hon. Mem., Advocacy Resources Centre for the Handicapped. Hon. Bencher, Lincoln's Inn, 1984. Hon. Prof., Manitoba Univ., 1985; Hon. Fellow, Amer. Coll. of Trial Lawyers, 1985. Hon. degrees: St John's Coll.; Law Soc. of Upper Canada; Univs of Manitoba, Saskatchewan, Ottawa, Queen's, Dalhousie, York, Laurentian, British Columbia, Toronto, Yeshiva, McGill, Carleton, Mount Allison, Windsor, Winnipeg, Brock, Western Ontario, Law Soc. of Upper Canada, Univ. of Victoria. KStJ 1985. Churchill Soc. Award, 1990; Royal Bank Award, 1992; Order of the Buffalo Hunt, Manitoba, 1961. Order of Ste Agathe (San Marino), 1991; Comdr, Nat. Order of Merit (France). *Recreations:* riding, swimming. *Address:* 360 Berry Side Road, RR # 1, Dunrobin, Ont K0A 1T0, Canada. *Club:* Rideau (Ottawa).

DICKSON, David John Scott; News Editor, Nature; *b* 30 Aug. 1947; *s* of David and Rachel Mary Dickson; *m* 1973, Prudence Mary; one *s* one *d*. *Educ:* Westminster Sch.; Trinity Coll., Cambridge. Medical News, 1968–70; Sec., Brit. Soc. for Social Responsibility in Science, 1970–72; science corresp., 1973–75, features editor, 1975–77, THES; Washington corresp., Nature, 1977–82; European corresp., Science, 1982–89; news editor, 1989–90, Editor, 1990–92, New Scientist. Lectures organiser, ICA, 1976–77. Visiting Research Fellow: Univ. of Linköping, Sweden, 1981; Open Univ., 1989. *Publications:* Alternative Technology, 1974; The New Politics of Science, 1984; Het verval van de Geest (The Death of the Spirit), 1990; contribs to various jls on science, technology and society. *Recreations:* music, photography, travel.

DICKSON, Eileen Wadham, (Mrs C. F. Dickson); *d* of John Edward Latton, Librarian to Inner Temple, and Ethel Letitia Baker; *m* 1931, Charles Frederick Dickson, OBE (*d* 1994). *Educ:* Convent of the Sacred Heart, Roehampton; Bruges, Belgium. Served War of 1939–45 with WVS and on Executive Council of Stage Door Canteen. Joined Harper's Bazaar, 1949; Fashion Editor, 1951; Editor, 1953–65. *Recreations:* theatre, reading, racing, gardens. *Address:* Grimsdyke, Aldworth, Reading, Berks RG8 9RY; 4 Stack House, Ebury Street, SW1W 9JS.

DICKSON, George, CBE 1991 (OBE 1974); HM Diplomatic Service, retired; Consul General, Amsterdam, 1987–91; *b* 23 May 1931; *s* of late George James Stark Dickson and of Isobel (*née* Brown). *Educ:* Aberdeen Acad. DSIR, 1952; CRO, 1952–54; Karachi, 1954–56; Penang, 1957–59; Nicosia, 1960–62; Kampala, 1962–66; FCO, 1966–68; Manila, 1968–71; Jakarta, 1971–75; Stuttgart, 1975–76; Beirut, 1976–79; Baghdad, 1979–81; Asst Dir, Internat. Affairs, Commonwealth Secretariat, 1981–85; Dep. High Comr, Kingston, Jamaica, 1985–87. *Recreations:* friends, travel, walking. *Address:* c/o Royal Bank of Scotland, 12 Golden Square, Aberdeen AB9 8DU.

DICKSON, Prof. Gordon Ross; Professor of Agriculture, University of Newcastle upon Tyne, since 1973; Deputy Chairman, Home-Grown Cereals Authority, since 1982; Chairman, North England Regional Advisory Committee, Forestry Commission, since 1987; *b* 12 Feb. 1932; *s* of T. W. Dickson, Tynemouth; *m* 1st, 1956, Dorothy Stobbs (*d* 1989); two *s* one *d*; 2nd, 1991, Violet Adams. *Educ:* Tynemouth High Sch.; Durham Univ. BSc (Agric) 1st cl. hons 1953, PhD (Agric) 1958, Dunelm. Tutorial Research Student, Univ. Sch. of Agric., King's Coll., Newcastle upon Tyne, 1953–56; Asst Farm Dir, Council of King's Coll., Nafferton, Stocksfield-on-Tyne, 1956–58; Farms Director for the Duke of Norfolk, 1958–71; Principal, Royal Agric. Coll., Cirencester, 1971–73. Chm., Agricl Wages Bd for England and Wales, 1981–84. FRAgS; FIAgrM 1992. *Address:* Faculty of Agriculture, University of Newcastle upon Tyne, Newcastle upon Tyne NE1 7RU; The West Wing, Bolam Hall, Morpeth, Northumberland NE61 3ST.

DICKSON, Jennifer (Joan), (Mrs R. A. Sweetman), RA 1976 (ARA 1970); RE 1965; graphic artist, photographer and painter; *b* 17 Sept. 1936; 2nd *d* of late John Liston Dickson and Margaret Joan Turner, S Africa; *m* 1962, Ronald Andrew Sweetman; one *s*. *Educ:* Goldsmith's College Sch. of Art, Univ. of London; Atelier 17, Paris. Taught at Eastbourne Sch. of Art, 1959–62 (French Govt Schol., to work in Paris under S. W. Hayter). Directed and developed Printmaking Dept, Brighton Coll. of Art, 1962–68; developed and directed Graphics Atelier, Saidye Bronfman Centre, Montreal, 1970–72. Exhibn, L'Ultimo Silenzio, Palazzo Te, Mantua, Italy, 1993. Has held appointments of Vis. Artist at following Universities: Ball State Univ., Muncie, Indiana, 1967; Univ. of the West Indies, Kingston, Jamaica, 1968; Univ. of Wisconsin, Madison, 1972; Ohio State Univ., 1973; Western Illinois Univ., 1973; Haystack Mountain Sch. of Crafts, Maine, 1973; Vis. Artist, Queen's Univ., Kingston, Ont., 1977; part-time Instructor of Drawing, 1980–81, 1983, Sessional Instructor, 1980–85, Ottawa Univ.; Vis. Prof., 1987, Hon. LLD 1988, Univ. of Alberta. Founder Mem., Brit. Printmakers' Council. Prix des Jeunes Artistes (Gravure), Biennale de Paris, 1963; Major Prize, World Print Competition, San Francisco, 1974; Norwegian Print Biennale Prize, 1981. *Publications:* suites of original prints and photographs: Genesis, 1965; Alchemic Images, 1966; Aids to Meditation, 1967; Eclipse, 1968; Song of Songs, 1969; Out of Time, 1970; Fragments, 1971; Sweet Death and Other Pleasures, 1972; Homage to Don Juan, 1975; Body Perceptions, 1975; The Secret Garden, 1976; Openings, 1977; Three Mirrors to Narcissus, 1978; Il Paradiso Terrestre, 1980; Il Tempo Classico, 1981; Grecian Odes, 1983; Aphrodite Anadyomene, 1984; The Gardens of Paradise, part 1, 1984, part 2, 1985; Reflected Palaces, 1985; The Gilded Cage, 1986; Water Gardens, 1987; The Hospital for Wounded Angels, 1987; The Gardens of Desire, 1988; Pavane to Spring, 1989; Sonnet to Persephone, 1990; The Gardener's Journal, 1990; Cadence and Echo: the song of the garden, 1991; The Spirit of the Garden, 1992; The Haunted Heart, 1993; Sanctuaries and Paradeisos, 1994. *Address:* 20 Osborne Street, Ottawa, Ontario K1S 4Z9, Canada. *T:* (613) 730 2083, *Fax:* (613) 730 1818.

DICKSON, Leonard Elliot, CBE 1972; MC 1945; TD 1951; DL; Solicitor, Dickson, Haddow & Co., 1947–84; *b* 17 March 1915; *s* of Rev. Robert Marcus Dickson, DD, Lanark, and Cordelia Elliot; *m* 1950, Mary Elisabeth Cuthbertson; one *s* one *d*. *Educ:* Uppingham, Rutland; Univ. of Cambridge (BA 1936); Univ. of Glasgow (LLB 1947). Served War, with 1st Bn Glasgow Highlanders, HLI, 1939–46. Clerk to Clyde Lighthouses Trust, 1953–65. Chm., Lowland TAVR, 1968–70; Vice-Chm. Glasgow Exec. Council, NHS, 1970–74. DL Glasgow, 1963. *Publication:* Historical Sketch of Glasgow Society of Sons of the Clergy, 1990. *Recreations:* travel, gardening. *Address:* Bridge End, Gartmore, by Stirling FK8 3RR. *T:* Aberfoyle (01877) 382220. *Club:* Royal Scottish Automobile (Glasgow).

DICKSON, Murray Graeme, CMG 1961; *b* 19 July 1911; *s* of Norman and Anne Dickson. *Educ:* Rugby; New Coll., Oxford. Prison Service (Borstals), 1935–40. Served War of 1939–45, in Force 136. Entered Colonial Service, 1947; Education Officer, Sarawak, 1947, Deputy Dir of Education, 1952, Dir of Education, 1955–66; retd. Unesco adviser on educl planning to Govt of Lesotho, 1967–68. *Publications:* Understanding Kant's Critique of Pure Reason, 1986; Tales from Herodotus, 1989; The Best of Thucydides, 1991; trans. Froissart, Conflict and Chivalry in the Fourteenth Century, 1992. *Address:* 1 Hauteville Court Gardens, Stamford Brook Avenue, W6 0YF.

DICKSON, Prof. Peter George Muir, DPhil, DLitt; FBA 1988; Professor of Early Modern History, University of Oxford, 1989–Oct. 1996; Fellow, St Catherine's College, Oxford, since 1960; *b* 26 April 1929; *s* of William Muir Dickson, and Regina Dowdall-Nicolls; *m* 1964, Ariane Faye; one *d*. *Educ:* St Paul's Sch.; Worcester Coll., Oxford (Schol.; BA (1st Cl. Hons), MA, DPhil); DLitt Oxon 1992. FRHistS. Research Fellow, Nuffield Coll., Oxford, 1954–56; Tutor, St Catherine's Soc., Oxford, 1956–60; Vice-Master, St Catherine's Coll., 1975–77; Reader in Modern Hist., Oxford Univ., 1978–89. *Publications:* The Sun Insurance Office 1710–1960, 1960; The Financial Revolution in England 1688–1756, 1967; Finance and Government under Maria Theresia 1740–1780, 2 vols, 1987. *Recreations:* tennis, swimming, running, cinema. *Address:* Field House, Iffley, Oxford OX4 4EG. *T:* Oxford (01865) 779599.

DICKSON, Prof. Robert Andrew, DSc; FRCS, FRCSE; Professor and Head of Department of Orthopaedic Surgery, University of Leeds, since 1981; Consultant Surgeon, St James's University Hospital, Leeds, and Leeds General Infirmary, since 1981; *b* 13 April 1943; *s* of Robert Campbell Miller Dickson and late Maude Evelyn Dickson; *m* 1980, Ingrid Irene Sandberg; one *s*. *Educ:* Edinburgh Academy; Edinburgh Univ. (MB, ChB 1967, ChM 1973); MA 1979, DSc 1992, Oxon. FRCSE 1972; Moynihan Medal (Assoc. of Surgeons of GB and Ire.), 1977; FRCS *ad eund.* 1982. Lecturer, Nuffield Dept of Orthopaedic Surgery, Univ. of Oxford, 1972–75; Fellow in Spinal Surgery, Univ. of Louisville, Kentucky, 1975–76; Reader, Nuffield Dept of Orthopaedic Surgery, Univ. of Oxford, 1976–81. Arris and Gale Lectr, and Hunterian Prof., RCS. Fellow, Brit. Orthopaedic Assoc.; Member: Brit. Soc. for Surgery of the Hand; Brit. Orthopaedic Research Soc.; Brit. Scoliosis Soc. *Publications:* Surgery of the Rheumatoid Hand, 1979; Musculo-skeletal disease, 1984; Management of spinal deformities, 1984; Management of spinal deformities, 1988; papers on scoliosis, spinal surgery, hand surgery, and microsurgery. *Recreations:* squash, music. *Address:* 14A Park Avenue, Leeds LS8 2JH.

DICKSON, Rt. Hon. Robert George Brian; *see* Dickson, Rt Hon. B.

DICKSON, Robert Hamish, WS; Sheriff of South Strathclyde, Dumfries and Galloway, at Airdrie, since 1988; *b* 19 Oct. 1945; *s* of late Sheriff Ian Anderson Dickson, WS, and Mrs Margaret Forbes Ross or Dickson; *m* 1976, Janet Laird, *d* of late Alexander Campbell, Port of Menteith; one *s*. *Educ:* Glasgow Acad.; Drumtochty Castle; Glenalmond; Glasgow Univ. (LLB). WS 1969. Solicitor: Edinburgh, 1969–71; Glasgow, 1971–86 (Partner, Brown Mair Mackintosh, 1973–86); Sheriff of South Strathclyde, Dumfries and Galloway, at Hamilton, 1986–88 (floating). *Publications:* (jtly) Powers & Harris' Medical Negligence,

2nd edn 1994; articles in medical legal jls. *Recreations:* golf, music, reading. *Address:* Airdrie Sheriff Court, Airdrie ML6 6EE. *T:* Airdrie (01236) 751121. *Clubs:* Glasgow Golf, Elie Golf House.

DICKSON MABON, Rt. Hon. Jesse; *see* Mabon, Rt Hon. J. D.

DIEHL, John Bertram Stuart; QC 1987; **His Honour Judge Diehl;** a Circuit Judge, since 1990; *b* 18 April 1944; *s* of E. H. S. and C. P. Diehl; *m* 1967, Patricia L. Charman; two *s*. *Educ:* Bishop Gore Grammar Sch., Swansea; University Coll. of Wales, Aberystwyth (LLB 1965). Called to the Bar, Lincoln's Inn, 1968. Asst Lectr and Lectr in Law, Univ. of Sheffield, 1965–69; barrister, in practice on Wales and Chester Circuit, 1969–90; a Recorder, 1984–90.

DIESKAU, Dietrich F.; *see* Fischer-Dieskau.

DIGBY, family name of **Baron Digby.**

DIGBY, 12th Baron (Ire.) *cr* 1620, and 5th Baron (GB) *cr* 1765; **Edward Henry Kenelm Digby,** JP; Lord-Lieutenant, Dorset, since 1984 (Vice Lord-Lieutenant, 1965–84); Captain, late Coldstream Guards; *b* 24 July 1924; *o s* of 11th and 4th Baron Digby, KG, DSO, MC, and Hon. Pamela Bruce, OBE (*d* 1978), *y d* of 2nd Baron Aberdare; *S* father, 1964; *m* 1952, Dione Marian (*see* Lady Digby); two *s* one *d*. *Educ:* Eton; Trinity Coll., Oxford; RMC. Served War of 1939–45. Capt., 1947; Malaya, 1948–50; ADC to C-in-C: FARELF, 1950–51; BAOR, 1951–52. Director: Brooklyns Westbrick Ltd, 1970–83; Beazer plc, 1983–91; Kier Internat., 1986–91; Gifford-Hill Inc., 1986–91; PACCAR (UK) Ltd, 1990–. Dep. Chm., SW Economic Planning Council, 1972–77. Mem. Council, Royal Agricultural Soc. of England, 1954; Chm., Royal Agricultural Soc. of Commonwealth, 1966–77, Hon. Fellow 1977. Pres., 1976, Vice Pres., 1977, Royal Bath and West Soc. Dorchester Rural District Councillor, 1962–68; Dorset County Councillor, 1966–81 (Vice Chm. CC, 1977–81). President: Council, St John, Dorset; Wessex Br., Inst. of Dirs; Patron, Dorset Br., British Red Cross Soc. Churchwarden, St Andrews, Minterne Magna. Hon. Col, 4th Bn, Devonshire and Dorset Regt, 1992–. DL 1957, JP 1959, Dorset. KStJ 1985. *Recreations:* ski-ing, shooting, tennis. *Heir: s* Hon. Henry Noel Kenelm Digby, ACA [*b* 6 Jan. 1954; *m* 1980, Susan, *er d* of Peter Watts; one *s* one *d*]. *Address:* Minterne, Dorchester, Dorset DT2 7AU. *T:* Cerne Abbas (01300) 341370. *Club:* Pratt's.

DIGBY, Lady; Dione Marian Digby, DBE 1991; DL; Member, National Rivers Authority, since 1989 (Chairman, Southern Regional Advisory Board, since 1995); *b* 23 Feb. 1934; *d* of Rear-Adm. Robert St Vincent Sherbrooke, VC, CB, DSO, and Rosemary Neville Sherbrooke (*née* Buckley), Oxton, Notts; *m* 1952, Baron Digby, *qv*; two *s* one *d*. *Educ:* Talindert State Sch., Victoria, Australia; Southover Manor Sch., Lewes, Sussex. Chairman: Dorset Assoc. of Youth Clubs, 1966–73; Dorset Community Council, 1977–79; Standing Conf. of Rural Community Councils and Councils of Voluntary Service SW Region, 1977–79. Councillor (Ind.) W Dorset DC, 1976–86; Mem. Dorset Small Industries Cttee, CoSIRA, 1977 (Chm. 1981); Mem., Wessex Water Authority, 1983–89; Chm., Wessex Regl Adv. Bd, 1989–93, Co-Chm., S Western Adv. Bd, 1993–95, NRA. Dir, SW Regl Bd, then Western Adv. Bd, Nat. Westminster Bank, 1986–92. Mem. BBC/IBA Central Appeals Adv. Cttee, 1975–80. Governor: Dorset Coll. of Agriculture, 1978–83; Sherborne Sch., 1986–; Mem. Council, Exeter Univ., 1981–. Founder Chairman, Hon. Sec., Summer Music Soc. of Dorset, 1963–; Mem. Bath Festival Soc. Council of Management, 1971–81 (Chm. of the Society, 1976–81); Chm. Bath Fest. Friends Trust, 1982–87; Member: SW Arts Management Cttee, 1981–86; Arts Council of GB, 1982–86; South Bank Bd, 1985–88 (Gov., 1988–90); South and West Concerts Bd, 1986– (Chm., 1989–); Pres. of Council and Bd Mem., Bournemouth Orchs, 1991– (Mem. Bd of Management, Western Orchestral Soc., 1989–91). Mem., Council of Management, The Joseph Weld (formerly Dorset Respite) Hospice Trust, 1990– (Pres., 1993–). DL Dorset, 1983. *Recreations:* music and the arts, skiing, sailing, tennis; interest in local government, politics, history, people. *Address:* Minterne, Dorchester, Dorset DT2 7AU. *T:* Cerne Abbas (013003) 370.

DIGBY, Adrian, CBE 1964; MA Oxon; FSA; Keeper, Department of Ethnography, British Museum, 1953–69; excavated Maya site of Las Cuevas, British Honduras, 1957; *b* 13 June 1909; *s* of late William Pollard Digby, FInstP, MIME, MIEE; *m* 1939, Sylvia Mary, *d* of late Arnold Inman, OBE, KC; two *d*. *Educ:* Lancing; Brasenose Coll., Oxford. Entered British Museum as Asst Keeper, 1932. Hon. Asst Sec. of International Congress of Anthropological and Ethnological Sciences, London, 1934; Hon. Sec. of International Congress of Americanists, Cambridge, 1952. Served in Intelligence Division Naval Staff, Admiralty, 1942–44; Hydrographic Dept, Admiralty, 1944–45. Vis. Prof. in Archaeology, Univ. de Los Andes, Bogota, 1970. Pres. Sect. H of The British Association for the Advancement of Science, 1962; Vice-Pres. Royal Anthropological Inst., 1962–66. *Publications:* Ancient American Pottery (with G. H. S. Bushnell), 1955; Maya Jades, 1964; articles on anthropological subjects in Man and in Chambers's Encyclopædia. *Recreation:* sundials. *Address:* Greentrees, Eastcombe, Stroud, Glos GL6 7DR. *T:* Gloucester (01452) 770409.

DIGBY, Very Rev. Richard Shuttleworth W; *see* Wingfield Digby.

DIGBY, Simon Wingfield, TD 1946; DL; MA; *b* 1910; *s* of late Col F. J. B. Wingfield Digby, DSO; *m* 1936, Kathleen Elizabeth, *d* of late Hon. Mr Justice Courtney Kingstone, Toronto, Canada; one *s* one *d*. *Educ:* Harrow Sch.; Trinity Coll., Cambridge. Delegate to International Studies Conference, 1934. Prospective Conservative Candidate for West Dorset, Jan. 1937–June 1941; MP (U) West Dorset, 1941–Feb. 1974; a Conservative Whip, 1948–51. Barrister-at-law, Inner Temple; served in Army (TA), Aug. 1939–June 1945 in UK and NW Europe; Major, 1943; GSO II, 1944. Civil Lord of the Admiralty, 1951–57. Mem. of Empire Parl. Delegn to East Africa, 1948 and Inter-Parliamentary Union Delegation to Chile, 1962. Pres., Wessex Young Conservatives, 1947–50; Sec., Conservative Social Services Cttee, 1947; Chairman: Conservative Forestry Sub-Cttee, 1959–67; Shipping and Shipbuilding Cttee, 1964–74. Member: Coastal Pollution Select Cttee, 1966–68; Select Cttee on Procedure; Public Accounts Cttee. Delegate (C), Council of Europe Assembly and Assembly of WEU, 1968–74 (Leader, 1972–74). Pres., Soc. of Dorset Men, 1972–85. DL Dorset, 1953. Order of Leopold and Order of White Lion. Medal of Council of Europe Assembly, 1974. *Recreations:* fishing, bloodstock breeding. *Address:* Sherborne Castle, Sherborne, Dorset DT9 5NR. *T:* Gillingham (01747) 822650, (office) Sherborne (01935) 813182; Coleshill House, Coleshill, near Birmingham. *Club:* Carlton.

See also Sir Rupert Hardy, Bt.

DIGBY, Ven. Stephen Basil W.; *see* Wingfield-Digby.

DIGGLE, Prof. James, LittD; FBA 1985; Professor of Greek and Latin, University of Cambridge, since 1995; Fellow of Queens' College, since 1966; *b* 29 March 1944; *s* of James Diggle and Elizabeth Alice Diggle (*née* Buckley); *m* 1973, Sedwell Mary Chapman, *d* of late Rev. Preb. F. A. R. Chapman and K. A. Chapman (*née* Mill); three *s*. *Educ:* Rochdale Grammar School; St John's College, Cambridge (Major Scholar; Classical Tripos Pt I, first cl., 1964, Pt II, first cl. with dist., 1965; Pitt Scholar, Browne Scholar, Hallam Prize, Members' Latin Essay Prize, 1963; Montagu Butler Prize, Browne Medals for Greek Elegy and Latin Epigram, 1964; Porson Prize, First Chancellor's Classical Medal, Craven Student, Allen Scholar, 1965; BA 1965; MA 1969; PhD 1969; LittD 1985). Queens' College, Cambridge: Research Fellow, 1966–67; Official Fellow and Director of Studies in Classics, 1967–; Librarian, 1969–77; Praelector, 1971–73, 1978–; Cambridge University: Asst Lectr in Classics, 1970–75; Lectr, 1975–89; Reader in Greek and Latin, 1989–95; Chm., Faculty Bd of Classics, 1989–90; Orator, 1982–93. Hon. Sec., Cambridge Philological Soc., 1970–74 (Jt Editor, Procs, 1970–82); Chm., Classical Jls Bd, 1991– (Hon. Treas., 1979–91); Jt Editor, Cambridge Classical Texts and Commentaries, 1977–. *Publications:* The Phaethon of Euripides, 1970; (jtly) Flavii Cresconii Corippi Iohannidos, Libri VIII, 1970; (ed jtly) The Classical Papers of A. E. Housman, 1972; (ed jtly) Dionysiaca: nine studies in Greek poetry, presented to Sir Denys Page, 1978; Studies on the Text of Euripides, 1981; Euripidis Fabulae (Oxford Classical Texts), vol. ii 1981, vol. i 1984, vol. iii 1994; (ed jtly) Studies in Latin Literature and its Tradition, in honour of C. O. Brink, 1989; The textual tradition of Euripides' Orestes, 1991; (ed jtly) F. R. D. Goodyear, Papers on Latin Literature, 1992; Euripidea: collected essays, 1994; Cambridge Orations 1982–1993: a selection, 1994. *Recreation:* family life. *Address:* Queens' College, Cambridge CB3 9ET. *T:* Cambridge (01223) 335527.

DIGGLE, Judith Margaret, (Mrs P. J. Diggle); *see* Brown, J. M.

DIGGORY, Colin; Headmaster, Latymer Upper School, since 1991; *b* 22 July 1954; *s* of John Harold Diggory and late Olga Diggory; *m* 1976, Susan Janet Robinson; one *s* two *d*. *Educ:* Sir William Turner's Sch., Redcar; Univ. of Durham (BSc 1st cl. Hons Maths, PGCE). CMath, FIMA. Assistant Master: Manchester Grammar Sch., 1976–83; St Paul's Sch., Barnes, 1983–87; Head of Maths, Merchant Taylors' Sch., 1987–90; Second Master, Latymer Upper Sch., 1990–91. Chief Examr, A Level Maths, Univ. of London, 1989–91. FRSA. *Recreations:* walking, camping. *Address:* Latymer Upper School, King Street, W6 9LR. *Club:* East India, Devonshire, Sports and Public Schools.

DIGGORY, Elizabeth Mary; Head Mistress, Manchester High School for Girls, since 1994; *b* 22 Dec. 1945; *d* of Clarence Howard Diggory and Beatrice Mary Diggory. *Educ:* Shrewsbury High Sch. for Girls; Westfield Coll., Univ. of London (BA Hons Hist.); Hughes Hall, Univ. of Cambridge (PGCE). King Edward VI High School for Girls, Birmingham: Asst Teacher, 1968–73; Hd of History Dept, 1973–82; Head Mistress, St Albans High Sch. for Girls, 1983–94. Pres., GSA, 1991–92. FRSA 1993. *Recreations:* theatre, the arts in general, travel. *Address:* Manchester High School for Girls, Grangethorpe Road, Manchester M14 6HS. *T:* 0161–224 0447.

DIGNAN, Maj.-Gen. Albert Patrick, CB 1978; MBE 1952; FRCS, FRCSI; Director of Army Surgery and Consulting Surgeon to the Army, 1973–78; Hon. Consultant Surgeon, Royal Hospital, Chelsea, 1973–78; Hon. Consultant in Radiotherapy and Oncology, Westminster Hospital, 1974–78; *b* 25 July 1920; *s* of Joseph Dignan; *m* 1952, Eileen White; two *s* one *d*. *Educ:* Trinity Coll., Dublin (Med. Schol.). MB, BCh, BAO, BA 1943, MA, MD 1968, FRCSI 1947, FRCS 1976. Prof. of Physiol. Prize, TCD. Posts in Dublin, Belfast and Wigan; subseq. NS Sen. Specialist in Surgery, Major RAMC Malaya; Sen. Registrar in Surgery, Bristol Royal Infirmary and Wanstead Hosp.; Sen. Specialist in Surgery, BAOR Mil. Hosps and Consultant Surg., Brit. Mil. Hosps Singapore and Tidworth, 1953–68; Brig., and Consulting Surg., Farelf, 1969–70; Consultant Surg., Mil. Hosp. Tidworth, 1971–72; Consultant Surgeon, Queen Alexandra Mil. Hosp. Millbank, 1972–73; Consultant in Accident and Emergency, Ealing Dist, DHSS, 1978–79. Pres., Army Med. Bds, 1980–90. Fellow, Association of Surgeons of GB and Ireland; FRSocMed. Mem., Acad. of Medicine, Singapore, 1969–71. QHS, 1974–78. *Publications:* A Doctor's Experiences of Life (autobiog.), 1994; papers in Brit. Jl Surgery, BMJ, Jl of RAMC, Postgrad. Med. Jl, Univ. Singapore Med. Soc. Med. Gazette. *Recreations:* gardening, golf. *Address:* Ramridge Dene, 182 Beckenham Hill Road, Beckenham, Kent BR3 4JJ.

DILHORNE, 2nd Viscount *cr* 1964, of Green's Norton; **John Mervyn Manningham-Buller;** Bt 1866; Baron 1962; Barrister-at-Law; *b* 28 Feb. 1932; *s* of 1st Viscount Dilhorne, PC, and of Lady Mary Lilian Lindsay, 4th *d* of 27th Earl of Crawford, KT, PC; *S* father, 1980; *m* 1st, 1955, Gillian Evelyn (marr. diss. 1973), *d* of Colonel George Stockwell; two *s* one *d*; 2nd, 1981, Dr Susannah Jane Eykyn, MB BS, FRCPath. *Educ:* Eton; RMA Sandhurst. Called to the Bar, Inner Temple, 1979. Formerly Lieut, Coldstream Guards. Managing Director, Stewart Smith (LP&M) Ltd, 1970–74. Member, Wilts County Council, 1967–70. Mem., Jt Parly Cttee on Statutory Instruments, 1981–88. FTII (Mem. Council, 1967–82). *Heir: s* Hon. James Edward Manningham-Buller, formerly Captain Welsh Guards [*b* 20 Aug. 1956; *m* 1985, Nicola Marion, *e d* of Sven Mackie; one *s* one *d*. *Educ:* Harrow; Sandhurst]. *Address:* 4 Breams Buildings, EC4A 1AQ. *T:* 0171–353 5835; 164 Ebury Street, SW1W 8UP. *T:* 0171–730 0913. *Clubs:* Pratt's, Buck's, Beefsteak; Swinley Forest Golf.

DILKE; *see* Fetherston-Dilke.

DILKE, Sir John Fisher Wentworth, 5th Bt *cr* 1862; *b* 1906; *e s* of Sir Fisher Wentworth Dilke, 4th Bt, and Ethel Clifford (*d* 1959); *S* father, 1944; *m* 1st, 1934, Sheila (marr. diss. 1949), *d* of late Sir William Seeds, KCMG; two *s*; 2nd, 1951, Iris Evelyn, *d* of late Ernest Clark. *Educ:* Winchester; Oxford. Foreign Office, 1929; Editorial Staff, The Times, 1936; rejoined Foreign Service, 1939. *Heir: s* Charles John Wentworth Dilke, *b* 1937. *Address:* Ludpits, Etchingham, Sussex TN19 7DB.

DILKS, Prof. David Neville, FRHistS; FRSL; Vice-Chancellor, University of Hull, since 1991; *b* Coventry, 17 March 1938; *s* of Neville Ernest Dilks and Phyllis Dilks; *m* 1963, Jill Medlicott; one *s*. *Educ:* Royal Grammar Sch., Worcester; Hertford Coll., Oxford (BA Modern Hist., Class II, 1959); St Antony's Coll., Oxford (Curzon Prizeman, 1960). Research Assistant to: Rt Hon. Sir Anthony Eden (later Earl of Avon), 1960–62; Marshal of the RAF Lord Tedder, 1963–65; Rt Hon. Harold Macmillan, 1964–67; Asst Lectr, then Lectr, in International History, LSE, 1962–70; University of Leeds: Prof. of Internat. History, 1970–91; Chm., Sch. of History, 1974–79; Dean, Faculty of Arts, 1975–77. Vis. Fellow, All Souls' Coll., Oxford, 1973. Consultant, Sec.-Gen. of the Commonwealth, 1967–75; Chm., Commonwealth Youth Exchange Council, 1968–73. Member: Adv. Council on Public Records, 1977–85; Central Council, 1982–85, Library Cttee, 1982–91, Royal Commonwealth Soc.; British Nat. Cttee for History of Second World War, 1983– (Pres., Internat. Cttee, 1992–); Inst. of Contemporary British History, 1986–; Acad. Adv. Council, Hughenden Foundn, 1986–; UFC, 1989–91. Trustee: Edward Boyle Meml Trust, 1982– (Hon. Sec., 1981–82); Imperial War Museum, 1983–90; Lennox-Boyd Meml Trust, 1984–91; Nathaniel Trust, 1986–90. Pres., Worcester Old Elizabethans' Assoc., 1986–87. FRSL 1986. Liveryman, Goldsmiths' Co., 1984– (Freeman, 1979). Wrote and presented BBC TV series, The Loneliest Job, 1977; interviewer in BBC TV series, The Twentieth Century Remembered, 1982. Médaille de Vermeil, Acad. Française, 1994. *Publications:* Curzon in India, Vol. I, 1969, Vol. II, 1970; (ed) The Diaries of Sir Alexander Cadogan, 1971; (contrib.) The Conservatives (ed Lord Butler of Saffron Walden), 1977; (ed and contrib.) Retreat from Power, vol. 1, 1906–1939, Vol. 2, after 1939, 1981; (ed and contrib.) Britain and Canada (Commonwealth Foundn Paper), 1980;

(ed and contrib.) The Missing Dimension: governments and intelligence communities in the twentieth century, 1984; Neville Chamberlain, Vol. I: Pioneering and Reform 1869–1929, 1984; (ed jtly and contrib.) Grossbritannien und der deutsche Widerstand, 1994; (ed jtly) Barbarossa: the axis and the allies, 1994; reviews and articles in English Historical Rev., Survey, History, Scandinavian Jl of History, etc. *Recreations:* ornithology, painting, railways, Bentley cars. *Address:* University of Hull, Hull HU6 7RX. *T:* Hull (01482) 465131. *Clubs:* Brooks's, Commonwealth Trust.

DILKS, John Morris Whitworth; Director, Transportation System, BG TransCo, since 1994; *b* 10 Feb. 1950; *s* of John Amos Whitworth Dilks and Margaret (*née* Thraves); *m* 1971, Patricia Anne Roberts; one *s* one *d*. *Educ:* Oakham Sch.; Sheffield Univ. (BA Hons). ACMA; CIGasE. Audit Manager, British Gas E Midlands, 1980–85; Asst Dir of Finance, British Gas, 1985–86; Regl Dir of Finance, British Gas NE, 1986–91; Regl Chm., British Gas Eastern, 1991–93. *Recreations:* sailing, walking, gardening. *Address:* (office) 31 Homer Road, Solihull, W Midlands B91 3LT.

DILLAMORE, Ian Leslie, PhD, DSc; FEng 1985; FIM; Group Managing Director, INCO Engineered Products Ltd, since 1987; *b* 22 Nov. 1938; *s* of Arthur Leslie Dillamore and Louise Mary Dillamore; *m* 1962, Maureen Birch; two *s*. *Educ:* Birmingham Univ. (BSc, MSc, PhD, DSc). ICI Research Fellow, Birmingham Univ., 1962–63, Lectr in Physical Metallurgy, 1963–69; Head of Phys. Metallurgy, BISRA, 1969–72; Head of Metals Technology Unit, British Steel Corp., 1972–76; Head of Metallurgy Dept, Aston Univ., 1976–81, Dean of Engineering, 1980–81; Director of Research and Development, INCO Europe, 1981–82; Dir of Technology, INCO Engineered Products, 1982–87. Hon. Professor of Metallurgy, Birmingham Univ., 1981–. Mem. Council: Metals Soc., 1980–84; Instn of Metallurgists, 1981–84; Vice-Pres., Inst. of Metals, 1985–88; Mem. SRC Metallurgy Cttee, 1972–75, Materials Cttee, 1977–82; Chm., Processing Sub-Cttee, SRC, later SERC, 1979–82; Mem., DTI Non Ferrous Metals Exec. Cttee, 1982–85; Pres. Birmingham Metallurgical Assoc., 1980–81. Sir Robert Hadfield Medal and Prize, Metals Soc., 1976. *Publications:* numerous contribs to metallurgical and engrg jls. *Recreation:* industrial archaeology. *Address:* 28–30 Derby Road, Melbourne, Derbyshire DE7 1FE. *T:* Melbourne (01332) 864900.

DILLON, family name of **Viscount Dillon.**

DILLON, 22nd Viscount *cr* 1622, of Castello Gallen, Co. Mayo, Ireland; **Henry Benedict Charles Dillon;** Count in France, 1711; *b* 6 Jan. 1973; *s* of 21st Viscount Dillon and of Mary Jane, *d* of late John Young, Castle Hill House, Birtle, Lancs; *S* father, 1982. *Heir: uncle* Hon. Richard Arthur Louis Dillon [*b* 23 Oct. 1948; *m* 1975, Hon. Priscilla Frances Hazlerigg, *d* of 2nd Baron Hazlerigg, *qv*; one *s* one *d*].

DILLON, Hon. Sir Brian; *see* Dillon, Hon. Sir G. B. H.

DILLON, C(larence) Douglas; Chairman, US & Foreign Securities Corporation, 1967–84; Managing Director, Dillon, Read & Co. Inc., 1971–83; retired; *b* Geneva, Switzerland, 21 Aug. 1909; *s* of Clarence Dillon; *m* 1st, 1931, Phyllis Ellsworth (*d* 1982); two *d*; 2nd, 1983, Susan Sage. *Educ:* Groton Sch.; Harvard Univ. (AB). Mem., NY Stock Exchange, 1931–36; US and Foreign Securities Corporation and US and International Securities Corporation, 1937–53 (Dir, 1938–53; Pres., 1946–53); Dir, Dillon, Read & Co. Inc., 1938–53 (Chm. of Bd, 1946–53); American Ambassador to France, 1953–57; Under-Sec. of State for Economic Affairs, USA, 1957–59, Under-Sec. of State, USA, 1959–61; Sec. of the Treasury, USA, 1961–65. Served US Naval Reserve, 1941–45 (Lieut-Comdr; Air Medal, Legion of Merit). Dir, Council on Foreign Relations, 1965–78 (Vice-Chm. 1977–78); Pres., Board of Overseers, Harvard Coll., 1968–72; Chm., Rockefeller Foundn, 1971–75; Chm., Brookings Instn, 1971–75. Trustee Emeritus, Metropolitan Museum of Art (President, 1970–77; Chm., 1977–83). Hon. Dr of Laws: New York Univ., 1956; Lafayette Coll., 1957; Univ. of Hartford, Conn, 1958; Columbia Univ., 1959; Harvard Univ., 1959; Williams Coll., 1960; Rutgers Univ., 1961; Princeton Univ., 1961; University of Pennsylvania, 1962; Bradley Univ., 1964; Middlebury Coll., 1965; Tufts Univ., 1982; Marymount Manhattan Coll., 1984. US Presidential Medal of Freedom, 1989.

DILLON, Rt. Hon. Sir (George) Brian (Hugh), Kt 1979; PC 1982; a Lord Justice of Appeal, 1982–94; *b* 2 Oct. 1925; *s* of late Captain George Crozier Dillon, RN; *m* 1954, Alison, *d* of late Hubert Samuel Lane, MC and Dr Isabella Lane, MB, ChB Edin.; two *s* two *d*. *Educ:* Winchester College; New College, Oxford. Called to the Bar, Lincoln's Inn, 1948; QC 1965; a Judge of the High Court of Justice, Chancery Division, 1979–82. *Address:* Bridge Farm, Grundisburgh, Woodbridge, Suffolk IP13 6UF.

DILLON, Sir Max, Kt 1979; *b* 30 June 1913; *s* of Cyril and Phoebe Dillon; *m* 1940, Estelle Mary Jones; one *s* one *d*. *Educ:* Wesley Coll., Melbourne; Melbourne Univ. (Faculty of Commerce). FCPA (AASA (Sen.) 1939); ACIS 1940; FAIM 1947. General Manager, Cable Makers Australia Pty Ltd, 1957–70; Dep. Man. Dir, Metal Manufactures Ltd Gp, 1970–75. President: Aust. Council of Employer Fedns, 1967–69; Associated Chambers of Manufactures, 1974–77; Confedn of Aust. Industry, 1977–80; Chairman: Nat. Employers Policy Cttee, 1971–73 and 1975–78; Central Industrial Secretariat Council, 1972–77; Productivity Promotion Council, 1971–74; Member: Nat. Labour Adv. Council, 1966–72; Nat. Labour Consultative Council, 1977–80; Exec. Cttee, Aust. Manufacturing Council, 1978–80. *Recreations:* golf, swimming. *Address:* 33 Church Street, Pymble, NSW 2073, Australia. *T:* (02) 443160. *Clubs:* Australian, Elanora Country (Sydney).

DILLON, Thomas Michael; QC 1973; **His Honour Judge Dillon;** a Circuit Judge, since 1985; *b* 29 Nov. 1927; *yr s* of Thomas Bernard Joseph Dillon, Birmingham, and Ada Gladys Dillon (*née* Noyes); *m* 1956, Wendy Elizabeth Marshall Hurrell; two *s* one *d*. *Educ:* King Edward's Sch., Aston, Birmingham; Birmingham Univ. (LLB); Lincoln Coll., Oxford (BCL). Called to Bar, Middle Temple, 1952, Master of the Bench 1981. 2nd Lieut, RASC, 1953–54. In practice as barrister, 1954–85; a Recorder, 1972–85; Part-time Chm. of Industrial Tribunals, 1968–74. *Recreations:* reading, listening to music. *Address:* 1 Fountain Court, Birmingham B4 6DR. *T:* 0121–236 5721.

DILLWYN-VENABLES-LLEWELYN, Sir John Michael; *see* Venables-Llewelyn.

DILNOT, Mary, (Mrs Thomas Ruffle), OBE 1982; Director, IPC Women's Magazines Group, 1976–81; Editor, Woman's Weekly, 1971–81; *b* 23 Jan. 1921; 2nd *d* of George Dilnot, author, and Ethel Dilnot; *m* 1974, Thomas Ruffle. *Educ:* St Mary's Coll., Hampton. Joined Woman's Weekly, 1939. *Recreations:* home interests, reading, travel, golf. *Address:* 28 Manor Road South, Hinchley Wood, Esher, Surrey KT10 0QL.

DIMBLEBY, Bel, (Mrs Jonathan Dimbleby); *see* Mooney, Bel.

DIMBLEBY, David; broadcaster and newspaper proprietor; Chairman, Dimbleby & Sons Ltd, since 1986 (Managing Director, 1966–86); *b* 28 Oct. 1938; *e s* of (Frederick) Richard and Dilys Dimbleby; *m* 1967, Josceline Rose Gaskell (*see* J. R. Dimbleby); one *s* two *d*. *Educ:* Glengorse Sch.; Charterhouse; Christ Church, Oxford (MA); Univs of Paris and Perugia. News Reporter, BBC Bristol, 1960–61; Presenter and Interviewer on network programmes on: religion (Quest), science for children (What's New?), politics (In My Opinion), Top of the Form, etc, 1961–63; Reporter, BBC2 (Enquiry), and Dir films, incl.: Ku-Klux-Klan, The Forgotten Million, Cyprus: Thin Blue Line, 1964–65; Special Correspondent CBS News, New York; documentary film (Texas-England) and film reports for '60 minutes', 1966–68; Reporter, BBC1 (Panorama), 1967–69; Presenter, BBC1 (24 Hours), 1969–72; Yesterday's Men, 1971; Chm., The Dimbleby Talk-In, 1971–74; films for Reporter at Large, 1973; Presenter: BBC 1 (Panorama), 1974–77, 1980–82, 1989–; (People and Power), 1982–83; (This Week, Next Week), 1984–86; Chm., BBC Question Time, 1994–; Election Campaign Report, 1974; BBC Election and Results programmes, 1979, 1983, 1987, 1992; film series: The White Tribe of Africa, 1979 (Royal TV Soc. Supreme Documentary Award); An Ocean Apart, 1988; The Struggle for South Africa, 1990 (Emmy Award, 1991; Golden Nymph Award, 1991). *Publication:* An Ocean Apart (with David Reynolds), 1988. *Address:* 14 King Street, Richmond, Surrey TW9 1NF. *T:* 0181–940 6668.
See also J. Dimbleby.

DIMBLEBY, Jonathan; freelance broadcaster, journalist, and author; *b* 31 July 1944; *s* of Richard and Dilys Dimbleby; *m* 1968, Bel Mooney, *qv*; one *s* one *d*. *Educ:* University Coll. London (BA Hons Philosophy). TV and Radio Reporter, BBC Bristol, 1969–70; BBC Radio, World at One, 1970–71; for Thames TV: This Week, 1972–78, 1986–88; TV Eye, 1979; Jonathan Dimbleby in South America, 1979; documentary series, Witness (Editor), 1986–88; for Yorkshire TV: series, Jonathan Dimbleby in Evidence: The Police, 1980; The Bomb, 1980; The Eagle and the Bear, 1981; The Cold War Game, 1982; The American Dream, 1984; Four Years On—The Bomb, 1984; First Tuesday (Associate Editor/Presenter), 1982–86; for TV-am: Jonathan Dimbleby on Sunday (Presenter/ Editor), 1985–86; for BBC TV: On the Record, 1988–93; Election Call, 1992; Charles: the private man, the public role (documentary), 1994; for LWT: Jonathan Dimbleby, 1995–; Presenter: Any Questions?, BBC Radio 4, 1987–; Any Answers, BBC Radio 4, 1989–. Pres., CPRE, 1992–; Member: Richard Dimbleby Cancer Fund, 1966–; VSO. SFTA Richard Dimbleby Award, for most outstanding contribution to factual TV, 1974. *Publications:* Richard Dimbleby, 1975; The Palestinians, 1979; The Prince of Wales: a biography, 1994. *Recreations:* music, sailing, tennis. *Address:* c/o David Higham Associates Ltd, 5 Lower John Street, W1R 4HA.
See also D. Dimbleby.

DIMBLEBY, Josceline Rose; Cookery Editor, Sunday Telegraph, since 1982; *b* 1 Feb. 1943; *d* of late Thomas Josceline Gaskell and of Barbara Montagu-Pollock; *m* 1967, David Dimbleby, *qv*; one *s* two *d*. *Educ:* Cranborne Chase Sch., Dorset; Guildhall School of Music. Contributor, Daily Mail, 1976–78; cookery writer for Sainsbury's, 1978–. André Simon Award, 1979. *Publications:* A Taste of Dreams, 1976, 3rd edn 1984; Party Pieces, 1977; Josceline Dimbleby's Book of Puddings, Desserts and Savouries, 1979, 2nd edn 1983; Favourite Food, 1983, 2nd edn 1984; (for Sainsbury's): Cooking for Christmas, 1978; Family Meat and Fish Cookery, 1979; Cooking with Herbs and Spices, 1979; Curries and Oriental Cookery, 1980; Salads for all Seasons, 1981; Marvellous Meals with Mince, 1982; Festive Food, 1982; Sweet Dreams, 1983; First Impressions, 1984; The Josceline Dimbleby Collection, 1984; Main Attractions, 1985; A Traveller's Tastes, 1986; The Josceline Dimbleby Christmas Book, 1987; The Josceline Dimbleby Book of Entertaining, 1988; The Essential Josceline Dimbleby, 1989; The Cook's Companion, 1991; The Almost Vegetarian Cookbook, 1994; The Christmas Book, 1994. *Recreations:* singing, travel. *Address:* 14 King Street, Richmond, Surrey TW9 1NF. *T:* 0181-940 6668.

DIMECHKIÉ, Nadim, GCVO (Hon.) 1978; business and economic consultant; *b* Lebanon, 5 Dec. 1919; *s* of Badr and Julia Dimechkié; *m* 1946, Margaret Alma Sherlock; two *s*. *Educ:* American Univ. of Beirut (BA, MA Economics). Deleg., Jt Supply Bd for Syria and Lebanon, 1942–44; Dir Gen., Min. of Nat. Economy, 1943–44; Counsellor, Lebanese Embassy, London, 1944–49; Consul-Gen., Ottawa, 1950; Dir, Economic and Social Dept, Min. of Foreign Affairs, 1951–52; Chargé d'Affaires, Cairo, 1952; Minister, 1953–55; Minister, Switzerland, 1955–57; Ambassador to USA, 1958–62; Dir, Economic Affairs, Min. of Foreign Affairs, 1962–66; Ambassador to UK, 1966–78, and Doyen of the Diplomatic Corps, 1977–78; Ambassador at large, and Senior Adviser on foreign affairs to Foreign Sec., Beirut, 1979–80. Board Member and Consultant: Bank de Credit Populaire Union Nationale, 1985–; Union Foncier et Financing, 1985–; Sterling Drugs Internat., 1985–; Hon. Consultant, Arab Fedn of Chambers of Commerce and Industry, 1980. Lebanese Order of Cedars, UAR Order of Ismail and Order of Merit; Syrian Order of Merit; Tunisian Order of Merit; Greek Order of Phoenix. *Clubs:* Golf, Aero (Beirut); Cercle Interallié (Paris).

DIMMOCK, Peter, CVO 1968; OBE 1961; Chairman: Television Enterprise and Asset Management plc, since 1991; Peter Dimmock Associates, TV and Media Consultants, since 1991; *e s* of late Frederick Dimmock, OBE, and Paula Dimmock (*née* Hudd); *m* 1st, 1960, Mary Freya (Polly) (*d* 1987), *e d* of late Hon. Mr Justice Elwes, OBE, TD; three *d*; 2nd, 1990, Christabel Rosamund, *e d* of Sir John Bagge, 6th Bt, ED, and *widow* of James Hinton Scott. *Educ:* Dulwich Coll.; France. TA; RAF pilot, instr, and Air Ministry Staff Officer, 1939–45. After demobilisation became Press Association correspondent; joined BBC as Television Outside Broadcasts Producer and commentator, 1946; produced both studio and outside broadcasts, ranging from documentaries to sporting, theatrical and public events; has produced or commentated on more than 500 television relays, including Olympic Games 1948, Boat Race 1949, first international television relay, from Calais, 1950, King George VI's Funeral, Windsor, 1952. Produced and directed television outside broadcast of the Coronation Service from Westminster Abbey, 1953; first TV State Opening of Parliament, 1958; first TV Grand National, 1960; TV for Princess Margaret's Wedding, 1960. Created BBC Sportsview Unit and introduced new television programme Sportsview, 1954, regular host of this weekly network programme, 1954–64; Gen. Manager and Head of Outside Broadcasts, BBC TV, 1954–72; responsible for Liaison between BBC and Royal Family, 1963–77; Gen. Manager, BBC Enterprises, 1972–77; Vice-Pres., ABC Worldwide Sales and Marketing TV Sports, 1978–86; Vice-Pres. and Consultant, ABC Video Enterprises Div., Capital Cities/ABC Inc., NY, 1984–91; Dir, Entertainment and Sports Cable Network, 1984–90. Sports Adviser, European Broadcasting Union, 1959–72. Mem., Greater London and SE Sports Council, 1972–77; Chm., Sports Develt Panel, 1976–77. Fellow, Royal Television Soc., 1978. *Publications:* Sportsview Annuals, 1954–65; Sports in View, 1964; (contrib.) The BBC Book of Royal Memories, 1990. *Recreations:* flying, winter sports, golf. *Address:* c/o Coutts & Co., 440 Strand, WC2R 0QS. *Fax:* Bagshot (01276) 452202. *Clubs:* Garrick, Turf, Boodle's; Berkshire Golf; St Enedoc Golf; New York Athletic.

DIMMOCK, Rear-Adm. Roger Charles, CB 1988; Chairman, Archer Mullins Ltd, since 1989; *b* 27 May 1935; *s* of late Frank Dimmock and Ivy Dimmock (*née* Archer); *m* 1958, Lesley Patricia Reid; two *d* (and one *d* decd). *Educ:* Price's School. Entered Royal Navy, 1953; pilot's wings FAA, 1954, USN, 1955; qualified Flying Instructor, 1959; Master Mariner Foreign Going Cert. of Service, 1979. Served RN Air Sqdns and HM Ships Bulwark, Albion, Ark Royal, Eagle, Hermes, Anzio, Messina, Murray, Berwick (i/c), Naiad (i/c), to 1978; CSO to FO Carriers and Amphibious Ships, 1978–80; Comd RNAS Culdrose, 1980–82; Comd HMS Hermes, 1982–83; Dir, Naval Air Warfare,

MoD, 1983–84; Naval Sec., 1985–87; FONAC, 1987–88. Non-exec. Dir, Manufg and Marketing Services Ltd, 1993–. Mem. Cttee of Management, RNLI, 1987– (Pres., Denmead and Hambledon Br., 1981–). Chairman: Trustees, Fleet Air Arm Museum, 1987–88; Fleet Air Arm Benevolent Trust, 1987–88; First of June Appeal, 1987–88; Gov., Royal Naval Benevolent Trust, 1987–88; Chm., Naval Canteen Cttee, 1987–88. President: RN Hockey Assoc., 1985–89; CS Hockey Assoc., 1987–93. Mem., Royal Aero Club. *Recreations:* hockey (player and umpire), cricket, squash, golf, family, home and garden, RNLI. *Address:* Beverley House, Beverley Grove, Farlington, Portsmouth PO6 1BP. *T:* Portsmouth (01705) 386548. *Clubs:* Royal Navy of 1765 and 1785; Royal Naval and Royal Albert Yacht (Portsmouth).

DIMOND, Paul Stephen; HM Diplomatic Service; Deputy Head of Mission, The Hague, since 1994; *b* 30 Dec. 1944; *yr s* of late Cyril James Dimond and of Dorothy Mabel Louisa Hobbs (*née* Knight); *m* 1965, Carolyn Susan Davis-Mees, *er d* of late Dennis Charles Mees and of Eileen Lilian (*née* Barratt); two *s*. *Educ:* St Olave's and St Saviour's Grammar Sch. for Boys, Bermondsey. FCIM 1989; FIL 1988. British Bakeries Ltd, 1962–63; FO, 1963–65; Diplomatic Service Admin, 1965–66; Japanese lang. student, Tokyo, 1966–68; Vice-Consul (Commercial), 1968–70, Consul (Commercial), 1970–72, Osaka; Second Sec. (Commercial), Tokyo, 1972–73; seconded to Dept of Trade as assistant to Special Advr on Japanese Mkt, BOTB, 1973–75; FCO, 1975–76; First Secretary: (Economic), Stockholm, 1977–80; FCO, 1980–81; (Commercial), Tokyo, 1981–86; FCO, 1986–88; seconded to Smiths Industries plc as Strategic Marketing Advr, Smiths Industries Med. Systems, 1988–89; Commercial Counsellor, Tokyo, 1989–93. Sec., First Anglo–Mongolian Round Table, Ulaan Baatar, 1987. FRSA 1980. *Recreations:* the arts, manufactures and commerce, vintage Batsfords, walking. *Address:* c/o Foreign and Commonwealth Office, King Charles Street, SW1A 2AH. *Club:* Travellers'.

DIMSON, Gladys Felicia, (Mrs S. B. Dimson), CBE 1976; Member of GLC for Battersea North, 1973–85; Member, Inner London Education Authority, 1970–85; *o d* of late I. Sieve, BA; *m* 1936, Dr S. B. Dimson (*d* 1991), *e s* of late Rev. Z. Dimson; one *d*. *Educ:* Laurel Bank Sch., Glasgow; Glasgow Univ.; London Sch. of Economics. Voluntary social worker, mainly in E London, 1950–63; Co-opted Mem., Children's Cttee, LCC, 1958–65; Chm., gp of LCC Children's Homes and of a voluntary Hostel for Girls; Educn Counsellor, Marriage Guidance Council. Member: Home Office Advisory Cttee on Juvenile Delinquency, 1963–65 (Chm. Sub-Cttee on Transition from Sch. to Work); a Youth Employment Cttee, 1960–; Hendon Gp Hosp. Management Cttee, 1965–70; Exec., Greater London Labour Party, 1964–74; Toynbee Housing Soc., 1967– (Chm., 1976–87); Council, Toynbee Hall, 1983–90; Bd of Governors, Nat. Hosp. for Nervous Diseases, 1976–79; Board of Management, Shelter, 1976–89 (Trustee, Shelter Housing Aid Centre); London Local Adv. Cttee, IBA, 1979–83; Hampstead DHA, 1981–84; Trustee, Sutton Housing Trust, 1982–90; Chm., East London Housing Assoc., 1979–94. Mem., GLC Haringey, 1964–67, Wandsworth, 1970–73; (Vice-Chm.) GLC Ambulance Cttee; GLC Housing Cttee: Mem. (co-opted), 1968–70; Labour Spokesman, 1970–73, and 1977–81; Chm., 1973–75, 1981–82. Contested (Lab) Hendon South, at Gen. Election, 1970. Mem., Nat. and London Councils of Nat. Fedn of Housing Assocs, 1980–83. Co-Pres., Nat-amat UK (Internat. Orgn of Working Women and Volunteers), 1994–. FRSA 1977. *Recreations:* walking in the country, lazing in the sun; reading (incl. thrillers); theatre; watching TV.

See also O. W. Baron.

DINES, Peter Munn, CBE 1991; educational consultant; Secretary, School Examinations and Assessment Council, 1988–91; *b* 29 Aug. 1929; *e s* of Victor Edward Dines and Muriel Eleanor Dines (*née* Turner); *m* 1952, Kathleen Elisabeth Jones; two *s* one *d*. *Educ:* Palmer's Sch., Grays, Essex; Imperial Coll. London (ARCS; BSc 1st cl. 1949); Inst. of Education, London (PGCE 1950); Bristol Univ. (MEd 1968). RAF, 1950–53. Teaching maths, 1953–69; Headmaster, Cramlington High Sch., 1969–76; Jt Sec., Schools Council, 1976–78; Headmaster, Sir John Leman High Sch., Beccles, 1978–80; Examinations Officer, Schools Council, 1980–83; Dep. Chief Exec., 1983–87, Chief Exec., 1988, Secondary Examinations Council. Educn Consultant, British Council, Swaziland, 1993 and Pakistan, 1994. Mem., Schools Broadcasting Council, later Educn Broadcasting Council, 1982–91; occasional broadcaster on radio and TV. *Recreations:* sailing, esp. on W coast of Scotland; walking. *Club:* Clyde Cruising.

DINEVOR; *see* Dynevor.

DINGEMANS, Rear-Adm. Peter George Valentin, CB 1990; DSO 1982; Head of Benefits Payroll and Insurances, Slaughter and May, since 1992; *b* 31 July 1935; *s* of Dr George Albert and Marjorie Dingemans; *m* 1961, Faith Vivien Bristow; three *s*. *Educ:* Brighton College. Entered RN 1953; served HM Ships Vanguard, Superb, Ark Royal, 1953–57; qualified Torpedo Anti Submarine specialist, 1961; Comd, HMS Maxton, 1967; RAF Staff Course, 1968; Directorate of Naval Plans, 1971–73; Comd, HMS Berwick, HMS Lowestoft, 1973–74; Staff Asst, Chief of Defence Staff, 1974–76; Captain, Fishery Protection, 1977–79; Comd HMS Intrepid, 1980–83 (incl. service South Atlantic, 1982); Commodore, Amphibious Warfare, 1983–85; Flag Officer Gibraltar, 1985–87; COS to C-in-C Fleet, 1987–90, retd. Director: Administration, Argosy Asset Management PLC, 1990–91; Ivory and Sime, 1991–92. FIMgt (FBIM 1990). Freeman, City of London, 1984; Liveryman, Coach Makers and Coach Harness Makers Co., 1984. *Recreations:* family and friends, tennis, shooting. *Address:* c/o Lloyds Bank, Steyning, Sussex BN44 3ZA. *Clubs:* Naval and Military, City Livery.

DINGLE, John Thomas, PhD, DSc; President, Hughes Hall, Cambridge, since 1993; *b* 27 Oct. 1927; *s* of Thomas Henry and Violet Nora Dingle; *m* 1953, Dorothy Vernon Parsons; two *s*. *Educ:* King Edward Sch., Bath; London Univ. (BSc, DSc); Clare Coll., Cambridge (PhD). Royal National Hosp. for Rheumatic Diseases, Bath, 1951–59; Research Fellowship, Strangeways Research Laboratory, Cambridge, 1959–61; MRC External Staff, 1961–79; Strangeways Research Laboratory: Head of Tissue Physiology Dept, 1966; Dep. Dir, 1970–79; Dir, 1979–93; Fellow, Corpus Christi Coll., Cambridge, 1968–93; Bursar of Leckhampton, 1972–80, Warden, 1980–86. Visiting Professor: of Biochemistry, Royal Free Hosp. Med. Sch., 1975–78; of Rheumatology, New York Univ., 1977. Chm., British Connective Tissue Soc., 1980–87. Chm. Editorial Bd, Biochemical Jl, 1975–82. Pres., Cambridge Univ. RFC, 1990– (Treas., 1982–90). Heberden Orator and Medalist, 1978; American Orthopaedic Assoc. Steindler Award, 1980. *Publications:* communications to learned jls. *Recreations:* Rugby football (playing member, Bath, Bristol, Somerset RFCs, 1943–57), sailing. *Address:* Hughes Hall, Cambridge CB1 2EW. *Clubs:* Farmers'; Hawks (Cambridge); Royal Dart (Dartmouth).

DINGLE, Prof. Robert Balson, PhD; FRSE; Professor of Theoretical Physics, University of St Andrews, 1960–87, now Emeritus; *b* 26 March 1926; *s* of late Edward Douglas Dingle and Nora Gertrude Balson; *m* 1958, Helen Glenronnie Munro; two *d*. *Educ:* Bournemouth Secondary Sch.; Cambridge University. PhD 1951. Fellow of St John's Coll., Cambridge, 1948–52; Theoretician to Royal Society Mond Lab., 1949–52; Chief Asst in Theoretical Physics, Technical Univ. of Delft, Holland, 1952–53; Fellow, Nat. Research Council, Ottawa, 1953–54; Reader in Theoretical Physics, Univ. of WA, 1954–60. *Publications:* Asymptotic Expansions: their derivation and interpretation, 1973; contribs to learned journals. *Recreations:* music, local history, gastronomy. *Address:* 6 Lawhead Road East, St Andrews, Fife, Scotland KY16 9ND. *T:* St Andrews (01334) 474287.

DINGWALL, Baron; *see* Lucas of Crudwell and Dingwall.

DINGWALL, John James, OBE 1964; HM Inspector of Constabulary for Scotland, 1966–70; *b* 2 Sept. 1907; *s* of late James Dingwall, Bannockburn, Stirling; *m* 1932, Jane Anne (*d* 1980), *d* of late James K. Halliday, Falkirk; two *d*. *Educ:* Bridge of Allan and Stirling. Stirlingshire Constabulary, 1927–49; Stirling and Clackmannan Police Force, 1949–55; seconded to Directing Staff, Scottish Police Coll., 1953–55; Chief Constable of Angus, 1955–66. *Recreations:* angling, shooting, golf. *Address:* Tigh Na Muirn, 4 Victoria Street, Monifieth DD5 4HL.

DINGWALL-SMITH, Ronald Alfred, CB 1977; *b* 24 Feb. 1917; 2nd *s* of Robert Frederick Sydney Smith (*d* in action 1917) and Alice Olive Brookman; *m* 1946, Margaret Eileen Dingwall; adopted surname Dingwall-Smith; one *s* one *d*. *Educ:* Alleyn's Sch., Dulwich; London School of Economics (evening classes). Entered Civil Service as Clerical Officer, Ministry of Transport, 1934; Exchequer and Audit Dept, 1935–47; Scottish Educn Dept, 1947–65; Scottish Development Dept, 1965–70; Under-Sec. (Principal Finance Officer), Scottish Office, 1970–78. Sen. Res. Fellow, Glasgow Univ., 1979–81. Director: St Vincent Drilling Ltd, 1979–80; Hanover (Scotland) Housing Assoc. Ltd, 1979–92 (Chm., 1988–92); Heritage Housing Ltd, 1982–92 (Chm., 1988–92); Hanover (Caol) Housing Assoc. Ltd, 1986–92 (Chm., 1988–92). Mem., Commn for Local Auth. Accts in Scotland, 1980–85. Governor, Moray Hse Coll. of Educn, Edinburgh, 1980–87. *Recreations:* golf, bowls (Pres., Braid Bowling Club, Edinburgh, 1990 (Hon. Sec., 1980–89)), gardening. *Address:* 3 Frogston Terrace, Edinburgh EH10 7AD. *T:* 0131–445 2727.

DINKIN, Anthony David; QC 1991; barrister; *b* 2 Aug. 1944; *s* of Hyman Dinkin and Mary (*née* Hine); *m* 1968, Derina Tanya (*née* Green). *Educ:* Henry Thornton Grammar Sch., Clapham; Coll. of Estate Management, London (BSc (Est. Man.)). Called to the Bar, Lincoln's Inn, 1968. A Recorder of the Crown Court, 1989–. Examr in Law, Reading Univ., 1985–93. *Recreations:* gardening, theatre, music, travel. *Address:* 2–3 Gray's Inn Square, WC1R 5JH. *T:* 0171–242 4986. *Club:* Players.

DINSDALE, Richard Lewis; Chairman, West of England Newspapers Ltd, 1969–72; *b* 23 June 1907; *m* 1930, Irene Laverack (*d* 1984); one *d*. *Educ:* Hull Technical Coll. Joined Hull Daily Mail as reporter, 1926; Editorial posts: Newcastle Evening World; Chief Sub-editor, Manchester Evening News; Dep. Chief Sub-editor, Daily Express, Manchester; Evening News, London; Daily Mirror, 1940–42; War Service, 1942–46; Copy-taster, Daily Mirror, 1946, successively Chief Sub-editor, Dep. Night Editor, Night Editor; Dep. Editor, 1955; seconded Daily Herald as Editorial Adviser, 1961; Dep. Editor, Daily Herald, 1962; Dep. Editor, The Sun, 1964, Editor, 1965–69. *Recreation:* strolling. *Address:* Southlands Court, 33 Hastings Road, Bexhill-on-Sea, E Sussex TN40 2HJ.

DINWIDDY, Bruce Harry; HM Diplomatic Service; Head of African Department (Southern), Foreign and Commonwealth Office, since 1995; *b* 1 Feb. 1946; *s* of late Thomas Lutwyche Dinwiddy and of Ruth Dinwiddy (*née* Abbott); *m* 1974, Emma Victoria Llewellyn; one *s* one *d*. *Educ:* Winchester Coll.; New Coll., Oxford (MA). Economist, Govt of Swaziland (ODI Nuffield Fellow), 1967–70; Res. Officer, ODI, 1970–73; HM Diplomatic Service, 1973; First Sec., UK Deleg. to MBFR talks, Vienna, 1975–77; FCO, 1977–81; Head of Chancery, Cairo, 1981–83; FCO, 1983–86; Asst Sec., Cabinet Office, 1986–88; Counsellor, Bonn, 1989–91; Dep. High Comr, Ottawa, 1992–95. *Publication:* Promoting African Enterprise, 1974. *Recreations:* golf (captained Oxford *v* Cambridge, 1967), lawn tennis, music, travel. *Address:* c/o Foreign and Commonwealth Office, SW1A 2AH. *Clubs:* Vincent's (Oxford); Aldeburgh Golf, Royal Wimbledon Golf.

DIONISOTTI-CASALONE, Carlo, FBA 1972; Professor of Italian, Bedford College (formerly Bedford College for Women), University of London, 1949–70; *b* 9 June 1908; *s* of Eugenio Dionisotti-Casalone and Carla Cattaneo; *m* 1942, Maria Luisa Pinna-Pintor; three *d* (and one *d* decd). *Educ:* Turin, Italy. Dottore in lettere, Univ. of Turin, 1929; Libero Docente di Letteratura Italiana, Univ. of Turin, 1937; Asst di Letteratura Italiana, Univ. of Rome, 1943; Italian Lectr, Univ. of Oxford, 1947; MA Oxon, 1947. *Publications:* Indici del giornale storico della letteratura italiana (Turin), 1945; Guidiccioni-orazione ai nobili di Lucca (Rome), 1946; Bembo-Savorgnan, Carteggio d'amore (Florence), 1950; Oxford Book of Italian Verse (revised edn), 1952; Bembo, Prose e Rime (Turin), 1960; Geografia e storia della letter. ital. (Turin), 1967; Gli Umanisti e il Volgare (Florence), 1968; Machiavellerie (Turin), 1980; Appunti sui moderni (Bologna), 1988; Ricordo di A. Momigliano (Bologna), 1989. *Address:* 44 West Heath Drive, NW11 7QH.

DIOUF, Jacques, PhD; Director-General, United Nations Food and Agriculture Organization, since 1994; *b* 1 Aug. 1938; *m* 1963, Aïssatou Seye; one *s* four *d*. *Educ:* Ecole nationale d'agriculture, Grignon-Paris (BSc Agric.); Ecole nationale d'application d'agronomie tropicale, Nogent-Paris, (MSc Trop. Agronomy); Panthéon-Sorbonne, Paris (PhD Agricl Econs). Dir, European Office and Agricl Prog. of Mkting Bd, Dakar/Paris, 1963–64; Executive Secretary: African Groundnut Council, Lagos, 1965–71; W Africa Rice Develt Assoc., Liberia, 1971–77; Sec. of State for Sci. and Technol., Senegal, 1978–83; MP Senegambian Confedn, 1983–84: Chm. and Elected Sec., Foreign Relns Cttee, 1983–84; Chm., Friendship Parly Gp, Senegal–UK, 1983–84; Advr to Pres. and Regl Dir, Internat. Develt Res. Centre, Ottawa, 1984–85; Central Bank for W African States, Dakar: Sec.-Gen., 1985–90; Special Advr to Governor, 1990–91; Ambassador, Senegal Perm. Mission to UN, 1991–93. Légion d'Honneur (France), 1978; Grand Comdr, Order of Star of Africa (Liberia), 1977. *Publications:* contrib. to learned jls. *Address:* United Nations Food and Agriculture Organization, Viale della Terme di Caracalla, 00100 Rome, Italy.

DI PALMA, Vera June, (Mrs Ernest Jones), OBE 1986; FCCA, FTII; Chairman, Mobile Training Ltd (formerly Mobile Training & Exhibitions Ltd), since 1978; *b* 14 July 1931; *d* of late William Di Palma and of Violet Di Palma; *m* 1972, Ernest Jones. *Educ:* Haverstock Central Sch., London. Accountant in public practice, 1947–64; Taxation Accountant, Dunlop Co., 1964–67; Sen. Lectr in Taxation, City of London Polytechnic, 1967–71; taxation consultant, 1971–80. Pres., Assoc. of Certified Accountants, 1980–81 (Dep. Pres., 1979–80); Public Works Loan Comr, 1978–; Dep. Chm., Air Travel Trust Cttee, 1986–; Mem., VAT Tribunals, 1977–; Non-exec. Mem., S Warwicks HA, 1991–93. *Publications:* Capital Gains Tax, 1972, 5th edn 1981; Your Fringe Benefits, 1978. *Recreations:* dog-walking, golf, tennis, gardening. *Address:* Temple Close, Sibford Gower, Banbury, Oxon OX15 5RX. *T:* Swalcliffe (01295) 780222.

DIPLOCK, Prof. Anthony Tytherleigh; Professor, since 1977, Chairman of Division of Biochemistry, since 1984, and Co-Director, Free Radical Research Group, since 1991, United Medical and Dental Schools of Guy's and St Thomas' Hospitals (formerly Guy's Hospital Medical School); *b* 24 July 1935; *s* of Bernard and Elsie Diplock; *m* 1st, 1957,

Elisabeth Anne Price (marr. diss. 1979); one *s* one *d*; 2nd, 1980, Lynn Christine Richards; one *s*. *Educ:* Univ. of Bristol (BSc Physiol/Chemistry); Univ. of London (PhD Biochem.); DSc London 1976. Mem., then Hd, Biochem. Res. Dept, Vitamins Ltd, Tadworth, subseq. Beecham Res. Labs, 1956–67; Sen. Lectr, then Reader in Biochem., Royal Free Hosp. Med. Sch., Univ. of London, 1967–77. University of London: Mem., Senate, 1980–94; Mem. Ct, 1989–94; Mem., Council, 1994–; Dean, Faculty of Medicine, 1986–91; Chm., Academic Council Med. Cttee, 1984–91; Mem., numerous Univ. of London cttees and wkg parties, 1978–. Res. Prog. Manager, MAFF. Member, Council: BPMF, 1988–91; Hunterian Inst., RCS, 1989–92; Royal Free Hosp. Sch. of Medicine, 1989–95; Roedean Sch., 1989–; Mem., Council of Govs, 1987–, Chm., Academic Bd, 1991–95, UMDS; Advr, ACU, 1987–91; Mem., Commonwealth Scholarships Commn, 1991–. Hon. Prof. of Biochem., Xi'an Med. Univ., People's Republic of China, 1985–. Evian Health Award, 1986; Caroline Walker Award for Science, 1993. *Publications:* Fat-Soluble Vitamins, 1985; (solely or jtly) over 180 pubns on fat-soluble vitamins, trace elements, antioxidant nutrients in human health, nutritional prevention of cancer and cardiovascular disease. *Recreations:* renovating an old cottage, sailing, music, building long-case clocks, dogs. *Address:* Division of Biochemistry, United Medical and Dental Schools, Guy's Hospital, SE1 9RT. *T:* 0171–955 4521/2, *Fax:* 0171–403 7195.

DISBREY, Air Vice-Marshal William Daniel, CB 1967; CBE 1945 (OBE 1943); AFC 1939; *b* London, 23 Aug. 1912; *s* of Horace William Disbrey; *m* 1939, Doreen Alice, *d* of William Henry Ivory, Stevenage; two *d*. *Educ:* Minchenden Sch. Joined RAF as an Apprentice, 1928; gained Cadetship to RAF Coll., Cranwell, 1931; No 3 Fighter Sqdn, 1933–34; Fleet Air Arm, 1934–37; Engr Specialist Course, Henlow, 1937–39; Engr Officer, No 13 Group HQ, 1940–41; Engr Officer, HQ Fighter Comd, 1941–43; Chief Engr Officer, 2nd TAF, 1943–46; Staff Coll. Course, 1946; CO, No 12 Sch. of Technical Training, 1946–48; Sen. Technical Officer, Royal Indian Air Force, 1948–51; Min. of Supply, 1951–54; Chief Engr Officer, Bomber Comd, 1954–57; Imperial Defence Coll., 1957; Dir of Research and Development, Bombers, Min. of Aviation, 1958–61; Comdt, No 1 Radio Sch., Locking, 1961–64; Dir-Gen. of Engineering (RAF), 1964–67; AO Engineering, Bomber Comd, 1967, Strike Comd, 1968–70, retired. Manager, Tech. Trng Inst., Airwork Services, Saudi Arabia, 1970. CEng; FIMechE; FRAeS. *Recreations:* golf, sailing. *Address:* Old Heatherwode, Buxted, East Sussex TN22 4JW. *T:* Buxted (0182581) 2104. *Club:* Royal Air Force.

DISLEY, John Ivor, CBE 1979; Director: London Marathon Ltd, since 1980; Reebok UK Ltd, since 1985; *b* Gwynedd, 20 Nov. 1928; *s* of Harold Disley and Marie Hughes; *m* 1957, Sylvia Cheeseman; two *d*. *Educ:* Oswestry High Sch.; Loughborough Coll. (Hon. DCL). Schoolmaster, Isleworth, 1951; Chief Instructor, CCPR Nat. Mountaineering Centre, 1955; Gen. Inspector of Educn, Surrey, 1958; Dir, Ski Plan, 1971. Member: Adv. Sports Council, 1964–71; Mountain Leadership Trng Bd, 1965–; Canal Adv. Bd, 1965–66; Internat. Orienteering Fedn, 1972–78; Countryside Commn, 1974–77; Water Space Adv. Council, 1976–81; Royal Commn on Gambling, 1976–78. Vice-Chm., Sports Council, 1974–82; Chm., Nat. Jogging Assoc., 1978–80. Mem., British athletics team, 1950–59; Brit. record holder steeplechase, 1950–56; Welsh mile record holder, 1952–57; bronze medal, Olympics, Helsinki, 1952; Sportsman of the Year, 1955; Athlete of the Year, 1955. *Publications:* Tackle Climbing, 1959; Young Athletes Companion, 1961; Orienteering, 1966; Expedition Guide for Duke of Edinburgh's Award Scheme, 1965; Your Way with Map and Compass, 1971. *Recreations:* running games, mountain activities. *Address:* Hampton House, Upper Sunbury Road, Hampton, Mddx TW12 2DW. *T:* 0181–979 1707. *Clubs:* Climbers'; Ranelagh Harriers, Southern Navigators.

See also Rev. Canon B. L. Hebblethwaite.

DISNEY, Harold Vernon, CBE 1956; Manager, Engineering Division, Reactor Group, UK Atomic Energy Authority, 1969–72, retired; *b* 2 July 1907; *s* of Henry Disney and Julia Vernon; *m* 1936, Lucy Quinton; two *d*. *Educ:* Hallcroft Higher Standard Sch., Ilkeston; Nottingham Univ. Coll. Internat. Combustion, 1931–35; ICI (Alkali), 1935–46. On loan to Min. of Supply (RFF's), 1941–46. Dept of Atomic Energy, 1946–54; UKAEA: Asst Dir, Defence Projects, Industrial Gp, 1954; Dir of Engineering, Industrial Gp, 1958; Man. Dir, Engineering Gp, Risley, 1962. FIMechE 1947. *Recreation:* gardening. *Address:* 63 Vincent Drive, Westminster Park, Chester CH4 7RQ.

DISS, Eileen, (Mrs Raymond Everett), RDI 1978; freelance designer for theatre, film and television, since 1959; *b* 13 May 1931; *d* of Thomas and Winifred Diss; *m* 1953, Raymond Everett; two *s* one *d*. *Educ:* Ilford County High Sch. for Girls; Central Sch. of Art and Design. MSIAD; FRSA. BBC Television design, 1952–59. *Television* series and plays: Maigret, 1962–63; The Tea Party, 1964; Up the Junction, 1965; Somerset Maugham, 1969; Uncle Vanya, 1970; The Duchess of Malfi, and Candide, 1972; The Importance of Being Earnest, and Pygmalion, 1973; Caesar and Cleopatra, 1974; Moll Flanders, 1975; Ghosts, and The Winslow Boy, 1976; You Never Can Tell, 1977; The Rear Column, Hedda Gabler, 1980; The Potting Shed, 1981; Porterhouse Blue, 1987; Behaving Badly, 1989; Jeeves & Wooster, 1989, 1990, and 1992; Best of Friends, 1991; Head Over Heels, 1993; Love on a Branch Line, 1993. Television opera: The Merry Widow, 1968; Tales of Hoffmann, 1969; Die Fledermaus, 1971; Falstaff, 1972; The Yeomen of the Guard, 1974; television films: Cider with Rosie, 1971; Robinson Crusoe, 1974. *Theatre:* Exiles, 1969; Butley, 1971; The Caretaker, 1972 and 1991; Otherwise Engaged, 1975; The Apple-cart, 1977; The Rear Column, The Homecoming, 1978; The Hothouse, 1980; Translations, Quartermaine's Terms, Incident at Tulse Hill, 1981; Rocket to the Moon, 1982; The Communication Cord, 1983; The Common Pursuit, 1984; Other Places, The Seagull, Sweet Bird of Youth, 1985; Circe and Bravo, 1986; The Deep Blue Sea, 1988; Veterans Day, The Mikado, Steel Magnolias, 1989; Burn This, 1990; The Philanthropist, 1991; Private Lives, A Month in the Country, 1992; Oleanna, 1993; Pinter Fest., Dublin, 1994; Cell Mates, 1995; National Theatre: Blithe Spirit, 1976; The Philanderer, 1978; Close of Play, When We Are Married, 1979; Watch on the Rhine, 1980; The Caretaker, 1980; Measure for Measure, 1981; The Trojan War Will Not Take Place, 1983; Landscape, 1994. *Films:* Joseph Losey's A Doll's House, 1972; Sweet William, 1978; Harold Pinter's Betrayal, 1982; Secret Places, 1984; 84 Charing Cross Road, 1986; A Handful of Dust, 1988; August, 1994. BAFTA Television Design Award, 1962, 1965, 1974 and 1992. *Recreations:* music, cinema. *Address:* 4 Gloucester Walk, W8 4HZ. *T:* 0171–937 8794.

DIVER, Hon. Sir Leslie Charles, Kt 1975; President, Legislative Council, Western Australia, 1960–74; Member, Legislative Council (Country Party) for Central Province, Western Australia, 1952–74; *b* Perth, Australia, 4 Nov. 1899; *s* of late J. W. Diver; *m* 1st, 1922, Emma J. (decd), *d* of late F. Blakiston; one *s* two *d*; 2nd, 1971, Mrs Thelma May Evans (decd). Farmer and grazier. Chairman: Kellerberrin Road Bd, 1940, 1942–46; Hon. Royal Commn on Retailing of Motor Spirits, 1956. Chm., Sixth Aust. Area Conf., Commonwealth Parly Assoc., 1961; Rep. WA Parlt, Town Planning Adv. Cttee. Warden, State War Meml, 1967–68. *Publication:* From Plough to Politics (autobiog.). *Recreations:* bowls, Australian rules football. *Address:* Dryandra Hostel, Leake Street, Kellerberrin, WA 6410, Australia. *Clubs:* Eastern Districts (Kellerberrin); Manning Memorial Bowling.

DIVERRES, Prof. Armel Hugh; Professor of French and Head of Department of Romance Studies, University College of Swansea, 1974–81, now Emeritus; *b* Liverpool, 4 Sept. 1914; *o s* of late Paul Diverres and Elizabeth (*née* Jones); *m* 1945, Ann Dilys, *d* of late James and Enid Williams; one *s* two *d*. *Educ:* Swansea Grammar Sch.; University Coll., Swansea; Univ. of Rennes; Sorbonne, Paris. MA (Wales), LèsL (Rennes), Docteur de l'Université de Paris. Fellow of Univ. of Wales, 1938–40; served in RA and Int. Corps, 1940–46, Captain. Asst Lectr in French, 1946–49, Lectr, 1949–54, Univ. of Manchester; Sen. Lectr in French, 1954–57, Carnegie Prof., 1958–74, Dean, Faculty of Arts, 1967–70, Univ. of Aberdeen. Governor: Nat. Mus. of Wales, 1978–81; Centre for Information on Language Teaching and Res., 1977–82; Aberdeen Coll. of Education, 1971–74. Member: CNAA Lang. Board, 1965–78, Cttee for Res., 1975–82, Humanities Bd, 1978–81; Welsh Jt Educn Cttee, 1975–81. Pres., British Br., Internat. Arthurian Soc., 1978–80, Internat. Pres., 1979–81; Pres., Soc. French Stud., 1976–78. Officier des Palmes Académiques, 1971; Chevalier de l'Ordre National du Mérite, 1986. *Publications:* Voyage en Béarn by Froissart (ed), 1953; La Chronique métrique attribuée à Geffroy de Paris (ed), 1956; Chatterton by A. de Vigny (ed), 1967; articles and reviews in learned journals. *Recreation:* hill walking. *Address:* 23 Whiteshell Drive, Langland, Swansea, W Glamorgan SA3 4SY. *T:* Swansea (01792) 360322.

DIX, Alan Michael, OBE 1985; Director General, Motor Agents' Association Ltd, 1976–85; *b* 29 June 1922; *s* of late Comdr Charles Cabry Dix, CMG, DSO, RN, and Ebba Sievers; *m* 1955, Helen Catherine McLaren; one *s* one *d*. *Educ:* Stenhus Kostskole, Denmark. Escaped Nazi occupied Denmark to Scotland, 1943; joined RAF, commissioned 1944. President, Capitol Car Distributors Inc., USA, 1958–67; Gp Vice-Pres., Volkswagen of America, USA, 1967–68; Man. Dir, Volkswagen (GB) Ltd, London, 1968–72; Pres., Mid Atlantic Toyota Inc., USA, 1972–73; Dir Marketing, British Leyland International, 1973–74; Proprietor, Alan M. Dix Associates, 1974–76. Chm., Motor Agents Pensions Administrators Ltd, 1976–85; Dir, Hire Purchase Information Ltd, 1977–85. Freedom and Livery, Coachmakers' and Coach Harness Makers' Co., 1980. FIMI, FInstM, FIMH, FBIM. King Christian X war medal, 1947. *Publications:* contribs to automotive trade jls. *Recreations:* yachting, photography; the study of professional management (internat. speaker on management and organisation). *Address:* Tigh na Failte, Firhills, Letham Grange, near Arbroath, Angus DD11 4RL. *T:* Gowanbank (01241) 890421. *Clubs:* Danish, Royal Air Force, Burkes; Royal Air Force Yacht (Hamble).

DIX, Geoffrey Herbert, OBE 1979; Secretary-General, The Institute of Bankers, 1971–82; *b* 1 March 1922; *o s* of late Herbert Walter and Winifred Ada Dix; *m* 1945, Margaret Sybil Outhwaite, MA (Cantab) (*d* 1981); one *s*. *Educ:* Watford Grammar Sch.; Gonville and Caius Coll., Cambridge. MA (Mod. langs). Served War, 1942–45: commissioned into Royal Devon Yeomanry; later served with HQ 1st Airborne Corps. Inst. of Export, 1946–51; with Inst. of Bankers, 1951–: Asst Sec., 1956; Under-Sec. 1962; Dep. Sec. 1968. Mem., Jt Cttee for National Awards in Business Studies, 1960–76. *Recreations:* Mozart, theatre. *Address:* Tanglewood, Tally Road, Limpsfield Chart, Oxted, Surrey RH8 0TQ. *T:* Oxted (01883) 713163. *Club:* Caterham Players.

DIX, Prof. Gerald Bennett, RIBA; FRTPI; architect; Lever Professor of Civic Design, University of Liverpool, 1975–88; Professor Emeritus and Hon. Senior Fellow, Liverpool University, since 1988; Hon. Senior Research Fellow, Chinese Research Academy of Environmental Sciences, since 1989; *b* 12 Jan. 1926; *s* of late Cyril Dix and Mabel Winifred (*née* Bennett); *m* 1st, 1956 (marr. diss.); two *s*; 2nd, 1963, Lois Nichols; one *d*. *Educ:* Altrincham Grammar Sch.; Univ. of Manchester (BA (Hons Arch.), DipTP (dist.)); Harvard Univ. (MLA). Studio Asst, 1950–51, Asst Lectr in Town and Country Planning, 1951–53, Manchester Univ.; Asst Architect, 1954; Chief Architect-Planner, Addis Ababa, and chief asst to Sir Patrick Abercrombie, 1954–56; Planning Officer, Singapore, 1957–59; Acting Planning Adviser, 1959; Sen. Research Fellow, Univ. of Science and Technol., Ghana, 1959–63; UN Planning Mission to Ghana, 1962; Planner, later Sen. Planner, BRS/ODM, 1963–65 (adv. missions to W Indies, W Africa, Aden, Bechuanaland, Swaziland, Cyprus); Nottingham University: Lectr, 1966–68; Sen. Lectr, 1968–70; Prof. of Planning, and Dir, Inst. of Planning Studies, 1970–75; Liverpool University: Chm., Fac. of Social and Environmental Studies, 1983–84; Pro Vice-Chancellor, 1984–87. Dir, Cyprus Planning Project, 1967–71; adv. visits on planning educn, to Uganda 1971, Nigeria 1972, Sudan 1975, Mexico 1978, Egypt 1980; UK Mem., Adv. Panel on planning Canal towns, Egypt, 1974, and Western Desert, 1975; Jt Dir, Alexandria Comprehensive Master Plan Project, 1980–86. Member: Professional Literature Cttee, RIBA, 1966–80, 1981–88 (Chm. 1975–80); Library Management Cttee, 1969–72, 1975–80; Historic Areas Adv. Cttee, English Heritage, 1986–88. Vice-Pres., World Soc. for Ekistics, 1975–79, Pres., 1987–90. Editorial adviser, Ekistics (journal), 1972–; Chm., Bd of Management, Town Planning Rev., 1976–88; (Founder) Editor, Third World Planning Rev., 1978–90. FRSA. Hon. DEng Dong-A Univ., Korea, 1995. *Publications:* ed, C. A. Doxiadis, Ecology and Ekistics, 1977, Boulder, Colo, 1978, Brisbane, 1978; numerous planning reports to govts in various parts of world; articles and reviews in Town Planning Rev., Third World Planning Rev., Ekistics, RIBA Jl, Arch. Rev. *Recreations:* photography, listening to music, travel, cooking. *Address:* Department of Civic Design, University of Liverpool, PO Box 147, Liverpool L69 3BX. *T:* 0151–794 3108; 13 Friar's Quay, Norwich, Norfolk NR3 1ES. *T:* Norwich (01603) 632433. *Club:* Athenæum.

DIXEY, John, OBE 1976; Newspaper Consultant, since 1991; Development Co-ordinator, Evening Standard Company, since 1987; *b* 29 March 1926; *s* of John Dixey and Muriel Doris Dixey; *m* 1948, Pauline Seaden; one *s* one *d*. *Educ:* Battersea Grammar Sch. Served Royal Marines and Royal Fusiliers, 1944–47. Press Telegraphist, Yorkshire Post and Glasgow Herald, 1948–59; Asst to Gen. Sec., Nat. Union of Press Telegraphists, 1959; Labour Officer, Newspaper Soc., 1959–63; Labour Adviser, Thomson Organisation Ltd, 1963–64; Asst Gen. Man., Liverpool Daily Post & Echo, 1964–67; Executive Dir, Times Newspapers, 1967–74; Special Adviser to Man. Dir, Thomson Org., 1974; Dir, Newspaper Publishers Assoc. Ltd, 1975–76; Employment Affairs Advr, IPA, 1977–79; Sec., Assoc. of Midland Advertising Agencies, 1977–79; Production Dir and Bd Mem., The Guardian, 1979–84; Asst Man. Dir, Mirror Gp Newspapers, 1985; Newspaper Consultant, 1986. Chm., Advertising Assoc. Trade Union Liaison Group, 1975–84; Mem., TUC New Daily Newspaper Advisory Group, 1982–83. Ward-Perkins Vis. Fellow, Pembroke Coll., Oxford, 1978. Mem., Printing and Publishing Industry Trng Bd, 1975–76; Governor, London Coll. of Printing, 1975–76. *Recreations:* cooking, photography. *Address:* 23 West Hill, Sanderstead, Surrey CR2 0SB. *T:* 0181–657 7940.

DIXEY, Paul (Arthur Groser); Chairman of Lloyd's, 1973, 1974 (Deputy Chairman, 1967, 1969, 1972); *b* 13 April 1915; *e s* of late Neville Dixey, JP (Chairman of Lloyd's, 1931, 1934 and 1936), and Marguerite (*née* Groser); *m* 1939, Mary Margaret Baring, JP, 2nd *d* of late Geoffrey Garrod; four *s* one *d*. *Educ:* Stowe; Trinity Coll., Cambridge. Elected an Underwriting Mem. of Lloyd's, 1938. Served War of 1939–45, Royal Artillery. Member: London Insce market delegn to Indonesia, 1958; Dunmow RDC, 1958–64; Cttee, Lloyd's Underwriters' Assoc., 1962–74; Cttee, Salvage Assoc., 1962–74; Cttee, Lloyd's, 1964–70, 1972–75; Gen. Cttee, Lloyd's Register of Shipping, 1964–90; Chm., Salvage Assoc., 1964–65. Chairman: Paul Dixey Underwriting Agencies Ltd, 1973–76; Pieri Underwriting Agencies Ltd, 1976–94; Director, Merrett Dixey Syndicates Ltd, 1976–78. Mem. Council, Morley Coll., 1952–62; Chm. Governors, Vinehall Sch.,

1966–73. Leader, Barn Boys' Club, 1949–61. Chm., Essex Hunt Cttee, 1981–. *Recreations:* riding, fly-fishing. *Address:* Little Easton Spring, Dunmow, Essex CM6 2JB. *T:* Great Dunmow (01371) 872840.

DIXIT, Prof. Avinash Kamalakar; John J. F. Sherrerd '52 Professor of Economics, Princeton University, USA, since 1989 (Professor of Economics, 1981–89); *b* 8 June 1944; *s* of Kamalakar Ramchandra Dixit and Kusum Dixit (*née* Phadke). *Educ:* Bombay Univ. (BSc); Cambridge Univ. (BA, MA); Massachusetts Inst. of Technology (PhD). Acting Asst Professor, Univ. of California, Berkeley, 1968–69; Lord Thomson of Fleet Fellow and Tutor in Economics, Balliol Coll., Oxford, 1970–74; Professor of Economics, Univ. of Warwick, 1974–80. Guggenheim Fellowship, 1991–92. Fellow: Econometric Society, 1977; Amer. Acad. of Arts and Scis, 1992. Co-Editor, Bell Journal of Economics, 1981–83. *Publications:* Optimization in Economic Theory, 1976; The Theory of Equilibrium Growth, 1976; (with Victor Norman) Theory of International Trade, 1980; (with Barry Nalebuff) Thinking Strategically, 1991; (with Robert S. Pindyck) Investment Under Uncertainty, 1994; several articles in professional jls. *Recreations:* listening to music (pre-Schubert only), watching cricket (when possible). *Address:* Department of Economics, Princeton University, Princeton, NJ 08544, USA. *T:* (609) 2584013.

DIXON, family name of **Baron Glentoran.**

DIXON, Prof. Adrian Kendal, MD; FRCP; FRCR; Professor of Radiology, University of Cambridge, since 1994; Fellow of Peterhouse, Cambridge, since 1986; *b* 5 Feb. 1948; *s* of Kendal Cartwright Dixon and Anne Sybil (*née* Darley); *m* 1979, Anne Hazel Lucas; two *s* one *d. Educ:* Uppingham; King's Coll., Cambridge; St Bartholomew's Hosp. Med. Coll., London (MD 1988), FRCR 1978; FRCP 1991. Medical posts in: St Bartholomew's Hosp., 1972–79; Gen. Hosp., Nottingham, 1973–75; Hosp. for Sick Children, Gt Ormond St, 1978; Lectr, Dept of Radiology, Univ. of Cambridge, 1979–94; Hon. Cons. Radiologist, Addenbrooke's Hosp., Cambridge, 1979–. Visiting Professor: Md and Washington, 1988; Dublin, 1991; Univ. of Otago, NZ, 1992. *Publications:* Body CT, 1983; CT and MRI, Radiological Anatomy, 1991; Human Cross Sectional Anatomy, 1991; papers on computed tomography, magnetic resonance imaging and radiological strategies. *Recreations:* family, golf. *Address:* Peterhouse, Cambridge CB2 1RD. *T:* Cambridge (01223) 336890.

DIXON, Anthony Philip G.; *see* Graham-Dixon.

DIXON, Dr Bernard; science writer and consultant; *b* Darlington, 17 July 1938; *s* of late Ronald Dixon and Grace Peirson; *m* 1963, Margaret Helena Charlton (marr. diss. 1988); two *s* one *d. Educ:* Queen Elizabeth Grammar Sch., Darlington; King's Coll., Univ. of Durham; Univ. of Newcastle upon Tyne. BSc, PhD. Luccock Res. Fellow, 1961–64, Frank Schon Fellow, 1964–65, Univ. of Newcastle; Asst Editor, 1965–66, Dep. Editor, 1966–68, World Medicine; Editor, New Scientist, 1969–79; European Editor: The Scientist, 1986–89; Bio Technology, 1989–; Editor, Medical Science Research, 1989–; Mem. Editorial Board: Biologist, 1988–; World Jl of Microbiology and Biotechnology, 1988–; Columnist, BMJ, The Independent. Chm., Cttee, Assoc. of British Science Writers, 1971–72; Member: Soc. for General Microbiology, 1962–; Amer. Inst. of Biol Sci., 1986–; European Assoc. of Sci. Eds, 1980–; Amer. Assoc. for Advancement of Sci., 1980–; CSS 1982–91 (Vice-Chm., 1989–91); Soc. for Applied Bacteriol., 1989–; Internat Science Writers Assoc., 1988–; Amer. Soc. for Microbiology, 1995–; Council: BAAS, 1977–83 (Pres., Section X, 1979; Vice-Pres., 1986–); European Envtl Res. Orgn; Chm., Prog. Cttee, Edinburgh Internat. Science Fest., 1990–. FIBiol 1982; CBiol 1984. *Publications:* (ed) Journeys in Belief, 1968; What is Science For?, 1973; Magnificent Microbes, 1976; Invisible Allies, 1976; Beyond the Magic Bullet, 1978; (with G. Holister) Ideas of Science, 1984; Health and the Human Body, 1986; Engineered Organisms in the Environment, 1986; Recombinant DNA: what's it all about, 1987; The Science of Science: changing the way we think, 1989; The Science of Science: changing the way we live, 1989; (ed) From Creation to Chaos: classic writings in science, 1989; (with A. L. W. F. Eddleston) Interferons in the Treatment of Chronic Virus Infections of the Liver, 1989; (with E. Millstone) Our Genetic Future: the science and ethics of genetic technology, 1992; Genetics and the Understanding of Life, 1993; Power Unseen: how microbes rule the world, 1994; Enzymes Make the World Go Round, 1994; *contributor to:* Animal Rights—A Symposium, 1979; The Book of Predictions, 1980; Development of Science Publishing in Europe, 1980; Medicine and Care, 1981; From Biology to Biotechnology, 1982; Encyclopædia Britannica, 15th edn, 1984; Encyclopædia Britannica Yearbook, 1986–; Inquiry into Life, 1986; The Domesday Project, 1986; Industrial Biotechnology in Europe: issues for public policy, 1986; Biotechnology Information, 1987; Future Earth, 1989; Harrap's Illustrated Dictionary of Science, 1989; Biotechnology—A Brave New World?, 1989; Soundings from BMJ columnists, 1993; Taking Sides: clashing views on controversial issues in health and society, 1993; numerous articles in scientific and general press on microbiology, and other scientific topics; research papers in Jl of General Microbiology, etc, mostly on microbial biochemistry. *Recreation:* playing Scottish traditional music, collecting old books. *Address:* 130 Cornwall Road, Ruislip Manor, Middlesex HA4 6AW. *T:* Ruislip (01895) 632390, *Fax:* (01895) 678645.

DIXON, Bernard Tunbridge; solicitor; *b* 14 July 1928; *s* of Archibald Tunbridge Dixon and Dorothy Dixon (*née* Cardinal); *m* 1962, Jessie Netta Watson Hastie; one *s* three *d. Educ:* Owen's Sch.; University Coll. London (LLB). Admitted Solicitor, 1952 (Edmund Thomas Child Prize); Partner in Dixon & Co., Solicitors, 1952–59; Legal Asst/Sen. Legal Asst with Treasury Solicitor, 1959–67; Sen. Legal Asst with Land Commission, 1967–70; Sen. Legal Asst with Charity Comrs, 1970–74; Dep. Charity Comr, 1975–81; Charity Comr, 1981–84. *Recreation:* photography. *Address:* c/o Maxwell Entwistle & Byrne, 14 Castle Street, Liverpool L2 0SG.

DIXON, (David) Jeremy; architect in private practice; *b* 31 May 1939; *s* of Joseph Lawrence Dixon and Beryl Margaret Dixon (*née* Braund); *m* 1964, Fenella Mary Anne Clemens; one *s* two *d. Educ:* Merchant Taylors' School; Architectural Assoc. Sch. of Architecture (AA Dip. (Hons)). RIBA. Private practice with Edward Jones as Jeremy Dixon. Edward Jones; formed partnership of Jeremy Dixon. Edward Jones. BDP with William Jack, 1984. Work includes: Royal Opera House, Covent Garden; bus station for Venice (exhibn in Venice sponsored by FCO); housing in London at St Mark's Road, Lanark Road, Ashmill St, Compass Point, Isle of Dogs; Henry Moore Sculpture Inst., Leeds; work for Henry Moore Foundn, Perry Green; work for Tate Gall., London; study centre for Darwin Coll., Cambridge; university housing; work for J. Sainsbury plc. *Recreations:* walking in English landscape, contemporary sculpture and painting, music. *Address:* 47 North Hill, Highgate, N6 4BS; (office) 10–11 Percy Street, W1P 9FB.

DIXON, Donald; MP (Lab) Jarrow, since 1979; Deputy Chief Opposition Whip, since 1987 (an Opposition Whip, since 1984); *b* 6 March 1929; *s* of late Christopher Albert Dixon and Jane Dixon; *m* Doreen Morad; one *s* one *d. Educ:* Ellison Street Elementary School, Jarrow. Shipyard Worker, 1947–74; Branch Sec., GMWU, 1974–79. Councillor, South Tyneside MDC, 1963–. Mem. Select Cttee on H of C Services; Chm., PLP Shipbuilding Gp. Freeman of Jarrow, 1972. *Recreations:* football, reading. *Address:* 1 Hillcrest, Jarrow NE32 4DP. *T:* (0191) 897635; (office) 35 Park Road, Jarrow NE32 5JL. *T:* 0191–420 0648, *Fax:* 0191–489 7531. *Clubs:* Jarrow Labour, Ex Servicemens (Jarrow); Hastings (Hebburn).

DIXON, Prof. Gordon Henry, OC 1993; PhD; FRS 1978; FRSC; Professor of Medical Biochemistry, 1974–94, now Emeritus, and Head of the Department, 1983–88, Faculty of Medicine, University of Calgary; *b* 25 March 1930; *s* of Walter James Dixon and Ruth Nightingale; *m* 1954, Sylvia Weir Gillen; three *s* one *d. Educ:* Cambs High Sch. for Boys; Trinity Coll., Cambridge (Open Schol. 1948; BA Hons, MA); Univ. of Toronto (PhD). FRSC 1970. Res. Asst Prof., Dept of Biochem., Univ. of Washington, Seattle, USA, 1954–58; Mem. staff, MRC Unit for res. in cell metabolism, Univ. of Oxford, 1958–59; Univ. of Toronto: Res. Associate, Connaught Med. Res. Lab., 1959–60; Associate Prof., Dept of Biochem., 1960–63; Prof., Dept of Biochem., Univ. of BC, Vancouver, 1963–72; Prof., Biochem. Group, Univ. of Sussex, 1972–74. Vis. Fellow Commoner, Trinity Coll., Cambridge, 1979–80. Mem. Exec., IUBMB (formerly IUB), 1988–94; President: Canadian Biochemical Soc., 1982–83; Pan-American Assoc. of Biochemical Socs, 1987–90 (Vice-Pres., 1984–87; Past Pres., 1990–93). Ayerst Award, Canadian Biochemistry Soc., 1966; Steacie Prize, 1966; Flavelle Medal, RSC, 1980; Izaak Walton Killam Meml Prize, 1991. *Publications:* over 200 pubns in learned jls, incl. Jl Biol Chem., Proc. Nat. Acad. Sci. (US), Nature, and Biochemistry. *Recreations:* music, reading, gardening. *Address:* Department of Medical Biochemistry, University of Calgary, 3330 Hospital Drive NW, Calgary, Alberta T2N 4N1, Canada; 4402 Shore Way, Victoria, BC V8N 3T9, Canada.

DIXON, (Henry) Joly; Director for International Economic and Financial Affairs, European Commission, since 1992; *b* 13 Jan. 1945; *s* of Gervais Joly Dixon and Kay Dixon; *m* 1976, Mary Minch; three *s* two *d. Educ:* Shrewsbury Sch.; York Univ. Lecturer in: Econs and Stats, York Univ., 1970–72; Econs, Exeter Univ., 1972–74; European Commission, 1975–: Econ. Advr to Jacques Delors, 1987–92. Guest Scholar, Brookings Instn, Washington, 1980. *Recreations:* gardening, photography. *Address:* 70 rue Notre Dame, 1200 Brussels, Belgium. *T:* (2) 7706977.

DIXON, Jack Shawcross, OBE 1969; HM Diplomatic Service, retired 1976; *b* 8 March 1918; *s* of Herbert Dixon and Helen (*née* Woollacott); *m* 1941, Ida Hewkin; one *d. Educ:* Oldham Hulme Grammar Sch.; London Sch. of Economics (BScEcon). Served in Royal Welch Fusiliers and RAOC attached Indian Army, 1940–46. Colonial Office, 1948; entered HM Foreign (subseq. Diplomatic) Service, 1949; FO, 1949; HM Political Agency, Kuwait, 1950; Rep. of Polit. Agent, Mina al Ahmadi, 1951; FO, 1952; 1st Sec., Singapore, 1956; HM Consul, Barcelona, 1959; FO, 1962; 1st Sec., Rome, 1966; FCO, 1971; Head of Treaty and Nationality Dept, FCO, 1973–76. *Publications:* contribs to Jl of Imperial and Commonwealth History, Indica Jaipurensia. *Recreation:* art-historical research (India). *Address:* 26 Brook Court, 47 Meads Road, Eastbourne, E Sussex BN20 7PY. *Club:* Commonwealth Trust.

DIXON, Jeremy; *see* Dixon, D. J.

DIXON, Joly; *see* Dixon, H. J.

DIXON, Jon Edmund, CMG 1975; Under Secretary, Ministry of Agriculture, Fisheries and Food, 1971–85; *b* 19 Nov. 1928; *e s* of Edmund Joseph Claude and Gwendoline Alice Dixon; *m* 1953, Betty Edith Stone; two *s* one *d* (and one *d* decd). *Educ:* St Paul's Sch., West Kensington; Peterhouse, Cambridge (Natural Sciences Tripos Part I and Part II (Physiology); MA). Asst Principal, Min. of Agric. and Fisheries, 1952; Private Sec. to successive Parliamentary Secretaries, 1955–58; Principal, 1958; Asst Sec., 1966; Under-Sec., 1971; Minister in UK Delegn, subseq. Office of Permanent Rep., to EEC, 1972–75. Founded JOED Music (editing and publishing Renaissance polyphonic choral music), 1988. *Publications:* Calico Pie (suite for vocal sextet), 1988; The Leuven Carols, 1988; The Pobble Who Has No Toes (4 part-songs), 1989; editions of Renaissance choral music by Arcadelt, Byrd, Clemens, Ferrabosco, Festa, G. Gabrieli, Gombert, Hassler, Josquin, Lassus, de Monte, Morales, Mouton, Palestrina, Philips, Schütz, Tallis, de Silva, Victoria, Walther, White and Willaert; contribs to Early Music News. *Recreations:* musical composition (Choral, Organ and String Music: a selection of works by Jon Dixon, 1970–85 (two LPs)), oil painting, building harpsichords, gardening, walking.

DIXON, Sir Jonathan (Mark), 4th Bt *cr* 1919, of Astle, Chelford, Co. Chester; Technical and Development Director, Lawson Mardon Flexible, since 1989; *b* 1 Sept. 1949; *s* of Captain Nigel Dixon, OBE, RN (*d* 1978), and of Margaret Josephine Dixon; *S* uncle, 1990; *m* 1978, Patricia Margaret, *d* of James Baird Smith; two *s* one *d. Educ:* Winchester Coll.; University Coll., Oxford (MA). *Recreation:* fishing. *Heir: s* Mark Edward Dixon, *b* 29 June 1982. *Address:* 19 Clyde Road, Redland, Bristol BS6 6RJ.

DIXON, Kenneth Herbert Morley, DL; Chairman, Rowntree (formerly Rowntree Mackintosh) plc, 1981–89, retired; Vice-Chairman, Legal & General Group, 1986–94 (Director, 1984–94); Deputy Chairman, Bass PLC, since 1990; *b* 19 Aug. 1929; *yr s* of Arnold Morley Dixon and Mary Jolly; *m* 1955, Patricia Oldbury Whalley; two *s. Educ:* Cathedral Sch., Shanghai; Cranbrook Sch., Sydney, Australia; Manchester Univ. (BA(Econ) 1952); Harvard Business Sch. AMP, 1969. Lieut Royal Signals, 1947–49. Calico Printers Assoc., 1952–56; joined Rowntree & Co. Ltd, 1956; Dir, 1970; Chm., UK Confectionery Div., 1973–78; Dep. Chm., 1978–81. Dep. Chm., Bass, 1990– (Dir, 1988–); Dir, Yorkshire–Tyne Tees (formerly Yorks) TV Hldgs, 1989–; Mem., British Railways Bd, 1990–. Member: Council, Incorporated Soc. of British Advertisers, 1971–79; Council, Cocoa, Chocolate and Confectionery Alliance, 1972–79; Council, Advertising Assoc., 1976–79; BIM Econ. and Social Affairs Cttee, 1980–84; Council, CBI, 1981–90 (Mem., Companies Cttee, 1979–84; Mem., Employment Policy Cttee, 1983–90); Governing Council, Business in the Community, 1983–90; Council, Food from Britain, 1986–89; Exec. Cttee, Food and Drink Fedn, 1986–89 (Mem. Council, 1986–87); Council for Industry and Higher Educn, 1986–; Council, Nat. Forum for Management Educn & Develt, 1987–; HEQC (Chm., Quality Audit Steering Council, 1993–); Chm., Food Assoc., 1986. Treas., York Archaeol Trust, 1993–. Mem. Council, York Univ., 1983– (Chm., 1990–), Pro-Chancellor, 1987–; Chm., Vis. Cttee, Open Univ., 1990–92. FRSA; CIMgt. DL N Yorks, 1991. DUniv York, 1993. *Recreations:* reading, music, fell walking. *Address:* c/o Fairfax House, Castlegate, York YO1 1RN. *T:* York (01904) 655543. *Club:* Reform.

DIXON, Margaret Rumer Haynes; *see* Godden, Rumer.

DIXON, Peter Vibart; management consultant; Member, Merton, Sutton and Wandsworth Family Health Services Authority, since 1994; *b* 16 July 1932; *s* of late Meredith Vibart Dixon and Phyllis Joan (*née* Hemingway); *m* 1955, Elizabeth Anne Howie Davison; three *s. Educ:* Summer Fields; Radley Coll.; King's Coll., Cambridge (BA Classics and Law 1955, MA 1959). Royal Artillery, 1951–52. Asst Principal, HM Treasury, 1955; Office of Lord Privy Seal, 1956; Treasury, 1956–62: Private Sec. to Economic Sec., 1959; Principal, 1960; Colonial Office, 1963; CS Selection Bd, 1964–65; Treasury, 1965–72, Asst Sec., 1969; Counsellor (Economic), HM Embassy, Washington, 1972–75; Treasury, 1975–82: Press Sec., 1975–78; Under Sec., Industrial Policy, 1978–82; Sec., NEDC, 1982–87; Dir of Planning and Admin, Turner Kenneth Brown, solrs, 1988–92. Mem. Council, RIPA,

1976–82. FRSA 1984; FIMgt (FBIM 1988). *Address:* 17 Lauriston Road, Wimbledon SW19 4TJ. *T:* 0181–946 8931. *Club:* United Oxford & Cambridge University.

DIXON, Piers; *b* 29 Dec. 1928; *s* of late Sir Pierson Dixon (British Ambassador in New York and Paris) and Lady (Ismene) Dixon; *m* 1st, 1960, Edwina (marr. diss. 1973), *d* of Rt Hon. Lord Duncan-Sandys, CH, PC; two *s*; 2nd, 1976, Janet (marr. diss. 1981), *d* of R. D. Aiyar, FRCS, and *widow* of 5th Earl Cowley; 3rd, 1984, Anne (marr. diss. 1985), *d* of John Cronin; one *s*; 4th, 1994, Ann Mavroleon, *d* of John Davenport. *Educ:* Eton (schol.); Magdalene Coll., Cambridge (exhibnr); Harvard Business Sch. Grenadier Guards, 1948. Merchant banking, London and New York, 1954–64; Sheppards and Chase, stockbrokers, 1964–81. Centre for Policy Studies, 1976–78. Contested (C) Brixton, 1966; MP (C) Truro, 1970–Sept. 1974; Sec., Cons. Backbenchers' Finance Cttee, 1970–71, Vice-Chm., 1972–74; sponsor of Rehabilitation of Offenders Act, 1974. *Publications:* Double Diploma, 1968; Cornish Names, 1973. *Recreations:* tennis, modern history. *Address:* 22 Ponsonby Terrace, SW1P 4QA. *T:* 0171–828 6226. *Clubs:* Beefsteak, Brooks's, Pratt's.

DIXON, Prof. Richard Newland, PhD, ScD; FRS 1986; CChem, FRSC; Professor of Theoretical Chemistry, since 1969, Alfred Capper Pass Professor of Chemistry, since 1990, University of Bristol; *b* 25 Dec. 1930; *s* of late Robert Thomas Dixon and Lilian Dixon; *m* 1954, Alison Mary Birks; one *s* two *d*. *Educ:* The Judd Sch., Tonbridge; King's Coll., Univ. of London (BSc 1951); St Catharine's Coll., Univ. of Cambridge (PhD 1955; ScD 1976). FRSC 1976. Scientific Officer, UKAEA, 1954–56; Res. Associate, Univ. of Western Ontario, 1956–57; Postdoctoral Fellow, NRCC, Ottawa, 1957–59; ICI Fellow, Univ. of Sheffield, 1959–60, Lectr in Chem., 1960–69; Bristol University: Hd of Dept of Theoretical Chemistry, 1969–90; Dean, Faculty of Science, 1979–82; Pro-Vice-Chancellor, 1989–92. Sorby Res. Fellow, Royal Soc., 1964–69; Vis. Schol., Stanford Univ., 1982–83. Harkins Lectr, Univ. of Chicago, 1994. Mem. Council, Faraday Div., RSC, 1985–, Vice-Pres., 1989–; Mem., and Chm. sub-cttee, Laser Facility Cttee, SERC, 1987–90. Non-exec. Dir, United Bristol Healthcare NHS Trust, 1994– (Vice-Chm., 1995–). Corday-Morgan Medal, Chemical Soc., 1966; RSC Award for Spectroscopy, 1984; Liversidge Lectr and Medal, RSC, 1993–94. *Publications:* Spectroscopy and Structure, 1965; Theoretical Chemistry: Vol. 1, 1974, Vol. 2, 1975, Vol. 3, 1978; numerous articles in res. jls of chemistry and physics. *Recreations:* mountain walking, travel, theatre, concerts. *Address:* 22 Westbury Lane, Bristol BS9 2PE. *T:* Bristol (0117) 968 1691; School of Chemistry, The University, Bristol BS8 1TS. *T:* Bristol (0117) 928 7661.

DIXON, Maj.-Gen. Roy Laurence Cayley, CB 1977; CVO 1991; MC 1944; Chapter Clerk, College of St George, Windsor Castle, 1981–90; *b* 19 Sept. 1924; *s* of Lt-Col Sidney Frank Dixon, MC and Edith Mary (Sheena) (*née* Clark); *m* 1986, Anne Maureen Aspeslåen (marr. diss. 1988). *Educ:* Haileybury; Edinburgh Univ. Commnd Royal Tank Regt, 1944; served in armd units and on staff; psc 1956; Instructor, Staff Coll., 1961–64; comd 5th Royal Tank Regt, 1966–67; Royal Coll. of Defence Studies, 1971; Comdr Royal Armd Corps, Germany, 1968–70; qual. helicopter pilot, 1973; Dir, Army Air Corps, 1974–76; Chief of Staff, Allied Forces Northern Europe, 1977–80. Col Comdt, RTR, 1978–83. Chm., Salisbury Civic Soc., 1991–. Freeman, City of London, 1990. *Address:* c/o Lloyds Bank, Cox's & Kings Branch, PO Box 1190, 7 Pall Mall, SW1Y 5NA. *Club:* Army and Navy.

DIXON, Stanley; Chairman, Midland-Yorkshire Tar Distillers Ltd, 1968–71; *b* 12 Aug. 1900; *m* 1936, Ella Margaret Hogg; two *s*. *Educ:* Leeds Grammar Sch.; Queen's Coll., Oxford. Articled to Leather & Veale, Chartered Accountants in Leeds, 1924–27; Manager, Leather & Veale (later Peat, Marwick, Mitchell & Co.), Leeds, 1927–35; Sec., Midland Tar Distillers Ltd, 1935–66; Dir, Midland Tar Distillers Ltd (later Midland-Yorkshire Holdings Ltd), 1943–71. Pres., Inst. of Chartered Accountants in England and Wales, 1968–69. Hon. DSocSc Birmingham, 1972. *Publications:* The Case for Marginal Costing, 1967; The Art of Chairing a Meeting, 1975. *Recreations:* Church affairs, gardening and music. *Address:* 83 Norton Road, Stourbridge, West Midlands DY8 2TB. *T:* Stourbridge (01384) 395672.

DIXON, Group Captain William Michael, CBE 1972; DSO 1943; DFC 1941; AFC 1958; Bursar, Summer Fields School, Oxford, 1975–86; *b* 29 July 1920; *s* of late William Michael Dixon; *m* 1st, 1944, Mary Margaret (*d* 1957), *d* of late William Alexander Spence, MC, MM; three *s*; 2nd, 1988, Eileen Margaret Collinson, *d* of late Claud Henry Tucker, OBE. Served War of 1939–45, Bomber Comd; Air Staff, Rhodesian Air Trng Gp, 1946–49; psa 1949; comd No 2 (Bomber) Sqdn RAAF, 1952–55; comd No 192 Sqdn RAF, 1955–58; jssc 1958; comd RAF Feltwell, 1961–63; Sen. Officer Admin No 1 (Bomber) Gp, 1963–66; Sen. Personnel SO HQ Air Support Comd, 1966–68; DCAS, Royal Malaysian Air Force, 1968–71; Dir of Aircraft Projects (RAF), MoD, 1972–75; ADC to the Queen, 1968–73. *Recreation:* natural history. *Address:* Lower Farm, Duck End Lane, Sutton, Witney, Oxon OX8 1RX. *T:* Oxford (01865) 881553.

DIXON-LEWIS, Prof. Graham, DPhil; FRS 1995; Professor of Combustion Science, University of Leeds, 1978–87, now Emeritus; *b* Newport, Gwent, 1 July 1922; *s* of Daniel Watson Dixon-Lewis and Eleanor Jane Dixon-Lewis; *m* 1950, Patricia Mary Best; one *s* two *d*. *Educ:* Newport High Sch.; Jesus Coll., Oxford (MA; DPhil 1948). Research Chemist, Courtaulds, 1946–49; Sen. Scientific Officer, Gas Res. Bd, Beckenham, 1949–53; University of Leeds: Gas Council Sen. Res. Fellow, 1953–70; Reader, 1970–78. Vis. Prof., Applied Physics Lab., Johns Hopkins Univ., 1965; Vis. Scientist, Sandia Nat. Labs, Calif, 1987. Alfred Egerton Gold Medal 1990, Silver Medal 1990, Combustion Inst.; Award for Combustion and Hydrocarbon Oxidation Chemistry, RSC, 1993. *Publications:* numerous scientific papers on combustion topics, chemically reacting flows, and molecular transport processes. *Recreations:* walking, gardening. *Address:* 16 West Park Grove, Leeds LS8 2HQ. *T:* Leeds (0113) 266 2269.

DIXON-SMITH, family name of **Baron Dixon-Smith.**

DIXON-SMITH, Baron *cr* 1993 (Life Peer), of Bocking in Essex; **Robert William Dixon-Smith;** DL; farmer, since 1958; *b* 30 Sept. 1934; 2nd *s* of Dixon Smith, Braintree, Essex and Winifred Smith (*née* Stratton); Dixon Smith adopted by Deed Poll as surname, 1961; *m* 1960, Georgina Janet, *d* of George Cook, Halstead, Essex and Kathleen Cook; one *s* one *d*. *Educ:* Oundle; Writtle Coll. Nat. Service, 2nd Lt, King's Dragoon Guards, 1955–57. Member: Essex CC, 1965–93 (Chm., 1986–89); Association of County Councils, 1983–93 (Chm., 1992–93). Member: H of L EC Cttee sub-cttee C (Envmt), 1994–; H of L Select Cttee on Sci. and Technol., 1994–. Member: Local Govt Management Bd, 1991–93; Council, Essex Univ., 1991–94; Chm., Anglia Polytechnic Univ., 1992–93. Governor, Writtle Coll., 1967–94 (Chm., 1973–85; Fellow, 1993). Freeman, City of London, 1988; Liveryman, Farmers' Co., 1991. DL Essex, 1986. *Recreations:* shooting, fishing, golf. *Address:* Lyons Hall, Braintree, Essex CM7 6SH. *T:* Braintree (01376) 326834.

DIXON-WARD, Frank, CBE 1979; Member: Board of Directors, World Society for the Protection of Animals, since 1986; Board of Overseers, Massachusetts SPCA, since 1988; *b* 28 June 1922; *s* of late Cecil Ward, LRAM, and Helen Cecilia Ward (*née* Woodward), Eastbourne; *m* 1960, Claire Collasius (*d* 1985); one *s* one *d*. *Educ:* Eastbourne Grammar School. Solicitor (Hons), 1948. Articled to Town Clerk, Eastbourne, 1940. Served War, Royal Air Force, 1941–46. Solicitor posts, Peterborough, 1948–51, West Ham, 1952–54; Deputy Town Clerk, Hove, 1954–62; Chairman: Local Govt Legal Soc., 1957; Hove Round Table, 1961–62; Mem. Council, Sussex LTA, 1957–62; Town Clerk: Camberwell, 1963–65; Southwark, 1964–70; Chief Exec., Lambeth, 1970–81; Consultant, 1982. Exec. Dir, RSPCA, 1982–87. Lawyer/Chm., London Rent Assessment Cttees, 1982, 1986–93. Hon. Clerk: South London Housing Consortium, 1965–70; Social Service Cttee, London Boroughs Assoc., 1966–82; Hon. Legal Adviser: Age Concern (Gtr London), 1965–82; Eurogroup for Animal Welfare, 1986–92. Member official committees: London Welfare Services, 1963–65; NHS Reorganisation, 1969–74; Homelessness, 1970–72; Citizens Advice Bureaux, 1973–74; Jt Approach to Social Policies, 1975–76; Exec. Cttee, SOLACE, 1975–81. Chm., St Dunstan's College Soc., 1975–78. Eurogroup Medal, 1992. *Recreations:* music, lawn tennis. *T:* 0181–650 8312. *Club:* Royal Over-Seas League.

DIXSON, Maurice Christopher Scott, DPhil; FRAeS; FInstPS; Chief Executive, Simon Engineering, since 1993; Director: Higgs & Hill plc, since 1994; British Airways Engineering, since 1995; *b* 5 Nov. 1941; *s* of late Herbert George Muns Dixson and of Elizabeth Eileen Dixson; *m* 1965, Anne Beverley Morris. *Educ:* University Coll., Swansea (BA Jt Hons); Carleton Univ., Ottawa (MA); Pembroke Coll., Oxford (DPhil). Commercial Exec., Hawker Siddeley Aviation, 1969–74; Contracts Man., Export, later Commercial Man., Export, Mil. Aircraft Div., BAC, 1974–80; British Aerospace: Warton Division: Div. Commercial Man., 1980–81; Exec. Dir, Contracts, 1981–83; Divl Commercial Dir, 1983–86; Military Aircraft Division: Dir-in-Charge, Saudi Arabian Ops, March–Aug. 1986; Commercial Dir and Dir-in-Charge, Saudi Arabian Ops, 1986–87; Chief Exec., Royal Ordnance PLC, 1987–88; Man. Dir, British Aerospace (Commercial Aircraft), 1988–90; Supervisory Man. Dir, Electronic Metrology and Components Groups, and Main Bd Dir, GEC, 1990–93. *Recreations:* played representative soccer at school and university, supporter of Tottenham Hotspur Football Club, golf, fishing, shooting, sport, politics and current affairs. *Address:* (office) Simon House, 6 Eaton Gate, SW1W 9BJ. *T:* 0171–730 0777. *Club:* Royal Automobile.

DJANOGLY, Sir Harry Ari Simon, Kt 1993; CBE 1983; Chairman, Nottingham Manufacturing Co. Ltd; *b* 1 Aug. 1938. Former Man. Dir and Dep. Chm., Vantona Viyella; Dir, Coats Viyella. *Address:* Serck House, 60 Trafalgar Square, WC2N 5DS.

DOBB, Erlam Stanley, CB 1963; TD; *b* 16 Aug. 1910; *m* 1937, Margaret Williams; no *c*. *Educ:* Ruthin; University Coll. of N Wales. Chartered Surveyor and Land Agent, Anglesey, Denbigh and Merioneth, 1930–35; Asst Land Comr, to Dir, Agricultural Land Service, MAFF, 1935–70; a Dep. Dir-Gen., Agricl Develt and Adv. Service, MAFF, 1971–73; Dir-Gen., 1973–75. Mem., ARC, 1973–75; Vice-Chm., Adv. Council for Agriculture and Horticulture in England and Wales, 1974–75. Trustee, T. P. Price Charity, Markshall Estate, Essex, 1971–84 (Chm. Trustees, 1971–83). Governor, Royal Agricultural College, 1960–75. Royal Welch Fusiliers (TA), 1938–46, Major. FRICS; FRAgS. *Publications:* professional contributions to journals of learned societies. *Recreations:* golf, gardening. *Address:* Churchgate, Westerham, Kent TN16 1AS. *T:* Westerham (01959) 62294. *Clubs:* Farmers'; Crowborough Beacon Golf, Limpsfield Chart Golf.

DOBBIE, Dr Robert Charles; Head, Competitiveness (formerly Industrial Competitiveness) Division, Department of Trade and Industry, since 1992; *b* 16 Jan. 1942; *s* of Scott U. Dobbie and Isobel M. Dobbie; *m* 1964, Elizabeth Barbour; three *s*. *Educ:* Univ. of Edinburgh (BSc); Univ. of Cambridge (PhD). Res. Fellow, Univ. of Alberta, 1966–67; ICI Res. Fellow, Univ. of Bristol, 1967–68; Lectr in Inorganic Chemistry, Univ. of Newcastle upon Tyne, 1968–76; sabbatical, California State Univ., LA, 1974; Tutor, Open Univ., 1975–85; Principal, DTI, 1976–83; Asst Sec., Dept. of Industry, 1983–90; Under Sec., DTI, 1990–; Dir, Merseyside Task Force, 1990–92 (seconded to DoE). *Publications:* on inorganic and organometallic chemistry. *Recreations:* theatre, hill walking, malt whisky. *Address:* Department of Trade and Industry, Ashdown House, 123 Victoria Street, SW1E 6RB.

DOBBIN, Rev. Dr Victor, MBE 1980; QHC 1993; Chaplain General to the Forces, since 1995; *b* 12 March 1943; *s* of Vincent Dobbin and late Annie Dobbin (*née* Doherty); *m* 1967, Rosemary Gault; one *s* one *d*. *Educ:* Trinity Coll., Dublin (MA 1967); Queen's Univ., Belfast (MTh 1979; PhD 1984). Asst Minister, Rosemary Presbyterian Ch, Belfast, 1970–72; joined RAChD, 1972; Dep. Warden, RAChD Centre, 1982–86; Sen. Chaplain, 3rd Armd Div., 1986–89; Staff Chaplain, HQ BAOR, 1989–91; Sen. Chaplain, SE Dist, 1991–93; Asst Chaplain Gen., Southern Dist, 1993–94. *Recreations:* golf, walking. *Address:* c/o Ministry of Defence Chaplains (Army), Bagshot Park, Bagshot, Surrey GU19 5PL. *T:* Bagshot (01276) 471717.

DOBBING, Prof. John, DSc, FRCP, FRCPath; Professor of Child Growth and Development, Department of Child Health, University of Manchester, and Honorary Consultant, United Manchester Hospitals, 1968–84, now Professor Emeritus; *b* 14 Aug. 1922; *s* of Alfred Herbert Dobbing and May Gwendoline (*née* Cattell); *m* Dr Jean Sands. *Educ:* Bootham Sch., York; St Mary's Hosp., London (BSc 1st cl. hons, MB, BS). DSc Manchester, 1981. FRCPath 1976; FRCP 1981. Lectr in Path. and Gull Student, Guy's Hosp., 1954–61; Sen. Lectr in Physiol., London Hosp., 1961–64; Sen. Lectr, Inst. of Child Health, London, and Hon. Consultant, Hosp. for Sick Children, Gt Ormond Street, 1964–68. *Publications:* Applied Neurochemistry, 1968; (ed with J. A. Davis) Scientific Foundations of Paediatrics, 1974 (2nd edn 1981); Maternal Nutrition in Pregnancy: eating for two?, 1981; Prevention of Spina Bifida, 1983; pubns on undernutrition and developing brain in scientific literature. *Recreations:* writing, travel, France and the French. *Address:* Higher Cliff Farm, via Birch Vale, via Stockport, Cheshire SK12 5DL. *T:* New Mills (01663) 743220.

DOBBS, Bernard; *see* Dobbs, W. B. J.

DOBBS, Prof. (Edwin) Roland, PhD, DSc; Hildred Carlile Professor of Physics, University of London, 1973–90, and Head of Department of Physics, Royal Holloway and Bedford New College, 1985–90; Emeritus Professor of Physics, University of London, 1990; *b* 2 Dec. 1924; *s* of late A. Edwin Dobbs, AMIMechE, and Harriet Dobbs (*née* Wright); *m* 1947, Dorothy Helena, *o d* of late Alderman A. F. T. Jeeves, Stamford, Lincs; two *s* one *d*. *Educ:* Ilford County High Sch.; Queen Elizabeth's Sch., Barnet; University College London. BSc (1st cl. Physics) 1943, PhD 1949; DSc London 1977; FInstP 1964; FIOA 1977. Radar research, Admiralty, 1943–46; DSIR Res. Student, UCL, 1946–49; Lectr in Physics, QMC, Univ. of London, 1949–58; Res. Associate in Applied Maths, 1958–59, Associate Prof. of Physics, 1959–60, Brown Univ., USA; Mem., Gonville and Caius Coll., Cambridge, 1960–; AEI Fellow, Cavendish Lab., Univ. of Cambridge, 1960–64; Prof. and Head of Dept of Physics, Univ. of Lancaster, 1964–73; Bedford College, London University: Head of Dept of Physics, 1973–85; Vice-Principal, 1981–82; Dean, Faculty of Science, 1980–82; Chm., Bd of Studies in Physics, Univ. of London, 1982–85; Vice-Dean, 1986–88, Dean, 1988–90, Faculty of Science, Univ. of London. Member: Physics Cttee, SRC, 1970–73, SERC, 1983–86; Nuclear Physics Bd, SRC, 1974–77; Paul Instrument Fund Cttee, 1984–. Visiting Professor: Brown Univ., 1966; Wayne State Univ., 1969; Univ. of Tokyo, 1977; Univ. of Delhi, 1983; Cornell Univ.,

1984; Univ. of Florida, 1989; Univ. of Sussex, 1989–. Pres., Inst. of Acoustics, 1976–78; Hon. Sec., Inst. of Physics, 1976–84. Convenor, Standing Conf. of Profs of Physics of GB, 1985–88. Hon. Fellow, Indian Cryogenics Council, 1977. *Publications:* Electricity and Magnetism, 1984 (trans. Chinese 1990); Electromagnetic Waves, 1985 (trans. Chinese 1992); Basic Electromagnetism, 1993; Solid Helium Three, 1994; research papers on metals and superconductors in Procs of Royal Soc., on solid state physics and acoustics in Jl of Physics, Physical Rev. Letters, Physical Acoustics, and on superfluid helium 3 in Jl Low Temperature Physics, etc. *Recreations:* travel, theatre, gardening. *Address:* Mill Farm, Ripe, Lewes, E Sussex BN8 6AX. *T:* Ripe (01323) 811232. *Club:* Athenæum.

See also Prof. M. A. Jeeves.

DOBBS, Joseph Alfred, CMG 1972; OBE 1957 (MBE 1945); TD 1945; HM Diplomatic Service, retired; *b* Abbeyleix, Ireland, 22 Dec. 1914; *s* of John L. Dobbs and Ruby (*née* Gillespie); *m* 1949, Marie, *d* of Reginald Francis Catton, Sydney; four *s*. *Educ:* Worksop Coll.; Trinity Hall, Cambridge (Schol.). Pres., Cambridge Union Soc., 1936. Served War of 1939–45, Major, Royal Artillery (despatches). Joined Foreign Office, 1946; served Moscow, 1947–51, 1954–57 and 1965–68; FO, 1951–54; Delhi, 1957–61; Warsaw, 1961–64; Rome, 1964–65; Consul-Gen., Zagreb, 1969–70; Minister, Moscow, 1971–74. *Recreations:* reading, gardening. *Address:* The Coach House, Charlton Musgrove, Wincanton, Somerset BA9 8ES. *T:* Wincanton (01963) 33356.

DOBBS, Mattiwilda; Order of North Star (Sweden), 1954; opera singer (coloratura soprano); *b* 11 July 1925, Atlanta, Ga, USA; *d* of John Wesley and Irene Dobbs; *m* 1957, Bengt Janzon, retired Dir. of Information, Nat. Ministry of Health and Welfare, Sweden; no *c*. *Educ:* Spelman Coll., USA (BA 1946); Columbia Univ., USA (MA 1948). Studied voice in NY with Lotte Leonard, 1946–50; special coaching Paris with Pierre Bernac, 1950–52. Marian Anderson Schol., 1948; John Hay Whitney Schol., 1950; 1st prize in singing, Internat. Comp., Geneva Conservatory of Music, 1951. Appeared Royal Dutch Opera, Holland Festival, 1952. Recitals, Sweden, Paris, Holland, 1952; appeared in opera at La Scala, Milan, 1953; Concerts, England and Continent, 1953; Glyndebourne Opera, 1953–54, 1956, 1961; Covent Garden Opera, 1953, 1954, 1956, 1958; command performance, Covent Garden, 1954. Annual concert tours: US, 1954–; Australia, New Zealand, 1955, 1959, 1968; Australia, 1972, 1977; Israel, 1957 and 1959; USSR concerts and opera (Bolshoi Theater), 1959; San Francisco Opera, 1955; début Metropolitan Opera, 1956; there annually, 1956–64. Appearances Hamburg State Opera, 1961–63; Royal Swedish Opera, 1957 and there annually, 1957–73; Norwegian and Finnish Operas, 1957–64. Vis. Prof., Univ. of Texas at Austin, 1973–74; Professor: Univ. of Illinois, 1975–76; Univ. of Georgia, 1976–77; Howard Univ., Washington, 1977–91. Hon. Dr of Music: Spelman Coll., Atlanta, 1979; Emory Univ., Atlanta, 1980. *Address:* 1101 South Arlington Ridge Road, Apt 301, Arlington, VA 22202, USA.

DOBBS, Michael John; novelist and broadcaster; *b* 14 Nov. 1948; *s* of Eric William Dobbs and Eileen Dobbs (*née* Saunders); *m* 1981, Amanda Louise Collingridge; two *s*. *Educ:* Christ Church, Oxford (MA); Fletcher School of Law and Diplomacy, USA (PhD, MALD, MA). Govt Special Adviser, 1981–87; Chief of Staff, Conservative Party, 1986–87; Dep. Chm., Saatchi & Saatchi, 1983–86, 1988–91; Jt Dep. Chm., Cons. Party, 1994–95. *Publications:* House of Cards, 1989 (televised, 1990); Wall Games, 1990; Last Man to Die, 1991; To Play the King, 1992 (televised, 1993); The Touch of Innocents, 1994; The Final Cut, 1995. *Recreations:* genealogy, coming home. *Address:* Bilshay Dairy Farmhouse, Dottery, Bridport, Dorset DT6 5HR. *T:* Bridport (01308) 425808. *Club:* Royal Automobile.

DOBBS, Captain Sir Richard (Arthur Frederick), KCVO 1991; Lord-Lieutenant of County Antrim, 1975–94 (HM Lieutenant for County Antrim, 1959–75); *b* 2 April 1919; *s* of Senator Major Arthur F. Dobbs, DL, of Castle Dobbs, and Hylda Louisa Dobbs; *m* 1953, Carola Day, *d* of Christopher Clarkson, Old Lyme, Conn, USA; four *s* one *d*. *Educ:* Eton; Magdalene Coll., Cambridge (MA). Served War: 2nd Lieut Irish Guards (Supp. Reserve), 1939; Captain 1943. Called to Bar, Lincoln's Inn, 1947; Member, Midland Circuit, 1951–55. *Address:* Castle Dobbs, Carrickfergus, County Antrim, N Ireland BT38 9BX. *T:* Whitehead (01960) 372238. *Club:* Cavalry and Guards.

DOBBS, Roland; *see* Dobbs, E. R.

DOBBS, (William) Bernard (Joseph); HM Diplomatic Service, retired; Ambassador to Laos (Lao People's Democratic Republic), 1982–85; *b* 3 Sept. 1925; *s* of late William Evelyn Joseph Dobbs and Maud Clifford Dobbs (*née* Bernard); *m* 1952, Brigid Mary Bilitch; one *s* one *d*. *Educ:* Shrewsbury Sch.; Trinity Coll., Dublin (BA Hons Mod. History 1951; MA 1977). Served Rifle Bde/7th Gurkha Rifles, 1943–47 (Captain). Forbes Forbes Campbell and Co. Ltd, 1952–56; Examiner, Patent Office, 1957–61; British Trade Commission, 1961–65: Lagos, 1961–64; Freetown, 1964–66; HM Diplomatic Service: Freetown, London, Rangoon, Milan, Kinshasa, Vientiane, 1965–85. *Recreations:* reading, walking, writing. *Club:* Royal Automobile.

DOBEREINER, Peter Arthur Bertram; golf correspondent, The Observer, 1965–90; *b* 3 Nov. 1925; *s* of Major Arthur Dobereiner and Dorothy (*née* Hassall); *m* 1951, Betty Evelyn Jacob; two *s* two *d*. *Educ:* King's College, Taunton; Lincoln College, Oxford. RNVR 1942. Asst Manager, Parry & Co. (Madras), 1946; various newspaper appts, 1949–: East Essex Gazette, Oxford Times, News Chronicle, Daily Express, Daily Mail, The Guardian. Hon. Mem., Amer. Soc. of Golf Course Architects. Screen Writers Guild Award (jtly) (That Was the Week That Was), 1962; MacGregor writing awards, 1977, 1981; Donald Ross award, 1985; Irish Golf Fellowship Award, 1987. *Publications:* The Game With a Hole In It, 1970, 3rd edn 1973; The Glorious World of Golf, 1973, 3rd edn 1975; Stroke, Hole or Match?, 1976; Golf Rules Explained, 1980, 8th edn 1992; For the Love of Golf, 1981; Tony Jacklin's Golf Secrets, 1982; Down the Nineteenth Fairway, 1982; The World of Golf, 1982; (ed) The Golfers, 1982; The Book of Golf Disasters, 1983; The Fifty Greatest Post-War Golfers, 1985; Arnold Palmer's Complete Book of Putting, 1986; Preferred Lies, 1987; Golf a la Carte, 1990; Maestro, 1992. *Recreation:* golf. *Address:* Chelsfield Hill House, Pratts Bottom, Orpington, Kent BR6 7SL. *T:* Farnborough (Kent) (01689) 853849. *Clubs:* West Kent Golf; Pine Valley Golf; Hon. Ballybunion (Ireland).

DOBKIN, Ian James; His Honour Judge Dobkin; a Circuit Judge, since 1995; *b* 8 June 1948; *s* of Morris Dobkin, dental surgeon, Leeds, and Rhoda Dobkin; *m* 1980, Andrea, *d* of Jack and Rose Dante; two *s*. *Educ:* Leeds Grammar Sch.; Queen's Coll., Oxford (Hastings Exhibnr in Classics; BA Jurisp. 1970; MA 1974). Called to the Bar, Gray's Inn, 1971; barrister, North Eastern Circuit, 1971–95; Asst Recorder, 1986–90; Recorder, 1990–95. Mem., Adv. Cttee, Centre for Criminal Justice Studies, Univ. of Leeds, 1987–. United Hebrew Congregation, Leeds: Vice-Pres., 1981–84 and 1992–; Pres., 1984–88. *Recreations:* crosswords, reading, music. *Address:* 6 Sandmoor Drive, Leeds LS17 7DG. *Clubs:* Moor Allerton Golf (Leeds); Yorkshire County Cricket.

DOBLE, Denis Henry; HM Diplomatic Service; Consul-General, Amsterdam, since 1991; *b* 2 Oct. 1936; *s* of Percy Claud Doble and Dorothy Grace (*née* Petley); *m* 1975, Patricia Ann Robinson; one *d* one *s*. *Educ:* Dover Grammar School; New College, Oxford (MA Modern Hist.). RAF, 1955–57. Colonial Office, 1960–64; Asst Private Sec. to Commonwealth and Colonial Sec., 1963–64; HM Diplomatic Service, 1965; First Sec., Brussels, 1966–68, Lagos, 1968–72; S Asian and Defence Depts, FCO, 1972–75; First Sec. (Economic), Islamabad, 1975–78; Head of Chancery, Lima, 1978–82; E African Dept, FCO, 1982–84; Actg Dep. High Comr, Bombay, 1985; Deputy High Commissioner: Calcutta, 1985–87; Kingston, 1987–91. SBStJ. *Recreations:* travel, cinema, cricket, tennis, colonial history. *Address:* c/o Foreign and Commonwealth Office, SW1A 2AH. *Clubs:* MCC; Industrieele Groote (Amsterdam).

DOBLE, John Frederick, OBE 1981; HM Diplomatic Service; Consul General, Johannesburg, 1990–94; *b* 30 June 1941; *s* of Comdr Douglas Doble, RN and Marcella (*née* Cowan); *m* 1975, Isabella Margaret Ruth (marr. diss. 1992), *d* of late Col W. H. Whitbread, TD; one *d*. *Educ:* Sunningdale; Eton (Scholar); RMA Sandhurst; Hertford College, Oxford. 17th/21st Lancers, 1959–69 (Captain); attached Lord Strathcona's Horse (Royal Canadians), 1967–69; joined HM Diplomatic Service, 1969; Arabian Dept, FCO, 1969–72; Beirut, 1972–73; Brussels, 1973–77; Commonwealth Dept, FCO, 1977–78. Maputo, 1978–81; Inf. Dept, FCO, 1981–83; attached Barclays Bank International, 1983–85; Consul General, Edmonton, Canada, 1985–89. *Recreations:* horse and water sports, history, manual labour. *Address:* c/o Foreign and Commonwealth Office, SW1A 2AH. *Clubs:* Royal Over-Seas League; Poplar, Blackwall and District Rowing.

DOBREE, John Hatherley, MS, FRCS; Consulting Ophthalmic Surgeon, St Bartholomew's Hospital, London, EC1 (Consultant 1956); Honorary Ophthalmic Surgeon, North Middlesex Hospital, N18 (Senior Ophthalmic Surgeon 1947); *b* 25 April 1914; *s* of Hatherley Moor Dobree, OBE, and Muriel Dobree (*née* Hope); *m* 1941, Evelyn Maud Smyth; two *s*. *Educ:* Victoria Coll., Jersey; St Bartholomew's Hosp. MS London 1947; FRCS 1950. House Physician, Metropolitan Hosp., E8, 1938–39; House Surgeon, Western Ophthalm. Hosp., 1940. Served in RAMC, 1940–46, in MEF, as RMO and Ophthalmic Specialist. Chief Asst, Eye Dept, St Bartholomew's Hosp., 1946–51. FRSocMed (Past Sec., Sect. of Ophthalmology); Vice-Pres. and Past Hon. Sec. Ophthalmological Soc. of UK; Dep. Master, Oxford Ophth. Congress, 1976. *Publications:* The Retina, vol. x, in Sir Stewart Duke-Elder's System of Ophthalmology, 1967; (with E. S. Perkins) Differential Diagnosis of Fundus Conditions, 1971; (with E. Boulter) Blindness and Visual Handicap, the Facts, 1982; Soldiers of the Company, 1988. *Recreations:* archaeology, walking. *Address:* The Rosery, Great Bealings, Woodbridge, Suffolk IP13 6NW.

DOBROSIELSKI, Marian, PhD Zürich; Banner of Labour, 1st Class 1975 (2nd Class 1973); Knight Cross of the Order of Polonia Restituta, 1964; Professor of Philosophy, Warsaw University, 1974–88; Ambassador *ad personam*, since 1973; *b* 25 March 1923; *s* of Stanislaw and Stefania Dobrosielski; *m* 1950; one *d*. *Educ:* Univ. of Zürich; Univ. of Warsaw. Served in Polish Army in France, War of 1939–45. With Min. of Foreign Affairs, 1948–81; Polish Legation, Bern, 1948–50; Head of Section, Min. of Foreign Affairs, 1950–54; Asst Prof., Warsaw Univ. and Polish Acad. of Sciences, 1954–57; Mem. Polish delegn to UN Gen. Assembly, 1952, 1953, 1958, 1966, 1972, 1976. First Sec., Counsellor, Polish Embassy in Washington, 1958–64; Min. of Foreign Affairs: Counsellor to Minister, 1964–69; Acting Dir, Research Office, 1968–69; Polish Ambassador to London, 1969–71; Dir, Polish Inst. of Internat. Affairs, 1971–80; Dep. Minister of Foreign Affairs, 1978–81. Univ. of Warsaw: Associate Prof., 1966; Vice-Dean of Faculty of Philosophy, 1966–68; Dir, Inst. of Philosophy, 1971–73 (Chm. Scientific Council, 1969). Chm., Editorial Bd of Studia Filozoficzne, 1968–69; Sec., Polish Philos. Soc., 1955–57 and 1965–69. Chm., Polish Cttee for European Security and Co-operation, 1973–79 (Vice-Chm., 1971–73); Vice-Chm., Cttee on Peace Research, Polish Acad. of Scis, 1984–91; Chm., Scientific Council, Inst. of Peace Res. and Security Policy, Univ. of Hamburg, 1987–. Hon. Vice-Pres., Scottish-Polish Cultural Assoc., Glasgow, 1969–71; Chm., Polish delegn to: 2nd stage Conf. on Security and Co-operation in Europe, 1973–75; CSCE Belgrade Meeting, 1977–78; CSCE Meeting, Madrid, 1980–81. Chm., Polish Nat. Interest Club, 1991–. *Publications:* A Basic Epistemological Principle of Logical Positivism, 1947; The Philosophical Pragmatism of C. S. Peirce, 1967; On some contemporary problems: Philosophy, Ideology, Politics, 1970; (trans. and introd) Selection of Aphorisms of G. C. Lichtenberg, Oscar Wilde, Karl Kraus, M. von Ebner-Eschenbach, Mark Twain, C. Norwid, 1970–85; On the Theory and Practice of Peaceful Coexistence, 1976; Belgrad 77, 1978; Chances and Dilemmas, 1980; The Crisis in Poland, 1984; On Politics and Philosophy, 1988; Philosophy of Reason, 1988; Karl R. Popper's Philosophy of History and Politics, 1991; (jtly) Next Europe, 1993; numerous articles on philosophy and internat. problems in professional jls. *Recreation:* tennis. *Address:* Kozia Street 9–14, 00 070 Warszawa, Poland.

DOBRY, His Honour George Leon Severyn, CBE 1977; QC 1969; a Circuit Judge, 1980–92; international counsel and arbitrator; *b* 1 Nov. 1918; *m* 1948, Margaret Headley Smith (*d* 1978), *e d* of late Joseph Quartus Smith, JP, Bardfield Saling, Essex; two *d*. *Educ:* Gimnazium Mikolaja Reya, Warsaw; Warsaw Univ.; Edinburgh Univ. (MA). ACIArb. Served War of 1939–45: Army, France and Norway, 1939–42 (despatches); Air Force, 1942–46. Called to Bar, Inner Temple, 1946; Bencher 1977. A Recorder of the Crown Court, 1977–80. Legal Sec., Internat. Commn of Jurists at The Hague, 1955–57. Member Council: 'Justice', 1956–68; on Law Reporting, 1984–94. Adviser to Sec. of State for Environment and Sec. of State for Wales on Develt Control, 1973–75; Mem., Docklands Jt Cttee, 1974–76; Inspector, Inquiry into M25, 1978–79. Chairman: British Centre for English Legal Studies, Warsaw Univ., 1992–; Panel, Avon Structure Plan, 1992–93; Mem., Panel, Polish Arbitration Court. Jt Pres., British-Polish Legal Assoc., 1989–; UK Patron, Europ. Law Students Assoc. Hon. LLD Warsaw, 1994. Comdr, Order of Merit (Poland), 1993. *Publications:* Woodfall's Law of Landlord and Tenant, 25th edition (one of the Editors), 1952; Blundell and Dobry, Town and Country Planning, 1962; Blundell and Dobry Planning Appeals and Inquiries, 1962, 4th edn 1990; Review of the Development Control System (Interim Report), 1972 (Final Report), 1975; (ed jtly) Development Gains Tax, 1975; Hill and Redman, Landlord and Tenant (Cons. Editor), 16th edn, 1976; (Gen. Editor) Encyclopedia of Development Law, 1976. *Address:* 105 Whitelands House, Cheltenham Terrace, SW3 4RA. *T:* 0171–730 7335, *Fax:* 0171–259 0157; (chambers) 4 Bream's Buildings, EC4A 1AQ. *T:* 0171–353 5835, *Fax:* 0171–430 1677. *Clubs:* Garrick, Travellers'.

DOBRYNIN, Anatoly Fedorovich, Hero of Socialist Labour; Order of Lenin (five awards); Order of Red Banner of Labour; Secretary, Central Committee, Communist Party of the Soviet Union, 1986–91; Deputy, Supreme Soviet of the USSR, 1986–91; *b* 16 Nov. 1919; *m* Irina Nikolaevna Dobrynina; one *d*. *Educ:* Moscow Inst. of Aviation, 1942; Higher Sch. of Diplomacy, 1946 (doctorate in History). Asst to Dean of Faculty, Moscow Inst. of Aviation, engr-designer, 1942–44; Official, Min. of For. Affairs, 1946–52; Counsellor, Counsellor-Minister, Embassy to USA, 1952–54; Asst to Minister for For. Affairs, 1955–57; Dep. Sec. Gen., UN, 1957–60; Chief, Dept of Amer. Countries, Min. of For. Affairs, 1960–62; Amb. to USA, 1962–86. Mem., CPSU Central Cttee, 1971–91 (Candidate Mem., 1966–71); Chief, Internat. Dept, CPSU Central Cttee, 1986–91.

DOBSON, Christopher Selby Austin, CBE 1976; FSA; Librarian, House of Lords, 1956–77; *b* 25 Aug. 1916; *s* of late Alban Tabor Austin Dobson, CB, CVO, CBE; *m* 1941,

Helen Broughton (*d* 1984), *d* of late Capt. E. B. Turner, Holyhead; one *d* (one *s* decd). *Educ:* Clifton Coll.; Emmanuel Coll., Cambridge (BA). With National Council of Social Service, 1938–39. Served War of 1939–45, Lieut Middx Regt (despatches). Asst Principal (Temp.), Ministry of Education, 1946–47; Asst Librarian, House of Lords, 1947–56. *Publication:* (ed) Oxfordshire Protestation Returns 1641–42, 1955. *Recreations:* collecting books, stamps, etc. *Address:* Swan House, Symonds Lane, Linton, Cambridge CB1 6HY. *T:* Cambridge (01223) 893796. *Clubs:* Roxburghe; (Hon.) Rowfant (Cleveland).

DOBSON, Vice-Adm. Sir David (Stuart), KBE 1992; Chief of Staff to Commander Allied Naval Forces Southern Europe, 1991–94; *b* 4 Dec. 1938; *s* of Walter and Ethel Dobson; *m* 1962, Joanna Mary Counter; two *s* one *d*. *Educ:* English School, Nicosia, Cyprus; RN College, Dartmouth. Joined RN 1956; qualified Observer, 1961; served HM Ships Ark Royal, Protector, Eagle; BRNC Dartmouth, 1968–70; Flight Comdr, HMS Norfolk, 1970–72; Staff of FO Naval Air Comd, 1972–74; CO HMS Amazon, 1975–76; Naval Sec's Dept, MoD, 1976–78; Naval and Air Attaché, Athens, 1980–82; Senior Naval Officer, Falklands, 1982–83; Captain 5th Destroyer Sqdn (HMS Southampton), 1983–85; Captain of the Fleet, 1985–88; Naval Sec., 1988–90. Chm., RN Club of 1765 and 1785, 1995. Trustee, Hands Around the World, charity, 1995. FIPD (FIPM 1991). *Recreations:* tennis, hill walking, bird watching, choral singing. *Address:* c/o Lloyd's Bank, The Square, Petersfield, Hants GU32 3HL. *Club:* Army and Navy.

DOBSON, Sir Denis (William), KCB 1969 (CB 1959); OBE 1945; QC 1971; Clerk of the Crown in Chancery and Permanent Secretary to the Lord Chancellor, 1968–77; *b* 17 Oct. 1908; *s* of late William Gordon Dobson, Newcastle upon Tyne; *m* 1st, 1934, Thelma (marr. diss. 1947), *d* of Charles Swinburne, Newcastle upon Tyne; one *s* one *d*; 2nd, 1948, Mary Elizabeth, *d* of J. A. Allen, Haywards Heath; two *s* one *d*. *Educ:* Charterhouse; Trinity Coll., Cambridge (MA, LLB). Solicitor, 1933. Served in RAF, 1940–45 (Desert Air Force, 1942–45). Called to the Bar, Middle Temple, 1951; Bencher, 1968. Dep. Clerk of the Crown in Chancery and Asst Permanent Sec. to Lord Chancellor, 1954–68. Mem., Adv. Council on Public Records, 1977–83. *Address:* 50 Egerton Crescent, SW3 2ED. *T:* 0171–589 7990. *Club:* Athenæum.
See also M. W. R. Dobson, R. S. Dobson.

DOBSON, Frank Gordon; MP (Lab) Holborn and St Pancras, since 1983 (Holborn and St Pancras South, 1979–83); *b* 15 March 1940; *s* of James William and Irene Shortland Dobson, York; *m* 1967, Janet Mary, *d* of Henry and Edith Alker; three *c*. *Educ:* Dunnington County Primary Sch., York; Archbishop Holgate's Grammar Sch., York; London School of Economics (BScEcon). Administrative jobs with Central Electricity Generating Bd, 1962–70, and Electricity Council, 1970–75; Asst Sec., Commn for Local Administration (local Ombudsman's office), 1975–79. Member, Camden Borough Council, 1971–76 (Leader of Council, 1973–75); Chm., Coram's Fields and Harmsworth Meml Playground, 1977–. NUR sponsored MP; front bench spokesman on educn, 1981–83, on health, 1983–87; Shadow Leader of the Commons and Party Campaign Co-ordinator, 1987–89; opposition front bench spokesman on energy, 1989–92, on employment, 1992–93, on transport and London, 1993–. Chm., NHS Unlimited, 1981–89. Governor: LSE, 1986–; Inst. of Child Health, 1987–. *Address:* 22 Great Russell Mansions, Great Russell Street, WC1B 3BE. *T:* 0171–242 5760. *Club:* Covent Garden Community Centre.

DOBSON, Keith; *see* Dobson, W. K.

DOBSON, Michael William Romsey; Group Chief Executive, Morgan Grenfell Group plc, since 1989; *b* 13 May 1952; *s* of Sir Denis (William) Dobson, *qv*. *Educ:* Eton; Trinity Coll., Cambridge. Joined Morgan Grenfell, 1973: Morgan Grenfell NY, 1978–80, Man. Dir, 1984–85; Hd, Investment Div., 1987–88; Dep. Chief Exec., 1988–89. *Address:* 23 Great Winchester Street, EC2P 2AX.

DOBSON, Sir Patrick John H.; *see* Howard-Dobson.

DOBSON, Prof. Richard Barrie, FSA; FRHistS; FBA 1988; Professor of Medieval History, and Fellow of Christ's College, University of Cambridge, since 1988; *b* 3 Nov. 1931; *s* of Richard Henry Dobson and Mary Victoria Dobson (*née* Kidd); *m* 1959, Narda Leon; one *s* one *d*. *Educ:* Barnard Castle Sch.; Wadham Coll., Oxford (BA 1st cl. Modern Hist.; MA 1958; DPhil 1963). Senior demy, Magdalen Coll., Oxford, 1957–58; Lectr in Medieval History, Univ. of St Andrews, 1958–64; University of York: Lectr, Sen. Lectr, Reader, Prof. of History, 1964–88; Dep. Vice-Chancellor, 1984–87. British Acad. Fellow, Folger Shakespeare Liby, Washington, 1974; Cornell Vis. Prof., Swarthmore Coll., USA, 1987; Vis. Fellow, Trinity Coll., Toronto, 1994. FRHistS 1972 (Vice-Pres., 1985–89); FSA 1979; President: Surtees Soc., 1987; Jewish Historical Soc. of England, 1990–91; Ecclesiastical History Soc., 1991–92; Chm., York Archeol Trust, 1990. Life Mem., Merchant Taylors' Co, York. Gen. Editor, Yorks Archaeol. Soc., Record Series, 1981–86. *Publications:* The Peasants' Revolt of 1381, 1971, 2nd edn 1983; Durham Priory 1400–1450, 1973; The Jews of Medieval York and the Massacre of March 1190, 1974; (with J. Taylor) Rymes of Robyn Hood, 1977; (ed) York City Chamberlains' Accounts 1396–1500, 1980; (ed) The Church, Politics and Patronage in the Fifteenth Century, 1984; (contrib.) A History of York Minster, 1977; (contrib.) History of the University of Oxford, Vol. II, 1993; articles in learned jls. *Recreations:* hill walking, cinema, chess, modern jazz. *Address:* Christ's College, Cambridge CB2 3BU. *T:* Cambridge (01223) 334900.

DOBSON, Roger Swinburne, OBE 1987; FEng 1993; FICE; Director-General and Secretary, Institution of Civil Engineers, since 1990; *b* 24 June 1936; *s* of Sir Denis William Dobson, *qv* and Thelma Swinburne; *m* 2nd, Deborah Elizabeth Sancroft Burrough; one *s* one *d*. *Educ:* Bryanston Sch.; Trinity Coll., Cambridge (MA); Stanford Univ., Calif (DofEng). MBCS 1981; FICE 1990. Qualified pilot, RN, 1955. Binnie & Partners, 1959–69; Bechtel Ltd, 1969–90: Gen. Manager, PMB Systems Engrg, 1984–86; Man. Dir, Laing-Bechtel Petroleum Devélt, 1986–90. Deputy Chairman: Thomas Telford Ltd, 1990–; Thomas Telford Services Ltd, 1991–. Chairman: Computer Aided Design Computer Aided Manufacturing Gp, NEDC, 1981–85; Energy Industries Council, 1987–90; Mem., Construction Industry Sector Gp, NEDC, 1988–92. *Publications:* Applications of Digital Computers to Hydraulic Engineering, 1967; contrib. Procs of ICE and IMechE. *Recreations:* sailing, tennis, squash, gardening. *Address:* Penleigh House, Westbury, Wilts BA13 4EB. *Clubs:* Royal Ocean Racing; Shearwater Sailing.
See also M. W. R. Dobson.

DOBSON, Sue; Editor-in-Chief, Choice, since 1994; *b* 31 Jan. 1946; *d* of Arthur and Nellie Henshaw; *m* 1966, Michael Dobson (marr. diss. 1974). *Educ:* convent schs; BA Hons CNAA. From 1964, worked for a collection of women's magazines, including Femina and Fair Lady in S Africa, variously as fashion, cookery, beauty, home and contributing editor, editor at SA Institute of Race Relations and editor of Wedding Day and Successful Slimming in London, with breaks somewhere in between in PR and doing research into the language and learning of children; Editor, Woman and Home, 1982–94. *Publication:* The Wedding Day Book, 1981, 2nd edn 1989. *Recreations:* photography, reading, travelling, exploring. *Address:* Apex House, Oundle Road, Peterborough PE2 9NP.

DOBSON, (William) Keith, OBE 1988; Director, Germany, British Council, since 1993; *b* 20 Sept. 1945; *s* of Raymond Griffin Dobson and Margaret (*née* Wylie); *m* 1972, Valerie Guest; two *d*. *Educ:* King Edward's Grammar School, Camp Hill, Birmingham; Univ. of Keele (BA Internat. Relns 1968); Univ. of Essex (DipSoc 1972). With Clarks Ltd, Shoemakers, 1968–71; joined British Council: Lagos, 1972–75; London, 1975–77; Ankara, 1977–80; Caracas, 1980–84; Budapest, 1984–87; London, 1987–90; Europe Div., 1990–93. *Recreations:* music, cinema, bridge, woodworking. *Address:* British Council, Hahnenstrasse 6, 50667 Köln, Germany. *T:* (221) 206440.

DOCHERTY, Dr Daniel Joseph, JP; General Medical Practitioner, 1949–87, retired; Examining Medical Officer, Department of Social Security (formerly Department of Health and Social Security), 1982; *b* 24 Oct. 1924; *s* of Michael Joseph Docherty and Ellen Stewart; *m* 1952, Dr Rosemary Catherine Kennedy; eight *s* two *d*. *Educ:* St Aloysius' Coll.; Anderson Coll. of Medicine; Glasgow Univ. LRCP, LRCS, LRFPS. MO, King's Flight, RAF Benson, 1950. Glasgow Town Councillor, 1959–75; Sen. Magistrate, City of Glasgow, 1964–65; Chm. of Police Cttee, 1967–68; Chm. of Educn Cttee, 1971–74. Mem., MSC, 1974–77; Chm. in Scotland, Job Creation Programme, 1975–78. Member: Strathclyde Univ. Ct, 1971–72; Glasgow Univ. Ct, 1972–74; Council, Open Univ., 1972–75. JP Glasgow, 1961. *Recreation:* travel. *Address:* 92 Mansion House Gardens, Glasgow G41 3DN. *T:* 0141–649 0307.

DOCKER, Rt. Rev. Ivor Colin; Bishop Suffragan of Horsham, 1975–91; an Assistant Bishop, diocese of Exeter, since 1991; *b* 3 Dec. 1925; *s* of Colonel Philip Docker, OBE, TD, DL, and Doris Gwendoline Docker (*née* Whitehill); *m* 1950, Thelma Mary, *d* of John William and Gladys Upton; one *s* one *d*. *Educ:* King Edward's High Sch., Birmingham; Univ. of Birmingham (BA); St Catherine's Coll., Oxford (MA). Curate of Normanton, Yorks, 1949–52; Lecturer of Halifax Parish Church, 1952–54; CMS Area Sec., 1954–59; Vicar of Midhurst, Sussex, 1959–64; RD of Midhurst, 1961–64; Vicar and RD of Seaford, 1964–71; Canon and Prebendary of Colworth in Chichester Cathedral, 1966–81; Vicar and RD of Eastbourne, 1971–75; Proctor in Convocation, 1970–75. Chm., C of E Nat. Council for Social Aid, 1987–. *Recreations:* photography, travel, reading. *Address:* Braemar, Bradley Road, Bovey Tracey, Newton Abbot, Devon TQ13 9EU. *T:* Bovey Tracey (01626) 832468.

DOCTOROW, Edgar Lawrence; Glucksman Professor of American and English Letters, New York University, since 1987; *b* 6 Jan. 1931; *s* of David R. Doctorow and Rose Doctorow Buck; *m* 1954, Helen Setzer; one *s* two *d*. *Educ:* Kenyon College (AB 1952); Columbia Univ. (graduate study). Script-reader, Columbia Pictures, NY, 1956–59; sen. editor, New American Library, 1959–64; editor-in-chief, 1964–69, publisher, 1968–69, Dial Press; writer-in-residence, Univ. of California, Irvine, 1969–70; Mem., Faculty, Sarah Lawrence Coll., NY, 1971–78; Creative Writing Fellow, Yale Sch. of Drama, 1974–75; Vis. Sen. Fellow, Council on Humanities, Princeton, 1980–81. Hon. degrees from Brandeis Univ., Kenyon, Hobart and William Smith Colls. Guggenheim Fellowship, 1972; Creative Arts Service Fellow, 1973–74. *Publications:* Welcome to Hard Times, 1960; Big as Life, 1966; The Book of Daniel, 1971; Ragtime, 1975 (Amer. Acad. Award, Nat. Book Critics Circle Award); Drinks Before Dinner, 1979 (play, 1978); Loon Lake, 1980; Lives of the Poets, 1984; World's Fair, 1985 (American Book Award); Billy Bathgate, 1989 (Howells Medal, Amer. Acad.; PEN/Faulkner and Nat. Books Critics Awards; Premio Letterario Internationale, 1991); The Waterworks, 1994. *Address:* c/o Random House Publishers, 201 East 50th Street, New York, NY 10022, USA. *Club:* Century Association (NY).

DODD, Kenneth Arthur, (Ken Dodd), OBE 1982; entertainer, comedian, singer and actor; *b* 8 Nov. 1931; *s* of late Arthur and Sarah Dodd; unmarried. *Educ:* Holt High School, Liverpool. Made professional début at Empire Theatre, Nottingham, 1954; created record on London Palladium début, 1965, by starring in his own 42 week season; has also starred in more than 20 pantomimes. Now travels widely in quest to play every theatrical venue in British Isles. Shakespearean début as Malvolio, Twelfth Night, Liverpool, 1971. Record, Tears, topped British charts for six weeks; awarded two Gold, one Platinum, many Silver Discs (Love Is Like A Violin, Happiness, etc). *Relevant publication:* How Tickled I Am: Ken Dodd, by Michael Billington, 1977. *Recreations:* racing, soccer, reading, people. *Address:* 76 Thomas Lane, Knotty Ash, Liverpool L14 5NX.

DODD, Philip Kevin, OBE 1987; Stipendiary Magistrate, Cheshire, since 1991; *b* 2 April 1938; *s* of Thomas and Mary Dodd; *m* 1962, Kathleen Scott; one *s* one *d*. *Educ:* St Joseph's Coll., Dumfries; Leeds Univ. (BA, LLB). Admitted Solicitor, 1966. Articled Clerk, Ashton-under-Lyne Magistrates' Court, 1961–63; Dep. Justices' Clerk, 1963–67; Justices' Clerk: Houghton-le-Spring and Seaham, 1967–70; Wolverhampton, 1970–76; Manchester, 1976–91. Council Member: Justices' Clerks' Soc., 1974–89 (Pres., 1985–86); Manchester Law Soc., 1978–91 (Pres., 1987–88). Sec., Standing Conf., Clerks to Magistrates' Courts Cttees, 1974–82 (Chm., 1983–84). *Recreations:* growing mimosa, planning holidays. *Address:* Warrington Magistrates' Court, Winmarleigh Street, Warrington WA1 1PB. *T:* Warrington (01925) 53136.

DODD, William Atherton, CMG 1983; *b* 5 Feb. 1923; *s* of Frederick Dodd and Sarah Atherton; *m* 1949, Marjorie Penfold; two *d*. *Educ:* Chester City Grammar Sch.; Christ's Coll., Cambridge (MA, CertEd). Served War, 1942–45: Captain, 8 Gurkha Rifles. Sen. History Master, Ipswich Sch., 1947–52; Educn Officer, Dept of Educn, Tanganyika, 1952–61; Sen. Educn Officer, Min. of Educn, Tanzania, 1961–65; Lectr, Dept of Educn in Developing Countries, Univ. of London Inst. of Educn, 1965–70; Educn Adviser, ODM, 1970–77; Chief Educn Advr, 1978–83, and Under Sec. (Educn Div.), 1980–83, ODA. Consultant: UC Cardiff, 1983–87; Inst. of Educn, Univ. of London, 1983–91; Child-to-Child Trust, 1988–; AMAR (Marsh Arabs) Appeal, 1994–. UK Mem., Unesco Exec. Bd, 1983–85. Chm., Christopher Cox Meml Fund, 1983–. Trustee, Internat. Extension Coll., 1987–. *Publications:* A Mapbook of Exploration, 1965; Primary School Inspection in New Countries, 1968; Education for Self-Reliance in Tanzania, 1969; (with J. Cameron) Society, Schools and Progress in Tanzania, 1970; (ed) Teacher at Work, 1970; (with C. Criper) Report on the Teaching of the English Language in Tanzania, 1985. *Recreations:* walking, music, cricket. *Address:* 20 Bayham Road, Sevenoaks, Kent TN13 3XD. *T:* Sevenoaks (01732) 454238. *Clubs:* MCC; Sevenoaks Vine.

DODDERIDGE, Morris, CBE 1974 (OBE 1962); British Council Representative, Rome, 1970–75, retired; *b* 17 Oct. 1915; *s* of Reginald William Dodderidge and Amy Andrew; *m* 1941, Esme Williams; one *s* one *d* (and one *s* decd). *Educ:* Hertford Grammar Sch.; King's Coll., London; Inst. Educn, London. BA 1st cl. hons English 1937; Brewer Prize for Lit.; Teachers Dip. 1938; DipEd 1952. Asst Master, Hele's Sch., Exeter, 1938–40. War of 1939–45, Royal Signals; served N Africa, Italy, Austria (Captain, despatches). Joined British Council, 1946: Dir of Studies, Milan, 1947–53; Rep., Norway, 1953–57; Teaching of English Liaison Officer, 1957–59; Dir, Recruitment Dept, 1959–64; Controller: Recruitment Div., 1964–66; Overseas Div. A, 1966–67; Home Div. I, 1967–68; Appts Div., 1968–70. *Publications:* Man on the Matterhorn, 1940; (with W. R. Lee) Time for a Song, 1965. *Recreations:* golf, swimming. *Address:* River Cottage, Church Street, Presteigne, Powys LD8 2BU. *T:* Presteigne (01544) 267609.

DODDS, Denis George, CBE 1977; LLB (London); CompIEE; Solicitor; Chairman, British Approval Service for Electricity Cables Ltd, 1982–93; *b* 25 May 1913; *s* of Herbert Yeaman Dodds and Violet Katharine Dodds; *m* 1937, Muriel Reynolds Smith; two *s* three *d*. *Educ:* Rutherford Coll., Newcastle upon Tyne; King's Coll., Durham Univ. Asst Solicitor and Asst Town Clerk, Gateshead, 1936–41. Served Royal Navy (Lieut RNVR), 1941–46. Dep. Town Clerk and Dep. Clerk of the Peace, City of Cardiff, 1946–48; Sec., S Wales Electricity Board, 1948–56; Chief Industrial Relations Officer, CEA and Industrial Relations Adviser, Electricity Council, 1957–59; Dep. Chm., 1960–62, Chm., 1962–77, Merseyside and N Wales Electricity Bd. Chairman: Merseyside Chamber of Commerce and Industry, 1976–78; Port of Preston Adv. Bd, 1978; Assoc. of Members of State Industry Boards, 1976–89. Member: CBI Council for Wales, 1960–78; NW Economic Planning Council, 1971; Dir, Development Corporation for Wales, 1970–83. Mem., Nat. Adv. Council for Employment of the Disabled, 1978–91. *Recreations:* music and gardening. *Address:* Corners, 28 Grange Park, Westbury on Trym, Bristol BS9 4BP. *T:* Bristol (0117) 962 1440.

DODDS, James Pickering, CB 1954; Under-Secretary, Department of Health and Social Security, 1968–73; *b* 7 Feb. 1913; *s* of James Thompson and Elizabeth Fingland Dodds; *m* 1942, Ethel Mary Gill (*d* 1987); two *d*. *Educ:* Queen Elizabeth's Grammar Sch., Darlington; Jesus Coll., Cambridge. Entered Ministry of Health, 1935; Nuffield Home Civil Service Travelling Fellowship, 1950; Under-Sec., 1951; Dir of Establishments and Orgn, 1965–68. *Address:* 17 Herne Road, Oundle, Peterborough PE8 4BS.

DODDS, Nigel Alexander; barrister; Lord Mayor of Belfast, 1988–89 and 1991–92; *b* 20 Aug. 1958; *s* of Joseph Alexander and Doreen Elizabeth Dodds; *m* 1985, Diana Jean Harris; two *s*. *Educ:* Portora Royal Sch., Enniskillen; St John's Coll., Cambridge (MA); Inst. of Professional Legal Studies, Belfast (Cert. of Professional Legal Studies). Called to the Bar, NI, 1981. Mem., Belfast City Council, 1985– (Chm., F and GP Cttee, 1985–87); Alderman, Castle Area, 1989–. Vice Pres., Assoc. of Local Authorities of NI, 1988–89. Mem., Senate, QUB, 1987–93. *Address:* City Hall, Belfast BT1 5GS.

DODDS, Sir Ralph (Jordan), 2nd Bt *cr* 1964; *b* 25 March 1928; *o s* of Sir (Edward) Charles Dodds, 1st Bt, MVO, FRS, and Constance Elizabeth (*d* 1969), *o d* of late J. T. Jordan, Darlington; *S* father, 1973; *m* 1954, Marion, *er d* of late Sir Daniel Thomas Davies, KCVO; two *d*. *Educ:* Winchester; RMA, Sandhurst. Regular commission, 13/18th Royal Hussars, 1948; served UK and abroad; Malaya, 1953 (despatches); resigned, 1958. Underwriting Member of Lloyd's, 1964. *Address:* 49 Sussex Square, W2 2SP. *Clubs:* Cavalry and Guards, Hurlingham.

DODDS-PARKER, Sir (Arthur) Douglas, Kt 1973; MA (Oxford); company director since 1946; *b* 5 July 1909; *o s* of A. P. Dodds-Parker, FRCS, Oxford; *m* 1946, Aileen, *d* of late Norman B. Coster and late Mrs Alvin Dodd, Grand Detour, Ill., USA; one *s*. *Educ:* Winchester; Magdalen Coll., Oxford. BA in Modern History, 1930; MA 1934. Entered Sudan Political Service, 1930; Kordofan Province, 1931–34; Asst Private Sec. to Governor-General, Khartoum, 1934–35; Blue Nile Province, 1935–38; Public Security Dept, Khartoum, 1938–39; resigned 1938; joined Grenadier Guards, 1939; employed on special duties, March 1940; served in London, Cairo, East African campaign, North Africa, Italy and France, 1940–45; Mission Comdr, SOE, Western and Central Mediterranean, 1943–44; Col, 1944 (despatches, French Legion of Honour, Croix de Guerre). MP (C): Banbury Div. of Oxon, 1945–Sept. 1959; Cheltenham, 1964–Sept. 1974; Jt Parly Under-Sec. of State for Foreign Affairs, Nov. 1953–Oct. 1954, Dec. 1955–Jan. 1957; Parly Under-Sec. for Commonwealth Relations, Oct. 1954–Dec. 1955. Chairman: British Empire Producers Organisation; Joint East and Central Africa Board, 1947–50; Conservative Commonwealth Council, 1960–64; Cons. Parly Foreign and Commonwealth Cttee, 1970–73; Europe Atlantic Gp, 1976–79; Delegate to Council of Europe, North Atlantic and W European Assemblies, 1965–72; led Parly Delegn to China, 1972; Mem., British Parly Delegn to European Parlt, Strasbourg, 1973–75. Mem., Regtl Bd, FANY, 1945–. Freeman, City of London, 1983. *Publications:* Setting Europe Ablaze, 1983; Political Eunuch, 1986. *Address:* 9 North Court, Great Peter Street, SW1P 3LL. *Clubs:* Special Forces (Pres., 1977–81), Institute of Directors; Vincent's (Oxford); Leander.

DODSON, family name of **Baron Monk Bretton.**

DODSON, Sir Derek (Sherborne Lindsell), KCMG 1975 (CMG 1963); MC 1945; DL; HM Diplomatic Service, retired; Special Representative of Secretary of State for Foreign and Commonwealth Affairs, since 1981; *b* 20 Jan. 1920; *e* and *o* surv. *s* of late Charles Sherborne Dodson, MD, and Irene Frances Lindsell; *m* 1952, Julie Maynard Barnes (*d* 1992); one *s* one *d*. *Educ:* Stowe; RMC Sandhurst. Commissioned as 2nd Lieut in Royal Scots Fusiliers, 1939, and served in Army until Feb. 1948. Served War of 1939–45 (MC): India, UK, Middle East, and with Partisans in Greece and N Italy. Mil. Asst to Brit. Comr, Allied Control Commn for Bulgaria, July 1945–Sept. 1946; GSO 3, War Office, Oct. 1946–Nov. 1947; apptd a Mem. HM Foreign Service, 1948; 2nd Sec., 1948; Acting Vice-Consul at Salonika, Sept. 1948; Acting Consul Gen. there in 1949 and 1950; Second Sec., Madrid, 1951; promoted First Sec., Oct. 1951; transferred to Foreign Office, Sept. 1953; apptd Private Sec. to Minister of State for Foreign Affairs, 1955; First Sec. and Head of Chancery, Prague, Nov. 1958; Chargé d'Affaires there in 1959, 1960, 1961, 1962; promoted and apptd Consul at Elisabethville, 1962; Transf. FO and apptd Head of the Central Dept, 1963; Counsellor, British Embassy, Athens, 1966–69; Ambassador: to Hungary, 1970–73; to Brazil, 1973–77; to Turkey, 1977–80. Chm., Beaver Guarantee Ltd, 1984–86; Dir, Benguela Rly Co., 1984–. Chm., Anglo-Turkish Soc., 1982–. Mem., Bd of Governors, United World College of the Atlantic, 1982–95. DL Lincoln, 1987. Order of the Southern Cross, Brazil. *Recreations:* shooting, fishing, walking. *Address:* 47 Ovington Street, SW3 2JA. *T:* 0171–589 5055; Gable House, Leadenham, Lincoln LN5 0PN. *T:* Loveden (01400) 272212. *Clubs:* Boodle's, Travellers'.

DODSON, Joanna; QC 1993; *b* 5 Sept. 1945; *d* of Jack Herbert Dodson and Joan Muriel (*née* Webb); *m* 1974, John Alan Donne Reeve Hopkin (marr. diss. 1981). *Educ:* James Allen's Girls' Sch.; Newnham Coll., Cambridge (BA 1967; MA 1971). Called to the Bar, Middle Temple, 1971. *Address:* 14 Gray's Inn Square, Gray's Inn, WC1R 5JP. *T:* 0171–242 0858.

DODSON, Robert North; *see* North, R.

DODSWORTH, Geoffrey Hugh, JP; FCA; Chairman: Dodsworth & Co. Ltd, since 1988; Jorvik Finance Corporation Ltd, since 1986; Director, First International Leasing Corp., since 1990; *b* 7 June 1928; *s* of late Walter J. J. Dodsworth and Doris M. Baxter; *m* 1st, 1949, Isabel Neale (decd); one *d*; 2nd, 1971, Elizabeth Ann Beeston; one *s* one *d*. *Educ:* St Peter's Sch., York. MP (C) Herts SW, Feb. 1974–Oct. 1979, resigned. Mem. York City Council, 1959–65; JP York 1961, later JP Herts. Dir, Grindlays Bank Ltd, 1976–80; Chief Exec., Grindlay Brandts Ltd, 1977–80; Pres. and Chief Exec., Oceanic Finance Corp., 1980–85, Dep. Chm., 1985–86; Chm., Oceanic Financial Services, 1985–86; Dir, County Properties Group, 1987–88. *Recreation:* riding. *Address:* Well Hall, Well, Bedale, N Yorks DL8 2PX. *T:* Bedale (01677) 70223; 78 Cliffords Inn, Fetter Lane, EC4A 1BX. *Club:* Carlton.

DODSWORTH, Prof. (James) Martin; Professor of English, Royal Holloway (formerly Royal Holloway and Bedford New College), University of London, since 1987; *b* 10 Nov. 1935; *s* of Walter Edward and Kathleen Ida Dodsworth; *m* 1967, Joanna Rybicka; one *s*. *Educ:* St George's Coll., Weybridge; Univ. of Fribourg, Switzerland; Wadham Coll., Oxford (MA). Asst Lectr and Lectr in English, Birkbeck Coll., London, 1961–67; Lectr and Sen. Lectr, Royal Holloway Coll., later Royal Holloway and Bedford New Coll., London, 1967–87. Vis. Lectr, Swarthmore Coll., Pa, 1966. Chairman: English Assoc., 1987–; Cttee for University English, 1988–90. Editor, English, 1976–87. *Publications:* (ed) The Survival of Poetry, 1970; Hamlet Closely Observed, 1985; (ed) English Economis'd, 1989; (ed) The Penguin History of Literature, vol. 7: The Twentieth Century, 1994; contribs to The Guardian, Essays in Criticism, The Review, etc. *Recreations:* reading, eating and drinking, short walks. *Address:* 59 Temple Street, Brill, Bucks HP18 9SU. *T:* Brill (01844) 237106.

DODSWORTH, Sir John Christopher S.; *see* Smith-Dodsworth.

DODSWORTH, Martin; *see* Dodsworth, J. M.

DODWORTH, Air Vice-Marshal Peter, CB 1994; OBE 1982; AFC 1971; Senior Directing Staff (Air), Royal College of Defence Studies, since 1994; *b* 12 Sept. 1940; *e s* of Eric and Edna Dodworth; *m* 1963, Kay Parry; three *s*. *Educ:* Southport Grammar Sch.; Leeds Univ. (BSc Physics, 1961). Served: 54 Sqn Hunters, 1963–65; 4 FTS Gnats, 1965–67; Central Flying Sch., 1967–68; Harrier Conversion Team, 1969–72; Air Staff RAF Germany, 1972–76; OC Ops, RAF Wittering, 1976–79; ndc 1980; Air Comdr, Belize, 1980–82; staff, RAF Staff Coll., 1982–83; Stn comdr, RAF Wittering, 1983–85; Command Group Exec., HQ AAFCE, Ramstein, 1985–87; RCDS, 1987; Dir of Personnel, MoD, 1988–91; Defence Attaché and Hd, British Defence Staff (Washington), 1991–94. *Recreations:* squash, golf, DIY, reading. *Address:* RCDS, Seaford House, Belgrave Square, SW1X 8NS. *Club:* Royal Air Force (Chm.).

DOE, Rt Rev. Michael David; *see* Swindon, Bishop Suffragan of.

DOERR, Michael Frank, FIA; Group Chief Executive, Friends Provident Life Office, since 1992; *b* 25 May 1935; *s* of Frank and May Doerr; *m* 1958, Jill Garrett; one *s* one *d*. *Educ:* Rutlish Sch. FIA 1959. Actuarial student, Friends Provident Life Office, 1954; Pensions Actuary, 1960–66; Life Manager, 1966–73; Gen. Manager, Marketing, 1973–80; Gen. Manager, Ops, and Dir, 1980–87; Dep. Man. Dir, 1987–92. *Recreations:* golf, tennis, chess, theatre, sailing. *Address:* Pixham End, Dorking, Surrey RH4 1QA. *T:* Dorking (01306) 740123. *Clubs:* Royal Automobile, Carlton; Chichester Yacht, Goodwood Park Country.

DOGGART, George Hubert Graham, OBE 1993; Headmaster, King's School, Bruton, 1972–85; *b* 18 July 1925; *e s* of late Alexander Graham Doggart and Grace Carlisle Hannan; *m* 1960, Susan Mary, *d* of R. I. Beattie, Eastbourne; one *s* two *d*. *Educ:* Winchester; King's Coll., Cambridge. BA History, 1950; MA 1955. Army, 1943–47 (Sword of Honour, 161 OCTU, Mons, 1944); Coldstream Guards. On staff at Winchester, 1950–72 (exchange at Melbourne C of E Grammar Sch., 1963); Housemaster, 1964–72. HMC Schools rep. on Nat. Cricket Assoc., 1964–75; President: English Schools Cricket Assoc., 1965–; Quidnuncs, 1983–88; Cricket Soc., 1983–; Member: Cricket Council, 1968–71, 1972, 1983–92; MCC Cttee, 1975–78, 1979–81, 1982–92 (Pres., 1981–82; Treas., 1987–92). Captain, Butterflies CC, 1986–. Chm., Friends of Arundel Castle CC, 1992–. *Publications:* (ed) The Heart of Cricket: memoir of H. S. Altham, 1967; (jtly) Lord Be Praised: the story of MCC's bicentenary celebrations, 1988; (jtly) Oxford and Cambridge Cricket, 1989. *Recreations:* literary and sporting (captained Cambridge v Oxford at cricket, Association football, rackets and squash, 1949–50; played in Rugby fives, 1950; played for England v W Indies, two tests, 1950; captained Sussex, 1954). *Address:* 19 Westgate, Chichester, West Sussex PO19 3ET. *Clubs:* MCC, Lord's Taverners', Hawks (Cambridge).

DOHA, Aminur Rahman S.; *see* Shams-ud Doha, A. R.

DOHERTY, Prof. Peter Charles; FRS 1987; FAA 1983; Chairman, Department of Immunology, St Jude Children's Research Hospital, since 1988; *b* 15 Oct. 1940; *s* of Eric C. and Linda M. Doherty; *m* 1965, Penelope Stephens; two *s*. *Educ:* Univ. of Queensland (BVSc, MVSc); Univ. of Edinburgh (PhD). Veterinary Officer, Queensland Dept of Primary Industries, 1962–67; Scientific Officer, Moredun Research Inst., Edinburgh, 1967–71; Research Fellow, Dept of Microbiology, John Curtin Sch. of Med. Research, Canberra, 1972–75; Associate Prof., later Prof., Wistar Inst., Philadelphia, 1975–82; Prof. of Experimental Pathology, John Curtin Sch. of Medical Res., ANU, 1982–88. Bd Mem., Internat. Lab. for Res. on Animal Disease, Nairobi, 1987–92. Paul Ehrlich Prize and Medal for Immunology, 1983; Gairdner Internat. Award for Med. Research, 1987; Alumnus of Year, Univ. of Queensland, 1993. *Publications:* papers in scientific jls. *Recreations:* walking, reading, ski-ing. *Address:* c/o St Jude Children's Research Hospital, Memphis, TN 38105–0318, USA. *T:* (901) 5220473, *Fax:* (901) 5228570.

DOHMANN, Barbara; QC 1987; a Recorder, since 1990; *b* Berlin; *d* of Paul Dohmann and Dora Dohmann (*née* Thiele). *Educ:* schools in Germany and USA; Univs of Erlangen, Mainz and Paris. Called to the Bar, Gray's Inn, 1971. Mem., Learned Soc. for Internat. Civil Procedure Law, 1991–. Mem. Bd of Govs, London Inst. Higher Educn Corp., 1993–. *Recreations:* gardening, opera, fiction. *Address:* 2 Hare Court, Temple, EC4Y 7BH. *T:* 0171–583 1770. *Club:* CWIL.

DOIG, Very Rev. Dr Andrew Beveridge; *b* 18 Sept. 1914; *s* of George and Hannah Doig; *m* 1st, 1940, Nan Carruthers (*d* 1947); one *d*; 2nd, 1950, Barbara Young; one *s* one *d*. *Educ:* Hyndland Secondary Sch., Glasgow; Glasgow Univ. (MA, BD; Hon. DD 1974); Union Theol Seminary, New York (STM). Ordained, 1938; Church of Scotland Missionary to Nyasaland, 1939–63; service included: Dist Missionary and Sec. of Mission Council; Sen. Army Chaplain, E Africa Comd, 1941–45; Mem., Legislative Council; Mem., Adv. Cttee on African Educn, and Coll. Council, Univ. of Rhodesia and Nyasaland; Regional Sec., Nyasaland and N Rhodesia; seconded to represent African interests in Fed. Parlt, Rhodesias and Nyasaland, 1953–58; Gen. Sec., Synod of Ch. of Central Africa (Presbyterian), 1958–63; Minister, St John's and King's Park, Dalkeith, Scotland, 1963–72; Gen. Sec., National Bible Soc. of Scotland, 1972–82; Moderator of the Gen. Assembly of the Church of Scotland, 1981–82. *Address:* The Eildons, Moulin, Pitlochry PH16 5EW. *T:* Pitlochry (01796) 472892.

DOIG, Peter Muir; *b* 27 Sept. 1911; *m* 1938, Emily Scott; two *s*. *Educ:* Blackness Sch., Dundee. Served RAF, 1941–46. Sales Supervisor with T. D. Duncan Ltd, Bakers, Dundee, until 1963. Mem., TGWU; joined Labour Party, 1930; Mem. of Dundee Town Council, 1953–63, Hon. Treasurer, 1959–63. Contested (Lab) S Aberdeen, 1959; MP (Lab) Dundee West, Nov. 1963–1979. *Recreation:* chess. *Address:* 2 Westwater Place, Wormit, Newport-on-Tay, Fife DD6 8NS.

DOIG, Ralph Herbert, CMG 1974; CVO 1954; *b* 24 Feb. 1909; *s* of late William and Rose Doig; *m* 1937, Barbara Crock; two *s* four *d*. *Educ:* Guildford Grammar Sch.; University of Western Australia (BA, DipCom). Entered Public Service of WA, 1926;

Private Sec. to various Premiers, 1929–41; Asst Under-Sec., Premier's Dept, 1941; Under-Sec., Premier's Dept, and Clerk of Executive Council, Perth, Western Australia, 1945–65; Public Service Comr, W Australia, 1965–71; Chm., Public Service Board, WA, 1971–74. State Director: visit to Western Australia of the Queen and the Duke of Edinburgh, 1954; visit of the Duke of Edinburgh for British Empire and Commonwealth Games, 1962; visit of the Queen and the Duke of Edinburgh, 1963. *Recreation:* bowls. *Address:* 44 Hamersley Street, North Beach, WA 6020, Australia. *T:* (9) 4486843.

DOLBY, Ray Milton, Hon. OBE 1986; PhD; engineering company executive; electrical engineer; Owner and Chairman, Dolby Laboratories Inc., San Francisco and London, since 1965; *b* Portland, Ore, 18 Jan. 1933; *s* of Earl Milton Dolby and Esther Eufemia (*née* Strand); *m* 1966, Dagmar Baumert; two *s*. *Educ:* San Jose State Coll.; Washington Univ.; Stanford Univ. (Beach Thompson award, BS Elec. Engrg); Pembroke Coll., Cambridge (Marshall schol., 1957–60, Draper's studentship, 1959–61, NSF Fellow, 1960–61; PhD Physics 1961; Fellow, 1961–63; research in long-wave length x-rays, 1957–63; Hon. Fellow 1983). Electronic technician/jun. engr, Ampex Corp., Redwood City, Calif, 1949–53. Served US Army 1953–54. Engr, 1955–57; Sen. Engr, 1957; UNESCO Advr, Central Sci. Instruments Org., Punjab, 1963–65; Cons., UKAEA, 1962–63. Inventions, research, pubns in video tape rec., x-ray microanalysis, noise reduction and quality improvements in audio and video systems; 50 UK patents. Trustee, Univ. High Sch., San Francisco, 1978–84; Mem., Marshall Scholarships Selection Cttee, 1979–85; Dir, San Francisco Opera; Governor, San Francisco Symphony. Fellow: Audio Engrg Soc. (Silver Medal, 1971; Gold Medal, 1992; Governor, 1972–74, 1979–84; Pres., 1980–81); Brit. Kinematograph, Sound, TV Soc.; Soc. Motion Picture, TV Engrs (S. L. Warner award, 1978; Alexander M. Poniatoff Gold Medal, 1982; Progress Medal, 1983; Hon. Mem., 1992); Inst. of Broadcast Sound, 1987. MIEEE; Tau Beta Pi. Other Awards: Emmy, for contrib. to Ampex video recorder, 1957, and for noise reduction systems on video recorder sound tracks, 1989; Trendsetter, Billboard, 1971; Lyre, Inst. High Fidelity, 1972; Emile Berliner Assoc. Maker of Microphone award, 1972; Top 200 Execs Bi-Centennial, 1976; Sci. and Engrg, 1979, Oscar, 1989, Acad. of Motion Picture Arts and Scis; Man of the Yr, Internat. Tape Assoc., 1987; Pioneer Award, Internat. Teleproduction Soc., 1988; Eduard Rhein Ring, Eduard Rhein Foundn, 1988; Life Achievement Award, Cinema Audio Soc., 1989. *Recreations:* yachting, skiing, flying. *Address:* (home) 3340 Jackson Street, San Francisco, CA 94118, USA. *T:* (415) 563–6947; (office) 100 Potrero Avenue, San Francisco, CA 94103. *T:* (415) 5580200.

DOLCI, Danilo; Coordinator, Centro Studi e Iniziative, since 1958 (Founder); *b* Sesana, Trieste, 1924; *s* of Enrico Dolci and Mely Kontely. *Educ:* University of Rome; University of Milan. Came to Sicily to work for improvement of social conditions, 1952; arrested and tried for non-violent "reverse strike" to find work for unemployed, 1958. Mem. Internat. Council of War Resisters' International, 1963. Hon. DPhil, Univ. of Berne, 1968; Lenin Peace Prize, 1958; Gold Medal, Accademia Nazionale dei Lincei, 1969; Sonning Prize, 1971; Etna Taormina Poetry Prize, 1975; Viareggio Internat. Prize, 1979. *Publications:* Banditi a Partinico, 1955; Inchiesta a Palermo, 1956; Spreco, 1960; Racconti siciliani, 1963; Verso un mondo nuovo, 1964 (trans. A New World in the Making, 1965); Chi Gioca Solo, 1966; Chissá se i pesci piangono (documentazione di un'esperienza educativa), 1973; Non esiste il silenzio, 1974; Esperienze e riflessioni, 1974; Creatura di creature, 1983; Palpitare di nessi, 1985; The World is One Creature, 1986; Se gli occhi fioriscono, 1990; Nessi fra esperiènza, etica e politica, 1993; Gente semplice, 1993; Communicare, legge della vita, 1993; La legge come germe musicale, 1993; La comunicazione di masse non existe, 1995. *Address:* Centro Studi, Largo Scalia 5, Partinico 90047 (Palermo), Italy. *T:* (91) 8781905.

DOLE, Bob; *see* Dole, R. J.

DOLE, John Anthony; Controller and Chief Executive of HM Stationery Office, and the Queen's Printer of Acts of Parliament, 1987–89, retired; *b* 14 Oct. 1929; *s* of Thomas Stephen Dole and Winifred Muriel (*née* Henderson); *m* 1952, Patricia Ivy Clements; two *s*. *Educ:* Bideford Grammar Sch.; Berkhamsted Sch. Air Ministry: Exec. Officer, 1950; Higher Exec. Officer, 1959; Principal, 1964; Ministry of Transport: Principal, 1965; Asst Sec. (Roads Programme), 1968; Administrator of Sports Council, 1972–75; Under Sec., Freight Directorate, 1976–78; Dir, Senior Staff Management, Depts of the Environment and Transport, 1978–82; Controller of Supplies, PSA, DoE, 1982–84; Controller of the Crown Suppliers, 1984–86. *Publications: plays:* Cat on the Fiddle, 1964; Shock Tactics, 1966; Lucky for Some, 1968; Once in a Blue Moon, 1972; Top Gear, 1976; *verse:* Odd Bodikins, 1992. *Recreations:* writing, philately.

DOLE, Robert Joseph, (Bob Dole); Purple Heart; United States Senator, since 1968; Leader, United States Senate, since 1995 (Senate Republican Leader, since 1985); Leader, Republican Party, United States, since 1992; *b* Russell, Kansas, 22 July 1923; *s* of Doran and Bina Dole; *m* 1975, Elizabeth Hanford; one *d*. *Educ:* Univ. of Kansas (AB); Washburn Municipal Univ. (LLB). Served US Army, 1943–48; Platoon Ldr, 10th Mountain Div., Italy; wounded and decorated twice for heroic achievement; Captain. Kansas Legislature, 1951–53; Russell County Attorney, Kansas, 1953–61; US House of Representatives, 1960–68. *Address:* Office of the Republican Leader, United States Senate, Washington, DC 20510, USA. *T:* (202) 2243135.

DOLL, Sir Richard; *see* Doll, Sir W. R. S.

DOLL, Prof. Sir (William) Richard (Shaboe), Kt 1971; OBE 1956; FRS 1966; DM, MD, FRCP, DSc; Hon. Consultant, Imperial Cancer Research Fund Cancer Studies Unit, Radcliffe Infirmary, Oxford, since 1983; first Warden, Green College, Oxford, 1979–83; *b* Hampton, 28 Oct. 1912; *s* of Henry William Doll and Amy Kathleen Shaboe; *m* 1949, Joan Mary Faulkner, MB, BS, MRCP, DPH; one *s* one *d*. *Educ:* Westminster Sch. (Hon. Fellow, 1991); St Thomas's Hosp. Med. Sch., London. MB, BS 1937; MD 1945; FRCP 1957; DSc London 1958. RAMC, 1939–45. Appts with Med. Research Council, 1946–69; Mem. Statistical Research Unit, 1948; Dep. Dir, 1959; Dir, 1961–69; Hon. Associate Physician, Central Middlesex Hosp., 1949–69; Teacher in Medical Statistics and Epidemiology, University Coll. Hosp. Med. Sch., 1963–69; Regius Prof. of Medicine, Oxford Univ., 1969–79. Member: MRC, 1970–74; Royal Commn on Environmental Pollution, 1973–79; Standing Commn on Energy and the Environment, 1978–81; Scientific Council of Internat. Cancer Research Agency, 1966–70 and 1975–78; Council, Royal Society, 1970–71 (a Vice-Pres., 1970–71); Chairman: Adverse Reaction Sub-Cttee, Cttee on Safety of Medicines, 1970–77; UK Co-ordinating Cttee on Cancer Research, 1972–77. William Julius Mickle Fellow, Univ. of London, 1955. Hon. Lectr London Sch. of Hygiene and Tropical Med., 1956–62 (Hon. Fellow 1982); Milroy Lectr, RCP, 1953; Marc Daniels Lectr, RCP, 1969; Harveian Orator, RCP, 1982. Emeritus Fellow, Academia Europaea, 1990; Hon. Fellow: FPHM, 1974; RCGP, 1978; FOM, 1987; RCOG, 1992; UMDS, 1992; RCR, 1993; Hon. Foreign Member: Norwegian Acad. of Scis, Amer. Acad. of Arts and Scis. Hon DSc: Newcastle, 1969; Belfast, 1972; Reading, 1973; Newfoundland, 1973; Stony Brook, 1988; Harvard, 1988; London, 1988; Oxon, 1989; Oxford Brookes, 1994; Hon. DM Tasmania, 1976; Hon. MD Birmingham, 1994. David Anderson Berry Prize (jt), RSE 1958; Bisset Hawkins Medal, RCP, 1962; UN award for cancer research, 1962; Gairdner Award, Toronto, 1970; Buchanan Medal, Royal Soc., 1972; Presidential award, NY Acad. Sci., 1974; Prix Griffuel, Paris, 1976; Gold Medal, RIPH&H, 1977; Mott Award, Gen. Motors' Cancer Res. Foundn, 1979; Bruce Medal, Amer. Coll. of Physicians, 1981; National Award, Amer. Cancer Soc., 1981; Gold Medal, BMA, 1983; Conrad Röntgen prize, Accademia dei Lincei, 1984; Johann-Georg-Zimmermann Prize, Hanover, 1985; Royal Medal, Royal Soc., 1986; Ettore Majorana Erice Science for Peace Prize, 1990; first Helmut Horten Award, Lugano, 1991; first Prince Mahidol Award, Bangkok, 1992. *Publications:* Prevention of Cancer: pointers from epidemiology, 1967; (jtly) Causes of Cancer, 1982; articles in scientific journals on aetiology of lung cancer, leukaemia and other cancers, also aetiology and treatment of peptic ulcer, effects of ionizing radiations, oral contraceptives; author (jt) Med. Research Council's Special Report Series, 1951, 1957, 1964. *Recreations:* food and conversation. *Address:* 12 Rawlinson Road, Oxford OX2 6UE.

DOLLERY, Sir Colin (Terence), Kt 1987; FRCP; Dean, Royal Postgraduate Medical School, since 1991, Pro-Vice-Chancellor for Medicine and Dentistry, since 1992, University of London; *b* 14 March 1931; *s* of Cyril Robert and Thelma Mary Dollery; *m* 1958, Diana Myra (*née* Stedman); one *s* one *d*. *Educ:* Lincoln Sch.; Birmingham Univ. (BSc, MB,ChB); FRCP 1968. House officer: Queen Elizabeth Hosp., Birmingham; Hammersmith Hosp., and Brompton Hosp., 1956–58; Hammersmith Hospital: Med. Registrar, 1958–60; Sen. Registrar and Tutor in Medicine, 1960–62; Consultant Physician, 1962–; Lectr in Medicine, 1962–65, Prof. of Clinical Pharmacology, 1965–87, Prof. of Medicine, 1987–91, Royal Postgrad. Med. Sch. Member: MRC, 1982–84; UGC, subseq. UFC, 1984–92. Hon. Mem., Assoc. of Amer. Physicians, 1982. Chevalier de l'Ordre National du Mérite (France), 1976. *Publications:* The Retinal Circulation, 1971 (New York); Therapeutic Drugs, 1991; numerous papers in scientific jls concerned with high blood pressure and drug action. *Recreations:* travel, amateur radio, work. *Address:* 101 Corringham Road, NW11 7DL. *T:* 0181–458 2616. *Club:* Athenæum.

DOLLEY, Christopher; Chairman, Damis Agencies Ltd, since 1983; *b* 11 Oct. 1931; *yr s* of late Dr Leslie George Francis Dolley and of Jessie, Otford, Kent; *m* 1966, Christine Elizabeth Cooper; three *s*. *Educ:* Bancrofts Sch.; Corpus Christi Coll., Cambridge. Joined Unilever, 1954; with Unilever subsidiaries, 1954–62: G. B. Ollivant Ltd, 1954–59; United Africa Co., 1959–62. Joined Penguin Books Ltd as Export Manager, 1962; became Dir, 1964, Man. Dir, 1970–73, Chm., 1971–73; Dir for Book Develt, IPC, 1973–77. Exec. Vice-Pres., Penguin Books Inc., Baltimore, 1966; Director: Penguin Publishing Co., 1969–73 (Jt Man. Dir, 1969); Pearson Longman Ltd, 1970–73; The Hamlyn Group, 1971–81. Mem., Nat. Film Finance Corp., 1971–81; Dir, Nat. Film Trustee Corp., 1971–81. *Publication:* (ed) The Penguin Book of English Short Stories, 1967. *Recreations:* golf, gardening, collecting. *Address:* Le Bosq, Taminage, 47120 Duras, France. *T:* 53837788. *Clubs:* Savile; 14 West Hamilton Street (Baltimore, Md).

DOLMETSCH, Carl Frederick, CBE 1954; Director of Haslemere Festival since 1940; specialist and authority on early music and instruments; recording artist i.. England and America; *b* 23 Aug. 1911; *s* of Arnold Dolmetsch and Mabel Johnston; *m*; one *s* two *d* (and one *s* decd). *Educ:* privately. Began studying music with Arnold Dolmetsch at age of 4; first performed in public at 7, first concert tour at 8, first broadcast on violin and viol, 1925, at 14 years of age; virtuoso recorder-player at 15. Toured and broadcast in America, 1935 and 1936; recorder recitals, Wigmore Hall, Feb. and Nov. 1939, and annually, 1946–; toured and broadcast on radio and TV in Holland, 1946; Italy and Switzerland, 1947; Sweden, 1949; New Zealand, 1953; France, 1956; America, 1957; Switzerland, Austria, Germany, Holland, 1958; Belgium, America, 1959; Sweden, Austria, Germany, 1960; Australia, 1965; Colombia, 1966; France, Sweden, 1967; Alaska, Canada and Italy, 1969; Japan, 1974; Denmark, 1983; Colombia, 1984; Italy, 1985; France, 1991; America (yearly), 1961–81. Frequent broadcasts in this country and abroad. Chm. and Man. Dir, Arnold Dolmetsch Ltd, 1963–78; Chm., Dolmetsch Musical Instruments, 1982–. Musical Dir of Soc. of Recorder Players, 1937–; Musical Dir, Dolmetsch Internat. Summer School, 1970–; Mem. Incorporated Soc. of Musicians; Mem. Art Workers' Guild, 1953 (Master, 1988); Patron Early Music Soc., University of Sydney. Hon. Fellow of Trinity Coll. of Music, 1950. Hon. DLitt University of Exeter, 1960. Hon. Fellow London Coll. of Music, 1963. *Publications:* Recorder Tutors, 1957, 1962, 1970, 1977; edited and arranged numerous publications of 16th-, 17th- and 18th-century music; contrib. to many music jls. *Recreations:* ornithology, natural history. *Address:* Jesses, Haslemere, Surrey GU27 2BS. *T:* Haslemere (01428) 643818.

DOLTON, David John William; management consultant, since 1989; *b* 15 Sept. 1928; *e s* of Walter William and Marie Frances Duval Dolton; *m* 1959, Patricia Helen Crowe (marr. diss. 1985); one *s* one *d*; *m* 1986, Rosalind Jennifer Chivers. *Educ:* St Lawrence Coll., Ramsgate. FCIS, FIPD, FIMgt. 2nd Lt RA, 1946–48. Various appointments in Delta Metal Co. Ltd, 1950–76, incl. Commercial Director, Extrusion Division, and Director of Administration and Personnel, Rod Division, 1967–76; Chief Exec., Equal Opportunities Commn, 1976–78; Asst Gen. Manager, Nat. Employers Mutual Gen. Insce Assoc. Ltd, 1979–89. Governor, The Queen's Coll., Birmingham, 1974–88. Reader, Dio. Gloucester. Liveryman, Worshipful Co. of Gold and Silver Wyre Drawers. *Recreations:* music, reading, formerly mountaineering, now mountain and hill walking, swimming, travel. *Address:* Arrabon, Cirencester Road, South Cerney, Cirencester, Glos GL7 6HT. *T:* Cirencester (01285) 862600.

DOMB, Prof. Cyril, PhD; FRS 1977; Professor of Physics, Bar-Ilan University, 1981–89, now Emeritus; *m* Shirley Galinsky; three *s* three *d*. *Educ:* Hackney Downs Sch.; Pembroke Coll., Cambridge. Major Open Schol., Pembroke Coll., 1938–41; Radar Research, Admiralty, 1941–46; MA Cambridge, 1945; Nahum Schol., Pembroke Coll., 1946; PhD Cambridge, 1949; ICI Fellowship, Clarendon Laboratory, Oxford, 1949–52; MA Oxon, 1952; University Lecturer in Mathematics, Cambridge, 1952–54; Prof. of Theoretical Physics, KCL, 1954–81; FKC 1978. Max Born Prize, Inst. of Physics and German Physical Soc., 1981. *Publications:* (ed) Clerk Maxwell and Modern Science, 1963; (ed) Memories of Kopul Rosen, 1970; Phase Transitions and Critical Phenomena, (ed with M.S. Green) vols 1 and 2, 1972, vol. 3, 1974, vols 5a, 5b, 6, 1976, (ed with J. L. Lebowitz) vols 7 and 8, 1983, vol. 9, 1984, vol. 10, 1986, vol. 11, 1987, vol. 12, 1988, vol. 13, 1989, vol. 14, 1991, vol. 15, 1992, vol. 16, 1994; (ed with A. Carmell) Challenge, 1976; articles in scientific journals. *Recreations:* walking, swimming. *Address:* Department of Physics, Bar-Ilan University, 52 100 Ramat-Gan, Israel; 28 St Peter's Court, Queens Road, NW4 2HG.

DOMINGO, Placido; tenor singer, conductor; Artistic Director, Washington Opera, since 1994; *b* Madrid, 21 Jan. 1941; *s* of Placido Domingo and Pepita (*née* Embil), professional singers; *m* Marta Ornelas, lyric soprano; three *s*. *Educ:* Instituto, Mexico City; Nat. Conservatory of Music, Mexico City. Operatic début, Monterrey, as Alfredo in La Traviata, 1961; with opera houses at Dallas, Fort Worth, Israel, to 1965; NY City Opera, 1965–; débuts: at NY Metropolitan Opera, as Maurizio in Adriana Lecouvreur, 1968; at La Scala, title role in Ernani, 1969; at Covent Garden, Cavaradossi in Tosca, 1971. Has conducted in Vienna, Barcelona, NY and Frankfurt; début as conductor in UK, Covent Garden, 1983. *Films:* La Traviata, 1983; Carmen, 1984; Otello, 1986; appears on TV, makes recordings, throughout USA and Europe. FRCM; FRNCM. Officer, Legion of Honour, 1983; Medal of City of Madrid. *Publication:* My First Forty Years (autobiog.), 1983. *Recreations:* piano, swimming.

DOMINIAN, Dr Jacobus, (Jack), MBE 1994; FRCPEd, FRCPsych; DPM; Hon. Consultant, Central Middlesex Hospital, since 1988 (Senior Consultant Psychiatrist, 1965–88); *b* 25 Aug. 1929; *s* of late Charles Joseph Dominian and Mary Dominian (*née* Scarlatou); *m* 1955, Edith Mary Smith; four *d*. *Educ:* Lycée Leonin, Athens; St Mary's High Sch., Bombay; Stamford Grammar Sch., Lincs; Cambridge Univ.; Oxford Univ. MA, MB BChir (Cantab). Postgraduate work in medicine, various Oxford hosps, 1955–58, Maudsley Hosp. (Inst. of Psychiatry), 1958–64; training as psychiatrist at Maudsley Hosp.; Dir, One Plus One: Marriage and Partnership Research, 1971–. Hon. DSc Lancaster, 1976. *Publications:* Psychiatry and the Christian, 1961; Christian Marriage, 1967; Marital Breakdown, 1968; The Church and the Sexual Revolution, 1971; Cycles of Affirmation, 1975; Depression, 1976; Authority, 1976; (with A. R. Peacocke) From Cosmos to Love, 1976; Proposals for a New Sexual Ethic, 1977; Marriage, Faith and Love, 1981; Make or Break, 1984; The Capacity to Love, 1985; Sexual Integrity: the answer to AIDS, 1987; Passionate and Compassionate Love, 1991; (with Edmund Flood) The Everyday God, 1993; Marriage, 1995; contribs to Lancet, BMJ, the Tablet, TLS. *Recreations:* enjoyment of the theatre, music, reading and writing. *Address:* Pefka, The Green, Croxley Green, Rickmansworth, Herts WD3 3JA. *T:* Rickmansworth (01923) 720972.

DOMINIC, Zoë Denise, FBIPP, FRPS; professional photographer; *b* 4 July 1920; *d* of Lionel J. Levi and Dora Jane Macdonald; name changed to Dominic by Deed Poll, 1960. *Educ:* Francis Holland Sch., Regent's Park. FRPS 1972 (Hood Medal, 1986); FBIPP 1993. Photographer, stage, opera and ballet: English Stage Co. at Royal Court Theatre, 1957–67; National Theatre, 1963–70; Royal Shakespeare Co., 1958; Royal Ballet; Royal Opera Co.; ENO; English Music Theatre; WNO; Stratford, Ontario, 1975. Chm., Avenue Productions, 1987– (Dir, 1986); produced: A Private Treason, Watford, 1986; Blithe Spirit, Vaudeville, 1987; Noël and Gertie, Donmar Warehouse 1987, Comedy, 1989; specialist photographer on films: Dr Zhivago, Nijinsky, Reds, Travels With My Aunt, Victor Victoria; exhibns of ballet photographs, Photographers' Gallery, 1971, Riverside Studios, 1979. Mem. Council, LAMDA, 1989– (Mem., Finance Cttee (Chm., 1991–94)). Trustee, Theatre Projects Trust, 1970 (Chm., 1983–92). *Publications:* Frederick Ashton, 1971; (jtly) John Cranko and the Stuttgart Ballet, 1973; Theatre at Work (text Jim Hiley), 1981; Full Circle (text Dame Janet Baker), 1982; The Best of Plays and Players 1953–68, 1987. *Recreation:* gardening. *Address:* 3 Lexham Walk, W8 5JD. *T:* 0171–373 6461.

DOMOKOS, Dr Mátyás; General Director, Diplomatic Service Directorate, Ministry of Foreign Affairs, Hungary, since 1989; *b* 28 Oct. 1930; *m* 1956, Irén Beretyán; one *d*. *Educ:* Karl Marx Univ. of Econs, Budapest. Foreign trading enterprises, 1954–57; Commercial Sec., Damascus and Trade Comr, Khartoum, 1958–61; various posts in Ministry for Foreign Trade, Hungary, 1961–74; Ambassador to UN, Geneva, 1974–79; Head of Dept of Internat. Organisations, Ministry of Foreign Affairs, 1979–84; Ambassador to UK, 1984–89. *Recreations:* gardening, chess. *Address:* Diplomatic Corps Service Directorate (DTEI), 1024 Budapest, Mártirok u. 43–45, Hungary.

DON-WAUCHOPE, Sir Roger Hamilton; *see* Wauchope.

DONAHOE, Arthur Richard; QC (Can.) 1982; Secretary-General, Commonwealth Parliamentary Association, since 1993; *b* 7 April 1940; *s* of Richard A. Donahoe and Eileen (*née* Boyd); *m* 1972, Carolyn Elizabeth MacCormack. *Educ:* public schools in Halifax, NS; St Mary's Univ. (BComm 1959); Dalhousie Univ. (LLB 1965). Admitted to Bar of Nova Scotia, 1966; Exec. Asst to Leader of Opposition, Senate of Canada, 1967; barrister and solicitor, 1968–81; Lectr in Commercial Law, St Mary's Univ., 1972–75; MLA (PC), Nova Scotia, 1978–92, Speaker, 1981–91. Canadian Regl Rep., CPA Exec. Cttee, 1983–86. *Publications:* contrib. articles to Parliamentarian and Canadian Parly Rev. *Recreations:* golf, running, reading. *Address:* Suite 700, Westminster House, 7 Millbank, Westminster, SW1P 3JA. *T:* 0171–799 1460; 128 Kenilworth Court, Lower Richmond Road, Putney, SW15 1HB. *T:* 0181–788 2208. *Clubs:* Royal Mid-Surrey Golf; Ashburn Golf (Pres., 1982–83), Halifax (Halifax, NS).

DONALD, Sir Alan (Ewen), KCMG 1988 (CMG 1979); Director: Fleming Far Eastern Investment Trust, since 1991; China Fund Inc. (New York), since 1992; China Aeronautical Technology Fund, since 1993; HSBC China Fund Ltd, since 1994; Adviser on Chinese Affairs: Rolls-Royce; Willis, Faber and Dumas; Lloyd's Register of Shipping; *b* 5 May 1931; 2nd *s* of Robert Thomson Donald and Louise Turner; *m* 1958, Janet Hilary Therese Blood; four *s*. *Educ:* Aberdeen Grammar Sch.; Fettes Coll., Edinburgh; Trinity Hall, Cambridge. BA, LLM. HM Forces, RA (L Battery, 2nd Regt RHA), 1949–50. Joined HM Foreign Service, 1954: Third Sec., Peking, 1955–57; FO, 1958–61: Private Sec. to Parly Under-Sec., FO, 1959–61; Second, later First Sec., UK Delegn to NATO, Paris, 1961–64; First Sec., Peking, 1964–66; Personnel Dept, Diplomatic Service Admin. Office, later FCO, 1967–71; Counsellor (Commercial), Athens, 1971–73; Political Advr to Governor of Hong Kong, 1974–77; Ambassador to: Republics of Zaire, Burundi and Rwanda, 1977–80; People's Republic of the Congo, 1978–80; Asst Under-Sec. of State (Asia and the Pacific), FCO, 1980–84; Ambassador to: Republic of Indonesia, 1984–88; People's Republic of China, 1988–91. Hon. LLD Aberdeen, 1991. *Recreations:* music, military history, water colour sketching, films, golf. *Address:* Applebys, Chiddingstone Causeway, Kent TN11 8JH. *Clubs:* United Oxford & Cambridge University; Aula (London/Cambridge).

DONALD, Dr Alastair Geoffrey, CBE 1993 (OBE 1982); FRCGP, FRCPE, FRCPSGlas; General Medical Practitioner, 1952–92; Assistant Director, Edinburgh Postgraduate Board for Medicine, 1970–91; Regional Adviser in General Practice, SE Scotland, 1972–91; President, Royal College of General Practitioners, 1992–94; *b* 24 Nov. 1926; *s* of Dr Pollok Donald and Henrietta Mary (*née* Laidlaw); *m* 1952, Patricia Ireland; two *s* one *d*. *Educ:* Edinburgh Academy; Corpus Christi Coll., Cambridge (MA); Edinburgh Univ. (MB, ChB); Member: Cambridge and Edinburgh Univs Athletic Teams, RAF Medical Branch, 1952–54; general medical practice, Leith and Cramond (Edin.), 1954–92; Lectr, Dept of General Practice, Univ. of Edinburgh, 1960–70. Royal College of General Practitioners: Vice-Chm. of Council, 1976–77, Chm., 1979–82; Chm., Bd of Censors, 1978–79; past Chm. and Provost, SE Scotland Faculty. Chairman: UK Conf. of Postgrad. Advisers in Gen. Practice, 1978–80; Jt Cttee on Postgrad. Trng for Gen. Practice, 1982–85; Armed Services Gen. Practice Approval Bd, 1987–. Vice-Chm., Medical and Dental Defence Union of Scotland, 1992–. Specialist Advr, H of C Social Services Select Cttee, 1986–87. Radio Doctor, BBC (Scotland), 1976–78. Chm., Scottish Cttee, ASH, 1985–92. Chm. Court of Directors, Edinburgh Acad., 1978–85 (Dir, 1955–85); President: Edinburgh Academical Club, 1978–81; Rotary Club of Leith, 1957–58. Lectures: James Mackenzie, RCGP, 1985; David Bruce, RAMC, 1987; Robert Campbell, Ulster Med. Soc., 1989; Ian Murray Scott, 1991, Pinsent, 1993, RCGP. James Mackenzie Medal, RCPE, 1983; Defence Med. Services Medal, 1993; Hippocrates Medal, SIMG, 1994. *Publications:* contribs to medical jls. *Recreations:* golf, family life, reading The Times. *Address:* 30 Cramond Road North, Edinburgh EH4 6JE. *T:* 0131–336 3824. *Clubs:* Hawks (Cambridge); University of Edinburgh Staff (Edinburgh).

DONALD, Craig Reid Cantlie, CMG 1963; OBE 1959; *b* 8 Sept. 1914; *s* of Rev. Francis Cantlie and Mary Donald, Lumphanan, Aberdeenshire; *m* 1945, Mary Isabel Speid (*d* 1989); one *d*. *Educ:* Fettes; Emmanuel Coll., Cambridge (Scholar; BA 1937, MA 1947). Administrative Officer, Cyprus, 1937; Military Service, 1940–46, Lieut-Col. Commissioner, Famagusta, 1948; Registrar, Cooperative Societies, 1951; Deputy Financial Sec., Uganda, 1951; MLC, 1954–62; Sec. to the Treasury, 1956–63. Fellow, Econ. Devlt Inst., World Bank, 1956. Bursar, Malvern Coll., 1964–79. Governor: Hillstone Sch., 1979–86; Ellerslie, 1979–93; Downs Sch., Colwall, 1979–92. *Recreation:* country pursuits. *Address:* 55 Geraldine Road, Malvern WR14 3NU. *T:* Malvern (01684) 561446. *Club:* Travellers'.

See also I. G. Gilbert.

DONALD, George Malcolm, RSA 1992 (ARSA 1975); RSW 1976; SSA 1976; Lecturer, School of Drawing and Painting, Edinburgh College of Art, since 1972; *b* 12 Sept. 1943; *s* of George Donald and Margaret (*née* Tait); *m* 1966 (marr. diss.); one *s* one *d*. *Educ:* Edinburgh Coll. of Art (DA 1966; Post Grad. Dip. 1967); Hornsey Coll. of Art, London Univ. (ATC 1969); Edinburgh Univ. (MEd 1980). Tutor and Asst to Vice Principal (Art and Design), Edinburgh Coll. of Art, 1984–87. Dir., Edinburgh Coll. of Art Summer Sch., 1991–. Printmaker in Residence, Soulisquoy Print Workshop, Orkney Is, 1988; Visiting Artist: Szechuan Fine Art Inst., China, 1989; Silpakorn Univ., Thailand, 1989; Chulalongkorn Univ., Thailand, 1989; Vis. Prof., Zhejiang Acad. Fine Art, China, 1994–. Solo exhibitions include: Art Dept Gall., Univ. of Central Florida, 1985; Dept of Fine Art, Univ. of Georgia, 1987; Open Eye Gall., Edinburgh, 1987 and 1990; Galerija Fakulteta Likovnih Umetnosti, Belgrade, 1987; World Trade Centre, Dubai, 1994; touring exhibn, UK and France, 1990; Christopher Hull Gall., London, 1992; Open Eye Gall., Edinburgh, 1993; commissions: portrait, Glasgow Univ. and Scottish Arts Council, 1985; window design, New Scottish Nat. Lib., Edinburgh, 1986; portrait: Edinburgh Chamber of Commerce, 1986; St John's Hosp., Livingston, 1994; public collections include: Scottish Arts Council; Edinburgh, Aberdeen and Leeds CCs; Hunterian Mus., Glasgow Univ.; Heriot Watt Univ.; Victoria and Albert Mus.; IBM; BBC; Nat. Library of Scotland; private collections in UK, Europe, Canada and USA, Asia and Australia. Latimer Award 1970, Guthrie Award 1973, Royal Scottish Acad.; Scottish Arts Council Bursary, 1973; Gillies Bequest Travel Award to India, Royal Scottish Acad., 1978. *Publications:* The New Maths, 1969; An Account of Travels in Turkey, Iran, Afghanistan, Pakistan, India, Kashmir and Nepal, 1969; An Indian Diary, 1980; Aims and Objectives in Teaching Drawing and Painting, 1980; The Day Book, 1987. *Recreations:* pottering, fiddling, travelling. *Address:* Edinburgh College of Art, Lauriston Place, Edinburgh EH3 9DF.

DONALD, Air Marshal Sir John (George), KBE 1985 (OBE 1972); Medical Adviser, AMI Middle East Services Ltd, since 1989; *b* 7 Nov. 1927; *s* of John Shirran Donald and Janet Knox (*née* Napier); *m* 1954, Margaret Jean Walton; one *s* two *d*. *Educ:* Inverurie Acad.; Aberdeen Univ. (MB, ChB 1951); DTM&H Edin 1964; MRCGP 1971, FRCGP 1977; MFCM 1972, FFCM 1985; MFOM 1982 (AFOM 1980); FRCPE 1986. Commnd RAF, 1953; Senior Medical Officer: Colombo, Ceylon, 1954–57; RAF Stafford, 1957–60; RAF Waddington, 1960–63; student, RAF Staff Coll., 1965; SMO, HQ AFCENT, France and Holland, 1966–68; Dep. Dir, Medical Personnel (RAF), 1969–72; OC, The Princess Mary's RAF Hosp., Akrotiri, Cyprus, 1972–76; OC, RAF Hosp., Ely, 1976–78; PMO, RAF Germany, 1978–81; PMO, RAF Strike Comd, 1981–84; Dir-Gen., RAF Med. Services, 1984–85; Dep. Surg. Gen. (Ops), MoD, and Dir Gen., RAF Med. Services, 1985–86; Med. Dir, Security Forces Hosp., 1986–89. QHS, 1983–86. CStJ 1984. *Recreations:* golf, skiing, camping, ornithology. *Address:* Curzon House, Drews Park, Knotty Green, Beaconsfield, Bucks HP9 2TT. *T:* Beaconsfield (014946) 4621. *Clubs:* Royal Air Force, Royal Society of Medicine.

DONALDSON, family name of **Barons Donaldson of Kingsbridge** and **Donaldson of Lymington.**

DONALDSON OF KINGSBRIDGE, Baron *cr* 1967 (Life Peer), of Kingsbridge; **John George Stuart Donaldson,** OBE 1943; retired farmer; *b* 9 Oct. 1907; *s* of Rev. S. A. Donaldson, Master of Magdalene, Cambridge, and Lady Albinia Donaldson (*née* Hobart-Hampden); *m* 1935, Frances Annesley Lonsdale (*d* 1994), writer, *d* of Frederick Lonsdale; one *s* two *d*. *Educ:* Eton; Trinity Coll., Cambridge. Pioneer Health Centre, Peckham, 1935–38; Road Transport, 1938–39. Royal Engineers, 1939–45. Farmed in Glos, and later Bucks. Member: Glos Agric. Exec. Cttee, 1953–60; SE Regional Planning Council, 1966–69. Parly Under-Sec. of State, NI Office, 1974–76; Minister for the Arts, DES, 1976–79. Joined: SDP, 1981; Soc and Lib Dem, 1987. Hon. Secretary: Nat. Assoc. Discharged Prisoners Aid Socs, 1961; All Party Penal Affairs Gp, 1981–; Chairman: Nat. Assoc. for the Care and Resettlement of Offenders, 1966–74; Bd of Visitors, HM Prison, Grendon, 1963–69; Consumer Council, 1968–71; EDC for Hotel and Catering Industry, 1972–74; Nat. Cttee Family Service Units, 1968–74; Cttee of Enquiry into conditions of service for young servicemen, 1969; Assoc. of Arts Instns, 1980–83; Confedn of Art and Design Assocs, 1982–84; British Fedn of Zoos, 1970–74; Pres., RSPB, 1975–80. Director: Royal Opera House, Covent Garden, 1958–74; Sadler's Wells, 1963–74; British Sugar Corp., 1966–74. *Recreations:* music in general, opera in particular. *Address:* 17 Edna Street, SW11 3DP. *Club:* Brooks's.

See also N. D. Deakin.

DONALDSON OF LYMINGTON, Baron *cr* 1988 (Life Peer), of Lymington in the County of Hampshire; **John Francis Donaldson;** Kt 1966; PC 1979; Master of the Rolls, 1982–92; *b* 6 Oct. 1920; *er s* of late Malcolm Donaldson, FRCS, FRCOG, and late Evelyn Helen Marguerite Maunsell; *m* 1945, Dorothy Mary (*see* Dame Mary Donaldson); one *s* two *d*. *Educ:* Charterhouse; Trinity Coll., Cambridge (Hon. Fellow, 1983); MA Oxon 1982. Sec. of Debates, Cambridge Union Soc., 1940; Chm. Federation of University Conservative and Unionist Assocs, 1940; BA (Hons) 1941; MA 1959. Commissioned Royal Signals, 1941; served with Guards Armoured Divisional Signals, in UK and NW Europe, 1942–45; and with Military Government, Schleswig-Holstein, 1945–46; Hon. Lieut-Col, 1946. Called to Bar, Middle Temple, 1946; Harmsworth Law Scholar, 1946; Bencher 1966; Treas. 1986; Mem. Gen. Council of the Bar, 1956–61, 1962–66, Junior Counsel to Registrar of Restrictive Trading Agreements, 1959–61; QC 1961; Dep. Chm., Hants QS, 1961–66; Mem. Council on Tribunals, 1965–66; Judge of the High Court, Queen's Bench Div., 1966–79; Pres., Nat. Industrial Relations Court, 1971–74; a Lord Justice of Appeal, 1979–82. Chm., inquiry into prevention of pollution from merchant shipping, 1993–94. Pres. Council, Inns of Court, 1987–90. Mem. Croydon County Borough Council, 1949–53. President: Carthusian Soc., 1978–82; British Maritime Law Assoc., 1979–95 (Vice-Pres., 1969–78); British Insurance Law Assoc., 1979–81 (Dep. Pres., 1978–79); British Records Assoc., 1982–92; Chairman: Adv. Council on Public Records, 1982–92; Magna Carta Trust, 1982–92; Financial Law Panel, 1992–. FCIArb 1980 (Pres., 1980–83). Hon. Member: Assoc. of Average Adjusters, 1966 (Chm., 1981); Grain and Feed Trade Assoc., 1979; Liverpool Cotton Assoc., 1979; Law Soc., 1994. Governor, Sutton's Hosp. in Charterhouse, 1981–84. Visitor: UCL, 1982–92;

Nuffield Coll., Oxford, 1982–92; London Business Sch., 1986–92. Hon. Freeman, Worshipful Co. of Drapers, 1984. DU Essex, 1983; Hon. LLD: Sheffield, 1984; Nottingham Trent, 1992. Silver Medal, Thomas Gray Meml Trust, 1995. *Publications:* Jt Ed., Lowndes and Rudolf on General Average and the York-Antwerp Rules (8th edn), 1955, (9th edn), 1964 and (10th edn), 1975; contributor to title Insurance, in Halsbury's Laws of England (3rd edn), 1958. *Recreations:* sailing, do-it-yourself. *Address:* House of Lords, SW1A 0PW. *T:* (home) 0171–588 6610. *Clubs:* Royal Cruising, Royal Lymington Yacht.

See also Hon. J. M. Williams.

DONALDSON OF LYMINGTON, Lady; *see* Donaldson, Dame D. M.

DONALDSON, Dr Alexander Ivan; Head, Pirbright Laboratory, Institute for Animal Health, since 1989; *b* 1 July 1942; *s* of Basil Ivan Donaldson and Dorothy Cunningham Donaldson; *m* 1966, Margaret Ruth Elizabeth Swan; one *s* one *d. Educ:* High Sch., Dublin; Trinity Coll., Univ. of Dublin (BA, MA, ScD); Ontario Veterinary Coll., Univ. of Guelph (PhD). MRCVS. Post-doctoral research, 1969–71, Vet. Res. Officer, 1973–76, Principal Vet. Res. Officer, 1976–89, Animal Virus Res. Inst., subseq. AFRC. Inst. for Animal Health, Pirbright Lab.; Head, World Ref. Lab. for Foot-and-Mouth Disease, 1985–89. Vis. Prof., Ontario Vet. Coll., Univ. of Guelph, 1972–73. Research Medal, RASE, 1988. *Publications:* numerous articles on animal virology in learned jls. *Recreations:* jogging, windsurfing, photography. *Address:* Institute for Animal Health, Pirbright Laboratory, Ash Road, Pirbright, Woking, Surrey GU24 0NF. *T:* Guildford (01483) 232441.

DONALDSON, Prof. (Charles) Ian (Edward), FBA 1993; Grace I Professor of English, and Fellow, King's College, University of Cambridge, since 1995; *b* 6 May 1935; *s* of Dr William Edward Donaldson and Elizabeth Donaldson (*née* Weigall); *m* 1st, 1962, Tamsin Jane Procter (marr. diss. 1990); one *s* one *d*; 2nd, 1991, Grazia Maria Therese Gunn. *Educ:* Melbourne Grammar Sch.; Melbourne Univ. (BA 1st cl. Hons English 1957); Magdalen Coll., Oxford (BA 1st cl. Hons English 1960; MA 1964). Sen. Tutor in English, Univ. of Melbourne, 1958; Oxford University: Harmsworth Sen. Scholar, Merton Coll., 1960–62; Fellow and Lectr in English, Wadham Coll., 1962–69; CUF Lectr in English, 1963–69; Chm., English Faculty, 1968–69; Prof. of English, ANU Canberra, 1969–91; Foundn Dir, Humanities Res. Centre, ANU, 1974–90; Regius Prof. of Rhetoric and English Lit., Univ. of Edinburgh, 1991–95. Vis. appts, Univ. of California Santa Barbara, Gonville and Caius Coll., Cambridge, Cornell Univ., Melbourne Univ. FAHA 1975; corresp. FBA 1987; FRSA 1993. *Publications:* The World Upside-Down: comedy from Jonson to Fielding, 1970; (ed) Ben Jonson Poems, 1975; The Rapes of Lucretia, 1982; (ed) Jonson and Shakespeare, 1983; (ed) Transformations in Modern European Drama, 1983; (ed with Tamsin Donaldson) Seeing the First Australians, 1985; (ed) Ben Jonson, 1985; (ed jtly) Shaping Lives: reflections on biography, 1992; (ed) Ben Jonson: Selected Poems, 1995. *Address:* King's College, Cambridge CB2 1ST. *T:* Cambridge (01223) 331100.

DONALDSON, David Abercrombie, RSA 1962 (ARSA 1951); RP 1964; RGI 1977; Painter; Head of Painting School, Glasgow School of Art, 1967–81; Her Majesty's Painter and Limner in Scotland, since 1977; *b* 29 June 1916; *s* of Robert Abercrombie Donaldson and Margaret Cranston; *m* 1st, 1942, Kathleen Boyd Maxwell; one *s*; 2nd, 1949, Maria Krystyna Mora-Szorc; two *d. Educ:* Coatbridge Sec. Sch.; Glasgow Sch. of Art. Travelling Scholarship, 1938. Joined Staff of Glasgow Sch. of Art, 1940. Paintings in private collections in America, Canada, Australia, South Africa and Europe and public collections in Scotland. Sitters include: The Queen, 1968; Sir Hector Hetherington; Dame Jean Roberts; Sir John Dunbar; Lord Binning; Rev. Lord McLeod; Mrs Winifred Ewing; Miss Joan Dickson; Earl of Haddo; Sir Samuel Curran; Roger Ellis; Sir Norman Macfarlane; Rt Hon. Margaret Thatcher; Dr Steven Watson; Rt Hon. David Steel, Sir Alwyn Williams. Hon. LLD Strathclyde, 1971; Hon. DLitt Glasgow, 1988. *Recreations:* music, cooking. *Address:* 5 Cleveden Drive, Glasgow G12 0SU. *T:* 0141–334 1029; 7 Chelsea Manor Studios, Flood Street, SW3 5SR. *T:* 0171–352 1932; St Roman de Malegarde, 84290 Vaucluse en Provence, France. *T:* 90289265. *Club:* Art (Glasgow).

DONALDSON, David Torrance; QC 1984; a Recorder, since 1994; *b* 30 Sept. 1943; *s* of Alexander Walls Donaldson and Margaret Merry Bryce. *Educ:* Glasgow Academy; Gonville and Caius College, Cambridge (Maj. Schol.; MA); University of Freiburg i. Br., West Germany (Dr jur). Fellow, Gonville and Caius College, Cambridge, 1965–69. Called to the Bar, Gray's Inn, 1968, Bencher, 1995. *Address:* 2 Hare Court, Temple, EC4Y 7BH. *T:* 0171–583 1770.

DONALDSON, Dame (Dorothy) Mary, GBE 1983; JP; Lord Mayor of London for 1983–84; Alderman, City of London Ward of Coleman Street, 1975–91; *b* 29 Aug. 1921; *d* of late Reginald George Gale Warwick and Dorothy Alice Warwick; *m* 1945, John Francis Donaldson (*see* Baron Donaldson of Lymington); one *s* two *d. Educ:* Portsmouth High Sch. for Girls (GPDST); Wingfield Morris Orthopædic Hosp.; Middlesex Hosp., London. SRN 1946. Chairman: Women's Nat. Cancer Control Campaign, 1967–69; Interim Licensing Authy for Human In Vitro Fertilisation and Embryol., 1985–91; Vice-Pres., British Cancer Council, 1970; Member: NE Met. Regional Hosp. Bd, 1970–74; NE Thames RHA, 1976–81. Governor: London Hosp., 1971–74; Gt Ormond Street Hosp. for Sick Children, 1978–80; Member: Cities of London and Westminster Disablement Adv. Cttee, 1974–79; Inner London Educn Authority, 1968–71; City Parochial Foundn, 1969–75; Cttee, Royal Humane Soc., 1968–83; Cttee, AA, 1985–89; Press Complaints Commn, 1991–; Chm. Council, Banking Ombudsman, 1985–94; Vice-Pres., Counsel and Care for the Elderly, 1980–; Pres., BACUP, 1985–93. Governor: City of London Sch. for Girls, 1971–83; Berkhamsted Schools, 1976–80; Mem., Governing Body, Charterhouse Sch., 1980–85; Mem., Court of Common Council, 1966–75, Sheriff, 1981–82, HM Lieutenant, 1983, City of London; Mem. Guild of Freemen, City of London, 1970 (Mem. Court, 1983–86); Liveryman, Gardeners' Co., 1975; Hon. Freeman, Shipwrights' Co., 1985. JP Inner London, 1960; Mem., Inner London Juvenile Court Panel, 1960–65. Hon. Mem., CIArb, 1981; Hon. Fellow: Girton Coll., Cambridge, 1983; Portsmouth Univ. (formerly Poly.), 1984. FRSH 1984; Hon. FRCOG 1991. Hon. DSc City, 1983. DStJ 1984. Freedom, City of Winnipeg, 1968. Order of Oman, 1982; Order of Bahrain, 1984. Grand Officier, Ordre Nat. du Mérite, 1984. *Recreations:* gardening, sailing, geriatric ski-ing. *T:* (home) 071–588 6610. *Clubs:* Reform; Royal Cruising, Royal Lymington Yacht.

See also Hon. J. M. Williams.

DONALDSON, Hamish; corporate adviser and company director; Chairman, Gresham Telecomputing plc, since 1993; *b* 13 June 1936; *s* of late James Donaldson and Marie Christine Cormack; *m* 1965, Linda, *d* of late Dr Leslie Challis Bousfield; three *d. Educ:* Oundle School; Christ's College, Cambridge (MA). De La Rue Bull, 1960–66; Urwick, Orr & Partners, 1966–73; Hill Samuel & Co., 1973–91; Man. Dir, Hill Samuel Merchant Bank (SA), 1985–86; Chief Exec., Hill Samuel Bank, 1987–91. Chm., London Bridge Finance, 1993–95 (Dir, 1992–95); Director: TSB Bank, 1988–91; TSB Group, 1990–91; Macquarie Bank, 1989–91; South African Business News, 1991–94; RSH Trading Ltd, 1994–; Sanlic (UK) Ltd, 1994–. Mem., Co. Affairs Cttee, Inst. of Dirs, 1991–. Chm., Guildford DAC for the Care of Churches and Churchyards, 1992–; Dir, Prior's Field Sch. Trust, 1992–94; Governor: Prior's Field Sch., 1992–94; Royal Naval Sch., 1994–95; Royal Sch., Hindhead, 1995–. Freeman, City of London, 1988; Liveryman, Information Technologists' Co., 1992–. *Publication:* a Guide to the Successful Management of Computer Projects, 1978. *Recreation:* amateur operatics. *Address:* Edgecombe, Hill Road, Haslemere, Surrey GU27 2JN. *T:* Haslemere (01428) 644473.

DONALDSON, Ian; *see* Donaldson, C. I. E.

DONALDSON, Dame Mary; *see* Donaldson, Dame D. M.

DONALDSON, Air Vice-Marshal Michael Phillips, MBE 1973; Commandant, Royal Air Force Staff College, since 1993; *b* 22 July 1943; *s* of George Millar Donaldson and Mabel Donaldson (*née* Phillips); *m* 1970, Mavis Cornish; one *s* one *d. Educ:* Chislehurst and Sidcup Grammar Sch. for Boys. RAF Gen. Duties; Pilot and Weapons Instructor; No 23 Sqn (Lightning), 1965–68; No 226 OCU, 1969; USAF Florida (F106), 1970–73; No 29 Sqn (Phantom), 1974–76; No 228 OCU, 1977; Army Staff Coll., 1978; PSO to Dep. Comdr in Chief AFCENT, Brunssum, 1979–80; MoD, 1980–83; OC 19 Sqn, 1983–85; OC 23 Sqn (Falkland Is), 1985; Dep. PSO to CDS, 1986–87; OC RAF Wattisham, 1987–89; RCDS 1990; SASO, 11 Group, 1990–93. Pres., RAF Squash Rackets Assoc., 1993–. *Recreations:* music, history, squash, tennis, golf. *Address:* RAF Staff College, Bracknell, Berks RG12 3DD. *T:* Bracknell (01344) 54593. *Club:* Royal Air Force.

DONALDSON, Patricia Anne; *see* Hodgson, P. A.

DONALDSON, Prof. Simon Kirwan, DPhil; FRS 1986; Wallis Professor of Mathematics, and Fellow of St Anne's College, University of Oxford, since 1985; *b* 20 Aug. 1957; *m* 1986, Ana Nora Hurtado; one *s* one *d. Educ:* Sevenoaks Sch., Kent; Pembroke Coll., Cambridge (BA 1979; Hon. Fellow, 1992); Worcester Coll., Oxford (DPhil 1983). Jun. Res. Fellow, All Souls Coll., Oxford, 1983–85. *Publications:* (with P. B. Kronheimer) The Geometry of Four-manifolds, 1990; papers in mathematical jls. *Recreation:* sailing. *Address:* St Anne's College, Oxford OX2 6HS.

DONCASTER, Bishop Suffragan of, since 1993; **Rt. Rev. Michael Frederick Gear;** *b* 27 Nov. 1934; *s* of Frederick Augustus and Lillian Hannah Gear; *m* 1961, Daphne, *d* of Norman and Millicent Earl; two *d. Educ:* St John's College and Cranmer Hall, Durham. BA Social Studies, 1st cl., 1959; DipTh 1961. Assistant Curate: Christ Church, Bexleyheath, 1961–64; St Aldate, Oxford, 1964–67; Vicar of St Andrew, Clubmoor, Liverpool, 1967–71; Rector, Avondale, Salisbury, Rhodesia, 1971–76; Tutor, Wycliffe Hall, Oxford, 1976–80; Team Rector, Macclesfield, 1980–88; Archdeacon of Chester, 1988–93. *Recreations:* photography, golf, history and contemporary politics of Southern Africa. *Address:* Bishop's Lodge, Hooton Roberts, Rotherham S65 4PF. *T:* Rotherham (01709) 853370.

DONCASTER, Archdeacon of; *see* Holdridge, Ven. B. L.

DONDELINGER, Jean; Ambassador of Luxembourg to Greece, since 1993; *b* Luxembourg, 4 July 1930; *m*; one *s. Educ:* Nancy Univ.; Paris Univ.; St Antony's Coll., Oxford. Barrister, Luxembourg, 1954–58; Asst to Head, Internat. Economic Relations Service, Dept of Foreign Affairs, 1958–61; Dep. Permanent Rep. of Luxembourg to EEC, 1961–70, Ambassador and Permanent Rep., 1970–84; Sec.-Gen., Min. of Foreign Affairs, 1984; Mem., EEC, 1989–92. Rep. of Pres. of Govt, Cttee on Institutional Affairs (Dooge Cttee), 1984–85; Chm., Negotiating Gp on Single Act, 1986; Vice-Pres., ITU World Conf. on Fixing of Orbital Frequencies of Satellites, 1988. *Address:* c/o Ministry of Foreign Affairs, 5 rue Notre Dame, 2911 Luxembourg.

DONEGALL, 7th Marquess of, *cr* 1791; **Dermot Richard Claud Chichester,** LVO 1986; Viscount Chichester and Baron of Belfast, 1625; Earl of Donegall, 1647; Earl of Belfast, 1791; Baron Fisherwick (GB), 1790; Baron Templemore, 1831; Hereditary Lord High Admiral of Lough Neagh; late 7th Queen's Own Hussars; Standard Bearer, Honourable Corps of Gentlemen at Arms, 1984–86 (one of HM Bodyguard, since 1966); *b* 18 April 1916; 2nd *s* of 4th Baron Templemore, PC, KCVO, DSO, and Hon. Clare Meriel Wingfield, 2nd *d* of 7th Viscount Powerscourt, PC Ireland (she *d* 1969); *S* father 1953, and to Marquessate of Donegall, 1975; *m* 1946, Lady Josceline Gabrielle Legge (*d* 1995), *y d* of 7th Earl of Dartmouth, GCVO, TD; one *s* two *d. Educ:* Harrow; RMC, Sandhurst. 2nd Lt 7th Hussars, 1936; Lt 1939; served War of 1939–45 in Middle East and Italy (prisoner); Major, 1944; retired, 1949. *Recreations:* hunting, shooting, fishing. *Heir: s* Earl of Belfast, *qv. Address:* Dunbrody Park, Arthurstown, Co. Wexford, Eire. *T:* Waterford (51) 389104. *Clubs:* Cavalry and Guards; Kildare Street and University (Dublin).

DONERAILE, 10th Viscount *cr* 1785 (Ire.); **Richard Allen St Leger;** Baron Doneraile, 1776; Food Marketing Analyst since 1974; *b* 17 Aug. 1946; *s* of 9th Viscount Doneraile and of Melva, Viscountess Doneraile; *S* father, 1983; *m* 1970, Kathleen Mary Simcox, Churchtown, Mallow, Co. Cork; one *s* one *d. Educ:* Orange Coast College, California; Mississippi Univ. Served US Army. Air Traffic Control specialist; antiquarian book appraiser, 1970–73. *Recreations:* outdoor sports, skiing, golf, sailing. *Heir: s* Hon. Nathaniel Warham Robert St John St Leger, *b* 13 Sept. 1971. *Club:* Yorba Linda Country (California).

DONIACH, Prof. Israel, MD (London); FRCPath 1963; FRCP 1968; Professor of Morbid Anatomy in University of London, London Hospital, 1960–76, now Emeritus Professor; Hon. Lecturer in Histopathology, St Bartholomew's Hospital Medical School, since 1976; *b* 9 March 1911; *yr s* of late Aaron Selig and late Rahel Doniach; *m* 1933, Deborah Abileah; one *s* (one *d* decd). *Educ:* University Coll. and Hosp., London. Asst Pathologist, St Mary's Hosp., London, 1935–37; Clinical Pathologist and Cancer Research Asst, Mount Vernon Hosp., Northwood, 1937–43; Senior Lecturer in Morbid Anatomy, Postgraduate Medical Sch. of London, 1943–59, Reader, 1959–60. Hon. FRSocMed 1990; Hon. Member: Pathol. Soc., 1987; Soc. for Endocrinol., 1985. *Publications:* papers in morbid anatomy and experimental pathology in various journals. *Address:* 25 Alma Square, NW8 9PY. *T:* 0171–286 1617.

DONKIN, Alexander Sim; HM Diplomatic Service, retired; Counsellor (Administration), UK Mission to United Nations, and Deputy Consul-General, New York, 1977–82; *b* 14 July 1922; *s* of Matthew Henderson Donkin and Margaret Donkin; *m* 1944, Irene Florence (*née* Willis) (*d* 1988); two *d. Educ:* Monkwearmouth Sch., Co. Durham. Served War, RAF, 1941–46; Sqdn Ldr. Civil Service, 1947–66; HM Diplomatic Service, 1966; FCO, 1966–70; Washington, 1970–74; FCO, 1974–77. *Recreations:* music, walking, photography. *Address:* 1 Amberley Road, Eastbourne, East Sussex BN22 0EH.

DONKIN, Air Cdre Peter Langloh, CBE 1946; DSO 1944; retired; *b* 19 June 1913; *s* of Frederick Langloh and Phyllis Donkin; *m* 1941, Elizabeth Marjorie Cox; two *d. Educ:* Sherborne; RAF Coll., Cranwell. Commissioned RAF, 1933; No. 16 Sqdn, 1933–38; British Mission in Poland, 1939; CO 225 Sqdn, 1940; CO 239 Sqdn, 1941–42; CO 35 Wing, 1943–44; Sch. Land Air Warfare, 1945; HQ, RAF Levant, 1946; RCAF Staff Coll., 1948–49; Exchange USAF, 1950; CO, RAF Chivenor, 1951–53; Air Attaché, Moscow, 1954–57; Asst Chief of Staff, HQ Allied Air Forces, Central Europe, 1957–58;

idc, 1959; AOC, RAF, Hong Kong, 1960–62. *Recreations:* shooting, yachting. *Address:* Coombe Cross Cottage, Horsington, Templecombe, Som BA8 0DD. *Club:* Carlton.

DONKIN, Dr Robin Arthur, FBA 1985; Reader in Historical Geography, since 1990, and Fellow of Jesus College, since 1972, University of Cambridge; *b* Morpeth, 28 Oct. 1928; *s* of Arthur Donkin and Elizabeth Jane Kirkup; *m* 1970, Jennifer Gay Kennedy; one *d. Educ:* Univ. of Durham (BA 1950; PhD 1953); MA Cantab 1971; LittD Cantab 1993. Lieut, Royal Artillery, 1953–55 (Egypt). King George VI Meml Fellow, Univ. of California, Berkeley, 1955–56; Asst Lectr, Dept of Geography, Univ. of Edinburgh, 1956–58; Lectr, Dept of Geography, Univ. of Birmingham, 1958–70; Lectr in the Geography of Latin America, Univ. of Cambridge, 1971–90; Tutor, Jesus Coll., Cambridge, 1975–. Leverhulme Research Fellow, 1966; Vis. Associate Prof. of Geography, Univ. of Toronto, 1969; field work in Middle and S America, NW Africa, India, China, Turkestan. *Publications:* The Cistercian Order in Europe: a bibliography of printed sources, 1969; Spanish Red: cochineal and the Opuntia cactus, 1977; The Cistercians: studies in the geography of medieval England and Wales, 1978; Agricultural Terracing in the Aboriginal New World, 1979; Manna: an historical geography, 1980; The Peccary, 1985; The Muscovy Duck, 1986; Meleagrides: an historical and ethnogeographical study of the Guinea fowl, 1991; articles in geographical, historical and anthropological jls. *Address:* Jesus College, Cambridge CB5 8BL; 13 Roman Hill, Barton, Cambridge. *T:* Cambridge (01223) 262572.

DONLEAVY, James Patrick; author and artist; *b* 23 April 1926; *m* Valerie Heron (marr. diss.); one *s* one *d*; *m* Mary Wilson Price (marr. diss.); one *s* one *d. Educ:* schs in USA; Trinity Coll., Dublin. Evening Standard Drama Critics' Award, 1961; Brandeis Univ. Creative Arts Award, 1962; AAAL Grantee, 1975. *Art exhibitions:* Painter's Gall., Dublin, 1950, 1951; Bronxville, NY, 1959; Langton Galls, London, 1975; Caldwell Galls, Belfast, 1987; Anna Mei Chadwick Gall., London, 1989, 1991; Alba Fine Art Gall., London, 1991. *Publications:* The Ginger Man (novel), 1955; Fairy Tales of New York (play), 1960; What They Did In Dublin With The Ginger Man (introd. and play), 1961; A Singular Man (novel), 1963 (play, 1964); Meet My Maker The Mad Molecule (short stories), 1964; The Saddest Summer of Samuel S (novella), 1966 (play, 1967); The Beastly Beatitudes of Balthazar B (novel), 1968 (play, 1981); The Onion Eaters (novel), 1971; The Plays of J. P. Donleavy, 1972; A Fairy Tale of New York (novel), 1973; The Unexpurgated Code: a complete manual of survival and manners, 1975; The Destinies of Darcy Dancer, Gentleman (novel), 1977; Schultz (novel), 1980; Leila (novel), 1983; De Alfonce Tennis: the superlative game of eccentric champions, its history, accoutrements, rules, conduct and regimen (sports manual), 1984; J. P. Donleavy's Ireland, in all her Sins and in some of her Graces, 1986; Are You Listening Rabbi Low (novel), 1987; A Singular Country, 1989; That Darcy, That Dancer, That Gentleman (novel), 1990; The History of the Ginger Man (autobiog.), 1994; The Lady Who Liked Clean Rest Rooms, 1995; contribs to jls etc., incl. The Observer, The Times (London), New York Times, Washington Post, Esquire, Envoy, Punch, Guardian, Saturday Evening Post, Holiday, Atlantic Monthly, Saturday Review, The New Yorker, Queen, Vogue, Penthouse, Playboy, Architectural Digest, Vanity Fair, Rolling Stone, Liberation (Paris). *Address:* Levington Park, Mullingar, Co. Westmeath, Ireland.

DONN, Mary Cecilia; *see* Spinks, M. C.

DONNACHIE, Prof. Alexander, FInstP; Professor of Physics since 1969, and Director of the Physical Laboratories since 1989, University of Manchester; *b* 25 May 1936; *s* of John Donnachie and Mary Ramsey Donnachie (*née* Adams); *m* 1960, Dorothy Paterson; two *d. Educ:* Kilmarnock Acad.; Glasgow Univ. (BSc, PhD). DSIR Res. Fellow 1961–63, Lectr 1963–65, UCL; Res. Associate, CERN, Geneva, 1965–67; Sen. Lectr, Univ. of Glasgow, 1967–69; Hd of Theoretical Physics 1975–85, Dean of Faculty of Science 1985–87, Chm., Dept of Physics, 1988–94, Dean, Faculty of Science and Engrg, 1994–, Univ. of Manchester. Mem., SERC, 1989–94 (Chm., Nuclear Phys Bd, 1989–93); CERN: Chairman: Super Proton Synchrotron Cttee, 1988–90; Super Proton Synchrotron and LEAR Cttee, 1991–93; Member: Res. Bd, 1988–; Sci. Policy Cttee, 1988–93; Council, 1989–94; Particle, Space and Astronomy Bd, 1993–94; Sec., C11 Commn, IUPAP, 1989–91. *Publications:* Electromagnetic Interactions of Hadrons, vols I and II, 1978; over 100 articles in learned jls of Particle Physics. *Recreations:* sailing, walking. *Address:* Department of Physics and Astronomy, University of Manchester, Manchester M13 9PL. *T:* 0161–273 4200.

DONNE, David Lucas; Chairman: Argos PLC, 1990–95; Sphere Investment Trust, since 1989 (Director, since 1982); *b* 17 Aug. 1925; *s* of late Dr Cecil Lucas Donne, Wellington, NZ, and of Marjorie Nicholls Donne; *m* 1st, 1957, Jennifer Margaret Duncan (*d* 1975); two *s* one *d*; 2nd, 1978, Clare, *d* of Maj. F. J. Yates. *Educ:* Stowe; Christ Church, Oxford (MA Nat. Science). Called to the Bar, Middle Temple, 1949. Studied Business Admin, Syracuse Univ., 1952–53; Charterhouse Group, 1953–64; William Baird, 1964–67. Chairman: Crest Nicholson, 1973–92; Dalgety, 1977–86 (Dep. Chm., 1975–77); Steetley, 1983–92 (Dep. Chm., 1979–83); ASDA-MFI, 1986–87; Dir, Royal Trust Bank, 1972–93 (Dep. Chm., 1989–93). Member: Nat. Water Council, 1980–83; Bd, British Coal (formerly NCB), 1984–87; Stock Exchange Listed Cos Adv. Cttee, 1987–91. Trustee, BACUP, 1993–. Fellow, Game Conservancy, 1987. *Recreations:* shooting, opera, sailing. *Address:* 8 Montagu Mews North, W1H 1AH. *Club:* Royal Thames Yacht.

DONNE, Hon. Sir Gaven (John), KBE 1979; Chief Justice: of Nauru, since 1985; of Tuvalu, since 1986; Member, Kiribati Court of Appeal, since 1987; *b* 8 May 1914; *s* of Jack Alfred Donne and Mary Elizabeth Donne; *m* 1946, Isabel Fenwick, *d* of John Edwin Hall; two *s* two *d. Educ:* Palmerston North Boys' High Sch.; Hastings High Sch.; Victoria Univ., Wellington; Auckland Univ. (LLB New Zealand). Called to the Bar and admitted solicitor, 1938. Military Service, 2nd NZEF, Middle East and Italy, 1941–45. Stipendiary Magistrate, NZ, 1958–75; Puisne Judge, Supreme Court of Western Samoa, 1970–71; Chief Justice, Western Samoa, 1972–75, Mem. Court of Appeal of Western Samoa, 1975–82; Judge, High Court of Niue, 1973; Chief Justice of the Cook Islands, 1975–82, and of Niue, 1974–82; Queen's Rep. in the Cook Islands, 1982–84. Hon. Counsellor, Internat. Assoc. of Youth Magistrates, 1974–. Member: Takapuna Bor. Council, 1957–58; Auckland Town Planning Authority, 1958; Bd of Governors, Westlake High Sch., 1957–58. Grand Cross 2nd Cl., Order of Merit of Fed. Republic of Germany, 1978. *Recreations:* golf, fishing, walking. *Address:* Meneng Drive, Nauru, Central Pacific. *T:* 4443713; RD4, Otaramarae, Lake Rotoiti, Rotorua, New Zealand. *T:* Rotorua (73) 624861. *Club:* University (Auckland).

DONNE, Sir John (Christopher), Kt 1976; Chairman, National Health Service Training Authority, 1983–86; *b* 19 Aug. 1921; *s* of late Leslie Victor Donne, solicitor, Hove, and Mabel Laetitia Richards (*née* Pike); *m* 1945, Mary Stuart (*née* Seaton); three *d. Educ:* Charterhouse. Royal Artillery, 1940–46 (Captain); served Europe and India. Solicitor, 1949; Notary Public; Consultant, Donne Mileham & Haddock, 1985–92; Pres., Sussex Law Soc., 1969–70. Chairman: SE (Metropolitan) Regional Hosp. Bd, 1971–74; SE Thames RHA, 1973–83. Governor, Guy's Hosp., 1971–74, Guy's Hosp. Med. Sch., 1974–82; Dep. Chm., RHA Chairmen, 1976–78 (Chm., 1974–76); Mem., Gen. Council, King Edward's Hosp. Fund for London, 1972–91 (Mem., Management Cttee, 1978–84); a Governing Trustee, Nuffield Provincial Hosp. Trust, 1975–; Dir, Nuffield Health and Soc. Services Fund, 1976–. Member: Council, Internat. Hosp. Fedn, 1979–85; Council, Inst. for Med. Ethics (formerly Soc. for Study of Medical Ethics), 1980–86; Court of Univ. of Sussex, 1979–87. FRSA 1985–92; FRSocMed 1985. Mem. Ct of Assts, Hon. Company of Broderers, 1979– (Master, 1983–84). Mem., Editorial Bd, Jl Medical Ethics, 1977–79. *Recreations:* genealogy, gardening, photography, listening to music. *Address:* The Old School House, Acton Burnell, Shrewsbury SY5 7PG. *T:* Acton Burnell (01694) 731647. *Clubs:* Army and Navy, Pilgrims, MCC; Butterflies, Sussex Martlets.

DONNELLY, Alan John; Member (Lab) Tyne and Wear, European Parliament, since 1989; *b* 16 July 1957; *s* of John and Josephine Donnelly; *m* 1979 (marr. diss. 1982); one *s. Educ:* Valley View Primary School and Springfield Comprehensive School, Jarrow; Sunderland Poly. (Hon. Fellow, Sunderland Univ., 1993). GMBATU Northern Region: Health and Safety Officer, 1978–80; Education Officer, 1980–84; Finance and Admin. Officer, 1984–87; GMB Central Finance Manager, 1987–89. Mem., S Tyneside MBC, 1979–82. B Director, Unity Trust Bank, 1987–89. Kt Comdr, Order of Merit (Germany), 1991. *Recreations:* tennis, swimming, reading. *Address:* 1 South View, Jarrow, Tyne and Wear NE32 5JP. *T:* 0191–489 7643.

DONNELLY, Brendan Patrick; Member (C) Sussex South and Crawley, European Parliament, since 1994; *b* 25 Aug. 1950; *s* of Patrick Aloysius Donnelly and late Mary Josephine Donnelly (*née* Barrett). *Educ:* Christ Church, Oxford (BA Classics 1972; MA 1976). Theodor Heuss Travelling Scholar, Munich, 1974–76; FCO, 1976–82; Private Sec. to Sir Henry Plumb, 1983–86; on staff of Lord Cockfield, a Vice-Pres. of CEC, 1986–87; Political Consultant on EC, 1987–90; Special Advr to Leader of Conservatives in EP, 1990–94. *Recreations:* watching cricket, modern languages, modern history. *Address:* c/o 72 High Street, Brighton BN2 1RP. *T:* Brighton (01273) 571199. *Clubs:* Carlton; Middlesex County Cricket, Sussex County Cricket.

DONNELLY, (Joseph) Brian; HM Diplomatic Service; Minister and Deputy Permanent Representative, UK Delegation to NATO, Brussels, since 1995; *b* 24 April 1945; *s* of Joseph Donnelly and Ada Agnes (*née* Bowness); *m* 1966, Susanne Gibb (marr. diss. 1994); one *d. Educ:* Workington Grammar Sch.; Queen's Coll., Oxford (Wyndham Scholar, MA); Univ. of Wisconsin (MA). Joined HM Diplomatic Service, 1973; 2nd Sec., FCO, 1973; 1st Sec., UK Mission to UN, NY, 1975–79; Head of Chancery, Singapore, 1979–82; Asst Head, Personnel Policy Dept, FCO, 1982–84; Dep. to Chief Scientific Adviser, Cabinet Office, 1984–87; Counsellor and Consul General, Athens, 1988–91; RCDS, 1991; Head of Non-Proliferation Dept, FCO, 1992–95. *Recreations:* MG cars, flying kites, reading, cooking, films. *Address:* c/o Foreign and Commonwealth Office, King Charles Street, SW1A 2AH. *Club:* MG Owners'.

DONNISON, David Vernon; Research Fellow and Professor Emeritus, Glasgow University, since 1991; *b* 19 Jan. 1926; *s* of late Frank Siegfried Vernon Donnison, CBE and Ruth Seruya Singer, MBE, JP; *m* 1st, Jean Kidger; two *s* two *d*; 2nd, 1987, Catherine McIntosh, (Kay), Carmichael, *qv. Educ:* Marlborough Coll., Wiltshire; Magdalen Coll., Oxford. Asst Lecturer and Lecturer, Manchester Univ., 1950–53; Lecturer, Toronto Univ., 1953–55; Reader, London Sch. of Economics, 1956–61; Prof. of Social Administration, 1961–69; Dir, Centre for Environmental Studies, 1969–75; Chm., Supplementary Benefits Commn, 1975–80; Prof. of Town and Regl Planning, Glasgow Univ., 1980–91. Chm., Public Schs Commn, 1968–70. Hon. doctorates: Bradford, 1973; Hull, 1980; Leeds, Southampton, 1981. *Publications:* The Neglected Child and the Social Services, 1954; Welfare Services in a Canadian Community, 1958; Housing since the Rent Act, 1961; The Government of Housing, 1967; An Approach to Social Policy, 1975; Social Policy and Administration Revisited, 1975; (with Paul Soto) The Good City, 1980; The Politics of Poverty, 1982; (with Clare Ungerson) Housing Policy, 1982; (ed with Alan Middleton) Regenerating the Inner City: Glasgow's Experience, 1987; (ed with D. Maclennan) The Housing Service of the Future, 1991; A Radical Agenda, 1991. *Address:* 23 Bank Street, Glasgow G12 8JQ. *T:* 0141–334 5817.

DONNISON, Kay; *see* Carmichael, C. M.

DONOGHUE, Prof. Denis, MA, PhD; literary critic; Henry James Professor of Letters, New York University, since 1979; *b* 1 Dec. 1928. *Educ:* University College, Dublin. BA 1949, MA 1952, PhD 1957; MA Cantab 1965. Admin. Office, Dept of Finance, Irish Civil Service, 1951–54. Asst Lectr, Univ. Coll., Dublin, 1954–57; Coll. Lectr, 1957–62; Visiting Schol., Univ. of Pennsylvania, 1962–63; Coll. Lectr, Univ. Coll., Dublin, 1963–64; University Lectr, Cambridge Univ., 1964–65; Fellow, King's Coll., Cambridge, 1964–65; Prof. of Modern English and American Literature, University Coll., Dublin, 1965–79. Mem. Internat. Cttee of Assoc. of University Profs of English. Mem. BBC Commn to monitor the quality of spoken English on BBC Radio, 1979. Reith Lectr, BBC, 1982. *Publications:* The Third Voice, 1959; Connoisseurs of Chaos, 1965; (ed jtly) An Honoured Guest, 1965; The Ordinary Universe, 1968; Emily Dickinson, 1968; Jonathan Swift, 1969; (ed) Swift, 1970; Yeats, 1971; Thieves of Fire, 1974; (ed) W. B. Yeats, Memoirs, 1973; Sovereign Ghost: studies in Imagination, 1978; Ferocious Alphabets, 1981; The Arts without Mystery, 1983; We Irish (selected essays), 1987; Pure Good of Theory, 1992; contribs to reviews and journals. *Address:* New York University, 19 University Place, New York, NY 10003, USA; Gaybrook, North Avenue, Mount Merrion, Dublin, Ireland.

DONOHOE, Brian Harold; MP (Lab) Cunninghame South, since 1992; *b* 10 Sept. 1948; *s* of late George Joseph Donohoe and Catherine Sillars Donohoe (*née* Ashworth); *m* 1973, Christine Pawson; two *s. Educ:* Irvine Royal Academy; Kilmarnock Technical Coll. Apprentice fitter-turner, 1965–69; draughtsman, 1969–81; Trade Union Official, NALGO, 1981–92. Mem., Select Cttee on transport, 1993–. *Recreation:* gardening. *Address:* 5 Greenfield Drive, Irvine KA12 0ED. *T:* Irvine (01294) 274419. *Club:* NALGO Staff Social.

DONOHOE, Peter Howard; pianist; *b* 18 June 1953; *s* of Harold Donohoe and Marjorie Donohoe (*née* Travis); *m* 1980, Elaine Margaret Burns; one *d. Educ:* Chetham's School of Music, Manchester; Leeds Univ.; Royal Northern Coll. of Music; Paris Conservatoire. BMus; GRNCM, ARCM; Hon. FRNCM 1983. Professional solo pianist, 1974–; London début, 1978; concert tours in Europe, USA, Canada, Australia, Asia, USSR; regular appearances at Royal Festival Hall, Barbican Hall, Queen Elizabeth Hall, Henry Wood Promenade concerts, 1979–; numerous TV and radio broadcasts, UK and overseas; recordings include music by Rachmaninov, Stravinsky, Prokofiev, Britten, Messiaen, Muldowney, Tchaikovsky. Competition finalist: British Liszt, London, 1976; Liszt-Bartok, Budapest, 1976; Leeds International Piano, 1981; winner, Internat. Tschaikovsky competition, Moscow, 1982. Concerto Recording Award, Gramophone, 1988. *Recreations:* jazz, golf, helping young musicians, clock collecting. *Address:* c/o IMG Artists (Europe), Media House, 3 Burlington Lane, W4 2TH.

DONOUGHMORE, 8th Earl of, *cr* 1800; **Richard Michael John Hely-Hutchinson;** Baron Donoughmore, 1783; Viscount Hutchinson (UK), 1821; Chairman, Hodder

Headline (formerly Headline Book Publishing) PLC, since 1986; *b* 8 Aug. 1927; *er s* of 7th Earl of Donoughmore and of Dorothy Jean (MBE 1947), *d* of late J. B. Hotham; *S* father, 1981; *m* 1951, Sheila, *o c* of late Frank Frederick Parsons and Mrs Learmond Perkins; four *s*. *Educ:* Winchester; New College, Oxford (MA; BM, BCh). *Heir: s* Viscount Suirdale, *qv*. *Address:* The Manor House, Bampton, Oxon OX8 2LQ. *Club:* Jockey (Paris).
See also Hon. T. M. Hely Hutchinson.

DONOUGHUE, family name of **Baron Donoughue**.

DONOUGHUE, Baron *cr* 1985 (Life Peer), of Ashton in the County of Northamptonshire; **Bernard Donoughue;** *b* 1934; *s* of late Thomas Joseph Donoughue and of Maud Violet Andrews; *m* 1959, Carol Ruth Goodman (marr. diss. 1989); two *s* two *d*. *Educ:* Secondary Modern Sch. and Grammar Sch., Northampton; Lincoln Coll. and Nuffield Coll., Oxford. BA (1st class hons), MA, DPhil (Oxon). FRHistS. Henry Fellow, Harvard, USA. Mem., Editorial Staff: The Economist, Sunday Times, Sunday Telegraph. Sen. Res. Officer, PEP, 1960–63; Lectr, Sen. Lectr, Reader, LSE, 1963–74; Sen. Policy Advr to the Prime Minister, 1974–79; Development Dir, Economist Intelligence Unit, 1979–81; Asst Editor, The Times, 1981–82; Partner, 1983–86, Head of Res. and Investment Policy, 1984–86, Grieveson, Grant & Co; Dir, 1986–88, Head of Res., 1986–87, of Internat. Res. and Investment Policy, 1987–88, Kleinwort Grieveson Securities; Exec. Vice-Chm., London and Bishopsgate Internat. Investment Holdings, 1988–91. Opposition spokesman on Treasury, 1991–92, on Energy, 1991–93, on Nat. Heritage, 1992–. Member: Sports Council, 1965–71; Commn of Enquiry into Association Football, 1966–68; Ct of Governors, LSE, 1968–74, 1982–; Civil Service Coll. Adv. Council, 1976–79; Adv. Bd, Wissenschaftzentrum, Berlin, 1978–91; Bd, Centre for European Policy Studies, Brussels, 1982–87; London Arts Bd, 1991–. Trustee, Inst. for Policy Res., 1990–. Exec., London Symphony Orch., 1979–91 (Patron, 1989–); Vice-Pres., Newbury Music Fest., 1993–. Associate Mem., Nuffield Coll., Oxford, 1982–87; Mem., Sen. Common Room, Lincoln Coll., Oxford, 1985– (Hon. Fellow, 1986); Patron, Inst. of Contemporary British History, 1988–. FRSA. Hon. Fellow, LSE, 1989. Hon. LLD Leicester, 1990. *Publications:* (ed jtly) Oxford Poetry, 1956; Wage Policies in the Public Sector, 1962; Trade Unions in a Changing Society, 1963; British Politics and the American Revolution, 1964; (with W. T. Rodgers) The People into Parliament, 1966; (with G. W. Jones) Herbert Morrison: portrait of a politician, 1973; Prime Minister, 1987. *Recreations:* politics, sport, economics, music. *Address:* 71 Ebury Mews East, SW1W 9QA.

DONOVAN, Charles Edward; Board Member, 1981–92, and Senior Managing Director, Corporate Activities, 1991–92, British Gas plc; *b* 28 Jan. 1934; *s* of Charles and Sarah Donovan; *m* 1963, Robina Evelyn (*née* Anderson); three *s*. *Educ:* Camphill Sch., Paisley; Royal Technical Coll., Glasgow. FIPM 1990; CIGasE 1985; CIMgt (CBIM 1991). Personnel Officer: HQ, BEA, 1962; London and SE, Richard Costain Ltd, Constr. and Civil Engrs, 1963; Sen. Personnel Officer, Engrg, W Midlands Gas Bd, 1966; Southern Gas, 1970–77: Personnel Manager, 1973; Personnel Dir, 1975; British Gas: Dir, Indust. Relations, 1977–81; Man. Dir, Personnel, 1981–91, also Group Services, 1989–91. Dir, Inst. of Citizenship Studies, 1992. FRSA 1992. *Recreations:* sailing, hill walking. *Address:* 65 Moss Lane, Pinner, Middx HA5 3AZ.

DONOVAN, Prof. Desmond Thomas; Yates-Goldsmid Professor of Geology and Head of Department of Geology, University College, London, 1966–82; Hon. Curator, Wells Museum, Somerset, 1982–85; *b* 16 June 1921; *s* of T. B. Donovan; *m* 1959, Shirley Louise Saward; two *s* one *d*. *Educ:* Epsom Coll.; University of Bristol. BSc 1942; PhD 1951; DSc 1960. Asst Lectr in Geology, University of Bristol, 1947; Lectr in Geology, Bristol, 1950; Prof. of Geology, University of Hull, 1962. Pres., Palaeontographical Soc., 1979–84. *Publications:* Stratigraphy: An Introduction to Principles, 1966; (ed) Geology of Shelf Seas, 1968; papers on fossil cephalopods, Jurassic stratigraphy, Pleistocene deposits, marine geology. *Address:* 52 Willow Road, NW3 1TP. *T:* 0171–794 8626. *Club:* Athenæum.

DONOVAN, Ian Edward, FCMA; Director and Group Controller, Smiths Industries Aerospace & Defence Ltd, since 1988; *b* 2 March 1940; *s* of late John Walter Donovan and Ethel Molyneux; *m* 1969, Susan Betty Harris; two *s*. *Educ:* Leighton Park, Reading. FCMA 1985. Gen. Factory Manager, Lucas CAV, 1969–72; Finance Man., Lucas Girling, 1972–78; Finance Director: Lucas Girling, Koblenz, 1978–81; Lucas Electrical Ltd, 1982–84; Mem., 1985–88, Gp Dir, Finance and Central Services, 1986–88, CAA. Mem. Council, SBAC, 1994–. *Recreations:* golf, fly fishing, sailing, gardening, music. *Address:* Lawn Farm, Church Lane, Tibberton, Droitwich, Worcs WR9 7NW.

DONOVAN, Terence Daniel, FRPS, FBIPP; photographer; film director, since 1957; *b* 14 Sept. 1936; *s* of Daniel Donovan and Constance Donovan (*née* Wright); *m* 1st, 1961, Janet Cohen (marr. diss.); one *s*; 2nd, 1970, Diana St Felix Dare; one *s* one *d*. FRPS 1968; FBIPP 1968. Photography: has worked for Vogue, Harpers & Queen, Elle, and Marie Claire; exhibn, Albemarle Gall., 1990. Films: has directed TV commercials, 1967–; also produced plays for CBS, documentaries for LWT, and pop promos; dir. feature film, Yellow Dog, 1972. Trustee, Arts Foundn, 1991–. FRSA. *Publications:* Glances, 1983; Fighting Judo, 1985. *Recreations:* judo (black belt), photography, painting abstract expressionism. *Address:* 47/48 New Bond Street, W1Y 9HA. *T:* 0171–491 4477. *Clubs:* Victory Service Men's; Budokwai Judo.

DOOGE, Prof. James Clement Ignatius; Professor of Civil Engineering, University College, Dublin, 1970–84, now Professor Emeritus; research consultant; Consultant: United Nations specialised agencies; European Commission; President, Royal Irish Academy, 1987–90; *b* 30 July 1922; *s* of Denis Patrick Dooge and Veronica Catherine Carroll; *m* 1946, Veronica O'Doherty; two *s* three *d*. *Educ:* Christian Brothers' Sch., Dun Laoghaire; University Coll., Dublin (BE, BSc 1942, ME 1952); Univ. of Iowa (MSc 1956). FICE; FASCE. Jun. Civil Engr, Irish Office of Public Works, 1943–46; Design Engr, Electricity Supply Bd, Ireland, 1946–58; Prof. of Civil Engrg, UC Cork, 1958–70. Irish Senate: Mem., 1965–77 and 1981–87; Chm., 1973–77; Leader, 1983–87; Minister for Foreign Affairs, Ireland, 1981–82. President: ICEI, 1968–69 (Hon. FICEI; Kettle Premium and Plaque, 1948, 1985; Mullins Medal, 1951, 1962); Internat. Assoc. for Hydrologic Scis, 1975–79; Member: Exec. Bureau, Internat. Union for Geodesy and Geophysics, 1979–87; Gen. Cttee, ICSU, 1980–86, 1988– (Sec. Gen., 1980–82; Pres., 1993–Sept. 1996). Fellow, Amer. Geophysical Union (Horton Award, 1959; Bowie Medal, 1986); Hon. Mem., Eur. Geophysical Soc., 1993. Foreign Member: Polish Acad. of Scis, 1985; Russian Acad. of Scis, 1994. Hon. DrAgrSc Wageningen, 1978; Hon. DrTech. Lund, 1980; Hon. DSc Birmingham, 1986; Hon. ScD Dublin, 1988. Internat. Prize for Hydrology, 1983. *Address:* Centre for Water Resources Research, University College, Earlsfort Terrace, Dublin 2, Ireland.

DOOKUN, Sir Dewoonarain, Kt 1984; Chairman and Managing Director, Mauritius Cosmetics Ltd, since 1966; *b* 7 Dec. 1929; *s* of Jadoonath Dookun; *m* 1959, Henriette Keupp; two *s*. *Educ:* St Joseph College; Univ. of Edinburgh. Manufacturing, marketing, business administration and accounts, Mainz, West Germany; founder of: Mauritius Cosmetics, 1966; Paper Converting Co., 1967; Jet Industries, 1967; FDG Garments Industries, 1968; Agri-Pac, 1979; Deramann, 1979; Gumboots Manufacturers, 1976; DG Rubber, 1979; Elite Textiles, 1982; Deodan Textile, 1984. *Recreations:* reading, walking, golf. *Address:* Queen Mary Avenue, Floreal, Mauritius. *T:* 86-2361; *telex:* 4239 Dookun IW. *Clubs:* Institute of Directors; Mauritius Gymkhana; Swastika.

DORAN, Frank; *b* 13 April 1949; *s* of Francis Anthony Doran and Betty Hedges or Doran; *m* 1967, Patricia Ann Govan or Doran; two *s*. *Educ:* Ainslie Park Secondary Sch.; Leith Acad.; Dundee Univ. (LLB Hons). Admitted Solicitor, 1977. Eur. Parly Cand. (Lab) NE Scotland, 1984. MP (Lab) Aberdeen South, 1987–92; contested (Lab) Aberdeen S, 1992. Asst Editor, Scottish Legal Action Group Bulletin, 1975–78. *Recreations:* cinema, art, sports. *Clubs:* Aberdeen Trades Council; Dundee Labour.

DORAN, John Frederick, CEng, FInstGasE, MInstM; Chairman, East Midlands Gas Region, 1974–77; *b* 28 July 1916; *s* of Henry Joseph and Clara Doran; *m* 1940, Eileen Brotherton; two *s*. *Educ:* Wandsworth Technical Coll.; Wimbledon Technical Coll. Served War, Fleet Air Arm, 1943–46. Various appts Gas Light & Coke Co. (subseq. North Thames Gas Bd), 1935–53; Dist Manager, Hornsey Dist, North Thames Gas Bd, 1953; Regional Sales Manager, North Western Div., North Thames Gas Bd, 1955–57. Southern Gas Board: Regional Sales and Service Manager, Southampton Region and Dorset and Bournemouth Regions, 1957–65; Marketing Manager, 1965–67; Commercial Manager, 1968–69; Commercial Dir, 1970–71; Commercial Dir and Bd Mem., 1971–73. Dep. Chm., East Midlands Gas Region, 1973. Founder, John Doran Gas Museum, Leicester. *Publications:* technical papers to Instn Gas Engrs. *Recreations:* golf, gardening. *Address:* 14 Oberfield Road, Brockenhurst, Hants SO42 7QF. *T:* Lymington (01590) 623185.

DORCHESTER, Area Bishop of, since 1988; **Rt. Rev. Anthony John Russell,** DPhil; *b* 25 Jan. 1943; *s* of Michael John William and Beryl Margaret Russell; *m* 1967, Sheila Alexandra, *d* of Alexander Scott and Elizabeth Carlisle Ronald; two *s* two *d*. *Educ:* Uppingham Sch; Univ. of Durham (BA); Trinity Coll., Oxford (DPhil); Cuddesdon Coll., Oxford. Deacon 1970, Priest 1971; Curate, Hilborough Group of Parishes, 1970–73; Rector, Preston on Stour, Atherstone on Stour and Whitchurch, 1973–88; Chaplain, Arthur Rank Centre (Nat. Agricl Centre), 1973–82, Director, 1983–88; Chaplain to the Queen, 1983–88. Canon Theologian, Coventry Cathedral, 1977–88. Mem., Gen. Synod, 1980–88. Chaplain, Royal Agricl Soc., 1982–91, Vice-Pres., 1991–; Hon. Chaplain, RABI, 1983–. Comr, Rural Develt Commn, 1991–. Trustee, Rural Housing Trust, 1983–. *Publications:* Groups and Teams in the Countryside (ed), 1975; The Village in Myth and Reality, 1980; The Clerical Profession, 1980; The Country Parish, 1986; The Country Parson, 1993. *Address:* Holmby House, Sibford Ferris, Banbury, Oxfordshire OX15 5RG. *T:* Swalcliffe (01295) 780583.

DORE, Prof. Ronald Philip, CBE 1989; FBA 1975; Research Associate, Centre for Economic Performance, London School of Economics and Political Science, since 1991; Adjunct Professor, Massachusetts Institute of Technology, since 1989; *b* 1 Feb. 1925; *s* of Philip Brine Dore and Elsie Constance Dore; *m* 1957, Nancy Macdonald; one *s* one *d*. *Educ:* Poole Grammar Sch.; SOAS, Univ. of London (BA). Lectr in Japanese Instns, SOAS, London, 1951; Prof. of Asian Studies, Univ. of BC, 1956; Reader, later Prof. of Sociol., LSE, 1961 (Hon. Fellow, 1980); Fellow IDS, 1969–82; Asst Dir, Technical Change Centre, 1982–86; Dir, Japan–Europe Industry Res. Centre, ICSTM, 1986–91. Mem., Academia Europaea, 1989. Hon. Foreign Mem., Amer. Acad. of Arts and Scis, 1978; Hon. Foreign Fellow, Japan Acad., 1986–. Order of the Rising Sun (Third Class), Japan, 1988. *Publications:* City Life in Japan, 1958; Land Reform in Japan, 1959, 2nd edn 1984; Education in Tokugawa Japan, 1963, 2nd edn 1983; (ed) Aspects of Social Change in Modern Japan, 1967; British Factory, Japanese Factory, 1973; The Diploma Disease, 1976; Shinohata: portrait of a Japanese village, 1978; (ed with Zoe Mars) Community Development, Comparative Case Studies in India, The Republic of Korea, Mexico and Tanzania, 1981; Energy Conservation in Japanese Industry, 1982; Flexible Rigidities: structural adjustment in Japan, 1986; Taking Japan Seriously: a Confucian perspective on leading economic issues, 1987; (ed jtly) Japan and World Depression, Then and Now: essays in memory of E. F. Penrose, 1987; (with Mari Sako) How the Japanese Learn to Work, 1988; (ed jtly) Corporatism and Accountability: organized interests in British public life, 1990; Will the 21st Century be the Age of Individualism?, 1991. *Address:* 157 Surrenden Road, Brighton, East Sussex BN1 6ZA. *T:* Brighton (01273) 501370. *Club:* Reform.

DOREY, Sir Graham (Martyn), Kt 1993; Bailiff of Guernsey, since 1992 (Deputy Bailiff, 1982–92); a Judge of the Court of Appeal of Jersey, since 1992; President, Guernsey Court of Appeal, since 1992; *b* 15 Dec. 1932; *s* of late Martyn Dorey and Muriel (*née* Pickard); *m* 1962, Penelope Cecile, *d* of Maj. E. A. Wheadon, ED; two *s* two *d*. *Educ:* Kingswood Sch., Bath; Ecole des Roches, Verneuil; Univs of Bristol and Caen. Admitted Solicitor, 1959; Advocate, Royal Court of Guernsey, 1960; called to the Bar, Gray's Inn, 1992; People's Deputy, States of Guernsey, 1970; Solicitor Gen., 1973, Attorney Gen., 1977, Guernsey. *Recreations:* sailing, maritime history, music. *Address:* La Hougue ès Pies, Vale, Guernsey. *T:* Guernsey (01481) 44868, *Fax:* (01481) 43833. *Clubs:* Royal Ocean Racing; Royal Yacht Squadron.

DORIN, Bernard Jean Robert, Hon. GCVO; Officier de la Légion d'Honneur; Officier de l'Ordre National du Mérite; Ambassadeur de France; Conseiller d'Etat, since 1993; *b* 25 Aug. 1929; *s* of Robert Dorin and Jacqueline Dorin (*née* Goumard); *m* 1971, Christine du Bois de Meyrignac; two *s* two *d*. *Educ:* Inst. d'Etudes Politiques, Paris; Ecole Nat. d'Administration. Attaché, French Embassy, Ottawa, 1957–59; Min. of Foreign Affairs, 1959–64; technical adviser: for sci. research, nuclear and space, 1966–67; to Minister of Nat. Educn, 1967–68; to Minister for sci. research, 1968–69; Harvard Univ., 1969–70; Min. of Foreign Affairs, 1970–71; Ambassador in Port-au-Prince, 1972–75; Head of Francophone Affairs Dept, 1975–78; Ambassador in Pretoria, 1978–81; Dir for America, Min. of Foreign Affairs, 1981–84; Ambassador, Brazil, 1984–87, Japan, 1987–90, UK, 1990–93. *Recreation:* collections of naïve paintings. *Address:* 6 rue Guy de Maupassant, 75016 Paris, France; Conseil d'Etat, Palais Royal, 75001 Paris, France. *Club:* Richelieu (Paris).

DORKEN, (Anthony) John; Head of Consumer Affairs Division, Department of Trade and Industry, since 1993; *b* 24 April 1944; *s* of Oscar Roy Dorken, OBE and Margaret Dorken (*née* Barker); *m* 1972, Satanay Mufti; one *s* one *d*. *Educ:* Mill Hill Sch.; King's Coll., Cambridge (BA Classics 1965; MA 1969). VSO, Libya, 1965–66; Asst Principal, BoT, 1967–71; Private Sec. to Parly Under Sec. of State for Industry, 1971–72; Principal, DTI, later Dept of Energy, 1972–77; seconded to Cabinet Office, 1977–79; Asst Sec., Dept of Energy, 1980–86; seconded to Shell UK Exploration and Prodn, 1986–89; Dir of Resource Management, Dept of Energy, 1989–92; Dep. Dir Gen., Office of Gas Supply, 1992–93. *Publications:* articles on gas regulation in specialist jls. *Recreations:* reading, walking, music, squash, tennis. *Address:* Department of Trade and Industry, 1 Victoria Street, SW1. *T:* 0171–215 3280. *Club:* Stormont Lawn Tennis and Squash Rackets (Highgate) (Hon. Treas.).

DORKING, Suffragan Bishop of; *no new appointment at time of going to press.*

DORKING, Archdeacon of; *no new appointment at time of going to press.*

DORMAN, Lt-Col Sir Charles (Geoffrey), 3rd Bt *cr* 1923; MC 1942; *b* 18 Sept. 1920; *o s* of Sir Bedford Lockwood Dorman, 2nd Bart, CBE and Lady Constance Phelps Dorman (*née* Hay), (*d* 1946); *S* father, 1956; *m* 1954, Elizabeth Ann (marr. diss. 1972; she *d* 1993), *d* of late George Gilmour Gilmour-White, OBE; one *d*. *Educ:* Rugby Sch.; Brasenose Coll., Oxford (MA). Commissioned, 1941; served with 3rd The King's Own Hussars at Alamein (MC) and in Italian Campaign; Commissioned to 13th/18th Royal Hussars (QMO), 1947; GSO1, 1961–70; retired. *Recreation:* gliding. *Heir: cousin* Philip Henry Keppel Dorman [*b* 19 May 1954; *m* 1982, Myriam Jeanne Georgette, *d* of late René Bay; one *d*]. *Address:* Hutton Grange Cottage, Great Rollright, Chipping Norton, Oxon OX7 5SN.

DORMAN, Richard Bostock, CBE 1984; HM Diplomatic Service, retired; High Commissioner to Vanuatu, 1982–85; Chairman, the British Friends of Vanuatu, since 1986; *b* 8 Aug. 1925; *s* of late John Ehrenfried and Madeleine Louise Dorman; *m* 1950, Anna Illingworth; one *s* two *d*. *Educ:* Sedbergh Sch.; St John's Coll., Cambridge. Army Service (Lieut, S Staffs Regt), 1944–48; Asst Principal, War Office, 1951; Principal, 1955; transferred to Commonwealth Relations Office, 1958; First Sec., British High Commission, Nicosia, 1960–64; Dep. High Commissioner, Freetown, 1964–66; SE Asia Dept, FO, 1967–69; Counsellor, Addis Ababa, 1969–73; Commercial Counsellor, Bucharest, 1974–77; Counsellor, Pretoria, 1977–82. *Address:* 67 Beresford Road, Cheam, Surrey SM2 6ER. *T:* 0181–642 9627. *Club:* Commonwealth Trust.

DORMAND, family name of **Baron Dormand of Easington.**

DORMAND OF EASINGTON, Baron *cr* 1987 (Life Peer), of Easington in the county of Durham; **John Donkin Dormand;** *b* 27 Aug. 1919; *s* of Bernard and Mary Dormand; *m* 1963, Doris Robinson; one step *s* one step *d*. *Educ:* Bede Coll., Durham; Loughborough Coll.; St Peter's Hall, Oxford (Hon. Fellow, St Peter's Coll., 1993); Univ. of Harvard. Teacher, 1940–48; Education Adviser, 1948–52 and 1957–63; District Education Officer, Easington RDC, 1963–70. MP (Lab) Easington, 1970–87. An Asst Govt Whip, 1974; a Lord Comr of HM Treasury, 1974–79; Chm., PLP, 1981–87. *Recreations:* music, sport.

DORMENT, Richard, PhD; Art Critic, Daily Telegraph, since 1986; *b* 15 Nov. 1946; *s* of James Dorment and Marguerite Dorment (*née* O'Callaghan); *m* 1st, 1970, Kate S. Ganz (marr. diss. 1981); one *s* one *d*; 2nd, 1985, Harriet Mary Waugh. *Educ:* Georgetown Prep. Sch.; Princeton Univ. (BA 1968); Columbia Univ. (MA 1969, MPhil, PhD 1975). Faculty Fellow, Columbia Univ., 1968–72; Asst Curator, European Painting, Philadelphia Mus. of Art, 1973–76; Curator, Alfred Gilbert: Sculptor and Goldsmith, RA, 1985–86; Art Critic, Country Life, 1986; Co-curator, James McNeill Whistler, Tate Gall., 1994–95. Member: Judging Panel, Turner Prize, 1989; Hayward Gall. Adv. Gp, 1995–. Hawthornden Prize for art criticism in Britain, 1992. *Publications:* Alfred Gilbert, 1985; British Painting 1750–1900: A Catalogue of the British Paintings in the Philadelphia Museum of Art, 1986; Alfred Gilbert Sculptor and Goldsmith, 1986; (with Margaret McDonald) James McNeill Whistler, 1994; reviews for NY Rev. of Books, TLS, Literary Rev.; contribs to exhibn catalogues and to Burlington Magazine. *Address:* 10 Clifton Villas, W9 2PH. *T:* 0171–266 2057.

DORMER, family name of **Baron Dormer.**

DORMER, 16th Baron *cr* 1615; **Joseph Spencer Philip Dormer;** Bt 1615; landowner and farmer; *b* 4 Sept. 1914; *s* of 14th Baron Dormer, CBE, and Caroline May (*d* 1951), *y d* of Sir Robert Cavendish Spencer Clifford, 3rd Bt; *S* brother, 1975. *Educ:* Ampleforth; Christ Church, Oxford. Served World War II, Scots Guards. Consultant, Thomas Comely & Sons Ltd. Pres., Warwick and Leamington Conservative Assoc., 1983–. Formerly Mem. Council, West Midlands Area Conservative Assoc. Hon. Vice-Pres., Worcs Br., Grenadier Gds Assoc. Kt of Honour and Devotion, SMO Malta, 1989. *Heir: cousin* Geoffrey Henry Dormer [*b* 13 May 1920; *m* 1st, 1947, Janet (marr. diss. 1957), *yr d* of James F. A. Readman; two *d*; 2nd, 1958, Pamela, *d* of late Wallace Levick Simpson; two *s*]. *Address:* Grove Park, Warwick CV35 8RF. *Club:* Cavalry and Guards.

DORNHORST, Antony Clifford, CBE 1977; MD, FRCP; Professor of Medicine, St George's Hospital Medical School, 1959–80; Civilian Consultant in Aviation Medicine to RAF, 1973–85; *b* 2 April 1915; *s* of Ernst Dornhorst and Florence, *née* Partridge; *m* 1946, Helen Mary Innes; three *d*. *Educ:* St Clement Danes Sch.; St Thomas's Hosp. Medical Sch. MB BS London 1937; MD London 1939; FRCP 1955. Junior Appointments, St Thomas' Hosp., 1937–39. Served with RAMC, mostly in Mediterranean theatre, 1940–46. Reader in Medicine, St Thomas's Hosp. Medical Sch., 1949–59. Member: MRC, 1973–77; SW Thames RHA, 1974–82. *Publications:* papers in various journals on normal and abnormal physiology. *Recreation:* music. *Address:* 8 Albert Place, W8 5PD. *T:* 0171–937 8782.

DORR, Noel; Secretary, Department of Foreign Affairs, Ireland, since 1987; *b* Limerick, 1933; *m* 1983, Caitríona Doran. *Educ:* St Nathy's Coll., Ballaghaderreen; University Coll., Galway (BA, BComm, HDipEd); Georgetown Univ., Washington, DC (MA). Entered Dept of Foreign Affairs, 1960; Third Sec., 1960–62; Third Sec., Brussels, 1962–64; First Sec., Washington, 1964–70; First Sec., Dept of For. Affairs, 1970–72; Counsellor (Press and Inf.), Dept of For. Affairs, 1972–74; Asst Sec., Political Div., and Political Dir, 1974–77, Dep. Sec. and Political Dir, 1977–80; Perm. Rep. of Ireland to UN, New York, 1980–83; Rep of Ireland, Security Council, 1981–82; Ambassador of Ireland to UK, 1983–87. *Address:* Department of Foreign Affairs, 80 St Stephen's Green, Dublin 2, Ireland.

DORRANCE, Dr Richard Christopher; Chief Executive, Council for Awards in Children's Care and Education, since 1994; *b* 25 Feb. 1948; *s* of Eric and Joan Dorrance. *Educ:* Wolverhampton GS; Aylesbury GS; Univ. of East Anglia (BSc Chem. 1969; PhD 1973). FRSC. Res. into properties of detergents, Unilever and UEA, 1969–72; taught chemistry and geology, Royal GS, High Wycombe (and i/c stage lighting), 1972–80; Head of Science, Monks Walk Sch., Welwyn Garden City, 1980–83; Gen. Advr, Berks CC, 1983–88; Asst Chief Exec., Nat. Curriculum Council, 1989–91; Dep. Chief Exec., Sch. Exams and Assessment Council, 1991–93 (acting Chief Exec., 1991–92). *Publications:* Eye (computer prog.), 1983; GAS 81, 1982; papers in professional jls. *Recreations:* walking, foreign travel, natural history, bowling, gardening, model making, photography. *Address:* 1 Crewe Curve, Berkhamsted, Herts HP4 1SE. *T:* Berkhamsted (01442) 876689.

DORRELL, Ernest John; Secretary, Headmasters' Conference, 1975–79; General Secretary, Secondary Heads Association, 1978–79 (Secretary, Incorporated Association of Headmasters, 1975–77); *b* 31 March 1915; *s* of John Henry Whiting Dorrell and Amy Dorrell (*née* Roberts); *m* 1940, Alwen Irvona Jones; one *s* one *d*. *Educ:* Taunton Sch.; Exeter Coll., Oxford (Exhibr). Hon. Mods and Lit. Hum., MA. Served with 71 Field Regt and HQ 46 Div. RA, 1940–46. Asst Master, Dauntsey's Sch., 1937–40 and 1946–47; Admin. Asst, WR Educn Dept, 1947; Dep. Dir of Educn, Oxfordshire CC, 1950; Dir of Educn, Oxfordshire CC, 1970; Report on Educn in St Helena, 1974. Member: BBC Schs Broadcasting Council, 1975–79; Thames TV Educn Adv. Council, 1976–79. *Recreations:* walking, travel, golf. *Address:* Lynfield, 2 Gravel Lane, Warborough, Wallingford, Oxon OX10 7SD. *T:* Warborough (01865) 858342.

DORRELL, Rt. Hon. Stephen James, PC 1994; MP (C) Loughborough, since 1979; Secretary of State for Health, since 1995; *b* 25 March 1952; *s* of Philip Dorrell; *m* 1980, Penelope Anne Wears, *y d* of Mr and Mrs James Taylor, Windsor; one *s* one *d*. *Educ:* Uppingham; Brasenose Coll., Oxford. BA 1973. RAFVR, 1971–73. Personal asst to Rt Hon. Peter Walker, MBE, MP, Feb. 1974; contested (C) Kingston-upon-Hull East, Oct. 1974; PPS to the Secretary of State for Energy, 1983–87; Asst Govt Whip, 1987–88; a Lord Comr of HM Treasury (Govt Whip), 1988–90; Parly Under-Sec. of State, DoH, 1990–92; Financial Sec. to HM Treasury, 1992–94; Sec. of State for Nat. Heritage, 1994–95. Sec., Cons. Backbench Trade Cttee, 1980–81. Bd Mem., Christian Aid, 1985–87. *Recreations:* aviation, reading. *Address:* House of Commons, SW1A 0AA.

DORSET, Archdeacon of; *see* Walton, Ven. G. E.

DORWARD, William, OBE 1977; Commissioner for Hong Kong Economic Affairs, United States, 1983–87, retired; *b* 25 Sept. 1929; *s* of Alexander and Jessie Dorward; *m* 1960, Rosemary Ann Smith; one *s*. *Educ:* Morgan Academy, Dundee. Colonial Office, 1951–53; Commerce and Industry Dept, Hong Kong Govt, 1954–74; Counsellor (Hong Kong Affairs) UK Mission, Geneva, 1974–76; Hong Kong Government: Dep. Dir of Commerce and Industry, 1974–77; Comr of Industry and Customs, 1977–79; Dir of Trade, Industry and Customs, 1979–82, Sec. for Trade and Industry, 1982–83; MLC, 1979–83. Mem., GATT Dispute Settlement Panel, 1991–. *Address:* Waulkmill House, Skirling, by Biggar ML12 6HB. *Clubs:* Carlton, Royal Over-Seas League; Hong Kong.

DOSSER, Prof. Douglas George Maurice; Professor of Economics, University of York, 1965–81; retired, 1981; *b* 3 Oct. 1927; *s* of George William Dosser; *m* 1954, Valerie Alwyne Elizabeth, *d* of Leslie Jack Lindsey; three *d*. *Educ:* Latymer Upper School; London School of Economics. Lecturer in Economics, Univ. of Edinburgh, 1958–62; Vis. Prof. of Economics, Univ. of Washington, Seattle, 1960; Vis. Res. Prof. of Economics, Columbia Univ., NY, 1962; Reader in Economics, Univ. of York, 1963–65. *Publications:* Economic Analysis of Tax Harmonisation, 1967; (with S. Han) Taxes in the EEC and Britain, 1968; (with F. Andic) Theory of Economic Integration for Developing Countries, 1971; European Economic Integration and Monetary Unification, 1973; (with K. Hartley) The Collaboration of Nations, 1981; articles in Economic Jl, Economica, Rev. of Economic Studies. *Recreations:* art and antiques.

DOTRICE, Roy; actor (stage, films and television); *b* 26 May 1925; *m* 1946, Kay Newman, actress; three *d*. *Educ:* Dayton and Intermediate Schs, Guernsey, CI. Served War of 1939–45: Air Gunner, RAF, 1940; PoW, 1942–45. Acted in Repertory, 1945–55; formed and directed Guernsey Theatre Co., 1955; Royal Shakespeare Co., 1957–65 (Caliban, Julius Caesar, Hotspur, Firs, Puntila, Edward IV, etc); World War 2½, New Theatre, London, 1966; Brief Lives, Golden Theatre, New York, 1967; Latent Heterosexual and God Bless, Royal Shakespeare Co., Aldwych, 1968; Brief Lives (one-man play), Criterion, 1969 (over 400 perfs, world record for longest-running solo perf.), toured England, Canada, USA, 1973, Mayfair, 1974 (over 150 perfs), Broadway season, and world tour (over 1,700 perfs), 1974, Australian tour, 1975; Peer Gynt, Chichester Festival, 1970; One At Night, Royal Court, 1971; The Hero, Edinburgh, 1970; Mother Adam, Arts, 1971; Tom Brown's Schooldays, Cambridge, 1972; The Hollow Crown, seasons in USA 1973 and 1975, Sweden 1975; Gomes, Queen's, 1973; The Dragon Variation, Duke of York's, 1977; Australian tour with Chichester Festival, 1978; Passion of Dracula, Queen's, 1978; Oliver, Albery, 1979; Mister Lincoln (one-man play on Abraham Lincoln), Washington, NY and TV special, 1980, Fortune, 1981; A Life, NY, 1980–81; Henry V, and Falstaff in Henry IV, American Shakespeare Theatre, Stratford, Conn, 1981; Murder in Mind, Strand, 1982; Winston Churchill (one-man play), USA 1982 (also CBS TV); Kingdoms, NY, 1982; The Genius, Los Angeles, 1984 (Dramalogue Best Perf. Award); Down an Alley, Dallas, 1984; Great Expectations, Old Vic, 1985; Enemy of the People, NY, 1985; Hay Fever, NY and Washington, 1986; The Homecoming, NY, 1991; The Best of Friends, NY, 1993; *films include:* Heroes of Telemark, Twist of Sand, Lock up Your Daughters, Buttercup Chain, Tomorrow, One of Those Things, Nicholas and Alexandra, Amadeus, Corsican Brothers, The Eliminators, Camilla, L-Dopa, The Lady Forgets, Lounge People, The Cutting Edge. *Television:* appearances in: Dear Liar, Brief Lives, The Caretaker (Emmy award), Imperial Palace, Misleading Cases, Clochemerle, Dickens of London, Stargazy on Zummerdown, Family Reunion (USA), Tales of the Gold Monkey (USA), The Wizard (USA), A Team (USA), Tales from the Dark-Side (USA), Beauty and the Beast (USA), series, Going to Extremes (USA), The Good Policeman (USA). TV Actor of the Year Award, 1968; Tony Nomination for A Life, 1981. *Recreations:* fishing, riding. *Club:* Garrick.

DOUBLEDAY, John Vincent; sculptor since 1968; *b* 9 Oct. 1947; *s* of late Gordon V. and Margaret E. V. Doubleday; *m* 1969, Isobel J. C. Durie; three *s*. *Educ:* Stowe; Goldsmiths' College School of Art. *Exhibitions include:* Waterhouse Gallery, 1968, 1969, 1970, 1971; Galerie Sothmann, Amsterdam, 1969, 1971, 1979; Richard Demarco Gallery, Edinburgh, 1973; Laing Art Gallery, Newcastle, Bowes Museum, Barnard Castle, 1974; Pandion Gallery, NY, Aldeburgh Festival, 1983; *works include:* Baron Ramsey of Canterbury, 1974; King Olav of Norway, 1975; Prince Philip, Duke of Edinburgh, Earl Mountbatten of Burma, Golda Meir, 1976; Maurice Bowra, 1979; Charlie Chaplin (Leicester Square), Lord Olivier, Mary and Child Christ, 1981; Caduceus (Harvard, Mass), Lord Feather (TUC Congress House), Isambard Kingdom Brunel (two works), Charlie Chaplin (Vevey), 1982; Beatles (Liverpool), Dylan Thomas, 1984; Royal Marines Commando Meml, Lympstone, Devon, 1986; Sherlock Holmes (Meiringen), 1991; Graham Gooch (Chelmsford), 1992; Dorothy L. Sayers (Witham), J. B. Pflug (Biberach), 1994, *works in public collections:* Ashmolean Mus., British Mus., Herbert F. Johnson Mus., USA, Tate Gall., V & A, Nat. Mus. of Wales. *Recreation:* enthusiasm for the unnecessary. *Address:* Goat Lodge, Goat Lodge Road, Great Totham, Maldon, Essex CM9 8BX. *T:* Maldon (01621) 891329.

DOUCE, Prof. John Leonard, FEng 1991; FIEE; Professor of Electrical Science, Warwick University, 1965–94 (part-time 1989–94), now Emeritus; *b* 15 Aug. 1932; *s* of John William and Florrie Douce; *m* 1959, Jean Shanks; one *s* one *d*. *Educ:* Manchester Grammar Sch.; Manchester Univ. (BSc, MSc, PhD, DSc). SMIEEE. Lectr, Sen. Lectr, Reader, Queen's Univ., Belfast, 1958–65. Member: Technology Sub-Cttee, UGC, 1980–89; Engrg Bd, 1987–91, Science Bd, 1989–91, SERC; Contract Assessor, HEFCE, 1993–94. Sir Harold Hartley Silver Medal, Inst. of Measurement and Control, 1989. *Publications:* Introduction to Mathematics of Servomechanisms, 1963, 2nd edn 1972; papers on control engineering. *Recreations:* bridge, boating, home-brewing. *Address:* 259 Station Road, Balsall Common, Coventry CV7 7EG. *T:* Berkswell (01676) 532070.

DOUEK, Ellis Elliot, FRCS; Consultant Otologist since 1970, and Chairman, Hearing Research Group, since 1974, Guy's Hospital; *b* 25 April 1934; *s* of Cesar Douek and Nelly Sassoon; *m* 1993, Gill Green; two *s* by former marriage. *Educ:* English School, Cairo; Westminster Medical School. MRCS, LRCP 1958; FRCS 1967. House appts, St Helier Hosp., 1959, and Whittington Hosp., 1963; nat. service, RAMC, 1960–62; ENT Registrar, Royal Free Hosp., 1966; Sen. Registrar, King's College Hosp., 1968. Mem., MRC working party on Hearing Research, 1975; MRC Rep. to Europ. Communities on Hearing Res., 1980; UK Rep. to Europ. Communities on Indust. Deafness, 1983; Mem., Scientific Cttee, Inst. de Recherche sur la surdité, Paris, 1989–. Dalby Prize for hearing research, RSM, 1978. *Publications:* Sense of Smell—Its Abnormalities, 1974; Eighth Nerve, in Peripheral Neuropathy, 1975; Olfaction, in Scientific Basis of Otolaryngology, 1976; Cochlear Implant, in Textbook of ENT, 1980; papers on hearing and smell. *Recreations:* drawing and painting; studying history. *Address:* (home) 24 Reynolds Close, NW11 7EA. *T:* 0181–455 6427; 97 Harley Street, W1N 1DF. *T:* 0171–935 7828. *Club:* Athenæum.

DOUGAL, Malcolm Gordon; HM Diplomatic Service; HM Consul General, San Francisco, since 1994; *b* 20 Jan. 1938; *s* of Eric Gordon Dougal and Marie (*née* Wildermuth); *m* 1964, Elke (*née* Urban); one *s*. *Educ:* Ampleforth Coll., Yorkshire; The Queen's Coll., Oxford (MA Mod. History). National Service in Korea and Gibraltar with Royal Sussex Regt, 1956–58; Oxford, 1958–61; Contracts Asst, De Havilland Aircraft, Hatfield, 1961–64; Asst to Export Manager, Ticket Equipment Ltd (Plessey), 1964–66; Export Manager, Harris Lebus Ltd, 1967–69; entered HM Diplomatic Service, 1969; Foreign Office, 1969–72; 1st Secretary (Commercial): Paris, 1972–76; Cairo, 1976–79; Foreign Office, 1979–81; Consul Gen., Lille, 1981–85; Dep. High Comr and Head of Chancery, Canberra, 1986–89; RCDS, 1990; Dir, Jt FCO/DTI Directorate of Overseas Trade Services, FCO, 1991–94. *Publication:* (contrib.) The Third Battle of Ypres (Seaford House Papers), 1990. *Recreations:* natural history, walking, books, sport, wine. *Address:* c/o Foreign and Commonwealth Office, Whitehall, SW1A 2AH.

DOUGAN, (Alexander) Derek; company director and marketing consultant; *b* 20 Jan. 1938; *s* of John and Josephine Dougan; *m* 1963, Jutta Maria; two *s*. *Educ:* Mersey Street primary sch., Belfast; Belfast Technical High School. Professional footballer with: Distillery, NI, 1953–57; Portsmouth, 1957–59; Blackburn Rovers, 1959–61; Aston Villa, 1961–63; Peterborough, 1963–65; Leicester, 1965–67; Wolverhampton Wanderers, 1967–75. Represented N Ireland at all levels, from schoolboy to full international, more than 50 times. Chm., PFA, 1970–78. Chief Exec., Kettering Town FC, 1975–77; Chm. and Chief Exec., Wolverhampton Wanderers' FC, 1982–85. Sports Presenter, Yorkshire Television. Mem. Council, Co-Operation North, 1987–. *Publications:* Attack! (autobiog.), 1969; The Sash He Never Wore (autobiog.), 1972; The Footballer (novel), 1974; On the Spot (football as a profession), 1974; Doog (autobiog.), 1980; How Not to Run Football, 1981; (with Patrick Murphy) Matches of the Day 1958–83, 1984. *Recreations:* watching football, playing squash. *Address:* Bayern House, 40 Keepers Lane, Codsall, Wolverhampton, West Midlands WV8 2DP.

DOUGAN, Dr David John; Arts Development Officer, Essex County Council, since 1989; *b* 26 Sept, 1936; *s* of William John Dougan and Blanche May; *m* 1st, 1959, Eileen Ludbrook (marr. diss. 1985); one *s*; 2nd, 1986, Barbara Taylor; one *s* one *d*. *Educ:* Durham Univ. (BA, MA); City Univ. (PhD). Reporter, Tyne Tees Television, 1963; presenter, BBC, 1966; Director, Northern Arts, 1970; Dir, Crafts Council, 1984–88. Chm., Nat. Youth Dance Trust, 1985–91. *Publications:* History of North East Shipbuilding, 1966; Great Gunmaker, 1968; Shipwrights Trade Union, 1971. *Recreations:* theatre, crafts, running. *Address:* Grovelands, 1 Grove Road, Bury St Edmunds, Suffolk IP33 3BE. *T:* Bury St Edmunds (01284) 752588.

DOUGHERTY, Maj.-Gen. Sir Ivan Noel, Kt 1968; CBE 1946; DSO 1941 (bar, 1943); ED; *b* Leadville, NSW, 6 April 1907; *m* 1936, Emily Phyllis Lofts; two *s* two *d* (and one *d* decd). *Educ:* Leadville Primary Sch.; Mudgee High Sch.; Sydney Teachers' Coll.; Sydney Univ. (BEc). NSW Education Dept: Asst Teacher, 1928–32; Dep. Headmaster, 1933–39; Headmaster, 1946–47; Dist Inspector of Schs, 1948–53; Staff Inspector 1953–55. Commissioned Sydney Univ. Regt, 1927. Capt. 1931; Unattached List, 1932–34; transf. to 33/41 Bn. 1934; Major, 1938; Command, 33rd Bn, 1938; Lieut-Col 1939. Served War of 1939–45 (DSO and Bar, CBE, despatches thrice); Australian Imperial Force, Second-in-Command, 2/2 Inf. Bn, 1939–40; Commanded 2/4 inf. Bn (Libya, Greece, Crete campaigns), 1940–42; Brig. 1942; commanded 23 Bde, 1942; commanded 21 Bde, South-West Pacific, 1942–45; R of O, 1946–47; commanded 8th Bde, Austr. Mil. Forces, 1948–52; Maj.-Gen., 1952; commanded 2nd Div., 1952–54; Citizen Military Forces Member, Australian Mil. Bd, 1954–57; R of O, 1957–64; Retired List, 1964. Hon. ADC to Governor-Gen. of Australia, 1949–52; Hon. Col, Australian Cadet Corps, Eastern Command, 1964–70; Representative Hon. Col, Australian Cadet Corps, 1967–70. Dir of Civil Defence for NSW, 1955–73. Mem. Council, Nat. Roads and Motorists' Assoc., 1969–79. Mem. Senate, 1954–74, Dep. Chancellor, 1958–66, Hon. LLD 1976, Univ. of Sydney. *Address:* 4 Leumeah Street, Cronulla, NSW 2230, Australia. *T:* (2) 5235465.

DOUGHTY, George Henry; General Secretary, Technical and Supervisory Section, Amalgamated Union of Engineering Workers, 1971–74, retired; Member, Central Arbitration Committee, 1976–85; *b* 17 May 1911; British; *m* 1941, Mildred Dawson; two *s*. *Educ:* Handsworth Tech. Sch.; Aston Technical Coll. Draughtsman; trained at General Electric Co., Birmingham, 1927–32; employed as Design Draughtsman: English Electric, Stafford 1932–33; GEC Birmingham, 1934–46. With Draughtsmen's & Allied Technician's Assoc., 1946–71, General Secretary, 1952–71. Member: Gen. Council of TUC, 1968–74; Independent Review Cttee, 1976–89; Chm., EDC for Electrical Engrg, 1974–82. Mem., Royal Commn on Distribution of Income and Wealth, 1974–78. Industrial Relns Advr, SIAD, 1977–88. *Publications:* various technical and Trade Union publications. *Recreation:* photography.

DOUGHTY, Sir William (Roland), Kt 1990; Chairman, North West Thames Regional Health Authority, 1984–94; Deputy Chairman, Britannia Refined Metals Ltd, since 1982 (Director, since 1978); *b* 18 July 1925; *s* of Roland Gill Doughty and Gladys Maud Doughty (*née* Peto); *m* 1952, Patricia Lorna Cooke; three *s*. *Educ:* Headstone Sch.; Acton Technical Coll.; Trinity Coll., Dublin (MA); Harvard Business Sch. (AMP). Metal Box Co. Ltd, 1953–66; Molins Ltd, 1966–69, Dir, 1967; Cape Industries, 1969–84, Dir, 1972, Man. Dir, 1980–84. Member: SE Economic Planning Council, 1966–79 (Chm., Industry and Employment Cttee, 1972–79); CBI Council, 1975–86 (Chm., London Region, 1981–83). Founder and Chm., Assoc. for Conservation of Energy, 1981–85, Pres., 1985–. Governor: SE Tech. Coll., 1967–69; Gt Ormond St Hosp. for Sick Children, 1978–90; Mem., Gen. Council, King Edward VII's Hosp. Fund for London, 1984– (Mem., Management Cttee, 1987–95); Chairman: King's Fund Centre Cttee, 1991–95; Adv. Cttee on Distinction Awards, 1994–. LHSM 1986. CIMgt; FRSA. *Recreations:* cricket, theatre, golf, horse racing. *Clubs:* Savile, MCC, Middlesex County Cricket; Kildare Street and University (Dublin).

DOUGILL, John Wilson, FEng 1990; FICE; FIStructE; FASCE; Chief Executive and Secretary, Institution of Structural Engineers, since 1994 (Director of Engineering, 1987–94); *b* 18 Nov. 1934; *s* of William John Dougill and Emily Firmstone Wilson; *m* 1959, Daphne Maude Weeks; one *s* one *d*. *Educ:* Trinity Sch. of John Whitgift, Croydon; King's Coll., London; Imperial Coll. of Science and Technology. MScEng, DIC, PhD. Engineer with George Wimpey, 1956–58 and 1960–61; Research Asst to Prof. A. L. L. Baker, Imperial Coll., 1961–64; King's College London: Lectr in Civil Engrg, 1964–73; Reader in Engrg Science, 1973–76; Prof. of Engrg Science, 1976–81; Prof. of Concrete Structures and Technology, Imperial Coll., 1981–87. Vis. Res. Engineer, Univ. of California, Berkeley, 1967–68; Vis. Prof., Dept of Civil Engrg, Imperial Coll., 1991–. Chm., SERC Civil Engrg Sub-Cttee, 1982–83; Mem., NEDO Res. Strategy Cttee, 1983–85. Sec. Gen., Fedn Internat. de la Precontrainte, 1992–. Mem. Court of Governors, Whitgift Foundn, 1981–. *Publications:* papers in jls of engrg mech., materials and struct. engrg. *Recreations:* coarse gardening, travel, good food, walking. *Address:* Ashcroft, Larch Close, The Glade, Kingswood, Surrey KT20 6JF. *T:* Mogador (01737) 833283.

DOUGLAS, family name of **Viscount Chilston, Earl of Morton,** and **Marquess of Queensberry.**

DOUGLAS AND CLYDESDALE, Marquess of; Alexander Douglas-Hamilton; *b* 31 March 1978; *s* and *heir* of Duke of Hamilton, *qv*.

DOUGLAS, Prof. Alexander Stuart; Regius Professor of Medicine, University of Aberdeen, 1970–85, now Emeritus; Senior Research Fellow, Department of Medicine, Aberdeen Royal Infirmary, since 1992; *b* 2 Oct. 1921; *s* of late Dr R. Douglas, MOH for Moray and Nairn; *m* 1954, Christine McClymont Stewart; one *s* one *d*. *Educ:* Elgin Academy, Morayshire. Mil. Service, RAMC, 1945–48 (despatches 1947). Research Fellow, Radcliffe Infirmary, Oxford, and Postgrad. Med. Sch., London, 1951–53; Lectr, Sen. Lectr and Reader in Medicine, Univ. Dept of Med., Royal Infirmary, Glasgow, 1953–64; Hon. Consultant status, 1957; Prof. of Med., Univ. of Glasgow, 1964–70; secondment to Univ. of East Africa with hon. academic rank of Prof., 1965; Hon. Consultant Physician in Administrative Charge of wards, Royal Infirmary, Glasgow, 1968–70. Leverhulme Sen. Res. Fellow, 1990–92. *Publications:* scientific papers on haemostasis and thrombosis and seasonal variation in health and disease. *Recreations:* curling, travel. *Address:* University Department of Medicine, Aberdeen Royal Infirmary, Foresterhill, Aberdeen AB9 2ZD. *T:* Aberdeen (01224) 681818 (ext. 53014).

DOUGLAS, Barry; concert pianist; *b* 23 April 1960; *m* Deirdre O'Hara; one *d*. *Educ:* Royal College of Music; private study with Maria Curcio. ARCM, LRAM. Gold Medal, Tchaikovsky International Piano Competition, Moscow, 1986; Berlin Philharmonic début, 1987; engagements incl. regular appearances in major European, US and Far East cities. Recordings incl. Tchaikovsky's Concerto No 1 and Sonata in G, Mussorgsky's Pictures at an Exhibition, Brahms' Piano Quintet in F minor and Piano Concerto No 1, Liszt Concertos Nos 1 and 2, Beethoven Sonata Op 106, Prokofiev Sonatas 2 and 7, Rachmaninov Concerto No 2. Vis. Fellow, Oriel Coll., Oxford, 1992–93. Hon. DMus QUB, 1986. *Recreations:* driving, reading, food and wine. *Address:* c/o Terry Harrison Artists Management, The Orchard, Market Street, Charlbury, Oxon OX7 3PJ.

DOUGLAS, Prof. Charles Primrose, FRCOG; Professor of Obstetrics and Gynæcology, University of Cambridge, 1976–88, now Emeritus; Fellow, Emmanuel College, Cambridge, 1979–88; *b* 17 Feb. 1921; *s* of Dr C. Douglas, Ayr, Scotland; *m* 1948, Angela Francis; three *s* one *d*. *Educ:* Loretto Sch.; Peterhouse; Edinburgh Univ. Surg. Lieut RNVR, 1944–47. Registrar and Sen. Registrar, Victoria Infirmary, Glasgow, 1950–59; William Waldorf Astor Foundn Fellow, 1957; Visiting Fellow, Duke Univ., NC, 1957; Sen. Lectr, Univ. of the West Indies, 1959–65; Prof. of Obst. and Gyn., Royal Free Hosp. Sch. of Medicine, 1965–76. Member: Bd of Governors, Royal Free Hosp., 1972–74; Camden and Islington AHA, 1974–76, Cambridge AHA, 1981–82; Cambridge DHA, 1983–88. Mem., Council, RCOG, 1980–86. Hon. FACOG, 1983. *Publications:* contribs to BMJ, Amer. Heart Jl, Jl of Obst. and Gynæc. of Brit. Commonwealth, etc. *Recreations:* travel, art. *Address:* Old Mill House, Linton Road, Balsham, Cambs CB1 6HA. *Club:* Royal Over-Seas League.

DOUGLAS, Sir (Edward) Sholto, Kt 1977; Solicitor of the Supreme Court of Queensland, since 1934; *b* 23 Dec. 1909; *s* of Hon. Mr Justice E. A. Douglas and Annette Eileen Power; *m* 1939, Mary Constance Curr. *Educ:* St Ignatius Coll., Riverview, Sydney. Queensland Law Society Incorporated: Mem. Council, 1954–76; Actg Pres., 1960; Pres., 1962–64; Mem., Statutory Cttee, 1976–81; Member: Legal Assistance Cttee, Qld, 1965–80; Solicitors' Bd, 1969–75; Exec. Mem., Law Council of Aust., 1973–75. President: Taxpayers Assoc. of Qld, 1955–58; Federated Taxpayers of Aust., 1957–58; Mem. Adv. Cttee, Terminating and Permanent Building Socs, 1966–77. Pres., Qld Div., Nat. Heart Foundn, 1976–77 (Vice-Pres., 1966–75); Vice-Pres., RSPCA, 1965–86; Chm., Management Cttee, Currumbin Bird Sanctuary and Wildlife Reserve, 1978–80. *Recreations:* racing, gardening. *Address:* 81 Markwell Street, Hamilton, Brisbane, Qld 4007, Australia. *T:* (7) 32682759. *Clubs:* Queensland, Brisbane (Pres. 1965), Tattersalls, Royal Queensland Golf, Queensland Turf, Tattersalls Racing, Brisbane Amateur Turf (all Brisbane).

DOUGLAS, Gavin Stuart, RD 1970; QC (Scot.) 1971; *b* 12 June 1932; *y s* of late Gilbert Georgeson Douglas and Rosena Campbell Douglas. *Educ:* South Morningside Sch.; George Heriot's Sch.; Edinburgh Univ. MA 1953, LLB 1955. Qual. as Solicitor, 1955; nat. service with RN, 1955–57. Admitted to Faculty of Advocates, 1958; Sub-editor (part-time), The Scotsman, 1957–61; Mem. Lord Advocate's Dept in London (as Parly Draftsman), 1961–64; returned to practice at Scots Bar, 1964; Junior Counsel to BoT, 1965–71; Counsel to Scottish Law Commn, 1965–; Hon. Sheriff in various sheriffdoms, 1965–71; a Chm. of Industrial Tribunals, 1966–78; Counsel to Sec. of State for Scotland under Private Legislation Procedure (Scotland) Act 1936, 1969–75, Sen. Counsel under that Act, 1975–; Temporary Sheriff, 1990–. Mem., Lothian Health Bd, 1981–85. Mem. Bd, Leith Nautical Coll., 1981–84. Editor, Session Cases, 7 vols, 1976–82. *Recreations:* golf, ski-ing. *Address:* Parliament House, Parliament Square, Edinburgh EH1 1RF. *Clubs:* Army and Navy; University Staff (Edinburgh); Rolls-Royce Enthusiasts'; Hon. Company of Edinburgh Golfers (Muirfield).

DOUGLAS, Henry Russell, FJI; Media law consultant; Legal Manager, News Group Newspapers, 1976–89; *b* Bishopbriggs, Lanarkshire, 11 Feb. 1925; 2nd *s* of late Russell Douglas and Jeanie Douglas Douglas (*née* Drysdale); *m* 1951, Elizabeth Mary, *d* of late Ralph Nowell, CB; two *s* three *d*. *Educ:* various Scottish and English Grammar Schools; Lincoln Coll., Oxford (MA Hons). Served RNVR, 1943–46 (Sub-Lt, submarines). Merchant Navy, 1946–47; Oxford Univ., 1947–50; Liverpool Daily Post, 1950–69; The Sun, 1969–76. Inst of Journalists, 1956: Fellow, 1969; Pres., 1972–73; Chm. of Executive, 1973–76; Member: Press Council, 1972–80; Council, Newspaper Press Fund, 1972–76, 1986– (Chm., 1990–91); Founder Mem., Media Society, 1973 (Treas., 1973–86, Vice-Pres., 1987–89); Founder, Soc. of Fleet Street Lawyers, 1989. *Recreations:* chess, travel, history. *Address:* Austen Croft, 31 Austen Road, Guildford, Surrey GU1 3NP. *T:* Guildford (01483) 576960.

DOUGLAS, James Murray, CBE 1985; Director-General, Country Landowners' Association, 1970–90; *b* 26 Sept. 1925; *s* of Herbert and Amy Douglas, Brechin; *m* 1950, Julie Kemmner; one *s* one *d*. *Educ:* Morrison's Acad., Crieff; Aberdeen Univ.; Balliol Coll., Oxford. Entered Civil Service, 1950; Treasury, 1960–63; Asst Sec., Min. of Housing and Local Govt, 1964; Sec. to Royal Commn on Local Govt, 1966–69. Dir, Booker Countryside, 1990–93; Public Affairs Consultant, John Kendall Associates, 1990–93. Vice-Pres., Confedn of European Agriculture, 1971–88 (Chm., Environment Cttee, 1988–90); Mem., Econ. Develt Cttee for Agriculture, 1972–90; Sec., European Landowning Orgns

Gp, 1972–87. Mem., Council, CBI, 1986–89. *Publications:* various articles on local govt planning, agriculture and landowning. *Address:* 1 Oldfield Close, Bickley, Kent BR1 2LL. *T:* 0181–467 3213. *Club:* United Oxford & Cambridge University.

DOUGLAS, Kenneth, CBE 1991; CEng; Managing Director, Austin and Pickersgill Ltd, 1958–69, and 1979–83; Chairman, Kenton Shipping Services, Darlington, 1968–83; *b* 28 Oct. 1920; British; *m* 1942, Doris Lewer; one *s* two *d. Educ:* Sunderland Technical Coll. (Dip. Naval Architecture). CEng. Dep. Shipyard Manager, Vickers Armstrong Naval Yard, Newcastle-upon-Tyne, 1946–53; Dir and Gen. Manager, Wm Gray & Co. Ltd, West Hartlepool, 1954–58; Man. Dir, Upper Clyde Shipbuilders Ltd, Chm., Simons Lobnitz Ltd and Chm., UCS Trng Co., 1969–73; Dep. Chm., Govan Shipbuilders, 1971–73; Chm., Douglas (Kilbride) Ltd, 1972–77; Chm. and Man. Dir, Steel Structures Ltd, 1974–76; Shiprepair Marketing Dir, British Shipbuilders, 1978–79; Mem. Bd, PCEF, 1988–91. Mem., Tyne and Wear Residuary Body, DoE, 1985–89. Hon. Fellow, Sunderland Univ., 1993 (Fellow, 1980 and 1992–93, Chm. of Govs, 1982–93, Sunderland Poly., subseq. Univ.). Formerly: FRINA, MBIM, MInstD. *Recreations:* fishing, golf. *Address:* 60 Durham Road, Sunderland, Tyne and Wear SR3 3LZ. *Clubs:* Sunderland, Ashbrooke Cricket and Rugby Football (Sunderland).

DOUGLAS, Margaret Elizabeth, OBE 1994; Supervisor of Parliamentary Broadcasting, since 1993; *b* 22 Aug. 1934; *d* of Thomas Mincher Douglas and Dorothy Jones. *Educ:* Parliament Hill Grammar Sch., London. Joined BBC as sec., 1951; subseq. researcher, dir and producer in Current Affairs television, working on Panorama, Gallery, 24 Hours and on special progs with Lord Avon and Lord Stockton; Editor, Party Conf. coverage, 1972–83; Chief Asst to Dir-Gen., 1983–87; Chief Political Advr, BBC, 1987–93. *Recreations:* watching politics and football. *Address:* House of Commons, SW1A 0AA.

DOUGLAS, Prof. (Margaret) Mary, CBE 1992; FBA 1989; Avalon Foundation Professor in the Humanities, Northwestern University, 1981–85, Professor Emeritus, since 1985; *b* 25 March 1921; *d* of Gilbert Charles Tew and Phyllis Twomey; *m* 1951, James A. T. Douglas, OBE; two *s* one *d. Educ:* Sacred Heart Convent, Roehampton; St Anne's Coll., Oxford (MA, BSc, DPhil; Hon. Fellow, 1992). Returned to Oxford, 1946, to train as anthropologist; fieldwork in Belgian Congo, 1949–50, 1953 and 1987; Lectr in Anthropology, Univ. of Oxford, 1950; Univ. of London, 1951–78, Prof. of Social Anthropology, UCL, 1970–78. Res. Scholar, Russell Sage Foundn, NY, 1977–81; Vis. Prof., Princeton Univ., 1986–88. Gifford Lectr, Univ. of Edinburgh, 1989. Mem., Academia Europaea, 1988. Hon. Fellow, UCL, 1994. Hon. Dr of Philosophy, Univ. of Uppsala, 1986; Hon. LLD Univ. of Notre Dame, 1988; Hon. DLitt: UEA, Jewish Theol Soc. of America, 1992; Hon. Dr Essex, 1992. *Publications:* The Lele of the Kasai, 1963; Purity and Danger, 1966; Natural Symbols, 1970; Implicit Meanings, 1975; (with Baron Isherwood) The World of Goods: towards an anthropology of consumption, 1979; Evans-Pritchard, 1980; (with Aaron Wildavsky) Risk and Culture, 1982; In the Active Voice, 1982; Risk Acceptability, 1986; How Institutions Think, 1986; Risk and Blame, 1992; In the Wilderness, 1993. *Address:* 22 Hillway, Highgate, N6 6QA. *Club:* United Oxford & Cambridge University.

DOUGLAS, Richard Giles; *b* 4 Jan. 1932; *m* 1954, Jean Gray, *d* of Andrew Arnott; two *d. Educ:* Co-operative College, Stanford Hall, Loughborough; Univ. of Strathclyde; LSE. Engineer (Marine). Tutor organiser in Adult Educn, Co-operative movement, 1957; Sectional Educn Officer, Scotland, 1958–61; Lectr in Economics, Dundee Coll. of Technol., 1964–70. Contested (Lab): South Angus, 1964, Edinburgh West, 1966, Glasgow Pollok, March 1967; (Lab and Co-op) Clackmannan and E Stirlingshire, Oct. 1974; MP (Lab and Co-op) Clackmannan and E Stirlingshire, 1970–Feb. 1974; MP Dunfermline, 1979–83, Dunfermline West, 1983–92 (Lab and Co-op, 1979–90, SNP, 1990–92); contested (SNP) Glasgow, Garscadden, 1992. Contested (SNP) Scotland Mid and Fife, Euro. Parly elecns, 1994. Hon. Lectr, Strathclyde, 1980–. *Address:* Braehead House, High Street, Auchtermuchty, Fife KY14 7AR.

DOUGLAS, Sir Robert (McCallum), Kt 1976; OBE 1956; President, Tilbury Douglas PLC, since 1991 (Director, 1930–88, Chairman, 1952–77, President, 1980–91, Robert M. Douglas Holdings); *b* 2 Feb. 1899; *s* of John Douglas and Eugenia McCallum; *m* 1927, Millicent Irene Tomkys Morgan (*d* 1980); one *s* one *d. Educ:* Terregles Sch.; Dumfries Academy. Served Army, 1916–19. Served 10 years with civil engineering contracting co., 1920–30; founded Douglas Group of Companies, 1930. Mem., MPBW Midland Regional Jt Adv. Cttee, 1940–46. Federation of Civil Engineering Contractors: Chm., Midland Section, 1942–43 and 1947–48; Chm. Council, 1948–49; Pres., 1958–60. Patron, Staffs Agric. Soc.; Pres., Burton Graduate Med. Centre, 1988–. Hon. DSc Aston, 1977. *Recreation:* farming. *Address:* Dunstall Hall, Barton-under-Needwood, Burton-on-Trent, Staffordshire DE13 8BE. *T:* Barton-under-Needwood (01283) 712471. *Club:* Caledonian.

DOUGLAS, Hon. Sir Roger (Owen), Kt 1991; Director, Brierley Investments Ltd, since 1990; *b* 5 Dec. 1937; *s* of Norman and Jenny Douglas; *m* 1961, Glennis June Anderson; one *s* one *d. Educ:* Auckland Grammar Sch.; Auckland Univ. (Accountancy Degree). Company Sec. and Acct. MP (Lab) Manurewa, 1969–90; Cabinet Minister, NZ, 1972–75; Minister in Charge of Inland Revenue Dept and Minister in Charge of Friendly Societies, 1984; Minister of Finance, 1984–88; Minister of Immigration and Minister of Police, 1989–90. *Publications:* There's Got to be a Better Way, 1981; papers on NZ economy: An Alternative Budget, 1980; Proposal for Taxation, 1981; Toward Prosperity, 1987; Unfinished Business, 1993. *Recreations:* cricket, rugby, reading. *Address:* 411 Redoubt Road, Papatoetoe RD1, Auckland, New Zealand. *T:* (9) 2639596.

DOUGLAS, Prof. Ronald Walter, DSc, FInstP, FSGT; Professor of Glass Technology, University of Sheffield, 1955–75; *b* 28 March 1910; *s* of John H. P. and A. E. Douglas; *m* 1933, Edna Maud Cadle; two *s. Educ:* Latymer Upper Sch.; Sir John Cass Coll., London. Mem., Research Staff, Research Laboratories of General Electric Company, 1927–55. Pres., Internat. Commn on Glass, 1972–75. *Publications:* (with S. Frank) A History of Glassmaking, 1972; many papers on the physics of glass and semiconductors. *Address:* Otter Close, Perrys Gardens, West Hill, Ottery St Mary, Devon EX11 1XA.

DOUGLAS, Sir Sholto; *see* Douglas, Sir E. S.

DOUGLAS, Prof. Thomas Alexander; Professor of Veterinary Biochemistry and Head of Department of Veterinary Biochemistry (Clinical), University of Glasgow, 1977–90; *b* 9 Aug. 1926; *s* of Alexander and Mary Douglas; *m* 1957, Rachel Ishbel McDonald; two *s. Educ:* Battlefield Public Sch.; High Sch. of Glasgow; Glasgow Vet. Coll., Univ. of Glasgow (BSc; Animal Health Schol., 1950–54; PhD). MRCVS. General Veterinary Practice: Ulverston, 1948–49; Lanark, 1949–50; University of Glasgow: Asst Lectr, Biochemistry, 1954–57; Lectr 1957–71, Sen. Lectr 1971–77, in Vet. Biochem., Vet. Sch.; Dean of Faculty of Vet. Medicine, 1982–85. Mem. Council, RCVS, 1982–85. Mem., UGC, 1986–89 (Chm., Agriculture and Veterinary Studies Sub-Cttee, 1986–89). *Publications:* sci. articles in vet. and biochem. jls. *Recreations:* golf, hill walking. *Address:* 77 South Mains Road, Milngavie, Glasgow G62 6DE. *T:* 0141–956 2751.

DOUGLAS, Rt. Hon. Sir William (Randolph), KCMG 1983; Kt 1969; PC 1977; High Commissioner for Barbados in London, 1991–93; *b* Barbados, 24 Sept. 1921; *e s* of William P. Douglas and Emily Frances Douglas (*née* Nurse); *m* 1951, Thelma Ruth (*née* Gilkes) (*d* 1992); one *s* one *d. Educ:* Bannatyne Sch. and Verdun High Sch., Verdun, Que., Canada; McGill Univ. (BA, Hons); London Sch. of Economics (LLB). Private Practice at Barbados Bar, 1948–50; Dep. Registrar, Barbados, 1950; Resident Magistrate, Jamaica, 1955; Asst Attorney-Gen., Jamaica, 1959; Solicitor-Gen., Jamaica, 1962; Puisne Judge, Jamaica, 1962; Chief Justice of Barbados, 1965–86; Ambassador to USA, 1987–91. Chm., Commonwealth Caribbean Council of Legal Education, 1971–77; Mem., ILO Cttee of Experts on the Application of Conventions and Recommendations, 1975–; Dep. Judge, ILO Administrative Tribunal, 1982–. *Club:* Barbados Yacht.

DOUGLAS, Prof. William Wilton, MD; FRS 1983; Professor of Pharmacology, Yale University School of Medicine, New Haven, USA, 1968–94, now Professor Emeritus; *b* 15 Aug. 1922; *s* of Thomas Hall James Douglas and Catherine Dorward (*née* Wilton); *m* 1954, Jeannine Marie Henriette Dumoulin; two *s. Educ:* Glasgow Acad.; Univ. of Glasgow (MB, ChB 1946, MD 1949). Resident House Surgeon: Glasgow Western Infirm., 1946; Law Hosp., Carluke, 1947; Demonstr in Physiology, Univ. of Aberdeen, 1948; served RAMC, 1949–50: Chemical Defence Res. Estab., Porton Down, Wilts (Major); Mem. Staff, National Inst. for Med. Res., Mill Hill, 1950–56; Prof. of Pharmacol., Albert Einstein Coll. of Medicine, New York, 1956–68. *Publications:* papers on cellular mechanisms of secretion in Jl of Physiol., Brit. Jl of Pharmacol., Nature, and Science. *Recreations:* yachting, skiing. *Address:* 76 Blake Road, Hamden, CT 06517, USA. *T:* (203) 7761800.

DOUGLAS-HAMILTON, family name of **Duke of Hamilton and Brandon** and **Earl of Selkirk.**

DOUGLAS-HAMILTON, Lord James Alexander; MP (C) Edinburgh West since Oct. 1974; Minister of State for Home Affairs and Health, Scottish Office, since 1995; *b* 31 July 1942; 2nd *s* of 14th Duke of Hamilton, and *b* of 15th Duke of Hamilton, *qv*; *m* 1974, Hon. Priscilla Susan Buchan, *d* of Baron Tweedsmuir, *qv* and late Baroness Tweedsmuir of Belhelvie, PC; four *s* (incl. twins). *Educ:* Eton College; Balliol Coll., Oxford (MA, Mod. History; Oxford Boxing Blue, 1961; Pres., Oxford Univ. Cons. Assoc., 1963; Pres., Oxford Union Soc., 1964); Edinburgh Univ. (LLB, Scots Law). Advocate at Scots Bar, 1968. Town Councillor, Murrayfield-Cramond, Edinburgh, 1972. Scottish Conservative Whip, 1977; a Lord Comr of HM Treasury, and Govt Whip for Scottish Cons. Mems, 1979–81; PPS to Foreign Office Minister, 1983–86, to Sec. of State for Scotland, 1986–87; Parly Under-Sec. of State for Home Affairs and the Envmt, 1987–92, for Educn and Housing, 1992–95, Scottish Office. Captain Cameronian Co., 2 Bn Low Vols RARO, 1974–92. Hon. Pres., Scottish Amateur Boxing Assoc., 1975–; President: Royal Commonwealth Soc. in Scotland, 1979–87; Scottish Council, UNA, 1981–87. *Publications:* Motive for a Mission: The Story Behind Hess's Flight to Britain, 1971; The Air Battle for Malta: the diaries of a fighter pilot, 1981, 2nd edn 1990; Roof of the World: man's first flight over Everest, 1983; The Truth About Rudolf Hess, 1993. *Recreations:* golf, forestry. *Address:* House of Commons, SW1A 0AA. *Clubs:* New (Edinburgh); Hon. Company of Edinburgh Golfers.

DOUGLAS-HOME, family name of **Baroness Dacre** and **Baron Home of the Hirsel.**

DOUGLAS-HOME, Hon. David Alexander Cospatrick, CBE 1991; Chairman: Morgan Grenfell (Scotland), since 1986 (Director, since 1978); Morgan Grenfell International Ltd, since 1987; Director, Morgan Grenfell & Co. Ltd, since 1974; *b* 20 Nov. 1943; *o s* of Baron Home of the Hirsel, *qv*; *heir* to Earldom of Home; *m* 1972, Jane Margaret, *yr d* of Col J. Williams-Wynne, *qv*; one *s* two *d. Educ:* Eton College; Christ Church, Oxford (BA 1966). Chm., Morgan Grenfell Export Services, 1984–; Director: Morgan Grenfell Egyptian Finance Co. Ltd, 1975–77; Morgan Grenfell (Asia) Ltd, 1978–82 (Dep. Chm., 1979–82); Arab Bank Investment Co., 1979–87; Agricultural Mortgage Corp., 1979–93; Arab-British Chamber of Commerce, 1975–84; EFG (formerly Economic Forestry Group), 1981– (Chm., 1993–); Credit for Exports, 1984–; Morgan Grenfell (Hong Kong), 1989–; Morgan Grenfell Asia Holdings Pte Ltd, 1989–; Morgan Grenfell Thai Co., 1990–; Chm., Cegelec Controls Ltd, 1991–94; K & N Kenanga Sdn Bhd, 1993–; Grosvenor Estate Hldgs, 1993–; Trustee, Grosvenor Estate, 1993–. Chairman: Committee for Middle East Trade, 1986–92 (Mem., 1973–75). Governor: Ditchley Foundn, 1977–; Commonwealth Inst., 1988–. *Recreations:* outdoor sports. *Address:* 99 Dovehouse Street, SW3 6JZ. *T:* 0171–352 9060. *Club:* Turf.

DOUGLAS-MANN, Bruce Leslie Home; Solicitor, in practice since 1954; Senior Partner, Douglas-Mann & Co.; *b* 23 June 1927; *s* of late Leslie John Douglas-Mann, MC and Alice Home Douglas-Mann; *m* 1955, Helen Tucker; one *s* one *d. Educ:* Upper Canada Coll., Toronto; Jesus Coll., Oxford. Leading Seaman, RN, 1945–48; Oxford, 1948–51. Admitted solicitor, 1954. Contested (Lab): St Albans, 1964; Maldon, 1966; MP North Kensington, 1970–74, Merton, Mitcham and Morden, 1974–May 1982, resigned (Lab 1970–81, Ind 1981, SDP Jan.-May 1982); contested: Merton, Mitcham and Morden (SDP), June 1982; Mitcham and Morden (SDP), 1983 (SDP/Alliance), 1987. Chairman: PLP Housing and Construction Gp, 1974–79; PLP Environment Gp, 1979–81 (Vice-Chm., 1972–79); Parly Select Cttee on Environment, 1979–82. Member: SDP Council, 1984–88; Steering Cttee, Yes to Unity, 1987–88; Mem., England Co-ordinating Cttee, SLD, 1988–89; Chm., Hammersmith SLD, 1988–89. Vice-Pres., Soc. of Lab. Lawyers, 1980–81 (Chm., 1974–80). Mem., Kensington or Kensington and Chelsea Borough Council, 1962–68. Chairman: Arts Council Trust for Special Funds, 1981–; Common Voice, 1990–92; Bd Mem., Shelter, 1974– (Chm., 1990–93; Chm., Exec. Cttee, 1987–90). *Publications:* pamphlets: (ed) The End of the Private Landlord, 1973; Accidents at Work—Compensation for All, 1974. *Address:* 33 Furnival Street, EC4A 1JQ. *T:* 0171–405 7216.

DOUGLAS MILLER, Robert Alexander Gavin; Chairman and Managing Director, Jenners (Princes St Edinburgh) Ltd; Director: Kennington Leasing Ltd; Chamber Developments Ltd; Bain Clarkson Ltd; First Scottish American Investment Trust; Northern American Trust; *b* 11 Feb. 1937; *s* of F. G. Douglas Miller and Mora Kennedy; *m* 1963, Judith Madeleine Smith; three *s* one *d. Educ:* Harrow; Oxford Univ. (MA). 9th Lancers, 1955–57; Oxford, 1958–61. Treasurer, Queen's Body Guard for Scotland (Royal Company of Archers). Pres., Edinburgh Chamber of Commerce & Manufactures, 1985–87. Member, Council: Assoc. of Scottish Salmon Fishery Bds, 1984–; Atlantic Salmon Trust, 1989–; Chm., Game Conservancy (Scotland), 1990–. Chm., Outreach Trust, 1976–. *Recreations:* shooting, fishing. *Address:* Bavelaw Castle, Balerno, Midlothian EH14 7JS. *T:* 0131–449 3972. *Club:* New (Edinburgh).
See also Ian MacArthur.

DOUGLAS-PENNANT, family name of **Baron Penrhyn.**

DOUGLAS-SCOTT, Douglas Andrew Montagu; *see* Scott.

DOUGLAS-SCOTT-MONTAGU, family name of **Baron Montagu of Beaulieu.**

DOUGLAS-WILSON, Ian, MD; FRCPE; Editor of the Lancet, 1965–76; *b* 12 May 1912; *o s* of late Dr H. Douglas-Wilson; *m* 1939, Beatrice May, *e d* of late R. P. Bevan; one *s* two *d. Educ:* Marlborough Coll.; Edinburgh Univ. MB ChB 1936; MD (commended) Edinburgh 1938; FRCP Edinburgh 1945. Served with RAMC, 1940–45 (temp. Major). House-physician, Royal Infirmary, Edinburgh, 1937; joined the Lancet staff, 1946; Asst Ed., 1952–62; Dep. Ed., 1962–64. Corresp. Mem., Danish Soc. of Int. Med., 1965. Dr (*hc*) Edinburgh, 1974. *Address:* 10 Homan Court, Friern Watch Avenue, N12 9HW. *T:* 0181–446 9047.

DOUGLAS-WITHERS, Maj.-Gen. John Keppel Ingold, CBE 1969; MC 1943; *b* 11 Dec. 1919; *s* of late Lt-Col H. H. Douglas-Withers, OBE, MC, FSA, and late Mrs V. G. Douglas-Withers; *m* 1945, Sylvia Beatrice Dean, Croydon, Surrey; one *s* one *d*. *Educ:* Shrewsbury Sch.; Christ Church, Oxford. Diploma in French, Univ. of Poitiers, 1938; Associate of Inst. of Linguists, in French and German, 1939. Commissioned into RA, 1940; Service in UK, Iraq, Western Desert, N Africa and Italy, 1940–45. Instr in Gunnery, Sch. of Artillery, Larkhill, 1945–47; service in Canal Zone, 1948–49; attended Staff Coll., Camberley, 1950; Staff appt in WO (Mil. Ops), 1951–53; service in The King's Troop, RHA, 1954–55; Instr, Staff Coll., Camberley, 1956–58; Battery Comdr, G Bty, Mercers Troop, RHA, 1959–60; Staff appt in WO (Mil. Sec. Dept), 1961; commanded 49 Field Regt in BAOR and Hong Kong, 1962–64; student at IDC, 1965; Comd 6 Inf. Bde in BAOR, 1966–67; Chief of Staff, 1st Brit. Corps, 1968–69; GOC SW District, 1970–71; Asst Chief of Personnel and Logistics, MoD, 1972–74; retired 1974. Col Comdt, RA, 1974–82. Asst Dir and Gp Personnel Man., Jardine Matheson & Co. Ltd, Hong Kong, 1974–80; Consultant, Matheson & Co. Ltd, London, 1980–94. MPIM (Hong Kong), 1976. *Recreations:* history, military music, gardening. *Address:* Lloyds Bank, 25 High Street, Shipston-on-Stour, Warwickshire CV36 4AJ. *Clubs:* East India, Devonshire, Sports and Public Schools; MCC.

DOULTON, Alfred John Farre, CBE 1973 (OBE 1946); TD 1954; psc 1943; MA Oxon; Head of Statistical Team and Comptroller, Independent Schools Information Service, 1974–80, Consultant, 1980–81; *b* 9 July 1911; *s* of H. V. Doulton, Housemaster, Dulwich Coll., and Constance Jessie Farre, Dulwich; *m* 1940, Vera Daphne, *d* of A. R. Wheatley, Esher; four *s* one *d*. *Educ:* Dulwich Coll.; Brasenose Coll., Oxford (Classical Scholar). Asst Master, Uppingham School, 1934–40. Served War, 1940–46 (despatches twice); DAAG 11 Army Group, 1944; active service, Burma, Malaya, Java, 1945–46; DAQMG 4 Corps, AA&QMG 23 Indian Division, 1945–46. Burma Star, Far East and GS Medal with Java Clasp. Head of Classics and Housemaster of The Lodge, Uppingham Sch., 1946; Headmaster, Highgate Sch., 1955–74. Vice-Chm., HMC, 1967 (Hon. Treasurer, 1964–74). Alderman, Haringey, 1968–71 (Vice-Chm. Educn Cttee). Mem., Governing Bodies Assoc., 1977–80. Vice-Chm. and Chm. Finance Cttee, Kelly Coll., 1974–86; Trustee, Uppingham Sch., 1966–85. Mem., Indep. Schools Careers Orgn Council, 1978–81. *Publications:* The Fighting Cock, 1951; Highgate School 1938–1944: the story of a wartime evacuation, 1976. *Recreations:* music, cricket, books, dinghy sailing, ornithology. *Address:* Field Cottage, Beadon Lane, Salcombe, Devon TQ8 8JS. *T:* Salcombe (0154884) 2316. *Clubs:* Athenæum, MCC; Salcombe Yacht (Cdre, 1987–90).
See also *J. H. F. Doulton.*

DOULTON, John Hubert Farre; Principal, Elizabeth College, Guernsey, since 1988; *b* 2 Jan. 1942; *s* of Alfred John Farre, *qv*; *m* 1986, Margaret Anne (*née* Ball); two step *d*. *Educ:* Rugby School; Keble College, Oxford (1st Mods, 2nd Greats). Teacher: Rugby, 1965–66; Radley, 1966–88. *Recreations:*music, walking, boats, foreign travel, carpentry. *Address:* Brantwood, Forest Road, St Martin's, Guernsey. *T:* Guernsey (01481) 38995.

DOUNE, Lord; John Douglas Stuart; *b* 1966; *s* and *heir* of 20th Earl of Moray, *qv*. *Educ:* Loretto School, Musselburgh; University Coll. London (BA Hist. of Art). *Address:* Doune Park, Doune, Perthshire; Darnaway Castle, Forres, Moray.

DOURO, Marquess of; Arthur Charles Valerian Wellesley; Chairman: Framlington Group plc, since 1994; Deputy Chairman, Vendôme Luxury Group plc, since 1993; Director: Transatlantic Holdings PLC, since 1983; Global Asset Management Worldwide Inc., since 1984; Sun Life Corporation plc, since 1988; *b* 19 Aug. 1945; *s* and *heir* of 8th Duke of Wellington, *qv*; *m* 1977, Antonia von Preussen, *d* of late Prince Frederick of Prussia and Lady Brigid Ness; two *s* three *d*. *Educ:* Eton; Christ Church, Oxford. Chm., Deltec Securities (UK) Ltd, 1985–89; Deputy Chairman: Thames Valley Broadcasting, 1975–84; Deltec Panamerica SA, 1985–89; Guinness Mahon Hldgs, 1988–91; Director: Antofagasta and Bolivia Railway Co., 1977–80; Eucalyptus Pulp Mills, 1979–88; Continental and Industrial Trust plc, 1987–90; Rothmans International, 1990–93; Chm., Dunhill Holdings, 1991–93. MEP (C): Surrey, 1979–84, Surrey West, 1984–89; contested (C) Islington N, Oct. 1974; Mem., Basingstoke Borough Council, 1978–79. Kt Comdr, Order of Isabel the Catholic (Spain), 1986. *Heir:* *s* Earl of Mornington, *qv*. *Address:* Apsley House, Piccadilly, W1V 9FA; The Old Rectory, Stratfield Saye, Reading RG7 2DA.

DOVE, Arthur Allan, CEng, CStat; Chairman, Council for Registered Gas Installers; *b* 20 May 1933; *s* of William Joseph Dove and Lucy Frances Dove; *m* 1958, Nancy Iris Powell; two *s* one *d*. *Educ:* Taunton's Sch., Southampton; King's Coll. and London Sch. of Econs and Pol. Science, Univ. of London (BSc; AKC 1954). CEng, FIGasE 1974; MIS 1962. Asst Statistician, 1958, Marketing Officer, 1961, Southern Gas; Controller of Sales and Marketing, Scottish Gas, 1965; Commercial Sales Manager, Gas Council, 1969; Dep. Chm., South Eastern Gas, 1973; Regl Chm., British Gas plc, S Eastern, 1982–87, N Thames, 1988–91; Managing Director: Regions, 1991–92; Regl Services, 1992–93. *Recreation:* sailing. *Address:* 19 Sunning Avenue, Sunningdale, Berks SL5 9PN.

DOVER, Suffragan Bishop of, since 1992; **Rt. Rev. John Richard Allan Llewellin;** *b* 30 Sept. 1938; *s* of John Clarence Llewellin and Margaret Gwenllian Llewellin; *m* 1965; Jennifer Sally (*née* House); one *s* two *d*. *Educ:* Clifton College, Bristol; Westcott House and Fitzwilliam Coll., Cambridge (MA). Solicitor, 1960. Ordained deacon, 1964; priest, 1965; Curate at Radlett, Herts, 1964–68; Curate at Johannesburg Cathedral, 1968–71; Vicar of Waltham Cross, 1971–79; Rector of Harpenden, 1979–85; Suffragan Bishop of St Germans, 1985–92. Chm., USPG, 1994–. *Recreations:* sailing, DIY. *Address:* Upway, 52 St Martin's Hill, Canterbury, Kent CT1 1PR. *T:* Canterbury (01227) 464537.

DOVER, Den; MP (C) Chorley, since 1979; *b* 4 April 1938; *s* of Albert and Emmie Dover; *m* 1st, 1959, Anne Marina Wright (marr. diss. 1986); one *s* one *d*; 2nd, 1989, Kathleen Edna Fisher. *Educ:* Manchester Grammar Sch.; Manchester Univ. BSc Hons. CEng, MICE. John Laing & Son Ltd, 1959–68; National Building Agency: Dep. Chief Executive, 1969–70; Chief Exec., 1971–72; Projects Dir, Capital and Counties Property Co. Ltd, 1972–75; Contracts Manager, Wimpey Laing Iran, 1975–77. Director of Housing Construction, GLC, 1977–79. Member, London Borough of Barnet Council, 1968–71. Mem., Commons Select Cttee on Transport, 1979–87. *Recreations:* cricket, hockey, golf; Methodist. *Address:* 166 Furzehill Road, Boreham Wood, Herts WD6 2DS. *T:* 0181–953 5945; 30 Countess Way, Euxton, Chorley, Lancs PR7 6PT.

DOVER, Sir Kenneth James, Kt 1977; DLitt; FRSE 1975; FBA 1966; Chancellor, University of St Andrews, since 1981; *b* 11 March 1920; *o s* of P. H. J. Dover, London, Civil Servant; *m* 1947, Audrey Ruth Latimer; one *s* one *d*. *Educ:* St Paul's Sch. (Scholar); Balliol Coll., Oxford (Domus Scholar); Gaisford Prize, 1939; 1st in Classical Hon. Mods., 1940; Ireland Scholar, 1946; Cromer Prize (British Academy), 1946; 1st in Lit. Hum., Derby Scholar, Amy Mary Preston Read Scholar, 1947; Harmsworth Sen. Scholar, Merton Coll., 1947 (Hon. Fellow, 1980); DLitt Oxon 1974. Served War of 1939–45: Army (RA), 1940–45; Western Desert, 1941–43, Italy, 1943–45 (despatches). Fellow and Tutor, Balliol Coll., 1948–55 (Hon. Fellow, 1977); Prof. of Greek, 1955–76, Dean of Fac. of Arts, 1960–63, 1973–75, Univ. of St Andrews; Pres., Corpus Christi Coll., Oxford, 1976–86 (Hon. Fellow, 1986); Prof. of Classics (Winter Quarter), Stanford Univ., 1988–92. Vis. Lectr, Harvard, 1960; Sather Prof. of Classical Literature, Univ. of California, 1967; Prof.-at-large, Cornell Univ., 1984–89. President: Soc. for Promotion of Hellenic Studies, 1971–74; Classical Assoc., 1975; Jt Assoc. of Classical Teachers, 1985. Pres., British Acad., 1978–81. For. Hon. Mem., Amer. Acad. of Arts and Sciences, 1979; For. Mem., Royal Netherlands Acad. of Arts and Sciences, 1979. Hon. LLD: Birmingham, 1979; St Andrews, 1981; Hon. DLitt: Bristol, 1980; London, 1980; St Andrews, 1981; Durham, 1984; Hon. LittD Liverpool, 1983; Hon. DHL Oglethorpe, 1984. Kenyon Medal, British Acad., 1993. *Publications:* Greek Word Order, 1960; Commentaries on Thucydides, Books VI and VII, 1965; (ed) Aristophanes' Clouds, 1968; Lysias and the Corpus Lysiacum, 1968; (with A. W. Gomme and A. Andrewes) Historical Commentary on Thucydides, vol. IV, 1970, vol. V, 1981; (ed) Theocritus, select poems, 1971; Aristophanic Comedy, 1972; Greek Popular Morality in the Time of Plato and Aristotle, 1974; Greek Homosexuality, 1978; (ed) Plato, Symposium, 1980; (ed and co-author) Ancient Greek Literature, 1980; The Greeks, 1980 (contrib., The Greeks, BBC TV series, 1980); Greek and the Greeks, 1987; The Greeks and their Legacy, 1989; (ed) Aristophanes, Frogs, 1993; Marginal Comment (memoirs), 1994; articles in learned journals; Co-editor, Classical Quarterly, 1962–68. *Recreations:* historical linguistics, country walking. *Address:* 49 Hepburn Gardens, St Andrews, Fife KY16 9LS. *Club:* Athenæum.

DOW, Andrew Richard George; Commercial Director, Eastern Track Renewals Co., since 1995; *b* 1 Dec. 1943; *s* of George Dow and Doris Mary Dow (*née* Soundy); *m* 1973, Stephanie Brenda Murphy; one *s* one *d*. *Educ:* The Hall, Hampstead; Brighton Coll. Chartered Secretary; ACIS. Commercial Apprentice, Bristol Siddeley Engines, 1962–67; appts in Bristol Siddeley and Rolls-Royce Commercial Depts, Bristol, Coventry and New Jersey, 1967–89; Commercial Exec., 1989; Head of Business (Mil.), 1990; Head, Nat. Railway Mus., 1992–94; Commercial Man., BR Infrastructure Services, 1994–95. Dir, Fastline Rail Services Plc, 1995–. Director: York Visitor and Conf. Bureau, 1992–94; FNRM Enterprises Ltd, 1992–94; A1 Steam Locomotive Trust, 1994–. President: Leighton Buzzard Narrow Gauge Rly Soc., 1994–; Lynton and Barnstaple Rly Assoc., 1994–. Vice-President: Stephenson Locomotive Soc., 1992–; Great Central Rly Soc., 1994–; British Overseas Rly Historical Trust, 1994–. Fellow, Permanent Way Instn, 1994. FRSA. *Publications:* book reviews, monthly column, and articles in British and American railway jls. *Recreations:* family life, railways, travel, photography, collecting. *Address:* Sycamore House, Station Lane, Shipton-by-Beningbrough, York YO6 1AG. *T:* York (01904) 471915.

DOW, Christopher; *see* Dow, J. C. R.

DOW, Rear-Adm. Douglas Morrison, CB 1991; Director, National Trust for Scotland, since 1992; *b* 1 July 1935; *s* of George Torrance Dow and Grace Morrison MacFarlane; *m* 1959, Felicity Margaret Mona Napier, *d* of John Watson Napier and Beatrix Mary Carson; two *s*. *Educ:* George Heriot's School; BRNC Dartmouth. Joined RN, 1952; served Staff of C-in-C Plymouth, 1959–61; HMS Plymouth, 1961–63; RN Supply Sch., 1963–65; Staff of Comdr FEF, 1965–67; HMS Endurance, 1968–70; BRNC Dartmouth, 1970–72; Asst Dir, Officer Appointments (S), 1972–74; Sec. to Comdr British Navy Staff, Washington, 1974–76; HMS Tiger, 1977–78; NDC Latimer, 1978–79; CSO(A) to Flag Officer Portsmouth, 1979; Sec. to Controller of the Navy, 1981; Captain, HMS Cochrane, 1983; Commodore, HMS Centurion, 1985; RCDS 1988; Dir Gen., Naval Personal Services, 1989–92. Hon. ADC to the Queen, 1986–89. FIMgt. *Recreations:* Royal Navy Rugby Union (Chairman, 1985–91), fly fishing, shooting, golf, gardening. *Address:* 5 Charlotte Square, Edinburgh EH2 4DU. *Club:* New (Edinburgh).

DOW, Rt. Rev. Geoffrey Graham; *see* Willesden, Area Bishop of.

DOW, Harold Peter Bourner; QC 1971; *b* 28 April 1921; *s* of late Col H. P. Dow and P. I. Dow; *m* 1943, Rosemary Merewether, *d* of late Dr E. R. A. Merewether, CB, CBE, FRCP; two *s* one *d*. *Educ:* Charterhouse; Trinity Hall, Cambridge (MA). Served RAF (Air Crew), 1941–42. Min. of Supply, 1943–45. Barrister, Middle Temple, 1946. *Publications:* Restatement of Town and Country Planning, 1947; National Assistance, 1948; Rights of Way (with Q. Edwards), 1951; ed, Hobsons Local Government, 1951 and 1957 edns. *Recreations:* music, painting. *Address:* Mustow House, Mustow Street, Bury St Edmunds, Suffolk IP33 1XL. *T:* Bury St Edmunds (01284) 725093.

DOW, (John) Christopher (Roderick), FBA 1982; Visiting Fellow, National Institute of Economic and Social Research, since 1984; *b* 25 Feb. 1916; *s* of Warrender Begernie and Amy Langdon Dow; *m* 1960, Clare Mary Keegan; one *s* three *d*. *Educ:* Bootham Sch., York; Brighton, Hove and Sussex Grammar Sch.; University College London, Fellow 1973. Economic Adviser, later Senior Economic Adviser, HM Treasury, 1945–54; on staff, and Dep. Dir, National Inst. for Economic and Social Research, 1954–62; Treasury, 1962–63; Asst Sec.-Gen., OECD, Paris, 1963–73; Exec. Dir, Bank of England, 1973–81; an Advr to the Governor of the Bank of England, 1981–84. *Publications:* The Management of the British Economy, 1945–1960, 1964; Fiscal Policy for a Balanced Economy (jointly), 1968; (with I. D. Saville) A Critique of Monetary Policy: Theory and British Experience, 1988. Various articles in learned jls. *Clubs:* Garrick, Reform.

DOWD, James Patrick; MP (Lab) Lewisham West, since 1992; *b* Germany, 5 March 1951; *s* of late James Patrick Dowd and Elfriede Anna Dowd (*née* Janocha). *Educ:* Dalmain JM&I Sch., London; Sedgehill Comprehensive, London; London Nautical School. Apprentice telephone engineer, GPO, 1967–72; Station Manager, Heron petrol stations, 1972–73; Telecomms Engineer, Plessey Co., later GPT, 1973–92. Group Rep. and Br. Cttee, PO Engrg Union, 1967–72; Sen. Negotiator, ASTMS, then MSF. Lewisham Council: Councillor, 1974–94: Chief Whip; Chm. of Cttees; Dep. Leader; Dep. Mayor, 1987, 1991; Mayor, 1992. Former Mem., Lewisham and Southwark DHA. Contested (Lab): Beckenham, 1983; Lewisham W, 1987. An Opposition Whip, 1993–. Former school governor. *Recreations:* music, reading, theatre, Cornwall, being with friends. *Address:* House of Commons, SW1A 0AA. *T:* 0171–219 4617. *Club:* Lewisham Labour.

DOWDALL, John Michael; Comptroller and Auditor-General for Northern Ireland, since 1994; *b* 6 Sept. 1944; *s* of W. Dowdall, MBE, and late E. Dowdall; *m* 1964, Aylerie (*née* Houston); three *s* one *d*. *Educ:* King Edward's Sch., Witley, Surrey; Queen's Univ., Belfast (BScEcon). Lectr in Economics, Royal Univ. of Malta, 1966–69; Lectr in Political Econ., King's Coll., Univ. of Aberdeen, 1969–72; Economic Advr, Dept of Commerce, N Ireland, 1972–78, Principal, Dept of Commerce, 1978–82; Asst Sec., Dept of Finance and Personnel, N Ireland, 1982–85; Dep. Chief Exec., Industrial Develt Bd, NI, 1986–89; Under Sec., Dept of Finance and Personnel, NI, 1989–94.

DOWDEN, Richard George; journalist; Diplomatic Editor, The Independent, since 1994 (Africa Editor, 1986–94); *b* 20 March 1949; *s* of Peter Dowden and Eleanor Dowden; *m* 1976, Penny Mansfield; two *d*. *Educ:* St George's Coll., Weybridge, Surrey; London Univ.

(BA History). Volunteer Teacher, Uganda, 1971–72; Asst Sec., Justice and Peace Commn, 1973–76; Editor, Catholic Herald, 1976–79; journalist, The Times, 1980–86. *Address:* 7 Highbury Grange, N5 2QB.

DOWDESWELL, Lt-Col (John) Windsor, MC 1943; TD 1947; Chairman, Gateshead Health Authority, 1984–93; Vice Lord-Lieutenant of Tyne and Wear, 1987–93; *b* 11 June 1920; *s* of Thomas Reginald Dowdeswell and Nancy Olivia Pitt Dowdeswell; *m* 1948, Phyllis Audrey Horsfield; one *s* one *d*. *Educ:* Malvern Coll. Commnd RA (TA), 1938; served War, RA 50 (N) Division: France, 1940; Western Desert, 1941–43; Sicily, 1943; NW Europe, 1944–46; Lt-Col Comdg 272 (N) Field Regt, RA (TA), 1963–66; Hon. Col, 101 (N) Field Regt, RA (TA), 1981–86. Emerson Walker Ltd, 1946–68 (Man. Dir, 1961–68); Clarke Chapman Ltd, 1968–77; NEI plc, 1977–83. JP Gateshead, 1955–90 (Chm., 1979–86); DL Tyne and Wear, 1976. *Address:* 40 Oakfield Road, Gosforth, Newcastle upon Tyne NE3 4HS. *T:* 0191–285 2196. *Club:* Northern Counties (Newcastle upon Tyne).

DOWDING, family name of **Baron Dowding.**

DOWDING, 3rd Baron *cr* 1943, of Bentley Priory, Middlesex; **Piers Hugh Tremenheere Dowding;** Associate Professor of English, Okayama University, Japan, since 1977; *b* 18 Feb. 1948; *s* of 2nd Baron Dowding and of his 2nd wife, Alison Margaret, *d* of Dr James Bannerman and widow of Major R. W. H. Peebles; *S* father, 1992; *m* Noriko Shiho; two *d*. *Educ:* Fettes. *Heir: b* Hon. Mark Denis James Dowding, *b* 11 July 1949.

DOWDING, Hon. Peter M'Callum, barrister; *b* 6 Oct. 1943; *m*; five *c*. *Educ:* Hale School, Perth; Univ. of Western Australia (LLB 1964). Churchill Fellowship, 1974, UK and Canada. In practice as solicitor and barrister until 1983 and as barrister, 1990–. MLC North Province, WA, 1980–86; MLA (ALP) Maylands, 1986–90; Cabinet Member, 1983–90; Minister for: Mines, Fuel and Energy, 1983; Planning, and Employment and Training, 1983–84; Consumer Affairs, 1983–86; Minister assisting the Minister for Public Sector Management, 1984–88; Minister for Works and Services, Labour, Productivity and Employment, and assisting the Treasurer, 1987–88; Treasurer, and Minister for Productivity, 1988–89; Leader, WA Parly Lab Party, 1987–90; Premier, WA, 1988–90; Minister, Public Sector Management, and Women's Interests, 1989–90. *Recreations:* sailing, bushwalking. *Address:* Level 31, 52 Martin Place, Sydney, NSW 2000, Australia. *T:* Australia (2) 2238088.

DOWELL, Sir Anthony (James), Kt 1995; CBE 1973; Senior Principal, since 1967, Director, since 1986, Royal Ballet, Covent Garden (Assistant to Director, 1984–85; Associate Director, 1985–86); *b* 16 Feb. 1943; *s* of late Catherine Ethel and Arthur Henry Dowell; unmarried. *Educ:* Hampshire Sch., St Saviour's Hall, Knightsbridge; Royal Ballet Sch., White Lodge, Richmond, Surrey; Royal Ballet Sch., Barons Court. Joined Opera Ballet, 1960, Royal Ballet, for Russian Tour, 1961; promoted Principal Dancer, 1966. *Principal roles with Royal Ballet include:* La Fête Etrange, 1963; Napoli, 1965; Romeo and Juliet, 1965; Song of the Earth, 1966; Card Game, Giselle, Swan Lake, 1967; The Nutcracker, Cinderella, Monotones, Symphonic Variations, new version of Sleeping Beauty, Enigma Variations, Lilac Garden, 1968; Raymonda Act III, Daphnis and Chloe, La Fille Mal Gardée, 1969; Dances at a Gathering, 1970; La Bayadère, Meditation from Thaïs, Afternoon of a Faun, Anastasia, 1971; Triad, Le Spectre de la Rose, Giselle, 1972; Agon, Firebird, 1973; Manon, 1974; Four Schumann Pieces, Les Sylphides, 1975; Four Seasons, 1975; Scarlet Pastorale, 1976; Rhapsody, 1981; A Month in the Country, The Tempest, Varii Capricci, 1983; Sons of Horus, Frankenstein: the modern Prometheus, 1986; Ondine, 1988. Guest Artist with Amer. Ballet Theater, 1977–79; *performed in:* The Nutcracker; Don Quixote; Other Dances; *created:* The Dream, 1964; Shadow Play, 1967; Pavane, 1973; Manon, 1974; Contredanses; Solor in Makarova's La Bayadère; Fisherman in Le Rossignol (Ashton's choreography), NY Metropolitan Opera, 1981; Winter Dreams, 1991. Narrator in A Wedding Bouquet (first speaking role), Joffrey Ballet, 1977; guest appearances with Nat. Ballet of Canada (The Dream, Four Schumann Pieces), 1979 and 1981; Anthony Dowell Ballet Gala, Palladium, 1980 (for charity); narrated Oedipus Rex, NY Metropolitan Opera, 1981. *Television performances:* La Bayadère (USA); Swan Lake, Cinderella, Sleeping Beauty, A Month in the Country, The Dream, Les Noces (all BBC); Winter Dreams; All the Superlatives (personal profile), Omnibus, BBC. Dance Magazine award, NY, 1972. *Recreations:* painting, paper sculpture, theatrical costume design. *Address:* Royal Opera House, Covent Garden, WC2E 9DD.

DOWELL, Ian Malcolm; Editor, Birmingham Evening Mail, since 1987; *b* 15 Nov. 1940; *s* of late James Mardlin and Lilian Dowell; *m* 1st, 1967, Maureen Kane; two *d*; 2nd, 1980, Pauline Bridget Haughian. *Educ:* Exmouth Grammar Sch., Devon. Reporter, Exmouth and East Devon Journal, 1958; Sub-Editor, Woodrow Wyatt Newspapers, 1960; Editor, Wallingford News, Berks, 1962; Dep. Editor, Birmingham Planet, 1964–66; Birmingham Evening Mail: Sub-Editor, 1966; Dep. Features Editor, 1972; Chief Sub-Editor, 1976; Asst Editor, 1981; Dep. Editor, 1985. Bd Mem., Birmingham Post & Mail Ltd, 1992–. Mem., W Midlands Reg. Guild of Editors, 1994. Pres., Black Country Olympics Cttee, 1992–; Mem. Foundn Bd, Solihull Coll., 1994–. Chm., Birmingham Christmas Tree Fund, 1992–. Fellow, RSPB, 1987. *Recreations:* the countryside, gardening. *Address:* The Birmingham Post & Mail Ltd, 28 Colmore Circus, Birmingham B4 6AX. *T:* 0121–236 3366.

DOWELL, Prof. John Derek, FRS 1986; Professor of Elementary Particle Physics, University of Birmingham, since 1980; *b* 6 Jan. 1935; *s* of William Ernest Dowell and Elsie Dorothy Dowell (*née* Jarvis); *m* 1959, Patricia Clarkson; one *s* one *d*. *Educ:* Coalville Grammar Sch., Leics; Univ. of Birmingham (BSc, PhD). Research Fellow, Univ. of Birmingham, 1958–60; Res. Associate, CERN, Geneva, 1960–62; Lectr, 1962–70, Sen. Lectr, 1970–75, Reader, 1975–80, Univ. of Birmingham. Vis. Scientist, Argonne Nat. Lab., USA, 1968–69. CERN, Geneva: Scientific Associate, 1973–74, 1985–87; Mem., Scientific Policy Cttee, 1982–90, 1993–; Chairman: Large Electron Positron Collider Cttee, 1993–; ATLAS Collaboration Bd, 1996–. Mem., Nuclear Physics Bd, 1974–77, 1981–85, Chm., Particle Physics Cttee, 1981–85, SERC. Member: Europ. Cttee for Future Accelerators, 1989–93; BBC Science Consultative Gp, 1992–94; Deutsches Elektronen Synchrotron Extended Scientific Council, 1992–; Particle Physics and Astronomy Res. Council, 1994–. Mem. Court, Univ. of Warwick, 1992–. Rutherford Prize and Medal, InstP, 1988. *Publications:* numerous, in Phys. Letters, Nuovo Cimento, Nuclear Phys., Phys. Rev., Proc. Royal Soc., and related literature. *Recreations:* piano, amateur theatre, squash, ski-ing. *Address:* 57 Oxford Road, Moseley, Birmingham B13 9ES; School of Physics and Space Research, University of Birmingham, Birmingham B15 2TT.

DOWER, Michael Shillito Trevelyan; Director-General, Countryside Commission, since 1992; *b* 15 Nov. 1933; *s* of late John Gordon Dower and Pauline Dower; *m* 1960, Agnes Done; three *s*. *Educ:* Leys Sch., Cambridge; St John's Coll., Cambridge (MA); University Coll. London (DipTP). MRTPI, ARICS. Town Planner: LCC, 1957–59; Civic Trust, 1960–65; Amenity and Tourism Planner, UN Develt Prog., Ireland, 1965–67; Dir, Dartington Amenity Res. Trust and Dartington Inst., Devon, 1967–85; Nat. Park Officer, Peak Park Jt Planning Bd, 1985–92. Member: Sports Council, 1965–72; English Tourist Bd, 1969–76; Founder Chm., Rural Voice, 1980; Pres., European Council for Village and Small Town, 1986–90. Hon. FLI 1995. Hon. DSc Plymouth, 1994. *Publications:* Fourth Wave, 1965; Hadrian's Wall, 1976; (jtly) Leisure Provision and People's Needs, 1981; research and consultancy reports. *Recreations:* walking, landscape painting, dry-stone walling, travel. *Address:* Countryside Commission, John Dower House, Crescent Place, Cheltenham, Glos GL50 3RA. *T:* Cheltenham (01242) 521381.

DOWLING, Prof. Ann Patricia, (Mrs T. P. Hynes), PhD; CEng, FIMechE; Professor of Mechanical Engineering, University of Cambridge, since 1993; Fellow, Sidney Sussex College, Cambridge, since 1979; *b* 15 July 1952; *d* of Mortimer Joseph Patrick Dowling and Joyce Dowling (*née* Barnes); *m* 1974, Dr Thomas Paul Hynes. *Educ:* Ursuline Convent Sch., Westgate, Kent; Girton Coll., Cambridge (BA 1973; MA 1977; PhD 1978). CEng, FIMechE 1990; Fellow, Inst. Acoustics, 1989. Cambridge University: Res. Fellow, 1977–78, Dir of Studies in Engrg, 1979–90, Sidney Sussex Coll.; Asst Lectr in Engrg, 1979–82; Lectr, 1982–86; Reader in Acoustics, 1986–93; Dep. Hd, Engrg Dept, 1990–93. Member: AIAA, 1990; Defence and Aerospace Technology Foresight Panel, 1994–. Vice-Pres., Cambridge Philosophical Soc., 1995–. Trustee, Ford of Britain Trust, 1993–. Governor: Centre for Inf. on Lang. Teaching and Res., 1993–; Felsted Sch., 1994–. A. B. Wood Medal, Inst. of Acoustics, 1990. *Publications:* (with J. E. Ffowcs Williams) Sound and Sources of Sound, 1983; (with D. G. Crighton *et al.*) Modern Methods in Analytical Acoustics, 1992; contribs to scientific and engrg jls, mainly on fluid mechanics, vibration and acoustics. *Recreations:* opera, flying light aircraft. *Address:* Engineering Department, Cambridge University, Trumpington Street, Cambridge CB2 1PZ. *T:* Cambridge (01223) 332739.

DOWLING, Dame Jean (Elizabeth); DCVO 1978 (CVO 1976; MVO 4th Cl. 1971, 5th Cl. 1964); retired; *b* 7 Nov. 1916; *d* of late Captain William Taylor (killed in action, 1917); *m* 1993, Ambrose Francis Dowling, MVO, MBE, TD. *Educ:* Tunbridge Wells High School (GPDST). Entered Office of Private Secretary to the Queen, 1958; Chief Clerk, 1961–78. *Recreations:* music, walking, looking at old buildings. *Address:* Church Cottage, Frittenden, Cranbrook, Kent TN17 2DD.

DOWLING, Kenneth, CB 1985; Deputy Director of Public Prosecutions, 1982–85; *b* 30 Dec. 1933; *s* of Alfred and Maria Dowling; *m* 1957, Margaret Frances Bingham; two *d*. *Educ:* King George V Grammar Sch., Southport. Called to the Bar, Gray's Inn, 1960. RAF, 1952–54. Immigration Branch, Home Office, 1954–61; joined DPP Dept: Legal Asst, 1961; Sen. Legal Asst, 1966; Asst Solicitor, 1972; Asst Dir, 1976; Princ. Asst Dir, 1977. *Recreations:* reading, golf.

DOWLING, Rt. Rev. Owen Douglas; Bishop of Canberra and Goulburn, 1983–92; Rector of St James's, New Town, Hobart, since 1993; *b* 11 Oct. 1934; *s* of Cecil Gair Mackenzie Dowling and Winifred Hunter; *m* 1958, Beverly Anne Johnston (*d* 1985); two *s* one *d*; *m* 1993, Gloria Helen Goodwin. *Educ:* Melbourne High School; Trinity Coll., Melbourne Univ. (BA, DipEd, ThL). Victorian Education Dept, Secondary Teacher, 1956–60; ordained to ministry of Anglican Church, 1960; Asst Curate, Sunshine/Deer Park, Dio. Melbourne, 1960–62; Vicar of St. Philip's, W Heidelberg, 1962–65; Precentor and Organist, St Saviour's Cathedral, Goulburn, 1965–67; Rector of South Wagga Wagga, 1968–72; Rector of St John's, Canberra, 1972–81; Archdeacon of Canberra, 1974–81; Asst Bishop, Dio. Canberra and Goulburn, 1981–83. Comr, Australian Heritage Commn, 1993–. *Recreations:* pipe organ and piano playing, squash. *Address:* New Town St James Anglican Church, 24 Bedford Street, New Town, Tas 7008, Australia. *Club:* Southern Cross (Canberra).

DOWLING, Prof. Patrick Joseph, PhD; FEng 1981; Vice Chancellor and Chief Executive, University of Surrey, since 1994; Partner, Chapman and Dowling, Consulting Engineers, 1981–94; *b* 23 March 1939; *s* of John Dowling and Margaret McKittrick, Dublin; *m* 1966, Grace Carmine Victoria Lobo, *d* of Palladius Lobo and Marcilia Moniz, Zanzibar; one *s* one *d*. *Educ:* Christian Brothers Sch., Dublin; University Coll., Dublin (BE NUI 1960); Imperial Coll. of Science and Technol., London (PhD 1968). DIC 1961; FRINA 1985; FIStructE 1978; FICE 1979; FCGI 1989. Demonstr in Civil Engrg, UC Dublin, 1960–61; Post-grad. studies, Imperial Coll., London, 1961–65; Bridge Engr, British Constructional Steelwork Assoc., 1965–68; Imperial Coll., London: Res. Fellow, 1968–74; Reader in Structural Steelwork, 1974–79; British Steel Prof. of Steel Structures, 1979–94; Hd of Civil Engrg Dept, 1985–94. Chm., Eurocode 3 (Steel Structures) Drafting Cttee, 1981–84. Mem. Council, RHBNC, 1990–. Institution of Structural Engineers: Vice-Pres., 1991–94; Pres., 1994–95; Oscar Faber Award, 1971; Henry Adams Medal, 1976; Guthrie Brown Medal, 1979; Oscar Faber Medal, 1985; Telford Premium, ICE, 1976; Gustave Trasenster Medal, Assoc. des Ingénieurs sortis de l'Univ. de Liège, 1984; Silver Medal, RINA, 1993; Curtin Medal, ICE, 1993. Editor, Jl of Constructional Steel Research, 1980–. Hon. LLD NUI, 1995. *Publications:* Steel Plated Structures, 1977; Buckling of Shells in Offshore Structures, 1982; Structural Steel Design, 1988; Constructional Steel Design, 1992; technical papers on elastic and inelastic behaviour and design of steel and composite land-based and offshore structures. *Recreations:* travelling, sailing, reading, the enjoyment of good company. *Address:* University of Surrey, Guildford GU2 5XH. *Clubs:* Athenæum, Chelsea Arts; National Yacht of Ireland.

DOWN AND CONNOR, Bishop of, (RC), since 1991; **Most Rev. Patrick Joseph Walsh;** *b* 9 April 1931; *s* of Michael and Nora Walsh. *Educ:* Queen's Univ. Belfast (MA); Christ's Coll., Cambridge (MA); Pontifical Lateran Univ., Rome (STL). Ordained 1956; Teacher, St MacNissi's Coll., Garron Tower, 1958–64; Chaplain, Queen's Univ., Belfast, 1964–70; Pres., St Malachy's Coll., Belfast, 1970–83; Auxiliary Bishop of Down and Connor, 1983–91. *Recreations:* walking, music, theatre. *Address:* 73 Somerton Road, Belfast BT15 4DE. *T:* Belfast (01232) 776185.

DOWN AND DROMORE, Bishop of, since 1986; **Rt. Rev. Gordon McMullan;** *b* 1934; *m* 1957, Kathleen Davidson; two *s*. *Educ:* Queen's Univ., Belfast (BSc Econ 1961, PhD 1971); Ridley Hall, Cambridge. ACIS 1957. Dipl. of Religious Studies (Cantab) 1978; ThD Geneva Theol Coll., 1988; MPhil TCD, 1990. Deacon 1962, priest 1963, dio. Down; Curate of Ballymacarrett, 1962–67; Central Adviser on Christian Stewardship to Church of Ireland, 1967–70; Curate of St Columba, Knock, Belfast, 1970–71; Rector of St Brendan's, East Belfast, 1971–76; Rector of St Columba, Knock, Belfast, 1976–80; Archdeacon of Down, 1979–80; Bishop of Clogher, 1980–86. *Publications:* A Cross and Beyond, 1976; We are called . . ., 1977; Everyday Discipleship, 1979; Reflections on St Mark's Gospel, 1984; Growing Together in Prayer, 1990; Reflections on St Luke's Gospel, 1994. *Address:* The See House, 32 Knockdene Park South, Belfast BT5 7AB.

DOWN, Sir Alastair (Frederick), Kt 1978; OBE 1944 (MBE 1942); MC 1940; TD 1951; Chairman, The Burmah Oil Co. PLC, 1975–83 (Chief Executive, 1975–80); *b* 23 July 1914; *e s* of Frederick Edward Down and Margaret Isobel Down (*née* Hutchison); *m* 1947, Bunny Mellon; two *s* two *d*. *Educ:* Edinburgh Acad.; Marlborough Coll. Commissioned in 7th/9th Bn, The Royal Scots (TA), 1935. CA 1938. Joined British Petroleum Co. Ltd in Palestine, 1938. Served War of 1939–45 (despatches twice, MC, MBE, OBE, Kt Comdr, Order of Orange Nassau, with swords, 1946): Middle East, N Africa, Italy and Holland, with Eighth Army and 1st Canadian Army as Lt-Col and full Col. Rejoined BP, in Iran, 1945–47; Head Office, 1947–54; Canada, 1954–62 (Chief Rep. of BP in Canada, 1954–57; Pres., BP Group in Canada, 1957–62); Pres. BP Oil Corp., 1969–70; Man. Dir, 1962–75 and Dep. Chm., 1969–75, British Petroleum Co. Ltd; Director: TRW Inc., USA, 1977–86; Scottish American Investment Co. Ltd, 1980–85; Royal Bank of Canada, 1981–85; Chairman: British-North American Res. Assoc., 1980–84; London American Energy NV, 1981–85. Member: Review Body for pay of doctors and dentists, 1971–74; Television Adv. Cttee, 1971–72; Council, Marlborough Coll., 1979–87 (Chm. Council, 1982–87); Hon. Treasurer, Field Studies Council, 1977–81. FRSA 1970; FIMgt (FBIM 1972); JDipMA (Hon.), 1966. Hambro British Businessman of the Year Award, 1980; Cadman Meml Medal, Inst. of Petroleum, 1981. *Recreations:* shooting, golf, fishing. *Address:* Brieryhill, Hawick, Roxburghshire TD9 7LL. *Club:* New (Edinburgh).

DOWN, Antony Turnbull L.; *see* Langdon-Down.

DOWN, Barbara Langdon; *see* Littlewood, Lady (Barbara).

DOWN, Rt Rev. William John Denbigh; Assistant Bishop of Leicester and Priest-in-charge, St Mary, Humberstone, since 1995; *b* 15 July 1934; *s* of William Leonard Frederick Down and Beryl Mary Down (*née* Collett); *m* 1960, Sylvia Mary Aves; two *s* two *d. Educ:* Farnham Grammar School; St John's Coll., Cambridge (BA 1957; MA 1961); Ridley Hall, Cambridge. Deacon 1959, priest 1960, Salisbury; Asst Curate, St Paul's Church, Salisbury, 1959–63; Chaplain, Missions to Seamen, 1963–74: South Shields, 1963–65; Hull, 1965–71; Fremantle, WA, 1971–74; Dep. Gen. Secretary, Missions to Seamen, 1975, Gen. Sec. 1976–90; Chaplain, St Michael Paternoster Royal, 1976–90; Hon. Asst Curate, St John's, Stanmore, 1975–90; Bishop of Bermuda, 1990–95. Hon. Canon of Gibraltar, 1985–90, of Kobe, 1987–. Chaplain RANR, 1972–74. Hon. Chaplain, Worshipful Co. of Carmen, 1977–90 (Hon. Chaplain Emeritus, 1990), of Farriers, 1983–90 (Hon. Chaplain Emeritus, 1990), of Innholders, 1983–90. Freeman, City of London, 1981. Hon. FNI 1991. *Publications:* On Course Together, 1989; contrib. to Internat. Christian Maritime Assoc. Bulletin. *Recreations:* sport (keen follower of soccer, cricket, golf), ships and the sea, travel, walking. *Address:* St Mary's Vicarage, 56 Vicarage Lane, Humberstone, Leicester LE5 1EE. *Clubs:* Commonwealth Trust; MCC.

DOWNE, 11th Viscount, *cr* 1680; **John Christian George Dawnay;** Bt 1642; Baron Dawnay of Danby (UK) *cr* 1897; DL; technology manager; *b* Wykeham, 18 Jan. 1935; *s* of 10th Viscount Downe, OBE and Margaret Christine (*d* 1967), *d* of Christian Bahnsen, NJ; *S* father, 1965; *m* 1965, Alison Diana, *d* of I. F. H. Sconce, OBE; one *s* one *d. Educ:* Eton Coll.; Christ Church, Oxford. 2nd Lieut, Grenadier Guards, 1954–55. Non-marine broker at Lloyd's, 1958–65. Part-time Mem., Electronics Res. Gp, J. J. Thomson Physical Lab., Univ. of Reading, 1964–78; Brookdeal Electronics Ltd: Man. Dir. 1965–68; Vice-Chm., 1968–71; Chm., 1971–84; Director: Dawnay Faulkner Associated Ltd (Consultants), 1968–; Allen Bradley Electronics Ltd, 1970–81; George Rowney & Co. Ltd, 1978–83; York Ltd, 1980– (Chm., 1980–93; Pres., 1993–); Yorkshire Bank PLC, 1990–; SensorDynamics Ltd, 1990–; Aaston Ltd, 1992–; Aaston Inc., 1992–; Dir, Scarborough Theatre Trust, 1981– (Vice-Chm., 1986–). Member: CLA Yorks Br. Cttee, 1966– (Chm., 1988–90); CLA Exec. Cttee, 1990–94; N Yorks Moors Nat. Park Cttee, 1969– (Vice-Chm., 1982–85); N Riding/N Yorks County Council, 1969–85; Nat. Railway Mus. Cttee, 1974– (Chm., 1985–); N Yorks Rural Develt Commn County Cttee, 1978– (Chm., 1986–); President: N York Moors Hist. Railway Trust, 1970–; Yorks Rural Community Council,. 1977–; Aston Martin Owners Club, 1980–; Friends of the Nat. Railway Mus., 1988–; Trustee: Nat. Mus. of Science and Industry, 1985–; Burton Constable Foundn, 1992–. Hon. Col, 150 (Yorkshire) Regt RLC(V) (formerly 150 (Northumbrian) Regt RCT(V)), 1984–. Freeman, Co. of the Staple of England, 1979; Liveryman, Co. of Scientific Instrument Makers, 1991–. DL N Yorks, 1981. *Publications:* contributions to various journals. *Recreations:* linear circuit design, railways (selectively). *Heir: s* Hon. Richard Henry Dawnay, *b* 9 April 1967. *Address:* Wykeham Abbey, Scarborough, North Yorks YO13 9QS. *T:* Scarborough (01723) 862404; 5 Douro Place, W8 5PH. *T:* 0171–937 9449. *Club:* Pratt's.

DOWNER, Dame Jocelyn Anita; *see* Barrow, Dame J. A.

DOWNER, Prof. Martin Craig; Professor and Head of Department of Dental Health Policy, Hon. Consultant in Dental Public Health, Eastman Dental Institute, since 1990; *b* 9 March 1931; *s* of Dr Reginald Lionel Ernest Downer and Mrs Eileen Maud Downer (*née* Craig); *m* 1961, Anne Catherine (*née* Evans); four *d. Educ:* Shrewsbury Sch.; Univ. of Liverpool; Univ. of Manchester (PhD 1974; DDS 1989); Univ. of London. LDSRCS 1958; DDPH RCS 1969. Dental Officer, St Helens Local Authority, 1958–59; gen. dental practice, 1959–64; Dental Officer, Bor. of Haringey, 1964–67; Principal Dental Officer, Royal Bor. of Kensington and Chelsea, 1967–70; Res. Fellow in Dental Health, Univ. of Manchester, 1970–74; Area Dental Officer, Salford HA (also Hon. Lectr, Univ. of Manchester), 1974–79; Chief Dental Officer, SHHD (also Hon. Sen. Lectr, Univs of Edinburgh and Dundee), 1979–83; Chief Dental Officer (Under Sec.), Dept of Health (formerly DHSS), 1983–90. *Publications:* contribs to books and papers in learned jls in gen. field of dental public health, incl. epidemiology and biostatistics, clin. trials and trial methodology, inf. systems, health services res., and econs of dental care. *Recreations:* music, reading, cookery, natural history, vintage aviation, walking. *Address:* Institute of Dental Surgery, Eastman Dental Hospital, 256 Gray's Inn Road, WC1X 8LD.

DOWNES, Prof. David Malcolm; Professor of Social Administration, London School of Economics, since 1987; *b* 26 Aug. 1938; *s* of Bernice Marion Downes and Herman Leslie Downes; *m* 1961, Susan Onaway Correa-Hunt; one *s* two *d. Educ:* King Edward VII Grammar Sch., Sheffield; Keble Coll., Oxford (BA Hons Mod. Hist. 1959); LSE (PhD Criminology 1964). Asst Lectr, Lectr, Sen. Lectr in Social Admin, 1963–82, Reader, 1982–87, LSE. Sen. Res. Fellow, Nuffield Coll., Oxford, 1970–72. Visiting Professor/Academic Visitor: Univ. of California at Berkeley, 1975; Univ. of Toronto, 1977; Free Univ. of Amsterdam, 1981; Univ. of Bologna, 1991. British Mem., Harvard Internat. Seminar, 1966. Mem., BFI. Editor, British Jl of Criminology, 1985–90. *Publications:* The Delinquent Solution, 1966, 3rd edn 1973; Gambling, Work and Leisure, 1976; (ed with Paul Rock) Deviant Interpretations, 1979; (with Paul Rock) Understanding Deviance, 1982, 2nd edn 1988; Contrasts in Tolerance: postwar penal policy in the Netherlands and England and Wales, 1988; (ed) Crime and the City: essays in memory of John Mays, 1989; (ed) Unravelling Criminal Justice, 1992. *Recreations:* modern literature, cinema, theatre. *Address:* 25 Rosehill Road, Wandsworth, SW18 2NY. *T:* 0181–870 3410.

DOWNES, Sir Edward (Thomas), Kt 1991; CBE 1986; Associate Music Director and Principal Conductor, Royal Opera House, Covent Garden, since 1991; *b* 17 June 1924. FRCM. Royal Opera House, Covent Garden, 1952–69; Music Dir, Australian Opera, 1972–76; Prin. Conductor, BBC Northern Symphony Orch., subseq. BBC Philharmonic Orch., 1980–91. *Address:* c/o Royal Opera House, Covent Garden, WC2E 7QA.

DOWNES, George Robert, CB 1967; Director of Studies, Royal Institute of Public Administration, 1972–94; *b* 25 May 1911; *o s* of late Philip George Downes; *m* Edna Katherine Millar; two *d. Educ:* King Edward's Grammar School, Birmingham; Grocers', London. Entered GPO, 1928; Assistant Surveyor, 1937; Asst Principal, 1939. Served War of 1939–45: RNVR, in destroyers, 1942–45. Principal, GPO, 1946; Principal Private Sec. to: Lord President of the Council, 1948–50, Lord Privy Seal, 1951; Assistant Secretary, 1951; Imperial Defence College, 1952; Deputy Regional Director, GPO London, 1955; Dir, London Postal Region, 1960–65; Dir of Postal Services, 1965–67; Dir, Operations and Overseas, PO, 1967–71. *Recreations:* music, gardening. *Address:* Orchard Cottage, Frithsden, Berkhamsted, Herts HP4 1NW.

DOWNES, George Stretton, CBE 1976; Deputy Receiver for the Metropolitan Police District, 1973–76; retired; *b* London, 2 March 1914; *e s* of late George and Rosalind S. Downes; *m* 1st, 1939, Sheilah Gavigan (*d* 1986); two *s* two *d*; 2nd, 1991, Barbara (*née* Haydon). *Educ:* Cardinal Vaughan Sch., Kensington. Joined Metropolitan Police Office, 1934; Secretary, 1969. *Recreations:* golf, gardening. *Address:* 13 Ember Gardens, Thames Ditton, Surrey KT7 0LL.

See also J. S. Higgins.

DOWNES, Prof. Kerry John, OBE 1994; FSA; Professor of History of Art, University of Reading, 1978–91, now Emeritus; *b* 8 Dec. 1930; *s* of late Ralph William Downes, CBE and Agnes Mary Downes (*née* Rix); *m* 1962, Margaret Walton. *Educ:* St Benedict's, Ealing; Courtauld Institute of Art. BA, PhD London. Library, Courtauld Inst. of Art, 1954–58; Librarian, Barber Inst. of Fine Arts, Univ. of Birmingham, 1958–66; Lectr in Fine Art, Univ. of Reading, 1966–71, Reader, 1971–78. Vis. Lectr, Yale Univ., 1968; Hon. Vis. Prof., Univ. of York, 1994–. Mem., Royal Commission on Historical Monuments of England, 1981–93; Pres., Soc. of Architectural Historians of GB, 1984–88. Hon. DLitt Birmingham, 1995. *Publications:* Hawksmoor, 1959, 2nd edn 1979; English Baroque Architecture, 1966; Hawksmoor, 1969; Christopher Wren, 1971; Whitehall Palace, in Colvin and others, History of the King's Works, V, 1660–1782, 1976; Vanbrugh, 1977; The Georgian Cities of Britain, 1979; Rubens, 1980; The Architecture of Wren, 1982, 2nd edn 1988; Sir John Vanbrugh, a Biography, 1987; Sir Christopher Wren: Design for St Paul's Cathedral, 1988; contribs to Burlington Magazine, Architectural History, Architectural Rev., TLS, etc. *Recreations:* drawing, making music, learning electronics, procrastination. *Address:* c/o Department of History of Art, University of Reading, Blandford Lodge, Whiteknights, PO Box 217, Reading RG6 2AN. *T:* Reading (01734) 318890.

DOWNES, M. P.; *see* Panter-Downes.

DOWNEY, Anne Elisabeth; Her Honour Judge Downey; a Circuit Judge, since 1986; *b* 22 Aug. 1936; *d* of John James Downey and Ida May Downey. *Educ:* Notre Dame Convent, Liverpool; Liverpool Univ. LLB (Hons.). Called to the Bar, Gray's Inn, 1958. A Recorder, 1980–86. *Recreations:* antiques, reading. *Address:* Copperfield, 4 Pine Walk, Prenton, Merseyside. *T:* 0151–608 2404.

DOWNEY, Sir Gordon (Stanley), KCB 1984 (CB 1980); Comptroller and Auditor General, 1981–87; *b* 26 April 1928; *s* of Stanley William and Winifred Downey; *m* 1952, Jacqueline Goldsmith; two *d. Educ:* Tiffin's Sch.; London Sch. of Economics (BSc(Econ)). Served RA, 1946–48. Ministry of Works, 1951; entered Treasury, 1952; Asst Private Sec. to successive Chancellors of the Exchequer, 1955–57; on loan to Ministry of Health, 1961–62; Asst Sec., 1965, Under-Sec., 1972, Head of Central Unit, 1975; Dep. Sec., Treasury, 1976–81; on loan as Dep. Head, Central Policy Review Staff, Cabinet Office, 1978–81. Special Advr, Ernst & Young (formerly Ernst & Whinney), 1988–90; Complaints Comr, The Securities Assoc., 1989–90; Chairman: FIMBRA, 1990–93; PIA, 1993. Readers' Rep., The Independent, 1990–95. Chm., Delegacy, King's College Med. and Dental Sch., 1989–91. *Recreations:* reading, visual arts, tennis. *Address:* Chinley Cottage, 1 Eaton Park Road, Cobham, Surrey KT11 2JG. *T:* Cobham (01932) 867878. *Club:* Army and Navy.

DOWNEY, Air Vice-Marshal John Chegwyn Thomas, CB 1975; DFC 1945, AFC; Deputy Controller of Aircraft (C), Ministry of Defence, 1974–75, retired; *b* 26 Nov. 1920; *s* of Thomas Cecil Downey and Mary Evelyn Downey; *m* Diana, (*née* White); one *s* two *d. Educ:* Whitgift Sch. Entered RAF 1939; served War of 1939–45 in Coastal Command (DFC 1945 for his part in anti-U-boat ops). Captained Lincoln Aries III on global flight of 29,000 miles, during which London-Khartoum record was broken. RAF Farnborough 1956–58; commanded Bomber Comd Develt Unit 1959–60; head of NE Defence Secretariat, Cyprus, 1960–62; Comd RAF Farnborough, 1962–64; a Dir, Op. Requirements (RAF) MoD, 1965–67; IDC, 1968; Comdt, RAF Coll. of Air Warfare, Manby, Jan./Oct. 1969; Comdr Southern Maritime Air Region, 1969–71; Senior RAF Mem., RCDS, 1972–74. *Publications:* Management in the Armed Forces: an anatomy of the military profession, 1977; (contrib.) Yearbook of World Affairs, 1983. *Recreations:* sailing, ski-ing. *Address:* c/o Lloyds Bank, 7 Pall Mall, SW1Y 5NA. *Club:* Royal Air Force.

DOWNEY, William George, CB 1967; *b* 3 Jan. 1912; *s* of late William Percy Downey; *m* 1936, Iris, *e d* of late Ernest Frederick Pickering; three *d. Educ:* Southend Grammar Sch. ACWA 1935, ACA 1937, FCA 1960. Ministry of Aircraft Production, 1940; Ministry of Supply, 1946 (Director of Finance and Administration, Royal Ordnance Factories, 1952–57); Ministry of Aviation, 1959; Under-Secretary, 1961; Chm., Steering Gp, Develt Cost Estimation, 1964–66; Min. of Technology, 1967, Min. of Aviation Supply, 1970; DTI, 1971; Management Consultant to Procurement Exec., MoD, 1972–74; Under Sec., NI Office, 1974–75; Dir, Harland and Wolff, 1975–81; Consultant to CAA, 1976–79, to Dept of Energy, 1980. *Address:* Starvelarks, Dawes Heath Road, Rayleigh, Essex SS6 7NL. *T:* Rayleigh (01268) 774138.

DOWNIE, Prof. Robert Silcock, FRSE 1986; Professor of Moral Philosophy, Glasgow University, since 1969; *b* 19 April 1933; *s* of late Robert Mackie Downie and late Margaret Barlas Downie; *m* 1958, Eileen Dorothea Flynn; three *d. Educ:* The High Sch. of Glasgow; Glasgow Univ.; The Queen's Coll., Oxford. MA, first cl. hons, Philosophy and Eng. Lit., Glasgow, 1955; Russian linguist, Intelligence Corps, 1955–57; Ferguson Schol., 1958; BPhil Oxford Univ., 1959. Glasgow University: Lectr in Moral Philosophy, 1959; Sen. Lectr in Moral Philosophy, 1968; Stevenson Lectr in Med. Ethics, 1985–88. Vis. Prof. of Philosophy, Syracuse Univ., NY, USA, 1963–64. *Publications:* Government Action and Morality, 1964; (jtly) Respect for Persons, 1969; Roles and Values, 1971; (jtly) Education and Personal Relationships, 1974; (jtly) Values in Social Work, 1976; (jtly) Caring and Curing, 1980; Healthy Respect, 1987; (jtly) Health Promotion: models and values, 1990; (jtly) The Making of a Doctor, 1992; (ed) Francis Hutcheson: selected writings, 1994; (ed) The Healing Arts: an Oxford anthology, 1994; Go Gentle: ethics in palliative care, 1995; contribs to: Mind, Philosophy, Analysis, Aristotelian Society, Political Studies. *Recreation:* music. *Address:* Department of Moral Philosophy, University of Glasgow G12 8QQ. *T:* 0141–339 8855.

DOWNING, Dr Anthony Leighton, FEng; Consultant, Binnie & Partners, Consulting Engineers, since 1986 (Partner, 1973–86); *b* 27 March 1926; *s* of Sydney Arthur Downing and Frances Dorothy Downing; *m* 1952, Kathleen Margaret Frost; one *d. Educ:* Arnold Sch., Blackpool; Cambridge and London Universities. BA Cantab. 1946; BSc Special

Degree 2 (1) Hons. London, 1950; DSc London 1967. Joined Water Pollution Research Lab., 1946; seconded to Fisheries Research Lab., Lowestoft, 1947–48; granted transfer to Govt Chemist's Lab., 1948; returned to WPRL as Scientific Officer, 1950; subsequently worked mainly in field of biochemical engrg; Dir, Water Pollution Res. Lab., 1966–73. Vis. Prof., Imperial Coll. of Science and Technology, 1978–82. FIChemE 1975; FIWPC 1965 (Pres., 1979); FIBiol 1965; FIWES 1975; Hon. FIPHE 1965; FIWES 1975; Hon. FIWEM 1987; FEng 1991. FRSA. Freeman, City of London, 1988. *Publications:* papers in scientific and technical journals. *Recreations:* golf, snooker, gardening. *Address:* 2 Tewin Close, Tewin Wood, Welwyn, Herts AL6 0HF. *T:* Bulls Green (01438) 798474. *Clubs:* United Oxford & Cambridge University; Knebworth Golf.

DOWNING, David Francis, PhD; part-time Chairman, Civil Service Science Recruitment Boards; *b* 4 Aug. 1926; *e s* of late Alfred William and Violet Winifred Downing; *m* 1948, Margaret Joan Llewellyn; one *s* one *d*. *Educ:* Bristol Grammar Sch.; Univ. of Bristol (BSc 1952, PhD 1955). Served Coldstream Gds and Royal Welch Fusiliers, 1944–48 (Lieut RWF, 1947). Student Mem. of delegn from Brit. univs to Soviet univs, 1954; Eli Lilley Res. Fellow, Univ. of Calif, LA, and Fulbright Travel Scholarship, 1955–56; Long Ashton Res. Stn, Univ. of Bristol, 1957–58; Chem. Def. Estab., 1958–63; Def. Res. Staff, Washington, 1963–66; Chem. Def. Estab., 1966–68; Counsellor (Scientific), British High Commn, Ottawa, 1968–73; Head, Management Services, RARDE, 1973–75, and Head, Pyrotechnics Br., 1975–78; Counsellor (Scientific), British Embassy, Moscow, 1978–81; Asst Dir, Resources and Programmes B, MoD, 1981–83; Head, Land Systems Group, British Defence Staff, British Embassy, Washington, 1983–87. Reader, Salisbury Cathedral, 1990–. Governor: Salisbury and Wells Theological Coll., 1987–94 (Chm., 1990–94); Sarum Coll., 1994–. FRSA 1969. *Publications:* scientific papers, mainly in Jl of Chem. Soc., and Qly Revs of Chem. Soc. *Recreations:* cathedral music, travel, bird watching, skiing. *Address:* 13 The Close, Salisbury, Wilts SP1 2EB. *T:* Salisbury (01722) 323910. *Club:* Army and Navy.

DOWNING, Henry Julian; HM Diplomatic Service, retired; *b* 22 March 1919; *o s* of Henry Julian Downing and Kate Avery; *m* 1951, Ruth Marguerite Ambler. *Educ:* Boys' High Sch., Trowbridge; Hertford Coll., Oxford. Indian Civil Service (Madras) 1941–47. Joined HM Foreign Service, 1947; 2nd Secretary, Madras and Dacca, 1947–50; Foreign Office, 1950–52; 1st Secretary (Commercial), Istanbul, 1952–56; Foreign Office, 1956–58; 1st Secretary and Head of Chancery, Kabul, 1958–62; Foreign Office, 1963–65; HM Consul-General, Lourenço Marques, 1965–69; Head of Claims Dept, 1969–71, of Migration and Visa Dept, 1971–73, FCO; Consul-Gen., Cape Town, 1973–77. *Recreations:* swimming, walking, bird watching. *Address:* 8b Greenaway Gardens, Hampstead, NW3 7DJ. *T:* 0171–435 2593. *Club:* United Oxford & Cambridge University.

DOWNPATRICK, Lord; Edward Edmund Maximilian George Windsor; *b* 2 Dec. 1988; *s* and *heir* of Earl of St Andrews, *qv*.

DOWNS, Sir Diarmuid, Kt 1985; CBE 1979; FRS 1985; FEng, FIMechE; Managing Director, 1967–84, Chairman, 1976–87, Ricardo Consulting Engineers plc; *b* 23 April 1922; *s* of John Downs and Ellen McMahon; *m* 1951, Mary Carmel Chillman; one *s* three *d*. *Educ:* Gunnersbury Catholic Grammar Sch.; Northampton Poly. (BScEng London Univ., 1942). CEng, FIMechE 1961. Ricardo Consulting Engineers Ltd, 1942–87: Head, Petrol Engine Dept, 1947; Dir, 1957. Mem., Adv. Council for Applied R&D, 1976–80; Member: SERC, 1981–85 (Chm., Engineering Bd); Design Council, 1981–89; Bd of Dirs, Soc. of Automotive Engineers Inc., 1983–86; Bd of British Council, 1987–93; Council, Motor Industry Res. Assoc., 1987–89. President: Fédération Internationale des Sociétés d'Ingénieurs des Techniques de L'Automobile, 1978 (Vice-Pres., 1975); IMechE, 1978–79 (Vice-Pres., 1971–78); Assoc. of Indep. Contract Res. Organisations, 1975–77; Section G, British Assoc. for Advancement of Science, 1984; Royal Commn for Exhibn of 1851. Chm., Technology Activities Cttee, Royal Soc., 1989–; Mem., Adv. Bd, Parly Office of Science and Technology, 1988–93. Dir, Gabriel Communications (formerly Universe Publications) Ltd, 1986–93. Vis. Fellow, Lincoln Coll. Oxford, 1987–88. Hinton Lecture, Fellowship of Engrg, 1987. Foreign Associate, Nat. Acad. of Engrg, USA, 1987; Hon. Mem., Hungarian Acad. of Scis, 1988. Liveryman, Co. of Engineers, 1984–. Pro Chancellor, Surrey Univ., 1992–94 (Mem. Council, 1983–94, Chm., 1989–92); Mem. Council, City Univ., 1980–82. Hon. Fellow, St Mary's UC, Strawberry Hill, 1995. Hon. DSc: City, 1978; Cranfield Inst. of Technol., 1981. George Stephenson Research Prize, 1951, Crompton Lanchester Medal, 1951 and Dugald Clerk Prize, 1952, IMechE; James Alfred Ewing Medal, ICE, 1985; Medal, Internat. Fedn of Automobile Engrs' and Technicians' Assocs, 1986. KSG 1993. *Publications:* papers on internal combustion engines in British and internat. engrg jls and conf. proc. *Recreation:* theatre. *Address:* The Downs, 143 New Church Road, Hove, East Sussex BN3 4DB. *T:* Brighton (01273) 419357. *Clubs:* St Stephen's Constitutional; Hove (Hove).

DOWNS, Mrs George Wallingford; *see* Tureck, Rosalyn.

DOWNSHIRE, 8th Marquess of, *cr* 1789 (Ire.); **Arthur Robin Ian Hill;** Viscount Hillsborough, Baron Hill 1717; Earl of Hillsborough, Viscount Kilwarlin 1751; Baron Harwich (GB) 1756; Earl of Hillsborough, Viscount Fairford (GB) 1772; Hereditary Constable of Hillsborough Fort; farmer, since 1963; *b* 10 May 1929; *s* of Lord Arthur Francis Henry Hill (*d* 1953) (*yr s* of 6th Marquess) and Sheila (*d* 1961), *d* of Col Stewart MacDougall of Lunga; *S* uncle, 1989; *m* 1st, 1957, Hon. Juliet Mary (*d* 1986), *d* of 7th Baron Forester; two *s* one *d*; 2nd, 1989, Mrs Diana Hibbert (*née* Cross). *Educ:* Eton. 2nd Lieut Royal Scots Greys, 1948–50. Articled clerk, 1950–55; Chartered Accountant (ACA 1959). *Recreations:* shooting, travel. *Heir: s* Earl of Hillsborough, *qv*. *Address:* Clifton Castle, Ripon, North Yorks HG4 4AB. *T:* Ripon (01765) 689326. *Club:* White's.

DOWNSIDE, Abbot of; *see* Fitzgerald-Lombard, Rt Rev. Charles.

DOWNWARD, Maj.-Gen. Peter Aldcroft, CB 1979; DSO 1967; DFC 1952; Governor, Military Knights of Windsor, since 1989; *b* 10 April 1924; *s* of late Aldcroft Leonard and Mary Downward; *m* 1st, 1953, Hilda Hinckley Wood (*d* 1976); two *s*; 2nd, 1980, Mrs Mary Boykett Procter (*née* Allwork). *Educ:* King William's Coll., Isle of Man. Enlisted 1942; 2nd Lieut, The South Lancashire Regt (Prince of Wales's Volunteers), 1943; served with 13th Bn (Lancs) Parachute Regt, NW Europe, India, Far East, 1944–46, Greece and Palestine, 1947; transf. to Glider Pilot Regt, 1948; Berlin Airlift, 1949, Korea, 1951–53; 1st Bn The South Lancs Regt (PWV) in Egypt and UK, 1953–54; instructor at Light Aircraft Sch., 1955–56; RAF Staff Coll., 1958; War Office, 1959–60; BAOR, 1961–63; Brigade Major 127 Bde, 1964; Comd 4th Bn The East Lancs Regt, 1965–66; Comd 1st Bn The Lancs Regt (PWV), Aden, 1966–67; Allied Forces N Europe, Oslo, 1968–69; instructor, Sch. of Infantry, 1970–71; Comd Berlin Inf. Bde. 1971–74; Comdt, Sch. of Infantry, 1974–76; GOC West Midland District, 1976–78; Lt-Governor and Sec., The Royal Hosp., Chelsea, 1979–84. Col, The Queen's Lancashire Regt, 1978–83; Col Comdt, The King's Division, 1979–83; Hon. Col, Liverpool Univ. OTC, 1980–89. Dir, Oxley Develts Co. Ltd, 1984–89. Chm., Museum of Army Flying, 1984–88; President: British Korean Veterans Assoc., 1986–; Assoc. of Service Newspapers, 1986–; Trustee, Princess Christian Hosp., Windsor, 1989–94. *Recreations:* sailing, skiing, shooting. *Address:* The Mary Tudor Tower, Windsor Castle, Berks SL4 1NJ. *Club:* Army and Navy.

DOWNWARD, Sir William (Atkinson), Kt 1977; JP; Lord-Lieutenant of Greater Manchester, 1974–87; Councillor, Manchester City Council, 1946–75; Alderman, Manchester, 1971–74; *b* 5 Dec. 1912; *s* of late George Thomas Downward; *m* 1946, Enid, *d* of late Ald. Charles Wood. *Educ:* Manchester Central High Sch.; Manchester Coll. of Technology. Dir, Royal Exchange Theatre Co., 1976–89; Chairman: Manchester Overseas Students Welfare Conf., 1972–87; Peterloo Gall., 1974–76. Chm., Pat Seed Appeal Fund, 1977–; President: Manchester Opera Soc., 1977–; Gtr Manchester Fedn of Boys' Clubs, 1978–; Broughton House Home for Disabled Ex-Servicemen, 1978–. Mem. Court of Governors: Manchester Univ., 1969–; Salford Univ., 1974–87. Hon. LLD Manchester, 1977. Hon. RNCM 1982; FRSA 1978. Lord Mayor of Manchester, 1970–71; DL Lancs, 1971; JP Manchester, 1973. KStJ 1974. *Address:* 23 Kenmore Road, Northenden, Manchester M22 4AE. *T:* 0161–998 4742.

DOWSETT, Prof. Charles James Frank, MA, PhD Cantab; FBA 1977; Calouste Gulbenkian Professor of Armenian Studies, University of Oxford, 1965–91, now Emeritus Professor, and Fellow of Pembroke College, Oxford, 1965–91, now Emeritus Fellow; *b* 2 Jan. 1924; *s* of late Charles Aspinall Dowsett and Louise (*née* Stokes); *m* 1949, Friedel (*d* 1984), *d* of Friedrich Lapuner, Kornberg, E Prussia. *Educ:* Owen's Sch.; St Catherine's Society, Oxford, 1942–43; Peterhouse, Cambridge (Thomas Parke Scholar), 1947–50 (Mod. and Mediaeval Languages Tripos, Part I, 1st Class Russian, 1st Class German, 1948, Part II, Comparative Philology, 1st Class with distinction, 1949). Treasury Studentship in Foreign Languages and Cultures, 1949–54. Ecole Nationale des Langues Orientales Vivantes, Univ. de Paris, 1950–52 (diplôme d'arménien); Ecole des Langues Orientales Anciennes, Institut Catholique de Paris, 1950–53 (diplôme de géorgien); Lecturer in Armenian, School of Oriental and African Studies, University of London, 1954; Reader in Armenian, 1965. Vis. Prof., Univ. of Chicago, 1976. Member: Council, RAS, 1972–76; Philological Soc., 1973–77; Marjory Wardrop Fund for Georgian Studies, 1966–. *Publications:* The History of the Caucasian Albanians by Movses Dasxuranci, 1961; The Penitential of David of Ganjak, 1961; (with J. Carswell) Kütahya Armenian Tiles, vol. 1, The Inscribed Tiles, 1972; (contrib.) Iran and Islam: Vladimir Minorsky Memorial Volume, 1971; (contrib.) Hayg Berberian Memorial Volume, 1986; articles in Bulletin of the School of Oriental and African Studies, Le Muséon, Revue des Etudes Arméniennes, Jl of Soc. for Armenian Studies,The Geographical Journal, W. B. Henning Memorial Volume, 1970, Raft, etc; translations from Flemish (Felix Timmermans' Driekoningentryptiek: "A Christmas Triptych", 1955, Ernest Claes' De Witte: "Whitey", 1970); as Charles Downing (children's books): Russian Tales and Legends, 1956; Tales of the Hodja, 1964; Armenian Folktales and Fables, 1972. *Address:* 21 Hurst Rise Road, Cumnor Hill, Oxford OX2 9HE.

DOWSON, Prof. Duncan, CBE 1989; FRS 1987; FEng 1982; Professor of Engineering Fluid Mechanics and Tribology, 1966–93, now Professor Emeritus and Hon. Fellow; Head of Department of Mechanical Engineering, 1987–92, and Dean for International Relations, 1987–93, Leeds University; *b* 31 Aug. 1928; *o s* of Wilfrid and Hannah Dowson, Kirkbymoorside, York; *m* 1951, Mabel, *d* of Mary Jane and Herbert Strickland; one *s* (and one *s* decd). *Educ:* Lady Lumley's Grammar Sch., Pickering, Yorks; Leeds Univ. (BSc Mech Eng. 1950; PhD 1952; DSc 1971). FIMechE; Fellow ASME 1973; Fellow ASLE 1983. Research Engineer, Sir W. G. Armstrong Whitworth Aircraft Co., 1953–54; Univ. of Leeds: Lecturer in Mechanical Engineering, 1954; Sen. Lecturer, 1963; Reader, 1965; Prof. 1966; Dir, Inst. of Tribology, Dept of Mech. Engrg, 1967–87; Pro-Vice-Chancellor, 1983–85. Pres., IMechE, 1992–93 (Chm., Tribology Group Cttee, 1967–69). Chm., Yorks Region, RSA, 1992–. Foreign Mem., Royal Swedish Acad. of Engrg Sciences, 1986. Hon. DSc INSA, Lyon, 1991. James Clayton Fund Prize (jtly), IMechE, 1963; Thomas Hawksley Gold Medal, IMechE, 1966; Gold Medal, British Soc. of Rheology, 1969; Nat. Award, ASLE, 1974; ASME Lubrication Div. Best Paper Awards (jt), 1975, 1976; ASME Melville Medal (jt), 1976; James Clayton Prize, IMechE, 1978; ASME Mayo D. Hersey Award, 1979; Tribology Gold Medal, IMechE, 1979. Hon. DTech Chalmers Univ. of Technology, Göteborg, 1979; Hon. DSc Institut Nat. des Sciences Appliquées de Lyon, 1991. *Publications:* Elastohydrodynamic Lubrication—the fundamentals of roller and gear lubrication (jtly), 1966, 2nd edn 1977; History of Tribology, 1979; (jtly) An Introduction to the Biomechanics of Joints and Joint Replacement, 1981, (jtly) Ball Bearing Lubrication: The Elastohydrodynamics of Elliptical Contacts, 1981; papers on tribology and bio-medical engrg, published by: Royal Society; Instn of Mech. Engineers; Amer. Soc. of Mech. Engineers; Amer. Soc. of Lubrication Engineers. *Recreations:* travel, photography. *Address:* Ryedale, 23 Church Lane, Adel, Leeds LS16 8DQ. *T:* Leeds (0113) 267 8933.

DOWSON, Graham Randall; Partner, Graham Dowson and Associates, since 1975; Chairman, Dowson Shurman (formerly Dowson-Salisbury) Associates Ltd, since 1987; *b* 13 Jan. 1923; *o s* of late Cyril James Dowson and late Dorothy Celia (*née* Foster); *m* 1954, Fay Weston (marr. diss. 1974); two *d*; *m* 1975, Denise Shurman. *Educ:* Alleyn Court Sch.; City of London Sch.; Ecole Alpina, Switzerland. Served War of 1939–45 (1939–43 and Africa Stars, Atlantic, Defence and Russian Arctic Medals, etc); RAF, 1941–46 (Pilot, Sqdn-Ldr). Sales, US Steel Corporation (Columbia Steel), Los Angeles, 1946–49; Sales and Senior Commentator, Mid South Network (MBS), radio, US, 1949–52; Dir, Rank Organization Ltd, 1960–75, Chief Exec., 1974–75; Chairman: Erskine House Investments, 1975–83; Mooloya Investments, 1975–78; Pincus Vidler Arthur Fitzgerald Ltd, 1979–83; Marinex Petroleum, 1981–83; Nash Industries, 1988–90; Premier Speakers, 1987–91; Chm. and Chief Exec., Teltech Ltd, 1984–87; Deputy Chairman: Nimslo European Hldgs, 1978–87; Nimslo International Ltd, 1981–87; Nimslo Ltd, 1979– (Dir, 1978); Paravision (UK) Ltd, 1988–91; Director: A. C. Nielsen Co., Oxford, 1953–58; Carron Co. (Holdings) Ltd, 1976–; Carron Investments Ltd, 1976–; RCO Holdings PLC (formerly Barrowmill Ltd), 1979–; Nimslo Corp., 1978–87; Filmbond plc, 1985–88; Fairhaven Internat. Ltd, 1988–; Grovewood Securities, 1990–91. Chm., 1972–84, Pres., 1984–, European League for Econ. Co-operation (British Section). Dep. Chm., 1974–87, Vice-Pres., 1987–, NPFA; Chm., Migraine Trust, 1985–88; Patron, Internat. Centre for Child Studies. Liveryman, Distillers' Co.; Mem., Court of Common Council, City of London, 1992–. FInstD 1957; CIMgt (CBIM 1969); FInstM 1971. *Recreation:* sailing. *Address:* 193 Cromwell Tower, Barbican, EC2Y 8DD. *Clubs:* Athenæum, Carlton, City Livery, Royal Air Force, Saints and Sinners, Thirty; Royal London Yacht (Ex-Commodore).

DOWSON, Sir Philip (Manning), Kt 1980; CBE 1969; MA; PRA (RA 1986; ARA 1979); RIBA, FCSD; a Senior Partner, Ove Arup Partnership, 1969–90, Consultant, since 1990; Architectural Founder Partner, Arup Associates, architects and engineers; President, Royal Academy of Arts, since 1993; *b* 16 Aug. 1924; *m* 1950, Sarah Crewdson; one *s* two *d*. *Educ:* Gresham's Sch.; University Coll., Oxford; Clare Coll., Cambridge (Hon. Fellow, 1991); Architectural Association. AA Dip. Lieut, RNVR, 1943–47. Award-winning work includes: university and college buildings in Oxford, Cambridge, Birmingham and Leicester; headquarter buildings for IBM, Lloyd's of London and CEGB; buildings for music and the arts, incl.: extension for Imperial War Mus.; reconstruction of Snape Maltings as concert hall; urban and landscape projects. Member: Royal Fine Art Commn, 1971–; Craft Adv. Cttee, 1972–75. Governor, St Martin's Sch. of Art, 1975–82. Trustee:

The Thomas Cubitt Trust, 1978–; Royal Botanic Gdns, Kew, 1983–; Royal Armouries, 1984–89. Hon. Fellow, Duncan of Jordanstone Coll. of Arts; Hon. FAIA; Hon. FRCA. Royal Gold Medal for Architecture, RIBA, 1981. *Recreation:* sailing. *Address:* 13 Fitzroy Street, W1P 6BQ. *T:* 0171–636 1531. *Clubs:* Garrick, MCC.

DOYLE, Dr Anthony Ian, FBA 1992; Hon. Reader in Bibliography, Durham University, since 1985; *b* 24 Oct. 1925; *s* of Edward Doyle and Norah Keating. *Educ:* St Mary's Coll., Great Crosby, Liverpool; Downing Coll., Cambridge (BA 1945; MA 1949; PhD 1953). Durham University: Asst Librarian, 1950–59; Keeper of Rare Books, 1959–82; Reader in Bibliography, 1972–85. Chm., Assoc. for Manuscripts and Archives in Res. Collections, 1992. Corresp. Fellow, Mediaeval Academy of America, 1991. Israel Gollancz Prize, British Academy, 1983. *Publications:* Palaeographical introductions to facsimiles of the Hengwrt Manuscript, 1979, Vernon Manuscript, 1987, and Ellesmere Manuscript, 1995, of Chaucer's Canterbury Tales; articles on medieval MSS, early printed books and collectors. *Address:* University Library, Palace Green, Durham DH1 3RN. *T:* 0191–374 3001, 3029.

DOYLE, Bernard; *see* Doyle, F. B.

DOYLE, Brian André; Judge, Botswana Court of Appeal, 1973–79 and 1988–91; *b* 10 May 1911; *s* of John Patrick Doyle, ICS and Louise Doyle (*née* Renard); *m* 1937, Nora (*née* Slattery) (*d* 1992); one *s* one *d*. *Educ:* Douai Sch.; Trinity Coll., Dublin. BA, LLB. British Univs and Hosps Boxing Champion, 1929, 1930, 1931 (Flyweight), 1932 (Bantamweight); Irish Free State Army Boxing Champion, 1930 (Flyweight). Called to Irish Bar, 1932; Magistrate, Trinidad and Tobago, 1937; Resident Magistrate, Uganda, 1942; Solicitor-Gen., Fiji, 1948; Attorney-Gen., Fiji, 1949; KC (Fiji), 1950, later QC; Attorney-Gen., N Rhodesia, 1956; Minister of Legal Affairs and Attorney-Gen., Northern Rhodesia (Zambia, 1964), 1959–65, retired as minister, 1965; Chm., Local Govt Service Commn, Zambia, 1964; Justice of Appeal, 1965; Chief Justice and Pres., Supreme Court of Zambia, 1969–75. Dir, Law Develt Commn, Zambia, 1976–79; Chm., Delimitation Commn, Botswana, 1981–82. *Recreations:* fishing, golf. *Address:* 26 Choumert Square, Peckham Rye, SE15 4RE. *Clubs:* Lusaka, Chainama Hills Golf; Dulwich and Sydenham Hill Golf.

DOYLE, (Frederick) Bernard; Director, MSL International, since 1994 (Director, Public Sector Operations, 1988–90); *b* 17 July 1940; *s* of James Hopkinson Doyle and Hilda Mary Doyle (*née* Spotsworth); *m* 1963, Ann Weston; two *s* one *d*. *Educ:* St Bede's Coll.; Univ. of Manchester (BSc Hons); Harvard Business Sch., 1965–67 (MBA). CEng, FICE, FIWEM (FIWES 1986); CIMgt (CBIM 1987). Resident Civil Engineer with British Rail, 1961–65; Management Consultant with Arthur D. Little Inc., 1967–72; Booker McConnell Ltd: Secretary to Executive Cttee, 1973; Director, Engineering Div., 1973–76; Chairman, General Engineering Div., 1976–78; Chm. and Chief Exec., Booker McConnell Engineering, and Director, Booker McConnell, 1978–81; Chief Executive: SDP, 1981–83; Welsh Water Authy, 1983–87; Man. Dir, Hamptons, 1990–92; Gen. Manager, Bristol & West Building Soc., 1992–94. FRSA. *Recreations:* sport, theatre, reading, walking, bird watching. *Address:* 15 Oldfield Place, Hotwells, Bristol BS8 4QJ. *T:* Bristol (0117) 922 7976.

DOYLE, Air Comdt Dame Jean (Lena Annette) C.; *see* Conan Doyle.

DOYLE, Dr Peter, CBE 1992; FRSE; Director, Zeneca Group, since 1993; *b* 6 Sept. 1938; *s* of late Peter and Joan Penman Doyle; *m* 1962, Anita McCulloch; one *s* one *d*. *Educ:* Univ. of Glasgow (BSc Hons 1st class 1960; PhD 1963). FRSE 1993. Research Chemist, ICI Pharmaceuticals, 1963; Manager, Quality Control Dept, 1973–75; Manager, Chemistry Dept, 1975–77; Research Dir, ICI Plant Protection, 1977–86; Business Dir, ICI Seeds, 1985–86; Dep. Chm. and Technical Dir, ICI Pharmaceuticals, 1986–88; Res. and Technol. Dir, ICI Gp, 1989–93. Dir, AFRC Rothamsted Experimental Station, 1992–. Member: ACOST, 1989–93; MRC, 1990–94; Royal Commn on Envmtl Pollution, 1994–; Central R&D Cttee for NHS, 1995–. Foreign Mem., Royal Swedish Acad. of Engineering Scis, 1990. Mem. Council, UCL, 1984–. Liveryman, Salters' Co., 1983. Hon. DSc: Glasgow, 1992; Nottingham, 1993. *Publications:* contribs to Chemical Communications and Jl Chem. Soc. *Recreation:* golf. *Address:* Zeneca Corporate Office, 15 Stanhope Gate, W1Y 6LN. *T:* 0171–304 5000. *Club:* Mill Ride Golf (Ascot).

DOYLE, Sir Reginald (Derek Henry), Kt 1989; CBE 1980; HM Chief Inspector of Fire Services, since 1987; *b* 13 June 1929; *s* of John Henry and Elsie Doyle; *m* 1953, June Margretta (*née* Stringer); two *d*. *Educ:* Aston Commercial College. RN 1947–54. Fire Brigades, 1954–84; Chief Fire Officer: Worcester City and County, 1973; Hereford and Worcester County, 1974; Kent County, 1977; Home Office Fire Service Inspector, 1984–87. Warden, Guild of Fire Fighters. OStJ 1990. *Recreations:* shooting, swimming, badminton, horses. *Address:* Glebecroft, Marley Road, Harrietsham, Kent ME17 1BS. *T:* Maidstone (01622) 859259. *Club:* Rotary (Weald of Kent).

DOYLE, Prof. William, DPhil; FRHistS; Professor of History, University of Bristol, since 1986; *b* 4 March 1942; *s* of Stanley Joseph Doyle and Mary Alice Bielby; *m* 1968, Christine Thomas. *Educ:* Bridlington Sch.; Oriel Coll., Oxford (BA 1964; MA, DPhil 1968). FRHistS 1976. University of York: Asst Lectr, 1967; Lectr, 1969; Sen. Lectr, 1978; Prof. of Modern History, Univ. of Nottingham, 1981–85. Visiting Professor: Univ. of S Carolina, 1969–70; Univ. de Bordeaux III, 1976; Ecole des Hautes Etudes en Sciences Sociales, Paris, 1988; Vis. Fellow, All Souls Coll., Oxford, 1991–92. Dr *hc* Bordeaux, 1987. *Publications:* The Parlement of Bordeaux, 1974; The Old European Order 1660–1800, 1978; Origins of the French Revolution, 1980; The Ancien Régime, 1986; (ed jtly) The Blackwell Dictionary of Historians, 1988; The Oxford History of the French Revolution, 1989; Officers, Nobles and Revolutionaries, 1995; contribs to Past and Present, Historical Jl, French Historical Studies, Studies on Voltaire. *Recreations:* books, decorating, travelling about. *Address:* Department of Historical Studies, University of Bristol, 13 Woodland Road, Bristol BS8 1TB. *T:* Bristol (0117) 930 7932. *Clubs:* Athenæum, United Oxford & Cambridge University.

DOYLE, William Patrick, PhD; CIMgt; President, Texaco Middle East/Far East, since 1991; *b* 15 Feb. 1932; *s* of James W. Doyle and Lillian I. Doyle (*née* Kime); *m* 1957, Judith A. Gosha; two *s* one *d* (and one *s* decd). *Educ:* Seattle Univ. (BS 1955); Oregon State Univ. (PhD 1959). CIMgt (FBIM 1980); MInstD 1982. Texaco, USA: Chemist, 1959; Res. Supervisor, 1966; Asst to Vice Pres. of Petrochemicals, 1968; Asst to Sen. Vice Pres. of Supply and Distribn, 1971; Asst Manager, Producing, 1972; Asst Regional Man., Marketing, 1974; Texaco Ltd: Dep. Man. Dir, 1977; Man. Dir, Exploration and Production, 1981; Vice President: Texaco Europe, 1987; Texaco Latin America and Africa, 1989. Pres., UK Offshore Operators Assoc., 1985 (Vice Pres., 1984). *Publications:* contrib. Jl of Amer. Chem. Soc. *Recreations:* tennis, music, theatre. *Address:* 2000 Westchester Avenue, White Plains, NY 10650, USA.

D'OYLY, Sir Nigel Hadley Miller, 14th Bt *cr* 1663, of Shottisham, Norfolk; *b* 6 July 1914; *s* of Sir Hastings Hadley D'Oyly, 11th Bt, and Evelyn Maude, *d* of George Taverner Miller; *S* half-brother, 1986; *m* 1940, Dolores (*d* 1971), *d* of R. H. Gregory; one *s* two *d*. *Educ:* Radley; RMC Sandhurst. Formerly Major, Royal Scots; served War of 1939–45, Hong Kong, France and War Office. *Heir:* *s* Hadley Gregory D'Oyly [*b* 29 May 1956; *m* 1991, Annette Frances Elizabeth, *yr d* of Maj. Michael White; one *d*]. *Address:* New Lodge, Crowhurst, near Battle, East Sussex TN33 9AB.

DRABBLE, Jane; Director of Education, BBC, since 1994; *b* 15 Jan. 1947; *d* of Walter Drabble and Molly (*née* Boreham). *Educ:* Bristol Univ. (BA Hons 1968). BBC: Studio Manager, 1968–72; Producer, Radio Current Affairs, 1972–75; Asst Producer, then Producer, TV Current Affairs, 1975–87; Editor, Everyman, 1987–91; Head of Factual Progs, 1993–94, Asst Man. Dir, 1991–94, Network TV. *Recreations:* music, theatre, walking, sailing. *Address:* BBC White City, 201 Wood Lane, W12 7TS. *T:* 0181–752 5252.

DRABBLE, Margaret, (Mrs Michael Holroyd), CBE 1980; author; *b* 5 June 1939; 2nd *d* of His Honour J.F. Drabble, QC and late Kathleen Marie Bloor; *m* 1st, 1960, Clive Walter Swift, *qv* (marr. diss. 1975); two *s* one *d*; 2nd, 1982, Michael Holroyd, *qv*. *Educ:* The Mount Sch., York; Newnham Coll., Cambridge. Lives in London. Chm., Nat. Book League, 1980–82 (Dep. Chm., 1978–80). E. M. Forster Award, Amer. Acad. of Arts and Scis, 1973; Hon. Fellow, Sheffield City Polytechnic, 1989. Hon. DLitt: Sheffield, 1976; Manchester, 1987; Keele, 1988; Bradford, 1988; Hull, 1992; UEA, 1994; York, 1995. *Publications:* A Summer Birdcage, 1962; The Garrick Year, 1964; The Millstone, 1966 (filmed, as A Touch of Love, 1969); Wordsworth, 1966; Jerusalem the Golden, 1967; The Waterfall, 1969; The Needle's Eye, 1972; (ed with B. S. Johnson) London Consequences, 1972; Arnold Bennett, a biography, 1974; The Realms of Gold, 1975; (ed) The Genius of Thomas Hardy, 1976; (ed jtly) New Stories 1, 1976; The Ice Age, 1977; For Queen and Country, 1978; A Writer's Britain, 1979; The Middle Ground, 1980; (ed) The Oxford Companion to English Literature, 5th edn, 1985; The Radiant Way, 1987; (ed with Jenny Stringer) The Concise Oxford Companion to English Literature, 1987; A Natural Curiosity, 1989; Safe as Houses, 1989; The Gates of Ivory, 1991; Angus Wilson: a biography, 1995. *Recreations:* walking, dreaming. *Address:* c/o A. D. Peters, Fifth Floor, The Chambers, Chelsea Harbour, Lots Road, SW10 0XF.

DRABBLE, Richard John Bloor; QC 1995; *b* 23 May 1950; *s* of John Frederick and Kathleen Marie Drabble; *m* 1980, Sarah Madeleine Hope Lewis; two *s* (and one *s* decd). *Educ:* Leighton Park Sch., Reading; Downing Coll., Cambridge (BA Hons). Called to the Bar, Inner Temple, 1975; Junior Counsel to the Crown, Common Law, 1992. *Publications:* contrib. on Social Security to Halsbury's Laws of England, 4th edn; various articles. *Recreations:* reading, walking. *Address:* 4 Bream's Buildings, EC4A 1AQ. *T:* 0171–353 5835.

DRACE-FRANCIS, Charles David Stephen, CMG 1987; HM Diplomatic Service; Government Affairs Director, British Aerospace, since 1991 (on secondment); *b* 15 March 1943; *m* 1967, Griselda Hyacinthe Waldegrave; two *s* one *d*. *Educ:* Magdalen Coll., Oxford. Third Sec., FO, 1965; Tehran, 1967; Second, later First Sec., FCO, 1971; Asst Political Advr, Hong Kong, 1974; First Sec., Office of UK Rep. to EEC, Brussels, 1978; FCO, 1980; All Souls Coll., Oxford, 1983; Chargé d'affaires, Kabul, 1984; Counsellor, Lisbon, 1987. *Address:* c/o Foreign and Commonwealth Office, SW1A 2AH.

DRAKE, Sir (Arthur) Eric (Courtney), Kt 1970; CBE 1952; DL; *b* 29 Nov. 1910; *e s* of Dr A. W. Courtney Drake; *m* 1st, 1935, Rosemary Moore; two *d*; 2nd, 1950, Margaret Elizabeth Wilson; two *s*. *Educ:* Shrewsbury; Pembroke Coll., Cambridge (MA; Hon. Fellow 1976). With The British Petroleum Co. Ltd, 1935–75, Chm., 1969–75, Dep. Chm., P&O Steam Navigation Co., 1976–81. Pres., Chamber of Shipping, 1964; Hon. Mem., General Council of British Shipping, 1975–; Member: Gen. Cttee, Lloyd's Register of Shipping, 1960–81, 1985–87; MoT Shipping Adv. Panel, 1962–64; Cttee on Invisible Exports, 1969–75; Bd of Governors, Pangbourne Nautical Coll., 1958–69; Court of Governors, London Sch. of Economics and Political Science, 1963–74; Governing Body of Shrewsbury Sch., 1969–83; Cttee of Management, RNLI, 1975–85; Life Mem., Court of City Univ., 1969–; Pres., City and Guilds Insignia Award Assoc., 1971–75; Hon. Petroleum Adviser to British Army, 1971–. Hon. Mem., Honourable Co. of Master Mariners, 1972; Elder Brother of Trinity House, 1975–. Vice Pres., Mary Rose Trust, 1984– (Chm., 1979–83). Freeman of City of London, 1974; one of HM Lieutenants, City of London. DL Hants, 1983. Hon. DSc Cranfield, 1971; Hon. Fellow, UMIST, 1974. Hambro British Businessman of the Year award, 1971; Cadman Meml Medal, Inst. of Petroleum, 1976. Comdr, Ordre de la Couronne, Belgium, 1969; Kt Grand Cross of Order of Merit, Italy, 1970; Officier, Légion d'Honneur, 1972; Order of Homayoun, Iran, 1974; Comdr, Ordre de Leopold, Belgium, 1975. *Address:* Meadow Cottage, Cheriton, Alresford, Hants SO24 0PP. *T:* Bramdean (01962) 771334. *Clubs:* London Rowing; Royal Yacht Squadron (Trustee), Leander, Royal Cruising.

DRAKE, Hon. Sir (Frederick) Maurice, Kt 1978; DFC 1944; **Hon. Mr Justice Drake;** a Judge of the High Court of Justice, Queen's Bench Division, since 1978; *b* 15 Feb. 1923; *o s* of late Walter Charles Drake and Elizabeth Drake; *m* 1954, (Alison) May, *d* of late W. D. Waterfall, CB; two *s* three *d*. *Educ:* St George's Sch., Harpenden; Exeter Coll., Oxford. MA Hons 1948. Served War of 1939–45, RAF 96 and 255 Squadrons. Called to Bar, Lincoln's Inn, 1950, QC 1968, Bencher, 1976. Dep. Chm., Beds QS, 1966–71; a Recorder of the Crown Court, 1972–78; Dep. Leader, Midland and Oxford Circuit, 1975–78, Presiding Judge, 1979–83. Standing Senior Counsel to RCP, 1972–78. Nominated Judge for appeals from Pensions Appeal Tribunal, 1985–95. Vice-Chm., Parole Bd, England and Wales, 1985–86 (Mem., 1984–86). Chm. Governors, Aldwickbury Prep. Sch. (Trust), 1969–80; Governor, St George's Sch., Harpenden, 1975–79. Hon. Alderman, St Albans DC, 1976–. *Recreations:* music, opera, gardening, sea-fishing. *Address:* The White House, West Common Way, Harpenden, Herts AL5 2LH. *T:* Harpenden (01582) 712329; Royal Courts of Justice, Strand, WC2A 2LL.

DRAKE, Jack Thomas Arthur H.; *see* Howard-Drake.

DRAKE, Brig. Dame Jean Elizabeth R.; *see* Rivett-Drake.

DRAKE, John Gair; Chief Registrar and Chief Accountant, Bank of England, 1983–90; *b* 11 July 1930; *s* of John Nutter Drake and Anne Drake; *m* 1957, Jean Pamela Bishop; one *s* one *d*. *Educ:* University College School; The Queen's College, Oxford. MA. Joined Bank of England, 1953; editor, Quarterly Bulletin, 1971; Asst Chief Cashier, 1973; Management Development Manager, 1974; Dep. Chief, Economic Intell. Dept, 1977; Dep. Chief Cashier and Dep. Chief, Banking Dept, 1980. Governor, South Bank Univ. (formerly Poly.), 1987–. *Address:* 114 Stanstead Road, Caterham, Surrey CR3 6AE. *T:* Caterham (01883) 346130. *Club:* Chaldon Cricket.

DRAKE, Hon. Sir Maurice; *see* Drake, Hon. Sir F. M.

DRAPER, Alan Gregory; Director, Defence Procurement Management Group, Royal Military College of Science, 1988–91; *b* 11 June 1926; *e s* of late William Gregory Draper and Ada Gertrude (*née* Davies); *m* 1st, 1953, Muriel Sylvia Cuss, FRSA (marr. diss.); three *s*; 2nd, 1977, Jacqueline Gubel. *Educ:* Leeds Grammar Sch.; The Queen's Coll., Oxford (Scholar 1944; MA 1951). RNVR, 1945; Sub-Lt, 1946–47. Admiralty: Asst Principal, 1950; Private Sec. to Civil Lord of the Admiralty, 1953–55; MoD, 1957–60; Head of

Polit. Sect., Admiralty 1960–64; First Sec., UK Delegn to NATO, 1964–66; Asst Sec., MoD, 1966; Counsellor, UK Delegn to NATO, 1974–77; Chm., NATO Budget Cttees, 1977–81; Royal Ordnance Factories: Personnel Dir, 1982–84; Dir Gen., Personnel, 1984; Dir, Management/Career Develt, Royal Ordnance plc, 1985; Sen. Lectr, Defence Procurement, RMCS, 1986–91. MIPM 1985. *Publication:* British Involvement in Major European Collaborative Defence Projects: 1957–1987, 1990. *Recreations:* reading, music, nostalgia. *Address:* 93 avenue Prince Bavdovin, Brussels 1150, Belgium.

DRAPER, Gerald Carter, OBE 1974; Chairman: G. Draper Consultancy, since 1988; Draper Associates Ltd, 1982–88; *b* 24 Nov. 1926; *s* of Alfred Henderson Draper and Mona Violanta (*née* Johnson); *m* 1951, Winifred Lilian Howe; one *s* three *d*. *Educ:* Univ. of Dublin, Trinity Coll. (MA). FInstM, FCIT. Joined Aer Lingus, 1947; Advertising and PR Manager, 1950; Commercial Man., Central Afr. Airways, 1959; British European Airways: Advertising Man., 1964; Asst Gen. Man. (Market Develt), 1966; Gen. Man. and Dir, Travel Sales Div., 1970; British Airways: Dir, Travel Div., 1973; Marketing Dir, 1977; Dir, Commercial Ops, 1978; Mem. Bd, 1978–82; Man. Dir, Intercontinental Services Div., 1982. Chairman: British Air Tours Ltd, 1978–82; Silver Wing Surface Arrangements Ltd, 1971–82; Deputy Chairman: Trust Houses Forte Travel Ltd, 1974–82; ALTA Ltd, 1977–82; Hoverspeed, 1984–87; Member Board: Internat. Aeradio Ltd, 1971–82; British Airways Associated Cos Ltd, 1972–82; British Intercontinental Hotels Ltd, 1976–82; Communications Strategy Ltd, 1984–86; AGB Travel Research Internat. Ltd, 1984–86; Centre for Airline and Travel Marketing Ltd, 1986–; BR (Southern Region), 1990–92. Chm., Outdoor Advertising Assoc., 1985–92. Mem., Samuel Pepys Club. Master, Co. of Marketors, 1990; Mem., Guild of Freemen, 1991. FRSA 1979. Chevalier de l'Ordre du Tastevin, 1980; Chambellan de l'Ordre des Coteaux de Champagne, 1982. *Recreations:* shooting, golf. *Address:* Old Chestnut, Onslow Road, Burwood Park, Walton-on-Thames, Surrey KT12 5AY; 13B La Frenaie, Cogolin, Var, France. *Clubs:* Livery; Burhill Golf (Weybridge).

DRAPER, (John Haydn) Paul; Senior Planning Inspector, Department of Environment, 1977–86, retired; *b* 14 Dec. 1916; *o c* of late Haydn Draper, clarinet player, and Nan Draper; *m* 1941, Nancy Allum, author and journalist; one *s* one *d* (and one *d* decd). *Educ:* LCC primary sch.; Bancroft's Sch.; University Coll. London. Engr in Post Office, 1939–48; Royal Signals, Signalman to Major, Middle East, N Africa, Sicily, NW Europe (despatches), 1940–46; MoT, 1948–64 and 1968–70; Jt Principal Private Sec. to Minister, 1956–58; Asst Sec., 1959; Counsellor (Shipping), British Embassy, Washington, 1964–67; BoT, 1967–68; Under-Sec., 1968; DoE, 1970–74; Senior Planning Inspector, 1973–74; Resident Chm., Civil Service Selection Bd, 1975–76. *Address:* 24 Gordon Mansions, Huntley Street, WC1E 7HF.

DRAPER, Michael William; Under Secretary, Department of Health and Social Security, 1976–78, retired; *b* 26 Sept. 1928; *s* of late John Godfrey Beresford Draper and Aileen Frances Agatha Draper (*née* Masefield); *m* 1952, Theodora Mary Frampton, *o d* of late Henry James Frampton, CSI, CIE; one *s* two *d*. *Educ:* St Edward's Sch., Oxford. FCA. Chartered Accountant, 1953; various posts in England, Ireland, Burma, Nigeria, Unilever Ltd, 1953–64; joined Civil Service, 1964; Principal, Min. of Power, 1964; Asst Sec., DHSS, 1972–76. Sec., Diocese of Bath and Wells, 1978–88; mem. of staff team, Lamplugh House, Christian Renewal Conf. Centre, 1988–89; working with Anglican Church in Zambia, 1991; associated with Sharing of Ministries Abroad, 1992–. *Recreations:* mountain walking, church affairs. *Address:* 21 Kent Park Avenue, Kendal, Cumbria LA9 5JT.

DRAPER, Paul; *see* Draper, J. H. P.

DRAPER, Peter Sydney, CB 1994; Principal Establishment and Finance Officer, Property Services Agency, Department of the Environment, since 1993; *b* 18 May 1935; *s* of late Sydney George Draper and Norah Draper; *m* 1959, Elizabeth Ann (*née* French); three *s*. *Educ:* Haberdashers' Aske's; Regent Polytechnic Sch. of Management (Dip. in Management Studies). AMBIM 1966. Joined GCHQ, Cheltenham, 1953; Min. of Transport, 1956–70; Principal, 1969; Department of the Environment, 1970–: Directorate of Estate Management Overseas, PSA, 1970; Asst Sec., 1975; Head of Staff Resources Div., 1975–78; Asst Dir, Home Regional Services, 1978–80; RCDS, 1981; Dir, Eastern Reg., 1982–84, Under Sec., Dir of Defence Services II, 1985–87, Principal Establishment Officer, 1987–93, PSA. *Recreations:* gardening, golf, walking. *Address:* c/o Lambeth Bridge House, Albert Embankment, SE1 7SB. *Clubs:* Civil Service; Saffron Walden Golf.

DRAPER, Prof. Ronald Philip, PhD; Regius Chalmers Professor of English, University of Aberdeen, 1986–94, now Professor Emeritus; *b* 3 Oct. 1928; *s* of Albert William and Elsie Draper; *m* 1950, Irene Margaret Aldridge; three *d*. *Educ:* Univ. of Nottingham (BA, PhD). Educn Officer, RAF, 1953–55. Lectr in English, Univ. of Adelaide, 1955–56; Lectr, Univ. of Leicester, 1957–68, Sen. Lectr, 1968–73; Prof., Univ. of Aberdeen, 1973–86. *Dramatic scripts:* (with P. A. W. Collins) The Canker and the Rose, Mermaid Theatre, 1964; (with Richard Hoggart) D. H. L., A Portrait of D. H. Lawrence, Nottingham Playhouse, 1967 (televised 1980). *Publications:* D. H. Lawrence, 1964, 3rd edn 1984; (ed) D. H. Lawrence, The Critical Heritage, 1970, 3rd edn 1986; (ed) Hardy, The Tragic Novels, 1975, rev. edn 1991; (ed) George Eliot, The Mill on the Floss and Silas Marner, 1977, 3rd edn 1984; (ed) Tragedy, Developments in Criticism, 1980; Lyric Tragedy, 1985; The Winter's Tale, Text and Performance, 1985; (ed) Hardy, Three Pastoral Novels, 1987; (ed) The Literature of Region and Nation, 1989; (with Martin Ray) An Annotated Critical Bibliography of Thomas Hardy, 1989; (ed) The Epic: developments in criticism, 1990; (ed jtly) A Spacious Vision: essays on Hardy, 1994; articles and reviews in Archiv für das Studium der Neueren Sprachen und Literaturen, Critical Qly, Essays in Criticism, Etudes Anglaises, English Studies, Jl of D. H. Lawrence Soc., Lit. of Region and Nation, Longman Critical Essays, MLR, New Lit. Hist., Notes and Queries, Revue des Langues Vivantes, Rev. of English Studies, Shakespeare Qly, Studies in Short Fiction, THES, Thomas Hardy Annual, Thomas Hardy Jl. *Recreations:* reading, listening to music. *Address:* Maynestay, Chipping Camden, Glos GL55 6DJ. *T:* Chipping Camden (01386) 840796.

DRAYCOTT, Douglas Patrick, MA Oxon; QC 1965; a Recorder, since 1972 (Recorder of Shrewsbury, 1966–71); *b* 23 Aug. 1918; *s* of George Draycott and Mary Ann Draycott (*née* Burke); *m* Elizabeth Victoria Hall (marr. diss. 1974); two *s* three *d*; *m* 1979, Margaret Jean Brunton (*née* Speed). *Educ:* Wolstanton Grammar Sch.; Oriel Coll., Oxford (MA). War Service: Royal Tank Regiment and General Staff, 1939–46. Barrister, Middle Temple, 1950, Master of the Bench, 1972. Joined Oxford Circuit, 1950; Leader, Midland and Oxford Circuit, 1979–83. *Recreation:* cruising on inland waterways. *Address:* 4 King's Bench Walk, Temple, EC4Y 7DL. *T:* 0171–353 3581; 11 Sir Harry's Road, Edgbaston, Birmingham B15 2UY. *T:* 0121–440 1050; 5 Fountain Court, Steelhouse Lane, Birmingham, B4 6DR. *T:* 0121–606 0500.

DRAYCOTT, Gerald Arthur; a Recorder of the Crown Court, 1972–86; *b* 25 Oct. 1911; *s* of Arthur Henry Seely Draycott and Maud Mary Draycott; *m* 1939, Phyllis Moyra Evans; two *s* one *d*. *Educ:* King Edward's Sch., Stratford-on-Avon. FCII. Called to Bar, Middle Temple, 1938. Served in RAF, 1939–46 (Sqdn Ldr; despatches). Practised at Bar, SE Circuit, 1946–90; Dep. Recorder, Bury St Edmunds and Great Yarmouth, 1966–72. Chairman: Eastern Rent Assessment Panel, 1965–77; Nat. Insurance Tribunal, Norwich, 1970–84; E Anglia Med. Appeal Tribunal, 1978–84. *Address:* Nethergate House, Saxlingham Nethergate, Norwich NR15 1PB. *T:* Hempnall (01508) 498306.

DRAYSON, Robert Quested, DSC 1943; MA; *b* 5 June 1919; *s* of late Frederick Louis Drayson and late Elsie Mabel Drayson; *m* 1943, Rachel, 2nd *d* of Stephen Spencer Jenkyns; one *s* two *d*. *Educ:* St Lawrence Coll., Ramsgate; Downing Coll., Cambridge. Univ. of Cambridge: 1938–39, 1946–47; History Tripos, BA 1947, MA 1950. Served RNVR, 1939–46; Lieut in command HM Motor Torpedo Boats. Asst Master and Housemaster, St Lawrence Coll., 1947–50; Asst Master, Felsted Sch., 1950–55; Headmaster, Reed's Sch., Cobham, 1955–63; Headmaster of Stowe, 1964–79; Resident Lay Chaplain to Bishop of Norwich, 1979–84; Lay Reader, 1979. Member: HMC Cttee, 1973–75 (Chm., Midland Div., 1974–75); Council, McAlpine Educnl Endowments Ltd, 1979–; Allied Schools Council, 1980–94; Gen. Council, S Amer. Missionary Soc. (and Chm. Selection Cttee), 1980–; Scholarship Cttee, Indep. Schs Travel Assoc., 1982–; Martyrs' Meml and C of E Trust, 1983–94. Treas., Swifts Sports Trust, 1988–. Chm. of Govs, Riddlesworth Hall, 1980–84; Governor: Parkside, 1958–63; Beachborough, 1965–79; Bilton Grange, 1966–79; Beechwood Park, 1967–79; Monkton Combe, 1976–85; Felixstowe Coll., 1981–84; Vice President: Reed's Sch., 1991–; St Lawrence Coll., 1993– (Gov., 1977–93). FRSA 1968. *Recreations:* formerly hockey (Cambridge Blue, 1946, 1947; Kent XI (Captain), 1947–56; England Final Trial, 1950); now golf, walking, watching cricket. *Address:* Three Gables, Linkhill, Sandhurst, Cranbrook, Kent TN18 5PQ. *T:* Sandhurst (01580) 850447. *Clubs:* Hawks (Cambridge); Rye Golf; Band of Brothers.

DREHER, Derek; conducting review of pay and grading of Ministry of Defence senior staff, since 1995; *b* 12 Jan. 1938; *s* of Frederick Charles Dreher and Mary Emily Dreher (*née* Rutherford); *m* 1961, Patricia Audrey Dowsett; one *s* one *d*. *Educ:* Roan Grammar Sch., Greenwich. Joined War Office as Exec. Officer, 1956; Nat. Service, RAF, 1956–58 (trained as Russian linguist); with War Office, 1958–64, then MoD: postings include: Cyprus, 1962–65; NI, 1969–71; on secondment to Treasury, 1976–79; Asst Sec., 1980; Asst Under Sec. of State, 1992; Command Sec., UKLF, 1992–95. *Recreations:* all forms of sport, but particularly tennis, theatre, foreign travel, reading, particularly political works. *Address:* Kantara, Church Road, Hartley, Kent DA3 8DL.

DREW, Prof. George Charles, MA; London University Professor of Psychology, University College, 1958–79, now Professor Emeritus; Honorary Fellow, 1979; *b* 10 Dec. 1911; *e s* of George Frederick Drew; *m* 1936, Inez Annie, *d* of F. Hulbert Lewis; one *s* one *d*. *Educ:* St George's Sch., Bristol; Bristol, Cambridge and Harvard Univs. Viscount Haldane of Cloan studentship, Cambridge, 1935–36; Rockefeller Fellowship, Harvard Univ., 1936–38; Rockefeller Research Fellowship, Cambridge, 1938–42; Psychological Adviser, Air Ministry, 1942–46; Lecturer in Psychology, University of Bristol, 1946–49, Reader, 1949–51, Prof. of Psychology, 1951–58. Mem. Science Research Council, 1965–67. Vis. Prof., University of Calif, Berkeley, USA, 1967–68. C. S. Myers Lectr, 1973. Founder Mem., Exper. Psych. Soc., 1946 (Pres. 1950–51, 1959–60); Pres., British Psych. Soc., 1962–63; Pres. and Chm., Org. Cttee, 19th Internat. Congress of Psychology, 1969. Dean of Science, UCL, 1973–76. *Publications:* articles on animal behaviour, learning, vision, and other psychological problems, in various British and American journals.

DREW, Jane Beverly, FRIBA; architect; Partner in firm of Fry Drew and Partners, since 1946; *b* 24 March 1911; *m* 1st; two *d*; 2nd, 1942, Edwin Maxwell Fry, CBE, RA (*d* 1987). *Educ:* Croydon. Was in partnership with J. T. Alliston, 1934–39; independent practice, 1939–45; in partnership with Maxwell Fry, 1945–. Asst Town Planning Adviser to Resident Minister, West African Colonies, 1944–45; Senior Architect to Capital project of Chandigarh, Punjab, India, 1951–54; Beamis Prof. Mass Inst. of Techn., Jan.-June, 1961; Vis. Prof. of Architecture, Harvard, Feb.-March 1970; Bicentennial Prof., Utah Univ., 1976. Completed work includes housing, hospitals, schools, and colleges in UK, West Africa, including Univs in Nigeria, Middle East and India; a section of Festival of Britain, 1951; town planning, housing and amenity buildings in Iran, W Africa and India. Past Pres., Architectural Association (1969). Hon. FAIA 1978; Hon. FNIA 1985; Hon. Fellow: Humberside Polytechnic, 1991; Yorks Br., RIBA, 1993; S African Inst. of Architects. Hon LLD Ibadan, 1966; DUniv Open, 1973; Hon. DLitt Newcastle, 1987; Hon. DArch Witwatersrand, 1994. *Publications:* (with Maxwell Fry) Architecture for Children, 1944; (with Maxwell Fry and Harry Ford) Village Housing in the Tropics, 1945; (Founder Editor, 1945–) Architects' Year Book; (with Maxwell Fry) Architecture in the Humid Tropics; Tropical Architecture, 1956; (with Maxwell Fry) Architecture and the Environment, 1976. *Recreations:* reading, writing, friends. *Address:* West Lodge, Cotherstone, Barnard Castle, Co. Durham DH12 9PF. *T:* Teesdale (01833) 650217. *Club:* Institute of Contemporary Arts.

DREW, Joanna Marie, CBE 1985; Director, Hayward and Regional Exhibitions, South Bank Centre, 1987–92; *b* Naini Tal, India, 28 Sept. 1929; *d* of Brig. Francis Greville Drew, CBE, and Sannie Frances Sands. *Educ:* Dartington Hall; Edinburgh Univ. (MA Hons Fine Art); Edinburgh Coll. of Art (DA). Arts Council of GB, 1952–88: Asst Dir of Exhibns, 1970; Dir of Exhibns, 1975; Dir of Art, 1978–86. Mem. Council, RCA, 1979–82. Officier: l'Ordre des Arts et Lettres, 1988 (Chevalier, 1979); l'Ordre Nat. du Mérite, 1994 (Chevalier, 1990).

DREW, John Sydney Neville; Visiting Professor of European Business, and Co-Director, Institute for Study of Change, Durham University, since 1995; Chairman, DSL Ltd, since 1995; *b* 7 Oct. 1936; *s* of late John William Henry Drew and Kathleen Marjorie (*née* Wright); *m* 1962, Rebecca Margaret Amanda (*née* Usher); two *s* one *d*. *Educ:* King Edward's Sch., Birmingham; St John's Coll., Oxford (MA); Fletcher School of Law and Diplomacy, Tufts Univ. (AM). Sloan Fellow of London Business Sch., 1971. Lieut, Somerset LI, 1955–57. HM Diplomatic Service, 1960–73; Dir of Marketing and Exec. Programmes, London Business Sch., 1973–79; Dir of Corporate Affairs, Rank Xerox, 1979–84; Dir of European Affairs, Touche Ross Internat., 1984–86; Head of UK Offices, EEC, 1987–93; Dir, Europa Times, 1993–94; Dep. Chm., ESG, 1993–95. Associate Fellow, Templeton Coll., Oxford, 1982–86; Visiting Professor of European Management: Imperial Coll. of Science and Technology, 1987–91; Open Univ., 1993–. Special Advr, Howlands Trust, Durham Univ., 1994–. Pres., Inst. of Linguists, 1993–. FRSA 1991. Hon. Editor, European Business Jl, 1987–. Hon. MBA Univ. of Northumbria, 1991. *Publications:* Doing Business in the European Community, 1979, 3rd edn 1991 (trans. Spanish and Portuguese 1987); Networking in Organisations, 1986; (ed) Readings in International Enterprise, 1995; articles on European integration and management development. *Recreations:* travel, reading, golf. *Address:* 49 The Ridgeway, NW11 8PQ. *Club:* United Oxford & Cambridge University.

DREW, Peter Robert Lionel, OBE 1979; Hon. Director, World Trade Centers Association, New York, since 1992; Chairman, Taylor Woodrow Group of Companies, 1990–92; *b* 4 Sept. 1927; *s* of Edith Mary Drew (*née* Ball) and Sydney Herbert Drew; *m* 1st, 1952, June Durham; one *s* one *d*; 2nd, 1966, Monica Margaret Mary Allman (marr. diss. 1993); one *d*; 3rd, 1993, Wendy Ferris. *Educ:* Kingston College (Dip. Eng., later Architecture). Helicopter research, Don Juan de la Cierva enterprise, 1949; archit. studies and practice, London, 1951; started housing co., Lytham St Anne's, for Sir Lindsay Parkinson & Co., 1954; Willetts and Bernard Sunley Investment Trust, 1962–90; Taylor Woodrow Property Co., 1965, Dir, 1979–92; Founder Chm., St Katharine by the Tower Ltd (pioneer, London Docks redevelt), 1970; founded World Trade Centre, London, 1973. Chm. and Vice-Pres., internat. WTCA movement; Pres., London World Trade Centre Assoc., 1985–. First Master, Co. of World Traders, 1993 (Founding Master, Guild of World Traders in London, 1982). Dir, Develt Bd, 1990–, Gov., 1992–, Museum of London; Trustee, Silver Jubilee Walkway Trust, 1977–. Gov., Sadler's Wells, 1990–. CIMgt (CBIM 1990). FRSA. Church Warden, All Hallows by the Tower, 1972–94. Liveryman, Painter-Stainers' Co., 1984–; Freeman, Co. of Watermen and Lightermen, 1975. *Publications:* Buy Your Own Home!, 1957; papers on world trade and urban renewal. *Recreations:* water colour painting, sailing, public speaking. *Address:* 18 Westgate Street, Bury St Edmunds, Suffolk IP33 1QG. *T:* Bury St Edmunds (01284) 725990; 43 Trinity Square, EC3N 4DJ.

DREW, Philippa Catherine; Director of Personnel and Office Services, 1995–March 1996, of Corporate Resources, from April 1996, Home Office; *b* 11 May 1946; *d* of Sir Arthur Charles Walter Drew, KCB and Rachel Anna Drew (*née* Lambert). *Educ:* St Paul's Girls' Sch.; St Anne's Coll., Oxford (MA Hons 1968 PPE); Univ. of Pennsylvania (MA Hons 1969 Internat. Relations). Foreign and Commonwealth Office: Central and Southern Africa Dept, 1969; New Delhi, 1970–74; First Sec., S Asia Dept, 1974–75; Home Office: EEC Referendum Count Unit, 1975; Criminal Dept, 1975–78; Police Dept, 1978–81; Gen. Dept, 1981–84; Prison Dept, 1984–85; Field Dir, SCF, Nepal, 1985–87; Head, Probation Service Div., 1987–91; Dir of Custody, HM Prison Service, 1992–95. *Recreations:* opera, travel, talk. *Address:* Home Office, Grenadier House, 99–105 Horseferry Road, SW1P 2DD.

DREWITT, (Lionel) Frank; Managing Director, Harrods Ltd, since 1984; *b* 24 Sept. 1932; *s* of William and Jeanne Drewitt; *m* 1959, Doris Else Heybrok; three *d. Educ:* London Univ. (Bsc Econ). FCA. National Service, 1951–53. Wells & Partners, later Thornton Baker, 1956–64; Chartered Accountant, 1961; joined Harrods Store group, 1964; positions incl. Asst Internal Auditor, Chief Accountant, Company Sec., Asst Man. Dir. *Recreation:* cottages. *Address:* 23 Hertford Avenue, East Sheen, SW14 8EF. *T:* 0181–876 9348.

DREWRY, Dr David John; Director, Science and Technology, Natural Environment Research Council, since 1994; *b* 22 Sept. 1947; *s* of late Norman Tidman Drewry and Mary Edwina Drewry (*née* Wray); *m* 1971, Gillian Elizabeth (*née* Holbrook). *Educ:* Havelock School, Grimsby; Queen Mary Coll., Univ. of London (BSc 1st cl. hons 1969; Fellow, QMW, 1992); Emmanuel College, Cambridge (PhD 1973). FRGS 1972. Queen Mary Coll. E Greenland Expdn, 1968; UK-US Antarctic Expdns, 1969–70 and 1971–72; Cambridge E Greenland Expdn, 1972; Sir Henry Strakosh Fellow, 1974; UK-US Antarctic Expdns, 1974–75, 1977–78 (leader), 1978–79 (leader); Sen. Res. Asst, Univ. of Cambridge, 1978–83; leader, UK-Norwegian Svalbard Expdns, 1980, 1983, 1985, 1986; Asst Dir of Research, Univ. of Cambridge, 1983; Director: Scott Polar Res. Inst., Univ. of Cambridge, 1984–87; British Antarctic Survey, 1987–94. Vice-President: Council, RGS, 1990–93 (Mem., 1986–93); Council, Internat. Glaciological Soc., 1990– (Mem., 1980–82); Comité Arctique Internat., 1989–; Member: Transantarctic Assoc., 1982–; Council of Managers, Nat. Antarctic Programmes, 1988– (Chm., 1988–91); European Cttee on Ocean and Polar Science, 1989–; Royal Soc. Interdisciplinary Science Cttee on Antarctic Res., 1990–; Royal Soc. Envmtl Res. Cttee, 1990–. Hon. Sec., Arctic Club, 1976–83; UK alternate deleg., Sci. Cttee on Antarctic Res., 1985–. Hon. DSc Robert Gordon Univ., 1993. US Antarctic Service Medal, 1979; Cuthbert Peek Award, RGS, 1979; Polar Medal, 1986. *Publications:* Antarctica: glaciological and geophysical folio, 1983; Glacial Geologic Processes, 1986; papers on polar glaciology, geophysics, remote sensing in learned jls. *Recreations:* music, skiing, walking, gastronomy. *Address:* Natural Environment Research Council, Polaris House, North Star Avenue, Swindon SN2 1EU. *Clubs:* Geographical, Antarctic, Arctic.

DREYER, Adm. Sir Desmond (Parry), GCB 1967 (KCB 1963; CB 1960); CBE 1957; DSC; JP; DL; *b* 6 April 1910; *yr s* of late Adm. Sir Frederic Dreyer, GBE, KCB; *m* 1st, 1934, Elisabeth (*d* 1958), *d* of late Sir Henry Chilton, GCMG; one *s* one *d* (and one *s* decd); 2nd, 1959, Marjorie Gordon, *widow* of Hon. R. G. Whiteley. Served War of 1939–45 (DSC). Cdre First Class, 1955. Chief of Staff, Mediterranean, 1955–57; Asst Chief of Naval Staff, 1958–59; Flag Officer (Flotillas) Mediterranean, 1960–61; Flag Officer Air (Home), 1961–62; Comdr, Far East Fleet, 1962–65; Second Sea Lord, 1965–67; Chief Adviser (Personnel and Logistics) to Sec. of State for Defence, 1967–68. Principal Naval ADC to the Queen, 1965–68. Gentleman Usher to the Sword of State, 1973–80. Member: Nat. Bd for Prices and Incomes, 1968–71; Armed Forces Pay Review Body, 1971–79. President: RN Benevolent Trust, 1970–78; Officers' Pension Soc., 1978–84; Regular Forces Employment Assoc., 1978–82; Not Forgotten Assoc., 1973–91. JP 1968, High Sheriff, 1977–78, DL 1985, Hants. *Recreations:* fishing, golf. *Address:* Brook Cottage, Cheriton, near Alresford, Hants SO24 0QA. *T:* Bramdean (01962) 771215. *Club:* Army and Navy.

DREYFUS, John Gustave, FIOP; typographical consultant and historian; *b* 15 April 1918; *s* of late Edmond and Marguerite Dreyfus; *m* 1948, Irène Thurnauer; two *d* (one *s* decd). *Educ:* Oundle Sch.; Trinity Coll., Cambridge (MA). FIOP 1977. Served War, Army, 1939–45. Joined Cambridge University Press as graduate trainee, 1939; Asst Univ. Printer, 1949–56; Typographical Adviser, 1956–82; Typographical Adviser to Monotype Corp., 1955–82; European Consultant to Limited Editions Club, USA, 1956–77; Dir, Curwen Press, 1970–82; Sandars Reader in Bibliography, Univ. of Cambridge, 1979–80. Helped plan exhibn, Printing and the Mind of Man, 1963 (also designed catalogues). President: Assoc. Typographique Internationale, 1968–73 (organised internat. congresses for Assoc.); Printing Historical Soc., 1991 (org. Caxton Internat. Congress, 1976). FRSA. Sir Thomas More Award, Univ. of San Francisco, 1979; Laureate, Amer. Printing Historical Soc., 1984; Frederic W. Goudy Award, Rochester Inst. of Technology, NY, 1984. *Publications:* The Survival of Baskerville's Punches, 1949; The Work of Jan van Krimpen, 1952; (ed series) Type Specimen Facsimiles, 1963–71; Italic Quartet, 1966; (ed with François Richaudeau) La Chose Imprimée (French encyc. on printing), 1977; A History of the Nonesuch Press, 1981; French Eighteenth Century Typography, 1982; A Typographical Masterpiece, 1990; Into Print, 1994; contrib. The Library. *Recreations:* travel, theatre-going. *Address:* 38 Lennox Gardens, SW1X 0DH. *T:* 0171–584 3510. *Club:* Garrick.

DRIELSMA, Claude Dunbar H.; *see* Hankes Drielsma.

DRIFE, Prof. James Owen, MD; FRCOG, FRCSE; Professor of Obstetrics and Gynaecology, University of Leeds, since 1990; *b* 8 Sept. 1947; *s* of late Thomas Drife and Rachel Drife (*née* Jones); *m* 1973, Diana Elizabeth, *d* of Ronald Haxton Girdwood, *qv*; one *s* one *d. Educ:* Cumnock Acad.; Univ. of Edinburgh (BSc Hons; MB ChB 1971; MD 1982). Hosp. appts, Edinburgh, 1971–79; MRC Res. Fellow in Reproductive Biology, Edinburgh, 1974–76; Lectr in Obst. and Gyn., Univ. of Bristol, 1979–82; Dept of Surgery, Frenchay Hosp., Bristol, 1980–81; Sen. Lectr, Obst. and Gyn., Univ. of Leicester, 1982–90. Non-Exec. Dir, United Leeds Teaching Hosps NHS Trust, 1991–. Mem., Cases Cttee, Medical Protection Soc., 1985–94; Assessor for England, Enquiries into Maternal Deaths, 1992–; Mem., Midwifery Cttee, UKCC, 1993–; Mem. Council, RCOG, 1993– (Convenor of Study Gp, 1989–92; Chm., Liby Cttee, 1994–); Mem., GMC, 1994–. Hon. FASPOG. Editor or co-editor, obst. and gyn. jls, 1985–. *Publications:* Dysfunctional Uterine Bleeding and Menorrhagia, 1989; (jtly) Micturition, 1990;(with J. Studd) HRT and Osteoporosis, 1990; (with D. Donnai) Antenatal Diagnosis of Fetal Abnormalities, 1991; (with A. Calder) Prostaglandins and the Uterus, 1992; (with A. Templeton) Infertility, 1992; (with D. Baird) Contraception, 1993; The Benefits and Risks of Oral Contraceptives, 1994; contribs to The Times, BMJ. *Recreations:* songwriting, theatregoing, visiting the pub with wife. *Address:* School of Medicine, Clarendon Wing, Belmont Grove, Leeds LS2 9NS. *T:* Leeds (0113) 292 3888. *Clubs:* National Liberal, Royal Society of Medicine.

DRING, Richard Paddison; Editor of Official Report (Hansard), House of Commons, 1972–78; *b* 6 Nov. 1913; *s* of late Fred Dring and late Florence Hasleham Dring, East Sheen; *m* 1939, Joan Wilson, St Albans; one *s. Educ:* St Paul's School. Commd in British Army during the War, serving in Europe and later in India with IA. Herts Advertiser, 1932; Press Association, 1936; Official Report (Hansard), House of Commons, 1940: Asst Editor, 1954; Dep. Editor, 1970. *Recreation:* golf. *Address:* 24 Vicarage Drive, SW14 8RX. *T:* 0181–876 2162. *Club:* Richmond Golf.

DRINKALL, John Kenneth, CMG 1973; HM Diplomatic Service, retired; High Commissioner to Jamaica, and Ambassador (non-resident) to Haiti, 1976–81; *b* 1 Jan. 1922; *m* 1961, Patricia Ellis; two *s* two *d. Educ:* Haileybury Coll.; Brasenose Coll., Oxford. Indian Army, 1942–45. Entered HM Foreign Service, 1947; 3rd Sec., Nanking, 1948; Vice-Consul, Tamsui, Formosa, 1949–51; Acting Consul, 1951; Foreign Office, 1951–53; 1st Sec., Cairo, 1953–56; Foreign Office, 1957–60; 1st Sec., Brasilia, 1960–62; Foreign Office, 1962–65. Appointed Counsellor, 1964; Counsellor: Nicosia, Cyprus, 1965–67; British Embassy, Brussels, 1967–70; FCO, 1970–71; Canadian Nat. Defence Coll., 1971–72; Ambassador to Afghanistan, 1972–76. *Recreations:* lawn tennis, golf, racquets and squash. *Address:* 68 Rivermead Court, Ranelagh Gardens, SW6 3RZ. *Clubs:* Hurlingham, Royal Automobile, All England Lawn Tennis.

DRINKROW, John; *see under* Hardwick, Michael.

DRINKWATER, Sir John (Muir), Kt 1988; QC 1972; a Commissioner of Income Tax, since 1983; *b* 16 March 1925; *s* of late Comdr John Drinkwater, OBE, RN (retd); *m* Jennifer Marion (*d* 1990), *d* of Edward Fitzwalter Wright, Morley Manor, Derbs; one *s* four *d. Educ:* RNC Dartmouth. HM Submarines, 1943–47; Flag Lieut to C-in-C Portsmouth and First Sea Lord, 1947–50; Lt-Comdr 1952; invalided 1953. Called to Bar, Inner Temple, 1957, Bencher, 1979; a Recorder, 1972–90. Mem., Parly Boundary Commn for England, 1977–80. Mem. Bd, British Airports Authy, 1985–87, Dir, BAA plc, 1987–94. Life Mem. Council, SPAB, 1982. Chm., Cotswold Cons. Assoc., 1995–. Governor, St Mary's Hosp., 1960–64. *Recreations:* swimming, reading, travel. *Address:* Meysey Hampton Manor, Cirencester, Glos GL7 5JS. *T:* Cirencester (01285) 851366; 27 Kilmaine Road, SW6 5JU. *T:* 0171–381 1279; Lohitzun, 64120 St Palais, France. *Clubs:* Garrick, Pratt's.

DRISCOLL, James; Policy Adviser, Nationalised Industries' Chairmen's Group, since 1990 (Director, 1976–90); Senior Partner, Woodcote Consultancy Services, since 1990; *b* 24 April 1925; *s* of Henry James Driscoll and Honorah Driscoll; *m* 1955, Jeanne Lawrence Williams, BA, CertEd; one *s* one *d. Educ:* Coleg Sant Illtyd, Cardiff; University Coll., Cardiff. BA (1st Cl. Hons). Chm., Welsh Young Conservatives, 1948–49; Nat. Dep. Chm., Young Conservatives, 1950; Dep. Chm., Univ. Cons. Fedn, 1949–50; Dep. Chm., NUS, 1951–53. Vice-Chm., European Youth Campaign, 1951–53. Contested (C) Rhondda West, 1950. Asst Lectr, UC Cardiff, 1950–53; Council of Europe Res. Fellowship, 1953. Joined British Iron and Steel Fedn, 1953; various econ. and internat. posts; Econ. Dir and Dep. Dir-Gen., 1963–67; various posts, British Steel Corporation, 1967–80; Man. Dir, Corporate Strategy, 1971–76, Adviser, 1976–80; Chm. and Man. Dir, Woodcote Consultants Ltd, 1980–90. Chm., Lifecare NHS Trust, 1990–94. Member: Grand Council, FBI, 1957–65; CBI Council, 1970–93; Observer, NEDC, 1977–91; Lay Mem., Investigation Cttee, ICA, 1991–. Chm., Econ. Studies Cttee, Internat. Iron and Steel Inst., 1972–74. Mem., Court of Governors, Univ. of Wales Coll. of Cardiff (formerly UC, Cardiff), 1970– (Fellow, 1986). FREconS; FRSA. *Publications:* various articles and pamphlets on econ. and internat. affairs, esp. steel affairs, European integration, wages policy and financing of world steel investment. *Recreations:* travel, reading. *Address:* Foxley Hatch, Birch Lane, Purley, Surrey CR8 3LH.

DRISCOLL, Dr James Philip, CEng; Partner, Coopers & Lybrand (formerly Coopers & Lybrand Deloitte), since 1990; *b* 29 March 1943; *s* of Reginald Driscoll and Janetta Bridget Driscoll; *m* 1969, Josephine Klapper, BA; two *s* two *d. Educ:* St Illtyd's Coll., Cardiff; Birmingham Univ. (BSc 1964; PhD 1972); Manchester Business Sch. MIChemE 1975; MIGasE 1975; MInstF 1975. Taught at St Illtyd's Coll., Cardiff, 1964; res. posts with Joseph Lucas, Solihull, 1968–69; British Steel Corporation: res. posts, 1969–70; commercial posts, 1971–79, incl. Manager, Divl Supplies, 1973; Reg. Manager, BSC (Industry), 1979–82; Dir, S Wales Workshops, 1980–82; Industrial Dir, Welsh Office, 1982–85; Associate Dir, 1985–87, Dir, 1987–90, Coopers & Lybrand Associates. *Publications:* various technical papers. *Recreations:* family, sport. *Address:* 6 Cory Crescent, Wyndham Park, Peterston-super-Ely, S Glam CF5 6LS. *T:* Peterston-super-Ely (01446) 760372. *Clubs:* Cardiff Athletic, Peterston Football (Cardiff).

DRISCOLL, Michael John; QC 1992; *b* 22 Feb. 1947; *s* of John and Gladys Mary Driscoll; *m* 1970, Heather Edyvean Nichols; two *s* two *d. Educ:* Rugby Sch.; St John's Coll., Cambridge (BA, LLB). Asst Lectr, Manchester Univ., 1969–70; called to the Bar, Middle Temple, 1970. *Recreation:* family. *Address:* 9 Old Square, Lincoln's Inn, WC2A 3SR. *T:* 0171–405 4682.

DRIVER, Sir Antony (Victor), Kt 1986; Chairman, South West Thames Regional Health Authority, 1982–88; *b* London, 20 July 1920; *s* of late Arthur William Driver and Violet Clementina Driver (*née* Browne); *m* 1948, Patricia (née Tinkler); three *s. Educ:* King's Coll., Univ. of London (BScEng Hons); Dip., Graduate Sch. of Industrial Admin., Carnegie-Mellon Univ., Pittsburgh. CEng; FIMechE, FInstPet; FIMgt. In oil industry with Shell-Mex and BP Ltd, until 1975, and BP Oil Ltd, 1976–80: seconded to British Petroleum Co., as Marketing Manager, N Europe, 1969–71; General Manager, Sales, 1971–78; Director, Personnel and Admin, 1979–80. Non-executive Director: Candles Ltd, 1976–80; Rockwood Ltd, 1978–80; Baxter Fell & Co. Ltd, 1980–85; Chm., Hoogovens (UK) Ltd, 1985–88. Director: Inst. of Cancer Research, 1981–; Oil Industries Club Ltd, 1981–; Surrey Assoc. of Youth Clubs and Surrey PHAB Ltd, 1991–. Liveryman, Tallow Chandlers' Co., 1977–; Freeman, City of London. *Recreations:* travel, gardening, wine, pyrotechnics. *Address:* Winterdown, Holmbury St Mary, Dorking, Surrey RH5 6NL. *T:* Dorking (01306) 730238.

DRIVER, Bryan, FCIT 1976; Bryan Driver Associates, Management Consultants; *b* 26 August 1932; *s* of Fred and Edith Driver; *m* 1955, Pamela Anne (*née* Nelson); two *d. Educ:* Wath-upon-Dearne Grammar School. Joined British Railways (Junior Clerk), 1948; Royal Air Force, 1950–52; management training with BR, 1958–59; posts in London, Doncaster, Newcastle, 1959–69; Divisional Operating Manager, Norwich, 1969–71, Liverpool Street, 1971–72; Divisional Manager, West of England, 1972–75, South Wales, 1975–77; Dep. Gen. Manager, Eastern Region, 1977–82; Man. Dir, 1982–87, Chm., 1985–87, Freightliners Ltd; Consultant Advr, 1987–88, Ops Dir, then Dir, Ops and Rolling Stock, 1988–93, Transmanche-Link (Channel Tunnel Contractors). *Recreations:* cricket, Rugby football, golf. *Address:* Riverds Lea, 4 Shilton Garth Close, Old Earswick, York YO3 9SQ. *T:* York (01904) 762848. *Clubs:* Savile, MCC; Yorkshire CC, York Golf.

DRIVER, Charles Jonathan, MPhil; Master of Wellington College, since 1989; *b* 19 Aug. 1939; *s* of Rev. Kingsley Ernest Driver and Phyllis Edith Mary (*née* Gould); *m* 1967, Ann Elizabeth Hoogewerf; two *s* one *d. Educ:* St Andrews Coll., Grahamstown; Univ. of Cape Town (BA Hons, BEd, STD); Trinity Coll., Oxford (MPhil). Pres., National Union of S African Students, 1963–64; Asst Teacher, Sevenoaks Sch., 1964–65 and 1967–68; Housemaster, Internat. Sixth Form Centre, Sevenoaks Sch., 1968–73; Dir of Sixth Form Studies, Matthew Humberstone Sch., 1973–78; Res. Fellow, Univ. of York, 1976; Principal, Island Sch., Hong Kong, 1978–83; Headmaster, Berkhamsted Sch., 1983–89. Mem., HMC. FRSA. Trustee, Lomans Trust; Governor: Benenden Sch.; Shiplake Coll.; Eagle House Prep. Sch.; Visitor, Scaitcliffe Sch. Editor, Conference and Common Room, 1993–. *Publications: novels:* Elegy for a Revolutionary, 1968; Send War in Our Time, O Lord, 1969; Death of Fathers, 1972; A Messiah of the Last Days, 1974; *poetry:* I Live Here Now, 1979; (with Jack Cope) Occasional Light, 1979; Hong Kong Portraits, 1986; In the Water-Margins, 1994; *biography:* Patrick Duncan, 1980. *Recreations:* long-distance running, reading, writing, Rugby. *Address:* Wellington College, Crowthorne, Berks RG11 7PU.

DRIVER, Christopher Prout; writer and broadcaster; Personal Page consultant, The Guardian, since 1994 (Personal Page Co-Editor, 1988–94); *b* 1 Dec. 1932; *s* of Dr Arthur Herbert Driver and Elsie Kathleen Driver (*née* Shepherd); *m* 1958, Margaret Elizabeth Perfect; three *d. Educ:* Dragon Sch., Oxford; Rugby Sch.; Christ Church, Oxford (MA). Friends Ambulance Unit Internat. Service, 1955–57; Reporter, Liverpool Daily Post, 1958–60; Reporter, 1960–64, Features Editor, 1964–68, Food and Drink Ed., 1984–88, The Guardian; Editor, Good Food Guide, 1969–82. Member: Christian Aid Bd, 1972–84; Highgate URC, 1962–. *Publications:* A Future for the Free Churches?, 1962; The Disarmers: a study in protest, 1964; The Exploding University, 1971; The British at Table 1940–1980, 1983; (publisher and co-ed) Shaftesbury, 1983; (jtly) Pepys at Table, 1984; Twelve Poems, 1985; Music for Love, 1994; contribs on various topics to The Guardian and other serious jls. *Recreations:* cooking, playing violin and viola, avoiding cars, accumulating books. *Address:* 6 Church Road, Highgate, N6 4QT; The Guardian, 119 Faringdon Road, EC1R 3ER. *T:* 0171–278 2332.

DRIVER, Sir Eric (William), Kt 1979; retired; Chairman, Mersey Regional Health Authority, 1973–82; Chairman, National Staff Committee, (Works), 1979–82; *b* 19 Jan. 1911; *s* of William Weale Driver and Sarah Ann Driver; *m* 1st, 1938, Winifred Bane; two *d*; 2nd, 1972, Sheila Mary Johnson. *Educ:* Strand Sch., London; King's Coll., London Univ. (BSc). FICE. Civil Engr with ICI Ltd, 1938–73, retd as Chief Civil Engr Mond Div. *Recreations:* hill walking, gardening, travel. *Address:* Conker Tree Cottage, South Bank, Great Budworth, Cheshire CW9 6HG. *Club:* Budworth Sailing.

DRIVER, Olga Lindholm; *see* Aikin, O. L.

DROGHEDA, 12th Earl of, *cr* 1661 (Ireland); **Henry Dermot Ponsonby Moore;** Baron Moore of Mellifont, 1616; Viscount Moore, 1621; Baron Moore of Cobham (UK), 1954; photographer; *b* 14 Jan. 1937; *o s* of 11th Earl of Drogheda, KG, KBE and of Joan *o d* of late William Henry Carr; *S* father, 1989; *m* 1st, 1968, Eliza Lloyd (marr. diss. 1972), *d* of Stacy Barcroft Lloyd, Jr, and Mrs Paul Mellon; 2nd, 1978, Alexandra, *d* of Sir Nicholas Henderson, *qv*; two *s* one *d. Educ:* Eton; Trinity College, Cambridge. *Publications:* (as Derry Moore): (with Brendan Gill) The Dream Come True, Great Houses of Los Angeles, 1980; (with George Plumptre) Royal Gardens, 1981; (with Sybila Jane Flower) Stately Homes of Britain, 1982; (with Henry Mitchell) Washington, Houses of the Capital, 1982; (with Michael Pick) The English Room, 1984; (with Alvilde Lees-Milne) The Englishwoman's House, 1984; (with Alvilde Lees-Milne) The Englishman's Room, 1986; (with the Marchioness of Salisbury) The Gardens of Queen Elizabeth the Queen Mother, 1988; (with Sarah Hollis) The Shell Guide to the Gardens of England and Wales, 1989. *Heirs: s* Viscount Moore, *qv. Address:* 40 Ledbury Road, W11 2AB. *Club:* Brooks's.

DROMGOOLE, Jolyon; MA Oxon; Director (Council Secretariat), Institution of Civil Engineers, 1985–91; Deputy Under-Secretary of State (Army), Ministry of Defence, 1984–85; *b* 27 March 1926; 2nd *s* of late Nicholas and Violet Dromgoole; *m* 1956, Anthea, *e d* of Sir Anthony Bowlby, 2nd Bt; five *d* (incl. triplets). *Educ:* Christ's Hospital; Dulwich Coll.; University Coll., Oxford, 1944. 2nd Cl. Hons (History), MA. Entered HM Forces, 1944; commissioned 14/20 King's Hussars, 1946. University Coll., 1948–50. Entered Administrative Cl., Civil Service; assigned to War Office, 1950; Private Sec. to Permanent Under-Sec., 1953; Principal, 1955; Private Sec. to Sec. of State, 1964–65; Asst Sec., 1965; Command Sec., HQ FARELF, Singapore, 1968–71; Royal Coll. of Defence Studies, 1972; Under-Sec., Broadcasting Dept, Home Office, 1973–76; Asst Under-Sec. of State, Gen. Staff, 1976–79, Personnel and Logistics, 1979–84, MoD. Trustee and Gov., Royal Sch., Hampstead, 1985–. *Recreations:* polo, literature, publisher. *Address:* 13 Gladstone Street, SE1 6EY. *T:* 0171–928 2162, Montreal House, Barnsley, Glos GL7 5EL. *T:* Cirencester (01285) 740331. *Club:* Athenæum.
See also P. S. B. F. Dromgoole.

DROMGOOLE, Patrick Shirley Brookes Fleming; Chairman, PDP Ltd, since 1992; *b* 30 Aug. 1930; *s* of late Nicholas and Violet Dromgoole; *m* 1st, 1960, Jennifer Veronica Jill Davis (marr. diss. 1991); two *s* one *d*; 2nd, 1991, June Kell Morrow. *Educ:* Dulwich Coll.; University Coll., Oxford (MA). Actor and various employments in London and Paris, 1947–51; BBC Drama Producer/Dir, 1954–63; freelance theatre, film and television dir (directed first plays in West End of Orton, Wood, Welland, Halliwell and others), 1963–69; directed regularly Armchair Theatre for ABC TV and Thames TV; made number of films for cinema; joined HTV Ltd as Programme Controller, 1969; Asst Man. Dir, 1981; Man. Dir, HTV, 1987; Chief Exec., HTV Gp, 1988–91. Various awards incl. Pye Oscar, RTS, for Thick as Thieves, 1971; Best Play of the Year, for Machinegunner, 1973; Amer. Emmy, for D.P., 1985. FRTS 1978; FRSA 1989. *Recreations:* travel, œnophilia, pre-Raphaelite art, reading. *Address:* Penkill Castle, Old Dailly, Girvan, Ayrshire KA26 9TQ. *Clubs:* Savile, Groucho; Castel's (Paris).
See also J. Dromgoole.

DROMORE, Bishop of, (RC), since 1976; **Most Rev. Francis Gerard Brooks,** DD, DCL; *b* Jan. 1924. Priest, 1949. Formerly President, St Colman's Coll., Violet Hill, Newry. *Address:* Bishop's House, Newry, Co. Down, N Ireland BT35 6PN. *T:* Newry (01693) 62444, *Fax:* Newry (01693) 60496.

DRONFIELD, Ronald; Chief Insurance Officer for National Insurance, Department of Health and Social Security, 1976–84, retired; *b* 21 Dec. 1924; *m* 1966, Marie Renie (*née* Price). *Educ:* King Edward VII Sch., Sheffield; Oriel Coll., Oxford. RN, 1943–46. Entered Min. of National Insurance, 1949; Principal Private Sec. to Minister of Pensions and Nat. Insurance, 1964–66; Cabinet Office, 1970–71. *Recreation:* reading, biography. *Address:* 8 Beechrow, Ham Common, Richmond, Surrey TW10 5HE.

DRONKE, Prof. (Ernst) Peter (Michael), FBA 1984; Fellow of Clare Hall, since 1964, and Professor of Medieval Latin Literature, since 1989, University of Cambridge; *b* 30 May 1934; *s* of Senatspräsident A. H. R. Dronke and M. M. Dronke (*née* Kronfeld); *m* 1960, Ursula Miriam (*née* Brown); one *d. Educ:* Victoria University, NZ (MA 1st Cl. Hons 1954); Magdalen College, Oxford (BA 1st Cl. Hons 1957; MA 1961); MA Cantab 1961. Research Fellow, Merton Coll., Oxford, 1958–61; Lectr in Medieval Latin, 1961–79, Reader, 1979–89, Univ. of Cambridge. Guest Lectr, Univ. of Munich, 1960; Guest Prof., Centre d'Etudes Médiévales, Poitiers, 1969; Leverhulme Fellow, 1973; Guest Prof., Univ. Autónoma, Barcelona, 1977; Vis. Fellow, Humanities Res. Centre, Canberra, 1978; Vis. Prof. of Medieval Studies, Westfield Coll., 1981–86. Lectures: W. P. Ker, Univ. of Glasgow, 1976; Matthews, Birkbeck Coll., 1983; Jackson, Harvard Univ., 1992; O'Donnell, Univ. of Toronto, 1993; Barlow, UCL, 1995. Corresp. Fellow, Real Academia de Buenas Letras, 1976. Hon. Pres., Internat. Courtly Literature Soc., 1974. Co-Editor, Mittellateinisches Jahrbuch, 1977–. Premio Internazionale Ascoli Piceno, 1988. *Publications:* Medieval Latin and the Rise of European Love-Lyric, 2 vols, 1965–66; The Medieval Lyric, 1968; Poetic Individuality in the Middle Ages, 1970; Fabula, 1974; Abelard and Heloise in Medieval Testimonies, 1976; (with Ursula Dronke) Barbara et antiquissima carmina, 1977; (ed) Bernardus Silvestris, Cosmographia, 1978; Introduction to Francesco Colonna, Hypnerotomachia, 1981; Women Writers of the Middle Ages, 1984; The Medieval Poet and his World, 1984; Dante and Medieval Latin Traditions, 1986; Introduction to Rosvita, Dialoghi drammatici, 1986; (ed) A History of Twelfth-Century Western Philosophy, 1988; Hermes and the Sibyls, 1990; Latin and Vernacular Poets of the Middle Ages, 1991; Intellectuals and Poets in Medieval Europe, 1992; Verse with Prose: from Petronius to Dante, 1994; Nine Medieval Latin Plays, 1994; (ed) Hildegard of Bingen, *Liber divinorum operum*, 1995; essays in learned jls and symposia. *Recreations:* music, film, Brittany. *Address:* 6 Parker Street, Cambridge CB1 1JL. *T:* Cambridge (01223) 359942.

DRU DRURY, Martin; *see* Drury.

DRUCKER, Henry Matthew, PhD; Managing Director, Oxford Philanthropic, since 1994; *b* 29 April 1942; *s* of Arthur and Frances Drucker; *m* 1975, Nancy Livia Newman. *Educ:* Allegheny Coll., Meadville, Penn (BA Philosophy); London School of Economics (PhD PolPhil). Lectr in Politics 1964–76, Sen. Lectr in Politics 1976–86, Univ. of Edinburgh; Dir, Univ. Develt Office, Oxford Univ., 1987–93; Dir, Campaign for Oxford, 1988–93. Vis. Prof. of Govt, LSE, 1994–. *Publications:* Political Uses of Ideology, 1974; (ed with M. G. Clarke) Our Changing Scotland, 1977; Breakaway—The Scottish Labour Party, 1978; (ed with Nancy Drucker) Scottish Government Yearbook, 1978–82; Doctrine and Ethos in the Labour Party, 1979; (ed) Multi-Party Britain, 1979; (with Gordon Brown) The Politics of Nationalism and Devolution, 1980; (ed) John P. Mackintosh on Scotland, 1982; (general ed.) Developments in British Politics, 1983; (general ed.) Developments in British Politics 2, 1986, revd edn 1988. *Recreations:* reading aloud to wife, walking. *Address:* Oxford Philanthropic Ltd, 36 Windmill Road, Oxford OX3 7BX. *T:* Oxford (01865) 744300.

DRUCKER, Prof. Peter (Ferdinand); writer and consultant; Clarke Professor of Social Science, Claremont Graduate School, Claremont, Calif, since 1971; *b* 19 Nov. 1909; *s* of Adolph B. Drucker and Caroline (*née* Bond); *m* 1937, Doris Schmitz; one *s* three *d. Educ:* Austria, Germany, England. Investment banker, London, 1933–36; newspapers, 1937–41; Professor of Philosophy and Politics, Bennington Coll., Bennington, Vt, USA, 1942–49; Prof. of Management, NY Univ., 1950–72; Professorial Lectr in Oriental Art, Claremont Colls, 1980–86. Management Consultant (internat. practice among businesses and govts) (as well as Professorships), 1943–. Has recorded audio-cassettes on management practice. Holds hon. doctorates from Univs in Belgium, GB, Japan, Spain, Switzerland, USA. Hon. FIMgt; FAAAS; Fellow: Amer. Acad. of Management; Internat. Acad. of Management. Godkin Lectr, Harvard Univ., 1994. Order of Sacred Treasure, Japan; Grand Cross, Austria. *Publications:* End of Economic Man, 1939, 1995; Future of Industrial Man, 1942, 1994; Concept of the Corporation, 1946, 1992; The New Society, 1950, 1992; Practice of Management, 1954, 1992; America's Next Twenty Years, 1959; Landmarks of Tomorrow, 1960; Managing for Results, 1964, 1992; The Effective Executive, 1966, 1992; The Age of Discontinuity, 1969, 1992; Technology, Management and Society, 1970; Men, Ideas and Politics, 1971; The New Markets . . . and other essays, 1971; Management: tasks, responsibilities, practices, 1974, 1992; The Unseen Revolution: how pension fund socialism came to America, 1976; Adventures of a Bystander, 1979, 1994; Managing in Turbulent Times, 1980, 1992; Toward the New Economics, 1981; The Changing World of the Executive (essays), 1982; Innovation and Entrepreneurship, 1985, 1992; The Frontiers of Management, 1986; The New Realities, 1989; Managing the Non-Profit Organisation, 1990; Managing for the Future, 1992; The Ecological Vision, 1993; Post Capitalist Society, 1993; Managing at a Time of Great Change, 1995; *novels:* The Last of All Possible Worlds, 1982; The Temptation to Do Good, 1984. *Recreations:* mountaineering; Japanese history and paintings. *Address:* 636 Wellesley Drive, Claremont, CA 91711, USA. *T:* (909) 6211488.

DRUMLANRIG, Viscount; Sholto Francis Guy Douglas; *b* 1 June 1967; *s* and *heir* of 12th Marquess of Queensberry, *qv.*

DRUMM, Rt. Rev. Mgr. Walter Gregory; Rector, Pontifical Beda College, Rome, 1987–91; *b* 2 March 1940; *s* of Owen and Kathleen Drumm. *Educ:* St Joseph's Sch. and St Aloysius' Coll., Highgate; Balliol Coll., Oxford (MA). Tutor, The Grange, Warlingham, 1962–66; studied at Beda Coll., 1966–70; ordained, Westminster Dio., 1970; Asst Priest, Wood Green, 1970–73; Chaplain, Oxford Univ., 1973–83; Parish Priest, Our Lady of Victories, Kensington, 1983–87. Prelate of Honour to the Pope, 1988. *Address:* Westminster Cathedral Clergy House, Francis Street, SW1P 1QW. *Club:* United Oxford & Cambridge University.

DRUMMOND, family name of **Earl of Perth** and **Baroness Strange.**

DRUMMOND, Maj.-Gen. Anthony John D.; *see* Deane-Drummond.

DRUMMOND, David Classon, FIBiol; Deputy Director, Research and Development Service, Agricultural Development Advisory Service, Ministry of Agriculture, Fisheries and Food, 1987–88, retired; *b* 25 July 1928; *s* of Roger Hamilton Drummond and Marjorie Holt Drummond; *m* 1952, Barbara Anne, *d* of late Prof. Alfred Cobban; three *d. Educ:* St Peter's Sch., York; University Coll., London (BSc 1952); Pennsylvania State Univ., USA (Kellogg Fellow; MS 1962). FIBiol 1975. Project Manager, FAO, UN, Karachi, 1971–72; Agricultural Science Service, MAFF: Head of Rodent Res. Dept, and Officer i/c Tolworth Lab., 1974–82; Head of Biol. Div., and Officer i/c Slough Lab.,

1982–85; Sen. Agricl Scientist with special responsibilities for R&D, 1985–87. Mem., WHO Expert Adv. Panel on Vector Biology and Control, 1980–. *Publications:* scientific papers and reviews mainly concerned with rodent biology and control and develt of agricl and urban rat control programmes. *Recreations:* travel, gardening, history of rat catching. *Address:* 22 Knoll Road, Dorking, Surrey RH4 3EP.

DRUMMOND, Sir John (Richard Gray), Kt 1995; CBE 1990; writer and broadcaster; *b* 25 Nov. 1934; *s* of late Captain A. R. G. Drummond and Esther (*née* Pickering), Perth, WA. *Educ:* Canford; Trinity Coll., Cambridge (MA History). RNVR, 1953–55. BBC Radio and Television, 1958–78, latterly as Asst Head, Music and Arts; programmes produced incl.: Tortelier Master Classes, 1964; Leeds Piano Comp., 1966 (1st Prize, Prague Fest., 1967); Diaghilev, 1967; Kathleen Ferrier, 1968; Music Now, 1969; Spirit of the Age, 1975; The Lively Arts, 1976–78; Dir, Edinburgh Internat. Fest., 1978–83; Controller of Music, 1985–92, and of Radio 3, 1987–92, BBC; Dir, BBC Prom. Concerts, 1986–95. Dir, European Arts Fest., 1992. Pres., Kensington Soc., 1985–; Vice Pres., British Arts Festivals Assoc., 1993– (Vice-Chm., 1981–83); Chm., Nat. Dance Co-ordinating Cttee, 1986–94; Mem. various adv. councils and cttees concerning music, theatre and dance; Governor, Royal Ballet, 1986–; Mem., Theatres Trust, 1989–. Hon. GSM 1988; Hon. RAM 1994; Hon. FRNCM 1994; Hon. FTCL 1994. FRSA. *Publications:* (with Joan Bakewell) A Fine and Private Place, 1977; (with N. Thompson) The Turn of Dance?, 1984. *Recreations:* conversation, looking at architecture, browsing in bookshops. *Address:* 61c Campden Hill Court, W8 7HL. *T:* 0171–937 2257. *Club:* New (Edinburgh).

DRUMMOND, Kevin; *see* Drummond, T. A. K.

DRUMMOND, Maldwin Andrew Cyril, OBE 1990; JP; DL; farmer and author; *b* 30 April 1932; *s* of late Maj. Cyril Drummond, JP, DL, and Mildred Joan Quinnell; *m* 1st, 1955, Susan Dorothy Cayley (marr. diss. 1977); two *d*; 2nd, 1978, Gillian Turner Laing; one *s*. *Educ:* Eton Coll.; Royal Agricl Coll., Cirencester; Univ. of Southampton (Cert. in Environmental Sci., 1972). 2nd Lieut, Rifle Bde, 1950–52; Captain, Queen Victoria's, later Queen's, Royal Rifles (TA), retd 1967. Verderer of New Forest, 1961–90; Chairman: Heritage Coast Forum, 1989–; New Forest Cttee, 1990– (Consultative Panel, 1982–); Mem., Countryside Commn, 1980–86. Member: Southampton Harbour Bd, 1967; British Transport Docks Bd, Southampton, 1968–74; Southern Water Authority, 1984–87. Chairman: Sail Training Assoc., 1967–72; Maritime Trust, 1979–89; Cutty Sark Soc., 1979–89; Warrior (formerly Ships) Preservation Trust, 1979–91; Vice-Pres., 1983–, and Chm. Boat Cttee, 1983–92, RNLI; Trustee, World Ship Trust, 1980–91; Chm., Hampshire Bldgs Preservation Trust, 1986–92. Younger Brother of Trinity House, 1991–. Mem., New Forest RDC, 1957–66; Hampshire: County Councillor, 1967–75; JP 1964 (Chm., New Forest Bench, 1992–); DL 1975; High Sheriff, 1980–81. FRGS 1978; FRSA 1987. Hon. DSc. *Publications:* Conflicts in an Estuary, 1973; Tall Ships, 1976; Salt-Water Places, 1979; (with Paul Rodhouse) Yachtsman's Naturalist, 1980; (with Philip Allison) The New Forest, 1980; The Riddle, 1985; West Highland Shores, 1990. *Recreations:* cruising under sail and wondering about the sea. *Address:* Cadland House, Fawley, Southampton SO45 1AA. *T:* (office) Fawley (01703) 892039, (home) (01703) 891543; Wester Kames Castle, Port Bannatyne, Isle of Bute PA20 0QW. *T:* Rothesay (01700) 3983. *Clubs:* White's, Pratt's, Royal Cruising; Royal Yacht Squadron (Cdre, 1991–) (Cowes); Leander (Henley).

DRUMMOND, Rev. Norman Walker, MA; BD; Scottish Governor, BBC, and Chairman, Broadcasting Council for Scotland, since 1994; Chaplain to the Queen in Scotland, since 1993; *b* 1 April 1952; *s* of late Edwin Payne Drummond and Jean (*née* Walker); *m* 1976, Lady Elizabeth Helen Kennedy, *d* of 7th Marquess of Ailsa, OBE; three *s* two *d*. *Educ:* Merchiston Castle Sch.; Fitzwilliam Coll., Cambridge (MA Law); New Coll., Univ. of Edinburgh (BD). Ordained as Minister of the Church of Scotland, and commnd to serve as Chaplain to HM Forces in the Army, 1976; Chaplain: Depot, Parachute Regt and Airborne Forces, 1977–78; 1st Bn The Black Watch (Royal Highland Regt), 1978–82; to the Moderator of the Gen. Assembly of the Church of Scotland, 1980; Fettes Coll., 1982–84; Headmaster, Loretto Sch., 1984–95. Chaplain to Gov. of Edinburgh Castle, 1991–93. Chairman: Musselburgh and Dist Council of Social Service; Ronald Selby Wright Christian Leadership Trust; Member: Queen's Bodyguard for Scotland (Royal Co. of Archers); Court, Heriot-Watt Univ.; Scottish Council, ISCO; Scottish Cttee, ICRF, 1995; Trustee: Arthur Smith Meml Trust; Foundn for Skin Res., 1995; Governor: St Mary's Sch., Melrose; Croftinloan Sch., Pitlochry; Gordonstoun Sch., 1995–. President: Edinburgh Bn, Boys' Bde, 1993; Victoria League in Scotland, 1995. Cambridge Univ. Rugby Blue, 1971; Captain: Scottish Univs XV, 1974; Army XV and Combined Services XV, 1976–77. FRSA 1993. *Publications:* The First Twenty-five Years: official history of The Black Watch Kirk Session, 1979; Mother's Hands (collection of short stories for children, parents and teachers), 1992. *Recreations:* Rugby football, cricket, golf, curling, traditional jazz, Isle of Skye. *Address:* BBC Scotland, Broadcasting House, Queen Margaret Drive, Glasgow G12 8DG. *Clubs:* MCC, Free Foresters; New (Edinburgh); Hawks (Cambridge).

DRUMMOND, (Thomas Anthony) Kevin; QC (Scot.) 1987; *b* 3 Nov. 1943; *s* of Thomas Drummond, BSc, and Mary (*née* Hughes); *m* 1966, Margaret Evelyn Broadley; one *d* (and one *d* decd). *Educ:* Blair's Coll., Aberdeen; St Mirin's Acad., Paisley; Edinburgh Univ. (LLB). Estate Duty Office, CS, 1963–70; Solicitor, 1970; admitted Faculty of Advocates, 1974; Advocate-Depute, Crown Office, Edinburgh, 1985–90. Member: Criminal Injuries Compensation Bd, 1990–; Firearms Consultative Cttee, 1990–. Cartoonist, Scots Law Times, 1981–. *Publications:* legal cartoons under name of TAK: The Law at Work, 1982; The Law at Play, 1983. *Recreations:* shooting, hill-walking, fishing, under water hang-gliding. *Address:* Pomathorn House, Howgate, Midlothian EH26 8PJ. *T:* Penicuik (01968) 74046.

DRUMMOND YOUNG, James Edward; QC (Scot.) 1988; *b* 17 Feb. 1950; *s* of Duncan Drummond Young, MBE, DL, Edinburgh, and Annette (*née* Mackay); *m* 1991, Elizabeth Mary, *d* of John Campbell-Kease, Connel, Argyll. *Educ:* John Watson's Sch.; Sidney Sussex Coll., Cambridge (BA 1971); Harvard Univ. (Joseph Hodges Choate Meml Fellow, 1971–72; LLM 1972); Edinburgh Univ. (LLB 1974). Admitted to Faculty of Advocates, 1976. Standing Jun. Counsel in Scotland to Bd of Inland Revenue, 1986–88. *Publications:* (with J. B. St Clair) The Law of Corporate Insolvency in Scotland, 1988, 2nd edn 1992; (contrib.) Stair Memorial Encyclopaedia of Scots Law, 1989. *Recreations:* music, travel. *Address:* 14 Ainslie Place, Edinburgh EH3 6AS. *T:* 0131–225 6393. *Club:* New (Edinburgh).

DRUON, Maurice Samuel Roger Charles, Hon. CBE 1988; Grand Officier de la Légion d'Honneur; Commandeur des Arts et Lettres; author; Member of the French Academy since 1966, Permanent Secretary, since 1986; Member: French Parliament (Paris), 1978–81; Assembly of Council of Europe, 1978–81; European Parliament, 1979–80; Franco-British Council, since 1972; *b* Paris, 23 April 1918; *s* of René Druon de Reyniac and Léonilla Jenny Samuel-Cros; *m* 1968, Madeleine Marignac. *Educ:* Lycée Michelet and Ecole des Sciences Politiques, Paris. Ecole de Cavalerie de Saumur, aspirant, 1940; joined Free French Forces, London, 1942; Attaché Commissariat à l'Intérieur et Direction de l'Information, 1943; War Correspondent, 1944–45; Lieut de réserve de cavalerie. Journalist, 1946–47; Minister for Cultural Affairs, France, 1973–74. Awarded Prix Goncourt, 1948, for novel Les Grandes Familles; Prix de Monaco, 1966. Member: Acad. of Morocco, 1980; Athènes' Acad., 1981; Acad. de Lisbonne, 1994; Pres., Franco-Italian Assoc., 1985–. Dr *hc* York Univ., Ontario, 1987. Commandeur du Phénix de Grèce; Grand Officer de l'Ordre de l'Honneur de Grèce; Grand Officier du Mérite de l'Ordre de Malte; Commandeur de l'Ordre de la République de Tunisie; Grand Officier du Lion du Sénégal; Grand Croix du Mérite de la République Italienne; Grand Croix de l'Aigle Aztèque du Mexique; Grand Officier Ouissam Alaouite (Morocco); Commandeur du Mérite de Monaco; Commandeur du Cruseiro del Sul (Brazil); Commandeur de l'ordre du Cèdre (Lebanon); Comdr, Ordre de Léopold (Belgium); Grand Croix, l'ordre du Christ (Portugal), 1994. *Publications:* Lettres d'un Européen, 1944; La Dernière Brigade (The Last Detachment), 1946 (publ. in England 1957); Les Grandes Familles, La Chute des Corps, Rendez-Vous aux Enfers, 1948–51 (trilogy publ. in England under title The Curtain falls, 1959); La Volupté d'Etre (Film of Memory), 1954 (publ. in England 1955); Les Rois Maudits (The Accursed Kings), 1955–60 (six vols: The Iron King, The Strangled Queen, The Poisoned Crown, The Royal Succession, The She-Wolf of France, The Lily and the Lion, publ. in England 1956–61); Tistou les pouces verts (Tistou of the green fingers), 1957 (publ. in England 1958); Alexandre le Grand (Alexander the God), 1958 (publ. in Eng. 1960); Des Seigneurs de la Plaine- (The Black Prince and other stories), 1962 (publ. in Eng. 1962); Les Mémoires de Zeus I (The Memoirs of Zeus), 1963 (in Eng. 1964); Bernard Buffet, 1964; Paris, de César à Saint Louis (The History of Paris from Caesar to St Louis), 1964 (in Eng. 1969); Le Pouvoir, 1965; Les Tambours de la Mémoire, 1965; Le Bonheur des Uns, 1967; Les Mémoires de Zeus II (The Memoirs of Zeus II), 1967; L'Avenir en désarroi, 1968; Vézelay, colline éternelle, 1968; Nouvelles lettres d'un Européen, 1970; Une Eglise qui se trompe de siècle, 1972; La Parole et le Pouvoir, 1974; Oeuvres complètes, 25 vols, 1973–79; Quand un roi perd la France (Les Rois Maudits 7), 1977; Attention la France!, 1981; Réformer la Démocratie, 1982; Lettre aux Français sur leur langue et leur âme, 1994; *plays:* Mégarée, 1942; Un Voyageur, 1953; La Contessa, 1962; *song:* Le Chant des Partisans (with Joseph Kessel and Anna Marly), 1943 (London). *Recreations:* riding, travel. *Address:* Palais Mazarin, 1 rue de Seine, 75006 Paris, France; Abbaye de Faise, Les Artigues de Lussac, 33570 Lussac, France. *Clubs:* Savile, Garrick; Travellers' (Paris).

DRURY, Allen Stuart; author; *b* Houston, Texas, 2 Sept. 1918; *s* of Alden M. and Flora A. Drury. *Educ:* Stanford Univ. (BA). Served with US Army, 1942–43. Ed., The Tulare (Calif) Bee, 1939–41; county ed., The Bakersfield Californian, Bakersfield, Calif, 1941–42; United Press Senate Staff, Washington, DC, 1943–45; freelance correspondent, 1946; Nation Ed., Pathfinder Magazine, Washington, DC, 1947–53; National Staff, Washington Evening Star, 1953–54; Senate Staff, New York Times, 1954–59. Mem., National Council on the Arts (apptd by Pres. Reagan), 1982–88. Sigma Delta Chi Award for Editorial Writing, 1942; Hon. LitD, Rollins Coll., Winter Park, Fla, 1961. *Publications:* Advise and Consent, 1959 (Pulitzer Prize for Fiction, 1960); A Shade of Difference, 1962; A Senate Journal, 1963; That Summer, 1965; Three Kids in a Cart, 1965; Capable of Honor, 1966; "A Very Strange Society", 1967; Preserve and Protect, 1968; The Throne of Saturn, 1971; Courage and Hesitation: inside the Nixon administration, 1972; Come Nineveh, Come Tyre, 1973; The Promise of Joy, 1975; A God Against the Gods, 1976; Return to Thebes, 1977; Anna Hastings, 1977; Mark Coffin, USS, 1978; Egypt: the eternal smile, 1980; The Hill of Summer, 1981; Decision, 1983; The Roads of Earth, 1984; Pentagon, 1986; Toward What Bright Glory?, 1990; Into What Far Harbor?, 1992. *Address:* PO Box 941, Tiburon, CA 94920, USA. *Clubs:* Cosmos, University (Washington, DC); Bohemian (San Francisco).

DRURY, Very Rev. John Henry; Dean of Christ Church, Oxford, since 1991; *b* 23 May 1936; *s* of Henry and Barbara Drury; *m* 1972, (Frances) Clare Nineham, *d* of Rev. Prof. D. E. Nineham, *qv*; two *d*. *Educ:* Bradfield; Trinity Hall and Westcott House, Cambridge. MA (Hist. Pt 1, Cl. 1; Theol. Pt 2, Cl. 2/1). Curate, St John's Wood Church, 1963; Chaplain of Downing Coll., Cambridge, 1966; Chaplain and Fellow of Exeter Coll., Oxford, 1969 (Hon. Fellow, 1991); Res. Canon of Norwich Cathedral and Examining Chaplain to Bp of Norwich, 1973–79; Vice-Dean of Norwich, 1978; Fleck Resident in Religion, Bryn Mawr Coll., USA, 1978; Lectr in Religious Studies, Sussex Univ., 1979–81; Dean, 1981–91, Fellow, 1982–91, King's College, Cambridge. Syndic, Fitzwilliam Museum, Cambridge, 1988–91. Examining Chaplain to Bp of Chichester, 1980–82. Mem., Doctrine Commn for C of E, 1978–82. Jt Editor, Theology, 1976–86. *Publications:* Angels and Dirt, 1972; Luke, 1973; Tradition and Design in Luke's Gospel, 1976; The Pot and The Knife, 1979; The Parables in the Gospels, 1985; Critics of the Bible 1724–1873, 1989; The Burning Bush, 1990; articles and reviews in Jl of Theol. Studies, Theology, Expository Times, TLS. *Recreations:* drawing, carpentry, reading. *Address:* Christ Church, Oxford OX1 1DP.

DRURY, Martin Dru, FSA; Director-General, National Trust, since 1996 (Deputy Director-General, 1992–95); *b* 22 April 1938; *s* of Walter Neville Dru Drury, TD; *m* 1971, Elizabeth Caroline, *d* of Hon. Sir Maurice Bridgeman, KBE; two *s* one *d*. *Educ:* Rugby. Commissioned, 3rd The King's Own Hussars, 1957. Insurance Broker at Lloyd's, 1959–65; Mallett & Son, 1965–73 (Associate Dir, 1970–73); joined National Trust as Historic Buildings Rep., SE, and Furniture Advr, 1973; Historic Buildings Sec., 1981–95. Chm., Landmark Trust, 1992–; Vice-Chm., Attingham Summer Sch. Trust, 1982–. Mem., Exec. Cttee, Georgian Group, 1976–94. *Address:* c/o Lloyds Bank, 8/10 Waterloo Place, SW1Y 4BE. *Clubs:* Pratt's, Brooks's; Seaview Yacht.

DRURY, Sir Michael; *see* Drury, Sir V. W. M.

DRURY, Sir (Victor William) Michael, Kt 1989; OBE 1978; FRCP; FRCGP; FRACGP; Professor of General Practice, University of Birmingham, 1980–91, now Emeritus; Chairman, Age Concern England, since 1993; *b* 5 Aug. 1926; *s* of Leslie and Beatrice Drury; *m* 1950, Joan (*née* Williamson); three *s* one *d*. *Educ:* Bromsgrove Sch.; Univ. of Birmingham (MB ChB Hons); MRCS LRCP 1949; FRCGP 1970 (MRCGP 1963); FRCP 1988; FRACGP 1988. Ho. Surg., Birmingham Gen., 1949–50; RSO, Kidderminster, 1950–51; Major, RAMC, 1951–53; Principal in Gen. Practice, Bromsgrove, 1953; Nuffield Trav. Fellow, 1965; Clarkson Sen. Clin. Tutor, Univ. of Birmingham, 1973–80. Lectures: James MacKenzie, 1983, Eli Lilley, 1984; Sir David Bruce, 1985; Gale, 1986. Royal College of General Practitioners: Mem. Council, 1971–85 (Vice-Chm. 1980); Chm., Practice Org., 1966–71, Cttee and Res. Div., 1983–85; Pres., 1985–88. Member: Cttee on Safety of Medicines (Adverse Drug Reaction), 1975–79; Prescription Pricing Authy, 1981–86; DHA, 1981–85; Res. Cttee, RHA, 1982–86; GMC, 1984–94; Standing Cttee, Post Grad. Med. Educn, 1988–93. Civilian Advr in Gen. Practice to Army, 1984. Mem. Ct, Liverpool Univ., 1980–87. *Publications:* Introduction to General Practice, 1974; (ed) Treatment, 1978–; Medical Secretaries Handbook, 6th edn 1992; Treatment and Prognosis, 1990; The New Practice Manager, 1990, 3rd edn 1994; various chapters in books on Drug Safety, Gen. Practice, etc; res. articles in Lancet, BMJ, Brit. Jl of Surgery, Jl RCGP. *Recreations:* gardening, reading, bridge, talking and listening.

Address: Rossall Cottage, Church Hill, Belbroughton, near Stourbridge DY9 0DT. *T:* Belbroughton (01562) 730229.

DRYDEN, Sir John (Stephen Gyles), 8th and 11th Bt *cr* 1795 and 1733; *b* 26 Sept. 1943; *s* of Sir Noel Percy Hugh Dryden, 7th and 10th Bt, and Rosamund Mary (*d* 1994), *e d* of late Stephen Scrope; *S* father, 1970; *m* 1970, Diana Constance, *o d* of Cyril Tomlinson, Highland Park, Wellington, NZ; one *s* one *d*. *Educ:* Oratory School. *Heir: s* John Frederick Simon Dryden, *b* 26 May 1976. *Address:* Spinners, Fairwarp, Uckfield, East Sussex TN22 3BE.

DRYSDALE, Thomas Henry, WS; Deputy Keeper of HM Signet, since 1991; *b* 23 Nov. 1942; *s* of Ian Drysdale and late Rosalind Marion Drysdale (*née* Gallie); *m* 1967, Caroline, *d* of Dr Gavin B. Shaw; one *s* two *d*. *Educ:* Cargilfield; Glenalmond; Edinburgh Univ. (LLB). Partner, Shepherd & Wedderburn WS, 1967, Managing Partner, 1988–94; Dir, Edinburgh Solicitors' Property Centre, 1976–89 (Chm., 1981–88). *Recreations:* ski-ing, walking, reading. *Address:* Shepherd & Wedderburn WS, Saltire Court, 20 Castle Terrace, Edinburgh EH1 2ET. *T:* 0131–228 9900. *Clubs:* New (Edinburgh); Scottish Ski.

DRYSDALE WILSON, John Veitch, CEng, FIMechE, FCIArb; Deputy Secretary, Institution of Mechanical Engineers, 1979–90; *b* 8 April 1929; *s* of Alexander Drysdale Wilson and Winifred Rose (*née* Frazier); *m* 1954, Joan Lily, *e d* of Mr and Mrs John Cooke, Guildford; one *s* one *d*. *Educ:* Solihull School; Guildford Technical Coll. Dennis Bros Ltd, Guildford: Engineer Apprentice, 1946–50; MIRA Research Trainee, 1949–50; Jun. Designer, 1950–51. National Service Officer, REME, 1951–53, Captain on Staff of CREME, 6th Armd Div. Management Trainee, BET Fedn, 1953–55; Technical Sales Engr, subseq. Head of Mechanical Laboratories, Esso Petroleum Co. Ltd, 1955–66; Chief Engr, R&D, Castrol Ltd, subseq. Burmah Oil Trading Ltd and Edwin Cooper Ltd, 1966–77; Projects and Res. Officer, Instn of Mechanical Engineers, 1977–79. Director: Mechanical Engineering Publications Ltd, 1979–90; Professional Engineers Insurance Bureau Ltd, 1989–90. Freeman, City of London, 1986; Liveryman: Co. of Engineers, 1987; Co. of Arbitrators, 1987. *Publications:* numerous papers to learned societies in USA and Europe on subjects related to engine lubrication. *Recreations:* travel, genealogy, horology. *Club:* Caravan.

D'SOUZA, Most Rev. Henry Sebastian; *see* Calcutta, Archbishop of, (RC).

DUBE, Alfred Uyapo Majaye; High Commissioner for Botswana in London, since 1993; *b* 8 June 1949; *s* of Mbangwa Edison Majaye and Phakela Majaye; *m* 1977, Elvyn Jones; three *s*. *Educ:* Poly. of North London; Univ. of Essex (BA Hons Govt). Librarian, Nat. Liby Service, 1971–74; Foreign Service Officer, Dept of Ext. Affairs, Botswana, 1977–79; First Sec., Botswana Embassy and Mission to EC, Brussels, 1979–80; Counsellor, London, 1980–81; Under-Sec., Min. of Mineral Resources and Water Affairs, 1981–83; Minister Counsellor, Brussels, 1983–87; Under-Sec., Dept of Ext. Affairs, 1987–89; Ambassador to Sweden, all Nordic countries and USSR/Russia, 1989–93. *Recreations:* reading, jazz, wine. *Address:* Botswana High Commission, 6 Stratford Place, W1N 9AE. *T:* 0171–499 0031.

DUBLIN, Archbishop of, and Primate of Ireland, since 1985; **Most Rev. Donald Arthur Richard Caird;** *b* Dublin, 11 Dec. 1925; *s* of George Robert Caird and Emily Florence Dreaper, Dublin; *m* 1963, Nancy Ballantyne, *d* of Prof. William Sharpe, MD, and Gwendolyn Hind, New York, USA; one *s* two *d*. *Educ:* Wesley Coll., Dublin, 1935–44; Trinity Coll., Dublin Univ., 1944–50. Sen. Exhibn, TCD, 1946; elected Schol. of the House, TCD, 1948; 1st cl. Moderatorship in Mental and Moral Science, 1949; Prizeman in Hebrew and Irish Language, 1946 and 1947; Lilian Mary Luce Memorial Prize for Philosophy, 1947; BA 1949; MA and BD 1955; HDipEd 1959. Curate Asst, St Mark's, Dundela, Belfast, 1950–53; Chaplain and Asst Master, Portora Royal Sch., Enniskillen, 1953–57; Lectr in Philosophy, University Coll. of St. David's, Lampeter, 1957; Rector, Rathmichael Parish, Shankill, Co. Dublin, 1960–69; Asst Master, St Columba's Coll., Rathfarnham, Co. Dublin, 1960–67; Dept Lectr in Philosophy, Trinity Coll., Dublin, 1962–63; Lectr in the Philosophy of Religion, Church of Ireland Theol Coll., Dublin, 1964–70; Dean of Ossory, 1969–70; Bishop of Limerick, Ardfert and Aghadoe, 1970–76; Bishop of Meath and Kildare, 1976–85. Fellow of St Columba's Coll., Dublin, 1971. Mem., Bord na Gaeilge, 1974. Hon. DD TCD, 1988. *Publication:* The Predicament of Natural Theology since the Criticism of Kant, in Directions, 1970 (Dublin). *Recreations:* swimming, tennis. *Address:* The See House, 17 Temple Road, Milltown, Dublin 6.

DUBLIN, Archbishop of, and Primate of Ireland, (RC), since 1988; **Most Rev. Desmond Connell,** DD; *b* 24 March 1926; *s* of John Connell and Maisie Connell (*née* Lacy). *Educ:* St Peter's National School, Phibsborough; Belvedere College; Clonliffe College; University Coll., Dublin (MA); St Patrick's Coll., Maynooth; Louvain Univ., Belgium (DPhil); DLitt NUI, 1981. University College, Dublin: Dept of Metaphysics, 1953–72; Prof. of General Metaphysics, 1972–88; Dean, Faculty of Philosophy and Sociology, 1983–88. Chaplain: Poor Clares, Donnybrook, 1953–55; Carmelites, Drumcondra, 1955–66; Carmelites, Blackrock, 1966–88. Prelate of Honour, 1984. *Publications:* The Vision in God, 1967; articles in reviews. *Address:* Archbishop's House, Drumcondra, Dublin 9. *T:* Dublin 373732.

DUBLIN, Auxiliary Bishop of, (RC); *see* Dunne, Most Rev. Patrick.

DUBLIN, (Christ Church), Dean of; *see* Paterson, Very Rev. J. T. F.

DUBLIN, (St Patrick's), Dean of; *see* Stewart, Very Rev. M. E.

du BOULAY; *see* Houssemayne du Boulay.

DU BOULAY, Prof. (Francis) Robin (Houssemayne), FBA 1980; Emeritus Professor of Mediæval History in the University of London, 1982; *b* 19 Dec. 1920; *er s* of late Philip Houssemayne Du Boulay and Mercy Tyrrell (*née* Friend); *m* 1948, Cecilia Burnell Matthews; two *s* one *d*. *Educ:* Christ's Hospital; Phillip's Academy, Andover, Mass., USA; Balliol Coll., Oxford. Williams Exhibitioner at Balliol Coll., 1939; Friends' Ambulance Unit and subsequently Royal Artillery, 1940–45; MA 1947; Asst Lecturer at Bedford Coll., 1947, Lecturer, 1949; Reader in Mediæval History, in University of London, 1955, Prof., 1960–82. Hon. Sec., RHistS, 1961–65. Mem. Court, Univ. of Hull, 1992–95. *Publications:* The Register of Archbishop Bourgchier, 2 vols, 1953–55; Medieval Bexley, 1961, 2nd edn 1994; Documents Illustrative of Medieval Kentish Society, 1964; The Lordship of Canterbury, 1966; An Age of Ambition, 1970; (ed jtly) The Reign of Richard II, 1972; Germany in the later Middle Ages, 1983; Legion, and other poems, 1983; The England of Piers Plowman, 1991; various essays and papers on late medieval subjects, English and German, in specialist journals and general symposia. *Address:* 23 Molescroft Road, Beverley, E Yorks HU17 7DX.

DUBOWITZ, Prof. Victor, MD, PhD; FRCP; Professor of Paediatrics, University of London, at the Royal Postgraduate Medical School, since 1972; Consultant Paediatrician, Hammersmith Hospital, since 1972; Director, Muscle Research Centre, Royal Postgraduate Medical School, since 1975; *b* 6 Aug. 1931; *s* of late Charley and Olga Dubowitz (*née* Schattel); *m* 1960, Dr Lilly Magdalena Suzanne Sebok; four *s*. *Educ:* Beaufort West Central High Sch., S Africa; Univ. of Cape Town (BSc, MB, ChB, 1954; MD 1960). PhD Sheffield, 1965; DCH 1958; FRCP 1972. Intern, Groote Schuur Hosp., Cape Town, 1955; Sen. House Officer, Queen Mary's Hosp. for Children, Carshalton, 1957–59; Res. Associate in Histochem., Royal Postgrad. Med. Sch., 1958–59; Lectr in Clin. Path., National Hosp. for Nervous Diseases, Queen Square, London, 1960; Lectr in Child Health, 1961–65, Sen. Lectr, 1965–67, and Reader, 1967–72, Univ. of Sheffield; Res. Associate, Inst. for Muscle Diseases, and Asst Paediatrician, Cornell Med. Coll., New York, 1965–66. Several lectureships and overseas vis. professorships. Comdr, Order of Constantine the Great, 1980. Arvo Ylppö Gold Medal, Finland, 1982; Baron ver Heyden de Lancey Prize, Med. Art Soc., 1980 and 1982. *Publications:* Developing and Diseased Muscle: a histochemical study, 1968; The Floppy Infant, 1969, 2nd edn 1980; (with M. H. Brooke) Muscle Biopsy: a modern approach, 1973, 2nd edn 1985; (with L. M. S. Dubowitz) Gestational Age of the Newborn: a clinical manual, 1977; Muscle Disorders in Childhood, 1978, 2nd edn 1995; (with L. M. S. Dubowitz) The Neurological Assessment of the Preterm and Full-term Newborn Infant, 1981; Colour Atlas of Muscle Disorders in Childhood, 1989; (jtly) A Colour Atlas of Brain Lesions in the Newborn, 1990; chapters in books and articles in learned jls on paediatric topics, partic. muscle disorders and newborn neurology. *Recreation:* sculpting. *Address:* 25 Middleton Road, Golders Green, NW11 7NR. *T:* 0181–455 9352.

DUBS, family name of **Baron Dubs**.

DUBS, Baron *cr* 1994 (Life Peer), of Battersea in the London Borough of Wandsworth; **Alfred Dubs;** Director, Refugee Council, since 1988; Member, Broadcasting Standards Council, 1988–93; *b* Prague, Czechoslovakia, Dec. 1932; *m*; one *s* one *d*. *Educ:* LSE. BSc (Econs). Local govt officer. Mem., Westminster CC, 1971–78; Chm., Westminster Community Relns Council, 1972–77; Mem., Kensington, Chelsea and Westminster AHA, 1975–78. Member: TGWU; Co-operative Party. Contested (Lab): Cities of London and Westminster, 1970; Hertfordshire South, Feb. and Oct. 1974; Battersea, 1987 and 1992. MP (Lab): Wandsworth, Battersea S, 1979–83; Battersea, 1983–87. Mem., Home Affairs Select Cttee, 1981–83 (Mem., Race Relations and Immigration Sub-Cttee, 1981–83); opposition front bench spokesman on home affairs, 1983–87. *Recreation:* walking in the Lake District. *Address:* 56 Westbourne Park Villas, W2 5EB. *T:* 0171–727 2149.

DU CANE, John Peter, OBE 1964; Director, Amax Inc., 1966–91; *b* 16 April 1921; *s* of Charles and Mathilde Du Cane; *m* 1945, Patricia Wallace (*née* Desmond); two *s*. *Educ:* Canford Sch., Wimborne. Pilot, Fleet Air Arm, RN, 1941–46. De Beers Consolidated Mines, 1946–54; Sierra Leone Selection Trust, 1955–63; Director: Consolidated African Selection Trust, 1963–81; Selection Trust Ltd, 1966–81 (Man. Dir, 1975–80; Chm., 1978–81); BP International Ltd, 1981; Chief Exec., BP Minerals Internat. Ltd, 1980–81; Director: Australian Consolidated Minerals Pty, 1981–86 (Dep. Chm., 1983–86); Ultramar Plc, 1983–87; Austamax Resources Ltd, 1984–86 (Dep. Chm., 1984–86). Mem., RNSA. *Recreations:* sailing, fishing, photography. *Address:* Castel du Prieuré, La Vicomté, 8 avenue de Bizeux, 35800 Dinard , France. *Club:* Naval and Military.

du CANN, Col Rt. Hon. Sir Edward (Dillon Lott), KBE 1985; PC 1964; Chairman, Lonrho Plc, 1984–91 (Director, 1972–92; Joint Deputy Chairman, 1983–84); *b* 28 May 1924; *er s* of late C. G. L. du Cann, Barrister-at-Law, and Janet (*née* Murchie); *m* 1st, 1962, Sallie Innes (marr. diss. 1990), *e d* of late James Henry Murchie, Caldy, Cheshire; one *s* two *d*; 2nd, 1990, Jenifer Patricia Evelyn (*d* 1995), *yr d* of late Evelyn Mansfield King, and *widow* of Sir Robert Cooke. *Educ:* Colet Court; Woodbridge Sch.; St John's Coll., Oxford (MA, Law). Served with RNVR, 1943–46 (CO, HMMTB 5010). Vice-Pres., Somerset and Wilts Trustee Savings Bank, 1956–75; Founder, Unicorn Group of Unit Trusts, 1957 (pioneered equity linked life assurance); Chairman: Barclays Unicorn Ltd and associated cos, 1957–72; Keyser Ullman Holdings Ltd, 1970–75, Cannon Assurance Ltd, 1972–80. Chm., Association of Unit Trust Managers, 1961. Contested: West Walthamstow Div., 1951; Barrow-in-Furness Div., 1955. MP (C) Taunton Div. of Somerset, Feb. 1956–1987. Economic Sec. to the Treasury, 1962–63; Minister of State, Board of Trade, 1963–64. Mem., Lord Chancellor's Adv. Cttee on Public Records, 1960–62; Joint Hon. Sec.: UN Parly Group, 1961–62; Conservative Parly Finance Group, 1961–62; Mem., Select Cttee on House of Lords Reform, 1962; Founder Chairman: Select Cttee on Public Expenditure, 1971–73; All-Party Maritime Affairs Parly Gp, 1984–87; Mem., Select Cttee on Privilege, 1972–87; Chairman: Select Cttee on Public Accounts, 1974–79; 1922 Cttee, 1972–84; Liaison Cttee of Select Cttee Chairmen, 1974–83; (founder) Select Cttee on Treasury and Civil Service Affairs, 1979–83; (first) Public Accounts Commn, 1984–87; Cons. Party Organisation, 1965–67; Burke Club, 1968–79. President: (founder) Anglo-Polish Cons. Soc., 1972–74; Nat. Union of Conservative and Unionist Assocs, 1981–82; Cons. Parly European Community Reform Gp, 1985–87; Vice-Chm., British American Parly Gp, 1978–81. Jt Leader, British-American Parly Gp delegns to USA, 1978, 1980; Leader, Jt British Parly Gp delegn to China, IPU, 1982. Dir, James Beattie Ltd, 1965–79. Pres., Inst. of Freight Forwarders Ltd, 1988–89; Vice-Pres., British Insurance Brokers Assoc., 1978–; Patron, Assoc. of Insurance Brokers, 1974–77. Visiting Fellow, Univ. of Lancaster Business School, 1970–82. Member: Panel of Judges, Templeton Foundn, 1984–; Management Council, GB-Sasa Kawa Foundn, 1984–. Patron, Human Ecology Foundn, 1987–. Mem. Governing Council, Taunton Sch., 1972–93; Governor, Hatfield Coll., Durham Univ., 1988–92. Commodore, 1962, Admiral, 1974–87, House of Commons Yacht Club. Hon. Col, 155 (Wessex) Regt, RCT (Volunteers), 1972–82, Hon. Life Mem., Instn of RCT, 1983. Lecturer, broadcaster. Mem. Court of Assts, Fruiterers' Co. (Master, 1990); elected first Freeman of Taunton Deane Borough, 1977. FRSA 1986. *Publications:* Investing Simplified, 1959; Two Lives: the political and business careers of Edward du Cann, 1995; pamphlets, and articles on financial and international affairs (incl. The Case for a Bill of Rights, How to Bring Government Expenditure within Parliamentary Control, A New Competition Policy, Hoist the Red Ensign). *Recreations:* travel, gardening, sailing.

DUCAT, Dawn, (Mrs Thomas Ducat); *see* Primarolo, D.

DUCAT-AMOS, Air Comdt Barbara Mary, CB 1974; RRC 1971; Director of Royal Air Force Nursing Services and Matron-in-Chief, Princess Mary's Royal Air Force Nursing Service, 1972–78; Nursing Sister, Medical Department, Cable and Wireless plc, 1978–85; *b* 9 Feb. 1921; *d* of late Captain G. W. Ducat-Amos, Master Mariner, and late Mrs M. Ducat-Amos. *Educ:* The Abbey Sch., Reading; St Thomas's Hosp., London (The Nightingale Trng Sch.). SRN 1943; CMB Pt 1 1948. PMRAFNS, 1944–47: served in RAF Hosps, UK and Aden; further training; nursing in S Africa and SW Africa, 1948–52; rejoined PMRAFNS, 1952: served in RAF Hosps as General Ward and Theatre Sister, UK, Germany, Cyprus, Aden and Changi (Singapore); Matron 1967; Sen. Matron 1968; Principal Matron 1970. QHNS 1972–78. Vice-Pres., Girls' Venture Corps Air Cadets, 1991– (Nat. Chm., 1982–91). CStJ 1975. *Recreations:* music, theatre, travel. *Address:* c/o Barclays Bank, Wimbledon Common Branch, 75 High Street, SW19 5EQ. *Club:* Royal Air Force.

duCHARME, Gillian Drusilla Brown; Headmistress, Benenden School, since 1985; *b* 23 Jan. 1938; *d* of Alfred Henry Brown and Alice Drusilla Grant; *m* 1969, Jean Louis duCharme (marr. diss.). *Educ:* Girton College, Cambridge. BA 1960, MA 1964. Visitors'

Dept, British Council, London and Oxford, 1964–66; Chm., French Dept and Head of Upper Sch., Park Sch., Brookline, Mass, 1969–77; Dir of Admissions, Concord Acad., Concord, Mass, 1977–80; Headmistress, The Town Sch., New York City, 1980–85. *Recreations:* tennis, cross-country skiing, photography, theatre, film, travel. *Address:* Benenden School, Cranbrook, Kent TN17 4AA. *T:* Cranbrook (01580) 240592.

DUCHÊNE, Louis-François; author; *b* 17 Feb. 1927; *s* of Louis Adrien Duchêne and Marguerite Lucienne Duchêne (*née* Lainé); *m* 1952, Anne Margaret Purves; one *d*. *Educ:* St Paul's Sch.; London Sch. of Economics. Leader writer, Manchester Guardian, 1949–52; Press attaché, High Authority, European Coal and Steel Community, Luxembourg, 1952–55; Correspondent of The Economist, Paris, 1956–58; Dir, Documentation Centre of Action Cttee for United States of Europe (Chm. Jean Monnet), Paris, 1958–63; Editorial writer, The Economist, London, 1963–67. Director: Internat. Inst. for Strategic Studies, 1969–74; European Res. Centre, Sussex Univ., 1974–82. *Publications:* (ed) The Endless Crisis, 1970; The Case of the Helmeted Airman, a study of W. H. Auden, 1972; New Limits on European Agriculture, 1985; (ed with G. Shepherd) Managing Industrial Change in Western Europe, 1987; Jean Monnet: first statesman of interdependence, 1994. *Address:* 3 Powis Villas, Brighton, East Sussex BN1 3HD. *T:* Brighton (01273) 329258.

DUCHESNE, Brig. (Peter) Robin, OBE 1978; Secretary General, Royal Yachting Association, since 1986; *b* 25 Sept. 1936; *s* of late Herbert Walter Duchesne and Irene Duchesne (*née* Cox); *m* 1968, Jennifer Maclean Gouldsbury; one *s* one *d*. *Educ:* Colwyn Bay Grammer Sch.; RMA Sandhurst. FIMgt. Commissioned RA 1956; Battery Comdr, 101 Airborne Div., USA, 1963–64; Instructor, RMA, 1965–67; RN Staff Coll., 1969; CO 49 Field Regt, RA, 1975–77; Directing Staff, Army Staff Coll., 1977–79; Comdr, Commonwealth Adv. Team, Ghana, 1979–81; CRA 1 Armd Div., 1981–83; Dep. Comdr and COS UNFICYP, 1984–86. Vice-Chm., Sail Trng Assoc., Tall Ships Races, 1986–; Chm. Council, Marine Conservation Soc., 1993–. *Recreations:* sailing, most sports, organising Tall Ships Races. *Address:* Lake Lodge, Churt, Farnham, Surrey GU10 2QB. *T:* (home) Farnham (01252) 793901, (office) Southampton (01703) 627400. *Clubs:* Royal Ocean Racing, Royal Thames Yacht.

DUCIE, 7th Earl of *cr* 1837; **David Leslie Moreton;** Baron Ducie, 1763; Baron Moreton, 1837; *b* 20 Sept. 1951; *e s* of 6th Earl of Ducie and of Alison May, *d* of L. A. Bates; *S* father, 1991; *m* 1975, Helen, *er d* of M. L. Duchesne; one *s* one *d*. *Educ:* Cheltenham College; Wye Coll., London Univ. (BSc 1973). *Heir: s* Lord Moreton, *qv*. *Address:* Talbots End Farm, Cromhall, Glos GL12 8AJ.

DUCK, Hywel Ivor; Director of Fisheries, Secretariat General, Council of Ministers of European Communities, since 1987; *b* 12 June 1933; *s* of Dr Ernest Frank Duck and Minnie Isabel Duck (*née* Peake); *m* 1980, Dr Barbara Elisabeth Huwe (decd); one *s* one *d*. *Educ:* King's School, Canterbury; Trinity College, Cambridge (MA); Diplôme d'Etudes Supérieures Européennes, Nancy. Called to the Bar, Gray's Inn, 1956. Foreign Office, 1956; served Warsaw, FO, Cairo, Khartoum, Damascus; Second later First Sec., Bonn, 1964; DSAO, later FCO, 1968; Consul (Commercial), Zürich and Dep. Dir, British Export Promotion in Switzerland, 1970–73; Head of Div., Secretariat Gen., Council of Ministers, EC, 1973–75; Dir of Ops and Translation, 1975–84; Dir, Directorate-Gen. for Agriculture and Fisheries, 1984–87. *Recreation:* classical music. *Address:* 175 rue de la Loi, 1048 Brussels, Belgium. *T:* (2) 2856267. *Clubs:* United Oxford & Cambridge University; American and Common Market (Brussels).

DUCKWORTH, Brian Roy; His Honour Judge Duckworth; a Circuit Judge, since 1983; *b* 26 July 1934; *s* of Roy and Kathleen Duckworth; *m* 1964, Nancy Carolyn Duckworth, JP, *d* of late Chris and Annie Holden; three *s* one *d*. *Educ:* Sedbergh Sch.; Worcester Coll., Oxford (MA). Called to Bar, Lincoln's Inn, 1958; a Recorder of the Crown Court, 1972–83; Member: Northern Circuit; Bar Council, 1979–82. Councillor, Blackburn RDC, 1960–74 (Chm. 1970–72). Liaison Judge and Hon. Pres., South Cumbria Magistracy, 1987–92; Liaison Judge, SW Lancs Magistracy, 1993–. Member: Lord-Lieut's Magistracy Adv. Cttee, 1993–; Lancs Probation Cttee, 1991–. Chm., Samlesbury Hall Charitable Trust, 1993–. *Recreations:* golf, gardening, motor sport. *Address:* c/o The Crown Court, Lancaster Road, Preston PR1 2PD. *T:* Preston (01772) 23431. *Clubs:* St James's (Manchester); Pleasington Golf.

DUCKWORTH, Eric; *see* Duckworth, W. E.

DUCKWORTH, John Clifford; FEng 1975; FIEE, FInstP, FInstE; Chairman, Lintott plc, 1980–93; *b* 27 Dec. 1916; *s* of late H. Duckworth, Wimbledon, and of Mrs A. H. Duckworth (*née* Woods); *m* 1942, Dorothy Nancy Wills; three *s*. *Educ:* KCS, Wimbledon; Wadham Coll., Oxford (MA). FIEE 1957; FInstP 1957; SFInstE 1957. Telecommunications Research Establishment, Malvern: Radar Research and Development, 1939–46; National Research Council, Chalk River, Ont., 1946–47; Atomic Energy Research Establishment, Harwell, 1947–50; Ferranti Ltd: Chief Engineer, Wythenshawe Laboratories, 1950–54; Nuclear Power Engineer, Brit. Electricity Authority, 1954–58; Central Electricity Authority, 1957–58; Chief Research and Development Officer, Central Electricity Generating Board, 1958–59; Man. Dir., Nat. Research Develt Corp., 1959–70. Mem. Bd, AEA, 1963–68. Mem., Defence Res. Adv. Council, 1955–65. Chm. or non-exec. dir of various public cos, 1970–83. Pres., Institute of Fuel, 1963–64; Vice-Pres., Parliamentary and Scientific Cttee, 1964–67. Chm., Science Mus. Adv. Council, 1972–84; Trustee, Science Mus., 1984–90. Vice-Pres., IEE, 1974–77. *Address:* Huefield, Helford Passage, Falmouth TR11 5LD. *Club:* Athenæum.

DUCKWORTH, Sir Richard Dyce, 3rd Bt, *cr* 1909; *b* 30 Sept. 1918; *s* of Sir Edward Dyce Duckworth, 2nd Bt, and Cecil Gertrude, *y d* of Robert E. Leman; *S* father, 1945; *m* 1942, Violet Alison, *d* of Lieut-Col G. B. Wauchope, DSO; two *s*. *Educ:* Marlborough Coll. Started business in 1937, retired 1969. *Recreations:* sailing, golf, squash, shooting. *Heir: s* Edward Richard Dyce Duckworth [*b* 13 July 1943; *m* 1976, Patricia, *o d* of Thomas Cahill; one *s* one *d*]. *Address:* Dunwood Cottage, Shootash, Romsey, Hants SO51 6GA. *T:* Romsey (01794) 513228.

DUCKWORTH, Prof. Roy, CBE 1987; MD; FRCS, FDSRCS, FRCPath; Emeritus Professor of Oral Medicine, University of London; Dean, The London Hospital Medical College, 1986–94; *b* Bolton, 19 July 1929; *s* of Stanley Duckworth and Hilda Evelyn Moores; *m* 1953, Marjorie Jean Bowness, Flimby; two *s* one *d*. *Educ:* King George V Sch., Southport; Univ. of Liverpool (BDS; MD 1964); Univ. of London. FDSRCS 1957; FRCPath 1973; FRCS 1986. Served RAF Dental Br., 1953–55. Nuffield Fellow, RPMS and Guy's Hosp. Dental Sch., 1959–61; The London Hospital Medical College: Sen. Lectr in Oral Medicine, 1961; Reader in Oral Medicine, 1965; Dean of Dental Studies, 1969–75; Prof. and Head, Dept of Oral Medicine, 1968–90. Consultant in Oral Medicine, The London Hosp., 1965–90. Dean, Faculty of Dental Surgery, RCS, 1983–86. Civil Consultant: in Dental Surg., to Army, 1977–90; in Oral Medicine and Oral Path., to RN, 1982–90; Temp. Consultant, WHO, 1973; British Council Visitor, 1977. Vis. Prof. in many countries. President: British Soc. of Periodontology, 1972–73; British Soc. for Oral Medicine, 1986–87; BDA, 1990–91. Chm., Standing Dental Adv. Cttee, Dept of Health, 1988–92 (Mem., 1984–88); Member: Adv. Council on Misuse of Drugs, 1977–85; Medicines Commn, 1980–83; Council, Fédération Dentaire Internationale, 1981–90 (Mem., List of Honour, 1993); GDC, 1984–89. Scientific Adviser, British Dental Jl, 1975–82; Editor, Internat. Dental Jl, 1981–90. *Publications:* contrib. professional jls. *Recreation:* sailing.

DUCKWORTH, (Walter) Eric, OBE 1991; PhD; FEng 1980; FIM, FInstP; Managing Director, Fulmer Ltd (formerly Fulmer Research Institute), 1969–90; Chairman, Bournville Consultants Ltd, since 1994; *b* 2 Aug. 1925; *s* of Albert Duckworth and Rosamund (*née* Biddle); *m* 1949, Emma Evans; one *s*. *Educ:* Cambridge Univ. (MA, PhD). Research Manager, Glacier Metal Co., 1955; Asst Director, BISRA, 1966; Chm., Yarsley Technical Centre, 1973–89; Director: Ricardo Consulting Engineers plc, 1978–85; H. Darnell Ltd, 1982–94; Fleming Technol. Investment Trust plc, 1984–90. Chm., Council of Science and Technology Insts, 1977–78; first Charter Pres., Instn of Metallurgists, 1974–75; Pres., Assoc. of Independent Res. and Technol. Organisations (formerly Assoc. of Indep. Contract Res. Organs), 1978–79, 1988–89; Hon. Treas., Metals Soc., 1981–84; Chm., Professional Affairs Bd, Inst. of Metals, 1985–88. Member: Parly and Scientific Cttee, 1968–; Res. and Technol. Cttee, 1979–88, and Indust. Policy Cttee, 1983–88, Council, 1988–89, CBI; Nominations Cttee, 1983–88, Standing Cttee on Industry, 1988–94, Engrg Council; Engrg Bd, SERC, 1985–87; Council, Standing Conf. on Schools' Sci. and Technol., 1994–. Chm., Christian Nationals Evangelism Commn, 1974–93; Trustee: Comino Foundn, 1981–; FMI, 1995– (Mem. Council, 1995–); Vice-Pres., St Mary's Hosp. Med. Sch., 1976–; Mem. Court, Brunel Univ., 1978–85, and 1991–. Liveryman: Worshipful Co. of Scientific Instrument Makers; Co. of Engineers; Freeman, City of London. First Edwin Liddiard Meml Lectr, London Metallurgical Soc. of Inst. of Metals, 1982. Hon. DTech Brunel, 1976; DUniv Surrey, 1980. Editor, 1978–85, Chm., Editorial Bd, 1985–92, Materials and Design. *Publications:* A Guide to Operational Research, 1962, 3rd edn 1977; Statistical Techniques in Technological Research, 1968; Electroslag Refining, 1969; Manganese in Ferrous Metallurgy, 1976; Contract Research, 1991; *circa* 100 contribs to learned and other jls on many topics. *Recreations:* gardening, photography, changing other people's attitudes. *Address:* Orinda, Church Lane, Stoke Poges, Bucks SL2 4PB. *T:* Farnham Common (01753) 645778. *Club:* Stoke Park Golf.

du CROS, Sir Claude Philip Arthur Mallet, 3rd Bt *cr* 1916; *b* 22 Dec. 1922; *s* of Sir (Harvey) Philip du Cros, 2nd Bt, and of Dita, *d* of late Sir Claude Coventry Mallet, CMG; *S* father, 1975; *m* 1st, 1953, Mrs Christine Nancy Tordoff (marr. diss. 1974), *d* of late F. R. Bennett, Spilsby, Lincs; one *s*; 2nd, Mrs Margaret Roy Cutler (marr. diss. 1982), *d* of late R. J. Frater, Gosforth, Northumberland. *Heir: s* Julian Claude Arthur Mallet du Cros [*b* 23 April 1955; *m* 1984, Patricia, *o d* of Gerald Wyatt, Littlefield School, Liphook; one *s* one *d*]. *Address:* Long Meadow, Ballaugh Glen, IoM.

DUDA, Dr Karel; Ambassador of the Czech and Slovak Federal Republic to the Court of St James's, 1990–92; *b* 31 May 1926; *s* of Karel Duda and Marie Dudová; *m* 1952, Danuše Barešová; one *s* two *d*. *Educ:* Charles Univ., Prague (LLD). Ministry of Finance, 1950–54; Min. of Foreign Affairs, 1954–92; Ambassador to USA, 1963–69. *Address:* Oravska 3, Prague 10, 10000, Czech Republic.

DUDBRIDGE, Bryan James, CMG 1961; retired from HM Overseas Civil Service, Nov. 1961; Deputy Director, formerly Associate Director, British Council of Churches Department of Christian Aid, 1963–72; *b* 2 April 1912; *o s* of late W. Dudbridge, OBE, and of Anne Jane Dudbridge; *m* 1943, Audrey Mary, *o d* of late Dr and Mrs Heywood, Newbury; two *s* one *d*. *Educ:* King's Coll. Sch., Wimbledon; Selwyn Coll., Cambridge. Appointed to Colonial Administrative Service as Cadet in Tanganyika, 1935; Asst Dist Officer, 1937; Dist Officer, 1947; Sen. Dist Officer, 1953; Actg Provincial Commr, Southern Province; Administrative Officer (Class IIA), 1955, and Actg Provincial Commissioner (Local Government); Provincial Commissioner, Western Province, 1957; Minister for Provincial Affairs, 1959–60, retd. *Publications:* contrib. Journal of African Administration, Tanganyika Notes and Records, and Avon and Gloucestershire Family History Socs. *Recreations:* family history, natural history, beagling, wildfowl. *Address:* Red Rock Bungalow, Elm Grove Road, Topsham, Exeter EX3 0EJ. *T:* Exeter (01392) 874468. *Club:* Commonwealth Trust.

DUDBRIDGE, Prof. Glen, PhD; FBA 1984; Shaw Professor of Chinese and Fellow of University College, Oxford, since 1989; *b* 2 July 1938; *s* of George Victor Dudbridge and Edna Kathleen Dudbridge (*née* Cockle); *m* 1965, Sylvia Lo (Lo Fung-young); one *s* one *d*. *Educ:* Bristol Grammar School; Magdalene College, Cambridge (MA, PhD); New Asia Institute of Advanced Chinese Studies, Hong Kong. MA Oxon. Nat. Service, RAF, 1957–59. Research Fellow, Magdalene College, Cambridge, 1965; Lectr in Modern Chinese, 1965–85 and Fellow, Wolfson Coll., 1966–85, Univ. of Oxford; Prof. of Chinese and Fellow, Magdalene Coll., Univ. of Cambridge, 1985–89. Visiting Professor: Yale Univ., 1972–73; Univ. of California, Berkeley, 1980. *Publications:* The Hsi-yu chi: a study of antecedents to the sixteenth century Chinese novel, 1970; The Legend of Miao-shan, 1978 (Chinese edn, 1990); The Tale of Li Wa: study and critical edition of a Chinese story from the ninth century, 1983; Religious experience and lay society in T'ang China, 1995; contribs to Asia Major, Harvard Jl of Asiatic Studies, New Asia Jl. *Address:* Institute for Chinese Studies, Walton Street, Oxford OX1 2HG.

DUDDING, Richard Scarbrough; Director, Pollution Control and Wastes, Department of the Environment, since 1993; *b* 29 Nov. 1950; *s* of Sir John Scarbrough Dudding and of Lady (Enid Grace) Dudding; *m* 1987, Priscilla Diana Russell; two *s*. *Educ:* Cheltenham Coll.; Jesus Coll., Cambridge (MA 1st Cl. Hons History). Joined DoE, 1972; Private Sec. to John Smith, MP, 1976–78; Principal, 1977; Asst Sec., 1984; Sec., Cttee of Inquiry into Conduct of Local Govt Business, 1985–86; Under Sec., 1990; Finance Dir, 1990–93. *Recreations:* gardening, walking, golf. *Address:* 3 Dora Road, SW19 7EZ. *T:* 0181–879 7441.

DUDGEON, Air Vice-Marshal Antony Greville, CBE 1955; DFC 1941; *b* 6 Feb. 1916; *s* of late Prof. Herbert William Dudgeon, Guy's Hosp. and Egyptian Government Service; *m* 1942, Phyllis Margaret (*d* 1994), *d* of late Group Capt. John McFarlane, OBE, MC, AFC, Lowestoft, Suffolk; one *s* one *d*. *Educ:* Eton; RAF Cranwell. RAF Service, 1933–68, in UK, Europe, Near, Middle and Far East, USA; personnel work, training, operations, flight safety, organisation of new formations, liaison with civilian firms and youth organisations; courses at Staff Coll., Flying Coll., and London Polytechnic (Dip.); NATO Staff; 6 command appointments; 3,500 hours on over 70 types of aircraft as pilot. Manager, Professional Staff Services, McKinsey & Co., Paris, 1968–78; representative, France, Grangersol Ltd, 1978–81. *Publications: autobiographical works:* A Flying Command (under pen-name Tom Dagger), 1962; The Luck of the Devil (1929–41), 1985; Wings Over North Africa (1941–43), 1987; The War That Never Was (1941), 1991; stories and articles contributed to Blackwood's Magazine and to other jls. *Recreations:* writing, lecturing, photography, swimming; languages (French, Egyptian). *Address:* 43 Winchendon Road, SW6 5DH. *Clubs:* Royal Air Force, Hurlingham.

DUDLEY, 4th Earl of, *cr* 1860; **William Humble David Ward;** Baron Ward, 1644; Viscount Ednam, 1860; *b* 5 Jan. 1920; *e s* of 3rd Earl of Dudley, MC, TD, and Rosemary Millicent, RRC (*d* 1930), *o d* of 4th Duke of Sutherland; *S* father, 1969; *m* 1st, 1946,

Stella (marr. diss., 1961), *d* of M. A. Carcano, KCMG, KBE; one *s* twin *d*; 2nd, 1961, Maureen Swanson; one *s* five *d*. *Educ:* Eton; Christ Church, Oxford. Joined 10th Hussars, 1941, Adjt, 1944–45; ADC to Viceroy of India, 1942–43. Served War of 1939–45 (wounded). Pres., Baggeridge Brick Co. Ltd. *Heir: s* Viscount Ednam, *qv*. *Address:* 6 Cottesmore Gardens, W8 5PR; Vention House, Putsborough, N Devon. *Clubs:* White's, Pratt's; Royal Yacht Squadron.

DUDLEY, Baroness (14th in line), *cr* 1439–1440 (called out of abeyance, 1916); **Barbara Amy Felicity Hamilton;** *b* 23 April 1907; *o d* of 12th Baron Dudley and Sybil Augusta (*d* 1958), *d* of late Rev. Canon Henry William Coventry; *S* brother, 1972; *m* 1929, Guy Raymond Hill Wallace (*d* 1967), *s* of late Gen. Hill Wallace, CB, RHA; three *s* one *d*; *m* 1980, Charles Anthony Crosse Hamilton. *Recreations:* floral water-colours (has exhibited Royal Watercolour Society, Conduit St); gardening. *Heir: e s* Hon. Jim Anthony Hill Wallace [*b* 9 Nov. 1930; *m* 1962, Nicola Jane, *d* of Lt-Col Philip William Edward Leslie Dunsterville; two *s*]. *Address:* Hill House, Kempsey, Worcestershire WR5 3PY. *T:* Worcester (01905) 820253.

DUDLEY, Bishop Suffragan of, since 1993; **Rt. Rev. Rupert William Noel Hoare;** *b* 3 March 1940; *s* of Julian Hoare and Edith Hoare (*née* Temple); *m* 1965, Gesine (*née* Pflüger); three *s* one *d*. *Educ:* Rugby School; Trinity Coll., Oxford (BA 1961, MA 1967); Westcott House and Fitzwilliam House, Cambridge (BA 1964); Birmingham Univ. (PhD 1973). Deacon 1964, priest 1965, Dio. Manchester; Curate of St Mary, Oldham, 1964–67; Lecturer, Queen's Theological Coll., Birmingham, 1968–72; Rector, Parish of the Resurrection, Manchester, 1972–78; Residentiary Canon, Birmingham Cathedral, 1978–81; Principal, Westcott House, Cambridge, 1981–93. Canon Theologian of Coventry Cathedral, 1970–75. *Publications:* (trans. jtly) Bultmann's St John, 1971; (contrib.) Queen's Sermons, 1973, Queen's Essays, 1980; The Trial of Faith, 1988; articles in Theology. *Recreations:* hill walking, sailing, gardening, listening to music. *Address:* Bishop's House, 366 Halesowen Road, Cradley Heath, West Midlands B64 7JF. *T:* 0121–550 3407.

DUDLEY, Archdeacon of; *see* Gathercole, Ven. J. R.

DUDLEY, Prof. Hugh Arnold Freeman, CBE 1988; FRCSE, FRCS, FRACS; Professor of Surgery, St Mary's Hospital, London University, 1973–88, now Emeritus; *b* 1 July 1925; *s* of W. L. and Ethel Dudley; *m* 1947, Jean Bruce Lindsay Johnston; two *s* one *d*. *Educ:* Heath Grammar Sch., Halifax; Edinburgh and Harvard Univs. MB, ChB Edin. 1947; ChM (Gold Medal and Chiene Medal) Edin. 1958; FRCSE 1951; FRACS 1965; FRCS 1974. Research Fell., Harvard Univ., 1953–54; Lecturer in Surgery, Edinburgh Univ., 1954–58; Sen. Lectr, Aberdeen Univ., 1958–63; Foundation Prof. of Surgery, Monash Univ., Melbourne, 1963–72. President: Surgical Res. Soc. of Australasia, 1968 (Corresp. Mem.); Biol. Engrg Soc. of GB, 1978–80; Surgical Res. Soc. of GB, 1981. Regl Research Co-ordinator, NW Thames RHA, 1989–92. Chairman, Independent Ethics Committee: Army Personnel Res. Estabt, Farnborough, 1989–94; Chemical and Biological Defence Estabt, Porton Down, 1988– (Mem. Council, 1992–94). Chm., Med. Writers Gp, 1980–83, Mem. Cttee, 1984–87, Soc. of Authors. Corresponding Member: Surgical Res. Soc. of SA; Vascular Soc. of SA; Hon. Member: Hellenic Soc. of Experimental Medicine; Aberdeen Medico-Chirurgical Soc.; Hon. Fellow: Amer. Surgical Assoc.; Amer. Assoc. for the Surgery of Trauma; S African Coll. of Surgeons. Chm. Editorial Board of Br. Jl of Surgery and of Br. Jl Surgery Soc. Ltd, 1980–88; Associate Editor, BMJ, 1988–91. *Publications:* Principles of General Surgical Management, 1958; (jtly) Access and Exposure in Abdominal Surgery, 1963; (jtly) Guide for House Surgeons in the Surgical Unit, 5th edn 1974, to 8th edn 1988; (ed) Rob and Smith's Operative Surgery, 3rd and 4th edns, 1976–; Hamilton Bailey's Emergency Surgery, 10th edn 1977, 11th edn 1986; Communication in Medicine and Biology, 1977; (ed) Aid to Clinical Surgery, 1978, 4th edn 1988; (jtly) Practical Procedures for House Officers, 1988; (jtly) The People's Hospital of North East Scotland, 1992; papers in med. and sci. jls. *Recreations:* missing pheasants; annoying others; surgical history. *Address:* House of Broombrae, Glenbuchat, Strathdon, Aberdeenshire AB3 8UA. *T:* Glenkindie (019756) 41341.

DUDLEY, Prof. Norman Alfred, CBE 1977; FEng; Lucas Professor of Engineering Production, 1959–80, Emeritus Professor 1981, University of Birmingham; Head of Department of Engineering Production and Director of Lucas Institute of Engineering Production, 1956–80; *b* 29 Feb. 1916; *s* of Alfred Dudley; *m* 1940, Hilda Florence, *d* of John Miles; one *s* two *d*. *Educ:* Kings Norton Grammar Sch.; Birmingham Coll. of Technology. BSc London, PhD Birmingham. FEng 1981. Industrial training and appts: H. W. Ward & Co. Ltd, 1932–39; Imperial Typewriter Co. Ltd, 1940–45; Technical Coll. Lectr, 1945–52; Sen. Lectr, Wolverhampton and Staffs, 1948–52; Lectr in Eng. Prod., 1952, Reader, 1956, University of Birmingham. Chm., Manufacturing Processes Div., Birmingham Univ. Inst. for Advanced Studies in Engineering Sciences, 1965–68. Director: Birmingham Productivity Services Ltd; West Midlands Low Cost Automation Centre. Member: SRC Manufacturing Technol. Cttee; SRC and DoI Teaching Company Cttee, 1977–80. Chm., Cttee of Hds of Univ. Depts of Production Studies, 1970–80. Governor: Dudley and Staffs Tech. Coll., and Walsall and Staffs Tech. Coll., 1955–60; Letchworth Coll. of Technol., 1964–66. Member: Council, West Midlands Productivity Assoc.; Council Internat. Univ. Contact for Management Education, 1957; Council, Instn of Prod. Engineers, 1959–61 (Chm., Research Cttee, 1965–66; Viscount Nuffield Meml Lectr, 1969); UK Delegn to UNCSAT Geneva, 1963; W Midlands Economic Planning Council, 1970–78; Adv. Panel on Economic Develt, West Midlands Metropolitan CC, 1976–77; Council, Nat. Materials Handling Centre. Pres., Midlands Operational Research Soc., 1966–80. Mem., Ergonomics Res. Soc.; Emeritus Mem., Internat. Inst. of Production Engrg Research. FIMgt; Hon. FIMfgE; Hon. FIEE. Hon. Member: Japanese Industrial Management Assoc.; Internat. Foundn of Prodn Research. Hon. DTech Loughborough, 1981. Editor, International Journal of Production Research, 1961–80. J. D. Scaife Medal, 1958. Granted armorial bearings, 1994. *Publications:* Work Measurement: Some Research Studies, 1968; (co-ed) Production and Industrial Systems, 1978; The Bulstrodes alias Bolstridges of Bedworth, 1991; The Dudleys of Northwich Hundred, 1994; various papers on Engineering Production. *Address:* 37 Abbots Close, Knowle, Solihull, West Midlands B93 9PP. *T:* Knowle (01564) 775976.

DUDLEY, William Stuart; Associate Designer of the National Theatre, since 1981; *b* 4 March 1947; *s* of William Dudley and Dorothy Stacey. *Educ:* Highbury Sch., London; St Martin's School of Art; Slade School of Art. DipAD, BA Fine Art; UCL Postgrad. Dip. Fine Art. First production, Hamlet, Nottingham Playhouse, 1970; subseq. prodns include: The Duchess of Malfi and Man is Man, Royal Court, 1971; *National Theatre*, 1971–: Tyger, 1974; The Good-Natured Man, 1974; The Passion, 1977; Lavender Blue, 1977; The World Turned Upside Down, Has Washington Legs?, 1978; Dispatches, Lost Worlds, Lark Rise, Candleford, Undiscovered Country (SWET award, Designer of the Year, 1980), 1979; Good Soldier Schweyk, 1982; Cinderella, 1983; The Mysteries, Real Inspector Hound/The Critic, 1985 (Laurence Olivier (formerly SWET) Award, Designer of the Year, 1985); Futurists, 1986; Waiting for Godot, 1987; Cat on a Hot Tin Roof, The Shaugraun, and The Changeling, 1988; Bartholemew Fair, 1988; The Crucible, 1990; The Coup, 1991; Pygmalion, 1992; On the Ledge, 1993; Under Milk Wood, 1995; *Royal Court:* Live Like Pigs, 1972; Merry-Go-Round, 1973; Magnificence, 1975; The Fool, 1975; Small Change, 1976; Hamlet, 1980; Kafka's Dick, 1986; Etta Jenks, 1990; *RSC:* Twelfth Night, 1974; Ivanov, 1976; That Good Between Us, 1977; Richard III, The Party, Today, 1984; Merry Wives of Windsor, 1985, 1992; A Midsummer Night's Dream, Richard II, 1986; Kiss Me Kate, 1987; *West End:* Mutiny, Piccadilly, 1985; Heartbreak House, Theatre Royal, Haymarket, 1992; The Deep Blue Sea, Almeida, 1993; *opera:* WNO: Il barbiere di Siviglia, 1976; Idomeneo, 1991; Metropolitan, NY: Billy Budd, 1978; Glyndebourne: Die Entführung aus dem Serail, 1980; Il barbiere di Siviglia, 1981; Royal Opera: Les Contes d'Hoffman (sets), 1980, 1986; Don Giovanni, 1981; The Cunning Little Vixen, 1990; Bayreuth: Der Ring des Nibelungen, 1983; Der Rosenkavalier, 1984; Salzburg Festival: Un ballo in maschera, 1989; *other productions:* The Ship, Glasgow, 1990; The Big Picnic, Glasgow, 1994. Designer of the Year, Laurence Olivier Awards, 1986. *Recreation:* playing the concertina. *Address:* Flat D, 30 Crooms Hill, SE10 8ER. *T:* 0181–858 8711.

DUDLEY-SMITH, Rt. Rev. Timothy; Bishop Suffragan of Thetford, 1981–92; *b* 26 Dec. 1926; *o s* of Arthur and Phyllis Dudley Smith, Buxton, Derbyshire; *m* 1959, June Arlette MacDonald; one *s* two *d*. *Educ:* Tonbridge Sch.; Pembroke Coll., and Ridley Hall, Cambridge. BA 1947, MA 1951; Certif. in Educn 1948. Deacon, 1950; priest, 1951; Asst Curate, St Paul, Northumberland Heath, 1950–53; Head of Cambridge Univ. Mission in Bermondsey, 1953–55; Hon. Chaplain to Bp of Rochester, 1953–60; Editor, Crusade, and Editorial Sec. of Evangelical Alliance, 1955–59; Asst Sec. of Church Pastoral-Aid Soc., 1959–65, Sec., 1965–73; Archdeacon of Norwich, 1973–81; Commissary to Archbp of Sydney, 1971–92; Exam. Chap. to Bp of Norwich, 1971–85. President: Evangelical Alliance, 1987–91; C of E Evangelical Council, 1990–93. MLitt Lambeth, 1991. *Publications:* Christian Literature and the Church Bookstall, 1963; What Makes a Man a Christian?, 1966; A Man Named Jesus, 1971; Someone who Beckons, 1978; Lift Every Heart, 1984; A Flame of Love, 1987; Songs of Deliverance, 1988; Praying with the English Hymn Writers, 1989; A Voice of Singing, 1992; contributor to various hymn books. *Recreations:* reading, verse, woodwork, family and friends. *Address:* 9 Ashlands, Ford, Salisbury, Wilts SP4 6DY. *T:* Salisbury (01722) 326417.

DUDLEY-WILLIAMS, Sir Alastair (Edgcumbe James), 2nd Bt *cr* 1964, of Exeter; Director, Wildcat Consultants, since 1986; *b* 26 Nov. 1943; *s* of Sir Rolf Dudley Dudley-Williams, 1st Bt and of Margaret Helen, *er d* of F. E. Robinson, OBE; *S* father, 1987; *m* 1972, Diana Elizabeth Jane, twin *d* of R. H. C. Duncan; three *d*. *Educ:* Pangbourne College. Hughes Tool Co. (Texas), 1962–64; Bay Drilling Corp. (Louisiana), 1964–65; Bristol Siddeley Whittle Tools Ltd, 1965–67; Santa Fe Drilling Co., 1967–72; Inchcape plc, 1972–86. *Recreations:* shooting, fishing. *Heir: b* Malcolm Philip Edgcumbe Dudley-Williams [*b* 10 Aug. 1947; *m* 1973, Caroline Anne Colina, twin *d* of R. H. C. Duncan; two *s* one *d*]. *Address:* c/o The Old Manse, South Petherton, Somerset TA13 5DB. *Club:* Royal Cornwall Yacht.

DUE, Ole; Grand Cross, Order of Dannebrog 1994 (Kt 1970); President, Court of Justice of European Communities, 1988–94; *b* 10 Feb. 1931; *s* of Stationmaster H. P. Due and Jenny Due (*née* Jensen); *m* 1954, Alice Maud Halkier Nielsen; three *s* one *d*. *Educ:* Copenhagen Univ. (Law degree, 1955). Ministry of Justice, Copenhagen: civil servant, 1955; Head of Div., 1970; Head of Dept, 1975; Appeal Court Judge *ai*, 1978; Judge, Court of Justice of EC, 1979–88. Legal Counsellor to Danish Delegn, negotiations of adhesion to EC, 1970–72; Mem., Danish Delegn to Hague Conf. on private internat. law, 1964–76. Hon. Member: Gray's Inn; King's Inn, Dublin. Hon. Prof., Copenhagen, 1994. Dr *hc* Stockholm, 1991. *Publications:* (ed jtly) EF-Karnov 1973, 1975; (ed) EF-lovregister, 1973–75; (jtly) Juridisk Grundbog, 1975; (jtly) Kommenteret færdselslov, 1979; articles on community law, private internat. law and legal technique. *Recreation:* hiking. *Address:* Mördrupvej 116, 3060 Espergærde, Denmark.

DUFF, Anthony Michael; Director General, International House, since 1990; *b* 7 Aug. 1946; *s* of Anthony Duff and Alice Mary Duff (*née* Conway). *Educ:* St Conleth's Coll., Dublin; University Coll., Dublin (BA Hons). LGSM (Drama) 1968; LRAM (Drama) 1970; RSA Dip. TEFLA 1972. Dir, Teacher Trng and Foundn Dir, Câfê Théatre Anglais, Internat. House, Paris, 1971–74; Vis. Lectr in Drama, Thomond Coll., Co. Limerick, 1975–76; Pedagogic Advr to Longman Italia, 1977–79; International House, London: Dir of Educn, 1979–83; Dir, 1984–89. FRSA 1993. *Publications:* English For You, 2 vols, 1979, 1981; (ed) Explorations in Teacher Training, 1989. *Recreations:* music, reading, the theatre, walking, being solitary. *Address:* 8 Scholar's Road, SW12 0PG.

DUFF, Rt. Hon. Sir (Arthur) Antony, GCMG 1980 (KCMG 1973; CMG 1964); CVO 1972; DSO 1944; DSC; PC 1980; Deputy Secretary, Cabinet Office, 1980–85, retired 1987; *b* 25 Feb. 1920; *s* of late Adm. Sir Arthur Allen Morison Duff, KCB; *m* 1944, Pauline Marion, *d* of Capt. R. H. Bevan, RN, and *widow* of Flt-Lieut J. A. Sword; one *s* two *d* (and one step *s*). *Educ:* RNC, Dartmouth. Served in RN, 1937–46. Mem., Foreign (subseq. Diplomatic) Service, 1946; 3rd Sec., Athens, Oct. 1946; 2nd Sec., 1948; 2nd Sec., Cairo, 1949; 1st Sec., 1952; transferred Foreign Office, Private Sec. to Minister of State, 1952; 1st Sec., Paris, 1954; Foreign Office, 1957; Bonn, 1960; Counsellor, 1962; British Ambassador to Nepal, 1964–65; Commonwealth Office, 1965–68; FCO, 1968–69; Dep. High Comr, Kuala Lumpur, 1969–72; High Comr, Nairobi, 1972–75; Dep. Under-Sec. of State, 1975–80, Dep. to Perm. Under-Sec. of State, 1976–80, FCO. Dep. Governor, Southern Rhodesia, 1979–80. *Address:* c/o National Westminster Bank, PO Box 25, 130 Commercial Road, Portsmouth PO1 1ES. *Club:* Army and Navy.

DUFF, Graham; Director (Operations), Crown Prosecution Service, since 1990; *b* 7 Jan. 1947; *s* of Norman Alexander Duff and Doris Duff; *m* 1st, 1969, Lalage Ann Ibbotson (marr. diss. 1978); 2nd, 1987, Jacqueline Tremble; one *s* one *d*. *Educ:* Newcastle Royal Grammar Sch.; Univ. of Durham (BA (Hons) Law); Univ. of Newcastle upon Tyne (Grad. Cert Ed). Called to the Bar, Lincoln's Inn, 1976. Asst Dir of Public Prosecutions, 1986; Br. Crown Prosecutor, Inner London, 1986; Chief Crown Prosecutor, Northumbria and Durham, 1987. *Recreations:* breeding foreign birds, old Riley motor cars, riding, target shooting, Northumbrian countryside. *Address:* Crown Prosecution Service, 50 Ludgate Hill, EC4M 7EX. *T:* 0171–273 8146.

DUFF, Patrick Craigmile, CMG 1982; *b* 6 Jan. 1922; *o s* of late Archibald Craigmile Duff, ICS, and Helen Marion (*née* Phillips); *m* 1st, 1947, Pamela de Villeneuve Graham (*osp*); 2nd, 1950, Elizabeth Rachel, *d* of late Rt Rev. R. P. Crabbe (Bishop of Mombasa, 1936–53) and Mrs Crabbe; two *d*. *Educ:* Wellington Coll., Berks; New Coll., Oxford (MA 1946). War service, 1941–42. HMOCS, 1942–63: Tanganyika; Kenya; CRO, 1964–65; ODM/ODA, 1966–74; Head, West Indian and Atlantic Dept, FCO, 1975–80; Head, British Develt for E Africa, FCO, 1980–82. *Recreations:* making music, fell walking, ball games. *Address:* 6 Christchurch Road, Winchester, Hants SO23 9SR. *T:* Winchester (01962) 865200. *Club:* Commonwealth Trust.

DUFF, Col Thomas Robert G.; *see* Gordon-Duff.

DUFF GORDON, Sir Andrew (Cosmo Lewis), 8th Bt, *cr* 1813; *b* 17 Oct. 1933; *o s* of Sir Douglas Duff Gordon, 7th Bt and Gladys Rosemary (*d* 1933), *e d* of late Col Vivien

Henry, CB; *S* father, 1964; *m* 1st, 1967, Grania Mary (marr. diss. 1975), *d* of Fitzgerald Villiers-Stuart, Ireland; one *s*; 2nd, 1975, Eveline Virginia, BA, *d* of S. Soames, Newbury; three *s*. *Educ:* Repton. Served with Worcs Regiment and 1st Bn Ches Regt, 1952–54. Mem. of Lloyd's, 1962–91. *Recreations:* golf, shooting, skiing. *Heir:* *s* Cosmo Henry Villiers Duff Gordon, *b* 18 June 1968. *Address:* Downton House, Walton, Presteigne, Powys LD8 2RD. *T:* New Radnor (0154421) 223; 27 Cathcart Road, SW10 9JG. *T:* 0171–351 1170. *Clubs:* City University; Kington Golf; Sunningdale Golf.

DUFFELL, Lt-Gen. Peter Royson, KCB 1992; CBE 1988 (OBE 1981); MC 1966; Inspector General Doctrine and Training, Ministry of Defence, 1992–95; *b* 19 June 1939; *s* of late Roy John Duffell, Lenham, Kent, and of Ruth Doris (*née* Gustaffson); *m* 1982, Ann Murray, *d* of late Col Basil Bethune Neville Woodd, Rolvenden, Kent; one *s* one *d*. *Educ:* Dulwich Coll. psc, rcds. FRGS 1975; FRAS 1992. Commnd 2nd KEO Gurkha Rifles, 1960; Staff Coll., Camberley, 1971; Bde Major 5 Bde, 1972–74; MA to C-in-C UKLF, 1976–78; Comdt 1st Bn 2nd KEO Gurkha Rifles, 1978–81; Col GS, MoD, 1981–83; Comdr Gurkha Field Force, 1984–85; COS 1 (BR) Corps, 1986–87; RCDS, 1988; Cabinet Office Efficiency Unit, 1989; Comdr, British Forces Hong Kong, and Maj.-Gen. Brigade of Gurkhas, 1989–92. *Recreations:* travel, reading, golf, collecting pictures, photography, elephant polo, wine. *Address:* c/o Drummonds, 49 Charing Cross, SW1A 2DX. *Club:* Travellers'.

DUFFERIN AND CLANDEBOYE, 11th Baron *cr* 1800 (Ire.); **John Francis Blackwood;** Bt (Ire.) 1763; Bt (UK) 1814; architect; *b* 18 Oct. 1944; *s* of 10th Baron and of Margaret Alice, *d* of Hector Kirkpatrick; *S* father, 1991 (claim to peerage not yet established); *m* 1971, Annette Kay, *d* of Harold Greenhill; one *s* one *d*. *Educ:* Barker Coll., Hornsby; Univ. of NSW (BArch). ARAIA. *Recreations:* antiques, building conservation, fishing. *Heir:* *s* Hon. Francis Senden Blackwood, *b* 6 Jan. 1979. *Address:* 169 Anson Street, Orange, NSW 2800, Australia. *T:* (63) 625399.

DUFFETT, Roger Hugh Edward; Secretary, Royal College of Surgeons of England, since 1988; *b* 20 Jan. 1936; *s* of Dr Edward Cecil Duffett and Cicely Duffett (*née* Haw); *m* 1959, Angela Julie Olden; one *d* (one *s* decd). Educ: Sherborne Sch. (Scholar); Peterhouse, Cambridge (Scholar; MA). Commissioned RA (Nat. Service), 1954–56; British Petroleum Co.: joined 1956; refinery process foreman, 1959–60; research, molecular sieve properties of synthetic zeolites and reactions of frozen free radicals, 1960–64; creation of computerised manpower planning models, 1964–68; creation and operation of computerised linear programming models for integrated oil ops, 1968–71; application of mathematical models to corporate planning, 1971–73; planning, internat. ops for lubricants, 1973–78; negotiation and op., crude oil contracts, 1978–79; consultancy for analysis and resolution of orgnl problems: in shipping, research, engrg, marketing and personnel; for management of secondary schools, Cambs; Unicef (UK); employment of secondees to Enterprise Bds, 1979–87; orgn and systems consultant for BP Oil Internat., for Riding for Disabled, 1987–88. Member: Management Cttee, Clare Park, 1979–83; Riding for Disabled, 1990–; Dir, Quinta Nursing Home, Farnham, 1983–88. *Publications:* contribs to learned jls. *Recreations:* golf, coarse gardening, creating brain teasers, writing, reading. *Address:* Royal College of Surgeons of England, 35–43 Lincoln's Inn Fields, WC2A 3PN. *T:* 0171–405 3474.

DUFFIELD, Vivien Louise, CBE 1989; *b* 26 March 1946; *d* of Sir Charles Clore and Mrs Francine Clore (née Halphen); *m* 1969, John Duffield (marr. diss. 1976); one *s* one *d*. *Educ:* Cours Victor Hugo, Paris; Lycée Français de Londres; Heathfield Sch.; Lady Margaret Hall, Oxford (MA). Member: NSPCC Centenary Appeal Cttee, 1983; NSPCC Financial Develt Cttee, 1985; Vice-Chairman: Great Ormond Street Hosp. Wishing Well Appeal, 1987; Royal Marsden Hosp. Cancer Appeal, 1990; Director: Royal Opera House Trust, 1985– (Dep. Chm., 1988); Royal Opera House, 1990–; Mem., Royal Ballet Bd, 1990–; Trustee, Dulwich Coll. Picture Gall., 1993–. Hon. DLitt Buckingham, 1990; Hon. DPhil Weizmann Inst., 1985; Hon. RCM, 1987. *Recreations:* ski-ing, opera, ballet, shooting. *Address:* c/o Clore Foundation, 3 Chelsea Manor Studies, Flood Street, SW3 5SR; 39 Quai Wilson, Geneva 1201, Switzerland.

DUFFUS, Sir Herbert (George Holwell), Kt 1966; *b* 30 Aug. 1908; *e s* of William Alexander Duffus, JP, and Emily Henrietta Mary (*née* Holwell); *m* 1939, Elsie Mary (*née* Hollinsed); no *c*. *Educ:* Cornwall Coll., Jamaica. Admitted as Solicitor: Jamaica, 1930, England, 1948. Resident Magistrate, Jamaica, 1946–58; Called to the Bar, Lincoln's Inn, 1956; acted as Puisne Judge, Jamaica, 1956–58; Puisne Judge, Jamaica, 1958–62; Judge of Appeal, Jamaica, 1962–64; Pres. Court of Appeal, 1964–67; Chief Justice of Jamaica, 1968–73; Acting Governor General of Jamaica, 1973. Chairman: Commn of Enquiry into Prisons of Jamaica, 1954; Commn of Enquiry into the administration of justice and police brutality in Grenada, WI, 1974; Police Service Commission (Jamaica), 1958–68. Sole Commissioner, Enquiries into: Maffesanti Affair, 1968; Operations of Private Land Developers in Jamaica, 1975–76; Barbados Govt's Private Enterprises, 1977–78; Electoral Malpractices (Jamaican Local Govt Elecns), 1986. Pres., Boy Scouts Assoc., Jamaica, 1967–70. Chm., Western Regl Council, Cheshire Homes, 1975–89. Chancellor of the Church (Anglican) in Jamaica, 1973–76. *Address:* 6 Braywick Road, PO Box 243, Liguanea PO, Kingston 6, Jamaica. *T:* 9270171; 119 Main Street, Witchford, Ely, Cambs CB6 2HQ. *T:* Ely (01353) 663281.

DUFFY, Sir (Albert Edward) Patrick, Kt 1991; PhD; *b* 17 June 1920. *Educ:* London Sch. of Economics (BSc(Econ.), PhD); Columbia Univ., Morningside Heights, New York, USA. Served War of 1939–45, Royal Navy, incl. flying duties with FAA. Lecturer, University of Leeds, 1950–63, 1967–70. Visiting Professor: Drew Univ., Madison, NJ, 1966–70; Amer. Grad. Sch. of Internat. Business, 1982–. Contested (Lab) Tiverton Division of Devon, 1950, 1951, 1955. MP (Lab): Colne Valley Division of Yorks, 1963–66; Sheffield, Attercliffe, 1970–92. PPS to Sec. of State for Defence, 1974–76; Parly Under-Sec. of State for Defence (Navy), MoD, 1976–79; opposition spokesman on defence, 1979–80, 1983–84. Chairman: PLP Economic and Finance Gp, 1965–66, 1974–76; Trade and Industry Sub-Cttee of Select Cttee on Expenditure, 1972–74; PLP Defence Cttee, 1984; Vice-Chairman: PLP Defence Gp, 1979–84; Anglo-Irish Gp, 1979–92. Pres., N Atlantic Assembly, 1988–90 (Mem. 1979–92; Chm., Defence Co-op. sub-cttee, 1983–87); Dep. Chm., Atlantic Council of UK, 1994–. Hon. DHL Rosary Coll., Illinois, 1993. *Publications:* contrib. to Economic History Review, Victorian Studies, Manchester School, Annals of Amer. Acad. of Pol. and Soc. Sci., etc. *Address:* 153 Bennetthorpe, Doncaster, South Yorks DN2 6AH. *Clubs:* Naval; Trades and Labour (Doncaster).

DUFFY, Antonia Susan, (Mrs P. J. Duffy); *see* Byatt, A. S.

DUFFY, Carol Ann, OBE 1995; poet and freelance writer; *b* 23 Dec. 1955; *d* of Frank Duffy and May Black. *Educ:* St Joseph's Convent, Stafford; Stafford Girls' High Sch.; Univ. of Liverpool (BA Hons Philosophy 1977). *Awards:* Eric Gregory, 1983; Somerset Maugham, 1987; Dylan Thomas, 1990; Cholmondeley, 1992; Whitbread Poetry, 1993; Forward Poetry, 1993. *Plays:* Take My Husband, 1982; Cavern of Dreams, 1984; Little Women, Big Boys, 1986; Loss (radio), 1986; Grimm Tales, 1995. *Publications:* Standing Female Nude, 1985; Selling Manhattan, 1987, 4th edn 1994; (ed) Home and Away, 1988; The Other Country, 1990; (ed) I Wouldn't Thank You for a Valentine, 1992; Mean Time, 1993; Selected Poems, 1994; (ed) Anvil New Poets, 1995; (ed) Stopping for Death, 1995. *Recreations:* poker, holidays. *Address:* c/o Anvil Press, 69 King George Street, SE10 8PX. *T:* 0181–858 2946.

DUFFY, Daniel; Chairman, Transport and General Workers' Union, since 1988; *b* 3 Oct. 1929; *s* of late William and Mary Duffy; *m* Susan (*née* Salton). *Educ:* St Mungo's Academy. Transport Driver, 1947; joined S. H. & M. Assoc., 1947. Member: Exec. Council, Scottish Commercial Motormen's Union, 1960–71 (Pres., 1969–71); TGWU Exec. Council, 1971–; TUC General Council, 1988–. *Recreation:* bowls. *Address:* TGWU, Transport House, Smith Square, SW1P 3JB. *T:* 0171–828 7788.

DUFFY, Dr Francis Cuthbert, PPRIBA; Chairman, DEGW International, since 1989; President, Royal Institute of British Architects, 1993–95; *b* 3 Sept. 1940; *s* of late John Austin Duffy and of Annie Margaret Duffy (*née* Reed); *m* 1965, Jessica Bear; three *d*. *Educ:* Architectural Assoc. Sch. (AA Dip Hons); Univ. of California at Berkeley (MArch); Princeton Univ. (MA, PhD). Asst Architect, Nat. Building Agency, 1964–67; Commonwealth Fund Harkness Fellow, Berkeley and Princeton, 1967–70; established London office, JFN Associates (of NY), 1971; estab. architectural practice, DEGW, 1974. Mem. Council, 1989–; Pres., Architects' Council of Europe, 1994. Editor, AA Jl, 1965–67; founder Editor, Facilities, 1985–90. *Publications:* Office Landscaping, 1966; (jtly) Planning Office Space, 1976; (jtly) The Changing City, 1989; The Changing Workplace, 1992; (jtly) The Responsible Workplace, 1993. *Recreations:* walking, talking, reading. *Address:* DEGW International, 8 Crinan Street, N1 9SQ. *T:* 0171–239 7777; 195 Liverpool Road, N1 0RF. *T:* 0171–837 3064. *Clubs:* Athenæum; Princeton (NY).

DUFFY, Most Rev. Joseph; *see* Clogher, Bishop of, (RC).

DUFFY, Joseph Michael; Hon. Mr Justice Duffy; High Court Judge, Hong Kong, since 1987; *b* 6 Dec. 1936; *s* of John Joseph Duffy and Mary Frances Mullaney; *m* 1962, Patricia Ann Scott; one *s* two *d*. *Educ:* St Andrews Univ. (MA, LLB). Solicitor, Scotland, 1965, Hong Kong, 1976; Advocate, Scotland, 1981; QC Hong Kong, 1983. Apprentice, then Solicitor, Dundee, 1963–72; Crown Counsel and Sen. Crown Counsel, Hong Kong, 1972–76 and 1978–80 (Solicitor, Hong Kong, 1976–78); Dep. Dir and Dir of Public Prosecutions, Hong Kong, 1980–86; Solicitor-General, Hong Kong, 1986–87. *Recreations:* golf, tennis, running, music. *Address:* 53 Mount Nicholson Road, Hong Kong. *T:* 8910446; 7 Bonspiel Gardens, Broughty Ferry, Dundee DD5 2LH. *T:* Dundee (01382) 775492. *Clubs:* Shek O Country, Ladies Recreation, Royal Hong Kong Jockey (Hong Kong); Panmure Golf (Scotland).

DUFFY, Maureen Patricia, FRSL 1985; author; *b* 1933; *o c* of Grace Rose Wright. *Educ:* Trowbridge High Sch. for Girls; Sarah Bonnell High Sch. for Girls; King's College, London (BA). Chairman: Greater London Arts Literature Panel, 1979–81; Authors Lending and Copyright Soc., 1982–94; British Copyright Council, 1989– (Vice Chm., 1981–86); Vice Chm., Copyright Licensing Agency, 1994–. Pres., Writers' Guild of GB, 1985–88 (Jt Chm., 1977–78); Co-founder, Writers' Action Group, 1972–79; Vice-President: European Writers Congress, 1992–; Beauty Without Cruelty, 1975–. *Publications:* That's How It Was, 1962; The Single Eye, 1964; The Microcosm, 1966; The Paradox Players, 1967; Lyrics for the Dog Hour (poetry), 1968; Wounds, 1969; Rites (play), 1969; Love Child, 1971; The Venus Touch, 1971; The Erotic World of Faery, 1972; I want to Go to Moscow, 1973; A Nightingale in Bloomsbury Square (play), 1974; Capital, 1975; Evesong (poetry), 1975; The Passionate Shepherdess, 1977; Housespy, 1978; Memorials of the Quick and the Dead (poetry), 1979; Inherit the Earth, 1980; Gorsaga, 1981 (televised as First Born, 1988); Londoners: an elegy, 1983; Men and Beasts, 1984; Collected Poems 1949–84, 1985; Change (novel), 1987; A Thousand Capricious Chances: Methuen 1889–1989, 1989; Illuminations (novel), 1991; Occam's Razor (novel), 1993; Henry Purcell, 1994 (biog.); *visual art:* Prop art exhibn (with Brigid Brophy), 1969. *Address:* 18 Fabian Road, SW6 7TZ. *T:* 0171–385 3598.

DUFFY, Sir Patrick; *see* Duffy, Sir A. E. P.

DUFFY, Peter Clarke, QPM 1979; Director General, Federation Against Copyright Theft, 1985–89, retired; *b* Hamilton, Scotland, 10 May 1927; *s* of Hugh Duffy and Margaret Archibald; *m* 1958, S. M. Joyce (marr. diss.); one *s* two *d*. *Educ:* Our Lady's High Sch., Motherwell. MInstAM 1983. Served Army, Western Arab Corps, Sudan Defence Force, 1945–48 (War Medal). Joined Metropolitan Police, 1949; Criminal Investigation Dept, 1954; Comdr, New Scotland Yard, 1976–83; Dir, Investigations, Fedn Against Copyright Theft, 1983–85. *Recreations:* golf, living. *Club:* Royal Automobile.

DUGARD, Arthur Claude, CBE 1969; Chairman, Cooper & Roe Ltd, 1952–79, retired (formerly Joint Managing Director); *b* 1 Dec. 1904; *s* of Arthur Thomas Turner Dugard, Nottingham; *m* 1931, Christine Mary Roe, Nottingham; two *s*. *Educ:* Oundle Sch., Northants. Joined Cooper & Roe Ltd, Knitwear manufacturers, 1923 (Dir, 1936; Man. Dir, 1947). President: Nottingham Hosiery Manufrs Assoc., 1952–53; Nat. Hosiery Manufrs Fedn, 1959–61; Nottingham Chamber of Commerce, 1961–62. First Chm., CBI North Midland Regional Council, 1965–66; Chm. British Hosiery & Knitwear Export Gp, 1966–68; Mem. East Midlands Economic Planning Council, 1967–72. *Recreation:* golf. *Address:* 16 Hollies Drive, Edwalton, Nottingham NG12 4BZ. *T:* Nottingham (0115) 923 3217.

DUGDALE, family name of **Baron Crathorne.**

DUGDALE, Mrs John; *see* Dugdale, K. E. H.

DUGDALE, Kathryn Edith Helen, (Lady Dugdale), DCVO 1984 (CVO 1973); JP; DL; a Lady-in-Waiting to the Queen, since 1985; *b* 4 Nov. 1923; *d* of Rt Hon. Oliver Stanley, PC, MC, MP and Lady Maureen Vane-Tempest Stewart; *m* 1956, Sir John Robert Stratford Dugdale, *qv*; two *s* two *d*. *Educ:* many and varied establishments. Served with WRNS. Temp. Woman of the Bedchamber to The Queen, 1955–60, Extra Woman of the Bedchamber 1960–72; Woman of the Bedchamber, 1972–. Pres., Shropshire Community Council. JP Salop, 1964; DL Shropshire, 1995. Employee of Greater London Fund for the Blind. *Recreations:* gardening, reading. *Address:* Tickwood Hall, Much Wenlock, Salop TF13 6NZ. *T:* Telford (01952) 882644.

DUGDALE, Norman, CB 1974; Trustee, The Pushkin Prizes, since 1987; Permanent Secretary, Department (formerly Ministry) of Health and Social Services, Northern Ireland, 1970–84; *b* 6 Feb. 1921; *yr s* of William and Eva Dugdale, Burnley, Lancs; *m* 1949, Mary Whitehead. *Educ:* Burnley Grammar Sch.; Manchester Univ. (BA). Asst Principal, Bd of Trade, 1941; Min. of Commerce, NI, 1948; Asst Sec., Min. of Health and Local Govt, NI, 1955; Sen. Asst Sec., Min. of Health and Local Govt, NI, 1964; Second Sec., Min. of Health and Social Services, 1968. Chm., Bryson House, Belfast, 1985–93. Mem. Bd, British Council, 1986–92 (founder Mem., 1987–, Chm., 1988–92, NI Cttee). Governor, Nat. Inst. for Social Work, London, 1965–84; Mem. Court, NUU, 1971–84. Hon. DLitt NUU, 1983. *Publications:* *poems:* The Disposition of the Weather, 1967; A Prospect of the West, 1970; Night-Ferry, 1974; Corncrake in October, 1978; Running Repairs, 1983;

Limbo, 1991; contribs to various literary periodicals. *Recreations:* procrastinating; next week-end.

DUGDALE, Peter Robin, CBE 1987; Chairman, Trade Indemnity plc, 1980–93; *b* 12 Feb. 1928; *s* of late Dr James Norman Dugdale and Lilian (*née* Dolman); *m* 1957, Esmé Cyraine, *d* of L. Norwood Brown; three *s*. *Educ:* Canford; Magdalen Coll., Oxford (MA). Joined Union Insurance Soc. of Canton, Hong Kong, 1949; merged with Guardian Assurance, London, 1960; Marine and Aviation Underwriter, 1965–73; Pres., Guardian Insurance Company of Canada, 1973–76; Guardian Royal Exchange: Gen. Manager, 1976; Dir, 1977–91; Man. Dir, 1978–90. Chm., Aviation and General Insurance Co. Ltd, 1982–84. Chairman: British Insurance Assoc., 1981–82; Assoc. of British Insurers, 1987–89. Master, Worshipful Co. of Insurers, 1989–90; Hon. Life Mem., Inst. of London Underwriters, 1985. Hon. Treas., GDBA, 1992–. Gov., Canford Sch., 1980– (Chm. Govs, 1995–). *Recreations:* military and naval history, flatcoated retrievers. *Address:* Cherry Copse, Broad Lane, Hambledon, Hants PO7 4QS. *T:* Hambledon (01705) 632462. *Club:* Oriental.

DUGDALE, Sir William (Stratford), 2nd Bt *cr* 1936; CBE 1982; MC 1943; JP; DL; Director and Chairman, General Utilities PLC, since 1988; *b* 29 March 1922; *er s* of Sir William Francis Stratford Dugdale, 1st Bt, and Margaret, 2nd *d* of Sir Robert Gordon Gilmour, 1st Bt, of Liberton and Craigmillar; *S* father, 1965; *m* 1st, 1952, Lady Belinda Pleydell-Bouverie (*d* 1961), 2nd *d* of 6th Earl of Radnor; one *s* three *d*; 2nd, 1967, Cecilia Mary, *e d* of Sir William Malcolm Mount, 2nd Bt; one *s* one *d*. *Educ:* Eton; Balliol Coll., Oxford. Served War of 1939–45, Grenadier Guards (Captain), Admitted as Solicitor, 1949. Director: Phoenix Assurance Co., 1968–85; Lee Valley Water Co., 1989–90; North Surrey Water Co., 1989–; Chairman: Severn Trent Water Authority, 1974–83; National Water Council, 1982–83; Birmingham Diocesan Board of Finance, 1979–92. Steward, Jockey Club, 1985–87. Chm., Wolverhampton Racecourse PLC, 1965–91. Governor, Lady Katherine Leveson's Hosp., Temple Balsall. Mem., Warwicks CC, 1964–76; High Steward, Stratford upon Avon, 1977. JP 1951, DL 1955, High Sheriff 1971, Warwicks. *Publications:* contrib. DNB. *Heir: s* William Matthew Stratford Dugdale [*b* 22 Feb. 1959; *m* 1990, Paige Sullivan; one *s* two *d*]. *Address:* Blyth Hall, Coleshill, near Birmingham B46 2AD. *T:* Coleshill (01675) 462203; Merevale Hall, Atherstone CV9 2HG. *T:* Atherstone (01827) 713143; 24 Bryanston Mews West, W1H 7FR. *T:* 0171–262 2510. *Clubs:* Brooks's, White's, MCC; Jockey (Newmarket).

See also Baron Hazlerigg.

DUGGAN, Gordon Aldridge; HM Diplomatic Service; High Commissioner in Singapore, since 1991; *b* 12 Aug. 1937; *s* of late Joseph Nathan Duggan and Elizabeth Aldridge; *m* 1969, Erica Rose Anderssen; one *s* two *d*. *Educ:* Liverpool Collegiate Sch.; Lincoln Coll., Oxford. BA, BPhil. FO, 1963–66; Canberra, 1966–69; FCO, 1969–72; Information Officer, Bonn, 1972–74; Head of Chancery, Jakarta, 1974–76; Canberra, 1976–79; FCO, 1979–80; Commercial and Economic Counsellor, Lagos, 1981–84; Consul-Gen., Zürich, Dir of British Export Promotion in Switzerland, and Consul-Gen., Liechtenstein, 1985–88; Hd of Commercial Management and Exports Dept, FCO, 1988–89; (on secondment) Dir, Project Develt, NEI, 1989–90. *Recreations:* armchair sport, jazz, theatre, walking, string quartets. *Address:* c/o Foreign and Commonwealth Office, King Charles Street, SW1A 2AH. *Club:* United Oxford & Cambridge University.

DUGGAN, Rt. Rev. John Coote; *b* 7 April 1918; *s* of Rev. Charles Coote Whittaker Duggan, BD and Ella Thackeray Duggan (*née* Stritch); *m* 1948, Mary Elizabeth Davin; one *s* one *d* (and one *d* decd). *Educ:* High School, Dublin; Trinity Coll., Dublin (Schol.). Moderator (1st cl.)Men. and Moral Sci., 1940; Bernard Prize, Div. Test. (2nd cl.); BA 1940; BD 1946. Deacon 1941; Priest 1942. Curate Asst: St Luke, Cork, 1941–43; Taney, Dublin, 1943–48; Hon. Clerical Vicar, Christ Church Cath., 1944–48; Incumbent: Portarlington Union, Kildare, 1948–55; St Paul, Glenageary, Dublin, 1955–69; Westport and Achill Union, Tuam, 1969–70; Archdeacon of Tuam, 1969–70; Bishop of Tuam, Killala and Achonry, 1970–85. Exam. Chaplain to Archbp of Dublin, 1958–69; Examiner in BD Degree, Univ. of Dublin, 1960–69. Editor, Irish Churchman's Almanack, 1958–69. *Publications:* A Short History of Glenageary Parish, 1968. *Recreation:* fishing. *Address:* 15 Beechwood Lawn, Rochestown Avenue, Dun Laoghaire, Co. Dublin.

DUGGIN, Thomas Joseph; HM Diplomatic Service; Counsellor, Foreign and Commonwealth Office, since 1995; *b* 15 Sept. 1947; *s* of late Joseph Duggin and of Alice Lilian (*née* Mansfield); *m* 1st, 1968 (marr. diss.); two *s*; 2nd, 1983, Jittip Dunlop (*née* Charernnaimuang). *Educ:* Thornleigh Salesian Coll. Joined HM Diplomatic Service, 1967; Third Sec., Oslo, 1969–73; Third, later Second Sec. (Commercial), Bucharest, 1973–75; FCO, 1976–79; Second Sec., Bangkok, 1979–82; FCO, 1982–85; Head of Chancery and HM Consul, La Paz, 1985–88; Head of Chancery, Mexico City, 1989–91; High Comr, Vanuatu, 1992–95. MSM, Order of Vanuatu, 1992. *Recreations:* golf, reading, music. *Address:* c/o Foreign and Commonwealth Office, King Charles Street, SW1A 2AH.

DUGGLEBY, (Charles) Vincent (Anstey); freelance broadcaster and financial journalist, since 1989; *b* 23 Jan. 1939; *s* of late Bernard Waldby Duggleby and of Vivien Duggleby (*née* Hawkins); *m* 1964, Elizabeth Nora Frost; two *d*. *Educ:* Blundell's Sch.; Worcester Coll., Oxford (BA 1963). FRPSL 1979. Reporter, Bristol Evening Post, 1957–59; Sub-editor, Daily Express, 1960; BBC, 1963–89: sub-editor and sports presenter, 1963–67; Asst Sports Editor, 1967–70; Asst Editor, Current Affairs, 1970–80; Financial Editor, 1980–89. Mem., Royal Mint Adv. Cttee, 1987–94. Royal Philatelic Society: Mem. Council, 1979–; Hon. Treas., 1988–93; Vice-Pres., 1994–. Numerous awards incl. Broadcasting Financial Journalist of Year, Harold Wincott Foundn, 1992. *Publications:* Highlights from 21 Years of Sports Report, 1969; English Paper Money, 1975, 5th edn 1994; (with Louise Botting) Making the Most of Your Money, 1984, 2nd edn 1985. *Recreations:* philately, genealogy, classic jazz. *Address:* 41 Devonshire Place, W1N 1PE. *T:* 0171–486 1044.

DUGUID, Andrew Alexander; Director, Policy and Planning, Lloyd's of London, since 1994; *b* 22 June 1944; *s* of Wing Comdr (retd) Alexander Gordon Duguid and Dorothy Duguid (*née* Duder); *m* 1967, Janet Hughes; two *s* one *d*. *Educ:* Whitby Dist High Sch.; Ashbury Coll., Ottawa; Sidcot Sch.; LSE (BSc Econs); Univ. of Lancaster (MA Marketing). Res. Assistant, Brunel Univ., 1967–69; Marketing Executive: Interscan Ltd, 1969–72; Ogilvy Benson and Mather, 1972–73; joined DTI as Principal, 1973; Prin. Pvte Sec. to Sec. of State for Industry, 1977–79; Asst Sec., seconded to Prime Minister's Policy Unit, 1979; returned to set up Policy Planning Unit, Dept of Industry, later DTI, 1982; Under Sec., DTI, 1985–86; Lloyd's of London: Head of Regulatory Services, 1986–88; Head of Market Services, 1988–92; Dir, Marketing Services, 1993–94. Non-exec. Dir, Kingsway Public Relations, 1982–85. *Publication:* (with Elliott Jaques) Case Studies in Export Organisation, 1971. *Recreations:* tennis, ski-ing, walking, canoeing. *Address:* 1 Binden Road, W12 9RJ. *T:* 0181–743 7435. *Club:* Hartswood.

DUGUID, Prof. James Paris, CBE 1979; MD, BSc; FRCPath; Professor of Bacteriology, University of Dundee, 1967–84; Consultant, Tayside Health Board, 1963–84; *b* 10 July 1919; *s* of late Maj.-Gen. David Robertson Duguid, CB, and Mary Paris; *m* 1944, Isobel Duff; one *s* three *d*. *Educ:* Edinburgh Academy; Univ. of Edinburgh (MB ChB Hons 1942; BSc 1st Cl. Hons 1943; MD (Gold Medal) 1949); FRCPath 1966. Lectr, Sen. Lectr and Reader, Univ. of Edinburgh, 1944–62; Prof. of Bacteriology, Univ. of St Andrews, 1963–67; Director of Postgrad. Medical Educn, Univ. of Dundee, 1968–71, Dean of Faculty of Medicine, 1971–74, Mem. Univ. Court, 1977–81. Cons. Adviser in Microbiology, Scottish Home and Health Dept, 1967–85, Mem. Adv. Cttee on Medical Research, 1967–71; Member: Eastern Regional and Tayside Health Bds, 1967–77; Adv. Cttee on Laboratory Services, Scottish Health Serv. Council, 1967–74 (Chm., Epidemiology Sub-cttee, 1966–71); Scottish Health Services Planning Council, 1974–77 (Member: Adv. Cttee on New Developments in Health Care, 1976–84; Scientific Services Adv. Gp, 1975–79; Chm., Microbiology and Clin. Immunology Cttees, 1975–77); Jt Cttee on Vaccination and Immunisation, Health Services Councils, 1967–74; GMC, 1975–81; Council for Professions Supp. to Medicine, 1978–86; Independent Adv. Gp on Gruinard Island, 1986–87. Hon. Mem., Pathol Soc. of GB and Ireland, 1985. Co-Editor: Jl of Pathology and Bacteriology, 1959–68; Jl of Medical Microbiology, 1968–71. *Publications:* (co-ed) Mackie and McCartney, Medical Microbiology, 11th edn 1969, 12th edn 1973, 13th edn 1978; (ed) Mackie and McCartney, Practical Medical Microbiology, 1989; scientific papers on bacterial fimbriae, adhesins, biotyping and phylogeny, airborne infection, and the action of penicillin. *Recreations:* grandchildren, gardening, atheism. *Address:* 69 Dalkeith Road, Dundee DD4 7HF. *T:* Dundee (01382) 456956; Hillside, Glenborrodale, Argyll PH36 4JP.

DUKAKIS, Michael Stanley; Governor, Commonwealth of Massachusetts, 1975–79, and 1983–90; teacher, Florida Atlantic University, since 1991; *b* 3 Nov. 1933; *s* of Panos Dukakis and Euterpe Boukis-Dukakis; *m* 1963, Katharine Dickson; one *s* two *d*. *Educ:* Brookline High Sch. (Dip. 1951); Swarthmore Coll., Pa (BA 1955); Harvard Law Sch. (JD 1960). Attorney, Hill & Barlow, Boston, Mass, 1960–74; Lectr and Dir, Intergovtl Studies, John F. Kennedy Sch. of Govt, Harvard Univ., 1979–82. Moderator of public television's The Advocates, 1971–73. State Representative, Brookline, Mass, 1963–71; Democratic Candidate for the Presidency of the USA, 1988. *Publication:* (with Rosabeth Moss Kanter) Creating the Future: Massachusetts comeback and its promise for America, 1988. *Recreations:* walking, playing tennis, gardening. *Address:* Florida Atlantic University, Boca Raton, FL 33437, USA.

DUKE, family name of **Baron Merrivale.**

DUKE, Cecil Howard Armitage; Director of Establishments and Organisation, Ministry of Agriculture, Fisheries and Food, 1965–71; *b* 5 May 1912; *s* of late John William Duke and Gertrude Beatrice (*née* Armitage); *m* 1st, 1939, Eleanor Lucy (*née* Harvie) (*d* 1992); one *s* one *d*; 2nd, 1994, Joan Gladys Haig Daly (*née* Seymour). *Educ:* Selhurst Gram. Sch.; LSE. RNVR, 1942–45 (Corvettes). Entered Civil Service, 1929; Asst Princ., 1940; Princ., 1945; Private Sec. to Lord Presidents of the Council, 1951–53; Asst Sec., Land Drainage Div. and Meat Div., 1953; Under-Sec., 1965. *Recreations:* walking, gardening, watching Sussex cricket. *Address:* 22 Fairways Road, Seaford, East Sussex BN25 4EN. *T:* Seaford (01323) 894338.

DUKE, Rt. Rev. Michael Geoffrey H.; *see* Hare Duke.

DUKE, Neville Frederick, DSO 1943; OBE 1953; DFC and Two Bars, 1942, 1943, 1944; AFC 1948; MC (Czech) 1946; Managing Director, Duke Aviation; Technical Adviser and Consultant Test Pilot; *b* 11 Jan. 1922; *s* of Frederick and Jane Duke, Tonbridge, Kent; *m* 1947, Gwendoline Dorothy Fellows. *Educ:* Convent of St Mary and Judds Sch., Tonbridge, Kent. Joined Royal Air Force (cadet), 1940, training period, 1940; 92 Fighter Sqdn, Biggin Hill, 1941; Desert Air Force: 112 Fighter Sqdn, Western Desert, 1941–42, 92 Fighter Sqdn, Western Desert, 1943, Chief Flying Instructor, 73 Operational Training Unit, Egypt, 1943–44, Commanding 145 Sqdn Italy (Fighter), 1944, 28 enemy aircraft destroyed. Hawker Aircraft Ltd test flying, 1945; Empire Test Pilots Sch., 1946; RAF high speed flight, 1946 (world speed record); test flying Aeroplane and Armament Experimental Estab., Boscombe Down, 1947–48; resigned from RAF as Sqdn Leader, 1948; test flying Hawker Aircraft Ltd, 1948; Commanding 615 (County of Surrey) Sqdn, Royal Auxiliary Air Force, Biggin Hill, 1950; Chief Test Pilot, Hawker Aircraft Ltd, 1951–56 (Asst Chief, 1948–51). FRSA 1970; FRAeS 1993 (ARAeS 1948). World records: London-Rome, 1949; London-Karachi, 1949; London-Cairo, 1950. World Speed Record, Sept. 1953. Closed Circuit World Speed Record, 1953. Gold Medal Royal Danish Aero Club, 1953; Gold Medal, Royal Aero Club, 1954; two De la Vaux Medals, FAI, 1954; Segrave Trophy, 1954; Queen's Commendation, 1955. Member: RAF Escaping Soc.; United Service & Royal Aero Club (Associate). Hon. Fellow, Soc. of Experimental Test Pilots, 1991. Hon. Pres., Tangmere Mil. Aviation Mus., 1988. *Publications:* Sound Barrier, 1953; Test Pilot, 1953; Book of Flying, 1954; Book of Flight, 1958; The Crowded Sky (anthology), 1959. *Recreations:* sporting flying, yachting. *Address:* 3 Vitre Gardens, Lymington, Hants SO41 3NA. *Clubs:* Royal Air Force; Royal Cruising, Royal Naval Sailing, Royal Lymington Yacht.

DUKES, Alan M.; TD (FG) Kildare, since 1981; President, Fine Gael Party, since 1987 (Leader, 1987–90); *b* 22 April 1945; *s* of James and Rita Dukes; *m* 1968, Fionnuala Corcoran; two *d*. *Educ:* Colaiste Mhuire, Dublin; University College Dublin (MA). Chief Economist, Irish Farmers' Assoc., 1967–72; Dir, Irish Farmers' Assoc., Brussels, 1973–76; Personal Advr to Comr of European Communities, 1977–80. Minister for Agriculture, 1981–82; opposition spokesman on agric., March-Dec. 1982; Minister for Finance, 1982–86; Minister for Justice, 1986–87. Vice-President: European Movt, 1991– (Pres., Irish Council, 1987–91); European People's Party, 1987–; Mem., Council of State, 1988–90. Adjunct Prof. of Public Admin/Management, Univ. of Limerick, 1991–. Governor: EIB, 1982–86; IMF. *Address:* (office) Dáil Éireann, Dublin 2.

DUKES, Justin Paul; Chairman, European Communications Industries Consortium, since 1990; Director: VTR plc, since 1993; Herald Investment Trust plc, since 1994; *b* 19 Sept. 1941; *s* of late John Alexander Dukes and Agnes Dukes; *m* 1990, Jane Macallister; one *s*, and two *s* one *d* by a previous marriage. *Educ:* King's Coll., Univ. of Durham. Dir, Financial Times Ltd, 1975–81; Chairman: Financial Times (Europe) Ltd and Fintel Ltd, 1978–81; C. S. & P. International Inc., NY, 1980–83; Man. Dir, Channel Four TV Co., 1981–88; Chief-Exec., Galileo Co., 1988–89. Pres., Inst. of Information Scientists, 1982–83; Mem. Council, Foundn for Management Educn, 1979–90. Member: British Screen Adv. Council, 1986–88; Nat. Electronics Council, 1986–. Trustee, Internat. Inst. of Communications, 1986–91. FRTS 1986; FRSA 1986; CIMgt (CBIM 1988). Chevalier, Ordre des Arts et des Lettres (France), 1988. *Recreations:* changing institutions, walking. *Address:* 15 St Mark's Crescent, NW1 7TS.

DULBECCO, Dr Renato; Distinguished Research Professor, since 1977, Senior Clayton Foundation Investigator, since 1979, and President Emeritus, since 1993, The Salk Institute for Biological Studies (President, 1989–93); *b* Italy, 22 Feb. 1914; USA citizen; *s* of late Leonardo Dulbecco and late Maria Virdia; *m* 1963, Maureen R. Muir; one *d*; and one *d* (one *s* decd) by previous marriage. *Educ:* Univ. of Turin Medical Sch. (MD). Assistente, Univ. of Turin: Inst. Pathology, 1940–46; Anatomical Inst., 1946–47; Res. Assoc., Indiana Univ., 1947–49; Sen. Res. Fellow, 1949–52, Assoc. Prof., 1952–54, Prof. 1954–63, California Inst. Technology; Vis. Prof., Rockefeller Inst., 1962; Royal Soc. Vis. Prof. at

Univ. of Glasgow, 1963–64; Resident Fellow, Salk Inst., Calif, 1963–72, Fellow, 1972–77; Imperial Cancer Research Fund: Asst Dir of Res., 1972–74; Dep. Dir of Res., 1974–77; Prof. of Pathology and Medicine, Univ. of Calif San Diego Med. Sch., 1977–81. MNAS; Member: Fedn of Amer. Scientists; Amer. Assoc. for Cancer Research; Cancer Center, Univ. of Calif at San Diego; Bd of Scientific Counselors, Dept of Cancer Etiology, NCI; Amer. Acad. of Arts and Scis; Internat. Physicians for Prevention of Nuclear War, Inc.; Pres., Amer.-Ital. Foundn for Cancer Res. Trustee: Amer.-Italian Foundn for Cancer Res.; La Jolla Country Day School. Foreign Member: Academia dei Lincei, 1969; Royal Society, 1974; Hon. Member: Accademia Ligure di Scienze a Lettere, 1982; Società Medico-Chirugica di Modena, 1985; Tissue Culture Assoc., 1988. Has given many lectures to learned instns. Hon. DSc Yale, 1968; Hon. LLD Glasgow, 1970; *hc* Dr Med., Vrije Universiteit Brussel, Brussels, 1978; Hon. DSc Indiana, 1984. (Jtly) Nobel Prize for Physiology or Medicine, 1975; Premio Fregene, Italy, 1988; numerous other prizes and awards. *Publications:* (jtly) Microbiology, 1967; numerous in sci. jls. *Recreation:* music. *Address:* The Salk Institute, PO Box 85800, San Diego, CA 92186-5800, USA. *Club:* Athenæum.

DULVERTON, 3rd Baron *cr* 1929, of Batsford; **Gilbert Michael Hamilton Wills;** Bt 1897; farmer, forester and industrialist; *b* 2 May 1944; *s* of 2nd Baron and his 1st wife, Judith Betty (*d* 1983), *d* of Lt-Col Hon. Ian Leslie Melville, TD; *S* father, 1992; *m* 1980, Rosalind van der Velde-Oliver; one *s* one *d*. *Educ:* Gordonstoun. Dep. Chm., Thwaites Ltd; Director: W Highland Woodlands Ltd; Batsford Estate Co.; Cotswold Houses Ltd. Trustee: Dulverton Trust; Batsford Foundn. *Heir: s* Hon. Robert Anthony Hamilton Wills, *b* 20 Oct. 1983.

DUMAS, Roland; Officier de la Légion d'Honneur; Croix de Guerre (1939–45); Croix du Combattant Volontaire; Minister of Foreign Affairs, France, 1988–93; *b* Limoges, Haute-Vienne, 23 Aug. 1922; *s* of Georges Dumas and Elisabeth (*née* Lecanuet); *m* 1964, Anne-Marie Lillet; two *s* one *d*. *Educ:* Lycée de Limoges; Faculté de Droit de Paris; Ecole des Sciences Politiques de Paris; Univ. of London; Ecole de langues orientales de Paris. LLL; Diplomas: in Advanced Studies in Laws; in Political Science, Paris, and London School of Economics. Counsel, Court of Appeal, Paris; journalist; Sen. Political Dir, Journal Socialiste Limousin; Political Dir of weekly, La Corrèze Républicaine et Socialiste; Deputy: UDSR, Haute Vienne, 1956–58; FGDS, Corrèze, 1967–68; Socialiste de la Dordogne, 1981–83, 1986–88; Minister for European Affairs, 1983–84; Govt spokesman, 1984; Minister for External Relations, 1984–86; Pres. Commn for Foreign Affairs, Nat. Assembly, 1986–87. Grand Cross, Order of Isabel (Spain), 1982. *Publications:* J'ai vu vivre la Chine, 1960; Les Avocats, 1970; Le Droit de l'Information et de la Presse, 1981; Plaidoyer pour Roger Gilbert Lecomte, 1985; Le droit de la propriété littéraire et artistique, 1986; Le Peuple Assemblé, 1989. *Address:* 28 rue de Bièvre, 75005 Paris, France.

DUMBELL, Dr Keith Rodney; Senior Specialist in Microbiology, Medical School, University of Cape Town, 1982–90, retired; *b* 2 Oct. 1922; *s* of late Stanley Dumbell and Dorothy Ellen (*née* Hewitt); *m* 1st, 1950, Brenda Margaret (*née* Heathcote) (*d* 1971); two *d*; 2nd, 1972, Susan (*née* Herd); two *s*. *Educ:* Wirral Gram. Sch.; University of Liverpool, MB, ChB 1944; MD (Liverpool), 1950. FRCPath 1975. Asst Lecturer, Dept of Bacteriology, University of Liverpool, 1945–47; Mem. of Scientific Staff, MRC, 1947–50; Junior Pathologist, RAF, 1950–52; Asst in Pathology and Microbiology, Rockefeller Inst. for Medical Research (Dr Peyton Rous' laboratory), 1952–53; Lecturer in Bacteriology, University of Liverpool, 1952–58; Senior Lecturer, 1958–64; Prof. of Virology, Univ. of London at St Mary's Hosp. Med. Sch., 1964–81. *Publications:* articles in various medical and scientific journals. *Address:* c/o National Westminster Bank, Berkhamsted, Herts HP4 1AW.

DUMBUTSHENA, Hon. Enoch; Chief Justice of Zimbabwe, 1984–90; Vice-President, International Commission of Jurists, since 1992 (Commissioner, since 1990); *b* 25 April 1920; *s* of late Job Matabasi Dumbutshena and Sarah Dumbutshena; *m* 1st, 1948, Alphosina (*née* Mahlangu) (marr. diss.; she *d* 1989); one *s* one *d*; 2nd, 1964, Miriam Masango (marr. diss.); one *s* two *d*. *Educ:* Univ. of South Africa (BA, BEd, UED). Called to the Bar, Gray's Inn, 1963, Hon. Bencher, 1989. Teacher, 1946–56; journalist, 1956–59; barrister, Southern Rhodesia, 1963–67; Zambia: founded Legal Aid Scheme, 1967–70; private practice, 1970–78; Zimbabwe: private practice, 1978–80; Judge of High Court, 1980; Judge President, 1983. Judge of Appeal, Transkei, 1991–; Acting Judge of Appeal, Namibia, 1991–. Exec. Mem., Centre for the Independence of Judges and Lawyers. Pres., Forum Party, Zimbabwe, 1993–. Chairman: Modus Publications; Art Printers Employees Trust, Harare. President: Boy Scouts; Zimbabwe Conservation Trust; Chairman: Moleli-Marshall Hartley Trust; Legal Resources Foundn Trust; Old Age Zimbabwe; Trustee, Omay Develt Trust, Harare. Governor: Arundel Sch., Harare; Moleli Secondary Sch. (Chm., Bd of Govs); Trustee, Chisipite Jun. Sch., Harare, 1985–91. Hon. DCL Oxford, 1990. *Publication:* Zimbabwe Tragedy, 1986. *Recreations:* mountain climbing (average height), reading, formerly tennis. *Address:* PO Box CH70, Chisipite, Harare, Zimbabwe. *T:* (office) (4) 724778, (residence) (4) 884147. *Club:* Harare.

DUMFRIES, Earl of; John Bryson Crichton-Stuart; *b* 21 Dec. 1989; *s* and *heir* of 7th Marquess of Bute, *qv*.

DUMMETT, (Agnes Margaret) Ann; Consultant (part-time) on European Policies to Commission for Racial Equality, since 1990; *b* 4 Sept. 1930; *d* of Arthur William Chesney and late Kitty Mary Chesney; *m* 1951, Michael Anthony Eardley Dummett, *qv*; three *s* two *d* (and one *s* one *d* decd). *Educ:* Guildhouse Sch., Pimlico; Ware Grammar Sch. for Girls; Somerville Coll., Oxford (MA). Pres., Oxford Univ. Liberal Club, 1949. Community Relations Officer, Oxford, 1966–69; teaching in further education, 1969–71; Research Worker: Inst. of Race Relations, 1971–73; Runnymede Trust, 1975, 1977; Jt Council for the Welfare of Immigrants, 1978–84; Dir, Runnymede Trust, 1984–87. *Publications:* A Portrait of English Racism, 1973; Citizenship and Nationality, 1976; A New Immigration Policy, 1978; (with Ian Martin) British Nationality: a guide to the new law, 1982; (ed) Towards a Just Immigration Policy, 1986; chapters in: Justice First (with Michael Dummett), 1969; Colloque de la Société Française pour le Droit International, 1979; Moral Philosophy, 1979; (with Andrew Nicol) Subjects, Citizens, Aliens and Others, 1990; Free Movement, 1992; numerous articles and pamphlets. *Recreations:* walking about cities, theatregoing, popular music. *Address:* 54 Park Town, Oxford OX2 6SJ. *T:* Oxford (01865) 58698. *Club:* Commonwealth Trust.

DUMMETT, George Anthony, FEng 1977; FIChemE; Chairman, Council of Engineering Institutions, 1976–77 (Vice-Chairman, 1975); *b* 13 Oct. 1907; *s* of George Herbert Dummett and Gertrude (*née* Higgins); *m* 1st, 1931, Peggy Schaeffer; 2nd, 1939, Ursula Margarete Schubert; two *s* one *d*. *Educ:* Rugby Sch.; Birmingham Univ.; Pembroke Coll., Cambridge. MA. Research in phys. chem., Cambridge Univ., 1930–32; Research Asst, Thorncliffe Coal Distillation Ltd, 1932–35; APV Co. Ltd (then Aluminium Plant and Vessel Co. Ltd): Technical Res. Asst, 1935; Laboratory Man., 1943; Chem. Engrg Dept Man., 1948; Scientific Man., 1949; Res. Dir, 1956; Dep. Man. Dir, 1965–72; Dir, APV (Holdings) Ltd, 1962–72; Dep. Chm., APV Internat., 1965–72. Chm., Res. Cttee, FBI, 1958–65; Pres., IChemE, 1968–69, Hon. Fellow, 1981. Chm., European Fedn Chemical Engrng, 1977–78. Hon. Member: Soc. de Chimie Ind., 1969; Dechema, 1976. *Publications:* From Little Acorns: a history of the APV company, 1981; numerous papers on chemical and biochemical engrg, metallurgy, etc. *Recreations:* music, mountaineering, gardening, stamp collecting. *Address:* 10 Priory Crescent, Lewes, East Sussex BN7 1HP. *T:* Lewes (01273) 473731. *Clubs:* Alpine, Climbers.

See also M. A. E. Dummett.

DUMMETT, Michael Anthony Eardley, FBA; Wykeham Professor of Logic in the University of Oxford, 1979–92, Professor Emeritus 1992; Emeritus Fellow: All Souls College, Oxford, 1979; New College, Oxford, 1992; *b* 27 June 1925; *s* of George Herbert Dummett and Iris Dummett (*née* Eardley-Wilmot); *m* 1951, Ann Chesney (*see* A. M. A. Dummett); three *s* two *d* (one *s* one *d* decd). *Educ:* Sandroyd Sch.; Winchester Coll. (1st Schol.); Christ Church, Oxford. Major hist. schol. (Ch. Ch.), 1942. Served in Army, 1943–47: in RA and Intell. Corps (India, 1945, Malaya, 1946–47, Sgt). Ch. Ch., Oxford, 1947–50, First Class Hons, PPE, 1950. Asst Lectr in Philosophy, Birmingham Univ., 1950–51; Commonwealth Fund Fellow, Univ. of California, Berkeley, 1955–56; Reader in the Philosophy of Mathematics, Univ. of Oxford, 1962–74; All Souls College, Oxford: Fellow, 1950–79, Senior Research Fellow, 1974–79; Sub-Warden, 1974–76; Fellow, New Coll., Oxford, 1979–92. Vis. Lectr, Univ. of Ghana, 1958; Vis. Professor: Stanford Univ., several occasions, 1960–66; Univ. of Minnesota, 1968; Princeton Univ., 1970; Rockefeller Univ., 1973; William James Lectr in Philosophy, Harvard Univ., 1976; Alex. von Humboldt-Stiftung Vis. Res. Fellow, Münster Univ., 1981. Founder Mem., Oxford Cttee for Racial Integration, 1965 (Chm., Jan.-May 1966); Member: Exec. Cttee, Campaign Against Racial Discrimination, 1966–67; Legal and Civil Affairs Panel, Nat. Cttee for Commonwealth Immigrants, 1966–68; Chairman: Jt Council for the Welfare of Immigrants, 1970–71 (Vice-Chm., 1967–69, 1973–75); unofficial cttee of enquiry into events in Southall 23 April 1979, 1979–80; shadow board, Barclays Bank, 1981–82. FBA 1968–84, re-elected 1995. For. Hon. Mem., Amer. Acad. of Arts and Scis, 1985. Hon. PhD Nijmegen, 1983; Hon. DLitt: Caen, 1993; Aberdeen, 1993. Lakatos Award in Phil. of Sci., 1994. *Publications:* Frege: philosophy of language, 1973, 2nd edn 1981; The Justification of Deduction, 1973; Elements of Intuitionism, 1977; Truth and other Enigmas, 1978; Immigration: where the debate goes wrong, 1978; Catholicism and the World Order, 1979; The Game of Tarot, 1980; Twelve Tarot Games, 1980; The Interpretation of Frege's Philosophy, 1981; Voting Procedures, 1984; The Visconti-Sforza Tarot Cards, 1986; Ursprünge der analytischen Philosophie, 1988, rev. edn as Origins of Analytical Philosophy, 1993; Frege and Other Philosophers, 1991; The Logical Basis of Metaphysics, 1991; Frege: Philosophy of Mathematics, 1991; Grammar and Style for Examination Candidates and Others, 1993; The Seas of Language, 1993; Il Mondo e l'Angelo, 1993; contributions to: Mind and Language, 1975; Truth and Meaning, 1976; Studies on Frege, 1976; Contemporary British Philosophy, 1976; Meaning and Use, 1979; Perception and Identity, 1979; Perspectives on the Philosophy of Wittgenstein, 1981; Approaches to Language, 1983; Frege: tradition and influence, 1984; Reflections on Chomsky, 1989; Meaning and Method, 1990; contrib. entry on Frege, to Encyclopedia of Philosophy (ed P. Edwards), 1967; (with Ann Dummett) chapter on Rôle of the Government, in Justice First (ed L. Donnelly), 1969; preface to R. C. Zaehner, The City Within the Heart, 1980; articles in: Aristotelian Soc. Proceedings, Philos. Review, Bull. of London Math. Soc., Synthese, Inquiry, Econometrica, Jl of Symbolic Logic, Zeitschrift für mathematische Logik, Dublin Review, New Blackfriars, Clergy Review, Jl of Warburg and Courtauld Insts, Jl of Playing-Card Soc. *Recreations:* listening to the blues, investigating the history of card games, reading science fiction. *Address:* 54 Park Town, Oxford OX2 6SJ. *T:* Oxford (01865) 58698. *Club:* Commonwealth Trust.

See also G. A. Dummett.

DUMPER, Rt. Rev. Anthony Charles; Hon. Assistant Bishop, diocese of Birmingham, since 1993; Hon. Tutor, Centre of Anglican Communion Studies, Selly Oak, since 1993; *b* 4 Oct. 1923; *s* of Charles Frederick and Edith Mildred Dumper; *m* 1948, Sibylle Anna Emilie Hellwig; two *s* one *d*. *Educ:* Surbiton Grammar School; Christ's Coll., Cambridge (MA); Westcott House, Cambridge. Relief Worker, Germany, 1946–47; ordained, 1947; Curate, East Greenwich, 1947–49; Vicar of South Perak, Malaya, 1949–57; Archdeacon of North Malaya, 1955–64; Vicar of Penang, Malaya, 1957–64; Dean of St Andrew's Cathedral, Singapore, 1964–70; Vicar of St Peter's, Stockton on Tees, and Rural Dean of Stockton, 1970–77; Bishop Suffragan of Dudley, 1977–93. *Publication:* Vortex of the East, 1963. *Recreations:* walking, gardening. *Address:* 117 Berberry Close, Bournville, Birmingham B30 1TB.

DUNALLEY, 7th Baron *cr* 1800 (Ire.), of Kilboy, Tipperary; **Henry Francis Cornelius Prittie;** Probation Officer with Oxfordshire Probation Service, since 1983; *b* 30 May 1948; *s* of 6th Baron Dunalley and of Mary Philippa, *o c* of late Hon. Philip Cary; *S* father, 1992; *m* 1978, Sally Louise, *er d* of Ronald Vere; one *s* three *d*. *Educ:* Gordonstoun Sch.; Trinity Coll., Dublin (BA); Bedford Coll., Univ. of London (CQSW). Probation Officer: Inner London Probation Service, 1977–80; Buckinghamshire Probation Service, 1980–83. *Heir: s* Hon. Joel Henry Prittie, *b* 29 April 1981. *Address:* 25 Stephen Road, Oxford OX3 9AY. *T:* Oxford (01865) 61914.

DUNANT, Sarah; novelist and broadcaster; *b* 8 Aug. 1950; *d* of David Dunant and Estelle (*née* Joseph); two *d* by Ian Willox. *Educ:* Godolphin and Latymer Girls' Sch.; Newnham Coll., Cambridge (BA Hons 1972). Actress, 1972–73; producer, Radio 4, 1974–76; freelance writer, TV and radio broadcaster and journalist, 1977–; sometime Presenter: Woman's Hour, Radio 4, 1986–; The Late Show, BBC 2, 1989–. *Publications:* as Peter Dunant, (with Peter Busby): Exterminating Angels, 1983; Intensive Care, 1986; as Sarah Dunant: Snow Storms in a Hot Climate, 1988; Birth Marks, 1991; Fatlands, 1993 (Silver Dagger Award); (ed) The War of the Words, 1994; Under my Skin, 1995. *Recreation:* travel. *Address:* c/o Gillon Aitken, Aitken, Stone & Wylie, 29 Fernshaw Road, SW10 0TG. *T:* 0171-351 7561.

DUNBAR, Alexander Arbuthnott, DL; farmer; *b* 14 March 1929; *yr s* of Sir Edward Dunbar, 9th Bt; *m* 1965, Elizabeth Susannah, *d* of Rev. Denzil Wright; one *s* one *d*. *Educ:* Wellington Coll., Berks; Pembroke Coll., Cambridge (MA); Edinburgh Sch. of Agriculture, 1980–81. Mil. Service, Lieut QO Cameron Highlanders, 1947–49. Called to the Bar, Inner Temple, 1953. Joined ICI, 1954: Asst Sec., Wilton Works, 1959–63. Joined North Eastern Assoc. for the Arts, 1963, Sec. 1964, Dir 1967; Director: Northern Arts Assoc., 1967–69; UK and British Commonwealth Branch, Calouste Gulbenkian Foundn, 1970–71; Scottish Arts Council, 1971–80. DL Moray, 1987. *Publications:* contribs to various jls. *Recreations:* art, theatre, conservation, history, cycling. *Address:* Pitgaveny, Elgin, Moray IV30 2PQ.

DUNBAR of Northfield, Sir Archibald (Ranulph), 11th Bt *cr* 1700; *b* 8 Aug. 1927; *er s* of Sir (Archibald) Edward Dunbar, 9th Bt (by some reckonings 10th Bt) and Olivia Douglas Sinclair (*d* 1964), *d* of Maj.-Gen. Sir Edward May, KCB, CMG; *S* father, 1969; *m* 1974, Amelia Millar Sommerville, *d* of Horace Davidson; one *s* two *d*. *Educ:* Wellington Coll.; Pembroke Coll., Cambridge; Imperial Coll. of Tropical Agriculture, Trinidad. Mil. Service, 2nd Lt, Cameron (att. Gordon) Highlanders, 1945–48. Entered Colonial Agricultural Service, Uganda, as Agricultural Officer, 1953; retired, 1970. Hon. Sheriff,

Sheriff Court District of Moray, 1989–. Kt of Honour and Devotion, SMO Malta, 1989. *Publications:* A History of Bunyoro-Kitara, 1965; Omukama Chwa II Kabarega, 1965; The Annual Crops of Uganda, 1969; various articles in Uganda Jl. *Recreations:* swimming, military modelling, model railways. *Heir: s* Edward Horace Dunbar, Younger of Northfield, *b* 18 March 1977. *Address:* The Old Manse, Duffus, Elgin, Scotland IV30 2QD. *T:* Hopeman (01343) 830270. *Club:* New (Edinburgh).

DUNBAR, Charles, CB 1964; Director, Fighting Vehicles Research and Development Establishment, Ministry of Defence, 1960–67; *b* 12 Jan. 1907; *s* of John Dunbar, Barrow-in-Furness, Lancs; *m* 1933, Mary Alice (*née* Clarke), Barnes, SW; two *d. Educ:* Grammar Sch., Barrow-in-Furness; Manchester Univ. (MSc). National Physical Laboratory, Dept of Scientific and Industrial Research, 1929–43; Tank Armament Research Establishment, Min. of Supply, 1943–47; Fighting Vehicles Research and Development Establishments, 1947–67, retired. *Publications:* contribs to learned journals. *Recreations:* golf, fishing. *Address:* 3 Invereoch Court, Arrochar, Dunbartonshire G83 7AB.

See also Peter Graham.

DUNBAR, Sir David H.; *see* Hope-Dunbar.

DUNBAR of Durn, Sir Drummond Cospatrick Ninian, 9th Bt, *cr* 1697; MC 1943; Major Black Watch, retired; *b* 9 May 1917; *o s* of Sir George Alexander Drummond Dunbar, 8th Bt and Sophie Kathleen (*d* 1936), *d* of late J. Benson Kennedy; *S* father, 1949; *m* 1957, Sheila Barbara Mary, *d* of John B. de Fonblanque, London; one *s. Educ:* Radley Coll.; Worcester Coll., Oxford. BA 1938. Served War of 1939–45, Middle East, North Africa, Sicily, Normandy (wounded twice, MC). Retired pay, 1958. *Heir: s* Robert Drummond Cospatrick Dunbar, Younger of Durn [*b* 17 June 1958; *m* 1994, Sarah, *yr d* of Robert Anthony Brooks; one *s. Educ:* Harrow; Christ Church, Oxford; BA 1979]. *Address:* Town Hill, Westmount, Jersey, Channel Islands JE2 3LP. *Club:* Naval and Military.

DUNBAR, Ian Duncan; Partner, since 1972, and Chairman, since 1994, Miller Hendry, Perth and Dundee (formerly Sneddon Campbell & Munro, Perth, and Miller Sneddon, WS); President, Law Society of Scotland, 1993–94 (Vice President, 1992–93); *b* 31 Oct. 1948; *s* of John Duncan Dunbar and Mary Golden; *m* 1973, Sue Young. *Educ:* Lawside Acad., Dundee; Queen's Coll., Dundee (St Andrews Univ., subseq. Dundee Univ.) (LLB 1969). Apprentice Solicitor, Soutar Reid & Mill, Dundee, 1969–71; Asst Solicitor, Sneddon Campbell & Munro, Perth, 1971–72. *Recreations:* golf, Rugby, cooking, food, wine. *Address:* Craigrownie, Bridge of Earn, Perth PH2 9HA. *T:* Perth (01738) 812255, (office) (01738) 637311. *Clubs:* County and City (Perth); Royal Perth Golfing Society; Blairgowrie Golf.

DUNBAR, Ian Malcolm, CB 1993; Director of Inmate Administration, Prison Service, Home Office, 1990–94; *b* 6 Jan. 1934; *s* of Thomas Dunbar and Rose (*née* Hook); *m* 1966, Sally Ann Hendrickson; two *s* one *d. Educ:* Buckhurst Hill County High Sch.; Keele Univ.; Reed Coll., Portland, USA; LSE. Joined Prison Service, 1959; Leyhill Prison, 1960; Prison Service Coll., 1965; Dep. Gov., Long Lartin, 1970; Gov., Usk Borstal and Detention Centre, 1972; Prison Dept 4 Div., Home Office, 1974; Governor: Feltham Borstal, 1978; Wakefield Prison, 1979; Wormwood Scrubs, 1983; seconded to HM Inspectorate of Prisons, 1985; Regl Dir, SW Reg., Prison Service, 1985. *Publication:* A Sense of Direction, 1985. *Recreations:* bee-keeping, gardening, photography, walking, reading.

DUNBAR of Mochrum, Colonel Sir James Michael, 14th Bt *cr* 1694 (NS), of Mochrum, Wigtownshire, *b* 17 Jan. 1950; *s* of Sir Jean Ivor Dunbar, 13th Bt and of Rose Jeanne, *d* of Henry William Hertsch; *S* father, 1993; *m* 1st, 1978, Margaret Jacobs (marr diss. 1989; she *d* 1991); two *s* one *d*; 2nd, 1989, Margaret, *d* of Roger Gordon Talbot; one *d*. Colonel, USAF. *Heir: s* Michael Joseph Dunbar, *b* 5 July 1980. *Address:* 49 Spruce Street, Box 1000, Langley AFB, VA 23665, USA.

DUNBAR, John Greenwell; Secretary, Royal Commission on the Ancient and Historical Monuments of Scotland, 1978–90; *b* 1 March 1930; *o s* of John Dunbar and Marie Alton; *m* 1974, Elizabeth Mill Blyth. *Educ:* University College Sch., London; Balliol Coll., Oxford (MA). FSA, FSAScot. Joined staff of Royal Commission on the Ancient and Historical Monuments of Scotland, 1953; Mem., Ancient Monuments Board for Scotland, 1978–90. Vice-President: Soc. for Medieval Archaeology, 1981–86; Soc. of Antiquaries of Scotland, 1983–86. Lindsay-Fischer Lectr, Oslo, 1985. Hon. FRIAS. *Publications:* The Historic Architecture of Scotland, 1966, revd edn 1978; (ed with John Imrie) Accounts of the Masters of Works 1616–1649, 1982; numerous articles in archaeological jls, etc. *Address:* Patie's Mill, Carlops, By Penicuik, Midlothian EH26 9NF. *T:* West Linton (01968) 660250. *Club:* New (Edinburgh).

DUNBAR of Hempriggs, Dame Maureen Daisy Helen, (Lady Dunbar of Hempriggs), Btss (8th in line) *cr* 1706 (NS); *b* 19 Aug. 1906; *d* of Courtenay Edward Moore and Janie King Moore (*née* Askins); assumed the name of Dunbar, in lieu of Blake, on claiming succession to the Hempriggs baronetcy after death of kinsman, Sir George Cospatrick Duff-Sutherland-Dunbar, 7th Bt, in 1963; claim established and title recognised by Lyon Court, 1965; *m* 1940, Leonard James Blake (*d* 1989); one *s* one *d. Educ:* Headington Sch.; Royal Coll. of Music. LRAM 1928. Music teacher at: Monmouth Sch. for Girls, 1930–33; Oxford High Sch., 1935–40; Malvern Coll., 1957–68. *Heir:* (to mother's Btcy) *s* Richard Francis Dunbar of Hempriggs, younger [*b* 8 Jan. 1945 (assumed the name of Dunbar, 1965); *m* 1969, Elizabeth Margaret Jane Lister; two *d*]. *Address:* 51 Gloucester Street, Winchcombe, Cheltenham, Glos GL54 5LX. *T:* Cheltenham (01242) 602122.

DUNBAR-NASMITH, Rear-Adm. David Arthur, CB 1969; DSC 1942; retired 1972; Vice Lord-Lieutenant, Morayshire, since 1980; *b* 21 Feb. 1921; *e s* of late Admiral Sir Martin Dunbar-Nasmith, VC, KCB, KCMG, DL, and of late Justina Dunbar-Nasmith, CBE, DStJ; *m* 1951, Elizabeth Bowlby; two *s* two *d. Educ:* Lockers Park; RNC, Dartmouth. To sea as Midshipman, 1939. War Service, Atlantic and Mediterranean, in HM Ships Barham, Rodney, Kelvin and Petard. In comd: HM Ships Haydon 1943, Peacock 1945–46, Moon 1946, Rowena 1946–48, Enard Bay 1951, Alert 1954–56, Berwick, and 5th Frigate Squadron, 1961–63; Commodore, Amphibious Forces, 1966–67. RN and Joint Service Staff Colls, 1948–49; Staff of Flag Officer 1st Cruiser Squadron, 1949–51; NATO HQ, SACLANT, 1952–54 and SACEUR, 1958–60; Dir of Defence Plans, Min. of Defence, 1963–65; Naval Secretary, 1967–70; Flag Officer, Scotland and N Ireland, 1970–72. Comdr 1951; Capt. 1958; Rear-Adm. 1967. Chm., Moray and Nairn Newspaper Co., 1982–91. Member: Highlands and Islands Devel Bd, 1972–83 (Dep. Chm., 1972–81; Chm., 1981–82); Countryside Commn for Scotland, 1972–76; British Waterways Bd, 1980–87; N of Scotland Hydro-Electric Bd, 1982–85. Mem. Queen's Body Guard for Scotland (Royal Company of Archers), 1974–; Gentleman Usher of the Green Rod to the Order of the Thistle, 1979–. DL Moray, 1974. *Recreations:* sailing, ski-ing and shooting. *Address:* Glen of Rothes, Rothes, Moray. *T:* Rothes (01340) 831216. *Clubs:* Royal Ocean Racing; New (Edinburgh).

See also J. D. Dunbar-Nasmith.

DUNBAR-NASMITH, Prof. James Duncan, CBE 1976; RIBA; PPRIAS; FRSA, FRSE; Partner: Law & Dunbar-Nasmith, architects, Edinburgh, Forres, founded 1957; Hilger, Law & Dunbar-Nasmith, architects, Innenarchitekten, Wiesbaden, Germany, founded 1993; Professor Emeritus, Heriot-Watt University, since 1988; *b* 15 March 1927; *y s* of late Adm. Sir Martin Dunbar-Nasmith, VC, KCB, KCMG, DL and of late Justina Dunbar-Nasmith, CBE, DStJ. *Educ:* Lockers Park; Winchester. Trinity Coll., Cambridge (BA); Edinburgh Coll. of Art (DA). ARIBA 1954. Architekten Kammer Hessen. Lieut, Scots Guards, 1945–48. Prof. and Hd of Dept. of Architecture, Heriot-Watt Univ. and Edinburgh Coll. of Art, 1978–88. President: Royal Incorporation of Architects in Scotland, 1971–73; Edinburgh Architectural Assoc., 1967–69. Member: Council, RIBA, 1967–73 (a Vice-Pres., 1972–73; Chm., Bd of Educn, 1972–73); Council, ARCUK, 1976–84 (Vice-Chm., Bd of Educn, 1977); Royal Commn on Ancient and Historical Monuments of Scotland, 1972–; Ancient Monuments Bd for Scotland, 1969–83 (interim Chm., 1972–73); Historic Buildings Council for Scotland, 1966–93; Council, Europa Nostra, 1986–; Dep. Chm., Edinburgh Internat. Festival, 1981–85; Trustee: Scottish Civic Trust, 1971–; Architectural Heritage Fund, 1976–; Theatres Trust, 1983–. *Recreations:* music, theatre, ski-ing, sailing. *Address:* (office) 16 Dublin Street, Edinburgh EH1 3RE. *T:* 0131–556 8631. *Clubs:* Royal Ocean Racing; New (Edinburgh).

See also D. A. Dunbar-Nasmith.

DUNBOYNE, 28th Baron by Prescription, 18th Baron by Patent; **Patrick Theobald Tower Butler; His Honour The Lord Dunboyne;** VRD; a Circuit Judge, 1972–86; *b* 27 Jan. 1917; *e s* of 27th Baron Dunboyne and Dora Isolde Butler (*d* 1977), *e d* of Comdr F. F. Tower; *S* father, 1945; *m* 1950, Anne Marie, *d* of late Sir Victor Mallet, GCMG, CVO; one *s* three *d. Educ:* Winchester; Trinity Coll., Cambridge (MA). Pres. of Cambridge Union. Lieut Irish Guards (Suppl. Res.); served European War, 1939–44 (King's Badge) (prisoner, then repatriated); Foreign Office, 1945–46. Barrister-at-Law, Middle Temple (Harmsworth Scholar), Inner Temple, South-Eastern Circuit, King's Inns, Dublin. In practice 1949–71. Recorder of Hastings, 1961–71; Dep. Chm., Quarter Sessions: Mddx, 1963–65; Kent, 1963–71; Inner London 1971–72. Legal Aid No 2 Area Cttee, 1954–64. Commissary Gen., Diocese of Canterbury, 1959–71. Home Sec's Ward-boundaries Comr, 1960–70. Irish Genealogical Research Society: Fellow, 1982; Pres., 1971–91; Vice-Pres., 1992–; Founder Hon. Sec., Bar Lawn Tennis Soc., 1950 (Vice-Pres. 1963–), and of Irish Peers Assoc., 1963–71 (Chm., 1987–90); Pres., Wireless Telegraphy Appeal Tribunal for Eng. and Wales, 1967–70. Mem. Council, Friends of Canterbury Cathedral, 1953–71. Lt, RNVR, 1951–58, RNR, 1958–60. *Publications:* The Trial of J. G. Haigh, 1953; (with others) Cambridge Union, 1815–1939, 1953; Butler Family History, 1966, 7th edn 1990. *Recreations:* rowing, lawn tennis, chess. *Heir: s* Hon. John Fitzwalter Butler [*b* 31 July 1951; *m* 1975, Diana Caroline, *yr d* of Sir Michael Williams, KCMG; one *s* three *d*]. *Address:* 36 Ormonde Gate, SW3 4HA. *T:* 0171–352 1837. *Clubs:* Irish; International Lawn Tennis of Great Britain (Vice-Pres., Pres. 1973–83) and (hon.) of Australia, France, Germany, Monaco, Netherlands and USA; Forty Five Lawn Tennis (Pres., 1974–91); All England Lawn Tennis (Wimbledon); Pitt, Union (Cambridge).

DUNCAN, Agnes Lawrie Addie, (Laura); Sheriff of Glasgow and Strathkelvin, since 1982; *b* 17 June 1947; *d* of late William Smith, District Clerk, and of Mary Marshall Smith McClure; *m* 1990, David Cecil Duncan, farmer, cricket coach, *y s* of late Dr and Mrs H. C. Duncan, Edinburgh. *Educ:* Hamilton Acad.; Glasgow Univ. (LLB 1967). Admitted Solicitor, 1969; called to the Scottish Bar, 1976. Solicitor, private practice, 1969–71; Procurator Fiscal Depute, 1971–75; Standing Junior Counsel to Dept of Employment, 1982. RYA dinghy sailing instructor, and racing coach; Mem. Council, RYA, Scotland, 1992–. Winner, Scottish Ladies Single handed Dinghy Championship, 1990. *Recreation:* sailing. *Address:* Glasgow Sheriff Court, 1 Carlton Place, Glasgow G5 9DA.

DUNCAN, Alan James Carter; MP (C) Rutland and Melton, since 1992; *b* 31 March 1957; 2nd *s* of late Wing Comdr J. G. Duncan, OBE and Anne Duncan (*née* Carter). *Educ:* Merchant Taylors' Sch.; St John's Coll., Oxford. Pres., Oxford Union, 1979. With Shell Internat. Petroleum, 1979–81; Kennedy Schol., Harvard Univ., 1981–82; oil trader, Marc Rich & Co., 1982–88; self-employed oil broker, 1988–. PPS to Min. of State, DoH, 1993–94. Mem., Select Cttee on Social Security, 1993–. Contested (C) Barnsley W and Penistone, 1987. Freeman, City of London, 1980; Liveryman, Merchant Taylors' Co., 1987. *Publications:* An End to Illusions, 1993; (with D. Hobson) Saturn's Children: how the state devours liberty, prosperity and virtue, 1995. *Address:* House of Commons, SW1A 0AA. *Clubs:* Carlton, Beefsteak.

DUNCAN, Prof. Archibald Alexander McBeth, FBA 1985; Professor of Scottish History and Literature, Glasgow University, 1962–93; *b* 17 Oct. 1926; *s* of Charles George Duncan and Christina Helen McBeth; *m* 1954, Ann Hayes Sawyer, *d* of W. E. H. Sawyer, Oxford; two *s* one *d. Educ:* George Heriot's Sch.; Edinburgh Univ.; Balliol Coll., Oxford. Lecturer in History, Queen's Univ., Belfast, 1951–53; Lecturer in History, Edinburgh Univ., 1953–61; Leverhulme Research Fellow, 1961–62. Clerk of Senate, Glasgow Univ., 1978–83. Mem., Royal Commn on the Ancient and Historical Monuments of Scotland, 1969–92. *Publications:* Scotland: The Making of the Kingdom, 1975; (ed and revised) W. Croft Dickinson's Scotland from the Earliest Times to 1603, 3rd edn 1977; Regesta Regum Scottorum, v, The Acts of Robert I, 1306–29, 1988. *Address:* 17 Campbell Drive, Bearsden, Glasgow G61 4NF.

DUNCAN, Brian Arthur Cullum, CB 1972; CBE 1963 (MBE 1949); QC 1972; Judge Advocate General of the Forces, 1968–72; *b* 2 Feb. 1908; *yr s* of late Frank Hubert Duncan, LDS, RCS, and late Edith Jane Duncan (*née* Cullum); *m* 1934, Irene Flora Templeman (*d* 1983), *o c* of late John Frederick Templeman and late Flora Edith Templeman; two *s* two *d. Educ:* Queens' Coll., Cambridge (MA). Called to the Bar, Lincoln's Inn, 1931. Practised South Eastern Circuit, Central Criminal Court, North London Sessions, and Herts and Essex Sessions. Commissioned RAF, April 1940; relinqd commn, 1950 (Wing Comdr). Joined JAG's Dept, 1945. Dep. Judge Advocate Gen. (Army and RAF): Middle East, 1950–53; Germany, 1954–57; Far East, 1959–62; Vice Judge Advocate Gen., 1967–68. *Address:* Culverlands, Neville Park, Baltonsborough, Glastonbury, Som BA6 8PY.

DUNCAN, David Francis; HM Diplomatic Service, retired; *b* 22 Feb. 1923; *s* of late Brig. William Edmonstone Duncan, CVO, DSO, MC, and Mrs Magdalene Emily Duncan (*née* Renny-Tailyour). *Educ:* Eton; Trinity Coll., Cambridge. Served War, RA, 1941–46 (despatches). Entered Foreign (later Diplomatic) Service, 1949; Foreign Office, 1949–52; Bogotá, 1952–54; UK Delegn to ECSC, Luxembourg, 1954–55; FO, 1955–58; Baghdad, 1958; Ankara, 1958–60; FO, 1960–62; Quito, 1962–65; Phnom Penh, 1965 (as Chargé d'Affaires); FO (later Foreign and Commonwealth Office), 1965–70; Islamabad, 1970–71; Counsellor, UK Delegn to Geneva Disarm. Conf., 1971–74; Ambassador to Nicaragua, 1974–76; retired 1976. *Recreations:* walking, photography, travel. *Address:* 133 Rivermead Court, Ranelagh Gardens, SW6 3SE. *T:* 0171–736 1576.

DUNCAN, Rev. Denis Macdonald, MA, BD; Managing Director, Arthur James Ltd (Publishers), since 1983; *b* 10 Jan. 1920; *s* of late Rev. Reginald Duncan, BD, BLitt and late Clarice Ethel (*née* Hodgkinson); *m* 1942, Henrietta Watson McKenzie (*née* Houston) (*d* 1993); one *s* one *d*. *Educ:* George Watson's Boys' Coll., Edinburgh; Edinburgh Univ.; New Coll., Edinburgh. Minister of: St Margaret's, Juniper Green, Edinburgh, 1943–49; Trinity Duke Street Parish Church, Glasgow, 1949–57; Founder-editor, Rally, 1956–67; Managing Editor, British Weekly, 1957–70 (Man. Dir, 1967–70); Man. Dir, DPS Publicity Services Ltd, 1967–74; broadcaster and scriptwriter, Scottish Television, 1963–68; concert promotion at Edinburgh Festival and elsewhere, 1966–; Concert series "Communication through the Arts" poetry/music anthologies (with Benita Kyle), 1970–80. Dir, Highgate Counselling Centre, 1969–86; Associate Dir and Trng Supervisor, Westminster Pastoral Foundn, 1971–79; Chm., Internat. Cttee of World Assoc. of Pastoral Care and Counselling, 1977–79; Dir, Churches' Council for Health and Healing, 1982–88; Moderator of the Presbytery of England, Church of Scotland, 1984. FIBA (FIICS) 1976. PhD Somerset Univ., 1989. *Publications:* (ed) Through the Year with William Barclay, 1971; (ed) Through the Year with Cardinal Heenan, 1972; (ed) Daily Celebration, vol. 1, 1972, vol. 2, 1974; Marching Orders, 1973; (ed) Every Day with William Barclay, 1973; (ed) Through the Year with J. B. Phillips, 1974; Marching On, 1974; Here is my Hand, 1977; Creative Silence, 1980; A Day at a Time, 1980; Love, the Word that Heals, 1981; The Way of Love, 1982; Victorious Living, 1982; Health and Healing: a ministry to wholeness, 1988; Be Still and Know . . .: 100 Daily Telegraph meditations, 1994. *Recreations:* cricket, badminton. *Address:* 1 Cranbourne Road, N10 2BT. *T:* 0181–883 1831, *Fax:* 0181–883 8307.

DUNCAN, Douglas John Stewart; freelance legal/legislative draftsman, since 1993; *b* 9 March 1945; *o s* of J. M. Duncan and Helen Stewart Collins; *m* 1972, Claire Isobel Callaghan; four *s*. *Educ:* Aberdeen Univ. (LLB Hons 1966). Asst Lectr in Law, Univ. of Sheffield, 1966–68; Lectr, Scots Law, Univ. of Aberdeen, 1968–70; Lectr, Evidence, Univ. of Edinburgh, 1972–74; Advocate, 1972; practice at the Scottish Bar, 1972–75; Lord Advocate's Dept, 1975–92, Scottish Parly Counsel and Sen. Asst Legal Sec. to Lord Advocate, 1979–92; called to the Bar, Inner Temple, 1990. Developed Statlaw system for electronic origination and publication of legislation (with D. C. Macrae), 1983–84; Chm., Statute Law Database Group, 1986–90. *Publications:* professional articles. *Recreations:* painting, racing. *Address:* Troodos, Crowder Terrace, Winchester, Hants SO22 4PT. *Club:* Hampshire (Winchester).

DUNCAN, Geoffrey Stuart; General Secretary, General Synod Board of Education and National Society for Promoting Religious Education, since 1990; *b* 10 April 1938; *s* of Alexander Sidney Duncan and Gertude Ruth (*née* Page); *m* 1962, Shirley Bernice Matilda Vanderput; one *s* one *d*. *Educ:* Hemel Hempstead Grammar Sch.; Univ. of London (BScEcon); Univ. of Exeter (MA). Served RAEC, 1960–64. School and technical coll. teaching, 1964–72; LEA Advr and Officer, 1972–82; Schs Sec. and Dep. Sec., Gen. Synod Bd of Educn and Nat. Soc. for Promoting Religious Educn, 1982–90. Part-time WEA Tutor, 1966–70; part-time Open Univ. Counsellor, 1971–72. *Publications:* contributor to: Faith for the Future, 1986; Schools for Tomorrow, 1988; various educn jls. *Recreations:* campanology, travel. *Address:* 17 Carlton Road, Seaford, East Sussex BN25 2LE. *T:* Seaford (01323) 893587. *Club:* Naval and Military.

DUNCAN, George; Chairman: ASW Holdings PLC (formerly Allied Steel and Wire (Holdings) Ltd), since 1986; Whessoe PLC, since 1987; Rubicon Group plc, since 1992; Higgs and Hill PLC, since 1993 (Director, 1992); *b* 9 Nov. 1933; *s* of William Duncan and Catherine Gray Murray; *m* 1965, Frauke Ulrike Schnuhr; one *d*. *Educ:* Holloway County Grammar Sch.; London Sch. of Economics (BSc(Econ)); Wharton Sch.; Univ. of Pennsylvania (MBA). Mem., Inst. of Chartered Accountants (FCA). Chief Executive, Truman Hanbury Buxton and Co. Ltd, 1967–71; Chief Executive, Watney Mann Ltd, 1971–72; Vice-Chm., Internat. Distillers and Vintners Ltd, 1972; Chm., Lloyds Bowmaker Finance Ltd (formerly Lloyds and Scottish plc), 1976–86; Dir, Lloyds Bank Plc, 1982–87. Chairman: Humberclyde Finance Gp, 1987–89; Household Mortgage Corp., 1986–94; Director: BET plc, 1981–; Haden plc, 1974–85 (Dep. Chm., 1984–85); TR City of London Trust PLC, 1977–; Associated British Ports PLC, 1986–; Newspaper Publishing plc, 1986–93; Laporte plc, 1987–; Crown House PLC, 1987; Dewe Rogerson Gp Ltd, 1987–; Calor Gp, 1990–. Chm., CBI Companies Cttee, 1980–83; Mem., CBI President's Cttee, 1980–83. Freeman, City of London, 1971. *Recreations:* opera, ski-ing. *Address:* Higgs & Hill, Crown House, Kingston Road, New Malden, Surrey KT3 3ST. *T:* 0181–942 8921. *Club:* Brooks's.

DUNCAN, George Alexander; Fellow Emeritus of Trinity College, Dublin, since 1967; *b* 15 May 1902; *s* of Alexander Duncan and Elizabeth Linn; *m* 1932, Eileen Stone, MSc, *d* of William Henry Stone and Sarah Copeland; one *d*. *Educ:* Ballymena Academy; Campbell Coll., Belfast; Trinity Coll., Dublin; University of North Carolina. BA, LLB 1923, MA 1926; Research Fellow on the Laura Spelman Rockefeller Memorial Foundation, 1924–25; Prof. of Political Economy in the University of Dublin, 1934–67; Registrar of TCD, 1951–52, and Bursar, 1952–57; Pro-Chancellor, Univ. of Dublin, 1965–72. Leverhulme Research Fellow, 1950; Visiting Fellow, Princeton Univ., 1963–64. Mem. of IFS Commissions of Inquiry into Banking, Currency and Credit, 1934–38; Agriculture, 1939; Emigration and Population, 1948. Planning Officer (temp.) in Ministry of Production, London, 1943–45; Economic Adviser to British National Cttee of Internat. Chambers of Commerce, 1941–47. Past Vice-Pres., Royal Dublin Society; Life Mem., Mont Pelerin Soc. Formerly Member: Irish National Productivity Cttee; Council Irish Management Inst.; Exec. Bd, Dublin Economic Research Inst.; Internat. Inst. of Statistics; Bd of Visitors, Nat. Mus. of Ireland. *Publications:* numerous papers in the economic periodicals. *Recreations:* travel, walking. *Address:* 7 Braemor Park, Churchtown, Dublin 14. *T:* Dublin 4922442.

DUNCAN, Dr George Douglas; Regional Medical Officer, East Anglian Regional Health Authority, 1973–85; *s* of late George Forman Duncan and of Mary Duncan (*née* Davidson); *m* 1949, Isobel (*née* Reid); two *s* one *d*. *Educ:* Robert Gordon's Coll., Aberdeen; Aberdeen Univ. MB, ChB 1948; DPH 1952; FFCM 1972; BA (Hons) Open Univ., 1992. Various hosp. appts; Asst MOH Stirlingshire, Divisional MO Grangemouth, 1953–57; Asst Sen. MO, Leeds RHB, 1957–60; Dep. Sen. Admin. MO, Newcastle RHB, 1960–68; Sen. Admin. MO, East Anglian RHB, 1968–73. Member: Nat. Nursing Staff Cttee and Nat. Staff Cttee for Nurses and Midwives, 1970–74; PHLS Bd, 1973–75; Central Cttee for Community Medicine, 1974–81; Chm., English Regl MOs Gp, 1981–83; Vice-Pres., FCM RCP, 1979–83. QHP 1984–87. Hon. Mem., BPA, 1988–. Hon. MA Cambridge, 1986. *Address:* 12 Storey's Way, Cambridge CB3 0DT. *T:* Cambridge (01223) 63427.

DUNCAN, Jacqueline Ann, JP; Principal of Inchbald Schools of Design and Fine Arts, since 1960; *b* 16 Dec. 1931; *d* of Mrs Donald Whitaker; *m* 1st, 1955, Michael Inchbald, *qv* (marr. diss. 1964); one *s* one *d*; 2nd, 1974, Brig. Peter Trevenen Thwaites (*d* 1991); 3rd, 1994, Col Andrew Tobin Warwick Duncan, LVO, OBE. *Educ:* Convent of the Sacred Heart, Brighton; House of Citizenship, London. FIIDA 1994. Founded: Inchbald Sch. of Design, 1960; Inchbald Sch. of Fine Arts, 1970; Inchbald Sch. of Garden Design, 1972. Member: Monopolies Commn, 1972–75; Whitfield Cttee on Copyright and Design, 1974–76; London Electricity Cons. Council, 1973–76; Westminster City Council (Warwick Ward), 1974–78. Mem., Vis. Cttee, RCA, 1986–90; International Society of Interior Designers: Acting Pres., London Chapter, 1987–90; Chm., 1990–92. Trustee, St Peters' Research Trust, 1987–90. JP South Westminster, 1976. *Publications:* Directory of Interior Designers, 1966; Bedrooms, 1968; Design and Decoration, 1971. *Recreations:* fishing, travel. *Address:* The Manor, Ayot St Lawrence, Herts AL6 9BP; (office) 32 Eccleston Square, SW1V 1PB.

DUNCAN, Sir James (Blair), Kt 1981; Chairman: Transport Development Group, 1975–92; Boalloy Industries Ltd, since 1992; *b* 24 Aug. 1927; *s* of late John Duncan and Emily MacFarlane Duncan; *m* 1974, Dr Betty Psaltis, San Francisco. *Educ:* Whitehill Sch., Glasgow. Qualified as Scottish Chartered Accountant. Joined Transport Development Group, 1953; Dir, 1960; Chief Exec., 1970–90; retd, 1992. Mem., LTE (part-time), 1979–82. Scottish Council: Mem. 1976–, and Chm. 1982–, London Exec. Cttee; Vice Pres., 1983–. Confedn of British Industry: Mem. Council, 1980–82; Mem. 1979–90, and Chm. 1983–88, London Region Roads and Transportation Cttee; Mem., Transport Policy Cttee, 1983–92. London Chamber of Commerce: Mem. Council, 1982–; Mem., Gen. Purposes Cttee, 1983–90; Dep. Chm., 1984–86; Chm., 1986–88; Chm., Commercial Educn Trust, 1992–. Pres., IRTE, 1984–87. FCIT (Pres., 1980–81; Spurrier Meml Lectr, 1972; Award of Merit, 1973; Herbert Crow Medal, 1978); CIMgt; FRSA 1977. *Publications:* papers on transport matters. *Recreations:* travel, reading, walking, swimming, theatre, golf. *Address:* 17 Kingston House South, Ennismore Gardens, SW7 1NF. *T:* 0171–589 3545. *Clubs:* Caledonian, Royal Automobile.

DUNCAN, Prof. James Playford, ME Adelaide, DSc Manchester; Professor of Mechanical Engineering, University of British Columbia, 1966–84, now Emeritus; Adjunct Professor, University of Victoria, 1985–87; *b* 10 Nov. 1919; *s* of late Hugh Sinclair Duncan and late Nellie Gladys Duncan; *m* 1942, Jean Marie Booth; three *s* one *d*. *Educ:* Scotch Coll., Adelaide; University of Adelaide, S Australia. Executive Engineer, Richards Industries Ltd, Keswick, S Australia, 1941–46; Senior Physics Master, Scotch Coll., Adelaide, 1946–47; Lecturer in Mechanical Engineering, University of Adelaide, 1948–49, Senior Lecturer, 1950–51 and 1953–54; Turbine Engineer, Metropolitan Vickers Electrical Co., Trafford Park, Manchester, 1952; Turner and Newall Research Fellow, University of Manchester, 1955; Lecturer in Mechanical Engineering, University of Manchester, 1956; Prof. of Mechanical Engineering, University of Sheffield, 1956–66. *Publications:* Sculptured Surfaces in Engineering and Medicine, 1983; Computer Aided Sculpture, 1989. *Recreations:* sailing, flautist. *Address:* 3568 Handley Crescent, Port Coquitlam, BC V3B 2Y5, Canada.

DUNCAN, Ven. John Finch, MBE 1991; Archdeacon of Birmingham, since 1985; *b* 9 Sept. 1933; *s* of John and Helen Maud Duncan; *m* 1965, Diana Margaret Dewes; one *s* two *d*. *Educ:* Queen Elizabeth Grammar School, Wakefield; University Coll., Oxford; Cuddesdon Coll. MA (Oxon). Curate, St John, South Bank, Middlesbrough, 1959–61; Novice, Society of St Francis, 1961–62; Curate, St Peter, Birmingham, 1962–65; Chaplain, Univ. of Birmingham, 1965–76; Vicar of All Saints, Kings Heath, Birmingham, 1976–85. Chairman: Copec Housing Trust, 1970–91; Focus Housing Assoc., 1991–. *Recreations:* golf, theatre, convivial gatherings. *Address:* 122 Westfield Road, Edgbaston, Birmingham B15 3JQ. *T:* 0121–454 3402. *Club:* Harborne Golf (Birmingham).

DUNCAN, John Spenser Ritchie, CMG 1967; MBE 1953; HM Diplomatic Service, retired; High Commissioner in the Bahamas, 1978–81; *b* 26 July 1921; *s* of late Rev. J. H. Duncan, DD; *m* 1950, Sheila Conacher, MB, ChB, DObstRCOG; one *d*. *Educ:* George Watson's Boys' Coll.; Glasgow Acad.; Dundee High Sch.; Edinburgh Univ. Entered Sudan Political Service, 1941. Served in HM Forces, 1941–43. Private Sec. to Governor-Gen. of the Sudan, 1954; Dep. Adviser to Governor-Gen. on Constitutional and External Affairs, 1955; appointed to Foreign (subseq. Diplomatic) Service, 1956; seconded to Joint Services Staff Coll., 1957; Political Agent, Doha, 1958; Dep. Dir-Gen., British Information Services, New York, 1959–63; Consul-Gen., Muscat, 1963–65; Head of Personnel Dept, Diplomatic Service, 1966–68; Minister, British High Commn, Canberra, 1969–71; High Comr, Zambia, 1971–74; Ambassador to Morocco, 1975–78. *Publications:* The Sudan: A Record of Achievement, 1952; The Sudan's Path to Independence, 1957. *Address:* 9 Blackford Road, Edinburgh EH9 2DT. *Club:* New (Edinburgh).

See also K. P. Duncan.

DUNCAN, Dr Kenneth Playfair, CB 1985; FRCP; FRCPE; Assistant Director (Biomedical Sciences), National Radiological Protection Board, 1985–88; *b* 27 Sept. 1924; *s* of late Dr J. H. Duncan, MA, BPhil, DD, and H. P. Duncan (*née* Ritchie); *m* 1950, Dr Gillian Crow, OBE, JP, MB, ChB; four *d*. *Educ:* Kilmarnock Acad.; Glasgow Acad.; Dundee High Sch.; St Andrews Univ. BSc, MB, ChB; DIH. FFOM 1978. House Surg., Dundee Royal Infirmary, 1947; RAMC, 1948–50; Gen. Practice, Brighton, 1950–51; Area MO, British Rail, 1951–54; Chief Medical Officer: SW Gas Bd, 1954–58; UKAEA, 1958–69; Head of Health and Safety, BSC, 1969–75; Dir of Medical Services, HSE, 1975–82; Dep. Dir-Gen., HSE, 1982–84. External Examiner in Occupational Health, Univ. of Dundee, 1970–74; Examiner in Occupational Health, Soc. of Apothecaries, 1974–79. Vis. Prof., London Sch. of Hygiene and Tropical Medicine, 1977–82. Member: Industrial Health Adv. Cttee, Dept of Employment, 1960–74; MRC, 1975–83. Pres., Soc. of Occupational Medicine, 1970. *Publications:* contrib. medical and scientific jls on radiological protection and gen. occupational health topics. *Recreation:* gardening. *Address:* Westfield, Steeple Aston, Oxon OX6 3SD. *T:* Steeple Aston (01869) 340277.

See also J. S. R. Duncan.

DUNCAN, Laura; *see* Duncan, A. L. A.

DUNCAN, Malcolm McGregor, OBE 1987; WS; Chief Executive, City of Edinburgh District Council, 1980–87; *b* 23 Jan. 1922; *s* of Rev. Reginald Duncan, BD, BLitt, and Clarice Ethel (*née* Hodgkinson); *m* 1954, Winifred Petrie (*née* Greenhorn); two *s* one *d*. *Educ:* George Watson's Coll., Edinburgh; Edinburgh Univ. (MA 1942; LLB 1948). Admitted Writer to the Signet, 1949. Served RAFVR, Flt Lieut, 1942–46. Edinburgh Corporation, 1952; Depute Town Clerk, 1971; Director of Administration, City of Edinburgh District Council, 1975–80. *Recreations:* playing golf, watching other sports, listening to music. *Address:* 52 Glendevon Place, Edinburgh EH12 5UJ. *T:* 0131–337 2869.

See also Rev. D. M. Duncan.

DUNCAN, Sean Bruce; His Honour Judge Duncan; a Circuit Judge, since 1988; *b* 21 Dec. 1942; *s* of Joseph Alexander Duncan and Patricia Pauline Duncan; *m* 1974, Dr Diana Bowyer Courtney; three *s* one *d*. *Educ:* Shrewsbury Sch.; St Edmund Hall, Oxford (MA). Called to the Bar, Inner Temple, 1966; Northern Circuit (Hon. Sec., Circuit Cttee, 1985–88); a Recorder, 1984–88. Served with Cheshire Yeomanry (TA), 1963–68 (Lieut). Chairman: Old Swan Boys Club, Liverpool, 1974–79; Liverpool Youth Organisations Cttee, 1977–83; Vice-Chm., Liverpool Council of Voluntary Service, 1982–88. *Recreations:* farming, sport, music. *Address:* c/o Queen Elizabeth II Law Courts, Derby Square, Liverpool. *Clubs:* Royal Liverpool Golf; Liverpool Ramblers AFC (Vice Pres.); Royal Chester Rowing.

DUNCAN, Stanley Frederick St Clare, CMG 1983; HM Diplomatic Service, retired; *b* 13 Nov. 1927; *yr s* of late Stanley Gilbert Scott and Louisa Elizabeth Duncan; *m* 1967, Jennifer Jane Bennett; two *d*. *Educ:* Latymer Upper Sch. FRGS. India Office, 1946; CRO,

1947; Private Sec. to Parly Under-Sec. of State, 1954; Second Sec., Ottawa, 1954–55; Brit. Govt Information Officer, Toronto, 1955–57; Second Sec., Wellington, 1958–60; First Sec., CRO, 1960; seconded to Central African Office, 1962–64; Mem., Brit. Delegn to Victoria Falls Conf. on Dissolution of Fedn of Rhodesia and Nyasaland, 1963; First Sec., Nicosia, 1964–67; FCO, 1967–70; FCO Adviser, Brit. Gp, Inter-Parly Union, 1968–70; Head of Chancery and First Sec., Lisbon, 1970–73; Consul-General and subsequently Chargé d'Affaires in Mozambique, 1973–75; Counsellor (Political), Brasilia, 1976–77; Head of Consular Dept, FCO, 1977–80; Canadian Nat. Defence Coll., 1980–81; Ambassador to Bolivia, 1981–85; High Comr in Malta, 1985–87. Mem., UN Observer Mission to S African elections, 1994. Officer, Military Order of Christ (Portugal), 1973. *Recreations:* countryside pursuits. *Address:* Tucksmead, Longworth, Oxon OX13 5ET.

DUNCAN-JONES, Richard Phare, PhD; FBA 1992; Fellow, Gonville and Caius College, Cambridge, since 1963; *b* 14 Sept. 1937; *s* of Austin Ernest Duncan-Jones and Elsie Elizabeth Duncan-Jones; *m* 1986, Julia Elizabeth Poole. *Educ:* King Edward's Sch., Birmingham; King's Coll., Cambridge (MA, PhD). Gonville and Caius College, Cambridge: W. M. Tapp Res. Fellow, 1963–67; Domestic Bursar, 1967–84; Official Fellow, 1967–; College Lectr and Dir of Studies in Classics, 1984–. Mem., Inst. for Advanced Study, Princeton, 1971–72. *Publications:* The Economy of the Roman Empire, 1974, 2nd edn 1982; Structure and Scale in the Roman Economy, 1990; Money and Government in the Roman Empire, 1994; articles in learned jls. *Recreations:* wine tasting, walking, continental cinema. *Address:* Caius College, Cambridge CB2 1TA. *T:* Cambridge (01223) 332394.

DUNCAN MILLAR, Ian Alastair, CBE 1978; MC; CEng, MICE; DL; Member, Tay District Salmon Fisheries Board, 1962–80 and 1986–93; Member, Royal Company of Archers (Queen's Body Guard for Scotland), since 1956; *b* 22 Nov. 1914; *s* of late Sir James Duncan Millar and Lady Duncan Millar (*née* Forester Paton); *m* 1945, Louise Reid McCosh; two *s* two *d*. *Educ:* Gresham's Sch., Holt; Trinity Coll., Cambridge (MA). Served with Corps of Royal Engineers, 1940–45 (Major; wounded; despatches): 7th Armoured Div., N Africa and Normandy; 51 (Highland) Div., France and Germany. Contested Parly Elections (L): Banff, 1945; Kinross and W Perthshire, 1949 and 1963. Depute Chm., North of Scotland Hydro-Electric Bd, 1970–72 (Mem., 1957–72). Chm., United Auctions (Scotland) Ltd, 1967–74; Dir, Macdonald Fraser & Co. Ltd, Perth, 1961–85. Dir, Hill Farming Research Organisation, 1966–78; Chm., Consultative Cttee to Sec. of State for Scotland under 1976 Freshwater and Salmon Fisheries Act, 1981–86. Vice-Pres., Scottish Landowners Fedn, 1985–90. Mem. Ct, Dundee Univ., 1975–78. Perth CC, 1945–75: Chm. Planning Cttee, 1954–75; Convener, 1970–75; Chm. Jt CC of Perth and Kinross, 1970–75; Tayside Regional Council: Councillor and Chm., 1974–75; Convener, 1975–78. Fellow, Inst. of Fisheries Management, 1988. DL 1963, JP 1952, Perthshire. *Publications:* A Countryman's Cog, 1990; A Bit of Breadalbane, 1995. *Recreations:* studying and catching salmon, land management. *Address:* Reynock, Remony, Aberfeldy, Perthshire PH15 2HR. *T:* Kenmore (01887) 830400. *Club:* Royal Golfing Society (Perth).

DUNCAN SMITH, (George) Iain; MP (C) Chingford, since 1992; *b* 9 April 1954; *s* of Group Captain W. G. G. Duncan Smith, DSO (Bar), DFC (2 Bars) and Pamela Mary Duncan Smith (*née* Summers); *m* 1982, Elizabeth Wynne (*née* Fremantle); two *s* two *d*. *Educ:* HMS Conway (Cadet School); Univ. di Perugia; RMA Sandhurst; Dunchurch Coll. of Management. Scots Guards, 1975–81; ADC to Gen. Sir John Acland, 1979–81; GEC, 1981–88; Dir, Bellwinch (Property), 1988; Dir, Jane's Inf. Group, 1989–92. Vice-Chm., Fulham Cons. Assoc., 1991; contested (C) Bradford West, 1987. Sec., Cons. Backbench Cttee on Foreign and Commonwealth Affairs, 1992–. Trustee, Lygon Almshouse, 1985–91. *Publications:* various pamphlets on social security, European and defence issues; occasional journalism. *Recreations:* family, painting, fishing, cricket, tennis, shooting, opera, reading. *Address:* House of Commons, SW1A 0AA. *T:* 0171–219 2664 and 3000.

DUNCANNON, Viscount; Myles Fitzhugh Longfield Ponsonby; *b* 16 Feb. 1941; *e s* and *heir* of Earl of Bessborough, *qv*; *m* 1972, Alison, *d* of William Storey, OBE; two *s* one *d*. *Heir:* *s* Hon. Frederick William Arthur Ponsonby, *b* 1974. *Address:* 19 Crescent Grove, SW4 7AF.

DUNCOMBE, family name of **Baron Feversham.**

DUNCOMBE, Sir Philip (Digby) Pauncefort-, 4th Bt *cr* 1859; DL; one of HM Body Guard, Honorable Corps of Gentlemen-at-Arms, since 1979 (Harbinger, since 1993); *b* 18 May 1927; *o s* of Sir Everard Pauncefort-Duncombe, 3rd Bt, DSO, and Evelyn Elvira (*d* 1986), *d* of Frederick Anthony Denny; *S* father, 1971; *m* 1951, Rachel Moyra, *d* of Major H. G. Aylmer; one *s* two *d*. *Educ:* Stowe. 2nd Lieut, Grenadier Guards, 1946; served in Palestine, 1947–48; Malaya, 1948–49; Cyprus, 1957–59; Hon. Major, retired 1960, Regular Army Reserve. County Comdt, Buckinghamshire Army Cadet Force, 1967–70. DL Bucks 1971, High Sheriff, 1987–88. CStJ 1992. *Heir:* *s* David Philip Henry Pauncefort-Duncombe [*b* 21 May 1956; *m* 1987, Sarah, *d* of late Reginald Battrum and of Mrs Reginald Battrum; one *s* one *d*]. *Address:* Great Brickhill Manor, Milton Keynes, Bucks MK17 9BE. *T:* Great Brickhill (01525) 261205. *Club:* Cavalry and Guards.

DUNCOMBE, Roy, VRD 1957; Chairman, Nationwide Building Society, 1989–91; *b* 7 June 1925; *s* of Joseph William Duncombe and Gladys May Duncombe (*née* Reece); *m* 1946, Joan Thornley Pickering; one *s* two *d*. *Educ:* Hinckley Grammar School. RNR, 1943–68 (Lt-Comdr (A); Pilot, Fleet Air Arm). Financial Dir, Ferry Pickering Gp, 1965–87; Chm., Anglia Building Soc., 1985–87; following merger with Nationwide Bldg Soc., Vice Chm., Nationwide Anglia Bldg Soc., 1987–89; name changed to Nationwide Bldg Soc., 1989. *Recreations:* walking, swimming, photography, ornithology. *Address:* Westways, Market Bosworth, Nuneaton, Warwickshire CV13 0LQ. *T:* Market Bosworth (01455) 291728. *Club:* Naval and Military.

DUNCUMB, Dr Peter, FRS 1977; Director, Research Centre in Super-conductivity, Cambridge University, 1988–89; *b* 26 Jan. 1931; *s* of late William Duncumb and of Hilda Grace (*née* Coleman); *m* 1955, Anne Leslie Taylor; two *s* one *d*. *Educ:* Oundle Sch.; Clare Coll., Cambridge (BA 1953, MA 1956, PhD 1957). DSIR Res. Fellow, Cambridge Univ., 1957–59; Tube Investments, subseq. TI Group, Research Laboratories: Res. Scientist and Gp Leader, 1959–67, Head, Physics Dept, 1967–72; Asst Dir, 1972–79; Dir and Gen. Manager, 1979–87. Hon. Prof., Warwick Univ., 1990–. Hon. Mem., Microbeam Analysis Soc. of America, 1973. C. V. Boys Prize, Inst. of Physics, 1966. *Publications:* numerous on electron microscopy and analysis in various jls. *Recreations:* hill walking, orienteering, family genealogy. *Address:* 5A Woollards Lane, Great Shelford, Cambridge CB2 5LZ. *T:* Cambridge (01223) 843064.

DUNDAS, family name of **Viscount Melville,** and of **Marquess of Zetland.**

DUNDEE, 12th Earl of, *cr* 1660 (Scotland); **Alexander Henry Scrymgeour;** Viscount Dudhope and Lord Scrymgeour, 1641 (Scotland); Lord Inverkeithing, 1660 (Scotland); Lord Glassary (UK), 1954; Hereditary Royal Standard-Bearer for Scotland; *b* 5 June 1949; *s* of 11th Earl of Dundee, PC, and of Patricia Katherine, *d* of late Col Lord Herbert Montagu Douglas Scott; *S* father, 1983; *m* 1979, Siobhan Mary, *d* of David Llewellyn, Gt Somerford, Wilts; one *s* three *d*. *Educ:* Eton; St Andrews Univ. Contested (C) Hamilton, by-election May 1978. A Lord in Waiting (Govt Whip), 1986–89. *Heir:* *s* Lord Scrymgeour, *qv*. *Address:* Farm Office, Birkhill, Cupar, Fife. *Clubs:* White's; New (Edinburgh).

DUNDEE (St Paul's Cathedral), Provost of; *see* Bunce, Very Rev. M. J.

DUNDONALD, 15th Earl of, *cr* 1669; **Iain Alexander Douglas Blair Cochrane;** Lord Cochrane of Dundonald, 1647; Lord Cochrane of Paisley and Ochiltree, 1669; Chairman, Duneth Securities and associated companies, since 1986; *b* 17 Feb. 1961; *s* of 14th Earl of Dundonald and Aphra Farquhar (*d* 1972), *d* of late Comdr George Fetherstonhaugh; *S* father, 1986; *m* 1987, Beatrice, *d* of Adolphus Russo; one *s*. *Educ:* Wellington College; RAC Cirencester. DipREM. Hon. Consul in Scotland for Chile, 1993–. *Recreations:* shooting, fishing, skiing, sailing. *Heir:* *s* Lord Cochrane, *qv*. *Address:* Lochnell Castle, Ledaig, Argyll PA37 1QT.

DUNEDIN, Bishop of, since 1990; **Rt. Rev. Penelope Ann Bansall Jamieson,** PhD; *b* Chalfont St Peter, Bucks, 21 June 1942; *m* 1964, Ian William Andrew Jamieson; three *d*. *Educ:* St Mary's Sch., Gerrards Cross; High Sch., High Wycombe; Edinburgh Univ. (MA 1964); Victoria Univ., Wellington (PhD 1977); Otago Univ. (BD 1983). Deacon 1982; priest 1983; Asst Curate, St James', Lower Hutt, 1982–85; Vicar, Karori West with Makara, dio. Wellington, 1985–90. *Address:* c/o Diocesan Office, PO Box 5445, Dunedin, New Zealand.

DUNGARVAN, Viscount; John Richard Boyle, (Jonathan); Director, E. D. & F. Man Sugar Ltd, London; *b* 3 Nov. 1945; *e s* and *heir* of Earl of Cork and Orrery, *qv*; *m* 1973, Hon. Rebecca Juliet Noble, *y d* of Baron Glenkinglas (Life Peer), PC; one *s* two *d* (of whom one *s* one *d* are twins). *Educ:* Harrow; RNC Dartmouth. Lt-Comdr RN, retd. Mem., Baltic Exchange, 1979–. *Recreations:* country pursuits, sailing, ski-ing, classic cars. *Address:* Lickfold House, Petworth, West Sussex GU28 9EY. *Club:* Boodle's.

DUNGEY, Prof. James Wynne, PhD; Professor of Physics, Imperial College, University of London, 1965–84; *b* 30 Jan. 1923; *s* of Ernest Dungey and Alice Dungey; *m* 1950, Christine Scotland (*née* Brown); one *s* one *d*. *Educ:* Bradfield; Magdalene Coll., Cambridge (MA, PhD). Res. Fellow, Univ. of Sydney, 1950–53; Vis. Asst Prof., Penn State Coll., 1953–54; ICI Fellow, Cambridge, 1954–57; Lectr, King's Coll., Newcastle upon Tyne, 1957–59; Sen. Principal Scientific Officer, AWRE, Aldermaston, 1959–63; Res. Fellow, Imperial Coll., London, 1963–65. Fellow, Amer. Geophysical Union, 1973. Hon. Mem., European Geophysical Soc., 1994. Chapman Medal, RAS, 1982; Gold Medal for Geophysics, RAS, 1990; Fleming Medal, Amer. Geophysical Union, 1991. *Publications:* Cosmic Electrodynamics, 1958; papers on related topics. *Recreations:* music, sailing. *Address:* Long Roof, Leverett's Lane, Walberswick, Southwold, Suffolk IP18 6UF. *T:* Southwold (01502) 722242.

DUNGLASS, Lord (courtesy title used by heirs to Earldom of Home before title was disclaimed); *see under* Douglas-Home, Hon. D. A. C.

DUNHAM, Sir Kingsley (Charles), Kt 1972; PhD Dunelm, 1932; SD Harvard, 1935; FRS 1955; FRSE; FGS; FEng; Hon. FIMM; Director, Institute of Geological Sciences, 1967–75; *b* Sturminster Newton, Dorset, 2 Jan. 1910; *s* of Ernest Pedder and Edith Agnes Dunham; *m* 1936, Margaret, *d* of William and Margaret Young, Choppington, Northumberland; one *s*. *Educ:* Durham Johnston Sch.; Hatfield Coll., Durham Univ. (Sen. Fellow, 1990); Adams House, Harvard Univ. Temporary Geologist, New Mexico Bureau of Mines, 1934; HM Geological Survey of Great Britain; Geologist, 1935–45; Senior Geologist 1946; Chief Petrographer, 1948; Prof. of Geology, Univ. of Durham, 1950–66, Emeritus, 1968–; Sub-Warden of Durham Colls, 1959–61. Miller Prof., University of Ill., 1956. Director: Weardale Minerals Ltd, 1982–86; Blackdene Minerals Ltd, 1983–86. Member: Council, Royal Society, 1965–66 (Foreign Sec., a Vice-Pres., 1971–76; Royal Medal, 1970); Council for Scientific Policy (Min. of Ed. & Sci.), 1965–66. President: Instn Mining and Metallurgy, 1963–64 (Gold Medal, 1968); Yorks Geological Soc., 1958–60 (Sorby Medal, 1964); Internat. Union of Geological Sciences, 1969–72; Geological Soc. of London, 1966–68 (Council 1949–52, 1960–64; Bigsby Medal, 1954; Murchison Medal, 1966; Wollaston Medal, 1976); BAAS, 1972–73; Mineralogical Soc., 1975–77; NE Region, Inst. of Geologists, 1981–. Institution of Geology: Founder Mem., 1976; Fellow, 1985; Aberconway Medal, 1986. Trustee, British Museum (Natural History), 1963–66. Member Geology-Geophysics Cttee (NERC) 1965–70; Chairman: Internat. Geol. Correlation Project (IUGS-UNESCO), 1973–76; Council for Environmental Science and Engineering, 1973 75. Mem. Council and UK Rep., 1972–77, Hon. Scholar, 1977–, Internat. Inst. for Applied Systems Analysis, Laxenburg, Vienna. President: Durham Univ. Soc., 1973–75; City, Dunelm and Palatinate Probus; Hon. Pres., Friends of Killhope, 1985–. Founder FEng, 1976. Hon. Member: Royal Geol Soc. Cornwall (Bolitho Medal 1972); Geol. Soc. of India, 1972; Hon. Foreign Fellow, Geol. Soc. of America; Corr. Foreign Mem., Austrian Acad. of Scis, 1971; Hon. Foreign Member: Société Géologique de Belge, 1974; Bulgarian Geological Soc., 1975. Fellow, Imperial Coll., 1976; Hon. Fellow, St John's Coll., Durham, 1991. Hon. DSc: Dunelm, 1946; Liverpool, 1967; Birmingham, 1970; Illinois, 1971; Leicester, 1972; Michigan, 1973; Canterbury, 1973; Edinburgh, 1974; Exeter, 1975; Hull, 1978; Hon. ScD Cantab, 1973; DUniv Open, 1982. Mitchell Meml Medal, City of Stoke on Trent, 1974; Haidinger Medaille der Geologischen Bundesanstalt, 1976; von Buch Medal, Deutsche Geologische Gesellschaft, 1981. Hon. Citizen of Texas, 1975. *Publications:* Geology of the Organ Mountains, 1935; Geology of the Northern Pennine Orefield, Vol. 1, 1948, 2nd edn 1990, Vol. 2 (with A. A. Wilson), 1985; (as Editor) Symposium on the Geology, Paragenesis and Reserves of the Ores of Lead & Zinc, 2nd edn, 1950; Fluorspar, 1952; Geology of Northern Skye (with F. W. Anderson) 1966; (with W. C. C. Rose) Geology and Hermatite Deposits of South Cumbria, 1977; articles in Quarterly Jl of Geological Soc., Mineralogical Magazine, Geological Magazine, American Mineralogist, etc. *Recreations:* music (organ and pianoforte); gardening. *Address:* Charleycroft, Quarryheads Lane, Durham DH1 3DY. *T:* Durham (0191) 348977. *Club:* Geological Society's.

DUNITZ, Prof. Jack David, FRS 1974; Professor of Chemical Crystallography at the Swiss Federal Institute of Technology (ETH), Zürich, 1957–90; *b* 29 March 1923; *s* of William Dunitz and Mildred (*née* Gossman); *m* 1953, Barbara Steuer; two *d*. *Educ:* Hillhead High Sch., Glasgow; Hutchesons' Grammar Sch., Glasgow; Glasgow Univ. (BSc, PhD). Post-doctoral Fellow, Oxford Univ., 1946–48, 1951–53; California Inst. of Technology, 1948–51, 1953–54; Vis. Scientist, US Nat. Insts of Health, 1954–55; Sen. Res. Fellow, Davy Faraday Res. Lab., Royal Instn, London, 1956–57. Overseas Fellow, Churchill Coll., Cambridge, 1968; Vis. Professor: Iowa State Univ., 1965; Tokyo Univ., 1967; Technion, Haifa, 1970; Hill Vis. Prof., Univ. of Minnesota, 1983; Fairchild Distinguished Scholar, CIT, 1985; Hooker Distinguished Vis. Prof., McMaster Univ., 1987; Alexander Todd Vis. Prof., Cambridge Univ., 1990; Oscar K. Rice Vis. Prof., Univ. of N Carolina, Chapel Hill, 1991; Robert B. Woodward Vis. Prof., Harvard Univ., 1992. Lectures: British Council, 1965; Treat B. Johnson Meml, Yale Univ., 1965; 3M Univ. of Minnesota, 1966; Reilly, Univ. Notre Dame, US, 1971; Kelly, Purdue Univ., 1971; Gerhard Schmidt Meml, Weizmann Inst. of Sci., 1973; George Fisher Baker, Cornell Univ., 1976;

Centenary, Chem. Soc., 1977; Appleton, Brown Univ., 1979; H. J. Backer, Gröningen Univ., 1980; Havinga, Leiden Univ., 1980; Karl Folkers, Wisconsin Univ., 1981; A. L. Patterson Meml, Inst. for Cancer Res., Philadelphia, 1983; C. S. Marvel, Illinois Univ., 1987; Birch, Canberra, 1989; Dwyer, Sydney, 1989; Bijvoet, Utrecht Univ., 1989. For. Mem., Royal Netherlands Acad. of Arts and Sciences, 1979; Member: Leopoldina Acad., 1979; European Acad. of Scis and Arts, 1991; Foreign Associate, US Nat. Acad. of Scis, 1988; Mem., Academia Europaea, 1989; Hon. Mem., Swiss Soc. of Crystallography, 1990; Fellow AAAS, 1981. Hon. DSc: Technion, Haifa, 1990; Weizmann Inst. of Sci., 1992. Tishler Award, Harvard Univ., 1985; Paracelsus Prize, Swiss Chem. Soc., 1986; Gregori Aminoff Prize, Swedish Royal Acad., 1990; Martin Buerger Award, Amer. Crystallographic Assoc., 1991. Jt Editor, Perspectives in Structural Chemistry, 1967–71; Mem. Editorial Bd: Helvetica Chimica Acta, 1971–85; Structure and Bonding, 1971–81. *Publications:* X-ray Analysis and the Structure of Organic Molecules, 1979; (with E. Heilbronner) Reflections on Symmetry in Chemistry . . . . and Elsewhere, 1993; papers on various aspects of crystal and molecular structure in Acta Crystallographica, Helvetica Chimica Acta, Jl Chem. Soc., Jl Amer. Chem. Soc., etc. *Recreation:* walking. *Address:* Obere Heslibachstrasse 77, 8700 Küsnacht, Switzerland. *T:* (1) 9101723; (office) Chemistry Department, CHNI23, ETH-Zentrum, 8092 Zürich, Switzerland. *T:* (1) 6322892.

DUNKEL, Arthur; Chairman, Arthur Dunkel consultancy, Geneva, since 1993; *b* 28 Aug. 1932; *s* of Walter Dunkel and Berthe Lerch; *m* 1957, Christiane Müller-Cerda; one *s* one *d*. *Educ:* Univ. of Lausanne (LèsSc écon. et comm.). Federal Office for external economic affairs, 1956: successively Head of sections for OECD matters, 1960; for cooperation with developing countries, 1964; for world trade policy, 1971; Permanent Representative of Switzerland to GATT, 1973; Delegate of Federal Council for Trade Agreements, rank of Ambassador, 1976; in this capacity, head of Swiss delegations to multilateral (GATT, UNCTAD, UNIDO, etc) and bilateral negotiations in the fields of trade, development, commodities, transfer of technology, industrialisation, agriculture, etc.; Dir Gen., GATT, 1980–93. Prof. at Univs of Geneva, 1983, and Fribourg, 1987. Pres., a Future for Geneva Foundn, 1994. Dr *hc* rer. pol.: Fribourg, 1980; Basle, 1992. Freedom Prize, Max Schmidheiny Foundn, 1989; Consumers Prize for World Trade, USA, 1990; Assoc. of Swiss Holding Cos Prize, 1993; Prize, Max Petitpierre Foundn, 1993. *Publications:* various articles and studies in economic, commercial, agricl and development fields. *Address:* Boulevard du Théâtre 6-4, 1204 Geneva, Switzerland.

DUNKELD, Bishop of, (RC), since 1981; **Rt. Rev. Vincent Logan;** *b* 30 June 1941; *s* of Joseph Logan and Elizabeth Flannigan. *Educ:* Blairs College, Aberdeen; St Andrew's Coll., Drygrange, Melrose. Ordained priest, Edinburgh, 1964; Asst Priest, St Margaret's, Davidson's Mains, Edinburgh, 1964–66; Corpus Christi Coll., London, 1966–67 (DipRE); Chaplain, St Joseph's Hospital, Rosewell, Midlothian, 1967–77; Adviser in Religious Education, Archdiocese of St Andrews and Edinburgh, 1967; Parish Priest, St Mary's, Ratho, 1977–81; Episcopal Vicar for Education, Archdiocese of St Andrews and Edinburgh, 1978. *Address:* Bishop's House, 29 Roseangle, Dundee DD1 4LS. *T:* Dundee (01382) 224327.

DUNKLEY, Christopher; journalist and broadcaster; Television Critic, Financial Times, since 1973; Presenter, Feedback, Radio 4, since 1986; *b* 22 Jan. 1944; 2nd *s* of late Robert Dunkley and Joyce Mary Dunkley (*née* Turner); *m* 1967, Carolyn Elizabeth, *e d* of Col A. P. C. Lyons; one *s* one *d*. *Educ:* Haberdashers' Aske's (expelled). Various jobs, incl. theatre flyman, cook, hospital porter, 1961–63; general reporter, then cinema and theatre critic, Slough Observer, 1963–65; feature writer and news editor, UK Press Gazette, 1965–68; night news reporter, then mass media correspondent and TV critic, The Times, 1968–73. Frequent radio broadcaster, 1963–, esp. on Kaleidoscope, Critics' Forum, Meridian, LBC. Occasional television presenter/script writer/chairman; series incl. Edition, Real Time, In Vision (all BBC2), Whistle Blowers (BBC1), This Week, Viewpoint (ITV). Critic of the Year, British Press Awards, 1976, 1986; Broadcast Journalist of the Year, 1989, Judges' Award, 1990, TV-am Awards. *Publications:* Television Today and Tomorrow: Wall to Wall Dallas?, 1985; many articles in The Listener, Television World, Stills, Electronic Media, Telegraph Magazine, etc. *Recreations:* motorcycling, reading in secondhand bookshops, collecting almost everything, especially dictionaries, tin toys, Victorian boys' books. *Address:* 38 Leverton Street, NW5 2PG. *T:* 0171-485 7101.

DUNLAP, Air Marshal Clarence Rupert, CBE 1944; CD; RCAF retired; *b* 1 Jan. 1908; *s* of late Frank Burns Dunlap, Truro, Nova Scotia; *m* 1935, Hester, *d* of late Dr E. A. Cleveland, Vancouver, BC; one *s*. *Educ:* Acadia Univ.; Nova Scotia Technical Coll. Joined RCAF 1928 as Pilot Officer; trained as pilot and specialised in aerial survey; later specialised in armament; Dir of Armament, RCAF HQ Ottawa on outbreak of War; commanded: RCAF Station, Mountain View, Ont., Jan.-Oct. 1942; RCAF Station, Leeming, Yorks, Dec. 1942–May 1943; 331 Wing NASAF, Tunisia, May-Nov. 1943; 139 Wing TAF, Nov. 1943–Feb. 1945; 64 Base, Middleton St George, Feb.-May 1945; Dep., AMAS, AFHQ, Ottawa, 1945–48; Air Mem. for Air Plans, AFHQ, Ottawa, 1948–49; AOC North-West Air Command, Edmonton, Alberta, 1949–51; Commandant of National Defence Coll., Kingston, Ont., 1951–54; Vice Chief of the Air Staff, AFHQ, Ottawa, 1954–58; Dep. Chief of Staff, Operations, SHAPE, Paris, 1958–62; Chief of Air Staff, AFHQ, Ottawa, 1962–64; Dep. C-in-C, N Amer. Air Def. Comd, 1964–67. Hon. DCL Acadia Univ., 1955; Hon. DEng Nova Scotia Technical Coll., 1967. *Address:* 203–1375 Newport Avenue, Victoria, BC V8S 5E8, Canada. *Clubs:* Union (Victoria); Victoria Golf; Royal Ottawa Golf (Ottawa).

DUNLEATH, 5th Baron *cr* 1892; **Michael Henry Mulholland;** Bt 1945; retired; *b* 15 Oct. 1915; *s* of Rt Hon. Sir Henry George Hill Mulholland, 1st Bt, 3rd *s* of 2nd Baron Dunleath, and Sheelah (*d* 1982), *d* of Sir Douglas Brooke, 4th Bt; *S* to baronetcy of father, 1971; *S* to Barony of cousin, 1993; *m* 1st, 1942, Rosemary Ker (marr. diss. 1948); 2nd, 1949, Elizabeth (*d* 1989), *d* of Laurence B. Hyde; one *s*. *Educ:* Eton; Pembroke College, Cambridge (BA). Regular Army Commission, 1937, Oxford and Bucks Light Infantry; retired, 1951, with rank of Major. *Heir: s* Hon. Brian Henry Mulholland [*b* 25 Sept. 1950; *m* 1976, Mary Joana, *y d* of Major R. J. F. Whistler; two *s* one *d*]. *Address:* Storbrooke, Massey Avenue, Belfast BT4 2JT. *T:* Belfast (01232) 763394. *Clubs:* Light Infantry (Shrewsbury); Green Jackets (Winchester).

DUNLEAVY, Philip, CBE 1983 (OBE 1978); JP; Leader, Cardiff City Council, 1974–76 and 1979–82; Lord Mayor of Cardiff, 1982–83; *b* 5 Oct. 1915; *s* of Michael and Bridget Dunleavy; *m* 1936, Valerie Partridge; two *s* two *d*. *Educ:* St Cuthbert's Sch., Cardiff. Served War, TA (Sgt), 1939–46. Post Office, 1930–39 and 1946–75 (Executive Officer, 1960–75). Member: Cardiff City Council, 1962–83; South Glamorgan County Council, 1974–81. Hon. Freeman, City of Cardiff, 1993. JP 1960. *Recreations:* youth, conservation, local historical research, local govt political activity. *Address:* 35 Merches Gardens, Grangetown, Cardiff CF1 7RF.

DUNLOP, Rear-Adm. Colin Charles Harrison, CB 1972; CBE 1963; DL; *b* 4 March 1918; *s* of late Engr Rear-Adm. S. H. Dunlop, CB; *m* 1941, Moyra Patricia O'Brien Gorges (*d* 1991); two *s* (and one *s* decd). *Educ:* Marlborough Coll. Joined RN, 1935; served War of 1939–45 at sea in HM Ships Kent, Valiant, Diadem and Orion; subseq. HMS Sheffield, 1957–59; Sec. to 1st Sea Lord, 1960–63; comd HMS Pembroke, 1964–66; Programme Evaluation Gp, MoD, 1966–68; Director, Defence Policy (A), MoD, 1968–69; Comdr, British Navy Staff, Washington, 1969–71; Chief Naval Supply and Secretariat Officer, 1970–74; Flag Officer, Medway, and Port Adm., Chatham, 1971–74, retd 1974. Director General: Cable TV Assoc., 1974–83; Nat. TV Rental Assoc., 1974–83. DL Kent 1976. *Recreations:* cricket, country pursuits. *Address:* Chanceford Farm, Sand Lane, Frittenden, near Cranbrook, Kent TN17 2BA. *T:* Frittenden (01580) 852242. *Clubs:* Army and Navy; MCC, I Zingari, Free Foresters, Incogniti, RN Cricket, Band of Brothers.

DUNLOP, Frank, CBE 1977; theatre director; Director, Edinburgh International Festival, 1983–91; *b* 15 Feb. 1927; *s* of Charles Norman Dunlop and Mary Aarons. *Educ:* Kibworth Beauchamp Grammar Sch.; University Coll., London (Fellow, 1979). BA Hons, English. Postgrad. Sch. in Shakespeare, at Shakespeare Inst., Stratford-upon-Avon; Old Vic Sch., London. Served with RAF before going to University. Director: (own young theatre co.) Piccolo Theatre, Manchester, 1954; Arts Council Midland Theatre Co., 1955; Associate Dir, Bristol Old Vic, 1956; Dir, Théâtre de Poche, Brussels, 1959–60; Founder and Dir, Pop Theatre, 1960; Dir, Nottingham Playhouse, 1961–63; New Nottingham Playhouse, 1963–64; (dir.) The Enchanted, Bristol Old Vic Co., 1955; (wrote and dir.) Les Frères Jaques', Adelphi, 1960; Director: London Première, The Bishop's Bonfire, Mermaid, 1960; Schweyk, Mermaid, 1963; The Taming of the Shrew, Univ. Arts Centre, Oklahoma, 1965; Any Wednesday, Apollo, 1965; Too True to be Good, Edinburgh Fest., also Strand and Garrick, 1965; Saturday Night and Sunday Morning, Prince of Wales, 1966; The Winter's Tale and The Trojan Women, Edin. and Venice Festivals, also Cambridge Theatre, London, 1966; The Burglar, Vaudeville, 1967; Getting Married, Strand, 1967; A Midsummer Night's Dream and The Tricks of Scapin, Edin. Fest. and Saville Theatre, London, 1967; A Sense of Detachment, Royal Court, 1972; Sherlock Holmes, Aldwych, 1974, NY 1974; Habeas Corpus, NY 1975; The New York Idea, The Three Sisters, NY 1977; The Devil's Disciple, LA and NY, 1978; The Play's the Thing, Julius Caesar, NY, 1978; The Last of Mrs Cheyney, USA, 1978; Rookery Nook, Birmingham and Her Majesty's, 1979; Camelot, USA, 1980; Sherlock Holmes, Norwegian Nat. Th., Oslo, 1980; Lolita, NY, 1981; L'Elisir d'Amore, Opéra de Lyon, 1992; *National Theatre:* Assoc. Dir, 1967–71 and Admin. Dir, 1968–71; productions: *Nat. Theatre:* Edward II (Brecht and Marlowe); Home and Beauty; Macrune's Guevara; The White Devil; Captain of Kopenick; *Young Vic:* Founder, 1969; Mem. Bd, 1969–; Dir, 1969–78 and 1980–83; Consultant, 1978–80; productions: (author and Dir) Scapino 1970, 1977, NY 1974, LA 1975, Australia 1975, Oslo 1975; The Taming of the Shrew, 1970, 1977; The Comedy of Errors, 1971; The Maids, Deathwatch, 1972; The Alchemist, 1972; Bible One, 1972; French Without Tears, 1973; Joseph and the Amazing Technicolor Dreamcoat (Roundhouse and Albery Theatre), 1973, NY 1976; Much Ado About Nothing, 1973; Macbeth, 1975; Antony and Cleopatra, 1976; King Lear, 1980; Childe Byron, 1981; Masquerade, 1982; *for Théâtre National de Belgique:* Pantagleise, 1970; Antony and Cleopatra, 1971; Pericles, 1972. Mem., Arts Council Young People's Panel, 1968. Governor, Central School of Arts and Crafts, 1970. Hon. Fellow of Shakespeare Inst. Hon. Dr of Theatre, Philadelphia Coll. of Performing Arts, 1978; DUniv Heriot-Watt, 1989; Dr *hc* Edinburgh, 1990. Chevalier, Order of Arts and Literature (France), 1987. *Recreations:* reading and looking. *Address:* c/o Piccolo Theatre Co., 6 Langley Street, WC2H 9JA; c/o E. Nives, Suite 1400, 157 West 57th Street, New York, NY 10019, USA. *T:* (212) 2658787.

DUNLOP, Rev. Canon Ian Geoffrey David, FSA; Canon and Chancellor of Salisbury Cathedral, 1972–92, Canon Emeritus, since 1992; *b* 19 Aug. 1925; *s* of late Walter N. U. Dunlop and Marguerite Irene (*née* Shakerley); *m* 1957, Deirdre Marcia, *d* of late Dr Marcus Jamieson; one *s* one *d*. *Educ:* Winchester Coll.; New Coll., Oxford (MA); Strasbourg Univ. (Diploma); Lincoln Theol Coll. FSA 1965. Served Irish Guards, 1944–46 (Lieut). Curate, Hatfield, 1956–60; Chaplain, Westminster Sch., 1960–62; Vicar of Bures, Suffolk, 1962–72. Member: Gen. Synod, 1975–85; Cathedrals' Adv. Commn, 1981–86. Trustee, Historic Churches Preservation Trust, 1969–. *Publications:* Versailles, 1956, 2nd edn 1970; Palaces and Progresses of Elizabeth I, 1962; Châteaux of the Loire, 1969; Companion Guide to the Ile de France, 1979, 2nd edn 1985; Cathedrals Crusade, 1981; Royal Palaces of France, 1985; Thinking It Out, 1986; (contrib.) Oxford Companion to Gardens, 1986; Burgundy, 1990; Marie-Antoinette: a portrait, 1993; weekly column in Church Times, 1970–90. *Recreations:* painting, bird watching. *Address:* Gowanbrae, The Glebe, Selkirk TD7 5AB. *T:* Selkirk (01750) 20706; Hill Cottages, Marsh Lane, Felixstowe, Suffolk IP11 9RP. *T:* Felixstowe (01394) 286118. *Club:* Army and Navy.

DUNLOP, John; *b* 20 May 1910; *s* of Martin T. and Agnes Dunlop, Belfast; *m* 1st, 1936, Ruby Hunter; two *s* (and one *s* decd); 2nd, 1970, Joyce Campbell. *Educ:* primary sch. and techn. college. Apprentice multiple grocers, 1926; assumed management, 1934; acquired own business, 1944. Mem. (VULC), Mid-Ulster, NI Assembly, 1973–74. MP (UUUP) Mid-Ulster, 1974–83. Civil Defence Medal and ribbon 1945. *Recreations:* music, choral singing, amateur soccer. *Address:* Turnaface Road, Moneymore, Magherafelt, Co. Londonderry BT45 7YP. *T:* Moneymore (016487) 48594.

DUNLOP, John Leeper; racehorse trainer, since 1965; *b* 10 July 1939; *s* of Dr John Leeper Dunlop and Margaret Frances Mary Dunlop; *m* 1965, Susan Jennifer Page; two *s* (and one *s* decd). *Educ:* Marlborough Coll. Royal Ulster Rifles, 1959–61. Leading trainer, 1984; wins include: Shirley Heights, Derby, 1978; Circus Plume, Oaks, 1984; Salsabil, Oaks, 1990; Moon Madness, St Leger, 1980; Erhaab, Derby, 1994; One Thousand Guineas: Quick as Lightning, 1980; Salsabil, 1990; Shadayid, 1991. *Recreations:* breeding race horses and show horses. *Address:* House on the Hill, Arundel, West Sussex BN18 9LJ. *T:* Arundel (01903) 882106. *Club:* Turf.

DUNLOP, Richard B.; *see* Buchanan-Dunlop.

DUNLOP, Sir Thomas, 3rd Bt, *cr* 1916; Partner, Thomas Dunlop & Sons, Ship and Insurance Brokers, Glasgow, 1938–86; *b* 11 April 1912; *s* of Sir Thomas Dunlop, 2nd Bt; *S* father, 1963; *m* 1947, Adda Mary Alison, *d* of T. Arthur Smith, Lindsaylands, Biggar, Lanarks; one *s* one *d* (and one *d* decd). *Educ:* Shrewsbury; St John's Coll., Cambridge (BA). Chartered Accountant, 1939. Former Chm., Savings Bank of Glasgow. Member: Cttee of Princess Louise Scottish Hosp., Erskine; Vice-Pres., Royal Alfred Seafarers' Soc. OStJ 1965. *Recreations:* shooting, fishing, golf. *Heir: s* Thomas Dunlop [*b* 22 April 1951; *m* 1984, Eileen, *er d* of A. H. Stevenson; one *s* one *d*]. *Address:* The Corrie, Kilmacolm, Renfrewshire PA13 4NY. *T:* Kilmacolm (01505) 873239. *Club:* Western (Glasgow).

DUNLOP, Sir William (Norman Gough), Kt 1975; JP; Managing Director, Dunlop Farms Ltd, retired 1990; *b* 9 April 1914; *s* of Norman Matthew Dunlop and Alice Ada Dunlop (*née* Gough); *m* 1940, Ruby Jean (*née* Archie); three *s* three *d*. *Educ:* Waitaki Boys' High Sch. Farmer in Canterbury, NZ. President: Federated Farmers, NZ, 1973–74; Coopworth Sheep Soc., NZ, 1971–74; Member: Agriculture Adv. Council, NZ, 1970–74; Immigration Adv. Council, NZ, 1971–; Transport Adv. Council, NZ, 1971–76; Chm., Neurological Foundn (Canterbury), 1975–88; Dep. Chm., NZ Meat and Wool Board Electoral Coll., 1973; Director: Rural Bank & Finance Corp., NZ, 1974–81; New Zealand Light Leathers, 1973–80. Trustee: Todd Foundn, 1973–81; Lincoln Coll. Foundn,

1977–88 (Chm. Bd). Anniv. Medal, NZ Animal Production Soc., 1991. Internat. Visitors Award, US Dept of State, 1971. JP 1972. *Recreations:* music, gardening. *Address:* 242 Main Road, Monks Bay, Christchurch 8, New Zealand. *T:* (8) 849056. *Club:* Canterbury (Christchurch).

DUNLUCE, Viscount; Randal Alexander St John McDonnell; *b* 2 July 1967; *o s* and heir of Earl of Antrim, *qv.*

DUNMORE, 11th Earl of, *cr* 1686; **Kenneth Randolph Murray;** Viscount Fincastle, Lord Murray of Blair, Moulin and Tillemett, 1686; retired; *b* 6 June 1913; *s* of Arthur Charles Murray (*d* 1964) (*g g s* of 4th Earl), and Susan Maud (*d* 1922), *d* of Edward Richards, Tasmania; *S* brother, 1981; *m* 1938, Margaret Joy (*d* 1976), *d* of late P. D. Cousins, Burnie, Tasmania; two *s*. *Educ:* Tasmanian State School. Sgt, 12th/50th Bn, AIF, 1939–45. Former Post-master, Tasmania. Past Master, Tamar Valley Masonic Lodge 42 Tasmanian Constitution, 1957–58. Patron: NSW Combined Scottish Soc.; Exeter RSL Bowls Club. JP Beaconsfield, Tasmania, 1963. *Heir: s* Viscount Fincastle, *qv. Address:* c/o PO Box 100E, East Devonport, Tas 7310, Australia. *Club:* Exeter RSL (Exeter, Tasmania).

DUNN, Baroness *cr* 1990 (Life Peer), of Hong Kong Island in Hong Kong and of Knightsbridge in the Royal Borough of Kensington and Chelsea; **Lydia Selina Dunn,** DBE 1989 (CBE 1983; OBE 1978); JP; Executive Director, John Swire & Sons Ltd, from June 1996; Deputy Chairman: Hongkong and Shanghai Banking Corporation, since 1992 (Director, 1981–92); HSBC Holdings plc (formerly Hong Kong and Shanghai Banking Corporation Holdings (London)), since 1992 (Director, 1990–92); *b* 29 Feb. 1940; *d* of Yencheun Yeh Dunn and Chen Yin Chu; *m* 1988, Michael David Thomas, *qv. Educ:* St Paul's Convent Sch., Hong Kong; Univ. of Calif, Berkeley (BS). MLC, Hong Kong, 1976–88 (Sen. Mem., 1985–88); MEC, 1982–95 (Sen. Mem., 1988–95). Director: John Swire & Sons (HK) Ltd, 1978–; Swire Pacific Ltd, 1982–; Cathay Pacific Airways Ltd, 1985–; Volvo AB, 1991–93 (Mem. Internat. Adv. Bd, 1985–91). Chairman: Hong Kong/Japan Business Co-operation Cttee, 1988–95 (Mem., 1983–88); Hong Kong Trade Develt Council, 1983–91; Mem., Hong Kong/US Econ. Co-op. Cttee, 1984–93. Chm., Lord Wilson Heritage Trust, 1993–95. Hon. LLD: Chinese Univ. of Hong Kong, 1984; Univ. of Hong Kong, 1991; Univ. of British Columbia, 1991; Leeds Univ., 1994; Hon. DSc Univ. of Buckingham, 1995. Prime Minister of Japan's Trade Award, 1987; USA Sec. of Commerce's To Peace and Commerce Award, 1988. *Publication:* In the Kingdom of the Blind, 1983. *Recreation:* collecting antiques. *Address:* John Swire & Sons Ltd, Swire House, 59 Buckingham Gate, SW1E 6AJ. *Clubs:* Hong Kong, Royal Hong Kong Jockey (Hong Kong); China.

DUNN, Anderson; Assistant Commissioner, Metropolitan Police, since 1994; *b* 6 May 1944; *s* of William Rennie and Wilma Rennie (*née* Turner); *m* 1967, Margaret Docherty; one *s* one *d*. *Educ:* Queen Mary Coll., London (LLB Hons). Joined Metropolitan Police, 1963; transf. to Thames Valley Police as Chief Supt, 1987; Asst Chief Constable, Operations, 1988–93; Dep. Chief Constable, Northants, 1993–94. *Recreations:* walking, reading, most sports. *Address:* Metropolitan Police Service, 3 Area (NE) Headquarters, 462 Fore Street, N9 0PW.

DUNN, Prof. Douglas Eaglesham, FRSL; poet and short-story writer; Professor of English, since 1991, Director, St Andrews Scottish Studies Institute, since 1992, Head of School of English, since 1994, St Andrews University; *b* 23 Oct. 1942; *s* of William Douglas Dunn and Margaret McGowan; *m* 1st, 1964, Lesley Balfour Wallace (*d* 1981); 2nd, 1985, Lesley Jane Bathgate; one *s* one *d*. *Educ:* Univ. of Hull (BA). Became full-time writer, 1971. Hon. Vis. Prof., Dundee Univ., 1987–89; Fellow in Creative Writing, Univ. of St Andrews, 1989–91. Mem., Scottish Arts Council, 1992–94. FRSL 1981. Hon. Fellow, Humberside Coll., 1987. Hon. LLD Dundee, 1987. Cholmondeley Award, 1989. *Publications:* Terry Street, 1969 (Somerset Maugham Award, 1972); The Happier Life, 1972; (ed) New Poems, 1972–73, 1973; Love or Nothing, 1974 (Geoffrey Faber Meml Prize, 1976); (ed) A Choice of Byron's Verse, 1974; (ed) Two Decades of Irish Writing, 1975 (criticism); (ed) The Poetry of Scotland, 1979; Barbarians, 1979; St Kilda's Parliament, 1981 (Hawthornden Prize, 1982); Europa's Lover, 1982; (ed) A Rumoured City: new poets from Hull, 1982; (ed) To Build a Bridge: celebration of Humberside in verse, 1982; Elegies, 1985 (Whitbread Poetry Prize, 1985; Whitbread Book of the Year Award, 1986); Secret Villages, 1985 (short stories); Selected Poems 1964–1983, 1986; Northlight, 1988 (poetry); New and Selected Poems 1966–1988, 1989; Andromache, 1990; (ed) The Essential Browning, 1990; (ed) Scotland: an anthology, 1991; (ed) Faber Book of 20th Century Scottish Poetry, 1992; Dante's Drum-Kit, 1993; Boyfriends and Girlfriends, 1994 (short stories); Oxford Book of Scottish Short Stories, 1995; contrib. to Counterblast pamphlet series, Glasgow Herald, New Yorker, TLS, etc. *Recreations:* playing the clarinet and saxophone, listening to jazz music, gardening. *Address:* School of English, St Andrews University, St Andrews, Fife KY16 9AL.

DUNN, Air Marshal Sir Eric (Clive), KBE 1983; CB 1981; BEM 1951; *b* 27 Nov. 1927; *s* of late W. E. and of K. M. Dunn; *m* 1951, Margaret Gray; three *d*. *Educ:* Bridlington Sch. CEng, FRAeS. RAF aircraft apprentice, 1944–47; commnd Engr Br., 1954; Staff Coll., 1964; Jt Services Staff Coll., 1967; Sen. Engrg Officer, RAF Boulmer, 1968; MoD, 1969–70; Comd Electrical Engr, NEAF, 1971–72; Dir of Engrg Policy (RAF), 1973–75; RCDS, 1976; AO Wales, and Stn Comdr RAF St Athan, 1977; Air Officer Maintenance, RAF Support Comd, 1977–81; Air Officer Engineering, HQ Strike Comd, 1981–83; Chief Engr, RAF, 1983–86. Dir, Hellermann Deutsch, 1986–90; Engrg Consultant, Dowty Gp, 1986–90. *Recreations:* golf. *Club:* Royal Air Force.

DUNN, John Churchill; broadcaster, host of own daily radio programme; *b* 4 March 1934; *s* of late John Barrett Jackson Dunn and of Dorothy Dunn (*née* Hiscox); *m* 1958, Margaret Jennison; two *d*. *Educ:* Christ Church Cathedral Choir School, Oxford; The King's School, Canterbury. Nat. Service, RAF, 1953–55. Joined BBC as studio manager, External Service, 1956; announcer/newsreader, Gen. Overseas Service, 1958, Domestic Services, 1959; worked all radio networks before joining Light Programme/Radio 2, and subseq. freelance; *radio series include:* Just For You; Housewives' Choice; Music Through Midnight; Roundabout; Jazz at Night; Saturday Sport; Sunday Sport; 4th Dimension; Breakfast Special; It Makes Me Laugh; Nat. and European Brass Band Championships; Light Music Festivals; The John Dunn Show, 1972–; numerous TV appearances. TV and Radio Industries Club Personality of the Year, 1971, 1984, 1986; Variety Club of GB Radio Personality of the Year, 1983; Daily Mail Silver Microphone, 1988. *Publication:* John Dunn's Curious Collection, 1982; Answers Please. *Recreations:* music, skiing, wine. *Address:* c/o Jo Gurnett Personal Management, 45 Queen's Gate Mews, SW7 5QN. *T:* 0171–584 7642.

DUNN, Prof. John Montfort, FBA 1989; Professor of Political Theory, University of Cambridge, since 1987; Fellow of King's College, Cambridge, since 1966; *b* 9 Sept. 1940; *s* of Col. Henry George Montfort Dunn and Catherine Mary Dunn; *m* 1st, 1965, Susan Deborah Fyvel (marr. diss. 1971); 2nd, 1973, Judith Frances Bernal (marr. diss. 1987); one *s* (and one *s* decd) by Dr Heather Joan Glen. *Educ:* Winchester Coll.; King's Coll., Cambridge (BA 1962). Harkness Fellow, Graduate Sch. of Arts and Sciences, Harvard Univ., 1964–65; Official Fellow in History, Jesus Coll., Cambridge, 1965–66; Dir of Studies in History, King's Coll., Cambridge, 1966–72; Lectr in Pol Science, 1972–77, Reader in Politics, 1977–87, Cambridge Univ. Vis. Lectr, Dept of Pol Science, Univ. of Ghana, 1968–69; Visiting Professor: Dept of Civics and Politics, Univ. of Bombay, 1979–80; Faculty of Law, Tokyo Metropolitan Univ., 1983–84; Distinguished Vis. Prof., Murphy Inst. of Pol Economy, Tulane Univ., New Orleans, 1986; Benjamin Evans Lippincott Dist. Prof., Minnesota Univ., 1990; Olmsted Vis. Prof., Yale Univ., 1991. Foreign Hon. Mem., Amer. Acad. of Arts and Scis, 1991. Bd of Consultants, Dae-Jung Peace Foundn for the Asia Pacific Region, 1994–. FRSA 1993. *Publications:* The Political Thought of John Locke, 1969; Modern Revolutions, 1972; Dependence and Opportunity: political change in Ahafo, 1973; (ed) West African States: failure and promise, 1978; Western Political Theory in the Face of the Future, 1979; Political Obligation in its Historical Context, 1980; Locke, 1984; The Politics of Socialism, 1984; Rethinking Modern Political Theory, 1985; (ed) The Economic Limits to Modern Politics, 1989; (ed) Contemporary West African States, 1989; Interpreting Political Responsibility, 1990; (ed) Democracy: the unfinished journey, 1992; Contemporary Crisis of the Nation State?, 1995. *Address:* The Merchant's House, 31 Station Road, Swavesey, Cambridge CB4 5QJ. *T:* Swavesey (01954) 231451.

DUNN, Martin; Editor-in-Chief, The New York Daily News, since 1993; *b* 26 Jan. 1955. *Educ:* Dudley Grammar Sch., Worcs. Dudley Herald, 1974–77; Birmingham Evening Mail, 1977; Birmingham Post, 1978; Daily Mail, 1978–79; freelance journalist, 1979–83; New York Correspondent, The Sun, 1983–84; The Sun, London, 1984–88; Deputy Editor: News of the World, 1988–89; The Sun, 1989–91; Editor: Today, 1991–93; The Boston Herald, 1993. *Recreations:* squash, running, golf. *Address:* The New York Daily News, 220 East 42nd Street, New York, NY 10017, USA.

DUNN, Air Marshal Sir Patrick Hunter, KBE 1965 (CBE 1950); CB 1956; DFC 1941; FRAeS; *b* 31 Dec. 1912; *s* of late William Alexander Dunn, Ardentinny, Argyllshire; *m* 1939, Diana Ledward Smith; two *d*. *Educ:* Glasgow Academy; Loretto; Glasgow Univ. Commissioned, 1933, Pre-war service in flying boats; as flying instructor 500 (County of Kent) Sqdn, AAF; with the Long Range Development Unit and as instructor at the Central Flying Sch. War service included command of 80 and 274 Fighter Squadrons and 71 OTU, all in Middle East (1940–42); at Air Ministry, and in Fighter Command, Sector Commander, 1945–46. Post-war service in Air Ministry, 1947–48; Malaya, 1949–50; NATO Defence Coll., 1950–52; Fighter Command, 1953–56; ADC to the Queen, 1953–58. AOC and Commandant, RAF Flying Coll., 1956–58; Deputy Air Sec., 1959–61; AOC No. 1 Group, Bomber Command, 1961–64; AOC-in-Chief, Flying Training Command, 1964–66; retired from RAF, 1967. Director i/c Management Services, British Steel Corp., 1967–68; resigned to become Dep. Chm., British Eagle Internat. Airlines Ltd; Chm., Eagle Aircraft Services, 1969; Aviation Consultant, British Steel Corporation, 1969–76. Mem. Council, Air League, 1968–73 and 1975–79 (Dep. Chm., 1972–73; Chm., Defence Cttee, 1968–73); Member: British Atlantic Cttee, 1976–; Atlantic Council, 1993–. Dir, Gloucester, Coventry, Cricklewood and Kingston Industrial Trading Estates, 1969–75 and 1977–81. A Trustee and Governor of Loretto, 1959–81; President: Fettesian-Lorettonian Club, 1972–75; Lorettonian Soc., 1980–81; Mem. Cttee, Assoc. of Governing Bodies of Public Schs, 1976–79. *Recreations:* tennis, sailing, shooting. *Address:* Little Hillbark, Hockett Lane, Cookham Dean, Berks SL6 9UF. *Clubs:* Royal Air Force, Hurlingham.

See also Sir N. J. D. Marsden, Bt.

DUNN, Richard Johann, CBE 1995; Executive Director, News International Television, since 1995; Chairman, Production Design Co., since 1994; Director, Dorling Kindersley Holdings, since 1994; *b* 5 Sept. 1943; *s* of late Major Edward Cadwalader Dunn, MBE, TD, and of Gudlaug Johannesdóttir; *m* 1972, Virginia Gregory Gaynor, USA; two *s* one *d*. *Educ:* Forest Sch., St John's Coll., Cambridge. Writer and Producer, Associated British Pathe, 1967–70; Exec. Producer, EMI Special Films Unit, 1970–72; Man. Dir, Swindon Viewpoint Ltd, cable community television service, 1972–76; EMI Film and Th. Corp., 1976–77; joined Thames Television, 1978: Dir of Prodn, 1981–85; Chief Exec., 1985–95; Man. Dir, Pearson Television Hldgs, 1993–95. Director: ITCA, subseq. ITV Assoc., 1985–92 (Chm., 1988–90); ITN, 1985–93 (Chm., 1991–93); ITV Publications, 1985–89. Chairman: Euston Films Ltd, 1985–91; Cosgrove Hall Productions, 1985–93; Thames Television Internat., 1985–95; Teddington Studios, 1992–95; Financial Times Television, 1993–95; UK Living, 1993–95; British Transport Advertising Ltd, 1994–95; Director: Thames Valley Broadcasting Plc, 1985–89; Starstream Ltd (The Children's Channel), 1986–90; Channel Four TV, 1988–91; UK Gold Television Ltd, 1992–95; Eur. Channel Management Ltd, 1995. Director: Internat. Council of Nat. Acad. of Television Arts and Scis, NY, 1985– (Vice Chm., 1990–93); BARB, 1986–88; Société Européenne des Satellites, 1987–95; Association des Télévisions Commerciales en Europe, 1989–91. Vice Chm., Independent Broadcasting Telethon Trust, 1987–94. Vice Pres. and Fellow, RTS, 1988–. Chm., Film and Video Panel, GLAA, 1978–82; Pres., Battersea Arts Centre, 1989– (Chm., 1984–88). Internat. Emmy (Founders) Award, 1993. *Address:* Lovel Dene, Woodside, Windsor Forest, Berks SL4 2DP. *T:* Winkfield Row (01344) 884968. *Clubs:* Garrick, Royal Automobile; Hawks (Cambridge).

DUNN, Robert John; MP (C) Dartford, since 1979; *b* July 1946; *s* of late Robert and of Doris Dunn, Swinton, Lancs; *m* 1976, Janet Elizabeth Wall, BD, JP, *d* of late Denis Wall, Dulwich; two *s*. *Educ:* State schs. Senior Buyer, J. Sainsbury Ltd, 1973–79. Councillor, London Borough of Southwark, 1974–78 (Opposition Minority Gp spokesman on Housing and Finance Matters). Vice-Pres., Eccles Conservative Assoc., 1974–; contested (C): Eccles, Gen. Elections, Feb. and Oct. 1974; adopted as Parly Candidate (C) Dartford, 1975. PPS to Parly Under-Secs of State at DES, 1981–82, to Paymaster General and Chancellor of the Duchy of Lancaster, 1982–83; Parly Under-Sec. of State, DES, 1983–88. Mem., Parly Select Cttee on the Environment, 1981–82, on Selection, 1991–; Jt Sec., Cons backbench Educn Cttee, 1980–81; Chairman: Cons. backbench Social Security Cttee, 1988–89; Cons. backbench Transport Cttee, 1992–; Vice-Chm., Cons. backbench Party Organization Cttee, 1989–; Mem. Exec. Cttee, 1922 Cttee, 1988–. President: Dartford Young Conservatives, 1976–; Kent Gp Young Conservatives, 1982–85; SE Area Young Conservatives, 1989–; SE Area Educn Adv. Cttee, 1982–93; Dartford branch, Kent Assoc. for the Disabled, 1983–. *Recreations:* canvassing; American politics. *Address:* House of Commons, SW1A 0AA. *T:* 0171–219 5209. *Club:* Dartford Rotary (Hon. Mem.).

DUNN, Rt. Hon. Sir Robin Horace Walford, Kt 1969; MC 1944; PC 1980; a Lord Justice of Appeal, 1980–84; *b* 16 Jan. 1918; *s* of late Brig. K. F. W. Dunn, CBE, and of Ava, *d* of Brig.-Gen. H. F. Kays, CB; *m* 1941, Judith (*d* 1995), *d* of late Sir Gonne Pilcher, MC; one *s* one *d* (and one *d* decd). *Educ:* Wellington; Royal Military Academy, Woolwich (Sword of Honour). First Commissioned, RA, 1938; RHA, 1941; Staff Coll., 1946; retired (hon. Major), 1948. Served War of 1939–45; France and Belgium, 1939–40; Western Desert and Libya, 1941–42; Normandy and NW Europe, 1944–45 (wounded thrice, despatches twice, MC); Hon. Col Comdt, RA, 1980–84, Hon. Col 1984–. Called to Bar (Inner Temple), 1948; Master of the Bench, Inner Temple, 1969. Western Circuit, Junior Counsel to Registrar of Restrictive Trading Agreements, 1959–62; QC 1962;

Judge of the High Court of Justice, Family Division (formerly Probate, Divorce and Admiralty Division), 1969–80; Presiding Judge, Western Circuit, 1974–78. Treas., Gen. Council of the Bar, 1967–69 (Mem., 1959–63); Chm. Betting Levy Appeal Tribunal, 1964–69; Dep. Chm., Somerset QS, 1965–71; Mem., Lord Chancellor's Cttee on Legal Educn, 1968–69. *Publication:* Sword and Wig: memoirs of a Lord Justice, 1994. *Recreation:* hunting. *Address:* Lynch Mead, Allerford, Somerset TA24 8HJ. *T:* Minehead (01643) 862509.

DUNN, William Francis N.; *see* Newton Dunn.

DUNN, William Hubert, QC 1982; **His Honour Judge Dunn;** a Circuit Judge, since 1993; *b* 8 July 1933; *s* of William Patrick Millar Dunn and Isabel (*née* Thompson); *m* 1971, Maria Henriqueta Theresa d'Arouje Perestrello de Moser; one *s* one *d*. *Educ:* Rockport, Co. Down, N Ireland; Winchester Coll.; New Coll., Oxford (Hons degree PPE) (Half-Blue fencing 1954–55). 2nd Lieut, Life Guards, 1956–57; Household Cavalry Reserve of Officers, 1957–64. Cholmondeley Scholar, Lincoln's Inn, 1958, called to Bar, 1958; Bencher, Lincoln's Inn, 1990. A Recorder, 1980–93. *Recreations:* travel, literature. *Address:* 19 Clarendon Street, SW1V 2EN. *Club:* Boodle's.

DUNNACHIE, James Francis, (Jimmy), JP; MP (Lab) Glasgow, Pollok, since 1987; *b* 17 Nov. 1930; *s* of William and Mary Dunnachie; *m* 1974, M. Isobel Payne. Councillor, City of Glasgow Corp., 1972–74 (Chm., Clearance and Rehabilitation); District Councillor, City of Glasgow, 1974–77 (Chm., C and R Cttee); Councillor, Strathclyde Regional Council, 1978–87 (Vice-Chm., Social Work Cttee). An Opposition Whip, 1988–92, Scottish Whip, 1989–92. *Recreations:* gardening, reading, junior football. *Address:* 15 Loganswell Gardens, Glasgow G46 8HU. *T:* 0141–638 9756.

DUNNE, Sir Thomas (Raymond), KCVO 1995; JP; HM Lord-Lieutenant, County of Hereford and Worcester, since 1977; *b* 24 Oct. 1933; *s* of Philip Dunne, MC, and Margaret Walker; *m* 1957, Henrietta Crawley; two *s* two *d*. *Educ:* Eton; RMA Sandhurst. Served Army, 1951–59: Royal Horse Guards. Herefordshire CC, 1962–68. President: 3 Counties Agric. Soc., 1977; W Midlands TA Assoc., 1988–; National Vice Pres., Royal British Legion, 1982–89. Mem., West Mercia Police Authy, 1980–; Dir, West Regional Bd, Central TV, 1981–92. Trustee, Dyson Perrins Mus. Trust, 1980–. Colonel: 4th Worcester and Sherwood Foresters (formerly 2nd Mercian Volunteers), 1987–93; 5th Bn LI, 1993–. High Sheriff 1970, DL 1973, Herefordshire; JP Hereford and Worcester, 1977. KStJ 1978. *Address:* c/o County Hall, Spetchley Road, Worcester WR5 2NP.

DUNNETT, Sir Alastair (MacTavish), Kt 1995; *b* 26 Dec. 1908; *s* of David Sinclair Dunnett and Isabella Crawford MacTavish; *m* 1946, Dorothy Halliday; two *s*. *Educ:* Overnewton Sch.; Hillhead High Sch., Glasgow. Commercial Bank of Scotland, Ltd, 1925; Co-founder of The Claymore Press, 1933–34; Glasgow Weekly Herald, 1935–36; The Bulletin, 1936–37; Daily Record, 1937–40; Chief Press Officer, Sec. of State for Scotland, 1940–46; Editor, Daily Record, 1946–55; Editor, The Scotsman, 1956–72; Man. Dir, The Scotsman Publications Ltd, 1962–70, Chm., 1970–74; Mem. Exec. Bd, The Thomson Organisation Ltd, 1974–78; Director: Scottish Television Ltd, 1975–79; Thomson Scottish Petroleum Ltd, 1979–87 (Chm., 1972–79). Smith-Mundt Scholarship to USA, 1951. Governor, Pitlochry Festival Theatre, 1958–84. Member: Scottish Tourist Board, 1956–69; Press Council, 1959–62; Council of Nat. Trust for Scotland, 1962–69; Council of Commonwealth Press Union, 1964–78; Edinburgh Univ. Court, 1964–66; Edinburgh Festival Council, 1967–80. Hon. Mem., Saltire Soc., 1991. FRSA 1987. Hon. LLD Strathclyde, 1978. *Publications:* Treasure at Sonnach, 1935, repr. 1995, as The Canoe Boys; Heard Tell, 1946; Quest by Canoe, 1950, repr. 1967, as It's Too Late in the Year; Highlands and Islands of Scotland, 1951; The Donaldson Line, 1952; The Land of Scotch, 1953; (as Alec Tavis) The Duke's Day, 1970; (ed) Alistair Maclean Introduces Scotland, 1972; No Thanks to the Duke, 1978; Among Friends (autobiog.), 1984; (with Dorothy Dunnett) The Scottish Highlands, 1988; End of Term, 1989; *plays:* The Original John Mackay, Glasgow Citizens, 1956; Fit to Print, Duke of York's, 1962. *Recreations:* sailing, riding, walking. *Address:* 87 Colinton Road, Edinburgh EH10 5DF. *T:* 0131–337 2107. *Clubs:* Caledonian; Scottish Arts, New (Edinburgh).

DUNNETT, Denzil Inglis, CMG 1967; OBE 1962; HM Diplomatic Service, retired; *b* 21 Oct. 1917; *s* of late Sir James Dunnett, KCIE and late Annie (*née* Sangster); *m* 1946, Ruth Rawcliffe (*d* 1974); two *s* (one *d* decd). *Educ:* Edinburgh Acad.; Corpus Christi Coll., Oxford. Served with RA, 1939–45. Diplomatic Service: Foreign Office, 1947–48; Sofia, 1948–50; Foreign Office, 1950–53; UK Delegn to OEEC, Paris, 1953–56; Commercial Sec., Buenos Aires, 1956–60; Consul, Elisabethville, 1961–62; Commercial Counsellor, Madrid, 1962–67; seconded to BoT, 1967–70; Counsellor, Mexico City, 1970–73; Ambassador to Senegal, Mauritania, Mali and Guinea, 1973–76, and to Guinea-Bissau, 1975–76; Diplomatic Service Chm., CS Selection Bd, 1976–77. London Rep., Scottish Develt Agency, 1978–82. *Publication:* Bird Poems, 1989. *Recreations:* chess, music. *Address:* 11 Victoria Grove, W8 5RW. *T:* 0171–584 7523. *Club:* Caledonian.

DUNNETT, Jack; President, Football League, 1981–86 and 1988–89 (Member, Management Committee, 1977–89); *b* 24 June 1922; *m* 1951; two *s* three *d*. *Educ:* Whitgift Middle Sch., Croydon; Downing Coll., Cambridge (MA, LLM). Served with Cheshire Regt, 1941–46 (Capt.). Admitted Solicitor, 1949. Middlesex CC, 1958–61; Councillor, Enfield Borough Council, 1958–61; Alderman, Enfield Borough Council, 1961–63; Councillor, Greater London Council, 1964–67. MP (Lab) Central Nottingham, 1964–74, Nottingham East, 1974–83; former PPS to: Minister of State, FCO; Minister of Transport. Mem. FA Council, 1977–89, Vice-Pres., 1981–86, 1988–89; Mem., Football Trust, 1982–89; Chm., Notts County FC, 1968–87; Vice-Chm., Portsmouth FC, 1989–90. *Recreation:* watching professional football. *Address:* Whitehall Court, SW1A 2EP. *T:* 0171–839 6962.

DUNNETT, Sir (Ludovic) James, GCB 1969 (KCB 1960; CB 1957); CMG 1948; Permanent Under-Secretary of State, Ministry of Defence, 1966–74; *b* 12 Feb. 1914; *s* of late Sir James Dunnett, KCIE; *m* 1st, 1944, Olga Adair (*d* 1980); no *c*; 2nd, 1984, Lady Clarisse Grover. *Educ:* Edinburgh Acad.; University Coll., Oxford. Entered Air Ministry, 1936; Private Sec. to Permanent Sec., 1937–44; transferred to Ministry of Civil Aviation, 1945; Under Sec., 1948; Under Sec., Min. of Supply, 1951, Deputy Sec., 1953; Deputy Sec., Min. of Transport, 1958; Permanent Secretary: Min. of Transport, 1959–62; Min. of Labour, 1962–66. Mem., SSRC, 1977–82. Visiting Fellow, Nuffield Coll., Oxford, 1964–72. Chm., Internat. Maritime Industries Forum, 1976–79; Pres., Inst. of Manpower Studies, 1977–80. Trustee, Charities Aid Foundn, 1974–88. *Recreation:* golf. *Address:* 85 Bedford Gardens, W8 7EQ. *T:* 0171–727 5286. *Club:* Reform.

DUNNILL, Prof. Peter, DSc, PhD; FEng 1985; FRSC, FIChemE; Director, BBSRC (formerly SERC) Interdisciplinary Research Centre for Biochemical Engineering, since 1991; Professor, University College London, since 1984; *b* 20 May 1938; *s* of Eric and Marjorie Dunnill; *m* 1962, Patricia Mary Lievesley; one *s*. *Educ:* University College London (BSc; DSc 1978; Fellow, 1991). Royal Instn MRC staff, 1963–64; Lectr, 1964–79, Reader, 1979–84, UCL. Member: Internat. Cttee on Econ. and Applied Microbiol., 1974–82; Scientific and Technical Cttee, Central Lab. of Nat. Blood Transfusion Service, 1978–82; Biotechnol. Directorate Management Cttee, SERC, 1982–88, 1993–94; Biotechnol. Adv. Gp to Heads of Res. Councils, 1987–90; Biotechnol. Jt Adv. Bd, 1989–92; BBSRC, 1994–. *Publications:* c 150 pubns in learned jls. *Recreation:* music. *Address:* Advanced Centre for Biochemical Engineering, University College London, Torrington Place, WC1E 7JE. *T:* 0171–380 7031.

DUNNING, Prof. John Harry, PhD; Emeritus Professor of International Business, University of Reading, since 1992; State of New Jersey Professor of International Business, Rutgers University, US, since 1989; *b* 26 June 1927; *m* 1st, 1948, Ida Teresa Bellamy (marr. diss. 1975); one *s*; 2nd, 1975, Christine Mary Brown. *Educ:* Lower Sch. of John Lyon, Harrow; University Coll. London (BSc (Econ); PhD). Research Asst, University Coll. London, 1951–52; Lectr and Sen. Lectr, Univ. of Southampton, 1952–64; University of Reading: Prof. of Economics, 1964–74; Hd of Dept of Economics, 1964–87; Esmée Fairburn Prof. of Internat. Investment and Business Studies, 1975–87; ICI Res. Prof. of Internat. Business, 1988–92. Visiting Prof.: Univ. of Western Ontario, Canada; Univ. of California (Berkeley), 1968–69; Boston Univ., USA, 1976; Stockholm Sch. of Economics, 1978; HEC, Univ. of Montreal, Canada, 1980; Walker-Ames Prof., Univ. of Washington, Seattle, 1981; Seth Boyden Distinguished Prof., Rutgers Univ., 1987; Univ. of Berkeley, 1987. Consultant to UN, 1974–, OECD, 1975–, and EC, 1985–. Member: SE Economic Planning Council, 1966–68; Chemicals EDC, 1968–77; UN Study Gp on Multinational Corps, 1973–74. Chm., Economists Advisory Gp Ltd. Pres., Internat. Trade Assoc., 1994. Fellow, Acad. of Internat. Business (Pres., 1987–88). Hon. PhD: Uppsala, 1975; Universidad Autónoma de Madrid, 1990. *Publications:* American Investment in British Manufacturing Industry, 1958; (with C. J. Thomas) British Industry, 1963; Economic Planning and Town Expansion, 1963; Studies in International Investment, 1970; (ed) The Multinational Enterprise, 1971; (with E. V. Morgan) An Economic Study of the City of London, 1971; (ed) International Investment, 1972; (ed) Economic Analysis and the Multinational Enterprise, 1974; US Industry in Britain, 1976; (with T. Houston) UK Industry Abroad, 1976; International Production and the Multinational Enterprise, 1981; (ed with J. Black) International Capital Movements, 1982; (with J. Stopford) Multinationals: Company Performance and Global Trends, 1983; (with R. D. Pearce) The World's Largest Industrial Companies 1962–83, 1985; (ed) Multinational Enterprises, Economic Structure and International Competitiveness, 1985; Japanese Participation in British Industry, 1986; (with J. Cantwell) World Directory of Statistics on International Direct Investment and Production, 1987; Explaining International Production, 1988; Multinationals, Technology and Competitiveness, 1988; (ed with A. Webster) Structural Change in the World Economy, 1990; Multinational Enterprises and the Global Economy, 1992; Global Business and the Challenge of the 1990s, 1993; (ed with R. Narula) Catalysts for Change, 1995; (ed with K. Hamdani) Globalization and Developing Countries, 1995; numerous articles in learned and professional jls. *Address:* Department of Economics, University of Reading, Whiteknights Park, Reading, Berks RG6 2AA. *T:* Reading (01734) 875123. *Club:* Athenæum.

DUNNING, Joseph, CBE 1977; Chairman, Lothian Health Board, 1983–84; Principal, Napier College of Commerce and Technology, Edinburgh, 1963–81, retired; *b* 9 Oct. 1920; *s* of Joseph and Elizabeth Ellen Dunning; *m* 1948, Edith Mary Barlow (*d* 1972); one *s* one *d*; *m* 1992, Eileen Murdoch, OBE. *Educ:* London University (BSc Hons); Durham University (MEd); Manchester College of Technology (AMCT). Metallurgical Industry and lecturing, 1936–56; Principal, Cleveland Technical College, 1956–63. MA Open Univ.; FEIS. Hon. Fellow, Napier Polytech. of Edinburgh, 1989. Hon. DEd CNAA, 1983. *Recreations:* silversmithing, photography. *Address:* 2 Thorpe Field, Sockbridge, Penrith, Cumbria CA10 2JN. *Club:* New (Edinburgh).

DUNNING, Sir Simon (William Patrick), 3rd Bt, *cr* 1930; *b* 14 Dec. 1939; *s* of Sir William Leonard Dunning, 2nd Bt, and Kathleen Lawrie (*d* 1992), *d* of J. P. Cuthbert, MC; *S* father, 1961; *m* 1975, Frances Deirdre Morton, *d* of Major Patrick Lancaster; one *d*. *Educ:* Eton. *Recreation:* shooting. *Address:* Low Auchengillan, Blanefield, by Glasgow G63 9AU. *T:* Blanefield (01360) 70323. *Clubs:* Turf; Western (Glasgow).

DUNNINGTON-JEFFERSON, Sir Mervyn (Stewart), 2nd Bt *cr* 1958; Company Director, since 1968; *b* 5 Aug. 1943; *s* of Sir John Alexander Dunnington-Jefferson, 1st Bt, DSO, and of Frances Isobel, *d* of Col H. A. Cape, DSO; *S* father, 1979; *m* 1971, Caroline Anna, *o d* of J. M. Bayley; one *s* two *d*. *Educ:* Eton College. Joined Charrington & Co. Ltd (Brewers), 1961; left in 1968 to become joint founder and director of Hatton Builders Ltd, specialising in building contracting and property development. *Recreations:* sport—cricket, skiing, golf, etc. *Heir:* *s* John Alexander Dunnington-Jefferson, *b* 23 March 1980. *Address:* 7 Bolingbroke Grove, SW11 6ES. *T:* 0181–675 3395. *Clubs:* MCC, Queen's.

DUNPHIE, Maj.-Gen. Sir Charles (Anderson Lane), Kt 1959; CB 1948; CBE 1942; DSO 1943; *b* 20 April 1902; *s* of late Sir Alfred Dunphie, KCVO, Rotherfield Greys, Oxon; *m* 1st, 1931, Eileen (*d* 1978), *d* of late Lieut-Gen. Sir Walter Campbell, KCB, KCMG, DSO; one *s* one *d*; 2nd, 1981, Susan, *widow* of Col P. L. M. Wright. *Educ:* RN Colls Osborne and Dartmouth; RMA Woolwich. Commissioned into Royal Horse and RFA, 1921; served War of 1939–45 (wounded, despatches); Brig. RAC, 1941; Comdr 26 Armoured Bde, 1942–43; Dep. Dir RAC, War Office, 1943–45; Temp. Maj.-Gen., Dir Gen. Armoured Fighting Vehicles 1945–48; retired 1948. Joined Vickers Ltd, 1948; Chm., 1962–67. One of HM's Honourable Corps of Gentlemen-at-Arms, 1952–62. US Legion of Merit (Commander); US Silver Star. *Address:* Roundhill, Wincanton, Somerset BA9 8HH. *Club:* Army and Navy.

DUNRAVEN and MOUNT-EARL, 7th Earl of, *cr* 1822; **Thady Windham Thomas Wyndham-Quin;** Baron Adare, 1800; Viscount Mountearl, 1816; Viscount Adare, 1822; Bt 1871; *b* 27 Oct. 1939; *s* of 6th Earl of Dunraven and Mount-Earl, CB, CBE, MC, and Nancy (*d* 1994), *d* of Thomas B. Yuille, Halifax County, Va; *S* father 1965; *m* 1969, Geraldine, *d* of Air Commodore Gerard W. McAleer, CBE, MB, BCh, DTM&H, Wokingham; one *d*. *Educ:* Ludgrove; Le Rosey. *Heir:* none. *Address:* Kilcurly House, Adare, Co. Limerick, Ireland. *T:* Limerick 86201. *Club:* Kildare Street and University (Dublin).

See also Sir F. G. W. Brooke, Bt.

DUNROSSIL, 2nd Viscount, *cr* 1959; **John William Morrison,** CMG 1981; JP; HM Diplomatic Service, retired; Lord-Lieutenant, Western Isles, 1993–94 (Vice Lord-Lieutenant, 1992–93); *b* 22 May 1926; *e s* of William Shepherd Morrison, 1st Viscount Dunrossil, GCMG, MC, PC, QC; *S* father, 1961; *m* 1st, 1951, Mavis (marr. diss. 1969), *d* of A. Ll. Spencer-Payne, LRCP, MRCS, LDS; three *s* one *d*; 2nd, 1969, Diana Mary Cunliffe, *d* of C. M. Vise; two *d*. *Educ:* Fettes; Oriel Coll., Oxford (Hon. Fellow, 1994). Royal Air Force, 1945–48, Flt-Lieut (Pilot). Joined Commonwealth Relations Office, 1951; Asst Private Sec. to Sec. of State, 1952–54; Second Sec., Canberra, 84211954–56; CRO, 1956–58; First Sec. and Acting Deputy High Commissioner, Dacca, East Pakistan, 1958–60; First Sec., Pretoria/Capetown, 1961–64; FO, 1964–68; seconded to Intergovernmental Maritime Consultative Org., 1968–70; Counsellor and Head of Chancery, Ottawa, 1970–74; Counsellor, Brussels, 1975–78; High Comr in Fiji, and High

Comr (non-resident) to Republic of Nauru and to Tuvalu, 1978–82; High Comr, Bridgetown, Antigua, Barbuda, Dominica, Grenada, St Vincent and the Grenadines, and British Govt Rep. to WI Associated States, 1982–83; Governor and C-in-C, Bermuda, 1983–88. Chm., Bison Books Ltd, 1990–; Dep. Chm., Bank of Bermuda (Luxembourg) SA, 1990–; Bd, Internat. Registries Inc.; Consultant, Bank of Bermuda Ltd. Chm., Bermuda Soc., London, 1989–. JP 1994; DL Western Isles, 1990. Liveryman, Merchant Taylor's Co., 1984. KStJ. *Heir: s* Hon. Andrew William Reginald Morrison [*b* 15 Dec. 1953; *m* 1986, Carla Brundage; two *d*]. *Address:* 7 Ringmer Avenue, Fulham, SW6 5LP. *T:* 0171–736 8896; Dunrossil House, Trunisgarry, by Lochmaddy, North Uist, Hebrides HS6 5AY. *T:* Lochmaddy (01876) 500213. *Clubs:* Royal Air Force, Commonwealth Trust.

DUNSANY, 19th Baron of, *cr* 1439; **Randal Arthur Henry Plunkett;** Lieut-Col (retd) Indian Cavalry (Guides); *b* 25 Aug. 1906; *o s* of 18th Baron Dunsany, DL, LittD, and Rt Hon. Beatrice, Lady Dunsany (*d* 1970); *S* father, 1957; *m* 1st, 1938, Mrs Vera Bryce (from whom he obtained a divorce, 1947, she *d* 1986), *d* of Señor G. De Sà Sottomaior, São Paulo, Brazil; one *s*; 2nd, 1947, Sheila Victoria Katrin, *widow* of Major John Frederick Foley, Baron de Rutzen, DL, JP, CC, Welsh Guards (killed in action, 1944), *o d* of Sir Henry Philipps, 2nd Bt; one *d*. *Educ:* Eton. Joined the 16th/5th Lancers (SR), 1926; transferred to the Indian Army, 1928, Guides Cavalry, Indian Armoured Corps, retired, 1947. *Heir: s* Hon. Edward John Carlos Plunkett [*b* 10 Sept. 1939. *Educ:* Eton; Slade Sch. of Fine Art]. *Address:* (Seat) Dunsany Castle, Co. Meath, Ireland. *T:* 046–25198. *Clubs:* Beefsteak, Cavalry and Guards; Kildare Street and University (Dublin).

DUNSTAN, (Andrew Harold) Bernard, RA 1968 (ARA 1959); RWA; painter; *b* 19 Jan. 1920; *s* of late Dr A. E. Dunstan; *m* 1949, Diana Maxwell Armfield, *qv*; three *s*. *Educ:* St Paul's; Byam Shaw Sch.; Slade Sch. Has exhibited at RA since 1945. Many one-man exhibitions; now exhibits regularly at Agnews, Bond St. Pictures in public collections include London Museum, Bristol Art Gall., Nat. Gall. of NZ, Arts Council, Nat. Portrait Gall., and many in private collections. Mem., New English Art Club; Chm., Artists' General Benevolent Instn, 1987–91; Pres., Royal West of England Acad., 1980–84. Trustee, RA, 1989–95. *Publications:* Learning to Paint, 1970; Painting in Progress, 1976; Painting Methods of the Impressionists, 1976; (ed) Ruskin, Elements of Drawing, 1991; The Paintings of Bernard Dunstan, 1993. *Recreation:* music. *Address:* 10 High Park Road, Kew, Richmond, Surrey TW9 4BH. *T:* 0181–876 6633. *Club:* Arts.

DUNSTAN, Hon. Donald Allan, AC 1979; QC 1965; Chairman, Community Aid Abroad Freedom From Hunger, 1992–93; *b* Suva, Fiji, 21 Sept. 1926; *s* of late Francis Vivian Dunstan, MBE, sometime Branch Manager, Morris Hedstrom Ltd, and Ida May Dunstan (*née* Hill); *m* 1st, 1949, Gretel Ellis (marr. diss.); two *s* one *d*; 2nd, 1976, Adele Koh (*d* 1978). *Educ:* Murray Bridge Infant and Primary Schs, SA; Suva Grammar Sch.; St Peter's Coll., Adelaide; St Mark's Coll., Univ. of Adelaide (LLB 1948). Admitted to S Australian Bar, 1948, to Fiji Bar, 1949; in practice: Fiji, 1949–50; Adelaide, 1951–. MHA (Labor) South Australia, for Norwood, 1953–79; Attorney-Gen., Minister for Social Welfare, for Aboriginal Affairs, 1965–67; Premier, Treasurer, Attorney-Gen. and Minister for Housing, 1967–68; Leader of Opposition, 1968–70; Premier, Treasurer, 1970–79; Minister for Develt and Mines, 1970–76, for Ethnic Affairs, 1976–79. Dir of Tourism, Victoria, 1982–83; Chm., Victorian Tourism Commn, 1983–86; Dep. Chm., Alpine Resorts Commn, 1983–86; Mem. Bd, Victorian Econ. Develt Corp., 1983–86. Nat. Pres., 1982–87, Chm., 1987–91, Australian Freedom from Hunger Campaign; President: Mus. of Chinese Aust. History, 1984–86; Movement for Democracy in Fiji, 1987–; Chairman: Chinatown Statutory Cttee, 1983–86; Mandela Foundn, 1987–93; Jam Factory Craft Workshops, 1990–94. Author and presenter, TV series, Australia: a personal view, 1981. DUniv Flinders, 1991. *Publications:* Don Dunstan's Cookbook, 1976; Don Dunstan's Australia, 1978; Felicia: the political memoirs of Don Dunstan, 1981; Australia: a personal view, 1981. *Address:* 15 Clara Street, Norwood, SA 5067, Australia.

DUNSTAN, Lt-Gen. Sir Donald (Beaumont), AC 1991; KBE 1980 (CBE 1969; MBE 1954); CB 1972; Governor of South Australia, 1982–91; *b* 18 Feb. 1923; *s* of late Oscar Reginald Dunstan and Eileen Dunstan; *m* 1948, Beryl June Dunningham; two *s*. *Educ:* Prince Alfred Coll., South Australia; RMC, Duntroon. Served War of 1939–45: Regimental and Staff appts in SW Pacific Area, 1942–45. Served in Korea, 1954; Instructor: RMC Duntroon, 1955–56, 1963; Staff Coll., Queenscliff, 1958; Staff Coll., Camberley, 1959–60; Dep. Comdr 1 Task Force, Vietnam, 1968–69; Comdr, 10th Task Force, Holsworthy, NSW, 1969; idc 1970; Commander Aust. Force, Vietnam, 1971; Chief of Materiel, 1972–74; GOC Field Force Comd, 1974–77; CGS, 1977–82. KStJ 1982. *Recreations:* golf, fishing. *Address:* 52 Martin Court, West Lakes, SA 5021, Australia. *Clubs:* Australian (Sydney); Royal Sydney Golf, Royal Adelaide Golf.

DUNSTAN, Rev. Prof. Gordon Reginald, CBE 1989; F. D. Maurice Professor of Moral and Social Theology, King's College, London, 1967–82, now Emeritus; Honorary Research Fellow, University of Exeter, since 1982; Chaplain to the Queen, 1976–87; *b* 25 April 1917; *yr s* of late Frederick John Menhennet and Winifred Amy Dunstan (*née* Orchard); *m* 1949, Ruby Maud (*née* Fitzer); two *s* one *d*. *Educ:* Plymouth Corp. Gram. Sch.; University of Leeds; College of the Resurrection, Mirfield. BA, 1st cl. Hist., 1938, Rutson Post-Grad. Schol. 1938, MA w dist. 1939, Leeds Univ.; FSA 1957; FKC 1974. Deacon 1941, priest 1942; Curate, King Cross, Halifax, 1941–45; Huddersfield, 1945–46; Sub Warden, St Deiniol's Library, Hawarden, 1945–49; Vicar of Sutton Courtney with Appleford, 1949–55; Lecturer, Wm Temple Coll., 1947–49; Ripon Hall, Oxford, 1953–55; Minor Canon, St George's Chapel, Windsor Castle, 1955–59; Westminster Abbey, 1959–67; Canon Theologian, Leicester Cathedral, 1966–82, Canon Emeritus, 1982–. Sec., C of E Council for Social Work, 1955–63; Sec., Church Assembly Jt Bd of Studies, 1963–66; Editor of Crucible, 1962–66; Editor of Theology, 1965–75; Dep. Priest in Ordinary to the Queen, 1959–64, Priest in Ordinary, 1964–76; Select Preacher: University of Cambridge 1960, 1977; Leeds, 1970; Hulsean Preacher, 1977. Lectures: Prideaux, Univ. of Exeter, 1968; Moorhouse, Melbourne, 1973; Stephenson, Sheffield, 1980. Gresham's Prof. in Divinity, City Univ., 1969–71. Consultant, Lambeth Conf., 1988. Mem. Council, Canterbury and York Soc., 1950–85 (Vice-Pres., 1985–). Mem. or Sec. cttees on social and ethical problems; Vice-Pres., 1965–66, and Chm. Brit. Cttee, of Internat. Union of Family Organizations, 1964–66; Vice-Pres., London Medical Gp and Inst. of Medical Ethics, 1985–; Pres., Tavistock Inst. of Med. Psychology, 1991–; Member: Adv. Gp on Transplant Policy, Dept of Health, 1969; Council of Tavistock Inst. of Human Relations (Vice-Pres., 1977–82), and Inst. of Marital Studies, 1969–88; Adv. Gp on Arms Control and Disarmament, FCO, 1970–74; Adv. Cttee on Animal Experiments, Home Office, 1975–89; Council, Advertising Standards Auth., 1981–93; MRC/RCOG Voluntary Licensing Authority, 1985–91; Cttee on Ethics of Gene Therapy, DoH, 1989–93; Nuffield Council on Bioethics, 1991–95. Hon. FRSM 1985; Hon. MRCP 1987; FRCOG *ad eundem* 1991; Hon. FRCGP 1993; Hon. FRCP 1995. Pres., Devon and Cornwall Record Soc., 1984–87; Vice-Pres., UFAW, 1985–. Hon. DD Exeter, 1973; Hon. LLD Leicester, 1986. *Publications:* The Family Is Not Broken, 1962; The Register of Edmund Lacy, Bishop of Exeter 1420–1455, 5 vols, 1963–72; A Digger Still, 1968; Not Yet the Epitaph, 1968; The Sacred Ministry, 1970; The Artifice of Ethics, 1974; A Moralist in the City, 1974; (ed) Duty and Discernment, 1975; (ed with M. J. Seller) Consent in Medicine, 1983; (ed with M. J. Seller) The Status of the Human Embryo: perspectives from moral tradition, 1988; (ed with D. Callahan) Biomedical Ethics: an Anglo-American dialogue, 1988; (ed with E. A. Shinebourne) Doctors' Decisions: ethical conflicts in medical practice, 1989; (ed) The Human Embryo: Aristotle and the Arabic and European Traditions, 1990. *Recreations:* small islands, *domus* and *rus*. *Address:* 9 Maryfield Avenue, Pennsylvania, Exeter EX4 6JN. *T:* Exeter (01392) 214691.

DUNSTAN, Ivan, PhD; CChem, FRSC; Director-General International, British Standards Institution, 1991–93; *b* 27 Aug. 1930; *s* of Edward Ernest and Sarah Kathleen Dunstan; *m* 1955, Monica Jane (*née* Phillips); two *s* one *d*. *Educ:* Falmouth Grammar Sch.; Bristol Univ. (BSc). Joined Scientific Civil Service, working at Explosives Research and Development Estabt, Waltham Abbey, 1954; became Supt of Gen. Chemistry Div., 1967; Warren Spring Laboratory (DTI) as Dep. Dir (Resources), 1972–74; Dir, Materials Quality Assurance, MoD (PE), 1974–79; Dir, Bldg Res. Estabt, DoE, 1979–83; Standards Dir, 1983–86, Dir-Gen., 1986–91, BSI. Chm., UK Nat. Forum for Quality Policy and Conformity Assessment, 1993–. President: RILEM, 1988; European Standards Organ, 1990; European Orgn for Testing and Certification, 1990–92; Vice-Pres., Inst. of Quality Assurance, 1988; Mem., British Bd of Agrément, 1987. CIMgt (CBIM 1986). *Recreations:* golf, badminton, gardening. *Address:* 6 High Oaks Road, Welwyn Garden City, Herts AL8 7BH. *T:* Welwyn Garden (01707) 322272. *Club:* Athenæum.

DUNSTER, (Herbert) John, CB 1979; consultant in radiation protection; *b* 27 July 1922; *s* of Herbert and Olive Grace Dunster; *m* 1945, Rosemary Elizabeth, *d* of P. J. Gallagher; one *s* three *d*. *Educ:* University Coll. Sch.; Imperial College of Science and Technology (ARCS, BSc). FSRP 1988. Scientist, UK Atomic Energy Authority, 1946–71; Asst Dir, Nat. Radiological Protection Bd, 1971–76; Dep. Dir Gen., HSE, 1976–82; Dir, NRPB, 1982–87. Member: Internat. Commn on Radiological Protection, 1977–; Sci. and Tech. Cttee, Euratom, 1982–93; Sci. Adv. Cttee, IAEA, 1982–87. *Publications:* numerous papers in technical jls. *Recreations:* music, photography. *Address:* 142 Andrewes House, Barbican, EC2Y 8BA.

DUNT, Vice Adm. John Hugh, CEng, FIEE; Deputy Chief of Defence Staff (Systems), Ministry of Defence, since 1995; *b* 14 Aug. 1944; *s* of Harris Hugh Dunt and Margaret Rea Dunt (*née* Morgan); *m* 1972, Alynne Margaret Wood; two *d*. *Educ:* Duke of York Sch., Nairobi; RNEC Manadon (BScEng). Joined RN at BRNC Dartmouth, 1963; served in HM Ships Kent, Ajax, Dundas, Collingwood, Nubian; MoD (PE); Staff, C-in-C Fleet, 1980; Naval Operational Requirements, 1980–82; HMS Invincible, 1982–84; Staff Weapon Engr Officer to FO Sea Training, 1984; Naval Staff Duties, 1985–87; RCDS 1988; Higher Command and Staff Course, Camberley, 1989; Captain, HMS Defiance, 1989–90; Dir, Defence Systems, MoD, 1991–93; Dir, Gen. Fleet Support (Ops and Plans), 1993–95. Gov., Royal Naval Sch., Haslemere, 1992–. *Publications:* articles in naval and professional jls. *Recreations:* sport (cricket, squash), gardening, travel. *Address:* Ministry of Defence, Main Building, Whitehall, SW1A 2HB. *Clubs:* MCC; Royal Navy Cricket (Pres.).

DUNTZE, Sir Daniel (Evans), 8th Bt *cr* 1774, of Tiverton, Devon; graphics art consultant; *b* 4 April 1926; *s* of George Douglas Duntze (*d* 1946) and of Mabel Lillian, *d* of Daniel Evans; *S* cousin, 1987; *m* 1954, Marietta Welsh; one *s* two *d*. *Educ:* Washington Univ. Sch. of Fine Arts, St Louis, Mo. Served in US Army Air Force, World War II. *Heir: s* Daniel Evans Duntze, *b* 11 Aug. 1960. *Address:* 8049 Gannon Avenue, University City, Missouri 63130, USA.

But his name does not, at time of going to press, appear on the Official Roll of Baronets.

DUNWICH, Viscount; Robert Keith Rous; *b* 17 Nov. 1961; *s* and *heir* of Earl of Stradbroke, *qv*.

DUNWICH, Bishop Suffragan of, since 1995; **Rt Rev. Timothy John Stevens;** *b* 31 Dec. 1946; *s* of Ralph and Jean Ursula Stevens; *m* 1973, Wendi Kathleen; one *s* one *d*. *Educ:* Chigwell Sch.; Selwyn Coll., Cambridge (BA 1968; MA 1972); Ripon Hall, Oxford (DipTh). BOAC, 1968–72; FCO, 1972–73. Ordained priest, 1976; Curate, East Ham, 1976–79; Team Vicar, Upton Park, 1979–80; Team Rector, Canvey Island, 1980–88; Bp of Chelmsford's Urban Officer, 1988–91; Archdeacon of West Ham, 1991–95. Hon. Canon of Chelmsford, 1987–95. *Recreations:* golf, cricket. *Address:* The Old Vicarage, Stowupland, Stowmarket, Suffolk IP14 4BQ. *T:* Stowmarket (01449) 678234, *Fax:* (01449) 771148.

DUNWOODY, Gwyneth (Patricia); MP (Lab) Crewe and Nantwich, since 1983 (Crewe, Feb. 1974–1983); *b* 12 Dec. 1930; *d* of late Morgan Phillips and Baroness Phillips; *m* 1954, Dr John Elliott Orr Dunwoody, *qv* (marr. diss. 1975); two *s* one *d*. MP (Lab) Exeter, 1966–70; Parly Sec. to BoT, 1967–70; Mem., European Parlt, 1975–79; Front Bench Spokesman on Foreign Affairs, 1980, on Health Service, 1980–83, on Transport, 1984–85; Parly Campaign Co-ordinator, 1983–84; Member: Labour Party NEC, 1981–88; Chairmen's Panel, 1992–. Pres., Labour Friends of Israel, 1993– (Chm., 1988–93); Vice-Pres., Socialist Internat. Women, 1986–92. Dir, Film Production Assoc. of GB, 1970–74. *Address:* c/o House of Commons, SW1A 0AA.

DUNWOODY, Dr John (Elliott Orr), CBE 1986; general practitioner; Chairman, Bloomsbury District Health Authority, 1982–90; *b* 3 June 1929; *s* of Dr W. O. and late Mrs F. J. Dunwoody; *m* 1st, 1954, Gwyneth Patricia (*née* Phillips), *qv* (marr. diss. 1975); two *s* one *d*; 2nd, 1979, Evelyn Louise (*née* Borner). *Educ:* St Paul's Sch.; King's Coll., London Univ.; Westminster Hosp. Med. Sch. MB, BS London; MRCS, LRCP 1954. House Surgeon, Westminster (Gordon) Hosp., 1954; House Physician, Royal Berks Hosp., 1954–55; Sen. House Physician, Newton Abbot Hosp., 1955–56; Family Doctor and Medical Officer, Totnes District Hosp, 1956–66; MO, Staff Health Service, St George's Hosp., 1976–77. MP (Lab) Falmouth and Camborne, 1966–70; Parly Under-Sec., Dept of Health and Social Security, 1969–70. Vice-Chm., 1974–77, Chm., 1977–82, Kensington, Chelsea and Westminster AHA (T). Member: Exec. Cttee, British Council, 1967–69; Council, Westminster Med. Sch., 1974–82; (co-opted) Social Services Cttee, Westminster City Council, 1975–78; Nat. Exec. Council, FPA, 1979–87 (Dep. Chm., 1980, Chm., 1981–87). Council Mem., UCL, 1982–90. Hon. Dir, Action on Smoking and Health, 1971–73. Governor, Pimlico Sch., 1972–75. *Publication:* (jtly) A Birth Control Plan for Britain, 1972. *Recreations:* travel, cooking. *Address:* 9 Cautley Avenue, SW4 9HX. *T:* 0181–673 7471.

DUNWOODY, (Thomas) Richard, MBE 1993; National Hunt jockey; Vice-President, Jockeys' Association, since 1993; *b* 19 Jan. 1964; *s* of George Rutherford and Gillian Margaret Dunwoody; *m* 1988, Carol Ann Abraham. *Educ:* Rendcomb Coll., Glos. Wins include: Grand National, on West Tip, 1986, on Miinnehoma, 1994; Cheltenham Gold Cup, on Charter Party, 1988; Champion Hurdle, on Kribensis, 1990; Breeders' Cup Steeplechase, on Highland Bud, 1989 and 1992; Champion National Hunt Jockey, 1992–93 and 1993–94. *Publications:* (with Marcus Armytage) Hell for Leather, 1993; (with S. Magee) Duel, 1994. *Recreations:* squash, golf. *Address:* Hyperion House, Sparsholt, Wantage, Oxon OX12 9PU.

DUNWORTH, John Vernon, CB 1969; CBE 1955; President, International Committee of Weights and Measures, Sèvres, France, 1975–85; *b* 24 Feb. 1917; *o c* of late John Dunworth and Susan Ida (*née* Warburton); *m* 1967, Patricia Noel Boston; one *d*. *Educ:* Manchester Grammar Sch.; Clare Coll., Cambridge; Denman Baynes Research Studentship, 1937, Robins Prize, 1937; MA, PhD; Twisden Studentship and Fellowship, Trinity Coll., 1941. War Service: Ministry of Supply on Radar Development, 1939–44; National Research Council of Canada, on Atomic Energy Development, 1944–45. Univ. Demonstrator in Physics, Cambridge, 1945. Joined Atomic Energy Research Establishment, Harwell, 1947; Dir, NPL, 1964–76. Alternate United Kingdom Member on Organising Cttee of UN Atoms for Peace Confs in Geneva, 1955 and 1958. Pres., 1975–85, Vice-Pres., 1968–75, Internat. Cttee of Weights and Measures; Mem., Manx Communications Commn, 1985–. Fellow Amer. Nuclear Soc. 1960. Chm., British Nuclear Energy Soc., 1964–70; Vice-President, Institute of Physics: Physical Soc., 1966–70. CEng 1966. Comdr (with Star), Order of Alfonso X el Sabio, Spain, 1960. *Address:* The Warbuck, Kirk Michael, Isle of Man IM6 1AR. *T:* Kirk Michael (IOM) (01624) 878359. *Club:* Athenæum.

DU PLESSIS, Barend Jacobus; Minister of Finance, Republic of South Africa, 1984–92; MP (National Party) Florida, 1974–92; Leader of National Party of Transvaal, 1989–92; *b* 19 Jan. 1940; *s* of late Jan Hendrik and of Martha J. W. (*née* Botha); *m* 1962, Antoinette (*née* Van Den Berg); three *s* one *d*. *Educ:* Potchefstroom Univ. for Christian Higher Educn (BSc); Potchefstroom Teachers' Trng Coll. (THED). Mathematics Teacher, Hoër Seunskool Helpmekaar, Johannesburg and Johannesburg Technical Coll., 1962; Engineering Div., Data Processing and Admin. Sec., SABC, 1962–68; Systems Engineering and Marketing in Banking and Finance, IBM (SA), 1968–74. Dep. Minister of Foreign Affairs and Information, 1982; Minister of Educn and Trng, 1983.

du PLESSIS, Prof. Daniel Jacob, FRCS; Vice-Chancellor and Principal, University of the Witwatersrand, 1978–83; *b* 17 May 1918; *s* of D. J. du Plessis and L. du Plessis (*née* Carstens); *m* 1946, Louisa Susanna Wicht; two *s*. *Educ:* Univ. of Cape Town (MB ChB 1941); Hon. MD, 1986; Hon. Fellow, Smuts Hall, 1986); Univ. of the Witwatersrand (ChM 1951). Served, SA Medical Corps, 1942–46. Postgraduate study, 1947–51; Surgeon and Lectr, Univ. of Cape Town, 1952–58; Prof. of Surgery, Univ. of the Witwatersrand, 1958–77 (Hon. LLD, 1984). Trustee, S African Blood Transfusion Service, 1985–. Dir, Transvaal Bd, Provincial Bldg Soc., 1984–91. Pres., S Transvaal Br., Medical Assoc. of S Africa, 1986–87; Chairman of Council: B. G. Alexander Nursing Coll., 1985–95; Bonalesedi (formerly Natalspruit) Nursing Coll., 1985–92; Member: Council, Med. Univ. of Southern Africa, 1986–95; Adv. Council for Univs and Technikons, 1984–92; Council, Johannesburg Coll. of Educn, 1984–92; Council, Univ. of Transkei, 1989–94. Governor, Amer. Coll. of Surgeons, 1988–94. Hon. FACS 1974; Hon. Fellow: Assoc. of Surgeons of GB and Ireland, 1979; Amer. Surgical Assoc., 1981; Hon. FCSSA 1982. Hon. Life Vice-President: Assoc. of Surgeons of S Africa; Surgical Res. Soc. of Southern Africa. Paul Harris Fellowship, Rotary Club, Orange Grove, Johannesburg, 1984. Hon. Mem., Alpha Omega Alpha Honor Med. Soc. (USA), 1986. Hon. DSc Med. Univ. of Southern Africa, 1995. Order for Meritorious Service Cl. 1 (Gold), RSA, 1989. *Publications:* Principles of Surgery, 1968, 2nd edn 1976; Synopsis of Surgical Anatomy, 10th edn (with A. Lee McGregor) 1969, 11th edn 1975, 12th edn (with G. A. G. Decker) 1986; numerous articles in learned jls on surgical topics, espec. on diseases of parotid salivary gland and gastric ulcers. *Address:* 17 Chateau Road, Richmond, Johannesburg, 2092, South Africa.

DUPPLIN, Viscount; Charles William Harley Hay, MA; barrister; Underwriter, Hiscox Syndicates (formerly Roberts & Hiscox) Ltd, since 1990; *b* 20 Dec. 1962; *s* and *heir* of 15th Earl of Kinnoull, *qv*. *Educ:* Summer Fields; Eton; Christ Church, Oxford (Scholar); City Univ. (Dip. in Law); Inns of Court Sch. of Law. Called to the Bar, Middle Temple, 1990. Associate, Credit Suisse First Boston Ltd, 1985–88. Lieut, Atholl Highlanders, 1993–. Trustee, Royal Caledonian Ball, 1992–. *Publication:* contrib. Jl of Chem. Soc. *Recreations:* cricket, Cresta Run, skiing, philately. *Address:* 59 Scarsdale Villas, W8 6PU. *T:* 0171–938 4265; Pitkindie House, Abernyte, Perthshire PH14 9RE. *T:* Inchture (01828) 686342. *Clubs:* White's, Turf, MCC; Royal Perth (Perth).

DUPRE, Sir Tumun, Kt 1993; MBE 1987; President, South Wahgi Local Government Council, Papua New Guinea, 1967–88 and 1990–93 (Councillor, 1988–90); *b* 1923; *s* of Awil Dupre and Dop Amban Ai; *m* 1st, Abamp; 2nd, Kawil; 3rd, Danamp; 4th, Muru; 5th, Wai; thirteen *s* two *d*. *Educ:* no formal schooling. Government interpreter, 1948–63; Luluai (people's representative, apptd by govt), 1956–63. PNG Independence Medal, 1975; 10th Anniversary Medal, 1985; Provincial Medal, 1988. *Recreation:* village life. *Address:* c/o South Wahgi Local Government Council, Post Office Box, Minj, Papua New Guinea. *T:* 565512.

DUPREE, Sir Peter, 5th Bt *cr* 1921; *b* 20 Feb. 1924; *s* of Sir Victor Dupree, 4th Bt and of Margaret Cross; *S* father, 1976; *m* 1947, Joan, *d* of late Captain James Desborough Hunt. *Heir: cousin* Thomas William James David Dupree, *b* 5 Feb. 1930. *Address:* 15 Hayes Close, Chelmsford, Essex CM2 0RN.

DURAND, Sir Edward (Alan Christopher David Percy), 5th Bt *cr* 1892, of Ruckley Grange, Salop; student; *b* 21 Feb. 1974; *s* of Rev. Sir (Henry Mortimer) Dickon (Marion St George) Durand, 4th Bt and of Stella Evelyn Durand (*née* L'Estrange); *S* father, 1993. *Educ:* St Columba's Coll., Dublin; Milltown Inst., Dublin. *Recreations:* music, surfing. *Heir: b* David Michael Dickon Percy Durand, *b* 6 June 1978. *Address:* Lisnalurg House, Sligo, Eire. *T:* (71) 45819.

DURANT, Sir Anthony; *see* Durant, Sir R. A. B.

DURANT, John Robert, PhD; Assistant Director (Head of Science Communication (formerly Research and Information)), Science Museum, since 1989; Professor of Public Understanding of Science, Imperial College, London, since 1993; *b* 8 July 1950; *s* of Kenneth Albert James Durant and Edna Kathleen Durant (*née* Norman); *m* 1977, Nirmala Naidoo; two *s* one *d*. *Educ:* Queens' College, Cambridge (MA Nat. Scis; PhD Hist. of Sci.). Staff Tutor in Biological Scis, Dept of Extramural Studies, UC Swansea, 1976–82; Staff Tutor in Biol Scis, Dept for External Studies, Univ. of Oxford, 1983–89. Vis. Prof. of History and Public Understanding of Science, Imperial College London, 1989–93. *Publications:* (ed) Darwinism and Divinity, 1985; (with P. Klopfer and S. Oyama) Aggression: conflict in animals and humans reconsidered, 1988; (ed) Museums and Public Understanding of Science, 1992; articles in professional jls. *Recreations:* family, writing, broadcasting. *Address:* Science Museum Library, South Kensington, SW7 5NH. *T:* 0171–938 8201, *Fax:* 0171–938 8213. *Club:* Athenæum.

DURANT, Sir (Robert) Anthony (Bevis), Kt 1991; MP (C) Reading West, since 1983 (Reading North, Feb. 1974–1983); *b* 9 Jan. 1928; *s* of Captain Robert Michael Durant and Mrs Violet Dorothy Durant (*née* Bevis); *m* 1958, Audrey Stoddart; two *s* one *d*. *Educ:* Dane Court Prep. Sch., Pyrford, Woking; Bryanston Sch., Blandford, Dorset. Royal Navy, 1945–47. Coutts Bank, Strand, 1947–52; Cons. Party Organisation, 1952–67 (Young Cons. Organiser, Yorks; Cons. Agent, Clapham; Nat. Organiser, Young Conservatives). PPS to Sec. of State for Transport and to Sec. of State for Employment, 1983–84; Asst Govt Whip, 1984–86; a Lord Comr of HM Treasury, 1986–88; Vice-Chamberlain of HM Household, 1988–90. Member: Select Cttee Parly Comr (Ombudsman), 1973–83, 1990–93; Select Cttee on Members' Interests, 1993–; Exec., 1922 Cttee, 1990–; Chairman: All Party Gp on Widows and One Parent Families, 1977–85; All Party Gp on Inland Waterways, 1992–; Cons. Nat. Local Govt Adv. Cttee, 1981–84; Backbench Envmt Cttee, 1991–; All Party Gp on Film Industry, 1991–; Vice-Chm., Parly Gp for World Govt, 1979–84. Mem., UK delegn to Council of Europe, 1992–; Chm., British Br., CPA, 1988–90; Mem., Council of Europe, 1981–83. Former Consultant: The Film Production Association of Great Britain Ltd; Delta Electrical Div. of Delta Metal Co. Ltd; Allied Industrial Designers. Mem., Inland Waterways Adv. Council, 1975–84. Dir, British Industrial Scientific Film Assoc., 1967–70; Mem. Bd of Govs, BFI, 1992–. *Recreations:* boating, golf. *Address:* House of Commons, SW1A 0AA.

DURANTE, Viviana; Principal Dancer, Royal Ballet Company, since 1989; *b* Italy, 8 May 1967. *Educ:* Royal Ballet School. Came to England in 1977; first major rôle, Swan Lake, Covent Garden, 1988; rôles include Manon, Ondine, La Bayadère, Giselle, Kitri (in Don Quixote), Aurora, Cinderella. Evening Standard Award, 1989. *Address:* Royal Ballet Company, Royal Opera House, Covent Garden, WC2E 9DD.

DURÃO BARROSO, José Manuel; MP (PSD) Viseu, since 1987 (Lisbon, 1985–87); Minister for Foreign Affairs, Portugal, since 1992; *b* 23 March 1956; *s* of Luis Barroso and Marie Elisabete Durão; *m* Marie Margaride Pinto Riberio de Souse Uve Barroso; three *s*. *Educ:* Univ. of Lisbon (LLD Hons 1978); Univ. of Geneva (Master in Pol Sci. 1981); European Univ. Inst., Univ. of Geneva (Dip.). Lecturer: Faculty of Law, Lisbon Univ.; Pol Sci. Dept, Geneva Univ.; Vis. Scholar, Univ. of Georgetown, Washington. Ed., Revista de Ciência Política. Secretary of State for: Home Affairs; Foreign Affairs and Co-operation. Mem., Nat. Council, PSD. Scholarship Fellow: Swiss Confedn; CEC; Volkswagenwerk Foundn; NATO; Swiss Nat. Fund for Scientific Res. *Publications:* (jtly) Governmental System and Party System, 1980; Le Système Politique Portugais face à l'Intégration Européenne, 1983; Política de Cooperacão, 1990; contrib. to collective works, encyclopaedias and internat. scientific jls. *Address:* Ministry for Foreign Affairs, Lisbon, Portugal.

DURAS, Marguerite; French author and playwright; *b* Gia Dinh, Indochina; *d* of Henri Donnadieu and Marie (*née* Legrand). *Educ:* Lycée de Saigon; Faculté de droit de Paris; Ecole libre des sciences politiques. Sec., Colonies Ministry, 1935–41. *Screenplays:* also directed: Hiroshima, mon Amour, 1960; Jaune le soleil, 1971; India Song, 1973; Nathalie Granger, 1973; La femme du Gange, 1974; Aurélia Steiner, 1979; L'homme assis dans le couloir, 1980; L'homme atlantique, 1981; Agatha et les lectures illimitées, 1981; Dialogue de Rome, 1982; Les Enfants, 1985; directed and appeared in Le Camion, 1977. Grand Prix du théâtre de l'Académie Française, 1983. *Publications:* Les Impudents, 1943; La vie tranquille, 1944; Un barrage contre le Pacifique, 1950; Le marin de Gibraltar, 1952; Les petits chevaux de Tarquinia, 1953; Des journées entières dans les arbres (short stories), 1954 (Prix Jean Cocteau) (adapted for stage, 1964); Le square, 1955; Moderato Cantabile, 1958; Les viaducs de la Seine-et-Oise, 1960; Dix heures et demi du soir en été, 1960 (filmed, 1967); L'après-midi de Monsieur Andesmas, 1962; Le ravissement de Lol V. Stein, 1964; L'amante anglaise, 1967; Détruire, dit-elle, 1969 (filmed), 1970 (also dir)); L'amour, 1972; L'été 80, 1980; Outside, 1981; La Maladie de la mort, 1983; L'amant, 1984 (Prix Goncourt; Ritz Paris Hemingway Award, 1986; filmed); La douleur (short stories), 1985; Les yeux bleus cheveux noirs, 1986; La Pute de la côte normande, 1986; Practicalities, 1990; Summer Rain, 1992; Yann Andrea Steiner, 1994; *plays:* Les eaux et les forêts, 1965; Théâtre I, le vice-consul, 1965; Théâtre II (5 plays), 1968; Susanna Andler, 1969; Yes, Peut-être, 1976; Abahn Sabana David, 1976; La Musica, 1976; Baxter Vera Baxter, 1977; L'Eden cinéma, 1977. *Address:* 5 rue le Benoît, 75006 Paris, France.

DURBIN, Prof. James; Professor of Statistics, University of London (London School of Economics), 1961–88, now Emeritus; *b* 30 June 1923; *m* 1958, Anne Dearnley Outhwaite; two *s* one *d*. *Educ:* Wade Deacon GS, Widnes; St John's Coll., Cambridge. Army Operational Research Group, 1943–45. Boot and Shoe Trade Research Assoc., 1945–47; Dept of Applied Economics, Cambridge, 1948–49; Asst Lectr, then Lecturer, in Statistics, London Sch. of Economics, 1950–53; Reader in Statistics, 1953–61. Visiting Professor: Univ. of North Carolina, 1959–60; Stanford Univ., 1960; Johns Hopkins Univ., 1965–66; Univ. of Washington, 1966; ANU, 1970–71; Univ. of Calif, Berkeley, 1971; Univ. of Cape Town, 1978; UCLA, 1984; Univ. of Calif, Santa Barbara, 1989; Nat. Univ. of Singapore, 1989–90; Univ. of Trento, Italy, 1991; Ohio State Univ., 1993. Research Fellow: US Bureau of the Census, 1992; Statistics Canada, 1994. Member: ESRC, 1983–86 (Chm., Res. Resources and Methods Cttee, 1982–85); Internat. Statistical Inst., 1955 (Pres., 1983–85); Bd of Dirs, Amer. Statistical Assoc., 1980–82 (Fellow, 1960); Fellow, Inst. of Mathematical Statistics, 1958; Fellow, Econometric Soc., 1967; Royal Statistical Society: Vice Pres., 1969–70 and 1972–73; Pres. 1986–87; Guy Medal in Bronze, 1966, in Silver, 1976. *Publications:* Distribution Theory for Tests based on the Sample Distribution Function, 1973; articles in statistical journals, incl. Biometrika, Jl of Royal Statistical Society, etc. *Recreations:* skiing, mountain walking, travel, opera, theatre. *Address:* 31 Southway, NW11 6RX. *T:* 0181–458 3037.

DURBIN, Leslie, CBE 1976; MVO 1943; silversmith; *b* 21 Feb. 1913; *s* of late Harry Durbin and of Lillian A. Durbin; *m* 1940, Phyllis Ethel Durbin (*see* Phyllis E. Ginger); one *s* one *d*. *Educ:* Central Sch. of Arts and Crafts, London. Apprenticed to late Omar Ramsden, 1929–39; full-time schol., 1938–39, travelling schol., 1939–40, both awarded by Worshipful Co. of Goldsmiths. Started working on own account in workshop of Francis Adam, 1940–41. RAF, Allied Central Interpretation Unit, 1941–45. Wkg partnership with Leonard Moss, 1945–75. Commissioned by Jt Cttee of Assay Offices of GB to design Silver Jubilee Hall Mark; designed regional variants of pound coin for Royal Mint, 1983. Retrospective exhibn, Leslie Durbin, 50 years of Silversmithing, Goldsmiths' Hall, 1982. Hon. LLD Cambridge, 1963. Council of Industrial Design Awards for Silver for the 70's. MVO awarded for work on Stalingrad Sword.

DURBRIDGE, Francis (Henry); playwright and author; *b* 25 Nov. 1912; *s* of late Francis and Gertrude Durbridge; *m* 1940, Norah Elizabeth Lawley; two *s*. *Educ:* Bradford Grammar Sch.; Wylde Green Coll.; Birmingham Univ. After period in stockbroker's office, began to write (as always intended); short stories and plays for BBC; many subseq. radio plays, including Promotion, 1933; created character of Paul Temple. Entered Television with The Broken Horseshoe, 1952 (the first adult television serial); other serials followed; Portrait of Alison, 1954; My Friend Charles, 1955; The Other Man, 1956; The Scarf 1960; The World of Tim Frazer (Exec. Prod.), 1960–61; Melissa, 1962; Bat Out of Hell, 1964; Stupid Like a Fox, 1971; The Doll, 1976; Breakaway, 1980. The television serials have been presented in many languages, and are continuing; novels, based on them, have been published in USA, Europe, etc. The European Broadcasting Union asked for a radio serial for an internat. market (La Boutique, 1967, broadcast in various countries); German, French and Italian productions, 1971–72. Films include two for Korda and Romulus, 1954–57. Stage plays: Suddenly at Home, 1971; The Gentle Hook, 1974; Murder With Love, 1976; House Guest, 1980; Nightcap, 1983; Murder Diary, 1986; A Touch of Fear, 1987; The Small Hours, 1989; Sweet Revenge, 1991. *Publications:* include contribs to newspapers and magazines, at home and abroad. *Recreations:* family, reading, travel. *Address:* c/o Harvey Unna and Stephen Durbridge Ltd, 24 Pottery Lane, Holland Park, W11 4LZ. *Club:* Royal Automobile.

DURHAM, 6th Earl of, *cr* 1833; Baron Durham, 1828; Viscount Lambton, 1833; peerages disclaimed, 1970; *see under* Lambton.

DURHAM, Baron; a subsidiary title of Earldom of Durham (disclaimed 1970), used by Hon. Edward Richard Lambton, *b* 19 Oct. 1961, *heir* to disclaimed Earldom.

DURHAM, Bishop of, since 1994; **Rt. Rev. Michael Turnbull;** *b* 27 Dec. 1935; *s* of George Ernest Turnbull and Adeline Turnbull (*née* Awty); *m* 1963, Brenda Susan Merchant; one *s* two *d*. *Educ:* Ilkley Grammar Sch.; Keble Coll., Oxford (MA); St John's Coll., Durham (DipTh). Deacon, 1960; priest, 1961; Curate: Middleton, 1960–61; Luton, 1961–65; Domestic Chaplain to Archibishop of York, 1965–69; Rector of Heslington and Chaplain, York Univ., 1969–76; Chief Secretary, Church Army, 1976–84; Archdeacon of Rochester, also Canon Residentiary of Rochester Cathedral and Chm., Dio. Bd for Mission and Unity, 1984–88; Bishop of Rochester, 1988–94. Mem., General Synod, C of E, 1970–75, 1987–; Vice-Chm., Central Bd of Finance, C of E, 1990–; Member: Bd, Church Commissioners, 1989–; Archbps' Commn on Cathedrals, 1992–; Chm., Archbps' Commn on orgn of C of E, 1994–. Chm., Coll. of Preachers, 1990–. Examining Chaplain to Bishop of Norwich, 1982–84. *Publications:* (contrib.) Unity: the next step?, 1972; God's Front Line, 1979; Parish Evangelism, 1980; Learning to Pray, 1981. *Recreations:* cricket, family life. *Address:* Auckland Castle, Bishop Auckland, Co. Durham DL14 7NR. *T:* Bishop Auckland (01388) 602576. *Clubs:* Athenæum, MCC.

DURHAM, Dean of; *see* Arnold, Very Rev. J. R.

DURHAM, Archdeacon of; *see* Hodgson, Ven. J. D.

DURHAM, Sir Kenneth, Kt 1985; Chairman: Unilever, 1982–86; Kingfisher (formerly Woolworth Holdings) plc, 1986–90 (non-executive Deputy Chairman, 1985–86); Deputy Chairman, British Aerospace, 1986–90 (Board Member, 1980–90); *b* 28 July 1924; *s* of late George Durham and Bertha (*née* Aspin); *m* 1946, Irene Markham; one *s* one *d*. *Educ:* Queen Elizabeth Grammar Sch., Blackburn; Univ. of Manchester (Hatfield Schol.; BSc Hons, Physics). Flight Lieut, RAF, 1942–46. ARE, Harwell, 1950; Unilever: joined Res. Lab., Port Sunlight, 1950, Head of Lab., 1961; Head, Res. Lab., Colworth, Bedford, 1965; assumed responsibility for animal feed interests, 1970; Chm., BOCM Silcock Ltd, 1971; Dir, Unilever Ltd, 1974, Vice-Chm., 1978; Dir, Unilever NV, 1974–86. Board Mem., Delta PLC, 1984–; Dir, Morgan Grenfell Hldgs, 1986–90. Chairman: Food, Drink and Packaging Machinery EDC, NEDO, 1981–86; Trade Policy Res. Centre, 1982–89; Industry and Commerce Liaison Cttee, Royal Jubilee Trusts, 1982–87; Economic and Financial Policy Cttee, CBI, 1983–86; Priorities Bd for Govt Agricl Depts and AFRC, 1984–87; Member: British-N America Cttee, 1982–87; British Shippers Council, 1982–86; Bd, British Exec. Service Overseas, 1982–86; Adv. Cttee, CVCP, 1984–; Governing Body, ICC UK, 1984–88; ACARD, 1984–86; European Adv. Council, NY Stock Exchange, 1985–; Council for Industry and Higher Educn, 1985–; Adv. Panel, Science Policy Res. Unit, Sussex Univ., 1985–; Adv. Bd, Industrial Res. Labs, Durham Univ., 1985–; President: ABCC, 1986–87; BAAS, 1986–87. Attended Harvard Advanced Management Program, 1962; Member: Council, PSI, 1978–85; Council, Royal Free Hosp. Sch. of Med., 1984–. Vice-President: Liverpool Sch. of Tropical Medicine, 1982–; Opportunities for the Disabled, 1982–88; Help the Aged, 1986–; Trustee: Leverhulme Trust, 1974–; Civic Trust, 1982–. Governor, NIESR, 1983–. CIMgt (CBIM 1978); FIGD 1983. Hon. LLD Manchester, 1984; Hon. DSc Loughborough, 1984; QUB. Comdr, Order of Orange Nassau (Netherlands), 1985. *Publications:* Surface Activity and Detergency, 1960; various scientific papers. *Recreations:* walking, golf. *Club:* Athenæum.

DURHAM HALL, Jonathan David; QC 1995; a Recorder, since 1995; *b* 2 June 1952; *s* of Peter David Hall and Muriel Ann Hall, Sheffield; *m* 1973, Patricia Helen Bychowski, *d* of Stefan Bychowski, Whitehaven; one *s* one *d*. *Educ:* King Edward VII Sch., Sheffield; Nottingham Univ. (LLB Hons). Called to the Bar, Gray's Inn, 1975; joined North Eastern Circuit, 1976: Junior, 1982; Cryer, 1990–95; Asst Recorder, 1991–95. Mem., Bar Council, 1994–95. *Recreations:* the creation and preservation of woodland, Roman Britain, the plays of Shakespeare, ski-ing. *Address:* Old Bank House, Hartshead, Sheffield S1 2EL. *T:* Sheffield (0114) 275 1223. *Clubs:* Kandahar; Ski of Great Britain.

DURIE, Sir Alexander (Charles), Kt 1977; CBE 1973; Vice-President, The Automobile Association, since 1977 (Director-General, 1964–77); *b* 15 July 1915; *er s* of late Charles and Margaret Durie (*née* Gardner), Shepton Mallet, Somerset; *m* 1941, Joyce, *o c* of late Lionel and Helen Hargreaves (*née* Hirst), Leeds and Bridlington, Yorks; one *s* one *d*. *Educ:* Queen's Coll., Taunton. Joined Shell-Mex and BP Ltd, 1933. Served War of 1939–45, Royal Artillery; Gunnery Staff Course (IG), 1941; Lieut-Col 1945. Dir Shell Co. of Australia Ltd, 1954–56; Dir, 1962, Man. Dir, 1963–64, Shell-Mex and BP Ltd; Director: Mercantile Credit Co. Ltd, 1973–80; Thomas Cook Group Ltd, 1974–79; Private Patients Plan Ltd, 1977–87 (a Vice-Pres., 1987–); H. Clarkson (Holdings) Ltd, 1978–85; Chelsea Building Soc., 1979–87. Mem. Council, Motor and Cycle Trades Benevolent Fund, 1959–73; Vice-Pres. British Assoc. of Industrial Editors, 1959–71; Gen. Commissioner of Income Tax, 1960–85; Member Govt Inquiries into: Civilianisation of Armed Forces, 1964; Cars for Cities, 1964; Road Haulage Operators' Licensing, 1978. FBIM, 1959, Council Mem., 1962–73, Chm. Exec. Cttee, 1962–65, Vice-Chm. Council, 1962–67, Chm., Bd of Fellows, 1970–73 (Verulam Medal 1973); Member: Nat. Road Safety Adv. Council, 1965–68; Adv. Council on Road Res., 1965–68; Brit. Road Fedn Ltd, 1962– (Vice-Pres., 1978); Council, Internat. Road Fedn Ltd, London, 1962–64; Marketing Cttee, BTA, 1970–77; Adv. Cttee on Traffic and Safety, TRRL, 1973–77; Vice-Pres., Alliance Internationale de Tourisme, 1965–71, Pres., 1971–77; Chm., Indep. Schs Careers Orgn, 1969–73 (Vice-Pres., 1973–); Governor: Ashridge Coll., 1963–78 (Vice Pres., 1978–93); Queen's Coll., Taunton, 1969–83. Chm. Council, Imperial Soc. of Knights Bachelor, 1986–88 (Mem., 1978–); Pres., Surrey CCC, 1984–85 (Mem. Cttee, 1970–80; Vice-Pres., 1980–84, 1985–); Vice-Pres., Hampshire CCC, 1984–. Freeman of City of London and Liveryman, Worshipful Co. of Paviors, 1965. FCIT; Hon. FInstHE 1969. Spanish Order of Touristic Merit Silver Medal, 1977. *Recreations:* cricket, golf, racing. *Address:* The Garden House, Windlesham, Surrey GU20 6AD. *T:* Bagshot (01276) 472035. *Clubs:* MCC; Royal and Ancient; Berkshire Golf.

DURIE, David Robert Campbell, CMG 1995; Deputy Secretary, Regional and Small Firms, Department of Trade and Industry, since 1995; *b* 21 Aug. 1944; *s* of Frederick Robert Edwin Durie and Joan Elizabeth Campbell Durie (*née* Learoyd); *m* 1966, Susan Frances Weller; three *d*. *Educ:* Fettes Coll., Edinburgh; Christ Church, Oxford (MA Physics). Asst Principal, 1966, Pvte Sec. to Perm. Sec., 1970, Min. of Technology; Principal, DTI, 1971; First Sec., UK Delegn to OECD, 1974; Dept of Prices and Consumer Protection, 1977; Asst Sec., 1978; Dept of Trade, 1979; Cabinet Office, 1982; DTI, 1984; Under Sec., 1985–91; Dep. Sec., 1991; Minister and Dep. UK Perm. Rep. to EC/EU, Brussels, 1991–95. *Recreations:* moderately strenuous outdoor exercise, theatre, family. *Address:* c/o Department of Trade and Industry, 1 Victoria Street, SW1.
See also Maj.-Gen. I. G. C. Durie.

DURIE, Maj. Gen. Ian Geoffrey Campbell, CBE 1991 (OBE 1987); Director, Royal Artillery, 1994–April 1996; *b* 21 Aug. 1944; *s* of Frederick Robert Edwin Durie and Joan Elizabeth Campbell Durie (*née* Learoyd); *m* 1968, Carolyn Jane Whitehead; one *d*. *Educ:* Fettes Coll., Edinburgh; RMA, Sandhurst; St John's Coll., Cambridge (MA Mech. Sci.). Commnd, RA; Adjt, 27 Field Regt, RA, 1973; sc 1974; Battery Comd, 29 Commando Regt, RA, 1979; SO1 Plans, Falklands Is, 1984; CO, 29 Commando Regt, RA, 1984; Instr, Staff Coll., 1987; Chief Instr, Tactics, Royal Sch. of Artillery, 1988; Commander: RA 1st Armd Div., 1989; RA 1st (UK) Armd Div. Artillery Gp, Op. Desert Sabre (Gulf War), 1991; rcds, 1992; Dir, Land Warfare, 1992. *Recreations:* Church and Christian societies, golf (just started), orienteering (nearly finished), garden, fishing, family. *Address:* (until April 1996) HQ Royal Artillery, Larkhill, Salisbury, Wilts SP4 8QT; (from April 1996) c/o Bank of Scotland, 44 Court Street, Haddington, East Lothian EH41 3NP. *Club:* Army and Navy.
See also D. R. C. Durie.

DURIE, Thomas Peter, MBE 1958; GM 1951; Chairman, United Bristol Healthcare NHS Trust, 1991–94; *b* 1 Jan. 1926; *s* of Col Thomas Edwin Durie, DSO, MC, late RA and Madeleine Louise Durie; *m* 1st, 1952, Pamela Mary Bowlby (*d* 1982); one *s* one *d*; 2nd, 1983, Constance Christina Mary Linton. *Educ:* Fettes Coll.; Queen's Univ., Belfast. Commissioned RA 1945, served with RHA and Airborne Forces, India, Palestine, Cyprus, BAOR; Lt Col Directing Staff, Staff Coll., Camberley; retired 1964; Courage Ltd, 1964–86 (Main Bd Dir and Group Asst Man. Dir, 1974); Chm., Bristol & Weston DHA, 1986–90. University of Bristol: Mem. Court and Council, 1982–; Chm., Buildings Cttee, 1992–; Pro-Chancellor, 1994–. Master, Soc. of Merchant Venturers, 1988–89. DL Avon, 1992. *Recreations:* gardening, music, ski-ing, tennis. *Address:* Gatesgarth, Wrington, Avon BS18 7QA. *Club:* Army and Navy.

DURKIN, Air Marshal Sir Herbert, KBE 1976; CB 1973; MA; CEng, FIEE, FRAeS; Controller of Engineering and Supply (RAF), 1976–78; *b* 31 March 1922; *s* of Herbert and Helen Durkin, Burnley, Lancs; *m* 1951, Dorothy Hope, *d* of Walter Taylor Johnson, Burnley; one *s* two *d*. *Educ:* Burnley Grammar Sch.; Emmanuel Coll., Cambridge (MA). Commissioned into Tech. Br., RAF, Oct. 1941. Served War, with No 60 Gp, until 1945. India, 1945–47, becoming ADC to AOC-in-C India; Central Bomber Estabt, 1947–50; Sqdn Ldr, 1950; Atomic Weapons Research Estabt, 1950–52; RAF Staff Coll., 1953; Chief Signals Officer, AHQ, Iraq, 1954–56; Wing Comdr, Chief Instr of Signals Div. of RAF Tech. Coll., 1956–58; Air Ministry, 1958–60; jssc, 1961; HQ, 2 ATAF, 1961–63; Gp Capt 1962; Sen. Tech. Staff Officer, HQ Signals Command, 1964–65; Comdt, No 2 Sch. of Tech. Trg, Cosford, 1965–67; Air Cdre, 1967; Director of Eng (Policy), MoD, 1967–69; IDC, 1970; AOC No 90 Group, RAF, 1971–73; Dir-Gen. Engineering and Supply Management, 1973–76. Pres., IEE, 1980 (Dep. Pres., 1979). Pres., Assoc. of Lancastrians in London, 1988–90. Freeman, City of London, 1988. *Recreation:* golf. *Address:* Willowbank, Drakes Drive, Northwood, Middlesex HA6 2SL. *T:* Northwood (01923) 823167. *Club:* Royal Air Force.

DURLACHER, Nicholas John, CBE 1995; Director, London International Financial Futures and Options Exchange, since 1984 (Chairman, 1992–95); *b* 20 March 1946; *s* of late John Sidney Durlacher, MC and of Alma Gabrielle (*née* Adams); *m* 1971, Mary Caroline Mclaren; one *s*. *Educ:* Stowe; Magdalene Coll., Cambridge (BA Econs). Mem., Stock Exchange, 1970–; Partner, Wedd Durlacher, 1972–86; Director: BZW Ltd, 1986–; BZW Futures, 1986–. Director: Securities Futures Authy, 1987–; Investor's Compensation Scheme, 1992–. *Recreations:* ski-ing, shooting, golf, tennis. *Address:* 10 Rutland Street, SW7 1EH. *Clubs:* White's, City of London; Hawks.

DURMAN, David John; Editor-in-Chief, IPC Magazines, since 1994; *b* 10 July 1948, *s* of late John Durman and of Joan Durman; *m* 1973, Hilary Pamela Aldrick. *Educ:* Leeds Univ. (BA). Editor, Woman, 1988–94; Dep. Editor, Woman's Own, 1992–94. *Recreations:* reading, theatre, life. *Address:* IPC Magazines, Stamford Street, SE1 9LS. *T:* 0171–261 6401.

DURR, Kent Skelton; Chairman: Fuel-Tech NV, since 1995; Clean Diesel Technologies, Inc., since 1995; *b* 28 March 1941; *s* of Dr John Michael Durr and Diana (*née* Skelton); *m* 1966, Suzanne Wiese; one *s* two *d*. *Educ:* South African Coll. Schs; Cape Town Univ. Dir, family publishing co., 1966–68; Founder and later Man. Dir, Durr Estates, 1968–84. Elected to Provincial Council of Cape, 1974; MP for Maitland, SA, 1977–91; Dep. Minister, Trade and Industry, 1984–86, Finance, 1984–88; Minister of Budget and Public Works in Ministers' Council, 1988–89; Cabinet Minister of Trade and Industry and Tourism, 1989–91; S African Ambassador to UK, 1991–94; High Comr for S Africa in London, 1994–95. Mem., SA Nat. Foundn for Conservation of Coastal Birds, 1985 (Award of Honour, 1987). Freeman: City of London, 1995; Vintners' Co., 1995. *Publications:* numerous articles in newspapers and jls on econs, foreign affairs, constitutional affairs, urban renewal, conservation and real estate. *Recreations:* history, country pursuits, field sports, mountaineering, conservation. *Address:* (office) 28a Cadogan Square, SW1X 0JH. *Clubs:* Royal Automobile; City and Civil Service, Kelvin Grove (Cape Town, SA).

DURRANDS, Prof. Kenneth James, CBE 1992; DGS (Birm), MSc, CEng, FIMechE, FIEE; Vice-Chancellor and Rector, University of Huddersfield, 1992–95 (Rector, The Polytechnic, Huddersfield, 1970–92; Professor, 1985); *b* 24 June 1929; *s* of A. I. Durrands, Croxton Kerrial; *m* 1956 (marr. diss. 1971), one *s*; *m* 1983, Jennifer Jones; one *s*. *Educ:* King's Sch., Grantham; Nottingham Technical Coll.; Birmingham Univ. Min. of Supply Engrg Apprentice, ROF, Nottingham, 1947–52; Techn. Engr, UKAEA, Risley, 1954–58; Lecturer in Mechanical and Nuclear Engrg, Univ. of Birmingham, 1958–61; Head of Gen. Engrg Dept, Reactor Engrg Lab., UKAEA, Risley, 1961–67; Technical Dir, Vickers Ltd, Barrow Engrg Works, 1967–70. Vis. Lectr, Manchester Univ., 1962–68. Member: DoI Educn and Training Cttee, 1973–75 (Chm., 1975–80); DoI Garment & Allied Industries Requirements Bd, 1975–79 (Chm. Computer Cttee, 1975–79); BEC Educn Cttee, 1975–79; BEC Business Studies Bd, 1976–79; Inter-Univ. and Polytech. Council, 1978–81; Yorks Consumers' Cttee, Office of Electricity Regulation, 1990–; British Council: Higher Educn Cttee, 1981–91; Engrg and Technology Adv. Cttee, 1981–90; Cttee, CICHE, 1985–; Council for the Accreditation of Teacher Educn, 1991–92; Hon. Sec./Treas., Cttee of Dirs of Polytechnics, 1970–79. Educn Comr, MSC, subseq. Training Commn, 1986–89. Mem. Council, IMechE, 1963–66. Preliminary Judge, Prince of Wales Award for Industrial Innovation and Production, 1982–. Member, Court: Leeds Univ., 1970–; Bradford Univ., 1973–. *Publications:* technical and policy papers. *Recreations:* gardening, squash rackets. *Address:* Church Cottage, Croxton Kerrial, Grantham, Lincolnshire NG32 1PY. *Club:* Athenæum.

DURRANT, Anthony Harrisson; His Honour Judge Durrant; a Circuit Judge, since 1991; *b* 3 Jan. 1931; *s* of Frank Baston Durrant and Irene Maud Durrant; *m* 1956, Jacqueline Ostroumoff; one *s* two *d*. *Educ:* Sir Joseph Williamson Mathematical Sch., Rochester. Admitted Solicitor, 1956; Partner, 1960, Sen. Partner, 1976–91, Horwood & James, Aylesbury; a Recorder, 1987–91. Dep. Chm., Agricl Land Tribunal, 1987–91.

Pres., Berks, Bucks and Oxon Incorp. Law Soc., 1977–78; Chm., Berks, Bucks and Oxon Jt Consultative Cttee of Barristers and Solicitors, 1985–91. *Recreations:* reading, boating. *Club:* Phyllis Court (Henley).

DURRANT, Jennifer Ann, RA 1994; painter; part-time Lecturer: Royal College of Art, since 1979; Royal Academy Schools, since 1991; *b* 17 June 1942; *d* of Caleb John Durrant and Winifred May (*née* Wright); *m* 1964, William Alistair Herriot Henderson (marr. diss. 1976). *Educ:* Varndean Grammar Sch. for Girls, Brighton; Brighton Coll. of Art; Slade Sch. of Fine Art; University Coll. London (Dip. Fine Art). FRCA 1993. Postgrad. Scholar, Slade Sch. of Fine Art, 1965–66. Artist in Residence, Somerville Coll., Oxford, 1979–80. *Solo exhibitions* include: Arnolfini Gall., Bristol, 1979; Mus. of Modern Art, Oxford, 1980; Nicola Jacobs Gall., London, 1982 and 1983; Serpentine Gall., 1987; Concourse Gall., Barbican, 1992; Salander-O'Reilly Galls, NY, 1993; *group exhibitions* include: Hayward Gall., 1976, 1979, 1980 and 1990; Mus. of Fine Art, Boston, Mass and Royal Acad., 1977; Salander-O'Reilly Galls, NY, 1981; Tate Gall. and Carnegie Inst., Pittsburgh, 1982; Serpentine Gall., 1983 and 1984; Royal Acad., 1985; Mall Galls, London, 1990–92; also in provincial galls in UK, and in Europe; has exhibited at Royal Acad. Summer Exhibn, 1986, 1987 and annually, 1989–; *works in public collections* including: Arts Council, British Council; Contemporary Art Soc.; Mus. of Fine Arts, Boston, Mass; Tate Gall.; Govt Art Collection; Neue Galerie, Aachen; *commissions:* Newham Hosp.; R. P. Scherer 50th Anniv., Swindon, 1987; Thomas Neal, Covent Gdn, 1992; Glaxo UK, Stevenage, 1994. Arts Council Award, 1976; Arts Council Major Award, 1978; Gtr London Arts Assoc. Award, 1980; Athena Art Award, 1988. *Recreations:* classical music, opera, archaeology, museums, painting and sculpture, looking at nature. *Address:* 9–10 Holly Grove, SE15 5DF. *T:* 0171-639 6424.

DURRANT, Sir William Alexander Estridge, 8th Bt *cr* 1784, of Scottow, Norfolk; *b* 26 Nov. 1929; *o s* of Sir William Henry Estridge Durrant, 7th Bt and Georgina Beryl Gwendoline (*d* 1968), *d* of Alexander Purse; *S* father, 1994; *m* 1953, Dorothy, *d* of Ronal Croker, Quirindi, NSW; one *s* one *d*. *Heir: s* David Alexander Durrant, *b* 1 July 1960. *Address:* Red Hill, Nundle Road, Nemingha, NSW 2340, Australia.

DURWARD, (Alan) Scott; Director, 1985–91, and Group Chief Executive, 1989–91, Alliance & Leicester Building Society; Chairman, Girobank Plc, 1990–91; *b* 30 Aug. 1935; *o c* of late Prof. Archibald Durward, MD and Dorothy Durward; *m* 1962, Helen Gourlay; two *s*. *Educ:* Stowe; St John's Coll., Cambridge (MA). Imperial Tobacco Co. Ltd, 1958–65; Rowntree & Co. Ltd, 1965–67; Cheltenham & Gloucester Bldg Soc., 1967–75; Leicester Building Society: Dep. Gen. Man., 1975–77; Gen. Man., 1977–81; Dir and Chief Gen. Man., 1981–85; merger with Alliance Bldg Soc. to form Alliance & Leicester Bldg Soc., 1985; Jt Chief Gen. Manager, 1985–86; Chief Gen. Manager, 1986–89. Chm., Midland Assoc. of Bldg Socs, 1984–85; Member: Council, Bldg Socs Assoc., 1981–85 and 1987–91; Council, Eur. Fedn of Bldg Socs, 1987–91. Underwriting Mem. of Lloyd's. Director: Gourlay Properties, 1985–; John Laing plc, 1987–89; Mem. Bd, BR (London Midland), 1990–92. Dir, Leics Ambulance and Paramedic Service NHS Trust, 1993–. Chm., Peterborough Diocesan Bd of Finance, 1993–. Mem. Council, Loughborough Univ. of Technology, 1984– (Treas., 1991–). *Recreations:* tennis, fishing. *Address:* The Old House, Medbourne, Market Harborough, Leics LE16 8DX.

DUTHIE, Prof. Sir Herbert Livingston, Kt 1987; MD; FRCS, FRCSEd; Provost of the University of Wales College of Medicine (formerly the Welsh National School of Medicine, University of Wales), 1979–94; *b* 9 Oct. 1929; *s* of Herbert William Duthie and Margaret McFarlane Livingston; *m* 1959, Maureen McCann; three *s* one *d*. *Educ:* Whitehill Sch., Glasgow; Univ. of Glasgow (MB, ChB 1952; MD Hons 1962; ChM Hons 1959). FRCSEd 1956; FRCS 1957. Served RAMC, 1954–56. Sen. House Officer, Registrar, and Lectr in Surgery, Western Infirmary, Glasgow, 1956–59; Rockefeller Travelling Fellow, Mayo Clinic, Rochester, Minn, USA, 1959–60; Lectr in Surg., Univ. of Glasgow, 1960–61; Sen. Lectr in Surg., Univ. of Leeds, 1961–63, Reader, 1964; Prof. of Surg., Univ. of Sheffield, 1964–79 (Dean, Faculty of Medicine, 1976–78). Mem., S Glam HA, 1980–94. Chm., Med. Adv. Cttee, CVCP, 1992–93. President: Surgical Res. Soc., 1978–80; Assoc. of Surgeons of GB and Ireland, 1989–90; Member: GMC, 1976– (Treas., 1981–94); Welsh Med. Cttee, 1980–94. Hon. LLD Sheffield, 1990. *Publications:* articles on gastroenterological topics. *Address:* St Curig, Windsor Road, Radyr, Cardiff CF4 8BQ. *T:* Cardiff (01222) 843472. *Club:* Army and Navy.

DUTHIE, Prof. Robert Buchan, CBE 1984; MA Oxon, MB, ChM; FRCSE, FRCS; Nuffield Professor of Orthopædic Surgery, Oxford University, 1966–92, now Emeritus; Professorial Fellow, Worcester College, Oxford, 1966–92, now Emeritus Fellow; Surgeon, Nuffield Orthopædic Centre, Oxford, 1966–92; Civilian Consultant Adviser in Orthopaedic Surgery to Royal Navy, since 1978; *b* 4 May 1925; 2nd *s* of late James Andrew Duthie and late Elizabeth Jean Duthie, Edinburgh; *m* 1956, Alison Ann Macpherson Kittermaster, MA; two *s* two *d*. *Educ:* Aberdeen Grammar Sch.; King Edward VI Gram. Sch., Chelmsford; Heriot-Watt Coll., Edinburgh; University of Edinburgh Med. Sch. Robert Jones Prize 1947, MB, ChB 1948, ChM (with dist.) (Gold Medal for Thesis) 1956, University of Edinburgh; FRCSE 1953; Hon. FACS 1987. Ho. Surg. Royal Infirmary, 1948–49; Ho. Phys., Western Gen. Hosp., Edinburgh, 1949. Active service in Malaya, RAMC, 1949–51. Registrar, Royal Infirmary, Edinburgh, 1951–53; David Wilkie Res. Schol. of University of Edinburgh, 1953; Res. Fellow of Scottish Hosps Endowment Research Trust, Edinburgh, 1953–56; Res. Fellow, Nat. Cancer Inst., Bethesda, USA, 1956–57; Extern. Mem. of MRC in Inst. of Orthopædics, London and Sen. Registrar, 1957–58; Prof. of Orthopædic Surg., University of Rochester Sch. of Medicine and Dentistry and Orthopædic Surg.-in-Chief, University of Rochester Med. Centre, 1958–66. Consultant Adviser in Orthopaedics and Accident Surgery to DHSS, 1971–80. Mem., Royal Commn on Civil Liability and Compensation for Personal Injury, 1973–78; Chairman: Adv. Cttee of Res. in Artificial Limbs and Appliances, DHSS, 1975; Working Party on Orthopaedic Services to Sec. of State for Social Services, 1980–81. Governor, Oxford Sch. for Boys, 1967–91 (Chm., 1986–91). Fellow Brit. Orthopædic Assoc. (Pres., 1983–84); Pres., Internat. Soc. of Research in Orthopaedics and Trauma, 1987–90; Member: Internat. Soc. for Orthopædic Surgery and Traumatology; Orthopædic Research Soc.; Inter-urban Orthopædic Club: Internat. Orthopædic Club. Amer. Rheumatism Assoc.; Hon. Member: Portuguese Soc. of Orthopaedic Surgery and Traumatology; Japanese Orthopaedic Assoc.; Corresponding Member: Assoc. of Orthopaedic Surgery and Traumatology, Yugoslavia; German Soc. of Orthopaedics and Traumatology; Hon. Fellow, Austrian Traumatology Assoc. Hon. DSc Rochester, NY, 1982. President's Prize, Soc. Internat. de Chirurgie, 1957. Commander, SMO, Malta. *Publications:* (co-author) Textbook of Orthopædic Surgery, 7th edn, 1982; contribs to med. and surg. jls relating to genetics, histochemistry, transplantation, pathology, neoplasia of musculo-skeletal tissues, and clinical subjects. *Recreations:* writing, stained glass. *Address:* Barna Brow, Harberton Mead, Headington, Oxford OX3 0DB. *T:* Oxford (01865) 62745.

DUTHIE, Sir Robert Grieve, (Sir Robin), Kt 1987; CBE 1978; CA; Chairman: Tay Residential Investment Ltd, since 1989; Neill Clerk Group plc; Vice Chairman, Advisory Board for Scotland, British Petroleum, since 1990; *b* 2 Oct. 1928; *s* of George Duthie and Mary (*née* Lyle); *m* 1955, Violetta Noel Maclean; two *s* one *d*. *Educ:* Greenock Academy. Apprentice Chartered Accountant with Thomson Jackson Gourlay & Taylor, CA, 1946–51 (CA 1952); joined Blacks of Greenock, 1952: Man. Dir, 1962; Chairman: Black & Edgington Ltd, 1972–83; Insight Internat. Tours Ltd, 1979–94; Bruntons (Musselburgh), 1984–86; Britoil, 1988–90; Director: British Assets Trust, 1977–; Royal Bank of Scotland, 1978–; Investors Capital Trust, 1985–94; Carclo Engineering Gp, 1986–; British Polythene Industries (formerly Scott & Robinson), 1989–; Devol Engineering Ltd, 1994–. Chm., Greenock Provident Bank, 1974; Dir, Greenock Chamber of Commerce, 1967–68; Tax Liaison Officer for Scotland, CBI, 1976–79. Chm., SDA, 1979–88; Member: Scottish Telecommunications Bd, 1972–77; E Kilbride Develt Corp., 1976–78; Clyde Port Authority, 1971–83 (Chm., 1977–80); Council, Inst. of Chartered Accountants of Scotland, 1973–78; Scottish Econ. Council, 1980–; Council, Strathclyde Business Sch., 1986–; Governing Council, Scottish Business in the Community, 1987–. Chm., Made Up Textiles Assoc. of GB, 1972; Pres., Inverkip Soc., 1966; Mem. of Council, Royal Caledonian Curling Club, 1985–88. Commissioner: Queen Victoria Sch., Dunblane, 1972–89; Scottish Congregational Ministers Pension Fund, 1973–; Treasurer, Nelson Street Evangelical Union Congregational Church, Greenock, 1970–. Fellow, Scottish Vocational Council, 1988. CIMgt (CBIM 1976); FRSA 1983. Hon. FRIAS, 1989. Hon. Fellow, Paisley Coll., 1990. Hon. LLD Strathclyde, 1984; Hon. DTech Napier Coll., 1989. *Recreations:* curling, golf. *Address:* Fairhaven, Finnart Street, Greenock PA16 8JA. *T:* Greenock (01475) 722642. *Club:* Greenock Imperial (Greenock).

DUTTON, Maj.-Gen. Bryan Hawkins; CBE 1990 (OBE 1984; MBE 1978); Commander British Forces, Hong Kong, since 1994; *b* 1 March 1943; *s* of late Ralph Dutton and Honor Badcoe (formerly Dutton, *née* Morris); *m* 1972, Angela Margaret Wilson; one *s* one *d*. *Educ:* Lord Weymouth Sch.; RMA Sandhurst. Commissioned, Devonshire and Dorset Regt, 1963; served NI, British Guiana, Libya, Belize, Germany, UK; Instructor, Sch. of Infantry, 1969–71; RMCS and Staff Coll., 1974–75; C-in-C's Mission to Soviet Forces in Germany, 1976–78; Co. Comdr, 1st Devonshire and Dorset, 1978–79 (despatches 1979); Planning Staff, NI Office, 1979–81; Instructor, Staff Coll., 1981–82; MA to Adjutant-Gen., 1982–84; CO 1st Bn Devonshire and Dorset Regt, 1984–87; Ops Staff, UKLF, 1987; Comdr 39 Infantry Brigade, 1987–89; Dir, Public Relations (Army), 1990–92; Dir of Infantry, 1992–94. *Recreations:* offshore sailing, fishing, wild-life, Rugby spectator, history, classical music. *Address:* c/o Barclays Bank, 32 Market Place, Warminster, Wilts. *Club:* Army and Navy.

DUTTON, James Macfarlane; HM Diplomatic Service, retired; *b* 3 June 1922; *s* of late H. St J. Dutton and Mrs E. B. Dutton; *m* 1958, Jean Mary McAvoy; one *s*. *Educ:* Winchester Coll.; Balliol Coll., Oxford. Dominions Office, 1944–46; Private Sec. to Permanent Under Sec., 1945; Dublin, 1946–48; CRO, 1948–50; Asst Private Sec. to Sec. of State, 1948; 2nd Sec., New Delhi, 1950–53; CRO, 1953–55; 1st Sec., Dacca and Karachi, 1955–58, Canberra, 1958–62; Head of Constitutional and Protocol Dept, CRO, 1963–65; Canadian Nat. Defence Coll., 1965–66; Dep. High Comr and Counsellor (Commercial), Colombo, 1966–70; Head of Rhodesia Econ. Dept, FCO, 1970–72; attached CSD, 1972–73; seconded to: British Electrical & Allied Manufacturers Assoc. (Dir, Overseas Affairs), 1973–74; Wilton Park and European Discussion Centre, 1974–75; Consul-Gen., Gothenburg, 1975–78. *Recreations:* golf, trout-fishing. *Address:* Cockerhurst, Tyrrells Wood, Leatherhead, Surrey KT22 8QH.

DUTTON, Prof. Peter Leslie, FRS 1990; Professor of Biochemistry and Biophysics, since 1981, and Director, Johnson Foundation for Molecular Biophysics, since 1991, University of Pennsylvania; *b* 12 March 1941; *s* of Arthur Bramwell Dutton and Mary Dutton; *m* 1965, Dr Julia R. Dwyer; two *s* one *d*. *Educ:* Univ. of Wales (BSc Hons Chem.; PhD Biochem.). PD Fellow, Dept of Biochem. and Soil Science, Univ. of Wales, 1967–68; University of Pennsylvania: PD Fellow, 1968–71, Asst Prof., 1971–76, Johnson Res. Foundn; Associate Prof., Dept of Biochem. and Biophysics, 1976–81; Hon. MA 1976. *Recreations:* painting (several one-man and group shows in Wales and USA), sailing. *Address:* B501 Richards Building, 37th and Hamilton Walk, University of Pennsylvania, Philadelphia, PA 19104, USA; 654 West Rose Tree Road, Media, PA 19063, USA. *T:* (215) 5650863, *Fax:* (215) 8980465. *Clubs:* Mantoloking Yacht (NJ); Corinthian Yacht (Philadelphia).

DUTTON, Reginald David Ley; *b* 20 Aug. 1916; *m* 1951, Pamela Jean (*née* Harrison); two *s* one *d*. *Educ:* Magdalen Coll. Sch., Oxford. Joined OUP; subseq. joined leading British advertising agency, London Press Exchange (now Lopex plc), 1937. During War of 1939–45 served in Royal Navy. Returned to agency after his service; there, he worked on many of major accounts; Dir, 1954; Man. Dir and Chief Exec., 1964–71; Chm., 1971–76; retired 1976. Pres. Inst. Practitioners in Advertising, 1969–71; Chm., Jt Ind. Council for TV Advertising Research, 1973–75; Mem. Council, BIM, 1970–74; FIPA 1960. Councillor, Canterbury CC, 1976–77. *Recreations:* fishing, amateur radio. *Address:* Butts Fold, Stalham Road, Hoveton, Norwich NR12 8DU. *T:* Norwich (01603) 783145.

DUVAL, Sir (Charles) Gaetan, Kt 1981; QC 1975; barrister; Deputy Prime Minister, 1983–88, and Minister of Employment and Tourism, 1986–88, Mauritius; *b* 9 Oct. 1930. *Educ:* Royal Coll., Curepipe; Faculty of Law, Univ. of Paris. Called to the Bar, Lincoln's Inn. Entered politics, 1958; Member: Town Council, Curepipe, 1960, re-elected 1963 (Chm., 1960–61, 1963–68); Legislative Council, Curepipe, 1960, re-elected, 1963; Municipal Council, Port Louis, 1969 (Mayor, 1969–71; Lord Mayor, 1971–74, 1981); Minister of Housing, 1964–65; Leader, Parti Mauritien Social Démocrate, 1966–; first MLA for Grand River NW and Port-Louis West, 1967; Minister of External Affairs, Tourism and Emigration, 1969–73; Leader of Opposition, 1973–76, 1982; Minister of Justice, 1983–86. Comdr, Legion of Honour, France, 1973; Grand Officer, Order of the Lion, Senegal, 1973. *Address:* Chambers, Place Foch, Port-Louis, Mauritius.

DUVAL, Sir Gaetan; *see* Duval, Sir C. G.

DUXBURY, Air Marshal Sir (John) Barry, KCB 1986; CBE 1981 (MBE 1967); Director and Chief Executive, Society of British Aerospace Companies, since 1990; Secretary, Defence Industries Council, since 1990; *b* 23 Jan. 1934; *s* of Lloyd Duxbury and Hilda Robins; *m* 1954, Joan Leake; one *s*. *Educ:* Lancashire County Grammar Schs. Commnd 1954; served Maritime Sqdns, Aeroplane and Armament Exptl Estab., Canadian Forces Staff Coll., and Central Tactics and Trials Orgn, 1955–70; CO 201 Sqdn, 1971; PSO to CAS, 1971–74; CO RAF St Mawgan, 1976–77; Sec., Chiefs of Staff Cttee, 1978–80; RAF Dir, RCDS, 1982; Air Sec. (RAF), 1983–85; AOC No 18 Gp, RAF, and Comdr Maritime Air Eastern Atlantic and Channel, 1986–89, retd. ADC to the Queen, 1977. FRIN 1989; FRAeS 1992. *Recreations:* painting, photography. *Club:* Royal Air Force.

DUXBURY, Philip Thomas; Chairman, Bradford and Bingley Building Society, 1988–91; *b* 4 Sept. 1928; *s* of Tom Duxbury and Ellen Duxbury (*née* Hargreaves); *m* 1952, Katherine Mary Hagley; three *s*. *Educ:* Bradford Grammar School. Magnet and Southerns plc, 1944–84 (Dir, 1963; Man. Dir, 1975); Dir, Bradford and Bingley Building Soc., 1980–91. *Recreations:* DIY, travel. *Address:* High Court, East Morton, near Keighley BD20 5SE. *T:* Bradford (01274) 564894.

DWEK, Prof. Raymond Allen, DPhil, DSc; CChem, FRSC; Professor of Glycobiology, and Director of Glycobiology Institute (formerly Unit), University of Oxford, since 1988; Professorial Fellow, Exeter College, Oxford, since 1988 (Fellow, 1974–88); *b* 10 Nov. 1941; *s* of Victor Joe Dwek and Alice Liniado; *m* 1964, Sandra (*née* Livingstone); two *s* two *d*. *Educ:* Carmel Coll.; Manchester Univ. (BSc 1st Cl. Hons Chemistry and Mercer Scholar, 1963; MSc 1964); Lincoln Coll., Oxford (DPhil 1966); Exeter Coll., Oxford (DSc 1985). Christ Church, Oxford: Res. Lectr in Physical Chemistry, 1966–68, in Biochem., 1975–76; Lectr in Inorganic Chem., 1968–75; Deptl Demonstrator, 1969–74, Lectr, 1976–88, Biochem. Dept, Oxford; Royal Soc. Locke Res. Fellow, 1974–76; Lectr in Biochem., Trinity Coll., Oxford, 1976–84. Vis. Royal Soc. Res. Fellow, Weizmann Inst., Rehovot, Israel, 1969; Visiting Professor: Duke Univ., NC, seconded to Inst. of Exploratory Res., Fort Monmouth, NJ, 1968; Univ. of Trieste, Italy, 1974; Univ. of Lund, Sweden, 1977; Inst. of Enzymology, Budapest, 1980. Dir and Founding Scientist, Oxford Glycosystems Ltd, 1988–. Member: Oxford Enzyme Gp, 1971–88; MRC AIDS Antiviral Steering Cttee, 1987–89; Founder Mem., Oxford Oligosaccharide Gp, 1983. Mem., editl bds. Wellcome Trust Award, for research in biochemistry related to medicine, 1994. *Publications:* Nuclear Magnetic Resonance (NMR) in Biochemistry, 1973; (jtly) Physical Chemistry Principles and Problems for Biochemists, 1975, 3rd edn 1983; (jtly) NMR in Biology, 1977; (jtly) Biological Spectroscopy, 1984; articles in books and jls on physical chemistry, biochemistry and medicine; various patents. *Recreations:* family, Patent Law, sport, sailing, listening to music. *Address:* Exeter College, Oxford OX1 3DP. *T:* Oxford (01865) 275344; Glycobiology Institute, Department of Biochemistry, University of Oxford, South Parks Road, Oxford OX1 3QU.

DWIGHT, Reginald Kenneth; *see* John, E. H.

DWORKIN, Prof. Gerald; Herbert Smith Professor of European Law and Director, Centre of European Law, King's College, University of London, since 1993; *b* 8 July 1933; *s* of Louis and Rose Dworkin; *m* 1960, Celia Sharon Levin; two *s* one *d*. *Educ:* Raines Grammar Sch., London; Univ. of Nottingham (LLB 1954). Admitted solicitor of Supreme Court, 1957; Asst Lectr, Lectr, then Reader, LSE, 1958–67; Prof. of Law, Univ. of Southampton, 1968–86; Herchel Smith Prof. of Intellectual Property Law, QMW, Univ. of London, 1986–92. Visiting Professor: Univ. of Monash, 1965–67, 1980, 1987; Univ. of NSW, 1975; Nat. Univ. of Singapore, 1985, 1991; Arizona State Univ., 1985. Member: EC Cttee, Academic Experts on Copyright Law; Working Party on Human Tissue, Nuffield Council on Bioethics. Member: Council, Common Law Inst. of Intellectual Property; Brit. Literary and Artistic Copyright Soc.; Law Soc. Sub-cttee on Intellectual Property; Ethical Cttee, RCP. FRSA 1993. Member of Board: Mod. Law Rev.; European Intellectual Property Law Rev.; Intellectual Property Jl. *Publication:* (with R. Taylor) Guide to Copyright Law, 1989. *Address:* Rosebery, 7A Branksome Wood Road, Bournemouth, Dorset BH2 6BT. *T:* Bournemouth (01202) 555522.
See also P. D. Dworkin.

DWORKIN, Paul David, FSS; an Assistant Director, Central Statistical Office, 1989–91; *b* 7 April 1937; *s* of Louis and Rose Dworkin; *m* 1959, Carole Barbara Burke; two *s*. *Educ:* Hackney Downs Grammar Sch., London; LSE (BScEcon 1958). FSS 1969. E Africa High Commn, Dar es Salaam, Tanganyika, 1959; E African Common Services Org., Nairobi, Kenya, 1961; Asst Statistician, BoT, 1962, Stat. 1965; Chief Statistician: DTI, 1972; Dept of Employment, 1977; Under Secretary: Depts of Trade and Industry, 1977–81; Central Statistical Office, 1982–83; Dir of Stats, Dept of Employment, 1983–89. *Recreations:* golf, skiing, theatre. *Club:* Stanmore Golf.
See also G. Dworkin.

DWORKIN, Prof. Ronald Myles, FBA 1979; Professor of Jurisprudence, Oxford University, since 1969; Fellow of University College, Oxford, since 1969; *b* 11 Dec. 1931, *s* of David Dworkin and Madeline Talamo; *m* 1958, Betsy Celia Ross; one *s* one *d*. *Educ:* Harvard Coll.; Oxford Univ.; Harvard Law Sch. Legal Sec. to Judge Learned Hand, 1957–58; Associate, Sullivan & Cromwell, New York, 1958–62; Yale Law School: Associate Prof. of Law, 1962–65; Prof. of Law, 1965–68; Wesley N. Hohfeld Prof. of Jurisprudence, 1968–69. Vis. Prof. of Philosophy, Princeton Univ., 1974–75; Prof. of Law, NY Univ. Law Sch., 1975–; Prof.-at-Large, Cornell Univ., 1976–80; Vis. Prof. of Philosophy and Law, Harvard Univ., 1977, Vis. Prof. of Philosophy, 1979–82. Member: Council, Writers & Scholars Educnl Trust, 1982–; Programme Cttee, Ditchley Foundn, 1982–. Co-Chm., US Democratic Party Abroad, 1972–76. Fellow, Amer. Acad. of Arts and Scis, 1979. Hon. LLD: Williams Coll., 1981; John Jay Coll. of Criminal Justice, 1983; Claremont Coll., 1987; Kalamazoo Coll., 1987. *Publications:* Taking Rights Seriously, 1977; (ed) The Philosophy of Law, 1977; A Matter of Principle, 1985; Law's Empire, 1986; Philosophical Issues in Senile Dementia, 1987; A Bill of Rights for Britain, 1990; Life's Dominion, 1993; several articles in legal and philosophical jls. *Address:* University College, Oxford OX1 4BH. *Club:* Oxford American Democrats (Oxford).

DWYER, Joseph Anthony; Group Chief Executive, George Wimpey plc, since 1991; *b* 20 June 1939. CEng, FICE, FCIOB. Director: Exec. Bd, 1983, Main Bd, 1988, George Wimpey. *Address:* George Wimpey, Hammersmith Grove, W6 7EN. *T:* 0181–748 2000.

DYE, Maj.-Gen. Jack Bertie, CBE 1968 (OBE 1965); MC; Vice Lord-Lieutenant of Suffolk, 1983–94; Director, Volunteers, Territorials and Cadets, 1971–74; Major-General late Royal Norfolk Regiment; *b* 1919. Served War of 1939–45 (MC). Brigadier, 1966; psc. Commanded South Arabian Army, 1966–68; GOC Eastern District, 1969–71. Col Comdt, The Queen's Division, 1970–74; Col, Royal Anglian Regt, 1976–82 (Dep. Col, 1974–76). DL Suffolk, 1979.

DYER, Alexander Patrick; Chief Executive and Deputy Chairman, BOC Group plc, 1993–96; Chairman, Bunzl plc, since 1993; *b* 30 Aug. 1932; *m* 1954, Shirley Shine; one *s* (and one *s* decd). *Educ:* US Military Acad. (BSc Engrg); Harvard Business Sch. (MBA). US Army, 1954–57; Esso Corp., 1959–63; Air Products, 1963–89; Gp Vice Pres., Gases, 1978–87; Exec. Vice Pres., Gas and Equipment, 1987–88; Bd Dir, 1988–89; Man. Dir, Gases, BOC Gp, 1989–93. *Recreations:* golf, skeet. *Address:* 5 Lowndes Court, Lowndes Square, SW1X 9JJ. *T:* 0171–235 4634. *Clubs:* Guards' Polo; Wentworth Golf; Saucon Valley Country; Loblolly Pines Golf; Loblolly Bay Yacht.

DYER, Charles; playwright and novelist; actor-director (as Raymond Dyer); *b* 7 July 1928; *s* of James Sidney Dyer and Florence (*née* Stretton); *m* 1959, Fiona Thomson, actress; three *s*. *Educ:* Queen Elizabeth's Sch., Barnet. *Plays:* Clubs Are Sometimes Trumps, 1948; Who On Earth!, 1951; Turtle in the Soup, 1953; The Jovial Parasite, 1954; Single Ticket Mars, 1955; Time, Murderer, Please, and Poison In Jest, 1956; Wanted—One Body!, 1958; Prelude to Fury, 1959 (also wrote theme music); Rattle of A Simple Man, 1962 (also in Berlin, Paris, NY, Rome and London), 1981, USA, 1985, 1990, Netherlands, 1988, Germany, 1993, Scandinavia, 1993, 1995; Staircase, 1966 (for RSC; also in NY, Paris (1968, 1982, 1986, 1992), Amsterdam, Berlin, Rome, 1988, 1992, Vienna, Brazil, 1992, trans-Germany, 1992–95); Mother Adam, Paris, Berlin, 1970, London, 1971, 1973, NY, 1974; The Loving Allelujah, 1974; Circling Dancers, 1979; Lovers Dancing, 1981, 1983; Futility Rites, 1981; as R. Kraselchik: Red Cabbage and Kings, 1960 (also wrote theme music); *screenplays:* Rattle, 1964; Insurance Italian Style, 1967; Staircase, 1968; Brother Sun and Sister Moon, 1970. Also directed plays for the stage and television. *Acted in: plays:* Worm's Eye View, 1948; Room For Two, 1955; Dry Rot, 1958; *films:* Cuptie Honeymoon, 1947; Britannia Mews, 1949; Road Sense, 1950; Off The Record, 1952; Pickwick Papers, 1952; Dockland Case, 1953; Strange Case of Blondie, 1953; Naval Patrol, 1959; Loneliness of the Long Distance Runner, 1962; Mouse On The Moon, 1962; Knack, 1964; Rattle of A Simple Man, 1964; How I Won The War, 1967; Staircase, 1968; *television:* Charlie in Staircase, BBC, 1986; *television series:* Hugh and I, 1964. *Publications:* (as Charles Dyer): plays: Wanted—One Body!, 1961; Time, Murderer, Please, 1962; Rattle Of A Simple Man, (Fr.) 1963; Staircase, 1966; Mother Adam, 1970; The Loneliness Trilogy, 1972; Hot Godly Wind, 1973; novels: Rattle Of A Simple Man, 1964; Charlie Always Told Harry Almost Everything, 1969 (USA and Europe, 1970); The Rising of our Herbert, 1972. *Recreations:* amateur music and carpentry. *Address:* Old Wob, Austenwood Common, Gerrards Cross, Bucks SL9 8SF.

DYER, Prof. Christopher Charles, PhD; FBA 1995; Professor of Medieval Social History, University of Birmingham, since 1991; *b* 24 Dec. 1944; *s* of Charles James Dyer and Doris Mary Dyer; *m* 1967, Jenifer Ann Dent; one *s* one *d*. *Educ:* Univ. of Birmingham (BA, PhD). Asst Lectr in History, Univ. of Edinburgh, 1967–70; Sen. Lectr and Reader, Univ. of Birmingham, 1970–90. *Publications:* Lords and Peasants in a Changing Society, 1980; Standards of Living in the later Middle Ages, 1989; Everyday Life in Medieval England, 1994. *Address:* School of History, The University, Birmingham B15 2TT. *T:* 0121–414 5741.

DYER, Sir Henry Peter Francis S.; *see* Swinnerton-Dyer.

DYER, Lois Edith, OBE 1984; FCSP; international physiotherapy consultant; *b* 18 March 1925; *d* of Richard Morgan Dyer and Emmeline Agnes (*née* Wells). *Educ:* Middlesex Hospital. FCSP 1986. Variety of posts as physiotherapist in Britain, Southern, Central and North Africa, 1948–71; extensive travel world wide, visiting and lecturing at national and internat. conferences. First Physiotherapist Member, NHS Health Adv. Service, 1971; first Advr in Physiotherapy, DHSS, 1976–85; first non-medical Chm., Chartered Society of Physiotherapy, 1972–75; Founder Mem., Soc. for Res. in Rehabilitation, 1978–; Hon. Life Vice-Pres., S African Soc. of Physiotherapy. Editor-in-Chief, Physiotherapy Practice, 1985–90. *Publications:* Care of the Orthopaedic Patient (jtly), 1977; numerous papers in professional jls. *Recreations:* music, country pursuits, bird watching, bridge, ecology, wildlife, conservation. *Address:* Garden Flat, 6 Belsize Grove, NW3 4UN. *T:* 0171–722 1794.

DYER, Mark; His Honour Judge Dyer; a Circuit Judge, since 1977; *b* 20 Nov. 1928; *er s* of late Maj.-Gen. G. M. Dyer, CBE, DSO, and of Evelyn Mary (*née* List); *m* 1953, Diana, *d* of Sir Percy Lancelot Orde, CIE; two *d*. *Educ:* Ampleforth Coll.; Christ Church, Oxford (MA). 2nd Lieut, Royal Scots Greys, 1948–49; The Westminster Dragoons (2nd CLY) TA, 1950–58, Captain. Called to the Bar, Middle Temple, 1953; Mem., Gen. Council of the Bar, 1965–69. Dep. Chm., Isle of Wight QS, 1971. A Recorder of the Crown Court, 1972–77; Hon. Recorder of Devizes, 1988. Liaison Judge for Wiltshire, 1981. Member: Judicial Studies Bd, 1986–91; Parole Bd, 1992–. Pres., Council of HM Circuit Judges, 1992 (Hon. Sec., 1989–91). *Address:* Swindon Combined Court Centre, The Law Courts, Islington Street, Swindon, Wiltshire SN1 2HG. *Club:* Cavalry and Guards.
See also S. Dyer.

DYER, Simon, CBE 1995; MA; FCA; Director General, Automobile Association, since 1987; *b* 19 Oct. 1939; *s* of late Maj.-Gen. G. M. Dyer, CBE, DSO, and of Evelyn Dyer; *m* 1967, Louise Gay Walsh; two *d*. *Educ:* Ampleforth Coll., Univ. of Paris; Univ. of Oxford (MA Jurisprudence). FCA 1978 (ACA 1967); FIMI 1992 (Vice-Pres., 1992–). Coopers and Lybrand, 1963–67; Automobile Association, 1967–: Dir, 1973; Asst Man. Dir, 1977; Man. Dir, 1983. Member: Exec. Cttee, British Road Fedn, 1987–92; Management Cttee, Alliance Internationale de Tourisme, 1987– (Pres., 1992–95); Council, Inst. of Advanced Motorists, 1989–; Council, CBI, 1989–. Trustee, Nat. Motor Mus., Beaulieu, 1992–. Gov., Queen Mary's Coll., Basingstoke, 1987–93. Freedom, City of London, 1984; Liveryman, Co. of Coachmakers and Coach Harness Makers, 1984– (Mem. Court, 1991–). CIMgt 1989. *Recreations:* gardening, tennis, ski-ing. *Address:* Norfolk House, Priestley Road, Basingstoke, Hants RG24 9NY. *Club:* Cavalry and Guards.
See also M. Dyer.

DYER-SMITH, Rear-Adm. John Edward, CBE 1972; Director-General Aircraft (Naval), Ministry of Defence, 1970–72, retired; *b* 17 Aug. 1918; *s* of Harold E. Dyer-Smith and Emily Sutton; *m* 1940, Kathleen Powell; four *s* one *d*. *Educ:* Devonport High Sch.; RN Engineering Coll.; Imperial Coll. of Science. Served War of 1939–45: Engineer Officer, HMS Prince of Wales, 1940–41; Asst Fleet Engr Officer, Eastern Fleet, 1942–43; HMS Illustrious, 1943. Various MAP and Min. of Aviation appts, 1946–54; Head of Naval Air Dept, RAE, 1957–61; Dir of RN Aircraft/Helicopters, Min. of Aviation, 1961–64; Defence and Naval Attaché, Tokyo, 1965–67; Superintendent, RN Aircraft Yard, Belfast, 1968–70. *Recreations:* wood sculpting, piano, flute. *Address:* Carrer Ample 31, Cala Alcaufar, 07713 Menorca, Baleares. *T:* (9) 71150605.

DYKE; *see* Hart Dyke.

DYKE, Gregory; Chairman and Chief Executive, Pearson Television, since 1995; *b* 20 May 1947; *s* of Joseph and Denise Dyke; two *s* two *d*. *Educ:* Hayes Grammar Sch.; York Univ. (BA Politics). Varied career, 1965–83; Editor in Chief, TV-am, 1983–84; Dir of Programmes, TVS, 1984–87; London Weekend Television: Dir of Progs, 1987–91; Dep. Man. Dir, 1989–90; Man. Dir, subseq. Gp Chief Exec., 1990–94; Chm., GMTV, 1993–94; Director: Channel Four Television, 1988–91; BSkyB, 1995–. Chm., ITV Council., 1991–94. *Recreations:* football, squash, tennis. *Address:* Pearson Television, Teddington Studios, Teddington Lock, Mddx TW11 9NT.

DYKES, David Wilmer, MA, PhD; Director, National Museum of Wales, 1986–89; *b* 18 Dec. 1933; *s* of late Captain David Dykes, OBE and Jenny Dykes; *m* 1967, Margaret Anne George; two *d*. *Educ:* Swansea Grammar Sch.; Corpus Christi Coll., Oxford (MA); PhD (Wales). FSA 1973; FRHistS 1965; FRNS 1958 (Parkes-Weber Prize, 1954). Commnd RN, 1955–58. Civil Servant, Bd of Inland Revenue, 1958–59; administrative appts, Univ. of Bristol and Univ. Coll. of Swansea, 1959–63; Dep. Registrar, Univ. Coll. of Swansea, 1963–69; Registrar, Univ. of Warwick, 1969–72; Sec., Nat. Museum of Wales, 1972–86, Acting Dir, 1985–86. Hon. Lectr in History, University Coll., Cardiff, later Univ. of Wales Coll. of Cardiff, 1975–. Mem. Council, Royal Instn of S Wales, 1962–69 and 1985–91. FRSA 1990. Liveryman: Worshipful Co. of Tin Plate Workers, 1985; Welsh Livery Guild, 1993; Freeman, City of London, 1985. KStJ 1993 (CStJ 1991; Chancellor, Priory for Wales, 1991–). *Publications:* Anglo-Saxon Coins in the National Museum of Wales, 1977; (ed and contrib.) Alan Sorrell: Early Wales Re-created, 1980; Wales in Vanity Fair, 1989; The University College of Swansea: an illustrated history, 1992; articles and reviews in numismatic, historical and other jls. *Recreations:* numismatics, writing, gardening. *Address:* Cherry Grove, Welsh St Donats, near Cowbridge, South Glam CF7 7SS. *Clubs:* Athenæum; Cardiff and County (Cardiff); Bristol Channel Yacht (Swansea).

DYKES, Hugh John; MP (C) Harrow East since 1970; Associate Member, Quilter, Hilton, Goodison, Stockbrokers, since 1978; *b* 17 May 1939; *s* of Richard Dykes and Doreen Ismay Maxwell Dykes; *m* 1965, Susan Margaret Dykes (*née* Smith); three *s*. *Educ:* Weston super Mare Grammar Sch.; Pembroke Coll. Cambridge. Partner, Simon & Coates, Stockbrokers, 1968–78. MSI, 1993. Dir, Dixons Stores Far East Ltd, 1985–. Contested (C) Tottenham, Gen. Elec., 1966. PPS: to three Parly Under-Secs of State for Defence, 1970; to Parly Under-Sec. of State in Civil Service Dept attached to Cabinet Office, 1973; Mem., H of C EEC Select Cttee, 1983–. Mem., European Parlt, Strasbourg, 1974; Chairman: Cons. Parly European Cttee, 1979–80 (Vice-Chm., 1974–79); Commons Euro-Gp, 1988–; Vice-Pres., Cons. Gp for EEC, 1982–86 (Chm., 1978–81). Chm., European Movement, 1990– (Jt Hon. Sec., 1982–87). Research Sec., Bow Gp, 1965; Chm., Coningsby Club, 1969. Governor: Royal Nat. Orthopaedic Hosp., 1975–82; N London Collegiate Sch., 1982–. *Publications:* (ed) Westropp's "Invest £100", 1964, and Westropp's "Start Your Own Business", 1965; many articles and pamphlets on political and financial subjects. *Recreations:* music, theatre, swimming, travel. *Address:* House of Commons, SW1A 0AA. *T:* 0171–219 3000. *Clubs:* Garrick, Carlton, Beefsteak.

DYKES, Richard Thornton Booth; Managing Director, Post Office Counters Ltd, since 1993; *b* 7 April 1945; *s* of Alan Thornton Dykes and Myra McFie Dykes (*née* Booth); *m* 1970, Janet Rosemary Cundall; one *s*. *Educ:* Rossall Sch. Articled clerk, Dehn & Lauderdale, solicitors, 1965–67; EO, later HEO, Min. of Labour, 1967–73; Private Sec. to Sec. of State for Employment, 1974–76; Principal, Econ. Policy Div., Dept of Employment, 1976–77; Dir, Industrial Relns, British Shipbuilders, 1977–80; Non-exec. Dir, Austin & Pickersgill Ltd, Sunderland, 1979–80; Principal Private Sec. to Sec. of State for Employment, 1980–82; Department of Employment: Hd, Unemployment Benefit Service, 1982–85; Sec., Sen. Mgt Gp, 1985–86; Hd, Inner Cities Central Unit, 1986; Post Office Counters Ltd: Gen. Manager for Gtr London, 1986–87; Dir of Ops, 1987–92. Member: Forensic Sci. Service Adv. Bd, Home Office, 1991–; EDC, BITC, 1994–; Design Council, 1994–. *Recreations:* travel, hill-walking. *Address:* Post Office Counters Ltd, Head Office, Drury House, 1/16 Blackfriars Road, SE1 9UA. *T:* 0171–922 1100; 30 Wimbledon Close, The Downs, Wimbledon, SW20 8HL. *T:* 0181–947 6369.

DYKSTRA, Ronald Gerrit Malcolm; Senior Partner, Addleshaw Sons & Latham, solicitors, 1987–94, retired; *b* 4 March 1934; *s* of Gerrit Abe Dykstra and Margaret Kirk Dykstra (*née* McDonald); *m* 1st, 1960, Jennifer Mary Cramer (marr diss. 1985); three *s*; 2nd, 1986, Sonia Hoole. *Educ:* Edinburgh Academy. FCIArb. Admitted Solicitor, 1957; Asst Solicitor, 1957, Partner, 1961, Addleshaw Sons & Latham, Manchester. Mem., Wilmslow Green Room Soc. *Recreations:* swimming, cycling, amateur drama, walking. *Address:* 7 Racecourse Road, Wilmslow, Cheshire SK9 5LF. *T:* Wilmslow (01625) 525856.

DYMOKE, Lt-Col John Lindley Marmion, MBE 1960; Vice Lord-Lieutenant of Lincolnshire, since 1991; 34th Hereditary Queen's Champion, 1946; *b* 1 Sept. 1926; *s* of late Lionel Marmion Dymoke and Rachel, *d* of Hon. Lennox Lindley; *m* 1953, Susan Cicely Fane; three *s*. *Educ:* Christ's Hosp. Commnd Royal Lincs Regt, 1946; Staff Coll., 1957; Armed Forces Staff Coll., USA, 1964; Coll. Chief Instructor, RMA Sandhurst, 1961–64; Comd 3rd Bn, Royal Anglian Regt, 1966–69; military service included: India, Sumatra, Malaya, Egypt, Jordan, Aden, France, Germany, USA and UK; retired 1972. Farmer and landowner, 1972–. Dist Councillor, 1973–. Chairman: Lincs Br, CLA, 1982–85; Horncastle Grammar Sch., 1979–91. Master, Grocers' Co., 1977–78. DL 1976, High Sheriff 1979, Lincs. *Recreation:* care of Scrivelsby Estate. *Address:* Scrivelsby Court, near Horncastle, Lincolnshire LN9 6JA. *T:* Horncastle (01507) 523325.

DYMOKE, Rear-Adm. Lionel Dorian, CB 1974; *b* 18 March 1921; *s* of Henry Lionel Dymoke and Dorothy (*née* Briscoe); *m* 1st, 1952, Patricia Pimlott (*d* 1968); one *s*; 2nd, 1970, Iris Hemsted (*née* Lamplough). *Educ:* Nautical Coll., Pangbourne. Entered Royal Navy, 1938; Comdr 1953; Captain 1961; Rear-Adm. 1971; retired 1976. *Address:* 3 Woodland Place, Bath, Avon BA2 6EH. *T:* Bath (01225) 464228.

DYMOND, Michael John; Chief Executive (formerly Director General), Defence Accounts Agency, Ministry of Defence, 1989–95; *b* 11 Aug. 1936; *s* of Archibald William John Dymond and Violet Eileen Mary Dymond (*née* Young); *m* 1963, Angela Rosalind Terry; one *s* one *d*. *Educ:* Colston's Sch., Bristol; Merton Coll., Oxford (BA Jurisp. 1960; MA). ACA 1963, FCA 1973. Chartered Accountant and Auditor, Deloitte & Co., 1960–66; Passenger Fares Officer, Audit, British Railways, 1966–70; Group Financial Controller, Metals Research Ltd, 1970–73; Asst Dir, Audit, MoD, 1973–76; Careers Officer for Accountants, DTI, 1976–81; Dep. Dir Gen. Management Audit, MoD, 1981–88. *Recreations:* singing, music, cricket, stamps. *Address:* Laburnum Cottage, 4 Hughes Court, High Street, Rode, Bath BA3 6NX. *T:* Frome (01373) 830149.

DYNEVOR, 9th Baron *cr* 1780; **Richard Charles Uryan Rhys;** *b* 19 June 1935; *s* of 8th Baron Dynevor, CBE, MC; *S* father, 1962; *m* 1959, Lucy (marr. diss. 1978), *d* of Sir John Rothenstein, CBE; one *s* three *d*. *Educ:* Eton; Magdalene Coll., Cambridge. *Heir:* *s* Hon. Hugo Griffith Uryan Rhys, *b* 19 Nov. 1966. *Address:* House of Lords, SW1A 0PW.

DYSART, Countess of (11th in line), *cr* 1643; **Rosamund Agnes Greaves;** Baroness Huntingtower, 1643; *b* 15 Feb. 1914; *d* of Major Owain Greaves (*d* 1941), RHG, and Wenefryde Agatha, Countess of Dysart (10th in line); *S* mother, 1975. *Heir:* *sister* Lady Katherine Grant of Rothiemurchus [*b* 1 June 1918; *m* 1941, Colonel John Peter Grant of Rothiemurchus, MBE (*d* 1987); one *s* one *d*]. *Address:* Bryn Garth, Grosmont, Abergavenny, Gwent.

DYSON, Rev. Anthony Oakley, DPhil; Samuel Ferguson Professor of Social and Pastoral Theology, Manchester University, since 1980; Academic Director, Centre for Social Ethics and Policy, Manchester University, since 1987; *b* 6 Oct. 1935; *s* of Henry Oakley Leslie Dyson and Lilian Dyson; *m* 1960, Edwina Anne Hammett; two *s*. *Educ:* William Hulme's Grammar Sch., Manchester; Univs of Cambridge (BA 1959, MA 1963) and Oxford (MA, BD 1964, DPhil 1968). 2nd Lieut, West Yorks Regt, 1954–56; Emmanuel Coll., Cambridge, 1956–59; Exeter Coll., Oxford and Ripon Hall, Oxford, 1959–61; Curate of Putney, Dio. Southwark, 1961–63; Chaplain of Ripon Hall, Oxford, 1963–69; Principal of Ripon Hall, 1969–74; Canon of St George's Chapel, Windsor Castle, 1974–77, Custodian, 1975–77; Lectr in Theology, Univ. of Kent, 1977–80. Vis. Prof., Univ. of Essex, 1992–93. Licensed to Officiate Dio. Oxford, 1965–75, Dio. Canterbury, 1978–80, Dio. Chester, 1980–, Dio. Manchester, 1980–. Examng Chaplain to Bishop of Carlisle; Select Preacher, Univ. of Oxford, 1971; University Preacher, Cambridge, 1985; Lectures: Hensley Henson, Univ. of Oxford, 1972–73; Pollock, Halifax, NS, 1973; Shann, Hong Kong, 1983. Associate Dir, Centre for the Study of Religion and Society, Canterbury, 1978–80. Hon. MA(Theol) Manchester, 1982. Editor: The Teilhard Review, 1966–72; The Modern Churchman, 1982–93. *Publications:* Existentialism, 1965; Who is Jesus Christ?, 1969; The Immortality of the Past, 1974; We Believe, 1977; (ed with J. Harris) Experiments on Embryos, 1990; Ethics and the New Reproductive Technologies, 1992; The Ethics of In-Vitro Fertilisation, 1994; (ed with J. Harris) Biotechnology and Ethics, 1994; *contributions to:* Evolution Marxism and Christianity, 1967; What Kind of Revolution?, 1968; A Dictionary of Christian Theology, 1969, 2nd edn, 1983; The Christian Marxist Dialogue, 1969; Teilhard Reassessed, 1970; Oxford Dictionary of the Christian Church, 2nd edn, 1974; Education and Social Action, 1975; Ernst Troeltsch and the Future of Theology, 1976; The Language of the Church in Higher and Further Education, 1977; England and Germany: studies in theological diplomacy, 1981; The Nature of Religious Man, 1982; A New Dictionary of Christian Theology, 1983; The Church of England and Politics, 1986; A Dictionary of Pastoral Care, 1987; The British and their Religions, 1988; The Nuclear Weapons Debate: theological and ethical issues, 1989; The Ethics of IVF, 1995; contrib. Theology, The Modern Churchman, Study Encounter, The Month, Contact, The Way, TLS, Bull. of John Rylands Library, Studia Theologica, Jl of Med. Ethics, etc. *Recreations:* literature, sport. *Address:* Department of Religions and Theology, University of Manchester, Manchester M13 9PL. *T:* 0161–275 3597 (ext. 3545); 33 Danesmoor Road, West Didsbury, Manchester M20 3JT. *T:* 0161–434 5410.

DYSON, Prof. Freeman John, FRS 1952; Professor, School of Natural Sciences, Institute for Advanced Study, Princeton, New Jersey, 1953–94, Professor Emeritus since 1994; *b* 15 Dec. 1923; *s* of late Sir George Dyson, KCVO; *m* 1st, 1950, Verena Esther (*née* Huber) (marr. diss. 1958); one *s* one *d*; 2nd, 1958, Imme (*née* Jung); four *d*. *Educ:* Winchester; Cambridge; Cornell University. Operational research for RAF Bomber Command, 1943–45. Fellow of Trinity Coll., Cambridge, 1946–50, Hon. Fellow, 1989; Commonwealth Fund Fellow at Cornell and Princeton, USA, 1947–49; Mem. of Institute for Advanced Study, Princeton, USA, 1949–50; Professor of Physics, Cornell Univ., Ithaca, NY, USA, 1951–53. Mem. of National Academy of Sciences (USA), 1964; For. Associate, Acad. des Scis, Paris, 1989. Gifford Lectr, Aberdeen, 1985; Radcliffe Lectr, Oxford, 1990. Lorentz Medal, Royal Netherlands Acad. of Sciences, 1966; Hughes Medal, Royal Soc., 1968; Max Planck Medal, German Physical Soc., 1969. *Publications:* Disturbing the Universe, 1979; Weapons and Hope, 1984; Origins of Life, 1986; Infinite in All Directions, 1988; From Eros to Gaia, 1991; contrib. to The Physical Review, Annals of Mathematics, etc. *Address:* School of Natural Sciences, Institute for Advanced Study, Olden Lane, Princeton, NJ 08540, USA.

DYSON, Hon. Sir John (Anthony), Kt 1993; **Hon. Mr Justice Dyson;** a Judge of the High Court of Justice, Queen's Bench Division, since 1993; *b* 31 July 1943; *s* of Richard and Gisella Dyson; *m* 1970, Jacqueline Carmel Levy; one *s* one *d*. *Educ:* Leeds Grammar Sch.; Wadham Coll., Oxford (Open Classics Scholar; MA). Harmsworth Law Scholar, 1968, called to Bar, Middle Temple, 1968, Bencher, 1990; QC 1982; a Recorder, 1986–93. Mem., Council of Legal Educn, 1992–. *Recreations:* piano playing, gardening, walking. *Address:* Royal Courts of Justice, Strand, WC2A 2LL.

DYSON, John Michael; Chief Master of the Supreme Court of Judicature (Chancery Division), since 1992 (a Master, since 1973); a Recorder, since 1994; *b* 9 Feb. 1929; *s* of late Eric Dyson, Gainsborough and Hope Patison (*née* Kirkland). *Educ:* Bradfield Coll.; Corpus Christi Coll., Oxford. 2nd Lieut, Royal Tank Regt, 1948. Admitted Solicitor, 1956; Partner, Field Roscoe & Co., 1957 (subseq. Field Fisher & Co. and Field Fisher & Martineau). *Address:* 20 Keats Grove, NW3 2RS. *T:* 0171–794 3389. *Club:* United Oxford & Cambridge University.

DYSON, Prof. Roger Franklin, PhD; Honorary Professor and Director of Clinical Management Unit Centre for Health Planning and Management, University of Keele, since 1989; *b* 30 Jan. 1940; *s* of John Franklin Dyson and Edith Mary Jobson; *m* 1964 (marr. diss. 1994); one *s* one *d*. *Educ:* Counthill Grammar Sch., Oldham; Keele Univ. (BA Hons 1st cl. Hist. and Econs, 1962); Leeds Univ. (PhD 1971). Asst Lectr, 1963, Lectr, 1966, Adult Educn Dept, Leeds Univ.; Dep. Dir and Sen. Lectr in Ind. Relations, Adult Educn Dept, 1974, Prof. and Dir of Adult and Continuing Educn, 1976–89, Keele Univ. Consultant Advr on Ind. Relations to Sec. of State, DHSS, 1979–81. Chm., N Staffs HA, 1982–86. Mem., RSocMed. Editor, Health Manpower Management (formerly Health Services Manpower Review), 1975–91. *Publications:* (ed jtly) Management for Hospital Doctors, 1994; contribs to BMJ. *Recreations:* gardening, gastronomy. *Address:* 4 Huskards, Fryerning, Ingatestone, Essex CM4 0HR. *T:* Brentwood (01277) 354841. *Club:* Carlton.

DYVIG, Peter; Comdr (1st cl.), Order of the Dannebrog, 1986; Ambassador of Denmark in Washington, since 1989; *b* 23 Feb. 1934; *m* 1959, Karen Dyvig (*née* Møller); one *s* one *d*. *Educ:* Copenhagen Univ. (grad. in Law). Entered Danish For. Service, 1959; bursary at Sch. of Advanced Internat. Studies, Washington, 1963–64; First Secretary: Danish Delegn to NATO, Paris, 1965–67; Brussels, 1967–69; Min. of For. Affairs, Copenhagen, 1969–74; Minister Counsellor, Washington, 1974–76; Ambassador, Asst Under-Sec. of State, Min. of For. Affairs, Copenhagen, 1976–79; Under-Sec. for Pol. Affairs, 1980; State Sec., 1983–86; Ambassador to UK, 1986–89. *Address:* Royal Danish Embassy, 3200 Whitehaven Street, NW, Washington, DC 20008–3683, USA.

E

EABORN, Prof. Colin, PhD, DSc (Wales); FRS 1970; FRSC; Professor of Chemistry, University of Sussex, since 1962; *b* 15 March 1923; *s* of Tom Stanley and Caroline Eaborn; *m* 1949, Joyce Thomas. *Educ:* Ruabon Grammar Sch., Denbighshire; Univ. Coll. of N Wales, Bangor. Asst Lecturer, 1947, Lecturer, 1950, and Reader 1954, in Chemistry, Univ. of Leicester. Research Associate, Univ. of California at Los Angeles, 1950–51; Robert A. Welch Visiting Scholar, Rice Univ., Texas, 1961–62; Erskine Fellow, Univ. of Canterbury (NZ), 1965; Pro-Vice Chancellor (Science), Univ. of Sussex, 1968–72; Dist. Prof., New Mexico State Univ., 1973; Canadian Commonwealth Fellow, Univ. of Victoria, BC, 1976; Lectures: Riccoboni, Univ. of Padua, 1977; Gilman, Iowa State Univ., 1978; R. A. Welch Vis., Texas, 1983. Hon. Sec., Chemical Society, 1964–71, Vice-Pres., Dalton Div., 1971–75: Mem. Council, Royal Soc., 1978–80, 1988–89; Chm., British Cttee on Chemical Educn, 1967–69; Mem., Italy/UK Mixed Commn, 1972–80. Hon. DSc Sussex, 1990. F. S. Kipping Award, Amer. Chem. Soc., 1964; Organometallic Award, Chem. Soc., 1975; Ingold Lectureship and Medal, Chem. Soc., 1976; Main Gp Award, Chem. Soc., 1989. *Publications:* Organosilicon Compounds, 1960; Organometallic Compounds of the Group IV Elements, Vol. 1, Part 1, 1968; numerous research papers, mainly in Jl of Chem. Soc. and Jl of Organometallic Chemistry (Regional Editor). *Address:* School of Chemistry and Molecular Sciences, University of Sussex, Brighton BN1 9QJ. *T:* Brighton (01273) 606755, *Fax:* Brighton (01273) 677196.

EADIE, Alexander, BEM 1960; JP; *b* 23 June 1920; *m* 1941; one *s*. *Educ:* Buckhaven Senior Secondary Sch. Coal-miner from 1934. Chm., Fife County Housing Cttee, 9 yrs; Chm., Fife County Educn Cttee, 18 mths; Governor, Moray House Teachers' Training Coll., Edinburgh, 5 years; Exec. Committee: Scottish Council of Labour Party, 9 yrs; NUM Scottish Area, 2 yrs; Mem., Eastern Regional Hosp. Bd (Scotland), 14 yrs. Contested Ayr, 1959 and 1964; MP (Lab) Midlothian, 1966–92. Former PPS to Miss M. Herbison, MP, Minister of Social Security, and Mem. of Parly Select Cttee on Scottish Affairs; Opposition Front Bench Spokesman on Energy (incl. N Sea Oil), 1973–74; Parly Under-Sec. of State, Dept of Energy, 1974–79; Shadow Front Bench Spokesman on Energy, 1979–92. Chm., All Party Energy Studies Gp, 1991–92; Chm., Parly Labour Party Power and Steel Gp, 1972–74; Sec., Miners' Parly Gp, 1983–92; Vice-Chm., Parly Trade Union Group, 1972–74. JP Fife, 1951. *Recreations:* bowling, gardening. *Address:* Balkerack, The Haugh, East Wemyss, Fife KY1 4SB. *T:* Buckhaven (01592) 3636.

EADIE, Douglas George Arnott, FRCS; Consulting Surgeon, The Royal London Hospital (Consultant Surgeon, 1969–87); Consultant Surgeon, King Edward VII Hospital, London, 1978–94; *b* 16 June 1931; *s* of Dr Herbert Arnott Eadie and Hannah Sophia (*née* Wingate); *m* 1957, Gillian Carlyon Coates; two *s* two *d*. *Educ:* Epsom Coll.; London Hosp. Med. Coll. (MB BS; MS 1969). Jun. Specialist in Surgery and Captain RAMC, Far East Land Forces, 1957–60; Hugh Robertson Exchange Fellow, Presbyterian St Luke's Hosp., Chicago, 1962; Surgical Registrar, London Hosp., 1963–67. Cons. to Royal Masonic Hosp., 1980–82; Hon. Cons., Osborne House, IoW, 1980. Chm. of Council, Medical Protection Soc., 1976–83 (Mem. Council, 1974; Treasurer, 1986–90); Mem., Med. Adv. Cttee, Cromwell Hosp. (Chm., 1991). Examiner in Surgery: Soc. of Apothecaries of London, 1976–80; Univ. of London, 1976–84; Professional Linguistic Assessment Bd, 1992–94. Member: London Adv. Cttee, Barnardos, 1990; Court, Bradford Univ., 1991–94. Master, Soc. of Apothecaries, 1990–91 (Mem. Ct of Assts, 1980); rep. on GMC, 1983–88. FRSM 1956. *Publications:* contribs to med. jls on topics relating to vascular disease. *Recreations:* golf, gardening, shooting. *Address:* Monks Lodge, Great Maplestead, Halstead, Essex CO9 2RN. *T:* Halstead (01787) 460440. *Clubs:* Sloane, MCC.

EADIE, Mrs Ellice (Aylmer), CBE 1966; Standing Counsel to General Synod of Church of England, 1972–80; *b* 30 June 1912; *d* of late Rt Rev. R. T. Hearn, LLD, sometime Bishop of Cork, and Dr M. E. T. Hearn, MD, FRCPI; *m* 1946, John Harold Ward Eadie (*d* 1995). *Educ:* Cheltenham Ladies' Coll.; St Hugh's Coll., Oxford. Called to Bar, Gray's Inn, 1936. Flt Officer, WAAF, 1941–46. Parliamentary Counsel Office, 1949–72, Parly Counsel, 1968–72. *Address:* 74 Roebuck House, Palace Street, SW1E 5BD. *T:* 0171–828 6158.

EADY, family name of **Baron Swinfen.**

EADY, David, QC 1983; a Recorder, since 1986; *b* 24 March 1943; *s* of late Thomas William Eady and of Kate Eady; *m* 1974, Catherine, *yr d* of J. T. Wiltshire, Bath, Avon; one *s* one *d*. *Educ:* Brentwood Sch.; Trinity Coll., Cambridge (Exhibnr; Pt I Moral Science Tripos, Pt II Law Tripos; MA, LLB). Called to the Bar, Middle Temple, 1966, Bencher, 1991. Mem., Cttee on Privacy and Related Matters (Calcutt Cttee), 1989–90. *Publication:* The Law of Contempt (with A. J. Arlidge, QC), 1982. *Address:* 1 Brick Court, Temple, EC4Y 9BY. *T:* 0171–353 8845.

EAGERS, Derek; Under-Secretary, Department of Trade and Industry (formerly Department of Trade), 1975–84; *b* 13 Sept. 1924; *s* of late Horace Eagers and Florence (*née* Green); *m* 1953, Hazel Maureen Henson; two *s*. *Educ:* King Edward VII Sch., Sheffield; Brasenose Coll., Oxford. RNVR, 1943–47. Min. of Fuel and Power, 1949; UK Atomic Energy Authority, 1955–57; British Embassy, Washington, 1958–60; Principal Private Sec. to successive Ministers of Power, 1963–65; Petroleum Counsellor, Washington, 1966–68; Min. of Power (subseq. Min. of Technology, Dept of Trade and Industry), 1969; Dept of Industry, 1974. *Recreation:* concealing his true ignorance of cricket, gardening and railway history. *Address:* Bryniau Golau, Llangower, Bala, Gwynedd LL23 7BT. *T:* Bala (01678) 520517.

EAGLAND, (Ralph) Martin; Director, Martin Eagland Economic Development Consultancy, since 1995; *b* 1 May 1942; *s* of Norman Albert Eagland and Jessie Eagland; *m* 1963, Patricia Anne Norton; one *s* one *d*. *Educ:* Hipperholme Grammar Sch.; Leeds Sch. of Town Planning; Univ. of Bradford (MSc); Univ. of Birmingham. FRTPI, MIHT, SOLACE, CIMgt, MIPR. Jun. planning posts, Huddersfield, Dewsbury and Halifax, 1959–67; Principal Planning Officer, City of Gloucester, 1967–72; Asst Co. Planning Officer, Northants CC, 1972–74; Chief Planner (Envmt), W Yorks CC, 1974–79, Head of Econ. Develt Unit, 1979–84; Chief Executive: Kettering Borough Council, 1984–88; Leeds Develt Corp., 1988–95. Mem., W Yorks Cttee, CoSIRA, 1985–88; Sec., Kettering Enterprise Agency, 1986–88. Hon. Public Relns Officer, RTPI (Yorks Br. Exec. Cttee), 1990–92. Member: Colne and Holme Valley Jt Cttee for the Blind, 1992–94; Yorks Contract Bridge Assoc., Wakefield; Rotary Club of Leeds. *Publications:* contribs to RTPI Jl, Instn of Highways and Transportation Jl and various property jls and publications. *Recreations:* environmental studies, ballroom dancing, bridge, writing, gardening. *T:* (office) Huddersfield (01484) 686859. *Club:* Yorkshire Society (Leeds).

EAGLE, Angela; MP (Lab) Wallasey, since 1992; *b* 17 Feb. 1961; *d* of André and late Shirley Eagle. *Educ:* Formby High Sch.; St John's Coll., Oxford (BA, PPE). Economic Directorate, CBI, 1984; Confederation of Health Service Employees: Researcher, 1984; Press Officer, 1986; Parly Officer, 1987–92. Mem., Labour Party Nat. Women's Cttee, 1989–. Mem., BFI. *Recreations:* chess (Jun. Internat. Hons), cricket, cinema. *Address:* House of Commons, SW1A 0AA. *T:* 0171–219 4074.

EAGLES, Lt-Col (Charles Edward) James, LVO 1988; Member, HM Body Guard of the Honourable Corps of Gentlemen-at-Arms, 1967–88 (Harbinger, 1981–86; Standard Bearer, 1986–88); *b* 14 May 1918; *o s* of late Major C. E. C. Eagles, DSO, RMLI and Esmé Field; *m* 1941, Priscilla May Nicolette, *d* of late Brig. A. F. B. Cottrell, DSO, OBE; one *s* three *d*. *Educ:* Marlborough Coll. 2nd Lieut RM, 1936; served: HMS Sussex, Mediterranean and S Atlantic, 1938–40; Mobile Naval Base Def. Orgn, UK, ME, Ceylon and India, 1940–43; 1 HAA Regt RM, India, UK and NW Europe, 1943–45; Asst Mil. Sec., 1945; Amphibious Trng Wing, 1945–47; Staff of Maj.-Gen. RM, Portsmouth, 1947–50; HMS Devonshire, 1951–52; RN Staff Course, 1952; DS, Amphibious Warfare Sch., 1952–55; HMS Afrikander, SO (Intell.), S Atlantic, 1955–57; Dep. Dir, PRORM, 1957–59; CSO, Plymouth Gp, 1960; AAG, Staff of CGRM, 1960–62; Dir, PRORM, 1962–65; retd 1965; Civil Service, MoD, 1965–83. Pres., T. S. Churchill Sea Cadet Corps, 1988–. *Recreations:* shooting, genealogy. *Address:* Fallowfield, Westwell, Ashford, Kent TN25 4LQ. *T:* Charing (01233) 712552. *Club:* Army and Navy.

EAGLETON, Prof. Terence Francis, PhD; Thomas Warton Professor of English Literature, and Fellow of St Catherine's College, University of Oxford, since 1992; *b* 22 Feb. 1943; *s* of Francis Paul Eagleton and Rosaleen (*née* Riley); *m* 1966, Elizabeth Rosemary Galpin; two *s*. *Educ:* Trinity Coll., Cambridge (MA, PhD). Fellow in English, Jesus Coll., Cambridge, 1964–69; Oxford University: Tutorial Fellow, Wadham Coll., 1969–89; Lectr in Critical Theory, 1989–92; Fellow, Linacre Coll., 1989–92. Hon. DLitt Salford, 1993. *Publications:* Criticism and Ideology, 1976; Marxism and Literary Criticism, 1976; Literary Theory: an introduction, 1983; The Function of Criticism, 1984; The Ideology of the Aesthetic, 1990; Ideology: an introduction, 1993; Heathcliff and the Great Hunger: studies in Irish culture, 1995. *Recreation:* Irish music. *Address:* St Catherine's College, Oxford OX1 3UJ. *T:* Oxford (01865) 271700. *Club:* Irish.

EAGLING, Wayne John; dancer and choreographer; Artistic Director, Dutch National Ballet, since 1991; *s* of Eddie and Thelma Eagling. *Educ:* P. Ramsey Studio of Dance Arts; Royal Ballet Sch. Sen. Principal, Royal Ballet, 1975–91; has danced lead rôles in major classics including Sleeping Beauty, Swan Lake, Cinderella; first rôle created for him was Young Boy in Triad, 1972; subsequent created rôles include: Solo Boy in Gloria; Ariel in The Tempest; Woyzeck in Different Drummer. Choreographed: The Hunting of the Snark by Michael Batt; (for Royal Ballet) Frankenstein, The Modern Prometheus, 1985; Beauty and the Beast, 1986; The Wall, Berlin, 1990; (for Dutch Nat. Ballet) Ruins of Time, 1993, Symphony in Waves, 1994; choreographed, produced and directed various galas. *Publication:* (with Ross MacGibbon and Robert Jude) The Company We Keep, 1981. *Recreations:* golf, scuba diving, tennis, antique cars. *Address:* Dutch National Ballet, Het Muziektheater, Waterlooplein 22, 1011 PG Amsterdam, The Netherlands.

EALES, Victor Henry James, CEng, MIMechE; Director of Weapons Production and Quality (Naval), 1980–81, and Head of Naval Weapons Professional and Technical Group, 1979–81, Ministry of Defence; *b* 11 Dec. 1922; *s* of William Henry and Frances Jean Eales; *m* 1949, Elizabeth Gabrielle Irene James; two *s* one *d*. *Educ:* Wimbledon Central Sch.; Guildford Technical Coll.; Portsmouth Polytechnic. Ministry of Defence: Asst Director, Weapons Production (Naval), 1970; Dep. Director, Surface Weapons Projects (Naval), 1975; Director, Weapons Production (Naval), 1979. *Recreation:* golf. *Address:* 11 Penrhyn Avenue, East Cosham, Portsmouth, Hants PO6 2AX.

EALING, Abbot of; *see* Soper, Rt Rev. A. L.

EAMES, family name of **Baron Eames** (*see under* Archbishop of Armagh and Primate of All Ireland).

EAMES, Lady; Ann Christine Eames; World-Wide President, Mothers' Union, since 1995; *b* 21 Jan. 1943; *d* of Captain William Adrian Reynolds Daly and Olive Margaret Daly; *m* 1966, Most Rev. Robert Henry Alexander Eames, Baron Eames (*see* Archbishop of Armagh); two *s*. *Educ:* Ashleigh House Sch., Belfast; Queen's Univ., Belfast (LLB Hons, MPhil). *Recreations:* sailing, reading. *Address:* The See House, Cathedral Close, Armagh, Co. Armagh BT61 7EE. *T:* Armagh (01681) 522851.

EAMES, Eric James, JP; Lord Mayor of Birmingham, 1974–75, Deputy Lord Mayor, 1975–76; *b* Highley, Shropshire, 13 April 1917; *s* of George Eames; *m* (marr. diss.); one *s*. *Educ:* Highley Sch., Highley, Shropshire. Member (Lab): Birmingham City Council,

1949–92; W Midlands CC, 1974–77. Mem., Governing Board, Internat. Center for Information Co-operation and Relationship among World's Major Cities. Dir, Assoc. for Neighbourhood Democracy (formerly Councils), 1992–. Governor, Harper Adams Agric. Coll., 1953–90. JP Birmingham, 1972. *Recreations:* gardening, do-it-yourself enthusiast. *Address:* 78 Westley Road, Acocks Green, Birmingham B27 7UH. *T:* 0121–706 7629.

EAMES, Most Rev. Robert Henry Alexander; *see* Armagh, Archbishop of, and Primate of All Ireland.

EARDLEY-WILMOT, Sir John (Assheton), 5th Bt *cr* 1821; LVO 1956; DSC 1943; Staff of Monopolies Commission, 1967–82; *b* 2 Jan. 1917; *s* of Commander Frederick Neville Eardley-Wilmot (*d* 1956) (*s* of 3rd Bt) and Dorothy Little (*d* 1959), formerly of Brooksby, Double Bay, Sydney; *S* uncle, 1970; *m* 1939, Diana Elizabeth, *d* of Commander Aubrey Moore, RN, and Mrs O. Bassett; one *s* one *d*. *Educ:* Stubbington; RNC, Dartmouth. Motor Torpedo Boats, 1939–43; served HMS Apollo, 1944; HMS Fencer, 1945–46; RN Staff Course, 1950; Commander 1950; HMS Opossum, 1951–53; Cabinet Office, 1954–57; Admiralty, 1958–67; retired 1967, as Deputy Director Naval Administrative Planning. MIMgt (MBIM 1978); FRSA 1970. Freeman, City of London (by Redemption). Norwegian War Medal. *Recreation:* fishing. *Heir: s* Michael John Assheton Eardley-Wilmot [*b* 13 Jan. 1941; *m* 1971, Wendy (marr. diss. 1987), *y d* of A. J. Wolstenholme; two *s* one *d*; *m* 1987, Diana Margaret, *d* of Robert Graham Wallis; one *d*]. *Address:* 41 Margravine Gardens, W6 8RN. *T:* 0181–748 3723.

EARL, Christopher Joseph, MD, FRCP; Hon. Consultant Physician to: Neurological Department, Middlesex Hospital, since 1988 (Physician, 1971–88); National Hospital, Queen Square, since 1988 (Physician, 1958–88); Moorfields Eye Hospital, since 1988 (Physician, 1959–88); Consultant Neurologist: King Edward VII Hospital for Officers, since 1966; Hospital of St John and St Elizabeth, 1967–88; *b* 20 Nov. 1925; *s* of Christopher and Winifred Earl, Ashbourne, Derbyshire; *m* 1951, Alma Patience Hopkins, Reading; two *s* three *d*. *Educ:* Cotton Coll.; Guy's Hosp. House phys. and house surg., Guy's Hosp., and MO, RAF, 1948–50. Lecturer in Chemical Pathology, Guy's Hosp., 1950–52; Research Fellow, Harvard Med. Sch., and Neurological Unit, Boston City Hosp., 1952–54; Resident MO, Nat. Hosp., Queen Square, 1954–56; Chief Asst, Neurological Dept, Guy's Hosp., 1956–58; Physician, Neurological Dept, London Hosp., 1961–71. Civil Consultant in Neurol., RAF, 1976–88. Director: Medical Sickness Annuity & Life Assce Soc. Ltd, 1981– (Chm., 1993–); Permanent Insurance Co., 1985–95. Hon. Dir of Photography, Royal Society of Medicine, 1967–73. Hon. Sec., 1968–74, Pres., 1989–90, Assoc. British Neurologists; Mem. Council, 1967–91, Vice Chm. Bd of Management, 1993–, Med. Defence Union; Chm., Cttee on Neurology, RCP (Censor, 1983–85). Corresp. Mem., Amer. Neurological Assoc., 1978. *Publications:* papers in learned jls on Biochemistry and Neurology. *Recreation:* reading history. *Address:* 23 Audley Road, Ealing, W5 3ES. *T:* 0181–997 0380; 149 Harley Street, W1N 1HG. *Club:* Garrick.

EARL, Eric Stafford; Clerk to the Worshipful Company of Fishmongers, 1974–88, retired; *b* 8 July 1928; *s* of late Alfred Henry Earl and Mary Elizabeth Earl; *m* 1951, Clara Alice Alston. *Educ:* SE Essex Technical Coll.; City of London Coll. Served with RA, 1946–48. Joined Fishmongers' Co. 1948: Accountant, 1961–68; Asst Clerk, 1969–73; Actg Clerk, 1973–74; Liveryman, 1977. Clerk to Governors of Gresham's Sch., 1974–88; formerly: Sec., City and Guilds of London Art School Ltd; Sec., Atlantic Salmon Res. Trust Ltd; Mem. Exec. and Mem. Council, Salmon and Trout Assoc.; Mem., Nat. Anglers' Council (Chm., 1983–85). Hon. Sec., Shellfish Assoc. of GB, 1974–88; Jt Hon. Sec., Central Council for Rivers Protection, 1974–88; Hon. Asst River Keeper of River Thames, 1968–88; Mem. Council, Anglers' Co-operative Assoc., 1974– (Vice Chm., 1988–). Director: Hulbert Property Co. Ltd, 1975–88; Hulbert Property Holdings Ltd, 1975–88. FZS 1988. Hon. Freeman, Watermen's Co., 1984. *Recreations:* fishing, gardening, tennis, cricket. *Address:* Dolphins, Watling Lane, Thaxted, Essex CM6 2RA. *T:* Thaxted (01371) 830758. *Club:* Flyfishers'.

EARL, John, FSA; Director, Theatres Trust, since 1986; *b* 11 April 1928; *s* of Philip Haywood Earl and May Florence (*née* Walsh); *m* 1952, Valerie Atkins; one *s* (one *d* decd). *Educ:* Roan Sch.; Brixton Sch. of Building. ARICS 1952; FSA 1978. Nat. Service, RE, 1947–49. London County Council: Architect's Dept, 1954–56; Historic Bldgs Section, 1956–61; MPBW (Special Services), 1961–65; Section Leader, GLC Historic Bldgs Div., 1965–86. Private consultancy, 1986–. Lectr, various bldg conservation courses, 1970–; Ext. Examr, RICS Conservation course, 1990–95. *Publications:* (with J. Stanton) Canterbury Hall and Palace of Varieties, 1982; Philosophy of Building Conservation, 1995; Dr Langdon-Down and the Normansfield Theatre, 1995; contrib. numerous books and jls on building conservation and theatre buildings. *Recreations:* avoiding organised sport. *Address:* The Theatres Trust, 22 Charing Cross Road, WC2H 0HR. *T:* 0171–836 8591.

EARLE, Arthur Frederick; management and economic consultant, since 1983; *b* Toronto, 13 Sept. 1921; *s* of Frederick C. Earle and Hilda M. Earle (*née* Brown); *m* 1946, Vera Domini Lithgow; two *s* one *d*. *Educ:* Toronto; London Sch. of Economics (BSc (Econ.), PhD; Hon. Fellow 1980). Royal Canadian Navy (Rating to Lieut Comdr), 1939–46. Canada Packers Ltd, 1946–48; Aluminium Ltd cos in British Guiana, West Indies and Canada, 1948–53; Treas., Alumina Jamaica Ltd, 1953–55; Aluminium Union, London, 1955–58; Vice-Pres., Aluminium Ltd Sales Inc., New York, 1958–61; Dir, 1961–74, Dep. Chm., 1961–65, Man. Dir, 1963–65, Hoover Ltd; Principal, London Graduate Sch. of Business Studies, 1965–72. Pres., Internat. Investment Corp. for Yugoslavia, 1972–74; Pres., Boyden Consulting Group Ltd, 1974–82; Associate, 1974–82, Vice-Pres., 1975–82, Boyden Associates, Inc.; Advisor to the Pres., Canada Develt Investment Corp., 1983–86; Director: Rio Algom Ltd, 1983–92; National Sea Products Ltd, 1984–86; Bathpaul Ltd, UK, 1984–86; Monkwells Ltd, UK, 1984. Sen. Res. Fellow, Nat. Centre for Management R & D, Univ. of Western Ontario, 1987–90. Member: Commn of Enquiry, Jamaican Match Industry, 1953; Consumer Council, 1963–68; NEDC Cttee on Management Educn, Training and Develt, 1967–69; NEDC for Electrical Engineering Industry. Chm., Canadian Assoc. of Friends of LSE, 1975–. Dir, Nat. Ballet of Canada, 1982–85. Governor: Ashridge Management Coll., 1962–65; LSE, 1968; NIESR, 1968–74; Governor and Mem. Council, Ditchley Foundn, 1967. Fellow, London Business Sch., 1988. Thomas Hawksley Lecture, IMechE, 1968. *Publications:* numerous, on economics and management. *Recreations:* hill climbing, model ship building. *Address:* 1234 Rushbrooke Drive, Oakville, Ont L6M 1K9, Canada. *T:* (905) 8476459. *Club:* Royal Canadian Military Institute (Toronto).

EARLE, Sir George; *see* Earle, Sir H. G. A.

EARLE, Very Rev. George Hughes, SJ; MA; *b* 20 Sept. 1925; *s* of late Lieut-Col F. W. Earle, DSO, JP, Morestead House, Winchester, and late Marie Blanche Lyne-Stivens. *Educ:* Pilgrims' Sch., Winchester; Westminster Sch.; Peter Symonds' Sch., Winchester; Balliol Coll., Oxford. Served with RAF, 1943–47. Joined Soc. of Jesus, 1950. Taught at Beaumont Coll., 1955–57, and Stonyhurst Coll., 1962–63; Headmaster, Stonyhurst Coll., 1963–72; Superior of Southwell House, 1972–75; Educnl Asst to Provincial, 1972–75; Co-editor, The Way, 1974–78; Rector of St Aloysius, Glasgow, 1978–81; Superior, English Province, SJ, 1981–87. Co-ordinator of Seminaries, S African Bishops' Conf., 1993. *Recreations:* none; wasting time. *Address:* 493 Marshall Street, Belgravia, Johannesburg 2094, South Africa.

EARLE, Sir (Hardman) George (Algernon), 6th Bt *cr* 1869; *S* father, 1979; *m*; one *s* one *d*. *Heir: s*.

EARLE, Ion, TD 1946; Assistant to the Directors, Clive Discount Co., 1973–81, retired; *b* 12 April 1916; *s* of late Stephen Earle and of E. Beatrice Earle (*née* Blair White); *m* 1946, Elizabeth Stevens, US citizen; one *s* one *d*. *Educ:* Stowe Sch.; University Coll., Oxford; Université de Grenoble. Federation of British Industries, Birmingham, 1938–51, London, 1952–60; Chief Executive, Export Council for Europe, 1960–64; Dep. Dir-Gen., BNEC, 1965–71 (Dir, 1964–65); Head of Personnel, Kleinwort Benson Ltd, 1972. Royal Artillery, TA, 1939–46 (Major). *Recreations:* golf, gardening. *Address:* 69 Sea Avenue, Rustington, West Sussex BN16 2DP. *T:* Rustington (01903) 773350. *Club:* West Sussex Golf.

EARLE, Joel Vincent, (Joe); arts management consultant, since 1990; Head of Public Services, Victoria and Albert Museum, 1987–89; *b* 1 Sept. 1952; *s* of late James Basil Foster Earle and Mary Isabel Jessie Weeks; *m* 1980, Sophia Charlotte Knox; two *s*. *Educ:* Westminster Sch.; New Coll., Oxford (BA 1st Cl. Hons Chinese). Far Eastern Department, Victoria & Albert Museum: Res. Asst, 1974–77; Asst Keeper, 1977–82; Keeper, 1982–87. Exhibns Co-ordinator, Japan Fest. 1991, 1990–91; *other exhibitions include:* Japan Style, V&A, 1980; Japanese Lacquer, V&A, 1980; Great Japan Exhibition, RA, 1981; Japanese Ceramics Today, V&A, 1983; The Toshiba Gall. of Japanese Art, V&A, 1986; British Design, South Coast Plaza, 1990; Visions of Japan, V&A, 1991–92; Songs of My People, RFH, 1992–93; London Transport Posters, 1994. Trustee, Design Mus., 1988–. *Publications:* An Introduction to Netsuke, 1980, 2nd edn 1982; An Introduction to Japanese Prints, 1980; (contrib.) Japan Style, 1980; (contrib.) The Great Japan Exhibition, 1981; (trans.) The Japanese Sword, 1983; The Toshiba Gallery: Japanese art and design, 1986; Shibata Zeshin, 1995; Flower Bronzes of Japan, 1995; articles in learned jls. *Address:* 123 Middleton Road, E8 4LL. *T:* 0171–923 2662.

EARLE, John Nicholas Francis, (Nick); Headmaster, Bromsgrove School, 1971–85; *b* 14 Nov. 1926; *s* of John William Arthur Earle and Vivien Constance Fenton (*née* Davies); *m* 1959, Ann Veronica Lester; one *s* two *d*. *Educ:* Winchester Coll.; Trinity Coll., Cambridge. 1st cl. Maths Tripos pt 2, 1st cl. Theol. Tripos pt 1; MA. Deacon, 1952; Priest, 1953; relinquished Holy Orders, 1994. Curate, St Matthew, Moorfields, 1952–57; PARS Fellow, Union Theol Seminary, New York, 1957–58; Lectr, St Botolph, Aldgate, 1958–61; Asst Master, Dulwich Coll., 1961–71. *Publications:* What's Wrong With the Church?, 1961; Culture and Creed, 1967; Logic, 1973. *Recreations:* travel, gardening. *Address:* 1 Red Post Hill, Pond Mead, SE21 7BX.

EARLES, Prof. Stanley William Edward, PhD, DScEng; FEng 1992; FIMechE; Professor of Mechanical Engineering, King's College, University of London, 1976–94, Emeritus since 1994; *b* 18 Jan. 1929; *s* of late William Edward Earles and Winnifred Anne Cook; *m* 1955, Margaret Isabella Brown; two *d*. *Educ:* King's Coll., Univ. of London (BScEng, PhD, DScEng; AKC; FKC 1993). FIMechE 1976. Nuffield Apprentice, Birmingham, 1944–50; King's Coll., Univ. of London, 1950–53; Scientific Officer, Royal Naval Scientific Service, 1953–55; University of London: Queen Mary College: Lectr in Mech. Eng, 1955–69; Reader in Mech. Eng, 1969–75; Prof. of Mech. Eng, 1975–76; King's College: Head, Dept of Mech. Engrg, 1976–90, 1991–94; Dean of Engrg, 1986–90; Hd of Sch. of Phys. Scis and Engrg, 1990–91. James Clayton Fund prize, IMechE, 1967; Engineering Applied to Agriculture Award, IMechE, 1980. *Publications:* papers and articles in Proc. IMechE, Jl of Mech. Eng Science, Jl of Sound and Vibration, Wear, Proc. ASME and ASLE, and Eng. *Recreations:* real tennis, gardening. *Address:* Woodbury, Church Lane, Wormley, Broxbourne, Herts EN10 7QF. *T:* Hoddesdon (01992) 464616.

EARNSHAW, (Thomas) Roy, CBE 1978 (OBE 1971); Director and General Manager of Division, TBA Industrial Products Ltd, Rochdale, 1966–76; retired; *b* 27 Feb. 1917; *s* of Godfrey Earnshaw and Edith Annie (*née* Perry); *m* 1953, Edith Rushworth; two *d*. *Educ:* Marlborough Coll., Liverpool. MICS. Served War, Army, 1940–46: Major Lancs Fusiliers. Shipbroking, Liverpool, 1933–39; appts with subsid. cos of Turner & Newall Ltd: Turner Brothers Asbestos Co. Ltd, Rochdale (mainly Export Sales Manager), 1939–40 and 1946–53; Dir, AM&FM Ltd, Bombay, 1954–59; Export Dir, Ferodo Ltd, Chapel-en-le-Frith, 1959–66. British Overseas Trade Board: Mem. Adv. Council, 1975–82; Export Year Advr, 1976–77; Export United Advr, 1978–83. Director: Actair Holdings Ltd, 1979–83; Actair Internat. Ltd, 1979–83; Unico Finance Ltd, 1979–81. Formerly: Pres., Rochdale Chamber of Commerce; Chm., NW Region Chambers of Commerce; UK Delegate to European Chambers of Commerce. London Economic Adviser to Merseyside CC, 1980–82. Vis. Fellow, Henley Management Coll. (formerly ASC), 1981–90. Chm., Henley Crime Prevention Panel, 1992–94; Mem., Bd of Managers, Henley YMCA, 1989–91. FRSA. *Publication:* Glad Hearts in Export Year, 1991. *Recreations:* gardening, oil painting, hill walking, cycling. *Club:* Leander (Henley-on-Thames).

EASMON, Prof. Charles Syrett Farrell, MD, PhD; Director of Education and Training, North Thames Region, since 1994, and Dean of Postgraduate Medicine for Northwest Thames, since 1993, British Postgraduate Medical Federation, University of London; *b* 20 Aug. 1946; *s* of Dr McCormack Charles Farrell Easmon and Enid Winifred Easmon; *m* 1977, Susan Lynn (*née* Peach). *Educ:* Epsom Coll.; St Mary's Hospital Med. Sch. (Open Schol.; MB BS; MD); PhD London. MRCP; FRCPath. Pathology trng, St Bartholomew's Hosp., 1970–71; St Mary's Hospital Medical School: Research Asst, 1971; Lectr, 1973; Sen. Lectr, 1976; Reader and Actg Head of Dept, 1980; Personal Chair, 1983; Fleming Prof. of Med. Microbiol., 1984–92. *Publications:* (ed) Medical Microbiology, vol. 1 1982, vols 2 and 3 1983, vol. 4 1984; (ed) Infections in the Immunocompromised Host, 1983; (ed) Staphylococci and Staphylococcal Infections, 1983; numerous papers in learned jls. *Recreations:* music, history, fishing. *Address:* 21 Cranes Park Avenue, Surbiton, Surrey KT5 8BS.

EASON, Anthony Gordon, CBE 1995; Secetary for Planning, Environment and Lands, Hong Kong, 1992–95; *b* 30 May 1938; *s* of Aubrey Eason and Helen Eason (*née* Hajj); *m* 1962, Teresa Wong; two *d*. *Educ:* Chatham House Grammar Sch., Ramsgate; RMA, Sandhurst. Served RA, 1959–62. Hong Kong Civil Service: Exec. Officer, 1962–68; Admin. Service, 1968–89; Dir, Buildings and Lands, 1989–92. *Recreations:* reading, walking. *Address:* Flat 7E, Clapham Court, Stanley Fort, Hong Kong.

EASON, Henry, CBE 1967; JP; a Vice-President of the Institute of Bankers, 1969–75, and Consultant with special reference to overseas relationships, 1971–74 (Secretary-General, 1959–71); *b* 12 April 1910; *s* of late H. Eason and F. J. Eason; *m* 1939 (at Hexham Abbey), Isobel (*d* 1992), *d* of Wm and late Dorothy Stevenson; one *s* two *d*. *Educ:* Yarm (Schol.); King's Coll., University of Durham. BCom (with distinction). Barrister-at-law, Gray's Inn. Served Lloyds Bank until 1939; Asst Sec., Institute of Bankers, 1939. Served War of 1939–45 and until 1946, with Royal Air Force (Wing Commander, despatches twice). Asst Dir, Military Gov. (Banking), NW Europe, 1944–46; United Nations Adviser (Banking) to Pakistan Govt, 1952; Deputy Sec., Institute of Bankers, 1956; Governor,

City of London Coll., 1958–69; Mem., British National Cttee, Internat. Chamber Commerce, 1959–74. Director: Internat. Banking Summer Sch., Christ Church, Oxford, 1961, 1964, 1970; Cambridge Banking Seminar, Christ's Coll., Cambridge, 1968 and 1969. Editor, Jl Inst. of Bankers, 1959–71. Hon. Fellow, Inst. of Bankers, 1971. JP Bromley 1967. Gen. Comr of Income Tax, Bromley, 1973–76. *Publications:* contributions to professional journals. *Recreations:* golf, walking, gardening, world travel. *Address:* 12 Redgate Drive, Hayes Common, Bromley BR2 7BT. *T:* 0181–462 1900. *Clubs:* Gresham, Bankers'; Langley Park Golf.

EAST, David Albert, QPM 1982; Secretary, Welsh Rugby Union, 1989; *b* 5 June 1936; *s* of Albert East and Florence Emily East; *m* 1957, Gloria (*née* Swinden); one *d*. *Educ:* King Alfred Grammar Sch., Wantage, Berks; University Coll. London (LLB Hons). Berks Constabulary, 1958–65 (constable to sergeant); First Special Course, Police Coll., Bramshill, 1962 (Johnson Prize and Cert. of Distinction); Inspector, York City Police, 1965–68; UCL, 1965–68; Metropol. Police Chief Inspector to Chief Supt, 1968–75; Eight Sen. Comd Course, Bramshill, 1971; Asst Chief Constable, Avon and Somerset Constab., 1975–78; RCDS, 1978; Dep. Chief Constable, Devon and Cornwall Constab., 1978–82, Chief Constable, 1982–83; seconded to Cyprus, 1981 and to Singapore, 1982; Chief Constable, S Wales Constab., 1983–88. Chm., British Police Athletic Assoc. OStJ 1985. Police Long Service and Good Conduct Medal, 1980. *Recreations:* Rugby, cricket.

EAST, Frederick Henry, CB 1976; FEng 1984; FIEE, FRAeS; Deputy Secretary, and Chief Weapon System Engineer (Polaris), Ministry of Defence, 1976–80, retired; *b* 15 Sept. 1919; *s* of Frederick Richard East; *m* 1st, 1942, Pauline Isabel Veale Horne (*d* 1972); 2nd, 1990, Christine Grace Veale Horne. *Educ:* Skinners' Company's Sch., Tunbridge Wells; University Coll., Exeter (Visc. St Cyres Schol., Tucker and Franklin Prize, 1939). BSc London 1940; MInstP. Joined Research Dept, Min. of Aircraft Production, 1940; various appts in RAE, 1942–57; Asst Dir of Air Armament Research and Develt, Min. of Supply/Aviation, 1957–62; Head of Weapon Project Gp, RAE, 1962–67; Student, IDC, 1968; Asst Chief Scientific Adviser (Projects), MoD, 1969–70; Dir, Royal Armament Res. and Develt Establishment, 1971–75. Reader, C of E, 1969–; Mem., Candidates Cttee, ACCM, 1981–86. *Publications:* contrib. to: Application of Critical Path Techniques, 1968; official reports, and articles in jls. *Address:* The Folly, Mill Street, Prestbury, Cheltenham GL52 3BG. *T:* Cheltenham (01242) 230749.

EAST, John Anthony, OBE 1982; Chief Executive, English Tourist Board, 1985–95; Chairman, Watermark, since 1995; *b* 25 May 1930; *s* of John East and Jessie Mary East; *m* 1st, 1957, Barbara Collins; two *s* one *d*; 2nd, 1982, Susan Finch; two *d*. *Educ:* Bromley Grammar School. Reuter's, 1954–58; Notley Advertising, 1958–60; Director: French Government Tourist Office, 1960–70; English Tourist Bd, 1970–95. *Publications:* History of French Architecture, 1968; Gascony and the Pyrenees, 1969; articles on France and French architecture. *Recreations:* walking, gardening, studying things French. *Address:* (office) 12 Hands Road, SW3.

EAST, Kenneth Arthur, CMG 1971; HM Diplomatic Service, retired; Ambassador to Iceland, 1975–81; *b* 9 May 1921; *s* of H. F. East; *m* 1946, Katherine Blackley; two *s* three *d*. *Educ:* Taunton's Sch; Southampton Univ. Served HM Forces, 1942–46. India Office/Commonwealth Relations Office, 1946–50; Asst Private Sec. to Sec. of State; First Secretary: Ottawa, 1950–53; Colombo, 1956–60; Head of East and General Africa Dept, CRO, 1961–63; Head of Personnel Dept, CRO, 1963–64; Counsellor, Diplomatic Service Administration, 1965; Counsellor and Head of Chancery, Oslo, 1965–70; Minister, Lagos, 1970–74. *Club:* Commonwealth Trust.

EAST, Sir (Lewis) Ronald, Kt 1966; CBE 1951; retired as Chairman, State Rivers and Water Supply Commission, Victoria (1936–65) and as Commissioner, River Murray Commission, Australia (1936–65); *b* 17 June 1899; *s* of Lewis Findlay East, ISO, Evansford, Vic., Australia and Annie Eleanor (*née* Burchett) Brunswick, Vic.; *m* 1927, Constance Lilias Keil, MA, Kilwinning, Ayrshire; three *d*. *Educ:* Scotch Coll., Melbourne; Melbourne Univ. BCE (Melbourne) 1922; MCE (Melbourne) 1924. Mem., Snowy Mountains Coun., until 1965; Pres., Instn of Engrs, Austr., 1952–53; Mem. Coun., Instn of Civil Engrs, 1960–62; Vice-Pres., Internat. Commn on Irrigation and Drainage, 1959–62. Hon. Fellow, Instn of Engineers, Australia, 1969; FRHSV 1983. Coopers Hill War Meml Prize and Telford Premium, ICE, 1932; Kernot Memorial Medal, University of Melbourne, 1949; Peter Nicol Russell Memorial Medal, Instn of Engineers, Australia, 1957. Hon. DEng Melbourne, 1981. *Publications:* River Improvement, Land Drainage and Flood Protection, 1952; A South Australian Colonist of 1836 and his Descendants, 1972; The Kiel Family and related Scottish Pioneers, 1974; More Australian Pioneers: the Burchetts and related families, 1976; (ed) The Gallipoli Diary of Sergeant Lawrence, 1981; More About the East Family and Related Pioneers, 1988; many technical papers on water conservation and associated subjects in Proc. Instn Engs, Austr., Proc. Instn Civil Engrs, Amer. Soc. Civil Engrs and other jls. *Recreation:* handicrafts (model engineering). *Address:* 57 Waimarie Drive, Mt Waverley, Victoria 3149, Australia. *T:* Melbourne (3) 2774315.

EAST, Hon. Paul Clayton; MP (N) Rotorua, New Zealand, since 1978; Attorney-General, since 1990; Minister for Crown Health Enterprises, since 1991; Minister of State Services, since 1993; *b* 4 Aug. 1946; *s* of Edwin Cuthbert East and Edith Pauline Addison East; *m* 1972, Marilyn Kottman; three *d*. *Educ:* King's Coll., Auckland; Auckland Univ. (LLB 1970); Univ. of Virginia, USA (LLM 1972). Law Clerk, Morpeth Gould & Co., Solicitors, Auckland, 1968–70; barrister and solicitor, Auckland, 1971; Graduate Fellow, Univ. of Va Sch. of Law, 1971–72; Solicitor, 1973, Partner, 1974–78, Consultant, 1978–, East Brewster, Solicitors, Rotorua. City Councillor, and Dep. Mayor of Rotorua, 1974–79 (Chm., Finance Cttee, 1977–79). Opposition Spokesman, NZ Parliament: for Commerce and Customs, 1984; on Justice, Attorney-Gen. and Constitutional Affairs, 1985; on Health, 1986; on Justice and Attorney-Gen., 1990. Leader of House of Representatives, 1990–93. Chm., Parly Select Cttee on Official Information, 1982; Member: Parly Select Cttee for Justice and Law Reform, 1987–90; Nat. Exec., NZ Nat. Party, 1985; NZ Delegn, Council of Europe and Eur. Parlt, 1985; NZ Delegn, Eur. Parlt, 1985. Chm., Rotorua Airport Cttee, 1977–78; Mem. Exec., Airport Authorities of NZ, 1974–79. Trustee, Rotorua Hospice; Patron: Rotorua Racing Club; Rotorua Multiple Sclerosis Soc.; Patron, Rotorua Branch: NZ Crippled Children Soc.; SPCA; NZ Riding for Disabled Assoc. Fellow, Australia/NZ Foundn, 1983. *Publications:* numerous articles. *Recreations:* ski-ing, fishing, golf. *Address:* 23 Sophia Street, Rotorua, New Zealand. *T:* (4) 4992677. *Club:* Rotorua (NZ).

EAST, Sir Ronald; *see* East, Sir L. R.

EAST, Ronald Joseph; Director: Kleinwort Charter Investment Trust PLC; Kleinwort Development Fund PLC; *b* 17 Dec. 1931; *s* of Joseph William and Marion Elizabeth Emma East; *m* 1955, Iris Joyce Beckwith; two *d*. *Educ:* Clare Coll., Cambridge Univ. (MA). Engineering Apprenticeship, Ford Trade Sch., Ford Motor Co. Ltd, 1945–52. Troop Comdr, RA (Lieut), 1953–55. Managerial posts in economics, product planning, finance, and engineering areas of Ford Motor Co. Ltd, 1959–65; Guest, Keen & Nettlefolds Ltd: Corporation Staff Dir of Planning, 1965–70; Planning Exec., Automotive and Allied Products Sector, 1972–73; Chairman: GKN Castings Ltd, 1974–77; GKN Kent Alloys Ltd, 1974–77; GKN Shotton Ltd, 1974–77; Dir, GKN (UK) Ltd, 1974–77; Corporate Staff Dir, Group Supplies, GKN Ltd, 1976–77. Dir, Programme Analysis and Review (PAR) and Special Advisor to Chief Sec. to the Treasury, 1971–72. Chairman: Hale Hamilton Hldgs, 1981–89; Hale Hamilton (Valves), 1981–89. *Recreations:* walking, ski-ing, ethnology, dramatic art. *Address:* The Waldrons, Feckenham, Worcs B96 6JP. *T:* Astwood Bank (01527) 892486.

EAST, William Gordon; Professor of Geography in the University of London at Birkbeck College, 1947–70, now Emeritus Professor; *b* 10 Nov. 1902; *s* of George Richard East and Jemima (*née* Nicoll); *m* 1934, Dorothea Small; two *s* two *d*. *Educ:* Sloane Sch., Chelsea; Peterhouse, Cambridge. Open scholarship in History, 1921, and research studentship, 1924, at Peterhouse. BA (Hons), Cambridge Univ. (History), 1924. MA 1928; Thirlwall Prizeman of Cambridge Univ., 1927. Asst in historical geography, London Sch. of Economics, 1927; temp. administrative officer in Ministry of Economic Warfare and Foreign Office, 1941–45; Reader in Geography in University of London, 1946. Visiting Professor: Univ. of Minnesota, 1952; Univ. of California, Los Angeles, 1959–60; Univ. of Michigan, 1966–67; Univ. of Wisconsin, 1969–70; Univ. of Saskatchewan, 1971. Myres Memorial Lectr, Oxford Univ., 1970–71. Mem., RGS Council, 1956–59 (Hon. Fellow, 1992); Pres., Inst. of British Geographers, 1959. Murchison Award, RGS, 1972. *Publications:* The Union of Moldavia and Wallachia, 1859, 1929, repr. 1973; An Historical Geography of Europe, 1935; The Geography Behind History, 1938; Mediterranean Problems, 1940; (ed jtly) The Changing Map of Asia, 1950, 1971; (Jt) The Spirit and Purpose of Geography, 1951; (ed jtly) The Changing World, 1956; (ed) The Caxton Atlas, 1960; (ed) Regions of The British Isles, 1960–; The Soviet Union, 1963, 2nd edn 1976; (jt) Our Fragmented World, 1975; contributions to journals of geography, history and foreign affairs. *Address:* Wildwood, 17 Danes Way, Oxshott, Surrey KT22 0LU. *T:* Oxshott (01372) 842351.

EAST ANGLIA, Bishop of, (RC), since 1995; **Rt Rev. Peter David Smith;** *b* 21 Oct. 1943. *Educ:* Clapham Coll.; Univ. of Exeter (LLB 1966); St John's Seminary, Wonersh; Angelicum Univ., Rome (Dr *summa cum laude* 1977). Coutts Bank, London; ordained priest, 1972; Asst Priest, Larkhall Lane, London, 1972–74; Prof. of Canon Law, St John's Seminary, Wonersh, 1977–84; Parish Priest, St Andrew's, Thornton Heath, 1984–85; Rector, St John's Seminary, Wonersh, 1985–95. Vice-Officialis and Judge, Diocesan Marriage Tribunal, 1977; Officialis, Metropolitan Tribunal, 1980–85; Mem., Cttee for Ministerial Formation, Bishops' Conf., 1989–. *Address:* The White House, 21 Upgate, Poringland, Norwich, Norfolk NR14 7SH. *T:* Framingham Earl (01508) 492202.

EASTCOTT, Harry Hubert Grayson, MS; FRCS; FRCOG; Consulting Surgeon, St Mary's Hospital; Consultant in Surgery and Vascular Surgery to the Royal Navy, 1957–82, now Emeritus; *b* 17 Oct. 1917; *s* of Harry George and Gladys Eastcott; *m* 1941, Doreen Joy, *e d* of Brenchley Ernest and Muriel Mittell; four *d*. *Educ:* Latymer Sch.; St Mary's Hosp. Medical School and Middlesex Hospital Medical Sch., University of London; Harvard Med. Sch. War of 1939–45, Junior surgical appts and service as Surgeon Lieut, RNVR up till 1946. Surg. Lieut Comdr RNVR, London Div., until 1957. MRCS; LRCP; MB, BS (Hons), 1941; FRCS 1946; MS (London), 1951. Sen. Registrar, 1950 as Hon. Cons. to St Mary's and Asst Dir Surgical Unit; Research Fellow in Surgery, Harvard Med. Sch., and Peter Bent Brigham Hosp., Boston, Mass, 1949–50; recognised teacher, 1953, and Examr, 1959, in surgery, University of London; Cons. Surgeon, St Mary's Hosp. and Lectr in Surgery, St Mary's Hosp. Med. Sch., 1955–82; Surgeon, Royal Masonic Hosp., 1964–80; Cons. Surgeon, King Edward VII Hosp. for Officers, 1965–87; Hon. Surg., RADA, 1959–; External Examr in Surgery: Queen's Univ., Belfast, 1964–67; Cambridge Univ., 1968–84; Univ. of Lagos, Nigeria, 1970–71. Editorial Sec., British Jl of Surgery, 1972–78. Royal College of Surgeons: Hunterian Prof., 1953; Mem. Court of Examrs, 1964–70; Mem. Council, 1971 83; Bradshaw Lectr, 1980; Vice-Pres., 1981–83; Cecil Joll Prize, 1984; RCS Visitor to RCOG Council, 1972–80. FRSocMed (Hon. Sec., Section of Surgery, 1963–65, Vice-President, 1966, Pres., 1977; Pres., United Services Section, 1981–83, Hon. Mem., 1992). Fellow Medical Soc. of London (Hon. Sec., 1962–64, Vice-Pres. 1964, Pres., 1976, Fothergill Gold Medal, 1974, Trustee 1988). Pres., Assoc. of Surgeons of GB and Ireland, 1982–83. Mem., Soc. Apothecaries, 1967 (Galen Medal, 1993). Hon. FACS, 1977; Hon. FRACS, 1978; Hon. Fellow: Amer. Surgical Assoc., 1981; Amer. Heart Assoc.; Stroke Council, 1981; Hon. Mem., Purkinje Med. Soc., Czechoslovakia, 1984. Editor, Brit. Jl of Surg., 1973–79. *Publications:* Arterial Surgery, 1969, 3rd edn 1992; A Colour Atlas of Operations on the Internal Carotid Artery, 1984; various articles on gen. and arterial surgery, Lancet, Brit. Jl of Surg., etc.; contrib. chap. of peripheral vascular disease, Med. Annual, 1961–80; various chaps in textbooks on these subjects. *Recreations:* music, travel, and a lifelong interest in aeronautics. *Address:* 47 Chiltern Court, Baker Street, NW1 5SP. *T:* 0171–935 2020. *Club:* Garrick.

EASTERLING, Prof. Patricia Elizabeth; Regius Professor of Greek, Cambridge University, and Fellow of Newnham College, Cambridge, since 1994; *b* 11 March 1934; *d* of Edward Wilson Fairfax and Annie Smith; *m* 1956, Henry John Easterling; one *s*. *Educ:* Blackburn High School for Girls; Newnham College, Cambridge (BA 1955, MA 1959). Asst Lectr, Univ. of Manchester, 1957–58; University of Cambridge: Asst Lectr, 1968; Lectr, 1969–87; Newnham College, Cambridge: Asst Lectr, 1958–60; Fellow and Lectr, 1960–87; Dir of Studies in Classics, 1979–87; Vice-Principal, 1981–86; Hon. Fellow, 1987–94; Prof. of Greek, UCL, 1987–94. Townsend Lectr, Cornell Univ., 1990. Pres., Classical Assoc., 1988–89. Chm., Council of Univ. Classical Depts, 1990–93. *Publications:* (with E. J. Kenney) Ovidiana Graeca, 1965; (ed) Sophocles, Trachiniae, 1982; (with B. M. W. Knox, ed and contrib.) Cambridge History of Classical Literature, vol I, 1985; (ed with J. V. Muir) Greek Religion and Society, 1985; articles and reviews in classical jls. *Recreation:* hill walking. *Address:* Newnham College, Cambridge CB3 9DF. *T:* Cambridge (01223) 335700.

EASTHAM, Kenneth; MP (Lab) Manchester, Blackley, since 1979; *b* 11 Aug. 1927; *s* of late James Eastham; *m* 1951, Doris, *d* of Albert Howarth; one *d*. Planning engr, GEC, Trafford Park. Mem., Manchester CC, 1962–80 (Dep. Leader 1975–79; Chairman: Planning Cttee, 1971–74; Educn Cttee, 1978–79); Mem., NW Econ. Planning Council, 1975–79. An Opposition Whip, 1987–92. *Address:* House of Commons, SW1A 0AA; 12 Nan Nook Road, Manchester M23 9BZ.

EASTON, David John; HM Diplomatic Service; Foreign and Commonwealth Office, since 1989; *b* 27 March 1941; *o s* of Air Cdre Sir James Easton, KCMG, CB, CBE, and Anna, *d* of Lt-Col J. A. McKenna, Ottawa; *m* 1964, Alexandra Julie, *er d* of K. W. Clark, London, W8; two *s* two *d*. *Educ:* Stone House, Broadstairs; Stowe (Exhbnr); Balliol Coll., Oxford (Trevelyan Schol.; BA Hons Jurisprudence 1963, MA 1973). Apprentice, United Steel Cos, Workington, 1960. TA, 1959–65; 2nd Lieut, Oxford Univ. OTC, 1962; Lieut, Inns of Court and City Yeo., 1964. Entered Foreign Office, 1963; Third Sec., Nairobi, 1965–66; Second Sec., UK Mission to UN, Geneva, 1967–70; MECAS, Lebanon, 1970–72; First Sec., FCO, 1972–73; First Sec. (Information), Tripoli, 1973–77; Defence Dept, FCO, 1977–80; First Sec. (Chancery), later Political Counsellor, Amman, 1980–83; Counsellor, FCO, 1984–86; Counsellor (Political), New Delhi, 1986–89. Director, Internat. Community Sch. (Jordan) Ltd, 1980–83 (Chm. 1981–83). Pres., Delhi Diplomatic

Assoc., 1988–89; Chm., Lansdowne Residents' Assoc., 1990–95. *Recreations:* swimming, tennis, travel, antiques and antiquities. *Address:* c/o Foreign and Commonwealth Office, King Charles Street, SW1A 2AH.

EASTON, James, OBE 1986; HM Diplomatic Service, retired; Feature Writer, Accordion Times, since 1992; *b* 1 Sept. 1931; *s* of John Easton and Helen Easton (*née* Whitney); *m* 1960, Rosemary Hobbin; one *s* two *d. Educ:* St John Cantius Catholic Sch., Broxburn. Served 3rd Hussars, 1952–55. Admiralty, 1957–60; FO, 1960; Prague, 1960–62; Paris, 1963–65; FO, 1965–68; Vice-Consul: Belgrade, 1968–71; La Paz, 1971–74; Second Sec. (Commercial), New York, 1974–78; FCO, 1978–83; First Sec., Rome, 1983–87; Counsellor (Admin) and Consul-Gen., Brussels, 1987–89. *Recreation:* music. *Address:* 6 Cedar Gardens, Sutton, Surrey SM2 5DD. *T:* 0181–643 2432.

EASTON, Robert Alexander, PhD; Chief Executive, Delta plc, since 1989; *b* 24 Oct. 1948; *s* of Malcolm Edward George Easton and Violet May Liddell Easton (*née* Taylor); *m* 1983, Lynden Anne Welch; two *d. Educ:* St Lawrence Coll.; Univ. of Manchester (BSc Hons); Univ. of Aston (PhD). Delta plc, 1974–: Dir of Planning, 1980–83; Man. Dir, Industrial Services Div., 1984–87; Dep. Chief Exec., 1988–89. Director: G. E. Crane (Holdings), 1986–91; Harrisons & Crosfield plc, 1991–. *Recreations:* golf, travel, medieval art and architecture. *Address:* c/o Delta plc, 1 Kingsway, WC2B 6XF. *T:* 0171–836 3535.

EASTON, Sir Robert (William Simpson), Kt 1990; CBE 1980; CEng, FIMechE, FIMarE, FRINA; Chairman: Yarrow Shipbuilders Ltd, 1979–94; GEC Scotland, since 1990; *b* 30 Oct. 1922; *s* of James Easton and Helen Agnes (*née* Simpson); *m* 1948, Jean, *d* of H. K. Fraser and Jean (*née* Murray); one *s* one *d. Educ:* Royal Technical Coll., Glasgow. Fairfield Shipbuilding Co., 1939–51; Yarrow Shipbuilders Ltd: Manager, 1951; Director, 1965; Dep. Managing Director, 1970; Managing Director, 1977–91; Main Board Director, Yarrow & Co. Ltd, 1970–77. Vice Pres., Clyde Shipbuilders, 1972–79; Chm., Clyde Port Authy, 1983–93. Chm., GEC Naval Systems, 1991–94; Director: Genships (Canada), 1979–80; Supermarine Consortium Ltd, 1986–90. Chancellor, Paisley Univ., 1993–. Pres., Inst. of Welding, 1991–93; Member: Council, RINA, 1983–91 (Hon. Vice Pres., 1991–); Worshipful Company of Shipwrights, 1982–; Merchants House of Glasgow, 1989–; Incorporation of Hammermen, 1989–. *Recreations:* walking, sailing, golf, gardening. *Address:* Springfield, Stuckenduff, Shandon, Dunbartonshire G84 8NW. *T:* Rhu (01436) 820677. *Clubs:* Caledonian; RNVR (Glasgow).

EASTWOOD, Basil Stephen Talbot; HM Diplomatic Service; Director of Research and Analysis, Foreign and Commonwealth Office, since 1991; *b* 4 March 1944; *s* of late Christopher Gilbert Eastwood, CMG and Catherine Emma (*née* Peel); *m* 1970, Alison Faith Hutchings; four *d. Educ:* Eton (KS); Merton College, Oxford. Entered Diplomatic Service, 1966; Middle East Centre for Arab Studies, 1967; Jedda, 1968; Colombo, 1969; Cairo, 1972; Cabinet Office, 1976; FCO, 1978; Bonn, 1980; Khartoum, 1984; Athens, 1987. *Recreation:* theatre. *Address:* c/o Foreign and Commonwealth Office, SW1A 2AH.
See also M. L. Cahill.

EASTWOOD, John Stephen; a Recorder, 1987–92; Regional Chairman of Industrial Tribunals, Nottingham Region, 1983–92; *b* 27 April 1925; *s* of Rev. John Edgar Eastwood and Elfreda Eastwood; *m* 1949, Nancy (*née* Gretton); one *s* two *d. Educ:* Denstone College, Uttoxeter. Solicitor. RN (Coder), 1943–46. Articles, and Asst Sol. to Leics CC, 1946–50; Asst Sol., Salop CC, 1950–53; Sen. Asst Sol., Northants CC, 1953–58; Partner, Wilson & Wilson, Solicitors, Kettering, 1958–76; Chm., Industrial Tribunals, 1976–83; Asst Recorder, 1983–87. *Recreations:* music, painting, photography, walking, gardening, exploring British Isles, grandchildren. *Address:* 4 Gate Lane, Broughton, Kettering, Northants NN14 1ND. *T:* Kettering (01536) 790169.

EASTWOOD, Noel Anthony Michael, MA; CEng, MRAeS; Chairman, InterData Group, 1981–93; *b* 7 Dec. 1932; *s* of Edward Norman Eastwood and Irene Dawson; *m* 1965, Elizabeth Tania Gresham Boyd, *d* of Comdr Thomas Wilson Boyd, CBE, DSO, DL and Irene Barbara Gresham; three *s. Educ:* The Leys School, Cambridge; Christ's College, Cambridge. Lieut RA, 1951–53; Pilot Officer, RAFVR, 1954–57; de Havilland Aircraft Co., 1956–60; RTZ Group, 1960–61; AEI Group, 1961–64; Director: Charterhouse Development, 1964–69; Charterhouse Japhet, 1969–79 (Pres., Charterhouse Japhet Texas, 1974–77); Charterhouse Middle East, 1975–79; Wharton Crane & Hoist, 1967–70 (Chm.); Daniel Doncaster & Son, 1971–81; The Barden Corp., 1971–82; Hawk Publishing (UAE), 1981–87; Oryx Publishing (Qatar), 1981–87; Falcon Publishing (Bahrain), 1981–84; Caribbean Publishing, 1981–84; IDP InterData (Australia), 1984–92; European Public Policy Advisers Gp, 1987–; Spearhead Communications, 1988–; Seafish Falklands Ltd, 1990–. Sec., RAeS, 1983. Member: London Cttee, Yorkshire & Humberside Development Assoc., 1975–; Management Cttee, Offshore Europe Conf. and Exhibn, 1990–; S Atlantic Council, 1991–. Hon. Treas., Herts Conservation Soc., 1992–. *Recreations:* vintage sportscars, family picnics, desert travel. *Address:* Palace House, Much Hadham, Herts SG10 6HW. *T:* Much Hadham (0127984) 2409. *Club:* Royal Thames Yacht.

EASTWOOD, Dr Wilfred, PhD; FEng, FICE, FIStructE, FIMechE; Senior Partner, Eastwood and Partners, Consulting Engineers, since 1972; *b* 15 Aug. 1923; *s* of Wilfred Andrew Eastwood and Annice Gertrude Eastwood; *m* 1947, Dorothy Jean Gover; one *s* one *d*. Road Research Laboratory, 1945–46; University of Manchester, 1946–47; University of Aberdeen, 1947–53; University of Sheffield, 1954–70: Head, Dept of Civil Engrg, 1964–70; Dean, Faculty of Engrg, 1967–70. Pres., IStructE, 1976–77; Chairman: CEI, 1983–84; Commonwealth Engrg Council, 1983–85. Hon. DEng Sheffield, 1983. *Publications:* papers in Proc. ICE and Jl IStructE, etc. *Address:* 45 Whirlow Park Road, Sheffield S11 9NN. *T:* Sheffield (0114) 236 4645. *Club:* Yorkshire County Cricket (Leeds).

EASTY, Prof. David Leonello, MD; FRCS, FCOphth; Professor of Ophthalmology and Head of Department of Ophthalmology, University of Bristol, since 1982; *b* 1933; *s* of Arthur Victor Easty and Florence Margaret (*née* Kennedy); *m* 1963, Božana Martinović; three *d. Educ:* King's Sch., Canterbury; Univ. of Manchester. MD 1963; FRCS 1969; FCOphth 1988. Capt., RAMC, 1959; Med. Officer, British Antarctic Survey, 1960. Moorfield's Eye Hospital: Resident, 1966–69; Lectr, 1969–72; Consultant, Bristol Eye Hosp., 1972–82. Dir, Corneal Transplant Service Eye Bank, 1986–. Member: BMA; RSocMed; Internat. Soc. for Eye Res.; Assoc. for Res. in Vision and Ophthalmology; British Soc. for Immunology. Member: Antarctic Club; Piscatorial Soc. *Publications:* Virus Disease of the Eye, 1985; (with G. Smolim) External Eye Disease, 1985; (ed) Current Ophthalmic Surgery, 1990; (with N. Ragge) Immediate Eye Care, 1990. *Recreations:* fishing, squash, running, opera. *Address:* Bristol Eye Hospital, Lower Maudlim Street, Bristol BS1 2LX. *T:* Bristol (0117) 923 0060. *Clubs:* Army and Navy; Clifton (Bristol).

EATES, Edward Caston, CMG 1968; LVO 1961; QPM 1961; CPM 1956; Commissioner, The Royal Hong Kong Police, 1967–69, retired; re-employed at Foreign and Commonwealth Office, 1971–76; *b* London, 8 April 1916; *o s* of late Edward Eates and Elizabeth Lavinia Issac Eates (*née* Caston); *m* 1941, Maureen Teresa McGee (*d* 1987); no *c. Educ:* Highgate Sch.; King's Coll., London (LLB). Asst Examr, Estate Duty Office, 1935. Army, 1939–46 (RAC): Western Desert and NW Europe; Adjt 2nd Derby Yeo., 1943; Temp. Maj. 1944; Staff Coll. Quetta (sc), 1945. Apptd to Colonial Police Service, Nigeria, 1946; Sen. Supt, Sierra Leone, 1954; Comr, The Gambia, 1957; Asst Comr, 1963, Dep. Comr, 1966, Hong Kong. *Recreations:* cricket and association football (inactive); travel, motoring. *Address:* 2 Riverside Court, Colleton Crescent, Exeter EX2 4BZ. *T:* Exeter (01392) 436434. *Clubs:* Commonwealth Trust, East India; Surrey County Cricket.

EATOCK TAYLOR, Prof. (William) Rodney, FEng 1990; Professor of Mechanical Engineering, University of Oxford, and Fellow of St Hugh's College, Oxford, since 1989; *b* 10 Jan. 1944; *s* of late William Taylor, Hadley Wood, Herts and Norah O'Brien Taylor (*née* Ridgeway); *m* 1971, Jacqueline Lorraine Cannon, *d* of late Desmond Cannon Brookes; two *s. Educ:* Rugby Sch.; King's Coll., Cambridge (BA, MA); Stanford Univ. (MS, PhD). FRINA 1986; FIMechE 1989. Engineer, Ove Arup and Partners, 1968–70; University College London: Res. Asst, 1970; Lectr, 1972; Reader, 1980; Prof. of Ocean Engineering, 1984–89; Dean, Faculty of Engineering, 1988–89. Dir, Marine Technology Directorate Ltd, 1990–; Chm., Marine Technology Trust, 1991–. Member, Editorial Boards: Engineering Structures, 1978–; Applied Ocean Research, 1984–; Jl of Fluids and Structures, 1990–. *Publications:* numerous contribs to learned jls of structural dynamics and marine hydrodynamics. *Recreations:* walking, music. *Address:* St Hugh's College, Oxford OX2 6LE. *T:* Oxford (01865) 274900. *Club:* Athenæum.

EATON, Rt. Rev. Derek Lionel; *see* Nelson, NZ, Bishop of.

EATON, Fredrik Stefan, OC 1990; Chairman of Executive Committee, Eaton's of Canada Ltd, since 1994; *b* 26 June 1938; *s* of late John David Eaton and Signy Hildur Eaton (*née* Stephenson); *m* 1962, Catherine Howard (Nicky) Martin; one *s* one *d. Educ:* Univ. of New Brunswick (BA). T. Eaton Co. Ltd: joined 1962; positions in Victoria, London, England and Toronto, 1962–67; Dir, 1967; Pres. and Dir, Eaton's of Canada, 1969; Chm., Pres. and Chief Exec. Officer, 1977; Chm., 1988–91; High Comr for Canada in the UK, 1991–94. Director: Baton Broadcasting, 1994–; Hollinger, 1994–; Maple Leaf Foods, 1994–; Premdor, 1994–; Trizec Corp., 1994–. Member: CIIA; Ontario Ex-Presidents Assoc. Chm., Toronto Hosp.; Director: Bata Shoe Museum Foundn; WWF (Canada); Member: ICBP Rare Bird Club; Polite Soc. Gov., Eaton Foundn. FRSA. Chancellor, Univ. of New Brunswick, 1993–. Internat. Retailer of the Year Award, Nat. Retail Merchants Assoc., NY, 1978; McGill Univ. Management Award, 1987. Hon. LLD New Brunswick, 1983. *Recreations:* art, music, shooting, yachting. *Address:* Eaton's of Canada, 250 Yonge Street, Toronto, Ont M5B 1C8; Canada.

EATON, James Thompson, CBE 1992; TD 1963; Lord-Lieutenant, County Borough of Londonderry, since 1986; *b* 11 Aug. 1927; *s* of late J. C. Eaton, DL, and Mrs E. A. F. Eaton, MBE; *m* 1954, Lucy Edith Smeeton, OBE 1986; one *s* one *d. Educ:* Campbell Coll., Belfast; Royal Technical Coll., Glasgow. Man. Dir, Eaton & Co. Ltd, 1965–80. Mem., Londonderry Devolt Commn, 1969–73 (Chm., Educn Cttee, 1969–73); Chm., Londonderry Port and Harbour Comrs, 1989–95 (Mem., 1977–95; Vice Chm., 1985). Served North Irish Horse (TA), 1950–67 (Major, 1961). Hon. Col, 1st (NI) Bn, ACF, 1992–. High Sheriff, Co. Londonderry, 1982. *Recreations:* military history, gardening. *Address:* Cherryvale Park, Limavady, Co. Londonderry, Northern Ireland BT49 9AH.

EATON, Adm. Sir Kenneth (John), GBE 1994; KCB 1990; FEng, FIEE; Controller of the Navy, 1989–94; *b* 12 Aug. 1934; *s* of John and May Eaton; *m* 1959, Sheena Buttle; two *s* one *d. Educ:* Borden Grammar Sch.; Fitzwilliam Coll., Cambridge (BA). FIEE 1989; FEng 1994. HMS Victorious, 1959–61; ASWE, 1961–65; HM Ships Eagle, Collingwood and Bristol, 1965–71; Defence Communications Network, 1971–72; ASWE, 1972–76; HMS Ark Royal, 1976–78; MoD, 1978–81; ASWE, 1981–83; Dir Torpedoes, 1983–85; Dir-Gen. Underwater Weapons (Navy), 1985–87; Flag Officer, Portsmouth, and Naval Base Comdr, Portsmouth, 1987–89. Non-exec. Dir, Govt Div., UKAEA, 1995–. *Recreations:* countryside, theatre, opera, classical music. *Address:* c/o Naval Secretary, Victory Building, HM Naval Base, Portsmouth PO1 3LS.

EATON, Martin Roger, CMG 1993; HM Diplomatic Service; Deputy Legal Adviser, Foreign and Commonwealth Office, since 1991; *b* 10 Nov. 1940; *m* 1972, Sylvia White; two *s* one *d*. Admitted Solicitor, 1968; FCO, 1970; Bonn, 1977; FCO, 1981; Legal Counsellor: FCO, 1982; UKREP Brussels, 1987; FCO, 1991. *Recreations:* choral singing, gardening. *Address:* c/o Foreign and Commonwealth Office, SW1A 2AH.

EATON, Robert James; Chairman and Chief Executive, Chrysler Corporation, since 1993; *b* 13 Feb. 1940; *s* of Gene and Mildred Eaton; *m* 1964, Cornelia Cae Drake; two *s. Educ:* Univ. of Kansas (BS Mech Eng). Joined General Motors, 1963, transf. to English staff, 1971; Chevrolet Div., 1975; Oldsmobile, 1979; Vice-Pres. in charge of Tech. Staffs, 1986; Pres., General Motors Europe, 1988–92; Mem., Bd of Dirs, Lotus Group, 1986–; Chm., Saab Auto, 1990–. Member: Industrial Adv. Board, Stanford Univ.; Business Roundtable and Business Council; President's Adv. Council on Trade and Policy Negotiations. Mem. Bd, Dama. Mem., Nat. Acad. of Engrg; FSAE. *Address:* Chrysler Corporation, 12000 Chrysler Drive, Highland Park, MI 48288, USA.

EATWELL, family name of **Baron Eatwell.**

EATWELL, Baron *cr* 1992 (Life Peer), of Stratton St Margaret in the County of Wiltshire; **John Leonard Eatwell;** Fellow of Trinity College, Cambridge, since 1970; Lecturer, Faculty of Economics and Politics, Cambridge University, since 1977; *b* 2 Feb. 1945; *s* of Harold Jack and Mary Eatwell; *m* 1970, Hélène Seppain; two *s* one *d. Educ:* Headlands Grammar Sch., Swindon; Queens' Coll., Cambridge (BA 1967; MA 1971); Harvard Univ. (PhD 1975). Teaching Fellow, Grad. Sch. of Arts and Scis, Harvard Univ., 1968–69; Res. Fellow, Queens' Coll., Cambridge, 1969–70; Asst Lectr, Faculty of Econs and Politics, Cambridge Univ., 1975–77. Vis. Prof. of Economics, New Sch. for Social Res., NY, 1982–. Econ. Advr to Rt Hon. Neil Kinnock, MP, Leader of the Labour Party, 1985–92. Opposition spokesman on Treasury affairs, and on trade and industry, HoL, 1992–93; Principal Opposition spokesman on Treasury and econ affairs, HoL, 1993–. Trustee and Sec., Inst. for Public Policy Res., 1988–. Chm., Crusaid, 1993–. Non-exec. Dir, Anglia Television Gp, 1994–. Chm., Extemporary Dance Theatre, 1990; Governor, Contemporary Dance Trust, 1991–; Dir, Arts Theatre Trust, Cambridge, 1991–. *Publications:* (with Joan Robinson) An Introduction to Modern Economics, 1973; Whatever Happened to Britain?, 1982; (ed with Murray Milgate) Keynes's Economics and the Theory of Value and Distribution, 1983; (ed with Murray Milgate and Peter Newman): The New Palgrave: A Dictionary of Economics, 4 vols, 1987; The New Palgrave Dictionary of Money and Finance, 3 vols, 1992; articles in sci. jls and other collected works. *Recreations:* classical and contemporary dance, Rugby Union football. *Address:* Trinity College, Cambridge CB2 1TQ. *T:* Cambridge (01223) 338406.

EAVES, Caroline Sarah; *see* Raphael, C. S.

EAYRS, Prof. John Thomas, PhD, DSc; Sands Cox Professor of Anatomy, University of Birmingham, 1968–77; *b* 23 Jan. 1913; *e s* of late Thomas William Eayrs, AMICE, and late Florence May (*née* Clough); *m* 1941, Frances Marjorie Sharp; one *s* two *d. Educ:* King Edward's, Birmingham; University of Birmingham. In industry until 1938. War service:

Pte Royal Warwicks Regt, 1939–40; 2nd Lieut Manchester Regt, 1940; Lieut 1940; Capt. 1941; Major 1942; Worcester Regt, 1943; sc Staff Coll., Camberley, 1944. University of Birmingham: Peter Thompson Prize, 1947; John Barritt Melson Memorial Gold Medal, 1947; Lectr in Anatomy, 1948; Bertram Windle Prize, 1950; Sen. Lectr 1955; Research Fellow, Calif. Inst. of Technology, 1956–57; Reader in Comparative Neurology, Birmingham, 1958; Henry Head Research Fellow, Royal Society, London, 1957–62; Prof. of Neuroendocrinology, Birmingham, 1961; Fitzmary Prof. of Physiology, London Univ., 1963–68. Governor, King Edward's Foundn, Birmingham, 1968–77. *Publications:* Scientific Papers dealing with developmental neuroendocrinology and behaviour in Jl Endocrin., Jl Anat. (London), Anim. Behav., etc. *Recreations:* cruising, foreign travel and languages. *Address:* 51 Old Street, Upton upon Severn, Worcester WR8 0HN.

EBAN, Abba; a Member of the Knesset, 1959–88; Minister of Foreign Affairs, Israel, 1966–74; *b* 2 Feb. 1915, Cape Town, SA; *s* of Avram and Alida Solomon; *m* 1945, Susan Ambache; one *s* one *d*. *Educ:* Cambridge Univ. (MA). Res. Fellow and Tutor for Oriental Languages, Pembroke Coll., Cambridge, 1938. Liaison officer of Allied HQ with Jewish population in Jerusalem, 1942–44; Chief Instructor, Middle East Arab Centre, Jerusalem, 1944–46; Jewish Agency, 1946–47; Liaison Officer with UN Special Commn on Palestine, 1947; UN: Representative of provisional govt of Israel, 1948; Permanent rep., 1949–59; Vice-Pres., General Assembly, 1953; Ambassador to USA, 1950–59; Minister without Portfolio, 1959–60; Minister of Educn and Culture, 1960–63; Dep. Prime Minister, 1963–66. Pres., Weizmann Inst. of Science, 1958–66; Vice-Pres., UN Conf. on Science and Technology in Advancement of New States, 1963; Mem., UN Adv. Cttee on Science and Technology for Develt. Fellow: World Acad. of Arts and Sciences; Amer. Acad. of Arts and Sciences; Amer. Acad. of Pol Science. Hon. Doctorates include: New York; Boston; Maryland; Cincinnati; Temple; Brandeis; Yeshiva. *Publications:* The Modern Literary Movement in Egypt, 1944; Maze of Justice, 1946; Social and Cultural Problems in the Middle East, 1947; The Toynbee Heresy, 1955; Voice of Israel, 1957; Tide of Nationalism, 1959; Chaim Weizmann: a collective biography, 1962; Reality and Vision in the Middle East (Foreign Affairs), 1965; Israel in the World, 1966; My People, 1968; My Country, 1972; An Autobiography, 1978; The New Diplomacy: international affairs in the modern age, 1983; Heritage, Civilisation and the Jews, 1985; Personal Witness: Israel through my eyes, 1993; articles in English, French, Hebrew and Arabic. *Address:* PO Box 394, Herzliya, Israel.

EBBSFLEET, Bishop Suffragan of, since 1994; **Rt. Rev. John Richards;** Episcopal Visitor for the Province of Canterbury, since 1994; Assistant Bishop, diocese of Lichfield, since 1994; *b* 4 Oct. 1933; *s* of William and Ethel Mary Richards; *m* 1958, Ruth Haynes; two *s* three *d*. *Educ:* Reading School; Wyggeston Grammar School, Leicester; Sidney Sussex Coll., Cambridge (MA); Ely Theological Coll. Asst Curate, St Thomas, Exeter, 1959–64; Rector of Holsworthy with Hollacombe and Cookbury, 1964–74; RD of Holsworthy, 1970–74; Rector of Heavitree with St Paul's, Exeter, 1974–81; RD of Exeter, 1978–81. Archdeacon of Exeter and Canon Res. of Exeter Cathedral, 1981–94. Chm. of House of Clergy, Exeter Diocesan Synod, 1979–82; Mem. Gen. Synod, 1985–94. Mem., C of E Pensions Bd, 1989–. A Church Commissioner, 1988–94 (Mem. Bd of Govs, 1993–94). *Recreations:* gardening, fishing, walking. *Address:* The Rectory, Leigh, Stoke-on-Trent ST10 4PT. *T:* Field (01889) 502366.

EBERHART, Richard (Ghormley); Professor Emeritus of English and Poet in Residence, Dartmouth College, USA; Florida Ambassador of the Arts, since 1984; *b* Austin, Minn, 5 April 1904; *s* of late Alpha La Rue Eberhart and late Lena Eberhart (*née* Lowenstein); *m* 1941, Helen Elizabeth Butcher, Christ Church, Cambridge, Mass; one *s* one *d*. *Educ:* Dartmouth Coll., USA (AB); St John's Coll., Cambridge Univ., England (BA, MA; Hon Fellow, 1986); Harvard Univ. Grad. Sch. of Arts and Sciences. Taught English, 1933–41, also tutor to son of King Prajadhipok of Siam for a year. Served War in USN Reserve finishing as Lieut-Comdr, 1946; subseq. entered Butcher Polish Co., Boston, Mass, as Asst Man., finishing as Vice-Pres. (now Hon. Vice-Pres. and Mem. Bd of Directors). Founder (and first Pres.) Poets' Theatre Inc., Cambridge, Mass, 1950. Called back to teaching, 1952, and has served as Poet in Residence, Prof., or Lecturer at University of Washington, University of Conn., Wheaton Coll., Princeton, and in 1956 was apptd Prof. of English and Poet in Residence at Dartmouth Coll. Class of 1925 Chair, 1968 (being absent as Consultant in Poetry to the Library of Congress, 1959–61). Visiting Professor: Univ. of Washington, 1967, Jan.–June 1972; Columbia Univ., 1975; Distinguished Vis. Prof., Florida Univ., 1974 (President's Medallion, 1977); Regents Prof., Univ. of California, Davis, 1975; First Wallace Stevens Fellow, Timothy Dwight Coll., Yale, 1976. Shelley Memorial Prize; Bollingen Prize, 1962; Pulitzer Prize, 1966; Fellow, Acad. of Amer. Poets, 1969 (Nat. Book Award, 1977). Advisory Cttee on the Arts, for the National Cultural Center (later John F. Kennedy Memorial Center), Washington, 1959; Member: Amer. Acad. and Inst. of Arts and Letters, 1960; Nat. Acad. of Arts and Sciences, 1967; Amer. Acad. of Arts and Letters, 1982; Elliston Lecturer on Poetry, University of Cincinnati, 1961. Poet Laureate of New Hampshire, 1979–84. Apptd Hon. Consultant in American Letters, The Library of Congress, 1963–66, reapptd, 1966–69. Hon. Pres., Poetry Soc. of America, 1972. Participant, Poetry International, London, 1973; Exhibn, Dartmouth Coll. Library, 1984. Hon. LittD: Dartmouth Coll., 1954; Skidmore Coll., 1966; Coll. of Wooster, 1969; Colgate Univ., 1974; St Lawrence Univ., 1985; Hon. DHL, Franklin Pierce, 1978. Phi Beta Kappa poem, Harvard, 1967; Hon. Mem., Alpha Chapter, Mass, 1967; New York Qly Poetry Day Award, 1980; Sarah Josepha Hale Award, Richards Library, Newport, NH, 1982; Robert Frost Medal, Poetry Soc. of America, 1986. Diploma: World Acad. of Arts and Culture, Republic of China, 1981; Internat. Poets Acad., Madras, India, 1987. Richard Eberhart Day: 14 July 1982, RI; 14 Oct. 1982, Dartmouth; Eberhart at Eighty, celebration at Univ. of Florida, 4–6 April 1984. *Publications:* (concurrently in England and America): A Bravery of Earth, 1930; Reading the Spirit, 1936; Selected Poems, 1951; Undercliff, Poems, 1946–53, also Great Praises, 1957; Collected Poems, 1930–60, 1960; Collected Verse Plays, 1962; The Quarry, 1964; Selected Poems, 1930–65, New Directions, 1965; Thirty One Sonnets, 1967; Shifts of Being, 1968; Fields of Grace, 1972 (Nat. Book Award nominee, 1973); Poems to Poets, 1975; Collected Poems 1930–1976, 1976; Collected Poems 1930–86, 1988; To Eberhart from Ginsberg: a letter about 'Howl', 1956, 1976; Of Poetry and Poets (criticism), 1979; Ways of Light, 1980; Survivors, 1980; Four Poems, 1980; New Hampshire/Nine Poems, 1980; Chocorua, 1981; Florida Poems, 1981; The Long Reach, 1984; Maine Poems, 1989; New and Collected Poems, 1990; Recorded Readings of his Poetry, 1961, 1968; four documentary films, 1972, 1975, 1986, 1987; *Festschriften:* (in New England Review, 1980) Richard Eberhart: A Celebration; (in Negative Capability, 1986) Richard Eberhart. *Recreations:* swimming, cruising, tennis, flying 7–ft kites. *Address:* 80 Lyme Road #161, Hanover, NH 03755–1230, USA. *Clubs:* Century (New York); Buck's Harbor Yacht (S Brooksville, Maine); Signet (Harvard).

EBERLE, Adm. Sir James (Henry Fuller), GCB 1981 (KCB 1979); Vice Admiral of the United Kingdom, since 1994; Director, Royal Institute of International Affairs, 1984–90; writer on international affairs and security; *b* 31 May 1927; *s* of late Victor Fuller Eberle and of Joyce Mary Eberle, Bristol; *m* 1950, Ann Patricia Thompson (*d* 1988), Hong Kong; one *s* two *d*. *Educ:* Clifton Coll.; RNC Dartmouth and Greenwich. Served War of 1939–45 in MTBs, HMS Renown, HMS Belfast; subseq. in Far East; qual. Gunnery Specialist 1951; Guided Missile Develt and trials in UK and USA, 1953–57; Naval Staff, 1960–62; Exec. Officer, HMS Eagle, 1963–65; comd HMS Intrepid, 1968–70; Asst Chief of Fleet Support, MoD (RN), 1971–74; Flag Officer Sea Training, 1974–75; Flag Officer Carriers and Amphibious Ships, 1975–77; Chief of Fleet Support, 1977–79; C-in-C, Fleet, and Allied C-in-C, Channel and Eastern Atlantic, 1979–81; C-in-C, Naval Home Comd, 1981–82, retired 1983. Rear Adm. of the UK, 1990–94. Vice-Pres., RUSI, 1979. Chm. Council, Clifton Coll., 1984–94; Devon Rural Skills Trust, 1992–93. Freeman: Bristol, 1946; London, 1982. Hon. LLD: Bristol, 1989; Sussex, 1992. *Publications:* Management in the Armed Forces, 1972; Jim, First of the Pack, 1982; Britain's Future in Space, 1988. *Recreations:* hunting (Master of Britannia Beagles), tennis. *Address:* c/o Royal Institute of International Affairs, St James's Square, SW1Y 4LE. *Clubs:* Farmers'; Society of Merchant Venturers (Bristol); All England Lawn Tennis.

EBERT, Peter; producer; *b* 6 April 1918; *s* of Carl Ebert, CBE, and Lucie Oppenheim; *m* 1st, 1944, Kathleen Havinden; two *d*; 2nd, 1951, Silvia Ashmole; five *s* three *d*. *Educ:* Salem Sch., Germany; Gordonstoun, Scotland. BBC Producer, 1948–51; 1st opera production, Mefistofele, Glasgow, 1951; Mozart and Rossini guest productions: Rome, Naples, Venice, 1951, 1952, 1954, 1955: Wexford Festival: 12 prods, 1952–65; 1st Glyndebourne Fest. prod., Ariecchino, 1954, followed by Seraglio, Don Giovanni, etc.; 1st Edinburgh Fest. prod., Forza del Destino, 1955; Chief producer: Hannover State Opera, 1954–60; Düsseldorf Opera, 1960–62; directed opera class, Hannover State Conservatory, 1954–60; Head of Opera studio, Düsseldorf, 1960–62. Guest productions in Europe, USA, Canada. TV productions of Glyndebourne operas, 1955–64; 1st TV studio prod., 1963; Opera Adviser to BBC TV, 1964–65; Dir of Productions, 1965–77, Gen. Administrator, 1977–80, Scottish Opera Co. First drama prod., The Devils, Johannesburg, 1966; first musical, Houdini, London, 1966. Dir, Opera Sch., University of Toronto, 1967–68; Intendant: Stadttheater, Augsburg, 1968–73; Stadttheater Bielefeld, 1973–75; Staatstheater Wiesbaden, 1975–77. Hon. DMus St Andrews, 1979. *Recreation:* building. *Address:* Col di Mura, Lippiano, 06010 (PG), Italy.

EBERTS, John David, (Jake); Founder, 1985, and Chief Executive, since 1985, Allied Filmmakers; *b* 10 July 1941; *s* of Edmond Howard Eberts and Elizabeth Evelyn MacDougall; *m* 1968, Fiona Louise Leckie; two *s* one *d*. *Educ:* McGill Univ. (BChemEng 1962); Harvard Univ. (MBA 1966). Project Engr, l'Air Liquide, Paris, 1962–64; Marketing Manager, Cummins Engine Co., Brussels, 1966–68; Vice Pres., Laird Inc., NY, 1968–71; Man. Dir, Oppenheimer and Co. Ltd, London, 1971–76; Founder, 1976, and Chief Exec., 1976–83 and 1985–86, Goldcrest Films and Television Ltd; Pres., Embassy Communications International, 1984–85. Involved in prodn of many BAFTA and Amer. Acad. award-winning films, including: Chariots of Fire; Gandhi; The Dresser; The Killing Fields; The Name of the Rose; Hope and Glory; Driving Miss Daisy; Dances with Wolves; A River Runs Through It. Film Producers' Award of Merit, 1986; Evening Standard Special Award, 1987. *Publication:* (with Terry Ilott) My Indecision is Final, 1990. *Recreations:* tennis, skiing, photography. *Clubs:* Queen's; North Hatley (Quebec).

EBRAHIM, Sir (Mahomed) Currimbhoy, 4th Bt, *cr* 1910; BA, LLB, Advocate, Pakistan; Member, Standing Council of the Baronetage, 1961; *b* 24 June 1935; *o s* of Sir (Huseinali) Currimbhoy Ebrahim, 3rd Bt, and Alhaja Lady Amina Khanum, *d* of Alhaj Cassumali Jairajbhoy; *S* father 1952; *m* 1958, Dur-e-Mariam, *d* of Minuchehir Ahmud Ghulamaly Nana; three *s* one *d*. *Recreations:* tennis (Karachi University No 1, 1957, No 2, 1958), cricket, table-tennis, squash, reading (literary), art, poetry writing, debate, quotation writing. *Heir: s* Zulfiqar Ali Currimbhoy Ebrahim, *b* 5 Aug. 1960.

EBRAHIM, Prof. Shaheen Brian John; Professor of Clinical Epidemiology, Royal Free Hospital School of Medicine, University of London, since 1992; *b* 19 July 1952; *s* of Dr Donald William Ebrahim and Marjorie Sybil (*née* Evans); *m* 1984, Julia Lesley Shaw. *Educ:* King Henry VIII Sch., Coventry; Nottingham Univ. Med. Sch. (BMed Sci; BM BS 1975; DM 1985). Wellcome Trust Clinical Epidemiology Trng Fellow, Nottingham Univ. Med. Sch., 1981–83; Lectr in Geriatric Medicine, Univ. of Nottingham, 1983–85; Wellcome Trust Lectr in Epidemiology, Dept of Social Medicine and Gen. Practice, St George's Hosp. Med. Sch., London, 1985–86; Cons. Physician and Sen. Lectr, Dept of Geriatric Medicine, Royal Free Hosp. Sch. of Medicine, 1987–89; Prof. of Geriatric Medicine, London Hosp. Med. Coll. and St Bartholomew's Hosp. Med. Coll., 1989–92. Vis. Prof., Christchurch Med. Sch., NZ, 1990; Nat. Heart Foundn of NZ Vis. Prof. in Stroke, 1991; Australian Veterans Vis. Prof., 1995. *Publications:* Clinical Epidemiology of Stroke, 1990; (ed jtly) The Health of Older Women, 1992; (with G. Bennett) Essentials of Health Care in Old Age, 1992, 2nd edn 1995; (ed jtly) Epidemiology and Ageing, 1995; scientific papers on clinical epidemiology and geriatric medicine. *Recreations:* coarse fishing, music of Velvet Underground and Don Van Vliet. *Address:* Royal Free Hospital School of Medicine, Rowland Hill Street, NW3 2PF. *T:* 0171–794 0500. *Club:* Royal Society of Medicine.

EBSWORTH, Hon. Dame Ann (Marian), DBE 1992; **Hon. Mrs Justice Ebsworth;** a Judge of the High Court of Justice, Queen's Bench Division, since 1992; *b* 19 May 1937; *d* of late Arthur E. Ebsworth, OBE, BEM, RM and Hilda Mary Ebsworth. *Educ:* Notre Dame Convent, Worth, Sussex; Portsmouth High Sch., GPDST; London Univ. BA Hons (History). Called to Bar, Gray's Inn, 1962; Bencher, 1992. A Recorder of the Crown Court, 1978–83; a Circuit Judge, 1983–92. Mental Health Review Tribunal, 1975–83, 1984–90; Parole Bd, 1989–92; Civil and Family Cttee, Judicial Studies Bd, 1991–92. *Recreations:* Italian travel, medieval history, needlework. *Address:* Royal Court of Justice, Strand, WC2A 2LL.

EBSWORTH, Prof. Evelyn Algernon Valentine, PhD, ScD; FRCS, FRSE; Vice-Chancellor, Durham University, since 1990; *b* 14 Feb. 1933; *s* of Wilfred Algernon Ebsworth and Cynthia (*née* Blech); *m* 1st, 1955, Mary Salter (*d* 1987); one *s* three *d*; 2nd, 1990, Rose Zuckerman. *Educ:* King's Coll., Cambridge (BA 1st Cl., 1954; PhD 1957; MA 1958; ScD 1967). FRSE 1969. Fellow, King's Coll., Cambridge, 1957–59; Res. Associate, Princeton Univ., 1958–59; Cambridge University: Demonstrator, 1959–63; Lectr, 1963–67; Fellow, 1959–67, Tutor, 1963–67, Christ's Coll.; Crum Brown Prof. of Chemistry, Edinburgh, 1967–90. Corresp. Mem., Acad. of Scis, Göttingen. *Publications:* Volatile Silicon Compounds, 1963; (with S. Cradock and D. W. H. Rankin) Structural Methods in Inorganic Chemistry, 1988; papers in learned jls. *Recreations:* opera, gardening. *Address:* University of Durham, Old Shire Hall, Durham DH1 3HP.

EBURY, 6th Baron, *cr* 1857; **Francis Egerton Grosvenor;** *b* 8 Feb. 1934; *s* of 5th Baron Ebury, DSO and Ann Acland-Troyte; *heir-pres.* to 7th Earl of Wilton, *qv*; *S* father 1957; *m* 1st, 1957, Gillian Elfrida (Elfin) (marr. diss. 1962), *d* of Martin Soames, London; one *s*; 2nd, 1963, Kyra (marr. diss. 1973), *d* of late L. L. Aslin; 3rd, 1974, Suzanne Jean, *d* of Graham Suckling, Christchurch, NZ; one *d*. *Educ:* Eton. *Recreation:* ornithology. *Heir: s* Hon. Julian Francis Martin Grosvenor [*b* 8 June 1959; *m* 1987, Danielle, sixth *d* of Theo Rossi, Sydney, Australia]. *Address:* PO Box 53, Mt Macedon, Vic 3441, Australia. *Clubs:* Oriental; Melbourne, Melbourne Savage (Melbourne); Hong Kong.

ECCLES, family name of **Viscount Eccles** and **Baroness Eccles of Moulton.**

ECCLES, 1st Viscount, *cr* 1964; 1st Baron, *cr* 1962; **David McAdam Eccles,** CH 1984; KCVO 1953; PC 1951; MA Oxon; *b* 18 Sept. 1904; *s* of late W. McAdam Eccles, FRCS and Anna Coralie, *d* of E. B. Anstie, JP; *m* 1st, 1928, Sybil (*d* 1977), *e d* of Viscount Dawson of Penn, PC, GCVO, KCB, KCMG; two *s* one *d;* 2nd, 1984, Mrs Donald Hyde, Somerville, NJ. *Educ:* Winchester, New Coll., Oxford. Joined Ministry of Economic Warfare, Sept. 1939; Economic Adviser to HM Ambassadors at Madrid and Lisbon, 1940–42; Ministry of Production, 1942–43. MP (C) Chippenham Div. of Wilts, 1943–62; Minister of Works, 1951–54; Minister of Education, 1954–57; Pres. of the Board of Trade, 1957–59; Minister of Education, Oct. 1959–July 1962; Paymaster-General, with responsibility for the arts, 1970–73. Trustee, British Museum, 1963–, Chm. of Trustees, 1968–70; Chm., British Liby Bd, 1973–78. Dir, Courtaulds, 1962–70. Chm., Anglo-Hellenic League, 1967–70. Pres., World Crafts Council, 1974–78. Hon. Fellow, RIBA; Sen. Fellow, RCA. *Publications:* Half-Way to Faith, 1966; Life and Politics: A Moral Diagnosis, 1967; On Collecting, 1968; By Safe Hand: Letters of Sybil and David Eccles 1939–42, 1983. *Heir: s* Hon. John Dawson Eccles, *qv. Address:* Dean Farm, Chute, near Andover, Hants SP11 9ET. *T:* Chute Standen (01264) 730210; 6 Barton Street, SW1P 3NG. *T:* 0171–222 1387. *Clubs:* Brooks's, Roxburghe; Knickerbocker, Grolier (New York).

ECCLES OF MOULTON, Baroness *cr* 1990 (Life Peer), of Moulton in the County of North Yorkshire; **Diana Catherine Eccles;** Chairman, Ealing, Hammersmith and Hounslow Health Authority, since 1993 (Chairman, Ealing District Health Authority, 1988–93); *b* 4 Oct. 1933; *d* of late Raymond Sturge and of Margaret Sturge; *m* 1955, Hon. John Dawson Eccles, *qv;* one *s* three *d. Educ:* St James's Sch., West Malvern; Open Univ. (BA). Voluntary work, Middlesbrough Community Council, 1955–58; Partner, Gray Design Associates, 1963–77. Director: Tyne Tees Television, 1986–94; J . Sainsbury, 1986–; Yorkshire Electricity Gp, 1990–; National & Provincial Building Soc., 1991–; Member: North Eastern Electricity Bd, 1974–85; British Railways Eastern Bd, 1986–92; Teesside Urban Develt Corp., 1987–; Yorkshire Electricity Bd, 1989–90. Member: Adv. Council for Energy Conservation, 1982–84; Widdicombe Inquiry into Local Govt, 1985–86; Home Office Adv. Panel on Licences for Experimental Community Radio, 1985–86; Unrelated Live Transplant Regulatory Authority, 1990–. Vice Chairman: Nat. Council for Voluntary Orgns, 1981–87; Durham Univ. Council, 1985– (Lay Mem., 1981–85); Chm., Tyne Tees Television Programme Consultative Council, 1982–84. Trustee, Charities Aid Foundn, 1982–89. Hon. DCL Durham, 1995. *Address:* Moulton Hall, Richmond, N Yorks DL10 6QH. *T:* Darlington (01325) 377227; 6 Barton Street, Westminster SW1P 3NG. *T:* 0171–222 7559.

ECCLES, Geoffrey, OBE 1986; CEng; Regional Chairman, British Gas plc, Eastern, 1987–90; *b* 25 Dec. 1925; *s* of George William Eccles and Elsie Eccles (*née* Hepworth); *m* 1946, Marjorie Jackson; one *s. Educ:* Halifax and Bradford Colls of Technol. MIGasE. West Midlands Gas Board: various technical and managerial appts, incl. Asst Regl Distribution Engr, 1964; Grid Engr, 1967; Dep. Pipelines Engr, Gas Council, 1971; Pipelines Engr, British Gas Corp., 1980; Dep. Chm., Eastern Gas, 1984. *Recreations:* hill walking, reading, music. *Address:* 3 Little Gaddesden House, Little Gaddesden, Berkhamsted, Herts HP4 1PL. *T:* Little Gaddesden (01442) 842731.

ECCLES, (Hugh William) Patrick; QC 1990; a Recorder, since 1987; *b* 25 April 1946; *s* of Gp Captain (retd) Hugh Haslett Eccles and Mary Eccles; *m* 1972, Rhoda Ann Eccles (*née* Moroney); three *d. Educ:* Stonyhurst Coll.; Exeter Coll., Oxford (MA). Called to the Bar, Middle Temple, 1968; practising barrister, head of chambers, 1985–. Mem., County Court Rule Cttee, 1986–91. Asst Parly Boundary Comr, 1992–. *Recreations:* tennis, wine, P. G. Wodehouse. *Address:* Grapevine Cottage, High Street, Long Wittenham, Oxon OX14 4QQ. *T:* Oxford (01865) 407436.

ECCLES, Jack Fleming, CBE 1980; retired trade union official; *b* 9 Feb. 1922; *s* of Tom and Dora Eccles; *m* 1952, Milba Hartley Williamson; one *s* one *d. Educ:* Chorlton High Sch.; Univ. of Manchester. BA (Com). Gen. and Municipal Workers Union: District Organiser, 1948–60; Nat. Industrial Officer, 1960–66; Regional Sec. (Lancs), 1966–86. Trades Union Congress: Gen. Council, 1973–86; Chm., 1984–85; Pres., 1985. Non-Executive Director: Remploy Ltd, 1976–90; English Industrial Estates, 1976–92; Plastics Processing ITB, 1982–88 (Chm.); British Steel plc (formerly BSC), 1986–91. *Recreations:* motoring, ciné photography. *Address:* Terange, 11 Sutton Road, Alderley Edge, Cheshire SK9 7RB. *T:* Alderley Edge (01625) 583684.

ECCLES, Sir John Carew, AC 1990; Kt 1958; FRS 1941; FRSNZ; FAA; *b* 27 Jan. 1903; *s* of William James and Mary Eccles; *m* 1st, 1928, Irene Frances Miller (marr. diss. 1968); four *s* five *d;* 2nd, 1968, Helena Táboříková. *Educ:* Melbourne Univ.; Magdalen Coll., Oxford. Melbourne University: 1st class Hons MB, BS 1925; Victorian Rhodes Scholar, 1925. Univ. of Oxford: Christopher Welch Scholar; 1st class Hons Natural Science (Physiology), 1927; MA 1929; DPhil 1929; Gotch Memorial Prize, 1927; Rolleston Memorial Prize, 1932. Junior Res. Fellow, Exeter Coll., Oxford, 1927–32; Staines Med. Fellow, Exeter Coll., 1932–34; Fellow and Tutor of Magdalen Coll., and Univ. Lectr in Physiology, 1934–37; Dir, Kanematsu Memorial Inst. of Pathology, Sydney, 1937–44; Prof. of Physiology: Univ. of Otago, Dunedin, NZ, 1944–51; ANU, Canberra, 1951–66; Mem., Inst. for Biomedical Res., Chicago, 1966–68; Dist. Prof. and Head of Res. Unit of Neurobiology, Health Sci. Faculty, State Univ. of NY at Buffalo, 1968–75, now Dist. Prof. Emeritus. Lectures: Waynflete, Magdalen Coll., Oxford, 1952; Herter, Johns Hopkins Univ., 1955; Ferrier, Royal Soc., 1959; Sherrington, Liverpool Univ., 1966; Patten, Indiana Univ., 1972; Pahlavi, Iran, 1976; Gifford, Edinburgh, 1978, 1979; Carroll, Georgetown, 1982; Idreos, Manchester Coll., Oxford, 1990. Pres., Australian Acad. of Science, 1957–61. Member: Pontifical Acad. of Science; Deutsche Akademie der Naturforscher Leopoldina. Foreign Hon. Member: Amer. Acad. of Arts and Sciences; Amer. Philosophical Soc.; Amer. Neurological Soc.; Accademia Nazionale dei Lincei. Hon. Life Mem., New York Acad. of Sciences, 1965; Foreign Associate, Nat. Acad. of Sciences; For. Mem., Max-Planck Soc. Hon. Fellow: Exeter Coll., Oxford, 1961; Magdalen Coll., Oxford, 1964; Amer. Coll. of Physicians, 1967. Hon. ScD Cantab; Hon. DSc: Oxon; Tasmania; British Columbia; Gustavus Adolphus Coll., Minnesota; Marquette Univ., Wisconsin; Loyola, Chicago; Yeshiva, NY; Fribourg; Georgetown, Washington DC; Hon. LLD Melbourne; Hon. MD: Charles Univ., Prague; Torino; Basel; Hon. Dr: Madrid; Ulm, 1994. (Jointly) Nobel Prize for Medicine, 1963; Baly Medal, RCP, 1961; Royal Medal, Royal Soc., 1962; Cothenius Medal, Deutsche Akademie der Naturforscher Leopoldina, 1964; (first) Golden Medal, Charles Univ., Prague, 1993. Order of the Rising Sun, Gold and Silver Stars (Japan), 1987. *Publications:* (jtly) Reflex Activity of Spinal Cord, 1932; Neuro-physiological Basis of Mind, 1953; Physiology of Nerve Cells, 1957; Physiology of Synapses, 1964; (jtly) The Cerebellum as a Neuronal Machine, 1967; The Inhibitory Pathways of the Central Nervous System, 1969; Facing Reality, 1970; The Understanding of the Brain, 1973; (jtly) Molecular Neurobiology of the Mammalian Brain, 1977, 2nd edn 1987; (jtly) The Self and Its Brain, 1977; The Human Mystery, 1979; (jtly) Sherrington, his Life and Thought, 1979; The Human Psyche, 1980; (jtly) The Wonder of Being Human: our brain, our mind, 1984; Evolution of the Brain: creation of the self, 1989; How the Self Controls its Brain, 1993; contrib. to Can Scientists Believe, 1991; papers in Proc. Royal Soc., Jl of Physiology, Jl of Neurophysiology, Experimental Brain Research. *Recreation:* European travel. *Address:* Ca' a la Gra', 6646 Contra (Locarno), Ticino, Switzerland. *T:* 093–672931.

ECCLES, Hon. John Dawson, CBE 1985; Chairman, Courtaulds Textiles plc, since 1995 (Director, since 1992); *b* 20 April 1931; *er s* and *heir* of 1st Viscount Eccles, *qv; m* 1955, Diana Catherine Sturge (*see* Baroness Eccles of Moulton); one *s* three *d. Educ:* Winchester Coll.; Magdalen Coll., Oxford (BA). Director: Glynwed International plc, 1972–; Investors in Industry plc, 1974–88; Chairman: Head Wrightson & Co. Ltd, 1976–77 (Man. Dir, 1968–77); Chamberlin & Hill plc, 1982–; Director: The Nuclear Power Gp Ltd, 1968–74; Davy Internat. Ltd, 1977–81; Chamberlain Phipps Group, 1994–. Member: Monopolies and Mergers Commn, 1976–85 (Dep. Chm., 1981–85); Industrial Develt Adv. Bd, 1989–93; Gen. Manager, subseq. Chief Exec., Commonwealth Develt Corp., 1985–94 (Mem., 1982–85). Chm., Bd of Trustees, Royal Botanic Gardens, Kew, 1983–91. Hon DSc Cranfield Inst. of Technology, 1989. *Recreation:* industrial psychology. *Address:* 6 Barton Street, SW1P 3NG. *T:* 0171–222 7559; Moulton Hall, Richmond, N Yorks DL10 6QH. *T:* Darlington (01325) 377227. *Club:* Brooks's.

ECCLES, Patrick; *see* Eccles, H. W. P.

ECCLES-WILLIAMS, Hilary a'Beckett, CBE 1970; Vice-President, West Midlands Conservative Council, since 1985 (Deputy Chairman, 1982–85); *b* 5 Oct. 1917; *s* of late Rev. Cyril Eccles-Williams and Hermione (*née* Terrell); *m* 1941, Jeanne, *d* of W. J. Goodwin; two *s* four *d. Educ:* Eton; Brasenose Coll., Oxford (MA). Served War of 1939–45, Major RA (anti-tank), Dunkirk and Normandy (wounded). Consul: for Nicaragua, 1951–59; for Cuba, 1952–60; for Costa Rica, 1964–93; for Bolivia, 1965–82. Chairman of companies; Chm., 1978–82, non-exec. Dir, 1982–87, Rabone Petersen; has travelled 900,000 miles on export business. Chairman: Brit. Export Houses Assoc., 1958–59; Guardians of Birmingham Assay Office, 1979–88 (Guardian, 1970–); President: Birmingham Chamber of Commerce, 1965–66; Assoc. of Brit. Ch. of Commerce (93 Chambers), 1970–72. Comr of Income Tax, 1966–70. Chairman: Birmingham Cons. Assoc., 1976–79 (Pres., 1979–84); W Midlands Metropolitan Co. Co-ordinating Cttee, Cons. Party, 1980–86; European Parlt constituency of Birmingham S Cons. Assoc., 1978–82 (Pres., 1982–84); Latin Amer. Gp, Cons. Foreign and Overseas Council, 1986–89; President: Eur. Parlt constituency of Birmingham E Cons. Assoc., 1984–95; Sparkbrook Constituency Cons. Assoc., 1988–92; Anglo-Asian Cons. Soc., 1984–87; Cons. Party One Nation Forum, 1990–; Mem., National Union Exec. Cttee, Cons. Party, 1975–85. Mem., Brit. Hallmarking Council, 1976–88; Pres., Birmingham Consular Assoc., 1973–74; Chairman: Asian Christian Colls Assoc., 1960–66; Brit. Heart Foundn, Midland Counties, 1973–74; Golden Jubilee Appeal Cttee, Queen Elizabeth Hosp., Birmingham, 1987–90; W Midlands Macmillan Nurse Appeal, 1991–94; Mem., Nat. Council, Cancer Relief Macmillan Fund, 1992–94. Governor, Birmingham Univ., 1966–; Trustee, Birmingham Centre for Drama, 1994–. Liveryman, Worshipful Co. of Glaziers, 1974; Freeman, Goldsmiths' Co., 1988. Hon. Captain, Bolivian Navy, 1969. Numerous TV appearances. *Recreations:* sailing, golf. *Address:* 36 St Bernard's Road, Solihull, West Midlands B92 7BB. *T:* 0121–706 0354. *Clubs:* Olton Mere Sailing; North Warwickshire Golf.

ECCLESTON, Harry Norman, OBE 1979; PPRE (RE 1961; ARE 1948); RWS 1975 (ARWS 1964); RWA 1991; Artist Designer at the Bank of England Printing Works, 1958–83; *b* 21 Jan. 1923; *s* of Harry Norman Eccleston and Kate Pritchard, Coseley, Staffs; *m* 1948, Betty Doreen Gripton (*d* 1995); two *d. Educ:* Sch. of Art, Bilston; Coll. of Art, Birmingham; Royal College of Art. ATD 1947; ARCA (1st Class) 1950. Studied painting until 1942. Served in Royal Navy, 1942–46; Temp. Commn, RNVR, 1943. Engraving Sch., Royal College of Art, 1947–51; engraving, teaching, free-lance graphic design, 1951–58. Pres., Royal Soc. of Painter-Etchers and Engravers, 1975–89. Hon. RBSA 1989. *Recreation:* reading. *Address:* 110 Priory Road, Harold Hill, Romford, Essex RM3 9AL. *T:* Ingrebourne (01708) 340275. *Club:* Arts.

ECCLESTONE, Jacob Andrew; Deputy General Secretary, National Union of Journalists, since 1981; *b* 10 April 1939; *s* of late Rev. Alan Ecclestone and Delia Reynolds Abraham; *m* 1966, Margaret Joan Bassett; two *s* one *d. Educ:* High Storrs Grammar Sch., Sheffield; Open Univ. (BA). Journalism: South Yorkshire Times, 1957–61; Yorkshire Evening News, 1961–62; The Times, 1962–66, 1967–81. Member: Nat. Exec., NUJ, 1977 (Vice-Pres. 1978, Pres., 1979); Press Council, 1977–80; Exec., Nat. Council for Civil Liberties, 1982–86. *Recreations:* gardening, climbing, music. *Address:* 40 Chatsworth Way, SE27 9HN. *T:* 0181–670 8503.

ECHENIQUE, Prof. Marcial Hernan, DArch; Professor of Land Use and Transport Studies, University of Cambridge, since 1993; Fellow, Churchill College, Cambridge, since 1972; *b* 23 Feb. 1943; *s* of Marcial Echenique and Rosa de Echenique (*née* Talavera); *m* 1963, Maria Luisa Holzmann; two *s* one *d. Educ:* Catholic Univ. of Chile; Univ. of Barcelona (DArch). MA Cantab 1972. MRTPI 1990. Asst Lectr, Univ. of Barcelona, 1964–65; University of Cambridge: Research Officer, 1967–70; Lectr, 1970–80; Reader in Architecture and Urban Studies, 1980–93. Founder and Mem., Bd of Applied Res., Cambridge, 1969–83. Chm., Marcial Echenique & Partners Ltd, England, 1978–; Pres., Marcial Echenique y Compañía SA, Spain, 1988–; Member Board: Trasporti e Territorio SRL, Italy, 1992–; Autopista Vasco-Aragonesa SA, Spain, 1994–; Tecnologica SA, Spain, 1994–. Bank of Bilbao-Vizcaya of Spain: Mem. Bd, 1988–94; Trustee of Foundn, 1990–94. *Publications:* (ed jtly) La Estructura del Espacio Urbano, 1975; (ed jtly) Urban Development Models, 1975; (ed) Modelos Matematicos de la Estructura Espacial Urbana: aplicaciones en America Latina, 1975; (with L. Piemontese) Un Modello per lo Sviluppo del Sistema Grecia-Italia Meridionale, 1984. *Recreations:* music, reading, gardening. *Address:* Department of Architecture, University of Cambridge, 1 Scroope Terrace, Cambridge CB2 1PX. *T:* Cambridge (01223) 332950; Farm Hall, Godmanchester, Cambs PE18 8HQ.

ECHLIN, Sir Norman David Fenton, 10th Bt, *cr* 1721; Captain 14/1st Punjab Regiment, Indian Army; *b* 1 Dec. 1925; *s* of Sir John Frederick Echlin, 9th Bt, and Ellen Patricia (*d* 1971), *d* of David Jones, JP, Dublin; *S* father, 1932; *m* 1953, Mary Christine, *d* of John Arthur, Oswestry, Salop. *Educ:* Masonic Boys' School, Dublin. *Heir:* none. *Address:* Nartopa, 36 Marina Avenue, Appley, Ryde, IoW.

ECKERBERG, (Carl) Lennart, Hon. KCMG 1983; Officer of Royal Northern Star 1970; Swedish Ambassador to the Court of St James's, 1991–94; *b* 2 July 1928; *s* of late Enar Lars Eckerberg and of Dagmar Liljedahl; *m* 1965, Willia Fales; two *s* one *d. Educ:* Univ. of Stockholm (law degree 1953). Swedish Foreign Service in Stockholm, London, Warsaw and Washington, 1954–71; Disarmament Ambassador, Geneva, 1971; Minister Plenipotentiary, Washington, 1975; Ambassador, Dar es Salaam, 1977; Under Sec., Political Affairs, Stockholm, 1979; Ambassador, Bonn, 1983–91. Orders from Finland, Germany, Iceland, Spain and Mexico. *Recreations:* golf, tennis, bridge. *Address:* Martornsvägen 3, 230 11 Falsterbo, Sweden; (winter) 3812 Klingle Place, NW,

Washington, DC 20016, USA. *T:* (202) 9660594. *Clubs:* Chevy Chase (Washington); Falsterbo (Sweden).

ECKERSLEY, Sir Donald (Payze), Kt 1981; OBE 1977; farmer, since 1946; Inaugural President, National Farmers' Federation of Australia, 1979–81; *b* 1 Nov. 1922; *s* of Walter Roland Eckersley and Ada Gladys Moss; *m* 1949, Marjorie Rae Clarke; one *s* two *d*. *Educ:* Muresk Agricl Coll. (Muresk Diploma in Agriculture). Aircrew, RAAF, 1940–45. Pres., Milk Producers' Assoc., 1947–50; Farmers' Union of WA: Executive, 1962–67; Pres., Milk Sect., 1965–70; Vice-Pres., 1969–72; Gen. Pres., 1972–75; Pres., Australian Farmers' Fedn, 1975–79; Austr. Rep., Internat. Fedn of Agric., 1979–81. Pres., Harvey Shire Council, 1970–79; Director: Chamberlain John Deere, 1980–; Br. Bd. Australian Mutual Provident Soc., 1983–. Chairman: Leschenault Inlet Management Authority, 1977–; Artificial Breeding Bd of WA, 1981–; SW Develt Authority, 1989–; Bd, Muresk Inst. of Agric., 1984–88; Member: WA Waterways Commn, 1977–; Nat. Energy Adv. Cttee, 1979–; Comr, WA State Housing Commn, 1982–. Mem., Senate, Univ. of WA, 1981–. Mem., Harvey Rotary Club. JP WA, 1982–86. Hon. DTech Curtin, 1989. WA Citizen of Year award, 1976; Man of Year, Austr. Agriculture, 1979. *Publication:* (contrib.) Farm Focus: the '80s, 1981. *Recreations:* golf, fishing. *Address:* Korijedale, Harvey, WA 6220, Australia. *T:* (97) 291472. *Clubs:* Weld (Perth); Harvey Golf.

ECKERSLEY, Thomas, OBE 1948; RDI 1963; AGI; graphic designer; Head of Department of Design, London College of Printing, 1958–76; *b* Sept. 1914; *s* of John Eckersley and Eunice Hilton; *m* Daisy Eckersley; three *s*; *m* 1966, Mary Kessell, painter. *Educ:* Salford Sch. of Art. Free-lance Graphic Designer for London Transport, Shell Mex, BBC, GPO, MOI, Unicef, CoID and other leading concerns since 1936. Work exhibited in Sweden, USA, Paris, Hamburg, Lausanne, Milan, Amsterdam; permanent collections of work in V&A Museum, Imperial War Museum, London Transport Museum, Nat. Gall. of Australia, Museum of Modern Art, USA, Library of Congress, USA and Die Neue Sammlung Staatliches Museum München. One-man exhibitions: Soc. of Artists and Designers, 1976; Camden Arts Centre, British Arts Centre, Yale, 1980; Peel Park Gall., Salford, Edinburgh, 1981; Newcastle upon Tyne Polytechnic Gall., 1983; London Transport Museum, 1985; Maidstone Coll. of Art, 1985; Oxford Polytechnic, 1986; Emmerich Poster Museum, Germany, 1987. Mem. of Alliance Graphique Internationale; Hon. Fellow: Manchester Coll. of Art and Design; Humberside Coll. of Higher Educn, 1985; RCA, 1991. FSTD. Medal of CSD, 1990. *Publications:* contribs to Graphis, Gebrauchsgraphik, Form und Technik, Art and Industry, Print Design and Production, Penrose Annual; *relevant publication:* F. H. K. Henrion, Top Graphic Designers, 1983. *Recreation:* cricket. *Address:* 53 Belsize Park Gardens, NW3 4JL. *T:* 0171–586 3586.

ECKERSLEY-MASLIN, Rear Adm. David Michael, CB 1984; retired, RN; *b* Karachi, 27 Sept. 1929; *e s* of Comdr C. E. Eckersley-Maslin, OBE, RN, Tasmania, and late Mrs L. M. Lightfoot, Bedford; *m* 1955, Shirley Ann, *d* of late Captain H. A. Martin; one *s* one *d*. *Educ:* Britannia Royal Naval Coll. Qual. Navigation Direction Officer, 1954; rcds 1977. Far East Malayan Campaign, 1950–53; Australian Navy, 1954–56; BRNC Dartmouth, 1959–61; commanded HM Ships Eastbourne, Euryalus, Fife and Blake, 1966–76; Captain RN Presentation Team, 1974; Dir, Naval Operational Requirements, 1977–80; Flag Officer Sea Training, 1980–82; ACNS (Operational Planning) (Falklands), 1982; ACDS (CIS), 1982–84; Asst Dir (CIS), IMS, NATO, Brussels, 1984–86; Dir Gen., NATO Communications and Inf. Systems Agency, 1986–91. ADC to the Queen, 1980. Vice Pres., AFCEA, 1987–90 (Gold Medal, 1991); Chm., AFCEA (UK) Academic Trust, 1992–. Mem. Council, Shipwrecked Mariners Soc., 1992–. Naval Gen. Service Decoration, Palestine, 1948, and Malaya, 1951. *Recreations:* tennis, squash, cricket. *Address:* Dunningwell, Hall Court, Shedfield, near Southampton SO32 2HL. *T:* Wickham (01329) 832350. *Club:* MCC.

EDDERY, Patrick James John; jockey; *b* 18 March 1952; *s* of Jimmy and Josephine Eddery; *m* 1978, Carolyn Jane (*née* Mercer); two *d*. Rode for Peter Walwyn, 1972–80; Champion Jockey, 1974, 1975, 1976, 1977, 1986, 1988, 1989, 1990; 1993; Champion Jockey in Ireland, 1982; won the Oaks, 1974, 1979, the Derby, on Grundy, 1975, on Golden Fleece, 1982, on Quest for Fame, 1990; Prix de l'Arc de Triomphe, 1980, 1985, 1986, 1987; St Leger on Moon Madness, 1986, on Moonax, 1994. *Recreations:* swimming, golf, snooker. *Address:* Musk Hill Farm, Lower Winchendon, Aylesbury, Bucks HP18 0DT. *T:* Haddenham (01844) 290282. *Club:* The Subscription Rooms (Newmarket).

EDDEY, Prof. Howard Hadfield, CMG 1974; FRCS, FRACS, FACS; Foundation Professor of Surgery, University of Melbourne, at Austin Hospital and Repatriation General Hospital, 1967–75, now Emeritus; also Dean of Austin Hospital and Repatriation General Hospital Clinical School, 1971–75; *b* Melbourne, 3 Sept. 1910; *s* of Charles Howard and Rachel Beatrice Eddey; *m* 1940, Alice Paul (decd); two *s* one *d*. *Educ:* Melbourne Univ.; St Bartholomew's Hosp. Med. Sch. BSc, MB BS, 1934; FRCS 1938; FRACS 1941; FACS 1964; Hallett Prize of RCS, 1938. Served War, 1941–45: AAMC, Major and Surgical Specialist; served in PoW camps: Changi (Singapore); Sandakan and Kuching (Borneo). Hon. Surgeon: Prince Henry Hosp., Melbourne, 1946–47; Alfred Hosp., Melbourne, 1947; Royal Melbourne Hosp., 1947–67; Cons. Surg., 1967, Royal Melbourne and Royal Women's Hosps; Peter MacCallum Clinic. Mem. AMA, 1935; Mem., Faculty of Med., Univ. of Melbourne, 1950–75 (Mem. Convocation, 1965–67); Indep. Lectr in Surgical Anatomy, Univ. of Melb., 1950–65; Dean, Royal Melb. Hosp. Clin. Sch., 1965–67; Colombo Plan Visitor to India, 1960–65; Cons. in Surg., Papuan Med. Coll., 1965–68; Mem. Cancer Inst. Bd, 1958–67; Mem. Med. and Sci. Cttee, Anti-Cancer Council of Vic., 1958–67; Chm., Melb. Med. Postgrad. Cttee, 1963–71; Vice-Pres., Aust. Postgrad. Fedn in Med., 1965–71 (Life Governor, 1972). Mem. Council, RACS, 1967–75 (Mem. Bd of Examrs, 1958–75, Chm. Bd, 1968–73; Hon. Librarian, 1968–75). Mem. Med. Bd of Vic., 1968–77; Mem. Austin Hosp. Bd of Management, 1971–77 (Vice-Pres., 1975–77; Life Governor, 1977). Hunterian Prof., RCS, 1960; Vis. Prof. of Surg., 1962, External Examr in Surg., 1970, Univ. of Singapore; Leverhulme Fellow, Univ. of Melb., 1974; Vis. Prof. of Surg., Univ. of Hong Kong, 1974. Howard Eddey Medal, named in 1972 by RACS and awarded to most successful cand., Part I exam (surgery) for FRACS in SE Asia, in recognition of dist. service to RACS. Hon. Surgeon to HRH Prince Charles on his visit to Victoria, 1974. Melbourne and Australian Universities Lacrosse Blue. *Publications:* many, in sci. jls, particularly in relation to diseases of salivary glands and cancer of mouth. *Recreation:* reading. *Address:* 5/45 Vanessa Avenue, Highton, Geelong, Vic 3216, Australia. *T:* (52) 435645.

EDDINGTON, Paul Clark-, CBE 1987; actor; *b* 18 June 1927; *s* of Albert Clark Eddington and Frances Mary (*née* Roberts); *m* 1952, Patricia Scott; three *s* one *d*. *Educ:* Holy Child Convent, Cavendish Sq., W1; Friends (Quaker) Sch., Sibford Ferris, Banbury, Oxon; RADA. First appearance on stage with ENSA, 1944; joined Birmingham Repertory Th., 1945; has played with several other rep. theatres during subseq. 30 years; first appearance in West End in The 10th Man, Comedy Th., 1961; first (and only, so far) appearance in New York in A Severed Head, 1964; joined National Theatre to play in revival of Who's Afraid of Virginia Woolf?, 1981; Noises Off, Savoy, 1982; Lovers Dancing, Albery, 1983; Forty Years On, Queen's, 1984; Jumpers, Aldwych, 1985; HMS Pinafore, Victoria State Opera, Australia, 1987 (tour); The Browning Version, and Harlequinade (double-bill), Royalty, 1988, subseq. Australia; London Assurance, Chichester Fest., 1989, transf. Theatre Royal, Haymarket, 1989; The Double Dealer, Ipswich, 1990; Tartuffe, Playhouse, 1991; No Man's Land, Almeida, 1992, transf. Comedy, 1993 (Critics' Circle Best Actor Award, 1993); Home, Wyndhams, 1994. Many TV appearances, including series, The Good Life, Yes Minister, Yes, Prime Minister and The Camomile Lawn. Chm., Internat. Cttee for Artists' Freedom, Equity, 1985–; Member: Council, Equity, 1972–75; Artistic Bd, Internat. Shakespeare Globe Centre, 1993–; Council, Howard League for Penal Reform, 1993–. Governor, Bristol Old Vic Theatre Trust, 1975–84. Hon. Prof. of Drama, Sheffield Univ., 1993–94. Hon. MA Sheffield, 1987. *Publication:* So Far So Good (autobiog.), 1995. *Recreations:* listening to music, reading, washing up, lying down and thinking what ought to be done in the garden. *Address:* c/o ICM Ltd, 388/396 Oxford Street, W1N 9HE. *T:* 0171–629 8080. *Club:* Garrick.

EDDLEMAN, Gen. Clyde Davis; DSM with oak leaf cluster (US); Silver Star; Legion of Merit; Bronze Star; Philippines Distinguished Service Star; Vice-Chief of Staff, US Army, 1960–62; *b* 17 Jan. 1902; *s* of Rev. W. H. Eddleman and Janie Eddleman (*née* Tureman); *m* 1926, Lorraine Heath; one *s* (and one *s* decd). *Educ:* US Military Academy, West Point, New York. Commissioned 2nd Lieut of Infantry upon graduation from US Military Academy, 1924. Advanced, through the ranks, and reached grade of Gen. 1959. Comdr, Central Army Group (NATO), and C-in-C, US Army, Europe, at Heidelberg, Germany, 1959–60. Knight Commander's Cross, Order of Merit (Germany); Kt Grand Cross of the Sword (Sweden). *Recreations:* hunting, fishing.

EDDY, Prof. Alfred Alan; Professor of Biochemistry, University of Manchester Institute of Science and Technology, 1959–94, Emeritus since 1994; *b* 4 Nov. 1926; Cornish parentage; *s* of late Alfred and Ellen Eddy; *m* 1954, Susan Ruth Slade-Jones; two *s*. *Educ:* Devonport High Sch.; Open scholarship Exeter Coll., Oxford, 1944; BA 1st Class Hons, 1949. ICI Research Fellow, 1950; DPhil 1951. Joined Brewing Industry Research Foundation, Nutfield, 1953. *Publications:* various scientific papers. *Recreations:* walking, talking, wining and dining. *Address:* Larchfield, Buxton Road, Disley, Cheshire SK12 2LH.

EDE, Ven. Dennis; Archdeacon of Stoke-upon-Trent, since 1990; *b* 8 June 1931; *m* 1956, Angela Horsman; one *s* two *d*. *Educ:* Univ. of Nottingham (BA Theology 1955); Barnett House, Oxford (Cert. of Social Studies); Ripon Hall, Oxford; MSocSc Birmingham, 1972. Nat. Service, RAF, 1950–52; Pilot Officer, Admin. Branch. Asst Curate, St Giles, Shelds, dio. Birmingham, 1957–60; Asst Curate-in-charge, St Philip and St James, Hodge Hill, Birmingham, 1960–64, Priest-in-charge 1964–70, Team Rector 1970–76; Part-time Chaplain, East Birmingham Hosp., 1961–76; Vicar of All Saints Parish Church, West Bromwich, dio. Lichfield, 1976–90. Mem., Gen. Synod of C of E, 1975–76, 1980–90. Diocese of Lichfield: Chm. House of Clergy, 1985–90; Chm. of Communications, 1983–; Prebendary of Lichfield Cathedral, 1983–90; Hon. Canon, 1990–. Chairman: Sandwell Volunteer, 1980–86; Faith in Sandwell, 1986–90; Shallowford House, 1990–; Diocesan Clergy Retirement Cttee, 1990–; Widows (Diocesan) Officers Cttee, 1990–. Co-ordinator for religious bodies in Staffs in major disasters. *Recreations:* walking, cycling, squash. *Address:* Archdeacon's House, 39 The Brackens, Clayton, Newcastle-under-Lyme ST5 4JL. *T:* Newcastle-under-Lyme (01782) 663066, *Fax:* (01782) 711165.

EDE, Jeffery Raymond, CB 1978; Keeper of Public Records, 1970–78; *b* 10 March 1918; *e s* of late Richard Arthur Ede; *m* 1944, Mercy, *d* of Arthur Radford Sholl; one *s* one *d*. *Educ:* Plymouth Coll.; King's Coll., Cambridge (MA). Served War of 1939–45, Intell. Corps (despatches); GSO2 HQ 8 Corps District, BAOR, 1945–46. Asst Keeper, Public Record Office, 1947–59; Principal Asst Keeper, 1959–66; Dep. Keeper, 1966–69. Lectr in Archive Admin., Sch. of Librarianship and Archives, University Coll., London, 1956–61; Unesco expert in Tanzania, 1963–64. Chm., British Acad. Cttee on Oriental Documents, 1972–78; Vice Pres., Internat. Council on Archives, 1976–78. Pres., Soc. of Archivists, 1974–77. FRHistS 1969. Hon. Mem., L'Institut Grand-Ducal de Luxembourg, 1977. Freeman: Goldsmiths' Company, 1979; City of London, 1979. *Publications:* Guide to the Contents of the Public Record Office, Vol. II (major contributor), 1963; articles in archival and other professional jls. *Recreations:* theatre, countryside. *Address:* Lambourn House, Apple Court Mews, Silver Street, Ilminster, Som TA19 0DW.

EDEL, (Joseph) Leon; Citizens Professor of English, University of Hawaii, 1970–78, now Emeritus; *b* 9 Sept. 1907; *e s* of Simon Edel and Fanny (*née* Malamud), Pittsburgh, Pa; *m* 1st, 1935, Bertha Cohen (marr. diss. 1950); 2nd, 1950, Roberta Roberts (marr. diss. 1979); 3rd, 1980, Marjorie Sinclair; no *c*. *Educ:* McGill Univ., Montreal (BA 1927, MA 1928); Univ. of Paris (Docteur-ès-Lettres 1932). Served with US Army in France and Germany, 1943–46: Bronze Star Medal (US), 1945; Chief of Information Control, News Agency, US Zone, 1946–47. Asst Prof., Sir George Williams Coll., Montreal, 1932–34; miscellaneous writing and journalism, 1934–43; Christian Gauss Seminar in Criticism, Princeton Univ., 1951–52; New York University: Vis. Prof., 1952–53; Associate Prof., 1953–55; Prof. of English, 1955–66; Henry James Prof. of English and American Letters, 1966–72. Guggenheim Fellow, 1936–38, 1965–66; Alexander Lectures, Toronto, 1956; Visiting Professor: Indiana, 1954; Hawaii, 1955, 1969, 1970; Harvard, 1959–60; Purdue, 1970; Centenary, Toronto, 1967; Vernon, in Biography, Dartmouth, 1977; Vis. Fellow, Humanities Res. Centre, Canberra, 1976. Westminster Abbey Address, Henry James Meml in Poets' Corner, 1976. Mem., Educnl Adv. Cttee, Guggenheim Foundn, 1968–80. Pres., US Center of PEN, 1957–59. Pres., Hawaii Literary Arts Council, 1978–79. Fellow, Amer. Acad. of Arts and Sciences, 1959; Bollingen Fellow, 1959–61. Member: Nat. Inst. of Arts and Letters, 1964– (Sec., 1965–67); Amer. Acad. of Arts and Letters, 1972; Council, Authors' Guild, 1965–68 (Pres., 1969–70); Soc. of Authors, 1968; Adv. Council, Amer. Trust for British Liby. FRSL 1970. Hon. Member: W. A. White Psychiatric Inst., 1966; Amer. Acad. Psychoanalysis, 1975; Hon. DLitt: McGill, 1963; Union Coll., Schenectady, 1963; Univ. of Saskatchewan, 1983; Hawaii Loa Coll., Honolulu, 1988. Nat. Inst. of Arts and Letters Award, 1959; US Nat. Book Award for non-fiction, 1963; Pulitzer Prize for biography, 1963; AAAL Gold Medal for biography, 1976; Hawaii Literary Arts Award, 1978; Nat. Arts Club Medal for Literature, 1981; Nat. Book Critics Circle Award (Biography), 1985. *Publications:* Henry James: les années dramatiques, 1932; The Prefaces of Henry James, 1932; James Joyce: The Last Journey, 1947; (with E. K. Brown) Willa Cather, 1953; The Life of Henry James: The Untried Years, 1953, The Conquest of London, 1962, The Middle Years, 1963, The Treacherous Years, 1969, The Master, 1972, rev. edn in 2 vols, 1978, rewritten, rev. into 1 vol., Henry James, a life, 1985; The Psychological Novel, 1955; Literary Biography, 1957; (with Dan H. Laurence) A Bibliography of Henry James, 1957; Thoreau, 1970; Bloomsbury: A House of Lions, 1979; Stuff of Sleep and Dreams (essays), 1982; Writing Lives: Principia Biographica, 1984; Some Memories of Edith Wharton, 1993; *edited:* The Complete Plays of Henry James, 1949, rev. edn 1991; Selected Letters of Henry James, 1956, 1987; (with Gordon N. Ray) James and H. G. Wells, Letters, 1958; The Complete Tales of Henry James, 12 vols, 1962–65; The Diary of Alice James, 1964; Literary History and Literary Criticism, 1965; Henry James: Stories of the Supernatural, 1971; Harold Goddard Alphabet of the Imagination, 1975; Henry James Letters: vol. I, 1843–1875, 1975; vol. II, 1875–1883,

1980; vol. III, 1883–1895, 1981; vol. IV, 1895–1916, 1984; Edmund Wilson: The Twenties, 1975; Edmund Wilson: The Thirties, 1980; Edmund Wilson: The Forties, 1983; (with Mark Wilson) Henry James, Critical Essays, 1984 (two vols); Edmund Wilson: The Fifties, 1986; (ed with Lyall H. Powers) The Complete Notebooks of Henry James, 1986. *Recreations:* music, swimming. *Address:* 3817 Lurline Drive, Honolulu, HI 96816, USA. *Club:* Century (New York).

EDELL, Stephen Bristow; Personal Investment Authority Ombudsman, since 1994; *b* 1 Dec. 1932; *s* of late Ivan James Edell and late Hilda Pamela Edell; *m* 1958, Shirley Ross Collins; two *s* one *d*. *Educ:* St Andrew's Sch., Eastbourne; Uppingham. LLB London. Legal Mem., RTPI, 1971–92. Commnd RA, 1951. Articled to father, 1953; qual. Solicitor 1958; Partner, Knapp-Fishers (Westminster), 1959–75; Law Comr, 1975–83; Partner, Crossman Block and Keith (Solicitors), 1983–87; Building Societies Ombudsman, 1987–94. Mem. Cttee, 1973–85, Vice-Pres., 1980–82, Pres., 1982–83, City of Westminster Law Soc. Oxfam: Mem., Retailing and Property Cttee, 1984–93 (Chm., 1989–93); Mem. Council, 1985–93; Mem., Exec., 1987–93. Makers of Playing Cards' Company: Liveryman, 1955–; Mem., Ct of Assts, 1978–; Sen. Warden, 1980–81; Master, 1981–82. FRSA. *Publications:* Inside Information on the Family and the Law, 1969; The Family's Guide to the Law, 1974; articles in Conveyancer, Jl of Planning and Environmental Law, and newspapers. *Recreations:* family life; music, opera, theatre; early astronomical instruments; avoiding gardening; interested in problems of developing countries. *Address:* The Old Farmhouse, Twineham, Haywards Heath, Sussex RH17 5NP. *T:* Hurstpierpoint (01273) 832058; Personal Investment Authority Ombudsman Bureau, 3rd Floor, Centre Point, 103 New Oxford Street, WC1A 1QH. *T:* 0171–240 3838. *Club:* City Livery.

EDELMAN, Colin Neil; QC 1995; *b* 2 March 1954; *s* of Gerald Bertram Edelman and Lynn Queenie Edelman (*née* Tropp); *m* 1978, Jacqueline Claire Seidel; one *s* one *d*. *Educ:* Haberdashers' Aske's Sch., Elstree; Clare Coll., Cambridge (MA). Called to the Bar, Middle Temple, 1977; Asst Recorder, 1993. *Publications:* articles for internat. Insurance Law Review and British Insurance Law Assoc. Jl. *Recreations:* badminton, ski-ing, walking. *Address:* Devereux Chambers, Devereux Court, WC2R 3JJ. *T:* 0171–353 7534, *Fax:* 0171–353 1724.

EDELMAN, Prof. Gerald Maurice, MD, PhD; Vincent Astor Distinguished Professor of Biochemistry, The Rockefeller University, New York, since 1974; Chairman, Department of Neurobiology, Scripps Research Institute, since 1992; *b* NYC, 1 July 1929; *s* of Edward Edelman and Anna Freedman; *m* 1950, Maxine Morrison; two *s* one *d*. *Educ:* Ursinus Coll. (BS); University of Pennsylvania (MD); The Rockefeller University (PhD). Med. Hse Officer, Massachusetts Gen. Hosp., 1954–55; Asst Physician, Hosp. of The Rockefeller Univ., 1957–60; The Rockefeller University: Asst Prof. and Asst Dean of Grad. Studies, 1960–63; Associate Prof. and Associate Dean of Grad. Studies, 1963–66; Prof., 1966–74. Trustee, Rockefeller Brothers Fund, 1972–82; Associate, Neurosciences Res. Program, 1965– (Scientific Chm., 1980–; Dir, Neurosciences Inst., 1981–). Mem., Adv. Bd, Basel Inst. Immunology, 1970–77 (Chm., 1975–77); Member Emeritus, Weizmann Inst. of Science, 1987 (Mem., Bd of Governors, 1971–87); non-resident Fellow and Mem. Bd Trustees, Salk Inst. for Biol. Studies, 1973–85; Member: Biophysics and Biophys. Chem. Study Section, Nat. Insts of Health, 1964–67; Sci. Council, Center for Theoretical Studies, 1970–72; Bd of Overseers, Faculty Arts and Scis, Univ. of Pa, 1976–83; Board of Trustees, Carnegie Inst. of Washington (Mem., Adv. Cttee). Member: Nat. Acad. Scis; Amer. Acad. Arts Scis; Amer. Philosophical Soc.; Fellow: AAAS; NY Acad. Scis; NY Acad. of Medicine; Member: Amer. Soc. Biol Chemists; Amer. Assoc. Immunologists; Genetics Soc. of America; Harvey Soc. (Pres., 1975–76); Amer. Chem. Soc.; Amer. Soc. Cell Biol.; Soc. for Developmental Biol.; Sigma XI; Alpha Omega Alpha; Council of Foreign Relations. Hon. Member: Pharmaceutical Soc. of Japan; Japanese Biochem. Soc.; Foreign Mem., Academie des Sciences, Institut de France. Hon. DSc: Pennsylvania, 1973; Gustavus Adolphus Coll., Minn., 1975; Paris, Cagliari, Georgetown Univ. Sch. of Med., 1989; Univ. degli Studi di Napoli Federico II, 1990; Tulane, 1991; Hon. ScD: Ursinus Coll., 1974; Williams Coll., 1976; Hon. MD Univ. Siena, Italy, 1974. Spencer Morris Award, Univ. of Pennsylvania, 1954; Eli Lilly Award in Biol Chem., Amer. Chem. Soc., 1965; Annual Alumni Award, Ursinus College, 1969; (jtly) Nobel Prize in Physiology or Medicine, 1972; Albert Einstein Commemorative Award, Yeshiva Univ., 1974; Buchman Meml Award, Caltech, 1975; Rabbi Shai Shacknai Meml Prize in Immunology and Cancer Res., Hebrew Univ. Hadassah Med. Sch., 1977; Regents Medal of Excellence, New York State, 1984; Hans Neurath prize, Washington Univ., 1986; Sesquicentennial Commem. Award, Nat. Liby of Medicine, 1986; Cécile and Oskar Vogt award, Dusseldorf Univ., 1988; Dist. Grad. Award, Pennsylvania Univ., 1990; Personnelité de l'année, Paris, 1990. *Publications:* Neural Darwinism, 1987; Topobiology, 1988; The Remembered Present, 1989; Bright Air, Brilliant Fire, 1992. *Recreation:* music. *Address:* Scripps Research Institute, 10666 N Torrey Pines Road, La Jolla, CA 92037, USA.

EDELMAN, Keith Graeme; Chief Executive, Storehouse and BHS, since 1993; *b* 10 July 1950; *m* 1974, Susan Brown; two *s*. *Educ:* Haberdashers' Aske's Sch.; UMIST (BSc). IBM, 1971–73; Rank Xerox, 1973–78; Bank of America, 1978–83; Grand Metropolitan, 1983–84; Corporate Planning Dir and Chm., Texas Homecare, Ladbroke Group, 1984–91; Man. Dir, Carlton Communications, 1991–93. . *Recreations:* tennis, ski-ing. *Address:* Storehouse plc, Marylebone House, 129–137 Marylebone Road, NW1 5QD. *T:* 0171–262 3456.

EDELSTEIN, Victor Arnold; couturier; founded Victor Edelstein Ltd, 1978; *b* 10 July 1945; *s* of Israel and Rebecca Edelstein; *m* 1973, Anna Maria Succi. Trainee Designer, Alexon, 1962–66; Asst Designer, Biba, 1966–68; formed own small dress designing co., 1968–72; Salvador, 1972–76; Designer, Christian Dior, 1976–78. Ballet design, Rhapsody in Blue, 1989. *Recreations:* painting, ski-ing, music. *Address:* 3 & 4 Stanhope Mews West, SW7 5RB. *T:* 0171–244 7481.

EDEN, family name of **Barons Auckland, Eden of Winton** and **Henley.**

EDEN OF WINTON, Baron *cr* 1983 (Life Peer), of Rushyford in the County of Durham; **John Benedict Eden;** Bt (E) 1672 and Bt (GB) 1776; PC 1972; Chairman, WonderWorld plc, since 1982; Director, Lady Eden's Schools Ltd, 1949–70 and since 1974; *b* 15 Sept. 1925; *s* of Sir Timothy Calvert Eden, 8th and 6th Bt and Patricia (*d* 1990), *d* of Arthur Prendergast; *S* father, 1963; *m* 1st, 1958, Belinda Jane (marr. diss. 1974), *o d* of late Sir John Pascoe; two *s* two *d*; 2nd, 1977, Margaret Ann, Viscountess Strathallan. Lieut Rifle Bde, seconded to 2nd KEO Goorkha Rifles and Gilgit Scouts, 1943–47. Contested (C) Paddington North, 1953; MP (C) Bournemouth West, Feb. 1954–1983. Mem. House of Commons Select Cttee on Estimates, 1962–64; Vice-Chm., Conservative Parly Defence Cttee, 1963–66 (formerly: Chm., Defence Air Sub-Cttee; Hon. Sec., Space Sub-Cttee); Vice-Chm., Aviation Cttee, 1963–64; Additional Opposition Front Bench Spokesman for Defence, 1964–66; Jt Vice-Chm., Cons. Parly Trade and Power Cttee, 1966–68; Opposition Front Bench Spokesman for Power, 1968–70; Minister of State, Min. of Technology, June-Oct. 1970; Minister for Industry, DTI, 1970–72; Minister of Posts and Telecommunications, 1972–74; Mem., Expenditure Cttee, 1974–76; Chairman: House of Commons Select Cttee on European Legislation, 1976–79; Home Affairs Cttee, 1981–83. Vice-Chm., Assoc. of Conservative Clubs Ltd, 1964–67, Vice-Pres., 1970–; President: Wessex Area Council, Nat. Union of Conservative and Unionist Assocs, 1974–77; Wessex Area Young Conservatives, 1978–80. UK Deleg. to Council of Europe and to Western European Union, 1960–62; Mem., NATO Parliamentarians' Conf., 1962–66. Chm., Royal Armouries, 1986–94. Chairman: Gamlestaden plc, 1987–92; Bricom Gp, 1990–93. Pres., Independent Schs Assoc., 1969–71; a Vice-Pres., Nat. Chamber of Trade, 1974–86; Vice-Pres., Internat. Tree Foundn. Hon. Vice-Pres., Nat. Assoc. of Master Bakers, Confectioners & Caterers, 1978–82. Mem., British Lebanese Assoc. *Heir* (to baronetcies only)*:* *s* Hon. Robert Frederick Calvert Eden, *b* 30 April 1964. *Address:* 41 Victoria Road, W8 5RH. *Clubs:* Boodle's, Pratt's.

EDEN, Prof. Richard John, OBE 1978; Professor of Energy Studies, Cavendish Laboratory, University of Cambridge, 1982–89, now Emeritus; Fellow of Clare Hall, Cambridge, 1966–89, now Emeritus (Vice-President, 1987–89; Hon. Fellow, 1993); *b* 2 July 1922; *s* of James A. Eden and Dora M. Eden; *m* 1949, Elsie Jane Greaves; one *s* one *d* and one step *d*. *Educ:* Hertford Grammar Sch.; Peterhouse, Cambridge. BA 1943, MA 1948, PhD 1951. War service, 1942–46, Captain REME, Airborne Forces. Cambridge University: Bye-Fellow, Peterhouse, 1949–50; Stokes Student, Pembroke Coll., 1950–51; Clare College: Research Fellow, 1951–55; Official Fellow, 1957–66; Dir of Studies in Maths, 1951–53, 1957–62; Royal Soc. Smithson Res. Fellow, 1952–55; Sen. Lectr in Physics, Univ. of Manchester, 1955–57; Cambridge University: Lectr in Maths, 1957–64 (Stokes Lectr, 1962); Reader in Theoretical Physics, 1964–82; Head of High Energy Theoretical Physics Gp, 1964–74, Hd of Energy Res. Gp, 1974–89, Cavendish Lab. Mem., Princeton Inst. for Advanced Study, 1954, 1959, 1973, 1989; Vis. Scientist: Indiana Univ., 1954–55; Univ. of California, Berkeley, 1960, 1967; Vis. Professor: Univ. of Maryland, 1961, 1965; Columbia Univ., 1962; Scuola Normale Superiore, Pisa, 1964; Univ. of Marseilles, 1968; Univ. of California, 1969. Member: UK Adv. Council on Energy Conservation, 1974–83; Eastern Electricity Bd, 1985–93; Energy Adviser to UK NEDO, 1974–75. Syndic, CUP, 1984–. Chm., Cambridge Energy Res. Ltd, subseq. Caminus Energy Ltd, 1985–91. Companion, Inst. of Energy, 1985. Smiths Prize, Univ. of Cambridge, 1949; Maxwell Prize and Medal, Inst. of Physics, 1970; Open Award for Distinction in Energy Economics, BIEE, 1989. *Publications:* (jtly) The Analytic S Matrix, 1966; High Energy Collisions of Elementary Particles, 1967; Energy Conservation in the United Kingdom (NEDO report), 1975; Energy Prospects (Dept of Energy report), 1976; World Energy Demand to 2020 (World Energy Conf. report), 1977; (jtly) Energy Economics, 1981; (jtly) Electricity's Contribution to UK Energy Self Sufficiency, 1984; (jtly) UK Energy, 1984; papers and review articles on nuclear physics and theory of elementary particles. *Recreations:* painting, reading, gardening, travel. *Address:* Cavendish Laboratory, Cambridge CB3 0HE. *T:* Cambridge (01223) 337231; 6 Wootton Way, Cambridge CB3 9LX. *T:* Cambridge (01223) 355591.

EDER, (Henry) Bernard; QC 1990; *b* 16 Oct. 1952; *s* of Hans and Helga Eder; *m* 1976, Diana Levin; four *s* one *d*. *Educ:* Haberdashers' Aske's School, Elstree; Downing College, Cambridge (BA 1974). Called to the Bar, Inner Temple, 1975. *Recreations:* tennis, ski-ing. *Address:* Essex Court Chambers, 24–26 Lincoln's Inn Fields, WC2A 3ED. *T:* 0171–813 8000.

EDES, (John) Michael, CMG 1981; HM Diplomatic Service, retired; Ambassador and Head, UK Delegation to Conventional Arms Control Negotiations, Vienna, 1989–90; *b* 19 April 1930; *s* of late Lt-Col N. H. Edes and Mrs Louise Edes; *m* 1978, Angela Mermagen; two *s*. *Educ:* Blundell's Sch.; Clare Coll., Cambridge (Scholar; BA); Yale Univ. (MA). HM Forces, 1948–49; Mellon Fellow, Yale Univ., 1952–54; FO, 1954; MECAS, 1955; Dubai, 1956–57; FO, 1957–59 (Moscow, 1959); Rome, 1959–61; FO, 1961–62; UK Delegn to Conf. on Disarmament, Geneva, 1962–65 (UK Mission to UN, NY, 1963); FO, 1965–68; Cabinet Office, 1968–69; FCO, 1969–71; Ambassador to Yemen Arab Republic, 1971–73; Mem., UK Delegn to CSCE, Geneva, 1973–74; FCO, 1974–77; RIIA, 1977–78; Paris, 1978–79; Ambassador to Libya, 1980–83; Hd, UK Delegn to Conf. on Confidence and Security Building Measures and Disarmament in Europe, Stockholm, 1983–86; Hd, UK team at conventional arms control mandate talks, 1987–89. Vis. Fellow, IISS, 1987. *Recreations:* listening to music, gardening. *Address:* c/o Lloyds Bank, 7 Pall Mall, SW1Y 5NA. *Clubs:* Athenæum; Hawks (Cambridge).

EDEY, Prof. Harold Cecil, BCom (London), FCA; Professor of Accounting, London School of Economics, University of London, 1962–80, now Emeritus; *b* 23 Feb. 1913; *s* of Cecil Edey and Elsie (*née* Walmsley); *m* 1944, Dilys Mary Pakeman Jones; one *s* one *d*. *Educ:* Croydon High Sch. for Boys; LSE (Hon. Fellow, 1986). Chartered Accountant, 1935. Commnd in RNVR, 1940–46. Lectr in Accounting and Finance, LSE, 1949–55; Reader in Accounting, Univ. of London, 1955–62; Pro-Dir, LSE, 1967–70. Mem., UK Adv. Coun. on Educn for Management, 1961–65; Mem., Academic Planning Bd for London Grad. Sch. of Business Studies, and Governor, 1965–71; Chm., Arts and Social Studies Cttee, CNAA, 1965–71, and Mem. Council, 1965–73; Chm., Bd of Studies in Econs, 1966–71, Mem. Senate, 1975–80, University of London; Mem. Council, Inst. of Chartered Accountants in England and Wales, 1969–80. Hon. Freeman, 1981, Hon. Liveryman, 1986, Co. of Chartered Accountants in England and Wales. Hon. Professor, UCW, Aberystwyth, 1980–; Patron, Univ. of Buckingham, 1984–. Hon. LLD CNAA, 1972. Bard of the Cornish Gorsedd, 1933. Chartered Accountants Founding Socs' Centenary Award, 1987. *Publications:* (with A. T. Peacock) National Income and Social Accounting, 1954; Business Budgets and Accounts, 1959; Introduction to Accounting, 1963; (with B. S. Yamey and H. Thomson) Accounting in England and Scotland 1543–1800, 1963; (with B. V. Carsberg) Modern Financial Management, 1969; (with B. S. Yamey) Debits, Credits, Finance and Profits, 1974; (with L. H. Leigh) The Companies Act 1981, 1981; Accounting Queries, 1982; articles in various jls. *Address:* 10 The Green, Southwick, Brighton BN42 4DA.

EDGAR, David Burman; author and playwright; Chair, MA in Playwriting Studies, University of Birmingham, since 1989, Hon. Professor, since 1992; (Hon. Senior Research Fellow, 1988–92); *b* 26 Feb. 1948; *s* of Barrie Edgar and Joan (*née* Burman); *m* 1979, Eve Brook; two *s*. *Educ:* Oundle Sch.; Univ. of Manchester (BA 1969). Fellow in Creative Writing, Leeds Polytechnic, 1972–74; Resident Playwright, Birmingham Rep. Theatre, 1974–75, Board Mem., 1985–; UK/US Bicentennial Arts Fellow, USA, 1978–79; Literary Consultant, 1984–88, Hon. Associate Artist, 1989, RSC. Hon. Fellow, Birmingham Polytechnic, 1991. Hon. MA Bradford, 1984; DUniv Surrey, 1993. *Plays:* The National Interest, 1971; Excuses Excuses, Coventry, 1972; Death Story, Birmingham Rep., 1972; Baby Love, 1973; The Dunkirk Spirit, 1974; Dick Deterred, Bush Theatre, 1974; O Fair Jerusalem, Birmingham Rep., 1975; Saigon Rose, Edinburgh, 1976; Blood Sports, incl. Ball Boys, Bush Theatre, 1976; Destiny, Other Place, 1976, Aldwych, 1977; Wreckers, 1977; Our Own People, 1977; (adaptation) The Jail Diary of Albie Sachs, Warehouse Theatre, 1978; (adaptation) Mary Barnes, Birmingham Rep., then Royal Court, 1978–79; (with Susan Todd) Teendreams, 1979; (adaptation) Nicholas Nickleby, Aldwych, 1980, Plymouth Theatre, NY, 1981; Maydays, Barbican, 1983; Entertaining Strangers, 1985, Nat. Theatre, 1987; That Summer, Hampstead, 1987; (with Stephen Bill and Anne Devlin) Heartlanders, Birmingham Rep., 1989; The Shape of the Table, NT, 1990;

(adaptation) Dr Jekyll and Mr Hyde, Barbican, 1991; Pentecost, Other Place, 1994; *TV and radio:* The Eagle has Landed, 1973; Sanctuary, 1973; I know what I meant, 1974; Ecclesiastes, 1977; (with Neil Grant) Vote for Them, 1989; A Movie Starring Me, 1991; Buying a Landslide, 1992; Citizen Locke, 1994; *film:* Lady Jane, 1986. *Publications:* Destiny, 1976; Wreckers, 1977; The Jail Diary of Albie Sachs, 1978; Teendreams, 1979; Mary Barnes, 1979; Nicholas Nickleby, 1982; Maydays, 1983; Entertaining Strangers, 1985; Plays One, 1987; That Summer, 1987; The Second Time as Farce, 1988; Vote for Them, 1989; Heartlanders, 1989; Edgar Shorts, 1990; Plays Two, 1990; The Shape of the Table, 1990; Plays Three, 1991, Dr Jekyll and Mr Hyde, 1992. *Recreation:* correspondence. *Address:* c/o Michael Imison Playwrights Ltd, 28 Almeida Street, N1 1TD.

EDGAR, William, FIMechE; Chief Executive, National Engineering Laboratory, since 1990; *b* 16 Jan. 1938; *s* of William Edgar and Alice Anderson McKerrell; *m* 1961, June Gilmour; two *s*. *Educ:* Royal Coll. of Science and Technology (Strathclyde Univ.); ARCST 1961; Birmingham Univ. (MSc 1962). Develt Engr, BSC, Motherwell and Glasgow, 1954–62; Principal Aeromech. Engr, BAC, Warton, 1963–67; Chief Develt Engr, Gen. Manager Sales and Service, Gen. Works Manager, Weir Pumps, Glasgow, 1967–73; Chief Exec., Seaforth Engineering and Corporate Develt Dir, Seaforth Maritime, Aberdeen, 1973–86; Business Develt Dir, Vickers Marine Engineering, Edinburgh, 1986–88; Exec. Chm., Cochrane Shipbuilders, Yorks, 1988–90. *Recreations:* golf, squash, football, walking, reading. *Address:* Rusteph, 7 Glasclune Gardens, North Berwick, East Lothian EH39 4RB. *T:* North Berwick (01620) 4640. *Clubs:* Sloane; Glen Golf.

EDGCUMBE, family name of **Earl of Mount Edgcumbe.**

EDGE, Geoffrey; Senior Associate, P-E International (formerly P-E Inbucon), since 1987; Chairman, West Midlands Enterprise Board, since 1982; *b* 26 May 1943; single. *Educ:* London Sch. of Econs (BA); Birmingham Univ. Asst Lectr in Geography, Univ. of Leicester, 1967–70; Lectr in Geog., Open Univ., 1970–74. Bletchley UDC, 1972–74 (Chm. Planning Sub-cttee 1973–74); Milton Keynes District Councillor, 1973–76 (Vice-Chm. Planning Cttee, 1973–75); Mem. Bucks Water Bd, 1973–74. MP (Lab) Aldridge-Brownhills, Feb. 1974–1979; PPS to Minister of State for Educn, Feb.-Oct. 1974, 1976–77, to Minister of State, Privy Council Office, Oct. 1974–76. Research Fellow, Dept of Planning Landscape, Birmingham Polytechnic, 1979–80; Senior Research Fellow: Preston Polytechnic, 1980–81; NE London Polytechnic, 1982–84; Hon. Res. Fellow, Birmingham Polytechnic, 1980–81; New Initiatives Co-ordinator, COPEC Housing Trust, 1984–87. Mem., W Midlands CC, 1981–86 (Chm., Econ. Develt Cttee); Mem., Walsall MBC, 1983–90 (Leader, 1988–90). *Publications:* (ed jtly) Regional Analysis and Development, 1973; Open Univ. booklets on industrial location and urban development. *Recreations:* music, reading, touring. *Address:* 5 Sedgefield Close, Milking Bank, Dudley DY1 2UY.

EDGE, Captain Sir (Philip) Malcolm, KCVO 1995; FNI; Deputy Master and Chairman, Board of Trinity House, 1988–July 1996; *b* 15 July 1931; *s* of Stanley Weston Edge and Edith Edge (*née* Liddell); *m* 1967, (Kathleen) Anne Greenwood (*d* 1994); one *s* one *d*. *Educ:* Rockferry High School; HMS Conway. Master Mariner. Apprenticed to Shipping subsidiary of British Petroleum, 1949, and served in all ranks; in command, world wide, 1969–78. Elder Brother and Mem. Board, Trinity House, 1978; Mem., PLA, 1980–. Dir, Standard Steamship Owners' Protection & Indemnity Assoc. Ltd, 1988– (Chm., 1992–). Mem. Council, Internat. Assoc. of Lighthouse Authies, 1988– (Pres., 1988–90); Ex officio Mem., Cttee of Management, RNLI, 1988–; Vice-President: Royal Alfred Seafarers Soc., 1988–; Shipwrecked Mariners Royal Benevolent Soc., 1988–. Hon. Mem., London Flotilla, 1989–. Freeman, City of London, 1980; Liveryman, 1980–, Hon. Mem., 1988–, Hon. Co. of Master Mariners; Liveryman, Shipwrights' Co., 1990–. Warden, Watermen and Lightermen's Co., 1993– . *Recreations:* sailing, family. *Address:* c/o Trinity House, Tower Hill, EC3N 4DH. *T:* 0171–480 6601. *Clubs:* Royal Thames Yacht; Samuel Pepys (Oxford).

EDGE, Maj.-Gen. Raymond Cyril Alexander, CB 1968; MBE 1945; FRICS 1949; FRGS; Director General, Ordnance Survey, 1965–69, retired; *b* 21 July 1912; *s* of Raymond Clive Edge and Mary (*née* Masters); *m* 1st, 1939, Margaret Patricia (*d* 1982), *d* of William Wallace McKee; one *s* one *d*; 2nd, 1983, Audrey Anne, *d* of Sir Lewis Richardson, 1st Bt, CBE, and *widow* of Jonathan Muers-Raby. *Educ:* Cheltenham Coll.; RMA; Caius Coll., Cambridge (BA). Commissioned in RE, 1932. Served in India, Royal Bombay Sappers and Miners and Survey of India, 1936–39. War Service in India, Burma (despatches), and Malaya. Lt-Col 1951; Col 1954; Dir (Brig.) Ordnance Survey, 1961; Maj.-Gen. 1965. Col Comdt, RE, 1970–75 (Representative Col Comdt, 1974). Mem., Sec. of State for the Environment's Panel of Independent Inspectors, 1971–82. Chairman: Assoc. British Geodesists, 1963–65; Geodesy Sub-Cttee, Royal Soc., 1968–75; Field Survey Assoc., 1968–70. Pres., Section E, British Assoc., 1969. Member: Council, RGS, 1966–69; Council, RICS, 1966–72 (Vice-Pres. 1970–72); Land Surveyors Council (Chm. 1970–72). *Publications:* contrib. A History of the Ordnance Survey, 1980; various papers on geodetic subjects in Bulletin Géodesique and other publications. *Recreation:* music. *Address:* Brook Farm, North Curry, near Taunton, Som TA3 6DJ. *T:* North Curry (01823) 490444. *Club:* Army and Navy.

EDGE, William, (3rd Bt *cr* 1937); *S* father, 1984. *Heir: s* Edward Knowles Edge. Does not use the title and his name is not on the Official Roll of Baronets.

EDIE, His Honour Thomas Ker; a Circuit Judge, South Eastern Circuit, 1972–84; *b* 3 Oct. 1916; *s* of H. S. Ker Edie, Kinloss, Morayshire; *m* 1945, Margaret, *d* of Rev. A. E. Shooter, TD; four *s* one *d*. *Educ:* Clifton; London Univ. Called to Bar, Gray's Inn, 1941. Metropolitan Magistrate, 1961–70; Dep. Chm. Middlesex QS, 1970–71.

EDINBURGH, Bishop of, since 1986; **Most Rev. Richard Frederick Holloway;** Primus of the Episcopal Church in Scotland, since 1992; *b* 26 Nov. 1933; *s* of Arthur and Mary Holloway; *m* 1963, Jean Elizabeth Kennedy, New York; one *s* two *d*. *Educ:* Kelham Theol Coll.; Edinburgh Theol Coll.; Union Theol Seminary, New York (STM); BD (London). FRSE 1995. Curate, St Ninian's, Glasgow, 1959–63; Priest-in-charge, St Margaret and St Mungo's, Glasgow, 1963–68; Rector, Old St Paul's, Edinburgh, 1968–80; Rector, Church of the Advent, Boston, Mass, USA, 1980–84; Vicar, St Mary Magdalen's, Oxford, 1984–86. Mem., Human Fertilisation and Embryo Authority, 1991–; Chm., Edinburgh Voluntary Orgns Council, 1991–. FRSA 1992. DUniv Strathclyde, 1994; Hon. DD Aberdeen, 1995. *Publications:* Let God Arise, 1972; New Vision of Glory, 1974; A New Heaven, 1978; Beyond Belief, 1982; Signs of Glory, 1983; The Killing, 1984, 2nd edn as Behold Your King, 1995; (ed) The Anglican Tradition, 1984; Paradoxes of Christian Faith and Life, 1984; The Sidelong Glance, 1985; The Way of the Cross, 1986; Seven to Flee, Seven to Follow, 1987; Crossfire: faith and doubt in an age of certainty, 1988; Another Country, Another King, 1991; Who Needs Feminism?, 1991; Anger, Sex, Doubt and Death, 1992; The Stranger in the Wings, 1994; (jtly) Churches and How to Survive Them, 1994; Limping Towards the Sunrise, 1995. *Recreations:* long-distance walking, reading, cinema, music. *Address:* 3 Eglinton Crescent, Edinburgh EH12 5DH. *T:* 0131–226 5099.

EDINBURGH, Dean of; *see* Morris, Very Rev. T. D.

EDINBURGH, (St Mary's Cathedral), Provost of; *see* Forbes, Very Rev. G. J. T.

EDIS, Richard John Smale, CMG 1994; HM Diplomatic Service; Ambassador to Mozambique, since 1992; *b* 1 Sept. 1943; *s* of Denis Edis and Sylvia (*née* Smale); *m* 1971, Geneviève Cérisoles; three *s*. *Educ:* King Edward's Sch., Birmingham (schol.); St Catharine's Coll., Cambridge (Exhibnr; MA). British Centre, Stockholm, 1965–66; entered HM Diplomatic Service, 1966; FO, 1966–68; Third, later Second Sec., Nairobi, 1968–70; Second, later First Sec., Lisbon, 1971–74; FCO, 1974–77; First Sec., UK Mission to UN, New York, 1977–80; Alternate UK Rep. to UN Human Rights Commn, 1978–81; Asst Head of Southern African Dept, FCO, 1981–82; Counsellor 1982; on secondment to Northern Ireland Office as Asst Sec., 1982–84; Dep. Leader, UK Disarmament Delegn, Geneva, 1984–88; Comr, British Indian Ocean Territory, and Head, E Africa Dept, FCO, 1988–91; Vis. Fellow, Centre of Internat. Studies, Univ. of Cambridge, 1991–92. FRGS. Special Constabulary Medal, 1991. Officer, Military Order of Christ, Portugal, 1973. *Publications:* Peak of Limuria: the story of Diego Garcia, 1993; contrib. Cambridge Review of Internat. Affairs, and other academic jls. *Recreations:* sport, history, reading. *Address:* c/o Foreign and Commonwealth Office, SW1A 2AH. *Clubs:* Travellers'; The Union (Cambridge).

EDMOND, Prof. John Marmion, PhD; FRS 1986; Professor of Marine Geochemistry, Massachusetts Institute of Technology, since 1970; *b* 27 April 1943; *s* of late Andrew John Shields Edmond and Christina Marmion Edmond; *m* 1978, Massoudeh Vafai; two *s*. *Educ:* Univ. of Glasgow (BSc 1st class Hons, Pure Chemistry, 1965); Univ. of California at San Diego, Scripps Instn of Oceanography (PhD, Marine Chemistry, 1970). Massachusetts Institute of Technology: Asst Prof., 1970; Associate Prof., 1975; Full Prof., 1981. Mackelwane Award, Amer. Geophysical Union, 1976. *Publications:* over 80 scientific papers in professional jls. *Recreations:* reading, gardening. *Address:* 21 Robin Hood Road, Arlington, MA 02174, USA. *T:* (617) 2535739.

EDMONDS, David Albert; General Manager, Group Property and Central Services, National Westminster Bank, since 1991; *b* 6 March 1944; *s* of Albert and Gladys Edmonds; *m* 1966, Ruth Beech; two *s* two *d*. *Educ:* Helsby County Grammar School; University of Keele. BA Hons Political Institutions and History. Asst Principal, Min. of Housing and Local Govt, 1966–69; Private Sec. to Parly Sec., MHLG and DoE, 1969–71; Principal, DoE, 1971–73; Observer, CSSB, 1973–74; Vis. Fellow, Centre for Metropolitan Planning and Research, Johns Hopkins Univ., 1974–75; Private Sec. to Perm. Sec., DoE, 1975–77; Asst Sec., DoE, 1977–79; Principal Private Sec. to Sec. of State, DoE, 1979–83; Under Sec., Inner Cities Directorate, DoE, 1983–84; Chief Exec., Housing Corporation, 1984–91. Dir, Housing Finance Corp., 1988–91. Pres., Internat. New Town Assoc., 1987–91; Mem. Cttee, Notting Hill Housing Trust, 1991–94. Dep. Chm., New Statesman and Society, 1988–90 (Chm., New Society, 1986–88); Mem. Editl Adv. Bd, Building, 1986–93. *Recreations:* films, theatre, opera, walking, golf. *Address:* National Westminster Bank, 41 Lothbury, EC2P 2BP. *T:* 0171–726 1000. *Clubs:* Wimbledon Park Golf; Wimbledon Wanderers Cricket.

EDMONDS, John Christopher, CMG 1978; CVO 1971; HM Diplomatic Service, retired; *b* 23 June 1921; *s* of late Captain A. C. M. Edmonds, OBE, RN, and late Mrs. Edmonds; *m* 1st, 1948, Elena Tornow (marr. diss., 1965); two *s*; 2nd, 1966, Armine Williams. *Educ:* Kelly College. Entered Royal Navy, 1939; psc, 1946. Staff: of NATO Defence Coll., Paris, 1953–55; of C-in-C Home Fleet, 1956–57 (Comdr, 1957); of Chief of Defence Staff, 1958–59. Entered Diplomatic Service, 1959; Foreign Office, 1959–60; 1st Secretary (Commercial), Tokyo, 1960–62; FO, 1963–67; 1st Secretary and Head of Chancery, Ankara, 1967–68; Counsellor: Ankara, 1968–71; Paris, 1972–74; Head of Arms Control and Disarmament Dept, FCO, 1974–77; Leader, UK Delegn to Comprehensive Test Ban Treaty Negotiations, Geneva, with personal rank of Ambassador, 1978–81. Chm., Jt SDP-Liberal Alliance Commn on Defence and Disarmament, 1984–86. Vis. Fellow in Internat. Relations, Reading Univ., 1981–; Vis. Prof., Westminster Univ., 1992–. *Recreations:* gardening, travel. *Address:* North Lodge, Sonning, Berks RG4 0ST. *Club:* Army and Navy.

EDMONDS, John Christopher Paul, CBE 1993; Chief Executive, Railtrack, since 1993; *b* 22 April 1936; *s* of Frank Winston Edmonds and late Phyllis Mary Edmonds; *m* 1962, Christine Elizabeth Seago; one *s* one *d*. *Educ:* Lowestoft Grammar School; Trinity College, Cambridge. Nat. Service Commission, RAF, 1955–57. Joined British Rail, 1960; Chief Freight Manager, London Midland Region, 1981; Nat. Business Manager, Coal, 1982; Dir, Provincial, 1984; Gen. Manager, Anglia Region, 1987, Bd Mem., and Man. Dir, Gp Services, 1989–93. *Recreations:* gardening, music. *Address:* Railtrack Group plc, 40 Bernard Street, WC1N 1BY.

EDMONDS, John Walter; General Secretary, GMB (formerly General, Municipal, Boilermakers and Allied Trades Union), since 1986; *b* 28 Jan. 1944; *s* of Walter and Rose Edmonds; *m* 1967, Linden (*née* Callaby); two *d*. *Educ:* Brunswick Park Primary; Christ's Hosp.; Oriel Coll., Oxford (BA 1965, MA 1968). General and Municipal Workers' Union: Res. Asst, 1966; Dep. Res. Officer, 1967; Reg. Officer, 1968; Nat. Industrial Officer, 1972. Director: National Building Agency, 1978–82; Unity Trust Bank, 1986–. Mem., Royal Commn on Environmental Pollution, 1979–89; a Forestry Comr, 1994–. Vis. Fellow, Nuffield Coll., Oxford, 1986–94. Mem. Council, Consumers' Assoc., 1991–. Trustee, Inst. of Public Policy Research, 1988–. Gov., LSE, 1986–. Hon. LLD Sussex, 1994. FRSA. *Recreations:* cricket, carpentry. *Address:* 50 Graham Road, Mitcham, Surrey CR4 2HA. *T:* 0181–648 9991.

EDMONDS, Robert Humphrey Gordon, CMG 1969; MBE 1944; writer; HM Diplomatic Service, retired; *b* 5 Oct. 1920; *s* of late Air Vice-Marshal C. H. K. Edmonds, CBE, DSO; *m* 1st, 1951, Georgina Combe (marr. diss.); four *s*; 2nd, 1976, Mrs Enid Balint (*d* 1994), *widow* of Dr Michael Balint. *Educ:* Ampleforth; Brasenose Coll., Oxford. Pres., Oxford Union, 1940. Served Army, 1940–46; attached to Political Div., Allied Commn for Austria, 1945–46. Entered Foreign Service, Dec. 1946; served Cairo, 1947; FO, 1949; Rome, 1953; Warsaw, 1957; FO, 1959; Caracas, 1962; FO, CO and FCO, 1966–69; Minister, Moscow, 1969–71; High Comr, Nicosia, 1971–72; Asst Under Sec. of State, FCO, 1974–77, retd 1978. Vis. Fellow, Glasgow Univ., 1973–74; Fellow, Woodrow Wilson Internat. Centre for Scholars, Washington, 1977; Leverhulme Res. Fellow, 1989–91; Hon. Fellow, Glasgow Inst. of Soviet and E European Studies, 1988–91. Adviser, Kleinwort Benson, 1978–83, consultant, 1984–86. Mem. Council, RIIA, 1986–92. *Publications:* Soviet Foreign Policy: the paradox of superpower, 1975; Soviet Foreign Policy: the Brezhnev years, 1983; Setting the Mould: the United States and Britain 1945–1950, 1986; The Big Three, 1990; (contrib.) Churchill, ed Blake and Louis, 1992; Pushkin: the man and his age, 1994; articles and review articles in International Affairs, TLS and Survival. *Address:* Raven House, Ramsbury, Wilts SN8 2PA. *Club:* Turf.

EDMONDS, Sheila May, MA, PhD; Fellow, and Lecturer in Mathematics, Newnham College, Cambridge, 1945–82 (Vice-Principal, 1960–81); Fellow Emerita, Newnham College, since 1982; *b* 1 April 1916; *d* of Harold Montagu Edmonds and Florence Myra

Edmonds (*née* Lilley). *Educ:* Wimbledon High Sch.; Newnham Coll., Cambridge. Research Student of Westfield Coll., 1939–40, and of Newnham Coll., 1940–41; Research Fellow of Newnham Coll., 1941–43; Asst Lecturer, Newnham Coll., 1943–45. *Publications:* papers in mathematical journals. *Recreations:* travel, photography. *Address:* 5 Cross Lane Close, Orwell, Royston, Herts SG8 5QW. *T:* Cambridge (01223) 207789.

EDMONDS, Winston Godward, CBE 1966; ERD 1945; Managing Director, Manchester Ship Canal Co., 1961–70; *b* 27 Nov. 1912; *s* of Wilfred Bell Edmonds and Nina (*née* Godward); *m* 1940, Sheila Mary (*née* Armitage); one *s*. *Educ:* Merchant Taylors'. Joined LNER, first as traffic apprentice and then in various positions, 1930–46; Manchester Ship Canal Co.: Commercial Manager, 1947–58; Manager, 1959–61. *Recreations:* golf, philately. *Address:* Herons Wood, 22 Castlegate, Prestbury, Cheshire SK10 4AZ. *T:* Prestbury (01625) 828966.

EDMONDS-BROWN, (Cedric Wilfred) George; HM Diplomatic Service; First Secretary, United Kingdom Mission to the United Nations, Geneva, since 1995; *b* 24 April 1939; *s* of late Maj. W. R. E. Edmonds-Brown and E. M. Edmonds-Brown; *m* 1st, 1964, Everild A. V. Hardman (*d* 1988); one *s* two *d*; 2nd, 1990, Teiko Watanabe; one *s*. *Educ:* Dame Allan's Boys' Sch., Newcastle; King's Coll., Durham Univ. Joined CRO, 1962; Lagos, 1963; Karachi, 1964–68; 3rd Sec., Buenos Aires, 1968–73; FCO, 1973–76; 2nd Sec., Bucharest, 1976–80; 1st Sec. and HM Consul, Caracas, 1980–85; ODA, 1985–88; Head of Chancery, Ottawa, 1988; Dep. High Comr, Barbados, 1989–91; First Sec., Rome, 1991–95. *Recreations:* writing, art, travel, cricket. *Address:* c/o Foreign and Commonwealth Office, King Charles Street, SW1A 2AH.

EDMONDSON, family name of **Baron Sandford.**

EDMONDSON, His Honour Anthony Arnold; a Circuit Judge (formerly County Court Judge and Commissioner, Liverpool and Manchester Crown Courts), 1971–91; *b* 6 July 1920; *s* of late Arnold Edmondson; *m* 1947, Dorothy Amelia Wilson, Gateshead-on-Tyne; three *s* one *d*. *Educ:* Liverpool Univ. (LLB Hons); Lincoln Coll., Oxford (BCL Hons). Served RA (Adjutant), 1940–44; RAF (Pilot), 1944–46; thereafter RA (TA) and TARO. Called to the Bar, Gray's Inn, 1947; William Shaw Schol. 1948; practised on Northern Circuit, 1948–71; Chairman, Liverpool Dock Labour Bd Appeal Tribunal, 1955–66; Mem. Court of Liverpool Univ., 1960–. Dep. Chm., Lancashire QS, 1970–71; Pres., S Cumbria Magistrates' Assoc., 1977–87; JP Lancs, 1970. *Recreations:* walking, fishing. *Address:* County Sessions House, Preston, Lancs PR1 2PD.

EDMONDSON, Leonard Firby; Executive Council Member, Amalgamated Union of Engineering Workers, 1966–77; *b* 16 Dec. 1912; *s* of Arthur William Edmondson and Elizabeth Edmondson; unmarried. *Educ:* Gateshead Central Sch. Served apprenticeship as engr, Liner Concrete Machinery Co. Ltd, Newcastle upon Tyne, 1929–34; worked in a number of engrg, ship-bldg and ship-repairing firms; shop steward and convener of shop stewards in several firms. AUEW: Mem., Tyne Dist Cttee, 1943–53; Tyne Dist Sec., 1953–66. CSEU: Mem., Exec. Council, 1966–78; Pres., 1976–77. Member: Shipbldg Industry Trng Bd, 1966–79; Council, ACAS, 1976–78; Royal Commn on Legal Services, 1976–79; Council on Tribunals, 1978–84; Cttee of Inquiry into Prison Services, 1978–79; Gen. Council of TUC, 1970–78. Mem., Birtley Canine Soc. *Recreation:* exhibiting Shetland sheep dogs. *Address:* 6 Kenwood Gardens, Low Fell, Gateshead, Tyne and Wear NE9 6PN. *T:* 0191–487 9167. *Clubs:* Northern Counties Shetland Sheep Dog; Manors Social (Newcastle-upon-Tyne).

EDMONSTONE, Sir Archibald (Bruce Charles), 7th Bt *cr* 1774; *b* 3 Aug. 1934; *o* surv. *s* of Sir Charles Edmonstone, 6th Bt, and Gwendolyn Mary (*d* 1989), *d* of late Marshall Field and Mrs Maldwin Drummond; *S* father, 1954; *m* 1st, 1957, Jane (marr. diss. 1967), *er d* of Maj.-Gen. E. C. Colville, CB, DSO; two *s* one *d*; 2nd, 1969, Juliet Elizabeth, *d* of Maj.-Gen. C. M. F. Deakin, CB, CBE; one *s* one *d*. *Educ:* St Peter's Court; Stowe Sch. *Heir: s* Archibald Edward Charles Edmonstone [*b* 4 Feb. 1961; *m* 1988, Ursula, *e d* of late Benjamin Worthington]. *Address:* Duntreath Castle, Blanefield, Stirlingshire G63 9AJ.

See also Sir A. R. J. B. Jardine, Captain Sir C. E. McGrigor.

EDMONTON, Area Bishop of, since 1984; **Rt. Rev. Brian John Masters;** *b* 17 Oct. 1932; *s* of late Stanley William and Grace Hannah Masters; unmarried. *Educ:* Collyers School, Horsham; Queens' Coll., Cambridge (MA 1955); Cuddesdon Theological Coll. Lloyd's broker, 1955–62. Asst Curate, S Dunstan and All Saints, Stepney, 1964–69; Vicar, Holy Trinity with S Mary, Hoxton, N1, 1969–82; Bishop Suffragan of Fulham, 1982–84. Chm. Exec. Cttee, Church Union, 1984–88. *Recreations:* theatre, squash. *Address:* 1 Regent's Park Terrace, NW1 7EE. *T:* 0171–267 4455, *Fax:* 0171–267 4404. *Club:* United Oxford & Cambridge University.

EDMONTON (Alberta), Archbishop of, (RC), since 1973; **Most Rev. Joseph Neil MacNeil;** *b* 15 April 1924; *s* of John Martin MacNeil and Kate MacNeil (*née* MacLean). *Educ:* St Francis Xavier Univ., Antigonish, NS (BA 1944); Holy Heart Seminary, Halifax, NS; Univs of Perugia, Chicago and St Thomas Aquinas, Rome (JCD 1958). Priest, 1948; pastor, parishes in NS, 1948–55; Chancery Office, Antigonish, 1958–59; admin, dio. Antigonish, 1959–60; Rector, Antigonish Cathedral, 1961; Dir of Extension Dept, St Francis Xavier Univ., Antigonish, 1961–69; Vice-Pres., 1962–69; Bishop of St John, NB, 1969–73. Pres., Canadian Conf. of Catholic Bishops, 1979–81 (Vice-Pres., 1977–79; Member: Commn on Ecumenism, 1985–91; Commn on Mission, 1991–); Chm., Alberta Bishops' Conf., 1973–. Chancellor, Univ. of St Thomas, Fredericton, NB, 1969. Founding Mem., Inst. for Res. on Public Policy, 1968–80; Mem., Bd of Directors: The Futures Secretariat, 1981–; Centre for Human Develt, Toronto, 1985–. Chairman: Bd, Newman Theol Coll., Edmonton, 1973–; Bd, St Joseph's Coll., Alberta Univ., 1973–. Member, Bd of Management: Edmonton Gen. Hosp., 1983–92; Edmonton Caritas Health Gp, 1992–. *Address:* 8421–101 Avenue, Edmonton, Alberta T6A 0L1, Canada.

EDMONTON (Alberta), Bishop of, since 1988; **Rt. Rev. Kenneth Lyle Genge;** *b* 25 Oct. 1933; *s* of Nelson Simms Genge and Grace Winifred Genge; *m* 1959, Ruth Louise Bate; two *s* one *d*. *Educ:* Univ of Saskatchewan (BA 1958); Emmanuel Coll., Saskatoon (LTh 1957; BD 1959). Parish priest, 1959–85; Conference Retreat Centre Director, 1985–88. Hon. DD Emmanuel Coll. and St Chad, 1989. *Recreations:* sports, physical fitness, music. *Address:* 12324 52 Avenue, Edmonton, Alberta T6H 0P4.

EDNAM, Viscount; William Humble David Jeremy Ward; *b* 27 March 1947; *s* and heir of Earl of Dudley, *qv* and of Stella Viscountess Ednam, *d* of M. A. Carcano, KCMG, KBE; *m* 1st, 1972, Sarah (marr. diss. 1976), *o d* of Sir Alastair Coats, Bt, *qv*; 2nd, 1976, Debra Louise (marr. diss. 1980), *d* of George Robert and Marjorie Elvera Pinney; one *d*. *Educ:* Eton; Christ Church, Oxford.

EDSBERG, John Christian; Director for Execution of the Budget, Directorate General for Budgets, European Commission, since 1986; *s* of Flight Lt Jørgen Palle Christian Edsberg and Olivia Alice Mary (*née* Gulland); *m* 1966, Rosalyn (*née* Padfield); two *s*. *Educ:* Westminster School; Brasenose College, Oxford (MA Hons Maths and Engrg Science). MICE. Civil engineer with Sir Alexander Gibb & Partners, 1961–66; Engineer and Contracts Manager, Soil Mechanics Ltd, 1966–67; Consultant and Senior Consultant, P. A. Management Consultants Ltd, 1967–74; Commission of the European Communities: Principal Administrator, 1974–81; Directorate Gen. for Transport, 1974–81; Directorate Gen. for Develt, 1981–82; Head of Div., Directorate Gen. for Financial Control, 1982–86. *Recreation:* architecture. *Address:* European Commission, 200 rue de la Loi, 1049 Brussels, Belgium. *T:* (2) 2955529; 46 Sydney Street, SW3 6PS. *T:* 0171–351 0685.

EDSON, Ven. Michael; Archdeacon of Leicester, since 1994; *b* 2 Sept, 1942; *s* of Joseph Pratt and Elsie (*née* Edson); name changed to Edson, 1989; *m* 1968, (Ann) Frances Tuffley; three *s* one *d*. *Educ:* Univ. of Birmingham (BSc Hons 1964); Univ. of Leeds (BA Hons 1971); College of Resurrection, Mirfield. Management Consultant, 1966–68. Ordained deacon, 1972, priest, 1973; Curate, Barnstaple, Devon, 1972–77; Team Vicar, Barnstaple, 1977–82; Chaplain, N Devon Dist Hosp., 1976–82; Vicar, Roxbourne, Harrow, 1982–89; Area Dean of Harrow, 1985–89; Warden of Lee Abbey Fellowship, Devon, 1989–94. *Publications:* The Renewal of the Mind, 1988; Loved into Life, 1993. *Recreations:* hill-walking, interesting people, writing. *Address:* 13 Stoneygate Avenue, Leicester LE2 3HE. *T:* Leicester (0116) 2704441.

EDWARD, Judge David Alexander Ogilvy, CMG 1981; QC (Scotland) 1974; FRSE; Judge of the Court of Justice of the European Communities, since 1992 (Judge of the Court of First Instance, 1989–92); *b* 14 Nov. 1934; *s* of J. O. C. Edward, Travel Agent, Perth; *m* 1962, Elizabeth Young McSherry; two *s* two *d*. *Educ:* Sedbergh Sch.; University Coll., Oxford; Edinburgh Univ. Sub-Lt RNVR (Nat. Service); HMS Hornet, 1956–57. Admitted Advocate, 1962; Clerk of Faculty of Advocates, 1967–70, Treasurer, 1970–77. Pres., Consultative Cttee of Bars and Law Societies, EC, 1978–80; Salvesen Prof. of European Instns, 1985–89, Hon. Prof., 1990, Univ. of Edinburgh. Trustee, Nat. Library of Scotland, 1966–; Mem. Law Adv. Cttee, British Council, 1974–88; Specialist Advr, H of L Select Cttee on EC, 1985, 1986 and 1987. Mem., Panel of Arbitrators, Internat. Centre for Settlement of Investment Disputes, 1981–89; Chm., Scottish Council for Internat. Arbitration, 1988–89 (Hon. Pres. 1989–). Director: Continental Assets Trust plc, 1985–89 (Chm.); Adam & Co. Group plc, 1983–89; Harris Tweed Association Ltd, 1984–89. Hon. Bencher, Gray's Inn, 1992. Member: Foundation Senate, Europa Universität Viadrina, Frankfurt/Oder, 1991–93; Bd of Trustees, Acad. of European Law, Trier, 1993–. FRSE 1990. Hon. LLD Edinburgh, 1993. Distinguished Cross, First Class, Order of St Raymond of Penafort, Spain, 1979. *Publications:* The Professional Secret, Confidentiality and Legal Professional Privilege in the EEC, 1976; (with R. C. Lane) European Community Law: an introduction, 1991, 2nd edn 1995; articles in legal jls, etc. *Address:* Court of Justice of the EC, L-2925 Luxembourg; 20 Rue Principale, Flaxweiler, L-6925 Luxembourg; 32 Heriot Row, Edinburgh EH3 6ES. *Clubs:* Athenæum; New (Edinburgh); Royal Scottish Automobile (Glasgow).

EDWARDES, family name of **Baron Kensington.**

EDWARDES, Sir Michael (Owen), Kt 1979; Chairman: Charter Consolidated PLC, since 1988; Tryhorn Investments Ltd, since 1987; ARC International Ltd, since 1991; *b* 11 Oct. 1930; *s* of Denys Owen Edwardes and Audrey Noel (*née* Copeland); *m* 1st, 1958, Mary Margaret (*née* Finlay) (marr. diss.); three *d*; 2nd, 1988, Sheila Ann (*née* Guy). *Educ:* St Andrew's Coll., Grahamstown, S Africa; Rhodes Univ., Grahamstown (BA; Hon. LLD). Chairman: BL Ltd (formerly British Leyland), 1977–82; Mercury Communications Ltd, 1982–83; ICL PLC, 1984; Dunlop Hldgs plc, 1984–85; Exec. Dir, Chloride Gp PLC, 1969–77 and 1986. Dep. Chm., R K Carvill (Internat. Hldgs) Ltd; Chm., Porth Gp, 1991; Director: Hill Samuel Gp, 1980–87; Minorco SA, 1984–; Standard Securities PLC, 1985–87; Delta Motor Corp. (Pty) Ltd, 1986–; Flying Pictures Ltd, 1987–; Kaye Organisation, 1987–88; Jet Press Hldgs BV, 1990–; Hi-Tec Sports, 1993–. Dir, Internat. Management Develt Inst., Washington, 1978–. CIMgt (Vice-Chm., BIM, 1977–80); Hon. FIMechE, 1981. President: Squash Rackets Assoc., 1991–94; Veterans Squash Club of GB; Trustee, Thrombosis Res. Inst., 1991–. *Publication:* Back From the Brink, 1983. *Recreations:* sailing, squash, water ski-ing, tennis. *Clubs:* Royal Automobile; Jesters; Rand and Country (Johannesburg).

EDWARDS, family name of **Barons Chelmer** and **Crickhowell.**

EDWARDS, (Alfred) Kenneth, CBE 1989 (MBE 1963); Deputy Director-General, Confederation of British Industry, 1982–88; Director: Polar Electronics PLC, since 1989; Reliance Bank Ltd, since 1992; *b* 24 March 1926; *s* of late Ernest Edwards and Florence Edwards (*née* Branch); *m* 1949, Jeannette Lilian, *d* of David Speeks, MBE; one *s* two *d*. *Educ:* Latymer Upper Sch.; Magdalene Coll., Cambridge; University Coll. London. Served RAF, 1944–47; RAF Coll., Cranwell, 1945, FO (Pilot). Entered HMOCS, Nigeria, 1952; Provincial Administration, Warri and Benin, 1952–54; Lagos Secretariat, 1954; Sen. Asst Sec., Nigerian Min. of Communications and Aviation, 1959; retired, 1962. Secretary, British Radio Equipment Manufrs' Assoc., 1962; Gp Marketing Manager, Thorn Elec. Industries Ltd, 1965; Internat. Dir, Brookhirst Igranic Ltd (Thorn Gp), 1967; Gp Marketing Dir, Cutler Hammer Europa, 1972; Dep. Chm., BEAMA Overseas Trade Cttee, 1973; Chief Exec., BEAMA, 1976–82. CBI: Member: Council, 1974, 1976–82; Finance and Gen. Purposes Cttee, 1977–82; Vice-Chm., Eastern Reg. Council, 1974; Chm., Working Party on Liability for Defective Products, 1978–82; Mem., President's Cttee, 1979–82. Chm., Facilities & Properties Management Plc, 1989–91. Member: Elec. Engrg EDC, 1976; Council, Elec. Res. Assoc. Ltd, 1976–82; Exec. Cttee, ORGALIME, 1976–82; Management Bd, Eur. Cttee for Develt of Vocational Training, 1988–; BSI Bd, 1978–82, 1984–89 (Chm., British Electrotechnical Cttee and Electrotechnical Divisional Council, 1981–82; Chm., Quality Policy Cttee, 1988–); BOTB, 1982–88; BTEC, 1983–89; BBC Consultative Gp on Indust. and Business Affairs, 1983–88; Bd and Exec. Cttee, Business in the Community, 1987–88; President: CENELEC, 1977–79; Liaison Cttee for Electrical and Electronic Industries, ORGALIME, 1979–82 (Chm., 1980–82); Mem. Exec. Cttee, 1982–89, and Chm. Finance Cttee, 1983–89, UNICE. Dep. Chm., Salvation Army Adv. Bd. Mem. Court, Cranfield Inst. of Technol., 1970–75. *Publications:* contrib. technical jls; lectures and broadcasts on industrial subjects. *Recreations:* music, books, walking. *Address:* 53 Bedford Road, Rushden, Northants NN10 0ND. *Clubs:* Athenæum, Royal Air Force.

EDWARDS, Andrew John Cumming, CB 1994; Director (Deputy Secretary), HM Treasury, 1990–95; writer and consultant, since 1995; *b* 3 Nov. 1940; *s* of John Edwards and Norah Hope Edwards (*née* Bevan); *m* 1969, Charlotte Anne Chilcot (marr. diss. 1987); one *s* two *d*; *m* 1994, Ursula Mary Richardson; one *s*. *Educ:* Fettes Coll., Edinburgh; St John's Coll., Oxford (MA); Harvard Univ. (AM, MPA). Asst master, Malvern Coll., 1962–63; HM Treasury: Asst Principal, 1963–67; Pvte Sec. to Jt Perm. Sec., 1966–67; Principal, 1967–75; Harkness Fellow, Harvard Univ., 1971–73; Asst Sec., 1975–83; RCDS, 1979; Asst Sec., DES, 1983–85; Under Sec., HM Treasury, 1985–89. Gov., British Inst. of Recorded Sound, 1974–79; Sec., Bd of Dirs, Royal Opera House, 1988– (Sec., Develt Bd, 1984–87). Conductor, Acad. of St Mary's, Wimbledon, 1980–. *Publications:* Nuclear Weapons, the balance of terror, the quest for peace, 1986; articles on European Community Budget. *Recreations:* music, writing, walking.

EDWARDS, Arthur Frank George; Vice-Chairman, Thames Water Authority, 1973–83; *b* 27 March 1920; *o s* of Arthur Edwards and Mabel (Elsie) Edwards; *m* 1946, Joyce May

Simmons; one *s* one *d*. *Educ:* West Ham Grammar Sch.; Garnett Coll., London; West Ham Coll. of Technology; City of London Polytechnic (MSc 1990); King's College London. CEng, FIChemE, MSE; Hon. FIWM. Various posts with Ever Ready (GB) Ltd, 1936–50; Prodn Man., J. Burns & Co. Ltd, 1950–53; various lectrg posts, 1954–65; Organiser for science and techn. subjects, London Boroughs of Barking and Redbridge, 1965–82. Member: West Ham Co. Borough Council, 1946–65; Newham Council, 1964–86 (Mayor, 1967–68); GLC, 1964–86 (Dep. Chm., 1970–71; Chm., Public Services Cttee, 1973–77); Chm. of Governors, NE London Polytechnic, 1972–87. Mem., Fabian Soc. *Recreations:* reading, Association football (watching West Ham United). *Address:* 18 Wanstead Park Avenue, E12 5EN. *T:* 0181–530 6436. *Club:* West Ham Supporters'.

EDWARDS, Brian, CBE 1988; Chief Executive, West Midlands Regional Health Authority, since 1993; Regional Director, NHS Executive, since 1994; *b* 19 Feb. 1942; *s* of John Albert Edwards and Ethel Edwards; *m* 1964, Jean (*née* Cannon); two *s* two *d*. *Educ:* Wirral Grammar Sch. Jun. Administrator, Clatterbridge Hosp., 1958–62; Dep. Hosp. Sec., Cleaver Hosp., 1962–64; National Trainee, Nuffield Centre, Leeds, 1964–66; Administrator, Gen. Infirmary, Leeds, 1966–67; Hosp. Sec., Keighley Victoria Hosp., 1967–68; Administrator, Mansfield HMC, 1969–70; Lectr, Univ. of Leeds, 1970–72; Dep. Gp Sec., Hull A HMC, 1972–74; Nuffield Travelling Fellow, USA, 1973; Dist Administrator, Leeds AHA(T), 1974–76; Area Administrator, Cheshire AHA, 1976–81; Regional Administrator, 1981–84, Regl Gen. Man., 1984–93, Trent RHA. Chm., Clinical Pathology Accreditation Ltd, 1992–. Vis. Lectr, Health Care Studies, 1973–, and Associate Fellow, Nuffield Inst., 1987–, Univ. of Leeds; Vis. Prof., Health Care Studies, Univ. of Keele, 1989; Queen Elizabeth Nuffield Fellow, Nuffield Provincial Hosps Trust, 1991. Adviser to WHO, 1982–; Chairman: NHS Manpower Planning Adv. Gp, 1983–86; Regional Gen. Managers Gp, 1986–87, 1991–94; NHS Patient Empowerment Gp, 1991–94; Patient's Charter Team, 1992; Clinical Pathology Accreditation Ltd, 1992–; Member: Steering Cttee on Future of Nursing, 1988; Standing Cttee on Medical Audit, RCP, 1989–94; Leader, Sec. of State's Task Force on Quality in NHS, 1993. Inst. of Health Service Administrators: Mem., 1964–; Pres., 1982–83; Mem. Editorial Cttee, Health Care in the UK: its organisation and management, 1982–83. Jt Editor, Health Services Manpower Review, 1970–91. CIMgt (CBIM 1988). *Publications:* Si Vis Pacem—preparations for change in the NHS, 1973; Profile for Change, 1973; Bridging in Health, Planning the Child Health Services, 1975; Industrial Relations in the NHS: managers and industrial relations, 1979; Manpower Planning in the NHS, 1984; Employment Policies for Health Care, 1985; Distinction Awards for Doctors, 1987; (contrib.) Doctors' Contracts, 1992; (contrib.) Public Sector Managers' Handbook, 1992; The NHS: a manager's tale, 1993; (contrib.) Management for Doctors, 1994; conf. papers presented in UK, Norway, Germany, USA, India, USSR, Czechoslavakia, Mexico and Guyana; contrib. prof. jls. *Recreations:* golf, stage management. *Address:* 3 Royal Croft Drive, Baslow, Derbyshire DE45 1SN. *T:* Baslow (01246) 583459, *Fax:* (01246) 582583. *Clubs:* Baslow Cricket (Vice-Pres.); Bakewell Golf (Captain, 1991).

EDWARDS, Charles Harold, FRCP; Dean of St Mary's Hospital Medical School, Paddington, 1973–79; *b* 1913; *m* 1959; one *s* two *d*. *Educ:* Blundell's Sch., Tiverton; Guy's Hosp. Med. Sch. MRCS 1937; LRCP 1937; MRCP 1946; FRCP 1961. Formerly: Resident Medical Appts, Guy's Hosp.; Resident Med. Officer, Nat. Hosp., Queen Square; Neurological Registrar, St Mary's Hosp., Paddington; Consultant Physician, Dept Nervous Diseases, St Mary's Hosp., 1954–78; Consultant Neurologist: Royal Nat. Throat, Nose and Ear Hosp., 1955–78; King Edward VII Hosp., Windsor, 1952–78; Canadian Red Cross Meml Hosp., Taplow, 1952–78; Maidenhead Hosp., 1952–78. Co-ordinator, Special Progs, Wellcome Trust, 1979–85. Mem., British Assoc. of Neurologists, 1952–; FRSocMed. *Publications:* Neurology of Ear, Nose and Throat, 1973; Neurological Section: Synopsis of Otolaryngology, 1967; Scott-Brown, Diseases of Ear, Nose and Throat, 1971; contrib. Qly Jl Medicine, Lancet, etc. *Recreations:* words, gardening. *Address:* Cardinal House, The Green, Hampton Court, Surrey KT8 9BW. *T:* 0181–979 6922. *Club:* Garrick.

EDWARDS, (Charles) Marcus; His Honour Judge Marcus Edwards; a Circuit Judge, since 1986; *b* 10 Aug. 1937; *s* of John Basil Edwards, *qv*; *m* 1st, 1963, Anne Louise Stockdale (*d* 1970), *d* of Sir Edmund Stockdale, 1st Bt; 2nd, 1975, Sandra Wates (*née* Mouroutsos); one *d* and three step *d*. *Educ:* Dragon Sch., Oxford; Rugby Sch.; Brasenose Coll., Oxford (scholar; BA Jurisprudence). Trooper, RAC, 1955; 2nd Lieut, Intelligence Corps, Cyprus, 1956–57. HM Diplomatic Service, 1960–65; Third Sec., 1960, Spain, 1961, FO, 1961–62, South Africa and High Commn Territories, 1962–63, Laos, 1964; Second Sec., FO, 1965, resigned. Called to the Bar, Middle Temple, 1962; practised, London, 1966–86; Mem., Midland and Oxford Circuit; a Recorder, 1985–86. Chm., Pavilion Opera, 1987–. *Recreations:* gardening, walking, talking, food and drink. *Address:* Melbourne House, South Parade, W4 1JU. *T:* 0181–995 9146. *Club:* Beefsteak.

EDWARDS, Sir Christopher (John Churchill), 5th Bt *cr* 1866; Director, Ohmeda, BOC Group, Louisville, Colorado, 1989–92; *b* 16 Aug. 1941; *s* of Sir (Henry) Charles (Serrell Priestley) Edwards, 4th Bt and of Lady (Daphne) Edwards (*née* Birt); *S* father, 1963; *m* 1972, Gladys Irene Vogelgesang; two *s*. *Educ:* Frensham Heights, Surrey; Loughborough, Leics. Gen. Manager, Kelsar Inc., American Home Products, San Diego, Calif, 1979–84; Vice-Pres., Valleylab Inc., Boulder, Colorado, 1981–89. *Heir:* *s* David Charles Priestley Edwards, *b* 22 Feb. 1974. *Address:* 11637 Country Club Drive, Westminster, CO 80234, USA. *T:* (303) 4693156. *Club:* Ranch Country (Westminster, Colorado).

EDWARDS, Prof. Christopher Richard Watkin, MD; FRCP, FRCPE; FRSE; Moncrieff Arnott Professor of Clinical Medicine, University of Edinburgh, since 1980; *b* 12 Feb. 1942; *s* of Thomas Archibald Watkin Edwards and Beatrice Elizabeth Ruby Watkin Edwards; *m* 1968, Sally Amanda Kidd; two *s* one *d*. *Educ:* Marlborough Coll.; Christ's Coll., Cambridge (BA, MB, BChir, MA, MD). St Bartholomew's Hospital: Lectr in Medicine, 1969–75; Sen. Lectr in Medicine and MRC Sen. Res. Fellow, 1975–80; Hon. Consultant Physician, 1975–80; University of Edinburgh: Dean, Faculty of Medicine, 1991–; Provost, Faculty Group of Medicine and Veterinary Medicine, 1992–. Mem., MRC, 1991–. Gov., Wellcome Trust, 1994–. *Publications:* (ed) Clinical Physiology, 5th edn, 1984; (ed) Essential Hypertension as an Endocrine Disease, 1985; Endocrinology, 1986; (ed) Recent Advances in Endocrinology Metabolism, vol. 3, 1989; (ed) Davidson's Principles and Practice of Medicine, 16th edn, 1991; 367 scientific papers and communications. *Recreations:* running, reading, golf, ski-ing. *Address:* 2 Ellersly Road, Edinburgh EH12 6HZ. *T:* 0131–337 1681. *Club:* Athenæum.

EDWARDS, Sir Clive; *see* Edwards, Sir J. C. L.

EDWARDS, David; Director, John Laing plc, since 1982; Chairman, Londondome Ltd, 1988–93; *b* 27 Oct. 1929; *s* of Col Cyril Edwards, DSO, MC, DL and Jessie Edwards; *m* 1966, Gay Clothier; two *s* one *d*. *Educ:* Felsted Sch.; Trinity Hall, Cambridge (MA, LLM). Called to the Bar, Middle Temple, 1952; Harmsworth Scholar, Middle Temple, 1955; admitted Solicitor, 1958. Partner, E. Edwards Son & Noice, 1959–75; Sec., Legal Aid, 1976–86, and Dep. Sec.-Gen., 1982–86, Law Soc. Dir, Laing Properties, 1988–90. Chm., Offshore Racing Council, 1970–78; Dep. Chm., Royal Yachting Assoc., 1976–81. *Recreation:* sailing. *Address:* Olivers, Colchester, Essex CO2 0HJ. *Clubs:* Royal Ocean Racing; Royal Yacht Squadron (Cowes).

See also Baron Chelmer, J. T. Edwards.

EDWARDS, (David) Elgan (Hugh); His Honour Judge Elgan Edwards; a Circuit Judge, since 1989; *b* 6 Dec. 1943; *s* of Howell and Dilys Edwards; *m* 1982, Carol Anne Smalls; two *s* two *d*. *Educ:* Rhyl Grammar Sch.; University Coll. of Wales, Aberystwyth (LLB Hons 1966; Pres., Students Union, 1967). Called to the Bar, Gray's Inn, 1967; a Recorder (Wales and Chester Circuit), 1983–89. Conservative Parly Candidate: Merioneth, 1970; Stockport South, Feb. 1974. Sheriff, City of Chester, 1977–78. *Recreation:* swimming. *Address:* The Crown Court, Chester Castle, Chester CH1 2AN. *T:* Chester (01244) 317606. *Club:* Chester City (Chester).

EDWARDS, Very Rev. David Lawrence, OBE 1995; Provost of Southwark Cathedral, 1983–94, Emeritus since 1994; *b* 20 Jan. 1929; *s* of late Lawrence Wright and Phyllis Boardman Edwards; *m* 1st, 1960, Hilary Mary (*née* Phillips) (marr. diss. 1984); one *s* three *d*; 2nd, 1984, Sybil, *d* of Michael and Kathleen Falcon. *Educ:* King's Sch., Canterbury; Magdalen Coll., Oxford. Lothian Prize, 1951; 1st cl. hons Mod. Hist., BA 1952; MA 1956. Fellow, All Souls Coll., Oxford, 1952–59. Deacon, 1954; Priest, 1955. On HQ staff of Student Christian Movement of Gt Brit. and Ireland, 1955–66; Editor and Man. Dir, SCM Press Ltd, 1959–66; Gen. Sec. of Movt, 1965–66. Curate of: St John's, Hampstead, 1955–58; St Martin-in-the-Fields, 1958–66; Fellow and Dean of King's College, Cambridge, 1966–70; Asst Lectr in Divinity, Univ. of Cambridge, 1967–70; Rector of St Margaret's, Westminster, 1970–78; Canon of Westminster, 1970–78; Sub-Dean, 1974–78; Speaker's Chaplain, 1972–78; Dean of Norwich, 1978–82. Exam. Chaplain: to Bp of Manchester, 1965–73; to Bp of Durham, 1968–72; to Bp of Bradford, 1972–78; to Bp of London, 1974–78; to Archbishop of Canterbury, 1975–78. Hulsean Lectr, 1967; Six Preacher, Canterbury Cathedral, 1969–76. Chairman: Churches' Council on Gambling, 1970–78; Christian Aid, 1971–78. Hon. Fellow, South Bank Univ. (formerly Poly.), 1990. DD Lambeth, 1990. *Publications:* A History of the King's School, Canterbury, 1957; Not Angels But Anglicans, 1958; This Church of England, 1962; God's Cross in Our World, 1963; Religion and Change, 1969; F. J. Shirley: An Extraordinary Headmaster, 1969; The Last Things Now, 1969; Leaders of the Church of England, 1971; What is Real in Christianity?, 1972; St Margaret's, Westminster, 1972; The British Churches Turn to the Future, 1973; Ian Ramsey, Bishop of Durham, 1973; Good News in Acts, 1974; What Anglicans Believe, 1974; Jesus for Modern Man, 1975; A Key to the Old Testament, 1976; Today's Story of Jesus, 1976; The State of the Nation, 1976; A Reason to Hope, 1978; Christian England: vol 1, Its story to the Reformation, 1981; vol. 2, From the Reformation to the Eighteenth Century, 1983; vol. 3, From the Eighteenth Century to the First World War, 1984; The Futures of Christianity, 1987; Essentials: a Liberal-Evangelical dialogue with John Stott, 1988; The Cathedrals of Britain, 1989; Tradition and Truth, 1989; Christians in a New Europe, 1990; The Real Jesus, 1992; What is Catholicism?, 1994; (ed) The Honest to God Debate, 1963; (ed) Collins Children's Bible, 1978; (ed) Christianity and Conservatism, 1990; (ed) Robert Runcie: a portrait by his friends, 1990. *Address:* 19 Cripstead Lane, Winchester SO23 9SF. *T:* Winchester (01962) 862597. *Club:* Athenæum.

See also M. G. Falcon.

EDWARDS, David Michael, CMG 1990; Law Officer (International Law), Hong Kong Government, since 1990; *b* 28 Feb. 1940; *s* of late Ernest William Edwards and of Thelma Irene Edwards; *m* 1966, Veronica Margaret Postgate; one *s* one *d*. *Educ:* The King's Sch., Canterbury; Univ. of Bristol. LLB Hons. Admitted to Roll of Solicitors, 1964. Solicitor of Supreme Court, 1964–67; Asst Legal Adviser, Foreign Office, 1967; Legal Adviser: British Military Govt, Berlin, 1972; British Embassy, Bonn, 1974; Legal Counsellor, 1977; Dir, Legal Div., IAEA, Vienna, 1977–79; Legal Counsellor, FCO, 1979; Agent of the UK Govt in cases before European Commn and Court of Human Rights, 1979–82; Counsellor (Legal Adviser), UK Mission to UN, New York, and HM Embassy, Washington, 1985–88; Legal Counsellor, 1988–89, Dep. Legal Advr, 1989–90, FCO; Sen. Counsel, Bechtel Ltd, 1990. *Recreations:* reading, travel, antique clocks. *Address:* 3rd Floor, Central Government Offices, Lower Albert Road, Hong Kong. *Club:* Royal Over-Seas League.

EDWARDS, Prof. David Olaf, DPhil; FRS 1988; University Professor of Physics, Ohio State University, since 1988; *b* 27 April 1932; *s* of Robert Edwards and Margaret Edwina (*née* Larsen); *m* 1967, Wendy Lou Townsend; one *s* one *d*. *Educ:* Holt High Sch., Liverpool; Brasenose Coll., Oxford (BA 1st cl. Hons, 1953; Sen. Hulme Schol., 1953–56; MA; DPhil 1957). FAPS. Pressed Steel Co. Res. Fellow, Clarendon Lab., Oxford Univ., 1957–58; Ohio State University: Vis. Asst Prof., 1958–60; Asst Prof., 1960–62; Associate Prof., 1962–65; Prof., 1965–88. Visiting Professor: Imperial Coll., London, 1964; Sussex Univ., 1964, 1968; Technion, Israel, 1971–72; Ecole Normale Supérieure, Paris, 1978, 1982, 1986; Vis. Scientist, Brookhaven Nat. Lab., 1975. Consultant: Brookhaven Nat. Lab., 1975–77; Los Alamos Scientific Lab., 1979–81. Sir Francis Simon Prize, British Inst. of Phys, 1983; Dist. Schol. Award, Ohio State Univ., 1984; Special Creativity Awards, US Nat. Sci. Foundn, 1981, 1986; Oliver E. Buckley Condensed Matter Physics Prize, APS, 1990. Mem. Editl Bd, Jl of Low Temperature Physics, 1990–. *Publications:* (ed jtly) Proceedings of the Ninth International Conference on Low Temperature Physics (LT9), 1966; numerous articles on low temp. physics in scientific jls. *Recreations:* beagling (Master, Rocky Fork Beagles, 1975–90), snorkeling (Grand Cayman), crossword puzzles, reading detective stories, watching old British TV programs. *Address:* 2345 Dorset Road, Columbus, OH 43221, USA. *T:* (614) 4864553; Department of Physics, Ohio State University, 174 W 18th Avenue, Columbus, OH 43210–1106, USA. *T:* (614) 2927275.

EDWARDS, Douglas John; Consultant, Argyll Foods Ltd (formerly Louis C. Edwards & Sons (Manchester) Ltd), 1979–84 (Joint Chairman and Managing Director, 1966–79); Chairman and Managing Director, Imexport Meats Ltd, since 1979; *b* 18 March 1916; *s* of Louis Edwards and Catherine Edwards; *m* 1st, 1941, Emmeline H. Haslam (*d* 1964); two *s*; 2nd, 1973, Valerie Barlow-Hitchen. *Educ:* De La Salle Coll., Salford. Served in Grenadier Guards, 1940–45. Member of Lloyd's, 1965–: Joined Manchester Conservative Party, 1947; Mem. Manchester City Council, 1951–74; Alderman, 1967–74; Lord Mayor of City of Manchester, 1971–72; Greater Manchester Metropolitan CC, 1974–78; High Sheriff, 1975–76. President: Manchester Cttee, Grenadier Guards Assoc., 1968–81 (Life Mem.); Greater Manchester Youth Assoc., 1973–80; Chairman: Manchester Br., Variety Club of GB, 1969–70; Northern Cttee, Hotel and Catering Benev. Assoc., 1976–81. Governor: De La Salle Teacher Training Coll., Greater Manchester, 1972–81; De La Salle Coll., Salford, 1972–81. DL Greater Manchester, 1979–81. Freeman and Liveryman, Makers of Playing Cards Co., 1974. Polonia Restituta, First Cl., 1972. KCHS (Papal knighthood) 1993 (KHS 1986). *Recreations:* golf, sailing, shooting. *Address:* Apt 10A, The Marbella, 250 South Ocean Boulevard, Boca Raton, FL 33432, USA. *T:* (407) 3928203. *Clubs:* Carlton; Royal Thames Yacht; Lloyd's Yacht; Lancs County Cricket (Life Mem.); Cheshire Polo; Altrincham Rifle; Antibes Yacht; St Francis Yacht, (Hon. Mem.) Royal Palm Yacht and Country (USA).

EDWARDS, Prof. Edward George, PhD, BSc, FRSC; Vice-Chancellor and Principal, University of Bradford, 1966–78, Hon. Professor, since 1978; Principal of Bradford

Institute of Technology, 1957–66; *b* 18 Feb. 1914; *m* 1940, Kathleen Hewitt; two *s* two *d.* *Educ:* Cardiff High Sch.; University of South Wales; Cardiff Coll. of Technology. Lecturer in Chemistry, University of Nottingham, 1938–40; Research Chemist (ICI Ltd), 1940–45; Head of Dept of Chemistry and Applied Chemistry, Royal Technical Coll., Salford, 1945–54; Principal, Coll. of Technology, Liverpool, 1954–57. Hon. DTech Bradford, 1980; Fellow, University Coll., Cardiff, 1981. *Publications:* Higher Education for Everyone, 1982; various research papers in chemical jls; articles and papers on higher educn, technological innovation, university planning. *Recreations:* philosophy, music, walking, travel. *Address:* Corner Cottage, Westwood Drive, Ilkley, West Yorks LS29 9QX. *T:* Ilkley (01943) 607112.

EDWARDS, Elgan; *see* Edwards, D. E. H.

EDWARDS, Elizabeth Alice, OBE 1995; Chairman, Dumfries and Galloway Community NHS Trust, since 1995; *b* 26 May 1937. *Educ:* Coleraine High Sch.; Univ. of Edinburgh (BSc Soc. Sci.); SRN, SCM. Staff Nurse, Midwife, Ward Sister and nurse management posts, 1958–72; Principal Nursing Officer, Edinburgh Northern Hosps Gp, 1972–74; Dist Nursing Officer, N Lothian, Lothian Health Bd, 1974–80; Chief Area Nursing Officer: Dumfries and Galloway Health Bd, 1980–88; Tayside Health Bd, 1988–94. Mem., Nat. Bd for Nursing, Midwifery and Health Visiting, Scotland, 1983–93 (Dep. Chm., 1985–93). Hon. Sen. Lectr, Univ. of Dundee, 1988–94. *Publications:* papers on nursing. *Address:* 19 Suffolkhill Avenue, Dumfries DG2 7PQ.

EDWARDS, Very Rev. Erwyd; *see* Edwards, Very Rev. T. E. P.

EDWARDS, Frederick Edward, LVO 1992; RD 1968 and Clasp, 1977; Director of Social Work, Strathclyde Region, 1976–93; *b* 9 April 1931; *s* of Reginal Thomas Edwards and Jessie Howard Simpson; *m* 1st, 1957, Edith Jocelyn Price (marr. diss. 1990); two *s* one *d*; 2nd, 1990, Mary Olds (*née* Ellis). *Educ:* St Edward's Coll., Liverpool; Univ. of Glasgow (Dip. Applied Soc. Studies 1965). BA Open Univ., 1973. FIMgt. Merchant Navy Deck Officer, 1948–58; Perm. Commn, RNR, 1953, Lt-Comdr 1963; sailed Barque Mayflower to USA, 1957. Morgan Refractories, 1958–60; Probation Service, Liverpool, 1960–69; Dir of Social Work: Moray and Nairn, 1969–74; Grampian, 1974–76. Vis. Prof., Dept of Social Policy (formerly Social Admin.) and Social Work, Univ. of Glasgow, 1988–93. Member: Scottish Marriage Guidance Council, 1970– (Chm., 1980–83); Scottish Council on Crime, 1972–75; Adv. Council on Social Work, 1976–81. Chm., Carnegie Third Age Prog. Cttee, 1993–; Pres., Volunteer Develt Scotland, 1994–; Trustee, New Lanark Trust, 1993–. MUniv Open, 1988; DUniv Paisley, 1993. *Recreations:* sailing, natural history, reading. *Address:* Gardenfield, Ninemileburn, Midlothian EH26 9LT.

EDWARDS, Gareth Owen; QC 1985; **His Honour Judge Gareth Edwards;** a Circuit Judge, since 1991; *b* 26 Feb. 1940; *s* of Arthur Wyn Edwards and Mair Eluned Edwards; *m* 1967, Katharine Pek Har Goh; two *s* one *d.* *Educ:* Herbert Strutt Grammar Sch., Belper; Trinity Coll., Oxford (BA,BCL). Called to the Bar, Inner Temple, 1963; Army Legal Service, 1963–65; Commonwealth Office, 1965–67. Practised, Wales and Chester Circuit, 1967–; Recorder, Crown Court, 1978–91. *Recreations:* climbing, chess. *Address:* 58 Lache Lane, Chester CH4 7LS. *T:* Chester (01244) 677795. *Club:* Army and Navy.

EDWARDS, Gareth Owen, MBE 1975; retired 1978 as Welsh Rugby footballer; chairman of leisure company in S Wales; *b* 12 July 1947; *s* of Granville and Anne Edwards; *m* 1972, Maureen Edwards; two *s.* *Educ:* Pontardawe Tech. Sch.; Millfield Sch.; Cardiff College of Educn. Rugby Football: 1st cap for Wales, 1967 (*v* France); Captain of Wales on 13 occasions; youngest Captain of Wales (at 20 years), 1968; British Lions Tours: 1968, 1971, 1974; Barbarians, 1967–78. Member of Cardiff RFC, 1966–; a record 53 consecutive caps, to 1978. *Publications:* Gareth: an autobiography, 1978; (jtly) Rugby Skills, 1979; Rugby Skills for Forwards, 1980; Gareth Edwards on Fishing, 1984; Rugby, 1986; Gareth Edwards' 100 Great Rugby Players, 1987. *Recreations:* fishing, golf. *Address:* 211 West Road, Nottage, Porthcawl, Mid-Glamorgan CF36 3RT. *T:* Porthcawl (01656) 785669.

EDWARDS, Geoffrey Francis, CBE 1975 (OBE 1968; MBE 1956); TD; HM Diplomatic Service, retired; *b* 28 Sept. 1917; *s* of late Oliver and Frances Margaret Edwards, Langley, Bucks; *m* 1st, 1949, Joyce Black (*d* 1953); one *d*; 2nd, 1961, Johanna Elisabeth Franziska Taeger. *Educ:* Brighton Coll. Joined Pixley & Abell, Bullion Brokers, 1936. Commissioned RA (TA), June 1939; served with 117 Fd Regt and 59 (Newfoundland) Heavy Regt RA in NW Europe, 1939–45; joined Control Commn for Germany, 1945; joined British Military Govt, Berlin, 1949; Economic Adviser, 1956; Consul-General, Berlin, 1966–75. Ernst Reuter Silver Plaque, Berlin, 1975. *Recreations:* gardening, fishing, golf. *Address:* Am Kurgarten 105, 53489 Sinzig-Bad Bodendorf, Germany. *T:* (2642) 44821.

EDWARDS, Sir George (Robert), OM 1971; Kt 1957; CBE 1952 (MBE 1945); FRS 1968; FEng; DL; now retired; Chairman, British Aircraft Corporation Ltd, 1963–75; Pro-Chancellor, University of Surrey, 1964–79, now Pro-Chancellor Emeritus; *b* 9 July 1908; *m* 1935, Marjorie Annie (*née* Thurgood) (*d* 1994); one *d.* *Educ:* S West Essex Tech. Coll.; London Univ. (BScEng). Gen. engineering, 1928–35; joined Design Staff, Vickers-Aviation Ltd, Weybridge, 1935; Experimental Manager, Vickers-Armstrongs Ltd, Weybridge Works, 1940. Chief Designer, Weybridge Works, 1945; Dir, Vickers Ltd, 1955–67. Pres., Royal Aeronautical Soc., 1957–58; Vice-Pres., Royal Society of Arts, 1958–61. Mem., Royal Instn, 1971–. Pres., Surrey CCC, 1979 (Vice-Pres., 1974). DL Surrey, 1981. FEng; Hon. Fellow: RAeS 1960; IMechE; Manchester Coll. of Science and Technology; Hon. FAIAA. Hon. DSc: Southampton, 1962; Salford, 1967; Cranfield Inst. of Technology, 1970; City Univ., 1975; Stirling, 1979; Surrey, 1979; Hon. DSc(Eng) London, 1970; Hon. LLD Bristol, 1973. George Taylor Gold Medal, 1948; British Gold Medal for Aeronautics, 1952; Daniel Guggenheim Medal, 1959; Air League Founders Medal, 1969; Albert Gold Medal (RSA), 1972; Royal Medal, Royal Soc., 1974. *Publications:* various papers and lectures in Jl RAeS, Amer. Inst. of Aeronautical Sciences and Amer. Soc. of Automotive Engrs. *Recreation:* painting. *Address:* Albury Heights, White Lane, Guildford, Surrey GU4 8PR. *T:* Guildford (01483) 504488. *Clubs:* Athenæum; Royal Air Force Yacht.

EDWARDS, Griffith; *see* Edwards, James G.

EDWARDS, Huw William Edmund; Senior Lecturer in Social Policy, University of Brighton (formerly Brighton Polytechnic), 1988–91, and since 1992; *b* 12 April 1953; *s* of Rev. Dr Ifor M. Edwards and Esme Edwards. *Educ:* Eastfields High Sch., Mitcham; Manchester Polytechnic; Univ. of York (BA, MA, MPhil). Lecturer in Social Policy: Coventry (Lanchester) Poly., 1980–81; Univ. of Sheffield, 1983–84; Poly. of the South Bank, 1984–85; Manchester Poly., 1985–88. Res. Associate, Low Pay Unit, 1985–; Tutor with Open Univ., 1987–. MP (Lab) Monmouth, May 1991–1992; contested (Lab) Monmouth, 1992. Mem., Select Cttee on Welsh Affairs, 1991–92. Member: Parlt for Wales Campaign, 1992–; Labour campaign for Electoral Reform, 1991–; Fabian Soc., 1992–. Pres., Chepstow Mencap, 1992–; Mem. Exec., Shelter Cymru, 1988–91. Mem., Boro' Welsh Congregational Chapel, London. *Publications:* Low Pay in South Wales, 1989; Wales in the 1990s: land of low pay, 1994; articles in professional jls. *Recreations:* sport, football, Rugby, tennis, cricket, Welsh choral music (Member, Gwalia Male Voice Choir). *Address:* 8 College Street, Kemptown, Brighton, E Sussex BN2 1JG. *T:* Brighton (01273) 625125. *Club:* London Welsh Association.

EDWARDS, Iorwerth Eiddon Stephen, CMG 1973; CBE 1968; MA, LittD; FSA; FBA 1962; Keeper of Egyptian Antiquities, British Museum, 1955–74; *b* 21 July 1909; *s* of late Edward Edwards, Orientalist, and Ellen Jane (*née* Higgs); *m* 1938, Elizabeth, *y d* of late Charles Edwards Lisle; one *d* (one *s* decd). *Educ:* Merchant Taylors'; Gonville and Caius Coll., Cambridge (Major Scholar; Merchant Taylors' Sch. Exhibitioner and John Stewart of Rannoch Univ. Scholar, Cambridge, 1928; 1st Cl. Oriental Languages Tripos (Arabic and Hebrew), Parts I and II, 1930–31; Mason Prize, Tyrwhitt Scholarship and Wright Studentship, 1932). FSA 1942. Entered Dept of Egyptian and Assyrian Antiquities, British Museum, 1934; seconded to Foreign Office; attached to British Embassies, Cairo and Baghdad, and to Secretariat, Jerusalem, 1942–45. T. E. Peet Prize, Liverpool Univ., 1947. Visiting Prof., Brown Univ., Providence, RI, USA, 1953–54. Glanville Meml Lectr, Cambridge Univ., 1980; Foreign Guest Lectr, Coll. de France, 1982. Pioneered and chose objects for Tutankhamun Exhibition, London, 1972; Consultant to Australian Govt, Gold of the Pharaohs Exhibn, 1988. Member, Unesco-Egyptian Min. of Culture Cttees for saving monuments of Philae, 1973–80, for planning Nat. Mus., Cairo, 1985, for re-organising Egyptian Mus. Cairo, 1985, for protection of monuments of Giza, 1990. Vice-Pres. Egypt Exploration Soc., 1962–88; Member: German Archæological Inst.; Austrian Archæol Inst.; Associate Mem., Inst. of Egypt; Mem., Cttee of Visitors of Metropolitan Museum of Art, NY; Corres. Mem., Fondation Egyptologique Reine Elisabeth; Correspondant étranger de L'Institut, Académie des Inscriptions et Belles-Lettres. *Publications:* Hieroglyphic Texts in the British Museum, Vol. VIII, 1939; The Pyramids of Egypt, 1947, 5th edn 1993; Hieratic Papyri in the British Museum, 4th Series (Oracular Amuletic Decrees of the Late New Kingdom), 1960; The Early Dynastic Period in Egypt, 1964; Joint Editor of The Cambridge Ancient History (3rd edn), vols I-III, 1970–91; Treasures of Tutankhamun (Catalogue of London exhibn), 1972; Treasures of Tutankhamun (Catalogue of US exhibn), 1976; Tutankhamun's Jewelry, 1976; Tutankhamun: his tomb and its treasures, 1976; articles in Journal of Egyptian Archæology and other scientific periodicals. *Recreations:* watching cricket, gardening. *Address:* Dragon House, The Bullring, Deddington, Oxon OX15 0TT. *T:* Deddington (01869) 338481. *Club:* Athenæum.

EDWARDS, Jack Trevor, CBE 1985; CEng, FICE; FCIT; Chairman, Halcrow Fox and Associates, 1986–92; Consultant, Freeman Fox & Partners, since 1986 (Senior Partner, 1979–86, retired); *b* 23 June 1920; *s* of late Col Cyril Ernest Edwards, DSO, MC, JP, and Jessie Boyd; *m* 1959, Josephine, (Sally), *d* of late S. W. Williams; one *d.* *Educ:* Felsted Sch.; City and Guilds Coll., Imperial Coll. London (BScEng, FCGI). RAF Armament and Airfield Construction Branches, Sqdn Ldr, 1941–46. Civil Engr on hydro-electric and thermal power stations, James Williamson and Partners, 1946–50; Freeman Fox & Partners: Engineer, 1951–64; Partner, 1965–79; special field: civil engrg and building works associated with thermal power stations and railways at home and overseas; major projects: Hong Kong Mass Transit Railway, opened 1980; Baghdad and Taipei Metros; Engineer to Dean and Chapter of St Paul's Cathedral, 1969–86. Mem. Council, British Consultants Bureau, 1979–85 (Chm., 1982–83). Liveryman, Worshipful Co. of Painter-Stainers, 1969–. *Publications:* Civil Engineering for Underground Rail Transport, 1990; contrib. Proc. Instn of Civil Engrs. *Recreation:* sailing. *Address:* Keepers, 77 Brentwood Road, Ingrave, Brentwood, Essex CM13 3NU. *T:* Brentwood (01277) 810285. *Clubs:* Royal Cruising, Royal Burnham Yacht.

See also Baron Chelmer, D. Edwards.

EDWARDS, Prof. (James) Griffith, CBE 1989; DM, DSc, FRCP, FRCPsych; Professor of Addiction Behaviour, Institute of Psychiatry, University of London, 1979–94, Professor Emeritus since 1994; Hon. Director, Addiction Research Unit, since 1970 (Principal Investigator, 1967–70); Hon. Consultant, Bethlem and Maudsley Hospitals, 1967–94; *b* 3 Oct. 1928; *yr s* of late Dr J. T. Edwards and late Constance Amy (*née* McFadyean); *m* 1st, 1969, Evelyn Morrison (marr. diss. 1981); one *s* one *d* (and one *d* decd); 2nd, 1981, Frances Susan Stables. *Educ:* Andover Grammar Sch.; Balliol Coll., Oxford (BA Physiology 1952; MA; Theodore Williams Schol. in Anatomy); St Bartholomew's Hosp. (Kirkes Schol. and Gold Medal); DM Oxford, 1966; DPM London, 1962; DSc London, 1990; FRCP 1976; FRCPsych 1976. Served RA, 1948–49 (2nd Lieut). Jun. hosp. appts, King George, Ilford, St Bartholomew's, Hammersmith and Maudsley Hosps, 1956–62; Inst. of Psychiatry: res. worker, 1962; Lectr, 1966; Sen. Lectr, 1967; Reader, 1973. Chm., RC Psych. Special Cttee on Drug Dependence, 1983–87 (on Alcohol and Alcoholism, 1975–78); Medical Dir, Alcohol Educn Centre, 1980–83; Member: Home Office Working Party on Drunkenness Offenders, 1967–70; WHO Expert Adv. Cttee on Drug Dependence, 1969–; DoE Cttee on Drinking and Driving, 1974–75; Home Office Adv. Council on Misuse of Drugs, 1972–; DHSS Adv. Cttee on Alcoholism, 1975–78; ESRC (formerly SSRC), 1981–89; S African Adv. Cttee on Drug Abuse, 1995. Consultant Advisor: on Alcoholism, DHSS, subseq. DoH, 1986–94; Huntercombe Manor, 1995–; ODA Consultant in Bolivia, 1987. Chm., Nat. Addiction Centre, 1991–94; Vice-Patron, Phoenix House, 1990–. Roche Vis. Prof., Aust. and NZ, 1982; Hon. Prof., Univ. of Chile, 1992; Vis. Prof., Amer. Coll. of Neuropsychopharmacology, 1993. Steven's Lectr and Gold Medallist, RSM, 1971; Lectures: Dent, King's Coll., 1980; Pollak, 1988, Okey, 1995, Inst. of Psychiatry. Jellinek Meml Award, 1980; Evian Award, 1986; Prize, Assoc. for Med. Educn and Res. on Substance Abuse, USA, 1990. Editor, Addiction (formerly British Jl of Addiction), 1978–; Editor-in-Chief, Internat. Research Monographs on the Addictions, 1995–. *Publications:* Unreason in an Age of Reason, 1971; (jtly) Alcohol Control Policies, 1975; (ed jtly) Drugs in Socio-Cultural Perspective, 1980; (jtly) Opium and the People, 1981; Treatment of Drinking Problems, 1982 (trans. into 5 langs), 2nd edn 1987; (ed) Drug Scenes, 1987; (ed jtly) Nature of Dependence, 1990; (ed) Personal Influences and Scientific Movements, 1991; (ed) Nature of Alcohol and Drug Problems, 1992; (ed jtly) Drugs, Alcohol and Tobacco: strengthening the science and policy connections, 1993; (ed jtly) Addiction: processes of change, 1994; (ed jtly) Alcohol and Alcohol Problems, 1994; (jtly) Alcohol Policy and the Public Good, 1994; (jtly) Alcohol and Public Policy, Evidence and Issues, 1995; (jtly) Psychotherapy, Psychological Treatments and the Addictions, 1995; articles in jls on scientific and policy aspects of alcohol and drug dependence. *Recreations:* frequenting junk shops, putting drink down, smoking the devils out. *Address:* 32 Crooms Hill, SE10 8ER. *T:* 0181–858 5631. *Club:* Athenæum.

See also J. M. McF. Edwards.

EDWARDS, James Valentine, CVO 1978; MA; *b* 4 Feb. 1925; *s* of late Captain Alfred Harold Edwards, OBE, and Mrs Eleanor Edwards; *m* 1965, Barbara, Princess Cantacuzene, Countess Speransky, *d* of late Sir John Hanbury-Williams, CVO, and Lady Hanbury-Williams; two *d*, and one step *s* one step *d.* *Educ:* St Edmund's, Hindhead; Radley; Magdalen Coll., Oxford (MA). Served RN, 1943–47. Oxford, 1943 and 1947–49. *Address:* Almonry House, Muchelney, Langport, Somerset TA10 0DG. *T:* Langport (01458) 252174. *Clubs:* MCC, Free Foresters; Vincent's (Oxford).

EDWARDS, Jeremy John Cary; Group Managing Director, Henderson Administration Group, since 1989; *b* 2 Jan. 1937; *s* of late William Philip Neville Edwards, CBE, and

Hon. Mrs Sheila Edwards; *m* 1st, 1963, Jenifer Graham (*née* Mould) (decd); one *s* one *d*; 2nd, 1974, April Philippa Harding (marr. diss. 1993); one *s*; 3rd, 1994, Mrs Amanda Barber. *Educ:* Ridley Coll, Ontario; Vinehall Sch., Sussex; Haileybury and Imperial Service Coll. Unilever, 1955–57; Hobson Bates & Co., 1957–59; Overseas Marketing and Advertising, 1959–61; Courtaulds, 1961–63; Vine Products, 1963–66; Loewe SA, 1966–68; Jessel Securities, 1968–70; Man. Dir, Vavasseur Unit Trust Management, 1970–74; Henderson Admin Gp, 1974–: Jt Man. Dir, 1983–89. Hon. Treas., WWF, 1984–; Mem. Council, 1987–, Chm., Appeals Cttee, 1989– (Mem., 1983–), C of E Children's Soc. *Recreations:* Italy, music. *Address:* (office) 3 Finsbury Avenue, EC2M 2PA. *Clubs:* Boodle's, City of London; Brook (NY).

EDWARDS, John Basil, CBE 1972; JP; Chairman, Magistrates Association, 1976–79; *b* 15 Jan. 1909; *s* of Charles and Susan Edwards; *m* 1935, Molly Patricia Philips (*d* 1979); one *s* two *d*. *Educ:* King's Sch., Worcester; Wadham Coll., Oxford (BA Hons Jurisprudence, MA). Commnd Royal Warwickshire Regt (RE) TA, 1938. Admitted Solicitor, 1933. Worcester CC, 1936; Mayor of Worcester, 1947–49; Alderman, City of Worcester, 1948. Magistrates Association: Mem. Council, 1960; Chm., Worcestershire Br., 1960–66; Hon. Treasurer, 1968–70; Dep. Chm., 1970–76. Mem., James Cttee on Distribution of Criminal Business, 1973–75. Chm., Worcester Three Choirs Festival, 1947–72. Freeman, City of London. Liveryman: Haberdashers Company; Distillers Company. JP Worcs 1940; Chm., Worcester City Justices, 1951–79. *Recreation:* gardening. *Address:* 21 Britannia Square, Worcester WR1 3DH. *T:* Worcester (01905) 29933.

See also C. M. Edwards.

EDWARDS, John Charles, JP; Lord Mayor of Cardiff, 1980–81; *b* 3 April 1925; *s* of John Robert Edwards and Elsie Florence Edwards; *m* 1946, Cynthia Lorraine Bushell; one *s* two *d*. *Educ:* Lansdowne Road Sch., Cardiff; Ruskin Coll., Oxford. Served War of 1939–45, RM (1939–45 Star, France and Germany Star, War Medal 1939–45); TA, 1948–62, RASC (TEM). Postal Exec. Officer, GPO. Member: Cardiff CC, 1962–83 (Dep. Lord Mayor, 1978–79); S Glam CC, 1974–78; Associate Mem., Inst. of Transport Admin, 1982. Freeman of City of London, 1981. JP S Glam, 1979. Mem., St John's Council for S Glam; OStJ 1980. *Recreations:* athletics, football. *Address:* 61 Cosmeston Street, Cathays, Cardiff CF2 4LQ. *T:* Cardiff (01222) 221506. *Clubs:* Civil Service; United Services Mess; Cardiff Athletic.

EDWARDS, Sir (John) Clive (Leighton), 2nd Bt *cr* 1921; *b* 11 Oct. 1916; *s* of 1st Bt and Kathleen Ermyntrude (*d* 1975) *d* of late John Corfield, JP; *S* father, 1922. *Educ:* Winchester Coll. Volunteered and served in the Army, 1940–46. *Recreations:* motoring, gardening. *Heir:* none. *Address:* Milntown, Lezayre, Ramsey, Isle of Man. *Clubs:* Royal Automobile (Hon. Mem.); Midland Automobile (Hon. Life Mem.), Bugatti Owners.

EDWARDS, John Coates, CMG 1989; HM Diplomatic Service, retired; High Commissioner, Botswana, 1991–94; *b* 25 Nov. 1934; *s* of late Herbert John and Doris May Edwards; *m* 1959, Mary Harris; one *s* one *d*. *Educ:* Skinners' Co. Sch., Tunbridge Wells, Kent; Brasenose Coll., Oxford (MA). Military Service, 1953–55: Lieut, RA. Asst Principal: Min. of Supply, 1958; Colonial Office, 1960; Private Sec. to Parly Under Sec. of State for the Colonies, 1961; Principal: Nature Conservancy, 1962; Min. of Overseas Develt, 1965; First Sec. (Develt), and UK Perm. Rep. to ECAFE, Bangkok, Thailand, 1968; Asst Sec., Min. of Overseas Develt, 1971; Head of E Africa Develt Div., Nairobi, Kenya, 1972; Asst Sec., Min. of Overseas Develt, 1976; Head of British Develt Div. in the Caribbean, Barbados, and UK Dir, Caribbean Develt Bank, 1978; Hd, West Indian and Atlantic Dept, FCO, 1981–84; Dep. High Comr, Kenya, 1984–88; High Comr, Lesotho, 1988–91. *Address:* Fairways, Back Lane, Ightham, Sevenoaks, Kent TN15 9AU. *Clubs:* Commonwealth Trust, Royal Over-Seas League, Muthaiga Country (Life Mem.) (Nairobi).

EDWARDS, Prof. John Hilton, FRCP; FRS 1979; Professor of Genetics, and Fellow of Keble College, University of Oxford, 1979–95; *b* 26 March 1928; *s* of late Harold Clifford Edwards, CBE, FRCS, FRCOG; *m* 1953, Felicity Clare, *d* of Dr C. H. C. Toussaint; two *s* two *d*. *Educ:* Univ. of Cambridge (MB, BChir). FRCP 1972. MO, Falkland Islands Dependency Survey, 1952–53; Mem., MRC Unit on Population Genetics, Oxford, 1958–60; Geneticist, Children's Hosp. of Philadelphia, 1960–61; Lectr, Sen. Lectr, and Reader, Birmingham Univ., 1961–67; Hon. Consultant Paediatrician, Birmingham Regional Bd, 1967; Vis. Prof. of Pediatrics, Cornell Univ., and Sen. Investigator, New York Blood Center, 1967–68; Consultant, Human Genetics, Univ. of Iceland, 1967–; Prof. of Human Genetics, Birmingham Univ., 1969–79. *Publications:* Human Genetics, 1978; scientific papers. *Recreations:* gliding, skiing. *Address:* 78 Old Road, Headington, Oxford OX3 7LP. *Club:* Athenæum.

EDWARDS, John Lionel; retired civil servant; *b* 29 Aug. 1915; *s* of Rev. Arthur Edwards and Constance Edwards; *m* 1948, Cecily Miller (*d* 1993); one *s* two *d*. *Educ:* Marlborough; Corpus Christi Coll., Oxford. Entered Scottish Office, 1938. Served War, (Army), 1940–45. Min. of Labour, 1945: Principal Private Sec. to Minister of Labour, 1956; Asst Sec., 1956; Sec., NEDC, 1968–71; Under-Sec., Dept of Employment, 1971–75; Certification Officer for Trade Unions and Employers' Assocs, 1976–81. *Address:* Little Bedwyn, The Ridgway, Pyrford, Surrey GU22 8PN. *T:* Byfleet (01932) 343459. *Club:* United Oxford & Cambridge University.

EDWARDS, (John) Michael (McFadyean), CBE 1986; QC 1981; barrister; *b* 16 Oct. 1925; *s* of Dr James Thomas Edwards and Constance Amy Edwards, *yr d* of Sir John McFadyean; *m* 1st, 1952, Morna Joyce Piper (marr. diss.); one *s* one *d*; 2nd, 1964, Rosemary Ann Moore; two *s*. *Educ:* Andover Grammar Sch. (schol.); University Coll., Oxford (BCL, MA). Called to the Bar, Middle Temple, 1949, Bencher, 1993; Asst Parly Counsel, HM Treasury, 1955–60; Dep. Legal Advr and Dir of certain subsid. cos, Courtaulds Ltd, 1960–67; British Steel Corporation: Dir, Legal Services, 1967–71; Man. Dir, BSC (Internat.) Ltd, 1967–81; Chm. and Man. Dir, BSC (Overseas Services) Ltd, 1973–81; Provost, City of London Polytechnic, 1981–88. Dir, 1982–90, and Man. Dir, 1988–89, Bell Group Internat. Ltd; Director: Bell Resources Ltd (Australia), 1983–88; Bell Group Ltd (Australia); West Australian Newspapers Ltd, 1990–92. Member: Overseas Projects Bd, 1973–81; E European Trade Council, 1973–81; Educn Assets Bd, 1988–. Deputy Chairman: Appeal Cttee, Assoc. of Certified Accountants, 1990– (Chm., 1987–90); Independent Appeals Authy for Sch. Exams, 1991–. Member: Bar Council, 1971–79, 1980–83; Senate of Inns of Court and Bar, 1974–79, 1980–83; Gen. Cttee, Bar Assoc. for Commerce, Finance and Industry, 1967–92 (Vice-Pres., 1980–82, 1992–; Chm., 1972–74); Acad. Council, Inst. of Internat. Business Law and Practice, ICC, Paris, 1982–88. Chairman: Eastman Dental Hosp., 1983– (Gov., 1981–83); Management Cttee, Eastman Dental Inst. (formerly Inst. of Dental Surgery), Univ. of London, 1984–; Mem., Governing Body, BPMF, 1988–. Mem., Council, Regional Opera Trust, (Kent Opera), 1981–88 (Chm., 1983–86). CIMgt (Mem. Council, BIM, 1978–81); FCIArb, 1984. Freeman, City of London; Master, Ironmongers' Co., 1994–95. *Recreations:* family (numerous), other people. *Address:* Verulam Chambers, Peer House, Verulam Street, Gray's Inn, WC1X 8LZ. *T:* 0171–813 2400. *Club:* Garrick.

See also J. G. Edwards.

EDWARDS, Rear Adm. John Phillip, CB 1984; LVO 1972; CEng, FIMechE 1982; Emeritus Fellow and Development Director, Wadham College, Oxford, since 1994 (Domestic Bursar and Fellow, 1984–94); *b* 13 Feb. 1927; *s* of Robert Edwards and Dilys (*née* Phillips); *m* 1951, Gwen Lloyd Bonner; three *d*. *Educ:* Brynhyfryd Sch., Ruthin, Clwyd; HMS Conway; Royal Naval Engrg Colls, Keyham and Manadon. MA 1984. FBIM 1980. Served, 1948–72: HMS Vengeance, Mauritius, Caledonia, Torquay, Lion, Diamond, Defender, HMCS Stadacona, and HMY Britannia; Mechanical Trng Estab., Portsmouth; Personnel Panel; Staff of C-in-C Fleet; SOWC; Dep. Dir, RN Staff Coll., 1972–74; Asst Dir, Dir Gen. Ships, 1974–76; RCDS, 1977; Captain of Portland Naval Base, 1978–80; Dir Gen., Fleet Support Policy and Services, 1980–83. Comdr 1964, Captain 1971, Rear Adm. 1980. Mem. (non-exec.), Welsh Office Health Policy Bd, 1985–90. President: Oxford Royal Naval Assoc., 1984–90; Oxford Royal Naval and Royal Marine Assoc., 1994–; Midland Naval Officers Assoc., 1985–; Vice-Pres., N Oxfordshire SSAFA, 1984–. Trustee, Oxford Preservation Trust, 1994–. Freeman: Co. of Engineers, 1984; City of London, 1984. Hon. FISTC 1976. *Recreations:* golf, tennis. *Address:* Wadham College, Oxford OX1 3PN. *Club:* Frilford Heath Golf.

EDWARDS, Joseph Robert, CBE 1963; JP; Consultant, Canewdon Consultants plc, Southend-on-Sea, since 1989 (Chairman, 1986–89); Deputy Chairman, Theale Estates Ltd (formerly Martin Electrical Equipment (Theale) Ltd), since 1979; Director, Creative Industries Group Inc., Detroit, since 1985; *b* 5 July 1908; *y s* of late Walter Smith Edwards and Annie Edwards, Gt Yarmouth; *m* 1st, 1936, Frances Mabel Haddon Bourne (*d* 1975); three *s* one *d*; 2nd, 1976, Joan Constance Mary Tattersall. *Educ:* High Sch., Great Yarmouth. Joined Austin Motor Co., Birmingham, 1928; Hercules factory, 1939; rejoined Austin Motor Co., 1941; Gen. Works Manager, 1951; Local Dir, 1953; Works Dir, 1954; Dir of Manufacturing, British Motor Corp., 1955; Managing Director: British Motor Corp., 1966–68; Pressed Steel/Fisher Ltd, 1956–67; Dep. Chm., Harland & Wolff Ltd, 1968–70, Chm. 1970; Dep. Chm., Associated Engrg, 1969–78; Dir, BPC Ltd, 1973–81; Vice-Chm., Lucas (Industries) Ltd, 1976–79; Chm., Penta Motors Ltd, Reading, 1978–87; Dir, CSE Aviation Ltd, 1973–87. Pres., Motor Industry Research Assoc. Mem., Commn on Industrial Relations to 1974. JP Oxford, 1964. Hon. MA Oxon, 1968. *Recreation:* golf. *Address:* Flat 16, Shoreacres, Banks Road, Sandbanks, Poole, Dorset BH13 7QH. *T:* Canford Cliffs (01202) 709315. *Club:* Royal Motor Yacht.

EDWARDS, Julie Andrews; *see* Andrews, J.

EDWARDS, Kenneth; *see* Edwards, A. K.

EDWARDS, Dr Kenneth John Richard; Vice-Chancellor, University of Leicester, since 1987; *b* 12 Feb. 1934; *s* of John and Elizabeth May Edwards; *m* 1958, Janet Mary Gray; two *s* one *d*. *Educ:* Market Drayton Grammar Sch.; Univ. of Reading (BSc 1st class 1958); University Coll. of Wales, Aberystwyth (PhD 1961). Nat. Service, RAF, 1952–54. Fellow, Univ. of California, 1961–62; ARC Fellow, Welsh Plant Breeding Station, Aberystwyth, 1962–63, Sen. Sci. Officer, 1963–66; Cambridge University: Lectr in Genetics, 1966–84; Head of Dept of Genetics, 1981–84; Sec. Gen. of Faculties, 1984–87; St John's College: Fellow, 1971–87; Lectr, 1971–84; Tutor, 1980–84. Vis. Lectr in Genetics, Univ. of Birmingham, 1965; Vis. Prof., INTA, Buenos Aires, 1973; Leverhulme Res. Fellow, Univ. of California, 1973. Chm., CVCP, 1993–95; Member: Marshall Aid Commemoration Commn, 1991–; Council, ACU, 1994–; Bd, CRE, 1994–. Mem. Bd, USS Ltd, 1994–. Chm. Governing Body, Inst. of Grassland and Envmtl Res., 1994–. Hon. LLD QUB, 1994; Hon. DSc Reading, 1994. *Publications:* Evolution in Modern Biology, 1977; articles on genetics in sci. jls. *Recreations:* music, gardening. *Address:* Knighton Hall, Leicester LE2 3WG. *T:* Leicester (0116) 270 6677.

EDWARDS, Lionel Antony, (Tony), CEng, FRAeS; Chief Executive, Dowty, TI Group PLC, since 1992, Chairman and Chief Executive, Messier-Dowty, since 1994; *b* 4 Nov. 1944; *s* of Lionel Victor and Marjorie Edwards; *m* 1993, Sheena Jolley. *Educ:* Abingdon Sch.; Univ. of Birmingham (BSc Hons 1966); Harvard Business Sch. (MBA 1972). CEng 1991; FRAeS 1991. Apprentice Engr, Rolls-Royce, Derby, 1962–68; Mfg Engr, General Electric, Lynn, Mass, 1968–71; Lectr, Harvard Univ., 1972–73; Manager/Dir, General Electric, Lynn and Cincinatti, Ohio, 1973–82; Gen. Manager, Storno A/S, Copenhagen, 1983–86; Corporate Vice-Pres., Motorola, Copenhagen, 1986–88; President: Challenger Exec. Jet Div., Montreal, 1988–89; Canadair Aerospace Gp, Montreal, 1989; Man. Dir, Lucas Aerospace Ltd, Solihull, 1989–92; Gp Man. Dir, Lucas Industries, 1992. Member: Council, SBAC, 1989– (Vice-Pres. 1990–91, Pres. 1991–92, Dep. Pres. 1992–93); DTI Aviation Cttee, 1992–; Council, Air League, 1992–; Council, RAeS, 1992–; NDIC, 1992–. *Recreations:* photography, building sports cars, preservation of historic aircraft. *Address:* TI Group PLC, Lambourn Court, Abingdon OX14 1UH. *T:* Abingdon (01235) 555570.

EDWARDS, Hon. Sir Llewellyn (Roy), AC 1989; Kt 1984; FRACMA; Executive Consultant, Jones Lang Wootton, Brisbane, since 1989; *b* 2 Aug. 1935; *s* of Roy Thomas Edwards and Agnes Dulcie Gwendoline Edwards; *m* 1st, 1958, Leone Sylvia Burley (decd); two *s* one *d*; 2nd, 1989, Jane Anne Brumfield. *Educ:* Raceview State Sch.; Silkstone State Sch.; Ipswich Grammar Sch.; Univ. of Queensland (MB, BS 1965). Qualified Electrician, 1955. RMO and Registrar in Surgery, Ipswich Hosp., 1965–68; gen. practice, Ipswich, 1968–74. MLA (L) Ipswich, Qld Parlt, 1972–83; Minister for Health, Qld, 1974–78; Dep. Premier and Treasurer, Qld, 1978–83; Dep. Med. Supt, Ipswich Hosp., 1983–85. Chairman: Ansvar Australia Insurance Ltd, 1984–; World Expo 88 Authority 1984–89; Australian Coachline Holdings Ltd, 1992–; Micromedical Industries, 1993–; Director: Westpac Banking Corp., 1984–; James Hardie Industries Pty Ltd, 1990–; Peregrine Capital Australia Ltd, 1992–. Chm., Pacific Film and Television Commn, 1991–; Mem., Australia Japan Foundn Bd, 1992–. Chancellor, Univ. of Queensland, 1993– (Mem. Senate, 1984–). FRACMA 1984. Hon. FAIM 1988. Hon. LLD Queensland, 1988. *Recreations:* tennis, walking, cricket, Rugby Union. *Address:* 8 Ascot Street, Ascot, Qld 4007, Australia. *Clubs:* Brisbane (Brisbane, Qld); United Services (Qld); Ipswich (Ipswich, Qld); Brisbane Polo.

EDWARDS, Malcolm John, CBE 1985; Chairman, Coal Investments Plc, since 1993; founded Edwards Energy Ltd, 1992; Commercial Director, British Coal (formerly National Coal Board), 1985–92; Member of the Board, British Coal, 1986–92; *b* 25 May 1934; *s* of John J. Edwards and Edith (*née* Riley); *m* 1967, Yvonne, *d* of Mr and Mrs J. A. W. Daniels, Port Lincoln, S Australia; two *s*. *Educ:* Alleyn's Sch., Dulwich; Jesus Coll., Cambridge (MA). Joined NCB as trainee, 1956; Industrial Sales Manager, 1962; Dir of Domestic and Industrial Sales, 1969; Dir Gen. of Marketing, 1973; responsible for coal utilisation R & D, 1984–92; Chm., British Fuels Gp, 1988–92; Dep. Chm., Inter Continental Fuels, 1989–92. *Publication:* (with J. J. Edwards) Medical Museum Technology, 1959. *Recreations:* book collecting, arts and crafts movement, music, gardening. *Address:* Lodge Farm, Moot Lane, Downton, Salisbury, Wilts SP5 3LN.

EDWARDS, Marcus; *see* Edwards, C. M.

EDWARDS, Michael; *see* Edwards, J. M. McF.

EDWARDS, Dr Michael Frederick, OBE 1993; FEng, FIChemE; Principal Engineer, Unilever, since 1987; *b* 27 April 1941; *s* of H. S. Edwards and J. Edwards (*née* Wallwork); *m* 1964, Margaret Roberta Thorne; one *s* one *d*. *Educ:* University Coll., Swansea (BSc, PhD). FIChemE 1980; FEng 1992. Lectr in Engrg Scis, Univ. of Warwick, 1966–69; Lectr, Sen. Lectr in Chem. Engrg, 1969–81, Prof. of Chemical Engrg, 1981–87, Bradford Univ. Mem., various research council bds and cttees. *Publication:* Mixing in the Process Industries, 1985, 2nd edn 1992. *Recreations:* hill-walking, classical music. *Address:* 44 Long Meadow, Gayton, Wirral L60 8QQ. *T:* 0151–342 5602.

EDWARDS, Norman L.; *see* Lloyd-Edwards.

EDWARDS, Owen; Director, Sianel 4 Cymru (Welsh Fourth Channel Authority), 1981–89; *b* 26 Dec. 1933; *s* of Sir Ifan ab Owen Edwards and Eirys Mary Edwards; *m* 1st, 1958; two *d*; 2nd, 1994. *Educ:* Ysgol Gymraeg, Aberystwyth; Leighton Park, Reading; Lincoln Coll., Oxford (MA). Cataloguer, Nat. Library of Wales, 1958–60; BBC Wales: Compère, TV Programme Heddiw, 1961–66; Programme Organiser, 1967–70; Head of Programmes, 1970–74; Controller, 1974–81. Chairman: Assoc. for Film and TV in Celtic Countries, later Celtic Film and TV Assoc., 1983–85, 1989–91; Royal Nat. Eisteddfod of Wales, 1986–89 (Vice-Chm., 1985–86). Hon LLD Wales, 1989. Gold Medal, RTS, 1989; BAFTA Cymru Special Award, 1995. *Recreations:* walking, fishing. *Address:* 2 Riversdale, Llandaff, Cardiff CF5 2QL. *T:* Cardiff (01222) 555392.

EDWARDS, Patricia Anne, (Mrs Roger Cox); Deputy Parliamentary Commissioner for Administration, since 1994; *b* 29 May 1944; *d* of late Maurice James Edwards and of Marion Edwards (*née* Lewis); *m* 1970, Roger Charles Cox, *qv*. *Educ:* Barry and Purley County Grammar Schools; King's College London (LLB). Called to the Bar, Middle Temple, 1967; Criminal Appeal Office, 1965–74; Law Officers' Dept, 1974–77; Home Office: Sen. Legal Asst, 1977–80; Asst Legal Adviser, 1980–88; Principal Asst Legal Advr, 1988–94. *Recreations:* music, travel, reading, domestic pursuits. *Address:* Office of Parliamentary Commission for Administration, Church House, Great Smith Street, SW1P 3BW.

EDWARDS, Peter Robert; Director, Personal Investment Authority, since 1992; *b* 30 Oct. 1937; *s* of Robert and Doris Edith Edwards; *m* 1st, 1967, Jennifer Ann Boys; one *s*; 2nd, 1970, Elizabeth Janet Barrett; one *d*. *Educ:* Christ's Hospital. Chartered Accountant. Ernst & Young (and predecessor firms), 1955–90; Chief Exec., Secretan, 1990–92. Indep. Mem. Council, FIMBRA, 1990–. Dir, Blackwall Green Ltd, 1992–. *Recreations:* ornithology, gardening. *Address:* Glebe Cottage, Church Lane, Bury, Pulborough, West Sussex RH20 1PB. *T:* Pulborough (01798) 831774. *Club:* Caledonian.

EDWARDS, Prof. Philip Walter, PhD; FBA 1986; King Alfred Professor of English Literature, University of Liverpool, 1974–90, now Emeritus; *b* 7 Feb. 1923; *er s* of late R. H. Edwards, MC, and late Mrs B. Edwards; *m* 1st, 1947, Hazel Margaret (*d* 1950), *d* of late Prof. C. W. and late Mrs E. R. Valentine; 2nd, 1952, Sheila Mary, *d* of late R. S. and late Mrs A. M. Wilkes, Bloxwich, Staffs; three *s* one *d*. *Educ:* King Edward's High Sch., Birmingham; Univ. of Birmingham. MA, PhD Birmingham; MA Dublin. Royal Navy, 1942–45 (Sub-Lieut RNVR). Lectr in English, Univ. of Birmingham, 1946–60; Commonwealth Fund Fellow, Harvard Univ., 1954–55; Prof. of English Lit., TCD, 1960–66; Fellow of TCD, 1962–66; Prof. of Lit., Univ. of Essex, 1966–74; Pro-Vice-Chancellor, Liverpool Univ., 1980–83. Visiting Professor: Univ. of Michigan, 1964–65; Williams Coll., Mass, 1969; Otago Univ., NZ, 1980; Internat. Christian Univ., Tokyo, 1989; Visiting Fellow: All Souls Coll., Oxford, 1970–71; Huntington Liby, Calif., 1977, 1983. *Publications:* Sir Walter Ralegh, 1953; (ed) Kyd, The Spanish Tragedy, 1959; Shakespeare and the Confines of Art, 1968; (ed) Pericles Prince of Tyre, 1976; (ed with C. Gibson) Massinger, Plays and Poems, 1976; Threshold of a Nation, 1979; (ed jtly) Shakespeare's Styles, 1980; (ed) Hamlet Prince of Denmark, 1985; Shakespeare: a writer's progress, 1986; Last Voyages, 1988; The Story of the Voyage, 1994; numerous articles on Shakespeare and literature of his time in Shakespeare Survey, Proc. British Acad., etc. *Recreations:* walking, gardening. *Address:* High Gillinggrove, Gillinggate, Kendal, Cumbria LA9 4JB.

EDWARDS, Quentin Tytler, QC 1975; **His Honour Judge Quentin Edwards;** a Circuit Judge, since 1982; Chancellor, Diocese of Chichester, since 1978; *b* 16 Jan. 1925; *s* of Herbert Jackson Edwards and Juliet Hester Edwards; *m* 1948, Barbara Marian Guthrie; two *s* one *d*. *Educ:* Bradfield Coll.; Council of Legal Educn. Royal Navy, 1943–46. Called to Bar, Middle Temple, 1948; Bencher, 1972. A Recorder of the Crown Court, 1974–82; Chancellor, Dio. of Blackburn, 1977–90. Licensed Reader, Dio. of London, 1967; Chm., Ecclesiastical Law Soc., 1990–; Member: Legal Adv. Commn of General Synod of Church of England, 1973; Dioceses Commn, 1978–. Pres., Highgate Literary and Scientific Instn, 1988–93. Hon. MA (Archbp of Canterbury), 1961. *Publications:* (with Peter Dow) Public Rights of Way and Access to the Countryside, 1951; (with K. Macmorran, et al) Ecclesiastical Law, 3rd edn, Halsbury's Laws of England, 1955; What is Unlawful?, 1959; (with J. N. D. Anderson, et al) Putting Asunder, 1966. *Recreations:* the open air; the table; architecture. *Address:* Central London County Court, 13–14 Park Crescent, W1N 3PD. *Club:* Athenæum.

EDWARDS, Prof. Richard Humphrey Tudor, FRCP; Professor and Head of Department of Medicine, since 1984, Director, Magnetic Resonance Research Centre, since 1985, and Director, Muscle Research Centre, since 1986, University of Liverpool; *b*. 28 Jan. 1939; *s* of Hywel Islwyn Edwards and Menna Tudor Edwards (*née* Davies); *m* 1964, Eleri Wyn Roberts; one *d* (one *s* decd). *Educ:* Llangollen Grammar Sch.; Middlesex Hosp. Med. Sch., London (BSc, PhD, MB, BS). Ho. appts, Middlesex, National Heart and Hammersmith Hosps, 1964–65; Res. Fellow, Asst Lectr, then Lectr (Wellcome Sen. Res. Fellow in Clin. Science), Hon. Cons. Physician (Respiratory Med.), Royal Postgrad. Med. Sch., Hammersmith Hosp., 1966–76; Wellcome Swedish Res. Fellow, Karolinska Inst., Stockholm, 1970; Prof. of Human Metabolism, UCH Med. Sch., 1976–84; Hd of Dept of Medicine, UCL, 1982–84; Hon. Consultant Physician: Royal Liverpool Hosp., 1984–; Robert Jones and Agnes Hunt Orthopaedic Hosp., Oswestry, 1979–. *Publications:* Clinical Exercise Testing, 1975; Muscle Weakness and Fatigue, 1980; sci. papers on human muscle in health and disease in Jl of Physiology, Clinical Sci., Clinical Physiol., Muscle and Nerve, etc. *Recreations:* Wales—planting trees, mountain walking, gardening, music. *Address:* Department of Medicine, University of Liverpool, PO Box 147, Liverpool L69 3BX. *T:* 0151–706 4072.

EDWARDS, Prof. Robert Geoffrey, CBE 1988; FRS 1984; Professor of Human Reproduction, Cambridge University, 1985–89, now Emeritus; Extraordinary Fellow, Churchill College, Cambridge; *b* 27 Sept. 1925; *s* of Samuel and Margaret Edwards; *m* 1956, Ruth Eileen Fowler; five *d*. *Educ:* Manchester Central High Sch.; Univs of Wales and Edinburgh. PhD (Edin); DSc (Wales); MA (Cantab). Service in British Army, 1944–48; commnd 1946. UC North Wales, Bangor, 1948–51; Univ. of Edinburgh, 1951–57; Res. Fellow at California Inst. of Tech., 1957–58; Scientist at Nat. Inst. of Medical Research, Mill Hill, NW7, 1958–62; Glasgow Univ. 1962–63; in Dept of Physiology, Cambridge Univ., 1963–89; Ford Foundation Reader in Physiology, 1969–85. Scientific Dir, Bourn Hallam Clinics, Cambridgeshire and London, 1988–91. Founder Chm., European Soc. of Human Reproduction and Embryology, 1984–86. Vis. Scientist: in Johns Hopkins Hosp., Baltimore, 1965; Univ. of N Carolina, 1966; Vis. Prof., Free Univ., Brussels, 1984. Hon. Pres., British Fertility Soc., 1988–. Hon. FRCOG 1985; Hon. MRCP 1986. Hon. Mem. French Soc. for Infertility, 1983. Life Fellow, Australian Fertility Soc., 1985. Hon. Citizen of Bordeaux, 1985. Hon. DSc: Hull, 1983; York; Vrije Univ., Brussels. Spanish Fertility Soc. Gold Medal, 1985; King Faisal Award, 1989. Chief Editor, Human Reproduction, 1986–. *Publications:* A Matter of Life (with P. C. Steptoe), 1980; Conception in the Human Female, 1980; (with C. R. Austin) Mechanisms of Sex Differentiation in Animals and Man; (with J. M. Purdy) Human Conception in Vitro, 1982; (with J. M. Purdy and P. C. Steptoe) Implantation of the Human Embryo, 1985; (with M. Seppälä) In Vitro Fertilisation and Embryo Transfer, 1985; Life Before Birth, 1989; editor of several scientific textbooks on reproduction; numerous articles in scientific and medical jls, organiser of conferences, etc. *Recreations:* farming, politics, music. *Address:* Duck End Farm, Dry Drayton, Cambridge CB3 8DB. *T:* Crafts Hill (01954) 780602.

EDWARDS, Robert John, CBE 1986; Deputy Chairman, Mirror Group Newspapers, 1985–86 (Senior Group Editor, 1984–85); *b* 26 Oct. 1925; *m* 1st, 1952, Laura Ellwood (marr. diss. 1972); two *s* two *d*; 2nd, 1977, Brigid Segrave. *Educ:* Ranelagh Sch., Bracknell. Editor, Tribune, 1951–54; feature writer, London Evening Standard, 1954–57; Dep. Editor, Sunday Express, 1957–59; Man. Editor, Daily Express, 1959–61; Editor: Daily Express, 1961, 1963–65; Evening Citizen, Glasgow, 1962–63; Sunday People, 1966–72; Sunday Mirror, 1972–84; Dir, Mirror Group Newspapers, 1976–88. Ombudsman to Today newspaper, 1990–. *Publication:* Goodbye Fleet Street (autobiog.), 1988. *Address:* Georgian Wing, Williamscot House, near Banbury, Oxon OX17 1AE. *T:* Banbury (01295) 750809. *Clubs:* Garrick, Reform, Kennel, Groucho's.

EDWARDS, Robert Septimus Friar, CVO 1964; CBE 1963; *b* 21 Oct. 1910; *y s* of late Augustus C. Edwards and of Amy Edwards; *m* 1946, Janet Mabel Wrigley; one *s* two *d*. *Educ:* Hereford Cathedral Sch. Chief Engineering Asst, Hereford, until 1936; Min. of Transport, Highway Engineering, 1936–43; Principal, Min. of War Transport, 1943; Mem. British Merchant Shipping Mission, Washington, DC, 1944–46. Sec. Gen. Internat. Conf. on Safety of Life at Sea, 1948; Principal Private Sec. to Minister of Transport, 1949–51; Shipping Attaché, British Embassy, Washington, DC, 1951–54; Dir of Sea Transport, 1954–57; Gen. Manager, London Airports, 1957–63; Gen. Manager, 1967–69, Dir-Gen., 1969–71, Mersey Docks and Harbour Board. Chm., Morris & David Jones Ltd, 1973–74. Called to the Bar, Middle Temple, 1941. *Address:* 3 Simon Court, Hoscote Park, West Kirby, Wirral, Merseyside L48 0RX. *T:* 0151–625 2629.

EDWARDS, Robin Anthony, CBE 1981; Partner with Dundas & Wilson, CS (formerly Davidson & Syme, WS), since 1965; *b* 7 April 1939; *s* of Alfred Walton Edwards and Ena Annie Ruffell; *m* 1963, Elizabeth Alexandra Mackay (marr. diss.); one *s* one *d*; *m* 1986, Janet Cant Pow. *Educ:* Daniel Stewart's Coll., Edinburgh; Edinburgh Univ. (MA, LLB (distinction), Cl. Medallist). Former Lectr in Conveyancing, Edinburgh Univ.; Admitted Member, WS Society, 1964; Mem. Council, Law Society of Scotland, 1969–84, Vice-Pres., 1978–79, Pres., 1979–80 (youngest Pres. ever, at that time). Mem., Lands Tribunal for Scotland, 1991–. *Recreations:* French travel and cuisine. *Address:* 7/6 Rocheid Park, East Fettes Avenue, Edinburgh EH4 1RP; (office) Saltire Court, 20 Castle Terrace, Edinburgh EH1 2EN.

EDWARDS, Dr Roger Snowden, CBE 1964; JP; Chairman, Gas Industry Training Board, 1965–74, retired; *b* 19 Dec. 1904; *s* of late Herbert George Edwards and late Margaret Alice Edwards; *m* 1935, Eveline Brunton, MBE (*d* 1986); two *s* one *d*. *Educ:* Enfield Grammar Sch.; Imperial Coll. of Science. Junior Staff, Imperial Coll. of Science, 1925–28; Physicist, British Xylonite Co., 1928–29; Physicist, Boot Trade Research Association, 1929–39; Dir, Co-operative Wholesale Soc., 1939–49. Chairman: Council of Industrial Design, 1947–52 (Mem., 1944–47); NE Gas Board, 1949–66; Mem., Gas Council, 1966–70. JP Harrogate, 1960; Surrey, 1966. *Recreation:* golf. *Address:* 23 Manor Way, Letchworth, Herts SG6 3NL.

EDWARDS, Prof. Ronald Walter, CBE 1992; DSc; FIBiol, FIWEM, FIFM; Professor and Head of Department of Applied Biology, University of Wales Institute of Science and Technology, 1968–90, now Emeritus; *b* 7 June 1930; *s* of Walter and Violet Edwards. *Educ:* Solihull Sch., Warwicks; Univ. of Birmingham (BSc, DSc). FIBiol 1965; FIWEM (FIWPC 1981). Biologist, Freshwater Biol Assoc., 1953–58; Sen., Principal, and Sen. Principal Scientific Officer, Water Pollution Res. Lab., 1958–68. Chm., Nat. Parks Rev. Panel, 1989–91; Dep. Chm., Welsh Water Authority, 1983–89 (Mem., 1974–89); Member: NRA, 1988–94; NERC, 1970–73 and 1982–85; Nat. Cttee, European Year of the Environment, 1987–88; Adv. Cttee, Envmt Agency, 1995–; Council, RSPB, 1988–92; Brecon Beacons Nat. Park Cttee, 1993–95; Vice Pres., Council for Nat. Parks, 1993–. *Publications:* (co-ed) Ecology and the Industrial Society, 1968; (co-ed) Conservation and Productivity of Natural Waters, 1975; (with Dr M. Brooker) The Ecology of the River Wye, 1982; Acid Waters in Wales, 1990; about 90 papers in learned jls. *Recreations:* music, collecting Staffordshire pottery. *Address:* Rivers House, St Mellons Business Park, Cardiff CF3 0LT.

EDWARDS, Prof. Sir Samuel Frederick, (Sir Sam Edwards), Kt 1975; FRS 1966; Cavendish Professor of Physics, 1984–95, Professor Emeritus since 1995 (John Humphrey Plummer Professor, 1972–84), and Pro-Vice-Chancellor, 1992–95, Cambridge University; Fellow, Gonville and Caius College, Cambridge, since 1972 (President, since 1992); *b* 1 Feb. 1928; *s* of Richard and Mary Jane Edwards, Manselton, Swansea; *m* 1953, Merriell E. M. Bland; one *s* three *d*. *Educ:* Swansea Grammar Sch.; Gonville and Caius Coll., Cambridge (MA, PhD); Harvard University. Inst. for Advanced Study, Princeton, 1952; Univ. of Birmingham, 1953; Univ. of Manchester, 1958, Prof. of Theoretical Physics, 1963–72. Chief Scientific Adviser, Department of Energy, 1983–88. Chm., SRC, 1973–77. UK Deleg. to NATO Science Cttee, 1974–79; Mem., Planning Cttee, Max-Planck Gesellschaft, 1974–77. Vice-Pres., Institute of Physics, 1970–73 (Mem. Council, 1967–73); Mem. Council, Inst. of Mathematics and its Applications, 1976– (Vice-Pres., 1979, Pres., 1980–81). Member: Physics Cttee, SRC, 1968–73 (Chm. 1970–73); Polymer Cttee, SRC, 1968–73; Science Bd, SRC, 1970–73; Council, European Physical Soc., 1969–71 (Chm., Condensed Matter Div., 1969–71); UGC, 1971–73; Defence Scientific Adv. Council, 1973– (Chm., 1977–80); Metrology and Standards Req. Bd, Dept of Industry, 1974–77; AFRC, 1990–94; HEFCW, 1992–. Chm., Adv. Council on R&D, Dept of Energy, 1983–88 (Mem., 1974–77); Member Council: European R&D (EEC), 1976–80; Royal Soc., 1982–83 (a Vice-Pres., 1982–83); Pres., BAAS, 1988–89 (Chm. Council, 1977–82); Foreign Mem., Académie des Sciences, France, 1989. Non-exec. Director: Lucas Industries, 1981–93; Steetley plc, 1985–93; Chm., Sen. Adv. Gp, Unilever, 1992–; Mem., Adv. Gp, BP, 1992–. FInstP; FIMA; FRSC. Hon. DTech Loughborough, 1975; Hon. DSc: Salford, Edinburgh, 1976; Bath, 1978; Birmingham, 1986; Wales, 1987; Sheffield, 1989; Dublin, 1991; Leeds, 1994; UEA, 1995; DUniv Strasbourg, 1986. Hon. Fellow, UC Swansea, 1994. Maxwell Medal and Prize, Inst. of Physics, 1974; High Polymer Physics Prize, Amer. Phys. Soc., 1982; Davy Medal, Royal Soc., 1984; Gold Medal, Inst. of Maths, 1986; Guthrie Medal and Prize, Inst. of Physics, 1987; Gold Medal, Rheological Soc., 1990; Louis Vaillon Moët Hennessy Prize (Science pour l'Art), 1993.

Publications: Technological Risk, 1980; (with M. Doi) Theory of Polymer Dynamics, 1986; (with S. M. Aharoni) Networks of Liquid Crystal Polymers, 1994; contribs to learned jls. *Address:* 7 Penarth Place, Cambridge CB3 9LU. *T:* Cambridge (01223) 66610. *Club:* Athenæum.

EDWARDS, Sian; conductor; Music Director, English National Opera, since 1993; *b* 27 Aug. 1959. *Educ:* Royal Northern Coll. of Music; Leningrad Conservatoire. Since 1985 has conducted many orchestras incl. LPO, RPO, Royal Scottish Orch., City of Birmingham SO, Hallé, English Chamber Orch. and Docklands Sinfonietta; conducted Orchestre de Paris and Philharmonique de Lille in France, and St Paul Chamber Orch., San Francisco Symphony and Los Angeles Philharmonic in USA, 1989; has also conducted orchestras in Canada, Belgium, Germany, Austria, Russia and Australia. Operatic début with Mahagonny (Weill), then Carmen, Scottish Opera, 1986; world première of Greek (Turnage), Munich Biennale and Edinburgh Fest., 1988; Glyndebourne: La Traviata, 1987; Katya Kabanova, 1988; New Year (Tippett), 1990; Royal Opera, Covent Garden: The Knot Garden (Tippett), 1988; Rigoletto, 1989; Il Trovatore, 1990; Madam Butterfly, 1992; English National Opera: The Gambler (Prokofiev), 1990; The Queen of Spades, 1993; La Bohème, Marriage of Figaro, Jenufa, The Mikado, Khovanshchina, 1994; Mahagonny, 1995. Recordings incl. orchestral works by Tchaikovsky, Prokofiev, Ravel and Britten. *Address:* c/o Ingpen & Williams Ltd, 14 Kensington Court, W8 5DN. *T:* 0171–937 5158.

EDWARDS, Stewart Leslie, CMG 1967; Under-Secretary, Department of Trade, retired; *b* 6 Nov. 1914; *s* of late Walter James and Lilian Emma Edwards; *m* 1940, Dominica Jeanne Lavie, *d* of Joseph Lavie and Jeanne Jauréguiberry; two *s*. *Educ:* King's Sch., Canterbury; Corpus Christi Coll., Cambridge (Foundn Scholar). BA 1936; MA 1943. Appointed to War Office, 1937. Military service, 1942–44. Called to the Bar, Inner Temple, 1947. Seconded from War Office to OEEC, 1948–51; Board of Trade, 1951–65; Minister (Economic), Bonn, 1965–70; Under-Sec., DTI later Dept of Trade, 1970–74. *Recreations:* music, reading, hill-walking, wine. *Address:* B51 Résidence La Pastourelle, Bât. A, 20 Avenue Daniel-Hedde, 17200 Royan, France. *T:* 46392203.

EDWARDS, Very Rev. (Thomas) Erwyd (Pryse); Dean of Bangor, since 1988; *b* 26 Jan. 1933; *s* of Richard and Gwladys Edwards; *m* 1961, Mair (*née* Roberts); two *s*. *Educ:* St David's University College, Lampeter (BA 1956); St Michael's College, Llandaff. Curate of Caernarfon, 1958–63; Asst Chaplain, St George's Hosp., London, 1963–66; Chaplain, King's College Hosp., London, 1966–72; Vicar: Penmon, Anglesey, 1972–75; Menai Bridge, 1975–61; St David's, Bangor, 1981–85; St David's and St James's, Bangor, 1985–88; Canon of Bangor Cathedral, 1988. *Address:* The Deanery, Cathedral Close, Bangor, Gwynedd LL57 1LH. *T:* Bangor (01248) 370693.

EDWARDS, Tony; *see* Edwards, L. A.

EDWARDS, Vero C. W.; *see* Wynne-Edwards.

EDWARDS, William (Henry); solicitor; *b* 6 Jan. 1938; *s* of Owen Henry Edwards and S. Edwards; *m* 1961, Ann Eleri Rogers; one *s* three *d*. *Educ:* Sir Thomas Jones' Comprehensive Sch.; Liverpool Univ. LLB. MP (Lab) Merioneth, 1966–Feb. 1974; contested (Lab) Merioneth, Oct. 1974; Prospective Parly Cand. (Lab), Anglesey, 1981–83. Mem., Historic Building Council for Wales, 1971–76. Editor, Solicitors Diary. *Recreations:* golf, Association football (from the terraces).

EDWARDS-MOSS, (Sir) David John, (5th Bt *cr* 1868); *S* father, 1988, but does not use the title.

EDWARDS-STUART, Antony James Cobham; QC 1991; an Assistant Recorder, since 1991; *b* 2 Nov. 1946; *s* of Lt-Col Ivor Arthur James Edwards-Stuart and Mrs Elizabeth Aileen Le Mesurier Edwards-Stuart (*née* Deck); *m* 1973, Fiona Ann, *d* of late Paul Weaver, OBE; two *s* two *d*. *Educ:* Sherborne Sch.; RMA Sandhurst; St Catharine's Coll., Cambridge. Called to the Bar, Gray's Inn, 1976. Commnd 1st RTR, 1966; Adjutant: 1st RTR, 1973–75; Kent and Sharpshooters Sqn, Royal Yeomanry, 1976–77. *Recreations:* woodwork, fishing, shooting. *Address:* 4 Aberdeen Park, Highbury, N5 2BN. *T:* 0171–359 7224; 2 Crown Office Row, Temple, EC4Y 7HJ.

EDWARDSON, Prof. James Alexander, PhD; Director, Medical Research Council Neurochemical Pathology Unit, since 1979; Professor of Neuroendocrinology, Newcastle University, since 1982; Director, Institute for the Health of the Elderly, Newcastle University, since 1994; *b* 18 March 1942; *s* of James Thompson Hewson Edwardson and Isabel Ann Edwardson; *m* 1965, Caroline Hunter; one *s* two *d*. *Educ:* South Shields Grammar-Technical Sch. for Boys; Univ. of Nottingham (BSc Hons Zoology 1963); Inst. of Psychiatry, Univ. of London (PhD 1966). MRC Junior Res. Fellow, Inst. of Psychiatry, 1966–67; Lectr in Physiology, Aberdeen Univ., 1967–69; MRC Scientist and Lectr in Biochem., Imperial Coll., London, 1970–75; Sen. Lectr, then Reader, in Physiology, St George's Hosp. Med. Sch., 1975–79. Vice-Pres., Alzheimer's Disease Soc., 1989–. *Publications:* numerous papers on brain biochem., physiology and behaviour and on Alzheimer's Disease and related neurodegenerative disorders. *Recreations:* bird watching, religions, Labour Party, poetry, gardening. *Address:* 24 Harton Grove, South Shields, Tyne and Wear NE34 6LT. *T:* 0191–456 3628.

EDZARD, Christine; film director; Managing Director, Sands Film Studios, since 1975; *b* 15 Feb. 1945; *d* of Dietz Edzard and Susanne Eisendieck, painters; *m* 1968, Richard Goodwin; one *d*, and one step *s* one step *d*. *Educ:* Ecole National de Science Politique, Paris (Econ degree). Asst designer to Lila de Nobili and Rostislav Doboujinsky, Paris; asst on Zefirelli's Romeo and Juliet, 1966; designer for Hamburg Opera, WNO and Camden Town Fest.; designer, costumes and sets and wrote (with Richard Goodwin) script of film, Tales of Beatrix Potter, 1971; directed short films, The Little Match Girl, The Kitchen and Little Ida, released as Tales from a Flying Trunk; dir, The Nightingale, 1979; wrote and directed: Biddy, 1981 (first feature film); Little Dorrit, 1987 (BAFTA Award, Best Screenplay; LA Critics Award, Best Film; Orson Welles Award, Best Director); The Fool, 1991; Directed and Producer, As You Like It, 1992. *Address:* Sands Films, Grice's Wharf, 119 Rotherhithe Street, SE16 4NF. *T:* 0171–231 2209.

EFFINGHAM, 6th Earl of, *cr* 1837; **Mowbray Henry Gordon Howard;** 16th Baron Howard, of Effingham, *cr* 1554; *b* 29 Nov. 1905; *er s* of 5th Earl and Rosamond Margaret, *d* of late E. H. Hudson; *S* father, 1946; *m* 1st, 1938, Manci Maria Malvina Gertler (marr. diss. 1946); 2nd, 1952, Gladys Irene Kerry (marr. diss. 1971); 3rd, 1972, (Mabel) Suzanne Mingay Cragg, *d* of late Maurice Jules-Marie Le Pen, Paris, and *widow* of Wing Comdr Francis Talbot Cragg. *Educ:* Lancing. Served War 1939–45, RA and 3rd Maritime Reg. *Recreations:* shooting, fishing, philately. *Heir:* *n* Comdr David Peter Mowbray Algernon Howard, RN [*b* 29 April 1939; *m* 1st, 1964, Anne Mary Sayer (marr. diss. 1975); one *s*; 2nd, 1992, Mrs Elizabeth J. Turner]. *Address:* House of Lords, SW1A 0PW.

EFSTATHIOU, Prof. George Petros, FRS 1994; Savilian Professor of Astronomy, Oxford, since 1988; Fellow of New College, Oxford, since 1988; PPARC Senior Fellow, since 1994; *b* 2 Sept. 1955; *s* of Petros Efstathiou and Christina (*née* Parperi); *m* 1976, Helena Jane (*née* Smart); one *s* one *d*. *Educ:* Somerset Comprehensive Sch.; Keble Coll., Oxford (BA); Univ. of Durham (Dept of Physics) (PhD). Res. Asst, Astronomy Dept, Univ. of California, Berkeley, 1979–80; SERC Res. Asst, Inst. of Astronomy, Univ. of Cambridge, 1980–83; Jun. Res. Fellow, 1980–84, Sen. Res. Fellow, 1984–88, King's Coll., Cambridge; Institute of Astronomy, Cambridge: Sen. Asst in Res., 1984–87; Asst Dir of Res., 1987–88; Head of Astrophysics, 1988–94. Maxwell Medal and Prize Inst. of Physics, 1990; Bodossaki Foundn Academic and Cultural Prize for Astrophysics, 1994. *Publications:* articles in astronomical jls. *Recreations:* playing with his children, running. *Address:* Astrophysics, Department of Physics, Nuclear and Astrophysics Laboratory, University of Oxford, Keble Road, Oxford OX1 3RH. *T:* Oxford (01865) 273300.

EGAN, Sir John (Leopold), Kt 1986; DL; FRAeS, FCIT, FCIPS; Chief Executive, BAA plc, since 1990; *b* 7 Nov. 1939; *m* 1963, Julia Emily Treble; two *d*. *Educ:* Bablake Sch., Coventry; Imperial Coll., London Univ., 1958–61 (BSc Hons; FIC 1985); London Business Sch., London Univ., 1966–68 (MScEcon). Petroleum Engineer, Shell International, 1962–66; General Manager, AC-Delco Replacement Parts Operation, General Motors Ltd, 1968–71; Managing Director, Leyland Cars Parts Div., Parts and Service Director, Leyland Cars, BLMC, 1971–76; Corporate Parts Director, Massey Ferguson, 1976–80; Chm. and Chief Exec., Jaguar Cars Ltd, 1980–85, Jaguar plc, 1985–90. Director: Foreign and Colonial Investment Trust, 1985–; Legal & General Group, 1987–. Chm., London Tourist Bd, 1993–; Dir, BTA, 1994–. DL Warwicks, 1988. Hon. Professor: Dept of Engrg, Warwick Univ., 1990; Aston Univ., 1990. Sen. Fellow, RCA, 1987; FCIPS 1993; FRAeS 1994. Hon. FCIM 1989. Hon. Fellow: London Business Sch., 1988; Wolverhampton Poly., 1989. Dr *hc* Cranfield Inst. of Technology, 1986; Hon. DTech Loughborough, 1987; Hon. DBA Internat. Business Sch., 1988; Hon. LLD Bath, 1988; Hon. DSc Aston, 1992. Hon. Insignia for Technology, CGLI, 1987. Internat. Distinguished Entrepreneur Award, Univ. of Manitoba, 1989. MBA Award of the Year, 1988. *Recreations:* music, squash, tennis. *Address:* c/o BAA plc, 130 Wilton Road, SW1V 1LQ. *Clubs:* Royal Automobile; Warwick Boat.

EGAN, Patrick Valentine Martin; Chairman, Fisons plc, 1992–94; *b* 17 July 1930; *s* of Eric and Sandy Egan; *m* 1953, Tessa Coleman; three *d*. *Educ:* Worth Prep. Sch., Crawley; Downside Sch., Bath. Signals Instructor, RA, 1948–50; joined Unilever, 1951; appts UK and abroad; joined main board, 1978; retired from Unilever, 1992; joined board of Fisons plc, 1985. Chairman: English Hops Ltd, 1993–; English Hop Products Ltd, 1993–. *Recreations:* fishing, shooting, gardening. *Address:* Whiteways, Sissinghurst, Cranbrook, Kent TN17 2JA.

EGAN, Seamus; Hon. Mr Justice Egan; Judge of the Supreme Court of Ireland, since 1991; *b* 1924; *m* Ada Leahy; two *s* five *d*. *Educ:* Blackrock College; University College Dublin. Called to the Bar, 1945; practised on Western Circuit; Judge of the High Court, Ireland, 1964. *Recreations:* golf, classical music, theatre; represented Connaught at tennis and table tennis. *Address:* Killowen, Shrewsbury Road, Dublin 4, Ireland.

EGAN, Rt Rev. Mgr Thomas; Vicar General, Archdiocese of Westminster, since 1993; *b* 15 Feb. 1942; *s* of Frank and Mary Egan. *Educ:* St Edmund's Coll., Ware; Inst. of Educn (BEd). Asst priest, Our Lady and St Joseph, Hanwell, 1967–72; Home Mission Team, 1972–73; asst priest, St Joan of Arc, Highbury, 1973–78; Parish Priest, St Pius X, St Charles Square, 1978–86; Pastoral Dir, Allen Hall Seminary, 1986–90; Parish Priest, Our Lady of Hal, Camden Town, 1990–93. *Recreations:* fishing, swimming, football. *Address:* Archbishop's House, Westminster, SW1P 1QJ. *T:* 0171–798 9043.

EGDELL, Dr John Duncan; Consultant in Public Health Medicine (formerly Community Physician), Clwyd Health Authority, 1986–92, now Hon. Consultant; *b* 5 March 1938; *s* of late John William Egdell and of Nellie (*née* Thompson); *m* 1963, Dr Linda Mary Flint; two *s* one *d*. *Educ:* Clifton Coll.; Univ. of Bristol. MB, ChB (Bristol) 1961; DipSocMed (Edin.) 1967; FFPHM 1990 (MFCM 1973, FFCM 1979). Ho. Phys. and Ho. Surg., Bristol Gen. Hosp., 1961–62; gen. practice, 1962–65; Med. Administration: with Newcastle Regional Hosp. Bd, 1966–69; with South Western Regional Hosp. Bd, 1969–74; Regional Specialist in Community Med., South Western Regional Health Authority, 1974–76; Regional Medical Postgrad. Co-ordinator, Univ. of Bristol, 1973–76; Regl MO, Mersey RHA, 1977–86; Hon. Lectr in Community Health, Univ. of Liverpool, 1980–86. *Recreations:* delving into the past, nature conservation. *Address:* Gelli Gynan Lodge, Llanarmon-yn-Ial, near Mold, Clwyd CH7 4QX. *T:* Llanarmon-yn-Ial (01824) 780345.

EGELAND, Leif; *b* 19 Jan. 1903; *s* of late J. J. Egeland, Consul for Norway in Natal, and Ragnhild Konsmo; *m* 1942, Marguerite Doreen (*d* 1984), *d* of late W. J. de Zwaan, Waterkloof, Pretoria; one *d*. *Educ:* Durban High Sch.; Natal University Coll.; Oxford Univ. MA English Lang. and Literature, Natal Univ. Coll.; MA, Hons BA, Jurisprudence, BCL Oxon; Rhodes Scholar (Natal), Trinity Coll., Oxford, 1924–27; official Fellow in Law and Classics, Brasenose Coll., 1927–30 (Hon. Fellow, 1984); Harmsworth Scholar, Middle Temple, 1927–30; Barrister, Middle Temple, 1930, Hon. Bencher, 1948; Hon. LLD Cambridge, 1948. Admitted as Advocate of Supreme Court of S Africa, 1931; Vice-Consul for Norway, Natal, 1931–44; MP (House of Assembly) for Durban (Berea), 1933–38, for Zululand, 1940–43; SA Minister to Sweden, 1943, to Holland and Belgium, 1946. Served War of 1939–45, as AJAG, in UDF, 1940–43; Middle East with 6th Armoured Div. of UDF, 1943. SA Delegate to San Francisco Conf., 1945, to 1st Gen. Assembly of UN, London, 1946, to Final Assembly of League of Nations, 1946; SA delegate and Pres. of Commn on Italian Political and Territorial Questions at Peace Conf., Paris, 1946–47. High Comr in London for the Union of South Africa, 1948–50. Vice-Pres., Royal Commonwealth Soc., 1948–; Hon. Pres., South Africa Inst. of Internat. Affairs; Chm., Smuts Memorial Trust; Life Trustee, South Africa Foundn. Hon. Pres., SA Guide-dogs Assoc. for the Blind (Life Mem., 1994). LLD *hc* Univ. of Natal, 1990. FRSA 1948. Knight Commander with Star of St Olav (Norway), 1943; Knight Grand Cross of North Star (Sweden), 1946; Order of Meritorious Services (Class I) Gold (S Africa), 1987. *Publication:* (autobiog.) Bridges of Understanding, 1978. *Recreation:* bridge. *Address:* 41 The Guild, 213 Rivonia Road, Morningside, South Africa. *Clubs:* Rand, Inanda, South African International Lawn Tennis (Hon. Mem., 1950) (S Africa).

EGERTON, family name of **Duke of Sutherland** and **Earl of Wilton.**

EGERTON, Maj.-Gen. David Boswell, CB 1968; OBE 1956; MC 1940; *b* 24 July 1914; *s* of Vice-Admiral W. de M. Egerton, DSO, and late Anita Adolphine (*née* David); *m* 1946, Margaret Gillian, *d* of Canon C. C. Inge; one *s* two *d*. *Educ:* Stowe; RMA Woolwich. Commissioned Royal Artillery, Aug. 1934; served in India, 1935–39; ops in Waziristan, 1937; France and Belgium, 1940 (MC); Egypt 1942, Italy 1944. Technical Staff course, RMCS, 1946; BJSM, Washington, DC, 1950–52; Asst Chief Engineer in charge of ammunition development, Royal Armament R&D Estabt, 1955–58; idc 1959; Army Mem., Defence Research Policy Staff, 1959–62; Comdt, Trials Estabt Guided Weapons, RA, 1962–63; Army Mem., Air Defence Working Party, 1963–64; Dir-Gen. of Artillery, Army Dept, 1964–67; Vice-Pres., Ordnance Board, 1967–69, President, 1969–70; retired 1970. Col Comdt, RA, 1970–74. Gen. Sec., Assoc. of Recognised Eng. Lang. Schs, 1971–79. *Recreations:* gardening, travel. *Address:* Campion Cottage,

Cheselbourne, Dorchester DT2 7NT. *T:* Milborne St Andrew (01258) 837641. *Club:* Army and Navy.

EGERTON, Sir John Alfred Roy, (Jack Egerton), Kt 1976; *b* Rockhampton, 11 March 1918; *s* of J. G. Egerton, Rockhampton; *m* 1940, Moya, *d* of W. Jones; one *s*. *Educ:* Rockhampton High Sch.; Mt Morgan High Sch.; Australian Admin. Staff Coll. A Union Exec. Officer, 1941–76; Federal Officer of Boilermakers' Union, 1951–66 (Vice-Pres. Fed. Council; rep. Union in China, 1956); Official, Metal Trades Fedn, 1951–67; Mem., ACTU Interstate Exec., 1969; former Pres., Qld Trades and Labor Council. Aust. Rep. ILO Congresses, Geneva: 1960, 1966, 1968, 1974; Qld Rep. to ACTU Congress and ALP Fed. Conf.; Pres., ALP Qld Exec., 1968–76 (Mem. Qld Central Exec., 1958); Mem., Fed. Exec. of ALP, 1970, Sen. Vice-Pres. 1972. Alderman and Dep. Mayor, Gold Coast City Council. Director: Qantas Airways Ltd, 1973–84; Mary Kathleen Uranium; SGIO Building Soc.; Beenleigh Rum. Member: Duke of Edinburgh Study Conf. Cttee, 1967–74; Griffith Univ. Council. *Recreations:* reading, Rugby League (Vice-Pres. and Dir, Qld), golf, trotting. *Address:* 14 Anne Avenue, Broadbeach, Qld 4218, Australia. *Clubs:* NSW and Queensland League, Virginia Golf, Albion Park Trotting.

EGERTON, Sir Philip John Caledon G.; *see* Grey Egerton.

EGERTON, Sir Seymour (John Louis), GCVO 1977 (KCVO 1970); Director, Coutts & Co., Bankers, 1947–85 (Chairman, 1951–76); *b* 24 Sept. 1915; *s* of late Louis Egerton and Jane, *e d* of Rev. Lord Victor Seymour; unmarried. *Educ:* Eton. Served War of 1939–45, in Grenadier Guards. Governor, St George's Hosp., 1958–73. Treasurer, Boy Scouts' Assoc., 1953–64; Vice-Pres., Corporation of the Church House, 1954–81. Sheriff of Greater London, 1968. *Address:* Flat A, 51 Eaton Square, SW1W 9BE. *T:* 0171–235 2164. *Clubs:* Boodle's, Beefsteak, Pratt's.

EGERTON, Sir Stephen (Loftus), KCMG 1988 (CMG 1978); HM Diplomatic Service, retired; Consultant, Enterprise Oil plc, since 1992; Director, St Andrew's Trust, Lambeth Palace, since 1994; *b* 21 July 1932; *o s* of late William le Belward Egerton, ICS, and late Angela Doreen Loftus Bland; *m* 1958, Caroline, *er d* of Major and late Mrs E. T. E. Cary-Elwes, Laurel House, Bergh Apton, Norfolk; one *s* one *d*. *Educ:* Summer Fields; Eton; Trinity Coll., Cambridge. BA 1956, MA 1960. 2nd Lieut, 60th Rifles (KRRC), 1952–53. Entered Foreign Service, 1956; Middle East Centre for Arab Studies, Lebanon, 1956–57; Political Officer and Court Registrar, Kuwait, 1958–61; Private Sec. to Parliamentary Under-Secretary, FO, 1961–62; Northern Dept, FO, 1962–63; Oriental Sec. and later also Head of Chancery, Baghdad, 1963–67; First Sec., UK Mission to the UN, New York, 1967–70; Asst Head of Arabian and Near Eastern Depts, FCO, 1970–72; Counsellor and Head of Chancery, Tripoli, 1972–73; Head of Energy Dept, FCO, 1973–77; Consul-Gen., Rio de Janeiro, 1977–80; Ambassador to Iraq, 1980–82; Asst Under-Sec. of State, FCO, 1982–85; Ambassador: to Saudi Arabia, 1986–89; to Italy, 1989–92; (non-resident) to Republic of Albania, May–July 1992. Pres., Soc. for Libyan Studies, 1994–; Vice-Pres., British Sch. of Archaeology in Iraq, 1994; Mem. Council, Keats-Shelley Meml House, Rome, 1992–. Order of King Feisal bin Abdul Aziz, 1st class, 1987; Grand Cross of the Italian Republic, 1990. *Recreations:* topiary, argument. *Address:* c/o Barclays Bank, 8 High Street, Eton, Windsor SL4 6AU. *Clubs:* Brooks's; Greenjackets, Eton Ramblers.

EGGAR, Rt Hon. Timothy (John Crommelin), (Tim); PC 1995; MP (C) Enfield North, since 1979; Minister of State, Department of Trade and Industry (Minister for Energy, since 1992, also for Industry, since 1994); *b* 19 Dec. 1951; *s* of late John Drennan Eggar and of Pamela Rosemary Eggar; *m* 1977, Charmian Diana Minoprio; one *s* one *d*. *Educ:* Winchester Coll.; Magdalene Coll., Cambridge (MA). Called to the Bar, Inner Temple, 1976. European Banking Co., 1975–83; Dir, Charterhouse Petroleum, 1984–85. Chm., Cambridge Univ. Cons. Assoc., 1972; Vice-Chm., Fedn of Cons. Students, 1973–74. PPS to Minister for Overseas Develt, 1982–85; Parly Under-Sec. of State, FCO, 1985–89; Minister of State: Dept of Employment, 1989–90; DES, 1990–92. *Recreations:* ski-ing, village cricket, simple gardening. *Address:* House of Commons, SW1A 0AA. *Clubs:* Bush Hill Park Conservative, Enfield Highway Conservative, Ponders End Conservative, North Enfield Conservative, Enfield Town Conservative.

EGGINGTON, Dr William Robert Owen; Medical Adviser, Benefits Agency, since 1994; *b* 24 Feb. 1932; *s* of Alfred Thomas Eggington and Phyllis Eggington (*née* Wynne); *m* 1961, Patricia Mary Elizabeth, *d* of Henry David and Elizabeth Grant; one *s* one *d*. *Educ:* Kingswood School, Bath; Guy's Hosp. MB, BS 1955, DTM&H 1960, DPH 1962, DIH 1963; MFCM 1970. House Surgeon, Guy's Hosp., 1955; House Physician, St John's Hosp., Lewisham, 1956. RAMC, 1957–73, retired as Lt-Col, Senior Specialist Army Health. DHSS, later DSS, 1973–92; Chief Med. Advr (Social Security), DHSS, later Chief Med. Advr, DSS, 1986–92. *Recreations:* Goss heraldic china, military history, football spectator. *Address:* 65 Frobisher Drive, Lytham St Annes, Lancs FY8 2RG.

EGGINTON, Anthony Joseph, CBE 1991; consultant; Visiting Professor, University College London, since 1991; *b* 18 July 1930; *s* of Arthur Reginald Egginton and Margaret Anne (*née* Emslie); *m* 1957, Janet Leta, *d* of late Albert and Florence Herring; two *d*. *Educ:* Selhurst Grammar Sch., Croydon; University Coll., London (BSc 1951; Fellow, 1992). Res. Assoc., UCL, 1951–56; AERE Harwell (Gen. Physics Div.), 1956–61; Head of Beams Physics Gp, NIRNS Rutherford High Energy Lab., 1961–65; DCSO and Head of Machine Gp, SRC Daresbury Nuclear Physics Lab., 1965–72; Head of Engrg Div., 1972–74, Under Sec. and Dir of Engineering and Nuclear Physics, 1974–78, Dir of Science and Engrg Divs, 1978–83, SRC; Science and Engineering Research Council: Dir of Engrg, 1983–88; Dir Progs, and Dep. Chm., 1988–91. Head, UK Delegn, 1978–83, Chm., 1982–83, Steering Cttee, Inst. Laue-Langevin, Grenoble. *Publications:* papers and articles in jls and conf. proceedings on particle accelerators and beams. *Recreations:* sport, cinema, music. *Address:* Witney House, West End, Witney, Oxon OX8 6NQ. *T:* Witney (01993) 703502. *Club:* Lansdowne.

EGGLESTON, Anthony Francis, OBE 1968; Headmaster, Campion School, Athens, 1983–88, retired; *b* 26 Jan. 1928; *s* of late J. F. Eggleston and late Mrs J. M. Barnard, Harrow, Middx; *m* 1957, Jane Morison Buxton, JP, *d* of late W. L. Buxton, MBE and late Mrs F. M. M. Buxton, Stanmore, Middx; one *s* two *d*. *Educ:* Merchant Taylors' Sch., Northwood (Schol.); St John's Coll., Oxford (Sir Thomas White Schol.). BA 1949, MA 1953; 2nd cl. hons Chemistry. National Service, 1950–52; 2nd Lieut, RA, Suez Canal Zone. Asst Master, Cheltenham Coll., 1952–54; Sen. Science Master, English High Sch., Istanbul, 1954–56; Asst Master, Merchant Taylors' Sch., Northwood, 1956–62; Principal, English Sch., Nicosia, 1962–68; Headmaster, Felsted Sch., 1968–82. *Recreation:* looking at and lecturing about buildings of all periods. *Address:* Garden House, Chester Place, Norwich NR2 3DG. *T:* Norwich (01603) 616025.

EGGLESTON, Prof. Harold Gordon; Professor Emeritus of Mathematics, London University; *b* 27 Nov. 1921; 2nd *s* of H. T. and E. M. Eggleston, Bents Green, Sheffield; *m* 1955, Elizabeth, *o d* of F. R. and C. A. W. Daglish, Beamish, County Durham; two *s* one *d*. *Educ:* High Storrs Grammar Sch., Sheffield; Trinity Coll., Cambridge. Lecturer and Senior Lecturer, University Coll. of Swansea, 1948–53; Lecturer, University of Cambridge, 1953–58; Prof. of Mathematics, University of London at Bedford Coll., 1958–66, at Royal Holloway Coll., 1966–81. *Publications:* Problems in Euclidean Space, 1957; Convexity, 1958; Elementary Real Analysis, 1962. *Address:* 22 Windsor Square, Exmouth, Devon EX8 1JY.

EGGLESTON, Prof. James Frederick; Professor of Education, University of Nottingham, 1972–84, now Emeritus; *b* 30 July 1927; *s* of Frederick James and Anne Margaret Eggleston; *m* 1956, Margaret Snowden; three *s* two *d*. *Educ:* Appleby Grammar Sch.; Durham Univ. (King's Coll., Newcastle upon Tyne). BSc Hons Zoology; DipEd; FIBiol 1975. School teacher, 1953–64, Head of Biol., later Head of Sci., Hinckley Grammar Sch.; Res. Fellow, Res. Unit for Assessment and Curriculum Studies, Leicester Univ. Sch. of Educn, 1964; team leader, later consultant, Nuffield Sci. Teaching Project, 1964–68; Lectr in Educn, Leicester Univ. Sch. of Educn, 1966; apptd to Colls and Curriculum Chair of Educn, Nottingham Univ., 1973, Dean of Educn, 1975–81. *Publications:* A Critical Review of Assessment Procedures in Secondary School Science, 1965; Problems in Quantitative Biology, 1968; (with J. F. Kerr) Studies in Assessment, 1970; (jtly) A Science Teaching Observation Schedule, 1975; (jtly) Processes and Products of Science Teaching, 1976; contributions to: The Disciplines of the Curriculum, 1971; The Art of the Science Teacher, 1974; Frontiers of Classroom Research, 1975; Techniques and Problems of Assessment, 1976; (with Trevor Kerry) Topic Work in the Primary School, 1988; articles in professional jls. *Recreations:* fell walking, golf, photography. *Address:* The Old Chapel, Church Street, Fritchley, Derbys DE56 2FQ.

EGGLESTON, Prof. (Samuel) John, BScEcon, MA, DLitt; Professor, since 1985, and Chairman, 1985–91, Department of Education, University of Warwick; *b* 11 Nov. 1926; *s* of Edmund and Josephine Eggleston, Dorchester. *Educ:* Chippenham Grammar Sch.; LSE (BScEcon 1957); Univ. of London Inst. of Educn (MA 1965). DLitt Univ. of Keele, 1977. Teacher, Suffolk and Worcs, 1950–54; Leverhulme Scholarship, LSE, 1954–57; Teacher, Beds, and Headteacher, Oxfordshire, 1957–60; Lectr, Loughborough Coll. of Educn, 1960–63; Lectr, later Sen. Lectr, Leicester Univ., 1963–67; Keele University: Prof. and Head of Dept of Educn, 1967–84; Chm., Bd of Soc. Scis, 1976–79; Chm., Higher Degree and Res. Cttee, 1981–84. Vis. Commonwealth Fellow, Canada, 1973–74; Leverhulme Fellow, 1994–; Vis. Res. Prof., Univ. of Central England, 1994–. Director: DES Res. Project, Structure and Function of Youth Service, 1968–74; Schs Council Project, Design and Craft Educn, 1968–74; DES Research Projects: Training for Multi-Racial Educn, 1978–80; Minority Gp Adolescence, 1981–84. Chairman: Council of Europe Workshop on Multi-Cultural Higher Educn, 1981–86; Education Cttee, Central Television, 1987–; Technol. Exams Cttee, RSA, 1993–; Trustees and Judges, Young Electronic Designer Awards, 1988–; Vice-Chm., Design & Technology Assoc., 1992–; Member: Council of Europe Working Party, Diversif. of Tertiary Educn, 1972–78; Cheshire Educn Cttee, 1981–83; Council, Eur. Inst. of Educn and Social Policy, 1983–93; Educnl Res. Bd, SSRC, 1973–77; Panel on Public Disorder and Sporting Events, SSRC, 1976–77; Assessment of Performance Unit, DES, Consultative Cttee, 1980–88; Res. Consultancy Cttee, DES, 1981–83; Arts Council Cttee on Trng for the Arts, 1982–87; Academic Adv. Cttee, EEC Erasmus Project, 1990–92. Hon. FEICDT 1987; Hon. FCP. Editor: Design and Technology Teaching (formerly Studies in Design Education and Craft), 1968–; Sociological Rev., 1982– (Chm., Editorial Bd, 1970–82); Chm., Editorial Bd, European Jl of Educn (formerly Paedagogica Europaea), 1976– (Editor in Chief, 1968–76); Founding Chm., Editorial Bd, Multicultural Teaching, 1982–. Hon. FCollH 1968. DUniv Middlesex, 1994. *Publications:* The Social Context of the School, 1967; (with G. N. Brown) Towards an Education for the 21st Century, 1969; (ed with A. R. Pemberton) International Perspectives of Design Education, 1973; (ed) Contemporary Research in the Sociology of Education, 1974; Adolescence and Community, 1976; New Developments in Design Education, 1976; The Sociology of the School Curriculum, 1977; The Ecology of the School, 1977; (ed) Experimental Education in Europe, 1978; Teacher Decision Making in the Classroom, 1979; School Based Curriculum Development, 1980; Work Experience in Secondary Schools, 1982; Education for Some, 1986; The Challenge for Teachers, 1992; Teaching Design & Technology, 1992; (ed) Re-education for Employment, 1992; articles in books and jls, incl. Sociol., Brit. Jl of Sociol., New Soc., Educnl Res. *Recreations:* work in design and craft, skiing, riding, travel, gardening. *Address:* Institute of Education, University of Warwick, Coventry CV4 7AL. *T:* Coventry (01203) 524104.

EGGLETON, Anthony, AO 1991; CVO 1970; Federal Director, Liberal Party of Australia, 1975–90; Secretary-General, CARE International, since 1991; *b* 30 April 1932; *s* of Tom and Winifred Eggleton; *m* 1953, Mary Walker, Melbourne; two *s* one *d*. *Educ:* King Alfred's Sch., Wantage. Journalist, Westminster Press Group, 1948–50; Editorial Staff, Bendigo Advertiser, Vic, 1950–51; Australian Broadcasting Commn, 1951–60 (Dir of ABC-TV News Coverage, 1956–60); Dir of Public Relations, Royal Australian Navy, 1960–65; Press Sec. to Prime Ministers of Australia, 1965–71 (Prime Ministers Menzies, Holt, Gorton, McMahon); Commonwealth Dir of Information, London, 1971–74; Special Advr to Leader of Opposition, and Dir of Communications, Federal Liberal Party, 1974–75; Campaign Dir, Federal Elections, 1975, 1977, 1980, 1983, 1984, 1987, 1990. Exec. Sec., Pacific Democrat Union, 1982–84, 1985–87, Dep. Chm., 1987–90. Australian Public Relations Inst.'s 1st Award of Honour, 1968; Outstanding Service Award, Liberal Party of Australia, 1990. *Address:* PO Box 648, Civic Square, ACT 2608, Australia; Boulevard du Regent 58, B-1000 Brussels, Belgium. *Clubs:* (Foundn Pres.) National Press (Canberra), Commonwealth (Canberra).

EGILSSON, Ólafur; Ambassador of Iceland to Denmark, since 1994, and concurrently to Japan, since 1990, also to Italy, Israel, Lithuania and Turkey; *b* 20 Aug. 1936; *s* of Egill Kristjánsson and Anna Margrjet Thuríður Ólafsdóttir Briem; *m* 1960, Ragna Sverrisdóttir Ragnars; one *s* one *d*. *Educ:* Commercial College, Iceland (grad. 1956); Univ. of Iceland, Faculty of Law (grad. 1963). Reporter on Vísir, 1956–58, Morgunblaðið, 1959–62; publishing Exec., Almenna bókafélagið, 1963–64; Head, NATO Regional Inf. Office, Iceland, 1964–66, and Gen. Sec., Icelandic Assoc. for Western Co-operation and Atlantic Assoc. of Young Political Leaders of Iceland; Icelandic Foreign Service, 1966; Foreign Ministry, 1966–69; First Sec., later Counsellor, Icelandic Embassy, Paris, and Dep. Perm. Rep. to OECD, UNESCO, 1969–71, and Council of Europe, Strasbourg, 1969–70; Dep. Perm. Rep., N Atlantic Council and Dep. Head, Icelandic Delegn to EEC, Brussels, 1971–74; Counsellor, later Minister Counsellor, Political Div., Min. of Foreign Affairs, 1974–80; Chief of Protocol, with rank of Ambassador, 1980–83; Acting Principal Private Sec. to President of Iceland, Oct. 1981–June 1982; Dep. Perm. Under Sec. and Dir Gen. for Political Affairs, Min. of Foreign Affairs, 1983–87; Ambassador to UK, 1986–89, and concurrently to the Netherlands, Ireland and Nigeria; Ambassador to USSR, later Russia, 1990–94, and concurrently to Bulgaria, Mongolia and Romania; also to Georgia and Ukraine, 1992–94. Chm., Governing Bd, Icelandic Internat. Develt Agency, 1982–87; Sec., Commn revising Foreign Service Act, 1968–69. President: Nat. Youth Council of Iceland, 1963–64; Acad. Assoc. of Reykjavík, 1967–68; Exec. Mem., Bible Soc., 1977–87, History Soc., 1982–88. Commander, Icelandic Order of the Falcon, 1981; holds numerous foreign orders. *Publications:* (jtly) Iceland and Jan Mayen, 1980; (ed) Bjarni Benediktsson: Contemporaries' views, 1983; (jtly) NATO's Anxious Birth: the prophetic vision of the 1940's, 1985. *Recreations:* walking, ski-ing, music (opera), history. *Address:* Krathusvej 32, 2920 Charlottenlund, Denmark. *T:* 33159604, *Fax:* 33930506.

EGLINGTON, Charles Richard John; Director, since 1986, Vice-Chairman, since 1990, S. G. Warburg Securities; *b* 12 Aug. 1938; *s* of Richard Eglington and Treena Margaret Joyce Eglington. *Educ:* Sherborne. Dir, Akroyd & Smithers, 1978–86. Mem. Council, Stock Exchange, 1975–86, Dep. Chm., 1981–84 (Chairman: Quotations Cttee, 1978–81; Property and Finance Cttee, 1983–86); Mem., Gp of Thirty Working Cttee on Clearance and Settlement Systems, 1988–89. Governor: Sherborne Sch., 1980–; Twyford Sch., 1984–. *Recreations:* golf, cricket. *Address:* S.G. Warburg Securities, 1 Finsbury Avenue, EC2M 2PA. *T:* 0171–606 1066. *Clubs:* MCC; Royal and Ancient Golf (St Andrews); Walton Heath Golf; Rye Golf.

EGLINTON and WINTON, 18th Earl of, *cr* 1507; **Archibald George Montgomerie;** Lord Montgomerie, 1448; Baron Seton and Tranent, 1859; Baron Kilwinning, 1615; Baron Ardrossan (UK), 1806; Earl of Winton (UK), 1859; Hereditary Sheriff of Renfrewshire; Chairman, Edinburgh Investment Trust plc, since 1994; *b* 27 Aug. 1939; *s* of 17th Earl of Eglinton and Winton and Ursula (*d* 1987), *er d* of Hon. Ronald Watson, Edinburgh; *S* father, 1966; *m* 1964, Marion Carolina, *o d* of John Dunn-Yarker; four *s*. *Educ:* Eton. Man. Dir, Gerrard & National Hldgs, 1972–92 (Dep. Chm., 1980–92); Chm., Gerrard Vivian Gray Ltd, 1992–94. Asst Grand Master, United Grand Lodge of England, 1989–. *Heir: s* Lord Montgomerie, *qv*. *Address:* Balhomie, Cargill, Perth PH2 6DS.

EGLINTON, Prof. Geoffrey, PhD, DSc; FRS 1976; Professor of Organic Geochemistry, University of Bristol, 1973–93, now Emeritus; Adjunct Scientist, Woods Hole Oceanographic Institution, Massachusetts, since 1991; *b* 1 Nov. 1927; *s* of Alfred Edward Eglinton and Lilian Blackham; *m* 1955, Pamela Joan Coupland; two *s* (one *d*. decd). *Educ:* Sale Grammar Sch.; Manchester Univ. (BSc, PhD, DSc). Post-Doctoral Fellow, Ohio State Univ., 1951–52; ICI Fellow, Liverpool Univ., 1952–54; Lectr, subseq. Sen. Lectr and Reader, Glasgow Univ., 1954–67; Sen. Lectr, subseq. Reader, Bristol Univ., 1967–73. Mem., NERC, 1984–90. Hon. Fellow, Plymouth Polytechnic, 1981. Gold Medal for Exceptional Scientific Achievement, NASA, 1973; Hugo Müller Silver Medal, Chemical Soc., 1974; Alfred Treibs Gold Medal, Geochem. Soc., 1981; Coke Medal, Geol Soc. of London, 1985. *Publications:* Applications of Spectroscopy to Organic Chemistry, 1965; Organic Geochemistry: methods and results, 1969; 'Chemsyn', 1972, 2nd edn 1975; contrib. Nature, Geochim. Cosmochim. Acta, Phytochem., Chem. Geol., Sci. American. *Recreations:* gardening, walking, sailing. *Address:* Oldwell, 7 Redhouse Lane, Bristol BS9 3RY. *T:* Bristol (0117) 968 3833. *Club:* Rucksack (Manchester).

EGMONT, 11th Earl of, *cr* 1733; **Frederick George Moore Perceval;** Bt 1661; Baron Perceval, 1715; Viscount Perceval, 1722; Baron Lovell and Holland (Great Britain), 1762; Baron Arden, 1770; Baron Arden (United Kingdom), 1802; *b* 14 April 1914; *o s* of 10th Earl and Cecilia (*d* 1916), *d* of James Burns Moore, Montreal; *S* father, 1932; *m* 1932, Ann Geraldine, *d* of D. G. Moodie; one *s* one *d* (and two *s* decd). *Heir: s* Viscount Perceval, *qv*. *Address:* Two-dot Ranch, Nanton, Alberta, Canada.

EGREMONT, 2nd Baron *cr* 1963, **AND LECONFIELD,** 7th Baron *cr* 1859; **John Max Henry Scawen Wyndham,** DL; *b* 21 April 1948; *s* of John Edward Reginald Wyndham, MBE, 1st Baron Egremont and 6th Baron Leconfield, and of Pamela, *d* of late Captain the Hon. Valentine Wyndham-Quin, RN; *S* father, 1972; *m* 1978, Caroline, *er d* of A. R. Nelson, Muckairn, Taynuilt, Argyll, and Hon. Lady Musker; one *s* three *d*. *Educ:* Eton; Christ Church, Oxford (MA Modern History). Mem., Royal Commn on Historical MSS, 1989–. Chm., Friends of the Nat. Libraries, 1985–; Trustee: Wallace Collection, 1988–; British Museum, 1990–; Nat. Manuscripts Conservation Trust, 1995–. Pres., ACRE, 1993–. DL W Sussex, 1988. *Publications:* (as Max Egremont) The Cousins, 1977 (Yorkshire Post First Book Award); Balfour: a life of Arthur James Balfour, 1980; *novels:* The Ladies' Man, 1983; Dear Shadows, 1986; Painted Lives, 1989; Second Spring, 1993. *Heir: s* Hon. George Ronan Valentine Wyndham, *b* 31 July 1983. *Address:* Petworth House, Petworth, West Sussex GU28 0AE. *T:* Petworth (01798) 342447.

EHRMAN, John Patrick William, FBA 1970; historian; *b* 17 March 1920; *o s* of late Albert and Rina Ehrman; *m* 1948, Elizabeth Susan Anne, *d* of late Vice-Adm. Sir Geoffrey Blake, KCB, DSO; four *s*. *Educ:* Charterhouse; Trinity Coll., Cambridge (MA). Served Royal Navy, 1940–45. Fellow of Trinity Coll., Cambridge, 1947–52; Historian, Cabinet Office, 1948–56; Lees Knowles Lectr, Cambridge, 1957–58; James Ford Special Lectr, Oxford, 1976–77. Hon. Treas., Friends of the National Libraries, 1960–77; Trustee of the Nat. Portrait Gall., 1971–85; Member: Reviewing Cttee on Export of Works of Art, 1970–76; Royal Commn on Historical Manuscripts, 1973–94; Chairman: Adv. Cttee to British Library Reference Div., 1975–84; Nat. Manuscripts Conservation Trust, 1989–94; Vice-Pres., Navy Records Soc., 1968–70, 1974–76. FSA 1958; FRHistS. *Publications:* The Navy in the War of William III, 1953; Grand Strategy, 1943–5 (2 vols, UK Official Military Histories of the Second World War), 1956; Cabinet Government and War, 1890–1940, 1958; The British Government and Commercial Negotiations with Europe, 1783–1793, 1962; The Younger Pitt, vol. 1, The Years of Acclaim, 1969, vol. 2, The Reluctant Transition, 1983. *Address:* The Mead Barns, Taynton, near Burford, Oxfordshire OX18 4UH. *Clubs:* Army and Navy, Beefsteak, Garrick.
See also W. G. Ehrman.

EHRMAN, William Geoffrey; HM Diplomatic Service; UK Member, Bosnia Contact Group, since 1994; *b* 28 Aug. 1950; *s* of J. P. W. Ehrman, *qv* and Susan (*née* Blake); *m* 1977, Penelope Anne, *d* of late Brig. H. W. Le Patourel, VC and of Babette Le Patourel; one *s* three *d*. *Educ:* Eton; Trinity Coll., Cambridge (MA). Joined Diplomatic Service, 1973; language student, Hong Kong, 1975–76; Third/Second Sec., Peking, 1976–78; First Secretary: UK Mission to UN, NY, 1979–83; Peking, 1983–84; FCO, 1985–89; Pol Advr, Hong Kong, 1989–93; Head, Near East and N Africa Dept, FCO, 1993–94. *Recreations:* sailing, walking, ski-ing. *Address:* c/o Foreign and Commonwealth Office, SW1A 2AH. *Club:* Royal Cruising.

EICHELBAUM, Rt. Hon. Sir (Johann) Thomas, GBE 1989; PC 1989; Chief Justice of New Zealand, since 1989; *b* 17 May 1931; *s* of Dr Walter and Frida Eichelbaum; *m* 1956, Vida Beryl Franz; three *s*. *Educ:* Hutt Valley High School; Victoria University College (LLB). Partner, Chapman Tripp & Co., Wellington, 1958–78; QC 1978; Judge of High Court of NZ, 1982–88. Pres., NZ Law Soc., 1980–82. *Publication:* (Editor in Chief) Mauet's Fundamentals of Trial Techniques, NZ edn, 1989. *Recreations:* reading, music, tennis, beachcombing. *Address:* 17 Cheviot Road, Lowry Bay, Eastbourne, New Zealand. *T:* (4) 5685200; Chief Justice's Chambers, High Court, PO Box 1091, Wellington, New Zealand. *Clubs:* Wellington (Wellington); Northern (Auckland).

EIGEN, Manfred; Director at Max-Planck-Institut für biophysikalische Chemie, Göttingen, since 1964; *b* 9 May 1927; *s* of Ernst and Hedwig Eigen; *m* 1952, Elfriede Müller; one *s* one *d*. *Educ:* Göttingen Univ. Dr rer. nat. (Phys. Chem.) 1951. Research Asst, Inst. für physikal. Chemie, Göttingen Univ., 1951–53; Asst, Max-Planck-Institut für physikal. Chemie, 1953; Research Fellow, Max-Planck-Gesellschaft, 1958; Head of separate dept of biochemical kinetics, Max-Planck-Inst., 1962. Andrew D. White Prof. at Large, Cornell Univ., 1965; Hon. Prof., Technische Hochschule Braunschweig, 1965. For. Hon. Mem., Amer. Acad. of Arts and Sciences, 1964; Mem. Leopoldina, Deutsche Akad. der Naturforscher, Halle, 1964; Mem., Akad. der Wissenschaften, Göttingen, 1965; Hon. Mem., Amer. Assoc. Biol Chemists, 1966; For. Assoc., Nat. Acad. of Scis, Washington, 1966; For. Mem., Royal Soc., 1973. Dr of Science *hc*, Washington, Harvard and Chicago Univs, 1966. Has won prizes, medals and awards including Nobel Prize for Chemistry (jointly), 1967. *Publications:* numerous papers in Z. Elektrochem., Jl Phys. Chem., Trans Faraday Soc., Proc. Royal Soc., Canad. Jl Chem., ICSU Rev., and other learned jls. *Address:* Max-Planck-Institut für biophysikalische Chemie, Karl-Friedrich Bonhoeffer Institut, Postfach 2841, 37018 Göttingen-Nikolausberg, Germany.

EILLEDGE, Elwyn Owen Morris, FCA; Senior Partner, Ernst & Young, Chartered Accountants, 1989–95; Joint Chairman, Ernst & Young International, 1989–95; *b* 20 July 1935; *s* of Owen and Mary Elizabeth Eilledge; *m* 1962, Audrey Ann Faulkner Ellis; one *s* one *d*. *Educ:* Merton College, Oxford (BA, MA). FCA 1968. Articled with Farrow, Bersey, Gain, Vincent & Co. (now Binder Hamlyn), 1959–66; Whinney Murray & Co. subseq. Ernst & Whinney, now Ernst & Young, Liberia, 1966–68; Ernst & Whinney: Audit Manager, Hamburg, 1968–71; Partner, London, 1972; Managing Partner, London office, 1983–86; Dep. Sen. Partner, 1985; Sen Partner, 1986–89; Chm., Ernst & Whinney Internat., 1988–89 and 1993–95. *Recreations:* gardening, swimming, tennis, listening to classical music. *Address:* Whitethorn House, Long Grove, Seer Green, Beaconsfield, Bucks HP9 2QH. *Club:* Brooks's.

EILON, Prof. Samuel, FEng; Senior Research Fellow and Emeritus Professor, Imperial College of Science, Technology and Medicine, University of London, since 1989; Member, Monopolies and Mergers Commission, since 1990; industrial consultant on corporate performance and strategy; *b* 13 Oct. 1923; *s* of Abraham and Rachel Eilon; *m* 1946, Hannah Ruth (*née* Samuel); two *s* two *d*. *Educ:* Reali Sch., Haifa; Technion, Israel Inst. of Technology, Haifa; Imperial Coll., London. PhD London, 1955; DSc(Eng) London, 1963. Founder FEng, FIMechE, FIEE. Engr, Palestine Electric Co. Ltd, Haifa, 1946–48; Officer, Israel Defence Forces, 1948–52; CO of an Ordnance and workshop base depot (Major); Res. Asst, Imperial Coll., 1952–55; Lectr in Production Engrg, Imperial Coll., 1955–57; Associate Prof. in Industrial Engrg, Technion, Haifa, 1957–59; Imperial College: Head of Section, 1955–57; Reader, 1959–63; Head of Dept, 1959–87; Prof. of Management Sci., 1963–89. Consultant and Lectr, European Productivity Agency, Paris, 1960–62. Professorial Research Fellow, Case Western Reserve Univ., Cleveland, Ohio, 1967–68. Vis. Fellow, University Coll., Cambridge, 1970–71. Past Mem. of several cttees of IProdE and DES. Member: Council, Operational Res. Soc., 1965–67; Council, Inst. of Management Scis, 1970–72, 1980–82; Exec. Cttee, British Acad. of Management, 1985–89. Adviser, P-E Consulting Gp, 1961–71; Principal and Dir, Spencer Stuart and Associates, 1971–74; Director: Amey Roadstone Corp., subseq. ARC, 1974–88; Campari Internat., 1978–80. Chief Editor, OMEGA, Internat. Jl of Management Science, 1972–94; Deptl Editor, Management Science, 1969–77. CBIM; Hon. FCGI 1978. Two Joseph Whitworth Prizes for papers, IMechE, 1960; Silver Medal, ORS, 1982. *Publications:* Elements of Production Planning and Control, 1962; Industrial Engineering Tables, 1962; (jtly) Exercises in Industrial Management, 1966; (jtly) Industrial Scheduling Abstracts, 1967; (jtly) Inventory Control Abstracts, 1968; (jtly) Distribution Management, 1971; Management Control, 1971, 2nd edn 1979; (jtly) Applications of Management Science in Banking and Finance, 1972; (jtly) Applied Productivity Analysis for Industry, 1976; Aspects of Management, 1977, 2nd edn 1979; The Art of Reckoning: analysis of performance criteria, 1984; Management Assertions and Aversions, 1985; (jtly) The Global Challenge of Innovation, 1991; Management Practice and Mispractice, 1992; some 300 papers and articles in the field of management. *Recreations:* theatre, tennis, walking. *Address:* Mechanical Engineering Building, Imperial College, Exhibition Road, SW7 2BX. *T:* 0181–458 6650.

EKLUND, Dr (Arne) Sigvard; Director General (now Emeritus), International Atomic Energy Agency, Vienna, 1961–81; *b* Kiruna, Sweden, 1911; *m* 1941, Anna-Greta Johansson; one *s* two *d*. *Educ:* Uppsala Univ., Sweden (DSc). Assoc. Prof. in Nuclear Physics, Royal Inst. of Technology, Stockholm, 1946–56; Dir of Research, later Reactor development Div., AB Atomenergi, 1950–61. Conference Sec.-Gen., 2nd Internat. UN Conf. on Peaceful Uses of Atomic Energy, 1958. Fellow, Amer. Nuclear Soc., 1961 (Hon. Life Mem., 1992); Member: Royal Swedish Acad. of Engineering Sciences, 1953; Royal Swedish Acad. of Sciences, 1972; Hon. Member: British Nuclear Energy Soc., 1963; European Nuclear Soc., 1982; Assoc. for Nuclear Technique, Stockholm, 1992; For. Associate, Nat. Acad. of Engineering, USA, 1979. Dr *hc*: Univ. of Graz, 1968; Acad. of Mining and Metallurgy, Cracow, 1971; Univ. of Bucarest, 1971; Chalmers Inst. of Technol., Gothenberg, 1974; Buenos Aires, Budapest, Columbia and Moscow Univs, 1977; Dresden Technical and Yon-sei, Seoul Univs, 1978; Nat. Agrarian Univ. of La Molina, Peru, 1979; Royal Inst. of Technol., Stockholm, 1980. (Jointly) Atoms for Peace Award, 1968; Golden Medal of Honour, Vienna, 1971; Henry DeWolf Smyth Nuclear Statesman Award, 1976; Exceptional Service Award, Amer. Nuclear Soc., 1980; Swedish Energy Prize, 1991. Hon. Senator, Univ. of Vienna, 1977. Comdr, Order of St Gregory, bestowed by His Holiness Pope John Paul II, 1982. Kt Comdr, Order of North Star, Sweden, 1971; Das Grosse Goldene Ehrenzeichen am Bande für Verdienste, Austria, 1981; Das Grosse Verdienstkreuz mit Stern und Schulterband, FRG, 1981; Aquila Azteca en el Grado de Banda, Mexico, 1981; SPk, 1987; Grand Cordon, Order of the Sacred Treasure, Japan, 1991. *Publications:* Studies in Nuclear Physics, 1946 (Sweden); preface to Light Water Reactor Safety, by Bengt Pershagen, 1989; (contrib.) Future of Nuclear Power, ed Bo Södersten, 1991; articles on peaceful uses of nuclear energy. *Address:* Krapfenwaldgasse 48, 1190–Vienna, Austria. *T:* (1) 322424, *Fax:* (1) 328492. *Club:* Sällskapet (Stockholm).

ELAM, Caroline Mary; Editor, Burlington Magazine, since 1987; *b* 12 March 1945; *d* of John Frederick Elam and Joan Barrington Elam (*née* Lloyd). *Educ:* Colchester County High Sch.; Lady Margaret Hall, Oxford (BA); Courtauld Inst. of Art, Univ. of London. MA London and Cantab. Lectr, Fine Art Dept, Univ. of Glasgow, 1970–72; Jun. Res. Fellow, King's Coll., Cambridge, 1972–76 (Hon. Fellow, 1992); Lectr, History of Art Dept, Westfield Coll., Univ. of London, 1976–87. Fellow, Harvard Univ. Center for Renaissance Studies, Villa I Tatti, Florence, 1981–82. Member: Exec. Cttee, NACF, 1988–; Bd, Warburg Inst., 1992–; Bd, Courtauld Inst. of Art, 1993–. Syndic, Fitzwilliam Mus., Cambridge, 1993–. *Publications:* articles in Art History, Burlington Magazine, I Tatti Studies, Mitteilungen des Kunsthistorischen Insts in Florenz, Jl of RSA, etc. *Address:* Burlington Magazine, 14 Dukes Road, WC1H 9AD. *T:* 0171–388 1228.
See also J. N. Elam.

ELAM, (John) Nicholas, CMG 1994; HM Diplomatic Service; Ambassador to Luxembourg, since 1994; *b* 2 July 1939; *s* of John Frederick Elam, OBE and Joan Barrington Elam (*née* Lloyd); *m* 1967, Florence Helen, *d* of P. Lentz; two *s* one *d*. *Educ:* Colchester Royal Grammar Sch.; New Coll., Oxford (schol.). Frank Knox Fellow, Harvard Univ., 1961–62. Entered HM Diplomatic Service, 1962; FO, 1962–64; Pretoria and Cape Town, 1964–68; Treasury Centre for Admin. Studies, 1968–69; FCO, 1969–71; First Sec., Bahrain, 1971; Commercial Sec., Brussels, 1972–76; FCO, 1976–79, Dep. Head of News Dept, 1978–79; Counsellor and Dep. British Govt Rep., Salisbury, 1979; Dep. High Comr, Salisbury (later Harare), 1980–83; Consul-General, Montreal, 1984–87; Hd of Cultural Relations Dept, FCO, 1987–94. Chm., Cultural Co-operation Council,

Council of Europe, 1993–94. Mem., British Council, 1994. *Recreations:* travel, the arts. *Address:* c/o Foreign and Commonwealth Office, SW1A 2AH.
See also C. M. Elam.

ELAND, Michael John; Commissioner, HM Customs and Excise, since 1992; *b* 26 Sept. 1952; *s* of George Eland and Betty Eland (*née* Middleton-Walker); *m* 1981, Luned Rhiannon Wynn Jones; one *s* one *d*. *Educ:* Worksop Coll.; Trinity Coll., Oxford (BA Jurisp, MA). Called to the Bar, Middle Temple, 1975. Administration Trainee, HM Customs and Excise, 1975; Private Sec. to Chm., 1979–81; Cabinet Office, 1982–87; Private Sec. to Lord President of the Council (Viscount Whitelaw), 1987–88; Asst. Sec., HM Customs and Excise, 1988–92. *Recreations:* walking, theatre. *Address:* HM Customs and Excise, New King's Beam House, Upper Ground, SE1 9PJ. *T:* 0171–865 5087.

ELCOAT, Rev. Canon George Alastair; Vicar of Tweedmouth, Berwick-upon-Tweed, 1987–91 (Priest-in-charge, 1981–87); Chaplain to The Queen, 1982–92; Rural Dean of Norham, 1982–91; *b* 4 June 1922; *s* of George Thomas Elcoat and Hilda Gertrude Elcoat. *Educ:* Tynemouth School; Queen's College, Birmingham. Served RAF, 1941–46. Asst Master, Newcastle Cathedral Choir School, 1947–48. Deacon 1951, priest 1952; Asst Curate, Corbridge, 1951–55; Vicar: Spittal, 1955–62; Chatton with Chillingham, 1962–70; Sugley, 1970–81; RD, Newcastle West, 1977–81; Hon. Canon, Newcastle, 1979–91, Hon. Canon Emeritus, 1991–. *Recreations:* fell walking, photography, gardening, music. *Address:* 42 Windsor Crescent, Berwick-upon-Tweed, Northumberland TD15 1NT.

ELDER, David Renwick, MC 1940; CA; *b* 4 Jan. 1920; *s* of John Kidd Elder and Mary Kinnear Swanley; *m* 1947, Kathleen Frances Duncan; two *s* two *d*. *Educ:* Dundee High School. Served 1939–46, The Black Watch (RHR) and Sea Reconnaissance Unit (Major). Royal Dutch Shell Group, 1948–71; Ocean Transport & Trading Ltd, 1971–80 (Dep. Chm., 1975–80; Chm., Ocean Inchcape, 1974–80); Director: Letraset International Ltd, 1975; Capital & Counties Property Ltd, 1979; Whessoe Ltd, 1980. *Recreation:* golf. *Clubs:* Wentworth Golf (Virginia Water); Panmure Golf (Carnoustie).

ELDER, Mark Philip, CBE 1989; conductor; *b* 2 June 1947; *s* of John and Helen Elder; *m* 1980, Amanda Jane Stein; one *d*. *Educ:* Bryanston Sch.; Corpus Christi Coll., Cambridge (Music Scholar, Choral Scholar; BA, MA). Music staff, Wexford Festival, 1969–70; Chorus Master and Asst Conductor, Glyndebourne, 1970–71; music staff, Covent Garden, 1970–72; Staff Conductor, Australian Opera, 1972–74; Staff Conductor, ENO, 1974, Associate Conductor, 1977, Music Dir, 1979–93; Music Dir, Rochester Philharmonic Orch., USA, 1989–94. Principal Guest Conductor: London Mozart Players, 1980–83; BBC Symphony Orchestra, 1982–85; CBSO, 1992–95. *Publication:* (with Peter Jonas and David Pountney) Power House, 1992. *Address:* c/o Ingpen and Williams Ltd, 14 Kensington Court, W8 5DN.

ELDER, Prof. Murdoch George, MD, DSc; FRCS, FRCOG; Professor of Obstetrics and Gynaecology, University of London, at Institute of Obstetrics and Gynaecology, since 1978, and Dean, Institute of Obstetrics and Gynaecology, since 1985, Royal Postgraduate Medical School; *b* 4 Jan. 1938; *s* of late Archibald James and of Lotta Annie Elder; *m* 1964, Margaret Adelaide McVicker; two *s*. *Educ:* Edinburgh Acad.; Edinburgh Univ. (MB ChB 1961, MD 1973). DSc London, 1994. FRCS 1968; FRCOG 1978. Junior posts, Edinburgh and Bristol, 1961–68; Lectr, Inst. of Obst. and Gyn. and Royal Univ. of Malta, 1968–71; Sen. Lectr and Reader, Charing Cross Hosp. Med. Sch., Univ. of London, 1971–78. Green Armytage Scholarship, RCOG, 1976; WHO Travelling Scholarship, 1977; Dir, Clinical Res. Centre, WHO, 1980–94; Mem., Steering Cttee on Contraception, WHO, 1980–86. Mem., Hammersmith and Queen Charlotte's Special Health Authy, 1982–90. Mem. Council, RPMS, 1979–. Vis. Prof., UCLA, Singapore Univ., Natal Univ., 1990. Ext Examr for DSc, PhD, Masters and MB, BS degrees of 15 univs in several countries. Silver Medal, Hellenic Obstetrical Soc., 1983. Mem., Editl Bds, Jl of Obst. and Gyn. and Clinical Reproduction, 1985–. *Publications:* Human Fertility Control, 1979; (ed) Preterm Labour, 1980; (ed) Reproduction, Obstetrics and Gynaecology, 1988; chapters in books and learned articles on steroid and prostaglandin biochemistry in reproduction, clinical obstetrics, gynaecology and contraception. *Recreations:* travel, golf. *Address:* 4 Stonehill Road, SW14 8RW. *T:* 0181–876 4332. *Clubs:* Roehampton; 1942.

ELDERFIELD, John, PhD; Chief Curator at Large, Museum of Modern Art, New York, since 1993; Adjunct Professor of Fine Arts, Institute of Fine Arts, New York University, since 1994; *b* 25 April 1943; *s* of Henry Elderfield and Rhoda May (*née* Risbrough); *m* 1st, 1965, Joyce Davey (marr. diss.); two *s*; 2nd, 1989; Jill Elizabeth Moser (marr. diss.). *Educ:* Univ. of Manchester; Univ. of Leeds (BA 1966; MPhil 1970); Univ. of London (PhD 1975). Lectr in Hist. of Art, Winchester Sch. of Art, 1966–70; Harkness Fellow, Yale Univ., 1970–72; John Simon Guggenheim Meml Fellow, 1972–73; Lectr in Hist. of Art, Univ. of Leeds, 1973–75; Museum of Modern Art, New York: Curator of Painting and Sculpture, 1975–93; Dir, Dept of Drawings, 1980–93. Editor, Studies in Modern Art, 1991–. Chevalier des Arts et Lettres (France), 1989. *Publications:* Hugo Ball: the flight out of time, 1974; The Wild Beasts: Fauvism and its affinities, 1976; European Master Paintings from Swiss Collections: Post Impressionism to World War II, 1976; The Cut-outs of Henri Matisse, 1978; Matisse in the Collection of the Museum of Modern Art, 1978; The Modern Drawing, 1983; The Drawings of Henri Matisse, 1984; Kurt Schwitters, 1985; Morris Louis, 1986; The Drawings of Richard Diebenkorn, 1988; Helen Frankenthaler, 1988; (jtly) Matisse in Morocco, 1990; Henri Matisse: a retrospective, 1992; Pleasuring Painting: Matisse's feminine representations, 1995. *Recreation:* gardening. *Address:* Museum of Modern Art, 11 West 53 Street, New York, NY 10019, USA. *T:* (212) 7089550. *Club:* Century (New York).

ELDERFIELD, Maurice; Chairman and Chief Executive, Berfield Associates Ltd, 1980–92; Chairman: Midland Industrial Leasing Ltd, 1979–90; Saga Ltd, 1979–90; Sheldon & Partners Ltd, 1981–91; *b* 10 April 1926; *s* of Henry Elderfield and Kathleen Maud Elderfield; *m* 1953, Audrey June (*née* Knight); one *s* three *d*. *Educ:* Southgate Grammar Sch. FCA. Fleet Air Arm, 1944–47. Thomson, Kingdom & Co., Chartered Accountants (qual. 1949), 1947–49; Personal Asst to Man. Dir, Forrestell, Land, Timber & Railway Co., 1949–57; Group Chief Accountant, Stephens Group, 1957–60; various posts, Segas, culminating in Board Mem. and Dir for Finance, 1960–73; Dir of Finance, Southern Water Authority, 1973–75; PO Board Mem. for Finance and Corporate Planning, 1975–76; Dir of Finance, Ferranti Ltd, 1977; Finance Mem., British Shipbuilders, 1977–80. Director: S. P. International Ltd, Hong Kong, 1987–90; PV Ltd, 1987–90. Chairman: Throgmorton Trust, 1972–84; Throgmorton Investment Management, 1981–84; Capital for Industry Ltd, 1980–84. *Recreations:* golf, tennis, squash. *Address:* Hadleigh, Keeill Pharick Park, Glen Vine, Isle of Man IM4 4EW. *Club:* Gravetye Manor Country.

ELDON, 5th Earl of, *cr* 1821; **John Joseph Nicholas Scott;** Baron Eldon 1799; Viscount Encombe 1821; *b* 24 April 1937; *s* of 4th Earl of Eldon, GCVO, and Hon. Magdalen Fraser, OBE (*d* 1969), *d* of 16th Baron Lovat; *S* father, 1976; *m* 1961, Comtesse Claudine de Montjoye-Vaufrey et de la Roche, Vienna; one *s* two *d*. *Educ:* Ampleforth; Trinity Coll., Oxford. 2nd Lieut Scots Guards (National Service). Lieut AER. *Heir:* *s* Viscount Encombe, *qv*.

ELDRIDGE, John Barron; Chairman, Matthews Wrightson Holdings Ltd, 1971–77; *b* 28 May 1919; *s* of William John Eldridge and Jessie Winifred (*née* Bowditch); *m* 1940, Marjorie Potier; one *s* two *d*. *Educ:* Lancing Coll. FIA 1950. Dir, Matthews Wrightson Holdings Ltd, 1964. Croix de Guerre 1944. *Address:* Castleton, Warwicks Bench Road, Guildford, Surrey GU1 3TL. *T:* Guildford (01483) 62687.

ELEY, Bridget Katharine C.; *see* Cracroft-Eley.

ELEY, Prof. Daniel Douglas, OBE 1961; ScD, PhD Cantab; MSc, PhD Manchester; FRS 1964; CChem, FRSC; Professor of Physical Chemistry, University of Nottingham, 1954–80, now Emeritus; Dean of Faculty of Pure Science, 1959–62; *b* 1 Oct. 1914; *s* of Daniel Eley and Fanny Allen Eley, *née* Ross; *m* 1942, Brenda May Williams, MA, MB, BChir (Cantab) (*d* 1992), 2nd *d* of Benjamin and Sarah Williams, Skewen, Glam; one *s*. *Educ:* Christ's Coll., Finchley; Manchester Univ.; St John's Coll., Cambridge. Manchester Univ.: Woodiwiss Schol. 1933, Mercer Schol. 1934, Darbishire Fellow 1936, DSIR Sen. Award 1937; PhD 1937; PhD 1940, ScD 1954, Cambridge. Bristol Univ.: Lectr in Colloid Chemistry, 1945; Reader in Biophysical Chemistry, 1951. Leverhulme Emeritus Fellow, 1981. Lectures: Reilly, Univ. of Notre Dame (USA), 1950; Royal Aust. Chem. Inst., 1967; Sir Jesse Boot Foundn, Nottingham Univ., 1955, 1981; Sir Eric Rideal, Soc. of Chem. Industry, 1975. Mem. Council of Faraday Soc., 1951–54, 1960–63; Vice-Pres., 1963–66. Corresp. Mem., Bavarian Acad. of Sciences, 1971. Meetings Sec., British Biophysical Soc., 1961–63, Hon. Sec., 1963–65, Hon. Mem., 1983. Scientific Assessor to Sub-Cttee on Coastal Pollutions, House of Commons Select Cttee on Science and Technology, 1967–68. Medal of Liège Univ., 1950. *Publications:* (ed) Adhesion, 1961; papers in Trans Faraday Soc., Proc. Royal Soc., Jl Chem. Soc., Biochem. Jl, etc. *Recreations:* hill walking, gardening, ski-ing. *Address:* Brooklands, 35 Brookland Drive, Chilwell, Nottingham NG9 4BD; Chemistry Department, Nottingham University, University Park, Nottingham NG7 2RD.

ELEY, John L.; *see* Lloyd-Eley.

ELFER, David Francis, QC 1981; a Recorder of the Crown Court, since 1978; *b* 15 July 1941; *s* of George and Joy Elfer; *m* 1968, Karin Ursula Strub; two *s*; *m* 1988, Alexandra Smith-Hughes; one *s*. *Educ:* St Bede's Coll., Manchester; Emmanuel Coll., Cambridge (MA). Called to the Bar, Inner Temple, 1964, Bencher, 1989; Western Circuit. Bar Col rep. for W Circuit, 1987–89. *Recreation:* music. *Address:* (chambers) 1 Paper Buildings, Temple, EC4Y 7EP. *T:* 0171–353 3728.

ELGIN, 11th Earl of, *cr* 1633, **AND KINCARDINE,** 15th Earl of, *cr* 1647; **Andrew Douglas Alexander Thomas Bruce,** KT 1981; CD 1981; JP; Lord Bruce of Kinloss, 1604, Lord Bruce of Torry, 1647; Baron Elgin (UK), 1849; 37th Chief of the Name of Bruce; Lord-Lieutenant of Fife, since 1987; late Scots Guards; Ensign of Royal Company of Archers, HM Body Guard for Scotland; Hon. Colonel, Elgin Regiment, Canada; *b* 17 Feb. 1924; *e s* of 10th Earl of Elgin, KT, CMG, TD and Hon. Katherine Elizabeth Cochrane (DBE 1938) (*d* 1989), *er d* of 1st Baron Cochrane of Cults; *S* father, 1968; *m* 1959, Victoria, *o d* of Dudley Usher, MBE and Mrs Usher of Larach Bhan, Kilchrennan, Argyll; three *s* two *d*. *Educ:* Eton; Balliol College, Oxford (BA Hons, MA Hons). Served War of 1939–45 (wounded). Dir, Royal Highland and Agricultural Soc., 1973–75; Pres., Scottish Amicable Life Assurance Soc., 1975–94. Chm., Nat. Savings Cttee for Scotland, 1972–78; Mem., Scottish Post Office Bd (formerly Scottish Postal Bd), 1980–. Chm., Scottish Money Management Assoc., 1981–. Lord High Comr, Gen. Assembly of Church of Scotland, 1980–81. County Cadet Commandant, Fife, 1952–65. Hon. Col, 153(H) Regt RCT(V), TAVR, 1976–86. JP 1951, DL 1955, Fife. Grand Master Mason of Scotland, 1961–65. Brigade Pres. of the Boys' Brigade, 1966–85; Pres., Royal Caledonian Curling Club, 1968–69. Hon. LLD: Dundee, 1977; Glasgow, 1983; Hon. DLitt St Mary's, Halifax, NS. Freeman: Bridgetown, Barbados; Regina; Port Elgin; Winnipeg; St Thomas, Ont; Moose Jaw. *Heir:* *s* Lord Bruce, *qv*. *Address:* Broomhall, Dunfermline KY11 3DU. *T:* Limekilns (01383) 872222. *Clubs:* Beefsteak, Caledonian, Pratt's; New (Edinburgh); Royal Scottish Automobile (Pres.) (Glasgow).
See also Hon. J. M. E. Bruce.

ELIAS, Gerard, QC 1984; a Recorder of the Crown Court, since 1984; *b* 19 Nov. 1944; *s* of Leonard Elias and Patricia Elias, JP; *m* 1970, Elisabeth Kenyon; three *s*. *Educ:* Cardiff High School; Exeter University (LLB). Barrister; called to the Bar, Inner Temple, 1968, Bencher, 1993; Wales and Chester Circuit (Circuit Treasurer, 1990–92; Leader, 1993–); Asst Comr, Boundary Commission for Wales, 1981–83, 1985–. Mem., Bar Council, 1985–89, 1993–; Dir, Bar Mutual Insurance Fund, 1987–. Governor and Mem. Council, Malvern Coll., 1988–; Dep. Chm., Glam CCC, 1993– (Mem. Exec. Cttee, 1986–93). *Recreations:* music, cricket. *Address:* 13 The Cathedral Green, Llandaff, Cardiff, South Glamorgan CF5 2EB. *T:* Cardiff (01222) 578857. *Club:* Cardiff and County.

ELIAS, Patrick; QC 1990; *b* 28 March 1947; *s* of Leonard and Patricia Mary Elias; *m* 1970, Wendy; three *s* one *d*. *Educ:* Cardiff High Sch.; Univ. of Exeter (LLB 1969); King's Coll., Cambridge (MA; PhD 1973). Called to the Bar, Inner Temple, 1973; Bencher, 1995. Fellow of Pembroke Coll., Cambridge, 1973–84; Lectr, Univ. of Cambridge, 1975–84. *Publications:* (jtly) Labour Law: cases and materials, 1979; Editor, Harvey on Industrial Relations and Employment Law, 1976; (with Keith Ewing) Trade Union Democracy, Members' Rights and the Law, 1987. *Recreations:* literature, music, sport. *Address:* 13 Madingley Road, Cambridge CB3 0EG. *T:* Cambridge (01223) 67214.

ELIASSEN, Kjell, Hon. GCMG 1981; Commander with Star, Royal Order of Saint Olav, 1982; Norwegian Ambassador to Germany, since 1994; *b* 18 Aug. 1929; *s* of Carl August Eliassen and Bergljot (*née* Store); *m* 1953, Vesla Skretting; one *s* one *d*. *Educ:* Oslo Univ. (law degree). Entered Norwegian Foreign Service 1953; served Belgrade, Moscow, London; Counsellor, Min. of Foreign Affairs, 1963–67; Moscow, 1967–70; Dep. Dir-Gen., Min. of Foreign Affairs, 1970–72; Dir-Gen., 1972–77; Ambassador to Yugoslavia, 1977–80; Perm. Under-Sec., Min. of Foreign Affairs, 1980–84; Ambassador: to USA, 1984–89; to UK, 1989–94. Numerous foreign decorations. *Address:* (office) Königlich Norwegische Botschaft, Mittelstrasse 43, 53175 Bonn, Germany; (private) Tannenallee 16, 53179 Bonn.

ELIBANK, 14th Lord *cr* 1643 (Scotland); **Alan D'Ardis Erskine-Murray;** Bt (Nova Scotia) 1628; personnel consultant; Deminex UK Oil and Gas, 1981–86; *b* 31 Dec. 1923; *s* of Robert Alan Erskine-Murray (*d* 1939) and Eileen Mary (*d* 1970), *d* of late John Percy MacManus; *S* cousin, 1973; *m* 1962, Valerie Sylvia, *d* of late Herbert William Dennis; two *s*. *Educ:* Bedford Sch.; Peterhouse, Cambridge (MA Law). Barrister-at-Law. RE, 1942–47; Cambridge Univ., 1947–49; Practising Barrister, 1949–55; Shell International Petroleum Co., 1955–80. *Recreations:* golf, tennis. *Heir:* *s* Master of Elibank, *qv*. *Address:* House of Lords, SW1A 0PW. *Club:* MCC.

ELIBANK, Master of; Hon. Robert Francis Alan Erskine-Murray; *b* 10 Oct. 1964; *s* and *heir* of 14th Lord Elibank, *qv*. *Educ:* The Grove, Harrow School; Reading Univ. (BA

(Hons) History and Politics, 1987). *Recreations:* soccer, tennis and photography. *Address:* 34 Richmond Hill Court, Richmond upon Thames, Surrey TW10 6BD.

ELION, Prof. Gertrude Belle; Research Professor of Pharmacology and Medicine, Duke University, North Carolina, since 1983; *b* 23 Jan. 1918; *d* of Robert and Bertha Elion. *Educ:* Hunter Coll., New York (AB 1937); New York Univ. (MS 1941). Lab. Asst in Biochemistry, NY Hosp. Sch. of Nursing, 1937; Res. Asst in Organic Chem., Denver Chemical Manufg Co., NY, 1938–39; teacher, secondary schs, NYC, 1940–42; Food Analyst, Quaker Maid Co., 1942–43; Res. Asst in Organic Synthesis, Johnson and Johnson, 1943–44; Wellcome Research Laboratories: Biochemist, 1944–50; Sen. Res. Chemist, 1950–55; Asst to the Associate Res. Dir, 1955–63; Asst to Res. Dir (Chemotherapy), 1963–67; Head, Dept of Experimental Therapy, 1967–83; Scientist Emeritus, 1983–. Hon. Mem., Acad. of Pharmaceutical Sciences, 1983. Member: Nat. Acad. of Scis, 1990; Inst. of Medicine, 1991; Fellow, Amer. Acad. of Arts and Scis, 1991; For. Mem., Royal Soc., 1995. DStJ 1992. Hon. DSc: George Washington, 1969; Michigan, 1983; Hunter Coll. (CUNY), New York Univ., Polytechnic Univ., Brooklyn, NC State Univ., and Ohio State Univ., 1989; Univ. of NC/Chapel Hill, Russell Sage Coll., 1990; Duke, 1991; Columbia, McMaster and SUNY at Stony Brook, 1992; Washington Coll., S Florida, Wisconsin, E Carolina, 1993; Wake Forest, 1994; Hon. DMS: Brown Univ., 1969; Utah State, 1994. Garvan Medal, Amer. Chemical Soc., 1968; President's Medal, 1970, Hall of Fame, 1973, Hunter Coll.; Distinguished NC Chemist Award, NC Inst. of Chemists, 1981; Judd Award, Sloan-Kettering Inst., 1983; (jtly) Cain Award, Amer. Assoc. for Cancer Res., 1984; NC Distinguished Chemist Award, NC Section, Amer. Chemical Soc., 1985; (jtly) Nobel Prize in Physiology or Medicine, 1988; Bertner Award, Univ. of Texas, 1989; Medal of Honor, Amer. Cancer Soc., 1990; City of Medicine Award, Durham, NC, 1990; (jtly) Discoverer's Award, Pharmaceutical Manufrs Assoc., 1990; Third Century Award, Foundn for a Creative America, 1990; Nat. Inventors Hall of Fame, 1991; Nat. Women's Hall of Fame, 1991; Nat. Medal of Science, 1991; Engrg and Sci. Hall of Fame, 1992. *Publications:* contribs to scientific jls on chemistry, pharmacology and cancer research. *Recreations:* photography, travel, music. *Address:* 1 Banbury Lane, Chapel Hill, NC 27514, USA. *T:* (919) 9674102.

ELIOT, family name of **Earl of St Germans.**

ELIOT, Lord; Jago Nicholas Aldo Eliot; *b* 24 March 1966; *s* and *heir* of Earl of St Germans, *qv*.

ELIOT, Ven. Canon Peter Charles, MBE 1945; TD 1945; Archdeacon of Worcester, 1961–75; now Archdeacon Emeritus; Residentiary Canon, Worcester Cathedral, 1965–75; now Canon Emeritus; *b* 30 Oct. 1910; *s* of late Hon. Edward Granville Eliot and late Mrs Eliot; *m* 1934, Lady Alethea Constance Dorothy Sydney Buxton, *d* of 1st and last Earl Buxton, PC, GCMG, and late Countess Buxton; no *c*. *Educ:* Wellington Coll.; Magdalene Coll., Cambridge. Commissioned in Kent Yeomanry (Lt-Col Comdg, 1949–52), 1933. Admitted Solicitor, 1934; Partner in City firm until 1953. Studied at Westcott House, Cambridge, 1953–54; made Deacon to serve in Parish of St Martin-in-the-Fields, London, 1954; Priest, 1955; Vicar of Cockermouth, 1957–61; Rural Dean of Cockermouth and Workington, 1960–61; Vicar of Cropthorne with Charlton, 1961–65. *Recreations:* amateur acting, sketching, sight-seeing, gardening. *Address:* The Old House, Kingsland, Leominster, Herefordshire HR6 9QS. *T:* Kingsland (01568) 708285. *Club:* Travellers'.

ELIOTT OF STOBS, Sir Charles (Joseph Alexander), 12th Bt *cr* 1666 (NS); *b* 9 Jan. 1937; *s* of Charles Rawdon Heathfield Eliott (*d* 1972) and Emma Elizabeth Harris; *S* cousin, 1989; *m* 1959, Wendy Judith, *d* of Henry John Bailey; one *s* four *d* (and one *s* decd). *Educ:* St Joseph's Christian Brothers' College, Rockhampton. *Heir:* *s* Rodney Gilbert Charles Eliott [*b* 15 July 1966; *m* 1988, Andrea Therese Saunders; one *d*]. *Address:* 27 Cohoe Street, Toowoomba, Queensland 4350, Australia.

ELIS-THOMAS, family name of **Baron Elis-Thomas.**

ELIS-THOMAS, Baron *cr* 1992 (Life Peer), of Nant Conwy in the County of Gwynedd; **Dafydd Elis Elis-Thomas;** President, Plaid Cymru, 1984–91; Chairman, Welsh Language Board, since 1993; *b* 18 Oct. 1946; name changed from Thomas to Elis-Thomas by deed poll, 1992; *m* 1st, 1970, Elen M. Williams (marr. diss.); three *s*; 2nd, 1993, Mair Parry Jones. *Educ:* Ysgol Dyffryn Conwy; UC North Wales. Research worker, Bd of Celtic Studies, 1970; Tutor in Welsh Studies, Coleg Harlech, 1971; Lectr, Dept of English, UC North Wales, 1974. MP (Plaid Cymru) Merioneth, Feb. 1974–1983, Meirionnydd Nant Conwy, 1983–92. Mem., Arts Council for Wales; Chm., Screen Wales. Part-time freelance broadcaster, BBC Wales, HTV, S4C and Radio Wales, 1970–73. *Recreations:* hill walking, camping. *Address:* 2 Stryd Ralant, Caernarfon, Gwynedd LL55 1EH. *Club:* Sport and Social (Trawsfynydd).

ELKAN, Prof. Walter; Professor of Economics, and Head of Economics Department, Brunel University, 1978–88, now Emeritus Professor; *b* Hamburg, 1 March 1923; *s* of Hans Septimus Elkan and Maud Emily (*née* Barden); *m* Susan Dorothea (*née* Jacobs) (marr. diss. 1982); one *s* two *d*. *Educ:* Frensham Heights; London Sch. of Economics. BSc (Econ), PhD. Army, 1942–47; Research Asst, LSE, 1950–53; Sen. Res. Fellow, E African Inst. of Social Research, 1954–58; Vis. Res. Assoc., MIT and Lectr, N Western Univ., 1958; Lectr in Econs, Makerere UC, 1958–60; Lectr in Econs, Durham Univ., 1960; Prof. of Econs, 1966–78, and rotating Head of Dept, 1968–78, Durham Univ. Vis. Res. Prof., Nairobi Univ., 1972–73. Member: Council, Overseas Develt Inst.; Econ. and Social Cttee, EEC, 1982–86; Bd of Management, Sch. of Hygiene and Trop. Med., 1982–86; Econ. and Social Cttee for Overseas Res., 1977–92; Associate, Inst. of Development Studies. Former Pres., African Studies Assoc.; former Member: Northern Economic Planning Council; REconS. Sometime consultant to Govts of Basutoland, Mauritius, Solomon Is, Fiji, Kenya and others. *Publications:* An African Labour Force, 1956; Migrants and Proletarians, 1960; Economic Development of Uganda, 1961; Introduction to Development Economics, 1973, 1995; articles mainly on contemp. African econ. history in econ. and other social science jls; ILO, UNESCO, IBRD and British Govt reports. *Recreation:* music. *Address:* 98 Boundary Road, NW8 0RH. *T:* 0171–624 5102.

ELKES, Prof. Joel, MD, ChB; FACP, FAPA; Distinguished Service Professor Emeritus, The Johns Hopkins University, since 1975; Emeritus Professor, University of Louisville; Fellow and Senior Scholar-in-Residence, Fetzer Institute, Kalamazoo; *b* 12 Nov. 1913; *s* of Dr Elchanan Elkes and Miriam (*née* Malbin); *m* 1943, Dr Charmian Bourne; one *d*; *m* 1975, Josephine Rhodes, MA. *Educ:* private schools; Lithuania and Switzerland; St Mary's Hosp., London; Univ. of Birmingham Med. Sch. (MB, ChB 1947; MD Hons 1949). MRCS, LRCP 1941. University of Birmingham: Sir Halley Stewart Research Fellow, 1942–45; Lectr, Dept of Pharmacology, 1945–48; Senior Lectr and Actg Head of Dept, 1948–50; Prof. and Chm., Dept of Experimental Psychiatry, 1951–57; Clinical Professor of Psychiatry, George Washington Univ. Med. Sch., Washington, 1957–63; Chief of Clinical Neuropharmacology Research Center, Nat. Inst of Mental Health, Washington, 1957–63; Dir, Behavioral and Clinical Studies Center St Elizabeth's Hosp., Washington, 1957–63; Henry Phipps Prof. and Dir, Dept of Psychiatry and Behavioural Scis, Johns Hopkins Univ. Sch. of Medicine, and Psychiatrist-in-Chief, Johns Hopkins Hosp., 1963–74; Samuel McLaughlin Prof.-in-residence, McMaster Univ., 1975; Professor of Psychiatry: McMaster Univ., 1976–80; Univ. of Louisville, 1980–84 (Director: Div. of Behavioral Medicine, 1982; Arts in Medicine Prog.). Dir, Foundns Fund for Research in Psychiatry, 1964–68; Consultant, WHO, 1957. Vis. Fellow, New York Univ. and New England Med. Center, Boston, 1950; Benjamin Franklin Fellow, RSA, 1974. Lectures: Harvey, 1962; Salmon, 1963; Jacob Bronowski Meml, 1978, etc. President: (first) Amer. Coll. of Neuropsychopharmacology, 1962; Amer. Psychopathological Assoc., 1968; Chairman: Bd, Israel Inst. of Psychobiol., 1961–; Foundns Fund Prize Bd for Res. in Psychiatry, 1977–81; Board Member: Inst. for Advancement of Health, 1982; Govs, Hebrew Univ. of Jerusalem. Formerly Member: Council, Internat. Collegium N Psychopharm; Central Council, Internat. Brain Research Organisation, UNESCO (Chm., Sub-Cttee on Educn); RSM. Life Fellow, Amer. Psych. Assoc.; Charter Fellow, RCPsych, GB; Fellow: Amer. Acad. of Arts and Scis; Amer. Coll. of Psychiatry; Amer. Coll. of Neuropsychopharmacol; Amer. Acad. of Behavioral Medicine Res. and Soc. of Behavioral Medicine; Fetzer Inst., 1990; Fellow and Mem. Exec. Cttee, World Acad. of Art and Sci., 1985; Member: Physiological Soc., GB; Pharmacological Soc., GB; Amer. Soc. for Pharmacology and Experimental Therapeutics; New York Acad. of Science; Sigma Xi; Scientific Assoc.; Acad. of Psychoanalysis. Hon. DPhil Hebrew Univ. of Jerusalem, 1989. Distinguished Practitioner, Nat. Acads of Practice, 1985. Joel Elkes Res. Labs, Dept of Psychiatry, Johns Hopkins Univ., dedicated 1989. *Publications:* papers to various jls and symposia. *Recreation:* painting. *Address:* Fetzer Institute, 9292 WKL Avenue, Kalamazoo, MI 49009, USA. *Clubs:* Cosmos (Washington); West Hamilton, Johns Hopkins (Baltimore).

ELKIN, Alexander, CMG 1976; international law consultant, retired; *b* St Petersburg, 2 Aug. 1909; *o c* of Boris and Anna Elkin; *m* 1937, Muriel Solomons, Dublin. *Educ:* Grunewald Gymnasium and Russian Academic Sch., Berlin; Univs of Berlin, Kiel and London. DrJur Kiel 1932, LLM London 1935. Called to the Bar, Middle Temple, 1937; practised at English Bar, 1937–39; BBC Monitoring Service, 1939–42; war-time govt service, 1942–45; Associate Chief, Legal Service, UN Interim Secretariat, London, 1945–46; Asst Dir, UN European Office, Geneva, 1946–48; Legal Adviser to UNSCOB, Salonica, 1948; Dep. Legal Adviser, later Legal Adviser, OEEC (OECD 1960–), Paris, 1949–61; UNECA Legal Consultant, formation of African Develt Bank and Econ. Council for Africa, 1962–64; Actg Gen. Counsel of ADB, 1964–65; UNDP Legal Consultant, formation of Caribbean Develt Bank, 1967–68; Special Adviser on European Communities Law, FCO, 1970–79. Legal consultancies for: WHO, 1948; IBRD, 1966; W Afr. Regional Gp, 1968; OECD, 1975. Lectured: on Europ. payments system and OEEC/OECD activs, Univ. of the Saar, 1957–60, and Univ. Inst. of Europ. Studies, Turin, 1957–65; on drafting of treaties, UNITAR Seminars, The Hague, Geneva and NY, for legal advisers and diplomats, 1967–84; on language and law, Univ. of Bath, 1979–95; Univ. of Bradford, 1979–84. Hon. Vis. Prof., Bradford Univ., 1982–84. Mem., RIIA. Hon. LLD Bath, 1990. Ford Foundn Leadership Grant, 1960. *Publications:* contrib. European Yearbook, Jl du Droit Internat., Revue Générale de Droit Internat. Public, Survey of Internat. Affairs 1939–1946, Travaux pratiques de L'Institut de Droit Comparé de la Faculté de Droit de Paris, etc. *Recreations:* reading, visiting art collections, travel. *Address:* 70 Apsley House, Finchley Road, NW8 0NZ. *Club:* Travellers'.

ELKIN, Sonia Irene Linda, OBE 1981 (MBE 1966); Director for Regions and Smaller Firms, Confederation of British Industry, 1985–92; *b* 15 May 1932; *d* of Godfrey Albert Elkin and Irene Jessamine Archibald. *Educ:* Beresford House Sch., Eastbourne. Association of British Chambers of Commerce, 1950–66: Overseas Director, 1956–66; Lloyds Bank Overseas Dept, 1966–67; Confederation of British Industry, 1967–92. Commissioner, Manpower Services Commission, 1982–85. Non-executive Director: Greggs, 1992–; Kall Kwik Printing (UK), 1993–. *Publications:* What about Europe?, 1967; What about Europe Now?, 1971. *Club:* United Oxford & Cambridge University (Lady Associate).

ELKINGTON, Prof. Andrew Robert, FRCS; FRCOphth; Professor of Ophthalmology, University of Southampton, since 1990; Consultant Ophthalmic Surgeon, Southampton General Hospital, since 1974; President, Royal College of Ophthalmologists, since 1994; *b* 12 Dec. 1935; *s* of late Dr George Ernest Elkington, MC, FRCS, Newport, Salop and Kathleen Mary Elkington (*née* Budgen); *m* 1964, Patricia Kathleen Wright, *er d* of late R. M. Wright, MC and Bar and Joan Wright; four *s*. *Educ:* Repton Sch., Derbys; Clare Coll., Cambridge (MA); St Thomas' Hosp. (BChir, MB). FRCS 1969; FRCOphth 1988; DRCOG 1965; DO 1968. Moorfields Eye Hospital: Hse Surgeon and Sen. Resident Officer, 1967–70; Chief Clinical Asst, 1970–74; Sen. Registrar in Ophthalmol., Westminster Hosp., 1970–74. European Vis. Prof., RSocMed, 1992–93. Examnr, DO, 1977–83 (Chm., Examng Bd, 1981–83); Mem., Ct of Examnrs (Ophthalmol.), RCS, 1984–89 (Chm., 1988–89); Ext. Examnr, RCPSG (Ophthalmol.), 1984–89; Examnr in ophthalmol., Univs. of Glasgow, 1991, Leicester, 1992, Bristol, 1987, London, 1988, Nottingham, 1993; Examnr to Ophthalmic Nursing Bd, 1980–. Section of Ophthalmology, Royal Society of Medicine: Mem. Council, 1980–92; Hon. Sec., 1980–83; Vice Pres., 1983–86; Pres., 1990–92; Faculty of Ophthalmologists, subseq. Royal College of Ophthalmologists: Mem. Council, 1985–88; Hon. Sec., 1986–91; Vice-Pres., 1991–94; Ophthalmological Society of UK: Mem. Council, 1979–82; Vice Pres., 1987–88; Mem. Council, RCS, 1994–. Member: Council, Oxford Ophthalmol. Congress, 1982–; Senate, Royal Surgical Colls, 1994–; Conf. and Scottish Conf. of Med. Royal Colls and their Faculties, 1994–; Standing Med. Adv. Cttee, 1994–. Govt of Hong Kong Commnd Trainer in ophthalmol., 1991–. Mem., Bd of Govs, Moorfields Eye Hosp., 1988–94. *Publications:* (jtly) Clinical Optics, 1984, 2nd edn 1991; Ophthalmology for Nurses, 1986; ABC of Eyes, 1988, 2nd edn 1994; Aids to Ophthalmology, 1989; contribs on trauma, glaucoma and retinal detachment to ophthalmic jls. *Recreations:* wildlife, tending vegetables. *Address:* Southampton Eye Unit, Southampton University Hospitals NHS Trust, Southampton General Hospital, Tremona Road, Southampton SO9 4XY. *Club:* Travellers'.

ELLACOMBE, Air Cdre John Lawrence Wemyss, CB 1970; DFC 1942 (Bar 1944); FBIM; *b* Livingstone, N Rhodesia, 28 Feb. 1920; *s* of Dr Gilbert H. W. Ellacombe; *m* 1951, Wing Officer Mary Hibbert, OBE, WRAF; one *s* two *d*. *Educ:* Diocesan Coll., Rondebosch, Cape. War of 1939–45: RAF, 1939; Fighter Comd and Two ATA Force, 1940–45 (Pilot, Battle of Britain). Aden, 1946–48; RAF Staff Coll., 1948–49; Fighter Command, 1949–57; BJSM, Washington, 1959. JSSC, 1959–60; Gp Captain, CO RAF Linton on Ouse, to Nov 1962; CFE, to Aug. 1965; Defence Operational Analysis Estabt, West Byfleet, 1965–68; Air Cdre, Commander Air Forces Gulf, 1968–70; Dir of Ops (Air Defence and Overseas), MoD (Air), 1970–73; St Thomas' Hospital: Dir, Scientific Services, 1973–80; Administrator to Special Trustees, 1980–85. *Recreations:* photography, golf, cricket. *Address:* 33 The Drive, Northwood, Middlesex HA6 1HW. *Club:* Royal Air Force.

ELLEN, Eric Frank, QPM 1980; LLB; CIMgt; Executive Director, International Chamber of Commerce Commercial Crime Services (formerly ICC Corporate Risk Management Services), since 1994 (First Director: International Maritime Bureau, since 1981; Counterfeiting Intelligence Bureau, since 1985; Commercial Crime Bureau, since 1992;

Regional Piracy Centre, Kuala Lumpur, since 1992); *b* London, 30 Aug. 1930; *s* of late Robert Frank Ellen and of Jane Lydia Ellen; *m* 1949, Gwendoline Dorothy Perkins; one *s* one *d*. *Educ:* Wakefield Central Sch., East Ham; Holborn Coll. of Law, Univ. of London (LLB Hons, London Univ. Certificate in Criminology). CIMgt (FBIM 1978). Joined PLA Police, 1951; Sgt 1956; Inspector 1961; Chief Insp. 1972; Supt and Chief Supt 1973; attended 11th Sen. Comd Course, Bramshill Police Coll., 1974; Dep. Chief Constable 1975; Chief Constable, 1975–80. Adviser on security to Ports Div. of Dept of Environment; advised Barbados Govt on formation of Barbados Port Authy Police Force, 1983; reviewed port security at Jeddah and Dammam. Sec., Internat. Assoc. of Airport and Seaport Police, 1980–88 (Pres., 1977–78 and 1978–79); Founder, Chm. and Life Mem., EEC Assoc. of Airport and Seaport Police, 1975–78; Chm., Panel on Maritime Fraud, Commonwealth Secretariat, 1982–90; Consultant, Commercial Crime Unit. Member: Internat. Assoc. of Ports and Harbours Standing Cttee on Legal Protection of Port Interests, 1977–79 (Chm., Sub-Cttee on Protection of Ports against Sabotage and Terrorism, 1977–79); Cttee of Conservative Lawyers, 1985–; Shipbrokers Cttee on Maritime Fraud; British Acad. of Forensic Sciences; Hon. Soc. of Middle Temple. Police Long Service and Good Conduct Medal, 1974. Freeman of the City of London, 1978. Police Medal Republic of China, 1979. *Publications:* (co-author) International Maritime Fraud, 1981; (ed) Violence at Sea, 2nd edn, 1987; (ed) Piracy at Sea, 1989; Ports at Risk, 1993; professional articles on marine fraud and counterfeiting, terrorism, piracy and port policing (has lectured on these topics at seminars in over 50 countries). *Recreations:* golf, swimming. *Address:* (office) Maritime House, 1 Linton Road, Barking, Essex IG11 8HG. *T:* 0181–591 3000. *Club:* Wig and Pen.

ELLEN, Patricia Mae Hayward; *see* Lavers, P. M.

ELLENBOROUGH, 8th Baron *cr* 1802; **Richard Edward Cecil Law;** Director: Towry Law & Co., since 1958; Towry Law Group; *b* 14 Jan. 1926; *s* of 7th Baron and Helen Dorothy, *o d* of late H. W. Lovatt; *S* father, 1945; *m* 1st, 1953, Rachel Mary (*d* 1986), *o d* of late Major Ivor Hedley; three *s*; 2nd, 1994, Mrs Frances Kimberley. *Educ:* Eton Coll.; Magdalene Coll., Cambridge. Pres., Nat. Union of Ratepayers' Associations, 1960–90. *Heir: s* Major the Hon. Rupert Edward Henry Law, Coldstream Guards, retd [*b* 28 March 1955; *m* 1981, Hon. Grania, *d* of Baron Boardman, *qv*; two *s* one *d*]. *Address:* Withypool House, Observatory Close, Church Road, Crowborough, East Sussex TN6 1BN. *T:* Crowborough (01892) 663139. *Club:* Turf.

ELLERAY, Anthony John; QC 1993; *b* 19Aug. 1954; *s* of late Alexander John Elleray and of Sheila Mary Elleray (*née* Perkins); *m* 1982, Alison Elizabeth Potter; one *s* one *d*. *Educ:* Bishop's Stortford Coll.; Trinity Coll., Cambridge (MA). Called to the Bar, Inner Temple, 1977. *Recreations:* pictures, garden, wine. *Address:* St James's Chambers, 68 Quay Street, Manchester M3 3EL. *T:* 0161–834 7000. *Club:* Manchester Tennis and Racquets.

ELLERTON, Sir Geoffrey (James), Kt 1992; CMG 1963; MBE 1956; Chairman, Local Government Boundary Commission for England, 1983–92; *b* 25 April 1920; *er s* of late Sir Cecil Ellerton; *m* 1946, Peggy Eleanor, *d* of late F. G. Watson; three *s*. *Educ:* Highgate Sch.; Hertford Coll., Oxford (MA). Military Service, 1940–45. Apptd Colonial Administrative Service as District Officer, Kenya, 1945. Acted as Minister for Internal Security and Defence, 1960 and 1962. Retired as Permanent Sec., Prime Minister's Office and Sec. to the Cabinet, at time of Kenya's Independence, Dec. 1963. Sec. to the Maud and Mallaby Cttees on Management and Staffing in Local Government, 1964. Joined Elder Dempster Lines, 1965, Chm., 1972–74; an Exec. Dir, Ocean Transport & Trading Ltd, 1972–80; Dir, Overseas Containers Ltd, 1975–80; Chm., Globe Management Ltd, 1981–83; Dir, Globe Investment Trust PLC, 1983–86. Mem. Council, Liverpool Univ., 1974–78; a Vice-Pres., Liverpool Sch. of Tropical Medicine, 1978–87. Hakluyt Society: Mem. Council, 1984–86; Hon. Treas., 1986–94; Trustee, 1994–. *Recreations:* music, books. *Address:* Briar Hill House, Broad Campden, Chipping Campden, Glos GL55 6XB. *T:* Evesham (01386) 841003. *Clubs:* Brooks's, MCC.

ELLES, family name of **Baroness Elles.**

ELLES, Baroness *cr* 1972 (Life Peer), of the City of Westminster; **Diana Louie Elles;** *b* 19 July 1921; *d* of Col Stewart Francis Newcombe, DSO and Elisabeth Chaki; *m* 1945, Neil Patrick Moncrieff Elles, *qv*; one *s* one *d*. *Educ:* private Schs, England, France and Italy; London University (BA Hons). Served WAAF, 1941–45. Barrister-at-law. Care Cttee worker in S London, 1956–72. UK Delegn to UN Gen. Assembly, 1972; Mem., UN Sub-Commn on Prevention of Discrimination and Protection of Minorities, 1973–75; UN special rapporteur on Human Rights, 1973–75; Mem., British delegn to European Parlt, 1973–75. Mem., Cripps Cttee on legal discrimination against women; Chm., Sub-cttee of Women's Nat. Adv. Cttee (Conservative Party) on one-parent families (report publ. as Unhappy Families); Internat. Chm., European Union of Women, 1973–79; Chm., Cons. Party Internat. Office, 1973–78; Opposition front bench spokesman on foreign and Eur. affairs, H of L, 1975–79; Mem., H of L Europ. Communities Select Cttee, 1989–94 (Chm., Law and Institutions Sub-Cttee, 1992); Mem, 1996 16C Sub-Cttee, 1995. European Parliament: MEP (C) Thames Valley, 1979–89; EDG spokesman on NI, 1980–87; Vice-Pres., 1982–87; Chm., Legal Affairs Cttee, 1987–89. Vice-Pres., UK Assoc. of European Lawyers, 1985–. Mem. Council, Caldecott Community, 1990–; Trustee: Cumberland Lodge, 1982–; Industry and Parlt Trust, 1985–; Vice Chm. Bd, British Inst., Florence, 1994– (Gov., 1986–); Gov., Reading Univ., 1986–. Hon. Bencher, Lincoln's Inn, 1993. *Publications:* The Housewife and the Common Market (pamphlet), 1971; Human Rights of Aliens, 1980; articles, etc. *Address:* 75 Ashley Gardens, SW1P 1HG; Villa Fontana, Ponte del Giglio, Lucca, Italy.

ELLES, James Edmund Moncrieff; Member (C) European Parliament, Buckinghamshire and Oxfordshire East, since 1994 (Oxford and Buckinghamshire, 1984–94); *b* 3 Sept. 1949; *s* of N. P. M. Elles, *qv* and Baroness Elles, *qv*; *m* 1977, Françoise Le Bail; one *s* one *d*. *Educ:* Ashdown House; Eton College; Edinburgh University. External Relations Div., EEC, 1976–80; Asst to Dep. Dir Gen. of Agriculture, EEC, 1980–84. EPP spokesman on the Budget, 1994–; Mem., Institutional Cttee, European Parlt. Co-Founder and Patron, Thames Action and Resource Gp for Educn and Trng; Chm., Transatlantic Policy Network, 1993–. *Address:* Conservative Centre, 100 Walton Street, Aylesbury, Bucks HP21 7QP; c/o European Parliament, 97–113 Rue Belliard, 1040 Brussels, Belgium. *Clubs:* Carlton; Royal and Ancient Golf (St Andrews).

ELLES, Neil Patrick Moncrieff; Chairman, Value Added Tax Appeals Tribunal, 1972–92; *b* 8 July 1919; *s* of Edmund Hardie Elles, OBE and Ina Katharine Hilda Skene; *m* 1945, Diana Louie Newcombe (*see* Baroness Elles); one *s* one *d*. *Educ:* Eton; Christ Church, Oxford (MA). War Service, RAF, 1939–45. Called to the Bar, Inner Temple, 1947; Sec., Inns of Court Conservative and Unionist Taxation Cttee, 1957–71; Mem., Special Study Gp, Commn on Law of Competition, Brussels, 1962–67. *Publications:* The Law of Restrictive Trade Practices and Monopolies (with Lord Wilberforce and Alan Campbell), 1966; Community Law through the Cases, 1973. *Recreations:* fishing, listening to music, the cultivation of vines. *Address:* 75 Ashley Gardens, SW1P 1HG. *T:* 0171–828 0175; Villa Fontana, Ponte del Giglio, Lucca, Italy. *Clubs:* Flyfishers', MCC.

ELLETSON, Harold Daniel Hope; MP (C) Blackpool North, since 1992; *b* 8 Dec. 1960; *m* 1987, Fiona Margaret Ferguson; one *s*. *Educ:* Eton Coll.; Exeter Univ.; Voronezh Univ., USSR; Poly. of Central London; Bradford Univ. Mem. (C) Lancashire CC, 1984–88; worked in journalism and public affairs, 1984–88; CBI and Illingworth Morris plc, 1988–90; consultant to cos trading in Eastern Europe, 1990–. Contested (C) Burnley, 1987. *Address:* House of Commons, SW1A 0AA.

ELLINGWORTH, Richard Henry; HM Diplomatic Service, retired; *b* 9 March 1926; *s* of Vincent Ellingworth; *m* 1952, Joan Mary Waterfield; one *s* three *d*. *Educ:* Uppingham; Aberdeen Univ.; Magdalen Coll., Oxford (Demy); Exeter Univ. (certificates in French, 1989, Theology, 1991, and Russian, 1993). Served War of 1939–45: RA, and Intelligence Corps, 1944–47. Oxford, 1947–50 (first Lit. Hum.); HM Embassy, Japan, 1951–55; FO, 1955–59; HM Embassy: Belgrade, 1959–63; Japan, 1963–68 (Olympic Attaché, 1964); Head of Oil Dept., FCO, 1969–71; Research Associate, Internat. Inst. for Strategic Studies, 1971–72; Counsellor, Tehran, 1972–75; seconded to Dept of Energy, 1975–77. Course Dir (European Training), Civil Service Coll., 1978–83. Mem., Farningham Parish Council, 1979–83; pt-time Agent, Sevenoaks Liberal Assoc., 1983–84; Hon. Organiser, Farmingham, Royal British Legion, 1982–87. *Publications:* (with A. N. Gilkes) An Anthology of Oratory, 1946; Japanese Economic Policy and Security, 1972. *Recreations:* gardening, music. *Address:* 29 Carlton Mews, Wells BA5 1SG.
See also Sir J. C. King, Bt.

ELLIOT; *see* Elliot-Murray-Kynynmound, family name of Earl of Minto.

ELLIOT; *see* Scott-Elliot.

ELLIOT, Sir Gerald (Henry), Kt 1986; FRSE; Chairman, Christian Salvesen plc, 1981–88; *b* 24 Dec. 1923; *s* of late Surg. Captain J. S. Elliot, RN, and Magda Salvesen; *m* 1950, Margaret Ruth Whale (MBE 1993); two *s* one *d*. *Educ:* Marlborough Coll.; New Coll., Oxford (BA PPE 1948). FRSE 1978. Captain FF Rifles, Indian Army, 1942–46. Christian Salvesen Ltd, 1948–88, Dep. Chm. and Man. Dir, 1973–81. Dir, Scottish Provident Instn, 1971–89, Chm., 1983–89; Chairman: Chambers and Fargus, 1975–79; Scottish Br., RIIA, 1973–77 (Sec., 1963–73); FAO Fishery Industries Develt Gp, 1971–76; Forth Ports Authority, 1973–79; Scottish Arts Council, 1980–86. Chairman: Scottish Unit Managers Ltd, 1984–88; Martin Currie Unit Trusts, 1988–90; Biotal, 1987–90. Sec., National Whaling Bd, 1953–62; Mem., Nat. Ports Council, 1978–81. Chm., Scottish Div., Inst. of Dirs, 1989–92; Vice-Chm., Scottish Business in the Community, 1987–89. Chairman: Prince's Scottish Youth Business Trust, 1987–94; Scottish Opera, 1987–92 (Vice-Pres., 1994–). A Vice-Pres., RSE, 1988–91. Pres., UN 50 Scotland, 1993–. Trustee: Nat. Museums of Scotland, 1987–91; The Prince's Trust, 1992–94; Edinburgh Fest. Th., 1995–; Chm., Trustees, David Hume Inst., 1985–95. Pres., Edinburgh Univ. Develt Trust, 1990–94. Member Court: Edinburgh Univ., 1984–93; Regents, RCSE, 1990–. Dr *hc* Edinburgh, 1989; Hon. LLD Aberdeen, 1991. Consul for Finland in Edinburgh, 1957–89; Dean, Consular Corps in Edinburgh-Leith, 1986–88. Kt 1st Cl., Order of White Rose of Finland, 1975. *Publications:* papers on control of whaling and fishing, arts administration and economic management. *Address:* 39 Inverleith Place, Edinburgh EH3 5QD.

ELLIOT, Prof. Harry, CBE 1976; FRS 1973; Emeritus Professor of Physics, University of London; Professor of Physics at Imperial College, London, 1960–80 (Assistant Director of Physics Department, 1963–71); *b* 28 June 1920; *s* of Thomas Elliot and Hannah Elizabeth (*née* Littleton), Weary Hall, Cumberland; *m* 1943, Betty Leyman; one *s* one *d*. *Educ:* Nelson Sch., Wigton; Manchester Univ. MSc, PhD. Served War, Signals Branch, RAF, incl. liaison duties with USAAF and USN, 1941–46. Manchester University: Asst Lectr in Physics, 1948–49; Lectr in Physics, 1949–54; Imperial College, London: Lectr in Physics, 1954–56; Sen. Lectr in Physics, 1956–57; Reader in Physics, 1957–60; Sen. Res. Fellow, 1982–87. Member: Science Research Council, 1971–77; Council, Royal Soc., 1978–79; Science Adv. Cttee, ESA, 1979–81. Hon. Prof., Universitad Mayor de San Andres, 1957; Hon. ARCS, 1965. Fellow, World Acad. of Arts and Scis, 1978. Holweck Prize and Medal, Inst. of Physics and Société Française de Physique, 1976. *Publications:* papers on cosmic rays, solar physics and magnetospheric physics in scientific jls; contrib. scientific reviews and magazine articles. *Recreation:* painting. *Address:* Rosan, Broadwater Down, Tunbridge Wells, Kent TN2 5PE.

ELLIOT, Virginia Helen Antoinette, MBE 1986; equestrian event rider; *b* 1 Feb. 1955; *d* of late Col Ronald Morris Holgate, RM and of Heather Holgate; *m* 1st, 1985, Hamish Julian Peter Leng (marr. diss. 1989), *s* of Gen. Sir Peter Leng, *qv*; 2nd, 1993, Michael Elliot. *Educ:* Bedgebury Park, Goudhurst, Kent. Three day event wins: Junior European Champion, 1973 (Dubonnet); Mini Olympics, 1975 (Jason); Burghley, 1983 (Priceless), 1984 (Nightcap), 1985 (Priceless), 1986 (Murphy Himself), 1989 (Master Craftsman); Badminton, 1985 (Priceless), 1989 (Master Craftsman), 1993 (Houdini); European Championship, 1985 (Priceless), 1987 (Nightcap), 1989 (Master Craftsman); World Championship, 1986 (Priceless); Team Silver Olympic Medal, 1984 and 1988; Bronze Individual Olympic Medal, 1984 (Priceless), and 1988 (Master Craftsman). *Publications:* (with Genevieve Murphy) Ginny, 1986; (with Nancy Roberts) Priceless, 1987; (with Genevieve Murphy) Ginny and Her Horses, 1987; (with Genevieve Murphy) Training the Event Horse, 1990. *Recreations:* ski-ing, cooking, art, theatre. *Address:* Ivyleaze, Acton Turville, Badminton, Avon GL9 1HJ. *T:* Badminton (0145421) 8633.

ELLIOT-MURRAY-KYNYNMOUND, family name of **Earl of Minto.**

ELLIOT-SMITH, Alan Guy, CBE 1957; *b* 30 June 1904; *s* of late F. Elliot-Smith; *m* 1939, Ruth Kittermaster; no *c*. *Educ:* Charterhouse; Oriel Coll., Oxford. Hons Mod. Lang. Sch., 1925; Asst Master, Harrow Sch., 1925–40; Headmaster, Cheltenham Coll., 1940–51; Mem., Harrow UDC, 1933–36; Deleg. to Inst. of Pacific Relations Conf., Calif., 1936; lectured to German teachers on Education, 1947 and 1948; lectured to Service units in the Middle East, 1949; Head-master of Victoria Coll., Cairo, 1952–56; Representative in Nigeria of the West Africa Cttee, 1957–58; Headmaster, Markham Coll., Lima, Peru, 1960–63. *Recreations:* travel, reading. *Address:* Bevois Mount, Rowsley Road, Eastbourne, Sussex BN20 7XS.

ELLIOTT, family name of **Baron Elliott of Morpeth**.

ELLIOTT OF MORPETH, Baron *cr* 1985 (Life Peer), of Morpeth in the County of Northumberland and of the City of Newcastle-upon-Tyne; **Robert William Elliott;** Kt 1974; DL; Vice-Chairman, Conservative Party Organisation, 1970–74; *b* 11 Dec. 1920; *s* of Richard Elliott; *m* 1956, Jane Morpeth; one *s* four *d* (of whom two are twin *d*). *Educ:* Morpeth Grammar Sch. Farmer, 1939–, at Low Heighley, Morpeth, Northumberland. MP (C) Newcastle-upon-Tyne North, March 1957–1983; Parliamentary Private Secretary: to joint Parliamentary Secs, Ministry of Transport and Civil Aviation, April 1958–Oct. 1959; to Under-Sec., Home Office, Nov. 1959–60; to Minister of State, Home Office, Nov. 1960–61; to Sec. for Technical Co-operation, 1961–63; Asst Govt Whip (unpaid), 1963–64; Opposition Whip, 1964–70; Comptroller of the Household, June-Sept. 1970. Chm., Select Cttee on Agric., Fisheries and Food, 1980–83. DL Northumberland, 1985.

Address: Lipwood Hall, Haydon Bridge, Northumberland NE47 6DY. *T:* Hexham (01434) 684777. *Clubs:* Carlton; Northern Counties (Newcastle upon Tyne).

ELLIOTT, Hon. Lord; Walter Archibald Elliott, MC 1943; Chairman, Scottish Land Court, 1978–92; President, Lands Tribunal for Scotland, 1971–92; *b* 6 Sept. 1922; 2nd *s* of late Prof. T. R. Elliott, CBE, DSO, FRS, Broughton Place, Broughton, Peeblesshire; *m* 1954, Susan Isobel Mackenzie Ross, Kaimend, North Berwick; two *s*. *Educ:* Eton; Trinity Coll., Cambridge; Edinburgh Univ. Active service in Italy and North West Europe with 2nd Bn Scots Guards, 1943–45 (MC); demobilised, Staff Capt., 1947. Barrister-at-law, Inner Temple, 1950; Advocate at Scottish Bar, 1950; QC (Scotland) 1963. Chm., Med. Appeal Tribunals, 1971–78. Brigadier, Royal Company of Archers (Queen's Body Guard for Scotland). *Publications:* Us and Them: a study of group consciousness, 1986; articles in legal periodicals. *Recreations:* gardening, travelling. *Address:* Morton House, Fairmilehead, Edinburgh EH10 7AW. *T:* 0131–445 2548. *Clubs:* New, Arts (Edinburgh).

ELLIOTT, Anthony Michael Manton, (Tony Elliott); Founder, 1968 and Chairman, Time Out Group; *b* 7 Jan. 1947; *s* of late Katherine and Alan Elliott; *m* 1st, 1976, Janet Street-Porter, *qv* (marr. diss. 1978); 2nd, 1989, Jane L. Coke; three *s* (incl. twins). *Educ:* Stowe; Keele Univ. Time Out Group titles include: Time Out; i-D; Modern Painters; annual guides. Time Out Trust formed 1989. *Recreations:* travel, watching television, cinema going, eating out with friends, reading newspapers and magazines, being with family. *Address:* Time Out Group, Universal House, 251 Tottenham Court Road, W1P 0AB. *T:* 0171–813 3000, *Fax:* 0171–813 6001.

ELLIOTT, Rev. Dr Charles Middleton; Fellow, Dean and Chaplain of Trinity Hall, since 1990, Affiliated Lecturer in Theology, since 1991, University of Cambridge; *b* 9 Jan. 1939; *s* of Joseph William Elliott and Mary Evelyn Elliott; *m* 1962, Hilary Margaret Hambling; three *s* (one *d* decd). *Educ:* Repton; Lincoln and Nuffield Colls, Oxford (MA, DPhil). Deacon, 1964; priest, 1965. Lectr in Econs, Univ. of Nottingham, 1963–65; Reader in Econs, Univ. of Zambia, 1965–69; Asst Sec., Cttee on Society, Develt and Peace, Vatican and World Council of Churches, 1969–72; Sen. Lectr in Develt Econs, Univ. of E Anglia, 1972–73; Dir, Overseas Develt Gp, UEA, 1973–77; Minor Canon, Norwich Cathedral, 1974–77; Prof. of Develt Policy and Planning, and Dir, Centre of Develt Studies, Univ. of Wales, 1977–82; Director of Christian Aid, 1982–84; Asst Gen. Sec., BCC, 1982–84; Benjamin Meaker Prof., Bristol Univ., 1985–86; Sen. Consultant, ODI, 1986–87. G. E. M. Scott Fellow, Univ. of Melbourne, 1984–85; Hon. Vis. Prof. of Christian Ethics, Univ. of Edinburgh, 1985–87; Vis. Prof. in Theology, KCL, 1986–88. Chm., Indep. Gp on British Aid, 1981–89. Prebendary of Lichfield Cathedral, 1987–. *Publications:* The Development Debate, 1972; Inflation and the Compromised Church, 1973; Patterns of Poverty in the Third World, 1975; Praying the Kingdom: an introduction to political spirituality, 1985 (Biennial Collins Prize for Religious Lit., 1985); Comfortable Compassion, 1987; Praying through Paradox, 1987; Signs of Our Times, 1988; Sword and Spirit, 1989; articles in Jl of Develt Studies, Econ. Hist. Rev., Theology, World Health Forum, World Develt and in Proc. Royal Soc. *Recreations:* sailing, fly-fishing, walking, chatting to rural craftsmen. *Address:* 11 Perowne Street, Cambridge CB1 2AY.

ELLIOTT, Charles Thomas, CBE 1994; PhD; FRS 1988; Chief Scientific Officer, Defence Research Agency, Electronics Sector, since 1991; *b* 16 Jan. 1939; *s* of Charles Thomas and Mary Jane Elliott; *m* 1962, Brenda Waistell; one *s* two *d*. *Educ:* Washington Grammar Sch.; Manchester Univ. (BSc 1960; PhD 1965). Univ. of Manchester: Research student, 1960–63; Asst Lectr/Lectr, 1963–67 (research on dielectric breakdown); joined RSRE 1967, to study electrical transport in semiconductors; Vis. Scientist, MIT, Lincoln Lab., USA, 1970–71; research into infrared detectors, 1972–; DCSO, RSRE, 1986–91. Vis. Prof. of Physics, Heriot-Watt Univ., 1992–. Rank Prize for optoelectronics and IEE Electronics Div. Premium Award, 1982; Churchill Medal, Soc. of Engineers, 1986; MacRobert Award for Engineering, 1991. *Publications:* numerous papers and patents. *Recreations:* reading, golf. *Address:* DRA Electronics Sector, St Andrews Road, Malvern, Worcs WR14 3PS. *T:* Malvern (01684) 894820.

ELLIOTT, Sir Clive (Christopher Hugh), 4th Bt *cr* 1917, of Limpsfield, Surrey; Country Projects Officer, Eastern and Southern Africa, Food and Agriculture Organization of the UN, Rome, since 1989; *b* Moshi, Tanganyika, 12 Aug. 1945; *s* of Sir Hugh Elliott, 3rd Bt, OBE and of Elizabeth Margaret, *d* of A. G. Phillipson; *S* father, 1989; *m* 1975, Marie-Thérèse, *d* of H. Rüttimann; two *s*. *Educ:* Dragon Sch., Oxford; Bryanston Sch., Dorset; University Coll., Oxford (BA Hons Zoology); Univ. of Cape Town, S Africa (PhD Zoology 1973). University of Cape Town: Research Officer, FitzPatrick Inst. of Ornithology, 1968–71; first Officer i/c National Unit for Bird-ringing Admin, 1972–75; ornithologist/ecologist, crop protectionist/project manager, FAO: Chad, 1975–78; Tanzania, 1978–86; Kenya, 1986–89. Member: South African Ornithological Soc.; Field Staff Assoc. of FAO (Chm., 1992). *Publications:* (ed jtly with R. L. Bruggers) Quelea Quelea: Africa's Bird Pest, 1989; contrib. to books and jls on ornithology. *Recreations:* tennis, fishing, bird-watching, wildlife conservation, everything African. *Heir: s* Ivo Antony Moritz Elliott, *b* 9 May 1978. *Address:* FAO/AGOE, Via delle terme di Caracalla, Rome, Italy. *Club:* British Ornithologists' Union.

ELLIOTT, Sir David Murray, KCMG 1995; CB 1987; Director General (Internal Market, Industry, Telecommunications), General Secretariat of Council of European Union, 1991–95; *b* 8 Feb. 1930; *s* of late Alfred Elliott, ISM, and Mabel Kathleen Emily Elliott (*née* Murray); *m* 1956, Ruth Marjorie Ingram; one *d* (one *s* decd). *Educ:* Bishopshalt Grammar Sch.; London Sch. of Economics and Political Science (BScEcon); Kitchener Scholar. National Service, RAF, 1951–54; Gen. Post Office, 1954–57; seconded to Federal Ministry of Communications, Nigeria, 1958–62; GPO, 1962–69; Asst Secretary: Min. of Posts and Telecommunications, 1969–74 (Dep. Leader, UK Delegn to Centenary Congress, UPU, Lausanne, 1974); Dept of Industry, 1974–75; Counsellor at UK Representation to the European Communities, Brussels, 1975–78; Under Sec., Cabinet Office, 1978–82; Minister and Dep. UK Perm. Rep. to the Eur. Communities, Brussels, 1982–91. *Recreation:* reading The Times. *Address:* 31 Ailsa Road, St Margarets, Twickenham, Middlesex TW1 1QW. *Club:* Travellers'.

ELLIOTT, David Stuart; Director, Museum of Modern Art, Oxford, since 1976; *b* 29 April 1949; *s* of Arthur Elliott and May Elliott; *m* 1974, Julia Alison; two *d*. *Educ:* Loughborough Grammar Sch.; Durham Univ. (BA Hons Mod. Hist.); Univ. of London (MA Hist. of Art, Courtauld Inst.). Asst Stage Manager, Phoenix Theatre, Leicester, 1966; Asst, City Art Gallery, Leicester, 1971; Regional Art Officer, Arts Council, 1973–76. Contribs to radio and TV. NACF Award, 1988. *Publications:* Alexander Rodchenko, 1979; José Clemente Orozco, 1980; New Worlds: Russian Art and Society 1900–1937, 1986; (ed with Ian Christie) Eisenstein at 90, 1988; (ed with Valery Dudakov) 100 Years of Russian Art 1889–1989, 1989; (ed with A. Lavrentiev) Alexander Rodchenko: Works on Paper, 1991; (ed with M. Cullerne Bown) Engineers of the Human Soul: Soviet Socialist Realism, 1992; Photography in Russia 1840–1940, 1992; Art from Argentina 1920–1940, 1994; contribs to arts magazines. *Recreations:* keeping fit, travelling. *Address:* Museum of Modern Art, 30 Pembroke Street, Oxford OX1 1BP. *T:* Oxford (01865) 722733, *Fax:* (01865) 722573, (home) (01865) 57043.

ELLIOTT, Frank Abercrombie, MD, FRCP; Emeritus Professor of Neurology, University of Pennsylvania, since 1979; Consultant, Elliott Neurology Centre, Pennsylvania Hospital, Philadelphia, since 1975; *b* 18 Dec. 1910; *s* of Arthur Abercrombie Elliott and Kathleen Gosselin; *m* 1st, 1940, Betty Kathleen Elkington; two *d*; 2nd, 1970, Mrs Josiah Marvel (*née* Hopkins). *Educ:* Rondebosch; Univ. of Cape Town. Univ. entrance schol., 1928; Lewis Memorial schol., 1930–34; MB, ChB Cape Town, with Hons and Gold Medal; Hiddingh Travelling Fellowship, 1936–39. House Surg. and House Phys. to professorial units, Cape Town; House Physician, British Postgrad. Sch. of Medicine and Nat. Hosp. for Nervous Diseases, London; Resident MO, Nat. Heart Hosp. RAMC, 1943–48, Lt-Col; Adviser in Neurology, India and War Office. FRCP 1948; FACP 1973. Physician to Charing Cross Hosp., 1947–58; to Moorfields Eye Hospital, 1949–58; Prof. of Neurology, Univ. of Pennsylvania, 1963–78. Lecturer and Examiner, London Univ. Member: Assoc. of British Neurologists; Assoc. of British Physicians; Internat. Soc. of Internal Medicine; Am. Acad. of Neurology; Philadelphia Neurological Soc. *Publications:* (ed) Clinical Neurology, 1952; Clinical Neurology, 1964 (2nd edn, 1971); papers on neurological subjects and the origins of aggressive behaviour. *Address:* Pennsylvania Hospital, Philadelphia, Pa 19107, USA. *Club:* Philadelphia.

ELLIOTT, Frank Alan, CB 1991; Permanent Secretary, Department of Health and Social Services, Northern Ireland, since 1987; *b* 28 March 1937; *s* of Frank Elliott and Doreen Allen; *m* 1964, Olive Lucy O'Brien; one *s* two *d*. *Educ:* Royal Belfast Academical Inst.; Trinity Coll., Dublin (BA (Mod.) 1st cl.). Entered NI Civil Service, 1959; Principal, Min. of Health, 1966, Asst Sec., 1971; Sen. Asst Sec., Dept of Health and Social Services, 1975, Under Sec., 1981. Gov., Sullivan Upper Sch., 1982–. *Recreations:* music and the arts, motoring. *Address:* Department of Health and Social Services, Dundonald House, Upper Newtownards Road, Belfast, Northern Ireland BT4 3SF. *T:* Belfast (01232) 524615.

ELLIOTT, George, FRICS; Senior Partner, Edmond Shipway and Partners, 1985–93; *b* 20 Aug. 1932; *s* of Harry Elliott and Nellie Elizabeth Elliott; *m* 1st, 1958, Winifred Joan (marr. diss. 1990); one *s* one *d*; 2nd, 1992, Hazel Ann Willis. *Educ:* Sir George Monoux Grammar Sch.; SW Essex Technical Coll. FRICS 1966. Founder Partner, Edmond Shipway, 1963; Chief Exec., British Urban Develt Services Unit, 1975–78. *Recreation:* travel. *Address:* 6 Olinda Avenue, City Beach, Perth, WA 6015, Australia. *T:* (9) 3858031.

ELLIOTT, Hugh Percival, CMG 1959; retired, 1967; *b* 29 May 1911; *s* of late Major P. W. Elliott, IA; *m* 1951, Bridget Rosalie (*d* 1981), *d* of late Rev. A. F. Peterson. *Educ:* St Lawrence Coll., Ramsgate; Hertford Coll., Oxford. Joined Colonial Administrative Service, Nigeria, 1934; seconded Colonial Office, 1946; Supervisor, Colonial Service Courses, London, 1948–50; Senior District Officer, 1954; Permanent Sec., 1956; Adviser, Govt of Eastern Nigeria, 1962–67. Many visits to Ethiopia, Zimbabwe, Kenya, Uganda and Nigeria to support the initiatives for Moral Re-Armament by African friends, 1968–. Companion, Order of the Niger, Nigeria, 1964. *Publications:* Darkness and Dawn in Zimbabwe, 1978; Dawn in Zimbabwe, 1980. *Recreations:* the countryside, watercolour painting, Africa. *Address:* Flat 8, Rosewood Lodge, 79 Wickham Road, Shirley, Croydon CR0 8TB.

ELLIOTT, Prof. James Philip, PhD; FRS 1980; Professor of Theoretical Physics, University of Sussex, 1969–94, now Professor Emeritus; *b* 27 July 1929; *s* of James Elliott and Dora Kate Smith; *m* 1955, Mavis Rosetta Avery; one *s* two *d*. *Educ:* University College, Southampton; London External degrees: BSc 1949, PhD 1952. Senior Scientific Officer, AERE Harwell, 1951–58; Vis. Associate Prof., Univ. of Rochester, USA, 1958–59; Lecturer in Mathematics, Univ. of Southampton, 1959–62; Reader in Theoretical Physics, Univ. of Sussex, 1962–69. Fellow of former Physical Soc. Rutherford Medal, Inst. of Physics, 1994. *Publications:* Symmetry in Physics, 1979; contribs include: The Nuclear Shell Model, Handbuch der Physik, vol 39, 1957; many papers, mostly published in Proc. Roy. Soc. and Nuclear Phys. *Recreations:* gardening, sport and music. *Address:* 36 Montacute Road, Lewes, Sussex BN7 1EP. *T:* Lewes (01273) 474783.

ELLIOTT, John Dorman; Chairman, Australian Product Traders Pty Ltd, since 1992; Deputy Chairman, Foster's Brewing Group (formerly Elders IXL Ltd), 1990–92 (Chairman and Chief Executive, 1985–90); *b* 3 Oct. 1941; *s* of Frank Faithful Elliott and Anita Caroline Elliott; *m* 1st, 1965, Lorraine Clare (*née* Golder); two *s* one *d*; 2nd, 1987, Amanda Mary Drummond Moray (*née* Bayles); one *d*. *Educ:* Carey Baptist Grammar School, Melbourne; BCom (Hons) 1962, MBA Melbourne 1965. With BHP, Melbourne, 1963–65; McKinsey & Co., 1966–72; formed consortium and raised $30 million to acquire Henry Jones (IXL), and became Man. Dir, 1972; Elder Smith Goldsbrough Mort merged with Henry Jones (IXL) to form Elders IXL, 1981; Elders IXL acquired Carlton & United Breweries, 1983, largest takeover in Aust. history. Pres., Liberal Party of Australia, 1987–90. Pres., Carlton FC, 1983–. *Recreations:* football, tennis, Royal tennis. *Address:* 1 Towers Road, Toorak, Vic 3142, Australia. *T:* (3) 96211411. *Clubs:* Melbourne, Australian, Savage (Melbourne); Royal Melbourne Tennis, Royal South Yarra Tennis.

ELLIOTT, Sir John (Huxtable), Kt 1994; FBA 1972; Regius Professor of Modern History, and Fellow of Oriel College, Oxford, since 1990; *b* 23 June 1930; *s* of late Thomas Charles Elliott and Janet Mary Payne; *m* 1958, Oonah Sophia Butler. *Educ:* Eton College; Trinity College, Cambridge (MA, PhD). Fellow of Trinity Coll., Cambridge, 1954–67, Hon. Fellow, 1991; Asst Lectr in History, Cambridge Univ., 1957–62; Lectr in History, Cambridge Univ., 1962–67; Prof. of History: KCL, 1968–73; Inst. for Advanced Study, Princeton, NJ, 1973–90. King Juan Carlos Vis. Prof., New York Univ., 1988. Wiles Lectr, QUB, 1969; Trevelyan Lectr, Cambridge Univ., 1982–83. Corresp. Fellow, Real Academia de la Historia, Madrid, 1965; Fellow, Amer. Acad. Arts and Scis, 1977. Mem., Amer. Philosophical Soc., 1982; Corresponding Member: Hispanic Soc. of America, 1975; Real Academia Sevillana de Buenas Letras, 1976; Royal Acad. of Letters, Barcelona, 1992; Nat. Acad. of History, Venezuela, 1992. Dr *hc* Universidad Autónoma de Madrid, 1983; Genoa, 1992; Barcelona, 1994; Hon. DLitt: Portsmouth, 1993; Warwick, 1995. Medal of Honour, Universidad Internacional Menéndez y Pelayo, 1987; Medalla de Oro al Mérito en las Bellas Artes, Spain, 1990; Premio Antonio de Nebrija, Univ. of Salamanca, 1993. Visitante Ilustre de Madrid, 1983; Comdr, 1984, Grand Cross, 1988, Order of Alfonso X El Sabio; Comdr, Order of Isabel la Católica, 1987. *Publications:* The Revolt of the Catalans, 1963; Imperial Spain, 1469–1716, 1963; Europe Divided, 1559–1598, 1968; The Old World and the New, 1492–1650, 1970; ed (with H. G. Koenigsberger) The Diversity of History, 1970; (with J. F. de la Peña) Memoriales y Cartas del Conde Duque de Olivares, 2 vols, 1978–80; (with Jonathan Brown) A Palace for a King, 1980; Richelieu and Olivares, 1984 (Leo Gershoy Award, Amer. Hist. Assoc., 1985); The Count-Duke of Olivares, 1986 (Wolfson Lit. Prize for History); Spain and its World 1500–1700, 1989; (ed) The Hispanic World, 1991. *Recreation:* looking at paintings. *Address:* Oriel College, Oxford OX1 4EW; 122 Church Way, Iffley, Oxford OX4 4EG. *T:* Oxford (01865) 716703.

ELLIOTT, Mark, CMG 1988; HM Diplomatic Service; Ambassador to Norway, since 1994; *b* 16 May 1939; *s* of William Rowcliffe Elliott, *qv*, and Karin Tess Elliott (*née* Classen); *m* 1964, Julian Richardson; two *s*. *Educ:* Eton Coll. (King's Scholar); New Coll., Oxford. HM Forces (Intell. Corps), 1957–59. FO, 1963; Tokyo, 1965; FCO, 1970;

Private Sec. to Perm. Under-Sec. of State, 1973–74; First Sec. and Head of Chancery, Nicosia, 1975–77; Counsellor, 1977–81, Head of Chancery, 1978–81, Tokyo; Hd of Far Eastern Dept, FCO, 1981–85; Under-Sec. on secondment to N Ireland Office, 1985–88; Ambassador to Israel, 1988–92; Dep. Under-Sec. of State, FCO, 1992–94. Grand Cross, Order of Merit (Norway), 1994. *Recreations:* photography, walking, music. *Address:* c/o Foreign and Commonwealth Office, SW1A 2AH.

ELLIOTT, Dr Michael, CBE 1982; FRS 1979; Lawes Trust Senior Fellow, Rothamsted Experimental Station, since 1989; *b* 30 Sept. 1924; *s* of Thomas William Elliott and Isobel Constance (*née* Burnell); *m* 1950, Margaret Olwen James; two *d. Educ:* Skinners Co.'s Sch., Tunbridge Wells, Kent; The Univ., Southampton (BSc, PhD); King's Coll., Univ. of London (DSc; FKC 1984). FRSC. Postgrad. res., University Coll., Southampton, 1945–46, and King's Coll., Univ. of London, 1946–48; Rothamsted Experimental Station: Organic Chemist, Dept of Insecticides and Fungicides, 1948–85; SPSO 1971–79; DCSO 1979–83 (Hd of Dept of Insecticides and Fungicides, 1979–83, and Dep. Dir, 1980–83); Hon. Scientist and Consultant, Chemistry of Insecticides, 1983–85. Vis. Res. Scientist, Div. of Entomology, Univ. of Calif at Berkeley, 1969, 1974 and 1986–88; Vis. Prof., Imperial Coll. of Sci. and Tech., 1978–. Hon. DSc Southampton, 1985. Burdick and Jackson Internat. Award for Res. in Pesticide Chemistry, 1975; Holroyd Medal and Lectureship, Soc. of Chem. Ind., 1977; John Jeyes Medal and Lectureship, Chem. Soc., 1978; Mullard Medal, Royal Soc., 1981; Grande Médaille de la Société Française de Phytiatrie et de Phytopharmacie, 1983; Fine Chemicals and Medicinals Gp Award, RSC, 1984; British Crop Protection Council Award, 1986; Wolf Foundn Prize in Agriculture, 1989; Prix de la Fondation de la Chimie, Paris, 1989; Envmt Medal, SCI, 1993. *Publications:* Synthetic Pyrethroids, 1977; papers on chemistry of insecticides and relation of chemical structure with biological activity; chapters in books on insecticides. *Recreations:* photography, designing insecticides. *Address:* 9 Long Ridge, Aston, Stevenage, Herts SG2 7EW. *T:* Shephall (01438) 880328. *Club:* Camera.

ELLIOTT, Michael Alwyn; theatre consultant, actor; *b* 15 July 1936; *s* of W. A. Edwards and Mrs J. B. Elliott (assumed stepfather's name); *m* Caroline Margaret McCarthy; two *s* one *d. Educ:* Raynes Park Grammar School. AMP INSEAD, 1976. Journalist, 1955–59; Public Relations, Avon Rubber Co. Ltd, 1959–63; Marketing, CPC International, 1963–68; Kimberly-Clark Ltd: Product Manager, 1968; Marketing Manager, 1969; Marketing and Development Manager, 1975; General Manager, 1976; Director, 1977; Gen. Administrator, Nat. Theatre, 1979–85; Dir of Admin, Denton, Hall, Burgin and Warrens, Solicitors, 1985–88; Head, Theatres Div., Bill Kenwright Ltd, 1992–93. Mem., Executive Council, Soc. of West End Theatre, 1980–85. *Recreations:* golf, walking. *Address:* Blurtings, 149 Forest Road, Tunbridge Wells, Kent TN2 5EX. *T:* Tunbridge Wells (01892) 530615, *Fax:* (01892) 532318.

ELLIOTT, Michael Norman; Member (Lab) London West, European Parliament, since 1984; *b* 3 June 1932. *Educ:* Brunel College of Technology. Formerly res. chemist in food industry. Mem., Ealing Borough Council, 1964–86 (former Leader of Council and Chm., Educn Cttee). Vice-Chair, Parly delegn to Norway; Member: Culture, Educn and Media Parly Cttee; Civil Liberties Parly Cttee; Parly Cttee of Inquiry into Racism and Xenophobia. Pres., Local Authority Aircraft Noise Council. Member: CND, 1961–; Friends of the Earth, 1985–. Hon. Fellow, Ealing Coll. of Higher Educn, 1988. *Address:* 358 Oldfield Lane North, Greenford, Middx UB6 8PT. *T:* 0181–578 1303.

ELLIOTT, Nicholas Blethyn; QC 1995; *b* 11 Dec. 1945; *s* of Col Blethyn William Treharne Elliott, late South Wales Borderers, and Zara Elliott; *m* 1976, Penelope, (Nemmy), Margaret Longbourne Browne; two *s. Educ:* Kelly Coll.; Bristol Univ. (LLB Hons). Called to the Bar, Gray's Inn, 1972. *Recreations:* tennis, cycling, swimming, bridge, rock and roll dancing. *Address:* Old Whistley Farmhouse, Potterne, Devizes, Wilts SN10 5TD.

ELLIOTT, Oliver Douglas; British Council Representative in Yugoslavia, 1979–85; *b* 13 Oct. 1925; *y s* of late Walter Elliott and Margherita Elliott, Bedford; *m* 1954, Patience Rosalie Joan Orpen; one *s. Educ:* Bedford Modern Sch.; Wadham Coll., Oxford (MA); Fitzwilliam House, Cambridge. Served RNVR (Sub-Lt), 1944–47. Colonial Educn Service, Cyprus, 1953–59; joined British Council, 1959; served Lebanon, 1960–63; Dep. Rep., Ghana, 1963; Dir, Commonwealth I Dept, 1966; Dir, Service Conditions Dept, 1970; Dep. Educn Advr, India, 1973; Representative in Nigeria, 1976–79. *Recreation:* golf.

ELLIOTT, Ven. Peter; Archdeacon of Northumberland, since 1993; *b* 14 June 1941; *s* of James Reginald and Hilda Elliott; *m* 1967, Evelyn Embleton; one *d. Educ:* Queen Elizabeth Grammar Sch., Horncastle; Hertford Coll., Oxford (MA Mod. History); Lincoln Theological Coll. Assistant Curate: All Saints, Gosforth, 1965–68; St Peter, Balkwell, 1968–72; Vicar: St Philip, High Elswick, 1972–80; North Gosforth, 1980–87; Embleton with Rennington and Rock, 1987–93. RD of Alnwick, 1989–93; Hon. Canon, Newcastle Cathedral, 1990–93. *Recreations:* water-colour painting, travel, railway timetables. *Address:* 80 Moorside North, Fenham, Newcastle upon Tyne NE4 9DU. *T:* 0191–273 8245.

ELLIOTT, Sir Randal (Forbes), KBE 1977 (OBE 1976); President, New Zealand Medical Association, 1976; *b* 12 Oct. 1922; *s* of Sir James Elliott and Lady (Ann) Elliott (*née* Forbes), MBE; *m* 1949, Pauline June Young; one *s* six *d. Educ:* Wanganui Collegiate Sch.; Otago Univ. MB, ChB (NZ), 1947; DO, 1953; FRCS, FRACS. Group Captain, RNZAF. Ophthalmic Surgeon, Wellington Hospital, 1953–. Chm. Council, NZ Med. Assoc. GCStJ 1987 (KStJ 1978). *Publications:* various papers in medical jls. *Recreations:* sailing, skiing, mountaineering. *Address:* Wakefield House, 90 The Terrace, Wellington, New Zealand. *T:* (4) 721375. *Club:* Wellington (NZ).

ELLIOTT, Robert Anthony K.; *see* Keable-Elliott.

ELLIOTT, Air Vice-Marshal Robert D.; *see* Deacon Elliott.

ELLIOTT, Sir Roger (James), Kt 1987; FRS 1976; Secretary to the Delegates and Chief Executive of Oxford University Press, 1988–93; Professor of Physics, Oxford University, 1989–Oct. 1996; Fellow of New College, Oxford, since 1974; *b* Chesterfield, 8 Dec. 1928; *s* of James Elliott and Gladys Elliott (*née* Hill); *m* 1952, Olga Lucy Atkinson; one *s* two *d. Educ:* Swanwick Hall Sch., Derbyshire; New Coll., Oxford (MA, DPhil). Research Fellow, Univ. of California, Berkeley, 1952–53; Research Fellow, UKAEA, Harwell, 1953–55; Lectr, Reading Univ., 1955–57; Fellow of St John's College, Oxford, 1957–74, Hon. Fellow, 1988; University Reader, Oxford, 1964–74; Wykeham Prof. of Physics, 1974–89; Senior Proctor, 1969; Delegate, Oxford Univ. Press, 1971–88. Chm., Computer Bd for Univs and Research Councils, 1983–87; Vice-Chm., Parly Office of Sci. and Technol., 1990–93; Member: Adv. Bd for Res. Councils, 1987–90; (part-time) UKAEA, 1988–94; British Council Bd, 1990–. Physical Sec. and Vice-Pres., Royal Soc., 1984–88; Pres., Publishers Assoc., 1993–94 (Treas., 1990–92). Visiting Prof., Univ. of California, Berkeley, 1961; Miller Vis. Prof., Univ. of Illinois, Urbana, 1966; Vis. Dist. Prof., Florida State Univ., 1981. Hon. DSc: Paris, 1983; Bath, 1991; Essex, 1993. Maxwell Medal, 1968, Guthrie Medal, 1990, Inst. of Physics. *Publications:* Magnetic Properties of Rare Earth Metals, 1973; Solid State Physics and its Applications (with A. F. Gibson), 1973; papers in Proc. Royal Soc., Jl Phys., Phys. Rev., etc. *Address:* 11 Crick Road, Oxford OX2 6QL. *T:* Oxford (01865) 273997. *Club:* Athenæum.

ELLIOTT, Sir Ronald (Stuart), Kt 1981; Director: International Board, Security Pacific National Bank, USA, 1983–91; Security Pacific Australia Ltd, 1985–91; *b* 29 Jan. 1918; *s* of Harold J. W. Elliott and Mercedes E. Manning; *m* 1944, Isabella Mansbridge Boyd; one *s* one *d. Educ:* C of E Grammar Sch., Ballarat, Victoria. ABIA; FAIM. Commonwealth Banking Corporation: Sec., 1960–61; Dep. Manager for Queensland, 1961–63; Chief Manager, Foreign Div., 1963–64; Chief Manager, Queensland, 1964–65; Gen. Manager, Commonwealth Develt Bank of Australia, 1966–75; Dep. Man. Dir, 1975–76, Man. Dir, 1976–81, Commonwealth Banking Corp.; Chm., Australian European Finance Corp. Ltd, 1976–81. Director: Australian Bd, Internat. Commodities Clearing House Ltd, 1981–88; Brambles Industries, 1981–90. Mem., Sci. and Industry Forum, Australian Acad. of Sci., 1978–81. Dir., Australian Opera, 1980–87; Mem., Australian Film Develt Corp., 1970–75. *Recreations:* golf, reading, music, particularly opera. *Address:* PO Box 1401, Armidale, NSW 2350, Australia. *T:* (67) 722387. *Clubs:* Union, Australian Golf (Sydney) (Pres., 1982–87, Capt., 1987–88); Armidale Golf.

ELLIOTT, Timothy Stanley; QC 1992; *b* 2 April 1950; *s* of John Edwin Elliott and Annie Elizabeth Stanley (*née* Lowe); *m* 1973, Katharine Barbara Lawrance; one *s* one *d. Educ:* Marlborough Coll.; Trinity Coll., Oxford (Exhibnr, MA Lit. Hum. 1973). Called to the Bar, Middle Temple, 1975. *Address:* 10 Essex Street, WC2R 3AA. *T:* 0171–240 6981.

ELLIOTT, Walter Archibald; *see* Elliott, Hon. Lord.

ELLIOTT, William Rowcliffe, CB 1969; Senior Chief Inspector, Department of Education and Science, 1968–72, retired; *b* 10 April 1910; *s* of Thomas Herbert Elliott and Ada Elliott (*née* Rowcliffe); *m* 1937, Karin Tess, *d* of Ernest and Lilly Classen; one *s. Educ:* St Paul's Sch.; The Queen's Coll., Oxford. Schoolmaster, 1933–36; HM Inspector of Schools: in Leeds, 1936–39; in Leicestershire, 1940–44; in Liverpool, 1944–48; Staff Inspector: for Adult Education, 1948–55; for Secondary Modern Education, 1955–57; Chief Inspector for Educational Developments, 1957–59; for Secondary Educn, 1959–66; Dep. Sen. Chief Insp., 1966–67. Pres., Section L, British Assoc., 1969; Mem., Oxfam Governing Council, 1974–80. Chm. of Governors, Friends' Sch., Saffron Walden, 1982–84. Governor of The Retreat, York, 1984–90. *Publications:* Monemvasia, The Gibraltar of Greece, 1971; Chest-tombs and 'tea caddies' by Cotswold and Severn, 1977. *Recreations:* village life, photography, gardenage. *Address:* Malthus Close, Farthinghoe, Brackley, Northants NN13 5NY. *T:* Banbury (01295) 710388. *Club:* Royal Over-Seas League.
See also Mark Elliott.

ELLIS; *see* Scott-Ellis.

ELLIS, Dr Adrian Foss, FEng 1995; Director of Technology and Health Sciences Division, Health and Safety Executive, since 1991; *b* 15 Feb. 1944; *s* of Henry James Ellis and Marjorie Foss Ellis (*née* Smith); *m* 1st, 1968, Lesley Maxted Smith (*d* 1970); 2nd, 1973, Hilary Jean Miles; two *d* one *s. Educ:* Dean Close Sch., Cheltenham; Univ. of London (1st cl. Hons Chem. Eng.); Loughborough Univ. of Technology (PhD). FIChemE 1977; FInstE 1977. Student Apprentice, Richard Thomas & Baldwins, 1962–66; British Steel Corp., 1966–71; DoE (Alkali and Clean Air), 1971–83; Health and Safety Executive: Major Hazards Assessment Unit, 1983–86; Dep. Chief Inspector (Chemicals), 1986; Regl Dir, 1990; Dir of Technology and Dir of Hazardous Installations Policy, 1990. ILO Consultant on major hazards control in India, Pakistan, Thailand, Indonesia. Vis. Prof., Dept of Applied Energy, Cranfield Univ. (formerly Inst. of Technology), 1992–. Mem. Council, IChemE, 1993–. *Publications:* papers on risk assessment and major hazards control. *Recreations:* bridge, Swindon Town FC, exploring car boot sales. *Address:* Health and Safety Executive, St Anne's House, Stanley Precinct, Bootle, Merseyside L20 3RA. *T:* 0151–951 4574. *Clubs:* Athenæum; Southport Bridge.

ELLIS, Alice Thomas; *see* Haycraft, A. M.

ELLIS, Andrew Steven, OBE 1984; political affairs and governmental relations consultant; Central and Eastern European Director, GJW Government Relations Ltd, since 1990; *b* 19 May 1952; *s* of Peter Vernon Ellis and Kathleen Dawe; *m* 1st, 1975, Patricia Ann Stevens (marr. diss. 1987); 2nd, 1990, Helen Prudence Drummond. *Educ:* Trinity Coll., Cambridge (BA Mathematics); Univ. of Newcastle upon Tyne (MSc Statistics); Newcastle upon Tyne Polytechnic (BA Law). Proprietor, Andrew Ellis (Printing and Duplicating), Newcastle upon Tyne, 1973–81; freelance Election Agent/Organizer, 1981–84; Sec.-Gen., Liberal Party, 1985–88; Chief Exec., Social and Liberal Democrats, 1988–89; freelance political consultant, 1989–93. Consultant Nat. Agent, Welsh Liberal Party, 1984–88. Contested (L): Newcastle upon Tyne Central, Oct. 1974, Nov. 1976, 1979; Boothferry, 1983; Leader, Liberal Gp, Tyne & Wear CC, 1977–81; Vice-Chm., Liberal Party, 1980–86. *Publications:* Algebraic Structure (with Terence Treeby), 1971; Let Every Englishman's Home Be His Castle, 1978. *Recreation:* travel. *Address:* 19 Hayle Road, Maidstone, Kent ME15 6PD. *T:* Maidstone (01622) 678443; Porth House, Powell Street, Aberystwyth, Ceredigion SY23 1QQ. *Club:* National Liberal.

ELLIS, Arthur John, CBE 1986; Chief Executive Officer, since 1969, and Chairman, since 1984, Fyffes Group Ltd; *b* 22 Aug. 1932; *s* of Arthur Ellis and Freda Jane Ellis; *m* 1956, Rita Patricia Blake; two *s* one *d. Educ:* Chingford Jun. High Sch.; South West Essex Technical Coll. FCCA; FCMA; FCIS; MBCS. Joined Fyffes Gp Ltd as qual. accountant in Finance and Admin Dept, 1954; Chief Financial Officer, 1965; Financial Dir, 1967; Dir, Fyffes plc, 1991–. Chm., Nat. Seed Develt Organisation Ltd, 1982–87. Chm., Intervention Bd for Agricl Produce, later Intervention Bd Exec. Agency, 1986–95. *Recreations:* golf, reading, gardening. *Address:* 12 York Gate, Regent's Park, NW1 4QJ. *T:* 0171–487 4472. *Clubs:* Reform, Farmers'.

ELLIS, His Honour Arthur Robert Malcolm, DL; a Circuit Judge (formerly Judge of County Courts), 1971–86; *b* 27 June 1912; *s* of David and Anne Amelia Ellis, Nottingham; *m* 1938, Brenda Sewell (*d* 1983); one *d. Educ:* Nottingham High Sch. Admitted Solicitor, 1934; called to the Bar, Inner Temple, 1953. Chm., Nottingham Council of Social Service, 1950–55; Dep. Chm., E Midland Traffic Area, 1955–71; Chm., Ministry of Pensions and National Insurance Tribunal, Sutton-in-Ashfield, Notts, 1961–64, resigned; Chm., Min. of Pensions and Nat. Insce Tribunal, Notts, 1964–71; Chm., Medical Appeals Tribunal, 1971–76. Chm., Notts QS, 1963–71 (Dep.-Chm., 1962–63); Chm., Derbyshire QS, 1966–71 (Dep.-Chm., 1965–66). DL Notts, 1973. *Recreations:* golf, bridge, reading. *Address:* Byways, 5 Manvers Grove, Radcliffe-on-Trent, Notts NG12 2FT. *Club:* United Services (Nottingham).

ELLIS, Bryan James; Under-Secretary, Department of Health and Social Security, later Department of Social Security, 1977–93; *b* 11 June 1934; *s* of late Frank and Renée Ellis; *m* 1960, Barbara Muriel Whiteley; one *s* one *d. Educ:* Merchant Taylors' Sch.; St John's Coll., Oxford. Sec., Oxford Union Soc., 1956. Joined Min. of Pensions and National Insurance as Asst Principal, 1958; Principal, 1963; Asst Sec., DHSS, 1971; served in CSSB as Chm., 1986, and in OPCS as Dep. Dir, 1987–90. Chm., Assoc. of First Div. Civil Servants, 1983–85. Chm., Trustees of Leopardstown Park Hosp., Dublin, 1979–84. *Publication:* Pensions in Britain 1955–75, 1989. *Recreations:* walking, theatre and cinema, bridge. *Address:* Cheshunt, Dennett Road, Bembridge, Isle of Wight PO35 5XF. *Club:* MCC.

ELLIS, Carol Jacqueline, (Mrs Ralph Gilmore), CBE 1995; QC 1980 (practises as Miss Ellis); JP (sits as Mrs Gilmore); Editor, The Law Reports, since 1976; Consultant Editor, Weekly Law Reports, since 1990; *b* 6 May 1929; *d* of Ellis W. Ellis and Flora Bernstein; *m* 1957, Ralph Gilmore; two *s*. *Educ:* Abbey Sch., Reading; La Ramée, Lausanne; Univ. of Lausanne; University Coll. London (LLB). Called to the Bar, Gray's Inn, 1951; supernumerary law reporter for The Law Reports, The Times, and other legal jls, 1952; law reporter to The Law Reports and Weekly Law Reports, 1954; Asst Editor, Weekly Law Reports, 1969; Managing Editor, The Law Reports and Weekly Law Reports, 1970; Editor, Weekly Law Reports, 1976–90. Mem., Inner London Probation Cttee, 1989–. JP W Central Div. Inner London, 1972–. *Recreations:* travel, music, theatre. *Address:* 11 Old Square, Lincoln's Inn, WC2A 3TS. *T:* 0171–403 0341.

ELLIS, (Dorothy) June; Headmistress, The Mount School, York, 1977–86; Clerk to Central Committee, Quaker Social Responsibility and Education, 1987–90; *b* 30 May 1926; *d* of Robert Edwin and Dora Ellis. *Educ:* La Sagesse, Newcastle upon Tyne; BSc Pure Science, Durham; DipEd Newcastle upon Tyne. Assistant Mistress: Darlington High Sch., 1947–49; Rutherford High Sch., 1949–50; La Sagesse High Sch., 1950–53; Housemistress, 1953–61, Sen. Mistress, 1961–64, St Monica's Sch.; Dep. Head, Sibford Sch., 1964–77. Clerk, 1986–90, Mem., 1990–, Swerford Parish Council. Mem. Cttee, Bray d'Oyley Housing Assoc., 1993–. Mem. Council, Woodbrooke Coll., 1987–93; Governor: Ellerslie Sch., Malvern, 1987–92; Friends' Sch., Saffron Walden, 1990–93. *Recreations:* walking, gardening, home-making. *Address:* Willowside, Swerford, Oxford OX7 4BQ. *T:* Hook Norton (01608) 737334.

ELLIS, Rear-Adm. Edward William, CB 1974; CBE 1968; *b* 6 Sept. 1918; *s* of Harry L. and Winifred Ellis; *m* 1945, Dilys (*née* Little); two *s*. Joined RN, 1940; War service afloat in HM Ships Broadwater and Eclipse, and liaison duties in USS Wichita and US Navy destroyer sqdn; psc 1952; Staff of Flag Officer Flotillas, Mediterranean, 1954–55; Sec. to 4th Sea Lord, 1956–58; Sec. to C-in-C South Atlantic and South America, 1959–60; HM Ships Bermuda and Belfast, 1960–62; Head of C-in-C Far East Secretariat, 1963–65; Sec. to C-in-C Portsmouth and Allied C-in-C Channel, 1965–66; Sec. to Chief of Naval Staff and 1st Sea Lord, 1966–68; Cdre RN Barracks Portsmouth, 1968–71; Adm. Pres., RNC Greenwich, 1972–74. Comdr 1953; Captain 1963; Rear-Adm. 1972. Private Sec. to Lord Mayor of London, 1974–82. Freeman of the City of London, 1974; Liveryman, Shipwrights' Co., 1980. OStJ 1981. Commander, Royal Order of Danebrog, 1974. *Recreations:* fishing, gardening. *Address:* South Lodge, Minstead, Lyndhurst, Hants SO43 7FR. *Club:* Army and Navy.

ELLIS, Eileen Mary, RDI 1984; freelance textile designer; *b* 1 March 1933; *m* 1954, Julian Ellis; one *s* two *d*. *Educ:* Huyton College; Leicester, Central and Royal Colleges of Art. Des RCA 1957; FCSD (FSIAD 1976). Designer of contract and decorative woven furnishing fabrics, carpets and wall coverings; designed for Ascher & Co., 1957–59; Partner, Orbit Design Group, 1960–73; formed Weaveplan as design consultancy, 1973–; design consultant: Tintawn Carpets, 1969–; Abbotsford Fabrics, 1982–; Botany Weaving Mill, Ireland, 1984–; Earlys of Witney. Recent projects include work for Herman Miller Inc., British Airways, BAA, Intercity. Lectr, Hornsey Coll. of Art/Middlesex Polytechnic, 1965–74; Vis Lectr, RCA (Lectr, 1974–82). RSA Bursary in Dress Textiles, 1953; RSA Travel Bursary for established designer in textile industry, 1973. Textile Inst. Design Medal, 1985. *Recreations:* country life, reading. *Address:* c/o Weaveplan, The Glasshouse, 11/12 Lettice Street, SW6 4EH. *T:* 0171–736 3085.

ELLIS, Prof. George Francis Rayner, PhD; FRSSAf; Professor of Applied Mathematics, University of Cape Town, since, 1989; President, Royal Society of South Africa, 1992–96; *b* 11 Aug. 1939; *s* of George Rayner Ellis and Gwendoline Hilda Ellis (*née* MacRobert); *m* 1st, 1963, Jane Mary Sue Parkes; one *s* one *d*; 2nd, 1978, Mary MacDonald Wheeldon. *Educ:* Univ. of Cape Town (BSc Hons 1960; Fellow, 1982); St John's Coll., Cambridge (PhD 1964). FRSSAf 1983. Lectr, Cambridge Univ., 1968–73; Prof., Univ. of Cape Town, 1973–87; Prof., Scuola Internazionale Superiore di Studi Avanzati Trieste, 1987–89. Vis. Prof., Univs of Texas, Hamburg, Chicago, Alberta, and QMC London. Clerk, S Africa Yearly Meeting of Quakers, 1982–86; Chairman: Quaker Service, W Cape, 1978–86; Quaker Peace Work Cttee, W Cape, 1989–. Herschel Medal, Royal Soc. of S Africa, 1978; Medal, SA Assoc. for Advancement of Science, 1993. *Publications:* (with S. W. Hawking) The Large Scale Structure of Space-Time, 1973; (with D. Dewar) Low Income Housing Policy, 1979; Before the Beginning, 1993. *Recreations:* mountain climbing, gliding. *Address:* Department of Applied Mathematics, University of Cape Town, Rondebosch 7700, Cape Town, South Africa; 3 Marlow Road, Kenilworth, Cape Town 7700, South Africa. *T:* 7612313. *Club:* Mountain of South Africa (Cape Town).

ELLIS, Prof. Harold, CBE 1987; MA, MCh, DM; FRCS; FRCOG; Clinical Anatomist, University of London, at Guy's campus, since 1993; *b* 13 Jan. 1926; *s* of Samuel and Ada Ellis; *m* 1958, Wendy Mae Levine; one *s* one *d*. *Educ:* Queen's Coll. (State Scholar and Open Scholar in Natural Sciences), Oxford; Radcliffe Infirmary, Oxford. BM, BCh, 1948; FRCS, MA, 1951; MCh 1956; DM 1962; FRCOG *ad eundem*, 1987; Hon. FACS 1989. House Surgeon, Radcliffe Infirmary, 1948–49; Hallett Prize, RCS, 1949. RAMC, 1949–51. Res. Surgical Officer, Sheffield Royal Infirm., 1952–54; Registrar, Westminster Hosp., 1955; Sen. Registrar and Surgical Tutor, Radcliffe Infirm., Oxford, 1956–60; Sen. Lectr in Surgery, 1960–62, Hon. Consultant Surgeon, 1960–89, Westminster Hosp.; Prof. of Surgery, Univ. of London, 1962–89; Clinical Anatomist, Univ. of Cambridge and Fellow, Churchill Coll., Cambridge, 1989–93. Hon. Consultant Surgeon to the Army, 1978–89. Mem. Council, RCS, 1974–86. Member: Association of Surgeons; British Soc. of Gastroenterol.; Surgical Research Soc.; Council: RSocMed; British Assoc. of Surgical Oncology; Associé étranger, L'Academie de Chirurgie, Paris, 1983. *Publications:* Clinical Anatomy, 1960; Anatomy for Anaesthetists, 1963; Lecture Notes on General Surgery, 1965; Principles of Resuscitation, 1967; History of the Bladder Stone, 1970; General Surgery for Nurses, 1976; Intestinal Obstruction, 1982; Notable Names in Medicine and Surgery, 1983; Famous Operations, 1984; Wound Healing for Surgeons, 1984; Maingot's Abdominal Operations, 1985; Research in Medicine, 1990; Cross-sectional Anatomy, 1991; Surgical Case-Histories from the Past, 1994; numerous articles on surgical topics in medical journals. *Recreation:* medical history. *Address:* 16 Bancroft Avenue, N2 0AS. *T:* 0181–348 2720.

ELLIS, Herbert; *see* Ellis, W. H. B.

ELLIS, Humphry Francis, MBE 1945; MA; writer; *b* 1907; 2nd *s* of late Dr John Constable Ellis, Metheringham, Lincs and Alice Marion Raven; *m* 1933, Barbara Pauline Hasseldine; one *s* one *d*. *Educ:* Tonbridge Sch.; Magdalen Coll., Oxford (Demy). 1st cl. Hon. Mods, 1928; 1st cl. Lit. Hum., 1930. Asst Master, Marlborough Coll., 1930–31. Contributor to Punch, 1931–68; Editorial staff, 1933; Literary and Dep. Ed., 1949–53. Privilege Mem., RFU, 1952–. Served War of 1939–45 in RA (AA Command). *Publications:* So This is Science, 1932; The Papers of A. J. Wentworth, 1949; Why the Whistle Went (on the laws of Rugby Football), 1947; Co-Editor, The Royal Artillery Commemoration Book, 1950; Editor, Manual of Rugby Union Football, 1952; Twenty Five Years Hard, 1960; Mediatrics, 1961; A. J. Wentworth, BA (Retd), 1962; The World of A. J. Wentworth, 1964 (re-issued as A. J. Wentworth, BA, 1980); Swansong of A. J. Wentworth, 1982; A Bee in the Kitchen, 1983; contribs to The New Yorker. *Recreation:* fishing. *Address:* Hill Croft, Kingston St Mary, Taunton, Somerset TA2 8HT. *T:* Kingston St Mary (01823) 451264. *Clubs:* Garrick, MCC.

ELLIS, John; Steel Worker, British Steel plc, Scunthorpe, 1980–89; *b* Hexthorpe, Doncaster, 22 Oct. 1930; *s* of George and Hilda Ellis; *m* 1953, Rita Butters; two *s* two *d*. *Educ:* Rastrick Gram. Sch., Brighouse. Laboratory technician, Meteorological Office, 1947–63; Vice-Chm., Staff side, Air Min. Whitley Council, 1961–63; Member Relations Offr, Co-op. Retail Services, Bristol/Bath Region, 1971–74. Member: Easthampstead RDC, 1962–66; Bristol City Council, 1971–74; Humberside County Council, 1987–. Vice-Chm., Humberside Social Service Council, 1990–; Chm., Social Services Children's Cttee, 1992–; Member: Scunthorpe HA, 1988–91 (Chm., Jt Consultative Cttee, 1990–); NRA (formerly Lincs Land Drainage Cttee), 1988– (Member: Anglian Regl Flood Defence cttee; Lincs Flood Defence cttee). Contested (Lab) Wokingham, 1964; MP (Lab) Bristol North-West, 1966–70, Brigg and Scunthorpe, Feb. 1974–1979; PPS to Minister of State for Transport, 1968–70; an Asst Govt Whip, 1974–76. JP, North Riding Yorks, 1960–61. *Recreations:* gardening, watching cricket. *Address:* 102 Glover Road, Scunthorpe, South Humberside DN17 1AS.

ELLIS, John, CB 1985; independent technical consultant; Head of Royal Armament Research and Development Establishment, Chertsey, 1984–85, retired; *b* 9 Jan. 1925; *s* of Frank William and Alice Ellis; *m* 1958, Susan Doris (*née* Puttock). *Educ:* Leeds Univ. BSc, 1st cl. hons. Mech. Eng; CEng, MIMechE. Hydro-Ballistic Research Estabt, Admty, 1945–47; David Brown & Sons Ltd, Huddersfield, 1948; RAE, Min. of Supply (Structures Dept, Armament Dept, Weapons Dept), 1948–68; MVEE (formerly FVRDE), MoD, 1968–84; Dir, MVEE, Chertsey, 1978–84, when MVEE and RARDE amalgamated. *Recreations:* motoring, golf. *Address:* Foresters, 1 Kitchers Close, Sway, Lymington, Hants SO41 6DS. *T:* Lymington (01590) 682410.

ELLIS, John Norman, OBE 1995; Secretary to Council of Civil Service Unions, 1992–95; *b* 22 Feb. 1939; *s* of Margaret and Albert Ellis; *m* 1st; one *s* one *d*; 2nd, Diane Anderson; two step *s*. *Educ:* Osmondthorpe; Leeds Secondary Modern; Leeds College of Commerce. Post Office Messenger and Postman, 1954–58; Clerical Officer and Executive Officer, MPBW, 1958–67; Civil and Public Services Association: Asst Sec., 1968–82; Dep. Gen. Sec., 1982–87; Gen. Sec., 1987–92. Member: Gen. Council, TUC, 1988–92 (Mem. Economic, Social Services, Industrial Welfare, Public Services and Pensions Specialists Cttees); CS Occupational Health Service Adv. Bd.; Exec. Cttee, Inst. of Employment Rights; Industrial Tribunals Panel; Public Sector Res. Foundn Steeering Cttee. Dir, CS Housing Assoc., 1988–. *Recreations:* reading, watching sport, gardening, listening to music. *Address:* 26 Harestone Valley Road, Caterham, Surrey CR3 6HD.

ELLIS, Sir John (Rogers), Kt 1980; MBE 1943; MA, MD, FRCP; Physician, 1951–81, Consulting Physician, since 1981, The London Hospital; Chairman, Graves Educational Resources, since 1982; *b* 15 June 1916; 3rd *s* of late Frederick William Ellis, MD, FRCS; *m* 1942, Joan, *d* of late C. J. C. Davenport; two *s* two *d*. *Educ:* Oundle Sch.; Trinity Hall, Cambridge; London Hosp. Served RNVR, 1942–46, Mediterranean and Far East, Surg-Lieut. Gen. Practice, Plymouth, 1946; Sen. Lectr, Med. Unit, London Hosp., 1948–51; Sub-Dean, London Hosp. Med. Coll., 1948–58, Vice-Dean, 1967–68, Dean, 1968–81, Fellow, 1986; Asst Registrar, RCP, 1957–61, Mem. Council 1969–72, Streatfield Schol., 1957; Physician to Prince of Wales Gen. Hosp., 1958–68; PMO (part-time), Min. of Health, 1964–68. Mem., City and E London AHA, 1974–81; Vice-Chm., Newham DHA, 1981–85. Vice-Chm., Med. Council on Alcoholism, 1983–; Member: UGC's Med. Sub-cttee, 1959–69; WHO Expert Adv. Panel on Health Manpower, 1963–82; Jt Bd of Clinical Nursing Studies, 1969–74; formerly Member: Porritt (Med. Services) Cttee; Royal Commn on Med. Educn; UK Educn Cttee, RCN. Sec., Assoc. for Study of Med. Educn, 1956–71, Vice-Pres., 1971–; Pres., Medical Protection Soc., 1985–88. Lectures: Goulstonian, RCP, 1956; Wood-Jones, Univ. of Manchester, 1960; Porter, Univ. of Kansas, 1960; Sir Charles Hastings, BMA, 1964; Anders, Coll. of Physicians, Pa, 1965; Adams, RCSI, 1965; Shattuck, Massachusetts Med. Soc., 1969; Shorstein, 1979, 1985, Sprawson, 1980, 1985, London Hosp. Med. Coll.; Attlee Meml, Attlee Foundn, 1993; Visiting Lecturer: Assoc. of Amer. Med. Colls, 1957, 1960 and 1963; Ghana Acad. of Sciences, 1967. Former examr in Med., Univs of Birmingham, Bristol, Cambridge, E Africa, London, Nairobi, Ireland, Newcastle upon Tyne, St Andrews. Corr. Mem., Royal Flemish Acad. of Medicine; Hon. Member: Swedish Med. Soc.; AOA Honor Med. Soc., USA; Sect. of Med. Educn, RSocMed (former Pres.). Pres., Waltham Forest Sea Cadet Unit, 1977–; Chairman of Governors: Inst. of Educn, London Univ., 1983–93; Woodford Co. High Sch. for Girls, 1992–; Member Bd of Governors, Atlantic Coll.; formerly Member Board of Governors: Inst. of Psychiatry; Bethlem Royal and Maudsley Hosps; London Hosp.; British Postgrad. Med. Fedn; Queen Mary Coll.; CARE for Mentally Handicapped. Pres., London Hosp. League of Friends, 1980–. Formerly Mem. Court, Univ. of Essex. Editor, British Jl of Medical Education, 1966–75. Hon. Fellow: QMC, 1985; London Hosp. Med. Coll., 1986. Hon. MD Uppsala, 1977. *Publications:* LHMC 1785–1985, 1986; articles on medical education in medical and scientific journals. *Recreations:* painting, gardening. *Address:* Little Monkhams, Monkhams Lane, Woodford Green, Essex IG8 0NP. *T:* 0181–504 2292.

ELLIS, Prof. John Romaine; Professor of Automobile Engineering, 1960–82 and Director, 1960–76, School of Automotive Studies, Cranfield; *b* 30 Sept. 1922; *m* 1947, Madelaine Della Blaker; one *s* one *d*. *Educ:* Tiffin Sch., Kingston-on-Thames. Royal Aircraft Establishment, 1944–56; Fairey Aviation Company, 1946–48; Royal Military Coll. of Science, Shrivenham, near Swindon, Wilts, 1949–60. *Recreations:* golf, music. *Address:* Upper Watkins, Lower Road, Edington, Wilts BA13 4QW.

ELLIS, John Russell; Managing Director, ScotRail, since 1995; *b* 21 May 1938; *s* of Percy Macdonald Ellis and Winifred Maud (*née* Bunker); *m* 1962, Jean Eileen Taylor; two *d*. *Educ:* Rendcomb Coll., Cirencester; Pembroke Coll., Oxford (BA Hons PPE). Joined BR as Grad. Management Trainee, 1962; various posts, 1963–80; Chief Freight Manager, 1980–83, Divl Manager, 1983–84, Asst Gen. Manager, 1984–85, Eastern Region; Dep. Gen. Manager, Southern Region, 1985–87; Gen. Manager, ScotRail, 1987–90; Gen. Manager, Southern Region, 1990–91; Dep. Man. Dir, InterCity, 1992–93; Dir, Production, Railtrack, 1993–95. *Recreations:* hockey, cricket, walking, gardening, music. *Address:* St Anne's, Chipping Campden, Glos GL55 6AL. *T:* Evesham (01386) 841253; (office) Caledonian Chambers, 87 Union Street, Glasgow.

ELLIS, Dr Jonathan Richard, FRS 1985; Leader, Theoretical Studies Division, CERN, Geneva, since 1988; *b* 1 July 1946; *s* of Richard Ellis and Beryl Lilian Ellis (*née* Ranger); *m* 1985, Maria Mercedes Martinez Rengifo; one *s* one *d*. *Educ:* Highgate Sch.; King's Coll.,

Cambridge. BA; PhD. Postdoctoral research, SLAC, Stanford, 1971–72; Richard Chase Tolman Fellow, Caltech, 1972–73; Staff Mem., CERN, Geneva, 1973–. Maxwell Medal, Inst. of Physics, 1982. *Recreations:* movies, hiking in the mountains, horizontal jogging. *Address:* 5 Chemin du Ruisseau, Tannay, 1295 Mies, Vaud, Switzerland. *T:* (22) 7764858.

ELLIS, June; *see* Ellis, D. J.

ELLIS, Laurence Edward, MA; Rector, The Edinburgh Academy, 1977–92; *b* 21 April 1932; *s* of Dr and Mrs E. A. Ellis; *m* 1961, Elizabeth Ogilvie; two *s* one *d.* *Educ:* Winchester Coll.; Trinity Coll., Cambridge (MA). AFIMA. 2/Lieut Rifle Bde, 1950–52. Marlborough Coll., 1955–77 (Housemaster, 1968). FRSA. *Publications:* (part-author) texts on school maths, statistics, computing, and calculating; articles in jls. *Recreations:* writing, music, woodwork. *Address:* Glendene, Wick Lane, Devizes, Wilts SN10 5DW.

ELLIS, Martin Arthur; Taxing Master of the Supreme Court, since 1990; *b* 10 Jan. 1933; *s* of Walter Ellis and Phoebe Alicia Ellis; *m* 1961, Moira Herbert; two *s.* *Educ:* Beckenham Grammar School. Solicitor, admitted 1956; 2nd Lieut, 4th Regt, Royal Horse Artillery, 1957–58; Partner, Simmons & Simmons, 1973–90. *Recreations:* sport, golf, cricket. *Address:* Birch Lawn, 5 Westwood Close, Bromley, Kent BR1 2JJ. *T:* 0181–460 4299. *Clubs:* MCC; Kent CC, The Addington Golf, Royal St George's Golf.

ELLIS, Mary; actress; singer; authoress; *b* New York City, 15 June 1900; *m* 1st, L. A. Bernheimer (decd); 2nd (marr. diss.); 3rd, Basil Sydney (marr. diss.); 4th, J. Muir Stewart Roberts (decd). *Educ:* New York. Studied art for three years; studied singing with Madame Ashforth. First Stage appearance, Metropolitan Opera House, New York, in Sœur Angelica, 1918; with Metropolitan Opera House, 1918–22; first appearance dramatic stage, as Nerissa in Merchant of Venice, Lyceum, New York, 1922; was the original Rose Marie (in the musical play, Rose Marie), Imperial, 1924; The Dybbuk, New York, 1925–26; Taming of the Shrew, 1927, and many New York leads followed; first appearance on London stage, as Laetitia in Knave and Quean, Ambassadors', 1930; after appearance in Strange Interlude in London, remained in London, giving up US citizenship in 1946; London: Strange Interlude, 1932; Double Harness, 1933; Music in the Air, 1934; Glamorous Night, Drury Lane, 1935; Innocent Party, St James's, 1937; Dancing Years, Drury Lane, 1939. From 1939–43: doing hospital welfare work and giving concerts for troops. Re-appeared on stage as Marie Foret in Arc de Triomphe, Phœnix, London, 1943; Old Vic (at Liverpool Playhouse), 1944 (Ella Rentheim in John Gabriel Borkman; Linda Valaine in Point Valaine; Lady Teazle in The School for Scandal); Maria Fitzherbert in The Gay Pavilion, Piccadilly, 1945; Season at Embassy: Mrs Dane's Defence, also tour and première of Ian Hay's Hattie Stowe, 1946–47; post-war successes include: Playbill, Phœnix, 1949; Man in the Raincoat, Edinburgh, 1949; If this be Error, Hammersmith, 1950. Stratford-on-Avon Season, 1952: Volumnia in Coriolanus. London: After the Ball (Oscar Wilde-Noel Coward), Globe, 1954–55; Mourning Becomes Electra, Arts, 1955–56; Dark Halo, Arts, 1959; Look Homeward Angel, Pembroke Theatre, Croydon, 1960, Phœnix, 1962; Yvonne Arnaud, Guildford: Silver Cord (revival), 1971; Mrs Warren's Profession, 1972. *Films:* Bella Donna, 1934; Hollywood, 1935–36: Paris in the Spring; The King's Horses; Fatal Lady; Glamorous Night, 1937; Gulliver's Travels, 1961. Since 1972 has devoted time to writing, radio and television; has made several major television appearances, also many radio programmes and interviews; television, 1956–: Shaw's Great Catherine, Van Druten's Distaff Side, Memoirs of Sherlock Holmes and numerous others. Theatre lectures in USA, 1977. *Publications:* Those Dancing Years (autobiog.), 1982; Moments of Truth, 1986. *Recreations:* painting, travel, writing. *Address:* c/o Chase Manhattan Bank, Woolgate House, Coleman Street, EC2P 2HD.

ELLIS, Maxwell (Philip), MD, MS, FRCS; retired; Dean of the Institute of Laryngology and Otology, University of London, 1965–71; Consulting Surgeon, Royal National Throat, Nose and Ear Hospital, 1937–71; Consulting Ear, Nose and Throat Surgeon, Central Middlesex Hospital, 1937–74; *b* 28 Feb. 1906; *s* of Louis Ellis; *m* 1st, 1935, Barbara Gertrude Chapman (*d* 1977); 2nd, 1979, Mrs Clarice Adler (*d* 1989). *Educ:* University Coll., London (Exhibitioner), Fellow 1975; University Coll. Hosp. (Bucknill Exhbnr). Liston and Alexander Bruce Gold Medals, Surgery and Pathology, UCH, 1927–29. MB, BS (London), Hons Medicine, 1930; MD 1931; FRCS 1932; MS 1937; Geoffrey Duveen Trav. Student, Univ. of London, 1934–36; Leslie Pearce Gould Trav. Schol., 1934, Perceval Alleyn Schol. (Surg. research), 1936, UCH; Hunterian Prof., RCS, 1938. RAFVR, 1940–45 (Wing-Comdr). FRSM, also Mem. Council; Past Pres., Section of Otology; Trustee, Hon. Fellow and Mem. Council, Med. Soc. London (Hon. Sec. 1961–63; Pres., 1970–71); Hon. Member: Assoc. of Otolaryngologists of India; Salonika Soc. of Otolaryngology; Athens Soc. of Otolaryngology; Corresp. Mem., Société Française d'Oto-Rhino-Laryngologie; Hon. Corresp. Mem., Argentine Soc. of Otolaryngology. Lectr on Diseases of Ear, Nose and Throat, Univ. of London, 1952. *Publications:* Modern Trends in Diseases of the Ear, Nose and Throat (Ed. and part author), 1954, 2nd edn 1971; Operative Surgery (Rob and Smith), Vol. 8 on Diseases of the Ear, Nose and Throat (Ed. and part author), 1958; 2nd edn 1969; Clinical Surgery (Rob and Smith), Vol. 11, Diseases of the Ear, Nose and Throat (Ed. and part author), 1966; Sections in Diseases of the Ear, Nose and Throat (Ed. Scott-Brown), 1952, new edns 1965, 1971; Sections in Cancer, Vol. 4 (Ed. Raven), 1958; Section in Modern Trends in Surgical Materials (Ed. Gillis), 1958; papers in various medical and scientific jls. *Recreations:* golf, gardening; formerly bridge and squash rackets. *Address:* 48 Townshend Road, NW8 6LE. *T:* 0171–722 2252. *Clubs:* Royal Automobile; Sunningdale Golf.

ELLIS, Norman David; Under Secretary, British Medical Association, since 1980 (Senior Industrial Relations Officer, 1978–82); *b* 23 Nov. 1943; *s* of late George Edward Ellis and late Annie Elsie Scarfe; *m* 1966, Valerie Ann Fenn, PhD; one *s.* *Educ:* Minchenden Sch.; Univ. of Leeds (BA); MA (Oxon), PhD. Research Officer, Dept of Employment, 1969–71; Leverhulme Fellowship in Industrial Relations, Nuffield Coll., Oxford, 1971–74; Gen. Sec., Assoc. of First Division Civil Servants, 1974–78. *Publications:* (with W. E. J. McCarthy) Management by Agreement, 1973; Employing Staff, 1984; (with J. Chisholm) Making sense of the Red Book, 1993; (with T. Stanton) Making sense of Partnerships, 1994; Making sense of General Practice, 1994; (with J. Lindsay) Making sense of Pensions and Retirement, 1995; various contribs to industrial relations literature. *Recreations:* reading, swimming. *Address:* 33 Foxes Dale, SE3 9BH. *T:* 0181–852 6244.

ELLIS, Osian Gwynn, CBE 1971; harpist; Professor of Harp, Royal Academy of Music, London, since 1959; *b* Ffynnongroew, Flints, 8 Feb. 1928; *s* of Rev. T. G. Ellis, Methodist Minister; *m* 1951, Rene Ellis Jones, Pwllheli; two *s.* *Educ:* Denbigh Grammar Sch.; Royal Academy of Music. Has broadcast and televised extensively. Has given recitals/concertos all over the world; shared poetry and music recitals with Dame Peggy Ashcroft, Paul Robeson, Burton, C. Day-Lewis, etc. Mem., Melos Ensemble; solo harpist with LSO. Former Mem., Music and Welsh Adv. Cttees, British Council. Works written for him include Harp Concertos by Hoddinott, 1957 and by Mathias, 1970, Jersild, 1972, Robin Holloway, 1985; chamber works by Gian Carlo Menotti, 1977; William Schuman, 1978; from 1960 worked with Benjamin Britten who wrote for him Harp Suite in C (Op. 83) and (for perf. with Sir Peter Pears) Canticle V, Birthday Hansel, and folk songs; accompanied the late Sir Peter Pears on recital tours, Europe and USA, 1974–; records concertos, recitals, folk songs, etc. Film, The Harp, won a Paris award; other awards include Grand Prix du Disque and French Radio Critics' Award. FRAM 1960. Hon. DMus Wales, 1970. *Publication:* Story of the Harp in Wales, 1991. *Address:* 90 Chandos Avenue, N20 9DZ. *T:* 0181–445 7896.

ELLIS, Prof. Reginald John, PhD; FRS 1983; Professor of Biological Sciences, University of Warwick, since 1976; *b* 12 Feb. 1935; *s* of Francis Gilbert Ellis and Evangeline Gratton Ellis; *m* 1963, Diana Margaret Warren; one *d.* *Educ:* Highbury County Sch.; King's Coll., London (BSc, PhD). ARC Fellow, Univ. of Oxford, 1961–64; Lectr in Botany and Biochemistry, Univ. of Aberdeen, 1964–70; Sen. Lectr, 1970–73, Reader, 1973–76, Dept of Biol Sciences, Univ. of Warwick; SERC Senior Res. Fellow, 1983–88. Sen. Vis. Fellow, St John's Coll., Oxford, 1992–93. Mem. EMBO, 1986–. LRPS 1987. Tate & Lyle Award (for contribs to plant biochem.), 1980. *Publications:* 120 papers in biochem. jls. *Recreations:* photography, hill walking. *Address:* 44 Sunningdale Avenue, Kenilworth, Warwicks CV8 2BZ. *T:* Kenilworth (01926) 56382.

ELLIS, Richard Peter; Principal Assistant Treasury Solicitor, Legal Advisory Division, Ministry of Defence, 1988–91; *b* 25 Oct. 1931; *s* of late Comdr Thomas Ellis, RN and Kathleen Mary Ellis (*nee* Lewis); *m* 1963, Penelope Jane, *yr d* of late Captain J. B. Hall, RN; two *s* two *d.* *Educ:* Sherborne; RMA Sandhurst. Commissioned Royal Irish Fusiliers, 1952; served 1st Bn, BAOR, Berlin, Korea, Kenya; resigned commission 1957. Called to the Bar, Lincoln's Inn, 1960; Practised Common Law Bar, 1960–65, Oxford Circuit; Treasury Solicitor's Dept, 1965–91. *Recreations:* country pursuits, travel, reading. *Address:* c/o Lloyds Bank, Somerton, Somerset TA11 7NB. *Club:* Army and Navy.

ELLIS, Prof. Richard Salisbury, FRS 1995; Plumian Professor of Astronomy and Experimental Philosophy, Cambridge University, since 1993; Director, Institute of Astronomy, Cambridge, since 1994; Professorial Fellow, Magdalene College, Cambridge, since 1994; *b* 25 May 1950; *s* of Capt. Arthur Ellis, MBE and Marion Ellis (*née* Davies); *m* 1972, Barbara Williams; one *s* one *d.* *Educ:* Abergele GS; University Coll. London (BSc Hons 1971); Wolfson Coll., Oxford (DPhil 1974). FRAS 1974. Durham University: Sen. Demonstrator in Physics, 1974–77; Res. Asst, 1977–81; Lectr in Astronomy, 1981–83; Principal Res. Fellow, Royal Greenwich Observatory, 1983–85; Prof. of Astronomy, Durham Univ., 1985–93; SERC Sen. Res. Fellow, 1989–94. Chm., SERC Large Telescope Panel, 1986–90; Mem., Anglo-Australian Telescope Bd, 1991–95. Associate, Canadian Inst. of Advanced Res., 1993–; Space Telescope Science Inst. Council, 1995–. Visiting Professor: Space Telescope Science Inst., 1985; Anglo-Australian Observatory, 1991; Caltech, 1991; Princeton, 1992. Lectures: J. L. Bishop, Princeton, 1992; Halley, Oxford, 1993. *Publications:* Epoch of Galaxy Formation, 1988; Observational Tests of Cosmological Inflation, 1991; numerous articles in astronomical jls. *Recreations:* exploration, photography, music, ski-ing. *Address:* Institute of Astronomy, Madingley Road, Cambridge CB3 0HA. *T:* Cambridge (01223) 337548.

ELLIS, (Robert) Thomas; *b* 15 March 1924; *s* of Robert and Edith Ann Ellis; *m* 1949, Nona Harcourt Williams; three *s* one *d.* *Educ:* Universities of Wales and Nottingham. Works Chemist, ICI, 1944–47; Coal Miner, 1947–55; Mining Engineer, 1955–70; Manager, Bersham Colliery, N Wales, 1957–70. MP Wrexham, 1970–83 (Lab, 1970–81; SDP, 1981–83). Contested: Clywd South West (SDP) 1983, (SDP/Alliance) 1987; Pontypridd (SLD) Feb. 1989. Mem., European Parlt, 1975–79. *Publication:* Mines and Men, 1971. *Recreations:* golf, reading, music. *Address:* 3 Old Vicarage, Ruabon, Clwyd LL14 6LG. *T:* Wrexham (01978) 821128.

ELLIS, Ven. Robin Gareth; Archdeacon of Plymouth, since 1982; *b* 8 Dec. 1935; *s* of Walter and Morva Ellis; *m* 1964, Anne Ellis (*née* Landers); three *s.* *Educ:* Worksop Coll., Notts; Pembroke Coll., Oxford (BCL, MA). Curate of Swinton, 1960–63; Asst Chaplain, Worksop Coll., 1963–66; Vicar of Swaffham Prior and Reach, and Asst Director of Religious Education, Diocese of Ely, 1966–74; Vicar of St Augustine, Wisbech, 1974–82; Vicar of St Paul's, Yelverton, 1982–86. *Recreations:* cricket, theatre, prison reform. *Address:* 33 Leat Walk, Roborough, Plymouth, Devon PL6 7AT. *T:* Plymouth (01752) 793397.

ELLIS, Roger Henry, MA; FSA; FRHistS; Secretary, Royal Commission on Historical Manuscripts, 1957–72; *b* 9 June 1910; *e s* of late Francis Henry Ellis, Debdale Hall, Mansfield; *m* 1939, Audrey Honor (*d* 1993), *o d* of late H. Arthur Baker, DL; two *d.* *Educ:* Sedbergh (scholar); King's College, Cambridge (scholar, Augustus Austen Leigh Student). 1st Cl. Class. Tripos, Pts I and II. Asst Keeper, Public Record Office, 1934; Principal Asst Keeper, 1956. Served War of 1939–45: Private, 1939; Major, 5th Fusiliers, 1944; Monuments, Fine Arts and Archives Officer in Italy and Germany, 1944–45. Lectr in Archive Admin, Sch. of Librarianship and Archives, University Coll. London, 1947–57. Mem. London Council, British Inst. in Florence, 1947–55; Hon. Editor, British Records Assoc., and (first) Editor of Archives, 1947–57, Chm. Council, 1967–73, Vice-Pres., 1971–. Vice-Pres., Business Archives Council, 1958–; Member: Adv. Council on Export of Works of Art, 1964–72; Jt Records Cttee of Royal Soc. and Historical MSS Commn, 1968–76; ICA Cttee on Sigillography, 1962–77; Pres., Soc. of Archivists, 1964–73. Chm., Drafting Cttee, British Standard 5454 (The Storage and Exhibition of Archival Documents), 1967–76. A Manager, 1973–76, a Vice-Pres., 1975–76, Royal Instn. Corresp. Mem., Indian Historical Records Commn. *Publications:* The Principles of Archive Repair, 1951; (ed) Manual of Archive Administration by Sir Hilary Jenkinson, 2nd edn 1965; Manuscripts and Men (Royal Commn on Hist. MSS centenary exhibn cat.), 1969; Catalogue of Seals in the Public Record Office: Personal Seals, vol. I, 1978, vol. II, 1981, Monastic Seals, vol. I, 1986; Ode on St Crispin's Day, 1979; (ed jtly) Select Writings of Sir Hilary Jenkinson, 1980; Walking Backwards, 1986; opuscula and articles in British and foreign jls and compilations on care, study and use of archives and MSS. *Recreations:* poetry, travel, the arts. *Address:* 7 Straffan Lodge, Belsize Grove, NW3 4XE. *Club:* Athenæum.

ELLIS, Roger Wykeham, CBE 1984; Director, Asquith Court Schools Ltd, since 1992; *b* 3 Oct. 1929; *s* of Cecil Ellis, solicitor, and Pamela Unwin; *m* 1964, Margaret Jean Stevenson; one *s* two *d.* *Educ:* St Peter's Sch., Seaford; Winchester Coll.; Trinity Coll., Oxford (Schol., MA). Royal Navy, 1947–49. Asst Master, Harrow Sch., 1952–67, and Housemaster of the Head Master's House, 1961–67; Headmaster of Rossall Sch., 1967–72; Master of Marlborough College, 1972–86. Graduate Recruitment Manager, Barclays Bank, 1986–91. Chm., HMC, 1983. Member: Harrow Borough Educn Cttee, 1956–60; Wilts County Educn Cttee, 1975–86. Governor: Campion Sch., Athens, 1981–; Cheam Sch., 1975–93 (Chm. of Govs, 1987–93); Hawtreys Sch., 1975–86; Sandroyd Sch., 1982–86; Fettes Coll., 1983–94; St Edward's Sch., Oxford, 1985– (Chm., 1992–); Harrow Sch., 1987–. *Recreations:* golf, fishing. *Address:* 18 North Avenue, Ealing, W13 8AP. *Clubs:* East India; Denham Golf.

ELLIS, Sir Ronald, Kt 1978; BSc Tech; FEng, FIMechE; FCIT; Chairman, EIDC Ltd, 1981–93; *b* 12 Aug. 1925; *s* of William Ellis and Besse Brownbill; *m* 1st, 1956, Cherry Hazel Brown (*d* 1978); one *s* one *d*; 2nd, 1979, Myra Ann Royle. *Educ:* Preston Grammar Sch.; Manchester Univ. (BScTech Hons 1949). FIMechE 1949; FCIT 1975; FEng 1981. Gen. Man., BUT Ltd, 1954; Gen. Sales and Service Man., 1962, Gen. Man., 1966, Leyland Motors Ltd; Man. Dir, British Leyland Truck and Bus, 1968; Dir, British Leyland Motor Corp. Ltd, 1970. Head of Defence Sales, MoD, 1976–81. Chm., Bus Manufacturers

Hldg Co., 1972–76. Dir of corp. develt, Wilkinson Sword Gp, 1981–82; Pres. and Man. Dir, Industrial Div., 1982–85, Dir, Internat. Gp, 1981–86, Allegheny International. Director: Yarrow & Co., 1981–86; Redman Heenan Internat., 1981–86; Bull Thompson Associates, 1987–89; IDRH Ltd, 1987–89; R. L. Holdings Ltd, 1989–90. Vice-Pres., SMMT, 1972–73; Dir, ROFs, 1976–81. Mem., Engineering Council, 1988–92. Governor, UMIST, 1970–92, Vice-Pres., 1983–92, Hon. Fellow, 1981. Pres., Manchester Technology Assoc., 1982. Liveryman, Engineers' Co., 1984–; Freeman, City of London, 1984. FRSA; CIMgt (CBIM 1984). *Recreations:* fishing, sailing. *Address:* West Mead, Church Lane, Shilton, Burford, Oxon OX18 4AE. *Clubs:* Turf, Naval, City Livery, Royal Thames Yacht; Royal Naval Sailing Assoc.

ELLIS, Tom; *see* Ellis, R. T.

ELLIS, Vivian, CBE 1984; Lt-Comdr RNVR; composer, author; President, Performing Right Society, since 1983 (Deputy President, 1975–83); *s* of Harry Ellis and Maud Isaacson. *Educ:* Cheltenham Coll. (Musical Exhibition). Commenced his career as concert pianist after studying under Myra Hess; studied composition at the Royal Academy of Music; first song published when fifteen; his first work for the theatre was the composition of additional numbers for The Curate's Egg, 1922; contributed to The Little Revue and The Punch Bowl Revue, 1924; to Yoicks, Still Dancing, and Mercenary Mary, and composer of By the Way, 1925; to Just a Kiss, Kid Boots, Cochran's Revue, My Son John, Merely Molly and composer of Palladium Pleasures, 1926; to Blue Skies, The Girl Friend, and Clowns in Clover, 1927; to Charlot, 1928; and composer of Peg o' Mine, Will o' The Whispers, Vogues and Vanities, 1928; to A Yankee at the Court of King Arthur, The House that Jack Built, and (with Richard Myers) composer of Mister Cinders, 1929, new production, Fortune Theatre, 1983; part-composer of Cochran's 1930 Revue, and composer of Follow a Star and Little Tommy Tucker, 1930; part-composer of Stand Up and Sing, and Song of the Drum (with Herman Finck), and composer of Folly to be Wise, and Blue Roses, 1931; part-composer of Out of the Bottle, 1932; composer of Cochran's revue Streamline, 1934; Jill Darling, 1935; music and lyrics of Charlot Revue, The Town Talks, 1936; Hide and Seek, 1937; The Fleet's Lit Up, Running Riot, Under Your Hat, 1938; composer (to Sir A. P. Herbert's libretto) Cochran light operas: Big Ben, 1946; Bless the Bride, 1947 (new prodn, Exeter, 1985; Sadler's Wells, 1987); Tough at the Top, 1949; Water Gipsies, 1955; music and lyrics of And So To Bed, 1951; music for The Sleeping Prince, 1953; music and lyrics of Listen to the Wind, 1954; Half in Earnest (musical adaptation of The Importance of Being Earnest), 1958; Spread a Little Happiness: a Celebration, King's Head, 1992; composer of popular songs, incl. Spread a Little Happiness, This is My Lovely Day, Ma Belle Marguerite, Other People's Babies and I'm on a See-Saw; many dance items; Coronation Scot; also music for the films Jack's the Boy, Water Gipsies, 1932; Falling for You, 1933; Public Nuisance No 1, 1935; Piccadilly Incident, 1946, etc. Hon. GSM, 1990. Ivor Novello Award for outstanding services to British music, 1973; Ivor Novello Award for Lifetime Achievement in British Music, 1983. Vivian Ellis Prize instituted by PRS in collab. with GSMD, to celebrate his 80th birthday. *Publications: novels:* Zelma; Faint Harmony; Day Out; Chicanery; *travel:* Ellis in Wonderland; *autobiography:* I'm on a See-Saw; *humour:* How to Make your Fortune on the Stock Exchange; How to Enjoy Your Operation; How to Bury Yourself in the Country; How to be a Man-about-Town; Good-Bye, Dollie; contrib: The Rise and Fall of the Matinée Idol; Top Hat and Tails: biography of Jack Buchanan; *for children:* Hilary's Tune; Hilary's Holidays; The Magic Baton; *song book:* Vivian Ellis: a composer's jubilee, 1982. *Recreations:* gardening, painting, operations. *Club:* Garrick.

ELLIS, Dr (William) Herbert (Baxter), AFC 1954; Medical Adviser, Department of Health and Social Security, 1972–92; Underwriting Member of Lloyd's; *b* 2 July 1921; *er s* of William Baxter Ellis and Georgina Isabella Ellis (*née* Waller); *m* 1st, 1948, Margaret Mary Limb (marr. diss.); one *s* one *d*; 2nd, 1977, Mollie Marguerite Clarke (marr. diss.); 3rd, 1994, Jean Stanley Stawell Gross, *widow* of Ken Gross. *Educ:* Oundle Sch.; Durham Univ. (MD, BS). Royal Navy, 1945–59: Surg. Comdr, Fleet Air Arm Pilot. Motor industry, 1960–71; research into human aspects of road traffic accidents, 1960–71; Dir-Gen., Dr Barnardo's, 1971–73; dir of various companies. Industrial Medical Consultant: Wellworthy, 1979–87; Telephone Manufacturing Co., 1980–87; Plessey Co., 1981–87. Part-time Mem., Employment Medical Adv. Service, 1973–81. Freeman, City of London, 1994. St John Ambulance: Chief Comdr, 1989–91; County Surgeon, 1979–87, Comdr, 1987–89, Glos Br. KStJ 1989 (CStJ 1988). Gilbert Blane Medal, RCP, 1954. *Publications:* Physiological and Psychological Aspects of Deck Landings, 1954; Hippocrates, RN—memoirs of a naval flying doctor (autobiog.), 1988; Why Not Live a Little Longer?, 1995; various on the human factor in industrial management. *Recreations:* memories of walking, observing humanity, mending fences. *Address:* Little Dalling, Rocks Lane, High Hurstwood, East Sussex TN22 4BH. *T:* Uckfield (01825) 733139. *Clubs:* Army and Navy, Naval and Military.

ELLIS-REES, Hugh Francis, CB 1986; Member, Black Country Development Corporation, since 1990; *b* 5 March 1929; *s* of late Sir Hugh Ellis-Rees, KCMG, CB and Lady (Eileen Frances Anne) Ellis-Rees; *m* 1956, Elisabeth de Mestre Gray; three *s* one *d*. *Educ:* Ampleforth Coll.; Balliol Coll., Oxford. Served Grenadier Guards, 1948–49. Joined War Office, 1954; transf. to DoE, 1970; Cabinet Office, 1972–74; Under Sec., DoE, 1974; Regl Dir, West Midlands, Depts of the Environment and Transport, 1981–89.

ELLISON, Prof. Arthur James, DSc(Eng); CEng, FIMechE, FIEE; Professor of Electrical and Electronic Engineering, and Head of Department, The City University, London, 1972–85, now Professor Emeritus; *b* 15 Jan. 1920; *s* of late Lawrence Joseph and Elsie Beatrice Ellison, Birmingham; *m* 1st, 1952, Marjorie Cresswell (*d* 1955); 2nd, 1963, Marian Elizabeth Gumbrell; one *s* one *d*. *Educ:* Solihull Sch., Warwicks; Birmingham Central Tech. Coll. (now Univ. of Aston); Northampton Polytechnic (now City Univ.), as ext. student of Univ. of London BSc(Eng) (1st Cl. Hons); DSc(Eng). Sen. MIEEE. Design Engr, Higgs Motors, Birmingham, 1938–43; Tech. Asst, RAE, 1943–46; Graduate apprentice with British Thomson-Houston Co., Rugby, 1946, Design Engr, 1947–58; Lectr, Queen Mary Coll. (Univ. of London), 1958–65, Sen. Lectr, 1965–72. Visiting Prof., MIT, USA, 1959; lecture tour of Latin Amer. for Brit. Council, 1968; Hon. Prof., Nat. Univ. of Engrg, Lima, Peru, 1968; numerous overseas lectures and conf. contribs. Ext. Examiner to many UK and overseas univs and polytechnics; Founder and Chm., biennial Internat. Conf. on Elec. Machines, 1974–84 (Pres. of Honour). Consultant to industrial cos and nationalised industry on elec. machines, noise and vibration problems; Director: Landspeed, 1975–; Landspeed University Consultants, 1975–82; Landspeed International, 1975–83; Cotswold Research, 1983–; Building Health Consultants, 1989–94. Pres., Soc. for Psychical Research, 1976–79, 1981–84; Chm., Theosophical Res. Centre, 1976–87. Member: Council, Scientific and Med. Network, 1973–; Council, IEE, 1981–84; Bd, Eta Kappa Nu Assoc., USA, 1984–86 (Hon. Mem.); Trustee, Res. Council for Complementary Med., 1983–90. *Publications:* Electromechanical Energy Conversion, 1965, 2nd edn 1970; Generalized Electric Machines, 1967; Generalized Electric Machine Set Instruction Book (AEI), 1963, 2nd edn 1968; (jtly) Machinery Noise Measurement, 1985; The Reality of the Paranormal, 1988; ed, Proc. Queen Mary Coll. Conf., The Teaching of Electric Machinery Theory, 1961; jt ed, Proc. Queen Mary Coll. Conf., Design of Electric Machines by Computer, 1969; contribs to: Psychism and the Unconscious Mind, 1968; Intelligence Came First, 1975; numerous papers in engrg and sci. jls on elec. machines, noise and vibration, future guided land transport (IEE premium, 1964); also papers in Jl Soc. for Psych. Res. *Recreations:* reading, meditation, psychical research, travel. *Address:* 10 Foxgrove Avenue, Beckenham, Kent BR3 2BA. *T:* 0181–402 3399; Department of Electrical Engineering, The City University, EC1V 0HB. *T:* 0171–253 4399. *Club:* Athenæum.

ELLISON, Rt. Rev. John Alexander; *see* Paraguay, Bishop of.

ELLISON, His Honour John Harold, VRD 1948; a Circuit Judge, 1972–87; Chancellor of the Dioceses of Salisbury and Norwich, since 1955; *b* 20 March 1916; *s* of late Harold Thomas Ellison, MIMechE, and late Mrs Frances Amy Swithinbank, both of Woodspeen Grange, Newbury; *m* 1952, Margaret Dorothy Maud, *d* of late Maynard D. McFarlane, Sun City, Arizona; three *s* one *d*. *Educ:* Uppingham Sch.; King's Coll., Cambridge (MA). Res. Physicist, then Engr, Thos Firth & John Brown Ltd, Sheffield; Lieut, RE, TA (49th WR) Div., 1937–39; Officer in RNVR, 1939–51 (retd as Lt-Comdr): Gunnery Specialist, HMS Excellent, 1940; Sqdn Gunnery Officer, 8 Cruiser Sqdn, 1940–42; Naval Staff, Admty, 1942–44; Staff Officer (Ops) to Flag Officer, Western Mediterranean, 1944–45. Called to Bar, Lincoln's Inn, 1948; practised at Common Law Bar, 1948–71. Pres., SW London Br., Magistrates' Assoc., 1974–87. Former Governor, Forres Sch. Trust, Swanage. FRAS. *Publications:* (ed) titles Allotments and Smallholdings, and Courts, in Halsbury's Law of England, 3rd edn, and Allotments and Smallholdings, 4th edn. *Recreations:* organs and music, sailing, ski-ing, shooting. *Address:* Goose Green House, Egham, Surrey TW20 8PE. *Clubs:* Army and Navy; Bar Yacht; Ski Club of GB, Kandahar Ski.

ELLISON, Sir Ralph Henry C.; *see* Carr-Ellison, Sir R. H.

ELLMAN, Louise Joyce; Leader, Lancashire County Council, since 1981 (Chairman, 1981–85; Leader, Labour Group, since 1977); *b* 14 Nov. 1945; *d* of late Harold and Annie Rosenberg; *m* 1967, Geoffrey David Ellman; one *s* one *d*. *Educ:* Manchester High Sch. for Girls; Hull Univ. (BA Hons); York Univ. (MPhil). Worked in further educn and on Open Univ., 1970–76. Member: Lancs CC, 1970–; W Lancs DC, 1974–87; Local Govt Adv. Cttee, Labour Party's NEC, 1977–; Regl Exec., NW Labour Party, 1985– (Chm., 1993–). Contested (Lab) Darwen, 1979. Vice-Chm., Lancashire Enterprises, 1982–; Founder Mem., Co-operative Enterprises NW, 1979–; Founder Chm., NW Regl Assoc., 1992–93. Youngest mem., Lancs CC, 1970; youngest mem. and first woman to be Chm., 1981. *Recreations:* reading, travel. *Address:* 40 Elmers Green, Skelmersdale, Lancs WN8 6SB. *T:* Skelmersdale (01695) 23669. *Club:* Upholland Labour (Skelmersdale).

ELLSWORTH, Robert; President, Robert Ellsworth & Co. Inc., since 1977; Deputy Secretary of Defense, USA, 1975–77; *b* 11 June 1926; *s* of Willoughby Fred Ellsworth and Lucile Rarig Ellsworth; *m* 1956, Vivian Esther Sies; one *s* one *d*. *Educ:* Univs of Kansas (BSME) and Michigan (JD). Active service, US Navy, 1944–46, 1950–53 (Lt-Comdr). Mem. United States Congress, 1961–67; Asst to President of US, 1969; Ambassador and Permanent Representative of US on N Atlantic Council, 1969–71; Asst Sec. of Defense (Internat. Security Affairs), 1974–75. Chm. Council, IISS, 1990– (Mem., 1973–). Licensed Lay Reader, Episcopal Dio. of Washington. Hon. LLD: Ottawa, 1969; Boston, 1970. *Recreations:* single sculling, swimming, music. *Address:* 24120 Old Hundred Road, Dickerson, MD 20842, USA. *Clubs:* Brook (New York); Army and Navy (Washington).

ELLWOOD, Peter Brian; Group Chief Executive, TSB Group, since 1992; *b* 15 May 1943; *s* of Isaac and Edith Ellwood; *m* 1968, Judy Ann Windsor; one *s* two *d*. *Educ:* King's Sch., Macclesfield. FCIB. Barclays, Bristol, 1961–89; Controller, Barclaycards Ops, 1983–85; Chief Exec., Barclaycard, 1985–89; Chief Exec., Retail Banking, TSB, 1989–92; Chief Exec., TSB Bank, 1992–; Chm., Visa International, 1994– (Dir, 1993–; Chm., Eur., ME and Africa Bd, 1992–94). Former Chm., UDT; Director: Barclays Bank UK; Sears, 1994–. Trustee, Royal Theatre, Northampton, 1982–. Mem. Court, Nene Coll., Northampton, 1989–. CIMgt; FRSA. Hon. LLD Leicester, 1994; DUniv Central England, 1995. *Recreations:* theatre, music. *Address:* TSB Bank, Victoria House, Victoria Square, Birmingham B1 1BZ. *T:* 0121–600 6101; Catesby House, Lower Catesby, near Daventry, Northants NN11 6LF. *Club:* Royal Automobile.

ELLY, (Richard) Charles; Partner, Reynolds, Parry-Jones & Crawford, solicitors, since 1968; a Recorder, since 1995; *b* 20 March 1942; *s* of Harold Elly and Dora Ellen Elly (*née* Luing); *m* 1967, Marion Rose Blackwell; one *s* one *d*. *Educ:* Sir William Borlase's Sch., Marlow; Hertford Coll., Oxford (MA); Coll. of Law, London. Admitted solicitor, 1966. Sec., Southern Assoc. of Law Socs, 1975–82; Law Society: Sec., 1975–82, Pres., 1988–89, Berks, Bucks and Oxon Br.; Mem. Council, 1981–; Dep. Vice-Pres., 1992–93; Vice-Pres., 1993–94; Pres., 1994–95. Mem., Berks CC, 1980–81. Chairman: Maidenhead Deanery Synod, 1972–79; High Wycombe and Dist CAB, 1983–88. Pres., Cookham Soc., 1987–. *Recreations:* ornithology, theatre, walking, gardening. *Address:* Court Cottage, Dean Lane, Cookham Dean, Maidenhead, Berks SL6 9AF. *T:* Marlow (01628) 482637; (office) 10 Easton Street, High Wycombe HP11 1NP. *Club:* United Oxford & Cambridge University.

ELMES, Dr Peter Cardwell; Director, Medical Research Council Pneumoconiosis Unit, Llandough Hospital, Penarth, 1976–81, retired from MRC 1982; Consultant in Occupational Lung Diseases, since 1976; *b* 12 Oct. 1921; *s* of Florence Romaine Elmes and Lilian Bryham (*née* Cardwell); *m* 1957, Margaret Elizabeth (*née* Staley); two *s* one *d*. *Educ:* Rugby; Oxford Univ. (BM, BCh 1945); Western Reserve Univ., Cleveland, Ohio (MD 1943). MRCP 1951. Mil. Service, RAMC, 1946–48. Trng posts, Taunton and Oxford, 1948–50; Registrar, then Sen. Registrar in Medicine, Hammersmith Hosp., 1950–58; Dept of Therapeutics, Queen's Univ., Belfast: Sen. Lectr, 1959–63; Reader, 1963–67; Prof. of Therapeutic Sciences, 1967–71; Whitla Prof. of Therapeutics and Pharmacology, 1971–76. Member: Medicines Commn, 1976–79; Industrial Injuries Adv. Council, 1982–87; Indep. Scientific Cttee on Smoking and Health, 1982–92. *Publications:* contrib. med. jls on chronic chest disease, treatment and control of infection, occupational lung disease asbestosis, and mesothelioma. *Recreation:* working on house and garden. *Address:* Dawros House, St Andrews Road, Dinas Powys, South Glamorgan CF64 4HB. *T:* Dinas Powys (01222) 512102; *Fax:* Dinas Powys (01222) 515975.

ELMSLIE, Maj.-Gen. Alexander Frederic Joseph, CB 1959; CBE 1955; psc; CEng; FIMechE; FCIT; *b* 31 Oct. 1905; *er s* of Captain A. W. Elmslie, RAEC and Florence Edith Elmslie (*née* Kirk); *m* 1931, Winifred Allan Wright; one *d* one *s*. *Educ:* Farnham Grammar Sch.; RMC Sandhurst; Staff Coll., Camberley. Commissioned in Royal Army Service Corps, 29 Jan. 1925, and subsequently served in Shanghai, Ceylon, E Africa and Singapore; Lieutenant 1927; Captain 1935; served War of 1939–45 (despatches) in Madagascar, India (Combined Ops) and Europe (SHAEF); Major, 1942; Lt-Col 1948; Temp. Brig. 1943; Brig. 1953; Maj.-Gen. 1958. Dep. Dir of Supplies and Transport, War Office, 1953–55; Dir of Supplies and Transport, GHQ Far East Land Forces, 1956–57; Inspector, RASC, War Office, 1957–60, retired. Chairman Traffic Commissioners: NW Traffic Area, 1962–64; SE Traffic Area, 1965–75. Hon. Col 43 (Wessex) Inf. Div. Coln, RASC, TA, 1960–64; Col Comdt, RASC, 1964–65; Col Comdt, Royal Corps of

Transport, 1965–69. Fellow, Royal Commonwealth Soc. *Address:* 9 Stanmer House, Furness Road, Eastbourne, E Sussex BN21 4EY.

ELPHICK, Michael John; actor; *b* 19 Sept. 1946; *s* of Herbert Frederick Elphick and Joan Mary (*née* Haddow); one *d*. *Educ:* Lancastrian Sch. for Boys, Chichester; Central Sch. of Speech and Drama. *Theatre* includes: The Changing Room, Royal Court; Hamlet, Royal Court; The Ticket of Leave Man, National; *films* include: Blind Terror; Phyliss Dixie; The Knowledge; The Elephant Man; Quadrophenia; The Curse of the Pink Panther; Gorky Park, 1983; Privates on Parade, 1983; Little Dorritt, 1987; The Krays; Buddy's Song, 1992; *television* includes: The Nearly Man; Holding On; Blue Remembered Hills; Bloomfield; Private Schultz, 1982; Smiley's People; Oxbridge Blues, 1984; *series:* Pull the Other One, 1984; Three Up, Two Down, 1985–88; Boon, 1986–93; Harry, 1993–94. *Publication:* Absolute Beginner's Guide to Cookery. *Recreation:* boats. *Address:* c/o Dennis Selinger, ICM, Oxford House, 76 Oxford Street, W1N 0AX. *T:* 0171–636 6565, *Fax:* 0171–323 0101. *Clubs:* Groucho, Gerry's.

ELPHIN, Bishop of, (RC), since 1994; **Most Rev. Christopher Jones,** DD; *b* 3 March 1936; *s* of Christopher Jones and Christina Hanley. *Educ:* Maynooth Coll. (BA Classics 1958); UC Galway, NUI (Higher DipEd 1963); UC Dublin, NUI (DipSoc 1973). Teacher, St Muireadach's, Ballina, 1962–65; Teacher, 1965–71, Spiritual Dir, 1972–79, Summerhill Coll., Sligo; Archivist, Diocesan Office, 1971–72; Dir, Sligo Social Service Council, 1973–87; Administrator, Cathedral Parish, Sligo, 1987–94. Freeman, Sligo City, 1995. *Publication:* Child, Adolescent and Adult in Family and Community, 2nd edn 1978. *Recreations:* walking, golfing, music, reading. *Address:* St Mary's, Sligo, Ireland. *T:* (71) 62670, (71) 69434. *Clubs:* Strandhill Golf; Co. Sligo Golf.

ELPHINSTONE, family name of **Lord Elphinstone.**

ELPHINSTONE, 19th Lord *cr* 1509; **Alexander Mountstuart Elphinstone;** Baron (UK) 1885; *b* 15 April 1980; *e s* of 18th Lord Elphinstone and of Willa Mary Gabriel, 4th *d* of Major David Chetwode; *S* father, 1994. *Heir: b* Hon. Angus John Elphinstone, *b* 1982.

ELPHINSTONE, Sir Douglas; *see* Elphinstone, Sir M. D. W.

ELPHINSTONE of Glack, Sir John, 11th Bt *cr* 1701, of Logie Elphinstone and Nova Scotia; Land Agent, retired; *b* 12 Aug. 1924; *s* of Thomas George Elphinston (*d* 1967), and of Gladys Mary Elphinston, *d* of late Ernest Charles Lambert Congdon; *S* uncle, 1970; *m* 1953, Margaret Doreen, *d* of Edric Tasker; four *s*. *Educ:* Eagle House, Sandhurst, Berks; Repton; Emmanuel College, Cambridge (BA). Lieut, Royal Marines, 1942–48. Chartered Surveyor; Land Agent with ICI plc, 1956–83; Consultant, Gandy & Son, Northwich, 1983–88. Past Pres., Cheshire Agricultural Valuers' Assoc.; Past Chm., Land Agency and Agric. Div., Lancs, Cheshire and IoM Branch, RICS; Mem., Lancs River Authority, 1970–74. *Recreations:* country pursuits, cricket. *Heir: s* Alexander Elphinston [*b* 6 June 1955; *m* 1986, Ruth, *er d* of Rev. Robert Dunnett; one *s* one *d*]. *Address:* Pilgrims, Churchfields, Sandiway, Northwich, Cheshire CW8 2JS. *T:* Sandiway (01606) 883327.

ELPHINSTONE, Sir (Maurice) Douglas (Warburton), 5th Bt *cr* 1816; TD 1946; retired, 1973; *b* 13 April 1909; *s* of Rev. Canon Maurice Curteis Elphinstone (4th *s* of 3rd Bt) (*d* 1969), and Christiana Georgiana (*née* Almond); *S* cousin, 1975; *m* 1943, Helen Barbara, *d* of late George Ramsay Main; one *s* one *d*. *Educ:* Loretto School, Musselburgh; Jesus Coll., Cambridge (MA). FFA; FRSE. Actuary engaged in Life Assurance companies until 1956 (with the exception of the war); Member of Stock Exchange, London, 1957–74. War service with London Scottish and Sierra Leone Regt, RWAFF, mainly in W Africa and India. *Publications:* technical papers mainly in Trans Faculty of Actuaries and Jl Inst. of Actuaries. *Heir: s* John Howard Main Elphinstone, *b* 25 Feb. 1949. *Address:* 11 Scotby Green Steading, Scotby, Carlisle CA4 8EH. *T:* Scotby (01228) 513141.

ELRINGTON, Prof. Christopher Robin, FSA, FRHistS; Editor, Victoria History of the Counties of England, 1977–94; Professor of History, Institute of Historical Research, University of London, 1992–94, now Professor Emeritus; *b* 20 Jan. 1930; *s* of late Brig. Maxwell Elrington, DSO, OBE, and Beryl Joan (*née* Ommanney); *m* 1951, Jean Margaret (*née* Buchanan), RIBA; one *s* one *d*. *Educ:* Wellington Coll., Berks; University Coll., Oxford (MA); Bedford Coll., London (MA). FSA 1964; FRHistS 1969. Asst to Editor, Victoria County History, 1954; Editor for Glos, 1960; Dep. Editor, 1968. British Acad. Overseas Vis. Fellow, Folger Shakespeare Library, Washington DC, 1976. Mem., Adv. Bd for Redundant Churches, 1982–. Pres., Bristol and Glos Archaeol Soc., 1984–85. Hon. Gen. Editor, 1962–72, Pres., 1983–, Wilts Record Soc. *Publications:* Divers Letters of Roger de Martival, Bishop of Salisbury, 2 vols, 1963, 1972; Wiltshire Feet of Fines, Edward III, 1974; articles in Victoria County History and in learned jls. *Address:* 34 Lloyd Baker Street, WC1X 9AB. *T:* 0171–837 4971.

ELSDEN, Sidney Reuben, BA, PhD (Cambridge); Professor of Biology, University of East Anglia, 1965–85; *b* 13 April 1915; *er s* of late Reuben Charles Elsden, Cambridge; *m* 1st, 1942, Frances Scott Wilson (*d* 1943); 2nd, 1948, Erica Barbara Scott, *er d* of late Grahame Scott Gardiner, Wisbech, Cambs; twin *s*. *Educ:* Cambridge and County High Sch. for Boys; Fitzwilliam House, Cambridge (Exhibn, Goldsmiths' Co.). Lecturer, Biochemistry, University of Edinburgh, 1937–42; Mem. Scientific Staff of ARC Unit for Animal Physiology, 1943–48; Sen. Lectr in Microbiology, 1948–59, West Riding Prof. of Microbiology, 1959–65, Sheffield Univ.; Hon. Dir, ARC Unit for Microbiology, Univ. of Sheffield, 1952–65; Dir, ARC Food Research Inst., 1965–77. Visiting Prof. of Microbiology, Univ. of Illinois, Urbana, Ill, USA, 1956. Pres., Soc. for General Microbiology, 1969–72, Hon. Mem. 1977. Hon. DSc Sheffield, 1985. *Publications:* contribs to scientific jls on metabolism of micro-organisms. *Recreations:* gardening, angling. *Address:* 26a The Street, Costessey, Norwich NR8 5DB.

ELSE, John, MBE 1946; TD 1946; Regional Chairman of Industrial Tribunals, Eastern Region, Bury St Edmunds, 1980–84; *b* 9 Aug. 1911; *s* of late Mr and Mrs A. G. Else; *m* 1937, Eileen Dobson; one *d*. *Educ:* Cowley Sch., St Helens; Liverpool Univ. (LLB 1930). Admitted as solicitor, 1932. Commnd TA, 1932; served War: UK and BEF, 1939–41 (despatches, 1940); Iraq, 1942; India, 1942–45 (ADS GHQ, 1944–45). Practised in St Helens, London and Birmingham, 1932–39; Partner, Beale & Co., London and Birmingham, 1946–61; Mem., Mental Health Review Tribunal, 1960–61; Chm., Traffic Comrs and Licensing Authority for Goods Vehicles, W Midlands Traffic Area, 1961–72; Indust. Tribunals Chm., Birmingham, 1972–76, Cambridge, 1976–80. *Recreations:* photography, gardening. *Address:* The Cottage, Long Lane, Fowlmere, Royston, Herts SG8 7TA. *T:* Fowlmere (01763) 208367.

ELSMORE, Sir Lloyd, Kt 1982; OBE 1977; JP; Mayor of Manukau City, since 1968; *b* 16 Jan. 1913; *s* of George and Minnie Elsmore; *m* 1935, Marie Kirk; two *s* two *d*. *Educ:* Greymouth High Sch. Commenced grocery business on own account, 1933; President: Grocers' Assoc., 1949, 1950, 1952, Life Member, 1954; NZ Grocers' Federation, 1955, Life Member, 1959. Mem., Auckland Harbour Bd, 1971–83. Local Body involvement, 1953–; Mayor of Ellerslie Borough Council, 1956–62. *Recreations:* boating, fishing, gardening. *Address:* 18 Sanctuary Point, Pakuranga, New Zealand. *T:* 567–025. *Club:* Rotary (Pakuranga).

ELSOM, Cecil Harry, CBE 1976; Consultant, EPR Partnership (formerly Elsom Pack & Roberts, Architects), since 1980 (Senior Partner, 1947–80); *b* 17 Jan. 1912; *s* of Julius Israelson and Leah Lazarus; name changed by deed poll to Elsom, 1930; *m* 1940, Gwyneth Mary Buxton Hopkin; two *s*. *Educ:* Upton Cross Elem. Sch.; West Ham Polytechnic; Northern Polytechnic Architectural School. FRIBA. Started practice by winning competition for town hall, Welwyn Garden City, 1933; partner in Lyons Israel & Elsom, 1936; won two more competitions, Town Hall, Consett, Co. Durham and Health Clinic in Bilston, Staffs. Served with Ordnance Corps, RE, 1940–46, ending war as Captain. Began new practice, as Sen. Partner, Elsom Pack & Roberts, 1947. Works include housing, schools and old people's homes for GLC, Lambeth BC and Westminster CC; office buildings and flats for Church Commissioners, Crown Estate Commissioners, BSC, LWT (Eternit Prize for offices, Victoria St, 1977); stores in Wolverhampton, Guildford and London for Army & Navy Stores; town centres in Slough, Chesterfield, Derby and Tamworth (three Civic Trust Awards, four Commendations). Adviser to DoE on Lyceum Club, Liverpool; Assessor for Civic Trust Awards, 1980. Pres., Nightingale House Old People's Home, 1973–. Liveryman, Clockmakers' Co., 1979. FSA 1979. *Recreation:* horology. *Address:* 14 Ferrings, College Road, Dulwich, SE21 7LU. *Club:* Arts.

ELSON, Graham Peel; General Secretary, Liberal Democrats, since 1989; *b* 21 Aug. 1949; *s* of George Ernest Elson and Rhoda (*née* Atkinson); *m* 1975, Jane Rosamunde Isaac. *Educ:* Palmers Endowed Sch. for Boys, Grays, Essex; NE London Polytechnic (BA Business Studies). Brand Manager, Rank Hovis McDougall Foods, 1972–74; Gen. Manager, Wilkinson Sword Gp, 1974–85. Councillor and Leader, Oxfordshire CC, 1985–89. *Recreations:* boating, gardening, supporting West Ham United FC. *Address:* (office) 4 Cowley Street, SW1P 3NB. *T:* 0171–233 2093. *Club:* National Liberal.

ELSTEIN, David Keith; Head of Programmes, BSkyB, since 1993; *b* 14 Nov. 1944; *s* of late Albert Elstein and Millie Cohen; *m* 1978, Jenny Conway; one *s*. *Educ:* Haberdashers' Aske's; Gonville and Caius Coll., Cambridge (BA, MA). BBC: The Money Programme, Panorama, Cause for Concern, People in Conflict, 1964–68; Thames Television: This Week, The Day Before Yesterday, The World At War, 1968–72; London Weekend Television: Weekend World, 1972; Thames Television, 1972–82: This Week (ed., 1974–78); Exec. Producer, Documentaries; founded Brook Prodns, 1982: Exec. Producer, A Week in Politics, 1982–86; Exec. Producer, Concealed Enemies, 1983; Man. Dir, Primetime Television, 1983–86; Dir of Programmes, Thames Television, 1986–92. *Recreations:* theatre, cinema, bridge, politics, reading. *Address:* BSkyB, 6 Centaurs Business Park, Grant Way, Syon Lane, Isleworth, Mddx TW7 5QD.

ELSTOB, Peter (Frederick Egerton); Vice-President: International PEN, since 1981 (Secretary-General, 1974–81); English PEN, since 1978; Managing Director, Archive Press Ltd, since 1964 (co-founder 1963); writer and entrepreneur; *b* London, 22 Dec. 1915; *e s* of Frederick Charles Elstob, chartered accountant, RFC, and Lillian Page, London; *m* 1st, 1937, Medora Leigh Smith (marr. diss. 1953); three *s* one *d* (and one *d* decd); 2nd, 1953, Barbara Zacheisz (*d* 1992); one *s* one *d*. *Educ:* private schs, London, Paris, Calcutta; state schs, NY and NJ; Univ. of Michigan, 1934–35. Reporter, salesman, tourist guide, 1931–36; volunteer, Spanish Civil War, 1936 (imprisoned and expelled); RTR, 1940–46 (despatches); founded Yeast-pac Co. Ltd with A. B. Eiloart, 1938, Dir, 1938–70, Man. Dir, 1970–93; with A. B. Eiloart: bought Arts Theatre Club, London, 1941; founded Peter Arnold Studios (artists' and writers' colony, Mexico), 1951–52, and Archives Designs Ltd, 1954–62; Director: MEEC Prodns (Theatre), 1946–54; Peter Arnold Properties, 1947–61; City & Suffolk Property Ltd, 1962–70; ABC Expedns, 1957–61; Manager, Small World Trans-Atlantic Balloon Crossing, 1958–59. Chm., Dorking Divl Lab. Party, 1949–50. Bulgarian Commemorative Medal, 1982; Normandy Freedom Medal, 1994. *Publications:* (autobiog.) Spanish Prisoner, 1939; (with A. B. Eiloart) The Flight of the Small World, 1959; novels: Warriors for the Working Day, 1960; The Armed Rehearsal, 1964; Scoundrel, 1986; military history: Bastogne the Road Block, 1968; The Battle of the Reichswald, 1970; Hitler's Last Offensive, 1971; Condor Legion, 1973; (ed) The Survival of Literature, 1979; (ed series) PEN International Books; PEN Broadsheet, 1977–82. *Recreations:* playing the Stock Exchange, travelling. *Address:* Ponds Cottage, Burley Lawn, Ringwood, Hants BH24 4DL. *T:* Burley (01425) 403406; 14 Knivet Road, Fulham, SW6 1JH. *Clubs:* Savage, Garrick, PEN, Society of Authors.

ELSTON, Christopher David; Chief Executive, London Bullion Market Association, since 1995; *b* 1 Aug. 1938; *s* of Herbert Cecil Elston and Ada Louisa (*née* Paige); *m* 1964, Jennifer Isabel Rampling; one *s* two *d*. *Educ:* University Coll. Sch., Hampstead; King's Coll., Cambridge (BA Classics, 1960, MA 1980); Yale Univ. (MA Econs, 1967). Bank of England, 1960–94: seconded to Bank for Internat. Settlements, Basle, Switzerland, 1969–71; Private Sec. to Governor of Bank of England, 1974–76; Asst to Chief Cashier, 1976–79; seconded to HM Diplomatic Service, as Counsellor (Financial), British Embassy, Tokyo, 1979–83; Advr, later Sen. Advr (Asia and Australasia), 1983–94. Advr, Koram Bank London Rep. Office, 1995–. *Recreations:* serious music, photography, walking, garden. *Address:* 23 Grasmere Avenue, Harpenden, Herts AL5 5PT. *T:* Harpenden (01582) 760147.

ELTIS, Walter Alfred, DLitt; Chief Economic Adviser to President of the Board of Trade, since 1992; *b* 23 May 1933; *s* of Rev. Martin Eltis and Mary (*née* Schnitzer); *m* 1959, Shelagh Mary, *d* of Rev. Preb. Douglas Owen; one *s* two *d*. *Educ:* Wycliffe Coll.; Emmanuel Coll., Cambridge (BA Econs 1956); Nuffield Coll., Oxford. MA Oxon 1960; DLitt Oxon 1990. Nat. Service, Navigator, RAF, 1951–53. Res. Fellow, Exeter Coll., Oxford, 1958–60; Lectr in Econs, Exeter and Keble Colls, Oxford, 1960–63; Fellow and Tutor in Econs, Exeter Coll., Oxford, 1963–88, Emeritus Fellow, 1988; National Economic Development Office: Econ. Dir, 1986–88; Dir Gen., 1988–92. Vis. Reader in Econs, Univ. of WA, 1970; Visiting Professor: Univ. of Toronto, 1976–77; European Univ., Florence, 1979; Reading Univ., 1992–; Gresham Prof. of Commerce, Gresham Coll., 1993–. Mem. Council, 1987–93, Chm., Social Scis Cttee, 1987–88, CNAA; Member Council: European Policy Forum, 1992–; Foundn for Manufacturing and Industry, 1993–. Gov., Wycliffe Coll., 1972–88. Gen. Ed., Oxford Economic Papers, 1975–81. *Publications:* Economic Growth: analysis and policy, 1966; Growth and Distribution, 1973; (with R. Bacon) The Age of US and UK Machinery, 1974; (with R. Bacon) Britain's Economic Problem: too few producers, 1976, 2nd edn 1978; The Classical theory of Economic Growth, 1984; (with P. Sinclair) Keynes and Economic Policy, 1988; Classical Economics, Public Expenditure and Growth, 1993; contribs to econ. jls. *Recreations:* chess, music. *Address:* Danesway, Jarn Way, Boars Hill, Oxford OX1 5JF. *T:* Oxford (01865) 735440. *Clubs:* Reform (Chm., 1994–95), Royal Automobile.

ELTON, family name of **Baron Elton.**

ELTON, 2nd Baron *cr* 1934, of Headington; **Rodney Elton,** TD 1970; Deputy Chairman, Andry Montgomery Ltd, 1978–79 and since 1986; *b* 2 March 1930; *s* of 1st Baron Elton and of Dedi (*d* 1977), *d* of Gustav Hartmann, Oslo; *S* father, 1973; *m* 1958, Anne Frances (divorced, 1979), *e d* of late Brig. R. A. G. Tilney, CBE, DSO, TD; one *s* three *d*; *m* 1979, S. Richenda Gurney, *y d* of late Sir Hugh Gurney, KCMG, MVO, and Lady Gurney. *Educ:* Eton; New Coll., Oxford (MA). Farming, 1954–64. Assistant Master, Loughborough

Grammar Sch., 1962–67; Assistant Master, Fairham Comprehensive School for Boys, Nottingham, 1967–69; Lectr, Bishop Lonsdale College of Education, 1969–72. Contested (C) Leics, Loughborough, 1966, 1970. Cons. Whip, House of Lords, Feb. 1974–76, an Opposition spokesman, 1976–79; Parly Under Sec. of State, NI Office, 1979–81, DHSS, 1981–82, Home Office, 1982–84; Minister of State: Home Office, 1984–85; DoE, 1985–86. Mem., H of L Delegated Powers Scrutiny Cttee, 1993–. Chm., FIMBRA, 1987–90; Mem., Panel on Takeovers and Mergers, 1987–90. Formerly Director: Overseas Exhibition Services Ltd; Building Trades Exhibition Ltd. Mem. Exec. Cttee, Assoc. of Cons. Peers, 1986–93, 1994– (Dep. Chm., 1991–93). Dep. Sec., Cttee on Internat. Affairs, Synod of C of E, 1976–78. Mem. Boyd Commn to evaluate elections in Rhodesia, 1979; Chm., Cttee of Enquiry into discipline in schools, 1988. Chm., Intermediate Treatment Fund, 1990–93; Vice-Pres., Inst. of Trading Standards Administrators, 1990–; Member of Council: CGLI, 1987–91 (now Hon. Mem.); Rainer Foundn, 1990–; Founding Chm., DIVERT Trust, 1993–; Pres., Building Conservation Trust, 1990–; Trustee: City Parochial Foundn, 1990–; Trust for London, 1990–. Late Captain, Queen's Own Warwickshire and Worcs Yeo.; late Major, Leics and Derbys (PAO) Yeo. Lord of the Manor of Adderbury, Oxon. *Heir:* *s* Hon. Edward Paget Elton, *b* 28 May 1966. *Address:* House of Lords, SW1A 0PW. *Clubs:* Pratt's, Beefsteak, Cavalry and Guards.

See also Master of Gray.

ELTON, Sir Arnold, Kt 1987; CBE 1982; MS; FRCS; Consultant Surgeon: Northwick Park Hospital and Clinical Research Centre, since 1970; British Airways, since 1981; *b* 14 Feb. 1920; *s* of late Max Elton and of Ada Elton; *m* 1952, Billie Pamela Briggs; one *s*. *Educ:* University Coll. London (exhibnr; MB BS 1943); UCH Med. Sch. (MS 1951); Jun. and Sen. Gold Medal in Surgery. LRCP 1943; MRCS 1943, FRCS 1946. House Surg., House Physician and Casualty Officer, UCH, 1943–45; Sen. Surgical Registrar, Charing Cross Hosp., 1947–51 (Gosse Res. Schol.); Consultant Surgeon: Harrow Hosp., 1951–70; Mount Vernon Hosp., 1960–70. First Chm., Med. Staff Cttee, Chm., Surgical Div. and Theatre Cttee, Mem., Ethical Cttee, Northwick Park Hosp. Mem., Govt Wkg Party on Breast Screening for Cancer, 1985–. Examiner: GNC; RCS, 1971–83; Surgical Tutor, RCS, 1970–82. Pres., Cons. Med. Soc., 1992– (Nat. Chm., 1975–92; Eur. Rep., 1994–; Chm., Eur. Gp; Ed., Eur. Bull., 1994–); Mem., Cons. Central Council and Nat. Exec. Cttee, 1976–. Founder Mem., British Assoc. of Surgical Oncology; Mem. Ct of Patrons, RCS, 1986–. Fellow: Assoc. of Surgeons of GB; Hunterian Soc.; FRSocMed; FICS; Associate Fellow, British Assoc. of Urological Surgeons. Liveryman: Apothecaries' Soc.; Carmen's Co. Jubilee Medal, 1977. *Publications:* contribs to med. jls. *Recreations:* tennis, music. *Address:* 58 Stockleigh Hall, Prince Albert Road, NW8 7LB; The Consulting Rooms, Wellington Hospital, Wellington Place, NW8 9LR. *T:* 0171-935 4101. *Clubs:* Carlton, Royal Automobile, MCC.

ELTON, Benjamin Charles; author and performer; *b* 3 May 1959; *s* of Prof. Lewis Richard Benjamin Elton, *qv* and Mary Elton (*née* Foster); *m* 1994, Sophie Gare. *Educ:* Godalming Grammar Sch.; S Warwicks Coll. of Further Educn; Manchester Univ. (BA Drama). First professional appearance, Comic Strip Club, 1981; writer for television: Happy Families, 1985; Filthy Rich and Catflap, 1986; jointly: The Young Ones, 1983; Blackadder II, 1987; Blackadder the Third, 1988; Blackadder goes Forth, 1989; writer and performer: Friday Live, 1987–88; Saturday Live, 1987; The Man from Auntie, 1990, 1994; Stark, 1993; writer and director: Gasping, Theatre Royal, Haymarket, 1990; Silly Cow, Theatre Royal, Haymarket, 1991; actor: Much Ado About Nothing (film), 1993; numerous tours as a stand-up comic, 1986, 1987, 1989, 1993. *Publications: novels:* Stark, 1989; Gridlock, 1991; This Other Eden, 1993; *plays:* Gasping, 1990; Silly Cow, 1991. *Recreations:* walking, reading, socialising. *Address:* c/o Phil McIntyre, 15 Riversway, Navigation Way, Preston, Lancs PR2 2YP. *Clubs:* Groucho, Globe.

ELTON, Sir Charles (Abraham Grierson), 11th Bt *cr* 1717; *b* 23 May 1953; *s* of Sir Arthur Hallam Rice Elton, 10th Bt, and Margaret Ann (*d* 1995), *d* of Olafur Bjornson; *S* father, 1973; *m* 1990, Lucy Lauris, *d* of late Lukas Heller; one *d*. *Address:* Clevedon Court, Somerset BS21 6QU.

ELTON, Dr George Alfred Hugh, CB 1983; consultant in biochemistry, since 1985; *b* 27 Feb. 1925; *s* of Horace and Violet Elton; *m* 1951, Theodora Rose Edith Kingham; two *d*. *Educ:* Sutton County Sch.; London Univ. (evening student). BSc 1944, PhD 1948, DSc 1956; FRSC (FRIC 1951); CChem 1974; Eur Chem 1993; FIFST 1968; FIBiol 1976; CBiol 1984. Mem. Faculty of Science, and Univ. Examnr in Chemistry, Univ. of London, 1951–58; Dir, Fog Res. Unit, Min. of Supply, 1954–58; Reader in Applied Phys. Chemistry, Battersea Polytechnic, 1956–58; Dir, British Baking Industries Res. Assoc., 1958–66; Dir, Flour Milling and Baking Res. Assoc., 1967–70; Ministry of Agriculture, Fisheries and Food: Chief Sci. Adviser (Food), 1971–85; Head of Food Science Div., 1972–73; Dep. Chief Scientist, 1972; Under-Sec. 1974; Chief Scientist (Fisheries and Food), 1981–85. Vis. Prof., Surrey Univ., 1982–. Consultant, FAO, 1992. Chairman: National Food Survey Cttee, 1978–85; Adv. Bd, Inst. of Food Res. (Bristol), 1985–88; Scientific Advr, BFMIRA, 1986–92; Scientific Governor: British Nutrition Foundn, 1971–; Internat. Life Scis Inst. (Europe), 1987–; Vice-Chm., EEC Scientific Cttee for Food, 1987–92; Member: Cttee on Medical Aspects of Food Policy, 1971–85; UK Delegn, Tripartite Meetings on Food and Drugs, 1971–85; AFRC (formerly ARC), 1981–85; NERC, 1981–85; Fisheries Res. and Develt Bd, 1982–85; Adv. Bd for Research Councils, 1981–84; Council: Chemical Soc., 1972–75; BIBRA, 1990– (Chm., 1993–). Co-inventor, Chorleywood Bread Process (Queen's Award to Industry 1966); Silver Medallist, Royal Soc. of Arts, 1969. Hon. DSc Reading, 1984; DUniv Surrey, 1991. *Publications:* research papers in jls of various learned societies. *Recreation:* golf. *Address:* Green Nook, Bridle Lane, Loudwater, Rickmansworth, Herts WD3 4JH. *Club:* MCC.

ELTON, John; *see* Elton, P. J.

ELTON, Prof. Lewis Richard Benjamin, MA, DSc; CPhys; FInstP, FIMA, FSRHE; University Professor of Higher Education, University of Surrey, 1987–90, now Emeritus; Professor of Higher Education, University College London, since 1994; *b* 25 March 1923; *yr s* of late Prof. Victor Leopold Ehrenberg, PhD, and Eva Dorothea (*née* Sommer); *m* 1950, Mary, *d* of late Harold William Foster and Kathleen (*née* Meakin); three *s* one *d*. *Educ:* Stepanska Gymnasium, Prague; Rydal Sch., Colwyn Bay; Christ's Coll., Cambridge (Exhibr); Univ. Correspondence Coll., Cambridge, and Regent Street Polytechnic; University Coll. London (Univ. Research Studentship). BA 1945, Certif.Ed 1945, MA 1948, Cantab; BSc (External) 1st Cl. Hons Maths 1947, PhD 1950, London. Asst Master, St Bees Sch., 1944–46; Asst Lectr, then Lectr, King's Coll., London, 1950–57; Head of Physics Dept, Battersea Coll. of Technology, 1958–66; University of Surrey: Prof. of Physics, 1964–71; Head of Physics Dept, 1966–69; Prof. of Sci. Educn, 1971–86; Hd, Inst. of Educnl Develt (formerly Educnl Technol.), 1967–84; Associate Head, Dept of Educnl Studies, 1983–86. Research Associate: MIT, 1955–56; Stanford Univ., 1956; Niels Bohr Inst., Copenhagen, 1962; Visiting Professor: Univ. of Washington, Seattle, 1965; UCL, 1970–77; Univ. of Sydney, 1971; Univ. of Sao Paulo, 1975; Univ. of Science, Malaysia, 1978, 1979; Univ. of Malaya, 1982, 1983; Asian Inst. of Technology, 1985, 1986; Fundaçao Armando Alvares Penteado, São Paulo, 1985–89. Higher Educn Advr, Trng, Enterprise and Educn Directorate (formerly Trng Agency), DoE, 1989–. Member: Governing Body, Battersea Coll. of Technology, 1962–66; Council, Univ. of Surrey, 1966–67, 1981–83; Council for Educational Technology of UK, 1975–81; Army Educn Adv. Bd, 1976–80; Convener, Standing Conf. of Physics Profs, 1971–74; Chairman: Governing Council, Soc. for Research into Higher Educn, 1976–78. Vice-Pres., Assoc. for Educnl and Trng Technology, 1976–. Fellow, Amer. Physical Soc., 1978. FRSA. *Publications:* Introductory Nuclear Theory, 1959, 2nd edn 1965 (Spanish edn 1964); Nuclear Sizes, 1961 (Russian edn 1962); Concepts in Classical Mechanics, 1971; (with H. Messel) Time and Man, 1978; Teaching in Higher Education: appraisal and training, 1987 (Japanese edn 1989); contribs to sci. jls on nuclear physics, higher education, science educn and educnl technology. *Recreation:* words. *Address:* 3 Great Quarry, Guildford, Surrey GU1 3XN. *T:* Guildford (01483) 576548.

See also B. C. Elton.

ELTON, Michael Anthony; Director General, National Association of Pension Funds, 1987–95; *b* 20 May 1932; *s* of late Francis Herbert Norris Elton and of Margaret Helen Elton (*née* Gray); *m* 1955, Isabel Clare, *d* of late Thomas Gurney Ryott and Clare Isabel Ryott; two *s* two *d*. *Educ:* Peter Symonds Sch.; Brasenose Coll., Oxford (Class. Mods 1952, BA 1st cl. Jurisp. 1954; MA, BCL 1955). Articled to Sir Andrew Wheatley, Clerk of Hants County Council, 1954; solicitor; Cumberland CC, 1958–61; Surrey CC, 1961–65; Asst Clerk, Bucks CC, 1965–70, Dep. Clerk of the Peace, 1967–70; Chief Exec., Assoc. of British Travel Agents, 1970–86; Dir Gen., European Fedn for Retirement Provision, 1987–91. FRSA. CIMgt. *Publications:* (with Gyles Brandreth) Future Perfect: how to profit from your pension planning, 1988; Travelling to Retirement: plus ça change, plus c'est la même chose, 1989; articles in professional jls. *Recreations:* tennis (geriatric mixed doubles), golf (unhandicapped), squash (lapsed-former Hants County player), music (choral singing, opera and lieder), bridge (friendly), gardening (esp. ponds). *Address:* 80 Old Kennels Lane, Oliver's Battery, Winchester, Hants SO22 4JT. *T:* Winchester (01962) 868470. *Club:* United Oxford & Cambridge University.

ELTON, (Peter) John, MC 1944: Director, British Alcan Aluminium (formerly Alcan Aluminium (UK) Ltd), since 1962; *b* 14 March 1924; 2nd *s* of Sydney George Elton; *m* 1948, Patricia Ann Stephens; two *d*. *Educ:* Eastbourne Coll.; Clare Coll., Cambridge. Indian Army: 14th Punjab Regt, 1942–45 (twice wounded). Hons Degree, Econs and Law, Cambridge. Man. Dir, Alcan Aluminium (UK) Ltd, 1967–74, Exec. Chm. 1974–76, non-Exec. Chm., 1976–78; Chm., Alcan Booth Industries Ltd, 1968–76; Director: Alcan Aluminium Ltd, 1972–77; Hill Samuel Group, 1976–87; Consolidated Goldfields, 1977–88; Spillers, 1978–80; TVS Entertainment, 1988–90. *Recreations:* sailing, shooting. *Address:* Salternshill Farm, Buckler's Hard, Beaulieu, Hants SO42 7XE. *T:* Buckler's Hard (01590) 616206. *Clubs:* Bucks; Royal Yacht Squadron (Cowes).

ELVIDGE, John William; Under Secretary, Scottish Office, since 1993; *b* 9 Feb. 1951; *s* of Herbert William Elvidge and Irene Teresa Elvidge. *Educ:* Sir George Monoux Sch., Walthamstow; St Catherine's Coll., Oxford (BA English Lang. and Lit.). Joined Scottish Office, 1973: Principal, 1978–84; Asst Sec., 1984–88 and 1989–93; Dir, Scottish Homes, 1988–89. *Recreations:* painting, film, theatre, music, modern novels, food and wine. *Address:* Scottish Office, Victoria Quay, Edinburgh EH6 6QQ. *T:* 0131–244 0781.

ELVIN, Herbert Lionel; Emeritus Professor of Education; Director of the University of London Institute of Education, 1958–73 (Professor of Education in Tropical Areas, 1956–58, Hon. Fellow, 1993); Director, Department of Education, UNESCO, Paris, 1950–56; *b* 7 Aug. 1905; *e s* of late Herbert Henry Elvin; *m* 1934, Mona Bedortha, *d* of Dr C. S. S. Dutton, San Francisco; one *s*. *Educ:* elementary schs; Southend High Sch.; Trinity Hall, Cambridge (1st Class Hons, History and English; Hon. Fellow, 1980). Commonwealth Fellow, Yale Univ., USA, Fellow of Trinity Hall, Cambridge, 1930–44; Temporary Civil Servant (Air Min., 1940–42, MOI, 1943–45); Principal, Ruskin Coll., Oxford, 1944–50. Parliamentary candidate (Lab), Cambridge Univ., 1935, Formerly Pres., English New Education Fellowship; Pres., Council for Education in World Citizenship; Chm., Commonwealth Educn Liaison Cttee. Member: Cttee on Higher Education; Govt of India Educn Commn; University Grants Cttee, 1946–50; Central Advisory Council for Education (England) and Secondary School Examinations Council. *Publications:* Men of America (Pelican Books), 1941; An Introduction to the Study of Literature (Poetry), 1949; Education and Contemporary Society, 1965; The Place of Commonsense in Educational Thought, 1977; (ed) The Educational Systems in the European Community, 1981; Encounters with Education, 1987. *Recreations:* formerly most games indifferently, athletics (half-mile, Cambridge *v* Oxford, 1927). *Address:* 4 Bulstrode Gardens, Cambridge CB3 0EN. *T:* Cambridge (01223) 358309.

ELVIN, Violetta, (Violetta Prokhorova), (Signora Fernando Savarese); ballerina; a prima ballerina of Sadler's Wells Ballet, Royal Opera House, London (now The Royal Ballet), 1951–56; Director, Ballet Company, San Carlo Opera, Naples, 1985–87; *b* Moscow, 3 Nov. 1925; *d* of Vassilie Prokhorov, engineer, and Irena Grimouzinskaya, former actress; *m* 1st, 1944, Harold Elvin (divorced 1952), of British Embassy, Moscow; 2nd, 1953, Siegbert J. Weinberger, New York; 3rd, 1959, Fernando Savarese, lawyer; one *s*. *Educ:* Bolshoi Theatre Sch., Moscow. Trained for ballet since age of 8 by: E. P. Gerdt, A. Vaganova, M. A. Kojuchova. Grad, 1942, as soloist; made mem. Bolshoi Theatre Ballet; evacuated to Tashkent, 1943; ballerina Tashkent State Theatre; rejoined Bolshoi Theatre at Kuibishev again as soloist, 1944; left for London, 1945. Joined Sadler's Wells Ballet at Covent Garden as guest-soloist, 1946; later became regular mem. Has danced all principal rôles, notably, Le Lac des Cygnes, Sleeping Beauty, Giselle, Cinderella, Sylvia, Ballet Imperial, etc. Danced four-act Le Lac des Cygnes, first time, 1943; guest-artist Stanislavsky Theatre, Moscow, 1944, Sadler's Wells Theatre, 1947; guest-prima ballerina, La Scala, Milan, Nov. 1952–Feb. 1953 (Macbeth, La Gioconda, Swan Lake, Petrouchka); guest artist, Cannes, July 1954; Copenhagen, Dec. 1954; Teatro Municipal, Rio de Janeiro, May 1955 (Giselle, Swan Lake, Les Sylphides, Nutcracker, Don Quixote and The Dying Swan); Festival Ballet, Festival Hall, 1955; guest-prima ballerina in Giselle, Royal Opera House, Stockholm (Anna Pavlova Memorial), 1956; concluded stage career when appeared in Sleeping Beauty, Royal Opera House, Covent Garden, June 1956. *Appeared in films:* The Queen of Spades, Twice Upon a Time, Melba. Television appearances in Russia and England. Has toured with Sadler's Wells Ballet, France, Italy, Portugal, United States and Canada. *Recreations:* reading, painting, swimming. *Address:* Marina di Equa, 80066 Seiano, Bay of Naples, Italy. *T:* (81) 8798520.

ELWES, Henry William George, JP; Lord-Lieutenant of Gloucestershire, since 1992; *b* 24 Oct. 1935; *s* of John Hargreaves Elwes, MC, Major, Scots Guards (killed in action, N Africa, 1943) and late Isabel Pamela Ivy Beckwith, *g d* of 7th Duke of Richmond and Gordon, KG, GCVO, CB; *m* 1962, Carolyn Dawn Cripps; two *s* (and one *s* decd). *Educ:* Eton; RAC, Cirencester. Served Army, Lieut, Scots Guards, 1953–56. Member: Cirencester RDC, 1959–74; Glos CC, 1970–91 (Vice-Chm., 1976–83 and 1991; Chm., 1983–85). Regl Dir, Lloyds Bank, 1985–91. Mem., Nat. Jt Council for Fire Brigades, 1979–91; Dir, Cirencester Benefit Soc. Trustee Co. Ltd, 1985–. Member: Prince's Trust for Glos; Prince's Youth Business Trust for Glos. Trustee: Glos Arthritis Trust; Cheltenham and N Glos Eye Therapy Trust; Barnwood House Trust; President: Western Woodland Owners Ltd; Glos Historic Bldgs Trust. Gloucestershire: High Sheriff, 1979–80; DL 1982;

JP 1992. Confrèrie des Chevaliers du Tastevin. *Address:* Colesbourne Park, near Cheltenham, Glos GL53 9NP.

ELWES, Captain Jeremy Gervase Geoffrey Philip; Vice Lord-Lieutenant of Humberside, since 1983; *b* 1 Sept. 1921; *s* of Rev. Rolf Elwes, OBE, MC; *m* 1955, Clare Mary Beveridge; four *s*. *Educ:* Avisford Sch.; Ampleforth Coll.; RMC Sandhurst. Joined Lincolnshire Regt, 1940; commissioned KRRC 1941; served until 1946, S Africa, Middle East, 8th Army, Yugoslavia, Southern Albania (despatches), Dalmatia and Greece; Moulton Agricultural Coll., 1947; farmer, 1949–; founder Dir, Linvend Ltd, 1960–, later J. S. Linder Ltd; founder Dir, Universal Marine Ltd, 1965–71; founder, Elwes Enterprises, 1970–; founder Dir, Euro-Latin Aviation Ltd, 1975–88. Opened country park to the public, Conservation Year, 1970; Mem., BBC Northern Adv. Council, 1966–69; Vice-Chm., BBC Radio Humberside, 1970–73; founder Chm., Lincs and Humberside Arts and Heritage Assoc., 1964–69; Co-Founder, Mus. of Lincolnshire Life, 1969; Pres., Lincs Branch, CPRE, 1980–89 (Chm., 1959–80); Mem. Council, Vice-Pres. and Steward, Lincs Agric. Soc., 1964–; Mem., Lincs Branch Exec., CLA, 1966–69. Pres., Shrievalty Assoc. of GB (founder Chm., 1971–92); joint founder, Scarbank Trust Charity, 1978–; Vice-Chm., Environmental Medicine Foundn, 1987–. Mem., Brigg and Scunthorpe Cons. Assoc. Exec. Cttee, 1948–73; Mem., Brigg RDC, 1957–73, Lindsey CC, 1961–71. High Sheriff, Lincs, 1969; DL Lincs 1970, Humberside 1975. Kt of SMO Malta, 1959. *Recreations:* the arts and countryside. *Address:* Elsham Hall, near Brigg, South Humberside DN20 0QZ. *T:* Barnetby (01652) 688738.

ELWES, Sir Jeremy (Vernon), Kt 1994; CBE 1984; Chairman, St Helier NHS Trust, since 1990; *b* 29 May 1937; *s* of late Eric Vincent Elwes and of Dorothea Elwes (*née* Bilton); *m* 1963, Phyllis Marion Relf, 2nd *d* of George Herbert Harding Relf and late Rose Jane Relf (*née* Luery); one *s*. *Educ:* Wirral Grammar Sch.; Bromley Grammar Sch.; City of London Coll. ACIS 1963. Technical Journalist, Heywood & Co., 1958–62; Accountant and Co. Sec., Agricultural Press, 1962–70; Sec. and Dir, East Brackland Hill Farming Development Co., 1967–70; IPC Business Press: Pensions Officer, 1966–70; Divl Personnel Manager, 1970–73; Manpower Planning Manager, 1973–78; Exec. Dir (Manpower), 1978–82; Personnel Dir, Business Press Internat., then Reed Business Publishing, 1982–93; Human Resources Dir, Reed Publishing Europe, 1993–94. Director: Periodicals Trng Council, 1986–92; Sutton Enterprise Agency Ltd, 1987– (Chm., 1987–90). Chairman: Cons. Political Centre Nat. Adv. Cttee, 1981–84; Cons. SE Area, 1986–90; Member: Nat. Union Exec. Cttee; Gen. Purposes Cttee; Cons. Group for Europe. Chm. of Governors, Walthamstow Hall; Governor, Eltham College. Member Judge, Internat. Wine and Spirit Competition; Mem., Wine Guild of UK. FRSA 1994. Liveryman, Stationers' and Newspapermakers' Co., 1991–. Chevalier, Ordre des Chevaliers Bretvins (Chancelier to 1992). *Recreations:* wine and food, reading, walking, golf. *Address:* Crispian Cottage, Weald Road, Sevenoaks, Kent TN13 1QQ. *T:* Sevenoaks (01732) 454208. *Clubs:* Carlton; Edenbridge Golf and Country.

ELWOOD, Sir Brian (George Conway), Kt 1990; CBE 1985; Chief Ombudsman: Chairman, Local Government Commission, New Zealand, 1985–92; Commissioner, Wellington Area Health Board, 1991–92; Chairman, Survey Industry Review Commission; *b* 5 April 1933; *s* of Jack Philip Elwood and Enid Mary Elwood; *m* 1956, Dawn Barbara Elwood (*née* Ward); one *s* two *d*. *Educ:* Victoria Univ., Wellington (LLB); Trinity Coll., London (ATCL). Barrister and Solicitor, 1957; Mayor, Palmerston North City, 1971–85. Hon. Mem., NZ Inst. of Surveyors. Hon. DLitt Massey, 1994. Medal for Distinguished Public Service, Lions Club Internat., 1985. *Recreations:* golf, fishing, gardening. *Address:* 38 Leeward Drive, Whitby, Wellington, New Zealand. *T:* (4) 2359255. *Club:* Wellington.

ELWORTHY, Sir Peter (Herbert), Kt 1988; farmer; *b* 3 March 1935; *s* of Harold Herbert Elworthy and June Mary Elworthy (*née* Batchelor); *m* 1960, Fiona Elizabeth McHardy; two *s* two *d*. *Educ:* Waihi Prep. Sch.; Christ's Coll.; Lincoln Agric. Coll. Nuffield Scholarship, UK, 1970; McMeekan Meml Award, 1978; Bledisloe Award, Lincoln, 1987. FNZIAS. Director: Reserve Bank of NZ, 1985–; Landcorp, 1986–88; BP NZ Ltd, 1986–; Ascot Management Corp. (NZ) Ltd, 1991–; Enerco NZ Ltd, 1992–; Huttons Kiwi Ltd, 1992–; Skellerup Gp Ltd, 1993–; Chm., Timaru Port Co., 1988–. Mem., NZ Adv. Cttee on Overseas Aid, 1986–89 (Chm., 1988–89). President: NZ Deer Farmers Assoc., 1974–81; Federated Farmers of NZ, 1984–88; Chairman: Ravensdown Co-op, 1977–82; Electricity Distribution Reform Unit, 1990–92; The Power Co., 1990–; Rural Electrical Reticulation Council, 1990–; QEII National Trust, 1987–93; NZ Rural Property Trust, 1988–; Opihi (SC) River Develt Co, 1992–; Sky Tower Co. (Auckland), 1992–; Sealoil (NZ) Ltd, 1994–. Trustee: Lincoln Univ. Foundn, 1989–; Waitingi Foundn, 1990–; NZ Inst. Econ. Res. (Inc.), 1991–; Alan Duff Charitable Foundn, 1994–; Chm., Salvation Army Inaugural Community Support Cttee, 1994–; Patron, Internat. Organic Agric. Conf., Lincoln, 1994–. NZ Commemoration Medal, 1990. *Recreations:* riding, fishing, flying (licensed pilot), reading. *Address:* Craigmore Farm, Maungati, 2RD, Timaru, New Zealand. *T:* Maungati (036129) 809. *Clubs:* Farmers'; Christchurch (Canterbury, NZ); Wellington (Wellington).

ELWORTHY, Air Cdre Hon. Timothy Charles, CVO 1995; CBE 1986; Her Majesty's Senior Air Equerry, since 1995; Extra Equerry to the Queen, since 1991; *b* 27 Jan. 1938; *e s* of Marshal of the RAF Baron Elworthy, KG, GCB, CBE, DSO, LVO, DFC, AFC and late Audrey Elworthy; *m* 1st, 1961, Victoria Ann (marr. diss.), *d* of Lt Col H. C. W. Bowring; two *d*; 2nd, 1971, Anabel, *d* of late Reginald Harding, OBE; one *s*. *Educ:* Radley; RAF Coll., Cranwell. CO 29 (Fighter) Sqn, 1975 (Wing Comdr); PSO to AO Commanding-in-Chief, Strike Comd, 1979; CO RAF Stn Leuchars, 1983 (Gp Capt.); RCDS, 1986; Dir, Operational Requirements, (Air), MoD, 1987 (Air Cdre); Captain of The Queen's Flight, 1989–95. Mem. Central Council, Royal Over-Seas League, 1994– (Mem. Exec. Cttee, 1995). Liveryman, GAPAN, 1995. QCVSA 1968. *Recreations:* country pursuits, wine, travel. *Address:* The Office of HM's Senior Air Equerry, RAF Northolt, Ruislip, Mddx HA4 6NG. *T:* 0171–636 0844. *Club:* Boodle's.

ELY, 8th Marquess of, *cr* 1801; **Charles John Tottenham;** Bt 1780; Baron Loftus, 1785; Viscount Loftus, 1789; Earl of Ely, 1794; Baron Loftus (UK), 1801; Headmaster, Boulden House, Trinity College School, Port Hope, Ontario, 1941–81; *b* 30 May 1913; *s* of G. L. Tottenham, BA (Oxon), and Cécile Elizabeth, *d* of J. S. Burra, Bockhanger, Kennington, Kent; *g s* of C. R. W. Tottenham, MA (Oxon), Woodstock, Newtown Mount Kennedy, Co. Wicklow, and Plâs Berwyn, Llangollen, N Wales; *S* cousin, 1969; *m* 1st, 1938, Katherine Elizabeth (*d* 1975), *d* of Col W. H. Craig, Kingston, Ont; three *s* one *d*; 2nd, 1978, Elspeth Ann, *o d* of late P. T. Hay, Highgate. *Educ:* Collège de Genève, Internat. Sch., Geneva; Queen's Univ., Kingston, Ont (BA). Career as Schoolmaster. *Recreation:* gardening. *Heir: e s* Viscount Loftus, *qv*. *Address:* Trinity College School, Port Hope, Ontario L1A 3W2, Canada. *T:* (905) 8855209; 20 Arundel Court, Jubilee Place, SW3 3TJ. *T:* 0171–352 9172. *Club:* University (Toronto).

ELY, Bishop of, since 1990; **Rt. Rev. Stephen Whitefield Sykes,** MA; *b* 1939; *m* 1962; one *s* two *d*. *Educ:* St John's Coll., Cambridge. BA (Cantab) 1961; MA (Cantab) 1964. Univ. Asst Lectr in Divinity, Cambridge Univ., 1964–68, Lectr. 1968–74; Fellow and Dean, St John's Coll., Cambridge, 1964–74; Van Mildert Canon Prof. of Divinity, Durham Univ., 1974–85; Regius Prof. of Divinity, and Fellow, St John's College, Cambridge, 1985–90. Mem., Archbishop's Cttee on Religious Educn, 1967. Hon. Canon of Ely Cathedral, 1985–90. Examining Chaplain to Bishop of Chelmsford, 1970–75. Edward Cadbury Lectr, Univ. of Birmingham, 1978; Hensley Henson Lectr, Univ. of Oxford, 1982–83. Chm., North of England Inst. for Christian Educn, 1980–85. Pres., Council of St John's Coll., Durham, 1984–. *Publications:* Friedrich Schleiermacher, 1971; Christian Theology Today, 1971; (ed) Christ, Faith and History, 1972; The Integrity of Anglicanism, 1978; (ed) Karl Barth: studies in his theological method, 1980; (ed) New Studies in Theology, 1980; (ed) England and Germany, Studies in Theological Diplomacy, 1982; The Identity of Christianity, 1984; (ed) Authority in the Anglican Communion, 1987; (ed) The Study of Anglicanism, 1988; (ed) Karl Barth: Centenary Essays, 1989; (ed) Sacrifice and Redemption, 1991; Unashamed Anglicanism, 1995. *Recreation:* walking. *Address:* The Bishop's House, Ely, Cambs CB7 4DW. *T:* Ely (01353) 662749, *Fax:* (01353) 669477.

ELY, Dean of; *see* Higgins, Very Rev. M. J.

ELY, Archdeacon of; *see* Watson, Ven. J. J. S.

ELY, Keith; *see* Ely, S. K.

ELY, Philip Thomas; Senior Partner, Paris Smith & Randall, Southampton, since 1981 (Partner, since 1961); *b* 22 March 1936; *s* of Eric Stanley Ely and Rose Josephine Ely; *m* 1966, Diana Mary (*née* Gellibrand); two *s* three *d*. *Educ:* Douai Sch.; LLB (external) London Univ. Admitted Solicitor, 1958. National Service, RN, 1958–60 (commnd, 1959). Articled Hepherd Winstanley & Pugh, Southampton, 1953–58; joined Paris Smith & Randall, Southampton, as Asst Solicitor, 1960. Law Society: Mem. Council, 1979–; Vice-Pres., 1990–91; Pres., 1991–92; Hampshire Incorporated Law Society: Asst Hon. Sec., 1961–66; Hon. Sec., 1966–74; Hon. Treasurer, 1974–79; Pres., 1979. Hon. LLD Southampton, 1992. *Recreations:* fly-fishing, gardening, music, reading. *Address:* Lansdowne House, Castle Lane, Southampton SO9 4FD. *T:* Southampton (01703) 635191.

ELY, (Sydney) Keith; Editor, Daily Post, Liverpool, since 1989; *b* 17 April 1949; *s* of Charles Rodenhurst Ely and Dorothy Mary Ely (*née* Rowlands); *m* 1970, Patricia Davies (marr. diss. 1994); three *d*. *Educ:* Maghull Grammar Sch.; Open Univ. (BA). Journalist: Liverpool Daily Post & Echo, 1968–78; Reuters, 1978–80; Daily Post, Liverpool: Business Editor, 1980–84; Acting Asst Editor, 1984; Systems Develt, 1985–86; Features Editor, 1987; Dep. Editor, 1987. Director: Corporate Culture Ltd, 1988; Liverpool Daily Post & Echo Ltd, 1989–. *Recreations:* music, computing. *Address:* 6 Harington Close, Formby, Merseyside L37 1XP. *T:* Formby (017048) 78344.

ELYAN, Prof. Sir (Isadore) Victor, Kt 1970; Professor of Law, and Dean of the Faculty of Law, Durban-Westville University, 1973–77, retired; Chief Justice of Swaziland, 1965–70, retired; *b* 5 Sept. 1909; *s* of Jacob Elyan, PC, JP and Olga Elyan; *m* 1939, Ivy Ethel Mabel Stuart-Weir (*d* 1965); no *c*; *m* 1966, Rosaleen Jeanette O'Shea. *Educ:* St Stephen's Green Sch., Dublin; Trinity Coll., Dublin Univ. BA 1929, LLB 1931, MA 1932, TCD. Admitted a Solicitor of Supreme Court of Judicature, Ireland, 1930; Barrister-at-Law, King's Inns 1949, Middle Temple, 1952. Resident Magistrate, HM Colonial Legal Service, Gold Coast, 1946–54; Senior Magistrate, 1954–55; Judge of Appeal of the Court of Appeal for Basutoland, the Bechuanaland Protectorate and Swaziland, 1955–66; Judge, High Courts of Basutoland and the Bechuanaland Protectorate, 1955–65; on occasions acted as Judge between 1953 and 1955, Gold Coast; as Justice of Appeal, West African Court of Appeal; and as Chief Justice of Basutoland, the Bechuanaland Protectorate and Swaziland, also Pres. Court of Appeal, during 1956, 1961 and 1964; Judge of Appeal: Court of Appeal for Botswana, 1966–70; Court of Appeal for Swaziland, 1967–70; Court of Appeal, Lesotho, 1968–70. Served War, 1942–46; attached to Indian Army, 1944–46; GSO2 Military Secretary's Branch (DAMS), 1945–46 in rank of Major. Mem., Internat. Adv. Bd, The African Law Reports, 1969. *Publications:* Editor, High Commission Territories Law Reports, 1956, 1957, 1958, 1959, 1960. *Recreation:* sailing. *Address:* PO Box 22001, Fish Hoek 7975, Cape, South Africa.

ELYSTAN-MORGAN, family name of Baron Elystan-Morgan.

ELYSTAN-MORGAN, Baron *cr* 1981 (Life Peer), of Aberteifi in the County of Dyfed; **Dafydd Elystan Elystan-Morgan; His Honour Judge Elystan-Morgan;** a Circuit Judge, since 1987; *b* 7 Dec. 1932; *s* of late Dewi Morgan and late Mrs Olwen Morgan; *m* 1959, Alwen, *d* of William E. Roberts; one *s* one *d*. *Educ:* Ardwyn Grammar Sch., Aberystwyth; UCW, Aberystwyth. LLB Hons Aberystwyth, 1953. Research at Aberystwyth and Solicitor's Articles, 1953–57; admitted a Solicitor, 1957; Partner in N Wales (Wrexham) Firm of Solicitors, 1958–68; Barrister-at-law, Gray's Inn, 1971; a Recorder, 1983–87. MP (Lab) Cardiganshire, 1966–Feb. 1974; Chm., Welsh Parly Party, 1967–68, 1971–74; Parly Under-Secretary of State, Home Office, 1968–70; front-bench spokesman on Home Affairs, 1970–72, on Welsh Affairs, 1972–74, on Legal and Home Affairs, House of Lords, 1981–85. Contested (Lab): Cardigan, Oct. 1974; Anglesey, 1979. Pres., Welsh Local Authorities Assoc., 1967–73. *Address:* Carreg Afon, Dolau, Bow Street, Dyfed SY24 5AE.

ELYTIS, Odysseus; Order of the Phoenix, 1965; Grand Commander, Order of Honour, 1979; poet; *b* Crete, 2 Nov. 1911; *y c* of Panayiotis and Maria Alepoudelis. *Educ:* Athens Univ. (Law); Sorbonne (Lettres). First publication, 1940; Broadcasting and Program Director, National Broadcasting Inst., 1945–47 and 1953–54; Administrative Board, Greek National Theatre, 1974–76. President, Admin. Board, Greek Broadcasting and Television, 1974. Hon. DLitt: Salonica, 1976; Sorbonne, 1980; Hon. DLit London, 1981. First National Prize in Poetry, 1960; Nobel Prize for Literature, 1979; Benson Silver Medal, RSL, 1981. Commander de la Légion d'Honneur (France), 1989. *Publications:* Orientations, 1940; Sun the First, 1943; The Axion Esti, 1959; Six, but one remorses for the Sky, 1960; The Light Tree, 1971; The Monogram, 1972; Villa Natacha, 1973; The Painter Theophilos, 1973; The Open Book, 1974; The Second Writing, 1976; Maria Nefeli, 1978; Selected Poems, 1981; Three Poems, 1982; Journal of an Unseen April, 1984; Saphfo, 1984; The Little Mariner, 1985; Private Way, 1991. *Address:* Skoufa Street 23, Athens, Greece. *T:* (1) 3626458.

EMANUEL, Aaron, CMG 1957; Consultant to OECD, 1972–83; *b* 11 Feb. 1912; *s* of Jack Emanuel and Jane (*née* Schaverien); *m* 1936, Ursula Pagel; two *s* one *d*. *Educ:* Henry Thornton Sch., Clapham; London Sch. of Economics (BSc Econ.). Economist at International Institute of Agriculture, Rome, 1935–38; Board of Trade, 1938; Ministry of Food, 1940; Colonial Office, 1943; Ministry of Health, 1961; Dept. of Economic Affairs, 1965; Under Secretary: Min. of Housing and Local Govt, 1969; Dept of the Environment, 1970–72. Chm., West Midlands Econ. Planning Bd, 1968–72; Vis. Sen. Lectr, Univ. of Aston in Birmingham, 1972–75. *Publication:* Issues of Regional Policies, 1973. *Address:* 119 Salisbury Road, Moseley, Birmingham B13 8LA. *T:* 0121–449 5553.

EMANUEL, David, FCSD; Joint Partner/Director, Emanuel, since 1977; *b* 17 Nov. 1952; *s* of John Lawrence Morris Emanuel and late Elizabeth Emanuel; *m* 1975, Elizabeth

Weiner (*see* E. Emanuel) (separated 1990); one *s* one *d*. *Educ:* Cardiff Coll. of Art (Diploma); Harrow Sch. of Art (Diploma); Royal College of Art (MA). Final Degree show at RCA, 1977. Emanuel (couture business) commenced in Mayfair, W1, 1977; The Emanuel Shop (retail), London, SW3, 1986–90; ready-to-wear business partnership in USA, 1988; formed David Emanuel Couture, 1990. Designed: wedding gown for the Princess of Wales, 1981; ballet productions, incl. Frankenstein, the Modern Prometheus, Royal Opera House, Covent Garden, 1985 and La Scala, Milan, 1987; uniforms for Virgin Atlantic Airways, 1990; prodns for theatre and operatic recitals. FCSD (FSIAD 1984). *Publication:* (with Elizabeth Emanuel) Style for All Seasons, 1983. *Recreations:* horse-riding, jet-ski-ing, tennis, opera. *T:* 0171–482 6486, *Fax:* 0171–267 6627. *Clubs:* White Elephant; Royal Ascot Tennis (Berks).

EMANUEL, Elizabeth Florence, FCSD; *b* 5 July 1953; *d* of Samuel Charles Weiner and Brahna Betty Weiner; *m* 1975, David Leslie Emanuel, *qv* (separated 1990); one *s* one *d*. *Educ:* City of London Sch. for Girls; Harrow Sch. of Art (Diploma with Hons); Royal Coll. of Art (MA 1977; DesRCA 1977). FCSD 1984. Emanuel (couture) commenced in Mayfair, W1, 1977; The Emanuel Shop (retail), London, SW3, 1986–90; launched internat. fashion label, Elizabeth Emanuel, 1991. Design Consultant, Wensum Corporate, 1990–. Designed: wedding gown for the Princess of Wales, 1981; ballet productions, incl. Frankenstein, the Modern Prometheus, Royal Opera House, Covent Garden, 1985 and La Scala, Milan, 1987; costumes for film Diamond Skulls, 1990; uniforms for Virgin Atlantic Airways, 1990; prodns for theatre and operatic recitals. *Publication:* (with David Emanuel) Style for All Seasons, 1983. *Recreations:* ballet, films, writing. *Address:* Elizabeth Emanuel, Studio 7, 44 Grove End Road, NW8 9NE. *T:* 0171–266 1233.

EMANUEL, Richard Wolff, MA, DM Oxon, FRCP; Physician to Department of Cardiology, Middlesex Hospital, 1963–87; Lecturer in Cardiology, Middlesex Hospital Medical School, 1963–87; Physician to National Heart Hospital, 1963–90; Lecturer to National Heart and Lung Institute (formerly Institute of Cardiology), 1963–90; *b* 13 Jan. 1923; *s* of Prof. and Mrs J. G. Emanuel, Birmingham; *m* 1950, Lavinia Hoffmann; three *s*. *Educ:* Bradfield Coll.; Oriel Coll., Oxford; Middlesex Hospital. House Appts at Middx Hospital, 1948 and 1950. Captain RAMC, 1948–50; Med. Registrar, Middx Hosp., 1951–52; Sen. Med. Registrar, Middx Hosp., 1953–55; Sen. Med. Registrar, Nat. Heart Hosp., 1956–58; Fellow in Med., Vanderbilt Univ., 1956–57; Sen. Med. Registrar, Dept of Cardiology, Brompton Hosp., 1958–61; Asst Dir, Inst. of Cardiology and Hon. Asst Physician to Nat. Heart Hosp., 1961–63. Advr in Cardiovascular Disease to Sudan Govt, 1969–; Civil Consultant in Cardiology, RAF, 1979–89. Vis. Lecturer: Univ. of Med. Sciences and Chulalongkorn Univ., Thailand; Univ. of the Philippines; Univ. of Singapore; Univ. of Malaya; Khartoum Univ.; St Cyre's Lectr, London, 1968; Ricardo Molina Lectr, Philippines, 1969. Has addressed numerous Heart Socs in SE Asia. Member: British Cardiac Soc., 1955– (Asst Sec., 1966–68; Sec., 1968–70; Mem. Council, 1981–85); Council, British Heart Foundn, 1967–73, 1979–92 (Chm., Cardiac Care Cttee, 1987–92); Cardiol Cttee, RCP, 1967–85 (Sec., 1972–79; Chm., 1979–85); Brit. Acad. of Forensic Sciences (Med.); Assoc. of Physicians of GB and Ireland; Chest, Heart and Stroke Assoc., 1978–91. FACC; Hon. Fellow, Philippine Coll. of Cardiology; Hon. Mem., Heart Assoc. of Thailand. Gov., National Heart and Chest Hosps Bd, 1972–75; Mem. Trustees and Exec. Cttee, Gordon Meml Coll. Trust Fund, 1987–. Mem., Editl Cttee, British Heart Journal, 1964–72. Grand Comdr of Most Distinguished Order of Crown of Pahang, 1990. *Publications:* various articles on diseases of the heart in British and American jls. *Recreations:* XVIIIth century glass, fishing. *Address:* 48 Wimpole Street, W1M 7DG. *T:* 0171–486 4337; 6 Lansdowne Walk, W11 3LN. *T:* 0171–727 6688; Canute Cottage, Old Bosham, near Chichester, West Sussex PO18 8LR. *T:* Bosham (01243) 573318. *Club:* Oriental.

EMBLING, John Francis, CB 1967; Deputy Under-Secretary of State, Department of Education and Science, 1966–71; *b* 16 July 1909; *m* 1940, Margaret Gillespie Anderson; one *s*. *Educ:* University of Bristol. Teaching: Dean Close, 1930; Frensham Heights, 1931; Lecturer: Leipzig Univ., 1936; SW Essex Technical Coll., 1938 (Head of Dept, 1942); Administrative Asst, Essex LEA, 1944; Ministry of Education: Principal, 1946; Asst Secretary, 1949; Under-Secretary of State for Finance and Accountant-General, Dept of Education and Science, 1960–66. Research Fellow in Higher Educn, LSE, 1972–73, Univ. of Lancaster, 1974–76. Mem. Council, Klagenfurt Univ., 1972–. Grand Cross, Republic of Austria, 1976.

EMBREY, Derek Morris, OBE 1986; CEng, FIEE, FIMechE, MIGasE; consultant electrical engineer, since 1991; Group Technical Director, AB Electronic Products Group PLC, 1973–91; *b* 11 March 1928; *s* of Frederick and Ethel Embrey; *m* 1951, Frances Margaret Stephens; one *s* one *d*. *Educ:* Wolverhampton Polytechnic (Hon. Fellow, 1987). Chief Designer (Electronics), Electric Construction Co. Ltd, 1960–65, Asst Manager Static Plant, 1965–69; Chief Engineer, Abergas Ltd, 1969–73. Member: Engineering Council, 1982–87; Welsh Industrial Develt Adv. Bd, 1982–85; NACCB, 1985–87; Council, IERE, 1984–88 (Vice Pres., 1985–88); National Electronics Council, 1985–; Welsh Adv. Bd, 1986–90 (Chm., 1987–90). Vis. Prof., Univ. of Technology, Loughborough, 1978–84 (External Examr, Dept of Mechanical Engrg, 1984–88); Visiting Lecturer: Loughborough Univ., 1988–; Birmingham Univ., 1989–. Member: Council, UWIST, Cardiff, 1984–88; Bd, Inst. of Transducer Technol., Southampton Univ., 1986–; Council, IEE, 1992– (Chm., Management and Design Divl Bd, 1993–94); Air Cadet Council, 1988–; Regl Civilian Chm., ATC, Wales, 1988–; Dir and Mem. Council, BTEC, 1993–. Freeman, City of London, 1986; Liveryman, Scientific Instrument Makers' Co., 1992–. *Publications:* contribs to various jls. *Recreations:* flying and navigating powered aircraft, gliding, music, archaeology. *Address:* 21 Rockfield Glade, Parc Seymour, Penhow, Newport, Gwent NP6 3JF. *T:* Penhow (01633) 400995. *Clubs:* Royal Air Force; Birmingham Electric.

EMECHETA, Buchi; writer and lecturer, since 1972; *b* 21 July 1944; *d* of Alice and Jeremy Emecheta; *m* 1960, Sylvester Onwordi; two *s* three *d*. *Educ:* Methodist Girls' High Sch., Lagos, Nigeria; London Univ. (BSc Hons Sociol.). Librarian, 1960–69; Student, 1970–74; Youth Worker and Res. Student, Race, 1974–76; Community Worker, Camden, 1976–78. Visiting Prof., 11 Amer. univs, incl. Penn. State, Pittsburgh, UCLA, Illinois at Urbana-Champaign, 1979; Sen. Res. Fellow and Vis. Prof. of English, Univ. of Calabar, Nigeria, 1980–81; lectured: Yale, Spring 1982; London Univ., 1982. Proprietor, Ogwugwn Afo Publishing Co. Included in twenty 'Best of Young British', 1983. Member: Arts Council of GB, 1982–83; Home Sec's Adv. Council on Race, 1979. *Publications:* In the Ditch, 1972; Second Class Citizen, 1975; The Bride Price, 1976; The Slave Girl, 1977; The Joys of Motherhood, 1979; Destination Biafra, 1982; Naira Power, 1982; Double Yoke, 1982; The Rape of Shavi, 1983; Head Above Water (autobiog.), 1984; Gwendolen, 1989; *for children:* Titch the Cat, 1979; Nowhere to Play, 1980; The Moonlight Bride, 1981; The Wrestling Match, 1981; contribs to New Statesman, TLS, The Guardian, etc. *Recreations:* gardening, going to the theatre, listening to music, reading. *Club:* Africa Centre.

EMERSON, Michael Ronald, MA; FCA; Ambassador and Head of Delegation of the European Communities to the Commonwealth of Independent States, since 1991; *b* 12 May 1940; *s* of James and Priscilla Emerson; *m* 1966, Barbara Brierley; one *s* two *d*. *Educ:* Hurstpierpoint Coll.; Balliol Coll., Oxford (MA (PPE)). Price Waterhouse & Co., London, 1962–65; Organisation for Economic Cooperation and Development, Paris: several posts in Develt and Economics Depts, finally as Head of General Economics Div., 1966–73; EEC, Brussels: Head of Division for Budgetary Policy, Directorate-General II, 1973–76; Economic Adviser to President of the Commission, 1977; Dir for Nat. Economies and Economic Trends, 1978–81; Dir for Macroecon. Analyses and Policies, 1981–86; Dir, Economic Evaluation of Community Policies, Directorate-General II, 1987–90. Fellow, Centre for Internat. Affairs, Harvard Univ., 1985–86. Hon. DLitt Keele, 1993; Hon. DCL Kent, 1993. *Publications:* (ed) Europe's Stagflation, 1984; What Model for Europe, 1987; The Economics of 1992, 1988; One Market, One Money, 1991; contribs to various economic jls and edited volumes on internat. and European economics. *Address:* Delegation of the European Union, 2/10 Astakhovsky Pereulok, 109028 Moscow, Russia. *T:* (095) 9563441; 128 avenue de Tervuren, 1150 Brussels, Belgium. *T:* (2) 7361283.

EMERSON, Dr Peter Albert, FRCP; Hon. Consultant Physician, Chelsea and Westminster Hospital (formerly Westminster and Charing Cross Hospitals), since 1988; *b* 7 Feb. 1923; *s* of Albert Emerson and Gwendoline (*née* Davy); *m* 1947, Ceris Hood Price; one *s* one *d*. *Educ:* The Leys Sch., Cambridge; Clare Coll., Univ. of Cambridge (MA); St George's Hosp., Univ. of London (MB, BChir 1947; MD 1954). FRCP 1964; Hon. FACP 1975. House Physician, St George's Hosp., 1947; RAF Med. Bd, 1948–52 (Sqdn Leader); Registrar, later Sen. Registrar, St George's Hosp. and Brompton Hosp., London, 1952–57; Asst Prof. of Medicine, Coll. of Medicine, State Univ. of New York, Brooklyn, USA, 1957–58; Consultant Phys., Westminster Hosp., 1959–88; Civilian Consultant Phys. in Chest Diseases to RN, 1974–88; Dean, Westminster Medical Sch., London, 1981–84. Hon. Consultant Phys., King Edward VII Hosp., Midhurst, 1969–88. Royal Coll. of Physicians: Asst Registrar, 1965–71; Procensor and Censor, 1978–80; Vice-Pres. and Sen. Censor, 1985–86; Mitchell Lectr, 1969. *Publications:* Thoracic Medicine, 1981; articles in med. jls and chapters in books on thoracic medicine and the application of decision theory and medical audit to clinical medicine. *Recreations:* tennis, restoring old buildings. *Address:* 3 Halkin Street, SW1X 7DJ. *T:* 0171–235 8529. *Club:* Royal Air Force.

EMERTON, Dame Audrey (Caroline), DBE 1989; DL; DStJ; RGN, RM, RNT; Chief Nursing Officer, since 1988, and Chairman of Medical Board, since 1993, St John Ambulance; Chairman, Brighton Health Care NHS Trust, since 1994 (Vice Chairman, 1993–94); *b* 10 Sept, 1935; *d* of late George Emerton and of Lily (*née* Squirrell). *Educ:* Tunbridge Wells GS; St George's Hosp.; Battersea Coll. of Technol. Sen. Tutor, Experimental 2 year and 1 year Course, St George's Hosp., SW1, 1965–68; Principal Nursing Officer, Educn, Bromley HMC, 1968–70; Chief Nursing Officer, Tunbridge Wells and Leybourne HMC, 1970–73; Regl Nursing Officer, SE Thames RHA, 1973–91. St John Ambulance, Kent: Co. Nursing Officer, 1967–85; Co. Comr, 1985–88. Pres., Assoc. of Nurse Administrators, 1979–82; Hon. Vice Pres., RCN, 1994–. Chairman: English Nat. Bd for Nursing, Midwifery and Health Visiting, 1983–85; UKCC, 1985–93. Trustee, Kent Community Housing Trust, 1993–. DL Kent, 1992. Hon. DCL Kent, 1989. *Address:* St John Ambulance HQ, 1 Grosvenor Crescent, SW1X 7EF.

EMERTON, Rev. Prof. John Adney, FBA 1979; Regius Professor of Hebrew, Cambridge, 1968–95, Emeritus Professor since 1995; Fellow of St John's College, since 1970; Honorary Canon, St George's Cathedral, Jerusalem, since 1984; *b* 5 June 1928; *s* of Adney Spencer Emerton and Helena Mary Emerton; *m* 1954, Norma Elizabeth Bennington; one *s* two *d*. *Educ:* Minchenden Grammar Sch., Southgate; Corpus Christi Coll., Oxford; Wycliffe Hall, Oxford. BA (1st class hons Theology), 1950; 1st class hons Oriental Studies, 1952; MA 1954. Canon Hall Jun. Greek Testament Prize, 1950; Hall-Houghton Jun. Septuagint Prize, 1951, Senior Prize, 1954; Houghton Syriac Prize, 1953; Liddon Student, 1950; Kennicott Hebrew Fellow, 1952. Corpus Christi Coll., Cambridge, MA (by incorporation), 1955; BD 1960; DD 1973. Deacon, 1952; Priest, 1953. Curate of Birmingham Cathedral, 1952–53; Asst Lecturer in Theology, Birmingham Univ., 1952–53; Lecturer in Hebrew and Aramaic, Durham Univ., 1953–55; Lecturer in Divinity, Cambridge Univ., 1955–62; Reader in Semitic Philology and Fellow of St Peter's Coll., Oxford, 1962–68. Visiting Professor: of Old Testament and Near Eastern Studies, Trinity Coll., Toronto Univ., 1960; of Old Testament, Utd Theol Coll., Bangalore, 1986; Fellow, Inst. for Advanced Studies, Hebrew Univ. of Jerusalem, 1982–83. Select Preacher before Univ. of Cambridge, 1962, 1971, 1986. President: Internat. Orgn for the Study of the Old Testament, 1992–95 (Sec., 1971–89); SOTS, 1979. Mem. Editorial Bd, Vetus Testamentum, 1971–. Corresp. Mem., Akademie der Wissenschaften, Göttingen, 1990. Hon. DD Edinburgh, 1977. Burkitt Medal for Biblical Studies, British Acad., 1991. *Publications:* The Peshitta of the Wisdom of Solomon, 1959; The Old Testament in Syriac: Song of Songs, 1966; (ed) Studies in the Historical Books of the Old Testament, 1979; (ed) Prophecy: essays presented to Georg Fohrer, 1980; (ed) Studies in the Pentateuch, 1990; Editor, Congress Volumes (International Organization for Study of the Old Testament): Edinburgh 1973, 1974; Göttingen 1977, 1978; Vienna 1980, 1981; Salamanca 1983, 1985; Jerusalem 1986, 1988; Leuven 1989, 1991; articles in Journal of Semitic Studies, Journal of Theological Studies, Theology, Vetus Testamentum, Zeitschrift für die Alttestamentliche Wissenschaft. *Address:* 34 Gough Way, Cambridge CB3 9LN.

EMERY, Prof. Alan Eglin Heathcote; MD, PhD, DSc; FRSE, FRCP, FRCPE; FRSocMed; FLS; Research Director, European Neuromuscular Center, Baarn, The Netherlands, since 1990; Professor of Human Genetics, University of Edinburgh and Hon. Consultant Physician, Lothian Health Board, 1968–83, now Emeritus Professor and Honorary Fellow; Hon. Visiting Fellow, Green College, Oxford, since 1986; *b* 21 Aug. 1928; *s* of Harold Heathcote Emery and Alice Eglin. *Educ:* Chester Coll.; Manchester Univ.; Johns Hopkins Univ., Baltimore (PhD). MD, DSc; FRIPHH 1965; FRCPE 1970; MFCM 1974; FRSE 1972; FLS 1985; FRSocMed 1992. Formerly Resident in Medicine and Surgery, Manchester Royal Infirmary; Fellow in Medicine, Johns Hopkins Hosp., Baltimore, 1961–64; Reader in Medical Genetics, Univ. of Manchester, 1964–68 and Hon. Consultant in Medical Genetics, United Manchester Hosps; Sen. Res. Fellow, Green Coll., Oxford, 1985–86. Visiting Professor: Univ. of NY, 1968; Heidelberg, 1972; Hyderabad, 1975; California (UCLA), 1980; Padua, 1984; Medical Coll., Peking, 1985; RPMS, 1986; Duke Univ. (N Carolina), 1987; Univ. of London (Inst. of Neurology), 1988; St George's Univ., Grenada, 1991. Lectures: Harveian, 1970; Woodhull, Royal Instn, 1972; Boerhaave, 1984. Pres., British Clinical Genetics Soc., 1980–83; Council Mem., British Genetic Soc.; Member: Soc. of Authors, 1989; Royal Soc. of Lit., 1993. Hon. Mem., Gaetano Conte Acad., Italy, 1991. Hon. Fellow, Muscular Dystrophy Assoc. of Brazil, 1982; Hon. FACMG 1993; For. Associate, Royal Soc. of South Africa, 1989. Hon. MD Naples, 1993. Nat. Foundn (USA) Internat. Award for Research, 1980; Wilfred Card Medal, 1985. Exec. Editor, Procs B, RSE, 1986–90. Hon. MD Naples, 1993. *Publications:* Elements of Medical Genetics, 1968, 8th edn 1992; Methodology in Medical Genetics, 1976, 2nd edn 1986; Recombinant DNA—an introduction, 1984; Duchenne Muscular Dystrophy, 1987, 2nd edn 1993; Muscular Dystrophy: the facts, 1994; The History of a Genetic Disease, 1995; editor: Modern Trends in Human Genetics, vol. 1, 1970, vol. 2, 1975; Antenatal Diagnosis of Genetic Disease, 1973; Registers for the

Detection and Prevention of Genetic Disease, 1976; Principles and Practice of Medical Genetics, 1983, 2nd edn 1990; Psychological Aspects of Genetic Counselling, 1984; Diagnostic Criteria for Neuromuscular Disorders, 1994; numerous scientific papers. *Recreations:* writing poetry, marine biology, oil painting. *Address:* Ingleside Court, Upper West Terrace, Budleigh Salterton, Devon EX9 6NZ. *T:* Budleigh Salterton (01395) 445847.

EMERY, Eleanor Jean, CMG 1975; HM Diplomatic Service, retired; *b* 23 Dec. 1918; *d* of Robert Paton Emery and Nellie Nicol (*née* Wilson). *Educ:* Western Canada High Sch., Calgary, Alberta; Glasgow Univ. MA Hons in History, 1941. Dominions Office, 1941–45; Asst Private Sec. to Sec. of State, 1942–45; British High Commn, Ottawa, 1945–48; CRO, 1948–52; Principal Private Sec. to Sec. of State, 1950–52; First Sec., British High Commn, New Delhi, 1952–55; CRO, 1955–58; First Sec., British High Commn, Pretoria/Cape Town, 1958–62; Head of South Asia Dept, CRO, 1962–64; Counsellor, British High Commn, Ottawa, 1964–68; Head of Pacific Dependent Territories Dept, FCO, 1969–73; High Comr, Botswana, 1973–77. Chm., UK Botswana Soc., 1984–88, Vice-Chm., 1981–84 and 1988–92. Governor, Commonwealth Inst., 1980–85. *Recreations:* walking, gardening. *Address:* 17 Winchmore Drive, Cambridge CB2 2LW. *Club:* Commonwealth Trust.

See also J. M. Zachariah.

EMERY, Fred; author and broadcaster; Presenter, Panorama, BBC TV, 1978–80 and 1982–92; *b* 19 Oct. 1933; *s* of Frederick G. L. Emery and Alice May (*née* Wright); *m* 1958, E. Marianne Nyberg; two *s*. *Educ:* Bancroft's Sch.; St John's Coll., Cantab (MA). RAF fighter pilot, 266 & 234 Squadrons, National Service, 1953. Radio Bremen, 1955–56; joined The Times, 1958, Foreign Correspondent, 1961; served in Paris, Algeria, Tokyo, Indonesia, Vietnam, Cambodia, Malaysia and Singapore until 1970; Chief Washington Corresp., 1970–77; Political Editor, 1977–81; Home Editor, 1981–82; Exec. Editor (Home and Foreign), 1982. Reporter, Watergate (TV series), 1994. *Publication:* Watergate: the corruption and fall of Richard Nixon, 1994. *Recreations:* skiing, hill walking, tennis. *Address:* 5 Woodsyre, SE26 6SS. *T:* 0181–761 0076. *Club:* Garrick.

EMERY, George Edward, CB 1980; Director General of Defence Accounts, Ministry of Defence, 1973–80, retired; *b* 2 March 1920; *s* of late Frederick and Florence Emery; *m* 1946, Margaret (*née* Rice); two *d*. *Educ:* Bemrose Sch., Derby. Admiralty, 1938; Min. of Fuel and Power, 1946; Min. of Supply, 1951; Min. of Aviation, 1959; Min. of Technology, 1967; Principal Exec. Officer, 1967; Asst Sec., Min. of Aviation Supply, 1970; Ministry of Defence: Asst Sec., 1971; Exec. Dir, 1973; Under-Sec., 1973. *Recreations:* amateur dramatics, gardening. *Address:* 3 The Orchard, Freshford, Bath BA3 6EW.

EMERY, Joan Dawson, (Mrs Jack Emery); *see* Bakewell, J. D.

EMERY, Joyce Margaret; *see* Zachariah, J. M.

EMERY, Lina, (Mrs Ralph Emery); *see* Lalandi-Emery, L.

EMERY, Rt. Hon. Sir Peter (Frank Hannibal), Kt 1982; PC 1993; MA; FCIPS; MP (C) Honiton, since 1967 (Reading, 1959–66); *b* 27 Feb. 1926; *s* of late F. G. Emery, Highgate; *m* 1st, 1954 (marr. diss.); one *s* one *d*; 2nd, 1972, Elizabeth, *y d* of late G. J. R. Monnington; one *s* one *d*. *Educ:* Scotch Plains, New Jersey, USA; Oriel Coll., Oxford (MA). Joint Founder and First Secretary of the Bow Group. Parliamentary Private Secretary in Foreign Office, War Dept and Min. of Labour, 1960–64; Jt Hon. Secretary, 1922 Cttee, 1964–65; Opposition Front Bench Spokesman for Treasury, Economics and Trade, 1964–66; Parliamentary Under-Secretary of State: DTI, 1972–74; Dept of Energy, 1974; Member: Select Cttee on Industry and Trade, 1979–87; Select Cttee on Procedure, 1972– (Chm., 1983–). Jt Vice-Chm., Conservative Finance Cttee, 1970–72; Chairman: Cons. Housing and Construction Cttee, 1974–75. Member, Delegation to CPA Conference: Westminster, 1961; Canada, 1962; Fiji, 1981; Leader, Delegn to Kenya, 1977; Delegate: Council of Europe and WEU, 1962–64, 1970–72; North Atlantic Assembly, 1983– (Chm., Science and Technology Cttee, 1985–89; Rapporteur, 1989–); Deleg. and Treas., OSCE (formerly CSCE), 1992–. Chm., Winglaw Gp; Director: Property Growth Insurance, 1966–72; Phillips Petroleum-UK Ltd, 1963–72; Institute of Purchasing and Supply, 1961–72; Secretary-General, European Federation of Purchasing, 1962–72; Chairman, Consultative Council of Professional Management Organisations, 1968–72. Founding Chm., Nat. Asthma Campaign, 1990–; Mem. Adv. Bd, Center for Strategic and Internat. Studies, Washington DC, 1990–. *Recreations:* sliding down mountains, tennis, cricket, golf and bridge (Capt., H of C team, 1984–). *Address:* Tytherleigh Manor, near Axminster, Devon EX13 7BD. *T:* South Chard (01460) 220309; 8 Ponsonby Terrace, SW1P 4QA. *T:* 0171–222 6666; (office) 0171–219 4497, *Fax:* 0171–219 2300. *Clubs:* Carlton, Portland; Leander (Henley-on-Thames).

EMERY-WALLIS, Frederick Alfred John, DL; FSA; Member, Hampshire County Council, since 1973 (Vice-Chairman, 1975–76; Leader, 1976–93); Vice-President, Southern Tourist Board, since 1988 (Chairman, 1976–88); *b* 11 May 1927; *o s* of Frederick Henry Wallis and Lillian Grace Emery Coles; *m* 1960, Solange, *o d* of William Victor Randall, London, and Albertine Beaupère, La Guerche-sur-l'Aubois; two *d*. *Educ:* Blake's Academy, Portsmouth. Royal Signals SCU4 (Middle East Radio Security), 1945–48. Portsmouth City Council, 1961–74; Lord Mayor, 1968–69; Alderman, 1969–74. Chm., Recreation Cttee, 1982–85, Mem., Exec. and Policy Cttees, ACC, 1974–93. Chairman: Portsmouth Develt and Estates Cttee, 1965–74; Portsmouth Papers Editorial Bd, 1966–82; S Hampshire Plan Adv. Cttee, 1969–74; Portsmouth South Cons. and Unionist Assoc., 1971–79, 1982–85; Portsmouth Record Series Adv. Panel, 1982–; Hampshire Archives Trust, 1986–; Exec. Cttee, Hampshire Sculpture Trust, 1988–; Director: Warrior Preservation Trust, 1988–91; WNO, 1990–; Learning Through Landscapes Trust, 1991–; Member: Economic Planning Council for the South East, 1969–74; British Library Adv. Council, 1979–84, 1986–91; Council, British Records Assoc., 1979–; Library and Information Services Council, 1980–83; Mary Rose Develt Trust, 1980–90; Arts Council of GB Reg. Adv. Bd, 1984–88; Hampshire Gardens Trust, 1984–; Nat. Council on Archives, 1992–; Victoria County History Cttee, 1993–. President: Hampshire Field Club, 1971–74; Hatrics, the Southern Information Network, 1978–. Gov., Univ. of Portsmouth, 1992– (Mem., 1961–92, Vice-Chm., 1967–75, Portsmouth Polytechnic); Chm. of Govs, Portsmouth High Sch. for Girls, 1982–92. Trustee: New Theatre Royal, Portsmouth, 1982–92; Royal Naval Mus., Portsmouth, 1987–; Royal Marines Mus., Portsmouth, 1993–. Vice-Pres., Mottisfont Soc., 1978–. Pres., Portsmouth YMCA, 1978–88. DL Hants 1988. Hon. Fellow, Portsmouth Polytechnic, 1972. FSA 1980. Hon. FRIBA 1985. *Publications:* various publications concerning history and develt of Portsmouth and Hampshire. *Recreations:* book collecting, music. *Address:* Froddington, Craneswater Park, Portsmouth PO4 0NR. *T:* Portsmouth (01705) 731409.

EMLYN JONES, John Hubert, CBE 1986 (MBE (mil.) 1941); FRICS; JP; Member of the Lands Tribunal, 1968–86; *b* 6 Aug. 1915; *s* of late Ernest Pearson Jones and Katharine Cole Jones (*née* Nicholas); *m* 1954, Louise Anne Montague, *d* of late Raymond Ralph Horwood Hazell; two *s* one *d*. *Educ:* Dulwich. FRICS 1939. Served War, RE, 1939–46: Major 1943. Partner, Rees-Reynolds and Hunt, and Alfred Savill & Sons, Chartered Surveyors, 1950–68. President: Rating Surveyors Assoc., 1965–66 (Hon. Mem. 1968); Climbers' Club, 1966–69 (Hon. Mem. 1970); Alpine Club, 1980–82. Mem. Council, RICS, 1964–69. Mem. Bureau, 1964–72, Treasurer 1967–69, Fédération Internationale des Géomètres. Mem., expedns to Himalayas: Annapurna, 1950; Ama Dablam, 1959 (Leader). High Sheriff, Bucks, 1967–68, JP 1968. *Publications:* articles and revs in mountaineering jls. *Recreations:* mountaineering, music. *Address:* Ivinghoe Manor, Leighton Buzzard, Beds LU7 9EH. *T:* Cheddington (01296) 668202. *Clubs:* Garrick, Alpine.

EMMERSON, David, CBE 1989; AFC 1982; Chief Executive, Elizabeth FitzRoy Homes, since 1991; *b* 6 Sept. 1939; *s* of late Alfred Robert and Sarah Helen Emmerson; *m* 1961, Martha (Marie) Katherine Stuart. *Educ:* Colchester Royal Grammar Sch. Operational and instructional flying, 1959–65; specialist navigation course, 1966; Nimrod aircraft develt team, 1967–69; sqn navigation ldr, 1970–72; Canadian Forces Staff Coll., 1973–74; High Commn, Ottawa, 1975–76; SO to ACAS (Pol), MoD, 1977; Air 3 British Defence Staff, Washington, USA, 1978–80; OC 206 Sqn, 1981–82; Gp Capt. Ops, Northwood, 1983; Stn Comdr, RAF Kinloss, 1984–85; RCDS, 1986; Principal Staff Officer to CDS, 1987–88; Chief of Staff, HQ 18 Gp, Northwood, 1989–90; retired in rank of Air Vice-Marshal. Chm., Assoc. for Residential Care, 1995–. *Recreations:* travel, world politics, all sports. *Address:* c/o Caxton House, Station Approach, Haslemere, Surrey GU27 2PE. *T:* Haslemere (01428) 656766. *Club:* Royal Air Force.

EMMERSON, Rt. Rev. Ralph; an Assistant Bishop, Diocese of Ripon, since 1986; *b* 7 June 1913; *s* of Thomas and Alys Mary Emmerson; *m* 1942, Ann Hawthorn Bygate (*d* 1982); no *c*. *Educ:* Leeds Grammar Sch.; King's Coll., London (BD, AKC); Westcott House, Cambridge. Leeds Educn Authority Youth Employment Dept, 1930–35; Curate, St George's, Leeds, 1938–41; Priest-in-Charge, Seacroft Estate, 1941–48; Rector of Methley and Vicar of Mickletown, 1949–56; Vicar of Headingley, 1956–66; Hon. Canon of Ripon Cath., 1964; Residentiary Canon and Canon Missioner for Dio. Ripon, 1966–72; Bishop Suffragan of Knaresborough, 1972–79; Asst Bishop, Dio. Wakefield, 1980–86. *Address:* Flat 1, 15 High Saint Agnesgate, Ripon HG4 1QR. *T:* Ripon (01765) 601626.

EMMET, Dorothy Mary, MA Oxon, Cantab and Manchester; *b* 1904; *d* of late Rev. C. W. Emmet, Fellow of University Coll., Oxford, and late Gertrude Julia Emmet (*née* Weir). *Educ:* St Mary's Hall, Brighton; Lady Margaret Hall, Oxford. Classical Exhibitioner, Lady Margaret Hall, Oxford, 1923; Hon. Mods Class I, 1925; Lit. Hum. Class I, 1927. Tutor, Maesyrhaf Settlement, Rhondda Valley, 1927–28 and 1931–32; Commonwealth Fellow, Radcliffe Coll., Cambridge, Mass, USA, 1928–30; Research Fellow, Somerville Coll., Oxford, 1930–31; lecturer in Philosophy, Armstrong Coll., Newcastle upon Tyne, 1932–38 (now Newcastle Univ.); lecturer in Philosophy of Religion, University of Manchester, 1938–45; Reader in Philosophy, 1945–46; Prof. of Philosophy, University of Manchester, 1946–66; Prof. Emeritus, 1966. Stanton Lecturer in Philosophy of Religion, University of Cambridge, 1950–53. Visiting Professor: Barnard Coll., Columbia Univ., New York, 1960–61; Univ. of Ibadan, Nigeria, 1974. President Aristotelian Society, 1953–54. Dean of the Faculty of Arts, University of Manchester, 1962–64. Hon. Fellow, Lady Margaret Hall, Oxford. Fellow, Lucy Cavendish Coll., Cambridge, 1967, Emeritus Fellow, 1981. Hon. DLitt: Glasgow, 1974; Leicester, 1976. *Publications:* Whitehead's Philosophy of Organism, 1932, 2nd edn 1982; Philosophy and Faith, 1936; The Nature of Metaphysical Thinking, 1945; Function, Purpose and Powers, 1958, 2nd edn 1972; Rules, Roles and Relations, 1966; (ed with Alasdair MacIntyre) Sociological Theory and Philosophical Analysis, 1970; The Moral Prism, 1979; The Effectiveness of Causes, 1984; The Passage of Nature, 1992; The Role of the Unrealisable, 1994; contributions to philosophical journals. *Recreations:* listening to music, reading. *Address:* 11 Millington Road, Cambridge CB3 9HW.

EMMETT, Bryan David; Administrator, EAGA Charitable Trust, since 1993; *b* 15 Feb. 1941; *m* 1960, Moira Miller (marr. diss. 1995); one *s*. *Educ:* Tadcaster Grammar Sch. Clerical Officer, Min. of Labour, and National Service, 1958–59; Exec. Officer, War Dept, 1959–64; Asst Principal, MOP, 1965–69 (Asst Private Sec. to Ministers of Power, 1968–69); Principal, Electricity Div., DTI, 1969–74; Department of Energy: Principal, and Private Sec. to Minister of State, 1974–75; Asst Sec., and Principal Private Sec. to Sec. of State for Energy, 1975–76; Asst Sec., Petroleum Engrg Div., 1977–80; Under Sec., and Principal Estab. Officer, 1980–81; Principal Estab. and Finance Officer, 1981–82; Chief Exec., Employment Div., MSC, 1982–85; Department of Energy: Head, Energy Policy Div., 1985–86; Head of Oil Div., 1986–87; Dir Gen., Energy Efficiency Office, 1987–88; seconded as Chief Exec., Educn Assets Bd, Leeds, 1988–90; compulsorily retired, 1991. NEXD Energy Action Grants Agency, 1991–. *Recreations:* National Hunt racing, horseriding, golf. *Address:* Hayside Farm, Low Street, Sancton, E Yorks Y04 3QY.

EMMOTT, William John, (Bill); Editor, The Economist, since 1993; *b* 6 Aug. 1956; *s* of Richard Anthony Emmott and Audrey Mary Emmott; *m* 1st, 1982, Charlotte Crowther (marr. diss.); 2nd, 1992, Carol Barbara Mawer. *Educ:* Latymer Upper Sch., Hammersmith; Magdalen Coll., Oxford (BA Hons PPE); Nuffield Coll., Oxford. The Economist: Brussels corresp., 1980–82; Economics corresp., 1982–83; Tokyo corresp., 1983–86; Finance Editor, 1986–88; Business Affairs Editor, 1989–93; Editorial Dir, Economist Intelligence Unit, May–Dec. 1992. *Publications:* The Pocket Economist (with Rupert Pennant-Rea), 1983; The Sun Also Sets, 1989; Japan's Global Reach, 1992. *Address:* The Economist Newspaper, 25 St James's Street, SW1A 1HG. *T:* 0171–830 7000. *Clubs:* Reform, Lansdowne.

EMMS, David Acfield, OBE 1995; MA; Director, The London Goodenough Trust (formerly London House) for Overseas Graduates, 1987–95; *b* 16 Feb. 1925; *s* of late Archibald George Emms and Winifred Gladys (*née* Richards); *m* 1950, Pamela Baker Speed; three *s* one *d*. *Educ:* Tonbridge Sch.; Brasenose Coll., Oxford. BA Hons Mod. Langs Oxford, 1950, Diploma in Education, 1951; MA 1954. Rugby football, Oxford *v* Cambridge, 1949, 1950. Served War of 1939–45, RA, 1943–47. Undergraduate, 1947–50; Asst Master, Uppingham Sch. (Head of Mod. Languages Dept, CO, CCF Contingent), 1951–60; Headmaster of: Cranleigh School, 1960–70; Sherborne School, 1970–74; Master, Dulwich Coll., 1975–86. Chm., HMC, 1984; Vice-Pres., ISCO, 1973–. Dep. Chm., E-SU, 1984–89; Chm., Jt Educnl Trust, 1987–90; Mem. Cttee, GBA, 1989–92. Vice-Chm. Council and Dep. Pro-Chancellor, City Univ., 1989–91; Governor: Bickley Park, 1978–81; Feltonfleet, 1967–86; Brambletye, 1982–88; St Felix Sch., Southwold, 1981–88; Portsmouth Grammar Sch., 1987–; Tonbridge, 1988–; St. George's, Montreux, 1989–; St Dunstan's Coll., 1992–. President: Alleyn Club, 1985; Brasenose Soc., 1987; Vice-Pres., Dulwich Soc. Mem. Council, Fairbridge Soc., 1984–. FRSA 1988. Freeman, City of London; Master, Skinners' Co., 1987–88. Hon. Col, 39th (City of London) Signal Regt (Special Communications) (Volunteers), 1988–91. *Publication:* HMC Schools and British Industry, 1981. *Recreations:* radical gardening, travel. *Address:* Seaforth, Spinney Lane, Itchenor, W Sussex PO20 7DJ. *Clubs:* East India, Devonshire, Sports and Public Schools; Vincent's (Oxford); Itchenor Sailing.

EMMS, Peter Fawcett; Know How Fund advisory team to Ukrainian government, since 1994; *b* 25 April 1935; *s* of late Reginald Emms and of Hetty Emms; *m* 1960, Carola

Wayne; three *d*. *Educ:* Derby Sch., Derby; Magdalen Coll., Oxford, 1956–59 (John Doncaster Open Schol. in Mod. Langs; MA French and German). National Service, Jt Services Russian Course, 1954–56. Assistant Master: Abingdon Sch., 1959–62; Rugby Sch., 1962–74; Vis. Master, Groton Sch., Mass, 1967–68; Hd of Mod. Langs 1969–71, Housemaster of Town House 1971–74, Rugby Sch.; joined DoE as Principal, 1974, with posts in Road Safety, Construction Industries and Housing; Asst Sec., 1979; Hd of Greater London Housing, 1979–81; seconded to DES, Further and Higher Educn Br., 1981–83; Hd of Housing Management Div., and of Estate Action Unit, 1983–87; Nuffield Leverhulme Travelling Fellowship, 1987–88; Hd, Dept of Transport Internat. Transport Div., Mem., Central Rhine Commn, 1988–89; Under Sec., 1989; Regl Dir, Eastern Reg., DoE and Dept of Transport, 1989–94. *Publications:* Social Housing: a European dilemma?, 1990; (contrib.) Changing Housing Finance Systems, 1991. *Recreation:* the civilizations of Europe. *Address:* 2 Thorncroft, Hemel Hempstead HP3 8HP; 71800 Vauban, France.

EMPEY, Reginald Norman Morgan, OBE 1994; Member, Belfast City Council, since 1985; Lord Mayor of Belfast, 1989–90 and 1993–94; *b* 26 Oct. 1947; *s* of Samuel Frederick Empey and Emily Winifred (*née* Morgan); *m* 1977, Stella Ethna Donnan; one *s* one *d*. *Educ:* The Royal Sch., Armagh; Queen's Univ., Belfast (BSc (Econ)). Cons. & Unionist Assoc., QUB, 1967; Publicity Officer, 1967–68, Vice-Chm., 1968–72, Ulster Young Unionist Council; Chm., Vanguard Unionist Party, 1974–75; Mem., E Belfast, NI Constitutional Convention, 1975–76. Member: Belfast Harbour Comrs, 1985–89; Eastern Health and Social Services Bd, 1985–86; Ulster Unionist Council, 1987– (Hon. Sec., 1990–); Bd, Laganside Corp., 1992–; Police Authy for NI, 1992–; European Cttee of the Regions for NI, Brussels, 1994–; Standing Adv. Commn on Human Rights, 1994–. *Recreations:* walking, gardening. *Address:* Knockvale House, 205 Sandown Road, Belfast BT5 6GX. *T:* Belfast (01232) 795569.

EMPEY, Most Rev. Walton Newcombe Francis; *see* Meath and Kildare, Bishop of.

EMPSON, Adm. Sir (Leslie) Derek, GBE 1975; KCB 1973 (CB 1969); Commander-in-Chief Naval Home Command and Flag Officer Portsmouth Area, 1974–75; *b* 29 Oct. 1918; *s* of Frank Harold Empson and Madeleine Norah Empson (*née* Burge); *m* 1958, Diana Elizabeth Kelly; one *s* one *d*. *Educ:* Eastbourne Coll.; Clare Coll., Cambridge (Class. Exhibn). Athletics Blue, 1939; BA 1940. Joined Royal Navy for pilot duties, 1940; commd as Sub-Lieut (A) RNVR, 1940; flew as Fleet Air Arm pilot, 1940–45; perm. commn in RN, 1944; Naval Asst to First Sea Lord, 1957–59; Comd HMS Eagle, 1963–65; Imp. Def. Coll., 1966; Flag Officer, Aircraft Carriers, 1967–68; Asst Chief of Naval Staff (Operations and Air), 1968–69; Comdr, Far East Fleet, 1969–71; Second Sea Lord and Chief of Naval Personnel, 1971–74; Flag ADC to The Queen, 1974–75. Rear-Adm. of the UK, 1984–86; Vice-Adm. of the UK, 1986–88. Comdr 1952; Captain 1957; Rear-Adm. 1967; Vice-Adm. 1970; Adm. 1972. Chm., Roymark, 1985–92; Consultant: Thorn EMI, 1976–86; Warner Communications, 1987–88; Astra Hldgs, 1987–90. Chm. of Governors, Eastbourne Coll., 1972–88.

EMSLIE, family name of **Baron Emslie.**

EMSLIE, Baron *cr* 1980 (Life Peer), of Potterton in the District of Gordon; **George Carlyle Emslie,** PC 1972; MBE 1946; FRSE 1987; Lord Justice-General of Scotland and Lord President of the Court of Session, 1972–89; *b* 6 Dec. 1919; *s* of late Alexander and Jessie Blair Emslie; *m* Lilias Ann Mailer Hannington; three *s*. *Educ:* The High School of Glasgow; The University of Glasgow (MA, LLB). Commissioned A&SH, 1940; served War of 1939–45 (despatches): North Africa, Italy, Greece, Austria, 1942–46; psc Haifa, 1944; Brigade Major (Infantry), 1944–46. Advocate, 1948; Advocate Depute (Sheriff Courts), 1955; QC (Scotland) 1957; Sheriff of Perth and Angus, 1963–66; Dean of Faculty of Advocates, 1965–70; Senator of Coll. of Justice in Scotland and Lord of Session, 1970–72. Chm., Scottish Agricultural Wages Bd, 1969–73; Mem., Council on Tribunals (Scottish Cttee), 1962–70. Vice-Chm., Bd of Trustees, Nat. Library of Scotland, 1975–. Hon. Bencher: Inner Temple, 1974; Inn of Court of N Ireland, 1981. Hon. LLD Glasgow, 1973. *Recreation:* golf. *Address:* 47 Heriot Row, Edinburgh EH3 6EX. *T:* 0131–225 3657. *Clubs:* New (Edinburgh); The Honourable Company of Edinburgh Golfers.

See also Hon. D. R. A. Emslie, Hon. G. N. H. Emslie.

EMSLIE, Hon. Derek Robert Alexander; QC (Scot.) 1987; *b* 21 June 1949; *s* of Baron Emslie, *qv*; *m* 1974, Elizabeth Jane Cameron Carstairs, *d* of Andrew McLaren Carstairs; one *s* two *d*. *Educ:* Edinburgh Acad.; Trinity Coll., Glenalmond; Gonville and Caius Coll., Cambridge (Hist. Schol.; BA); Edinburgh Univ. (LLB). Advocate 1974; Standing Jun. Counsel, DHSS, 1979–87; Advocate Depute, 1985–88; part time Chairman: Pension Appeal Tribunal (Scotland), 1988–; Medical Appeal Tribunal (Scotland), 1990–. *Recreations:* golf, cinema, wine, watching football. *Address:* 35 Ann Street, Edinburgh EH4 1PL. *T:* 0131–332 6648. *Clubs:* Hawks; Hon. Co. of Edinburgh Golfers.

See also Hon. G. N. H. Emslie.

EMSLIE, Hon. (George) Nigel (Hannington); QC (Scot.) 1986; *b* 17 April 1947; *s* of Lord Emslie, *qv*; *m* 1973, Heather Ann Davis; one *s* two *d*. *Educ:* Edinburgh Acad.; Trinity Coll., Glenalmond; Gonville and Caius Coll., Cambridge (BA); Edinburgh Univ. (LLB). Admitted to Faculty of Advocates, 1972; Standing Junior Counsel: to Forestry Commn in Scotland and to Dept of Agric. and Fisheries for Scotland, 1981–82; to Inland Revenue in Scotland, 1982–86. Part-time Chm., Med. Appeal Tribunals, 1988–. *Address:* 20 Inverleith Place, Edinburgh EH3 5QB. *T:* 0131–552 4091. *Clubs:* Hawks (Cambridge); New (Edinburgh).

See also Hon. D. R. A. Emslie.

EMSLIE, Prof. Ronald Douglas, FDSRCS; Dean of Dental Studies, Guy's Hospital Medical and Dental Schools, 1968–80, retired; Professor of Periodontology and Preventive Dentistry, University of London, 1970–80, now Emeritus; *b* 9 March 1915; *s* of late Alexander G. H. Emslie and Elizabeth Spence; *m* 1951, Dorothy, *d* of William A. Dennis, Paris, Ill, USA; four *s*. *Educ:* Felsted Sch.; Guy's Hosp. Dental Sch., London (BDS); Univ. of Illinois, Chicago (MSc). FDSRCS Eng., 1950; DRD (Edin), 1978. Served War: Surg. Lt (D) RNVR, 1943–46; Surg. Lt Comdr (D) RNVR, 1946. Half-time Asst in Dept of Preventive Dentistry, Guy's Hosp., 1946–48, also in private practice with Mr E. B. Dowsett; Research Fellow, Univ. of Illinois, Chicago, 1948–49; Head of Dept of Preventive Dentistry, Guy's Hosp., 1949–55; Reader in Preventive Dentistry, Univ. of London (Guy's Hosp. Dental Sch.), 1956–62; Prof. of Preventive Dentistry, Univ. of London (Guy's Hosp. Dental Sch.), 1963–70. Pres., Brit. Soc. of Periodontology, 1959–60; Chm., Dental Health Cttee of BDA, 1963–69; Member: Internat. Dental Fedn; Internat. Assoc. for Dental Research; Dental Educn Adv. Council (Chm., 1978–80); Bd of Faculty of Dental Surgery, RCS, 1966–81 (Vice-Dean, 1976–77); Fluoridation Soc. (Chm. 1970–80); Bd of Studies in Dentistry, Univ. of London (Chm., 1975–77). Past Pres., Odontological Section, RSM; Vis. Lectr, Univ. of Illinois, 1956; Nuffield Grant to study dental aspects of facial gangrene, in Nigeria, Sept.–Dec. 1961; Sci. Advr, Brit. Dental Jl, 1961–80 (Sci. Asst Ed., 1951–61); Consultant in Periodontology to RN, 1971–80. Fellow, BDA. *Publications:* various contribs to dental literature. *Recreations:* tennis, sailing, old motor cars. *Address:* Little Hale, Woodland Way, Kingswood, Surrey KT20 6NW. *T:* Mogador (01737) 832662.

ENCOMBE, Viscount; John Francis Thomas Marie Joseph Columba Fidelis Scott; *b* 9 July 1962; *s* and *heir* of 5th Earl of Eldon, *qv*.

ENDERBY, Prof. John Edwin, FRS 1985; H. O. Wills Professor of Physics, University of Bristol, since 1981; *b* 16 Jan. 1931; *s* of late Thomas Edwin Enderby and Rheita Rebecca Hollinshead (*née* Stather); *m* Susan, *yr d* of late Harold Vincent Bowles, OBE and of Colleen Bessie Bowles; one *s* two *d*, and one *d* (one *s* decd) of previous marriage. *Educ:* Chester Grammar Sch.; London Univ. (BSc, PhD). Lecturer in Physics: Coll. of Technology, Huddersfield, 1957–60; Univ. of Sheffield, 1960–67; Reader in Physics, Univ. of Sheffield, 1967–69; Prof. in Physics and Head of the Dept, Univ. of Leicester, 1969–76; Prof. of Physics, Bristol Univ., 1976–94; Head of Dept of Physics, and Dir, H. H. Wills Physics Lab., Bristol Univ., 1981–94; Directeur-Adjoint, Institut Laue-Langevin, Grenoble, 1985–88. Fellow, Argonne Nat. Lab., Ill., USA, 1989–91; Visiting Fellow, Battelle Inst., 1968–69; Visiting Professor: Univ. of Guelph, Ont., 1978; Univ. of Leiden, 1989. Member: Physics Cttee, SRC, 1974–77; Neutron Beam Res. Cttee, SRC, 1974–80 and 1988–91 (Chm., 1977–80 and 1988–91); PPARC, 1994–. Chm., Liquids Bd, Eur. Physical Soc., 1991–. Member: Council, Institut Laue-Langevin, Grenoble, 1973–80; Council, Royal Soc., 1990–92; Academia Europaea, 1989. FInstP 1970 (Chm., SW Br., 1979–83; Guthrie Medal, 1995). Associate Editor, Philosophical Magazine, 1975–81. Editor, Proc. Royal Soc. A, 1989–94. *Publications:* (jointly): Physics of Simple Liquids, 1968; Amorphous and Liquid Semiconductors, 1974; many publications on the structure and properties of liquids in: Phil. Mag. Adv. Phys, Jl Phys, Proc. Royal Soc., etc. *Recreations:* gardening, watching Association football. *Address:* H. H. Wills Physics Laboratory, Tyndall Avenue, Bristol BS8 1TL. *T:* Bristol (0117) 928 8737; 7 Cotham Lawn Road, Bristol BS6 6DU. *T:* Bristol (0117) 973 3411.

ENDERBY, Kenneth Albert; General Manager, Runcorn Development Corporation, 1978–81; *b* 7 Aug. 1920; *s* of Albert William Enderby and Frances Enderby; *m* 1946, Mary Florence; one *s* two *d*. *Educ:* Nottingham High Sch.; London Univ. (BSc Econs). IPFA. Served War, Royal Corps of Signals (TA), 1939–46: BEF, MEF, CMF (mentioned in despatches, 1944); Captain. Local Govt Finance: Nottingham, 1936–51; Buckingham, 1951–53; Chief Auditor, City of Sheffield, 1953–56; Dep. City Treasurer, Coventry, 1956–64; Chief Finance Officer, Runcorn Develt Corp., 1964–78. *Recreations:* gardening, camping, fresh air, zymology. *Address:* Four Winds, 2 Helmeth Road, Church Stretton, Salop SY6 7AS. *T:* Church Stretton (01694) 722328.

ENDERBY, Col Samuel, CVO 1977; DSO 1943; MC 1939; JP; *b* 15 Sept. 1907; *s* of Col Samuel Enderby and Mary Cuninghame; *m* 1936, Pamela, *e d* of Major Charles Beck Hornby, DSO; two *s* one *d*. *Educ:* Uppingham Sch.; RMC Sandhurst. Regular soldier, commissioned 5th Fusiliers, 1928. Served War, 1939–46: MEF, CMF, comd 2/4th KOYLI and 2/5 Leicester Regt; Commandant, Sch. of Infantry: ACRE, 1945–46; Netheravon, 1947–48; comd, 7th Bn Royal Northumberland Fusiliers, 1949; retd 1949. JP 1956; High Sheriff of Northumberland, 1968. Mem., Hon. Corps of Gentlemen at Arms, 1954–77, Standard Bearer, 1976–77. *Address:* The Riding, Hexham, Northumberland NE46 4PF. *T:* Hexham (01434) 2250. *Club:* Army and Navy.

ENFIELD, Viscount; William Robert Byng; computer programmer, British Gas, since 1989; *b* 10 May 1964; *s* and *heir* of 8th Earl of Strafford, *qv*; *m* 1994, Karen Elizabeth, *d* of S. Graham Lord, Prestatyn. *Educ:* Winchester Coll.; Durham Univ. *Address:* 5 Brierville, Durham DH1 4QE.

ENFIELD, Harry; comedy actor; *b* 30 May 1961. *Educ:* York Univ. (BA Hons Politics). TV programmes include: Sir Norbert Smith: a life, 1989 (Silver Rose of Montreux, Emmy Award); Radio Fab FM: the end of an era, 1994; series: Harry Enfield's Television Programme, 2 series, 1992; Harry Enfield's Guide to the Opera, 1993; Harry Enfield and Chums, 1994; also appeared regularly in: Saturday Night Live, 1987, 1988; Gone to the Dogs, 1991; Men Behaving Badly, 1992. *Address:* c/o PBJ Management Ltd, 5 Soho Square, W1V 5DE. *T:* 0171–287 1112.

ENGEL, Matthew Lewis; journalist, The Guardian, since 1979; Editor, Wisden Cricketers' Almanack, since 1992; *b* 11 June 1951; *s* of Max David and Betty Ruth Engel; *m* 1990, Hilary Davies; one *s*. *Educ:* Manchester Univ. (BA Econ). Reporter, Chronicle and Echo, Northampton, 1972–75; Reuters, 1977–79; Guardian, 1979–: cricket corresp., 1982–87; feature writer, sports columnist, occasional political and foreign corresp., 1987–. Member: Nothing Writers; Golden Valley Organic Vegetable Co-op. Sports Writer of the Year, What the Papers Say, 1985; Sports Journalist of the Year, British Press Awards, 1991. *Publications:* Ashes '85, 1985; (ed) Guardian Book of Cricket, 1986; (ed) Sportswriter's Eye, 1989; (ed) Sportspages Almanac, 1990, 1991, 1992; (with A. Radd) History of Northamptonshire CCC, 1993; Tickle the Public, 1996. *Recreations:* not writing, not watching sport. *Address:* The Oaks, Newton St Margarets, Herefordshire HR2 0QN. *T:* Michaelchurch (01981) 510250. *Clubs:* Cricket Writers'; Northamptonshire CCC (Vice-Pres.).

ENGEL, Dame Sister Pauline Frances, DBE 1995 (CBE 1986); Vicar for Education, Diocese of Auckland (RC), New Zealand, since 1994; *b* 10 Sept. 1930; *d* of John Edmond Engel and Eileen Frances Engel (*née* McDavitt). *Educ:* St Mary's Coll., Wellington; Univ. of Auckland (MA Hons). Registered Teacher. Entered Sisters of Mercy Congregation, 1960; Dep. Principal, McAuley High Sch., 1978–79; Principal, Carmel Coll., 1983–91. Gen. Exec. Sec. to Major Superiors Conference, NZ, 1992–93. Sisters of Mercy Leadership Council, 1995–. *Publication:* The Abolition of Capital Punishment in New Zealand 1935–61, 1976. *Recreations:* classical music, reading. *Address:* Mount Carmel Convent, Box 31142, Milford, Auckland 9, New Zealand; Pompallier Diocesan Centre, Private Bag 47–904, Ponsonby, Auckland 2, New Zealand. *T:* (9) 3784380.

ENGESET, Jetmund, FRCSE; FRCSG; Consultant Surgeon, Grampian Health Board, since 1987; Surgeon to the Queen in Scotland, since 1985; *b* 22 July 1938; *s* of Arne K. Engeset and Marta Engeset; *m* 1966, Anne Graeme (*née* Robertson); two *d*. *Educ:* Slemdal and Ris Skole, Oslo, Norway; Oslo University; Aberdeen University (MB ChB, ChM Hons). House Officer (Surgical and Medical), Aberdeen Royal Infirmary, 1964–65; Aberdeen University: Res. Assistant, Dept of Surgery, 1965–67; Surgical Registrar, 1967–70; Lectr in Surgery, 1970–74; Sen. Lectr in Surgery, 1974–87; Head of Dept of Surgery, 1982–85 (seconded to Salgrenska Hosp. Surgical Unit, Gothenburg, Sweden, 1972–74). *Publications:* papers on microcirculation, vascular surgery, organ preservation and tissue transplantation. *Recreations:* skiing, angling, squash, gardening. *Address:* Pine Lodge, 315 North Deeside Road, Milltimber, Aberdeen, Aberdeenshire AB1 0DL. *T:* Aberdeen (01224) 733753.

ENGLAND, Prof. George Leslie, DScEng; CEng, FICE, FINucE; Professor of Mechanics and Structures, Imperial College, London, since 1989; *b* 9 Oct. 1935; *s* of John Edward Philip England and Rose Gladys England; *m* 1968, W. Margaret Landon. *Educ:* East Barnet Grammar Sch.; King's Coll., London (Sambrooke Schol.; BScEng 1st Cl. Hons; Jameson Prize (Eng); Eng. Soc. Centenary Prize, Tennant Medal (Geol); PhD 1961; DScEng

1974). MIStructE. King's College, London: Lectr, 1961; Reader in Engrg Mechanics, 1975; Dean, 1983–85; Vice-Dean, 1985–86; Prof. of Mechanics and Structures, 1986–89. Consultant to: HSE, NII, 1971–; UN Develt Project, Central Soils and Materials Res. Station, India, 1992–. Mem., British Orthop. Res. Soc.; MASCE. *Publications:* contribs to learned jls on time-dependent service-life performance of concrete structures and behaviour of structures at high temperatures. *Recreations:* landscape gardening, mountain walking. *Address:* Civil Engineering Department, Imperial College of Science, Technology and Medicine, SW7 2BU. *T:* 0171–594 6109, *Fax:* 0171 5844220.

ENGLAND, Glyn, BSc(Eng); FEng, FIEE, FIMechE, CIMgt; Chairman: Silvanus Services (formerly Woodlands Initiatives) Ltd, since 1988; Windcluster Ltd, since 1991; Consultant, World Bank; *b* 19 April 1921; *m* 1942, Tania Reichenbach; two *d. Educ:* Penarth County Sch.; Queen Mary Coll., London Univ. (BSc (Eng)); London School of Economics. Department of Scientific and Industrial Research, 1939. War service, 1942–47. Chief Ops Engr, CEGB, 1966–71; Dir-Gen., SW Region, 1971–73; Chm., SW Electricity Bd, 1973–77; part-time Mem., 1975–77, Chm., 1977–82, CEGB. Director: F. H. Lloyd (Hldgs), 1982–87; Triplex Lloyd, 1987–90; The Wind Fund PLC, 1994–. Mem., British Nat. Cttee, World Energy Conf., 1977–82; Vice-Pres., Internat. Union of Producers and Distributors of Electrical Energy, 1981–82. Mem., Bd of Dirs, UK CEED, 1984–. Chairman: Council for Envmtl Conservation, 1983–88; Bd of Trustees, Silvanus Trust (formerly Dartington Action Res. Trust), 1985–94. Sometime Labour Mem., Herts CC; Mem. Council, Magistrates' Assoc. JP Welwyn, Herts, 1962–71. Hon. DSc Bath, 1981. *Publications:* (with Rex Savidge) Landscape in the Making; papers on: Economic Growth and the Electricity Supply Industry, Security of Electricity Supplies, Planning for Uncertainty, Railways and Power (IMechE Tritton Lecture), Efficiency Audits, Industrial Ecology. *Recreation:* actively enjoying the countryside. *Address:* Woodbridge Farm, Ubley, Bristol BS18 6PX. *T:* Mendip (01761) 462479.

ENGLAND, Rear-Adm. Timothy John, FIEE; Chief Staff Officer (Support) to Commander-in-Chief Fleet, 1992–94; Harbour Master, River Hamble, since 1995; *b* Llandudno, 6 Feb. 1942; *s* of Wilfred James England and Kathleen Helen England (*née* Stacey); *m* 1966, Margaret Ann Cullen; one *s* one *d. Educ:* Trinity Sch. of John Whitgift, Croydon; RNEC Manadon. BScEng ext. London Univ. CEng. Joined RN at BRNC Dartmouth as Weapon Engineering specialist, 1960; served HM Ships Alert, Collingwood, London, Salisbury; Staff of DG Ships; HM Dockyard, Devonport; HMS Bristol; Staff of C-in-C Fleet; Directorate of Naval Operational Requirements, 1978–80; Weapon Engineer Officer, HMS Invincible, incl. Falklands Campaign, 1981–82; Staff Weapon Engineer Officer to FO Sea Training, 1982–84; Defence Operational Requirements, 1984–86; RCDS 1987; Fleet Weapon Engineer Officer, 1988–89; WRNS Sea Service Implementation Team Leader, 1990; Captain, RNEC, Manadon, 1990–92. MInstD. *Publications:* articles in Naval and professional jls. *Recreations:* gardening, photography, information technology. *Address:* 22 Sennen Place, Port Solent, Portsmouth PO6 4SZ. *Club:* Thunderers.

ENGLE, Sir George (Lawrence Jose), KCB 1983 (CB 1976); QC 1983; First Parliamentary Counsel, 1981–86; *b* 13 Sept. 1926; *m* 1956, Irene, *d* of late Heinz Lachmann; three *d. Educ:* Charterhouse (scholar); Christ Church, Oxford (Marjoribanks and Dixon schols, MA). Served RA, 1945–48 (2nd Lt, 1947). Firsts in Mods and Greats; Cholmeley Schol., Lincoln's Inn, 1952. Called to Bar, Lincoln's Inn, 1953, Bencher, 1984. Joined Parly Counsel Office, 1957; seconded as First Parly Counsel, Fedn of Nigeria, 1965–67; Parly Counsel, 1970–80; Second Parly Counsel, 1980–81; with Law Commn, 1971–73. Pres., Commonwealth Assoc. of Legislative Counsel, 1983–86. *Publications:* Law for Landladies, 1955; (ed jtly) Cross on Statutory Interpretation, 2nd edn 1987, 3rd edn 1995; contributor to: Ideas, 1954; O Rare Hoffnung, 1960; The Oxford Companion to English Literature, 1985. *Recreations:* books, travel, theatre, bricolage. *Address:* 32 Wood Lane, Highgate, N6 5UB. *T:* 0181–340 9750.

ENGLEFIELD, Dermot John Tryal; Librarian, House of Commons, 1991–93; *b* 27 Aug. 1927; *o s* of Major Henry Wotton Englefield and Blanchfield Bernardine Englefield (*née* O'Halloran); *m* 1962, Dora, *o d* of Josip and Maca Grahovac, Karlovac, Croatia; one *s* one *d. Educ:* Mount St Mary's Coll.; Trinity Coll. Dublin (MA); Sarah Purser Scholarship (Hist. of Art) 1951. ALA 1966. Served RAF, 1946–48. St Marylebone Ref. Liby, 1952–54; House of Commons Liby, 1954–93; Asst Librarian (Parly Div.), 1967; Dep. Librarian, 1976. H of C corresp. to European Centre of Parly Res. and Documentation, 1977–93; Consultant to: Council of Europe, 1970; European Parlt, 1973; proposed Scottish Assembly, 1978; NI Assembly, 1982; Hong Kong Legislative Council, 1988; Romanian Parlt, 1993; Slovakian Parlt, 1993; Eur. Parlt, 1993–94; Swaziland, 1994; Malaŵi, 1994. Member: Parly Libraries Sect., IFLA (Sec., 1981–85; Chm., 1985–89); Study of Parlt Gp, 1970– (Chm., 1987–90). Gov., Dulwich Coll., 1985–. Editor for Industry and Parlt Trust, 1984–. Silver Jubilee Medal, 1977. *Publications:* The Printed Records of the Parliament of Ireland 1613–1800, 1978; Parliament and Information, 1981; Whitehall and Westminster, 1985; The Study of Parliament Group, 1985; (jtly) Facts About the British Prime Ministers, 1995; *edited:* (with G. Drewry) Information Sources in Politics and Political Science, 1984; Commons Select Committees, 1984; Today's Civil Service, 1985; Legislative Libraries and Developing Countries, 1986; Local Government and Business, 1987; Parliamentary Libraries and Information Services, 1990; Workings of Westminster, 1991; Getting the Message Across: the media, business and government, 1992; Guidelines for Legislative Libraries, 1993; chapters in books and contribs to jls. *Recreations:* travel, theatre. *Address:* 38 Crystal Palace Park Road, SE26 6UG. *T:* 0181–659 0731. *Clubs:* Arts, Authors'.

ENGLEHART, Robert Michael; QC 1986; a Recorder, since 1987; *b* 1 Oct. 1943; *s* of G. A. F. and K. P. Englehart; *m* 1971, Rosalind Mary Foster; one *s* two *d. Educ:* St Edward's Sch., Oxford; Trinity Coll., Oxford (MA); Harvard Law School (LLM); Bologna Centre (Dip. in Internat. Relns). Assistente, Univ. of Florence, 1968. Called to the Bar, Middle Temple, 1969; practising barrister, 1969–. Chm., London Common Law and Commercial Bar Assoc., 1990–91. *Publication:* (contrib.) Il Controllo Giudiziario: a comparative study of civil procedure, 1968. *Recreations:* shooting, cricket, windsurfing. *Address:* 2 Hare Court, Temple, EC4Y 7BH. *T:* 0171–583 1770. *Clubs:* Garrick, MCC.

ENGLISH, Cyril; President, Nationwide Housing Trust, since 1991 (Chairman, 1987–90); Director, Nationwide, then Nationwide Anglia, Building Society, 1978–90 (Deputy Chairman, 1989–90); *b* 18 Feb. 1923; *s* of Joseph and Mary Hannah English; *m* 1945, Mary Brockbank; two *d. Educ:* Ashton-under-Lyne Grammar School. ALCM; CIMgt. Joined Nationwide Building Society, 1939; Asst Secretary, 1961; Asst General Manager, 1967; General Manager, 1971; Deputy Chief General Manager, 1974; Chief Gen. Manager, 1981–85. *Recreations:* golf, music. *Address:* Ashton Grange, Cedar Drive, Pangbourne, Berks RG8 7BH. *T:* Pangbourne (01734) 843841. *Club:* Calcot Park Golf (Reading).

ENGLISH, Sir Cyril (Rupert), Kt 1972; retired; Director-General, City and Guilds of London Institute, 1968–76; *b* 19 April 1913; *m*; two *s. Educ:* Northgate Sch., Ipswich. BScEng Ext. London, 1934. Technical teacher, 1935–39. Served Royal Navy, 1939–46, Lieut-Commander (E). HM Inspector of Schools, 1946–55; Staff Inspector (Engineering), 1955–58; Chief Inspector of Further Education, in connection with Industry and Commerce, 1958–65; Senior Chief Inspector, Dept of Education and Science, 1965–67. Member, Anglo-American Productivity Team, 1951; attended Commonwealth Education Conferences, Delhi, 1962, Ottawa, 1964. Chairman: British Assoc. for Commercial and Industrial Educn, 1970–71, 1971–72; RAF Educn Adv. Cttee; Member: Services Colleges Cttee, 1965–66; Adv. Bd, RAF Coll., Cranwell; Academic Adv. Council, Royal Defence Acad.; Bd of Dirs, Industrial Training Service; Central Training Council; CTC Gen. Policy Cttee; Nat. Adv. Council for Educn in Industry and Commerce; Council for Tech. Educn and Training for Overseas Countries (Bd Mem., Chm. Educn Cttee); Reg. Adv. Council for Technol. Educn (London and Home Counties); Schools Science and Technology Cttee; Educn Cttee, IMechE; Associated Examining Bd; Cttee of Inquiry into Training of Teachers (James Cttee); Standing Conf. on Schs' Science and Technology; Cttee on Regular Officer training (Army). Vice-Pres., Soc. Electronic and Radio Technicians, 1972–74, Pres., 1975. Governor, Imperial Coll. FIMechE; FIProdE; FIMarE. Hon. Fellow, Inst. of Road Transport Engrs, 1971. Hon. Fellow, Manchester Polytechnic, 1976. Hon. DTech Brunel, 1970; Hon. DSc Loughborough, 1973; DUniv Open, 1974. *Address:* 12 Pineheath Road, High Kelling, Holt, Norfolk NR25 6QF.

ENGLISH, Sir David, Kt 1982; Editor, Daily Mail, 1971–92; Editor in Chief, since 1989, and Chairman, since 1992, Associated Newspapers (Joint Deputy Chairman, 1989–92; Vice-Chairman, Associated Newspapers Group, 1986–88); *b* 26 May 1931; *m* 1954, Irene Mainwood; one *s* two *d. Educ:* Bournemouth Sch. Daily Mirror, 1951–53; Feature Editor, Daily Sketch, 1956; Foreign Correspondent: Sunday Dispatch, 1959; Daily Express, 1960; Washington Correspdt, Express, 1961–63; Chief American Correspdt, Express, 1963–65; Foreign Editor, Express, 1965–67; Associate Editor, Express, 1967–69; Editor: Daily Sketch, 1969–71; Mail on Sunday, 1982. Chairman: Burlington Magazines, 1988–; New Era TV, 1988–; Teletext UK, 1993–; Channel One TV, 1993–. Member: Bd, Assoc. of British Editors, 1985–; Press Complaints Commn, 1993–. Pres., CPU, 1994–. *Publication:* Divided They Stand (a British view of the 1968 American Presidential Election), 1969. *Recreations:* reading, ski-ing, boating. *Address:* Northcliffe House, 2 Derry Street, W8 5TT. *T:* 0171–938 6000. *Clubs:* London Press; Ski of Great Britain.

ENGLISH, Rev. Donald; General Secretary, Methodist Church Division of Home Mission, since 1982; Moderator, Free Church Federal Council, 1986–87; President of the Methodist Conference, 1978–79 and 1990–91; *b* 20 July 1930; *s* of Robert and Ena Forster English; *m* 1962, Bertha Forster Ludlow; two *s. Educ:* Consett Grammar Sch.; University Coll., Leicester; Wesley House, Cambridge. BA London; DipEd Leicester; MA Cantab. Education Officer, RAF, 1953–55; Travelling Sec., Inter-Varsity Fellowship, 1955–58; Asst Tutor, Wesley Coll., Headingley, 1960–62; ordained into Methodist Ministry, 1962; New Testament Tutor, Trinity Coll., Umuahia, E Nigeria, 1962–66; Circuit Minister, Cullercoats, Northumberland, 1966–72; Tutor in Historical Theology, Hartley Victoria Coll., Manchester (Lord Rank Chair), 1972–73; Tutor in Practical Theol. and Methodism, Wesley Coll., Bristol (Lord Rank Chair), 1973–82. Chm., World Methodist Council Exec. Cttee, 1991–Aug. 1996 (Mem., 1976–86, Vice-Chm., 1986–91); Mem., Central Religious Adv. Cttee, 1987–93. Hon. Fellow, Roehampton Inst. of Educn, 1989. Hon. DD Asbury, USA, 1979; DUniv Surrey, 1990; Hon. DLitt Leicester, 1994. *Publications:* Evangelism and Worship, 1971; God in the Gallery, 1975; Christian Discipleship, 1977; Windows on the Passion, 1978; From Wesley's Chair: Presidential Addresses, 1979; Why Believe in Jesus?: evangelistic reflections for Lent, 1986; Evangelistic Counselling, 1987; Evangelism Now, 1987; The Meaning of the Warmed Heart, 1988; Everything in Christ, 1988; The Message of Mark, 1992; (ed) Windows on Salvation, 1994. *Recreations:* gardening, reading. *Address:* 44 Anne Boleyn's Walk, Cheam, Surrey. *T:* 0181–643 3679.

ENGLISH, Gerald; Australian Artists Creative Fellow, since 1994; *b* 6 Nov. 1925; *m* 1954, Jennifer Ryan; two *s* two *d*; *m* 1974, Linda Jacoby; one *s. Educ:* King's Sch., Rochester. After War service studied at Royal College of Music and then began career as lyric tenor; subsequently travelled in USA and Europe, appeared at Sadler's Wells, Covent Garden and Glyndebourne and recorded for major gramophone companies; Professor, Royal Coll. of Music, 1960–77; Director, Opera Studio, Victorian Coll. for the Arts, Melbourne, 1977–89. *Address:* PO Box 4177, Geelong, Vic 3220, Australia.

ENGLISH, Michael; Member: Lambeth Borough Council, since 1990; London Fire and Civil Defence Authority, since 1992; *b* 24 Dec. 1930; *s* of late William Agnew English; *m* 1976, Carol Christine Owen; one *s* one *d. Educ:* King George V Grammar Sch., Southport; Liverpool Univ. (LLB). Joined Labour Party, 1949; Rochdale County Borough Council, 1953–65 (Chairman Finance Cttee until 1964). Employed until 1964 as Asst Manager of department concerned with management services in subsidiary of large public company. Chm., Lambeth CHC, 1993–94. Contested (Lab) Shipley Div., WR Yorks, 1959; MP (Lab) Nottingham West, 1964–83. Parliamentary Private Secretary, Board of Trade, 1966–67; Chairman: Parly Affairs Gp of Parly Lab. Party, 1970–76; Gen. Sub-Cttee of House of Commons Expenditure Cttee, 1974–79; Chm., E Midlands Gp, PLP, 1976–78; formerly Mem., Chairmen's Panel, Treasury and Civil Service, Procedure (Finance) and Sound Broadcasting Cttees, House of Commons. Chm., E Midlands Regional Lab. Party, 1979–80. *Recreation:* reading history. *Address:* 12 Denny Crescent, Kennington, SE11 4UY. *T:* 0171–582 9970.

ENGLISH, Sir Terence (Alexander Hawthorne), KBE 1991; FRCS; FRCP; Master of St Catharine's College, Cambridge, since 1993; Consultant Cardiothoracic Surgeon, Papworth and Addenbrooke's Hospitals, Cambridge, 1973–95; *b* 3 Oct. 1932; *s* of late Arthur Alexander English and Mavis Eleanor (*née* Lund); *m* 1963, Ann Margaret, *e d* of late Frederick Mordaunt Dicey and Ann Gwendoline (*née* Smartt); two *s* two *d. Educ:* Hilton Coll., Natal; Witwatersrand Univ. (BSc(Eng) 1954); Guy's Hosp. Med. Sch. (MB, BS 1962); MA Cantab 1977. FRCSE 1967; FRCS 1967; FRCP 1990. House appointments, Guy's Hosp., 1962–63; Demonstrator, Anatomy Dept, Guy's Hosp., 1964–65; Surgical Registrar: Bolingbroke Hosp., 1966; Brompton Hosp., 1967–68; Res. Fellow, Dept of Surgery, Univ. of Alabama, 1969; Sen. Registrar, Brompton, National Heart and London Chest Hosps, 1968–72; Dir, Papworth Heart Transplant Res. Unit, 1980–88. Chief Med. Advr, BUPA, 1991–. Mem., Audit Commn, 1993–. Mem., Specialists Adv. Cttee in Cardiothoracic Surgery, 1980–87. Member: British Cardiac Soc., 1973–; British Transplantation Soc., 1980–; Soc. of Thoracic and Cardiovascular Surgeons, 1972– (Exec. Council, 1975–77); Thoracic Soc., 1971– (Exec. Council, 1978–81). Member: Council, British Heart Foundn; GMC, 1983–89; Standing Med. Adv. Cttee, 1989–92; Jt Consultants Cttee, 1989–92; Supraregional Services Adv. Gp, 1990–92; Clinical Standards Adv. Gp, 1991–94. President: Internat. Soc. of Heart Transplantation, 1984–85; Soc. of Perfusionists of GB and Ireland, 1985–86; RCS, 1989–92 (Mem. Council, 1981–93; Court of Patrons, 1994); Cardiothoracic Sect., RSM, 1992–93; BMA, 1995–96. Upjohn Lectr, Royal Soc., 1988. Capt., Guy's Hosp. RFC, 1959–60. Gov., Leys Sch., Cambridge. Hon. Freeman, Barbers' Co., 1993. FACC 1986. Hon. FRCSCan 1990; Hon. FRACS 1991; Hon. FCSSA 1991; Hon. FRCS (Thailand) 1991; Hon. FCP&S (Pakistan), 1991; Hon. FRCAnaes, 1991; Hon. FDSRCS 1992; Hon. FACS 1992; Hon. FRCSI 1992; Hon. FCOphth 1993; Hon. Fellow: St Catharine's Coll., Cambridge, 1992; Hughes Hall, Cambridge, 1993; UMDS, Guy's and St Thomas' Hosps, 1993. Hon. DSc Sussex, 1992;

Hon. MD: Nantes, 1992; Mahidol, Thailand, 1993. Man of the Year, RADAR, 1980; Clement Price Thomas Award, RCS, 1986. *Publications:* (jtly) Principles of Cardiac Diagnosis and Treatment: a surgeons' guide, 1992; chapter on Surgery of the Thorax and Heart in Bailey and Love's Short Practice of Thoracic Surgery, 1980; numerous articles in medical jls on matters relating to the practice of heart transplantation and cardiothoracic surgery. *Recreations:* reading, music, walking, tennis. *Address:* St Catharine's College, Cambridge CB2 1RL. *Club:* Athenæum.

ENGLISH, Terence Michael; a Metropolitan Stipendiary Magistrate, since 1986; Chairman, Inner London Juvenile Court Panel, since 1989; a Recorder, since 1994; *b* 3 Feb. 1944; *s* of John Robert English and Elsie Letitia English; *m* 1966, Ivy Joan Weatherley; one *s* one *d*. *Educ:* St Ignatius' Coll., London N15; London Univ. (external LLB 1967). Admitted Solicitor of the Supreme Court, 1970. Assistant, Edmonton PSD, 1962–71; Dep. Clerk to Justices, Bullingdon, Bampton E, Henley and Watlington PSDs, 1972–76; Clerk to the Justices: Newbury and Hungerford and Lambourn PSDs, 1977–85; Slough and Windsor PSDs, 1985–86. Chm., Family Panel, 1991–92. *Recreations:* golf, philately.

ENNALS, Kenneth Frederick John, CB 1983; Member, Local Government Commission for England, since 1992; Deputy Secretary, Department of the Environment, 1980–87; *b* 10 Jan. 1932; *s* of Ernest Ennals and Elsie Dorothy Ennals; *m* 1958, Mavis Euphemia; one *s* two *d*. *Educ:* Alleyn's Sch., Dulwich; LSE. Joined Export Credits Guarantee Dept, 1952; Principal, DEA, 1965–69; Min. of Housing and Local Govt, later DoE, 1969; Asst Sec., 1970, Under Sec., 1976–80, DoE. Mem., Local Govt Boundary Commn for England, 1987–92 (Chm., 1992). *Recreations:* reading, painting. *Address:* Skitreadons, Petworth Road, Haslemere, Surrey GU27 3AU. *T:* Haslemere (01428) 642733. *Clubs:* Commonwealth Trust, Royal Over-Seas League.

ENNISKILLEN, 7th Earl of, *cr* 1789 (Ire.); **Andrew John Galbraith Cole;** Baron Mountflorence 1760; Viscount Enniskillen 1776; Baron Grinstead (UK) 1815; pilot and company director; Captain Irish Guards, 1965; *b* 28 April 1942; *s* of 6th Earl of Enniskillen, MBE and Sonia (*d* 1982), *d* of Major Thomas Syers, RA; *S* father, 1989; *m* 1964, Sarah, *o d* of Maj.-Gen. J. Keith-Edwards, CBE, DSO, MC, Nairobi; three *d*. *Educ:* Eton. Man. Dir, Kenya Airways, 1979–81. *Heir: uncle* Arthur Gerald Cole [*b* 15 Nov. 1920; *m* 1949, Prudence Tobina, *d* of late A. R. A. Cartright; three *s* one *d*]. *Address:* c/o Royal Bank of Scotland, 9 Pall Mall, SW1.

ENNISMORE, Viscount; Francis Michael Hare; *b* 28 June 1964; *s* and *heir* of 5th Earl of Listowel, *qv*.

ENRICI, Most Rev. Domenico, JCD; former Apostolic Nuncio; *b* 9 April 1909; *s* of late Domenico Enrici and Maria Dalmasso Enrici. *Educ:* Diocesan Seminary, Cuneo; Pontifical Gregorian Univ. and Pontifical Ecclesiastical Academy, Rome. Ordained, 1933; parochial work in Dio. Cuneo, 1933–35. Served at various Apostolic Nunciatures and Delegations: Ireland, 1938–45; Egypt, 1946–48; Palestine and Jordan, 1948–53; Formosa, Free China, 1953–55; apptd Titular Archbp of Ancusa, 1955; Apostolic Internuncio to Indonesia, 1955–58; Apostolic Nuncio to Haiti and Apostolic Delegate to West Indies, 1958–60; Apostolic Internuncio to Japan, 1960–62; Apostolic Delegate to Australia, New Zealand and Oceania, 1962–69; Apostolic Delegate to GB and Gibraltar, 1969–73; Pro-Pres., Pontifical Ecclesiastical Acad., 1974–75; Delegate for Pontifical Representations, 1973–79; retired, 1979. Commander, Order of the Nile (Egypt), 1948; Order of the Sacred Treasure, 1st class (Japan), 1962; Assistant to the Pontifical Throne, Vatican City, 1979. *Publication:* Mistero e Luce (Mystery and Light), 1984. *Address:* Via Senatore Toselli, 8, 12100 Cuneo, Italy. *T:* (0171) 631120.

ENRIGHT, Dennis Joseph, OBE 1991; freelance writer; *b* 11 March 1920; *s* of late George and Grace Enright; *m* 1949, Madeleine Harders; one *d*. *Educ:* Leamington Coll.; Downing Coll., Cambridge. MA Cantab; DLitt Alexandria. Lecturer in English, University of Alexandria, 1947–50; Organising Tutor, University of Birmingham Extra-Mural Dept, 1950–53; Vis. Prof., Kōnan Univ., Japan, 1953–56; Vis. Lecturer, Free University of Berlin, 1956–57; British Council Professor, Chulalongkorn Univ., Bangkok, 1957–59; Prof. of English, Univ. of Singapore, 1960–70; Hon. Prof. of English, Univ. of Warwick, 1975–80. Dir, Chatto and Windus, 1974–82. Co-Editor, Encounter, 1970–72. FRSL 1961. Cholmondeley Poetry Award, 1974; Queen's Gold Medal for Poetry, 1981. Hon. DLitt Warwick, 1982; DUniv. Surrey, 1985. *Publications: poetry:* The Laughing Hyena, 1953; Bread Rather Than Blossoms, 1956; Some Men Are Brothers, 1960; Addictions, 1962; The Old Adam, 1965; Unlawful Assembly, 1968; Selected Poems, 1969; Daughters of Earth, 1972; The Terrible Shears, 1973; Rhyme Times Rhyme (for children), 1974; Sad Ires, 1975; Paradise Illustrated, 1978; A Faust Book, 1979; Collected Poems, 1981; Instant Chronicles, 1985; Collected Poems 1987, 1987; Selected Poems 1990, 1990; Under the Circumstances, 1991; Old Men and Comets, 1993; *novels:* Academic Year, 1955; Heaven Knows Where, 1957; Insufficient Poppy, 1960; Figures of Speech, 1965; The Way of the Cat, 1992; *novels for children:* The Joke Shop, 1976; Wild Ghost Chase, 1978; Beyond Land's End, 1979; *criticism:* The Apothecary's Shop, 1957; English Critical Texts (co-editor), 1962; Conspirators and Poets, 1966; Shakespeare and the Students, 1970; Man is an Onion, 1972; (ed) A Choice of Milton's Verse, 1975; Samuel Johnson: Rasselas, 1976; (ed) The Oxford Book of Contemporary Verse 1945–1980, 1980; A Mania for Sentences, 1983; (ed) Fair of Speech: the uses of euphemism, 1985; The Alluring Problem: an essay on irony, 1986; Fields of Vision: essays on literature, language and television, 1988; Interplay: a kind of commonplace book; *travel:* The World of Dew: Japan, 1955; Memoirs of a Mendicant Professor, 1969; *translation:* The Poetry of Living Japan (co-editor), 1957; *anthologies:* (ed) The Oxford Book of Death, 1983; (ed) The Faber Book of Fevers and Frets, 1989; (ed jtly) The Oxford Book of Friendship, 1991; The Oxford Book of the Supernatural, 1994; contributor to: Scrutiny, Encounter, London Review of Books, TLS, etc. *Recreations:* reading, writing, television, listening to music. *Address:* 35A Viewfield Road, SW18 5JD.

ENRIGHT, Derek Anthony; MP (Lab) Hemsworth, since Nov. 1991; *b* 2 Aug. 1935; *s* of Lawrence and Helen Enright; *m* 1963, Jane Maureen (*née* Simmons); two *s* two *d*. *Educ:* St Michael's Coll., Leeds; Wadham Coll., Oxford (BA, DipEd). Head of Classics, John Fisher Sch., Purley, Surrey, 1959–67; Dep. Head of St Wilfrid's, North Featherstone, W Yorks, 1967–79; Mem. (Lab) Leeds, Eur. Parlt, 1979–84; Brit. Labour Group Spokesman on third world affairs and women's rights, 1979–84; EEC deleg. in Guinea Bissau, 1985–87; Special Advr to EEC on The Third World, 1988–91. Contested (Lab) Kent East, European elecn, 1984. Mem., Select Cttee on European Legislation, 1991–. Chm., Lab Movt in Europe, 1994–; Mem., Exec. Cttee, European Movt. Order of Merit (Guinea Bissau), 1987. *Publications:* reports on: fishing agreements in West Africa; EEC relations with non ACP developing countries; Namibia after independence. *Recreations:* reading the Guardian, Staffordshire Bull Terriers, watching Featherstone Rovers Rugby league. *Address:* The Hollies, 112 Carleton Road, Pontefract, W Yorks WF8 3NQ. *T:* Pontefract (01977) 702096.

ENSOM, Donald, FRICS, FCIArb; Chartered Surveyor; Consultant, Debenham Tewson & Chinnocks, 1986–92 (Partner, 1962–86); *b* 8 April 1926; *s* of Charles R. A. W. Ensom and Edith (*née* Young); *m* 1951, Sonia (*née* Sherrard); one *s* one *d*. *Educ:* Norbury Manor Sch., Croydon. Qualified as Chartered Surveyor, 1951; FRICS 1958; FCIArb 1970. Served RA, 1943–47. Partner, Nightingale, Page & Bennett/Debenham Tewson & Chinnocks (after merger), 1958–86. Chm., Bldg Conservation Trust, 1981–83; Royal Institution of Chartered Surveyors: Pres., Bldg Surveyors Div., 1975–76; Chm., Professional Practice Cttee, 1978–83; Hon. Sec., 1983–90; Vice-Pres., 1988–90. Pres., Land Economy Soc., Univ. of Cambridge, 1990–91. *Publications:* (jtly) Party Walls, 1993; numerous professional papers. *Recreations:* reading, opera and music, caravanning, canals. *Address:* Saxons, 102 Grange Road, Cambridge CB3 9AA. *Clubs:* East India, Royal Over-Seas League, Chartered Surveyors (1913), Pyramus and Thisbe (Chm. 1987–89).

ENSOR, David, OBE 1986; Managing Director, Croydon Advertiser Ltd, 1979–85; *b* 2 April 1924; *s* of Rev. William Walters and Constance Eva Ensor; *m* 1947, Gertrude Kathleen Brown; two *s*. *Educ:* Kingswood Sch., Bath; London Coll. of Printing. Served Royal Signals, 1942–46, Captain; ADC to GOC Bengal Dist. Managing Director: George Reveirs, 1947–59; Charles Skipper & East, 1959–69; Knapp Drewett & Sons, 1969–79; Chairman: Methodist Newspaper Co., 1975–94; Methodist Publishing House, 1981–. A Vice-Chm., Press Council, 1987–90 (Mem., 1982–90); Mem. Council, Newspaper Soc., 1979–94. Pres., London Printing Industries Assoc., 1976. Vice-Pres., Methodist Conf., 1981. *Address:* Milborne Lodge, Dinton Road, Fovant, Salisbury, Wilts SP3 5JW. *T:* Fovant (01722) 714521.

ENSOR, George Anthony; Senior Partner, Weightman Rutherfords (formerly Rutherfords), Solicitors, Liverpool, since 1992 (Partner, 1962–92); a Recorder of the Crown Court, since 1983; *b* 4 Nov. 1936; *s* of George and Phyllis Ensor; *m* 1968, Jennifer Margaret Caile, MB, ChB; two *d*. *Educ:* Malvern College; Liverpool University (LLB). Solicitor, 1961 (Atkinson Conveyancing Medal, 1962; Rupert Bremner Medal, 1962). Deputy Coroner, City of Liverpool, 1966–; part-time Chairman, Industrial Tribunals, 1975–; Asst Parly Boundary Comr, 1992–. Mem., Judicial Studies Bd, 1987–89; President, Liverpool Law Society, 1982. Trustee, Empire Theatre (Merseyside) Trust, Ltd, 1986–. Dir, Liverpool FC, 1985–93. *Recreations:* golf, theatre. *Address:* 23 Far Moss Road, Blundellsands, Liverpool L23 8TG. *T:* 0151–924 5937. *Clubs:* Artists (Liverpool); Formby Golf; Waterloo Rugby Union.

ENSOR, Michael de Normann, CMG 1980; OBE 1958; Head, East Africa Development Division, Overseas Development Administration, 1975–80; *b* 11 June 1919; *s* of Robert Weld Ensor and Dr Beatrice Ensor; *m* 1945, Mona Irene Blackburn; two *s*. *Educ:* Bryanston School; St. John's Coll., Oxford. Military service, 1940; Colonial Service, Gold Coast/Ghana Civil Service, 1940–58; Secretary, Foundation for Mutual Assistance in Africa South of the Sahara, 1958–64; Dept of Technical Cooperation/Min. of Overseas Development/Overseas Development Administration, 1964–80. Chairman: Paragon Management Co., 1983–86; Overseas Service Pensioners' Benevolent Soc., 1986–91. *Address:* Flat 1, 12 The Paragon, Blackheath, SE3 0NZ. *T:* 0181–852 5345. *Clubs:* Travellers'; Royal Blackheath Golf.

ENTWISTLE, Prof. Kenneth Mercer; Professor of Metallurgy and Materials Science, University of Manchester Institute of Science and Technology, 1962–90, now Emeritus; *b* 3 Jan. 1925; *s* of William Charles and Maude Elizabeth Entwistle; *m* 1949, Alice Patricia Mary Johnson; two *s* two *d*. *Educ:* Urmston Grammar Sch.; Univ. of Manchester (BSc Elect. Eng. 1945, MSc 1946, PhD 1948). FIM, CEng. University of Manchester: Lectr in Metallurgy, 1948; Sen. Lectr, 1954; Reader, 1960; Dean, Faculty of Technology, 1976–77; Pro-Vice-Chancellor, 1982–85; Vice-Principal, UMIST, 1972–74. Chairman: Materials Cttee, CNAA, 1972–74; Educn Cttee, Instn of Metallurgists, 1977–79; Metallics Sub-Cttee, SRC, 1979–81; Mem., UGC, 1985–89 (Chm., Technology Sub-Cttee, 1985–89); Engrg Advr to Chief Exec. of UFC, 1989–92. Comp. UMIST, 1991. Hon. Fellow, Sheffield Polytechnic, 1971. *Publications:* numerous papers in scientific jls. *Recreations:* Scottish dancing, choral singing. *Address:* Greenacre, Bridge End Lane, Prestbury, Macclesfield, Cheshire SK10 4DJ. *T:* Prestbury (01625) 829269. *Club:* Athenæum.

EÖTVÖS, Peter; composer and conductor; *m* 1968, Piroska Molnar; one *s*; *m* 1976, Pi-Hsien Chen; one *d*; *m* 1995, Maria Mezei. *Educ:* Acad. of Music, Budapest; Musik Hochschule, Cologne. Composer, chamber music, electronic music, opera and orchestral music; conductor and musical director, Ensemble Intercontemporain, Paris, 1979–91; principal guest conductor, BBC Symphony Orchestra, 1985–88; first Guest Conductor, Budapest Fest. Orch., 1992–95; Chief Conductor, Radio Chamber Orch. Hilversum, 1994–. Prof., Musikhochschule Karlsruhe, 1992–; Founder, Internat. Eötvös Inst., for young professional conductors, 1991. *Recreations:* walking, pipe smoking, jazz. *Address:* c/o Allied Artists, 42 Montpelier Square, SW7 1JZ. *T:* 0171–589 6243.

EPHRAUMS, Maj.-Gen. Roderick Jarvis, CB 1977; OBE 1965; DL; Major-General Royal Marines, Commando Forces, 1976–78, retired; *b* 12 May 1927; *s* of Hugh Cyril Ephraums and Elsie Caroline (*née* Rowden); *m* 1955, Adela Mary (*née* Forster); two *s* one *d*. *Educ:* Tonbridge. Commnd 2nd Lieut, RM, 1945; HMS Mauritius, 1946–48; 3 Commando Bde, RM, 1952–54; Staff Coll., Camberley, 1960; Bde Major, 3 Commando Bde, 1962–64; CO, 45 Commando RM, 1969–71; Royal Coll. of Defence Studies, 1972; Comdr, 3 Commando Bde, 1973–74; NATO Defense Coll., Rome, 1975. A Col Comdt, RM, 1985–, Rep. Col Comdt, 1987 and 1988. DL Angus, 1985. CStJ 1993. *Recreations:* painting, gardening. *Club:* Army and Navy.

EPSTEIN, Sir (Michael) Anthony, Kt 1991; CBE 1985; FRS 1979; Fellow, Wolfson College, Oxford, since 1986; Professor of Pathology, 1968–85 (now Emeritus), and Head of Department, 1968–82, University of Bristol; Hon. Consultant Pathologist, Bristol Health District (Teaching), 1968–82; *b* 18 May 1921; *yr s* of Mortimer and Olga Epstein; *m* 1950, Lisbeth Knight; two *s* one *d*. *Educ:* St Paul's Sch., London; Trinity Coll., Cambridge (Perry Exhibr, 1940); Middlesex Hosp. Medical Sch. MA, MD, DSc, PhD; FRCPath. Ho. Surg., Middlesex Hosp., London, and Addenbrooke's Hosp., Cambridge, 1944; Lieut and Captain, RAMC, 1945–47; Asst Pathologist, Bland Sutton Inst., Mddx Hosp. Med. Sch., 1948–65, with leave as: Berkeley Travelling Fellow, 1952–53; French Govt Exchange Scholar at Institut Pasteur, Paris, 1952–53; Vis. Investigator, Rockefeller Inst., NY, 1956; Reader in Experimental Pathology, Mddx Hosp. Med. Sch., 1965–68; Hon. Consultant in Experimental Virology, Mddx Hosp., 1965–68. Member: Cttee, Pathological Soc. of GB and Ire., 1969–72 (Hon. Mem., 1987); Council, and Vice-Pres., Pathology Section of RSM, 1966–72 (Hon. Mem., 1988); Study Gp on Classification of Herpes Viruses, of Internat. Commn for Nomenclature of Viruses, 1971–; Scientific Adv. Bd, Harvard Med. Sch.'s New England Regional Primate Center, 1972–; Cancer Research Campaign MRC Jt Cttee, 1973–77, 1982–87 (Chm. 1983–87); Cttee, British Soc. for Cell Biology, 1974–77; MRC, 1982–86 (Mem. 1979–84, Chm. 1982–84, Cell Bd; Mem., 1984–85, Chm., 1985–88, Tropical Medicine Res. Bd); Council, Royal Soc., 1983–85, 1986–91 (Foreign Sec. and a Vice-Pres., 1986–91; Assessor on MRC, 1987–91); Medical and Scientific Panel, Leukaemia Research Fund, 1982–85; Scientific Adv. Cttee, Lister Inst., 1984–87; Expert Working Party on Bovine Spongiform Encephalopathy, DoH, 1988; Exec. Bd, ICSU, 1990–93 (Chm., Cttee on Sci. in Central and Eastern Europe, 1992–); Exec. Council, ESF, 1990–93; Program Adv. Gp, World Bank China Key Studies Project, 1992–; Special Rep. of Dir Gen. UNESCO for Sci. in Russia, 1992. Discovered in 1964 a new human herpes virus, now known as Epstein-Barr virus, which causes infectious mononucleosis and is also causally implicated in some forms of human cancer (Burkitt's lymphoma and nasopharyngeal carcinoma). Fellow, UCL, 1992. Mem., Academia Europaea, 1988. Mem. d'honneur, Belgian Soc. for Cancer Res., 1979. Hon. Professor: Sun Yat-Sen Med. Univ., Guangzhou, 1981; Chinese Acad. of Preventive Medicine, Beijing, 1988. Hon. Fellow, Queensland Inst. of Med. Research, 1983; Hon. FRCP 1986; Hon. FRSE 1991; Hon. FRCPA 1995; Hon. MD Edinburgh, 1986. Paul Ehrlich and Ludwig Darmstaedter Prize and Medal, Paul Ehrlich Foundn, W Germany, 1973; Markham Skerrit Prize, 1977; (jtly) Bristol-Myers Award, NY, 1982; Leeuwenhoek Prize Lectr, Royal Soc., 1983; Prix Griffuel, Assoc. pour la recherche sur le cancer, Paris, 1986; Samuel Weiner Distinguished Visitor Award, Univ. of Manitoba, 1988; John H. Lattimer Award, Amer. Urol Assoc., 1988; Internat. Award, Gairdner Foundn, Toronto, 1988; Royal Medal, Royal Soc., 1992. *Publications:* over 225 scientific papers in internat. jls on tumour cell structure, viruses, tumour viruses, Burkitt's lymphoma, and the EB virus. Jt Founder Editor, The Internat. Review of Experimental Pathology (vols 1–28, 1962–86); (ed jtly) The Epstein-Barr Virus, 1979; (ed jtly) The Epstein-Barr Virus: recent advances, 1986. *Address:* Nuffield Department of Clinical Medicine, University of Oxford, John Radcliffe Hospital, Oxford OX3 9DU. *T:* Oxford (01865) 221334, *Fax:* Oxford (01865) 222901.

ERAUT, Prof. Michael Ruarc, PhD; Professor of Education, University of Sussex, since 1986; *b* 15 Nov. 1940; *s* of Lt-Col Ruarc Bertrand Sorel Eraut and Frances Mary (*née* Hurst); *m* 1964, (Mary) Cynthia Wynne; two *s*. *Educ:* Winchester Coll. (Scholar); Trinity Hall, Cambridge (Scholar; BA Nat. Sci.; PhD Chem.). Fulbright Scholar, 1965–67; Res. Assistant, 1965–66, Vis. Asst Prof., 1966–67, Univ. of Illinois, Chicago; University of Sussex: Fellow, 1967–71; Sen. Fellow, 1971–73; Dir, Centre for Educnl Technol., 1973–76; Reader in Educn, 1976–86; Dir, Inst. of Continuing and Professional Educn, 1986–91. Chm. of Corporation, Lewes Tertiary Coll., 1992–. *Publications:* (with N. Mackenzie and H. C. Jones) Teaching and Learning: new methods and resources in higher education, 1970, 3rd edn 1976 (trans. French, German, Spanish and Portuguese); In-Service Education for Innovation, 1972; (with L. Goad and G. Smith) The Analysis of Curriculum Materials, 1975 (trans. German 1976); Accountability in the Middle Years of Schooling, 1980; (with B. Connors and E. Hewton) Training in Curriculum Development and Educational Technology in Higher Education, 1980; (with T. Becher and J. Knight) Policies for Educational Accountability, 1981; Curriculum Development in Further Education, 1985; Evaluation of Management Courses, 1986; (with J. Burke) Improving the Quality of YTS, 1986; (with D. Pennycuick and H. Radnor) Local Evaluation of INSET, 1988; (ed) International Encyclopaedia of Educational Technology, 1989; (with G. Cole) Business Education: a handbook for schools, 1990; Education and the Information Society, 1991; (with C. Nash and M. Fielding) Flexible Learning in Schools, 1991; (with G. Cole) Assessing Competence in the Professions, 1993; Developing Professional Knowledge and Competence, 1994; chapters in books and numerous conference papers. *Recreation:* travel. *Address:* 49 St Anne's Crescent, Lewes, E Sussex BN7 1SD. *T:* Lewes (01273) 475955.

ERDMAN, Edward Louis, FSVA; FRSA; Founder, 1934, and Senior Consultant, since 1974, Edward Erdman, Surveyors, later Erdman Lewis International; *b* 4 July 1906; *s* of David and Pauline Erdman; *m* 1949, Pamela (*née* Mason); one *s*. *Educ:* former Grocers' Co. Sch. Founded practice, 1934. TA KRRC, 1937; war service, N Africa and Italy, 1939–45. Re-opened practice, 1945; Director: Chesterfield Properties Plc, 1960–; Warnford Investments Plc, 1962; retired from practice, 1974. WPHT Housing Association (subseq. re-named Sanctuary Housing Association): Mem., Central Council, 1974–; Chm., 1978–87; Pres. 1987–; Mem., Property Adv. Panel to Treasury, 1975–77. FRSA 1957. *Publication:* People and Property, 1982. *Recreations:* football, cycling, farming. *Address:* (office) 6 Grosvenor Street, W1X 0AD. *T:* 071–629 8191. *Club:* Naval and Military.

EREAUT, Sir (Herbert) Frank (Cobbold), Kt 1976; Bailiff of Jersey, 1975–85; Judge of the Court of Appeal of Guernsey, 1976–89; *b* 6 May 1919; *s* of Herbert Parker Ereaut and May Julia Cobbold; *m* 1942, Kathleen FitzGibbon; one *d*. *Educ:* Tormore Sch., Upper Deal, Kent; Cranleigh Sch., Surrey; Exeter Coll., Oxford. BA 1946, MA 1966. RASC, 1940–46: N Africa, Italy and NW Europe; 2nd Lieut 1940; Lieut 1941; Captain 1943. Called to Bar, Inner Temple, 1947; Solicitor-General, Jersey, 1958–62, Attorney-General, 1962–69; Dep. Bailiff of Jersey, 1969–74. Chm., TSB Foundn for CI, 1986–90; Director: Standard Chartered Bank (CI), 1986–90; Standard Chartered Offshore, 1990–93. KStJ 1983 (CStJ 1978). *Recreations:* music, gardening, travel. *Address:* Les Cypres, St John, Jersey, Channel Islands. *T:* Jersey (01534) 22317.

EREMIN, Prof. Oleg, MD, FRCSE, FRACS; Regius Professor of Surgery, University of Aberdeen, since 1985; *b* 12 Nov. 1938; *s* of Theodor and Maria Eremin; *m* 1963, Jennifer Mary Ching; two *s* one *d*. *Educ:* Christian Brothers' Coll., St Kilda, Melbourne; Univ. of Melbourne. MB BS 1964; MD 1985. FRACS 1971; FRCSE 1983. Clinical posts: Royal Melbourne Hosp., 1965–72; Norfolk and Norwich Hosps, 1972–74; Research Asst-Associate, Dept of Pathology, Univ. of Cambridge, 1974–80; Sen. Lectr, Dept Clinical Surgery, Univ. of Edinburgh, 1981–85. Hon. Professorial Fellow, Rowett Res. Inst., 1992. *Publications:* articles in surgical, oncological and immunological jls. *Recreations:* music, sport, reading. *Address:* 3 The Chanonry, Old Aberdeen AB2 1RP. *T:* Aberdeen (01224) 484065. *Club:* Royal Northern and University (Aberdeen).

ERICKSON, Prof. Charlotte Joanne; Paul Mellon Professor of American History, University of Cambridge, 1983–90, now Professor Emeritus; Fellow of Corpus Christi College, Cambridge, since 1982; *b* 22 Oct. 1923; *d* of Knut Eric Erickson and Lael A. R. Johnson; *m* 1952, G. L. Watt; two *s*. *Educ:* Augustana Coll., Rock Island, Ill (BA 1945); Cornell Univ., Ithaca, NY (MA 1947; PhD 1951). Instructor in History, Vassar Coll., Poughkeepsie, NY, 1950–52; Research Fellow, NIESR, 1952–55; Lillian Gilmore Fellow, Cornell Univ., April-Sept. 1954; Asst Lectr, 1955, Lectr, 1958, Sen. Lectr, 1966, Reader, 1975, Prof., 1979–82, in Economic History, London School of Economics. Guggenheim Fellow, Washington, DC, 1966–67; Sherman Fairchild Distinguished Scholar, Calif Inst. of Technology, 1976–77; MacArthur Fellow, John D. and Dorothy MacArthur Foundn, Chicago, 1990–95. Hon. DHumLet Augustana College, 1977. *Publications:* British Industrialists, Steel and Hosiery 1850–1950, 1958; American Industry and the European Immigrant 1860–1885, 1969; Invisible Immigrants, The Adaptation of English and Scottish Immigrants in Nineteenth Century America, 1972; Leaving England: essays on British emigration in the Ninteenth Century, 1994; articles in professional jls and collective works. *Recreations:* music, gardening. *Address:* Corpus Christi College, Cambridge CB2 1RH; 8 High Street, Chesterton, Cambridge CB4 1NG.

ERICKSON, Prof. John, FRSE 1982; FBA 1985; University Endowment Fellow, and Director, Centre for Defence Studies, University of Edinburgh, since 1988; *b* 17 April 1929; *s* of Henry Erickson and Jessie (*née* Heys); *m* 1957, Ljubica (*née* Petrović); one *s* one *d*. *Educ:* South Shields High Sch.; St John's Coll., Cambridge (MA). Research Fellow, St Anthony's Coll., Oxford, 1956–58; Lectr, Dept of History, St Andrews Univ., 1958–62; Lectr, Sen. Lectr and Reader, Dept of Government, Univ. of Manchester, 1962–67; Edinburgh University: Reader, Lectr in Higher Defence Studies, 1967; Prof. of Politics (Defence Studies), 1969–88. Visiting Professor: Russian Res. Center, Univ. of Indiana, 1967; Texas A&M Univ., 1981; Dept. of History, Yale Univ., 1987. Pres., Assoc. of Civil Defence and Emergency Planning Officers, 1981–. FRSA 1991; Hon. Fellow, Aerospace Acad., Ukraine, 1995. *Publications:* The Soviet High Command 1918–1941, 1962; Storia dello Stato Maggiore Sovietico, 1963; ed, The Military-Technical Revolution, 1966; (ed) The Armed Services and Society, 1970; Soviet Military Power, 1971; The Road to Stalingrad, 1975 (reprinted, 1993); (ed) Soviet Military Power and Performance, 1979; The Road to Berlin, 1983; (ed) Barbarossa, The Axis and the Allies, 1994; (jtly) The Soviet Armed Forces 1918–1992: research guide to Soviet sources, 1995. *Recreations:* military models and music. *Address:* 13 Ravelston House Road, Edinburgh EH4 3LP. *T:* 0131–332 1787. *Club:* Edinburgh University Staff, Scottish Arts (Edinburgh).

ERLEIGH, Viscount; Julian Michael Rufus Isaacs; *b* 26 May 1986; *s* and *heir* of Marquess of Reading, *qv*.

ERMISCH, Prof. John Francis, FBA 1995; Professor, ESRC Research Centre on Micro-Social Change, University of Essex, since 1994; *b* 1 July 1947; *s* of Elmer and Frances Ermisch; *m* 1977, Dianne M. Monti. *Educ:* Univ. of Wisconsin (BSc); Univ. of Kansas (MA, PhD). Res. Economist, US Dept of Housing and Urban Develt, 1974–76; Res. Fellow, Centres for Environmental Studies and for the Study of Social Policy, London, 1976–78; Sen. Res. Fellow, PSI, 1978–86; Sen. Res. Officer, NIESR, 1986–91; Bonar-Macfie Prof., Univ. of Glasgow, 1991–94. *Publications:* Lone Parenthood: an economic analysis, 1991; The Political Economy of Demographic Change, 1983; contribs to economic and demographic jls. *Recreations:* films, tennis, golf, interior decoration. *Address:* ESRC Research Centre, University of Essex, Wivenhoe Park, Colchester CO4 3SQ. *T:* Colchester (01206) 872335.

ERNE, 6th Earl of, *cr* 1789; **Henry George Victor John Crichton,** JP; Baron Erne 1768; Viscount Erne (Ireland), 1781; Baron Fermanagh (UK), 1876; Lord Lieutenant of Co. Fermanagh, Northern Ireland, since 1986; *b* 9 July 1937; *s* of 5th Earl and Lady Katharine Cynthia Mary Millicent (Davina) Lytton (who *m* 1945, Hon. C. M. Woodhouse, *qv*), *yr d* of 2nd Earl of Lytton, KG, PC, GCSI, GCIE; *S* father, 1940; *m* 1958, Camilla Marguerite (marr. diss. 1980), *er d* of late Wing-Comdr Owen G. E. Roberts and Mrs Roberts; one *s* four *d*; *m* 1980, Mrs Anna Carin Hitchcock (*née* Bjork). *Educ:* Eton. Page of Honour to the Queen, 1952–54 (to King George VI, 1952). Lieut, North Irish Horse, 1959–66. Member: Royal Ulster Agricultural Society; Royal Forestry Society. JP Co. Fermanagh. *Recreations:* sailing, fishing, shooting. *Heir:* *s* Viscount Crichton, *qv*. *Address:* Crom Castle, Newtownbutler, Co. Fermanagh BT92 8AP. *T:* Newtownbutler (0136573) 8208. *Clubs:* White's; Lough Erne Yacht.

ERNST, Prof. Richard Robert; Professor of Physical Chemistry, Swiss Federal Institute of Technology (ETH-Z), since 1976; *b* 14 Aug. 1933; *s* of Prof. Robert Ernst, architect, and Irma Ernst (*née* Brunner); *m* 1963, Magdalena Kielholz; one *s* two *d*. *Educ:* Winterthur schools; ETH-Zentrum (DipChemEng 1956; PhD 1962). Mil. Service, 1956–57. Scientist, Instrument Div., Varian Associates, Calif., 1963–68; Swiss Federal Institute of Technology (ETH-Z): Lectr in Phys. Chem., 1968–70 (Group Leader in Magnetic Resonance Spectroscopy); Asst Prof., 1970; Associate Prof., 1972–76; Pres., Research Council, 1990. Mem. Bd, Spectrospin AG (Vice-Pres., 1989). Fellow, Amer. Phys. Soc.; For. Mem., Royal Soc., 1993; Member: internat. scientific bodies; editl bds of learned jls. Hon. doctorates: ETH Lausanne; Technical Univ., Munich; Univ. of Zürich. Numerous medals and prizes, Swiss and foreign; Nobel Prize in Chemistry, 1991; Wolf Prize, 1991; Louisa Gross Horwitz Prize, 1991. *Address:* Laboratorium für Physikalische Chemie, ETH-Zentrum, 8092 Zürich, Switzerland. *T:* (1) 2564368; Kurlistasse 24, 8404 Winterthur, Switzerland. *T:* (52) 277807.

ERNSTING, Air Vice-Marshal John, CB 1992; OBE 1959; PhD; FRCP, FFOM, FRAeS; Hon. Civil Consultant in Aviation Medicine to RAF, since 1993; *b* 21 April 1928; *s* of late Reginald James Ernsting and of Phyllis May Josephine Ernsting (*née* Allington); *m* 1st, 1952, Patricia Mary Woolford (decd); two *s* one *d*; 2nd, 1970, Joyce Marion Heppell. *Educ:* Chislehurst and Sidcup County Grammar Sch. for Boys; Guy's Hosp. Med. Sch. (BSc 1949; MB BS 1952; PhD 1964). MFOM 1981, FFOM 1993; MRCP 1985. Guy's Hosp., 1952–53; Guy's-Maudsley Neurosurgical Unit, 1953–54; RAF Medical Branch, 1954; Lectr in Physiology, Guy's Hosp. Med. Sch., 1961–85; RAF Consultant in Aviation Physiology, 1964; RAF Consultant Adviser in Aviation Medicine, 1971–89; Dep. Dir and Dir of Research, 1976–88, Comdt, 1988–92, RAF Inst. of Aviation Medicine; Dean of Air Force Medicine, 1990–91; Sen. Consultant (RAF) 1991–93, retd. QHS, 1989–93. Visiting Professor: Guy's Hosp. Med. Sch., 1985–; KCL, 1987–; Imperial Coll., 1993–; Hon. Dir of Studies MSc in Human and Applied Physiology, KCL, 1984–. *Publications:* (ed) Aviation Medicine, 1978, 2nd edn 1988; papers and chapters in books on aviation physiology and aviation medicine. *Recreations:* music, reading, travel. *Address:* White Gables, 2A Greenways, Fleet, Hants GU13 9UG. *T:* Fleet (01252) 621788. *Club:* Royal Air Force.

ERRÁZURIZ, (Talavera) Hernán; Ambassador of Chile to the Court of St James's, since 1993; *b* 14 Feb. 1941; *s* of Ladislao Errázuriz Pereira and Amelia Talavera Balmaceda; *m* 1964, Carmen Cruzat Amunategui; three *s* five *d*. *Educ:* German Sch. and Military Sch. Santiago; Univ. of Chile (Law degree, 1965); New York Sch. of Law. Admitted to legal practice, 1965; Sen. Partner, Errázuriz & Co. (estab. 1905 by grandfather); Legal Advr, Chilean Copper Corp., 1962–68; University of Chile: Prof. of Economic law, 1968–93; Dir, Inst. of Internat. Studies, 1974–83. Legal Advr to Confedn of Chilean Entrepeneurs, 1973–76. President: Assoc. of Chilean Industries, 1968–73; Latin American Assoc. of Industries, 1970–72; Chilean Council of Econ. Law, 1988–; Mem., Cttee of Foreign Investment of Chile, 1968–73. Mem., Internat. Gp of Lawyers, SGL, 1988–93. President: Liberal Youth Party, 1960–64; Chilean Liberal Party (PAC), 1991–93. *Publications:* Chilean Economic Law 1968–1974; The Chilean Economy in a Democratic Framework, 1984. *Recreations:* horse riding, theatre, opera. *Address:* Chilean Embassy, 12 Devonshire Street, W1N 2DS; Enrique Mac-Iver 125, P16, Santiago, Chile. *T:* (2) 6335134/397309. *Clubs:* Royal Automobile; De La Union (Santiago); Los Leones Golf, Sto Domingo Golf.

ERRINGTON, Viscount; Alexander Rowland Harmsworth Baring; *b* 5 Jan. 1994; *s* and *heir* of Earl of Cromer, *qv*.

ERRINGTON, Col Sir Geoffrey (Frederick), 2nd Bt *cr* 1963; Chairman, Harefield Hospital NHS Trust, since 1991; *b* 15 Feb. 1926; *er s* of Sir Eric Errington, 1st Bt, JP, and Marjorie (*d* 1973), *d* of A. Grant Bennett; *S* father, 1973; *m* 1955, Diana Kathleen Forbes, *o d* of late E. Barry Davenport, Edgbaston, Birmingham; three *s*. *Educ:* Rugby Sch.; New Coll., Oxford. psc 1958. GSO 3 (Int.), HQ 11 Armd Div., 1950–52; GSO 3, MI3 (b), War Office, 1955–57; Bde Major 146 Inf. Bde, 1959–61; Coy Comdr, RMA Sandhurst, 1963–65; Military Assistant to Adjutant-General, 1965–67; CO 1st Bn, The King's Regt, 1967–69; GSO 1, HQ 1st British Corps, 1969–71; Col. GS, HQ NW District, 1971–74; AAG MI (Army), MoD, 1974–75; retired 1975. Col, The King's Regt, 1975–86; Chm., The King's and Manchester Regts Assoc., 1971–86. Director: Personnel Services, British Shipbuilders, 1977–78; Executive Appointments, 1979–90 (Chm., 1982–90). Employer Bd Mem., Shipbuilding ITB, 1977–78. Chm., Assoc. for Prevention of Addiction, 1994–

(Vice-Chm., 1991–94); Mem. Gen. Cttee, Not Forgotten Assoc., 1991–. Chm., Woodroffe's Club, 1988–94. Freeman, City of London, 1980; Liveryman, Coachmakers' and Coach Harness Makers' Co. *Recreations:* travelling, gardening. *Heir:* *s* Robin Davenport Errington, *b* 1 July 1957. FRSA 1994. *Address:* Stone Hill Farm, Sellindge, Ashford, Kent TN25 6AJ; 203A Gloucester Place, NW1 6BU. *Clubs:* Boodle's, United Oxford & Cambridge University.

See also S. G. Errington.

ERRINGTON, Sir Lancelot, KCB 1976 (CB 1962); Second Permanent Secretary, Department of Health and Social Security, 1973–76; *b* 14 Jan. 1917; *e s* of late Major L. Errington; *m* 1939, Katharine Reine, *o d* of late T. C. Macaulay; two *s* two *d*. *Educ:* Wellington Coll.; Trinity Coll., Cambridge. Entered Home Office, 1939. Served RNVR, 1939–45. Transferred to Ministry of National Insurance, 1945; Principal Private Sec. to Minister of National Insurance, 1951; Asst Sec., 1953; Under-Sec., 1957–65; Cabinet Office, 1965–68; Min. of Social Security, 1968; Asst Under-Sec. of State, DHSS, 1968–71, Dep. Under-Sec. of State, 1971–73. *Recreation:* sailing. *Address:* St Mary's, Fasnacloich, Appin, Argyll PA38 4BJ. *T:* Appin (01631) 730331.

ERRINGTON, Stuart Grant, CBE 1994; JP; Chairman, National Association of Citizens' Advice Bureaux, 1989–94; *b* 23 June 1929; *yr s* of Sir Eric Errington, 1st Bt and late Marjorie Lady Errington; *m* 1954, Anne, *d* of late Eric and Eileen Baedeker; two *s* one *d*. *Educ:* Rugby; Trinity College, Oxford (MA). National Service, 2nd Lieut Royal Artillery, 1947–49. Ellerman Lines, 1952–59; Astley Industrial Trust, 1959–70; Exec Dir, 1970, Man. Dir, 1977, Chm., 1985, Mercantile Credit Co., Chm. and Chief Exec., Mercantile Gp, 1988–89. Chairman: Equipment Leasing Assoc., 1976–78; European Fedn of Leasing Assocs, 1978–80; Finance Houses Assoc., 1982–84; Director: Barclays Merchant Bank, Barclays Bank UK, 1979–86; Kleinwort Overseas Investment Trust, 1982–; Municipal Mutual Insurance, 1989–; Northern Electric, 1989–; Nationwide Building Soc., 1989–. Mem. Council, RHBNC, 1989–. Chm., Sportsmatch England Award Panel, Dept of Nat. Heritage, 1992–. JP Windsor Forest, 1970. *Recreations:* fishing, golf, splitting logs, avoiding telephones. *Address:* Earleywood Lodge, Ascot SL5 9JP. *T:* Ascot (01344) 21977. *Club:* Boodle's.

ERRITT, (Michael) John (Mackey), CB 1991; Deputy Director, Central Statistical Office, 1989–91; *b* 15 Feb. 1931; *s* of late William Albert Erritt, MBE, and Anna Erritt; *m* 1957, Marian Elizabeth Hillock; two *s*. *Educ:* St Andrews Coll., Dublin; Prince of Wales Sch., Nairobi; Queen's Univ., Belfast. BSc(Econ). Research Officer, Science and Industry Cttee, 1953; Asst Statistician, Central Statistical Office, 1955; Statistician: Board of Trade, 1960; Treasury, 1964; Board of Trade, 1967; Chief Statistician: Inland Revenue, 1968; Central Statistical Office, 1973; Depts of Industry, Trade and Prices and Consumer Protection, 1975; MoD, 1979; Asst Under-Sec. of State (Statistics), MoD, 1981; Asst Dir, Central Statistical Office, 1985. *Publications:* articles in official, academic and trade jls. *Recreations:* gardening, golf, travel. *Address:* Green Tiles, 14 Brook Lane, Lindfield, Sussex RH16 1SG. *Club:* Paxhill Park Golf.

ERROLL, 24th Earl of, *cr* 1452; **Merlin Sereld Victor Gilbert Hay;** Lord Hay, 1429; Baron of Slains, 1452; Bt 1685; 28th Hereditary Lord High Constable of Scotland, *cr* 1314; Celtic title, Mac Garadh Mor; 33rd Chief of the Hays (from 1171); Senior Great Officer, Royal Household in Scotland; computer consultant; *b* 20 April 1948; *er s* of 23rd Countess of Erroll and Sir Iain Moncreiffe of that Ilk, 11th Bt, CVO, QC; *S* mother, 1978 (and to baronetcy of father, 1985); *m* 1982, Isabelle Astell, *o d* of late T. S. Astell Hohler, MC; two *s* two *d*. *Educ:* Eton; Trinity College, Cambridge. Page to the Lord Lyon, 1956. Lieut, Atholl Highlanders, 1974. OStJ 1977. Member, Queen's Body Guard for Scotland, Royal Company of Archers, 1978. *Recreations:* skiing, climbing. *Heir:* *s* Lord Hay, *qv*. *Address:* Woodbury Hall, Sandy, Beds SG19 2HR. *T:* Sandy (01767) 650251. *Clubs:* White's, Pratt's; Puffin's (Edinburgh).

ERROLL OF HALE, 1st Baron, *cr* 1964; **Frederick James Erroll,** PC 1960; MA, FIEE; FIMechE; Chairman, Bowater Corporation, 1973–84; *b* 27 May 1914; *s* of George Murison Erroll, engineer, and Kathleen Donovan Edington, both of Glasgow and London; *m* 1950, Elizabeth, *o d* of R. Sowton Barrow, Exmouth, Devon. *Educ:* Oundle Sch.; Trinity Coll., Cambridge. Engineering Apprenticeship, 1931–32; Cambridge Univ., 1932–35; Engineer at Metropolitan-Vickers Electrical Co. Ltd, Manchester, 1936–38; Commissioned into 4th County of London Yeomanry (Sharpshooters), TA, 1939; technical appointments in connection with Tank Construction and Testing, 1940–43; service in India and Burma, 1944–45; Col 1945. MP (C) Altrincham and Sale, 1945–64. A Dir of Engineering and Mining Companies until April 1955; Parly Sec., Min. of Supply, April 1955–Nov. 1956; Parly Sec., BoT, 1956–58; Economic Sec. to the Treasury, Oct. 1958–59; Minister of State, BoT, 1959–61; Pres., BoT, 1961–63; Minister of Power, 1963–64. Mem., H of L Select Cttee on Science and Technology, 1985–91. Pres., Consolidated Gold Fields, 1982–89 (Chm., 1976–82); Chairman: Bowater Corporation Ltd; Whessoe plc, 1970–87 (Consultant, 1987–90); ASEA Ltd, 1965–84; Fläkt Ltd, 1971–85; Gen. Advr, ASEA, Sweden, 1965–86. Member: Council Inst. Directors, 1949–55, and 1965–87 (Chm. Council, 1973–76, Pres., 1976–84, Chancellor, 1984–87); NEDC, 1962–63. President: Hispanic and Luso-Brazilian Councils, 1969–73; British Export Houses Assoc., 1969–72; British Exec. Service Overseas, 1972–85; UK South Africa Trade Assoc., 1979–84; World Travel Market, 1986–; Vice-President: London Chamber of Commerce, 1969– (Pres., 1966–69); Inst. of Marketing, 1983–92; Automobile Assoc., 1986– (Chm., 1974–86). Dep. Chm., Decimal Currency Board, 1966–71; Chm., Cttee on Liquor Licensing, 1971–72; Pres., Electrical Research Assoc., 1971–74. Trustee, Westminster Abbey Trust, 1978–86. FRSA 1971. *Heir:* none. *Address:* House of Lords, SW1A 0PW. *Club:* Carlton.

ERSHAD, Lt-Gen. Hussain Muhammad; President of Bangladesh, 1983–90; President of the Council of Ministers, 1982–90; Minister of Defence, Establishment, Health and Population Control, 1986–90; *b* 1 Feb. 1930; *s* of late Makbul Hussain, Advocate, and of Mojida Begum; *m* 1956, Begum Raushad Ershad; one *s* one adopted *d*. *Educ:* Carmichael Coll., Rangpur; Dhaka Univ. (BA 1st Div.). Staff Course, Defence Service Command and Staff Coll., Quetta, Pakistan, 1966; War Course, National Defence Coll., New Delhi, India, 1975. Infantry Regimental Service, 1953–58; Adjt, E Bengal Regimental Centre (Basic Inf. Trng Centre), 1960–62; E Pakistan Rifles, 1962–65; Bde Major/Dep. Asst Adjt and Quarter Master General, 1967–68; CO, Inf. Bn, 1969–71; Adjt General, Bangladesh Army, 1973–74; Dep. Chief of Army Staff, Bangladesh Army, Chm., Coordination and Control Cell for National Security, 1975–78; Chief of Army Staff, Bangladesh Army, 1978–86; C-in-C, Bangladesh Armed Forces, 1982; Chief Martial Law Administrator, Bangladesh, 1982–86. Chm., National Sports Control Bd. *Publications:* poems in Bengali contributed occasionally to literary jls. *Address:* c/o Office of the President, Bangabhaban, Dhaka, Bangladesh. *Club:* Kurmitola Golf (Dhaka).

ERSKINE; *see* St Clair-Erskine.

ERSKINE, family name of **Earls of Buchan** and **Mar and Kellie.**

ERSKINE, Sir David; *see* Erskine, Sir T. D.

ERSKINE, Ralph, CBE 1978; architect; own practice (in Sweden since 1939); *b* 24 Feb. 1914; *s* of late George and Mildred Erskine; *m* 1939, Ruth Monica Francis; one *s* two *d*. *Educ:* Friends' Sch., Saffron Walden, Essex; Regent Street Polytechnic (architecture). ARIBA 1936; AMTPI 1938; SAR 1965. Won number of prizes in arch. comps in Sweden; one year's study at Academy for Fine Arts, Sweden, 1945. *Work executed:* town plans; workers' houses; co-operative housing and industrial housing; flats; hostels; factories; ski-hotel; shopping centre; school; town hall; hall of residence at Clare Coll., Cambridge; churches; housing estates at Newmarket and Killingworth; clearance scheme, Byker, Newcastle upon Tyne; design of new town, Resolute Bay, Canada; University Library, Allhuset and Sports Hall, Stockholm Univ. Lecturing: in America, Canada, Japan and many countries in Europe. Hon. Dr, Lund Univ., Sweden, 1975; Hon. DLitt, Heriot-Watt Univ., 1982. For. Mem., Royal Acad. of Arts, Sweden, 1972; Hon. Mem., Bund Deutscher Architekten, 1983. Hon Fellow of AIA, 1966; SAR's Kasper Sahlin prize for 1971 and 1981; Ytong Prize, 1974; Guld medal, Litteris et Artibus, 1980; Canadian Gold Medal, RAIC, 1983; Wolf Prize for Architecture, 1984; Royal Gold Medal, RIBA, 1987. *Publications:* for several arch. magazines, on building in northern climates, etc. *Relevant publication:* Ralph Erskine, by Mats Egelius, 1978. *Recreations:* ski-ing, skating, swimming, yachting, ice yachting. *Address:* Gustav III's väg, Drottningholm, Sweden. *T:* 7590352.

ERSKINE, Sir (Thomas) David, 5th Bt, *cr* 1821; JP; Vice Lord-Lieutenant, Fife Region, 1981–87; Convener, Fife County Council, 1970–73; *b* 31 July 1912; *o surv. s* of Sir Thomas Wilfred Hargreaves John Erskine, 4th Bt, and late Magdalen Janet, *d* of Sir Ralph Anstruther, 6th Bt of Balcaskie; *S* father, 1944; *m* 1947, Ann, *er d* of late Lt-Col Neil Fraser-Tytler, DSO, MC, and late Christian Helen Fraser-Tytler, CBE; two *s* (and one *d* decd). *Educ:* Eton; Magdalene Coll., Cambridge. Employed by Butterfield & Swire, London and China, in 1934 and served with them in China, 1935–41. Joined HM Forces in India and commissioned into Indian Corps of Engineers. Served with them in Mid-East, India and Malaya, being demobilised in 1945 with rank of Major. JP Fife, 1951; DL Fife, 1955–81. *Heir:* *s* Thomas Peter Neil Erskine [*b* 28 March 1950; *m* 1972, Catherine, *d* of Col G. H. K. Hewlett; two *s* two *d*]. *Address:* West Newhall House, Kingsbarns, Fife KY16 8QD. *T:* Crail (01333) 450228. *Club:* New (Edinburgh).

ERSKINE, Thomas Ralph, CB 1986; First Legislative Counsel, Northern Ireland, 1979–93; *b* 14 Oct. 1933; *m* 1966, Patricia Joan Palmer; one *s* one *d*. *Educ:* Campbell College; Queen's University, Belfast. Called to the Bar, Gray's Inn, 1962. *Publications:* contribs to Cryptologia, Annals of the History of Computing, legal periodicals, etc. *Recreations:* ski-ing, gardening, modern naval history. *Address:* c/o Office of the Legislative Counsel, Parliament Buildings, Belfast BT4 3SW.

ERSKINE CRUM, Douglas Vernon, CBE 1994; Racecourse Director, Ascot, since 1994; *b* 31 May 1949; *s* of Lt-Gen. Vernon Forbes Erskine Crum, CIE, MC and Rosemary Aimée Douglas Dawson; *m* 1980, Jacqueline Margaret Wilson; one *s* two *d*. *Educ:* Eton. Commissioned Scots Guards 1970; Staff Coll., Camberley, 1982; Co. Comdr 1 SG, 1983–84; Army Plans, MoD, 1984–87; Brigade Major, Household Div., 1987–89; CO 2 SG, 1989–91; ACOS Ops, HQ N Ireland, 1991–92; Comdr 3 Inf. Brigade, 1992–94; retired 1994. *Recreations:* most sports. *Address:* Ascot Racecourse, Ascot, Berks SL5 7JN. *T:* Ascot (01344) 22211. *Club:* Turf.

ERSKINE-HILL, Sir (Alexander) Roger, 3rd Bt *cr* 1945, of Quothquhan, Co. Lanark; *b* 15 Aug. 1949; *s* of Sir Robert Erskine-Hill, 2nd Bt and of Christine Alison, *o d* of late Capt. (A) Henry James Johnstone of Alva, RN; *S* father, 1989; *m* 1984, Sarah Anne Sydenham (marr. diss. 1994), *er d* of late Dr R. J. Sydenham Clarke and of Mrs Charles Clarke; one *s* one *d*. *Educ:* Eton; Aberdeen Univ. (LLB). Director: Salestrac Ltd, 1985–; Map Marketing Ltd, 1988–; The Offer Shop Ltd, 1990–. *Heir:* *s* Robert Benjamin Erskine-Hill, *b* 6 Aug. 1986. *Address:* c/o Salestrac Ltd, Cowley Bridge Road, Exeter EX4 5HQ.

ERSKINE-HILL, Prof. (Henry) Howard, PhD; FBA 1985; Professor of Literary History, since 1994, and Fellow of Pembroke College, since 1980, Cambridge University; *b* 19 June 1936; *s* of late Henry Erskine-Hill and Hannah Lilian Poppleton. *Educ:* Ashville Coll.; Nottingham Univ. (BA, PhD); MA Cantab; LittD Cantab 1988. University of Wales, Swansea: Tutor, 1960; Asst Lectr, 1961; Lectr in Eng. Lit., 1962; Sen. Fellow, 1964–65; University of Cambridge: Lectr in English, 1969–84; Reader in Literary Hist., 1984–94; Fellow, 1969–80, Tutor, 1970–76, Jesus Coll.; Tutor for Graduates, Pembroke Coll., 1983–84. Olin Fellow, Nat. Humanities Center, NC, USA, 1988–89. Taught at British Council seminars in Britain, 1962–69; invited lectr, univs of Alberta, Adelaide, Berkeley (Calif), Bristol, Davis (Calif), Essex, Flinders (S Australia), Liverpool, London, Monash, Nantes, Oxford, Saskatchewan, Stanford, Singapore, Wales (Swansea), Victoria (BC), Warwick, W Australia and York; also at David Nichol Smith Seminar, Canberra, Inter-Univ. Centre, Dubrovnik, Inst. of Hist. Res., London, and Herzog-August Library, Wolfenbüttel. *Publications:* (ed) Alexander Pope: Horatian Satires and Epistles, 1964; Pope: The Dunciad, 1972; The Social Milieu of Alexander Pope, 1975; (ed with Anne Smith) The Art of Alexander Pope, 1978; (ed with Graham Storey) Revolutionary Prose of the English Civil War, 1983; The Augustan Idea, 1983; contributions to: Renaissance and Modern Essays, ed G. R. Hibbard, 1966; English Drama: forms and Development, ed Marie Axton and Raymond Williams, 1977; Ideology and Conspiracy, ed Eveline Cruickshanks, 1982; jls incl. Essays in Criticism, Eighteenth-Century Studies, Jl of the Warburg and Courtauld Insts, Modern Language Review, Rev. of English Studies, Renaissance and Modern Studies. *Recreation:* fell walking. *Address:* Pembroke College, Cambridge CB2 1RF. *T:* Cambridge (01223) 338100. *Club:* United Oxford & Cambridge University.

ERSKINE-HILL, Sir Roger; *see* Erskine-Hill, Sir A. R.

ERSKINE-MURRAY, family name of **Lord Elibank.**

ESAKI, Leo; President, University of Tsukuba, since 1992; *b* 12 March 1925; *s* of Soichiro Esaki and Niyoko Ito; *m* 1986, Masako Kondo (one *s* two *d* by previous *m*). *Educ:* Univ. of Tokyo. MS 1947, PhD 1959. Sony Corp., Japan, 1956–60; IBM Research, 1960–92; IBM Fellow, 1967–92. Director: IBM-Japan, 1976–92; Yamada Science Foundn, 1976–. Research in tunnelling in semiconductor junctions which led to the discovery of the Esaki tunnel diode; subsequently research on man-made semiconductor superlattice in search of predicted quantum mechanical effect. Sir John Cass sen. vis. res. fellow, London Poly, 1982. Councillor-at-Large, Amer. Phys. Soc., 1971–75; Dir, Amer. Vacuum Soc., 1972–76; Member: Japan Academy, 1975; Max-Planck-Ges., 1989; For. Associate, Nat. Acad. of Sciences, USA, 1976; For. Associate, Nat. Acad. of Engineering, USA, 1977; Corresp. Mem., Academia Nacional De Ingenieria, Mexico, 1978. Nishina Meml Award, 1959; Asahi Press Award, 1960; Toyo Rayon Foundn Award, 1961; Morris N. Liebmann Meml Prize, 1961; Stuart Ballantine Medal, Franklin Inst., 1961; Japan Academy Award, 1965; (jtly) Nobel Prize for Physics, 1973; Science Achievement Award, US-Asia Inst., 1983; Centennial Medal, IEEE, 1984; Internat. Prize for New Materials, Amer. Physical Soc., 1985; Distinguished Foreign-born Individual Award, Internat. Center, NY, 1986; IEEE Medal of Honor, 1991. Order of Culture (Japan), 1974. *Publications:* numerous papers in learned jls. *Address:* The Office of the President, University of Tsukuba, Tsukuba, Ibaraki 305, Japan.

ESCHENBACH, Christoph; pianist and conductor; Music Director, Houston Symphony Orchestra, since 1988; Music Director, Ravinia Festival, since 1994; *b* 20 Feb. 1940. *Educ:* Hamburg Conservatory; State Music Conservatory, Cologne. Winner: Internat. Piano Competition, Munich, 1962; Concours Clara Haskil, 1965. Canadian début, Montreal Expo, 1967; US début, Cleveland Orch., 1969; has toured Europe, N and S America, USSR, Israel, Japan; and has performed as pianist with leading orchs incl. Concertgebouw Amsterdam, Orch. de Paris, London Symphony, Berlin Philharmonic, and Cleveland Orch.; festivals incl. Salzburg, Lucerne, Bonn, and Aix-en-Provence. Chief Conductor, Tonhalle Orch., Zürich, and Artistic Dir, Tonhalle-Gesellschaft, Zürich, 1982–86; guest appearances with NY Philharmonic, Boston Symphony, Chicago Symphony, Cleveland Orch., Pittsburgh Symphony, Los Angeles Philharmonic, London Symphony, BBC Philharmonia, Berlin Philharmonic, Bavarian Radio Symphony Munich, Munich Philharmonic, Vienna Symphonic, Czech Philharmonic and New Japan Philharmonic. *Address:* c/o Columbia Artists Management Inc., 165 West 57th Street, New York, NY 10019, USA.

ESCOTT COX, Brian Robert; *see* Cox.

ESDALE, Patricia Joyce, (Mrs G. P. R. Esdale); *see* Lindop, P. J.

ESER, Prof. Dr Günter Otto; Director General, International Air Transport Association, Montreal/Geneva, 1985–92; *b* 10 Sept. 1927; *s* of Ernst Eser and Martha Siering; *m* 1976, Florida Huisman; two *s*. *Educ:* Bonn Univ.; Federal Acad. of Finance, Siegburg; Harvard (Management Programme). Auditor, Fed. German Min. of Finance, 1953–55; Lufthansa German Airlines, 1955–84: Head, Persian subsidiary, Teheran; Head, Munich Dist Office for Southern Germany; Sales Dir, Germany; Gen. Man., N and Central America; Mem., Chief Exec. Bd. Member: Adv. Bd, Europäische Reiseversicherung, 1978–; Adv. Bd, Amer. Univ., 1982–. Vis. Prof., Pace Univ., NY, 1978–. Bundesverdienstkreuz 1st Class (FRG), 1985; Commendatore Officiale (Italy), 1967. *Recreations:* trekking, ocean-fishing, literature, music. *Address:* ch. de Sodome, 1261 Givrins, Vaud, Switzerland.

ESHER, 4th Viscount, *cr* 1897; Baron *cr* 1885; **Lionel Gordon Baliol Brett,** CBE 1970; MA; PPRIBA; DistTP; Rector and Vice-Provost, Royal College of Art, 1971–78; *b* 18 July 1913; *o s.* of 3rd Viscount Esher, GBE; *S* father, 1963; *m* 1935, Christian, *e d* of late Col Ebenezer Pike, CBE, MC; five *s* one *d*. *Educ:* Eton (Scholar); New Coll., Oxford (Scholar); BA (1st Class), 1935; Hon. Fellow, 1980; RIBA Ashpitel Prizeman, 1939. Served War in RA, 1940–45; France and Germany, 1944–45 (despatches); Major. Architect Planner, Hatfield New Town, 1949–59; major housing projects: Hatfield, Stevenage, Basildon; consultant architect: Downside Abbey; Maidenhead Town Centre; Abingdon Town Centre; Portsmouth City Centre; York City Centre; Santiago, Chile and Caracas, Venezuela (both for UNDP); principal buildings include: (with Francis Pollen): High Comr's House, Lagos; 82 and 190 Sloane St, London; Pall Mall Ct, Manchester; Downside Sch. extensions; Exeter Coll., and Oxenford Hall, Oxford; (with Teggin & Taylor) Civic Offices, Portsmouth. Lecture tours: USA 1953; India, 1954; Australia, 1959; S America, 1970. Governor, Museum of London, 1970–77; Member: Royal Fine Art Commn, 1951–69; Adv. Bd for Redundant Churches (Chm., 1977–83); Advisory Council, Victoria and Albert Museum, 1967–72; Arts Council of GB, 1972–77 (Chm., Art Panel); Environment Panel, British Rail, 1977–85; National Trust (Chm., Thames and Chilterns Reg., 1979–83); Vice-Pres., RIBA, 1962–65; Pres., 1965–67; Trustee, Soane Museum, 1976–94. Hon. DLitt Strathclyde Univ., 1967; Hon. DUniv York, 1970; Hon. DSc Edinburgh, 1981. Hon. Fellow: Amer. Inst. of Architects, 1967; Portsmouth Polytechnic, subseq. Portsmouth Univ., 1984; Chartered Inst. of Designers, 1975. *Publications:* Houses, 1947; The World of Architecture, 1963; Landscape in Distress, 1965; York: a study in conservation, 1969; Parameters and Images, 1970; (with Elisabeth Beazley) Shell Guide to North Wales, 1971; A Broken Wave, 1981; The Continuing Heritage, 1982; Our Selves Unknown (autobiog.), 1985; The Glory of the English House, 1991. *Recreation:* landscapes. *Heir:* *s* Hon. Christopher Lionel Baliol Brett [*b* 23 Dec. 1936; *m* 1st, 1962, Camilla Charlotte (marr. diss. 1970), *d* of Sir (Horace) Anthony Rumbold, 10th Bt, KGMG, KCVO, CB; one *s* two *d*; 2nd, 1971, Valerie Harrington; two *s* twin *d*]. *Address:* Snowball Hill, Russell's Water, Henley on Thames RG9 6EU. *Club:* Arts.

See also Sir Martyn G. Beckett.

ESIRI, Dr Margaret Miriam, FRCPath; Clinical Reader in Neuropathology, Departments of Neuropathology and Neurology, Oxford University, since 1988; Professorial Fellow, St Hugh's College, Oxford, since 1988; *b* 5 Oct. 1941; *d* of William Alfred Evans and Doreen Mary (*née* Bates); *m* 1963, Frederick Obukowho Uruemuowho Esiri; two *s* one *d*. *Educ:* Croydon High Sch. (GPDST); St Hugh's Coll., Oxford (BSc, MA, DM). FRCPath 1988. University of Oxford: preregistration med. and surgical posts and scholarship for trng in research methods, 1967–69; Jun. Res. Fellow in Neuropathology, 1970–72; trng posts in Histopathology, 1973–79; MRC Sen. Clinical Fellow in Neuropathology, 1980–85; Consultant Neuropathologist, Radcliffe Infirmary, Oxford, 1986–88. *Publications:* (with J. Booss) Viral Encephalitis, 1986; (with D. R. Oppenheimer) Diagnostic Neuropathology, 1986. *Recreation:* assisting in my husband's clinic in Nigeria. *Address:* Neuropathology Department, Radcliffe Infirmary, Oxford OX2 6HE. *T:* Oxford (01865) 224403.

ESKDAILL, Lord; Walter John Francis Montagu Douglas Scott; *b* 2 Aug. 1984; *s* and *heir* of Earl of Dalkeith, *qv*.

ESKENAZI, Giuseppe, (J. E. Eskenazi); Managing Director, Eskenazi Ltd, since 1969; *b* 8 July 1939; *s* of late Isaac Eskenazi and of Lea Eskenazi; *m* 1963, Laura (*née* Bandini); one *s* one *d*. *Educ:* King's School, Sherborne; The Polytechnic, Regent Street; University College London. Art dealer, primarily Chinese and Japanese, 1962–; Eskenazi Ltd founded by father in 1960. *Publications:* numerous exhibition catalogues. *Recreations:* sailing, diving, opera. *Address:* 12 Carlyle Square, Chelsea, SW3 6EX. *T:* 0171–352 7461; Eskenazi, 10 Clifford Street, W1X 1RB. *T:* 0171–493 5464.

ESMONDE, Sir Thomas (Francis Grattan), 17th Bt *cr* 1629 (Ire.), of Ballynastragh, Wexford; Senior Registrar in Neurology, Royal Victoria Hospital, Belfast, since 1992; *b* 14 Oct. 1960; *s* of Sir John Henry Grattan Esmonde, 16th Bt and of Pamela Mary, *d* of late Francis Stephen Bourke, FRCPI; *S* father, 1987; *m* 1986, Pauline Loretto Kearns; one *s* one *d*. *Educ:* Sandford Park Secondary School, Ranelagh, Dublin; Medical School, Trinity College, Dublin. MB, BCh, BAO, MRCPI, MRCP (UK). Junior House Officer, Whiteabbey Hosp., 1984–85; SHO, Royal Victoria, Musgrave Park and Whiteabbey Hosps, 1985–87, Altnagelvin Hosp., Londonderry, 1987–88; Med. Registrar, Royal Gwent Hosp., Newport, 1988–89; Registrar in Neurology, Univ. Hosp. of Wales, 1989–90; Clinical Res. Fellow, Dept of Neurosci., Western General Hosp., Edinburgh, 1990–92. *Recreations:* chess, judo. *Heir:* *s* Sean Vincent Grattan Esmonde, *b* 8 Jan. 1989. *Address:* 6 Nutley Avenue, Donnybrook, Dublin 4. *T:* Dublin 2693040.

ESPIE, Sir Frank (Fletcher), Kt 1979; OBE 1971; FTS, FIMM, MAIMM, MAIME; company director, retired; *b* 8 May 1917; *s* of late Frank Fancett Espie and Laura Jean Espie; *m* 1st, 1941, Madeline Elizabeth Robertson (decd); one *s* three *d*; 2nd, 1985, Jean Primrose Angove. *Educ:* St Peter's Coll., Adelaide; Univ. of Adelaide (BEng). FTS 1978; FIMM 1958. CRA Ltd: Dir, 1968; Dep. Chm., 1974–79; non-exec. Dir, 1979–85; Bougainville Copper Ltd: Gen. Man., 1965; Man. Dir, 1969; Chm., 1971–79; non-exec. Dir, 1979–85. Director: ICI Aust. Ltd, 1979–87; Tubemakers of Australia, 1980–87; Westpac Banking Corporation, 1981–90; Woodside Petroleum, 1981–89. Chairman: Nat. Petroleum Adv. Cttee, 1979–87; Australian Mineral Foundn Inc., 1988–91. Member: Exec. Cttee, Aust. Mining Industry Council, 1973–81 (Pres., 1978–80); Council: Australasian Inst. of Mining and Metallurgy, 1970–88 (Pres., 1975; Inst. Medal, 1980); Aust. Acad. of Technological Scis, 1980–90. *Recreations:* swimming, golf. *Address:* 31 The Righi, South Yarra, Vic 3141, Australia. *T:* (3) 8662062. *Clubs:* Melbourne, Athenæum, Royal Melbourne Golf (Melbourne); Union (Sydney); Adelaide (Adelaide).

ESPLEN, (Sir) John Graham, (3rd Bt *cr* 1921, of Hardres Court, Canterbury, but does not use the title); *b* 4 Aug. 1932; *s* of Sir William Graham Esplen, 2nd Bt and of Aline Octavia, *d* of late A. Octavius Hedley; *S* father, 1989; *m*; one *s* three *d*. *Educ:* Harrow; St Catharine's Coll., Cambridge. *Heir:* *s* William John Harry Esplen, *b* 24 Feb. 1967. *Address:* The Mill House, Moorlands Road, Merriott, Somerset TA16 5NF.

ESPLIN, Air Vice-Marshal Ian (George), CB 1963; OBE 1946; DFC 1943; retired (voluntarily) 1965; *b* 26 Feb. 1914; *s* of late Donald Thomas Esplin and Emily Freame Esplin; *m* 1944, Patricia Kaleen Barlow; one *s* one *d*. *Educ:* Sydney Univ.; Oxford Univ. BEc 1936; MA 1939. Rowing Blue, 1934 and 1935. NSW Rhodes Schol., 1937. Entered RAF from Oxford, 1939. Served War of 1939–45, as Pilot in Night-Fighters; destroyed three enemy aircraft at night; also served at CFS and in HQ, SEAC; Air Min. (Policy), 1945; Comd RAF Desford, 1947; Dep. Senior Personnel Staff Officer, HQ Reserve Comd, 1948; Directing Staff, RAF Staff Coll., 1950–51; Comd first Jet All Weather Wing, Germany (No 148), 1952–54; Flying Coll. Course, 1954; Dep. Dir of Operational Requirements, Air Min., 1955–58; Comd RAF Wartling, 1958–60; Dir of Operational Reqts, 1960–62; Comdr, RAF Staff and Air Attaché, Washington, DC, 1963–65; Dean, Air Attaché Corps, 1964–65. *Recreations:* golf, tennis, swimming. *Address:* c/o National Westminster Bank, West End Office, 1 St James's Square, SW1Y 4JX. *Clubs:* Vincent's (Oxford); Leander (Henley-on-Thames)

ESQUIVEL, Rt. Hon. Manuel; PC 1986; Prime Minister of Belize, 1984–89 and since 1993; Member, House of Representatives, Belize, since 1984; Leader, United Democratic Party, since 1982; *b* 2 May 1940; *s* of John and Laura Esquivel; *m* 1971, Kathleen Levy; one *s* two *d*. *Educ:* Loyola Univ., New Orleans (BSc Physics); Bristol Univ. (Cert Ed.). Instructor in Physics, St John's Coll., Belize City, 1967–82. Member: Belize City Council, 1974–80; Nat. Senate, 1979–84; Leader of the Opposition, Belize, 1989–93. Chm., Utd Democratic Party, 1976–82. Hon. DHL Loyola Univ., 1986. *Recreation:* electronics. *Address:* Office of the Prime Minister, Belmopan, Belize.

ESSAAFI, M'hamed, Grand Officier, Order of Tunisian Republic, 1963; United Nations Disaster Relief Co-ordinator, 1982–92; *b* 26 May 1930; *m* 1956, Hedwige Klat; one *s* one *d*. *Educ:* Sadiki Coll., Tunis; Sorbonne, Paris. Secretariat of State for For. Affairs, 1956; 1st Sec., Tunisian Embassy, London, 1956; 1st Sec., Tunisian Embassy, Washington, 1957; Secretariat of State for For. Affairs, Tunis: Dir of Amer. Dept, 1960; America and Internat. Confs Dept, 1962; Ambassador to London, 1964–69; Ambassador to Moscow, 1970–74; Ambassador to Bonn, 1974–76; Sec.-Gen., Ministry of Foreign Affairs, Tunis, 1969–70 and 1976–78; Ambassador to Belgium and EEC, 1978–79; Permanent Rep. of Tunisia to the UN, and Special Rep. of the Sec.-Gen., 1980–81, Chef de Cabinet 1982. *Address:* c/o Ministère des Affaires Etrangères, Tunis, Tunisia.

ESSAME, Enid Mary, MA Cantab; Headmistress of Queenswood School, 1943–71; 2nd *d* of Oliver Essame. *Educ:* Wyggeston Gram. Sch., Leicester; Girls' High Sch., Newark; Newnham Coll., Cambridge (Hist. Tripos, 1928); King's Coll., University of London (Certificate of Education, 1929). Mary Ewart Travelling Scholar, Newnham Coll., 1934–35; AM in Education, American Univ., Washington, DC, USA, 1935. Asst Headmistress Queenswood Sch., 1935–43. British Council lecturer, India and Pakistan, 1953, Nigeria, 1961. Governor, Chorleywood Coll. for Girls with Little or No Sight, 1962. Hon. Sec. Assoc. of Headmistresses of Boarding Schools, Pres. 1962–64. Chm., Assoc. of Ind. and Direct Grant Schools. Bd Mem., Schoolmistresses and Governesses Benevolent Instn, 1974–; Hon. Adviser, Nat. Assoc. for Gifted Children, 1974–. Governor: St Helen's Sch., Northwood; Channing Sch., Highgate; Trustee, Stormont Sch., Potters Bar. Mem., Overseas Grants Cttee, Help the Aged, 1981. JP Herts 1952–76. *Address:* 4 Elmroyd Avenue, Potters Bar, Herts EN6 2ED. *T:* Potters Bar (01707) 653255. *Clubs:* Royal Over-Seas League, Arts Theatre.

ESSAYAN, Michael, QC 1976; *b* 7 May 1927; *s* of late Kevork Loris Essayan and Rita Sirvarte (*née* Gulbenkian); *m* 1956, Geraldine St Lawrence Lee Guinness, *d* of K. E. L. Guinness, MBE; one *s* one *d*. *Educ:* France; Harrow; Balliol Coll., Oxford (1st Cl. Class. Hon. Mods 1949, 1st Cl. Lit. Hum. 1951, MA). Served with RA, 1945–48 (Palestine, 1947–48). Iraq Petroleum Co., London and ME, 1951–56. Called to the Bar, Middle Temple 1957 (Bencher 1983), joined Lincoln's Inn *ad eundem* 1958. Mem., Gen. Council of the Bar, 1987–88. Mem., Bd of Administration, Calouste Gulbenkian Foundn, Lisbon, 1981–, Hon. Pres., 1992–. Comdr, Order of Merit (Portugal), 1993. *Publications:* The New Supreme Court Costs (with M. J. Albery, QC), 1960; (ed with Hon. Mr Justice Walton) Adkin's Landlord and Tenant, 15th, 16th, 17th and 18th edns. *Recreations:* wine and wife. *Address:* 6 Chelsea Square, SW3 6LF. *T:* 0171–352 6786. *Club:* Brooks's.

ESSEN, Louis, OBE 1959; FRS 1960; DSc, PhD; retired; *b* 6 Sept. 1908; *s* of Fred Essen and Ada (*née* Edson); *m* 1937, Joan Margery Greenhalgh; four *d*. *Educ:* High Pavement Sch., Nottingham; London Univ. (Ext.). BSc 1928, PhD 1941, DSc 1948, London. Joined the National Physical Laboratory, 1929; Senior Principal Scientific Officer, 1956–60; Deputy Chief Scientific Officer, 1960–72. Charles Vernon Boys Prize, Phys. Soc. 1957; Tompion Gold Medal, Clockmakers' Company, 1957; Wolfe Award, 1959; A. S. Popov Gold Medal, USSR Acad. of Sciences, 1959. Hon. FUMIST, 1971. *Publications:* Velocity of Light and Radio Waves, 1969; The Special Theory of Relativity, 1971; scientific papers. *Recreations:* walking, gardening, music. *Address:* High Hallgarth, 41 Durleston Park Drive, Great Bookham, Surrey KT23 4AJ. *T:* Bookham (01372) 454103.

ESSER, Robin Charles; editorial and media consultant, since 1990; *b* 6 May 1935; *s* of late Charles and Winifred Eileen Esser; *m* 1959, Irene Shirley Clough (decd); two *s* two *d*; 1981, Tui (*née* France); two *s*. *Educ:* Wheelwright Grammar School, Dewsbury; Wadham College, Oxford (BA Hons, MA). Edited Oxford Univ. newspaper, Cherwell, 1954. Commissioned, King's Own Yorkshire Light Infantry, 1956. Freelance reporter, 1957–60; Daily Express: Staff Reporter, 1960; Editor, William Hickey Column, 1963; Features Editor, 1965; New York Bureau, 1969; Northern Editor, 1970; Exec. Editor, 1985; Consultant Editor, Evening News, 1977; Editor, Sunday Express, 1986–89; Gp Editl Consultant, Express Newspapers, 1989–90. *Publications:* The Hot Potato, 1969; The Paper Chase, 1971. *Recreations:* lunching, sailing, talking, reading. *Address:* 35 Elthiron Road, SW6 4BW. *Club:* Garrick.

ESSERY, David James; Under Secretary, Scottish Office Home and Health Department, since 1991; *b* 10 May 1938; *s* of Lawrence and Edna Essery; *m* 1963, Nora Sim; two *s* one *d. Educ:* Royal High Sch., Edinburgh. Entered Dept of Health for Scotland, 1956; Private Sec. to Minister of State, Scottish Office, 1968; Principal, Scottish Develt Dept, 1969; Assistant Secretary: Scottish Economic Planning Dept, 1976; Scottish Develt Dept, 1981–85; Under Sec., Scottish Office Agric. and Fisheries Dept, 1985–91.*Recreations:* reading, music, cricket. *Address:* (office) St Andrew's House, Edinburgh EH1 3DE. *T:* 031–244 2127.

ESSEX, 10th Earl of, *cr* 1661; **Robert Edward de Vere Capell;** Baron Capell, 1641; Viscount Malden, 1661; *b* 13 Jan. 1920; *s* of Arthur Algernon de Vere Capell (*d* 1924) and Alice Mabel (*d* 1951), *d* of James Currie, Wimbledon; *S* kinsman, 1981; *m* 1942, Doris Margaret, *d* of George Frederick Tomlinson, Morecambe; one *s*. *Heir: s* Viscount Malden, *qv*.

ESSEX, Francis; author, producer and composer; *b* 24 March 1929; *s* of Harold and Beatrice Essex-Lopresti; *m* 1956, Jeanne Shires; one *s* (and one *s* decd). *Educ:* Cotton Coll., N Staffs. Light Entertainment Producer, BBC Television, 1954–60; Sen. Prod., ATV Network Ltd, 1960–65; Controller of Progs, Scottish Television, 1965–69; ATV Network Ltd: Prodn Controller, 1969–76; Mem., Bd of Dirs, 1974; Dir of Production, 1976–81. Chaiman: Children's Network Cttee, ITV, 1976–81; Children's Adv. Cttee, TV-am, 1988–90. Chm., Conservatives Abroad, Javea, 1990–92. Wrote and presented, The Bells of St Martins, St Martin's Theatre, 1953; devised and directed, Six of One, Adelphi, 1964; author, Jolson, Victoria Palace, 1995; *television film scripts include:* Shillingbury Tales; Gentle Flame, Silent Scream; Cuffy series; *scores:* Luke's Kingdom; Seas Must Live; The Lightning Tree; Maddie With Love, etc; writer of plays and songs. Fellow, Royal Television Soc., 1974. British Acad. Light Entertainment Award, 1964, and Leonard Brett Award, 1964, 1981. *Publications:* Shillingbury Tales, 1983; Skerrymor Bay, 1984. *Recreations:* tennis, gardening. *Address:* Punta Vista, Aldea de las Cuevas, 03759 Benidoleig, Prov. de Alicante, Spain.

ESSEX-CATER, Dr Antony John, LRCP, MRCS; FFPHM; FRAI; Medical Officer of Health, States of Jersey, Channel Islands, 1974–88; Venereologist, General Hospital, Jersey, 1974–88; Vice President, National Association for Maternal and Child Welfare, since 1988 (Chairman, 1975–88); *b* 28 Sept. 1923; *s* of Herbert Stanley Cater and Helen Marjorie Essex; *m* 1947, Jane Mary Binning; three *s* one *d*. *Educ:* Solihull Sch.; King's Coll., Univ. of London; Charing Cross Hosp.; School of Hyg. and Trop. Med., Univ. of London. Bygott Postgrad. Schol., Univ. of London, 1952–53. DPH, DIH, DCH; FRSH; AFOM. Medical Br., RAF, 1948–50. Dep. MOH, Swansea, 1953–58; Admin. MOH, Birmingham, 1958–61; Dep. MOH, Manchester, 1961–68; County MOH, Monmouthshire, 1968–74. Part-time Lectr in Child Health, Univ. of Birmingham, 1958–61; Council of Europe Medical Fellow, 1968. Short-term Consultant, WHO, 1988–89. Mem. Exec. Cttee 1958, Vice-Chm. 1969, Nat. Assoc. for Maternal and Child Welfare; Member: Public Health Lab. Services Bd, 1969–75; Steering Cttee, Nat. Health Service Reorganization (Wales), 1971–72; Founder Fellow and Mem. First Bd, Fac. of Community Med., Royal Colls of Physicians of UK, 1972–73. Member: BMA; Med. Soc. for Study of Venereal Diseases. *Publications:* Synopsis of Public Health and Social Medicine, 1960, 2nd edn 1967; Manual of Public Health and Community Medicine, 3rd edn 1979; numerous papers on medical and allied subjects. *Recreations:* literary, music, sport. *Address:* Honfleur, La Vallette, Mont Cambrai, St Lawrence, Jersey, CI. *T:* Jersey (01534) 872438. *Club:* Society of Authors.

ESSIG, Philippe Louis Charles Marie; Officier de l'Ordre National du Mérite, 1984; Commandeur de la Légion d'Honneur, 1994; international consultant, since 1991; Chairman, Board of Transmanche-Link, 1988–91; *b* 19 July 1933; *s* of Jean Essig and Germaine Olivier; *m* 1960, Isabelle Lanier; one *s* three *d*. *Educ:* Lycée Janson-de Sailly; Ecole Polytechnique; Engineer, Ponts et Chaussées. Engr, Dakar-Niger railway, 1957–59; Asst Dir, Régie du chemin de fer Abidjan-Niger, 1960–61; Dir, Régie des chemins de fer du Cameroun, 1961–66; Régie autonome des transports parisiens (RATP): Chief Engr, Research Dept, 1966–71; Chief Op. Officer, Ops Dept, 1971–73; Man. Dir, Railways, Paris, 1973–81; Gen. Man., 1982–85; Pres., SNCF, 1985–88. Sec. of State for Housing, 1988. Officier de l'Ordre de la Valeur Camerounaise, 1966. *Recreations:* walking, ski-ing, shooting. *Address:* 5 Avenue Fourcault de Pavant, 78000 Versailles, France.

ESSLIN, Martin Julius, OBE 1972; Professor of Drama, Stanford University, California (for two quarters annually), 1977–88, now Emeritus; *b* 8 June 1918; *s* of Paul Pereszlenyi and Charlotte Pereszlenyi (*née* Schiffer); *m* 1947, Renate Gerstenberg; one *d*. *Educ:* Gymnasium, Vienna; Vienna Univ.; Reinhardt Seminar of Dramatic Art, Vienna. Joined BBC, 1940; Producer and Scriptwriter, BBC European Services, 1941–55; Asst Head, BBC European Productions Dept, 1955; Asst Head, Drama (Sound), BBC, 1961; Head of Drama (Radio), BBC, 1963–77. Awarded title Professor by Pres. of Austria, 1967; Vis. Prof. of Theatre, Florida State Univ., 1969–76. Hon. DLitt Kenyon Coll., Ohio, 1978. *Publications:* Brecht, A Choice of Evils, 1959; The Theatre of the Absurd, 1962; (ed) Beckett (anthology of critical essays), 1965; Harold Pinter, 1967; The Genius of the German Theatre, 1968; Reflections, Essays on Modern Theatre (NY), 1969 (UK, as Brief Chronicles, 1970); The Peopled Wound: the plays of Harold Pinter, 1970, rev. edn as Pinter: a study of his plays, 1973, 4th edn as Pinter: the Playwright, 1982, 5th edn 1992; (ed) The New Theatre of Europe, 1970; Artaud, 1976; An Anatomy of Drama, 1976; (ed) Illustrated Encyclopaedia of World Theatre, 1977; Mediations, Essays on Brecht, Beckett and the Media, 1981; The Age of Television, 1982; The Field of Drama, 1987; trans. Horváth, Judgement Day, 1986. *Recreations:* reading, book collecting. *Address:* 64 Loudoun Road, NW8 0NA. *T:* 0171–722 4243; Ballader's Plat, Winchelsea, Sussex TN36 4EN. *T:* Rye (01797) 226 392. *Club:* Garrick.

ESSWOOD, Paul Lawrence Vincent; singer (counter-tenor); Professor, Royal Academy of Music, since 1985; *b* West Bridgford, Nottingham, 6 June 1942; *s* of Alfred Walter Esswood and Freda Garratt; *m* 1st, 1966, Mary Lillian Cantrill, ARCM (marr. diss.), two *s*; 2nd, 1990, Aimée Désirée Blattmann; one *d*. *Educ:* West Bridgford Grammar Sch.; Royal Coll. of Music (ARCM). Lay-Vicar, Westminster Abbey, 1964–71. Prof., RCM, 1973–85; Specialist in baroque performance; first broadcast, BBC, 1965; co-founder: Pro Cantione Antiqua; A Cappella Male Voice Ensemble for Performance of Old Music, 1967; operatic debut in Cavalli's L'Erismena, Univ. of California, Berkeley, 1968; debut at La Scala, Milan with Zurich Opera in L'Incoronazione di Poppea and Il Ritorno d'Ulisse, 1978; Scottish Opera debut in Dido and Aeneas, 1978; world premieres: Penderecki's Paradise Lost, Chicago Lyric Opera, 1979; Philip Glass's Echnaton, Stüttgart Opera, 1984; performed in major festivals: Edinburgh, Leeds Triennial, English Bach, Vienna, Salzburg, Zurich, Hamburg, Berlin, Naples, Israel, Lucerne, Flanders, Wexford, Holland. Has made over 100 recordings for major cos, incl. solo recitals of Purcell, Schumann and English lute songs. Hon. RAM 1990. *Recreations:* gardening (organic), apiculture. *Address:* Jasmine Cottage, 42 Ferring Lane, Ferring, West Sussex BN12 6QT. *T:* and *Fax:* Worthing (0903) 504480.

ESTEVE-COLL, Dame Elizabeth Anne Loosemore, DBE 1995; Vice-Chancellor, University of East Anglia, since 1995; *b* 14 Oct. 1938; *o d* of P. W. and Nora Kingdon; *m* 1960, José Alexander Timothy Esteve-Coll (*d* 1980). *Educ:* Darlington Girls High Sch.; Birkbeck Coll., London Univ. (BA 1976). Head of Learning Resources, Kingston Polytechnic, 1977; University Librarian, Univ. of Surrey, 1982; Keeper, National Art Library, 1985, Dir, 1988–95, V&A Museum. *Recreations:* reading, music, foreign travel. *Address:* University of East Anglia, Norwich NR4 7TJ.

ESTEY, Hon. Willard Zebedee, CC 1990; Counsel, McCarthy Tétrault, Toronto, since 1988; Chancellor, Wilfrid Laurier University, Waterloo, Ont, since 1990; *b* 10 Oct. 1919; *s* of James Wilfred Estey and Muriel Baldwin Estey; *m* 1946, Marian Ruth McKinnon; three *s* one *d*. *Educ:* Univ. of Saskatchewan (BA, LLB); Harvard Law Sch. (LLM). Mem., Bar of Sask., 1942 and of Ont, 1947; QC Ont 1960. Prof., Coll. of Law, Univ. of Sask., 1946–47; Lectr, Osgoode Hall Law Sch., 1947–51. Practised law, Toronto, 1947–72. Pres., Canadian Bar Assoc., Ont, 1972. Mem. Court of Appeal, 1973, and Chief Justice of High Court, Supreme Court of Ont, 1975; Chief Justice of Ontario, 1976; Justice of Supreme Court of Canada, 1977–88. Commissioner: Steel Profits Inquiry, Royal Commn of Inquiry, 1974; Air Canada Inquiry, 1975; Inquiry into certain banking operations, 1985–86. Special Advr to Chm., Bank of Nova Scotia, 1990–. Hon. LLD: Wilfrid Laurier Univ., Waterloo, Ont, 1977; Univ. of Toronto, 1979; Univ. of W Ont, 1980; Law Soc. of Upper Canada, 1981; Univ. of Saskatchewan, 1984; Univ. of Lethbridge, 1985. *Address:* Suite 4700, Toronto Dominion Bank Tower, Toronto Dominion Centre, Toronto, Ont M5K 1E6, Canada.

ETCHELLS, (Dorothea) Ruth, MA, BD; Principal, St John's College with Cranmer Hall, University of Durham, 1979–88 (Hon. Fellow, St John's College, Durham, 1991); *b* 17 April 1931; *d* of late Walter and Ada Etchells. *Educ:* Merchant Taylor's School for Girls, Crosby, Liverpool; Universities of Liverpool (MA) and London (BD). Head of English Dept, Aigburth Vale High Sch., Liverpool, 1959; Lectr in English, 1963, Sen. Lectr in English and Resident Tutor, 1965, Chester College of Education; Trevelyan College, Univ. of Durham: Resident Tutor and part-time Lectr in English, 1968; Vice Principal, 1972; Sen. Lectr, 1973; Mem. Council, Durham Univ., 1985–88. Examining Chaplain to Bishop of Bath and Wells, 1984–88. Member: Gen. Synod, 1985–; Doctrine Commn, 1986–91; Crown Appointments Commn, 1987–; Bishop's Council and Standing Cttee of Durham Diocesan Synod (Chm., House of Laity, 1988–94); Hon. Vice-Pres., CMS, 1992–. Vice-Chm., Durham FHSA, 1990– (Chm., Med. Services Cttee, 1990–). Mem., Governing Council, Ridley Coll., Cambridge. Trustee, Anvil, 1983–92. DD Lambeth, 1992. *Publications:* Unafraid To Be, 1969; The Man with the Trumpet, 1970; A Model of Making, 1983; (ed) Poets and Prophets, 1988; Praying with the English Poets, 1990; Just as I am: personal prayers for every day, 1994. *Recreations:* friends, quiet, country walking, pets. *Address:* 12 Dunelm Court, South Street, Durham DH1 4QX. *T:* Durham (091) 3841497.

ETHERINGTON, Stuart James; Chief Executive, Royal National Institute for Deaf People, since 1991; *b* 26 Feb. 1955; *s* of Ronald Etherington and Dorothy Etherington (*née* West). *Educ:* Sondes Place Sch., Dorking; Brunel Univ. (BSc Politics); Essex Univ. (MA Soc. Sci. Planning); London Business Sch. (MBA). Social Worker, London Borough of Hillingdon, 1977–79; Sen. Res. Officer, Joseph Rowntree Meml Trust, Circle 33, 1980–82; Policy Advr, BASW, 1982–84; Director: Good Practices in Mental Health, 1984–87; Public Affairs, RNID, 1987–91. *Publications:* Mental Health and Housing, 1984; Emergency Duty Teams, 1985; The Sensitive Bureaucracy, 1986; Social Work and Citizenship, 1987. *Recreations:* reading, gliding. *Address:* Royal National Institute for Deaf People, 105 Gower Street, WC1E 6AH; 40 Walnut Tree Road, Greenwich, SE10 9EU. *T:* 0181–305 1379.

ETHERINGTON, William; MP (Lab) Sunderland North, since 1992; *b* 17 July 1941; *m* 1963, Irene; two *d*. *Educ:* Monkwearmouth Grammar Sch.; Durham Univ. Apprentice fitter, Austin & Pickersgill shipyard, 1957–63; fitter, Dawdon Colliery, 1963–83; full-time NUM official, 1983–92. Mem., NUM, 1963– (Vice-Pres., NE Area, 1988–92). *Address:* House of Commons, SW1A 0AA.

ETHERINGTON-SMITH, (Raymond) Gordon (Antony), CMG 1962; HM Diplomatic Service, retired; *b* 1 Feb. 1914; *o s* of late T. B. Etherington-Smith and Henriette de Pitner; *m* 1950, Mary Elizabeth Besly (*d* 1989); one *s* three *d*. *Educ:* Downside; Magdalen Coll., Oxford; Sch. of Oriental and African Studies, London Univ. Entered FO, 1936. Served at: Berlin, 1939; Copenhagen, 1939–40; Washington, 1940–42; Chungking, 1943–45; Kashgar, 1945–46; Moscow, 1947; Foreign Office, 1947–52; Holy See, 1952–54; Counsellor, Saigon, 1954–57; The Hague, 1958–61; Office of UK Commissioner-Gen. for South-East Asia, Singapore, 1961–63; Ambassador to Vietnam, 1963–66; Minister, and Dep. Commandant, Berlin, 1966–70; Ambassador to Sudan, 1970–74. *Publication:* Maximilian's Lieutenant, 1993. *Recreations:* physical and mental exercise. *Address:* Lower Cottage, 30 High Street, Hindon, Salisbury, Wilts SP3 6DR. *T:* Tisbury (01747) 820301. *Club:* Oriental.

ETHERTON, Terence Michael Elkan Barnet; QC 1990; FCIArb; *b* 21 June 1951; *s* of Alan Kenneth Etherton and Elaine Myrtle (*née* Maccoby). *Educ:* Holmewood House Sch., Tunbridge Wells; St Paul's Sch., London (Sen. Foundn Schol.); Corpus Christi Coll., Cambridge (Open Exhibnr; MA (History and Law); LLM). FCIArb 1993. Called to the Bar, Gray's Inn, 1974 (Uthwatt Schol., 1972; Holker Sen. Award, 1974; Arden Atkin and Mould Prize, 1975); in practice, 1975–; Mem., Gray's Inn and Lincoln's Inn. Mem., Bar Council, 1978–81; Chm., Young Barristers' Cttee of Bar Council, 1980–81; Mem., Lord Rawlinson's Cttee on the Constitution of the Senate of the Inns of Court and the Bar, 1985–86; Mem., Mental Health Review Tribunal, 1994–. Dir (non-exec.), Riverside Mental Health NHS Trust, 1992– (Chm., Ethics Forum, 1994–). Claims Adjudicator, Savings and Investment Bank (Iom) Depositors' Compensation Scheme, 1993–94. Chm., DoE/MAFF Indep. Review Panel on designation of nitrate vulnerable zones under EC Nitrate Directive, 1995. Mem. Council, RHBNC, 1992– (Chm., Academic Staff Dismissal Appeals Tribunal, 1994–). Captain, Cambridge Univ. Fencing Team, 1971–72; Mem., GB Sen. Internat. Fencing Team (Sabre), 1977–80 (World Championships, 1977, 1978, 1979); England Sabre Team Gold Medal, Commonwealth Fencing Championships, 1978; selected for Moscow Olympics, GB Fencing Team, 1980. *Address:* 8 New Square, Lincoln's Inn, WC2A 3QP. *Club:* Hawks (Cambridge).

ETIANG, Paul Orono, BA London; Minister of Information, Uganda, since 1991; *b* 15 Aug. 1938; *s* of late Keziron Orono and Mirabu Achom Orono; *m* 1967, Zahra Ali Foum; two *s* two *d*. *Educ:* Makerere Univ. Coll. Uganda Admin. Officer, 1962–64; Asst Sec., Foreign Affairs, 1964–65; 3rd Sec., 1965–66, 2nd Sec., 1966–67, Uganda Embassy, Moscow; 1st Sec., Uganda Mission to UN, New York, 1968; Counsellor, 1968–69, High Commissioner, 1969–71, Uganda High Commission, London; Chief of Protocol and Marshal of the Diplomatic Corps, Uganda, 1971; Permanent Sec., Uganda Min. of Foreign Affairs, 1971–73; Minister of State for Foreign Affairs, 1973; Minister of State in the President's office, 1974; Minister of Transport and Communications, July 1976, of Transport, Communications and Works, Mar. 1977, of Transport and Works, 1978; an Asst. Sec.-Gen., OAU, Addis Ababa, 1978–87; Minister for Regl Co-operation, March–Dec. 1988; Minister of Commerce, 1989–91. *Recreations:* chess, classical music, billiards. *Address:* Ministry of Information, PO Box 7142, Kampala, Uganda.

EUSTACE, Dudley Graham, FCA; Vice President and Chief Financial Officer, Philips Electronics NV, Eindhoven, since 1992; *b* 3 July 1936; *s* of Albert and Mary Eustace; *m* 1964, Carol Diane Zakrajsek; two *d*. *Educ:* Cathedral Sch., Bristol; Univ. of Bristol (BA Econ). FCA 1972. John Barritt & Son, Hamilton, Bermuda, 1962; Internat. Resort Facilities, Ont, 1963; Aluminium Securities Ltd, Montreal, 1964–65; Aluminium Co. of Canada Ltd, Vancouver, 1966–69, Montreal, 1969–73; Alcan Aluminio America Latina, Buenos Aires, 1973–76, Rio de Janeiro, 1976–79; Empresa Nacional del Aluminio, Madrid, 1979–83; Alcan Aluminium Ltd, Montreal, 1983–84; British Alcan Aluminium PLC, Gerrards Cross, Bucks, 1984–87; BAe, 1987–92 (Finance Dir, 1988–92). Member: Council, ECGD, 1988–92; Board, Assoc. for Monetary Union in Europe, 1992–. *Recreations:* jogging, gardening, reading. *Address:* Residence de Karpen #137, Javalaan, Eindhoven, The Netherlands.

EUSTACE, Sir (Joseph) Lambert, GCMG 1985; GCVO 1985; Governor-General, St Vincent and the Grenadines, since 1985; *b* 28 Feb. 1908; *s* of Reynold Lambert Eustace and Beatrice Alexandrine Eustace (*née* St Hilaire); *m* 1945, Faustina Eileen Gatherer; one *s* one *d* (and one *d* decd). *Educ:* St Vincent Grammar School. Founded Intermediate High Sch., 1926; teacher of English, Maths and French, incl. latterly at St Vincent Grammar Sch., 1926–52; Manager, St Vincent Cotton Ginnery, 1952–59; Manager of own factory (oil, soap and feeds), 1959–66; MP South Leeward, 1966–71; Speaker, House of Assembly, 1972–74. Deleg. to overseas confs, 1957–74. *Recreations:* reading, gardening, woodwork. *Address:* Government House, Montrose, St Vincent and the Grenadines, West Indies. *T:* 61401.

EUSTON, Earl of; James Oliver Charles FitzRoy, MA, FCA; *b* 13 Dec. 1947; *s* and *heir* of 11th Duke of Grafton, *qv*; *m* 1972, Lady Clare Kerr, BA, *d* of Marquess of Lothian, *qv*; one *s* four *d*. *Educ:* Eton; Magdalene Coll., Cambridge (MA). Dir, Smith St Aubyn & Co. (Holdings) plc, 1980–86; Executive Director: Enskilda Securities, 1982–87; Jamestown Investments, 1987–91; Finance Director: Central Capital Hldgs, 1988–91; Capel-Cure Myers Capital Management, 1988–. *Heir: s* Viscount Ipswich, *qv*. *Address:* 6 Vicarage Gardens, W8 4AH; The Racing Stables, Euston, Thetford, Norfolk IP24 2QT.

EVANS; *see* Parry-Evans and Parry Evans.

EVANS, family name of **Baroness Blackstone** and **Baron Mountevans.**

EVANS, A. Briant; Hon. Consulting Gynæcological Surgeon, Westminster Hospital and Chelsea Hospital for Women; Hon. Consulting Obstetric Surgeon, Queen Charlotte's Maternity Hospital; *b* 26 June 1909; *e s* of late Arthur Evans, OBE, MD, MS, FRCS; *m* 1939, Audrey Marie, *er d* of late Roland Eveleigh Holloway; three *s*. *Educ:* Westminster Sch.; Gonville and Caius Coll., Cambridge; Westminster Hosp. MA, MB, BCh Cantab; FRCS; FRCOG. Sometime Examiner in Obstetrics to Univs of Cambridge and London and to Royal College of Obstetricians and Gynæcologists. Temp. Lieut-Col RAMC, served in Egypt, Italy and Austria; OC No. 9 Field Surgical Unit. *Address:* 8 New Court, Sutton Manor, Sutton Scotney, Winchester, Hants SO21 3JX. *T:* Winchester (01962) 760214.

EVANS, Alun; *see* Evans, T. A.

EVANS, Alun S.; *see* Sylvester-Evans.

EVANS, Amanda Louise Elliot, (Mrs A. S. Duncan); Editor, Homes & Gardens, since 1986; *b* 19 May 1958; *d* of Brian Royston Elliot Evans and June Annabella (*née* Gilderdale); *m* 1989, Andrew Sinclair Duncan; one *s* one *d*. *Educ:* Tonbridge Girls' Grammar Sch. Editorial writer, Interiors magazine, 1981–83; Consultant Editor, Mitchell Beazley Publishers, 1983–84; freelance writer and stylist on A la carte, Tatler, Country Homes & Interiors, Sunday Times, 1984–86; Dep. Editor, Homes & Gardens, April–Oct. 1986. *Recreations:* mountain walking, opera, camping. *Address:* c/o Homes & Gardens, IPC, King's Reach Tower, Stamford Street, SE1 9LS. *T:* 0171–261 5678.

EVANS, Anne Celia; *see* Segall, A. C.

EVANS, Anthony; *see* Evans, D. A.

EVANS, Sir Anthony (Adney), 2nd Bt, *cr* 1920; *b* 5 Aug. 1922; *s* of Sir Walter Harry Evans, 1st Bt, and Margaret Mary, *y d* of late Thomas Adney Dickens; *S* father 1954; married; two *s* one *d*. *Educ:* Shrewsbury; Merton Coll., Oxford.

EVANS, Rt. Hon. Sir Anthony (Howell Meurig), Kt 1985; RD 1968; PC 1992; **Rt. Hon. Lord Justice Evans;** a Lord Justice of Appeal, since 1992; *b* 11 June 1934; *s* of late His Honour David Meurig Evans and Joy Diedericke Sander; *m* 1963, Caroline Mary Fyffe Mackie, *d* of late Edwin Gordon Mackie; one *s* two *d*. *Educ:* Bassaleg Sec. Grammar Sch., Mon; Shrewsbury Sch.; St John's Coll., Cambridge. Nat. Service, RNVR, 1952–54 (Lt-Comdr RNR). BA 1957, LLB 1958, Cantab. Called to Bar, Gray's Inn, 1958 (Arden Scholar and Birkenhead Scholar; Bencher, 1979); QC 1971; a Recorder, 1972–84; a Presiding Judge, Wales and Chester Circuit, 1986–88; a Judge of the High Court of Justice, QBD, 1984–92; Judge in charge of the Commercial Court, 1991–92. Mem. Melbourne, Vic, Bar, 1975–84, Hon. Mem., 1985. Dep. Chm., Boundary Commn for Wales, 1989–92. Hon. Fellow, Internat. Acad. of Trial Lawyers, 1985; FCIArb 1986 (Patron, Wales Br., 1988). *Publication:* (Jt Editor) The Law of the Air (Lord McNair), 1964. *Recreations:* sailing, music. *Address:* c/o Royal Courts of Justice, Strand, WC2A 2LL. *Clubs:* Royal Lymington Yacht, Royal Southampton Yacht; Royal Welsh Yacht.

EVANS, Prof. Anthony John, PhD, FLA; Professor in Department of Information and Library Studies (formerly Library and Information Studies), 1973–95, and Director, Alumni Office, 1992–95, Loughborough University of Technology; *b* 1 April 1930; *s* of William John and Marian Audrey (*née* Young); *m* 1954, Anne (*née* Horwell); two *d*. *Educ:* Queen Elizabeth's Hosp., Bristol; Sch. of Pharmacy and University College, Univ. of London. BPharm, PhD. Lectr in Pharm. Eng. Sci., Sch. of Pharmacy, Univ. of London, 1954–58; Librarian, Sch. of Pharmacy, Univ. of London, 1958–63; University Librarian, 1964–91, and Dean, Sch. of Educnl Studies, 1973–76, Loughborough Univ. of Technology. Pres., IATUL, 1970–75 (Bd Mem. and Treasurer, 1968–70; Hon. Life Mem., 1976–); Mem. Exec. Bd, IFLA, 1983–89 (Treas., 1985–89; Consultative Cttee, 1968–76; Standing Cttee on Sci. and Tech. Libraries, 1977–87; Standing Cttee on Univ. Libraries, 1989–93); Pres., Commonwealth Library Assoc., 1994–; ASLIB: Vice-Pres., 1985–88; Mem. Council, 1970–80, 1985–88; Internat. Relations Cttee, 1974–85; Annual Lecture, 1985; BSI: Mem. Bd, 1984–86; Chm., Documentation Standards Cttee, 1980–86 (Mem., 1976–86); Member: Inf. Systems Council, 1980–86. Member: Adv. Cttee, Sci. Ref. Library, 1975–83; Vice-Chancellors and Principals Cttee on Libraries, 1972–77; Jt UNESCO/ICSU Cttee for establishment of UNISIST, 1968–71; Internat. Cttee, LA, 1985–; Adv. Council to Bd of Dirs of Engineering Information Inc., USA, 1986–; Chm., Adv. Gp on Documentation Standards, ISO, 1983–85; consultancy work for British Council, ODA, UNESCO, UNIDO, World Bank in Africa, Asia and Latin America, especially China, Kenya and Mexico. Hon. FLA, 1990. Medal IFLA, 1989. *Publications:* (with D. Train) Bibliography of the tabletting of medicinal substances, 1964, suppl. 1965; (with R. G. Rhodes and S. Keenan) Education and training of users of scientific and technical information, 1977; articles in librarianship and documentation. *Recreations:* canal cruising, sport, model railways. *Address:* 78 Valley Road, Loughborough, Leics LE11 3QA. *T:* Loughborough (01509) 215670. *Club:* Commonwealth Trust.

EVANS, Anthony Thomas; Metropolitan Stipendiary Magistrate, since 1990; *b* 29 Sept. 1943; *s* of late Emlyn Roger Evans and Dorothy Evans; *m* 1st, 1965, Gillian Celia Mather (*d* 1988); one *s*; 2nd, 1991, Margaret Elizabeth Ryles (*née* Howorth); one step *s* one step *d*. *Educ:* Bishop Gore Grammar Sch., Swansea; Univ. of Manchester (LLB 1965; LLM 1968). Asst Lectr, Univ. of Manchester, 1965–68; admitted Solicitor, 1971; Partner: Haye & Reid, 1971–85; Evans & Co., 1985–89; sole practitioner, 1989–90. Chairman: Inner London Family Courts, 1991–; Inner London Youth Courts, 1993–. Mem., British Acad. of Forensic Scis. *Recreations:* reading, music, theatre. *Address:* Highbury Corner Magistrates' Court, 51 Holloway Road, N7 8JA.

EVANS, (Arthur) Mostyn; General Secretary, Transport and General Workers Union, 1978–85; Member, TUC General Council, 1977–85; *b* 13 July 1925; *m* 1947, Laura Bigglestone; two *s* three *d* (and one *s* decd). *Educ:* Cefn Coed Primary Sch., S Wales; Church Road Secondary Modern Sch., Birmingham. District Officer, Birmingham, Chem. and Eng. Industries, 1956; Regional Officer, Midlands, 1960; Nat. Officer, Eng., 1966; National Secretary: Chem., Rubber, and Oil Industries, 1969; Engineering Industries, 1969; (Automotive Section), TGWU, 1969–73; Nat. Organiser, TGWU, 1973–78. Part-time Mem., Nat. Bus Co., 1976–78; Member: BOTB, 1978–79; NEDC, 1978–84; Exec., ITF, 1980–; Council, ACAS, 1982–; Pres., ICEF, 1982– (Vice-Pres., 1980–82). Councillor (Lab), Borough of Kings Lynn and W Norfolk, 1991–. *Recreation:* music. *Address:* Cheney House, Cheney Hill, Heacham, King's Lynn, Norfolk PE31 7BX. *T:* Heacham (01485) 70477.

EVANS, Briant; *see* Evans, A. B.

EVANS, Sir Charles; *see* Evans, Sir R. C.

EVANS, Christina Hambley; *see* Brown, Tina.

EVANS, Rev. Prof. Christopher Francis, FBA 1991; MA; Professor of New Testament Studies, King's College, London, 1962–77, now Emeritus Professor, University of London; *b* 7 Nov. 1909; 2nd *s* of Frank and Beatrice Evans; *m* 1941, Elna Mary (*d* 1980), *d* of Walter and Elizabeth Burt; one *s*. *Educ:* King Edward's Sch., Birmingham; Corpus Christi Coll., Cambridge. Asst Curate, St Barnabas, Southampton, 1934–38; Tutor Schol. Canc. Linc., 1938–44; Chaplain and Divinity Lecturer, Lincoln Training Coll., 1944–48; Chaplain, Fellow and Lecturer in Divinity, Corpus Christi Coll., Oxford, 1948–58, Emeritus Fellow, 1977; Lightfoot Prof. of Divinity in the University of Durham and Canon of Durham Cathedral, 1959–62; Vis. Fellow, Trevelyan Coll., Durham, 1982–83. Select Preacher, University of Oxford, 1955–57; Proctor in Convocation for University of Oxford, 1955–58; Exam. Chaplain: to Bishop of Bristol, 1948–58; to Bishop of Durham, 1958–62; to Archbishop of Canterbury, 1962–74; to Bishop of Lichfield, 1969–75. FKC, 1970. Hon. DLitt Southampton, 1977; Hon. DD Glasgow, 1987. *Publications:* Christology and Theology, 1961; The Lord's Prayer, 1963; The Beginning of the Gospel, 1968; Resurrection and the New Testament, 1970; (ed jtly) The Cambridge History of the Bible: vol. I, From the Beginnings to Jerome, 1970; Is 'Holy Scripture' Christian?, 1971; Explorations in Theology 2, 1977; The Theology of Rhetoric, 1988; Saint Luke, 1990; contribs to Journal of Theological Studies, Theology and Religious Studies, to Studies in the Gospels and to Christian Faith and Communist Faith. *Recreation:* fishing. *Address:* 4 Church Close, Cuddesdon, Oxford OX44 9HD. *T:* Wheatley (01865) 874406.

EVANS, Dr Christopher Paul; Director, Housing and Urban Monitoring and Analysis and Housing Policy, Department of the Environment, since 1993; *b* 25 Dec. 1948; *s* of Colwyn and Margery Evans; *m* 1971, Margaret Beckett; two *d*. *Educ:* St Julian's High Sch., Newport; Trinity Coll., Cambridge (MA, DipArch, PhD). Department of the Environment, 1975–: Private Sec. to Permanent Sec.,1978–80; Principal, 1980; Asst Sec., 1985; Under Sec., 1993. *Address:* 2 Marsham Street, SW1P 3EB. *T:* 0171–276 5594.

EVANS, Air Vice-Marshal Clive Ernest, CBE 1982; Senior Directing Staff (Air), Royal College of Defence Studies, 1988–91, retired; *b* 21 April 1937; *s* of Leslie Roberts Evans and Mary Kathleen Butcher; *m* 1963, Therese Goodrich; one *s* one *d*. *Educ:* St Dunstan's Coll., Catford. Flying training, RAF, 1955–56; graduated as pilot, 1956, as qualified flying instr, 1960; served on Vampires, Jet Provosts, Canberras, Lightnings and F111s (exchange tour with USAF), 1960–72; RAF Staff Coll., 1972; PSO to Controller Aircraft, 1973; OC No 24 Sqn (Hercules), 1974–76; Nat. Defence Coll., 1976–77; DS RAF Staff Coll., 1977–79; Head of RAF Presentation Team, 1979–81; OC RAF Lyneham, 1981–83; RCDS, 1984; COS and Dep. Comdr, British Forces Falkland Is, 1985; Dep. Air Sec., 1985–88. *Recreations:* reading, cricket, golf, gardening. *Address:* 43 Purley Bury Close, Purley, Surrey CR8 1HW. *T:* 0181–660 8115. *Club:* Royal Air Force.

EVANS, Colin Rodney; Director, Weapon Systems Research Laboratory, Defence Science and Technology Organisation, Adelaide, 1989–91; *b* 5 June 1935; *s* of John Evans and Annie (*née* Lawes); *m* 1963, Jennifer MacIntosh; two *d*. *Educ:* Bridlington Sch.; Woolwich Polytechnic; Imperial Coll., London. BSc(Eng); HND; MIMechE. Scientific Officer, ARDE (now RARDE), 1959–60; Lectr, RNC, Greenwich, 1960–61; Scientific Officer, then Sen. Scientific Officer and PSO, ARDE, 1961–69; SO to Chief Scientist (Army), MoD, 1969–71; British Defence Staff, Washington, 1971–73; SPSO, RARDE, 1973–79; Dep. Dir, Scientific and Technical Intell., MoD, 1979–81; seconded to Sir Derek Rayner's study team on efficiency in govt, 1981; RCDS, 1982; Dep. Dir (1), RARDE, 1983–84; Asst Under Sec. of State, MoD, Dep. Dir (Vehicles) and Hd of RARDE (Chertsey), 1985–89. President: Kent Squash Rackets Assoc., 1992–; Maudslay Soc., 1993–. *Recreations:* squash, tennis, bird watching, stamp collecting. *Address:* c/o Midland Bank, 86 High Street, Tunbridge Wells TN1 1YE.

EVANS, Dr (Daniel) John (Owen); Head of Music Department, BBC Radio 3, since 1993; *b* 17 Nov. 1953; *s* of John Leslie Evans and Avis Evans (*née* Jones). *Educ:* Gowerton Boys' Grammar Sch.; University Coll., Cardiff (BMus 1975; MA 1976; PhD 1984). ATCL 1974. First Res. Schol., Britten-Pears Liby and Archive, Aldeburgh, Suffolk, 1980–84; Music Producer, BBC Radio 3, 1985–89; Sen. Producer, BBC Singers, 1989–92; Chief Producer, Series, 1992–93. Artistic Director: Volte Face Opera, 1986–89; Covent Garden Chamber Orch., 1990–94; Mem., South Bank Music Adv. Panel, 1994–. Exec. Trustee, Peter Pears Award, 1989–92. Prix Italia Award and Charles Heidsieck Award, 1989; Royal Philharmonic Soc. Award, 1994. *Publications:* (with D. Mitchell) Benjamin Britten: pictures from a life 1913–1976, 1978; (ed) Benjamin Britten: his life and operas, by Eric Walter White, rev. edn 1982; contributions to: A Britten Companion, 1984; A Britten Source Book, 1987; ENO, Royal Opera Hse and Cambridge Opera guides on Britten's Peter Grimes, Gloriana, The Turn of the Screw and Death in Venice. *Recreations:* theatre, musicals, cooking, entertaining, travel. *Address:* 114 Lauderdale Mansions, Lauderdale Road, Maida Vale, W9 1NF. *T:* 0171–286 1876.

EVANS, Dr David; *see* Evans, Dr W. D.

EVANS, David, CBE 1992; Director-General, National Farmers' Union, since 1985 (Deputy Director-General, 1984–85); *b* 7 Dec. 1935; *yr s* of William Price Evans and late Ella Mary Evans; *m* 1960, Susan Carter Connal, *yr d* of late Dr John Connal and Antoinette Connal; one *s* one *d*. *Educ:* Welwyn Garden City Grammar Sch.; University Coll. London (BScEcon). Joined Min. of Agriculture, Fisheries and Food, 1959; Private Sec. to Parliamentary Sec. (Lords), 1962–64; Principal, 1964; Principal Private Sec. to Ministers, 1970–71; Asst Sec., 1971; seconded to Cabinet Office, 1972–74; Under-Sec., MAFF, 1976–80; joined NFU as Chief Economic and Policy Adviser, 1981. *Address:* 6 Orchard Rise, Kingston upon Thames, Surrey KT2 7EY. *T:* 0181–942 7701.

EVANS, Rev. David; Rector of Heyford with Stowe-Nine-Churches, since 1989; *b* Llanglydwen, Dyfed, 15 Feb. 1937; *o s* of late Rev. W. Noel Evans, JP, and Frances M. Evans; *m* 1962, Jenifer Margaret (*née* Cross); three s. Educ: Sherborne; Keble Coll., Oxford (MA); Wells Theological Coll. (BD London). 2nd Lieut, Royal Signals, 1956–57. Minor Canon, Brecon Cath., and Asst Curate, Brecon St Mary with Battle, 1964–68; Bishop's Chaplain to Students, UC, Swansea, and Asst Curate, Swansea St Mary with Holy Trinity, 1968–71; Bishop of Birmingham's Chaplain for Samaritan and Social Work, 1971–75; Dir, Samaritans of Swansea, 1969–71, of Birmingham, 1971–75; Jt Gen. Sec., 1975–84, Gen. Sec., 1984–89, The Samaritans; Chaplain, Northamptonshire Police, 1990–. Licensed Priest, Dio. of Oxford, 1975–89. Mem., Church in Wales Liturgical Commn, 1969–75. *Recreations:* music, railways. *Address:* The Rectory, Church Lane, Nether Heyford, Northampton NN7 3LQ. *T:* Weedon (01327) 340487.

EVANS, Prof. David Alan Price, FRCP; Director of Medicine, Riyadh Armed Forces Hospital, Saudi Arabia, since 1983; Hon. Professor of Medicine, King Saud University, since 1988; *b* 6 March 1927; *s* of Owen Evans and Ellen (*née* Jones). *Educ:* Univ. of Liverpool (MD, PhD, DSc); Johns Hopkins Univ. RAMC, Jun. Med. Specialist, BMH Kure, Field Hosp. Korea, BMH Singapore and BMH Kinrara, Malaysia, 1953–55; Capt. RAMC, 1954–55. House Physician and House Surg. 1951–52, and Med. Registrar, 1956–58 and 1959–60, United Liverpool Hosps; Res. Fellow, Div. of Med. Genetics, Dept of Medicine, Johns Hopkins Hosp., 1958–59; Lectr 1960–62, Sen. Lectr 1962–68, Personal Chair, 1968–72, Dept of Medicine, Univ. of Liverpool; Prof. and Chm., Dept of Medicine and Dir, Nuffield Unit Medical Genetics, Univ. of Liverpool, 1972–83; Cons. Physician, Royal Liverpool Hosp. (formerly Royal Liverpool Infirmary) and Broadgreen Hosp., Liverpool, 1965–83. Visiting Professor: Karolinska Univ., Stockholm, 1968; Johns Hopkins Univ, 1972. Lectures: Poulson Meml, Oslo Univ., 1972; first Sir Henry Dale, and Medallist, Johns Hopkins Univ., 1972; first Walter Idris Jones, Univ. of Wales, 1974; Watson Smith, RCP, 1976. Member: BMA, 1951; Assoc. of Physicians of GB and Ireland, 1964; Gastroenterological Soc., 1964. University of Liverpool: Roberts Prize, 1959; Samuels Prize, 1965; Thornton Prize, Eastern Psychiatric Assoc., 1964. Life Mem., Johns Hopkins Soc. of Scholars, 1972. Scientific Ed., Saudi Med. Jl, 1983–93; Editl Bd, Pharmacogenetics, 1991–. *Publications:* medical and scientific, principally concerned with genetic factors determining responses to drugs. *Recreation:* country pursuits. *Address:* 28 Montclair Drive, Liverpool L18 0HA. *T:* 0151–722 3112; Pen-yr-Allt, Paradwys, Llangristiolus, Bodorgan, Gwynedd LL62 5PD. *T:* Holyhead (01407) 840346.

EVANS, (David) Anthony; QC 1983; a Recorder of the Crown Court, since 1980; *b* 15 March 1939; *s* of Thomas John Evans, MD and May Evans; *m* 1974, Angela Bewley, *d* of John Clive Bewley, JP and Cynthia Bewley; two *d*. *Educ:* Clifton Coll., Bristol; Corpus Christi Coll., Cambridge (BA). Called to the Bar, Gray's Inn, 1965; in practice at the Bar, Swansea, 1965–84, London, 1984–. DTI Inspector, 1988–92. *Recreations:* sport of all kinds. *Address:* Carey Hall, Neath, W Glamorgan SA10 7AU. *T:* Neath (01639) 643859; 8 Coleherne Mews, SW10 9EA. *T:* 0171–370 1025; 9–12 Bell Yard, WC2A 2JR. *T:* 0171–404 1400. *Clubs:* Turf, MCC; Cardiff and County (Cardiff); Swansea Cricket and Football (Swansea).

EVANS, Ven. David Eifion; Archdeacon of Cardigan, 1967–79; *b* 22 Jan, 1911; *e s* of John Morris and Sarah Pryse Evans, Borth, Cards, Dyfed; *m* 1st, 1941, Iris Elizabeth Gravelle (*d* 1973); one *s*; 2nd, 1979, Madeleine Kirby. *Educ:* Ardwyn, Aberystwyth; UCW, Aberystwyth; St Michael's Coll., Llandaff. BA 1932; MA 1951. Deacon, 1934; Priest, 1935. Curate: Llanfihangel-ar-Arth, 1934–36; Llanbadarn Fawr, 1936–40; Chaplain to the Forces, 1940–45; Vicar, Llandeloy with Llanrheithan, 1945–48; Penrhyncoch, 1948, with Elerch, 1952–57; St Michael, Aberystwyth, 1957–67; Rural Dean, Llanbadarn Fawr, 1957–67; Chaplain, Anglican Students, 1966–67; Canon of St David's Cathedral (Caerfai), 1963–67; Chaplain, Earl of Lisburne, 1967–69; Vicar: Llanafan with Llanwnnws, 1967–69; Newcastle Emlyn, 1969–79. Member: Governing Body of Church in Wales, 1956–79; Representative Body of Church in Wales, 1967–79; Court of Governors, and Council, UCW, Aberystwyth, 1958–69; Sub-Visitor, St David's Univ. Coll., Lampeter, 1972–79. *Publications:* Influence of Tractarianism in Wales, 1952 (Welsh Nat. Eisteddfod, Aberystwyth, Special Prize); contributions to: Llên Cymru Yn Y Bedwaredd Ganrif Ar Bymtheg, 1968; Jl of Hist. Soc. of Church in Wales and other Welsh Church periodicals. *Recreations:* soccer, athletics, reading. *Address:* 31 Bryncastell, Bow Street, Dyfed SY24 5DE. *T:* Aberystwyth (01970) 828747.

See also Very Rev. J. W. Evans.

EVANS, Prof. (David) Ellis, DPhil; FBA 1983; Jesus Professor of Celtic, University of Oxford, and Fellow of Jesus College, since 1978; *b* Llanfynydd, 23 Sept. 1930; *yr s* of David Evans and Sarah Jane (*née* Lewis); *m* 1957, Sheila Mary, *er d* of David and Evelyn Jeremy; two *d*. *Educ:* Llandeilo Grammar Sch.; University Coll. of Wales, Aberystwyth (Hon. Fellow, 1992), and University Coll., Swansea (Hon. Fellow, 1985) (BA Wales, 1952; MA Wales, 1954); Jesus Coll., Oxford (Meyricke Grad. Scholar, 1952–54; DPhil 1962, MA 1978). University College of Swansea: Asst Lectr in Welsh, 1957; Lectr, 1960; Reader, 1968; Prof. of Welsh Lang. and Lit. and Head of Dept of Welsh, 1974; Hon. Prof., 1990; Chm., Faculty of Medieval and Modern Langs, Oxford Univ., 1985–86. Lectures: Sir John Rhys Meml, British Acad., 1977; Rudolf Thurneysen Meml, Univ. of Bonn, 1979, 1994; O'Donnell, Univ. of Wales, 1980; G. J. Williams Meml, UC Cardiff, 1986; Sir Thomas Parry-Williams Meml, UCW, Aberystwyth, 1990; Hallstatt, Mus. of Modern Art, Wales, 1995. Pres. and Organizing Sec., Seventh Internat. Congress of Celtic Studies, Oxford, 1983; President: Cymdeithas Dafydd ap Gwilym, 1978–; Irish Texts Soc., 1983–92 (Mem. Council, 1978–); Cambrian Archaeol Assoc., 1990–91; Vice President: N Amer. Congress of Celtic Studies, Ottawa, 1986; Nat. Liby of Wales, 1987–91 (Mem. Court and Council, 1974–91). Chairman: Welsh Dialect Studies Group, 1977–80; Council for Name Studies of GB and Ireland, 1980–84 (Mem. Council, 1962–); Member: Bd of Celtic Studies, Univ. of Wales, 1968–; Internat. Cttee of Onomastic Sciences, 1975–; Welsh Arts Council, 1981–87; Royal Commn on Ancient and Hist. Monuments in Wales, 1984–; Court, University of Wales, 1978–; Court, UC Swansea, 1980–; Court, Univ. of Wales Coll. of Cardiff, 1983–; UNESCO Internat. Cttee for the Study of Celtic Cultures, 1984– (Provisional Cttee, 1981–83); Council, Hon. Soc. Cymmrodorion, 1984–; Celtic Commn, Austrian Acad. of Scis, 1987–; Welsh Cttee, UFC, 1989–92. Hon. Mem., Druidic Order of Gorsedd of Bards, 1976–; Correspondant étranger, Etudes celtiques, 1982–; For. Hon. Mem., Amer. Acad. of Arts and Scis, 1992. Editor, Lang. and Lit. Section, Bull. of Bd of Celtic Studies, 1972– (Editor-in-Chief, 1988–); Mem. Editorial Bd: Geiriadur Prifysgol Cymru/A Dictionary of the Welsh Language, 1973–; Nomina, 1980–85; Welsh Acad. English-Welsh Dictionary, 1981–. Hon. DLitt Wales, 1993. *Publications:* Gaulish Personal Names: a study of some continental Celtic formations, 1967; Gorchest y Celtiaid yn yr Hen Fyd, 1975; (ed) Cofiant Agricola, Rheolwr Prydain, 1975; Termau Gwleidyddiaeth, 1976; (ed) Proc. 7th Internat. Congress of Celtic Studies, Oxford (1983), 1986; (ed with R. Brinley Jones) Cofio'r Dafydd, 1987; *contributed:* Swansea and its Region, ed W. G. V. Balchin, 1971; Homenaje a Antonio Tovar, 1972; (contrib.) The Anatomy of Wales, ed R. Brinley Jones, 1972; Indogermanisch und Keltisch, ed K. H. Schmidt, 1977; Aufstieg und Niedergang der römischen Welt, ed H. Temporini and W. Haase, 1983; Proc. 6th Internat. Congress of Celtic Studies, Galway (1979), 1983; Geschichte und Kultur der Kelten, ed K. H. Schmidt, 1986; Y Gwareiddiad Celtaidd, ed Geraint Bowen, 1987; Cell Gymysg o'r Genedlaethol, 1989; Britain 400–600: Language and History, 1990; Cof Cenedl, 1992; Lengua y Cultura en la Hispania Prerromana, 1993; (jtly) The Celtic Languages, ed M. J. Ball, 1993; Indogermanica et Caucasica, ed R. Bielmeier, 1994; The World of the Celts, ed M. Aldhouse Green, 1995; contrib. colloquia; articles and revs in learned journals. *Recreations:* music, walking. *Address:* Jesus College, Oxford OX1 3DW. *T:* Oxford (01865) 279700.

EVANS, Air Chief Marshal Sir David (George), GCB 1979 (KCB 1977); CBE 1967 (OBE 1962); Bath King of Arms, since 1985; Chairman, Arabian Gold plc, since 1989; Deputy Chairman, NAAFI (Director, since 1984; President of Council, 1981–83); *b* Windsor, Ont, Canada, 14 July 1924; *s* of William Stanley Evans, Clive Vale, Hastings, Sussex; *m* 1949, Denise Marson Williamson-Noble, *d* of late Gordon Till, Hampstead, London; two *d* (and two step *s*). *Educ:* Hodgson Sch., Toronto, Canada; North Toronto Collegiate. Served War, as Pilot, in Italy and NW Europe, 1944–45. Sqdn Pilot, Tactics Officer, Instructor, 1946–52; Sqdn Comdr, Central Flying Sch., 1953–55; RAF Staff Coll. course, 1955; OC No 11 (F) Sqdn, in Germany, 1956–57; Personal Staff Officer to C-in-C, 2nd Allied TAF, 1958–59; OC Flying, RAF, Coltishall, 1959–61; Coll. of Air Warfare course, 1961; Air Plans Staff Officer, Min. of Defence (Air), 1962–63; OC, RAF Station, Gutersloh, Germany, 1964–66; IDC, 1967; AOC, RAF Central Tactics and Trials Organisation, 1968–70; ACAS (Ops), 1970–73; AOC No 1 (Bomber) Group, RAF, 1973–76; Vice-Chief of Air Staff, 1976–77; C-in-C, RAF Strike Command, and UK NATO Air Forces, 1977–80; VCDS (Personnel and Logistics), 1981–83. Mil. Advr and Dir, BAe, 1983–92, and dir several BAe subsids; Chm., BAe Canada Ltd, 1987–92; Dir, Intermin Resource Corp. Ltd, 1986 (Chm., 1989–93); Chairman: Officers Pensions Soc. Ltd; OPS Investment Co. Ltd; Trustees, OPS Widows' Fund; Carroll Aircraft Corp. Ltd; Farnborough Aerospace Develt Corp.; Dir, Airshow Canada. Queen's Commendation for Valuable Service in the Air (QCVSA), 1955. CIMgt (CBIM 1978; Mem. Bd of Companions, 1983–; Dep. Chm., 1989–). *Recreations:* rep. RAF at Rugby football and winter sports (President: RAF Winter Sports Assoc.; Combined Services Winter Sports Assoc.); has rep. Gt Brit. at Bobsleigh in World Championships, Commonwealth Games and, in 1964, Olympic Games. *Address:* Royal Bank of Canada Europe Ltd, 71A Queen Victoria Street, EC4V 4DE. *Club:* Royal Air Force.

EVANS, David Howard; QC 1991; a Recorder, since 1992; *b* 27 July 1944; *s* of David Hopkin Evans and Phoebe Dora Evans (*née* Reading); *m* 1973, Anne Celia Segall, *qv*; two *s*. *Educ:* London Sch. of Economics (BSc Econ 1965; MSc 1967); Wadham Coll., Oxford (BA 1970). Asst Economic Adviser, HM Treasury, 1967–68; called to the Bar, Middle Temple, 1972; Asst Recorder of the Crown Court, 1987. *Recreations:* tennis, swimming, listening to music. *Address:* Queen Elizabeth Buildings, Temple, EC4Y 9BS. *T:* 0171–583 5766. *Clubs:* Roehampton; Riviera Golf.

EVANS, David John; MP (C) Welwyn, Hatfield, since 1987; *b* 23 April 1935; *s* of Violet Edith Evans and Arthur Thomas Evans; *m* 1956, Janice Hazel (*née* Masters); two *s* one *d*. *Educ:* Raglan Road School; Tottenham Tech. College. Professional cricketer (Glos and Warwicks) and footballer (Aston Villa); founded Exclusive Office Cleaning Ltd, 1960; Chm. and Man. Dir, Brengreen (Holdings), first co. with contract for refuse collection and street cleansing services (Southend-on-Sea Borough Council), 1960–86 (Brengreen (Holdings) acquired by BET plc, 1986); Chairman: Bradnam Enterprises Ltd, 1989–; Broadreach Group (formerly Broadreach Services) Ltd, 1990–. Parliamentary Private Secretary: to Minister of State for Industry, DTI, 1990–91; to Minister for Corporate Affairs, DTI, 1991–92; to Minister of State for Local Govt and Inner Cities, DoE, 1992–93; to Sec. of State for Wales, 1993–. Member: Select Cttee on Members' Interests, 1990; Exec., 1922 Cttee, 1993–. Chm., Luton Town Football and Athletic Co. Ltd, 1984–89 (Dir, 1977–90); Mem. Council, Lord's Taverners, 1978– (Chm., 1982–84; Chm., Finance Cttee, 1992–). *Address:* Little Radley, Mackerye End, Harpenden, Herts AL5 5DS. *T:* Harpenden (01582) 460302. *Clubs:* Carlton; MCC, Lord's Taverners, Middlesex CC; Harpenden Golf.

EVANS, David Lloyd C.; *see* Carey Evans.

EVANS, David Marshall, QC 1981; **His Honour Judge Marshall Evans;** a Circuit Judge, since 1987; *b* 21 July 1937; *s* of Robert Trevor and Bessie Estelle Evans; *m* 1961, Alice Joyce Rogers; two *s*. *Educ:* Liverpool Coll.; Trinity Hall, Cambridge (MA, LLM); Law Sch., Univ. of Chicago (JD). Called to the Bar, Gray's Inn, 1964. Teaching Fellow, Stanford University Law Sch., 1961–62; Asst Professor, Univ. of Chicago Law Sch., 1962–63; Lectr in Law, University Coll. of Wales, Aberystwyth, 1963–65; joined Northern Circuit, 1965; a Recorder, 1984–87. *Recreations:* walking, photography, visual arts, bird-watching, motorsport. *Address:* Queen Elizabeth II Law Courts, Derby Square, Liverpool L2 1XA. *T:* 0151–473 7373. *Clubs:* Athenæum, Artists' (Liverpool).

EVANS, David Milne; Cabinet Office, 1977–81; *b* 8 Aug. 1917; *s* of Walter Herbert Evans, MSc and Florence Mary Evans (*née* Milne); *m* 1946, Gwynneth May (*née* Griffiths), BA. *Educ:* Charterhouse (Scholar); Gonville and Caius Coll., Cambridge (Schol.; Wrangler, Math. Tripos). Administrative Class, Home Civil Service (War Office), 1939. Served in Army (Major, RA), 1940–45. Asst Sec., 1954; Imp. Def. Coll., 1954; Asst Under-Sec. of State, MoD, 1967–77 (Under-Sec., CS Dept, 1972). Coronation Medal, 1953; Silver Jubilee Medal, 1977. *Address:* 1 Church Rise, Walston Road, Wenvoe, Cardiff, South Glamorgan CF5 6DE. *T:* Cardiff (01222) 597129.

EVANS, David Philip, CBE 1968; MSc, PhD, FRSC; Principal, Glamorgan Polytechnic, Treforest, Pontypridd, Glam, 1970–72; *b* 28 Feb. 1908; *s* of D. C. and J. Evans, Port Talbot, Glam; *m* 1938, Vura Helena (*née* Harcombe); one *s*. *Educ:* Port Talbot County Grammar Sch.; University Coll., Cardiff (Fellow, 1981). Lectr in Chemistry, Cardiff Technical Coll., 1934–44; Principal: Bridgend Technical Coll., Glam, 1944–52; Glamorgan Coll. of Technology, Treforest, 1952–70. Hon. Fellow, Polytechnic of Wales, 1984. *Publications:* numerous papers in various chemical jls. *Recreations:* gardening, music. *Address:* Tree Tops, St Bride's Road, Ewenny Cross, Ewenny, Bridgend, Mid Glam CF35 5RG. *T:* Bridgend (01656) 661354.

EVANS, Rt. Rev. David Richard John; General Secretary, South American Missionary Society, since 1993; an Assistant Bishop, dioceses of Chichester, Canterbury and Rochester, since 1994; *b* 5 June 1938; *s* of William Henry Reginald Evans and Beatrix Catherine Mottram; *m* 1964, Dorothy Evelyn Parsons; one *s* two *d*. *Educ:* Caius College, Cambridge

(Hons degree in Mod. Langs and Theology, 1963; MA 1966). Curate, Christ Church, Cockfosters, 1965–68; Missionary Pastor and Gen. Sec., Argentine Inter-Varsity Christian Fellowship, in Buenos Aires, Argentina, 1969–77; Chaplain, Good Shepherd Church, Lima, Peru, 1977–82; Bishop of Peru, 1978–88 (with delegated jurisdiction of Bolivia from 1980); Asst Bishop, dio. of Bradford, 1988–93. Internat. Co-ordinator, Evangelical Fellowship of the Anglican Communion, 1989–. *Publication:* En Diálogo con Dios, 1976. *Recreations:* golf, philately. *Address:* (office) Allen Gardiner House, Pembury Road, Tunbridge Wells, Kent TN2 3QU. *T:* Tunbridge Wells (01892) 538647; The Rectory, Maresfield, Uckfield TN22 2HB. *T:* Uckfield (01825) 763817.

EVANS, (David) Roderick; QC 1989; **His Honour Judge Roderick Evans;** a Circuit Judge, since 1992; Resident Judge, Merthyr Tydfil Crown Court, since 1994; *b* 22 Oct. 1946; *s* of Thomas James and Dorothy Evans; *m* 1971, Kathryn Rebecca Lewis; three *s* one *d.* *Educ:* Bishop Gore Grammar School, Swansea; University College London (LLB 1967; LLM 1968). Called to the Bar, Gray's Inn, 1970; a Recorder, 1987–92. *Recreations:* reading, walking. *Address:* The Crown Court, Swansea. *T:* Swansea (01792) 459621.

EVANS, Derek; *see* Evans, John D.

EVANS, Eben, OBE 1976; Controller, Books Division, British Council, 1976–80; *b* 1 Nov. 1920; *s* of John Evans and Mary Evans; *m* 1946, Joan Margaret Howells; two *s* two *d.* *Educ:* Llandovery Grammar Sch.; University Coll. of Wales, Aberystwyth (BA 1948). Served War, 1941–46 (Army, Captain). Appointed to British Council, 1948; Cardiff, 1948–55; Thailand, 1955–59; Gambia, 1959–62; Ghana, 1962–64; Personnel Dept, London, 1964–68; Representative: Algeria, 1968–73; Yugoslavia, 1973–76. *Recreations:* walking, music. *Address:* Gorddinog Isaf, Llanfairfechan, Gwynedd LL33 0HS.

EVANS, Rt. Rev. Edward Lewis, BD, MTh; *b* 11 Dec. 1904; *s* of Edward Foley Evans and Mary (*née* Walker). *Educ:* St Anselm's, Croydon; Tonbridge Sch.; Bishops' Coll., Cheshunt. BD London 1935, MTh 1938. Deacon, 1937; priest 1938; Curate of St Mary's, Prittlewell, Essex, 1937–39; Warden of St Peter's, Theological Coll., Jamaica, 1940–49; Rector, Kingston Parish Church, Jamaica, 1949–52; Rector of Woodford and Craigton, 1952–57; Archdeacon of Surrey, Jamaica, 1950–57; Bishop Suffragan of Kingston, 1957–60; Bishop of Barbados, 1960–71. *Publications:* A History of the Diocese of Jamaica, 1977; Legends of West Indian Saints, 1984. *Address:* Terry's Cross, Woodmancote, Henfield, Sussex BN5 9SX.

EVANS, Edward Stanley Price, FRTPI; City Planning Officer, Liverpool, 1974–84, retired; *b* 13 April 1925; *s* of late Bernard James Reuben Evans and of Nellie Evans; *m* 1948, Eva Magdalena Emma Fry; one *s* (and one *s* decd). *Educ:* Wolverhampton Grammar Sch.; Nottingham Coll. of Art and Crafts (DipTP). FRTPI 1966 (MTPI 1954). Chief Town Planning Officer, Norwich, 1957; City Planning Officer, Nottingham, 1966–74. Member: DoE Environmental Bd, 1977–79; DoE Panel of Local Plan Inspectors, 1985–94. FRSA 1980. *Recreations:* travel, gardening, bridge (social). *Address:* Willow Cottage, The Ridgeway, Heswall, Wirral, Merseyside L60 8NB. *T:* 0151–342 4546.

EVANS, Ven. Eifion; *see* Evans, Ven. D. E.

EVANS, Ellis; *see* Evans, D. E.

EVANS, Emrys; *see* Evans, W. E.

EVANS, Ena Winifred; Headmistress, King Edward VI High School for Girls, Birmingham, 1977–Aug. 1996; *b* 19 June 1938; *d* of Frank and Leonora Evans. *Educ:* The Queen's Sch., Chester; Royal Holloway Coll., Univ. of London (BSc); Hughes Hall, Cambridge (CertEd). Asst Mistress, Bolton Sch. (Girls' Div.), 1961–65; Bath High School (GPDST): Head of Mathematics Dept, 1965–72; Second Mistress, 1970–72; Dep. Head, Friends' Sch., Saffron Walden, 1972–77. Pres., GSA, 1987–88. Mem., Central Birmingham DHA, 1988–90. Mem. Council, Aston Univ., 1989–. FRSA 1986. *Recreation:* music. *Address:* (until Aug. 1996) King Edward VI High School for Girls, Edgbaston Park Road, Birmingham B15 2UB. *T:* 0121–472 1834; (from Aug. 1996) 26 Weoley Hill, Selly Oak, Birmingham B29 4AD.

EVANS, Very Rev. Eric; *see* Evans, Very Rev. T. E.

EVANS, Fabyan Peter Leaf; His Honour Judge Fabyan Evans; a Circuit Judge, since 1988; *b* 10 May 1943; *s* of late Peter Fabyan Evans and Catherine Elise Evans; *m* 1967, Karen Myrtle (*née* Balfour), *g d* of 1st Earl Jellicoe; two *s* one *d.* *Educ:* Clifton College. Called to the Bar, Inner Temple, 1969. A Recorder, 1985–88. *Recreations:* sailing, singing. *Club:* Brooks's.

EVANS, Frederick Anthony, CVO 1973; General Secretary, The Duke of Edinburgh's Award Scheme, 1959–72 (Adviser for the Handicapped, 1972–84); *b* 17 Nov. 1907; *s* of Herbert Anthony Evans, mining engineer, and Pauline (*née* Allen); *m* 1934, Nancy (*née* Meakin); two *s* one *d.* *Educ:* Charterhouse; Corpus Christi, Cambridge. Manager Doondu Coffee Plantation, Kenya, 1927–31; Colonial Service, 1934; Asst District Officer, Nigeria, 1935–39; Provincial Commissioner and Asst Colonial Sec., Gambia, 1940–47; Colonial Sec., Nassau, Bahamas, 1947–51; Acting Governor, 1950; Permanent Sec., Gold Coast (later Ghana), 1951–57. Dir, Anglo-Gambian Archæological Expedition, 1965–66. *Publication:* The State Apartments at Buckingham Palace, 1985; St James's Palace, 1991. *Recreation:* gardening. *Address:* Bellsfield, South Ridge, Odiham, Hants RG25 1NG. *Club:* Commonwealth Trust.

EVANS, Senator Hon. Gareth (John); QC (Vic and ACT) 1983; Senator (Lab) for Victoria, since 1978; Minister for Foreign Affairs, Australia, since 1988; Leader of Government in Senate, since 1993; *b* 5 Sept. 1944; *m* 1969, Merran Anderson; one *s* one *d.* *Educ:* Melbourne Univ. (law and arts); Oxford Univ. (PPE). Lectr in Law, 1971–74, Sen. Lectr, 1974–76, Melbourne Univ.; practising Barrister, 1977–78; Shadow Attorney-General, 1980–83; Attorney-General, 1983–84; Minister for Resources and Energy, 1984–87, for Transport and Communications, 1987–88, for Trade, 1988–93; Dep. Leader of Govt in Senate, 1987–93. *Publications:* (ed) Labor and the Constitution, 1972; (ed) Law, Politics and the Labor Movement, 1980; (ed) Labor Essays, 1980, 1981, 1982; (jtly) Australia's Constitution, 1983; (jtly) Australia's Foreign Relations, 1991; Co-operating for Peace, 1993. *Recreations:* reading, writing, golf, football. *Address:* Parliament House, Canberra, ACT 2600, Australia. *T:* (62) 777500.

EVANS, Gareth Robert William; QC 1994; a Recorder, since 1993; *b* 19 Jan. 1947; *s* of David M. J. Evans and Megan Evans; *m* 1971, Marion Green; one *s* one *d.* *Educ:* Caerphilly Grammar Sch.; Birmingham Poly.; LLB Hons London. Called to the Bar, Gray's Inn, 1973. *Recreations:* Rugby, reading poetry, outdoor pursuits. *Address:* 5 Fountain Court, Steelhouse Lane, Birmingham B4 6DR. *T:* 0121–606 0500.

EVANS, George James; Sheriff of Glasgow and Strathkelvin at Glasgow, since 1983; *b* 16 July 1944; *s* of Colin Evans and Caroline Catherine Kennedy MacPherson Harris; *m* 1973, Lesley Jean Keir Cowie; two *d.* *Educ:* Ardrossan Acad.; Glasgow Univ. (MA Hons); Edinburgh Univ. (LLB). Advocate, 1973; Standing Jun. Counsel, Dept of Energy, Scotland, 1982. *Publications:* contribs to legal periodicals. *Recreations:* playing geriatric tennis, learning to sing, raiding public libraries, enjoying fine wine, good music and lively company. *Address:* 14 Dalkeith Avenue, Glasgow G41 5BJ. *T:* 0141–427 3709.

EVANS, Godfrey; *see* Evans, T. G.

EVANS, Gwynfor; Honorary President, Plaid Cymru, since 1982 (President, 1945–81, Vice-President, 1943–45); *b* 1 Sept. 1912; *s* of Dan Evans and Catherine Mary Richard; *m* 1941, Rhiannon Prys Thomas; four *s* three *d.* *Educ:* Gladstone Road Elementary Sch.; County Sch., Barry; University of Wales, Aberystwyth (Fellow, 1991); St John's Coll., Oxford. Qual. Solicitor, 1939. Hon. Sec. Heddychwyr Cymru (Welsh Pacifist movement), 1939–45; Chm. Union of Welsh Independents, 1954. MP (Plaid Cymru) Carmarthen, July 1966–1970 and Oct. 1974–1979. Contested (Plaid Cymru) Carmarthen, 1979 and 1983. Member: Carmarthen CC, 1949–74; Ct of Govs, UC, Aberystwyth; Council, UC Aberystwyth. Past Mem. Welsh Broadcasting Council. Hon. LLD Wales, 1973; Soc. of Cymmrodorion Medal, 1984. *Publications:* Plaid Cymru and Wales, 1950; Rhagom i Ryddid, 1964; Aros Mae, 1971; Wales can Win, 1973; Land of My Fathers, 1974; A National Future for Wales, 1975; Diwedd Prydeindod, 1981; Bywyd Cymro, 1982; Seiri Cenedl, 1986; Welsh Nation Builders, 1987; Pe Bai Cymru'n Rhydd, 1989; Fighting for Wales, 1990; Heddychiaeth Gristnogol yng Nghymru, 1991; Cymru o Hud, 1992. *Address:* Talar Wen, Pencarreg, Llanybydder, Dyfed SA40 9QQ. *T:* Llanybydder (01570) 480907.

EVANS, Harold Matthew; President and Publisher, Random House Trade Group, since 1990; *b* 28 June 1928; *s* of late Frederick and late Mary Evans; *m* 1st, 1953, Enid (marr. diss. 1978), *d* of late John Parker and of Susan Parker; one *s* two *d*; 2nd, 1981, Christina Hambley Brown (*see* Tina Brown); one *s* one *d.* *Educ:* St Mary's Road Central Sch., Manchester; Durham Univ. BA 1952, MA Dunelm 1966. Ashton-under-Lyne, Lancs, Reporter Newspapers, 1944–46 and 1949; RAF, 1946–49; Durham Univ., 1949–52; Manchester Evening News, 1952; Commonwealth Fund Fellow in Journalism, Chicago and Stanford Univs, USA, 1956–57; Asst Ed, Manchester Evening News, 1958–61; Ed., Northern Echo, 1961–66; Editor-in-Chief, North of England Newspaper Co., 1963–66; Sunday Times: Chief Asst to Editor, 1966; Managing Editor, 1966; Editor, 1967–81; Editor, The Times, 1981–82. Member, Executive Board: Times Newspapers Ltd, 1968–82 (Mem. Main Bd, 1978); International Press Inst., 1974–80; Director: The Sunday Times Ltd, 1968–82; Times Newspapers Ltd, 1978–82. Editor-in-Chief, Atlantic Monthly Press, NY, 1984–86; Founding Editor, Condé-Nast Traveler Magazine, 1986–90; Editl Dir, 1984–86, Contributing Editor, 1986–, US News and World Report, Washington, DC; Vice-Pres. and Sen. Editor, Weidenfeld & Nicolson, NY, 1986–87. Writer and Presenter, Evans on Newspapers, BBC TV, 1981. Hon. Vis. Prof. of Journalism, City Univ., 1978–; Vis. Prof., Inst. of Public Affairs, Duke Univ., N Carolina, 1984. Hon. FSIAD. Internat. Editor of the Year, 1975; Gold Medal Award, Inst. of Journalists, 1979; Hood Medal, RPS, 1981; Editor of the Year, 1982; Lotos Club Medal, NY, 1993. DUniv Stirling, 1982. *Publications:* The Active Newsroom, 1961; Editing and Design (five volumes): vol. 1, Newsman's English, 1972; vol. 5, Newspaper Design, 1973; vol. 2, Newspaper Text, 1974; vol. 3, Newspaper Headlines, 1974; vol. 4, Pictures on a Page, 1977; Good Times, Bad Times, 1983; (jointly): We Learned To Ski, 1974; The Story of Thalidomide, 1978; (ed) Eye Witness, 1981; How We Learned to Ski, 1983; Front Page History, 1984. *Recreations:* swimming, ski-ing, Sunday in the park with George and Isabel. *Address:* Random House, 201 East 50th Street, New York, NY 10022, USA. *Clubs:* Garrick, Royal Automobile; Century, Yale (New York).

EVANS, Sir Haydn T.; *see* Tudor Evans.

EVANS, Prof. (Henry) John, PhD; FRCPE; FRCSE; FIBiol; FRSE; Director, Medical Research Council Human Genetics (formerly Clinical and Population Cytogenetics) Unit, Edinburgh, 1969–94; *b* 24 Dec. 1930; *s* of David Evans and Gwladys Evans (*née* Jones); *m* 1st, 1957, Gwenda Rosalind (*née* Thomas) (*d* 1974); 2nd, 1976, Roslyn Rose (*née* Angell); four *s.* *Educ:* Llanelli Boys Grammar Sch.; UCW, Aberystwyth (BSc, PhD 1955). FRSE 1969; FIBiol 1982; FRCPE 1988; FRCSE 1992. Res. Scientist, MRC Radiobiology Unit, Harwell, 1955–65, Head of Cell Biology Section, 1962–65; Vis. Fellow, Brookhaven Nat. Laboratory, Brookhaven, NY, USA, 1960–61; Prof. of Genetics, Univ. of Aberdeen, 1965–69. Chm., Assoc. Radiation Research, 1970–72; Mem., MRC Biological Res. Bd, 1968–72; Council Mem., MRC, 1978–82. Member: Cttee on Biological Effects of Ionizing Radiation, US Nat. Acad. Sci., 1972; Genetic Manipulation Adv. Gp, 1976–80; DHSS Cttee, Mutagenicity of Foods and Chemicals, 1978–; Nat. Radiology Protection Bd, 1982–94; Lister Scientific Adv. Council, 1982–90; Sci. Council, Internat. Agency for Research on Cancer, 1982–86 (Chm., 1985–86); Scientific Cttee, CRC, 1983–95 (Chm., 1990–95); Chief Scientist Cttee, SHHD, 1983–87; Council, Imperial Cancer Res. Fund, 1985–90; Cttee on Med. Aspects of Radiation in the Environment, DHSS, 1985–94; Scientific Rev. Cttee, Alberta Heritage Foundn for Med. Res., 1986–; Internat. Commn for Protection of Envmt from Mutagens and Chemicals, 1986–91; Radiation Waste Management Adv. Cttee, DoE, 1988–92; Hong Kong Cancer Inst., 1994–. Member, Board of Governors: Beatson Inst. Cancer Res., 1985– (Chm., 1991–); Lister Inst. of Preventive Medicine, 1988–; Inveresk Res. Foundn, 1988–89; Caledonian Res. Foundn, 1989–; Inst. Cancer Res., 1990–94. Hon. Prof., Univ. of Edinburgh; Vis. Prof., Kyoto Univ., Japan, 1981; Boerhaave Prof., Univ. of Leiden, 1994–95. Hon. Fellow: UK Clinical Cytogenetics Soc., 1984; UK Environmental Mutagen Soc., 1984. Lectures include: Douglas Lea Meml, 1979; Railford Robinson, Adelaide, 1981; Honeyman-Gillespie, 1984; Woodhull, Royal Instn, 1992. Lilly Prize, 1985, Ballantyne Prize, 1990, RCPE; Frits Sobels EEMS Award, 1995. *Publications:* papers on radiation cytology, mutagenesis, chromosome structure and human cytogenetics in various internat. jls; editor of various books and jls in the field of genetics and radiobiology. *Recreations:* golf, music, fishing. *Address:* 45 Lauder Road, Edinburgh EH9 1UE. *T:* 0131–667 2437. *Club:* New (Edinburgh).

EVANS, (Henry) Nicholas; a Metropolitan Stipendiary Magistrate, since 1994; *b* 7 Nov. 1945; 3rd *s* of Gilbert Arthur Evans and Muriel Elaine Evans (*née* Oxford); *m* 1980, Diana Claire Smith; one *s* one *d.* *Educ:* Highgate Sch. Called to the Bar, Middle Temple, 1971, Lincoln's Inn, *ad eundem*, 1975. *Address:* 2 Pump Court, Temple, EC4Y 7AH. *Club:* Bar Yacht.

EVANS, Huw Prideaux, CB 1993; UK Executive Director, International Monetary Fund and World Bank, and Economic Minister, Washington, since 1994; *b* 21 Aug. 1941; *s* of late Richard Hubert Evans and of Kathleen Annie Evans; *m* 1966, Anne (*née* Bray); two *s.* *Educ:* Cardiff High Sch.; King's Coll., Cambridge (MA); London Sch. of Econs and Polit. Science (MSc). Economist: HM Treasury, 1964–72; European Commn, 1972–73; Asst Econ. Sec., Hong Kong Govt, 1973–75; Sen. Econ. Adviser (Econ. Forecasting), 1976–79, Under Sec., 1980–89, Dep. Sec., 1989–94, HM Treasury. *Address:* c/o British Embassy, 3100 Massachusetts Avenue, Washington, DC 2008, USA. *Club:* United Oxford & Cambridge University.

EVANS, Hywel Eifion, CB 1974; Welsh Secretary, Ministry of Agriculture, Fisheries and Food, 1968–75; *b* 24 Jan. 1910; *s* of late Gruffydd Thomas and Winnifred Evans, Felin Rhydhir, Pwllheli, Caernarvonshire; *m* 1st, 1939, Mary Elizabeth (*d* 1977), *d* of late

Richard and Hannah Jones, Gilfach, Glanywydden, Llandudno; one *s* one *d*; 2nd, 1978, Mrs Mair Lloyd Jones, *d* of late David Lloyd and Amelia Davies, Ceinfan, Narbeth, Dyfed. *Educ:* Pwllheli Grammar Sch.; University Coll. of North Wales, Bangor. BSc (Hons) (Agric.). Research Asst, Dept of Agricultural Economics, UCW, Aberystwyth, 1934–40; Dist and Dep. Exec. Officer, Leicester WAEC, 1940–46; County Advisory Officer: Radnor AEC, 1946–47; Carmarthen AEC, 1947–57; Dep. Regional Dir, Nat. Agricl Advisory Service for Wales, 1957–59, Regional Dir, 1959–66; Dep. Dir, Nat. Agricl Adv. Service (London), 1967–68. FRAgS 1972. *Publications:* articles on agricultural, economic and sociological topics in Welsh Jl of Agriculture, Agriculture, and other jls. *Recreations:* idling, fishing, shooting. *Address:* Llawryglyn, Lôn Tyllyd, Llanfarian, Aberystwyth, Wales SY23 4UH. *Club:* Farmers'.

EVANS, Iain Richard, FCA; Chairman: Welsh Water plc, since 1993; The L/E/K Partnership, since 1991; *b* 17 May 1951; *s* of Alan Caradog Crawshay Evans and late Barr Hargreave Bell (*née* Dalglish); *m* 1st, 1973, Zoe Dorothy Valentine; two *s*; 2nd, 1988, Jayne Doreen Almond; one *d*. *Educ:* John Lyon Sch.; Rotherham Sixth Form Coll.; Bristol Univ. (BSc Hons 1972); Harvard Univ. Grad. Sch. of Business Admin (MBA with High Distinction, Baker Scholar, Loeb Rhoades Fellow, 1978). ACA 1975, FCA 1977. Arthur Young McClelland Moores & Co., 1972–76; Bain & Co., 1978–83, Partner 1982; Founding Partner, L/E/K Partnership, 1983. Dir (non-exec.), Welsh Water plc (formerly Welsh Water Authy), 1989– (Dep. Chm., 1992–93); Mem. Adv. Bd, Welsh Develt Internat., 1989–. *Recreations:* tennis, golf, fishing, marine paintings. *Address:* The L/E/K Partnership, Adelphi Building, 1–11 John Adam Street, WC2N 6BW. *T:* 0171–930 1244. *Clubs:* Cardiff and County, Crawshays Rugby Football (Cardiff); Sandford Springs Golf (Kingsclere, Hants).

EVANS, Dr Ian Philip, FRSC; Head Master, Bedford School, since 1990; *b* 2 May 1948; *s* of Joseph Emlyn Evans and Beryl Evans; *m* 1972, Sandra Veronica Waggett; two *s*. *Educ:* Ruabon Boys' Grammar Sch.; Churchill College, Cambridge (BA 1970; MA 1973; 1st cl. hons Nat. Scis Tripos); Imperial College of Science and Technology (PhD, DIC). CChem, FRSC 1994. Post-Doctoral Fellow, Res. Sch. of Chemistry, ANU, 1973–75; Asst Master, St Paul's Sch, 1975–90 (Head of Chemistry Dept, 1984–90). Member: Schs Exams and Assessment Council, 1991–93; SCAA, 1993–. Chief Examr, A-level Chem., Univ. of London Schs Exam. Bd, 1987–90. *Publications:* papers in learned jls. *Recreations:* music, cricket, poetry. *Address:* Bedford School, Burnaby Road, Bedford MK40 2TU. *T:* Bedford (01234) 353436.

EVANS, James, CBE 1995; Member, Monopolies and Mergers Commission, since 1989; *b* 27 Nov. 1932; *s* of late Rex Powis Evans and Louise Evans; *m* 1961, Jette Holmboe; two *d*. *Educ:* Aldenham School; St Catharine's College, Cambridge (MA). Called to the Bar, Gray's Inn, 1959; admitted Solicitor, 1972; recalled to the Bar, Gray's Inn, 1991, Bencher, 1993. Commissioned 26th Field Regt RA, 1951–53. Legal Dept, Kemsley Newspapers Ltd, 1956–59; practised at Bar, 1959–65; Legal Adviser: Thomson Newspapers Ltd, 1965–73; Times Newspapers Ltd, 1967–73; Sec. and Mem. Exec. Bd, 1973–78, Dir, 1978–86, Thomson Organisation Ltd; Dir, 1977–81, Chm., 1980–81, Times Newspapers Ltd; Chm., Thomson Withy Grove Ltd, 1979–84; International Thomson Organisation plc: Dir, 1978; Jt Dep. Man. Dir, 1982–84; Man. Dir and Chief Exec., 1985–86; Chm., 1986. Chm. and Chief Exec., 1982–84, Dir, 1982–, Thomson Regional Newspapers Ltd. Dir, 1983–90, Chm., 1987–89, Press Assoc.; Dir, Reuters Holdings, 1984–92. Dir, Press Standards Bd of Finance, 1990–. Trustee, Visnews, 1985–. Member: Council, Newspaper Soc., 1984–; Press Council, 1987–90; Council of Legal Educn, 1992–94. Mem., Home Office Deptl Cttee on Official Secrets Act (Franks Cttee), 1971. *Recreations:* various. *Address:* c/o MMC, New Court, 48 Carey Street, WC2A 2JT. *Club:* Garrick.

EVANS, James Donald; retired; Special Correspondent, Westminster Press Ltd, 1983–86; Acting Editor, UK Press Gazette, 1986; freelance columnist, The Citizen, Gloucester, since 1987; *b* 12 Nov. 1926; *yr s* of Arthur Evans and Isabella McKinnon Evans; *m* 1946, Freda Bristow; two *s* three *d*. *Educ:* Royal Grammar Sch., High Wycombe. Jun. Reporter, Bucks Free Press, 1943–45; Army, 1945–48; Chief Reporter, Maidenhead Advertiser, 1948–50; Northern Echo: District Chief Reporter, 1950–60; Industrial Corresp., 1961–65; Industrial Editor, 1965–66; Editor and Editor-in-Chief, 1966–82; Dir, North of England Newspapers, 1971–82. *Recreations:* driving, reading. *Address:* 11 Onslow Road, Newent, Glos GL18 1TL. *T:* Newent (01531) 822001. *Club:* Presscala.

EVANS, Col J(ames) Ellis, CBE 1973 (OBE 1952); TD 1947; JP; Lord-Lieutenant of Clwyd, 1979–85; *b* 6 Aug. 1910; *s* of James William Evans and Eleanor Evans, MBE, JP; unmarried. *Educ:* Epworth Coll., Rhyl. Chartered Accountant (FCA). Joined TA, 1937; served War of 1939–45, RA: France, 1940; N Africa, 1941–44; Italy, 1944–45; comd 384 Light Regt RA (RWF), TA, 1947–52; Dep. CRA, 53 (Welsh) Div., 1953–57; Chm. Denbigh and Flint TA Assoc., 1961–68; Chm., Wales and Mon TA&VRA, 1971–74 (Vice-Chm., 1968–71); Pres., Wales TA&VRA, 1981–85. Mem., Prestatyn UDC, 1939–74 (Chm. 1947); Mayor, Prestatyn Town Council, 1974–75. Clwyd, formerly Flintshire: JP 1951; DL 1953; High Sheriff, 1970–71; Vice-Lieut, 1970–74, Vice Lord-Lieut, 1977–79. Chm., North Wales Police Authority, 1976–78. *Recreations:* lawn tennis (played for Wales and Lancashire, 1936–48), gardening. *Address:* Trafford Mount, Gronant Road, Prestatyn, Clwyd LL19 9DT. *T:* Prestatyn (01745) 854119. *Club:* City (Chester).

EVANS, James Humphrey R.; *see* Roose-Evans.

EVANS, Jeremy David Agard; Director, Public Affairs, British Rail, since 1990; *b* 20 June 1936; *s* of Arthur Burke Agard Evans and Dorothy (*née* Osborne); *m* 1964, Alison Mary (*née* White); one *s* two *d*. *Educ:* Whitgift Sch.; Christ's Coll., Cambridge (BA Hons). Ministry of Power: Asst Principal, 1960–64 (Private Sec. to Parly Sec., 1963–64); Principal, 1964–69; Sloan Fellow, London Business Sch., 1969–70; Principal, 1970–73, and Private Sec. to Minister for Industry, 1971–73, DTI; Asst Sec., DTI, 1973, Dept of Energy, 1974 (Offshore Supplies Office, 1973); seconded as Sec. to BNOC on its foundn, 1976–78; a Man. Dir, 1978; Man. Dir Corporate Develt, and Sec., 1980–82, Mem. Bd 1981–82; Dir, Britoil plc, 1982–88. Mem., GDC, 1989–94. *Recreations:* opera, skiing, walking, golf. *Address:* Dormans House West, Dormans Park, East Grinstead, West Sussex RH19 2LY. *T:* Dormans Park (01342) 870518.

EVANS, John; *see* Evans, D. J. O.

EVANS, Prof. John; *see* Evans, Prof. H. J.

EVANS, Dr John; *see* Evans, Dr N. J. B.

EVANS, John; MP (Lab) St Helens, North, since 1983 (Newton, Feb. 1974–1983); Member, National Executive Committee of the Labour Party, since 1982 (Chairman of Labour Party, 1991–92); *b* 19 Oct. 1930; *s* of late James Evans, miner and Margaret (*née* Robson); *m* 1959, Joan Slater; two *s* one *d*. *Educ:* Jarrow Central School. Apprentice Marine Fitter, 1946–49 and 1950–52; Nat. Service, Royal Engrs, 1949–50; Engr, Merchant Navy, 1952–55; joined AUEW (later AEU), 1952; joined Labour Party, 1955; worked in various industries as fitter, ship-building and repairing, steel, engineering, 1955–65, 1968–74. Mem. Hebburn UDC, 1962, Leader 1969, Chm. 1972; Sec./Agent Jarrow CLP, 1965–68. An Asst Govt Whip, 1978–79; Opposition Whip, 1979–80; PPS to Leader of Labour Party, 1980–83; opposition spokesman on employment, 1983–87. Mem., European Parlt, 1975–78; Chm., Regional Policy, Planning and Transport Cttee, European Parlt, 1976–78. Political Sec., Nat. Union of Labour and Socialist Clubs. *Recreations:* watching football, reading, gardening. *Address:* 6 Kirkby Road, Culcheth, Warrington, Cheshire WA3 4BS. *T:* (H of C) 0171–219 5203; (constituency) St Helens (01744) 27862. *Clubs:* Labour (Earlestown); Daten (Culcheth).

EVANS, Prof. John, PhD; Professor of Chemistry, University of Southampton, since 1990; *b* 2 June 1949; *s* of Leslie and Eleanor Evans; *m* 1972, Hilary Jane Fulcher; two *d*. *Educ:* Rutherford Grammar Sch., Newcastle upon Tyne; Imperial Coll. London (BSc 1970; ARCS); Sidney Sussex Coll., Cambridge (PhD 1973). Research Fellow, Princeton Univ., 1973–74; Cambridge University: ICI Res. Fellow, 1974–75; Royal Soc. Pickering Res. Fellow, 1975–76; Southampton University: Res. Fellow, 1976–78; Lectr, 1978–84; Sen. Lectr, 1984–87; Reader, 1987–90. Science and Engineering Research Council: Chm., Synchrotron Radiation Cttee, 1991–94; UK Deleg. to Council of European Synchrotron Radiation Facility, 1991–94 (Mem., Scientific Adv. Cttee, 1995–); Mem., Facilities Commn, 1993–94. Royal Society of Chemistry: Sec. and Treas., Dalton Div., 1993–June 1996; Council Mem., 1994–. Tilden Lectr, RSC, 1994. Editor, Inorganic Chemistry Series, Oxford Chemistry Primers Text Book Series, 1991–. Meldola Medal, RSC, 1978. *Publications:* contrib. scientific jls, incl. Jl RSC. *Recreations:* cycling, watching football, travel. *Address:* Department of Chemistry, University of Southampton, Southampton SO17 1BJ. *T:* Southampton (01703) 593307.

EVANS, Maj.-Gen. John Alan Maurice, CB 1989; Vice-Chairman, AEI Cables, since 1993 (Managing Director, 1992–93); *b* 13 Feb. 1936; *s* of John Arthur Mortimer Evans and Margaret (*née* Lewis); *m* 1958, Shirley Anne May; one *s* one *d*. *Educ:* Grammar schs in Wales and England; RMA Sandhurst; Trinity Coll., Cambridge (MA). Various Staff and RE appointments; CO, 22 Engr Regt, 1976–78; Comd, Berlin Inf. Bde, 1980–82; RCDS, 1983; Comdt, RMCS, Shrivenham, 1985–87; Sen. Army Mem., RCDS, 1988–90. Col Comdt, RE, 1991–. With GEC Wire and Cables Gp, 1990. Pres., Inst. of Royal Engineers, 1990–93. *Recreations:* music, reluctant DIY, travel. *Address:* c/o Midland Bank, 29 High Street, Camberley GU15 3RE. *Club:* Army and Navy.

EVANS, John Alfred Eaton; Headmaster, Brentwood School, 1981–93; *b* 30 July 1933; *s* of John Eaton Evans and Millicent Jane Evans (*née* Righton); *m* 1958, Vyvyan Margaret Mainstone; two *s* one *d*. *Educ:* Bristol Grammar Sch.; Worcester Coll., Oxford. MA (Lit. Hum.). Nat. Service, 1952–54, commnd RAOC. Assistant Master: Blundell's Sch., 1958–63; Rugby Sch., 1963–73; Housemaster: Phillips Acad, Andover, Mass, USA, 1968–69; Rugby Sch., 1973–81. Chm., London Div., HMC, 1993. Member selection panels: CMS, 1983–91; Admiralty, 1985–; Army Scholarship Bd, 1990–; ABM, 1992–. FRSA 1983. *Publications:* various articles on community service in education. *Recreations:* cricket, Rugby fives, piano, singing, drama, walking. *Address:* Manor Farm House, Easton, near Wells, Somerset BA5 1ED. *Clubs:* East India, Devonshire, Sports and Public Schools; Vincent's (Oxford); Jesters; Cryptics Cricket.

EVANS, Prof. John Davies, FBA 1973; Director, University of London Institute of Archæology, and Professor of Archæology in the University of London, 1973–89, now Professor Emeritus; *b* 22 Jan. 1925; *o s* of Harry Evans and Edith Haycocks; *m* 1957, Evelyn Sladdin. *Educ:* Liverpool Institute High Sch. (open schol. in English to Pemb. Coll.); Pembroke Coll., Cambridge. War Service, 1943–47. BA 1948, MA 1950, PhD 1956, LittD 1979; Dr *hc* Lyon 2, 1983. Fellow of British Institute of Archæology at Ankara, 1951–52; Research Fellow of Pembroke Coll., Cambridge, 1953–56; Prof. of Prehistoric Archæology, London Univ., 1956–73. President: Prehistoric Soc., 1974–78; Council for British Archæology, 1979–82; Member: Permanent Council, Internat. Union of Prehistoric and Protohistoric Scis, 1975– (Pres., 1982–86); Royal Commn on Historical Monuments (England), 1985–92; Chairman: Area Archaeol Adv. Cttee for SE England, 1975–79; Treasure Trove Reviewing Cttee, 1988–. FSA 1955 (Dir, 1975–80, 1983–84, Pres., 1984–87); Member: German Archaeological Inst., 1979– (Corr. Mem., 1968–79); Instituto Italiano di Preistoria e Protostoria, 1983–. *Publications:* Malta (Ancient Peoples and Places Series), 1959; (with Dr A. C. Renfrew) Excavations at Saliagos, near Antiparos, 1968; The Prehistoric Antiquities of the Maltese Islands, 1971; papers and reports in archæological journals. *Recreations:* walking, listening to music. *Address:* Melbury Cottage, 5 Love Lane, Shaftesbury, Dorset SP7 8BG.

EVANS, (John) Derek; Chief Conciliation Officer, Advisory, Conciliation and Arbitration Service, since 1992; *b* 11 Sept. 1942; *s* of late Leslie and Mary Evans, *m* 1964, Betty Wiseman; two *d*. *Educ:* Roundhay Sch., Leeds. FIPD. Dept of Employment, 1962–74; Advisory, Conciliation and Arbitration Service: Midlands, 1974–78; Head Office, 1978–82; Dir, Wales, 1982–88; Dir, Adv. Services, 1988–91; Dir, Conciliation and Arbitration, 1991–92. Industrial Fellow, Kingston Univ. *Recreations:* golf, driving, music. *Address:* ACAS, 27 Wilton Street, SW1X 7AZ. *T:* 0171–210 3669; 2 Tamarisk Rise, Wokingham, Berks RG11 1WG. *T:* Wokingham (01734) 789655. *Club:* Sand Martins Golf (Berks).

EVANS, His Honour John Field, QC 1972; a Circuit Judge, 1978–93; *b* 27 Sept. 1928; 2nd *s* of late John David Evans, Llandaff, and Lucy May Evans (*née* Field). *Educ.* Cardiff High Sch.; Exeter Coll., Oxford (MA). Pilot Officer, RAF, 1948–49. Called to Bar, Inner Temple, 1953; Dep. Chm., Worcestershire QS, 1964–71; a Recorder of the Crown Court, 1972–78.

EVANS, John G.; *see* Grimley Evans.

EVANS, John Kerr Q.; *see* Quarren Evans.

EVANS, John Marten Llewellyn, CBE 1956 (MBE 1945); JP; Official Solicitor to the Supreme Court of Judicature, 1950–70; *b* 9 June 1909; *s* of late Marten Llewellyn Evans, Solicitor, and Edith Helena (*née* Lile); *m* 1943, Winifred Emily, *y d* of late Austin Reed; one *s* one *d*. *Educ:* Rugby Sch.; Trinity Coll., Oxford. Admitted Solicitor, 1935; Legal Asst to the Official Solicitor, 1937. Served War of 1939–45, Major RA. Senior Legal Asst to the Official Solicitor, 1947; Asst Master in Lunacy, 1950. Vice-Chm., Austin Reed Group Ltd, 1969–77. Master of Worshipful Company of Cutlers, 1967–68. JP City of London, 1969. *Recreations:* the theatre, cricket, golf, tennis.

EVANS, Rev. Canon John Mascal; *b* 17 May 1915; *s* of Rev. Edward Foley Evans and Mary Evans; *m* 1941, Mary Elizabeth (*née* Rathbone); three *s* two *d*. *Educ:* St John's Sch., Leatherhead; Brasenose Coll., Oxford; Wells Theological Coll. Asst Curate, St Martin's, Epsom, 1938; Perpetual Curate, Stoneleigh, Epsom, 1942, All Saints, Fleet, 1952; Vicar, St Mary, Walton-on-Thames, 1960–68; Archdeacon of Surrey, 1968–80; Hon. Canon of Guildford, 1963–80, Canon Emeritus, 1980–; Mem. of Ridgeway Team Ministry, Dio. Salisbury, 1980–84. Member: General Synod of C of E, 1977–80; C of E Pensions Bd, 1977–85; Council of Cremation Soc., 1969–80. *Address:* 6 Gracey Court, Woodland Road, Broadclyst, Exeter EX5 3LP.

EVANS, John Robert, CC 1978; OO 1991; MD, DPhil, FRCP, FRCP (C), FRSC; Chairman: Allelix Inc. (Biotechnology), Mississauga, Ont, since 1983 (Chief Executive Officer, 1983–89); Torstar Corporation, since 1993; *b* 1 Oct. 1929; *s* of William Watson Evans and Mary Thompson; *m* 1954, Gay Glassco; four *s* two *d. Educ:* Univ. of Toronto (MD); University Coll., Oxford (Rhodes Schol.; Hon. Fellow, 1990) (DPhil). MACP; FRCP 1980. Jr interne, Toronto Gen. Hosp., 1952–53; Hon. Registrar, Nat. Heart Hosp., London, 1955; Asst Res.: Sunnybrook Hosp., Toronto, 1956; Toronto Gen. Hosp., 1957; Ontario Heart Foundn Fellow, Hosp. for Sick Children, Toronto, 1958; Chief Res. Physician, Toronto Gen. Hosp., 1959; Research Fellow, Baker Clinic Research Lab., Harvard Med. Sch., 1960; Markle Schol. in Acad. Med., Univ. of Toronto, 1960–65; Associate, Dept of Med., Faculty of Med., Univ. of Toronto, 1961–65; Asst Prof., 1965–66; Dean, Faculty of Med., McMaster Univ., 1965–72, Vice-Pres., Health Sciences, 1967–72; Pres., Univ. of Toronto, 1972–78; Dir, Dept of Population, Health and Nutrition, IBRD, Washington DC, 1979–83. Member: Council RCP (Can.), 1972–78; Inst. of Medicine, Nat. Acad. Sci., USA, 1972– (Mem. Council, 1976–80); Adv. Cttee Med. Res., WHO, 1976–80; Chm. Trustees, Rockefeller Foundn. Director: Dominion Foundries and Steel Ltd; Royal Bank of Canada; Alcan Aluminium Ltd (Montreal); Connaught Labs Ltd, Toronto; Pasteur Merieux Serums and Vaccins, Lyon; Trimark Investment Management Inc., Toronto. Fellow, LSHTM, 1989. Hon. LLD: McGill, 1972; Dalhousie, 1972; McMaster, 1972; Queen's, 1974; Wilfred Laurier, 1975; York, 1977; Yale, 1978; Toronto, 1980; Hon. DSc: Meml Univ. of Newfoundland, 1973; Montreal, 1977; Hon. DU Ottawa, 1978; Hon. DHL Johns Hopkins, 1978. *Recreations:* ski-ing, fishing, farming. *Address:* 58 Highland Avenue, Toronto, Ontario M4W 2A3, Canada.

EVANS, John Roger W.; *see* Warren Evans.

EVANS, John Stanley, QPM 1990; Chief Constable, Devon and Cornwall Constabulary, since 1989; *b* 6 Aug. 1943; *s* of late William Stanley and of Doris Evans; *m* 1965, Beryl Smith; one *s* one *d. Educ:* Wade Deacon Grammar Sch., Widnes; Liverpool Univ. (LLB Hons 1972). Liverpool City, then Merseyside Police, 1960–80; Asst Chief Constable, Greater Manchester Police, 1980–84; Dep. Chief Constable, Surrey Constabulary, 1984–88. Mem., ACPO (Mem., various cttees incl. Terrorism and Allied Matters (Sec.), Complaints and Discipline (Chm.)). Sec., Police Athletic Assoc., 1989–. *Recreations:* most sports (ran London Marathon, 1988, 1989), service and charitable activities. *Address:* Police Headquarters, Middlemoor, Exeter, Devon EX2 7HQ. *T:* Exeter (01392) 52101.

EVANS, Very Rev. (John) Wyn, FSA; FRHistS; Dean and Precentor of St Davids Cathedral, since 1994; *b* 4 Oct. 1946; *o s* of Ven. David Eifion Evans, *qv. Educ:* Ardwyn Grammar Sch., Aberystwyth; University Coll., Cardiff (BA); St Michael's Theol Coll., Llandaff (BD); Jesus Coll., Oxford. FSA 1989; FRHistS 1994. Deacon 1971, priest 1972; Curate, St Davids, 1971–72; Minor Canon, St Davids Cathedral, 1972–75; grad. student, Jesus Coll., Oxford, 1975–77, permission to officiate Oxford diocese, 1975–77; Diocesan Adviser on Archives, St Davids, 1976–82; Rector, Llanfallteg with Castell Dwyran and Clunderwen with Henllan Amgoed and Llangan, 1977–82; Exam. Chaplain to Bishop of St Davids, 1977; Diocesan Warden of Ordinands, 1978–83; Chaplain and Lectr, Trinity Coll., Carmarthen, 1982–90; Diocesan Dir of Educn, 1982–92; Hon. Canon, St Davids Cathedral, 1988–90, Canon (4th Cursal), 1990–94; Dean of Chapel, Trinity Coll., Carmarthen, 1990–94; Head, Dept of Theology and Religious Studies, 1991–94. *Publications:* (with Roger Worsley) St Davids Cathedral 1181–1981, 1981; contribs to jls, including Jl Welsh Ecclesiastical History, Carmarthen Antiquary, Diwinyddiaeth. *Recreations:* reading, music, antiquities. *Address:* The Deanery, The Close, St Davids, Dyfed SA62 6RH. *T:* St Davids (01437) 720202.

EVANS, (John) Wynford, CBE 1995; Chairman, South Wales Electricity plc (formerly South Wales Electricity Board), since 1984; *b* 3 Nov. 1934; *s* of late Gwilym Everton and Margaret Mary Elfreda Evans; *m* 1957, Sigrun Brethfeld; three *s. Educ:* Llanelli Grammar Sch.; St John's Coll., Cambridge (MA). CEng, CompIEE; FBCS. Served RAF (Flying Officer), 1955–57. IBM, 1957–58; NAAFI, W Germany, 1959–62; Kayser Bondor, 1962–63; various posts, inc. Computer and Management Services Manager, S Wales Electricity Bd, 1963–76; ASC, Henley, 1968; Dep. Chm., London Electricity Bd, 1977–84. Dir, Bank of Wales, 1989–. Member: Milton Keynes IT Adv. Panel, 1982–84; Welsh Regional Council, CBI, 1984– (Chm., 1991–93); Council, CBI, 1988–; Welsh Language Bd, 1988–89; Dep. Chm., Prince of Wales Cttee, 1989–; Chm., SE Wales Cttee, Industry Year 1986. Director: 1992 Nat. Garden Festival Ltd, 1987–88; Welsh Nat. Opera Ltd, 1988–93. Member: Hon. Soc. of Cymmrodorion, 1978–; Court, Cranfield Inst. of Technol., 1980–88; Civic Trust Bd for Wales, 1984–88; Nat. Trust Cttee for Wales, 1985–90; Trustee and Dep. Chm., Cardiff Bay Opera House Trust, 1994–; Governor, Polytechnic of Wales, 1987–88. FInstD 1988; FRSA; CIMgt. Liveryman, Tin Plate Workers alias Wireworkers' Co. High Sheriff, S Glamorgan, 1995. *Recreations:* fishing, cross-country ski-ing, golf, riding. *Address:* SWALEC plc, St Mellons, Cardiff CF3 9XW. *T:* Cardiff (01222) 792111. *Clubs:* City Livery, Flyfishers', London Welsh; Cardiff and County, Radyr Golf (Cardiff).

EVANS, John Yorath Gwynne; Deputy Director (Air), Royal Aircraft Establishment, 1972–76, retired; medical engineering consultant, 1980–88; *b* 10 Feb. 1922; *s* of Randell and Florence Evans, Carms; *m* 1948, Paula Lewis, *d* of late Roland Ford Lewis; two *s* one *d. Educ:* UCW Aberystwyth. Royal Aircraft Estabt, 1942; attached to RAF, Germany, 1945–46; Supt Wind Tunnels, RAE Bedford, 1958; Head of Aerodynamics Dept, RAE, 1971. *Publications:* contrib. various sci. and techn. jls. *Recreations:* sailing, travel, reading. *Address:* Rushmoor Cottage, Tilford, Farnham, Surrey GU10 2EP. *T:* Frensham (01252) 792275; 10 West Street, Ditchling, E Sussex BN6 8TS.

EVANS, Jonathan Peter; MP (C) Brecon and Radnor, since 1992; Parliamentary Under-Secretary of State for Corporate Affairs, Department of Trade and Industry, since 1994; *b* 2 June 1950; *s* of David John Evans and Harriet Mary Drury; *m* 1975, Margaret Thomas; one *s* two *d. Educ:* Lewis Sch., Pengam; Howardian High Sch., Cardiff; Coll. of Law, Guildford and London. Solicitor and Managing Partner, Leo Abse & Cohen, Cardiff, 1968–92. Dep. Chm., Tai Cymru (Welsh Housing Corp.), 1988–92. Chairman: Welsh Cons. Parly Candidates, 1985–91; Welsh Cons. Policy Gp, 1987–91. Contested (C): Ebbw Vale, Feb. and Oct., 1974; Wolverhampton NE, 1979; Brecon and Radnor, 1987. PPS to Minister of State, NI Office, 1992–94. Sec., Cons. Parly Agric. Cttee, 1992–94; Vice-Chm., Cons. Parly Party Orgn Cttee, 1992–94. Vice-Chm., Welsh NSPCC Council, 1991–; Pres., Cardiff and Dist NSPCC, 1992–. *Recreations:* watching Rugby Union, cricket and ice-hockey; reading. *Address:* House of Commons, SW1A 0AA. *Clubs:* Carlton; Cardiff and County (Cardiff); London Welsh RFC.

EVANS, Rt. Rev. Kenneth Dawson; Assistant Bishop of Guildford, 1986–90; *b* 7 Nov. 1915; *s* of late Dr Edward Victor Evans, OBE; *m* 1939, Margaret, *d* of J. J. Burton; one *s. Educ:* Dulwich Coll.; Clare Coll., Cambridge. Ordained, 1938; Curate of: St Mary, Northampton, 1938–41; All Saints', Northampton, 1941–45; Rector of Ockley, 1945–49; Vicar of Dorking, 1949–63; Archdeacon of Dorking and Canon Residentiary of Guildford Cathedral, 1963–68; Bishop Suffragan of Dorking, 1968–85. Hon. Canon of Guildford, 1955–63 and 1979–85. Mem., Bishop's Finance Commn, 1957. *Address:* 3 New Inn Lane, Burpham, Guildford, Surrey GU4 7HN. *T:* Guildford (01483) 67978.

EVANS, Kim; Head of Music and Arts, BBC Television, since 1993; *b* 3 Jan. 1951; *d* of Jon Evans and Gwendolen (*née* McLeod). *Educ:* Putney High Sch.; Our Lady of Sion Convent; Warwick Univ. (BA Hons Eng. and Amer. Lit.); Leicester Univ. (MA Hons Victorian Lit. and Society). Press Asst, Design Council, 1973–74; Asst Editor, Crafts mag., 1974–76; Chief Sub-Editor, Harpers & Queen, 1976–78; South Bank Show, LWT: researcher, 1978–82; Producer/Dir, 1982–89; BBC Television: Producer, Omnibus, 1989–92; Asst Hd, Music and Arts, 1992–93. Huw Wheldon Award for Best Arts Prog., BAFTA, 1993. *Recreations:* travelling, dreaming, cinema, reading. *Address:* Room EMO6, BBC Television, Wood Lane, W12 7RJ. *T:* 0181–895 6770.

EVANS, Lloyd Thomas; AO 1979; DSc, DPhil; FRS 1976; FAA; Hon. Research Fellow, Commonwealth Scientific and Industrial Research Organization Division of Plant Industry, Canberra, Australia, since 1992; *b* 6 Aug. 1927; *s* of C. D. Evans and G. M. Fraser; *m* 1954, Margaret Honor Newell; two *s* one *d* (and one *d* decd). *Educ:* Wanganui Collegiate Sch., NZ; Univ. of NZ (BSc, MAgrSc, DSc); Univ. of Oxford (DPhil). FAA 1971. Rhodes Scholar, Brasenose Coll., Oxford, 1950–54; Commonwealth Fund Fellow, Calif Inst. of Technol., 1954–56; res. scientist, CSIRO Div. of Plant Industry, Canberra, 1956–92 (Chief Res. Scientist, 1970–72; Chief, Div. of Plant Industry, 1971–78). National Acad. of Sciences (USA) Pioneer Fellow, 1963; Overseas Fellow, Churchill Coll., Cambridge, 1969–70; Vis. Fellow, Wolfson Coll., Cambridge, 1978. President: ANZAAS, 1976–77; Aust. Acad. of Science, 1978–82. Member, Board of Trustees: Internat. Foundn for Sci., Stockholm, 1982–87; Internat. Rice Res. Inst., Philippines, 1984–89; Internat. Center for Improvement of Wheat and Maize, 1990–. Mem., Norwegian Acad. of Sci. and Letters, 1990. Hon. Member: Royal Soc., NZ, 1986; RASE, 1987. Hon. LLD Canterbury, 1978. *Publications:* Environmental Control of Plant Growth, 1963; The Induction of Flowering, 1969; Crop Physiology, 1975; Daylength and the Flowering of Plants, 1976; Wheat Science: today and tomorrow, 1981; Policy and Practice, 1987; Crop Evolution, Adaptation and Yield, 1993; more than 180 scientific papers in jls. *Recreations:* windsurfing, chopping wood, Charles Darwin. *Address:* 3 Elliott Street, Canberra, ACT 2601, Australia. *T:* Canberra (6) 2477815.

EVANS, Madelaine Glynne Dervel, CMG 1992; HM Diplomatic Service; Head of United Nations Department, Foreign and Commonwealth Office, since 1990; *b* 23 Aug. 1944. Second Sec., FCO, 1971; Buenos Aires, 1972; First Sec., FCO, 1975; on loan to UN Secretariat, NY, 1978; First Sec., UKMIS NY, 1979; First Sec., subseq. Counsellor, FCO, 1982; Counsellor, Brussels, 1987. *Address:* c/o Foreign and Commonwealth Office, SW1A 2AH.

EVANS, Mark; QC 1995; *b* 21 March 1946; *s* of Rev. Clifford Evans and Mary (*née* Jones); *m* 1971, Dr Barbara Skew; one *s* one *d. Educ:* Christ Coll., Brecon; King's Coll., London (LLB Hons). Called to the Bar, Gray's Inn, 1971; practice in Bristol, 1973–; founded St John's Chambers, 1978. *Recreations:* music, vintage cars. *Address:* St John's Chambers, Small Street, Bristol. *T:* Bristol (0117) 9213456. *Club:* Savage.

EVANS, Mark Armstrong, CVO 1994; Director, British Council, and Cultural Counsellor, Russia, Armenia, Belarus, Georgia, Kazakhstan, Kyrgyzstan, Moldova, Tajikistan, Turkmenistan and Uzbekistan, since 1992; *b* 5 Aug. 1940; *s* of late Charles Tunstall Evans, CMG, Birmingham, and Kathleen Armstrong, Newcastle; *m* 1965, Katharine, *d* of Alfred Bastable, Brecon; one *s* one *d. Educ:* Marlborough Coll.; Clare Coll., Cambridge (BA 1962; MA 1966); Moscow State Univ.; Bristol Univ. (PGCE 1964). Head, Russian and German, Chichester High Sch. for Boys, 1964–69; apptd to British Council, 1969; Bahrain, 1969–71; Frankfurt, 1971–73; MECAS, Lebanon, 1973–74; Dir, UAE in Dubai, 1974–77; temp. posting, Kabul, 1977; Asst Dir, Educnl Contracts, 1977–79; Dep. Rep. and Cultural Attaché, France, 1979–85; Head, Office Services, 1985–88; Dir, Canada, and Cultural Counsellor, Ottawa, 1988–92. Mem., RSAA. *Recreations:* building models, gardening, household chores. *Address:* c/o Foreign and Commonwealth Office, King Charles Street, SW1A 2AH. *Club:* Union (Cambridge).
See also D. M. A. Stokes.

EVANS, Prof. Martin John, PhD; FRS 1993; Professor of Mammalian Genetics, University of Cambridge, since 1994 (Reader, 1991–94); *b* 1 Jan. 1941; *s* of Leonard Wilfred Evans and Hilary Joyce (*née* Redman); *m* 1966, Judith Clare Williams, MBE; two *s* one *d. Educ:* St Dunstan's Coll., Catford; Christ's Coll., Cambridge (BA Pt II in Biochem., MA); PhD London 1969. University College London: Res. Assistant, Dept of Anatomy and Embryology, 1963–66; Asst Lectr, 1966–69; Lectr, 1969–78; Univ. Lectr, Dept of Genetics, Univ. of Cambridge, 1978–91. *Publications:* numerous contribs to scientific works. *Recreations:* family, walking two Norfolk terriers. *Address:* Wellcome/CRC Institute, Tennis Court Road, Cambridge CB2 1QR. *T:* Cambridge (01223) 334132.

EVANS, Matthew; Chairman, Faber & Faber Ltd, since 1981 (Managing Director, 1972–93); *b* 7 Aug. 1941; *s* of late George Ewart Evans, and of Florence Ellen Evans; *m* 1st, 1966, Elizabeth Amanda (*née* Mead) (marr. diss. 1991); two *s*; 2nd, 1991, Caroline (*née* Michel); two *s. Educ:* Friends' Sch., Saffron Walden; London Sch. of Econs and Polit. Science (BScEcon). Bookselling, 1963–64; Faber & Faber, 1964–. Chairman: National Book League, 1982–84; English Stage Company, 1984–90; Library and Information Commn, 1995–. Member: Council, Publishers Assoc., 1978–84; Literary Adv. Panel, British Council, 1986–; Franco-British Soc., 1981–. Governor, BFI, 1982–. FRSA 1990. *Recreation:* cricket. *Address:* c/o Faber & Faber, 3 Queen Square, WC1N 3AU. *Club:* Groucho (Dir).

EVANS, Michael; *see* Evans, T. M.

EVANS, Michael Nordon, CMG 1964; Permanent Secretary, Ministry of Health and Housing, Kenya, 1960–64, retired; *b* 27 April 1915; *s* of late Christmas and Lilian Margaret Louise Evans, Tunbridge Wells; *m* 1st, 1939, Mary Stockwood; one *d*; 2nd, 1951, Mary Josephine Suzette van Vloten; one *d. Educ:* Eastbourne Coll.; Queens' Coll., Cambridge. Apptd District Officer in Colonial Administrative Service, Kenya, 1939; African Courts Officer, Kenya, 1953; Dep. Commissioner for Local Government, 1954; Permanent Sec., 1958. *Recreation:* tennis. *Address:* Hugon Lodge, 13 Hugon Road, Claremont, Cape, 7700, Republic of South Africa. *Clubs:* Hawks (Cambridge); Kelvin Grove (Cape Town).

EVANS, Mostyn; *see* Evans, Arthur M.

EVANS, Nicholas; *see* Evans, H. N.

EVANS, Nigel Martin; MP (C) Ribble Valley, since 1992; *b* 10 Nov. 1957. *Educ:* Swansea Univ. (BA Hons). Retail Newsagent, family business, 1979–90. West Glamorgan County Council: Councillor (C), 1985–91; Dep. Leader, 1989. Chm., Welsh Cons. Candidates Policy Gp, 1990; Pres., Cons. NW Parly Gp, 1991. Contested (C): Swansea West, 1987; Pontypridd, Feb. 1989; Ribble Valley, March 1991. PPS to Sec. of State for Employment, 1993–94, to Chancellor of Duchy of Lancaster, 1994–95. Mem., Select Cttee on Transport, 1993; Secretary: NW Gp of Cons. MPs, 1992–; Manufacturing Cttee; All-

Party Tourism Cttee; Vice Chm., All-Party Music Gp; Treas., Parly Food and Health Forum. Director: Made in the UK Ltd; Small Business Bureau. Chm., Central Lancs, Marie Curie Cancer Care Fund, 1991–. *Recreations:* tennis, swimming, theatre, tourism, new technology, defence, broadcasting. *Address:* 6 Crumpax Avenue, Longridge, Preston PR3 3JQ. *T:* Preston, Lancs (01772) 786224. *Clubs:* Carlton, Commonwealth Trust, Royal Over-Seas League.

EVANS, Dr (Noel) John (Bebbington), CB 1980; Deputy Secretary, Department of Health and Social Security, 1977–84; *b* 26 Dec. 1933; *s* of William John Evans and Gladys Ellen (*née* Bebbington); *m* 1st, 1960, Elizabeth Mary Garbutt (marr. diss.); two *s* one *d*; 2nd, 1974, Eileen Jane McMullan. *Educ:* Hymers Coll., Hull; Christ's Coll., Cambridge (scholar; 1st cl., Nat. Sci. Tripos); Westminster Medical Sch., London; London Sch. of Hygiene and Tropical Med. (Newsholme prize, Chadwick Trust medal and prize). MA, MB, BChir; FRCP, DPH (Dist.), FFPHM. Called to Bar, Gray's Inn, 1965. House officer posts at: Westminster, Westminster Children's, Hammersmith, Central Middlesex and Brompton Hosps, 1958–60; Medical Registrar and Tutor, Westminster Hosp., 1960–61; Asst MoH, Warwickshire CC, 1961–65; Dept of Health and Social Security (formerly Min. of Health), 1965–84, DCMO 1977–82; Sir Wilson Jameson Travelling Fellowship, 1966. Chairman: Welsh Cttee on Drug Misuse, 1986–91; Nat. Biological Standards Bd, 1988– (Mem., 1975–); UK Transplant Support Service, 1991–; Member: Welsh Cttee, Countryside Commn, 1985–89; Welsh Health Promotion Authority, 1987–89. Privy Council Mem., Council of Royal Pharmaceutical Soc., 1988–. *Publications:* The Organisation and Planning of Health Services in Yugoslavia, 1967; Health and Personal Social Service Research in Wales, 1986; (with P. Benner) Isle of Man Health Services Inquiry, 1986; (with P. Cunliffe) Study of Control of Medicines, 1987; Postgraduate Medical and Dental Education in Wales, 1991; Review of External Advice to the Department of Health, 1995; contribs to med. jls. *Recreations:* canals, photography. *Address:* Providence House, Wyre Lane, Long Marston, Stratford-upon-Avon, Warwickshire CV37 8RQ. *T:* Stratford-upon-Avon (01789) 721509.

EVANS, Ven. Patrick Alexander Sidney; Archdeacon of Maidstone, since 1989; *b* 28 Jan. 1943; *m* 1969, Jane Kemp; two *s* one *d*. *Educ:* Clifton College, Bristol; Lincoln Theological Coll. Curate: Holy Trinity, Lyonsdown, Barnet, 1973–76; Royston, 1976–78; Vicar: Gt Gaddesden, 1978–82; Tenterden, 1982–89; RD of West Charing, 1988–89; Diocesan Dir of Ordinands, 1989–93. *Address:* Archdeacon's House, Charing, Kent TN27 0LU. *T:* Charing (0123371) 2294.

EVANS, Peter, CBE 1986; National Secretary, General Workers' Trade Group, Transport & General Workers' Union, 1974–90; *b* 8 Nov. 1929; *m* 1st, 1957, Christine Pamela (marr. diss.); one *d*; 2nd, 1975, Gillian Rosemary (decd); two *s* one *d*; 3rd, 1980, Joy Elizabeth. *Educ:* Culvert Road Secondary School, Tottenham. London bus driver, 1955–62; District Officer, TGWU, 1962–66; Regional Trade Group Sec., Public Services, 1966–74. *Recreations:* talking, swimming in deep water, golf. *Address:* 19 Uffington Road, SE27 0RW. *T:* 0181–670 5143. *Clubs:* Victoria, Players' Theatre.

EVANS, Prof. Peter Angus, DMus; FRCO; Professor of Music, University of Southampton, 1961–90; *b* 7 Nov. 1929; *y s* of Rev. James Mackie Evans and Elizabeth Mary Fraser; *m* 1953, June Margaret Vickery. *Educ:* West Hartlepool Grammar Sch.; St Cuthbert's Soc., University of Durham. BA (1st cl. hons Music), 1950; BMus, MA 1953; DMus 1958; FRCO 1952. Music Master, Bishop Wordsworth's Sch., Salisbury, 1951–52; Lecturer in Music, University of Durham, 1953–61. Conductor: Palatine Opera Group, 1956–61; Southampton Philharmonic Soc., 1965–90. *Publications:* Sonata for Oboe and Piano, 1953; Three Preludes for Organ, 1955; Edns of 17th Century Chamber Music, 1956–58; The Music of Benjamin Britten, 1979, 2nd edn 1989; contributor to Die Musik, in Geschichte und Gegenwart, to A Concise Encyclopædia of Music, 1958, to New Oxford History of Music, 1974, to New Grove Dictionary of Music, 1981, and to Blackwell History of Music in Britain, 1995; writer and reviewer, especially on twentieth century music. *Address:* Pye's Nest Cottage, Parkway, Ledbury, Herefordshire HR8 2JD. *T:* Ledbury (01531) 633256.

EVANS, Richard Jeremy; Racing Correspondent, The Times, since 1991; *b* 28 June 1953; *s* of late George Evans and of Helen Maud Evans; *m* 1976, Alison Mary Thom. *Educ:* Ipswich Sch., Suffolk. Journalist: East Anglian Daily Times, 1974–78; Cambridge Evening News, 1978–79; with The Times, 1979–. *Recreations:* golf, croquet, wine. *Address:* Marymead House, Chieveley, Berks RG16 8UX. *T:* Newbury (01635) 247256.

EVANS, Prof. Richard John, FBA 1993; FRHistS; Professor of History, since 1989, and Vice-Master, since 1993, Birkbeck College, London; *b* 29 Sept. 1947; *s* of late Ieuan Trefor Evans and of Evelyn Evans (*née* Jones); *m* 1976, Elín Hjaltadóttir (marr. diss. 1993); lives with Christine L. Corton; one *s*. *Educ:* Forest Sch., London; Jesus Coll., Oxford (Open Schol.; 1st Cl. Hons Mod. Hist. 1969; Stanhope Hist. Essay Prize 1969); St Antony's Coll., Oxford (MA, DPhil 1973); Hamburg Univ. (Hanseatic Schol.); LittD East Anglia, 1990. Lectr in History, Univ. of Stirling, 1972–76; University of East Anglia: Lectr, 1976; Prof. of European History, 1983–89. Vis. Associate Prof. of European History, Columbia Univ., 1980; Vis. Fellow, Humanities Res. Centre, ANU, Canberra, 1986; Alexander von Humboldt Fellow, Free Univ. of Berlin, 1981, 1985, 1989. Wolfson Literary Award for History, 1988; William H. Welch Medal, Amer. Assoc. for Hist. of Medicine, 1989; Medaille für Kunst und Wissenschaft der Hansestadt Hamburg, 1993; Fraenkel Prize in Contemporary History, 1994. *Publications:* The Feminist Movement in Germany 1894–1933, 1976; The Feminists, 1977; (ed) Society and Politics in Wilhelmine Germany, 1978; Sozialdemokratie und Frauenemanzipation im deutschen Kaiserreich, 1979; (ed jtly) The German Family, 1981; (ed) The German Working Class, 1982; (ed jtly) The German Peasantry, 1986; (ed jtly) The German Unemployed, 1987; Comrades and Sisters, 1987; Rethinking German History, 1987; Death in Hamburg, 1987; (ed) The German Underworld, 1988; (ed) Kneipengespräche im Kaiserreich, 1989; In Hitler's Shadow, 1989; Proletarians and Politics, 1990; (ed jtly) The German Bourgeoisie, 1992; Szenen aus der deutschen Unterwelt, 1995; Rituals of Retribution: capital punishment in Germany 1600–1987, 1996. *Recreations:* playing the piano (Beethoven, Chopin), reading (not history books), cooking for friends. *Address:* 33 Lupton Street, NW5 2HS. *T:* (day) 0171–631 6268.

EVANS, Richard Llewellyn; Director of Social Services, Birmingham City Council, since 1994; *b* 1 June 1949; *s* of Robert Ellis Evans and Sarah Christine (*née* Cassidy); *m*; one *s* one *d*. *Educ:* Chiswick Poly.; Dundee Univ. (Dip. Social Work; CQSW; Dip. TMHA). Aircraft engr, BAC, 1964–69; Surrey County Council: Instructor, 1969–72; Dep. Manager, 1972–73; Trng Officer, Lothian Regl Council, 1973–77; Manager, Emergency Duty Team, Wilts CC, 1977–79; Principal Officer, Lothian Regl Council, 1979–81; Develt Officer, London Boroughs' Regl Children's Planning Cttee, 1981–83; Avon County Council: Asst Dir of Social Services, 1983–90; Dir, Social Services, 1990–94. Hon. Fellow, Birmingham Univ. *Recreations:* music, cinema, entertaining. *Address:* Louisa Ryland House, 44 Newhall Street, Birmingham B3 3PL. *T:* 0121–235 2992.

EVANS, Sir Richard (Mark), KCMG 1984 (CMG 1978); KCVO 1986; HM Diplomatic Service, retired; Emeritus Fellow, Wolfson College, Oxford (Senior Research Fellow, 1988–95); *b* 15 April 1928; *s* of late Edward Walter Evans, CMG; *m* 1973, Rosemary Grania Glen Birkett; two *s*. *Educ:* Dragon Sch., Oxford; Repton Sch.; Magdalen Coll., Oxford (BA 1949; MA 1992). Joined HM Foreign (now Diplomatic) Service: Third Sec., London, 1952–55; Third Sec., Peking, 1955–57; Second Sec., London, 1957–62; First Sec.: Peking, 1962–64; Berne, 1964–68; London, 1968–70; Counsellor, 1970; Head of Near Eastern Dept, FCO, 1970–72, Head of Far Eastern Dept, 1972–74; Fellow, Centre for Internat. Affairs, Harvard Univ., 1974–75; Commercial Counsellor, Stockholm, 1975–77; Minister (Economic), Paris, 1977–79; Asst Under-Sec. of State, 1979–82, Dep. Under-Sec. of State, 1982–83, FCO; Ambassador to People's Republic of China, 1984–88. Non-Exec. Dir, China Investment Trust, 1993–. *Publication:* Deng Xiaoping and the Making of Modern China, 1993. *Recreations:* travel, reading, music. *Address:* Sevenhampton House, Sevenhampton, near Highworth, Wilts SN6 7QA. *Club:* United Oxford & Cambridge University.

EVANS, Sir Robert, Kt 1994; CBE 1987; FEng; FIMechE, FInstE; Chairman, British Gas plc, 1989–93 (Chief Executive, 1983–92 and Member of the Board, 1983–89); *b* 28 May 1927; *s* of Gwilym Evans and Florence May Evans; *m* 1950, Lilian May (*née* Ward); one *s* one *d*. *Educ:* Old Swan Coll., Liverpool; Blackburn Coll.; City of Liverpool Coll. (Tech.). FEng 1991. D. Napier & Son Ltd, 1943–49; North Western Gas Bd, 1950–56; Burmah Oil Co., 1956–62; Dir of Engrg, Southern Gas Bd, 1962–70; Dep. Dir (Ops), Gas Council, 1972; Dir of Operations, British Gas, 1972–75; Dep. Chm., North Thames Gas, 1975–77; Chm., E Midlands Gas Region, 1977–82; Man. Dir, Supplies, British Gas Corp., 1982–83. President: Instn of Gas Engrs, 1981–82; Inst. of Energy, 1991–92; Pipeline Industries Guild, 1990–92. Chm., Nat. Council for Hospice and Specialist Palliative Care Services. FInstE (MInstE 1988); Hon. FIGasE 1961; CIMgt (CBIM 1983); Hon. FCGI. Freeman, City of London, 1974; Mem., Engineers' Co., 1984. *Recreations:* reading, golf.

EVANS, Sir (Robert) Charles, Kt 1969; MA, FRCS; Principal, University College of North Wales, 1958–84; Vice-Chancellor, University of Wales, 1965–67, and 1971–73; *b* 19 Oct. 1918; *o s* of late R. C. Evans and Mrs Charles Evans; *m* 1957, Denise Nea Morin; three *s*. *Educ:* Shrewsbury Sch.; University Coll., Oxford. BM, BCh Oxon 1943; MA Oxon 1947; FRCS 1949. RAMC, 1943–46 (despatches). Surgical Registrar, United Liverpool Hosps, and Liverpool Regional Hosps, 1947–57. Hunterian Prof., Royal College Surg. Eng., 1953. Dep. Leader, Mt Everest Expedition, 1953; Leader, Kangchenjunga Expedition, 1955; Pres., Alpine Club, 1967–70; Mem. Council, Royal Geog. Society, 1960–61. Hon. DSc Wales, 1956. Cullum Medal, American Geog. Soc., 1954; Livingstone Medal, Scottish Geog. Soc., 1955; Founder's Medal, Royal Geog. Society, 1956. *Publications:* Eye on Everest, 1955; On Climbing, 1956; Kangchenjunga—The Untrodden Peak, 1956; articles in Alpine Journal, Geographical Journal, etc. *Address:* Ardincaple, Capel Curig, N Wales LL24 0EU. *Club:* Alpine.

EVANS, Robert John Emlyn; Member (Lab) London North West, European Parliament, since 1994; *b* 23 Oct. 1956; *s* of T. F. Evans and late Marjorie Evans. *Educ:* County Sch., Ashford, Middlesex; Shoreditch Coll. of Educn; Inst. of Educn, London Univ. (BEd 1978; MA 1983). Teacher: Thames Ditton Middle Sch., 1978–83; Woodville Middle Sch., Leatherhead, 1983–85; Dep. Headteacher, Town Farm Middle Sch., 1985–89; Headteacher, Crane Jun. Sch., Hanworth, 1990–94. Member: Youth, Culture, Educn and Media Cttee, 1994–, Rules of Procedure Cttee, 1994–, EP. Contested (Lab): Berkshire East, 1987; Uxbridge, 1992; London South and Surrey, European Parly election, 1989. Member: NUT (Pres., Leatherhead Br., 1984–85); Nat. Exec., Socialist Educnl Assoc., 1989–. *Recreations:* cricket, hockey, swimming, theatre, travel, history of education. *Address:* European Parliament, 97 Rue Belliard, 1040 Brussels, Belgium; Pavitt Hall, Union Road, Wembley, Middlesex HA0 4AU. *T:* 0181–900 0065, *Fax:* 0181–900 9412. *Clubs:* MCC; Ruskin House Labour (Croydon); Ashford Hockey, Ashford Cricket (Middlesex); Middlesex County Cricket, Incogniti Cricket.

EVANS, Prof. Robert John Weston, PhD; FBA 1984; Fellow, Brasenose College, since 1968 and Professor of European History, since 1992, Oxford; *b* 7 Oct. 1943; *s* of Thomas Frederic and Margery Evans (*née* Weston), Cheltenham; *m* 1969, Kati Róbert; one *s* one *d*. *Educ:* Dean Close School; Jesus College, Cambridge (BA 1st Cl. with distinction 1965, PhD 1968). Lectr, 1969–90, Reader in Modern History of E Central Europe, 1990–92, Oxford Univ. Mem., Inst. for Advanced Study, Princeton, 1981–82. František Palacký Medal, Czechoslovakia, 1991. Jt Editor, English Historical Review, 1985–. *Publications:* Rudolf II and his World, 1973; The Wechel Presses, 1975; The Making of the Habsburg Monarchy, 1979 (Wolfson Literary Award for History, 1980; Anton Gindely Preis, Austria, 1986); (ed with H. Pogge von Strandmann) The Coming of the First World War, 1988; (ed with T. V. Thomas) Crown, Church and Estates: Central European politics, 1991. *Recreations:* music, walking, natural (and unnatural) history. *Address:* Brasenose College, Oxford OX1 4AJ. *T:* Oxford (01865) 277890; 83 Norreys Road, Cumnor, Oxford OX2 9PU.

EVANS, Maj.-Gen. Robert Noel, CB 1981; Postgraduate Dean and Commandant, Royal Army Medical College, 1979–81; *b* 22 Dec. 1922; *s* of William Evans and Norah Moynihan; *m* 1950, Mary Elizabeth O'Brien; four *s* one *d*. *Educ:* Christian Brothers Sch., Tralee, Co. Kerry; National University of Ireland (MB, BCh, BAO 1947). DTM&H 1961; FFARCS 1963. Commnd RAMC 1951; Consultant Anaesthetist, 1963; CO BMH Rinteln, 1969–71; ADMS 4th Div., 1971–73; DDMS HQ BAOR, 1973–75; Comdt, RAMC Trng Centre, 1975–77; DMS, HQ BAOR, 1977–79; QHP 1976–81. Col Comdt, RAMC, 1981–86. MFCM 1978. OStJ 1978. *Recreations:* gardening, walking, music. *Address:* 32 Folly Hill, Farnham, Surrey GU9 0BH. *T:* Farnham (01252) 726938.

EVANS, Roderick; *see* Evans, D. R.

EVANS, Roger Kenneth; MP (C) Monmouth, since 1992; Parliamentary Under-Secretary of State, Department of Social Security, since 1994; *b* 18 March 1947; *s* of G. R. Evans of Mere, Wilts and late Dr A. M. Evans; *m* 1973, June Rodgers, MA, barrister; two *s*. *Educ:* The Grammar Sch., Bristol; Trinity Hall, Cambridge (MA). President: Cambridge Union, 1970; Cambridge Georgian Gp, 1970; Chm., Cambridge Univ. Conservative Assoc., 1969. Called to the Bar: Middle Temple, 1970 (Astbury Schol.); Inner Temple, *ad eundem*, 1979; in practice, 1970–94. Contested (C): Warley West, Oct. 1974, 1979; Ynys Môn, 1987; Monmouth, May 1991. Member: Welsh Affairs Select Cttee, 1992–94; Ecclesiastical Cttee of Parlt. Mem. Exec. Cttee, Friends of Friendless Churches, 1983–. Member: Ecclesiastical Law Soc.; Exec. Cttee, Soc. of Cons. Lawyers. Freeman, City of London. *Recreations:* gardening, architectural history. *Address:* 2 Harcourt Buildings, Temple, EC4Y 9DB; House of Commons, SW1A 0AA. *Clubs:* Carlton, Coningsby (Chm., 1976–77; Treas., 1983–87); Abergavenny Constitutional, Chepstow Conservative, Monmouth Conservative, Usk Conservative.

EVANS, Roger W.; *see* Warren Evans.

EVANS, Roy Lyon, OBE 1993; General Secretary, Iron and Steel Trades Confederation, 1985–93; *b* 13 Aug. 1931; *s* of David Evans and Sarah (*née* Lyon); *m* 1960, Brenda Jones; one *s* two *d*. *Educ:* Gowerton Grammar Sch., Swansea. Employed in Tinplate Section of Steel Industry, 1948. Iron and Steel Trades Confederation: Divl Organiser, NW Area,

1964–69; Divl Organiser, W Wales Area, 1969–73; Asst Gen. Sec., 1973–85. Mem., Gen. Council, TUC, 1985–93. Jt Sec., Jt Industrial Council for the Slag Industry, 1975–85; Mem., ECSC Consultative Cttee, 1985–93 (Pres., 1986–88); Hon. Sec., British Section, IMF, 1985–93 (Pres., Iron and Steel Dept (World), 1986). Member: Jt Accident Prevention Adv. Cttee, 1974–93 (Chm., 1983); NEC of Labour Party, 1981–84. Bd Mem., British Steel (Industry) Ltd, 1986–94. *Recreations:* reading, walking.

EVANS, Russell Wilmot, MC 1945; Chairman, Rank Organisation, 1982–83; *b* 4 Nov. 1922; *s* of William Henry Evans and Ethel Williams Wilmot; *m* 1956, Pamela Muriel Hayward (*d* 1989); two *s* one *d*. *Educ:* King Edward's Sch., Birmingham; Birmingham Univ. LLB Hons. Served HM Forces, 1942–47; commnd Durham LI, 1942, Major, 1945. Admitted Solicitor, Birmingham, 1949; Solicitor with Shakespeare & Vernon, Birmingham, 1949–50; Asst Sec., Harry Ferguson, 1951; Sec., Massey-Ferguson (Hldgs) and UK subsids, 1955–62; Dir, gp of private cos in construction industry, 1962–67; joined Rank Organisation, 1967: Dep. Sec., 1967–68; Sec., 1968–72; Dir, 1972–83; Man. Dir, 1975–82; Dep. Chm., 1981; Dir, principal subsid. and associated cos incl. Rank Xerox, 1975–83; Fuji Xerox, 1976–83; Chm., Rank City Wall, 1976–83. Director: Eagle Star Holdings, 1982–87; Oxford Economic Forecasting Ltd, 1986–; Medical Cyclotron Ltd, 1988–. *Recreations:* tennis, golf, photography. *Address:* Walnut Tree, Roehampton Gate, SW15 5JR. *T:* 0181–876 2433. *Clubs:* English-Speaking Union, Roehampton (Dir 1971–87, Chm., 1984–87, Pres., 1991–).

EVANS, Ruth Elizabeth; Director, National Consumer Council, since 1992; *b* 12 Oct. 1957; *d* of Peter Evans and Dr Anne Evans. *Educ:* Girton Coll., Cambridge (MA Hist.). Dir, Maternity Alliance, 1981–86; Dep. Dir, then Actg Dir, Nat. Assoc. for Mental Health (MIND), 1986–90; Gen. Sec., War On Want, 1990; Mgt Consultant, 1990–91. FRSA 1991. *Recreations:* writing, music, swimming. *Address:* National Consumer Council, 20 Grosvenor Gardens, SW1W 0DH. *T:* 0171–730 3469.

EVANS, Simon John; His Honour Judge Simon Evans; a Circuit Judge, since 1991; *b* 18 Jan. 1937; *s* of Dr Thomas Evans and late Dr Enid Allardice Evans (*née* Taylour); *m* 1968, Heather Wendy Champion; one *s* one *d*. *Educ:* Diocesan Coll., Cape Town. Apprentice motor mechanic, Lusaka, Northern Rhodesia, 1954; GCE student, Guildford, 1955–56; Bar student, London, 1956–59; called to the Bar, Middle Temple, 1959; barrister, Temple, 1959–91; a Recorder, South Eastern Circuit, 1989–91. *Recreations:* Balinese cats, French studies, English footpaths. *Address:* c/o Isleworth Crown Court, 36 Ridgeway Road, Isleworth, Mddx TW7 5LP. *T:* 0181–568 8811.

EVANS, (Thomas) Alun, CMG 1994; HM Diplomatic Service; Counsellor, Foreign and Commonwealth Office, since 1982; *b* 8 June 1937; *s* of late Thomas Evans and Mabel Elizabeth (*née* Griffiths); *m* 1964, Bridget Elisabeth, *d* of Peter Lloyd, *qv* and Nora Kathleen Williams (*née* Patten); three *s*. *Educ:* Shrewsbury Sch.; University Coll., Oxford (MA). Army, 1956–58. Entered HM Foreign Service, 1961; Third Sec., Rangoon, 1962–64; Second Sec., Singapore, 1964–66; FO, 1966–70; First Sec., Geneva, 1970–74; FCO, 1974–79; Counsellor, Pretoria, 1979–82. *Recreations:* music, fishing. *Address:* c/o Foreign and Commonwealth Office, SW1A 2AH. *Club:* Travellers'.

EVANS, Very Rev. (Thomas) Eric; Dean of St Paul's, since 1988; *b* 1928; *s* of late Eric John Rhys Evans and Florence May Rogers; *m* 1957, Linda Kathleen Budge; two *d*. *Educ:* St David's Coll., Lampeter (BA); St Catherine's Coll., Oxford (MA); St Stephen's House, Oxford. Ordained, 1954; Curate, Margate Parish Church, 1954–58; Sen. Curate, St Peter's, Bournemouth, 1958–62; first Dir, Bournemouth Samaritans; Diocesan Youth Chaplain, dio. Gloucester, 1962–69; Residentiary Canon of Gloucester Cathedral, 1969–88; Archdeacon of Cheltenham, 1975–88. Wing Chaplain, ATC, 1963–69; Hon. Chaplain: Gloucester Coll. of Educn, 1968–75; Gloucestershire Constabulary, 1977–88. Chm., Glos Trng Cttee, 1967–69; Proctor in Convocation and Mem. Gen. Synod of C of E, 1970–; a Church Comr, 1978– (Mem., Bd of Governors, 1978–, Assets Cttee, 1985–88). Canon Missioner, dio. Gloucester, 1969–75; Chairman: House of Clergy, dio. Gloucester, 1979–82; Bd of Social Responsibility, dio. Gloucester, 1982–83; Glos Assoc. for Mental Health, 1983–85 (Vice-Chm., 1965–78); Glos Diocesan Adv. Cttee, 1984–88. Mem. Exec. Cttee, 1975–88, Chm., 1981–88, Council for Places of Worship, subseq. Council for the Care of Churches. Dean, Order of St Michael and St George, 1988–; Dean, Order of the British Empire, 1988–; Chaplain to Guild of Freemen of City of London, 1988–; ChStJ 1988, Sub-Prelate, 1991. Dir, Ecclesiastical Insurance Office Ltd, 1979–. Mem. Council, Cheltenham Ladies' College, 1982–93. Freeman, City of London, 1988; Liveryman, Gardeners' Co., 1993–. Hon. DD City, 1993. *Recreation:* travel, esp. Middle East. *Address:* The Deanery, 9 Amen Court, EC4M 7BU. *Clubs:* Carlton; Downhill Only (Wengen).

EVANS, (Thomas) Godfrey, CBE 1960; public relations officer; *b* Finchley, 18 Aug. 1920; *s* of A. G. L. Evans; *m* 1973, Angela Peart; one *d*. *Educ:* Kent Coll., Canterbury. Joined Kent County Staff at age of 16; first kept wicket for England in Test *v* India, 1946; first overseas Test tour, Australia and New Zealand, 1946–47; also played in Test matches in W Indies and S Africa; played in 91 Test matches (world record 1959); dismissed 218 batsmen in Test cricket from behind the stumps, 88 more than Oldfield, the previous record-holder, and retained the record until 1976; the first wicket-keeper to have dismissed more than 200 victims and scored over 2000 runs in Test cricket; held world record for not conceding a bye while 1,054 runs were scored in a Test series (Australia, 1946); holds record for longest Test innings without scoring (95 minutes *v* Australia, Adelaide, 1947); holds jointly, with Charles Barnett, record for fastest score before lunch in a Test match (98 *v* India, Lord's, 1952); in making 47 in 29 minutes was three runs off the fastest 50 in Test cricket (*v* Australia, Old Trafford, 1956); first Englishman to tour Australia with MCC four times after War of 1939–45. *Publications:* Behind the Stumps, 1951; Action in Cricket, 1956; The Gloves Are Off, 1960; Wicket Keepers of the World, 1984. *Recreations:* real tennis, golf, squash. *Address:* 51 Delaware Mansions, Delaware Road, W9 2LH. *Club:* MCC (Hon. Life Mem.).

EVANS, (Thomas) Michael, QC 1973; **His Honour Judge Michael Evans;** a Circuit Judge, since 1979; *b* 7 Sept. 1930; *s* of late David Morgan Evans, Barrister, and of Mary Gwynydd Lloyd; *m* 1957, Margaret Valerie Booker; one *s* four *d*. *Educ:* Brightlands Prep. Sch., Newnham, Glos; Marlborough Coll., Wilts; Jesus Coll., Oxford (MA (Juris.)). Called to the Bar, Gray's Inn, 1954; Wales and Chester Circuit, 1955; a Recorder of the Crown Court, 1972–79. Legal Chm., Mental Health Review Tribunal for Wales, 1970. Chancellor, Diocese of St Davids, 1986–. *Recreations:* walking, gardening, genealogy. *Address:* The Old Rectory, Reynoldston, Gower, Swansea SA3 1AD. *T:* Gower (01792) 390129.

EVANS, Prof. Trevor, FRS 1988; Personal Professor, University of Reading, 1968–92, Emeritus Professor, 1992; *b* 26 April 1927; *s* of late Henry and Margaret Evans; *m* Patricia Margaret Booth (*née* Johnson); two *s* and two step *s*. *Educ:* Bridgend Grammar Sch.; Univ. of Bristol (BSc, PhD, DSc). FInstP. Physicist: British Nylon Spinners, 1955–56; Tube Investments Res. Lab., 1956–58; Physics Department, University of Reading, 1958–92: Res. Physicist, 1958–61; successively, Lectr, Reader, Personal Prof., 1961–92; Hd of Dept, 1984–88; Warden of Wantage Hall, Reading Univ., 1971–84. *Publications:* papers in Proc. Royal Soc. and Phil. Mag., almost entirely concerning synthetic and natural diamond. *Recreation:* pottering in the garden. *Address:* Aston, Tutts Clump, Reading, Berks RG7 6JZ. *T:* Bradfield (01734) 744498.

EVANS, Dr Trevor John; Chief Executive and Secretary, Institution of Chemical Engineers, since 1994 (General Secretary, 1976–94); *b* 14 Feb. 1947; *o s* of Evan Alban Evans and Margaret Alice Evans (*née* Hilton); *m* 1973, Margaret Elizabeth (*née* Whitham); three *s* one *d*. *Educ:* King's Sch., Rochester; University Coll., London (BSc (Eng) 1968, PhD 1972); CEng, FIChemE, FIMgt. Res. Officer, CSIR, Pretoria, 1968–69; Ford Motor Co., Aveley, Essex, 1972–73; Institution of Chemical Engineers: Asst Sec., Technical, 1973–75; Dep. Sec., 1975–76. Member: Bd, Council of Science and Technology Institutes, 1976–87; Exec. Cttee, Commonwealth Engineers Council, 1976–; Jt Hon. Sec., European Fedn of Chem. Engrg, 1976–. Kurnakov Meml Medal, Russian Acad. of Scis, 1991. *Publications:* scientific papers and general articles in Chemical Engrg Science, The Chem. Engr, etc. *Recreations:* home renovation, drama. *Address:* The Institution of Chemical Engineers, 12 Gayfere Street, SW1P 3HP. *T:* 0171–222 2681.

EVANS, Sir Vincent; *see* Evans, Sir W. V. J.

EVANS, Maj.-Gen. William Andrew, CB 1993; Secretary, Council of TAVRAs, since 1993; *b* 5 Aug. 1939; *s* of late Maj.-Gen. Roger Evans, CB, MC and Eileen (*née* Stanton); *m* 1964, Virginia Susan, *e d* of late William Robert Tomkinson; two *d*. *Educ:* Sherborne; RMA Sandhurst; Christ Church, Oxford (MA). Commnd 5th Royal Inniskilling Dragoon Guards, 1959; served in BAOR, Middle East, Cyprus, Libya, N Ireland; Staff Coll., Bracknell, 1971; Army Instructor, RAF Cranwell, 1974–75; Instructor, Army Staff Coll., 1978–80; CO 5th Royal Inniskilling Dragoon Guards, 1980–82 (despatches, 1981); Col, Asst Dir (Policy), Defence Policy Staff, 1982–83; Comdr 4 Armd Bde, 1983–85; RCDS 1986; DCS, HQ BAOR, 1987–89; GOC Eastern Dist, 1989–92, retired. Council, Essex Univ., 1994–. FIMgt. Liveryman, Broderers' Co., 1992–. *Recreations:* tennis, fishing, birdwatching, cricket (Pres., Army Cricket Assoc., 1989–91; Chm., Combined Services Cricket Assoc., 1990). *Address:* Council of TAVRAs, Duke of York's Headquarters, Chelsea, SW3 4SG. *Club:* Cavalry and Guards.

EVANS, Dr (William) David; Head of Technology and Innovation Policy, Department of Trade and Industry, since 1994; *b* 20 April 1949; *s* of late Harold Evans and Gladys Evans (*née* Webber); *m* 1980, Elizabeth Crowe; three *s* one *d*. *Educ:* Haberdashers' Aske's School, Elstree; St Catherine's College, Oxford (BA 1971; DPhil 1974; Senior Scholar). FRAS 1975. Dept of Energy, 1974–80; First Sec., Science and Technology, British Embassy, Bonn, 1980–83; Asst Sec., 1984–89, Chief Scientist, 1989–92, Dept of Energy; Hd of Envmt Div., DTI, 1992–94. Member: NERC, 1989–92; EPSRC, 1994–; PPARC, 1994–; Assessor, SERC, ACORD, 1989–92. *Publications:* scientific papers in professional jls. *Recreations:* music, reading, history of technology. *Address:* Department of Trade and Industry, 151 Buckingham Palace Road, SW1W 9SS.

EVANS, (William) Emrys, CBE 1981; Senior Regional Director, Wales, Midland Bank Ltd, 1976–84; *b* 4 April 1924; *s* of late Richard and Mary Elizabeth Evans; *m* 1946, Mair Thomas; one *d*. *Educ:* Llanfair Caereinion County Sch. FCIB. Served War, RN, 1942–46 (despatches 1944). Entered Midland Bank Ltd, 1941; Asst Gen. Manager (Agric.), 1967–72; Reg. Dir, S Wales, 1972–74; Reg. Dir, Wales, 1974–76. Director: Executive Secondment Ltd, 1983–90 (Vice Chm., 1983–90); Align-Rite Ltd, 1984–; National Welsh Omnibus Services Ltd, 1989–92; Floridan Ltd, 1991–; Faircheck Ltd; Chairman: Menter a Busnes, 1988–; Cwmni Dilysu Cyf. Chairman: Welsh Cttee for Economic and Industrial Affairs, 1984–91; Midland Bank Adv. Council for Wales, 1984–. Director: Develt Corp. for Wales, 1973–77; Welsh Industrial Develt Adv. Bd, 1975–86; Develt Bd for Rural Wales, 1976–89; Royal Welsh Agricl Soc., 1973–; Mem. Council, CBI, Wales, 1975–86 (Chm., 1979–81). Pres., Royal Nat. Eisteddfod of Wales, 1980–83. Vice President: Tenovus Cancer Res. Unit, 1980–; Kidney Res. Unit for Wales Foundn, 1980–; Chm., Dr Barnardo's Centenary in Wales Appeal, 1988; Trustee: Catherine and Lady Grace James Foundn, 1973–; John and Rhys Thomas James Foundn, 1973–; Welsh Sports Aid Trust, 1980– (Vice Chm., 1988–); Llandovery Coll., 1982–93; Council for the Protection of Rural Wales, 1991–. Chm., Welsh Sports Aid Foundn, 1988–94 (Gov., 1980–); Member: Council for the Welsh Lang., 1973–78; Design Council Wales Adv. Cttee, 1981–86; Prince of Wales Cttee, 1975–87; Dairy Produce Quota Tribunal, 1984–92. Pres., Welsh Congregational Church in Wales, 1989 (Treasurer, 1975–86); Treasurer, Mansfield Coll., Oxford, 1977–89 (Trustee, 1989–); Member, Court and Council: UC Swansea, 1972– (Chm. Council, 1982–); UC Aberystwyth, 1979–84; Univ. of Wales, 1980–. Hon. LLD Wales, 1983. FRSA 1982. High Sheriff, S Glamorgan, 1985–86. *Recreations:* golf, gardening, music. *Address:* Maesglas, Pen-y-turnpike, Dinas Powis, S Glam CF64 4HH. *T:* Cardiff (01222) 512985. *Club:* Cardiff and County (Cardiff).

EVANS, Sir (William) Vincent (John), GCMG 1976 (KCMG 1970; CMG 1959); MBE 1945; QC 1973; Barrister-at-Law; a Judge of the European Court of Human Rights, 1980–91; *b* 20 Oct. 1915; *s* of Charles Herbert Evans and Elizabeth (*née* Jenkins); *m* 1947, Joan Mary Symons; one *s* two *d*. *Educ:* Merchant Taylors' Sch., Northwood; Wadham Coll., Oxford (Hon. Fellow 1981). 1st Class Hons, Jurisprudence, 1937; BCL, 1938; MA, 1941; elected Cassel Scholar, Lincoln's Inn, 1937; called to Bar, Lincoln's Inn, 1939 (Hon. Bencher, 1983). Served in HM Forces, 1939–46. Legal Adviser (Lt-Col) to British Military Administration, Cyrenaica, 1945–46; Asst Legal Adviser, Foreign Office, 1947–54; Legal Counsellor, UK Permanent Mission to the United Nations, 1954–59; Legal Counsellor, FO, 1959–60; Dep. Legal Adviser, FO, 1960–68; Legal Adviser, FCO, 1968–75, retired. Chm., Bryant Symons & Co. Ltd, 1964–85. Chm., European Cttee on Legal Cooperation, Council of Europe, 1969–71; UK Rep. Council of Europe Steering Cttee on Human Rights, 1976–80 (Chm., 1979–80); Mem., Human Rights Cttee set up under Internat. Covenant on Civil and Political Rights, 1977–84 (Vice-Chm., 1979–80); Mem., Permanent Court of Arbitration, 1987–. Vice-Pres., British Inst. of Human Rights, 1992–; Member: Adv. Bd, Centre for Internat. Human Rights Law, Univ. of Essex, 1983–94; Council of Management, British Inst. of Internat. and Comparative Law, 1969–; Diplomatic Service Appeals Bd, 1976–86; Sch. Cttee, Merchant Taylors' Co., 1985–93. Pres., Old Merchant Taylors' Soc., 1984–85; Vice-Pres., Hon. Soc. of Cymmrodorion, 1987–. DUniv Essex, 1986. *Recreation:* gardening. *Address:* (home) 4 Bedford Road, Moor Park, Northwood, Mddx HA6 2BB. *T:* Northwood (01923) 824085. *Club:* Athenæum.

EVANS, Very Rev. Wyn; *see* Evans, Very Rev. J. W.

EVANS, Wynford; *see* Evans, J. W.

EVANS-ANFOM, Emmanuel, FRCSE 1955; Commissioner for Education and Culture, Ghana, 1978; Member, Council of State, 1979; Chairman, National Education Commission, since 1984; *b* 7 Oct. 1919; *m* 1952, Leonora Francetta Evans (*d* 1980); three *s* one *d*; *m* 1984, Elise Henkel. *Educ:* Achimota School; Edinburgh University (MB; ChB; DTM&H). House Surgeon, Dewsbury Infirmary, 1948–49; Medical Officer, Gold Coast Medical Service, 1950–56, Specialist Surgeon, 1956–67; Senior Lecturer, Ghana Medical School, 1966–67; Vice-Chancellor, Univ. of Science and Technology, Kumasi, 1967–74.

Mem., WHO Expert Panel on Med. and Paramed. Educn, 1972–; Chairman: Nat. Council for Higher Educn, 1974–78; W African Exams Council, 1991–94; Chairman: Med. and Dental Council; Akrofi-Christaller Centre for Mission Res. and Applied Theology, 1986–; Inter-church and Ecumenical Relations Cttee, Presbyterian Church of Ghana, 1990–. Titular Mem., Internat. Assoc. Surgeons; Past President: Ghana Medical Assoc.; Assoc. of Surgeons of W Africa; FICS. Fellow: Ghana Acad. Arts and Sciences, 1971 (Pres., 1987–); African Acad. of Scis, 1986. Chm., Ghana Hockey Assoc. Pres., Ghana Boys' Brigade Council, 1987–. Hon. DSc Salford, 1974. *Publications:* Aetiology and Management of Intestinal Perforations, Ghana Med. Jl, 1963; Traditional Medicine in Ghana: practice problems and prospects, 1986. *Recreations:* hockey, music, art. *Address:* PO Box M135, Accra, Ghana.

EVANS-BEVAN, Sir Martyn Evan, 2nd Bt *cr* 1958; *b* 1 April 1932; *s* of Sir David Martyn Evans-Bevan, 1st Bt, and of Eira Winifred, *d* of late Sidney Archibald Lloyd Glanley; *S* father, 1973; *m* 1957, Jennifer Jane Marion, *d* of Robert Hugh Stevens; four *s*. *Educ:* Uppingham. Entered family business of Evan Evans Bevan and Evans Bevan Ltd, 1953; High Sheriff of Breconshire, 1967; Liveryman, Worshipful Co. of Farmers; Freeman, City of London. *Recreations:* shooting and fishing. *Heir:* *s* David Gawain Evans-Bevan; [*b* 16 Sept. 1961; *m* 1987, Philippa, *y d* of Patrick Sweeney; one *s* one *d*]. *Address:* Felinnewydd, Llandefalle, Brecon, Powys LD3 0NE. *Club:* Carlton.

EVANS-FREKE, family name of **Baron Carbery.**

EVANS-LOMBE, Hon. Sir Edward (Christopher), Kt 1993; **Hon. Mr Justice Evans-Lombe;** a Judge of the High Court of Justice, Chancery Division, since 1993; *b* 10 April 1937; *s* of Vice-Adm. Sir Edward Evans-Lombe, KCB, and Lady Evans-Lombe; *m* 1964, Frances Marilyn MacKenzie; one *s* three *d*. *Educ:* Eton; Trinity Coll., Cambridge (MA). National Service, 1955–57: 2nd Lieut Royal Norfolk Regt. Called to the Bar, Inner Temple, 1963, Bencher, 1985. Standing Counsel to Dept of Trade in Bankruptcy matters, 1971; QC 1978; a Recorder, 1982–93. Chm., Agricultural Land Tribunal, S Eastern Region, 1983–93. *Recreations:* fishing, falconry, forestry. *Address:* Royal Courts of Justice, Strand, WC2A 2LL. *Club:* Norfolk (Norwich).

EVANS-TIPPING, (Sir) David Gwynne, (5th Bt *cr* 1913, of Oaklands Park, Awre, Co. Gloucester); *b* 25 Nov. 1943; *e s* of Sir Francis Loring Gwynne-Evans, 4th Bt (who assumed name of Evans-Tipping, 1943–58), and of his 1st wife, Elisabeth Fforde, *d* of J. Fforde-Tipping; *S* father, 1993, but does not use the title. *Educ:* Trinity Coll., Dublin (BAgricSci). *Heir:* *b* Christopher Evan Evans-Tipping [*b* 27 Feb. 1946; *m* 1974, Fenella Catherine Morrison; one *s* one *d*]. *Address:* 11 rue Angelique-Verien, Neuilly-sur-Seine, France.

EVATT, Hon. Elizabeth Andreas, AO 1982; President, Australian Law Reform Commission, 1988–93; *b* 11 Nov. 1933; *d* of Clive Raleigh Evatt, QC and Marjorie Hannah (*née* Andreas); *m* 1960, Robert J. Southan, *qv*; one *d* (one *s* decd). *Educ:* Sydney Univ. (LLB); Harvard Univ. (LLM). Called to the Bar: NSW, 1955; Inner Temple, 1958. Chief Judge, Family Court of Australia, 1976–88. Dep. Pres., Australian Conciliation and Arbitration Commn, 1973–89; Chairperson, Royal Commn on Human Relationships, 1974–77; Dep. Pres., Australian Ind. Relns Commn, 1989–. Member: UN Cttee on Elimination of Discrimination against Women, 1984–92 (Chairperson, 1989–91); UN Human Rights Cttee, 1993–; Australian Law Reform Commn, 1993–94. Chancellor, Univ. of Newcastle, 1988–94. Hon. LLD: Sydney, 1985; Macquarie, 1989; Queensland, 1992; Flinders, 1994; Hon. Dr Newcastle, 1988. *Publication:* Guide to Family Law, 1986, 2nd edn 1991. *Recreation:* music. *Address:* 67 Brown Street, Paddington, NSW 2021, Australia. *Club:* Royal Corinthian Yacht.

EVE, family name of **Baron Silsoe.**

EVELEIGH, Rt. Hon. Sir Edward Walter, PC 1977; Kt 1968; ERD; MA; a Lord Justice of Appeal, 1977–85; *b* 8 Oct. 1917; *s* of Walter William and Daisy Emily Eveleigh; *m* 1940, Vilma Bodnar; *m* 1953, Patricia Helen Margaret Bury (decd); two *s* (and one *s* decd). *Educ:* Peter Symonds; Brasenose Coll., Oxford (Hon. Fellow 1977). Commissioned in the Royal Artillery (Supplementary Reserve), 1936; served War of 1939–45 (despatches, 1940). Called to Bar, Lincoln's Inn, 1945, Bencher 1968, Treas., 1988; QC 1961. Recorder of Burton-on-Trent, 1961–64, of Gloucester, 1964–68; Chm., QS, County of Oxford, 1968–71 (Dep. Chm., 1963–68); a Judge of the High Court of Justice, Queen's Bench Div., 1968–77; Presiding Judge, SE Circuit, 1971–76. Mem., General Council of the Bar, 1965–67. Mem., Royal Commn on Criminal Procedure, 1978–80; Chm., Statute Law Soc., 1985–89; President: British-German Jurists' Assoc., 1974–85; Bar Musical Soc., 1980–89. Hon. Citizen: Texas, 1980; Austin, 1985; Dallas, 1985. *Address:* Royal Courts of Justice, Strand, WC2 6TW. *Club:* Garrick.

EVELEIGH, Air Vice-Marshal Geoffrey Charles, CB 1964; OBE 1945; RAF retired; *b* 25 Oct. 1912; *s* of Ernest Charles Eveleigh, Henley-on-Thames; *m* 1939, Anthea Josephine, *d* of F. H. Fraser, Ceylon; one *s* one *d*. *Educ:* Brighton Coll.; RAF Coll., Cranwell. Joined RAF, 1932; served War of 1939–45 in Bomber Command and No 2 Group; Dep. Chief of Air Staff, Royal New Zealand Air Force, 1955–57; Air Commodore, 1957; Dir-Gen. of Signals, Air Ministry, 1959–61; Air Vice-Marshal, 1961; Air Officer, Administration, Fighter Command, 1961–64; retd 1965. *Address:* 22 Rosehill Park, Emmer Green, Reading RG4 8XE. *Club:* Royal Air Force.

EVENNETT, David Anthony; MP (C) Erith and Crayford, since 1983; *b* 3 June 1949; *s* of Norman Thomas Evennett and Irene Evennett; *m* 1975, Marilyn Anne Smith; two *s*. *Educ:* Buckhurst Hill County High School for Boys; London School of Economics and Political Science. BSc (Econ) Upper Second Hons, MSc (Econ). School Master, Ilford County High School for Boys, 1972–74; Marine Insurance Broker, Lloyd's, 1974–81; Mem., Lloyd's, 1976–; Dir, Lloyd's Underwriting Agency, 1982–91. Redbridge Borough Councillor, 1974–78. Contested (C) Hackney South and Shoreditch, 1979. PPS to Minister of State, Dept of Educn, 1992–93, to Sec. of State for Wales, 1993–95. Mem., Select Cttee on Educn, Science and the Arts, 1986–92. Mem., Bow Gp, 1971–; Vice-Chm., H of C Motor Club, 1992– (Sec., 1985–86). Vice-Pres., Hackney S and Shoreditch Cons. Assoc., 1985–. *Recreations:* my family, reading, history, theatre and cinema. *Address:* House of Commons, SW1A 0AA. *Club:* Priory Conservative (Belvedere).

EVERALL, Mark Andrew; QC 1994; *b* 30 June 1950; *s* of John Everall, FRCP and Pamela Everall; *m* 1978, Anne Perkins; two *d*. *Educ:* Ampleforth Coll., York; Lincoln Coll., Oxford (MA). Called to the Bar, Inner Temple, 1975; Asst Recorder, 1993–. *Publication:* (ed jtly) Rayden and Jackson on Divorce and Family Matters, qly Service to 16th edn. *Recreations:* walking, music, architecture. *Address:* 1 Mitre Court Buildings, Temple, EC4Y 7BS. *T:* 0171–797 7070.

EVERARD, Maj.-Gen. Sir Christopher E. W.; *see* Welby-Everard.

EVERARD, John Vivian; HM Diplomatic Service; Ambassador to the Republic of Belarus, since 1993; *b* 24 Nov. 1956; *s* of William Ralph Everard and Margaret Nora Jennifer Everard (*née* Massey); *m* 1990, Heather Ann Starkey. *Educ:* King's Sch., Chester; King Edward VI Sch., Lichfield; Emmanuel Coll., Cambridge (BA 1978; MA 1986); Peking Univ.; Manchester Business Sch. (MBA 1986). Joined HM Diplomatic Service, 1979: FCO, 1979–81; Third (later Second) Sec., Peking, 1981–83; Second Sec., Vienna, 1983–84; Manchester Business Sch., 1984–86; Metapraxis Ltd, 1986–87; FCO, 1987–90; First Sec., Santiago, 1990–93; Chargé d'Affaires, Minsk, 1993. *Recreations:* reading, travel, cats. *Address:* c/o Foreign and Commonwealth Office, King Charles Street, SW1A 2AH.

EVERARD, Sir Robin (Charles), 4th Bt *cr* 1911; Management Consultant, since 1976; *b* 5 Oct. 1939; *s* of Sir Nugent Henry Everard, 3rd Bt and Frances Audrey (*d* 1975), *d* of J. C. Jesson; *S* father, 1984; *m* 1963, Ariel Ingrid, *d* of late Col Peter Cleasby-Thompson, MBE, MC; one *s* two *d*. *Educ:* Sandroyd School; Harrow; RMA Sandhurst. Short service commn, Duke of Wellington's Regt, 1958–61. Money Broker; Managing Director, P. Murray-Jones, 1962–76; Consultant, 1976–91. *Heir:* *s* Henry Peter Charles Everard, *b* 6 Aug. 1970. *Address:* Church Farm, Shelton, Long Stratton, Norwich NR15 2SB.

EVERARD, Simon, TD 1968; DL; Chairman, Alliance and Leicester Building Society, since 1994; *b* 30 Oct. 1928; *s* of Charles Miskin Everard and Monica Mary Everard (*née* Barford); *m* 1955, Joceline Margaret Holt; three *s* one *d*. *Educ:* Uppingham Sch.; Clare Coll., Cambridge (Hons History). Served TA, Leics Yeomanry, subseq. Leics and Derbys Yeomanry. Ellis & Everard: joined 1952; Chm., 1980–90 and 1991–92; joined Leicester Temperance Building Soc., 1967; merged with Leicester Permanent Bldg Soc., 1974, with Alliance Bldg Soc., 1984; Dep. Chm., 1984–94. Non-Exec. Dir, Croda International, 1991–. DL Leics, 1984. *Recreations:* shooting, tennis, golf, bridge. *Address:* Sludge Hall, Cold Newton, Billesdon, Leics LE7 9DA. *Club:* Cavalry and Guards.

See also T. J. Everard.

EVERARD, Timothy John, CMG 1978; HM Diplomatic Service, retired; Secretary General, Order of St John, 1988–93; *b* 22 Oct. 1929; *s* of late Charles M. Everard and late Monica M. Everard (*née* Barford); *m* 1955, Josiane Romano; two *s* two *d*. *Educ:* Uppingham Sch.; Magdalen Coll., Oxford. BA (Mod. Langs). Banking: Barclays Bank DCO, 1952–62, in Egypt, Sudan, Kenya, Zaire. Entered Foreign (later Diplomatic) Service: First Sec., FO, 1962–63; First Sec., Commercial, Bangkok, 1964–66; resigned to take up directorship in Ellis & Everard Ltd, 1966–67. Rejoined Foreign and Commonwealth Office, Oct. 1967: First Sec., FO, 1967–68; Bahrain, 1969–72 (First Sec. and Head of Chancery, HM Political Residency); seconded to Northern Ireland Office, FCO, April–Aug. 1972; Consul-Gen., then Chargé d'Affaires, Hanoi, 1972–73; Economic and Commercial Counsellor, Athens, 1974–78; Commercial Counsellor, Paris, 1978–81; Minister, Lagos, 1981–84; Ambassador to GDR, 1984–88. Trustee, Dresden Trust. KStJ 1988. *Recreations:* golf, tennis. *Address:* Leagues, Stonecross, Crowborough, Sussex TN6 3SD. *Club:* Reform.

EVERED, David Charles; Second Secretary, Medical Research Council, since 1988; *b* 21 Jan. 1940; *s* of late Thomas Charles Evered and Enid Christian Evered; *m* 1964, Anne Elizabeth Massey Lings, (Kit), *d* of John Massey Lings, Manchester; one *s* two *d*. *Educ:* Cranleigh Sch., Surrey; Middlesex Hosp. Med. Sch. (BSc 1961, MB 1964, MRCP 1967, MD 1971). Junior hospital appointments, London and Leeds, 1964–70; First Asst in Medicine, Wellcome Sen. Res. Fellow and Consultant Physician, Univ. of Newcastle upon Tyne and Royal Victoria Infirmary, 1970–78; Dir, Ciba Foundn, 1978–88. Member: British Library Medical Information Review Panel, 1978–80; Council, St George's Hosp. Med. Sch. 1983–91; Cttee, Assoc. of Med. Res. Charities, 1981–84, 1987–88 (Vice-Chm., 1987–88); Public Understanding of Science Cttee, Royal Soc., 1986–88; Media Resource Service Adv. Cttee, NY, 1986–; NW Thames RHA, 1988–90; Hammersmith & Queen Charlotte's SHA, 1989–94; Council, Internat. Agency for Res. into Cancer (Lyon), 1988–; Council, RPMS, 1994–; Vice-Pres., Science Cttee, Louis Jeantet Fondation de Médecine, 1984–91. FRCP 1978; FIBiol 1978; FRSM; Scientific Fellow, Zool Soc. of London (Mem. Council, 1985–89). Member: Soc. for Endocrinology; Eur. Thyroid Assoc. (Mem. Exec. Cttee, 1977–81, Sec.-Treas., 1983–89). *Publications:* Diseases of the Thyroid, 1976; (with R. Hall and R. Greene) Atlas of Clinical Endocrinology, 1979, 2nd edn 1990; (with M. O'Connor) Collaboration in Medical Research in Europe, 1981; numerous papers on medicine, education and science policy. *Recreations:* reading, history, tennis, sailing. *Address:* Medical Research Council, 20 Park Crescent, W1N 4AL. *T:* 0171–636 5422.

EVEREST, David Anthony, PhD; FRSC; Research Associate, UK Centre for Economic and Environmental Development, since 1987; Editor, Energy and Environment, since 1989; *b* 18 Sept. 1926; *s* of George Charles and Ada Bertha Everest; *m* 1956, Audrey Pauline (*née* Sheldrick); three *s*. *Educ:* John Lyon Sch., Harrow; University Coll. London (Bsc, PhD). Lecturer in Chemistry, Battersea Polytechnic, 1949–56; Sen. Scientific Officer, 1956–58, PSO, 1958–64, National Chemical Laboratory; SPSO, 1964–70, Dep. Chief Scientific Officer, 1970–77, National Physical Laboratory; DCSO, RTP Div., Dept of Industry, 1977–79; Chief Scientist, Environmental Protection Gp, 1979–86, and Dir of Sci. Res. Policy, 1983–86, DoE. Vis. Res. Fellow, UEA, 1986–92. *Publications:* Chemistry of Beryllium, 1962; section on Beryllium in Comprehensive Inorganic Chemistry, 1972; The Greenhouse Effect: issues for policy makers, 1988; The Provision of Expert Advice to Government on Environmental Matters: the role of advisory committees, 1990; (contrib.) Science and Technology in the UK, 1991; (contrib.) Environmental Dilemmas: ethics and decisions, 1993; papers in Inorganic Chemistry, Extractive Metallurgy and Material Science. *Recreations:* astronomy, reading, walking. *Address:* Talland, Chorleywood Road, Chorleywood, Herts WD3 4ER. *T:* Rickmansworth (01923) 773253.

EVERETT, Bernard Jonathan; HM Diplomatic Service; Consul-General, Houston, 1991–95; *b* 17 Sept. 1943; *s* of Arnold Edwin Everett and Helene May Everett (*née* Heine); *m* 1970, Maria Olinda, *d* of Raul Correia de Albuquerque and Maria de Lourdes Gonçalves de Albuquerque; two *s* one *d* (and one *d* decd). *Educ:* King's Coll. Sch., Wimbledon; Lincoln Coll., Oxford (BA 1965). Researcher, Reader's Digest, 1965; entered HM Diplomatic Service, 1966; Third, later Second Sec., Lisbon, 1967; FCO, 1971; Consul, Luanda, 1975; FCO, 1976; Head of Chancery, Lusaka, 1978; Consul (Commercial), Rio de Janeiro, 1980; Asst Head, Information Dept, FCO, 1983; on secondment as Head, Sub-Saharan Africa Br., DTI, 1984; Ambassador to Guatemala, 1987–91. *Recreations:* sport, performing arts, numismatics. *Address:* c/o Foreign and Commonwealth Office, SW1A 2AH.

EVERETT, Charles William Vogt; Director of Finance and Administration, The Court Service, since 1994; *b* 15 Oct. 1949; *s* of Dr Thomas Everett and Ingeborg Everett (*née* Vogt); *m* 1978, Elizabeth Vanessa Ellis; three *s*. *Educ:* Bryanston Sch.; Reading Univ. Admin. trainee, Lord Chancellor's Dept, 1971; Asst Private Sec. to Lord Chancellor, 1974–76; Dept of Transport, 1982–84; Lord Chancellor's Dept, 1984–; Asst Sec., 1984; Under Sec., 1991; Head of Policy and Legal Services Gp, 1991–94. *Address:* The Court Service, Southside, 105 Victoria Street, SW1E 6QT.

EVERETT, Christopher Harris Doyle, CBE 1988; MA; Director General and Secretary, Daiwa Anglo-Japanese Foundation, since 1990; *b* 20 June 1933; *s* of late Alan Doyle Everett, MBE, MS, FRCS, and Annabel Dorothy Joan Everett (*née* Harris); *m* 1955, Hilary (Billy) Anne (*née* Robertson); two *s* two *d*. *Educ:* Winchester College; New

College, Oxford. MA (Class. Mods and Lit. Hum.). Grenadier Guards, Nat. Service, 1951–53. HM Diplomatic Service, 1957–70: posts included Beirut, Washington and Foreign Office; Headmaster: Worksop Coll., 1970–75; Tonbridge Sch., 1975–89. Chm., 1986, Vice-Chm., 1987, HMC. JP Tonbridge and W Malling, 1976–89. Hon. FCP 1988. *Recreations:* reading, walking, tennis. *Address:* (office) Condor House, 14 St Paul's Churchyard, EC4M 8BD. *T:* 0171–548 8302, *Fax:* 0171–334 9314; (home) Lavender House, 12 Madeira Park, Tunbridge Wells, Kent TN2 5SX. *T:* Tunbridge Wells (01892) 525624.

EVERETT, Douglas Hugh, MBE 1946; FRS 1980; Leverhulme Professor of Physical Chemistry, University of Bristol, 1954–82, now Emeritus; Dean of Faculty of Science, 1966–68; Pro-Vice-Chancellor, 1973–76; *b* 26 Dec. 1916; *e s* of late Charles Everett and Jessie Caroline; *m* 1942, Frances Elizabeth Jessop; two *d. Educ:* Grammar Sch., Hampton-on-Thames; University of Reading; Balliol Coll., Oxford. Wantage Scholar, Reading Univ., 1935–38; Kitchener Scholar, 1936–39; BSc, 1938; Ramsay Fellow, 1939–41; DPhil 1942. Special Scientific Duties, WO, 1942–45. ICI Fellow, Oxford Univ., 1945–47; Chemistry Lecturer, Dundee Univ. Coll., 1947; MA 1947; Fellow, Lecturer and Tutor, Exeter Coll., Oxford, 1947–48; Prof. of Chemistry, Dundee Univ. Coll., University of St Andrews, 1948–54. Chm., Internat. Union of Pure and Applied Chemistry Commn on Colloid and Surface Chemistry, 1969–73. FRSE 1950; DSc 1956. Mem., Building Research Board, DSIR, 1954–61; a Vice-Pres., Faraday Soc., 1958–61, 1963–65, 1968–70, Pres., 1976–78; Mem. Chemical Soc. Council, 1961–64, 1972–74 (Tilden Lectr, 1955; Award in Colloid and Surface Chemistry, 1971); Pres., Section B, BAAS, 1979–80; a Vice-Pres. and Gen. Sec., BAAS, 1983–88; Pres., Internat. Assoc. of Colloid and Interface Scientists, 1988–90. *Publications:* Introduction to Chemical Thermodynamics, 1959, 2nd edn, 1971; Basic Principles of Colloid Science, 1988; (with W. Rudzinski) Adsorption of Gases on Heterogeneous Surfaces, 1991; papers on Physical Chemistry in scientific jls. *Recreations:* walking, painting. *Address:* School of Chemistry, The University, Bristol BS8 1TS; 35 Downleaze, Bristol BS9 1LX.

EVERETT, Eileen, (Mrs Raymond Everett); *see* Diss, E.

EVERETT, Oliver William, CVO 1991 (LVO 1980); Librarian, Windsor Castle and Assistant Keeper of The Queen's Archives, since 1985; *b* 28 Feb. 1943; *s* of Charles Everett, DSO, MC and Judy Rothwell; *m* 1965, Theffania Vesey Stoney; two *s* two *d. Educ:* Felsted Sch.; Christ's Coll., Cambridge; Fletcher Sch. of Law and Diplomacy, Mass, USA. HM Diplomatic Service, 1967–81: First Sec., New Delhi, 1969–73; Head of Chancery, Madrid, 1980–81; Asst Private Sec. to HRH The Prince of Wales, 1978–80; Private Sec. to HRH The Princess of Wales, 1981–83, and Comptroller to TRH The Prince and Princess of Wales, 1981–83; Dep. Librarian, Windsor Castle, 1984. *Recreations:* skiing, rackets, windsurfing, baseball. *Address:* Garden House, Windsor Castle, Berks SL4 1NG. *T:* Windsor (01753) 833711; The East Wing, Kirtlington Park, Oxon OX5 3JN. *T:* Bletchington (01869) 350589. *Club:* Ski Club of Great Britain.

EVERETT, Thomas Henry Kemp; Special Commissioner of Income Tax, since 1983; *b* 28 Jan. 1932; *s* of late Thomas Kemp Everett and Katharine Ida Everett (*née* Woodward); *m* 1954, June (*née* Partridge); three *s. Educ:* Queen Elizabeth's Hospital, Bristol; Univ. of Bristol. LLB Hons 1957. Solicitor (Hons), admitted 1960; Partner, Meade-King & Co., 1963–83. Clerk to General Commissioners, Bedminster Div., 1965–83. Chairman: Service 9, 1972–75; Bristol Council of Voluntary Service, 1975–80; St Christopher's Young Persons' Residential Trust, 1976–83; Mem., Governing Council, St Christopher's School, Bristol, 1983–89; Gov., Queen Elizabeth's Hosp., 1974–92 (Vice-Chm. Govs, 1980–91); Pres., Queen Elizabeth's Hosp. Old Boys' Soc., 1990–91. Hon. Treasurer and Vice-Chm., Rowberrow PCC; Mem., Axbridge Deanery Synod. *Recreations:* music, reading, walking. *Address:* Dolebury Cottage, Dolberrow, Churchill, near Bristol BS19 5NS. *T:* Churchill (01934) 852329; 15–19 Bedford Avenue, WC1B 3AS. *T:* 0171–631 4242. *Club:* Lansdowne.

EVERITT, Prof. Alan Milner, PhD; FRHistS; FBA 1989; Hatton Professor and Head of Department of English Local History, University of Leicester, 1968–82, now Professor Emeritus (Associate Professor, 1982–84); *b* 17 Aug. 1926; *s* of Robert Arthur Everitt and Grace Beryl Everitt (*née* Milner); unmarried. *Educ:* Sevenoaks Sch.; Univ. of St Andrews (MA 1951); Inst. of Historical Res., London Univ. (Carnegie Scholar; PhD 1957). FRHistS 1969. Editorial Assistant, ACU, 1951–54; Department of English Local History, University of Leicester: Res. Assistant, 1957–59; Res. Fellow in Urban Hist., 1960–65; Lectr in Eng. Local Hist., 1965–68. Lectures: Gregynog, Univ. of Wales, 1976; Helen Sutermeister, UEA, 1982; James Ford Special, Univ. of Oxford, 1983. *Publications:* The County Committee of Kent in the Civil War, 1957; Suffolk and the Great Rebellion 1640–1660, 1960; The Community of Kent and the Great Rebellion 1640–60, 1966, 3rd edn 1986; Change in the Provinces: the seventeenth century, 1969; The Pattern of Rural Dissent: the nineteenth century, 1972; Perspectives in English Urban History, 1973; (with Margery Tranter) English Local History at Leicester 1948–1978, 1981; Landscape and Community in England, 1985; Continuity and Colonization: the evolution of Kentish settlement, 1986; contribs to: The Agrarian History of England and Wales; Past and Present, Trans of RHistS, Agricl Hist. Rev., Urban History Yearbook, Jl of Histl Geog., Jl of Transport Hist., Archaeologia Cantiana, Local Historian, TLS, Nomina. *Address:* Fieldedge, Poultney Lane, Kimcote, Lutterworth, Leics LE17 5RX.

EVERITT, Anthony Michael; writer; Secretary-General, Arts Council of Great Britain, 1990–94 (Deputy Secretary-General, 1985–90); *b* 31 Jan. 1940; *s* of late Michael Anthony Hamill Everitt and Simone Dolores Cathérine (*née* de Vergriette; she *m* 2nd, John Brunel Cohen). *Educ:* Cheltenham Coll.; Corpus Christi Coll., Cambridge (BA Hons English, 1962). Lectured variously at National Univ. of Iran, Teheran, SE London Coll. of Further Educn, Birmingham Coll. of Art, and Trent Polytechnic, 1963–72; The Birmingham Post: Art Critic, 1970–75; Drama Critic, 1974–79; Features Editor, 1976–79; Director: Midland Gp Arts Centre, Nottingham, 1979–80; E Midlands Arts Assoc., 1980–85. Chairman: Ikon Gall., Birmingham, 1976–79; Birmingham Arts Lab., 1977–79; Vice-Chm., Council of Regional Arts Assocs, 1984–85; Member: Drama Panel, 1974–78, and Regional Cttee, 1979–80, Arts Council of GB; Cttee for Arts and Humanities, 1986–87, Performing Arts Cttee, 1987–92, CNAA; General Adv. Council, IBA, 1987–90. *Publications:* Abstract Expressionism, 1974; contribs to The Guardian, Financial Times, Studio Internat., Country Life, etc. *Address:* Westerlies, Anchor Hill, Wivenhoe, Essex CO7 9BL.

EVERITT, William Howard, FEng 1988; FIMechE, FIEE; Managing Director, Automotive T & N plc, since 1990; *b* 27 Feb. 1940; *s* of H. G. H. Everitt and J. S. Everitt; *m* Antha Cecilia; two *s. Educ:* Leeds Univ. (BSc). Director of Operations, IBM Europe, 1974; Managing Director: Wellworthy, AE, 1975–76; Bearings, AE, 1977–79; AE plc, 1983–86 (Dir, 1978); Dir, T. & N. plc, 1987–. *Recreation:* golf. *Address:* Horley House, Hornton Lane, Horley, near Banbury, Oxon OX15 6BL. *T:* Banbury (01295) 730603.

EVERSON, Sir Frederick (Charles), KCMG 1968 (CMG 1956); *b* 6 Sept. 1910; *s* of Frederick Percival Everson; *m* 1937, Linda Mary Clark (*d* 1984); two *s* one *d* (and one *s* decd). *Educ:* Tottenham County Sch., Middlesex. BSc (Econ.) London. Entered Civil Service, July 1928; Consular Service, Dec. 1934. Chief Administrative Officer, British Embassy, Bonn, Germany, 1953–56; Ambassador to El Salvador, 1956–60; Commercial Counsellor, British Embassy, Stockholm, 1960–63; Minister (Economic), British Embassy, Paris, 1963–68. *Address:* Apt 17, Aynhoe Park, Aynho, Banbury, Oxon OX17 3BQ. *T:* Croughton Brackley (01869) 811362.

EVERSON, John Andrew; education consultant; *b* 26 Oct. 1933; *s* of Harold Leslie Everson and Florence Jane Stone; *m* 1961, Gilda Ramsden; two *s. Educ:* Tiffin Boys' Sch., Kingston-upon-Thames; Christ's Coll., Cambridge (MA); King's Coll., London (PGCE). Teacher: Haberdashers' Aske's Sch., Elstree, 1958–65; City of London Sch., 1965–68; Schools Inspectorate, DES, later Dept for Educn, 1968–92; Chief Inspector for Secondary Educn, 1981–89; seconded to Peat Marwick McLintock, 1989; Chief Inspector for Teacher Training, 1990–92. *Publications:* (with B. P. FitzGerald) Settlement Patterns, 1968; (with B. P. FitzGerald) Inside the City, 1972. *Recreations:* opera, walking, theatre, chess. *Address:* 74 Longdown Lane North, Epsom, Surrey KT17 3JF. *T:* Epsom (01372) 721556. *Club:* Athenæum.

EVERT, Christine Marie; American tennis player, retired 1989; founder, Chris Evert Charities Inc., 1989; *b* 21 Dec. 1954; *d* of James and Colette Evert; *m* 1st, 1979, John Lloyd (marr. diss. 1987); 2nd, 1988, Andy Mill; two *s. Educ:* St Thomas Aquinas High Sch., Fort Lauderdale. Amateur tennis player, 1970–72, professional player, 1972–89. Semi-finalist in US Open at age of 16; won numerous titles, including: Wimbledon: 1974, 1976, 1981 (doubles, 1976); French Open: 1974–75, 1979–80, 1983, 1985–86; US Open: 1975–78, 1980, 1982; Australian Open: 1982, 1984. Represented USA in Wightman Cup, 1971–73, 1975–82, and in Federation Cup, 1977–82. Pres., Women's Tennis Assoc., 1982–91. *Address:* c/o International Management Group, 1 Erieview Plaza, Suite 1300, Cleveland, OH 44114, USA; 7200 West Camino Real, Suite 310, Boca Raton, FL 33433, USA.

EVERY, Sir Henry (John Michael), 13th Bt *cr* 1641, of Egginton, Derbyshire; Partner, Touche Ross, Chartered Accountants, Birmingham; *b* 6 April 1947; *s* of Sir John Simon Every, 12th Bt and of Janet Marion, *d* of John Page; *S* father, 1988; *m* 1974, Susan Mary, *er d* of Kenneth Beaton, JP, Eastshotte, Hartford, Cambs; three *s. Educ:* Malvern College. FCA. Qualified as Chartered Accountant, 1970; worked in South Africa, 1970–74. Pres., Birmingham and West Midlands Dist Soc. of Chartered Accountants, 1995–96 (Chm., Dist Trng Bd, 1991–93). Mem., Egginton Parish Council, 1987–. Mem. Cttee, Lunar Soc., 1993–. *Recreations:* tennis, squash, gardening; supporter of Nottingham Forest FC. *Heir: s* Edward James Henry Every, *b* 3 July 1975. *Address:* Cothay, Egginton, near Derby DE65 6HJ. *Club:* Speakers' (Burton-on-Trent).

EVES, David Charles Thomas, CB 1993; Deputy Director General and HM Chief Inspector of Factories, Health and Safety Executive; *b* 10 Jan. 1942; *s* of Harold Thomas Eves and Violet Eves (*née* Edwards); *m* 1964, Valerie Ann Carter; one *d. Educ:* King's Sch., Rochester; University Coll., Durham. Teacher, Kent CC, 1963–64; HM Inspector of Factories, Min. of Labour, 1964; Under Sec., 1985–89, Dep. Sec., and Dep. Dir Gen., 1989–, HSE, Dept of Employment Gp; HM Chief Inspector of Factories, 1985–88, 1992–; Dir, Resources and Planning Div., HSE, 1988–89. *Recreations:* sailing, fishing, music, would-be painter. *Address:* Health and Safety Executive, Rose Court, 2 Southwark Bridge, SE1 9HS. *T:* 0171–717 6450, *Fax:* 0171–717 6616. *Club:* Athenæum.

EVISON, Dame (Helen June) Patricia, DBE 1993 (OBE 1980); freelance actress on stage, film, radio and television in New Zealand and Australia; *b* 2 June 1924; *d* of Rev. Ernest Oswald Blamires and Annie (*née* Anderson); *m* 1948, Roger Douglas Evison; two *s* one *d. Educ:* Solway Coll., Masterton; Victoria Univ. (BA 1943); Auckland Teachers Training Coll. (postgrad. course 1944); Auckland Univ. (DipEd 1944); LTCL (speech) 1942). Directors course, Old Vic Theatre Centre, 1947–48 (first NZ bursary); Assistant to Michel Saint-Denis, Young Vic Theatre Co., 1947–48; freelance director, Wellington, 1949–52; tutor for NZ Opera and NZ Ballet Schs, 1953–79. *Theatre includes:* Happy Days, 1964, 1974; Father's Day, 1966; The Killing of Sister George, 1968; An Evening with Katherine Mansfield (one-woman show), 1972; Awatea, 1974; Home, 1976; Juno and the Paycock, 1977; Hot Water, 1983; Last Days in Woolloomooloo, 1983; Ring Round the Moon, 1990; Steel Magnolias, 1991; Lettice and Lovage, 1993; *films:* Tim, 1979 (Best Supporting Actress, Aust. Film Inst, 1979); The Earthling, 1981; Starstruck, 1982; Bad Blood, 1982; The Silent One, 1983; The Clinic, 1983; What the Moon Saw, 1988; Moonrise, 1992; *television:* All Earth to Love, 1963; Pukemanu, 1971 (Cummings award for Best NZ Actress, 1972); Pig in a Poke, 1974 (Logie award for best individual acting perf., 1974); They Don't Clap Losers, 1974; Close to Home (series), 1975–82; The Emigrants, 1977; A Town Like Alice, 1982; Flying Doctors (series), 1984–87. Charter Member: Wellington Zonta Club; Zonta Club for Port Nicholson. *Recreations:* music, watching cricket and soccer, reading, swimming, travel. *Address:* 11 Beerehaven Road, Seatoun Heights, Wellington 3, New Zealand. *T:* (4) 3888766.

EWANS, Sir Martin Kenneth, KCMG 1987 (CMG 1980); HM Diplomatic Service, retired; *b* 14 Nov. 1928; *s* of late John Ewans; *m* 1953, Mary Tooke; one *s* one *d. Educ:* St Paul's; Corpus Christi Coll., Cambridge (major scholar, MA). Royal Artillery, 1947–49, 2nd Lt. Joined Commonwealth Relations Office, 1952; Second Sec., Karachi, 1954–55; First Sec.: Ottawa, 1958–61; Lagos, 1962–64; Kabul, 1967–69. Counsellor, Dar-es-Salaam, 1969–73; Head of East African Dept, FCO, 1973–77; Minister, New Delhi, 1978–82; Sen. Civilian Instructor, RCDS, 1982–83; High Commissioner: in Harare, Zimbabwe, 1983–85; Nigeria, 1986–88. *Publications:* Bharatpur, Bird Paradise, 1989; The Battle for the Broads, 1992. *Recreations:* bird watching, writing. *Address:* 24 Crockwell Street, Long Compton, Warwicks CV36 5JN.

EWART, Gavin Buchanan, FRSL; freelance writer (poet), since 1971; *b* 4 Feb. 1916; *s* of George Arthur Ewart and Dorothy Hannah (*née* Turner); *m* 1956, Margaret Adelaide Bennett; one *s* one *d. Educ:* Wellington Coll.; Christ's Coll., Cambridge (BA Hons 1937, MA 1942). FRSL 1981. Salesman, Contemporary Lithographs, 1938; served War, Royal Artillery, 1940–46; Production Manager, Editions Poetry, London, 1946; British Council, 1946–52; Advertising copywriter in London advertising agencies, 1952–71. Cholmondeley Award for Poetry, 1971; Michael Braude Award for Light Verse, AAIL, 1991. *Publications:* Poems and Songs, 1939; Londoners, 1964; Pleasures of the Flesh, 1966; The Deceptive Grin of the Gravel Porters, 1968; The Gavin Ewart Show, 1971; Be My Guest!, 1975; No Fool Like An Old Fool, 1976; Or Where a Young Penguin Lies Screaming, 1978; All My Little Ones, 1978; The Collected Ewart 1933–1980, 1980, 2nd edn 1982; The New Ewart, 1982; More Little Ones, 1983; Other People's Clerihews, 1983; The Ewart Quarto, 1984; The Young Pobble's Guide to His Toes, 1985; The Complete Little Ones of Gavin Ewart, 1986; The Learnèd Hippopotamus, 1987; Late Pickings, 1987; Penultimate Poems, 1989; Caterpillar Stew, 1990; Collected Poems 1980–1990, 1991; Like It Or Not, 1992; 85 Poems, 1993. *Recreations:* reading, listening to music. *Address:* 57 Kenilworth Court, Lower Richmond Road, SW15 1EN. *T:* 0181–788 7071.

EWART, Sir (William) Ivan (Cecil), 6th Bt, *cr* 1887; DSC 1945; JP; *b* 18 July 1919; *s* of late Major William Basil Ewart (*y s* of late Frederick William Ewart, 7th *s* of 1st Bt); *S* kinsman (Sir Talbot Ewart, 5th Bt), 1959; *m* 1948, Pauline Chevallier (*d* 1964), *e d* of late

Wing Comdr Raphael Chevallier Preston, OBE, AFC, JP; one *s* two *d*. *Educ:* Radley. Ulster Div., RNVR, 1938. Served War of 1939–45; Lieut, RNVR; service in Coastal Forces (Motor Torpedo-Boats), 1939–42 (DSC); POW, Germany, 1942–45. Chairman: William Ewart & Son Ltd, Linen Manufacturers, 1968–73 (Dir, 1954–73); William Ewart Investments Ltd, Belfast, 1973–77; Ewart New Northern Ltd, Belfast, 1973–77; E Africa Resident Rep., Royal Commonwealth Soc. for the Blind, 1977–84; Administrator, Ngora Freda Carr Hosp., Uganda (Assoc. of Surgeons of E Africa), 1985–89. Non-exec. Dir, Ewart plc, Belfast, 1986–92. Pres., NI Chamber of Commerce and Industry, 1974. A Northern Ireland Delegate to the Duke of Edinburgh's Study Conf. on the Human Problems of Industrial Communities within the Commonwealth and Empire, Oxford, 1956; Pres., Church of Ireland's Young Men's Soc., 1951–61 and 1975–77; Chm. Flax Spinners Assoc., 1961–66; Pres., Oldpark Unionist Assoc., 1950–68. Belfast Harbour Comr, 1968–77. High Sheriff for County Antrim, 1976. *Heir: s* William Michael Ewart, *b* 10 June 1953. *Address:* Hill House, Hillsborough, Co. Down BT26 6AE. *T:* Hillsborough (01846) 683000; PO Box 30171, Nairobi, Kenya. *T:* 725726. *Clubs:* Naval; Ulster Reform (Belfast); Nairobi.

EWBANK, Sir Anthony (Bruce), Kt 1980; Judge of the High Court of Justice, Family Division, 1980–95; *b* 30 July 1925; *s* of late Rev. Harold Ewbank and Gwendolen Ewbank (*née* Bruce); *m* 1958, Moya McGinn; four *s* one *d*. *Educ:* St John's Sch., Leatherhead; Trinity Coll., Cambridge, Natural Sciences Tripos (MA). Sub Lieut RNVR, 1945–47. Maths Master, Stamford School, 1947–50; Physics Master, Epsom Coll., 1950–53. Permanent RNVR, 1951–56. Called to Bar, Gray's Inn, 1954; Bencher, 1980. Junior Counsel to Treasury in Probate matters, 1969; QC 1972; a Recorder of the Crown Court, 1975–80. Chm., Family Law Bar Assoc., 1978–80. *Address:* 1 Chetwynd House, The Green, Hampton Court KT8 9BS.

EWBANK, Prof. Inga-Stina; Professor of English Literature, University of Leeds, since 1985; *b* 13 June 1932; *d* of Gustav and Ingeborg Ekeblad; *m* 1959, Roger Ewbank; one *s* two *d*. *Educ:* Högre Allänna Läroverket för Flickor, Gothenburg; Univs of Carleton (BA), Gothenburg (Fil.kand.), Sheffield (MA) and Liverpool (PhD). William Noble Fellow, Univ. of Liverpool, 1955–57; Res. Fellow at Shakespeare Inst., Univ. of Birmingham, 1957–60; Univ. of Liverpool: Asst Lectr, 1960–63; Lectr, 1963–70; Sen. Lectr, 1970–72; Reader in English Literature, Bedford Coll., Univ. of London, 1972–74, Hildred Carlile Prof., 1974–84. Vis. Lectr, Univ. of Munich, 1959–60; Vis. Assoc. Prof., Northwestern Univ., 1966; Visiting Professor: Harvard Univ., 1974; Univ. of Maryland, 1981; Georgetown Univ., 1982; Columbia Univ., 1984. Mem., Univ. and Poly. Grants Cttee, Hong Kong, 1982–. *Publications:* Their Proper Sphere: A Study of the Brontë Sisters as Early-Victorian Female Novelists, 1966; Shakespeare, Ibsen and the Unspeakable (Inaugural Lecture), 1975; chapter in, A New Companion to Shakespeare Studies, 1971; (with Peter Hall) Ibsen's John Gabriel Borkman: An English Version, 1975; (ed with Philip Edwards and G. K. Hunter) Shakespeare's Styles, 1980; chapter in, The Cambridge Companion to Shakespeare Studies, 1986; Strindberg and the Intimate Theatre, 1987; chapters in other books; contrib. Shakespeare Survey, Ibsen Yearbook, Rev. Eng. Studies, Mod. Lang. Rev., English Studies, etc. *Recreations:* same as work: reading, theatre; children. *Address:* 19 Woodfield Road, Ealing, W5. *T:* 0181–997 2895.

EWBANK, Ven. Walter Frederick; Archdeacon Emeritus and Canon Emeritus of Carlisle Cathedral; *b* Poona, India, 29 Jan. 1918; *er s* of late Sir Robert Benson Ewbank, CSI, CIE, and Frances Helen, *d* of Rev. W. F. Simpson; *m* 1st, 1941, Ida Margaret, 3rd *d* of late John Haworth Whitworth, DSO, MC, Inner Temple; three *d*, 2nd, 1976, Mrs Josephine Alice Williamson, MD, ChB, FRCOG. *Educ:* Shrewsbury Sch.; Balliol Coll., Oxford. Classical Scholar of Balliol, 1936; 1st, Classical Hon. Mods, 1938; 2nd, Hon. Sch. of Theology, 1946; BA and MA 1946; Bishops' Coll., Cheshunt, 1946; BD 1952. Friends' Ambulance Unit, 1939–42; Deacon, 1946; Priest, 1947; Asst Curate, St Martin's, Windermere, 1946–49; Dio. Youth Chaplain and Vicar of Ings, 1949–52; Chap. to Casterton Sch. and Vicar of Casterton, 1952–62; Domestic Chap. to Bp of Carlisle and Vicar of Raughtonhead, 1962–66; Vicar of St Cuthbert's, Carlisle, and Chap. to Corporation, 1966–71; Rural Dean of Carlisle, 1970–71; Archdeacon of Westmorland and Furness and Vicar of Winster, 1971–77; Archdeacon of Carlisle, 1977–84; Administrator of Church House, Carlisle and Chm., Diocesan Glebe Cttee, 1977–84; Canon Residentiary of Carlisle Cathedral, 1977–82; Hon. Canon, 1966–77 and 1982–84. Proctor in Convocation and Mem. Ch Assembly, 1957–70; Member: Canon Law Standing Commn, 1968–70; Faculty Jurisdiction Commn, 1979–83; Diocesan Dir: of Ordinands, 1962–70; of Post Ordination Trng, 1962–66; Vice-Chm., Diocesan Synod, 1970–79; Chm., Diocesan Board of Finance, 1977–82. Chm., Carlisle Tithe Barn Restoration Cttee, 1968–70. Winter War Remembrance Medal (Finland), 1940. *Publications:* Salopian Diaries, 1961; Morality without Law, 1969; Charles Euston Nurse—A Memoir, 1982; Thomas Bloomer—A Memoir, 1984; Poems of Cumbria and of the Cumbrian Church, 1985; Ellen Margaret Cartwright—A Memoir, 1991; Memories of the Border Regiment in the First World War, 1991; Faith of Our Fathers, 1992; articles in Church Quarterly Review. *Recreation:* classical studies. *Address:* 7 Castle Court, Castle Street, Carlisle CA3 8TP.
See also Baron Renfrew of Kaimsthorn.

EWER, Prof. Tom Keightley, OBE 1978; HDA; BVSc; PhD; MRCVS; Professor of Animal Husbandry, Bristol University, 1961–77, now Emeritus; retired; *b* 21 Sept. 1911; *s* of William Edward Frederick Ewer and Maria Louisa Keightley; *m* 1st, 1937, Iva Rosalind Biddle; three *s*; 2nd, 1959, Margaret June Fischer; three *d* one step *s* two step *d*. *Educ:* Fowey Grammar Sch.; Sydney Univ. (BVSc); Cambridge Univ. (PhD). Veterinary research with NZ Govt, 1938–45; Senior Lecturer, Univ. of NZ, 1945–47; Wellcome Research Fellow, University of Cambridge, 1947–50; Prof. of Animal Husbandry, University of Queensland, 1950–61; Prof. of Animal Resources, King Faisal Univ., Saudi Arabia, 1978–80. *Publications:* Practical Animal Husbandry, 1982; contrib. to scientific publications, on animal nutrition and veterinary education. *Recreation:* music. *Address:* Oakridge, Winscombe, Avon BS25 1LZ. *T:* Winscombe (01934) 843279.

EWIN, Sir David Ernest Thomas F.; *see* Floyd Ewin.

EWING; *see* Orr-Ewing and Orr Ewing.

EWING, family name of **Baron Ewing of Kirkford.**

EWING OF KIRKFORD, Baron *cr* 1992 (Life Peer), of Cowdenbeath in the District of Dunfermline; **Harry Ewing;** DL; *b* 20 Jan. 1931; *s* of Mr and Mrs William Ewing; *m* 1954, Margaret Greenhill; one *s* one *d*. *Educ:* Fulford Primary Sch., Cowdenbeath; Beath High Sch., Cowdenbeath. Contested (Lab) East Fife, 1970; MP (Lab) Stirling and Falkirk, Sept. 1971–Feb. 1974, Stirling, Falkirk and Grangemouth, Feb. 1974–83, Falkirk East, 1983–92. Parly Under-Sec. of State, Scottish Office, 1974–79. Chm., Ewing Inquiry into availability of housing for wheelchair and other disabled, 1993 (report, 1994). Jt Chm., Scottish Const. Convention, 1990–. Hon. Pres., Girls' Brigade, Scotland, 1993–. Member: Union of Post Office Workers; UCW. Patron, Scottish Overseas Aid. DL Fife, 1995. *Recreations:* bowls, gardening. *Address:* Gowanbank, 45 Glenlyon Road, Leven, Fife KY8 4AA. *T:* Leven (01333) 26123.

EWING, Vice-Adm. Sir Alastair; *see* Ewing, Vice-Adm. Sir R. A.

EWING, Margaret Anne; MP (SNP) Moray, since 1987; *b* 1 Sept. 1945; *d* of John and Peggie McAdam; *m* 1983, Fergus Stewart Ewing, *s* of Stewart Martin Ewing and Winifred Margaret Ewing, *qv*. *Educ:* Univs of Glasgow and Strathclyde. MA Glasgow 1967, BA Hons Strathclyde 1973. Asst Teacher, Our Lady's High, Cumbernauld, 1968–70; St Modan's High, Stirling: Special Asst Teacher, 1970–73; Principal Teacher, Remedial Educn, 1973–74. MP (SNP) East Dunbartonshire, Oct. 1974–1979; contested (SNP) Strathkelvin and Bearsden, 1983. Sen. Vice-Chm., SNP, 1984–87; Leader, SNP Parly Gp, 1987–. *Recreations:* the arts in general, folk music in particular. *Address:* Burns Cottage, Tulloch's Brae, Lossiemouth, Morayshire IV31 6QY. *T:* Lossiemouth (0134381) 2222.

EWING, Maria Louise; soprano; *b* Detroit, 27 March 1950; *y d* of Norman Ewing and Hermina Ewing (*née* Veraar); *m* 1982, Sir Peter Hall, *qv* (marr. diss. 1990); one *d*. *Educ:* High School; Cleveland Inst. of Music. Studied with Marjorie Gordon, Eleanor Steber, Jennie Tourel, Otto Guth. First public performance, Meadowbrook, 1968 (Rigoletto); débuts Metropolitan Opera and La Scala, 1976; sings at Covent Garden, Glyndebourne, Salzburg, Paris, Metropolitan Opera, LA Opera, La Scala and other major venues; rôles include Blanche, Carmen, Cherubino, Dorabella, Lady Macbeth, Mélisande, La Périchole, Poppea, Rosina, Salomé, Susanna, Tosca, Zerlina; concerts and recitals. *Address:* c/o Harold Holt Ltd, 31 Sinclair Road, W14 0NS.

EWING, Vice-Adm. Sir (Robert) Alastair, KBE 1962; CB 1959; DSC 1942; *b* 10 April 1909; *s* of Major Ian Ewing and Muriel Adèle Child; *m* 1st, 1940, Diana Smeed (*d* 1980), *d* of Major Harry Archer, DSO; one *s*; 2nd, 1984, Anne, *d* of Captain C. G. Chichester, DSO, RN and *widow* of Comdr Henry Wilkin. *Educ:* Royal Naval Coll., Dartmouth. In command of Destroyers during War of 1939–45; NATO Standing Group Staff, 1950–51; Imperial Defence Coll., 1952; in command of HMS Vanguard, 1953–54; Dir of Naval Staff Coll., Greenwich, 1954–56; Naval Sec. to First Lord of the Admiralty, 1956–58; Flag Officer Flotillas (Mediterranean), 1958–60; Adm. Commanding Reserves and Inspector of Recruiting, 1960–62; retd list, 1962. *Address:* 19 Reyntiens View, Odiham, Hants RG25 1AF. *T:* Odiham (01256) 703509. *Clubs:* Army and Navy; Royal Yacht Squadron (Naval Mem.).

EWING, Mrs Winifred Margaret; Member (SNP) European Parliament, since 1975, elected for Highlands and Islands, 1979, 1984, 1989 and 1994; *b* 10 July 1929; *d* of George Woodburn and Christina Bell Anderson; *m* 1956, Stewart Martin Ewing, CA; two *s* one *d*. *Educ:* Queen's Park Sen. Sec. Sch.; University of Glasgow (MA, LLB). Qual. as Solicitor, 1952. Lectr in Law, 1954–56; Solicitor, practising on own account, 1956–. Sec., Glasgow Bar Assoc., 1961–67, Pres., 1970–71. MP (SNP): Hamilton, Nov. 1967–70; Moray and Nairn, Feb. 1974–1979; contested (SNP) Orkney and Shetland, 1983. President: Scottish National Party; European Free Alliance, 1991–; Vice-Pres., Animal Welfare Intergroup, European Parliament, 1989–. Mem., Lomé Assembly, 1981–. Pres., Glasgow Central Soroptimist Club, 1966–67. FRSA. DUniv Open, 1993. *Address:* Goodwill, Milton Duff, Morayshire IV30 3TL. *T:* Elgin (01343) 541154, *Fax:* (01343) 540011.
See also M. A. Ewing.

EWINS, Prof. David John, CEng; FIMechE; Professor of Vibration Engineering, Mechanical Engineering Department, Imperial College of Science, Technology and Medicine, since 1983; *b* 25 March 1942; *s* of W. J. and P. Ewins; *m* 1964, Brenda Rene (*née* Chalk); three *d*. *Educ:* Kingswood Grammar Sch., Bristol; Imperial Coll., London (BScEng, ACGI, DScEng); Trinity Coll., Cambridge (PhD). MASME; FIMechE 1990. Res Asst for Rolls-Royce Ltd, Cambridge Univ., 1966–67; Lectr, then Reader, in Mech. Engrg, Imperial Coll., 1967–83; formed Modal Testing Unit at Imperial Coll., 1981; Dir, Rolls-Royce sponsored Centre of Vibration Engrg, Imperial Coll., 1990–. Sen. Lectr, Chulalongkorn Univ., Bangkok, 1968–69; Maître de Conférences, INSA, Lyon, 1974–75; Visiting Professor: Virginia Poly and State Univ., USA, 1981; ETH, Zürich, 1986; Inst. Nat. Polytechnique de Grenoble, 1990; Nanyang Technol Univ., Singapore, 1994; Hon. Professor: Nanjing Aero Inst., 1988; Shandong Polytechnic Inst., 1991. Consultant to: Rolls-Royce, 1969–; MoD, 1977–, and other organisations in Europe, S America and USA. Chm., Dynamic Testing Agency, 1990–. Governor: Cranleigh Sch., 1990–; Parmiter's Sch., 1993–. *Publications:* Modal Testing: Theory and Practice, 1984, 8th edn 1995; papers on vibration engrg in technical jls in UK, USA, France. *Recreations:* music (esp. piano duets), hill walking, travel, good food, French, bridge. *Address:* Imperial College, Exhibition Road, SW7 2BX. *T:* 0171–594 7068. *Club:* Executive.

EWINS, Peter David; Chief Scientist, Ministry of Defence, since 1994; *b* 20 March 1943; *s* of John Samuel Ewins and Kathleen Ewins; *m* 1968, Barbara Irene Howland; two *s* one *d*. *Educ:* Imperial College London (BSc Eng); Cranfield Inst. of Technology (MSc). CEng. MRAeS. Joined RAE Farnborough, 1966, research on structl applications of composite materials; section head, 1974; staff of Chief Scientist, RAF, MoD, 1978; Head of Helicopters Res. Div., RAE, 1981; seconded to Cabinet Office (Civil Service personnel policy), 1984; Dir, Nuclear Projects, MoD, 1987; Dir, ARE, MoD (PE), 1988; Man. Dir (Maritime and Electronics), 1991, Man. Dir, Command and Maritime Systems Gp, 1992, Man. Dir (Ops), 1993–94, Defence Res. Agency. *Publications:* technical papers on structural composite materials in learned jls. *Recreations:* horticulture, walking, occasional tennis. *Address:* Ministry of Defence, Main Building, Whitehall, SW1A 2HB.

EWUSIE, Prof. Joseph Yanney; Chief Policy Adviser and Hon. Fellow, Ghana Council for Scientific and Industrial Research; *b* 18 April 1927; *s* of Samuel Mainsa Wilson Ewusie and Elizabeth Dickson; *m* 1st, 1959, Stella Turkson (*d* 1989); four *s*, and one adopted *d*; 2nd, 1992, Emma (*née* Ghampson). *Educ:* Winneba Anglican Sch.; Mfantsipim Sch.; University Coll. of the Gold Coast; Univ. of Cambridge. BSc (London), PhD (Cantab). Lectr in Botany, Univ. of Ghana, 1957–62; Gen. Sec. (Chief Exec.), Ghana Academy of Sciences (highest learned and res. org. in Ghana), 1963–68; University of Cape Coast: Associate Prof. of Botany, 1969–72, Prof., 1973–79; Head, Dept of Botany, 1969–73; Dean, Faculty of Science, 1971–74; Pro-Vice Chancellor, 1971–73; Vice Chancellor, 1973–78. Vis. Prof./Prof., Univs of Nairobi and Ahmadu Bello, Nigeria, 1979–80; Sec.-Gen., Pan African Inst. for Development, 1980–83; Professor of Biology: Univ. of Swaziland, 1984–90; Univ. of Bophuthatswana, 1989–92. Mem. Exec. Cttee, ICSU, 1964–67. Founder and First Pres., Bophuthatswana Assoc. for Scientific Advancement, 1990; first Pres., Ghana Inst. of Biology, 1994 (Fellow). Member: Bimillenium Foundn, Washington DC, 1984–; NY Acad. of Sciences, 1984–. FWA 1963. Co-Founder and First Editor, Swaziland Jl of Sci. and Technol. Hon. DSc Cape Coast, 1994. Medal (Govt of Hungary) for internat. understanding between Ghana and Hungary, 1964; Dipl. of Merit, Internat. Acad. of Science, Letters and Arts, Rome, 1968; Dipl. of Honour, Internat. Inst. of Community Service, 1975; Ghana Scientist of the Year, Ghana Science Assoc., 1985. *Publications:* School Certificate Biology for Tropical Schools, 1964, 4th edn 1974; Tropical Biological Drawings, 1973; Elements of Tropical Ecology, 1980; Phenology in Tropical Ecology, 1992. *Address:* PO Box 8143 North, Accra, Ghana.

EXETER, 8th Marquess of, *cr* 1801; **William Michael Anthony Cecil;** Baron Burghley 1571; Earl of Exeter 1605; *b* 1 Sept. 1935; *s* of 7th Marquess of Exeter and Edith Lilian

Csanady de Telegd (*d* 1954); *S* father, 1988; *m* 1967, Nancy Rose (marr. diss. 1992), *d* of Lloyd Arthur Meeker; one *s* one *d*. *Educ:* Eton. Rancher and businessman in 100 Mile House, 1954–. *Publications:* (jtly) Spirit of Sunrise, 1979; The Long View, 1985; The Rising Tide of Change, 1986; Living at the Heart of Creation, 1990. *Heir: s* Lord Burghley, *qv*. *Address:* Box 8, 100 Mile House, BC V0K 2E0, Canada. *T:* (604) 3952767; Mickleton House, Mickleton, Glos GL55 6RY. *T:* Mickleton (01386) 438251.

EXETER, Bishop of, since 1985; **Rt. Rev. (Geoffrey) Hewlett Thompson;** *b* 14 Aug. 1929; *o s* of late Lt-Col R. R. Thompson, MC, RAMC; *m* 1954, Elisabeth Joy Fausitt, BA (Oxon), *d* of late Col G. F. Taylor, MBE and Dr Frances Taylor; two *s* two *d*. *Educ:* Aldenham Sch.; Trinity Hall, Cambridge (MA); Cuddesdon Theol College. 2nd Lieut, Queen's Own Royal West Kent Regt, 1948–49 (Nat. Service). Ordained 1954. Curate, St Matthew, Northampton, 1954; Vicar: St Augustine, Wisbech, 1959; St Saviour, Folkestone, 1966; Bishop Suffragan of Willesden, 1974. Chairman: Community and Race Relations Unit, BCC, 1980–84 (Vice-Chm., 1976–80); Hospital Chaplaincies Council, 1991–. Introduced into House of Lords, 1990. *Recreations:* fell walking, reading, gardening, music. *Address:* The Palace, Exeter EX1 1HY. *T:* Exeter (01392) 72362. *Club:* United Oxford & Cambridge University.

EXETER, Dean of; *see* Jones, Very Rev. K. B.

EXETER, Archdeacon of; *see* Tremlett, Ven. A. F.

EXMOUTH, 10th Viscount *cr* 1816; **Paul Edward Pellew;** Bt 1796 (Pellew of Treverry); Baron 1814; *b* 8 Oct. 1940; *s* of 9th Viscount Exmouth and Maria Luisa (*d* 1994), Marquesa de Olias (Spain, *cr* 1652; *S* 1940), *d* of late Luis de Urquijo, Marques de Amurrio, Madrid; *S* father, 1970; *m* 1st, 1964 (marr. diss. 1974); one *d*; 2nd, 1975, Rosemary Countess of Burford; twin *s*. *Educ:* Downside. Mem. Cons. Party, House of Lords. Mem., Inst. of Dirs. *Heir: er twin s* Hon. Edward Francis Pellew, *b* 30 Oct. 1978. *Address:* House of Lords, SW1A 0PW.

EXNER, Most Rev. Adam; *see* Vancouver, Archbishop of.

EXTON, Clive; scriptwriter and playwright; *b* 11 April 1930; *s* of late J. E. M. Brooks and Marie Brooks (*née* Rolfe); *m* 1951, Patricia Fletcher Ferguson (marr. diss. 1957); two *d*; *m* 1957, Margaret Josephine Reid; one *s* two *d*. *Educ:* Christ's Hospital. *TV plays:* No Fixed Abode, 1959; The Silk Purse; Where I Live; Some Talk of Alexander; Hold My Hand, Soldier; I'll Have You to Remember; The Big Eat; The Trial of Doctor Fancy; Land of my Dreams; The Close Prisoner; The Bone Yard; Conceptions of Murder (series); Are You Ready for the Music?; The Rainbirds; Killers (series); Stigma; Henry Intervenes; (with Tom Stoppard) The Boundary; The Crezz (series); Dick Barton—Special Agent (series); Wolf to the Slaughter, A Guilty Thing Surprised, Shake Hands for Ever (dramatizations of novels by Ruth Rendell); many scripts and script consultant for: Agatha Christie's Poirot; Jeeves and Wooster (Writers' Guild Award, 1992); Take No Farewell; Best Endeavours. *Stage plays:* Have You Any Dirty Washing, Mother Dear?; Twixt; Murder is Easy; Jeeves and the Last of the Woosters. *Films:* Night Must Fall; Isadora; Entertaining Mr Sloane; Ten Rillington Place; Running Scared; Doomwatch; The House in Nightmare Park; The Awakening; Radio Romance. *Publications:* No Fixed Abode (in Six Granada Plays, anthol.), 1960; Have You Any Dirty Washing, Mother Dear? (in Plays of the Year, vol. 37), 1970. *Recreation:* panification. *Address:* c/o Rochelle Stevens & Co., 2 Terret's Place, N1 1QZ. *T:* 0171–359 3900.

EXTON, Rodney Noel, JP; MA; Editor, Johansens Hotel Guides, since 1993; *b* 28 Dec. 1927; *s* of Noel Exton and Winifred (*née* Stokes); *m* 1961, Pamela Sinclair (*née* Hardie); two step *s* two step *d*. *Educ:* Clifton Coll.; Lincoln Coll., Oxford (MA Mod. Langs); Corpus Christi Coll., Cambridge (PGCE). FInstD. Served Royal Hampshire Regt, 1946–48. Asst Master, Eton, 1951–52; Internat. Research Fund Schol. to USA, 1952; Asst Master, Mill Hill Sch., 1953–63; Royal Commonwealth schol. to Australia, 1959–60; Headmaster, Reed's Sch., 1964–77; Walter Hines Page schol. to USA, 1971; Dir, ISCO, 1978–88. Vice-Chm., British Atlantic Educn Cttee, 1972–78; Chm., Exec. Cttee, GAP, 1982–87. Man. Dir, Exton Hotels Co. Ltd, 1966–80; Chm., Kandic Ltd, 1972–82; Dep. Chm., Johansens Ltd, 1989–93; Dir, Purbeck Properties Ltd, 1986–88. Dir, Vocational Guidance Assoc., 1988–90. Fellow, Atlantic Council of UK, 1993. Gov., Clifton Coll., 1986–; Vice-Pres., Reed's Sch., 1991–. Pres., Flycatchers CC, 1989–. Hampshire County Cricket XI, 1946. JP Surrey, 1968. *Publication:* Industrial Cadets, 1972. *Address:* 43 Temple Road, Kew Gardens, Surrey TW9 2EB. *T:* 0181–940 0305. *Clubs:* MCC; Royal Mid-Surrey Golf; Vincent's (Oxford).

EYERS, Patrick Howard Caines, CMG 1985; LVO 1966; HM Diplomatic Service; Ambassador to Jordan, 1991–93; *b* 4 Sept. 1933; *s* of late Arthur Leopold Caines Eyers and Nora Lilian Eyers; *m* 1960, Heidi, *d* of Werner Rüsch, Dipl. Ing, and Helene (*née* Feil); two *s* one *d*. *Educ:* Clifton Coll.; Gonville and Caius Coll., Cambridge (BA Hons 1957); Institut Universitaire de Hautes Etudes Internationales, Geneva. RA, 1952–54. Asst Editor, Grolier Soc. Inc., New York, 1957; HM Foreign (now Diplomatic) Service, 1959; ME Centre for Arabic Studies, 1960; Dubai, 1961; Brussels, 1964; FO, 1966; Aden, 1969; Abidjan, 1970; British Mil. Govt, Berlin, 1971; FCO, 1974; Counsellor, Bonn, 1977; Head, Republic of Ireland Dept, FCO, 1981; RCDS, 1984; Ambassador: to Zaire, the Congo, Rwanda and Burundi, 1985–87; to Algeria, 1987–89; to GDR, 1990. Officer, Order of Leopold, Belgium, 1966. *Recreations:* music, skiing, sailing. *Address:* c/o Barclays Bank, 86 Queens Road, Bristol BS6 1RB. *Clubs:* Ski of GB, Kandahar Ski, Hurlingham.

EYNON, Prof. John Marles, OBE 1990; RIBA; FSA; Professor of Architecture, University of Wales, and Head, Welsh School of Architecture, 1980–87, now Professor Emeritus; *b* 3 Jan. 1923; *s* of Philip Stanley Eynon and Gwendoline Eynon (*née* Marles); *m* 1950, Yvonne Marie, *e d* of Claire Faber (*née* Vermuse) and Vivian Valdemar Faber. *Educ:* Cardiff High Sch.; Welsh Sch. of Architecture, Univ. of Wales (MA, Dip. Arch.) ARIBA 1950, FRIBA 1963, FSA 1974. Military service: Captain RE, regtl duties, wounded, training, staff work. Chartered and Registered Architect, 1950; with Alwyn Lloyd & Gordon, later Alex Gordon & Partners, 1950–70; private practice and consultancy (historic buildings and conservation), 1970–. Lectr, Sen. Lectr, Prof. of Architecture, Welsh Sch. of Architecture, Univ. of Wales, 1956–87. Member: Historic Buildings Council for Wales, 1970–95; Welsh Arts Council, 1978–89; Craft Cttee for Wales (Chm.), Craft Council, 1970–89; Cambrian Archaeol. Assoc., 1969–; Assoc. of Artists and Designers in Wales, 1970–; Royal Welsh Agricl Soc., 1977; Llandaff Diocesan Adv. Cttee, Church in Wales, 1988–; Cardiff Castle Management Cttee, 1990–. Prince of Wales Awards, 1976, 1977; Europa Nostra Award, 1985. *Publications:* contribs to learned jls. *Recreation:* painter (retrospective exhibition, Cardiff, 1976). *Address:* 39 Waterloo Road, Penylan, Cardiff CF3 7BJ. *T:* Cardiff (01222) 485098.

EYRE, Brian Leonard, CBE 1993; DSc; FEng 1992; CPhys; Board Member, since 1987, and Deputy Chairman, since 1989, United Kingdom Atomic Energy Authority (Chief Executive, 1990–94); *b* 29 Nov. 1933; *s* of Leonard George and Mabel Eyre; *m* 1965, Elizabeth Caroline (*née* Rackham); two *s*. *Educ:* Greenford Grammar Sch.; Univ. of Surrey (BSc, DSc). FIM; FInstP. Research Officer, CEGB, 1959–62; Gp Leader, UKAEA, Harwell, 1962–79; Prof., Materials Science, Univ. of Liverpool, 1979–84; Dir, Fuel and Engrg Technology, UKAEA, Risley, 1984–87. Visiting Professor: Univ. of Illinois, 1969–70; Univ. of Wisconsin, 1976. FRSA 1984; CIMgt (CBIM 1992). *Publications:* over 100 papers in Procs Royal Soc., Philosophical Magazine, Acta Metallurgica, etc. *Recreations:* sailing, walking, mountaineering. *Address:* AEA Technology, Corporate Headquarters, Harwell, Didcot, Oxon OX11 0RA. *Club:* Athenæum.

EYRE, Hon. Dean Jack; New Zealand High Commissioner to Canada, 1968–73 and 1976–80; *b* Westport, NZ, 1914; *m*; two *s* one *d*. *Educ:* Hamilton High Sch.; Auckland University Coll. Served War of 1939–45, Lieut in RNVR. Electrical importer and manufacturer. MP (Nat) North Shore, 1949–66; Minister of Customs, Industries and Commerce, 1954–57; Minister of Social Security and Tourist and Health Resorts, 1956–57; Minister of Housing, State Advances and Defence, New Zealand, 1957; Minister in Charge of Police, 1960–63; Minister of Defence, 1960–66; Minister i/c Tourism, 1961–66. *Recreations:* yachting, fishing. *Address:* 517 Wilbrod Street, Ottawa, Ontario K1N 5R4, Canada. *Clubs:* Royal New Zealand Yacht Squadron, Northern, Officers (Auckland); Wellington (Wellington); Royal Ottawa Golf.

EYRE, Sir Graham (Newman), Kt 1989; QC 1970; a Recorder of the Crown Court, since 1975; Justice of Appeal for British Indian Ocean Territory, since 1992; *b* 9 Jan. 1931; *s* of Newman Eyre; *m* 1954, Jean Dalrymple Walker; one *s* three *d*. *Educ:* Marlborough Coll.; Trinity Coll., Cambridge. BA 1953, LLB 1954, MA 1958. Council Prizewinner, 1954. Called to Bar, Middle Temple, 1954, Harmsworth Law Schol., 1955, Bencher, Middle Temple, 1979; Mem., Lincoln's Inn, 1971; Head of Chambers, 1981. Inspector, The London Airports Inquiries, 1981–84. *Publications:* Rating Law and Valuation, 1963; contrib. Jl Planning Law. *Address:* Walberton House, Walberton, Arundel, West Sussex BN18 0PJ; 2–3 Gray's Inn Square, Gray's Inn, WC1R 5JH. *Club:* Athenæum.

EYRE, Maj.-Gen. Sir James (Ainsworth Campden Gabriel), KCVO 1986 (CVO 1978); CBE 1980 (OBE 1975); Director, Westminster Associates International Ltd, since 1989; *b* 2 Nov. 1930; *s* of Edward Joseph Eyre and Hon. Dorothy Elizabeth Anne Pelline (*née* Lyon-Dalberg-Acton); *m* 1967, Monica Ruth Esther Smyth; one *s* one *d*. *Educ:* Harvard Univ. (BA, LLB). Commissioned RHG, 1955; Commanding Officer, The Blues and Royals, 1970–73; GSO 1 HQ London District, 1973–75; Officer Commanding Household Cavalry and Silver Stick, 1975–78; Col GS HQ Northern Ireland, 1978–80; Sec., Chiefs of Staff Cttee, MoD, 1980–82; Dir of Defence Programmes Staff (Concepts), MoD, 1982–83; GOC London Dist and Maj. Gen. Comdg Household Div., 1983–86. *Recreations:* racing, shooting. *Address:* Somerville House, East Garston, Berks RG16 7EY. *Club:* Turf.

See also P. G. A. Eyre.

EYRE, Patrick Giles Andrew; Master of the Supreme Court, Queen's Bench Division, since 1992; *b* 11 March 1940; *s* of Edward Joseph Eyre and Hon. Dorothy Elizabeth Anne Pelline Lyon-Dalberg-Acton; *m* 1977, Victoria Mary Bathurst Barthorp; one *s*, and one step *d*. *Educ:* Downside; Trinity Coll., Oxford (MA). Farmer, 1965–72. Called to the Bar, Inner Temple, 1974. *Publications:* articles on law, horses and country pursuits. *Recreations:* books, horses, music, science. *Address:* Royal Courts of Justice, Strand, WC2A 2LL.

See also Maj.-Gen. Sir J. A. C. G. Eyre.

EYRE, Sir Reginald (Edwin), Kt 1984; Chairman: Birmingham Heartlands Development Corporation (formerly Birmingham Heartlands Ltd (East Birmingham Urban Development Agency)), since 1987; Birmingham Cable Corporation Ltd, since 1988; *b* 28 May 1924; *s* of late Edwin Eyre; *m* 1978, Anne Clements; one *d*. *Educ:* King Edward's Camp Hill Sch., Birmingham; Emmanuel Coll., Cambridge (MA). Midshipman and Sub-Lieut, RNVR, War of 1939–45. Admitted a Solicitor, 1950; Senior Partner, Eyre & Co., solicitors, Birmingham, 1951–91. Dep. Chm., Commn for New Towns, 1988–92. Hon. Consultant, Poor Man's Lawyer, 1948–58. Conservative Political Centre: Chm., W Midlands Area, 1960–63; Chm., National Advisory Cttee, 1964–66. Contested (C) Birmingham (Northfield) 1959; MP (C) Birmingham Hall Green, May 1965–87. Opposition Whip, 1966–70; a Lord Comr of the Treasury, June-Sept. 1970; Comptroller of HM Household, 1970–72; Parliamentary Under-Secretary of State: DoE, 1972–74; Dept of Trade, 1979–82; Dept of Transport, 1982–83. A Vice Chm., Cons. Party Organisation, 1975–79; Founder Chm., Cons. Parly Urban Affairs Cttee, 1974–79. Freeman, City of Birmingham, 1991. *Publication:* Hope for our Towns and Cities, 1977. *Address:* 7 Wallside, Monkwell Square, Barbican, EC2Y 8BH; 1041 Stratford Road, Hall Green, Birmingham B28 8AS. *Clubs:* Carlton; Birmingham (Birmingham).

EYRE, Richard Anthony; Group Managing Director, Capital Radio plc, since 1991; *b* 3 May 1954; *s* of Edgar Gabriel Eyre and Marjorie (*née* Corp); *m* 1977, Sheelagh Colquhoun; one *s* one *d*. *Educ:* King's Coll. Sch., Wimbledon; Lincoln Coll., Oxford (MA). Media buyer, Benton & Bowles, 1975–79; TV airtime salesman, Scottish TV, 1979–80; media planner, Benton & Bowles, 1980–84; Media Director: Aspect, 1984–86; Bartle Bogle Hegarty, 1986–91. *Recreations:* music, church, Wimbledon Football Club. *Address:* Capital Radio plc, Euston Tower, Euston Road, NW1 3DR. *T:* 0171–608 6161. *Club:* Thirty.

EYRE, Richard Charles Hastings, CBE 1992; theatre, film and TV director; Artistic Director, Royal National Theatre, since 1988 (Associate Director, 1981–88); *b* 28 March 1943; *m* 1973, Susan Elizabeth Birtwistle; one *d*. *Educ:* Sherborne Sch.; Peterhouse, Cambridge (BA). Asst Dir, Phoenix Theatre, Leicester, 1966; Lyceum Theatre, Edinburgh: Associate Dir, 1967–70; Dir of Productions, 1970–72; freelance director: Liverpool, 7:84 Co., West End; tours for British Council: W Africa, 1971; SE Asia, 1972; Artistic Dir, Nottingham Playhouse, 1973–78; Prod./Dir, Play for Today, BBC TV, 1978–80; Director: The Churchill Play, Nottingham, 1974; Comedians, Old Vic and Wyndhams, 1976; Touched, Nottingham, 1977; Hamlet, Royal Court, 1980; Edmond, Royal Court, 1985; Kafka's Dick, Royal Court, 1986; National Theatre: Guys and Dolls (SWET Director of the Year, 1982, Standard Best Director, 1982), The Beggar's Opera, and Schweyk in the Second World War, 1982; The Government Inspector, 1985; Futurists, 1986 (Best Production Award, Time Out, 1986); The Changeling, Bartholomew Fair, 1988; Hamlet, The Voysey Inheritance, 1989; Racing Demon, Richard III, 1990; White Chameleon, Napoli Milionaria, Murmuring Judges, 1991; Night of the Iguana, 1992; Macbeth, The Absence of War, 1993; Johnny on a Spot, Sweet Bird of Youth, 1994; Skylight, La Grande Magia, 1995. *Opera:* La Traviata, Covt Gdn, 1994. *Films:* The Ploughman's Lunch (Evening Standard Award for Best Film, 1983), Loose Connections, 1983; Laughterhouse, 1984, released as Singleton's Pluck, USA, 1985 (TV Prize, Venice Film Fest.); films for TV: The Imitation Game, Pasmore, 1980; Country, 1981; The Insurance Man, 1986 (Special Prize, Tokyo TV Fest., 1986); Past Caring, 1986; Tumbledown, 1988 (BAFTA Award for best single drama, Italia RAI Prize, RTS Award, Press Guild Award, Tokyo Prize); v., 1988 (RTS Award); Suddenly Last Summer, 1992; The Absence of War, 1995. Hon. Fellow: Goldsmiths' Coll., 1993; King's Coll., 1994. Hon. DLitt: Nottingham Trent, 1992; South Bank, 1994. STV Awards for Best Production, 1969, 1970 and 1971; De Sica Award, Sorrento Film Fest., 1986. *Publication:* Utopia and Other Places, 1993. *Address:* c/o Royal National Theatre, South Bank, SE1 9PX. *T:* 0171–928 2033.

EYRE, Very Rev. Richard Montague Stephens; Dean of Exeter, 1981–95; *b* 1929; *s* of Montague Henry and Ethel Mary Eyre; *m* 1963, Anne Mary Bentley; two *d*. *Educ:* Charterhouse; Oriel Coll. and St Stephen's House, Oxford. MA Oxon. Deacon 1956, priest 1957; Curate, St Mark's Church, Portsea, 1956–59; Tutor and Chaplain, Chichester Theological Coll., 1959–62; Chaplain, Eastbourne Coll., 1962–65; Vicar of Arundel, 1965–73; Vicar of Good Shepherd, Brighton, 1973–75; Archdeacon of Chichester, 1975–81; Treasurer of Chichester Cathedral, 1978–81. Mem., Gen. Synod of C of E, 1985–95. *Publication:* Faith in God?, 1990. *Recreations:* golf, music, travel, gardening. *Address:* Hathersage, Enmore Road, Enmore, Bridgwater, Som TA5 2DP. *Club:* United Oxford & Cambridge University.

EYSENCK, Prof. Hans Jürgen, PhD, DSc; Professor of Psychology, University of London, Institute of Psychiatry, 1955–83, Professor Emeritus, since 1983; Director, Psychological Department, Maudsley Hospital, 1946–83; *b* 4 March 1916; *s* of Eduard Anton and Ruth Eysenck; *m* 1st, 1938, Margaret Malcolm Davies (decd); one *s*; 2nd, 1950, Sybil Bianca Giuletta Rostal; three *s* one *d*. *Educ:* school in Germany, France and England; Univ. of London. BA 1938, PhD 1940, DSc 1964. Senior Research Psychologist, Mill Hill Emergency Hosp., 1942–46; Reader in Psychology, Univ. of London (Inst. of Psychiatry), 1950–54; Visiting Prof., Univ. of Pennsylvania, 1949–50; Visiting Prof., Univ. of California, Berkeley, 1954. Pres., Internat. Soc. for Study of Individual Differences, 1983–85. Dist. Scientist Award, Amer. Psychol Assoc., 1988. *Publications:* Dimensions of Personality, 1947; The Scientific Study of Personality, 1952; The Structure of Human Personality, 1953; Uses and Abuses of Psychology, 1953; The Psychology of Politics, 1954; Sense and Nonsense in Psychology, 1957; Dynamics of Anxiety and Hysteria, 1957; Perceptual Processes and Mental Illness, 1957; (ed) Handbook of Abnormal Psychology, 1960, 2nd edn, 1972; (ed) Behaviour Therapy and the Neuroses, 1960; (ed) Experiments in Personality, 1960; (ed) Experiments with Drugs, 1963; (ed) Experiments in Behaviour Therapy, 1964; (ed) Experiments in Motivation, 1964; Crime and Personality, 1964; Causes and Cures of Neurosis, 1965; Fact and Fiction in Psychology, 1965; Smoking, Health and Personality, 1965; The Biological Basis of Personality, 1968; Personality Structure and Measurement, 1969; Race, Intelligence and Education, 1971; Psychology is about People, 1972; (ed) Readings in Introversion-Extraversion, 3 vols, 1971; (ed) Lexikon der Psychologie, 3 vols, 1972; The Measurement of Intelligence, 1973; The Inequality of Man, 1973; (ed jtly) The Experimental Study of Freudian Theories, 1973; (ed jtly) Encyclopaedia of Psychology, 1973; (with Glenn Wilson) Know Your Own Personality, 1975; (ed) Case Studies in Behaviour Therapy, 1976; Sex and Personality, 1976; (with S. B. G. Eysenck) Psychoticism as a Dimension of Personality 1976; You and Neurosis, 1977; Die Zukunft der Psychologie, 1977; (with D. K. B. Nias) Sex, Violence and the Media, 1978; The Structure and Measurement of Intelligence, 1979; (with Glenn Wilson) The Psychology of Sex, 1979; The Causes and Effects of Smoking, 1980; (with M. W. Eysenck) Mindwatching, 1981; (ed) A Model for Personality, 1981; (with J. Kamin) Intelligence: the battle for the mind, 1981 (US as The Intelligence Controversy, 1981); (with D. K. B. Nias) Astrology: Science or Superstition?, 1982; Personality, Genetics and Behaviour, 1982; (ed) A Model for Intelligence, 1982; (with Carl Sargent) Explaining the Unexplained, 1982; I Do: your guide to happy marriage, 1983; (with Carl Sargent) Know your own psi-Q, 1984; (with M. W. Eysenck) Personality and Individual Differences, 1985; Decline and Fall of the Freudian Empire, 1985; (with L. Eaves and N. Martin) Genes, Culture and Personality, 1989; (with G. Gudjousson) Causes and Cures of Criminality, 1989; Rebel with a Cause (autobiog.), 1990; Smoking, Personality and Stress: environmental factors in the prevention of cancer and coronary heart disease, 1991; Genius: the natural history of creativity, 1995; Editor-in-Chief: Behaviour Research and Therapy, 1963–78; Personality and Individual Differences, 1980–; (ed) International Monographs of Experimental Psychology; some 1000 articles in British, American, German, Spanish and French Jls of Psychology. *Recreations:* walking, tennis, chess, detective stories, squash. *Address:* 10 Dorchester Drive, SE24 0DQ.

See also M. W. Eysenck.

EYSENCK, Prof. Michael William; Professor and Head of Department of Psychology, Royal Holloway (formerly Royal Holloway and Bedford New College), University of London, since 1987; *b* 8 Feb. 1944; *s* of Hans Jürgen Eysenck, *qv* and late Margaret Malcolm Eysenck (*née* Davies); *m* 1975, Mary Christine Kabyn; one *s* two *d*. *Educ:* Dulwich Coll.; University College London (BA Psych, 1st cl. Hons; Rosa Morrison Medal for outstanding arts graduate, 1965); Birkbeck Coll., London (PhD Psych). Asst Lectr, Lectr and Reader in Psychology, Birkbeck Coll., Univ. of London, 1965–87. Vis. Prof., Univ. of S Florida, Tampa, 1980. Chm., Cognitive Psych. Section, BPsS, 1982–87. Editor, European Jl of Cognitive Psych., 1989–91. *Publications:* Human Memory, 1977; (with H. J. Eysenck) Mindwatching, 1981; Attention and Arousal: cognition and performance, 1982; A Handbook of Cognitive Psychology, 1984; (with H. J. Eysenck) Personality and Individual Differences, 1985; (with J. T. Richardson and D. W. Piper) Student Learning: research in education and cognitive psychology, 1987; (with H. J. Eysenck) Mindwatching: why we behave the way we do, 1989; Happiness: facts and myths, 1990; (ed) The Blackwell Dictionary of Cognitive Psychology, 1990; International Review of Cognitive Psychology, 1990; (with M. T. Keane) Cognitive Psychology: a student's handbook, 1990; Anxiety: the cognitive perspective, 1992; (with M. Weller) The Scientific Basis of Psychiatry, 1992; (with A. Gale) Handbook of Individual Differences: biological perspectives, 1992; Principles of Cognitive Psychology, 1993; Perspectives on Psychology, 1994; Individual Differences: normal and abnormal, 1994; numerous book chapters and contribs to Qly Jl of Exptl Psychology, Jl of Exptl Psychology, Jl of Abnormal Psychology, British Jl of Clin. Psychology, Psychol Bull., and others. *Recreations:* travel, tennis, golf, walking, bridge, boules. *Address:* Department of Psychology, Royal Holloway, University of London, Egham Hill, Egham, Surrey TW20 0EX. *T:* Egham (01784) 443530, *Fax:* (01784) 434347.

EYTON, Anthony John Plowden, RA 1986 (ARA 1976); RWS 1988 (ARWS 1985); RWA 1984; RCA 1993; NEAC 1985; Visiting Teacher, Royal Academy Schools, since 1963; *b* 17 May 1923; *s* of late Captain John Seymour Eyton, ICS, author, and of Phyllis Annie Tyser; *m* 1960, Frances Mary Capell, MA (marr. diss.); three *d*. *Educ:* Twyford Sch.; Canford Sch.; Dept of Fine Art, Reading Univ.; Camberwell Sch. of Art (NDD). Served War, 1939–45, Cameronians (Scottish Rifles), Hampshire Regt, and Army Educn Corps. Abbey Major Scholarship in Painting, 1950–51. Elected Mem., London Gp, 1958. One Man Exhibitions: St George's Gall., 1955; Galerie de Seine, 1957; New Art Centre, 1959, 1961, 1968; New Grafton Gall., 1973; William Darby Gall., 1975; Newcastle Polytechnic Art Gall., 1978; Browse and Darby, 1978, 1981, 1985, 1987, 1990, 1993; Austin Desmond Gall., 1990; Retrospective Exhibn, S London Art Gall., Towner Art Gall., Eastbourne, and Plymouth Art Gall., 1981; Hong Kong and the New Territories exhibn, Imperial War Museum, 1983 (subsequent to commission); work included in British Painting 1945–77, RA. Work in public collections: Tate Gall.; Arts Council; Plymouth Art Gall.; Towner Art Gall., Eastbourne; Carlisle Art Gall.; DoE; RA; Government Picture Coll.; BR; Contemp. Art Soc.; Guildhall Art Gall. Fellowship awarded by Grocers' Co. (for work and travel in Italy), 1974. Hon. Mem., Pastel Soc., 1986; Hon. ROI 1988. Prize, John Moore's Exhibn, Liverpool, 1972; First Prize, Second British Internat. Drawing Biennale, Middlesbrough, 1975; Charles Wollaston Award, RA, 1981. *Recreation:* gardening. *Address:* 166 Brixton Road, SW9 6AU.

EZEILO, Prof. James Okoye Chukuka, CON 1979; PhD; Professor of Mathematics, University of Nigeria; Director, National Mathematical Centre, Abuja, since 1988; *b* 17 Jan. 1930; *s* of Josiah Ezeilo and Janet Ezeilo; *m* 1960, Phoebe Uchechuku; two *s* two *d*. *Educ:* Dennis Memorial Grammar Sch., Onitsha; University Coll., Ibadan (MSc London); Queens' Coll., Cambridge (PhD). University of Ibadan: Lectr in Maths, 1958–62; Sen. Lectr in Maths, 1962–64; Prof. of Maths, 1964–66; University of Nigeria: Prof. of Maths, 1966–75, 1980–; Vice-Chancellor, 1975–78. Vice-Chancellor, Bayero Univ., Nigeria, 1978–79. Benedict Dist. Prof. of Maths, Carleton Coll., 1979; Vis. Prof. of Maths, Howard Univ., 1979–80. President: Math. Assoc. of Nigeria, 1972–74; Nigerian Math. Soc., 1984–; Mem., Nigerian Council for Science and Technol., 1970–75; Fellow and Foundation Mem., Nigerian Acad. of Science. Hon. DSc Maiduguri, 1989. *Publications:* numerous papers on differential equations in math. jls. *Recreation:* gardening. *Address:* Department of Mathematics, University of Nigeria, Nsukka, Nigeria. *Clubs:* Oxford and Cambridge (Lagos); Rotary (Nsukka) (Charter Pres.).

EZRA, family name of **Baron Ezra.**

EZRA, Baron *cr* 1983 (Life Peer), of Horsham in the County of West Sussex; **Derek Ezra;** Kt 1974; MBE 1945; Chairman: Associated Heat Services plc, since 1966; Energy and Technical Services Group Plc, since 1990; Associated Gas Supplies Ltd, since 1987; Sheffield Heat and Power Ltd, since 1985; *b* 23 Feb. 1919; *s* of David and Lillie Ezra; *m* 1950, Julia Elizabeth Wilkins. *Educ:* Monmouth Sch.; Magdalene Coll., Cambridge (MA, Hon. Fellow, 1977). Army, 1939–47. Joined NCB, 1947; representative of NCB at Cttees of OEEC and ECE, 1948–52; Mem. of UK Delegn to High Authority of European Coal and Steel Community, 1952–56; Dep. Regional Sales Manager, NCB, 1956–58; Regional Sales Manager, 1958–60; Dir-Gen. of Marketing, NCB, 1960–65; NCB Bd Mem., 1965–67; Dep. Chm., 1967–71; Chm., 1971–82. Chairman: J. H. Sankey & Son Ltd, 1977–82; Petrolex PLC, 1982–85; Throgmorton Trust PLC, 1984–91; Director: British Fuel Co., 1966–82; Solvay SA, 1979–90; Redland PLC, 1982–89; Supervisory Bd, Royal Boskalis Westminster NV, 1982–85. Industrial Advr, Morgan Grenfell & Co. Ltd, 1982–88. Chm., NICG, 1972 and 1980–81; President: Nat. Materials Handling Centre, 1979; Coal Industry Soc., 1981–86 (Chm., 1961); W European Coal Producers' Assoc., 1976–79; BSI, 1983–86; Economic Res. Council, 1985–; Inst. of Trading Standards Admin, 1987–92; Vice-Pres., BIM, 1978 (Chm., 1976–78); Chm., British Iron and Steel Consumers' Council, 1983–86; Member: BOTB, 1972–82 (Chm., European Trade Cttee); Cons. Cttee, ECSC, 1973–82 (Pres., 1978–79); Adv. Council for Energy Conservation, 1974–79; Adv. Bd, Petrofina SA, 1982–90; Internat. Adv. Bd, Creditanstalt Bankverein, 1982–90; Energy Commn, 1977–79; Ct of Governors, Administrative Staff Coll., 1971–82; Internat. Adv. Bd, Banca Nazionale del Lavoro, 1984–; Governor, London Business Sch., 1973–82. Pres., Keep Britain Tidy Gp, 1985–89 (Chm., 1979–85). Hon. DSc Cranfield, 1979; Hon. LLD Leeds, 1982. Bronze Star (USA), 1945; Grand Officer, Italian Order of Merit, 1979; Comdr, Luxembourg Order of Merit, 1981; Officer of Légion d'Honneur, 1981. *Publications:* Coal and Energy, 1978; The Energy Debate, 1983. *Address:* House of Lords, Westminster, SW1A 0PW. *T:* 0171-219 3180.

F

FABER, David James Christian; MP (C) Westbury, since 1992; *b* 7 July 1961; *s* of Julian Tufnell Faber, *qv*; *m* 1988, Sally Elizabeth Gilbert; one *s*. *Educ:* Summer Fields, Oxford; Eton Coll.; Balliol Coll., Oxford (MA Mod. Langs). Conservative Central Office, 1985–87 (Personal Asst to Dep. Chm., 1985–86); Dir, Sterling Marketing Ltd, 1987– (Chm., 1991–). Contested (C) Stockton North, 1987. PPS to Min. of State, Foreign Office, 1994–. Mem., Social Security Select Cttee, 1992–; Sec., Cons. back bench Educn Cttee, 1992–94. Trustee: Addictive Diseases Trust; Life-Anew Trust. *Recreations:* spending time with my son, Henry; cricket, golf. *Address:* House of Commons, SW1A 0AA. *T:* 0171–219 3000. *Clubs:* White's, MCC; Vincent's (Oxford); Royal St George's Golf.

FABER, Diana; a Law Commissioner, since 1994; *b* 23 Oct. 1955; *d* of T. G. Faber and Mrs D. Swan. *Educ:* Putney High Sch.; University Coll. London (LLB Hons). Called to the Bar, Gray's Inn, 1977; practised at Common Law Bar, 1977–82; admitted solicitor, 1983; joined Richards Butler, 1982, Partner, 1988–94. *Publications:* numerous articles in legal and commercial jls and newspapers. *Recreations:* theatre, reading, walking. *Address:* The Law Commission, Conquest House, 37–38 John Street, Theobalds Road, WC1N 2BQ. *T:* 0171–411 1204/1243.

FABER, Julian Tufnell; Chairman: Willis Faber Ltd, 1972–77; Cornhill Insurance plc, 1986–88 (Director, 1972–88); *b* 6 April 1917; *s* of late Alfred and Edith Faber; *m* 1944, Lady (Ann) Caroline, *e d* of 1st Earl of Stockton, OM, PC, FRS, and late Lady Dorothy Macmillan; three *s* one *d* (and one *s* decd). *Educ:* Winchester; Trinity Coll., Cambridge. Joined Willis, Faber & Dumas Ltd, 1938. Served Welsh Guards (Major 2nd Bn), 1939–45. Director: Willis, Faber & Dumas Ltd, 1952; Willis, Faber & Dumas (Agencies) Ltd, 1965; Taisho Marine & Fire Insurance Co. (UK) Ltd, 1972 (Chm.); Willis Faber (Middle East) SAL, 1973; Morgan Grenfell Ltd, 1974–77; Allianz International Insurance Co., 1974. Former Mem. Bd of Governors, Summer Fields Sch., Oxford. Member: MCC Cttee, 1981–84; Kent CCC Cttee, 1977–84. *Address:* Fisher's Gate, Withyham, E Sussex TN7 4BB; Flat 4, 17 Sloane Court West, SW3 4TD. *Clubs:* White's, City of London, MCC.
See also D. J. C. Faber.

FABER, Michael Leslie Ogilvie; Professorial Fellow, Institute of Development Studies, Sussex University, since 1982 (Director, 1982–87); *b* 12 Aug. 1929; *s* of George and Kathleen Faber; *m* 1956, Diana Catriona Howard; two *s* twin *d*. *Educ:* Avon Old Farms, USA; Eton; Magdalen Coll., Oxford (MA); Univ. of Michigan. MA Cantab. Served 11th Hussars, PAO, Germany, 1948–49. Merchant Seaman, 1953–54. Claims Adjuster, Amer. Internat. Underwriters, Japan and Korea, 1954; Foreign Correspondent for Sunday Times, Observer, and Economist in FE, ME, N and Central Africa, 1954–60; Lectr in Econs, UCRN, 1958–60; community develt worker with Danilo Dolci in Sicily, 1961; Lectr in Econs, UWI, 1962–63; Sen. Economist and Under-Sec., Govt of Zambia, 1964–67; Dept of Applied Econs, Cambridge, 1968; Overseas Develt Gp, UEA, 1969–78; Dir, Tech. Assistance Gp, Commonwealth Secretariat, 1972–75 and 1978–82. Member: Council, Overseas Develt Inst., 1982–; Bd, Commonwealth Develt Corp., 1988–. Pres., UK Chapter, Soc. for Internat. Develt, 1986–91. Leader, UNDP/IBRD Mission to PNG, 1972; specialist negotiator of debt and resource agreements. *Publications:* Economic Structuralism and its Relevance, 1965; (with J. Potter) Towards Economic Independence, 1971; (ed with Dudley Seers) The Crisis in Economic Planning, 1972; (with R. Brown) Mining Agreements: law and policy, 1977; (with R. Brown) Changing the Rules of the Game, 1980; Conciliatory Debt Reduction: why it must come and how it could come, 1988; Beware of Debtspeak, 1988. *Address:* The Combe, Glynde, Lewes, Sussex BN8 6RP. *Clubs:* Brooks's; Lewes Golf.

FABER, Sir Richard (Stanley), KCVO 1980; CMG 1977; FRSL; HM Diplomatic Service, retired; Ambassador to Algeria, 1977–81; *b* 6 Dec. 1924; *er s* of late Sir Geoffrey Faber and Enid, *d* of Sir Henry Erle Richards, KCSI, KC; unmarried. *Educ:* Westminster Sch.; Christ Church, Oxford (MA). RNVR, 1943–46. 1st cl. Lit. Hum. Oxon; Pres., Oxford Union Soc., 1949. Joined HM Foreign (subseq. Diplomatic) Service, 1950; service in FO and in Baghdad, Paris, Abidjan, Washington; Head of Rhodesia Political Dept, FCO, 1967–69; Counsellor: The Hague, 1969–73; Cairo, 1973–75; Asst Under Sec. of State, FCO, 1975–77. Hon. Treas., RSL, 1986–91. *Publications:* Beaconsfield and Bolingbroke, 1961; The Vision and the Need: Late Victorian Imperialist Aims, 1966; Proper Stations: Class in Victorian Fiction, 1971; French and English, 1975; The Brave Courtier (biog. of Sir William Temple), 1983; High Road to England, 1985; Young England, 1987; A Brother's Murder, 1992. *Address:* 4 De L'Angle House, The Green, Chartham, Kent CT4 7JW. *T:* Canterbury (01277) 738973. *Club:* Travellers'.
See also T. E. Faber.

FABER, Thomas Erle, PhD; Chairman, Geoffrey Faber Holdings Ltd (formerly Faber & Faber (Publishers) Ltd), since 1977 (Director since 1969); Fellow of Corpus Christi College, Cambridge, since 1953; *b* 25 April 1927; *s* of Sir Geoffrey Faber; *m* 1st, 1959, Penelope (*d* 1983), *d* of Clive Morton, actor; two *s* two *d*; 2nd, 1986, Dr Elisabeth van Houts; one *s* one *d*. *Educ:* Oundle Sch.; Trinity Coll., Cambridge (MA, PhD). University of Cambridge: Res. Fellow, Trinity Coll., 1950–53; Univ. Demonstr, 1953–58; Armourers' and Brasiers' Fellow, 1958–59; Lectr in Physics, 1959–93; Treasurer, Corpus Christi Coll., 1963–76. *Publications:* Introduction to the Theory of Liquid Metals, 1972; Fluid Dynamics for Physicists, 1995; papers on superconductivity, liquid metals and liquid crystals. *Recreations:* walking, shooting. *Address:* The Old Vicarage, Thompson's Lane, Cambridge CB5 8AQ. *T:* Cambridge (01223) 356685.
See also Sir R. S. Faber.

FABIAN, Prof. Andrew Christopher; Royal Society Research Professor, Institute of Astronomy, University of Cambridge, since 1982; Fellow of Darwin College, Cambridge, since 1983; *b* 20 Feb. 1948; *s* of John Archibald and Daphne Monica Fabian; *m* 1st, 1971 (marr. diss. 1991); one *s* one *d*; 2nd, 1991, Dr Carolin Susan Crawford; one *s*. *Educ:* Daventry Grammar Sch.; King's Coll., London (BSc Physics); University Coll. London (PhD). SRC post doctoral research asst, University Coll. London, 1972–73; Institute of Astronomy, Cambridge: SRC post doctoral Fellow, 1973–75; SRC PDRA, 1975–77; Radcliffe Fellow in Astronomy, 1977–81. *Publications:* contribs to Monthly Notices RAS, Astrophys. Jl, Nature, etc. *Address:* Institute of Astronomy, Madingley Road, Cambridge CB3 0HA.

FABIAN, (Andrew) Paul; HM Diplomatic Service, retired; Chief Secretary, Turks and Caicos Islands, 1990–91; *b* 23 May 1930; *s* of late Andrew Taggart Fabian and Edith Mary Whorwell; *m* 1st, Elisabeth Vivien Chapman; one *s* two *d*; 2nd, 1983, Eryll Francesca Dickinson. *Educ:* Mitcham County School; Reading; St Paul's; Wadham College, Oxford (scholar; MA). Singapore Engineer Regt, 1953–54; Tanganyika, 1955–64 (on secondment to Foreign Office, serving at Usumbura, 1961–64); HM Diplomatic Service, 1964; served Lusaka, Ankara, New Delhi, Islamabad, Karachi; High Comr, Nuku'alofa, Tonga, 1987–90. *Publication:* Delhi Post Bedside Book (ed), 1977. *Recreations:* chess, reading, bird-watching. *Address:* La Guionie, 24600, France. *Clubs:* United Oxford & Cambridge University; Tunbridge Wells Chess.

FABIUS, Laurent; Deputy for Seine Maritime, French National Assembly, 1978–81, re-elected 1981, 1986, 1993; (President, 1988–92); *b* 20 Aug. 1946; *s* of André Fabius and Louise Fabius (*née* Mortimer); *m* 1981, Françoise Castro; two *s*. *Educ:* Lycée Janson-de-Sailly; Lycée Louis-le-Grand; Ecole Normale Supérieure, Paris; Institut d'Etudes Politiques, Paris (Agrégé des lettres); Ecole Nationale d'Administration. Conseil d'Etat, 1973–81; First Deputy Mayor, Grand-Quevilly, 1977–81; Nat. Sec., Parti Socialiste (responsible for the press), 1979–81; Junior Minister, Ministry of Economy and Finance (responsible for the budget), 1981–83; Minister of Industry and Research, 1983–84; Prime Minister of France, 1984–86; First Sec., Socialist Party, 1992–93. Mem., Conseil d'Etat, 1981–93. Pres., Regional Council, Haute Normandie, 1981–. *Publications:* La France inégale, 1975; Le Coeur du Futur, 1985; C'est en allant vers la mer, 1990. *Address:* 15 place du Panthéon, 75005 Paris, France.

FABRICANT, Michael Louis David; MP (C) Mid-Staffordshire, since 1992; *b* 12 June 1950; *s* of Isaac Nathan Fabricant and Helena (*née* Freed). *Educ:* Loughborough Univ. (BA Law and Econs); Univ. of Sussex (MSc Systems); PhD. CEng, FIEE. FIMgt. Postgrad. doctoral res., mathematical econs, London Univ., Oxford Univ. and Univ. of S California, LA. Formerly: Broadcaster, current affairs, BBC Radio; Man. Dir, Commercial Radio Gp; Founder Dir, Internat. Broadcast Electronics and Investment Gp, 1979–91. Member: Nat. Heritage Select Cttee, 1993–; European Legislation Scrutiny Cttee B, 1993–; Dep. Chm., Cons. Parly Media Cttee, 1992–. *Publications:* various newspaper articles and pamphlets. *Recreations:* fell-walking, reading, music (Mozart to rock), ski-ing. *Address:* House of Commons, SW1A 0A. *Club:* Rottingdean (Sussex).

FACER, Roger Lawrence Lowe, CB 1992; Deputy Under-Secretary of State, Ministry of Defence, 1988–93; *b* 28 June 1933; *s* of late John Ernest Facer and Phyllis Facer; *m* 1960, Ruth Margaret, *o d* of late Herbert Mostyn Lewis, PhD, Gresford, Clwyd; three *d*. *Educ:* Rugby; St John's Coll., Oxford (MA). HM Forces, 2nd Lieut, East Surrey Regt, 1951–53. War Office, 1957; Asst Private Sec. to Secretary of State, 1958; Private Sec. to Permanent Under-Sec., 1958; Principal, 1961; Cabinet Office, 1966; Ministry of Defence, 1968–93: Private Sec. to Minister of State (Equipment), 1970; Asst Sec., 1970; Internat. Inst. for Strategic Studies, 1972–73; Counsellor, UK Delegn, MBFR Vienna, 1973–75; Private Sec. to Sec. of State for Defence, 1976–79; Asst Under-Sec. of State, 1979–81; Under Sec., Cabinet Office, 1981–83; Rand Corporation, Santa Monica, USA, 1984; Asst Under-Sec. of State, MoD, 1984–87. Dir Gen., Carroll Inst., 1993–95. *Publications:* Weapons Procurement in Europe—Capabilities and Choices, 1975; Conventional Forces and the NATO Strategy of Flexible Response, 1985; articles in Alpine Garden Soc. Bulletin. *Recreations:* Alpine gardening, hill-walking, opera. *Address:* Kennett Lodge, Hambledon, Hants PO7 4SA.

FACK, Robbert; Commander, Order of Orange-Nassau, 1979; Chevalier, Order of Netherlands Lion 1971; Netherlands diplomat, retired; Ambassador of the Netherlands to the Court of St James's, 1976–82; also, concurrently, Ambassador to Iceland, 1976–82; *b* 1 Jan. 1917; *m* 1943, Patricia H. Hawkins; four *s*. *Educ:* Univ. of Amsterdam. Military service, 1937–45. Min. of Foreign Affairs, The Hague, 1945–46; New York (UN), 1946–48; Min. of Foreign Affairs, 1948–50; Rome, 1950–54; Canberra, 1954–58; Bonn, 1958–63; Min. of Foreign Affairs, 1963–68; Ambassador-at-large, 1968–70; Perm. Rep. to UN, New York, 1970–74. Holds various foreign decorations. *Publication:* Gedane Zaken (Finished Business), (reminiscences), 1984. *Address:* Widden Hill House, Horton, near Bristol BS17 6QU. *Club:* Dutch.

FAGAN, (Florence) Mary, JP; Lord Lieutenant of Hampshire, since 1994; *b* 11 Sept. 1939; *o d* of Col George Vere-Laurie, JP, DL, Carlton Hall, Newark, Notts; *m* 1960, Capt. Christopher Fagan, Grenadier Guards; one *s* (and one *s* decd). *Educ:* St Elphin's Sch., Matlock; Southover Manor, Sussex. Dir, Andover Dist Community Health Care NHS Trust, 1993–94; Chm., Countess of Brecknock Hospice and Home Care Service Appeal, Andover, 1989–; Vice-Pres., Hospital Saving Assoc., 1990–; Mem., Central Adv. Cttee, Cancer Relief Macmillan Fund (Chm., Hants Br.). Former Mem., Sch. Adv. Cttee, N Hants. President: ESU, 1994–; Hants Council of Community Service, 1994–; Hants and IoW Youth Options, 1994–; Hants Br., Army Benevolent Fund, 1994–; Vice-President: Southern Regl Assoc. for the Blind, 1994–; Mary Rose Trust, 1994–; Fortune Centre of Riding Therapy, 1994–; Patron: Rowans Hospice, Portsmouth, 1994–; Hants Music Trust, 1994–; Hants Br., BRCS, 1994–; Trustee: Andover Med. Fund, 1994–; Marwell Zool Park, 1994–; Hants Gardens Trust, 1994–. Freeman, Saddlers' Co., 1962.

JP Hants, 1994. DStJ 1994 (Pres. Council, Hants, 1994–; former County Pres., Hants). *Recreations:* country sports. *Address:* Deane Hill House, Deane, near Basingstoke, Hants RG25 3AX. *T:* Basingstoke (01256) 780591.

FAGAN, Maj.-Gen. Patrick Feltrim, CB 1990; MBE (mil.) 1966; FRICS 1971; FRGS 1966; independent consultant on mapping matters; *b* 8 Dec. 1935; *s* of Air Cdre Thomas Patrick Feltrim Fagan and Hon. Isabel Mairi, *yr d* of 15th Baron Arundell of Wardour; *m* 1967, Veronica Thompson (*née* Lorant), *widow* of Captain C. J. C. Thompson, RE; two *s*. *Educ:* Stonyhurst Coll.; RMA, Sandhurst; University Coll. London (MSc (Hons) 1969). FBIM 1971. Commnd RE, 1955; served in Gibraltar, Germany, Aden and Oman. Internat. Scientific Expedn to Karakoram, 1961–62; UAE-Oman Border Survey, 1964; Jt Services Expedn to S Georgia, 1964–65; Ordnance Survey, 1969–73; Geographic Advr, AFCENT, 1979–83; Chief Geographic Officer, SHAPE, 1983–85; Dir, Survey Operations and Prodn, 1985–87; Dir Gen. of Military Survey, 1987–90. Member: Council, RGS, 1987–92 and 1993–95 (Vice-Pres., 1990–92); Council, BSES, 1987–90; Cttee of Management, Mt Everest Foundn, 1989–95 (Dep. Chm., 1990; Chm., 1992–94); Nat. Cttee for Photogrammetry and Remote Sensing, 1987–91; Adv. Bd, Inst. of Engrg, Surveying and Space Geodesy, Nottingham Univ., 1987–91; Council, RICS Land Surveyors, 1988–91; RICS Pres's Disciplinary and Appeals Tribunal, 1989–95. Dep. Pres., Army RU, 1989–91. Col Comdt, RE, 1991–, Rep. Col Comdt, 1992. *Publications:* articles on surveying and mapping in Geographical Jl, Photogrammetric Record, Survey Rev., Chartered Surveyor, and on ski mountaineering in subject jls. *Recreations:* mountain sports, boats, cricket, reading, photography, music, travel. *Address:* c/o Lloyds Bank, 7 Pall Mall, SW1Y 5NA. *Clubs:* Alpine, Alpine Ski, Eagle Ski (Pres., 1988–90), MCC, Geographical, Royal Over-Seas League.

FAGE, Prof. John Donnelly, MA, PhD; Professor of African History, 1963–84, now Emeritus, Pro-Vice-Chancellor, 1979–84, and Vice-Principal 1981–84, University of Birmingham; *b* 3 June 1921; *s* of late Arthur Fage, CBE, FRS, and Winifred Eliza Donnelly; *m* 1949, Jean, *d* of late Fred Banister, MBE; one *s* one *d*. *Educ:* Tonbridge Sch.; Magdalene Coll., Cambridge (scholar, MA, PhD). Served War, Pilot with RAFVR (Flt Lt), 1941–45. Bye-Fellow, Magdalene Coll., Cambridge, 1947–49; Lectr and Sen. Lectr, Univ. Coll. of the Gold Coast, 1949–55; Prof. of History, 1955–59, and Dep. Principal, 1957–59; Lectr in African History, SOAS, Univ. of London, 1959–63. Visiting Prof., Univ. of Wisconsin, Madison, 1957, and Smith Coll., Northampton, Mass, 1962; Dir, Centre of West African Studies, Univ. of Birmingham, 1963–82, Dep. Dean, Faculty of Arts, 1973–75, Dean, 1975–78; Founding Hon. Sec., African Studies Assoc. of the UK, 1963–66 (Vice-Pres. 1967–68, Pres. 1968–69); Council Mem., Internat. African Inst., 1965–75, and Consultative Dir, 1975–80; Member: UNESCO Scientific Cttee for Gen. History of Africa, 1971–80; Culture Adv. Cttee of UK Nat. Commn for UNESCO, 1967–85 (Chm., 1978–85); Co-ordinating Council of Area Studies Associations, 1980–86 (Vice-Chm. 1980–84, Chm., 1984–86); Chm., Birmingham Jt Cttee for Adult Educn Inf. and Advice Services, 1985–88. FRHistS. Hon. Fellow, SOAS, Univ. of London. Editor (with Roland Oliver), The Jl of African History, 1960–73; Gen. Editor (with Roland Oliver), The Cambridge History of Africa, 8 vols, 1975–86. *Publications:* An Introduction to the History of West Africa, 1955, 3rd edn 1962; An Atlas of African History, 1958, 2nd edn, 1978; Ghana, a Historical Interpretation, 1959; A Short History of Africa (with Roland Oliver), 1962, 6th edn 1988; A History of West Africa, 1969, reprinted 1993; (ed) Africa Discovers Her Past, 1970; (ed with Roland Oliver) Papers on African Prehistory, 1970; A History of Africa, 1978, 3rd edn 1995; A Guide to Sources for Western Africa, 1987; articles in historical and Africanist jls. *Recreations:* doing things to houses and gardens. *Address:* Hafod Awel, Pennal, Machynlleth, Powys SY20 9DP. *T:* Machynlleth (01654) 791207. *Club:* Athenæum.

FAGGE, Sir John William Frederick, 11th Bt, *cr* 1660; *b* 28 Sept. 1910; *s* of late William Archibald Theodore Fagge (*b* of 9th Bt) and Nellie (*d* 1924), *d* of H. T. D. Wise; *S* uncle, 1940; *m* 1940, Ivy Gertrude, *d* of William Edward Frier, 15 Church Lane, Newington, Kent; one *s* one *d*. *Heir:* *s* John Christopher Fagge [*b* 30 April 1942; *m* 1974, Evelyn Joy Golding]. *Address:* c/o 11 Forbes Road, Faversham, Kent ME13 8QF.

FAHEY, Hon. John Joseph; MP (L) Southern Highlands, NSW, since 1988; Premier of New South Wales, 1992–95; Minister for Economic Development, 1993–95; *b* 10 Jan. 1945; *s* of Stephen Fahey and Annie (*née* Fahey); *m* 1968, Colleen Maree McGurren; one *s* two *d*. *Educ:* St Anthony's Convent, Picton, NSW; Chevalier Coll., Bowral, NSW; Univ. of Sydney Law Extension Cttee (Dip. Law). Practised law, Camden, NSW, 1971–86. MP (L) Camden, 1984–88; Minister for Ind. Relns and Minister assisting the Premier, NSW, 1988–90; Minister for Ind. Relns, Further Educn, Trng and Employment, 1990–92; Treasurer, 1992–93. *Recreations:* tennis, Rugby, cricket, gardening, reading. *Address:* 24 Wingecarribee Street, Bowral, NSW 2576, Australia. *Fax:* (48) 613546.

FAINT, John Anthony Leonard; Under Secretary (Eastern Europe and Western Hemisphere), Overseas Development Administration, since 1993; *b* 24 Nov. 1942; *s* of Thomas Leonard Faint and Josephine Rosey Faint (*née* Dunkerley); *m* 1978, Elizabeth Theresa Winter. *Educ:* Chigwell Sch.; Magdalen Coll., Oxford (BA LitHum 1965); MA Development Economics, Fletcher Sch., Mass, 1969. Ministry of Overseas Development (later Overseas Development Administration), London, 1965–71 (study leave in Cambridge, Mass, 1968–69); First Secretary (Aid), Blantyre, Malawi, 1971–73; ODM/ODA, London, 1974–80; Head of SE Asia Develt Div., Bangkok, 1980–83; Head of Finance Dept, ODA, FCO, 1983–86; Alternate Exec. Dir, World Bank, Washington, 1986–89; Head, E Asia Dept, 1989–90, Under Sec., Internat. Div., 1990–91, ODA; on secondment as UK Dir, EBRD, 1991–92; Under Sec. (Eastern Europe), ODA, 1991–93. *Recreations:* music, bridge, chess, computers. *Address:* Overseas Development Administration, 94 Victoria Street, SW1E 5JL.

FAIR, Donald Robert Russell, OBE (mil.) 1945; Board Member, Central Electricity Generating Board, 1975–77; *b* 26 Dec. 1916; *s* of Robert Sidney Fair and Mary Louie Fair; *m* 1941, Patricia Laurie Rudland; one *s*. *Educ:* Roan Sch., Blackheath; King's Coll., London Univ. (BSc, AKC). CEng, FInstE; CPhys, FInstP. Served War of 1939–45, RAF (Wing Comdr; despatches 1944; USAAF Commendation 1944). Lectr, RMA Sandhurst, 1948–50; UK AEA, 1950–62; Central Electricity Generating Bd, 1962–77. *Recreations:* sailing, cricket. *Address:* 22 Carlton Leas, The Leas, Folkestone, Kent CT20 2DJ. *T:* Folkestone (01303) 250573.

FAIRBAIRN, Sir Brooke; *see* Fairbairn, Sir J. B.

FAIRBAIRN, Hon. Sir David Eric, KBE 1977; DFC 1944; Australian Ambassador to the Netherlands, 1977–80; grazier, 1939–71; *b* 3 March 1917; *s* of Clive Prell Fairbairn and Marjorie Rose (*née* Jowett); *m* 1945, Ruth Antill (*née* Robertson); three *d*. *Educ:* Geelong Grammar Sch.; Cambridge Univ. (MA). Served RAAF, 1940–45, England and New Guinea. MP (L) Commonwealth of Australia, 1949–75; Minister: for Air, 1962–64; for Nat. Develt, 1964–69; for Educn and Science, March–Aug. 1971; for Defence, 1971–72. *Recreations:* golf, gardening. *Address:* 18 Yarralumla Bay, 51 Musgrave Street, Yarralumla, ACT 2600, Australia. *T:* (6) 2814659. *Clubs:* Melbourne (Melbourne); Commonwealth (Canberra); Royal Canberra Golf.

FAIRBAIRN, David Ritchie, OBE 1990; Vice-Chairman, James Martin Holdings Ltd, since 1994; Managing Director, James Martin Management Associates Ltd, since 1995; *b* 4 July 1934; *s* of G. F. Fairbairn; *m* 1958, Hon. Susan Hill, *d* of Baron Hill of Luton, PC; one *s* two *d*. *Educ:* Mill Hill Sch.; Gonville and Caius Coll., Cambridge (BAEcon). FBCS; FIDPM, FInstD. President, Cambridge Union Soc. Overseas Marketing Manager, Arthur Guinness Son & Co. Ltd, 1960; President, Guinness-Harp Corp., New York, 1964; Marketing Dir, Guinness Overseas Ltd, 1969; Man. Dir, Dataset Ltd (ICL), 1970; Manager, Retail and Distribution Sector, International Computers Ltd, 1975; Dir of Marketing, EMI Medical Ltd, 1976; Dir, Nat. Computing Centre, 1980–86; Man. Dir, James Martin Associates UK, 1985–89; Gp Man. Dir, James Martin Associates Ltd, 1989–92; Man. Dir, JMA Information Engineering Ltd, 1992–94; Vice Pres., Europe, Texas Instruments Inc., 1993–94. Pres., Inst. of Data Processing Management, 1982– (Vice-Pres., 1980–82). Vice-Chm., Parly IT Cttee, 1982. Member: Monopolies and Mergers Commn, 1985–; Patent Office Steering Bd, 1989–. Freeman, City of London, 1990. FRSA. *Recreations:* sailing, water-ski-ing, ski-ing. *Address:* 11 Oak Way, West Common, Harpenden, Herts AL5 2NT. *T:* Harpenden (01582) 715820, *Fax:* (01582) 468339.

FAIRBAIRN, Sir (James) Brooke, 6th Bt *cr* 1869, of Ardwick; *b* 10 Dec. 1930; *s* of Sir William Albert Fairbairn, 5th Bt, and of Christine Renée Cotton, *d* of late Rev. Canon Robert William Croft; *S* father, 1972; *m* 1960, Mary Russell (*d* 1992), *d* of late William Russell Scott, MB, ChB, FFARCS; two *s* one *d*. *Educ:* Stowe. Proprietor of J. Brooke Fairbairn & Co., textile converters and wholesalers dealing in furnishing fabrics. Upper Bailiff, Weavers' Co., 1992–93. *Heir:* *s* Robert William Fairbairn [*b* 10 April 1965; *m* 1990, Sarah, *e d* of Roger Griffin, BVSc, MRCVS]. *Address:* Barkway House, Bury Road, Newmarket, Suffolk CB8 7BT. *T:* Newmarket (01638) 662733; J. Brooke Fairbairn & Co., The Railway Station, Newmarket CB8 9BA. *T:* Newmarket (01638) 665766.

FAIRBAIRN, John Sydney; Chairman, Esmée Fairbairn Charitable Trust, since 1988; Deputy Chairman, M & G Group plc, 1979–89 (non-executive Director, since 1989); *b* 15 Jan. 1934; *s* of late Sydney George Fairbairn, MC and Angela Maude Fairbairn (*née* Fane); *m* 1968, Mrs Camilla Fry, *d* of late G. N. Grinling; one *s* two *d* and two step *s* two step *d*. *Educ:* Eton; Trinity College, Cambridge (MA). FCA. National Service, 2nd Lieut 17/21 Lancers, 1952–54. Monkhouse Stoneham & Co., 1957–60; joined M & G Group, 1961, Dir, 1974. Chm., Central European Growth Fund plc, 1994–; Dir, ITS Gp, 1993–. Dep. Chm., Lautro, 1986–89; Chm., Unit Trust Assoc., 1989–91. Trustee: Monteverdi Trust, 1991–; Royal Pavilion, Art Gall. and Museums of Brighton, 1993– (Gov. of Friends, 1990–); Comeback, 1993–; Dulwich Picture Gall., 1994– (Mem., Governing Cttee, 1991–); Council Mem. and Treasurer, King's College London, 1972–84 (Fellow 1978); Council Member: Univ. of Buckingham, 1986–; Policy Studies Inst. DUniv Buckingham, 1992. *Address:* Harvest Hill, Cuckfield, West Sussex RH17 5AH. *T:* Haywards Heath (01444) 412200. *Clubs:* White's, Brooks's, MCC.

FAIRBANKS, Douglas (Elton), (Jr), KBE 1949; DSC 1944; Captain, USNR, retired; actor, writer, producer, company director; Chairman, Fairtel, Inc. (US), since 1946; formerly Chairman, Douglas Fairbanks Ltd; Director or Special Consultant: Fairbanks Co. Inc.; Norlantic Development; Boltons Trading; Alcoa Inc.; Dougfair Corp. (US); Scripto Pens Ltd (US and UK), 1952–73; Golden Cycle and subsidiaries, 1965–73; Rambagh Palace Hotel, Ltd (Jaipur, India); Cavalcade Film Co. Ltd (UK), etc; *b* New York City, 9 Dec. 1909; *s* of Douglas Elton Fairbanks, Denver, Colorado, and Anna Beth Sully, Providence, RI; *m* 1st, 1929, Lucille Le Sueur (Joan Crawford) (marr. diss. 1933); 2nd, 1939, Mary Lee Epling (*d* 1988), Keystone, W Virginia; three *d*. 3rd, 1991, Vera Shelton. *Educ:* Bovée Sch., Knickerbocker Greys, Collegiate Mil. Sch., NY; Pasadena Polytechnic, Harvard Mil. Sch., Los Angeles; tutored privately in London and Paris. Began career as film actor, 1923, on stage 1926. Organised own producing company, UK, 1935. Studied painting and sculpture, Paris, 1922–24; began writing, professionally, 1928; articles, fiction and essays on public affairs, etc., 1936–. Vice-Pres. Franco-British War Relief and National Vice-Pres. Cttee "Defend America by Aiding the Allies", 1939–40; Presidential Envoy, Special Mission to Latin America, 1940–41; one-time Consultant to Office of the Presidency (Washington, DC); Lieut (jg), USNR, 1941; promoted through grades to Capt., 1954. National Chm., CARE Cttee, 1947–50; Nat. Vice-Pres. Amer. Assoc. for the UN, 1946–60; Pres. Brit.-Amer. Alumni Assoc. 1950; Bd Gov., English-Speaking Union of the US, 1949–60; Nat. Chm., Amer. Relief for Korea, 1950–54; Trustee, Edwina Mountbatten Trust; Mem., Bd of Dirs, Mountbatten Meml Trust (US); Mem. Bd of Dirs, Amer. Friends of RSC and RSC Trust; Dir, Shakespeare Globe Theater; Mem. Council, American Museum in Brit.; a Governor and Exec. Cllr, Royal Shakespeare Theatre; Governor: United World Colleges, 1951–; Ditchley Foundations; Co-Chm., US Capitol Bicentenary 1776–1976; Guild of St Bride's Church, Fleet Street, EC; Mem., Council on Foreign Relations (NY); US Naval Mem., US Mil. Delegn, SEATO Conf., 1971; Mem., Bd of Dirs, Pilgrims Soc. of US, 1985–; Vis. Fellow, St Cross Coll., Oxford; MA Oxon; Senior Churchill Fellow, Westminster Coll., Fulton, Mo; Hon. DFA Westminster Coll., Fulton, Mo, USA; Hon. LLD Univ. of Denver, Colo; Silver Star Medal (US); Legion of Merit ("Valor" clasp) (US), Special Naval Commendation (US), KJStJ 1950 (Hon. Dep. Chancellor, Amer. Friends, Order of St John), etc; Officer Legion of Honour (Fr.), Croix de Guerre with Palm (Fr.); Knight Comdr Order of George I (Greece); Knight Grand Officer, Order del Merito (Chile); Grand Officer, Order of Merit (Italy); Comdr Order of Orange Nassau (Neth.); Officer of: Orders of Crown (Belg.), of Star of Italy, Cross of Mil. Valour (Italy), Southern Cross (Brazil); Grand Comdr Order of Merit (West Germany); Murmansk Convoys Campaign (USSR); Hon. Citizen and National Medal of Korea, etc. *Films include:* Stella Dallas; Little Caesar; Outward Bound; Morning Glory; Catherine the Great; The Amateur Gentleman; The Prisoner of Zenda; Gunga Din; The Corsican Brothers; Sinbad the Sailor; The Exile; The Fighting O'Flynn; State Secret; The Young in Heart; Having Wonderful Time; The Rage of Paris; The Joy of Living; L'Athlète Malgré Lui (French); A Woman of Affairs; Lady in Ermine; Stephen Steps Out; The Barker; Chances; The Life of Jimmy Dolan; Mimi; Angels Over Broadway. *Plays include:* Young Woodley; Romeo and Juliet; The Jest; Man in Possession; The Winding Journey; Moonlight is Silver; My Fair Lady; The Pleasure of his Company; The Secretary Bird; Present Laughter; Sleuth; The Youngest; The Dummy; Towards the Light; produced over 160 TV plays, acted in over 50; also recordings etc. *Publications: autobiography:* The Salad Days, 1988; A Hell of a War, 1993; short stories, poems, articles, to periodicals; *relevant publications:* Knight Errant, by Brian Connell; The Fairbanks Album, by Richard Schickel; The Fourth Musketeer, by Letitia Fairbanks-Milner. *Recreations:* swimming, tennis, golf, travel. *Address:* The Beekman, 575 Park Avenue, New York, NY 10021, USA; (office) Inverness Corporation, 545 Madison Avenue, New York, NY 10022, USA. *Clubs:* White's, Naval and Military, Garrick, Beefsteak; Puffin's (Edinburgh); Brook, Knickerbocker, Century (NY); Metropolitan (Washington, DC); Racquet (Chicago); Myopia Hunt (Hamilton, Mass) (Hon. Mem.).

FAIRCLOUGH, Anthony John, CMG 1990; Special Adviser and Hon. Director General, European Commission (formerly Commission of the European Communities), since 1989; Director, Environmental Resources Management, since 1989; *b* 30 Aug. 1924; *m* 1957, Patricia Monks; two *s*. *Educ:* St Philip's Grammar Sch., Birmingham; St Catharine's Coll., Cambridge. Scholar 1944, BA Cantab 1945, MA 1950. Ministry of Aircraft

Production and Ministry of Supply, 1944–48; Colonial Office, 1948; Secretary, Nyasaland Commn of Inquiry, 1959; Private Secretary to Minister of State for Commonwealth Relations and for the Colonies, 1963–64; Assistant Secretary, 1964; Head of Pacific and Indian Ocean Dept, Colonial Office, subseq. Commonwealth Office, 1964–68; Head of W Indian Dept, FCO, 1968–70; Head of New Towns 1 Div., DoE, 1970–72; Under-Sec., 1973; Head of Planning, Minerals and Countryside Directorate, 1973, of Planning, Sport and Countryside Directorate, 1973–74; Dir, Central Unit on Environmental Pollution, 1974–78; Dir, Internat. Transport, Dept of Transport, 1978–81; Dir for the Environment, CEC, 1981–85; Actg Dir Gen. for the Environment, Consumer Protection and Nuclear Safety, CEC, 1985–86; Dep. Dir-Gen. for Develt, CEC, 1986–89. Senior UK Commissioner at Sessions of South Pacific Commn, 1965–67; Minister's Deputy, European Conf. of Mins of Transport, 1978–81; Chm., Environment Cttee, OECD, 1976–79; British Channel Tunnel Co., 1978–81; British Co-Chm., Jt UK/USSR Cttee established under UK/USSR Agreement on cooperation in field of Environmental Protection, 1974–78; Chm., Network for Envmtl Technology Transfer, asbl, Belgium, 1989–; Dir, Groundwork Foundn, 1989–. Consultant to European Orgn for Res. and Treatment of Cancer, 1989–. Member: Royal Soc.'s British Nat. Cttee on Problems of Environment, 1974–78; EDC for Internat. Freight Movement, 1978–80; Governing Body, Chiswick Sch., 1973–79. Comp. ICE, 1989–93. FRSA. *Address:* 6 Cumberland Road, Kew, Richmond, Surrey TW9 3HQ; Appt 12, 32 Quai aux Briques, 1000 Brussels, Belgium.

FAIRCLOUGH, Rt. Hon. Ellen Louks, PC (Can.) 1957; CC 1995 (OC 1979); FCA 1965; UE; Member of Progressive Conservative Party, Canada; *b* Hamilton, Ont, 28 Jan. 1905; *d* of Norman Ellsworth Cook and Nellie Bell Louks; *m* 1931, David Henry Gordon Fairclough; one *s*. *Educ:* Hamilton Public and Secondary Schs. Certified Public Accountant, public practice, 1935–57 (Fellow, Chartered Accountants of Ontario, 1965). Hamilton City Council, Alderman, 1946–49; Controller, 1950. Elected to House of Commons as Progressive Conservative mem. for Hamilton West, 1950; re-elected at gen. elections, 1953, 1957, 1958, 1962, defeated in 1963 election. Sec. of State for Canada, 1957–58; Minister of Citizenship and Immigration, 1958–62; Postmaster-Gen., 1962–63. Patron, Huguenot Soc. of Canada, 1969–; Chancellor, Royal Hamilton College of Music, 1978–80. Mem. Bd, Ontario Bicentennial Commn, 1983–84; Hon. Treas. and Exec. Dir, Chedoke-McMaster Hosps Foundn, 1982–86; Patron: United Empire Loyalists Assoc., Hamilton Br., 1980–; Huguenot Soc. of Canada. Internat. Treasurer, Zonta Internat. HQ, Chicago, 1972–76 (Hon. Life Mem.). Ontario Govt Bldg named Ellen Fairclough Bldg, 1982. LLD (*hc*), McMaster Univ., 1975. *Recreations:* music, reading and photography. *Address:* 25 Stanley Avenue, Hamilton, Ont L8P 2K9, Canada. *T:* (416) 5225248. *Clubs:* Albany (Toronto); Hamilton, Zonta I (Hamilton); Faculty (McMaster).

FAIRCLOUGH, Sir John (Whitaker), Kt 1990; FEng, FIEE, FBCS; Chief Scientific Adviser to Cabinet Office, 1986–90; *b* 23 Aug. 1930; *m* Margaret Ann; two *s* one *d*. *Educ:* Manchester Univ. (BScTech). Ferranti, 1954; IBM: Poughkeepsie Lab., US, 1957; Hursley Lab., UK, 1958; Director of Development, IBM UK Ltd, 1964; Asst Gen. Manager and Dir Data Processing IBM UK, 1968; Dir, Raleigh Development Lab., USA, 1970; System Develt Div. Vice Pres., Raleigh, USA, 1972; System Communication Div. Vice Pres. and Man. Dir, Director of Development, Hursley Lab., UK, 1974; System Product Div. Vice Pres. and Man. Dir, Hursley Lab., UK, 1982; Dir of Manufacturing & Development, IBM UK Ltd, and Chm, IBM UK Laboratories Ltd, 1983. Chairman: Systematica Ltd, 1990–92; Rothschild Ventures Ltd, 1990–; Non-exec. Director: Oxford Instruments Gp, 1990–; N. M. Rothschild & Sons Ltd, 1990–; Infolink plc, 1991–93; DSC (Europe), 1992–; DSC Communication Corp., 1992–; Lucas Industries, 1992–; Psion plc, 1995–. Chairman: Engineering Council, 1990– (Mem., 1982–90); CEST, 1990–95; Prince Charles' Innovation Initiative, 1991–. Pres., BCS, 1987; Vice Pres., UMIST, 1992–95. Freeman, City of London, 1989. Fellow, Nat. Acad. of Engrg, USA, 1990. Hon. Fellow: Portsmouth Polytechnic, 1991; Manchester Metropolitan Univ., 1992. Hon. DSc: Southampton, 1983; Cranfield, 1987; Manchester, 1988; Aston, 1990; Polytechnic of Central London, 1991; City, 1992; Hon. DTech Loughborough, 1990. Mensford Gold Medal, IProdE, 1989. *Recreations:* gardening, carpentry. *Address:* The Old Blue Boar, St John's Street, Winchester, Hants SO23 8HF.

FAIRCLOUGH, Wilfred, RE; RWS; ARCA (London); Assistant Director, Kingston Polytechnic, and Head of the Division of Design, 1970–72, retired; Principal of Kingston College of Art, Surrey, 1962–70; *b* 13 June 1907; *s* of Herbert Fairclough and Edith Amy Milton; *m* 1936, Joan Cryer; one *s* one *d*. *Educ:* Royal College of Art, London, 1931–34 (Diploma 1933); British Sch. at Rome, Italy, 1934–37; Rome Scholar in Engraving, 1934–37. Army and Royal Air Force, 1942–46. Rome Scholarships, Faculty of Engraving, 1951 (Chm., 1964–73); Leverhulme Research Award, 1961. RE 1946 (ARE 1934); RWS 1968 (ARWS 1961). Chairman: Assoc. of Art Instns, 1965–66; Assessors, Vocational Courses of Surrey CC. *Work in public and private collections: paintings:* Min. of Supply; Min. of Works; Surrey CC; Scottish Modern Art Assoc.; Beaumont Coll.; *drawings:* British Museum; V&A Museum; Arts Council; Contemporary Art Soc.; Wye Coll., London Univ.; English Electric Co.; Art Galls at Blackburn, Kingston-upon-Thames, Worthing; Graves Art Gall., Sheffield; Atkinson Art Gall., Southport; *prints:* British Museum, V&A Museum; Ashmolean Museum, Oxford; Contemporary Art Soc.; British Sch. at Rome; South London Art Gall.; Stoke Educn Authority; Wye Coll., London Univ.; Gottenburg Museum; Print Collectors Club. *Publications:* The Etchings of Wilfrid Fairclough, 1990; work reproduced: Recording Britain; Londoners' England; Royal Academy Illustrated; Studio; Fine Prints of the Year; Print Collectors Quarterly; illustrated article, Leisure Painter, 1969; paintings, drawings and prints. *Address:* 12 Manorgate Road, Kingston-upon-Thames, Surrey KT2 7AL.

FAIREY, Michael John, CB 1989; Chief Executive, The Royal London Hospital and Associated Community NHS Trust, 1991–94; *b* 20 Sept. 1933; *s* of late Ernest John Saunder Fairey and Lily Emily (*née* Pateman); *m* 1st, 1958 (marr. diss. 1989); two *s* one *d*; 2nd, 1990, Victoria Frances Hardman. *Educ:* Queen Elizabeth's Sch., Barnet; Jesus Coll., Cambridge (MA). Served RA, 1952–53. Jun. Administrator, St Thomas' Hosp., 1957–60; Gp Develt Sec., Westminster Hosp., 1960–62; Deputy House Governor, The London Hosp., 1962, House Governor 1972; Regional Administrator, NE Thames RHA, 1973; Dir, Planning and Inf, NHS Management Bd, DHSS, later Dept of Health, 1984–89; Dir of Information Systems, NHS Management Exec., Dept of Health, 1989–91. *Publications:* various articles in med. and computing jls. *Recreations:* church music, history of medieval exploration, Rugby football. *Club:* Athenæum.

FAIRFAX, family name of **Lord Fairfax of Cameron.**

FAIRFAX OF CAMERON, 14th Lord *cr* 1627; **Nicholas John Albert Fairfax;** *b* 4 Jan. 1956; *e s* of 13th Lord and of Sonia, *yr d* of late Capt. Cecil Gunston, MC; *S* father, 1964; *m* 1982, Annabel, *er d* of late Nicholas and of Sarah Gilham Morriss; three *s*. *Educ:* Eton; Downing Coll., Cambridge (LLB in international law subjects, 1981). Called to the Bar, Gray's Inn, 1977. Director, Thomas Miller P and I, and Thomas Miller Defence, 1987–90. *Recreations:* sailing, tennis. *Heir: s* Hon. Edward Nicholas Thomas Fairfax, *b* 20 Sept. 1984. *Address:* 10 Orlando Road, SW4 0LF.

FAIRFAX, James Oswald, AO 1993; Chairman, John Fairfax Ltd, Sydney, 1977–87; *b* 27 March 1933; *s* of Sir Warwick Oswald Fairfax and late Marcie Elizabeth Fairfax (*née* Wilson). *Educ:* Geelong Grammar School; Balliol College, Oxford (MA; Hon. Fellow, 1992). Director, John Fairfax, 1957–87; Chm., Amalgamated Television Services Pty Ltd, 1975–87 (Dir, 1958); Chm., David Syme & Co., 1984–87 (Dir, 1977). Member: Bd of Management, Royal Alexandra Hosp. for Children, 1967–85 (Bd, Children's Med. Res. Foundn, 1986–88); Council, International House, Sydney Univ., 1967–79; Internat. Council, Museum of Modern Art, NY, 1971–; Council, Australian Nat. Gallery, 1976–84. Life Governor: Art Gallery of NSW, 1991; Australian Nat. Gall. Foundn, 1992. *Publication:* My Regards to Broadway: a memoir, 1991. *Address:* Retford Park, Old South Road, Bowral, NSW 2576, Australia; Stanbridge Mill, Gussage All Saints, near Wimborne, Dorset BH21 5EP. *Clubs:* Garrick; Union, Australian (Sydney); Melbourne (Melbourne).

FAIRFAX-LUCY, Sir Edmund (John William Hugh Cameron-Ramsay-), 6th Bt *cr* 1836; painter; *b* 4 May 1945; *s* of Sir Brian Fulke Cameron-Ramsay-Fairfax-Lucy, 5th Bt and Hon. Alice Caroline Helen Buchan (*d* 1993), *o d* of 1st Baron Tweedsmuir, PC, GCMG, GCVO, CH; *S* father, 1974; *m* 1994, Erica, *d* of Warren Loane, Crocknaerieve, Enniskillen; one *s*. *Educ:* City and Guilds of London Art Sch.; Royal Academy Schs of Art. Regular exhibitor, RA Summer Exhibn, 1967–; one-man shows, numerous mixed exhibitions. *Heir: s* Patrick Samuel Thomas Fulke Cameron-Ramsay-Fairfax-Lucy, *b* 3 April 1995. *Address:* Charlecote Park, Warwick CV35 9ER.

FAIRGRIEVE, Sir (Thomas) Russell, Kt 1981; CBE 1974; TD 1959; JP; *b* 3 May 1924; *s* of late Alexander Fairgrieve, OBE, MC, JP, and Myma Margaret Fairgrieve; *m* 1954, Millie Mitchell; one *s* three *d*. *Educ:* St Mary's Sch., Melrose; Sedbergh School; Scottish Coll. of Textiles. Major 8th Gurkha Rifles (Indian Army), 1946. Major, KOSB, 1956–72. Man. Dir, Laidlaw & Fairgrieve Ltd, 1958; Director: Joseph Dawson (Holdings) Ltd, 1961–72; William Baird and Co. PLC, 1975–79, 1982–; Bain Dawes (Scotland) Ltd, 1985–; Bain Clarkson Ltd; Chm., Quality Guaranteed PLC. Formerly: Chairman: Hall Advertising; Aberdeen Construction Group PLC; Dir, Hall & Tawse Group Ltd. Indust. consultant on exec. selection, textile problems and marketing. Selkirk County and Galashiels Town Councillor, 1949–59; Pres., Scottish Conservative Assoc., 1965, Vice-Chm., 1971; Chm., Conservative Party in Scotland, 1975–80. MP (C) Aberdeenshire West, Feb. 1974–83; Parly Under Sec. of State, Scottish Office, 1979–81. Formerly Mem., Council of Europe. JP Selkirkshire, 1962. *Recreation:* golf. *Address:* Pankalan, Boleside, Galashiels, Selkirk TD1 3NX. *T:* Galashiels (01896) 2278. *Clubs:* Carlton; New (Edinburgh); Royal and Ancient (St Andrews).

FAIRHALL, Hon. Sir Allen, KBE 1970; FRSA; Member, House of Representatives, 1949–69; *b* 24 Nov. 1909; *s* of Charles Edward and Maude Fairhall; *m* 1936, Monica Clelland, *d* of James and Ellen Ballantyne; one *s*. *Educ:* East Maitland Primary and High Sch.; Newcastle Tech. Inst. Founded commercial broadcasting stn 2KO, 1931; Supervising Engr, Radio and Signals Supplies Div., Min. of Munitions, 1942–45; Pres., Austr. Fedn of Commercial Broadcasting Stns, 1942–43. Mem. Australian Delegn to UN Gen. Assembly, 1954; Minister for Interior and Works, 1956–58; Minister for Supply, 1961–66; Minister for Defence, 1966–69. Mem. Newcastle CC, 1941. FRSA 1970. Hon. DSc Univ. of Newcastle, 1968. *Recreations:* amateur radio; deep sea fishing. *Address:* 7 Parkway Avenue, Newcastle, NSW 2300, Australia. *T:* (4) 9292295. *Clubs:* Tattersall's, National (Sydney); Newcastle (Newcastle).

FAIRHAVEN, 3rd Baron *cr* 1929 and 1961 (new creation); **Ailwyn Henry George Broughton;** JP; Vice Lord-Lieutenant, Cambridgeshire, 1977–85; *b* 16 Nov. 1936; *s* of 2nd Baron Fairhaven and Hon. Diana Rosamond (*d* 1937), *o d* of late Captain Hon. Coulson Fellowes; *S* father, 1973; *m* 1960, Kathleen Patricia, *d* of Col James Henry Magill, OBE; four *s* two *d*. *Educ:* Eton; RMA, Sandhurst. Royal Horse Guards, 1957–71. Mem., Jockey Club, 1977– (Steward, 1981–82, Sen. Steward, 1985–89). DL Cambridgeshire and Isle of Ely, 1973; JP South Cambridgeshire, 1975. KStJ 1992. *Recreations:* gardening, cooking. *Heir: s* Major Hon. James Henry Ailwyn Broughton [*b* 25 May 1963; *m* 1990, Sarah Olivia, *d* of H. D. F. Creighton, *qv*; two *d*]. *Address:* Anglesey Abbey, Cambridge CB5 9EJ. *T:* Cambridge (01223) 811746. *Club:* White's.

FAIRLEY, John Alexander; Chairman, ITV Broadcast Board, 1995; *s* of Alexander Miller Fairley and Madge Irene Fairley; *m*; three *d*. *Educ:* Merchant Taylors' Sch., Crosby; Queen's Coll., Oxford (MA). Midshipman, RNVR. Journalist: Bristol Evening Post, 1963; London Evening Standard, 1964; Producer: BBC Radio, 1965–68; Yorkshire TV, 1968–78; freelance writer and broadcaster, 1979–84; Dir of Programmes, Yorkshire TV, 1984–92; Managing Director: Yorkshire TV Programmes, 1992–93; Yorkshire TV, 1993–95. *Publications:* (jtly) The Monocled Mutineer, 1978; (jtly) Arthur C. Clarke's Mysterious World, 1980, and subseq. vols, 1984, 1987; Great Racehorses In Art, 1984; Racing In Art, 1990; (jtly) The Cabinet of Curiosities, 1991; The Art of the Horse, 1995. *Recreations:* writing, racing, hunting. *Address:* Trainer's House, Eddlethorpe, Malton, Yorks YO17 9QS; 539 Willoughby House, Barbican, EC2Y 8BN.

FAIRLIE-CUNINGHAME, Sir William Henry, 16th Bt *cr* 1630, of Robertland, Ayrshire; *b* 1 Oct. 1930; *s* of Sir William Alan Fairlie-Cuninghame, 15th Bt, MC, and Irene Alice (*d* 1970), *d* of Henry Margrave Terry; *S* father, 1981; *m* 1972, Janet Menzies, *d* of late Roy Menzies Saddington; one *s*. *Heir: s* Robert Henry Fairlie-Cuninghame, *b* 19 July 1974. *Address:* 29A Orinoco Street, Pymble, NSW 2073, Australia.

FAIRTLOUGH, Gerard Howard, CBE 1989; Chairman: Therexsys Ltd, since 1992; Landmark Information Group Ltd, since 1994; *b* 5 Sept. 1930; *s* of late Maj.-Gen. Eric V. H. Fairtlough, DSO, MC, and A. Zoë Fairtlough (*née* Barker); *m* 1954, Elizabeth A. Betambeau; two *s* two *d*. *Educ:* Cambridge Univ. (BA Biochemistry, Pt II). Royal/Dutch Shell Group, 1953–78; Managing Director, Shell Chemicals UK Ltd, 1973–78; Divisional Director, NEB, 1978–80; Chief Exec., Celltech Ltd, 1980–90; Dir, Cantab Pharmaceuticals plc, 1990–. Chm., Coverdale Orgn, 1974–93. Mem., SERC, 1989–94. Hon. DSc: City, 1987; CNAA, 1990. *Publication:* Creative Compartments, 1994. *Recreations:* walking, yoga, theatre. *Address:* 5 Belmont Grove, SE13 5DW. *T:* 0181–852 3228.

FAIRWEATHER, Brig. Claude Cyril, CB 1967; CBE 1965 (OBE 1944); TD 1944; JP; Vice Lord-Lieutenant, County of Cleveland, 1977–82; Chairman, North of England TA&VRA, 1968–71; *b* 17 March 1906; *s* of Nicholas Fairweather, Middlesborough; *m* 1930, Alice Mary, *e d* of late Sir William Crosthwaite; one *s* one *d*. *Educ:* St Peter's Sch., York. 2nd Lieut, Royal Corps of Signals, 1928; Lt-Col 1941; Col 1943; Brig. 1945. Chm., North Riding T&AFA, 1950–53 and 1962–68; Member: TA Advisory Cttee and TA Exec. Cttee, 1968–71. Chm., St John Council, N Yorks (Vice-Pres., N Yorks St John Amb. Bde); Hon. Col, 34 (N) Signal Regt (V), 1967–75; Chairman: N Riding Co. Cadet Cttee, 1947–52; St Luke's Hosp. Man. Cttee, Middlesborough, 1959–74; Cleveland AHA, 1973–76. Retd Company Dir. Hon. Trust Representative for Cleveland, Royal Jubilee Trusts, 1977–81. DL 1949, JP 1963, NR Yorks. KStJ 1978. *Recreations:* golf, cricket, Rugby football. *Address:* The White Lodge, Hutton Rudby, Yarm, Cleveland TS15 0HY. *T:* Stokesley (01642) 700598. *Clubs:* Army and Navy; Cleveland (Middlesborough); Royal and Ancient (St Andrews).

FAIRWEATHER, Prof. Denys Vivian Ivor, MD; FRCOG; Secretary-General of International Federation of Gynaecology and Obstetrics, 1985–94; Professor and Head of Department of Obstetrics and Gynaecology, 1966–90, and Vice-Provost, 1984–90, University College London; Pro-Vice-Chancellor for Medicine and Dentistry, University of London, 1989–92; *b* 25 Oct. 1927; *s* of late Albert James Ivor Fairweather and Gertrude Mary Forbes; *m* 1956, (Gwendolen) Yvonne Hubbard; one *s* two *d*. *Educ:* Forfar Acad.; Websters Seminary, Kirriemuir; St Andrews Univ. (MB, ChB 1949; MD 1966). FRCOG 1967 (MRCOG 1958). Served RAF Med. Br., 1950–55, Sqn Leader. Sen. Lectr, Univ. of Newcastle upon Tyne, 1959–66; Fulbright Scholar, Western Reserve Univ., USA, 1963–64; Dean, Faculty of Clinical Science, UCL, 1982–84; Vice Provost (Medicine) and Head, University Coll. London Sch. of Medicine, later University Coll. and Mddx Sch. of Medicine of UCL, 1984–89; Hon. Fellow, UCL, 1985. Member: GMC, 1988–92; Internat. Med. Adv. Panel, IPPF, 1988–94; Vice Pres., FPA, 1985–. Hon. FAARM 1969. Freeman, City of Krakow, 1989. *Publications:* Amniotic Fluid Research and Clinical Applications, 1973, 2nd edn 1978; Labour Ward Manual, 1985; over 160 pubns in scientific jls, on perinatal mortality, rhesus disease, genetics, antenatal diagnosis, very low birthweight, medical education. *Recreations:* gardening, fishing, do-it-yourself. *Address:* 37 Lyndhurst Avenue, Mill Hill, NW7 2AD.

FAIRWEATHER, Eric John, FCIB; Regional General Manager North, Co-operative Bank PLC, since 1995; *b* 9 Nov. 1942; *s* of late John Walter William Fairweather and Lilian Emma Fairweather; *m* 1st, 1966, Frances Mary Ewer (marr. diss.); two *d*; 2nd, 1991, Deborah Chubb; two *s*. *Educ:* Carlisle Grammar Sch. Entered Midland Bank at Carlisle, 1961; Manager, Corporate Finance Div., 1978–81; Sen. Asst Man., Poultry and Princes Street, 1981–84; on secondment as Dir, Industrial Develt Unit, DTI (Under Sec.), 1984–86; Manager, UK Business Sector, Midland Bank, 1986; Manager, Central Management and Planning, 1986–87; Corporate Banking Area Manager, Manchester, 1987–93; Area Manager: Manchester, 1993–94; Sheffield, 1994–95. Dir, Sheffield TEC, 1994–95. *Recreations:* classical music, Association football (Bolton Wanderers), golf. *Address:* Co-operative Bank, PO Box 101, 1 Balloon Street, Manchester M60 4EP.

FAIRWEATHER, Dr Frank Arthur; Environmental Safety Officer, Research Division, Unilever House, since 1982; *b* 2 May 1928; *s* of Frank and Maud Harriet Fairweather; *m* 1953, Christine Winifred Hobbs; two *s*. *Educ:* City of Norwich Sch.; Middlesex Hospital. MB, BS 1954; MRCPath 1963, FRCPath 1975; FIBiol 1972. Clinical house appts, Ipswich Gp of Hosps, 1955–56; Pathologist, Bland Sutton Inst. of Pathology, and Courtauld Inst. of Biochem., Middlesex Hosp., Soho Hosp. for Women, 1956–60; Jt Sen. Registrar in Histopathology, Middlesex and West Middlesex Hosps, 1961–62; Chief Med. Adviser and Cons. Pathologist, Benger Labs, 1962–63; Chief Pathologist, British Industrial Biological Res. Assoc., Carshalton, and Hon. Sen. Lectr, RCS, 1963–65; Associate Res. Dir, Wyeth Labs, Taplow, 1965–69; Sen. Med. Officer, DHSS, and Principal Med. Officer, Cttee on Safety of Medicines, 1969–72; SPMO, DHSS, 1972–82. Member: Expert Panels on Environmental Pollution, Food Toxicology, and Safety, to WHO; EEC Scientific Cttee for Food, 1976– (Chm., Sci. Cttee for Cosmetology); Consultant Adviser in Toxicology to DHSS, 1978–81; Dir, DHSS Toxicological Lab., St Bartholomew's Hosp., 1978–82, Hon. Dir, 1982–84; Hon. Lectr in Path., Middlesex Hosp., 1972–; Hon. Prof. of Toxicology, Dept of Biochemistry, Univ. of Surrey, 1978–84; Hon. Prof. of Toxicology and Pathology, Sch. of Pharmacy, Univ. of London, 1982. Chief Examiner in Toxicology, Inst. of Biology, 1989–. Chm., BIBRA, 1987–. Hon. FFOM 1991. QHP, 1977–80. *Publications:* various toxicological and medical papers. *Recreations:* angling, gardening, painting. *Address:* 394 London Road, Langley, Slough, Berks SL3 7HX.

FAIRWEATHER, Sir Patrick (Stanislaus), KCMG 1992 (CMG 1986); HM Diplomatic Service; Ambassador to Italy and to Albania (non-resident), since 1992; *b* 17 June 1936; *s* of John George Fairweather and Dorothy Jane (*née* Boanus); *m* 1962, Maria (*née* Merica); two *d*. *Educ:* Ottershaw Sch., Surrey; Trinity Coll., Cambridge (Hons History). National Service in Royal Marines and Parachute Regt, 1955–57. Entered FCO, 1965; 2nd Secretary, Rome, 1966–69; FCO, 1969–70; 1st Secretary (Economic), Paris, 1970–73; FCO, 1973–75; 1st Sec. and Head of Chancery, Vientiane, 1975–76; 1st Sec., UK Representation to EEC, Brussels, 1976–78; Counsellor (Economic and Commercial), Athens, 1978–83; Head of European Community Dept (Internal), FCO, 1983–85; Ambassador to Angola, 1985–87; Asst Under-Sec. of State, FCO, 1987–90; Dep. Under-Sec. of State (ME/Africa), FCO, 1990–92. *Recreations:* travel, gardening, photography, sailing. *Address:* c/o Foreign and Commonwealth Office, SW1A 2AH. *Club:* Garrick.

FAITH, (Irene) Sheila; JP; Dental Surgeon; *b* 3 June 1928; *yr d* of late I. Book; *m* 1950, Dennis Faith. *Educ:* Central High School, Newcastle upon Tyne; Durham Univ. LDS 1950. Practised as schools dental surgeon, Northumberland. Member: Northumberland CC, 1970–74 (Mem., Health and Social Services Cttees; Rep., S Northumberland Youth Employment Bd); Newcastle City Council, 1975–77 (Mem., Educn Cttee). Vice-Chm., Jt Consultative Cttee on Educn for District of Newcastle during local govt reorganisation, 1973–74. Mem., Parole Bd, 1991–. Contested (C) Newcastle Central, Oct. 1974; MP (C) Belper, 1979–83. Mem., Select Cttee on Health and Social Services, 1979–83; Sec., Conservative backbench Health and Social Services Cttee, 1982–83. MEP (C) Cumbria and Lancs N, 1984–89; Member: Transport Cttee, 1984–87; Cttee on Energy, Res. and Technol., 1987–89. Mem., Exec. Cttee, Cons. Medical Soc., 1981–84; Pres., Cumbria and Lancs N Cons. Euro Constituency Council, 1989–; Dep. Chm., Hampstead and Highgate Cons. Assoc., 1991–92. Has served as Chm. or Mem. several school governing bodies and Manager of Community Homes and with CAB, Newcastle upon Tyne. JP: Northumberland County, 1972–74; Newcastle upon Tyne, 1974–78; Inner London, 1978–. *Recreations:* reading, music. *Address:* 11 Merlin House, Oak Hill Park, Hampstead, NW3 7LJ. *T:* 0171–435 3702.

FAITHFULL, family name of **Baroness Faithfull.**

FAITHFULL, Baroness *cr* 1975 (Life Peer), of Wolvercote, Oxfordshire; **Lucy Faithfull,** OBE 1972; *b* 26 Dec. 1910; *d* of Lt Sydney Leigh Faithfull, RE (killed 1916) and late Elizabeth Adie Faithfull (*née* Algie); unmarried. *Educ:* Talbot Heath Sch. (formerly Bournemouth High Sch.). Social Science Dipl., Birmingham Univ., 1933; Family case work training (Charity Welfare Organisation, now Family Welfare Assoc.), 1936, and Cert. in Child Care, 1969. Club Leader and Sub-Warden, Birmingham Settlement, 1932–35; Asst Organiser, Child Care, LCC Education Dept, 1935–40; Regional Welfare Officer (Evacuation Scheme), Min. of Health, 1940–48; Inspector in Children's Br., Home Office, 1948–58; Oxford City Council: Children's Officer, 1958–70; Director of Social Services, 1970–74; retired, 1974. Chm., All Party Parly Gp for Children. Pres., Nat. Children's Bureau, 1984–; Vice President: Barnardo's, 1989–; Nat. Assoc. of Voluntary Hostels, 1978–; Chm., Faithfull Foundn dealing with child sexual abuse; Mem., Nursery and Family Care Assoc. Hon. Mem. Council, NSPCC, 1989–; Hon. Fellow BPA; Hon. FRCPsych. Chm. Council, Caldecott Community Kent Sch. for Distracted and Deliquent Children, 1975; Gov., Bessel Leigh Sch. for children experiencing emotional behavioural difficulties; Trustee, Gracewell Inst., Birmingham. Patron, Nat. Mediation and Conciliation Council. Hon. MA Oxford, 1974; Hon. DLitt Warwick, 1978. *Recreations:* friends, travel, garden. *Address:* 303 Woodstock Road, Oxford OX2 7NY. *T:* Oxford (01865) 55389.

FAKLEY, Dennis Charles, OBE 1973; retired; *b* 20 Nov. 1924; *s* of Charles Frederick and Ethel May Fakley; *m* 1976, Louise Grace Swindell. *Educ:* Chatham House Grammar Sch., Ramsgate; Queen Mary Coll., Univ. of London (BSc Special Physics). Royal Naval Scientific Service, 1944–63; Min. of Defence, 1963–84. *Recreations:* reading, cricket. *Address:* 14 Coval Gardens, SW14 7DG. *T:* 0181–876 6856.

FALCON, David; public sector consultant, since 1992; *b* 3 Jan. 1946; *s* of Arnold and Barbara Falcon; *m* 1967 (marr. diss. 1991); two *s*. *Educ:* Helston County Grammar Sch.; University College London (BSc); Lancaster Univ. (MA); Univ. of Pennsylvania. Research Associate, Univ. of Lancaster, 1969–72; Lectr, Leeds Polytechnic, 1972–74; Sen. Lectr, Sheffield Polytechnic, 1974–76; Asst Dir, Sen. Asst Dir, Dep. Dir of Education, Humberside CC, 1976–85; Dir of Education, ILEA, 1985–88; Dir-Gen., RIPA, 1988–92. FRSA. *Publications:* articles in educn and management jls. *Recreations:* music, opera, photography, travel. *Address:* 32 Oakey Lane, King Edward Walk, SE1 7HL. *T:* 0171–928 2556, *Fax:* 0171–401 9306.

FALCON, Michael Gascoigne, CBE 1979; JP, DL; Chairman: Norwich Union Insurance Group, 1981–94 (Director, 1963–94; Vice Chairman, 1979–81); Norwich Winterthur Holdings Ltd, 1984–94; Norfolk and Norwich Health Care NHS Trust, since 1994; *b* 28 Jan. 1928; *s* of late Michael Falcon and Kathleen Isabel Frances Gascoigne; *m* 1954, April Daphne Claire Lambert; two *s* one *d*. *Educ:* Stowe Sch., Bucks; Heriot-Watt Coll., Edinburgh. National Service, Grenadier Gds and Royal Norfolk Regt, 1946–48. Head Brewer and Jt Man. Dir, E. Lacon & Co. Ltd, Great Yarmouth, 1952–68; Exec. Dir, Edgar Watts, Willow Merchants, 1968–73; Chairman: National Seed Develt Orgn Ltd, 1972–82; Pauls & Whites PLC, 1976–85 (Dir, 1973–85); Eastern Counties Regional Bd, Lloyds Bank Plc, 1979–91 (Dir, 1972–91); Director: Securicor (East) Ltd, 1969–72; Lloyds Bank UK Management Ltd, 1979–85; Matthew Brown plc, 1981–87; National Bus Properties Ltd, 1983–86; Greene King & Sons PLC, 1988–; British Railways (Anglia) Bd, 1988–92. Chm., Norwich HA, 1988–93. Trustee, E Anglian Trustee Savings Bank, 1963–75. Chm., Trustees, John Innes Foundn, 1990–. Mem., Norwich Prison Bd of Visitors, 1969–82. JP 1967, High Sheriff 1979, DL 1981, Co. of Norfolk; High Steward, Great Yarmouth, 1984–. CStJ 1986. Hon. LLD Nottingham, 1988. *Recreation:* country pursuits. *Address:* Keswick Old Hall, Norwich, Norfolk NR4 6TZ. *T:* Norwich (01603) 454348; Kirkgate, Loweswater, Cockermouth, Cumbria. *Clubs:* Norfolk (Norwich); Royal Norfolk and Suffolk Yacht (Lowestoft).
See also Ven. D. L. Edwards.

FALCON, Norman Leslie, FRS 1960; *b* 29 May 1904; 2nd *s* of late Thomas Adolphus Falcon, MA, RBA; *m* 1938, Dorothy Muriel, 2nd *d* of late F. G. Freeman, HM Consular Service; two *s* one *d*. *Educ:* Exeter Sch.; Trinity Coll., Cambridge (Sen. Exhibitioner 1925, Natural Science Tripos Pt I 1925, 1st cl., Part II 1927, 1st cl.; MA Cantab). Joined Anglo-Persian Oil Company as geologist, 1927; FGS, FRGS, 1927; Geological Exploration in Persia, UK and elsewhere, 1927–40. Served War of 1939–45, Intelligence Corps, 1940–45. Rejoined Anglo-Iranian Oil Company as Geologist on Head Office staff, 1945; Chief Geologist, 1955–65, Geological Adviser, 1965–72, British Petroleum Co Ltd. FInstPet, 1959; Geological Soc. of London: Mem. Council, 1954–58, 1967–71; Foreign Sec. 1967–70; Murchison Medal, 1963; Hon. Mem. 1988; Royal Geographical Society: Mem. Council, 1966–69; Vice-Pres. 1973; Founder's Medal, 1973. Mem., NERC, 1968–71. Hon. Mem., American Assoc. Petroleum Geologists, 1973. Bronze Star Medal (USA), 1945. *Publications:* geological papers. *Recreations:* outdoor pursuits. *Address:* 2 Mansell Close, Church Hanborough, Witney, Oxon OX8 8AU.

FALCONER, Alexander, (Alex); Member (Lab) Mid Scotland and Fife, European Parliament, since 1984; *b* Dundee, 1 April 1940; *s* of John Falconer, labourer, and Margaret McFarlane Falconer, canteen assistant; *m* Margaret Cavell Falconer, canteen assistant; one *s* one *d*. Former foundry worker; served with RN, 1959–68; insulator, Rosyth dockyard, 1969–84. Shop Steward, TGWU, 1970–84; Chm., Fife Fedn of Trades Councils. Mem., CND. *Address:* 25 Church Street, Inverkeithing, Fife KY11 1LH.

FALCONER, Charles Leslie; QC 1991; *b* 19 Nov. 1951; *s* of John Leslie Falconer and of late Anne Mansel Falconer; *m* 1985, Marianna Catherine Thoroton Hildyard, *d* of Sir D. H. T. Hildyard, *qv*; three *s* one *d*. *Educ:* Trinity Coll., Glenalmond; Queens' Coll., Cambridge. Called to the Bar, Inner Temple, 1974. *Address:* Fountain Court, Temple, EC4Y 6DP.

FALCONER, Prof. Douglas Scott, FRS 1973; FRSE 1972; *b* 10 March 1913; *s* of Gerald Scott Falconer and Lillias Harriet Gordon Douglas; *m* 1942, Margaret Duke; two *s*. *Educ:* Edinburgh Academy; Univ. of St Andrews (BSc); Univ. of Cambridge (PhD. ScD). Scientific Staff of Agricultural Research Council, 1947–68; Prof. of Genetics, Univ. of Edinburgh, and Dir, ARC Unit of Animal Genetics, 1968–80. *Publications:* Introduction to Quantitative Genetics, 1960, 3rd edn 1989; Problems on Quantitative Genetics, 1983; papers in scientific jls. *Recreations:* music, walking, sailing. *Address:* 21 Mansionhouse Road, Edinburgh EH9 1TZ.

FALCONER, Hon. Sir Douglas (William), Kt 1981; MBE 1946; a Judge of the High Court of Justice, Chancery Division, 1981–89; *b* 20 Sept. 1914; *s* of late William Falconer, S Shields; *m* 1941, Joan Beryl Argent (*d* 1989), *d* of late A. S. Bishop, Hagley, Worcs; one *s* one *d*. *Educ:* South Shields; King's Coll., Durham Univ.; BSc (Hons) Physics, 1935. Served War of 1939–45 (Hon. Major): commissioned E Yorks Regt, 1939. Called to Bar, Middle Temple, 1950, Bencher 1973; QC 1967. Apptd to exercise appellate jurisdiction of BoT, later DoT, under Trade Marks Act, 1970–81; Member: of Departmental Cttee to review British trade mark law and practice, 1972–73; Standing Adv. Cttee on Patents, 1975–79; Standing Adv. Cttee on Trade Marks, 1975–79; Senate of Four Inns of Court, 1973–74; Senate of Four Inns of Court and the Bar, 1974–77; Chm., Patent Bar Assoc., 1971–80. *Publications:* (Jt Editor) Terrell on the Law of Patents (11th and 12th edns), 1965 and 1971. *Recreations:* music, theatre. *Address:* Ridgewell House, West Street, Reigate, Surrey RH2 9BZ. *T:* Reigate (01737) 244374.

FALCONER, Peter Serrell, FRIBA, FRSA; Founder of The Falconer Partnership, Architects and Consultants, and of Handling Consultants Ltd, Stroud and Johannesburg; *b* 7 March 1916; *s* of Thomas Falconer, FRIBA, and Florence Edith Falconer; presumed heir to the Barony (1206) and Lordship (1646) of Halkerton, vacant since 1966; *m* 1941, Mary Hodson; three *s* one *d*. *Educ:* Bloxham Sch., Banbury. Commenced practice in Stroud, as partner in Ellery Anderson Roiser & Falconer, 1944; Sen. Partner of Peter Falconer and Partners, 1959–82 (with br. office in Adelaide, SA, 1970). Specialist in materials handling and industrial architecture; Mem., Materials Handling Inst. *Publications:* Building and Planning for Industrial Storage and Distribution, 1975; contributor to: Architectural Review; Architects' Jl; Material Handling magazines. *Recreations:* restoring historic buildings, garden planning, motor sport. *Address:* St Francis, Lammas Park, Minchinhampton, Stroud, Glos GL6 9HA. *T:* Brimscombe (01453) 882188.

FALDO, Nicholas Alexander, MBE 1988; professional golfer; *b* 18 July 1957; *s* of George and Joyce Faldo; *m* 1st, Melanie (marr. diss.); 2nd, 1986, Gill; one *s* two *d*. *Educ:* Welwyn Garden City. Won English Amateur Golf Championship, 1975; Professional golfer, 1976;

Mem., Ryder Cup team, 1977–; many championship titles include: Open, Muirfield, 1987, 1992, St Andrews, 1990; US Masters, 1989, 1990; French Open 3 times; GA Europ. Open, 1992; World Match Play Championship, 1992; Irish Open, 1991, 1992, 1993. *Publications:* Golf: the winning formula, 1989; In Search of Perfection, 1994; A Swing for Life, 1995. *Recreations:* fly fishing, DIY, snooker, motor sports. *Address:* c/o IMG, Pier House, Strand on the Green, Chiswick, W4 3NN.

FALETAU, 'Inoke Fotu, CVO 1993; Director, Commonwealth Foundation, 1985–93; *b* 24 June 1937; 2nd *s* of 'Akau'ola Sateki Faletau and Celia Lyden; *m* 'Evelini Ma'ata Hurrell; three *s* three *d*. *Educ:* St Peter's, Cambridge, NZ; Tonga High Sch.; Auckland Grammar Sch.; UC Swansea (Hon. Fellow 1990); Manchester Univ. Joined Tonga Civil Service, 1958; Asst Sec., Prime Minister's Office, 1965; Sec. to Govt, 1969; seconded to Univ. of South Pacific, 1971; Sec. to Govt, 1972; High Comr, UK, 1972–82; Ambassador to: France, 1972–82; Germany, 1976–82; Belgium, Luxembourg, Netherlands, EEC, 1977–82; USA, 1979–82; USSR, 1980–82; Denmark, 1981–82; Dir, Management Develt Programme, Commonwealth Secretariat, 1983–84. *Recreations:* Rugby, tennis, reading, bridge, fishing. *Address:* c/o Commonwealth Foundation, Marlborough House, Pall Mall, SW1Y 5HY. *Clubs:* Royal Over-Seas League; Nuku'alofa Yacht and Motor Boat.

FALK, Sir Roger (Salis), Kt 1969; OBE (mil.) 1945; Hon. DLitt; FIMC; CIMgt; Vice President, Sadler's Wells Foundation and Trust, since 1986 (Chairman, 1976–86); *b* 22 June 1910; *s* of Lionel David Falk; *m* 1938, Margaret Helen (*née* Stroud) (*d* 1958); one *s* two *d*. *Educ:* Haileybury (Life Governor, 1971–; Council Mem., 1978–92); Geneva Univ. Gen. Manager's Office, Rhodesia Railways, Bulawayo, 1931; D. J. Keymer & Co: Manager in Bombay and Calcutta, 1932–35; Dir, 1935–49; Managing Dir, 1945–49; Vice-Chm., 1950; formerly: Dir, P-E International Ltd (Chm., 1973–76); Chm., London Bd, Provincial Insurance Co. Ltd. Shoreditch Borough Council, 1937–45. Dir-Gen. British Export Trade Research Organisation (BETRO) from 1949 until disbandment. Chairman: Furniture Development Council, 1963–82; Central Council for Agric. and Hort. Cooperation, 1967–75; British European Associated Publishers, 1976–79; Action for Dysphasic Adults (ADA), 1982–85 (Vice-Pres., 1985–); Dep. Chm., Gaming Bd, 1978–81; Member: Council of Industrial Design, 1958–67; Monopolies and Mergers Commn, 1965–80; Council, RSA, 1968–74; Council, Imp. Soc. of Knights Bachelor, 1979–; Pres., Design and Industries Assoc., 1971–72. Served War of 1939–45, RAFVR; Wing-Comdr, 1942. Hon. DLitt City Univ. *Publication:* The Business of Management, 1961, 5th rev. edn 1976. *Recreations:* writing, music, reading, theatre. *Address:* 603 Beatty House, Dolphin Square, SW1V 3PL. *T:* 0171–828 3752. *Clubs:* Garrick, MCC.

FALKENDER, Baroness *cr* 1974 (Life Peer), of West Haddon, Northants; **Marcia Matilda Falkender,** CBE 1970; Private and Political Secretary to Lord Wilson of Rievaulx, 1956–83 (at 10 Downing Street, 1964–70 and 1974–76); *b* March 1932; *d* of Harry Field. *Educ:* Northampton High School; Queen Mary Coll., Univ. of London. BA Hons Hist. Secretary to Gen. Sec., Labour Party, 1955–56. Member: Prime Minister's Film Industry Working Party, 1975–76; Interim Cttee on Film Industry, 1977–82; British Screen Adv. Council, 1985–. Pres., UNIFEM (formerly UN Develt Fund for Women) (UK Cttee Trust), 1990–. Chm., Canvasback Productions, 1989–91. Director: Peckham Building Soc., 1986–91; South London Investment and Mortgage Corp., 1986–91; Milford Dock Co., 1986–87. Political columnist, Mail on Sunday, 1982–88. Trustee, Silver Trust, 1988–. Mem., External Relations Cttee, QMW (formerly QMC), London Univ., 1987 (Lay Gov., 1987–93). *Publications:* Inside Number 10, 1972; Downing Street in Perspective, 1983. *Address:* 3 Wyndham Mews, Upper Montagu Street, W1H 1RS. *Club:* Reform.

FALKINER, Sir Edmond (Charles), 9th Bt *cr* 1778, of Annemount, Cork; Probation Officer since 1969; *b* 24 June 1938; *s* of Sir Terence Edmond Patrick Falkiner, 8th Bt and Mildred Katherine (*d* 1989), *y d* of Sir John Cotterell, 4th Bt; *S* father, 1987; *m* 1960, Janet Iris, *d* of Arthur E. B. Darby; two *s*. *Educ:* Downside. CQSW. Various jobs, 1956–68. Home Office Probation Training Course, 1968; Hon. Chm., Drugcare (St Albans), 1986–. *Recreations:* jazz, and playing a variety of saxophones. *Heir: s* Benjamin Simon Patrick Falkiner, *b* 16 Jan. 1962. *Address:* 111 Wood Street, Barnet, Herts EN5 4BX. *T:* 0181–440 2426. *Club:* Ronnie Scott's.

FALKINGHAM, Ven. John Norman; Warden, Community of the Holy Name, 1969–85; *b* 9 Feb. 1917; 2nd *s* of Alfred Richard Falkingham and Amy Grant (*née* Macallister); *m* 1947, Jean Dorothy Thoren; two *d*. *Educ:* Geelong Gram. Sch., Corio, Vic.; Trinity Coll., Univ. of Melbourne. BA (Hons) Melbourne 1940; ThL (1st Cl. Hons), ThD 1978, Australian Coll. of Theol.; prizes for Divinity and Biblical Greek. Deacon, 1941; Priest, 1942. Curate of Holy Trinity, Surrey Hills, Vic., 1941–44; Chaplain, Trinity Coll., Univ. of Melbourne, 1944–50; Incumbent, St Paul's, Caulfield, Vic., 1950–61. Exam. Chaplain to Archbishop of Melbourne, 1947–61; Lectr in Theol. Faculty, Trinity Coll., Melbourne, 1950–60; Canon of St Paul's Cath., Melbourne, 1959–61; Dean of Newcastle, NSW, 1961–75; Rector of St Paul's, Manuka, ACT, 1975–82; Canon of St Saviour's Cath., Goulburn, 1976–81; Archdeacon of Canberra, 1981–82, Archdeacon Emeritus, 1982. Sec., Liturgical Commn of Gen. Synod, 1966–78; Mem. Bd of Delegates, Aust. Coll. of Theology, 1962–88; Lecturer: Canberra Coll. of Ministry, 1975–84; St Mark's Library, Canberra, 1982–87; Chm., Bd of Dirs, Canberra C of E Girls' Grammar Sch., 1983–90. *Publications:* articles in various jls. *Recreation:* walking. *Address:* 4 Serra Place, Stirling, ACT 2611, Australia.

FALKLAND, 15th Viscount *cr* 1620 (Scot.), of Falkland, Co. Fife; **Lucius Edward William Plantagenet Cary;** Lord Cary 1620; Premier Viscount of Scotland on the Roll; *b* 8 May 1935; *s* of 14th Viscount Falkland, and Constance Mary(*d* 1995), *d* of late Captain Edward Berry; *S* father, 1984; *m* 1st, 1962, Caroline Anne (marr. diss. 1990), *o d* of late Lt-Comdr Gerald Butler, DSC, RN, and late Mrs Patrick Parish; one *s* two *d* (and one *d* decd); 2nd, 1990, Nicole, *o d* of late Milburn Mackey; one *s*. *Educ:* Wellington Coll.; Alliance Française, Paris. Late 2nd Lieut 8th Hussars. Export marketing consultant, formerly Chief Executive, C. T. Bowring Trading (Holdings) Ltd. Mem., H of L Select Cttee on Overseas Trade, 1984–85. Dep. Whip, Lib Dem, H of L, 1989–. *Recreations:* golf, motorcycling, cinema. *Heir: s* Master of Falkland, *qv*. *Address:* c/o House of Lords, SW1A 0PW. *Clubs:* Brooks's; Sunningdale Golf.

FALKLAND, Master of; Hon. Lucius Alexander Plantagenet Cary; late Captain, 2nd Battalion, Scots Guards; *b* 1 Feb. 1963; *s* and *heir* of 15th Viscount Falkland, *qv*; *m* 1993, Linda, *d* of Raymond Purl, Colorado City, USA; one *s*. *Educ:* Loretto School; RMA Sandhurst. *Recreations:* ski-ing, golf.*Club:* Cavalry and Guards.

FALKUS, Hugh Edward Lance; naturalist, independent writer, film director, broadcaster; now engaged in teaching salmon fishing and speycasting, and writing autobiography; *b* 15 May 1917; *s* of James Everest Falkus and Alice Musgrove; *m* 1957, Kathleen Armstrong. Served War of 1939–45 (Fighter Pilot). Films include: Drake's England, 1950; Shark Island, 1952; TV films include: Salmo—the Leaper; (with Niko Tinbergen) Signals for Survival (Italia Prize, 1969; Amer. Blue Ribbon, New York Film Fest., 1971); Highland Story; The Gull Watchers; The Signreaders; The Beachcombers; The Riddle of the Rook (Venice Film Festival, 1972); Tender Trap (Certificate of Merit, BAAS, 1975); Self-Portrait of a Happy Man. Cherry Kearton Medal and Award, RGS, 1982. *Publications:* Sea Trout Fishing, 1962, 2nd edn 1975, revised 2nd edn 1981; The Stolen Years, 1965, 2nd edn 1979; (with Niko Tinbergen) Signals for Survival, 1970; (with Fred Buller) Freshwater Fishing, 1975, 9th edn 1987; (jtly) Successful Angling, 1977; Nature Detective, 1978, 2nd edn 1987; (with Joan Kerr) From Sydney Cove to Duntroon, 1982; Master of Cape Horn, 1982; Salmon Fishing, 1984; The Sea Trout, 1987; Speycasting: a new technique, 1994. *Recreations:* fishing, shooting, sailing, oil painting. *Address:* Cragg Cottage, near Ravenglass, Cumbria CA18 1RT. *T:* Ravenglass (01229) 717247.

FALL, Sir Brian (James Proetel), GCVO 1994; KCMG 1992 (CMG 1984); HM Diplomatic Service, retired; Principal, Lady Margaret Hall, Oxford, since 1995; *b* 13 Dec. 1937; *s* of John William Fall, Hull, Yorkshire, and Edith Juliette (*née* Proetel); *m* 1962, Delmar Alexandra Roos; three *d*. *Educ:* St Paul's Sch.; Magdalen Coll., Oxford; Univ. of Michigan Law Sch. Joined HM Foreign (now Diplomatic) Service, 1962; served in Foreign Office UN Dept, 1963; Moscow, 1965; Geneva, 1968; Civil Service Coll., 1970; FO Eastern European and Soviet Dept and Western Organisations Dept, 1971; New York, 1975; Harvard Univ. Center for Internat. Affairs, 1976; Counsellor, Moscow, 1977–79; Head of Energy, Science and Space Dept, FCO, 1979–80; Head of Eastern European and Soviet Dept, FCO, 1980–81; Prin. Private Sec. to Sec. of State for Foreign and Commonwealth Affairs, 1981–84; Dir, Cabinet, Sec. Gen. of NATO, 1984–86; Asst Under-Sec. of State (Defence), FCO, 1986–88; Minister, Washington, 1988–89; High Comr to Canada, 1989–92; Ambassador to Russian Fedn, 1992–95, and to Republics of Armenia, Georgia, Moldova and Turkmenistan. *Address:* Lady Margaret Hall, Oxford OX2 6QA.

FALL, David William; HM Diplomatic Service; Deputy High Commissioner, Canberra, since 1993; *b* 10 March 1948; *s* of George William Fall and Susan Fall; *m* 1973, Margaret Gwendolyn Richards; three *s*. *Educ:* St Bartholmew's Grammar Sch., Newbury; New Coll., Oxford (MA Mod. Hist.). VSO, Papua-New Guinea, 1970–71; joined FCO, 1971; language student, later 2nd then 1st Sec., Bangkok, 1973–77; seconded to Cabinet Office, 1977–78; FCO, 1978–80; 1st Sec., Cape Town and Pretoria, 1980–85; FCO, 1985–90; Counsellor, 1989; Head of Narcotics Control and AIDS Dept, FCO, 1989–90; Dep. Hd of Mission, Bangkok, 1990–93. *Recreations:* cartooning, jogging, walking, golf, reading, Monty Python. *Address:* c/o Foreign and Commonwealth Office, King Charles Street, SW1A 2AH.

FALLA, Paul Stephen; *b* 25 Oct. 1913; *s* of Norris Stephen Falla and Audrey Frances Stock, Dunedin, New Zealand; *m* 1958, Elizabeth Shearer; one *d*. *Educ:* Wellington and Christ's Colls, NZ; Balliol Coll., Oxford (Scholar). Appointed to Foreign Office, 1936; served HM Embassies, Warsaw, 1938–39, Ankara, 1939–43, Tehran, 1943; Foreign Office, 1943–46; UK Delegation to UN, New York, 1946–49; Foreign Office, 1949–67 (Dep. Dir of Research, 1958–67). Member: Exec. Cttee, Translators' Assoc., Soc. of Authors, 1971–73 and 1984–86 (Vice-Chm., 1973); Council, Inst. Linguists, 1975–81 (FIL 1984); Cttee, Translators' Guild, 1975–81. Fellow, Inst. of Translation and Interpreting, 1989. Scott Moncrieff prize, 1972 and 1981; Schlegel-Tieck Prize, 1983. *Publications:* (ed) The Oxford English-Russian Dictionary, 1984; about 50 book translations from French, German, Dutch, Russian, Polish and other languages, 1967–. *Recreation:* reading (history, philosophy, poetry, language matters). *Address:* 63 Freelands Road, Bromley, Kent BR1 3HZ. *T:* 0181–460 4995. *Club:* Travellers'.

FALLE, Sir Sam, KCMG 1979 (CMG 1964); KCVO 1972; DSC 1945; HM Diplomatic Service, retired; *b* 19 Feb. 1919; *s* of Theodore and Hilda Falle; *m* 1945, Merete Rosen; one *s* three *d*. *Educ:* Victoria Coll., Jersey, CI. Served Royal Navy, 1937–48; joined Foreign (subseq. Diplomatic) Service, 1948; British Consulate, Shiraz, Iran, 1949–51; British Embassy, Tehran, 1952; British Embassy, Beirut, 1952–55; FO, 1955–57; British Embassy, Baghdad, 1957–61; Consul-Gen., Gothenburg, 1961–63; Head of UN Dept, FO, 1963–67; with Lord Shackleton's mission to Aden 1967; Deputy High Comr, Kuala Lumpur, 1967–69; Ambassador to Kuwait, 1969–70; High Comr, Singapore, 1970–74; Ambassador to Sweden, 1974–77; High Comr in Nigeria, 1977–78; Delegate, Commn of the European Communities, Algiers, 1979–82; carried out evaluation of EEC aid to Zambia, 1983–84, and Swedish aid to Swaziland, 1986. Kt Grand Cross, Order of Polar Star, Sweden, 1975. *Recreations:* swimming, ski-ing, jogging. *Address:* Slättna, 57030 Mariannelund, Sweden.

FALLON, Hazel Rosemary; *see* Counsell, H. R.

FALLON, Ivan Gregory; Editorial Director, Argus Group, since 1994; Director, N. Brown Holdings, since 1994; *b* 26 June 1944; *s* of Padraic and Dorothea Fallon; *m* 1967, Susan Mary Lurring; one *s* two *d*. *Educ:* St Peter's Coll., Wexford; Trinity Coll., Dublin (BBS). Irish Times, 1964–66; Thomson Provincial Newspapers, 1966–67; Daily Mirror, 1967–68; Sunday Telegraph, 1968–70; Deputy City Editor, Sunday Express, 1970–71; Sunday Telegraph, 1971–84: City Editor, 1979–84; Dep. Editor, Sunday Times, 1984–94. Member: Council, Univ. of Buckingham, 1982–94; Council of Governors, United Med. and Dental Schs of Guy's and St Thomas's Hosps, 1985–94; Trustee: Project Trust, 1984–94; Generation Trust, Guy's Hosp., 1985–94. FRSA 1989. *Publications:* (with James L. Srodes) DeLorean: the rise and fall of a dream-maker, 1983; (with James L. Srodes) Takeovers, 1987; The Brothers: the rise of Saatchi and Saatchi, 1988; Billionaire: the life and times of Sir James Goldsmith, 1991; Paper Chase, 1993; The Player: the life of Tony O'Reilly, 1994. *Recreations:* squash, tennis. *Address:* Clare Cottage, Mill Street, East Malling, Kent ME19 6BU. *T:* West Malling (01732) 843091. *Clubs:* Beefsteak, Royal Automobile.

See also P. M. Fallon.

FALLON, Martin; *see* Patterson, Harry.

FALLON, Michael; Director, Quality Care Homes plc, since 1992; *b* 14 May 1952; *s* of late Martin Fallon, OBE, FRCSI and of Hazel Fallon; *m* 1986, Wendy Elisabeth, *e d* of Peter Payne, Holme-on-Spalding Moor, Yorks; two *s*. *Educ:* St Andrews Univ. (MA Hons 1974). European Educnl Res. Trust, 1974–75; Opposition Whips Office, House of Lords, 1975–77; EEC Officer, Cons. Res. Dept, 1977–79; Jt Man. Dir, European Consultants Ltd, 1979–81. Sec., Lord Home's Cttee on future of House of Lords, 1977–78; Assistant to Baroness Elles, 1979–83. MP (C) Darlington, 1983–92; contested (C) Darlington, 1992. PPS to Sec. of State for Energy, 1987–88; an Asst Govt Whip, 1988–90; a Lord Comr of HM Treasury, 1990; Parly Under-Sec. of State, DES, 1990–92. Member: HEFCE, 1993–; Adv. Council, Social Market Foundn, 1994–. *Publications:* The Quango Explosion (jtly), 1978; Sovereign Members?, 1982; The Rise of the Euroquango, 1982; Brighter Schools, 1993; contribs to journals. *Recreations:* tennis, ski-ing. *Club:* Academy.

FALLON, Padraic Matthew; Chairman, Euromoney Publications PLC, since 1992; *b* 21 Sept. 1946; *s* of Padraic Fallon and Dorothea (Don) (*née* Maher); *m* 1972, Gillian Elizabeth Hellyer; one *s* three *d*. *Educ:* St Peter's Coll., Wexford; Blackrock Coll., Co. Dublin; Trinity Coll., Dublin (BBS, MA). Reporter: Thomson Newspapers City office, 1969–70; Daily Mirror, 1970–72; Daily Mail City pages, 1972–74; Managing Editor, Middle East Money, Beirut, 1974; Editor, Euromoney, 1974–85; Euromoney Publications PLC: Dir, 1975–; Man. Dir, 1985–89; Chief Exec., 1989–92. Non-exec. Dir, Allied Irish Banks plc,

1988–. Mem., Internat. Adv. Bd, Creditanstalt-Bankverein, Vienna, 1990–. FRSA. *Recreation:* country sports. *Address:* Euromoney Publications PLC, Nestor House, Playhouse Yard, EC4V 5EX. *T:* 0171–779 8888; 20 Lower Addison Gardens, W14 8BQ. *T:* 0171–602 1253. *Club:* Kildare Street and University (Overseas Member) (Dublin).

See also I. G. Fallon.

FALLON, Peter, QC 1971; **His Honour Judge Fallon;** a Circuit Judge, since 1979, a Senior Circuit Judge, since 1980; *b* 1 March 1931; *s* of Frederick and Mary Fallon; *m* 1st, 1955, Zina Mary (*née* Judd); one *s* two *d*; 2nd, 1980, Hazel Rosemary Counsell, *qv*. *Educ:* Leigh Grammar Sch.; St Joseph's Coll., Blackpool; Bristol Univ. (LLB Hons). Called to Bar, Gray's Inn, 1953. Commissioned in RAF for three years. A Recorder of the Crown Court, 1972–79. *Publications:* Crown Court Practice: Sentencing, 1974; Crown Court Practice: Trial, 1978; contrib. Proc. RSM. *Recreations:* golf, fishing, painting. *Address:* The Crown Court, The Guildhall, Bristol BS1 1DA.

FALLOWS, Albert Bennett, CB 1987; FRICS; Hon. FSVA; Chief Valuer, Inland Revenue Valuation Office and Commissioner of Inland Revenue, 1984–88; *b* 7 Dec. 1928; *s* of Bennett and May Fallows; *m* 1955, Maureen James; two *d*. *Educ:* Leek High School. Private practice, surveying, 1945–56; Stoke City Council, 1956–58; Staffs County Council, 1958–62; District Valuer's Office, Kidderminster, 1962–68; Chief Valuer's Office, 1968–73; District Valuer, Basingstoke, 1973–75; Superintending Valuer, Liaison Officer, DoE/Dept of Transport, 1975–77; Board of Inland Revenue: Superintending Valuer, North West, Preston, 1977–80; Asst Chief Valuer, 1980–83; Dep. Chief Valuer, 1983. Hon. FSVA 1987. *Recreation:* golf. *Address:* 110 Whitedown Lane, Alton, Hants GU34 1QR. *T:* Alton (01420) 82818. *Club:* Blackmoor Golf.

FALLOWS, Geoffrey Michael; Headteacher, Camden School for Girls, since 1989; *b* 28 Sept, 1941; *er s* of Rt Rev. William Gordon Fallows and Edna (*née* Blakeman); *m* 1968, Carolyn, *d* of Dr William Brian Littler, *qv* and Pearl Littler; two *d*. *Educ:* Shrewsbury Sch.; Wadham Coll., Oxford (MA); London Univ. Inst. of Education (PGCE). Vis. Classics Fellow, Marlboro Coll., Vermont, 1964–65; Asst Master, Latymer Upper Sch., 1966–69; Head of Classics, Crown Woods Sch., 1969–75; Dep. Head, Camden Sch. for Girls, 1975–89. Exec. Sec., Jt Assoc. of Classical Teachers, 1978–81. Co-founder, Omnibus magazine, 1981. FRSA 1994. *Recreations:* theatre, gardening, Lake District. *Address:* Camden School for Girls, Sandall Road, NW5 2DB. *T:* 0171–485 3414; 53 Byng Road, Barnet, Herts EN5 4NW. *T:* 0181–449 2980.

FALMOUTH, 9th Viscount, *cr* 1720; **George Hugh Boscawen;** 26th Baron Le Despencer, 1264; Baron Boscawen-Rose, 1720; Lord-Lieutenant of Cornwall, 1977–94; *b* 31 Oct. 1919; 2nd but *e* surv. *s* of 8th Viscount; *S* father, 1962; *m* 1953, Elizabeth Price Browne, DL; four *s*. *Educ:* Eton Coll.; Trinity Coll., Cambridge. Served War, 1939–46, Italy. Capt., Coldstream Guards. DL Cornwall, 1968. *Heir: s* Hon. Evelyn Arthur Hugh Boscawen [*b* 13 May 1955; *m* 1977, Lucia Vivian-Neal, *e d* of R. W. Vivian-Neal; one *s* one *d*]. *Clubs:* Athenæum, Army and Navy.

See also Rt Hon. R. T. Boscawen.

FANE, family name of **Earl of Westmorland.**

FANE TREFUSIS, family name of **Baron Clinton.**

FANNER, His Honour Peter Duncan; a Circuit Judge, 1986–95; *b* 27 May 1926; *s* of late Robert William Hodges Fanner, solicitor, and Doris Kitty Fanner; *m* 1949, Sheila Eveline England; one *s* one *d*. *Educ:* Pangbourne Coll. Admitted Solicitor of the Supreme Court, 1951 (holder Justices' Clerks' Society's prize). Served War of 1939–45, Pilot in Fleet Air Arm, Lieut (A) RNVR, 1944–47. Asst Clerk to Bromley Justices, 1947–51; Dep. Clerk to Gore Justices, 1951–56; Clerk to Bath Justices, 1956–72; Metropolitan Stipendiary Magistrate, 1972–86; a Dep. Circuit Judge, 1974–80; a Recorder, 1980–86. Mem. Council of Justices' Clerks' Society, 1966–72; Assessor Mem. of Departmental Cttee on Liquor Licensing, 1971–72. Chm., Bath Round Table, 1963–64. *Publications:* Stone's Justices' Manual; contrib. to Justice of the Peace, The Magisterial Officer, The Lawyer's Remembrancer. *Recreations:* travel, railways. *Address:* c/o The Law Courts, Small Street, Bristol BS1 1DA. *T:* Bristol (0117) 976 3030.

FANSHAWE OF RICHMOND, Baron *cr* 1983 (Life Peer), of South Cerney in the County of Gloucestershire; **Anthony Henry Fanshawe Royle,** KCMG 1974; *b* 27 March 1927; *s* of Sir Lancelot Royle, KBE; *m* 1957, Shirley Worthington; two *d*. *Educ:* Harrow; Sandhurst. Captain, The Life Guards (Germany, Egypt, Palestine and Transjordan), 1945–48; 21st Special Air Service Regt (TA), 1948–51. MP (C) Richmond, 1959–83; Parliamentary Private Secretary: to Under-Sec. of State for the Colonies, 1960; to Sec. of State for Air, 1960–62; to Minister of Aviation, 1962–64; Vice-Chm., Cons. Parly Foreign Affairs Cttee, 1965–67; Tory Whip, 1967–70; Parly Under-Sec. of State for Foreign and Commonwealth Affairs, 1970–74. Vice-Chm., Cons. Party Orgn, 1979–84 (Chm., Internat. Office, 1979–84). Mem., Assembly of Council of Europe and WEU, 1965. Chairman: Wilkinson Sword Gp, 1980–83; Sedgwick Gp, 1993– (Dir, 1984–); Director: Westland Gp, 1985–; Rank Xerox UK, 1988–; TI Group, 1990–. Esteemed Family Order (1st cl.), Brunei, 1975. *Address:* House of Lords, SW1A 0PW. *Clubs:* Pratt's, White's, Brooks's.

See also T. L. F. Royle.

FANSHAWE, Captain Thomas Evelyn, CBE 1971; DSC 1943; RN retd; Captain of the Sea Cadet Corps, 1972–81; *b* 29 Sept. 1918; *s* of Rev. Richard Evelyn Fanshawe and Mrs Isobel Fanshawe (*née* Prosser Hale); *m* 1944, Joan Margaret Moxon; one *s* two *d*. *Educ:* Dover Coll.; Nautical Coll., Pangbourne. FRHS. Served 1939–45 in destroyers and frigates and comdg HMS Clover (DSC, despatches 1943 and 1944); HM Ships Ocean, Constance and Phoenix, 1945–51; comd HM Ships: Zest and Obedient, 1951–54; Loch Insh, 1955–57; Temeraire, 1957–59; Tyne, 1959–61; NATO Defence Coll. and Liaison Officer with C-in-C Southern Europe, 1961–64; comd HMS Plymouth and Captain (D) 29th Escort Sqdn, 1964–66; Sen. Naval Officer Persian Gulf and Comdr Naval Forces Gulf, 1966–68 (Cdre); SBNO and Naval Attaché, S Africa (Cdre), 1969–71; ADC to the Queen, 1970–71; retd 1971. Cmdr 1955; Captain 1961. *Recreations:* gardening, golf, general interest in sport. *Address:* Freshwater House, Stroud, Petersfield, Hants GU32 3PN. *T:* Petersfield (01730) 62430. *Clubs:* Royal Navy of 1765 and 1785, MCC.

FANTONI, Barry Ernest; novelist, broadcaster, cartoonist, jazz musician; Member of editorial staff of Private Eye, since 1963; Director, Snartz Ltd, since 1988; *b* 28 Feb. 1940; *s* of late Peter Nello Secondo Fantoni and of Sarah Catherine Fantoni; *m* 1972, Teresa Frances, (Tessa), Reidy. *Educ:* Archbishop Temple Sch.; Camberwell Sch. of Arts and Crafts (Wedgwood Scholar). Cartoonist of The Listener, 1968–88; contrib. art criticism to The Times, 1973–77; record reviewer, Punch, 1976–77; Diary cartoonist, The Times, 1983–90; Dir, Barry Fantoni Merchandising Co., 1985–93; designer of film and theatre posters and illustrator of book jackets; mural for Queen Elizabeth II Conf. Centre, London, 1985; film and television actor; An Evening with Barry Fantoni (one-man show for stage), 1991–; presenter and writer, Barry Fantoni's Chinese Horoscopes, BBC Radio 4 series, 1986. One-man shows: Woodstock Gall., London, 1963; Comara Gall., LA, 1964; Brunel Univ., 1974; Times cartoon exhibition, Charlotte Lampard Gall., 1990; retrospective: Cadogan Contemporary Gall., 1991; two-man shows (with Peter Fantoni): Langton Gall., London, 1977; Annexe Gall., London, 1978; Katherine House Gall., 1983; Fulford Cartoon Gall., 1983; New Grafton Gall., 1985; Green & Stone, Cirencester, 1986; work exhibited: AIA Gall., London, 1958, 1961 and 1964; D and AD Annual Exhibn, London, 1964; Royal Acad. Summer Exhibn, 1963 (as Stuart Harris, with William Rushton), 1964, 1975 and 1978 (with Richard Napper); Tate Gall., 1973; Bradford Print Biennale, 1974; National Theatre, 1977; Browse and Darby, 1977; Gillian Jason Gall., 1983; Three Decades of Art Schools, RA, 1983. Musical compositions include: popular songs (also popular songs with Marianne Faithfull and with Stanley Myers); The Cantors Crucifixion (musical improvisation for 13 instruments), 1977; (with John Wells) Lionel (musical), 1977. Created Barry Fantoni's Jazz Circus, 1992 (a performance jazz trio). Male TV Personality of the Year, 1966. Editor, St Martin's Review, 1969–74; weekly columnist on Chinese Horoscopes: Today, 1986–87; Woman, 1987–88; Plus magazine, 1989; The Guardian, 1990. *Publications:* (with Richard Ingrams) Private Pop Eye, 1968; (as Old Jowett, with Richard Ingrams) The Bible for Motorists, 1970; Tomorrow's Nicodemus, 1974; (as Sylvie Krin, with Richard Ingrams) Love in the Saddle, 1974; Private Eye Cartoon Library 5, 1975; (as E. J. Thribb, with Richard Ingrams) So Farewell Then . . . and Other Poems, 1978; Mike Dime, 1980; (as Sylvie Krin, with Richard Ingrams) Born to be Queen, 1981; Stickman, 1982; (ed) Colemanballs, 1982; (ed) Colemanballs 2, 1984; The Times Diary Cartoons, 1984; Barry Fantoni's Chinese Horoscope, annually 1985–, retitled Barry Fantoni's Complete Chinese Horoscope, 1991; (ed) Colemanballs 3, 1986; Barry Fantoni Cartoons: a personal selection from The Times and The Listener, 1987; The Royal Family's Chinese Horoscopes, 1988; (ed) Colemanballs 4, 1988; Chinese Horoscope Guide to Love, Marriage and Friendship, 1989; (ed) Colemanballs 5, 1990; (ed) Colemanballs 6, 1992; (ed) Colemanballs 7, 1994; *illustrations for:* How To Be a Jewish Mother, 1966; The BP Festivals and Events in Britain, 1966; (with George Melly) The Media Mob, 1980; The Best of Barry Fantoni Cartoons, 1990. *Recreations:* road running, animal welfare. *Address:* c/o Abner Stein, 10 Roland Gardens, SW7 3PH. *T:* 0171–373 0456. *Clubs:* Chelsea Arts (Chm., 1978–80), Arts.

FARHI, Nicole, (Mrs David Hare); fashion designer; Founder, 1983 and Designer, Nicole Farhi Co.; *b* 25 July 1946; *d* of Ephraim Farhi and Marcelle (*née* Babani); one *d* by Stephen Marks; *m* 1992, David Hare, *qv*. *Educ:* Lycée Calmette, Nice; Cours Berçot Art Sch., Paris. First designed for Pierre d'Albi, 1968; founded French Connection with Stephen Marks, 1973; launched Nicole Farhi For Men, 1989; opened Nicole's Restaurant, 1994. *Recreation:* sculpture. *Address:* 16 Foubert's Place, W1V 1HH. *T:* 0171–287 8787.

FARINGDON, 3rd Baron *cr* 1916; **Charles Michael Henderson;** Bt 1902; Partner, Cazenove & Co., since 1968; Chairman, Witan Investment Company plc, since 1980; *b* 3 July 1937; *s* of Hon. Michael Thomas Henderson (*d* 1953) (2nd *s* of Col Hon. Harold Greenwood Henderson, CVO, and *g s* of 1st Baron) and Oonagh Evelyn Henderson, *er d* of late Lt-Col Harold Ernest Brassey; *S* uncle, 1977; *m* 1959, Sarah Caroline, *d* of J. M. E. Askew, *qv*; three *s* one *d*. *Educ:* Eton College; Trinity College, Cambridge (BA). Treasurer, Nat. Art Collections Fund, 1984–91; Chm., RCHM, 1994–. Chm. Bd of Governors, Royal Marsden Hosp., 1980–85; Mem. Bd of Management, Inst. of Cancer Res., 1990–. *Heir: s* Hon. James Harold Henderson [*b* 14 July 1961; *m* 1986, Lucinda, *y d* of Desmond Hanson, Knipton, Lincs; two *s* one *d*]. *Address:* Buscot Park, Faringdon, Oxon SN7 8BU; Barnsley Park, Cirencester, Glos GL7 5EG.

FARLEY, Prof. Francis James Macdonald, FRS 1972; Professor Emeritus, Royal Military College of Science (Dean, 1967–82); *b* 13 Oct. 1920; *er s* of late Brig. Edward Lionel Farley, CBE, MC; *m* 1945, Josephine Maisie Hayden; three *s* one *d*; *m* 1977, Margaret Ann Pearce. *Educ:* Clifton Coll.; Clare Coll., Cambridge. MA 1945; PhD 1950; ScD Cantab 1967; FInstP. Air Defence Research and Development Establishment, 1941–45 (first 3cm ground radar, Doppler radar), Chalk River Laboratories, 1945–46; Research Student, Cavendish Lab., Cambridge, 1946–49; Auckland Univ. Coll., NZ, 1950–57; attached AERE, 1955; CERN, Geneva, 1957–67 (muon g-2 experiment). Vis. Lectr, Univ. of Bristol, 1965–66; Vis. Scientist, CERN, 1967– (muon storage ring, tests of relativity); Vis. Scn. Res. Physicist, Yale Univ., 1984–92; Visiting Professor: Swiss Inst. of Nuclear Research, 1976–77; Reading, 1982–86; Consultant, Centre Antoine Lacassagne, Nice, 1986–92. Rep. NZ at UN Conf. on Atomic Energy for Peaceful Purposes, 1955. Governor: Clifton Coll., to 1994; Welbeck Coll., 1970–82; Member Court: Univ. of Bath, 1974–82; Cranfield Inst. of Technology, 1989–93. Hon. Mem., Instn of Royal Engineers. Hon. Fellow, TCD, 1986. Hughes Medal, Royal Soc., 1980. *Publications:* Elements of Pulse Circuits, 1955; Progress in Nuclear Techniques and Instrumentation, Vol. I, 1966, Vol. II, 1967, Vol. III 1968; scientific papers on nuclear physics, electronics, high energy particle physics, wave energy. *Recreations:* gliding (FAI gold and diamond), ski-ing. *Address:* Le Masage, chemin de Saint Pierre, 06620 Le Bar sur Loup, France. *T:* 93424512, *Fax:* 93429407.

FARLEY, Henry Edward, (Rob); Group Deputy Chief Executive, Royal Bank of Scotland Group, 1986–90; Director, Nationwide Building Society, since 1990; *b* 28 Sept. 1930; *s* of late William and Frances Elizabeth Farley; *m* 1955, Audrey Joyce Shelvey; one *s* one *d*. *Educ:* Harrow County Sch. for Boys. FCIB (FIB 1966). Entered National Bank, 1947; Head of UK Banking, 1978, Dir, 1981, Williams & Glyn's Bank; Chairman: Williams & Glyn's Bank (IOM) Ltd, 1973–76; Joint Credit Card Co. Ltd, 1982–84; Royal Bank of Scotland Gp Insce, 1988–90; Mem. Bd, Mastercard International Inc., 1982–84; Director: Royal Bank of Scotland Group plc, 1985–90; Royal Bank of Scotland, 1985–90 (Man. Dir, 1985–86); Charterhouse Japhet, 1985–86; Charterhouse Development, 1985–86; Charterhouse plc, 1986–90; Chm., Royscot Finance Gp, 1987–90; Dep. Chm., Supervisory Bd of CC Bank, Germany, 1989–90. Director: EFT-POS (UK) Ltd, 1986–88; A. T. Mays Gp, 1987–90; (Alternate) Citizens Financial Gp (USA), 1989–90; John Maunders Gp, 1989–; Banque Rivaud, Paris, 1990–; High Table Ltd, 1991–; Davenham Gp, 1992–. Member: Council, Inst. of Bankers, 1985–90; APACS Council, 1983–90; Exec. Cttee, British Bankers Assoc., 1983–90. Gov. and Mem. Council, UMIST, 1990–; Mem. Bd, Manchester Federal Sch. of Business and Management, 1994–. FRSA 1995. Liveryman, Marketors' Co., 1987– (Dir, Marketors' Hall Ltd, 1992–). *Publications:* The Clearing Banks and Housing Finance, 1983; Competition and Deregulation: branch networks, 1984; The Role of Branches in a Changing Environment, 1985; Deregulation and the Clearing Banks, 1986. *Recreations:* all forms of rough sport, travel, modern literature. *Address:* 13 Montagu Square, W1H 1RB. *Clubs:* Bankers', MCC; Pickwick Bicycle; St James (Manchester).

FARLEY, Prof. Martyn Graham, CEng, FRAeS, FIMechE, FIEE; Emeritus Professor, Royal Military College of Science, Shrivenham and Cranfield Institute of Technology, since 1986; Chairman, Harwell Computer Power Ltd, since 1991 (Director, since 1986); *b* 27 Oct. 1924; *s* of Herbert Booth Farley and Hilda Gertrude (*née* Hendey); *m* 1948, Freda Laugharne; two *s* one *d*. *Educ:* Merchant Venturers Tech. Coll., Bristol; Bristol Aeroplane Co. Tech. Coll. CEng, FRAeS 1968; FIMechE 1969; FIEE (FIProdE 1975); FIIM 1988; CIMgt (CBIM 1980). Engine Div., Bristol Aeroplane Co.: Design Apprentice, 1939–45; Engine Design, 1945–46; Develt Engr, 1946–51; Bristol Aero Engines Ltd: Sen. Designer, Gas Turbine Office, 1951–55; Asst Chief Develt Engr, 1955–59; Bristol Siddeley

Engines: Asst Chief Mech. Engr, 1959–62; Chief Develt Engr, Small Engines Div., 1962–65, Chief Engr, 1965–67; Small Engines Div., Rolls-Royce: Chief Engr, 1967–68; Gen. Works Manager, 1968–72; Manufg and Prodn Dir, 1972–74; HQ Exec. to Vice-Chm. of Rolls-Royce (1971) Ltd, 1974–75; Prof. and Head of Dept of Management Sciences, RMCS, 1975–84; Vice-Chm., Sch. of Management and Maths, RMCS Faculty of Cranfield Inst. of Technology, 1984–86. Dir, World Tech Ventures, 1984–86; Chm., RECSAM Components Ltd, 1986–89. Royal Aeronautical Society: Mem. Council, 1972–92; Vice Pres., 1980–83; Pres., 1983–84; Dir, Aeronautical Trusts, 1975–88; Hon. Treasurer, 1984–88. Vice Pres., Instn of Indust. Engrs, 1981–92; Pres., IProdE, 1984–85 (Mem. Council, 1973–; Chm. Council, 1978–80; Vice-Pres., 1982–83); Chm., British Management Data Foundn Ltd, 1978–; Founder Chm., Alliance of Manufg and Management Orgns, 1981; Member: EEF Manufg Trng Cttee, 1975–91; Guggenheim Medal Bd of Award, 1983; Adv. Council, RN Engrg Coll., Manadon, 1988–; Court, Brunel Univ., 1977–80, Loughborough Univ., 1977–, Cranfield Inst. of Technol., 1977–, Bath Univ., 1983–. Mem., Sen. Awards Cttee, 1979–, and Hon. Mem. Council, 1985–, City and Guilds of London Inst.; Hon. CGIA 1981 (Pres., CGIA Assoc., 1984–); Hon. FCGI 1990; Designer and Project Co-ordinator, EITB Manufg Fellowships, 1977–91. Hon. Fellow, Indian IProdE, 1979; Hon. Member: Amer. Inst. of Indust. Managers, 1979; Australian Inst. of Indust. Engrs, 1981; Amer. Soc. of Manufg Engrs, 1985 (elected Charter Fellow, 1986). Freeman, City of London, 1981; Mem., Co. of Coachmakers and Coach Harness Makers. Internat. Archimedes Award, Amer. Soc. of Prof. Engrs, 1979; Internat. Award, LA Council of Engrs and Scientists, 1981; First Shuttle Contributions Medal, 1981; Educn Award, ASME, 1983; Amer. Instn Advanced Engr Medal, 1984; NASA/Rocketdyne Tech. Award, 1984; California State Engrg Commendation, 1985; NASA Contribs Award, 1985; W. B. Johnson Award, ASME, 1988. *Publications:* articles and technical pubns; procs of conferences. *Address:* Willow End, Vicarage Lane, Shrivenham, Swindon, Wilts SN6 8DT. *T:* Swindon (01793) 782319. *Clubs:* Athenæum, Advanced Class; Shrivenham (Shrivenham); Ariel Rowing (Bristol).

FARLEY, Mary-Rose Christine, (Mrs R. D. Farley); *see* Bateman, M.-R. C.

FARLEY, Rob; *see* Farley, H. E.

FARMBROUGH, Rt. Rev. David John; Bishop Suffragan of Bedford, 1981–93; *b* 4 May 1929; 2nd *s* of late Charles Septimus and late Ida Mabel Farmbrough; *m* 1955, Angela Priscilla Hill, DL; one *s* three *d. Educ:* Bedford Sch.; Lincoln Coll., Oxford (BA 1951, MA 1953); Westcott House, Cambridge, 1951–53. Deacon, 1953, priest, 1954; Curate of Bishop's Hatfield, 1953–57; Priest-in-charge, St John's, Hatfield, 1957–63; Vicar of Bishop's Stortford, 1963–74; Rural Dean of Bishop's Stortford, 1973–74; Archdeacon of St Albans, 1974–81. Mem., Gen. Synod, 1972–81. *Publications:* In Wonder, Love and Praise, 1966; Belonging, Believing, Doing, 1971. *Recreations:* sailing, gardening. *Address:* St Michael Mead, 110 Village Road, Bromham, Beds MK43 8HU. *T:* Bedford (01234) 825042.

FARMER, Bruce; *see* Farmer, E. B.

FARMER, Prof. Edward Desmond; Louis Cohen Professor of Dental Surgery, 1957–82, Director of Post-Graduate Dental Studies, 1972–77, Dean of the Faculty of Medicine, 1977–82, and Pro-Vice-Chancellor, 1967–70, University of Liverpool; *b* 15 April 1917; *s* of late S. R. and L. M. Farmer; *m* 1942, Mary Elwood Little; one *s* two *d. Educ:* Newcastle-under-Lyme High Sch.; Univ. of Liverpool (1936–41); Queens' Coll., Cambridge (1948–50). MA Cantab, 1955; MDS Liverpool, 1951; FDSRCS 1952; MRCPath 1967, FRCPath 1968; Hon. FRCR 1981. RNVR, Surgeon Lieut (D), 1942–45; Lectr in Parodontal Diseases, Univ. of Liverpool, 1950–57; Nuffield Fellow, 1948–50. Hon. Cons. Dent. Surg. to Bd of Governors of United Liverpool Hosps and Liverpool AHA (Teaching), formerly Liverpool Regional Hosp. Bd. Member Council: Brit. Soc. of Periodontology, 1954–59 (Pres. 1957–58); RSM, Odonto. Sect., 1965–68. Member: Central Cttee and Exec., Hosp. Dental Service, 1964–76; Negotiating Cttee of Central Cttee for Hosp. Medical Services, 1968–76; Bd of Govs, United Liverpool Hosps, 1968–71; UGC Dental Sect., 1968–77; Conf. and Exec., Dental Post-Grad. Deans, 1972–77; Cttee of Dental Teachers and Res. Workers Gp, BDA, 1974–79; Liverpool AHA(T) (and Chm., Regional Dental Cttee), 1975–77; RHA, 1977–82; Faculty of Dental Surgery, RCS, 1974–82; Dental Cttee of Medical Defence Union; Council, Medical Insurance Agency; Exec., Teaching Hospitals Assoc.; Chm., Commn of Dental Educn, Fedn Dentaire Internat., 1977–79 (Vice-Chm., 1974–77); Alternate, Dental Adv. Cttee to EEC, 1980–83; Vice-Chm., NW Cancer Research Fund, 1987– (Mem. Exec. Cttee, 1982–); President: NW Br. BDA, 1967–68; Hospitals' Gp, BDA, 1972–73; Assoc. for Dental Educn in Europe, 1976–78; British Soc. of Oral Medicine, 1982–83; Pres., Odontological Section, RSM, 1983–84. Chairman: Merseyside Conf. for Overseas Students, 1983–88; Age Concern, Liverpool, 1984–94; Member: Council, Liverpool Queen Victoria Dist Nursing Assoc., 1987–94; Exec. Cttee, Age Concern England, 1988–92. *Publications:* (with F. E. Lawton) Stones' Oral and Dental Diseases, 5th edn, 1966; papers in Proceedings Royal Society Med., Jl of Gen. Microbiology, Brit. Med. Jl, Dental Practitioner; Internat. Dental Jl. *Recreations:* golf, gardening, painting and enjoyment of the countryside. *Address:* Brookville, 44 Dawstone Road, Heswall, Wirral L60 0BS. *T:* 0151–342 3179. *Clubs:* Athenæum (Liverpool); Royal Liverpool Golf; Caldy Golf.

FARMER, Dr (Edwin) Bruce, CEng; FIM; Group Managing Director and Chief Executive, The Morgan Crucible Co., since 1983; *b* 18 Sept. 1936; *s* of Edwin Bruce Farmer and Doris Farmer (*née* Darby); *m* 1962, Beryl Ann, *d* of late William Alfred Griffiths, Birmingham; one *s* one *d. Educ:* King Edward's, Birmingham; Univ. of Birmingham (BSc, PhD). Dir and Gen. Manager, Brico Metals, 1967–69; Man. Dir, Brico Engineering, 1970–76; Man. Dir, Wellworthy, 1976–81; The Morgan Crucible Co.: Dir, 1981–83; Chm., Thermal Ceramics Div., 1981–83; Dir, Scapa plc. CIMgt, FRSA. Liveryman, Scientific Instrument Makers' Co. *Recreations:* music, cricket, squash. *Address:* The Morgan Crucible Co., Morgan House, Windsor, Berks SL4 1EP. *T:* Windsor (01753) 83700; Weston House, Bracken Close, Wonersh, Surrey GU5 0QS.

FARMER, Frank Reginald, OBE 1967; FRS 1981; *b* 18 Dec. 1914; *s* of Frank Henry Farmer and Minnie Godson; *m* 1939, Betty Smart; one *s* two *d. Educ:* St John's Coll., Cambridge (BA). Kestner Evaporator & Engineering Co., 1936–46; Director, Safety Reliability Directorate, Atomic Energy Authority (formerly Dept of Atomic Energy), 1947–79, retired. Editor, Reliability Engineering, 1980–. FInstP 1965; Hon. FSE 1974; Foreign Associate, Nat. Acad. of Engineers, USA, 1980. Churchill Gold Medal, 1974. *Publication:* Nuclear Reactor Safety, 1977. *Recreations:* golf, books. *Address:* The Long Wood, Lyons Lane, Appleton, Warrington WA4 5ND. *T:* Warrington (01925) 262503.

FARMER, Sir George; *see* Farmer, Sir L. G. T.

FARMER, George Wallace; President, Immigration Appeal Tribunal, since 1991 (Vice President, 1982–91); *b* 4 June 1929; *s* of George Lawrence Farmer and Blanche Amy (*née* Nicholls); *m* 1961, Patricia Mary Joyce; three *d. Educ:* The Lodge, Barbados; Harrison Coll., Barbados. Called to the Bar, Middle Temple, 1950. Private practice, Barbados, 1950–52; Magistrate, Barbados, 1952–56; Resident Magistrate, Uganda, 1956–63, Sen. Resident Magistrate, 1963–64; Dir of Public Prosecutions, Uganda, 1964–65; attached to Cottle Catford & Co., Solicitors, Barbados, 1965–67; Legal Manager, Road Transport Industry Trng Bd, 1967–70; Adjudicator, Immigration Appeals, 1970–82. *Recreations:* allotments (Britain), beach cricket (Barbados). *Address:* 40 South Croxted Road, West Dulwich, SE21 8BD. *T:* 0181–670 4828.

FARMER, Hugh Robert Macdonald, CB 1967; *b* 3 Dec. 1907; *s* of late Charles Edward Farmer and late Emily (*née* Randolph); *m* 1st, 1934, Penelope Frances (*d* 1963), *d* of late Capt. Evelyn Boothby, RN; one *s* three *d*; 2nd, 1966, Jean (*d* 1988), *widow* of Peter Bluett Winch. *Educ:* Cheam Sch.; Eton Coll.; New Coll., Oxford. House of Commons: Asst Clerk, 1931; Sen. Clerk, 1943; Clerk of Private Bills and Taxing Officer, and Examr of Petitions for Private Bills, 1958–60; Clerk of Cttees, 1960–65; Clerk/Administrator, 1965–72, retired 1972. *Recreations:* golf, gardening. *Address:* The Old Rectory, Iping, Midhurst, West Sussex GU29 0PE. *T:* Midhurst (01730) 815923. *Club:* MCC.

FARMER, Sir (Lovedin) George (Thomas), Kt 1968; LLD, MA, FCA, JDipMA; Coordinator, Rover and Triumph, 1972–73; Chairman: Rover Co. Ltd, 1963–73; Zenith Carburettor Co. Ltd, 1973–77; Deputy Chairman, British Leyland Motor Corporation, 1971–73; *b* 13 May 1908; *m* 1st, 1938, Editha Mary Fisher (*d* 1980); no *c*; 2nd, 1980, Muriel Gwendoline Mercer Pinfold. *Educ:* Oxford High Sch. 2nd Vice-Chm. and Mem. Adv. Cttee, Metalurgica de Santa Ana, Madrid, 1963–74; Director: Empresa Nacional de Automcamiones, 1968–73; ATV Network Ltd, 1968–75; Rea Brothers (Isle of Man) Ltd, 1976–88; Aero Designs (Isle of Man) Ltd, 1979–89. President: Birmingham Chamber of Commerce, 1960–61; Motor and Cycle Trades Benevolent Fund, 1962; SMMT, 1962–64 (Dep. Pres., 1964–65; Chm., Exec. Cttee, 1968–72); Fellowship of Motor Industry, 1965; Member: Midland Regl Bd for Industry, 1961–65; Midland Industrial Adv. Council, 1962; Engrg Adv. Council, 1962–66; Export Council for Europe, 1963; Iron, Steel Bd, 1964–66; Engrg ITB, 1964–66; EDC for Motor Industry, 1967; Past Member: Advisory Council, ECGD (Board of Trade); UK Committee of Federation of Commonwealth and British Chambers of Commerce; Vice-Pres., Inst. of Motor Industry, 1964; Vice-Chm., ABCC, 1964; Past Vice-Pres., West Midlands Engineering Employers' Assoc.; Governor, Chm. Finance Cttee, Dep. Chm. Executive Council (Chm., 1966–75), Royal Shakespeare Theatre; Pres., Loft Theatre, Leamington Spa. Pro-Chancellor, Birmingham Univ., 1966–75; Hon. LLD Birmingham, 1975. Past Pres., Automobile Golfing Soc. Mem., Worshipful Co. of Coach and Coach Harness Makers. *Recreations:* theatre, golf, fishing. *Address:* Longridge, The Chase, Ballakillowey, Colby, Isle of Man. *T:* Port St Mary (01624) 832603. *Club:* Royal and Ancient (St Andrews).

FARMER, Michael; *see* Farmer, P. M.

FARMER, Peter John; Circuit Administrator, North-Eastern Circuit, since 1994; *b* 5 Nov. 1952; *s* of Alec and Norah Farmer; *m* 1986, Christine Ann Tetley. *Educ:* King Edward VI Sch., Southampton; Gonville and Caius College, Cambridge (Maths; MA); London Univ. (Cert. Psych.). Joined HM Customs and Excise, 1975; HM Treasury, 1979; Lord Chancellor's Dept, 1981; Circuit Principal, Leeds, 1983; Asst Sec., 1987; Asst Public Trustee, 1988; Public Trustee and Accountant Gen. of Supreme Court, 1991. FIMgt. *Recreations:* English folk dancing, hill walking. *Address:* North-Eastern Circuit Office, West Riding House, Albion Street, Leeds LS1 5AA. *T:* Leeds (0113) 244 1841.

FARMER, (Pryce) Michael; QC 1995; *b* 20 May 1944; *er s* of Sarah Jane Farmer; *m* 1975, Olwen Mary, *d* of late Rev. Griffith John Roberts and of Margaret Morris Roberts; one *s* one *d. Educ:* Ysgol Dyffryn Nantlle, Penygroes; King's Coll., London (BA Hons); Inns of Court Sch. of Law. Schoolmaster, St David's Coll., Llandudno, 1968–71; called to the Bar, Gray's Inn, 1972; practice, Wales and Chester Circuit, 1973–; Junior, Wales and Chester Circuit, 1992; Asst Recorder, 1993. Contested (Plaid Cymru) Conwy, Feb. and Oct. 1974. Head of Chambers, Sedan House, Chester, 1995. *Recreations:* listening to classical music, reading, gardening, watching Rugby football. *Address:* Sedan House, Stanley Place, Chester CH1 2LU. *T:* Chester (01244) 348282; Goldsmith Building, Temple, EC4Y 7BL. *T:* 0171–353 7881. *Clubs:* Reform; Rygbi Yr Wyddgrug (Mold).

FARMER, Robert Frederick, OBE 1985; General Secretary, Institute of Journalists, 1962–87; Member of Council, Media Society, 1982–90 (Secretary, 1973–82); *b* 19 Aug. 1922; *s* of Frederick Leonard Farmer and Gladys Farmer (*née* Winney); *m* 1958, Anne Walton. *Educ:* Saltley Grammar Sch., Birmingham. Served War of 1939–45, Royal Armoured Corps, 1941–52 (commissioned 3rd Carabiniers, despatches, Burma campaign). Secretariat: Instn of Plant Engineers, 1952–59; Instn of Civil Engineers, 1959–62. Consultative Mem., Press Council, 1962–87; Mem., Cttee on Defamation, 1971–75. *Recreations:* cookery, walking, old churches. *Address:* c/o Institute of Journalists, Suite 2, Dock Offices, Surrey Quays, Lower Road, SE16 2XL.

FARMER, Thomas, CBE 1990; Chairman and Chief Executive, Kwik-Fit, since 1984; *b* 10 July 1940; *s* of John Farmer and Margaret (*née* Mackie); *m* 1966, Anne Drury Scott; one *s* one *d. Educ:* St Mary's Primary Sch., Edinburgh; Holy Cross Acad., Edinburgh. Founder, Kwik-Fit, 1971. Chairman: Scottish BITC, 1990–; Investors in People Scotland, 1991–; Mem. Bd, Scottish Enterprise, 1990–. *Recreations:* tennis, swimming, ski-ing. *Address:* (office) 17 Corstorphine Road, Edinburgh EH12 6DD. *T:* 0131–337 9200.

FARNCOMBE, Charles Frederick, CBE 1977; FRAM; Musical Director: Handel Opera Society, 1955–85; Malcolm Sargent Festival Choir, since 1985; *b* 29 July 1919; *o s* of Harold and Eleanor Farncombe, both of London; *m* 1963, Sally Mae (*née* Felps), Riverside, Calif, USA; one *d. Educ:* London Univ., 1936–40 (Archibald Dawnay Scholarship in Civil Engrg, 1936) (BSc Hons (Eng) 1940); Royal Sch. of Church Music, 1947–48; Royal Academy of Music, 1948–51 (RAM, Mann Prize). Civil Engr to John Mowlem & Co, 1940–42. Served War, 1942–47, as Captain in REME, in 21st Army Gp. Free Lance Conductor: formed Handel Opera Soc. 1955; Musical Dir, 1968–79, Chief Conductor, 1970–79, Royal Court Theatre, Drottningholm, Sweden; Chief Guest Conductor, 1979–85, Chief Conductor, annual Handel Fest., 1985–95, Badisches Staatstheater, Karlsruhe, 1979–. AMICE, 1945 (resigned later); FRAM 1963 (ARAM 1962); Hon. Fellow, Royal Swedish Acad. of Music, 1972. Hon DMus: Columbus Univ., Ohio, USA, 1959; City Univ., 1988. Gold Medal of the Friends of Drottningholm, 1971; Gold Medal, Karlsruhe Handel Fest. Cttee, 1992. Kt Comdr, Order of North Star, Sweden, 1982. *Recreations:* cajoling singers, swimming, farm on Offa's Dyke. *Address:* c/o Child & Co., 1 Fleet Street, EC4Y 1BD.

FARNDALE, Gen. Sir Martin (Baker), KCB 1983 (CB 1980); Master Gunner, St James's Park, since 1988; Director and Senior Defence Adviser, Short Brothers, since 1988; Defence Adviser, Touche Ross, since 1988; Consultant, Westland Helicopters, since 1989; *b* Alberta, Canada, 6 Jan. 1929; *s* of late Alfred Farndale and of Margaret Louise Baker; *m* 1955, Margaret Anne Buckingham; one *s. Educ:* Yorebridge Grammar Sch., Yorks. Joined Indian Army, 1946; RMA, Sandhurst, 1947; commnd RA, 1948; Egypt, 1949; 1st RHA, 1950–54 (Germany from 1952); HQ 7 Armoured Div., 1954–57; Staff College, 1959; HQ 17 Gurkha Div., Malaya, 1960–62; MoD, 1962–64; comd Chestnut Troop 1st RHA, Germany and Aden, 1964–66; Instructor, Staff Coll., 1966–69; comd 1st RHA, UK, N Ire., Germany, 1969–71; MoD, 1971–73; comd 7th Armoured Bde,

1973–75. Dir, Public Relations (Army), 1976–78; Dir of Mil. Ops, MoD (Army), 1978–80; Comdr 2nd Armoured Div., BAOR, 1980–83; Comdr 1st (British) Corps, BAOR, 1983–85; C-in-C, BAOR, and Comdr, Northern Army Gp, 1985–87; retired, 1988. Colonel Commandant: Army Air Corps, 1980–88; RA, 1982–; RHA, 1988–. Hon. Colonel: 3rd Bn Yorkshire Volunteers TA, 1983–90; 1st RHA, 1983–90. Chm., RUSI, 1989–93. Chairman: RA Historical Affairs Cttee, 1988; English Heritage Battlefields Adv. Panel, 1993–; Vice-Pres., Royal Patriotic Fund Corp., 1989–92. *Publications:* The History of the Royal Artillery France, 1914–18, 1987; Forgotten Fronts and the Home Base 1914–18, 1989; articles for British Army Rev. and Jl RA. *Recreations:* military history, gardening. *Address:* c/o Lloyds Bank, Cox's and King's Branch, 7 Pall Mall, SW1Y 5NA. *Club:* East India, Devonshire, Sports and Public Schools.

FARNDON, Prof. John Richard, MD; FRCS; Professor of Surgery, University of Bristol, since 1988; Hon. Consultant Surgeon, Bristol Royal Infirmary, since 1988; *b* 16 Feb. 1946; *s* of George Arthur Farndon and Margaret Cooper; *m* 1972, Christine Brenda Louet; two *s* one *d*. *Educ:* Woodhouse Grammar Sch., Sheffield; Univ. of Newcastle upon Tyne (BSc, MB BS, MD). Surgical training posts in Newcastle upon Tyne, 1971–79; Peel Travelling Fellow and Internat. Res. Fellow, Duke Univ., USA, 1979–81; Sen. Lectr in Surgery, Univ. of Newcastle upon Tyne and Consultant to Royal Infirmary, Newcastle, 1981–88. James IV Travelling Fellow, 1984; Hunterian Prof., RCS, 1985; Travelling Fellow, Australasian Coll. of Surgeons, 1985; British Council Scholar to India, 1991; Dist. Visitor, RCS of Australia, 1993; Penman Vis. Prof., Univ. of Cape Town, 1995. Ext. Examiner, Chinese Univ. of Hong Kong, 1994. Consultant to World Jl of Surgery, 1991–; Editor, British Jl of Surgery, 1992–. *Publications:* (ed with G. Keen) Operative Surgery and Management, 3rd edn 1992; numerous papers and chapters on surgical endocrinology and oncology. *Recreations:* gardening, Betjeman Society (founder member), classical music. *Address:* Department of Surgery, Bristol Royal Infirmary, Marlborough Street, Bristol BS2 8HW. *T:* Bristol (0117) 926 0601. *Club:* Royal Society of Medicine.

FARNELL, Graeme, FMA; Publishing Editor, IMS Publications Ltd, since 1994; *b* 11 July 1947; *s* of Wilson Elliot Farnell and Mary Montgomerie Wishart Farnell (*née* Crichton); *m* 1969, Jennifer Gerda (*née* Huddlestone); one *s*. *Educ:* Loughborough Grammar Sch.; Edinburgh Univ. (MA); London Film Sch. (DipFilm Studies). FMA 1989; FSAScot 1976; MBIM. Asst Keeper, Mus. of East Anglian Life, 1973–76; Curator, Inverness Mus. and Art Gall., 1976–79; Dir, Scottish Museums Council, 1979–86; Dir Gen., Museums Assoc., 1986–89; Man. Dir, The Development (formerly Museum Development) Co. Ltd, 1989. Publisher, Heritage Development. *Publications:* (ed) The American Museum Experience, 1986; The Handbook of Grants, 1990, 2nd edn, 1993; contribs to Museums Jl, Internat. Jl of Mus. Management and Curatorship, Museum (Unesco); Industrial Soc. *Recreations:* baroque opera, travel. *Address:* 8 Faraday Drive, Shenley Lodge, Milton Keynes, Bucks MK5 7DA. *T:* Milton Keynes (01908) 660629.

FARNHAM, 12th Baron, *cr* 1756; **Barry Owen Somerset Maxwell;** Bt (Nova Scotia) 1627; Chairman: Avon Rubber plc, since 1978 (Director, since 1966); Provident Mutual Life Assurance Association, since 1989 (Director, since 1967; Deputy Chairman, 1987–89); *b* 7 July 1931; *s* of Hon. Somerset Arthur Maxwell, MP (died of wounds received in action, 1942), and Angela Susan (*d* 1953), *o d* of late Capt. Marshall Owen Roberts; *S* grandfather, 1957; *m* 1959, Diana Marion, *er d* of Nigel Gunnis; two adopted *d*. *Educ:* Eton; Harvard Univ. Chairman: Brown, Shipley & Co. Ltd (Merchant Bankers), 1984–91 (Dir, 1959–91); Brown Shipley Hldgs plc, 1976–91. Pro. Grand Master, United Grand Lodge of England, 1991–. *Heir: b* Hon. Simon Kenlis Maxwell [*b* 12 Dec. 1933; *m* 1964, Karol Anne, *d* of Maj.-Gen. G. E. Prior-Palmer, CB, DSO, and Katherine Edith Bibby; two *s* one *d* (of whom one *s* one *d* are twins)]. *Address:* 11 Earl's Court Gardens, SW5 0TD, Farnham, Co. Cavan. *Clubs:* Boodle's, City of London; Kildare Street and University (Dublin).

FARNINGHAM, Alexander Ian, DSC; Managing Director, Industrial Relations and Personnel, British Shipbuilders, 1977–80; *b* 3 Nov. 1923; *s* of Alexander Farningham and Janet Leask Broadley; *m* 1st, 1949, Lois Elizabeth Halse (marr. diss. 1981); one *s* two *d*; 2nd, 1981, Susan Wyllie. *Educ:* Glebelands Primary Sch., Dundee; Morgan Academy, Dundee; St Andrews Univ. (MA). *Recreations:* walking, birdwatching, photography, sailing. *Address:* Ardriach, Lady Ileene Road, Tarbert, Argyll PA29 6TU. *T:* Tarbert (01880) 820343; Urbanizacao do Pimentão, Lote 2 e 3, R/C Dto, Estrada de Alvor, 8500 Portimao, Portugal. *T:* (82) 82182.

FARNSWORTH, Ian Ross; Deputy Chairman and Chief Executive, Coutts & Co., 1992–95; *b* 15 Feb. 1938; *s* of Frederick Sutcliffe and Winifred Ruby Bryan; *m* 1964, Rosalind Amanda Baker; one *s* one *d*. *Educ:* Nottingham High Sch. ACIB. Westminster Bank, later National Westminster Bank: joined 1954; seconded Nat. Bank of N America, 1979–80; Exec. Vice-Pres., NatWest N America, 1981–84; Asst Gen. Manager, NatWest, 1987–88; Dir, European Businesses, 1988–90; Gen. Manager, NatWest, 1990–91; Dep. Chm., Coutts & Co. AG, Zürich, 1991–94; Mem., Supervisory Bd, F. van Lanschot Bankiers, Holland, 1991–95. Liveryman, Information Technologists' Co., 1994–. *Recreations:* music, golf. *Address:* 15 Dellcroft Way, Harpenden, Herts AL5 2NQ. *T:* Harpenden (01582) 712518.

FARNWORTH, John David; His Honour Judge Farnworth; a Circuit Judge, since 1991; *b* 20 June 1935; *s* of George Arthur Farnworth and Mary Lilian Farnworth; *m* 1964, Carol Gay Mallett; one *s* two *d*. *Educ:* Bedford Sch.; St Edmund Hall, Oxford (BA). Bigelow Teaching Fellow, Univ. of Chicago Law Sch., 1958–59. Admitted Solicitor, 1962; a Recorder, 1986–91. *Recreations:* golf, cricket, snooker, art galleries. *Clubs:* MCC; Bedfordshire Golf.

FARQUHAR, Charles Don Petrie, JP; DL; engineer; *b* 4 Aug. 1937; *s* of late William Sandeman Farquhar and Annie Preston Young Farquhar; *m*; two *d*. *Educ:* Liff Road and St Michael's Primary Schs, Dundee; Stobswell Secondary Sch., Dundee. Served with Royal Engineers (Trng NCO); subseq. supervisory staff, plant engrg; Area Manager, Community Industry, Dundee/Fife, 1972–91. City Councillor, Dundee, 1965–74 (ex-Convener, Museums, Works and Housing Cttees); Mem., Dundee DC, 1974– (Chm., Leisure and Recreation Cttees, 1992–); Lord Provost and Lord Lieutenant of City of Dundee, 1975–77; Chairman: Dundee Dist Licensing Bd, Dundee Dist Licensing Cttee, 1984–93; Cttee for Employment of Disabled People (formerly Disabled Adv. Cttee), Tayside and Fife, 1979–94. JP Dundee, 1974; DL Dundee, 1977. *Recreations:* fresh-water angling, gardening, caravanning, numismatics, do-it-yourself. *Address:* 2 Killin Avenue, Dundee DD3 6EB. *T:* Dundee (01382) 229369.

FARQUHAR, Sir Michael (Fitzroy Henry), 7th Bt *cr* 1796, of Cadogan House, Middlesex; farmer; *b* 29 June 1938; *s* of Sir Peter Walter Farquhar, 6th Bt, DSO, OBE, and Elizabeth Evelyn (*d* 1983), *d* of Francis Cecil Albert Hurt; *S* father, 1986; *m* 1963, Veronica Geraldine Hornidge; two *s*. *Educ:* Eton; Royal Agricultural College. *Recreations:* fishing, shooting. *Heir: s* Charles Walter Fitzroy Farquhar, *b* 21 Feb. 1964. *Address:* Manor Farm, West Kington, Chippenham, Wilts SN14 7JG. *T:* Castle Combe (01249) 782671. *Club:* White's.

FARQUHARSON of Invercauld, Captain Alwyne Arthur Compton, MC 1944; JP; Head of Clan Farquharson; *b* 1 May 1919; *er s* of late Major Edward Robert Francis Compton, JP, DL, Newby Hall, Ripon, and Torloisk, Isle of Mull, and Sylvia, *y d* of A. H. Farquharson; recognised by Lord Lyon King of Arms as Laird of Invercauld (16th Baron of Invercauld; *S* aunt 1941), also as Chief of name of Farquharson and Head of Clan, since 1949; assumed (surname) Compton as a third forename and assumed surname of Farquharson of Invercauld, by warrant granted in Lyon Court, Edinburgh, 1949; *m* 1st, 1949, Frances Strickland Lovell (*d* 1991), *d* of Robert Pollard Oldham, Seattle, Washington, USA; 2nd, 1993, Patricia Gabrielle Estelle Parry de Winton, *d* of Henry Norman Simms-Adams, Brancaster Hall, Norfolk. *Educ:* Eton; Magdalen Coll., Oxford. Joined Royal Scots Greys, 1940. Served War, 1940–45, Palestine, N Africa, Italy, France (wounded); Captain 1943. County Councillor, Aberdeenshire, 1949–75, JP 1951. *Address:* Invercauld, Braemar, Aberdeenshire AB35 5TT. *T:* Braemar (013397) 41213.

See also R. E. J. Compton.

FARQUHARSON of Whitehouse, Captain Colin Andrew, FRICS; chartered surveyor and land agent; Lord Lieutenant of Aberdeenshire, since 1987 (Vice Lord Lieutenant, 1983–87); JP; *b* 9 Aug. 1923; *s* of late Norman Farquharson of Whitehouse; *m* 1st, 1948, Jean Sybil Mary (*d* 1985), *d* of late Brig.-Gen. J. G. H. Hamilton of Skene, DSO, JP, DL; two *d* (and one *d* decd); 2nd, 1987, Clodagh, *widow* of Ian Houldsworth of Dallas Lodge, Moray, and *d* of Sir Kenneth Murray of Geanies, Ross-shire; three step *s* two step *d*. *Educ:* Rugby. FLAS 1956, FRICS 1970. Served Grenadier Guards, 1942–48: ADC to Field Marshal Sir Harold Alexander (later (1st) Earl Alexander of Tunis), 1945. Member, Queen's Body Guard for Scotland (Royal Company of Archers), 1964–. Chartered surveyor and land agent in private practice in Aberdeenshire, 1953–; Director, MacRobert Farms (Douneside) Ltd, 1971–87. Member, Bd of Management for Royal Cornhill Hosps, 1962–74; Chm., Gordon Local Health Council, 1975–81; Mem., Grampian Health Bd, 1981–89. DL 1966, JP 1969, Aberdeenshire. *Recreations:* shooting, fishing, farming. *Address:* Whitehouse, Alford, Aberdeenshire AB33 8DP. *Clubs:* MCC; Royal Northern and University (Aberdeen).

See also Master of Arbuthnott.

FARQUHARSON, Rt Hon. Sir Donald (Henry), Kt 1981; PC 1989; DL; a Lord Justice of Appeal, 1989–95; *b* 1928; *yr s* of Charles Anderson Farquharson, Logie Coldstone, Aberdeenshire, and Florence Ellen Fox; *m* 1960, Helen Mary, *er d* of Comdr H. M. Simpson, RN (retd), Abbots Brow, Kirkby Lonsdale, Westmorland; three *s* (one *d* decd). *Educ:* Royal Commercial Travellers Sch.; Keble Coll., Oxford (MA; Hon. Fellow, 1989). Called to Bar, Inner Temple, 1952; Bencher, 1979. Dep. Chm., Essex QS, 1970; a Recorder of the Crown Court, 1972–81; QC 1972; Judge, High Court of Justice, QBD, 1981–89; Presiding Judge, SE Circuit, 1985–88. A Legal Assessor to GMC and GDC, 1978–81; Chairman: Disciplinary Cttee of Bar, 1983–85; Judicial Studies Bd, 1992–94 (Mem., 1984–85); Criminal Justice Consultative Council, 1992–94. DL Essex, 1990. *Recreations:* opera, walking. *Address:* Royal Courts of Justice, Strand, WC2A 2LL.

FARQUHARSON, Sir James (Robbie), KBE 1960 (CBE 1948; OBE 1944); retired, and is now farming; *b* 1 Nov. 1903; *s* of Frank Farquharson, Cortachy, Angus, Scotland, and Agnes Jane Robbie; *m* 1933, Agnes Binny Graham (*d* 1992); two *s*. *Educ:* Royal Technical College, Glasgow; Glasgow Univ. BSc Glasgow 1923. Asst Engineer, LMS Railway, 1923–25; Asst Engineer, Kenya and Uganda Railway, 1925–33; Senior Asst Engineer, Kenya and Uganda Railway, 1933–37; Asst to Gen. Manager, Tanganyika Railways, 1937–41; Chief Engineer, Tanganyika Railways, 1941–45; General Manager, Tanganyika Railways, 1945–48; Deputy General Manager, East African Railways, 1948–52; Gen. Manager, Sudan Railways, 1952–57; Gen. Manager, East African Railways and Harbours, 1957–61; Asst Crown Agent and Engineer-in-Chief of Crown Agents for Overseas Governments and Administrations, 1961–65. Chm., Millbank Technical Services Ordnance Ltd, 1973–75. Fellow, Scottish Council for Develt and Industry, 1986–. *Publication:* Tanganyika Transport, 1944. *Recreation:* cricket. *Address:* Kinclune, by Kirriemuir, Angus DD8 5HX. *T:* Kirriemuir (01575) 574710. *Club:* Nairobi (Kenya).

FARQUHARSON, Jonathan; Charity Commissioner, since 1985; *b* 27 Dec. 1937; *s* of Alan George Farquharson and Winifred Mary Farquharson (*née* Wilson); *m* 1963, Maureen Elsie Bright; two *d*. *Educ:* St Albans School; Manchester Univ. (LLB). Solicitor, 1962; with D. Herbert, Banbury, 1962–64; Charity Commission, 1964–. *Recreations:* geology, photography, reading, record collecting. *Address:* Charity Commission, 2nd Floor, 20 King's Parade, Queen's Dock, Liverpool L3 4DQ.

FARQUHARSON, Robert Alexander, CMG 1975; HM Diplomatic Service, retired; *b* 26 May 1925; *s* of late Captain J. P. Farquharson, DSO, OBE, RN, and late Mrs Farquharson (*née* Prescott-Decie); *m* 1955, Joan Elizabeth, *o d* of Sir (William) Ivo Mallet, GBE, KCMG; two *s* one *d* (and one *s* decd). *Educ:* Harrow; King's Coll., Cambridge. Served with RNVR, 1943–46. Joined Foreign (now Diplomatic) Service, 1949; 3rd Sec., Moscow, 1950; FO, 1952; 2nd Sec., Bonn, 1955; 1st Sec., Panama, 1958; Paris, 1960; FO, 1964; Counsellor, Dir of British Trade Develt, S Africa, 1967; Minister, Madrid, 1971; Consul-Gen., San Francisco, 1973; Ambassador to Yugoslavia, 1977–80. Lord of the Manor of Bockleton. *Address:* The Old Rectory, Tollard Royal, Wilts SP5 5PS. *Club:* Flyfishers'.

FARR, Dennis Larry Ashwell, CBE 1991; FMA; Director, Courtauld Institute Galleries, 1980–93; *b* 3 April 1929; *s* of late Arthur William Farr and Helen Eva Farr (*née* Ashwell); *m* 1959, Diana Pullein-Thompson (writer), *d* of Captain H. J. Pullein-Thompson, MC, and Joanna (*née* Cannan); one *s* one *d*. *Educ:* Luton Grammar Sch.; Courtauld Inst. of Art, London Univ. (BA, MA). Asst Witt Librarian, Courtauld Inst. of Art, 1952–54; Asst Keeper, Tate Gallery, 1954–64; Curator, Paul Mellon Collection, Washington, DC, 1965–66; Sen. Lectr in Fine Art, and Dep. Keeper, University Art Collections, Univ. of Glasgow, 1967–69; Dir, City Museums and Art Gallery, Birmingham, 1969–80. Fred Cook Meml Lecture, RSA, 1974. Hon. Art Adviser, Calouste Gulbenkian Foundation, 1969–73; Member: British Council Fine Arts Adv. Cttee, 1971–80; Wright Cttee on Provincial Museums and Galleries, 1971–73; Museums Assoc. Council, 1971–74 (Vice-Pres., 1978–79, 1980–81; Pres., 1979–80; Instnl Councillor, 1991–93); Art Panel, Arts Council, 1972–77; ICOM(UK) Exec. Bd, 1976–85; Cttee, Victorian Soc., 1980–; Exec. Cttee, Assoc. of Art Historians, 1981–87 (Chm. of Assoc., 1983–86); History of Art and Design Bd, CNAA, 1981–87; Comité Internat. d'Histoire de l'Art, 1983–94 (Hon. Mem., 1994); Registration Cttee, Museums and Galls Commn, 1993–. Trustee, Birmingham Mus. and Art Gall. Appeal Fund, 1980– (Chm. Trustees, 1978–80); Secretary: Home House Soc. Trustees, 1986–90; Samuel Courtauld Trust, 1990–93. FRSA 1970; FMA 1972. Hon. DLitt Birmingham, 1981. JP Birmingham, 1977–80. Gen. Editor, Clarendon Studies in the History of Art, 1985–. *Publications:* William Etty, 1958; Catalogue of the Modern British School Collection, Tate Gallery (with M. Chamot and M. Butlin), 1964; British Sculpture since 1945, 1965; New Painting in Glasgow, 1968; Pittura Inglese 1660–1840, 1975; English Art 1870–1940, 1978, 2nd edn 1984; (contrib.) British Sculpture in the Twentieth Century, 1981; (with W. Bradford) The Courtauld Collection (catalogue for exhibns in Tokyo and Canberra), 1984; (with W. Bradford) The Northern Landscape (catalogue for exhibn in New York), 1986; (contrib.) In Honor of Paul Mellon, Collector and Benefactor, 1986; (jtly) Impressionist and Post-Impressionist Masterpieces: the Courtauld Collection, 1987; (ed and contrib.) 100 Masterpieces from the Courtauld Collections: Bernardo Daddi to Ben Nicholson, 1987; (jtly) The Oxford Dictionary of Art, 1988; (with Eva Chadwick) Lynn Chadwick: Sculptor, a complete catalogue 1947–88, 1990; (ed and contrib.) Thomas Gambier Parry as Artist and Collector, 1993; articles in: Apollo, Burlington Magazine, TLS, etc. *Recreations:* riding, reading, foreign travel. *Address:* Orchard Hill, Swan Barn Road, Haslemere, Surrey GU27 2HY. *T:* Haslemere (01428) 641880. *Clubs:* Athenæum, Institute of Contemporary Arts.

See also Denis Cannan. J. M. W. Pullein-Thompson.

FARR, Sir John (Arnold), Kt 1984; Member of Lloyd's; *b* 25 Sept. 1922; *er s* of late Capt. John Farr, JP, and Mrs M. A. Farr, JP; *m* 1960, Susan Ann, *d* of Sir Leonard Milburn, 3rd Bt, and of Joan Lady Milburn, Guyzance Hall, Acklington, Northumberland; two *s*. *Educ:* Harrow. RN, 1940–46 serving in Mediterranean and S Atlantic; Lieut-Comdr RNVR. Executive Dir, Home Brewery and Apollo Productions Ltd, 1950–55. Contested Ilkeston, General Election, 1955; MP (C) Harborough, 1959–92. Sec., Cons. Parly Agric. Cttee, 1970–74, Vice-Chm., 1979–83; Sec., Parly Conservation Cttee, 1972–92. Member: Exec. Cttee, UK Branch CPA, 1972–74; UK Delegn to WEU and Council of Europe, 1973–78 (Vice-Chm., Cttee on Agric.); Chairman: Anglo-Irish Parly Gp, 1977–80; Parly Knitwear Ind. Gp, 1980–92; British-Zimbabwe Parly Gp, 1980–91; British-Korea Parly Gp, 1983–91. Vice-Pres., Shooting Sports Trust, 1972–86; Chm., British Shooting Sports Council, 1977–86. *Recreations:* cricket and shooting. *Address:* Shortwood House, Lamport, Northants NN6 9HN. *T:* Maidwell (0160128) 260; 11 Vincent Square, Westminster, SW1P 2LX. *Clubs:* Boodle's, Carlton.

FARR, Air Vice-Marshal Peter Gerald Desmond, CB 1968; OBE 1952; DFC 1942; retired; Director, Brain Research Trust, 1973–83; *b* 26 Sept. 1917; *s* of late Gerald Farr and Mrs Farr (*née* Miers); *m* 1949, Rosemarie (*d* 1983), *d* of late R. S. Haward; two *s* one *d*. *Educ:* Tonbridge Sch. Commnd in RAF, 1937; served War of 1939–45, Middle East, India and Burma; OC, No. 358 Sqdn, 1944–45; OC, RAF Pegu, 1945–46; OC, 120 Sqdn, 1950–51; Dep. Dir, Jt Anti-Submarine sch., 1952–54; OC, RAF Idris, 1954–55; Directing Staff, Jt Services Staff Coll., 1959; SASO, Malta, 1960–63; OC, RAF Kinloss, 1963–64; Air Officer Administration: RAF Germany, 1964–68; Strike Comd, 1969–72. *Recreations:* golf, fishing, music. *Address:* c/o Lloyds Bank, Great Missenden, Bucks HP16 0AT. *Club:* Royal Air Force.

FARRAN, Rt Rev. Brian George; an Assistant Bishop of Perth (Goldfields Region), Western Australia, since 1992; *b* 15 Dec. 1944; *s* of George Farran and Dorothy Barnes; *m* 1971, Robin Jeanne; one *s* two *d*. *Educ:* ANU (BA); St John's Theol Coll., Morpeth (ThL); Deakin Univ. (BLitt). Ordained deacon, 1967, priest, 1968; Curate: St Phillips, O'Connor, 1968; St Alban's, Griffith, 1969–71; Rector: Ch of the Epiphany, Lake Cargelligo, 1972–75; St Barnabas, N Rockhampton, 1975–79; St Saviour's, Gladstone, 1979–82; Dean of St Paul's Cathedral, Rockhampton, Queensland, 1983–89; Regl Dir, Australian Bd of Missions, Province of Victoria, 1989–92. Vice Chm., Gen. Bd of Religous Educn, Anglican Ch of Australia, 1984–. *Recreations:* gardening, music, films, reading. *Address:* Bishopsbourne, 41 Ward Street, Kalgoorlie, WA 6430, Australia. *T:* (90) 912944.

FARRANCE, Roger Arthur, CBE 1988; Chief Executive, Electricity Association, 1990–93; Chairman: Electricity Association Services Ltd, 1991–93; Electricity Association Technology Ltd, 1991–93; *b* 10 Nov. 1933; *s* of Ernest Thomas Farrance and Alexandra Hilda May (*née* Finch); *m* 1956, Kathleen Sheila (*née* Owen); one *d*. *Educ:* Trinity School of John Whitgift, Croydon; London School of Economics (BScEcon). CIPD; CIMgt; CompIEE. HM Inspector of Factories, Manchester, Doncaster and Walsall, 1956–64; Asst Sec., West of England Engineering Employers' Assoc., Bristol, 1964–67; Industrial Relations and Personnel Manager, Foster Wheeler John Brown Boilers Ltd, 1967–68; Dep. Director, Coventry and District Engineering Employers' Assoc., also Coventry Management Trng Centre, 1968–75; Electricity Council: Dep. Industrial Relations Adviser (Negotiating), 1975–76; Industrial Relations Adviser, 1976–79; Mem., 1979–88; Dep. Chm., 1989–90. Chm., Power Aid Logistics, 1993–94. Member Council: ACAS, 1983–89; CBI, 1983–93 (Chm., Health and Safety Policy Cttee, 1990–93); Mem., Directing Cttee, Union Internationale des Producteurs et Distributeurs d'Energie Electrique, 1991–94 (Chm., Human Factors Cttee, 1991–94). President: IPM, 1991–93; Electricity Supply Industry Ambulance Centre, St John's Amb. Assoc., 1979–93; St John's 210 (London Electricity) Combined Div., 1989–94. Chairman: Devonshire House Management Trustees, 1989–94; Management Bd, Electrical and Electronics Industry Benevolent Assoc., 1987–93. FRSA. Councillor, London Borough of Merton, 1994–. Freeman, City of London, 1985; Liveryman, Basketmakers' Co., 1986–. OStJ 1983. *Recreations:* photography, music, cycling, walking. *Address:* 14 Bathgate Road, Wimbledon, SW19 5PN.

FARRAND, Dame Brenda Marjorie; *see* Hale, Hon. Dame B. M.

FARRAND, Julian Thomas, LLD; Pensions Ombudsman, since 1994; *b* 13 Aug. 1935; *s* of J. and E. A. Farrand; *m* 1st, 1957, Winifred Joan Charles (marr. diss. 1992); one *s* two *d*; 2nd, 1992, Brenda Marjorie Hoggett (*see* Hon. Dame Brenda Hale). *Educ:* Haberdashers' Aske's Sch.; University Coll. London (LLB 1957, LLD 1966). Admitted Solicitor, 1960. Asst Lectr, then Lectr, KCL, 1960–63; Lectr, Sheffield Univ., 1963–65; Reader in Law, QMC, 1965–68; Prof. of Law, 1968–88, Dean of Faculty of Law, 1970–72, 1976–78, Manchester Univ. Vis. Prof., UCL, 1990–. A Law Comr, 1984–88; Insce Ombudsman, 1989–94. Chairman: Gtr Manchester and Lancs Area, 1973–90 (Vice-Pres., 1977–84), London Area, 1984–, Rent Assessment Panel; Supplementary Benefit Appeals Tribunal, 1977–80; Nat. Insce Local Tribunal, 1980–83; Social Security Appeal Tribunal, 1983–88; Govt Conveyancing Cttee, 1984–85. FCIArb 1994. Hon. QC 1994. Hon. LLD Sheffield, 1990. *Publications:* (ed with Dr J. Gilchrist Smith) Emmet on Title, 15th edn 1967 to 19th edn (as sole editor) 1986; Contract and Conveyance, 1963–64, 4th edn 1983; (ed) Wolstenholme and Cherry, Conveyancing Statutes, 13th edn (vols 1–6) 1972; The Rent Acts and Regulations, 1978, 2nd edn (with A. Arden) 1981. *Recreations:* chess, bridge, wine. *Address:* (office) 11 Belgrave Road, SW1V 1RB.

FARRANDS, Dr John Law, AO 1990; CB 1982; FTS, CEng; FInstP, FAIP; FIE (Aust); consultant to companies and government, since 1982; *b* 11 March 1921; *s* of Harold Rawlings Farrands and Hilda Elizabeth (*née* Bray); *m* 1946, Jessica (*née* Ferguson); three *s* one *d* (and one *s* decd). *Educ:* Melbourne Univ. (BSc); London Univ. (PhD); Imperial Coll. of Science and Technol. (DIC, CEng). FTS 1976; FInstP 1957; FAIP 1962; FIE(Aust) 1987. Served RAEME, AIF, 1941 (Captain). Scientific Adviser to Mil. Bd, 1957; Chief Supt, Aeronautical Res. Labs, 1967; Chief Def. Scientist, 1971; Permanent Head, Dept of Science and Environment, later Dept of Science and Technol., 1977–82. Chairman: Aust. Inst. of Marine Science, 1982–90; R&D Bd, Overseas Telecommunications Commn, 1983–89. Leader, Aust. Delegn to UNCSTD, 1980. Cllr, Nat. Energy Res., Develt and Demonstration Council, 1978–83. Director: Interscan Australia, 1980–84; Quest Investment, 1986–91; SCIRAD, 1987–. Hon. DSc Melbourne, 1994. *Publications:* (jtly) Changing Disease Patterns and Human Behaviour, 1981; Don't Panic, PANIC!, 1993; articles in scientific and engrg jls. *Recreations:* fishing, music. *Address:* 20 The Boulevard, Glen Waverley, Vic 3150, Australia. *T:* (3) 98028195.

FARRAR, Rex Gordon, LVO 1975; HM Diplomatic Service, retired; Regional Director (Tokyo), 1985–90, Consultant, since 1990, De La Rue Co. plc; *b* 22 Aug. 1925; *s* of late John Percival Farrar and Ethel Florence Farrar (*née* Leader); *m* 1978, Masako (*née* Ikeda); one *s* one *d*. *Educ:* Latymer's Sch., Edmonton; London Univ. (BA Hons History). Served Royal Navy, 1944–47. Joined HM Diplomatic Service, 1947; served, New Orleans, 1953–57; Jakarta, 1960–63; Caracas, 1964–68; San Salvador, 1968–71; Tokyo, 1971–75; Rangoon, 1978–80; Consul-Gen. and Dir of Trade Promotion, Osaka, Japan, 1980–85. *Recreations:* golf, tennis, studying Japanese. *Club:* Kobe (Japan).

FARRAR-HOCKLEY, Gen. Sir Anthony Heritage, GBE 1982 (MBE 1957); KCB 1977; DSO 1953 and bar 1964; MC 1944; author (military history), defence consultant and lecturer; Commander-in-Chief Allied Forces Northern Europe, 1979–82; ADC General to the Queen, 1981–83; retired 1983; *b* 8 April 1924; *s* of late Arthur Farrar-Hockley and Agnes Beatrice (*née* Griffin); *m* 1945, Margaret Bernadette Wells (*d* 1981); two *s* (and one *s* decd); *m* 1983, Linda Wood. *Educ:* Exeter Sch. War of 1939–45 (despatches, MC): enlisted under-age in ranks of The Gloucestershire Regt and served until Nov. 1942; commissioned into newly forming 1st Airborne Div., campaigning in Greece, Italy, S France, to 1945 (despatches 1943). Palestine, 1945–46; Korea, 1950–53 (despatches 1954); Cyprus and Port Said, 1956; Jordan, 1958; College Chief Instructor, RMA Sandhurst, 1959–61; commanded parachute bn in Persian Gulf and Radfan campaign, 1962–65; Principal Staff Officer to Dir of Borneo Ops, 1965–66; Comdr, 16 Parachute Bde, 1966–68; Defence Fellowship, Exeter Coll., Oxford, 1968–70 (BLitt); DPR (Army), 1970; Comdr, Land Forces, N Ireland, 1970–71; GOC 4th Div., 1971–73; Dir, Combat Development (Army), 1974–77; GOC SE District, 1977–79. Colonel Commandant: Prince of Wales's Div., 1974–80; Parachute Regt, 1977–83; Col, The Gloucestershire Regt, 1978–84. *Publications:* The Edge of the Sword, 1954; (ed) The Commander, 1957; The Somme, 1964; Death of an Army, 1968; Airborne Carpet, 1969; War in the Desert, 1969; General Student, 1973; Goughie: the Life of General Sir Hubert Gough, GCB, GCMG, KCVO, 1975; Opening Rounds, 1988; The British Part in the Korean War, vol. 1: A Distant Obligation, 1990, vol. 2: An Honourable Discharge, 1995; Army in the Air, 1994; (contrib. and associate ed.) The D-Day Encyclopaedia, 1994. *Recreations:* cricket, badminton, sailing, walking. *Address:* c/o National Westminster Bank, 30 Wellington Street, Aldershot, Hants GU11 1EB. *Club:* Savage.

FARRELL, James Aloysius; Sheriff of Lothian and Borders at Edinburgh, since 1986; *b* 14 May 1943; *s* of James Stoddart Farrell and Harriet Louise McDonnell; *m* 1967, Jacqueline Allen; two *d*. *Educ:* St Aloysius College; Glasgow University (MA); Dundee University (LLB). Admitted to Faculty of Advocates, 1974; Advocate-Depute, 1979–83; Sheriff: Glasgow and Strathkelvin, 1984; S Strathclyde, Dumfries and Galloway, 1985. *Recreations:* sailing, hillwalking, cycling. *Address:* c/o Advocates' Library, Parliament House, Edinburgh EH1 1RF.

FARRELL, M. J.; *see* Keane, M. N.

FARRELL, Michael Arthur; European Sales Manager, VCS Sport Ltd, since 1993; *b* 27 April 1933; *s* of Herbert and Marjorie Farrell; *m* 1st, 1957, Myra Shilton (*d* 1973); two *d*; 2nd, 1976, Beryl Browne. *Educ:* Beverley Grammar Sch., Yorks; Holly Lodge Grammar Sch., Birmingham. Design Draughtsman, 1949–51; Nat. Service, RASC, 1951–53; Planning Engineer, 1953–61; Representative, 1961–74; Sales Manager, Lillywhites Cantabrian, 1974–80; Sales Executive, En-Tout-Cas, 1908–82; Gen. Sec., AAA, subseq. British Athletic Fedn, 1982–91; Export Sales Dir, Cantabrian Athletics Ltd, 1992–93. *Recreations:* painting, walking, cycling. *Address:* PO Box 7, Royston, Herts SG8 6TE.

FARRELL, Terence, (Terry Farrell), OBE 1978; Chairman, Terry Farrell & Company, since 1987; *b* 12 May 1938; *s* of Thomas and Molly Farrell (*née* Maguire); *m* 1st, 1960, Angela Rosemarie Mallam; two *d*; 2nd, 1973, Susan Hilary Aplin; two *s* one *d*. *Educ:* St Cuthbert's Grammar Sch., Newcastle; Durham Univ. (BArch, 1st class hons); Univ. of Pennsylvania (MArch, MCP). ARIBA 1963; MRTPI 1970; FCSD (FSIAD 1981). Harkness Fellow, Commonwealth Fund, USA, 1962–64. Partner: in Farrell Grimshaw Partnership, 1965–80; in Terry Farrell Partnership, 1980–87. Major projects include: Headquarters and studios for TVam; Henley Royal Regatta Headquarters; redevelt of Charing Cross Station; Edinburgh Internat. Conf. Centre; British Consulate-Gen., Hong Kong. *Exhibitions:* RIBA Heinz Gall., London, 1987; British Architecture, Japan, 1989. *Publications:* Architectural Monograph, 1985; Urban Design Monograph, 1993; articles in numerous British and foreign jls. *Recreations:* walking, swimming. *Address:* 17 Hatton Street, NW8 8PL.

FARRELL, Timothy Robert Warwick; Organist, Liberal Jewish Synagogue, St John's Wood, since 1975; *b* 5 Oct. 1943; *m* 1975, Penelope Walmsley-Clark (marr. diss. 1995); one *s*. *Educ:* Diocesan Coll., Cape Town; Royal Coll. of Music, London; Paris, etc. FRCO, ARCM (piano and organ). Asst Organist, St Paul's, Knightsbridge, 1962–66; Asst Organist, St Paul's Cath., 1966–67; Sub-organist, Westminster Abbey, 1967–74; Organ Tutor at Addington Palace, RSCM, 1966–73; Organist, Choirmaster and Composer, HM Chapels Royal, 1974–79. Broadcaster, gramophone records, electronic and orchestral music, etc. *Recreations:* golf, walking, sailing, flying. *Address:* Liberal Jewish Synagogue, 28 St John's Wood Road, NW8 7HA. *T:* 0171–286 5181.

FARRER, (Arthur) Mark; Partner, Farrer & Co., since 1968; Chairman: Essex Water Co., since 1992 (Director, since 1986; Deputy Chairman, 1987); Suffolk Water Co., since 1992 (Director, since 1990); *b* 25 March 1941; *s* of Hugh Frederick Francis Farrer and Elizabeth Mary Cross; *m* 1969, Zara Jane Thesiger; one *d*. *Educ:* Eton. Admitted solicitor, 1966. Dir, Lyonnaise Europe, 1989–. Mem. Council, Lloyd's, 1988–91; Chm., Assoc. of Lloyd's Members Ltd, 1991–92. *Publications:* articles in learned jls. *Recreations:* gardening, salmon fishing, the steam railway. *Address:* The Brick House, Finchingfield, Essex CM7 4LB. *T:* Thaxted (01371) 810283; 56 Sangomore, Durness by Lairg, Sutherland. *Clubs:* Brooke's; Celer et Audax (Winchester).

FARRER, Brian Ainsworth; QC 1978; **His Honour Judge Farrer;** a Circuit Judge, since 1985; *b* 7 April 1930; *s* of A. E. V. A. Farrer and Gertrude (*née* Hall); *m* 1960, Gwendoline Valerie (*née* Waddoup), JP; two *s* one *d*. *Educ:* King's Coll., Taunton; University Coll., London (LLB). Called to the Bar, Gray's Inn, 1957. A Recorder, 1974–85. *Recreations:* golf, music, chess, bridge. *Address:* c/o Queen Elizabeth II Law Courts, Newton Street, Birmingham B4 7LU. *Club:* Aberdovey Golf.

FARRER, Sir (Charles) Matthew, GCVO 1994 (KCVO 1983; CVO 1973); Private Solicitor to the Queen, 1965–94; Partner in Messrs Farrer & Co, Solicitors, 1959–94; *b* 3 Dec. 1929; *s* of late Sir (Walter) Leslie Farrer, KCVO, and Hon. Lady Farrer; *m* 1962, Johanna Creszentia Maria Dorothea Bennhold; one *s* one *d*. *Educ:* Bryanston Sch.; Balliol Coll., Oxford (MA). A Trustee, British Museum, 1989–; Comr, Royal Commn on Historical Manuscripts, 1991–; Mem., British Library Bd, 1994–. Trustee, Lambeth Palace Library, 1991–. *Recreations:* travel, reading. *Address:* 6 Priory Avenue, Bedford Park, W4 1TX. *T:* 0181–994 6052.

FARRER, David John; QC 1986; a Recorder, since 1983; *b* 15 March 1943; *s* of John Hall Farrer and Mary Farrer; *m* 1969, Hilary Jean Bryson; two *s* one *d*. *Educ:* Queen Elizabeth's Grammar Sch., Barnet; Downing Coll., Cambridge (MA, LLB). Called to the Bar, Middle Temple, 1967; in practice, 1968–; Mem., Bar Council, 1986–; Chm., Bar Services Cttee, 1989–. Contested (L): Melton, 1979; Rutland and Melton, 1983. *Recreations:* tennis, cricket, Liberal Party politics. *Address:* The Grange, Hoby, Melton Mowbray, Leics LE14 3DT. *T:* Rotherby (01664) 434232. *Club:* National Liberal.

FARRER, Margaret Irene, OBE 1970; Chairman of Central Midwives Board, 1973–79; *b* 23 Feb. 1914; *e d* of Alfred and Emblyn Farrer. *Educ:* Poltimore Coll., Exeter; UCH London. SRN, SCM, DN (London), MTD, RST. Midwifery Tutor, General Lying-in Hosp., 1942–49; Matron: St Mary's Hosp., Croydon, 1949–56; Forest Gate Hosp., 1956–71; Chief Nursing Officer, Thames Gp, 1971–74. Member: Central Midwives Bd, 1952–; Central Health Services Council, 1963–74; NE Metropolitan Regional Hosp. Bd, 1969–74; NE Thames Regional Health Authority, 1973–76; Editorial Bd, Midwife and Health Visitor; Hon. Treas., Royal Coll. of Midwives, 1967–76. *Recreations:* gardening, walking. *Address:* Coombe Brook, Dawlish, South Devon EX7 0QN. *T:* Dawlish (01626) 863323.

FARRER, Mark; *see* Farrer, A. M.

FARRER, Sir Matthew; *see* Farrer, Sir C. M.

FARRER, William Oliver, CVO 1991; Senior Partner, Farrer & Co., Solicitors, 1976–91 (Partner, 1955–91); *b* 23 June 1926; *s* of John Oliver Farrer, MC, and Winifred Millicent Farrer; *m* 1st, 1955, Margery Hope Yates (*d* 1976); two *s* one *d*; 2nd, 1979, Hazel Mary Andrew. *Educ:* Eton Coll.; Balliol Coll., Oxford (MA). Lieut, Coldstream Guards, 1945–48. Admitted a Solicitor, 1953; Solicitor to the Duchy of Lancaster, 1984–91; Mem., Solicitors' Disciplinary Tribunal, 1986–94. Dir, Sotheby's, 1992–. Mem. Council, Inst. of Cancer Res., 1994–. *Recreations:* golf, music. *Address:* Popmoor, Fernhurst, Haslemere, Surrey GU27 3LL. *T:* Haslemere (01428) 642564. *Clubs:* Brooks's, MCC; Royal and Ancient (St Andrews); Honourable Company of Edinburgh Golfers.

FARRIMOND, Herbert Leonard, CBE 1977; retired; Adviser, The Associated Octel Company Ltd, 1982–88; Chairman, H. L. Farrimond & Associates Ltd, 1978–88; *b* 4 Oct. 1924; *s* of late George and Jane Farrimond, Newcastle upon Tyne; *m* 1951, Patricia Sara (*née* McGrath); one *s*. *Educ:* St Cuthbert's Grammar Sch., Newcastle upon Tyne; Durham Univ. BA (Hons) Politics and Economics. Lieut RM, 1943–46. Australian Dept of Labour and Nat. Service, 1948–50; Imperial Chemical Industries Ltd, and Imperial Metal Industries Ltd, 1950–68; Upper Clyde Shipbuilders Ltd, 1968–69; Dir of Personnel, Dunlop Ltd, 1969–72; Mem., British Railways Bd, 1972–77. Director: British Rail Engineering Ltd; British Rail Shipping and Internat. Services Div.; Transmark Ltd (Chm.); Portsmouth and Sunderland Newspapers Ltd, 1978–80; Chm., British Transport Hotels, 1976–78. Adviser to industrial and commercial cos, 1978–88. Mem. Council, Advisory, Conciliation and Arbitration Service, 1974–78. Part-time Mem., British Waterways Bd, 1980–82. Governor, British Transport Staff Coll. Ltd, 1972–77. FCIT; FIPM. *Recreations:* golf, gardening, music. *Address:* 9 Ardgare, Shandon, Helensburgh, Dunbartonshire G84 8NW. *T:* Helensburgh (01436) 820803.

FARRINGTON, family name of **Baroness Farrington of Ribbleton**.

FARRINGTON OF RIBBLETON, Baroness *cr* 1994 (Life Peer), of Fulwood in the County of Lancashire; **Josephine Farrington;** Chairman, Association of County Councils, since 1994 (Vice-Chairman, 1990–94); Member (Lab), Lancashire County Council, since 1977; *b* 29 June 1940; *m* 1960, Michael James Farrington; three *s*. Lancashire County Council: Chm., 1992; Chm., Educn Cttee, 1981–91. Association of County Councils: Chm., Policy Cttee, 1993–94; Leader, Labour Gp, 1987–94. Mem., Consultative Council for Local Govt Finance, 1987–. UK Rep., Cttee of the Regions, 1994– (Chm., Educn and Trng Cttee, 1994–). Pres., Council of Europe Cttee for culture, educn and the media, 1989–94. UK European Woman of the Year, 1994. *Address:* Association of County Councils, Eaton House, 66A Eaton Square, SW1W 9BH. *T:* 0171–201 1500; 114 Victoria Road, Fulwood, Preston, Lancs PR2 4NN. *T:* Preston (01772) 718836.

FARRINGTON, Prof. David Philip, PhD; Professor of Psychological Criminology, University of Cambridge, since 1992; *b* 7 March 1944; *s* of William Farrington and Gladys Holden (*née* Spurr); *m* 1966, Sally Chamberlain; three *d*. *Educ:* Clare Coll., Cambridge (BA, MA, PhD Psychology). On staff of Cambridge Univ. Inst. of Criminology, 1969–: Reader in Psychol Criminology, 1988–92; Fellow, Darwin Coll., Cambridge, 1980–83. Mem., Parole Bd for England and Wales, 1984–87. Chm., Div. of Criminological and Legal Psychology, British Psychological Soc., 1983–85; Pres., British Soc. of Criminology, 1990–93; Pres. elect, Europ. Assoc. of Psychology and Law, 1994–; Vice-Chm., US Nat. Acad. of Scis Panel on Violence, 1989–92. Sellin-Glueck Award, Amer. Soc. of Criminology, 1984. *Publications:* Who Becomes Delinquent? 1973; The Delinquent Way of Life, 1977; Behaviour Modification with Offenders, 1979; Psychology, Law and Legal Processes, 1979; Abnormal Offenders, Delinquency and the Criminal Justice System, 1982; Aggression and Dangerousness, 1985; Reactions to Crime, 1985; Prediction in Criminology, 1985; Understanding and Controlling Crime, 1986; Human Development and Criminal Behaviour, 1991; Offenders and Victims, 1992; Integrating Individual and Ecological Aspects of Crime, 1993; Psychological Explanations of Crime, 1994; Building a Safer Society, 1995. *Address:* Institute of Criminology, 7 West Road, Cambridge CB3 9DT. *T:* Cambridge (01223) 335384.

FARRINGTON, Sir Henry Francis Colden, 7th Bt, *cr* 1818; RA retired; *b* 25 April 1914; *s* of Sir Henry Anthony Farrington, 6th Bt, and Dorothy Maria (*d* 1969), *o d* of Frank Farrington; *S* father, 1944; *m* 1947, Anne, *e d* of late Major W. A. Gillam, DSO; one *s* one *d*. *Educ:* Haileybury. Retired from Army, 1960 (Major; now Hon. Col). *Heir: s* Henry William Farrington, ARICS [*b* 27 March 1951; *m* 1979, Diana Donne Broughton, *yr d* of Geoffrey Broughton, Somerset; two *s*]. *Address:* Higher Ford, Wiveliscombe, Taunton, Somerset TA4 2RL. *T:* Wiveliscombe (01984) 623219.

FARROW, Christopher John; Director General, London Investment Banking (formerly British Merchant Banking and Securities Houses) Association, since 1993; *b* 29 July 1937; *s* of late Thomas and Evangeline Dorothea Farrow; *m* 1961, Alison Brown; one *s* one *d*. *Educ:* Cranleigh Sch.; King's Coll., Cambridge (BA). Board of Trade, 1961; Harkness Fellowship and visiting scholar, Stanford Univ., USA, 1968–69; Private Sec. to Pres. of BoT and Minister for Trade, 1970–72; Dept of Trade and Industry, 1972–74; Cabinet Office, 1975–77; Dept of Industry, 1977–83; Asst Dir, Bank of England, 1983–87; Dir, Kleinwort, Benson Ltd, 1987–92. Director: London Metal Exchange Ltd, 1987–; Glynwed International, 1993–. Member: Engrg Council, 1984–86; Financial Reporting Review Panel, 1992–. *Recreation:* gardening. *Address:* LIBA, 6 Frederick's Place, EC2R 8BT.

FARROW, Christopher John; Chief Executive, Merseyside Development Corporation, since 1991; *b* 19 Nov. 1947; *s* of Sydney A. Farrow; *m* 1980, Susan Thomas; three *d*. *Educ:* Claysmore Sch., Dorset; Univ. of London (BA Hons); Polytechnic of Central London (DipTP Dist.). London Borough of Newham, 1974–81; Director: LDDC, 1981–91; Greenland Dock Develt Co., 1985–; Docklands Enterprise Centre, 1988–91; Mersey Partnership, 1992–. MRTPI. FRSA 1993. *Publications:* planning papers on urban develt and economy. *Address:* Merseyside Development Corporation, Royal Liver Building, Pier Head, Liverpool L3 1JH. *T:* 0151–236 6090.

FARROW, Mia (Villiers); actress; *b* 9 Feb. 1945; *d* of John Villiers Farrow and Maureen O'Sullivan; *m* 1970, André Previn (marr. diss. 1979), *qv*; three *s* two *d*; one *s* by Woody Allen, *qv*. *TV series:* Peyton Place, 1965; *films:* Secret Ceremony, 1968; Rosemary's Baby, 1969; John and Mary, 1970; The Public Eye, 1972; The Great Gatsby, 1974; Full Circle, Death on the Nile, A Wedding, 1978; Hurricane, 1980; A Midsummer Night's Sex Comedy, 1982; Zelig, 1983; Broadway Danny Rose, 1984; The Purple Rose of Cairo, 1985; Hannah and her Sisters, 1986; Radio Days, 1987; September, 1988; Another Woman, 1989; Crimes and Misdemeanours, 1990; Alice, 1990; Husbands and Wives, 1992; Shadows and Fog, 1992; Miami Rhapsody, 1995; *stage:* The Importance of Being Earnest, NY, 1963; Mary Rose, Shaw, 1973; The Three Sisters, Greenwich, 1974; The House of Bernarda Alba, Greenwich, 1974; Peter Pan, 1975; The Marrying of Ann Leete, RSC, 1975; The Zykovs, Ivanov, RSC, 1976; A Midsummer Night's Dream, Leicester, 1976; Romantic Comedy, NY, 1979. David Donatello Award, Italy, 1969; Best Actress awards: French Academy, 1969; San Sebastian, 1969; Rio de Janeiro, 1970. *Address:* Bridgewater, CT, USA.

FARTHING, (Richard) Bruce (Crosby); Deputy Director-General, General Council of British Shipping, 1980–83; Rapporteur, Sea Transport Commission, International Chamber of Commerce, since 1976; Consultant Director, International Association of Dry Cargo Shipowners, since 1984; *b* 9 Feb. 1926; *s* of late Col Herbert Hadfield Farthing and late Marjorie Cora (*née* Fisher); *m* 1st, 1959, Anne Brenda Williams (marr. diss. 1986), LLB, barrister, *d* of late Thomas Williams, solicitor; one *s* one *d*; 2nd, 1986, Moira Roupell, *o d* of late Lt-Col R. A. Curties and Mrs Ida Curties. *Educ:* Alleyns Sch., (Dulwich and Rossall) St Catharine's Coll., Cambridge (MA). Commissioned RA and RHA, 1944–48. Called to Bar, Inner Temple, 1954; Govt Legal Service, 1954–59; joined Chamber of Shipping of the United Kingdom, 1959; Asst General Manager, 1966; Secretary, Cttee of European Shipowners and Cttee of European National Shipowners' Assocs, 1967–74; Secretary-General, Council of European and Japanese National Shipowners' Assocs (CENSA), 1974–76; Director, General Council of British Shipping, 1976–80. Freeman, City of London, 1979; Liveryman, Shipwrights' Co., 1982–; Mem. Court of Common Council (Aldgate Ward), 1981–. Pres., Aldgate Ward Club, 1985 (Vice-Pres., 1984). Governor: City of London Sch., 1983– (Dep. Chm., 1988–89, 1993–94, Chm., 1990–93); SOAS, 1985–; Mem. Council, City Univ., 1994–. Mem. Court, Hon. Irish Soc., 1992–94. Trustee, Nautical Museums Trust, 1983–. Chm., King of Norway Reception Cttee, 1988. FIMgt. Commander, Royal Norwegian Order of Merit, 1988. *Publications:* ed, Vol. 20, Aspinalls Maritime Law Cases, 1961; International Shipping, 1987, 2nd edn 1993. *Recreations:* sailing, music, gardening. *Address:* 44 St George's Drive, SW1V 4BT; Snaylham House, Icklesham, E Sussex TN36 4AJ. *Clubs:* MCC, Incogniti Cricket, Royal Ocean Racing; Rye Golf.

FARVIS, Prof. William Ewart John, CBE 1978 (OBE 1972); BSc, BSc(Eng), CEng, Hon. FIEE; FRSE; engineering consultant; Professor Emeritus of Electrical Engineering, University of Edinburgh (Professor, 1961–77); *b* 12 Dec. 1911; *o s* of late William Henry Farvis and Gertrude Anne Farvis; *m* 1939, Margaret May Edmonstone Martin; one *s* one *d*. *Educ:* Queen Elizabeth's Hosp., Bristol; Bristol and London Univs. Lectr, University Coll., Swansea, 1937–40 and 1945–48; Air Ministry, Telecommunications Res. Estab., 1940–45; Lectr/Sen. Lectr, Edinburgh Univ., 1948–61, Prof. and Head of Dept of Electrical Eng., 1961–77, Chairman, Sch. of Engineering Sci. 1972–75. Mem., British Nat. Cttee for Radio Science, 1960–66; Science Research Council: Mem., Electrical and Systems Cttee, 1968–72, Engineering Board, 1972–75 and 1976–81; Polytechnics Cttee, 1975–78; Chm., Solid-state Devices Panel, 1972–75; Electrical and Systems Cttee 1972–75; Advanced Ground Transport Panel 1975–80; Mem. Council, 1976–81. Mem. Council, IEE, 1972–75 and 1976–79; Hon. FIEE 1987. Editor, Microelectronics Journal, 1976–78. *Recreation:* music. *Address:* 14 Cluny Terrace, Edinburgh EH10 4SW. *T:* 0131–447 4939. *Club:* Athenæum.

FASELLA, Prof. Paolo Maria; Director-General for Science, Research and Development, Commission of the European Communities, since 1981; *b* 16 Dec. 1930; *s* of Felice Fasella and Margherita Parazzoli; *m* 1957, Sheila Hauck Dionisi; four *d*. *Educ:* Univ. of Rome. PhD Biolog. Chem. and Applied Biochem. Asst, then Associate Prof. in Biol. Chem., Univ. of Rome, 1959–65; Associate, then Prof. in Biochem., Univ. of Parma, 1965–71; Prof. of Biol. Chem.,Univ. of Rome, 1971–81. Res. Associate, 1961–62, Vis. Scientist (part-time), 1963–64, MIT; Vis. Prof., Dept. of Chem., Cornell Univ., 1966. Member: Accademia Nazionale delle Scienze—detta dei XL; EMBO; Internat. Foundn for Artificial Intelligence, Tokyo; NY Acad. of Scis; MAE; Hon. Fellow: Inst. of Biology, 1990; Belgian Royal Acad. of Medicine, 1990. Hon. DSc NUI, 1990. Europe and Medicine Prize, Inst des Scis de la Santé, Paris, 1993. *Publications:* numerous papers on protein structure and functions, biological catalysis, biotechnology; articles on sci. res. policy and bioethics. *Address:* Directorate-General for Science, Research and Development, Commission of the European Communities, 200 rue de la Loi, 1049 Brussels, Belgium. *T:* (2) 2953570.

FASSETT, Kaffe; textile designer; *b* 7 Dec. 1937; *s* of William Elliot Fassett and Madeleine Fassett. Self-educated. Retrospective exhibn, Tokyo, 1986; V&A Museum, 1989; Copenhagen, Stockholm, Oslo, Melbourne, Toronto and Helsinki, 1990; Vancouver, 1993. *Publications:* Glorious Knitting, 1985; Glorious Needlepoint, 1987; Kaffe Fassett at the V & A, 1988, 4th edn, as Glorious Colour, 1991; Family Album, 1989; Glorious Inspiration, 1991; Kaffe's Classics, 1994; Glorious Interiors, 1995. *Address:* c/o Random Century, 20 Vauxhall Bridge Road, SW1V 2SA.

FATAYI-WILLIAMS, Hon. Atanda, GCON 1983; CFR 1980; Chief Justice of Nigeria, 1979–83; *b* 22 Oct. 1918; *s* of Alhaji Issa Williams and Alhaja Ashakun Williams; *m* 1948, Irene Violet Lofts; three *s*. *Educ:* Methodist Boys' High Sch., Lagos, Nigeria; Trinity Hall, Cambridge (BA 1946, LLM 1947, MA 1949; Hon. Fellow 1983). Called to the Bar, Middle Temple, 1948. Private practice, Lagos, 1948–50; Crown Counsel, Lagos, 1950–55; Dep. Comr for Law Revision, Western Nigeria, 1955–58; Chief Registrar, High Court of Western Nigeria, 1958–60; High Court Judge, 1960–67; Justice of Appeal, Western State Court of Appeal, 1967–69; Justice, Supreme Court of Nigeria, 1969–79. Mem., Council of State, 1983–84, 1990–. Chairman: Ports Arbitration Bd, 1971; All Nigeria Law Reports Cttee, 1972–75; Body of Benchers, 1979–80; Legal Practitioners' Privileges Cttee, 1979–83; Federal Judicial Service Commn, 1979–83; Judiciary Consultative Cttee, 1979–83; National Archives Cttee, 1979–83; Presidential Cttee on Medical Doctors' Remuneration, 1990; Bd of Trustees, The Van Leer Nigerian Educn Trust, 1973–85; Crescent Bearers, Lagos, 1978–84; Council of Legal Educn, 1984–. Mem., Nigerian Inst. of Internat. Affairs, 1972–. Trustee, Nigerian Youth Trust, 1979–84. Hon. Fellow, Nigerian Inst. of Advanced Legal Studies, 1983; Life FRSA 1949. Presidential Award for outstanding service to the Judiciary, Nigeria, 1992. *Publications:* (ed) Western Nigeria Law Reports, 1955–58; (with Sir John Verity) Revised Laws of the Western Region of Nigeria,

1959; Sentencing Processes, Practices and Attitudes, as seen by an Appeal Court Judge, 1970; Faces, Cases and Places (autobiog.), 1983. *Recreations:* reading, swimming, walking, speed-boats. *Address:* 8 Adetokunbo Ademola Street, Victoria Island, Lagos, Nigeria. *T:* Lagos 611315. *Clubs:* Athenæum, United Oxford & Cambridge University; Metropolitan, Motor Boat (Lagos).

FATCHETT, Derek John; MP (Lab) Leeds Central, since 1983; *b* 22 Aug. 1945; *s* of Herbert and Irene Fatchett; *m* 1969, Anita Bridgens (*née* Oakes); two *s*. *Educ:* Monks Road Primary School; Lincoln School; Birmingham University (LLB); LSE (MSc). Research Officer, LSE, 1968–70; Research Fellow, University College, Cardiff, 1970–71; Lectr in Industrial Relations, Univ. of Leeds, 1971–83. Labour Whip, 1986–87; Opposition spokesman on education (secondary and tertiary), 1987, on education and training, 1988–92; Opposition front bench spokesman on trade and industry, 1992–94, on defence, 1994–. Dep. Campaigns Co-ordinator, 1987–92. *Publications:* (jtly) Workers Participation in Management, 1972; (jtly) Worker Participation: industrial control and performance, 1974; (jtly) The Worker Directors, 1976; Trade Unions and Politics in the 1980's: the political fund ballots, 1987; articles in learned jls. *Recreations:* gardening, cricket, jogging. *Address:* 130 Bradford Road, Wakefield, Yorks WF1 2AN. *T:* Wakefield (01924) 375291.

FATEH, Abul Fazal Muhammad Abul; Hon. Representative of Royal Commonwealth Society in Bangladesh, 1985–94; *b* 28 Feb. 1926; *s* of Abdul Gafur and Zohra Khatun; *m* 1956, Mahfuza Banu; two *s*. *Educ:* Dhaka, Bangladesh. MA (English Lit.); special course, LSE, 1949–50. Carnegie Fellow in Internat. Peace, 1962–63. Entered Pakistan Foreign Service, 1949; 3rd Secretary: Paris, 1951–53; Calcutta, 1953–56; 2nd Sec., Washington, DC, 1956–60; Dir, Min. of Foreign Affairs, Karachi, 1961–65; 1st Sec., Prague, 1965–66; Counsellor, New Delhi, 1966–67; Dep. High Comr for Pakistan, Calcutta, 1968–70; Ambassador of Pakistan, Baghdad, 1971; Adviser to Actg President of Bangladesh, Aug. 1971; Foreign Sec., Bangladesh, Jan. 1972; Ambassador of Bangladesh to France and Spain, 1972–75; Permanent Deleg. to UNESCO, 1972–76; High Comr for Bangladesh in London, 1976–77; Ambassador, Algeria, 1977–82. Leader, Bangladesh Delegation: Commonwealth Youth Ministers' Conf., Lusaka, 1973; Meeting of UN Council on Namibia, Algiers, 1980; Ministerial Meeting of Non-aligned Countries Co-ordination Bureau on Namibia, Algiers, 1981. Chm., Commonwealth Human Ecology Council Symposium, 1977. *Address:* 9a Linhope Street, NW1 6ES.

FATT, Prof. Paul, FRS 1969; Emeritus Professor, University of London, since 1989. Professor of Biophysics, University College, London, 1976–89 (Reader, 1956–76); Fellow, UCL, 1973. *Publications:* papers in various scientific jls. *Address:* Department of Protein and Molecular Biology, Royal Free Hospital School of Medicine, Rowland Hill Street, NW3 2PF. *T:* 0171–794 0500.

FAULDS, Andrew Matthew William; MP (Lab) Warley East, since 1974 (Smethwick, 1966–74); *b* 1 March 1923; *s* of late Rev. Matthew Faulds, MA, and of Doris Faulds; *m* 1945, Bunty Whitfield; one *d*. *Educ:* George Watson's, Edinburgh; King Edward VI Grammar Sch., Louth; Daniel Stewart's, Edinburgh; High Sch., Stirling; Glasgow Univ. Three seasons with Shakespeare Memorial Co., Stratford-upon-Avon; BBC Repertory Co.: Jet Morgan in Journey into Space (BBC). Has appeared in over 35 films and many TV and radio performances. Parliamentary Private Secretary: to Minister of State for Aviation, Min. of Technology, 1967–68; to Postmaster General, 1968–69; Opposition spokesman for the Arts, 1970–73, 1979–82; Chairman: British br., Parly Assoc. for Euro-Arab Cooperation, 1974–; All-Party Parly Heritage Gp; Member: British Delegn to Council of Europe and WEU, 1975–80, and 1987–92; Exec. Cttee, GB China Centre, 1976–; Exec. Cttee, IPU, (British Section), 1983–92; Exec. Cttee, Franco-British Council. *Recreation:* cosseting his constituents. *Address:* 14 Albemarle Street, W1X 3HA. *T:* 0171–499 7589.

FAULKNER OF DOWNPATRICK, Lady; Lucy (Barbara Ethel) Faulkner, CBE 1985; *b* 1 July 1925; *d* of William John Forsythe and Jane Ethel Sewell; *m* 1951, Arthur Brian Deane Faulkner (MP (NI) 1949–73; PC 1959; *cr* Baron Faulkner of Downpatrick, 1977) (killed in a hunting accident, 1977); two *s* one *d*. *Educ:* Aubrey House; Bangor Collegiate Sch.; Trinity College Dublin. BA (Hons History). Journalist, Belfast Telegraph, 1947; Personal Secretary to Sir Basil Brooke, Prime Minister of N Ireland, 1949. Nat. Governor for NI, BBC, 1978–85; Chm., Broadcasting Council for NI, 1981–85; Researcher, 1977, Trustee 1980–, Ulster Historical Foundation; Mem., NI Tourist Bd, 1985–91. Governor, Linenhall Library, 1982–. Hon. LLD QUB, 1994. *Recreations:* hunting and dressage, genealogy, book collecting. *Address:* Toberdoney, Farranfad, Downpatrick BT30 8NH. *T:* Seaforde (0139687) 712. *Club:* Royal Over-Seas League.

FAULKNER, David Ewart Riley, CB 1985; Senior Research Associate, Oxford Centre for Criminological Research, and Fellow, St John's College, Oxford, since 1992; *b* 23 Oct. 1934; *s* of Harold Ewart and Mabel Faulkner; *m* 1961, Sheila Jean Stevenson; one *s* one *d*. *Educ:* Manchester Grammar Sch.; Merchant Taylors' Sch., Northwood; St John's Coll., Oxford (MA Lit Hum). Home Office: Asst Principal, 1959; Private Sec. to Parly Under-Sec. of State, 1961–63; Principal, 1963; Jt Sec. to Inter-Party Conf. on House of Lords Reform, 1968; Private Sec. to Home Sec., 1969–70; Asst Sec., Prison Dept, 1970, Establishment Dept, 1974, Police Dept, 1976; Asst Under-Sec. of State, 1976; Under Sec., Cabinet Office, 1978–80; Home Office; Asst Under-Sec. of State, Dir of Operational Policy, Prison Dept, 1980–82; Dep. Under-Sec. of State, 1982; Head of Criminal and Res. and Statistical Depts, 1982–90; Principal Estab. Office, 1990–92. Member: UN Cttee on Crime Prevention and Control, 1984–91; Adv. Bd, Helsinki Inst. for Crime Prevention and Control, 1988–93; Council, Magistrates' Assoc., 1992–; Council, Justice, 1993–. Trustee, Mental Health Foundn, 1992–, and other charities. *Recreations:* railways, birds. *Address:* St John's College, Oxford OX1 3JP.

See also R. O. Faulkner.

FAULKNER, Sir Dennis; *see* Faulkner, Sir J. D. C.

FAULKNER, Prof. Douglas, WhSch, BSc, PhD; FEng 1981, FRINA, FIStructE, FSNAME; RCNC; Head of Department of Naval Architecture and Ocean Engineering, University of Glasgow, 1973–95, now Emeritus Professor; *b* 29 Dec. 1929; *s* of Vincent and Florence Faulkner; *m* 1st, 1954, Jenifer Ann Cole-Adams (marr. diss. 1986); three *d*; *m* 2nd, 1987, Isobel Parker Campbell. *Educ:* Sutton High Sch., Plymouth; HM Dockyard Technical Coll., Devonport; RNC, Greenwich. Aircraft Carrier Design, 1955–57; Production Engrg, 1957–59; Structural Research at NCRE, Dunfermline, 1959–63; Asst Prof. of Naval Construction, RNC, Greenwich, 1963–66; Structural Adviser to Ship Dept, Bath, 1966–68; Naval Construction Officer att. to British Embassy, Washington DC, 1968–70, and Mem. Ship Research Cttee, Nat. Acad. of Scis, 1968–71; Res. Associate and Defence Fellow, MIT, 1970–71; Structural Adviser to Ship Dept, Bath, and to the Merrison Box Girder Bridge Cttee, 1971–73. UK Rep., Standing Cttee, Internat. Ship Structures Congress, 1973–85. Chm., Conoco-ABS cttee producing a design code for Tension Leg Platforms offshore, 1981–83; Dir, Veritec Ltd, 1985–88; Mem. Bd of Govs, BMT Quality Assessors Ltd, 1990–. FRSA 1983. Consulting Editor, Jl of Marine Structures, 1990– (Editor, 1987–90). Hon. DSc Technical Univ. of Gdansk, 1993. David W. Taylor Medal, SNAME, 1991; William Froud Medal, RINA, 1993; Peter the Great Medal, St Petersburg Univ. of Ocean Technology, 1993. *Publications:* (ed jtly) Integrity of Offshore Structures, 1981; Integrity of Offshore Structures—3, 1987; Integrity of Offshore Structures—4, 1990; Integrity of Offshore Structures—5, 1993; chapters in Ship Structural Design Concepts (Cornell Maritime Press), 1975; papers related to structural design of ships, in Trans RINA, Jl of Ship Res., Behaviour of Offshore Structures, etc. *Recreations:* hill walking, swimming, music, chess. *Address:* 4 Murdoch Drive, Milngavie, Glasgow G62 6QZ. *T:* 0141–956 5071.

FAULKNER, Hugh (Branston), OBE 1980; Hon. Director, Persistent Virus Disease Research Foundation, since 1992; Director, Help the Aged, from formation, 1961–83; *b* Lutterworth, 8 June 1916; *s* of Frank and Ethel Faulkner; *m* 1954, Anne Carlton Milner; one *s* one *d*. *Educ:* Lutterworth Grammar Sch. FCIS. Educn Administration, City of Leicester, 1936–46; Organising Sec., Fellowship of Reconciliation, 1946–54; business and charity career from 1954. Hon. Dir and later Dir, Voluntary and Christian Service, 1954–79; a Director: Helpage International Ltd, 1966–83; Help the Aged Housing Appeal, 1975–83; Dir, Asthma Res. Council and Asthma Soc., 1983–88. Christian peace delegate to USSR, 1952, followed by lecture tour in USA, 1953, on internat. relations; deleg. and speaker, UN World Assembly on Ageing, Vienna, 1982. Mem., Exec. Cttee, Council for Music in Hospitals, 1983–. Trustee: World in Need Trust; Lester Trust; Andrews Pension Trust; Voluntary and Christian Service; Nat. Asthma Training Centre; Advr, Elderly Accommodation Counsel; Member: Help the Aged Housing Assoc., 1966–; Voluntary Service Housing Assoc. (formerly Voluntary and Christian Service Housing Assoc.), 1980–. *Recreations:* music, gardening. *Address:* Longfield, 4 One Tree Lane, Beaconsfield, Bucks HP9 2BU. *T:* Beaconsfield (01494) 674769. *Club:* National Liberal.

FAULKNER, Sir (James) Dennis (Compton), Kt 1991; CBE 1980; VRD 1960; DL; Chairman, Marlowe Cleaners Ltd, since 1973; *b* 22 Oct. 1926; *s* of James and Nora Faulkner; *m* 1952, Janet Cunningham (*d* 1994); three *d*. *Educ:* College of St Columba, Co. Dublin. Served RNVR, 1946–71; UDR, 1971–92 (Col Comdt, 1986–92). Chairman: Belfast Collar Co. Ltd, 1957–63; Belfast Savings Bank, 1960–61; NI Develt Agency, 1978–82; Board Member: Gallaher NI, 1980–89 (Chm., 1982–89); Northern Bank Ltd, 1983–; Chm., Ladybird (NI) Ltd, 1963–88. Farming, 1946–. Chairman: Strangford Lough Management Cttee, 1992–; Ulster, North Down and Ards Hosp. Trust, 1993–94. DL County Down, 1988. *Recreations:* sailing, hunting, ocean racing. *Address:* Northern Ireland. *Clubs:* Royal Ocean Racing, Royal Cruising; Royal Yacht Squadron; Cruising Club of America (New York).

FAULKNER, John Richard Hayward; theatre and management consultant; international impresario; *b* 29 May 1941; *s* of Richard Hayward Ollerton and Lilian Elizabeth (*née* Carrigan); *m* 1970, Janet Gill (*née* Cummings) (*d* 1994); two *d* two step *d*. *Educ:* Archbishop Holgate's Sch., York; Keble Coll., Oxford (BA). Worked with a number of theatre companies, Prospect Productions, Meadow Players, Century Theatre, Sixty-Nine Theatre Co., Cambridge Theatre Co., toured extensively, UK, Europe, Indian Sub-Continent, Australia, 1960–72; Drama Director: Scottish Arts Council, 1972–77; Arts Council of GB, 1977–83; Head, Artistic Planning, Nat. Theatre, 1983–88. Director: Minotaur Films, 1988–; Visionhaven Ltd, 1991–; New Zoo Develts Ltd, 1992–. Mem. Bd, Pleasance Theatre Trust, 1995–. Trustee: The Arts Educational Schools, 1986–; The Arts for Nature, 1990–; Performing Arts Labs, 1991–. *Recreations:* intricacies and wildernesses. *Address:* 28 Ellesmere Road, Chiswick W4 4QH. *T:* 0181–995 3041.

FAULKNER, Most Rev. Leonard Anthony; *see* Adelaide, Archbishop of, (RC).

FAULKNER, Richard Oliver; First Deputy Chairman, Football Trust; Joint Managing Director, Westminster Communications Group Ltd, since 1989; *b* 22 March 1946; *s* of late Harold Ewart and Mabel Faulkner; *m* 1968, Susan Heyes; two *d*. *Educ:* Merchant Taylors' Sch., Northwood; Worcester Coll., Oxford (MA PPE). Research asst and journalist, Labour Party, 1967–69; PRO, Construction Ind. Trg Bd, 1969–70; Editor, Steel News, 1971; Account dir, F. J. Lyons (PR) Ltd, 1971–73; Dir, PPR International, 1973–76. Co-founder, parly jl The House Magazine; communications advisor: to Leader of the Opposition and Labour Party (unpaid), gen. elections, 1987, 1992; to the Bishop at Lambeth, 1990; Govt relations adviser: Fyffes Gp, 1973–; rly trade unions, 1975–76; C. A. Parsons & Co., 1976–77; Pool Promoters Assoc., 1977–; British Rlys Bd, 1977–; Prudential Assurance Co., 1978–88; TSB Gp, 1987–; IPU, 1988–90; Southampton City Council, 1989–91; CAMRA, 1989; Barclays de Zoete Wedd, 1990–92; Standard Life Assurance, 1990–; S Glam CC, 1991–94; Cardiff Bay Develt Corp., 1993–; Littlewoods Orgn, 1994–. Football Trust: Foundn Trustee, 1979–82; Sec., 1983–86; Dep. Chm., 1986–90; Chm., Sports Grounds Initiative, 1995–; Member: Sports Council, 1986–88; Football League enquiry into membership schemes, 1984, anti-hooliganism cttee, 1987–90; former dir, Wimbledon and Crystal Palace Football Clubs; Chm., Women's Football Assoc., 1988–91. Vice-Chm., Transport 2000 Ltd, 1986–. Mem., Merton Borough Council, 1971–78; contested (Lab) Devizes 1970, Feb. 1974, Monmouth, Oct. 1974, Huddersfield W, 1979. *Recreations:* collecting Lloyd George memorabilia, tinplate trains, watching Association Football, travelling by railway. *Address:* Cowley House, Little College Street, SW1P 3XS. *T:* 0171–222 0666. *Club:* Reform.

See also D. E. R. Faulkner.

FAULKS, Esmond James; His Honour Judge Faulks; a Circuit Judge, since 1993; *b* 11 June 1946; *s* of Hon. Sir Neville Faulks, MBE, TD and Bridget Marigold (*née* Bodley); *m* 1972, Pamela Margaret Ives; one *s* one *d*. *Educ:* Uppingham Sch.; Sidney Sussex Coll., Cambridge (MA). Called to the Bar, Inner Temple, 1968; a Recorder, 1987–93. *Recreations:* country pursuits. *Address:* Chesterwood, Haydon Bridge, Northumberland NE47 6HW. *T:* Hexham (01434) 684329.

FAULKS, His Honour Peter Ronald, MC 1943; a Circuit Judge, 1980–90; *b* 24 Dec. 1917; *s* of late M. J. Faulks and A. M. Faulks (*née* Ginner); *m* 1949, Pamela Brenda, *d* of Peter Lawless; two *s*. *Educ:* Tonbridge; Sidney Sussex Coll., Cambridge (MA). Served War of 1939–45, Duke of Wellington's Regt, Dunkirk, N Africa, Anzio, etc; Major 1943; wounded 3 times. Admitted a solicitor, 1949. A Recorder of the Crown Court, 1972–80. Dep. Chm., Agricultural Land Tribunal (SE England), 1972–80; Pres., Berks, Bucks and Oxon Law Soc., 1976–77. *Recreation:* country life. *Address:* Downs Cottage, Westbrook, Boxford, Newbury, Berks RG20 8DJ. *T:* Boxford (01488) 605382. *Clubs:* MCC, Farmers'.

See also S. C. Faulks.

FAULKS, Sebastian Charles; author and journalist; *b* 20 April 1953; *s* of His Honour Peter Ronald Faulks, *qv* and Pamela (*née* Lawless); *m* 1989, Veronica Youlten; one *s* one *d*. *Educ:* Wellington Coll.; Emmanuel Coll., Cambridge. Editor, New Fiction Society, 1978–81; Daily Telegraph, 1978–82; feature writer, Sunday Telegraph, 1983–86; Literary Editor, Independent, 1986–89; Dep. Editor, 1989–90, Associate Editor, 1990–91, Independent on Sunday; columnist, The Guardian, 1992–. *Publications:* A Trick of the Light, 1984; The Girl at the Lion d'Or, 1989; A Fool's Alphabet, 1992; Birdsong, 1993; contribs to newspapers and magazines. *Recreation:* cricket. *Address:* c/o Aitken and Stone, 29 Fernshaw Road, SW10 0TG.

FAULL, David Wenlock, OBE 1993; Consultant, Winckworth & Pemberton, since 1990 (Senior Partner, 1985–90); *b* 25 Feb. 1929. *Educ:* Taunton School. Qualified Solicitor, 1954; joined Winckworth & Pemberton, 1978; Diocesan Registrar: St Albans, 1960–79; Chelmsford, 1960–89; Southwark, 1960–93; London, 1969–; Dep. Registrar, Dio. of Europe, 1980; Legal Sec., Bishop of Rochester, 1960–; Chapter Clerk and Solicitor to St Paul's Cathedral, 1981–. Mem., Solicitors' Disciplinary Tribunal, 1992. Chm., Ecclesiastical Law Assoc., 1988–90; Treasurer, Ecclesiastical Law Soc., 1986. Founder Mem., Paddington Church's Housing Assoc., 1964; Bd Mem., Sutton and Hastoe Housing Assoc., 1987. Chm., Christian Children's Fund (GB), 1992. *Recreations:* walking, theatre, Cornish history. *Address:* Ayr House, Upper Basildon, near Pangbourne, Berks RG8 8LU. *T:* Upper Basildon (01491) 671323; (office) 0171–222 7811. *Club:* Athenæum.

FAUSET, Ian David; Assistant Under-Secretary of State, Civilian Management (Personnel), Ministry of Defence, since 1991; *b* 8 Dec. 1943; *s* of late George William Fauset and Margaret Fauset (*née* Davies); *m* 1972, Susan, *d* of Donald and Gwendolen Best; two *s* one *d. Educ:* Chester City Grammar Sch.; King Edward VI Sch., Lichfield; University of London (BSc); UCW Aberystwyth (Dip. Statistics). CEng, FRAeS. Dept of Chief Scientist (RAF), MoD, 1968–78; Head of Air Studies, Defence Optl Analysis Orgn, Germany, 1978–82; fast jet aircraft and helicopter projects, MoD (PE), 1982–87; Civilian Management (Specialists), MoD, 1987–89; Project Dir, Tornado Aircraft, 1989, EH 101 Helicopter, 1989–91, MoD (PE). Non-Exec. Dir, GEC Avery, 1991–94. *Recreations:* bridge, opera, cricket, tennis, squash, rowing (mainly watching now). *Address:* Ministry of Defence, Lacon House, Theobalds Road, WC1X 8RY. *Club:* Athenæum.

FAUVELLE, Major Michael Henry; barrister-at-law; *b* 12 Aug. 1920; *s* of Victor Edmond Fauvelle and Brigid Mary Fauvelle (*née* Westermann); *m* 1964, Marie-Caroline, *e d* of Count and Countess Stanislas d'Orsetti, Château de la Grènerie, Jarzé, France; one *s* one *d. Educ:* Stonyhurst Coll.; Royal Military Coll., Sandhurst. Commissioned, 2/Lieut The South Lancashire Regt, 1939, T/Major 1944; active service in N Africa, Italy and Palestine (wounded three times, arguably five); Staff employment as GSO 3 (Ops), Gibraltar, 1947; Staff Captain Q HQ Palestine, 1947–48; Staff Captain A HQ BMM to Greece and HQ 2 Inf. Bde, 1948–50; Adjt 1st Bn, 1951; Major 1952; retired, 1953. Called to the Bar, Lincoln's Inn, 1955; Western Circuit and Hampshire Sessions, 1955–; Dep. Recorder, Oxford, Bournemouth and Reading, 1971; a Dep. Circuit Judge, 1972–79; a Recorder, 1979–92; Hd of Chambers at 17 Carlton Crescent, Southampton, 1975–82. Pres., Pensions Appeal Tribunals for England and Wales, 1987–93 (a Chm., 1983–93; Dep. Pres., 1984–87). Lord Chancellor's Legal Visitor, 1983–90. *Recreation:* avoiding stress. *Address:* Tadley Cottage, Wherwell, Hampshire SP11 7JU. *T* and *Fax:* Chilbolton (01264) 860217. *Clubs:* Hampshire (Winchester); Home Guard (Wherwell, Hants).

FAVELL, Anthony Rowland; solicitor and company director; Chairman, Tameside and Glossop Acute Services NHS Trust, since 1993; *b* 29 May 1939; *s* of Arnold Rowland Favell and Hildegard Favell; *m* 1966, Susan Rosemary Taylor; one *s* one *d. Educ:* St Bees School, Cumbria; Sheffield University (LLB). MP (C) Stockport, 1983–92; contested (C) Stockport, 1992. *Recreations:* music, gardening, hill walking, dry stone walling. *Address:* Skinners Hall, Edale, Sheffield S30 2ZE. *T:* Hope Valley (01433) 670281. *Club:* Lansdowne.

FAWCETT, Colin, QC 1970; *b* 22 Nov. 1923; *s* of late Frank Fawcett, Penrith; *m* 1952, Elizabeth Anne Dickson; one *s* one *d. Educ:* Sedbergh. Commnd Border Regt, 1943. Called to Bar, Inner Temple, 1952, Bencher, 1978. Mem., Criminal Injuries Compensation Bd, 1983–. *Recreations:* fishing, music. *Address:* 6 Hubert Day Close, Beaconsfield, Bucks HP9 1TL. *T:* Beaconsfield (01494) 670755.

FAWCETT, John Harold, CMG 1986; HM Diplomatic Service, retired; *b* 4 May 1929; *yr s* of late Comdr Harold William Fawcett, OBE, RN, and of late Una Isobel Dalrymple Fawcett (*née* Gairdner); *m* 1961, Elizabeth Shaw; one *s. Educ:* Radley (Scholar); University Coll., Oxford (Scholar). 1st cl. Hon. Mods 1951, 2nd cl. Lit. Hum. 1953. Nat. Service, RN (Radio Electrician's Mate), 1947–49. British Oxygen Co., 1954–63 (S Africa, 1955–57). Entered Foreign Service, 1963; FO, 1963–66; 1st Sec. (Commercial), Bombay, 1966–69; 1st Sec. and Head of Chancery, Port-of-Spain, 1969–70; Asst, Caribbean Dept, FCO, 1971–72; Head of Icelandic Fisheries Unit, Western European Dept, FCO, 1973; Amb. to Democratic Republic of Vietnam, 1974; Counsellor and Head of Chancery, Warsaw, 1975–78; Dep. High Comr, Wellington, 1978–86; Counsellor (Commercial and Economic, 1978–83, Political and Economic, 1983–86), and Head of Chancery 1983–86, Wellington; Amb. to Bulgaria, 1986–89. Mem., 1989–94, Lay Chm., 1994–, Ewecross Deanery Synod, dio. of Bradford. Chm., Morecambe Bay Gp, CS Pensioners' Alliance, 1994–. Clerk, 1989–94, Chm. of Govs, 1994–, Dent Grammar Sch. Educnl Foundn; Governor, Dent C of E Primary Sch., 1994–. *Recreations:* gardening, collecting books, mathematical models. *Address:* Strait End, Dent, Cumbria LA10 5QL. *Clubs:* Savile; Wellington Racing (Wellington); Royal Bombay Yacht.

FAWCETT, Kay-Tee; *see* Khaw, Kay-Tee.

FAWCUS, Maj.-Gen. Graham Ben, CB 1991; Chief of Staff and Head of UK Delegation, Live Oak, SHAPE, 1989–91, retired; *b* 17 Dec. 1937; *s* of late Col Geoffrey Arthur Ross Fawcus, RE and Helen Sybil Graham (*née* Stronach); *m* 1966, Diana Valerie, *d* of Dr P. J. Spencer-Phillips of Bildeston, Suffolk; two *s* one *d. Educ:* Wycliffe College; RMA Sandhurst (Sword of Honour); King's College, Cambridge (BA 1963, MA 1968). Commissioned RE, 1958; served UK, Cyprus, BAOR, MoD; OC 39 Field Squadron RE, BAOR, 1973–74; MoD, 1975–76; GSO1 (DS), Staff College, 1977–78; CO 25 Engineer Regt, BAOR, 1978–81; Cabinet Office, 1981; Comdt, RSME, 1982–83; ACOS, HQ 1 (Br) Corps, 1984–85; Chief, Jt Services Liaison Orgn, Bonn, 1986–89. Col Comdt RE, 1991–. Chm., RE Widows Soc., 1992–. *Recreations:* ski-ing, tennis, Scottish country dancing, furniture restoration. *Address:* Flowton Hall, Flowton, Ipswich, Suffolk IP8 4LH.

FAWCUS, Sir (Robert) Peter, KBE 1964 (OBE 1957); CMG 1960; Overseas Civil Service, retd; *b* 30 Sept. 1915; *s* of late A. F. Fawcus, OBE; *m* 1943, Isabel Constance (*née* Ethelston); one *s* one *d. Educ:* Charterhouse; Clare Coll., Cambridge. Served RNVR, 1939–46 (Lt-Comdr). Joined Colonial Service (District Officer, Basutoland), 1946; Bechuanaland Protectorate: Govt Sec., 1954; Resident Commissioner, 1959; HM Commissioner, 1963–65; retd 1965. *Address:* Dochart House, Killin, Perthshire FK21 8TN.

FAWCUS, Simon James David; His Honour Judge Fawcus; a Circuit Judge, since 1985; *b* 12 July 1938; *s* of late Ernest Augustus Fawcus and of Jill Shaw; *m* 1966, Joan Mary (*née* Oliphant); one *s* four *d. Educ:* Aldenham Sch.; Trinity Hall, Cambridge (MA). Called to the Bar, Gray's Inn, 1961; in practice on Northern Circuit, 1962–85; a Recorder, 1980–85. *Recreations:* real tennis and other lesser sporting activities, music (listening). *Address:* Rosehill, Brook Lane, Alderley Edge, Cheshire SK9 7QG. *Clubs:* MCC; Manchester Tennis and Racquet, Big Four (Manchester); Circuit Judges Golfing Soc.

FAWKES, Sir Randol (Francis), Kt 1977; Attorney-at-Law, since 1948; *b* 20 March 1924; *s* of Edward Ronald Fawkes and Mildred Fawkes (*née* McKinney); *m* 1951, Jacqueline Fawkes (*née* Bethel); three *s* one *d. Educ:* public schools in the Bahamas. Called to the Bar, Bahamas, 1948. A founder: Citizen Cttee, 1949; People's Penny Savings Bank, 1951. Elected Mem. (Progressive Liberal Party), House of Assembly, 1956; promoted law establishing Labour Day as Public Holiday, 1961. Founder, and Pres. 1955–, Bahamas Fedn of Labour (led 19 day general strike which resulted in major labour and political reforms, 1958). Represented Labour Party at constitutional confs in London, 1963 and 1968; addressed UN Cttee of 24 on preparation of Bahamas for independence, 1966. Gen Sec., Bahamas Assoc. of former Mems of Parlt, 1990. *Publications:* You Should Know Your Government, 1949; The Bahamas Government, 1962; The New Bahamas, 1966; The Faith That Moved The Mountain: a memoir of a life and the times, 1977; Majority of One: the first 450 of the PLP–Labour Coalition, 1987. *Recreations:* swimming, music, Bible tract writing. *Address:* PO Box N-7625, John F. Kennedy Drive, Nassau, NP, Bahamas. *T:* (office) (32) 34053; (home) (32) 34855.

FAWKES, Wally; cartoonist, since 1945; *b* 21 June 1924; *m* 1st, 1949, Sandra Boyce-Carmichelle; one *s* two *d*; 2nd, 1965, Susan Clifford; one *s* one *d. Educ:* Sidcup Central Sch.; Sidcup Sch. of Art; Camberwell Sch. of Art. Came from Vancouver, BC, to England, 1931. Joined Daily Mail, 1945; started Flook strip, 1949, transferred to The Mirror, 1984. Political cartoons for: Spectator, 1959–; Private Eye, and New Statesman, 1965–; Observer, and Punch, 1971–; Today, 1986–87; London Daily News, 1987. Co-Founder, Humphrey Lyttelton Band, 1948. *Publications:* World of Trog, 1977; Trog Shots, 1984; Trog: 40 Graphic Years, 1987; collections of Flook strips. *Recreations:* playing jazz (clarinet and soprano saxophone), cooking, cricket. *Address:* 44 Laurier Road, NW5 1SJ. *T:* 0171–267 2979. *Clubs:* MCC, Middlesex County Cricket.

FAY, Dr Christopher Ernest; Chairman and Chief Executive, Shell UK, since 1993; *b* 4 April 1945; *s* of Harry Thomas Fay and Edith Margaret Fay (*née* Messenger); *m* 1971, Jennifer Olive Knight; one *s* two *d. Educ:* Leeds Univ. (BSc Civil Eng. 1967; PhD 1970). FICE 1994 (MICE 1973); CEng; FInstPet 1994. Joined Shell Internat. Petroleum Co., 1970, as offshore design engr; Shell-BP Develt Co., Nigeria, 1971–74; Head, Engrg Planning and Design and Offshore Construction, Sarawak Shell Berhad, Malaysia, 1974–78; Develt Manager, Dansk Undergrunds Consortium, Copenhagen, on secondment from Dansk Shell, 1978–81; Technical Manager, Norske Shell Exploration and Production, Stavanger, 1981–84; Dir, Exploration and Production, Norway, 1984–86; Gen. Manager and Chief Exec., Shell Cos, Turkey, 1986–89; Man. Dir, Shell UK Exploration and Production and a Man. Dir, Shell UK, 1989–93. Member: CBI President's Cttee, 1993–; INSEAD UK Cttee, 1993–; British Cttee, Det. Norske Veritas, 1994–; Bd, Oil and Gas Projects and Supplies Office, 1994–; Exec. Cttee, British Energy Assoc., 1994–; Chm., Oil Industries Emergency Cttee, 1993–. Mem. Council, Motability, 1993–. CIMgt 1994. FRSA 1994. *Recreations:* gardening, ski-ing, golf, squash, tennis, Rugby. *Address:* Shell UK, Shell-Mex House, Strand, WC2R 0DX. *Clubs:* Wentworth Golf, Bramley Golf, Royal Aberdeen Golf.

FAY, His Honour Edgar Stewart, QC 1956; FCIArb; a Circuit Judge (formerly an Official Referee of the Supreme Court of Judicature), 1971–80; *b* 8 Oct. 1908; *s* of late Sir Sam Fay; *m* 1st, Kathleen Margaret, *e d* of late C. H. Buell, Montreal, PQ, and Brockville, Ont; three *s*; 2nd, Jenny Julie Henriette (*d* 1990), *yr d* of late Dr Willem Roosegaarde Bisschop, Lincoln's Inn; one *s. Educ:* Courtenay Lodge Sch.; McGill Univ.; Pembroke Coll., Cambridge (MA). Called to Bar, Inner Temple, 1932; Master of the Bench, 1962. FCIArb 1981. Recorder: of Andover, 1954–61; of Bournemouth, 1961–64; of Plymouth, 1964–71; Dep. Chm., Hants QS, 1960–71. Member: Bar Council, 1955–59, 1966–70; Senate of Four Inns of Court, 1970–72. Chm., Inquiry into Crown Agents, 1975–77. *Publications:* Why Piccadilly?, 1935; Londoner's New York, 1936; Discoveries in the Statute Book, 1937; The Life of Mr Justice Swift, 1939; Official Referees' Business, 1983. *Address.* Knox End, Ashdon, Saffron Walden, Essex CB10 2HR. *T:* Ashdon (01799) 584275.

FAY, Sir (Humphrey) Michael (Gerard), Kt 1990; Chairman, Fay, Richwhite & Co. Ltd, Merchant Bankers, since 1975; *b* 10 April 1949; *s* of James and Margaret Fay; *m* 1983, Sarah Williams; one *s* two *d. Educ:* St Patrick's Coll., Silverstream, Wellington; Victoria Univ., Wellington (LLB 1971). Jt Chief Exec., Capital Markets, 1986–; Dir, Bank of New Zealand, 1989–92. Chairman: Australia/NZ Bicentennial Commn, 1988; Expo 1988 Commn, 1987–88; Expo 1992 Commn, 1989–. Chm., NZ Americas Cup Challenges, 1987, 1988, 1992. *Recreations:* yachting, horse breeding and racing, fishing, swimming. *Address:* PO Box 1650, Auckland, New Zealand. *T:* (649) 3663600. *Clubs:* Northern (Auckland); Royal New Zealand Yacht Squadron, Auckland Racing, Mercury Bay Boating.

FAY, Sir Michael; *see* Fay, Sir H. M. G.

FAYERS, Norman Owen; City Treasurer and Director of Financial Services, Bristol City Council, since 1990; *b* 8 Jan. 1945; *s* of Claude Lance Fayers and Winifred Joyce (*née* Reynolds); *m* 1966, Patricia Ann Rudd; two *s. Educ:* Northgate Grammar Sch. for Boys, Ipswich; BA Open Univ. IPFA; IRRV; MAAT. Ipswich CBC, 1961–66; Eastbourne CBC, 1966–70; Group Accountant (Educn), Royal Borough of Kingston upon Thames, 1970–73; Chief Accountant, RBK & C, 1973–77; Chief Officer, Finance, London Borough of Ealing, 1977–90. Chartered Institute of Public Finance and Accountancy: Mem. Council, 1991–92; Pres., S Wales and W England Reg., 1993–95 (Vice Pres., 1991–92); Mem. Council, Assoc. of Accounting Technicians, 1992–. *Recreations:* golf, squash, music, bridge. *Address:* The Council House, College Green, Bristol BS99 7BL. *T:* Bristol (0117) 922 2417.

FAYRER, Sir John (Lang Macpherson), 4th Bt *cr* 1896; research associate; *b* 18 Oct. 1944; *s* of Sir Joseph Herbert Spens Fayrer, 3rd Bt, DSC, and Helen Diana Scott (*d* 1961), *d* of late John Lang; *S* father, 1976. *Educ:* Edinburgh Academy; Scottish Hotel School, Univ. of Strathclyde. *Heir:* none. *Address:* Overhailes, Haddington, East Lothian EH41 3SB.

FEACHEM, Prof. Richard George Andrew, CBE 1995; PhD, DSc; FEng; Senior Adviser on population, health and nutrition, World Bank; *b* 10 April 1947; *s* of Charles George Paulin Feachem and Margaret Flora Denise Greenhow; *m* 1970, Zuzana Sedlarova; one *s* one *d. Educ:* Wellington Coll.; Univ. of Birmingham (BSc 1969); Univ. of NSW (PhD 1974); DSc (Med) London, 1991. MICE 1980; FIWEM 1987; FICE 1990; FEng 1994. Volunteer, Solomon Is, 1965–66; Research Fellow: Univ. of NSW, 1970–74; Univ. of Birmingham, 1974–76; London School of Hygiene and Tropical Medicine: Lectr and Sen. Lectr, 1976–82; Reader, 1983–87; Prof. of Tropical Envmtl Health, 1987–95; Dean, 1989–95; Vis. Prof., 1995–. Consultant, WHO, 1982–83; Principal Public Health Specialist, World Bank, 1988–89; Chairman, Advisory Committee: World Develt Report, 1992–93; TB Programme, WHO, 1992–95; Member: Adv. Cttee, Caribbean Epidemiology Centre, 1990–95; Mgt Cttee, Inst. of Child Health, 1989–91; Bd on Internat. Health, US Nat. Acad. of Scis, 1992–. Member Council: RSTM&H, 1978–81; VSO, 1991–; Water Aid, 1994–95; Patron, Assoc. for Promotion of Healthcare in former Soviet Union, 1992–. Trustee Internat. Centre for Diarrhoeal Diseases Research, Bangladesh, 1985–89. Hon. FFPHM 1990. Member, Editorial Board: Transactions of the

RSTM&H, 1979–88; Jl of Tropical Medicine and Hygiene, 1979–; Current Issues in Public Health, 1993–; Health and Human Rights, 1993–. *Publications:* Water, Wastes and Health in Hot Climates, 1977; Subsistence and Survival: rural ecology in the Pacific, 1977; Water, Health and Development, 1978; Evaluation for Village Water Supply Planning, 1980; Sanitation and Disease, 1983; Environmental Health Engineering in the Tropics, 1983; Evaluating Health Impact, 1986; Disease and Mortality in Sub-Saharan Africa, 1991; The Health of Adults in the Developing World, 1992; over 140 papers in scientific jls. *Recreations:* mountaineering, ski-ing. *Address:* London School of Hygiene and Tropical Medicine, Keppel Street, WC1E 7HT. *T:* 0171–927 2237. *Club:* Travellers'.

FEARN, John Martin, CB 1976; Secretary, Scottish Education Department, 1973–76, retired; *b* 24 June 1916; *s* of William Laing Fearn and Margaret Kerr Fearn; *m* 1947, Isobel Mary Begbie, MA, MB, ChB; one *d. Educ:* High Sch. of Dundee; Univ. of St Andrews; Worcester Coll., Oxford. Indian Civil Service, Punjab, 1940–47; District Magistrate, Lahore, 1946; Scottish Home Dept, 1947; Under-Sec., 1966; Under-Sec., Scottish Educn Dept, 1968. Chairmen's Panel, CSSB, 1977–85. *Recreation:* golf. *Address:* 31 Midmar Gardens, Edinburgh EH10 6DY. *T:* 0131–447 5301. *Club:* New (Edinburgh).

FEARN, Sir (Patrick) Robin, KCMG 1991 (CMG 1983); HM Diplomatic Service, retired; *b* 5 Sept. 1934; *s* of late Albert Cyprian Fearn and Hilary (*née* Harrison); *m* 1961, Sorrel Mary Lynne Thomas; three *s* one *d. Educ:* Ratcliffe Coll.; University Coll., Oxford (BA Hons, Mod. Langs). Nat. Service, Intelligence Corps, 1952–54. Overseas marketing, Dunlop Rubber Co. Ltd, 1957–61; entered Foreign Service, 1961; FO, 1961–62; Third, later Second Sec., Caracas, 1962–64; Havana, 1965; First Sec., Budapest, 1966–68; FCO, 1969–72; Head of Chancery, Vientiane, 1972–75; Asst Head of Science and Technol. Dept, FCO, 1975–76; Counsellor, Head of Chancery and Consul Gen., Islamabad, 1977–79; Head of S America Dept, FCO, 1979–82; Head of Falkland Islands Dept, FCO, 1982; RCDS, 1983; Ambassador to Cuba, 1984–86; Asst Under-Sec. of State (Americas), FCO, 1986–89; Ambassador to Spain, 1989–94. *Recreations:* tennis, golf, reading, family life. *Address:* c/o Barclays Bank, 5a Marylebone High Street, W1M 4AH. *Club:* United Oxford & Cambridge University.

FEARN, Ronald Cyril, (Ronnie), OBE 1985; *b* 6 Feb. 1931; *s* of James Fearn and Martha Ellen Fearn; *m* 1955, Joyce Edna Dugan; one *s* one *d. Educ:* King George V Grammar School. FCIB. Banker with Williams Deacons Bank, later Williams & Glyn's Bank, later Royal Bank of Scotland. MP Southport, 1987–92 (L 1987–88, Lib Dem, 1988–92); contested (Lib Dem) Southport, 1992. Lib Dem spokesman on health and tourism, 1988–89, on local govt, 1989–90, on transport, housing and tourism, 1990–92. Councillor, Sefton MBC, 1974–. *Recreations:* badminton, amateur dramatics, athletics. *Address:* Norcliffe, 56 Norwood Avenue, Southport, Merseyside PR9 7EQ. *T:* Southport (01704) 28577.

FEARNLEY, David; Vice Lord-Lieutenant, West Yorkshire, since 1992; Director, Allied Textiles plc, since 1971; *b* 20 Dec. 1924; *s* of late Wilfred Fearnley and Elizabeth (*née* Walker); *m* 1947, Patricia Bentley; one *s* one *d. Educ:* Pocklington Sch., York; Univs of Bradford and Leeds. Served RN, War of 1939–45. Joined family firm, Walter Walker & Sons Ltd, 1945; Dir, 1955; Man. Dir, 1960; co. purchased by Allied Textiles, 1971. Chm., Louis Latour Ltd, 1990–; Dir, WW Gp Ltd, 1990–. Gen. Comr of Inland Revenue, Wakefield Div., 1973– (Chm., 1987–). Mem. Bd, Wakefield Prison, 1979–94. Fellow, Woodard Corp., 1989–95. High Sheriff, W Yorks, 1982–83. *Recreations:* fell walking, wine, tennis (playing), Rugby football (watching). *Address:* The Grange, Hopton, Mirfield, W Yorks WF14 8EL. *Clubs:* Garrick; Leeds (Leeds).

FEATES, Prof. Francis Stanley, CB 1991; PhD; CEng, FIChemE; FRSC; CChem; Professor of Environmental Engineering, University of Manchester Institute of Science and Technology, 1991–95; *b* 21 Feb. 1932; *s* of Stanley James Feates and Dorothy Marguerite Jenny Feates (*née* Orford); *m* 1953, Gwenda Grace Goodchild; one *s* three *d. Educ:* John Ruskin Sch., Croydon; Birkbeck Coll. London (BSc Special Chem.; PhD). FRSC 1972; FIChemE 1991; CEng 1991. Wellcome Res. Foundn, 1949–52; Chester-Beatty Cancer Res. Inst., Univ. of London, 1952–54. Chemistry Lectr, Goldsmiths' Coll., London, 1954–56; AERE, Harwell, UKAEA, 1956–78; Argonne Nat. Lab., Univ. of Chicago, Illinois, 1965–67; Department of the Environment: Dir, Nuclear Waste Management, 1978–83; Chief Radiochemical Inspector, 1983–86; Chief Inspector, Radioactive Substances, HM Inspectorate of Pollution, 1986–88; Dir and Chief Inspector, HM Inspectorate of Pollution, 1989–91. Consultant to EEC on nuclear decommissioning, 1992–93. Director: Sir Alexander Gibb & Partners, 1991–; Siemens Plessey Controls Ltd, 1991–92; Grundon Waste Management, 1991–92. Expert Mem., Scientific and Technical Cttee, EEC, Brussels, 1989–; Member: Steering Cttee, Nuclear Energy Agency, OECD, Paris, 1988–91; Steering Bd, Lab. of Govt Chemist, 1991–; Observer Mem., NRPB, 1988–91. Founder Editor, Jl of Hazardous Materials, 1975–85. *Publications:* Hazardous Materials Spills Handbook, 1982; Integrated Pollution Management, 1995; numerous scientific papers on nuclear power, electrochemistry, thermodynamics, waste management, electron microscopy. *Recreations:* walking, cycling, travel. *Address:* The Kilns, Beggarsbush Hill, Benson, Oxon OX10 6PL. *T:* Wallingford (01491) 839276.

FEATHER, Prof. John Pliny, FLA; Professor of Information and Library Studies, since 1988, and Dean of Education and Humanities, since 1994, Loughborough University; *b* 20 Dec. 1947; *m* 1971, Sarah, *d* of late Rev. A. W. Rees and Mrs S. M. Rees. *Educ:* Heath Sch., Halifax; Queen's Coll., Oxford (BLitt, MA); MA Cambridge, PhD Loughborough. FLA 1986. Asst Librarian, Bodleian Liby, Oxford, 1972–79; Munby Fellow in Bibliography, Cambridge Univ., 1977–78; Loughborough University: Lectr, then Sen. Lectr, 1979–88; Head, Dept of Inf. and Liby Studies, 1990–94. Vis. Prof., UCLA, 1982. Pres., Oxford Bibliographical Soc., 1988–92. Mem., many nat. and internat. professional cttees; consultancy and teaching in many countries and for UNESCO, EEC and British Council, 1977–. *Publications:* The Provincial Book Trade in Eighteenth-Century England, 1985; A Dictionary of Book History, 1987; A History of British Publishing, 1988; Preservation and the Management of Library Collections, 1991; Index to Selected Bibliographical Journals 1971–1985, 1991; Publishing, Piracy and Politics: a history of copyright in the British book trade, 1994; The Information Society, 1994; articles and reviews in academic and professional jls, conf. procs, etc. *Recreations:* photography, music, travel, cooking (and eating) good food. *Address:* 36 Farnham Street, Quorn, Leicestershire LE12 8DR. *Clubs:* Athenæum; Grolier (New York).

FEATHERSTONE, Hugh Robert, CBE 1984 (OBE 1974); FCIS, FCIT; Director-General, Freight Transport Association, 1969–84; *b* 31 March 1926; *s* of Alexander Brown Featherstone and Doris Olive Martin; *m* 1948, Beryl Joan Sly; one *s* one *d. Educ:* Minchenden Sch., Southgate, London. FCIS 1956; FCIT 1970. Served War, RNVR, 1943–46 (Sub-Lt). Assistant Secretary: Nat. Assoc. of Funeral Dirs, 1946–48; Brit. Rubber Develt Bd, 1948–58; Asst Sec. 1958–60, Sec. 1960–68, Traders Road Transport Assoc. *Publications:* contrib. to jls concerned with transport and admin. *Recreations:* golf, gardening, languages, travel, bridge, cookery.

FEAVER, Rt. Rev. Douglas Russell; *b* 22 May 1914; *s* of late Ernest Henry Feaver, Bristol; *m* 1st, 1939, Katharine (*d* 1987), *d* of late Rev. W. T. Stubbs; one *s* two *d*; 2nd, 1988, Mary Frances Clare Harvey, *qv. Educ:* Bristol Grammar School; Keble College, Oxford (Scholar; 1st cl. Hons. Mod. History, 1935; 1st Cl. Hons. Theology, 1937; Liddon Student, 1935–37; MA); Wells Theological College. Deacon 1938, priest 1939, St Albans; Curate, St Albans Abbey, 1938–42. Chaplain, RAFVR, 1942–46. Canon and Sub-Dean of St Albans, 1946–58; Chaplain to St Albans School, 1946–58; Proctor in Convocation, 1951–58; Examining Chaplain to Bp of St Albans, 1948–58, to Bp of Portsmouth, 1960–72; Vicar of St Mary's, Nottingham and Rural Dean of Nottingham, 1958–72; Hon. Canon of Southwell, 1958–72; Treasurer, 1959–69; Proctor in Convocation for Southwell, 1970–72; Bishop of Peterborough, 1972–84. Chairman of Trent House Boys' Probation Hostel, 1967–72; Governor of Nottingham Bluecoat School, 1958–72. *Publications:* reviews and articles in Church Times. *Recreation:* conferences not attended. *Address:* 6 Mill Lane, Bruton, Somerset BA10 0AT.

See also W. A. Feaver.

FEAVER, William Andrew; art critic, The Observer, since 1975; *b* 1 Dec. 1942; *s* of Rt. Rev. Douglas Russell Feaver, *qv*; *m* 1st, 1964, Victoria Turton (marr. diss.); one *s* three *d*; 2nd, 1985, Andrea Rose; two *d. Educ:* St Albans School; Nottingham High School; Keble College, Oxford. Teacher: South Stanley Boys' Modern Sch., Co. Durham, 1964–65; Newcastle Royal Grammar Sch., 1965–71; Sir James Knott Res. Fellow, Newcastle Univ., 1971–73; art critic: The Listener, 1971–75; Financial Times, 1974–75; art adviser, Sunday Times Magazine, 1974–75. Critic of the Year, UK Press Awards, 1984. *Publications:* The Art of John Martin, 1975; When We Were Young, 1976; Masters of Caricature, 1981; Pitmen Painters, 1988. *Recreation:* painting. *Address:* 1 Rhodesia Road, SW9 9EJ. *T:* 0171–737 3386.

FEDDEN, (Adye) Mary, (Mrs J. O. Trevelyan), RA 1992; RWEA; painter; *b* 14 Aug. 1915; *d* of Harry Vincent Fedden and Ida Margaret Fedden; *m* 1951, Julian Otto Trevelyan, Sen. Hon. RA (*d* 1988). *Educ:* Badminton Sch., Bristol; Slade Sch. of Art (Schol). Exhibns yearly in London and provinces, 1948–; paintings in collections of the Queen, Crown Prince of Jordan, Tate Gall., city art galls in UK, Australia, USA, and in private collections in England and overseas. Tutor: Royal College of Art, 1956–64; Yehudi Menuhin Sch., 1964–74. Pres., Royal West of England Acad., 1984–88. *Recreation:* reading. *Address:* Durham Wharf, Hammersmith Terrace, W6 9TS.

FEDIDA, Sam, OBE 1980; independent consultant, information systems, retired; inventor of Prestel, viewdata system (first public electronic information service); *b* 1918; *m* 1942, Joan Iris Druce. Served Royal Air Force, Radar Officer, 1940–46. Became Asst Dir of Research, The English Electric Company; started research for the Post Office, 1970; Prestel first in use 1979, as public service; MacRobert Award, Council of Engineering Instns, 1979; Prestel sold in Europe, USA, Far East. *Address:* Constable Cottage, 23 Brook Lane, Felixstowe, Suffolk IP11 7JP.

FEESEY, Air Vice-Marshal John David Leonard, AFC 1977; Director General, Policy and Plans, National Air Traffic Services, since 1993; *b* 11 Oct. 1942; *s* of Leonard Ewart Feesey and Maisie Veronica Lillian Feesey; *m* 1968, Glenda Doris Barker; two *s. Educ:* Oldershaw Grammar Sch., Wallasey, Cheshire. MRAeS 1987. RAF Officer Cadet, 1961; commnd General Duties Br., 1962; RAF pilot (Hunter, Harrier), 1962–83; OC No 1 (Fighter) Sqdn (Harrier), 1983–86; Stn Comdr, RAF Wittering, 1986–88; Comnd Exec. Officer, HQ AAFCE, 1989–91; Dir Airspace Policy, HQ NATS, 1991–93. *Recreations:* hill walking, fishing, gardening. *Address:* HQ National Air Traffic Services, Room T1407, CAA House, 45–59 Kingsway, WC2B 6TE. *T:* 0171–832 5782. *Club:* Royal Air Force.

FEHR, Basil Henry Frank, CBE 1979; Life President, Frank Fehr & Co. Ltd UK and group of companies, 1992; Chairman, Fehr Bros (Industries) Inc., New York, 1992; *b* 11 July 1912; *s* of Frank E. Fehr, CBE and Jane (*née* Poulter); *m* 1st, 1936, Jane Marner (*née* Tallent) (marr. diss. 1951); two *s* one *d*; 2nd, 1951, Greta Constance (*née* Bremner) (marr. diss. 1971); one *d* one step *d*; 3rd, 1974, Anne Norma (*née* Cadman); one *d. Educ:* Rugby Sch.; Neûchatel Ecole de Commerce, Switzerland. Served War, 1939–45: HAC, later Instr, Gunnery Sch. of Anti-Aircraft, RA; retd Major. Joined father in family firm, Frank Fehr & Co., 1934; Partner, 1936; Governing Dir, Frank Fehr & Co. London, 1948; Pres., 1949, Chm., 1979–92, Fehr Bros (Manufactures) New York, later Fehr Bros Inc. New York; Chm. and Man. Dir, Frank Fehr & Co. Ltd London and group of cos, 1957–91. Chairman: Cocoa Assoc. of London, 1952; London Commodity Exchange, 1954; London Oil and Tallow Trades Assoc., 1955; Copra Assoc. of London, 1957; Inc. Oilseed Assoc., 1958; United Assocs Ltd, 1959. Elected to Baltic Exchange, 1936; Director: Baltic Mercantile and Shipping Exchange, 1963–69 and 1970–77 (Vice Chm. 1973–75, Chm. 1975–77, Hon. Mem. 1991); Colyer Fehr Hldgs Pty, Sydney, 1976– (Chm. 1984–89). Jurat of Liberty of Romney Marsh, 1979. *Recreations:* sports generally, farming. *Address:* Slodden Farm, Dymchurch, Romney Marsh, Kent TN29 0LW. *T:* Dymchurch (01303) 872241. *Clubs:* City Livery, Aldgate Ward, MCC, Royal Automobile, Little Ship; Ski Club of Great Britain; West Kent Cricket; Littlestone Golf.

FEIBUSCH, Hans; painter, mural painter, lithographer, sculptor, writer; *b* 15 Aug. 1898; *s* of Dr Carl Feibusch and Marianne Ickelheimer; *m* 1935, Sidonie (*d* 1963), *e d* of D. Gestetner. *Educ:* Frankfurt a/M and Munich Univs. Studied at the Berlin Academy, at Paris Art Schs, in Florence and Rome; received German State award and grant in 1931; pictures in German Public Galleries; work banned and destroyed by Nazis in 1933; since then in London; large mural paintings in churches: St Wilfred's, Brighton; St Elizabeth's, Eastbourne; St Martin's, Dagenham; St John's, Waterloo Road, SE1; St Ethelburga's, Bishopsgate; St Alban's, Holborn; Town Hall, Dudley; Civic Centre, Newport, Mon (designs bought by V&A for Newport Mus., 1991); Chichester Cathedral; Chichester Palace; Parish Churches, Egham, Goring, Wellingborough, Welling, Preston, Plumstead, Eltham, Portsmouth, Bexley Heath, Wembley, Merton, Southwark, Harrow, Exeter, Battersea, Rotherhithe, Plymouth, Coventry, Christchurch Priory, Bournemouth, Christ Church, St Laurence, Sydney, Portmeirion, Bath; West London Synagogue; statues: St John the Baptist, St John's Wood Church; Christ, Ely Cathedral; Risen Christ, St Alban's Church EC1; posthumous portrait of Bishop Bell, Bonhoeffer Church, Forest Hill, 1994. 80th birthday exhibn by GLC, Holland Park, 1978; 6 one-man exhibns, incl. Berlin 1980; retrospective exhibn 1925–85, Historisches Museum, Frankfurt, 1986; retrospective exhibitions: Frankfurt, 1987, 1988; Brighton Polytechnic, 1988; Pallant Gall., Chichester, 1995. Much portrait and figure sculpture, 1975–. Dr of Letters, Lambeth, 1985. German Cross of Merit, 1967, Grand Cross of Merit, 1989. *Publications:* Mural Painting, 1946; The Revelation of Saint John, 1946. *Recreations:* music and poetry. *Address:* 30 Wadham Gardens, NW3 3DP. *T:* 0171–586 1456, (studio) 0171–286 7420.

FEILDEN, Sir Bernard (Melchior), Kt 1985; CBE 1976 (OBE 1969); FRIBA 1968 (ARIBA 1949); Consultant, Feilden and Mawson, Chartered Architects (Partner, 1956–77); Member, Cathedrals Advisory Commission for England, since 1981; *b* 11 Sept. 1919; *s* of Robert Humphrey Feilden, MC, and Olive Feilden (*née* Binyon); *m* 1949, Ruth Mildred Bainbridge (*d* 1994); two *s* two *d. Educ:* Bedford Sch. Exhibr, Bartlett Sch. of Architecture, 1938 (Hon. Fellow, UCL, 1985). Served War of 1939–45: Bengal Sappers and Miners. AA Diploma (Hons), 1949; Bratt Colbran Schol., 1949. Architect, Norwich Cathedral, 1963–77; Surveyor to the Fabric: York Minster, 1965–77; St Paul's Cathedral, 1969–77;

Consultant Architect, UEA, 1969–77. Dir, Internat. Centre for the Preservation and Restoration of Cultural Property, Rome, 1977–81. Hoffman Wood Prof. of Architecture, Leeds Univ., 1973–74. Mem., Ancient Monuments Bd (England), 1964–77; Mem. Council, RIBA, 1972–77; President: Ecclesiastical Architects' and Surveyors' Assoc., 1975–77; Guild of Surveyors, 1976–77. FSA 1969; FRSA 1973; Hon. FAIA 1987. Corresp. Mem., Architectes en Chef, France. DUniv York, 1973; Hon. DLitt: Gothenburg, 1988; East Anglia, 1989. Aga Khan Award for Architecture, 1986. *Publications:* The Wonder of York Minster, 1976; Introduction to Conservation, 1979; Conservation of Historic Buildings, 1982; Between Two Earthquakes, 1987; Guidelines for Conservation, 1989; articles in Architectural Review, Chartered Surveyor, AA Quarterly. *Recreations:* painting, sailing, fishing, photography. *Address:* Stiffkey Old Hall, Stiffkey, near Wells-on-Sea, Norfolk NR23 1JQ. *T:* Fakenham (01328) 830585. *Club:* Norfolk (Norwich).

See also G. B. R. Feilden.

FEILDEN, Geoffrey Bertram Robert, CBE 1966; MA Cantab; FRS 1959; Founder FEng 1976, FIMechE, Hon. FIStructE; Hon. FIQA; CBIM; Hon. MIED; Principal Consultant, Feilden Associates, since 1981; *b* 20 Feb. 1917; *s* of Robert Humphrey Feilden, MC, and Olive Feilden (*née* Binyon); *m* 1st, Elizabeth Ann Gorton; one *s* two *d*; 2nd, Elizabeth Diana Angier (*née* Lloyd). *Educ:* Bedford Sch.; King's Coll., Cambridge (Scholar). Lever Bros. and Unilever Ltd, 1939–40; Power Jets Ltd, 1940–46; Ruston and Hornsby Ltd, 1946–59; Chief Engineer, Turbine Dept, 1949; Engineering Dir, 1954; Man. Dir, Hawker Siddeley Brush Turbines Ltd, and Dir of Hawker Siddeley Industries Ltd, 1959–61; Gp Technical Dir, Davy-Ashmore Ltd, 1961–68; Dep. Dir Gen., British Standards Instn, 1968–70, Dir Gen. 1970–81. Director: Averys Ltd, 1974–79; Plint & Partners Ltd, 1982–. Member: Cttees and Sub-Cttees of Aeronautical Research Council, 1947–62; BTC Res. Adv. Council, 1956–61; Council for Sci. and Indust. Res. of DSIR, 1961–65; Design Council (formerly CoID), 1966–78 (Dep. Chm., 1977–78); Central Adv. Council for Science and Technology, 1970–71; Vis. Cttee to RCA, 1968–84 (Chm., 1977–84); Res. Develt and Engrg Cttee, Industrial Develt Bd for NI, 1983–86; Chm., UK Panel for CODATA (formerly British Nat. Cttee on Data for Sci. and Technol.), 1988– (UK Deleg. to CODATA, 1989–); Pres., European Cttee for Standardisation, 1977–79. Member, Royal Society Delegation: to USSR, 1965; Latin America, 1968; People's Republic of China, 1975; Leader, BSI Delegn to People's Republic of China, 1980. Technical Adviser to Govt of India, 1968. DSIR Visitor to Prod. Engineering Res. Assoc. of Gt Brit., 1957–65, and to Machine Tool Industry Res. Assoc., 1961–65. Member Council: Royal Society (a Vice-Pres., 1967–69); IMechE, 1955–61, 1969–80; Univ. of Surrey, 1977–78. Trustee: Maurice Lubbock Meml Fund, 1973–; Smallpeice Trust, 1981–88. Senior Fellow, RCA, 1986. Hon. DTech Loughborough, 1970; Hon. DSc QUB, 1971. MacRobert Award for innovation (jt winner), 1983; Hodgson Prize, RAeS, 1994. *Publications:* Gas Turbine Principles and Practice (contributor), 1955; First Bulleid Memorial Lecture (Nottingham Univ.), 1959; Report, Engineering Design, 1963 (Chm. of Cttee); numerous papers and articles on engineering subjects. *Recreations:* sailing, skiing, driving kitchen and garden machines. *Address:* Verlands, Painswick, Glos GL6 6XP. *T:* Painswick (01452) 812112. *Club:* Athenæum.

See also Sir B. M. Feilden.

FEILDEN, Sir Henry (Wemyss), 6th Bt *cr* 1846; *b* 1 Dec. 1916; *s* of Col Wemyss Gawne Cunningham Feilden, CMG (*d* 1943) (3rd *s* of 3rd Bt) and Winifred Mary Christian (*d* 1980), *d* of Rev. William Cosens, DD; *S* cousin, Sir William Morton Buller Feilden, 5th Bt, 1976; *m* 1943, Ethel May, 2nd *d* of John Atkinson, Annfield Plain, Co. Durham; one *s* two *d*. *Educ:* Canford Sch.; King's Coll., London. Served War, RE, 1940–46. Clerical Civil Service, 1960–79. *Recreations:* watching cricket, reading. *Heir:* *s* Henry Rudyard Feilden, BVetSc, MRCVS [*b* 26 Sept. 1951; *m* 1982, Anne Shepperd; one *s*]. *Address:* Little Dene, Heathfield Road, Burwash, Etchingham, East Sussex TN19 7HN. *T.* Burwash (01435) 882205. *Club:* MCC.

FEILDING, family name of **Earl of Denbigh.**

FEINBERG, Peter Eric; QC 1992; a Recorder, since 1994; *b* 26 Oct. 1949; *s* of Leon and May Feinberg; *m* 1988, Tini Flannery; two *s*. *Educ:* Bradford Grammar Sch.; University College London (LLB Hons). Called to the Bar, Inner Temple, 1972; Asst Recorder, 1990. Pres., Mental Health Tribunals, 1995. *Recreations:* opera, music, jogging, Czechoslovakia. *Address:* 1 Crown Office Row, Temple, EC4Y 7HH. *T:* 0171–583 3724. *Club:* Lambs.

FEINSTEIN, Prof. Charles Hilliard, PhD; FBA 1983; Professor of Economic History, University of Oxford, since 1989; Fellow, All Souls College, since 1989; *b* 18 March 1932; *s* of Louis and Rose Feinstein; *m* 1st, 1958, Ruth Loshak; one *s* three *d*; 2nd, 1980, Anne Digby. *Educ:* Parktown Boys' High Sch., Johannesburg; Univ. of Witwatersrand (BCom 1950); Fitzwilliam Coll., Cambridge (PhD 1958). CA (SA) 1954. Cambridge University: Research Officer, Dept of Applied Econs, 1958–63; Univ. Lectr in Faculty of Econs, 1963–78; Clare College: Fellow, 1963–78, Hon. Fellow, 1994; Sen. Tutor, 1969–78; Prof. of Econ. and Social History, 1978–87, and Head, Dept of Econ. and Related Studies, 1981–86, Univ. of York; Reader in Recent Social and Econ. History, and Professorial Fellow, Nuffield Coll., 1987–89, Univ. of Oxford. Harvard University: Vis. Res. Fellow, Russian Res. Centre, 1967–68; Vis. Scholar, Dept of Econ., 1986–87; Vis. Lectr, Univ. of Delhi, 1972. W. D. Wilson Vis. Fellow, Univ. of Cape Town, 1994. Vice-Pres., British Acad., 1991–93 (Mem. Council, 1990–93); Mem. Council: Royal Economic Soc., 1980–94; Economic History Soc., 1980–; Mem., Economic Affairs Cttee, SSRC, 1982–86 (Chm., 1985–86). Governor, NIESR, 1985–. Man. Editor, The Economic Jl, 1980–86. *Publications:* Domestic Capital Formation in the United Kingdom 1920–1938, 1965; (ed) Socialism, Capitalism and Economic Growth, Essays presented to Maurice Dobb, 1967; National Income, Expenditure and Output of the United Kingdom 1855–1965, 1972; (ed) York 1831–1981, 1981; (jtly) British Economic Growth 1856–1973, 1982; (ed) The Managed Economy: Essays in British Economic Policy and Performance since 1929, 1983; Studies in Capital Formation 1750–1920, 1988. *Recreations:* reading, buying books. *Address:* Treetops, Harberton Mead, Headington, Oxford OX3 0DB.

FELDMAN, Sir Basil, Kt 1982; Chairman: National Union of Conservative Party, 1985–86 (Vice-Chairman, 1982–85; Vice-President, since 1986); National Union Executive Committee, since 1991 (Member, since 1975); Chairman: Better Made in Britain Campaign, since 1983; London Arts Season, since 1993; Festival of Arts and Culture, since 1994; *b* 23 Sept. 1926; *s* of late Philip and Tilly Feldman; *m* 1952, Gita Julius; two *s* one *d*. *Educ:* Grocers' School. National Union of Conservative and Unionist Associations, Greater London area: Dep. Chm., 1975–78; Chm., 1978–81; Pres., 1981–85; Vice Pres., 1985–; Jt Nat. Chm., Cons. Party's Impact 80s Campaign, 1982–87; Chm., Team 1000, 1989–93; Member: Policy Gp for London, 1975–81, 1984–87; Nat. Campaign Cttee, 1976 and 1978; Adv. Cttee on Policy, 1981–86; Cttee for London, 1984–87; Vice-Pres., Greater London Young Conservatives, 1975–77; President: Richmond and Barnes Cons. Assoc., 1976–84; Hornsey Cons. Assoc., 1978–82; Patron, Hampstead Cons. Assoc., 1981–86. Contested GLC Elections, Richmond, 1973; Member: GLC Housing Management Cttee, 1973–77; GLC Arts Cttee, 1976–81. Mem., Free Enterprise Loan Soc., 1977–84. Chairman: Martlet Services Gp Ltd, 1973–81; Solport Ltd, 1980–85; The Quality Mark, 1987–92. Chairman: Market Opportunities Adv. Gp, DTI, 1991–93; Shopping Hours Reform Council, 1988–94; Better Business Opportunities, 1990–; Watchpost Ltd, 1983–; Dir, Young Enterpreneurs Fund, 1985–95. Underwriting Mem. of Lloyds, 1979–. Membre Consultatif, Institut Internat. de Promotion et de Prestige, Geneva (affiliated to Unesco), 1978–. Member: Post Office Users National Council, 1978–81 (Mem., Tariffs Sub-Cttee, 1980–81); English Tourist Board, 1986–; Chairman: Clothing EDC (NEDO), 1978–85; Maker/User Working Party (NEDO), 1988–89. Gov., Sports Aid Foundn, 1990–. Mem., Internat. Council, Los Angeles Philharmonic, 1995–. FRSA 1987. *Publications:* Some Thoughts on Jobs Creation (for NEDO), 1984; Constituency Campaigning: a guide for Conservative Party workers; several other Party booklets and pamphlets. *Recreations:* golf, tennis, theatre, opera, travel. *Club:* Carlton.

FELDMAN, Prof. Stanley, FFARCS; Professor of Anaesthetics, Charing Cross and Westminster Medical School, University of London, since 1989; *b* 10 Aug. 1930; *s* of Israel and Lilly Feldman; *m* 1957, Carole Bowman; one *s* one *d*. *Educ:* London Univ. (BSc 1950); Westminster Med. Sch. (MB BS 1955). FFARCS 1962. Fellow, Univ. of Washington, Seattle, 1957–58; Westminster Hospital: Registrar, 1958–62; Consultant Anaesthetist, 1962–89; Sen. Lectr, RPMS, 1963–66. Postgrad. Advr in Anaesthetics, RCS, 1966–72; Res. Consultant, Royal Nat. Orthopaedic Hosp. NHS Trust, 1995–. Vis. Prof., Stanford Univ., 1967–68. Hon. Member: Australasian Soc. Anaesthetists; Spanish Portuguese Soc. Anaesth.; Belgian Soc. Anaesth.; Netherlands Soc. Anaesthetists; Israeli Soc. Anaesth. Editor, Review of Anaesthetic Pharmacology, 1992–. *Publications:* Anatomy for Anaesthetists, 1963, 6th edn 1991; Scientific Foundations of Anaesthesia, 1971, 4th edn 1990; Muscle Relaxants, 1973, 2nd edn 1981; Drug Mechanisms in Anaesthesia, 1981, 2nd edn 1993. *Recreations:* sailing, travel. *Address:* Magill Department of Anaesthetics, Chelsea Westminster Hospital, SW10 9NH. *T:* 0181–746 8024. *Clubs:* Royal Society of Medicine, Royal Thames Yacht.

FELDSTEIN, Prof. Martin Stuart; Professor, Harvard University, since 1969; *b* 25 Nov. 1939; *m* Kathleen Foley; two *d*. *Educ:* Harvard Coll. (AB *summa cum laude* 1961); Oxford Univ. (BLitt 1963, MA 1964, DPhil 1967). Nuffield College, Oxford University: Research Fellow, 1964–65; Official Fellow, 1965–67; Lectr in Public Finance, Oxford Univ., 1965–67; Harvard University: Asst Professor, 1967–68; Associate Professor, 1968–69. President, National Bureau of Economic Research, 1977–82 and 1984–; Chm., Council of Economic Advrs, 1982–84. Director: American International Gp; J. P. Morgan; TRW. Member: Amer. Philosophical Soc.; Amer. Acad. of Arts and Scis; Trilateral Commn; Council on Foreign Relations. *Publications:* (ed) The American Economy in Transition, 1980; Hospital Costs and Health Insurance, 1981; Inflation, Tax Rules, and Capital Formation, 1983; Capital Taxation, 1983; Effects of Taxation on Capital Formation, 1986; United States in the World Economy, 1988; International Economic Co-operation, 1988; American Economic Policy in the 1980s, 1994. *Address:* National Bureau of Economic Research, 1050 Massachusetts Avenue, Cambridge, MA 02138, USA.

FELL, Sir Anthony, Kt 1982; *b* 18 May 1914; *s* of Comdr David Mark Fell, RN; *m* 1938, June Warwick; one *s* one *d*. *Educ:* New Zealand. Contested (C) Brigg, 1948, South Hammersmith, 1949 and 1950. MP (C) Yarmouth, Norfolk, 1951–66 and 1970–83. *Address:* 11 Denny Street, SE11 4UX.

FELL, Sir David, KCB 1995 (CB 1990); Head of Northern Ireland Civil Service, and Second Permanent Under Secretary of State, Northern Ireland Office, since 1991; *b* 20 Jan. 1943; *s* of Ernest Fell and Jessie (*née* McCreedy); *m* 1967, Sandra Jesse (*née* Moore); one *s* one *d*. *Educ:* Royal Belfast Academical Instn; The Queen's University of Belfast (BSc: Pure and Applied Mathematics, also (1st Cl. Hons) Physics). Sales Manager, Rank Hovis McDougall Ltd, 1965–66; Teacher, 1966–67; Research Associate, 1967–69; Civil Servant, 1969–: Dept of Agriculture (NI), 1969–72; Dept of Commerce (NI), 1972–82 (Under Secretary, 1981); Under Secretary, Dept of Economic Development (NI), 1982; Dep. Chief Exec., Industrial Develt Bd for NI, 1982–84; Permanent Sec., Dept of Economic Develt (NI), 1984–91. CIMgt; FRSA. *Recreations:* music, reading, golf, Rugby Union. *Address:* Stormont Castle, Belfast BT4 3ST. *T:* Belfast (01232) 528145. *Club:* Old Instonians (Belfast).

FELL, Richard Taylor; HM Diplomatic Service; Counsellor and Deputy Head of Mission, Bangkok, since 1993; *b* 11 Nov. 1948; *s* of late Eric Whineray Fell and Margaret Farrer Fell (*née* Taylor); *m* 1981, Claire Gates; three *s*. *Educ:* Bootham Sch., York; Bristol Univ. (BSc); Univ. of London (MA). Joined HM Diplomatic Service, 1971; Ottawa, 1972–74; Saigon, 1974–75; Vientiane, 1975; First Sec. and Chargé d'Affaires *ai*, Hanoi, 1979; First Sec., UK Delegn to NATO, 1979–83; First Sec. and Head of Chancery, Kuala Lumpur, 1983–86; FCO, 1986–88; on secondment to Thorn EMI, 1988–89; Counsellor, Ottawa, 1989–93. *Publication:* Early Maps of South-East Asia, 1988. *Recreations:* antiques, reading, sport. *Address:* c/o Foreign and Commonwealth Office, SW1A 2AH.

FELL, Robert, CB 1972; CBE 1966; Commissioner of Banking, Hong Kong, 1984–87; *b* 6 May 1921; *s* of Robert and Mary Ann Fell, Cumberland; *m* 1946, Eileen Wicks; two *s* one *d*. *Educ:* Whitehaven Grammar School. War Office, 1939; military service, 1940–46 (despatches); BoT, 1947; Trade Comr, Qld, 1954–59; Asst Sec., Tariff Div., 1961; Commercial Counsellor, Delhi, 1961–66; Under-Sec. i/c export promotion, 1967–71; Sec., ECGD, 1971–74; Chief Exec., The Stock Exchange, 1975–82; Comr for Securities, Hong Kong, 1981–84. Mem., British Overseas Trade Board, 1972–75; Pres., City Branch, BIM, 1976–82. FRSA. *Recreations:* Rugby football (watching), gardening. *Club:* Travellers'.

FELLGETT, Prof. Peter Berners, PhD; FRS 1986; Professor of Cybernetics, University of Reading, 1965–87, now Emeritus; *b* 11 April 1922; *s* of Frank Ernest Fellgett and Rose, (Rowena), (*née* Wagstaffe); *m* 1947, Janet Mary, *o d* of late Prof. G. E. Briggs, FRS and Mrs Nora Briggs; one *s* two *d*. *Educ:* The Leys Sch., Cambridge; Univ. of Cambridge (BA 1943, MA 1947, PhD 1952). Isaac Newton Student, Cambridge Observatories, 1950–51; Lick Observatory, Calif, 1951–52; Cambridge Observatories, 1952–59; Royal Observatory, Edinburgh, 1959–65. *Publications:* approx. 75 pubns in learned jls and 32 gen. articles. *Recreations:* making musical instruments, high quality audio, gardening, fun-running, not being interrupted and not being hurried. *Address:* Little Brighter Farm, St Kew Highway, Bodmin, Cornwall PL30 3DU.

FELLNER, Dr Peter John; Chief Executive and Managing Director, Celltech Group plc, since 1990; *b* 31 Dec. 1943; *s* of Hans Julius Fellner and Jessica (*née* Thompson); *m* 1st, 1969, Sandra Head (*née* Smith); one *d* and one step *s*; 2nd, 1982, Jennifer Mary Zabel (*née* Butler); two step *s*. *Educ:* Sheffield Univ. (BSc Biochem. 1965); Trinity Coll., Cambridge (PhD 1968). Post-doctoral Res. Fellow, 1968–70, Associate Prof., 1970–73, Strasbourg Univ.; Searle UK Research Laboratories: Sen. Res. Investigator, 1973–77; Dir of Chem., 1977–80; Dir of Res., 1980–84; Dir of Res., Roche UK Res. Centre, 1984–86; Man. Dir, Roche UK, 1986–90; Director: Colborn Dawes Ltd, 1986–90; British Biotechnol. Gp plc, 1988–90. *Recreation:* country walking. *Address:* Celltech Group plc, 216 Bath Road, Slough, Berks SL1 4EN. *T:* Slough (01753) 534655.

FELLOWES, family name of **Baron De Ramsey.**

FELLOWES, Rt. Hon. Sir Robert, KCB 1991 (CB 1987); KCVO 1989 (LVO 1983); PC 1990; Private Secretary to the Queen and Keeper of the Queen's Archives, since 1990; *b* 11 Dec. 1941; *s* of Sir William Fellowes, KCVO; *m* 1978, Lady Jane Spencer, *d* of 8th Earl Spencer, LVO; one *s* two *d*. *Educ:* Eton. Scots Guards (short service commission), 1960–63. Director, Allen Harvey & Ross Ltd, Discount Brokers and Bankers, 1968–77; Asst Private Sec. to the Queen, 1977–86, Dep. Private Sec., 1986–90. *Recreations:* golf, shooting, watching cricket. *Clubs:* Athenæum, White's, Pratt's, MCC.

FELLOWS, Derek Edward, FIA; Executive Director, Securities and Investments Board, 1989–91; *b* 23 Oct. 1927; *s* of late Edward Frederick Fellows and of Gladys Fellows; *m* 1948, Mary Watkins; two *d*. *Educ:* Mercers' Sch. FIA 1956. Entered Prudential Assurance Co. Ltd, 1943; Gp Pensions Manager, 1973–81; Chief Actuary, 1981–88; Man. Dir, Gp Pension Div., 1984–88; Dir, Prudential Corp. plc, 1985–88; non-exec. Dir, Hambro Guardian Assurance, 1992–. Member: Occupational Pensions Bd, 1974–78; Audit Cttee, Church Comrs, 1994–; Chm., Bd of Trustees, South Bank Centre Retirement Plan, 1993–. FPMI 1976; Vice Pres., Inst. of Actuaries, 1980–83. *Publications:* contrib. Jl of Inst. of Actuaries. *Recreations:* music, gardening, bridge. *Club:* Actuaries'.

FELLOWS, Edward Frank; Managing Director, Fellows Associates, publishing consultants, since 1992; Features Editor, Shell Agriculture, 1993–94; *b* 25 Sept. 1930; *s* of Edward Fellows and Gladys Nora Fellows; *m* 1962, Christine Woolmore; three *s*. *Educ:* Ewell primary and secondary schs; Epsom Sch. of Art (schol.); Merrist Wood Agricl Inst. Nat. Service, CRMP, 1949. Joined editorial staff of Farmer and Stockbreeder, 1957; Editor, Power Farming, 1974; Dep. Editor, Farmers Weekly, 1982; Editor, Crops, 1984; Editor, Farmers Weekly, 1987–90; Editor-in-Chief, Reed Farmers Publishing Group, 1990–91. Hon. Mem., Falkland Islands Assoc., 1983–. *Publication:* Tim Chooses Farming, 1962. *Recreations:* Bernese mountain dogs, walking, photography, gardening, reading. *Address:* Braccate House, The Priory, Horsley, Nailsworth, Glos GL6 0QR. *T:* Stroud (01453) 834377, *Fax:* (01453) 834505. *Club:* Farmers'.

FELLOWS, Jeffrey Keith; Technical Planning Director, BAe plc, since 1995; *b* 17 Sept. 1940; *s* of Albert and Hilda May Fellows; *m* 1965, Mary Ewins; one *s*. *Educ:* Handsworth Grammar Sch.; Birmingham Univ. (BSc (Phys) Hons 1962). Royal Aircraft Establishment: joined Weapons Dept, 1962, Sect. Leader, 1973; Div. Leader, Systems Assessment Dept, 1976; Head of: Combat Mission Systems Div., 1981; Flight Systems Dept, 1983; seconded to BNSC as Dir (Projects and Technol.), 1986; Dep. Dir (Mission Systems), RAE, Farnborough, 1988–89; Asst Under Sec. of State, MoD, 1989–95. *Publications:* various, for AGARD, IBA, US Nat. Space Foundn, etc. *Recreations:* tennis, aeromodelling.

FELLOWS, John Walter, FICE, FIHT; Board Director–Road Programme (formerly Network), Highway Agency, since 1994; *b* 27 July 1938; *s* of William Leslie Fellows and Lavinia Keziah (*née* Chilton); *m* 1964, Maureen Joyce Lewis; two *s*. *Educ:* Dudley Technical High Sch.; Wolverhampton Polytechnic; Birmingham Univ. (MSc). FICE 1990; FIHT 1989. Civil Engineer (pupil), Contractors Wilson Lovatt & Sons Ltd, 1954–59; Civil Engineer: CBs of Wolverhampton, Coventry and Dudley, 1959–69; joined Department of Transport, 1969: Asst Sec., Highway Maintenance Div., 1984–88; Dir, SE, 1988–90; Regl Dir (SE), DoE/DoT, 1990–94. *Publications:* papers to ICE and IHT. *Recreations:* boating, sailing, golf, music, theatre. *Address:* Highway Agency, St Christopher House, Southwark Street, SE1 0TE. *T:* 0171–921 4669.

FELLS, Prof. Ian, FEng; Professor of Energy Conversion, University of Newcastle upon Tyne, since 1975; *b* 5 Sept. 1932; *s* of late Dr Henry Alexander Fells, MBE and Clarice Fells, Sheffield; *m* 1957, Hazel Denton Scott; four *s*. *Educ:* King Edward VII School, Sheffield; Trinity College, Cambridge. MA, PhD. FInstE, CChem, FRSC, FIChemE; FEng 1979. Chief Wireless Officer, British Troops in Austria, 1951–52; Lectr and Dir of Studies, Dept of Fuel Technology and Chem. Engineering, Univ. of Sheffield, 1958–62; Reader in Fuel Science, King's Coll., Univ. of Durham, 1962; Public Orator, Univ. of Newcastle upon Tyne, 1970–73. Lectures: Brough, Paisley Coll., 1977; Allerdale Wylde, Cumbria Science Socs, 1986; Fawley, Southampton Univ., 1987; Robert Spence, RSC, 1988 and 1990; Charles Parsons' Meml, Royal Soc., 1988; Clancey, City Univ., 1992. Pres., Inst. of Energy, 1978–79; Scientific Advr, World Energy Council, 1990–; Special Advisor: to H of L Select Cttee for the European Communities, 1991–92; to H of C Select Cttee on Envmt, 1993–94. Member: Electricity Supply Res. Council, 1979–90; Sci. Consultative Gp, BBC, 1976–81; Exec., David Davies Inst. of Internat. Affairs, 1975–; CNAA, 1987–93. Hatfield Meml Prize, 1974; Beilby Meml Medal and Prize, 1976; Faraday Award, Royal Soc., 1993. Participator in TV series: Young Scientist of the Year; The Great Egg Race; Men of Science; Earth Year 2050; Take Nobody's Word For It; QED; The Human Element. *Publications:* Energy for the Future, 1973, 2nd edn 1986; UK Energy Policy Post-Privatisation, 1991; contribs to professional jls. *Recreations:* sailing, cross-country ski-ing, energy conversation. *Address:* Department of Chemical and Process Engineering, The University, Newcastle upon Tyne NE1 7RU. *T:* 0191–222 7276; (home) 0191–285 5343. *Club:* Naval and Military.

FELWICK, Wing Comdr David Leonard, RAF retd; Director of Trading (Food), John Lewis Partnership and Managing Director, Waitrose Ltd, since 1991; *b* 9 Nov. 1944; *s* of Leonard Felwick and Mary J. Felwick (*née* Rolling); *m* 1970, Lynne Margaret Yeardley; two *s*. *Educ:* Devonport High Sch., Plymouth; RAF Coll., Cranwell. Served RAF, 1962–82. Joined John Lewis Partnership, 1982; Man. Dir, John Lewis, Welwyn, 1985–87; Dir of Selling, Waitrose Ltd, 1987–91. MInstD 1985. *Recreations:* ski-ing, shooting, tennis, golf. *Address:* John Lewis Partnership, 171 Victoria Street, SW1E 5NN. *T:* 0171–828 1000. *Club:* Royal Air Force.

FENBY, Eric William, OBE 1962; Professor of Harmony, Royal Academy of Music, 1964–77; *b* 22 April 1906; *s* of late Herbert Henry and Ada Fenby; *m* 1944, Rowena Clara Teresa Marshall; one *s* one *d*. *Educ:* Municipal Sch., Scarborough; privately. Amanuensis to Frederick Delius, 1928–34; Mus. Adv. Boosey & Hawkes, 1936–39; début as composer, BBC Promenade Concerts, 1942. Captain, RAEC Sch. of Educn, Cuerdon Hall, 1942–45. Mus. Dir, N Riding Coll. of Educn, 1948–62; Artistic Dir, Delius Centenary Festival, 1962; Pres. Delius Soc., 1964–; Chm., Composers' Guild of Great Britain, 1968, Mem. Council, 1970. Visiting Prof. of Music and Composer in Residence, Jacksonville Univ., Fla, USA, 1968. Mem. Cttee of Management, Royal Philharmonic Soc., 1972. FRCM 1985; Hon. FTCL 1986; Hon. Member: RAM, 1965; Royal Philharmonic Soc., 1984; Hon. DMus Jacksonville, 1978; Hon. DLitt Warwick, 1978; Hon. DLitt Bradford, 1978. *Publications:* Delius as I Knew Him, 1936, rev. edn 1966; a further rev. edn, 1981, packaged with own recordings of all works dictated to him by Delius, known as The Fenby Legacy; Menuhin's House of Music, 1969; Delius, 1971. *Recreations:* walking, chess. *Address:* 1 Raincliffe Court, Stepney Road, Scarborough, N Yorks YO12 5BT. *T:* Scarborough (01723) 372988. *Club:* Royal Academy of Music.

FENBY, Jonathan; Editor, The Observer, 1993–95; *b* 11 Nov. 1942; *s* of Charles Fenby and June (*née* Head); *m* 1967, Renée Wartski; one *s* one *d*. *Educ:* King Edward VI Sch., Birmingham; Westminster Sch.; New Coll., Oxford (BA). Reuters, 1963–77, Ed., Reuters World Service, 1973–77; correpondent in France and Germany, Economist, 1982–86; Asst Ed. and Home Ed., The Independent, 1986–88; Dep. Ed., The Guardian, 1988–93. Chevalier, Ordre de Mérite (France), 1992. *Publications:* Fall of the House of Beaverbrook, 1979; Piracy and the Public, 1983; International News Services, 1986. *Recreation:* walking. *Address:* 101 Ridgmount Gardens, WC1E 7AZ.

FENDALL, Prof. Neville Rex Edwards, MD; Professor of International Community Health, School of Tropical Medicine, University of Liverpool, 1971–81, now Emeritus Professor; Visiting Professor of Public Health, Boston University, since 1982; Adjunct Professor of Community Health, University of Calgary, since 1983; *b* 9 July 1917; *s* of Francis Alan Fendall and Ruby Inez Matthews; *m* 1942, Margaret Doreen (*née* Beynon). *Educ:* University College Hosp. (MD, BSc); London Sch. of Hygiene and Tropical Med. (DPH); FFPHM. Colonial Medical Service, 1944–64, Nigeria, Malaya, Singapore, Kenya; Brit. Mil. Admin, 1945–46; Dir of Med. Services, Kenya; Staff Mem., Rockefeller Foundn, 1964–66; Regional Dir, Population Council Inc., New York, 1966–71. Mem., Panel of Experts, WHO, 1957–83; Consultant: World Bank; UN Fund for Population Activities; ODM; Cento; Internat. Develt Res. Centre, Canada; APHA; USAID; Overseas govts. Visiting Lecturer: Harvard, 1966–83; Inst. of Tropical Medicine, Marseilles; Univ. of Glasgow; Univ. of Bradford; Vis. Consultant, Univ. of Hawaii; Commonwealth Foundn Travelling Lectr, 1976. Mem., Acad. of Med., Physical and Nat. Scis, Guatemala, 1986–. Gold Medal, Mrigendra Medical Trust, Nepal, 1983. *Publications:* Auxiliaries in Health Care, 1972 (English, French, Spanish edns); (with J. M. Paxman and F. M. Shattock) Use of Paramedicals for Primary Health Care in the Commonwealth, 1979; (with F. M. Shattock) Restraints and Constraints to Development, 1983; contribs on primary health care, epidemiology, population dynamics, in various books and jls. *Recreations:* gardening, travel. *Address:* The Coach House, Mill Street, Ludlow, Shropshire SY8 1BB. *Clubs:* Commonwealth Trust; Athenæum (Liverpool).

FENDER, Prof. Brian Edward Frederick, CMG 1985; Chief Executive, Higher Education Funding Council for England, since 1995; *b* 15 Sept. 1934; *s* of late George Clements and of Emily Fender; *m* 1st, 1956; one *s* three *d*; 2nd, 1986, Ann Linscott. *Educ:* Carlisle Grammar Sch.; Sale County Grammar Sch.; Imperial College London (ARCS, BSc 1956; DIC, PhD 1959); MA Oxon 1963; CChem, FRSC. Research Instructor, Univ. of Washington, Seattle, 1959–61; Senior Research Fellow, Nat. Chem. Lab. (now NPL), 1961–63; University of Oxford: Dept Demonstrator in Inorganic Chemistry, 1963–65; Lectr, 1965–84; Senior Proctor, 1975–76; Mem., Hebdomadal Council, 1977–80; St Catherine's College: Fellow, 1963–84 (Hon. Fellow 1986); Sen. Tutor, 1965–69; Chm., Management Cttee, Oxford Colls Admissions Office, 1973–80; Vice-Chancellor, Univ. of Keele, 1985–95. Institut Laue-Langevin, Grenoble: Asst Dir, 1980–82; Dir, 1982–85; Mem., Steering Cttee, 1974–77; Mem., Scientific Council, 1977–80. Member: SERC, 1985–90; CERN Review Cttee, 1986–87; Chairman: Science Board, SERC, 1985–90 (Mem., 1974–77); Neutron Beam Res. Cttee, 1974–77 (Mem., 1969–71); Science Planning Group for Rutherford Lab. Neutron Scattering Source, 1977–80; Keele Univ. Science Park, 1985–95; Member: Adv. Cttee, Tate Gall., Liverpool, 1988–93; Defence Meteorol Bd, 1991–; British Technol. Gp Bd, 1992–95. Member Council: Chem. Soc., 1973–76; CVCP, 1988–95. CIMgt (CBIM 1989). *Publications:* scientific articles on neutron scattering and solid state chemistry. *Recreations:* visiting France, modern art. *Address:* Higher Education Funding Council for England, Northavon House, Coldharbour Lane, Bristol BS16 1QD. *Club:* Athenæum.

FENECH-ADAMI, Hon. Dr Edward; MP Malta, since 1969; Prime Minister of Malta, since 1987 (also Foreign Minister, 1989–90); Leader of Nationalist Party, since 1977; *b* Birkirkara, Malta, 7 Feb. 1934; *s* of late Luigi Fenech-Adami and Josephine (*née* Pace); *m* 1965, Mary (*née* Sciberras); four *s* one *d*. *Educ:* St Aloysius Coll., Malta; Royal Univ. of Malta (BA 1955, LLD 1958). Entered legal practice in Malta, 1959. Mem. Nat. Exec., Nationalist Party, 1961, Asst Gen. Sec., 1962–75, Chm., Gen. Council and Admin. Council, 1975–77; Shadow Minister for Labour and Social Services, 1971–77; Leader of the Opposition, Malta, 1977–81 and 1982–87. Vice-Pres., European Union of Christian Democrat Parties, 1979–. Editor, Il-Poplu, 1962–69. *Address:* Auberge de Castille, Valletta, Malta. *T:* 242560.

FENHALLS, Richard Dorian; Chief Executive, Strand Partners Ltd, since 1993; *b* 14 July 1943; *s* of Roydon Myers and Maureen Rosa Fenhalls; *m* 1967, Angela Sarah Allen; one *s* one *d*. *Educ:* Hilton Coll., Univ. of Natal (BA); Christ's Coll., Cambridge (MA, LLM). Attorney, S Africa, 1969. Goodricke & Son, Attorney, S Africa, 1969–70; Citibank, 1970–72; Senior Vice President: Marine Midland Bank, 1972–77; American Express Bank, 1977–81; Dep. Chm. and Chief Exec., Guinness Mahon & Co. Ltd, 1981–85; Chief Exec., Henry Ansbacher Hldgs, 1985–93; Chm., Henry Ansbacher & Co. Ltd, 1985–93. *Recreations:* sailing, ski-ing. *Address:* 15 St James's Gardens, W11 4RE. *Clubs:* Royal Ocean Racing, Royal Thames Yacht, Ski Club of Great Britain; Royal Southern Yacht (Hamble).

FENN, Sir Nicholas (Maxted), GCMG 1995 (KCMG 1989; CMG 1980); HM Diplomatic Service; High Commissioner in New Delhi, 1991–Feb. 1996; *b* 19 Feb. 1936; *s* of late Rev. Prof. J. Eric Fenn and of Kathleen (*née* Harrison); *m* 1959, Susan Clare (*née* Russell); two *s* one *d*. *Educ:* Kingswood Sch., Bath; Peterhouse, Cambridge (MA). Pilot Officer, RAF, 1954–56. Third Sec., British Embassy, Rangoon, 1959–63; Asst Private Sec. to Sec. of State for Foreign and Commonwealth Affairs, 1963–67; First Secretary: British Interests Sect., Swiss Embassy, Algiers, 1967–69; Public Relations, UK Mission to UN, NY, 1969–72; Dep. Head, Energy Dept, FCO, 1972–75; Counsellor, Peking, 1975–77; Head of News Dept and FCO Spokesman, 1979–82; Spokesman to last Governor of Rhodesia, 1979–80; Ambassador: Rangoon, 1982–86; Dublin, 1986–91. *Recreation:* sailing. *Address:* c/o Foreign and Commonwealth Office, King Charles Street, SW1A 2AH.

FENNELL, Hon. Sir (John) Desmond (Augustine), Kt 1990; OBE 1982; a Judge of the High Court of Justice, Queen's Bench Division, 1990–92; *b* 17 Sept. 1933; *s* of late Dr A. J. Fennell, Lincoln; *m* 1966, Susan Primrose, *d* of late J. M. Trusted; one *s* two *d*. *Educ:* Ampleforth; Corpus Christi Coll., Cambridge. Served with Grenadier Guards, 1956–58. Called to the Bar, Inner Temple, 1959, Bencher, 1983; Dep. Chm., Bedfordshire QS, 1971; a Recorder of the Crown Court, 1972–89; QC 1974; Leader, Midland and Oxford Circuit, 1983–88; a Judge of the Courts of Appeal of Jersey and Guernsey, 1984–89; a Judge of the Employment Appeal Tribunal, 1991–92. Vice-Chm., 1988, Chm., 1989, Gen. Council of the Bar. Inspector, King's Cross Underground fire, 1988. Chm., Buckingham Div. Cons. Assoc., 1976–79 (Pres., 1983–89). *Clubs:* Boodle's, Pilgrims.

FENNER, Prof. Frank John, AC 1989; CMG 1976; MBE 1944; FRCP 1967; FRS 1958; FAA 1954; Visiting Fellow, John Curtin School of Medical Research, Australian National University, since 1983 (University Fellow, 1980–82); *b* 21 Dec. 1914; *s* of Charles and Emma L. Fenner; *m* 1944, Ellen Margaret Bobbie Roberts; one *d* (and one *d* decd). *Educ:* Thebarton Technical High Sch.; Adelaide High Sch.; Univ. of Adelaide. MB, BS (Adelaide) 1938; MD (Adelaide) 1942; DTM (Sydney) 1940. Served as Medical Officer, Hospital Pathologist, and Malariologist, AIF, 1940–46; Francis Haley Research Fellow, Walter and Eliza Hall Inst. for Medical Research, Melbourne, 1946–48; Rockefeller

Foundation Travelling Fellow, 1948–49; Prof. of Microbiology, 1949–73, Dir, John Curtin Sch. of Med. Research, 1967–73, Prof. of Environmental Studies and Dir, Centre for Resource and Environmental Studies, 1973–79, ANU; Overseas Fellow, Churchill Coll., Cambridge, 1962–63. Fogarty Schol., Nat. Insts of Health, USA, 1973–74, 1982–83. Chm., Global Commn for Certification of Smallpox Eradication, WHO, 1978–80. For. Associate, Nat. Acad. of Scis, USA, 1977; David Syme Prize, Univ. of Melbourne, 1949; Harvey Lecture, Harvey Soc. of New York, 1957; Royal Society: Leeuwenhoek Lecture, 1961, Florey Lecture, 1983; Australian Acad. of Science: Matthew Flinders Lecture, 1967; Burnet Lecture, 1985. Hon. MD Monash, 1966; Dr *hc* Univ. of Liège, 1992. Mueller Medal, Australian and New Zealand Assoc. for the Advancement of Science, 1964; Britannica Australia Award for Medicine, 1967; ANZAC Peace Award, 1980; ANZAAS Medal, 1980; Stuart Mudd Award, Internat. Union of Microbiol Socs; 1986; Japan Prize (Preventive Medicine), Sci. & Technol. Foundn of Japan, 1988. *Publications:* The Production of Antibodies (with F. M. Burnet), 1949; Myxomatosis (with F. N. Ratcliffe), 1965; The Biology of Animal Viruses, 1968, 2nd edn 1974; Medical Virology (with D. O. White), 1970, 4th edn 1994; Classification and Nomenclature of Viruses, 1976; (with A. L. G. Rees) The Australian Academy of Science: the First Twenty-five Years, 1980; (jtly) Veterinary Virology, 1987, 2nd edn 1993; (jtly) Smallpox and its Eradication, 1988; (with Z. Jezek) Human Monkeypox, 1988; (with A. Gibbs) Portraits of Viruses: a history of virology, 1988; (jtly) The Orthopoxviruses, 1989; History of Microbiology in Australia, 1990; numerous scientific papers, dealing with virology, epidemiology, bacteriology, and environmental problems. *Recreations:* gardening, tennis. *Address:* 8 Monaro Crescent, Red Hill, Canberra, ACT 2603, Australia. *T:* (6) 2959176.

FENNER, Dame Peggy, DBE 1986; DL; MP (C) Medway, since 1983 (Rochester and Chatham, 1970–Sept. 1974 and 1979–83); *b* 12 Nov. 1922; *m* 1940, Bernard Fenner; one *d. Educ:* LCC School, Brockley; Ide Hill, Sevenoaks. Contested (C) Newcastle-under-Lyme, 1966; Parly Sec., MAFF, 1972–74 and 1981–86; Mem., British Delegn to European Parlt, Strasbourg, 1974; UK rep. to Council of Europe and WEU, 1987–. Member: West Kent Divisional Exec. Educn Cttee, 1963–72; Sevenoaks Urban District Council, 1957–71 (Chairman, 1962 and 1963); Exec. of Kent Borough and Urban District Councils Assoc., 1967–71; a Vice-Pres, Urban District Councils Assoc., 1971. DL Kent, 1992. *Recreations:* reading, travel, theatre, gardening. *Address:* 12 Star Hill, Rochester, Kent ME1 1XB. *T:* Medway (01634) 42124.

FENNESSY, Sir Edward, Kt 1975; CBE 1957 (OBE 1944); BSc; FIEE, FRIN; *b* 17 Jan. 1912; *m* 1st, 1937, Marion Banks (*d* 1983); one *s* one *d*; 2nd, 1984, Leonora Patricia Birkett, *widow* of Trevor Birkett. *Educ:* Univ. of London. Telecommunications Research, Standard Telephones and Cables, 1934–38; Radar Research, Air Min. Research Station, Bawdsey Manor, 1938. War of 1939–45: commissioned RAFVR, 1940; Group Captain, 1945; staff No 60 Group, RAF, 1940–45; resp. for planning and construction radar systems for defence of UK, and Bomber Ops. Joined Bd of The Decca Navigator Co., 1946; Managing Director: Decca Radar Ltd, 1950–65; The Plessey Electronics Group, 1965–69. Chairman: British Telecommunications Research Ltd, 1966–69; Electronic Engineering Assoc., 1967–68; Man. Dir, Telecommunications, 1969–77, and Dep. Chm., 1975–77, Post Office Corp. Chairman: IMA Microwave Products Ltd, 1979–83; LKB Biochrom, 1978–87; British Medical Data Systems, 1981–91; Dep. Chm., LKB Instruments, 1978–87. Pres., Royal Institute of Navigation, 1975–78. DUniv Surrey, 1971. *Recreation:* sailing. *Address:* Northbrook, Littleford Lane, Shamley Green, Surrey GU5 0RH. *T:* Guildford (01483) 892444. *Club:* Royal Air Force.

FENNEY, Roger Johnson, CBE 1973 (MBE (mil.) 1945); Chairman, Special Trustees, Charing Cross Hospital, 1980–88; *b* 11 Sept. 1916; *s* of James Henry Fenney and Annie Sarah Fenney; *m* 1942, Dorothy Porteus (*d* 1989); two *d. Educ:* Cowley Sch., St Helens; Univ. of Manchester (BA Admin 1939). Served War, 1939–46: Gunner to Major, Field Artillery; served N Africa and Italy (mentioned in despatches). Secretary, Central Midwives Board, 1947–82; Governor, Charing Cross Hosp., 1958–74 (Chm., Clinical Res. Cttee, 1970–80; Mem. Council, Med. Sch., 1970–80); Governor, Hammersmith Hosp., 1956–74; Chm., W London Hosp., 1957–68; First Nuffield Fellow for Health Affairs, USA, 1968; Dep. Chm., Kennedy Inst. of Rheumatol., 1970–77. Member: Exec., Arthritis and Rheumatism Council, 1978–; Ealing, Hammersmith and Hounslow AHA, 1974–79; Field Dir, Jt Study Gp (FIGO/ICM), Accra, Yaounde, Nairobi, Dakar, San José and Bogotá, 1972–76. *Address:* 11 Gilray House, Gloucester Terrace, W2 3DF. *T:* 0171–262 8313.

FENTEM, Prof. Peter Harold, FRCP; Stroke Association Professor of Stroke Medicine, University of Nottingham, since 1992; Hon. Consultant, Nottingham City Hospital NHS Trust (formerly Nottingham Health Authority), since 1976; *b* 12 Sept. 1933; *s* of Harold and Agnes Fentem; *m* 1958, Rosemary Hodson; two *s* two *d. Educ:* Bury Grammar Sch.; Univ. of Manchester (BSc 1st cl. hons 1955; MSc 1956; MB ChB Hons 1959). FRCP 1989. Hosp. appts, Manchester Royal Inf., 1959–60; Demonstrator in Path., Univ. of Manchester, 1960–61; Manchester and Cardiff Royal Infs, 1961–64; Lectr in Physiol., St Mary's Hosp. Med. Sch., 1964–68; University of Nottingham: Sen. Lectr in Physiol., 1968; Reader, 1975; Prof. of Physiol., 1975–92; Dean of Medicine, 1987–93. Chm., BSI Tech. Sub-Cttee on Compression Hosiery, 1978–89; Sci. Sec., Fitness and Health Adv. Gp, Sports Council, 1981; Civil Consultant to RAF, 1983–; Hon. Consultant to Army, 1989–; Member: Army Personnel Res. Cttee, 1983– (Chm., Applied Physiol. Panel, 1986–93); GMC, 1988–93; Trent RHA, 1988–90; DoH Physical Activity Task Force, 1993–. *Publications:* (jt author): Exercise: the facts, 1981; Work Physiology, in Principles and Practice of Human Physiology, 1981; The New Case for Exercise, 1988; Benefits of Exercise: the evidence, 1990; (Adv. Editor) Physiology Integrated Clinical Science, 1983. *Recreations:* gardening, walking. *Address:* Division of Stroke Medicine, Nottingham City Hospital NHS Trust, Hucknall Road, Nottingham NG5 1PB. *Club:* Royal Society of Medicine.

FENTON, Prof. Alexander, CBE 1986; DLitt; Professor of Scottish Ethnology and Director, School of Scottish Studies, University of Edinburgh, 1990–94; Director, European Ethnological Research Centre, Edinburgh, since 1989; *b* 26 June 1929; *s* of Alexander Fenton and Annie Stirling Stronach; *m* 1956, Evelyn Elizabeth Hunter; two *d. Educ:* Turriff Academy; Aberdeen Univ. (MA); Cambridge Univ. (BA); Edinburgh Univ. (DLitt). Senior Asst Editor, Scottish National Dictionary, 1955–59; Asst Keeper, Nat. Museum of Antiquities of Scotland, 1959–75, Dep. Keeper, 1975–78, Director, 1978–85; Res. Dir, Nat. Museums of Scotland, 1985–89. Mem., Ancient Monuments Bd for Scotland, 1979–94. Member: Royal Gustav Adolf Acad., Uppsala, Sweden, 1978; Royal Danish Acad. of Scis and Letters, 1979; Jury, Europa Preis für Volkskunst (FVS Foundation, Hamburg) 1975–. Hon. DLitt Aberdeen, 1989. Co-editor, Tools and Tillage (Copenhagen), 1968–; Editor: Review of Scottish Culture, 1984–; Scottish Studies, 1992–. *Publications:* The Various Names of Shetland, 1973, 2nd edn 1977; Scottish Country Life, 1976, 2nd edn 1978; (trans.) S. Steensen Blicher, En Landsbydegns Dagbog (The Diary of a Parish Clerk, 1976); The Island Blackhouse, 1978; The Northern Isles: Orkney and Shetland, 1978; (with B. Walker) The Rural Architecture of Scotland, 1981; The Shape of the Past, 2 vols, 1985; (trans.) S. Weöres, Ha a Világ Rigó Lenne (If All the World were a Blackbird), 1985; Wird's an' Wark 'e Seasons Roon, 1987; Country Life in Scotland, 1987; The Turra Coo: a legal episode in the popular culture of NE Scotland, 1989; Scottish Country Life, 1989; numerous articles in learned jls. *Address:* 132 Blackford Avenue, Edinburgh EH9 3HH. *T:* 0131–667 5456. *Club:* New (Edinburgh).

FENTON, Ernest John; Director General, Association of Investment Trust Companies, since 1993; *b* 14 Oct. 1938; *s* of Forbes Duncan Campbell Fenton and Janet Burnfield Fenton (*née* Easson); *m* 1965, Ann Ishbel Ramsay; one *s* two *d. Educ:* Harris Acad., Scotland. CA 1961. Partner, W. Greenwell & Co., 1968–87; Chm. and Chief Exec., Greenwell Montagu Stockbrokers, 1987–92. Non-executive Director: Valetrue Ltd (Farmers), 1986–; Fleming Income & Capital Investment Trust PLC, 1991–; Cotesworth & Co. Ltd (Lloyd's Managing Agents), 1994–. Farmer, Kinross and Kent, 1973–. FRSA 1993; MInstD 1994. *Recreations:* shooting, ski-ing, curling. *Address:* 519 Ben Jonson House, Barbican, EC2Y 8NH; Dundale Farm, Tunbridge Wells, Kent TN3 9AQ. *Club:* City of London.

FENTON, Air Cdre Harold Arthur, CBE 1946; DSO 1943; DFC 1942; BA; AFRAeS; *b* Gallegos, Patagonia, Argentine, 9 Feb. 1909; *s* of Dr E. G. Fenton, FRCSI, DPH, Co. Sligo and J. Ormsby, Glen Lodge, Ballina, Co. Mayo; *m* 1935, H. de Carteret; no *c. Educ:* Sandford Park Sch.; Trinity Coll., Dublin (BA 1927). Joined RAF 1928. Served India, 1930–33. Flying Instructor at Air Service Training Ltd, Hamble, until outbreak of war. During war commanded: Fighter Sqdn, Battle of Britain; Fighter Wing, and Fighter Group, Western Desert and Libya; Fighter Sector, London Area. Finished war as Senior Staff Officer, Germany (83 Group) (despatches thrice). Managing Dir, Deccan Airways Ltd, Hyderabad, Deccan, until 1947; Gen. Manager of Airways Training Ltd, 1947–48; Operations Manager, BOAC, 1949–52; Managing Dir, Peter Jones, 1952–58. *Recreation:* gardening. *Address:* Le Vallon, St Brelade, Jersey, Channel Islands. *T:* Jersey (0534) 41172.

FENTON, James Martin, FRSL; writer; Professor of Poetry, University of Oxford, since 1994; *b* 25 April 1949; *s* of Rev. Canon J. C. Fenton, *qv* and Mary Hamilton (*née* Ingoldby). *Educ:* Durham Choristers Sch.; Repton Sch.; Magdalen Coll., Oxford (MA). FRSL 1983. Asst Literary Editor, 1971, Editorial Asst, 1972, New Statesman; freelance correspondent in Indo-China, 1973–75; Political Columnist, New Statesman, 1976–78; German Correspondent, The Guardian, 1978–79; Theatre Critic, Sunday Times, 1979–84; Chief Book Reviewer, The Times, 1984–86; Far East Corresp., 1986–88, columnist, 1993–, The Independent. *Publications:* Our Western Furniture, 1968; Terminal Moraine, 1972; A Vacant Possession, 1978; A German Requiem, 1980; Dead Soldiers, 1981; The Memory of War, 1982; (trans.) Rigoletto, 1982; You Were Marvellous, 1983; (ed) The Original Michael Frayn, 1983; Children in Exile, 1984; Poems 1968–83, 1985; (trans.) Simon Boccanegra, 1985; The Fall of Saigon, in Granta 15, 1985; The Snap Revolution, in Granta 18, 1986; (ed) Cambodian Witness: the autobiography of Someth May, 1986; (with John Fuller) Partingtime Hall (poems), 1987; All the Wrong Places: adrift in the politics of Asia, 1989; (ed) Underground in Japan, by Rey Ventura, 1992; Out of Danger (poems), 1993. *Address:* Peters Fraser & Dunlop, 5th Floor, The Chambers, Chelsea Harbour, Lots Road, SW10 0XF.

FENTON, Rev. Canon John Charles; Canon of Christ Church, Oxford, 1978–91, Hon. Canon, 1991–92, now Hon. Canon Emeritus and Emeritus Student; *b* 5 June 1921; *s* of Cornelius O'Connor Fenton and Agnes Claudine Fenton. *Educ:* S Edward's Sch., Oxford; Queen's Coll., Oxford (BA 1943, MA 1947, BD 1953); Lincoln Theol Coll. Deacon 1944, priest 1945. Asst Curate, All Saints, Hindley, Wigan, 1944–47; Chaplain, Lincoln Theol Coll., 1947–51, Sub-Warden, 1951–54; Vicar of Wentworth, Yorks, 1954–58; Principal: Lichfield Theol Coll., 1958–65; S Chad's Coll., Durham, 1965–78. *Publications:* Preaching the Cross, 1958; The Passion according to John, 1961; Crucified with Christ, 1961; Saint Matthew (Pelican Commentaries), 1963; Saint John (New Clarendon Bible), 1970; What was Jesus' Message?, 1971; (with M. Hare Duke) Good News, 1976; Finding the Way through John, 1988; Sunday Readings, 1991; Affirmations, 1993; Finding the Way through Mark, 1995; contrib. Theol., Jl of Theol Studies, and Church Times. *Recreations:* walking, camping, gardening. *Address:* 8 Rowland Close, Wolvercote, Oxford OX2 8PW. *T:* Oxford (01865) 54099.

FENWICK, Very Rev. Jeffery Robert; Dean of Guernsey, 1989–95; *b* 8 April 1930; *s* of Stanley Robert and Dorothy Fenwick; *m* 1955, Pamela Frances (*née* Galley); one *s* two *d. Educ:* Torquay and Selhurst Grammar Schools; Pembroke Coll., Cambridge (MA); Lincoln Theol Coll. Deacon 1955, priest 1956, Liverpool; Curate, St Thomas the Martyr, UpHolland, 1955; Priest-in-charge, Christ the King, Daramombe, Mashonaland, 1958; Secretary, USPG, Oxford, 1964; Rector, Gatooma 1965, Salisbury East 1967, Mashonaland; Dean, Bulawayo, Matabeleland, 1975; Canon Residentiary, Worcester Cathedral, 1978; Librarian and Treasurer, 1978–89. Examining Chaplain, Mashonaland and Matabeleland, 1966–78; Archdeacon of Charter, 1970–75, of Bulawayo 1975–78. Hon. Canon of Winchester Cathedral, 1989–. Chm., Cathedrals Finance Conf. for England, 1983–89. *Publications:* Chosen People, 1971; (contrib.) The Pattern of History, 1973. *Recreations:* painting, music, gardening, walking. *Address:* 4 Moffat Avenue, Hillside, Bulawayo, Zimbabwe.

FENWICK, John James, DL; Chairman, Fenwick Ltd, since 1979 (Deputy Chairman, 1972–79; Managing Director, 1972–82); Director, Northern Rock Building Society, since 1984; *b* 9 Aug. 1932; *e s* of James Frederick Trevor Fenwick; *m* 1957, Muriel Gillian Hodnett; three *s. Educ:* Rugby Sch.; Pembroke Coll., Cambridge (MA). Chairman: Northumberland Assoc. of Youth Clubs, 1966–71; Retail Distributors Assoc., 1977–79; Vice Chm., National Assoc. of Citizens Advice Bureaux, 1971–79; Regional Dir, Northern Bd, Lloyds Bank, 1982–85. Member: Newcastle Diocesan Bd of Finance, 1964–69; Retail Consortium Council, 1976–79; Post Office Users' Nat. Council, 1980–82; Civic Trust for NE, 1979–. Governor: Royal Grammar Sch., Newcastle upon Tyne, 1975– (Chm. of Govs, 1987–); Moorfields Eye Hosp., 1981–86; Royal Shakespeare Theatre, 1985–. Master, Mercers' Co., 1991–92. DL Tyne and Wear, 1986. Hon. DCL Northumbria, 1993. *Recreations:* travel, shooting, theatre. *Address:* 63 New Bond Street, W1A 3BS. *Clubs:* Garrick, MCC.

FENWICK, Justin Francis Quintus; QC 1993; *b* 11 Sept. 1949; *s* of David and Maita Fenwick; *m* 1975, Marcia Mary Dunn; one *s* three *d. Educ:* Ampleforth Coll., York; Clare Coll., Cambridge (MA Mod. Langs and Architectural Hist.). Commnd Grenadier Guards, 1968; Adjt, 2nd Battalion, 1977–79; Temp. Equerry to HRH the Duke of Edinburgh, 1979–81. Called to the Bar, Inner Temple, 1980. *Recreations:* wine, shooting, reading. *Address:* 2 Crown Office Row, Temple, EC4Y 7HJ. *T:* 0171–797 8000. *Clubs:* Garrick, Travellers'.

FERGUSON, Alexander Chapman, CBE 1995 (OBE 1984); Manager, Manchester United Football Club, since 1986; *b* 31 Dec. 1941; *s* of Alexander and Elizabeth Ferguson; *m* 1966, Catherine Holding; three *s. Educ:* Govan High Sch., Glasgow. Footballer; played for: Queen's Park, 1958–60; St Johnstone, 1960–64; Dunfermline Athletic, 1964–67; Glasgow Rangers, 1967–69; Falkirk, 1969–73; Ayr United, 1973–74; numerous championship wins as Manager of St Mirren, 1974–78, of Aberdeen, 1978–86; wins with Manchester United: Premier Div., 1993–94, 1994–95; FA Cup, 1990, 1994; European

Cup Winners, 1991; Super Cup, 1991, League Cup, 1992; Charity Shield, 1990, 1993, 1994. *Publications:* A Light in the North, 1984; Six Years at United, 1992; Just Champion, 1993. *Recreations:* golf, snooker. *Address:* Manchester United Football Club, Old Trafford, Manchester M16 0RA. *T:* 0161-872 1661.

FERGUSON, Ernest Alexander; Under-Secretary and Accountant-General, Department of Employment, 1973–77; *b* 26 July 1917; *s* of William Henry and Lilian Ferguson; *m* 1940, Mary Josephine Wadsworth; two *s*. *Educ:* Priory Sch., Shrewsbury; Pembroke Coll., Cambridge (Scholar, 1935–39; MA 1944). Served War, RA (Captain), 1940–45. Entered Ministry of Labour, 1945; Principal, 1948; Asst Sec., 1962. Chm., Central Youth Employment Executive, 1967–69; Sec. to NEDC, 1971–73; Dep. Chm., Central Arbitration Cttee, 1977–87. *Recreations:* sport, hill walking, reading. *Address:* 164 Balcombe Road, Horley, Surrey RH6 9DS. *T:* Horley (01293) 785254. *Club:* Civil Service.

FERGUSON, Air Vice-Marshal Gordon MacArthur, CB 1993; CBE 1990; Managing Director, Taylor Curnow Ltd; *b* 15 April 1938; *s* of James Miller Ferguson and Elizabeth Thomson Ferguson (*née* Barron); *m* 1966, Alison Mary Saxby; one *s* one *d*. *Educ:* King Edward VI Sch., Southampton. Commissioned, RAF, 1960; served Mobile Air Movements, RAF Pergamos and Nicosia, HQ 38 Group, RAF Stafford and Fylingdales, MoD Supply Policy, HQ 2nd ATAF; RAF Staff Coll., 1977; OC Tac Supply Wing, 1977–79; MoD Supply Policy, 1979–81; Air Warfare Course, 1981; MoD Supply Policy, 1981–85; Dep. Dir, Supply Management, 1985–87, Dir, 1987–89; Dir, AMSO Reorgn Implementation Team, 1989–91; AOA, HQ Strike Comd, 1991–94. *Recreations:* golf, bridge, gardening. *Address:* c/o National Westminster Bank, 12 High Street, Southampton SO9 5UL. *Club:* Royal Air Force.

FERGUSON, Sir Ian Edward J.; *see* Johnson-Ferguson.

FERGUSON, John Alexander; HM Senior Chief Inspector of Schools in Scotland, 1981–87, retired; *b* 16 Oct. 1927; *s* of George Ferguson and Martha Crichton Dykes; *m* 1953, Jean Stewart; two *s* one *d*. *Educ:* Royal Coll. of Science and Technology, Univ. of Glasgow (BSc Hons, Diploma). Teacher, Airdrie Central Sch., 1950–51; Lectr, 1951–55, Head of Dept of Engrg, 1955–61, Coatbridge Technical Coll.; HM Inspector of Schs, 1961–72, Asst Sec., 1972–75, Scottish Educn Dept; HM Depute Sen. Chief Inspector of Schs, 1975–81. *Recreations:* golf, bridge. *Clubs:* Craigmillar Park Lawn Tennis, Carlton Bridge (Edinburgh); Luffness New Golf.

FERGUSON, John McIntyre, CBE 1976; FEng 1978; FIEE, FIMechE; engineering consultant, 1973, retired 1986; *b* 16 May 1915; *s* of Frank Ferguson and Lilian (*née* Bowen); *m* 1941, Margaret Frances Tayler; three *s*. *Educ:* Armstrong Coll., Durham Univ. BScEng (1st Cl. Hons). English Electric Co., Stafford: Research, 1936; Chief Engr, 1953; Dir Engrg, Heavy Electric Products, 1965; Dir of Engrg, GEC Power Engrg Co., 1969. Member: Metrication Bd, 1969–76; Science Res. Council, 1972–76; UGC, 1977–82. President: IEE, 1977–78; IEETE, 1979–81. Hon. FIEEIE. Hon. DSc Birmingham, 1983. *Recreations:* golf, sailing. *Address:* 11 Appledore Close, Baswich, Stafford ST17 0EW. *T:* Stafford (01785) 664700. *Club:* Commonwealth Trust.

FERGUSON, Martin John; President, Australian Council of Trade Unions, since 1990; *b* 12 Dec. 1953; *s* of Laurie John Ferguson and Mary Ellen Clare Ferguson (*née* Bett); *m* 1981, Patricia Jane Waller; one *s* one *d*. *Educ:* St Patrick's Convent, Guildford; St Patrick's Coll., Strathfield; Sydney Univ. (BEc Hons). Federated Miscellaneous Workers Union of Australia: Federal Research Officer, 1975–81; Asst Gen. Sec., 1981–84; Gen. Sec., 1984–90. Mem., Governing Body, ILO, 1990–. Member: Trade Develt Council, 1990–; Econ. Planning Adv. Council, 1990–; Australian Govt's Agric. Food Council, 1992–; Exec. Bd, Construction Ind. Develt Agency, 1992–. *Address:* Australian Council of Trade Unions, 6th Floor, ACTU House, 393 Swanston Street, Melbourne, Vic 3000, Australia. *T:* (3) 96635266.

FERGUSON, Richard; QC 1986; QC (NI) 1973; SC (Ireland) 1983; *b* 22 Aug. 1935; *o s* of late Wesley Ferguson and Edith Ferguson (*née* Hewitt); *m* 1st, Janet Irvine Magowan (marr. diss.); three *s* one *d*; 2nd, Roma Felicity Whelan; one *s*. *Educ:* Methodist Coll., Belfast; Trinity Coll., Dublin (BA); Queen's Univ. of Belfast (LLB). Called to NI Bar, 1956, and to Bar of England and Wales, Gray's Inn, 1972 (Bencher, 1994). Chairman: NI Mental Health Review Tribunal, 1973–84; Criminal Bar Assoc. of England and Wales, 1993–95. MP (OU) S Antrim, 1969–70. FRGS 1980. *Recreations:* swimming, watching the Arsenal. *Address:* 1 Crown Office Row, EC4Y 7HH. *T:* 0171-583 3724; Sandhill House, Derrygonnelly, Co. Fermanagh. *T:* Derrygonnelly (0136564) 612. *Club:* Kildare Street and University (Dublin).

FERGUSON DAVIE, Sir Antony (Francis), 6th Bt *cr* 1847, of Creedy, Devonshire; *b* 23 March 1952; *s* of Rev. Sir (Arthur) Patrick Ferguson Davie, 5th Bt, TD, and Iris Dawn (*d* 1992), *d* of Captain Michael Francis Buller; *S* father, 1988. *Educ:* Stanbridge Earls Sch.; London University. BA (History). Writer. *Recreations:* art, travel. *Heir: cousin* John Ferguson Davie [*b* 1 May 1906; *m* 1942, Joan Zoe (*d* 1987), *d* of late Raymond Hoole; two *s*]. *Club:* Naval and Military.

FERGUSON-SMITH, Prof. Malcolm Andrew, FRS 1983; FRSE 1978; Professor of Pathology and Professorial Fellow, Peterhouse, University of Cambridge, since 1987; Director: Cambridge University Centre for Medical Genetics (formerly for Medical Generation), since 1989; East Anglian Regional Clinical Genetics Service, since 1987; *b* 5 Sept. 1931; *s* of John Ferguson-Smith, MA, MD, FRCP and Ethel May (*née* Thorne); *m* 1960, Marie Eva Gzowska; one *s* three *d*. *Educ:* Stowe Sch.; Univ. of Glasgow (MB ChB 1955). MRCPath 1966, FRCPath 1978; MRCPGlas 1972, FRCPGlas 1974. Registrar in Lab. Medicine, Dept of Pathology, Western Infirmary, Glasgow, 1958–59; Fellow in Medicine and Instructor, Johns Hopkins Univ. Sch. of Medicine, 1959–61; Lectr, Sen. Lectr and Reader in Med. Genetics, Univ. of Glasgow, 1961–73, Prof. of Med. Genetics, 1973–87; Hon. Consultant: in Med. Paediatrics, Royal Hosp. for Sick Children, Glasgow, 1966–73; in Clin. Genetics, Yorkhill and Associated Hosps, 1973–87; Dir, W of Scotland Med. Genetics Service, 1973–87. Pres., Clinical Genetics Soc., 1979–81. Mem., Johns Hopkins Univ. Soc. of Scholars, 1983; Foreign Mem., Polish Acad. of Scis, 1988. Hon. DSc Strathclyde, 1992. Bronze Medal, Univ. of Helsinki, 1968; Makdougall-Brisbane Prize, RSE, 1988; San Remo Internat. Prize for Genetic Res., 1990. Editor, Prenatal Diagnosis, 1980–. *Publications:* (ed) Early Prenatal Diagnosis, 1983; (jtly) Essential Medical Genetics, 1984, 4th edn 1993; (ed) Prenatal Diagnosis and Screening, 1992; papers on cytogenetics, gene mapping, human genetics and prenatal diagnosis in med. jls. *Recreations:* swimming, sailing, fishing. *Address:* Department of Pathology, University of Cambridge, Tennis Court Road, Cambridge CB2 1QP. *T:* Cambridge (01223) 333691.

FERGUSSON, Adam (Dugdale); consultant on European affairs, since 1989; *b* 10 July 1932; *yr s* of Sir James Fergusson of Kilkerran, 8th Bt, LLD, FRSE, and of Frances Dugdale; *m* 1965, Penelope, *e d* of Peter Hughes, Furneaux Pelham Hall; two *s* two *d*. *Educ:* Eton; Trinity Coll., Cambridge (BA History, 1955). Glasgow Herald, 1956–61: Leader-writer, 1957–58; Diplomatic Corresp., 1959–61; Statist, 1961–67: Foreign Editor, 1964–67; Feature-writer for The Times on political, economic and environmental matters, 1967–77. Special Advr on European Affairs, FCO, 1985–89. European Parliament: Member (C) West Strathclyde, 1979–84; Spokesman on Political Affairs for European Democratic Gp, 1979–82; Vice-Chm., Political Affairs Cttee, 1982–84; Mem., Jt Cttee of ACP/EEC Consultative Assembly, 1979–84; contested (C) London Central, European elecn, 1984. Vice-Pres., Pan-European Union, 1981–; Mem., Scotland Says No Referendum Campaign Cttee, 1978–79. Gov., Howick Trust, 1976–. *Publications:* Roman Go Home, 1969; The Lost Embassy, 1972; The Sack of Bath, 1973; When Money Dies, 1975; various pamphlets; articles in national and internat. jls and magazines. *Address:* 15 Warwick Gardens, W14 8PH. *T:* 0171-603 7900.

FERGUSSON of Kilkerran, Sir Charles, 9th Bt *cr* 1703; *b* 10 May 1931; *s* of Sir James Fergusson of Kilkerran, 8th Bt, and Frances (*d* 1988), *d* of Edgar Dugdale; *S* father, 1973; *m* 1961, Hon. Amanda Mary Noel-Paton, *d* of Lord Ferrier, ED; two *s*. *Educ:* Eton; Edinburgh and East of Scotland Coll. of Agriculture. *Heir: s* Major Adam Fergusson, AAC [*b* 29 Dec. 1962; *m* 1989, Jenifer, *yr d* of Adam Thomson; two *d*].

FERGUSSON, Sir Ewen (Alastair John), GCMG 1993 (KCMG 1987); GCVO 1992; HM Diplomatic Service, retired; Chairman: Coutts & Co. Group, since 1993; Savoy Hotel, since 1994; *b* 28 Oct. 1932; *er s* of late Sir Ewen MacGregor Field Fergusson; *m* 1959, Sara Carolyn, *d* of late Brig.-Gen. Lord Esmé Gordon Lennox, KCVO, CMG, DSO and *widow* of Sir William Andrew Montgomery-Cuninghame, 11th Bt; one *s* two *d*. *Educ:* Rugby; Oriel Coll., Oxford (MA; Hon. Fellow, 1988). Played Rugby Football for Oxford Univ., 1952 and 1953, and for Scotland, 1954. 2nd Lieut, 60th Rifles (KRRC), 1954–56. Joined Foreign (later Diplomatic) Service, 1956; Asst Private Sec. to Minister of Defence, 1957–59; British Embassy, Addis Ababa, 1960; FO, 1963; British Trade Development Office, New York, 1967; Counsellor and Head of Chancery, Office of UK Permanent Rep. to European Communities, 1972–75; Private Sec. to Foreign and Commonwealth Sec., 1975–78; Asst Under Sec. of State, FCO, 1978–82; Ambassador to S Africa, 1982–84; Dep. Under-Sec. of State (Middle East and Africa), FCO, 1984–87; Ambassador to France, 1987–92. Director, since 1993: British Telecom; Sun Alliance Gp; Savoy Gp of Cos. Governor, Rugby Sch., 1985– (Chm., 1995); Trustee, Nat. Gall., 1995. Grand Officier, Légion d'Honneur (France), 1992. *Address:* Coutts & Co., 440 Strand, WC2R 0QS. *T:* 0171-753 1000. *Clubs:* Royal Automobile, Beefsteak; Jockey (Paris).

FERGUSSON, Sir James H. H. C.; *see* Colyer-Fergusson.

FERMAN, James Alan; Director (formerly Secretary), British Board of Film Classification (formerly British Board of Film Censors), since 1975; *b* New York, 11 April 1930; *m* 1956, Monica Sophie (*née* Robinson); one *s* one *d*. *Educ:* Great Neck High Sch., NY; Cornell Univ. (BA Hons); King's Coll., Cambridge (MA Hons). Actor, writer and univ. lectr until 1957; author/adaptor, Zuleika (musical comedy), Saville Theatre, 1957; television director of drama and documentaries, 1957–75: trained on Armchair Theatre, then 7½ years in ITV, then freelance, chiefly at BBC, 1965–75; principal director: The Planemakers (SFTA Award, 1963); Miss Hanago; The Pistol; Kafka's America (Critics' Circle Award, 1966); Before the Party (BAFTA Award, 1970); also stage producer; wrote and dir., Drugs and Schoolchildren, documentary film series for teachers and social workers. Part-time Lectr in Community Studies, Polytechnic of Central London, 1973–76 (Dir and Chm., Community Mental Health Prog., in-service trng for social workers, health workers, teachers, etc, organised jtly with MIND); Educn Adviser, Standing Conf. on Drug Abuse; Vice-Pres., Assoc. for Prevention of Addiction. Chm. and organiser, internat. confs on standards in screen entertainment, BBFC, 1982–. *Recreations:* theatre, music, reading, hill-walking. *Address:* British Board of Film Classification, 3 Soho Square, W1V 5DE. *T:* 0171-439 7961.

FERMOR, Patrick Michael Leigh, DSO 1944; OBE (mil.) 1943; CLit 1991; author; Hon. Citizen of Herakleion, Crete, 1947, Gytheion, Laconia, 1966, and of Kardamyli, Messenia, 1967; *b* 11 Feb. 1915; *s* of late Sir Lewis Leigh Fermor, OBE, FRS, DSc, and Eileen, *d* of Charles Taaffe Ambler; *m* 1968, Hon. Joan Eyres-Monsell, *d* of 1st Viscount Monsell, PC, GBE. *Educ:* King's Sch., Canterbury. After travelling for four years in Central Europe, Balkans and Greece, enlisted in Irish Guards, 1939; "I" Corps, 1940; Lieut, British Mil. Mission, Greece, 1940; Liaison Officer, Greek GHQ, Albania; campaigns of Greece and Crete; 2 years in German occupied Crete with Resistance, commanded some minor guerilla operations; team-commander in Special Allied Airborne Reconnaissance Force, N Germany, 1945. Dep.-Dir British Institute, Athens, till middle 1946; travelled in Caribbean and Central American republics, 1947–48. Corres. Mem., Athens Acad., 1980. Hon. DLitt: Kent, 1991; Amer. Sch. of Greece, 1993. Municipality of Athens Gold Medal of Honour, 1988; Prix Jacques Audiberti, Ville d'Antibes, 1992. *Publications:* The Traveller's Tree (Heinemann Foundation Prize for Literature, 1950, and Kemsley Prize, 1951); trans. Colette, Chance Acquaintances, 1952; A Time to Keep Silence, 1953; The Violins of Saint Jacques, 1953; Mani, 1958 (Duff Cooper Meml Prize; Book Society's Choice); (trans.) The Cretan Runner (George Psychoundakis), 1955; Roumeli, 1966; A Time of Gifts, 1977 (W. H. Smith & Son Literary Award, 1978); Between the Woods and the Water, 1986 (Thomas Cook Travel Book Award, 1986; Internat. PEN/Time Life Silver Pen Award, 1986); Three Letters from the Andes, 1991. *Recreation:* travel. *Address:* c/o Messrs John Murray, 50 Albemarle Street, W1X 4BD. *Clubs:* White's, Travellers', Pratt's, Beefsteak, Special Forces, Puffins.

FERMOR-HESKETH, family name of **Baron Hesketh.**

FERMOY, 6th Baron *cr* 1856; **Patrick Maurice Burke Roche;** *b* 11 Oct. 1967; *s* of 5th Baron Fermoy and of Lavinia Frances Elizabeth, *o d* of late Captain John Pitman; *S* father, 1984. *Educ:* Eton. Blues and Royals, commissioned 1987; Capt. *Heir: b* Hon. (Edmund) Hugh Burke Roche, *b* 5 Feb. 1972. *Address:* Axford House, Axford, near Marlborough, Wilts SN8 2EY.

FERNANDES, Most Rev. Angelo; Archbishop of Delhi (RC), 1967–91, now Emeritus; President, International Catholic Education Organisation, since 1990; *b* 28 July 1913; *s* of late John Ligorio and Evelyn Sabina Fernandes. *Educ:* St Patrick's, Karachi; St Joseph's Seminary, Mangalore; Papal University, Kandy, Ceylon (STL). Secretary to Archbishop Roberts of Bombay, 1943–47; Administrator of Holy Name Cathedral, Bombay, 1947–59; Coadjutor Archbishop of Delhi, 1959–67; Sec. Gen., Catholic Bishops' Conf. of India, 1960–72 (Chm., Justice and Peace Commn, 1968–76, 1986–90). Pres., World Conf. of Religion for Peace, 1970–84, now Emeritus. Member: Vatican Secretariat for Non-Believers, 1966–71; Vatican Justice and Peace Acad., 1966–76; Secretariat of Synod of Bishops, 1971–74, 1980–83; Office of Human Develt of Fedn of Asian Bishops' Confs, 1973–78 (Chm., Exec. Cttee for Ecumenism and Inter-Religious Affairs, Asia, 1985–89). Founder Mem., Planetary Citizens, 1972. Hon. DD Vatican, 1959. *Publications:* Apostolic Endeavour, 1962; Religion, Development and Peace, 1971; Religion and the Quality of Life, 1974; Religion and a New World Order, 1976; Towards Peace with Justice, 1981; God's Rule and Man's Role, 1982 (Gandhi Meml Lect.); Summons to Dialogue, 1983; The Christian Way Today, 1987; As you Pray, so you Live, 1992; Building Bridges: the missing dimension in education, 1993; Experience of Dialogue, 1994; articles in Clergy Monthly, Vidyajyoti, World Justice, Religion and Society, Social Action, Reality, etc. *Recreations:* music, especially classical, and wide travel on the occasion of numerous meetings in many countries of the world. *Address:* Archbishop's House, Ashok Place, New Delhi 110001, India. *T:* 343457, 343593.

FERNANDO, Most Rev. Nicholas Marcus; *see* Colombo, Archbishop of, (RC).

FERNEYHOUGH, Prof. Brian John Peter; composer; Professor of Music, University of California at San Diego, since 1987; *b* 16 Jan. 1943; *s* of Frederick George Ferneyhough and Emily May (*née* Hopwood); *m* 1st, 1967, Barbara Joan Pearson; 2nd, 1980, Elke Schaaf; 3rd, 1984, Carolyn Steinberg. *Educ:* Birmingham Sch. of Music; RAM; Sweelinck Conservatory, Amsterdam; Musikakademie, Basle. Mendelssohn Schol., 1968; Stipend: City of Basle, 1969; Heinrich-Strobel-Stiftung des Südwestfunks, 1972; Composition teacher, Musikhochschule, Freiburg, 1973–86 (Prof., 1978–86); Principal Composition Teacher, Royal Conservatory, The Hague, 1986–87. Guest Artist, Artists' Exchange Scheme, Deutsche Akad. Austauschdienst, Berlin, 1976–77; Lectr, Darmstadt Summer Sch., 1976– (Comp. course co-ordinator, 1984–); Guest Prof., Royal Conservatory, Stockholm, 1981–83, 1985; Vis. Prof., Univ. of Chicago, 1986; Master Class, Civica Scuola di Musica di Milano, 1985–. Mem., ISCM Internat. Jury, 1977, 1988. Prizes, Gaudeamus Internat. Comp., 1968, 1969; First Prize, ISCM Internat. Comp., Rome, 1974; Koussevitsky Prize, 1978. Chevalier, l'Ordre des Arts et des Lettres, 1984. *Compositions include:* Sonatas for String Quartet, 1967; Epicycle, for 20 solo strings, 1968; Firecycle Beta, for large orch. with 5 conductors, 1971; Time and Motion Studies I–III, 1974–76; Unity Capsule, for solo flute, 1975; Funérailles, for 7 strings and harp, 1978; La Terre est un Homme, for orch., 1979; 2nd String Quartet, 1980; Lemma-Icon-Epigram, for solo piano, 1981; Carceri d'Invenzione, for various ensembles, 1981–86; 3rd String Quartet, 1987; Kurze Schatten II, for guitar, 1988; La Chute d'Icare, for clarinet ensemble, 1988; Trittico per G. S., 1989; 4th String Quartet, 1990; Bone Alphabet, for percussionist, 1991; Terrain, for violin and eight instruments, 1992. *Publications:* collected writings: in Quaderni della Civica Scuola di Musica, numero speciale (Italian lang.), 1984; in Contemporary Music Review, 1993; articles in Contrechamps, Musiktexte, and Contemp. Music Rev. *Recreations:* reading, wine, cats. *Address:* 7150-D Calabria Court, San Diego, CA 92122, USA. *T:* (619) 558 0276.

FERNIE, Prof. Eric Campbell, CBE 1995; FSA 1973; FRSE; Watson Gordon Professor of Fine Art, University of Edinburgh, since 1984 (Dean, Faculty of Arts, 1989–92); *b* Edinburgh, 9 June 1939; *s* of Sydney Robert and Catherine Reid Fernie; *m* 1964, Margaret Lorraine French; one *s* two *d*. *Educ:* Univ. of the Witwatersrand (BA Hons Fine Arts); Univ. of London (Academic Diploma). FRSE 1993. Lectr, Univ. of the Witwatersrand, 1963–67; University of East Anglia: Lectr and Sen. Lectr, 1967–84; Dean, Sch. of Fine Art and Music, 1977–81; Public Orator, 1982–84. Chm., Ancient Monuments Bd for Scotland, 1989–; Trustee: Nat. Galleries of Scotland, 1991–; Scotland Inheritance Fund, 1992–; Mem., Historic Bldgs and Monuments Commn, 1995–. Vice-Pres., Soc. of Antiquaries of London, 1992–95. *Publications:* An Introduction to the Communar and Pitcaner Rolls of Norwich Cathedral Priory (with A. B. Whittingham), 1973; The Architecture of the Anglo-Saxons, 1983; An Architectural History of Norwich Cathedral, 1993; contribs to British and overseas architectural jls. *Address:* 17 Buckingham Terrace, Edinburgh EH4 3AD. *T:* 0131–332 6858.

FERNYHOUGH, Ven. Bernard; Archdeacon of Oakham, since 1977; Non-Residentiary Canon of Peterborough Cathedral, 1974–77 and since 1989 (Canon Residentiary, 1977–89); Priest-in-charge, Empingham and Exton with Horn and Whitwell, since 1995; *b* 2 Sept. 1932; *s* of Edward and Edith Fernyhough; *m* 1957, Freda Malkin; one *s* one *d*. *Educ:* Wolstanton Grammar Sch.; Saint David's Coll., Lampeter (BA 1953). Precentor, Trinidad Cathedral, 1955–61; Rector of Stoke Bruerne with Grafton Regis and Alderton, 1961–67; Vicar of Ravensthorpe with East Haddon and Holdenby, 1967–77; Rural Dean: Preston, 1965–67; Haddon, 1968–70; Brixworth, 1971–77. *Address:* The Rectory, Empingham, Rutland LE15 8PT. *T:* Empingham (01780) 460345.

FEROZE, Sir Rustam Moolan, Kt 1983; MD; FRCS, FRCOG; retired; (first) President, European Association of Obstetrics and Gynaecology, 1985–88, now Hon. President; Consulting Obstetrician, Queen Charlotte's Maternity Hospital; Consulting Surgeon, Chelsea Hospital for Women; *b* 4 Aug. 1920; *s* of Dr J. Moolan-Feroze; *m* 1947, Margaret Dowsett; three *s* one *d*. *Educ:* Sutton Valence Sch.; King's Coll. and King's Coll. Hospital, London. MRCS, LRCP 1943; MB, BS 1946; MRCOG 1948; MD (Obst. & Dis. Wom.) London 1952; FRCS 1952; FRCOG 1962; Hon. FRCSI 1984; Hon. FRACOG 1985; Hon. FACOG 1986. Surg.-Lt, RNVR, 1943–46. King's Coll. Hosp., 1946; RMO, Samaritan Hosp. for Women, 1948; Sen. Registrar: Hosp. for Women, Soho Sq., and Middlesex Hosp., 1950–53; Chelsea Hosp. for Women, and Queen Charlotte's Maternity Hosp., 1953–54; Consultant Obstetrician and Gynaecologist, King's Coll. Hosp., 1952–85. Dean, Inst. of Obstetrics and Gynaecology, Univ. of London, 1954–67; Dir, Postgrad. Studies, RCOG, 1975–80; Pres., RCOG, 1981–84; Chm., Conf. of Royal Colls and Faculties, 1982–84. McIlrath Guest Prof., Royal Prince Alfred Hosp., Sydney, 1970. Lectures: Soc. of Obstetrics and Gynaecology of Canada, Winnipeg, 1978; Bartholomew Mosse, Dublin, 1982; Shirodkar Meml, Bombay, 1982; Charter Day, National Maternity Hosp., Dublin, 1984. Past Examiner: RCOG; Univs of London, Cambridge, Birmingham and Singapore. *Publications:* contributor: Integrated Obstetrics and Gynaecology for Postgraduates, 1981; Gynaecological Oncology, 1981, rev. edn 1992; Bonney's Gynaecological Surgery, 1986; contribs to med. jls. *Recreations:* gardening, Bonsai, music, swimming. *Address:* 21 Kenwood Drive, Beckenham, Kent BR3 2QX. *Club:* Royal Automobile.

FERRALL, Sir Raymond (Alfred), Kt 1982; CBE 1969; retired; *b* 27 May 1906; *s* of Alfred C. Ferrall and Edith M. Ferrall; *m* 1931, Lorna, *d* of P. M. Findlay; two *s* two *d*. *Educ:* Launceston C of E Grammar Sch. Chairman: Launceston Bank for Savings, 1976–82; Tasmanian Colls of Advanced Educn, 1977–81; Launceston C of E Grammar Sch. Bd, 1956–73; Master Warden, Port of Launceston Authority, 1960–80. Captain, Tasmanian Cricket team, 1934; Vice Captain, Tasmanian Amateur Football team, 1932. Freeman, City of Launceston, 1981. Queen's Silver Jubilee Medal, 1977. *Publications:* Partly Personal, 1976; Idylls of the Mayor, 1978; Notable Tasmanians, 1980; The Age of Chiselry, 1981; The Story of the Port of Launceston, 1984; A Proud Heritage, 1985. *Recreations:* writing, print collecting, sailing. *Address:* Elphin House, 3 Olive Street, Launceston, Tas 7250, Australia. *T:* (03) 317122. *Clubs:* Launceston, Northern, Tamar Yacht (Tasmania).

FERRANTI, Sebastian Basil Joseph Ziani de; *see* de Ferranti.

FERRERS, 13th Earl *cr* 1711; **Robert Washington Shirley;** Viscount Tamworth 1711; Bt 1611; PC 1982; DL; High Steward of Norwich Cathedral, since 1979; Minister of State (Minister for the Environment and the Countryside), Department of the Environment, since 1995; Deputy Leader of the House of Lords, since 1988; *b* 8 June 1929; *o s* of 12th Earl Ferrers and Hermione Morley (*d* 1969); *S* father, 1954; *m* 1951, Annabel Mary, *d* of late Brig. W. G. Carr, CVO, DSO; two *s* three *d*. *Educ:* Winchester Coll. (Fellow, 1988); Magdalene Coll., Cambridge. MA (Agric.). Lieut Coldstream Guards, 1949 (as National Service). A Lord-in-waiting, 1962–64, 1971–74; Parly Sec., MAFF, 1974; Jt Dep. Leader of the Opposition, House of Lords, 1976–79; Dep. Leader of House of Lords, 1979–83; Minister of State: MAFF, 1979–83; Home Office, 1988–94; DTI, 1994–95. Mem., Armitage Cttee on political activities of civil servants, 1976–. Chm., TSB of Eastern England, 1977–79; Mem., TSB Central Bd, 1977–79; Director: Central TSB, 1978–79; TSB Trustcard Ltd, 1978–79; Norwich Union Insurance Group, 1975–79 and 1983–88. Chairman: RCHM(Eng.), 1984–88; British Agricl Export Council, 1984–88; Mem. Council, Food From Britain, 1984–88; Director: Economic Forestry Gp, 1985–88; Chatham Historic Dockyard Trust, 1984–88. Mem. Council, Hurstpierpoint Coll., 1959–68. DL Norfolk, 1983. *Heir: s* Viscount Tamworth, *qv*. *Address:* Ditchingham Hall, Bungay, Suffolk NR35 2LE. *Club:* Beefsteak.

FERRIER, Prof. Robert Patton, FRSE 1977; Professor of Natural Philosophy, University of Glasgow, since 1973; *b* 4 Jan. 1934; *s* of William McFarlane Ferrier and Gwendoline Melita Edwards; *m* 1961, Valerie Jane Duncan; two *s* one *d*. *Educ:* Glebelands Sch. and Morgan Academy, Dundee; Univ. of St Andrews (BSc, PhD). MA Cantab, FInstP. Scientific Officer, AERE Harwell, 1959–61; Res. Assoc., MIT, 1961–62; Sen. Asst in Res., Cavendish Lab., Cambridge, 1962–66; Fellow of Fitzwilliam Coll., Cambridge, 1965–73; Asst Dir of Res., Cavendish Lab. 1966–71; Lectr in Physics, Univ. of Cambridge, 1971–73; Guest Scientist, IBM Res. Labs San José, Calif, 1972–73. Chm., SERC Semiconductor and Surface Physics Sub-Cttee, 1979–. *Publications:* numerous papers in Phil. Mag., Jl Appl. Physics, Jl Physics, etc. *Recreations:* do-it-yourself, tennis, gardening, reading novels. *Address:* Glencoe, 31 Thorn Road, Bearsden, Glasgow G61 4BS. *T:* 0141–942 3592, (office) 0141–330 5388.

FERRIS, *see* Grant-Ferris, family name of Baron Harvington.

FERRIS, Hon. Sir Francis (Mursell), Kt 1990; TD 1965; **Hon. Mr Justice Ferris;** Judge of the High Court of Justice, Chancery Division, since 1990; *b* 19 Aug. 1932; *s* of Francis William Ferris and Elsie Lilian May Ferris (*née* Mursell); *m* 1957, Sheila Elizabeth Hester Falloon Bedford; three *s* one *d*. *Educ:* Bryanston Sch.; Oriel Coll., Oxford. BA (Modern History) 1955, MA 1979. Served RA, 1951–52; 299 Field Regt (RBY QOOH and Berks) RA, TA 1952–67, Major 1964. Called to the Bar, Lincoln's Inn, 1956, Bencher, 1987; practice at Chancery Bar, 1958–90; Standing Counsel to Dir Gen. of Fair Trading, 1966–80; QC 1980; a Recorder, 1989–90. Member: Bar Council, 1966–70; Senate of Inns of Court and the Bar, 1979–82. *Recreation:* gardening. *Address:* Royal Courts of Justice, Strand, WC2A 2LL. *Club:* Marlow Rowing.

FERRIS, Paul Frederick; author and journalist; *b* 15 Feb. 1929; *o c* of late Frederick Morgan Ferris and of Olga Ferris; *m* 1953, Gloria Moreton; one *s* one *d*. *Educ:* Swansea Gram. Sch. Staff of South Wales Evening Post, 1949–52; Womans Own, 1953; Observer Foreign News Service, 1953–54. *Publications: novels:* A Changed Man, 1958; Then We Fall, 1960; A Family Affair, 1963; The Destroyer, 1965; The Dam, 1967; Very Personal Problems, 1973; The Cure, 1974; The Detective, 1976; Talk to Me About England, 1979; A Distant Country, 1983; Children of Dust, 1988; The Divining Heart, 1995; *non-fiction:* The City, 1960; The Church of England, 1962; The Doctors, 1965; The Nameless: abortion in Britain today, 1966; Men and Money: financial Europe today, 1968; The House of Northcliffe, 1971; The New Militants, 1972; Dylan Thomas, 1977; Richard Burton, 1981; Gentlemen of Fortune: the world's investment bankers, 1984; (ed) The Collected Letters of Dylan Thomas, 1986; Sir Huge: the life of Huw Wheldon, 1990; Sex and the British: a 20th century history, 1993; Caitlin, 1993; *television plays:* The Revivalist, 1975; Dylan, 1978; Nye, 1982; The Extremist, 1984; The Fasting Girl, 1984. *Address:* c/o Curtis Brown Ltd, 162–168 Regent Street, W1R 5TB. *T:* 0171–872 0331.

FERRIS, Rt Rev. Ronald Curry; *see* Algoma, Bishop of.

FERSHT, Prof. Alan Roy, MA, PhD; FRS 1983; Herchel Smith Professor of Organic Chemistry, and Fellow, Gonville and Caius College, Cambridge since 1988; Director: Cambridge Interdisciplinary Research Centre in Protein Engineering, since 1989; MRC Unit for Protein Function and Design, since 1989; *b* 21 April 1943; *s* of Philip and Betty Fersht; *m* 1966, Marilyn Persell; one *s* one *d*. *Educ:* Sir George Monoux Grammar Sch.; Gonville and Caius Coll., Cambridge (MA, PhD). Res. Fellow, Brandeis Univ., 1968; Scientific Staff, MRC Lab. of Molecular Biology, Cambridge, 1969–77; Fellow, Jesus Coll., Cambridge, 1969–72; Eleanor Roosevelt Fellow, Stanford Univ., 1978; Wolfson Res. Prof. of Royal Society, Dept of Chemistry, Imperial Coll. of Science and Technology, 1978–89. Lectures: Smith Kline & French, Berkeley, 1984; Edsall, Harvard, 1984; B. R. Baker, Univ. of California at Santa Barbara, 1986; Frank Mathers, Univ. of Indiana, 1986; Cornell Biotechnol Program, 1987; Ferdinand Springer, FEBS, 1988–89; Calvin, Berkeley, 1990; Walker, Edinburgh, 1990; Max Tishler Prize, Harvard Univ., 1991–92; Jubilee, Biochemical Soc., 1993; E. Gordon Young Meml, Canada, 1993; Brändström, Gothenberg, 1993; Sternbach, Yale, 1994; Sunner Meml, Lund, 1994; Heatley, Oxford, 1995; Chan, Berkeley, 1995. Mem., EMBO, 1980–. Hon. For. Mem., Amer. Acad. of Arts and Sci., 1988; Mem., Academia Europaea, 1989. Essex County Jun. Chess Champion, 1961; Pres., Cambridge Univ. Chess Club, 1964 (Half Blue, 1965). FEBS Anniversary Prize, 1980; Novo Biotechnology Prize, 1986; Charmian Medal, RSC, 1986; Gabor Medal, Royal Soc., 1991; Harden Medal, Biochemical Soc., 1993. *Publications:* Enzyme Structure and Mechanism, 1977, 2nd edn 1984; papers in scientific jls. *Recreations:* chess, horology. *Address:* University Chemical Laboratory, Lensfield Road, Cambridge CB2 1EW. *T:* Cambridge (01223) 336341, *Fax:* Cambridge (01223) 336445; 2 Barrow Close, Cambridge CB2 1AT.

FESSEY, Mereth Cecil, CB 1977; Director, Business Statistics Office, 1969–77, retired; *b* Windsor, Berks, 19 May 1917; *s* of late Morton Fessey and Ethel Fessey (*née* Blake), Bristol; *m* 1945, Grace Lilian, *d* of late William Bray, Earlsfield, London; one *s* two *d*. *Educ:* Westminster City Sch.; LSE, Univ. of London. London Transport, 1934; Army, 1940; Min. of Transport, 1947; Board of Trade, 1948; Statistician, 1956; Chief Statistician, 1965. Statistical Adviser to Syrian and Mexican Govts, 1979; Consultant, Statistical Office, Eur. Communities, 1990–. Chm. of Council, Inst. of Statisticians, 1970–73; Vice Pres. and Mem., Council, Royal Statistical Soc., 1974–78; Chm., Cttee of Librarians and Statisticians, LA/Royal Stat. Soc., 1978–. Hon. FLA 1984. *Publications:* articles and papers in: Economic Trends; Statistical News; Jl of Royal Statistical Soc.; The Statistician; Annales de Sciences Economiques Appliquées, Louvain; etc. *Recreations:* chess, walking. *Address:* Undy House, Undy, Gwent NP6 3BX. *T:* Magor (01633) 880478.

FETHERSTON-DILKE, Capt. Charles Beaumont; RN retired; Vice Lord-Lieutenant, Warwickshire, since 1990; *b* 4 April 1921; *s* of late Dr Beaumont Albany Fetherston-Dilke, MBE and Phoebe Stella (*née* Bedford); *m* 1943, Pauline Stanley-Williams; one *s* one *d*. *Educ:* RNC, Dartmouth. Entered RN, 1935; served throughout War of 1939–45 and Korean War, 1952–54 (underwater warfare specialist); Comdr 1955; Danish Naval Staff, 1955–58; staff of C-in-C S Atlantic and S America Station, 1960–61; Captain 1961; Naval Dep. to UK Nat. Mil. Rep., SHAPE, 1962–64; comd HMS St Vincent, 1964–66; Defence Policy Staff, MOD, 1966–68; retired 1968. Warwickshire: JP 1969–91; CC, 1970–81 (Chm., 1978–80); Chm., CLA, 1984–87; High Sheriff 1974; DL 1974. SBStJ 1986 (Mem. Council, 1977–92). Seigneur de Vangalême, Jersey. *Publication:* A Short History of Maxstoke Castle, 1985. *Recreations:* country pursuits. *Address:* Keeper's Cottage,

Maxstoke, Coleshill, Birmingham B46 2QA. *T:* Coleshill (01675) 465100. *Club:* Army and Navy.

See also M. S. Fetherston-Dilke.

FETHERSTON-DILKE, Mary Stella, CBE 1968; RRC 1966; Organiser, Citizens' Advice Bureau, 1971–83, retired; *b* 21 Sept. 1918; *d* of late B. A. Fetherston-Dilke, MBE. *Educ:* Kingsley Sch., Leamington Spa; St George's Hospital, London (SRN). Joined QARNNS, 1942; Matron-in-Chief, QARNNS, 1966–70, retired. OStJ 1966. *Recreation:* antiques. *Address:* 12 Clareville Court, Clareville Grove, SW7 5AT.

See also C. B. Fetherston-Dilke.

FETTIPLACE, Prof. Robert, FRS 1990; Steenbock Professor of Neural and Behavioral Sciences, University of Wisconsin, since 1991; *b* 24 Feb. 1946; *s* of George Robert Fettiplace and Maisie Fettiplace (*née* Rolson); *m* 1977, Merriel Cleone Kruse. *Educ:* Nottingham High Sch.; Sidney Sussex Coll., Cambridge (BA 1968; MA 1972; PhD 1974). Research Fellow: Sidney Sussex Coll., Cambridge, 1971–74, Stanford Univ., 1974–76; Elmore Res. Fellow, Cambridge, 1976–79; Howe Sen. Res. Fellow, Royal Soc., 1979–90. *Publications:* contribs to Jl Physiology and other learned jls. *Recreations:* bird watching, listening to music. *Address:* Department of Neurophysiology, University of Wisconsin, 273 Medical Sciences Building, 1300 University Avenue, Madison, WI 53706, USA. *T:* (608) 2629320.

FEUILLÈRE, Edwige; Commandeur de la Légion d'Honneur; Commandeur des Arts et Lettres; French actress; *b* 29 Oct.; *m* (divorced). *Educ:* Lycée de Dijon; Conservatoire National de Paris. *Plays include:* La Dame aux camélias, 1940–42, 1952–53; Sodome et Gomorrhe, 1943; L'Aigle a deux têtes, 1946; Partage de midi, Pour Lucrèce, La Parisienne, Phèdre, Lucy Crown, Constance, Rodogune, 1964; La Folle de Chaillot, 1965–66; Delicate Balance; Sweet Bird of Youth; Le bâteau pour Lipaïa, 1971; Leocadia, 1984–85; (with Jean Marais) La Maison du Lac, 1986. *Films include:* L'Idiot, 1946; L'Aigle a deux têtes, 1947; Olivia, 1950; Le Blé en herbe, 1952; En cas de malheur, 1958; La vie à deux, 1958; Les amours célèbres, 1961; Le crime ne paye pas, 1962; La chair de l'orchidée, 1975. *Television series:* Cinema, 1988. *Publications:* Les Feux de la Mémoire, 1977; Moi, La Clairon: biographie romancée de Mlle Clairon, 1984. *Address:* c/o Joëlle Bonnet, Agents Associés, 201 rue du Faubourg Saint-Honoré, 75008 Paris, France.

FEVERSHAM, 6th Baron *cr* 1826; **Charles Antony Peter Duncombe;** free-lance journalist; *b* 3 Jan. 1945; *s* of late Col Antony John Duncombe-Anderson and G. G. V. McNalty; *S* (to barony of) *kinsman,* 3rd Earl of Feversham (the earldom having become extinct), 1963; *m* 1st, 1966, Shannon (*d* 1976), *d* of late Sir Thomas Foy, CSI, CIE; two *s* one *d*; 2nd, 1979, Pauline, *d* of John Aldridge, Newark, Notts; one *s. Educ:* Eton; Middle Temple. Chairman: Standing Conf. of Regional Arts Assocs, 1969–76; Trustees, Yorkshire Sculpture Park, 1981–; President: Yorkshire Arts Assoc., 1987–91 (Chm., 1969–80); Soc. of Yorkshiremen in London, 1974; The Arvon Foundn, 1976–86; Yorks and Cleveland Local Councils Assoc., 1977–; Nat. Assoc. of Local Councils, 1986–. Governor, Leeds Polytechnic, 1969–76. *Publications:* A Wolf in Tooth (novel), 1967; Great Yachts, 1970. *Heir: s* Hon. Jasper Orlando Slingsby Duncombe, *b* 14 March 1968. *Address:* Duncombe Park, Helmsley, York Y06 5EB.

FFITCH, George Norman; Managing Director, London Broadcasting Company and Independent Radio News, 1979–85; *b* 23 Jan. 1929; *s* of late Robert George Ffitch; *m* 1958, Pamela Mary Lyle (*d* 1990); one *s* one *d. Educ:* state schools and London Univ. Industrial Correspondent, Political Correspondent and Output Editor, Independent Television News, 1955–62; interviewer and presenter, ITV, 1962–67; Political Editor and an Asst Editor, The Economist, 1967–74; Associate Editor, Daily Express, 1974–76; columnist and broadcaster, 1976–79. *Recreation:* playing at playing golf. *Address:* 13 Charlwood Terrace, SW15 1NZ. *T:* 0181–785 2460. *Club:* Reform.

FFOLKES, Sir Robert (Francis Alexander), 7th Bt *cr* 1774; OBE 1990; *b* 2 Dec. 1943; *o s* of Captain Sir (Edward John) Patrick (Boschetti) ffolkes, 6th Bt, and Geraldine (*d* 1978), *d* of late William Roffey, Writtle, Essex; *S* father, 1960. *Educ:* Stowe Sch.; Christ Church, Oxford. *Address:* Coast Guard House, Morston, Holt, Norfolk NR25 7BH. *Club:* Turf.

FFORDE, John Standish; official historian, Bank of England, 1984–92; *b* 16 Nov. 1921; 4th *s* of late Francis Creswell Fforde, Raughlan, Lurgan, Co. Armagh, and Cicely Creswell; *m* 1951, Marya, *d* of late Joseph Retinger; three *s* one *d. Educ:* Rossall Sch.; Christ Church, Oxford (1st cl. Hons PPE). Served RAF, 1940–46. Prime Minister's Statistical Branch, 1951–53; Fellow, Nuffield Coll., Oxford, 1953–56; entered Bank of England, 1957; Dep. Chief, Central Banking Information Dept, 1959–64; Adviser to the Governors, 1964–66; Chief Cashier, 1966–70; Exec. Dir (Home Finance), 1970–82; Advr to the Governors, 1982–84. Chm., Jt Mission Hosp. Equipment Bd Ltd, subseq. Echo Internat. Health Services, 1985–96 (Dir, 1979–93); Director: Mercantile House Hldgs, 1984–87; Halifax BS, 1984–92; CL-Alexanders Laing and Cruickshank, subseq. Credit Lyonnais Capital Markets, 1987–91. *Publications:* The Federal Reserve System, 1945–49, 1953; An International Trade in Managerial Skills, 1957; The Bank of England and Public Policy 1941–1958, 1992. *Recreations:* travel, walking.

FFOWCS WILLIAMS, Prof. John Eirwyn, FEng 1988; Rank Professor of Engineering (Acoustics), University of Cambridge, and Professorial Fellow, Emmanuel College, Cambridge, since 1972; *b* 25 May 1935; *m* 1959, Anne Beatrice Mason; two *s* one *d. Educ:* Friends Sch., Great Ayton; Derby Techn. Coll.; Univ. of Southampton. BSc; MA, ScD Cantab 1986; PhD Southampton. CEng, FRAeS, FInstP, FIMA, FInstAcoust, Fellow Acoustical Soc. of America, FAIAA. Engrg Apprentice, Rolls-Royce Ltd, 1951–55; Spitfire Mitchell Meml Schol. to Southampton Univ., 1955–60 (Pres., Students' Union, 1957–58); Aerodynamics Div., NPL, 1960–62; Bolt, Beranek & Newman Inc., 1962–64; Reader in Applied Maths, Imperial Coll. of Science and Technology, 1964–69; Rolls Royce Prof. of Theoretical Acoustics, Imperial Coll., 1969–72. Chairman: Concorde Noise Panel, 1965–75; Topexpress Ltd, 1979–89; Dir, VSEL Consortium plc, 1987–. Chm., Noise Research Cttee, ARC, 1969–76. FRSA. Honour Prof., Beijing Inst. of Aeronautics and Astronautics, 1992–. Foreign Hon. Mem., Amer. Acad. Arts and Scis, 1989; Foreign Associate, NAE, USA. Gov., Felsted Sch., 1980–94. AIAA Aero-Acoustics Medal, 1977; Rayleigh Medal, Inst. of Acoustics, 1984; Silver Medal, Société Française d'Acoustique, 1989; Gold Medal, RAeS, 1990. *Publications:* (with A. P. Dowling) Sound and Sources of Sound, 1983; articles in Philosophical Trans Royal Soc., Jl of Fluid Mechanics, Jl IMA, Jl of Sound Vibration, Annual Reviews of Fluid Mechanics, Random Vibration, Financial Times; (jtly) film on Aerodynamic Sound. *Recreations:* friends and cigars. *Address:* 298 Hills Road, Cambridge CB2 2QG. *T:* Cambridge (01223) 248275. *Clubs:* Athenæum, Danish.

FFRENCH, family name of **Baron ffrench.**

FFRENCH, 8th Baron *cr* 1798; **Robuck John Peter Charles Mario ffrench;** Bt 1779; *b* 14 March 1956; *s* of 7th Baron ffrench and of Sonia Katherine, *d* of late Major Digby Cayley; *S* father, 1986; *m* 1987, Dörthe Marie-Louise, *d* of Captain Wilhelm Schauer; one *d. Educ:* Blackrock, Co. Dublin; Ampleforth College, Yorks. *Heir: uncle* John Charles Mary Joseph Francis ffrench [*b* 5 Oct. 1928; *m* 1963, Sara-Primm, *d* of James A. Turner; three *d*]. *Address:* Castle ffrench, Ballinasloe, Co. Galway, Ireland. *T:* Roscommon (903) 4226.

FFYTCHE, Timothy John, FRCS; Surgeon-Oculist to HM Household, since 1980; Ophthalmic Surgeon to St Thomas's Hospital, since 1973; Consultant Ophthalmologist, Moorfields Eye Hospital, since 1975; Hospital of Tropical Diseases, since 1988; Consultant Ophthalmic Surgeon to King Edward VIIth Hospital for Officers, since 1980; *b* 11 Sept. 1936; *s* of late Louis ffytche and of Margaret (*née* Law); *m* 1961, Bärbl, *d* of late Günther Fischer; two *s. Educ:* Lancing Coll.; St George's Hosp., London. MB, BS; DO 1961; FRCS 1968. Registrar, Moorfields Eye Hosp., 1966–69; Wellcome Lectr, Hammersmith Hosp., 1969–70; Sen. Registrar, Middlesex Hosp., 1970–73. Sec., OSUK, 1980–82. Mem., Medical Adv. Bd, LEPRA, 1982–; Vice-Pres., Ophthalmol Sect., RSocMed, 1985–88; UK rep. to Internat. Fedn of Ophthalmic Socs, 1985–89; Mem., Adv. Cttee to Internat. Council of Ophthalmology, 1985–. Founder, Ophthalmic Aid to Eastern Europe, 1990–; Co-chm., European Sect., Internat. Agency for Prevention of Blindness, 1994–. Clayton Meml Lectr, LEPRA, 1984. Editorial Committee: Ophthalmic Literature, 1968–; Transactions of OSUK, 1984–89, Eye, 1989–; European Jl of Ophthalmology, 1990–. *Publications:* articles on retinal diagnosis and therapy, retinal photography and the ocular complications of leprosy, in The Lancet, British Jl of Ophthalmol., Trans OSUK, Proc. Roy. Soc. Med., Leprosy Review and other specialist jls. *Recreations:* travel, cricket, occasional fishing. *Address:* 149 Harley Street, W1N 2DE; (home) 1 Wellington Square, SW3 4NJ.

FICKLING, Benjamin William, CBE 1973; FRCS, FDS RCS; Honorary Consultant Dental Surgeon, since 1974, formerly Dental Surgeon: St George's Hospital, SW1, 1936–74; Royal Dental Hospital of London, 1935–74; Mount Vernon Centre for Plastic and Jaw Surgery (formerly Hill End), 1941–74; *b* 14 July 1909; *s* of Robert Marshall Fickling, LDS RCS, and Florence (*née* Newson); *m* 1943, Shirley Dona, *er d* of Albert Latimer Walker, FRCS; two *s* one *d. Educ:* Framlingham; St George's Hosp. Royal Dental Hospital. William Brown Senior Exhibition, St George's Hosp., 1929; LDS RCS, 1932; MRCS, LRCP, 1934; FRCS 1938; FDS, RCS 1947, MGDS RCS 1979. Lectures: Charles Tomes, RCS, 1956; Everett Magnus, Melbourne, 1971; Webb-Johnson, RCS, 1978. Examiner (Chm.), Membership in Gen. Dental Surgery, 1979–83; formerly Examiner: in Dental Surgery, RCS; Univ. of London and Univ. of Edinburgh. Dean of Faculty of Dental Surgery, 1968–71, and Mem. Council, Royal College of Surgeons, 1968–71 (Vice-Dean, 1965; Colyer Gold Medal, 1979); Fellow Royal Society of Medicine (Pres. Odontological Section, 1964–65); Pres., British Assoc. of Oral Surgeons, 1967–68; Mem. GDC, 1971–74. Director: Med. Sickness Annuity and Life Assurance Soc. Ltd, 1967–86; Permanent Insurance Co. Ltd, 1974–86; Medical Sickness Finance Corp. Ltd, 1977–86. Civilian Dental Consultant to RN, 1954–76. *Publications:* (joint) Injuries of the Jaws and Face, 1940; (joint) Chapter on Faciomaxillary Injuries and Deformities in British Surgical Practice, 1951. *Address:* 29 Maxwell Road, Northwood, Mddx HA6 2YG. *T:* Northwood (01923) 822035. *Club:* Ski Club of Great Britain.

FIDDES, James Raffan, QC (Scot.) 1965; Sheriff of South Strathclyde, Dumfries and Galloway at Hamilton, 1977–88; *b* 1 Feb. 1919; *er s* of late Sir James Raffan Fiddes, CBE; *m* 1st, 1954, Edith Margaret (*d* 1979), 2nd *d* of late Charles E. Lippe, KC; 2nd, 1985, Jiřina (marr. diss. 1991), *d* of late Jan Kuchař, Brno, Czechoslovakia. *Educ:* Aberdeen Gram. Sch.; Glasgow Univ. (MA, 1942; LLB 1948); Balliol Coll., Oxford, (BA 1944). Advocate, 1948. *Address:* 23 South Learmonth Gardens, Edinburgh EH4 1EZ. *T:* 0131–332 1431. *Club:* Scottish Arts (Edinburgh).

FIDDICK, Peter Ronald; journalist and broadcaster; *b* 21 Oct. 1938; *s* of Wing-Comdr Ronald Fiddick and Phyllis (*née* Wherry); *m* 1966, Jane Mary Hodlin; one *s* one *d. Educ:* Reading Sch.; Magdalen Coll., Oxford (BA English Lang. and Lit.). Journalist, Liverpool Daily Post, 1962–65; Leader writer, Westminster Press, 1965–66; Asst Editor, Nova, 1968; The Guardian: reporter, 1966–67 and 1969; Asst Features Editor, 1970–75; Television Columnist, 1971–84; Media Editor, 1984–88; Editor: The Listener, 1989–91; Television (RTS), 1991–; Research (Market Res. Soc.), 1992–. FRTS 1992; Mem., BAFTA. Wrote and presented television series: Looking at Television, 1975–76; The Television Programme, 1979–80; Soviet Television—Fact and Fiction, 1985. *Publication:* (with B. Smithies) Enoch Powell on Immigration, 1969. *Recreations:* music, food, Saturdays.

FIDLER, Jan; Ambassador of the Czechoslovak Socialist Republic to the Court of St James's, 1986–90; *b* 14 May 1927; *s* of Marie and Josef Fidler; *m* 1950, Alena (*née* Oulehlová); two *s. Educ:* Higher School of Economics. Manager in woollen industry, 1950–60; Min. of Foreign Affairs, 1960–63; Second Sec., Stockholm, 1963–67; Min. of Foreign Affairs, 1967–70; Counsellor, Helsinki, 1970–77; Head, Office of First Dep. Minister, 1977–80; Minister Counsellor, Warsaw, 1980–83; Chief of Diplomatic Protocol, Min. of Foreign Affairs, 1984–86. Holder of State distinctions. *Address:* Sněženkova 3095, Prague 10, Czechoslovakia. *T:* 753440.

FIDLER-SIMPSON, John Cody; *see* Simpson.

FIELD, Brig. Anne, CB 1980; Deputy Controller Commandant, Women's Royal Army Corps, 1984–92 (Director, 1977–82); *b* 4 April 1926; *d* of Captain Harold Derwent and Annie Helena Hodgson. *Educ:* Keswick Sch.; St George's, Harpenden; London Sch. of Economics. Joined ATS, 1947; commissioned: ATS, 1948; WRAC, 1949; Lt-Col, 1968; Col, 1971. Hon. ADC to the Queen, 1977–82. Dep. Col Comdt, AGC, 1992–93. Dir, London Regl Bd, Lloyds Bank, 1982–91 (Dep. Chm., 1990–91). Special Comr, Duke of York's Royal Mil. Sch., 1989–. Freeman, City of London, 1981; Liveryman, Spectacle Makers' Co., 1990. CIMgt (FBIM 1978). *Address:* c/o Lloyds Bank Plc, PO Box 1190, 7 Pall Mall, SW1Y 5NA. *Club:* Lansdowne.

FIELD, Arnold, OBE 1965; aerospace consultant/technical journalist; Joint Field Commander, National Air Traffic Services, 1974–77; *b* 19 May 1917; *m* 1943, Kathleen Dulcie Bennett; one *s* one *d. Educ:* Sutton Coldfield Royal Sch.; Birmingham Technical Coll. RAF, 1940–46 (Sqdn Ldr). Civil Air Traffic Control Officer, 1946; Centre Supt, Scottish Air Traffic Control Centre, 1954; Centre Supt, London Air Traffic Control Centre, 1957; Divisional Air Traffic Control Officer, Southern Div., 1963; Dir, Civil Air Traffic Ops, 1969. Master, Guild of Air Traffic Control Officers, 1958; Pres., Internat. Fedn of Air Traffic Control Officers, 1970; Mem., Aviation/Space Writers' Assoc., 1986–. Gp Editor, Internat. Defence Newsletter, Law Enforcement Industry Digest, 1988–. *Publications:* The Control of Air Traffic, 1981; International Air Traffic Control, 1985; From Take-off to Touchdown—A Passenger's Guide, 1984; articles in Interavia, Times Supplement, Flight, Controller. *Recreations:* vintage cars, flying. *Address:* Footprints, Stoke Wood, Stoke Poges, Bucks. SL2 4AU. *T:* Farnham Common (01753) 642710. *Club:* Bentley Drivers (Long Crendon).

FIELD, Barry John Anthony, TD 1984; MP (C) Isle of Wight, since 1987; *b* 4 July 1946; *s* of Ernest Field and late Marguerite Eugenie Field; *m* 1969, Jaqueline Anne Miller; one *s* one *d. Educ:* Collingwood Boys' Sch.; Mitcham Grammar Sch.; Bembridge Sch.; Victoria Street Coll. Chm., J. D. Field & Sons Ltd, 1993–94 (Dir, 1981–); Dir, Great Southern Cemetery & Crematorium Co. Ltd, 1969–94. Mem. of Lloyd's. Councillor, Horsham

Dist. Council, 1983–86 (Vice-Chm., Housing, 1984–85, Chm., Housing, 1985–86); Mem., IoW CC, 1986–89. Chm., H of C Select Cttee on the Envmt, 1994–. Major RCT TA; Liveryman, Turners' Co.; Mem., Watermen and Lightermen's Co. *Recreations:* sailing, theatre, ski-ing. *Address:* Medina Lodge, 25 Birmingham Road, Cowes, Isle of Wight PO31 7BH. *T:* Cowes (01983) 291787. *Club:* Island Sailing (Cowes).

FIELD, (Edward) John, CMG 1991; HM Diplomatic Service; High Commissioner, Sri Lanka, since 1991; *b* 11 June 1936; *s* of Arthur Field, OBE, MC, TD, and late Dorothy Agnes Field; *m* 1960, Irene Sophie du Pont Darden; one *s* one *d.* *Educ:* Highgate Sch.; Corpus Christi Coll., Oxford; Univ. of Virginia. Courtaulds Ltd, 1960–62; FCO, 1963–: 2nd, later 1st Sec., Tokyo, 1963–68; Amer. Dept, FCO, 1968–70; Cultural Attaché, Moscow, 1970–72; 1st Sec. (Commercial), Tokyo, 1973–76; Asst Head, S Asian Dept, FCO, 1976–77; Dept of Trade, 1977–79 (Head, Exports to Japan Unit); Counsellor: (Commercial), Seoul, 1980–83; at Harvard Univ., 1983–84; UK Mission to UN, 1984–87; Minister, Tokyo, 1988–91. *Recreations:* tennis, listening to music. *Address:* c/o Foreign and Commonwealth Office, SW1A 2AH. *Clubs:* Travellers'; Tokyo (Tokyo).

FIELD, Frank; MP (Lab) Birkenhead, since 1979; *b* 16 July 1942; *s* of late Walter and of Annie Field. *Educ:* St Clement Danes Grammar Sch.; Univ. of Hull (BSc (Econ)). Director: Child Poverty Action Gp, 1969–79; Low Pay Unit, 1974–80. Chairman: Select Cttee on Social Services, 1987–90; Select Cttee on Social Security, 1991–. *Publications:* (ed, jtly) Twentieth Century State Education, 1971; (ed, jtly) Black Britons, 1971; (ed) Low Pay, 1973; Unequal Britain, 1974; (ed) Are Low Wages Inevitable?, 1976; (ed) Education and the Urban Crisis, 1976; (ed) The Conscript Army: a study of Britain's unemployed, 1976; (jtly) To Him Who Hath: a study of poverty and taxation, 1976; (with Ruth Lister) Wasted Labour, 1978 (Social Concern Book Award); (ed) The Wealth Report, 1979; Inequality in Britain: freedom, welfare and the state, 1981; Poverty and Politics, 1982; The Wealth Report—2, 1983; (ed) Policies against Low Pay, 1984; The Minimum Wage: its potential and dangers, 1984; Freedom and Wealth in a Socialist Future, 1987; The Politics of Paradise, 1987; Losing Out: the emergence of Britain's underclass, 1989; An Agenda for Britain, 1993; (jtly) Europe Isn't Working, 1994; (jtly) Beyond Punishment: pathways from workfare, 1994; Making Welfare Work, 1995. *Address:* House of Commons, SW1A 0AA. *T:* 0171–219 5193.

FIELD, Maj.-Gen. Geoffrey William, CB 1993; OBE 1983 (MBE 1976); Resident Governor, HM Tower of London, since 1994; *b* 30 Nov. 1941; *s* of William Edwin Field and Ellen Campbell Field (*née* Forsyth); *m* 1966, Janice Anne Olsen; one *s* two *d.* *Educ:* Daniel Stewart's College, Edinburgh; RMA Sandhurst; RMCS Shrivenham; Australian Staff College; RCDS. Commissioned RE 1961; OC 59 Indep. Cdo Sqn, RE, 1976–78; CO 36 Engr Regt, 1980–83 (served in Falkland Islands campaign); Asst Dir Defence Policy, MoD, 1983–85; Comd 11 Engr Gp, 1986–87; Dir Defence Programmes, MoD, 1989–90; Dir Gen., Logistic Policy (Army), 1990–93; Engr-in-Chief (Army), 1993–94. Colonel Commandant: RPC, 1991–93; RLC, 1993–; Hon. Col, RE Vols (Specialist Units), 1992–. CompICE 1994. Freeman, City of London, 1995. *Recreation:* golf. *Address:* Queen's House, HM Tower of London, EC3N 4AB. *T:* 0171–488 5630.

FIELD, Dr Ian Trevor, CBE 1994; General Secretary, World Medical Association, since 1994; *b* 31 Oct. 1933; *s* of late Major George Edward Field, MBE, IA, and Bertha Cecilia Field; *m* 1960, Christine Mary Osman, JP; three *s.* *Educ:* Shri Shivaji School, Poona; Bournemouth School; Guy's Hosp. Med. School. MB, BS; FFPHM; FFOM. Royal Engineers, 1952–54; Med. Sch., 1954–60; house posts, 1960–62; general practice, 1962–64; Asst Sec., later Under Sec., BMA, 1964–75; SMO, 1975–78, SPMO/Under Sec., 1978–85, DHSS, (Internat. Health and Communicable Disease Control, later NHS Regional Orgn); Chief Med. and Health Services Advr, ODA, 1978–83; Dep. Sec., 1985–89, Sec., 1989–93, BMA. Member: Council, Liverpool Sch. of Trop. Med., 1979–83, 1993–; Bd of Management, London Sch. of Hygiene and Trop. Med., 1979–83; Council, Royal Vet. Coll., 1982–88; WHO Global Adv. Cttee on Malaria Control, 1979–82 (Chm., 1981). Liveryman, Soc. of Apothecaries, 1971– (Ct of Assistants, 1986–). *Publications:* contribs to medical jls. *Recreations:* military history, opera, watching cricket and rugby. *Address:* 22 chemin de Vessy, 01210 Ferney-Voltaire, France. *Club:* Athenæum.

FIELD, Brig. Jill Margaret, CBE 1992; RRC 1988; Matron-in-Chief (Army) and Director of Defence Nursing Services, 1989–92; *b* 20 June 1934; *d* of late Major Charles Euston Field, Royal Signals, and Mrs Eva Gladys Field (*née* Watson). *Educ:* High School for Girls, Southend-on-Sea; St Bartholomew's Hosp., London (SRN). Joined QARANC, 1957; appointments include: service in Mil. Hosps in UK, BAOR, N Africa, Cyprus, Singapore; Instructor, QARANC Trng Centre, 1971–74; Liaison Officer QARANC, MoD, 1980–83; Matron, BMH Hannover, 1984–85; Dep. Medical (Nursing), BAOR, 1985–87; Matron, Cambridge Mil. Hosp., Aldershot and Chief Medical (Nursing) SE and SW Dist, 1987–89. QHNS 1989–92. *Recreations:* gardening, reading, music. *Address:* c/o Royal Bank of Scotland, Holt's Farnborough Branch, Lawrie House, Victoria Road, Farnborough, Hants GU14 7NR.

FIELD, John; *see* Field, E. J.

FIELD, Prof. John Edwin, OBE 1987; PhD; FRS 1994; Professor of Applied Physics, Department of Physics, University of Cambridge, since 1994; Head of Physics and Chemistry of Solids Section, Cavendish Laboratory, Cambridge, since 1987; Fellow of Magdalene College, Cambridge, since 1964; *b* 20 Sept. 1936; *s* of William Edwin Field and Madge (*née* Normansell); *m* 1963, Ineke Tjan; two *s* one *d.* *Educ:* Univ. of London (BSc); Univ. of Cambridge (PhD 1962). Graduate Tutor, Magdalene Coll., Cambridge, 1974–87; Asst Lectr, 1966–71, Lectr, 1971–90, Reader, 1990–94, Dept of Physics, Univ. of Cambridge. Hon. DSc Univ. of Luleå, Sweden, 1989. Duddell Medal, Inst. of Physics, 1990. *Publications:* (ed) The Properties of Diamond, 1979, 2nd edn 1991; (ed) The Properties of Natural and Synthetic Diamond, 1992; (ed) 3 conf. proc.; over 200 scientific papers. *Recreations:* mountain walking, running, ski-ing. *Address:* 1 Babraham Road, Cambridge CB2 2RB. *T:* Cambridge (01223) 575847.

FIELD, Sir Malcolm (David), Kt 1991; Chief Executive, W. H. Smith Group PLC, 1994–mid 1996; *b* 25 Aug. 1937; *s* of Stanley Herbert Raynor Field and Constance Frances (*née* Watson); *m* (marr. diss.); one *d.* *Educ:* Highgate Sch.; London Business Sch. National Service, commnd Welsh Guards (2nd Lieut), 1955–57 (served in Cyprus and Germany). PA to Dir, ICI (Paints Div.), 1957; joined family wholesale newspaper distributors business, 1960 (taken over by W. H. Smith, 1963); Wholesale Dir, 1970–82, Man. Dir, Retail Gp, 1978–82, Gp Man. Dir, 1982–93, W. H. Smith. Chm., Bd of Management, NAAFI, 1986–93 (Mem., Bd of Management, 1973–86; Dep. Chm., 1985–86); Non-executive Director: MEPC, 1989–; Scottish & Newcastle Breweries, 1993–; Phoenix Group Ltd, 1995. Mem. Council, RCA, 1991–; Gov., Highgate Sch., 1994. CIMgt (CBIM 1988); FRSA 1989. *Recreations:* cricket, tennis, golf, gardening in Portugal, reading biographies. *Address:* 61 Eaton Terrace, SW1W 8NR. *T:* 0171–730 5782. *Clubs:* Garrick, MCC.

FIELD, Marshall Hayward, CBE 1985; Consultant to Bacon & Woodrow, since 1986; *b* 19 April 1930; *s* of Harold Hayward Field and Hilda Maud Field; *m* 1960, Barbara Evelyn Harris; two *d.* *Educ:* Dulwich College. FIA 1957. With Pearl Assce, 1948–58; Phoenix Assurance: Actuary, 1964–85; Gen. Manager, 1972–85; Dir, 1980–85. Director: TSB Trust Co. Ltd, 1985–89; TSB Gp, 1990–; Ark Life Assurance Co., Dublin, 1991–. Institute of Actuaries: Hon. Sec., 1975–77; Vice-Pres., 1979–82; Pres., 1986–88; Vice Pres., International Actuarial Assoc., 1984–90; Chm., Life Offices' Assoc., 1983–85. Mem., Fowler Inquiry into Provision for Retirement, 1984; Consultant, Marketing of Investments Bd Organising Cttee, 1985–86. Mem., Dulwich Picture Gall. Cttee, 1985–94; Trustee, Dulwich Picture Gall., 1994–; Governor: Dulwich Coll. Estates, 1973–95 (Chm., 1988–90); Dulwich Coll., 1987–; James Allen's Girls' School, 1981–. Mem., Ct of Assistants, Actuaries' Co., 1989– (Jun. Warden, 1994). *Recreations:* theatre, architecture. *Address:* 12 Gainsborough Court, College Road, SE21 7LT; Bembridge, Isle of Wight.

FIELD, Hon. Michael Walter; Leader of the Opposition, Tasmania, 1988–89 and since 1992; MHA (Lab) Braddon, since 1976; *b* 28 May 1948; *s* of William Field and Blanche (*née* Burrows); *m* 1975, Janette Elizabeth Mary Fone; one *s* two *d.* *Educ:* Railton Primary Sch., Tasmania; Devonport High Sch., Tasmania; Univ. of Tasmania (BA Pol. Sci./History). Teacher, 1971–75; Community Develt Officer, 1975–76. Minister for Transport, Main Roads, Construction and Local Govt, 1979–82; Shadow Minister for: Transport, 1982–83; Education and Ind. Relns, 1982–86; Dep. Leader of Opposition and Shadow Minister for Forestry, Ind. Relns and Energy, 1986–88; Premier of Tasmania, 1989–92. *Recreations:* running, reading, music. *Address:* Parliament House, Hobart, Tasmania 7000, Australia. *T:* (02) 332385.

FIELD, Richard Alan; QC 1987; *b* 17 April 1947; *s* of Robert Henry Field and Ivy May Field; *m* 1968, Lynne Hauskind; two *s* two *d.* *Educ:* Ottershaw Sch.; Bristol Univ. (LLB); London School of Economics (LLM with Dist.). Asst Prof., Univ. of British Columbia, 1969–71; Lectr in Law, Hong Kong Univ., 1971–73; Associate Prof., McGill Univ., Montreal, 1973–77; called to the Bar, Inner Temple, 1977. *Publications:* articles and book reviews in UBC Law Rev., Hong Kong Law Jl, McGill Law Jl. *Recreations:* cricket, opera, theatre. *Address:* 11 King's Bench Walk, Temple, EC4Y 7EQ. *Clubs:* Garrick, Roehampton.

FIELD, William James; *b* 22 May 1909; *s* of late Frederick William Field, Solicitor; unmarried. *Educ:* Richmond County Sch.; London Univ; abroad. Joined Labour Party, 1935; Parliamentary Private Sec. to Sec. of State for War, May–Oct. 1951 (to Under-Sec. for War, 1950–51); Chm. South Hammersmith Divisional Labour Party, 1945–46; contested Hampstead Div., General Election, 1945; MP (Lab) North Paddington, Nov. 1946–Oct. 1953. Mem. Hammersmith Borough Council, 1945–53, and Leader of that Council, 1946–49; a Vice-Pres. of Assoc. of Municipal Corporations, 1952–53; for several years, mem. Metropolitan Boroughs' Standing Joint Cttee and of many local govt bodies. Volunteered for Army, Sept. 1939 and served in ranks and as officer in Intelligence Corps and RASC.

FIELD-FISHER, Thomas Gilbert, TD 1950; QC 1969; a Recorder of the Crown Court, 1972–87; *b* 16 May 1915; *s* of Caryl Field-Fisher, Torquay; *m* 1945, Ebba, *d* of Max Larsen, Linwood, USA. *Educ:* King's Sch., Bruton; Peterhouse, Cambridge. BA 1937, MA 1942. Called to Bar, Middle Temple, 1942, Bencher, 1976. Served Queen Victoria's Rifles, KRRC, 1939–47; BEF 1940 (POW; despatches). Judge Advocate Gen.'s Dept, 1945–47 (i/c War Crimes Dept, CMF); joined Western Circuit, 1947. Mem., Bar Council, 1962–66; Deputy Chairman: SW Agricultural Land Tribunal, 1967–82; Cornwall QS, 1968–71; Chm., Maria Colwell Inquiry, 1973–74. Vice-Chm., London Council of Social Service, 1966–79; Vice-Pres., London Voluntary Service Council, 1979–. Mem., Home Secretary's Adv. Cttee on Animal Experiments, 1980–89. Chm., Dogs' Home, Battersea, 1982–; Founder and Chm., Assoc. of British Dogs' Homes, 1985–; Vice-Pres., UFAW, 1989–. Pres., Cornwall Magistrates' Assoc., 1985–. Autumn Reader, Middle Temple, 1991. *Publications:* Animals and the Law, 1964; Rent Regulation and Control, 1967; contribs to Halsbury's Laws of England, 3rd and 4th edns, Law Jl, and other legal publications. *Recreations:* tennis, dogs, collecting watercolours, MG cars, gardening. *Address:* 38 Hurlingham Court, SW6 3UW. *T:* 0171–736 4627; 2 King's Bench Walk, Temple, EC4Y 7DE. *T:* 0171–353 1746. *Clubs:* Hurlingham, International Lawn Tennis of Great Britain.

FIELDEN, Frank, MA (Dunelm); Secretary, Royal Fine Art Commission, 1969–79; *b* 3 Oct. 1915; *s* of Ernest and Emma Fielden, Greenfield, Yorks; *m* 1939, Margery Keeler; two *d.* *Educ:* University of Manchester. Graduated, 1938. Served 1939–45 with Royal Engineers (Special Forces), France, N Africa, Italy, Germany. Town Planning Officer to Nigerian Government, 1945–46; Lecturer and Sen. Lectr, University of Durham, 1946–59; Prof. of Architecture, Univ. of Strathclyde, 1959–69. Mem., Royal Fine Art Commn for Scotland, 1965–69. RIBA Athens Bursar, 1950, Bronze Medallist 1960. Chairman: Soc. of Architectural Historians of Great Britain, 1965–67; Richmond Soc., 1971–74. *Publications:* articles in professional journals and national press. *Recreations:* music, gardening. *Address:* 28 Caledonian Road, Chichester, W Sussex PO19 2LQ.

FIELDHOUSE, Brian; Chief Executive, West Sussex County Council, 1990–95; *b* 1 May 1933; *s* of late Harry and Florence Fieldhouse; *m* 1959, Sonia J. Browne; one *s* one *d.* *Educ:* Barnsley Holgate Grammar Sch.; Keble Coll., Oxford (MA PPE). IPFA 1960. Formerly, Treasurer's Departments: Herts CC; Hants CC; Flints CC; County Treasurer: Lincs parts of Lindsey CC, 1970–73; W Sussex CC, 1973–90. Comr, Public Works Loans Bd, 1988–92. Principal Financial Advr, ACC, 1980–85. Pres., Soc. of Co. Treasurers, 1983. Trustee, Chichester Fest. Theatre, 1992–; Mem. Council, Univ. of Sussex, 1994–. FRSA 1984. *Recreations:* hill farming, theatre going. *Address:* 13 The Avenue, Chichester PO19 4PX. *Club:* Farmers'.

FIELDHOUSE, Prof. David Kenneth; Vere Harmsworth Professor of Imperial and Naval History, Cambridge University, 1981–92; Fellow, Jesus College, Cambridge, 1981–92, subseq. Emeritus; *b* 7 June 1925; *s* of Rev. Ernest Fieldhouse and Clara Hilda Beatrice Fieldhouse; *m* 1952, Sheila Elizabeth Lyon; one *s* two *d.* *Educ:* Dean Close Sch., Cheltenham; Queen's Coll., Oxford (MA, DLitt). War Service: RN, Sub-Lt (A), 1943–47. History master, Haileybury Coll., 1950–52; Lectr in Modern History, Univ. of Canterbury, NZ, 1953–57; Beit Lectr in Commonwealth History, Oxford Univ., 1958–81; Fellow, Nuffield Coll., Oxford, 1966–81. *Publications:* The Colonial Empires, 1966, 2nd edn, 1982; The Theory of Capitalist Imperialism, 1967, 2nd edn 1969; Economics and Empire, 1973, 2nd edn 1984; Unilever Overseas, 1978; Colonialism 1870–1945, 1981; Black Africa 1945–80, 1986; Merchant Capital and Economic Decolonization, 1994. *Recreations:* music, golf, sailing, writing fiction. *Address:* Jesus College, Cambridge CB5 8BL. *T:* Cambridge (01223) 68611.

FIELDING, Sir Colin (Cunningham), Kt 1986; CB 1981; Chairman, Microturbo Ltd, since 1988; consultant in defence systems, information technology and electronics, since 1986; *b* 23 Dec. 1926; *s* of Richard Cunningham and Sadie Fielding; *m* 1953, Gillian Aerona (*née* Thomas); one *d.* *Educ:* Heaton Grammar Sch., Newcastle upon Tyne; Durham Univ. BSc Hons Physics. British Scientific Instruments Research Assoc., 1948–49; RRE Malvern, 1949–65; Asst Dir of Electronics R&D, Min. of Technology, 1965–68; Head of Electronics Dept, RRE Malvern, 1968–73; RCDS, 1973–74; Dir of Scientific and

Technical Intelligence, MoD, 1975–77; Dir, Admiralty Surface Weapons Estabt, 1977–78; Dep. Controller, R&D Estabts and Res. A, and Chief Scientist (RN), MoD, 1978–80; Dep. Chief of Defence Procurement (Nuclear), and Dir, AWRE, MoD, 1980–82; Controller of R&D Estabts, Res. and Nuclear Progs, MoD, 1982–86. Dir, Cray Research (UK), 1988–. *Publications:* papers in Proc. IEE, Proc. IERE, Nature. *Recreations:* yachting, tennis, music, golf. *Address:* Cheviots, Rosemount Drive, Bickley, Kent BR1 2LQ.

FIELDING, Fenella Marion; actress; *b* London, 17 Nov. 1934. *Educ:* North London Collegiate School. Began acting career in 1954; *plays include:* Cockles and Champagne, Saville, 1954; Pay the Piper, Saville, 1954; Jubilee Girl, Victoria Palace, 1956; Valmouth, Lyric, Hammersmith, 1958, Saville, 1959, and Chichester Fest., 1982; Pieces of Eight, Apollo, 1959; Five Plus One, Edinburgh Fest., 1961; Twists, Arts, 1962 (Best Revue Performance of the Year in Variety); Doctors of Philosophy, New Arts, 1962; Luv, New Arts, 1963; So Much to Remember—The Life Story of a Great Lady, Establishment, transf. to Vaudeville, 1963; Let's Get a Divorce, Mermaid, transf. to Comedy, 1966; The Beaux Stratagem and The Italian Straw Hat, Chichester Fest., 1967; The High Bid, Mermaid, 1967; Façade, Queen Elizabeth Hall, 1970; Colette, Ellen Stewart, NY, 1970 (first appearance in NY); Fish Out of Water, Greenwich, 1971; The Old Man's Comforts, Open Space, 1972; The Provok'd Wife, Greenwich, 1973; Absurd Person Singular, Criterion, 1974, transf. to Vaudeville, 1975; Fielding Convertible, Edinburgh Fest., 1976; Jubilee Jeunesse, Royal Opera House, 1977; Look After Lulu, Chichester Fest., transf. to Haymarket, 1978; A personal Choice, Edinburgh Fest., 1978; Fenella on Broadway, W6, Studio, Lyric, Hammersmith, 1979; Valmouth, Chichester, 1982; Wizard of Oz, Bromley, 1983; The Jungle Book, Adelphi, 1984; The Country Wife, Mermaid, 1990; *films include:* Drop Dead, Darling; Lock Up Your Daughters; Carry On Screaming; Carry On Regardless; Doctor in Clover; Doctor in Distress; Doctor in Trouble; No Love for Johnnie; Robin Hood; *television series:* That Was The Week That Was; A Touch of Venus; Ooh La La; Stories from Saki; Dean Martin and the Gold-Diggers; Comedy Tonight; Rhyme and Reason; numerous appearances in UK and USA. *Recreations:* reading, diarising. *Address:* CCA Management, 4 Court Lodge, 48 Sloane Square, SW1W 8AT.

FIELDING, Sir Leslie, KCMG 1988; Vice-Chancellor, University of Sussex, 1987–92; *b* 29 July 1932; *o s* of late Percy Archer Fielding and of Margaret (*née* Calder Horry); *m* 1978, Dr Sally P. J. Harvey, FSA, FRHistS, sometime Fellow of St Hilda's Coll., Oxford; one *s* one *d*. *Educ:* Queen Elizabeth's Sch., Barnet; Emmanuel Coll., Cambridge (First in History; MA; Hon. Fellow 1990); School of Oriental and African Studies, London; St Antony's Coll., Oxford (MA; Vis. Fellow, 1977–78). Served with Royal Regt of Artillery, 1951–53. Entered HM Diplomatic Service, 1956; served in: Tehran, 1957–60; Foreign Office, 1960–64; Singapore, 1964; Phnom Penh (Chargé d'Affaires), 1964–66; Paris, 1967–70; Dep. Head of Planning Staff, FCO, 1970–73; seconded for service with European Commn in Brussels, 1973; Dir (External Relns Directorate Gen.), 1973–77; permanent transfer 1979; Head of Delegn of Commn in Tokyo, 1978–82; Dir-Gen. for External Relns, 1982–87. UK Mem., High Council of European Univ. Inst. in Florence, 1988–92. Chm., Nat. Curriculum Geography Wkg Gp, 1989–90. Hon. Pres., Univ. Assoc. for Contemporary European Studies, 1990–; Founder Mem., Japan–EC Assoc., 1988–; Mem., UK–Japan 2000 Gp, 1993–. Mem., Gen. Synod, C of E, 1990–92. Admitted to office of Reader by Bishop of Exeter, 1981. FRSA 1989; FRGS 1991 (Mem. Council, 1992–95); FIAM 1992. Hon. Fellow, Sussex European Inst., 1993. Hon. LLD Sussex, 1992. Grand Officer, Order of St Agatha (San Marino), 1987; Knight Commander Order of the White Rose (Finland), 1988; Grosse Silbenes Ehrenzeichen mit dem Stern (Austria), 1989. *Publications:* Europe as a global partner: the external relations of the European Community, 1991; articles on internat. relations, higher educn and ecclesiastical matters. *Recreations:* life in the country, theology. *Address:* Sutton Court, Stanton Lacy, Ludlow, Salop SY8 2AJ. *Clubs:* Travellers'; Sussex.

FIELDING, Richard Walter; Chairman: Richard Fielding Ltd, since 1992; Sharelink PLC, since 1993; *b* 9 July 1933; *s* of Walter Harrison Fielding, MBE, and Marjorie Octavia Adair (*née* Roberts); *m* 1st, 1961, Felicity Ann Jones; one *s* three *d*; 2nd, 1983, Jacqueline Winifred Digby (*née* Hussey). *Educ:* Clifton Coll., Bristol. National Service, Royal Engineers (Lieut), 1951–53. Broker to Dir, Bland Welch & Co. Ltd, 1954–68; Dir to Man. Dir, C. E. Heath & Co. Ltd, 1968–75; Founder and Chm., Fielding and Partners, 1975–86; Chm., C. E. Heath PLC, 1987–92. Director: Hambros Insurance Services, 1993–; Syndicate Capital Trust, 1993–. *Recreations:* hunting, country sports. *Address:* 114 Middlesex Street, E1 7HY.

FIELDS, Terence; *b* 8 March 1937; *s* of late Frank Fields; *m* 1962, Maureen Mongan; two *s* two *d*. Served RAMC, 1955–57. Fireman, Merseyside County Fire Bde, 1957–83. Former Vice-Chm., Bootle Constit. Lab. Party; former Mem., NW Regl Exec. Cttee, Lab. Party. MP Liverpool, Broad Green, 1983–92 (Lab, 1983–91, Ind, 1991–92); contested (Soc. Lab) Liverpool, Broad Green, 1992. *Address:* 20 John Hunter Way, Bootle, Merseyside L30 5RJ.

FIELDSEND, John Charles Rowell; Member, Court of Appeal, St Helena, Falkland Islands and British Antarctic Territory, since 1985; President, Court of Appeal, Gibraltar, since 1991 (Member, since 1986); Chief Justice (non-resident), British Indian Ocean Territory, since 1987 (Principal Legal Adviser, 1984–87); *b* 13 Sept. 1921; *s* of C. E. Fieldsend, MC, and Phyllis (*née* Brucesmith); *m* 1945, Muriel Gedling; one *s* one *d*. *Educ:* Michaelhouse, Natal; Rhodes University Coll., Grahamstown, SA (BA 1942, LLB 1947). Served RA, 1943–45. Called to the Bar, S Rhodesia, 1947; advocate in private practice, 1947–63; QC S Rhodesia, 1959; Pres., Special Income Tax Court for Fedn of Rhodesia and Nyasaland, 1958–63; High Court Judge, S Rhodesia, 1963, resigned 1968; Asst Solicitor, Law Commn, 1968–78, Sec., 1978–80; Chief Justice: of Zimbabwe, 1980–83; of Turks and Caicos Islands, 1985–87. *Recreations:* home-making, travel. *Address:* Great Dewes, Ardingly, Sussex RH17 6UP.

FIENNES; *see* Twisleton-Wykeham-Fiennes.

FIENNES, family name of **Baron Saye and Sele.**

FIENNES, Very Rev. Hon. Oliver William Twisleton-Wykeham-; Dean of Lincoln, 1969–89, Dean Emeritus since 1989; *b* 17 May 1926; *yr s* of 20th Baron Saye and Sele, OBE, MC, and Hersey Cecilia Hester, *d* of late Captain Sir Thomas Dacres Butler, KCVO; *m* 1956, Juliet, *d* of late Dr Trevor Braby Heaton, OBE; two *s* two *d*. *Educ:* Eton; New College, Oxford; Cuddesdon College. Asst Curate, New Milton, Hants, 1954; Chaplain, Clifton College, Bristol, 1958; Rector of Lambeth, 1963. Church Comr, 1977–88. Chairman: Pilgrims Assoc., 1986–89; St Matthew Soc., 1994–. World Fellow, Thanksgiving Square, Dallas, 1980; Pres., Lincoln Br., Inst. of Advanced Motorists, 1973–; Chm., Radio Lincolnshire Adv. Cttee, 1992–. Governor, Marlborough Coll., 1970–89. Nat Patron, E-SU in USA, 1987. ChStJ 1971. *Recreations:* cricket, travel, country activities. *Address:* Home Farm House, Colsterworth, Grantham, Lincs NG33 5HZ. *T:* Grantham (01476) 860811.

FIENNES, Sir Ranulph Twisleton-Wykeham-, 3rd Bt, *cr* 1916; OBE 1993; *b* 7 March 1944; *s* of Lieut-Col Sir Ranulph Twisleton-Wykeham-Fiennes, DSO, 2nd Bt (died of wounds, 1943) and Audrey Joan (*d* 1995), *yr d* of Sir Percy Newson, 1st Bt; *S* father 1944; *m* 1970, Virginia Pepper (first female member of Antarctic Club, 1985; first woman to be awarded Polar Medal, 1987). *Educ:* Eton. Liveryman, Vintners' Company, 1960. French Parachutist Wings, 1965. Lieut, Royal Scots Greys, 1966, Captain 1968 (retd 1970). Attached 22 SAS Regt, 1966, Sultan of Muscat's Armed Forces, 1968 (Dhofar Campaign Medal, 1969; Sultan's Bravery Medal, 1970). T&AVR 1971, Captain RAC. Leader of British expeditions: White Nile, 1969; Jostedalsbre Glacier, 1970; Headless Valley, BC, 1971; (Towards) North Pole, 1977; Transglobe (first surface journey around the world's polar axis), 1979–82, reached South Pole, 15 Dec. 1980, reached North Pole, 11 April 1982; North Polar Unsupported Expeditions: reached 84°48′N on 16 April 1986; reached 88°58′N on 14 April 1990 (Furthest North Unsupported record); South Polar Unsupported Expedition: first crossing of Antarctic Continent and longest polar journey in history (1,345 miles), 1992–93. Hon. DSc Loughborough, 1986; DUniv Birmingham, 1995. Elected to Guinness Hall of Fame, 1987. Livingstone Gold Medal, RSGS, 1983; Explorers' Club of New York Medal (and Hon. Life Membership), 1983; Founder's Medal, RGS, 1984; Polar Medal, 1987; ITN Award, for the Event of the Decade, 1990. *Film:* (cameraman) To the Ends of the Earth, 1983. *Publications:* A Talent for Trouble, 1970; Ice Fall in Norway, 1972; The Headless Valley, 1973; Where Soldiers Fear To Tread, 1975; Hell on Ice, 1979; To the Ends of the Earth, 1983; (with Virginia Fiennes) Bothie, the Polar Dog, 1984; Living Dangerously (autobiog.), 1987; The Feather Men, 1991; Atlantis of the Sands, 1992; Mind Over Matter, 1993; Living Dangerously, 1994; The Sett, 1995. *Recreations:* langlauf, photography. *Heir:* none. *Address:* Greenlands, Exford, Som TA24 7NU. *T:* Exford (0164) 383350.

FIENNES-CLINTON, family name of **Earl of Lincoln.**

FIFE, 3rd Duke of, *cr* 1900; **James George Alexander Bannerman Carnegie;** Baron Carnegie, 1616; Earl of Southesk, 1633; Bt (NS), 1663; Baron Balinhard, 1869; Earl of Macduff, 1900; *b* 23 Sept. 1929; *o s* of 11th Earl of Southesk (*d* 1992), and Princess Maud (*d* 1945); *S* aunt, Princess Arthur of Connaught (Dukedom of Fife), 1959; *m* 1956, Hon. Caroline Cicely Dewar (marr. diss. 1966; she *m* 1980, Gen. Sir Richard Worsley), *er d* of 3rd Baron Forteviot, MBE; one *s* one *d*. *Educ:* Gordonstoun. Nat. Service, Scots Guards (Malayan Campaign), 1948–50. Royal Agricultural College. Clothworkers' Company, and Freeman City of London. Pres. of ABA, 1959–73, Vice-Patron, 1973–94; Ship's Pres., HMS Fife, 1967–87; a Vice-Patron, Braemar Royal Highland Soc.; a Vice-Pres., British Olympic Assoc. *Heir:* *s* Earl of Southesk, *qv*. *Address:* (seat) Kinnaird Castle, Brechin, Angus DD9 6TZ; Elsick House, Stonehaven, Kincardineshire AB3 2NT. *Club:* Turf.

FIFOOT, Paul Ronald Ninnes, CMG 1978; HM Diplomatic Service, retired; *b* 1 April 1928; *o s* of late Ronald Fifoot, Cardiff; *m* 1952, Erica, *er d* of late Richard Alford, DMD; no *c*. *Educ:* Monkton House Sch., Cardiff; Queens' Coll., Cambridge. BA 1948, MA 1952. Military Service, 1948–50. Called to Bar, Gray's Inn, 1953; Crown Counsel, Tanganyika, 1953; Asst to the Law Officers, 1960; Legal Draftsman (later Chief Parliamentary Draftsman), 1961; retd from Tanzania Govt Service, 1966; Asst Legal Adviser, Commonwealth Office, 1966; Legislative Counsel, Province of British Columbia, 1967; Asst Legal Adviser, Commonwealth (later Foreign and Commonwealth) Office, 1968; Legal Counsellor, 1971; Agent of the UK Govt in cases before the European Commn and Court of Human Rights, 1971–76; Counsellor (Legal Advr), UK Mission to UN, NY, 1976–79; Legal Counsellor, FCO, 1979–84; Dep. Leader, UK Delegation to 3rd UN Conference on the Law of the Sea, 1981–82; Leader, UK Delegation to Preparatory Commn for Internat. Sea Bed Authority, 1983–84; Dep. Legal Advr, FCO, 1984–88. Special Legal Advr, FCO, 1988, 1990, and 1992–; consultant and constitutional advr to various overseas govts, 1988–; consultant, Council on Tribunals, 1988–89. *Publications:* articles and reviews in journals, etc. *Address:* Zebrato, Lynwood Avenue, Epsom, Surrey KT17 4LQ.

FIGG, Sir Leonard (Clifford William), KCMG 1981 (CMG 1974); HM Diplomatic Service, retired; *b* 17 Aug. 1923; *s* of late Sir Clifford Figg and late Lady (Eileen) Figg (*née* Crabb); *m* 1955, Jane Brown, *d* of late Judge Harold Brown; three *s*. *Educ:* Charterhouse; Trinity Coll., Oxford. RAF, 1942–46 (Flt-Lt). HM Diplomatic Service, 1947; served in: Addis Ababa, 1949–52; FO, 1952–58; Amman, 1958–61; FO, 1961–67; Counsellor, 1965; Deputy Consul-General, Chicago, 1967–69; DTI, 1970–73; Consul General and Minister, Milan, 1973–77; Asst Under Sec. of State, FCO, 1977–80; Ambassador to Ireland, 1980–83. Mem. Council, Cooperation Ireland, 1985–95. A Vice-Chm., British Red Cross Soc., 1983–88; a Vice-Pres., Bucks Red Cross, 1988–. President: Aylesbury Divl Conservative Assoc., 1985–95; Bucks Assoc. of Youth Clubs, 1987–; Chiltern Soc., 1990–; Chm., Bucks Farming and Wildlife Adv. Gp, 1991–. *Recreations:* forestry, reading, tennis. *Address:* Court Field House, Great Missenden, Bucks HP16 9PP. *Club:* Brooks's.

FIGGESS, Sir John (George), KBE 1969 (OBE 1949); CMG 1960; a director of Christie, Manson and Woods Ltd, 1973–82; *b* 15 Nov. 1909; *e s* of Percival Watts Figgess and Leonora (*née* McCanlis); *m* 1948, Alette, *d* of Dr P. J. A. Idenburg, The Hague; two *d*. *Educ:* Whitgift Sch. In business in Japan, 1933–38. Commissioned, Intelligence Corps, 1939; Staff Coll., 1941; served with Intelligence Corps, India/Burma Theatre, 1942–45. Attached to UK Liaison Mission, Japan, 1945; Asst Mil. Adviser (Lt-Col), UKLM, Tokyo, 1947–52; GSO1, War Office (MI Directorate), 1953–56; Military Attaché, Tokyo, 1956–61; Information Counsellor, British Embassy, Tokyo, 1961–68; Comr Gen. for Britain, World Exposition, Osaka, Japan, 1968–70. Mem., Expert Adv. Council, Percival David Foundn of Chinese Art, 1984–90; Pres., Oriental Ceramic Soc., 1987–90. Gold and Silver Star, Order of the Sacred Treasure, Japan, 1986. *Publications:* (with Fujio Koyama) Two Thousand Years of Oriental Ceramics, 1960; The Heritage of Japanese Ceramics, 1973; contrib. to Oriental Art, Far Eastern Ceramic Bulletin, etc. *Address:* The Manor House, Burghfield, Berks RG3 3TG. *Club:* Army and Navy.

FIGGIS, Anthony St John Howard, CMG 1993; HM Diplomatic Service; Assistant Under-Secretary of State, Foreign and Commonwealth Office, and HM Vice-Marshal of the Diplomatic Corps, since 1991; *b* 12 Oct. 1940; *s* of Roberts Richmond Figgis and Philippa Maria Young; *m* 1964, Miriam Ellen Hardt; two *s* one *d*. *Educ:* Rugby Sch.; King's Coll., Cambridge (Mod Langs). Joined HM Foreign (later Diplomatic) Service, 1962; Third Sec., Belgrade, 1963–65; Commonwealth Office, 1965–68; Second Sec., Polit. Residency, Bahrain, 1968–70; FCO, 1970–71; First Sec. (Commercial), Madrid, 1971–74; CSCE delegn, Geneva, 1974–75; FCO, 1975–79; Madrid: Head of Chancery, 1979–80; Commercial Counsellor, 1980–82; Counsellor, Belgrade, 1982–85; Head of E European Dept, FCO, 1986–88; Counsellor and Head of Chancery, Bonn, 1988–89; Dir of Res., subseq. of Res. and Analysis, FCO, 1989–91. *Recreations:* fly-fishing, tennis, music (piano). *Address:* c/o Foreign and Commonwealth Office, SW1A 2AH.

FIGGIS, His Honour Arthur Lenox; a Circuit Judge (formerly Judge of County Courts), 1971–92; *b* 12 Sept. 1918; *s* of late Frank Fernesley Figgis and late Frances Annie Figgis; *m* 1953, Alison, *d* of late Sidney Bocher Ganthony and late Doris Ganthony; two *s* three *d*. *Educ:* Tonbridge; Peterhouse, Cambridge (MA). Served War, 1939–46, Royal Artillery. Barrister-at-Law, Inner Temple, 1947. *Recreations:* rifle shooting half-blue, 1939, and shot for Ireland (Elcho Shield), 1935–39; walking. *Address:* The Forge, Shamley Green, Guildford, Surrey GU5 0UB. *T:* Guildford (01483) 898360.

FIGURES, Sir Colin (Frederick), KCMG 1983 (CMG 1978); OBE 1969; HM Diplomatic Service, retired; Deputy Secretary, Cabinet Office, 1985–89; *b* 1 July 1925; *s* of Frederick and Muriel Figures; *m* 1956, Pamela Ann Timmis; one *s* two *d*. *Educ:* King Edward's Sch., Birmingham; Pembroke Coll., Cambridge (MA). Served Worcestershire Regt, 1943–48. Joined Foreign Office, 1951; attached Control Commn, Germany, 1953–56; Amman, 1956–58; FCO, 1958–59; Warsaw, 1959–62; FCO, 1962–66; Vienna, 1966–69; FCO, 1969–85 (Dep. Sec.). *Recreations:* watching sport, gardening, beachcombing. *Address:* c/o Midland Bank, 130 New Street, Birmingham B2 4JU. *Club:* Old Edwardians (Birmingham).

FILBY, Ven. William Charles Leonard; Archdeacon of Horsham, since 1983; *b* 21 Jan. 1933; *s* of William Richard and Dorothy Filby; *m* 1958, Marion Erica, *d* of Prof. Terence Wilmot Hutchison, *qv*; four *s* one *d*. *Educ:* Ashford County Grammar School; London Univ. (BA); Oak Hill Theological Coll. Curate, All Souls, Eastbourne, 1959–62; Curate-in-charge, Holy Trinity, Knaphill, 1962–65; Vicar, Holy Trinity, Richmond-upon-Thames, 1965–71; Vicar, Bishop Hannington Memorial Church, Hove, 1971–79; Rector of Broadwater, 1979–83; RD of Worthing, 1980–83; Hon. Canon of Chichester Cathedral, 1981–83. Proctor in Convocation, 1975–90. Chm., Redcliffe Missionary Trng Coll., Chiswick, 1970–91; Mem., Keswick Convention Council, 1973–93; Pres., Chichester Diocesan Evangelical Union, 1978–84; Chairman: Diocesan Stewardship Cttee, 1983–89; Sussex Churches Broadcasting Cttee, 1984–; Diocesan Cttee for Mission and Renewal, 1989–93. Bishops Advr for Hosp. Chaplains, 1986–. Governor: St Mary's Hall, Brighton, 1984–; W Sussex Inst. of Higher Educn, 1985–. *Recreations:* sport, music. *Address:* The Archdeaconry, Itchingfield, Sussex RH13 7NX. *T:* Slinfold (01403) 790315.

FILDES, (David) Christopher, OBE 1994; financial journalist; *b* 10 Nov. 1934; *s* of late David Garland Fildes and of Shelagh Fildes (*née* Jones), Manley, Cheshire; *m* 1st, 1969, Susan Patricia Mottram (*d* 1978); one *d* decd; 2nd, 1986, Frederica Bement Lord (*d* 1992). *Educ:* Clifton; Balliol Coll., Oxford. Financial journalist, 1963–; columnist, editor and broadcaster (The Times, Spectator, Daily Mail, Euromoney, Evening News, Investors Chronicle, Business Prog.); financial columnist: Euromoney, 1969–; Daily Telegraph and Spectator, 1984–. Dir, The Spectator (1828) Ltd, 1990–. Wincott Award for financial journalism, 1978 and 1986. *Recreations:* racing, railways. *Address:* 4 Scarsdale Villas, W8 6PR. *Clubs:* Garrick, City of London.

FILER, Denis Edwin, CBE 1992; TD 1965 and 1977; FEng 1985; FIMechE; FIChemE; Chairman, Adwest Group plc, since 1994 (Director, since 1991); *b* 19 May 1932; *s* of Francis and Sarah Filer; *m* 1957, Pamela Armitage; one *s* two *d*. *Educ:* Manchester Central Grammar Sch.; Manchester Univ. (Hons BSc Mech. Eng.); BA Open 1987. Commissioned REME (Nat. Service); served in Germany; REME TA, 1955–: Col, 1975–77; Hon. Col, 1978–87. ICI: Works Maintenance Engineer, 1960–67; Project Manager, Manchester, 1967–71; Project Manager, Holland (ICI Europa), 1971–73; Div. Maintenance Advisor, Organics Div., 1973; Plastics Div., Wilton Works: Works Engineer, 1973–76; Engineering Manager, 1976–78; Engineering & Production Dir, 1978–81; Dir of Engrg, 1981–88; Dir.-Gen., Engrg Council, 1988–95 (Mem., 1986–88; Chm., Continuous Educn and Trng Cttee; Mem., Standing Cttee for Industry). Chm., Rolinx, 1978–81; Director: Bexford, 1978–80; Engineering Services Wilton, 1978–81; Electra Innvotec Ltd, 1989–. Member: Council, IMechE, 1983–89 (Vice-Pres., 1987–89; Chm., Process Industries Div. Bd, 1985–87); Board, Lloyd's Register of Quality Assurance, 1986–88, Gen. Cttee, Lloyd's Register, 1988–. CIMgt. *Recreations:* squash, tennis, Territorial Army. *Address:* Brambles, Watton Green, Watton-at-Stone, Hertford SG14 3RB. *T:* Ware (01920) 830207. *Club:* Army and Navy.

FILER, (Douglas) Roger, FCA; Managing Director, Mayfair Theatres and Cinemas Ltd (formerly Maybox Group), since 1993; *b* 25 Feb. 1942; *s* of Horace Filer and Raie (*née* Behrman); *m* 1979, Vivienne Sara Green; one *s* one *d*. *Educ:* Clifton Coll.; St John's Coll., Oxford (MA); FCA 1970. Called to the Bar, Gray's Inn, 1979. Joined Association Television Group, 1967; Chief Accountant, Ambassador Bowling, 1967–69; Financial Controller, Bentray Investments, 1969–70; Financial Dir, M. Berman then Bermans & Nathans, 1971–73; Financial Controller, Stoll Theatres Corp./Moss Empires, 1974; Dir, 1982–92, Man. Dir, 1990–92, Stoll Moss Theatres. Mem., Bd of Management, SOLT. *Recreations:* music, history, walking. *Address:* Four Brim Hill, Hampstead Garden Suburb, N2 0HF. *T:* 0171–304 7922.

FILKIN, (David) Geoffrey (Nigel); Secretary, Association of District Councils, since 1991; *b* 1 July 1944; *s* of Donald Geoffrey and Winifred Filkin; *m* 1974, Elizabeth Tompkins (*see* Elizabeth Filkin) (marr. diss. 1994); three *d*. *Educ:* King Edward VI Sch., Five Ways, Birmingham; Clare Coll., Cambridge (MA Hist.); Manchester Univ. (DipTP); Birmingham Univ. (postgrad. study). MRTPI. Teacher on VSO, Ghana, 1966–67; Planner, Redditch Develt Corp., 1969–72; Manager, Brent Housing Aid Centre, London Borough of Brent, 1972–75; Dep. Chief Exec., Merseyside Improved Houses, 1975–79; Borough Housing Officer, Ellesmere Port and Neston Council, 1979–82; Dir of Housing, London Borough of Greenwich, 1982–88; Chief Exec., Reading BC, 1988–91. Hon. Fellow, Inst. of Local Govt Studies, Birmingham Univ. *Publications:* articles on housing and local govt. *Recreations:* music, walking, swimming. *Address:* c/o Association of District Councils, 26 Chapter Street, SW1P 4ND.

FILKIN, Elizabeth; The Adjudicator, since 1995 (Revenue Adjudicator, 1993–95); *b* 24 Nov. 1940; *d* of Frances Trollope and John Tompkins; *m* 1974, David Geoffrey Nigel Filkin, *qv* (marr. diss. 1994); three *d*. *Educ:* Birmingham Univ. (BSocSci). Organiser, Sparkbrook Assoc., 1961–64; Whyndham Deedes Fellowship, Israel, 1964; Res. Asst, Res. Associate, Lectr, Birmingham Univ., 1964–68; Lectr and Community Worker, Nat. Inst. for Social Work, 1968–71; Community Work Services Officer, London Borough of Brent, 1971–75; Lectr in Social Studies, Liverpool Univ., 1975–83; Chief Exec., Nat. Assoc. of CABx, 1983–88; Dir of Community Services, 1988–90, Asst Chief Exec., 1990–92, LDDC. Non-executive Director: Britannia Bldg Soc., 1992–; Hay Management Consultants, 1992–; Logica, 1995–. Chm., Lord Chancellor's Adv. Cttee on Legal Aid, 1991–94. *Publications:* The New Villagers, 1968; What a Community Worker Needs to Know, 1974; Community Work and Caring for Children, 1979; Caring for Children, 1979; (ed) Women and Children First, 1984. *Recreations:* walking, swimming. *Address:* The Adjudicator's Office, Haymarket House, 28 Haymarket, SW1Y 4SP. *T:* 0171–930 2292.

FILKIN, Geoffrey; *see* Filkin, D. G. N.

FILLEUL, Peter Amy, MA; Head Master, William Hulme's Grammar School, Manchester, 1974–87; *b* 7 Aug. 1929; *s* of J. C. Filleul and L. A. Mundy; *m* 1963, Elizabeth Ann Talbot; one *s* one *d*. *Educ:* Victoria Coll., Jersey; Bedford Sch.; (Exhibnr) Exeter Coll., Oxford (MA, DipEd). Royal Air Force, 1952–55. Portsmouth GS, 1955–65; Stationers' Company's Sch., 1965–68; Cardiff High Sch. (Head Master), 1969–74. *Recreations:* rifle shooting, fishing. *Address:* Kirkliston, Midvale Close, Upper Midvale Road, St Helier, Jersey, Channel Islands JE2 3ZH. *T:* Jersey (01534) 59941.

FILON, Sidney Philip Lawrence, TD; Librarian and Secretary to the Trustees, National Central Library, 1958–71, retired; *b* 20 Sept. 1905; *s* of late Prof. L. N. G. Filon, FRS and late Anne Godet; *m* 1st, 1939, Doris Schelling; one *d*; 2nd, 1959, Liselotte Florstedt; one *d*. *Educ:* Whitgift Sch.; University Coll., London (BSc). Sch. of Librarianship, University Coll., London, 1929–30; FLA 1931. National Central Library, 1930–39. Military service, 1939–45. Dep. Librarian, National Central Library, 1946–58. Mem., Library Advisory Council (England), 1966–71. *Publication:* The National Central Library: an experiment in library cooperation, 1977. *Address:* 107 Littleheath Road, Selsdon, Surrey CR2 7SL.

FINCASTLE, Viscount; Malcolm Kenneth Murray; Electrical Technical Officer, Civil Aviation Authority; *b* 17 Sept. 1946; *er s* and *heir* of Earl of Dunmore, *qv*; *m* 1970, Joy Anne, *d* of A. Partridge; one *s* one *d*. *Educ:* Launceston Technical High School (Board A Certificate). Patron, Scottish Australian Heritage Council's annual Sydney Scottish Week; Patron and Member: St Andrew Soc., Tas; Clan Murray Soc., Vic. *Recreations:* flying (Tow Master for Soaring Club of Tasmania), astronomy. *Address:* PO Box 100E, East Devonport, Tasmania 7310, Australia. *Club:* Soaring Club of Tasmania.

FINCH, Janet Valerie, PhD; Vice Chancellor, Keele University, since 1995; *b* 13 Feb. 1946; *d* of Robert Bleakley Finch and Evelyn Muriel (*née* Smith); *m* 1st, 1967, Geoffrey O. Spedding (marr. diss. 1982); 2nd, 1994, David H. J. Morgan. *Educ:* Merchant Taylors' Sch. for Girls, Crosby; Bedford Coll., London (BA Hons Sociol.); Univ. of Bradford (PhD Sociol. 1975). Lectr, Endsleigh Coll., Hull, 1974–76; Lancaster University: Lectr, then Sen. Lectr, 1976–88; Prof. of Social Relations, 1988–95; Pro-Vice-Chancellor, 1992–95. Non-exec. Dir, NW Regl HA, 1992–96. Chm., Preston CRC, 1980–85. Economic and Social Research Council: Mem., 1993–; Chm., Res. Grants Bd, 1994–. Chm. Exec., Brit. Sociol. Assoc., 1983–84. *Publications:* Married to the Job, 1983; Education as Social Policy, 1984; Research and Policy, 1986; Family Obligations and Social Change, 1989; Negotiating Family Responsibilities, 1993. *Recreations:* theatre-going, hill-walking in the Languedoc. *Address:* The Clock House, Keele University, Keele, Staffs ST5 5BG. *Club:* University Women's.

FINCH, Stephen Clark, OBE 1989; independent consultant, since 1989; *b* 7 March 1929; *s* of Frank Finch and Doris Finch (*née* Lloyd), Haywards Heath; *m* 1975, Sarah Rosemary Ann, *d* of Adm. Sir A. T. F. G. Griffin, *qv*; two *d*. *Educ:* Ardingly; Sch. of Signals; RMCS. FInstAM; FIMgt; FTMA. Commnd Royal Signals 1948; served Korea, UK and BAOR; retired 1968. Joined British Petroleum Co. Ltd, 1968: Gp Telecommunications Manager, 1968–81; Sen. Adviser, Regulatory Affairs, 1981–84; Asst Co-ordinator, Inf. Systems Admin, 1984–89. Member: Adv. Panel on Licensing Value Added Network Services, 1982–87; Monopolies and Mergers Commn, 1985–. Member: Inst. of Administrative Management, 1968– (Mem. Council, 1981–84; Medallist, 1985); Telecommunications Managers Assoc., 1968– (Exec. Cttee, 1971–91; Chm., 1981–84; Regulatory Affairs Exec., 1984–87; Dir, External Affairs, 1988–91); Council, Internat. Telecommunications Users Gp, 1981–94 (Chm., 1987–89). *Publications:* occasional contribs to learned jls. *Recreations:* sailing, skiing, swimming, opera. *Address:* 97 Englefield Road, Canonbury N1 3LJ. *T:* 0171–226 2803. *Club:* National.

FINCH HATTON, family name of **Earl of Winchilsea and Nottingham.**

FINCH-KNIGHTLEY, family name of **Earl of Aylesford.**

FINCHAM, Prof. John Robert Stanley, FRS 1969; FRSE 1978; Arthur Balfour Professor of Genetics, University of Cambridge, 1984–91, now Emeritus; Professorial Fellow, Peterhouse, Cambridge, 1984–91, now Emeritus Fellow; Hon. Fellow, Division of Biology, University of Edinburgh, since 1992; *b* 11 Aug. 1926; *s* of Robert Fincham and Winifred Emily Fincham (*née* Western); *m* 1950, Ann Katherine Emerson; one *s* three *d*. *Educ:* Hertford Grammar Sch.; Peterhouse, Cambridge. BA 1946, PhD 1950, ScD 1964. Bye-Fellow of Peterhouse, 1949–50; Lectr in Botany, University Coll., Leicester, 1950–54; Reader in Genetics, Univ. of Leicester, 1954–60; Head of Dept of Genetics, John Innes Inst., 1960–66; Prof. of Genetics, Leeds Univ., 1966–76; Buchanan Prof. of Genetics, Univ. of Edinburgh, 1976–84. Vis. Associate Prof. of Genetics, Massachusetts Inst. of Technology, 1960–61. Pres., Genetical Soc., 1978–81. Editor, Heredity, 1971–78. *Publications:* Fungal Genetics (with P. R. Day), 1963, 4th edn, 1979; Microbial and Molecular Genetics, 1965; Genetic Complementation, 1966; Genetics, 1983; (jtly) Genetically Engineered Organisms, 1991; papers in Biochemical Jl, Jl Gen. Microbiol., Jl Biol. Chem., Heredity, Jl Molecular Biol., Genet. Res. *Recreations:* listening to music, walking. *Address:* 20 Greenbank Road, Edinburgh EH10 5RY.

FINDLAY, Alastair Donald Fraser; Under Secretary, Fisheries, Scottish Office Agriculture and Fisheries Department, since 1993; *b* 3 Feb. 1944; *s* of late Rev. Donald Fraser Findlay and Isobel Ellis Findlay (*née* Louden); *m* 1969, Morag Cumming Peden; one *s* three *d*. *Educ:* Pitlochry High Sch.; Kelso High Sch.; Univ. of Edinburgh (MA (Hons) Mental Philosophy). Asst Principal, Dept of Agriculture and Fisheries for Scotland, 1966–70; Private Sec. to Jt Parly Under Sec. of State, Scottish Office, 1970–71; Principal, Scottish Office, 1971–74; on loan to FCO as First Sec. (Agric. and Food), The Hague, 1975–78; Asst Sec., Higher Educn Div., Scottish Educn Dept, 1979–82; Fisheries Div., 1982–85, Livestock Products Div., 1985–88, Dept. of Agric. and Fisheries for Scotland; Under Sec., IDS, then Scottish Office Industry Dept, 1988–93. *Recreations:* golf, walking, motor cars, Rugby spectating. *Address:* (office) Pentland House, Edinburgh EH14 1TW. *T:* 0131–244 6034. *Club:* Commonwealth Trust.

FINDLAY, Donald Russell; QC (Scot.) 1988; *b* 17 March 1951; *s* of James Findlay and Mabel Findlay (*née* Muirhead); *m* 1982, Jennifer Edith (*née* Borrowman). *Educ:* Harris Academy, Dundee; Univ. of Dundee (LLB 1st cl. Hons); Univ. of Glasgow (MPhil). Mem., Faculty of Advocates, 1975–; Lectr in Law, Heriot Watt Univ., 1976–77. Mem., Lothian Health Bd, 1987–91. Vice Chm., Glasgow Rangers FC, 1992– (Dir, 1991–). Vice Chm., N Cunninghame Cons. and Unionist Assoc., 1989–92. Rector, St Andrews Univ., 1993–. *Publications:* contribs to Scots Law Times. *Recreations:* Glasgow Rangers FC, Egyptology, malt whisky, photography, cooking, drinking claret, politics, ethics. *Address:* 26 Barnton Park Crescent, Edinburgh EH4 6EP. *T:* 0131–336 3734. *Clubs:* Royal Scottish Automobile (Glasgow); Royal Burgess Golfing Society, Glasgow Rangers Bond.

FINDLAY, Ian Herbert Fyfe; Chairman, Lloyd's, 1978 and 1979 (Deputy Chairman, 1977); *b* 5 Feb. 1918; *s* of Prof. Alexander Findlay, CBE, Aberdeen, and Alice Mary (*née* de Rougemont); *m* 1950, Alison Mary Ashby; two *s* one *d*. *Educ:* Fettes Coll., Edinburgh. Served War, Royal Artillery, 1939–46. Mem. of Lloyd's, 1946. Chm., Price Forbes (Holdings) Ltd, 1967; Dep. Chm., Sedgwick Forbes Holdings Ltd, 1972, Chm., 1974–77. Mem. Cttee, Lloyd's Insurance Brokers Assoc., 1961–65 and 1966–69; Chm., Non-Marine Cttee, 1967–68; Chm. of Assoc., 1969–70; Mem., Cttee of Lloyd's, 1971–74, 1976–79; Chm., British Insurance Brokers Assoc., 1980–82. Trustee, St George's English Sch., Rome, 1980–91; Chm., Guide Dogs for the Blind, 1981–87; Governor, Brighton Coll., 1981–88. Pres., Senior Golfers' Soc., 1990–93. *Recreations:* golf, postal history. *Address:* 24 Forest Ridge, Keston Park, Kent BR2 6EQ. *T:* Farnborough (Kent) (01689)

852993. *Clubs:* City of London; Royal and Ancient Golf (St Andrews); Royal St George's (Sandwich); Addington (Surrey).

FINE, Anne; writer; *b* 7 Dec. 1947; *d* of Brian Laker and Mary Baker; *m* 1968, Kit Fine (marr. diss. 1991); two *d*. *Educ:* Northampton High School for Girls; Univ. of Warwick (BA Hons History and Politics). Guardian Children's Fiction Award, 1990; Carnegie Medal, 1990, 1993; Children's Author of the Year, Publishing News, 1990, 1993. *Publications: for older children:* The Summer House Loon, 1978; The Other Darker Ned, 1978; The Stone Menagerie, 1980; Round Behind the Icehouse, 1981; The Granny Project, 1983; Madame Doubtfire, 1987; Goggle-Eyes, 1989; The Book of the Banshee, 1991; Flour Babies, 1992 (Whitbread Award, 1993); Step by Wicked Step, 1995; *for younger children:* Scaredy-Cat, 1985; Anneli the Art Hater, 1986; Crummy Mummy and Me, 1988; A Pack of Liars, 1988; Stranger Danger, 1989; Bill's New Frock, 1989; The Country Pancake, 1989; A Sudden Puff of Glittering Smoke, 1989; A Sudden Swirl of Icy Wind, 1990; Only a Show, 1990; Design-a-Pram, 1991; A Sudden Glow of Gold, 1991; The Worst Child I Ever Had, 1991; The Angel of Nitshill Road, 1991; Same Old Story Every Year, 1992; The Chicken Gave it to Me, 1992; The Haunting of Pip Parker, 1992; *picture book:* Poor Monty, 1991; *novels:* The Killjoy, 1986; Taking the Devil's Advice, 1990; In Cold Domain, 1994. *Recreations:* reading, walking. *Address:* c/o Murray Pollinger, 222 Old Brompton Road, SW5 0BZ.

FINE, Prof. Leon Gerald, FRCP, FRCPGlas, FACP; Professor of Medicine and Head of Department, Joint Department of Medicine, University College London Medical School and Royal Free Hospital School of Medicine, since 1993; *b* 16 June 1943; *s* of Matthew Fine and Jeanette (*née* Lipshitz); *m* 1966, Brenda Sakinovsky; two *d*. *Educ:* Univ. of Cape Town, SA (MB, ChB). FACP 1978; FRCP 1986; FRCPGlas 1993. Internship and Residency in Internal Medicine, Tel Aviv Univ. Med. Sch., Israel, 1967–70; Asst Prof. of Medicine, Albert Einstein Coll. of Medicine, NY, 1975–76; University of Miami School of Medicine: Asst Prof., 1976–78; Associate Prof., 1978–82; Professor of Medicine: and Chief, Div. of Nephrology, UCLA, 1982–91; and Hd of Dept, UCL Med. Sch., 1991–. Editor: Internat. Yearbook of Nephrology, Dialysis, Transplantation, 1989–; Exptl Nephrology, 1993–. *Publications:* contribs on pathophysiology of chronic renal disease, renal growth control, and renal growth responses to acute and chronic injury in professional jls. *Recreations:* collecting rare books on the history of medicine and fine printing, book-binding. *Address:* Department of Medicine, University College London, The Rayne Institute, 5 University Street, WC1E 6JJ. *T:* 0171–380 9907. *Club:* Athenæum.

FINER, Dr Elliot Geoffrey; CChem, FRSC; Head of Chemicals and Biotechnology Division, Department of Trade and Industry, since 1992; *b* 30 March 1944; *s* of Reuben and Pauline Finer; *m* 1970, Viviane Kibrit; two *s*. *Educ:* Royal Grammar Sch., High Wycombe; Cheadle Hulme Sch.; East Barnet Grammar Sch.; St Catharine's Coll., Cambridge (BA 1965); Univ. of East Anglia (MSc 1966; PhD 1968). CChem, FRSC 1993. Unilever Research, Welwyn, 1968–75; Dept of Energy, 1975–90; Dir for Industry and Commerce, 1983–86, Dir Gen., 1988–90, Energy Efficiency Office; Under Secretary, 1988; Head of Management Develt Gp, Cabinet Office, 1990–92; Head of Enterprise Initiative Div., DTI, 1992. Dir, Spillers Foods Ltd, 1989–92. Mem., BBSRC, 1994–. *Publications:* scientific papers and articles on nuclear magnetic resonance spectroscopy and its applications, esp. to phospholipid systems, in learned jls. *Recreations:* home and family, reading, DIY, music. *Address:* Department of Trade and Industry, 151 Buckingham Palace Road, SW1W 9SS.

FINESTEIN, His Honour Israel, MA; QC 1970; a Circuit Judge, 1972–87; *b* 29 April 1921; *y c* of late Jeremiah Finestein, Hull; *m* 1946, Marion Phyllis, *er d* of Simon Oster, Hendon, Mddx. *Educ:* Kingston High School, Hull; Trinity Coll., Cambridge (Major Scholar and Prizeman). MA 1946. Called to the Bar, Lincoln's Inn, 1953. President: Jewish Hist. Soc. of England; Bd of Deps of British Jews, 1991–94. *Publications:* Short History of the Jews of England, 1956; Sir George Jessel, 1959, etc. *Recreation:* reading history. *Address:* 18 Buttermere Court, Boundary Road, NW8.

FINESTEIN, Jonathon Eli; Stipendiary Magistrate for Lancashire and Merseyside, since 1992; an Assistant Recorder, since 1992; *b* 9 April 1950; *s* of Gustav Finestein and Esther Finestein; *m* 1985, Elaine March; one *d*. *Educ:* Hull Grammar Sch.; Leeds Univ. (LLB). Called to the Bar, Gray's Inn, 1973; practice in Hull; Asst Stipendiary Magistrate, 1989–92. *Recreations:* watching all sports, walking. *Address:* Knowsley Magistrates' Court, The Court House, Lathom Road, Huyton, Merseyside L36 9XY. *T:* 0151–489 4558.

FINGERHUT, John Hyman; Consultant to the Pharmaceutical and Allied Industries; *b* 2 Nov. 1910; *s* of late Abraham Fingerhut and Emily (*née* Rowe); *m* 1950, Beatrice Leigh, FCA; two *s* two *d*. *Educ:* Manchester Grammar Sch.; Manchester Univ. FBOA 1931; Hon. FRPharmS (Hon. FPS 1971). Pharmaceutical Chemist, 1932. Served with RAC and Infantry, France, Mauritius and E Africa, 1942–46; commnd Royal Pioneer Corps, transf. to Queen's Royal Regt (seconded King's African Rifles); demobilised as Captain. Merck Sharp & Dohme Ltd: medical rep., 1937–42; Sales Man., 1946; Dep. Man. Dir, 1957; Man. Dir, 1963; Chm., 1967–72; Consultant, 1972–77; Regional Dir, Merck Sharp & Dohme International, 1967–72; Chm., Thomas Morson & Son Ltd, 1967–72; Mem., ABPI Working Party on Resale Price Maintenance, 1970; Associate: Bracken Kelner and Associates Ltd, 1976; Key Pharmaceutical Appointments, 1978–88. Admin. Staff Coll., Henley, 1960. Mem., New Southgate Group Hosp. Management Cttee, 1972–74. Associate Mem., Faculty of Homœopathy, 1974. *Recreations:* music, reading, gardening, washing up. *Address:* 76 Green Lane, Edgware, Mddx HA8 7QA. *T:* 0181–958 6163.

FINGLAND, Sir Stanley (James Gunn), KCMG 1979 (CMG 1966); HM Diplomatic Service, retired; High Commissioner to Kenya, 1975–79; UK Permanent Representative to the UN Environment Programme 1975–79, and to UN Centre for Human Settlements, 1979; *b* 19 Dec. 1919; *s* of late Samuel Gunn Fingland and late Agnes Christina (*née* Watson); *m* 1946, Nellie (*née* Lister); one *s* one *d*. *Educ:* Royal High Sch., Edinburgh. TA 1938. War service, 1939–46 as Major, Royal Signals; served N Africa, Sicily, Italy, Egypt. Commonwealth Relations Office, 1948–; British High Commission, India, 1948–51; Australia, 1953–56; Adviser on Commonwealth and External Affairs to Governor-Gen., Nigeria, 1958–60; British High Commission, Nigeria, 1960; Adviser on Commonwealth and External Affairs to Governor-Gen., Fedn of The W Indies, 1960–61, and to the Governor of Trinidad and Tobago, 1962; British Dep. High Commissioner: Trinidad and Tobago, 1962–63; Rhodesia, 1964–66; High Comr, Sierra Leone, 1966–69; Asst Under-Sec. of State, FCO, 1969–72; Ambassador to Cuba, 1972–75. *Recreation:* fishing.

FINGLETON, David Melvin; Metropolitan Stipendiary Magistrate, 1980–95; *b* 2 Sept. 1941; *s* of Laurence Fingleton and Norma Phillips (*née* Spiro); *m* 1975, Clare, *yr d* of late Ian Colvin. *Educ:* Aldwickbury Sch., Harpenden; Stowe Sch.; University Coll., Oxford (Exhibnr; BA Hons Modern History, MA). Called to Bar, Middle Temple, 1965; South Eastern Circuit. Mem. of Corp. and Board, Trinity Coll. of Music, 1986–; Trustee, Samuel Butler's Educnl Foundn, 1968–. Music Correspondent, Contemporary Review, 1969–92; Opera and Ballet Critic, Tatler and Bystander, 1970–78; Stage Design Corresp., Arts Review, 1976–; Associate Editor, Music and Musicians, 1977–80; Music Critic: Evening News, 1979–80; Daily Express, 1982–. *Publications:* Kiri, 1982; articles in Contemp. Rev., Tatler and Bystander, Music and Musicians, Arts Rev., Evening News, Daily Express. *Recreations:* listening to and writing about music, village life in France. *Address:* c/o John Johnson Agency, Clerkenwell House, 45/47 Clerkenwell Green, EC1R 0HT. *Clubs:* Garrick, MCC.

FINGRET, Peter; His Honour Judge Fingret; a Circuit Judge, since 1992; *b* 13 Sept. 1934; *s* of late Iser and Irene Fingret; *m* 1st, 1960, June Moss (marr. diss. 1980); one *s* one *d*; 2nd, 1980, Dr Ann Lilian Mary Hollingworth (*née* Field). *Educ:* Leeds Modern Sch.; Leeds Univ. (LLB Hons); Open Univ. (BA). President, Leeds Univ. Union, 1957–58. Admitted Solicitor, 1960. Partner: Willey Hargrave & Co., Leeds, 1964–75; Fingret, Paterson & Co., Leeds, 1975–82. Stipendiary Magistrate for Co. of Humberside sitting at Kingston-upon-Hull, 1982–85; Metropolitan Stipendiary Magistrate, 1985–92; a Recorder, 1987–92. Councillor, Leeds City Council, 1967–72; Member: Court, Univ. of Leeds, 1975–85; Cttee, Leeds Internat. Piano Competition, 1981–85. *Recreations:* golf, music, theatre. *Address:* Southwark Crown Court, 1 English Grounds, SE1 2HU. *Clubs:* Garrick, Reform, Royal Society of Medicine.

FINK, Prof. George, FRSE 1989; Director, MRC Brain Metabolism Unit, since 1980, Hon. Professor since 1984, University of Edinburgh; *b* 13 Nov. 1936; *s* of John H. Fink and Therese (*née* Weiss); *m* 1959, Ann Elizabeth Langsam; one *s* one *d*. *Educ:* Melbourne High Sch.; Univ. of Melbourne (MB BS 1960; MD 1978); Hertford Coll., Univ. of Oxford (DPhil 1967). Jun. and sen. house officer, Royal Melbourne and Alfred Hosps, Victoria, Australia, 1961–62; Demonstrator in Anatomy, Monash Univ., Victoria, 1963–64; Nuffield Dominions Demonstrator, Oxford Univ., 1965–67; Sen. Lectr in Anatomy, Monash Univ., 1968–71; Univ. Lectr 1971–80, Official Fellow in Physiology and Med., Brasenose Coll., 1974–80, Oxford Univ. Royal Soc.-Israel Acad. Exchange Fellow, Weizmann Inst., 1979; Walter Cottman Fellow and Vis. Prof., Monash Univ., 1985, 1989; Arthur Fishberg Prof., Mt Sinai Med. Sch., NY, 1988. Prosector in Anatomy, Melbourne Univ., 1956; Wolfson Lectr, Univ. of Oxford, 1982; first G. W. Harris Lectr, Physiol Soc., Cambridge, 1987. Pres., European Neuroendocrine Assoc., 1991–; Member: Council, European Neuroscience Assoc., 1980–82, 1994–; Mental Health Panel, Wellcome Trust, 1984–89; Steering Cttee, British Neuroendocrine Group, 1984–88 (Trustee, BNG, 1990–); Co-ordinating Cttee, ESF Network on Neuroimmunomodulation, 1990–. Trustee, Jl of Neuroendocrinology, 1990–. *Publications:* (ed with L. J. Whalley) Neuropeptides: Basic and Clinical Aspects, 1982; (ed with A. J. Harmar and K. W. McKerns) Neuroendocrine Molecular Biology, 1986; (ed with A. J. Harmar) Neuropeptides: A Methodology, 1989; numerous scientific publications mainly on neuroendocrinology and neuroendocrine molecular biology. *Recreations:* ski-ing, diving. *Address:* MRC Brain Metabolism Unit, University Department of Pharmacology, 1 George Square, Edinburgh EH8 9JZ. *T:* 0131–650 3548, *Fax:* 0131–662 0240.

FINKELSTEIN, Prof. Ludwik, OBE 1990; DSc; FEng 1986; FIEE; CPhys, FInstP; Professor of Measurement and Instrumentation, The City University, since 1980; *b* 6 Dec. 1929; *s* of Adolf and Amalia Finkelstein; *m* 1957, Mirjam Emma, *d* of Dr Alfred and Dr Margarethe Wiener; two *s* one *d*. *Educ:* Univ. of London (MSc). DSc City Univ., 1989. Physicist, Technical Staff, Electronic Tubes Ltd, 1951–52; Scientist, Instrument Br., NCB Mining Res. Estabt, 1952–59; Northampton Coll., London, and City University, London: Lectr, 1959–61; Sen. Lectr, 1961–63; Principal Lectr, 1963–67; Reader, 1967–70; Prof. of Instrument and Control Engineering, 1970–80; Head of Dept of Systems Science, 1974–79; Head of Dept of Physics, 1980–88; Dean, Sch. of Electrical Engrg and Applied Physics, 1983–88; Dean, Sch. of Engrg, 1988–93; Pro-Vice-Chancellor, 1991–94. Visiting Prof., Delft Univ. of Technology, 1973–74. Pres., Inst. of Measurement and Control, 1980 (Vice-Pres., 1972–75, 1977–79; Hartley Silver Medal, 1980); Chm., Management and Design Div., IEE, 1984–85 (Management and Design Divl Premium (jtly), 1984). Hon. FInstMC 1991. Hon. Dr St Petersburg Technical Univ., 1994. *Publications:* papers in learned jls and conference proc. *Recreations:* books, conversation, Jewish studies. *Address:* City University, Northampton Square, EC1V 0HB. *T:* 0171–253 4399; 9 Cheyne Walk, Hendon NW4 3QH. *T:* 0181–202 6966.

FINLAY, Alexander William; retired; *b* 28 Nov. 1921; *s* of late Robert Gaskin Finlay and late Alice Finlay; *m* 1949, Ona Margaret Lewis; no *c*. *Educ:* Tottenham County School. Flt-Lt RAF, 1941–47; various posts, BOAC and British Airways, 1947–78, Planning Dir, 1971–78, retd. Chm., Soc. for Long Range Planning, 1978–79; Mem. Council, Sussex Trust for Nature Conservation, 1982–89; Trustee, Charitable Trust, 1983–. Active interest in support for crime victims, 1989–. FCIT. *Recreations:* conservation, photography, gardening. *Address:* 12 Hunters Way, Chichester, West Sussex PO19 4RB. *Club:* Royal Air Force.

FINLAY, Sir David (Ronald James Bell), 2nd Bt *cr* 1964, of Epping, Co. Essex; *b* 16 Nov. 1963; *s* of Sir Graeme Bell Finlay, 1st Bt, ERD and of June Evangeline, *y d* of Col Francis Collingwood Drake, OBE, MC, DL; *S* father, 1987. *Educ:* Marlborough College; Bristol Univ. (BSc Hons Economics/Philosophy). Peat Marwick McLintock, 1986–91; Hill Samuel Financial Services, 1992–94; Gerrard Vivian Gray, 1994–. Freeman, City of London, 1991. *Recreations:* ski-ing, shooting. *Heir:* none. *Address:* c/o Gerrard Vivian Gray, Burne House, 88 High Holborn, WC1V 6LS. *T:* 0171–413 0881.

FINLAY, Frank, CBE 1984; actor; *b* Farnworth, Lancs, 6 Aug. 1926; *s* of Josiah Finlay; *m* 1954, Doreen Shepherd; two *s* one *d*. *Educ:* St Gregory the Great, Farnworth; RADA (Sir James Knott Schol.). *Stage:* repertory, 1950–52 and 1954–57; Belgrade, Coventry, 1958; Epitaph for George Dillon, NY, 1958; Royal Court, 1958, 1959–62: Sugar in the Morning; Sergeant Musgrave's Dance; Chicken Soup with Barley, Roots, I'm Talking About Jerusalem; The Happy Haven; Platonov; Chips with Everything, Royal Court, transf. to Vaudeville Theatre, 1962 (Clarence Derwent Best Actor Award); Chichester Festival, 1963: St Joan; The Workhouse Donkey; with National Theatre Co. 1963–70: St Joan, 1963; Willie Mossop in Hobson's Choice, and Iago in Othello (both also Chichester Fest., 1964, Berlin and Moscow, 1965), The Dutch Courtesan (also Chichester Fest.), 1964; Giles Corey in The Crucible, Dogberry in Much Ado About Nothing, Mother Courage, 1965; Joxer Daly in Juno and the Paycock, Dikoy in The Storm, 1966; Bernard in After Haggerty, Aldwych, Criterion, Jesus Christ in Son of Man, Leicester Theatre and Round House (first actor ever to play Jesus Christ on stage in English theatre), 1970; Kings and Clowns (musical), Phoenix, 1978; Filumena, Lyric, 1978, US tour, 1979–80, and NY, 1980; The Girl in Melanie Klein, 1980; The Cherry Orchard, tour and Haymarket, 1983; Mutiny (musical), Piccadilly, 1985–86; Beyond Reasonable Doubt, Queen's, 1987, Australian tour, 1988–89, UK tour, 1989–90; Black Angel, King's Head, Islington, 1990; A Slight Hangover, 1991, The Heiress, 1992, Bromley and UK tour; The Woman in Black, UK tour, 1993–94; Peter Pan, Chichester and UK tour; *with National Theatre Co.:* Peppino in Saturday, Sunday, Monday, 1973; Sloman in The Party, 1973; Freddy Malone in Plunder, Ben Prosser in Watch It Come Down, Josef Frank in Weapons of Happiness, 1976; Amadeus, 1982; *films include,* 1962–: The Longest Day, Private Potter, The Informers, A Life for Ruth, Loneliness of the Long Distance Runner, Hot Enough for June, The Comedy Man, The Sandwich Man, A Study in Terror, Othello (nominated for Amer. Acad. award; best actor award, San Sebastian, 1966), The Jokers, I'll Never Forget What's 'Is Name, The Shoes of the Fisherman, Deadly Bees, Robbery, Inspector Clouseau,

Twisted Nerve, Cromwell, The Molly Maguires (in Hollywood), Assault, Victory for Danny Jones, Gumshoe, Shaft in Africa, Van Der Valk and the Girl, Van Der Valk and the Rich; Van Der Valk and the Dead; The Three Musketeers; The Ring of Darkness, The Wild Geese, The Thief of Baghdad, Sherlock Holmes—Murder by Decree; Enigma; Return of the Soldier; The Ploughman's Lunch, 1982; La Chiave (The Key), Italy, 1983; Sakharov, 1983; Christmas Carol, Arch of Triumph, 1919, 1984; Lifeforce, 1985; Casanova, 1986; The Return of the Musketeers, 1988; Cthulhu Mansion, 1992; Charlemagne, 1993; The Sparrow, 1993; *TV appearances include:* Julius Caesar, Les Misérables, This Happy Breed, The Lie (SFTA Award), Casanova (series), The Death of Adolf Hitler, Don Quixote (SFTA Award), Voltaire, Merchant of Venice, Bouquet of Barbed Wire (series) (Best Actor Award), 84 Charing Cross Road, Saturday Sunday Monday, Count Dracula, The Last Campaign, Napoleon in Betzi, Dear Brutus, Tales of the Unexpected, Tales from 1001 Nights, Aspects of Love—Mona, In the Secret State, Verdict on Erebus (NZ), King of the Wind, Mountain of Diamonds (series), Stalin (US), Sherlock Holmes. Hon. Fellow, Bolton Inst., 1992. *Address:* c/o Ken McCready, 91 Regent Street, W1R 7TB. *Club:* Garrick.

FINLAY, Ian; *see* Finlay, W. I. R.

FINLAY, Rt. Rev. Terence Edward; *see* Toronto, Bishop of.

FINLAY, Thomas Aloysius; Chief Justice of Ireland, 1985–94; *b* 17 Sept. 1922; *s* of Thomas A. Finlay and Eva Finlay; *m* 1948, Alice Blayney; two *s* three *d. Educ:* Xavier Sch., Dublin; Clongowes Wood Coll.; University Coll. Dublin. BA Legal and Political Science, NUI. Called to the Bar, King's Inns, 1944 (Bencher, 1972); Hon. Bencher: Inn of Court of NI, 1985; Middle Temple, 1986. Mem., Dáil Éireann, 1954–57; Sen. Counsel, 1961; Judge of the High Court, 1972, Pres. of the High Court, 1974. *Recreations:* fishing, shooting, conversation. *Address:* 22 Ailesbury Drive, Dublin 4. *T:* Dublin 693395.

FINLAY, (William) Ian (Robertson), CBE 1965; MA; HRSA; Director of the Royal Scottish Museum, 1961–71 (Keeper of the Department of Art and Ethnography, 1955–61); Professor of Antiquities to the Royal Scottish Academy, since 1971; *b* Auckland, New Zealand, 2 Dec. 1906; *s* of William R. Finlay and Annie M. Somerville; *m* 1933, Mary Scott, *d* of late W. Henderson Pringle, barrister-at-law; two *s* one *d. Educ:* Edinburgh Academy; Edinburgh Univ. Joined staff of Royal Scottish Museum, 1932; Deputy Regional Officer for Scotland, Ministry of Information, 1942–44; Vice-Chairman, Scottish Arts Council, 1967; Secretary, Royal Fine Art Commission for Scotland, 1953–61. Guest of State Department in US, 1960. Freeman of City of London; Member of Livery, Worshipful Company of Goldsmiths, London; Mem., Edinburgh Festival Council, 1968–71. FRSA 1971. *Publications:* Scotland, World To-Day Series, 1945; Scottish Art (for British Council), 1945; Art in Scotland, 1948; Scottish Crafts, 1948; The Scottish Tradition in Silver (Saltire booklet), 1948; Scottish Architecture (for schools), 1951; Treasures in Edinburgh, 1951; Scotland, Young Traveller Series, 1953; A History of Scottish Gold and Silver Work, 1956, 2nd edn 1991; Scotland, 1957; The Lothians, 1960; The Highlands, 1963; The Young Robert Louis Stevenson, 1965; The Lowlands, 1967; Celtic Art: an introduction, 1973; The Central Highlands, 1976; Priceless Heritage: the future of museums, 1977; Columba, 1979, new edn 1990; articles, reviews and broadcast talks on art and general subjects. *Address:* Currie Riggs, Balerno, Midlothian EH14 5AG. *T:* 0131–449 4249.

FINLAY-MAXWELL, David Campbell, MBE 1994; PhD; CEng, MIEE; FTI, FSDC; Director: D. F. Maxwell Co., since 1991; John Gladstone & Co. Ltd, since 1993; *b* 2 March 1923; *s* of Luke Greenwood Maxwell and of Lillias Maule Finlay; *m* 1954, Constance Shirley Hood; one *s* one *d. Educ:* St Paul's; Heriot-Watt Coll. (Edinburgh Univ.) (Electronic and Control Engrg). CEng 1950; MIEE 1950; FTI 1974; FSDC 1985. PhD Leeds, 1983. Major Royal Signals, 1945. Harvard Univ. Advanced Management Programme, 1968. Man. Dir, 1946–86, Chm., 1960–89, John Gladstone & Co.; Chm. and Man. Dir, John Gladstone & Co. (Engrg), 1948–89. Chairman: Manpower Working Party, NEDO, 1970–73; Wool Industries Res. Assoc., 1974–77; Textile Res. Council, 1977–82; Wool Textile EDC, 1977–79, UK Rep., Consultative Cttee for R&D, Brussels, 1979–84. EEC Reviewer, ESPRIT Prog., 1986–. Dir, Wool Foundn (Internat. Wool Secretariat), 1985–. Member: Council, Textile Inst., 1972–74; British Textile Council, 1977–85; Textile Industry and Dyeing Adv. Cttee, Leeds Univ. Council, 1974–95; Soc. of Dyers and Colourists, 1950–. Pres., Comitextil Sci. Res. Cttee, Brussels. Hon. Lectr, Leeds Univ. Dir/Vice-Chm., Sound Recording Bd of Dirs, RNIB (also Mem., Scientific Develt Sub Cttee); Hon. Organiser for UK, Technical Volunteer Helpers for Blind. *Recreations:* radio propagation, satellite tracking. *Address:* D. F. Maxwell Co., Prospect House, Prospect Street, Huddersfield HD1 2NU. *T:* Huddersfield (01484) 450982. *Clubs:* Special Forces; Royal Scottish Automobile (Glasgow).

FINLAYSON, George; HM Diplomatic Service; Consul-General, Melbourne, since 1994; *b* 22 April 1943; *s* of late George Finlayson and Alison Boath (*née* Barclay); *m* 1966, Patricia Grace Ballantine; two *s. Educ:* Tynecastle High Sch., Edinburgh. Joined HM Diplomatic Service, 1965; Reykjavik, 1967–69; Prague, 1969–71; Lagos, 1971–75; FCO, 1975–78; 2nd Sec., New Delhi, 1978–81; 1st Sec., FCO, 1981–83; 1st Sec. and Head of Chancery, Montevideo, 1983–87; Consul (Commercial) and Dep. Dir for Trade Promotion, New York, 1987–90; Dep. High Comr, Dhaka, 1990–93. *Recreations:* golf, tennis, drawing, painting. *Address:* c/o Foreign and Commonwealth Office, SW1A 2AH. *Clubs:* Athenæum (Melbourne); Royal Melbourne Golf.

FINLAYSON, George Ferguson, CMG 1979; CVO 1983; HM Diplomatic Service, retired; *b* 28 Nov. 1924; *s* of late G. B. Finlayson; *m* 1st, 1951, Rosslyn Evelyn (*d* 1972), *d* of late E. N. James; one *d*; 2nd, 1982, Anthea Judith, *d* of F. D. Perry. *Educ:* North Berwick High Sch. Royal Air Force, 1943–47. Apptd HM Foreign (later Diplomatic) Service, 1949; 2nd Sec. (Inf.), HM Embassy, Rangoon, 1952–54; FO, 1955–59; First Sec., 1959; HM Consul, Algiers, 1959–61; First Sec., HM Embassy, Bamako, 1961–63; HM Consul (Commercial), New York, 1964–68; Counsellor, 1968; Counsellor (Commercial), British High Commn, Singapore, 1969–72; Head of Trade Relations and Exports Dept, FCO, 1972–73; Counsellor (Commercial) Paris, 1973–78; Consul-General: Toronto, 1978–81; Los Angeles, 1981–84. *Recreations:* travel, walking, tennis, swimming. *Address:* 141b Ashley Gardens, SW1P 1HN. T: 071–834 6227; 49 Westgate, North Berwick, East Lothian EH39 4AG. *T:* North Berwick (01620) 2522. *Club:* Oriental.

FINLAYSON, Maj.-Gen. Robert G.; *see* Gordon-Finlayson.

FINLEY, Michael John; Governor, International Press Foundation, since 1988; *b* 22 Sept. 1932; *s* of late Walter Finley and of Grace Marie Butler; *m* 1955, Sheila Elizabeth Cole (*d* 1992); four *s. Educ:* King Edward VII Sch., Sheffield. Editor, 1964–69, Sheffield Morning Telegraph (formerly Sheffield Telegraph); Chief Editorial Dir, 1972–79, and Dir and Gen. Man., 1979–82, Kent Messenger Gp; Exec. Dir, Periodical Publishers Assoc., 1983–88; Dir, Internat. Fedn of Periodical Publishers, 1989–92. Hon. Mem. and Past Chm., Parly and Legal Cttee, Guild of British Newspaper Editors. Chm., Inst. of Dirs (Kent branch), 1980–83. Member: BBC Regional Adv. Council, 1967–69; BBC Gen. Adv. Council, 1971–77; Exec. Cttee, Internat. Fedn of Periodical Publishers, 1983–89; Bd, Fedn of Periodical Publishers in EEC, 1984–92; Bd, Internat. Press Centre, London, 1984–88; Gov., Cranbrook Sch., 1978–. *Publication:* contrib. Advertising and the Community, 1968. *Recreations:* golf, Rugby (spectator), snooker. *Address:* Sorrento, Staplehurst, Kent TN12 0PZ.

FINNEY, Albert; actor, stage and film; film director; *m* 1957, Jane Wenham, actress (marr. diss.); one *s*; *m* 1970, Anouk Aimée (marr. diss.). Associate Artistic Dir, English Stage Co., 1972–75; a Dir, United British Artists, 1983–86. *Stage:* London appearance in The Party, New, 1958; Cassio in Othello, and Lysander, Stratford-on-Avon, 1959; subsequently in: The Lily White Boys, Royal Court, 1960; Billy Liar, Cambridge Theatre, 1960; Luther, in Luther: Royal Court Theatre and Phoenix Theatre, 1961–62; New York, 1963; Armstrong in Armstrong's Last Goodnight, Miss Julie and Black Comedy, Chichester, 1965, Old Vic, 1966; A Day in the Death of Joe Egg, NY, 1968; Alpha Beta, Royal Court and Apollo, 1972; Krapp's Last Tape, Royal Court, 1973; Cromwell, Royal Court, 1973; Chez Nous, Globe, 1974; Uncle Vanya, and Present Laughter, Royal Exchange, Manchester, 1977; Orphans, Hampstead, transf. to Apollo, 1986; J. J. Farr, Phoenix, 1987; Another Time, Wyndham's, 1989, Chicago, 1991; Reflected Glory, Vauderville, 1992; *National Theatre:* Love for Love, 1965; Much Ado About Nothing, 1965; A Flea in Her Ear, 1966; Hamlet, 1975; Tamburlaine, 1977; The Country Wife, 1977; The Cherry Orchard, Macbeth, Has "Washington" Legs?, 1978; *Directed for stage:* The Freedom of the City, Royal Court, 1973; Loot, Royal Court, 1975; *Directed for stage and appeared in:* The Biko Inquest, Riverside, 1984; Serjeant Musgrave's Dance, Old Vic, 1984; *Films include:* Saturday Night and Sunday Morning; Tom Jones; Night Must Fall; Two for the Road; Charlie Bubbles (also Director); Scrooge; Gumshoe; Alpha Beta; Murder on the Orient Express; Wolfen; Loophole; Looker; Shoot the Moon; Annie; The Dresser; Under the Volcano; Orphans; Millers Crossing; The Playboys; Rich in Love; The Browning Version; A Man of No Importance; The Run of the Country; *TV films:* John Paul II; The Endless Game; The Image; The Green Man (series), 1990. Hon. LittD: Sussex, 1965; Salford, 1979. *Address:* c/o Michael Simkins, 45/51 Whitfield Street, W1P 5RJ.

FINNEY, Prof. David John, CBE 1978; MA, ScD Cantab; FRS 1955; FRSE; consultant biometrician; Professor of Statistics, University of Edinburgh, 1966–84; Director, Agricultural and Food Research Council (formerly Agricultural Research Council) Unit of Statistics, 1954–84; *b* Latchford, Warrington, 3 Jan. 1917; *e s* of late Robert G. S. Finney and late Bessie E. Whitlow; *m* 1950, Mary Elizabeth Connolly; one *s* two *d. Educ:* Lymm and Manchester Grammar Schools; Clare Coll., Cambridge; Galton Laboratory, Univ. of London. Asst Statistician, Rothamsted Experimental Station, 1939–45; Lecturer in the Design and Analysis of Scientific Experiment, University of Oxford, 1945–54; Reader in Statistics, University of Aberdeen, 1954–63, Professor, 1963–66. Dir, ISI Res. Centre, Netherlands, 1987–88. Vis. Prof. of Biomathematics, Harvard Univ., 1962–63; Vis. Scientist, Internat. Rice Res. Inst., 1984–85. United Nations FAO expert attached to Indian Council of Agricultural Research, 1952–53; FAO Key Consultant, Indian Agricl Stats Res. Inst., 1984–90. Scientific Consultant, Cotton Research Corporation, 1959–75. Chm., Computer Bd for Univs and Research Councils, 1970–74 (Mem., 1966–74); Member: Adverse Reactions Sub-Cttee, Cttee on Safety of Medicines, 1963–81; BBC General Adv. Council, 1969–76. Trustee, Drug Safety Res. Trust, Bursledon Hall, Southampton, 1986–. President of Biometric Society, 1964–65 (Vice-President, 1963, 1966); Fellow: Royal Statistical Soc. (Pres., 1973–74); American Statistical Assoc.; Mem., Internat. Statistical Inst.; Hon. Fellow Eugenics Society; Hon. Mem., Société Adolphe Quetelet. Weldon Memorial Prize, 1956; Paul Martini Prize, Deutsche Ges. für Medizinische Dokumentation und Statistik, 1971. Dr *hc*, Faculté des Sciences Agronomiques de l'Etat à Gembloux, Belgium, 1967; Hon. DSc: City, 1976; Heriot-Watt, 1981; Hon. Dr Math Waterloo (Ont), 1989. *Publications:* Probit Analysis, 1947 (3rd edn 1971); Biological Standardization (with J. H. Burn, L. G. Goodwin), 1950; Statistical Method in Biological Assay, 1952 (3rd edn 1978); An Introduction to Statistical Science in Agriculture, 1953 (4th edn 1972); Experimental Design and its Statistical Basis, 1955; Tecnica y Teoria en el diseño de Experimentos, 1957; An Introduction to the Theory of Experimental Design, 1960; Statistics for Mathematicians: An Introduction, 1968; Statistics for Biologists, 1980. Numerous papers in statistical and biological journals. *Recreations:* travel (active), music (passive), and the 3 R's. *Address:* 13 Oswald Court, South Oswald Road, Edinburgh EH9 2HY. *T:* 0131–667 0135.

FINNEY, James; Chairman, Staff Commission for Education and Library Boards, 1981–85; Permanent Secretary, Department of Manpower Services for Northern Ireland, 1976–80, retired; *b* 21 Jan. 1920; *s* of James and Ellen Finney, Co. Armagh; *m* 1956, Barbara Ann Bennett, Wargrave, Berks; one *s* three *d. Educ:* Royal Belfast Academical Instn; Trinity Coll., Dublin Univ. BA 1st cl. Mods 1942. Royal Engrs, 1943–46. Min. of Educn for N Ireland, 1946–76. *Recreation:* gardening. *Address:* Honeypots, Ballyhanwood Road, Dundonald, Belfast, N Ireland BT16 0XR. *T:* Dundonald (012318) 3428.

FINNEY, Jarlath John; His Honour Judge Finney; a Circuit Judge, since 1986; *b* Hale, Cheshire, 1 July 1930; *s* of late Victor Harold Finney, MA, and Aileen Rose Finney (*née* Gallagher), Dorking, Surrey; *m* 1957, Daisy Emöke, *y d* of late Dr Matyas Veszy, formerly of Budapest; two *s* two *d. Educ:* Wimbledon College; Gray's Inn. Served, 2nd Lieut, 8th Royal Tank Regt, 1953–55 (Lieut 1955). Called to Bar, Gray's Inn, 1953; Member, SE Circuit, 1955–86; Member, Panel of Counsel for HM Customs and Excise before VAT Tribunals, 1973–86; a Recorder of the Crown Court, 1980–86. FLS 1990. *Publications:* Gaming, Lotteries, Fundraising and the Law, 1982; (jtly) Sales Promotion Law, 1986; articles. *Recreations:* wild flowers, books, walking in the country, pottering about looking things up. *Address:* The Law Courts, Woodall House, Lordship Lane, Wood Green, N22 5LF. *T:* 0181–881 1400. *Club:* Wig and Pen.

FINNEY, Rt. Rev. John Thornley; *see* Pontefract, Bishop Suffragan of.

FINNIS, Prof. John Mitchell, DPhil; FBA 1990; Professor of Law and Legal Philosophy, Oxford University, since 1989; Fellow and Praelector in Jurisprudence, since 1966, Stowell Civil Law Fellow, since 1973, University College, Oxford; *b* 28 July 1940; *s* of Maurice and Margaret Finnis; *m* 1964, Marie Carmel McNally; three *s* three *d* (and one *d* decd). *Educ:* St Peter's Coll., Adelaide, SA; St Mark's Coll., Univ. of Adelaide (LLB 1961); University Coll., Oxford (Rhodes Scholar for SA, 1962; DPhil 1965). Called to the Bar, Gray's Inn, 1970. Associate in Law, Univ. of Calif at Berkeley, 1965–66; Rhodes Reader in Laws of British Commonwealth and United States, Oxford Univ., 1972–89; Prof. and Head of Dept of Law, Univ. of Malawi, 1976–78; Matthews Prof. of Law, Univ. of Notre Dame, USA, 1995–. Huber Distinguished Vis. Prof., Boston Coll. Law Sch., 1993–94. Special Adviser to Foreign Affairs Cttee, House of Commons, on role of UK Parlt in Canadian Constitution, 1980–82; Consultor, Pontifical Commn, Iustitia et Pax, 1977–89; Member: Pontifical Council de Iustitia et Pace, 1990–; Catholic Bishops' Jt Cttee on Bio-Ethical Issues, 1981–88; Internat. Theol Commn, The Vatican, 1986–92. Governor, Linacre Centre, London, 1981– (Vice-Chm., 1987–). *Publications:* Commonwealth and Dependencies, in Halsbury's Laws of England, 4th edn, Vol. 6, 1974, revised 1991; Natural Law and Natural Rights, 1980; Fundamentals of Ethics, 1983; (with Joseph Boyle and Germain Grisez) Nuclear Deterrence, Morality and Realism, 1987; Moral Absolutes, 1991. *Address:* University College, Oxford OX1 4BH. *T:* Oxford (01865) 276602; 12

Gray's Inn Square, WC1R 5JP. *T:* 0171-404 4866; 12 Staverton Road, Oxford OX2 6XJ. *T:* Oxford (01865) 58660.

FINNISSY, Michael Peter; composer; *b* 17 March 1946; *s* of George Norman Finnissy and Rita Isolene Finnissy (*née* Parsonson). *Educ:* Hawes Down Jun. Sch.; Bromley Tech. High Sch.; Beckenham and Penge Grammar Sch.; Royal Coll. of Music. Lectr, Music Dept, London Sch. of Contemporary Dance, 1969–74; Artist-in-Residence, Victorian Coll. of the Arts, Melbourne, Australia, 1982–83; Lectr, Dartington Summer Sch., 1981, 1990, 1992–; Consultant Tutor in Composition, Winchester Coll., 1988–; Res. Fellow in Music, Univ. of Sussex, 1989–; Mem., Composition Faculty, Royal Acad. of Music, 1990–. Pres., ISCM, 1990–. *Compositions include:* Eighteen Songs, 1963–76; World (vocal/orchestral), 1968–74; Tsuru-Kame (stage work), 1971–73; Mysteries (stage work), 1972–79; Verdi Transcriptions (piano), 1972–88; Cipriano (choral), 1974; Seven Piano Concertos, 1975–81; Pathways of Sun & Stars (orchestral), 1976; English Country-Tunes (piano), 1977; Alongside (orchestral), 1979; Sea and Sky (orchestral), 1979–80; Kelir (choral), 1981; The Undivine Comedy (stage work), 1985–88; Thérèse Raquin (stage work), 1992; Folklore (piano), 1993–94; Shameful Vice (stage work), 1994. *Address:* c/o Oxford University Press, Walton Street, Oxford OX2 6DP. *T:* Oxford (01865) 56767.

FINSBERG, Baron *cr* 1992 (Life Peer), of Hampstead in the London Borough of Camden; **Geoffrey Finsberg,** Kt 1984; MBE 1959; JP; Deputy Chairman, Commission for New Towns, since 1992; *b* 13 June 1926; *o s* of late Montefiore Finsberg, MC, and May Finsberg (*née* Grossman); *m* 1st, 1969, Pamela Benbow Hill (*d* 1989); 2nd, 1990, (Yvonne) Elizabeth Sarch (*née* Wright). *Educ:* City of London Sch. National Chm., Young Conservatives, 1954–57; Mem., Exec. Cttee, Nat. Union of Cons. and Unionist Assocs, 1953–79 (Mem. Exec. Cttee, 1949–79, Pres., 1986–89, Gtr London Area); a Vice-Chm., Conservative Party Organisation, 1975–79 and 1983–87. Borough Councillor: Hampstead, 1949–65; Camden, 1964–74 (Leader, 1968–70). Chairman: Gtr London Area Cons. Local Govt Cttee, 1972–75. MP (C) Hampstead, 1970–83, Hampstead and Highgate, 1983–92. Opposition spokesman on Greater London, 1974–79; Mem. Exec., 1922 Cttee, 1974–75; Member, Select Cttee on Expenditure, 1970–79; Parly Under Sec. of State, DoE, 1979–81, DHSS, 1981–83; Mem., Parly Assembly of Council of Europe (Pres., 1991–92), and of WEU, 1983–, delegn leader, 1987–. Controller of Personnel and Chief Industrial Relations Adviser, Great Universal Stores, 1968–79; Dep. Chm., South East Reg. Bd, TSB, 1986–89 (Mem., 1983–86). Vice-Pres., Assoc. of Municipal Corporations, 1971–74 (Dep. Chm., 1969–71); Member: Post Office Users Nat. Council, 1970–77; Council, CBI, 1968–79 (Chm., Post Office Panel). Jt Nat. Treas., CCJ, 1993–. FIPD (FIPM 1975). Patron, Maccabi Assoc. of GB; Trustee, Marie Curie Cancer Foundn, 1993–. Governor, UCS. JP Inner London, 1962. Order of Merit, (Austria), 1989; Comdr, Order of Isabella the Catholic (Spain), 1990. *Recreations:* bridge, reading. *Address:* 18 Fairfax Road, NW6 4HA. *T:* 0171–586 9979.

FIRMSTON-WILLIAMS, Peter, CBE 1987 (OBE 1979); Chairman, Flowers and Plants Association, 1984–89; *b* 30 Aug. 1918; *s* of late Geoffrey and Muriel Firmston-Williams; *m* Margaret Beaulah; one *s* one *d*. *Educ:* Harrow. Served War, Infantry, Green Howards Regt, 1939–45 (Captain). J. Lyons & Co. Ltd, 1945–53; Marketing Director, United Canners Ltd, 1953–55; Associated British Foods Ltd, Director, Store Operations, Fine Fare, 1958–61; Fitch Lovell Ltd, Man. Dir, Key Markets Ltd, 1962–71; Associated Dairies Group Ltd, Man. Dir, ASDA Stores, and Dir, Associated Dairies, 1971–81, retired; Director: Woolworth Hdgs (formerly Paternoster Stores), 1981–85 (non-exec. Dir, 1985–86; Dep. Chm., 1982–85); Bredero Properties Ltd, 1986–; Chm., Bayfleet Hldgs Ltd, 1988–. Chairman: Covent Garden Market Authority, 1982–88; Retail Consortium, 1984–86. *Recreations:* golf, water skiing, gardening. *Address:* Oak House, 12 Pembroke Road, Moor Park, Northwood, Mddx HA6 2HR. *T:* Northwood (01923) 823052.

FIRNBERG, David; Chairman, DFA Ltd, since 1989; Chief Executive, Strategic Planning Society, since 1995; *b* 1 May 1930; *s* of L. B. Firnberg and K. L. E. Firnberg; *m* 1957, Sylvia Elizabeth du Cros; one *s* three *d*. *Educ:* Merchant Taylors' Sch., Northwood. FBCS. Went West, 1953–56; Television Audience Measurement Ltd, 1956–59; ICT/ICL, 1959–72; David Firnberg Associates Ltd, 1972–74; Dir, Nat. Computing Centre Ltd, 1974–79; Eosys Ltd: Man. Dir, 1980–88; Chm., 1989–91; The Networking Centre Ltd: Chm., 1985–90; Exec. Chm., 1990–91. President: UK Assoc. of Project Managers, 1978–84; British Computer Soc., 1983–84 (Chm., IT Support for Disabled People project, 1989–91); Chairman: UK Council for Computing Develt, 1990–91; Steering Cttee, RSA Design Bursaries for Communications and Computing, 1989–94; Member: Foundn for Sci. and Technology, 1987–94; Council, PITCOM, 1989– (Chm., Prog. Exec.); Quality Audit Steering Council, Higher Educn Quality Council, 1992–. Freeman, City of London, 1987. FInstD; FRSA. *Publications:* Computers Management and Information, 1973; Cassell's New Spelling Dictionary, 1976; Cassell's Spelling Dictionary, 1984. *Address:* Home Farm, Ludgershall, Aylesbury, Bucks HP18 9NY. *T:* Brill (01844) 238600. *Club:* Wig and Pen.

FIRTH, Andrew Trevor; Regional Chairman, Industrial Tribunals, Yorkshire/Humberside, 1982–88 (Chairman, Industrial Tribunals, 1972–82); *b* 4 June 1922; *s* of Seth Firth and Amy Firth; *m* 1946, Nora Cornforth Armitage; one *s* two *d*. *Educ:* Prince Henry's Grammar Sch.; Leeds Univ. (LLB). Served RA, 6th Airborne Div., Normandy, 1944, Lieut; Intelligence Officer, Potsdam Conf., 1945, Captain; Rhine Army Coll., 1946, Major. Partner, later Sen. Partner, Barret Chamberlain & McDonnell, Solicitors, Harrogate, Otley, Leeds, 1948–72. Pres., Harrogate and Dist Law Soc., 1965–66; Area Chm., Law Soc. Legal Aid Cttee, Yorkshire, 1969–72. Bronze Star Medal, USA, 1945. *Recreations:* Chippendale Soc., golf, grandchildren. *Address:* Chevin Close, Birdcage Walk, Otley, West Yorkshire LS21 3HB. *Club:* Otley Golf.

FIRTH, (David) Colin; Headmaster, Cheadle Hulme School, 1977–89, retired; *b* 29 Jan. 1930; *s* of Jack and Muriel Firth; *m* 1954, Edith Scanlan; three *s* one *d*. *Educ:* Rothwell Grammar Sch.; Sheffield Univ. (BSc, DipEd). Royal Signals, 1952–54; Stand Grammar Sch., 1954–57; East Barnet Grammar Sch., 1957–61; Bristol Grammar Sch., 1961–73; The Gilberd Sch., 1973–77. *Publications:* A Practical Organic Chemistry, 1966; Elementary Thermodynamics, 1969; (jtly) Introductory Physical Science, 1971. *Recreations:* golf, fell walking, talking about gardening, singing. *Address:* Hill House, Fell Lane, Penrith, Cumbria CA11 8BJ.

FIRTH, Mrs Joan Margaret, CB 1995; PhD; Deputy Director of NHS Finance, Department of Health, 1990–95; *b* 25 March 1935; *d* of Ernest Wilson and Ann (*née* Crowther); *m* 1955, Kenneth Firth. *Educ:* Lawnswood High Sch., Leeds; Univ. of Leeds (1st Cl. BSc Colour Chemistry; PhD Dyeing of Wool). Research Asst, Leeds Univ., 1958–60; Head of Science, Selby High Sch., 1960–62; Sen. Lecturer in General Science, Elizabeth Gaskell Coll., Manchester, 1962–66; Lectr in Organic Chemistry, Salford Univ., 1966–67; joined Civil Service as Direct Entry Principal, 1967; Asst Sec., 1974; Under-Sec., DHSS, 1981; Under-Sec., Social Security Div. C, DHSS, later DSS, 1987–90. Member: ESRC, 1988–92; Training Bd, 1990–92. Mem., Audit Cttee, Inst. Cancer Res., 1994–. *Publications:* contrib. Jl Textile Inst., 1958. *Recreations:* wine, walking.

FIRTH, Paul James; Stipendiary Magistrate for Merseyside, since 1995; *b* 2 June 1951; *s* of Albert and Violet Firth; *m* 1979, Ann Barbara Whitehead; one *s*. *Educ:* Bradford Grammar Sch.; Queen's Coll., Oxford (MA 1973). Admitted solicitor, 1980; Trainee Court Clerk, Keighley Magistrates' Court, 1973–74; Trainee Court Clerk, Court Clerk, then Sen. Court Clerk, Leeds Magistrates' Court, 1975–81; Dep. Clerk to Justices (Legal), Manchester City Magistrates' Court, 1981–86; Clerk to Justices, Rotherham Magistrates' Court, 1986–95; Actg Stipendiary Magistrate, 1991–95. *Recreations:* beginners' golf, various sports (reduced to watching), reading anything except law books. *Address:* Liverpool City Magistrates' Court, 107–111 Dale Street, Liverpool L2 2JQ. *T:* 0151–236 5871.

FIRTH, Rt. Rev. Peter James; Bishop Suffragan of Malmesbury, 1983–94; *b* 12 July 1929; *s* of Atkinson Vernon Firth and Edith Pepper; *m* 1955, Felicity Mary Wilding; two *s* two *d* (and one long-term foster *d*). *Educ:* Stockport Grammar School; Emmanuel Coll., Cambridge (Open Exhibnr, MA, DipEd); St Stephen's House Theol Coll., Oxford. Ordained, 1955; Assistant Curate, St Stephen's, Barbourne in Worcester, 1955–58; Priest-in-charge, Church of the Ascension, Parish of St Matthias, Malvern Link, Worcs, 1958–62; Rector of St George's, Abbey Hey, Gorton in Manchester, 1962–66; Religious Broadcasting Assistant, North Region, BBC, 1966–67; Religious Broadcasting Organiser and Senior Producer, Religious Programmes, BBC South and West, Bristol, 1967–83. Internat. Radio Festival winner, Seville, 1975. *Publication:* Lord of the Seasons, 1978. *Recreations:* theatre, photography, music, travel, Manchester United. *Address:* 7 Ivywell Road, Bristol BS9 1NX. *T:* Bristol (0117) 968 5931.

FIRTH, Prof. Sir Raymond (William), Kt 1973; MA; PhD; FBA 1949; Professor of Anthropology, University of London, 1944–68, now Emeritus; *b* 25 March 1901; *s* of late Wesley Hugh Bourne Firth and Marie Elizabeth Jane Cartmill; *m* 1936, Rosemary, *d* of late Sir Gilbert Upcott, KCB; one *s*. *Educ:* Auckland Grammar Sch.; Auckland University College; London School of Economics (Hon. Fellow, 1970). Anthropological research in British Solomon Islands, including one year on Tikopia, 1928–29; Lecturer in Anthropology, University of Sydney, 1930–31; Acting Professor of Anthropology, University of Sydney, 1931–32; Lecturer in Anthropology, London School of Economics, 1932–35; Reader, 1935–44; Hon. Secretary Royal Anthropological Institute, 1936–39 (President 1953–55); Research in peasant economics and anthropology in Malaya, as Leverhulme Research Fellow, 1939–40; served with Naval Intelligence Division, Admiralty, 1941–44; Secretary of Colonial Social Science Research Council, Colonial Office, 1944–45; Academic Advr, ANU, 1948–52; Fellow, Center for Advanced Study in the Behavioral Sciences, Stanford, 1958–59; Prof. of Pacific Anthropology, Univ. of Hawaii, 1968–69. Visiting Professor: British Columbia, 1969; Cornell, 1970; Chicago, 1971; Graduate Center, City Univ. of New York, 1971; Univ. of California, Davis 1974, Berkeley 1977; Auckland, 1978. Life Pres., Assoc. of Social Anthropologists, 1975. Foreign Hon. Member American Academy of Arts and Sciences, 1963; Hon. Member Royal Society, NZ, 1964; Foreign Member: American Philosophical Society, 1965; Royal Soc., NSW; Royal Danish Academy of Sciences and Letters, 1966; Internat. Union of Anthropol and Ethnol Sciences, 1983; European Assoc. of Social Anthropologists, 1990. Social research surveys: W Africa, 1945; Malaya, 1947; New Guinea, 1951; Tikopia, 1952, 1966; Malaya, 1963. Hon. degrees: DPh Oslo, 1965; LLD Michigan, 1967; LittD East Anglia, 1968; Dr Letters ANU, 1969; DHumLett Chicago, 1968; DSc British Columbia, 1970; DLitt Exeter, 1972; DLit Auckland, 1978; PhD Cracow, 1984; DSc Econ London, 1984. *Publications:* The Kauri Gum Industry, 1924; Primitive Economics of the New Zealand Maori, 1929 (new edn, 1959); Art and Life In New Guinea, 1936; We, The Tikopia: A Sociological Study of Kinship in Primitive Polynesia, 1936; Human Types, 1938 (new edn, 1975); Primitive Polynesian Economy, 1939 (new edn, 1964); The Work of the Gods in Tikopia, 1940 (new edn, 1967); Malay Fishermen: Their Peasant Economy, 1946 (enlarged edn, 1966); Elements of Social Organization, 1951 (new edn 1971); Two Studies of Kinship in London (ed.), 1956; Man and Culture: An Evaluation of the Work of Malinowski (ed.), 1957; Social Change in Tikopia, 1959; History and Traditions of Tikopia, 1961; Essays on Social Organization and Values, 1964; (with B. S. Yamey) Capital Saving and Credit in Peasant Societies, 1964; Tikopia Ritual and Belief, 1967; Rank and Religion in Tikopia, 1970; (with J. Hubert and A. Forge) Families and Their Relatives, 1970; Symbols Public and Private, 1973; Tikopia-English Dictionary, 1985; Tikopia Songs, 1990. *Recreations:* Romanesque art, early music. *Address:* 33 Southwood Avenue, N6 5SA. *Club:* Athenæum.

FIRTH, Tazeena Mary; designer; *b* 1 Nov. 1935; *d* of Denis Gordon Firth and Irene (*née* Morris). *Educ:* St Mary's, Wantage; Chatelard Sch. Theatre Royal, Windsor, 1954–57; English Stage Co., Royal Court, 1957–60; partnership in stage design with Timothy O'Brien estabd 1961; output incl.: The Bartered Bride, The Girl of the Golden West, 1962; West End prodns of new plays, 1963–64; London scene of Shakespeare Exhibn, 1964; Tango, Days in the Trees, Staircase, RSC, and Trafalgar at Madame Tussaud's, 1966; All's Well that Ends Well, As You Like It, Romeo and Juliet, RSC, 1967; The Merry Wives of Windsor, Troilus and Cressida (also Nat. Theatre, 1976), The Latent Heterosexual, RSC, 1968; Pericles (also Comédie Française, 1974), Women Beware Women, Bartholomew Fair, RSC, 1969; 1970: Measure for Measure, RSC; Madame Tussaud's in Amsterdam; The Knot Garden, Royal Opera; 1971: Enemies, Man of Mode, RSC; 1972: La Cenerentola, Oslo; Lower Depths, The Island of the Mighty, RSC; As You Like It, OCSC; 1973: Richard II, Love's Labour's Lost, RSC; 1974: Next of Kin, NT; Summerfolk, RSC; The Bassarids, ENO; 1975: John Gabriel Borkman, NT; Peter Grimes, Royal Opera (later in Paris); The Marrying of Ann Leete, RSC; 1976: Wozzeck, Adelaide Fest.; The Zykovs, RSC; The Force of Habit, NT; 1977: Tales from the Vienna Woods, Bedroom Farce, NT; Falstaff, Berlin Opera; 1978: The Cunning Little Vixen, Göteborg; Evita, London (later in USA, Australia, Vienna); A Midsummer Night's Dream, Sydney Opera House; 1979: Peter Grimes, Göteborg; The Rake's Progress, Royal Opera; Turandot, Vienna State Opera, 1983. Designed independently: The Two Gentlemen of Verona, RSC, 1969; Occupations, RSC, 1971; The Rape of Lucretia, Karlstad, 1982; Katherina Ismailova, Göteborg, 1984; La Traviata, Umeå, The Trojan Woman, Göteborg, and Bluebeard's Castle, Copenhagen, 1985; Il Seraglio, Göteborg, 1986; The Magic Flute, Rigoletto, Umeå, 1987; Romeo and Juliet, Malmö, 1988; The Rake's Progress, Göteborg, and, Dido and Aeneas, Copenhagen, 1989; From the House of the Dead, Göteborg, and, Barbarians, RSC, 1990; Macbeth, Göteborg, 1990; Lady Macbeth of Mtsensk, Copenhagen, La Bohème, Malmö, and Il Seraglio, Stockholm, 1991; Don Giovanni, Prague, 1991; Rigoletto, Oslo, and Carmen, Copenhagen, 1992; Carmen, Stockholm, Drot og Mask, Copenhagen, Magic Flute, Prague and Peter Grimes, Copenhagen, 1993; Vox Humana, Göteborg, 1994; Don Giovanni, Japan, 1995. (Jtly) Gold Medal for Set Design, Prague Quadriennale, 1975. *Recreation:* sailing. *Address:* 33 Lansdowne Gardens, SW8 2EQ. *T:* 0171–622 5384.

FISCHER, August Antonios; Chief Executive, News International plc, since 1994; *b* 7 Feb. 1939; *s* of August Fischer and Elisabeth Fischer (*née* Zanola); *m* 1961, Gillian Ann Streete; one *s* one *d*. *Educ:* Univ. of Zurich, Switzerland (BA Business Admin). E. I. Du Pont de Nemours & Co., 1962–78; Napp Systems (Europe) Ltd, 1978–81; Napp Systems Inc., 1981–88; News International plc, 1989–. *Address:* News International plc, Virginia Street, E1 9XY. *T:* 0171–782 6059.

FISCHER, Dr Edmond Henri; Professor Emeritus, University of Washington, since 1990; *b* Shanghai, China, 6 April 1920; *s* of Oscar Fischer and Renee Tapernoux; *m* 1963, Beverley Bullock; two *s*. *Educ:* Univ. of Geneva (Licencié ès Sciences 1943; Diplôme d'Ingenieur 1944; DSc 1947). Asst, Labs of Organic Chem., Univ. of Geneva, 1946–47; Fellow, Swiss Nat. Foundn, 1948–50; Res. Fellow, Rockefeller Foundn, 1950–53; Res. Associate, Div. of Biol., CIT, 1953; University of Washington: Asst Prof. of Biochem., 1953–56; Associate Prof., 1956–61; Prof., 1961–90. Mem., Biochem. Section, NIH, 1959–64; National Academy of Sciences: Mem., Food Protection Cttee, 1971–72; Mem., Membership Cttee, 1977–78. Mem., Editl Adv. Bd, 1961–66, Associate Editor, 1966–92, Biochemistry, Jl of ACS. Member: Adv. Bd, ACS, 1962; Council, Amer. Soc. Biol Chemists, 1980–83. Member: Scientific Council on Basic Sci., Amer. Heart Assoc., 1977–80; Scientific Adv. Cttee, Muscular Dystrophy Assoc., 1980–89; Chm., Task Force, Muscular Dystrophy Assoc. Res. Centres, 1985–89. Member: Amer. Soc. Biol Chemists; ACS; AAAS; Amer. Assoc. of Univ. Profs. Hon. PhD: Montpellier 1985; Basel 1988; Med. Coll. of Ohio, 1993; Ruhr-Univ., 1994. Numerous awards, medals and prizes; Nobel Prize in Physiology or Medicine, 1992. *Publications:* numerous. *Recreations:* playing classical piano, private pilot. *Address:* Department of Biochemistry, University of Washington, Seattle, WA 98195, USA. *T:* (206) 5431741.

FISCHER, Prof. Ernst Otto; Professor of Inorganic Chemistry, Munich University (Techn); *b* Munich, 10 Nov. 1918; *s* of Prof. Karl T. Fischer and Valentine (*née* Danzer); unmarried. *Educ:* Tech. Univ., Munich. Dip. Chem., 1949; Dr rer. nat., 1952, Habilitation 1954. Associate Prof. of Inorganic Chem., Univ. of Munich, 1957, Prof. 1959, Prof. and Dir, Inorganic Chem. Inst., Tech. Univ., Munich, 1964. Member: Bavarian Acad. of Sciences; Akad. deutscher Naturforscher Leopoldina, 1969; Austrian Acad. of Scis, 1976; Accad. dei Lincei, Italy, 1976; Göttingen Akad. der Wissenschaften, 1977; Rheinisch-Westfälische Akad. der Wissenschaften, 1987; Soc. of German Chemists, etc; Centennial For. Fellow, Amer. Chem. Soc., 1976. Hon. Dr rer. nat.: Munich, 1972; Erlangen, 1977; Veszprem, 1983; Hon. DSc Strathclyde, 1975. Has received many prizes and awards including the Nobel Prize for Chemistry, 1973 (jointly with Prof. Geoffrey Wilkinson) for their pioneering work, performed independently, on the chem. of organometallic "sandwich compounds". *Publications:* (with H. Werner) Metall-pi-Komplexe mit di- und oligoolefinischen Liganden, 1963 (trans. as Metal pi-Complexes Vol. 1, Complexes with di- and oligo-olefinic Ligands, 1966–); numerous contribs to learned jls on organometallic chem., etc. *Recreations:* art, history, travel. *Address:* 16 Sohnckestrasse, 81479 München, Germany.

FISCHER-DIESKAU, Dietrich; baritone; *b* Berlin, 28 May 1925; *s* of Dr Albert Fischer-Dieskau; *m* 1949, Irmgard Poppen (*d* 1963); three *s*. *Educ:* High Sch., Berlin; Music Academy, Berlin. First Baritone, Städtische Oper, Berlin, 1948–78, Hon. Mem., 1978–; Mem., Vienna State Opera, 1957–63. Extensive Concert Tours of Europe and USA; soloist in Festivals at Edinburgh, Salzburg, Bayreuth, Vienna, Berlin, Munich, Holland, Luzern, Prades, etc. Opera roles include: Wolfram, Jochanaan, Almaviva, Marquis Posa, Don Giovanni, Falstaff, Mandryka, Wozzeck, Danton, Macbeth, Hans Sachs. Many recordings. Prof., Music Acad., Berlin, 1983; Member: Acad. of Arts, Berlin; Acad. of Fine Arts, Munich; Hon. RAM, 1972; Honorary Member: Wiener Konzerthausgesellschaft, 1962; Königlich-Schwedische Akad., 1972; Acad. Santa Cecilia, Rome; Royal Philharmonic Soc., 1985. Hon. DMus Oxford, 1978; Dr *hc* Sorbonne, 1980; Yale, 1980. Kunstpreis der Stadt Berlin, 1950; Internationaler Schallplattenpreis, since 1955 nearly every year; Orfeo d'oro, 1955 and 1966; Bayerischer Kammersänger, 1959; Edison Prize, 1961, 1964, 1966, 1970; Naras Award, USA, 1962; Mozart-Medaille, Wien, 1962; Berliner Kammersänger, 1963; Electrola Award, 1970; Léonie Sonning Music Prize, Copenhagen, 1975; Golden Gramophone Award, Germany, 1975; Ruckert-Preis, Schweinfurth, 1979; President's Prize, Charles Gros Acad., Paris, 1980; Ernst Von Siemen Prize, 1980; Artist of the Year, Phonoakademie, Germany, 1980; Gold Medal, Royal Philharmonic Soc., 1988. Bundesverdienstkreuz (1st class), 1958, Grosses Verdienstkreuz, 1974, Stern zum Grossen Bundesverdienstkreuz, 1986; Pour le mérite, Deutschland (FRG), 1984; Chevalier de la Légion d'Honneur (France), 1990. *Publications:* Texte Deutscher Lieder, 1968 (The Fischer-Dieskau Book of Lieder, 1976); Auf den Spuren der Schubert-Lieder, 1971; Wagner und Nietzsche, 1974; Robert Schumann—Wort und Musik, 1981; Töne sprechen, Worte klingen, 1985; Nachklang, 1987; Wenn Musik der Liebe Nahrung ist: Künstlerschicksale im 19 Jahrhundert, 1990; Weil nicht alle Blütenträume reifen (Reichardt), 1991; Fern die Klage des Fauns (Debussy), 1993.

FISCHLER, Dr Franz; Member, European Commission, since 1995; *b* 23 Sept. 1946; *s* of Josef Fischler and Theodora Fischler; *m* 1973, Adelheid Hausmann; two *s* two *d*. *Educ:* Univ. for Soil Sci., Vienna (Dr in Natural Scis 1978). Univ. Asst, Dept of Regl Agricl Planning., Inst. for Farm Mgt, Vienna, 1973–79; Tyrol Chamber of Agriculture: Mem., 1979–84; Dir, 1985–89; elected Mem., Nationalrat, 1990, 1994; Fed. Minister of Agric. and Forestry, 1989–94. Grosse Goldene Ehrenzeichen am Bande (Austria), 1993. *Address:* European Commission, Breydel 7/16, Avenue d'Auderghem 45, 1040 Brussels, Belgium. *T:* (2) 959625.

FISH, Prof. Francis, OBE 1989; BPharm, PhD; FRPharmS; Dean, School of Pharmacy, 1978–88 (Hon. Fellow, 1992), Professor of Pharmacy, 1988, Professor Emeritus, 1989, University of London; *b* 20 April 1924; *s* of William Fish and Phyllis (*née* Griffiths); *m* 1949, Hilda Mary Brown; two *s*. *Educ:* Houghton-le-Spring Grammar Sch.; Technical Coll., Sunderland (now Univ. of Sunderland). BPharm (London) 1946; PhD (Glasgow) 1955. FPS 1946. Asst Lectr, 1946–48, Lectr, 1948–62, Royal Coll. of Science and Technology, Glasgow; University of Strathclyde: Sen. Lectr, 1962–69; Reader in Pharmacognosy and Forensic Science, 1969–76; Personal Prof., 1976–78; Dean, Sch. of Pharmaceutical Sciences, 1977–78; Supervisor, MSc course in Forensic Science, 1966–78. Mem. Editorial Bd, Jl Pharm. Pharmacol., 1964–70 and 1975–78. Member: Pharm. Soc. Cttee on Pharmacognosy, 1963–74; British Pharm. Codex Pharmacognosy Sub-Cttee A, 1968–73; Brit. Pharm. Conf. Sci. Cttee, 1973–78 (Science Chm., 1977); Brit. Pharmacopoeia Pharmacognosy Panel, 1974–77; Council, Forensic Science Soc., 1974–77 (Vice-Pres., 1981–82); Professional and Gen. Services Cttee, Scottish Council on Alcoholism, 1976–78; British Pharmacopœia Commn, 1980–91; Cttee on Safety of Medicines, 1980–83 (Mem., Herbal Sub-Cttee, 1978–80; Mem., Chemistry, Pharmacy and Standards Sub-Cttee, 1980–92); Univ. of London Senate, 1981–88; DHSS Standing Pharmaceutical Adv. Cttee, 1982–88; UGC Panel on Studies Allied to Medicine, 1982–89 (Chm., 1984–89); Nuffield Foundn Cttee of Inquiry into Pharmacy, 1983–86; Cttee on Review of Medicines, 1984–91; UGC Medical Subcttee, 1984–89. Chm., Post Qualification Bd for NHS Pharmacists in Scotland, 1989–92. Mem., Governing Body, Wye College, 1985–88. Harrison Meml Medal, 1982; Charter Gold Medal, RPSGB, 1987. *Publications:* (with J. Owen Dawson) Surgical Dressings, Ligatures and Sutures, 1967; research pubns and review articles in Pharmaceut., Phytochem. and Forensic Sci. jls. *Recreations:* gardening, golf. *Address:* Grianan, Hazel Avenue, Crieff, Perthshire PH7 3ER.

FISH, Sir Hugh, Kt 1989; CBE 1984 (OBE 1971); Chairman, National Environment Research Council, 1984–88 (Member, 1976–84); independent consultant on environmental management; *b* 6 Jan. 1923; *s* of Leonard Mark and Millicent Fish; *m* 1943, Nancy, *o d* of William and Louise Asquith; one *s* one *d* (and one *s* decd). *Educ:* Rothwell Grammar Sch.; Leeds Univ. (BSc). War Service, 1942–46, RNVR (Lieut). Chemist, W Riding Rivers Bd, 1949–52; Pollution and Fisheries Inspector, Essex River Bd, 1952–65; River Conservator, Essex River Authy, 1965–69; Chief Purification Officer, Thames Conservancy, 1969–74; Thames Water Authority: Dir of Scientific Services, 1974–78; Chief Exec., 1978–84; Mem., 1983–85. Chm., Water Engineering Ltd, 1988–91. Member: Central Adv. Water Cttee, 1970–72; OGDEN Cttee on Water Authority Management and Structure, 1973; Management Bd, BNSC, 1984–88; Nat. Rivers Authority, 1989–91 (Mem. Adv. Cttee, 1988–89). Pres., Inst. of Fisheries Management, 1987–. Member of Council: IWES, 1975–85 (Pres. 1984); Freshwater Biol Assoc., 1972–74. Vis. Prof., Univ. of Hertfordshire, 1994–. FRSC, FIWEM. *Publications:* Principles of Water Quality Management, 1973; contribs to various jls on natural science of water. *Recreations:* gardening, water sports, inventions, theatre. *Address:* Red Roofs, Shefford Woodlands, near Newbury, Berks RG16 7AJ. *T:* Great Shefford (01488) 648369.

FISH, John; formerly Under-Secretary, Head of Establishment General Services Division, Department of Industry, 1973–80; *b* 16 July 1920; *m* 1948, Frances; two *s*. *Educ:* Lincoln School. BA Open Univ., 1989. Entered Customs and Excise, 1937; Exchequer and Audit Dept, 1939; War service, Pilot in RAF, 1940–46; Exchequer and Audit Dept, 1946; BoT, 1949; Principal, 1950; Min. of Materials, 1951; Volta River Preparatory Commn, Accra, 1953; BoT, 1956; Asst Sec., 1960; Min. of Health, 1962; BoT, 1965; DTI, 1970; Under-Sec., 1973; Dept of Industry, 1974. *Address:* The Green, Stockton, Rugby, Warwicks CV23 8JF. *T:* Southam (01926) 812833. *Club:* Civil Service.

FISH, Peter Stuart; His Honour Judge Fish; a Circuit Judge, since 1994; *b* 18 Dec. 1938; *s* of Geoffrey Chadwick Fish and Emma (*née* Wood); *m* 1963, Nola Ann Worrall; two *s* one *d* (and one *d* decd). *Educ:* Rydal Sch.; Trinity Hall, Cambridge (MA). Admitted solicitor, 1963; practised in Southport, 1964–87; Dist Registrar, subseq. Dist Judge, Manchester, 1987–94; a Recorder, 1991–94. *Recreations:* music, gardening, golf. *Address:* c/o Circuit Administrator's Officer, Quay Street, Manchester M60 9FD. *Club:* Royal Birkdale Golf.

FISHBURN, (John) Dudley; MP (C) Kensington, since July 1988; *b* 8 June 1946; *s* of John Eskdale Fishburn and Bunting Fishburn; *m* 1981, Victoria, *y d* of Sir Jack Boles, *qv*; two *s* two *d*. *Educ:* Eton Coll.; Harvard Univ. (BA). Exec. Editor, The Economist, 1979–88. Parliamentary Private Secretary: FCO, 1989–90; DTI, 1990. Advr, J. P. Morgan, 1989–; non-executive Director: HFC Bank plc, 1990–; Business Post plc, 1993–; Euclidian plc; Chm., UCL College Accommodation plc, 1993–. Governor, English National Ballet, 1989–95; Chm. Trustees, Open Univ., 1995–; Mem., Bd of Overseers, Harvard Univ., 1990–; Chm., Standing Cttee on Social Scis, Harvard Univ., 1993–; Member Executive Committee: Nat. Trust, 1993–; Prison Reform Trust, 1993–. Editor, The Economist's World in 1993, 1994, 1995, 1996. *Recreations:* sailing, cooking. *Address:* House of Commons, SW1A 0AA. *Club:* Brooks's.

FISHER, family name of **Baron Fisher** and **Baroness Fisher of Rednal.**

FISHER, 3rd Baron, *cr* 1909, of Kilverstone; **John Vavasseur Fisher,** DSC 1944; JP; Director, Kilverstone Latin-American Zoo and Wild Life Park, 1973–91; *b* 24 July 1921; *s* of 2nd Baron and Jane (*d* 1955), *d* of Randal Morgan, Philadelphia, USA; *S* father, 1955; *m* 1st, 1949, Elizabeth Ann Penelope (marr. diss. 1969), *yr d* of late Herbert P. Holt, MC; two *s* two *d*; 2nd, 1970, Hon. Mrs Rosamund Anne Fairbairn, *d* of 12th Baron Clifford of Chudleigh. *Educ:* Stowe; Trinity Coll., Cambridge. Member: Eastern Gas Bd, 1962–71; East Anglia Economic Planning Council, 1971–77. DL Norfolk, 1968–82; JP Norfolk, 1970. *Heir:* *s* Hon. Patrick Vavasseur Fisher [*b* 14 June 1953; *m* 1977, Lady Karen Carnegie, *d* of 13th Earl of Northesk; two *s* three *d*]. *Address:* Marklye, Rushlake Green, Heathfield, Sussex TN21 9PN. *T:* Heathfield (01435) 830270.

See also Baron Clifford of Chudleigh.

FISHER OF REDNAL, Baroness *cr* 1974 (Life Peer), of Rednal, Birmingham; **Doris Mary Gertrude Fisher,** JP; Member of the European Parliament, 1975–79; Member, Warrington and Runcorn (formerly Warrington) Development Corporation, since 1974; *b* 13 Sept. 1919; *d* of late Frederick J. Satchwell, BEM; *m* 1939, Joseph Fisher (*d* 1978); two *d*. *Educ:* Tinker's Farm Girls Sch.; Fircroft Coll.; Bournville Day Continuation Coll. Member: Birmingham City Council, 1952–74; Labour Party, 1945–; UNESCO study group; Nat. Pres. Co-operative Women's Guild, 1961–62. Contested Ladywood, Birmingham, 1969 by-election; MP (Lab) Birmingham, Ladywood, 1970–Feb. 1974. Member: Gen. Medical Council, 1974–79; New Towns Staff Commn, 1976–79; Birmingham Civic Housing Assoc. Ltd, 1982–; Vice-President: Assoc. of Municipal Authorities, 1980–; Assoc. of Dist Councils, 1982–; Inst. of Trading Standards Admin. Pres., Birmingham Royal Inst. for the Blind, 1980–; Chm., W Midlands Macmillan Fund, 1995. Patron, St Basil's Centre for Young Homeless, Birmingham. Guardian, Birmingham Assay Office, 1979–89; Mem., Hallmarking Council, 1989–. Chm. Governors, Baskerville Special Sch., 1981–87; Governor, Hunter's Hill Special Sch., 1988–94. JP Birmingham 1961. Hon. Alderman, 1974, Birmingham District Council. *Recreations:* swimming, walking. *Address:* 60 Jacoby Place, Priory Road, Birmingham B5 7UW. *T:* 0121–471 2003.

FISHER, Arthur J.; *see* Jeddere-Fisher.

FISHER, David Richard; Assistant Under-Secretary of State (Systems), Ministry of Defence, since 1992; *b* 13 May 1947; *s* of William Horace and Margaret Catherine Fisher; *m* 1970, Sophia Josephine Hibbard; two *d*. *Educ:* Reading Sch.; St John's Coll., Oxford (BA 1969, 1st cl. LitHum, 1st cl. Hon. Mods). Ministry of Defence, 1970–: Private Sec. to successive RAF Ministers, 1973–74; naval programme and budget, 1976–79; Defence Budget, 1981–83; Vis. Res. Fellow, Nuffield Coll., Oxford, 1983–84; Head, Resources and Progs (Air), 1984–88; Defence Counsellor, UK Delegn to NATO, Brussels (on loan to FCO), 1988–92. Mem., Management Cttee, Council on Christian Approaches to Defence and Disarmament. *Publications:* Morality and the Bomb, 1985; (contrib.) Ethics and European Security, 1986; (contrib.) Just Deterrence, 1990; contribs to jls on defence and ethical issues. *Recreations:* philosophy, gardening. *Address:* Ministry of Defence, Whitehall, SW1A 2HB. *Clubs:* Royal Over-Seas League, Commonwealth Trust.

FISHER, Desmond (Michael); Chairman, Nationalist and Leinster Times, Carlow, since 1992 (Editor and Managing Director, 1984–89; Executive Director, 1989–92); *b* 9 Sept. 1920; *e s* of Michael Louis Fisher and Evelyn Kate Shier; *m* 1948, Margaret Elizabeth Smyth; three *s* one *d*. *Educ:* St Columb's Coll., Derry; Good Counsel Coll., New Ross, Co. Wexford; University Coll., Dublin (BA (NUI)). Asst Editor, Nationalist and Leinster Times, Carlow, 1945–48; Foreign Editor, Irish Press, Dublin, 1948–51; Economic Correspondent, Irish News Agency, Dublin, 1951–54; London Editor, Irish Press, 1954–62; Editor, Catholic Herald, 1962–66; Radio Telefis Eireann: Dep. Head of News, 1967–73; Head of Current Affairs, 1973–75; Dir of Broadcasting Develt, 1975–83. *Publications:* The Church in Transition, 1967; Broadcasting in Ireland, 1978; The Right to Communicate: a status report, 1981; The Right to Communicate: a new human right,

1983; contributor to The Economist, The Furrow, Irish Digest and to various Irish, US and foreign magazines. *Address:* Louvain 22, Dublin 14. *T:* Dublin 884608.

FISHER, Donald, CBE 1987; County Education Officer, Hertfordshire, 1974–90; *b* 20 Jan. 1931; *s* of John Wilfred and Mabel Fisher; *m* 1953, Mavis Doreen (*née* Sutcliffe); one *s* two *d. Educ:* Heckmondwike Grammar Sch.; Christ Church, Oxford (MA). Teacher, Hull GS, 1954–59; Admin. Asst, Cornwall LEA, 1959–61; Asst Educn Officer, W Sussex LEA, 1961–64; Headmaster: Helston GS, 1964–67; Midhurst GS, 1967–72; Dep. Educn Officer, W Sussex LEA, 1972–74. Chm., Assoc. of Educn Officers, 1982; Pres., Soc. of Educn Officers, 1984. Chm., Steering Cttee, Educn Policy Inf. Centre, Europe. Gov., Univ. of Hertfordshire, 1993–. Hon. DEd Hatfield Polytechnic, 1989. *Publications:* (contrib.) Educational Administration, 1980, 3rd edn 1989; articles and book reviews in Education. *Recreation:* reading. *Address:* 74 The Ryde, Hatfield, Herts AL9 5DL. *T:* Hatfield (01707) 271428.

FISHER, Doris G.; *b* 1907; *d* of Gathorne John Fisher, Pontypool. *Educ:* Farringtons, Chislehurst; Royal Holloway Coll., University of London (BA Hons (English) 1929, (French) 1931); Sorbonne. Senior English Mistress, Maidenhead County Gram. Sch. 1934–39; Second Mistress, Dover County Grammar Sch., 1945; Headmistress of Farringtons, Chislehurst, Kent, 1946–57, retired. Lecturer at Westminster Training Coll., 1957–59; Lecturer at Avery Hill Training Coll., 1959–62. *Address:* 9 The Ridgeway, Newport, Gwent NP9 5AF.

FISHER, Dudley Henry, CBE 1990; DL; IPFA; Chairman, Wales Region, British Gas Corporation, 1974–87, retired; *b* 22 Aug. 1922; *s* of Arthur and Mary Fisher; *m* 1st, 1946, Barbara Lilian Sexton (*d* 1984); one *s* two *d*; 2nd, 1985, Jean Mary Livingstone Miller, *d* of late Dr and Mrs Robert Brown Miller, Cowbridge, S Glam. *Educ:* City of Norwich Sch. Various accountancy positions in Local Govt and Eastern Electricity Bd, 1938–53. War service, RAF, 1942–46 (pilot; Flt Lt). Northern Gas Bd, 1953; Wales Gas Board: Asst Chief Accountant, Dep. Chief Accountant, Chief Accountant, Dir of Finance, 1956–69; Dep. Chm., 1970. Member: Adv. Cttee on Local Govt Audit, 1979–82; Audit Commn for Local Authorities in England and Wales, 1983–88; Broadcasting Council for Wales, 1986–90; Hon. Treasurer, British National Cttee, 1980–89, and Chm., Admin. Cttee, 1986–89, World Energy Conf. Chm., Welsh Council, CBI, 1987–89; Dep. Chm., Inst. of Welsh Affairs, 1991–. Mem. Council, 1983–88, Treas., 1987–88, UC Cardiff; Member of Council: Univ. of Wales Coll. of Cardiff, 1988–; Univ. of Wales Coll. of Medicine, 1992–; Chm., Audit Cttee, Univ. of Wales, 1995–. Governor, United World Coll. of the Atlantic, 1988–. Trustee, Help the Aged, 1987–; Vice Chm., Help Age Internat., 1993–. High Sheriff, 1988–89, DL 1991, S Glam. *Recreations:* golf, gardening, reading. *Address:* Norwood Edge, 8 Cyncoed Avenue, Cardiff CF2 6SU. *T:* Cardiff (01222) 757958. *Clubs:* Royal Air Force; Cardiff and County (Cardiff).

FISHER, Rt. Rev. Edward George K.; *see* Knapp-Fisher.

FISHER, Elisabeth Neill; Her Honour Judge Fisher; a Circuit Judge, since 1989; *b* 24 Nov. 1944; *d* of Kenneth Neill Fisher and Lorna Charlotte Honor Fisher. *Educ:* Oxford High Sch. for Girls (GPDST); Cambridge Univ. (MA). Called to the Bar, Inner Temple, 1968. A Recorder, 1982–89. Mem. Senate, 1983–86. *Address:* Queen Elizabeth II Law Courts, Newton Street, Birmingham B4 7NA.

FISHER, Francis George Robson, MA Oxon; Deputy Secretary, Headmasters' Conference and Secondary Heads' Association, 1982–86; *b* 9 April 1921; *m* 1965, Sheila Vernon Dunsire; one *s. Educ:* Liverpool Coll. (Schol.); Worcester Coll., Oxford (Classical Exhibitioner). Served War of 1939–45; Capt. in Ayrshire Yeomanry, North Africa and Italy, 1942–45. Kingswood Sch., Bath, 1948–59, Housemaster and Sen. English Master, 1950–59; Schoolmaster Fellow, Balliol Coll., Oxford, 1958; Headmaster, Bryanston Sch., 1959–74; Chief Master, King Edward's Sch., Birmingham, and Head Master, Schs of King Edward VI in Birmingham, 1974–82. Chairman: HMC Direct Grant Sub-Cttee, 1979–80; HMC Assisted Places Sub-Cttee, 1981. Life Governor, Liverpool Coll., 1969–; Governor: Harrow Sch., 1982–87; Bromsgrove Sch., 1985–95; Kelly Coll., Tavistock, 1985–. *Recreations:* music, reading, sailing. *Address:* Craig Cottage, Lower Street, Dittisham, S Devon TQ6 0HY. *T:* Dittisham (01803) 722309. *Club:* East India, Devonshire, Sports and Public Schools.

FISHER, Sir George Read, Kt 1967; CMG 1961; Mining Engineer; President, MIM Holdings Ltd, 1970–75; *b* 23 March 1903; *s* of George Alexander and Ellen Harriett Fisher; *m* 1st, 1927, Eileen Elaine Triggs (*d* 1966); one *s* three *d*; 2nd, 1973, Marie C. Gilbey. *Educ:* Prince Alfred Coll., Adelaide; Adelaide Univ. (BE). Formerly Gen. Manager of Operations for Zinc Corporation Ltd, Broken Hill, NSW; Chm., Mount Isa Mines Ltd, 1953–70. *Recreations:* shooting and bowling. *Address:* GPO Box 1433, Brisbane, Qld 4001, Australia. *Clubs:* Queensland, Brisbane (Brisbane).

FISHER, Harold Wallace; Director, 1959–69, and Vice-President, 1962–69, Exxon Corporation, formerly Standard Oil Company (New Jersey) New York, retired; *b* 27 Oct. 1904; *s* of Dean Wallace Fisher and Grace Cheney Fisher; *m* 1930, Hope Elisabeth Case (*d* 1989); one *s*; *m* 1989, Janet Wilson Sawyer. *Educ:* Massachusetts Institute of Technology (BSc). Joined Standard Oil Company (NJ), 1927; Dir Esso Standard Oil Co. and Pres. Enjay Co. Inc., 1945. Resided in London, 1954–59. UK Rep. for Standard Oil Co. (NJ) and Chm. of its Coordination Cttee for Europe, 1954–57; Joint Managing Dir, Iraq Petroleum Co. Ltd and Associated Companies, 1957–59. Mem., Marine Bd, Nat. Acad. of Engineering, 1971–74; Vice-Chm., Sloan-Kettering Inst. for Cancer Research, 1974–75 (Chm., 1970–74); Mem., MIT Corp. Develt Cttee, 1975–; Vice-Chm., and Chm. Exec. Cttee, Community Blood Council of Greater New York, 1969–71. Hon. DSc 1960, Clarkson Coll. of Technology, Nat. Acad. of Engrg. *Publications:* various patents and technical articles relating to the Petroleum Industry. *Recreations:* golf, photography, horology. *Address:* 68 Goose Point Lane, PO Box 1792, Duxbury, MA 02331, USA. *Club:* Duxbury Yacht.

FISHER, Hon. Sir Henry (Arthur Pears), Kt 1968; President, Wolfson College, Oxford, 1975–85, Hon. Fellow, 1985; *b* 20 Jan. 1918; *e s* of late Lord Fisher of Lambeth, PC, GCVO; *m* 1948, Felicity (BA Hons, Open Univ., 1987), *d* of late Eric Sutton; one *s* three *d. Educ:* Marlborough; Christ Church, Oxford (Schol.); Gaisford Greek Prose Prize, 1937; 1st Cl. Hon. Mods 1938; BA 1942; MA 1943. Served Leics Regt, 1940–46; Staff Coll., Quetta, 1943; GSO2, 1943–44; GSO1 HQ 14th Army, 1945. Hon. Lieut-Col 1946 (despatches). Fellow of All Souls Coll., 1946–73, 1991–, Emeritus, 1976–91, Estates Bursar, 1961–66, Sub-Warden, 1965–67. Barrister, Inner Temple, 1947, Bencher, 1966; QC 1960; Recorder of Canterbury, 1962–68; a Judge of the High Court of Justice, Queen's Bench Div., 1968–70; Director: J. Henry Schroder Wagg & Co. Ltd, 1970–75; Schroder International Ltd, 1973–75; Thomas Tilling plc, 1970–83; Equity and Law Life Assurance Soc. plc, 1975–87; Equity and Law plc, 1987. Mem., Gen. Council of the Bar, 1959–63, 1964–68, Vice-Chm., 1965–66, Chm., 1966–68; Vice-Pres., Senate of the Four Inns of Court, 1966–68; Vice-Pres., Bar Assoc. for Commerce, Finance and Industry, 1973–. Pres., Howard League, 1983–91; Chairman: Cttee of Inquiry into Abuse of the Social Security System, 1971; City Cttee on Company Law, 1974–76; Cttee of Inquiry into self-regulation at Lloyd's, 1979–80; Appeal Cttee, Panel on Take-overs and Mergers, 1981–87; Jt Commn on the Constitution (set up by Social Democratic and Liberal Parties), 1981–83; Investment Management Regulatory Orgn, 1986–89. Conducted inquiry into Confait case, 1976–77. Member: Private Internat. Law Cttee, 1961–63; Coun. on Tribunals, 1962–65; Law Reform Cttee, 1963–66; Council, Marlborough Coll., 1967–83 (Chm., 1977–82); BBC Programmes Complaints Commn, 1972–79; Governing Body, Imperial Coll., 1973–88 (Chm., 1975–88) (FIC 1974); Trustee, Pilgrim Trust, 1965–92 (Chm., 1979–83, 1989–92). Hon. Mem., Lloyd's, 1983. Hon. Fellow, Darwin Coll., Cambridge, 1984. Hon. LLD Hull, 1979. *Recreation:* music. *Address:* Garden End, Cross Lane, Marlborough, Wilts SN8 1LA. *T:* Marlborough (01672) 515420. *Club:* Travellers'.

FISHER, Rev. James Atherton; *b* 1 May 1909; *s* of Rev. Legh Atherton Fisher and Beatrice Edith Fisher; *m* 1938, Joan Gardiner Budden; two *s* one *d. Educ:* Haileybury; Sidney Sussex Coll., Cambridge (Scholar); 1st cl. Theological Tripos Pts I and II (Senior Scofield Prize); Cuddesdon Theological Coll; BA 1932, MA 1945; Deacon 1933; Priest, 1934; Asst Curate: St Matthew's, Oxhey, 1933–36; The Priory Church, Dunstable, 1936–39; Chaplain of Bedford Sch., 1939–43; Vicar of St Paul's, Peterborough, 1943–53; Religious Broadcasting Asst, BBC, 1953–58; Chaplain of St Christopher's Coll., Blackheath, 1954–58; Chaplain of Heathfield Sch., Ascot, 1959–64. Canon of St George's, Windsor, 1958–78; Treasurer, 1962–77; Founder Mem., Council of St George's House, Windsor Castle, 1966–78 (resp. for Clergy trng, 1966–74). *Address:* 32 High Lawn, Devizes, Wilts SN10 2BA. *T:* Devizes (01380) 724254.
See also Rev. P. T. Fisher.

FISHER, James Neil; Partner, Theodore Goddard & Co., Solicitors, 1951–83, Senior Partner, 1980–83; *b* 27 May 1917; *s* of Henry John Fisher and Ethel Marie Fisher; *m* 1953, Elizabeth Mary Preston, *d* of late Bishop Arthur and Mrs Nancy Preston; one *s* two *d. Educ:* Harrow Sch.; Balliol Coll., Oxford (MA). Served War, Royal Signals, 1940–46 (Major 1945; despatches). Admitted solicitor, 1949. Hon. Organizer, Legal Advice Centre, Toynbee Hall, 1983–93. Chm., Rochester DAC for the Care of Churches, 1984–90. *Recreations:* the piano, walking, sight-seeing. *Address:* Ridge Lea, Oak Avenue, Sevenoaks, Kent TN13 1PR.

FISHER, John Mortimer, CMG 1962; HM Diplomatic Service, retired; *b* 20 May 1915; *yr s* of late Capt. Mortimer Fisher (W Yorks Regt) and Mrs M. S. Fisher (*née* Bailey); *m* 1949, Helen Bridget Emily Caillard (*d* 1993); two *s. Educ:* Wellington; Trinity Coll., Cambridge. Entered Consular (subseq. Diplomatic) Service, 1937; Probationer Vice-Consul, Bangkok, 1938; served at Casablanca, 1942, Naples, 1944; 1st Sec. in Foreign Office, 1946, Mexico City, 1949; Detroit, Mich., USA, 1952; Counsellor in charge of British Information Services, Bonn, 1955; an Inspector in HM Foreign Service, 1959; Counsellor and Consul-Gen. at Bangkok, 1962; Consul-General, Düsseldorf, 1966–70; part-time Course Dir (Eur. Trng), Civil Service Coll., 1971–85. *Address:* 36 Franklin Place, Chichester, W Sussex PO19 1BL. *T:* Chichester (01243) 531832.

FISHER, Mark; MP (Lab) Stoke-on-Trent Central, since 1983; *b* 29 Oct. 1944; *s* of Sir Nigel Fisher, *qv* and Lady Gloria Flower; *m* 1971, Ingrid Geach; two *s* two *d. Educ:* Eton College; Trinity College, Cambridge. MA. Documentary film producer and script writer, 1966–75; Principal, Tattenhall Centre of Education, 1975–83. Chairman: PLP Educn Cttee, 1984–85; PLP Arts Cttee, 1984–85; Vice-Chm., PLP Treasury Cttee, 1983–84; Mem., Treas. and CS Select Cttee, 1983–85; an Opposition Whip, 1985–87; Opposition spokesman on the arts, 1987–92, 1993–, on Citizen's Charter, 1992–93. Contested (Lab) Leek, 1979. Staffordshire County Councillor, 1981–85 (Chm., Libraries Cttee, 1981–83). Dep. Pro-Chancellor, Keele Univ., 1989–. Member: BBC Gen. Adv. Council, 1988–; Council, PSI, 1989–. Hon. FRIBA 1992; Hon. FRCA 1993. Hon. LLD Keele, 1994. Author of stage plays: Brave New Town, 1974; The Cutting Room, 1990. *Publications:* City Centres, City Cultures, 1988; (ed jtly) Whose Cities?, 1991; A New London, 1992. *Address:* 110 Victoria Street, Hartshill, Stoke-on-Trent ST4 6DU. *T:* Stoke-on-Trent (01782) 713813.

FISHER, Maurice; RCNC; General Manager, HM Dockyard, Rosyth, 1979–83; retired; *b* 8 Feb. 1924; *s* of William Ernest Fisher and Lily Edith (*née* Hatch); *m* 1955, Stella Leslie Sumsion; one *d. Educ:* St Luke's Sch., Portsmouth; Royal Dockyard Sch., Portsmouth; Royal Naval Coll., Greenwich. Constructor-in-Charge, HM Dockyard, Simonstown, 1956–60; Staff of Director of Naval Construction, 1960–63; Staff of C-in-C Western Fleet, 1963–65; Dep. Supt, Admiralty Experiment Works, Haslar, 1965–68; Dep. Prodn Manager, HM Dockyard, Devonport, 1968–72; Personnel Manager, HM Dockyard, Portsmouth, 1972–74; Planning Manager, 1974–77, Prodn Manager, 1977–79, HM Dockyard, Devonport. *Recreation:* game fishing. *Address:* Waterside, The Street, Chilcompton, Bath BA3 4EN.

FISHER, Rt. Rev. Brother Michael, SSF, **(Reginald Lindsay Fisher);** Assistant Bishop, Diocese of Ely, since 1985; *b* 6 April 1918; *s* of late Reginald Watson Fisher and Martha Lindsay Fisher. *Educ:* Clapham Central School; Bolt Court; Westcott House, Cambridge. Member, Society of St Francis, 1942. Deacon 1953, priest 1954, dio. Ely; Licence to officiate: Diocese of Ely, 1954–62; Newcastle, 1962–67; Sarum, 1967–79; Bishop Suffragan of St Germans, 1979–85; Bishop to HM Prisons, 1985. Minister Provincial, 1967–79, Minister-Gen., 1985–91, SSF. MA Lambeth, 1978. *Publication:* For the Time Being (autobiog.), 1993. *Recreations:* painting, music, cinema, people. *Address:* 15 Botolph Lane, Cambridge, Cambs CB2 3RD. *T:* Cambridge (01223) 353903.

FISHER, Prof. Michael Ellis, FRS 1971; Distinguished University Professor and Regents' Professor, Institute for Physical Science and Technology, University of Maryland, since 1993 (Wilson H. Elkins Distinguished Professor, 1987–93); *b* 3 Sept. 1931; *s* of Harold Wolf Fisher and Jeanne Marie Fisher (*née* Halter); *m* 1954, Sorrel Castillejo; three *s* one *d. Educ:* King's Coll., London. BSc 1951, PhD 1957, FKC 1981. Flying Officer (Educn), RAF, 1951–53; London Univ. Postgraduate Studentship, 1953–56; DSIR Sen. Research Fellow, 1956–58. King's Coll., London: Lectr in Theoretical Physics, 1958–62; Reader in Physics, 1962–64; Prof. of Physics, 1965–66; Cornell University: Prof. of Chemistry and Maths, 1966–73; Horace White Prof. of Chemistry, Physics and Maths, 1973–89; Chm., Dept of Chemistry, 1975–78. Guest Investigator, Rockefeller Inst., New York, 1963–64; Vis. Prof. in Applied Physics, Stanford Univ., 1970–71; Walter Ames Prof., Univ. of Washington, 1977; Vis. Prof. of Physics, MIT, 1979; Sherman Fairchild Disting. Scholar, CIT, 1984; Vis. Prof. in Theoretical Physics, Oxford, 1985; Lorentz Prof., Leiden, 1993; Vis. Prof., Nat. Inst. of Sci. and Technol., USA, 1994. Lectures: Buhl, Carnegie-Mellon, 1971; 32nd Richtmyer Meml, 1973; 17th Fritz London Meml, 1975; Morris Loeb, Harvard, 1979; H. L. Welsh, Toronto, 1979; Bakerian, Royal Soc., 1979; Welch Foundn, Texas, 1979; Alpheas Smith, Ohio State Univ., 1982; Laird Meml, Univ. of Western Ontario, 1983; Fries, Rensselaer Polytechnic Inst., NY, 1984; Amos de-Shalit Meml, Weizmann Inst., Rehovoth, 1985; Cherwell-Simon, Oxford, 1985; Marker, Penn. State Univ., 1988; Nat. Sci. Council, Taiwan, 1989; Hamilton Meml, Princeton Univ., 1990; 65th J. W. Gibbs, Amer. Math. Soc., Condon, Univ. of Colorado, and M. S. Green Meml, Temple Univ., 1992; R. and B. Sackler, Tel Aviv, 1992; Lennard-Jones, RSC, 1995; Gibbs, UC Berkeley, 1995; Hirschfelder, Wisconsin Univ., 1995. Mem. Council and Vice-Pres., Royal Soc., 1993–95. Mem., Amer. Philos. Soc., 1993. John Simon Guggenheim Memorial Fellow, 1970–71, 1978–79; Fellow, Amer. Acad. of Arts and Scis, 1979; FAAAS 1986; For. Associate, National Acad. of Sciences, USA, 1983. Hon. FRSE 1986. Hon. DSc Yale, 1987; Hon. DPhil Tel Aviv, 1992. Irving Langmuir Prize in Chemical Physics, Amer. Phys. Soc., 1970; Award in Phys. and Math. Scis, NY Acad. of Scis, 1978; Guthrie Medal, Inst. of Physics, 1980; Wolf Prize in Physics, State of Israel, 1980; Michelson-Morely Award, Case-Western Reserve Univ., 1982; James Murray Luck Award, National Acad. of Sciences, USA, 1983; Boltzmann Medal, Internat. Union of Pure and Applied Physics, 1983; Lars Onsager Medal, Norwegian Inst. of Technol., 1993; Onsager Meml Prize, Amer. Phys. Soc., 1995; Hildebrand Award, Amer. Chem. Soc., 1995. *Publications:* Analogue Computing at Ultra-High Speed (with D. M. MacKay), 1962; The Nature of Critical Points, (Univ. of Colorado) 1964, (Moscow) 1968; contribs to Proc. Roy. Soc., Phys. Rev., Phys. Rev. Lett., Jl Sci. Insts, Jl Math. Phys., Arch. Rational Mech. Anal., Jl Chem. Phys., Commun. Math. Phys., Rept Prog. Phys., Rev. Mod. Phys., Physica, etc. *Recreations:* Flamenco guitar, travel. *Address:* Institute for Physical Science and Technology, University of Maryland, College Park, MD 20742–2431, USA. *T:* (301) 4054820.

FISHER, Nancy Kathleen; *see* Trenaman, N. K.

FISHER, Sir Nigel (Thomas Loveridge), Kt 1974; MC 1945; MA (Cambridge); *b* 14 July 1913; *s* of late Comdr Sir Thomas Fisher, KBE, Royal Navy and of late Lady Shakespeare; step *s* of Rt Hon. Sir Geoffrey Shakespeare, 1st Bt; *m* 1935, Lady Gloria Vaughan (marr. diss. 1952), *e d* of 7th Earl of Lisburne; one *s* one *d*; *m* 1956, Patricia (*d* 1995), *o d* of late Lieut-Col Sir Walter Smiles, CIE, DSO, DL, MP. *Educ:* Eton; Trinity Coll., Cambridge. Served War of 1939–45; volunteered Welsh Guards and commissioned as 2nd Lieut 1939; Hook of Holland, Boulogne, 1940 (despatches); Capt., 1940; Major, 1944; N West Europe, 1945 (wounded, MC). Mem., National Executive Cttee of Conservative Party, 1945–47 and 1973–83; contested Chislehurst (N Kent), Gen. Election, 1945. MP (C): Herts, Hitchin, 1950–55; Surbiton, 1955–74; Kingston-upon-Thames, Surbiton, 1974–83. Mem. British Parl. Deleg. to Sweden, 1950, W Indies 1955, Malta 1966, Canada 1966, Uganda 1967, special mission to St Kitts, Anguilla, 1967. Parly Private Sec. to Minister of Food, 1951–54, to Home Sec., 1954–57; Parly Under-Sec. of State for the Colonies, July 1962–Oct. 1963; Parly Under-Sec. of State for Commonwealth Relations and for the Colonies, 1963–64; Opposition Spokesman for Commonwealth Affairs, 1964–66. Treasurer, CPA, 1966–68 (Vice-Chm., 1975–76; Treasurer, 1977–79, Dep. Chm., 1979–83, UK Branch). Mem. Exec., 1922 Cttee, 1960–62, 1969–83; Pres., British Caribbean Assoc. Freedom of Kingston-upon-Thames, 1983. *Publications:* Iain Macleod, 1973; The Tory Leaders, 1977; Harold Macmillan, 1982. *Recreation:* reading. *Address:* 45 Exeter House, Putney Heath, SW15 3SX. *Clubs:* Boodle's, MCC.
See also M. Fisher.

FISHER, Rev. Peter Timothy; Principal, The Queen's College, Birmingham, since 1994; *b* 7 July 1944; *s* of Rev. James Atherton Fisher, *qv*; *m* 1968, Elizabeth Lacey; two *s*. *Educ:* City of London Sch.; Durham Univ., (BA, MA); Cuddesdon Coll., Oxford. Ordained deacon, 1970, priest 1971; Curate, St Andrew's, Bedford, 1970–74; Chaplain, Surrey Univ., 1974–78; Sub-Warden, Lincoln Theol Coll., 1978–83; Rector, Houghton-le-Spring, 1983–94. *Recreations:* piano and water-colours, both strictly incognito. *Address:* The Queen's College, Somerset Road, Edgbaston, Birmingham B15 2QH. *T:* 0121–454 1527.

FISHER, Roger Anthony, FRCO(CHM); Organist and Master of Choristers, Chester Cathedral, since 1967; *b* 18 Sept. 1936; *s* of Leslie Elgar Fisher and Vera Althea (*née* Salter); *m* 1st, 1967, Susan Mary Green (marr. diss. 1983); one *d*; 2nd, 1985, Gillian Rushforth (*née* Heywood). *Educ:* Bancroft's Sch., Woodford Green, Essex; Royal Coll. Music; Christ Church, Oxford (Organ schol.; MA). FRCO(CHM); ARCM; ATCL. Organist, St Mark's, Regent's Park, 1957–62; Asst Organist, Hereford Cathedral, 1962–67; Asst Lectr in Music, Hereford Coll. of Educn, 1963–67. Music Critic, Liverpool Echo, 1976–79. Recital tours, 1967–, incl. USA, Canada, France, Germany, Switzerland, Hungary and Italy, Denmark, Norway and Sweden. Recordings in GB and Europe; BBC broadcasts as organist and with Chester Cathedral Choir. Conductor, choral socs and orchestras; Organ Consultant to churches and cathedrals. Geoffrey Tankard Prize for Solo Organ, RCM, 1959. *Publications:* articles about the organ and related subjects in several periodicals. *Recreations:* railway interests, walking, cycling, motoring. *Address:* The Old Chapel, Trelogan, Holywell, Clwyd CH8 9BD.

FISHER, Sylvia Gwendoline Victoria, AM 1994; formerly Principal Soprano, Royal Opera House, London; *b* 18 April 1910; *d* of John Fisher and Margaret Fisher (*née* Frawley); *m* 1954, Ubaldo Gardini (marr. diss.). *Educ:* St Joseph's Coll., Kilmore, Australia; Conservatorium of Music, Melbourne. Won "Sun" Aria Competition, Melbourne, 1936; International Celebrity Concert in Australia, 1947; tour of Australia, 1955. Operatic Debut in Cadmus and Hermione, 1932; Covent Garden Debut in Fidelio (Leonora), 1948. Appeared in: Rome (Sieglinde), 1952; Cagliari (Isolde), 1954; Bologna (Gutrune), 1955; Covent Garden (Brunnhilde), 1956; Frankfurt Opera House (in Der Rosenkavalier), 1957, etc. *Recreations:* gardening and rare books on singing. *Address:* 25 Tintern Avenue, Toorak, Vic 3142, Australia.

FISHER, Thomas Gilbert F.; *see* Field-Fisher.

FISHLOCK, Dr David Jocelyn, OBE 1983; Editor, since 1991, and Publisher, since 1992, R&D Efficiency; Consulting Editor, Pharmaceutical Forum, since 1992; *b* 9 Aug. 1932; *s* of William Charles Fishlock and Dorothy Mary Turner; *m* 1959, Mary Millicent Cosgrove; one *s*. *Educ:* City of Bath Boys' Sch. (now Beechen Cliff Sch.); Bristol Coll. of Technol. FIBiol 1988; Companion, Inst. of Energy, 1987. National Service, REME, 1955–58. Westinghouse Brake & Signal Co. Ltd, 1948–55; McGraw-Hill, 1959–62; New Scientist, 1962–67; Science Editor, Financial Times, 1967–91. Glaxo Travelling Fellow, 1978. Member: R&D Soc.; Scientific Instrument Soc. Hon. DLitt Salford, 1982; Hon. DSc Bath, 1993. Chemical Writer of the Year Award, BASF, 1982; Worthington Pump Award, 1982; British Press Award, 1986. Silver Jubilee Medal, 1977. *Publications:* The New Materials, 1967; Man Modified, 1969; The Business of Science, 1975; The Business of Biotechnology, 1982; (with Elizabeth Antébi) Biotechnology: strategies for life, 1986. *Recreations:* writing, reading, collecting old medical/pharmaceutical equipment. *Address:* Traveller's Joy, Copse Lane, Jordans, Bucks HP9 2TA. *T:* Chalfont St Giles (01494) 873242. *Club:* Athenæum.

FISHLOCK, Trevor; journalist and author; roving foreign correspondent, The Daily Telegraph, 1986–89 and since 1993; *b* 21 Feb. 1941; *m* 1978, Penelope Symon. *Educ:* Churcher's Coll., Petersfield; Southern Grammar Sch., Portsmouth. Portsmouth Evening News, 1957–62; freelance and news agency reporter, 1962–68; The Times: Wales and W England staff correspondent, 1968–77; London and foreign staff, 1978–80; S Asia correspondent, Delhi, 1980–83; New York correspondent, 1983–86; Moscow correspondent, Daily Telegraph, 1989–91; roving foreign correspondent, The Sunday Telegraph, 1991–93. Fellow, World Press Inst., St Paul, Minnesota, 1977–78. Mem., Council for the Welsh Language, 1973–77. David Holden Award for foreign reporting (British Press Awards), 1983; Internat. Reporter of the Year (British Press Awards), 1986. *Publications:* Wales and the Welsh, 1972; Talking of Wales, 1975; Discovering Britain: Wales, 1979; Americans and Nothing Else, 1980; India File, 1983; The State of America, 1986; Indira Gandhi (for children), 1986; Out of Red Darkness: reports from the collapsing Soviet Empire, 1992. *Recreation:* sailing. *Address:* c/o The Daily Telegraph, 1 Canada Square, Canary Wharf, E14 5DT. *Club:* Travellers'.

FISHWICK, Avril; Vice Lord-Lieutenant of Greater Manchester, since 1988; *b* 30 March 1924; *yr d* of Frank Platt and Charlotte Winifred Young; *m* 1950, Thomas William Fishwick; two *d*. *Educ:* Woodfield; High Sch. for Girls, Wigan; Liverpool Univ. (LLB 1946; LLM 1947). Admitted Solicitor 1949. War service, Foreign Office, Bletchley Park, 1942–45; Partner, Frank Platt & Fishwick, 1958–94. Chm., Tidy Britain Enterprises Ltd, 1990–; Dir, Northern Adv. Bd, National Westminster Bank, 1984–92. Member: Wigan and Leigh HMC, 1960–73 (Mem., Exec. Council, 1966–73); NW RHA, 1985–88; Chm., Wigan AHA, 1973–82. Local President: Civic Trust, 1976–91; RSPCA, 1974–; Little Theatre, 1985–91; Hon. Mem., Soroptimists Internat., 1973–; Mem., Groundwork Trust, 1986–93. Trustee: Skelton Bounty, 1985–; GMP Community Charity, 1986–. Mem. Court, Manchester Univ., 1984–. DL 1982, High Sheriff 1983–84, Gtr Manchester. Hon. MA Manchester, 1993. *Recreations:* family, natural history. *Address:* Haighlands, Haigh Country Park, Haigh, Wigan WN2 1PB. *T:* Wigan (01942) 831291.

FISK, David John, ScD, PhD; Under Secretary, since 1987, Chief Scientist, since 1988, and Director, Air, Climate and Toxic Substances, since 1990, Department of the Environment; *b* 9 Jan. 1947; *s* of late John Howard Fisk and of Rebecca Elizabeth Fisk (*née* Haynes); *m* 1972, A. Anne Thoday; one *s* one *d*. *Educ:* Stationers' Company's Sch., Hornsey; St John's Coll., Cambridge (BA, MA, ScD); Univ. of Manchester (PhD). FCIBSE 1983. Joined Building Res. Estabt (traffic noise res.), 1972; Higher Sci. Officer, 1972–73; Sen. Sci. Officer (energy conservation res.), 1973–75; PSO, 1975–78; SPSO, Hd Mechanical and Elec. Engrg Div., 1978–84; Asst Sec., DoE, Central Directorate of Environmental Protection, 1984–87; Dep. Chief Scientist, DoE, 1987–88. Vis. Prof., Univ. of Liverpool, 1988–. *Publications:* Thermal Control of Buildings, 1981; numerous papers on technical innovation, bldg sci., systems theory and economics. *Recreations:* modern theatre, music. *Address:* c/o Department of the Environment, 43 Marsham Street, SW1 3PY.

FISON, Sir (Richard) Guy, 4th Bt *cr* 1905; DSC 1944; *b* 9 Jan. 1917; *er s* of Sir William Guy Fison, 3rd Bt; *S* father, 1964; *m* 1952, Elyn Hartmann (*d* 1987); one *s* one *d*. *Educ:* Eton; New Coll., Oxford. Served RNVR, 1939–45. Entered Wine Trade, 1948; Master of Wine, 1954; Dir, Saccone & Speed Ltd, 1952–82; Chairman: Saccone & Speed Internat., 1979–82; Percy Fox & Co. Ltd, 1982–83; Wine Develt Bd, 1982–83; Fine Vintage Wines Plc, 1985–; Pres., Wine and Spirit Assoc., 1977–78. Hon. Freeman, 1976, Renter Warden, 1981–82, Upper Warden, 1982–83, Master, 1983–84, Vintners' Co. *Heir: s* Charles William Fison, *b* 6 Feb. 1954. *Address:* Medwins, Odiham, Hants RG25 1NE. *T:* Odiham (01256) 704075. *Club:* MCC.

FITCH, Douglas Bernard Stocker, FRICS; FAAV; MRAC; Director, Land and Water Service, Agricultural Development and Advisory Service, Ministry of Agriculture, Fisheries and Food, 1980–87, retired; *b* 16 April 1927; *s* of William Kenneth Fitch and Hilda Barrington; *m* 1952, Joyce Vera Griffiths; three *s*. *Educ:* St Albans Sch.; Royal Agricl Coll. (Dip. 1951). FRICS 1977. Served Army, RE, 1944–48. Joined Land Service, MAFF, 1951; Divl Surveyor, Guildford, 1971; Regional Surveyor, SE Reg., 1979. Prof., Rural Planning and Natural Resource Management, European Faculty of Land Use and Develt, 1985–. Royal Institution of Chartered Surveyors: Mem., Agric. Divl Council, 1980–87; Mem., Gen. Council, 1980–86. Internat. Fedn. of Surveyors deleg., 1988–91, and Chm., Standing Conf. on Marine Resource Management, 1985–89. Chm. Adv. Cttee, Centre for Rural Studies, 1990–95, Mem., Bd of Governors, Royal Agricl Coll., 1981–95. *Recreation:* golf. *Address:* 71 Oasthouse Crescent, Hale, Farnham, Surrey GU9 0NP. *T:* Farnham (01252) 716742. *Clubs:* Farmers', Civil Service.

FITCH, Rodney Arthur, CBE 1990; PPCSD (FSIAD 1976); design consultant; formerly Chairman, Fitch (Design Consultants), largest design company in Europe; *b* 19 Aug. 1938; *s* of late Arthur and Ivy Fitch; *m* 1965, Janet Elizabeth, *d* of Sir Walter Stansfield, CBE, MC, QPM; one *s* four *d*. *Educ:* Willesden Polytechnic, Sch. of Building and Architecture; Central School of Arts and Crafts (Theatre, TV Design); Hornsey School of Art (Interior and Furniture Design). Trainee designer, Hickman Ltd, 1956–58; National Service, RAPC, 1958–60; Charles Kenrick Associates, 1960–62; Conran Design Gp Ltd, 1962–69; C.D.G. (Design Consultants) Ltd, 1969–71; Founder, 1971, Fitch and Company, subseq. Fitch-RS and Fitch, a multi-discipline design practice engaged on a wide range of UK and overseas projects from offices in Europe, USA and Tokyo. Mem., Design Council, 1988–. Dep. Chm., Court of Govs, London Inst., 1989–; Mem. Council, RCA, 1989–; Trustee, V & A Museum, 1991–. CSD (formerly SIAD): Pres., 1988–90; Vice-Pres., 1982–86; Hon. Treas., 1984–87; Past Pres., Designers and Art Dirs Assoc., 1983. FRSA 1976. *Publications:* (with L. Knobel) Fitch on Retail Design, 1990; regular contributor to design publications. *Recreations:* cricket, tennis, opera, theatre, his family. *Address:* Porters South, 4 Crinan Street, N1 9UE. *T:* 0171–278 7200.

FITCHEW, Geoffrey Edward, CMG 1993; Chairman and First Commissioner, Building Societies Commission, since 1994; *b* 22 Dec. 1939; *s* of Stanley Edward Fitchew and Elizabeth Scott; *m* 1966, Mary Theresa Spillane; two *s*. *Educ:* Uppingham School; Magdalen Coll., Oxford (MA); London Sch. of Economics (MScEcon). Asst Principal, HM Treasury, 1964; Private Sec. to Minister of State, 1968–69; Principal, 1969; Gwilym Gibbon Research Fellow, Nuffield Coll., Oxford, 1973–74; Asst Sec., Internat. Finance Div., HM Treasury, 1975–77; Counsellor (Economics and Finance), UK Perm. Rep. to EEC, 1977–80; Asst Sec., HM Treasury, 1980–83; Under Sec., HM Treasury, 1983–86; Dir-Gen. (for Banking, Financial Services and Company Law), Directorate Gen. XV, EC, Brussels, 1986–93; Dep. Sec, Cabinet Office, 1993–94. *Recreations:* tennis, golf. *Address:* Building Societies Commission, 15 Great Marlborough Street, W1V 2LL.

FITT, family name of **Baron Fitt.**

FITT, Baron *cr* 1983 (Life Peer), of Bell's Hill in the County of Down; **Gerard Fitt;** *b* 9 April 1926; *s* of George Patrick and Mary Ann Fitt; *m* 1947, Susan Gertrude Doherty; five *d* (and one *d* decd). *Educ:* Christian Brothers' Sch., Belfast. Merchant Seaman, 1941–53; various positions, 1953–. Councillor, later Alderman, Belfast Corp., 1958–81; MP (Eire Lab), Parlt of N Ireland, Dock Div. of Belfast, 1962–72; Mem. (SDLP), N Belfast, NI Assembly, 1973–75, NI Constitutional Convention, 1975–76; Dep. Chief Exec., NI Exec., 1974; elected MP (Repub. Lab) Belfast West, 1966, a founder and Leader, Social Democratic and Labour Party, and MP (SDLP), 1970–79, when resigned Leadership; MP (Socialist), 1979–83. Contested (Socialist) Belfast West, 1983. *Recreation:* full-time politics. *Address:* House of Lords, SW1A 0PW.

FITTALL, Betty Daphne C.; *see* Callaway-Fittall.

FITTER, Richard Sidney Richmond; author and naturalist; *b* 1 March 1913; *o s* of Sidney and Dorothy Fitter; *m* 1938, Alice Mary (Maisie) Stewart, *e d* of Dr R. S. Park,

Huddersfield; two *s* one *d*. *Educ:* Eastbourne Coll.; LSE. BSc(Econ). Research staff: PEP, 1936–40; Mass-Observation, 1940–42; Operational Research Section, Coastal Command, 1942–45; Sec., Wild Life Cons. Special Cttee of Hobhouse Cttee on Nat. Parks, 1945–46; Asst Editor, The Countryman, 1946–59; Open Air Corresp., The Observer, 1958–66; Dir, Intelligence Unit, Council for Nature, 1959–63; Editor, Kingfisher, 1965–72. Vice-Pres., Fauna and Flora Preservation Soc., 1988– (Hon. Secretary, 1964–81; Chm., 1983–87); Member: Species Survival Commn (formerly Survival Service Commn), Internat. Union for Cons. of Nature, 1963– (Chm., Steering Cttee, 1975–88); Conservation Adv. Cttee, World Wildlife Fund Internat., 1977–79; Scientific Authority for Animals, DoE, 1965–81; Trustee, World Wildlife Fund, UK, 1977–83; Past Pres., Berks, Bucks and Oxfordshire Naturalists' Trust; Chm., Council for Nature, 1979; Vice Pres., Falklands Conservation, 1994– (Vice Chm., 1986–94); Minister's Representative, Southern Council for Sport and Recreation, 1980–82; formerly Hon. Treasurer and Hon. Sec., British Trust for Ornithology; Chm., Gen. Purposes Cttee, Royal Soc. for Protection of Birds; Editor, The London Naturalist; and council or cttee mem. of numerous nat. history and conservation bodies. Scientific FZS. Officier, Order of the Golden Ark, The Netherlands, 1978. *Publications:* London's Natural History, 1945; London's Birds, 1949; Pocket Guide to British Birds, 1952; Pocket Guide to Nests and Eggs, 1954; (with David McClintock) Pocket Guide to Wild Flowers, 1956; The Ark in Our Midst, 1959; Six Great Naturalists, 1959; Guide to Bird Watching, 1963; Wildlife in Britain, 1963; Britain's Wildlife: rarities and introductions, 1966; (with Maisie Fitter) Penguin Dictionary of Natural History, 1967; Vanishing Wild Animals of the World, 1968; Finding Wild Flowers, 1972; (with H. Heinzel and J. Parslow) Birds of Britain and Europe, with North Africa and the Middle East, 1972; (with A. Fitter and M. Blamey) Wild Flowers of Britain and Northern Europe, 1974; The Penitent Butchers, 1979; (with M. Blamey) Handguide to the Wild Flowers of Britain and Northern Europe, 1979; (with M. Blamey) Gem Guide to Wild Flowers, 1980; (with N. Arlott and A. Fitter) The Complete Guide to British Wildlife, 1981; (ed with Eric Robinson) John Clare's Birds, 1982; (with A. Fitter and J. Wilkinson) Collins Guide to the Countryside, 1984; (with A. Fitter and A. Farrer) Grasses, Sedges, Rushes and Ferns of Britain and Northern Europe, 1984; (ed) The Wildlife of the Thames Counties, 1985; Wildlife for Man, 1986; (with R. Manuel) Field Guide to the Freshwater Life of Britain and NW Europe, 1986; (with A. Fitter) Guide to the Countryside in Winter, 1988. *Recreations:* botanising, observing wild and human life, exploring new habitats, reading. *Address:* Drifts, Chinnor Hill, Chinnor, Oxon OX9 4BS. *T:* Kingston Blount (01844) 351223. *Club:* Athenæum.

FITZALAN-HOWARD, family name of **Lady Herries of Terregles** and of **Duke of Norfolk.**

FITZALAN-HOWARD, Maj.-Gen. Lord Michael, GCVO 1981 (KCVO 1971; MVO 1952); CB 1968; CBE 1962; MC 1944; DL; Her Majesty's Marshal of the Diplomatic Corps, 1972–81; *b* 22 Oct. 1916; 2nd *s* of 3rd Baron Howard of Glossop, MBE, and Baroness Beaumont (11th in line), OBE; *b* of 17th Duke of Norfolk, *qv*; granted title and precedence of a Duke's son, 1975; *m* 1st, 1946, Jean (*d* 1947), *d* of Sir Hew Hamilton-Dalrymple, 9th Bt; one *d*; 2nd, 1950, Margaret, *d* of Capt. W. P. Meade-Newman; four *s* one *d*. *Educ:* Ampleforth Coll.; Trinity Coll., Cambridge. Joined Scots Guards, 1938. Served in: North West Europe, 1944–45; Palestine, 1945–46; Malaya, 1948–49; Egypt, 1952–53; Germany, 1956–57 and 1961–66; Commander Allied Command Europe Mobile Forces (Land), 1964–66; Chief of Staff, Southern Command, 1967–68; GOC London Dist, and Maj.-Gen. comdg The Household Division, 1968–71. Colonel: The Lancs Regt (Prince of Wales's Volunteers), 1966–70; The Queen's Lancashire Regiment, 1970–78; Colonel of The Life Guards, 1979–; Gold Stick to the Queen, 1979–; Joint Hon. Col, Cambridge Univ. OTC, 1968–71. Chm. Council, TAVR Assocs, 1973–81, Pres., 1981–84; Patron, Council, TA&VRA, 1984–; Hon. Recorder, British Commonwealth Ex-Service League, 1991–. Chm., Talisman Energy (UK) Ltd, 1994–. DL Wilts, 1974. Freeman, City of London, 1985. *Address:* Fovant House, Fovant, Salisbury, Wilts SP3 5LA. *T:* Fovant (01722) 714617. *Clubs:* Buck's, Pratt's.

FITZCLARENCE, family name of **Earl of Munster.**

FITZGERALD, family name of **Duke of Leinster.**

FITZGERALD, Rev. (Sir) Daniel Patrick, SSC, (4th Bt *cr* 1903, of Geraldine Place, St Finn Barr, Co. Cork, but does not use the title); *b* 28 June 1916; *S* brother, Rev. (Sir) Edward Thomas FitzGerald (3rd Bt), 1988. Roman Catholic priest. *Heir: cousin* John Finnbarr FitzGerald [*b* 1918; *m* 1949, Margaret Hogg; one *s* one *d*].

FITZ-GERALD, Desmond John Villiers, (29th Knight of Glin); Irish Agent, Christie, Manson & Woods Ltd, since 1975; *b* 13 July 1937; *s* of Desmond Windham Otho Fitz-Gerald, 28th Knight of Glin (*d* 1949), and Veronica (who *m* 2nd, 1954, Ray Milner, CC (Canada), QC, Edmonton, Alta, and Qualicum Beach, Vancouver Island, BC), 2nd *d* of late Ernest Amherst Villiers, MP, and of Hon. Elaine Augusta Guest, *d* of 1st Baron Wimborne; *m* 1st, 1966, Louise Vava Lucia Henriette (marr. diss. 1970), *d* of the Marquis de la Falaise, Paris; 2nd, 1970, Olda Ann, *o d* of T. V. W. Willes, 39 Brompton Sq., SW3; three *d*. *Educ:* Stowe Sch.; University of British Columbia (BA 1959); Harvard Univ. (MA 1961). FSA 1970. Asst Keeper, 1965–72, Dep. Keeper, 1972–75, Dept of Furniture and Woodwork, V&A. Pres., Irish Georgian Soc., 1991–; Chm., Irish Georgian Foundn, 1990– (Dir, 1974–); Director: Irish Heritage Properties (formerly Historic Irish Tourist Houses Assoc.), 1977– (Chm., 1982–86); Castletown Foundn, 1979–; Irish Architectural Archive, 1987–. *Publications:* (ed) Georgian Furniture, 1969; (with Maurice Craig) Ireland Observed, a handbook to the buildings and antiquities, 1970; The Music Room from Norfolk House, 1972; (with Edward Malins) Lost Demesnes: Irish Landscape Gardening 1660–1845, 1976; (with Anne Crookshank) The Painters of Ireland, 1978; Irish Furniture, 1978; (jtly) Vanishing Country Houses of Ireland, 1988; (jtly) The Watercolours of Ireland, 1994; *catalogues*, all jointly: Irish Houses and Landscapes, 1963; Irish Architectural Drawings, 1965; Irish Portraits 1660–1860, 1969; Mildred Anne Butler, 1981; articles and reviews on architecture and the decorative arts in many Art periodicals. *Address:* Glin Castle, Glin, Co. Limerick, Ireland. *TA:* Knight Glin. *T:* Listowel (068) 34173 and 34112, *Fax:* (068) 34364; 52 Waterloo Road, Dublin 4. *T:* Dublin 680585, *Fax:* Dublin 680271. *Clubs:* Beefsteak, White's; Kildare Street and University (Dublin).

FITZGERALD, Edward Hamilton; QC 1995; *b* 13 Aug. 1953; *s* of Carrol James Fitzgerald and Cornelia (*née* Claiburne); *m* 1988, Rebecca Fraser; three *d*. *Educ:* Downside; Corpus Christi Coll., Oxford (BA 1st cl. Hons Lit. Hum. 1975); MPhil Cantab 1979. Called to the Bar, Inner Temple, 1978. *Recreations:* reading history and novels, visiting the seaside, travel. *Address:* (chambers) 11 Doughty Street, WC1N 2DG. *T:* 0171–404 1313.

FITZGERALD, Frank, CBE 1989; PhD; FEng 1977; consultant, since 1992; Director, Sheffield Forgemasters Ltd, since 1993; *b* 11 Nov. 1929; *s* of George Arthur Fitzgerald and Sarah Ann (*née* Brook); *m* 1956, Dorothy Eileen Unwin; two *s* one *d*. *Educ:* Barnsley Holgate Grammar Sch.; Univ. of Sheffield (BScTech; PhD). FInstE, FIChemE. Ministry of Supply, RAE, Westcott, Bucks, 1955; United Steel Cos, Swinden Laboratories, Rotherham, 1960–68; British Steel plc (formerly British Steel Corporation), 1968–92: Process Res. Manager, Special Steels Div., 1970; Head Corporate Advanced Process Laboratory, 1972; Director, R&D, 1977; Man. Dir, Technical, 1981–92; Dir, 1986–92; Chairman: British Steel Corp. (Overseas Services), subseq. British Steel Consultants, 1981–89; British Steel Stainless, 1989–91. Hon. DEng Sheffield, 1993. Hadfield Medal, Iron and Steel Inst., for work on application of combustion and heat transfer science to industrial furnaces, 1972; Melchett Medal, Inst. of Energy, 1988; Bessemer Gold Medal, Inst. of Metals, 1991; Esso Energy Award, Royal Soc., 1991. *Publications:* papers in learned jls on heat and mass transfer and metallurgical processes. *Recreation:* rock climbing and mountaineering. *Clubs:* Alpine; Climbers'.

FITZGERALD, Garret, PhD; Barrister-at-Law; Member of the Dáil (TD) (FG) for Dublin South East, 1969–92; Taoiseach (Prime Minister of Ireland), June 1981–March 1982 and 1982–87; European Deputy Chairman, Trilateral Commission, since 1989; *b* Dublin, 9 Feb. 1926; *s* of late Desmond FitzGerald (Minister for External Affairs, Irish Free State, 1922–27, and Minister for Defence, 1927–32) and Mabel FitzGerald (*née* McConnell); *m* 1947, Joan, *d* of late Charles O'Farrell; two *s* one *d*. *Educ:* St Brigid's Sch., Bray; Coláiste na Rinne, Waterford; Belvedere Coll., University Coll., and King's Inns (Hon. Bencher, 1993), Dublin. Called to the Bar, 1947. Aer Lingus (Irish Air Lines), 1947–58; Rockefeller Research Asst, Trinity Coll., Dublin, 1958–59; College Lectr, Dept of Political Economy, University Coll., Dublin, 1959–87. Member: Seanad Eireann (Irish Senate), 1965–69; Dáil Cttee on Public Accounts, 1969–73; Minister for Foreign Affairs, Ireland, 1973–77; Leader and President, Fine Gael Party, 1977–87; Leader of the Opposition, 1977–June 1981, and March–Dec. 1982. President: Council of Ministers, EEC, Jan.–June 1975; European Council, July–Dec. 1984; Irish Council of Eur. Movement, 1977–81 and March–Dec. 1982; Mem., Internat. Exec. Cttee of Eur. Movement, 1972–73; Vice-Pres., Eur. People's Party, 1979–87. Mem., Oireachtas Library Cttee, 1965–69; Governor, Atlantic Inst. of Internat. Relations, Paris, 1972–73; Mem. Bd, Internat. Peace Acad., NY, 1990–; Chm., Council of Patrons, Saferworld, 1992–; Mem., Senate of National Univ. of Ireland, 1973–. Formerly: Irish Correspondent of BBC, Financial Times, Economist and other overseas papers; Economic Correspondent, Irish Times; also Past Managing Dir, Economist Intelligence Unit of Ireland; Economic Consultant to Fedn of Irish Industries and Construction Industry Fedn, and Rep. Body for Guards; Past Member: Exec. Cttee and Council, Inst. of Public Admin; Council, Statistical and Social Inquiry, Soc. of Ireland; Senate Electoral Law Commn; Workmen's Compensation Commn; Transport Advisory Cttee for Second Programme; Cttee on Industrial Organisation; Gen. Purposes Cttee of Nat. Industrial Economic Council; Dir, Trade Develt Inst., Dublin, 1987–; Mem., Adv. Bd, Centre for Economic Policy Res., 1992–. Lectures: Radcliffe, Warwick Univ., 1980; Richard Dimbleby, BBC, 1982; Heinz, Pittsburgh Univ., 1980; Dunbar, Tulane Univ., 1987; Bass, Univ. of Ulster, 1988; Gaitskell, Nottingham Univ., 1988; Centenary Reckitt, London, 1988; Boston Coll., 1988, 1989; Schumann, UC, Cork, 1989; Morrell, Univ. of York, 1989; Mackintosh, Edinburgh Univ., 1990; Williamson, Univ. of Stirling, 1990; White, QUB, 1990; 2500 Anniv. of Democracy, Manchester Univ., 1993. Hon. LLD: New York, 1974; St Louis, 1974; St Mary's, Halifax, NS, 1985; Keele, 1986; Boston Coll., 1987; Westfield Coll., Mass, 1990; Hon. DCL: Oxon, 1987; NUI, 1991. Grand Cordon, Order of Al-Kaubar Al-Undari (Jordan), 1975; Grand Officier, Ordre de la République (Tunisia), 1976; Grand Cross (1st Cl.), Order of Merit (FRG), 1986; Order of Christ (Portugal), 1986; Grand Cordon, Order of Rising Sun (Japan), 1989; Comdr, Légion d'Honneur (France), 1995. *Publications:* State-sponsored Bodies, 1959; Planning in Ireland, 1968; Towards a New Ireland, 1972; Unequal Partners (UNCTAD), 1979; Estimates for Baronies of Minimum Level of Irish Speaking Amongst Successive Decennial Cohorts 1771–1781 to 1861–1871, 1984; All in a Life: an autobiography, 1991. *Address:* 30 Palmerston Road, Dublin 6, Ireland. *T:* 4962600, *Fax:* 962126. *Clubs:* Reform; Royal Irish Yacht (Dun Laoghaire).

FitzGERALD, Sir George (Peter Maurice), 5th Bt *cr* 1880; 23rd Knight of Kerry; MC 1944; Major, Army, retired; *b* 27 Feb. 1917; *s* of Sir Arthur Henry Brinsley FitzGerald, 4th Bt, and Mary Eleanor (*d* 1967), *d* of late Capt. Francis Forester; *S* father 1967; *m* 1939, Angela Dora Mitchell; one *s* one *d*. *Educ:* Harrow; RMC, Sandhurst. Commnd into Irish Guards, 1937; 2nd in comd, 1st Bn, 1944; 2nd in comd, 2nd Bn, 1946; retired, 1948. *Heir: s* Adrian James Andrew Denis FitzGerald, *b* 24 June 1940. *Address:* Colin's Farm House, 55 High Street, Durrington, Salisbury, Wilts SP4 8AQ. *Club:* Army and Navy.

FITZGERALD, Gerald Edward, AC 1991; **Hon. Justice Fitzgerald;** President, Court of Appeal, Supreme Court of Queensland, since 1991; *b* Brisbane, 26 Nov. 1941; *m* 1968, Catherine Glynn-Connolly; one *s* two *d*. *Educ:* Univ. of Queensland (LLB). Admitted Queensland Bar, 1964; QC Queensland 1975 and subseq. QC NSW and Victoria; Judge of Federal Court of Australia, 1981–84; Judge of Supreme Court of ACT, 1981–84; Presidential Mem., Administrative Appeals Tribunal, 1981–84; Mem., Australian Law Reform Commn, 1981–84; Chairman, Commission of Inquiry: into possible illegal activities and associated police misconduct, Qld, 1987–89; into the Conservation, Management and Use of Fraser Is. and the Gt Sandy Reg., Qld, 1990–91; Chm., Litigation Reform Commn, Qld, 1991–92. Chm., Australian Heritage Commn, 1990–91. Chm., Nat. Inst. for Law, Ethics and Public Affairs, 1992–; Mem. Vis. Cttee, Faculty of Law, Griffith Univ., 1992–. Chancellor, Sunshine Coast UC, 1994–. Mem. Gov. Bd, Mater Health Services, 1994–. *Recreations:* tennis, reading, music. *Address:* 43 McCaul Street, Taringa East, Brisbane, Qld 4068, Australia. *T:* (7) 33717509. *Clubs:* Queensland, Brisbane (Brisbane).

FITZGERALD, Brig. (retd) Gerald Loftus, CBE 1956; DSO 1945; *b* 5 May 1907; *s* of late Col D. C. V. FitzGerald, MC, Nairobi Kenya; *m* 1937, Mary Stuart, *d* of late Charles E. Mills, Holbrook, Suffolk; one *s* one *d*. *Educ:* Wellington Coll.; Royal Military Academy, Woolwich. Commissioned 2nd Lieut RA, 1926; Regimental duty UK and overseas, 1926–39; staff and regimental duty in UK and NW Europe during War of 1939–45. Brit. Mil. Mission to Greece, 1946–48; Chief Instructor, Officer Cadet Sch., 1949–50; Brit. Joint Services Mission, Washington, USA, 1951–52; Comdr Trg Bde, RA, 1953–55; Dep. Dir, War Office, 1956–58; retired pay, 1959. OStJ 1982. Order of Leopold (with Palm), Belgium, 1944; Croix de Guerre (with Palm), 1944. *Recreations:* field sports, travel. *Club:* Army and Navy.

FITZGERALD, Dr Michael; Vice-Chancellor, Thames Valley University, since 1991; *b* 4 May 1951; *s* of Richard Michael Fitzgerald and Janet Kilpatrick Costine Fitzgerald; two *s*. *Educ:* St Mary's Coll., Liverpool; Selwyn Coll., Cambridge (MA); Univ. of Leicester (PhD). Univ. of Leicester, 1973–75; taught social sciences, and criminology, Open Univ., 1975–87; Coventry Polytechnic, 1987–91. FRSA. *Publications:* 8 books on criminology. *Recreations:* rock music, football, cricket, crime fiction, channel surfing. *Address:* Thames Valley University, St Mary's Road, Ealing, W5 5RF. *T:* 0181–231 2204. *Club:* Reform.

FitzGERALD, Michael Frederick Clive, QC 1980; *b* 9 June 1936; *s* of Sir William James FitzGerald, MC, QC, and Mrs E. J. Critchley; *m* 1966, Virginia Grace Cave (marr. diss. 1992); one *s* three *d*. *Educ:* Downside; Christ's Coll., Cambridge, 1956–59 (MA). 2nd Lieut 9th Queen's Royal Lancers, 1954–56. Called to the Bar, Middle Temple, 1961, Bencher, 1987. *Recreations:* opera, field sports. *Address:* 49 Cheval Place, SW7 1EW. *Club:* Athenæum.

FitzGERALD, Niall William Arthur; Executive Director, since 1987, and Vice-Chairman, since 1994, Unilever; *b* 13 Sept. 1945; *s* of William FitzGerald and Doreen Chambers; *m* 1970, Monica Cusack; two *s* one *d.* *Educ:* St Munchins Coll., Limerick; University College Dublin (MComm). FCT. Unilever, 1968–: North America, 1978–80; Chief Exec. Officer, Foods, S Africa, 1981–85; Group Treasurer, 1985–86; Financial Dir, 1987–89; Exec. Dir, Unilever Foods, 1990–91; Exec. Dir, Unilever Detergents, 1992–. Non-Executive Director: Bank of Ireland, 1991–; Prudential Corp., 1994–. FRSA. *Recreation:* observing humanity. *Address:* Unilever, Blackfriars, EC4P 4BQ. *Clubs:* Royal Automobile; Wisley Golf.

FITZGERALD, Prof. Patrick John; Professor of Law, Carleton University, Ottawa, since 1971; *b* 30 Sept. 1928; *s* of Dr Thomas Walter and Norah Josephine Fitzgerald; *m* 1959, Brigid Aileen Judge; two *s* one *d.* *Educ:* Queen Mary's Grammar Sch., Walsall; University Coll., Oxford. Called to the Bar, Lincoln's Inn, 1951; Ontario Bar, 1984. Fellow, Trinity Coll., Oxford, 1956–60. Professor of Law: Leeds Univ., 1960–66; Univ. of Kent at Canterbury, 1966–71. Visiting Prof., University of Louisville, 1962–63. Consultant, Law Reform Commn of Canada, 1973–92. *Publications:* Criminal Law and Punishment, 1962; Salmond on Jurisprudence (12th edn), 1966; This Law of Ours, 1977; Looking at Law, 1979, 4th edn 1994; (ed) Crime, Justice and Codification, 1986. *Recreations:* music, golf, bridge. *Address:* 246–3310 Southgate Road, Ottawa, Ont K1V 8X4, Canada.

FITZGERALD, Penelope Mary, (Mrs Desmond Fitzgerald); writer; *b* 1916; *d* of E. V. Knox and Christina Hicks; *m* 1941, Desmond Fitzgerald, MC; one *s* two *d.* *Educ:* Wycombe Abbey; Somerville Coll., Oxford (BA). *Publications:* Edward Burne-Jones, 1975; The Knox Brothers, 1977; The Golden Child, 1977; The Bookshop, 1978; Offshore, 1979 (Booker Prize); Human Voices, 1980; At Freddie's, 1982; (ed) William Morris's unpublished Novel on Blue Paper, 1982; Charlotte Mew and her Friends, 1984 (Rose Mary Crawshay Prize, 1985); Innocence, 1986; The Beginning of Spring, 1988; The Gate of Angels, 1990; The Blue Flower, 1995. *Recreations:* listening, talking, watching grandchildren. *Address:* c/o Harper Collins, 77 Fulham Palace Road, W6 8JB.

FitzGERALD, Presiley Lamorna, (Mrs R. K. FitzGerald); *see* Baxendale, P. L.

FitzGERALD, Rowanne; *see* Pasco. R.

FitzGERALD, Sylvia Mary Denise, FLS; Chief Librarian and Archivist, Royal Botanic Gardens, Kew, since 1979; *b* 7 May 1939; *d* of Audoen Aengus FitzGerald and Doris Winifred (*née* Dickinson). *Educ:* Our Lady of Sion Sch., Worthing; Open Univ. (BA Hons 1977). ALA 1962. Assistant: Science Mus. Liby, 1956–57; Brit. Mus. (Natural Hist.) Zool. Liby, 1957–63; Assistant Librarian: Patent Office Liby, 1963–65; MAFF, 1965–67; Librarian-in-charge: MAFF Food & Nutrition Liby, 1967–72; MAFF Tolworth Liby for State Vet. Service and Vertebrate Pest Control, 1972–78. FLS 1992. *Publications:* contrib. State Librarian, Aslib Proc., Archives, etc. *Recreations:* friends, music. *Address:* Library & Archives, Royal Botanic Gardens, Kew, Richmond, Surrey TW9 3AE.

FITZGERALD-LOMBARD, Rt. Rev. Charles, OSB, **(James Michael Hubert Fitzgerald-Lombard);** Abbot of Downside, since 1990; *b* 29 Jan. 1941; *s* of late Col James C. R. Fitzgerald-Lombard and of Winifred (*née* Woulfe Flanagan). *Educ:* Downside; Collegio Sant Anselmo, Rome; King's Coll., London (MPhil). Monk of Downside Abbey, 1962–; ordained priest, 1968; Teacher and Tutor, Downside Sch., 1968–75; Bursar and Sec. to the Trustees, 1975–90. *Publications:* Prayers and Meditations, 1967, 3rd edn 1974; A Guide to the Church of St Gregory the Great, Downside Abbey, 1981, 2nd edn 1988; English and Welsh Priests 1801–1914, 1993. *Recreations:* electrical and telecommunications engineering, historical research, swimming. *Address:* Downside Abbey, Stratton-on-the-Fosse, Bath BA3 4RH. *T:* Bath (01761) 232226.

FitzGIBBON, Louis Theobald Dillon; Comte Dillon in France; political writer; *b* 6 Jan. 1925; *s* of Comdr Francis Lee-Dillon FitzGibbon, RN, and Kathleen Clare (*née* Atchison), *widow* of Hon. Harry Lee-Dillon; *m* 1st, 1950, Josephine Miriam Maud (*née* Webb) (marr. diss.); 2nd, 1962, Madeleine Sally (*née* Hayward-Surry) (*d* 1980); one *s* two *d*; 3rd, 1980, Joan Elizabeth Jevons (marr. diss.). *Educ:* St Augustine's Abbey Sch.; Royal Naval Coll., Dartmouth. Royal Navy, 1942–54 (incl. War of 1939–45 and service in ex-German U-1171); Polish interpreter's course, 1950–52. Dir, De Leon Properties Ltd, 1954–72 and 1994–. Solicitor's articled clerk, 1960–63; Anglo-Polish Conf., Warsaw, 1963. Personal Asst to the then Rt Hon. Duncan Sandys, MP (later Lord Duncan-Sandys), 1967–68; Gen. Sec., British Council for Aid to Refugees, 1968–72; United Nations (UNHCR) Mission to South Sudan, 1972–73; Dir of a medical charity, 1974–76; Exec. Officer, Nat. Assoc. for Freedom, 1977–78; Gen. Sec. of a trade assoc., 1978–80; Hon. Sec., British Horn of Africa Council, 1984–92. Mem., RIIA, 1982, 1988. Won first Airey Neave Meml Scholarship (proj. on Somalia), 1981. Hon. Secretary: Jt Cttee for Preservation of Historic Portsmouth, 1956–61; Katyn Memorial Fund, 1971–77; Area Pres., St John Amb. Brigade (Hants East), 1974–76. SMHO Malta, 1985 (Kt of Honour and Devotion and Officer of Merit). Polish Gold Cross of Merit, 1969; Order of Polonia Restituta (Polish Govt in Exile) (Officer, 1971; Comdr, 1972; Kt Comdr, 1976); Officer, Order of Merit (FRG), 1990; Katyn Meml Medal Bronze, USA, 1977; Laureate van de Arbeid, Netherlands, 1982. *Publications:* Katyn—A Crime without Parallel, 1971; The Katyn Cover-up, 1972; Unpitied and Unknown, 1975; Katyn—Triumph of Evil (Ireland), 1975; The Katyn Memorial, 1976; Katyn Massacre (paper) 1977, 3rd edn 1989; Katyn (USA), 1979; Katyn (in German), 1979; The Betrayal of the Somalis, 1982 (commnd by Japan-Somalia Friendship Assoc. in Japanese, 1989); Straits and Strategic Waterways in the Red Sea, 1984; Ethiopia Hijacks the Hijack, 1985; The Evaded Duty, 1985. *Recreations:* travelling, politics, writing, reading, history, languages, refugee problems. *Address:* Flat 2, 8 Portland Place, Brighton BN2 1DG. *T:* Brighton (01273) 685661.

FitzHARRIS, Viscount; James Carleton Harris; *b* 19 June 1946; *o s* and *heir* of 6th Earl of Malmesbury, *qv*; *m* 1969, Sally Ann, *yr d* of Sir Richard Newton Rycroft, *qv*; three *s* two *d.* *Educ:* Eton; Queen's Coll., St Andrews (MA). *Heir: s* Hon. James Hugh Carleton Harris, *b* 29 April 1970. *Address:* Greywell Hill, Greywell, Basingstoke, Hants RG25 1DB. *T:* Odiham (01256) 703565.

FITZHERBERT, family name of **Baron Stafford.**

FitzHERBERT, Giles Eden, CMG 1985; HM Diplomatic Service, retired; *b* Dublin, 8 March 1935; *e s* of late Captain H. C. FitzHerbert, Irish Guards, and Sheelah, *d* of J. X. Murphy; *m* 1st, 1962, Margaret Waugh (*d* 1986); two *s* three *d*; 2nd, 1988, Alexandra Eyre; three *s* one *d.* *Educ:* Ampleforth Coll.; Christ Church Oxford; Harvard Business Sch. 2nd Lieut, 8th King's Royal Irish Hussars, 1957–58. Vickers da Costa & Co., 1962–66. First Secretary: Foreign Office, 1966; Rome, 1968–71; FCO, 1972–75; Counsellor: Kuwait, 1975–77; Nicosia, 1977–78; Head of Eur. Community Dept (Ext.), FCO, 1978–82; on sabbatical leave, LSE, 1982; Inspector, FCO, 1983; Minister, Rome, 1983–87; Ambassador to Venezuela and concurrently (non-resident) to the Dominican Republic, 1988–93. Contested (L) Fermanagh and South Tyrone, Gen. Elect., 1964. *Address:* Fenagh Rectory, Co. Carlow, Ireland. *Clubs:* White's, Beefsteak; Kildare Street and University (Dublin).

FitzHERBERT, Sir Richard (Ranulph), 9th Bt *cr* 1784, of Tissington, Derbyshire; *b* 2 Nov. 1963; *s* of Rev. David Henry FitzHerbert, MC (*d* 1976) and of Charmian Hyacinthe, *yr d* of late Samuel Ranulph Allsopp, CBE; *S* uncle, 1989; *m* 1993, Caroline Louise, *d* of Major and Mrs Patrick Shuter; one *s.* *Educ:* Eton College. *Recreations:* cricket, shooting, restoring family estate. *Heir: s* Frederick David FitzHerbert, *b* 23 March 1995. *Address:* Tissington Hall, Ashbourne, Derbys DE6 1RA. *Clubs:* White's, MCC; Bachelors', Stansted Hall Cricket, Parwich Royal British Legion Cricket.

FITZHERBERT-BROCKHOLES, Michael John, OBE 1989; JP; Vice Lord-Lieutenant of Lancashire, 1977–95; Constable of Lancaster Castle, since 1995; *b* 12 June 1920; *s* of John William Fitzherbert-Brockholes and Eileen Agnes; *m* 1950, Mary Edith Moore; four *s.* *Educ:* The Oratory Sch.; New Coll., Oxford. Scots Guards, 1940–46. Mem., Lancs CC, 1968–89; Chm., Educn Cttee, 1977–81. JP 1960, DL 1975, Lancs. KSG 1978. *Recreation:* gardening. *Address:* Claughton Hall, Garstang, near Preston, Lancs. PR3 0PN. *T:* Brock (01995) 640286.

FITZ-MAURICE, family name of **Earl of Orkney.**

FITZMAURICE; *see* Mercer Nairne Petty-Fitzmaurice, family name of Marquess of Lansdowne.

FitzPATRICK, Air Cdre David Beatty, CB 1970; OBE 1953; AFC 1949 and Bar, 1958; *b* 31 Jan. 1920; *s* of late Comdr D. T. FitzPatrick, RN and Beatrice Anne Ward; *m* 1941, Kathleen Mary Miles; one *d.* *Educ:* Kenilworth Coll., Exeter; Midhurst. Commnd RAF, 1938; served War of 1939–45, Atlantic, Mediterranean and Far East theatres; comd No 209 Sqdn (Far East), 1944; (GD Pilot) Sqdn flying duty, 1945–52; cfs, pfc and GW Specialist, RAF Henlow, 1952–57; GW (Trials) Project Officer, Min. of Supply, 1957–59; Base Comdr Christmas Island, 1959–60 (British Nuclear Trials); NATO Def. Coll., and jssc, 1960–61; Dep. Dir (Ops) Air Staff, 1961–64; comd RAF Akrotiri and Nicosia, 1964–66; Dir of (Q) RAF, MoD, 1966–69; attached NBPI for special duty, 1969; Dir, Guided Weapons (Trials and Ranges), Min. of Technology, 1969–72; Dir, Guided Weapons Trials, MoD (PE), 1972–74; retd RAF, 1975; Head, teaching dept of indep. sch., 1975–85, retd. FIMgt (FBIM 1970); FRMetS 1984; MRAeS 1971. *Recreations:* swimming (Life Vice-Pres., Royal Air Force Swimming Assoc.), deep-sea fishing, cricket. *Address:* Whistledown, 38 Courts Mount Road, Haslemere, Surrey GU27 2PP. *T:* Haslemere (01428) 644589.

FITZPATRICK, Gen. Sir (Geoffrey Richard) Desmond, GCB 1971 (KCB 1965; CB 1961); DSO 1945; MBE 1943; MC 1939; *b* 14 Dec. 1912; *o s* of late Brig.-Gen. Sir Richard Fitzpatrick, CBE, DSO, and Lady (G. E.) Fitzpatrick; *m* 1944, Mary Sara, *o d* of Sir Charles Campbell, 12th Bt; one *s* one *d.* *Educ:* Eton; RMC Sandhurst. Commissioned The Royal Dragoons, 1932. Served in Palestine, 1938–39 (MC); War of 1939–45 (despatches, MBE, DSO); in Middle East, Italy, NW Europe. Bt. Lieut-Col 1951; Col 1953; ADC to the Queen, 1959; Maj.-Gen. 1959; Asst Chief of Defence Staff, Ministry of Defence, 1959–61; Dir Mil. Ops, War Office, 1962–64; Chief of Staff, BAOR, 1964–65; Lt-Gen. 1965; GOC-in-C, N Ire., 1965–66; Vice-Chief of Gen. Staff, 1966–68; Gen. 1968; C-in-C, BAOR, and Commander N Army Gp 1968–70; Dep. Supreme Allied Comdr, Europe, 1970–73; ADC (General) to the Queen, 1970–73. Lieutenant-Governor and C-in-C, Jersey, 1974–79. Col, The Royal Dragoons, 1964–69; Dep. Col., 1969–74, Col, 1979–, The Blues and Royals, and Gold Stick to the Queen, 1979–; Col Comdt, RAC, 1971–74. *Address:* Belmont, Otley, Suffolk IP6 9PF. *Clubs:* Cavalry and Guards; Royal Yacht Squadron.

FITZPATRICK, James Bernard, CBE 1983; JP; DL; Chairman, Royal Liverpool and Broadgreen University Hospitals NHS Trust, since 1995; *b* 21 April 1930; *s* of late B. A. Fitzpatrick and Mrs J. E. Fitzpatrick; *m* 1965, Rosemary, *d* of late Captain E. B. Clark, RD and bar, RNR and late Mrs K. E. Clark, Claughton; one *s* one *d.* *Educ:* Bootle Grammar Sch.; London Univ. (LLB). Admitted Solicitor, 1962; FCIT 1973; CIMgt. Joined Mersey Docks and Harbour Bd, 1951: various management posts from 1965; Personnel and Industrial Relns Dir, 1971, on formation of Mersey Docks and Harbour Co.; Jt Man. Dir, 1974; Dep. Chief Exec., 1975; Man. Dir and Chief Exec., 1977; Chm., 1984–87. Director: Plan Invest Group plc, 1984–91; Teesside Hldgs, 1992–; Mem., 1979–89, Chm., 1988–89, Merseyside Enterprise Forum. Chairman: Nat. Assoc. of Port Employers, 1979–82 (Vice-Chm., 1973–79); Employers' Assoc. of Port of Liverpool, 1974–83; Member: Liverpool Dock Labour Bd, 1974–76 (Chm., 1976); Exec. Council, British Ports Assoc., 1976–87 (Dep. Chm., 1985–87); Nat. Dock Labour Bd, 1978–84. Chairman: Liverpool HA, 1986–91; Royal Liverpool Univ. Hosp. NHS Trust, 1991–95. Mem. Council, Industrial Soc., 1989–92. Liverpool University: Mem. Council, 1988–89, 1991–; Chm., Inst. of Irish Studies, 1990–. FRSA. JP Liverpool 1977. DL Merseyside, 1985. Hon. Fellow, Liverpool John Moores Univ. (formerly Liverpool Polytechnic), 1988. *Recreations:* fell walking, gardening, music, reading. *Address:* 57 Hilbre Road, West Kirby, Merseyside L48 3HB. *T:* 0151–625 9612; Royal Liverpool Hospital, Prescot Street, Liverpool L7 8XP. *T:* 0151–706 2000. *Clubs:* Oriental, Pilgrims.

FITZPATRICK, Air Marshal Sir John (Bernard), KBE 1984; CB 1982; Royal Air Force, retired; Independent Panel Inspector, Departments of the Environment and Transport, since 1986; *b* 15 Dec. 1929; *s* of Joseph Fitzpatrick and Bridget Fitzpatrick; *m* 1954, Gwendoline Mary Abbott; two *s* one *d.* *Educ:* St Patrick's School, Dungannon; RAF Apprentice Sch., Halton; RAF Coll. Cranwell. Officer Commanding: No 81 Sqdn, 1966–68; No 35 Sqdn, 1971–72; Gp Captain Plans to AOC No 18 Gp, 1973; OC, RAF Scampton, 1974–75; RCDS, 1976; Dir of Ops (Strike), RAF, 1977–79; SASO, HQ Strike Command, 1980–82; Dir Gen. of Organisation, RAF, 1982–83; AOC No 18 Gp, RAF, and Comdr Maritime Air Eastern Atlantic and Channel, 1983–86. *Recreations:* golf, reading, carpentry. *Club:* Royal Air Force.

FITZPATRICK, John Ronald; Solicitor and Parliamentary Officer, Greater London Council, 1977–85, Consultant, 1985–86; *b* 22 Sept. 1923; *s* of Henry Fitzpatrick and Mary Lister; *m* 1952, Beryl Mary Newton; two *s* one *d.* *Educ:* St Bede's Coll., Manchester; Univ. of Manchester (LLB). Admitted Solicitor, 1947; LMRTPI 1951. Asst Solicitor: Burnley, 1947; Stockport, 1948–51; Asst/Principal Asst Solicitor, Mddx CC, 1951–65; Asst Clerk/Asst Dir-Gen., GLC, 1965–69; Asst Dir, 1969–72, Dir, 1972–77, Planning and Transportation, GLC. *Recreations:* golf, bridge. *Address:* Courtlands, 2 Langley Grove, New Malden, Surrey KT3 3AL. *T:* 0181–942 8652.

FitzROY, family name of **Duke of Grafton** and of **Southampton Barony.**

FitzROY NEWDEGATE, family name of **Viscount Daventry.**

FITZSIMONS, Anthony; *see* Fitzsimons, P. A.

FITZSIMONS, Prof. James Thomas, FRS 1988; Professor of Medical Physiology, University of Cambridge, 1990–95, now Emeritus Professor; Fellow of Gonville and Caius College, Cambridge, since 1961; *b* 8 July 1928; *s* of Robert Allen Fitzsimons, FRCS and Dr Mary Patricia (*née* McKelvey); *m* 1961, Aude Irène Jeanne, *d* of Gén. Jean Etienne Valluy, DSO and Marie (*née* Bourdillon); two *s* one *d.* *Educ:* St Edmund's Coll., Ware;

Gonville and Caius Coll., Cambridge (1st cl. Pts I and II, Nat. Sci. Tripos; BA 1949; MB BChir 1953; MA 1954; PhD 1960; MD 1967, Sir Lionel Whitby Medal; ScD 1979); Charing Cross Hosp. House appts, Leicester Gen. and Charing Cross Hosps, 1954–55; RAF, Inst. of Aviation Medicine, 1955–57 (Flight Lieut); Cambridge University: MRC Scholar, Physiol. Lab., 1957–59; Univ. Demonstrator in Physiol., 1959–64, Lectr, 1964–76, Reader, 1976–90; Gonville and Caius College: Tutor, 1964–72; Coll. Lectr in Physiol, 1964–93; Dir of Studies in Medicine, 1978–93. Visiting Professor: CNRS Lab. des Régulations Alimentaires, Coll. de France, 1967; Inst. of Neurol Scis, Univ. of Pennsylvania, 1968, 1972; CNRS Lab. de Neurobiol., Coll. de France, 1975; Lectures: Stevenson Meml, Univ. of Western Ontario, 1979; Halliburton, KCL, 1982. Royal Soc. rep., British Nat. Cttee for Physiol. Scis, 1976–82; Mem., Physiol. Soc. Cttee, 1972–76 (Chm., 1975–76); Mem., IUPS Commn on Physiol. of Food and Fluid Intake, 1973–80 (Chm., 1979–80). Member, Editorial Boards: Jl of Physiol., 1977–84; Neuroendocrinology, 1979–84; Editor, Biological Reviews, 1984–95. Hon. MD Lausanne, 1978. *Publications:* The Physiology of Thirst and Sodium Appetite, 1979; scientific papers in professional jls. *Recreations:* Irish language and literature, cats, music, photography, grandchildren. *Address:* Physiological Laboratory, Downing Street, Cambridge CB2 3EG. *T:* Cambridge (01223) 333836; 91 Thornton Road, Girton, Cambridge CB3 0NR. *T:* Cambridge (01223) 276874.

FITZSIMONS, P. Anthony; Chairman, Ruton Management Ltd; *b* 16 March 1946; two *s. Educ:* LSE (BSc Econ.). Rank Xerox: Australia, 1972–75; Southern Europe, 1975–76; Australasia, Middle East, 1976–79; Regional Control Dir, London, 1979–81; Grand Metropolitan: Finance Systems and Strategy Dir, Brewing and Retail Div., 1981–83; Man. Dir, Host Group, 1983–85; Man. Dir, Personal Banking, Citibank, 1985–89; Chief Exec. and Man. Dir, Bristol & West Bldg Soc., 1989–93. Chm., Avon TEC. *Recreations:* squash, riding, music, sailing. *Address:* Hill House, Hannington, Wilts SN6 7RS.

FITZWALTER, 21st Baron, *cr* 1295; **(Fitzwalter) Brook Plumptre,** JP; Hon. Captain, The Buffs; *b* 15 Jan. 1914; *s* of late George Beresford Plumptre, Goodnestone, Canterbury, Kent; *S* uncle, 1943 (FitzWalter Barony called out of abeyance in his favour, 1953); *m* 1951, Margaret Melesina, *yr d* of (Herbert) William Deedes, JP, Galt, Hythe, Kent; five *s. Educ:* Diocesan Coll., Rondebosch, Cape; Jesus Coll., Cambridge. Served War of 1939–45, with the Buffs (Royal East Kent Regt) in France, Belgium, UK and India; attached RIASC, as Capt. JP Kent, 1949. Landowner and farmer; succeeded to family estate, 1943. *Heir: s* Hon. Julian Brook Plumptre [*b* 18 Oct. 1952; *m* 1988, Sally, *o d* of late I. M. T. Quiney; one *s*]. *Address:* Goodnestone Park, Canterbury, Kent CT3 1PL. *T:* Nonington (01304) 840218.

FLACK, Bertram Anthony, CMG 1979; HM Diplomatic Service, retired; *b* 3 Feb. 1924; *y s* of Dr F. H. Flack and Alice Cockshut, Nelson, Lancs; *m* 1948, Jean W. Mellor; two *s* two *d. Educ:* Epsom Coll.; Liverpool Univ. (LLB Hons). Enlisted Gren. Gds, 1942; commissioned E Lancashire Regt, 1943; served in NW Europe (Captain). Joined Foreign Service, 1948; served Karachi, 1948–50; Alexandria, 1950–52; Stockholm, 1955–58; Accra, 1958–61; Johannesburg, 1964–67; Dep. High Comr, E Pakistan, 1967–68; Inspector, Diplomatic Service, 1968–70; Head of Communications Dept, FCO, 1971–73; Commercial Counsellor, Stockholm, 1973–75; Canadian Nat. Defence Coll., 1975–76; Dep. High Comr, Ottawa, 1976–79; High Comr, Repub. of Uganda, 1979–80. *Recreations:* cricket, golf. *Address:* Ripple Cottage, Douglas Street, Castletown, Isle of Man IM9 1AY.

FLACK, Ven. John Robert; Archdeacon of Pontefract, since 1992; *b* 30 May 1942; *s* of Edwin John Flack and Joan Annie Flack; *m* 1968, Julia Clare Slaughter; one *s* one *d. Educ:* Hertford Grammar Sch.; Univ. of Leeds (BA 1964); Coll. of the Resurrection, Mirfield. Ordained, deacon, 1966, priest, 1967; Assistant Curate: St Bartholomew, Armley, Leeds, 1966–69; St Mary the Virgin, Northampton, 1969–72; Vicar: Chapelthorpe (Wakefield dio.), 1972–81; Ripponden with Rishworth and Barkisland with West Scammonden, 1981–85; Brighouse, 1985–92 (Team Rector, 1988–92); Rural Dean of Brighouse and Elland, 1986–92. Hon. Canon of Wakefield Cathedral, 1989–. *Recreations:* cricket, Mozart. *Address:* 10 Arden Court, Horbury, Wakefield WF4 5AH. *T:* Wakefield (01924) 276797, *Fax:* (01924) 261095.

FLAGG, Rt. Rev. John William Hawkins; Diocesan Adviser in rural ministry and stewardship, since 1993, and overseas relations, since 1994, Southwell; an Hon. Assistant Bishop of Southwell, since 1992; *b* 16 April 1929; *s* of Wilfred John and Emily Flagg; *m* 1954, Marjorie Lund; two *s* four *d. Educ:* All Nations Christian Coll.; Clifton Theological Coll. Agricultural missionary, Chile, 1951; Chaplain and Missionary Superintendent, St Andrew's, Asunción, Paraguay, 1959–64; Archdeacon, N Argentine, 1964–69; Diocesan Bishop of Paraguay and N Argentine, 1969–73; Asst Bishop for Chile, Peru and Bolivia, 1973–77; Bishop, Diocese of Peru, 1977; Asst Bishop, Diocese of Liverpool, 1978–86; Vicar, St Cyprian's with Christ Church, Edge Hill, 1978–85; Priest-in-Charge of Christ Church, Waterloo, 1985–86; Gen. Sec., S American Missionary Soc., 1986–93; Hon. Asst Bishop of Rochester, 1986–92. Member of Anglican Consultative Council, 1974–79; Presiding Bishop of Anglican Council of South America (CASA), 1974–77. *Address:* 8 Ransome Close, Beacon Heights, Notts NG24 2LQ.

FLANAGAN, Barry, OBE 1991; RA 1991 (ARA 1987); sculptor; *b* 11 Jan. 1941. *Educ:* Birmingham Coll. of Arts and Crafts; St Martin's Sch. of Art. Teacher, St Martin's Sch. of Art and Central Sch. of Art and Design, 1967–71. One-man exhibitions include: Rowan Gall., 1966, 1968, 1970–74; Fischbach Gall., NY, 1969; Galleria del Leone, Venice, 1971; Mus. of Modern Art, NY, Mus. of Modern Art, Oxford, 1974; Hogarth Galls, Sydney, 1975; Centro de Arte y Communicación, Buenos Aires, 1976; Van Abbemuseum, Eindhoven, Arnolfini Gall., Bristol, Serpentine Gall. (tour), 1977–79; Galerie Durand-Dessert, Paris, 1980, 1982, 1988; Waddington Galls, 1980–81, 1983, 1985, 1990–94; Inst. of Contemporary Arts (prints and drawings), 1981–82; British Pavilion, XL Venice Biennale, and tour, 1982–83; Centre Georges Pompidou, Paris, 1983; Pace Gall., NY, 1983, 1994; Fuji Television Gall., Tokyo, 1985, 1991; Tate Gall., 1986; Laing Art Gall., Newcastle upon Tyne, Mus. of Contemporary Art, Belgrade, City Gall., Zagreb, Mus. of Modern Art, Ljubljana (tour), 1987–88; Madrid and Nantes, 1993–94; Gallagher Gall., RHA, 1995. Work includes: outdoor sculpture for Sint Pietersplein, Ghent, 1980; Camdonian sculpture, Lincoln's Inn Fields, 1980; bronze sculptures, Baby Elephant and Hare on Bell, Equitable Life Tower West, NY, 1984; bronze sculpture, Nine Foot Hare, Victoria Plaza, London, 1984; bronze sculpture, The Boxing Ones, Capability Green, Luton Hoo Estate, Beds, 1986; bronze sculpture, Kouros horse, Stockley Park, Uxbridge, 1987; two bronze Leaping Hare sculptures for Kawakyo Co., Osaka, 1990. Choreographed two pieces for dance gp, Strider, 1972. Judge, Bath Sculpture Competition, 1985. *Address:* c/o Waddington Galleries, 11 Cork Street, W1X 1PD.

FLANAGAN, Michael Joseph; Director, Finance and Planning, Cheshire Constabulary, since 1995; *b* 21 Nov. 1946; *s* of Daniel and Margaret Constance Flanagan; *m* 1968, Patricia Holland; two *s* one *d. Educ:* St Joseph's Coll., Blackpool; Southampton Coll. of Higher Educn. IPFA 1972; DMS 1983. Trainee Accountant, Lancs CC, 1965–69; Preston County Borough, 1969–70; Southampton City Council, 1970–72; Accountant, 1972, Asst Dir of Finance, 1981–87, Telford Develt Corp.; Dir of Finance and Tech. Services, 1987–90, Chief Exec., 1990–95, Develt Bd for Rural Wales. *Recreations:* sport, esp. football, golf, tennis; family activities. *Address:* Tan-y-Fron, Pantyffridd, Berriew, Powys.

FLANNERY, Martin Henry; *b* 2 March 1918; *m* 1949; one *s* two *d. Educ:* Sheffield Grammar Sch.; Sheffield Teachers' Trng College. Served with Royal Scots, 1940–46. Teacher, 1946–74 (Head Teacher, 1969–74). MP (Lab) Hillsborough, Sheffield, Feb. 1974–1992. Chairman: Tribune Group, 1980–81; PLP's NI Cttee, 1983–92; PLP Consultant MP for NUT, 1974–92. *Recreations:* music, rambling. *Address:* 53 Linaker Road, Sheffield S6 5DS.

FLATHER, family name of **Baroness Flather.**

FLATHER, Baroness *cr* 1990 (Life Peer), of Windsor and Maidenhead in the Royal County of Berkshire; **Shreela Flather**; JP; DL; Councillor, Royal Borough of Windsor and Maidenhead, 1976–91 (first ethnic minority woman Councillor in UK), Mayor, 1986–87 (first Asian woman to hold this office); *b* Lahore, India; *née* Shreela Rai; *m* Gary Flather, *qv*; two *s. Educ:* University Coll. London (LLB; Fellow 1992). Called to the Bar, Inner Temple, 1962. Infant Teacher, ILEA, 1965–67; Teacher of English as a second lang., Altwood Comp. Sch., Maidenhead, 1968–74, Broadmoor Hosp., 1974–78. Chairman: Consortium for Street Children, 1993–; Disaster and Emergencies Cttee, 1994–; Vice Chm., Refugee Council, 1991–; Member: W Metropolitan Conciliation Cttee, Race Relations Bd, 1973–78; Cttee of Inquiry (Rampton, later Swann Cttee) into Educn of Children from Ethnic Minority Gps, 1979–85; CRE, 1980–86 (Chm., Educn, Housing and Services Cttee, and Welsh Consultative Cttee, 1980–86); Police Complaints Board, 1982–85; HRH Duke of Edinburgh's Inquiry into British Housing, 1984–85; Lord Chancellor's Legal Aid Adv. Cttee, 1985–88; Social Security Adv. Cttee, 1987–90; Econ. and Social Cttee, EC, 1987–90; Carnegie Inquiry into the Third Age, 1990–93; H of L Select Cttee on Med. Ethics, 1993–; UK Rep., EC Commn Enquiry into Racism and Xenophobia, 1994–. President: Cambs, Chilterns and Thames Rent Assessment Panel, 1983–; Community Council for Berks, 1991–; Chm., Maidenhead Community Consultative Council, 1987–90; Vice-Chm. and Founder Mem., Maidenhead CRC, 1969; Vice-Chm. and Mem., Management Cttee, Maidenhead CAB, 1982–88; Member: Thames and Chilterns Tourist Bd, 1987–88; Berks FPC, 1987–88. Member: Cons. Women's Nat. Cttee (formerly Cons. Women's Nat. Adv. Cttee), 1978–89; Exec. Cttee, Anglo-Asian Cons. Soc., 1979–83; NEC, Cons. Party, 1989–90; formerly: Vice-Chairman: Estates and Amenities and Leisure Cttees, Windsor and Maidenhead; Police Consultative Cttee; Maidenhead Volunteer Centre; Sec., Windsor and Maidenhead Cons. Gp. Chm., Star FM, 1992–; Director: Daytime Television, 1978–79; Thames Valley Enterprise, 1990–93; Meridian Broadcasting, 1991–. Member: BBC S and E Regl Adv. Cttee, 1987–89; Cttee of Management, Servite Houses Ltd, 1987–; LWT Prog. Adv. Bd, 1990–94. Vice-President: BSA, 1988–91; Assoc. of Dist Councils, 1990–; Commonwealth Countries League, 1990–; AMA, 1991–. Pres., League of Friends of Broadmoor Hosp., 1991–; Member: Bd of Visitors, Holloway Prison, 1981–83; Broadmoor Hosp. Bd, 1987–88; Council, Winston Churchill Meml Trust, 1993–; Trustee: Berks Community Trust, 1978–90; Hillingdon Hosp. Trust, 1990–. Gov., Commonwealth Inst., 1993–; Governor: Altwood Comp. Sch., Maidenhead, 1978–86; Slough Coll. of Higher Educn, 1984–89; Mem. Council, Atlantic Coll., 1993–. Sec./Organiser Maidenhead Ladies' Asian Club, 1968–78; started New Star Boys' Club for Asian Boys and Summer Sch. Project for Asian children, Maidenhead; prepared English Teaching Scheme for Asian adults 'Stepping Stone'. JP Maidenhead, 1971; DL Berks, 1994. DUniv Open, 1994. *Recreations:* travel, cinema, swimming. *Address:* House of Lords, SW1A 0PW. *T:* 0171–219 5353.

FLATHER, Gary Denis; QC 1984; a Recorder, since 1986; *b* 4 Oct. 1937; *s* of late Denis Flather and of Joan Flather; *m* Shreela Flather (*see* Baroness Flather); two *s. Educ:* Oundle Sch.; Pembroke Coll., Oxford (MA). Called to the Bar, Inner Temple, 1962, Bencher, 1995. National Service, Second Lieut 1st Bn York and Lancaster Regt, 1956–58; Lieut Hallamshire Bn, TA, 1958–61. Asst Parly Boundary Comr, 1982–; Asst Recorder, 1983–86. Mem., Panel of Chairmen: for ILEA Teachers' Disciplinary Tribunal, 1974–90 (Chm., Disciplinary ILEA Tribunal, William Tyndale Jun. Sch. teachers, 1976); for Disciplinary Tribunal for London Polytechnics, 1982–90; a Chairman: Police Disciplinary Appeals, 1987–; MoD (Police) Disciplinary Appeals, 1992–; Legal Mem., Mental Health Review Tribunal (restricted patients), 1987–; a Financial Services Act Inspector, employees of Coutts Bank, 1987–88; a legal assessor, GMC and GDC, 1987–; Mem., Sec. of State for Health's Tech. Adv. Cttee on Grants to Disabled, 1995–; Chairman: Bar Council's Disability Panel, 1992–; Statutory Cttee, RPharmS, 1990–; Disciplinary Cttee, Chartered Inst. of Marketing, 1993–; Mem., Chambers Arbitration Panel, Bar Council, 1995. Dir, W. Fearnehough (Bakewell) Ltd, 1991–. Pres., Maidenhead Rotary Club, 1990–91. Vice-Pres., Community Council for Berks, 1987–. Trustee, ADAPT, 1995–. Escort to the Mayor of the Royal Borough of Windsor and Maidenhead, 1986–87. *Recreations:* travel, music, coping with multiple sclerosis, being with friends. *Address:* 4/5 Gray's Inn Square, Gray's Inn, WC1R 5AY. *T:* 0171–404 5252.

FLAUX, Julian Martin; QC 1994; *b* 11 May 1955; *s* of Louis Michael Flaux and Maureen Elizabeth Brenda Flaux; *m* 1983, Matilda Christian (*née* Gabb); three *s. Educ:* King's Sch., Worcester; Worcester Coll., Oxford (BCL, MA). Called to the Bar, Inner Temple, 1978; in practice, 1979–. *Recreations:* opera, reading, walking. *Address:* 7 King's Bench Walk, Temple, EC4Y 7DS. *T:* 0171–583 0404.

FLAVELL, Prof. Richard Anthony, PhD; FRS 1984; Chairman and Professor of Immunobiology, and Professor of Biology, Yale University School of Medicine, and Investigator of the Howard Hughes Medical Institute, since 1988; *b* 23 Aug. 1945; *s* of John T. and Iris Flavell; *m* Madlyn (*née* Nathanson); one *d*; two *s* of former *m. Educ:* Dept of Biochemistry, Univ. of Hull (PhD 1970); Univ. of Amsterdam (Royal Soc. Eur. Fellow); Univ of Zürich (Post-doctoral Fellow). Wetenschappelijk Medewerker, Univ. of Amsterdam, 1973–79; Head, Lab. of Gene Structure and Expression, NIMR, Mill Hill, 1979–82; Pres., Biogen Res. Corp., 1982–88; Principal Res. Officer and CSO, Biogen Gp, 1984–88. Darwin Trust Vis. Prof., 1995. Mem., EMBO, 1978–. MRI 1984–; Mem., Amer. Assoc. of Immunologists, 1990–. Anniversary Prize, FEBS, 1980; Colworth Medal, Biochem. Soc., 1980. *Publications: chapters in:* Handbook of Biochemistry and Molecular Biology ed Fasman, 3rd edn 1976; McGraw-Hill Yearbook of Science and Technology, 1980; Eukaryotic Genes: their structure, activity and regulation, ed jtly with it Maclean and Gregory, 1983; articles in numerous scientific jls, incl. Nature, Cell, Proc. Nat. Acad. Sci., EMBO Jl, Jl Exp. Med. Sci., Science, Immunity; contrib. Proceedings of symposia. *Recreations:* music, tennis, horticulture. *Address:* Section of Immunobiology, Yale University School of Medicine, 310 Cedar Street, New Haven, CT 06510, USA; 283 Moose Hill Road, Guildford, CT 06437, USA.

FLAVELL, Prof. Richard Bailey; Director, John Innes Centre (formerly Institute), since 1988; Chairman, AFRC Institute of Plant Science Research Management Committee, since 1990; *b* 11 Oct. 1943; *s* of Sidney Flavell and Emily Gertrude Flavell (*née* Bailey); *m* 1966, Hazel New; two *d. Educ:* Univ. of Birmingham (BSc 1964); Univ. of East Anglia (PhD 1967). Research Associate, Univ. of Stanford, California, 1967; Plant Breeding Institute, 1969–88 (Head, Molecular Genetics Dept, 1985–88). Hon. Prof., King's College

London, 1986–. Fellow, EMBO, 1990; Pres., Internat. Soc. for Plant Molecular Biology, 1993–95. *Publications:* scientific papers and books. *Recreations:* music, gardening. *Address:* John Innes Centre, Norwich Research Park, Colney, Norwich NR4 7UH. *T:* Norwich (01603) 452571.

FLAXEN, David William; Director of Statistics, Department of Transport, since 1989; *b* 20 April 1941; *s* of late William Henry Flaxen and Beatrice Flaxen (*née* Laidlow); *m* 1969, Eleanor Marie Easton; two *d*. *Educ:* Manchester Grammar Sch.; Brasenose Coll., Oxford (MA Physics); University Coll. London (DipStat). Teacher, Leyton County High School for Boys, 1963; cadet statistician, 1963–64; statistical posts, Central Statistical Office and Min. of Labour, 1964–71; United Nations Adviser: Swaziland, 1971–72; Ghana, 1985–86; Statistician, Dept of Employment, 1973–75; Chief Statistician: Dept of Employment, 1975–76; Central Statistical Office, 1976–77 and 1981–83; Inland Revenue, 1977–81; Asst Dir (Under Sec.), Central Statistical Office, 1983–89. *Publications:* contribs to articles in Physics Letters, Economic Trends, Dept of Employment Gazette, etc. *Recreations:* bridge, wine, cooking, music. *Address:* 65 Corringham Road, NW11 7BS. *T:* 0181–458 5451.

FLECKER, James William, MA; Headmaster, Ardingly College, since 1980; *b* 15 Aug. 1939; *s* of Henry Lael Oswald Flecker, CBE, and Mary Patricia Flecker; *m* 1967, Mary Rose Firth; three *d*. *Educ:* Marlborough Coll.; Brasenose Coll., Oxford (BA, now MA Lit. Hum., 1962). Asst Master: Sydney Grammar Sch., 1962–63; Latymer Upper Sch., 1964–67; (and later Housemaster), Marlborough Coll., 1967–80. *Recreations:* hockey, cricket, flute playing, children's operas. *Address:* Ardingly College, Haywards Heath, West Sussex RH17 6SQ. *T:* Ardingly (01444) 892577.

FLEET, Kenneth George; journalist; *b* 12 Sept. 1929; *s* of late Fred Major Fleet and Elizabeth Doris Fleet; *m* 1953, (Alice) Brenda, *d* of late Captain H. R. Wilkinson, RD, RNR and Mrs Kathleen Mary Wilkinson; three *s* one *d*. *Educ:* Calday Grange Grammar Sch., Cheshire; LSE (BScEcons). Jl of Commerce, Liverpool, 1950–52; Sunday Times, 1955–56; Dep. City Editor, Birmingham Post, 1956–58; Dep. Financial Editor, Guardian, 1958–63; Dep. City Editor, Daily Telegraph, 1963; City Editor, Sunday Telegraph, 1963–66; City Editor, Daily Telegraph, 1966–77; Editor, Business News, Sunday Times, 1977–78; City Editor, Sunday Express, 1978–82; City Editor-in-Chief, Express Newspapers plc, 1982–83; Exec. Ed. (Finance and Industry), The Times, 1983–87. Dir, TVS Entertainment plc, 1990–93. Dir, Young Vic, 1976–83; Chm., Chichester Fest. Theatre, 1985–93 (Dir, 1984–). Wincott Award, 1974. *Publication:* The Influence of the Financial Press, 1983. *Recreations:* theatre, books, sport. *Address:* The Senate House, Canonbury Lane, N1 2AS. *T:* 0171–226 7950. *Clubs:* MCC, Lord's Taverners; Piltdown Golf.

FLEET, Stephen George, PhD; FInstP; Registrary, University of Cambridge, since 1983; Fellow, Downing College, Cambridge, since 1974 (Bursar, 1974–83; President, 1983–85; Vice Master, 1985–88, 1991–94); *b* 28 Sept. 1936; *er s* of late George Fleet and of Elsie Fleet, Lewes, Sussex. *Educ:* Brentwood Sch.; Lewes County Grammar Sch.; St John's Coll., Cambridge (Scholar; MA; PhD 1962). FInstP 1972. Res. Physicist, Mullard Res. Labs, Surrey, 1961–62; University of Cambridge: Demonstr in Mineralogy, 1962–67; Lectr in Mineralogy, 1967–83; Fellow, Fitzwilliam House, 1963–66; Fellow, Fitzwilliam Coll., 1966–73 (Jun. Bursar, 1967–73; Dir of Studies in Physical Sciences, 1971–74); Mem., Council of Senate, 1975–82; Mem., Financial Bd, 1979–83; Chm., Bd of Exams, 1974–83; Chm., Bursars' Cttee, 1980–83; President: Fitzwilliam Soc., 1977; Downing Assoc., 1991. Member: Finance Cttee, Internat. Union of Crystallography, 1987–; Jt Negotiating Cttee, Universities Superannuation Scheme, 1992–. Trustee: Mineralogical Soc. of GB, 1977–87; Foundn of Edward Storey, 1976– (Chm., 1984–88); Treasurer: Cambridge Commonwealth Trust, 1983–; Cambridge Overseas Trust, 1988–; Mem., Cttee of Management, Charities Property Unit Trust, 1983–88. *Publications:* res. pubns in scientific jls. *Recreations:* books, music, history of Sussex. *Address:* Downing College, Cambridge CB2 1DQ. *T:* Cambridge (01223) 334843. *Clubs:* Athenæum, Royal Over-Seas League.

FLEETWOOD, Susan Maureen; actress; Hon. Associate Member, Royal Shakespeare Company, since 1988 (Associate Member, 1980–88); *b* 21 Sept. 1944; *d* of John Joseph Kells Fleetwood and Bridget Maureen (*née* Brereton), St Andrews, Scotland. *Educ:* sixteen schs, incl. Convent of the Nativity, Sittingbourne, Kent; RADA (Bancroft Gold Medal). Rosalind, in As You Like It, and Lady Macbeth, in Macbeth, tour, Arizona, USA, 1964; Founder Mem., Liverpool Everyman, 1965–67: Lady Percy, in Henry IV; Gwendolen, in The Importance of Being Earnest; Alison, in Look Back in Anger; Liz, in Fando and Liz; Margaret, in The Great God Brown; chorus leader, in Murder in the Cathedral; The Woman, in The Four Seasons; Lady Macbeth, in Macbeth; RSC, 1967–68: Regan, in King Lear; Marina/Thaisa, in Pericles; Julia, in The Two Gentlemen of Verona (tour); Beba, in Criminals; Amanda, in The Relapse; RSC, 1972: Portia, in The Merchant of Venice; chorus leader, in Murder in the Cathedral; The Bondwoman, in The Island of the Mighty; RSC, 1975–76: Katharina, in The Taming of the Shrew; Kaleria, in Summerfolk; Princess of France, in Love's Labour's Lost (also US tour); Imogen, in Cymbeline; National Theatre, 1976–78: Pegeen Mike, in Playboy of the Western World; Ophelia, in Hamlet; Jo, in Watch it Come Down; Zenocrate, in Tamburlaine the Great; Nora, in The Plough and the Stars; Clare, in Lavender Blue; Ismene, in The Woman; RSC, 1980–82: Rosalind, in As You Like It; Varya, in The Cherry Orchard; wife, in La Ronde; National Theatre, 1982–83: June Taylor, in Way Upstream; Titania, in A Midsummer Night's Dream; National Theatre, 1988–89: Laura, in The Father; RSC, 1990–91: Beatrice, in Much Ado About Nothing; Madame Arkadina, in The Seagull; Ella, in Curse of the Starving Class; other roles: Nina, in The Seagull, Cambridge Theatre Co., 1970; Ophelia, in Hamlet, Prospect Theatre Co., 1970–71; Clara, in I'm NOT Rappaport, Apollo, 1986; Kitty Twombley, in The Cabinet Minister, Royal Exchange, Manchester, 1988. Films include: Clash of the Titans; Heat and Dust; Young Sherlock Holmes; The Sacrifice; White Mischief; Dream Demons; The Krays; television serials and series include: Eustace and Hilda; The Good Soldier; Strangers and Brothers; Murder of a Moderate Man; Summer's Lease; Inspector Alleyn; The Buddha of Suburbia; Chandler and Co.; TV plays: Watercress Girl; Don't be Silly; Dangerous Corner; Flying in the Branches; Six Characters in Search of an Author; A Landing on the Sun; A Few Short Journeys of the Heart; Persuasion; many radio plays. *Recreations:* listening to music, going to the theatre, travelling, doing everything I can't do when working. *Address:* c/o ICM, Duncan Heath, Oxford House, 76 Oxford Street, W1R 1RB. *T:* 0171–636 6565.

FLEGG, Dr James John Maitland, FZS; FIHort; Director of Information Services, since 1987 and Head of Station, since 1990, Horticulture Research International, East Malling; *b* Hong Kong, 23 April 1937; *s* of Jack Sydney Flegg and Lily Elizabeth (*née* Spooner); *m* 1976, Caroline Louise Coles; two *s*. *Educ:* Melbourne, Australia; Gillingham Grammar Sch.; Imperial Coll. of Science and Technol. (BSc, PhD). ARCS 1962; FZS 1969; FIHort 1993. Nematologist, E Malling Res. Stn, 1956–66; MAFF, 1966–68; Dir, Brit. Trust for Ornithology, Tring, 1968–75; Hd, Zool. Dept, E Malling Res. Stn, 1976–87. Presenter, Country Ways, ITV, 1984–. Sec., European Soc. of Nematologists, 1965–68; Mem. Council, RSPB, 1978–83; Pres., Kent Ornithol Soc., 1986–. MBOU 1966. Chm. Council, Heart of Kent Hospice, 1992–. Chm., Romney Marsh Res. Trust, 1990–. Freeman, City of London; Liveryman, Co. of Fruiterers. *Publications:* books include: In Search of Birds, 1983; Oakwatch, 1985; Birdlife, 1986; Field Guide to the Birds of Britain and Europe, 1990; Poles Apart, 1991; Deserts, 1993; Classic Birds (60 Years of Bird Photography): a biography of Eric Hosking, 1993; numerous papers and articles on nematological, ornithological and envmtl topics. *Recreations:* wildlife, rural history, environmental affairs, photography, gardening, music, communication. *Address:* Horticulture Research International, E Malling, Kent ME19 6BJ. *T:* W Malling (01732) 843833; Divers Farm, E Sutton, Maidstone, Kent ME17 3DT.

FLEISCHMANN, Prof. Martin, FRS 1986; FRSC 1980; Research Professor, Department of Chemistry, University of Southampton, since 1983; *b* 29 March 1927; *s* of Hans Fleischmann and Margarethe Fleischmann (*née* Srb); *m* 1950, Sheila Flinn; one *s* two *d*. *Educ:* Worthing High School; Imperial College of Science and Technology. ARCS 1947; BSc 1948; PhD 1951. ICI Fellow, King's College, Univ. of Durham, 1952–57; Lectr, then Reader, Univ. of Newcastle upon Tyne, 1957–67; Electricity Council Faraday Prof. of Electrochemistry, Univ. of Southampton, 1967–77; Senior Fellowship, SERC, 1977–82. Pres., Internat. Soc. of Electrochemistry, 1970–72; Palladium Medal, US Electrochemical Soc., 1985. *Publications:* numerous papers and chapters in books. *Recreations:* ski-ing, walking, music, cooking. *Address:* Bury Lodge, Duck Street, Tisbury, Wilts SP3 6LJ. *T:* Tisbury (01747) 870384; 107 Impasse de Pierrefeu, 06560 Valbonne, France.

FLEMING, Ven. David; Chaplain-General to HM Prisons and Archdeacon of Prisons, since 1993; *b* 8 June 1937; *s* of John Frederick Fleming and Emma (*née* Casey); *m* 1966, Elizabeth Anne Marguerite Hughes; three *s* one *d*. *Educ:* Hunstanton County Primary School; King Edward VII Grammar School, King's Lynn; Kelham Theological Coll. National Service with Royal Norfolk Regt, 1956–58. Deacon 1963; Asst Curate, St Margaret, Walton on the Hill, Liverpool, 1963–67; priest 1964; attached to Sandringham group of churches, 1967–68; Vicar of Great Staughton, 1968–76; Chaplain of HM Borstal, Gaynes Hall, 1968–76; RD of St Neots, 1972–76; RD of March, 1977–82; Vicar of Whittlesey, 1976–85; Priest-in-Charge of Pondersbridge, 1983–85; Archdeacon of Wisbech, 1984–93; Vicar of Wisbech St Mary, 1985–88. Hon. Canon of Ely Cathedral, 1982–. Chm. of House of Clergy, Ely Diocesan Synod, 1982–85. *Recreations:* tennis, chess, extolling Hunstanton. *Address:* Fair Haven, 123 Wisbech Road, Littleport, Ely, Cambs CB6 1JJ; Prison Service Chaplaincy, Abell House, John Islip Street, SW1P 4LH. *T:* 0171–217 5683, *Fax:* 0171–217 5090. *Club:* Whittlesey Rotary.

FLEMING, Prof. Graham Richard, PhD; FRS 1994; Arthur Holly Compton Distinguished Service Professor, Department of Chemistry, University of Chicago, since 1987; *b* 3 Dec. 1949; *s* of Maurice Norman Henry Fleming and Lovima Ena Winter; *m* 1977, Jean McKenzie; one *s*. *Educ:* Bristol Univ. (BSc Hons); Royal Instn (PhD London). Res. Fellow, CIT, 1974–75; Univ. Res. Fellow, Univ. of Melbourne, 1975–76; Leverhulme Fellow, Royal Instn, 1977–79; Asst Prof., 1979–83, Associate Prof., 1983–85, Univ. of Chicago; Prof., Univ. of Chicago, 1985–87. Fellow, Amer. Acad. of Arts and Scis, 1991. *Publications:* Chemical Applications of Ultrafast Spectroscopy, 1986; numerous articles in learned jls. *Recreation:* mountaineering. *Address:* Department of Chemistry, University of Chicago, 5735 S Ellis Avenue, Chicago, IL 60637, USA. *T:* (312) 7027068; *Fax:* (312) 7020805. *Club:* Quadrangle (Chicago).

FLEMING, Grahame Ritchie; QC (Scot.) 1990; Sheriff of Lothian and Borders, since 1993; *b* 13 Feb. 1949; *s* of Ian Erskine Fleming and Helen Ritchie Wallace or Fleming; *m* 1984, Mopsa Dorcas Robbins; one *d*. *Educ:* Forfar Acad.; Univ. of Edinburgh (MA, LLB). Admitted Faculty of Advocates, 1976. Standing Jun. Counsel to Home Office in Scotland, 1986–89. *Recreations:* food, travel, supporting the Scottish Rugby team. *Address:* Sheriff's Chambers, Sheriff Court House, Court Square, Linlithgow EH49 7EQ.

FLEMING, Dr Ian, FRS 1993; Reader in Organic Chemistry, University of Cambridge, since 1986; Fellow of Pembroke College, Cambridge, since 1964; *b* 4 Aug. 1935; *s* of David Alexander Fleming and Olwen Lloyd Fleming (*née* Jones); *m* 1st, 1959, Joan Morrison Irving (marr. diss. 1962); 2nd, 1965, Mary Lord Bernard. *Educ:* Pembroke Coll., Cambridge (MA, PhD 1963; ScD 1982). Cambridge University: Res. Fellow, Pembroke Coll., 1962; Univ. Demonstrator, 1964–65; Asst Dir of Research, 1965–80; Univ. Lectr, 1980–86. *Publications:* (with D. H. Williams) Spectroscopic Methods in Organic Chemistry, 1966, 4th edn 1989; (with D. H. Williams) Spectroscopic Problems in Organic Chemistry, 1967; Selected Organic Syntheses, 1973; Frontier Orbitals and Organic Chemical Reactions, 1976; numerous papers in chem. jls. *Recreations:* watching movies, photography, reading, walking, music. *Address:* Pembroke College, Cambridge CB2 1RF. *T:* Cambridge (01223) 336372.

FLEMING, John, FRSL; writer; *b* 12 June 1919; *s* of Joseph Fleming and Elizabeth Stawart. *Educ:* Rugby Sch.; Trinity Coll., Cambridge (BA). FRSL 1963. Editor of Style & Civilisation, Art in Context, and, Architect and Society, for Penguin Books, 1964–. *Publications:* Robert Adam and his Circle in Edinburgh and Rome, 1962; (with Sir Nikolaus Pevsner and Hugh Honour) The Penguin Dictionary of Architecture, 1966, 4th rev. edn 1991; (with Hugh Honour) The Penguin Dictionary of Decorative Arts, 1977, rev. edn 1989; (with Hugh Honour) A World History of Art, 1982 (Mitchell Prize, 1982), 4th edn 1994 (US edn, The Visual Arts: a history); (with Hugh Honour) The Venetian Hours of Henry James, Whistler and Sargent, 1991. *Recreation:* gardening.

FLEMING, John Bryden; retired; *b* 23 June 1918; *s* of W. A. Fleming, advocate, and Maria MacLeod Bryden; *m* 1942, Janet Louise Guthrie (*d* 1981); one *s* three *d*. *Educ:* Edinburgh Academy; Univs of Edinburgh and London. MA Hons Geog. Edinburgh, BScEcon London. Army, 1940–46, RASC and REME. Planning Officer, Dept of Health for Scotland, 1946; Principal, 1956; Asst Sec., Scottish Devélt Dept, 1963, Under Sec., 1974–78; Sec., Scottish Special Housing Assoc., 1978–83. *Recreations:* gardening, hill walking. *Address:* 54 India Street, Edinburgh EH3 6HD. *T:* 0131–226 3917. *Club:* Commonwealth Trust.

FLEMING, John Marley; General Director, Marketing and Product Planning, Cadillac Motor Car Division, General Motors, since 1988; *b* 4 April 1930; *s* of David A. Fleming and Mary L. Fleming (*née* Marley); *m* 1961, Jeanne (*née* Retelle); one *s* two *d*. *Educ:* Harvard Coll., Cambridge, Mass, USA (BA); Harvard Business Sch., Boston, Mass (MBA). Lieut US Navy, 1952–55. Dist Manager, Frigidaire Sales Corp., 1957–63; Sales Promotion Manager, Ford Motor Co., 1963–68; Vice-Pres., J. Walter Thompson Co., 1969; Dir of Marketing, Oldsmobile Div., GMC, 1970–76; Dir of Sales, Adam Opel AG, West Germany, 1977–79; Dir of Commercial Vehicles, 1980–81, and Chm. and Man. Dir, 1982–85, Vauxhall Motors Ltd; Vice Pres., Sales, General Motors, Europe, 1986–87. *Recreations:* ski-ing, sailing, golf. *Address:* 4056 Augusta Court, Bloomfield Hills, MI 48302, USA. *Clubs:* Harpenden Golf; Detroit Yacht.

FLEMING, Raylton Arthur; freelance journalist specialising in international affairs, Mallorca, music and restaurants; Liaison Officer, United Nations University, World Institute for Development Economics Research, Helsinki, 1984–86; *b* 1925; *s* of Arthur and Evelyn Fleming; *m* 1967, Leila el Doweini; one *s*. *Educ:* Worksop Coll. Associate Producer, World Wide Pictures Ltd, 1952; Head of Overseas Television Production, Central Office of Information, 1957; Dep. Dir, Films/Television Div., COI, 1961; Asst Controller (Overseas) COI, 1968; Actg Controller (Overseas), 1969; Dir, Exhibns Div. COI, 1971; Controller (Home), COI, 1972–76; Controller (Overseas), COI, 1976–78; Dir of Inf., UN Univ., Japan, 1978–83; Dir, UN Univ. Liaison Office, NY, 1983–84. *Recreations:* music, opera. *Address:* Camino del Castillo, Alaro, Mallorca, Spain.

FLEMING, Robert, (Robin); DL; Chairman, Robert Fleming Holdings, since 1990; *b* 18 Sept. 1932; *s* of late Major Philip Fleming and Joan Cecil Fleming (*née* Hunloke); *m* 1962, Victoria Margaret Aykroyd; two *s* one *d*. *Educ:* Eton College; Royal Military Academy, Sandhurst. Served The Royal Scots Greys, 1952–58. Joined Robert Fleming, 1958; Director: Robert Fleming Trustee Co., 1961– (Chm., 1985–91); Robert Fleming Investment Trust, 1968–; Robert Fleming Holdings, 1974– (Dep. Chm., 1986–90). Chm., White Corries Ltd, 1966– (Dir, 1965–). High Sheriff, 1980, DL 1990, Oxfordshire. *Recreations:* most country pursuits, esp. stalking and fishing; most types of music, esp. Scottish traditional. *Address:* Church Farm, Steeple Barton, Bicester, Oxon OX6 3QR. *T:* Bicester (01869) 347177; Black Mount, Bridge of Orchy, Argyll PA36 4AH. *T:* Tyndrum (01838) 400237.

FLEMMING, John Stanton, FBA 1991; Warden, Wadham College, Oxford, since 1993; *b* 6 Feb. 1941; *s* of Sir Gilbert Nicolson Flemming, KCB, and late Virginia Coit; *m* 1963, Jean Elizabeth (*née* Briggs); three *s* one *d*. *Educ:* Rugby Sch.; Trinity Coll., Oxford (Hon. Fellow, 1994); Nuffield Coll., Oxford. BA Oxon 1962, MA 1966. Lecturer and Fellow, Oriel Coll., Oxford, 1963–65 (Hon. Fellow, 1993); Official Fellow in Economics, 1965–80, Emeritus Fellow, 1980, and Bursar, 1970–79, Nuffield Coll., Oxford. Bank of England: Chief Adviser, 1980–84; Economic Adviser to the Governor, 1984–88; Exec. Dir, 1988–91; Chief Economist, EBRD, 1991–93. Member: Nat. Freight Corp., 1978–80; Council, Royal Economic Soc., 1980– (Treas., 1993–); Adv. Bd on Research Councils, 1986–91; Chm., Economic Affairs Cttee, SSRC, 1981–84. British Academy: Mem. Council, 1993–; Vice Pres., 1994–95; Hon. Treas., 1995–. Associate Editor: Oxford Economic Papers, 1970–73; Review of Economic Studies, 1973–76; Editor, Economic Jl, 1976–80. *Publications:* Inflation, 1976; contrib. economic jls. *Address:* Wadham College, Oxford OX1 3PN.

FLESCH, Michael Charles, QC 1983; *b* 11 March 1940; *s* of Carl and late Ruth Flesch; *m* 1972, Gail Schrire; one *s* one *d*. *Educ:* Gordonstoun Sch.; University College London (LLB 1st Cl. Hons). Called to the Bar, Gray's Inn, 1963 (Lord Justice Holker Sen. Schol.), Bencher, 1993. Bigelow Teaching Fellow, Univ. of Chicago, 1963–64; Lectr (part-time) in Revenue Law, University Coll. London, 1965–82. Practice at Revenue Bar, 1966–. Chairman: Taxation and Retirement Benefits Cttee, Bar Council, 1985–93; Revenue Bar Assoc., 1993–. Governor of Gordonstoun Sch., 1976–. *Publications:* various articles, notes and reviews concerning taxation, in legal periodicals. *Recreation:* all forms of sport. *Address:* (home) 38 Farm Avenue, NW2 2BH. *T:* 0181–452 4547; (chambers) Gray's Inn Chambers, Gray's Inn, WC1R 5JA. *T:* 0171–242 2642, *Fax:* 0171–831 9017. *Clubs:* MCC, Arsenal FC, Brondesbury Lawn Tennis and Cricket.

FLESHER, Timothy James; Grade 3, Immigration and Nationality Department, Home Office, and Chief Inspector, Immigration Service, since 1994; *b* 25 July 1949; *s* of James Amos Flesher and Evelyn May Flesher (*née* Hale); *m* 1986, Margaret McCormack; one *d*. *Educ:* Hertford Coll., Oxford (BA). Lectr, Cambridge Coll. of Arts and Technol., 1972–74; Admin Trainee/HEO, Home Office, 1974–79; Sec. to Prisons Bd, 1979–82; Private Sec. to Prime Minister, 1982–86; Home Office: Head of: After Entry and Refugee Div., 1986–89; Personnel Div., 1989–91; Probation Service Div., 1991–92; Dir of Admin, OFSTED, 1992–94. *Recreations:* psephology, child care. *Address:* Lunar House, 40 Wellesley Road, Croydon, Surrey CR9 2BY. *T:* 0181–760 2907.

FLETCHER; *see* Aubrey-Fletcher.

FLETCHER, Alan Gerard, RDI 1972; FCSD; designer; Founding Partner, Pentagram Design; *b* Nairobi, Kenya, 27 Sept. 1931; *s* of Bernard Fletcher and Dorothy Murphy; *m* 1956, Paola Biagi; one *d*. *Educ:* Christ's Hosp. Sch.; Central Sch. of Arts and Crafts; Royal Coll. of Art (ARCA); Sch. of Architecture and Design, Yale Univ. (Master of Fine Arts). FSIAD 1964. Designer, Fortune Magazine, New York, 1958–59; freelance practice, London, 1959–62; Partner: Fletcher Forbes Gill, 1962–65; Crosby Fletcher Forbes, 1965–72; Partner, Pentagram, 1972–92; own freelance practice, 1993. Pres., Designers and Art Dirs Assoc., 1973; Internat. Pres., Alliance Graphique Internat., 1982–85. Sen. Fellow, RCA, 1989. Designers and Art Dirs Assoc. Gold Award for Design, 1974, and President's Award for Outstanding Contribn to Design, 1977; One Show Gold Award for Design, New York, 1974; Design Medal, SIAD, 1983; Prince Philip Prize for Designer of the Year, 1993. *Publications:* (jtly) Graphic Design: a visual comparison, 1963; (jtly) A Sign Systems Manual, 1970; (jtly) Identity Kits, 1971; (jtly) Living by Design, 1978; (jtly) Ideas on Design, 1987; (jtly) Pentagram, The Compendium, 1993; Beware Wet Paint, 1995; (also illus.) Was Ich Sah, 1967. *Address:* 12 Pembridge Mews, W11 3EQ. *T:* 0171–229 7095.

FLETCHER, Alan Philip; QC 1984; *b* 28 June 1914; *s* of late Philip Cawthorne Fletcher, MC and Edith Maud Fletcher; *m* 1945, Annette Grace Wright; three *s* one *d*. *Educ:* Marlborough College; Trinity College, Oxford. MA; hockey blue, 1936 and 1937. War service, Army, England and India, 1939–45, ending as acting Lt-Col; called to the Bar, Inner Temple, 1940; bencher; Junior Counsel, Inland Revenue (Rating Valuation), 1969–84; Leader, Barnet London Borough Council, 1965–73. *Recreations:* walking, golf, architectural and garden history. *Address:* 26 Hollies Close, Royston, Herts SG8 7DZ. *T:* Royston (01763) 248580.

See also P. J. Fletcher, R. A. Fletcher.

FLETCHER, Ann Elizabeth Mary, (Mrs Michael Fletcher); *see* Leslie, A. E. M.

FLETCHER, Dr Archibald Peter; Medical Director, IMS International; Director, PMS International; Partner in Documenta Biomedica; *b* 24 Dec. 1930; *s* of Walter Archibald Fletcher and Dorothy Mabel Fletcher; *m* 1972, Patricia Elizabeth Samson (*née* Marr); three *s* two *d*. *Educ:* Kingswood Sch.; London Hosp. Med. Coll.; St Mary's Hosp. Med. Sch., London Univ. MB, BS; PhD (Biochemistry). Sen. Lectr in Chemical Pathology, St Mary's Hosp., London, 1961–69; Head of Biochemistry, American Nat. Red Cross, USA, 1970–73; Med. Dir, Upjohn, Scandinavia; PMO, Medicines Div., DHSS, 1977; Med. Assessor to Cttee on Safety of Medicines; Chief Sci. Officer and SPMO, DHSS, 1978–79; Res. Physician, Upjohn International Inc., Brussels, 1979. *Publications:* numerous papers in scientific and medical journals on glycoproteins, physical chemistry, metabolism of blood cells and safety evaluation of new drugs. *Recreations:* gardening, golf. *Address:* Hall Corner Cottage, Little Maplestead, Halstead, Essex CO9 2RU. *T:* Halstead (01787) 475465. *Clubs:* Wig and Pen, Royal Society of Medicine.

FLETCHER, Augustus James Voisey, OBE 1977; GM 1957; HM Diplomatic Service, retired; Foreign and Commonwealth Office, 1982–89; *b* 23 Dec. 1928; *s* of James Fletcher and Naomi Fletcher (*née* Dudden); *m* 1956, Enyd Gwynne Harries; one *s* one *d*. *Educ:* Weston-super-Mare Grammar Sch.; Oriental Language Institute, Malaya. Colonial Service, Palestine, 1946–48, Malaya, 1948–58; Min. of Defence, 1958–64; FCO, 1964–: Hong Kong (seconded HQ Land Forces), 1966–70; FCO, 1970–73; Hong Kong, 1973–76; FCO, 1976–79; Counsellor, New Delhi, 1979–82. *Recreations:* trout fishing, walking, food/wine, theatre. *Club:* Travellers'.

FLETCHER, Charles Montague, CBE 1952; MD, FRCP, FFPHM; Physician to Hammersmith Hospital, 1952–76; Professor of Clinical Epidemiology, University of London at Royal Postgraduate Medical School, 1973–76 (Reader, 1952–73), now Professor Emeritus; *b* 5 June 1911; *s* of late Sir Walter Morley Fletcher, FRS and late Mary Frances Fletcher (*née* Cropper); *m* Louisa Mary Sylvia Seely, *d* of 1st Baron Mottistone; one *s* two *d*. *Educ:* Eton Coll.; Trinity Coll., Cambridge (Sen. Schol.; rowed in Univ. Boat, 1933); St Bartholomew's Hospital. MA 1936, MD 1945, Cantab; MRCP 1942; FRCP 1947; FFPHM (FFCM 1974). Michael Foster Research Student, Trinity Coll., 1934–36; Nuffield Res. Student, Oxford, 1940–42. Asst Phys., EMS, 1943–44; Dir, MRC Pneumoconiosis Res. Unit, 1945–52; Sec., MRC Cttee on Bronchitis Res., 1954–76. Royal Coll. of Physicians: Mem. Council, 1959–62; 2nd Vice Pres., 1975; Sec., Cttee on Smoking and Health, 1961–71; Goulstonian Lectr, 1947; Bissett Hawkins Gold Medal, 1969. WHO Consultant: Pulmonary Heart Disease, 1960; Chronic Bronchitis, 1962; Smoking and Health, 1970. Mem., Central Health Services Council and Standing Med. Adv. Cttee, 1966–76; Vice-Chm., Health Educn Council, 1967; Pres., ASH, 1979– (Chm., 1971–78); Member: Exec. Cttee, Asthma Soc., 1980–89; Council, British Diabetic Assoc., 1983–88 (Chm., Educn Sect., 1983–88); Wkg Party on Prolonging Life and Assisting Death, Inst. of Med. Ethics, 1989–93. Introd. many TV med. programmes incl. Hurt Mind, 1955, Your Life in Their Hands, 1958–65, Television Doctor, 1969–70. Consulting Ed. Jl of Med. Ethics, 1975–81. *Publications:* Communication in Medicine, 1973; Natural History of Chronic Bronchitis and Emphysema, 1976; many papers on: first use of penicillin, 1941; dust disease of lungs, 1946–55; bronchitis and emphysema, 1952–76. *Recreations:* music, gardening. *Address:* 24 West Square, SE11 4SN. *T:* 0171–735 8753; 2 Coastguard Cottages, Newtown, IoW PO30 4PA. *T:* Calbourne (01983) 531321. *Club:* Brooks's.

FLETCHER, David Edwin, MBE 1986; Executive Director, Transpennine Campaign, since 1988; environmental consultant and regional development specialist; *b* 15 July 1933; *s* of Edwin and Winifred Fletcher; marr. diss. 1990; two *d*. *Educ:* Hebden Bridge Grammar Sch.; Calder High Sch.; Sheffield Univ. (BSc Jt Hons); Leeds Univ. (PGCE); Bradford Univ. (MSc). Schoolmaster and Head of Biology, Bingley GS, 1957–60, Calder High Sch., 1960–69; Manchester Polytechnic: Sen. Lectr, 1970–74; Principal Lectr, 1974–80; Head, Envmt and Geographical Dept, 1980–88. Mem., Hebden Royd UDC, 1967–74 (Chm., Planning Cttee, 1969–74). Founder Chairman: Calder Civic Trust, 1965–75; Pennine Heritage Envmtl Trust, 1979–; Dir, Adv. Services, Civic Trust NW, 1970–76. Commissioner: Countryside Commn, 1988–; Rural Develt Commn, 1993–. Mem., NW Council for Sport and Recreation, 1972–78. *Publications:* ASK – Amenity, Society Knowhow, 1976; Industry Tourism, 1988; England's North West: a strategic vision for a European region, 1992; research and consultancy reports; contribs to acad. jls; environmental pamphlets. *Recreations:* walking, ski-ing, travel, meeting interesting people in interesting situations, restoring and finding new uses for wonderful old mills in the Pennines. *Address:* c/o Transpennine, Birchcliffe, Hebden Bridge, W Yorks HX7 8DG. *T:* Hebden Bridge (01422) 844450.

FLETCHER, Geoffrey Scowcroft; artist and author; *o s* of Herbert Fletcher and Annie Talence Fletcher; *m* Mary Jean Timothy. *Educ:* University Coll., London Univ. (Dip. in Fine Art). Abbey Major Schol., British Sch. at Rome, 1948. Drawings appeared in Manchester Guardian, 1950; London drawings and articles featured in The Daily Telegraph, 1958–. Author of television features on unusual aspects of London; has been instrumental in saving a number of metropolitan buildings from demolition. Drawings and paintings in various public and private collections in England and abroad, including: exhibn of paintings and drawings in possession of Islington Council, 1972, 1978; exhibns of drawings and paintings, 1981, 1986, Lancashire industrial drawings and paintings, 1992–93, Bolton Art Gall.; drawings and sketchbooks acquired by British Museum, 1990; oil paintings and sketchbooks acquired by Guildhall Art Gall., 1990–91; drawings and sketchbooks acquired by Ashmolean Mus., 1991–92; oil paintings and drawings acquired by Bury Art Gall., 1993–94. Geoffrey Fletcher Room, decorated with the artist's drawings, opened Selfridge Hotel, London, 1973. Designed enamel box for St Paul's Cathedral Appeal, 1972; exhibitions of drawings: Miles Gall., St James's, 1980; East End Drawings and Paintings, Limehouse, 1984; London drawings, Guildhall, City of London, 1988; Genoese drawings, for City of Genoa promotion, London, 1988. *Publications:* The London Nobody Knows (filmed, 1968), 1962, 2nd edn 1989; Down Among the Meths Men, 1966; Geoffrey Fletcher's London, 1968; City Sights, 1963; Pearly Kingdom, 1965; London's River, 1966; Elements of Sketching, 1966 (Amer. edn, 1968); London's Pavement Pounders, 1967; London After Dark, 1969; Changing London (Drawings from The Daily Telegraph), 1969; The London Dickens Knew, 1970; London Souvenirs, 1973; Paint It In Water Colour, 1974; Italian Impressions, 1974; Sketch It In Black and White, 1975; London: a private view, 1989; The Spitalfields Prints, 1990; Daily Telegraph Series: London Prints, 1975, London Colour Prints, 1978, London Portraits, 1978, London at My Feet, 1979; London Alleys, 1980. *Address:* c/o Cassell plc, Villiers House, 41–47 Strand, WC2N 5JE; c/o R. Davis-Poynter, 118 St Pancras, Chichester, W Sussex.

FLETCHER, Hugh Alasdair; Chief Executive Officer, Fletcher Challenge Ltd, since 1987; *b* 28 Nov. 1947; *s* of Sir James Muir Cameron Fletcher, *qv*; *m* 1970, Sian Seerpoohi Elias, QC (NZ); two *s*. *Educ:* Auckland Univ. (MCom Hons, BSc); Stanford Univ., USA (MBA 1972). Fletcher Holdings: Asst to Ops Res., 1969–70; PA to Man. Dir, 1972–76; Dep. Man Dir, 1976–79; Chief Exec. Officer, 1979–81; Man. Dir, Fletcher Challenge Ltd, 1981–87. Non-exec. Chm., Air New Zealand Ltd, 1985–89. Member: Prime Minister's Enterprise Council, 1992–; Business Council for Sustainable Develt, Geneva, 1993–. *Recreations:* horse riding, horse breeding and racing, chess, Go. *Address:* Fletcher Challenge Ltd, Private Bag 92114, Auckland, New Zealand. *T:* (649) 5259000, *Fax:* (649) 5259033.

FLETCHER, Sir James Muir Cameron, Kt 1980; FCA; Managing Director, 1942–79, Chairman, 1972–80, Fletcher Holdings Ltd; *b* Dunedin, NZ, 25 Dec. 1914; *s* of Sir James Fletcher; *m* 1942, Margery Vaughan, *d* of H. H. Gunthorp; three *s*. *Educ:* Waitaki Boys' High School; Auckland Grammar School. South British Insurance Co., 1931–37; then Fletcher Construction Co. and Fletcher Holdings; Pres. and Dir, Fletcher Challenge Ltd, 1981–90. *Address:* Fletcher Challenge Ltd, Private Bag, Auckland, New Zealand; 119 St Stephens Avenue, Parnell, Auckland, NZ.

See also H. A. Fletcher.

FLETCHER, Major John Antony, MBE (mil.) 1953; RA retired; Secretary, Institute of Road Transport Engineers, 1963–85; *b* 4 May 1918; *s* of Alexander Ernest Fletcher and Abbie (*née* Wheeler); *m* 1st, 1951, Elizabeth Cross (marr. diss. 1979); one *s* three *d*; 2nd, 1980, Susan Mary Brown. *Educ:* Cheltenham Coll. Jun. Sch.; Abingdon Sch.; RMA, Woolwich; Army and RAF Staff Colls (psc, pac). 2nd Lieut, RA, 1938; war service,

Malta, Middle East, Malaya and Burma; Korea Commonwealth Div.; retired 1960. Secretariat, Powell Duffryn Gp, 1960–63. Chm., Assoc. of Care-Takers and Care-Seekers, 1985–88. Hon. FIRTE 1985. *Publications:* article in Gunner Jl; eight letters (out of twelve!) to The Times. *Recreations:* being ex!: ex-playing mem., MCC; ex-Stragglers of Asia; ex-United Hunts Club; ex-Sherringham and many other golf clubs. *Address:* Milford Cottage, 10 Cudnall Street, Charlton Kings, Cheltenham, Glos GL53 8HT. *T:* Cheltenham (01242) 522367.

FLETCHER, John Edwin; His Honour Judge Fletcher; a Circuit Judge, since 1986; *b* 23 Feb. 1941; *s* of late Sydney Gerald Fletcher and Cecilia Lane Fletcher. *Educ:* St Bees Sch., Cumbria; Clare Coll., Cambridge (MA). Called to the Bar, Inner Temple, 1964; Midland and Oxford Circuit, 1965–86; a Recorder, 1983–86. Mem. Panel of Chairmen, Medical Appeal Tribunals, 1981–86. *Recreations:* enjoying life and friends, walking towards Santiago de Compostela.

FLETCHER, Leslie; General Manager (Chief Executive Officer) Williams Deacon's Bank Ltd, 1964–70, Director, 1966–70, retired; *b* 30 Jan. 1906; *s* of late Edward Henry and Edith Howard Fletcher; *m* 1934, Helen, *d* of Frank Turton; one *s* one *d*. *Educ:* City Gram. Sch., Chester; Manchester Univ. (BA Com). Entered Williams Deacon's Bank Ltd 1922; Asst Gen. Man., 1957; Dep. Gen. Man., 1961. Fellow and Mem. Council, Inst. of Bankers. *Recreations:* lawn tennis, golf. *Address:* Axon View, 13 Honey Lane, Burley, near Ringwood, Hants BH24 4EN. *T:* Burley (01425) 403723.

FLETCHER, Sir Leslie, Kt 1983; DSC 1945; FCA; Deputy Chairman, RMC Group, since 1991 (Director, since 1983); *b* 14 Oct. 1922; *s* of Ernest and Lily Fletcher; *m* 1947, Audrey Faviell Jackson; one *s* one *d*. *Educ:* Nether Edge Secondary Sch., Sheffield. FCA 1952. Served War, RNVR (FAA), 1942–46 (Lieut). Helbert Wagg & Co. Ltd (subseq. J. Henry Schroder Wagg & Co. Ltd), 1955–71, Dir 1966–71; Chm., Glynwed Internat., 1971–86; Dep. Chm., Standard Chartered PLC, 1983–89 (Dir, 1972–89); Chairman: Westland Group, 1989–94; Rank Orgn, 1992–95 (Dir, 1984–95). Mem. Council, CBI, 1976–86. *Recreations:* gardening, golf, photography. *Address:* 32 Chesham Place, SW1X 8HB. *Clubs:* Brooks's, MCC, Royal Automobile; Royal & Ancient Golf (St Andrews).

FLETCHER, Malcolm Stanley, MBE 1982; FEng 1993; FICE, FGS; Chairman, Sir William Halcrow & Partners Ltd, Consulting Civil Engineers, since 1990; *b* 25 Feb. 1936; *s* of Harold and Clarice Fletcher; *m* 1965, Rhona Christina Wood; one *s* two *d*. *Educ:* Manchester Grammar Sch.; Manchester Univ. (MSc); Imperial Coll., London (DIC). FICE 1976; FGS 1968. Pupil, Binnie & Partners, 1957–60; Sir William Halcrow & Partners, 1968–: Partner, 1985–. Resident Engineer: Jhelum Bridge, Pakistan, 1965–67; Guiliana Bridge, Libya, 1968–74; Design Team Leader, Orwell Bridge, Ipswich, 1976–82; Dir of Design, Second Severn Crossing, 1988–; Adviser: Dartford River Crossing, 1985–90; Lantau Fixed Crossing, Hong Kong, 1990. *Recreations:* cycling. *Address:* Burderop Park, Swindon, Wilts SN4 0QD. *T:* Swindon (01793) 812479.

FLETCHER, Comdt Marjorie Helen (Kelsey), CBE 1988; Director, Women's Royal Naval Service, 1986–88; *b* 21 Sept. 1932; *d* of late Norman Farler Fletcher and Marie Amelie Fletcher (*née* Adams). *Educ:* Avondale High Sch.; Sutton Coldfield High Sch. for Girls. Solicitor's Clerk, 1948–53; joined WRNS as Telegraphist, 1953; progressively, 3rd Officer to Chief Officer, 1956–76; Supt, 1981; served in Secretariat, Careers Advisor, Intelligence and Staff appts; ndc 1979; Directing Staff, RN Staff Coll., 1980–81; psc 1981; Internat. Mil. Staff, NATO HQ, 1981–84; Asst Dir, Dir Naval Staff Duties, 1984–85. ADC to the Queen, 1986–88. *Publication:* The WRNS, 1989. *Recreations:* reading, needlework, entertaining, cookery, gardening, collecting paintings.

FLETCHER, Neil; management consultant; *b* 5 May 1944; *s* of Alan and Ruth Fletcher; *m* 1967, Margaret Monaghan; two *s*. *Educ:* Wyggeston Sch., Leicester; City of Leeds Coll. of Educn (Teachers' Cert.), London Univ. (BA Hons); London Business Sch. (MBA 1994). Charter FCP 1990. Schoolteacher, 1966–68; Lectr, 1969–76; Admin. Officer, 1976–91, Educn Officer, 1991–93, NALGO; Educn Officer, UNISON, 1993–94. Member: Camden Bor. Council, 1978–86 (Dep. Leader, 1982–84); ILEA, 1979–90 (Chair, Further and Higher Educn Sub-Cttee, 1981–87; Leader, 1987–90); Chair: Council of Local Educn Authorities, 1987–88, 1989–90; Educn Cttee, AMA, 1987–90 (Vice-Chair, 1986–87). Governor: London Inst., 1986–; LSE, 1990–. FRSA 1989. *Recreations:* cricket, soccer, theatre, cookery, walking. *Address:* 42 Narcissus Road, NW6 1TH. *T:* 0171–435 5306.

FLETCHER, Paul Thomas, CBE 1959; FEng; Deputy President, British Standards Institution, 1982–89 (Chairman, 1979–82); Consulting Engineer: NNC Ltd, since 1977; BGE Co., Tokyo, since 1986; *b* 30 Sept. 1912; *s* of Stephen Baldwin Fletcher and Jessie Carrie; *m* 1941, Mary Elizabeth King; three *s*. *Educ:* Nicholson Inst., Stornaway, Isle of Lewis; Maidstone Grammar Sch.; Medway Techn. Coll. BSc(Eng); FEng, FICE, FIMechE (Hon. FIMechE 1989), FIEE. Served 3–year apprenticeship with E. A. Gardner & Sons Ltd, Maidstone, remaining for 7 years; joined Min. of Works, 1939, initially in Test Br. of Engrg Div., later with responsibility for variety of engrg services in public bldgs and Govt factories and for plant and equipment for Govt civilian and service res. estabts; Chief Mech. and Elec. Engr, 1951. On formation of UKAEA in 1954, became Dep. Dir of Engrg in Industrial Gp, later Engrg Dir and Dep. Man. Dir; Dir, United Power Co., 1961; Man. Dir, GEC (Process Engrg) Ltd, 1965; Man. Dir, 1971–76, Dep. Chm., 1976–84, Atomic Power Constructions Ltd. Chm., Pressure Vessels Quality Assurance Bd, 1977–84. President: IMechE, 1975–76; ITEME, 1979–81, 1985–88; IMechIE, 1994–. *Publications:* papers to IMechE. *Recreations:* photography, motoring. *Address:* 26 Foxgrove Avenue, Beckenham, Kent BR3 2BA. *T:* 0181–650 5563.

FLETCHER, Air Chief Marshal Sir Peter Carteret, KCB 1968 (CB 1965); OBE 1945; DFC 1943; AFC 1952; FRAeS; aerospace consultant, since 1983; Director, Corporate Strategy and Planning, British Aerospace, 1977–82, retired; Director, Airbus Industry Supervisory Board, 1979–82; *b* 7 Oct. 1916; *s* of F. T. W. Fletcher, Oxford (sometime tobacco farmer, Southern Rhodesia), and Dora Clulee, New Zealand; *m* 1940, Marjorie Isobel Kotze; two *d*. *Educ:* St George's Coll., Southern Rhodesia; Rhodes Univ., S Africa. SR Law Dept, 1937. Served War of 1939–45: SR Air Force, 1939; trans. to RAF, 1941; commanded 135 and 258 Fighter Sqdns and RAF Station Belvedere. Directing Staffs at: RAF Staff Coll., 1945–46; Jt Services Staff Coll., 1946–48; Imp. Defence Coll., 1956–58; Mem. Jt Planning Staff, 1951–53; comdg RAF Abingdon, 1958–60; Dep. Dir Jt Planning Staff, 1960–61; Dir of Opl Requirements (B), Air Min., 1961–63; Asst Chief of Air Staff (Policy and Plans), 1964–66; AOC, No 38 Group, Transport Command, 1966–67; VCAS, 1967–70; Controller of Aircraft, Min. of Aviation Supply (formerly Min. of Technology), 1970–71; Air Systems Controller, Defence Procurement Executive, MoD, 1971–73; Dir, Hawker Siddeley Aviation Ltd, 1974–77. FRAeS 1986. *Recreations:* books, travel. *Address:* 85A Campden Hill Court, Holland Street, Kensington, W8 7HW. *T:* 0171–937 1982.

FLETCHER, Philip John; Deputy Secretary, Cities and Countryside Group, Department of the Environment, since 1994; *b* 2 May 1946; *s* of Alan Philip Fletcher, *qv*; *m* 1977, Margaret Anne Boys; one *d* (and one *d* decd). *Educ:* Marlborough College; Trinity College, Oxford (MA). Asst Principal, MPBW, 1968; Department of the Environment: Private Sec. to Permanent Sec., 1978; Asst Sec., Private Sector Housebuilding, 1980, local govt expenditure, 1982–85; Under Secretary: Housing, Water and Central Finance, 1986–90; Planning and Develt Control, 1990–93; Chief Exec., PSA Services, 1993–94, and Dep. Sec., Property Holdings, 1994. *Recreations:* Reader, Church of England; walking. *Address:* Department of the Environment, 2 Marsham Street, SW1P 3EB. *T:* 0171–276 3259, *Fax:* 0171–276 0625.

FLETCHER, Robin Anthony, OBE 1984; DSC 1944; DPhil; Warden of Rhodes House, Oxford, 1980–89; Professorial Fellow, Trinity College, Oxford, 1980–89, now Emeritus; *b* 30 May 1922; *s* of Philip Cawthorne Fletcher, MC, and Edith Maud Fletcher (*née* Okell); *m* 1950, Jinny May (*née* Cornish); two *s*. *Educ:* Marlborough Coll.; Trinity Coll., Oxford (MA, DPhil). Served Royal Navy (Lieut RNVR), 1941–46. University Lecturer in Modern Greek, 1949–79; Domestic Bursar, Trinity Coll., Oxford, 1950–74; Senior Proctor, 1966–67; Member, Hebdomedal Council, 1967–74. Represented England at hockey, 1949–55 and GB, 1952 Olympic Games (Bronze Medal). *Publications:* Kostes Palamas, Athens, 1984; various articles. *Recreations:* sport, music. *Address:* Binglea, Quoyloo, Stromness, Orkney KW16 3LU. *Clubs:* Naval; Vincent's (Oxford).

See also A. P. Fletcher.

FLETCHER, Prof. Ronald Stanley; FRAeS; Professor of Thermal Power, since 1972, and Deputy Vice-Chancellor, since 1994, Cranfield University (formerly Cranfield Institute of Technology); *b* 12 Dec. 1937; *s* of Reginald and Dorothy Fletcher; *m* 1965, Pamela Alys, *d* of Gwilym and Alys Treharne; one *s* twin *d*. *Educ:* Imperial College, London Univ. (PhD, DIC); UMIST (BSc Tech). FRAeS 1994. Senior Engineer, Northern Research & Engineering Corp., Cambridge, USA, 1965–70; Consultant, Northern Research & Engineering Corp., Herts, 1970–72; Cranfield Institute of Technology: Head of Mechanical Engineering, 1977–87; Dean of Engineering, 1982–85; Pro-Vice-Chancellor, 1985–93; Head of Cranfield Campus, 1989–94. Visiting Professor: Cairo, 1975; Brazil, 1977; China (Beijing Inst. of Aero. and Astro.), 1979. Member: ARC, 1974–77; Governing Body, AFRC Inst. of Engrg Res. (formerly Nat. Inst. of Agricl Engrg), 1978– (Chm., Finance Cttee, 1982–86); Council, British Hydro. Res. Assoc., 1979–89; AGARD (NATO) Propulsion and Energetics Panel, 1980–; Scientific Bd, Univ. de Technologie de Compiègne, 1989–; Conseil Scientifique, Inst. Méditerranéen de Technologie, 1989–. Governor, Bedford Modern Sch., 1986–89. Médaille Gustave Trasenter, Liège, 1990; Prix Formation Etranger, Acad. Nat. de l'Air et de l'Espace, France, 1991. Chevalier, Ordre des Palmes Académiques (France), 1990. *Publications:* papers on combustion. *Recreations:* sailing, music. *Address:* 34 Brecon Way, Bedford MK41 8DD. *T:* Bedford (01234) 358483. *Club:* Parkstone Yacht.

FLETCHER, Stuart Barron; Chief Executive, Pembrokeshire NHS Trust, since 1994; *b* 28 July 1945; *s* of Arthur Barron Fletcher and Bertha Fletcher; *m* 1970, Dilys Roberts; two *s* one *d*. *Educ:* King George V Grammar Sch., Southport; Oriel Coll., Oxford (MA). MHSM, DipHSM. Entered Health Service as Nat. Trainee Administrator, 1968; NHS posts include: Hosp. Sec., Broadgreen Hosp., Liverpool, 1972–74; Area Gen. Administrator, St Helens and Knowsley HA, 1974–78; Dist Administrator, E Birmingham HA, 1978–82; Chief Exec., N Staffs HA, 1982–91; Regl Man. Dir, subseq. Chief Exec., W Midlands RHA, 1992–93. Member: NHS Trng Authy, 1985–91; NHS Trng Adv. Bd, 1991–93. Pres., IHSM, 1991–92 (Mem., Nat. Council, 1981–). *Recreations:* Rugby, fell walking, photography, theatre. *Address:* Flat C, Sealyham Block, Withybush General Hospital, Haverfordwest, Pembrokeshire SA61 2PZ. *T:* Haverfordwest (01437) 773506.

FLETCHER-COOKE, Sir Charles (Fletcher), Kt 1981; QC 1958; *b* 5 May 1914; *yr s* of late Capt. C. A. and Gwendolen May Fletcher-Cooke; *m* 1959, Diana Lady Avebury (whom he divorced, 1967; she *d* 1993), *d* of late Capt. Edward King and of Mrs J. St Vincent Hand; no surv. *c*. *Educ:* Malvern Coll. (Scholar); Peterhouse, Cambridge (Schol., MA 1940). FCIArb 1981. Pres., Cambridge Union, 1936; Editor, The Granta, 1936. Called to Bar through Lincoln's Inn, 1938 (1st Class Hons, Bar Final Examination; Studentship and Certificate of Honour), Bencher 1969. Mem. Senate, Four Inns of Court, 1970–74. Served War of 1939–45, in Naval Intelligence Div. and on Joint Intelligence Staff, with rank of Lieut-Comdr, RNVR. MP (C) Darwen, Lancs, 1951–83; Joint Parly Under-Sec. of State, Home Office, 1961–63; Chm., Select Cttee on Parly Comr for Admin, 1974–77. Legal Adviser to British Delegation, Danube Conf., Belgrade, 1948; Deleg. to Consultative Assembly of Council of Europe, 1954–55; Mem., European Parlt, 1977–79. Mem., Statute Law Cttee, 1955–61, 1970–83. Dato SPMB, Brunei, 1978. *Publications:* (with others) The Rule of Law; (with M. J. Albery) Monopolies and Restrictive Trade Practices. *Recreation:* fishing. *Address:* The Red House, Clifton Hampden, Oxon OX14 3EW. *T:* Clifton Hampden (01865) 407754. *Clubs:* Garrick, Pratt's.

FLETCHER-VANE, family name of **Baron Inglewood.**

FLEW, Prof. Antony Garrard Newton; Emeritus Professor, University of Reading, since 1983; *b* 11 Feb. 1923; *o s* of Rev. Dr R. N. Flew; *m* 1952, Annis Ruth Harty; two *d*. *Educ:* St Faiths Sch., Cambridge; Kingswood Sch., Bath; Sch. of Oriental and African Studies, London; St John's Coll., Oxford (John Locke Schol., MA); DLitt Keele, 1974. Lecturer: Christ Church, Oxford, 1949–50; Univ. of Aberdeen, 1950–54; Professor of Philosophy: Univ. of Keele, 1954–71; Univ. of Calgary, 1972–73; Univ. of Reading, 1973–82; (part-time) York Univ., Toronto, 1983–85; Distinguished Res. Fellow (part-time), Social Philosophy and Policy Center, Bowling Green State Univ., Ohio, 1986–91. Many temp. vis. appts. Gavin David Young Lectr, Adelaide, 1963; Gifford Lectr, St Andrews, 1986. A Vice-Pres., Rationalist Press Assoc., 1973–88; Chm., Voluntary Euthanasia Soc., 1976–79. Fellow, Acad. of Humanism, 1983–. *Publications:* A New Approach to Psychical Research, 1953; Hume's Philosophy of Belief, 1961; God and Philosophy, 1966; Evolutionary Ethics, 1967; An Introduction to Western Philosophy, 1971; Crime or Disease?, 1973; Thinking About Thinking, 1975; The Presumption of Atheism, 1976; Sociology, Equality and Education, 1976; A Rational Animal, 1978; Philosophy: an introduction, 1979; The Politics of Procrustes, 1981; Darwinian Evolution, 1984; Thinking About Social Thinking, 1985; Hume, Philosopher of Moral Science, 1986; (with G. Vesey) Agency and Necessity, 1987; The Logic of Mortality, 1987; Power to the Parents, 1987; Equality in Liberty and Justice, 1989; Atheistic Humanism, 1993; Shephard's Warning: setting schools back on course, 1994; articles in philosophical and other jls. *Recreations:* walking, climbing, house maintenance. *Address:* 26 Alexandra Road, Reading, Berks RG1 5PD. *T:* Reading (01734) 261848. *Club:* Union Society (Oxford).

FLINDALL, Jacqueline; JP; Non-Executive Director, Royal National Orthopaedic Hospital Trust, Stanmore, since 1991; *b* 12 Oct. 1932; *d* of Henry and Lilian Flindall. *Educ:* St Davids Sch., Ashford, Mddx; University Coll. Hosp., London (DipN). SRN, SCM, UCH, 1950–54; Midwifery, St Luke's Mat. Hosp., Guildford and Watford, 1955; exchange student, Mount Sinai Hosp., NY, 1956; Ward Sister and Clinical Teacher, UCH, 1957–63; Asst Matron, Wexham Park Hosp., 1964–66; Dep. Supt of Nursing, Prince of Wales and St Anne's, 1967–69; Chief Nursing Officer: Northwick Park Hosp., 1969–73; Oxfordshire HA, 1973–83; Regional Nursing Officer, Wessex RHA, 1983–85. Associate Consultant, PA Management Consultants, 1986–94. Mem., Hosp. Chaplaincies Council. Professional Organization Mem., RCN; Hon. FRCN 1983. Mem., Most Hon.

and Loyal Soc. of Ancient Britons. JP Oxford, 1982, Salisbury, 1987. *Publications:* contribs to nursing press. *Recreation:* painting. *Address:* 4 Mill Lane, Romsey, Hants, SO51 8EU. *T:* Romsey (01794) 513926.

FLINT, Prof. Anthony Patrick Fielding, PhD, DSc; FIBiol; Professor of Animal Physiology, Department of Physiology and Environmental Science, University of Nottingham, since 1993; *b* 31 Aug. 1943; *s* of Maurice Fielding Flint and Patricia Joan (*née* Ince); *m* 1967, Chan Mun Kwun; two *s*. *Educ:* Hill Crest Sch., Swanage; King's Sch., Bruton; Univ. of St Andrews (Queen's Coll., Dundee) (BSc 1966); Univ. of Bristol (PhD 1969; DSc 1984). FIBiol 1982. Res. Fellow, Univ. of Western Ontario, 1969–72; Sen. Res. Biochemist in Obs and Gyn., Welsh Nat. Sch. of Medicine, Cardiff, 1972–73; Lectr, Nuffield Dept of Obs and Gyn., Oxford Univ., 1973–77; Staff Mem., AFRC Inst. of Animal Physiology and Genetics Res., Cambridge, 1977–87; Dir of Science and Dir of Inst. of Zool., Zool Soc. of London, 1987–93. Special Lectr, 1985–87, Special Prof. in Molecular Biol., 1987–93, Univ. of Nottingham Sch. of Agric.; Visiting Professor: Dept of Biology, UCL, 1989–; Biosphere Scis Div., KCL, 1989–. Member: Cttee, Soc. for Study of Fertility, 1981–89 (Sec., 1985–89); Steering Cttee, WHO Task Force on Plants for Fertility Regulation, 1982–87 (Chm., 1985). Member: Council of Management, Journals of Reproduction and Fertility Ltd, 1981–87 (Mem. Exec. Cttee, 1983–87); Bd of Scientific Editors, Jl of Endocrinology, 1983–87. Medal, Soc. for Endocrinology, 1985. *Publications:* (ed jtly) Embryonic Diapause in Mammals, 1981; Reproduction in Domestic Ruminants, 1991; papers in physiol, endocrinol and biochemical jls. *Recreations:* playing Bach on the organ or cello, coasting in small ships. *Address:* Department of Physiology and Environmental Science, University of Nottingham, Sutton Bonington, Loughborough, Leics LE12 5RD.

FLINT, Charles John Raffles; QC 1995. *Educ:* Trinity College, Cambridge (BA 1973; MA 1980). Called to the Bar, Middle Temple, 1975; Junior Counsel to the Crown (Common Law), 1991–95. *Address:* 2 Hare Court, EC4Y 7BH.

FLINT, Prof. David, TD, MA, BL, CA; Professor of Accountancy, 1964–85, (Johnstone Smith Chair, 1964–75), and Vice-Principal, 1981–85, University of Glasgow; *b* 24 Feb. 1919; *s* of David Flint, JP, and Agnes Strang Lambie; *m* 1953, Dorothy Mary Maclachlan Jardine; two *s* one *d*. *Educ:* Glasgow High Sch.; University of Glasgow. Served with Royal Signals, 1939–46, Major (despatches). Awarded distinction final examination of Institute of Chartered Accountants of Scotland, 1948. Lecturer, University of Glasgow, 1950–60; Dean of Faculty of Law, 1971–73. Partner, Mann Judd Gordon & Co. Chartered Accountants, Glasgow, 1951–71. Hon. Prof. of Accountancy, Stirling Univ., 1988–91. Hon. Pres. Glasgow Chartered Accountants Students Soc., 1959–60; Chm., Assoc. of Univ. Teachers of Accounting (now British Accounting Assoc.), 1969. Mem. Council, Scottish Business Sch., 1971–77; Vice-Pres., Scottish Economic Soc., 1977–; Vice-Pres., Inst. of Chartered Accountants of Scotland, 1973–75, Pres., 1975–76; Pres., European Accounting Assoc., 1983–84; Member: Management and Ind. Rel. Cttee, SSRC, 1970–72 and 1978–80; Commn for Local Authy Accounts in Scotland, 1978–80. FRSA. *Publications:* A True and Fair View in Company Accounts, 1982; Philosophy and Principles of Auditing: an introduction, 1988. *Recreation:* golf. *Address:* 16 Grampian Avenue, Auchterarder, Perthshire PH3 1NY.

FLINT, Michael Frederick, FSA; Consultant, Denton Hall (formerly Denton Hall Burgin & Warrens), Solicitors, since 1993 (Chairman, 1990–93); *b* 7 May 1932; *s* of Frederic Nelson La Fargue Flint and Nell Dixon Smith; *m* 1st, 1954, Susan Kate Rhodes (marr. diss.) two *s* one *d*; 2nd, 1984, Phyllida Margaret Medwyn Hughes. *Educ:* St Peter's Sch., York; Kingswood Sch., Bath. Admitted Solicitor 1954; Denton Hall & Burgin, subseq. Denton Hall Burgin & Warrens: Articled Clerk, 1951–56; Asst Solicitor, 1956–60; Partner, 1960–66; Paramount Pictures Corporation: Asst Vice-Pres., 1967; Vice-Pres., 1968–70; Consultant, Henry Ansbacher & Co., 1970; Chm., London Screen Enterprises, 1970–72 (Exec. Producer, feature film, Glastonbury Fayre, 1972); Denton Hall Burgin & Warrens: Partner, 1972–93; Managing Partner, 1979–82. Director: Majestic Film & Television Internat. Ltd, 1992–; Harmsworth Broadcasting, 1993–; Intellectual Property Inst.; Chm., Intellectual Property, Entertainment and Telecommunications Cttee, Internat. Bar Assoc., 1985–90. Vice-Pres., Brit. Archaeol Assoc., 1988–. Member: BAFTA, 1984–; RTS, 1990–; British Screen Adv. Council, 1991– (Dep. Chm., 1995–); Bd of Govs, London Internat. Film Sch., 1993–. FSA 1965. *Publications:* A User's Guide to Copyright, 1979, 3rd edn 1990; (jtly) Television by Satellite: Legal Aspects, 1987; (jtly) Intellectual Property: The New Law, 1989. *Recreations:* painting, tennis, archaeology, opera. *Address:* Five Chancery Lane, Clifford's Inn, EC4A 1BU. *T:* 0171–320 6539. *Clubs:* Savile, Wig and Pen, Lord's Taverners; Orford Sailing.

FLINT, Rachael H.; *see* Heyhoe Flint, R.

FLOOD, David Andrew; Organist and Master of the Choristers, Canterbury Cathedral, since 1988; *b* 10 Nov. 1955; *s* of Frederick Flood and June Flood (*neé* Alexander); *m* 1976, Alayne Nicholas; two *s* two *d*. *Educ:* Royal Grammar School, Guildford; St John's Coll., Oxford (MA); Clare Coll., Cambridge (PGCE). FRCO (CHM). Assistant Organist, Canterbury Cathedral, 1978–86; Organist and Master of Choristers, Lincoln Cathedral, 1986–88. *Recreations:* motoring, cooking, travel. *Address:* 6 The Precincts, Canterbury, Kent CT1 2EE. *T:* Canterbury (01227) 765219.

FLOOD, Prof. John Edward, OBE 1986; DSc, PhD; CEng, FIEE; FInstP; Professor of Electrical Engineering, 1965–90, now Emeritus, and Head of Department of Electrical and Electronic Engineering, 1967–81 and 1983–89, University of Aston in Birmingham; *b* 2 June 1925; *s* of Sydney E. Flood and Elsie G. Flood; *m* 1949, Phyllis Mary Groocock; two *s*. *Educ:* City of London Sch.; Queen Mary Coll., Univ. of London (BSc 1945; PhD 1951; DSc 1965). CEng, FIEE 1959; FIERE 1967; FInstP 1987. Admiralty Signals Estab., 1944–46; Standard Telephone and Cables Ltd, 1946–47; PO Res. Stn, 1947–52; Siemens Brothers Ltd, 1952–57; Chief Engr, Advanced Develt Labs, AEI Telecommunications Div., 1957–65; Dean, Faculty of Engrg, 1971–74, and Sen. Pro-Vice-Chancellor, 1981–83, Univ. of Aston in Birmingham. Chairman: IEE Professional Gp on Telecommunications, 1974–77; IEE S Midland Centre, 1978–79; Univs Cttee on Integrated Sandwich Courses, 1981–82; BSI Cttee on Telecommunications, 1981–92; Member: British Electrotechnical Council, 1981–86; Monopolies and Mergers Commn, 1985–. FCGI 1991 (CGIA 1962). Freeman, City of London, 1957. *Publications:* Telecommunication Networks, 1975; Transmission Systems, 1991; Telecommunications Switching, Traffic and Networks, 1995; papers in scientific and technical jls; patents. *Recreations:* swimming, wine-making. *Address:* 60 Widney Manor Road, Solihull, West Midlands B91 3JQ. *T:* 0121–705 3604. *Club:* Royal Over-Seas League.

FLOOD, John Martin, CEng; FRAeS; Non-executive director, Hunting Engineering Ltd, since 1994; *b* 3 Oct. 1939; *s* of late Harry Flood and Rita Flood (*née* Martin); *m* 1962, Irene Edwards; one *s*. *Educ:* Merchant Taylors' School, Crosby; Leeds Univ. (BSc Physics, 1st cl.).; CEng 1991; FRAeS 1991. Graduate Apprentice, English Electric, Stevenage, 1962; joined RAE, 1963; Asst Dir, Dir Air Guided Weapons and on Army Chief Scientist staff, 1978–83; Supt, air-launched anti-armour weapons, RAE, 1983–85; Head, Attack Weapons and Defensive Systems Depts, RAE, 1985–89; Dep. Dir (Mission Systems), RAE, 1989–91; Technical Dir, RAE, 1991–92; Dir, Weapon Systems Sector, 1991–93, Technical Dir, 1993–94, DRA. *Recreations:* bird watching, walking, theatre, reading (political biography). *Address:* Hunting Engineering Ltd, Reddings Wood, Ampthill, Bedford MK45 2HD. *T:* Ampthill (01525) 841000.

FLOOD, Michael Donovan, (Mik); Director, Institute of Contemporary Arts, since 1990; *b* 7 May 1949; *s* of late Gp Capt. Donovan John Flood, DFC, AFC and of Vivien Ruth (*née* Allison); *m* 1975, Julie Ward (marr. diss. 1989); one *d*. *Educ:* St George's Coll., Weybridge; Llangefni County Sch., Anglesey. Founder and Artistic Dir, Chapter Arts Centre, Cardiff, 1970–81; Develt Dir, Baltimore Theater Project, USA, 1981–82; Administrator, Pip Simmons Theatre Gp, 1982–83; Arts consultancy, 1983–85; Dir, Watermans Arts Centre, Brentford, 1985–90. Producer of large-scale events: Woyzeck, Cardiff, 1976; Deadwood, Kew Gdns, 1986; Offshore Rig, River Thames, 1987. Member: Film Cttee, Welsh Arts Council, 1976–80; Exec. Cttee, SE Wales Arts Assoc., 1980–81; Exec. Cttee, Informal Eur. Theatre Meeting, 1994–; Co-Founder, Nat. Assoc. of Arts Centres, 1976; Bd Dir, Pip Simmons Theatre Gp, 1977–81. Mem., Ct of Govs, RCA, 1990–. Silver Jubilee Medal, 1977. *Publications:* book reviews in nat. newspapers; contribs on arts and cultural politics to British and European periodicals. *Recreations:* sailing, ichthyology, travel. *Address:* ICA, The Mall, SW1Y 5AH. *T:* 0171–930 0493.

FLORENCE, Prof. Alexander Taylor, CBE 1994; PhD, DSc; FRSE; FRPharmS, FRSC; Dean, School of Pharmacy, University of London, since 1989; *b* 9 Sept. 1940; *s* of late Alexander Charles Gerrard Florence and of Margaret Florence; *m* 1964, Elizabeth Catherine McRae; two *s* one *d*. *Educ:* Royal Coll. of Science and Technology, Glasgow and Univ. of Glasgow (BSc Hons 1962; PhD 1965); DSc Strathclyde, 1984. FRSC 1977; FRPharmS 1987. University of Strathclyde: MRC Jun. Res. Fellow, 1965–66; Lectr in Pharmaceutical Chemistry, 1966–72; Sen. Lectr in Pharm. Chem., 1972–76; J. P. Todd Prof. of Pharmacy, 1976–88. Member: Cttee on Safety of Medicines, 1983– (Mem., Sub-cttee on Chemistry, Pharmacy and Standards of Cttee on Safety of Medicines, 1972–); Nuffield Inquiry into Pharmacy, 1984–86; Standing Pharmaceutical Adv. Cttee, 1989–. FRSE 1987; FRSA 1989. British Pharmaceutical Conf. Science Award, 1972; Harrison Meml Medal, Royal Pharmaceutical Soc., 1986; Scheele Prize, Swedish Acad. of Pharmaceutical Scis, 1993. Co-Editor in Chief, Jl of Drug Targeting, 1993–. *Publications:* Solubilization by Surface Active Agents, 1968; Physicochemical Principles of Pharmacy, 1981, 2nd edn 1988; Surfactant Systems, 1983; (ed) Materials Used in Pharmaceutical Formulation, 1985; (ed) Formulation Factors in Adverse Reactions, 1990; (ed jtly) Liposomes in Drug Delivery, 1992; pubns on drug delivery and targeting, surfactants and drug absorption, and polymeric systems. *Recreations:* music, writing, painting. *Address:* School of Pharmacy, University of London, 29/39 Brunswick Square, WC1N 1AX. *T:* 0171–753 5819.

FLOREY, Prof. Charles du Vé; Professor of Community Medicine, University of Dundee, since 1983; *b* 11 Sept. 1934; *s* of Howard Walter Florey and Mary Ethel Florey; *m* 1966, Susan Jill Hopkins; one *s* one *d*. *Educ:* Univ. of Cambridge (MD); Yale Univ. (MPH). FFCM 1977; FRCPE 1986. Instructor, 1965, Asst Prof., 1966–69, Yale Univ. School of Medicine; Mem. Scientific Staff, MRC, Jamaica, 1969–71; St Thomas's Hospital Medical School, London: Sen. Lectr, 1971–78; Reader, 1978–81; Prof., 1981–83. *Publications:* (with S. R. Leeder) Methods for Cohort Studies of Chronic Airflow Limitation, 1982; (with others) Introduction to Community Medicine, 1983; A European Concerted Action: maternal alcohol consumption and its relation to the outcome of pregnancy and child development at eighteen months, 1992; (ed) Epilex: a multilingual lexicon of epidemiological terms, 1993. *Recreations:* photography, sailing, walking, computing. *Address:* Ninewells Hospital and Medical School, Dundee DD1 9SY. *T:* Dundee (01382) 632124.

FLOUD, Mrs Jean Esther, CBE 1976; MA, BSc(Econ); Principal, Newnham College, Cambridge, 1972–83, Hon. Fellow, 1983; *b* 3 Nov. 1915; *d* of Annie Louisa and Ernest Walter McDonald; *m* 1938, Peter Castle Floud, CBE (*d* 1960), *s* of late Sir Francis Floud, KCB, KCSI, KCMG, and formerly Keeper of Circulation, Victoria and Albert Museum; two *d* (one *s* decd). *Educ:* public elementary and selective secondary schools; London School of Economics (BScEcon), Hon. Fellow, 1972. Asst Dir of Educn, City of Oxford, 1940–46; Teacher of Sociology in the University of London (London School of Economics and Inst. of Educn), 1947–62; Official Fellow of Nuffield College, Oxford, 1963–72, Hon. Fellow, 1983; Hon. Fellow, Darwin Coll., Cambridge, 1986. Member: Franks Commission of Inquiry into the University of Oxford, 1964–66; University Grants Cttee, 1969–74; Social Science Research Council, 1970–73; Exec. Cttee, PEP, 1975–77; Adv. Bd for the Res. Councils, 1976–81; Council, Policy Studies Inst., 1979–83. Hon. LittD Leeds, 1973; Hon. DLitt City, 1978. *Publications:* (with A. H. Halsey and F. M. Martin) Social Class and Educational Opportunity, 1956; (with Warren Young) Dangerousness and Criminal Justice, 1981; papers and reviews in sociological jls. *Recreations:* books, music. *Address:* Elderwick House, The Ridings, Shotover, Oxford OX3 8TB.

FLOUD, Prof. Roderick Castle; Provost, London Guildhall University (formerly City of London Polytechnic), since 1988; *b* 1 April 1942; *s* of late Bernard Francis Castle Floud, MP and Ailsa (*née* Craig); *m* 1964, Cynthia Anne (*née* Smith); two *d*. *Educ:* Brentwood Sch.; Wadham Coll., Oxford; Nuffield Coll., Oxford. MA, DPhil. Asst Lectr in Economic History, UCL, 1966–69; Lectr in Economic History, Univ. of Cambridge and Fellow of Emmanuel Coll., Cambridge, 1969–75; Prof. of Modern History, Birkbeck Coll., Univ. of London, 1975–88. Vis. Prof. of European History and of Economics, Stanford Univ., Calif, 1980–81. Research Associate, Nat. Bureau of Economic Research, USA, 1978–; Research Programme Dir, Centre for Economic Policy Research, 1983–88. Mem. Council, ESRC, 1993–. Mem., Lord Chancellor's Adv. Council on Public Records, 1978–84. Treas., Oxford Union Soc., 1966. Hon. Fellow, Birkbeck Coll., 1994. *Publications:* An Introduction to Quantitative Methods for Historians, 1973, 2nd edn 1980; (ed) Essays in Quantitative Economic History, 1974; The British Machine Tool Industry 1850–1914, 1976; (ed) The Economic History of Britain since 1700, 1981, 2nd edn 1994; (ed) The Power of the Past, 1984; (jtly) Height, Health and History, 1990; articles in Economic History Review, Social Science History, etc. *Recreations:* camping, walking, music. *Address:* London Guildhall University, 117–119 Houndsditch, EC3A 7BU. *T:* 0171–320 1310; 21 Savernake Road, NW3 2JT. *T:* 0171–267 2197. *Club:* Athenæum.

FLOWER, family name of **Viscount Ashbrook.**

FLOWER, Antony John Frank, (Tony), MA, PhD; Deputy Director, Institute of Community Studies and of Mutual Aid Centre, since 1994; *b* 2 Feb. 1951; *s* of late Frank Robert Edward Flower and of Dorothy Elizabeth (*née* Williams). *Educ:* Chipping Sodbury Grammar Sch.; Univ. of Exeter (BA Hons Philosophy and Sociology; MA Sociology); Univ. of Leicester (PhD Mass Communications). Graphic Designer, 1973–76; Co-founder with Lord Young of Dartington, and first Gen. Sec., Tawney Soc., 1982–88; Dir, Res. Inst. for Econ. and Social Affairs, 1982–92. Co-ordinator, Argo Venture (Nat. Space Mus.), 1984–, Dir, Argo Trust, 1986–; Director: Healthline Health Inf. Service, 1986–88; Health Information Trust, 1987–88 (Trustee, 1988–90); Environmental Concern Centre in Europe, 1990–92. Mem. Adv. Bd, The Earth Centre, 1990–; Sec., Ecological Studies

Inst., 1990–92. Associate: Redesign Ltd, 1989–92; Nicholas Lacey, Jobst & Partners (Architects), 1989–; Consultant: CIRIA, 1992–; Rocklabs Geochemical Analysis CC, 1993–; Joseph Rowntree Reform Trust Ltd, 1993–. Co-ordinator, Campaign for Educnl Choice, 1988–89. Council Mem., Gaia, 1988–. Trustee: Gaia, 1988–; Mutual Aid Centre, 1990–; Inst. of Community Studies, 1993–; Tower Hamlets Summer Univ. Trust, 1995–. Founder Mem., SDP, 1981–; Mem., Council for Social Democracy, 1982–84; Dir of Develt, Green Alliance, 1991–92. Associate: Open Coll. of the Arts, 1988–; Inst. for Public Policy Res., 1989–; Family Covenant Assoc., 1994–. Editor, Tawney Journal, 1982–88; Co-founder and Man. Editor, Samizdat Magazine, 1988–. FRSA 1991. *Publications:* (with Graham Mort) Starting to Write: a course in creative writing, 1990; (ed jtly) The Alternative, 1990. *Recreations:* collecting junk, sailing, making and restoring musical instruments. *Address:* (office) 18 Victoria Park Square, E2 9PF. *T:* 0181–980 6263.

FLOWER, Desmond John Newman, MC 1944; Chairman, Cassell & Co. Ltd, 1958–71; President, Cassell Australia Ltd, 1965–71; Editorial Consultant, Sheldon Press, 1973–85; *b* London, 25 Aug. 1907; *o s* of late Sir Newman Flower; *m* 1st, 1931, Margaret Cameron Coss (marr. diss., 1952); one *s*; 2nd, 1952, Anne Elizabeth Smith (marr. diss. 1972); one *s* two *d*; 3rd, 1987, Sophie Rombeyko. *Educ:* Lancing; King's Coll., Cambridge. Entered Cassell & Co. 1930; Dir, 1931; Literary Dir, 1938; Dep.-Chm., 1952; Chm. Cassell & Co. (Holdings) Ltd, 1958–70. Served War of 1939–45 (despatches, MC); commissioned 1941, 5 Bn Argyll and Sutherland Highlanders later 91 (A&SH) A/T-Regt. Chm., the Folio Society, 1960–71; Liveryman, Stationers' Co. Président des Comités d'Alliance Française en Grande Bretagne, 1963–72. Officier de la légion d'honneur, 1972 (Chevalier 1950). DLitt (*hc*) University of Caen, 1957. *Publications:* founder and editor (with A. J. A. Symons) Book Collector's quarterly, 1930–34; ed, Complete Poetical Works of Ernest Christopher Dowson, 1934; compiled (with Francis Meynell and A. J. A. Symons) The Nonesuch Century, 1936; (with A. N. L. Munby) English Poetical Autographs, 1938; The Pursuit of Poetry, 1939; Voltaire's England, 1950; History of 5 Bn Argyll and Sutherland Highlanders, 1950; (with James Reeves) The War, 1939–1945, 1960; (with Henry Maas) The Letters of Ernest Dowson, 1967; New Letters of Ernest Dowson, 1984; Fellows in Foolscap (memoirs), 1991; numerous translations, inc. Saint Simon, Voltaire, Maupassant, Morand. *Recreation:* book collecting. *Address:* 26 Grovedale Road, N19 3EQ. *T:* 0171–281 0080. *Clubs:* Roxburghe; Royal and Ancient (St Andrews).

FLOWER, Rear-Adm. Edward James William, CB 1980; Director, Post-Design (Ships), Ministry of Defence (Navy), 1977–80, retired; *b* 1923; *m*; three *d*. Joined RN, 1941; served in HM Ships Norfolk, Duke of York, Liverpool, Whitby, Urchin and Tenby; Canadian Nat. Defence Coll., 1966; Fleet Marine Engineering Officer, Western Fleet, 1967–69; commanded RN Nuclear Propulsion Test and Trng Estab., 1970–71; MoD (Navy), 1971–75; Flag Officer Portsmouth, and Port Admiral, Portsmouth, 1975–76; Dir of Engrg (Ships), MoD, 1976–77. *Address:* Fairmount, Hinton Charterhouse, Bath.

FLOWER, Hon. Michael Llowarch Warburton; JP; DL; Partner, 1986–92, Consultant, since 1992, Pannone & Partners (formerly March Pearson & Skelton, then Pannone, March Pearson), Manchester; Vice Lord-Lieutenant, Cheshire, since 1990; *b* 9 Dec. 1935; *s* and *heir* of Viscount Ashbrook, *qv*; *m* 1971, Zoë Mary Engleheart; two *s* one *d*. *Educ:* Eton; Worcester Coll., Oxford (MA Mod. Hist.). 2nd Lieut, Grenadier Guards, 1955. Solicitor, 1963; Partner, Farrer & Co., Solicitors, 1966–76. Landowner. Chm., Taxation Sub-Cttee, 1984–86, Pres., Cheshire Branch, 1990–, CLA. DL 1982, JP 1983, Cheshire. *Recreations:* gardening, the countryside, shooting. *Address:* The Old Parsonage, Arley Green, Northwich, Cheshire CW9 6LZ. *T:* Arley (01565) 777277. *Club:* Brooks's.

FLOWER, Robert Philip; HM Diplomatic Service; Counsellor, Foreign and Commonwealth Office, since 1994; *b* 12 May 1939; *s* of Philip Edward Flower and Dorothy Agnes Elizabeth (*née* Beukers); *m* 1964, Anne Daveen Tweddle; two *s*. *Educ:* Christ's Hosp.; Magdalene Coll., Cambridge (BA). Called to the Bar, Middle Temple, 1964. FCO, 1967–; served in Malawi, Malaysia, UK Delegn to NATO, Bonn and London; Dep. Head of Mission, The Hague, 1990–93. *Recreations:* fell-walking, reading, music. *Address:* c/o Foreign and Commonwealth Office, King Charles Street, SW1A 2AH; Riverside Cottages, Skelwith Bridge, Ambleside, Cumbria LA22 0BR.

FLOWERS, family name of **Baron Flowers.**

FLOWERS, Baron *cr* 1979 (Life Peer), of Queen's Gate in the City of Westminster; **Brian Hilton Flowers,** Kt 1969; FRS 1961; Chairman, Nuffield Foundation, since 1987 (a Managing Trustee, since 1982); *b* 13 Sept. 1924; *o s* of late Rev. Harold J. Flowers, Swansea; *m* 1951, Mary Frances, *er d* of late Sir Leonard Behrens, CBE; two step *s*. *Educ:* Bishop Gore Grammar Sch., Swansea; Gonville and Caius Coll. (Exhibitioner), Cambridge (MA); Hon. Fellow, 1974; University of Birmingham (DSc). Anglo-Canadian Atomic Energy Project, 1944–46; Research in nuclear physics and atomic energy at Atomic Energy Research Establishment, Harwell, 1946–50; Dept of Mathematical Physics, University of Birmingham, 1950–52; Head of Theoretical Physics Div., AERE, Harwell, 1952–58; Prof. of Theoretical Physics, 1958–61, Langworthy Prof. of Physics, 1961–72, Univ. of Manchester; on leave of absence as Chm., SRC, 1967–73; Rector of Imperial Coll. of Sci. and Technol., 1973–85; Vice-Chancellor, Univ. of London, 1985–90. Chairman: Royal Commn on Environmental Pollution, 1973–76; Standing Commn on Energy and the Environment, 1978–81; Univ. of London Working Party on future of med. and dent. teaching resources, 1979–80; Cttee of Vice-Chancellors and Principals, 1983–85; Select Cttee on Science and Technology, H of L, 1989–93 (Mem., 1980–93, 1994–). Chancellor, Manchester Univ., 1994–. President: Inst. of Physics, 1972–74; European Science Foundn, 1974–80; Nat. Soc. for Clean Air, 1977–79. Chm., Computer Bd for Univs and Research Councils, 1966–70. Member: Council, RPMS, 1990– (Vice Chm., 1991–); Bd of Management, LSHTM, 1992– (Chm., 1994–). Founding Mem. and Mem. Exec. Council, Academia Europaea, 1988. Founder Mem., SDP, 1981. FInstP 1961; Hon. FCGI, 1975; Hon. MRIA (Science Section), 1976; Hon. FIEE, 1975; Sen. Fellow, RCA, 1983; Hon. Fellow, UMIST, 1985; Hon. FRCP 1992; Corresp. Mem., Swiss Acad. of Engrg Sciences, 1986. MA Oxon, 1956; Hon. DSc: Sussex, 1968; Wales, 1972; Manchester, 1973; Leicester, 1973; Liverpool, 1974; Bristol, 1982; Oxford, 1985; NUI, 1990; Hon. DEng Nova Scotia, 1983; Hon. ScD Dublin, 1984; Hon. LLD: Dundee, 1985; Glasgow, 1987; Manchester, 1995. Rutherford Medal and Prize, 1968, Glazebrook Medal and Prize, 1987, IPPS; Chalmers Medal, Chalmers Univ. of Technol., Sweden, 1980. Officier de la Légion d'Honneur, 1981 (Chevalier, 1975). *Publications:* (with E. Mendoza) Properties of Matter, 1970; An Introduction to Numerical Methods in C++, 1995; contribs to scientific periodicals on structure of the atomic nucleus, nuclear reactions, science policy, energy and the environment. *Recreations:* music, walking, computing, gardening. *Address:* 53 Athenaeum Road, N20 9AL. *T:* 0181–446 5993.

FLOYD, Christopher David; QC 1992; *b* 20 Dec. 1951; *s* of David and Hana Floyd; *m* 1974, Rosalind Jane Arscott; one *s* two *d*. *Educ:* Westminster Sch.; Trinity Coll., Cambridge (MA Nat. Scis and Law). Called to the Bar, Inner Temple, 1975; called to the Bar of Republic of Ireland, 1988. An Asst Recorder, 1994. *Recreations:* Austin Sevens, cricket, ski-ing, walking. *Address:* 11 South Square, Gray's Inn, WC1R 5EU. *T:* 0171–405 1222.

FLOYD, Sir Giles (Henry Charles), 7th Bt *cr* 1816; Director, Burghley Estate Farms, since 1958; *b* 27 Feb. 1932; *s* of Sir John Duckett Floyd, 6th Bt, TD, and of Jocelin Evadne (*d* 1976), *d* of late Sir Edmund Wyldbore Smith; *S* father, 1975; *m* 1st, 1954, Lady Gillian Moyra Katherine Cecil (marr. diss. 1978), 2nd *d* of 6th Marquess of Exeter, KCMG; two *s*; 2nd, 1985, Judy Sophia Lane, *er d* of late W. L. Tregoning, CBE, and D. M. E. Tregoning. *Educ:* Eton College. High Sheriff of Rutland, 1968. *Heir: er s* David Henry Cecil Floyd [*b* 2 April 1956; *m* 1981, Caroline, *d* of John Beckly, Manor Farm, Bowerchalke, Salisbury, Wilts; two *d*]. *Address:* Tinwell Manor, Stamford, Lincs PE9 3UD. *T:* Stamford (01780) 62676. *Clubs:* Turf, Farmers'.

FLOYD, John Anthony; Chairman: Christie Manson & Woods Ltd, 1974–85; Christies International Ltd, 1976–88; *b* 12 May 1923; *s* of Lt-Col Arthur Bowen Floyd, DSO, OBE; *m* 1948, Margaret Louise Rosselli; two *d*. *Educ:* Eton. Served King's Royal Rifle Corps, 1941–46. *Address:* Ecchinswell House, Newbury, Berks. *Clubs:* Boodle's, White's, MCC.

FLOYD, Keith; cook, broadcaster; *b* 28 Dec. 1943; *s* of late Sydney Albert Floyd and of Winnifred Margaret Floyd; *m*; one *s* one *d*. *Educ:* Wellington Sch. Commnd, 3rd RTR 1963; journalist, 1961–; broadcaster, 1986–. *Publications:* Floyd's Food; Floyd on France; Floyd on Fish; Floyd Britain and Ireland; Floyd in the Soup; Floyd American Pie; Floyd on Oz; Floyd on Spain; Floyd on Fire; A Feast of Floyd; Far Flung Floyd; Floyd on Italy; Floyd on Africa. *Recreations:* Rugby, fishing, drinking, gardening. *Address:* Floyd's Inn, Bow Creek, Tuckenhay, Totnes, Devon TQ9 7EQ.

FLOYD EWIN, Sir David Ernest Thomas, Kt 1974; LVO 1954; OBE 1965; MA; Lay Administrator, 1939–44, Registrar and Receiver, 1944–78, Consultant to the Dean and Chapter, since 1978, St Paul's Cathedral; Notary Public; *b* 17 Feb. 1911; 7th *s* of late Frederick P. Ewin and Ellen Floyd; *m* 1948, Marion Irene, *d* of William R. Lewis; one *d*. *Educ:* Eltham. MA (Lambeth) 1962. Chairman: Tubular Exhibn, subseq. Tubular Edgington, Group, 1978–91; Stonebert Ltd and subsids, 1985–91. Freeman, City of London, 1948; Member of Court of Common Council for Ward of Castle Baynard, 1963– (Dep., 1972–); Vice-Pres., Castle Baynard Ward Club (Chm. 1962 and 1988); Chm., Gresham Cttee, 1975–76, Benevolent Cttee, 1991–, Corp. of London; Member: Lord Mayor and Sheriffs Cttee, 1976, 1978, 1984 (Chm., 1987); Court of Assts, Hon. Irish Soc., 1976–79; Surrogate for Province of Canterbury; Trustee: City Parochial Foundn, 1967–90 (Chm., Pensions Cttee, 1978–90); St Paul's Cathedral Trust, 1978–; Temple Bar Trust, 1979–; Dep. Chm., City of London's Endowment Trust for St Paul's Cathedral, 1982–. Hon. Dir, British Humane Assoc.; Governor and Member of Court: Sons of the Clergy Corp.; St Gabriel's Coll., Camberwell, 1946–72. Past Master, Scriveners' Co.; Sen. Past Master, Guild of Freemen of the City of London; Liveryman, Wax Chandlers' Co.; Gold Staff Officer at Coronation of HM Queen Elizabeth, 1953. KStJ 1970 (OStJ 1965). *Publications:* A Pictorial History of St Paul's Cathedral, 1970; The Splendour of St Paul's, 1973; numerous papers and articles. *Recreations:* tennis, gardening, fishing. *Address:* St Augustine's House, 4 New Change, EC4M 9AB. *T:* 0171–248 0683; Chapter House, St Paul's Churchyard, EC4M 8AD. *T:* 0171–248 2705; Silver Springs, Stoke Gabriel, South Devon TQ9 6SJ. *T:* Stoke Gabriel (01803) 782264. *Clubs:* City Livery, Guildhall.

FLOYER, Prof. Michael Antony, MD; FRCP; Professor of Medicine, The London Hospital Medical College, University of London, 1974–86, now Professor Emeritus; Consulting Physician, The Royal London Hospital, since 1986; *b* 28 April 1920; *s* of Comdr William Antony Floyer, RN and Alice Rosalie Floyer (*née* Whitehead); *m* 1946, Lily Louise Frances Burns; two *s* one *d*. *Educ:* Sherborne Sch.; Trinity Hall, Cambridge; The London Hosp. Med. Coll. MA; MB, BCh; MD; FRCP 1963. RAF Medical Service, Sqdn Leader, RAF Hosps, Karachi and Cawnpore, 1946–48. The London Hospital: House Officer, 1944–45; Registrar in Medicine, 1945–46, Hon. Registrar, 1948–51; Hon. Sen. Registrar, 1951–58; Hon. Consultant Physician, 1958–86; Consultant i/c Emergency and Accident Dept, 1975–86; The London Hospital Medical College: Lectr in Medicine, 1948–51; Sen. Lectr, 1951–67; Asst Dir, Medical Unit, 1953–86; Reader in Medicine, 1967–74; Acting Dean, 1982–83; Dean, 1983–86; Fellow, 1988; seconded to Nairobi Univ., Kenya, as Prof. of Medicine, 1973–75. Oliver-Sharpey Prize, RCP, 1980. *Publications:* chapters in books and papers in scientific jls on the aetiology and mechanism of hypertension and on the physiology of the interstitial fluid space. *Recreations:* wild places and wild things. *Address:* Flat 40, Free Trade Wharf, 340 The Highway, E1 9ET. *T:* 0171–702 7577; c/o The London Hospital Medical College, E1 2AD. *T:* 0171–377 7602.

FLUCK, Peter Nigel; freelance artist; sculptor; founded (with Roger Law) Spitting Image, 1982; *b* 7 April 1941; *s* of Herbert William Fluck and Ada Margaret (*née* Hughes); *m* 1963, Anne-Cécile de Bruyne; one *d* one *s*. *Educ:* Cambs High Sch. for Boys; Cambridge Sch. of Art. Artist-reporter, illustrator, 1961–70; cartoonist and caricaturist, 1970–82; Luck & Flaw (with Roger Law), 1974–82. *Recreation:* fly fishing. *Address:* 6 Chapel Street, Duxford, Cambs CB2 4RJ. *T:* Cambridge (01223) 503700.

FLUTE, Prof. Peter Thomas, TD 1970; MD; FRCP, FRCPath; Postgraduate Medical Dean, South West Thames Regional Health Authority and Assistant Director, British Postgraduate Medical Federation, 1985–93; *b* 12 Aug. 1928; *s* of Rev. Richard Prickett Flute and Katie Flute (*née* Click); *m* 1951, Ann Elizabeth Harbroe, *d* of late G. John Wright; two *s* two *d*. *Educ:* Southend High Sch.; King's College London; KCH Med. Sch. (Warc Prize; MB, BS; MRCS). KCH, 1951–52; RAMC, 1952–54; Demonstrator in Pathology, KCH Med. Sch., 1955–56; Elmore Res. Student, Dept of Medicine, Cambridge, 1957–58; Lectr, 1958–62, Sen. Lectr, 1962–68, Reader, 1968–72, Dept of Haematology, KCH Med. Sch.; Hon. Consultant in Haematology, KCH, 1966–72; Prof. of Haematology, St George's Hosp. Med. Sch. and Hon. Consultant, St George's Hosp., 1972–85. RAMC T&AVR: Pathologist, 24 Gen. Hosp., 1955–58, 308 Gen. Hosp., 1958–67; OC 380 Blood Supply Unit, 1967–73, Hon. Col, 1977–82; Hon. Consultant to the Army in Haematology, 1977–87. Mem., Mid-Downs DHA, 1984–90. Royal College of Pathologists: Mem. Council, 1981–84; Exec. Cttee, 1982–84; SW Thames Regional Adviser in Postgraduate Educn, 1975–85; Royal College of Physicians: Mem., Cttee of Haematology, 1981–87; Jt Cttee on Higher Med. Training; Mem., Specialist Adv. Cttee on Haematology, 1977–83; Sec., 1978–83; British Soc. for Haematology: Mem., 1960–; Cttee, 1975–87; Associate Sec., 1977–81; Sec., 1981–83; Pres., 1985–86; Section of Pathology, Royal Society of Medicine: Mem. Council, 1964–68; Sec., 1972–76; Pres., 1978. Mem., Editorial Bd, British Jl of Haematology, 1971–81. *Publications:* chapters and contribs on thrombosis and blood diseases to med. and sci. jls. *Recreations:* mountain walking, reading. *Address:* 17 Church Lane, East Grinstead, West Sussex RH19 3AZ. *T:* East Grinstead (01342) 326288.

FLYNN, Prof. Frederick Valentine, MD (Lond), FRCP, FRCPath; Professor of Chemical Pathology in University of London at University College School of Medicine, 1970–89, now Professor Emeritus; Civil Consultant in Chemical Pathology to Royal Navy, 1978–92; *b* 6 Oct. 1924; *e s* of Frederick Walter Flynn and Jane Laing Flynn (*née* Valentine); *m* 1955, Catherine Ann, *o d* of Dr Robert Walter Warrick and Dorothy Ann Warrick (*née* Dimock); one *s* one *d*. *Educ:* University Coll. London; University Coll.

Hosp. Med. Sch. (Fellow, UCL, 1974). Obstetric Ho. Surg. and various posts, incl. Research Asst and Registrar, Dept of Clin. Pathology, UCH, 1947–60; Associate in Clin. Path., Pepper Laboratory of Clin. Medicine, Univ. of Pennsylvania, and British Postgrad. Med. Fedn Travelling Fellow, 1954–55; Consultant Chemical Pathologist, UCH, 1960–70. Chairman: Assoc. of Clin. Biochemists Sci. and Technical Cttee, 1968–70; Dept of Health's Adv. Gp on Scientific and Clinical Applications of Computers, 1971–76; Organising Cttee for 1st, 2nd and 3rd Internat. Confs on Computing in Clinical Labs, 1972–80; Research Cttee, NE Thames RHA, 1984–88; Member: Min. of Health Lab. Equipment and Methods Adv. Gp, 1966–71; Min. of Technol. Working Party on Lab. Instrumentation, 1966–67; BMA Working Party on Computers in Medicine, 1968–69; Dept of Health's Adv. Cttee on Med. Computing, 1969–76, and Laboratory Develts Adv. Gp, 1972–75; MRC Working Party on Hypogammaglobulinaemia, 1959–70; MRC Adv. Panel on Applications for Computing Facilities, 1973–77; NW Thames RHA Sci. Cttee, 1973–74; Med. Lab. Techns Bd, Council for Professions Supplementary to Medicine, 1984–88; NHS Supraregional Assay Services Bd, 1990–92; Sir Jules Thorn Charitable Trust: Mem. Med. Adv. Cttee, 1983–; Trustee, 1988–; Section of Pathology, RSM: Mem. Council, 1968–72, 1986–93; Vice-Pres., 1971–72, 1989–91; Royal Coll. of Pathologists: Chm., Panel of Examrs in Chem. Path., 1972–82; Mem. Council, 1973–83 and 1984–87; Vice-Pres., 1975–78; Treas., 1978–83; Dir of Continuing Med. Educn, 1992–; College Medal, 1995; Association of Clinical Pathologists: Chm., Working Party on Data Processing in Labs, 1964–67; Mem. Council, 1988–90; Pres.-elect, 1988–89; Pres., 1989–90. *Publications:* numerous contribs to med. and sci. books and jls. *Recreations:* photography, woodwork, gardening. *Address:* 20 Oakleigh Avenue, Whetstone, N20 9JH. *T:* 0181–445 0882.

FLYNN, John Gerrard, CMG 1992; HM Diplomatic Service; Ambassador to Venezuela, and concurrently (non-resident) to the Dominican Republic, since 1993; *b* 23 April 1937; *s* of late Thomas Flynn and Mary Chisholm; *m* 1973, Drina Anne Coates; one *s* one *d*. *Educ:* Glasgow Univ. (MA). Foreign Office, 1965; Second Sec., Lusaka, 1966; First Sec., FCO, 1968; seconded to Canning House as Asst Dir-Gen., 1970; First Sec. (Commercial) and Consul, Montevideo, 1971; FCO, 1976; Chargé d'Affaires, Luanda, 1978; Counsellor and Consul-Gen., Brasilia, 1979; Counsellor, Madrid, 1982; High Comr, Swaziland, 1987; Ambassador to Angola and (non-resident) to São Tomé and Principe, 1990–93. *Recreations:* walking, golf. *Address:* c/o Foreign and Commonwealth Office, SW1A 2AH. *Club:* Travellers'.

FLYNN, Padraig; Member, European Commission (formerly Commission of the European Communities), since 1993; *b* 9 May 1939; *m* 1963, Dorothy Tynan; one *s* three *d*. *Educ:* St Gerald's Secondary Sch., Castlebar, Co. Mayo; St Patrick's Trng Coll., Dublin (DipEd). Mayo County Council: Mem., 1967–87; Vice-Chm., 1975–77. TD (FF), 1977–93; Minister of State, Dept of Transport and Power, 1980–81; Minister for: Gaeltacht, Mar.–Oct. 1982; Trade, Commerce and Tourism, Oct.–Dec. 1982; spokesman on trade, commerce and tourism, 1982–87; Minister for: the Envmt, 1987–91; Justice, Feb.–Dec. 1992; Industry and Commerce, Nov.–Dec. 1992. Mem., Irish Nat. Teachers' Orgn, 1957–. Mem., Gaelic Athletic Assoc., 1959–. *Recreations:* golf, reading, world affairs. *Address:* European Commission, 45 avenue d'Auderghem, 1040 Brussels, Belgium. *T:* (2) 2952111.

FLYNN, Paul Phillip; MP (Lab) Newport West, since 1987; *b* 9 Feb. 1935; *s* of James Flynn and Kathleen Williams; *m* 1st, 1962, Anne Harvey (marr. diss. 1984); one *s* (one *d* decd); 2nd, 1985, Samantha Morgan; one step-*s* one step-*d*. *Educ:* St Illtyd's Coll., Cardiff. Steelworker, 1955–84; Researcher, 1984–87. Mem., Gwent CC, 1974–82. Contested (Lab) Denbigh, Oct. 1974. Frontbench spokesman on Wales, 1987, on social security, 1988–90. Mem., Gorsedd of Bards, 1991. Campaign for Freedom of Information Parly Award, 1991. *Address:* House of Commons, SW1A 0AA. *Club:* Ringland Labour (Newport, Gwent).

FLYNN, Most Rev. Thomas; *see* Achonry, Bishop of, (RC).

FO, Dario; Italian playwright and actor; *b* 24 March 1926; *s* of Felice Fo and Pina (*née* Rota); *m* 1954, Franca Rame; one *c*. *Educ:* Acad. of Fine Arts, Milan. Joined a small theatre gp, 1950; wrote satirical radio series, Poer nano (Poor Dwarf), 1951, and performed selections from it, Teatro Odeon, Milan; appeared in Cocorico, Teatro Odeon, Milan, 1952; jt founder and performer, I Dritti (revue co.), 1953–55 (toured nationally); screenwriter, Rome, 1955–58; performer and writer, theatre gp, Compagnia Fo-Rame, 1958–68; artistic dir, Chi l'ha visto? (TV musical revue), 1959; performer and writer, Canzonissima (TV variety show); returned to theatre work, 1963; jt founder, theatre co-operative, Nuova Scena, 1968 (toured, 1968–69); jt founder, theatre gp, la Comune, 1970; Tricks of the Trade (TV series), 1985. Plays include: Gli Arcangeli non Giocano a Flipper, 1959 (Archangels Don't Play Pinball); Isabella, Tre Caravelle e un Cacciabelle, 1963 (Isabella, Three Sailing Ships and a Con Man); Mistero Buffo, 1969; Morte Accidentale di un Anarchico, 1970 (Accidental Death of an Anarchist); Non Si Paga, Non Si Paga!, 1974 (Can't Pay! Won't Pay!); (with Franca Rame) Tutta Casa Letto e Chiesa, 1977 (All House, Bed and Church); Storia Della Tigre ed Altre Storie, 1979 (Tale of a Tiger and Other Stories); Clacson, Trombette e Pernacchi, 1980 (Trumpets and Raspberries); (with Franca Rame) Coppia Aperta, 1983 (Open Couple); Il Papa e La Strega, 1989 (The Pope and the Witch); (with Franca Rame) L'Eroina – Grassa e' Bello, 1991; Johan Padan a la Descoverta de le Americhe, 1991; his plays have been translated into many languages and performed in many countries. *Publications:* The Tricks of the Trade, 1991; many plays. *Address:* CTFR Srl, Viale Piave 11, 20129 Milan, Italy.

FOAKES, Prof. Reginald Anthony; Professor of English, University of California at Los Angeles, 1983–93, now Emeritus; *b* 18 Oct. 1923; 2nd *s* of William Warren Foakes and Frances (*née* Poate); *m* 1st, 1951, Barbara (*d* 1988), *d* of Harry Garratt, OBE; two *s* two *d*; 2nd, 1993, Mary, *d* of Albert White. *Educ:* West Bromwich Grammar Sch.; Birmingham Univ. (MA, PhD). Fellow of the Shakespeare Inst., 1951–54; Lectr in English, Durham Univ., 1954–62; Sen. Lectr, 1963–64; University of Kent at Canterbury: Prof. of Eng. Lit., 1964–82, now Emeritus Prof. of Eng. and Amer. Lit.; Dean, Faculty of Humanities, 1974–77. Commonwealth Fund (Harkness) Fellow, Yale Univ., 1955–56; Visiting Professor: University Coll., Toronto, 1960–62; Univ. of California, Santa Barbara, 1968–69; UCLA, 1981. *Publications:* (ed) Shakespeare's King Henry VIII, 1957; The Romantic Assertion, 1958; (ed with R. T. Rickert) Henslowe's Diary, 1961; (ed) The Comedy of Errors, 1962; (ed) The Revenger's Tragedy, 1966; (ed) Macbeth and Much Ado About Nothing, 1968; Romantic Criticism, 1968; Coleridge on Shakespeare, 1971; Shakespeare, the Dark Comedies to the Last Plays, 1971; (ed) The Henslowe Papers, 2 vols, 1977; Marston and Tourneur, 1978; (ed) A Midsummer Night's Dream, 1984; Illustrations of the English Stage 1580–1642, and Visitor's Guide, 1985; (ed) S. T. Coleridge, Lectures 1808–19: On Literature, 2 vols, 1987; (ed) Troilus and Cressida, 1987; (ed) Coleridge's Criticism of Shakespeare, 1989; Hamlet versus King Lear: cultural politics and Shakespeare's art, 1993. *Address:* Department of English, University of California at Los Angeles, 405 Hilgard Avenue, Los Angeles, CA 90024, USA.

FOALE, Air Cdre Colin Henry; *b* 10 June 1930; *s* of late William Henry Foale and Frances M. (*née* Muse); *m* 1954, Mary Katherine Harding, Minneapolis, USA; two *s* one *d*. *Educ:* Wolverton Grammar Sch.; RAF Coll., Cranwell. 1951–74: 13 Sqdn Pilot, Egypt; 32 Sqdn Flt Comdr; Fighter Flt, RAF Flying Coll., Manby; Officer and Aircrew Selection, Hornchurch; OC 73 Sqdn, Cyprus (Sqdn Ldr); Staff Coll., Bracknell; Air Staff, HQ RAF Germany (Wing Comdr); Jt Services Staff Coll., Latimer; OC 39 Sqdn, Malta; SO Flying, MoD (PE) (Gp Captain); Stn Comdr, Luqa, Malta, 1974–76; RCDS, 1977 (Air Cdre); Dir of Public Relations (RAF), 1977–79; retired at own request, 1979. Trng Advr to Chm., Conservative Party, 1980–81; Pilot to Cttee for Aerial Photography, Univ. of Cambridge, 1981–90. FIMgt, FIWM. *Recreations:* sailing, swimming, flying, travel, music, drama, writing. *Address:* St Catharine's College, Cambridge; 37 Pretoria Road, Cambridge CB4 1HD. *Club:* Royal Air Force.

FOCKE, Paul Everard Justus; QC 1982; a Recorder, since 1986; *b* 14 May 1937; *s* of Frederick Justus Focke and late Muriel Focke; *m* 1973, Lady Tana Marie Alexander, *er d* of 6th Earl of Caledon; two *d*. *Educ:* Downside; Exeter Coll., Oxford; Trinity Coll., Dublin. National Service, 1955–57; Territorial Army, 1957–66, Cheshire Yeomanry (Captain). Called to the Bar, Gray's Inn, 1964 (Bencher, 1992), to the Bar of NSW and to the NZ Bar, 1982. QC NSW 1984. Dir, Bar Mutual Indemnity Fund, 1988–. *Recreations:* travelling, aeroplanes. *Address:* (chambers) 1 Mitre Court Buildings, Temple, EC4Y 7BS. *T:* 0171–797 7070; (home) 7 Cheyne Walk, SW3 5QZ. *T:* 0171–351 0299. *Clubs:* Pratt's, Turf, Beefsteak, Cavalry and Guards; St Botolph (Boston).

FOËX, Prof. Pierre, DPhil; FRCA, FANZCA; Nuffield Professor of Anaesthetics, and Fellow of Pembroke College, University of Oxford, since 1991; *b* 4 July 1935; *s* of Georges and Berthe Foëx; *m* 1958, Anne-Lise Schürch; two *s*. *Educ:* Univ. of Geneva (DM); professional qualifying Swiss State Exam. in Medicine and Surgery, 1960; DPhil Oxon 1973. FRCA (FFARCS 1985); FANZCA 1993. University Hospital, Geneva: Asst, 1961–62 and Chef de Clinique, 1962–63, Dept of Neurology; Asst, 1963–65, Chef de Clinique-adjoint, 1966–68 and Chef de Clinique, 1969–70, Dept of Medicine; Nuffield Department of Anaesthetics, University of Oxford: Res. Fellow, 1970–71; Lectr, 1971–73; Univ. Lectr, 1973–76; Clinical Reader and Hon. Consultant (Clinical Physiology), 1976–91; Emer. Fellow, Worcester Coll., Oxford (Fellow, 1976–91). Mem., Exec. Cttee, Anaesthetic Res. Soc., 1982–86; Senator, European Acad. of Anaesthesiology, 1988– (Vice-Pres., 1991–). Vis. Prof., univs in Australia, Canada, Europe, NZ, USA. *Publications:* Anaesthesia for the Compromised Heart, 1989; chapters and papers on cardiac physiology, cardiovascular physiology applied to anaesthesia, myocardial ischaemia, cardiovascular pharmacology, anaesthesia and hypertension. *Recreations:* walking, foreign travel. *Address:* Nuffield Department of Anaesthetics, Radcliffe Infirmary, Woodstock Road, Oxford OX2 6HE. *T:* Oxford (01865) 224770.

FOGARTY, Christopher Winthrop, CB 1973; Deputy Secretary, Overseas Development Administration, Foreign and Commonwealth Office, (formerly Ministry of Overseas Development), 1976–81; *b* 18 Sept. 1921; *s* of late Philip Christopher Fogarty, ICS, and late Hilda Spenser Fogarty; *m* 1961, Elizabeth Margaret Ince (*d* 1972). *Educ:* Ampleforth Coll.; Christ Church, Oxford. War Service (Lieut RA), 1942–45. Asst Principal, 1946, Principal, 1949, HM Treasury; Permanent Sec., Min. of Finance of Eastern Nigeria, 1956; Asst Sec., HM Treasury, 1959, Under-Sec., 1966; Treasury Rep., S Asia and FE, 1967–72; Dep. Sec., HM Treasury, and Dir, European Investment Bank, 1972–76. *Address:* 7 Hurlingham Court, Ranelagh Gardens, SW6 3SH. *Clubs:* Commonwealth Trust, Travellers'; Royal Selangor Golf.

See also M. P. Fogarty.

FOGARTY, Michael Patrick; Director, Institute for Family and Environmental Research, 1981–84; *b* 3 Oct. 1916; *s* of late Philip Christopher Fogarty, ICS, and Mary Belle Pye, Galway; *m* 1939, Phyllis Clark; two *s* two *d*. *Educ:* Ampleforth Coll.; Christ Church, Oxford. Lieut RA, 1940 (wounded, Dunkirk). Nuffield Coll., 1941–51 (Fellow, 1944); Montague Burton Prof. of Industrial Relations, University Coll. of S Wales and Mon, 1951–66; Dir and Prof., Econ. and Social Res. Inst., Dublin, 1968–72; Centre for Studies in Social Policy: Sen. Fellow, 1973; Dep. Dir, 1977–78; Dep. Dir, PSI, 1978–82. Also held posts in Administrative Staff Coll., Oxford Institute of Statistics, Nat. Institute of Economic and Social Research, Ministry of Town and Country Planning, and as Asst Editor, The Economist. Chairman: Cttee on Industrial Relations in the Electricity Supply Bd (Ireland), 1968–69; Banks Inquiry, 1970–71; Member: Commn on the Status of Women (Ireland), 1970–72; Commn on Insurance Industry (Ireland), 1970–72; Cttee on Aid to Political Parties, 1975–76. Pres., Newman Assoc., 1957–59; Chm., Catholic Social Guild, 1959–63; Mem., Social Welfare Commn, RC Bishops' Conf. (E&W); Vice-Pres. Assoc. of University Teachers, 1964–66. Prospective Parly candidate (Lab) Tamworth, 1938–44; Parliamentary Candidate (L): Devizes, 1964 and 1966; Abingdon, Feb. and Oct. 1974. Vice-Pres. of the Liberal Party, 1964–66. Contested (L) Thames Valley, European Parlt, 1979. District Councillor, Vale of White Horse, 1973–87; CC Oxfordshire, 1981–89 (Vice-Chm., 1985–86; Chm., 1986–87). Hon. Dr of Political and Social Science, Louvain, 1963. *Publications:* Prospects of the Industrial Areas of Great Britain, 1945; Plan Your Own Industries, 1947; (ed) Further Studies in Industrial Organisation, 1948; Town and Country Planning, 1948; Economic Control, 1955; Personality and Group Relations in Industry, 1956; Christian Democracy in Western Europe, 1820–1953, 1957; The Just Wage, 1961; Under-Governed and Over-Governed, 1962; The Rules of Work, 1963; Company and Corporation—One Law?, 1965; Companies Beyond Jenkins, 1965; Wider Business Objectives, 1966; A Companies Act 1970?, 1967; (with Allen, Allen and Walters) Women in Top Jobs, 1971; (with Rapoport and Rapoport) Sex, Career and Family, 1971; Women and Top Jobs: the next move, 1972; Irish Entrepreneurs Speak For Themselves, 1974; Forty to Sixty, 1975; Company Responsibility and Participation—A New Agenda, 1975; Pensions—where next?, 1976; (with Eileen Reid) Differentials for Managers and Skilled Manual Workers in the UK, 1980; Retirement Age and Retirement Costs, 1980; (with Allen and Walters) Women in Top Jobs 1968–79, 1981; (ed) Retirement Policy: the next fifty years, 1982; (with Ryan and Lea) Irish Values and Attitudes, 1984; (with D. Brooks) Trade Unions and British Industrial Development, 1986; (with Ian Christie) Companies and Communities, 1990; (jtly) More Than Money, 1993. *Recreations:* swimming, walking. *Address:* Red Copse, Boars Hill, Oxford OX1 5DG.

See also C. W. Fogarty.

FOGDEN, Michael Ernest George, CB 1994; Chief Executive, The Employment Service, Department of Employment, then Department for Education and Employment, 1987–May 1996; *b* 30 May 1936; *s* of late George Charles Arthur and of Margaret May Fogden; *m* 1957, Rose Ann Diamond; three *s* one *d*. *Educ:* High Sch. for Boys, Worthing. Nat. Service, RAF, 1956–58. Ministry of Pensions and National Insurance, later Department of Health and Social Security: Clerical Officer, 1958–59; Exec. Officer, 1959–67, Private Sec. to Parly Sec., 1967–68; Asst Private Sec. to Sec. of State for Social Services, 1968–70; Principal, 1970–76; Asst Sec., 1976–83; Under Sec., 1983–84; Under Sec., Dept of Employment, then Dept for Educn and Employment, 1984–May 1996. Chm., First Div. Assoc. of Civil Servants, 1980–83. Chairman: London Council, RIPA, 1989–93; London Inst. of Public Admin, 1994–. FRSA. *Recreations:* gardening, talking, music. *Address:* 59 Mayfield Avenue, Orpington, Kent BR6 0AH. *T:* Orpington (01689) 77395. *Clubs:* Commonwealth Trust, Institute of Directors.

FOGEL, Prof. Robert W.; Charles R. Walgreen Professor of American Institutions, University of Chicago, since 1981; *b* 1 July 1926; *s* of Harry G. Fogel and Elizabeth (*née* Mitnik); two *s*. *Educ:* Cornell, Columbia and Johns Hopkins Univs. AB Cornell 1948; AM Columbia 1960; PhD Johns Hopkins 1963. Instructor, Johns Hopkins Univ., 1958–59; Asst Prof., Univ. of Rochester, 1960–64; Assoc. Prof., Univ. of Chicago, 1964–65; Prof., Econs and History, Univ. of Chicago, 1965–75, Univ. of Rochester, 1968–75. Taussig Research Prof., Harvard Univ., 1973–74; Pitt Prof. of Amer. History and Instns, Cambridge Univ., 1975–76; Harold Hitchings Burbank Prof. of Econs and Prof. of History, Harvard Univ., 1975–81. President: Economic History Assoc., 1977–78; Soc. Sci. Hist. Assoc., 1980–81. Fellow: Econometric Soc., 1971; Amer. Acad. of Arts and Scis, 1972; Nat. Acad. of Scis, 1973; FAAAS, 1978; FRHistS 1975; Corresponding FBA, 1991. Hon. DSc Rochester, 1987. Phi Beta Kappa, 1963; Arthur H. Cole Prize, Economic History Assoc., 1968; Schumpeter Prize, Harvard Univ., 1971; Bancroft Prize, Columbia Univ., 1975; Gustavus Myers Prize, 1990; (jtly) Nobel Prize for Economics, 1993. *Publications:* The Union Pacific Railroad: a case in premature enterprise, 1960; Railroads and American Economic Growth: essays in econometric history, 1964 (Spanish edn 1972); (jtly) The Reinterpretation of American Economic History, 1971 (Italian edn 1975); (jtly) The Dimension of Quantitative Research in History, 1972; (jtly) Time on the Cross: the economics of American Negro slavery, 1974 (Japanese edn 1977, Spanish edn 1981); Ten Lectures on the New Economic History, 1977; (jtly) Which Road to the Past? Two Views of History, 1983; Without Consent or Contract: the rise and fall of American slavery, vol. 1, 1989, vols 2–4 (jtly), 1992; numerous papers in learned jls. *Address:* (home) 5321 S University Avenue, Chicago, IL 60615, USA; (office) 1101 E 58th Street, Chicago, IL 60637, USA.

FOGG, Alan, MBE 1994; Chairman, Royal Philanthropic Society, 1982–90; former Director, PA International; *b* 19 Sept. 1921; *o s* of John Fogg, Dulwich; *m* 1948, Mary Marsh; two *s* one *d*. *Educ:* Repton; Exeter Coll., Oxford (MA, BSc). Served with RN, 1944–47. *Publications:* (with Barnes, Stephens and Titman) Company Organisation: theory and practice, 1970; various papers on management subjects. *Recreations:* travel, gardening, youth charities. *Address:* Albury Edge, Merstham, Surrey RH1 3DB. *T:* Merstham (01737) 642023.

FOGG, Cyril Percival, CB 1973; Director, Admiralty Surface Weapons Establishment, Ministry of Defence (Procurement Executive), 1973–75, retired; *b* 28 Nov. 1914; *s* of Henry Fogg and Mabel Mary (*née* Orton); *m* 1st, 1939, Margaret Amie Millican (*d* 1982); two *d*; 2nd, 1983, June Adele McCoy. *Educ:* Herbert Strutt Sch., Belper; Gonville and Caius Coll., Cambridge (MA, 1st cl. Mechanical Sciences Tripos). Research Staff, General Electric Co., 1936–37; various positions in Scientific Civil Service from 1937 with Air Ministry, Ministries of Aircraft Production, Supply, Aviation and Technology. Head of Ground Radar Dept, RRE Malvern, 1956–58; Dir Electronics R&D (Ground), 1959–63; Imperial Defence Coll., 1961; Dir of Guided Weapons Research, 1963–64; Dir-Gen. of Electronics R&D, Min. of Aviation, 1964–67; Dep. Controller of Electronics, Min. of Technology, later MoD (Procurement Executive), 1967–72. *Address:* 10 Miles Cottages, Taylors Lane, Bosham, Chichester, West Sussex PO18 8QG.

FOGG, Prof. Gordon Elliott, CBE 1983; FRS 1965; Professor and Head of the Department of Marine Biology, University College of North Wales, Bangor, 1971–85, now Professor Emeritus; *b* 26 April 1919; *s* of Rev. L. C. Fogg; *m* 1945, Elizabeth Beryl Llechid-Jones; one *s* one *d*. *Educ:* Dulwich Coll.; Queen Mary Coll., London; St John's Coll., Cambridge. BSc (London), 1939; PhD (Cambridge), 1943; ScD (Cambridge), 1966. Sea-weed Survey of British Isles, 1942; Plant Physiologist, Pest Control Ltd, 1943–45; successively Asst Lectr, Lectr and Reader in Botany, University Coll., London, 1945–60; Rockefeller Fellow, 1954; Prof. of Botany, Westfield Coll., Univ. of London, 1960–71. Trustee, BM (Natural Hist.), 1976–85; Royal Botanic Gardens, Kew, 1983–89. Member, Royal Commn on Environmental Pollution, 1979–85; NERC, 1981–82. Royal Soc. Leverhulme Vis. Prof., Kerala, 1969–70; Leverhulme Emeritus Fellow, 1986. Botanical Sec., Soc. for Experimental Biology, 1957–60; President: British Phycological Soc., 1961–62; International Phycological Soc., 1964; Inst. of Biology, 1976–77; Chm. Council, Freshwater Biol Assoc., 1974–85; Joint Organizing Sec., X International Botanical Congress. Visiting research worker, British Antarctic Survey, 1966, 1974, 1979; Biological Gen. Sec., British Assoc., 1967–72, Pres., Section K, 1973. Fellow, Queen Mary and Westfield Coll., London (formerly QMC), 1976. Hon. LLD Dundee, 1974. *Publications:* The Metabolism of Algae, 1953; The Growth of Plants, 1963; Algal Cultures and Phytoplankton Ecology, 1965, 3rd edn (with B. Thake), 1987; Photosynthesis, 1968; (jointly) The Blue-green Algae, 1973; (with D. Smith) The Explorations of Antarctica, 1990; A History of Antarctic Science, 1992; papers in learned jls. *Recreations:* water colour painting, walking. *Address:* Bodolben, Llandegfan, Menai Bridge, Gwynedd LL59 5TA. *T:* Menai Bridge (01248) 712916. *Club:* Athenæum.

FOGGON, George, CMG 1961; OBE 1949 (MBE 1945); Director, London Office, International Labour Organisation, 1976–82, retired; *b* 13 Sept. 1913; *s* of late Thomas and Margaret Foggon; *m* 1st, 1938, Agnes McIntosh (*d* 1968); one *s*; 2nd, 1969, Audrey Blanch. Joined Min. of Labour, 1930. Served War of 1939–45 (MBE), Wing-Comdr, RAFVR, 1941–46. Seconded to FO, 1946; on staff of Mil. Gov., Berlin, 1946–49; Principal, CO, 1949; Asst Sec., W African Inter-Territorial Secretariat, Gold Coast (now Ghana), 1951–53; Comr of Labour, Nigeria, 1954–58; Labour Adviser: to Sec. of State for Colonies, 1958–61; to Sec. for Techn. Co-op., 1962–64; to Min. of Overseas Development, 1965–66; Overseas Labour Advr, FO later FCO, 1966–76, retd. *Recreations:* walking, photography. *Address:* 8 Churton Place, SW1V 2LN. *T:* 0171–828 1492. *Clubs:* Athenæum, Oriental.

FOLDES, Prof. Lucien Paul; Professor of Economics, University of London, at London School of Economics and Political Science, since 1979; *b* 19 Nov. 1930; *s* of Egon and Marta Foldes. *Educ:* Bunce Court Sch.; Monkton Wyld Sch.; London School of Economics (BCom, MScEcon, DBA). National Service, 1952–54. LSE: Asst Lecturer in Economics, 1954–55; Lectr, 1955–61; Reader, 1961–79. Rockefeller Travelling Fellow, 1961–62. *Publications:* articles in Rev. of Economic Studies, Economica, Jl of Mathematical Economics, Stochastics, Mathematical Finance, and others. *Recreation:* mathematical analysis. *Address:* London School of Economics, Houghton Street, WC2A 2AE. *T:* 0171–405 7686.

FOLEY, family name of **Baron Foley.**

FOLEY, 8th Baron *cr* 1776; **Adrian Gerald Foley;** *b* 9 Aug. 1923; *s* of 7th Baron and Minoru (*d* 1968), *d* of late H. Greenstone, South Africa; *S* father, 1927; *m* 1st, 1958, Patricia Meek (marr. diss. 1971); one *s* one *d*; 2nd, 1972, Ghislaine Lady Ashcombe. *Heir:* *s* Hon. Thomas Henry Foley, *b* 1 April 1961. *Address:* c/o Marbella Club, Marbella, Malaga, Spain. *Club:* White's.

FOLEY, Rt. Rev. Brian Charles; Former Bishop of Lancaster; *b* Ilford, 25 May 1910. *Educ:* St Cuthbert's Coll., Ushaw; English College and Gregorian Univ., Rome (PhL 1934, STL 1938). Priest, 1937; Assistant Priest, Shoeburyness; subseq. Assistant Priest, Romford; Parish Priest, Holy Redeemer, Harold Hill, and Holy Cross, Harlow. Canon of Brentwood Diocese, 1959. Bishop of Lancaster, 1962–85. President: Catholic Record Society, 1964–80; Catholic Archive Soc., 1979–. Hon. DLitt Lancaster, 1993. *Publications:* Some People of the Penal Times, 1991; Some Other People of the Penal Tinal Times, 1992. *Address:* Nazareth House, Ashton Road, Lancaster LA1 5AQ. *T:* Lancaster (01524) 382748.

FOLEY, Hugh Smith; Principal Clerk of Session and Justiciary, Scotland, since 1989; *b* 9 April 1939; *s* of late John Walker Foley and Mary Hogg (*née* Smith); *m* 1966, Isobel King Halliday; two *s*. *Educ:* Dalkeith High Sch. (Joint Dux). Student Actuary, Standard Life Assce Co., 1956–59; nat. service, RAF, 1959–61; entered Scottish Court Service, Court of Session Br., 1962; Asst Clerk of Session, 1962–71; Depute Clerk of Session, 1972–80; seconded to Sherriff Court, Edinburgh, 1980–81; Prin. Sheriff Clerk Depute, Glasgow, 1981–82; Sheriff Clerk, Linlithgow, 1982; Dep. Prin. Clerk of Session, 1982–86; Sen. Dep. Principal Clerk, 1986–89. Mem., Lord President's Cttee on Procedure in Personal Injuries Litigation in Court of Session, 1978–79. *Recreations:* walking, painting. *Address:* Parliament House, Edinburgh EH1 1RQ. *T:* 0131–225 2595.

FOLEY, Johanna Mary, (Jo); journalist; *b* 8 Dec. 1945; *d* of John and Monica Foley. *Educ:* St Joseph's Convent, Kenilworth; Manchester Univ. (BA Jt Hons English and Drama, 1968). Woman's Editor, Walsall Observer, 1968; Reporter, Birmingham Post, 1970; English Teacher, Monkwick Secondary Modern Sch., Colchester, and More House Sch., London, 1972–73; Dep. Beauty Editor, Woman's Own, 1973; launched and edited magazine, Successful Slimming, 1976; Sen. Asst Editor, Woman's Own, 1978; Woman's Editor, The Sun, 1980; Editor, Woman, 1982; Exec. Editor (Features), The Times, 1984–85; Man. Editor, The Mirror, 1985–86; Editor: Observer Magazine, 1986–87; Options, 1988–91. Editor of the Year, British Soc. of Magazine Editors, 1983. *Publication:* The Pick of Woman's Own Diets, 1979. *Recreations:* eating, reading, cinema, opera.

FOLEY, John Dominic; His Honour Judge Foley; a Circuit Judge, since 1994; *b* 17 Jan. 1944; *s* of Cyril Patrick Foley and Winifred Hannah (*née* McAweeny); *m* 1978, Helena Frances McGowan (marr. diss. 1986); two *d*. *Educ:* St Brendan's Coll., Bristol; Exeter Univ. (LLB Hons). Called to the Bar, Inner Temple, 1968; practised Western Circuit, 1969–; Asst Recorder, 1986–89; Recorder, 1989–94. *Recreations:* Rugby, cricket, travel, theatre. *Clubs:* Clifton Rubgy Football, Bristol Rugby Football; Somerset County Cricket.

FOLEY, Lt-Gen. Sir John (Paul), KCB 1994 (CB 1991); OBE 1979; MC 1976; Ministry of Defence, since 1994; *b* 22 April 1939; *s* of Henry Thomas Hamilton Foley, MBE and Helen Constance Margaret Foley (*née* Pearson); *m* 1972, Ann Humphries; two *d*. *Educ:* Bradfield College; Mons OCS; Army Staff College (psc). Lieut, Royal Green Jackets, 1959; RMCS and Army Staff Coll., 1970–71; Regimental Duty, 1972–74; Chief of Staff, 51 Inf. Bde, Hong Kong, 1974–76; Instructor, Army Staff Coll., 1976–78; CO 3rd Bn RGJ, 1978–80; Comdt Jun. Div., Staff Coll., 1981–82. Arms Dir, MoD, 1983–85; RCDS 1986; Chief, British Mission to Soviet Forces in Germany, 1987–89; ACDS, MoD, 1989–92; Comdr, British Forces Hong Kong, and Maj.-Gen. Brigade of Gurkhas, 1992–94. Col Comdt, 1st Bn, Royal Green Jackets, 1991–94, The Light Div., 1994–. Liveryman, Skinners' Co., 1972–. *Recreations:* tennis, walking, shooting, reading. *Address:* Ministry of Defence, Old War Office Building, Whitehall, SW1A 2EU. *Club:* Boodle's.

FOLEY, Maurice (Anthony), CMG 1987; Deputy Director General, Directorate General for Development, Commission of the European Communities, 1973–86; *b* 9 Oct. 1925; *s* of Jeremiah and Agnes Foley; *m* 1952, Catherine, *d* of Patrick and Nora O'Riordan; three *s* one *d*. *Educ:* St Mary's Coll., Middlesbrough. Formerly: electrical fitter, youth organiser, social worker. Member: ETU, 1941–46; Transport and General Workers Union, 1948–; Royal Arsenal Co-operative Soc. MP (Lab) West Bromwich, 1963–73; Joint Parliamentary Under-Sec. of State, Dept of Economic Affairs, 1964–66; Parly Under-Secretary: Home Office, 1966 67; Royal Navy, MoD, 1967–68; FCO, 1968–70. *Address:* Gillingham House, Gillingham Street, SW1V 1HU.

FOLEY, Sir Noel; *see* Foley, Sir T. J. N.

FOLEY, Rt. Rev. Ronald Graham Gregory; appointed Bishop Suffragan of Reading, 1982, Area Bishop, 1985, retired 1989; Assistant Bishop, Diocese of York, since 1989; *b* 13 June 1923; *s* of Theodore Gregory Foley and Cessan Florence Page; *m* 1944, Florence Redman; two *s* two *d*. *Educ:* King Edward's Grammar Sch., Aston, Birmingham; Wakefield Grammar Sch.; King's Coll., London; St John's Coll., Durham BA Hons Theol., LTh. Curate, South Shore, Blackpool, 1950; Vicar, S Luke, Blackburn, 1954; Dir of Educn, Dio. of Durham, and Rector of Brancepeth, 1960; Chaplain, Aycliffe Approved Sch., 1962; Vicar of Leeds, 1971–82; Chaplain to the Queen, 1977–82. Hon. Canon: Durham Cathedral, 1965–71; Ripon Cath., 1971–82. Dir, Yorks Electricity Bd, 1976–82. Chm. of Trustees, Dorothy Kerin Trust, Burrswood, 1983–89. *Publication:* (jtly) Religion in Approved Schools, 1969. *Recreations:* journalism, reading detective stories, watching other people mow lawns. *Address:* Ramsey Cottage, 3 Poplar Avenue, Kirkbymoorside, York YO6 6ES. *T:* Kirkbymoorside (01751) 32439.

FOLEY, Sir (Thomas John) Noel, Kt 1978; CBE 1967; Chairman: CSR Ltd, 1980–84; Allied Manufacturing and Trading Industries (AMATIL) Ltd, 1955–79 (retired); *b* 1914; *s* of late Benjamin Foley, Brisbane. *Educ:* Brisbane Grammar Sch., Queensland; Queensland Univ. (BA, BCom). Chm., Bank of NSW, 1978–82, Westpac Banking Corp., 1980–87 (Pres., 1982–86). Founding Pres., WWF, Australia, 1978–80. DUniv Sydney. *Address:* 45 Kintore Street, Wahroonga, NSW 2076, Australia.

FOLEY, Thomas Stephen; Hon. KBE 1995; Speaker, House of Representatives, USA, 1989–95; *b* 6 March 1929; *s* of Ralph E. Foley and Helen Marie (*née* Higgins); *m* 1968, Heather Strachan. *Educ:* Gonzaga High Sch.; Gonzaga Univ.; Washington Univ. (BA 1951; LLB 1957). Partner, Higgins and Foley, 1957–58; Lectr in Law, Gonzaga Univ., 1958–60; Dep. Prosecuting Attorney, Spokane County, 1958–60; Asst Attorney Gen., Washington State, 1960–61; Special Counsel, Senate Interior and Insular Affairs Cttee, 1961–64; Mem. of 89th–101st Congresses from 5th Dist Washington (Democrat), 1964–. Chm., 1975–80, Vice-Chm., 1981–86, Agriculture Cttee. Chm., House Democratic Caucus, 1976–80; House Majority Whip, 1981–87; Majority Leader, 1987–89. Mem., Bd of Advrs, Yale Univ. Council; Dir, Council on Foreign Relations. *Address:* Akin, Gump, Strauss, Hauer and Feld, 1333 New Hampshire Avenue, NW, Washington, DC 20036, USA.

FOLJAMBE, family name of **Earl of Liverpool.**

FOLKESTONE, Viscount; William Pleydell-Bouverie; *b* 5 Jan. 1955; *s* and *heir* of 8th Earl of Radnor, *qv*. *Educ:* Harrow; Royal Agricultural Coll., Cirencester. *Address:* Alward House, Alderbury, Salisbury, Wilts SP5 3DJ. *T:* Salisbury (01722) 710371.

FOLLETT, Sir Brian (Keith), Kt 1992; FRS 1984; Vice-Chancellor, University of Warwick, since 1993; *b* 22 Feb. 1939; *s* of Albert James Follett and Edith Annie Follett; *m* 1961, Deb (*née* Booth); one *s* one *d*. *Educ:* Bournemouth Sch.; Univ. of Bristol (BSc 1960, PhD 1964); Univ. of Wales (DSc 1975). Res. Fellow, Washington State Univ., 1964–65; Lectr in Zool., Univ. of Leeds, 1965–69; Lectr, subseq. Reader and Prof. of Zool.,

University Coll. of N Wales, Bangor, 1969–78; Bristol University: Prof. of Zool., 1978–93, AFRC Res. Prof., 1989–93; Hd of Dept of Zool., 1978–89; Chm., Sch. of Biol Scis, 1989–93. Chm., ESRC-British Acad. Working Party on the Future of Funding Res. in the Humanities, 1992; Member: Biol Sci. Cttee, SERC, 1981–84; AFRC, 1984–88 (Mem., Animals Cttee, 1984–88); Biol Sci. Cttee, UGC, 1985–88; UFC, 1989–93; HEFCE, 1992– (Chm., Libraries Review Gp, 1992–94); Council, BBSRC, 1994– (Chm., Sci. and Engrg Bd, 1994–); Trustee, BM (Natural Hist.), 1989–. Biol Sec. and Vice-Pres., Royal Soc., 1987–93; Member of Council: Soc. for Study of Fertility, 1972–87 (Prog. Sec., 1976–78; Treas., 1982–87); Soc. for Endocrinology, 1974–77; Bristol Zoo, 1978–; Wildfowl Trust, Slimbridge, 1983–86; Zool Soc. of London, 1983–86. Lectures: Amoroso, Soc. for Study of Fertility, 1985; Annual Zool., Liverpool Univ., 1991; Barrington Meml, Nottingham Univ., 1992. Mem., Academia Europaea, 1988. Hon. Fellow, UCNW, Bangor, 1990. Hon. LLD Wales, 1992. Scientific Medal, 1976, Frink Medal, 1993, Zool Soc. of London; Dale Medal, Soc. of Endocrinology, 1988. Editorial Bds: Jl of Endocrinology, 1971–78; Gen. & Comparative Endocrinology, 1974–82; Jl of Biol. Rhythms, 1986–; Proc. of Royal Soc., 1987–90. *Publications:* over 250 scientific papers on biol. clocks and reproductive physiology. *Address:* Vice-Chancellor's Lodge, Cryfield Old Farmhouse, University of Warwick, Coventry CV4 7AJ. *T:* Coventry (01203) 692078.

FOLLETT, Ken; author, since 1977; *b* 5 June 1949; *s* of Martin Dunsford Follett and Lavinia Cynthia (Veenie) Follett (*née* Evans); *m* 1st, 1968, Mary Elson (marr. diss. 1985); one *s* one *d*; 2nd, 1985, Barbara Broer. *Educ:* Harrow Weald Grammar Sch.; Poole Tech. Coll.; University Coll. London (BA; Fellow 1994). Trainee journalist, S Wales Echo, 1970–73; Reporter, London Evening News, 1973–74; Everest Books: Edtl Dir, 1974–76; Dep. Man. Dir, 1976–77. *Publications include:* Eye of the Needle (Edgar Award, Mystery Writers of Amer.), 1978; Triple, 1979; The Key to Rebecca, 1980; The Man from St Petersburg, 1982; On Wings of Eagles, 1983; Lie down with Lions, 1986; The Pillars of the Earth, 1989; Night over Water, 1991; Mrs Shiblak's Nightmare (pamphlet), 1992; A Dangerous Fortune, 1993; A Place Called Freedom, 1995; various articles, screenplays and short stories. *Recreations:* bass guitarist in a blues band; Labour Party supporter and campaigner. *Address:* PO Box 708, SW10 0DH. *Club:* Groucho.

FONTAINE, André Lucien Georges; Editor-in-Chief, le Monde, 1985–91; *b* 30 March 1921; *s* of Georges Fontaine and Blanche Rochon Duvigneaud; *m* 1943, Belita Cavaillé; two *s* one *d*. *Educ:* Paris Univ. (diplomes études supérieures droit public et économie politique, lic.lettres). Joined Temps Présent, 1946; with le Monde from 1947; Foreign Editor, 1951; Chief Editor, 1969. Editorialist, Radio Luxemburg, 1980–91. Chm. Adv. Gp, Internat. Strategy for the 9th Plan, 1982–84; Mem. Bd, Institut Français des Relations Internationales, 1982–92. Mem. Bd, Bank Indosuez, 1983–85. Grand Officer, Order of Dom Enrique (Portugal); Commander: German Merit; Italian Merit; Greek Phoenix; Officer, Orders of Vasa (Sweden), Leopold (Belgium) and Lion (Finland); Kt, Danebrog (Denmark) and Crown of Belgium; Order of Tudor Vladimirescu (Romania). Atlas' Internat. Editor of the Year, 1976. *Publications:* L'Alliance atlantique à l'heure du dégel, 1960; Histoire de la guerre froide, vol. 1 1965, vol. 2 1966 (English trans., History of the Cold War, 1966 and 1967); La Guerre civile froide, 1969; Le dernier quart du siècle, 1976; La France au bois dormant, 1978; Un seul lit pour deux rêves, 1981; (with Pierre Li) Sortir de l'Hexagonie, 1984; L'un sans l'autre, 1991. *Address:* 15 rue Falguière, 75501 Paris Cedex 15, France.

FOOKES, Dame Janet (Evelyn), DBE 1989; MP (C) Plymouth, Drake, since 1974 (Merton and Morden, 1970–74); Second Deputy Chairman of Ways and Means and Deputy Speaker, House of Commons, since 1992; *b* 21 Feb. 1936; *d* of late Lewis Aylmer Fookes and of Evelyn Margery Fookes (*née* Holmes). *Educ:* Hastings and St Leonards Ladies' Coll.; High Sch. for Girls, Hastings; Royal Holloway Coll., Univ. of London (BA Hons). Teacher, 1958–70. Councillor for County Borough of Hastings, 1960–61 and 1963–70 (Chm. Educn Cttee, 1967–70). Mem., Speaker's Panel of Chairmen, 1976–. Sec., Cons. Parly Educn Cttee, 1971–75; Chairman: Educn, Arts and Home Affairs Sub-Cttee of the Expenditure Cttee, 1975–79; Parly Gp for Animal Welfare, 1985–92 (Sec., 1974–82); Member: Unopposed Bills Cttee, 1973–75; Services Cttee, 1974–76; Select Cttee on Home Affairs, 1984–92. Chm., Cons. West Country Mems Cttee, 1976–77, Vice-Chm., 1977. Mem. Council, RSPCA, 1975–92 (Chm., 1979–81); Member: Nat. Art Collections Fund; Council, SSAFA, 1980–; Council, Stonham Housing Assoc., 1980–92; Commonwealth War Graves Commn, 1987–. Member: RHS; Nat. Trust. *Recreations:* theatre, gardening, gymnasium exercises, swimming. *Address:* House of Commons, SW1A 0AA.

FOOT, family name of **Baron Foot**.

FOOT, Baron *cr* 1967 (Life Peer), of Buckland Monachorum; **John Mackintosh Foot;** Chairman, United Kingdom Immigrants Advisory Service, 1970–78 (President, 1978–84); *b* 17 Feb. 1909; 3rd *s* of late Rt Hon. Isaac Foot, PC and Eva Mackintosh; *m* 1936, Anne, *d* of Dr Clifford Bailey Farr, Bryn Mawr, Pa; one *s* one *d*. *Educ:* Forres Sch., Swanage; Bembridge Sch., IoW; Balliol Coll., Oxford. Pres., Oxford Union, 1931; Pres., OU Liberal Club, 1931; BA Oxon (2nd cl. hons Jurisprudence), 1931. Admitted Solicitor, 1934. Served in Army, 1939–45 (Hon. Major); jsc 1944. Contested (L); Basingstoke, 1934 and 1935; Bodmin, 1945 and 1950. Member: Dartmoor National Park Cttee, 1963–74; Commn on the Constitution, 1969–73; President: Dartmoor Preservation Assoc., 1976–94; Commons, Open Spaces and Footpaths Preservation Soc., 1976–82. Chm. Council, Justice, 1984–89. *Recreations:* chess, crosswords, defending Dartmoor. *Address:* Yew Tree, Crapstone, Yelverton, Devon PL20 7PJ. *T:* Yelverton (01822) 853417. *Club:* Royal Western Yacht.

See also Rt Hon. Michael Foot.

FOOT, David Lovell, FICFor; Forestry Commissioner, since 1986; *b* 20 May 1939; *s* of late John Bartram Lovell Foot, MBE and of Bertha Lilian Foot; *m* 1964, Verena Janine Walton; one *s* one *d*. *Educ:* John Lyon Sch., Harrow; Edinburgh Univ. (BSc Hons 1961). FICFor 1980. Dist Officer, Forestry Commn, 1961–64; Silviculturist, Dept of Forestry and Game, Govt of Malawi, 1964–70; Forestry Commission: various appts in S Scotland, N Wales and E Scotland, 1970–82; Conservator, S Scotland, 1982; Dir, Harvesting and Marketing Div., Edinburgh, 1985. *Recreations:* walking, fishing, photography. *Address:* 36 Coltbridge Terrace, Edinburgh EH12 6AE. *T:* 0131–337 3874.

FOOT, Sir Geoffrey (James), Kt 1984; Chairman and Commissioner, Hydro Electric Commission of Tasmania, 1987–89 (Associate Commissioner, 1984–87); *b* 20 July 1915; *s* of James P. Foot and Susan J. Foot; *m* 1940, Mollie W. Snooks; two *s* one *d*. *Educ:* Launceston High Sch. AASA; ACIS. MLC, Tasmania, 1961–72 (Leader for Govt, 1969–72). Chairman: Tasmania Permanent Bldg Soc., 1982–85; Launceston Gas Co., 1982–84; Gas Corp. of Tasmania, 1984–87. Mem., Lilydale Commn—Local Govt, 1983–85. Mem. Council, Univ. of Tas, 1970–85. Freeman, City of Launceston, 1990. Hon. LLD Tasmania, 1988. *Recreations:* reading, music. *Address:* 85 Arthur Street, Launceston, Tas 7250, Australia. *T:* (03) 340573. *Club:* Launceston (Launceston).

FOOT, Rt. Hon. Michael, PC 1974; *b* 23 July 1913; *s* of late Rt Hon. Isaac Foot, PC; *m* 1949, Jill Craigie. *Educ:* Forres Sch., Swanage; Leighton Park Sch., Reading; Wadham Coll., Oxford (Exhibitioner). Pres. Oxford Union, 1933; contested (Lab) Mon, 1935; MP (Lab): Devonport Div. of Plymouth, 1945–55; Ebbw Vale, Nov. 1960–1983; Blaenau Gwent, 1983–92; Sec. of State for Employment, 1974–76; Lord President of the Council and Leader of the House of Commons, 1976–79; Leader of the Opposition, 1980–83. Mem., Labour Party Nat. Exec. Cttee, 1971–83; Deputy Leader of the Labour Party, 1976–80, Leader of the Labour Party 1980–83. Asst Editor, Tribune, 1937–38; Acting Editor, Evening Standard, 1942; Man. Dir, Tribune, 1945–74, Editor, 1948–52, 1955–60; political columnist on the Daily Herald, 1944–64; former Book Critic, Evening Standard. Hon. Fellow, Wadham Coll. 1969. *Publications:* Guilty Men (with Frank Owen and Peter Howard), 1940; Armistice 1918–39, 1940; Trial of Mussolini, 1943; Brendan and Beverley, 1944; Still at Large, 1950; Full Speed Ahead, 1950; Guilty Men (with Mervyn Jones), 1957; The Pen and the Sword, 1957; Parliament in Danger, 1959; Aneurin Bevan: Vol. I, 1897–1945, 1962; Vol. II, 1945–60, 1973; Debts of Honour, 1980; Another Heart and Other Pulses, 1984; Loyalists and Loners, 1986; The Politics of Paradise, 1988. *Recreations:* Plymouth Argyle supporter, chess, reading, walking. *Address:* 308 Gray's Inn Road, WC1X 8DY. *T:* 0171–713 7145.

See also Baron Foot.

FOOT, Michael Colin, OBE 1984; freelance teacher and lecturer, English as a foreign language; *b* 3 Feb. 1935; *s* of William Reginald Foot and Elsie (*née* Collins); *m* 1964, Heather Pearl Foot (*née* Beaton); two *s* two *d*. *Educ:* Taunton's Sch., Southampton; University Coll., Leicester (BA London); Leicester Univ. (PGCE); Univ. of Essex (MA 1994). Lycée Champollion, Grenoble, 1959–60; Ashlyn's Sch., Berkhamsted, 1960–63. Served RAF, 1963–66. British Council: Asst Rep., Chile, 1966–71; Hd of Overseas Recruitment, Personnel Div., 1971–75; Dep. Rep., Nigeria, 1975–78; Dep. Dir, Personnel, 1978–81; Rep., Bangladesh, 1981–83; Dir, Personnel, 1984–85; Controller, Personnel, 1986–89; Dir, Australia, 1989–93; retd 1993. *Recreations:* reading, theatre, music, botany, swimming. *Address:* c/o Midland Bank, Bitterne, Southampton SO9 3RZ. *Club:* Royal Air Force.

FOOT, Michael David Kenneth Willoughby; Deputy Director, Supervision and Surveillance, Bank of England, since 1994; *b* 16 Dec. 1946; *s* of Kenneth Willoughby Foot and Ruth Joan (*née* Cornah); *m* 1972, Michele Annette Cynthia Macdonald; one *s* two *d*. *Educ:* Pembroke Coll., Cambridge (MA); Yale Univ., USA (MA). Joined Bank of England, 1969; manager, 1978; sen. man., 1985; seconded to IMF, Washington, as UK Alternate Exec. Dir, 1985–87; Head: Foreign Exchange Div., 1988–90; European Div., 1990–93; Banking Supervision Div., 1993–94. *Publications;* contrib. essays on monetary econs to books and jls. *Recreations:* choral singing, voluntary youth work. *Address:* c/o Bank of England, Threadneedle Street, EC2R 8AH.

FOOT, Michael Richard Daniell; historian; *b* 14 Dec. 1919; *s* of late R. C. Foot and Nina (*née* Raymond); *m* twice; one *s* one *d*; 3rd, 1972, Mirjam Michaela, DLitt, *y d* of late Prof. C. P. M. Romme, Oisterwijk. *Educ:* Winchester (scholar); New Coll., Oxford (scholar). Served in Army, 1939–45 (Major RA, parachutist, wounded). Taught at Oxford, 1947–59; research, 1959–67; Prof of Modern Hist., Manchester, 1967–73; Dir of Studies, European Discussion Centre, 1973–75. French Croix de Guerre, 1945; Officer, Order of Orange Nassau (Netherlands), 1989. *Publications:* Gladstone and Liberalism (with J. L. Hammond), 1952; British Foreign Policy since 1898, 1956; Men in Uniform, 1961; SOE in France, 1966; (ed) The Gladstone Diaries: vols I and II, 1825–1839, 1968; (ed) War and Society, 1973; (ed with Dr H. C. G. Matthew) The Gladstone Diaries: vols III and IV, 1840–1854, 1974; Resistance, 1976; Six Faces of Courage, 1978; (with J. M. Langley) MI9, 1979; SOE: an outline history, 1984; Art and War, 1990; (ed) Holland at war against Hitler, 1990; (ed) Oxford Companion to the Second World War, 1995. *Recreations:* reading, talking. *Address:* 45 Countess Road, NW5 2XH. *Clubs:* Savile, Special Forces.

FOOT, Paul Mackintosh; writer; journalist; with Private Eye, since 1993; *b* 8 Nov. 1937; *m*; three *s*; one *d*. Editor of Isis, 1961; President of the Oxford Union, 1961. TUC delegate from Nat. Union of Journalists, 1967 and 1971. Contested (Socialist Workers Party) Birmingham, Stechford, March 1977. Editor, Socialist Worker, 1974–75; with The Daily Mirror, 1979–93. Journalist of the Year, What The Papers Say Awards, 1972, 1989; Campaigning Journalist of the Year, British Press Awards, 1980; (with Tim Laxton) George Orwell Prize for Journalism, 1994. *Publications:* Immigration and Race in British Politics, 1965; The Politics of Harold Wilson, 1968; The Rise of Enoch Powell, 1969; Who Killed Hanratty?, 1971; Why You Should Be a Socialist, 1977; Red Shelley, 1981; The Helen Smith Story, 1983; Murder at the Farm: who killed Carl Bridgewater?, 1986; Who Framed Colin Wallace?, 1989; Words as Weapons, 1990; contrib. Counterblasts, 1989. *Address:* c/o Private Eye, 6 Carlisle Street, W1V 5RG.

FOOT, Prof. Philippa Ruth, FBA 1976; Griffin Professor, University of California at Los Angeles, 1988–91, now Emeritus (Professor of Philosophy, 1974–91); *b* 3 Oct. 1920; *d* of William Sydney Bence Bosanquet, DSO, and Esther Cleveland Bosanquet, *d* of Grover Cleveland, Pres. of USA; *m* 1945, M. R. D. Foot (marr. diss. 1960), *qv*; no *c*. *Educ:* St George's Sch., Ascot; privately; Somerville Coll., Oxford (BA 1942, MA 1946). Somerville Coll., Oxford: Lectr in philosophy, 1947; Fellow and Tutor, 1950–69; Vice-Principal, 1967–69; Sen. Res. Fellow, 1970–88; Hon. Fellow, 1988. Formerly Vis. Prof., Cornell Univ., MIT, Univ. of California at Berkeley, Princeton Univ., City Univ. of NY; Fellow, Center for Advanced Studies in Behavioral Scis, Stanford, 1981–82. Pres., Pacific Div., Amer. Philos. Assoc., 1982–83. Fellow, Amer. Acad. of Arts and Scis, 1983. *Publications:* Theories of Ethics (ed), 1967; Virtues and Vices, 1978; articles in Mind, Aristotelian Soc. Proc., Philos. Rev., New York Rev., Philosophy and Public Affairs. *Address:* 15 Walton Street, Oxford OX1 2HG. *T:* Oxford (01865) 57130.

FOOTE, Prof. Peter Godfrey; Emeritus Professor of Scandinavian Studies, University of London; *b* 26 May 1924; 4th *s* of late T. Foote and Ellen Foote, Swanage, Dorset; *m* 1951, Eleanor Jessie McCaig, *d* of late J. M. McCaig and Margaret H. McCaig; one *s* two *d*. *Educ:* Grammar Sch., Swanage; University Coll., Exeter; Univ. of Oslo; University Coll., London. BA London 1948; MA London 1951; Fil. dr *hc* Uppsala, 1972; dr phil. *hc* Univ. of Iceland, 1987. Served with RNVR, 1943–46. University College London: Asst Lectr, Lectr and Reader in Old Scandinavian, 1950–63; Prof. of Scandinavian Studies, 1963–83; Fellow, 1989. Jt Sec., Viking Soc., 1956–83 (Pres., 1974–76; 1990–92); Hon. Life Mem., 1983). Member: Royal Gustav Adolfs Academy, Uppsala, 1967; Kungl. Humanistiska Vetenskapssamfundet, Uppsala, 1968; Vísindafélag Islands, 1969; Vetenskapssocieteten, Lund, 1973; Kungl. Vetenskaps-samhället, Göteborg; Det kongelige Norske Videnskabers Selskab, 1977; Societas Scientiarum Fennica, 1979; Det norske Videnskapsakademi, 1986; Hon. Member: Isl. Bókmenntafélag, 1965; Thjóðvinafélag Ísl. í Vesturheimi, 1975; Corresp. Mem., Kungl. Vitterhets Hist. och Antikvitets Akad., Stockholm, 1971. Crabtree Orator, 1968. Commander with star, Icelandic Order of the Falcon, 1984 (Comdr, 1973); Knight, Order of Dannebrog (Denmark); Comdr, Royal Order of North Star (Sweden), 1977; Comdr, Royal Order of Merit (Norway), 1993. *Publications:* Gunnlaugs saga ormstungu, 1957; Pseudo-Turpin Chronicle in Iceland, 1959; Laing's Heimskringla, 1961; Lives of Saints: Icelandic manuscripts in fascimile IV, 1962, and XIX, 1990; (with G. Johnston) The Saga of Gisli, 1963; (with D. M. Wilson) The Viking Achievement, 1970, 2nd edn 1980; Aurvandilstá (selected papers), 1984; Jt Editor, Mediæval Scandinavia;

Mem. of Ed. Board, Scandinavica; papers in Saga-Book, Arv, Studia Islandica, Islenzk Tunga, etc. *Recreations:* bell-ringing, walking. *Address:* 18 Talbot Road, N6 4QR. *T:* 0181–340 1860.

FOOTMAN, Charles Worthington Fowden, CMG 1952; *b* 3 Sept. 1905; *s* of Rev. William Llewellyn and Mary Elizabeth Footman; *m* 1947, Joyce Marcelle Law; one *s* two *d*. *Educ:* Rossall Sch.; Keble Coll., Oxford. Colonial Administrative Service, Zanzibar, 1930; seconded to East African Governors' Conference, 1942; seconded to Colonial Office, 1943–46; Financial Sec., Nyasaland, 1947; Chief Sec., Nyasaland, 1951–60. Retired from HM Overseas Civil Service, 1960. Chm., Public Service Commissions, Tanganyika and Zanzibar, 1960–61; Commonwealth Relations Office, 1962–64; Min. of Overseas Development, 1964–70.

FOOTS, Sir James (William), Kt 1975; AO 1992; mining engineer; Chairman: MIM Holdings Ltd, 1970–83 (Director, 1956–87); Westpac Banking Corporation, 1987–89 (Director, 1971–89); *b* 1916; *m* 1939, Thora H.Thomas; one *s* two *d*. *Educ:* Melbourne Univ. (BME). President: Austr. Inst. Mining and Metallurgy, 1974; Austr. Mining Industry Council, 1974 and 1975; 13th Congress, Council of Mining and Metallurgical Institns, 1986. Fellow, Australian Acad. of Technol Scis. University of Queensland: Mem. Senate, 1970–92; Chancellor, 1985–92. Hon. DEng Univ. of Qld, 1982. *Address:* PO Box 662, Kenmore, Qld 4069, Australia.

FOOTTIT, Ven. Anthony Charles; Archdeacon of Lynn, since 1987; *b* 28 June 1935; *s* of Percival Frederick and Mildred Foottit; *m* 1977, Rosamond Mary Alyson Buxton; one *s* two *d*. *Educ:* Lancing College; King's Coll., Cambridge (MA). Asst Curate, Wymondham, 1961–64; Vicar, Blakeney Group, 1964–71; Rector, Camelot Group, 1971–81; RD of Cary, 1979–81; St Hugh's Missioner for Lincolnshire, 1981–87; Hon. Canon of Lincoln Cathedral, 1986–87. *Publication:* Mission and Ministry in Rural France, 1967. *Recreations:* gardening, botany, rambling. *Address:* Ivy House, Whitwell Street, Reepham, Norwich NR10 4RA. *T:* Norwich (01603) 870340.

FOPP, Dr Michael Anton; Director, Royal Air Force Museum, since 1988; *b* 28 Oct. 1947; *s* of Sqdn Ldr Desmond Fopp and Edna Meryl (*née* Dodd); *m* 1968, Rosemary Ann Hodgetts; one *s*. *Educ:* Reading Blue Coat Sch.; City Univ., London (MA 1984; PhD 1989). FIMgt; FMA. Dep. Keeper 1979–82, Keeper 1982–85, Battle of Britain Mus.; Co. Sec., Hendon Mus. Trading Co. Ltd, 1983–85; Dir, London Transport Mus., 1985–88. Hon. Sec. 1976–86, Chm. 1986–88, Soc. of Friends of RAF Mus. President: London Underground Rly Soc., 1987; Internat. Assoc. of Transport Museums. Chairman: Museums' Documentation Assoc.; London Transport Flying Club Ltd, 1986–. Freeman: City of London, 1984; Guild of Air Pilots and Navigators, 1987. *Publications:* The Boeing Washington, 1980; The Battle of Britain Museum Guide, 1980; The Bomber Command Museum Guide, 1982; The RAF Museum Guide, 1985; (ed) A Junior Guide to the RAF Museum, 1985; (ed) Battle of Britain Project Book, 1989; Royal Air Force Museum, 1992; (ed) High Flyers, 1993; various articles on aviation, museums and management, in magazines and jls. *Recreations:* flying, computers, Chinese cookery, building light aircraft. *Address:* Royal Air Force Museum, Hendon, NW9 5LL. *T:* 0181–205 2266. *Club:* Royal Air Force.

FORAY, Prof. Cyril Patrick; High Commissioner for Sierra Leone in the United Kingdom, 1993–95; *b* 16 March 1934; *s* of Michael Kelema Foray and Mary Bridget Foray (*née* Alie); *m* 1958, Arabella Williams; two *s* two *d*. *Educ:* St Edward's Secondary Sch., Freetown, Sierra Leone; Fourah Bay Coll., Freetown; St Cuthbert's Soc.; Durham Univ.; UCLA. Asst Master, St Edward's Secondary Sch., Freetown, 1958–60, Sen. Asst Master, 1960–62; part-time Lectr, Dept of Hist., Fourah Bay Coll., 1959–60; Lectr, Njala UC, 1964–67; Department of History, Fourah Bay College: Temp. Lectr, 1968–69 and 1972–73; Lectr, 1973–77; Actg Hd, 1975–77; Hd of Dept, 1977–85; Sen. Lectr, 1977–81; Associate Prof., 1981–85; Vice Principal, 1984–85; Prof. and Principal, 1985–93. University of Sierra Leone: Public Orator, 1976–85; Dean, Faculty of Arts, 1978–82; Pro-Vice Chancellor, 1988–90. MP Bo Town I constituency, Sierra Leone, 1969–73; Minister of: Ext. Affairs, 1969–71; Health, May–Sept. 1971. *Publications:* Historical Dictionary of Sierra Leone, Vol. 12, 1977; articles on Sierra Leone in Encyclopaedia Africana, 1979; The Road to the One Party—The Sierra Leone Experience, 1988. *Recreations:* cricket, lawn tennis. *Address:* c/o Sierra Leone High Commission, 33 Portland Place, W1N 3AG.

FORBES, family name of **Lord Forbes** and of **Earl of Granard.**

FORBES, 22nd Lord *cr* 1445 or before; **Nigel Ivan Forbes,** KBE 1960; JP, DL; Premier Lord of Scotland; Representative Peer of Scotland, 1955–63; Major (retired) Grenadier Guards; Chairman, Rolawn Ltd, since 1975; *b* 19 Feb. 1918; *o s* of 21st Lord and Lady Mabel Anson (*d* 1972), *d* of 3rd Earl of Lichfield; *S* father, 1953; *m* 1942, Hon. Rosemary Katharine Hamilton-Russell, *o d* of 9th Viscount Boyne; two *s* one *d*. *Educ:* Harrow; RMC Sandhurst. Served War of 1939–45 (wounded); Adjt, Grenadier Guards, Staff Coll. Military Asst to High Comr for Palestine, 1947–48. Minister of State, Scottish Office, 1958–59. Member: Inter-Parly Union Delegn to Denmark, 1956; Commonwealth Parly Assoc. Delegn to Canada, 1961; Parly Delegn to Pakistan, 1962; Inter-Parly Union Delegn to Hungary, 1965; Inter-Parly Union Delegn to Ethiopia, 1971. Director: Grampian Television PLC, 1960–88; Blenheim Travel Ltd, 1981–88; Dep. Chm., Tenant Caledonian Breweries Ltd, 1964–74. Mem., Aberdeen and District Milk Marketing Bd, 1962–72; Mem. Alford District Council, 1955–58; Chm., River Don District Bd, 1962–73. Pres., Royal Highland and Agricultural Society of Scotland, 1958–59; Member: Sports Council for Scotland, 1966–71; Scottish Cttee, Nature Conservancy, 1961–67; Chm., Scottish Br., Nat. Playing Fields Assoc., 1965–80; Pres., Scottish Scout Assoc., 1970–88. JP 1955, DL 1958, Aberdeenshire. *Recreations:* wildlife, travel, photography. *Heir: s* Master of Forbes, *qv*. *Address:* Balforbes, Alford, Aberdeenshire AB33 8DR. *T:* Alford (Aberdeen) (019755) 62516, *Fax:* (019755) 62898. *Club:* Army and Navy.

FORBES, Viscount; Jonathan Peter Hastings Forbes; *b* 24 Dec. 1981; *e s* and *heir* of Earl of Granard, *qv*.

FORBES, Master of; Hon. Malcolm Nigel Forbes; landowner; *b* 6 May 1946; *s* and *heir* of 22nd Lord Forbes, *qv*; *m* 1st,1969, Carole Jennifer Andrée (marr. diss. 1982), *d* of N. S. Whitehead, Aberdeen; one *s* one *d*; 2nd, 1988, Jennifer Mary Gribbon, *d* of I. P. Whittington, Tunbridge Wells. *Educ:* Eton; Aberdeen Univ. Director, Instock Disposables Ltd, 1974–. *Address:* Castle Forbes, Alford, Aberdeenshire AB33 8BL. *T:* Alford (019755) 62574; 3 Steeple Close, SW6 3LE. *T:* 0171–736 0730. *Club:* Royal Northern and University (Aberdeen).

FORBES, Hon. Sir Alastair (Granville), Kt 1960; President, Courts of Appeal for St Helena, Falkland Islands and British Antarctic Territories, 1965–88, and British Indian Ocean Territory, 1986–88; *b* 3 Jan. 1908; *s* of Granville Forbes and Constance Margaret (*née* Davis); *m* 1936, Constance Irene Mary Hughes-White (*d* 1995); two *d*. *Educ:* Blundell's Sch.; Clare Coll., Cambridge. Called to the Bar, Gray's Inn, 1932; Magistrate and Govt Officer, Dominica, BWI, 1936; Crown Attorney, Dominica, 1939; Resident Magistrate, Fiji, 1940; Crown Counsel, Fiji, 1942; Solicitor-Gen., Fiji, and Asst Legal Adviser, Western Pacific High Commission, 1945; Legal Draftsman, Federation of Malaya, 1947; Solicitor-Gen., Northern Rhodesia, 1950; Permanent Sec., Ministry of Justice, and Solicitor-Gen., Gold Coast, 1951; Puisne Judge, Kenya, 1956; Justice of Appeal, Court of Appeal for Eastern Africa, 1957; Vice-Pres., Court of Appeal for Eastern Africa, 1958; Federal Justice, Federal Supreme Court of Rhodesia and Nyasaland, 1963–64; Pres., Ct of Appeal: for Seychelles, 1965–76; for Gibraltar, 1970–83. Mem., Panel of Chairmen of Industrial Tribunals (England and Wales), 1965–73; Pres., Pensions Appeal Tribunals for England and Wales, 1973–80 (Chm., 1965–73); Chairman: Constituencies Delimitation Commissions, N Rhodesia, 1962 and 1963, and Bechuanaland, 1964; Gibraltar Riot Inquiry, 1968. *Publications:* Index of the Laws, Dominica, 1940; Revised Edition of Laws of Fiji, 1944. *Recreations:* fishing, shooting. *Address:* Badgers Holt, Church Lane, Sturminster Newton, Dorset DT10 1DH. *T:* Sturminster Newton (01258) 473268.

FORBES, Anthony David Arnold William; Joint Senior Partner, Cazenove & Co., 1980–94; *b* 15 Jan. 1938; *s* of late Lt-Col D. W. A. W. Forbes, MC, and Diana Mary (*née* Henderson), later Marchioness of Exeter; *m* 1st, 1962, Virginia June Ropner; one *s* one *d*; 2nd, 1973, Belinda Mary Drury-Lowe. *Educ:* Eton. Served Coldstream Guards, 1956–59. Joined Cazenove & Co., 1960; Member of Stock Exchange, subseq. MSI, 1965–. Director: Carlton Communications Plc, 1994–; The Merchants Trust PLC, 1994–; Royal Insurance Hldgs plc, 1994–; RTZ Pension Investment Ltd, 1994–; Watmoughs (Hldgs) PLC, 1994–; Phoenix Group Ltd, 1995–. Chairman: Hospital and Homes of St Giles, 1975–; Wellesley House Educnl Trust, 1983–94; Hon. Trustee, Royal Botanic Gardens Kew Foundn, 1992–; Trustee, Botanic Gardens Conservation Internat., 1992–. Governor: Cobham Hall, 1975–94; Royal Choral Soc., 1979–. FRSA 1993. Hon. DBA De Montfort Univ., 1994. *Recreations:* music, shooting, gardening. *Address:* 57 Hollywood Road, SW10 9HX. *T:* 0171–351 9334.

FORBES, Bryan; *b* 22 July 1926; *m* 1958, Nanette Newman, *qv*; two *d*. *Educ:* West Ham Secondary Sch. Studied at RADA, 1941; entered acting profession, 1942, and (apart from war service) was on West End stage, then in films here and in Hollywood, 1948–60. Formed Beaver Films with Sir Richard Attenborough, 1959; wrote and co-produced The Angry Silence, 1960. Subseq. wrote, dir. and prod. numerous films; *films include:* The League of Gentlemen, Only Two Can Play, Whistle Down the Wind, 1961; The L-Shaped Room, 1962; Séance on a Wet Afternoon, 1963; King Rat (in Hollywood), 1964; The Wrong Box, 1965; The Whisperers, 1966; Deadfall, 1967; The Madwoman of Chaillot, 1968; The Raging Moon, 1970; The Tales of Beatrix Potter, 1971; The Stepford Wives, 1974 (USA); The Slipper and the Rose, 1975 (Royal Film Perf., 1976); International Velvet, 1978; (British segment) The Sunday Lovers, 1980; Better Late Than Never, 1981; The Naked Face, 1983; (narrator) I am a Dancer, 1971. *Stage:* Directed: Macbeth, Old Vic, 1980; Killing Jessica, Savoy, 1986; The Living Room, Royalty, 1987; directed and acted in Star Quality, Th. Royal, Bath, 1983. *Television:* produced and directed: Edith Evans, I Caught Acting Like the Measles, Yorkshire TV, 1973; Elton John, Goodbye Norma Jean and Other Things, ATV 1973; Jessie, BBC, 1980; The Endless Game, C4, 1989; acted in: December Flower, Granada, 1984; First Among Equals, Granada, 1986. Man. Dir and Head of Production, ABPC Studios, 1969–71; Man. Dir and Chief Exec., EMI-MGM, Elstree Studios, 1970–71; Dir, Capital Radio Ltd, 1973–. Member: BBC Gen. Adv. Council, 1966–69; BBC Schs Council, 1971–73; President: Beatrix Potter Soc., 1982–; Nat. Youth Theatre, 1984–; Writers' Guild of GB, 1988–91. Won British Acad. Award, 1960; Writers' Guild Award (twice); numerous internat. awards. *Publications:* Truth Lies Sleeping, 1950; The Distant Laughter, 1972; Notes for a Life, 1974; The Slipper and the Rose, 1976; Ned's Girl: biography of Dame Edith Evans, 1977; International Velvet, 1978; Familiar Strangers, 1979; That Despicable Race, 1980; The Rewrite Man, 1983; The Endless Game, 1986; A Song at Twilight, 1989; A Divided Life, 1992; The Twisted Playground, 1993; Partly Cloudy, 1995; contribs to: The Spectator, New Statesman, Queen, and other periodicals. *Recreations:* running a bookshop, reading, landscape gardening, photography. *Address:* The Bookshop, Virginia Water, Surrey GU25 4DW.

See also Sir John Leon, Bt.

FORBES, Colin, RDI 1974; Partner, Pentagram Design, since 1972; *b* 6 March 1928; *s* of Kathleen and John Forbes; *m* 1961, Wendy Schneider; one *s* two *d*. *Educ:* Sir Anthony Browne's, Brentwood; LCC Central Sch. of Arts and Crafts. Design Asst, Herbert Spencer, 1952; freelance practice and Lectr, LCC Central Sch. of Arts and Crafts, 1953–57; Art Dir, Stuart Advertising, London, 1957–58; Head of Graphic Design Dept, LCC Central Sch. of Arts and Crafts, 1958–61; freelance practice, London, 1961–62; Partner: Fletcher/Forbes/Gill, 1962–65; Crosby/Fletcher/Forbes, 1965–72. Mem., Alliance Graphique Internationale, 1965– (Internat. Pres. 1976–79); Pres., Amer. Inst. Graphic Arts, 1984–86. *Publications:* Graphic Design: visual comparisons, 1963; A Sign Systems Manual, 1970; Creativity and Communication, 1971; New Alphabets A to Z, 1973; Living by Design, 1978; Pentagram: the compendium, 1993. *Address:* Forbes Farm, 403A Route 2, Westfield, NC 27053, USA. *T:* (910) 3513941.

FORBES, Donald James, MA; Headmaster, Merchiston Castle School, 1969–81; *b* 6 Feb. 1921; *s* of Andrew Forbes; *m* 1945, Patricia Muriel Yeo; two *s* one *d*. *Educ:* Oundle; Clare Coll., Cambridge (Mod. Lang. Tripos). Capt. Scots Guards, 1941–46; 1st Bn Scots Guards, 1942–46, N Africa, Italy. Asst Master, Dulwich Coll., 1946–55; Master i/c cricket, 1951–55; Headmaster, Dauntsey's Sch., 1956–69. Diploma in Spanish, Univ. of Santander, 1954; Lectr in Spanish, West Norwood Tech. Coll., 1954–55. *Recreations:* cricket, Rugby football, tennis, Rugby fives, curling, golf; history, literature; instrumental and choral music. *Address:* 33 Coates Gardens, Edinburgh EH12 5LG; Breachacha Castle, Isle of Coll PA78 6TB. *Clubs:* Hawks (Cambridge); HCEG (Muirfield).

FORBES, Very Rev. Graham John Thomson; Provost, St Mary's Cathedral, Edinburgh, since 1990; *b* 10 June 1951; *s* of J. T. and D. D. Forbes; *m* 1973, Jane T. Miller; three *s*. *Educ:* George Heriot's School, Edinburgh; Univ. of Aberdeen (MA); Univ. of Edinburgh (BD). Curate, Old St Paul's Church, Edinburgh, 1976–82; Provost, St Ninian's Cathedral, Perth, 1982–90. Mem., Parole Bd for Scotland, 1990–. *Recreations:* climbing, running, dry rot. *Address:* 8 Lansdowne Crescent, Edinburgh EH12 5EQ. *T:* (home) 0131–225 2978; (office) 0131–225 6293.

FORBES, Major Sir Hamish (Stewart), 7th Bt *cr* 1823, of Newe; MBE 1945; MC 1945; Welsh Guards, retired; *b* 15 Feb. 1916; *s* of Lt-Col James Stewart Forbes (*d* 1957) (*g s* of 3rd Bt) and Feridah Frances Forbes (*d* 1953), *d* of Hugh Lewis Taylor; *S* cousin, 1984; *m* 1st, 1945, Jacynthe Elizabeth Mary, *d* of late Eric Gordon Underwood; one *s* three *d*; 2nd, 1981, Mary Christine, MBE, *d* of late Ernest William Rigby. *Educ:* Eton College; Lawrenceville, USA; SOAS. Served Welsh Guards, France, Germany, Turkey, 1939–58. Mem., Church Lads' and Church Girls' Bde Incorporated Soc., 1978–92; Pres., Church Lads' and Church Girls' Bde Assoc., 1974–. Patron, Lonach Highland and Friendly Soc., 1984–. KJStJ 1984. *Recreations:* shooting, sculpture. *Heir: s* James Thomas Stewart Forbes [*b* 28 May 1957; *m* 1986, Kerry Lynne, *o d* of Rev. Lee Toms; two *d*]. *Address:* Newe, Strathdon, Aberdeenshire AB36 8TY. *T:* Strathdon (019756) 51431. *Clubs:* Turf, Chelsea Arts, Pilgrims.

FORBES, Ian, QPM 1966; Deputy Assistant Commissioner, Metropolitan Police and National Co-ordinator, Regional Crime Squads (England and Wales), 1970–72, retired; *b*

30 March 1914; *y s* of John and Betsy Forbes, Auchlossan, Lumphanan, Aberdeenshire; *m* 1941, Lilian Edith Miller, Edgware, Mddx; two *s*. *Educ:* Lumphanan School, Aberdeenshire. Joined Metropolitan Police, 1939; served in East End, Central London Flying Squad, New Scotland Yard; Detective Superintendent, 1964; served on New Scotland Yard Murder Squad, 1966–69; Commander, No 9 Regional Crime Squad (London area), 1969. *Publication:* Squadman (autobiog.), 1973. *Recreations:* gardening, motoring, reading.

FORBES, James, FCA; Chairman and Treasurer, Council of Almoners, Christ's Hospital, since 1987; Forestry Commissioner, 1982–88; *b* 2 Jan. 1923; *s* of Donald Forbes and Rona Ritchie Forbes (*née* Yeats); *m* 1948, Alison Mary Fletcher Moffat; two *s*. *Educ:* Christ's Hospital; Officers' Training School, Bangalore. Chartered Accountant. Commissioned 15th Punjab Regt, Indian Army, 1942; transf. IAOC, released 1947 (hon. Major); Peat Marwick Mitchell Co., 1952–58; Chief Accountant, L. Rose, 1958; Group Operational Research Manager, Schweppes, 1960, Group Chief Accountant, 1963 (Dir, subsid. cos); Sec. and Financial Adviser, Cadbury Schweppes (on formation), 1969, Main Board Dir, 1971, Group Finance Dir to April 1978; Senior Exec. Dir, Tate & Lyle, 1978, Vice-Chm., 1980–84; Chm., Tate & Lyle Gp Pension Fund, 1978–85. Non-exec. Director: British Transport Hotels, 1978–83; British Rail Investments, 1980–84; Steetley plc, 1984–89; Compass Hotels, 1984–; Lautro Ltd, 1986–90. Mem. Council, Inst. of Chartered Accountants, 1971–88 (Treasurer, 1984–86). Gov., Christ's Hosp., 1983–. Mem., Highland Society. *Recreation:* golf. *Clubs:* Caledonian, Commonwealth Trust; Chiddingfold Golf.

FORBES of Craigievar, Sir John (Alexander Cumnock), 12th Bt *cr* 1630 (NS), of Craigievar, Aberdeenshire; JP; equestrian photo-journalist; *b* 29 Aug. 1927; *s* of Rear-Adm. the Hon. Arthur Lionel Ochoncar Forbes-Sempill (*d* 1962), *y s* of 17th Lord Sempill, and of Mary Cutting Holland (*d* 1940), *o d* of Arthur J. Cumnock; *S* kinsman, 1991; *m* 1st, 1956, Penelope Grey-Pennington (marr. diss. 1963); 2nd, 1966, Jane Carolyn, *o d* of C. Gordon Evans. *Educ:* Cheam; Stowe; Sandhurst. Captain, Seaforth Highlanders, 1945–49. Director: Garrick Theatre, 1951–65; The Cinema, Newton Stewart, 1966–94; ACE Centre of Equitation Ltd, 1972–94. Baillie, Newton Stewart Town Council, 1965–76. Founder Convenor, Cree Valley Community Council, 1976. Chm. PR and Promotions, Scottish Br., BSJA. JP Wigtown, 1978. *Heir: kinsman* Andrew Iain Forbes, *b* 28 Nov. 1945. *Address:* Benevean, Kendoon, St John's Town of Dalry, Castle Douglas DG7 3UB. *Clubs:* Naval and Military; Royal Scottish Automobile (Glasgow).

FORBES, Vice-Adm. Sir John Morrison, KCB 1978; *b* 16 Aug. 1925; *s* of late Lt-Col R. H. Forbes, OBE, and late Gladys M. Forbes (*née* Pollock); *m* 1950, Joyce Newenham Hadden; two *s* two *d*. *Educ:* RNC, Dartmouth. Served War: HMS Mauritius, Verulam and Nelson, 1943–46. HMS Aisne, 1946–49; Gunnery course and staff of HMS Excellent, 1950–51; served in RAN, 1952–54; Staff of HMS Excellent, 1954–56; HMS Ceylon, 1956–58; Staff of Dir of Naval Ordnance, 1958–60; Comdr (G) HMS Excellent, 1960–61; Staff of Dir of Seaman Officers' Appts, 1962–64; Exec. Officer, Britannia RN Coll., 1964–66; Operational Comdr and 2nd in Comd, Royal Malaysian Navy, 1966–68; Asst Dir, Naval Plans, 1969–70; comd HMS Triumph, 1971–72; comd Britannia RN Coll., Dartmouth, 1972–74; Naval Secretary, 1974–76; Flag Officer, Plymouth, Port Adm., Devonport, Comdr, Central Sub Area, Eastern Atlantic, and Comdr, Plymouth Sub Area, Channel, 1977–79. Naval ADC to the Queen, 1974. Kesatria Manku Negara (Malaysia), 1968. *Recreations:* country pursuits. *Address:* c/o National Westminster Bank, Waterlooville, Portsmouth, Hants. *Clubs:* Army and Navy, RN Sailing Association.

FORBES, John Stuart; Sheriff of Tayside, Central and Fife at Dunfermline, since 1980; *b* 31 Jan. 1936; *s* of late John Forbes and Dr A. R. S. Forbes; *m* 1963, Marion Alcock; one *s* two *d*. *Educ:* Glasgow High Sch.; Glasgow Univ. (MA, LLB). Solicitor, 1959–61; Advocate, Scottish Bar, 1962–76; Sheriff of Lothian and Borders, 1976–80. Pres., Glasgow Juridical Soc., 1963–64. Life Trustee, Carnegie, Dunfermline and Hero Fund Trusts, 1985–; Trustee, Carnegie UK Trust, 1990–. *Recreations:* tennis, golf. *Address:* Inglewood, Old Perth Road, Milnathort, Kinross KY13 7YA. *Club:* Edinburgh Sports.

FORBES, Nanette; *see* Newman, N.

FORBES, Hon. Sir Thayne (John), Kt 1993; **Hon. Mr Justice Thayne Forbes;** a Judge of the High Court of Justice, Queen's Bench Division, since 1993; *b* 28 June 1938; *s* of late John Thomson Forbes and Jessie Kay Robertson Stewart; *m* 1960, Celia Joan; two *s* one *d*. *Educ:* Winchester College (Quirister); Wolverton Grammar Sch.; University College London (LLB, LLM). Served Royal Navy (Instructor Lieutenant), 1963–66. Called to Bar, Inner Temple, 1966, Governing Bencher, 1991; QC 1984; a Recorder, 1986–90; a Circuit Judge (Official Referee), 1990–93. *Recreations:* music, reading, sailing, bird watching, astronomy. *Address:* Royal Courts of Justice, Strand, WC2A 2LL.

FORBES, Sir William (Daniel) Stuart-, 13th Bt *cr* 1626 (NS), of Pitsligo and of Monymusk, Aberdeenshire; *b* 21 Aug. 1935; *s* of William Kenneth Stuart-Forbes (*d* 1946), 3rd *s* of 10th Bt, and of Marjory Gilchrist; *S* uncle, 1985; *m* 1956, Jannette, *d* of late Hori Toki George MacDonald; three *s* two *d*. *Heir: s* Kenneth Charles Stuart-Forbes [*b* 26 Dec. 1956; *m* 1981, Susan, *d* of Len Murray; one *s* two *d*]. *Address:* 9 Churchill Street, Blenheim, New Zealand.

FORBES, Captain William Frederick Eustace; Vice Lord-Lieutenant of Stirling and Falkirk, since 1984; Forestry Commissioner, 1982–88; *b* 6 July 1932; *er s* of late Lt-Col W. H. D. C. Forbes of Callendar, CBE and Elizabeth Forbes; *m* 1st, 1956, Pamela Susan (*d* 1993), *er d* of Lord McCorquodale of Newton, KCVO, PC; two *d*; 2nd, 1995, Venetia, Hon. Lady Troubridge, *widow* of Sir Peter Troubridge, 6th Bt. *Educ:* Eton. Regular soldier, Coldstream Guards, 1950–59; farmer and company director, 1959–. Chairman: Scottish Woodland Owners' Assoc., 1974–77; Nat. Playing Fields Assoc., Scottish Branch, 1980–90. *Recreations:* country pastimes, golf, cricket, travel. *Address:* Dinning House, Gargunnock, Stirling FK8 3BQ. *T:* Gargunnock (01786) 860289. *Clubs:* MCC; New (Edinburgh); Royal and Ancient Golf.

FORBES-LEITH of Fyvie, Sir Andrew (George), 3rd Bt *cr* 1923; landed proprietor; *b* 20 Oct. 1929; *s* of Sir R. Ian A. Forbes-Leith of Fyvie, 2nd Bt, KT, MBE, and Ruth Avis (*d* 1973), *d* of Edward George Barnett; *S* father, 1973; *m* 1962, Jane Kate (*d* 1969), *d* of late David McCall-McCowan; two *s* two *d*. *Heir: s* George Ian David Forbes-Leith, *b* 26 May 1967. *Address:* Dunachton, Kingussie, Inverness-shire PH21 1LY. *T:* Kincraig (01540) 651226. *Clubs:* Royal Northern (Aberdeen); Highland (Inverness).

FORBES-MEYLER, John William, OBE 1990; HM Diplomatic Service; Deputy Head of Mission, Vienna, since 1992; *b* 3 July 1942; *s* of late J. J. C. Forbes and of Moira Patricia (*née* Garvey, who later *m* James Robert Meyler (now decd)); changed name by Deed Poll, 1963 to Forbes-Meyler; *m* 1st, 1964, Margaret Goddard (marr. diss. 1979); one *d*; 2nd, 1980, Mary Read (*née* Vlachou); one step *s*. *Educ:* grammar sch., etc. Joined HM Diplomatic Service, 1962: CRO, 1962–64; Lagos, 1964–68; Chicago, 1968–69; Boston, 1969–70; FCO, 1970–71; NY, 1971–72; FCO, 1972–75; Athens, 1975–80; FCO, 1980–83; 1st Sec. (Econ.), Bonn, 1983–86; on loan to MoD, 1986–88; Dep. Head of Mission, Bogota, 1988–92. *Recreations:* walking, music, reading. *Address:* c/o Foreign and Commonwealth Office, King Charles Street, SW1A 2AH. *T:* 0171–270 3000.

FORD, Rev. Adam; Chaplain, St Paul's Girls' School, London, since 1976 (Head of Lower School, 1986–92); *b* 15 Sept. 1940; *s* of John Ford and Jean Beattie Ford (*née* Winstanley); *m* 1969, Veronica Rosemary Lucia Verey (marr. diss. 1993); two *s* two *d*. *Educ:* Minehead Grammar Sch.; King's Coll., Univ. of London (BD Hons, AKC 1964); Lancaster Univ. (MA Indian Religion 1972). Asst, Ecumenical Inst. of World Council of Churches, Geneva, 1964; Curate, Cirencester Parish Church, Glos, 1965–69; Vicar of Hebden Bridge, W Yorkshire, 1969–76; Priest-in-Ordinary to the Queen, 1984–90. Regular contributor to Prayer for the Day, Radio 4, 1978–; writer and narrator, Whose World?, series of TV progs on sci. and religion, 1987. Hon. FRAS 1960. *Publications:* Spaceship Earth, 1981; Weather Watch, 1982; Star Gazers Guide to the Night Sky (audio guide to astronomy), 1982; Universe: God, Man and Science, 1986; The Cuckoo Plant, 1991; Mr Hi-Tech, 1993; articles in The Times and science jls on relationship between science and religion, also on dialogue between religions. *Recreations:* dry stone walling, astronomy, searching for neolithic flints. *Address:* 55 Bolingbroke Road, Hammersmith, W14 0AH. *T:* 0171–602 5902.

FORD, Sir Andrew (Russell), 3rd Bt *cr* 1929, of Westerdunes, Co. of East Lothian; Lecturer, Chippenham College, since 1974; *b* 29 June 1943; *s* of Sir Henry Russell Ford, 2nd Bt, TD and of Mary Elizabeth, *d* of late Godfrey F. Wright; *S* father, 1989; *m* 1968, Penelope Anne, *d* of Harry Relph; two *s* one *d*. *Educ:* Winchester; New Coll., Oxford (half-blue, athletics, 1962); Loughborough Coll. (DLC); London Univ. (BA external); Birmingham Univ. (MA external). Schoolmaster: Blairmore Sch., Aberdeens, 1967–71; St Peter's Sch., Cambridge, NZ, 1971–74. *Recreations:* taking exercise, reading. *Heir: s* Toby Russell Ford, *b* 11 Jan. 1973. *Address:* 20 Coniston Road, Chippenham, Wilts SN14 0PX. *T:* Chippenham (01249) 655442.

FORD, Anthony; *see* Ford, J. A.

FORD, Antony; HM Diplomatic Service; Chairman, Civil Service Selection Board, since 1994 (on secondment to Recruitment and Assessment Services Agency); *b* Bexley, 1 Oct. 1944; *s* of late William Ford and Grace Ford (*née* Smith); *m* 1970, Linda Gordon Joy; one *s* one *d*. *Educ:* St Dunstan's Coll., Catford; UCW, Aberystwyth (BA). Joined HM Diplomatic Service, 1967; Third, later Second, Sec., Bonn, 1968–71; Second Sec., Kuala Lumpur, 1971–73; First Secretary: FCO, 1973–77; Washington, 1977–81; FCO, 1981–84; Counsellor: East Berlin, 1984–87; FCO, 1987–90; Consul-Gen., San Francisco, 1990–94. *Recreations:* reading, gardening, cricket. *Address:* c/o Foreign and Commonwealth Office, King Charles Street, SW1A 2AH.

FORD, Benjamin Thomas; DL; *b* 1 April 1925; *s* of Benjamin Charles Ford and May Ethel (*née* Moorton); *m* 1950, Vera Ada (*née* Fawcett-Fancet); two *s* one *d*. *Educ:* Rowan Road Central Sch., Surrey. Apprenticed as compositor, 1941. War Service, 1943–47, Fleet Air Arm (Petty Officer). Electronic Fitter/Wireman, 1951–64; Convener of Shop Stewards, 1955–64. Pres., Harwich Constituency Labour Party, 1955–63; Mem., Clacton UDC, 1959–62; Alderman Essex CC, 1959–65; JP Essex, 1962–67. MP (Lab) Bradford N, 1964–83; contested (Lab Ind.) Bradford N, 1983. Mem., H of C Select Cttee (Services), 1970–83 (Chm., Accom. and Admin Sub-Cttee, 1979–83); Chm., Jt Select Cttee on Sound Broadcasting, 1976–77; Chairman: British-Portuguese Parly Gp, 1965–83; British-Argentinian Parly Gp, 1974–81; British-Brazilian Parly Gp, 1974–79; British-Malaysian Parly Gp, 1975–83; British-Venezuelan Parly Gp, 1977–83; All-Party Wool Textile Parly Gp, 1974–83; Vice-Chairman: British-Latin American Parly Gp, 1974–79; PLP Defence Cttee, 1979–82; Mem. Exec. Cttee, IPU British Gp, 1971–83 (Chm., 1977–79); Sec., British-Namibian Parly Gp, 1980–83. Chm., Leeds NW Lib Dems, 1988–91; Pres., Leeds Fedn of Lib Dems, 1991–. Bd Mem., Bradford & Northern Housing Assoc., 1975– (Chm., Yorks and Humberside Regl Cttee). Chm., English Shooting Council, 1982–; Mem. Council, Nat. Rifle Assoc., 1968– (Vice-Pres., 1984–); President: Yorks and Humberside Region, Mencap, 1986–91; Bradford Civic Soc., 1988–. Freeman, City of London, 1979; Liveryman, Gunmakers' Co., 1978–. DL W Yorks, 1982. Hon. FAIA 1983. Grand Officer, Order of the Southern Cross (Brazil), 1976. *Publication:* Piecework, 1960. *Recreations:* music, shooting, family. *Address:* 9 Wynmore Crescent, Bramhope, Leeds LS16 9DH. *Club:* Idle Working Men's.

FORD, Prof. Boris, MA; Emeritus Professor, University of Bristol; freelance editor and writer; *b* 1 July 1917; *s* of late Brig. G. N. Ford, CB, DSO; *m* 1st, 1950, Noreen; one *s* three *d*; 2nd, 1977, Inge. *Educ:* Gresham's Sch., Holt, Norfolk; Downing Coll., Cambridge. Army Education, finally OC Middle East School of Artistic Studies, 1940–46. Chief Ed. and finally Dir, Bureau of Current Affairs, 1946–51; Information Officer, Technical Assistance Bd, UN (NY and Geneva), 1951–53; Sec., Nat. Enquiry into Liberalising Technical Educn, 1953–55; Editor, Journal of Education, 1955–58; first Head of Sch. Broadcasting, Associated-Rediffusion, 1957–58; Educn Sec., Cambridge Univ. Press, 1958–60; Prof. of Education and Dir of the Inst. of Education, Univ. of Sheffield, 1960–63; Prof. of Education, Univ. of Sussex, 1963–73, Dean, Sch. of Cultural and Community Studies, 1963–71, Chm., Educn Area, and Dir, Sch. of Educn, 1971–73; Prof. of Educn, Univ. of Bristol, 1973–82. Chm., Nat. Assoc. for the Teaching of English, 1963–65; Educational Dir, Pictorial Knowledge, 1968–71. Editor: Pelican Guide to English Literature, 7 Vols, 1954–61; New Pelican Guide to English Literature, 11 Vols, 1982–88; Cambridge Guide to the Arts in Britain, 9 vols, 1988–91 (paperback edn as Cambridge Cultural History of Britain, 9 vols, 1992); Editor, Universities Qly, Culture, Education & Society, 1955–86. *Publications:* Discussion Method, 1949; Teachers' Handbook to Human Rights, 1950; Liberal Education in a Technical Age, 1955; (ed) Young Readers: Young Writers, 1960; Changing Relationships between Universities and Teachers' Colleges, 1975; Collaboration and Commitment, 1984; (ed) Benjamin Britten's Poets, 1994. *Recreations:* music and living. *Address:* 35 Alma Vale Road, Clifton, Bristol BS8 2HL.

See also R. H. Vignoles.

FORD, Sir Brinsley; *see* Ford, Sir R. B.

FORD, Charles Edmund, FRS 1965; DSc London, FLS, FZS, FIBiol; Member of Medical Research Council's External Staff, Sir William Dunn School of Pathology, Oxford, 1971–78, retired; *b* 24 Oct. 1912; *s* of late Charles Ford and late Ethel Eubornia Ford (*née* Fawcett); *m* 1940, Jean Ella Dowling; four *s*. *Educ:* Slough Grammar Sch.; King's Coll., University of London. Demonstrator, Dept of Botany, King's Coll., University of London, 1936–38; Geneticist, Rubber Research Scheme, Ceylon, 1938–41 and 1944–45. Lieut Royal Artillery, 1942–43. PSO Dept of Atomic Energy, Min. of Supply, at Chalk River Laboratories, Ont, Canada, 1946–49. Head of Cytogenetics Section, MRC, Radiobiology Unit, Harwell, 1949–71. *Publications:* papers on cytogenetics in scientific journals. *Recreations:* travel, friends. *Address:* 156 Oxford Road, Abingdon, Oxon OX14 2AF. *T:* Abingdon (01235) 520001.

FORD, Colin John, CBE 1993; Director, National Museums and Galleries of Wales, since 1993; lecturer, writer and broadcaster on films, theatre and photography; exhibition organiser; *b* 13 May 1934; *s* of John William and Hélène Martha Ford; *m* 1st, 1961, Margaret Elizabeth Cordwell (marr. diss.); one *s* one *d*; 2nd, 1984, Susan Joan Frances Grayson; one *s*. *Educ:* Enfield Grammar Sch.; University Coll., Oxford (MA). Manager and Producer, Kidderminster Playhouse, 1958–60; Gen. Man., Western Theatre Ballet, 1960–62; Vis. Lectr in English and Drama, California State Univ. at Long Beach and UCLA (Univ. Extension), 1962–64; Dep. Curator, Nat. Film Archive, 1965–72. Organiser, 30th Anniv. Congress of Internat. Fedn of Film Archives, London, 1968; Dir, Cinema City Exhibn, 1970; Programme Dir, London Shakespeare Film Festival, 1972; Keeper of Film and Photography, Nat. Portrait Gall., 1972–81; founding Hd, Nat. Mus. of Photography, Film and Television, 1982–93. Hon. MA Bradford, 1989. *Film:* Masks and Faces, 1966 (BBC TV version, Omnibus, 1968). *Publications:* (with Roy Strong) An Early Victorian Album, 1974, 2nd edn 1977; The Cameron Collection, 1975; (ed) Happy and Glorious: Six Reigns of Royal Photography, 1977; Rediscovering Mrs Cameron, 1979; People in Camera, 1979; (with Brian Harrison) A Hundred Years Ago (Britain in the 1880s), 1983; Portraits (Gallery of World Photography), 1983; (ed) The Story of Popular Photography, 1988; (with Karl Steinorth): You Press the Button, We Do the Rest: the birth of snapshot photography, 1988; Lewis Carroll: photographs, 1991; Ferenc Berko: 60 Years of Photography, 1991; (principal contrib.) Oxford Companion to Film; articles in many jls. *Recreations:* travel, music, small boats. *Address:* National Museum and Gallery, Cathays Park, Cardiff, CF1 3NP.

FORD, Prof. David Frank, PhD; Regius Professor of Divinity and Fellow of Selwyn College, Cambridge University, since 1991; *b* 23 Jan. 1948; *s* of George Ford and Phyllis (*née* Woodman); *m* 1982, Deborah Perrin Hardy, *d* of Rev. Canon Prof. Daniel Wayne Hardy, *qv*; one *s* two *d* (and one *d* decd). *Educ:* Trinity Coll. Dublin (BA (Mod) 1970); St John's Coll., Cambridge (MA 1976; PhD 1977); Yale Univ. (STM 1973); Tübingen Univ. Lectr in Theology, Birmingham Univ., 1976–91. Chm., Faculty Bd of Divinity, Cambridge Univ., 1993–95. Mem., CUP Syndicate, 1993–. *Publications:* Barth and God's Story: biblical narrative and the theological method of Karl Barth in the Church Dogmatics, 1981; (with Daniel W. Hardy) Jubilate: Theology in praise, 1984; (with Frances M. Young) Meaning and Truth in 2 Corinthians, 1987; (ed) The Modern Theologians, vols I and II, 1989. *Recreations:* gardening, poetry, drama, sports (especially ball games). *Address:* Divinity School, St John's Street, Cambridge CB2 1TW. *T:* Cambridge (01223) 332592.

FORD, Sir David (Robert), KBE 1988 (OBE 1976); LVO 1975; Hong Kong Commissioner in London, 1980–81 and since 1994; *b* 22 Feb. 1935; *s* of William Ewart and Edna Ford; *m* 1st, 1958, Elspeth Anne (*née* Muckart) (marr. diss. 1987); two *s* two *d*; 2nd, 1987, Gillian Petersen (*née* Monsarrat). *Educ:* Tauntons School. National Service, 1953–55; regular commn, RA, 1955; regimental duty, Malta, 1953–58; Lieut, UK, 1958–62; Captain, Commando Regt, 1962–66; active service: Borneo, 1964; Aden, 1966; Staff Coll., Quetta, 1967; seconded to Hong Kong Govt, 1967; retired from Army (Major), 1972. Dep. Dir, Hong Kong Govt Information Service, 1972–74, Dir, 1974–76; Dep. Sec., Govt Secretariat, Hong Kong, 1976; Under Sec., NI Office, 1977–79; Sec. for Information, Hong Kong Govt, 1979–80; RCDS, 1982; Hong Kong Government: Dir of Housing, 1983–84; Sec. for Housing, 1985; Sec. for the Civil Service, 1985–86; Chief Sec., 1986–93. *Recreations:* tennis, fishing, photography, theatre. *Address:* Hong Kong Government Office, 6 Grafton Street, W1X 3LB.

FORD, Rt Rev. Douglas Albert; Bishop of Saskatoon, 1970–81; *b* 16 July 1917; *s* of Thomas George Ford and Elizabeth Eleanor (Taylor), both English; *m* 1944, Doris Ada (Elborne); two *s* one *d*. *Educ:* primary and secondary schs, Vancouver; Univ. of British Columbia (BA); Anglican Theological Coll. of BC (LTh); General Synod (BD). Deacon, 1941; Priest, 1942; Curate, St Mary's, Kerrisdale, 1941–42; St George's, Vancouver, 1942–44; Vicar of Strathmore, 1944–49; Rector of: Okotoks, 1949–52; Vermilion, 1952–55; St Michael and All Angels, Calgary, 1955–62; St Augustine, Lethbridge, 1962–66; Dean and Rector, St John's Cath., Saskatoon, 1966–70; Asst Bishop of Calgary, 1981–87; Incumbent of All Saints', Cochrane, dio. Calgary, 1981–85. Hon. DD: Coll. of Emmanuel and St Chad, Saskatoon, 1970; Anglican Theological Coll. of BC, Vancouver, 1971. *Address:* 126 Hawkstone Manor NW, Calgary, Alberta T3G 3X2, Canada.

FORD, Rev. Preb. Douglas William C.; *see* Cleverley Ford.

FORD, Sir Edward (William Spencer), KCB 1967 (CB 1952); KCVO 1957 (MVO 1949); ERD 1987; OStJ 1976; MA; FRSA; DL; Secretary and Registrar of the Order of Merit, since 1975; Secretary to the Pilgrim Trust, 1967–75; *b* 24 July 1910; 4th (twin) *s* of late Very Rev. Lionel G. B. J. Ford, Headmaster of Repton and Harrow and Dean of York, and of Mary Catherine, *d* of Rt Rev. E. S. Talbot, Bishop of Winchester and Hon. Mrs Talbot; *m* 1949, Virginia, *er d* of 1st and last Baron Brand, CMG, and *widow* of John Metcalfe Polk, NY; two *s*. *Educ:* Eton (King's Schol.); New Coll., Oxford (Open Scholar; Hon. Fellow, 1982). 1st Class Hon. Mods; 2nd Class Lit. Hum. (Greats). Law Student (Harmsworth Scholar) Middle Temple, 1934–35; Tutor to King Farouk of Egypt, 1936–37; called to Bar, Middle Temple, 1937 and practised 1937–39; 2nd Lieut (Supplementary Reserve of Officers) Grenadier Guards, 1936; Lieut 1939; served in France and Belgium, 1939–40 (despatches), and in Tunisia and Italy, 1943–44 (despatches), Brigade Major 10th Infantry and 24th Guards Brigades; Instructor at Staff Coll., Haifa, 1944–45. psc†. Asst Private Secretary to King George VI, 1946–52, and to the Queen, 1952–67; Extra Equerry to the Queen, 1955. Dir, London Life Assoc., 1970–83. Mem., Central Appeals Adv. Cttee, BBC and IBA, 1969–72, 1976–78; Mem., Council, St Christopher's Hospice, Sydenham, 1980–90 (Pres., 1990–); Chairman: UK/USA Bicentennial Fellowships Cttee, 1975–80; St John Council for Northamptonshire, 1976–82; Grants Cttee, Historic Churches Preservation Trust, 1977–90. Trustee: York Glaziers' Trust, 1977–; Butler Trust, 1986–90; Hon. Treas., Children's Country Holidays Fund, 1958–73, Vice-Pres., 1973–; Governor, The Ditchley Foundn, 1966–89. Mem. Ct of Assts, Goldsmiths' Co., 1970–, Prime Warden, 1979. High Sheriff Northants 1970, DL 1972. *Address:* Canal House, 23 Blomfield Road, W9 1AD. *T:* 0171–286 0028. *Clubs:* White's, Beefsteak, Pratt's, MCC.

FORD, Geoffrey; *see* Ford, M. G.

FORD, Air Marshal Sir Geoffrey (Harold), KBE 1979; CB 1974; FEng 1987; Secretary, The Institute of Metals, 1985–88; *b* 6 Aug. 1923; *s* of late Harold Alfred Ford, Lewes, Sussex; *m* 1951, Valerie, *d* of late Douglas Hart Finn, Salisbury; two *s*. *Educ:* Lewes County Grammar Sch.; Bristol Univ. (BSc). Served War of 1939–45: commissioned, 1942; 60 Gp, 1943; Italy and Middle East, 1944–46. 90 (Signals) Gp, 1946–49; Bomber Development, 1954–57; Air Ministry, 1958–61; RAF Technical Coll., 1961–62; Min. of Aviation, 1963–64; Chief Signals Officer, RAF Germany, 1965–68; MoD, 1968–72; RCDS, 1972; AO Engineering, Strike Command, 1973–76; Dir-Gen. Engineering and Supply Management, RAF, 1976–78; Chief Engr (RAF), 1978–81. Dir, The Metals Soc., 1981–84. FIEE (Council, 1977–82). *Address:* c/o Barclays Bank, Lewes, East Sussex BN7 2JP. *Club:* Royal Air Force.

FORD, George Johnson, DL; Member, Cheshire County Council, 1962–87 (Chairman, 1976–82); *b* 13 March 1916; *s* of James and Esther Ford; *m* 1941, Nora Helen Brocklehurst; three *s* one *d*. *Educ:* Chester Coll. Qualified estate agent, 1938. FAI 1938. Member, Runcorn RDC, 1953 (Chm., 1962); Mem. Bd, Warrington and Runcorn Develt Corp., 1981–87 (Runcorn Develt Corp., 1964–81). Mem., West Mercia Cttee, Nat. Trust, 1982. Pres., Frodsham Conservative Assoc., 1962–; Vice Pres., Eddisbury Parly Div., 1984. DL Cheshire, 1979. *Recreations:* horse racing, music and drama. *Address:* Manley Old Hall, Manley, via Warrington, Cheshire WA6 9EA. *T:* Manley (01928) 740481. *Club:* City (Chester).

FORD, Gerald Rudolph; President of the United States of America, Aug. 1974–Jan. 1977; lawyer; company director; *b* Omaha, Nebraska, 14 July 1913; (adopted) *s* of Gerald R. Ford and Dorothy Gardner; *m* 1948, Elizabeth (*née* Bloomer); three *s* one *d*. *Educ:* South High Sch., Grand Rapids; Univ. of Michigan (BA); Law Sch., Yale Univ. (LLB). Served War: US Navy (Carriers), 1942–46. Partner in law firm of Ford and Buchen, 1941–42; Member, law firm of Butterfield, Keeney and Amberg, 1947–49; subseq. with Amberg, Law and Buchen. Member US House of Representatives for Michigan 5th District, 1948–73; Member: Appropriations Cttee, 1951; Dept of Defense Sub-Cttee, etc; House Minority Leader, Republican Party, 1965–73; Vice President of the United States, Dec. 1973–Aug. 1974. Attended Interparly Union meetings in Europe; Mem. US-Canadian Interparly Gp. Dir, The Travelers Inc.; Advisory Director: American Express Co.; Texas Commerce Bancshares. Holds Amer. Pol. Sci. Assoc.'s Distinguished Congressional Service Award, 1961; several hon. degrees. Delta Kappa Epsilon, Phi Delta Phi. *Publications:* (with John R. Stiles) Portrait of an Assassin, 1965; A Time to Heal, 1979; Humor and the Presidency, 1987. *Recreations:* outdoor sports (formerly football), ski-ing, tennis, golf. *Address:* PO Box 927, Rancho Mirage, CA 92270, USA.

FORD, Dr Gillian Rachel, (Mrs N. I. MacKenzie), CB 1981; FRCP, FFPHM; Medical Director, Marie Curie Memorial Foundation, since 1990; *b* 18 March 1934; *d* of Cecil Ford and Grace Ford; *m* 1988, Prof. Norman I. MacKenzie. *Educ:* Clarendon Sch., Abergele; St Hugh's Coll., Oxford; St Thomas' Hosp., London. MA, BM, BCh; FFCM 1976; FRCP 1985. Junior hospital posts, St Thomas', Oxford, Reading, 1959–64; Medical Officer, Min. of Health, 1965, Sen. Med. Officer, 1968; SPMO, 1974–77, Dep. Chief MO (Dep. Sec.), 1977–89, DHSS, later Dept of Health; on secondment as Dir of Studies, St Christopher's Hospice, Sydenham, 1985–88; Med. Sec., Standing Cttee on Postgrad. Med. Educn., 1989–90. *Publications:* papers on health services research, terminal care, audit, palliative medicine and care in sundry med. publications. *Recreations:* music, ski-ing, children's literature, gardening. *Address:* 9 Ryecotes Mead, Dulwich Common, SE21 7EP. *T:* 0181–693 6576.

FORD, Glyn; *see* Ford, J. G.

FORD, Prof. Sir Hugh, Kt 1975; FRS 1967; FEng 1977; Professor of Mechanical Engineering, 1969–80, Professor Emeritus, since 1980, Pro-Rector, 1978–80, University of London (Imperial College of Science and Technology); Chairman, Sir Hugh Ford & Associates Ltd, since 1982; Director: Air Liquide UK Ltd, since 1979; Ford & Dain Research Ltd, 1972–93; *b* 16 July 1913; *s* of Arthur and Constance Ford; *m* 1st, 1942, Wynyard (*d* 1991), *d* of Major F. B. Scholfield; two *d*; 2nd, 1993, Mrs Thelma Jensen. *Educ:* Northampton Sch.; City and Guilds Coll., Univ. of London. DSc (Eng); PhD. Practical trng at GWR Locomotive Works, 1931–36; researches into heat transfer, 1936–39; R&D Engrg, Imperial Chemical Industries, Northwich, 1939–42; Chief Engr, Technical Dept, British Iron and Steel Fedn, 1942–45, then Head of Mechanical Working Div., British Iron and Steel Research Assoc., 1945–47; Reader in Applied Mechanics, Univ. of London (Imp. Coll. of Science and Technology), 1948–51, Prof., 1951–69; Head of Dept of Mech. Engineering, 1965–78. Mem. Bd of Governors, Imperial Coll., 1982–89. Technical Dir, Davy-Ashmore Group, 1968–71; Director: Alfred Herbert Ltd, 1972–79; Ricardo Consulting Engrs Ltd, 1980–88; Chm., Adv. Bd, Prudential Portfolio Managers, 1985–88; Mem., Adv. Bd, Brown and Root (UK), 1983–92. John Player Lectr, 1973, Hugh Ford Management Lectr, 1988, IMechE. First Pres., Inst. of Metals, 1985–87 (merger of Inst. of Metallurgists and Metals Soc.); President: Section 6, British Assoc., 1975–76; Welding Inst., 1983–85; Fellow, 1977, Vice-Pres., 1981–84, Mem. Council, 1989–92, Fellowship of Engineering; Member Council, IMechE (Vice-Pres., 1972, 1975, Sen. Vice-Pres., 1976, Pres., 1977–78); SRC, 1968–72 (Chm. Engineering Bd); Council, Royal Soc., 1973–74; ARC, 1976–81. FICE; Whitworth Schol.; FCGI; FIC 1982; Sen. Fellow, RCA, 1987. Hon. MASME, 1980; Hon. FIMechE 1984; Hon. FIChemE 1987. Hon. DSc: Salford, 1976; QUB, 1977; Aston, 1978; Bath, 1978; Sheffield, 1984; Sussex, 1990. Thomas Hawksley Gold Medallist, IMechE, 1948, for researches into rolling of metals; Robertson Medal, Inst. of Metals, 1954; James Alfred Ewing Gold Medal, ICE, 1982; James Watt Internat. Gold Medal, 1985. *Publications:* Advanced Mechanics of Materials, 1963; papers to Royal Soc., IMechE, Iron and Steel Inst., Inst. of Metals, foreign societies, etc. *Recreations:* gardening, music, model engineering. *Address:* 18 Shrewsbury House, Cheyne Walk, SW3 5LN; Shamley Cottage, Stroud Lane, Shamley Green, Surrey GU5 0ST. *Club:* Athenæum.

FORD, James Allan, CB 1978; MC 1946; *b* 10 June 1920; 2nd *s* of Douglas Ford and Margaret Duncan (*née* Allan); *m* 1948, Isobel Dunnett; one *s* one *d*. *Educ:* Royal High School, Edinburgh; University of Edinburgh. Served 1940–46, Capt. Royal Scots. Entered Civil Service, 1938; Asst Sec., Dept of Agriculture and Fisheries for Scotland, 1958; Registrar Gen. for Scotland, 1966–69; Principal Establishment Officer, Scottish Office, 1969–79. A Trustee, Nat. Lib. of Scotland, 1981–91. *Publications:* The Brave White Flag, 1961; Season of Escape, 1963; A Statue for a Public Place, 1965; A Judge of Men, 1968; The Mouth of Truth, 1972. *Address:* 6 Hillpark Court, Edinburgh EH4 7BE. *T:* 0131–336 5398. *Clubs:* Royal Scots, Scottish Arts (Edinburgh).

FORD, (James) Glyn; Member (Lab) Greater Manchester East, European Parliament, since 1984; *b* 28 Jan. 1950; *s* of late Ernest Benjamin Ford and Matilda Alberta Ford (*née* James); *m* 1st, 1973, Hazel Nancy Mahy (marr. diss. 1992); one *d*; 2nd, 1992, Daniela Zannelli. *Educ:* Marling; Reading Univ. (BSc Geol. with Soil Sci.); UCL (MSc Marine Earth Sci.); Manchester Univ. Undergraduate Apprentice, BAC, 1967–68; Course Tutor in Oceanography, Open Univ., 1976–78; Teaching Asst, UMIST, 1977–78; Res. Fellow, Sussex Univ., 1978–79; Manchester University: Res. Asst, 1976–77; Res. Fellow, 1979; Lectr, 1979–80; Sen. Res. Fellow, Prog. of Policy Res. in Engrg Sci. and Technol., 1980–84; Hon. Vis. Res. Fellow, 1984–. Vis. Prof., Tokyo Univ., 1983. Tameside Borough Council: Mem., 1978–86; Chairman: Environmental Health and Control Cttee, 1979–80; Educn Services Cttee, 1980–85. Mem., Lab Party NEC, 1989–93 (Member: Sci. and Technol. Policy Sub-Cttee, 1981–83; Review Gp on Trade Union/Labour Party Links, 1992–93). European Parliament: Chm., Cttee of Inquiry into Growth of Racism and Fascism in Europe, 1984–86; Vice-Chm., Sub-Cttee on Security and Disarmament, 1987–89; first Vice-President: Group of Party of European Socialists, 1989–93; Delgn, Japanese Diet, 1992–94; Leader, Eur. PLP, 1989–93. Mem. Council, Cttee on Racism and Xenophobia, 1994–. Contested (Lab), Hazel Grove, 1987. *Publications:* (with C. Niblett and L. Walker) The Future for Ocean Technology, 1987; Fascist Europe, 1992; The Evolution of a European, 1994; contribs to learned jls on sci. and technol. policy. *Recreations:* Japan, travel, writing. *Address:* 46 Stamford Road, Mossley, Lancs OL5 0BE. *T:* (home) Mossley (01457) 837892; (office) Mossley (01457) 836276, *Fax:* (01457) 834927. *Clubs:* Groucho; Park Bridge Working Mens Institute (Ashton-under-Lyne).

FORD, (John) Anthony; Director, Crafts Council, since 1988 (Deputy Director, 1985–88); *b* 28 April 1938; *s* of Frank Everatt Ford and Dorothy Mary Ford; *m* 1st, 1963, Caroline

Rosemary Wharrad (marr. diss.); one *d*; 2nd, 1984, Sandra Edith Williams. *Educ:* Epsom Coll.; St Edmund's Hall, Oxford (MA). Admitted Solicitor, 1963. Dir, Art Services Grants, 1974–79; Crafts Council, 1979–. Mem., Visual Arts Adv. Cttee, British Council, 1988–. Vice-Pres. for Europe, World Crafts Council, 1987–93 (Advr, 1993–). Mem., Fabric Adv. Cttee, Rochester Cathedral, 1990–. Member: Court, RCA, 1989–; Court of Govs, London Inst., 1993–. FRSA 1989. *Recreations:* theatre, cinema. *Address:* Crafts Council, 44a Pentonville Road, Islington, N1 9BY. *T:* 0171–278 7700.

FORD, Sir John (Archibald), KCMG 1977 (CMG 1967); MC 1945; HM Diplomatic Service, retired; *b* 19 Feb. 1922; *s* of Ronald Mylne Ford and Margaret Jesse Coghill, Newcastle-under-Lyme, Staffs; *m* 1956, Emaline Burnette (*d* 1989), Leesville, Virginia; two *d*. *Educ:* St Michael's Coll., Tenbury; Sedbergh Sch., Yorks; Oriel Coll., Oxford. Served in Royal Artillery, 1942–46 (temp. Major); demobilised, 1947. Joined Foreign (subseq. Diplomatic) Service, 1947. Third Sec., British Legation, Budapest, 1947–49; Third Sec. and a Resident Clerk, FO, 1949–52; Private Sec. to Permanent Under-Sec. of State, FO, 1952–54; HM Consul, San Francisco, 1954–56; seconded to HM Treasury, 1956–59; attended Course at Administrative Staff Coll., 1959; First Sec. and Head of Chancery, British Residency, Bahrain, 1959–61; Asst, FO Personnel Dept, 1961–63; Asst, FO Establishment and Organisation Dept, 1963; Head of Diplomatic Service Establishment and Organisation Dept, 1964–66; Counsellor (Commercial), Rome, 1966–70; Asst Under-Sec., FCO, 1970–71; Consul-Gen., New York, and Dir-Gen., British Trade Develt in USA, 1971–75; Ambassador to Indonesia, 1975–78; British High Comr in Canada, 1978–81. Lay Administrator, Guildford Cathedral, 1982–84. Mem., Exec. Cttee, VSO, 1982–87; Chm. of Trustees, Voluntary and Christian Service, 1985–88; Chm., AIDS Care Educn and Trng, 1989–93; Trustee: World in Need, 1987–; Opportunity Trust, 1991–; Opportunity Internat. (USA), 1994–. *Publication:* Honest to Christ, 1988. *Recreations:* walking, gardening, sailing. *Address:* Loquats, Guildown, Guildford, Surrey GU2 5EN; Admiral 633, 8750 South Ocean Drive, Jensen Beach, Florida 34957, USA. *Clubs:* Farmers'; Vanbrugh (Guildford).

FORD, (John) Peter, CBE 1969; Chairman and Managing Director, International Joint Ventures Ltd; *b* 20 Feb. 1912; *s* of Ernest and Muriel Ford; *m* 1939, Phoebe Seys, *d* of Herbert McGregor Wood, FRIBA; one *s* two *d*. *Educ:* Wrekin Coll.; Gonville and Caius Coll., Cambridge. BA (Hons Nat. Sci. Tripos) 1934; MA Cantab 1937. Cambridge Univ. Air Sqdn, 1932–35 (Pilot's A Licence, 1933–). Air Ministry (subsequently FO, RAFVR), 1939–40; Coventry Gauge and Tool Co. Ltd (Asst to Chm.), 1941–45; Gen. Man., Brit. Engineers Small Tools and Equipment Co. Ltd, and Gen. Man. Scientific Exports (Gt Brit.) Ltd, 1945–48; Man. Dir, Brush Export Ltd, Associated British Oil Engines (Export) Ltd and National Oil Engines (Export) Ltd, and Dir of other associated cos of The Brush Group, 1949–55; Dir, Associated British Engineering Ltd and subsidiaries, 1957–58; Man. Dir, Coventry Climax International Ltd, 1958–63; Director: Plessey Overseas Ltd, 1963–70; Bryant & May (Latin America) Ltd, 1970–73; Chm., Metra Martech Ltd, 1988–. Chm. Institute of Export, 1954–56, 1965–67; President: Soc. of Commercial Accountants, 1970–74 (Vice-Pres., 1956–70); Soc. of Company and Commercial Accountants, 1974–75; Member: Council, London Chamber of Commerce, 1951–72 (Dep. Chm., 1970–72; Vice-Pres., 1972–); London Ct of Arbitration, 1970–73; FBI, Overseas Trade Policy Cttee, 1952–63; Council, British Internal Combustion Engine Manufacturers Assoc., 1953–55; BNEC Cttee for Exports to Latin America, 1964–71 (Chm. 1968–71); NEDO Cttee for Movement of Exports, 1972–75; British Overseas Trade Adv. Council, 1975–82. Chm., British Shippers' Council, 1972–75 (Dep. Chm., 1971–72). Chm., British Mexican Soc., 1973–77; Vice-Pres., Hispanic and Luso Brazilian Council, 1980–. Freeman of City of London, 1945; Mem. Ct of Assistants, Ironmongers' Co. (Master, 1981); Governor: Wrekin Coll., 1953–57; Oversea Service Coll., 1966–86. CEng, CIMechE, CIMarE, MIEE. Order of Rio Branco (Brazil), 1977. *Publications:* contributor to technical press and broadcaster on international trade subjects. *Recreations:* Athletics (Cambridge Univ. and Internat. Teams, 1932–35; held various county championships, 1932–37; Hon. Treas, 1947–58, Vice-Pres., 1990–, Achilles Club; Pres., London Athletic Club, 1964–66). *Address:* 40 Fairacres, Roehampton Lane, SW15 5LX. *T:* 0181–876 2146. *Clubs:* United Oxford & Cambridge University, City Livery, MCC; Hawks (Cambridge).

FORD, (Martin) Geoffrey; Librarian, University of Bristol, since 1990; *b* 24 Jan. 1942; *s* of George Frederick Ford and Muriel (*née* Dowding); *m* 1974, Elizabeth Jill Barker. *Educ:* Sir Joseph Williamson's Mathematical Sch., Rochester; Leicester Univ. (BSc 1963); Sheffield Univ. (DipLib 1965; MSc 1973). ALA 1967. Liby Asst, Leicester Univ., 1963–64; Durham University: Asst Librarian, 1965–67; Sen. Res. Asst, 1968–69; Res. Associate, Bristol Univ., 1969–72; Asst Dir, Liby Res. Unit, Lancaster Univ., 1972–75; Sen. Res. Officer and Dir, Centre for Res. on User Studies, Sheffield Univ., 1976–78; Southampton University: Sub-librarian, 1978–87; Dep. Librarian, 1987–89. Member: Res. Cttee, 1990–, Adv. Cttee on Bibliographic Services, 1991–94, British Library; SCONUL Council, 1992–. (Jtly) Robinson Medal, LA, 1972. *Publications:* Review of Methods for Determining the Use of Library Stock, 1990; res. reports, articles and reviews in learned jls. *Recreations:* travelling on trains, gentle walking, naval and transport history. *Address:* University Library, Tyndall Avenue, Bristol BS8 1TJ. *T:* Bristol (0117) 928 8004.

FORD, Peter; *see* Ford, J. P.

FORD, Peter; His Honour Judge Ford; a Circuit Judge, since 1990; *b* 30 Sept. 1930; *s* of late Rev. Cecil Henry Ford and Gwyneth Kathleen Ford (*née* Hall); *m* 1961, Jenifer Dekenah, Cape Town; one *d*. *Educ:* Ellesmere Coll.; Univ. of Manchester (LLB). Called to the Bar, Gray's Inn, 1952. In practice as barrister, Northern Circuit, 1952–55; legal advr in industry, 1956–59; in practice as barrister, Patent Bar, 1959–79; Mem., Bds of Appeal, European Patent Office, Munich, 1979–90; Chm., Legal Bd of Appeal, 1985–90; nominated Judge of Patents County Court, 1990. Reader in C of E, 1955–. MRI 1958; FRSA 1953. *Publications:* various articles in legal jls. *Recreations:* music, foreign languages, travel. *Address:* The Patents County Court, 26–29 Park Crescent, W1N 4HT. *T:* 0171–917 7860.

FORD, Peter George Tipping; Secretary, Medical Protection Society, 1983–90; *b* 18 Sept. 1931; *s* of late Raymond Eustace Ford, CBE; *m* 1958, Nancy Elizabeth Procter; four *d*. *Educ:* Epsom College; St Bartholomew's Hosp. Med. Coll., Univ. of London (MB, BS); MRCGP, DObst RCOG. Nat. Service, RAMC, 1957–59. Gen. practice, Hythe, 1960–68; Asst Sec., Med. Protection Soc., 1968–72, Dep. Sec., 1972–83. Sec., Jt Co-ordinating Cttee, UK Defence Organizations, 1985–89. Mem., Soc. of Apothecaries. FRSM. Medal of Honour, Med. Defence Soc. of Queensland, 1984. *Publications:* contribs to medico-legal periodicals. *Recreations:* baroque choral music, gardening, bridge. *Address:* Braeside Cottage, Cannongate Road, Hythe, Kent CT21 5PT. *T:* Hythe (Kent) (01303) 67896. *Club:* Carlton.

FORD, Peter John; Chairman, London Transport, since 1994; *b* 21 Nov. 1938; *s* of John Frederick Arthur Ford and Hazel Mary Ford; *m* 1966, Olivia Mary Temple; two *s* two *d*. *Educ:* King's Sch., Canterbury; Christ Church, Oxford (MA Chem.); Harvard Business Sch. (MBA). With Shell Chemical Co., 1961–65; McKinsey & Co., NY, 1967–70; Exec. Dir, Sterling Guarantee Trust, 1970–85; Exec. Dir, P&OSNCo., 1985–93. *Recreations:* walking, music. *Address:* 16 The Drive, Wimbledon, SW20 8TG. *T:* 0181–944 7207. *Club:* Royal Automobile.

FORD, Peter William; HM Diplomatic Service; Head, Near East and North Africa Department, Foreign and Commonwealth Office, since 1994; *b* 27 June 1947; *s* of Alec and Gertrude Ford; *m* 1st, 1974, Aurora Garcia Mingo (marr. diss. 1992); 2nd, 1992, Alganesh Haile Beyene. *Educ:* Helsby Grammar Sch.; Queen's Coll., Oxford (BA Hons). FCO, 1971–72; Beirut, 1972–73; Second, then First, Sec., Cairo, 1974–78; Eur. Integration Dept, FCO, 1978–80; First Sec., Paris, 1980–85; Asst Hd, EC Dept, FCO, 1985–87; Counsellor (Commercial), Riyadh, 1987–90; Vis. Fellow, Harvard Univ., 1990–91; Dep. High Comr and Counsellor (Econ. and Commercial), Singapore, 1991–94. *Recreations:* sport, reading, travel. *Address:* c/o Foreign and Commonwealth Office, King Charles Street, SW1A 2AH.

FORD, Sir (Richard) Brinsley, Kt 1984; CBE 1978; FSA; Member of National Art-Collections Fund since 1927 (Member: Executive Committee 1960–88; Vice-Chairman, 1974–75, Chairman 1975–80; Advisory Panel, since 1988); *b* 10 June 1908; *e s* of late Capt. Richard Ford, Rifle Brigade, and Rosamund, *d* of Sir John Ramsden, 5th Bt; *m* 1937, Joan, *d* of late Capt. Geoffrey Vyvyan; two *s* one *d*. *Educ:* Eton; Trinity Coll., Oxford. Joined TA 1939; served for one year as Troop Sergeant Major, RA; commissioned 1941, and transferred to Intelligence Corps (Major 1945). Selected works for Arts Council Festival of Britain and Coronation Exhibitions; a Trustee of the National Gallery, 1954–61; Trustee, Watts Gall., Compton, 1955– (Chm., 1974–84); great-grandson of Richard Ford (1796–1858) who wrote the Handbook for Spain; owner of the Ford Collection of Richard Wilsons. Dir, Burlington Magazine, 1952–86, Trustee, 1988–. Member: Soc. of Dilettanti, 1952– (Sec., 1972–88); Georgian Gp, from foundn, 1937–. Member: Council, Byam Shaw Sch., 1957–73; Exec. Cttee, City and Guilds of London Art Sch., 1976–94. President: St Marylebone Soc., 1974–77; Walpole Soc., 1986–; Vice-Pres., Anglo-Spanish Soc. Patron, Attingham Summer Sch. Trust, 1984–. Founder, Richard Ford Award, Royal Acad., 1976. Jt Hon. Adviser on Paintings to Nat. Trust, 1980 (Chm., Nat. Trust Foundn for Art Cttee, 1986–90); Hon. Fellow, Royal Acad., 1981; Companion, NEAC, 1988. Hon. Fellow, Ateneo Veneto, 1988; Corresponding Member: Hispanic Soc. of Amer., 1963; Royal Acad. of San Fernando, Madrid, 1980. Hon. LLD Exeter, 1990. Order of Isabel la Católica of Spain, First Class A, 1986; Officer, Belgian Order of Leopold II, 1945; US Bronze Star, 1946; Médaille d'Argent de la Reconnaissance Française, 1947. *Publications:* The Drawings of Richard Wilson, 1951; contributor to the Burlington Magazine and Apollo. *Address:* 14 Wyndham Place, Bryanston Square, W1H 1AQ. *T:* 0171–723 0826. *Club:* Brooks's.

FORD, Gen. Sir Robert (Cyril), GCB 1981 (KCB 1977; CB 1973); CBE 1971 (MBE 1958); Vice-Chairman, Commonwealth War Graves Commission, 1989–93 (Commissioner, 1981–93); *b* 29 Dec. 1923; *s* of late John Stranger Ford and Gladys Ford, Yealmpton, Devon; *m* 1949, Jean Claudia Pendlebury, *d* of late Gp Capt. Claude Pendlebury, MC, TD, FLAS, FRICS, and Muriel Pendlebury, Yelverton, Devon; one *s*. *Educ:* Musgrave's Coll. War of 1939–45: commissioned into 4th/7th Royal Dragoon Guards, from Sandhurst, 1943; served with Regt throughout NW European campaign, 1944–45 (despatches) and in Egypt and Palestine, 1947–48 (despatches). Instructor, Mons OCS, 1949–50; Training Officer, Scottish Horse (TA), 1952–54; Staff Coll., Camberley, 1955; GSO 2 Mil. Ops, War Office, 1956–57; Sqdn Ldr 4/7 RDG, 1958–59; Bde Major, 20th Armoured Bde, 1960–61; Brevet Lt-Col, 1962; Sqdn Ldr, 4/7 RDG, 1962–63; GSO1 to Chief of Defence Staff, 1964–65; commanded 4/7 RDG in S Arabia and N Ireland, 1966–67; Comdr, 7th Armd Bde, 1968–69; Principal Staff Officer to Chief of Defence Staff, 1970–71; Cmdr Land Forces, N Ireland, 1971–73; Comdt, RMA Sandhurst, 1973–76; Military Secretary, 1976–78; Adjutant-General, 1978–81; ADC General to the Queen, 1980–81; Governor, Royal Hosp., Chelsea, 1981–87. Colonel Commandant: RAC, 1980–82; SAS Regt, 1980–85; Col 4th/7th Royal Dragoon Gds, 1984–88. President: Services Kinema Corp., 1978–81; Army Boxing Assoc., 1978–81. Chm., 1981–87, and Pres., 1986–, Army Benevolent Fund; Chm., Royal Cambridge Home for Soldiers' Widows, 1981–87; Nat. Pres., Forces Help Soc. and Lord Roberts Workshops, 1981–91. Governor, Corps of Commissionaires, 1981–94. Freeman, City of London, 1981. CIMgt. *Recreations:* watching cricket, tennis, war studies, theatre. *Address:* c/o National Westminster Bank, 45 Park Street, Camberley, Surrey GU15 3PA. *Clubs:* Cavalry and Guards, MCC.

FORD, Robert Stanley; HM Diplomatic Service, retired; *b* 30 Nov. 1929; *s* of late Robert Hempstead Ford and of Janet Mabel Elliot; *m* 1957, Cynthia Valerie Arscott, *d* of late Ronald Prowse Arscott, Bexhill-on-Sea, Sussex; one *s* two *d*. *Educ:* Daniel Stewart's Coll., Edinburgh; Univ. of Edinburgh (MA). Joined HM Diplomatic Service, 1949; HM Forces, 1949; FCO, 1951; Third Sec., Moscow, 1955; Consul, Dakar, 1958; FCO, 1959; Information Officer, NY, 1963; First Sec., Managua, 1965; Consul, Naples, 1968; FCO, 1972; Consul-Gen., Madrid, 1978; FCO, 1982; Counsellor (Admin), Paris, 1984–86. *Recreations:* music, photography, gardening, travel. *Address:* 20 Heatherbank, Haywards Heath, W Sussex RH16 1HY. *T:* Haywards Heath (01444) 455321.

FORD, Robert Webster, CBE 1982; HM Diplomatic Service, retired; *b* 27 March 1923; *s* of late Robert Ford; *m* 1956, Monica Florence Tebbett; two *s*. *Educ:* Alleyne's Sch. Served RAF, 1939–45. Served with British Mission, Lhasa, Tibet and Political Agency in Sikkim and Bhutan, 1945–47; joined Tibetan Govt Service, 1947; advised on and installed Tibet's first radio communication system and broadcasting stn; travelled extensively in Northern and Eastern Tibet, 1947–50; taken prisoner during Chinese Occupation of Tibet, 1950; imprisoned in China, 1950–55; free-lance writer and broadcaster on Chinese and Tibetan affairs, 1955; entered Foreign Service, 1956; 2nd Sec., Saigon, 1957–58; 1st Sec. (Information), Djakarta, 1959; Washington, 1960–62; FO, 1962–67; Consul-Gen., Tangier, 1967–70; Counsellor, 1970; Consul-General; Luanda, 1970–74; Bordeaux, 1974–78; Gothenburg, 1978–80; Geneva, 1980–83. *Publication:* Captured in Tibet, 1956, repr. 1990. *Recreations:* ski-ing, gardening, travelling. *Address:* Cedar Garth, Latimer Road, Monken Hadley, Barnet, Herts EN5 5NU. *Clubs:* Commonwealth Trust, Royal Geographical Society.

FORD, Roy Arthur, MA; Director of Visits, Canterbury Cathedral, 1986–90; *b* 10 May 1925; *s* of Arthur Ford and Minnie Elizabeth Ford; *m* 1965, Christine Margaret Moore; two *s*. *Educ:* Collyer's Sch., Horsham; Corpus Christi Coll., Cambridge (Scholar; 1st Cl. Pts I and II, History Tripos; BA 1949, MA 1971). Asst Master: Uppingham Sch., 1951–54; Tonbridge Sch., 1954–66; Uppingham Sch., (also Head of History and Sixth Form Master), 1966–71; Headmaster: Southwell Minster Grammar Sch., 1971–75; King's Sch., Rochester, 1975–86. *Recreations:* walking, travel, music. *Address:* 28 West Street, Faversham, Kent ME13 7JG. *T:* Faversham (01795) 537614.

FORD, Rev. Wilfred Franklin, CMG 1974; *b* 9 Jan. 1920; *s* of Harold Franklin Ford and Sarah Elizabeth Ford; *m* 1st, 1942, Joan Mary Holland (*d* 1981); three *d*; 2nd, 1982, Hilda Mary Astley. *Educ:* Auckland Univ., NZ (BA); Trinity Theological Coll., NZ. Served War, NZ Army, 1942–44. Entered Methodist Ministry, 1945; Dir, Christian Educn, Methodist Church of NZ, 1956–68; President: Methodist Church of NZ, 1971; NZ

Marriage Guidance Council, 1981–84; Life Mem., Wellington Marriage Guidance Council. *Publications:* contribs to NZ and internat. jls, on Christian educn. *Recreations:* gardening, reading, bowls. *Address:* 122 Totara Drive, Hamilton, New Zealand.

FORDE, Harold McDonald, MD; consultant physician; High Commissioner for Barbados in UK, 1984–86; *b* 10 Jan. 1916; *s* of Gertrude and William McDonald Forde; *m* 1949, Alice Leslie; one *s* two *d. Educ:* Harrison College, Barbados; University College London; University College Hospital (MB BS 1942; MD); DPH, DTM&H. MO, Colonial Med. Service, Belize, 1947–52; First Lectr, Dept. of Medicine, Univ. of West Indies, Jamaica, 1952–57; Consultant Physician, Barbados, 1957–78; Med. Supt, Barbados Gen. Hosp., 1961–64; Senior Lectr, Dept of Medicine, Univ. of West Indies, 1967–78 (Associate Dean, 1967–73); Mem. Senate, Univ. of W Indies, 1973–75; Chief Med. Officer, Commonwealth of Bahamas, 1978–79; Consultant Physician, Barbados, 1980–84; Chief Med. Officer, Life of Barbados, 1973–84. Mem. Privy Council, Barbados, 1980–85; Senior Fellow, Commonwealth Fund, 1976; Tech. Expert, Commonwealth Fund for Tech Co-Opn, 1978–79; Governor, Commonwealth Foundn, 1984. Hon. Vice-President: West India Cttee; Commonwealth Inst. Past Dist Gov., Lions Clubs Internat., 1973 (Life Mem., 1988; Melvin Jones Fellow, 1992). Mem., NY Acad. of Scis. Hon. FRCPE 1972; Hon. FACP 1975. Silver Jubilee Medal, 1977. *Publications:* articles in WI med. jls. *Recreations:* cricket, soccer, bridge, chess, athletics, music. *Address:* Bethesda Medical Centre, Black Rock, St Michael, Barbados, WI. *Club:* Commonwealth Trust.

FORDE, (Mary Marguerite) Leneen, (Mrs Angus McDonald), AC 1993; Governor of Queensland, since 1992; *b* 12 May 1935; *d* of John Alfred Kavanagh and Evelyn Philomena Kavanagh (*née* Bujold); *m* 1st, 1955, Francis Gerard Forde (*d* 1966), *s* of Rt Hon. Francis Michael Forde, PC; three *s* two *d*; 2nd, 1983, (Albert) Angus McDonald. *Educ:* Lisgar Collegiate, Ottawa (Dip. Med. Lab. Technician); Univ. of Queensland (LLB). Student Med. Lab. Technician, Ottawa Gen. Hosp., 1952–53; Med. Lab. Technician, Drs Rousell and Gagne, Ottawa, 1953–54; Haematol. Dept, Royal Brisbane Hosp., 1954–56; part-time lab. work, 1956–66; articled Law Clerk, Alexander McGillivray, 1969–70; Solicitor, Cannan & Peterson, 1971–74; Partner, Sly, Weigall Cannan & Peterson, 1974–92. Founder, Qld Women Lawyers' Assoc., 1976; Member: Qld Law Soc., 1971–; Women Chiefs of Enterprise Internat., 1989–; Zonta Club of Brisbane Inc., 1971–; Pres., Zonta Internat., 1990–92. Paul Harris Fellow, Rotary Club of Brisbane, 1990; Woman of Substance Award, Qld Girl Guides' Assoc., 1990; Queenslander of the Year, 1991. DUniv: Griffith, 1992; Qld Univ. of Technology, 1993. DStJ 1992. *Publication:* Queensland Annual Law Review, 1991, 1992. *Recreations:* theatre, art, music, ballet, surfing. *Address:* Government House, Fernberg Road, Paddington, Qld 4064, Australia. *T:* (7) 3697744, *Fax:* (7) 3699419.

FORDER, Ven. Charles Robert; Archdeacon Emeritus, Diocese of York, since 1974; *b* 6 Jan. 1907; *s* of late Henry Forder, Worstead, Norfolk; *m* 1933, Myra, *d* of late Harry Peat, Leeds; no *c. Educ:* Paston Sch., North Walsham; Christ's Coll. and Ridley Hall, Cambridge. Exhibitioner of Christ's Coll. and Prizeman, 1926; 1st Cl. Math. Trip. Part I, 1926, BA (Sen. Opt. Part II) 1928, MA 1932; Ridley Hall, 1928. Curate: St Peter's, Hunslet Moor, 1930–33; Burley, 1933–34; Vicar: Holy Trinity, Wibsey, 1934–40; St Clement's, Bradford, 1940–47; Organising Sec., Bradford Church Forward Movement Appeal, 1945–47; Vicar of Drypool, 1947–55; Rector of Routh and Vicar of Wawne, 1955–57; Canon, and Prebendary of Fenton, York Minster, 1957–76; Rector of Sutton-on-Derwent, 1957–63; Rector of Holy Trinity, Micklegate, York, 1963–66; Archdeacon of York, 1957–72. Chaplain to HM Prison, Hull, 1950–53; Proctor in Convocation, 1954–72; Organising Sec., Diocesan Appeal, 1955–76; Church Comr, 1958–73. *Publications:* A History of the Paston Grammar School, 1934, 2nd edn 1975; The Parish Priest at Work, 1947; Synods in Action, 1970; Churchwardens in Church and Parish, 1976; contrib. to Encyclopædia Britannica. *Recreations:* reading and writing. *Address:* Dulverton Hall, St Martin's Square, Scarborough YO11 2DQ. *T:* Scarborough (01723) 379534.

FORDER, Kenneth John; Registrar of the Architects Registration Council of the United Kingdom (established under Architects Registration Acts 1931 to 1969), 1977–90; *b* 11 June 1925; *s* of late James A. Forder and Elizabeth Forder (*née* Hammond); *m* 1948, Dorothy Margôt Burles; two *d. Educ:* Westcliff Sch.; Hertford Coll., Oxford (MA); Queen's Coll., Cambridge. Called to Bar, Gray's Inn, 1963. RAF, Flt Lieut, Aircrew Navigator, 1943–47. District Officer, N Rhodesia, 1951–61; District Commissioner, N Rhodesia, 1962–64; General Secretary, National Federation of Meat Traders, 1964–73; Bar Practice, 1973–77. Freeman of the City of London, 1966. *Publications:* Architects in Europe, 1987; The Chittenden Legend, 1994; Fifty True Stories Never Before Told, 1995. *Recreations:* tennis, bridge, chess. *Address:* Napier Cottage, Napier Avenue, SW6 3NJ. *T:* 0171–736 3958. *Club:* Hurlingham.

FORDHAM, John Jeremy; His Honour Judge Fordham; a Circuit Judge, since 1986; *b* 18 April 1933; *s* of John Hampden Fordham, CBE and Rowena Langran; *m* 1962, Rose Anita (*née* Brandon), *d* of Philip Brandon, Wellington, New Zealand; one *s* one *d. Educ:* Gresham's Sch.; Univ. of New Zealand. LLB (NZ). Merchant Navy, 1950–55 (2nd Mate (Foreign Going) Cert.); labourer, fireman etc, 1955–60; Barrister and Solicitor, New Zealand, 1960–64; called to Bar, Inner Temple, 1965; practised 1965–71, 1976–78; Sen. Magistrate, Gilbert and Ellice Islands, 1971–75; a Metropolitan Stipendiary Magistrate, 1978–86; a Recorder, 1986. *Recreations:* boats, games. *Address:* 9 King's Bench Walk, Temple, EC4Y 7DX. *T:* 0171–353 5638. *Club:* Garrick.

FOREMAN, Michael; RDI 1985; AGI; writer and illustrator; *b* 21 March 1938; *s* of Walter and Gladys Mary Foreman; *m* 1st, 1959, Janet Charters (marr. diss. 1966); one *s*; 2nd, 1980, Louise Phillips; two *s. Educ:* Notley Road Secondary Modern Sch., Lowestoft; Royal College of Art, London (ARCA 1st Cl. Hons and Silver Medal). Freelance, 1963–; six animated films produced, 1967–68. Awarded Aigle d'Argent, Festival International du Livre, Nice, 1972; (jtly) Kurt Maschler Award, 1982; Graphics Prize, Bologna, 1982; Kate Greenaway Medal, Library Assoc., 1983 and 1989. *Publications:* author and illustrator: The Perfect Present, 1966; The Two Giants, 1966; The Great Sleigh Robbery, 1968; Horatio, 1969; Moose, 1971; Dinosaurs and all that Rubbish, 1972 (Francis Williams Prize, 1972); War and Peas, 1974; All The King's Horses, 1976; Panda and his Voyage of Discovery, 1977 (Francis Williams Prize, 1977); Trick a Tracker, 1980; Panda and the Odd Lion, 1981; Land of Dreams, 1982; Panda and the Bunyips, 1984; Cat and Canary, 1984; Panda and the Bushfire, 1986; Ben's Box, 1986; Ben's Baby, 1987; The Angel and the Wild Animal, 1988; War Boy (autobiog.), 1989; Oneworld, 1990; World of Fairytales, 1990; The Boy Who Sailed with Columbus, 1991; Jack's Fantastic Voyage, 1992; War Game, 1993; Grandfather's Pencil, 1993; illustrator of many books by other authors. *Recreations:* football, travelling. *Address:* 5 Church Gate, SW6 3LD. *Club:* Chelsea Arts.

FOREMAN, Sir Philip (Frank), Kt 1981; CBE 1972; DL; FEng, FIMechE, CIMgt; Member Council, since 1986, and President, since 1994, British Standards Institution (Chairman, 1988–91); *b* 16 March 1923; *s* of late Frank and Mary Foreman; *m* 1971, Margaret Cooke; one *s. Educ:* Soham Grammar Sch., Cambs; Loughborough Coll., Leics. (DLC (Hons)). Royal Naval Scientific Service, 1943–58. Short Bros, 1958–88: Man. Dir, 1967–88; Chm., 1983–88. Director: Simon Engrg Ltd, 1987–94 (Dep. Chm., 1992; Chm., 1993); Progressive Bldg Soc., 1987– (Chm., 1990–); Ricardo Group (formerly Ricardo International) plc, 1988– (Chm., 1992–); Consultant, Foreman Associates, 1988–. Member: Design Council, 1986–92; NI Economic Council, 1972–88; Chm., Teaching Co. Management Cttee, 1987–90; Trustee, Scotch-Irish Trust, 1980–. Mem. Senate, QUB, 1993. Pres., IMechE, 1985–86. Fellow: Irish Management Inst., 1986; Irish Inst. of Engrs, 1987; MInstD 1987. FRSA 1978. A Freeman, City of London, 1980; Liveryman, Engineers' Co., 1992–. Hon. FRAeS 1983. Hon. DSc QUB, 1976; Hon. DTech Loughborough, 1983; DUniv Open, 1985. DL Belfast, 1975. *Publications:* papers to: Royal Aeronautical Soc.; Instn of Mechanical Engineers. *Recreations:* golf, gardening. *Address:* Ashtree House, 26 Ballymenoch Road, Holywood, Co. Down BT18 0HH. *T:* Belfast (01232) 425767.

FORESTER; *see* Weld Forester, family name of Baron Forester.

FORESTER, 8th Baron *cr* 1821; **George Cecil Brooke Weld Forester;** DL; Director: Linley Farms, since 1974; Sipolilo Estates, since 1977; *b* 20 Feb. 1938; *s* of 7th Baron Forester and Marie Louise Priscilla (*d* 1988), *d* of Col Sir Herbert Perrott, 6th Bt, CH, CB; *S* father, 1977; *m* 1967, Hon. Elizabeth Catherine Lyttelton, 2nd *d* of 10th Viscount Cobham, KG, PC, GCMG, GCVO, TD; one *s* three *d. Educ:* Eton; Royal Agricultural College, Cirencester (MRAC). Member: CLA (Mem. Minerals Working Party, 1980; Mem. Council, 1987–; Mem. Exec., 1990–); W Midlands Council for Sport and Recreation, 1991–. President: The Greenwood Trust, 1990–; Shropshire Farming and Wildlife Adv. Gp, 1991–. Former Chairman: Shropshire CLA; Shropshire Tree Council; Forestry Commn Regl Adv. Cttee. DL Shropshire, 1995. *Recreations:* fishing, silviculture, fine arts, the environment. *Heir: s* Hon. Charles Richard George Weld Forester, *b* 8 July 1975. *Address:* Willey Park, Broseley, Salop TF12 5JJ. *T:* Telford (01952) 882146.

FORESTIER-WALKER, Sir Michael (Leolin), 6th Bt *cr* 1835; Teacher, Feltonfleet School, since 1975; *b* 24 April 1949; *s* of Lt-Col Alan Ivor Forestier-Walker, MBE (*d* 1954) (*g s* of 2nd Bt), and Margaret Joan Forestier-Walker (*née* Marcoolyn) (*d* 1988); *S* cousin, 1983; *m* 1988, Elizabeth Hedley, *d* of Joseph Hedley, Bellingham, Northumberland; one *s* one *d. Educ:* Wellington College, Crowthorne; Royal Holloway College, London Univ. (BA Hons). *Recreations:* sailing, electronics. *Heir: s* Joseph Alan Forestier-Walker, *b* 2 May 1992. *Address:* Bibury, 116 Hogshill Lane, Cobham, Surrey KT11 2AW.

FORFAR, Prof. John Oldroyd, MC; Professor of Child Life and Health, University of Edinburgh, 1964–82, now Professor Emeritus; *b* 16 Nov. 1916; *s* of Rev. David Forfar, MA and Elizabeth Edith Campbell; *m* 1942, Isobel Mary Langlands Fernback, MB, ChB, DPH, AFOM; two *s* one *d. Educ:* Perth Acad.; St Andrews Univ. BSc 1938, MB, ChB 1941, St Andrews; DCH (London) 1948; FRCPE 1953 (MRCPE 1948); MD (Commendation) St Andrews, 1958; FRCP 1964 (MRCP 1947); FRSE 1975; FRCPGlas 1979 (MRCPGlas 1978). House Officer, Perth Royal Infirmary, 1941; RAMC, 1942–46: Med. Off., 47 Royal Marine Commando, 1943–45 (MC 1944; despatches, 1945); Registrar and Sen. Registrar, Dundee Royal Infirmary, 1946–48; Sen. Lectr in Child Health, St Andrews Univ., 1948–50; Sen. Paediatric Phys., Edinburgh Northern Gp of Hosps, and Sen. Lectr in Child Life and Health, Edinburgh Univ., 1950–64. Chairman: Scottish Assoc. of Voluntary Child Care Organisations, 1965–69; Medical Gp, Assoc. of British Adoption Agencies, 1966–76; Jt Paediatric Cttee of Royal Colls of Physicians and British Paediatric Assoc., 1979–85; President: Scottish Paediatric Soc., 1972–74; Assoc. of Clinical Professors and Heads of Departments of Paediatrics, 1980–83; Pres., BPA, 1985–88. Fellow, Amer. Coll. of Nutrition, 1977; Hon. Member: Australian Coll. of Paediatrics, 1986; Faculty of Paediatrics, RCPI, 1986. James Spence Medallist, BPA, 1983. *Publications:* (ed) Textbook of Paediatrics, 1973, 3rd edn 1984; Child Health in a Changing Society, 1988; The British Paediatric Association 1928–1988, 1989; contribs to general medical and to paediatric jls and books. *Recreations:* walking, travelling, gardening. *Address:* 9 Ravelston Heights, Edinburgh EH4 3LX. *T:* 0131–315 2184.

FORGAN, Elizabeth Anne Lucy; Managing Director, Network Radio BBC, since 1993; *b* 31 Aug. 1944; *d* of Thomas Moinet Forgan and Jean Margaret Muriel. *Educ:* Benenden Sch.; St Hugh's Coll., Oxford (BA). Journalist: Teheran Journal, 1967–68; Hampstead and Highgate Express, 1969–74; Evening Standard, 1974–78; The Guardian, 1978–81; Channel Four TV: Sen. Commissioning Editor, 1981–86; Dep. Dir of Progs, 1987; Dir of Progs, 1988–93. Member: Scott Trust, 1988–93; Bd of Govs, BFI, 1989–91; Vis. Cttee, RCA, 1990–93; Human Fertilisation and Embryology Authority, 1990–. FRTS 1988; FRSA 1989. Hon. DLitt Keele, 1994. Chevalier de l'ordre des arts et des lettres, 1990. *Recreations:* church music, cheap novels, Scottish Islands. *Address:* c/o BBC, Broadcasting House, W1A 1AA.

FORGE, Andrew Murray; artist, writer; Professor of School of Art, University of Yale, Conn, USA (Dean, 1975–83); *b* Hastingleigh, Kent, 10 Nov. 1923; *s* of Sidney Wallace Forge and late Joanna Ruth Forge (*née* Bliss); *m* 1950, Sheila Deane (marr. diss.); three *d*; *m* 1974, Ruth Miller. *Educ:* Downs Sch.; Leighton Park; Camberwell Sch. of Art (NDD). Sen. Lectr, Slade Sch., UCL, 1950–64; Head of Dept of Fine Art, Goldsmith's Coll., 1964–70. Trustee: Tate Gallery, 1964–71 and 1972–74; National Gallery, 1966–72; Member: Nat. Council for Diplomas in Art and Design, 1964–72; Jt NCDAD/NACEA Cttee, 1968–70; Calouste Gulbenkian Foundn Cttee to report on future of conservation studies in UK, 1970–72; Pres., London Group, 1964–71. Trustee, Amer. Acad. in Rome, 1983–. *Publications:* Klee, 1953; Vermeer, 1954; Soutine, 1965; Rauschenberg, 1972; (with C. Joyes) Monet at Giverny, 1975; (ed) The Townsend Journals, 1976; Monet, 1983; (jtly) The Last Flower Paintings of Manet, 1986; Degas, 1987. *Recreation:* travel. *Address:* Malthouse, Elmsted, near Ashford, Kent TN25 5JZ.

FORMAN, Sir Denis, Kt 1976; OBE 1956; Chairman, Granada Television, 1974–87; Deputy Chairman, Granada Group, 1984–90 (Director, 1964–90); *b* 13 Oct. 1917; *s* of late Rev. Adam Forman, CBE, and Flora Smith; *m* 1st, 1948, Helen de Mouilpied (*d* 1987); two *s*; 2nd, 1990, Moni, *widow* of James Cameron, CBE; one step *s* one step *d. Educ:* at home; Loretto; Pembroke Coll., Cambridge. Served War, 1940–45: Argyll and Sutherland Highlanders; Commandant, Orkney and Shetland Defences Battle Sch., 1942 (wounded, Cassino, 1944). Chief Production Officer, Central Office of Information Films, 1947; Dir, British Film Inst., 1948–55 (Chm., Bd of Governors, 1971–73); Granada TV Ltd, 1955–87: Dir, 1959; Jt Man. Dir, 1965–81; Chm., Novello & Co., 1971–88. Dep. Chm., Royal Opera Hse, Covent Gdn, 1983– (Dir, 1981–); Chm., Scottish Film Production Fund, 1990–; Mem. Council, RNCM, 1975–84 (Hon. Mem., RNCM, 1981; FRNCM 1993). Fellow, BAFTA, 1977. DUniv: Stirling, 1982; Keele, 1990; DU Essex, 1986; Hon. LLD: Manchester, 1983; Lancaster, 1989. Ufficiale dell'ordine Al Merito della Repubblica Italiana. *Publications:* Mozart's Piano Concertos, 1971; Son of Adam (autobiog.), 1990; To Reason Why (autobiog.), 1991; (ed) The Good Opera Guide, 1994. *Recreation:* music. *Address:* The Mill House, Howe Street, Chelmsford, Essex CM3 1BG. *Clubs:* Garrick, Savile.

See also M. B. Forman.

FORMAN, (Francis) Nigel; MP (C) Carshalton and Wallington, since 1983 (Carshalton, March 1976–1983); *b* 25 March 1943; *s* of late Brig. J. F. R. Forman and of Mrs P. J. M.

Forman; *m.* *Educ:* Dragon Sch., Oxford; Shrewsbury Sch.; New Coll., Oxford; College of Europe, Bruges; Kennedy Sch. of Govt, Harvard; Sussex Univ. Information Officer, CBI, 1970–71; Conservative Research Dept, 1971–76. Contested (C) Coventry NE, Feb. 1974. PPS to Lord Privy Seal, 1979–81 and to Minister of State, FCO, 1979–83, to Chancellor of the Exchequer, 1987–89; Parly Under Sec. of State, Dept for Educn, 1992. Member: Select Cttee on Science and Technology, 1976–79; Select Cttee on Foreign Affairs, 1990–92; Vice-Chairman: Cons. Finance Cttee, 1983–87; All Party Social Sci. and Policy Cttee, 1984–; Secretary: Cons. Education Cttee, 1976–79; Cons. Energy Cttee, 1977–79. Mem. Exec., 1922 Cttee, 1990–92. Mem., ESRC, 1991–92. Chm., GB–E Europe Centre; Hon. Treas., Federal Trust; Hon. Dir, Job Ownership Ltd. *Publications:* Towards a More Conservative Energy Policy, 1977; Another Britain, 1979; Mastering British Politics, 1985, 2nd edn 1991; (with John Maples) Work to be Done, 1985. *Address:* House of Commons, SW1A 0AA.

FORMAN, Air Vice-Marshal Graham Neil, CB 1989; Director of Legal Services, Royal Air Force, 1982–89; *b* 29 Nov. 1930; *s* of Stanley M. Forman and Eva Forman (*née* Barrett); *m* 1957, Valerie Fay (*née* Shaw); one *s* two *d.* *Educ:* Boston Grammar School; Nottingham Univ. Law School; Law Society's School of Law; admitted solicitor 1953. Commissioned RAF Legal Branch, 1957; served HQ Far East Air Force, Singapore, 1960–63 and 1965–68; Dep. Dir, RAF Legal Services, HQ Near East Air Force, Cyprus, 1971–72 and 1973–76; Dep. Dir, RAF Legal Services, HQ RAF Germany, 1978; Dep. Dir, Legal Services (RAF), 1978–82. *Recreations:* tennis, reading, traditional jazz music, watching cricket. *Address:* c/o Lloyds Bank, High Street, Union Street, Ryde, Isle of Wight PO33 2LH. *Clubs:* Royal Air Force; MCC.

FORMAN, Sir John Denis; *see* Forman, Sir Denis.

FORMAN, Michael Bertram, TD 1945; Director of Personnel and Organisation, TI Group plc, 1973–84; retired; *b* 28 March 1921; *s* of late Rev. A. Forman, CBE, and Flora Smith; *m* 1947, Mary Railston-Brown, *d* of Rev. W. R. Railston-Brown; four *d.* *Educ:* Loretto Sch., Musselburgh; Manchester Coll. of Technology. TA commn, 7th KOSB, 1939. War Service in Inf. and Airborne Forces, 1939–46: UK, Holland, Germany (POW), India. Labour Management, Courtaulds Ltd, 1946–53; Dir, Inst. of Personnel Management, 1953–56; Head of Staff Planning, NCB, 1956–59; Chief Staff Officer, SW Div., NCB, 1959–62; TI Group plc (formerly Tube Investments Ltd): Personnel Relations Adviser and Dep. Dir of Personnel, 1962–68; Personnel Dir, Steel Tube Div., 1968–73. Mem. NBPI, 1968–70; Chm., CSAB, 1984–90. CIPD. FRSA. *Recreations:* reading, gardening, fishing, shooting. *Address:* The Priory, Stoke Prior, Bromsgrove, Worcs B60 4LY. *T:* Bromsgrove (01527) 832196. *Club:* Savile.

See also Sir D. Forman.

FORMAN, Miloš; film director; *b* Čáslav, 18 Feb. 1932. *Educ:* Acad. of Music and Dramatic Art, Prague. Director: Film Presentations, Czechoslovak Television, 1954–56; Laterna Magika, Prague, 1958–62. Co-chm. and Prof., Film Div., Columbia Univ. Sch. of Arts, 1978–. Films directed include: Talent Competition; Peter and Pavla, 1963 (Czech. Film Critics' Award; Grand Prix, Locarno, 1964; Prize, Venice Festival, 1965); A Blonde in Love (Grand Prix, French Film Acad., 1966); The Fireman's Ball, 1967; Taking Off, 1971; (co-dir) Visions of Eight, 1973; One Flew Over the Cuckoo's Nest, 1975 (Academy Award, 1976; BAFTA Award, 1977); Hair, 1979; Ragtime, 1982; Amadeus, 1985 (Oscar Award, 1985); Valmont, 1988. *Publication:* Turnaround: a memoir, 1993. *Address:* c/o Robert Lantz, The Lantz Office, 888 Seventh Avenue, New York, NY 10106, USA.

FORMAN, Nigel; *see* Forman, F. N.

FORMAN, Roy; Director, General Healthcare Group PLC, since 1994; Deputy Chairman, Age Concern Enteprises Ltd; *b* 28 Dec. 1931; *s* of Leslie and Ena Forman; *m* 1954, Mary (*née* Nelson); three *s* one *d.* *Educ:* Nunthorpe Grammar Sch., York; Nottingham Univ. (BA Hons). RAF, 1953–56. Business economist, 1956–61; electricity supply industry, 1961–80: Chief Commercial Officer, S Wales Elec. Bd, 1972–76; Commercial Adviser, Electricity Council, 1976–80; Private Patients Plan Ltd: Gen. Manager, Marketing and Sales, 1980–81; Marketing Dir, 1981–85; Man. Dir and Chief Exec., 1985–93. Mem. Cttee of Mgt, Horder Centre for Arthritis, 1994–. Chm., The Opera Co., 1995–. CIMgt 1991. FRSA 1992. *Recreations:* music, walking, reading. *Address:* The Beacon Cottage, Cripps Corner Road, Staplecross, East Sussex TN32 5QR.

FORMARTINE, Viscount; George Ian Alastair Gordon; *b* 4 May 1983; *s* and *heir* of Earl of Haddo, *qv.*

FORRES, 4th Baron *cr* 1922; **Alastair Stephen Grant Williamson;** Bt 1909; MARAC; Director: Agriscot Pty Ltd; Jaga Trading Pty Ltd; *b* 16 May 1946; *s* of 3rd Baron Forres and of Gillian Ann Maclean, *d* of Major John Maclean Grant, RA; *S* father, 1978; *m* 1969, Margaret, *d* of late G. J. Mallam, Mullumbimby, NSW; two *s.* *Educ:* Eton. Alderman, Orange City Council, 1987–. Pres., Big Brother Movt, 1986–. Patron, Sydney Scottish Week, 1981–. *Heir: s* Hon. George Archibald Mallam Williamson, *b* 16 Aug. 1972. *Address:* Kenso Park, Forest Road, Orange, NSW 2800, Australia. *Clubs:* Union, Australian Jockey, Sydney Turf (Sydney).

FORREST, Prof. Sir (Andrew) Patrick (McEwen), Kt 1986; Regius Professor of Clinical Surgery, University of Edinburgh, 1970–88, now Professor Emeritus; Associate Dean, International Medical College, Kuala Lumpur, 1993–March 1996; *b* 25 March 1923; *s* of Rev. Andrew James Forrest, BD, and Isabella Pearson; *m* 1955, Margaret Beryl Hall (*d* 1961); one *s* one *d*; *m* 1964, Margaret Anne Steward; one *d.* *Educ:* Dundee High Sch.; Univ. of St Andrews. BSc 1942; MB, ChB 1945; ChM hons, University Gold Medal, 1954; MD hons, Rutherford Gold Medal, 1958; FRCSE 1950; FRCS 1952; FRCSGlas 1962; FRSE 1976; FIBiol 1986. Surg.-Lt RNVR, 1946–48. Mayo Foundation Fellow, 1952–53; Lectr and Sen. Lectr, Univ. of Glasgow, 1955–62; Prof. of Surgery, Welsh Nat. Sch. of Medicine, 1962–70. Hon. Consultant Surgeon: Royal Inf. of Edinburgh, until 1988; Royal Prince Alfred Hosp., Sydney; Civilian Consultant to RN, 1977–88. Chief Scientist (pt-time), SHHD, 1981–87. McIlrath Vis. Prof., Royal Prince Alfred Hosp., Sydney, 1969; Nimmo Vis. Prof., Royal Adelaide Hosp., 1973; McLauchlin-Gallie Prof., RCP of Canada, 1974; numerous other visiting professorships; Vis. Scientist, Nat. Cancer Inst., 1989–90; eponymous lectures include: Lister Meml, Canadian Med. Assoc., 1970; Inaugural Bruce Wellesley Hosp., Toronto, 1970; Inaugural Peter Lowe, RCP Glas., 1980. Member: Medical sub-cttee, UGC, 1967–76; MRC, 1974–79; Scientific Adv. Cttee, Cancer Res. Campaign, 1974–83; ABRC, 1982–85. Asst Editor and Editor, Scottish Med. Jl, 1957–61; Hon. Secretary: Scottish Soc. for Experimental Medicine, 1959–62; Surgical Research Soc., 1963–66, Pres., 1974–76; Chairman: British Breast Gp, 1974–77; Working Gp on Breast Cancer Screening (reported, 1986). Member Council: Assoc. of Surgeons of GB and Ireland, 1971–74 (Pres., 1988–89); RCSE, 1976–84, 1986–89; Member: Internat. Surgical Gp, 1963–; James IV Assoc. of Surgeons Inc., 1981–; Scottish Hosp. Endowments Res. Trust, 1990–. Hon. Fellow, Amer. Surgical Assoc., 1981; Hon. FACS, 1978; Hon. FRACS, 1987; Hon. FRCR, 1988; Hon. FRCSCan, 1989. Hon. DSc: Wales, 1981; Chinese Univ. of Hong Kong, 1986; Hon. LLD Dundee, 1986. Lister Medal, RCS, 1987. *Publications:* (ed jtly) Prognostic Factors in Breast Cancer, 1968; (jtly) Principles and Practice of Surgery, 1985; Breast Cancer: the decision to screen, 1991; various papers in surgical jls, mainly on gastro-intestinal disease and breast cancer. *Address:* 19 St Thomas Road, Edinburgh EH9 2LR. *T:* 0131–667 3203.

FORREST, Geoffrey; Consultant Chartered Surveyor; *b* 31 Oct. 1909; *er s* of late George Forrest, CA, Rossie Lodge, Inverness; *m* 1st, 1951, Marjorie Ridehalgh; two *s*; 2nd, 1974, Joyce Grey. *Educ:* Marlborough Coll. Chartered Surveyor. Served War of 1939–45, in Lovat Scouts. Joined Forestry Commn, 1946; Chief Land Agent for Forestry Commn in Wales, 1958–64; Chief Land Agent for Forestry Commn in Scotland, 1964–65; Sen. Officer of Forestry Commn in Scotland, 1965–69. Scottish Partner, Knight, Frank & Rutley, 1973–76. *Publications:* papers on land use and estate management in professional jls. *Recreations:* fishing, shooting, lawn tennis. *Address:* Harelaw, Lilliesleaf, Melrose TD6 9JW.

FORREST, Cdre (Retd) Geoffrey Cornish; Master of P & O vessel Arcadia from her completion in Jan. 1954 until Oct. 1956; Commodore P & O Fleet, 1955–56; *b* 1898. *Educ:* Thames Nautical Training Coll. (the Worcester). *Recreations:* photography, chess, bridge.

FORREST, John Richard, DPhil; FEng 1985; FIEE; Deputy Chairman, National Transcommunications Ltd since 1994 (Chief Executive, 1991–94); Chairman, Brewton Ltd, since 1994; *b* 21 April 1943; *s* of late John Samuel Forrest, FRS and Ivy May Olding; *m* 1973, Jane Patricia Robey Leech; two *s* one *d.* *Educ:* Sidney Sussex Coll., Cambridge (MA); Keble Coll., Oxford (DPhil). Research Associate and Lectr, Stanford Univ., Calif, 1967–70; Lectr, later Prof., Electronic and Elect. Engrg Dept, University Coll. London, 1970–84; Technical Dir, Marconi Defence Systems Ltd, 1984–86; Dir of Engrg, IBA, 1986–90. Dir, Egan Internat. Ltd, 1994–. Vice-President: IEE, 1992–; RTS, 1994–. FRSA 1986; FRTS 1990; FInstD 1991. Hon. Fellow, BKSTS. Hon. DSc City, 1992; Hon. DTech Brunel, 1995. Chevalier de l'ordre des arts et des lettres, 1990. *Publications:* papers and contribs to books on phased array radar, satellite communications, broadcasting and optoelectronics. *Recreations:* travel, sailing, mountain walking, literature, study of mankind. *Address:* Hilfield Farm House, Hilfield Lane, Aldenham, Herts WD2 8DD. *T:* 0181–950 1820; 15 Carlyle Court, Chelsea Harbour, SW10 0UQ. *T:* 0171–376 5731. *Club:* Athenæum.

FORREST, Prof. Sir Patrick; *see* Forrest, Prof. Sir A. P. M.

FORREST, Very Rev. Robin Whyte; Dean of Moray, Ross and Caithness, since 1992; Canon of St Andrew's Cathedral, Inverness, since 1986; Rector of Forres, since 1979; *b* 1933. *Educ:* Edinburgh Theol Coll., 1958. Ordained deacon, 1961, priest, 1962; Asst Curate, St Mary, Glasgow, 1961–66; Rector: Renfrew, 1966–70; Motherwell, 1970–79, with Wishaw, 1975–79; Nairn, 1979–92. Synod Clerk, Moray, 1991–92. *Address:* St John's Rectory, Victoria Road, Forres, Morayshire IV36 0BN. *T:* Forres (01309) 672856.

FORREST, Rear-Adm. Sir Ronald (Stephen), KCVO 1975; JP; DL; *b* 11 Jan. 1923; *s* of Stephen Forrest, MD, and Maud M. McKinstry; *m* 1st, 1947, Patricia (*d* 1966), *e d* of Dr and Mrs E. N. Russell; two *s* one *d*; 2nd, 1967, June (*née* Weaver), *widow* of Lieut G. Perks, RN; one step *s* one step *d.* *Educ:* Belhaven Hill; RNC, Dartmouth. War Service at Sea, Lieut 1943 (despatches 1944); Comdr 1955; CO HMS Teazer, 1956; on loan to Pakistan Navy, 1958–60; Captain 1963; jssc 1963; Chief Staff Officer to Adm. Comdg Reserves, 1964; comd Dartmouth Trng Sqdn, 1966; Dir, Seaman Officers Appointments, 1968; CO, HMS London, 1970; Rear-Adm. 1972; Defence Services Secretary, 1972–75. Pres., Devon Co. Agricl Assoc., 1990–91. County Comr, St John Amb. Bde, Devon, 1976–81, Comdr, 1981–87. Naval Gen. Service Medal, 1949. KStJ 1987 (CStJ 1983). JP Honiton, 1978; DL Devon, 1985. Chevalier, Ordre du Mérite Agricole (France), 1990. *Recreation:* gardening. *Address:* Higher Seavington, Stockland, near Honiton, Devon EX14 9DE. *Clubs:* Naval, Army and Navy.

FORREST, Prof. William George Grieve; Wykeham Professor of Ancient History, Oxford University, 1977–92, now Emeritus; Fellow of New College, Oxford, 1977–92, now Emeritus; *b* 24 Sept. 1925; *s* of William and Ina Forrest; *m* 1956, Margaret Elizabeth Mary Hall; two *d.* *Educ:* University College Sch., Hampstead; New Coll., Oxford (MA). Served RAF, 1943–47; New Coll., Oxford, 1947–51; Fellow, Wadham Coll., Oxford, 1951–76, now Emeritus. Visiting Professor: Trinity and University Colls, Toronto, 1961; Yale, 1968; Vis. Fellow, British Sch. at Athens, 1986. Hon. DPhil Athens, 1991. *Publications:* Emergence of Greek Democracy, 1966; History of Sparta, 1968, 2nd edn 1980; articles in classical and archaeological periodicals. *Address:* 9 Fyfield Road, Oxford OX2 6QE. *T:* Oxford (01865) 56187.

FORREST, Surgeon Rear-Adm. (D) William Ivon Norman, CB 1970; Director of Naval Dental Services, Ministry of Defence, 1968–71; *b* 8 June 1914; *s* of late Eng. Lt James Forrest; *m* 1942, Mary Margaret McMordie Black; three *s.* *Educ:* Christ's Hospital. Guy's Hospital, 1931–36. LDS, RCS. Dental House Surgeon, Guy's Hosp., 1936–37. Royal Navy: Surg. Lieut (D), 1937; Surg. Lt-Comdr (D), 1943; Surg. Comdr (D), 1950; Surg. Capt. (D), 1960; Surg. Rear-Adm. (D), 1968. Consultant in Dental Surgery, 1963. *Recreations:* golf, gardening, photography. *Address:* 24 Staple Close, Waterlooville, Hants PO7 6AH. *T:* Waterlooville (01705) 263139.

FORRESTER, David Michael; Under Secretary, Further Education, Department for Education and Employment (formerly Department for Education), since 1994; *b* 22 June 1944; *s* of late Reginald Grant Forrester and Minnie Forrester (*née* Chaytow); *m* 1st, 1978, Diana Douglas (marr. diss. 1983); 2nd, 1993, Helen Mary Williams, *qv*; one *s* one *d.* *Educ:* St Paul's Sch.; King's Coll., Cambridge (BA Hons 1st Cl. 1966, MA); Kennedy Sch. of Govt, Harvard Univ. (an inaugural Kennedy Scholar, 1966–67). DES, 1967; Private Sec. to Parly Under Sec., 1971–72; Principal, DES, 1972–76; HM Treasury, 1976–78; Asst Sec., DES, 1979–85; DTI, 1985–87; Under Sec., DES, subseq. DFE, 1988; Hd of Schs Funding Br., 1994. *Recreations:* cricket, squash, music, esp. opera, mountain walking. *Address:* Department for Education and Employment, Sanctuary Buildings, Great Smith Street, SW1P 3BT. *T:* 0171–925 5800. *Club:* Pretenders'.

FORRESTER, Rev. Prof. Duncan Baillie; Professor of Christian Ethics and Practical Theology, since 1978, and Principal of New College, since 1986, University of Edinburgh; Director, Edinburgh University Centre for Theology and Public Issues, since 1984; *b* 10 Nov. 1933; *s* of Rev. Prof. William Forrester and Isobel McColl or Forrester; *m* 1964, Rev. Margaret R. McDonald or Forrester (Minister of St Michael's Parish Church, Edinburgh); one *s* one *d.* *Educ:* Madras Coll., St Andrews; Univ. of St Andrews (MA Hons Mod. Hist. and Pol. Sci.); Univ. of Chicago (Grad., Dept of Politics); Univ. of Edinburgh (BD); DPhil Sussex. Part-time Asst in Politics, Univ. of Edinburgh, 1957–58; Asst Minister, Hillside Church and Leader of St James Mission, 1960–61; Church of Scotland Missionary to S India, 1962, Lectr, then Prof. of Politics, Madras Christian Coll., Tambaram, 1962–70; ordained as Presbyter of Church of S India, part-time Lectr in Politics, Univ. of Edinburgh, 1966–67; Chaplain and Lectr in Politics and Religious Studies, Sch. of African and Asian Studies, Univ. of Sussex, 1970–78. Lectures: Lee, Edinburgh, 1980; Hensley Henson, Oxford, 1988; Bernard Gilpin, Durham, 1992; F. D. Maurice, KCL, 1995. Chm., Edinburgh Council of Social Service, 1983–87; Faith and

Order Commn, WCC, 1983–. President: Soc. for the Study of Theol., 1991–93; Soc. for the Study of Christian Ethics, 1991–94. Mem., Center of Theol Inquiry, Princeton, 1992–. *Publications:* chapters on Luther, Calvin and Hooker, in History of Political Philosophy, ed Strauss and Cropsey, 1963, 3rd edn 1986; Caste and Christianity, 1980; (with J. I. H. McDonald and G. Tellini) Encounter with God, 1983; (ed with D. Murray) Studies in the History of Worship in Scotland, 1984; Christianity and the Future of Welfare, 1985; (ed with D. Skene and co-author) Just Sharing, 1988; Theology and Politics, 1988; Beliefs, Values and Policies: conviction politics in a secular age, 1989; (ed jtly) Worship Now, Book 2, 1989; (ed) Theology and Practice, 1990; articles on Indian politics and religion, ethics and political theology. *Recreations:* hill-walking, ornithology. *Address:* 25 Kingsburgh Road, Edinburgh EH12 6DZ. *T:* 0131–337 5646.

FORRESTER, Giles Charles Fielding; His Honour Judge Forrester; a Circuit Judge, since 1986; *b* 18 Dec. 1939; *s* of Basil Thomas Charles Forrester and Diana Florence Forrester (*née* Sandeman); *m* 1966, Georgina Elizabeth Garnett; one *s* one *d*. *Educ:* Rugby School; Grenoble Univ.; Trinity College, Oxford (MA Jurisp.). Account Exec., Pritchard Wood and Partners (Advertising Agents), 1962–66. Mem., HAC Infantry Bn, 1963–67. Called to the Bar, Inner Temple, 1966; practised, SE Circuit, 1966–86; a Recorder of the Crown Court, 1986. *Recreations:* a wide variety, mainly sporting. *Address:* c/o The Crown Court, Canbury Park Road, Kingston upon Thames, Surrey KT2 6JU. *T:* 0181–549 5241. *Clubs:* Roehampton; Royal Western Yacht; St Enedoc Golf; New Zealand Golf (Weybridge).

FORRESTER, Helen Mary; *see* Williams, H. M.

FORRESTER, Ian Stewart; QC (Scot.) 1988; *b* 13 Jan. 1945; *s* of late Alexander Roxburgh Forrester and Elizabeth Richardson Forrester (*née* Stewart); *m* 1981, Sandra Anne Therese Keegan, Louisiana lawyer; two *s*. *Educ:* Kelvinside Acad., Glasgow; Univ. of Glasgow (MA 1965; LLB 1967); Tulane Univ. of Louisiana (MCL 1969). Mem., British Univs debating team, 1966; Commonwealth expedn to India, 1967. Admitted Faculty of Advocates, Scots Bar, 1972; admitted Bar of State of NY, following order of NY Court of Appeals, 1977. With Maclay, Murray & Spens, 1968–69; Davis Polk & Wardwell, 1969–72; Cleary Gottlieb Steen & Hamilton, 1972–81; estab. indep. chambers, Brussels, 1981; co-founder, Forrester & Norall, 1981 (Forrester Norall & Sutton, 1989), practising before European Commn and Court. Chairman: British Conservative Assoc., Belgium, 1982–86; European Trade Law Assoc., 1989–; Mem., Eur. Cttee, British Invisibles. Hon. Vis. Prof., European Law, Univ. of Glasgow, 1991–. Mem., European Adv. Bd, Tulane Univ., 1992–. Elder, St Andrew's Church of Scotland, Brussels. *Publications:* numerous articles on EEC customs, dumping and trade law, competition law, German civil and commercial codes. *Recreations:* politics, wine, cooking, restoring old houses. *Address:* Forrester Norall & Sutton, 1 Place Madou, Box 34, 1030 Brussels, Belgium; Advocates' Library, Parliament House, Edinburgh EH1 1RF. *Clubs:* Athenæum; International Château Ste-Anne (Brussels); Royal Yacht Club of Belgium.

FORRESTER, John Stuart; *b* 17 June 1924; *s* of Harry and Nellie Forrester; *m* 1945, Gertrude H. Weaver. *Educ:* Eastwood Council Sch.; City Sch. of Commerce, Stoke-on-Trent; Alsager Teachers' Training Coll. Teacher, 1946–66. MP (Lab) Stoke-on-Trent, N, 1966–87. Sec., Constituency Labour Party, 1961–84. Mem., Speaker's Panel of Chairmen, 1982–87; Member: NUT, 1949–87; APEX, 1942–43, 1946–49, 1984–. Councillor, Stoke-on-Trent, 1970–. Freedom of Stoke-on-Trent, 1992. *Address:* 13 Cadeby Grove, Milton, Stoke-on-Trent ST2 7BY.

FORRESTER, Maj.-Gen. Michael, CB 1969; CBE 1963 (OBE 1960); DSO 1943 and Bar, 1944; MC 1939 and Bar, 1941; retired 1970; *b* 31 Aug. 1917; 2nd *s* of late James Forrester, Chilworth, Hants, and Elsie (*née* Mathwin); *m* 1947, Pauline Margaret Clara (marr. diss. 1960), *d* of late James Fisher, Crossmichael; two *s*. *Educ:* Haileybury. 2nd Lieut, SRO, Queen's Royal Regt, 1936, Regular Commn, 1938; served in Palestine (Arab Rebellion), 1938–39; served War of 1939–45 in Palestine, Egypt, Greece, Crete, Western Desert, Syria, N Africa, Italy and France; Intell. Officer, GHQ Cairo, 1940; GSO3 (Ops) British Military Mission, Greece, 1940–41; GSO3 (Ops), HQ Western Desert Force and HQ 13 Corps, 1941–42; Staff Coll., Haifa, 1942; Bde Major, 132 Inf. Bde, 1942 (despatches); GSO2 (Ops), HQ 13 Corps and HQ 18 Army Gp, 1943; Comdr, 1st/6th Bn, Queen's Royal Regt, 1943–44; wounded, Normandy; GSO1 (Ops), HQ 13 Corps, 1945–46; Mil. Asst to Supreme Allied Comdr Mediterranean, 1947; Mil. Asst to Comdr Brit. Army Staff and Army Mem., Brit. Jt Services Mission, Washington, DC, 1947–50; Co. Comdr, 2nd Bn Parachute Regt, Cyprus and Canal Zone, 1951–52; Dirg Staff, Staff Coll., Camberley, 1953–55; GSO1 (Ops), GHQ East Africa, 1955–57; transf. to Parachute Regt, 1957; Comdr, 3rd Bn Parachute Regt, 1957–60 (incl. Jordan, 1958); Col, Military Operations (4), War Office, 1960–61; Comdr, 16 Parachute Bde Gp, 1961–63; Imp. Def. Coll., 1964; GOC 4th Div., BAOR, 1965–67; Dir of Infantry, MoD, 1968–70. Col Comdt, The Queen's Division, 1968–70. Lay Co-Chm., Alton Deanery Synod, 1984–88; Mem., Winchester Diocesan Synod, 1988–91. Vice-Pres., UK Crete Veterans' Assoc., 1993–. Hon. Citizen, Canea, Crete, 1966. *Address:* Hammonds, West Worldham, near Alton, Hants GU34 3BH. *T:* Alton (01420) 84470.

FORRESTER, Prof. Peter Garnett, CBE 1981; Director, Faculties Partnership, since 1983; (Chairman, 1983–87); Professor Emeritus, Cranfield Institute of Technology; *b* 7 June 1917; *s* of Arthur Forrester and Emma (*née* Garnett); *m* 1942, Marjorie Hewitt, Berks; two *d*. *Educ:* Manchester Grammar Sch.; Manchester Univ. (BSc, MSc). Metallurgist, Thomas Bolton & Son Ltd, 1938–40; Research Officer, later Chief Metallurgist, Tin Research Inst., 1940–48; Chief Metallurgist and Research Man., Glacier Metal Co. Ltd, 1948–63; Dep. Principal, Glacier Inst. of Management, 1963–64; Consultant, John Tyzack & Partners, 1964–66; Prof. of Industrial Management, Coll. of Aeronautics, Cranfield, 1966; Dir, Cranfield Sch. of Management, 1967–82, Dean of Faculty, 1972; Pro-Vice-Chancellor, Cranfield Inst. of Technol., 1976–82. Chm., Conf. of Univ. Management Schs, 1976–77. Chm., Rye and Winchelsea Centre, Nat. Trust, 1991–93. Mem., Bd of Trustees, European Foundation for Management Develt, 1976–82. CIMgt. Hon. DSc Cranfield Inst. of Technol., 1983. Burnham Medal, BIM, 1979. *Publications:* The British MBA, 1986; papers and reports on management educn; numerous scientific and technological papers on metallurgy, bearing materials, tribology. *Recreations:* sailing, walking. *Address:* Strawberry Hole Cottage, Ewhurst Lane, Northiam, near Rye, Sussex TN31 6HJ. *T:* Northiam (01797) 252255.

FORRESTER-PATON, His Honour Douglas Shaw; QC 1965; a Circuit Judge (formerly a Judge of County Courts), 1970–86; *b* 1921; 3rd *s* of late Alexander Forrester-Paton, JP; *m* 1948, Agnete, *d* of Holger Tuxen; one *s* two *d*. *Educ:* Gresham's Sch., Holt; Queen's Coll., Oxford (BA). Called to Bar, Middle Temple, 1947; North East Circuit. Served RAF, 1941–45. Recorder: Middlesbrough, 1963–68; Teesside, 1968–70. *Address:* 11 The Dorkings, Great Broughton, Middlesbrough, Cleveland TS9 7NA. *T:* Stokesley (01642) 712301; 5 King's Bench Walk, Temple, EC4.

FORSBERG, (Charles) Gerald, OBE 1955; Comdr RN (Retd); author; Assistant Director of Marine Services, Ministry of Defence (Navy Department), 1972–75 (Deputy Director, 1958–72); *b* Vancouver, 18 June 1912; *s* of Charles G. Forsberg and Nellie (*née* Wallman); *m* 1952, Joyce Whewell Hogarth (*d* 1987), *d* of Dr F. W. Hogarth; one *s* one *d*. *Educ:* Polytechnic School; Training Ship Mercury; Sir John Cass Coll. Merchant Navy: Cadet to Chief Officer, 1928–38; qual. Master Mariner; transf. RN, 1938. Norwegian campaign, 1940; Malta Convoys, Matapan, Tobruk, Crete, etc, 1940–42; comd HMS Vega as Convoy Escort Comdr, 1943–45 (despatches). Comd HMS Mameluke and HMS Chaplet, 1945–49; comd Salvage Sqdn off Elba in recovery of crashed Comet aircraft in 100 fathoms, 1954. Swam Channel (England-France) in record time, 1957; first person to swim Lough Neagh and Loch Lomond, 1959; British long-distance champion, 1957–58–59; swam Bristol Channel in record time, 1964; many long-distance championships and records, 1951–; BLDSA Veteran Swimmer of the Year, 1992. Younger Brother of Trinity House, 1958; Civil Service, 1962. President: Channel Swimming Assoc., 1963–; British Long Distance Swimming Assoc., 1982–83. Master of Navy Lodge, 1966; Liveryman, Hon. Co. of Master Mariners. Freeman, City of London, 1968. Hon. Life Mem., Scottish Amateur Swimming Assoc., 1988. Elected to Internat. Marathon Swimming Hall of Fame, 1971; The Observer newspaper's Sports Nut of the Year, 1982. *Publications:* Long Distance Swimming, 1957; First Strokes in Swimming, 1961; Modern Long Distance Swimming, 1963; Salvage from the Sea, 1977, new edn 1992; Pocket Book for Seamen, 1981; Navy Chapter: first 50 years of life, 1993; many short stories, articles, papers, and book reviews for general periodicals, technical jls and encyclopædia; regular monthly contribs to Swimming Times and Nautical Magazine. *Recreations:* motoring, Association football affairs, books. *Address:* c/o Barclays Bank PLC, 19 Euston Road, Morecambe, Lancs LA4 5DE. *Clubs:* Victory Services; Otter Swimming.

FORSHAW, Brig. Peter, CBE 1984 (OBE 1980); FCIPS; Under Secretary, HM Treasury, 1990–94 (Director of Purchasing Group and the Central Unit on Procurement); *b* 12 June 1936; *s* of Alfred Ogden Forshaw and Florence Clara Vera (*née* Taylor); *m* 1960, Helen Patricia Talbot Cliff; two *d*. *Educ:* Wimborne, Dorset; RMCS Shrivenham and Staff Coll., Camberley. FCIPS (FInstPS 1990). National Service, 1954; served Army, 1954–90: Cyprus, 1957–59; Hong Kong, 1965–67; Army Staff Course, 1967; Comd, Germany, 1974–76; on Staff, RMCS, 1976–79; DCS Cyprus, 1982–84; Commander Supply Germany, 1987–89; retired 1990. Mem., Bd of Management, CIPS, 1992–94. FIMgt (FBIM 1986). Liveryman, Broderers' Co. *Recreations:* field sports, glass engraving, water colours. *Address:* New Barn House, Ansty, Salisbury SP3 5PX. *T:* Donhead (01747) 828338. *Clubs:* Army and Navy; Ansty Polo (Vice Pres.).

FORSTER, Sir Archibald (William), Kt 1987; FEng, FIChemE, FInstPet; Chairman and Chief Executive: Esso UK plc, 1983–93; Esso Petroleum Co. Ltd, 1980–93; Esso Exploration & Production UK Ltd, 1983–93; *b* 11 Feb. 1928; *s* of William Henry and Matilda Forster; *m* 1954, Betty Margaret Channing; three *d*. *Educ:* Tottenham Grammar Sch.; Univ. of Birmingham (BSc (Hons) ChemEng 1949, Cadman Medallist). Served Royal Air Force, Pilot (FO), 1949–51. Joined Esso Petroleum Co. Ltd, 1951; Refinery Manager, Milford Haven, 1962–63; Supply Manager, London, 1963–64; Refinery Manager, Fawley, 1964–69; Manager, Refining Dept, Esso Europe Inc., 1969–71; Exec. Dir, Esso Petroleum Co. Ltd, 1971–73; Exec. Asst to Chm., Exxon Corp., 1973–74; Manager, Corporate Planning Co-ordination, Exxon Corp., 1974–75; Vice-Pres., Esso Europe Inc., 1975–78; Dir, Exxon Research & Engineering Co., 1975–78; Man. Dir, Esso Petroleum Co. Ltd, 1979–80; Chm., Esso Pension Trust, 1980–93 (Dir, 1979–80); Director: Esso Europe Inc., 1980–87; Esso Africa Inc., 1980–86; Rover Group, 1986–88; Midland Bank, 1986–; Esso Europe-Africa Services Inc., 1987–93; Trafalgar House, 1992–; United Newspapers, 1993–; Montagu Private Equity, 1993–; Engen Ltd, 1994–. Exec. Bd Mem., Lloyd's Register of Shipping, 1981–94; Mem., Monopolies and Mergers Commn, 1993–. President: Oil Industries Club, 1982–83; IChemE, 1985; Inst. of Petroleum, 1988–90. Governor, E-SU, 1981–87. Hon. DSc: Birmingham, 1981; Loughborough, 1986; Southampton, 1988.

FORSTER, Charles Ian Kennerley, CBE 1964; Under-Secretary, Department of Trade and Industry, 1970–72, retired; *b* 18 July 1911; *s* of Douglas Wakefield Forster; *m* 1942, Thelma Primrose Horton (marr. diss. 1974); one *s* one *d*; *m* 1975, Mrs Loraine Huxtable. *Educ:* Rossall Sch. FIA 1936. With Sun Life Assurance Soc., 1928–39, and 1946. Served RA, 1939–45. Statistics Branch, Admty, 1946–54; Ministry of Power, 1954 (Chief Statistician, 1955–65, Dir of Statistics, 1965–69); Min. of Technology, 1969. Energy consultant to NCB, 1972–81, retd. *Publications:* contribs to Jls of Inst. of Actuaries and Inst. of Actuaries Students Soc., Trans VII World Power Conf., Trans Manchester Statistical Soc., Statistical News. *Recreations:* bridge, stamps. *Address:* 140 Watchfield Court, Chiswick, W4 4NE. *T:* 0181–994 3128.

FORSTER, Donald, CBE 1988; Managing Director, 1945–81, and Chairman, 1981–86, B. Forster & Co. Ltd, Leigh (textile manufacturing company); *b* 18 Dec. 1920; *s* of Bernard and Rose Forster; *m* 1942, Muriel Steinman; one *s* two *d*. *Educ:* N Manchester Grammar School. Served War, RAF pilot (Flt Lieut), 1940–45. Mem., Skelmersdale Develt Corp., 1980–82; Chairman: Warrington/Runcorn Develt Corp., 1982–86; Merseyside Develt Corp., 1984–87. *Recreations:* golf, music, paintings. *Address:* 6 The Dell, South Downs Road, Hale, Cheshire WA14 3HU. *T:* 0161–926 9145. *Clubs:* Whitefield Golf; Dunham Forst Country.

See also L. C. Goldstone.

FORSTER, His Honour Donald Murray; a Circuit Judge, 1984–90; *b* 18 June 1929; *s* of John Cameron Forster and late Maisie Constance Forster. *Educ:* Hollylea Sch., Liverpool; Merton House Sch., Penmaenmawr; Wrekin Coll., Wellington, Shropshire; St Edmund Hall, Oxford. Honour Sch. of Jurisprudence (2nd Cl. Hons). Called to Bar, Gray's Inn, 1953; Head of Chambers, 1968; a Recorder of the Crown Court, 1978–83. *Recreation:* sport. *Address:* Flat 8, Sutcliffe House, Edmond Castle, Wetheral, Carlisle, Cumbria. *Clubs:* Liverpool Ramblers Association Football (Vice-Pres.); Liverpool Racquet; Mersey Bowmen Lawn Tennis (Liverpool).

FORSTER, Brig. Eric Brown, MBE 1952; General Manager, Potato Marketing Board, 1970–82; *b* 19 May 1917; *s* of late Frank and Agnes Forster; *m* 1943, Margaret Bessie Letitia, *d* of late Lt-Col Arthur Wood, MBE and late Edith Wood; one *s* two *d*.. *Educ:* Queen Elizabeth Grammar Sch., Hexham. Commnd from RASC ranks into RAPC, 1941. Dir of Cost and Management Accounting (Army Dept), 1967–68. *Recreations:* philately, gardening. *Address:* Therncroft, Malt Kiln Lane, Appleton Roebuck, York YO5 7DT. *T:* York (01904) 744393. *Club:* MCC.

FORSTER, Prof. Leonard Wilson, FBA 1976; Schröder Professor of German, University of Cambridge, 1961–79; Fellow of Selwyn College, Cambridge, 1937–50 and since 1961; *b* 30 March 1913; *o s* of Edward James Forster, merchant, and Linda Charlotte (*née* Rogers), St John's Wood, NW8; *m* 1939, Jeanne Marie Louise, *e d* of Dr Charles Otto Billeter, Basel; one *s* two *d*. *Educ:* Marlborough Coll.; Trinity Hall, Cambridge (Thomas Carlyle Student, 1934–35; MA 1938; LittD 1976; Hon. Fellow 1989); Bonn Univ.; Basel Univ. (Dr phil. 1938). English Lektor: Univ. of Leipzig, 1934; Univ. of Königsberg, 1935–36; Univ. of Basel, 1936–38. Naval Staff Admiralty, 1939–41; Foreign Office, 1941–45; Lt-Comdr RNVR (Sp.), 1945–46. Faculty Asst Lectr, 1937, Univ. Lectr in German, 1947–50, Cambridge; Lectr, 1937, Dean and Asst Tutor, 1946–50, Selwyn Coll.,

Cambridge; Prof. of German, UCL, 1950–61. Pres., Internat. Assoc. for Germanic Studies (IVG), 1970–75. Corresponding Member: Deutsche Akademie für Sprache und Dichtung, 1957; Royal Belgian Academy of Dutch Language and Literature, 1973; Member: Maatschappij der Nederlandse Letterkunde, Leiden, 1966; Royal Netherlands Acad. of Sciences and Letters, 1968. Visiting Professor: Univ. of Toronto, 1957; Univ. of Heidelberg, 1964, 1980; McGill Univ., 1967–68; Univ. of Otago, 1968; Univ. of Utrecht, 1976; Univ. of Kiel, 1980–81; Univ. of Basel, 1985–86. Sen. Consultant: Folger Shakespeare Lib., Washington, 1975; Herzog August Bibliothek, Wolfenbüttel, 1976–83. Co-Editor: German Life and Letters; Daphnis. Hon. DLitt: Leiden, 1975; Bath, 1979; Strasbourg, 1980; Heidelberg, 1986. Gold Medal, Goethe-Institut, Munich, 1966; Friedrich Gundolf-Preis für Germanistik im Ausland, 1981; J. A. Comenius Medal, Czechoslovak Republic, 1992. Grosses Verdienstkreuz (Germany), 1976. *Publications:* G. R. Weckherlin, zur Kenntnis seines Lebens in England, 1944; Conrad Celtis, 1948; German Poetry, 1944–48, 1949; The Temper of Seventeenth Century German Literature, 1952; Penguin Book of German Verse, 1957; Poetry of Significant Nonsense, 1962; Lipsius, Von der Bestendigkeit, 1965; Die Niederlande und die Anfänge der deutschen Barocklyrik, 1967; Janus Gruter's English Years, 1967; The Icy Fire, 1969; The Poet's Tongues: Multilingualism in Literature, 1971; Kleine Schriften zur deutschen Literatur im 17 Jahrhundert, 1977; Literaturwissenschaft als Flucht vor der Literatur?, 1978; Iter Bohemicum, 1980; The Man Who Wanted to Know Everything, 1981; Christian Morgenstern, Sämtliche Galgenlieder, 1985; Christoffel van Sichem in Basel und der frühe deutsche Alexandriner, 1986; articles in British and foreign jls. *Recreation:* foreign travel. *Address:* 1 Amhurst Court, Grange Road, Cambridge CB3 9BH. *T:* Cambridge (01223) 562472; Selwyn College, Cambridge.

FORSTER, Margaret; author; *b* 25 May 1938; *d* of Arthur Gordon Forster and Lilian (*née* Hind); *m* 1960, Edward Hunter Davies, *qv*; one *s* two *d*. *Educ:* Carlisle and County High Sch. for Girls; Somerville Coll., Oxford (BA). FRSL. Teacher, Barnsbury Girls' Sch., Islington, 1961–63. Member: BBC Adv. Cttee on Social Effects of Television, 1975–77; Arts Council Literary Panel, 1978–81. Chief non-fiction reviewer, Evening Standard, 1977–80. *Publications: non-fiction:* The Rash Adventurer: the rise and fall of Charles Edward Stuart, 1973; William Makepeace Thackeray: memoirs of a Victorian gentleman, 1978; Significant Sisters: grassroots of active feminism 1839–1939, 1984; Elizabeth Barrett Browning: a biography, 1988; (ed, introd. and prefaces) Elizabeth Barrett Browning: selected poems, 1988; Daphne du Maurier, 1993; Hidden Lives (memoir), 1995; *novels:* Dame's Delight, 1964; Georgy Girl, 1965 (filmscript with Peter Nichols, 1966); The Bogeyman, 1965; The Travels of Maudie Tipstaff, 1967; The Park, 1968; Miss Owen-Owen is At Home, 1969; Fenella Phizackerley, 1970; Mr Bone's Retreat, 1971; The Seduction of Mrs Pendlebury, 1974; Mother, can you hear me?, 1979; The Bride of Lowther Fell, 1980; Marital Rites, 1981; Private Papers, 1986; Have the Men Had Enough?, 1989; Lady's Maid, 1990; The Battle for Christabel, 1991; Mothers' Boys, 1994. *Recreations:* walking on Hampstead Heath, reading contemporary fiction. *Address:* 11 Boscastle Road, NW5 1EE. *T:* 0171–485 3785; Grasmoor House, Loweswater, near Cockermouth, Cumbria CA13 0RU. *T:* Cockermouth (01900) 85303.

FORSTER, Neil Milward; Chairman, Air UK Group, since 1990; *b* 29 May 1927; *s* of Norman Milward Forster and Olive Christina Forster (*née* Cockrell); *m* 1954, Barbara Elizabeth Smith; one *s* two *d*. *Educ:* Hurstpierpoint College, Sussex; Pembroke College, Cambridge. BA Law and Economics; Fellow Inst. of Transport. Joined Clan Line Steamers, 1952; Chm., Calcutta Liners Conf., 1962–66; Director: Clan Line, 1967; Group and Associated cos, British & Commonwealth Shipping Co., 1974–78; British and Commonwealth Hldgs PLC, 1974–88 (Gp Man. Dir, 1982–86); Chm., Air UK Ltd, 1982–90. Chairman: Europe/SA Shipping Confs, 1977–87; UK S Africa Trade Assoc., 1985–87. Rep. England and GB at hockey, 1951–58. *Recreations:* golf, gardening. *Address:* The Orchard, Upper Slaughter, Cheltenham, Glos GL54 2JB. *T:* Bourton-on-the-Water (01451) 822025. *Clubs:* Oriental, MCC.

See also Sir O. G. Forster.

FORSTER, Sir Oliver (Grantham), KCMG 1983 (CMG 1976); LVO 1961; HM Diplomatic Service, retired; *b* 2 Sept. 1925; 2nd *s* of Norman Milward Forster and Olive Christina Forster (*née* Cockrell); *m* 1953, Beryl Myfanwy Evans; two *d*. *Educ:* Hurstpierpoint; King's Coll., Cambridge. Served in RAF, 1944–48. Joined Commonwealth Relations Office, 1951. Private Sec. to Parly Under-Sec., 1953–54; Second Sec., Karachi, 1954–56; Principal, CRO, 1956–59; First Sec., Madras, 1959–62; First Sec., Washington, 1962–65; Private Sec. to Sec. of State for Commonwealth Relations, 1965–67; Counsellor, Manila, 1967–70; Counsellor, New Delhi, 1970–75, Minister, 1975; Asst Under-Sec. of State and Dep. Chief Clerk, FCO, 1975–79; Ambassador to Pakistan, 1979–84. HQA 1984. Chm., Royal Commonwealth Soc. and Commonwealth Trust, 1992–. *Address:* 71 Raglan Road, Reigate, Surrey RH2 0HP. *Clubs:* United Oxford & Cambridge University, Commonwealth Trust.

See also N. M. Forster.

FORSTER, Sir William (Edward Stanley), Kt 1982; Judge of the Federal Court of Australia, 1977–89; *b* 15 June 1921; *s* of F. B. Forster; *m* 1950, Johanna B., *d* of Brig. A. M. Forbes; one *s* two *d*. *Educ:* St Peter's Coll., Adelaide; Adelaide Univ. (Stowe Prize; David Murray Scholar; LLB). Served RAAF, 1940–46. Private legal practice, 1950–59; Magistrate, Adelaide Police Court, 1959–61; Master, Supreme Court of SA, and Dist Registrar, High Court of Aust., 1966–71 (Dep. Master, and Dep. Dist Registrar, 1961–66); Sen. Judge, 1971, Chief Judge, 1977, Chief Justice, 1979–85, Supreme Court of NT. Chancellor, dio. of NT, 1975–85. Adelaide University: Lectr in Criminal Law, 1957–58; Lectr in Law of Procedure, 1967–71; Mem., Standing Cttee of Senate, 1967–71. President: NT Div., Australian Red Cross, 1973–85; Aboriginal Theatre Foundn, 1972–75; Chairman: Museum and Art Galls Bd, NT, 1974–85; NT Parole Bd, 1976–85. Air Efficiency Award, 1953. *Address:* 169 Stephen Terrace, Walkerville, SA 5081, Australia. *Clubs:* Adelaide (Adelaide); Darwin Golf.

FORSYTE, Charles; *see* Philo, G. C. G.

FORSYTH OF THAT ILK, Alistair Charles William, JP; FSCA, FSAScot; FInstPet; Baron of Ethie; Chief of the Name and Clan of Forsyth; chairman and director of companies; *b* 7 Dec. 1929; *s* of Charles Forsyth of Strathendry, FCA, and Ella Millicent Hopkins; *m* 1958, Ann, OStJ, *d* of Col P. A. Hughes, IA; four *s*. *Educ:* St Paul's Sch.; Queen Mary Coll., London. FInstPet 1973; FSCA 1976; FSAScot 1979. National Service, 2nd Lieut The Queen's Bays, 1948–50; Lieut The Parachute Regt, TA, 1950–54. Chm., Hargreaves Reiss & Quinn Ltd, and associated cos, 1981–. Mem., Standing Council of Scottish Chiefs, 1978–. Freeman, City of London, 1993; Liveryman, Scriveners' Co., 1993–. CStJ 1982 (OStJ 1974). JP NSW, 1965; JP Angus, 1987. KHS 1992. *Recreations:* hill walking, Scottish antiquities. *Address:* Ethie Castle, by Arbroath, Angus DD11 5SP. *Clubs:* Cavalry and Guards; New (Edinburgh).

FORSYTH, Bill; film director and script writer; *b* Glasgow, 1947; one *s* one *d*. *Educ:* National Film School. *Films directed:* That Sinking Feeling, 1980; Gregory's Girl, 1981; Local Hero, 1983; Comfort and Joy, 1984; Housekeeping, 1988; Breaking In, 1990; Being Human, 1993. TV film, Andrina, 1981. BAFTA Award: best screenplay, 1982; best dir, 1983. Hon. DLitt Glasgow, 1984; DUniv Stirling, 1989. *Address:* c/o A. D. Peters, The Chambers, Chelsea Harbour, SW10 0XF.

FORSYTH, Bruce; *see* Forsyth-Johnson, B. J.

FORSYTH, Jennifer Mary; Under-Secretary, HM Treasury and Department of Transport, 1975–83, retired; Councillor (Lab) Borough of Kensington and Chelsea, since 1986; *b* 7 Oct. 1924; *o d* of late Matthew Forsyth, theatrical director, and late Marjorie Forsyth. *Educ:* Frensham Heights; London Sch. of Economics and Political Science (Pres. of Students' Union, 1944–45) (BScEcon). Joined Home Finance Div., HM Treasury, 1945; UN Economic Commn for Europe, 1949–51; Information Div., HM Treasury, 1951–53; Principal, Estabts, Overseas Finance and Planning Divs, 1954–62; UK Treasury Delegn, Washington, 1962–64; Assistant Secretary: DEA, 1965–69; Social Services Div., HM Treasury, 1969–75; Under Secretary: Home, Transport and Education Gp, HM Treasury, 1975–80; Dept of Transport (Roads), 1980–83. Governor, Frensham Heights, 1965–76. *Recreations:* going to the theatre and to the Mediterranean. *Address:* Flat 4, One Ladbroke Square, W11 3LX.

FORSYTH, Rt Hon. Michael (Bruce); PC 1995; MP (C) Stirling, since 1983; Secretary of State for Scotland and Lord Keeper of the Great Seal of Scotland, since 1995; *b* 16 Oct. 1954; *s* of John T. Forsyth and Mary Watson; *m* 1977, Susan Jane Clough; one *s* two *d*. *Educ:* Arbroath High School; St Andrews University. MA. Pres., St Andrews Univ. Cons. Assoc., 1972–75; Nat. Chm., Fedn of Cons. Students, 1976–77; PPS to Sec. of State for Foreign and Commonwealth Affairs, 1986–87; Parly Under-Sec. of State, 1987–90, Minister of State, 1990–92, Scottish Office; Minister of State: Dept of Employment, 1992–94; Home Office, 1994–95. Chm., Scottish Cons. Party, 1989–90. Mem., Westminster City Council, 1978–83. *Recreations:* photography, mountaineering, amateur astronomy. *Address:* House of Commons, SW1A 0AA.

FORSYTH, Prof. Murray Greensmith, FRHistS; Professor of Government and Political Science, Hong Kong Baptist University, since 1995; *b* 30 Oct. 1936; *s* of Maj. Henry Russell Forsyth and Marie Elaine Forsyth; *m* 1964, Marie Denise Edelin de la Praudière; one *s* two *d*. *Educ:* Wellington Coll.; Balliol Coll., Oxford (BA Mod. Hist. 1959; MA 1964); College of Europe, Bruges. FRHistS 1991. Research Officer, Political and Econ. Planning, London, 1960–64; University of Leicester: Lectr in Politics, 1964–70; Reader in Internat. Politics, 1971–90; Dir, Centre for Federal Studies, 1988–94; Prof. of Politics, 1990–94, Prof. Emeritus 1994. British Acad. Wolfson Fellow, Paris, 1977; Bradlow Fellow, S African Inst. of Internat. Affairs, 1983; Vis. Prof., Coll. of Europe, Bruges, 1993–94. Pres., European Consortium for Regl and Federal Studies, 1993–94. *Publications:* The Parliament of the European Communities, 1964; (jtly) Economic Planning and Policies in Britain, France and Germany, 1968; (ed jtly) The Theory of International Relations, 1970; Unions of States: the theory and practice of confederation, 1981; Reason and Revolution: the political theory of the Abbé Sieyes, 1987; The Political Classics: Plato to Rousseau, 1988; (ed) Federalism and Nationalism, 1989; (trans.) The Spirit of the Revolution of 1789, 1989; (ed jtly) The Political Classics: Hamilton to Mill, 1993. *Recreations:* collecting prints and watercolours, browsing in second-hand bookshops. *Address:* 1B Tower 1, 22 Sui Wo Road, Fo Tan, New Territories, Hong Kong. *T:* 26880734; 28 Stockerston Road, Uppingham, Rutland LE15 9UD. *Club:* Travellers'.

FORSYTH-JOHNSON, Bruce Joseph, (Bruce Forsyth); entertainer and comedian; *b* 22 Feb. 1928; *m* 1st, 1953, Penny Calvert; three *d*; 2nd, 1973, Anthea Redfern (marr. diss. 1982); two *d*; 3rd, 1983, Wilnelia Merced; one *s*. *Educ:* Higher Latimer Sch., Edmonton. Started stage career as Boy Bruce—The Mighty Atom, 1942; after the war, appeared in various double acts and did a 2 yr spell at Windmill Theatre; first television appearance, Music Hall, 1954; resident compère, Sunday Night at the London Palladium, 1958–60; own revue, London Palladium, 1962; leading role, Little Me, Cambridge Theatre, 1964; début at Talk of the Town (played there 7 times); compèred Royal Variety Show, 1971, and on subseq. occasions; London Palladium Show, 1973 (also Ottawa and Toronto) and 1980; commenced Generation Game, BBC TV series, 1971 (completed 7 series), and 1990–95; compèred Royal Windsor to mark BBC Jubilee Celebrations, 1977; One Man Show, Theatre Royal, Windsor, and Lakeside, 1977; Bruce Forsyth's Big Night, ITV, 1978; Play Your Cards Right, ITV, 1980–87; Slinger's Day, ITV, 1986, 1987; You Bet!, 1988. Films include: Star; Can Hieronymous Merkin Ever Forget Mercy Humppe and Find True Happiness?; Bedknobs and Broomsticks; The Magnificent 7 Deadly Sins; Pavlova. Numerous records. Show Business Personality of the Year, Variety Club of GB, 1975; TV Personality of the Year, Sun Newspaper, 1976 and 1977; Male TV Personality of the Year, TV Times, 1975, 1976, 1977 and 1978; Favourite Game Show Host, TV Times, 1984. *Recreation:* golf (handicap 10, Wentworth Golf Club). *Address:* Straidarran, Wentworth Drive, Virginia Water, Surrey GU25 4NY. *Clubs:* White Elephant, Crockfords, Empress, Tramp.

FORSYTHE, Clifford; MP (UU) Antrim South, since 1983, resigned seat Dec. 1985 in protest against Anglo-Irish Agreement; re-elected Jan. 1986; Member, Antrim South, Northern Ireland Assembly, 1982–86; plumbing and heating contractor; *b* 24 Aug. 1929. *Educ:* Glengormley public elementary sch. Formerly professional football player, Linfield and Derry City. Mem., Newtownabbey Borough Council, 1981–85; Mayor, 1983. Dep. Chm., DHSS Cttee, NI Assembly, 1982–86; UU Parly spokesman on transport, communications and local govt. Exec. Mem., Ulster Unionist Council, 1980–83; Chm., S Antrim Official Unionist Assoc., 1981–83. Mem., Select Cttee on Social Security, 1991–. Fellow, Industry and Parlt Trust, 1986. Chm., Glengormley Br., NI Chest, Heart and Stroke Assoc., 1987. *Recreations:* church choir, football, running. *Address:* House of Commons, SW1A 0AA.

FORSYTHE, Air Cdre James Roy, (Paddy), CBE 1966; DFC; Director of Development, 1976–81, Joint Chief Executive, 1981–86, Look Ahead Housing Association Ltd; *b* 10 July 1920; *s* of W. R. and A. M. Forsythe; *m* 1st, 1946, Barbara Mary Churchman (*d* 1983); two *s* two *d*; 2nd, 1989, Mrs W. P. Newbery. *Educ:* Methodist Coll., Belfast; Queen's Univ., Belfast. Bomber Comd, 1944–45; OC, Aberdeen Univ. Air Sqdn, 1952–54; psa 1955; Principal Staff Officer to Dir-Gen. Orgn (RAF), 1956–58; OC, 16 Sqdn, 1958–60; Directing Staff, Coll. of Air Warfare, Manby, 1960–62; Head of RAF Aid Mission to India, 1963; Stn Comdr, RAF Acklington, 1963–65; Dep. Dir Air Staff Policy, MoD, 1965–68; Dir Public Relations, Far East, 1968–70; Dir Recruiting, RAF, 1971–73; Dir, Public Relations, RAF, 1973–75. Chm., RAF RU, 1972, 1973, 1974; Chm., Combined Services RU, 1974; Vice-Pres., 1979, Chm., 1988–90, Pres., 1990–, London Irish RFC. MIPR. *Recreations:* Rugby, golf. *Address:* 104 Earls Court Road, W8 6EG. *T:* 0171–937 5291. *Club:* Royal Air Force.

FORSYTHE, Dr (John) Malcolm; Professorial Fellow in Public Health, Kent University, since 1992; Senior Lecturer, King's College School of Medicine and Dentistry, since 1992; *b* 11 July 1936; *s* of late Dr John Walter Joseph Forsythe and Dr Charlotte Constance Forsythe (*née* Beatty); *m* 1961, Delia Kathleen Moore (marr. diss. 1983); one *s* three *d*; *m* 1984, Patricia Mary Barnes. *Educ:* Repton Sch., Derby; Guy's Hosp. Med. Sch., London Univ. BSc(Hons), MB, BS, MSc; DObstRCOG, FRCP; FFPHM. Area Medical Officer,

Kent AHA, 1974–78; SE Thames Regional Health Authority: Dir of Planning, 1985–89; Regl MO, 1978–92; Regl Dir of Public Health and Service Develt, 1989–92. Hon. Consultant, Univ. of Kent Health Services Res. Unit, 1977–92. Vis. Prof., Univ. of N Carolina, Chapel Hill, 1973, 1976, 1993; Jack Masur Fellow, Amer. Hosp. Assoc., 1976. Head, UK Deleg., Hospital Cttee, EEC, 1980–85, 1989–90; Consultant, Urwick Orr Ltd; Member: Resource Allocation Wkg Pty and Adv. Gp on Resource Allocation, 1975–78; Technical Sub Gp, Review of Resource Allocation Working Party Formula, 1986–87; DHSS Med. Manpower Planning Review, 1986–88; NHS Computer Policy Cttee, 1981–85; Standing Med. Adv. Cttee to Sec. of State, 1982–86; PHLS Bd, 1986–; Central Council for Postgrad. Med. Educn, 1986–88; Health Services Res. Cttee, MRC, 1988–91; Bd of Governors, UMDS of Guy's and St Thomas', 1982–92; Delegacy, King's Coll. Hosp. Med. and Dental Schs, 1978–. External Examiner to Univ. of London, 1987–89. Mem. Bd of Management, Horder Centre for Arthritis, Crowborough, 1992–. FRSA 1985. Silver Core Award, IFIP, 1977. *Publications:* (ed jtly) Information Processing of Medical Records, 1969; Proceedings of First World Conference on Medical Informatics, 1975. *Recreations:* tennis, music, ornithology. *Address:* Buckingham House, 1 Royal Chase, Tunbridge Wells, Kent TN4 8AX. *T:* Tunbridge Wells (01892) 522359; Centre for Health Services Studies, George Allen Wing, The University, Canterbury, Kent CT2 7NF. *T:* Canterbury (01227) 823681; Department of Public Health, King's College Medical School, Bessemer Road, SE5 9PJ. *T:* 0171–346 3418. *Clubs:* Royal Society of Medicine; Chasers.

FORSYTHE, Air Cdre Paddy; *see* Forsythe, Air Cdre J. R.

FORT, Mrs Jean; Headmistress of Roedean School, Brighton, 1961–70; *b* 1915; *d* of G. B. Rae; *m* 1943, Richard Fort (*d* 1959), MP Clitheroe Division of Lancs; four *s* one *d.* *Educ:* Benenden Sch.; Lady Margaret Hall, Oxford (MA, DipEd). Asst Mistress, Dartford County Sch. for Girls, 1937–39; WVS Headquarters staff, 1939–40; Junior Civil Asst, War Office, 1940–41; Personal Asst to Sir Ernest Gowers, Sen. Regional Comr for Civil Def., London, 1941–44. *Address:* 6 King's Close, Henley-on-Thames, Oxon RG9 2DS.

FORT, Maeve Geraldine, CMG 1990; Ambassador to the Lebanese Republic, since 1992; *b* 19 Nov. 1940; *d* of late F. L. Fort. *Educ:* Trinity College, Dublin (MA); Sorbonne, Paris. Joined Foreign Service, 1963; UKMIS, NY, 1964; CRO, 1965; seconded to SEATO, Bangkok, 1966; Bonn, 1968; Lagos, 1971; Second, later First Sec., FCO, 1973; UKMIS, NY, 1978; Counsellor, FCO, 1982; RCDS, 1983; Counsellor, Hd of Chancery and Consul-Gen., Santiago, 1984–86; Head of W African Dept, FCO, 1986–89, and Ambassador (non-resident) to Chad, 1987–89; Ambassador to Mozambique, 1989–92. *Address:* c/o Foreign and Commonwealth Office, King Charles Street, SW1A 2AH.

FORTE, family name of **Baron Forte.**

FORTE, Baron *cr* 1982 (Life Peer), of Ripley in the county of Surrey; **Charles Forte;** Kt 1970; FRSA; President, Forte (formerly Trusthouse Forte) PLC, since 1992 (Chairman, 1982–92, Executive Chairman, 1978–81; Deputy Chairman, 1970–78, and Chief Executive, 1971–78); *b* 26 Nov. 1908; *m* 1943, Irene Mary Chierico; one *s* five *d.* *Educ:* Alloa Academy; Dumfries Coll.; Mamiani, Rome. Fellow and Mem. Exec. Cttee, Catering Inst., 1949; Member: Small Consultative Advisory Cttee to Min. of Food, 1946; London Tourist Board. Hon. Consul Gen. for Republic of San Marino. FIMgt (FBIM 1971). Grand Officier, Ordine al Merito della Repubblica Italiana; Cavaliere di Gran Croce della Repubblica Italiana; Cavaliere del Lavoro (Italy). *Publications:* Forte (autobiog.), 1986; articles for catering trade papers. *Recreations:* golf, fishing, shooting, fencing, music. *Address:* 166 High Holborn, WC1V 6TT. *Clubs:* Carlton, Caledonian, Royal Thames Yacht.
See also Hon. Sir R. J. V. Forte, Hon. O. Polizzi.

FORTE, Hon. Sir Rocco (John Vincent), Kt 1995; FCA; Chairman, Forte (formerly Trusthouse Forte) plc, since 1992 (Chief Executive, 1983–92); *b* 18 Jan. 1945; *s* of Lord Forte, *qv*; *m* 1986, Aliai, *d* of Prof. Giovanni Ricci, Rome; one *s* two *d.* *Educ:* Downside Coll.; Pembroke Coll., Oxford (MA). Trusthouse Forte: Dir of Personnel, 1973–78; Dep. Chief Exec., 1978–82; Jt Chief Exec., 1982–83. Pres., BHA. Vice-Pres., Commonwealth Games Council for England; Dir, BTA. *Address:* Forte, 166 High Holborn, WC1V 6TT.
See also Hon. Olga Polizzi.

FORTESCUE, family name of **Earl Fortescue.**

FORTESCUE, 8th Earl *cr* 1789; **Charles Hugh Richard Fortescue;** Baron Fortescue, 1746; Viscount Ebrington, 1789; *b* 10 May 1951; *s* of 7th Earl and his 1st wife, Penelope Jane (*d* 1959), *d* of Robert Evelyn Henderson; *S* father, 1993; *m* 1974, Julia, *er d* of Air Commodore J. A. Sowrey; three *d.* *Heir: uncle* Hon. Martin Denzil Fortescue [*b* 5 Jan. 1924; *m* 1954, Prudence Louisa (*d* 1992), *d* of Sir Charles Samuel Rowley, 6th Bt, TD; two *s* two *d*; *m* 1994, Mrs Caroline Loftie].

FORTESCUE, (John) Adrian, LVO 1972; Deputy Director General, European Commission, since 1994; *b* 16 June 1941; *s* of T. V. N. Fortescue, *qv*; *m* 1st, 1978, Jillian Sarah Montague-Evans (marr. diss. 1987); one *s*; 2nd, 1989, Marie Wolfcarius. HM Diplomatic Service, 1964–94: MECAS, 1964; served Amman, FCO and Paris, 1966–72; on loan to EC, 1973–75; FCO, 1976–79; Washington, 1979–81; Head of Presidency Unit, ECD, FCO, 1981–82; Counsellor, Budapest, 1983–84; on loan to Commn of Eur. Communities, 1985–94 (Chef de Cabinet to Lord Cockfield, Vice-Pres., 1985–88). *Address:* 44 Avenue Beau-Séjour, 1180 Brussels, Belgium.

FORTESCUE, Trevor Victor Norman, (Tim), CBE 1984; Secretary-General, Food and Drink Industries Council, 1973–83; *b* 28 Aug. 1916; *s* of Frank Fortescue; *m* 1st, 1939, Margery Stratford (marr. diss. 1975), *d* of Dr G. H. Hunt; two *s* one *d*; 2nd, 1975, Anthea Maureen, *d* of Robert M. Higgins. *Educ:* Uppingham Sch.; King's Coll., Cambridge. BA 1938; MA 1945. Colonial Administrative Service, Hong Kong, 1939–47 and Kenya, 1949–51 (interned, 1941–45); FAO, UN, Washington, DC, 1947–49 and Rome, 1951–54; Chief Marketing Officer, Milk Marketing Bd of England and Wales, 1954–59; Manager, Nestlé Gp of Cos, Vevey, Switz., 1959–63 and London, 1963–66. MP (C) Liverpool, Garston, 1966–Feb. 1974; an Asst Govt Whip, 1970–71; a Lord Comr of HM Treasury, 1971–73. Chairman: Conference Associates Ltd, 1978–87; Standing Cttee, Confedn of Food and Drink Industries of European Community (CIAA), 1982–84; Pres., British Food Manufg Industries Res. Assoc., 1984–92; Member: Meat Promotion Rev. Body, 1984; Council, British Industrial Biol. Res. Assoc., 1980–83. Develt Manager (with A. M. Fortescue), Winchester Cathedral, 1989–90; Dir, Winchester Cathedral Enterprises Ltd, 1990–. Trustee, Uppingham Sch., 1957–63; Patron and Trustee, The Quest Community, Birmingham, 1971–85. *Publication:* Lovelines, 1987. *Recreations:* marriage to Anthea; Napoleon. *Address:* Waynflete House, 25 St Swithun Street, Winchester, Hants SO23 9JP. *T:* Winchester (01962) 854693.
See also J.A. Fortescue.

FORTEVIOT, 4th Baron *cr* 1917 of Dupplin, Perthshire; **John James Evelyn Dewar;** Bt 1907; Director (non-executive), John Dewar & Sons Ltd, since 1977; farmer, landowner; *b* 5 April 1938; *s* of 3rd Baron Forteviot, MBE, and Cynthia Monica Starkie (*d* 1986); *S* father, 1993; *m* 1963, Lady Elisabeth Waldegrave, 3rd *d* of 12th Earl Waldegrave, KG, GCVO; one *s* three *d.* *Educ:* Eton. Nat. Service, Black Watch (RHR), 1956–58. John Dewar & Sons Ltd, 1959–62; ADC to Governor General of NZ, 1962–63; John Dewar & Sons, 1963–. *Recreations:* fishing, shooting, birdwatching, travel. *Heir: s* Hon. Alexander John Edward Dewar, *b* 4 March 1971. *Clubs:* Boodle's, Royal Perth Golfing and Country and City.

FORTH, Eric; MP (C) Mid Worcestershire, since 1983; Minister of State, Department of Education and Employment (formerly Department for Education), since 1994; *b* 9 Sept. 1944; *s* of late William and of Aileen Forth; *m* 1st, 1967, Linda St Clair (marr. diss. 1994); two *d*; 2nd, 1994, Mrs Carroll Goff; one step *s.* *Educ:* Jordanhill Coll. Sch., Glasgow; Glasgow Univ. (MA Hons Politics and Econs). Chm., Young Conservatives', Constituency CPC, 1970–73; Member: Glasgow Univ. Cons. Club, 1962–66; Brentwood UDC, 1968–72. Contested (C) Barking, Feb. and Oct. 1974. Member (C), North Birmingham, European Parlt, 1979–84; Chm., Backbench Cttee, European Democ. Gp, European Parlt, 1979–84. PPS to Minister of State, DES, 1986–87; Parly Under Sec. of State: DTI, 1988–90; Dept of Employment, 1990–92; DFE, 1992–94. Mem., Select Cttee on Employment, 1986; Chm., Cons. Backbench European Affairs Cttee, 1987–88 (Vice-Chm., 1983–86). *Publication:* Regional Policy—A Fringe Benefit?, 1983. *Recreation:* discussion and argument. *Address:* House of Commons, SW1A 0AA. *Club:* Carlton.

FORTIER, Most Rev. Jean-Marie; *see* Sherbrooke, Archbishop of, (RC).

FORTY, Prof. Arthur John, CBE 1991; PhD, DSc; FRSE; FRSA; Principal and Vice-Chancellor, Stirling University, 1986–94; *b* 4 Nov. 1928; *s* of Alfred Louis Forty and Elisabeth Forty; *m* 1950, Alicia Blanche Hart Gough; one *s.* *Educ:* Headlands Grammar Sch.; Bristol Univ. (BSc; PhD 1953; DSc 1967). FRSE 1988, FRSA 1989. Served RAF, 1953–56. Sen. Res. Scientist, Tube Investments Ltd, 1956–58; Lectr, Univ. of Bristol, 1958–64; University of Warwick: Foundn Prof. of Physics, 1964–86; Pro-Vice-Chancellor, 1970–86. Visiting scientist: Gen. Electric Co., USA; Boeing Co.; Nat. Bureau of Standards, Washington, USA. Member: SRC Physics Cttee, 1969–73; SRC Materials Cttee, 1970–73; Computer Bd, 1982–85; University Grants Committee: Mem., 1982–86, Vice-Chm., 1985–86; Chairman: Physical Sciences Sub-cttee, 1985–86; Equipment Sub-cttee, 1985–86; Chairman: Jt ABRC, Computer Bd and UGC Working Party on Future Facilities for Advanced Res. Computing (author, Forty Report), 1985; Management Cttee for Res. Councils' Supercomputer Facility, 1986–88; UFC Cttee for Information Systems (formerly Computer Bd for Univs and Res. Councils), 1988–91; Jt Policy Cttee for Advanced Res. Computing, 1988–94; Cttee of Scottish Univ. Principals, 1990–92; Edinburgh Parallel Computing Centre, 1994–. Mem., British Library Bd, 1987–94. Hon. Fellow, Edinburgh Univ., 1994. Hon. LLD St Andrew's, 1989; DUniv Stirling, 1995. *Publications:* papers in Proc. Royal Soc., Phil Magazine and other learned jls. *Recreations:* sailing, gardening, the ancient metallurgy of gold. *Address:* Port Mor, St Fillans, by Crieff, Perthshire. *Club:* Caledonian.

FORWELL, Dr George Dick, OBE 1993; PhD; FRCP; Hon. Professor, School of Biological and Medical Sciences, St Andrews University, since 1993; *b* 6 July 1928; *s* of Harold C. Forwell and Isabella L. Christie; *m* 1957, Catherine F. C. Cousland; two *d.* *Educ:* George Watson's Coll., Edinburgh; Edinburgh Univ. (MB, ChB 1950; PhD 1955). MRCPE 1957, DIH 1957, DPH 1959, FRCPE 1967, FFCM 1972, FRCPGlas 1974, FRCP 1985. House Officer and Univ. Clin. Asst, Edinburgh Royal Infirm., 1950–52; RAF Inst. of Aviation Med., 1952–54; MRC and RCPE grants, 1954–56; pneumoconiosis field res., 1956–57; Grad. Res. Fellow and Lectr, Edinburgh Univ. Dept of Public Health and Social Med., 1957–60; Asst Dean, Faculty of Med., Edinburgh Univ., 1960–63; Dep. Sen. and Sen. Admin. MO, Eastern Reg. Hosp. Bd, Dundee, 1963–67; PMO, Scottish Home and Health Dept, 1967–73; Chief Admin. MO, 1973–93, and Dir of Public Health, 1989–93, Greater Glasgow Health Bd. Hon. Lectr, 1973–90, and Vis. Prof., 1990–93, Dept of Public Health, Glasgow Univ. QHP, 1980–83. Mem., GMC, 1984–89. *Publications:* papers on clin. res. and on health planning and services, in med. and other jls. *Recreation:* running. *Address:* 20 Irvine Crescent, St Andrews, Fife KY16 8LG. *Club:* Royal Air Force.

FORWOOD, Sir Dudley (Richard), 3rd Bt *cr* 1895; Member of Lloyd's; *b* 6 June 1912; *s* of Sir Dudley Baines Forwood, 2nd Bt, CMG, and Norah Isabella (*née* Lockett) (*d* 1962); *S* father, 1961; *m* 1952, Mary Gwendoline (who *m* 1st, Viscount Ratendone, later 2nd Marquis of Willingdon; 2nd, Robert Cullingford; 3rd, Col Donald Croft-Wilcock), *d* of Basil S. Foster. *Educ:* Stowe Sch. Attaché, British Legation, Vienna, 1934–37; Equerry to the Duke of Windsor, 1937–39. Served War of 1939–45, Scots Guards (Major). Master, New Forest Buckhounds, 1956–65; Official Verderer of the New Forest, 1974–82; Chairman: New Forest Consultative Panel, 1970–82; Crufts, 1973–87; Hon. Vice Pres., RASE (Hon. Dir, 1973–78; Vice-Pres., 1979). *Recreation:* hunting. *Heir: cousin* Peter Noel Forwood [*b* 1925; *m* 1950, Roy Murphy; six *d*]. *Address:* 43 Addison Road, W14. *T:* 0171–603 3620; Uppacott, Bagnum, near Ringwood, Hants BH24 3BZ. *T:* Ringwood (01425) 471480.

FORWOOD, Nicholas James; QC 1987; *b* 22 June 1948; *s* of Lt-Col Harry Forwood and Wendy Forwood (*née* French-Smith); *m* 1971, Sally Diane Gerrard, *e d* of His Honour Basil Harding Gerrard; one *s* three *d.* *Educ:* Stowe Sch.; St John's Coll., Cambridge (Open Schol., MA, Pt I Mechanical Scis Tripos (1st Cl. Hons), Pt II Law Tripos). Called to the Bar, Middle Temple, 1970. Mem., Law Adv. Cttee, British Council, 1985–91. Hon. Vice-Pres., British Assoc. for Shooting and Conservation, 1992. *Recreations:* ski-ing, golf, sailing, opera. *Address:* Brick Court Chambers, 15 Devereux Court, WC2R 3JJ. *T:* 0171–583 0777; 11 Avenue Juliette, 1180 Brussels, Belgium. *T:* 3752542. *Clubs:* United Oxford & Cambridge University, Ski Club of Gt Britain.

FOSKETT, David Robert; QC 1991; FCIArb; a Recorder, since 1995; *b* 19 March 1949; *s* of Robert Frederick Foskett and Ruth (*née* Waddington); *m* 1975, Angela Bridget Jacobs; two *d.* *Educ:* Warwick Sch.; King's Coll., London (LLB Hons). FCIArb 1992. King's College, London: Pres., Faculty of Laws, 1969–70; Pres., Union Soc., 1970–71; Mem., Delegacy, 1970–72. Called to the Bar, Gray's Inn, 1972. Mem., Midland and Oxford Circuit; Asst Recorder, 1992–95. Mem., Fees Collection Cttee, Bar Council, 1991–93. *Publications:* The Law and Practice of Compromise, 1980, 3rd edn 1991; various articles. *Recreations:* theatre, reading poetry and composing verse, bird watching, cricket, golf. *Address:* 1 Crown Office Row, Temple, EC4Y 7HH. *T:* 0171–797 7500. *Clubs:* Athenæum, MCC; Woking Golf.

FOSKETT, Douglas John, OBE 1978; FLA; Director of Central Library Services and Goldsmiths' Librarian, University of London, 1978–83; *b* 27 June 1918; *s* of John Henry Foskett and Amy Florence Foskett; *m* 1948, Joy Ada (*née* McCann); one *s* two *d.* *Educ:* Bancroft's Sch.; Queen Mary Coll., Univ. of London (BA 1939); Birkbeck Coll., Univ. of London (MA 1954). Ilford Municipal Libraries, 1940–48; RAMC and Intell. Corps, 1940–46; Metal Box Co. Ltd, 1948–57; Librarian, Univ. of London Inst. of Educn, 1957–78. Chairman of Council, Library Assoc., 1962–63, Vice-Pres., 1966–73, Pres., 1976; Hon. Library Adviser, RNID, 1965–90; Mem., Adv. Cttee on Sci. and Techn. Information, 1969–73; Mem. and Rapporteur, Internat. Adv. Cttee on Documentation, Libraries and Archives, UNESCO, 1968–73; Cons. on Documentation to ILO and to

European Packaging Fedn; Cttee Mem., UNISIST/UNESCO and EUDISED/Council of Europe Projects; Member: Army Educn Adv. Bd, 1968–73; Library Adv. Council, 1975–77. Visiting Professor: Univ. of Michigan, 1964; Univ. of Ghana, 1967; Univ. of Ibadan, 1967; Brazilian Inst. for Bibliography and Documentation, 1971; Univ. of Iceland, 1974. FLA 1949, Hon. FLA, 1975; Hon. Fellow, Polytechnic of North London, 1981. *Publications:* Assistance to Readers in Lending Libraries, 1952; (with E. A. Baker) Bibliography of Food, 1958; Information Service in Libraries, 1958, 2nd edn 1967; Classification and Indexing in the Social Sciences, 1963, 2nd edn 1974; Science, Humanism and Libraries, 1964; Reader in Comparative Librarianship, 1977; Pathways for Communication, 1984; contrib. to many professional jls. *Recreations:* books, travel, writing, cricket. *Address:* 1 Daleside, Gerrard's Cross, Bucks SL9 7JF. *T:* Gerrard's Cross (01753) 882835. *Clubs:* MCC; Sussex CC.

FOSS, Kathleen, (Kate); Member of Board, since 1983 and Chairman, since 1989, Direct Mail Services Standards Board; *b* 17 May 1925; *d* of George Arden and May Elizabeth Arden; *m* 1951, Robert Foss; one *s. Educ:* Northampton High Sch.; Whitelands Coll. (Teaching Dip.). Teacher: Northants, 1945–47; Mddx, 1947–53 (Dep. Head); Westmorland, 1953–60 (History specialist). Chairman: Consumers in European Community Gp (UK), 1979–82; Insurance Ombudsman Bureau, 1986– (Mem. Council, 1984–91); Member: Nat. Consumer Council, 1980–83; Consumers' Consultative Cttee, Brussels, 1981–86; Law Commn Standing Cttee on Conveyancing, 1985–88; Data Protection Tribunal Panel, 1986–; Council for Licensed Conveyancers, 1986–88. Vice Pres., Keep Britain Tidy Gp, 1982–88 (Vice-Chm., 1979–82); Mem. Exec., National Fedn of Women's Insts, 1969–81 (National Treasurer, 1974–78); Chm., Bd of Dirs, WI Books Ltd, 1981–89. *Recreations:* golf, bridge. *Address:* Merston, 61 Back Lane, Knapton, York YO2 6QJ. *T:* York (01904) 782549.

FOSTER; *see* Hylton-Foster.

FOSTER, Prof. Allan (Bentham); Professor of Chemistry, University of London, 1966–86, now Emeritus; *b* 21 July 1926; *s* of late Herbert and Martha Alice Foster; *m* 1949, Monica Binns; two *s. Educ:* Nelson Grammar Sch., Lancs; University of Birmingham. Frankland Medal and Prize, 1947; PhD, 1950; DSc, 1957. University Res. Fellow, University of Birmingham, 1950–53; Fellow of Rockefeller Foundn, Ohio State Univ., 1953–54; University of Birmingham: ICI Res. Fellow, 1954–55; Lectr, 1955–62; Sen. Lectr, 1962–64; Reader in Organic Chemistry, 1964–66; Institute of Cancer Research: Head of Chemistry Div., Chester Beatty Res. Inst., 1966–82; Head, Drug Metabolism Team, Drug Develt Sect., 1982–86. Sec., British Technol. Gp, New Cancer Product Develt Adv. Bd, 1986–91. FChemSoc (Mem. Coun., 1962–65, 1967–70); Corresp. Mem., Argentinian Chem. Soc. Editor, Carbohydrate Research, 1965–92. *Publications:* numerous scientific papers mainly in Jl Chem. Soc., Carbohydrate Research and cancer jls. *Recreations:* golf, gardening. *Address:* 1 Pine Walk, Carshalton Beeches, Surrey SM5 4ES. *T:* 0181–642 4102. *Club:* Banstead Downs.

FOSTER, Andrew William; Controller, Audit Commission, since 1992; *b* 29 Dec. 1944; *s* of George William and Gladys Maria Foster; *m* 1967, Christine Marquiss; one *s* one *d. Educ:* Abingdon School; Newcastle Polytechnic (BSc Sociol.); LSE (Postgrad. Dip. Applied Social Studies). Social Worker, London, 1966–71; Area Social Services Officer, 1971–75; Asst Dir of Social Services, Haringey, 1975–79; Dir of Social Services, Greenwich, 1979–82, N Yorks, 1982–87; Regional Gen. Manager, Yorks RHA, 1987–91; Dep. Chief Exec., NHS Management Exec., 1991–92. *Recreations:* golf, squash, walking, travel, theatre, food, wine. *Address:* Audit Commission, 1 Vincent Square, SW1P 2PN.

FOSTER, Brendan, MBE 1976; television athletics commentator, since 1981; Managing Director, Nova International Ltd, since 1987; *b* 12 Jan. 1948; *s* of Francis and Margaret Foster; *m* 1972; one *s* one *d. Educ:* St Joseph's Grammar Sch., Hebburn, Co. Durham; Sussex Univ. (BSc); Carnegie Coll., Leeds (DipEd). School Teacher, St Joseph's Grammar Sch., Hebburn, 1970–74; Sports and Recreation Manager, Gateshead Metropolitan Bor. Council, 1974–81; UK Man. Dir, Nike Internat., 1981–87; Chm., Nike (UK), 1981–86; Man. Dir, Nike Europe, 1985–87; Vice Pres. Marketing, Nike Inc. Oregon, USA, 1986–87. Commonwealth Games: Bronze medal: 1500 metres, 1970; 5000 m, 1978; Silver medal, 5000 m, 1974; Gold medal, 10,000 m, 1978; European Games: Bronze medal, 1500 m, 1971; Gold medal, 5000 m, 1974; Olympic Games: Bronze medal, 10,000 m, 1976; World Records: 2 miles, 1973; 3000 metres, 1974. BBC Sports Personality of the Year, 1974. Hon. Fellow, Sunderland Polytechnic, 1977; Hon. MEd Newcastle, 1978; Hon. DLitt Sussex, 1982. *Publications:* Brendan Foster, 1978; Olympic Heroes 1896–1984, 1984. *Recreations:* running (now only a recreation), sport (as spectator).

FOSTER, Sir Christopher (David), Kt 1986; MA; Advisor to the Chairman, Coopers & Lybrand Associates, since 1994; *b* 30 Oct. 1930; *s* of George Cecil Foster and Phyllis Joan Foster (*née* Mappin); *m* 1958, Kay Sheridan Bullock; two *s* three *d. Educ:* Merchant Taylors' Sch.; King's Coll., Cambridge (Scholar). Economics Tripos 1954; MA 1959. Commnd into 1st Bn Seaforth Highlanders, Malaya, 1949. Hallsworth Research Fellow, Manchester Univ., 1957–59; Senior Research Fellow, 1959–64, Official Fellow and Tutor, 1964–66, Hon. Fellow, 1992, Jesus Coll., Oxford; Dir-Gen. of Economic Planning, MoT, 1966–70; Head of Unit for Res. in Urban Economics, LSE, 1970–76; Prof. of Urban Studies and Economics, LSE, 1976–78; a Dir and Head of Econ. and Public Policy Div., Coopers & Lybrand Associates, 1978–84; a Dir, Public Sector Practice Leader and Economic Advr, Coopers & Lybrand, 1984–86; Commercial Adviser to British Telecom, 1986–88; Sen. Public Sector and Econs Partner, Coopers & Lybrand Deloitte, later Coopers & Lybrand Associates, 1988–94. Governor, 1967–70, Dir, 1976–78, Centre for Environmental Studies; Visiting Professor: of Economics, MIT, 1970; LSE, 1978–86. Special Economic Adviser (part time), DoE, 1974–77; Special Advr on BR Privatisation to Sec. of State for Transport, 1992–94; Mem. Bd, Railtrack, 1994–. Member: (part time), PO Bd, 1975–77; Audit Commn, 1983–88; ESRC, 1985–89; Chm., NEDO Construction Industry Sector Gp, 1988–92. Chm., Cttee of Inquiry into Road Haulage Licensing, 1977–78; Mem., Cttee of Inquiry into Civil Service Pay, 1981–82; Economic Assessor, Sizewell B Inquiry, 1982–86. Mem., LDDC, 1988–. Chairman: Circle 33 Housing Assoc, 1986–90; Construction Round Table, 1993–; non-exec. Dir, RAC plc, 1994–. Gov., RSC, 1991–. *Publications:* The Transport Problem, 1963; Politics, Finance and the Role of Economics: an essay on the control of public enterprise, 1972; (with R. Jackman and M. Perlman) Local Government Finance, 1980; Privatisation, Public Ownership and the Regulation of Natural Monopoly, 1993; papers in various economic and other journals. *Address:* 6 Holland Park Avenue, W11 3QU. *T:* 0171–727 4757. *Clubs:* Reform, Royal Automobile.

FOSTER, Christopher Norman; Keeper of the Match Book, since 1983, and Executive Director, since 1993, The Jockey Club; *b* 30 Dec. 1946; *s* of Maj.-Gen. Norman Leslie Foster, CB, DSO; *m* 1981, Anthea Jane Sammons; two *s. Educ:* Westminster Sch. ACA 1969, FCA 1979. Cooper Brothers & Co., Chartered Accountants, 1965–73; Weatherbys, 1973–90; Sec., Jockey Club, 1983–90. Governor, Westminster Sch. Soc., 1990–. *Recreations:* racing, shooting, fishing, gardening. *Address:* 42 Portman Square, W1H 0EN. *T:* 0171–486 4921. *Club:* MCC.

FOSTER, Hon. Dennis (Haley), CVO 1983; CBE 1981; JP; Chief Secretary, Cayman Islands, 1976–86; *b* 26 March 1931; *s* of late Arnold and Agatha Foster; *m* 1955, Reba Raphael Grant; one *d. Educ:* Munro Coll., Kingston, Jamaica. Joined Cayman Is Civil Service, 1950; seconded as Asst Administrator, Turks and Caicos Is, 1959; Dist Comr, Lesser Is, 1960; Asst Administrator, Cayman Is, 1968. *Recreation:* gardening. *Address:* PO Box 860, George Town, Grand Cayman, Cayman Islands, WI. *T:* (94) 92236.

FOSTER, Rt. Hon. Derek; PC 1993; MP (Lab) Bishop Auckland, since 1979; *b* 25 June 1937; *s* of Joseph and Ethel Maud Foster; *m* 1972, Florence Anne Bulmer; three *s* one *d. Educ:* Bede Grammar Sch., Sunderland; Oxford Univ. (BA Hons PPE). In industry and commerce, 1960–70; Youth and Community Worker, 1970–73; Further Educn Organiser, Durham, 1973–74; Asst Dir of Educn, Sunderland Borough Council, 1974–79. Councillor: Sunderland Co. Borough, 1972–74; Tyne and Wear County Council, 1973–77 (Chm. Econ. Develt Cttee, 1973–76). Chm., North of England Develt Council, 1974–76. North Regional Whip, 1981–82; PPS to Leader of Opposition, 1983–85; Opposition Chief Whip, 1985–95. Mem., Select Cttee on Trade and Industry, 1980–82; opposition front bench spokesman on social security, 1982–83. Vice Chm., Youthaid, 1979–86. *Recreations:* brass bands, choirs, uniformed member Salvation Army. *Address:* 3 Linburn, Rickleton, Washington, Tyne and Wear NE38 9EB. *T:* Washington (0191) 4171580.

FOSTER, Donald Michael Ellison; MP (Lib Dem) Bath, since 1992; *b* 31 March 1947; *s* of Rev. J. A. Foster and late Iris Edith (*née* Ellison); *m* 1968, Victoria, 2nd *d* of Major Kenneth Pettegree, OBE, TD and Jean Pettegree; one *s* one *d. Educ:* Lancaster Royal Grammar Sch.; Univ. of Keele (BA Hons; Cert Ed 1969); Univ. of Bath (MEd 1982). CPhys, MInstP 1970). Science teacher, Sevenoaks Sch., Kent, 1969–75; Science Curriculum Proj. Dir, Avon LEA, 1975–81; Science Educn Lectr, Bristol Univ., 1981–89: Head, Science Educn Centre; teacher trainer; organiser of link with Univ. of Zambia; Managing Consultant, Pannell Kerr Forster, 1989–92. Mem., Avon CC, 1981–89 (Leader, Liberal Gp; Chm., Educn Cttee, 1987–89). Mem. Exec. Cttee, ACC, 1985–89. Contested (L) Bristol East, 1987. Treas., All-Party Yugoslav Gp, 1994. Vice-Chm., British Assoc. for Central and Eastern Europe, 1994–. Vice-Chm., Nat. Campaign for Nursery Educn; Hon. Pres., British Youth Council, 1992–; Trustee: Open Sch., 1992–; Educn Extra, 1992–. Hon. Fellow, Bath Coll. of Further Educn, 1994. *Publications:* Resource-based Learning in Science, 1979; Science with Gas, 1981; (jtly) Aspects of Science, 1984; (jtly) Reading about Science, 1984; (jtly) Nuffield Science, 1986; (ed) Teaching Science 11–13, 1987; science curriculum resources and educn papers. *Recreations:* watching all forms of sport (former rower and Rugby player), reading, films, music. *Address:* House of Commons, SW1A 0AA. *T:* 0171–219 5001; 26 Ambra Vale, Cliftonwood, Bristol BS8 4RW. *T:* Bristol (0117) 929 1272. *Club:* National Liberal.

FOSTER, Ian Hampden; a Master of the Supreme Court, Queen's Bench Division, since 1991; *b* 27 Feb. 1946; *s* of Eric Hampden Foster and Irene Foster (*née* Warman); *m* 1975, Fiona Jane, *d* of Rev. J. N. and Mrs Robertson-Glasgow; one *s* one *d. Educ:* Battersea Grammar Sch.; Univ. of Exeter (LLB Hons 1968). Called to the Bar, Inner Temple, 1969; practice at common law bar, 1969–91. Adv. Editor, Atkin's Court Forms, 1991–. *Publication:* (ed jtly) Supreme Court Practice, 1993. *Recreations:* gardening, watching cricket. *Address:* Royal Courts of Justice, Strand, WC2A 2LL. *Club:* Norfolk (Norwich).

FOSTER, Joan Mary; Under Secretary, Department of Transport, Highways Planning and Management, 1978–80, retired; *b* 20 January 1923; *d* of John Whitfield Foster and Edith Foster (*née* Levett). *Educ:* Northampton School for Girls. Entered Civil Service (HM Office of Works), Oct. 1939; Ministry of Transport, 1955; Asst Secretary, 1970. *Recreations:* gardening, cooking, good wine. *Address:* 3 Hallfields, Shouldham, King's Lynn, Norfolk PE33 0DN. *T:* Fincham (01366) 347809.

FOSTER, Joanna Katharine; Director, BT Forum, since 1995; *b* 5 May 1939; *d* of Michael and Lesley Mead; *m* 1961, Jerome Foster; one *s* one *d. Educ:* Benenden School; Univ. of Grenoble. Sec. and Editl Asst, Vogue Magazine, London and NY, 1958–59; journalist, San Francisco Chronicle, 1959; Head of Press Dept, Conservative Central Office, 1962–66; Management Adviser, Industrial Soc., 1966–72; Dir, Centre Actif Bilingue, Fontainebleau, 1972–79; Press Attachée and Editor, INSEAD, Fontainebleau, 1972–79; Educn and Trng Dir, Corporate Services Unit, Western Psychiatric Inst. and Clinic, Univ. of Pittsburgh, 1980–82; Management Adviser, 1982–85, Head of Pepperell Unit, 1985–88, Mem. Council, 1990, Industrial Soc.; Chair: Equal Opportunities Commn, 1988–93; UK Council, UN Internat. Year of the Family 1994, 1992–95. Pres., European Commn Adv. Cttee on Equal Opportunities, 1991–92 (Vice Pres., 1990, 1991, 1993); Member: Nat. Adv. Council for Careers and Educnl Guidance, 1993–94; Sec. of State for Employment's Women's Issues Adv. Gp, 1991–93; Target Team for Business in the Community's Opportunity 2000 Initiative, 1992–. Chair, Adv. Cttee, European Public Policy Inst., Warwick Univ., 1993–. Dep. Chm., TSB Foundn, 1991–. Dir, WNO, 1990–94; Mem., Central TV Adv. Bd. Pres., Relate, 1993–. Gov., Oxford Brookes Univ., 1993–. Hon. Fellow, St Hilda's Coll., Oxford, 1988. Hon. DLitt Kingston, 1993; DU Essex, 1993; Hon. LLD: Oxford Brookes, 1993; West of England, 1993; Strathclyde, 1994; Salford, 1994. *Recreations:* family, friends, food. *Address:* Confessor's Gate, Islip, Oxford OX5 2SN. *Clubs:* Reform, Forum UK.

FOSTER, Sir John (Gregory), 3rd Bt *cr* 1930; Consultant Physician, George, Cape Province; *b* 26 Feb. 1927; *s* of Sir Thomas Saxby Gregory Foster, 2nd Bt, and Beryl, *d* of late Dr Alfred Ireland; *S* father, 1957; *m* 1956, Jean Millicent Watts; one *s* three *d. Educ:* Michaelhouse Coll., Natal. South African Artillery, 1944–46; Witwatersrand Univ., 1946–51; MB, BCh 1951; Post-graduate course, MRCPE 1955; Medical Registrar, 1955–56; Medical Officer, Cape Town, 1957. DIH London, 1962; FRCPE 1981. *Recreation:* outdoor sport. *Heir: s* Saxby Gregory Foster, *b* 3 Sept. 1957. *Address:* 7 Caledon Street, PO Box 1325, George 6530, Cape Province, South Africa. *T:* George (441) 743333. *Club:* Johannesburg Country (S Africa).

FOSTER, (John) Peter, OBE 1990; Surveyor of the Fabric of Westminster Abbey, 1973–88, now Emeritus; *b* 2 May 1919; *s* of Francis Edward Foster and Evelyn Marjorie, *e d* of Sir Charles Stewart Forbes, 5th Bt of Newe; *m* 1944, Margaret Elizabeth Skipper; one *s* one *d. Educ:* Eton; Trinity Hall, Cambridge. BA 1940, MA 1946; ARIBA 1949. Commnd RE 1941; served Norfolk Div.; joined Guards Armd Div. 1943, served France and Germany; Captain SORE(2) 30 Corps 1945; discharged 1946. Marshall Sisson, Architect: Asst 1948, later Partner; Sole Principal 1971; Surveyor of Royal Academy of Arts, 1965–80. Partner with John Peters of Vine Press, Hemingford Grey, 1957–63. Art Workers' Guild: Mem., 1971; Master, 1980; Trustee, 1985. Pres., Surveyors Club, 1980. Member: Churches Cttee for Historic Building Council for England, 1977–84; Adv. Bd for Redundant Churches, 1979–91; Exec. Cttee, Georgian Gp, 1983–91; Fabric Cttee, Canterbury Cathedral, 1987–91 (Chm., 1990); Council, Ancient Monuments Soc., 1988–; Fabric Cttee, Ely Cathedral, 1990–. Chm., Cathedral Architects Assoc., 1987–90. Governor, Suttons Hosp., Charterhouse, 1982–. FSA 1973; FRSA 1994. *Recreations:* painting, books, travel. *Address:* Harcourt, Hemingford Grey, Huntingdon, Cambs PE18 9BJ. *T:* St Ives (01480) 462200. *Club:* Athenæum.

FOSTER, John Robert; National Organiser, Amalgamated Union of Engineering Workers, 1962–81, retired; *b* 30 Jan. 1916; *s* of George Foster and Amelia Ann (*née* Elkington); *m* 1938, Catherine Georgina (*née* Webb); one *s* one *d*. *Educ:* London County Council. Apprentice toolmaker, 1931–36; toolmaker, 1936–47; Amalgamated Engineering Union: Kingston District Sec. (full-time official), 1947–62. In Guyana for ILO, 1982. Lectr on industrial relns and trade union educn, WEA, 1981–. Mem., Industrial Tribunals (England and Wales), 1984–86. Mem., Engrg Industry Trng Bd, 1974–80; Vice-Chm., Electricity Supply Industry Trng Cttee, 1967–81; Mem., Adv. Council on Energy Conservation, 1978–82. Mem., Soc. of Industrial Tutors, 1981–. MRI 1978. *Recreations:* music, photography, angling, 17th Century English Revolution. *Address:* 10 Grosvenor Gardens, Kingston-upon-Thames KT2 5BE.

FOSTER, Rev. Canon John William, BEM 1946; Dean of Guernsey, 1978–88; Rector of St Peter Port, Guernsey, 1978–88; Canon Emeritus of Winchester Cathedral since 1988; *b* 5 Aug. 1921; *m* 1943, Nancy Margaret Allen (*d* 1992); one *s*. *Educ:* St Aidan's Coll., Birkenhead. Served Leicestershire Yeomanry, 1939–46; Chaplain, Hong Kong Defence Force, 1958–. Reserve of Officers, Hong Kong Defence Force, 1967–73. Priest 1955; Curate of Loughborough, 1954–57; Chaplain, St John's Cathedral, Hong Kong, 1957–60, Precentor, 1960–63; Dean of Hong Kong, 1963–73; Hon. Canon, St John's Cathedral, Hong Kong, 1973; Vicar of Lythe, dio. York, 1973–78; Hon. Canon of Winchester, 1979–88. *Address:* 14 Lightfoots Avenue, Scarborough, N Yorks YO12 5NS. *T:* Scarborough (01723) 379012.

FOSTER, Jonathan Rowe; QC 1989; a Recorder, since 1988; Deputy High Court Judge (Family Division), since 1994; *b* 20 July 1947; *s* of Donald Foster and Hilda Eaton; *m* 1978, Sarah Ann Mary da Cunha; four *s*. *Educ:* Oundle Sch.; Keble Coll., Oxford. Called to the Bar, Gray's Inn, 1970. Treas., Northern Circuit, 1992–. Mem., Criminal Injuries Compensation Bd, 1995–. Gov., Ryleys' Sch., 1990–. *Recreations:* outdoor pursuits, bridge. *Address:* (chambers) 18 St John Street, Manchester M3 4EA. *T:* 0161–834 9843. *Clubs:* St James's (Manchester); Hale Golf, Bowdon Lawn Tennis; Treaddur Bay Sailing.

FOSTER, Lawrence; conductor; Chief Conductor, Orchestre Philharmonique (formerly Orchestre National) of Monte Carlo, since 1978; Music Director, City of Barcelona Symphony Orchestra, since 1996; *b* Los Angeles, 23 Oct. 1941; *s* of Thomas Foster and Martha Wurmbrandt. *Educ:* Univ. of California, LA; studied under Fritz Zweig, Bruno Walter and Karl Böhm. Asst Conductor, Los Angeles Philharmonic, 1965–68; British début, Royal Festival Hall, 1968; Covent Garden début, Troilus and Cressida, 1976; Chief Guest Conductor, Royal Philharmonic Orchestra, 1969–74; Music Dir and Chief Conductor, Houston Symphony Orchestra, 1971–78; Gen. Music Dir, Duisberg concert series, 1982–86; Prin. Guest. Conductor, Düsseldorf Opera, 1982–86; Music Director: Lausanne Chamber Orch., 1985–90; Aspen Fest., 1991–. *Recreations:* reading European history, films. *Address:* c/o Christopher Tennant Artists Management, Unit 2, 39 Tadema Road, SW10 0PY.

FOSTER, Sir Norman (Robert), Kt 1990; RA 1991 (ARA 1983); RDI 1988; RIBA, FCSD, FAIA; architect; Director: Sir Norman Foster and Partners, London, Glasgow, Frankfurt, Berlin; Foster Japan; Foster Hong Kong Ltd; *b* Redditch, 1 June 1935; *s* of late Robert Foster and Lilian Smith; *m* 1964, Wendy Ann Cheesman (*d* 1989); four *s*. *Educ:* Univ. of Manchester Sch. of Architecture (DipArch 1961, CertTP); Yale Univ. Sch. of Architecture (Henry Fellow, Jonathan Edwards Coll., March 1962). Founded: Foster Associates, 1967; Sir Norman Foster and Partners, 1992; in collab. with Dr Buckminster Fuller, 1968–83; Cons. Architect: UEA, 1978–87; Imperial Coll., London. Mem. Council: AA, 1969–70, 1970–71 (Vice Pres., 1974); RCA, 1981–. Taught at: Univ. of Pennsylvania; AA, London; Bath Acad. of Arts; London Polytechnic. External Examr and Mem. Visiting Bd of Educn, RIBA. Major projects include: IBM Pilot Head Office, Hampshire, 1970, Head Office for Willis Faber & Dumas, Ipswich, 1975 (First Trustees', Medal, RIBA, 1990); Sainsbury Centre for Visual Arts, Univ. of E Anglia, Norwich, 1977; Technical Park for IBM, Greenford, 1979; UK headquarters for Renault, 1983; Nomos Furniture System, 1985; Civic Hall, Nancy, 1986; new HQ, Hongkong and Shanghai Banking Corp., Hong Kong, 1986 (internat. competition winner, 1979); Esprit Shop, London, 1987; Kings Cross London Master Plan, 1988; Stockley Park, 1989; Millennium Tower, Tokyo, 1990; viaduct, Rennes, 1990; Commerzbank HQ, Frankfurt, 1991; RA Sackler Galls, 1991; Terminal Zone, Stansted, 1991; ITN building, 1991; Century Tower, Tokyo, 1991; Barcelona Telecoms Tower, 1992; masterplan for Rotterdam, 1992; Micro-Electronics Centre, Duisburg, 1993; new airport, Hong Kong, 1992; Musée de la Préhistoire, Verdon, 1992; Arts Centre, Nîmes, 1993; school, Fréjus, 1993; German Parlt bldg (Reichstag), Berlin, 1993; British Mus. redevelt, 1994; inner harbour, Duisburg, 1994; Bilbao Metro System, 1995. Work exhibited: Mus. of Mod. Art, New York, 1979 and Permanent Exhibn, 1982; Three New Skyscrapers, Museum of Modern Art, NY, 1983; Summer Exhibn RA; Milan, 1983; Barcelona, 1976, 1988; Manchester, 1984; Berlin, 1984; Paris, 1985, 1986; Sainsbury Centre, 1985, 1991; Hannover, 1986; Nîmes, 1986; RA 1986; Tokyo, Seville, 1988; Madrid, 1988, 1989; Venice, 1991; Bordeaux, 1992; Zurich, 1993; Munich, 1995. IBM Fellow, Aspen Conference, 1980; Hon. FAIA 1980; Hon. Mem., Bund deutscher Architekten, 1983; Member: Internat. Acad. of Architecture, Sofia; French Order of Architects; Associate, Académie Royale de Belgique, 1990. Hon. LittD East Anglia, 1980; Hon. DSc Bath, 1986. Awards include: R. S. Reynolds Internat. Awards, USA, 1976, 1979, 1986; RIBA Awards and Commendations, 1969, 1972, 1977, 1978, 1981, 1992, 1993; Royal Gold Medal for Architecture, 1983; Financial Times Awards for outstanding Industrial Architecture and Commendations, 1967, 1970, 1971, 1974, 1984; Structural Steel Awards, 1972, 1978, 1984, 1986; Internat. Design Award, 1976, 1980; RSA Award, 1976; Ambrose Congreve Award, 1980; Civic Trust Award, 1984, 1992, 1995; Yale Arts Award for Outstanding Achievement, 1985; Constructa-European Award, 1986; IStructE Special Award, 1986, 1991; Premio Compasso d'Oro Award, 1987; Japan Design Foundn Award, 1987; Annual Interiors Award (USA), 1988, 1992; Kunstpreis Award, Berlin, 1989; British Construction Industry Award, 1989, 1991, 1992; Trustees Medal, RIBA, 1990; Mies van der Rohe Award, Barcelona, 1991; Gold Medal, French Academy, 1991; Aluminium Imagination Awards, 1991; Arnold W. Brunner Meml Award, AAIL, 1992; Sunday Times and Royal Fine Art Commn Best Building of the Year Award, 1992, 1993; RICS Award, 1992; ICE Award, 1992; Concrete Soc. Award, 1992; Architecture & Urbanism Award, City of Barcelona, 1993; Gold Medal, Amer. Inst. of Architects, 1994. Officer, Order of Arts and Letters (France), 1994. *Relevant publications:* The Work of Foster Associates, 1979; Norman Foster, 1988; Norman Foster Foster Associates Buildings and Projects, vol 2, 1971–78, 1989, vol 3, 1978–85, 1989, vol. 1, 1964–73 (Norman Foster Team Four and Foster Associates Buildings and Projects), 1991; (by Kenneth Powell) Stanstead: Norman Foster and the architecture of flight, 1992; Norman Foster Sketches, 1992; Foster Associates, 1992; Architecture as Building, 1993. *Recreations:* running, flying, ski-ing. *Address:* (office) Riverside Three, 22 Hester Road, SW11 4AN. *T:* 0171–738 0455, *Fax:* 0171–738 1107.

FOSTER, Peter; *see* Foster, J. P.

FOSTER, Maj.-Gen. Peter Beaufoy, MC 1944; Major-General Royal Artillery, British Army of the Rhine, 1973–76; retired June 1976; *b* 1 Sept. 1921; *s* of F. K. Foster, OBE, JP, Allt Dinas, Cheltenham; *m* 1947, Margaret Geraldine, *d* of W. F. Henn, sometime Chief Constable of Glos; two *s* one *d* (and one *s* decd). *Educ:* Uppingham School. Commnd RA, 1941; psc 1950; jssc 1958; OC Para. Light Battery, 1958–60; DAMS MS5, WO, 1960–63; Mil. Assistant to C-in-C BAOR, 1963–64; CO 34 Light Air Defence Regt RA, 1964–66; GSO1, ASD5, MoD, 1966–68; BRA Northern Comd, 1968–71; Comdt Royal Sch. of Artillery, 1971–73. Col Comdt, RA, 1977–82; Regimental Comptroller, RA, 1985–86. Vice President: RA Assoc.; RHA Assoc. Chapter Clerk, Salisbury Cathedral, 1978–85. *Recreations:* shooting, gardening, beagling, walking, reading. *Address:* Sherborn House, High Street, Chipping Campden, Glos GL55 6HB.

FOSTER, Peter Martin, CMG 1975; HM Diplomatic Service, retired; *b* 25 May 1924; *s* of Frederick Arthur Peace Foster, RN and Marjorie Kathleen Sandford; *m* 1947, Angela Hope Cross; one *s* one *d*. *Educ:* Sherborne; Corpus Christi Coll., Cambridge. Army (Horse Guards), 1943–47; joined Foreign (now Diplomatic) Service, 1948; served in Vienna, Warsaw, Pretoria/Cape Town, Bonn, Kampala, Tel Aviv; Head of Central and Southern Africa Dept, FCO, 1972–74; Ambassador and UK Rep. to Council of Europe, 1974–78; Ambassador to German Democratic Republic, 1978–81. Dir, Council for Arms Control, 1984–86; Chm., Internat. Social Service of GB, 1985–90. *Address:* Rew Cottage, Abinger Lane, Abinger Common, Surrey RH5 6HZ. *T:* Dorking (01306) 730114.

FOSTER, Richard Anthony, FSA, FMA; Director, National Museums and Galleries on Merseyside, since 1986; *b* 3 Oct. 1941; *s* of late Eric Kenneth Foster and of Sylvia Renee Foster (now Westerman); *m* 1964, Mary Browning James; two *s* one *d*. *Educ:* Kingswood Sch.; London Sch. of Economics (BSc Econ 1963); Manchester Univ. (MA 1968). Student Asst, Leicester Museum, 1964–66; Museum Asst, Bowes Museum, Barnard Castle, 1967–68; Keeper in Charge, Durham Light Infantry Museum and Arts Centre, Durham, 1968–70; Dir, Oxford City and County Museum, Woodstock, 1970–74; Dir, Museum Services, Oxfordshire County Museum Service, Woodstock, 1974–78; Dir of Museums, Merseyside County Museums, Liverpool, 1978–86. Mem., Museums and Galls Commn, 1993–; Member Board: NW Museums and Art Galls Service, 1986–; Inst. of Popular Music, Univ. of Liverpool, 1987–. Advr, Fabric Cttee, Liverpool Cathedral, 1988. *Recreations:* sailing, watching football. *Address:* National Museums and Galleries on Merseyside, Liverpool Museum, William Brown Street, Liverpool L3 8EN. *T:* 0151–207 0001.

FOSTER, Robert; Under Secretary, Head of Aerospace Division, Department of Trade and Industry, since 1993; *b* 12 May 1943; *s* of David and Amelia Foster; *m* 1967, Judy Welsh; one *s* one *d*. *Educ:* Oundle Sch.; Corpus Christi Coll., Cambridge (BA 1964; MA 1967). CEng. Research and Development Engineer: Parkinson Cowan, 1964–66; Automation Ltd, 1966–71; Exec. Engineer, Post Office Telecommunications, 1971–76; DTI, 1977–92; Under Sec., OST, Cabinet Office, 1992–93. *Recreations:* tennis, squash, music. *Address:* 9 Holmdene Avenue, SE24 9LB.

FOSTER, Prof. Robert Fitzroy, (Roy), PhD; FRSL; FRHistS; FBA 1989; Carroll Professor of Irish History, University of Oxford, since 1991; *b* 16 Jan. 1949; *s* of Frederick Ernest Foster and Elizabeth (*née* Fitzroy); *m* 1972, Aisling O'Conor Donelan; one *s* one *d*. *Educ:* Newtown Sch., Waterford; St Andrew's Sch., Middletown, Delaware, USA; Trinity Coll., Dublin (MA; PhD 1975). FRHistS 1979; FRSL 1992. Lectr, 1974, Reader, 1983, Professor of Modern British Hist., 1988–91, Birkbeck Coll., London Univ. Alistair Horne Fellow, St Antony's Coll., Oxford, 1979–80; British Acad. Res. Reader in the Humanities, 1987–89; Fellow, Inst. for Advanced Study, Princeton, and Vis. Fellow, Dept of English, Princeton Univ., 1988–89. Irish Post Community Award, 1982; Sunday Independent/Irish Life Arts Award, 1988. *Publications:* Charles Stewart Parnell: the man and his family, 1976, 2nd edn 1979; Lord Randolph Churchill: a political life, 1981, 3rd edn 1987; Political Novels and Nineteenth Century History, 1983; Modern Ireland 1600–1972, 1988; (ed) The Oxford Illustrated History of Ireland, 1989; (ed) The Sub-Prefect Should Have Held His Tongue and other essays, by Hubert Butler, 1990; Paddy and Mr Punch: connections in English and Irish history, 1993; numerous essays and reviews. *Recreation:* recreation. *Address:* Hertford College, Oxford OX1 3BW. *Club:* Kildare Street and University (Dublin).

FOSTER, Sir Robert (Sidney), GCMG 1970 (KCMG 1964; CMG 1961); KCVO 1970; Governor-General and Commander-in-Chief of Fiji, 1970–73 (Governor and C-in-C, 1968–70); retired 1973; *b* 11 Aug. 1913; *s* of late Sidney Charles Foster and late Jessie Edith (*née* Fry); *m* 1947, Margaret (*née* Walker) (*d* 1991); no *c*. *Educ:* Eastbourne Coll.; Peterhouse, Cambridge. MA. Appointed Cadet, Administrative Service, Northern Rhodesia, 1936; District Officer, N Rhodesia, 1938. War Service, 2nd Bn Northern Rhodesia Regt, 1940–43, Major. Provincial Commissioner, N Rhodesia, 1957; Sec., Ministry of Native Affairs, N Rhodesia, 1960; Chief Sec., Nyasaland, 1961–63; Dep. Governor, Nyasaland, 1963–64; High Comr for W Pacific, 1964–68. KStJ 1968. Officer of the Legion of Honour, 1966. *Recreation:* self-help. *Address:* 18 Windmill Lane, Histon, Cambridge CB4 4JF. *Clubs:* Royal Over-Seas League; Leander (Henley).

FOSTER, Roy; *see* Foster, Robert Fitzroy.

FOSTER, Simon Ridgeby; farmer; *b* 1 Sept. 1939; *s* of Sir Ridgeby Foster and of Lady Nancy Foster (*née* Godden); *m* 1st, 1966, Mairi Angela Chisholm (marr. diss); one *s* two *d*; 2nd, 1990, Philippa Back. *Educ:* Shrewsbury Sch.; Jesus Coll., Cambridge (MA Hist.); London Business Sch. (Sloane Fellow); Wye Coll., London Univ. Pres. and Dir. Gen., Dunlop France, 1983–88; Dir, SMMT, 1988–91; Man. Dir, Toyota GB, 1991–93. Liveryman, Coachmakers' Co., 1993–. Médaille d'Allier, 1987. *Publication:* Politique Industrielle, 1990. *Recreations:* farming, Dutch sailing barges. *Club:* Oriental.

FOSTER, Thomas Ashcroft; *b* 27 May 1934; *s* of Thomas Lawrence Foster and Ada May Foster (*née* Ashcroft); *m* 1959, Beryl Wilson; two *d*. *Educ:* Rivington and Blackrod Grammar Sch.; Univ. of Leicester (Dip. Social Studies 1957); University Coll. of South Wales and Momouthshire (Dip. Applied Social Studies 1963). Youth Employment Asst, Derbyshire CC, 1957–59; Child Care Officer, Manchester City Council, 1959–62; Senior Mental Welfare Officer, Carlisle City Council, 1963; Student Supervisor, Children's Dept, Glamorgan CC, 1963–67; Area Children's Officer, Lancs CC, 1967–71; Divl Dir, Social Services, Cheshire CC, 1971–73; Dir, Social Services, Tameside Met. Borough Council, 1973–86; Dir of Social Services, Lancs CC, 1986–90. Mem., Cttee of Inquiry into Mental Handicap Nursing and Care, 1975–79; Social Services Adviser, AMA, 1983–86. Sen. Vice-Pres., Assoc. of Dirs of Social Servs, 1990 (Hon. Sec., Mental Health sub-cttee, 1991–). Hon. Lectr, Univ. of Lancaster, 1990–. *Recreations:* theatre, archaeology, walking.

FOSTER-BROWN, Rear-Adm. Roy Stephenson, CB 1958; RN Retired; *b* 16 Jan. 1904; *s* of Robert Allen Brown and Agnes Wilfreda Stephenson; *m* 1933, Joan Wentworth Foster; two *s*. *Educ:* RNC, Osborne and Dartmouth. Specialised in Submarines, 1924–28; specialised in Signals, 1930. Fleet Signal Officer, Home Fleet, 1939–40; Staff Signal Officer, Western Approaches, 1940–44; Comdr HMS Ajax, 1944–46; Capt., 1946; Capt. Sixth Frigate Sqdn, 1951; Dir Signal Div., Admiralty, 1952–53; Capt. HMS Ceylon, 1954; Rear-Adm. 1955; Flag Officer, Gibraltar, 1956–59; retd 1959. Hon. Comdt, Girls Nautical Trng Corps, 1961–. Master, Armourers and Braziers Co., 1964–65, 1974–75. *Recreations:*

sailing, shooting, golf, tennis. *Address:* 13 Ravenscroft Road, Henley on Thames, Oxon RG9 2DH. *Club:* Army and Navy.

FOTHERBY, Gordon; Deputy Solicitor, HM Customs and Excise, since 1993; *b* 15 Nov. 1950; *m* 1974, Victoria Eloise. *Educ:* Hull GS; Sheffield Univ. (LLB Hons 1972). Called to the Bar, Inner Temple, 1973; Capt., Army Legal Corps, 1973–77; Solicitor's Office, HM Customs and Excise, 1977–. Asst Sec., Legal, 1986–93; on secondment to EC, 1989–91. *Address:* c/o Solicitor's Office, HM Customs and Excise, New King's Beam House, SE1 9PJ.

FOTHERGILL, Dorothy Joan; Director, Postal Pay and Grading, 1974–83, retired; *b* 31 Dec. 1923; *d* of Samuel John Rimington Fothergill and Dorothy May Patterson. *Educ:* Haberdashers' Aske's Sch., Acton; University Coll. London. BA (Hons) History. Entered Civil Service as Asst Principal, 1948; Principal, Overseas Mails branch, GPO, 1953; UPU Congress, Ottawa, 1957; Establishments work, 1958–62; HM Treasury, 1963–65; Asst Sec., Pay and Organisation, GPO, 1965; Director: Postal Personnel, 1970; London Postal Region, 1971. *Recreations:* gardening, walking, theatre. *Address:* 38 Andrewes House, Barbican, EC2Y 8AX.

FOTHERGILL, Richard Humphrey Maclean; Director, The Ceres Trust, since 1988; *b* 21 March 1937; *s* of late Col C. G. Fothergill, RM, and Mrs E. G. Fothergill; *m* 1962, Angela Cheshire Martin; three *d*. *Educ:* Sandle Manor, Fordingbridge; Clifton Coll., Bristol; Emmanuel Coll., Cambridge (BA Hons Nat. Sci. Tripos, 1958). Commnd RASC, National Service, 1959–61. Contemporary Films Ltd, 1961; Head of Biology, SW Ham Technical Sch., 1961–69; Res. Fellow, Nat. Council for Educnl Technol., 1970–72; Founder and Head of PETRAS (Educnl Develt Unit), Newcastle upon Tyne Polytechnic, 1972–80; Dir, Microelectronics Educn Prog., DES, 1980–86; Dir, CET, 1986–87. Co-founder, Sec. and Treasurer, Standing Conf. on Educnl Develt Services in Polytechnics, 1974–80; Member: London GCE Bd and Schools Council Science Cttee, 1968–72; Standards and Specifications Cttee, CET, 1972–80. *Publications:* A Challenge for Librarians, 1971; Resource Centres in Colleges of Education, 1973; (with B. Williams) Microforms in Education, 1977; Child Abuse: a teaching package, 1978; (with I. Butchart) Non-book Materials in Libraries: a practical guide, 1978, 3rd edn 1990; (with J. S. A. Anderson) Microelectronics Education Programme: policy and guidelines, 1983; Implications of the New Technology for the School Curriculum, 1988; articles in Visual Educn, Educn Libraries Bull., Educnl Media Internat., and Educnl Broadcasting Internat. *Recreations:* reading, television, films, walking. *Address:* 17 Grenville Drive, Brunton Park, Newcastle upon Tyne NE3 5PA. *T:* 0191–236 3380. *Club:* National Film Theatre.

FOU TS'ONG; concert pianist; *b* 10 March 1934; *m* 1st, 1960, Zamira Menuhin (marr. diss. 1970); one *s*; 2nd, 1973, Hijong Hyun (marr. diss. 1976); 3rd, 1987, Patsy Toh; one *s*. *Educ:* Shanghai and Warsaw. Debut, Shanghai, 1953. Concerts all over Eastern Europe including USSR up to 1958. Arrived in Great Britain, Dec. 1958; London debut, Feb. 1959, followed by concerts in England, Scotland and Ireland; subsequently has toured all five Continents. Hon. DLitt Hong Kong, 1983. *Recreations:* many different ones. *Address:* c/o Horowitz Music Management Ltd, Grosvenor Gardens House, 35–37 Grosvenor Gardens, SW1W 0BS. *T:* 0181–295 3985, *Fax:* 0181–295 3984.

FOULDS, (Hugh) Jon; Chairman, Halifax Building Society, since 1990 (Director, since 1986); Deputy Chairman, 3i Group plc (formerly Investors in Industry), 1988–92 (Director and Chief Executive, 1976–88); *b* 2 May 1932; *s* of late Dr E. J. Foulds and Helen Shirley (*née* Smith); *m* 1st, 1960, Berry Cusack-Smith (marr. diss. 1970); two *s*; 2nd, 1977, Hélène Senn, *d* of Edouard Senn, Paris. *Educ:* Bootham Sch., York. Director: Brammer plc, 1980–91 (Chm., 1988–90); London Smaller Companies (formerly London Atlantic) Investment Trust, 1983–; Pan-Holding SA, 1986–; Eurotunnel plc, 1988–; Mercury Asset Management Gp plc, 1989–. Mem. Bd of Banking Supervision, Bank of England, 1993–. Mem., Arts Council Lottery Bd for the Arts and Films. Hon. MA Salford, 1987. *Recreations:* tennis, ski-ing, shooting, pictures. *Address:* Halifax Building Society, 62 Cornhill, EC3V 3QT. *T:* 0171–839 9011. *Clubs:* Garrick, Hurlingham; Cercle Interallié (Paris).

FOULGER, Keith, BSc(Eng); CEng, MIMechE; FRINA, RCNC; Chief Naval Architect, Ministry of Defence, 1983–85, retired; *b* 14 May 1925; *s* of Percy and Kate Foulger; *m* 1951, Joyce Mary Hart; one *s* one *d*. *Educ:* Univ. of London (Mech. Eng.); Royal Naval Coll., Greenwich. Asst Constructor, 1950; Constructor, 1955; Constructor Commander: Dreadnought Project, 1959; C-in-C Western Fleet, 1965; Chief Constructor, 1967; Asst Director, Submarines, 1973; Deputy Director: Naval Construction, 1979; Naval Ship Production, 1979–81; Submarines, Ship Dept, 1981–83; Asst Under-Sec. of State, 1983. *Recreations:* travel, gardening, local community affairs, restoration of HMS Victory. *Address:* Masons, Grittleton, Chippenham, Wilts SN14 6AP. *T:* Castle Combe (01249) 782308.

FOULIS, Sir Iain (Primrose Liston), 13th Bt, *cr* 1634, of Colinton; Bt 1661, of Ravelston, but for the attainder; Language Tutor, Madrid, since 1966; *b* 9 Aug. 1937; *s* of Lieut-Colonel James Alistair Liston-Foulis, Royal Artillery (killed on active service, 1942), and Mrs Kathleen de la Hogue Moran (*d* 1991), 2nd *d* of Lt-Col. John Moran, Indian Army and Countess Olga de la Hogue, *yr d* of Marquis de la Hogue, Mauritius; *S* cousin, Sir Archibald Charles Liston Foulis, 12th Bt, 1961. *Educ:* Hodder; St Mary's Hall; Stonyhurst Coll.; Cannington Farm Inst., Somerset (Dip. Agr.); Madrid (Dip. in Spanish). National Service, 1957–59; Argyll and Sutherland Highlanders, Cyprus, 1958 (Gen. Service Medal). Landowner, 1961–. Language Teacher, Estremadura and Madrid, 1959–61; Trainee, Bank of London and South America, 1962; Trainee, Bank of London and Montreal (in Nassau, 1963, Guatemala City, 1963–64; Managua, Nicaragua, 1964–65); Toronto (Sales), 1965–66. Life Mem., Nat. Trust for Scotland. Member: Spanish Soc. of the Friends of Castles; Friends of the St James Way. Cert. from Archbishop of Santiago de Compostela for pilgrimage on foot, Somport to Santiago, Jubilee Year, 1971. *Recreations:* long-distance running, swimming, walking, mountaineering, travelling, foreign languages and customs, reading, Spanish medieval history (especially Muslim Spain), car racing and rallies, country pursuits, hunting. *Address:* Aptdo de Correos 7, San Agustin De Guadalix, 28750 Madrid, Spain. *T:* (91) 8418978.

FOULKES, Arthur Alexander; High Commissioner of the Commonwealth of the Bahamas to the United Kingdom and Ambassador to France, Italy, Germany, Belgium and the European Community, since 1992; *b* 11 May 1928; *s* of late Dr William Alexander Foulkes and Julie Blanche Foulkes (*née* Maisonneuve); *m* 1st, Naomi Louise Higgs; 2nd, Joan Eleanor Bullard. *Educ:* Public Sch., Inagua, Bahamas; Western Central Sch., Nassau, Bahamas; privately tutored in journalism. News Editor, The Tribune, 1950–62; Editor, Bahamian Times, 1962; Founder/Chm., Diversified Services (PR), 1967. MP Bahamas, 1967; Chm., Bahamas Telecommunications Corp., 1967; Cabinet Minister, 1968; Co-Founder, Free Nat. Movement, 1970; Mem., Senate, 1972. Delegate: Bahamas Petition to UN Cttee on Decolonization, 1965; Bahamas Constitutional Conf., London, 1972. *Recreations:* theatre, music, art, literature. *Address:* 10 Chesterfield Street, W1X 8AH. *T:* 0171–408 4488.

FOULKES, George, JP; MP (Lab Co-op) Carrick, Cumnock and Doon Valley, since 1983 (South Ayrshire, 1979–83); *b* 21 Jan. 1942; *s* of George and Jessie M. A. W. Foulkes; *m* 1970, Elizabeth Anna Hope; two *s* one *d*. *Educ:* Keith Grammar Sch., Keith, Banffshire; Haberdashers' Aske's Sch.; Edinburgh Univ. (BSc 1964). President: Edinburgh Univ. SRC, 1963–64; Scottish Union of Students, 1965–67; Manager, Fund for Internat. Student Cooperation, 1967–68. Scottish Organiser, European Movement, 1968–69; Director: European League for Econ. Cooperation, 1969–70; Enterprise Youth, 1970–73; Age Concern, Scotland, 1973–79. Councillor: Edinburgh Corp., 1970–75; Lothian Regional Council, 1974–79; Chairman: Lothian Region Educn Cttee, 1974–79; Educn Cttee, Convention of Scottish Local Authorities, 1975–78. Jt Chm., All Party Pensioners Cttee, 1983– (Sec./Treasurer 1979–83); Mem., H of C Select Cttee on Foreign Affairs, 1981–83; Opposition spokesman on European and Community Affairs, 1984–85, on Foreign Affairs, 1985–92, on Defence, 1992–93, on Overseas Develt, 1994–. UK Delegate to Parly Assembly of Council of Europe, 1979–81; Treas., Parliamentarians for Global Action, 1993– (Mem. Council, 1987–); Member: UK Exec., CPA, 1987–; IPU, 1989–. Mem., Scottish Exec. Cttee, Labour Party, 1981–89. Rector's Assessor, Edinburgh Univ. Court, 1968–70, Local Authority Assessor, 1971–79. Chairman: Scottish Adult Literacy Agency, 1976–79; John Wheatley Centre, 1990–. Mem. Exec., British/China Centre, 1987–93. Director: St Cuthbert's Co-op. Assoc., 1975–79; Co-op. Press Ltd, 1990–. JP Edinburgh, 1975. *Publications:* Eighty Years On: history of Edinburgh University SRC, 1964; (contrib.) A Claim of Right, ed Owen Dudley Edwards, 1989. *Recreations:* boating, watching Heart of Midlothian FC. *Address:* 8 Southpark Road, Ayr KA7 2TL. *T:* Ayr (01292) 265776. *Club:* Edinburgh University Staff (Edinburgh).

FOULKES, Sir Nigel (Gordon), Kt 1980; Chairman: ECI International Management Ltd, 1987–91; ECI Management (Jersey) Ltd, 1986–91; Equity Capital Trustee Ltd, 1983–90; *b* 29 Aug. 1919; *s* of Louis Augustine and Winifred Foulkes; *m* 1948, Elisabeth Walker (*d* 1995), *d* of Ewart B. Walker, Toronto; one *s* one *d* of former marr. *Educ:* Gresham's Sch., Holt; Balliol Coll., Oxford (Schol., MA). RAF, 1940–45. Subsequently executive, consulting and boardroom posts with: H. P. Bulmer; P. E. Consulting Gp; Birfield; Greaves & Thomas; International Nickel; Rank Xerox (Asst Man. Dir 1964–67, Man. Dir 1967–70); Charterhouse Group Ltd (Dir, 1972–83); Dir, Charterhouse J. Rothschild plc, 1984–85; Chm., Equity Capital for Industry, 1983–86 (Vice-Chm., 1982); Dir, Bekaert Gp (Belgium), 1973–85. Chairman: British Airports Authority, 1972–77; Civil Aviation Authority, 1977–82. CIMgt; FRSA. *Address:* Westway House, West Adderbury, Banbury, Oxon OX17 3EU. *Club:* Royal Air Force.

FOUNTAIN, Alan; Senior Commissioning Editor, Channel Four TV, 1982–94; *b* 24 March 1946; *s* of Harold Fountain and Winifred Cecily Brown. *Educ:* Nottingham Univ. (BA Hons Philosophy). Film Officer, E Midlands Arts, 1976–79; producer, 1979–81; Channel Four TV, 1981–94. *Publications:* (ed) Ruff's Guide to the Turf, 1980; contrib. film and TV pubns. *Recreations:* family, golf, watching sports.

FOURCADE, Jean-Pierre; Officier de l'ordre national du Mérite; Senator, French Republic, for Hauts-de-Seine, since 1977; *b* 18 Oct. 1929; *s* of Raymond Fourcade (Médecin) and Mme Fourcade (*née* Germaine Raynal); *m* 1958, Odile Mion; one *s* two *d*. *Educ:* Collège de Sorèze; Bordeaux Univ. Faculté de Droit, Institut des Etudes politiques (Dip.); Ecole nationale d'administration; higher studies in Law (Dip.). Inspecteur des Finances, 1954–73. Cabinet of M. Valéry Giscard d'Estaing: Chargé de Mission, 1959–61; Conseiller technique, 1962, then Dir Adjoint to chef de service, Inspection gén. des Finances, 1962; Chef de service du commerce, at Direction-Gén. du Commerce intérieur et des Prix, 1968–70; Dir-gén. adjoint du Crédit industriel et commercial, 1970; Dir-gén., 1972, and Administrateur Dir-gén., 1973; Ministre de l'Economie et des Finances, 1974–76; Ministre de l'Equipement et de l'Aménagement du Territoire, 1976–77. Mayor of Saint-Cloud, 1971–92; Conseiller général of canton of Saint-Cloud, 1973–89; Conseiller régional d'Ile de France, 1976– (Vice-Président, 1982). Président: Clubs Perspectives et Realités, 1975–82; Comité des Finances Locales, 1980; Commn des Affaires Sociales du Sénat, 1983; Vice-Pres., Union pour la Démocratie Française, 1978–86 (Mem. Bureau, 1986). *Publications:* Et si nous parlions de demain, 1979; La tentation social-démocrate, 1985; Remèdes pour l'Assurance-Maladie, 1989. *Address:* Palais du Luxembourg, 75006 Paris, France; 8 Parc de Béarn, 92210 Saint-Cloud, France.

FOURNIER, Bernard; Managing Director, Rank Xerox Ltd, since 1989; *b* 2 Dec. 1938; *s* of Jean Fournier and Solange Hervieu; *m* 1st; two *s*; 2nd, 1980, Françoise Chavailler; one *s*. *Educ:* Philo Lycée (Baccalauréat); Louis Le Grand, Paris; Ecole des Hautes Etudes Commerciales, Lille. Joined: Publiart SA, 1964; Sanglier SA, 1965; Rank Xerox, 1966: Regional Manager Africa, Eastern Europe, 1980; Gen. Manager, RX France, 1981; Pres., Amer. Ops, Xerox, 1988. *Recreations:* tennis, cooking, oenology, stamps, antiques. *Address:* 37 Brompton Square, SW3 2AF.

FOURNIER, Jean, OC 1987; CD 1972; retired diplomat; Commissioner of the Metric Commission, Canada, since 1981; *b* Montreal, 18 July 1914; *s* of Arthur Fournier and Emilie Roy; *m* 1942, May Coote; five *s*. *Educ:* High Sch. of Québec; Laval Univ. (BA 1935, LLB 1938). Admitted to Bar of Province of Quebec, 1939. Royal Canadian Artillery (NPAM) (Lieut), 1935; Canadian Active Service Force Sept. 1939; served in Canada and overseas; discharged 1944, Actg Lt-Col. Joined Canadian Foreign Service, 1944; Third Sec., Canadian Dept of External Affairs, 1944; Second Sec., Canadian Embassy, Buenos Aires, 1945; Nat. Defence Coll., Kingston, 1948 (ndc); Seconded: to Privy Council Office, 1948–50; to Prime Minister's Office, Oct. 1950–Feb. 1951; First Sec., Canadian Embassy, Paris, 1951; Counsellor, 1953; Consul Gen., Boston, 1954; Privy Council Office (Asst Sec. to Cabinet), 1957–61; Head of European Division (Political Affairs), Dept of External Affairs, 1961–64; Chm., Quebec Civil Service Commn, 1964–71; Agent Gen. for the Province of Quebec in London, 1971–78. Pres., Inst. of Public Administration of Canada, 1966–67; Pres., Centre Québecois de Relations Internationales; Chm. Bd, Canadian Human Rights Foundn, 1982–90; Member: Canadian Inst. of Strategic Studies; Canadian Inst. of Internat. Affairs. Freedom, City of London, 1976. Pres., Canadian Veterans Assoc. of the UK, 1976–77. *Address:* 201 Metcalfe Avenue, Apt 903, Westmount, Québec H3Z 2H7, Canada. *T:* (514) 9328633. *Clubs:* Canada; St James's, Montreal (Montreal), Royal Canadian Military Institute (Toronto).

FOUYAS, Metropolitan Methodios, of Pisidia; former Archbishop of Thyateira and Great Britain; Greek Orthodox Archbishop of Great Britain, 1979–88; *b* 14 Sept. 1925. BD (Athens); PhD (Manchester), 1962. Vicar of Greek Church in Munich, 1951–54; Secretary-General, Greek Patriarchate of Alexandria, 1954–56; Vicar of Greek Church in Manchester, 1960–66; Secretary, Holy Synod of Church of Greece, 1966–68; Archbishop of Aksum (Ethiopia), 1968–79. Member, Academy of Religious Sciences, Brussels, 1974–. Dist. Lectr, Univ. of Berkeley, 1992. Estabd Foundn for Hellenism in GB, 1982; Editor, Texts and Studies: a review of the Foundn for Hellenism in GB, Vols I–X, 1982–91; Founder-Editor, Abba Salama Review of Ethio-Hellenic Studies, 10 Volumes; Editor: Ekklesiastikos Pharos (Prize of Academy of Athens), 11 Volumes; Ecclesia and Theologia, vols I–XII, 1980–93. Hon. DD: Edinburgh, 1970; Gr. Th. School of Holy Cross, Boston, 1984. Grand Cordon: Order of Phoenix (Greece); of Sellassie (Ethiopia). *Publications:* Orthodoxy, Roman Catholicism and Anglicanism, 1972; The Person of Jesus Christ in the Decisions of the Ecumenical Councils, 1976; History of the Church in Corinth, 1968; Christianity and Judaism in Ethiopia, Nubia and Meroe, 1st Vol., 1979, 2nd Vol., 1982;

Theological and Historical Studies, Vols 1–13, 1979–94; Greeks and Latins, 1990; Hellenism, the Pedestal of Christianity, 1992; Hellenism, the Pedestal of Islam, 1994; Hellenism and Judaism, 1995; contrib. to many other books and treatises. *Recreation:* gardening. *Address:* 9 Riga Ferraiou Street, Khalandri, 15232 Athens, Greece. *T:* 6824793.

FOWDEN, Sir Leslie, Kt 1982; FRS 1964; Director of Arable Crops Research, Agricultural and Food Research Council, 1986–88; *b* Rochdale, Lancs, 13 Oct. 1925; *s* of Herbert and Amy D. Fowden; *m* 1949, Margaret Oakes; one *s* one *d*. *Educ:* University Coll., London. PhD Univ. of London, 1948. Scientific Staff of Human Nutrition Research Unit of the MRC, 1947–50; Lecturer in Plant Chemistry, University Coll. London, 1950–55, Reader, 1956–64, Prof. of Plant Chemistry, 1964–73; Dean of Faculty of Science, UCL, 1970–73; Dir, Rothamsted Exptl Station, 1973–86. Rockefeller Fellow at Cornell Univ., 1955; Visiting Prof. at Univ. of California, 1963; Royal Society Visiting Prof., Univ. of Hong Kong, 1967. Consultant Dir, Commonwealth Bureau of Soils, 1973–88. Chm., Agric. and Vet. Adv. Cttee, British Council, 1987–; Member: Advisory Board, Tropical Product Inst., 1966–70; Council, Royal Society, 1970–72; Scientific Adv. Panel, Royal Botanic Gardens, 1977–83 (Trustee, 1983–93); Radioactive Waste Management Adv. Cttee, 1983–91. Foreign Member: Deutsche Akademie der Naturforscher Leopoldina, 1971; Lenin All-Union Acad. of Agricultural Sciences of USSR, 1978–92; Acad. of Agricl Scis of GDR, 1986–91; Russian Acad. of Agricl Scis, 1992–; Corresponding Mem., Amer. Soc. Plant Physiologists, 1981; Hon. Mem., Phytochemical Soc. of Europe, 1985. Hon. DSc Westminster, 1993. *Publications:* contribs to scientific journals on topics in plant biochemistry. *Address:* 31 Southdown Road, Harpenden, Herts AL5 1PF. *T:* Harpenden (01582) 764628.

FOWELLS, Joseph Dunthorne Briggs, CMG 1975; DSC 1940; Deputy Director General, British Council, 1976–77, retired; *b* 17 Feb. 1916; *s* of late Joseph Fowells and Maud Dunthorne, Middlesbrough; *m* 1st, 1940, Edith Agnes McKerracher (marr. diss. 1966); two *s* one *d*; 2nd, 1969, Thelma Howes (*d* 1974). *Educ:* Sedbergh Sch.; Clare Coll., Cambridge (MA). School teaching, 1938; service with Royal Navy (Lt-Comdr), 1939–46; Blackie & Son Ltd, Educnl Publishers, 1946; British Council, 1947: Argentina, 1954; Representative Sierra Leone, 1956; Scotland, 1957; Dir Latin America and Africa (Foreign) Dept, 1958; Controller Overseas B Division (foreign countries excluding Europe), 1966; Controller Planning, 1968; Controller European Div., 1970; Asst Dir Gen. (Functional), 1972; Asst Dir Gen. (Regional), 1973–76. *Recreations:* golf, sailing. *Address:* 5/57 Palmeira Avenue, Hove, East Sussex BN3 3GE. *T:* Brighton (01273) 770349.

FOWKE, Sir David (Frederick Gustavus), 5th Bt *cr* 1814, of Lowesby, Leics; *b* 28 Aug. 1950; *s* of Lt-Col Gerrard George Fowke (*d* 1969) (2nd *s* of 3rd Bt) and of Daphne (*née* Monasteriotis); *S* uncle, 1987. *Educ:* Cranbrook School, Sydney; Univ. of Sydney (BA 1971). *Heir:* none.

FOWLER, Prof. Alastair David Shaw, FBA 1974; Professor of English, University of Virginia, since 1990; Regius Professor of Rhetoric and English Literature, University of Edinburgh, 1972–84, now Emeritus (University Fellow, 1985–87); *b* 17 Aug. 1930; *s* of David Fowler and Maggie Shaw; *m* 1950, Jenny Catherine Simpson; one *s* one *d*. *Educ:* Queen's Park Sch., Glasgow; Univ. of Glasgow; Univ. of Edinburgh; Pembroke Coll., Oxford. MA Edin. 1952 and Oxon 1955; DPhil Oxon 1957; DLitt Oxon 1972. Junior Res. Fellow, Queen's Coll., Oxford, 1955–59; Instructor, Indiana Univ., 1957; Lectr, UC Swansea, 1959; Fellow and Tutor in English Lit., Brasenose Coll., Oxford, 1962–71. Visiting Professor: Columbia Univ., 1964; Univ. of Virginia, 1969, 1979, 1985–90; Mem. Inst. for Advanced Study, Princeton, 1966, 1980; Visiting Fellow: Council of the Humanities, Princeton Univ., 1974; Humanities Research Centre, Canberra, 1980; All Souls Coll., Oxford, 1984. Mem., Scottish Arts Council, 1976–77. Adv. Editor, New Literary History, 1972–; Gen. Editor, Longman Annotated Anthologies of English Verse, 1977–80; Mem. Editorial Board: English Literary Renaissance, 1978–; Word and Image, 1984–91; The Seventeenth Century, 1986–; Connotations, 1990–; Translation and Literature, 1990–; English Review, 1990–. *Publications:* (trans. and ed) Richard Wills, De re poetica, 1958; Spenser and the Numbers of Time, 1964; (ed) C. S. Lewis, Spenser's Images of Life, 1967; (ed with John Carey) The Poems of John Milton, 1968; Triumphal Forms, 1970; (ed) Silent Poetry, 1970; (ed with Christopher Butler) Topics in Criticism, 1971; Seventeen, 1971; Conceitful Thought, 1975; Catacomb Suburb, 1976; Edmund Spenser, 1977; From the Domain of Arnheim, 1982; Kinds of Literature, 1982; A History of English Literature, 1987; The New Oxford Book of Seventeenth Century Verse, 1991; The Country House Poem, 1994; contribs to jls and books. *Address:* (Jan.–Aug.) Department of English, David Hume Tower, George Square, Edinburgh EH8 9JX; (Sept.–Dec.) Department of English, Bryan Hall, Charlottesville, VA 22903, USA.

FOWLER, Beryl, (Mrs H. Fowler); *see* Chitty, (Margaret) B.

FOWLER, Christopher B.; *see* Brocklebank-Fowler.

FOWLER, Dennis Houston, OBE 1979 (MBE 1963); HM Diplomatic Service, retired; *b* 15 March 1924; *s* of Joseph Fowler and Daisy Lilian Wraith Fowler (*née* Houston); *m* 1944, Lilias Wright Nairn Burnett; two *s* one *d*. *Educ:* Alleyn's Sch., Dulwich. Colonial Office, 1940; RAF, 1942–46; India Office (subseq. CRO), 1947; Colombo, 1951; Second Secretary, Karachi, 1955; CRO, 1959; First Secretary, Dar es Salaam, 1961; Diplomatic Service Administration (subseq. FCO), 1965; First Sec. and Head of Chancery, Reykjavik, 1969; FCO, 1973; First Sec., Head of Chancery and Consul, Kathmandu, 1977; Counsellor and Hd of Claims Dept, FCO, 1980–83. *Recreations:* golf, music, do-it-yourself. *Address:* 25 Dartnell Park Road, West Byfleet, Surrey KT14 6PN. *T:* Byfleet (01932) 341583. *Clubs:* West Byfleet Golf; Royal Nepal Golf (Kathmandu).

FOWLER, Derek, CBE 1979; Chairman: Railways (formerly BR) Pension Trustee Co., since 1986; Kier Group Pension Scheme, since 1992; *b* 26 Feb. 1929; *s* of late George Edward Fowler and Kathleen Fowler; *m* 1953, Ruth Fox; one *d*. *Educ:* Grantham, Lincs. Financial appointments with: Grantham Borough Council, 1944–50; Spalding UDC, 1950–52; Nairobi City Council, 1952–62; Southend-on-Sea CBC, 1962–64. British Railways Board: Internal Audit Manager, 1964–67, and Management Acct, 1967–69, W Region; Sen. Finance Officer, 1969–71; Corporate Budgets Manager, 1971–73; Controller of Corporate Finance, 1973–75; Finance Mem., 1975–78; a Vice-Chm., 1981–90; Dep. Chm., 1990. Dep. Chm., Capita Gp, 1990–; Dir, Kier Gp, 1992–. Mem., UK Accounting Standards Cttee, 1982–84. Freeman: City of London, 1981; Co. of Information Technologists, 1987 (Liveryman, 1992); Liveryman, Worshipful Co. of Loriners, 1981. FCCA; JDipMA. *Recreation:* cartophily. *Address:* (office) 55 Old Broad Street, EC2M 1RX.

FOWLER, Sir (Edward) Michael (Coulson), Kt 1981; Mayor of Wellington, New Zealand, 1974–83; Partner, Calder Fowler Styles and Turner, since 1960; company chairman and director; *b* 19 Dec. 1929; *s* of William Coulson Fowler and Faith Agnes Netherclift; *m* 1953, Barbara Hamilton Hall; two *s* one *d*. *Educ:* Christ's Coll., Christchurch, NZ; Auckland Univ. (MArch). Architect, London office, Ove Arup & Partners, 1954–56; own practice, Wellington, 1957–59. Director: New Zealand Sugar Co., 1983–; Cigna Insurance New Zealand Ltd, 1985–89. Chm., Queen Elizabeth II Arts Council, 1983–87. Wellington City Councillor, 1968–74. Nat. Pres., YHA of NZ, 1984–87. Medal of Honour, NZIA, 1983; Alfred O. Glasse Award, NZ Inst. of Planning, 1984. *Publications:* Wellington Sketches: Folio I, 1971, Folio II, 1974; Country Houses of New Zealand, 1972, 2nd edn 1977; The Architecture and Planning of Moscow, 1980; Eating Houses in Wellington, 1980; Wellington Wellington, 1981; Eating Houses of Canterbury, 1982; Wellington—A Celebration, 1983; The New Zealand House, 1983; Buildings of New Zealanders, 1984; Michael Fowler's University of Auckland, 1993. *Recreations:* sketching, reading, writing, history, politics. *Address:* Branches, Giffords Road, RD3 Blenheim, New Zealand. *T:* (3) 5728987. *Club:* Wellington (Wellington, NZ).

FOWLER, Henry Hamill; investment banker; Limited Partner, Goldman Sachs & Co., New York; *b* 5 Sept. 1908; *s* of Mack Johnson Fowler and Bertha Browning Fowler; *m* 1938, Trudye Pamela Hathcote; two *d* (one *s* decd). *Educ:* Roanoke Coll., Salem, Va; Yale Law Sch. Counsel, Tennessee Valley Authority, 1934–38, Asst Gen. Counsel, 1939; Special Asst to Attorney-Gen. as Chief Counsel to Sub-Cttee, Senate Cttee, Educn and Labor, 1939–40; Special Counsel, Fed. Power Commn, 1941; Asst Gen. Counsel, Office of Production Management, 1941, War Production Board, 1942–44; Econ. Adviser, US Mission Econ. Affairs, London, 1944; Special Asst to Administrator, For. Econ. Administration, 1945; Dep. Administrator, National Production Authority, 1951, Administrator, 1952; Administrator, Defense Prodn Administration, 1952–53; Dir Office of Defense Mobilization, Mem. Nat. Security Coun., 1952–53; Under-Sec. of the Treasury, 1961–64; Secretary of the US Treasury, 1965–68. Sen. Mem. of Fowler, Leva, Hawes & Symington, Washington, 1946–51, 1953–61, 1964–65; Gen. Partner, Goldman Sachs & Co., 1969–80; Chm., Goldman Sachs Internat. Corp., 1969–84. Chairman: Roanoke Coll., 1974–81; Atlantic Council of the US, 1972–77; Inst. of Internat. Educn, 1973–78; US Treasury Adv. Cttee on Reform of Internat. Monetary System, 1973–84; Cttee to Fight Inflation, 1981–89; Bretton Woods Cttee, 1985–89; Co-Chairman: Cttee on Present Danger, 1976–88; Citizens Network for Foreign Affairs, 1988–. Trustee: Lyndon B. Johnson Foundn; Franklin D. Roosevelt Four Freedoms Foundn; Carnegie Endowment for Peace, 1972–78; Alfred Sloan Foundn, 1970–80. Hon. Degrees: Roanoke Coll., 1961; Wesleyan Univ., 1966; Univ. of William and Mary, 1966. *Recreation:* bridge. *Address:* 209 South Fairfax Street, Alexandria, VA 22314, USA; 85 Broad Street, New York, NY 10004, USA. *Clubs:* Links, River (NYC); Metropolitan (Washington), Bohemian (San Francisco).

FOWLER, Ian, OBE 1993; Principal Chief Clerk and Clerk to the Committee of Magistrates for the Inner London area, 1979–94; *b* 20 Sept. 1932; *s* of Major Norman William Frederick Fowler, OBE, QPM, and late Alice May (*née* Wakelin); *m* 1961, Gillian Cecily Allchin, JP; two *s* one *d*. *Educ:* Maidstone Grammar Sch.; Skinners Sch., Tunbridge Wells; King's Sch., Canterbury; St Edmund Hall, Oxford (MA). National Service, commnd 2nd Bn The Green Howards, 1951–53. Called to Bar, Gray's Inn, 1957; entered Inner London Magistrates Courts Service, 1959. Dep. Traffic Comr, Eastern Traffic Area, 1987–. Councillor: Herne Bay UDC and Canterbury CC, 1961–83 (Mayor, 1976–77). Mem. Court, Univ. of Kent at Canterbury, 1976–. *Recreation:* reading. *Address:* 6 Dence Park, Herne Bay, Kent CT6 6BG.

FOWLER, John Francis, DSc, PhD; FInstP; Professor, Department of Human Oncology, University of Wisconsin, USA, 1988–94, Emeritus Professor since 1994; Director of Cancer Research Campaign's Gray Laboratory, at Mount Vernon Hospital, Northwood, 1970–88; *b* 3 Feb. 1925; *er s* of Norman V. Fowler, Bridport, Dorset; *m* 1st, 1953, Kathleen Hardcastle Sutton, MB, BS (marr. diss. 1984); two *s* five *d*; 2nd, 1992, Anna Edwards, BSc, MCSP, SRP. *Educ:* Bridport Grammar Sch.; University Coll. of the South-West, Exeter. BSc 1st class Hons (London) 1944; MSc (London) 1946; PhD (London) 1955; DSc (London) 1974; FInstP 1957. Research Physicist: Newalls Insulation Co., 1944; Metropolitan Vickers Electrical Co., 1947; Newcastle upon Tyne Regional Hosp. Board (Radiotherapy service), 1950; Principal Physicist at King's Coll. Hosp., SE5, 1956; Head of Physics Section in Medical Research Council Radiotherapeutic Res. Unit, Hammersmith Hosp., 1959 (later the Cyclotron Unit); Reader in Physics, London Univ. at Med. Coll. of St Bartholomew's Hosp., 1962; Prof. of Med. Physics, Royal Postgraduate Med. Sch., London Univ., Hammersmith Hosp., 1963–70, Vice-Dean, 1967–70. Visiting Professor: in Oncology, Mddx Hosp. Med. Sch., 1977–88; Dept. of Oncol., University Hosp. of Leuven, Belgium, 1994–; Bush Vis. Prof., Ontario Cancer Inst., Toronto, 1991. President: Hosp. Physicists Assoc., 1966–67; Europ. Soc. Radiat. Biol., 1974–76; British Inst. Radiol., 1977–78. Hon. Fellow, Amer. Coll. of Radiology, 1981; Hon. Member: Amer. Assoc. of Med. Physicists, 1983; Inst. of Physical Sci. Med., 1993. Hon. MD Helsinki, 1981; Hon. DSc Med. Coll. Wisconsin, 1989. Roentgen Award, BIR, 1965; Röntgen Plakette, Deutsches Röntgen Museum, 1978; Heath Meml Award, Univ. of Texas, Houston, 1981; Breur Medal, European Soc. Therapeutic Radiology and Oncology, 1983; Barclay Medal, BIR, 1985; Marie Sklodowska-Curie Medal, Polish Radiation Res. Soc., 1986. *Publications:* Nuclear Particles in Cancer Treatment, 1981; papers on radiation dosimetry, radio-biology, radioisotopes, in Brit. Jl Radiology, Brit. Jl Cancer, Radiotherapy and Oncology, etc. *Recreations:* theatre, ballroom dancing, getting into the countryside. *Address:* 150 Lambeth Road, SE1 7DF.

FOWLER, Sir Michael; *see* Fowler, Sir E. M. C.

FOWLER, Neil Douglas; Editor, The Western Mail, since 1994; *b* 18 April 1956; *s* of Arthur Vincent Fowler and late Helen Pauline Fowler; *m* 1989, Carol Susan (*née* Cherry); one *d*, and one step *s*. *Educ:* Southend High Sch. for Boys; Univ. of Leicester (BA Social Scis). Reporter, Leicester Mercury, 1978–81; Dep. News Editor, then Asst Chief Sub-editor, Derby Evening Telegraph, 1981–84; Asst to Editor, Asst Editor, then Editor, Lincolnshire Echo, 1984–87; Editor, Derby Evening Telegraph, 1987–91; Editor, The Journal, Newcastle upon Tyne, 1991–94. Regional Editor of Year, Newspaper Focus magazines, 1994. *Recreations:* cricket, cinema, music of Frank Zappa. *Address:* The Western Mail, Thomson House, Havelock Street, Cardiff CF1 1XR. *T:* Cardiff (01222) 583650.

FOWLER, Rt. Hon. Sir Norman; *see* Fowler, Rt Hon. Sir P. N.

FOWLER, Prof. Peter Howard, FRS 1964; DSc; private consultant in the application of physics to industry; Royal Society Research Professor in Physics, University of Bristol, 1964–88, now Emeritus; *b* 27 Feb. 1923; *s* of Sir Ralph Howard Fowler, FRS, and Eileen, *o c* of 1st and last Baron Rutherford; *m* 1949, Rosemary Hempson (*née* Brown); three *d*. *Educ:* Winchester Coll.; Bristol Univ. BSc 1948, DSc 1958. Flying Officer in RAF, 1942–46 as a Radar Technical Officer. Asst Lectr in Physics, 1948, Lectr, 1951, Reader, 1961, Bristol Univ. Visiting Prof., Univ. of Minnesota, 1956–57. Rutherford Meml Lectr, Royal Soc., 1971. Chairman: Jt Cttee on Radiol Protection, MRC, 1983–92; Neutron Facilities Review Panel, SERC, 1989; Mem., Meteorol Cttee, 1983–93. Governor: King's Sch., Bruton, 1982–; Jawaharlal Nehru Meml Trust, 1985–; Rutherford Foundn, 1991–. Hughes Medal, Royal Soc., 1974. *Publications:* (with Prof. C. F. Powell and Dr D. H. Perkins) The Study of Elementary Particles by the Photographic Method, 1959; (with Dr V. M. Clapham) Solid State Nuclear Track Detectors, 1981; (with Dr B. Foster) Forty Years of Particle Physics, 1988. *Recreations:* gardening, meteorology. *Address:* 320 Canford Lane, Westbury on Trym, Bristol BS9 3PL.

FOWLER, Peter James, CMG 1990; HM Diplomatic Service; High Commissioner to Bangladesh, since 1993; *b* 26 Aug. 1936; *s* of James and Gladys Fowler; *m* 1962, Audrey June Smith; one *s* three *d*. *Educ:* Nunthorpe Grammar Sch., York; Trinity Coll., Oxford (BA). Army Service, 1954–56. FCO, 1962–64; Budapest, 1964–65; Lisbon, 1965–67; Calcutta, 1968–71; FCO, 1971–75; East Berlin, 1975–77; Counsellor, Cabinet Office, 1977–80; Comprehensive Test Ban Delegn, Geneva, 1980; Counsellor, Bonn, 1981–85; Head of N America Dept, FCO, 1985–88; Minister and Dep. High Comr, New Delhi, 1988–93. *Recreations:* reading, opera. *Address:* c/o Foreign and Commonwealth Office, King Charles Street, SW1A 2AH. *Clubs:* Commonwealth Trust, Oriental.

FOWLER, Peter Jon, PhD; Professor of Archaeology, University of Newcastle upon Tyne, since 1985; *b* 14 June 1936; *s* of W. J. Fowler and P. A. Fowler; *m* 1959, Elizabeth (*née* Burley) (marr. diss. 1993); three *d*. *Educ:* King Edward VI Grammar Sch., Morpeth, Northumberland; Lincoln Coll., Oxford (MA 1961); Univ. of Bristol (PhD 1977). Investigator on staff of RCHM (England), Salisbury office, 1959–65; Staff Tutor in Archaeology, Dept of Extra-Mural Studies, 1965–79, and Reader in Arch., 1972–79, Univ. of Bristol; Sec., Royal Commn on Historical Monuments (England), 1979–85. Member: Historic Bldgs and Ancient Monuments Adv. Cttees, Historic Buildings and Monuments Commn, 1983–86 (Ancient Monuments Bd, 1979–83); Council, National Trust, 1983–; Pres., Council for British Archaeol., 1981–83 (Vice-Pres., 1979–81). Archaeological consultant, Forestry Commn, 1988–; Mem., Landscape Adv. Cttee, DoT, 1990–. *Publications:* Regional Archaeologies: Wessex, 1967; (ed) Archaeology and the Landscape, 1972; (ed) Recent Work in Rural Archaeology, 1975; (ed with K. Branigan) The Roman West Country, 1976; Approaches to Archaeology, 1977; (ed with H. C. Bowen) Early Land Allotment in the British Isles, 1978; (with S. Piggott and M. L. Ryder) Agrarian History of England and Wales, I, pt 1, 1981; The Farming of Prehistoric Britain, 1983; Farms in England, 1983; (with P. Boniface) Northumberland and Newcastle upon Tyne, 1989; (jtly) Who Owns Stonehenge?, 1990; (with M. Sharp) Images of Prehistory, 1990; The Past in Contemporary Society: then, now, 1992; (jtly) Cadbury Congresbury 1968–73: a late/post-Roman hilltop settlement in Somerset, 1992; (with P. Boniface) Heritage and Tourism in 'the global village', 1993; contribs to learned jls. *Recreations:* writing, sport. *Address:* Department of Archaeology, The University, Newcastle upon Tyne NE1 7RU.

FOWLER, Rt. Hon. Sir (Peter) Norman, Kt 1990; PC 1979; MP (C) Sutton Coldfield, since Feb. 1974 (Nottingham South, 1970–74); Chairman of the Conservative Party, 1992–94; *b* 2 Feb. 1938; *s* of late N. F. Fowler and Katherine Fowler; *m* 1979, Fiona Poole, *d* of John Donald; two *d*. *Educ:* King Edward VI Sch., Chelmsford; Trinity Hall, Cambridge (MA). Nat. Service commn, Essex Regt, 1956–58; Cambridge, 1958–61; Chm., Cambridge Univ. Conservative Assoc., 1960. Joined staff of The Times, 1961; Special Corresp., 1962–66; Home Affairs Corresp., 1966–70; reported Middle East War, 1967. Mem. Council, Bow Group, 1967–69; Editorial Board, Crossbow, 1962–69; Vice-Chm., North Kensington Cons. Assoc., 1967–68; Chm., E Midlands Area, Cons. Political Centre, 1970–73. Chief Opposition spokesman: Social Services, 1975–76; Transport, 1976–79; Opposition spokesman, Home Affairs, 1974–75; PPS, NI Office, 1972–74; Sec. of State for Transport, 1981 (Minister of Transport, 1979–81), for Social Services, 1981–87, for Employment, 1987–90. Mem., Parly Select Cttee on Race Relations and Immigration, 1970–74; Jt Sec., Cons. Parly Home Affairs Cttee, 1971–72, 1974 (Vice-Chm., 1974); Chm., Cons Parly Cttee on European Affairs, 1991–92. Chm., Midland Independent Newspapers, 1991–. Chm., NHBC, 1992–. *Publications:* After the Riots: the police in Europe, 1979; political pamphlets including: The Cost of Crime, 1973; The Right Track, 1977; Ministers Decide: a memoir of the Thatcher years, 1991. *Address:* House of Commons, SW1A 0AA.

FOWLER, Richard Nicholas; QC 1989; *b* 12 Oct. 1946; 2nd *s* of late Ronald Hugh Fowler and of Winifred Mary Fowler (*née* Hull). *Educ:* Bedford Sch.; Brasenose Coll., Oxford (BA). Called to the Bar, Middle Temple, 1969. Liveryman, Goldsmiths' Co., 1989–. *Recreations:* walking, opera, dogs. *Address:* 93 Cheyne Walk, SW10 0DQ. *T:* 0171–352 4966; 4 Raymond Buildings, Gray's Inn, WC1R 5BP. *T:* 0171–405 7211; 28 rue de Toulouse, 1040 Brussels, Belgium. *T:* (2) 2303545.

FOWLER, Robert Asa; Owner and Chairman, Fowler International, since 1986; Consul General for Sweden, since 1989; *b* 5 Aug. 1928; *s* of Mr and Mrs William Henry Fowler; *m* 1987, Monica Elizabeth Heden; three *s* one *d* by a previous marriage. *Educ:* Princeton Univ. (BA Econs); Harvard Business Sch. (MBA). Lieut USNR, 1950–53. Various appts with Continental Oil, 1955–75; Area Manager, Northwest Europe, Continental Oil Co., 1975–78; Chm. and Man. Dir, Conoco Ltd, 1979–81; Vice-Pres., Internat. Marketing, Conoco Inc., 1981–85. An Hon. Consul Gen. for Sweden. *Recreations:* tennis, skiing. *Address:* 49 Briar Hollow Lane 1205, Houston, TX 77027, USA. *T:* (713) 8718907. *Clubs:* Hurlingham; River, Knickerbocker (NY); Allegheny Country (Pa); Chagrin Valley Hunt (Ohio).

FOWLER, Prof. Robert Stewart; Principal and Chief Executive, Central School of Speech and Drama, since 1986; *b* 1 Feb. 1932; *s* of William Fowler and Breta Bell Fowler (*née* Hobbs); *m* 1965, Penelope Jessie Hobbs; two *s* one *d*. *Educ:* Queen's Coll., Oxford (MA); Queen's Univ., Belfast (DipEd); Guildhall Sch. of Music and Drama (LGSM). Served RAEC, 1950–52. Asst in English, Drama and Latin, Royal Belfast Acad. Instn, 1955–58; Hd of Dept, Forest Gate Sch., 1958–60; Warden, Bretton Hall Coll., Wakefield, 1960–66; Dep. Principal and Principal Elect, Sittingbourne Coll. of Educn, 1966–76; HMI with resp. for theatre, the arts in teacher trng and staff inspector, teacher trng, 1976–86. Vis. Prof., Univ. of Central England, 1995–. FRSA 1990. *Publications:* Themes in Life and Literature, 1967; (jtly) English 11/16, 5 books, 1971–73; The Hobbit Introduced for Schools, 1973; (jtly) English: a literary foundation course, 1975. *Recreations:* living, loving, life-saving, laughing, Lake District, Provence, family, friends, writing. *Address:* Central School of Speech and Drama, Embassy Theatre, Eton Avenue, NW3 3HY. *T:* 0171–722 8183.

FOWLER, Ronald Frederick, CBE 1950; *b* 21 April 1910; *e s* of late Charles Frederick Fowler and Amy Beatrice (*née* Hollyoak); *m* 1937, Brenda Kathleen Smith. *Educ:* Bancroft's Sch.; LSE, University of London; Universities of Lille and Brussels. BCom (hons) London, 1931. Sir Ernest Cassel Travelling Scholar, 1929–30; Asst, later Lectr in Commerce, LSE, 1932–40; Central Statistical Office, 1940–50; Dir of Statistics and Under-Sec., Min. of Labour, 1950–68; Dir of Statistical Res., Dept of Employment, 1968–72. Consultant, Prices Div., Statistics Canada, Ottawa, 1971–72; Statistical Consultant, Prices Commn, 1973–77. *Publications:* The Depreciation of Capital, 1934; The Duration of Unemployment, 1968; Some Problems of Index Number Construction, 1970; Further Problems of Index Number Construction, 1973; articles in British and US economic and statistical jls. *Address:* 10 Silverdale Road, Petts Wood, Kent BR5 1NJ. *Club:* Reform.

FOWLER HOWITT, William; *see* Howitt, W. F.

FOWLES, John; writer; *b* 31 March 1926; *s* of Robert John Fowles and Gladys May Richards; *m* 1956, Elizabeth Whitton (*d* 1990). *Educ:* Bedford Sch.; New Coll., Oxford. English Centre PEN Silver Pen Award, 1969; W. H. Smith Award, 1970. *Publications:* The Collector, 1963; The Aristos, 1965; The Magus, 1966, rev. edn 1977; The French Lieutenant's Woman, 1969; Poems, 1973; The Ebony Tower, 1974 (televised, 1984); Shipwreck, 1975; Daniel Martin, 1977; Islands, 1978; (with Frank Horvat) The Tree, 1979; (ed) John Aubrey's Monumenta Britannica, parts 1 and 2, 1980, part 3 and Index, 1982; The Enigma of Stonehenge, 1980; Mantissa, 1982; Thomas Hardy's England, 1984; Land, 1985; A Maggot, 1985. *Recreations:* mainly Sabine. *Address:* c/o Anthony Sheil Associates, 43 Doughty Street, WC1N 2LF.

FOX, Dr Alan Martin; Assistant Under-Secretary of State (Quartermaster), Ministry of Defence, since 1994; *b* 5 July 1938; *s* of Sidney Nathan Fox and Clarice Solov; *m* 1965, Sheila Naomi Pollard; one *s* two *d*. *Educ:* Bancroft's Sch., Essex; Queen Mary Coll., London (BSc Hons II 1, Physics 1959; PhD Math. Phys. 1963). Home Civil Service by Open Competition, 1963; Ministry of Aviation: Private Sec. to Parly Sec., 1965–67; 1st Sec. (Aviation and Defence) on loan to FCO, Paris, 1973–75; MoD, 1975–78; RCDS, 1979; MoD, 1980–; Asst Under Sec. of State (Ordnance), 1988–92; Vis. Fellow, Center for Internat. Affairs, Harvard, 1992–93. *Recreations:* bridge, chess, watching Rugby, cricket, TV. *Address:* c/o Headquarters Quartermaster General, Monxton Road, Andover, Hants SP11 8HT.

FOX, Dr (Anthony) John; Chief Medical Statistician, since 1988, and Deputy Director, since 1990, Office of Population Censuses and Surveys; *b* 25 April 1946; *s* of Fred Frank Fox, OBE, and Gertrude Price; *m* 1971, Annemarie Revesz; one *s* two *d*. *Educ:* Dauntsey's School; University College London (BSc); Imperial College London (PhD, DIC). Statistician: Employment Medical Adv. Service, 1970–75; OPCS, 1975–79; Prof. of Social Statistics, City Univ., 1980–88. Vis. Prof., LSHTM, 1990–. *Publications:* Occupational Mortality 1970–72, 1978; Socio-Demographic Mortality Differentials, 1982; Health Inequalities in European Countries, 1989; (jtly) Health and Class: The early years, 1991. *Recreations:* family, tennis, bridge, theatre. *Address:* Office of Population Censuses and Surveys, St Catherine's House, Kingsway, WC2 6JP. *T:* 0171–242 0262.

FOX, Brian Michael; Head of Senior and Public Appointments Group (Grade 3), Cabinet Office, since 1994; *b* 21 Sept. 1944; *s* of Walter Frederick and Audrey May Fox; *m* 1966, Maureen Ann Shrimpton; one *d*. *Educ:* East Ham Grammar School for Boys. Joined CS, HM Treasury, 1963–: Private Sec. to Financial Sec., 1967–69; secondment to 3i Gp, 1981–82; Dep. Estabt Officer, 1983–87; Head of Defence Policy and Materiel Div., 1987–89; Principal Estabt and Finance Officer, 1989–93. *Recreations:* table tennis, badminton, soccer. *Address:* Cabinet Office, Horse Guards Road, SW1P 3AL. *T:* 0171–270 6220.

FOX, Edward; actor; *b* 13 April 1937; *s* of Robin and Angela Muriel Darita Fox; *m* 1958, Tracy (*née* Pelissier) (marr. diss. 1961); one *d*; and one *s* one *d* by Joanna Fox. *Educ:* Ashfold Sch.; Harrow Sch. RADA training, following National Service, 1956–58; entry into provincial repertory theatre, 1958, since when, films, TV films and plays, and plays in the theatre, have made up the sum of his working life. *Theatre includes:* Knuckle, Comedy, 1973; The Family Reunion, Vaudeville, 1979; Anyone for Denis, Whitehall, 1981; Quartermaine's Terms, Queen's, 1981; Hamlet, Young Vic, 1982; Interpreters, Queen's, 1985; Let Us Go Then, You and I, Lyric, 1987; The Admirable Crichton, Haymarket, 1988; (also dir) Another Love Story, Leicester Haymarket, 1990; The Philanthropist, Wyndham's, 1991. *Films include:* The Go-Between, 1971 (Soc. of Film and Television Arts Award for Best Supporting Actor, 1971); The Day of the Jackal, A Doll's House, 1973; Galileo, 1976; The Squeeze, A Bridge Too Far (BAFTA Award for Best Supporting Actor, 1977), The Duellists, The Cat and the Canary, 1977; Force Ten from Navarone, 1978; The Mirror Crack'd, 1980; Gandhi, 1982; Never Say Never Again, The Dresser, 1983; The Bounty, 1984; The Shooting Party, 1985. *Television series include:* Hard Times, 1977; Edward and Mrs Simpson, 1978 (BAFTA Award for Best Actor, 1978; TV Times Top Ten Award for Best Actor, 1978–79; British Broadcasting Press Guild TV Award for Best Actor, 1978; Royal TV Soc. Performance Award, 1978–79); They Never Slept, 1991. *Recreations:* music, reading, walking. *Club:* Savile.

See also J. Fox.

FOX, Hazel Mary, (Lady Fox); Editor, British Institute of International and Comparative Law, since 1989 (Director, 1982–89); *b* 22 Oct. 1928; *d* of J. M. B. Stuart, CIE; *m* 1954, Rt Hon. Sir Michael Fox, *qv*; three *s* one *d*. *Educ:* Roedean Sch.; Somerville Coll., Oxford (1st Cl. Jurisprudence, 1949; MA). Called to the Bar, Lincoln's Inn, 1950 (Buchanan Prize; Bencher, 1989); practised at the Bar, 1950–54; Lectr in Jurisprudence, Somerville Coll., Oxford, 1951–58; Lectr, Council of Legal Educn, 1962–76; Fellow of Somerville Coll., 1976–81, Hon. Fellow 1988; Vis. Lectr in Law, Oxford Univ., 1992–. Chairman: London Rent Assessment Panel, 1977–; London Leasehold Valuation Tribunal, 1981–; Mem., Home Office Deptl Cttee on Jury Service, 1963–65. Hon. QC 1993. JP London, 1959–77; Chm., Tower Hamlets Juvenile Court, 1968–76. General Editor, Internat. and Comparative Law Qly, 1987–. *Publications:* (with J. L. Simpson) International Arbitration, 1959; (ed) International Economic Law and Developing States, Vol. I 1988, Vol. II 1992; (ed) Joint Development of Offshore Oil and Gas, vol. I 1989, vol. II 1990; (ed jtly) Armed Conflict and the New Law, vol. II: Effecting Compliance, 1993. *Address:* c/o British Institute of International and Comparative Law, 17 Russell Square, WC1B 5DR. *T:* 0171–636 5802.

FOX, Sir (Henry) Murray, GBE 1974; MA, FRICS; *b* 7 June 1912; *s* of late Sir Sidney Fox and Molly Button; *m* 1941, Helen Isabella Margaret (*d* 1986), *d* of late J. B. Crichton; one *s* two *d*. *Educ:* Malvern; Emmanuel Coll., Cambridge. Chairman: Trehaven Trust Group, 1963–; City of London Sinfonia, 1983–91; Pres., City & Metropolitan Building Society, 1985–91 (Dir, 1972–85; Chm., 1976–85); Managing Trustee, Municipal Mutual Insurance Ltd, 1977–91. Dir, Toye, Kenning & Spencer Ltd, 1976–91. Governor: Christ's Hosp., 1966–82; Bridewell Royal Hosp., 1966 (Vice-Pres. 1976–82); Trustee, Morden Coll., 1976–. Court of Common Council, 1963–82; Past Master: Wheelwrights' Co.; Coopers' Co.; Alderman, Ward of Bread Street, 1966–82; Sheriff, City of London, 1971–72; Lord Mayor of London, 1974–75; one of HM Lieutenants, City of London, 1976–83. Order of Rising Sun and Sacred Treasure (Japan), 1971; Order of Stor (Afghanistan), 1971; Order of Orange Nassau (Netherlands), 1972. *Recreations:* golf, reading. *Address:* 7 Aldford Street, W1Y 5PQ. *Clubs:* City of London, City Livery (Pres. 1966–67).

FOX, James; actor; *b* 19 May 1939; *s* of Robin and Angela Fox; changed forename from William to James, 1962; *m* 1973, Mary Elizabeth Piper; four *s* one *d*. *Educ:* Harrow Sch.; Central Sch. of Speech and Drama. National Service, 1959–61. Entered acting as child, 1950; left acting to pursue Christian vocation, 1970–79; returned to acting, 1980. Main films include: The Servant, 1963; King Rat, 1964; Thoroughly Modern Millie, 1965; The Chase, 1966; Isadora, 1968; Performance, 1969; A Passage to India, 1984; Runners, 1984; Farewell to the King, 1987; Finding Mawbee (video film as The Mighty Quinn), 1988; She's Been Away, 1989; The Russia House, 1990; Afraid of the Dark, 1991; The Remains of the Day, 1993. *Publication:* Comeback: an actor's direction, 1983. *Recreations:* windsurfing, tennis. *Address:* c/o Michael Whitehall, 125 Gloucester Road, SW7 4TE.

See also E. Fox.

FOX, John; *see* Fox, A. J.

FOX, Sir (John) Marcus, Kt 1986; MBE 1963; MP (C) Shipley, since 1970; Parliamentary Under Secretary of State, Department of the Environment, 1979–81; *b* 11 June 1927; *s* of late Alfred Hirst Fox; *m* 1954, Ann, *d* of F. W. J. Tindall; one *s* one *d*. *Educ:* Wheelright Grammar Sch., Dewsbury. Mem. Dewsbury County Borough Council, 1957–65; contested (C): Dewsbury, 1959; Huddersfield West, 1966. An Asst Govt Whip, 1972–73; a Lord Comr, HM Treasury, 1973–74; Opposition Spokesman on Transport, 1975–76; Mem., Parly Select Cttee on Race Relations and Immigration, 1970–72; Sec., Cons. Party's Transport Industries Cttee, 1970–72; a Vice-Chm., Cons. Party Orgn, 1976–79; Chairman: Cttee of Selection, 1984–92; 1922 Cttee, 1992– (a Vice-Chm., 1983–92). Chm., Nat. Assoc. of Cons. Clubs, 1988–. *Recreations:* reading, tennis, walking. *Address:* House of Commons, SW1A 0AA.

FOX, Kenneth Lambert; public sector consultant, since 1986; *b* 8 Nov. 1927; *s* of J. H. Fox, Grimsby, Lincolnshire; *m* 1959, P. E. Byrne; one *d*. *Educ:* City of London Coll.; Univ. of London. BSc (Hons); FInstPS, MIIM. Plant Man., Rowntree Gp, 1950–63; Supply Man., Ford Motor Co. (UK), 1963–67; Sen. Management Conslt, Cooper & Lybrand Ltd, 1967–70; Man. of Conslts (Europe), US Science Management Corp., 1971–72; Supply Management, British Gas Corp., 1972–75; Dir of Supplies, GLC, 1975–86. *Recreations:* tennis, painting, bird watching, DIY. *Address:* 39 Parkland Avenue, Upminster RM14 2EX. *T:* Upminster (01708) 228927.

FOX, Rt. Rev. Langton Douglas, DD; retired Bishop of Menevia; *b* 21 Feb. 1917; *s* of Claude Douglas Fox and Ethel Helen (*née* Cox). *Educ:* Mark Cross, Wonersh and Maynooth. BA 1938; DD 1945. Priest 1942. Lectr, St John's Seminary, Wonersh, 1942–55; Mem., Catholic Missionary Soc., 1955–59; Parish Priest, Chichester, 1959–65; Auxiliary Bishop of Menevia, 1965–72; Bishop of Menevia, 1972–81. *Address:* Nazareth House, Hillbury Road, Wrexham, Clwyd LL13 7EU.

FOX, Dr Liam; MP (C) Woodspring, since 1992; an Assistant Government Whip, since 1994; *b* 22 Sept. 1961; *s* of William Fox and Catherine Young. *Educ:* St Bride's High Sch., E Kilbride; Univ. of Glasgow (MB ChB 1983). MRCGP 1989. General Practitioner, Beaconsfield, 1987–91; Army MO (civilian), RAEC, 1981–91; Divl Surgeon, St John's Ambulance, 1987–91. Contested (C) Roxburgh and Berwickshire, 1987. PPS to Home Sec., 1993–94. Mem., Select Cttee on Scottish Affairs, 1992; Secretary: Cons. back bench Health Cttee, 1992–93; Cons. West Country Members Group, 1992–93. *Publications:* Making Unionism Positive, 1988; (contrib.) Bearing the Standard, 1991; contrib. to House of Commons Magazine. *Recreations:* tennis, swimming, cinema, theatre. *Address:* House of Commons, SW1A 0AA. *T:* 0171–219 4086.

FOX, Sir Marcus; *see* Fox, Sir J. M.

FOX, Rt. Hon. Sir Michael John, Kt 1975; PC 1981; a Lord Justice of Appeal, 1981–92; *b* 8 Oct. 1921; *s* of late Michael Fox; *m* 1954, Hazel Mary Stuart (*see* Hazel Mary Fox); three *s* one *d*. *Educ:* Drayton Manor Sch., Hanwell; Magdalen Coll., Oxford (BCL, MA). Admiralty, 1942–45. Called to the Bar, Lincoln's Inn, 1949, Bencher, 1975; QC 1968. Judge of the High Court of Justice, Chancery Div., 1975–81.

FOX, Ven. Michael John; Archdeacon of Harlow, since 1993; *b* 28 April 1942; *s* of John and Dorothy Fox; *m* 1966, Susan Cooper; one *s* one *d*. *Educ:* Barking Abbey GS; Hull Univ. (BSc); Coll. of the Resurrection, Mirfield. Ordained deacon, 1966, priest, 1967; Curate: St Elizabeth, Becontree, 1966–70; Holy Trinity, S Woodford, 1970–72; Vicar: Ch. of the Ascension, Victoria Docks, and Missioner, Felsted Sch., 1972–76; All Saints, Chelmsford, 1976–88; Asst RD and RD, Chelmsford, 1982–88; Rector, St James, Colchester, 1988–93. Hon. Canon, Chelmsford Cathedral, 1991–. *Recreations:* walking, photography, West Ham. *Address:* Archdeacon's Office, Church Lane, Sheering, Bishop's Stortford, Essex CM22 7NR. *T:* Sheering (01279) 734524.

FOX, Sir Murray; *see* Fox, Sir H. M.

FOX, Sir Paul (Leonard), Kt 1991; CBE 1985; Chairman: Stepgrades Consultants, since 1991; The Racecourse Association Ltd, since 1993; Racecourse Technical Services, since 1994; Director: Thames Television Ltd, since 1991; British Horseracing Board, since 1993; Horseracing Betting Levy Board, since 1993; *b* 27 Oct. 1925; *m* 1948, Betty Ruth (*née* Nathan); two *s*. *Educ:* Bournemouth Grammar Sch. Served War, Parachute Regt, 1943–46. Reporter, Kentish Times, 1946; Scriptwriter, Pathé News, 1947; joined BBC Television, 1950: Scriptwriter, Television Newsreel; Editor, Sportsview, 1953, Panorama, 1961; Head, Public Affairs, 1963, Current Affairs, 1965, Controller, BBC1, 1967–73, Dir of Progs, 1973–84, Man. Dir, 1977–88, Yorkshire Television; Man. Dir, BBC Network Television, 1988–91. Chairman: ITN, 1986–88 (Dir, 1980–86); BBC Enterprises Ltd, 1988–91; Director: Trident Television, 1973–80; Channel Four, 1985–88; World Television News, 1986–88. Member: Royal Commn on Criminal Procedure, 1978–80; Inquiry into Police Responsibilities and Rewards, 1992–93. Pres., RTS, 1985–92; Member Committee: Nat. Mus. of Film, Photography and TV, 1985–95; Cinema and Television Benevolent Fund, 1986–92 (Pres., 1992–95). BAFTA Fellow, 1990. CIMgt (CBIM 1987). Hon. LLD Leeds, 1984; Hon. DLitt Bradford, 1991. Cyril Bennett Award, for outstanding television programming, 1984; Founders Award, Internat. Council, US Nat. Acad. of TV Arts and Scis, 1989. *Recreations:* television, attending race meetings. *Address:* c/o Stepgrades Consultants, 10 Charterhouse Square, EC1M 6LQ. *Club:* Garrick.

FOX, Peter Kendrew; University Librarian, University of Cambridge, and Fellow of Selwyn College, Cambridge, since 1994; *b* 23 March 1949; *s* of Thomas Kendrew Fox and Dorothy (*née* Wildbore); *m* 1983, Isobel McConnell; two *d*. *Educ:* Baines GS, Poulton-le-Fylde; King's Coll., London (BA, AKC); Sheffield Univ. (MA). MA Cantab; MA Dublin. ALA; ALAI. Cambridge University Library: grad. trainee, 1971–72; Asst Liby Officer, 1973–77; Asst Under-Librarian, 1977–78; Under-Librarian, 1978–79; Trinity College Dublin: Dep. Librarian, 1979–84; Librarian and Coll. Archivist, 1984–94. Chm., SCONUL Adv. Cttee on Inf. Services, 1987–90; Member: An Chomhairle Leabharlanna, Dublin, 1982–94; Nat. Preservation Adv. Cttee, 1984–. *Publications:* Reader Instruction Methods in British Academic Libraries, 1974; Trinity College Library, Dublin, 1982; *edited:* Treasures of the Library: Trinity College Dublin, 1986; Book of Kells: commentary vol. to facsimile edn, 1990; Proc. Internat. Confs on Library User Education, 1980, 1982, 1984; contrib. learned jls. *Address:* University Library, West Road, Cambridge CB3 9DR. *T:* Cambridge (01223) 333045; Selwyn College, Cambridge CB3 9DQ. *Club:* United Oxford & Cambridge University.

FOX, Prof. Renée Claire, PhD; FAAAS; Annenberg Professor of the Social Sciences, University of Pennsylvania, since 1969 (also Professor of: Sociology in Psychiatry, since 1969; Sociology in Medicine, since 1972; Sociology, School of Nursing, since 1978); *b* 15 Feb. 1928; *d* of Paul Fred Fox and Henrietta Gold Fox. *Educ:* Smith Coll., Northampton, Mass (BA *summa cum laude* 1949); Harvard Univ. (PhD Sociol. 1954). Teaching Fellow, Harvard Univ., 1950–51; Columbia University: Res. Asst, Bureau of Applied Social Res., 1953–55; Res. Associate, 1955–58; Barnard College, New York: Lectr in Sociol., 1955–58; Asst Prof., 1958–64; Associate Prof., 1964–66; Harvard University: Lectr in Sociol., 1967–69; Res. Fellow, Center for Internat. Affairs, 1967–68; Res. Associate, Program on Technol and Soc., 1968–71; Consultant, Social Sci. Curriculum, Lincoln Center Coll., Fordham Univ., NY, 1968–70; University of Pennsylvania: Faculty Asst to Pres., 1971–72; Chm., Dept of Sociol., 1972–78. Numerous distinguished visiting appointments and lectureships; George Eastman Vis. Prof., Oxford Univ., 1996–97. Fellow, Amer. Acad. of Arts and Letters, 1971; FAAAS 1975. *Publications:* (with W. de Craemer) The Emerging Physician: a sociological approach to the development of a Congolese medical profession, 1968; Experiment Perilous: physicians and patients facing the unknown, 1974; (with J. P. Swazey) The Courage to Fail: a social view of organ transplants and dialysis, 1974, rev. edn 1978; Essays in Medical Sociology: journeys into the field, 1979, 2nd edn 1988; (ed) The Social Meaning of Death, 1980; L'Incertitude Médicale, 1988; (jtly) Spare Parts: organ replacement in American society, 1992; The Sociology of Medicine: a participant observer's view, 1989 (trans. Korean 1993); In the Belgian Château: the spirit and culture of European society in the age of change, 1994; contrib. numerous articles on medical sociology and especially on organ donation and transplantation to scientific and learned jls worldwide. *Address:* Sociology Department, University of Pennsylvania, 3718 Locust Walk, Philadelphia, PA 19104–6299, USA. *T:* (215) 8987933; The Wellington # 1104, 135 South 19th Street, Philadelphia, PA 19103, USA. *T:* (215) 5634912.

FOX, Prof. Robert, FSA; FRHistS; Professor of the History of Science, University of Oxford, and Fellow of Linacre College, since 1988; *b* 7 Oct. 1938; *s* of Donald Fox and Audrey Hilda Fox (*née* Ramsell); *m* 1964, Catherine Mary Lilian Roper Power; three *d*. *Educ:* Doncaster Grammar Sch.; Oriel Coll., Oxford (BA 1961; MA 1965; DPhil 1967). Asst Master, Tonbridge Sch., 1961–63; Clifford Norton Junior Res. Fellow, Queen's Coll., Oxford, 1965–66; University of Lancaster: Lectr, 1966; Sen. Lectr, 1972; Reader, 1975; Prof. of History of Science, 1987. Mem., Inst. for Advanced Study, Princeton, 1974–75 and 1985; Vis. Prof. and Mem., Davis Center for Historical Studies, Princeton Univ., 1978–79; Dir, Centre de Recherche en Histoire des Sciences et des Techniques, Cité des Sciences et de l'Industrie, Paris, and Dir de recherche associé, Centre Nat. de la Recherche Scientifique, 1986–88; Asst Dir, Science Museum, 1988. Pres., Div. of History of Science, IUHPS, 1993–. *Publications:* The caloric theory of gases from Lavoisier to Regnault, 1971; Sadi Carnot: Réflexions sur la puissance motrice du feu, 1978 (trans. English 1986, German 1987, Italian 1992); (ed with George Weisz) The organization of science and technology in France 1808–1914, 1980; The culture of science in France 1700–1900, 1992; (ed with Anna Guagnini) Education, technology and industrial performance in Europe 1850–1939, 1993; Science, technology, and the social order in post-revolutionary France, 1995. *Address:* Modern History Faculty, Broad Street, Oxford OX1 3BD. *T:* Oxford (01865) 277268. *Club:* Athenæum.

FOX, Dr Robert McDougall, FRCPE; Editor, The Lancet, 1990–95; *b* 28 Dec. 1939; *s* of Sir Theodore Fortescue Fox and Margaret Evelyn McDougall; *m* 1969, Susan Clark; two *s* one *d*. *Educ:* Univ. of Edinburgh (MB ChB). MRCP 1993; FRCPE 1990. House physician, Western Gen. Hosp., Edinburgh; house surgeon, Royal Infirmary, Edinburgh; joined staff of The Lancet, 1968, Dep. Editor, 1976–90. *Recreations:* the bassoon, the hoe. *Address:* Green House, Rotherfield, Crowborough, East Sussex TN6 3QU. *T:* Crowborough (01892) 852850.

FOX, Robert Trench, (Robin), CBE 1993; Vice-Chairman, Kleinwort Benson Group, since 1989; *b* 1 Jan. 1937; *s* of Waldo Trench Fox and Janet Mary Kennedy Fox (*née* Bassett); *m* 1962, Lindsay Garrett Anderson; two *s* two *d*. *Educ:* Winchester Coll.; University Coll., Oxford (MA). FCIB, ACMA. Kleinwort Benson Group, 1961–; Director: Centro Internationale Handelsbank, 1977–; Whiteaway Laidlaw Bank, 1992–. Chairman: Export Guarantees Adv. Council, 1992–; Exec. Cttee, BBA, 1992–; Member: Deposit Protection Bd, 1990–, Overseas Projects Bd, 1988–; Fedn Bancaire de la Communauté Européene, 1991–. Chm. Council, City Univ. Business Sch., 1991–. *Recreations:* sailing, shooting, theatre, reading. *Address:* Kleinwort Benson, 20 Fenchurch Street, EC3P 3DB. *T:* 0171–623 8000. *Clubs:* Brooks's; Royal Cornwall Yacht.

FOX, Robin James L.; *see* Lane Fox.

FOX, Roy, CMG 1980; OBE 1967; HM Diplomatic Service, retired; consultant with various companies; *b* 1 Sept. 1920; *s* of J. S. and A. Fox; *m* 1st, 1943, Sybil Verity; two *s* one *d*; 2nd, 1975, Susan Rogers Turner; 3rd, 1995, Jean Mary Hayes. *Educ:* Wheelwright Grammar Sch., Dewsbury; Bradford Technical Coll. Served in RNVR, 1940–46. Bd of Trade, 1947–58; British Trade Commissioner: Nairobi, 1958–60; Montreal, 1960–62; Winnipeg, 1962–64; Dep. Controller, Bd of Trade Office for Scotland, 1964–65. First Sec. Commercial, Karachi, 1965–68; Deputy High Comr, E Pakistan, 1968–70; Consul-Gen. and Comm. Counsellor, Helsinki, 1970–74; promoted to Minister, 1977; Consul-Gen., Houston, 1974–80. *Recreations:* golf, reading, tennis. *Club:* Royal Automobile.

FOX, Ruth W.; *see* Winston-Fox.

FOX, Prof. Wallace, CMG 1973; MD, FRCP, FFPHM; Professor of Community Therapeutics, Cardiothoracic Institute, Brompton Hospital, 1979–86, now Emeritus; Director, Medical Research Council Tuberculosis and Chest Diseases Unit, Brompton Hospital, 1965–86; Hon. Consultant Physician, Brompton Hospital, 1969–86; WHO Consultant, since 1961; *b* 7 Nov. 1920; *s* of Samuel and Esther Fox; *m* 1956, Gaye Judith Akker; three *s*. *Educ:* Cotham Grammar Sch., Bristol; Guy's Hosp. MB, BS (London) 1943; MRCS, LRCP, 1943; MRCP 1950; MD (Dist.) (London) 1951; FRCP 1962; FFPHM (FFCM 1976). Ho. Phys., Guy's USA Hosp., 1945–46; Resident Phys., Preston Hall Sanatorium, 1946–50; Registrar, Guy's Hosp., 1950–51; Asst Chest Physician, Hammersmith Chest Clinic, 1951–52; Mem. Scientific Staff of MRC Tuberculosis and Chest Diseases Unit, 1952–56, 1961–65; seconded to WHO, to establish and direct Tuberculosis Chemotherapy Centre, Madras, 1956–61; Dir, WHO Collaborating Centre for Tuberculosis Chemotherapy and its Application, 1976–87. Lectures: Marc Daniels, RCP, 1962; First John Barnwell Meml, US Veterans Admin, 1968; Philip Ellman, RSocMed, 1976; Martyrs Meml, Bangladesh Med. Assoc., 1977; first Quezon Meml, Philippine Coll. of Chest Physicians, 1977; Morriston Davies Meml, BTA, 1981; Mitchell, RCP, 1982; E. Merck Oration, Indian Chest Soc., 1983; A. J. S. McFadzean, Univ. of Hong Kong, 1986; Ranbaxy–Robert Koch Oration, Tuberculosis Assoc. of India, 1989. Waring Vis. Prof. in Medicine, Univ. of Colorado and Stanford Univ., 1974. Mem. Tropical Med. Research Bd, 1968–72; Mem., several MRC Cttees; Member: WHO Expert Adv. Panel on Tuberculosis, 1965–91; BCG Vaccination Sub-Cttee, Min. of Health, 1968–; Mem. Council, Chest, Heart & Stroke Assoc., 1974–90; International Union Against Tuberculosis: Mem., later Chm., Cttee of Therapy, 1964–71; Associate Mem., Scientific Cttees, 1973; Mem., Exec. Cttee, 1973–85 (Chm., 1973–77). Chm., Acid Fast Club, 1971–72. Editor, Advances in Tuberculosis Research. Elected Corresp. Mem., Amer. Thoracic Soc., 1962; Mem., Mexican Acad. of Medicine, 1976; Hon. Life Mem., Canadian Thoracic Soc., 1976; Corresp. Mem., Argentine Nat. Acad. of Medicine, 1977; Corresp. For. Member: Argentine Soc. of Phtisiol. and Thoracic Pathol., 1977; Coll. of Univ. Med. Phtisiologists of Argentine, 1978; Hon. Member: Argentine Med. Assoc., 1977; Singapore Thoracic Soc., 1978. Sir Robert Philip Medal, Chest and Heart

Assoc., 1969; Weber Parkes Prize, RCP, 1973; Carlo Forlanini Gold Medal, Fedn Ital. contra la Tubercolosi e le Malattie Polmonari Sociali, 1976; Hon. Medal, Czech. Med. Soc., 1980; Robert Koch Centenary Medal, Internat. Union against Tuberculosis, 1982; Presidential Citation Award, Amer. Coll. of Chest Physicians, 1982; Presidential Commendation, Amer. Thoracic Soc., 1989. *Publications:* Reports on tuberculosis services in Hong Kong to Hong Kong Government: Heaf/Fox, 1962; Scadding/Fox, 1975; Fox/Kilpatrick, 1990; contribs to med. jls: on methodology of controlled clinical trials, on epidemiology and on chemotherapy, particularly in tuberculosis, and carcinoma of the bronchus. *Address:* 28 Mount Ararat Road, Richmond, Surrey TW10 6PG. *T:* 0181–940 9662.

FOX, Winifred Marjorie, (Mrs E. Gray Debros); Under-Secretary, Department of the Environment, 1970–76; *d* of Frederick Charles Fox and Charlotte Marion Ogborn; *m* 1953, Eustachy Gray Debros (*d* 1954); one *d. Educ:* Streatham County Sch.; St Hugh's Coll., Oxford. Unemployment Assistance Board, 1937; Cabinet Office, 1942; Ministry of Town and Country Planning, 1944; Ministry of Housing and Local Govt, 1952 (Under-Sec., 1963); Dept of the Environment, 1970; seconded to CSD as Chm., CS Selection Bd, 1971–72. *Address:* 2 The Pryors, East Heath Road, Hampstead, NW3 1BS. *T:* 0171–435 4962.

FOX-ANDREWS, His Honour James Roland Blake; QC 1968; a Circuit Judge (Official Referee), 1985–94; *b* 24 March 1922; step *s* of late Norman Roy Fox-Andrews, QC; *m* 1950, Angela Bridget Swift (*d* 1991); two *s. Educ:* Stowe; Pembroke Coll., Cambridge. FCIArb. RNVR, 1940–46. Called to the Bar, Gray's Inn, 1949, Bencher, 1974. Dep. Chm., Devon QS, 1970–71; Recorder of Winchester, 1971, Hon. Recorder, 1972; a Recorder of Crown Court, 1972–85. Leader, Western Circuit, 1982–84. Member: Gen. Council of the Bar, 1968–72; Senate of Inns of Court and the Bar, 1976–79. Editor, Inst. of Arbitrators Jl, 1950–54. *Publications:* (jtly) Leasehold Property (Temporary Provisions) Act, 1951; contrib. Halsbury's Laws of England, 3rd edn, building contracts, architects and engineers; (jtly) Landlord and Tenant Act, 1954; Business Tenancies, 1970, 5th edn 1995; (jtly) Assured Tenancies, 1989. *Address:* 20 Cheyne Gardens, SW3 5QT. *T:* 0171–352 9484; Lepe House, Exbury, Hants SO4 1AD. *T:* Southampton (01703) 891648.

FOX BASSETT, Nigel; Commissioner, Building Societies Commission, since 1993; Director, London First, since 1993; Senior Partner, Clifford Chance, 1990–93; *b* 1 Nov. 1929; *s* of Thomas Fox Bassett and Catherine Adriana Wiffen; *m* 1961, Patricia Anne Lambourne; one *s* one *d. Educ:* Taunton Sch.; Trinity Coll., Cambridge (MA Hons History and Law). Articled, Coward Chance, 1953; admitted Solicitor, 1956; Partner, 1960. Member: Council, British Inst. of Internat. and Comparative Law, 1977– (Chm., Exec. Cttee, 1986–); Council, British Gp, Internat. Assoc. for Protection of Indust. Property, 1984–89; Council, British Branch, Internat. Law Assoc., 1971–86 (Chm., Cttee on Internat. Securities Regulation, 1989–93); Business Section, Internat. Bar Assoc., 1969–93; European Gp, Law Soc., 1969–93; Cttee, Amer. Bar Assoc., 1979–93; Deleg., Banking and Finance Mission to Poland, 1989. Mem. Council, London Chamber of Commerce and Industry, 1993–. Liveryman, City of London Solicitors' Co. Pres. Council, Taunton Sch., 1994– (Mem. Council, 1985–). Mem., charitable, sports, opera concerns. *Publications:* (contrib.) Branches and Subsidiaries in the European Common Market, 1976; (contrib.) Business Law in Europe, 1982, 2nd edn 1990; articles in law professional jls. *Recreations:* shooting, beagling, cricket, art, opera. *Address:* 200 Aldersgate Street, EC1A 4JJ. *T:* 0171–600 1000. *Clubs:* Garrick, City of London, Pilgrims, MCC; Seaview Yacht.

FOX-STRANGWAYS, family name of **Earl of Ilchester.**

FOXALL, Colin, CBE 1995; Managing Director and Chief Executive, NCM Credit Insurance Ltd, since 1991; *b* 6 Feb. 1947; *s* of Alfred George Foxall and Ethel Margaret Foxall; *m* 1980, Diana Gail Bewick; two *s. Educ:* Gillingham Grammar Sch., Kent. MIEx; MICM. Joined ECGD, 1966; Dept of Trade, 1974; ECGD, 1975–91: Underwriter, Eastern Bloc, 1975; Dep. Hd, For. Currency Branch, 1977; Hd, Financial Planning, 1979; Asst Sec., ME Project Gp, 1982; Under Sec., and Dir of Comprehensive Guarantee, subseq. Insce Services, Gp, 1986–91. *Recreations:* family, home, clay target shooting, cycling. *Address:* c/o NCM Credit Insurance Ltd, Crown Building, Cathays Park, Cardiff CF1 3PX.

FOXELL, Clive Arthur Peirson, CBE 1987; FEng 1985; consultant; Managing Director, Engineering and Procurement, and Board Member, British Telecom, 1986–89; *b* 27 Feb. 1930; *s* of Arthur Turner Foxell and Lillian (*née* Ellerman); *m* 1956, Shirley Ann Patey Morris; one *d. Educ:* Harrow High Sch.; Univ. of London. BSc; FIEE, FInstP, FCIPS. GEC Res. Labs, 1947; Man., GEC Semiconductor Labs, 1968; Man. Dir, GEC Semiconductors Ltd, 1971; Dep. Dir of Research, PO, 1975; Dep. Dir, PO Procurement Exec., 1978–79; Dir of Purchasing, PO, 1980; British Telecom: Dir of Procurement, 1981, Senior Dir, 1984, Chief Exec., Procurement, 1984; Dir, British Telecommunications Systems Ltd, 1982–89. Chairman: Fulcrum Communications Ltd, 1985–86; TSCR Ltd, 1986–88; Phonepoint Ltd, 1989–93; Dir, BT&D Technologies Ltd, 1986–88. Member: Council, IEE, 1975–78, 1982–85, and 1987– (Vice-Chm., Electronics Div., 1980–81, Dep. Chm., 1982–83, Chm., 1983–84); SERC (formerly SRC) Engrg Bd, 1977–80 (Chm., Silicon Working Party, 1980–81; Chm., Microelectronics, 1982–86); SERC, 1986–90; NEDC (electronics), 1987–90; ACARD Working Party on IT, 1981. Pres., Mobile Radio Trng Trust, 1991–95. President: IBTE, 1987–90; Inst. of Physics, 1992–94. Hon. Treas., Nat. Electronics Council, 1994–. Bulgin Premium, IERE, 1964. Liveryman, Engineers' Co. Hon. DSc Southampton, 1994. *Publications:* Low Noise Microwave Amplifiers, 1968; articles and papers on electronics. *Recreations:* photography, steam railways. *Address:* 4 Meades Lane, Chesham, Bucks HP5 1ND. *T:* Chesham (01494) 785737.

FOXLEE, James Brazier; Under Secretary, Ministry of Agriculture, Fisheries and Food, 1971–81, retired; *b* 20 Nov. 1921; *s* of late Arthur Brazier Foxlee and late Mary Foxlee (*née* Fisher); *m* 1952, Vera June (*née* Guiver); one *s* two *d. Educ:* Brentwood Sch. Entered Min. of Agric. and Fisheries (later MAFF) as Clerical Officer, 1938. Served War, RNVR, Ordinary Seaman, 1941; commissioned, 1942; Lieut, in comd Light Coastal Forces craft and mine-sweepers. MAFF: Exec. Officer, 1946; HEO, 1948; SEO, 1950; Principal, 1955 (Welsh Dept, 1955–57; Treas., 1961–62); Asst Sec., 1965 (Regional Controller, Leeds, 1965–69). Hon. Fellow, NIAB, 1982; Hon. Mem., Arable Res. Inst. Assoc., 1990. *Recreations:* watching cricket, camping, oenology. *Address:* Arran, 43 Foxley Lane, Purley, Surrey CR8 3EH. *T:* 0181–660 1085.

FOXLEY-NORRIS, Air Chief Marshal Sir Christopher (Neil), GCB 1973 (KCB 1969; CB 1966); DSO 1945; OBE 1956; Chairman: Cheshire Foundation, 1974–82, now Chairman Emeritus (Vice-Chairman, 1972–74); Battle of Britain Fighter Association, since 1978; Gardening for the Disabled, since 1980; *b* 16 March 1917; *s* of Major J. P. Foxley-Norris and Dorothy Brabant Smith; *m* 1948, Joan Lovell Hughes; no *c. Educ:* Winchester (schol.); Trinity Coll., Oxford (schol.; Hon. Fellow, 1973); Middle Temple (Harmsworth Schol.). Commissioned RAFO, 1936; France, 1940; Battle of Britain, 1940; various operational tours of duty in wartime. MA 1946. ACDS, 1963; AOC No 224 Gp, FEAF, 1964–67; Dir-Gen., RAF Organization, MoD, 1967–68; C-in-C, RAF Germany and Comdr, NATO 2nd Tactical Air Force, 1968–70; Chief of Personnel and Logistics, MoD, 1971–74; retd. Vice Pres., RUSI, 1979. Chairman: Trinity Coll. Oxford Soc., 1984–86; Ex RAF and Dependants Severely Disabled Holiday Trust, 1984. Pres., Leonard Cheshire Housing Assoc., 1978–. CIMgt. *Publications:* A Lighter Shade of Blue, 1978; various in RUSI and other service jls. *Recreations:* golf, philately. *Address:* Tumble Wood, Northend Common, Henley-on-Thames RG9 6LJ. *T:* Turville Heath (0149163) 8457. *Clubs:* Royal Air Force; Huntercombe (Oxon).

FOXON, David Fairweather, FBA 1978; Reader in Textual Criticism and Fellow of Wadham College, Oxford, 1968–82, now Emeritus Fellow; *b* 9 Jan. 1923; *s* of late Rev. Walter Foxon and Susan Mary (*née* Fairweather); *m* 1947, Dorothy June (marr. diss. 1963) (*d* 1988), *d* of late Sir Arthur Jarratt, KCVO; one *d. Educ:* Kingswood Sch., Bath; Magdalen Coll., Oxford. BA 1948, MA 1953. Foreign Office, 1942–45; Asst Keeper, Dept of Printed Books, British Museum, 1950–65; Harkness Fellow, 1959–61; Professor of English, Queen's Univ., Kingston, Ontario, 1965–67; Guggenheim Fellow, 1967–68. Sen. Res. Fellow, Clark Library, UCLA, 1974–75; Lyell Reader in Bibliography, Oxford, 1975–76; Sandars Reader in Bibliography, Cambridge, 1977–78. Pres., Bibliographical Soc., 1980–81 (Gold Medal, 1985). Hon. Mem., Bibliographical Soc. of America, 1986. John H. Jenkins Award for Bibliography, 1977. *Publications:* T. J. Wise and the Pre-Restoration Drama, 1959; Libertine Literature in England, 1660–1745, 1964; (ed) English Bibliographical Sources, 1964–67; English Verse 1701–1750: a catalogue, 1975; Pope and the Early Eighteenth-century Book Trade, ed J. McLaverty, 1991; contribs to bibliographical jls. *Recreation:* music. *Address:* 7 Fane Road, Marston, Oxford OX3 0RZ. *T:* Oxford (01865) 248350.

FOXON, Harold Peter, OBE 1976; Group Managing Director, Inchcape plc, 1981–84 (Director, since 1971; a Managing Director, 1978); *b* 7 April 1919; *s* of William Henry Foxon and Kathleen Avis (*née* Perry); *m* 1948, Elizabeth Mary Butterfield; one *s* three *d. Educ:* Bancroft's. Served War, 1939–46, Royal Signals, Captain. Insurance, 1935–39; Smith Mackenzie & Co. Ltd (East Africa), 1946–69; Chm., Mackenzie Dalgety Ltd, 1966–69; Man. Dir, Gilman & Co. Ltd, Hong Kong, and Chm., Inchcape Hong Kong Ltd, 1969–77. Director: Dodwell & Co., Ltd, 1978–81; Anglo-Thai Corpn, 1978–82; Berry Trust Ltd, 1977–88; Member: Hong Kong Trade Adv. Gp, 1978–84; South East Asia Trade Adv. Gp, 1978–82. Master, Barbers' Co., 1986–87. *Recreation:* golf. *Address:* 48 Abingdon Court, Abingdon Villas, W8 6BT. *T:* 0171–937 8713; Tanglin, Second Avenue, Frinton-on-Sea, Essex CO13 9LX. *T:* Frinton (01255) 672208. *Clubs:* City of London, Oriental; Muthaiga (Kenya); Hong Kong (Hong Kong).

FOXTON, Maj.-Gen. Edwin Frederick, CB 1969; OBE 1959; MA; Fellow and Domestic Bursar, Emmanuel College, Cambridge, 1969–79; *b* 28 Feb. 1914; *y s* of F. Foxton and T. Wilson; unmarried. *Educ:* Worksop Coll.; St Edmund Hall, Oxford. Commissioned from General List TA, 1937; served: India, 1939–42; Middle East, 1942–45; India, 1945–47 (Chief Educn Officer, Southern Comd, India); War Office, 1948–52; Chief Instructor, Army Sch. of Educn, 1952–55; Dist Educn Officer, HQ Northumbrian District, 1955–57; War Office, 1957–60; Commandant, Army Sch. of Educn, 1961–63; War Office, 1963–65; Chief Educn Officer, FARELF, 1965; Dir of Army Educn, 1965–69. *Address:* South Close, North Dalton, Driffield, East Yorks YO25 9XA.

FOYLE, Christina Agnes Lilian, (Mrs Ronald Batty); Managing Director, W. & G. Foyle Ltd; *d* of late William Alfred Foyle; *m* 1938, Ronald Batty (*d* 1994). *Educ:* Aux Villas Unspunnen, Wilderswil, Switzerland. Began Foyle's Literary Luncheons, 1930, where book lovers have been able to see and hear great personalities. Member: Ct, Univ. of Essex; Council, RSA, 1963–69; Chm. East Anglian Region, RSA, 1978; Pres. Chelmsford District, Nat. Trust, 1979. DUniv Essex, 1975. *Publications:* So Much Wisdom, 1984; articles in various books and journals. *Recreations:* bird-watching, gardening, playing the piano. *Address:* Beeleigh Abbey, Maldon, Essex CM9 6LL.

FOZARD, Prof. John William, OBE 1981; FRS 1987; FEng 1984; FRAeS, FAIAA; consultant, writer, teacher; *b* 16 Jan. 1928; *s* of John Fozard and Eleanor Paulkit; *m* 1st, 1951, Mary (marr. diss. 1985), *d* of Regtl Sgt-Major C. B. Ward, VC, KOYLI; two *s*; 2nd, 1985, Gloria Ditmars Stanchfield Roberts, *widow* of Alan Roberts, Alexandria, Va, USA. *Educ:* Univ. of London (1st Cl. Hons BScEng 1948); Coll. of Aeronautics, Cranfield (DCAe with distinction 1950). FIMechE 1971; FRAeS 1964; FAIAA 1981. Hawker Aircraft Ltd: Design Engr, 1950; Head of Proj. Office, 1960; Hawker Siddeley Aviation: Chief Designer, Harrier, 1963–78; Exec. Dir, 1971; Marketing Dir, Kingston Brough Div., BAe, 1978–84; Divl Dir, Special Projects, Mil. Aircraft Div., BAe, 1984–87, retd 1989. Visiting Professor: Sch. of Mechanical, Aeronautical and Production Engrg, Kingston Polytech., 1982–87; Aircraft Design, RMCS, Shrivenham, 1986–87; Lindbergh Prof. of Aerospace Hist., Nat. Air and Space Mus., Smithsonian Instn, Washington, 1988; Vis. Lectr, Univ. of Michigan, 1989; Lectures: 1st J. D. North Meml, RAeS Wolverhampton Br., 1969, and 16th, 1985; 23rd R. J. Mitchell Meml, RAeS Southampton Br., 1976; 32nd Barnwell Meml, RAeS Bristol Br., 1982; 2nd Lindbergh Meml, Nat. Air & Space Museum, Smithsonian Instn, 1978, 12th Lindbergh Meml, 1988; Friday Evening Discourse, Royal Instn, 1986; 9th Sir Sydney Camm Meml, RAeS, 1987; Sir Izaac Newton series to young people around UK, IMechE, 1979–80; over 200 learned soc. lectures in UK, USA, Europe, Australia, China, 1965–. Vice Pres., 1980–85, Pres.-elect, 1985–86, Pres., 1986–87, RAeS. Hon. DSc Strathclyde, 1983. Simms Gold Medal, Soc. of Engrs, 1971; British Silver Medal for Aeronautics, 1977; James Clayton Prize, IMechE, 1983; Mullard Award (with R. S. Hooper), Royal Soc., 1983. *Publications:* (ed) Sydney Camm and the Hurricane, 1991; papers in aeronautical jls and in specialist press, 1954–. *Recreations:* music, engineering history. *Address:* 306 North Columbus Street, Alexandria, VA 22314–2414, USA. *T:* (703) 5495142.

FRAENKEL, Prof. Ludwig Edward, FRS 1993; Professor of Mathematics, School of Mathematical Sciences, University of Bath, since 1988; *b* 28 May 1927; *s* of Eduard David Mortier Fraenkel and Ruth (*née* von Velsen); *m* 1954, Beryl Jacqueline Margaret Currie; two *d. Educ:* Dragon Sch., Oxford; Univ. of Toronto Schs; Univ. of Toronto (BASc 1947; MASc 1948); MA Cantab 1964. SO, RAE, Farnborough, 1948–52; Res. Fellow, Univ. of Glasgow, 1952–53; Imperial College, London: Lectr, Aeronautics Dept, 1953–58, Reader 1958–61; Reader, Mathematics Dept, 1961–64; Lectr in Applied Maths, Univ. of Cambridge, 1964–75; Fellow, Queens' Coll., Cambridge, 1964–68; Prof., Maths Div., Univ. of Sussex, 1975–88. Sen. Whitehead Prize, London Math. Soc., 1989. *Publications:* some 60 papers in jls ranging from Aeronautical Qly to Acta Mathematica. *Recreations:* ski-ing, cycling. *Address:* School of Mathematical Sciences, University of Bath, Bath BA2 7AY. *T:* Bath (01225) 826249. *Club:* Ski of Great Britain.

FRAENKEL, Peter Maurice, FEng, FICE, FIStructE, FIHT; Founder and Senior Partner, Peter Fraenkel & Partners, since 1972; Chairman, Peter Fraenkel Maritime Ltd, since 1995; Director, Peter Fraenkel BMT Ltd, since 1990 (Chairman, 1990–93); *b* 5 July 1915; *s* of Ernest Fraenkel and Luise (*née* Tessmann); *m* 1946, Hilda Muriel, *d* of William Norman; two *d. Educ:* Battersea Polytechnic; Imperial Coll., London. BSc(Eng). FICE 1954, FIStructE 1954, MConsE 1962; FEng 1984; FIHT 1992. Asst Engr with London firm of contractors, engaged on design and construction of marine and industrial structures, 1937–40; served in Army, 1941–42; Works Services Br., War Dept, 1942–45; Rendel, Palmer & Tritton, Cons. Engineers: Civil Engr, 1945; Sen. Engr, 1953; Partner, 1961–72. Dir, British Maritime Technology, 1990–. Has been responsible for, or closely associated with, technical and management aspects of many feasibility and planning studies, and planning, design and supervision of construction of large civil engrg projects, incl. ports, docks, offshore terminals, inland waterways, highways, power stations and tunnels in Gt Britain, Middle East, India, Far East and Australia, including: new Oil port at Sullom Voe, Shetland; new Naval Dockyard, Bangkok; Shatin to Tai Po coastal Trunk Road, Hong Kong; comprehensive study for DoE, of maintenance and operational needs of canals controlled by Brit. Waterways Bd (Fraenkel Report), and new port at Limassol, Cyprus. James Watt Medal, 1963, Telford Gold Medal, 1971, ICE. *Publications:* (jtly) papers to Instn of Civil Engrs: Special Features of the Civil Engineering Works at Aberthaw Power Station, 1962; Planning and Design of Port Talbot Harbour, 1970. *Address:* Little Paddock, Oxted, Surrey RH8 0EL. *T:* Oxted (01883) 712927. *Club:* Athenæum.

FRAGA-IRIBARNE, Manuel; Founder-Member, People's Party (formerly People's Alliance), Spain, 1976, Leader, 1979–86; Member of the Cortes, since 1977; *b* 23 Nov. 1922; *m* 1948, María del Carmen Estévez; two *s* three *d*. *Educ:* Insts of Coruña, Villalba and Lugo; Univs of Santiago de Compostela and Madrid. Prof. of Polit. Law, Univ. of Valencia, 1945; Prof. of Polit. Sci. and Constit. Law, Univ. of Madrid, 1953; Legal Adviser to the Cortes, 1945; entered Diplomatic Service, 1945; Sec.-Gen., Instituto de Cultura Hispánica, 1951; Sec.-Gen. in Min. of Educn, 1953; Head, Inst. of Polit. Studies, 1961; Minister of Information and Tourism, 1961–69; Ambassador to UK, 1973–75; Interior Minister, Spain, 1975–76; Leader of the Opposition, 1982–86. Pres., Galician Govt, 1979–. Holds numerous foreign orders. *Publications:* various books on law, polit. sci., history and sociology, incl. one on British Parlt. *Recreations:* shooting, fishing. *Address:* Pazo de Raxoi, Plaza del Obradoiro, Santiago de Compostela, La Coruña, Spain.

FRAME, David William; Chairman and Senior Executive, Usborne Grain (formerly Usborne & Son (London)), since 1968; Chief Executive and Deputy Chairman, Usborne plc (formerly Feedex), since 1987; Member, Baltic Exchange, since 1961 (Chairman, 1987–89); *b* 26 July 1934; *s* of William and Ursula Frame; *m* 1963, Margaret Anne Morrison; two *d*. *Educ:* Wellington College. Commissioned Royal Artillery, National Service. Qualified Chartered Accountant, 1960; joined Usborne & Son (London), 1961, Dir 1962; Dir, Usborne and Feedex subsid. cos and other cos. *Recreation:* golf (played for GB and Ireland in Walker Cup, 1961, for England, 1958–63). *Address:* Green Glades, Frensham Vale, Farnham, Surrey GU10 3HT. *T:* Frensham (01252) 793272. *Golf Clubs:* Royal and Ancient, Worplesdon, Trevose, Hankley Common, Old Thorns, Plettenberg Bay.

FRAME, Frank Riddell; Adviser to the Board, HSBC Holdings plc, since 1990; *b* 15 Feb. 1930; *s* of William Graham Frame; *m* 1958, Maureen Milligan; one *s* one *d*. *Educ:* Hamilton Academy; Univ. of Glasgow (MA, LLB); admitted solicitor, 1955. North of Scotland Hydro-Electric Board, 1955–60; UK Atomic Energy Authority, 1960–68; The Weir Group plc, 1968–76 (Dir, 1971–76); joined The Hongkong and Shanghai Banking Corp., as Gp Legal Adviser, 1977, Exec. Dir, 1985, Dep. Chm., 1986–90. Chm., Wallem Group Ltd, 1992–; Director: Baxter Internat. Inc., 1992–; Edinburgh Dragon Trust plc, 1994–; formerly Chairman: South China Morning Post Ltd; Far Eastern Economic Review Ltd; formerly Director: Marine Midland Banks Inc.; The British Bank of the Middle East; Swire Pacific Ltd; Consolidated Press Internat. Ltd; Securities and Futures Commn, Hong Kong. *Publication:* The Law relating to Nuclear Energy, 1966. *Address:* 43 Shrewsbury House, Cheyne Walk, SW3 5LW. *T:* 0171–352 3968. *Clubs:* Brooks's; Hong Kong (Hong Kong).

FRAME, Rt Rev. John Timothy, DD; Dean of Columbia and Rector of Christ Church Cathedral, Victoria, BC, 1980–95; *b* 8 Dec. 1930; *m*; three *d*. *Educ:* Univ. of Toronto. Burns Lake Mission, Dio. Caledonia, 1957; Hon. Canon of Caledonia, 1965; Bishop of Yukon, 1968–80. *Address:* 2173 Tull Avenue, Courtenay, BC V9N 7S1, Canada.

FRAME, Ronald William Sutherland; author; *b* 23 May 1953; *s* of Alexander D. Frame and Isobel D. Frame (*née* Sutherland). *Educ:* High Sch. of Glasgow; Univ. of Glasgow (MA Hons); Jesus Coll., Oxford (BLitt). Full-time author, 1981–; first Betty Trask Prize (jtly), 1984; Samuel Beckett Prize, 1986; Television Industries' Panel's Most Promising Writer New to TV Award, 1986. *Publications:* Winter Journey, 1984; Watching Mrs Gordon, 1985; A Long Weekend with Marcel Proust, 1986; Sandmouth People, 1987; Paris (TV play), 1987; A Woman of Judah, 1987; Penelope's Hat, 1989; Bluette, 1990; Underwood and After, 1991; Walking My Mistress in Deauville, 1992; The Sun on the Wall, 1994. *Recreations:* swimming, walking. *Address:* c/o Curtis Brown Ltd, 28/29 Haymarket, SW1Y 4SP. *Club:* Royal Scottish Automobile (Glasgow).

FRANCE, Sir Arnold William, GCB 1972 (KCB 1965; CB 1957); retired; *b* 20 April 1911; *s* of late W. E. France; *m* 1940, Frances Margaret Linton, *d* of late Dr C. J. L. Palmer; four *d*. *Educ:* Bishop's Stortford Coll. District Bank, Ltd, 1929–40. Served War of 1939–45, Army, 1940–43; Deputy Economic and Financial Adviser to Minister of State in Middle East, 1943; HM Treasury, 1945; Asst Sec., 1948; Under Sec., 1952; Third Sec., 1960; Ministry of Health: Dep. Sec., 1963–64; Permanent Sec., 1964–68; Chm., Bd of Inland Revenue, 1968–73. Director: Pilkington Bros, 1973–81; Tube Investments, 1973–81; Rank Organisation, 1973–83. Chm., Central Bd of Finance, C of E, 1973–78. Chm., Bd of Management, Lingfield Hosp. Sch., 1973–81. *Address:* Thornton Cottage, Lingfield, Surrey RH7 6BT. *T:* Lingfield (01342) 832278. *Club:* Reform.

See also J. N. B. Penny.

FRANCE, Sir Christopher (Walter), GCB 1994 (KCB 1989; CB 1984); Staff Counsellor for the Security and Intelligence Services, since 1995; *b* 2 April 1934; *s* of W. J. and E. M. France; *m* 1961, Valerie (*née* Larman) (*see* V. E. France); one *s* one *d*. *Educ:* East Ham Grammar Sch.; New College, Oxford (BA (PPE), DipEd). CDipAF. HM Treasury, 1959–84: Principal Private Secretary to the Chancellor of the Exchequer, 1973–76; Principal Establishment Officer, 1977–80; on secondment to Electricity Council, 1980–81; Dep. Sec., 1981; on secondment to MoD, 1981–84; Dep. Sec., 1984–86, Second Perm. Sec., 1986, Perm. Sec., 1987–92, DHSS, subseq. DoH; Perm. Sec., MoD, 1992–95. Mem. Council, QMW, 1994–. *Recreations:* keeping the house up and the garden down. *Address:* c/o Barclays Bank, 80 High Street, Sevenoaks TN13 1LR. *Club:* Reform.

FRANCE, Elizabeth Irene; Data Protection Registrar, since 1994; *b* 1 Feb. 1950; *d* of Ralph Salem and Elizabeth Joan Salem (*née* Bryan); *m* 1971, Dr Michael William France; two *s* one *d*. *Educ:* Beauchamp Sch., Leics; UCW, Aberystwyth. Home Office: Admin Trainee, 1971; Principal, 1977; Asst Sec., 1986; Police Dept, Criminal Justice and Constitutional Dept, IT and Pay Services, 1986–94. *Recreations:* ski-ing, squash, cooking. *Address:* Office of the Data Protection Registrar, Wycliffe House, Water Lane, Wilmslow, Cheshire SK9 5AF. *T:* Wilmslow (01625) 535711.

FRANCE, Prof. Peter, DPhil; FBA 1989; Professor of French, 1980–90, now Emeritus, and University Endowment Fellow, since 1990, University of Edinburgh; *b* 19 Oct. 1935; *s* of Edgar France and Doris Woosnam Morgan; *m* 1961, Siân Reynolds; three *d*. *Educ:* Bridlington Sch.; Bradford Grammar Sch.; Magdalen Coll., Oxford (MA; DPhil). Lectr, then Reader, in French, Univ. of Sussex, 1963–80. French Editor, MLR, 1979–85. Mem., Chuvash Nat. Acad. Officer de l'Ordre des Palmes Académiques (France). *Publications:* Racine's Rhetoric, 1965; Rhetoric and Truth in France, 1972; Poets of Modern Russia, 1982; Racine: Andromaque, 1977; Diderot, 1983; Rousseau: Confessions, 1987; trans., An Anthology of Chuvash Poetry, 1991; Politeness and its Discontents, 1992; (ed) New Oxford Companion to Literature in French, 1995. *Address:* 10 Dryden Place, Edinburgh EH9 1RP. *T:* 0131–667 1177.

See also Rev. R. T. France.

FRANCE, Rev. Richard Thomas; Rector, Wentnor with Ratlinghope, Myndtown, Norbury, More, Lydham and Snead, diocese of Hereford, since 1995; *b* 2 April 1938; *s* of Edgar and Doris Woosnam France; *m* 1965, Barbara Wilding; one *s* one *d*. *Educ:* Bradford Grammar School; Balliol Coll., Oxford (MA); BD London; PhD Bristol. Asst Curate, St Matthew's Church, Cambridge, 1966–69; Lectr in Biblical Studies, Univ. of Ife, Nigeria, 1969–73; Tyndale House, Cambridge: Librarian, 1973–76; Warden, 1978–81; London Bible College: Senior Lectr, 1981–88; Vice-Principal, 1983–88; Principal, Wycliffe Hall, Oxford, 1989–95. Hon. Canon Theologian, Ibadan Cathedral, 1994–. *Publications:* Jesus and the Old Testament, 1971; (ed with D. Wenham) Gospel Perspectives, vols 1–3, 1980–83; The Gospel According to Matthew: an introduction and commentary, 1985; The Evidence for Jesus, 1986; Matthew: evangelist and teacher, 1989; Divine Government, 1990; (ed with A. E. McGrath) Evangelical Anglicans, 1993; Women in the Church's Ministry, 1995. *Recreations:* mountains, wildlife, travel, music. *Address:* The Rectory, Wentnor, Bishop's Castle, Shropshire SY9 5EE. *T:* and *Fax:* Linley (01588) 650244.

See also P. France.

FRANCE, Valerie Edith, (Lady France), OBE 1994; MA; Headmistress, City of London School for Girls, 1986–95; *b* 29 Oct. 1935; *d* of Neville and Edith Larman; *m* 1961, Sir Christopher Walter France, *qv*; one *s* one *d*. *Educ:* St Hugh's Coll., Oxford (MA); CertEd Cantab. Deputy Headmistress, Bromley High Sch., GPDST, 1984–86. Freeman, City of London, 1988. *Recreations:* family, friends, places. *Address:* c/o Barclays Bank, 80 High Street, Sevenoaks, Kent TN13 1LR.

FRANCIS, Clare Mary, MBE 1978; *b* 17 April 1946; *d* of Owen Francis, *qv*; *m* 1977, Jacques Robert Redon (marr. diss. 1985); one *s*. *Educ:* Royal Ballet Sch.; University Coll. London (BScEcon; Hon. Fellow, 1979). Crossed Atlantic singlehanded, Falmouth to Newport, in 37 days, 1973; Round Britain Race, 1974; Azores Race, 1975; L'Aurore Race, 1975, 1976; Observer Transatlantic Singlehanded Race: women's record (29 days), 1976; Whitbread Round the World Race (fully-crewed), first woman skipper, 1977–78. Hon. Fellow, UMIST, 1981. *Television series:* The Commanding Sea (BBC), 1981 (co-writer and presenter). *Publications: non-fiction:* Come Hell or High Water, 1977; Come Wind or Weather, 1978; The Commanding Sea, 1981; *novels:* Night Sky, 1983; Red Crystal, 1985; Wolf Winter, 1987; Requiem, 1991; Deceit, 1993; Betrayal, 1995. *Recreations:* opera, theatre, catching up. *Address:* c/o John Johnson Agency, 45–47 Clerkenwell Green, EC1R 0HT.

FRANCIS, Dick, (Richard Stanley), OBE 1984; author; *b* 31 Oct. 1920; *s* of George Vincent Francis and Catherine Mary Francis; *m* 1947, Mary Margaret Brenchley; two *s*. *Educ:* Maidenhead County Boys' School. Pilot, RAF, 1940–45 (Flying Officer). Amateur National Hunt jockey, 1946–48, Professional, 1948–57; Champion Jockey, season 1953–54. Racing Correspondent, Sunday Express, 1957–73. Hon. LHD Tufts, 1991. *Publications:* Sport of Queens (autobiog.), 1957, 3rd updated edn, 1982; Dead Cert, 1962; Nerve, 1964; For Kicks, 1965; Odds Against, 1965; Flying Finish, 1966; Blood Sport, 1967; Forfeit, 1968 (Edgar Allan Poe Award, 1970); Enquiry, 1969; Rat Race, 1970; Bonecrack, 1971; Smoke Screen, 1972; Slay-Ride, 1973; Knock Down, 1974; High Stakes, 1975; In the Frame, 1976; Risk, 1977; Trial Run, 1978; Whip Hand, 1979 (Golden Dagger Award, Crime Writers' Assoc., 1980; Edgar Allan Poe Award, 1980); Reflex, 1980; Twice Shy, 1981; Banker, 1982; The Danger, 1983; Proof, 1984; Break In, 1985; Lester, the official biography, 1986; Bolt, 1986; Hot Money, 1987; The Edge, 1988; Straight, 1989; Longshot, 1990; Comeback, 1991; (ed jtly) Great Racing Stories, 1989; Driving Force, 1992; Decider, 1993; Wild Horses, 1994; Come to Grief, 1995. *Recreations:* boating, travel. *Address:* PO Box 30866 SMB, Grand Cayman, West Indies. *T:* 9475947, *Fax:* 9475949.

FRANCIS, Prof. Edward Howel, DSc; FRSE; CGeol; FGS; Professor of Earth Sciences, University of Leeds, 1977–89; *b* 31 May 1924; *s* of Thomas Howel Francis and Gwendoline Amelia (*née* Richards); *m* 1952, Cynthia Mary (*née* Williams); one *d*. *Educ:* Port Talbot County Sch.; Univ. of Wales, Swansea (BSc, DSc; Hon. Fellow 1989). FGS 1948; FRSE 1962. Served Army, 1944–47. Geological Survey of Great Britain (now incorporated in British Geol Survey): Field Geologist, Scotland, 1949–62; Dist Geologist, NE England, 1962–67, N Wales, 1967–70; Asst Dir, Northern England and Wales, 1971–77. Geological Society of London: Murchison Fund, 1963; Mem. Council, 1972–74; Pres., 1980–82; Pres., Section C (Geol.), BAAS, 1976; Mem., Inst. of Geol., 1978. Clough Medal, Edinburgh Geol Soc., 1983; Sorby Medal, Yorks Geol Soc., 1983; Major John Sacheverell A'Deane Coke Medal, Geol Soc. of London, 1989. *Publications:* memoirs, book chapters and papers on coalfields, palaeovolcanic rocks and general stratigraphy, mainly of Britain. *Recreations:* opera, golf. *Address:* Michaelston, 11 Millbeck Green, Collingham, near Wetherby, W Yorks LS22 5AJ. *Club:* Sand Moor Golf.

FRANCIS, Ven. Edward Reginald; Archdeacon of Bromley, 1979–94, Emeritus since 1994; *b* 31 Jan. 1929; *s* of Alfred John and Elsie Hilda Francis; *m* 1950, Joyce Noreen Atkins; three *s*. *Educ:* Maidstone and Dover Grammar Schools; Rochester Theological College. National Service, RAF, 1947–49. Insurance, including period at Chartered Insurance Inst. (ACII), 1950–59. Ordained, 1961; Chaplain, Training Ship Arethusa, and Curate of All Saints, Frindsbury, 1961–64; Vicar of St William's, Chatham, 1964–73; Vicar and Rural Dean of Rochester, 1973–78. Mem., General Synod of C of E, 1981–94. Mem., Kent Industrial Mission, 1979–89; Jt Chm., Council for Social Responsibility, Dioceses of Canterbury and Rochester, 1983–89; Dir of Continuing Ministry Educn, dio. of Rochester, 1989–94. *Recreations:* ornithology, walking, music. *Address:* 71 Ash Tree Drive, West Kingsdown, Sevenoaks, Kent TN15 6LW. *T:* West Kingsdown (01474) 853202.

FRANCIS, Gwyn Jones, CB 1990; Director-General and Deputy Chairman, Forestry Commission, 1986–90, retired; *b* 17 Sept. 1930; *s* of Daniel Brynmor Francis and Margaret Jane Francis; *m* 1st, 1954, Margaretta Meryl Jeremy (*d* 1985); one *s* one *d* (and one *s* decd); 2nd, 1986, Audrey Gertrude (*née* Gill). *Educ:* Llanelli Grammar Sch.; University Coll. of N Wales, Bangor (BSc Hons 1952); Univ. of Toronto (MSc 1965). Served RE, 1952–54. Forestry Commission: Dist Officer, 1954; Principal, Forester Training Sch., 1962; Asst Conservator, 1969; Head, Harvesting and Marketing Div., 1976; Comr, 1983–86. Chm., Scottish Adv. Cttee, RSPB, 1992–. FICFor 1982; FIWSc 1984. *Recreations:* ornithology, gardening, walking. *Address:* 21 Campbell Road, Edinburgh EH12 6DT. *T:* 0131–337 5037. *Club:* New (Edinburgh).

FRANCIS, Sir (Horace) William (Alexander), Kt 1989; CBE 1976; FEng 1977; FICE; Director, British Railways Board, since 1994; Chairman, Fitzpatrick International Ltd, since 1993; Director: Peakbeam Ltd, since 1985; Tysons, since 1988; J. F. Donelon, since 1989; Donelon Tyson PLC, since 1989; Universal Project Business Ltd, since 1992; Mining (Scotland) Ltd, since 1995; *b* 31 Aug. 1926; *s* of Horace Fairie Francis and Jane McMinn Murray; *m* 1949, Gwendoline Maud Dorricott; two *s* two *d*. *Educ:* Royal Technical Coll., Glasgow. Dir, Tarmac Civil Engineering Ltd, 1960; Man. Dir, Tarmac Construction Ltd, 1963; Dir, Tarmac Ltd, 1964, Vice-Chm., 1974–77; Director: Trafalgar House Ltd, 1978–84; Trafalgar House Construction Hldgs, 1979–84; Chm., Fitzpatrick plc, 1990–92. Member: Export Guarantees Adv. Council, 1974–80; British Overseas Trade Bd, 1977–80; Chairman: Overseas Projects Bd, 1977–80; Black Country UDC, 1987–94. Mem., Engrg Council, 1995–. Pres., ICE, 1987–88 (Vice-Pres., 1984–87). Lt-Col, Engr and Transport Staff Corps, TA, 1986. FRSA 1989. Hon. LLD Strathclyde, 1988; Hon. DSc Aston, 1990. *Recreations:* golf, shooting, fishing, construction. *Address:* The Firs, Cruckton, near Shrewsbury, Shropshire SY5 8PW. *T:* Shrewsbury (01743) 860796. *Clubs:* Livery, Royal Over-Seas League.

FRANCIS, Dr John Michael, FRSE; Assistant Secretary, The Scottish Office Environment Department, since 1992; *b* 1 May 1939; *s* of late William Winston Francis and of Beryl Margaret Francis (*née* Savage); *m* 1963, Eileen Sykes, Cyncoed, Cardiff; two *d*. *Educ:* Gowerton County Grammar Sch.; Royal Coll. of Sci., Imperial Coll. of Sci. and Tech., Univ. of London (BSc, ARCS, PhD, DIC). FRIC 1969; FRSGS 1990; FRSE 1991; FRZSScot 1992. Res. Officer, CEGB, R&D Dept, Berkeley Nuclear Labs, 1963–70; First Dir, Society, Religion and Tech. Project, Church of Scotland, 1970–74; Sen. Res. Fellow in Energy Studies, Heriot-Watt Univ., 1974–76; Scottish Office, Edinburgh, 1976–84; Dir Scotland, Nature Conservancy Council, 1984–91 (Mem., Adv. Cttee for Scotland, 1974–76); Chief Exec., NCC for Scotland, 1991–92. Member: Oil Develt Council for Scotland, 1973–76; Indep. Commn on Transport, 1974; Adv. Cttee on Marine Fishfarming Crown Estate Commn, 1989–92. Chm., Francis Group (Consultants), 1992–. Consultant on Sci., Tech. and Social Ethics, WCC, Geneva, 1971–83; Chm., Cttee on Society, Religion and Tech., Church of Scotland, 1980–94. Chm., Edinburgh Forum, 1984–93. Mem. Council, Nat. Trust for Scotland, 1985–92. Mem., St Giles' Cathedral, Edinburgh. Associate, Scottish Inst. of Human Relations, 1974–; Fellow, Inst. for Advanced Studies in the Humanities, Edinburgh Univ., 1988; Vis. Fellow, Centre for Values and Social Policy, Univ. of Colorado at Boulder, 1991. Professional Mem., World Futures Soc., Washington DC, 1991–. Mem., John Muir Trust, 1994–. *Publications:* Scotland in Turmoil, 1973; (jtly) Changing Directions, 1974; (jtly) The Future as an Academic Discipline, 1975; Facing up to Nuclear Power, 1976; (jtly) The Future of Scotland, 1977; (jtly) North Sea Oil and the Environment, 1992; contribs to scientific and professional jls and periodicals. *Recreations:* rethinking environmental values and ethics, ecumenical travels, hill walking, theatre. *Address:* 49 Gilmour Road, Newington, Edinburgh EH16 5NU. *T:* 0131–667 3996.

FRANCIS, Sir Laurie (Justice), Kt 1982; New Zealand High Commissioner to Australia, 1976–85; barrister and solicitor, High Court of New Zealand, as Consultant to Farry & Co., Solicitors, Dunedin, since 1985; Commissioner of Oaths for Australian States, including Northern Territory, since 1985; *b* 30 Aug. 1918; *m* 1952, Heather Margaret McFarlane; three *d*. *Educ:* Otago Boys High Sch.; Victoria University of Wellington; Univ. of Otago (LLB). Practised law as Barrister and Solicitor, Winton, Southland, until 1964; Senior Partner, Dunedin firm of Gilbert, Francis, Jackson and Co., Barristers and Solicitors, 1964–76. Hon. Life Mem., RSL, 1984. *Recreations:* golf occasionally, follower of Rugby and cricket, lover of jazz. *Address:* 42 Glengyle Street, Dunedin, New Zealand. *Club:* Dunedin (Fernhill).

FRANCIS, Norman; *see* Francis, W. N.

FRANCIS, Owen, CB 1960; Chairman, London Electricity Board, 1972–76; *b* 4 Oct. 1912; *yr s* of Sidney and Margaret Francis, The White House, Austwick, Yorks; *m* 1938, Joan St Leger (*née* Norman); two *d*. *Educ:* Giggleswick Sch., Yorks. Joined Govt Actuary's Dept, 1931. *Address:* Meadow Cottage, Stanford Dingley, Berks RG7 6LT. *T:* Bradfield (01734) 744394. *Clubs:* Royal Yacht Squadron; Seaview Yacht; St Moritz Tobogganing.
See also C. M. Francis.

FRANCIS, Very Rev. Peter Brereton; Provost and Rector of St Mary's Cathedral, Glasgow, since 1992; *b* 18 June 1953; *s* of Richard and Pauline Francis; *m* 1976, Denise Steele. *Educ:* Malvern Coll.; St Andrews Univ. (MTh 1977); Queen's Coll., Birmingham. Ordained deacon, 1978, priest, 1979; Curate, Hagley, Worcs, 1978–81; Chaplain, QMC, 1981–87; Rector, Holy Trinity, Ayr, 1987–92. *Recreations:* cinema, theatre, cricket. *Address:* 45 Rowallan Gardens, Glasgow G11 7LH. *T:* 0141–339 4956, *Fax:* 0141–357 4544.

FRANCIS, Richard Mark; art historian and consultant; Chief Curator, Museum of Contemporary Art, Chicago, since 1993; *b* 20 Nov. 1947; *s* of Ralph Lawrence and Eileen Francis; *m* 1976, Tamar Janine Helen Burchill; one *d*. *Educ:* Oakham Sch.; Cambridge Univ.; Courtauld Inst. Walker Art Gall., Liverpool, 1971–72; Arts Council of GB, 1973–80; Asst Keeper, Tate Gall., London, 1980–86; Curator, Tate Gall., Liverpool, 1986–90. *Publication:* Jasper Johns, 1984. *Address:* Museum of Contemporary Art, 237 East Ontario Street, Chicago, IL 60611, USA. *T:* (312) 2802668.

FRANCIS, Richard Stanley; *see* Francis, Dick.

FRANCIS, Robert Anthony; QC 1992; *b* 4 April 1950; *s* of John Grimwade Francis and Jean Isobel Francis; *m* 1976, Catherine Georgievsky; one *s* two *d*. *Educ:* Uppingham Sch.; Exeter Univ. (LLB Hons). Pres., Exeter Univ. Guild of Students, 1971–72. Called to the Bar, Inner Temple, 1973. Legal Assessor, Chartered Soc. of Physiotherapists, 1991. Trustee, Peper Harow Orgn, 1992. Churchwarden, St John's Parish Church, Milford, Surrey, 1984–92. *Recreation:* cricket. *Address:* 3 Serjeants' Inn, EC4Y 1BQ. *T:* 0171–353 5537. *Clubs:* Travellers; Brook Cricket, Chiddingfold Cricket.

FRANCIS, Sir William; *see* Francis, Sir H. W. A.

FRANCIS, William Lancelot, CBE 1961; *b* 16 Sept. 1906; *s* of G. J. Francis and Ethel, *d* of L. G. Reed, Durham; *m* 1st, 1937, Ursula Mary Matthew (*d* 1966); two *s* three *d*; 2nd, 1968, Margaret Morris (*d* 1978). *Educ:* Latymer Upper Sch., Hammersmith; King's Coll., Cambridge. MA, PhD. DSIR Sen. Research Award, Cambridge, 1931–33; Rockefeller Foundn Fellowship in Experimental Zoology, Rockefeller Institute, New York, 1933–34; Science Master, Repton Sch., 1935–40; Radar research and administration in Ministries of Supply and Aircraft Production (TRE Malvern), 1940–45; Dept of Scientific and Industrial Res. Headquarters, 1945–65; Secretary, Science Research Council, 1965–72; Consultant, Civil Service Dept, 1972–75. Member: Nat. Electronics Council, 1965–72; CERN, 1966–70; Advisory Councils: R&D, Fuel and Power, 1966–72; Iron and Steel, 1966–72. Mem. Council, Oxfam, 1975–83. *Publications:* papers on physical chemistry and experimental zoology in scientific jls, 1931–37. *Recreations:* gardening, travel. *Address:* 269 Sheen Lane, SW14 8RN. *T:* 0181–876 3029. *Club:* Athenæum.

FRANCIS, His Honour (William) Norman; a Circuit Judge (formerly Judge of County Courts), 1969–93; *b* 19 March 1921; *s* of Llewellyn Francis; *m* 1951, Anthea Constance (*née* Kerry); one *s* one *d*. *Educ:* Bradfield; Lincoln Coll., Oxford (BCL, MA). Served War of 1939–45, RA. Called to Bar, Gray's Inn, 1946. Dep. Chm., Brecknock QS, 1962–71. Member: Criminal Law Revision Cttee, 1977–; Policy Adv. Cttee on Sexual Offences, 1977–85; County Court Rule Cttee, 1983–88 (Chm., 1987–88). Pres., Council of HM Circuit Judges, 1987. Chancellor, dio. of Llandaff, 1979–. Mem. Governing Body, Church in Wales. Fellow, Woodard Corp. (Western Div.), 1985–91. *Recreation:* walking. *Address:* 2 The Woodlands, Lisvane, near Cardiff CF4 5SW. *T:* Cardiff (01222) 753070.

FRANCKLIN, Comdr (Mavourn Baldwin) Philip, DSC 1940; RN; JP; Lord-Lieutenant of Nottinghamshire, 1972–83 (Vice-Lieutenant, 1968–72); *b* 15 Jan. 1913; *s* of Captain Philip Francklin, MVO, RN (killed in action, 1914); *m* 1949, Xenia Alexandra, *d* of Alexander Davidson, Kilpedder, Co. Wicklow; two *s* one *d* (and one *s* decd). *Educ:* RNC Dartmouth. Joined RN, 1926. Served War of 1939–45: Norway, N and S Atlantic, Indian Ocean (despatches twice); Asst to 5th Sea Lord, 1947–49; Comdr 1950; Korean War, 1950–51; Asst Naval Attaché, Paris, 1952–53. DL, 1963, JP 1958, Notts; High Sheriff of Notts, 1965. KStJ 1973. Croix de Guerre (France). *Address:* Gonalston Hall, Nottingham NG14 7JA. *T:* Nottingham (0115) 966 3635. *Club:* Boodle's.

FRANÇOIS-PONCET, Jean André; Member of the French Senate, since 1983 (Chairman of the Economic Committee, since 1986); Director, FMC Corporation, since 1982; *b* 8 Dec. 1928; *s* of André François-Poncet, Grand'Croix de la Légion d'Honneur, and Jacqueline (*née* Dillais); *m* 1959, Marie-Thérèse de Mitry; two *s* one *d*. *Educ:* Paris Law Sch.; Ecole Nationale d'Administration; Wesleyan Univ.; Fletcher Sch. of Law and Diplomacy. Joined Ministry of Foreign Affairs, 1955; Office of Sec. of State, 1956–58; Sec. Gen. of French delegn to Treaty negotiations for EEC and Euratom, 1956–58; Dep. Head, European Orgns, Ministry of Foreign Affairs, 1958–60; Head of Assistance Mission, Morocco, 1961–63; Dep. Head, African Affairs, 1963–65; Counsellor, Tehran, 1969–71. Professor, Institut d'Etudes Politiques, Paris, 1960–. Chm. 1971, Vice-Pres. 1972, Pres. and Chief Exec. 1973–75, Carnaud SA. Sec. of State for Foreign Affairs, Jan.-July 1976; Sec.-Gen. to Presidency of France, 1976–78; Minister for Foreign Affairs, 1978–81. President: Conseil Général of Lot-et-Garonne, 1978– (Member, from Laplume, 1967–); Comité du bassin Adour-Garonne, 1980–. *Publication:* The Economic Policy of Western Germany, 1970. *Address:* 6 boulevard Suchet, 75116 Paris, France.

FRANCOME, John, MBE 1986; first jockey to F. T. Winter, 1975–85; *b* 13 Dec. 1952; *s* of Norman and Lillian Francome; *m* 1976, Miriam Strigner. *Educ:* Park Senior High School, Swindon. First ride, Dec. 1970; Champion Jockey (National Hunt), 1975–76, 1978–79, 1980–81, 1981–82, 1982–83, 1983–84, 1984–85; record number of jumping winners (1,036), May 1984; retired March 1985 (1138 winners). *Publications:* Born Lucky (autobiog.), 1985; How to Make Money Betting—or at least how not to lose too much, 1986; Twice Lucky: the lighter side of steeplechasing, 1988; *novels* (with James MacGregor): Eavesdropper, 1986; Riding High, 1987; Declared Dead, 1988; Bloodstock, 1989. *Recreations:* tennis, music. *Address:* Trabbs Farm, Seven Barrows, Lambourn, Berks RG16 7UF.

FRANK, Air Vice-Marshal Alan Donald, CB 1967; CBE 1962; DSO 1943; DFC 1941; Bursar, St Antony's College, Oxford, 1970–74; *b* 27 July 1917; *s* of late Major N. G. Frank and late M. H. Frank (*née* Donald); *m* 1941, Jessica Ann Tyrrell; two *s* two *d*. *Educ:* Eton; Magdalen Coll., Oxford. Commanded 51 Squadron Bomber Command, 1943; RAF Staff Coll., 1944; OC 83 Sqdn, 1957; OC RAF Honington, 1958–60; Group Captain Ops, Bomber Comd, 1960–62; Dir Operational Requirements, MoD, 1962–65; Air Attaché and OC, RAF Staff, Washington, 1965–68; SASO, RAF Air Support Command, 1968–70. *Recreations:* music, gardening. *Address:* Roundway House, Devizes, Wilts SN10 2EG.

FRANK, Sir Andrew; *see* Frank, Sir R. A.

FRANK, Sir Charles; *see* Frank, Sir F. C.

FRANK, Sir Douglas (George Horace), Kt 1976; QC 1964; Deputy Judge of the High Court, Queen's Bench Division, 1976–89; *b* 16 April 1916; *s* of late George Maurice Frank and late Agnes Winifred Frank; *m* 1979, Audrey, MA (Cantab), *yr d* of late Charles Leslie Thomas, Neath, Glam; one *s* four *d* by former marriage. War service in Royal Artillery (TA): BEF, France, 1939–40. Called to the Bar, Gray's Inn, 1946 (Master of the Bench, 1970; Master of Moots, 1978–83; Master of Estate, 1982–84); established first Barristers' Chambers in Gray's Inn, 1966. One time Asst Commissioner, Parly Boundary Commission for England; Pres., Lands Tribunal, 1974–88. Mem., Cttee Public Participation in Planning (Min. Housing and Local Govt), 1968. Conducted Brixham Marina Inquiry, 1987. Mem., Senate of Inns of Court and Bar, 1984–85. Chm., Planning and Local Govt Cttee of the Bar, 1966–73. Leader, Bar Delegn to IBA Conf., Tokyo, 1970. Hon. Pres., Anglo-American Real Property Inst., 1980–90. *Publications:* various legal. *Recreations:* theatre, music, walking. *Address:* La Mayne-Longue-Haute, Sauveterre-La-Lémance, 47500 Fumel, France. *T:* 53406898; 10 South Square, Gray's Inn, WC1R 5EU. *T:* 0171–242 2937.

FRANK, Sir (Frederick) Charles, Kt 1977; OBE 1946; FRS 1954; DPhil; Henry Overton Wills Professor of Physics and Director of the H. H. Wills Physics Laboratory, University of Bristol, 1969–76 (Professor in Physics, 1954–69); now Emeritus Professor; *b* 6 March 1911; *e s* of Frederick and Medora Frank; *m* 1940, Maia Maita Asché, *y d* of late Prof. B. M. Asché; no *c*. *Educ:* Thetford Grammar Sch.; Ipswich Sch.; Lincoln Coll., Oxford. BA, BSc, Oxon. 1933; DPhil Oxon. 1937; Hon. Fellow, Lincoln Coll., 1968. Research: Dyson Perrins Laboratory and Engineering Laboratory, Oxford, 1933–36; Kaiser Wilhelm Institut für Physik, Berlin, 1936–38; Colloid Science Laboratory, Cambridge, 1939–40; Scientific Civil Service (temp.), 1940–46; Chemical Defence Research Establishment, 1940, Air Ministry, 1940–46; Research, H. H. Wills Physical Laboratory, Bristol Univ., 1946–; Research Fellow in Theoretical Physics, 1948; Reader in Physics, 1951–54; Vis. Prof., Univ. of California, San Diego, Inst. of Geophysics and Planetary Physics, and Dept of Physics, 1964–65; Raman Prof., Raman Res. Inst., Bangalore, 1979–80. A Vice-Pres., Royal Society, 1967–69. Foreign Associate: US Nat. Acad. of Engineering, 1980; Royal Soc. of S Africa, 1986; US Nat. Acad. of Sci., 1987. Hon. FIP 1978; Hon. FIASc 1984; Hon. Fellow, Bristol Univ., 1986. Hon. DSc: Ghent, 1955; Bath, 1974; TCD, 1978; Warwick, 1981; Leeds, 1992; DUniv Surrey, 1977. Docteur *hc* Univ. de Paris-Sud, 1986. Holweck Prize, French Physical Soc., 1963; Crystal Growth Award, Amer. Assoc. for Crystal Growth, 1978; Royal Medal, Royal Soc., 1979; Grigori Aminoff Gold Medal, Royal Swedish Acad. of Sciences, 1981; Guthrie Medal and Prize, Inst. of Physics, 1982; Robert Mehl Award, Amer. Metallurgical Soc., 1987; Von Hippel Award, Amer. Materials Res. Soc., 1988; Copley Medal, Royal Soc., 1994. *Publications:* (ed and introd) Operation Epsilon: the Farm Hall transcripts, 1993; articles in various learned journals, mostly dealing either with dielectrics or the physics of solids, in particular crystal dislocations, crystal growth, mechanical properties of polymers and mechanics of the earth's crust. *Address:* Orchard Cottage, Grove Road, Coombe Dingle, Bristol BS9 2RL. *T:* Bristol (0117) 968 1708. *Club:* Athenæum.

FRANK, Sir (Robert) Andrew, 4th Bt *cr* 1920, of Withyham, Co. Sussex; producer, since 1986; *b* 16 May 1964; *s* of Sir Robert John Frank, 3rd Bt, FRICS, and of Margaret Joyce, *d* of Herbert Victor Truesdale; *S* father, 1987; *m* 1990, Zoë, *er d* of S. A. Hasan. *Educ:* Ludgrove Prep. School; Eton College. *Recreations:* travel, theatre, cinema. *Heir:* none.

FRANKEL, Dr Hans Ludwig, OBE 1993; FRCP; Consultant in Spinal Injuries, since 1966 and Clinical Director, since 1993, National Spinal Injuries Centre, Stoke Mandeville Hospital; *b* 7 April 1932; *s* of late Dr Paul Frankel, CBE and Helen Frankel; *m* 1956, Mavis Anne Richardson; two *s*. *Educ:* Dauntsey's Sch.; University Coll. London; University Coll. Hosp. Med. Sch. (MB BS 1956). MRCS 1956; LRCP 1956, MRCP 1964, FRCP 1977. Casualty officer, Hampstead Gen. Hosp., 1957; Stoke Mandeville Hospital, 1957–: Hse Physician, 1957–58; National Spinal Injuries Centre: Registrar, 1958–62; Sen. Registrar, 1962–66; Dep. Dir, 1969–77; Mem., Exec. Bd, 1991–. Hon. Consultant, Star & Garter Home, Richmond, 1979–. Member: Editorial Board: Paraplegia; Annales de Readaptation et de Medecine Physique; Clinical Autonomic Res.; Editl Adv. Bd, Annals of Sports Medicine. Buckinghamshire Area Health Authority: Vice-Chm., 1976–77, Chm., 1978–80, Med. Adv. Cttee. International Medical Society of Paraplegia: Hon. Treas., 1966–78; Hon. Sec., 1976–87; Vice Pres., 1987–91; Chm., Scientific Cttee, 1992–. President: Brit. Cervical Spine Soc., 1990–92; Chiltern Gp, Spinal Injuries Assoc., 1989–. Mem., Exec. Cttee, Brit. Paraplegic Sports Soc., 1977–91. Chm. Trustees, Internat. Spinal Res. Trust, 1983–; Mem., Mgt Council, Brit. Neurol Res. Trust, 1989–. Numerous lectures in UK, Europe, USA and throughout the world, incl. Arnott Demonstrator, RCS 1987, Sandoz Lectr, Inst. of Neurol., London, 1988 and 1992. *Publications:* (ed) volume on Spinal Cord Injuries in Handbook of Clinical Neurology, 1992; contrib. chapters on spinal cord injuries to text books. *Recreations:* ski-ing, opera. *Address:* National Spinal Injuries Centre, Stoke Mandeville Hospital, Mandeville Road, Aylesbury, Bucks HP21 8AL. *T:* Aylesbury (01296) 315852.

FRANKEL, Prof. Herbert; *see* Frankel, Prof. S. H.

FRANKEL, Sir Otto (Herzberg), Kt 1966; DSc; DAgr; FRS 1953; FRSNZ; FAA; Honorary Research Fellow, Division of Plant Industry, CSIRO, Canberra, Australia, since 1966; *b* 4 Nov. 1900; *m* 1939, Margaret Anderson. *Educ:* Vienna; Berlin; Cambridge. Plant Geneticist, 1929–42, and Chief Executive Officer, 1942–49, Wheat Research Institute, NZ; Dir, Crop Research Division, Dept of Scientific and Industrial Research, New Zealand, 1949–51; Chief, Division of Plant Industry, CSIRO, Australia, 1951–62; Member of Executive, Commonwealth Scientific and Industrial Research Organization, Melbourne, Aust, 1962–66. Hon. Mem., Japan Academy, 1983; For. Associate, US Nat. Acad. of Scis, 1988. *Publications:* (ed jtly) Genetic Resources in Plants: their exploration and conservation, 1970; (ed jtly) Crop Genetic Resources for Today and Tomorrow, 1975; (with M. E. Soulé) Conservation and Evolution, 1981; (ed jtly) The Use of Plant Genetic Resources, 1989; numerous articles in British, NZ and Australian scientific journals. *Recreations:* ski-ing, gardening, angling. *Address:* 4 Cobby Street, Campbell, Canberra, ACT 2601, Australia. *T:* (6) 2479460.

FRANKEL, Prof. (Sally) Herbert, MA Rand, PhD London, DScEcon London, MA Oxon; Emeritus Professor in the Economics of Underdeveloped Countries, University of Oxford, and Emeritus Fellow, Nuffield College, Oxford (Professor, and Professorial Fellow, 1946–71); *b* 22 Nov. 1903; *e s* of Jacob Frankel; *m* 1928, Ilse Jeanette Frankel; one *s* one *d*. *Educ:* St John's Coll., Johannesburg; University of the Witwatersrand; London Sch. of Economics. Prof. of Economics, University of Witwatersrand, Johannesburg, 1931–46; responsible for calculations of National Income of S Africa for the Treasury, 1941–48; Jt Editor of South African Journal of Economics from its inception to 1946; Mem. of Union of South Africa Treasury Advisory Council on Economic and Financial Policy, 1941–45; Mem. of Union of South Africa Miners' Phthisis Commission, 1941–42; Commissioner appointed by Govts of Southern and Northern Rhodesia and the Bechuanaland Protectorate to report upon Rhodesia Railways Ltd, 1942–43; Chm. Commission of Enquiry into Mining Industry of Southern Rhodesia, 1945; Mem. East Africa Royal Commission, 1953–55; Consultant Adviser, Urban African Affairs Commn, Govt of S Rhodesia, 1957–58. Vis. Prof. of Econs, Univ. of Virginia, until 1974. Mem., Mont Pellerin Soc., 1950–. Chm., Bd of Governors, Oxford Centre for Postgrad. Hebrew Studies, 1983–89. Hon. DSc Econ Rhodes Univ., 1969; Hon. DLitt Rand Univ., 1970. *Publications:* Co-operation and Competition in the Marketing of Maize in South Africa, 1926; The Railway Policy of South Africa, 1928; Coming of Age: Studies in South African Citizenship and Politics (with Mr J. H. Hofmeyr and others), 1930; Capital Investment in Africa: Its Course and Effects, 1938; The Economic Impact on Underdeveloped Societies: Essays on International Investment and Social Change, 1953; Investment and the Return to Equity Capital in the South African Gold Mining Industry 1887–1965: An International Comparison, 1967; Gold and International Equity Investment (Hobart Paper 45), 1969; Money: two philosophies, the conflict of trust and authority, 1977; Money and Liberty, 1980; An Economist's Testimony: the autobiography of S. Herbert Frankel, 1992. *Recreation:* gardening. *Address:* 62 Cutteslowe House, Park Close, Oxford OX2 8NP. *T:* Oxford (01865) 514748. *Club:* Reform.

FRANKEL, William, CBE 1970; Editor, Jewish Chronicle, 1958–77; *b* 3 Feb. 1917; *s* of Isaac and Anna Frankel, London; *m* 1st, 1939, Gertrude Freda Reed (marr. diss.); one *s* (one *d* decd); 2nd, 1973, Mrs Claire Neuman. *Educ:* elementary and secondary schs in London; London Univ. (LLB Hons). Called to Bar, Middle Temple, 1944; practised on South-Eastern circuit, 1944–55. General Manager, Jewish Chronicle, 1955–58. Special Adviser to The Times, 1977–81. Chm., Jewish Chronicle Ltd, 1991–94 (Dir, 1959–95). Chairman: Mental Health Review Appeal Tribunal, 1978–89; Social Security Appeal Tribunal, 1979–89. Vis. Prof., Jewish Theological Seminary of America, 1968–69. Vice-Pres., Inst. of Jewish Affairs, 1993–. Emeritus Gov., Oxford Centre for Hebrew Studies; Trustee, Jewish Youth Fund, 1979–94. JP Co. of London, 1963–69. *Publications:* (ed) Friday Nights, 1973; Israel Observed, 1980; (ed) Survey of Jewish Affairs (annual), 1982–92. *Address:* 30 Montagu Square, W1H 1RJ. *T:* (office) 0171–935 3052; (home) 0171–935 1202. *Clubs:* Athenæum, MCC.

FRANKHAM, Very Rev. Harold Edward; Provost of Southwark, 1970–82, now Provost Emeritus; *b* 6 April 1911; *s* of Edward and Minnie Frankham; *m* 1942, Margaret Jean Annear; one *s* two *d* (and one *s* decd). *Educ:* London Coll. of Divinity (LCD). Ordained, 1941; Curate: Luton, 1941–44; Holy Trinity, Brompton, 1944–46; Vicar of Addiscombe, 1946–52; Rector of Middleton, Lancs, 1952–61; Vicar of Luton, 1961–70. Hon. Canon of St Albans, 1967–70. Exec. Sec., Archbishops' Council on Evangelism, 1965–73. *Recreations:* music, travel. *Address:* 3 Harnleigh Green, 80 Harnham Road, Salisbury SP2 8JN. *T:* Salisbury (01722) 321846.

FRANKL, Peter; pianist; *b* Hungary, 2 Oct 1935; *s* of Laura and Tibor Frankl; *m* 1958, Annie Feiner; one *s* one *d*. *Educ:* Liszt Ferenc Acad. of Music, Budapest. First Prize, several internat. competitions; London début, 1962; New York début, with Cleveland Orch. under George Szell, 1967; performances with Berlin Philharmonic, Amsterdam Concertgebouw, Israel Phil., Leipzig Gewandhaus, and with all London and major Amer. orchs. Vis. Prof. of Piano, Yale Univ. Sch. of Music. Recordings include: complete works for piano by Schumann and Debussy; (with ECO) Mozart concerti; (with Tamás Vásáry) complete 4-hand works by Mozart; (with Lindsay Quartet) Brahms, Schumann, Dvorak and Martinu quintets. *Recreations:* football, opera, theatre. *Address:* 5 Gresham Gardens, NW11 8NX. *T:* 0181–455 5228.

FRANKLAND, family name of **Baron Zouche.**

FRANKLAND, (Anthony) Noble, CB 1983; CBE 1976; DFC 1944; MA, DPhil; historian and biographer; *b* 4 July 1922; *s* of late Edward Frankland, Ravenstonedale, Westmorland; *m* 1st, 1944, Diana Madeline Fovargue (*d* 1981), *d* of late G. V. Tavernor, of Madras and Southern Mahratta Rly, India; one *s* one *d*; 2nd, 1982, Sarah Katharine, *d* of His Honour the late Sir David Davies, QC and late Lady Davies (Margaret Kennedy). *Educ:* Sedbergh; Trinity Coll., Oxford. Served Royal Air Force, 1941–45 (Bomber Command, 1943–45). Air Historical Branch Air Ministry, 1948–51; Official Military Historian, Cabinet Office, 1951–58. Rockefeller Fellow, 1953. Deputy Dir of Studies, Royal Institute of International Affairs, 1956–60; Dir, Imperial War Museum (at Southwark, 1960–82, Duxford Airfield, 1976–82, and HMS Belfast, 1978–82). Lees Knowles Lecturer, Trinity Coll., Cambridge, 1963. Historical advisor, Thames Television series, The World At War, 1971–74. Vice-Chm., British Nat. Cttee, Internat. Cttee for Study of Second World War, 1976–82. Mem., Council, Morley Coll., 1962–66; Trustee: Military Archives Centre, KCL, 1963–82; HMS Belfast Trust, 1971–78 (Vice-Chm., 1972–78); HMS Belfast Bd, 1978–82. *Publications:* Documents on International Affairs: for 1955, 1958; for 1956, 1959; for 1957, 1960; Crown of Tragedy, Nicholas II, 1960; The Strategic Air Offensive Against Germany, 1939–1945 (4 vols) jointly with Sir Charles Webster, 1961; The Bombing Offensive against Germany, Outlines and Perspectives, 1965; Bomber Offensive: the Devastation of Europe, 1970; (ed jtly) The Politics and Strategy of the Second World War (8 vols), 1974–78; (ed jtly) Decisive Battles of the Twentieth Century: Land, Sea, Air, 1976; Prince Henry, Duke of Gloucester, 1980; general editor and contributor, Encyclopaedia of 20th Century Warfare, 1989; Witness of a Century: the life and times of Prince Arthur Duke of Connaught, 1993; Historical Chapter in Manual of Air Force Law, 1956; other articles and reviews; broadcasts on radio and TV. *Address:* Thames House, Eynsham, Witney, Oxfordshire OX8 1DA. *T:* Oxford (01865) 881327.

FRANKLAND, Noble; *see* Frankland, A. N.

FRANKLIN, Albert Andrew Ernst, CVO 1965; CBE 1961 (OBE 1950); HM Diplomatic Service, retired; *b* 28 Nov. 1914; *s* of Albert John Henry Franklin; *m* 1944, Henrietta Irene Barry; two *d*. *Educ:* Merchant Taylors' Sch.; St John's Coll., Oxford. Joined HM Consular Service, 1937; served in Peking, Kunming, Chungking, Calcutta, Algiers, Marseilles, Kabul, Basle, Tientsin, Formosa, Düsseldorf and in the FO; HM Consul-General, Los Angeles, USA, 1966–74. Member of Kitchener Association. FRSA 1971. *Recreation:* chinese ceramics and paintings. *Address:* 5 Dulwich Wood Avenue, SE19 1HB. *T:* 0181–670 2769.

FRANKLIN, Sir Eric (Alexander), Kt 1954; CBE 1952; *b* 3 July 1910; *s* of late William John Franklin; *m* 1936, Joy Stella, *d* of late George Oakes Lucas, Cambridge. *Educ:* The English Sch., Maymyo; Emmanuel Coll., Cambridge. Appointed to ICS in 1935 and posted to Burma; Subdivisional Officer, 1936–39. Deputy Registrar, High Court of Judicature at Rangoon, 1939–40; District and Sessions Judge, Arakan, 1941–42; Deputy Sec. to Government of Burma at Simla, 1942–45; Registrar, High Court of Judicature at Rangoon, 1946–47; retired prematurely from ICS, 1948. Appointed on contract as Deputy Sec. to Government of Pakistan. Cabinet Secretariat, 1949; Joint Sec., Cabinet Secretariat, 1952; Establishment Officer and Head of Central Organisation and Methods Office, 1953–55; Establishment Sec. to Government of Pakistan, 1956–57; Chm. Sudan Government Commission on terms of service, 1958–59, Civil Service Adviser to Government of Hashemite Kingdom of Jordan, 1960–63, acting Resident Representative, UN Technical Assistance Board, Jordan, 1961; Senior UN Administrative Adviser to Government of Nepal, 1964–66. Chm., Cambridgeshire Soc. for the Blind, 1969–74, Vice-Pres., 1974–93. El Kawkab el Urdoni (Star of Jordan), 1963. *Recreations:* reading, music. *Address:* 18 Cavendish Avenue, Cambridge CB1 4US.

FRANKLIN, George Henry, RIBA, FRTPI; Consultant, Third World planning and development; *b* 15 June 1923; *s* of late George Edward Franklin, RN, and Annie Franklin; *m* 1950, Sylvia D. Franklin (*née* Allen); three *s* one *d*. *Educ:* Hastings Grammar Sch.; Hastings Sch. of Art; Architectural Assoc. Sch. of Arch. (AADipl); Sch. of Planning and Research for Regional Develt, London (SPDip). Served War of 1939–45: Parachute Sqdn; RE, Europe; Bengal Sappers and Miners, RIE, SE Asia. Finchley Bor. Council, 1952–54; Architect, Christian Med. Coll., Ludhiana, Punjab, India, 1954–57; Physical Planning Adviser (Colombo Plan) to Republic of Indonesia, 1958–62, and Govt of Malaysia, 1963–64; Physical Planning Adviser, Min. of Overseas Develt, later Overseas Develt Admin, FCO, 1966–83 (Overseas Div., Building Research Station, 1966–73, ODM, later ODA, 1973–83). Hon. Prof., Dept of Town Planning, UWIST, 1982–88; Sen. Advr, Develt Planning Unit, UCL, 1983–. Chm., Overseas Sch., Town and Country Planning Summer Sch., 1970–75. Commonwealth Assoc. of Planners: Mem. Exec. Cttee, 1970–80; Pres., 1980–84; Hon. Sec., 1984–88; Member: Exec. Cttee, Commonwealth Human Ecology Council, 1970–90; Internat. Adv. Bd, Centre for Develt and Environmental Planning, Oxford Polytechnic, 1985–; World Service Cttee, United Bible Socs, 1968–77. Chm., Warminster Bible Soc. Action Gp, 1991–; Vice Chm., W Wilts, Leonard Cheshire Care-at-Home (formerly Family Support) Service, 1994– (Chm., Warminster and Westbury Dist, 1990–94). Co-ordinator, Christian Aid, Warminster Dist, 1991–. Member Editorial Board: Third World Planning Review, 1979–91; Cities, 1983–91. FRSA; AIIA, 1955; AITP India, 1956. *Publications:* papers to internat. confs and professional jls concerning planning, building and housing in the Third World. *Recreations:* Third World, Christian and environmental issues and interests, fly-fishing. *Address:* The Manse, Sutton Veny, Warminster, Wilts BA12 7AW. *T:* Warminster (01985) 840072. *Clubs:* Commonwealth Trust, Victory Services.

FRANKLIN, Gordon Herbert, CVO 1989 (LVO 1976; MVO 1965); a Serjeant-at-Arms to HM the Queen, 1990–93; Personnel Officer, Royal Household, 1988–93, retired; *b* 1 Sept. 1933; *s* of late Herbert and of Elsie Franklin; *m* 1959, Gillian Moffett; three *d*. *Educ:* Windsor County Boys' Sch. Barclays Bank, 1950. 2nd ATAF, Germany, 1952–54. Royal Household, 1956–93: Chief Clerk, Master of the Household's Dept, 1975; Chief Accountant of Privy Purse, 1982. Member: Central Finance Board and Council of Methodist Church, 1984–; Methodist Council Exec., 1993–. Vice-Pres., Friends of Wesley's Chapel, 1989–. Freeman, City of London, 1982; Liveryman, Painter Stainers' Co., 1983–. *Recreations:* theatre, walking, travel. *Address:* 10 Cumberland Lodge Mews, The Great Park, Windsor, Berks SL4 2JD. *Club:* Royal Over-Seas League.

FRANKLIN, John; *see* Franklin, W. J.

FRANKLIN, Sir Michael (David Milroy), KCB 1983 (CB 1979); CMG 1972; Director: Whessoe plc, since 1988; Whitbread plc, since 1991; *b* 24 Aug. 1927; *o s* of late Milroy Franklin; *m* 1951, Dorothy Joan Fraser; two *s* one *d*. *Educ:* Taunton Sch.; Peterhouse,

Cambridge (1st cl. hons Economics). Served with 4th RHA, BAOR. Asst Principal, Min. of Agric. and Fisheries, 1950; Economic Section, Cabinet Office (subseq. Treasury), 1952–55; Principal, Min. of Agric., Fisheries and Food, 1956; UK Delegn to OEEC (subseq. OECD), 1959–61; Private Sec. to Minister of Agric., Fisheries and Food, 1961–64; Asst Sec., Head of Sugar and Tropical Foodstuffs Div., 1965–68; Under-Sec. (EEC Gp), MAFF, 1968–73; a Dep. Dir Gen., Directorate Gen. for Agric., EC, Brussels, 1973–77; Dep. Sec., Head of the European Secretariat, Cabinet Office, 1977–81; Permanent Sec., Dept of Trade, 1982–83; Perm. Sec., MAFF, 1983–87. Director: Agricultural Mortgage Corp., 1987–93; Barclays Bank, 1988–93; Barclays PLC, 1988–93. Pres., West India Cttee, 1987–; Chm., Europe Cttee, British Invisibles (formerly BIEC), 1993– (Dep. Chm., 1988–93); Member: Council, Royal Inst. for Internat. Relations, 1988–; Internat. Policy Council on Agric. and Trade, 1988–. Governor, Henley Management Coll. (formerly Henley Administrative Staff Coll.), 1983–93. *Publications:* Rich Man's Farming: the crisis in agriculture, 1988; Britain's Future in Europe, 1990; The EC Budget, 1992. *Address:* 15 Galley Lane, Barnet, Herts EN5 4AR. *Club:* United Oxford & Cambridge University.

FRANKLIN, Prof. Raoul Norman, CBE 1995; FInstP, FIMA; FEng, FIEE; CIMgt; Vice Chancellor, since 1978, and Professor of Plasma Physics and Technology, since 1986, The City University, London; Fellow, Keble College, Oxford, since 1963; *b* 3 June 1935; *s* of Norman George Franklin and Thelma Brinley Franklin (*née* Davis); *m* 1961, Faith, *d* of Lt-Col H. T. C. Ivens and Eva (*née* Gray); two *s*. *Educ:* Howick District High Sch.; Auckland Grammar Sch., NZ; Univ. of Auckland (ME, DSc); Christ Church, Oxford (MA, DPhil, DSc). FInstP 1968; FIMA 1970; FEng 1990; FIEE 1986; CIMgt (CBIM 1986). Officer, NZ Defence Scientific Corps, 1957–75. Sen. Res. Fellow, RMCS, Shrivenham, 1961–63; Univ. of Oxford: Tutorial Fellow, 1963–78, Dean, 1966–71, Hon. Fellow, 1980, Keble Coll.; Univ. Lectr in Engrg Science, 1966–78; Mem., Gen. Bd, 1967–74 (Vice Chm., 1971–74); Mem., Hebdomadal Council, 1971–74, 1976–78. Chm., Associated Examining Bd, 1994–. Consultant, UKAEA Culham, 1968–. Member: UGC Equipment Sub Cttee, 1975–78; Plasma Physics Commn, IUPAP, 1971–79; Science Bd, SERC, 1982–85; Exec. Council, Business in the Community, 1982–; Management Cttee, Spallation Neutron Source, 1983–86; Technology Educn Project, 1986–88; UK–NZ 1990 Cttee, 1988–90; Internat. Scientific Cttee, Eur. Sectional Conf. on Atomic and Molecular Processes in Ionized Gases, 1993–. Chairman: Internat. Science Cttee, Phenomena in Ionized Gases, 1976–77; City Techology Ltd, 1978–93 (Queen's Award for Technol., 1982, 1985, for Export, 1988, 1991). Mem., London Pensions Fund Authority, 1989–94. Trustee: Ruskin School of Drawing, 1975–78; Lloyds Tercentenary Foundn, 1990–. Mem. Council, Gresham Coll., 1981–. Gov., Ashridge Management Coll., 1986–. Liveryman, Curriers' Co., 1984–. Hon. Mem. RICS, 1992; Hon. GSMD 1993. FRSA. Freeman, City of London, 1981. Dep. Editor, Jl of Physics D, 1986–90. *Publications:* Plasma Phenomena in Ionized Gases, 1976; papers on plasmas, gas discharges and granular materials. *Recreations:* tennis, walking, gardening. *Address:* The City University, Northampton Square, EC1V 0HB. *T:* 0171–477 8002. *Club:* Athenæum.

FRANKLIN, Rt. Rev. William Alfred, OBE 1964; Assistant Bishop (full time), Diocese of Peterborough, and Hon. Canon of the Cathedral, 1978–86, Canon Emeritus since 1986; *b* 16 July 1916; *s* of George Amos and Mary Anne Catherine Franklin; *m* 1945, Winifred Agnes Franklin (*née* Jarvis); one *s* one *d*. *Educ:* schools in London; Kelham Theol Coll. Deacon 1940, priest 1941, London; Curate, St John on Bethnal Green, Chaplain ATC and Univ. Settlements, 1941–43; Curate of St John's, Palmers Green, and Chm. for area Interdenominational Youth Activities, 1943–45; Asst Chaplain, St Saviour's, Belgrano, Buenos Aires, Argentina and teaching duties at Green's School, Buenos Aires, 1945–48; Rector of Holy Trinity, Lomas de Zamora, Buenos Aires, Domestic Chaplain to Bishop in Argentina, Sec. Dio. Bd of Missions, and Chaplain St Alban's Coll., Lomas, 1948–58; Rector, Canon and Sub-Dean of Anglican Cathedral, Santiago, Chaplain Grange School and Founder and Chm. Ecumenical Gp in Chile, 1958–65; Rector of St Alban's, Bogotá, Colombia, 1965–71; Archdeacon of Diocese, 1966–71; consecrated Bishop of Diocese, 1972; resigned, 1978, allowing a national to be elected. Hon. Asst Bishop of Canterbury, 1987–92. Founder and Editor of Revista Anglicana, official magazine of Arensa (Assoc. of Anglican Dioceses in North of S America). *Recreations:* fishing, tennis and cricket. *Address:* 26c The Beach, Walmer, near Deal, Kent CT14 7AJ. *T:* Deal (01304) 361807. *Club:* Anglo-American (Bogotá, Colombia).

FRANKLIN, (William) John, DL; Deputy Chairman, Chartered Trust plc, since 1986 (Director, since 1982); Chairman, Howells Motors Ltd, 1986–89; Powell Duffryn Wagon, 1986–89; *b* 8 March 1927; *s* of late William Thomas Franklin and Edith Hannah Franklin; *m* 1951, Sally (*née* Davies); one *d*. *Educ:* Monkton House Sch., Cardiff. W. R. Gresty, Chartered Accountants, 1947–50; Peat Marwick Mitchell, Chartered Accountants, 1950–55; Powell Duffryn, 1956–86: Director, Cory Brothers, 1964; Man. Dir, Powell Duffryn Timber, 1967–70; Dir, 1970–86; Man. Dir and Chief Exec., 1976–85; Dep. Chm., Jan.–July 1986. Treas., UC of Swansea, 1989–92. DL Mid Glamorgan, 1989. *Recreation:* golf. *Address:* 80 South Road, Porthcawl, Mid Glamorgan CF36 3DA. *Club:* Royal Porthcawl Golf.

FRANKLYN, Rear-Adm. Peter Michael, MVO 1978; Commander, United Kingdom Task Group, 1994–Feb. 1996; Flag Officer Sea Training, from March 1996; *b* 10 Sept. 1946; *s* of Roy Vernon Bolton Franklyn and Yvonne Beryl Franklyn (*née* Hooper); *m* 1977, Caroline Barbara Anne Jenks; one *s* one *d*. *Educ:* King's Coll., Taunton. Joined RN, 1963; Comdr, 1980; CO, HMS Active, 1980–82; Trng Comdr, BRNC, Dartmouth, 1982–84; SO Ops FO 3rd Flotilla, 1984–86; Captain, 1986; Naval Asst to 1st Sea Lord, 1986–88; CO, HMS Bristol, 1988–90; RCDS, 1991; Capt., Sch. of Maritime Ops, 1992–93; Dir Naval Officers' Appts (Seaman), 1993–94; Rear-Adm., 1994. Mem., RNSA, 1993–. *Recreations:* family, outdoor activities, antique furniture, old houses. *Address:* (until March 1996) 7/8 The Parade, HM Naval Base, Portsmouth, Hants PO1 3NA. *T:* Portsmouth (01705) 726622; (from March 1996) Grenville Block, HMS Drake, Devonport, Plymouth PL2 2BG. *Club:* Naval.

FRANKS, Sir Arthur Temple, (Sir Dick Franks), KCMG 1979 (CMG 1967); HM Diplomatic Service, retired; *b* 13 July 1920; *s* of late Arthur Franks, Hove; *m* 1945, Rachel Marianne, *d* of late Rev. A. E. S. Ward, DD; one *s* two *d*. *Educ:* Rugby; Queen's Coll., Oxford. HM Forces, 1940–46 (despatches). Entered Foreign Service, 1949; British Middle East Office, 1952; Tehran, 1953; Bonn, 1962; FCO, 1966–81. *Address:* Roefield, Alde Lane, Aldeburgh, Suffolk IP15 5DZ. *Clubs:* Travellers', Army and Navy; Aldeburgh Golf.

FRANKS, Cecil Simon; solicitor; company director; Chairman, Pryde Investments Ltd, residential property, since 1960; *b* 1 July 1935; *m* (marr. diss. 1978); one *s*. *Educ:* Manchester Grammar Sch.; Manchester Univ. (LLB). Admitted solicitor, 1958. Member: Salford City Council, 1960–74 (Leader, Cons. Gp); Manchester City Council, 1975–84 (Leader, Cons. Gp). Mem., North West RHA, 1973–75. MP (C) Barrow and Furness, 1983–92; contested (C) Barrow and Furness, 1992. Indep. Mem., Parole Bd, 1994–. *Recreations:* ski-ing, tennis, theatre, literature. *Address:* 200 Upper Chorlton Road, Manchester M16 7SF. *T:* 0161–861 9322.

FRANKS, His Honour Desmond Gerald Fergus; a Circuit Judge, 1972–93; *b* 24 Jan. 1928; *s* of F. Franks, MC, late Lancs Fus., and E. R. Franks; *m* 1952, Margaret Leigh (*née* Daniel); one *d*. *Educ:* Cathedral Choir Sch., Canterbury; Manchester Grammar Sch.; University Coll., London (LLB). Called to Bar, Middle Temple, 1952; Northern Circuit; Asst Recorder, Salford, 1966; Deputy Recorder, Salford, 1971; a Recorder of the Crown Court, 1972. Pres., SW Pennine Br., Magistrates' Assoc., 1977–93. Chm., Selcare (Gtr Manchester) Trust, 1978–84, Vice-Pres., 1984–. *Recreations:* gardening, music, photography. *Address:* 4 Beathwaite Drive, Bramhall, Cheshire SK7 3NY.

FRANKS, Sir Dick; *see* Franks, Sir A. T.

FRANKS, Jeremy Christopher Reynell; Chief Executive and Managing Director, DAKS Simpson Group plc, since 1992; *b* 26 April 1937; *s* of late Geoffrey Charles Reynell Franks and Molly (*née* McCulluch); *m* 1959, Elizabeth Brown; one *d*. *Educ:* Lancing Coll. 2nd Lt, 1st Kings Dragoon Guards, 1956–57, Aide de Camp to British High Comr for Fedn of Malaya. Man. Dir, Simpson (Piccadilly) Ltd, 1985–86; Dir, DAKS Simpson Gp plc, 1986–87; Man. Dir, DAKS Simpson (Menswear) Ltd, 1987–91; Gp Man. Dir, DAKS Simpson Gp plc, 1991–92; Dir, Sankyo Seiko Co. Ltd, Japan, 1992–; Pres. Dir (non-exec.), New Bond Street Ltd, Japan, 1994–. Chm., British Menswear Guild, 1989–91 and 1994–. Mem., Walpole Cttee, 1991–. *Recreations:* Rugby, cricket, antiques, theatre. *Address:* 28 Hyde Park Gardens, W2 2UA; (office) 34 Jermyn Street, SW1Y 6HS. *Club:* Cavalry and Guards.

FRANKS, Air Vice-Marshal John Gerald, CB 1954; CBE 1949; RAF retired, 1960; *b* 23 May 1905; *e s* of late James Gordon Franks, *e s* of Sir John Hamilton Franks, CB, and Margaret, *y d* of Lord Chief Justice Gerald Fitz-Gibbon, Dublin; *m* 1936, Jessica Rae West (decd); two *d*. *Educ:* Cheltenham Coll.; RAF Coll., Cranwell. RAF; commissioned from Cranwell, 1924; No 56 Fighter Sqdn, Biggin Hill, 1925–26; flying duties with FAA HMS Courageous, Mediterranean, 1928–29; India, 1930–35; Middle East, 1936; RAF Staff Coll., 1939; Air Armament Sch., Manby, 1941; Experimental Establishment, Boscombe Down, 1944; Dir Armament Research and Development, 1945–48; idc 1951; Comdt RAF Technical Coll., Henlow, 1952; Air Officer Commanding No 24 Group, Royal Air Force, 1952–55; Pres. of Ordnance Board, 1959–60. Comdr American Legion of Merit, 1948. *Recreations:* motoring and walking in the west of Ireland.

FRANZ, Very Rev. Dr Kevin Gerhard; Provost, St Ninian's Cathedral, Perth, since 1990; *b* 16 June 1953; *m* 1976, Veda Fairley; one *s* one *d*. *Educ:* Univ. of Edinburgh (MA 1974; BD 1979; PhD 1992); Edinburgh Theol Coll. Ordained deacon, 1979; priest 1980; Curate, St Martin, Edinburgh, 1979–83; Rector, St John's, Selkirk, 1983–90. *Address:* St Ninian's House, 40 Hay Street, Perth PH1 5HS.

FRASER, family name of **Barons Fraser of Carmyllie, Fraser of Kilmorack,** and **Lovat, Lady Saltoun,** and **Baron Strathalmond.**

FRASER OF CARMYLLIE, Baron *cr* 1989 (Life Peer), of Carmyllie in the District of Angus; **Peter Lovat Fraser;** PC 1989; Minister of State, Department of Trade and Industry, since 1995; *b* 29 May 1945; *s* of Rev. George Robson Fraser and Helen Jean Meiklejohn or Fraser; *m* 1969, Fiona Macdonald Mair; one *s* two *d*. *Educ:* St Andrews Prep. Sch., Grahamstown, S Africa; Loretto Sch., Musselburgh; Gonville and Caius Coll., Cambridge (BA Hons; LLM Hons); Edinburgh Univ. Legal apprenticeship, Edinburgh, 1968; called to Scottish Bar, 1969; QC (Scot.) 1982. Lectr in Constitutional Law, Heriot-Watt Univ., 1972–74; Standing Jun. Counsel in Scotland to FCO, 1979. Hon. Vis. Prof. of Law, Dundee Univ., 1986. Hon. Bencher, Lincoln's Inn, 1989. Chm., Scottish Conservative Lawyers Law Reform Group, 1976. Contested (C): N Aberdeen, Oct. 1974; Angus E, 1987. MP (C): S Angus, 1979–83; Angus E, 1983–87. PPS to Sec. of State for Scotland, 1981–82; Solicitor Gen. for Scotland, 1982–89; Lord Advocate, 1989–92; Minister of State, Scottish Office, 1992–95. *Recreations:* ski-ing, golf. *Address:* Slade House, Carmyllie, by Arbroath, Angus DD11 2RE. *T:* Carmyllie (01241) 860215.

FRASER OF KILMORACK, Baron *cr* 1974 (Life Peer), of Rubislaw, Aberdeen; **Richard Michael Fraser,** Kt 1962; CBE 1955 (MBE mil. 1945); *b* 28 Oct. 1915; *yr s* of late Dr Thomas Fraser, CBE, DSO, TD, DL, LLD, Aberdeen and Maria-Theresia Kayser, Hanover; *m* 1944, Elizabeth Chloë, *er d* of late Brig. C. A. F. Drummond, OBE and Muriel Kyrle Ottley; one *s* (and one *s* decd). *Educ:* Aberdeen Grammar Sch.; Fettes; King's Coll., Cambridge. Begg Exhibition, 1934; James Essay Prize, 1935; BA Hons History, 1937; MA 1945. Served War of 1939–45 (RA); 2nd Lieut 1939; War Gunnery Staff Course, 1940; Capt. Feb. 1941; Major, June 1941; Lieut-Col (GSO1) 1945. Joined Conservative Research Dept, 1946; Head of Home Affairs Sect., 1950–51, Jt Dir, 1951–59, Dir, 1959–64, Chm., 1970–74; Exec. Dep. Chm., Cons. Party Orgn, 1964–75; Dep. Chm., Conservative Party's Adv. Cttee on Policy, 1970–75 (Sec., Aug. 1951–Oct. 1964); Sec. to the Conservative Leader's Consultative Cttee (Shadow Cabinet), Oct. 1964–June 1970 and March 1974–75. Director: Glaxo Holdings plc, and subsid. cos, 1975–85; Glaxo Enterprises Inc., USA, 1983–86; Whiteaway Laidlaw Bank Ltd, 1981–94. Smith-Mundt Fellowship, USA, 1952. Mem. Council, Imperial Soc. of Knights Bachelor, 1971–94. President: Old Fettesian Assoc., 1977–80; London Old Fettesian Assoc., 1992–. *Publications:* (contrib.) Ruling Performance: British governments from Attlee to Thatcher, 1987; contribs to political and hist. jls. *Recreations:* reading, music, opera, ballet, travel; collecting and recollecting. *Address:* 18 Drayton Court, Drayton Gardens, SW10 9RH. *T:* 0171–370 1543. *Clubs:* Carlton, St Stephen's Constitutional (Hon. Mem.); Coningsby (Hon. Mem., Pres., 1988–).

See also A. S. J. Fraser.

FRASER, Alasdair MacLeod, CB 1992; QC 1989; Director of Public Prosecutions for Northern Ireland, since 1989; *b* 29 Sept. 1946; *s* of late Rev. Dr Donald Fraser and Ellen Hart McAllister; *m* 1975, Margaret Mary Glancy; two *s* one *d*. *Educ:* Sullivan Upper School, Holywood; Trinity College Dublin (BA (Mod.); LLB); Queen's Univ., Belfast (Dip. Laws). Called to the Bar of Northern Ireland, 1970. Director of Public Prosecutions for Northern Ireland: Court Prosecutor, 1973; Asst Dir, 1974; Senior Asst Dir, 1982; Dep. Dir, 1988. *Address:* Royal Courts of Justice, Belfast, Northern Ireland BT1 3NX. *T:* Belfast (01232) 235111.

FRASER, Andrew John; Chief Executive, Invest in Britain Bureau, since 1994; *b* 23 Oct. 1950; *s* of John and Mary Fraser; *m* 1976, Julia Savell (marr. diss. 1987); two *d*. *Educ:* Univ. of Sussex (BA). Account Dir, Young and Rubicam, London, 1972–76; Man. Dir, McCann Erickson, Thailand, 1976–80; Exec. Vice Pres., Dir of Business Develt, Saatchi and Saatchi Worldwide, 1981–92; Man. Dir, cdp Europe (Dentsu Worldwide), 1992–94. *Recreations:* sports, theatre, food and drink, conversation. *Address:* c/o Invest in Britain Bureau, 1 Victoria Street, SW1H 0ET. *Clubs:* Royal Automobile, MCC.

FRASER, Sir Angus (McKay), KCB 1985 (CB 1981); TD 1965; Adviser to the Prime Minister on Efficiency and Effectiveness in Government, 1988–92; *b* 10 March 1928; *s* of late Thomas Douglas Fraser; *m* 1st, 1955, Margaret Neilson (marr. diss. 1968); one *s* one *d*; 2nd, 1991, Gillian Fenwick (*née* Manning); one step *d*. *Educ:* Falkirk High Sch.; Bordeaux Univ.; Glasgow Univ. (MA 1950; DLitt 1993). Nat. Service in RA, 1950–52; 44 Parachute Bde (TA), 1953–66. Entered HM Customs and Excise, 1952; HM Treasury,

1961–64; Under-Sec. and Comr of Customs and Excise, 1972; Under-Sec., CSD, 1973; Comr of Customs and Excise, 1976; Dep. Chm., Bd of Customs and Excise, 1978; Dep. Sec., CSD, subseq. MPO, 1980–83; First CS Comr, 1981–83; Chm., Bd of Customs and Excise, 1983–87. Advr, European Patent Office, 1988–. Chm., Civil Service, PO and BT Lifeboat Fund, 1986–; Vice-Pres., 1994–, and Mem., Cttee of Management, 1986–, RNLI; President: Electronic Data Interchange Assoc., 1988–; George Borrow Soc., 1991–; Vice-Pres., RIPA, 1985–92; Mem. Adv. Council, British Internat. Freight Assoc., 1994– (Pres., 1993–95). Trustee: Bethlem Art and History Collections Trust, 1992–; CS Benevolent Fund, 1991–. FSA 1991; FRSA 1985; Hon. FCIPS 1993. *Publications:* (ed) A Journey to Eastern Europe in 1844, 1981; (ed) George Borrow's Letters to John Hasfeld 1835–1839, 1982, 1841–1846, 1984; George Borrow, a Bibliographical Study, 1984; The Gypsies, 1992, 2nd edn 1995; articles and reviews in jls and encyclopedias, 1950–. *Recreations:* literary research, book collecting. *Address:* 84 Ennerdale Road, Kew, Richmond, Surrey TW9 2DL. *T:* 0181–940 9913. *Clubs:* Reform, Caledonian; Norfolk (Norwich).

FRASER, Angus Simon James; Chief Executive, Scruttons plc, since 1995; *b* 28 Feb. 1945; *s* of Baron Fraser of Kilmorack, *qv*; *m* 1970, Jennifer Ann Craig; two *s* one *d*. *Educ:* Fettes Coll., Edinburgh; Selwyn Coll., Cambridge (MA); European Inst. of Business Admin (INSEAD), France (MBA); Dip. Finance Houses Assoc. Dunlop Co. Ltd, 1968–70; Mercantile Credit Co. Ltd, 1971–76; Chloride Group PLC, 1976–: Gen. Man., Malaysia, 1977–80, France, 1980–82; Man. Dir, Chloride Motive Power, 1982–83; Chm., Chloride Europe, 1983–85; Main Bd Mem., 1984; Exec. Dir, Industrial Operations, 1985–87, Corporate Operations, 1987–88; Non-Exec. Dir, 1988–; Man. Dir, 1989–94, Gov., 1990–94, Imperial Coll. of Sci., Technol. and Medicine. Mem. Adv. Cttee, European Business Foundn, 1991–. *Recreations:* music, opera, golf, tennis, fly-fishing, painting. *Address:* Applecote, Pilgrims Way, Boughton Aluph, Ashford, Kent TN25 4EX.

FRASER, Air Cdre Anthony Walkinshaw; consultant in public relations; *b* 15 March 1934; *s* of late Robert Walkinshaw Fraser and Evelyn Elisabeth Fraser; *m* 1st, 1955, Angela Mary Graham Shaw (marr. diss. 1990); one *s* three *d*; 2nd, 1990, Grania Ruth Eleanor Stewart-Smith. *Educ:* Stowe Sch. MIL. RAF Pilot and Flying Instructor, 1952–66; sc Camberley, 1967; MA/VCDS, MoD, 1968–70; Chief Instructor Buccaneer OCU, 1971–72; Air Warfare Course, 1973; Directing Staff, National Defence Coll., 1973; Dep. Dir, Operational Requirements, MoD, 1974–76; Comdt, Central Flying Sch., 1977–79. ADC to the Queen, 1977–79. Dir, SMMT, 1980–88. Chairman: Personal Guard, 1992–94; Nature's Balance Marketing, 1994–; Dir, Nissan UK Ltd, 1989–91. President: Comité de Liaison de la Construction Automobile, 1980–83; Organisation (formerly Bureau Perm.) Internat. des Constructeurs d'Automobiles, 1983–87 (Vice-Pres., 1981–83). FRSA; FIMgt; FIMI. *Recreations:* shooting, golf, fishing, languages. *Address:* 31 Grove End Road, NW8 9LY. *T:* 0171–286 0521. *Clubs:* Boodle's, Royal Air Force, Sunningdale.

FRASER, Lady Antonia, (Lady Antonia Pinter); writer; *b* 27 Aug. 1932; *d* of 7th Earl of Longford, *qv*, and Countess of Longford, *qv*; *m* 1st, 1956, Rt Hon. Sir Hugh Charles Patrick Joseph Fraser, MBE, MP (*d* 1984) (marr. diss. 1977); three *s* three *d*; 2nd, 1980, Harold Pinter, *qv*. *Educ:* Dragon School, Oxford; St Mary's Convent, Ascot; Lady Margaret Hall, Oxford (MA). General Editor, Kings and Queens of England series. Mem., Arts Council, 1970–72; Chairman: Soc. of Authors, 1974–75; Crimewriters' Assoc., 1985–86; Vice Pres., English PEN, 1990– (Mem. Cttee, 1979–88; Pres., 1988–89; Chm., Writers in Prison Cttee, 1985–88, 1990). Hon. DLitt: Hull, 1986; Sussex, 1990; Nottingham, 1993; St Andrews, 1994. *Publications:* (as Antonia Pakenham): King Arthur and the Knights of the Round Table, 1954 (reissued, 1970); Robin Hood, 1955 (reissued, 1971); (as Antonia Fraser): Dolls, 1963; A History of Toys, 1966; Mary Queen of Scots (James Tait Black Memorial Prize, 1969), 1969 (reissued illus. edn, 1978); Cromwell Our Chief of Men, (in USA, Cromwell the Lord Protector), 1973; King James: VI of Scotland, I of England, 1974, (ed) Kings and Queens of England, 1975 (reissued, 1988); (ed) Scottish Love Poems, a personal anthology, 1975 (reissued, 1988); (ed) Love Letters: an anthology, 1976, rev. edn 1989; Quiet as a Nun (mystery), 1977, adapted for TV series, 1978; The Wild Island (mystery), 1978; King Charles II, (in USA, Royal Charles), 1979; (ed) Heroes and Heroines, 1980; A Splash of Red (mystery), 1981 (basis for TV series Jemima Shore Investigates, 1983); (ed) Mary Queen of Scots: poetry anthology, 1981; (ed) Oxford and Oxfordshire in Verse: anthology, 1982; Cool Repentance (mystery), 1982; The Weaker Vessel: woman's lot in seventeenth century England, 1984 (Wolfson History Award, 1984; Prix Caumont-La Force, 1985); Oxford Blood (mystery), 1985; Jemima Shore's First Case (mystery short stories), 1986; Your Royal Hostage (mystery), 1987; Boadicea's Chariot: the Warrior Queens, 1988 (paperback, The Warrior Queens, 1989, in USA The Warrior Queens, 1989); The Cavalier Case (mystery), 1990; Jemima Shore at the Sunny Grave (mystery short stories), 1991; The Six Wives of Henry VIII, 1992 (USA, as The Wives of Henry VIII); (ed) The Pleasure of Reading, 1992; Political Death (mystery), 1994; various mystery stories in anthols, incl. Have a Nice Death, 1983 (adapted for TV, 1984); TV plays: Charades, 1977; Mister Clay, Mister Clay (Time for Murder series), 1985. *Recreation:* grandchildren. *Address:* c/o Curtis Brown, 162–168 Regent Street, W1R 5TB. *Clubs:* PEN, Detection, Vanderbilt.

FRASER, Bernard W.; Chairman and Governor, Reserve Bank of Australia, since 1989; *b* 26 Feb. 1941; *m* 1965, Edna Gallogly; one *s* two *d*. *Educ:* Univ. of New England; Australian Nat. Univ. Joined Aust. Treasury, 1963; Treasury Rep., London, 1969–72; First Asst Sec., 1979; Dir, Nat. Energy Office, 1981; Sec. to Treasury, 1984. *Address:* Reserve Bank of Australia, 65 Martin Place, Sydney, NSW 2000, Australia.

FRASER, Sir Campbell; *see* Fraser, Sir J. C.

FRASER, Sir Charles (Annand), KVCO 1989 (CVO 1985; LVO 1968); DL; WS; non-executive Vice Chairman, United Biscuits (Holdings), since 1986 (Director, since 1978); Partner, W & J Burness, WS, Edinburgh, 1956–92; *b* 16 Oct. 1928; *o s* of late Very Rev. John Annand Fraser, MBE, TD; *m* 1957, Ann Scott-Kerr; four *s*. *Educ:* Hamilton Academy; Edinburgh Univ. (MA, LLB). Purse Bearer to Lord High Commissioner to General Assembly of Church of Scotland, 1969–88. Chairman: Morgan Grenfell (Scotland), 1985–86; Adam & Co., 1989–; Lothian & Edinburgh Enterprise Ltd, 1991–94; NSM, 1992–94; Director: Scottish Widows' Fund, 1978–94; British Assets Trust, 1969–; Scottish Television Ltd, 1979–, and other companies. Mem. Council, Law Society of Scotland, 1966–72; Governor of Fettes, 1976–86; Mem. Court, Heriot-Watt Univ., 1972–78. WS 1959; DL East Lothian, 1984–. Dr *hc* Edinburgh, 1991; Hon. LLD Napier, 1992. *Recreations:* gardening, skiing, piping. *Address:* Shepherd House, Inveresk, Midlothian EH21 7TH. *T:* 0131–665 2570. *Clubs:* New, Hon. Co. of Edinburgh Golfers (Edinburgh); Royal and Ancient (St Andrews).

FRASER, Maj.-Gen. Colin Angus Ewen, CB 1971; CBE 1968; General Officer Commanding, Southern Command, Australia, 1971–74; retired March 1974; *b* Nairobi, Kenya, 25 Sept. 1918; *s* of A. E. Fraser, Rutherglen, Vic.; *m* 1942, Dorothy, *d* of A. Champion; two *s* one *d*. *Educ:* Johannesburg; Adelaide High Sch.; RMC, Duntroon (grad. 1938); Melbourne Univ. (BA). Served War of 1939–45: UK, Middle East, Pacific. Staff Coll., Camberley, 1946; Dep. Comdr, Commonwealth Div., Korea, 1955–56; Dir, Military Trng, 1957–58; Services Attaché, Burma, 1960–62; Chief of Staff, Northern Command, Brisbane, 1964–68; Commandant, Royal Military Coll., Duntroon, 1968–69; Commander, Australian Force, Vietnam, 1970–71. *Address:* 107 Orana Road, Ocean Shores, Brunswick Heads, NSW 2483, Australia. *Clubs:* Tasmanian (Hobart); United Services (Qld).

FRASER, Gen. Sir David (William), GCB 1980 (KCB 1973); OBE 1962; retired; Vice Lord-Lieutenant of Hampshire, since 1988; *b* 30 Dec. 1920; *s* of Brig. Hon. William Fraser, DSO, MC, *y s* of 18th Lord Saltoun and Pamela, *d* of Cyril Maude and *widow* of Major W. La T. Congreve, VC, DSO, MC; *m* 1st, 1947, Anne Balfour; one *d*; 2nd, 1957, Julia de la Hey; two *s* two *d*. *Educ:* Eton; Christ Church, Oxford. Commnd into Grenadier Guards, 1941; served NW Europe; comd 1st Bn Grenadier Guards, 1960–62; comd 19th Inf. Bde, 1963–65; Dir, Defence Policy, MoD, 1966–69; GOC 4 Div., 1969–71; Asst Chief of Defence Staff (Policy), MoD, 1971–73; Vice-Chief of the General Staff, 1973–75; UK Mil. Rep. to NATO, 1975–77; Commandant, RCDS, 1978–80; ADC General to the Queen, 1977–80. Col, The Royal Hampshire Regt, 1981–87. DL Hants, 1982. Hon. DLitt Reading, 1992. *Publications:* Alanbrooke, 1982; And We Shall Shock Them, 1983; The Christian Watt Papers, 1983; August 1988, 1983; A Kiss for the Enemy, 1985; The Killing Times, 1986; The Dragon's Teeth, 1987; The Seizure, 1988; A Candle for Judas, 1989; In Good Company, 1990; Adam Hardrow, 1990; Codename Mercury, 1991; Adam in the Breach, 1993; The Pain of Winning, 1993; Knight's Cross: a life of Field Marshal Erwin Rommel, 1993. *Recreation:* shooting. *Address:* Vallenders, Isington, Alton, Hants GU34 4PP. *T:* Bentley (01420) 23166. *Clubs:* Turf, Pratt's.

FRASER, Prof. Derek, FRHistS; Vice-Chancellor, University of Teesside, since 1992; *b* 24 July 1940; *s* of Jacob and Dorothy Fraser; *m* 1962, Ruth Spector; two *s* one *d*. *Educ:* Univ. of Leeds (BA, MA, PhD). Schoolteacher, 1962–65; Lectr, Sen. Lectr, Reader and Prof. of Modern History, Univ. of Bradford, 1965–82; Prof. of English History, UCLA, 1982–84; HMI (History and Higher Educn), 1984–88; Staff Inspector (Higher Educn), DES, 1988–90; Asst/Dep. Principal, Sheffield City Polytechnic, 1990–92. *Publications:* The Evolution of the British Welfare State, 1973, 3rd edn 1996; Urban Politics in Victorian England, 1976; Power and Authority in the Victorian City, 1979; (ed) A History of Modern Leeds, 1980; (ed jtly) The Pursuit of Urban History, 1980; (ed) Municipal Reform and the Industrial City, 1982; (ed) Cities, Class and Communication: essays in honour of Asa Briggs, 1990. *Recreations:* squash, bridge, music, spectator sports. *Address:* University of Teesside, Middlesbrough TS1 3BA. *T:* Middlesbrough (01642) 342002.

FRASER, Donald Blake, FRCS; FRCOG; Gynæcologist and Obstetrician, St Bartholomew's Hospital, 1946–75; retired 1978; *b* 9 June 1910; *o s* of Dr Thomas B. Fraser, Hatfield Point, NB, Canada; *m* 1939, Betsy, *d* of late Sir James Henderson, KBE; one *s* one *d*. *Educ:* University of New Brunswick; Christ Church, Oxford. Rhodes Scholar, 1930; BA 1st Cl. Hons, 1932, BM, BCh Oxon 1936; MRCS, LRCP, LMCC, 1936; FRCS, 1939; MRCOG, 1940, FRCOG, 1952. Former Examiner: Central Midwives Bd; Universities of Oxford and London; Conjoint Bd; Royal College of Obstetricians and Gynæcologists. *Publications:* (joint) Midwifery (textbook), 1956; articles in medical journals. *Recreation:* philately. *Address:* 13 Stanton Crest, 7 Hale Street, Townsville, Qld 4810, Australia.

FRASER, Donald Hamilton, RA 1985 (ARA 1975); artist; Member, Royal Fine Art Commission, since 1986; *b* 30 July 1929; *s* of Donald Fraser and Dorothy Christiana (*née* Lang); *m* 1954, Judith Wentworth-Sheilds; one *d*. *Educ:* Maidenhead Grammar Sch.; St Martin's Sch. of Art, London; Paris (French Govt Scholarship). Tutor, Royal Coll. of Art, 1958–83, Fellow 1970, Hon. FRCA 1984. Has held 60 one-man exhibitions in Britain, Europe, N America and Japan. Work in public collections includes: Museum of Fine Arts, Boston; Albright-Knox Gall., Buffalo; Carnegie Inst., Pittsburgh; City Art Museum, St Louis; Wadsworth Athenaeum, Hartford, Conn; Hirshhorn Museum, Washington, DC; Yale Univ. Art Museum; Palm Springs Desert Museum; Nat. Gall. of Canada, Ottawa; Nat. Gall. of Vic, Melbourne; many corporate collections and British provincial galleries; Arts Council, DoE, etc. Designed Commonwealth Day issue of postage stamps, 1983. Vice-Pres. Artists Gen. Benevolent Inst., 1981– (Chm., 1981–87); Vice-Pres., Royal Over-Seas League, 1986–. Trustee: British Instn Fund, 1982–; Royal Acad., 1993– (Hon. Curator, 1992–). *Publications:* Gauguin's 'Vision after the Sermon', 1969; Dancers, 1989. *Address:* Bramham Cottage, Remenham Lane, Henley-on-Thames, Oxon RG9 2LR. *T:* Henley-on-Thames (01491) 574253. *Club:* Arts.

FRASER, Dame Dorothy (Rita), DBE 1987; QSO 1978; JP; Australasian Chairman, Community Systems Foundation Australasia, 1991–94 (New Zealand Director, 1975–91); *b* 3 May 1926; *d* of Ernest and Kate Tucker; *m* 1947, Hon. William Alex Fraser; one *s* one *d*. *Educ:* Gisborne High Sch. Chm., Otago Hosp. Bd, 1974–86 (Mem., 1953–56, 1962–86); Member: Nursing Council of NZ, 1981–87; Grading Review Cttee (Health Service Personnel Commn), 1984–87; Hosps Adv. Council, 1984–86; NZ Health Service Personnel Commn, 1987–88; Otago Plunket-Karitane Hosp. Bd, 1979–87; NZ Lottery Bd, 1985–90; Vice-Pres., NZ Hosp. Bds Assoc., 1981–86; Chairman: Southern Region Health Services Assoc., 1984–86; Hosp. and Specialist Services Cttee, NZ Bd of Health, 1985–88. Consultant, ADT Ltd Australasia, later Command Pacific Group, 1988–91. Chm., Otago Jt Tertiary Educn Liaison Cttee, 1988–; Member: Council, Univ. of Otago, 1974–86; Otago High Schs Bd of Governors, 1964–85. Chm., Dunedin Airport Cttee, 1971–74; Member: Dunedin CC, 1970–74; NZ Exec. Marr. Guidance, 1969–75. Life Mem., NZ Labour Party; Gold Badge for Service to Labour Party. JP 1959. Hon. LLD Otago, 1994. Silver Jubilee Medal, 1977. *Recreations:* gardening, golf, reading. *Address:* 21 Ings Avenue, St Clair, Dunedin, New Zealand. *T:* (3) 4558663.

FRASER, Edward; *see* Fraser, J. E.

FRASER, George MacDonald; author and journalist; *b* 2 April 1925; *s* of late William Fraser, MB, ChB and Anne Struth Donaldson; *m* 1949, Kathleen Margarette, *d* of late George Hetherington, Carlisle; two *s* one *d*. *Educ:* Carlisle Grammar Sch.; Glasgow Academy. Served in British Army, 1943–47: Infantryman XIVth Army, Lieut Gordon Highlanders. Newspaperman in England, Canada and Scotland from 1947; Dep. Editor, Glasgow Herald, 1964–69. *Publications:* Flashman, 1969; Royal Flash, 1970; The General Danced at Dawn, 1970; The Steel Bonnets, 1971; Flash for Freedom!, 1971; Flashman at the Charge, 1973; McAuslan in the Rough, 1974; Flashman in the Great Game, 1975; Flashman's Lady, 1977; Mr American, 1980; Flashman and the Redskins, 1982; The Pyrates, 1983; Flashman and the Dragon, 1985; The Sheikh and the Dustbin, 1988; The Hollywood History of the World, 1988; Flashman and the Mountain of Light, 1990; Quartered Safe Out Here, 1992; The Candlemass Road, 1993; Flashman and the Angel of the Lord, 1994; *film screenplays:* The Three Musketeers, 1974; The Four Musketeers, 1975; Royal Flash, 1975; The Prince and the Pauper, 1977; Octopussy, 1983; Red Sonja, 1985; Casanova, 1987; The Return of the Musketeers, 1989. *Recreations:* snooker, talking to wife, history, singing. *Address:* Baldrine, Isle of Man.

See also S. W. H. Fraser.

FRASER, Air Marshal Rev. Sir (Henry) Paterson, KBE 1961 (CBE 1945); CB 1953; AFC 1937; RAF, retired; ordained 1977; Concrete Consultant; *b* 15 July 1907; *s* of late

Harry Fraser, Johannesburg, South Africa; *m* 1933, Avis Gertrude Haswell; two *s*. *Educ:* St Andrews Coll., Grahamstown, South Africa; Pembroke Coll., Cambridge (MA), RAFO, and Pres. University Air Sqdn, Cambridge; joined RAF, 1929; served in India; RAF Engineering Course, Henlow, 1933–34; Aerodynamic Flight, RAE, Farnborough, 1934–38; RAF Staff Coll., 1938; Directorate of War Organization, Air Ministry, 1939–40; commanded Experimental Flying Section, RAE, Farnborough, 1941; Mem. RAF Element, Combined Chiefs of Staff, Washington DC, 1942; Dep. Dir of War Organization, Air Ministry, 1943; Senior Administrative Planner, 2nd Tactical Air Force, 1943–44, and Dep. Air Officer in Charge of Administration, 2nd TAF, 1944–45; commanded Aircraft and Armament Experimental Establishment, Boscombe Down, 1945–46; Dep. Dir (Air Staff) Policy, Air Ministry, 1947–48; Defence Research Policy Staff, Ministry of Defence, 1948–51; idc 1951; Senior Air Staff Officer, Headquarters Fighter Command, 1952–53; Chief of Staff, Headquarters Allied Air Forces, Central Europe, 1954–56; AOC No. 12 Group, Fighter Command, 1956–58; Dir, RAF Exercise Planning, 1959; UK Representative on Permanent Military Deputies Group of Cento, 1959–62; Inspector-Gen., RAF, 1962–64. Taylor Gold Medal of RAeS, 1937; FRAeS. *Address:* 803 King's Court, Ramsey, Isle of Man IM8 1LP. *T:* Ramsey (01624) 813069.

FRASER, Sir Ian, Kt 1963; DSO 1943; OBE 1940; DL; FRSE, FRCS, FRCSI, FACS; Consulting Surgeon, Belfast; Senior Surgeon: Royal Victoria Hospital, Belfast, 1955–66; Royal Belfast Hospital for Sick Children, 1955–66; Director: Provincial Bank of Ireland; Allied Irish Bank; *b* 9 Feb. 1901; *s* of Robert Moore Fraser, BA, MD, Belfast; *m* 1931, Eleanor Margaret Mitchell (*d* 1992); one *s* one *d*. *Educ:* Royal Academical Institution, Belfast; Queen's Univ., Belfast. MB, BCh 1st Cl. Hons 1923; MD 1932; MCh 1927; FRCSI 1926; FRCS 1927; FRSE 1938; FACS 1945. Coulter Schol.; McQuitty Schol.; 1st place in Ire. as FRCSI. Resident Surgical Officer, St Helen's, Lancs; Surgeon: Royal Belfast Hosp. for Sick Children; Royal Victoria Hosp., Belfast, and former Asst Prof. of Surgery. Served War: (overseas) 1940–45: in W Africa, N. Africa, Sicily, Italy (OBE, DSO, Salerno); invasion of France, India; Officer in charge of Penicillin in Research Team, N Africa; Brig, 1945. Hon. Col (TA): No 204 Gen. Hosp., 1961–71; No 4 Field Amb., 1948–71; Surgeon in Ordinary to the Governor of Northern Ireland; Hon. Cons. Surg. to the Army in NI; Chm., Police Authority, Royal Ulster Constabulary, 1970–76; Mem. Adv. Council, Ulster Defence Regt. Past President: RCSI (1956–57); Assoc. of Surgeons GB and Ireland (1957); BMA (1962–63); Irish Med. Graduates Assoc., London, Queen's Univ. Assoc., London; Services Club, QUB; Ulster Med. Soc. President: Ulster Surgical Club; Queen's Univ. Assoc., Belfast; Chm of Convocation and Mem. Senate QUB. Visiting Lecturer: Leicester, Birmingham, Edinburgh, Bradford, London, Sheffield, Dublin, Cheltenham, Rochester, New York, Copenhagen, Glasgow, Manchester, Middlesex Hosp., Bristol, Barnsley, etc; Delegate to various assocs abroad. John Snow Oration, 1967; Downpatrick Hosp. Bi-Centenary Oration, 1967; Bishop Jeremy Taylor Lecture, 1970; Maj.-Gen. Philip Mitchiner Lecture, 1971; Robert Campbell Orator, 1973; David Torrens Lectr, NUU, 1981; Thos Vicary Lecture, RCS, 1983. Visiting Examiner in Surgery: Liverpool, Cambridge, and Manchester Univs; NUI; Apothecaries' Hall, Dublin; TCD; RCS in Ire.; RCS of Glasgow, Councillor, RCSI; Mem. and Trustee, James IV Assoc. of Surgeons; Mem., Health Educn Cttee, Min. of Health, London; Fellow: BMA; Roy. Soc. Med. Lond.; Roy. Irish Acad. of Med.; Hon. FRCPGlas 1972; Hon. FRCSE; Hon. FRCPI 1977; Hon. Fellow: Brit. Assoc. of Paediatric Surgeons; Ulster Med. Soc., 1977; Foreign Mem., L'Académie de Chirurgie, Paris; Hon. Mem., Danish Assoc. of Surgery, Copenhagen; Mem., Internat. Soc. of Surgeons. Hon. Life Governor, Royal Victoria Hosp., Belfast; Governor for GB, Amer. Coll. Surgeons. Hon. DSc: Oxon, 1963; New Univ. of Ulster, 1977; Hon. LLD QUB, 1992. GCStJ 1974 (KStJ 1940); Mem., Chapter General, London, and Knight Commander of Commandery of Ards, Ulster, Order of St John. DL Belfast, 1955. Gold Medal: Ulster Hosp. for Women and Children; Royal Belfast Hosp. for Sick Children. Commander: Ordre de la Couronne (Belgium) 1963; Order of Orange Nassau, 1969; Ordre des Palmes Académiques, 1970; Chevalier de la Legion d'Honneur, France, 1981. *Publications:* Blood, Sweat and Cheers (autobiog.), 1989; various monographs on surgical subjects. *Recreations:* golf, formerly hockey and rugby. *Address:* (residence) 19 Upper Malone Road, Belfast BT9 6TE. *T:* Belfast (01232) 668235.

FRASER, Lt-Comdr Ian Edward, VC 1945; DSC 1943; RD and Bar 1948; JP; (former Managing Director, Universal Divers Ltd, 1947–65 and since 1983 Chairman); *b* 18 Dec. 1920; *s* of S. Fraser, Bourne End, Bucks; *m* 1943, Melba Estelle Hughes; four *s* two *d*. *Educ:* Royal Grammar Sch., High Wycombe; HMS Conway. Merchant Navy, 1937–39; Royal Navy, 1939–47; Lt-Comdr, RNR, 1951–65; Younger Brother of Trinity House, 1980. JP Wallasey, 1957. Hon. Freeman, Metropolitan Bor. of Wirral, 1993. Officer, American Legion of Merit. *Publication:* Frogman VC, 1957. *Address:* Sigyn, 1 Lyndhurst Road, Wallasey, Merseyside L45 6XA. *T:* 0151–639 3355. *Clubs:* Hoylake Sailing (life mem.); New Brighton Rugby (life mem.); Leasowe Golf (life mem.; Captain, 1975).

FRASER, Sir Ian (James), Kt 1986; CBE 1972; MC 1945; Chairman, Lazard Brothers, 1980–85; Deputy Chairman: Vickers Ltd, 1980–89; TSB Group plc, 1985–91; *b* 7 Aug. 1923; 2nd *s* of late Hon. Alastair Thomas Joseph Fraser and Lady Sibyl Fraser (*née* Grimston); *m* 1st, 1958, Evelyn Elizabeth Anne Grant (*d* 1984); two *s* two *d*; 2nd, 1993, Fiona Margaret Douglas-Home. *Educ:* Ampleforth Coll.; Magdalen Coll., Oxford. Served War of 1939–45: Lieut, Scots Guards, 1942–45 (despatches, MC). Reuter Correspondent, 1946–56; S. G. Warburg & Co. Ltd, 1956–69; Dir-Gen., Panel on Take-overs and Mergers, 1969–72; Part-time Mem., CAA, 1972–74. Chairman, City Capital Markets Cttee, 1974–78; Accepting Houses Cttee, 1981–85; Member: Exec. Cttee, City Communications Centre, 1976–85; Cttee on Finance for Industry, NEDC, 1976–79; President's Cttee, CBI, 1979–81; Exec. Cttee, Jt Disciplinary Scheme of Accountancy Insts, 1979–81. Director: BOC International Ltd, 1972–85; Davy International Ltd, 1972–84; Chloride Gp Ltd, 1976–80; S. Pearson & Son Ltd, 1977–89; EMI Ltd, 1977–80; Eurafrance SA, 1979–85; Pearson-Longman Ltd, 1980–83; Chairman: Rolls-Royce Motors, 1971–80; Datastream Ltd, 1976–77. Chm., Lloyd's Syndicate 90 (1982) Names Assoc., 1990–. Mem. Exec., Help the Hospices, 1985–90; Vice-Pres., BBA, 1981–85. Trustee, Tablet Trust, 1976– (Chm., Finance Cttee, 1985–). Governor, More House Sch., 1970–75. FRSA 1970; CIMgt (FBIM 1974). Kt of Honour and Devotion, SMO of Malta, 1971. *Recreations:* fishing, gardening, Scottish history. *Address:* South Haddon, Skilgate, Taunton, Somerset TA4 2DR. *T:* Bampton (Devon) (01398) 331247. *Club:* White's.

FRASER, Very Rev. Dr Ian Watson, CMG 1973; Minister of St Stephen's Presbyterian Church, Lower Hutt, Wellington, NZ, 1961–73, retired; *b* 23 Oct. 1907; *s* of Malcolm Fraser (*b* Inverness; 1st NZ Govt Statistician) and Caroline (*née* Watson; *b* Napier, NZ); *m* 1932, Alexa Church Stewart; one *s* two *d*. *Educ:* Scots Coll., Wellington, NZ; Victoria Univ. of Wellington (MA (Hons)); Theol Hall, Dunedin; BD (Melb.); Univ. of Edinburgh; Univ. of Bonn, Germany; Union Theol Seminary, NY (STM, ThD). Minister: St Andrew's Presbyterian Church, Levin, 1933–39; Presbyterian Ch., Wyndham, 1939–42; Chaplain, St Andrew's Coll., Christchurch, 1942–48; Minister, St John's Pres. Ch., Papatoetoe, Auckland, 1948–61. Moderator, Presbyterian Church of NZ, 1968–69. Chm., Nansen Home Cttee, Presbyterian Support Services, 1984–86 (Chm., NZ Refugee Homes Bd, administering Nansen Home, 1962–84). Refugee Award of Nat. Council of Churches, 1970. Compiled biographical register of ministers in Presbyterian Church of NZ, 1840–1990. *Publications:* Understandest Thou? (Introd. to NT), 1946; Understanding the OT, 1958; The Story of Nansen Home, 1984; various booklets. *Recreations:* beekeeping, music, reading. *Address:* 19A Bloomfield Terrace, Lower Hutt 6301, Wellington, New Zealand. *T:* Wellington (4) 5697269.

FRASER, Sir (James) Campbell, Kt 1978; FRSE 1978; Chairman: Scottish Television plc, 1975–91; Director: Arlen PLC, 1991–95 (Chairman, 1993–95); Barkers Communications Scotland Ltd, 1992–95 (Chairman, 1994–95); *b* 2 May 1923; *s* of Alexander Ross Fraser and Annie McGregor Fraser; *m* 1950, Maria Harvey (*née* McLaren), JP (*d* 1995); two *d*. *Educ:* Glasgow Univ.; McMaster Univ.; Dundee Sch. of Economics. BCom. Served RAF, 1941–45. Raw Cotton Commn, Liverpool, 1950–52; Economist Intelligence Unit, 1952–57; Dunlop Rubber Co. Ltd, 1957–83: Public Relations Officer, 1958; Group Marketing Controller, 1962; Man. Dir, Dunlop New Zealand Ltd, 1967; Exec. Dir, 1969; Jt Man. Dir, 1971; Man. Dir, 1972; Chm., Dunlop Holdings, 1978–83; Chm. and Man. Dir, Dunlop Ltd, 1977–83; Chm., Dunlop Internat. AG, 1978–83. Director: British Petroleum, 1978–92 (Mem., Scottish Adv. Bd); BAT Industries, 1980–82; Charterhouse J. Rothschild, 1982–84; Bridgewater Paper Co., 1984–; Alexander Proudfoot PLC, 1987–95; Chairman: Green Park Health Care, 1985–89; Tandem Computers Ltd, 1985–; Tandem Inc., 1993–; Pauline Hyde & Assocs, 1991–93. Pres., CBI, 1982–84 (Dep. Pres., 1981–82). Founder Mem., Past Chm., and Pres., 1972–84, Soc. of Business Economists; Mem. Exec. Cttee, SMMT, 1973–82. Trustee, The Economist, 1978–. Vis. Professor: Strathclyde Univ., 1980–85; Stirling Univ., 1980–88. Chm., Strathclyde Univ. Business Sch., 1976–81; Mem. Court, St Andrews Univ., 1987–90. CIMgt (CBIM 1971); FPRI 1978. Hon. LLD Strathclyde, 1979; DUniv Stirling, 1979; Hon. DCL Bishop's Univ., Canada, 1990. *Publications:* many articles and broadcasts. *Recreations:* reading, theatre, cinema, gardening, walking. *Address:* Silver Birches, 4 Silver Lane, Purley, Surrey CR8 3HG. *Club:* Caledonian.

FRASER, Prof. Sir James (David), 2nd Bt, *cr* 1943; Postgraduate Dean, Faculty of Medicine, University of Edinburgh, 1981–89; retired; *b* 19 July 1924; *o s* of Sir John Fraser, 1st Bt, KCVO, MC, and Agnes Govane Herald (*d* 1983), The Manse, Duns, Berwickshire; *S* father 1947; *m* 1950, Maureen, *d* of Rev. John Reay, MC, Bingham Rectory, Nottingham; two *s*. *Educ:* Edinburgh Academy; Magdalen Coll., Oxford (BA); Edinburgh Univ. (MB, ChB); ChM 1961; FRCSE 1953; FRCS 1973; FRCPE 1980; FRCSI 1984; FRACS 1984. RAMC (Major), 1948–51. Senior Lectr in Clinical Surgery, Univ. of Edinburgh and Hon. Cons. Surgeon, Royal Infirmary, Edinburgh, 1951–70; Prof. of Surgery, Univ. of Southampton, 1970–80, and Hon. Cons. Surgeon, Southampton Univ. Hospital Gp, 1970–80. Pres., RCSEd, 1982–85. *Recreations:* golf, swimming. *Heir:* *s* Iain Michael Fraser [*b* 27 June 1951; *m* 1982, Sherylle (marr. diss. 1991), *d* of Keith Gillespie, New Zealand; one *s* one *d*]. *Address:* 2 Lennox Street, Edinburgh EH4 1QA.

FRASER, (James) Edward, CB 1990; Secretary of Commissions for Scotland, 1992–94; *b* 16 Dec. 1931; *s* of late Dr James F. Fraser, TD, Aberdeen, and late Dr Kathleen Blomfield; *m* 1959, Patricia Louise Stewart; two *s*. *Educ:* Aberdeen Grammar Sch.; Univ. of Aberdeen (MA); Christ's Coll., Cambridge (BA). FSAScot. RA, 1953; Staff Captain 'Q', Tel-el-Kebir, 1954–55. Asst Principal, Scottish Home Dept, 1957–60; Private Sec. to Permanent Under Sec. of State, 1960–62, and to Parly Under-Sec. of State, 1962; Principal: SHHD, 1962–64; Cabinet Office, 1964–66; HM Treasury, 1966–68; SHHD, 1968–69; Asst Sec., SHHD, 1970–76; Asst Sec., 1976, Under Sec., 1976–81, Local Govt Finance Gp, Scottish Office; Under Sec., SHHD, 1981–91. Pres., Scottish Hellenic Soc. of Edinburgh and Eastern Scotland, 1987–93. *Recreations:* reading, music, walking, Greece ancient and modern, DIY. *Address:* 59 Murrayfield Gardens, Edinburgh EH12 6DH. *T:* 0131-337 2274. *Club:* Scottish Arts (Edinburgh).

FRASER, James Owen Arthur; a Sheriff of Grampian, Highland and Islands, since 1984; *b* 9 May 1937; *s* of James and Effie Fraser; *m* 1961, Flora Shaw MacKenzie; two *s*. *Educ:* Glasgow High Sch. (Classical Dux 1954); Glasgow Univ. (MA 1958; LlB 1961). Qualified as Solicitor, 1961; employed as solicitor, Edinburgh, 1961–65, Glasgow, 1965–66; Partner, Bird Son & Semple, later Bird Semple & Crawford Herron, Solicitors, Glasgow, 1967–84. Part-time Lectr in Evidence and Procedure, Glasgow Univ., 1976–83. Temp. Sheriff, 1983–84. *Recreation:* golf. *Address:* Sheriff Court House, Ferry Road, Dingwall IV15 9QX. *T:* Dingwall (01349) 863153.

FRASER, Hon. John Allen; PC (Can.) 1979; QC (Can.) 1983; Ambassador for the Environment, Department of Foreign Affairs and International Trade, Canada; *b* Japan, 1931; *m* Catherine Findlay; three *d*. *Educ:* Univ. of British Columbia (LLB 1954). Law practice, Vancouver. MP (PC) Vancouver S, 1972–93; Opposition environment spokesman, 1972, labour spokesman, 1974; Minister of Environment and Postmaster General, 1979; Opposition spokesman on fisheries, Post Office, and Solicitor-General, 1980–84; Minister of Fisheries and Oceans, 1984–85; Speaker of H of C, Canada, 1986–93. *Address:* Lester B. Pearson Building, 125 Sussex Drive, Ottawa, Ont K1A 0G2, Canada. *T:* (613) 9440886, *Fax:* (613) 9440892; Suite 1700, 800 Burrard Street, Vancouver, BC V6Z 2J7, Canada. *T:* (604) 6665423, *Fax:* (604) 6665471.

FRASER, John Denis; MP (Lab) Norwood, since 1966; *b* 30 June 1934; *s* of Archibald and Frances Fraser; *m* 1960, Ann Hathaway; two *s* one *d*. *Educ:* Sloane Grammar Sch., Chelsea; Co-operative Coll., Loughborough; Law Soc. Sch. of Law (John Mackrell Prize). Entered Australia & New Zealand Bank Ltd, 1950; Army service, 1952–54, as Sergt, RAEC (educnl and resettlement work). Solicitor, 1960; practised with Lewis Silkin. Mem. Lambeth Borough Coun., 1962–68 (Chm. Town Planning Cttee; Chm. Labour Gp). PPS to Rt Hon. Barbara Castle, 1968–70; Opposition front bench spokesman on Home Affairs, 1972–74; Parly Under-Sec. of State, Dept of Employment, 1974–76; Minister of State, Dept of Prices and Consumer Protection, 1976–79; opposition spokesman on trade, 1979–83, on housing and construction, 1983–87, on legal affairs, 1987–94. *Recreations:* walking, music. *Address:* House of Commons, SW1A 0AA.

FRASER, Rt. Hon. (John) Malcolm, AC 1988; CH 1977; PC 1976; MA Oxon; Prime Minister of Australia, 1975–83; *b* 21 May 1930; *s* of late J. Neville Fraser, Nareen, Vic, Australia; *m* 1956, Tamara, *d* of S. R. Beggs; two *s* two *d*. *Educ:* Melbourne C of E Grammar Sch.; Magdalen Coll., Oxford (MA 1952; Hon. Fellow, 1982). MHR (L) for Wannon, Vic, 1955–83; Mem. Jt Party Cttee on Foreign Affairs, 1962–66; Minister: for the Army, 1966–68; for Educn and Science, 1968–69, 1971–72; for Defence, 1969–71; Leader of Parly Liberal Party, 1975–83; Leader of the Opposition, 1975. Sen. Adjunct Fellow, Center for Strategic and Internat. Studies, Georgetown Univ., Washington, 1983–86. Chairman: UN Sec. Gen's Expert Gp on African Commodity Problems, 1989–90; CARE Australia; Pres., CARE Internat., 1990–. Co-Chm., Commonwealth Eminent Persons Gp on S Africa, 1986. Consultant, Prudential Insurance Co., US; Director: First Australia Fund; First Australia Prime Income Fund; First Australia Prime Income Investment Fund. Member: InterAction Council for Former Heads of Govt; ANZ Internat. Bd of Advice, 1987–93. Distinguished Internat. Fellow, Amer. Enterprise Inst. for Public Policy Res., 1984–86; Fellow, Center for Internat. Affairs, Harvard Univ.,

1985. Mem. Council, Aust. Nat. Univ., 1964–66. Hon. Vice President: Oxford Soc., 1983; Royal Commonwealth Soc., 1983. Hon. LLD: Univ. of SC, 1981; Deakin Univ., 1989. *Recreations:* fishing, photography, vintage cars. *Address:* ANZ Tower, 55 Collins Street, Melbourne, Vic 3000, Australia. *Club:* Melbourne.

FRASER, John Stewart; Chairman and Chief Executive, Ciba-Geigy plc, 1990–March 1996; *b* 18 July 1931; *s* of Donald Stewart Fraser and Ruth (*née* Dobinson); *m* 1955, Diane Louise Witt; two *s* one *d*. *Educ:* Royal Melbourne Inst. of Technology. ARACI. Technical Rep., Australian Sales Manager and Australian Marketing Manager, Monsanto Australia Ltd, 1953–68; Marketing Manager, Ilford (Australia) Pty Ltd, 1968–73; Ilford Ltd, UK: Marketing Dir, 1973–78; Man. Dir and Chief Exec., 1978–84; Corporate Man. Dir, Ciba-Geigy Plastics and Additives Co., UK, 1982–84; Ciba-Geigy plc, UK: Gp Man. Dir, 1984–87; Gp Man. Dir and Chief Exec., 1987–90. Non-exec. Dir, Westminster Health Care, 1993–. Pres., Chemical Industries Assoc., 1994–. *Recreations:* tennis, golf. *Address:* (until March 1996) Ciba-Geigy plc, Hulley Road, Macclesfield, Cheshire SK10 2NX. *T:* Macclesfield (01625) 421933; (from April 1996) The Lodge, Forest Place, Warren Lane, Waldron, near Heathfield, West Sussex TN21 0TG. *Club:* City Livery.

FRASER, Kenneth John Alexander; international marketing consultant; *b* 22 Sept. 1929; *s* of Jack Sears Fraser and Marjorie Winifred (*née* Savery); *m* 1953, Kathleen Grace Booth; two *s* one *d*. *Educ:* Thames Valley Grammar Sch., Twickenham; London School of Economics (BScEcon Hons). Joined Erwin Wasey & Co. Ltd, 1953, then Lintas Ltd, 1958; Managing Director, Research Bureau Ltd, 1962; Unilever: Head of Marketing Analysis and Evaluation Group, 1965; Head of Marketing Division, 1976–79, 1981–89; Hd of Internat. Affairs, 1985–89; Hd of External Affairs, 1989–90; seconded to NEDO as Industrial Dir, 1979–81. Advr, European Assoc. of Branded Goods Manufacturers, 1991–93. Member: Consumer Protection Adv. Cttee, Dept of Prices and Consumer Protection, 1975; Management Bd, ADAS, MAFF, 1986–92; Chairman: CBI Marketing and Consumer Affairs Cttee, 1977; Internat. Chamber of Commerce Marketing Commn, 1978; Vice Chm., Advertising Assoc., 1981–90; Dir, Direct Mail Services Standards Bd, 1991–. Mem., Advocacy Cttee, Nat. Children's Home, 1987–. FRSA. *Recreations:* walking, music, reading. *Address:* 14 Coombe Lane West, Kingston, Surrey KT2 7BX. *T:* 0181–949 3760. *Club:* Wig and Pen.

FRASER, Rt. Hon. Malcolm; *see* Fraser, Rt Hon. J. M.

FRASER, Marion Anne, (Lady Fraser); Chair of the Board, Christian Aid, since 1990; Lord High Commissioner, then HM High Commissioner, General Assembly, Church of Scotland, 1994–95; *b* 17 Oct. 1932; *d* of Robert Forbes and Elizabeth Taylor Forbes; *m* 1956, Sir William (Kerr) Fraser, *qv*; three *s* one *d*. *Educ:* Hutchesons' Girls' Grammar Sch.; Univ. of Glasgow (MA); Royal Scottish Academy of Music. LRAM, ARCM. Chm. (elect), Scottish Internat. Piano Comp., 1995. Director: Friends of Royal Scottish Academy (Founder Chm., 1986–89); Scottish Opera, 1990–94; St Mary's Music School, 1989–95. Trustee, Scottish Churches Architectural Heritage Trust, 1989–95; Gov., Laurel Bank Sch. for Girls, 1988–95. Hon. LLD Glasgow, 1995. *Recreations:* family, friends, people and places. *Address:* Broadwood, Edinburgh Road, Gifford, East Lothian EH41 4JE. *Club:* New (Edinburgh).

FRASER, Air Marshal Rev. Sir Paterson; *see* Fraser, Air Marshal Rev. Sir H. P.

FRASER, Peter Marshall, MC 1944; MA; FBA 1960; Fellow of All Souls College, Oxford, 1954–85; now Emeritus, and Acting Warden, 1985–87 (Sub-Warden, 1980–82); Lecturer in Hellenistic History, 1948–64, Reader 1964–85; *b* 6 April 1918; *y s* of late Archibald Fraser; *m* 1st, 1940, Catharine, *d* of late Prebendary Heaton-Renshaw (marr. diss.); one *s* three *d*; 2nd, 1955, Ruth Elsbeth, *d* of late F. Renfer, Bern, Switzerland; two *s*; 3rd, 1973, Barbara Ann Stewart, *d* of late L. E. C. Norbury, FRCS. *Educ:* City of London Sch.; Brasenose Coll., Oxford (Hon. Fellow 1977). Seaforth Highlanders, 1941–45; Military Mission to Greece, 1943–45. Sen. Scholar, Christ Church, Oxford, 1946–47, Junior Proctor, Oxford Univ., 1960–61; Domestic Bursar, All Souls Coll., 1962–65. Dir, British Sch. at Athens, 1968–71. Vis. Prof. of Classical Studies, Indiana Univ., 1973–74. Chm., Managing Cttee, Soc. of Afghan Studies, 1972–82; Vice Pres., Soc. for S Asian Studies, 1985–90. Ordinary Mem., German Archaeol. Soc., 1979; Corresp. Fellow, Archaeolog. Soc. of Athens, 1971. Gen. Editor and Chm., British Acad. Cttee, Lexicon of Greek Personal Names, 1973–. Hon. Dr. phil Trier, 1984. *Publications:* (with G. E. Bean) The Rhodian Peraea and Islands, 1954; (with T. Rönne) Boeotian and West Greek Tombstones, 1957; Rostovtzeff, Social and Economic History of the Roman Empire, 2nd edn, revised, 1957; Samothrace, The Inscriptions, (Vol. ii, Excavations of Samothrace), 1960; E. Löfstedt, Roman Literary Portraits, trans. from the Swedish (Romare), 1958; The Wares of Autolycus; Selected Literary Essays of Alice Meynell (ed), 1965; E. Kjellberg and G. Säflund, Greek and Roman Art, trans. from the Swedish (Grekisk och romersk konst), 1968; Ptolemaic Alexandria, 1972; Rhodian Funerary Monuments, 1977; A. J. Butler, Arab Conquest of Egypt, 2nd edn, revised, 1978; (with E. Matthews) A Lexicon of Greek Personal Names, vol. 1, 1987, vol. 2, 1994; (ed) Memorial Addresses of All Souls College, 1989; Cities of Alexander, 1995. *Address:* All Souls College, Oxford OX1 4AL.

FRASER, Ronald Petrie, CB 1972; Secretary, Scottish Home and Health Department, 1972–77; *b* 2 June 1917; *yr s* of late T. Petrie Fraser, Elgin; *m* 1962, Ruth Wright Anderson, Edinburgh; one *d*. *Educ:* Daniel Stewart's Coll., Edinburgh; University of Edinburgh; The Queen's Coll., Oxford. Joined Dept of Health for Scotland for work on emergency hosp. service, 1940; Asst Private Sec. to Sec. of State for Scotland, 1944; Cabinet Office, 1947; Sec., Scottish Hosp. Endowments Commn, 1950; Asst Sec., Dept of Health for Scotland, 1954; Asst Sec., Scottish Education Dept, 1961; Under-Sec., 1963; Under-Sec., 1968–71, Dep. Sec., 1971, Min. of Agriculture, Fisheries and Food. Chief Counting Officer for Scotland Act Referendum, 1979. *Recreations:* walking, music. *Address:* 40A Lygon Road, Edinburgh EH16 5QA. *T:* 0131–667 8298. *Club:* New (Edinburgh).

FRASER, Simon William Hetherington; Sheriff of North Strathclyde at Dumbarton, since 1989; *b* 2 April 1951; *s* of George MacDonald Fraser, *qv*; *m* 1979, Sheena Janet Fraser; one *d*. *Educ:* Glasgow Acad.; Glasgow Univ. (LLB). Solicitor, 1973–89 (Partner, Flowers & Co., Glasgow, 1976–89). Temp. Sheriff, 1987–89. Pres., Glasgow Bar Assoc., 1981–82. *Recreation:* cricket. *Address:* Sheriff Court, Church Street, Dumbarton G82 1QR. *T:* Dumbarton (01389) 763266. *Club:* Avizandum (Glasgow).

FRASER, Veronica Mary; Diocesan Director of Education, Diocese of Worcester, 1985–93; *b* 19 April 1933; *o d* of late Archibald Fraser. *Educ:* Richmond County Sch. for Girls; St Hugh's Coll., Oxford. Head of English Department: The Alice Ottley Sch., Worcester, 1962–65; Guildford County Sch. for Girls, 1965–67 (also Librarian); Headmistress, Godolphin Sch., Salisbury, 1968–80; Adviser on Schools to Bishop of Winchester, 1981–85. Pres., Assoc. of Sen. Members, St Hugh's Coll., Oxford. Gov., SPCK.

FRASER, William James; JP; Lord Provost of Aberdeen, 1977–80; Member, City of Aberdeen District Council, until April 1996; *b* 31 Dec. 1921; *s* of late William and Jessie Fraser; *m* 1961, Mary Ann; three *s* one *d*. *Educ:* York Street Sch., Aberdeen; Frederick Street Sch., Aberdeen. Mem., Scottish Exec., Labour Party, 1949–74 (Chm., 1962–63). Pres., Aberdeen Trades Council, 1952. JP Aberdeen, 1950. *Address:* The Mill House, Brig O'Balgownie, Aberdeen AB2 8JN. *T:* Aberdeen (01224) 826916.

FRASER, Sir William (Kerr), GCB 1984 (KCB 1979; CB 1978); Principal and Vice-Chancellor, University of Glasgow, 1988–95; *b* 18 March 1929; *s* of A. M. Fraser and Rachel Kerr; *m* 1956, Marion Anne Forbes (*see* Lady Fraser); three *s* one *d*. *Educ:* Eastwood Sch., Clarkston; Glasgow Univ. (MA, LLB). Joined Scottish Home Dept, 1955; Private Sec. to Parliamentary Under-Sec., 1959, and to Secretary of State for Scotland, 1966–67; Civil Service Fellow, Univ. of Glasgow, 1963–64; Asst Sec., Regional Development Div., 1967–71; Under Sec., Scottish Home and Health Dept, 1971–75; Dep. Sec., 1975–78, Permanent Under-Sec. of State, 1978–88, Scottish Office. Dir, Scottish Mutual Assce, 1990–. Chm., Royal Commn on the Ancient and Historical Monuments of Scotland, 1995–. Gov., Caledonian Res. Foundn, 1990–. FRSE 1985. FRCPS (Hon.) 1992; FRSAMD 1995. Hon. LLD: Glasgow, 1982; Strathclyde, 1991; Aberdeen, 1993; Dr *hc* Edinburgh, 1995. *Address:* Broadwood, Edinburgh Road, Gifford, East Lothian EH41 4JE. *Club:* New (Edinburgh).

FRASER McLUSKEY, Rev. James; *see* McLuskey.

FRAYLING, Prof. Christopher John, MA, PhD; Professor and Head of Department of Cultural History, since 1979, Pro-Rector, since 1993, Royal College of Art, London; *b* 25 Dec. 1946; *s* of late Arthur Frederick Frayling and of Barbara Kathleen (*née* Imhof); *m* 1981, Helen Snowdon. *Educ:* Repton Sch.; Churchill Coll., Cambridge (BA, MA, PhD). FCSD 1994. Churchill Research Studentship, 1968–71; Lectr in Modern History, Univ. of Exeter, 1971–72; Tutor, Dept of General Studies, Royal College of Art, 1972–73, Vis. Lectr, 1973–79; Research Asst, Dept of Information Retrieval, Imperial War Mus., 1973–74; Lectr in the History of Ideas and European Social History, Univ. of Bath, 1974–79; founded Dept of Cultural History (ex General Studies), RCA, 1979, founded courses: History of Design, 1982; Conservation, 1987; Visual Arts Admin, 1991. Vis. Prof., Shanghai Univ. of Technol., 1991. Historian, lectr, critic; regular contributor, as writer and presenter, to radio (incl. Kaleidoscope, Stop the Week, Meridian, Critics' Forum, Third Opinion, Third Ear, Nightwaves; series: The American Cowboy; America: the movie (Silver Medal, NY Internat. Radio Fest., 1989); Britannia: the film) and TV (incl. series Scene, Art of Persuasion (Gold Medal, NY Internat. Film and TV Fest., 1985), Busting the Block—or the Art of Pleasing People, Design Classics, Timewatch, Movie Profiles, The Face of Tutankhamun, and Strange Landscape). Crafts Council: Mem., 1982–85; Mem., Educn Cttee, 1981–85; Chm., Pubns and Inf. Cttee, 1984–85. Arts Council of England (formerly of GB): Mem., 1987–; Mem., Art Panel, 1983–94 (Dep. Chm., 1984–87; Chm., 1987–94); Chm., Film, Video and Broadcasting Panel, 1994–; Mem., Photography Adv. Panel, 1983–85; Chm., Art Projects Cttee, 1986–87; Mem., Combined Arts Cttee, 1987–88; Chm., Combined Arts Cttee, 1989–; Chm., New Collaborations Cttee, 1990–94. Mem. Adv. Bd, ICA, 1989–; Chm., Curriculum Develt Bd, Arts Technol. Centre, 1989–. Chm. of Trustees, Crafts Study Centre, Bath, 1982–; Foundn Trustee, Holbourne of Menstrie Mus., Bath, 1985–; Chm., Free Form Arts Trust, 1984–88; Trustee: V&A Museum, 1984– (Member: Adv. Council, 1981–83; Sen. Staff Appts Cttee, 1987–91; S Kensington Jt Planning Cttee, 1989–; Educn and Res. Cttees, 1990–); Koestler Awards for Art in Prisons, 1992–. Governor, BFI, 1982–87 (Mem., 1982–86, Chm. 1984–86, Educn Cttee); Member: Art and Design Sect., Leverhulme Team on Arts in Higher Educn, 1982; Working Party on art and design advising NAB, 1985–87. FRSA 1984. Radio play, The Rime of the Bounty (Sony Radio Award, 1990). *Publications:* Napoleon Wrote Fiction, 1972; (ed) The Vampyre—Lord Ruthven to Count Dracula, 1978; Spaghetti Westerns: Cowboys and Europeans, from Karl May to Sergio Leone, 1981; The Schoolmaster and the Wheelwrights, 1983; The Royal College of Art: one hundred and fifty years of art and design, 1987; Vampyres, 1991; (ed) Beyond the Dovetail: essays on craft, skill and imagination, 1991; Clint Eastwood, 1992; The Face of Tutankhamun, 1992, (with Helen Frayling) The Art Pack, 1992; Research in Art and Design, 1994; Strange Landscape: a journey through the Middle Ages, 1995; Things to Come: a classic film, 1995; contribs to: Reappraisals of Rousseau—studies in honour of R. A. Leigh, 1980; Cinema, Politics and Society in America, 1981; Rousseau et Voltaire en 1978, 1981; Rousseau After Two Hundred Years: Proc. of Cambridge Bicentennial Colloquium, 1982; Eduardo Paolozzi: perspectives and themes, 1984; Eduardo Paolozzi—Lost Magic Kingdoms, 1986; Rape: an interdisciplinary study, 1987; 2D/3D—Art and Craft made and designed for the twentieth century, 1987; The Cambridge Guide to the Arts in Britain, Vol. IX (post 1945), 1988; Craft Classics since the 1940s, 1988; Eduardo Paolozzo: Noah's Ark, 1990; Ariel at Bay: reflections on broadcasting and the arts, 1990; Objects and Images; essay on design and advertising, 1992; articles on film, popular culture and the visual arts/crafts in Cambridge Rev., Cinema, Film, Sight & Sound, London Magazine, New Society, Crafts, Burlington Magazine, Art and Design, Designer, Design Week, Design, THES, TLS, Time Out, Punch, Designer, Craft History, Creative Review, Blueprint, Independent Magazine, Listener, Times, Sunday Times, Guardian, and various learned jls. *Recreation:* finding time. *Address:* Royal College of Art, Kensington Gore, SW7 2EU. *T:* 0171–584 5020.

See also Rev. N. A. Frayling.

FRAYLING, Rev. Canon Nicholas Arthur; Rector of Liverpool, since 1987; Hon. Canon, Liverpool Cathedral, since 1989; *b* 29 Feb. 1944; *s* of late Arthur Frederick Frayling, OBE and of Barbara Kathleen (*née* Imhof). *Educ:* Repton Sch.; Exeter Univ. (BA Theology 1969); Cuddesdon Theol Coll., Oxford. Management training, retail trade, 1962–64; Temp. Probation Officer (prison welfare), Inner London Probation and After-Care Service, 1965–66, pt-time, 1966–71. Deacon, 1971; priest, 1972; Asst Curate, St John, Peckham, 1971–74; Vicar, All Saints, Tooting Graveney, 1974–83; Canon Residentiary and Precentor, Liverpool Cathedral, 1983–87. Chaplain: St Paul's Eye Hosp., Liverpool, 1987–90; Huyton Coll., 1987–91; to High Sheriff of Merseyside, 1992–93. Chairman: Southwark Diocesan Adv. Cttee for Care of Churches, 1980–83; Religious Adv. Panel, BBC Radio Merseyside, 1988–; Welfare Orgns Cttee, Liverpool CVS, 1992–. *Recreations:* music, friends. *Address:* 25 Princes Park Mansions, Sefton Park Road, Liverpool L8 3SA. *T:* (home) 0151–727 4692, (office) 0151–236 5287. *Clubs:* Commonwealth Trust; Artists' (Hon.), Athenæum (Liverpool); Liverpool Racquet (Hon.).

See also C. J. Frayling.

FRAYN, Claire, (Mrs Michael Frayn); *see* Tomalin, C.

FRAYN, Michael; writer; *b* 8 Sept. 1933; *s* of late Thomas Allen Frayn and Violet Alice Lawson; *m* 1st, 1960, Gillian Palmer (marr. diss. 1989); three *d*; 2nd, 1993, Claire Tomalin, *qv*. *Educ:* Kingston Gram. Sch.; Emmanuel Coll., Cambridge (Hon. Fellow, 1985). Reporter, Guardian, 1957–59; Columnist, Guardian, 1959–62; Columnist, Observer, 1962–68. *Television:* plays: Jamie, 1968; Birthday, 1969; First and Last, 1989 (Internat. Emmy Award, 1990); A Landing on the Sun, 1994; *documentaries:* Imagine a City Called Berlin, 1975; Vienna—the Mask of Gold, 1977; Three Streets in the Country, 1979; The Long Straight, 1980; Jerusalem, 1984; Prague—the Magic Lantern, 1993; *stage plays:* The Two of Us, 1970; The Sandboy, 1971; Alphabetical Order, 1975 (Evening Standard Drama Award for Best Comedy); Donkeys' Years, 1976 (SWET Best Comedy Award);

Clouds, 1976; Liberty Hall, 1980; Make and Break, 1980 (New Standard Best Comedy Award); Noises Off, 1982 (Standard Best Comedy Award; SWET Best Comedy Award); Benefactors, 1984 (Standard Best Play Award; Laurence Olivier (formerly SWET) Award for Play of the Year; Plays and Players London Theatre Critics' Best New Play); Look Look, 1990; Here, 1993; Now You Know, 1995; *filmscript:* Clockwise, 1986. Nat. Press Award, 1970. *Publications:* collections of columns: The Day of the Dog, 1962; The Book of Fub, 1963; On the Outskirts, 1964; At Bay in Gear Street, 1967; The Original Michael Frayn, 1983; *non-fiction:* Constructions, 1974; *novels:* The Tin Men, 1965 (Somerset Maugham Award); The Russian Interpreter, 1966 (Hawthornden Prize); Towards the End of the Morning, 1967; A Very Private Life, 1968; Sweet Dreams, 1973; The Trick of It, 1989; A Landing On the Sun, 1991; Now You Know, 1992; *translations:* Tolstoy, The Fruits of Enlightenment, 1979 (prod. 1979); Anouilh, Number One, 1984; Chekhov: The Cherry Orchard, 1978 (prod. 1978, 1989); Three Sisters, 1983 (prod. 1985); Wild Honey, 1984 (prod. 1984); The Seagull, 1986 (prod. 1986); Uncle Vanya, 1988 (prod. 1988); The Sneeze (adapted from one-act plays and short stories), 1989 (prod. 1988); Trifonov, Exchange, 1986 (prod. 1986, 1990). *Address:* c/o Greene Heaton Ltd, 37a Goldhawk Road, W12 8QQ.

FRAYNE, Very Rev. David; Provost of Blackburn, since 1992; *b* 19 Oct. 1934; *s* of Philip John Frayne and Daisy Morris Frayne (*née* Eade); *m* 1961, Elizabeth Ann Frayne (*née* Grant); one *s* two *d. Educ:* Reigate Grammar Sch.; St Edmund Hall, Oxford (BA 1958 (2nd cl. Hons PPE); MA 1962); The Queen's Coll., Birmingham (DTh 1960). Pilot Officer, RAF, 1954–55. Ordained deacon, 1960, priest, 1961; Asst Curate, St Michael, East Wickham, 1960–63; Priest-in-charge, St Barnabas, Downham, Lewisham, 1963–67; Vicar of N Sheen, Richmond, 1967–73; Rector of Caterham, 1973–83; Vicar of St Mary Redcliffe with Temple, Bristol and St John the Baptist, Bedminster, 1983–92. Rural Dean of Caterham, 1980–83; Hon. Canon, Southwark Cathedral, 1982, Emeritus, 1983; Rural Dean of Bedminster, 1986–92; Proctor in Convocation, 1987–90; Hon. Canon of Bristol Cathedral, 1991. *Recreations:* walking, camping, music. *Address:* The Provost's House, Preston New Road, Blackburn BB2 6PS. *T:* Blackburn (01254) 52502, 51491. *Club:* Oxford Society.

FRAZER, Prof. Malcolm John, CBE 1992; PhD, FRSC; education consultant; *b* 7 Feb. 1931; *m* 1st, 1957, Gwenyth Ida Biggs (marr. diss. 1990), JP, MA; three *s*; 2nd, 1991, Aleksandra Kornhauser. *Educ:* Univ. of London; BSc 1952, PhD 1955. Royal Military Coll. of Science, 1956–57; Lecturer and Head of Dept of Chemistry, Northern Polytechnic, London, 1965–72; Prof. of Chemical Educn, 1972–86, and Pro-Vice Chancellor, 1976–81, Univ. of East Anglia, Norwich; Chief Executive: CNAA, 1986–93; HEQC, 1992–93; Chm., CATE, 1993–94. Vis. Prof., Open Univ., 1993–. Vice-President: RSC, 1973–74; Royal Instn, 1988–91; SHRE, 1993–; Gen. Sec./Vice-Pres., Chm. Council, BAAS, 1978–91. Hon. Fellow: N London Poly., 1988; SCOTVEC, 1990; Poly. South West, 1991; Brighton Poly., 1992; Manchester Metropolitan Univ., 1993; Bolton Inst., 1994. Hon. FCollP, 1988. Hon. Dr Leuven, 1985; Hon. DSc: Leicester, 1993; Luton, 1993; Hon. DEd: CNAA, 1992; Heriot-Watt, 1993; Hon. DLitt Glasgow Caledonian, 1993. Nyholm Medal, RSC, 1982. *Publications:* textbooks on chemistry, chemical educn, and problem solving; contribs to Jl Chem. Soc., etc. *Address:* Sora, Abingdon Road, Tubney, Oxon OX13 5QQ.

FREARS, Stephen Arthur; film director; *b* 20 June 1941; *s* of Dr Russell E. Frears and Ruth M. Frears; *m* 1968, Mary K. Wilmers (marr. diss. 1974); two *s*; lives with Anne Rothenstein; one *s* one *d. Educ:* Gresham's Sch., Holt; Trinity Coll., Cambridge (BA Law). Director: Gumshoe, 1971; Bloody Kids, 1980; Going Gently, 1981; Walter, 1982; Saigon, 1983; The Hit, 1984; My Beautiful Laundrette, 1985; Prick Up Your Ears, 1986; Sammy and Rosie Get Laid, 1987; Dangerous Liaisons, 1989; The Grifters, 1990; Accidental Hero, 1992; The Snapper, 1993. *Recreation:* reading. *Address:* Casarotto Company, National House, 60 Wardour Street, W1V 3TE. *T:* 0171–287 4450.

FREDE, Prof. Michael, Dr.phil; FBA 1994; Professor of the History of Philosophy, and Fellow of Keble College, Oxford University, since 1991; *b* Berlin, 31 May 1940. *Educ:* Univ. of Göttingen (Dr.phil 1966). Philosophy Res. Assistant, Univ. of Göttingen, 1966–71; Loeb Fellow, Harvard Univ., 1971; University of California at Berkeley: Vis. Lectr, 1968–69; Asst, then Associate, Professor of Philosophy, 1971–74; Prof. of Philosophy, 1974–76; Princeton University: Prof. of Philosophy, 1976–89; Stewart Prof. of Philosophy, 1989–91. *Publication:* Essays in Ancient Philosophy, 1987. *Address:* Keble College, Oxford OX1 3PG.

FREDERICK, Sir Charles Boscawen, 10th Bt *cr* 1723; *b* 11 April 1919; *s* of Sir Edward Boscawen Frederick, 9th Bt, CVO and Edith Katherine (Kathleen) Cortlandt (*d* 1970), *d* of late Col W. H. Mulloy, RE; *S* father, 1956; *m* 1949, Rosemary, *er d* of late Lt-Col R. J. H. Baddeley, MC; two *s* two *d. Educ:* Eton. 2nd Lieut Grenadier Guards, 1942; served N Africa and Italy, 1943–45 (despatches); Capt. 1945; Palestine, 1946–47 (despatches); Malaya, 1948–49; Egypt, 1952–53; Major, 1953. Member: London Stock Exchange, 1954–62; Provincial Brokers Stock Exchange, 1962 (Mem. Council, 1966; Dep. Chm. 1972); Stock Exchange Council, and Chm., Provincial Unit, 1973–75. JP 1960. General Commissioner of Income Tax, 1966. *Heir: s* Christopher St John Frederick [*b* 28 June 1950; *m* 1990, Camilla, *o d* of Sir Derek Gilbey, 3rd Bt; one *s* one *d*]. *Address:* Virginia Cottage, Stoke Trister, Wincanton, Somerset BA9 9PQ.

FREDERICTON, Bishop of, since 1989; **Rt. Rev. George Colborne Lemmon;** *b* 20 March 1932; *m* 1957, Lois Jean Foster; two *s* one *d. Educ:* Univ. of New Brunswick (BA 1959); Wycliffe Coll., Toronto (LTh 1962; BD 1965). Linotype operator, Globe Print, Telegraph Jl, Toronto Telegram, 1949–62. Deacon 1962, priest 1963; Incumbent, Canterbury with Benton, 1962; Rector of: Wilmot with Wicklow and Peel, 1965; Renforth, 1969; Sackville with Dorchester, dio. of Fredericton, 1972–84; Christ Church, Fredericton, 1984–89; Canon of Fredericton, 1983–89. Hon. DD: King's Coll., Halifax, 1990; Wycliffe Coll., Toronto, 1991. *Recreation:* golfing. *Address:* Diocesan Office, 115 Church Street, Fredericton, New Brunswick E3B 4C8, Canada. *T:* (506) 4591801, *Fax:* (506) 4598475.

FREE, Prof. John Brand, CMG 1995; ScD, DSc; Hon. Professor, School of Pure and Applied Biology, University of Wales, Cardiff, since 1984; *b* 21 Aug. 1927; *s* of Frederick Charles Free and Gladys Ellen Free; *m* 1953, Nancy Wilson Speirs; two *s* one *d. Educ:* Cambridge and County High Sch.; Jesus Coll., Cambridge. BA 1950, MA 1955, ScD 1982, Cantab; PhD 1954, DSc 1967, London. FIBiol 1970. Served Army, 1945–48, Suffolk Regiment: commnd RPC; seconded to High Commnd Territory Corps in ME. Rothamsted Experimental Station: ARC Scholar, 1951–54; on staff, 1954–87; SPSO 1983. NRCC Fellow, Apiculture Dept, Univ. of Guelph, Ontario, 1958–59; Nuffield/NRCC lecture tour of Canadian univs and res. centres, 1967; Leverhulme Emeritus Fellow, 1987, 1988. Visited several tropical countries for ODA and British Council to initiate and advise on bee-keeping and crop pollination projects, 1972–. Vice-Chm., Internat. Bee Res. Assoc., 1975–83 (Hon. Vice-Pres., 1993); President: Central Assoc. of Beekeepers, 1977–83; Apimondia Standing Commn on Pollination, 1985–89 (Hon. Mem. Apimondia, 1989); Chm., British Section, Internat. Union for Study of Social Insects, 1979–82 (Hon. Mem., 1988). Hon. Fellow, British Beekeepers' Assoc., 1990. *Publications:* Bumblebees (with C. G. Butler), 1959; Insect Pollination of Crops, 1970, 2nd edn 1993; The Social Organisation of Honeybees, 1977; Bees and Mankind, 1982; (ed) Honeybee Biology, 1982; Pheromones of Social Bees, 1987; (ed) Keeping Bees, 1992; *children's books:* Honeybees, 1978; Insects We Need, 1980; (with R. Dutton) Arab Village, 1980; Life Under Stones, 1981; contrib. res. papers and rev. papers to scientific jls on: social orgn of bees and their behaviour within the colony and in the field; improving honey prodn and bee pollination of agricl crops; use of pheromones (natural and synthetic) that control bee activities; insect pests of oil seed rape. *Recreations:* photography (produced many educational slide series and film-strips—mostly on insects and tropical agriculture), ancient civilisations, painting, walking. *Address:* 37 Plainwood Close, Summersdale, Chichester, West Sussex PO19 4YB. *T:* Chichester (01243) 533822.

FREEDBERG, Prof. David Adrian; Professor of Art History, Columbia University, since 1984; *b* 1 June 1948; *s* of William Freedberg and Eleonore Kupfer; *m*; one *s* one *d. Educ:* S African Coll. High Sch., Cape Town; Yale Univ. (BA); Balliol Coll., Oxford (DPhil). Rhodes Scholar, Oxford, 1969–72; Lectr in History of Art: Westfield Coll., Univ. of London, 1973–76; Courtauld Inst. of Art, Univ. of London, 1976–84; Slade Prof. of Fine Art, Univ. of Oxford, 1983–84. Baldwin Prof., Oberlin Coll., Ohio, 1979; Vis. Mem., Inst. for Advanced Study, Princeton, NJ, 1980–81; Gerson Lectr, Univ. of Groningen, 1983; VUB-Leerstoel, Brussels Univ., 1988–89. *Publications:* Dutch Landscape Prints of the Seventeenth Century, 1980; The Life of Christ after the Passion (Corpus Rubenianum Ludwig Burchard, VII), 1983; Iconoclasts and their Motives, 1985; The Power of Images, 1989; (ed) The Prints of Pieter Bruegel the Elder, 1989; Joseph Kosuth: The Play of the Unmentionable, 1992; articles in Burlington Magazine, Revue de l'Art, Gentse Bijdragen, Münchner Jahrbuch der Bildenden Kunst, Jl of Warburg and Courtauld Insts, Print Quarterly, Quaderni Puteani. *Address:* Department of Art History, Columbia University, Schermerhorn Hall, New York, NY 10027, USA.

FREEDMAN, Amelia, (Mrs Michael Miller), MBE 1989; FRAM 1986; Artistic Director and Founder, Nash Ensemble, since 1964; *b* 21 Nov. 1940; *d* of Miriam Freedman (*née* Claret) and Henry Freedman; *m* 1970, Michael Miller; two *s* one *d. Educ:* St George's Sch., Harpenden; Henrietta Barnet, London; RAM. LRAM (piano), ARCM (clarinet). Music teacher, 1961–72: King's Sch., Cambridge; Perse Sch. for Girls, Cambridge; Chorleywood College for the Blind; Sir Philip Magnus Sch., London. Artistic Dir, Bath Internat. Fest., 1984–93; Musical Adviser, Israel Fest., 1989–; Programme Adviser, Philharmonia Orch., 1992–; chamber music consultant for various projects at South Bank Centre and Barbican, and for LSO. Hon. DMus Bath, 1993. Chevalier, L'ordre des Arts et des Lettres (France), 1984; Czech Govt Medal for services to Czech music in UK, 1986. *Recreations:* theatre, cinema, ballet, opera; spectator sport—cricket, rugger, football; stamp-collecting, children. *Address:* 14 Cedars Close, Hendon, NW4 1TR. *T:* 0181–203 3025, *Fax:* 0181–203 9540.

FREEDMAN, Charles, CB 1983; Commissioner, Customs and Excise, 1972–84; *b* 15 Oct. 1925; *s* of late Solomon Freedman, OBE, and Lilian Freedman; *m* 1949, Sarah Sadie King; one *s* two *d. Educ:* Westcliff High Sch.; Cheltenham Grammar Sch.; Trinity Coll., Cambridge (Sen. Schol., BA). Entered HM Customs and Excise, 1947; Asst Sec., 1963. *Address:* 10 Cliff Avenue, Leigh-on-Sea, Essex SS9 1HF. *T:* Southend-on-Sea (01702) 73148. *Club:* Civil Service.

FREEDMAN, Dawn Angela, (Mrs N. J. Shestopal); Her Honour Judge Freedman; a Circuit Judge, since 1991; *b* 9 Dec. 1942; *d* of Julius and Celia Freedman; *m* 1970, Neil John Shestopal. *Educ:* Westcliff High Sch. for Girls; University Coll., London (LLB Hons). Called to the Bar, Gray's Inn, 1966; Metropolitan Stipendiary Magistrate, 1980–91; a Recorder, 1989–91. Mem. Parole Bd, 1992–. *Recreations:* theatre, television, cooking. *Address:* Harrow Crown Court, Hailsham Drive, Harrow HA1 4TU.

FREEDMAN, Prof. Lawrence David, DPhil; FBA 1995; Professor of War Studies, King's College, London, since 1982; *b* 7 Dec. 1948; *s* of late Lt-Comdr Julius Freedman and of Myra Freedman; *m* 1974, Judith Anne Hill; one *s* one *d. Educ:* Whitley Bay Grammar Sch. BAEcon Manchester; BPhil York; DPhil Oxford. Teaching Asst, York Univ., 1971–72; Research Fellow, Nuffield Coll., Oxford, 1974–75; Research Associate, International Inst. for Strategic Studies, 1975–76 (Mem. Council, 1984–92); Research Fellow, Royal Inst. of International Affairs, 1976–78; Head of Policy Studies, RIIA, 1978–82. Hon. Dir, Centre for Defence Studies, 1990–. Chm., Cttee on Internat. Peace and Security, Social Science Res. Council (US), 1993–. FKC 1992. FRSA 1991. *Publications:* US Intelligence and the Soviet Strategic Threat, 1977, 2nd edn 1986; Britain and Nuclear Weapons, 1980; The Evolution of Nuclear Strategy, 1981; (jtly) Nuclear War & Nuclear Peace, 1983, 2nd edn 1989; (ed) The Troubled Alliance, 1983; The Atlas of Global Strategy, 1985; The Price of Peace, 1986; Britain and the Falklands War, 1988; (jtly) Signals of War, 1990; (ed) Population Change and European Security, 1991; (ed) Britain in the World, 1991; (jtly) The Gulf Conflict 1990–1991, 1993; War: a Reader, 1994; (ed) Military Intervention in Europe, 1994. *Recreations:* tennis, political caricature. *Address:* c/o Department of War Studies, King's College, Strand, WC2R 2LS. *T:* 0171–873 2025.

FREEDMAN, Louis, CBE 1978; Proprietor, Cliveden Stud; *b* 5 Feb. 1917; 4th *s* of Sampson and Leah Freedman; *m* 1st, 1944, Cara Kathlyn Abrahamson (marr. diss.); one *s* one *d*; 2nd, 1960, Valerie Clarke; one *s. Educ:* University College School. FSVA. TA, RE, 1938; commnd RA, 1943; Devonshire Regt, 1944. Director: Land Securities Investment Trust, 1958–77; GRA Gp, then Wembley PLC, 1985–94. Mem., Race Relations Bd, 1968–77. Chm., Nat. Assoc. Property Owners, 1971–72; Pres., Racehorse Owners Assoc., 1972–74. Vice-Chm., NE Thames RHA, 1975–79; Chairman: Camden and Islington AHA, 1979–82; City and Hackney DHA, 1982–84. Governor: Royal Hosp. of St Bartholomew the Great, 1971–74; St Bartholomew's Hosp. Med. Coll., 1974– (Chm. Special Trustees, 1988–92). Owned and bred: Polygamy, winner of the Oaks, 1974; Reference Point, winner of the Derby, King George VI and Queen Elizabeth Stakes, and the St Leger, 1987. *Recreation:* gardening. *Address:* Cliveden Stud House, Taplow, Maidenhead, Berks SL6 0HL. *Clubs:* Garrick; Jockey (Newmarket) (Deputy Senior Steward, 1981–83).

FREELAND, Sir John Redvers, KCMG 1984 (CMG 1973); QC 1987; HM Diplomatic Service, retired; Judge, Arbitral Tribunal and Mixed Commission for Agreement on German External Debts, since 1988; Judge, European Court of Human Rights, since 1991; *b* 16 July 1927; *o s* of C. Redvers Freeland and Freda Freeland (*née* Walker); *m* 1952, Sarah Mary, *er d* of late S. Pascoe Hayward, QC; one *s* one *d. Educ:* Stowe; Corpus Christi Coll., Cambridge. Royal Navy, 1945 and 1948–51. Called to Bar, Lincoln's Inn, 1952, Bencher, 1985; Mem. *ad eundem,* Middle Temple. Asst Legal Adviser, FO, 1954–63, and 1965–67; Legal Adviser, HM Embassy, Bonn, 1963–65; Legal Counsellor, FCO (formerly FO), 1967–70; Counsellor (Legal Advr), UK Mission to UN, NY, 1970–73; Legal Counsellor, FCO, 1973–76; Second Legal Advr, 1976–84, Legal Advr, 1984–87, FCO. Agent of UK govt, cases before European Commn of Human Rights, 1966–70. Mem., US-Chile Internat. Commn of Investigation, 1989–. Member: Exec. Cttee, David Davies

Meml Inst. of Internat. Studies, 1974–; Council of Management, British Inst. of Internat. and Comparative Law, 1984–87; Cttee of Management, Inst. of Advanced Legal Studies, 1984–87; Bd of Govs, British Inst. of Human Rights, 1992–. *Address:* 1 Point House, 18 West Grove, SE10 8QR. *Club:* Travellers'.

FREELAND, Mary Graham; *see* McGeown, M. G.

FREELING, Nicolas; writer since 1960; *b* 1927, of English parents; *m* 1954, Cornelia Termes; four *s* one *d*. *Educ:* primary and secondary schs. Hotel-restaurant cook, throughout Europe, 1945–60; novelist, 1960–. *Publications:* (numerous trans.) Love in Amsterdam, 1961; Because of the Cats, 1962; Gun before Butter, 1962; Valparaiso, 1963; Double Barrel, 1963; Criminal Conversation, 1964; King of the Rainy Country, 1965; Dresden Green, 1966; Strike Out Where Not Applicable, 1967; This is the Castle, 1968; Tsing-Boum, 1969; Kitchen Book, 1970; Over the High Side, 1971; Cook Book, 1971; A Long Silence, 1972; Dressing of Diamond, 1974; What Are the Bugles Blowing For?, 1975; Lake Isle, 1976; Gadget, 1977; The Night Lords, 1978; The Widow, 1979; Castang's City, 1980; One Damn Thing After Another, 1981; Wolfnight, 1982; Back of the North Wind, 1983; No Part in Your Death, 1984; A City Solitary, 1985; Cold Iron, 1986; Lady Macbeth, 1987; Not as far as Velma, 1989; Sandcastles, 1989; Those in Peril, 1990; The Pretty How Town, 1992; You Who Know, 1993; Criminal Convictions, 1994; The Seacoast of Bohemia, 1994. *Address:* Grandfontaine, 67130 Schirmeck, France.

FREEMAN, Catherine; Founder Director, Dove Productions, since 1989; *b* 10 Aug. 1931; *d* of Harold Dove and Eileen Carroll; *m* 1st, 1958, Charles Wheeler, *qv*; 2nd, 1962, John Freeman, *qv*; two *s* one *d*. *Educ:* Convent of the Assumption; St Anne's Coll., Oxford (MA Hons). Joined BBC as trainee producer, 1954; Producer/director: Panorama, Brains Trust, Monitor, Press Conference, 1954–58; joined Thames Television as Sen. Producer in Features Dept, 1976; Editor, Daytime progs, 1976–82; originator and series producer of Citizen 2000 for Channel 4; Controller, Documentaries, Features and Religion, 1982–86; Controller, Features and Religion, 1986–89. Member: Devlin Cttee on Identification Procedures, 1974–76; Literature Panel, Arts Council, 1981–84; Broadcasting, Film and Video panel, Arts Council, 1986–88. Director: ICA, 1983–93; One World Broadcasting Trust, 1990–95. *Address:* 2 Chalcot Crescent, NW1 8YD.

FREEMAN, David Charles; Founder/Director of Opera Factory; freelance opera and theatre director; *b* 1 May 1952; *s* of Howard Wilfred Freeman and Ruth Adair Nott; *m* 1985, Marie Angel; one *s* one *d*. *Educ:* Sydney Univ., NSW (BA Hons). Opera Factory Sydney, 1973–76; Opera Factory Zürich, 1976–: directed 20 prodns, appearing in 5, writing the text of 4; Opera Factory London, 1981–: directed 18 prodns (7 televised by Channel Four), writing text of one; founded Opera Factory Films, 1991; Associate Artist, ENO, 1981–: prodns include world première of The Mask of Orpheus, 1986; directed: Goethe's Faust, Pts I and II, Lyric, Hammersmith, 1988; (also adapted) Malory's Morte d'Arthur, Lyric, Hammersmith, 1990; opera prodns in New York, Houston, Paris, Germany and St Petersburg. Chevalier de l'Ordre des Arts et des Lettres, France, 1985.

FREEMAN, David John; Founder, 1952, and Senior Partner, 1952–92, D. J. Freeman, Solicitors, subseq. Consultant; *b* 25 Feb. 1928; *s* of late Meyer Henry and Rebecca Freeman; *m* 1950, Iris Margaret Alberge; two *s* one *d*. *Educ:* Christ's Coll., Finchley. Lieut, Army, 1946–48. Admitted Solicitor, 1952. Dept of Trade Inspector into the affairs of AEG Telefunken (UK) Ltd, and Credit Collections Ltd, 1977. Governor, Royal Shakespeare Theatre, 1979–. *Recreations:* reading, theatre, gardening, golf. *Address:* 43 Fetter Lane, EC4A 1NA. *T:* 0171-583 4055. *Clubs:* Athenæum; Huntercombe Golf.

FREEMAN, Dr Ernest Allan, CEng, FIEE; CMath, FIMA; Director, Trent Polytechnic, 1981–83; *b* 16 Jan. 1932; *s* of William Freeman and Margaret Sinclair; *m* 1954, Mary Jane Peterson; two *d*. *Educ:* Sunderland Technical Coll.; King's Coll., Univ. of Durham (Mather Scholarship, 1955–57). BSc, PhD, Durham; DSc Newcastle upon Tyne; MA (Oxon) 1972. Sunderland Forge & Engineering Co. Ltd. 1949–55; English Electric Co., 1957–58; Ferranti Ltd (Edinburgh), 1958–59; Sunderland Polytechnic: Dir of Research, 1959–65; Head of Control Engrg Dept, 1965–72; Rector, 1976–80; Tutor and Fellow in Engrg, St Edmund Hall, Oxford Univ., 1972–76. FRSA. *Publications:* contribs mainly in the fields of control engrg, systems theory and computing, to Wireless Engr, Proc. IEE (Heaviside Prize, 1974), Jl of Electronics and Control, Trans AIEE, Electronic Technol., Control, Jl of Optimisation Theory and Application, Trans Soc. of Instrument Technol., Proc. Internat. Fedn for Analogue Computation, Internat. Jl of Control. *Recreations:* swimming, browsing around antique shops, playing bridge. *Address:* 12 Rolfe Place, Headington, Oxford OX3 0DS.

FREEMAN, Prof. Ernest Michael, PhD; FEng 1987; Professor of Applied Electromagnetics, Imperial College of Science, Technology and Medicine, London University, since 1980; *b* 10 Nov. 1937; *s* of Ernest Robert Freeman and Agnes Maud Freeman; *m* 1987, Helen Anne Rigby. *Educ:* Colfe's Grammar Sch., Lewisham; King's Coll., London (BScEng; PhD 1964). Lectr, King's Coll., London, 1960–63 and 1966–70; Engrg Designer, AEI, Rugby, 1964–65; Reader: Brighton Polytechnic, 1970–73; Imperial Coll. of Science and Technology, 1973–80. Chm., Infolytica Ltd, 1978–; Vice Pres., Infolytica Corp., 1978–. FRSA 1988. *Publications:* papers in learned society jls on magnetics. *Recreations:* architecture, military history, art, aristology. *Address:* Electrical Engineering Department, Imperial College of Science, Technology and Medicine, Exhibition Road, SW7 2BT. *T:* 0171-584 5413.

FREEMAN, George Vincent; Under-Secretary (Legal), Treasury Solicitor's Department, 1973–76, retired; *b* 30 April 1911; *s* of Harold Vincent Freeman and Alice Freeman; *m* 1945, Margaret Nightingale; one *d*. *Educ:* Denstone Coll., Rocester. Admitted Solicitor, 1934; in private practice Birmingham until 1940. Served RN, 1940–46, Lieut RNVR. Legal Asst, Treasury Solicitor's Dept, 1946; Sen. Legal Asst 1950; Asst Treasury Solicitor 1964. *Recreation:* gardening. *Address:* 8 Shelley Close, Ashley Heath, Ringwood, Hants BH24 2JA. *T:* Ringwood (01425) 477102. *Clubs:* Civil Service; Conservative (Ringwood).

FREEMAN, Hugh Lionel, FRCPsych; FFPHM; Hon. Consultant Psychiatrist, Salford Health Authority, University of Manchester School of Medicine, since 1988 (Consultant Psychiatrist, 1961–88); Visiting Fellow, Green College, Oxford, 1986; *b* Salford, 4 Aug. 1929; *s* of late Bernard Freeman, FBOA and Dora Doris Freeman (*née* Kahn); *m* 1957, Sally Joan Freeman, MEd, PhD, FBPsS, Prof. at Middlesex Univ., *er d* of Philip and late Rebecca Casket; three *s* one *d*. *Educ:* Altrincham Grammar Sch.; St John's Coll., Oxford (open schol.; BM BCh 1954; MA; DM 1988); MSc Salford 1980. DPM 1958; FRCPsych 1971; FFPHM (FFCM 1989). Captain, RAMC, 1956–58. House Surg., Manchester Royal Inf., 1955; Registrar, Bethlem Royal and Maudsley Hosps, 1958–60; Consultant Psychiatrist, Salford Royal Hosp., 1961–70; Hon. Consultant Psychiatrist: Salford Health Dept, 1961–74; Salford Social Services Dept, 1974–88. Hon. Med. Consultant, NAMH, 1963–74. Med. Advisor, NW Fellowship for Schizophrenia, 1980–88. Chairman: Psychiatric Sub-Cttee, NW Reg. Med. Adv. Cttee, 1978–83; Area Med. Cttee and Med. Exec. Cttee, Salford AHA, 1974–78. University of Manchester: Hon. Lectr, 1973–; Mem., Univ. Court, 1989–94; Hon. Res. Fellow, UC and Middlesex Sch. of Medicine, 1989; Centre for Psychoanalytic Studies, Kent Univ., 1993. Visiting Professor: Univ. of WI, 1970; Univ. of WA, 1990; Univ. of Bern, 1995; Rockefeller Foundn Vis. Fellow, Italy, 1980. Examiner: Univ. of Manchester, United Examg Bd, 1993; RCPsych. Med. Mem., Mental Health Rev. Tribunal, 1982–93. Member: Sex Educn Panel, Health Educn Council, 1968–72; Working Party on Behaviour Control, Council for Sci. and Society, 1973–76; Minister of State's Panel on Private Practice, DHSS, 1974–75; UK Delgn to EC Conf. on Mental Health in Cities, Milan, 1980; Mental Health Act Commn, 1983–84; Home Sec's Wking Party on Fear of Crime, 1989; Historic Building Panel, City of Manchester, 1981–89. WHO Consultant: Grenada, 1970; Chile, 1978; Philippines, 1979; Bangladesh, 1981; Greece, 1985; Rapporteur: WHO Conf. on Mental Health Services in Pilot Study Areas, Trieste, 1984; WHO Workshop on Nat. Mental Health Progs, Ruanda, 1985. Editor, British Jl of Clin. and Social Psych., 1982–84; Dep. Editor, Internat. Jl of Social Psych., 1980–83; Editor: British Jl of Psych., 1983–93 (Asst Editor, 1978–83); Current Opinion in Psychiatry, 1988–93; Co-Editor, Psychiatric Bulletin, 1983; Associate Editor, Internat. Jl of Mental Health, 1981–; Asst Editor, History of Psychiatry, 1993–. Mem. Internat. Res. Seminars, US National Inst. of Mental Health: Washington, 1966; Pisa, 1977; has lectured to and addressed univs, confs and hosps worldwide; advr on and participant in radio and TV progs. Exec. Cttees, Royal Medico-Psychol Assoc., 1965–69; Exec. Cttee, Soc. of Clin. Psychs. Royal College of Psychiatrists: Foundn Mem., 1971; Mem. Council, 1983–93; Chm., Journal Cttee; Vice-Chm., Social and Community Gp; External Assessor; Maudsley Lectr, 1993. FRSH (Hon. Sec., Mental Health Gp, 1973–76); Vice-Chm., 1983–87, Mem., Council, 1987–91, MIND. Corresp. Fellow, Amer. Psychiatric Assoc., 1993; Corresp. Member: US Assoc. for Clinical Psychosociol Res.; US Assoc. for Behavioral Therapies; Hon. Member: Chilean Soc. of Psych., Neurol. and Neurosurgery; Egyptian Psychiatric Assoc.; Polish Psychiatric Assoc., 1986; Hungarian Psychiatric Soc., 1991; Bulgarian Soc. for Neuroscis, 1991; Senior Common Room, Pembroke Coll., Oxford, 1981; Hon. Life Mem., Soc. of Clinical Psychiatrists, 1985. Vice-Chm., Manchester Heritage Trust, 1983–89; Mem., Mercian Regional Cttee, NT, 1986–92. Hon. Professorial Fellow, Salford Univ., 1986. Freeman, City of London; Liveryman, Soc. of Apothecaries, 1984 (Yeoman, 1979–84). Distinguished Service Commendation, US Nat. Council of Community Mental Health Centers, 1982. *Publications:* (ed jtly) Trends in the Mental Health Services, 1963; (ed) Psychiatric Hospital Care, 1965; (ed jtly) New Aspects of the Mental Health Service, 1968; (ed) Progress in Behaviour Therapy, 1969; (ed) Progress in Mental Health, 1970; (ed) Pavlovian Approach to Psychopathology, 1971; (ed jtly) Dangerousness, 1982; Mental Health and the Environment, 1985; (jtly) Mental Health Services in Europe, 1985; (ed jtly) Mental Health Services in Britain: the way ahead, 1985; (ed jtly) Interaction between Mental and Physical Illness, 1989; (ed jtly) Community Psychiatry, 1991; (ed jtly) 150 Years of British Psychiatry, 1991; La Malattie del Potere, 1994; contribs to national press and learned jls. *Recreations:* architecture, travel, music. *Address:* 21 Montagu Square, W1H 1RE. *Clubs:* United Oxford & Cambridge University, Whitefriars.

FREEMAN, Sir James Robin, 3rd Bt *cr* 1945; *S* father, 1981. *Heir:* none.

FREEMAN, Rt. Hon. John, PC 1966; MBE 1943. *Educ:* Westminster Sch.; Brasenose College, Oxford (Hon. Fellow, 1968). Active service, 1940–45. MP (Lab) Watford Div. of Herts, 1945–50; Borough of Watford, 1950–55; PPS to Sec. of State for War, 1945–46; Financial Sec., War Office, 1946; Parly Under Sec. of State for War, April 1947; Leader, UK Defence Mission to Burma, 1947; Parly Sec., Min. of Supply, 1947–51, resigned. Asst Editor, New Statesman, 1951–58; Deputy Editor, 1958–60; Editor, 1961–65. British High Commissioner in India, 1965–68; British Ambassador in Washington, 1969–71. Chairman: London Weekend Television Ltd, 1971–84; LWT (Holdings) plc, 1976–84; Page & Moy (Holdings) Ltd, 1976–84; Hutchinson Ltd, 1978–82 (Director till 1984); ITN, 1976–81. Vis. Prof. of Internat. Relns, Univ. of California, Davis, 1985–90. Governor, BFI, 1976–82. Vice-Pres., Royal Television Soc., 1975–85 (Gold Medal, 1981).

FREEMAN, John Allen, OBE 1958; PhD; FRES, CBiol, FIBiol, Director, Ministry of Agriculture, Fisheries and Food's Pest Infestation Control Laboratory, 1977–79; *b* 30 Sept. 1912; *s* of Laurence Freeman and Maggie Rentoul Freeman; *m* 1945, Hilda Mary Jackson; one *s* one *d*. *Educ:* City of London Sch. (Jun. Corp. Scholar, Travers Scholar); Imperial Coll. of Science and Technol., London Univ. (BSc Special 1st Cl. Hons 1933, PhD 1938). ARCS; FRES 1943; FIBiol 1963. Min. of Agric. Scholar in Entomology, 1934–37: Hull University Coll., 1934–35; Rothamsted Exper. Stn, 1936; Cornell Univ., USA, 1936–37; Vineland Exper. Stn, Ont, Canadian Dept of Agric., 1937. Res. Asst, Imp. Coll., London, 1938–40; Jun. Scientific Officer, Dept of Science and Indust. Res. Pest Infestation Lab., 1940; seconded Min. of Food Infest. Control, 1940–47; Chief Entomologist, 1944; Sen. Sci. Officer, 1946; transf. Min. of Agric., 1947; Principal Sci. Off., 1947; seconded OECD, 1954–55, and CENTO, 1957–58; Sen. Principal Sci. Off., 1958; Dep. Chief Sci. Off., and Dep. Dir Pest Infest. Control Lab., 1971; Chief Sci. Off., 1977. Member: British Ecol Soc.; Assoc. of Applied Biol. Treasurer, Royal Entomol Soc. of London, 1977–84; Hon. Treas., Inst. of Biol, 1965–69. Pres., Royal Coll. of Science Union and Imp. Coll. Union, 1934. Has travelled professionally in N and S America, Europe, Africa, ME and Far East. Freeman of City of London, 1947. *Publications:* scientific articles, mainly on pests of stored foods. *Recreations:* gardening, photography, travel, DIY. *Address:* 5 Woodmere Way, Park Langley, Beckenham, Kent BR3 2SJ. *T:* 0181-658 6970.

FREEMAN, John Anthony, FCA; Managing Director, Home Service Division, Prudential Corporation plc, 1984–94; *b* 27 May 1937; *o s* of late John Eric Freeman and Dorothy Mabel Freeman; *m* 1st, 1964, Judith Dixon (marr. diss. 1984); one *s* one *d*; 2nd, 1986, Margaret Joyce (*née* Langdon-Ellis). *Educ:* Queen Elizabeth Grammar Sch., Mansfield; Birmingham Univ. (BCom). FCA 1961; FCMA 1974. Mellors Basden & Mellors, Chartered Accountants, 1958–62; Peat Marwick Mitchell, Chartered Accountants, 1962–73; National Freight Corp., 1973–77; Prudential Corp., 1977–94. *Recreations:* golf, gardening, music.

FREEMAN, Joseph William, OBE 1968; Director of Social Service, Leeds, 1970–78; *b* 8 April 1914; *s* of Thomas and Emma Freeman; *m* 1939, Louise King (*d* 1986); one *s* one *d*. *Educ:* Liverpool Univ. (BSc (Soc.) 1938); Toynbee Hall; Open Univ. (BA Hons 1983). CQSW 1970. Qual. social worker; Probation Service, Birmingham, 1938; served War of 1939–45: Army, 1940, commnd RA, 1941; Probation Service, Liverpool, 1946; Children's Officer: Warrington, 1948; Bolton, 1951; Sheffield, 1955. Church organist. *Publications:* papers in social work jls. *Recreation:* music. *Address:* 15 Fairfield Gardens, Crank Road, St Helens WA11 7SL.

FREEMAN, Dr Marie Joyce, FFCM; Health Service Management Consultant, since 1988; *b* 14 April 1934; *d* of Wilfrid George Croxson and Ada Mildred (*née* Chiles); *m* 1958, Samuel Anthony Freeman (decd); one *s*. *Educ:* Royal Free Hospital Sch. of Medicine (MB BS, DPH). Specialist in Community Medicine, Avon AHA, 1974; District MO, Southmead HA, 1982; Actg Regl MD, SW RHA, 1986–88. *Recreations:* making reproduction antique dolls, embroidery, gardening. *Address:* Hadfield House, Darlington Place, Bath BA2 6BY. *T:* Bath (01225) 466670.

FREEMAN, Michael Alexander Reykers, MD; FRCS; Consultant Orthopaedic Surgeon, The London Hospital, since 1968; *b* 17 Nov. 1931; *s* of Donald George and Florence Julia

Freeman; *m* 1st, 1951, Elisabeth Jean; one *s* one *d*; 2nd, 1959, Janet Edith; one *s* one *d*; 3rd, 1968, Patricia; one *d* (and one *s* decd). *Educ:* Stowe Sch.; Corpus Christi Coll., Cambridge (open scholarship and closed exhibn); London Hospital Med. Coll. BA (1st cl. hons), MB BCh, MD (Cantab). FRCS 1959. Trained in medicine and surgery, London Hosp., and in orthopaedic and traumatic surgery, London, Westminster and Middlesex Hosps; co-founder, Biomechanics Unit, Imperial Coll., London, 1964; Cons. Surg. in Orth. and Traum. Surgery, London Hosp., also Res. Fellow, Imperial Coll., 1968; resigned from Imperial Coll., to devote more time to clinical activities, 1979. Special surgical interest in field of reconstructive surgery in lower limb, concentrating on joint replacement; originator of new surgical procedures for reconstruction and replacement of arthritic hip, knee, ankle and joints of foot; has lectured and demonstrated surgery, Canada, USA, Brazil, Japan, China, Australia, S Africa, continental Europe; guest speaker at nat. and internat. profess. congresses. Robert Jones Lectr, RCS, 1989. Past Member: Scientific Co-ordinating Cttee, ARC; MRC; Clin. Res. Bd, London Hosp. Bd of Governors; Brent and Harrow AHA; DHSS working parties. President: Internat. Hip Soc., 1982–85; British Hip Soc., 1989–91; British Orthopaedic Assoc., 1992–93; Eur. Fedn of Nat. Assocs of Orthopaedics and Traumatol., 1994–. Member: BMA; Amer. Acad. Orth. Surgs; Orth. Res. Soc.; SICOT; RSM; Health Unit, IEA; SIROT; European Orth. Res. Soc. Hon. Member: Danish Orth. Assoc.; Soc. Française de Chirurg. Orth. et Traum.; Canadian Orth. Assoc. Hon. Fellow, Soc. Belge de Chirurg. Orth. et de Traum. Bacon and Cunning Prizes and Copeman Medal, CCC; Andrew Clark and T. A. M. Ross Prize in Clin. Med., London Hosp. Med. Coll.; Robert Jones Medal, Brit. Orth. Assoc. *Publications:* editor and part-author: Adult Articular Cartilage, 1973, 2nd edn 1979; Scientific Basis of Joint Replacement, 1977; Arthritis of the Knee, 1980; chapters in: Bailey and Love's Short Practice of Surgery; Mason and Currey's Textbook of Rheumatology; papers in Proc. Royal Soc., Jl Bone and Joint Surgery, and med. jls. *Recreations:* gardening, reading, surgery. *Address:* 79 Albert Street, NW1 7LX. *T:* 0171–387 0817.

FREEMAN, Paul, ARCS, DSc (London), FRES; Keeper of Entomology, British Museum (Natural History), 1968–81; *b* 26 May 1916; *s* of Samuel Mellor Freeman and Kate Burgis; *m* 1942, Audrey Margaret Long; two *d*. *Educ:* Brentwood Sch., Essex; Imperial Coll., London. Demonstrator in Entomology, Imperial Coll., 1938. Captain, RA and Army Operational Research Group, 1940–45. Lecturer in Entomology, Imperial Coll., 1945–47. Asst Keeper, Dept of Entomology, British Museum (Nat. Hist.), 1947–64, Dep. Keeper, 1964–68, Keeper, 1968. Royal Entomological Soc. of London: Vice-Pres., 1956, 1957; Hon. Sec., 1958–62; Hon. Fellow, 1984. Sec., XIIth Internat. Congress of Entomology, London, 1964. *Publications:* Diptera of Patagonia and South Chile, Pt III-Mycetophilidae, 1951; Simuliidae of the Ethiopian Region (with Botha de Meillon), 1953; numerous papers in learned jls, on taxonomy of Hemiptera and Diptera. *Recreations:* gardening, natural history. *Address:* Briardene, 75 Towncourt Crescent, Petts Wood, Orpington, Kent BR5 1PH. *T:* Orpington (01689) 827296.

FREEMAN, Paul Illife, CB 1992; PhD; Controller and Chief Executive of HM Stationery Office, and the Queen's Printer of Acts of Parliament, 1989–95; *s* of late John Percy Freeman and of Hilda Freeman; *m* 1959, Enid Ivy May Freeman; one *s* one *d*. *Educ:* Victoria University of Manchester (BSc (Hons) Chemistry, PhD). Post Doctoral Fellow, Nat. Research Council of Canada, 1959–61; Research Scientist, Dupont De Nemours Co. Ltd, Wilmington, Del, USA, 1961–64; Nat. Physical Laboratory: Sen. Scientific Officer, 1964–70; Principal Scientific Officer, 1970–74; Exec. Officer, Research Requirements Bds, DoI, 1973–77; Director: Computer Aided Design Centre, 1977–83; National Engrg Lab., 1980–83; Central Computer and Telecommunications Agency, HM Treasury, 1983–88. Member: CS Coll. Adv. Council, 1983–88; Bd, NCC, 1983–88; Bd, DVLA, 1990–92; Council, UEA, 1994–. Vis. Prof. Univ. of Strathclyde, 1981–86. *Publications:* scientific papers. *Recreations:* reading, walking, gardening. *Address:* 12 Broadway, Wilburton, Ely, Cambridgeshire CB6 3RT. *T:* Ely (01353) 740576.

FREEMAN, Peter David Mark; Head of Personnel, Organisation and Services Division, Overseas Development Administration, since 1993; *b* 8 Dec. 1947; *s* of Dr Victor Freeman and Ethel (*née* Halpern); *m* 1980, Anne Tyndale; two *d*. *Educ:* Merton Coll., Oxford (BA Hons); Univ. of Toronto (MA). Asst Private Sec. to Minister for Overseas Develt, 1973–75; Office of UK Exec. Dir, World Bank, 1975–78; British High Commn, Zimbabwe, 1980–83; Asst Head, Econ. Relns Dept, FCO, 1983–84; Overseas Development Administration: Head: EC Dept, 1984–88; Central and Southern Africa Dept, 1988–90; Aid Policy Dept, 1990–91; Internat. Div., 1991–93. Governor, Stanford Jun. Sch., Brighton, 1988– (Chm., 1992–). *Address:* 94 Victoria Street, SW1 5JL. *T:* 0171–917 0380.

FREEMAN, Sir Ralph, Kt 1970; CVO 1964; CBE 1952 (MBE (mil.) 1945); FEng; FICE; FASCE; FWeldI; retired consulting engineer; Senior Partner, Freeman, Fox & Partners, 1963–79, (Partner, 1947–79); *b* 3 Feb. 1911; *s* of late Sir Ralph Freeman and late Mary (*née* Lines); *m* 1939, Joan Elizabeth, *er d* of late Col J. G. Rose, DSO, VD, FRIC, Wynberg, Cape, S Africa; two *s* one *d*. *Educ:* Uppingham Sch.; Worcester Coll., Oxford (MA; Hon. Fellow, 1980). Construction Engineer: Dorman Long & Co., S Africa, Rhodesia and Denmark, 1932–36 and 1937–39; Braithwaite & Co., 1936–37; on staff of Freeman, Fox & Partners, 1939–46, Admty and other war work; served RE, Exp. Bridging Estabt (later seconded as bridging adviser to CE 21 Army Gp HQ, NW Europe campaign, 1943–45 (Temp. Major, 1945)). Consulting Engr to the Queen for Sandringham Estate, 1949–76. Past Pres., Instn of Civil Engrs (Mem. Council, 1951–55 and 1957–61, Vice-Pres., 1962–66; Pres., 1966–67); Mem. Emeritus, Smeatonian Soc. of Civil Engrs, 1984 (Mem., 1960; Pres., 1978). Member: Governing Body, SE London Techn. Coll., 1952–58; Nat. Cons. Council to Min. of Works, 1952–56; Bd of Governors, Westminster Hosp., 1963–69; Council, Worcester Coll. Soc., 1964–87; Adv. Council on Scientific Res. and Develt (MoD), 1966–69; Defence Scientific Adv. Council, 1969–72; Royal Fine Art Commn, 1968–85; Council, Assoc. of Consulting Engrs, 1969–72, 1973–77, Chm., 1975–76; Governing Body, Imp. Coll. of Science and Technology, 1975–83; Chm., Limpsfield Common Local Management Cttee, 1957–82 (Chm. NT Local Mgt Cttee, 1972–82). Pres., Welding Inst., 1975–77. Col, Engr and Rly Staff Corps RE (T&AVR), 1963–76, Col comdg 1970–74. DUniv Surrey, 1978. Hon. Mem., Instn Royal Engrs, 1971; Hon. FIMechE, 1971; Hon. Fellow, Zimbabwe (formerly Rhodesian) Instn of Engrs, 1969; FRSA. Kt, Order of Orange Nassau (Netherlands), 1945. *Publications:* several papers in Proc. ICE. *Recreations:* wood and metal work, letter writing. *Address:* Ballards Shaw, Ballards Lane, Limpsfield, Oxted, Surrey RH8 0SN. *T:* Oxted (01883) 723284. *Clubs:* Army and Navy; Leander (Henley-on-Thames).

See also D. L. Pearson.

FREEMAN, Prof. Raymond, MA, DPhil, DSc (Oxon); FRS 1979; John Humphrey Plummer Professor of Magnetic Resonance, and Fellow of Jesus College, Cambridge University, since 1987; *b* 6 Jan. 1932; *s* of late Albert and Hilda Frances Freeman; *m* 1958, Anne-Marie Périnet-Marquet; two *s* three *d*. *Educ:* Nottingham High Sch. (scholar); Lincoln Coll., Oxford (open scholar). Ingénieur, Centre d'Etudes Nucléaires de Saclay, Commissariat à l'Energie Atomique, France, 1957–59; Sen. Scientific Officer, Nat. Phys. Lab., Teddington, Mddx, 1959–63; Man., Nuclear Magnetic Resonance Research, Varian Associates, Palo Alto, Calif, 1963–73; Lectr in Physical Chemistry, 1973–87, Aldrichian Praelector in Chemistry, 1982–87, and Fellow, Magdalen Coll., 1973–87, Oxford Univ. Chem. Soc. Award in Theoretical Chem. and Spectroscopy, 1978; Leverhulme Medal, Royal Soc., 1990. *Publications:* A Handbook of Nuclear Magnetic Resonance, 1987; articles on nuclear magnetic resonance spectroscopy in various scientific journals. *Recreations:* swimming, traditional jazz. *Address:* Department of Chemistry, University of Cambridge, Lensfield Road, Cambridge CB2 1EW; Jesus College, Cambridge CB5 8BL; 29 Bentley Road, Cambridge CB2 2AW. *T:* Cambridge (01223) 323958.

FREEMAN, His Honour Richard Gavin; a Circuit Judge (formerly County Court Judge), 1968–83; *b* 18 Oct. 1910; *s* of John Freeman, MD, and Violet Alice Leslie Hadden; *m* 1937, Marjorie Pear; one *s* two *d*; *m* 1961, Winifred Ann Bell. *Educ:* Charterhouse; Hertford Coll., Oxford. Called to Bar, Gray's Inn, 1947. Deputy Chairman, Warwick Quarter Sessions, 1963–71. Hon. Major, RA. *Recreations:* cricket, gardening. *Address:* 10 Rees Street, N1 7AR. *Club:* Streatley Cricket.

FREEMAN, Rt Hon. Roger Norman, PC 1993; MA; FCA; MP (C) Kettering, since 1983; Chancellor of the Duchy of Lancaster, since 1995; *b* 27 May 1942; *s* of Norman and Marjorie Freeman; *m* 1969, Jennifer Margaret (*née* Watson); one *s* one *d*. *Educ:* Whitgift Sch., Croydon; Balliol Coll., Oxford (MA PPE). Chartered Accountant, 1969; FCA 1979. Articled with Binder Hamlyn & Co., 1964–69 (Hons Prize, 1968); General Partner, Lehman Brothers, 1969–86. Parliamentary Under-Secretary of State: for the Armed Forces, 1986–88; DoH, 1988–90; Minister of State: Dept of Transport, 1990–94; MoD, 1994–95. *Publications:* Professional Practice, 1968; Fair Deal for Water, 1985. *Address:* House of Commons, SW1A 0AA. *Clubs:* Carlton, Kennel.

FREEMAN-GRENVILLE, family name of **Lady Kinloss.**

FREER, Charles Edward Jesse, DL; *b* 4 March 1901; *s* of late Canon S. Thorold Winckley, FSA and Elizabeth (*née* Freer); changed name to Freer by Deed Poll, 1922; *m* 1st, 1927, Violet Muriel (*d* 1944), *d* of H. P. Gee, CBE, Leicester; two *s* two *d*; 2nd, 1945, Cynthia Lilian, *d* of Leonard R. Braithwaite, FRCS, Leeds; two *d*. *Educ:* Radley Coll. Solicitor, 1924; served RA (TA) in France, 1940; DJAG in Iceland, 1941–42; at SHAEF, 1943–44, Lt-Col. Chm., Leicestershire QS, 1949–71. Chm. Leicester Diocesan Board of Finance, 1946–56; Chm. Mental Health Tribunal, Sheffield Regional Board, 1961–73. A Chm. of Industrial Tribunals, 1966–73. DL 1946, JP 1946–71, Leics. *Recreations:* reading, walking. *Address:* Elmstead Lodge, 3 Elmstead Road, Canford Cliffs, Poole, Dorset BH13 7EY. *T:* Canford Cliffs (01202) 709490. *Clubs:* East India, Devonshire, Sports and Public Schools; Parkstone Yacht.

FREER, Air Chief Marshal Sir Robert (William George), GBE 1981 (CBE 1966); KCB 1977; Commandant, Royal College of Defence Studies, 1980–82, retired; Director, Pilatus Britten-Norman Ltd, since 1988; *b* Darjeeling, 1 Sept. 1923; *s* of late William Freer, Stretton, Cirencester, Glos; *m* 1950, Margaret, 2nd *d* of late J. W. Elkington and Mrs M. Elkington, Ruskington Manor, near Sleaford, Lincs; one *s* one *d*. *Educ:* Gosport Grammar Sch. Flying Instructor, S Africa and UK, 1944–47; RAF Coll., Cranwell, 1947–50; served 54 and 614 Fighter Sqdns, 1950–52; Central Fighter Estabt, 1952–54; commanded 92 Fighter Sqdn, 1955–57 (Queen's Commendation, 1955); Directing Staff, USAF Acad., 1958–60; Staff of Chief of Defence Staff, 1961–63; Station Comdr, RAF Seletar, 1963–66; DD Defence Plans (Air), MoD, 1966–67. Air ADC to the Queen, 1969–71; Dep. Comdt, RAF Staff Coll., 1969–71; SASO, HQ Near East Air Force, 1971–72; AOC 11 Group, 1972–75; Dir-Gen., Organisation (RAF), April–Sept. 1975; AOC No 18 Group, RAF, 1975–78; Dep. C-in-C, Strike Command, 1978–79; psa, 1957; pfc, 1960; IDC, 1968. Director: Rediffusion, 1982–88; British Manufg & Res. Co., 1984–88; Rediffusion Simulation, 1985–88. Pres., RAF LTA, 1975–81; Mem., Sports Council, 1980–82. CIMgt (FBIM 1977); FRAeS 1995. *Recreations:* golf, tennis. *Address:* c/o Lloyds Bank, Farnham, Surrey. *Clubs:* Royal Air Force; All England Lawn Tennis and Croquet; Hankley Common Golf.

FREESON, Rt. Hon. Reginald, PC 1976; Director: Reg Freeson & Associates, urban renewal consultants, since 1987; Speedex (UK) Monitoring Services, since 1991; freelance writer and speaker; *b* 24 Feb. 1926; *m* (marr. diss.); one *s* one *d*. *Educ:* Jewish Orphanage, West Norwood. Served in Army, 1944–47. Middle East magazines and newspapers, 1946–48. Joined Labour Party on return to United Kingdom, 1948, Co-operative Party, 1958, Fabian Society, 1960, Poale Zion—Labour Zionists, 1964 and Labour Finance and Industry Gp, 1990. Journalist, 1948–64: magazines, newspaper agencies and television; John Bull Today, News Review, Everybody's Weekly, Tribune, News Chronicle, Daily Mirror. Asst Press Officer with Min. of Works, British Railways Board. Some short story writing, research and ghosting of books and pamphlets. Editor: Searchlight, against fascism and racialism, 1964–67; Jewish Vanguard, Labour–Zionist qly, 1987–94. Radio and television: housing, urban planning, race relations and foreign affairs. Elected Willesden Borough Council, 1952; Alderman, 1955; Leader of Council, 1958–65; Chm. of new London Borough of Brent, 1964–65 (Alderman, 1964–68). MP (Lab): Willesden E, 1964–74; Brent E, Feb. 1974–1987. PPS to Minister of Transport, 1964–67; Parly Secretary: Min. of Power, 1967–69; Min. of Housing and Local Govt, 1969–70; Labour front-bench spokesman: on housing and urban affairs, 1970–74; on social security, 1979–81; Minister for Housing and Construction and Urban Affairs, DoE, 1974–79; responsible for planning, land and local govt, 1976–79; Mem., Select Cttee on the Environment, 1981–84 (Chm., 1982–83). Member: Council of Europe Parly Assembly, 1984–87; Western Eur. Assembly, 1984–87. Dir, Labour Friends of Israel, 1992–93. Dir, JBG Housing Soc., 1981–83; Mem. Exec., Housing Centre Trust, 1987–. Mem., Internat. Voluntary Service and UNA International Service. Sponsor, three Willesden housing co-operatives, 1958–60. Founder-Chairman: Willesden (now Brent) Coun. of Social Service, 1960–62; Willesden Social Action, 1961–63; Willesden Internat. Friendship Council (now Brent Community Relns Council), 1959–63 (Vice-Pres., 1967); Chairman: Warsaw Memorial Cttee, 1964–71; Poale Zion, 1984–87; Vice-Pres., Campaign for Democracy in Ulster; Founder/Sponsor, Internat. Centre for Peace in ME; Mem., Jewish Welfare Bd, 1971–74 (Mem. Exec., 1973–74). Life Member: YHA, 1957; Nat. Trust, 1987. Writer and speaker on urban and envmtl regeneration, housing, construction industry and planning. *Publications:* policy papers, reports and articles for Borrie Commn on Social Justice, Lab. Party Commn on Envmt, Fabian Rev., Rowntree Foundn, Housing Rev. *Recreations:* gardening, music, theatre, reading, country walking, community action. *Address:* 159 Chevening Road, NW6 6DZ.

FREETH, Denzil Kingson; *b* 10 July 1924; *s* of late Walter Kingson and late Vera Freeth. *Educ:* Highfield Sch., Liphook, Hants; Sherborne Sch. (Scholar); Trinity Hall, Cambridge (Scholar). Served War, 1943–46: RAF (Flying Officer). Pres. Union Soc., Cambridge, 1949; Chm. Cambridge Univ. Conservative Assoc. 1949; debating tour of America, 1949, also debated in Ireland; Mem. Exec. Cttee Nat. Union, 1955. MP (C) Basingstoke Division of Hants, 1955–64. PPS to Minister of State, Bd of Trade, 1956, to Pres. of the Bd of Trade, 1957–59, to Minister of Educn, 1959–60; Parly Sec. for Science, 1961–63. Mem. Parliamentary Cttee of Trustee Savings Bank Assoc., 1956–61. Mem. Select Cttee on Procedure, 1958–59. Employed by and Partner in stockbroking firms, 1950–61 and

1964–89; Mem. of Stock Exchange, 1959–61, 1965–91. Chm. Finance Cttee, London Diocesan Fund, 1986–94. Churchwarden, All Saints' Church, Margaret St, W1, 1977–. *Recreations:* good food, wine and conversation. *Address:* 3 Brasenose House, 35 Kensington High Street, W8 5BA. *T:* 0171–937 8685. *Clubs:* Carlton; Pitt (Cambridge).

FREETH, Hon. Sir Gordon, KBE 1978; Chairman, Australian Consolidated Minerals, 1981–90; *b* 6 Aug. 1914; *s* of late Rt Rev. Robert Evelyn Freeth and Gladys Mary Snashall; *m* 1939, Joan Celia Carew Baker; one *s* two *d. Educ:* Sydney Church of England Grammar Sch.; Guildford Grammar Sch.; Univ. of Western Australia. Rowed for Australia in British Empire Games, Sydney, 1938. Admitted as Barrister and Solicitor, WA, 1938; practised Law at Katanning, WA, 1939–49. Served as Pilot, RAAF, 1942–45. Elected to House of Representatives as Member for Forrest, 1949; MP 1949–69; Minister: for Interior and Works, 1958–63; for Shipping and Transport, 1963–68; Assisting Attorney-Gen., 1962–64; for Air, and Minister Assisting the Treasurer, 1968; for External Affairs, 1969; Ambassador to Japan, 1970–73; practised law in Perth, WA, 1973–77; High Comr for Australia in UK, 1977–80. *Recreations:* gardening, golf. *Address:* Tingrith, 25 Owston Street, Mosman Park, WA 6012, Australia. *Club:* Weld (Perth).

FREETH, Peter Stewart, RA 1991 (ARA 1990); RE 1991 (ARE 1987); Tutor, Etching, Royal Academy Schools, since 1966; *b* 15 April 1938; *s* of Alfred William Freeth and Olive Walker;*m* 1967, Mariolina Meliadò; two *s. Educ:* King Edward's Grammar School, Aston; Slade School, London (Dip Fine Art). British Sch., Rome, 1960–62; Camden Inst. One man shows: Christopher Mendez Gall., London, 1987–89; Friends' Room, Royal Acad., 1991; represented in collections: British Museum; V&A; Fitzwilliam Mus., Cambridge; Arts Council; Metropolitan Mus., NY; Nat. Gall., Washington. Mem., Royal Soc. of Painter Printmakers. Prix de Rome, Engraving, 1960. *Recreations:* music, books, yet more work. *Address:* 83 Muswell Hill Road, N10 3HT.

FREMANTLE, family name of **Baron Cottesloe.**

FRÉMAUX, Louis Joseph Felix; conductor; *b* 13 Aug. 1921. *Educ:* Conservatoire National Supérieur de Musique de Paris. Chef d'Orchestre Permanent et Directeur, l'Orchestre National de l'Opéra de Monte Carlo, 1956–66; Principal Conductor, Orchestre de Lyon, 1968–71; Musical Dir and Principal Conductor, City of Birmingham Symphony Orch., 1969–78; Music Dir and Principal Conductor, 1979–81, Principal Guest Conductor, 1982–85, Sydney Symph. Orch. First concert in England, with Bournemouth Symph. Orch., 1964. Guest appearances with all symph. orchs in GB; many recording. Hon. RAM, 1978. Hon. DMus Birmingham, 1978. Légion d'Honneur; Croix de Guerre (twice). *Recreations:* walking, photography. *Address:* c/o Tennant Artists, Unit 2, 39 Tadema Road, SW10 0PY. *T:* 0171–376 3758.

FRENCH, family name of **Baron De Freyne.**

FRENCH, Prof. Anthony Philip, PhD; Professor of Physics, Massachusetts Institute of Technology, 1964–91, now Emeritus; *b* 19 Nov. 1920; *s* of Sydney James French and Elizabeth Margaret (*née* Hart); *m* 1946, Naomi Mary Livesay; one *s* one *d. Educ:* Varndean Sch., Brighton; Sidney Sussex Coll., Cambridge (major schol.; BA Hons 1942, MA 1946, PhD 1948). British atomic bomb project, Tube Alloys, 1942–44; Manhattan Project, Los Alamos, USA, 1944–46; Scientific Officer, AERE, Harwell, 1946–48; Univ. Demonstrator in Physics, Cavendish Laboratory, Cambridge, 1948–51, Lectr 1951–55; Dir of Studies in Natural Sciences, Pembroke Coll., Cambridge, 1949–55, Fellow of Pembroke, 1950–55; Visiting research scholar: California Inst. of Technology, 1951; Univ. of Michigan, 1954; Prof. of Physics, Univ. of S Carolina, 1955–62 (Head of Dept, 1956–62); Guignard Lectr, 1958; Vis. Prof., MIT, 1962–64; Vis. Fellow of Pembroke Coll., Cambridge, 1975. Member, Internat. Commn on Physics Educn, 1972–84 (Chm., 1975–81); Pres., Amer. Assoc. of Physics Teachers, 1985–86. FInstP 1986; Fellow, Amer. Physical Soc., 1987. Hon. ScD Allegheny Coll., 1989. Bragg Medal, Institute of Physics, 1988; Oersted Medal, 1989, Melba Newell Phillips Award, 1993, Amer. Assoc. of Physics Teachers. *Publications:* Principles of Modern Physics, 1958; Special Relativity, 1968; Newtonian Mechanics, 1971; Vibrations and Waves, 1971; Introduction to Quantum Physics, 1978; Einstein: a centenary volume, 1979; Niels Bohr: a centenary volume, 1985; Introduction to Classical Mechanics, 1986; Physics in a Technological World, 1988. *Recreations:* music, squash, reading, writing. *Address:* c/o Physics Department, Massachusetts Institute of Technology, Cambridge, MA 02139, USA.

FRENCH, Cecil Charles John, FEng 1982; Group Technology Director, Ricardo International, 1990–92, retired; *b* 16 April 1926; *s* of Ernest French and Edith Hannah French (*née* Norris); *m* 1st, 1956, Olive Joyce Edwards (*d* 1969); two *d*; 2nd, 1971, Shirley Frances Outten; one *s* one *d. Educ:* King's Coll., Univ. of London (MScEng; DSc Eng 1987); Columbia Univ., New York. FIMechE, FIMarE. Graduate apprentice, CAV Ltd, 1948–50; Marshall Aid scholar, MIT, USA (research into combustion in engines), 1950–52; Ricardo Consulting Engineers, subseq. Ricardo Internat., 1952–92, Director, 1969, Vice-Chm., 1982, Man. Dir, 1989; Man. Dir, 1979–83, Chm., 1984–87, G. Cussons Ltd. President, Instn of Mechanical Engineers, 1988–89 (Vice-Pres, 1981–86, Dep. Pres., 1986–88). *Publications:* numerous articles on diesel engines in learned soc. jls world wide. *Recreations:* folk dancing, photography. *Address:* 303 Upper Shoreham Road, Shoreham-by-Sea, Sussex BN43 5QA. *T:* Shoreham-by-Sea (01273) 452050.

FRENCH, Hon. Sir Christopher James Saunders, Kt 1979; **Hon. Mr Justice French;** Judge of the High Court of Justice, Queen's Bench Division, since 1982 (Family Division, 1979–82); Judge of Employment Appeals Tribunal, since 1985; *b* 14 Oct. 1925; 2nd *s* of late Rev. Reginald French, MC, MA, Hon. Chaplain to the Queen, and Gertrude Emily Mary (*née* Haworth); *m* 1957, Philippa, *d* of Philip Godfrey Price, Abergavenny; one *s* one *d. Educ:* Denstone Coll. (scholar); Brasenose Coll., Oxford (scholar). Coldstream Guards, 1943–48 (Capt.). Called to the Bar, Inner Temple, 1950; QC 1966; Master of the Bench, 1975. Dep. Chm., Bucks QS, 1966–71. Recorder of Coventry, 1971–72; a Recorder, and Hon. Recorder of Coventry, 1972–79; Presiding Judge, SE Circuit, 1982–85. Member: Gen. Council of the Bar, 1963–67; Senate of Inns of Court and Bar, 1978–79; Lord Chancellor's Adv. Cttee on Trng Magistrates, 1974–80. *Publication:* (contrib.) Agency, in Halsbury's Laws of England, 4th edn, 1973. *Recreations:* walking, music, painting, fishing. *Address:* Royal Courts of Justice, Strand, WC2A 2LL. *Clubs:* Garrick, Pilgrims.

FRENCH, David; Director, Relate (formerly National Marriage Guidance Council), since 1987; *b* 20 June 1947; *s* of late Captain Godfrey Alexander French, CBE, RN, and of Margaret Annis French; *m* 1974, Sarah Anne, *d* of Rt Rev. H. D. Halsey, *qv*; four *s. Educ:* Sherborne Sch.; Durham Univ. (BA). MIPM. Nat. Council of Social Service, 1971–74; Hd of Social Services Dept, RNID, 1974–78; Dir of Services, C of E Children's Soc., 1978–87. Chairman: London Corrymeela Venture, 1973–76; St Albans Internat. Organ Fest., 1985–87. Trustee, Charity Appts, 1985–89. Mem. Governing Council, Family Policy Studies Centre, 1989–. Liveryman, Glaziers' Co., 1990–. MRSocMed 1988. FRSA 1993. *Recreations:* children and families. *Address:* 21 Prospect Road, St Albans, Herts AL1 2AT. *T:* (office) Rugby (01788) 573241.

FRENCH, Air Vice-Marshal David Rowthorne, CB 1993; MBE 1976; engineering consultant, since 1994; *b* 11 Dec. 1937; *s* of Norman Arthur French and late Edna Mary French (*née* Rowthorne); *m* 1st, 1963, Veronica Margaret Mead (marr. diss. 1982); two *s* one *d*; 2nd, 1984, Philippa Anne Pym, *d* of Sir Alexander Ross; one *s* one *d. Educ:* Gosport County Grammar Sch.; RAF Technical Coll., Henlow. CEng, MRAeS 1969. Commnd Engr Br., RAF, 1960; various engrg appts, 1960–69; Sen. Engrg Officer, No 14 Sqn, RAF Bruggen, 1970–71; OC Airframe Systems Sqn, CSDE, RAF Swanton Morley, 1971–72; RAF Staff Coll., Bracknell, 1973; Sen. Engrg Officer, No 54 Sqn, RAF Coltishall, 1974–76; OC Engrg Wg, RAF Lossiemouth, 1976–79; Air Warfare Coll., RAF Cranwell, 1979; SO for Offensive Support Aircraft, HQ Strike Comd, 1980; Dep. Dir of Engrg Policy, MoD, 1981–82; Comd Mech. Engr, HQ RAF Germany, 1983–86; Dir of Policy, Directorate Gen., Defence Quality Assurance, MoD (PE), 1986–87; AO Wales and Stn Comdr, RAF St Athan, 1988–90; Comd Mech. Engr, HQ Strike Comd, 1990–91; AO Maintenance and Chief Exec. Maintenance Gp Defence Support Agency, RAF Support Comd, 1991–94, retd. Chairman: RAF Germany Golf, 1983–86; RAF Support Comd Golf, 1988–90; Capt., RAF Germany Golf Club, 1985–86. *Recreations:* golf, ski-ing, gardening, wine. *Address:* Milestone Piece, Yarmouth Road, Blofield, Norwich, Norfolk NR13 4LQ. *Clubs:* Royal Air Force; Royal Norwich Golf.

FRENCH, Douglas Charles; MP (C) Gloucester, since 1987; *b* London, 20 March 1944; *s* of Frederick Emil French and late Charlotte Vera French; *m* 1978, Sue, *y d* of late Philip Arthur Phillips; two *s* one *d. Educ:* Glyn Grammar Sch., Epsom; St Catharine's Coll., Cambridge (MA). Called to the Bar, Inner Temple. Exec., then Dir, P. W. Merkle Ltd, 1966–93. Asst to Rt Hon. Sir Geoffrey Howe, Shadow Chancellor, 1976–79; Special Advr to Chancellor of the Exchequer, 1982–83; PPS to Minister of State, FCO, 1988–89, ODA, 1989–90, MAFF, 1992–93, DoE, 1993–. Contested (C) Sheffield, Attercliffe, 1979. Chm., Bow Gp, 1978–79. *Publications:* articles and reviews. *Recreations:* gardening, renovating period houses, ski-ing, squash. *Address:* House of Commons, SW1A 0AA. *Clubs:* Royal Automobile, Coningsby.

FRENCH, Henry William, CBE 1971; BSc (London); CEng, FIEE, FInstP; FCP; Senior Chief Inspector (Deputy Secretary), Department of Education and Science, 1972–74; *b* 14 Feb. 1910; *s* of Henry Moxey French and Alice French (*née* Applegate); *m* 1936, Hazel Anne Mary Ainley; two *s. Educ:* Varndean School, Brighton; Woolwich Polytechnic. Engineering Technician, 1925–27; Armed Forces (Royal Corps of Signals, Army Educational Corps), 1927–38; Lecturer, Radar Engineering, Mil. Coll. of Science, 1938–46; Dep. Dir, Educn and Training, Electric and Musical Industries, 1946–48; HM Inspector of Schools (Further Education), 1948–56; Regional Staff Inspector (NW), 1956–59; Staff Inspector (Engineering), 1956–65; Chief Inspector for Further Educn for Industry and Commerce, DES, 1965–72. Pro-Chancellor, 1978–86, Sen. Pro-Chancellor and Chm., Council, 1981–86, Loughborough Univ.; Mem. Council, Brighton Polytechnic, 1976–87 (Hon. Fellow, 1987). Fellow, Woolwich Polytechnic, 1966; Hon. Fellow, Sheffield Polytechnic, 1975. Hon. DSc Loughborough Univ. of Technology, 1966. *Publications:* Technician Engineering Drawing 1, 1979; Engineering Technicians: some problems of nomenclature and classification, 1980. *Recreations:* polyphonic music, opera, travel. *Address:* High Gables, Furze Hill, Kingswood, Surrey KT20 6EP. *T:* Burgh Heath (01737) 360146.

FRENCH, Leslie Richard; actor; *b* Kent, 23 April 1904; *s* of Robert Gilbert French and Jetty Sands Leahy; unmarried. *Educ:* London Coll. of Choristers. Began stage work 1914; early Shakespearean training with Sir Philip Ben Greet; parts include Hansel in Hansel and Gretel, Bert in Derby Day; Shakespearean parts include Puck, Ariel, Feste, Costard, etc; The Spirit in Comus; played Feste in the ballet Twelfth Night with the International Ballet at His Majesty's Theatre. Joined the Royal Corps of Signals, 1942; Lord Fancourt Babberly in Charley's Aunt, Christmas 1943. Produced Much Ado About Nothing and The Tempest for OUDS; Everyman as a ballet for the International Ballet Co., Lyric Theatre, 1943, Comus for the International Ballet, London Coliseum, 1946. Productions include: Charles and Mary, Cheltenham Festival, 1948; The Servant of Two Masters; Aladdin (Widow Twanky); Mother Goose (Mother Goose); She Stoops to Conquer for Edinburgh Festival (Tony Lumpkin), 1949; pantomime, Cinderella, 1950; The Dish Ran Away, Whitehall, 1950; Midsummer Night's Dream (Puck), Open Air Theatre during Cheltenham Festival; Open Air Theatre, Regent's Park, 1951; pantomime, Nottingham, 1951–52; The Ghost Train, Huddersfield, 1952; Pisanio in Cymbeline, Attendant Spirit in Comus, Open Air Theatre, 1952; Dyrkin in Out of the Whirlwind, Westminster Abbey, 1953; Open Air Theatre, Cape Town: The Taming of the Shrew, 1956; Midsummer Night's Dream, 1957; As You Like It (Touchstone), 1958; Johannesburg: The Tempest, 1956; Hamlet, 1957; Shakespearean seasons in Cape Town, 1959, 1960, 1961, 1962, 1963, 1966, 1969; Tempest, E. Oppenheimer Theatre, OFS, 1968; The Tell Tale Heart, 1969; An Evening with Shakespeare (tour), 1969; Twelfth Night, Port Elizabeth, 1970; The Way of the World, S Africa, 1970; Co-dir, Open Air Theatre, Regent's Park, 1958. Prod., Twelfth Night (in Great Hall of Hampton Ct Palace), 1965; Le Streghe (for Visconti), 1966; toured USA, 1969–70 and 1970–71: One Man Shakespearean Recitals, and Shylock in Merchant of Venice; The Chaplain in The Lady's not for Burning, Chichester Festival, 1972; toured USA 1973; recitals and prod Twelfth Night; The Tempest, Cape Town, 1973; As You Like It, Port Elizabeth, 1973; Shakespear (one-man show), Cape Town, Port Elizabeth, 1991; prod Love's Labour's Lost, Maynardville Open Air Theatre, 1991; Caroline, Yvonne Arnaud Theatre; Directed: Saturday Sunday Monday, Nat. Arts Council, S Africa, 1976; Romeo and Juliet, Cape Town, 1980; numerous appearances on TV, incl.: Villette (serial), 1970; The Singing Detective, 1986; The Book Liberator, 1988. *Films:* Orders to Kill (M Lafitte), 1957; The Scapegoat (M Lacoste), 1958; The Singer not the Song (Father Gomez); The Leopard (Chevalley), 1963; The Witches, 1966; Happy Ever After, 1966; Joseph of Coppertino, 1966; Death in Venice (Visconti), 1970. First Exhibition of Paintings—oil and water colour, Parsons Gall. Presented with Key to City of Cape Town, Jan. 1963. Gold Medals: Port Elizabeth Shakespeare Society, 1973; 1820 Settlers, 1978; Grahamstown Festival, 1977; Hon. Life Mem., Mark Twain Soc., USA, 1976 (all in recognition of his contribution to art and culture in the theatre in England and overseas). *Recreations:* gardening and painting. *Address:* Flat D, 29 Elsworthy Road, NW3 3BT. *T:* 0171–586 5721; 11 Chesterfield Road, Ewell West, Surrey KT19 9QR. *T:* 0181–393 1333. *Club:* Garrick.

FRENCH, Neville Arthur Irwin, CMG 1976; LVO 1968; HM Diplomatic Service, retired; *b* Kenya, 28 April 1920; *s* of late Major Ernest French and Alice Irwin (*née* Powell); *m* 1945, Joyce Ethel, *d* of late Henry Robert Greene, Buenos Aires and Montevideo; one *s* two *d. Educ:* London Sch. of Economics (BSc (Econ)). Fleet Auxiliary and Special Duties, Min. of War Transport, 1939–45. Colonial Admin. Service, Tanganyika, 1948, later HMOCS; District Comr, 1949–61; Principal Asst Sec., (External Affairs), Prime Minister's Office, Dar es Salaam, 1961; retd from HMOCS, 1962; Central African Office, 1963–64; 1st Sec., British High Commn, Salisbury, 1964–66; Head of Chancery, British Embassy, Rio de Janeiro, 1966–69; Asst Head of Western Organisations Dept, FCO, 1970–72; Counsellor, and Chargé d'Affaires, Havana, 1972–75; Governor and C-in-C, Falkland Islands, and High Comr, British Antarctic Territory, 1975–77; Dep. High Comr, Madras, 1977–80. Mem., LSE Club. Comdr, Order of Rio Branco (Brazil), 1968. *Recreations:*

sailing, books. *Address:* c/o Barclays Bank, 84 High Street, Bideford, Devon. *Clubs:* Commonwealth Trust; Madras.

FRENCH, Philip Neville; writer and broadcaster; Film Critic, The Observer, since 1978; *b* Liverpool, 28 Aug. 1933; *s* of late John and Bessie French; *m* 1957, Kersti Elisabet Molin; three *s*. *Educ:* Bristol Grammar Sch.; Exeter Coll., Oxford (BA Law) (editor, The Isis, 1956); Indiana Univ. Nat. Service, 2nd Lieut Parachute Regt, 1952–54. Reporter, Bristol Evening Post, 1958–59; Producer, BBC N Amer. Service, 1959–61; Talks Producer, BBC Radio, 1961–67; New Statesman: Theatre Critic, 1967–68; Arts Columnist, 1967–72; Sen. Producer, BBC Radio, 1968–90: editor of The Arts This Week, Critics' Forum and other series, writer-presenter of arts documentaries, Radio 3. Vis. Prof., Univ. of Texas, 1972. Mem., BFI Prodn Bd, 1968–74; Jury Mem., Cannes Film Fest., 1986. *Publications:* Age of Austerity 1945–51 (ed with Michael Sissons), 1963; The Movie Moguls, 1969; Westerns: aspects of a movie genre, 1974, rev. 1977; Three Honest Men: Edmund Wilson, F. R. Leavis, Lionel Trilling, 1980; (ed) The Third Dimension: voices from Radio Three, 1983; (ed with Deac Rossell) The Press: observed and projected, 1991; (ed) Malle on Malle, 1992; (ed with Ken Wlaschin) The Faber Book of Movie Verse, 1993; (with Kersti French) Wild Strawberries, 1995; numerous articles and essays in magazines, newspapers and anthologies. *Recreations:* woolgathering in England, picking wild strawberries in Sweden. *Address:* 62 Dartmouth Park Road, NW5 1SN. *T:* 0171–485 1711.

FREND, Rev. Prof. William Hugh Clifford, TD 1959 (Clasp, 1966); DD, FRSE, FSA; FBA 1983; Priest-in-Charge of Barnwell with Thurning and Luddington, 1984–90; Professor of Ecclesiastical History, 1969–84, now Professor Emeritus, and Dean of Divinity Faculty, 1972–75, Glasgow University; *b* 11 Jan. 1916; 2nd *s* of late Rev. E. G. C. Frend, Shottermill, Surrey and late Edith (*née* Bacon); *m* 1951, Mary Grace, *d* of late E. A. Crook, FRCS; one *s* one *d*. *Educ:* Fernden Sch.; Haileybury Coll. (Schol.); Keble Coll., Oxford (Schol.). 1st cl. hons Mod. Hist., 1937; Craven Fellow, 1937; DPhil 1940; BD Cantab 1964; DD Oxon 1966. Asst Princ., War Office, 1940; seconded Cabinet Office, 1941; FO, 1942; service in N Africa, Italy and Austria, 1943–46 (Gold Cross of Merit with Swords, Polish Forces); Ed. Bd, German Foreign Min. Documents, 1947–51; Res. Fellow, Nottingham Univ., 1951; S. A. Cook Bye-Fellow, 1952, Fellow, 1956–69, Dir Studies, Archaeology, 1961–69, Gonville and Caius Coll.; University Asst Lectr, 1953, Lectr in Divinity, 1958–69; Birkbeck Lectr in Ecclesiastical History, 1967–68. Lay Mem., CSSB 1970–72. Chm., AUT (Scotland), 1976–78. Vice-Pres., Assoc. internat. d'Etudes patristiques, 1983–87; Président d'Honneur, Internat. Commn for Comparative Study of Ecclesiastical History (CIHEC), 1983 (Vice-Pres. 1975–80, Pres. 1980–83). Assoc. Dir, Egypt Exploration Soc. excavations at Q'asr Ibrim, Nubia, 1963–64; Guest Scholar at Rhodes Univ., 1964 and Peter Ainslie Meml Lecturer; Guest Prof., Univ. of S Africa, 1976; Vis. Prof. of Inter-religious Studies (Walter and Mary Tuohy Chair), John Carroll Univ., Cleveland, 1981; Vis. Fellow, Harvard Univ. Center for Byzantine Studies, Dumbarton Oaks, 1984. Licensed Lay Reader, 1956, Deacon, 1982, Priest, 1983, serving in Aberfoyle parish. Mem., Peterborough Diocesan Synod, 1988–90. Editor, Modern Churchman, 1963–82. British Mem., Editl Bd, Coptic Encyclopædia, 1980–91. Commission Queen's Royal Regt (TA), 1947–67. FSA 1952 (Mem. Council, 1992–94); FRHistS 1954; FRSE 1979. Hon. DD Edinburgh, 1974. *Publications:* The Donatist Church, 1952; Martyrdom and Persecution in the Early Church, 1965; The Early Church, 1965; (contrib.) Religion in the Middle East, 1968; The Rise of the Monophysite Movement, 1972; Religion Popular and Unpopular in the Early Christian Centuries, 1976; (contrib.) Cambridge History of Africa, vol. ii, 1978; Town and Country in the Early Christian Centuries, 1980; The Rise of Christianity, 1984; Saints and Sinners in the Early Church, 1985; History and Archaeology in the Study of Early Christianity, 1988; (contrib.) Agostino d'Ippona: quaestiones disputatae, 1989; Christian Archaeology: an historical study, 1995; articles in Jl Theol Studies, Jl Roman Studies, Jl Eccles. History, Jahrbuch für Antike und Christentum, etc. *Recreations:* archæology, occasional golf and tennis, writing, collecting old coins and stamps. *Address:* Clerk's Cottage, Little Wilbraham, Cambridge CB1 5LB. *Club:* Authors'.

FRERE, Vice-Adm. Sir Richard Tobias, (Sir Toby), KCB 1994; Chief of Fleet Support, since 1994; *b* 4 June 1938; *s* of Alexander Stewart Frere and Patricia Frere; *m* 1968, Jane Barraclough; two *d*. *Educ:* Eton College; Britannia Royal Naval College. Joined RNVR as National Serviceman; transf. RN 1957; commissioned 1958; submarines 1960; served Canada, 1961–62, Australia, 1966–67, 1973; commanded HM Submarines Andrew, Odin and Revenge and Frigate HMS Brazen. JSSC, Canberra, 1973; RCDS London, 1982; Dir Gen. Fleet Support, Policy and Services, 1988–91; Flag Officer Submarines, and Comdr Submarines Eastern Atlantic, 1991–93. *Recreation:* sailing. *Address:* c/o Ministry of Defence (Navy), Main Building, Whitehall, SW1A 2HB. *Clubs:* Garrick, MCC.

FRERE, Prof. Sheppard Sunderland, CBE 1976; FSA 1944; FBA 1971; Professor of the Archæology of the Roman Empire, and Fellow of All Souls College, Oxford University, 1966–83, now professor Emeritus and Emeritus Fellow; *b* 23 Aug. 1916; *e s* of late N. G. Frere, CMG; *m* 1961, Janet Cecily Hoare; one *s* one *d*. *Educ:* Lancing Coll.; Magdalene Coll., Cambridge. BA 1938, MA 1944, LittD 1976, DLitt 1977. Master, Epsom Coll., 1938–40. National Fire Service, 1940–45. Master, Lancing Coll., 1945–54; Lecturer in Archæology, Manchester Univ., 1954–55; Reader in Archæology of Roman Provinces, London Univ. Inst. of Archæology, 1955–62; Prof. of the Archæology of the Roman Provinces, London Univ., 1963–66. Dir, Canterbury Excavations, 1946–60; Dir, Verulamium Excavations, 1955–61. Vice-Pres., Soc. of Antiquaries, 1962–66; President: Oxford Architectural and Historical Soc., 1972–80; Royal Archæological Inst., 1978–81; Soc. for Promotion of Roman Studies, 1983–86. Hon. Corr. Mem. German Archæological Inst., 1964, Fellow, 1967; Member: Royal Commn on Hist. Monuments (England), 1966–83; Ancient Monuments Board (England), 1966–82. Hon. LittD: Leeds, 1977; Leicester, 1983; Kent, 1985. Gold Medal, Soc. of Antiquaries, 1989. Editor, Britannia, 1969–79. *Publications:* (ed) Problems of the Iron Age in Southern Britain, 1961; Britannia, a history of Roman Britain, 1967 (rev. edn 1987); Verulamium Excavations, vol. I, 1972, vol. II, 1983, vol. III, 1984; Excavations on the Roman and Medieval Defences of Canterbury, 1982; Excavations at Canterbury, vol. VII, 1983; (with J. K. St Joseph) Roman Britain from the Air, 1983; (with F. A. Lepper) Trajan's Column, 1988; (with J. J. Wilkes) Strageath: excavations within the Roman fort, 1989; (ed with R. Tomlin) The Roman Inscriptions of Britain, vol. II, fasc. 1, 1990, fascs 2–3, 1991, fasc. 4, 1992, fasc. 5, 1993, fasc. 6, 1994, fascs 7–8, and Epigraphic Indexes, 1995; papers in learned jls. *Recreation:* gardening. *Address:* Netherfield House, Marcham, Abingdon, Oxon OX13 6NP.

FRERE, Vice-Adm. Sir Toby; *see* Frere, Vice-Adm. Sir R. T.

FRESHWATER, Prof. Donald Cole, FEng 1986; Professor, Louisiana State University, 1986–94; Professor Emeritus, University of Technology, Loughborough, 1987; *b* 21 April 1924; *s* of Thomas and Ethel May Freshwater; *m* 1948, Margaret D. Worrall (marr. diss. 1977); one *s* three *d*; *m* 1980, Eleanor M. Lancashire (*née* Tether). *Educ:* Brewood Grammar Sch.; Birmingham Univ. (BSc, PhD); Sheffield Univ.; Loughborough Coll. (DLC). Fuel Engineer, Min. of Fuel and Power, 1944; Chemical Engr: APV Co. Ltd, 1948; Midland Tar Distillers Co. Ltd, 1950; Lectr, Dept of Chem. Engrg, Univ. of Birmingham, 1952–57; Loughborough College (later University) of Technology: Hd, Dept of Chem. Engrg, 1957–86; Dean of Pure and Applied Science, 1982–85; Sen. Pro Vice-Chancellor, 1972–74. Visiting Professor: Univ. of Delaware, USA, 1962; Georgia Inst. of Technology, 1980–81. Chm., Chem. Engrg Gp, Soc. of Chemical Industry, 1973–75; Mem. Council, IChemE, 1982–87 (Vice Pres., 1985–87). Hon. DSc Loughborough, 1989. *Publications:* Chemical Engineering Data Book, 1959; numerous papers on mass transfer, particle technology and educn in chem. engrg jls. *Recreations:* sailing, collecting watercolours. *Address:* Department of Chemical Engineering, Louisiana State University, Baton Rouge, LA 70810, USA. *Club:* Athenæum.

FRETWELL, Elizabeth Drina, OBE 1977; professional adjudicator and vocal coach; operatic and dramatic soprano; *b* Melbourne, Australia, 13 Aug. 1920; *m* 1958, Robert Simmons; one *s* one *d*. *Educ:* privately. Joined National Theatre, Melbourne, 1950; came to Britain, 1955; joined Sadler's Wells, 1956; Australia, Elizabethan Opera Co., 1963; tour of W Germany, 1963; USA, Canada and Covent Garden, 1964; tour of Europe, 1965; guest soprano with Cape Town and Durban Opera Cos, South Africa, 1970; Australian Opera, 1970–87. Rôles include Violetta in La Traviata, Leonora in Fidelio, Ariadne in Ariadne auf Naxos, Senta in The Flying Dutchman, Minnie in The Girl of the Golden West, Leonora in Il Trovatore, Aida, Ellen Orford in Peter Grimes, Leonora in Forza del Destino, Alice Ford in Falstaff, Amelia in Masked Ball, Georgetta in Il Tabarro, opening season of Sydney Opera Hse, 1973. Has sung in BBC Promenade Concerts and on TV. Mem., music bd, Opera Foundn Australia, 1982–. *Recreation:* rose-growing. *Address:* 47 Kananook Avenue, Bayview, NSW 2104, Australia.

FRETWELL, Sir (Major) John (Emsley), GCMG 1987 (KCMG 1982; CMG 1975); HM Diplomatic Service, retired; Political Director and Deputy to the Permanent Under-Secretary of State, Foreign and Commonwealth Office, 1987–90; *b* 15 June 1930; *s* of late Francis Thomas Fretwell and of Dorothy Fretwell; *m* 1959, Mary Ellen Eugenie Dubois; one *s* one *d*. *Educ:* Chesterfield Grammar Sch.; Lausanne Univ.; King's Coll., Cambridge (MA). HM Forces, 1948–50. Diplomatic Service, 1953; 3rd Sec., Hong Kong, 1954–55; 2nd Sec., Peking, 1955–57; FO, 1957–59; 1st Sec., Moscow, 1959–62; FO, 1962–67; 1st Sec. (Commercial), Washington, 1967–70; Commercial Counsellor, Warsaw, 1971–73; Head of European Integration Dept (Internal), FCO, 1973–76; Asst Under-Sec. of State, FCO, 1976–79; Minister, Washington, 1980–81; Ambassador to France, 1982–87. Specialist Advr, H of L, 1992–93. Mem., Council of Lloyd's, 1991–92. Chm., Franco-British Soc., 1995–. *Recreations:* skiing, walking, wine. *Club:* Brooks's.

FREUD, Sir Clement (Raphael), Kt 1987; writer, broadcaster, caterer; *b* 24 April 1924; *s* of late Ernst and Lucie Freud; *m* 1950, Jill, 2nd *d* of H. W. Flewett, MA; three *s* two *d*. Apprenticed, Dorchester Hotel, London. Served War, Royal Ulster Rifles; Liaison Officer, Nuremberg war crimes trials, 1946. Trained, Martinez Hotel, Cannes. Proprietor, Royal Court Theatre Club, 1952–62. Sports writer, Observer, 1956–64; Cookery Editor: Time and Tide, 1961–63; Observer Magazine, 1964–68; Daily Telegraph Magazine, 1968–. Sports Columnist, Sun, 1964–69; Columnist: Sunday Telegraph, 1963–65; News of the World, 1965; Financial Times, 1964–; Daily Express, 1973–75; Radio Times, 1992–; Times Diarist, 1988–, Columnist, 1992–. Consultant: Forte (formerly THF), 1988–; Intercity, 1990–. Contested (L) Cambridgeshire NE, 1987. MP (L): Isle of Ely, July 1973–1983; Cambridgeshire NE, 1983–87. Liberal spokesman on education, the arts and broadcasting; sponsor, Official Information Bill. Chm., Standing Cttee, Liberal Party, 1982–86. Rector, Univ. of Dundee, 1974–80. Pres., Down's Children Assoc., 1988–. £5,000 class winner, Daily Mail London-NY air race, 1969. Award winning petfood commercial: San Francisco, Tokyo, Berlin, 1967. BBC (sound) Just a Minute, 1968–. MUniv Open, 1989. *Publications:* Grimble, 1968; Grimble at Christmas, 1973; Freud on Food, 1978; Clicking Vicky, 1980; The Book of Hangovers, 1981; Below the Belt, 1983; No-one Else has Complained, 1988; The Gourmet's Tour of Great Britain and Ireland, 1989; contributor to, New Yorker, etc (formerly to Punch). *Recreations:* racing, backgammon, pétanque. *Address:* 22 Wimpole Street, W1M 7AD. *T:* 0171–580 2222; Westons, Walberswick, Suffolk IP18 6UH; Casa de Colina, Praia da Luz, Algarve. *Clubs:* MCC, Lord's Taverners', Groucho.

See also Lucian Freud.

FREUD, Lucian, OM 1993; CH 1983; painter; *b* 8 Dec. 1922; *s* of late Ernst and Lucie Freud; *m* 1st, 1948, Kathleen Garman Epstein (marr. diss. 1952), *d* of Jacob Epstein; two *d*; 2nd, 1953, Lady Caroline Maureen Blackwood (marr. diss. 1957), *d* of 4th Marquess of Dufferin and Ava. *Educ:* Central Sch. of Art; East Anglian Sch. of Painting and Drawing. Worked on merchant ship SS Baltrover as ordinary seaman, 1942. Teacher, Slade Sch. of Art, 1948–58; Vis. Asst, Norwich Sch. of Art, 1964–65. Painted mostly in France and Greece, 1946–48. Hon. Mem., Amer. Acad. and Inst. of Arts and Letters, 1988. *Exhibitions:* Lefevre Gall., 1944, 1946; London Gall., 1947, 1948; British Council and Galérie René Drouin, Paris, 1948; Hanover Gall., 1950, 1952; British Council and Vancouver Art Gall., 1951; British Council, Venice Biennale, 1954; Marlborough Fine Art, 1958, 1963, 1968; Anthony d'Offay, 1972, 1978 (subseq. Davis & Long, NY), 1982; Nishimura Gall., Tokyo, 1979, 1991; Thos Agnew & Sons, 1983; Scottish Nat. Gall. of Modern Art, 1988; Berggruen Gall., Paris, 1990; Saatchi Collection, 1990; Thomas Gibson Fine Art Ltd, 1991; Palazzo Ruspoli, Rome, 1991; Castello Sforzesca, Milan, 1991; Art Gall. of NSW, 1992; Tochigi Prefectural Mus. of Fine Arts, Otani Meml Art Mus., Nishinomiya, and Setaguya Art Museum, Tokyo, Japan, 1992; Whitechapel Art Gall., 1993; Metropolitan Mus. of Art, New York, 1993; Muses Nacional Centro de Arte Reina Sofia, Madrid, 1994; Astrup Fearnley Museet for Moderne Kunst, Oslo, 1994; Dulwich Picture Gall., 1994; *retrospectives:* Hayward Gall., 1974 (subseq. Bristol, Birmingham and Leeds), 1988 (also Washington, Paris and Berlin, 1987–88); Works on Paper, Ashmolean Mus., Oxford, 1988 (subseq. other towns in provinces and in USA); Tate Gall., Liverpool, 1992. *Works included in public collections:* London: Tate Gall.; Nat. Portrait Gall.; V & A Museum; Arts Council of GB; British Council; British Mus.; DoE; provinces: Cecil Higgins Museum, Bedford; Fitzwilliam Mus., Cambridge; Nat. Mus. of Wales, Cardiff; Scottish Nat. Gall. of Mod. Art, Edinburgh; Hartlepool Art Gall.; Walker Art Gall., Liverpool; Liverpool Univ.; City Art Gall. and Whitworth Gall., Manchester; Ashmolean Mus. of Art, Oxford; Harris Mus. and Art Gall., Preston; Rochdale Art Gall.; Southampton Art Gall.; Australia: Queensland Art Gall., Brisbane; Art Gall. of S Australia, Adelaide; Art Gall. of WA, Perth; France: Musée National d'Art Moderne, Centre Georges Pompidou, Paris; Beaverbrook Foundn, Fredericton, New Brunswick; USA: Art Inst. of Chicago; Mus. of Mod. Art, NY; Cleveland Mus. of Art, Ohio; Mus. of Art, Carnegie Inst., Pittsburgh; Achenbach Foundn for Graphic Arts and Fine Arts Mus. of San Francisco; Art Mus., St Louis; Hirshhorn Musum and Sculpture Garden, Smithsonian Instn, Washington. *Relevant publications:* Lucian Freud, by Lawrence Gowing, 1982; Lucian Freud, Paintings, by Robert Hughes, 1987; Lucian Freud, works on paper, by Nicholas Penney and Robert Flynn Johnson, 1988. *Address:* c/o Diana Rawstron, Goodman Derrick, 90 Fetter Lane, EC4A 1EQ.

See also Sir C. R. Freud.

FREYBERG, family name of **Baron Freyberg.**

FREYBERG, 3rd Baron *cr* 1951, of Wellington, New Zealand and of Munstead, Co. Surrey; **Valerian Bernard Freyberg;** *b* 15 Dec. 1970; *o s* of 2nd Baron Freyberg, OBE, MC, and of Ivry Perronelle Katharine, *d* of Cyril Harrower Guild, Aspall Hall, Debenham, Suffolk; *S* father, 1993. *Educ:* Eton Coll.; Camberwell Coll. of Art. *Address:* Munstead House, Godalming, Surrey GU8 4AR.

FRICKER, (Anthony) Nigel; QC 1977; **His Honour Judge Fricker;** a Circuit Judge, since 1984; *b* 7 July 1937; *s* of late Dr William Shapland Fricker and of Margaret Fricker; *m* 1960, Marilyn Ann, *d* of A. L. Martin, Pa, USA; one *s* two *d. Educ:* King's School, Chester; Liverpool Univ. (LLB 1958). President of Guild of Undergraduates, Liverpool Univ., 1958–59. Called to Bar, Gray's Inn, 1960. Conf. Leader, Ford Motor Co. of Australia, Melbourne, 1960–61. Recorder, Crown Court, 1975–84; Prosecuting Counsel to DHSS, Wales and Chester Circuit, 1975–77; an asst comr, Boundary Commn for Wales, 1981–84. Member: Bar Council, 1966–70; Senate and Bar Council, 1975–78; County Court Rule Cttee, 1988–92. Fellow, Internat. Acad. of Trial Lawyers, 1979–. Mem. Court: Liverpool Univ., 1977–; York Univ., 1984–. Confrérie des Chevaliers du Tastevin. *Publications:* (Gen. Ed. and jt author) Family Courts: Emergency Remedies and Procedures, 1990, 2nd edn 1993; (with David Bean) Enforcement of Injunctions and Undertakings, 1991; (consulting ed.) The Family Court Practice, (annually) 1993–; contrib. legal periodicals in UK and USA (Family and Conciliation Courts Rev.). *Address:* Sheffield County Court, Belgrave House, Bank Street, Sheffield S1 1EH. *T:* Sheffield (0114) 273 7511; Farrar's Building, Temple, EC4Y 7BD.

FRICKER, Rt. Rev. Joachim Carl; a Suffragan Bishop of Toronto (Bishop of Credit Valley), 1985–94; *b* Zweibrucken, Germany, 1 Dec. 1927; *s* of Carl and Caroline Fricker; *m* 1952, Shirley Joan (*née* Gill); three *s* two *d. Educ:* Niagara Falls Public Schools; Univ. of Western Ontario (BA); Huron College (LTh). Ordained deacon and priest, 1952; Rector: St Augustine's, Hamilton, 1952–59; St David's, Welland, 1959–65; St James, Dundas, 1965–73; Canon of Christ's Church Cathedral, Hamilton, 1964–73; Dean of Diocese of Niagara and Rector, Christ's Church Cathedral, 1973–85. Chm., Nat. Doctrine and Worship Cttee (Anglican Church of Canada), 1989–92. Hon. DD: Huron Coll., 1974; Trinity Coll., 1987; Hon. DSL, Wycliffe Coll., 1987. *Recreations:* theatre, gardening, reading, walking. *Address:* 2052 Mississauga Road, Mississauga, Ontario L5H 2K6, Canada. *T:* (416) 2745108.

FRIEDBERGER, Maj.-Gen. John Peter William, CB 1991; CBE 1986 (MBE 1975); Chief Executive, British Helicopter Advisory Board, since 1992; *b* 27 May 1937; *s* of late Brig. John Cameron Friedberger, DSO, DL and Phyllis Grace Friedberger, JP; *m* 1966, Joanna Mary, *d* of Andrew Thorne, ERD; one *s* two *d. Educ:* Red House School, York; Wellington College; RMA Sandhurst. Commissioned, 10th Royal Hussars (PWO), 1956; seconded to Northern Frontier Regt, Sultan's Armed Forces, Oman, 1961–63; Australian Army Staff Coll., 1969; CO The Royal Hussars (PWO), 1975–78; RCDS, 1978–79; Comdr, Royal Brunei Armed Forces, 1982–86; ACOS, HQ Northern Army Group, 1986–88; Administrator, Sovereign Base Areas and Commander, British Forces, Cyprus, 1988–90. Hon. Colonel: The Royal Hussars (PWO), 1991–92; The King's Royal Hussars, 1992–. FRGS 1990; ARAeS, 1992; Dato, DPKT (Negara Brunei Darussalam) 1984. *Recreation:* travel. *Address:* c/o Home HQ, The King's Royal Hussars, Peninsula Barracks, Winchester, Hants SO23 8TS. *Club:* Cavalry and Guards.

FRIEDLANDER, Frederick Gerard, (Friedrich Gerhart), PhD; FRS 1980; Reader Emeritus, University of Cambridge, since 1982; Hon. Research Fellow, Department of Mathematics, University College London; *b* Vienna, 25 Dec. 1917. *Educ:* Univ. of Cambridge (BA, PhD). Fellow of Trinity Coll., Cambridge, 1940; Temporary Experimental Officer, Admiralty, 1943; Faculty Asst Lectr, Cambridge, 1945; Lecturer: Univ. of Manchester, 1946; Univ. of Cambridge, 1954; Fellow of St John's Coll., Cambridge, 1961; Fellow of Wolfson Coll., Cambridge, 1968; Reader in Partial Differential Equations, Univ. of Cambridge, 1979. *Publications:* Sound Pulses, 1958; The Wave Equation on a Curved Space-Time, 1975; Introduction to the Theory of Distributions, 1982; papers in mathematical jls. *Address:* 28 Greenlands, Cambridge CB2 2QY.

FRIEDMAN, David Peter; QC 1990; *b* 1 June 1944; *s* of Wilfred Emanuel Friedman and Rosa Lees; *m* 1972, Sara Geraldine Linton. *Educ:* Tiffin Boys' School; Lincoln College, Oxford (BCL, MA). Called to the Bar, Inner Temple, 1968. *Recreations:* good food (cooked by others), reading. *Address:* 4 Pump Court, Temple, EC4Y 7AN. *T:* 0171–353 2656. *Club:* Lansdowne.

FRIEDMAN, Prof. Jerome Isaac, PhD; Professor of Physics, Massachusetts Institute of Technology, since 1967; *b* 28 March 1930; *m* Tania Baranovsky Friedman; two *s* two *d. Educ:* Univ. of Chicago (AB 1950; MS 1953; PhD Physics 1956). Research associate; Univ. of Chicago, 1956–57; Stanford Univ., 1957–60; MIT: Asst Prof. and Associate Prof., 1960–67; Dir, Nuclear Science Lab., 1980–83; Head of Dept of Physics, 1983–88. Fellow: Amer. Phys. Soc.; Nat. Acad. of Scis; Amer. Acad. of Arts and Scis. (jtly) W. H. K. Panofsky Prize for Physics, 1989; (jtly) Nobel Prize for Physics, 1990. *Publications:* numerous papers in learned jls on particle physics, esp. the division of protons and neutrons into smaller particles, leading to different types of quarks. *Address:* Department of Physics, Massachusetts Institute of Technology, Cambridge, MA 02139, USA.

FRIEDMAN, Prof. Milton, PhD; Economist, USA; Senior Research Fellow, Hoover Institution, Stanford University, since 1976; Professor Emeritus of Economics, University of Chicago, since 1982 (Professor of Economics, 1948–82); Member of Research Staff, National Bureau of Economic Research, 1948–81; Economic Columnist, Newsweek, 1966–84; *b* New York, 31 July 1912; *s* of Jeno Saul and Sarah E. Friedman; *m* 1938, Rose Director; one *s* one *d. Educ:* Rutgers (AB), Chicago (AM), and Columbia (PhD) Univs. Associate Economist, Natural Resources Cttee, Washington, 1935–37; Nat. Bureau of Economic Research, New York, 1937–45 (on leave 1940–45). During 1941–45: Principal Economist, Tax Research Div., US Treasury Dept, 1941–43; Associate Dir, Statistical Research Gp, Div. of War Research, Columbia Univ., 1943–45. Fulbright Lecturer, Cambridge Univ., 1953–54; Vis. Prof., Econs, Columbia Univ., 1964–65, etc. Member: President's Commn on an All-Volunteer Armed Force, 1969–70; Commn on White House Fellows, 1971–73. Mem. Bd of Editors, Econometrica, 1957–65; Pres., Amer. Economic Assoc., 1967; Pres., Mont Pelerin Soc., 1970–72. John Bates Clark Medal, Amer. Econ. Assoc., 1951; Member various societies, etc., incl. Royal Economic Soc. (GB). Fellowships and awards, in USA. Holds several Hon. doctorates. Nobel Memorial Prize for Economics, 1976; Nat. Medal of Sci., USA, 1988. Grand Cordon, Sacred Treasure (Japan), 1986; US Presidential Medal of Freedom, 1988. *Publications:* Income from Independent Professional Practice (with Simon Kuznets), 1946; Sampling Inspection (with others), 1948; Essays in Positive Economics, 1953; (ed) Studies in the Quantity Theory of Money, 1956; A Theory of the Consumption Function, 1957; A Program for Monetary Stability, 1960; Capitalism and Freedom, 1962; Price Theory: a Provisional Text, 1962; A Monetary History of the United States 1867–1960 (with Anna J. Schwartz), 1963; Inflation: Causes and Consequences, 1963; The Balance of Payments: Free versus Flexible Exchange Rates (with Robert V. Roosa), 1967; Dollars and Deficits, 1968; Optimum Quantity of Money and Other Essays, 1969; Monetary vs Fiscal Policy (with Walter W. Heller), 1969; Monetary Statistics of the United States (with Anna J. Schwartz), 1970; A Theoretical Framework for Monetary Analysis, 1971; Social Security: Universal or Selective? (with Wilbur J. Cohen), 1972; An Economist's Protest, 1972; Money and Economic Development, 1973; There's No Such Thing as a Free Lunch, 1975; Price Theory, 1976; Free to Choose (with Rose Friedman), 1980; Monetary Trends in the United States and the United Kingdom (with Anna J. Schwahtz), 1982; Bright Promises, Dismal Performance, 1983; (with Rose Friedman) Tyranny of the Status Quo, 1984; Money Mischief, 1992. *Recreations:* tennis, carpentry. *Address:* Hoover Institution, Stanford, CA 94305–6010, USA. *Club:* Quadrangle (Chicago).

FRIEDMANN, Jacques-Henri; Officier, Légion d'Honneur, 1988; Chevalier, Ordre du Mérite, 1970; Chairman, Union des Assurances de Paris, since 1993; *b* Paris, 15 Oct. 1932; *s* of André Friedmann and Marie-Louise Bleiweiss; *m* 1962, Cécile Fleur; two *s* one *d. Educ:* Inst. d'Etudes Politiques, Paris (law degree). Student, Ecole Nat. d'Admin, 1957–58; Inspector of Finance, 1959; Lectr, Inst. d'Etudes Politiques, 1964–68; Special Asst 1964, Tech. Advr 1965–66, Deptl Staff of Valéry Giscard d'Estaing, Minister of Finance; Special Asst, Gen Directorate of Domestic Trade and Pricing, 1966; Actg Dep. Sec. Gen., Interministerial Cttee on Europ. Econ. Co-op., 1966–67; Hd, Finance Dept, French Planning Org., 1967–68; Chief Executive Secretary: to Jacques Chirac, Sec. of State for Econ. Affairs and Finance, 1969–70, and Minister responsible for liaison with Parlt, 1971; Hd of Dept of Gen. Inspectorate of Finances and of Central Dept of Gen. Inspectorate for the Nat. Economy, 1971–72; Advr on Econ. and Financial Affairs to Pierre Messmer, Prime Minister, then Chief Exec. Sec., 1972–74; Special Asst to Jacques Chirac, Prime Minister, 1974; Chm., Co. Générale Maritime, 1974–82; Inspector Gen. of Finance, 1980; Chm. and Man Dir, Co. Parisienne de Chauffage Urbaine, 1983–87; Special Asst to Edouard Balladur, Minister of Econ. Affairs, Finance and Privatisation, 1986–87; Chairman: Caisse d'Epargne de Paris, 1985–95; Air France, 1987–88; SAGI, 1989–93. *Address:* 9 Place Vendôme, 75001 Paris, France. *T:* 42867500.

FRIEL, Brian; writer; *b* 9 Jan. 1929; *s* of Patrick Friel and Christina Friel (*née* MacLoone); *m* 1954, Anne Morrison; one *s* four *d. Educ:* St Columb's Coll., Derry; St Patrick's Coll., Maynooth; St Joseph's Trng Coll., Belfast. Taught in various schools, 1950–60; writing full-time from 1960. Lived in Minnesota during first season of Tyrone Guthrie Theater, Minneapolis. Member: Irish Acad. of Letters, 1972; Aosdana, 1983–. Hon. DLitt: Chicago, 1979; NUI, 1983; NUU, 1986. *Publications: collected stories:* The Saucer of Larks, 1962; The Gold in the Sea, 1966; *plays:* Philadelphia, Here I Come!, 1965; The Loves of Cass McGuire, 1967; Lovers, 1968; The Mundy Scheme, 1969; Crystal and Fox, 1970; The Gentle Island, 1971; The Freedom of the City, 1973; Volunteers, 1975; Living Quarters, 1976; Aristocrats, 1979; Faith Healer, 1979; Translations, 1981 (Ewart-Biggs Meml Prize, British Theatre Assoc. Award); (trans.) Three Sisters, 1981; The Communication Cord, 1983; (trans.) Fathers and Sons, 1987; Making History, 1988; London Vertigo, 1989; Dancing at Lughnasa, 1990; A Month in the Country, 1990; Wonderful Tennessee, 1993; Molly Sweeney, 1995. *Recreations:* reading, trout-fishing, slow tennis. *Address:* Drumaweir House, Greencastle, Co. Donegal, Ireland.

FRIEND, His Honour (Archibald) Gordon; a Circuit Judge, 1972–84, retired; *b* 6 July 1912; *m* 1940, Patricia Margaret Smith (*d* 1993); no *c. Educ:* Dulwich Coll.; Keble Coll., Oxford (MA). Called to the Bar, Inner Temple, 1933. Served War: enlisted RA, Feb. 1940, commnd Nov. 1940; on staff of JAG MEF and PAIFORCE, 1941–44 (Major); released 1945. Dep. Chm., Herts Quarter Sessions, 1963–71, Inner London, later Mddx, QS, 1965–71; Inner London Crown Court, 1972–74; Knightsbridge Crown Court, 1974–84. *Recreation:* gardening. *Address:* Amesbury Abbey, Amesbury, Wilts SP4 7EX.

FRIEND, Rev. Frederick James; Librarian, University College London, since 1982; *b* 7 April 1941; *s* of James Frederick Friend and Emily Mary Friend (*née* Giddens); *m* 1969, Margaret Rusholme; one *s* one *d. Educ:* Dover Grammar Sch. for Boys; King's Coll., London (BA 1963); University Coll. London (DipLib 1965); Oak Hill Coll. Asst Librarian, Manchester Univ. Library, 1965–71; Sub-Librarian, Leeds Univ., 1971–76; Dep. Librarian, Nottingham Univ., 1976–78; Librarian, Essex Univ., 1978–82. Deacon 1982, priest 1983; NSM, Dio. Oxford, 1982–. *Publications:* various articles in learned jls. *Recreations:* walking the dogs, prayer. *Address:* The Chimes, Cryers Hill Road, High Wycombe, Bucks HP15 6JS.

FRIEND, Lionel; Musical Director: Nexus Opera, since 1981; New Sussex Opera, since 1989; *b* 13 March 1945; *s* of Moya and Norman A. C. Friend; *m* 1969, Jane Hyland; one *s* two *d. Educ:* Royal Grammar School, High Wycombe; Royal College of Music; London Opera Centre. LRAM; ARCM. Glyndebourne Opera, 1969–72; Welsh National Opera, 1969–72; Kapellmeister, Staatstheater, Kassel, Germany, 1972–75; Staff Conductor, ENO, 1978–89. Guest Conductor: BBC orchestras; Nash Ensemble, etc. *Recreations:* reading, theatre. *Address:* 136 Rosendale Road, SE21 8LG. *T:* 0181–761 7845.

FRIEND, Dame Phyllis (Muriel), DBE 1980 (CBE 1972); Chief Nursing Officer, Department of Health and Social Security, 1972–82; *b* 28 Sept. 1922; *d* of Richard Edward Friend. *Educ:* Herts and Essex High Sch., Bishop's Stortford; The London Hospital (SRN); Royal College of Nursing (RNT). Dep. Matron, St George's Hospital, 1956–59; Dep. Matron, 1959–61, Matron, 1961–68, Chief Nursing Officer 1969–72, The London Hospital. *Address:* Barnmead, Start Hill, Bishop's Stortford, Herts CM22 7TA. *T:* Bishop's Stortford (01279) 654873.

FRIEND, Prof. Richard Henry, FRS 1993; Cavendish Professor of Physics, University of Cambridge, since 1995; Fellow, St John's College, Cambridge, since 1977; *b* 18 Jan. 1953; *s* of John Henry Friend and Dorothy Jean (*née* Brown); *m* 1979, Carol Anne Maxwell (*née* Beales); two *d. Educ:* Rugby Sch.; Trinity Coll., Cambridge (MA, PhD). Res. Fellow, St John's Coll., Cambridge, 1977–80; University of Cambridge: Demonstrator in Physics, 1980–85; Lectr, 1985–93; Reader in Experimental Physics, 1993–95. Vis. Prof., Univ. of Calif, Santa Barbara, 1986–87; Vis. Fellow, Royal Instn, 1992; Nuffield Science Res. Fellowship, 1992–93. C. V. Boys Prize, Inst. of Physics, 1988; Interdisciplinary Award, RSC, 1991. *Publications:* papers on chem. physics and solid-state physics in scientific jls. *Address:* Cavendish Laboratory, Madingley Road, Cambridge CB3 0HE. *T:* Cambridge (01223) 337218.

FRIES, Richard James; Chief Charity Commissioner, since 1992; *b* 7 July 1940; *s* of late Felix Theodore Fries and Joan Mary Fries (now Mrs John Harris); *m* 1970, Carole Anne Buick; one *s* two *d. Educ:* King's Coll., Cambridge. Home Office, 1965–92. *Recreations:* chess, walking. *Address:* c/o Charity Commission, 57/60 Haymarket, SW1Y 4QX. *T:* 0171–210 4409.

FRINDALL, William Howard, (Bill); freelance cricket statistician, broadcaster, writer, and editor, since 1965; *b* 3 March 1939; *s* of late Arthur Howard Frindall and of Evelyn Violet Frindall (*née* McNeill); *m* 1st, 1960, Maureen Doris Wesson (marr. diss. 1970); two *s* one *d*; 2nd, 1970, Jacqueline Rose Seager (marr. diss. 1980); 3rd, 1992, Deborah Margaret Brown. *Educ:* Reigate Grammar Sch.; Kingston upon Thames Sch. of Art. Asst Prodn Manager, Lutterworth Press, 1958; Royal Air Force, 1958–65, commnd Secretarial

Br., 1964. BBC cricket statistician, 1966–; Editor, Playfair Cricket Annual, 1986–; Cricket Corresp., Mail on Sunday, 1987–89. Pres., British Blind Sport, 1984–. *Publications:* The Wisden Book of Test Cricket, 1979, 4th edn 1995; The Wisden Book of Cricket Records, 1981, 3rd edn 1993; The Guinness Book of Cricket Fact and Feats, 1983, 3rd edn 1991; The Wisden Book of One-Day International Cricket, 1985; England Test Cricketers, 1989. *Recreations:* cricket, sketching, painting, photography, philately, elementary gardening (under supervision from my wife). *Address:* Urchfont, Wiltshire. *Clubs:* MCC, Lord's Taverners; Cricket Writers'; Forty.

FRIPP, Alfred Thomas, BM; FRCS; *b* 3 July 1899; *s* of late Sir Alfred Fripp, KCVO, and late Lady M. S. Fripp, *d* of late T. B. Haywood; *m* 1931, Kathleen Kimpton, (Jennie) (*d* 1986); one *s* two *d*. *Educ:* Winchester; Christ Church, Oxford. 2nd Lieut 1st Life Guards, 1917–18. Christ Church, Oxford, 1919–21; Guy's Hospital, 1921; Surg., Royal National Orthopædic Hospital, 1934–64. Mem., Pensions Appeal Tribunal, 1966–74. FRCS 1927. Pres. Orthopædic Section, RSocMed, 1950–51. *Recreations:* gardening, rowing. *Address:* Shalesbrook, Forest Row, Sussex RH18 5LS. *Club:* Leander (Henley-on-Thames).

FRISBY, Audrey Mary; *see* Jennings, A. M.

FRISBY, Roger Harry Kilbourne; QC 1969; a Recorder, 1972–78 and since 1986; *b* 11 Dec. 1921; 2nd *s* of late Herbert Frisby and Hylda Mary Frisby; *m* 1961, Audrey Mary (*see* A. M. Jennings) (marr. diss. 1980); two *s* one *d* (and one *s* one *d* by previous marriage). *Educ:* Bablake Sch.; Christ Church, Oxford; King's Coll., Univ. of London. Called to the Bar, Lincoln's Inn, 1950. *Address:* Queen Elizabeth Building, Temple, EC4Y 9BS. *T:* 0171–583 5766. *Club:* Hurlingham.

FRISBY, Terence; playwright, actor, producer, director; *b* 28 Nov. 1932; *s* of William and Kathleen Frisby; *m* 1963, Christine Vecchione (marr. diss.); one *s*. *Educ:* Dobwalls Village Sch.; Dartford Grammar Sch.; Central Sch. of Speech Training and Dramatic Art. Substantial repertory acting and directing experience, also TV, films and musicals, 1957–63; appeared in A Sense of Detachment, Royal Court, 1972–73 and X, Royal Court, 1974; Clive Popkiss, in Rookery Nook, Her Majesty's, 1979, and many since. Productions: Once a Catholic (tour), 1980–81; There's a Girl in My Soup (tour), 1982; Woza Albert!, Criterion, 1983; The Real Inspector Hound/Seaside Postcard (tour), 1983–84; Comic Cuts, 1984. Has written many TV scripts, incl. series Lucky Feller, 1976; That's Love, 1988–92 (Gold Award, Houston Film Festival); film, There's A Girl in My Soup, 1970 (Writers Guild Award, Best British Comedy Screenplay). *Publications: plays:* The Subtopians, 1964; There's a Girl in My Soup, 1966; The Bandwagon, 1970; It's All Right if I Do It, 1977; Seaside Postcard, 1978; Just Remember Two Things: it's not fair and don't be late, 1989 (radio play; Giles Cooper Award, 1988); Rough Justice, 1995. *Address:* c/o Lemon Unna & Durbridge Ltd, 24 Pottery Lane, Holland Park, W11 4LZ. *T:* 0171–727 1346. *Club:* Richmond Golf.

FRISCHMANN, Wilem William, CBE 1990; PhD; FEng 1985; FIStructE; FCGI; Chairman: Pell Frischmann Group: Pell Frischmann Consulting Engineers Ltd, since 1985; Pell Frischmann Consultants Ltd, since 1986; Pell Frischmann Milton Keynes Ltd, since 1988; Pell Frischmann Engineering, since 1988; Conseco International, since 1985; Deputy Chairman, Pell Frischmann Water Ltd, since 1990; *s* of Lajos Frischmann and Nelly Frischmann; *m* 1957, Sylvia Elvey; one *s* one *d*. *Educ:* Hungary; Hammersmith College of Art and Building; Imperial Coll. of Science and Technology (DIC); City University (PhD). MASCE, MSISdeFr, MConsE. FIStructE 1964; FCGI 1988. Engineering training with F. J. Samuely and Partners and W. S. Atkins and Partners; joined C. J. Pell and Partners, 1958, Partner, 1961. Dep. Chm., Building & Property Management Services Ltd, 1993–. Structural Engineer for Nat. Westminster Tower (ICE Telford Premium Award), Centre Point, Drapers Gardens tower (IStructE Oscar Faber Prize) and similar high buildings, leisure buildings, hotels and hospitals; Engineer for works at Bank of England, Mansion House and Alexandra Palace; particular interest and involvement in tall economic buildings, shear walls and diaphragm floors, large bored piles in London clay, deep basements, lightweight materials for large span bridges, monitoring and quality assurance procedures for offshore structures; advisory appts include: Hong Kong and Shanghai Bank HQ, Malayan Banking Berhad, Kuala Lumpur. *Publications:* The use and behaviour of large diameter piles in London clay (IStructE paper), 1962; papers to learned socs and instns, originator of concepts: English Channel free-trade port; industrial complex based on Varne and Colbart sandbanks; two-mile high vertical city. *Recreations:* ski-ing, jogging, chess, architecture, design. *Address:* (office) 5 Manchester Square, W1A 1AU. *T:* 0171–486 3661, *Fax:* 0171–487 4153; Haversham Grange, Haversham Close, Twickenham, Middx TW1 2JP. *Club:* Arts.

FRITCHIE, Irene Tordoff, (Rennie); Chair, South and West Regional Health Authority, since 1994; *b* 29 April 1942; *d* of Charles Fredrick Fennell and Eva (*née* Tordoff); *m* 1960, Don Jamie Fritchie; one *s* (and one *s* decd). *Educ:* Ribston Hall Grammar Sch. for Girls. Admin. Officer, Endsleigh Insce Brokers, 1970–73; Sales Trng Officer, Trident Insce Ltd, 1973–76; Head of Trng Confs and Specialist Trng Advr on Women's Devel, Food and Drink ITB, 1976–80; Consultant, Social Ecology Associates, 1980–81; Dir, Transform Ltd, 1981–85; Rennie Fritchie Consultancy, 1985–89; Man. Dir, Working Choices Ltd, 1989–91; Mainstream Develt Consultancy, 1991–; Mem. Bd, Stroud and Swindon Bldg Soc., 1995–. Chair, Gloucester HA, 1988–92. Member: NHS Policy Bd, 1994–; Board, British Quality Foundn, 1994–; Selection Panel, Glos Police Authy, 1994–. Mem., Forum UK, IHSM, 1993. Patron: Headway, 1989–; Healing Arts, 1995–. *Publications:* Working Choices, 1988; The Business of Assertiveness, 1991. *Recreations:* reading, gardening, swimming, theatre, cooking, the 'Archers', breeding Gloucester cows. *Address:* Vine Cottage, The Stream, Ashleworth, Glos GL19 4JH. *T:* Gloucester (01452) 700777.

FRITH, Anthony Ian Donald; Board Member, Bristol Water Holdings plc, since 1989; *b* 11 March 1929; *s* of Ernest and Elizabeth Frith; *m* 1952, Joyce Marcelle Boyce; one *s* one *d*. *Educ:* various grammar schs and techn. colls. CEng, FIGasE, MInstM. Various appts in North Thames Gas Bd and Gas Light & Coke Co., 1945–65; Sales Man. 1965–67, Dep. Commercial Man. 1967–68, North Thames Gas Bd; Marketing Man., Domestic and Commercial Gas, Gas Council, 1968–72; Sales Dir, British Gas Corp., 1972–73; Chm., SW Region, British Gas, 1973–90; Mem. Bd, Bath Dist HA, 1990–94; non-exec. Dir, Wilts and Bath Health Commn, 1992–94. CIMgt (CBIM 1983). *Publications:* various techn. and prof. in Gas Engineering and other jls. *Recreations:* fishing, golf. *Address:* Greenacres, Kingwell Hall, Timsbury, Avon BA3 1HH.

FRITH, David Edward John; Editorial Director, Wisden Cricket Monthly, since 1979; *b* 16 March 1937; *s* of Edward Frith and Patricia Lillian Ethel Frith (*née* Thomas); *m* 1957, Debbie Oriel Christina Pennell; two *s* one *d*. *Educ:* Canterbury High Sch., Sydney. First grade cricket, Sydney, 1960–64. Editor, The Cricketer, 1972–78; Founder and Editor, Wisden Cricket Monthly, 1979. Cricket Soc. Literary Award, 1970 and 1987; Cricket Writer of the Year, Wombwell Cricket Lovers Soc., 1984; Magazine Sports Writer of the Year, Sports Council, 1988. *Publications:* Runs in the Family (with John Edrich), 1969; My Dear Victorious Stod, 1977; (ed) Cricket Gallery, 1976; (with Greg Chappell) The Ashes '77, 1977; The Golden Age of Cricket 1890–1914, 1978; The Ashes '79, 1979; Thommo, 1980; The Fast Men, 1981; The Slow Men, 1984; (with Gerry Wright) Cricket's Golden Summer, 1985; (ed) England *v* Australia Test Match Records 1877–1985, 1986; Archie Jackson, 1987; Pageant of Cricket, 1987; Guildford Jubilee 1938–1988, 1988; England *v* Australia: A Pictorial History of the Test Matches since 1877, 1990; By His Own Hand, 1991; Stoddy's Mission, 1995. *Recreations:* playing cricket, collecting cricketana, watching documentaries, culling Queensland cane toads. *Address:* 6 Beech Lane, Guildford, Surrey GU2 5ES. *T:* Guildford (01483) 32573. *Club:* MCC.

FRITH, Donald Alfred, OBE 1980; MA; Secretary, Headmasters' Conference, and General Secretary, Secondary Heads' Association, 1979–83; *b* 13 May 1918; *yr s* of late Charles Henry Frith and Mabel (*née* Whiting); *m* 1941, Mary Webster Tyler (*d* 1989), *yr d* of late Raymond Tyler and Rosina Mary (*née* Wiles); four *s* one *d*. *Educ:* Whitgift Sch. (schol.); Christ's Coll., Cambridge (schol.). MA Cantab 1944. Served War, 1940–46; commnd RASC; served in Middle East, Italy and at WO. Deme Warden, University College Sch., 1946–52; Headmaster, Richmond Sch., Yorks, 1953–59; Headmaster, Archbishop Holgate's Grammar Sch., York, 1959–78. Asst Dir, Centre for Study of Comprehensive Schs, 1983–88; Chm., N Yorks Forum for Vol. Orgns, 1983–91; Dir, N Yorks TEC, 1990–93. Chm., School Curriculum (formerly Schools Council) Industry Project, 1979–86. Additional Mem., N Yorks CC Educn Cttee, 1973–77. Chm., York Community Council, 1971–79. JP York, 1966–79. *Publication:* (gen. ed.) School Management in Practice, 1985. *Recreations:* music, gardening, reading. *Address:* Kilburn, York YO6 4AQ. *Clubs:* Athenæum; Yorkshire (York).

FRITH, Air Vice-Marshal Edward Leslie, CB 1973; *b* 18 March 1919; *s* of late Charles Edward Frith, ISO. *Educ:* Haberdashers' Askes School. Gp Captain, 1961; Air Cdre, 1968; Dir of Personal Services (2) RAF, MoD, 1969–71; Air Vice-Marshal, 1971; Air Officer Administration, Maintenance Comd, later Support Comd, 1971–74. *Recreations:* lawn tennis, bridge. *Clubs:* All England Lawn Tennis and Croquet, International Lawn Tennis of GB.

FRITH, Ven. Richard Michael Cokayne; Archdeacon of Taunton, since 1992; *b* 8 April 1949; *s* of Roger Cokayne Frith and Joan Agnes Frith; *m* 1975, Jill Richardson; two *s* two *d*. *Educ:* Marlborough Coll., Wiltshire; Fitzwilliam Coll., Cambridge (BA 1972; MA 1976); St John's Coll., Nottingham. Ordained: deacon, 1974, priest 1975; Asst Curate, Mortlake with East Sheen, Southwark, 1974–78; Team Vicar, Thamesmead, Southwark, 1978–83; Team Rector, Keynsham, Bath and Wells, 1983–92. *Recreations:* cricket, squash, theatre. *Address:* 4 Westerkirk Gate, Staplegrove, Taunton, Somerset TA2 6BQ. *T:* Taunton (01823) 323838. *Club:* MCC.

FRITH, Hon. Royce Herbert; High Commissioner for Canada in the United Kingdom, since 1994; *b* 12 Nov. 1923; *s* of George Harry Frith and Annie Beatrice (*née* Royce); *m* 1948, Elizabeth Mary Davison (*d* 1976); one *d* (one *s* decd). *Educ:* Lachine High Sch., Quebec; Parkdale Coll. Inst., Toronto; Victoria Coll., Univ. of Toronto (BA); Osgoode Hall Law Sch. (LLB); Univ. of Ottawa (Dip. d'etudes supérieures). Practiced Law, Toronto and Perth, 1949–89. Mem. (L) Senate, Ontario, 1977–94; Dep. Govt Leader, 1980–84; Dep. Leader of Opposition in Senate, 1984–91, Leader, 1991–93; Leading Front Bench Liberal, 1993–94. Comr, Royal Commn on Bilingualism and Biculturalism, 1963–70; Legal Advr to Comr of Official Langs, 1971–77. Pres., Ontario Liberal Assoc., 1961–62. Former Mem., Law Soc. of Upper Canada. Part-time broadcaster. *Publications:* Hoods on the Hill, 1991; The Show Must Not Go On, 1993. *Recreations:* music, theatre, golf, tennis, squash. *Address:* Canadian High Commission, Macdonald House, 1 Grosvenor Square, W1X 0AB. *T:* 0171–258 6328.

FRITSCH, Elizabeth, CBE 1995; potter; *b* Shropshire, 1940; *d* of Welsh parents; one *s* one *d*. *Educ:* Royal Acad. of Music; Royal Coll. of Art (Silver Medallist, 1970). Established own workshop, E London, 1985. Mem., Crafts Council (Bursary awarded, 1980). *One-woman exhibitions* include: Crafts Council, 1974; CAA, 1976; Leeds City Art Galls, 1978, touring to Glasgow, Bristol, Bolton and Gateshead City Art Galls; V & A, 1980; RCA, 1984; Besson Gall., London, 1989; Royal Mus. of Scotland, 1990; Hetjens Mus., Dusseldorf, 1990; touring to British City Art Galls, 1992; NY Crafts Council, 1993; Crafts Council, 1994; *group exhibitions* include: Oxford Gall., 1974; ICA, 1985; Kunstler Haus, Vienna, 1986; Fischer Fine Art, London, 1987; Kyoto and Tokyo Nat. Museums of Modern Art, 1988; Crafts Council, touring to Amsterdam, 1988; Sotheby's, 1988; 35 Connaught Square, London (Lord Queensberry), 1991; Stuttgart, 1991; Oriel Gall., Cardiff, 1991; *works in public collections:* V & A; Crafts Council; Lotherton Hall, Leeds City Art Galls; Royal Mus. of Scotland; Glasgow, Bolton, Bristol and Birmingham City Art Galls. Judge, Fletcher Challenge Internat. Ceramics Competition, NZ, 1990. Major influences on work: music, fresco painting, topology. Sen. Fellow, RCA, 1995. Herbert Read Meml Prize, 1970; Winner, Royal Copenhagen Jubilee Competition, 1972; Gold Medal, Internat. Ceramics Competition, Sopot, Poland, 1976. *Recreations:* music, mountains, theatre.

FRIZZELL, Edward William; Under Secretary, Scottish Office, since 1991; Chief Executive, Scottish Prison Service, since 1991; *b* 4 May 1946; *s* of late Edward Frizzell and of Mary McA. Russell; *m* 1969, Moira Calderwood; two *s* one *d*. *Educ:* Paisley Grammar School, Glasgow Univ. (MA Hons). Scottish Milk Marketing Board, 1968–73; Scottish Council (Devélt and Industry), 1973–76; Scottish Office, 1976–78; First Sec., Fisheries, FCO UK Rep. Brussels, 1978–82; Scottish Office, 1982–: SED, 1982–86; Finance Div., 1986–89; Industry Dept/SDA (Dir, Locate in Scotland), 1989–91. *Recreations:* running, mountain biking, painting, sculpture. *Address:* Scottish Prison Service HQ, Calton House, 5 Redheughs Rigg, Edinburgh EH12 9HW. *T:* 0131–244 8522. *Club:* Mortonhall Golf.

FRODSHAM, Anthony Freer, CBE 1978; company director and management consultant, now retired; Director-General, Engineering Employers' Federation, 1975–82; *b* Peking, China, 8 Sept. 1919; *er s* of late George William Frodsham and Constance Violet Frodsham (*née* Neild); *m* 1953, Patricia Myfanwy, *o c* of late Cmdr A. H. Wynne-Edwards, DSC, RN; two *s*. *Educ:* Ecole Lacordaire, Paris; Faraday House Engineering Coll., London. DFH, CEng, FIMechE, FIMC, CBIM. Served War, 1940–46: Engineer Officer, RN, Asst Fleet Engr Officer on staff of C-in-C Mediterranean, 1944–46 (despatches, 1945). P-E Consulting Group Ltd, 1947–73: Man. Dir and Gp Chief Exec., 1963–72; Group Specialist Adviser, United Dominions Trust Ltd, 1973–74. Director: TACE Ltd, 1973–76; Arthur Young Management Services, 1973–79; F. Pratt Engrg Corp. Ltd, 1982–85; Greyfriars Ltd, 1984–88 (Dep. Chm., 1986–88). Chairman: Management Consultants Assoc., 1968–70; Machine Tools EDC, 1973–79; Independent Chm., Compressed Air and Allied Machinery Cttee, 1976–; Chairman: European Business Institute Adv. Cttee, 1982–; Council, European Business Sch., 1986–91 (Mem., 1983–91); Vice-Chm., British Export Finance Adv. Council, 1982–87; President: Inst. of Management Consultants, 1967–68; Inst. of Linguists, 1986–89; Member: CBI Grand Council, 1975–82; CBI President's Cttee, 1979–82; Engineering Industry Training Bd, 1975–79; W European Metal Working Employers' Assoc., 1975–82; Manadon Adv. Council, RNEC, 1988–94; Enterprise Counsellor, DTI, 1988–91. A General Commissioner of Tax, 1975–94. Conducted MoD Study into Provision of Engineer Officers for Armed Services, 1983. Hon. FIL 1986. Hon. DBA RNEC, 1991. *Publications:* contrib. to technical jls; lectures and broadcasts on management subjects. *Address:* 36 Fairacres, Roehampton Lane, SW15 5LX. *T:* 0181–878 9551. *Club:* Carlton.

FROGGATT, Sir Leslie (Trevor), Kt 1981; Chairman, Ashton Mining Ltd, 1981–94; *b* 8 April 1920; *s* of Leslie and Mary Helena Froggatt (*née* Brassey); *m* 1945, Jessie Elizabeth Grant; three *s.* *Educ:* Birkenhead Park Sch., Cheshire. Joined Asiatic Petroleum Co. Ltd, 1937; Shell Singapore, Shell Thailand, Shell Malaya, 1947–54; Shell Egypt, 1955–56; Dir of Finance, Gen. Manager, Kalimantan, Borneo, and Dep. Chief Rep., PT Shell Indonesia, 1958–62; Shell International Petroleum Co. Ltd: Area Co-ordinator, S Asia and Australia, 1962–63; assignment in various Shell cos in Europe, 1964–66; Shell Oil Co., Atlanta, 1967–69; Chm. and Chief Exec. Officer, Shell Gp in Australia, 1969–80; non-exec. Dir, Shell Australia Ltd, 1981–87. Chairman: Pacific Dunlop, 1986–90 (Vice-Chm., 1981; Dir, 1978–90); BRL Hardy, 1992–; Director: Australian Industry Develt Corp., 1978–90; Australian Inst. of Petroleum Ltd, 1976–80, 1982–84 (Chm., 1977–79); Moonee Valley Racing Club Nominees Pty Ltd, 1977–92; Tandem Australia, 1989– (Chm., 1992–); Amskan Ltd, 1991–. Member: Australian Nat. Airlines Commn (Australian Airlines), 1981–87 (Vice-Chm., 1984–87); Internat. Bd of Advice, ANZ Banking Gp, 1986–91; Internat. Adv. Council, Tandem Computers Inc., USA, 1988–; Bd, Care Australia, 1989–. *Recreations:* reading, music, racing, golf. *Address:* 20 Albany Road, Toorak, Vic 3142, Australia. *T:* (3) 98221357. *Clubs:* Melbourne, Australian, Victoria Racing, Victoria Amateur Turf, Moonee Valley Racing, Commonwealth Golf (Melbourne).

FROGGATT, Sir Peter, Kt 1985; MD; FRCP, FRCPI; Director: AIB Group plc, since 1984; First Trust Bank (formerly TSB Bank (Northern Ireland)), since 1991; Pro-Chancellor, University of Dublin, since 1985; President and Vice-Chancellor, Queen's University of Belfast, 1976–86; *b* 12 June 1928; *s* of Albert Victor and Edith (*née* Curran); *m* 1958, Norma Cochrane; four *s* (and one *s* decd). *Educ:* Royal Belfast Academical Institution; Royal Sch., Armagh (Schol.); Trinity Coll., Dublin (BA; MB; BCh; BAO 1952; MA 1956; MD 1957; Welland Prize; Cunningham Medal; Begley Schol.); Queen's Univ., Belfast (DPH 1956; PhD 1967; Carnwath Prize). MRCPI 1972; FRCPI 1973; FFPHM (FFCM 1973); MRCP 1974; FFOMI 1975; FFCMI 1976; MRIA 1978; FRCP 1980. House Surgeon and Physician, Sir Patrick Dun's Hosp., Dublin, 1952–53; Nuffield Res. Student, 1955–57; Med. Officer, Short Bros and Harland Ltd, 1957–59; Queen's University, Belfast: Lectr, 1959–65; Reader, 1965–68; Prof. of Epidemiology, 1968–76; Dean, Faculty of Medicine, 1971–76; Consultant, Eastern Health and Social Services Board, 1960–76. Hon. Prof., St Bartholomew's Hosp. Med. Sch., 1986–94. Chairman: Independent Scientific Cttee on Smoking and Health, 1980–91 (Mem., 1977–80); Tobacco Products Res. Trust, 1981–; ASME, 1987–92; Central Ethical Compliance Gp, Unilever, 1991–; Pres., Biol Scis Section, British Assoc., 1987–88; Member: Bd, 1983–85, Adv. Cttee, NI, 1988–94, British Council; Gen. Adv. Cttee, BBC, 1986–88; Supervisory Bd, NHS NI, 1986–92; British Occupational Health Res. Foundn, 1991–. Hon. Member: Soc. for Social Medicine; Soc. of Occupational Medicine. Lectures: Robert Adams, 1977, Kirkpatrick, 1984, Abrahamson, 1986, RCSI; Apothecaries, SOM, 1978; Freyer, NUI, 1984; Bayliss, RCP, 1989; Smiley, FOMI, 1989; Bartholomew Mosse, Rotunda Hosp., 1992. Trustee, Mater Infirmorum Hosp., Belfast, 1994–; Chm., Scots-Irish Trust of Ulster, 1990. Freeman, City of London, 1990. FSS 1963; Hon. FRCSI 1988; Hon. Fellow, Royal Acad. of Medicine in Ireland; CIMgt (CBIM 1986). Hon. LLD: Dublin, 1981; QUB, 1991; Hon. DSc NUI, 1982. Dominic Corrigan Gold Medal, RCPI, 1981. *Publications:* (jtly) Causation of Bus-driver Accidents: Epidemiological Study, 1963; (ed jtly) Nicotine, Smoking and the Low Tar Programme, 1988; articles in jls on human genetics, occupational medicine, med. history, med. educn, epidemiology and smoking policies. *Recreations:* golf, music, travel. *Address:* Rathganley, 3 Strangford Avenue, Belfast BT9 6PG.

FRÖHLICH, Prof. Albrecht, PhD; FRS 1976; Professor of Pure Mathematics, King's College, University of London, 1962–81, now Emeritus Professor; Senior Research Fellow, Imperial College, University of London, since 1982; Emeritus Fellow, Robinson College, Cambridge, (Fellow 1982–84); *b* 22 May 1916; *s* of Julius Fröhlich and Frida Fröhlich; *m* 1950, Dr Evelyn Ruth Brooks; one *s* one *d.* *Educ:* Realgymnasium, Munich; Bristol Univ. (BSc 1948, PhD 1951). Asst Lectr in Maths, University Coll., Leicester, 1950–52; Lectr in Maths, University Coll. of N Staffs, 1952–55; King's College, London: Reader in Pure Maths, 1955–62; Hd, Dept of Maths, 1971–81. Vis. Royal Soc.-Israeli Acad. Research Prof., 1978; George A. Miller Prof., Univ. of Illinois, 1981–82; Gauss Prof., Göttingen Acad. of Scis, 1983; vis. prof. at other univs in USA, Canada, Germany, France, Switzerland, China and India. Corres. Mem., Heidelberg Acad. of Scis, 1982. FKC 1977. Hon. DSc Bordeaux, 1986. Senior Berwick Prize, 1976, de-Morgan Medal, 1992, London Math. Soc.; Res. Prize, Alexander von Humboldt Foundn, 1992. *Publications:* Formal Groups, 1968; Module Structure of Algebraic Integers, 1983; Class Groups and Hermitian Modules, 1984; (with M. J. Taylor) Algebraic Number Theory, 1991; papers in math. jls. *Recreations:* cooking, eating, walking, music. *Address:* Robinson College, Cambridge CB3 9AN.

FROOD, Alan Campbell, CBE 1988; Managing Director, Crown Agents for Oversea Governments and Administrations, 1978–88; Crown Agent, 1980–88; *b* 15 May 1926; *s* of James Campbell Frood, MC and Margaret Helena Frood; *m* 1960, Patricia Ann Cotterell; two *s* two *d.* *Educ:* Cranleigh Sch.; Peterhouse, Cambridge. Royal Navy, 1944–47 (Sub-Lt RNVR). Bank of England, 1949; Colonial Admin. Service, 1952; Bankers Trust Co., 1962; Dir, Bankers Trust Internat. Ltd, 1967; Gen. Man., Banking Dept, Crown Agents, 1975; Dir of Financial Services, Crown Agents, 1976–78. Trustee, Queen's Nursing Inst., 1986– (Hon. Treas., 1973–94). *Recreations:* sailing, gardening. *Address:* The Dairy, Bystock, Exmouth, Devon EX8 5EQ. *T:* Exmouth (01395) 267744.

FROSSARD, Sir Charles (Keith), KBE 1992; Kt 1983; Bailiff of Guernsey, 1982–92; Judge of the Court of Appeal, Jersey, 1983–92; a Judge of the Courts of Appeal of Jersey and Guernsey, 1992–95; *b* 18 Feb. 1922; *s* of late Edward Louis Frossard, CBE, MA, Hon. CF, Dean of Guernsey, 1947–67, and Margery Smith Latta; *m* 1950, Elizabeth Marguerite, *d* of late J. E. L. Martel, OBE; two *d.* *Educ:* Elizabeth Coll., Guernsey; Univ. de Caen (Bachelier en Droit; D*hc* 1990). Enlisted Gordon Highlanders, 1940; commnd 1941, 17 Dogra Regt, Indian Army; seconded to Tochi Scouts and Chitral Scouts; served India and NW Frontier, 1941–46. Called to Bar, Gray's Inn, 1949; Advocate of Royal Court of Guernsey, 1949; People's Deputy, States of Guernsey, 1958–67; Conseiller, States of Guernsey, 1967–69; HM Solicitor General, Guernsey, 1969–73; HM Attorney General, Guernsey, 1973–76; Dep. Bailiff of Guernsey, 1977–82. Member, Church Assembly and General Synod, Church of England, 1960–82. Pres., Indian Army Assoc., 1993–. ACIArb 1987. KStJ 1985. Médaille de Vermeil, Paris, 1984. *Recreations:* hill walking, fishing. *Address:* Les Lierres, Rohais, St Peter Port, Guernsey. *T:* Guernsey (01481) 722076. *Clubs:* Army and Navy, Naval and Military; United (Guernsey).

FROST, Abraham Edward Hardy, CBE 1972; Counsellor, Foreign and Commonwealth Office, 1972–78; *b* 4 July 1918; *s* of Abraham William Frost and Margaret Anna Frost; *m* 1972, Gillian (*née* Crossley); two *d.* *Educ:* Royal Grammar Sch., Colchester King's Coll., Cambridge (MA); London Univ. (BScEcon). FCIS. RNVR, 1940–46 (Lieut). ILO, Geneva, 1947–48; HM Treasury, 1948–49; Manchester Guardian, City Staff, 1949–51; FO (later FCO), 1951–78. *Publication:* In Dorset Of Course (poems), 1976. *Address:* Hill View, Buckland Newton, Dorset DT2 7BS. *T:* Buckland Newton (01300) 345415.

FROST, Albert Edward, CBE 1983; Director, Marks & Spencer Ltd, 1976–87; Chairman: Remploy, 1983–87; Trustees, Remploy Pension Fund, since 1990; *b* 7 March 1914; *s* of Charles Albert Frost and Minnie Frost; *m* 1942, Eugénie Maud Barlow. *Educ:* Oulton Sch., Liverpool; London Univ. Called to the Bar, Middle Temple (1st Cl. Hons). HM Inspector of Taxes, Inland Revenue, 1937; Imperial Chemical Industries Ltd: Dep. Head, Taxation Dept, 1949; Dep. Treasurer, 1957; Treasurer, 1960; Finance Dir, 1968; retd 1976. Director: British Airways Corp., 1976–80; BL Ltd, 1977–80; S. G. Warburg & Co., 1976–83; British Steel, 1980–83 (Chm., Audit and Salaries Cttees); Guinness Peat Gp, 1983–84; Chairman: Guinness Mahon Hldgs Ltd, 1983–84; Guinness Mahon & Co., 1983–84; Billingsgate City Securities, 1989–90. Mem. Council, St Thomas's Med. Sch., London, 1974– (Chm., Finance Cttee, 1978–85); Governor, United Med. Schs of Guy's and St Thomas's Hosps, 1982– (Dep. Chm. of Govs, 1989–; Chm., Finance and Investment Cttees, 1982–85; Hon. Fellow, 1994). Member: Council and Finance Cttee, Morley Coll., London, 1975–85; Exec. Cttee for Develt Appeal, Royal Opera House, Covent Garden, 1975–87; Arts Council of GB, 1982–84; Vice Pres., ABSA, 1992– (Mem. Council, 1976–93; Jt Dep. Chm., 1985–92); Chairman: Robert Mayer Trust for Youth and Music, 1981–90 (Dir, 1977–90); Jury, and of Org. Cttee, City of London Carl Flesch Internat. Violin Competition. Trustee and Treas., Loan Fund for Mus. Instruments; Dir, City Arts Trust, 1982–93. FRSA. *Publications:* (contrib.) Simon's Income Tax, 1952; (contrib.) Gunns Australian Income Tax Law and Practice, 1960; articles on financial matters affecting industry and on arts sponsorship. *Recreations:* violinist (chamber music); swimming (silver medallist, Royal Life Saving Assoc.); athletics (county colours, track and cross country); walking; arts generally. *Club:* Royal Automobile.

FROST, Sir David (Paradine), Kt 1993; OBE 1970; author, producer, columnist; star of 'The Frost Report', 'The Frost Programme', 'Frost on Friday', 'The David Frost Show', 'The Frost Interview', etc; Joint Founder, London Weekend Television; Chairman and Chief Executive, David Paradine Ltd, since 1966; *b* 7 April 1939; *s* of late Rev. W. J. Paradine Frost, Tenterden, Kent; *m* 1983, Lady Carina Fitzalan-Howard, 2nd *d* of Duke of Norfolk, *qv*; three *s.* *Educ:* Gillingham Grammar Sch.; Wellingborough Grammar Sch.; Gonville and Caius Coll., Cambridge (MA). Sec., The Footlights; Editor, Granta. LLD, Emerson Coll., USA. Jt Founder and Dir, TV-am, 1981–93. BBC Television series: That Was the Week That Was, 1962–63 (in USA, 1964–65); A Degree of Frost, 1963, 1973; Not So Much a Programme, More a Way of Life, 1964–65; The Frost Report, 1966–67; Frost Over England, 1967; Frost Over America, 1970; Frost's Weekly, 1973; The Frost Interview, 1974; We British, 1975–76; Forty Years of Television, 1976; The Frost Programme, 1977; The Guinness Book of Records Hall of Fame, 1986, 1987, 1988; Breakfast with Frost, 1993–; BBC Radio series, Pull the Other One, 1987, 1988, 1990. David Frost at the Phonograph (BBC Sound), 1966, 1972; Frost on Thursday (LBC), 1974. ITV series and programmes: The Frost Programme, 1966–67, 1967–68; Frost on Friday, 1968–69, 1969–70; The Frost Programme, 1972, 1973; The Sir Harold Wilson Interviews, 1976; A Prime Minister on Prime Ministers, 1977–78; Are We Really Going to be Rich?, 1978; David Frost's Global Village, 1979, 1980, 1982; The 25th Anniversary of ITV, The Begin Interview, and Elvis—He Touched Their Lives, 1980; The BAFTA Awards, and Onward Christian Soldiers, 1981; A Night of Knights: a Royal Gala, 1982; The End of the Year Show, 1982, 1983; Frost on Sunday (TV-am), 1983–92; David Frost Presents Ultra Quiz, 1984; Twenty Years On, 1985, 1986; Through the Keyhole, 1987–; The Frost Programme, 1993–. Other programmes include: David Frost's Night Out in London (USA), 1966–67; The Next President (USA), 1968; Robert Kennedy the Man (USA), 1968; The David Frost Show (USA), 1969–70, 1970–71, 1971–72; The David Frost Revue (USA), 1971–72, 1972–73; That Was the Year That Was (USA), 1973, 1985; David Frost Presents the Guinness Book of Records (USA), 1973–76; Frost over Australia, 1972, 1973, 1974, 1977; Frost over New Zealand, 1973, 1974; The Unspeakable Crime (USA), 1975; Abortion—Merciful or Murder? (USA), 1975; The Beatles—Once Upon a Time (USA), 1975; David Frost Presents the Best (USA), 1975; The Nixon Interviews with David Frost, 1976–77; The Crossroads of Civilization, 1977–78; Headliners with David Frost, 1978; A Gift of Song—MUSIC FOR UNICEF Concert, The Bee Gees Special, and The Kissinger Interview, 1979; The Shah Speaks, and The American Movie Awards, 1980; Show Business, This Is Your Life 30th Anniversary Special, The Royal Wedding (CBS), 1981; David Frost Presents The Internat. Guinness Book of World Records, annually 1981–86; The American Movie Awards, Rubinstein at 95, and Pierre Elliott Trudeau, 1982; Frost over Canada, 1982, 1983; David Frost Live by Satellite from London, 1983; The Search for Josef Mengele, 1985; Spitting Image: Down and Out in the White House, 1986; The Spitting Image Movie Awards, 1987; The Spectacular World of Guinness Records, 1987–88; Entertainment Tonight, 1987, 1988; The Next President with David Frost, 1987–88; ABC Presents a Royal Gala, 1988; The President and Mrs Bush Talking with David Frost, 1989; Talking with David Frost (USA), 1991–. Produced films: The Rise and Rise of Michael Rimmer, 1970; Charley One-Eye, 1972; Leadbelly, 1974; The Slipper and the Rose, 1975; James A. Michener's Dynasty, 1975; The Ordeal of Patty Hearst, 1978; The Remarkable Mrs Sanger, 1979. Mem., British/USA Bicentennial Liaison Cttee, 1973–76; Pres., Lord's Taverners, 1985, 1986. Companion, TRIC, 1992. Hon. Prof., Thames Valley Univ., 1994. Golden Rose, Montreux, for Frost Over England, 1967; Royal Television Society's Silver Medal, 1967; Richard Dimbleby Award, 1967; Emmy Award (USA), 1970, 1971; Religious Heritage of America Award, 1970; Albert Einstein Award, Communication Arts, 1971. *Stage:* An Evening with David Frost (Edinburgh Fest.), 1966. *Publications:* That Was the Week That Was, 1963; How to Live under Labour, 1964; Talking with Frost, 1967; To England With Love, 1967; The Presidential Debate 1968, 1968; The Americans, 1970; Whitlam and Frost, 1974; I Gave Them a Sword, 1978; I Could Have Kicked Myself, (David Frost's Book of the World's Worst Decisions), 1982; Who Wants to be a Millionaire?, 1983; (jtly) The Mid-Atlantic Companion, 1986; (jtly) The Rich Tide, 1986; The World's Shortest Books, 1987; David Frost: an autobiography: part one: From Congregations to Audiences, 1993. *Address:* David Paradine Ltd, 5 St Mary Abbots Place, W8 6LS.

FROST, Ven. George; Archdeacon of Salop, since 1987; Vicar of Tong, since 1987; *b* 4 April 1935; *s* of William John Emson Frost and Emily Daisy Frost; *m* 1959, Joyce Pratt; four *s.* *Educ:* Hatfield Coll., Durham Univ. (BA 1956, MA 1961); Lincoln Theological Coll. Schoolmaster, Westcliff High School, 1956–57; labourer, Richard Thomas and Baldwin Steelworks, Scunthorpe, 1958–59; Asst Curate, St Margaret, Barking Parish Church, 1960–64; Minister, Ecclesiastical District of St Mark, Marks Gate, 1964–70; Vicar: St Matthew, Tipton, 1970–77; St Bartholomew, Penn, Wolverhampton, 1977–87; RD of Trysull, 1984–87; Prebendary of Lichfield Cathedral, 1985–87, Hon. Canon 1987–. *Recreations:* walking, wild flowers, photography. *Address:* Tong Vicarage, Shifnal TF11 8PW. *T:* Albrighton (01902) 372622.

FROST, Gerald Philip Anthony; Director, Centre for Policy Studies, 1992–95; *b* 8 Nov. 1943; *s* of Sidney and Flora Frost; *m* 1970, Margaret Miriam Freedman; two *s.* *Educ:* Univ. of Sussex (BA Hons; mature student). Junior reporter, Ilford and East London newspapers, 1960–64; reporter: Recorder Newspapers, Ilford, 1964–65; Yorkshire Post, 1965–67;

Chief reporter, Morning Telegraph, 1967–68; Sub-editor: Daily Express, Manchester, 1968–69; Press Assoc., 1969–71; research staff, Centre for Policy Studies, 1974–80 (Sec. and Mem Bd, 1977–80); Chief Leader Writer, Evening Standard, 1979–80; Dir, consultant Dir, 1992–, Inst. for European Defence and Strategic Studies, 1980–92. *Publications:* Protest and Perish: a critique of unilateralism (with P. Towle and I. Eliott), 1983; (ed and contrib.) Europe in Turmoil, 1991; (ed and contrib.) In search of Stability, 1992; (ed and contrib.) Hubris: the tempting of modern conservatives, 1992; contribs to British and US newspapers and jls. *Recreations:* family pursuits, reading, wine. *Club:* Reform.

FROST, Jeffrey Michael Torbet; Executive Director, London & Continental Bankers, 1983–89 (Associate Director, 1982–83); *b* 11 June 1938; *s* of late Basil Frost and Dorothy Frost. *Educ:* Diocesan Coll., Cape, South Africa; Radley Coll.; Oriel Coll., Oxford; Harvard Univ. Exec. Dir, Cttee on Invisible Exports, 1976–81. Hon. Sec., Anglo-Brazilian Soc., 1977–84. Liveryman, Worshipful Co. of Clockmakers. FRSA. *Recreations:* bridge, ballet, walking. *Address:* 34 Paradise Walk, SW3 4JL. *T:* 0171–352 8642; The Parish Room, Kintbury, near Hungerford, Berks RG17 9UP. *Club:* White's.

FROST, Michael Edward, LVO 1983; HM Diplomatic Service; Deputy Consul General and Director (Investment), British Trade and Investment Office, New York, since 1991; *b* 5 July 1941; *s* of Edward Lee Frost and Ivy Beatrice (*née* Langmead); *m* 1964, Carole Ann Beigel; three *s*. *Educ:* Torquay Grammar Sch. FCO, 1959–62; Algiers, 1962–67; Commercial Officer, Kuala Lumpur, 1967–71; 3rd Sec., later 2nd Sec. Commercial, Bucharest, 1972–75; FCO, 1975–78; Consul (Commercial), Seattle, 1978–83; FCO, 1983–84; on secondment to ICI, 1984–87; Dep. Head of Mission, Sofia, 1987–90. *Recreations:* watercolours, golf, travel. *Address:* c/o Foreign and Commonwealth Office, King Charles Street, SW1A 2AH.

FROST, Dame Phyllis Irene, AC 1992; DBE 1974 (CBE 1963); Chairman, Victorian Relief Committee, since 1979 (Member since 1964); *b* 14 Sept. 1917; *née* Turner; *m* 1941, Glenn Neville Frost (*d* 1987), LDS, BDSc, JP; three *d*. *Educ:* Croydon Coll., Vic.; St Duthus Coll.; Presbyterian Ladies' Coll.; Univ. of Melbourne. Dip. of Physiotherapy, 1939; studied Criminology, 1955–56. Chairman: Victorian (formerly Fairlea) Women's Prison Council, 1954–; Aust. Contact Emergency Service, 1984–; Vice-Chairman: Victorian Assoc. for Care and Resettlement of Offenders, 1977–; Clean World Internat., 1980–92; Mem., State Disaster Welfare Cttees, Vic, 1983–. Hon. Life Member: Aust. Crime Prevention Council, 1972; Aust. Freedom from Hunger Campaign, 1977; Nat. Council of Women of Victoria, 1979; Keep Australia Beautiful Nat. Council (former Chm.); Trustee, patron, hon. life mem., hon. convener, and life governor of many community service, health and welfare orgns. Has attended several internat. confs as Aust. delegate or representative, including: Internat. Council of Women; FAO; FFHC (Chm., 4th Session in Rome, 1969; Chm., 3rd Regional Congress for Asia and the Far East, at Canberra, 1970, and Rome, 1971). Fellow, Melvin Jones Internat. Foundn, 1991. Chm., Bd of Dirs, Brain Behaviour Res. Inst., La Trobe Univ., 1984–91. JP, Vic, 1957–84. Freedom, City of Croydon, 1989. DSocSc *hc*, Univ. of Technol., Melb., 1993. Woman of the Year, Sun News Pictorial, 1970; Humanitarian Award, Rosicrucian Order, USA, 1971; Community Service Award, Victorian Employers' Fedn, 1978; Distinguished Service to Children Award, Aust. Parents without Partners, Vic, 1984; Community Service Award, Seventh Day Adventists, 1985. *Address:* Llanberis, 4 Jackson Street, Croydon, Victoria 3136, Australia. *T:* (3) 97232382. *Club:* Royal Automobile (Vic.).

FROST, Ronald Edwin; Executive Chairman, Hays plc, since 1989; *b* 19 March 1936; *s* of Charles Henry Frost and Doris (*née* Foggin); *m* 1959, Beryl Ward; one *s* two *d*. Founded Farmhouse Securities, 1965, Chm., 1979–81; Farmhouse Securities purchased by Hays Gp, 1981: Chief Exec., Distribn Div., 1981–83; Chief Exec. and Man. Dir, 1983–89. MInstD 1975; CIMgt (CBIM 1989). Liveryman, Co. of Watermen & Lightermen, 1983–. *Recreations:* farming, game shooting, sailing. *Address:* Thorncombe Park, Thorncombe Street, Bramley, Guildford, Surrey GU5 0ND. *T:* Guildford (01483) 893338. *Clubs:* Carlton, Royal Thames Yacht.

FROST, Hon. Sir Sydney; *see* Frost, Hon. Sir T. S.

FROST, Terence, (Terry Frost), RA 1992; artist; Professor of Painting, University of Reading, 1977–81 (formerly Reader in Fine Art), Professor Emeritus 1981; *b* Oct. 1915; *m* 1945; five *s* one *d*. *Educ:* Leamington Spa Central Sch. Exhibitions: Leicester Galls, 1952–58; Waddington Galls, 1958–; B. Schaeffer Gallery, New York, 1960–62; Plymouth 1976; Bristol 1976; Serpentine Gall., 1977; Paris, 1978; Norway, 1979; Austin/Desmond Fine Art, 1989; Adelson Gall., New York, 1992–94; Mayor Gall., London, 1994; McGeary Gall., Brussels, 1995; Green on Red Gall., Dublin, 1995. Oil paintings acquired by Tate Gallery, National Gallery of Canada, National Gallery of NSW; also drawing acquired by Victoria and Albert Museum. Other work in public collections; Canada, USA, Germany, Australia, and in Edinburgh, Dublin, Leeds, Hull, Manchester, Birmingham, Liverpool, Bristol, etc. Gregory Fellow in Painting, Univ. of Leeds, 1954–56. Hon. LLD CNAA, 1978. *Publications:* (illus.) 11 Poems by Federico Garcia Lorca, 1989; (jtly) Terry Frost, 1994. *Address:* Gernick Field Studio, Tredavoe Lane, Newlyn, Penzance TR18 5DL. *T:* Penzance (01736) 65902.

FROST, Thomas Pearson, FCIB; Chairman: ICCH Ltd, since 1993; London Clearing House Ltd; *b* 1 July 1933; *s* of James Watterson Frost and Enid Ella Crawte (*née* Pearson); *m* 1958, Elizabeth (*née* Morton); one *s* two *d*. *Educ:* Ormskirk Grammar Sch. FCIB (FIB 1976). Joined Westminster Bank, 1950; Chief Exec. Officer and Vice Chm., NBNA (now National Westminster Bank USA), 1980; National Westminster Bank: Gen. Man., Business Develt Div., 1982; Dir, 1984–93; Dep. Gp Chief Exec., 1985–87; Gp Chief Exec., 1987–92; Dep. Chm., 1992–93. Non-executive Director: Five Oaks Investments PLC, 1993–; Fenchurch PLC, 1993–. Member: BOTB, 1986–93; UK Adv. Bd, British-American Chamber of Commerce, 1987–93; Business in the Cities, 1988–91; Policy Adv. Cttee, Tidy Britain Gp, 1988–92; Adv. Bd, World Economic Forum, 1990–93; Chairman: CBI Business & Urban Regeneration Task Force, 1987–88; Exec. Cttee, British Bankers' Assoc., 1991–92. Trustee, British Sports Trust, 1988–92; Gov., Royal Ballet Sch., 1988–. Fellow, World Scout Foundn, 1984. Freeman, City of London, 1978. CIMgt (FCIM 1987); CompOR 1987; Companion, BITC, 1993; FRSA 1993. OStJ 1991. *Recreations:* golf, orchids, theatre. *Address:* London Clearing House Ltd, Roman Wall House, 1–2 Crutched Friars, EC3N 2AN. *Clubs:* Carlton; Harpenden Golf.

FROST, Hon. Sir (Thomas) Sydney, Kt 1975; Chief Justice of Papua New Guinea, 1975–78, retired; *b* 13 Feb. 1916; *s* of late Thomas Frost, Redfern, NSW; *m* 1943, Dorothy Gertrude (*née* Kelly) (*d* 1990); two *s* one *d*. *Educ:* Univ. of Melbourne (Alexander Rushall Meml Scholarship; LLM). Served 2nd AIF, 1941–45. Barrister, Victoria, 1945–64; QC 1961; Judge of the County Court of Victoria, 1964; Judge of Supreme Court of Papua New Guinea, 1964–75. Chairman: Aust. Govt Inquiry into Whales and Whaling, 1978; Royal Commn of Inquiry into Housing Commn Land Purchases and Valuation Matters, Vic., 1979–81; Bd of Accident Inquiry into causes of crash of Beechcraft Super King Air, Sydney, 21 Feb. 1980, 1982. Pres., Medical Services Review Tribunal, 1979–84.

FROY, Prof. Martin; Professor of Fine Art, University of Reading, 1972–91, now Emeritus; *b* 9 Feb. 1926; *s* of late William Alan Froy and Helen Elizabeth Spencer. *Educ:* St Paul's Sch.; Magdalene Coll., Cambridge (one year); Slade Sch. of Fine Art. Dipl. in Fine Art (London). Visiting Teacher of Engraving, Slade Sch. of Fine Art, 1952–55; taught at Bath Acad. of Art, latterly as Head of Fine Art, 1954–65; Head of Painting Sch., Chelsea Sch. of Art, 1965–72. Gregory Fellow in Painting, Univ. of Leeds, 1951–54; Leverhulme Research Award, six months study in Italy, 1963; Sabbatical Award, Arts Council, 1965. Mem., Fine Art Panel, 1962–71, Mem. Council, 1969–71, Nat. Council for Diplomas in Art and Design; Trustee: National Gall., 1972–79; Tate Gall., 1975–79. Fellow, UCL, 1978. *One-Artist Exhibitions:* Hanover Gall., London, 1952; Wakefield City Art Gall., 1953; Belgrade Theatre, Coventry, 1958; Leicester Galls, London, 1961; Royal West of England Acad., Bristol, 1964; Univ. of Sussex, 1968; Hanover Gall., London, 1969; Park Square Gall., Leeds, 1970; Arnolfini Gall., Bristol, 1970; City Art Gall., Bristol (seven paintings), 1972; Univ. of Reading, 1979; New Ashgate Gall., Surrey, 1979; Serpentine Gall., 1983. *Other Exhibitions:* Internat. Abstract Artists, Riverside Mus., NY, 1950; ICA, London, 1950; Ten English Painters, Brit. Council touring exhibn in Scandinavia, 1952; Drawings from Twelve Countries, Art Inst. of Chicago, 1952; Figures in their Setting, Contemp. Art Soc. Exhibn, Tate Gall., 1953; Beaux Arts Gall., London, 1953; British Painting and Sculpture, Whitechapel Art Gall., London, 1954; Le Congrès pour la Liberté de la Culture Exhibn, Rome, Paris, Brussels, 1955; Pittsburgh Internat., 1955; Six Young Painters, Arts Council touring Exhibn, 1956; ICA Gregory Meml Exhibn, Bradford City Art Gall., Leeds, 1958; City Art Gall., Bristol, 1960; Malerei der Gegenwart ans Sudwestengland, Kunstverein, Hanover, 1962; Corsham Painters and Sculptors, Arts Council Touring Exhibn, 1965; Three Painters, Bath Fest. Exhibn, 1970; Park Square Gall., Leeds, 1978; Ruskin Sch., Univ. of Oxford, 1978; Newcastle Connection, Newcastle, 1980; Homage to Herbert Read, Canterbury, 1984. *Commissions, etc:* Artist Consultant for Arts Council to City Architect, Coventry, 1953–58; mosaic decoration, Belgrade Th., Coventry, 1957–58; two mural panels, Concert Hall, Morley Coll., London, 1958–59. *Works in Public Collections:* Tate Gall.; Mus. of Mod. Art, NY; Chicago Art Inst.; Arts Council; Contemp. Art Soc.; Royal W of England Acad.; Leeds Univ.; City Art Galls of Bristol, Carlisle, Leeds, Southampton and Wakefield; Reading Mus. and Art Gall. *Address:* Department of Fine Art, University of Reading, Earley Gate, Reading, Berks RG6 2AT.

FRY, Christopher; dramatist; *b* 18 Dec. 1907; *s* of Charles John Harris and Emma Marguerite Hammond, *d* of Emma Louisa Fry; *m* 1936, Phyllis Marjorie Hart (*d* 1987); one *s*. *Educ:* Bedford Modern Sch. Actor at Citizen House, Bath, 1927; Schoolmaster at Hazlewood Preparatory Sch., Limpsfield, Surrey, 1928–31; Dir of Tunbridge Wells Repertory Players, 1932–35; life too complicated for tabulation, 1935–39; The Tower, a pageant-play produced at Tewkesbury Fest., 1939; Dir of Oxford Repertory Players, 1940 and 1944–46, directing at Arts Theatre, London, 1945; Staff dramatist, Arts, 1947. FRSL. Hon. Fellow, Manchester Metrop. Univ. (formerly Manchester Poly.), 1988. DLitt Lambeth, 1988; Hon. DLitt: Sussex, 1994; De Montfort, 1994. Queen's Gold Medal (for Poetry), 1962. *Plays:* A Phoenix Too Frequent, Mercury, 1946, St George's Theatre, 1983; The Lady's Not for Burning, Arts, 1948, Globe, 1949, Chichester, 1972; The Firstborn, Edinburgh Festival, 1948; Thor, with Angels, Canterbury Festival, 1949; Venus Observed, St James's, 1950, Chichester, 1992; The Boy with a Cart, Lyric, Hammersmith, 1950; Ring Round the Moon (translated from French of Jean Anouilh), Globe, 1950; A Sleep of Prisoners, produced St Thomas' Church, Regent Street, W1, 1951; The Dark is Light Enough, Aldwych, 1954; The Lark (trans. from French of Jean Anouilh), Lyric, Hammersmith, 1955; Tiger at the Gates (trans. from French of Jean Giraudoux), Apollo, 1955; Duel of Angels (trans. from Pour Lucrèce, of Jean Giraudoux), Apollo, 1958; Curtmantle, Edinburgh Festival, 1962; Judith (trans. from Giraudoux), Her Majesty's, 1962; A Yard of Sun, National, 1970; Peer Gynt (trans.), Chichester, 1970; Cyrano de Bergerac (trans.), Chichester, 1975; One Thing More, or Caedmon Construed, Chelmsford Cathedral, 1986. *TV:* The Brontës of Haworth, four plays, 1973 (also performed on stage, 1985); Sister Dora, 1977; The Best of Enemies, 1977. *Film Commentary* for The Queen is Crowned (Coronation film, 1953); *Film scripts:* (participation) Ben Hur; Barabbas; The Bible; The Beggar's Opera. *Publications:* The Boy with a Cart, 1939; The Firstborn, 1946; A Phoenix Too Frequent, 1946; The Lady's Not for Burning, 1949; Thor, with Angels, 1949; Venus Observed, 1950, rev. edn 1992; (trans.) Ring Round the Moon, 1950; A Sleep of Prisoners, 1951; The Dark is Light Enough, 1954; (trans.) The Lark, 1955; (trans.) Tiger at The Gates, 1955; (trans.) Duel of Angels, 1958; Curtmantle, 1961 (Heinemann Award of RSL); (trans.) Judith, 1962; A Yard of Sun, 1970; (trans.) Peer Gynt, 1970 (this trans. included in The Oxford Ibsen, vol. III, Brand and Peer Gynt, 1972); Four television plays: The Brontës at Haworth, 1954; (trans.) Cyrano de Bergerac, 1975; Can You Find Me: a family history, 1978; (ed and introd) Charlie Hammond's Sketch Book, 1980; Selected Plays, 1985; Genius, Talent and Failure, 1986 (Adam Lecture); One Thing More, or Caedmon Construed, 1987; Looking for a Language (lecture), 1992. *Address:* The Toft, East Dean, Chichester, West Sussex PO18 0JA. *Club:* Garrick.

FRY, Dr Ian Kelsey, DM, FRCP, FRCR; Dean, Medical College of St Bartholomew's Hospital, 1981–89; Consultant Radiologist, St Bartholomew's Hospital, 1966–87; *b* 25 Oct. 1923; *s* of Sir William and Lady Kelsey Fry; *m* 1951, Mary Josephine Casey; three *s* (one *d* decd). *Educ:* Radley Coll.; New Coll., Oxford; Guy's Hosp. Medical Sch. BM BCh 1948, DM Oxon 1961; MRCP 1956, FRCP 1972; DMRD 1961; FFR 1963; FRCR 1975. RAF Medical Services, 1949–50 (Sqdn Ldr). Director, Dept of Radiology, BUPA Medical Centre, 1973–86; Dir of Radiology, London Independent Hosp., 1986–94; Mem. Council, Royal College of Radiologists, 1979–82; Pres. and Chm. Bd, Med. Defence Union, 1993– (Mem. Bd, 1991–93); President, British Institute of Radiology, 1982–83. Gov., Charterhouse Sch., 1984–94. *Publications:* chapters and articles in books and jls. *Recreations:* golf, walking, racing. *Address:* The Pines, Woodlands Road, Bickley, Bromley, Kent BR1 2AE. *T:* 0181–467 4150.

FRY, Jonathan Michael; Chief Executive, Burmah Castrol plc, since 1993; *b* 9 Aug. 1937; *s* of late Stephen Fry and of Gladys Yvonne (*née* Blunt); *m* 1970, Caroline Mary Dunkerly; four *d*. *Educ:* Repton Sch.; Trinity Coll., Oxford (Lit. Hum., MA). Engagement Manager and Consultant, McKinsey & Co., 1966–73; Unigate Foods Division: Man. Dir, 1973–76; Chm., 1976–78; Gp Planning Dir, Burmah Oil Trading Ltd, 1978–81; Chief Executive: Burmah Speciality Chemicals Ltd, 1981–87; Castrol Internat., 1987–93; Man. Dir, Burmah Castrol, 1990–93. Non-Exec. Dir, Northern Foods plc, 1991–. *Recreations:* cricket, skiing, archaeology. *Address:* Burmah Castrol House, Pipers Way, Swindon, Wilts SN3 1RE. *T:* Swindon (01793) 511521; Beechingstoke Manor, Pewsey, Wilts SN9 6HQ. *Clubs:* MCC; Vincent's (Oxford).

FRY, Dame Margaret (Louise), DBE 1989 (OBE 1982); Chairman, National Union of Conservative and Unionist Associations, 1990–91 (a Vice-Chairman, 1987–90); *b* 10 March 1931; *d* of Richard Reed Dawe and Ruth Dora Dawe; *m* 1955, Walter William John Fry; three *s*. *Educ:* Tavistock Grammar School. Conservative Women's Advisory Committee (Western Area): Vice-Chm., 1975–78; Chm., 1978–81; Conservative Women's National Committee: Vice-Chm., 1981–82; Chm., 1984–87; Chm., W Devon Cons. Assoc., 1982–85; Pres., Torridge and W Devon Cons. Assoc., 1992– (Pres.,

Women's Cttee, 1988–93). Member: Transport Users' Consultative Cttee; SW RHA. *Recreations:* farming, conservation, church, sport (former member, Devon County Hockey XI). *Address:* Thorne Farm, Launceston, Cornwall PL15 9SN. *T:* Launceston (01566) 784308.

FRY, Sir Peter (Derek), Kt 1994; MP (C) Wellingborough since Dec. 1969; *b* 26 May 1931; *s* of Harry Walter Fry and late Edith Fry; *m*; one *s* one *d*; *m* 1982, Helen Claire Mitchell. *Educ:* Royal Grammar School, High Wycombe; Worcester College, Oxford (MA). Tillotsons (Liverpool) Ltd, 1954–56; Northern Assurance Co., 1956–61; Political Education Officer, Conservative Central Office, 1961–63. Member Bucks County Council, 1961–67. Parliamentary Consultant to: Bingo Assoc. of GB; Parly Monitoring Services Ltd; Westminster Advisers Ltd. Contested (C) North Nottingham, 1964, East Willesden, 1966. Mem., Select Cttee on Transport, 1979–92; Joint Chairman: All-Party Roads Study Gp, 1974–; Parly Road Passenger Gp, 1992–; All-Party Aviation Gp, 1992–; Parly Transport Forum, 1992–; Vice. Chm., Cons. Aviation Cttee, 1994–; Chairman: All-Party Footwear and Leather Gp, 1979–87; Anglo-Bahamas Parly Gp, 1980–; British Slovenia Gp, 1993–; British Macedonia Gp, 1993–; formerly Chm., British Yugoslav Parly Gp; Vice-Chairman: British Bosnia Gp, 1993–95; British Croatia Gp, 1993–95; Vice Pres., British Southern Slav Soc. Mem., Delegn to Council of Europe/WEU. Played Rugby for Bucks County, 1956–58, Hon. Secretary, 1958–61. *Recreations:* watching Rugby football; reading history and biographies. *Address:* House of Commons, SW1A 0AA. *Club:* Royal Automobile.

FRY, Peter George Robin Plantagenet S.; *see* Somerset Fry.

FRY, Richard Henry, CBE 1965; Financial Editor of The Guardian, 1939–65; *b* 23 Sept. 1900; *m* 1929, Katherine (*née* Maritz); no *c. Educ:* Berlin and Heidelberg Univs. *Publications:* Zero Hour, 1936; A Banker's World: the revival of the City, 1957–70, 1970; Bankers in West Africa, 1976. *Address:* 8 Montagu Mews West, W1H 1TF. *T:* 0171–262 0817. *Club:* Reform.

FRY, Ronald Ernest, FSS; Director of Economics and Statistics, Departments of the Environment and Transport, 1975–80, retired; *b* 21 May 1925; *s* of Ernest Fry and Lilian (*née* Eveling); *m* 1954, Jeanne Ivy Dawson; one *s* one *d. Educ:* Wilson's Grammar Sch., Camberwell; Birkbeck Coll., Univ. of London (BSc (Special)). MIS. Telecommunications Technician, Royal Signals, 1944–47; Scientific Asst, CEGB (London Region), 1948–52; Statistician: Glacier Metal Co., London, 1952–54; CEGB HQ, London, 1954–64; Gen. Register Office, 1965–66; Asst Dir of Research and Intelligence, GLC, 1966–69; Chief Statistician: (Social Statistics) Cabinet Office, 1969–74; (Manpower Statistics) Dept of Employment, 1974–75. *Publications:* various technical pubns in statistical and other professional jls. *Recreations:* photography, reading, motoring. *Address:* 39 Claremont Road, Hadley Wood, Barnet, Herts EN4 0HR. *T:* 0181–440 1393.

FRY, Stephen John; writer, actor, comedian; *b* 24 Aug. 1957; *s* of Alan John Fry and Marianne Eve (*née* Newman). *Educ:* Uppingham Sch.; Queens' Coll., Cambridge (MA). *TV series:* Blackadder, 1987–89; A Bit of Fry and Laurie, 1989–95; Jeeves in Jeeves and Wooster, 1990–92; *theatre:* Forty Years On, Queen's, 1984; The Common Pursuit, Phoenix, 1988; *films:* Peter's Friends, 1992; I.Q., 1995. Columnist: The Listener, 1988–89; Daily Telegraph, 1990–. *Publications:* Me and My Girl, 1984 (musical performed in West End and on Broadway); A Bit of Fry and Laurie: collected scripts, 1990; *novels:* The Liar, 1991; The Hippopotamus, 1994. *Recreations:* smoking, drinking, swearing, pressing wild flowers. *Address:* c/o Lorraine Hamilton, 6th Floor, 76 Oxford Street, W1N 0AT. *T:* 0171–836 3941. *Clubs:* Savile, United Oxford & Cambridge University, Groucho, Chelsea Arts.

FRY, Hon. Sir William Gordon, Kt 1980; JP; President, Legislative Council of Victoria, Australia, 1976–79; *b* 12 June 1909; *s* of A. G. Fry, Ballarat; *m* 1936, Lilian G., *d* of A. W. Macrae; four *s. Educ:* Ballarat High School; Melbourne Univ. Served War of 1939–45, 2nd AIF (Lt-Col, despatches). Education Dept of Victoria for 40 years; Headmaster of various schools, including Cheltenham East, Windsor, Cheltenham Heights. Councillor, City of Moorabbin; Mayor, 1968; MLC (Lib) for Higinbotham, Vic, 1967–79. Past Chm., Parly Select Cttee, Road Safety. Vice-Pres., Victoria League; Mem., RSL. Formerly Dep. Chm., World Bowls. Life Governor: Melbourne and Dist Ambulance Soc.; Royal Women's Hosp.; Royal Melbourne Hosp.; Gen. Management Cttee, Royal Victoria Eye and Ear Hosp.; Management Bd, Cheltenham-Mordialloc Hosp. (18 years service); Committee Member: Melbourne Family Care Orgn; Richmond Foundn; Legacy Australia; Brighton Tech. Coll. JP Melbourne, 1968. *Recreations:* lawn bowls, golf, swimming. *Address:* 139 Atherton Road, Oakleigh, Victoria 3166, Australia. *Clubs:* West Brighton; Royal Commonwealth Society (Victoria); Returned Services League (Cheltenham-Moorabbin).

FRY, William Norman H.; *see* Hillier-Fry.

FRYBERG, Sir Abraham, Kt 1968; MBE 1941; retired; *b* 26 May 1901; *s* of Henry and Rose Fryberg; *m* 1939, Vivian Greensil Barnard; one *s. Educ:* Wesley Coll., Melbourne; Queen's Coll., University of Melbourne. MB, BS (Melbourne) 1928; DPH, DTM (Sydney) 1936; Hon. MD (Qld); Hon. FACMA. Served with 9 Australian Div. (Tobruk, Alamein), 1940–45. Resident Med. Officer, then Registrar, Brisbane Hosp. and Brisbane Children's Hosp., 1929–33; GP, Hughenden, 1934; Health Officer, Qld Health Dept, 1936–46 (except for war service); Dep. Dir-Gen., 1946, Dir-Gen. of Health and Medical Services, Qld, 1947–67, retired. Hon. Col, RAAMC Northern Comd, 1962–67. SBStJ 1958. *Recreation:* racing. *Address:* 19 Dublin Street, Clayfield, Qld 4011, Australia. *T:* (7) 32622549. *Club:* United Service (Brisbane).

FRYE, Michael John Ernest; Chief Executive, B. Elliott, since 1988 (Chairman, 1987–92); *b* 2 June 1945; *s* of late Jack Frye, CBE and Daphne Page-Croft; *m* 1st, 1970, Geraldine Elizabeth Kendall; one *s*; 2nd, 1989, Valerie Patricia Harfield-Simpson. *Educ:* Marlborough Coll.; MIT (SB Business Management, Mech. Eng. Minor). B. Elliott and subsidiaries, 1967–; Dir, Goldfields Industrial, 1973–76; Overseas Dir, B. Elliott, 1974–76, non-exec. Dir, 1976–87; Chm. and Chief Exec., Rotaflex Gp of Cos, 1975–87; Chm., Concord Lighting, 1976–87; non-exec. Dir, Thorn Lighting Group, 1993–. Chm. and Founder, Light and Health Res. Council, 1978; Member: NEDC Sub-Cttee, exports for luminaire manufrs, 1980–81; Council, Lighting Industry Fedn, 1980–87 (Vice-Pres., 1987); Illuminating Eng. Soc. of N America, 1979–; Chairman: Cttee to establish nat. lighting award, 1984–87; Lighting Div., CIBSE, 1987–88. Chairman: West London Leadership, 1990–; Business Link London, 1995–; Dep. Chm., Park Royal Partnership, 1993– (Chm., 1991–92); Dir, London First, 1992– (a Vice-Chm.). Chm. and Mem., numerous technical and arts organisations. Liveryman, Turners' Co. and Lightmongers' Co. FRAeS 1994; Fellow, RSPB, 1987; FRSA 1978(Chm., 1991–93; Dep. Chm., 1993–94). Hon. Fellow, RCA, 1987. *Recreations:* golf, tennis, chess, bird watching, collecting old or rare bird books. *Address:* B. Elliott, Elliott House, Victoria Road, NW10 6NY. *T:* 0181–961 7333. *Clubs:* Boodle's, City Livery, Royal Automobile; Royal Worlington and Newmarket Golf.

FRYER, David Richard, OBE 1994; Secretary-General, Royal Town Planning Institute, since 1976; *b* 16 May 1936; *s* of Ernest William Fryer and Gladys Edith Battey; *m* 1961, Carole Elizabeth Hayes; one *s* two *d. Educ:* Chesterfield Sch.; New Coll., Oxford (MA, BCL). LMRTPI. Admitted solicitor, 1961. Articled Clerk and Asst Solicitor, Chesterfield Bor. Council, 1958–61; Associate Lawyer, Messrs Jones, Day, Cockley & Reavis, Cleveland, Ohio, 1961–63; Asst Solicitor, N Riding CC, 1963–65; Sen. Asst Solicitor, Bucks CC, 1966–69; Dep. Sec., RICS, 1970–75. Sec., Brit. Chapter, Internat. Real Estate Fedn, 1970–75; Pres., Internat. Fedn for Housing and Planning, 1992– (Mem., Bureau and Council, 1976–; Dep. Pres., 1984–92); Sec.-Gen., European Council of Town Planners, 1987–. Member: Exec. Cttee and Council, Public Works Congress and Exhibn Council Ltd, 1976–90; Exec. Cttee, Nat. Council for Social Service, 1976–79 (Chm., Planning and Environment Gp); Council and Standards Cttee, Nat. House-Bldg Council, 1976–95; Exec. Cttee, Commonwealth Assoc. of Planners, 1984–88. FRSA 1981. *Recreations:* international affairs, architecture, the countryside. *Address:* Stairways, Portway Road, Hartwell, Aylesbury, Bucks HP17 8RP. *T:* Aylesbury (01296) 748538. *Club:* East India.

FRYER, Dr Geoffrey, FRS 1972; Deputy Chief Scientific Officer, Windermere Laboratory, Freshwater Biological Association, 1981–88; *b* 6 Aug. 1927; *s* of W. and M. Fryer; *m* 1953, Vivien Griffiths Hodgson; one *s* one *d. Educ:* Huddersfield College. DSc, PhD London. Royal Navy, 1946–48. Colonial Research Student, 1952–53; HM Overseas Research Service, 1953–60: Malawi, 1953–55; Zambia, 1955–57; Uganda, 1957–60; Sen., then Principal, then Sen. Principal Scientific Officer, Freshwater Biological Assoc., 1960–81. H. R. Macmillan Lectr, Univ. of British Columbia, 1963; Distinguished Vis. Schol., Univ. of Adelaide, 1985; Distinguished Lectr, Biol Scis Br., Dept. Fisheries and Oceans, Canada, 1987; Hon. Prof., Inst. of Environmental and Biol Scis, Lancaster Univ., 1988–. Mem. Council, Royal Soc., 1978–80. Mem., Adv. Cttee on Science, Nature Conservancy Council, 1986–91. Pres., Yorks Naturalists' Union, 1993. Frink Medal, Zool Soc. of London, 1983; Linnean Medal for Zoology, Linnean Soc., 1987. *Publications:* (with T. D. Iles) The Cichlid Fishes of the Great Lakes of Africa: their biology and evolution, 1972; A natural history of the lakes, tarns and streams of the English Lake District, 1991; The Freshwater Crustacea of Yorkshire: a faunistic and ecological survey, 1993; numerous articles in scientific jls. *Recreations:* natural history, walking, church architecture, photography. *Address:* Elleray Cottage, Windermere, Cumbria LA23 1AW.

FUAD, Kutlu Tekin, CBE 1993; **Hon. Mr Justice Fuad;** President, Court of Appeal, Negara Brunei Darussalam, since 1993; *b* 23 April 1926; *s* of Mustafa Fuad Bey, CMG, and Belkis Hilmi; *m* 1952, Inci Izzet; two *s* one *d. Educ:* Temple Grove; Marlborough Coll.; St John's Coll., Cambridge (MA). Called to the Bar, Inner Temple, 1952, Bencher, 1993. Mil. Service, Lieut KRRC, 1944–48. Colonial Legal Service, 1953–62: Magistrate, Cyprus; Resident Magistrate, Sen. Crown Counsel, Legal Draftsman, and Dir of Public Prosecutions, Uganda; Judge of the High Court, Uganda, 1963–72 (Pres., Industrial Court; Chm., Law Reform Cttee); Dir, Legal Div., Commonwealth Secretariat, 1972–80; Judge, High Court of Hong Kong, 1980–82; Justice of Appeal, 1982–88, Vice-Pres., 1988–93, Court of Appeal, Hong Kong. Comr, Supreme Ct of Negara Brunei Darussalam, 1983–86, 1988–92. Mem., Law Reform Commn, Hong Kong, 1983–89. Pres., Hong Kong Family Law Assoc., 1986–93. Formerly Chm., Visitation Cttee, Makerere University Coll. *Recreations:* music, Rugby football, tennis. *Address:* PO Box 415, Lefkoşa, Mersin 10, Turkey; 51 Earl's Court Road, Kensington, W8 6EE. *T:* 0171–937 9209.

FUCHS, Sir Vivian (Ernest), Kt 1958; MA, PhD; FRS 1974; Director of the British Antarctic Survey, 1958–73; Leader Commonwealth Trans-Antarctic Expedition, 1955–58; *b* 11 Feb. 1908; *s* of late E. Fuchs, Farnham, Surrey, and late Violet Anne Fuchs (*née* Watson); *m* 1st, 1933, Joyce (*d* 1990), 2nd *d* of late John Connell; one *s* one *d* (and one *d* decd); 2nd, 1991, Mrs Eleanor Honnywill. *Educ:* Brighton Coll.; St John's Coll., Cambridge (Hon. Fellow, 1983). Geologist with: Cambridge East Greenland Expedn, 1929; Cambridge Expdn to E African Lakes, 1930–31; E African Archæological Expdn, 1931–32; Leader Lake Rudolf Rift Valley Expedn, 1933–34; Royal Geog. Society Cuthbert Peek Grant, 1936; Leader Lake Rukwa Expedn, 1937–38. 2nd Lieut Cambs Regt, TA, 1939; served in W Africa, 1942–43; Staff Coll., Camberley, 1943; served NW Europe (despatches), 1944–46; demobilized (Major), 1946. Leader Falkland Islands Dependencies Survey (Antarctica), 1947–50; Dir FIDSc Bureau, 1950–55. President: Internat. Glaciological Soc., 1963–66; British Assoc. for Advancement of Science, 1972; Mem. Council, RGS, 1958–61, Vice-Pres. 1961–64, Pres., 1982–84, Hon. Vice-Pres., 1985–. Founder's Gold Medal, Royal Geog. Soc., 1951; Silver Medal RSA, 1952; Polar Medal, 1953, and Clasp, 1958; Special Gold Medal, Royal Geog. Soc., 1958; Gold Medal Royal Scottish Geog. Society 1958; Gold Medal Geog. Society (Paris), 1958; Richthofen Medal (Berlin), 1958; Kirchenpauer Medal (Hamburg), 1958; Plancius Medal (Amsterdam), 1959; Egede Medal (Copenhagen), 1959; Hubbard Medal, Nat. Geog. Soc. (Washington), 1959; Explorers Club Medal (New York), 1959; Geog. Soc. (Chicago) Gold Medal, 1959; Geol. Soc. of London Prestwich Medal, 1960. Hon. Fellow, Wolfson (formerly University Coll.), Cambridge, 1970. Hon. LLD Edinburgh 1958; Hon. DSc: Durham 1958; Cantab 1959; Leicester 1972; Hon. ScD Swansea, 1971; Hon. LLD Birmingham, 1974. *Publications:* The Crossing of Antarctica (Fuchs and Hillary), 1958; Antarctic Adventure, 1959; (ed) Forces of Nature, 1977; Of Ice and Men, 1982; (ed) The Physical World (Oxford Illustrated Encyclopedia), 1985; A Time to Speak (autobiog.), 1990; geographical and geological reports and papers in scientific jls. *Recreation:* gardening. *Address:* 106 Barton Road, Cambridge CB3 9LH. *T:* Cambridge (01223) 359238. *Club:* Athenæum.

FUENTES, Prof. Carlos; Robert F. Kennedy Professor of Latin American Studies, Harvard University, since 1987; *b* 11 Nov. 1928; *s* of Ambassador Rafael Fuentes and Berta Fuentes; *m* 1st, 1957, Rita Macedo; one *d*; 2nd, 1973, Sylvia Lemus; one *s* one *d. Educ:* Law School, Nat. Univ., Mexico; Inst. des Hautes Etudes Internat., Geneva. Sec., Mexican Deleg. to ILO, Geneva, 1950; Under Director of Culture, Nat. Univ., Mexico, 1952–54; Head, Cultural Relations Dept, Min. of Foreign Affairs, Mexico, 1955–58; Ambassador to France, 1975–77; Prof. of English and Romance Languages, Univ. of Pennsylvania, 1978–83; Prof. of Comparative Literature, Harvard, 1984–86; Simón Bolivar Prof., Cambridge, 1986–87. Member: El Colegio Nacional, Mexico, 1974–; Mexican Nat. Commn on Human Rights, 1989–; Fellow, Wilson Center, Washington DC, 1974; Mem., Amer. Acad. and Inst. of Arts and Letters, 1986; Trustee, NY Public Library, 1987. Hon. DLitt: Wesleyan, 1982; Warwick, 1992; Hon. LLD Harvard, 1983; Hon. LittD Cambridge, 1987; DUniv Essex, 1987; Dr *hc* Tufts, 1993; UCLA, 1993. Nat. Prize for Literature, Mexico, 1985; Miguel de Cervantes Prize, 1987; Menéndez Pelayo Prize, Univ. of Santander, 1992. Légion d'Honneur (France), 1992. *Publications:* Where the Air is Clear, 1958; The Good Conscience, 1959; The Death of Artemio Cruz, 1962; Aura, 1962; A Change of Skin, 1967 (Biblioteca Breve Prize, Barcelona); Terra Nostra, 1975 (Rómulo Gallegos Prize); Distant Relations, 1980; Burnt Water, 1982; The Old Gringo, 1984 (filmed, 1989); Cristóbal Nonato, 1987; Myself with Others: selected essays, 1988; The Campaign, 1991; Valiente Mundo Nuevo: essays, 1991; Constancia and other stories for virgins, 1991; The Buried Mirror, 1992 (televised); El Naranjo (The Orange Tree) (novellas), 1993; Geography of the Novel: essays, 1993. *Address:* 401 Boylston Hall, Harvard University, Cambridge, MA 02138, USA. *T:* (617) 4952543; c/o Brandt & Brandt, 1501 Broadway, New York, NY 10036, USA.

FUGARD, Athol; playwright, director, actor; *b* 11 June 1932; *s* of Harold David Fugard and Elizabeth Magdalene Potgieter; *m* 1956, Sheila Meiring; one *d. Educ:* Univ. of Cape Town. Directed earliest plays, Nongogo, No Good Friday, Johannesburg, 1960; acted in The Blood Knot, touring S Africa, 1961; Hello and Goodbye, 1965; directed and acted in The Blood Knot, London, 1966; Boesman and Lena, S Africa, 1969; directed Boesman and Lena, London, 1971; directed Serpent Players in various prodns, Port Elizabeth, from 1963, directed co-authors John Kani and Winston Ntshona in Sizwe Bansi is Dead, SA, 1972, The Island, 1973, and London, 1973–74; acted in film, Boesman and Lena, 1972; directed and acted in Statements after an Arrest under the Immorality Act, in SA, 1972, directed in London, 1973; wrote Dimetos for Edinburgh Fest., 1975; directed and acted in, A Lesson from Aloes, SA, 1978, London, 1980 (directed, NY 1981, winning NY Critics Circle Award for Best Play); directed: Master Harold and the Boys, NY, 1982 (Drama Desk Award), Johannesburg, 1983, Nat. Theatre, 1983 (Standard award for Best Play); The Road to Mecca, Yale Repertory Theatre, 1984; (also wrote) My Children! My Africa!, NY, 1990; (also wrote) Playland, SA, 1992, NY and London, 1993. Hon. DLitt: Natal, 1981; Rhodes, 1983; Cape Town, 1984; Emory, 1992; Port Elizabeth, 1993; Hon. DFA Yale, 1983; Hon. DHL Georgetown, 1984. *Films:* Boesman and Lena, 1973; The Guest, 1977; (acted in) Meetings with Remarkable Men (dir, Peter Brook), 1979; (wrote and acted in) Marigolds in August (Silver Bear Award, Berlin), 1980; (acted in) Gandhi, 1982; (co-dir and acted in) Road to Mecca, 1991. *Publications:* The Blood Knot, 1962; People Are Living There, Hello and Goodbye, 1973; Boesman and Lena, 1973; (jtly) Three Port Elizabeth Plays: Sizwe Bansi is Dead, The Island, Statements after an Arrest under the Immorality Act, 1974; Tsotsi (novel), 1980 (also USA); A Lesson from Aloes, 1981 (also USA); Master Harold and the Boys, US 1982, UK 1983; Notebooks 1960–1977, 1983 (also USA); Road to Mecca, 1985; A Place with the Pigs, 1988. *Recreations:* angling, skin-diving, bird-watching. *Address:* PO Box 5090, Walmer, Port Elizabeth 6065, South Africa.

FUGARD, Maj.-Gen. Michael Teape, CB 1990; an Adjudicator of Immigration Appeals, since 1990 (full-time since 1991); a Recorder, since 1992; *b* Chester, 27 March 1933; *s* of Rev. Theodore Teape Fugard and Lilian Teape Fugard (*née* Baker); *m* 1961, Theresia Hollensteiner; two *s* two *d. Educ:* Chester Cathedral Sch.; Sherborne Sch. Admitted Solicitor, 1957. Enlisted Army, RASC, 1957; commnd, Captain Army Legal Services (later Army Legal Corps), 1958; OC (Major) Army Legal Aid Far East Land Forces, 1960, Lt-Col 1971; Asst Dir Army Legal Services, MoD, 1973–78; Col Legal Staff HQ UKLF, 1979; Comdr Army Law Trng and Pubns Br., 1980; Comdr Army Legal Aid, BAOR, 1982; Comdr (Brig.) Army Legal Gp UK, 1983; Maj.-Gen. 1986; Dir, Army Legal Services, 1986–90. An Asst Recorder, 1986–92. Mem., Lord Chancellor's Panel of Independent Inspectors, 1990–91. Governor, Royal Sch., Bath, 1985–92; Chm., Leaden Hall Sch., Salisbury, 1988–. *Address:* Immigration Appeals, Thanet House, 231 Strand, WC2R 1DA.

FUJII, Hiroaki; Ambassador of Japan to the Court of St James's, since 1994; *b* 21 Aug. 1933; *m* 1963, Kiyoko Shimoda; three *d. Educ:* Tokyo Univ.; Amherst Coll., USA (BA 1958). Entered Min. of Foreign Affairs, Japan, 1956; Dir, Econ. Affairs Div., UN Bureau, 1971–72; Private Sec. to Minister for Foreign Affairs, 1972–74; Dir, 2nd Econ. Co-operation Div., Econ. Co-operation Bureau, 1974–75; Dir, 1st N American Div., American Affairs Bureau, 1975–76; Fellow, Center for Internat. Affairs, Harvard Univ., 1976; Counsellor, Embassy of Japan, Washington, 1977–79; Ministry of Foreign Affairs: Dir, Personnel Div., Minister's Secretariat, 1979–81; Dep. Dir Gen., Asian Affairs Bureau, 1981–83; Consul-Gen., Hong Kong, 1983–85; Ministry of Foreign Affairs: Dir Gen., N American Affairs Bureau, 1985–88; Dep. Vice-Minister, 1988–89; Ambassador to: OECD, Paris, 1989–92; Thailand, 1992–94. Kt Grand Cross (1st Cl.), Most Exalted Order of White Elephant (Thailand), 1994. *Address:* Embassy of Japan, 101–104 Piccadilly, W1V 9FN. *T:* 0171–465 6500.

FUKUI, Prof. Dr Kenichi; Order of Culture, Person of Cultural Merits (Japan), 1981; Grand Cordon, Order of the Rising Sun (Japan), 1988; Director, Institute for Fundamental Chemistry, Kyoto, Japan, since 1988; *b* 4 Oct. 1918; *s* of Ryokichi Fukui and Chie Fukui (*née* Sugizawa); *m* 1947, Tomoe Horie; one *s* one *d. Educ:* Kyoto Imperial Univ. (AB Engrg, PhD Engrg). Lecturer, 1943–45, Asst Professor, 1945–51, Professor, 1951–82, Kyoto University; Pres., Kyoto Inst. of Technology, 1982–88. Member: European Acad. of Arts, Sciences and Humanities, 1981–; Japan Acad., 1983–; Pontifical Acad. of Sciences, 1985–. Foreign Associate, Nat. Acad. of Sciences, Washington, 1981–; Foreign Hon. Mem., Amer. Acad. of Arts and Sciences, 1983–; Foreign Mem., Royal Soc., 1989. Hon. DSc Wales, 1992. Nobel Prize in Chemistry (jtly), 1981. *Address:* 23 Kitashirakawahiraicho, Sakyo-ku, Kyoto 606, Japan. *T:* (075) 7815785.

FULCHER, Derick Harold, DSC 1944; Assistant Under-Secretary of State, Department of Health and Social Security, 1969–70; *b* 4 Nov. 1917; *s* of late Percy Frederick Fulcher and Gertrude Lilian Fulcher; *m* 1943, Florence Ellen May Anderson; one *s* one *d. Educ:* St Olave's Grammar School. Served in Royal Navy, 1940–46 (Lieut, RNVR). Entered Civil Service (War Office), 1936; Asst Principal, Ministry of National Insurance, 1947; Principal, 1950; Admin. Staff Coll., Henley, 1952; Asst Sec. 1959; seconded to HM Treasury, 1957–59; served on an ILO mission in Trinidad and Tobago, 1967–69. Interviewer for CS Commn, 1971–79. UK Delegate to and Chairman: NATO Management Survey Cttee, 1970–71; Council of Europe Management Survey Cttee, 1971–72. Chm., Supplementary Benefit Appeal Tribunals, 1971–75; Head of UK res. project in W Europe into social security provision for disablement, 1971–72; Res. Consultant, Office of Manpower Econs, 1972–73; served on technical aid mission to Indonesia, 1973; ILO Res. Consultant on Social Security, 1973–80; Consultant to: EEC Statistical Office, 1974; Govt of Thailand on Social Security, 1978–79 and 1981. Fellow, Inst. for European Health Services Research, Leuven Univ., Belgium, 1974–. *Publications:* Medical Care Systems, 1974; Social Security for the Unemployed, 1976. *Recreations:* walking, photography, travel. *Address:* 100 Downs Road, Coulsdon, Surrey CR5 1AF. *T:* Downland (01737) 554231. *Club:* Civil Service.

FULFORD, Adrian Bruce; QC 1994; *b* 8 Jan. 1953; *s* of Gerald John Fulford and Marie Bettine (*née* Stevens). *Educ:* Elizabeth Coll., Guernsey; Southampton Univ. (BA Hons). Housing Advr, Shelter's Housing Aid Centre, 1974–75; called to the Bar, Middle Temple, 1978. *Publications:* (contrib.) Atkin's Court Forms, 1987; (ed) Archbold Criminal Pleadings and Practices, 1992. *Recreations:* riding, tennis, politics, golf. *Address:* 14 Took's Court, Cursitor Street, EC4A 1JY. *Club:* Reform.

FULFORD, Prof. Michael Gordon, PhD; FSA; FBA 1994; Professor of Archaeology, since 1993 and Dean, Faculty of Letters and Social Sciences, since 1994, University of Reading; *b* 20 Oct. 1948; *s* of Comdr E. G. J. D. Fulford, RN (retd) and E. Z. Fulford (*née* Simpson); *m* 1972, Charlotte Jane Hobbs; one *s* one *d. Educ:* St Edwards Sch., Oxford; Univ. of Southampton (BA Hons 1970; PhD 1975). DES Res. Student, 1970; Research Assistant: Univ. of Southampton, 1971–72; Univ. of Oxford, 1972–74; University of Reading: Lectr in Archaeol., 1974–85; Reader, 1985–88; Leverhulme Res. Fellow, 1987; Personal Prof., 1988–93. Editor, Britannia, 1994–. English Heritage: Chm., Hadrian's Wall Adv. Panel, 1989– (Mem., 1985–); Mem., Ancient Monuments Adv. Cttee, 1991–; Comr, RCHM, 1993–; Mem., Archaeology Adv. Cttee, Nat. Mus. of Wales, 1991–. FSA 1977. *Publications:* New Forest Roman Pottery, 1975; (with B. Cuncliffe) CSIR Great Britain I: Bath and the Rest of Wessex, 1982; Silchester Defences, 1984; (with D. Peacock) Excavations at Carthage: The British Mission, The Pottery and other Ceramics, Vol 1, 1984, Vol 2, 1994; The Silchester Amphitheatre, 1989; Excavations at Sabratha 1948–1951, Vol. 2, pt i (ed with M. Hall), 1989, pt ii (ed with R. Tomber), 1994; (ed jtly) Developing Landscape of Lowland Britain: the archaeology of the British gravels, 1992. *Recreations:* music, walking, sailing. *Address:* Department of Archaeology, University of Reading, PO Box 218, Reading, Berks RG6 2AA. *T:* Reading (01734) 318132.

FULFORD, Robert John; Keeper, Department of Printed Books, British Library (formerly British Museum), 1967–85; *b* 16 Aug. 1923; *s* of John Fulford, Southampton; *m* 1950, Alison Margaret Rees; one *s* one *d. Educ:* King Edward VI Sch., Southampton; King's Coll., Cambridge; Charles Univ., Prague. Asst Keeper, Dept of Printed Books, British Museum, 1945–65; Dep. Keeper, 1965–67 (Head of Slavonic Div., 1961–67); Keeper, 1967–85. *Address:* 7 Tulip Tree Close, Tonbridge, Kent TN9 2SH. *T:* Tonbridge (01732) 350356; Maumont, 24390 Hautefort, France. *T:* 53505007.

FULHAM, Bishop Suffragan of, since 1985; **Rt Rev. Charles John Klyberg;** (first) Archdeacon of Charing Cross, since 1989; *b* 29 July 1931; *s* of late Captain Charles Augustine Klyberg, MN and Ivy Lilian Waddington, LRAM; unmarried. *Educ:* Eastbourne College. Eaton Hall OCS, 1953; 2nd Lieut, 1st Bn The Buffs, Kenya Emergency, 1953–54; Lieut 1955. ARICS. Asst Estates Manager, Cluttons, 1954–57. Lincoln Theological Coll., 1957–60. Curate, S John's, East Dulwich, 1960–63; Rector of Fort Jameson, Zambia, 1963–67; Vicar, Christ Church and S Stephen, Battersea, 1967–77; Dean of Lusaka Cathedral, Zambia, and Rector of the parish, 1977–85, Dean Emeritus, 1985; Vicar General, 1978–85. UK Commissary for Anglican Church in Zambia, 1985–89. Chm., Church Property Development Gp, 1978–85. Pres., Guild of All Souls, 1988–. Guardian, Shrine of Our Lady of Walsingham, 1991–. Warden, Quainton Hall Sch., Harrow, 1992–. *Recreations:* reading, music, travel. *Address:* 4 Cambridge Place, W8 5PB. *T:* 0171-937 2560. *Club:* Athenæum.

FULLER, Brian Leslie, CBE 1989; QFSM 1981; Commandant Chief Executive, Fire Service College, 1990–94; *b* 18 April 1936; *s* of Walter Leslie Victor Fuller and Eliza May Fuller; *m* 1957, Linda Peters; three *s. Educ:* St Albans County Grammar Sch. for Boys. FIFirE 1975. Station Officer: Herts Fire Brigade, 1960–66; Warwicks Fire Brigade, 1966–68; Asst Divl Officer, Notts Fire Brigade, 1968–69; Divl Commander, Essex Fire Brigade, 1969–72; Dep. Chief Fire Officer, Glamorgan Fire Brigade, 1972–74; Chief Fire Officer: Mid Glamorgan Fire Brigade, 1974–80; Notts Fire Brigade, 1980–81; W Midlands Fire Service, 1981–90. Hon. DSc South Bank, 1993. *Recreations:* cricket, music, reading. *Address:* Newland, Aqueduct Lane, Alvechurch, Birmingham B48 7BP.

FULLER, Geoffrey Herbert, CEng, FRINA, FIMarE; RCNC; defence and maritime consultant; Director, British Maritime Technology Ltd, Teddington, since 1985 (Deputy Chairman, 1985–95); *b* 16 Jan. 1927; *s* of late Major Herbert Thomas Fuller and Clarice Christine Fuller; *m* 1952, Pamela-Maria Quarrell; one *d. Educ:* Merchant Taylors', Northwood, Mddx; Royal Naval Engrg Coll., Keyham; Royal Naval Coll., Greenwich. FRINA 1965; FIMarE 1974. Constructor Commander: Staff of Flag Officer (Submarines), 1958; British Navy Staff, Washington, 1960; Sen. Officers War Course, 1969; RCDS, 1973; Head of Ship Material Engrg, 1974; Support Manager Submarines, 1976; Dep. Dir, Submarines/Polaris, Ship Dept, MoD, 1979; Dir of Naval Ship Production, 1981–82; Mem. Bd, and Man. Dir, Warship Div., British Shipbuilders, 1983–85; Exec. Chm., 1984–86, Technical Adviser, 1986–87, Vickers Shipbuilding and Engrg Ltd, Barrow. Chm. Council, RINA, 1994–. *Address:* Casa Feliz, Weston Park, Bath BA1 4AL. *T:* Bath (01225) 466054.

FULLER, Hon. Sir John (Bryan Munro), Kt 1974; President: Arthritis Foundation of Australia, 1980–91 (Emeritus Vice-President, since 1991); Barnardo's Australia, since 1985 (Member, Management Committee, 1980–85); *b* 22 Sept. 1917; *s* of late Bryan Fuller, QC; *m* 1940, Eileen, *d* of O. S. Webb; one *s* one *d. Educ:* Knox Grammar Sch., Wahroonga. Chm., Australian Country Party (NSW), 1959–64; MLC, NSW, 1961–78; Minister for Decentralisation and Development, 1965–73; NSW Minister for Planning and Environment, 1973–76; Vice-Pres. of Exec. Council and Leader of Govt in Legis. Council,1968–76; Leader of Opposition, 1976–78; Leader, various NSW Govt trade missions to various parts of the world. Pres., Assoc. of Former Mems of NSW Parlt, 1988–92. Australian Institute of Export: Federal Pres., 1986–91; Mem., Federal Council, 1985–92; Pres., NSW, 1985; Fellow, 1969; Hon. Life Fellow, 1991. Vice-Pres., Graziers Assoc. of NSW, 1965; Member: Council, Univ. of NSW, 1967–78; Cttee, United World Colls Trust, NSW, 1978–; Bd, Foundn for Res. and Treatment Alcohol and Drug Dependence, 1980–85; Council, Nat. Heart Foundn, NSW, 1980–. Chm., Rushcutters Bay Maritime Reserve Trust, 1993–. *Recreations:* tennis, bowls. *Address:* 54/8 Fullerton Street, Woollahra, NSW 2025, Australia. *Clubs:* Australian (Sydney); Coolah Bowling, Royal Sydney Golf, Australian Jockey.

FULLER, John Leopold, FRSL 1980; writer; Fellow of Magdalen College, Oxford, and Tutor in English, since 1966; *b* 1 Jan. 1937; *s* of late Roy Broadbent Fuller, CBE, FRSL; *m* 1960, Cicely Prudence Martin; three *d. Educ:* St Paul's School; New Coll., Oxford (BLitt, MA). Vis. Lectr, State Univ. of NY at Buffalo, 1962–63; Asst Lectr, Univ. of Manchester, 1963–66. *Publications:* Fairground Music, 1961; The Tree that Walked, 1967; A Reader's Guide to W. H. Auden, 1970; The Sonnet, 1972; Cannibals and Missionaries, 1972, and Epistles to Several Persons, 1973 (Geoffrey Faber Meml Prize, 1974); Squeaking Crust, 1973; The Last Bid, 1975; The Mountain in the Sea, 1975; Lies and Secrets, 1979; The Illusionists (Southern Arts Lit. Prize), 1980; The Extraordinary Wool Mill and other stories, 1980; Waiting for the Music, 1982; Flying to Nowhere (Whitbread Prize for a First Novel), 1983; The Beautiful Inventions, 1983; (ed) The Dramatic Works of John Gay, 1983; Come Aboard and Sail Away, 1983; The Adventures of Speedfall, 1985; Selected Poems 1954–1982, 1985; (with James Fenton) Partingtime Hall, 1986; Tell It Me Again, 1988; The Grey Among the Green, 1988; The Burning Boys, 1989; (ed) The Chatto Book of Love Poetry, 1990; The Mechanical Body, 1991; Look Twice, 1991; The Worm and the Star, 1993. *Recreations:* printing, correspondence chess, music. *Address:* Magdalen College, Oxford OX1 4AU. *T:* Oxford (01865) 276070.

FULLER, Major Sir John (William Fleetwood), 3rd Bt *cr* 1910; Major, The Life Guards, retired; *b* 18 Dec. 1936; *s* of Major Sir John Gerard Henry Fleetwood Fuller, 2nd Bt, and Fiona, Countess of Normanton, (*d* 1985), *d* of 4th Marquess Camden, GCVO; *S* father, 1981; *m* 1968, Lorna Marian, *o d* of F. R. Kemp-Potter, Findon, Sussex; three *s. Heir: s* James Henry Fleetwood Fuller, *b* 1 Nov. 1970. *Address:* Neston Park, Corsham, Wilts SN13 9TG.

FULLER, Michael John; Chief Executive, Al Ahli Commercial Bank, Bahrain, since 1992; *b* 20 July 1932; *s* of Thomas Frederick and Irene Emily Fuller; *m* 1st, 1955, Maureen Rita Slade (marr. diss. 1989); two *s* two *d*; 2nd, 1990, Elizabeth Frost. *Educ:* Wallington County Grammar Sch. FCIB 1980. National Service, commnd RAF, 1950–52. Midland Bank, 1948–90: various branch, regl and head office posts; Gp Public Affairs Advr, 1977–79;

Regl Dir, Southampton, 1979–81; Gen. Manager, Midland and Wales, 1981–82; Gen. Manager, Business Develt Div., 1982–85; UK Operations Dir, 1985–87; Dep. Chief Exec., 1987–89, Chief Exec., 1989–90, UK Banking Sector; Gen. Man., Nat. Bank of Abu Dhabi, 1991–92. FRSA. *Recreations:* reading, travelling, rough golf. *Address:* c/o Al Ahli Commercial Bank, PO Box 5941, Manama, Bahrain. *Club:* Royal Air Force.

FULLER, Simon William John, CMG 1994; HM Diplomatic Service; Head of UK Delegation to Conference on Security and Co-operation in Europe, Vienna, since 1993; *b* 27 Nov. 1943; *s* of late Rowland William Bevis Fuller and Madeline Fuller (*née* Bailey); *m* 1984, Eleanor Mary Breedon; three *s*. *Educ:* Wellington College; Emmanuel College, Cambridge (BA Hist.). Served Singapore and Kinshasa, 1969–73; First Sec., Cabinet Office, 1973–75; FCO, 1975–77; UK Mission to UN, New York, 1977–80; FCO, 1980–86 (Counsellor, 1984); Dep. Hd of Mission, Tel Aviv, 1986–90; Hd of NE and N African Dept, FCO, 1990–93. *Recreations:* cooking and cricket. *Address:* c/o Foreign and Commonwealth Office, SW1A 2AH; 27 Carlisle Mansions, Carlisle Place, SW1P 1EZ. *T:* 0171-828 6494. *Clubs:* United Oxford & Cambridge University, MCC.

FULLERTON, William Hugh, CMG 1989; HM Diplomatic Service; Ambassador to Kuwait, since 1992; *b* 11 Feb. 1939; *s* of late Major Arthur Hugh Theodore Francis Fullerton, RAMC, and of Mary (*née* Parker); *m* 1968, Arlene Jacobowitz; one *d*. *Educ:* Cheltenham Coll.; Queens' Coll., Cambridge (MA Oriental Langs). Shell Internat. Petroleum Co., Uganda, 1963–65; FO, 1965; MECAS, Shemlan, Lebanon, 1965–66; Information Officer, Jedda, 1966–67; UK Mission to UN, New York, 1967; FCO, 1968–70; Head of Chancery, Kingston, Jamaica, 1970–73, and Ankara, 1973–77; FCO, 1977–80; Counsellor (Economic and Commercial), 1980–83 and Consul-Gen., 1981–83, Islamabad; Ambassador to Somalia, 1983–87; on loan to MoD, 1987–88; Gov., Falkland Is, and Comr for S Georgia and S Sandwich Is, 1988–92. High Comr, British Antarctic Territory, 1988–89. *Recreations:* travelling in remote areas, sailing, reading, walking. *Address:* c/o Foreign and Commonwealth Office, King Charles Street, SW1A 2AH. *Club:* Travellers'.

FULTHORPE, Henry Joseph, FRINA; RCNC; General Manager, HM Dockyard, Portsmouth (Deputy Director of Naval Construction), 1967–75; *b* Portsmouth, 2 July 1916; *s* of Joseph Henry and Clarissa Fulthorpe; *m* 1939, Bette May Forshew; two *s* one *d*. *Educ:* Royal Naval Coll., Greenwich. Ship Design and Production, Admiralty, London and Bath, 1939–43; Principal (Ship) Overseer, Vickers, Barrow-in-Furness, 1943–46; Dep. Manager, HM Dockyard, Malta, 1946–49; Sec., Radiological Defence Panel, 1949–52; Staff Constr, first British atom bomb, Montebello Is, 1952–53; Constr i/c Minesweeper Design, Admty, Bath, 1953–54; Chief Constr, Maintenance, Bath, 1954–56; Dep. Manager, HM Dockyard, Portsmouth, 1956–58; Chief Constructor: HM Dockyard, Singapore, 1958–61; Dockyard Dept, Bath, 1961–63; Asst Dir of Naval Construction, Bath, 1963–64; Production Manager, HM Dockyard, Chatham, 1964–67; Manager, Constructive Dept, HM Dockyard, Portsmouth, 1967. *Recreations:* travel, walking, cooking. *Address:* Gerard House, 60 Granada Road, Southsea PO4 0RJ. *T:* Portsmouth (01705) 750427.

FULTON, Hon. (Edmund) Davie, OC 1992; PC (Canada) 1957; QC (BC) 1957; Barrister and Solicitor; Associate Counsel, Swinton & Company, Vancouver, 1983–90, retired; *b* 10 March 1916; *s* of Frederick John Fulton, KC, and Winifred M. Davie; *m* 1946, Patricia Mary, *d* of J. M. Macrae and Christine Macrae (*née* Carmichael), Winnipeg; three *d*. *Educ:* St Michael's Sch., Victoria, BC; Kamloops High Sch.; University of British Columbia; St John's Coll., Oxford. BA (BC), BA Oxon (Rhodes Scholar, elected 1936). Admitted to Bar of British Columbia, 1940. Served in Canadian Army Overseas as Company Comdr with Seaforth Highlanders of Canada and as DAAG 1st Canadian Inf. Div., 1940–45, including both Italian and Northwest Europe campaigns (despatches); transferred to R of O with rank of Major, 1945. Practised law with Fulton, Verchere & Rogers, Kamloops, BC, 1945–68, and with Fulton, Cumming, Richards & Co., Vancouver, 1968–73; Judge, Supreme Court of British Columbia, 1973–81. A Comr, 1986–92, Chm., 1990–92, Canadian Sect., Internat. Jt Commn, Ottawa. Elected to House of Commons of Canada, 1945; re-elected in 1949, 1953, 1957, 1958, 1962, 1965. Mem. Senate, University of British Columbia, 1948–57, 1969–75. Acting Minister of Citizenship and Immigration, June 1957–May 1958; Minister of Justice and Attorney Gen., Canada, June 1957–Aug. 1962; Minister of Public Works, Aug. 1962–April, 1963. Mem., Vancouver Adv. Cttee, Guaranty Trust Co. of Canada, 1983–86. Member: Law Soc. of BC, 1940–; Law Soc. of Upper Canada, 1957–; Canadian Bar Assoc., 1940–. Dir, Western Recovery Foundn, Vancouver; Hon. Dir, Physical Medicine Res. Foundn. Hon. Colonel: Rocky Mountain Rangers, 1959; 419 Sqdn, RCAF, 1993–. Hon. LLD: Ottawa, 1960; Queen's, 1963. Human Relns Award, Canadian Council of Christians and Jews, 1985; Citation for meritorious service to country and profession, Trial Lawyers Assoc. of BC, 1986. *Address:* 1632 West 40th Avenue, Vancouver, BC V6M 1V9, Canada. *Clubs:* Vancouver, Shaughnessy Golf and Country (Vancouver).

FULTON, Prof. John Francis; Provost, Legal, Social and Educational Sciences, Queen's University of Belfast, since 1993; *b* 21 Sept. 1933; *s* of Robert Patrick Fulton and Anne Fulton (*née* McCambridge); *m* 1958, Elizabeth Mary Brennan; one *s* one *d*. *Educ:* St Malachy's College, Belfast; QUB (BA 1954, DipEd 1958, MA 1964); Univ. of Keele (PhD 1975). Lectr and Principal Lectr, St Joseph's Coll. of Educn, Belfast, 1961–73; Queen's University of Belfast: Lectr, Inst. of Educn, 1973–76; Prof. and Head of Dept of Educnl Studies, 1977–85; Dir, Sch. of Educn, 1985–93; Pro-Vice-Chancellor, 1987–92. Mem., IBA, subseq. ITC, 1987–94. Mem., Trng and Employment Agency, 1993–. FRSA. *Publications:* contribs to: Education in Great Britain and Ireland, 1973; Educational Research and Development in Great Britain, 1982; Willingly to School, 1987; articles in learned jls. *Recreations:* golf, music. *Address:* Provost's Office, Legal, Social and Educational Sciences, Queen's University of Belfast, BT7 1NN. *T:* Belfast (01232) 245133.

FULTON, Robert Andrew; HM Diplomatic Service; Counsellor, Washington, since 1995; *b* 6 Feb. 1944; *s* of late Rev. Robert M. Fulton and of Janet W. Fulton (*née* Mackenzie); *m* 1970, Patricia Mary Crowley; two *s* one *d*. *Educ:* Rothesay Academy; Glasgow University (MA, LLB). Foreign and Commonwealth Office, 1968; Third later Second Secretary, Saigon, 1969; FCO, 1972; First Sec., Rome, 1973; FCO, 1977; First Sec., E Berlin, 1978; FCO, 1981; Counsellor, Oslo, 1984; FCO, 1987; UK Mission to UN, NY, 1989; FCO, 1992. *Recreations:* golf, racing, reading, cinema. *Address:* c/o Foreign and Commonwealth Office, SW1A 2AH. *Club:* University (Washington).

FUNG, Hon. Sir Kenneth Ping-Fan, Kt 1971; CBE 1965 (OBE 1958); JP; Chairman: Fung Ping Fan & Co. Ltd; Fung Ping Fan (China) Ltd; Fung Ping Fan Holdings (China) Ltd; Fung Ping Fan Holdings (International) Ltd; Director, The Bank of East Asia Ltd, Hong Kong, since 1947 (Chief Manager, 1963–69); Senior Consultant for External Economy, Chongqing, Sichuan Province, China, since 1985; *b* 28 May 1911; *yr s* of late Fung Ping Shan, JP; *m* 1933, Ivy (*née* Kan) Shiu-Han, OBE, JP, *d* of late Kan Tong-Po, JP; four *s* one *d*. *Educ:* Government Vernacular Sch.; Sch. of Chinese Studies, Univ. of Hong Kong. Unofficial Mem., Urban Council, 1951–60; Unofficial MLC, 1959–65, MEC, 1962–72. Hon. Chm., Sui Fung Consultants Ltd; Hon. Dir, Beijing Municipal Develt Centre of Sci. and Technol. of Agric., Forestry and Animal Husbandry. Pres., Chm., Mem. etc of numerous social organisations, both present and past, including: Pres., WWF, Hong Kong; Chm., Hong Kong Nat. Cttee, United World Colleges; Member: HK Br., CPA; Bd of Trustees, Duke of Edinburgh Award; Rotary Internat. (Paul Harris Fellow; 50-Year Membership Award, 1985); Internat. Council, Asia Soc., NY; Overseer Emer., Univ. of Calif. Hosp. Med. Sch., San Francisco. Comr St John Ambulance Bde (first Chinese to serve), 1953–58; first Chinese Hon. ADC to 4 successive Governors and Officers Admin. Govt (rep. StJAB). Life Mem. Court, Univ. of Hong Kong; formerly Mem. Council, Chinese Univ. of Hong Kong. JP Hong Kong, 1952; KStJ 1958. Hon. degrees: LLD, Chinese Univ. of Hong Kong, 1968; DSocSc, Univ. of Hong Kong, 1969. Founder Mem., Royal Asiatic Soc.; Mem. other Socs and Assocs. Silver Acorn, Commonwealth Scout Council (UK), 1976; Gold Dragon, Scout Assoc. of Hong Kong, 1985. Order of the Sacred Treasure, II Class (Japan), 1985; Knight Grand Officer, 1984 (Knight Commander, 1979), Internat. Order of St Hubert (Austria). *Recreations:* racing, golf, swimming. *Address:* (home) 14 South Bay Road, Hong Kong. *T:* 8122514; (office) Fung Ping Fan & Co. Ltd, Fung House, 2/F 20 Connaught Road C., Hong Kong. *T:* 220311. *Clubs:* Oriental; Hong Kong, Royal Hongkong Jockey (Hon. Steward), Royal Hongkong Golf, Royal Hongkong Yacht, Hongkong Country, Shek O Country, Hongkong Squash (Life Mem.), Chinese Recreation (Hon. Pres.), American, Rotary (Hong Kong); Knickerbocker, Sky, Explorers' (New York); Bohemian (San Francisco); Tokyo, Hodogaya Country (Japan).

FUNNELL, Christina Mary; Director, National Eczema Society, since 1987; Chief Executive, National Eczema Society Skin Care Campaign, since 1995; *b* 24 Aug. 1947; *d* of Joanna Christina Beaumont (*née* Lenes) and Norman Beaumont; *m* 1970 (marr. diss. 1994); one *s* one *d*. *Educ:* Hull Univ. (BA Spec. Hons Soc. Admin. 1968). W Riding CC Social Services, 1964; Methodist Assoc. of Youth Clubs, 1965–68; London Council of Social Service, 1971; Herts CC Youth Service, 1973; Nat. Eczema Soc., 1982–. *Publication:* (contrib.) Clinical and Experimental Dermatology, 1993. *Address:* National Eczema Society, 163 Eversholt Street, NW1 1BU. *T:* 0171–388 5655. *Club:* New Cavendish.

FURBER, (Frank) Robert; retired solicitor; *b* 28 March 1921; *s* of late Percy John Furber and Edith Furber; *m* 1948, Anne Wilson McArthur; three *s* one *d*. *Educ:* Willaston Sch.; Berkhamsted Sch.; University College London. LLB. Articled with Slaughter and May; solicitor 1945; Partner, Clifford-Turner, 1952–86. Mem., Planning Law Cttee, Law Society, 1964–69. Chairman: Blackheath Soc., 1968–89; Blackheath Preservation Trust, 1972–; Film Industry Defence Organization, 1968–89; Governor: Yehudi Menuhin Sch., 1964–91; Live Music Now!, 1977–87; Berkhamsted Sch., and Berkhamsted Sch. for Girls, 1976–91 (Chm., 1986–91); Board Member: Trinity Coll. of Music, 1974–91; Nat. Jazz Centre, 1982–87; Common Law Inst. of Intellectual Property, 1982–87; Chm., Rules of Golf Cttee, Royal and Ancient Golf Club, 1976–80; Trustee, Robert T. Jones Meml Trust, 1982–86; Mem. and Hon. Sec., R & A Golf Amateurism Commn of Inquiry, 1984–85; Mem., CCPR Cttee of Enquiry into Amateurism in Sport, 1986–88. Hon. Fellow, Trinity College, London. *Recreations:* golf, music, books, writing a history of The Moles Golfing Society. *Address:* 8 Pond Road, Blackheath, SE3 9JL. *T:* 0181–852 8065. *Clubs:* Buck's; Royal Blackheath Golf, Royal St George's Golf, Royal and Ancient, Honourable Company of Edinburgh Golfers; Pine Valley (USA).

See also Ven. R. S. Brown, S. A. Coakley, R. J. Furber.

FURBER, (Robert) John; QC 1995; *b* 13 Oct. 1949; *s* of Frank Robert Furber, *qv*, and Anne Wilson Furber (*née* McArthur); *m* 1977, Amanda Cherry Burgoyne Varney; one *s* two *d*. *Educ:* Westminster Sch.; Gonville and Caius Coll., Cambridge (MA). Called to the Bar, Inner Temple, 1973. *Publications:* (ed jtly) Halsbury's Laws of England: Landlord and Tenant, 4th edn 1981; (ed jtly) Hill and Redman's Law of Landlord and Tenant, 17th edn 1982, 18th edn 1995. *Address:* 1 Bream's Buildings, EC4A 1AQ. *T:* 0171–353 5835; 52 Southbrook Road, Lee, SE12 8LL. *T:* 0181–852 5770. *Clubs:* Buck's, Beefsteak.

FURLONG, Mrs Monica; writer; *b* 17 Jan. 1930; *d* of Alfred Gordon Furlong and Freda Simpson; *m* 1953, William John Knights (marr. diss. 1977); one *s* one *d*. *Educ:* Harrow County Girls' Sch.; University College London. Truth, Spectator, Guardian, 1956–61; Daily Mail, 1961–68; Producer, BBC, 1974–78. Moderator, Movement for the Ordination of Women, 1982–85. Hon. DD Gen. Theol Seminary, NY, 1986. *Publications:* Travelling In, 1971; Contemplating Now, 1971; God's A Good Man (poems), 1974; Puritan's Progress, 1975; Christian Uncertainties, 1975; The Cat's Eye (novel), 1976; Merton (biography), 1980; Cousins (novel), 1983; (ed) Feminine in the Church, 1984; Genuine Fake: a biography of Alan Watts, 1986; Thérèse of Lisieux (biog.), 1987; Wise Child (novel), 1987; (ed) Mirror to the Church, 1988; A Year and a Day (novel), 1990, A Dangerous Delight, 1991; Bird of Paradise (memoir), 1995. *Address:* c/o Anthony Sheil Associates, 43 Doughty Street, WC1N 2LF. *T:* 0171–405 9351. *Club:* Society of Authors.

FURLONG, Hon. Robert Stafford, MBE (mil.) 1945; Chief Justice of Newfoundland, 1959–79; *b* 9 Dec. 1904; *o s* of Martin Williams Furlong, KC, and Mary Furlong (*née* McGrath). *Educ:* St Bonaventure's Coll., St John's, Newfoundland. Called to the Bar, 1926, appointed KC 1944. Temp. Actg Lt-Comdr (S) RNVR. OStJ 1937; Knight of St Gregory 1958. *Recreations:* golf and motoring. *Address:* 8 Winter Avenue, St John's, Newfoundland, Canada. *T:* (709) 7267228. *Clubs:* Bally Haly Golf and Country, Crow's Nest (St John's).

FURLONG, Ronald (John), FRCS; Hon. Consulting Orthopædic Surgeon: St Thomas' Hospital; King Edward VII Hospital for Officers; Queen Victoria Hospital, East Grinstead; and lately to the Army; *s* of Frank Owen Furlong and Elsie Muriel Taffs, Woolwich; *m* 1970, Eileen Mary Watford. *Educ:* Eltham Coll.; St Thomas's Hosp. MB, BS London 1931; MRCS, LRCP, 1931; FRCS 1934. Served with Royal Army Medical Corps, 1941–46. Home Commands, North Africa and Italy; Brigadier, Consulting Orthopædic Surgeon to the Army, 1946, Hon. Consulting Orthopædic Surgeon 1951; Orthopædic Surgeon, St Thomas' Hosp., 1946. Established Furlong Research Foundn, 1989. *Publications:* Injuries of the Hand, 1957; (trans.) Pauwel's Atlas of the Biomechanics of the Normal and Diseased Hip, 1978; (trans.) Pauwel's Biomechanics of the Locomotor Apparatus, 1980; (trans.) W. Braun, O. Fischer, On the Centre of Gravity of the Human Body, 1986; contrib. Jl of Bone and Joint Surgery. *Recreations:* reading, history, archæology. *Address:* Lister House, 11–12 Wimpole Street, W1N 7AB. *T:* 0171–637 1844. *Club:* Athenæum.

FURLONGER, Robert William, CB 1981; retired public servant, Australia; *b* 29 April 1921; *s* of George William Furlonger and Germaine Rose Furlonger; *m* 1944, Verna Hope Lewis; three *s* one *d*. *Educ:* Sydney High Sch.; Sydney Univ. (BA). Served War, AMF, 1941–45. Australian Dept of External (later Foreign) Affairs, 1945–69 and 1972–77 (IDC, 1960; Dir, Jt Intell. Org., Dept of Def., 1969–72); appointments included: High Comr, Nigeria, 1961; Aust. Perm. Rep. to the European Office of the UN, 1961–64; Minister, Aust. Embassy, Washington, 1965–69; Ambassador to Indonesia, 1972–74, and to Austria, Hungary and Czechoslovakia, 1975–77; Dir-Gen., Office of National Assessments, Canberra, 1977–81. *Recreations:* golf, cricket, music. *Address:* PO Box 548, Belconnen, ACT 2616, Australia. *T:* (6) 2531384. *Clubs:* Canberra; Royal Canberra Golf.

FURMSTON, Bentley Edwin, FRICS; Director of Overseas Surveys, Ordnance Survey, 1984–89; *b* 7 Oct. 1931; *s* of Rev. Edward Bentley Furmston and Mary Furmston (*née* Bennett); *m* 1957, Margaret (*née* Jackson); two *s* one *d*. *Educ:* The Nelson Sch., Wigton, Cumbria; Victoria Univ., Manchester (BSc Mathematics). Entered Civil Service as Surveyor, Directorate of Overseas Surveys, 1953, with service in Gambia, Swaziland, Basutoland, N Rhodesia; Sen. Surveyor, N Rhodesia, 1960; Sen. Computer, DOS, 1963; seconded to Govt of Malawi as Dep. Commissioner of Surveys, 1965; Principal Survey Officer, DOS, 1968: Overseas Supervisor, Sch. of Military Survey; Regional Survey Officer, W Africa; Asst Director (Survey), 1971; Asst Dir (Cartography), Ordnance Survey, 1973; Dep. Dir, Field Survey, Ordnance Survey, 1974; Dep. Dir (Survey), DOS, 1977; Dir, Overseas Surveys and Survey Advr, Min. of Overseas Develt, 1980. *Publications:* contribs to technical jls. *Recreations:* reading, gardening, hill walking, climbing. *Address:* The Orchards, Carter's Clay Road, Newtown, Romsey, Hants SO51 0GL.

FURMSTON, Prof. Michael Philip, TD 1966; Professor of Law, University of Bristol, since 1978; *b* 1 May 1933; *s* of Joseph Philip Furmston and Phyllis (*née* Clowes); *m* 1964, Ashley Sandra Maria Cope; three *s* seven *d*. *Educ:* Wellington Sch., Somerset; Exeter Coll., Oxford (BA 1st Cl. Hons Jurisprudence, 1956; BCL 1st Cl. Hons 1957; MA 1960). LLM Birmingham, 1962. Called to the Bar, Gray's Inn, 1960 (1st Cl. Hons), Bencher, 1989. National Service, RA, 1951–53 (2nd Lieut); Major, TA, 1966–78, TAVR. Lecturer: Univ. of Birmingham, 1957–62; QUB, 1962–63; Fellow, Lincoln Coll., Oxford, 1964–78 (Sen. Dean, 1967–68; Sen. Tutor and Tutor for Admissions, 1969–74); Univ. Lectr in Law, 1964–78, Curator, University Chest, 1976–78, Oxford; Lectr in Common Law, Council of Legal Educn, 1965–78; Dean, Faculty of Law, 1980–84, Pro-Vice-Chancellor, 1986–89, Univ. of Bristol. Visiting Professor: City Univ., 1978–82; Katholieke Universiteit, Leuven, 1980, 1986 and 1992; Nat. Univ. of Singapore, 1987. Liveryman, Arbitrators' Co. Jt Editor, Construction Law Reports, 1985–. *Publications:* (ed) Cheshire, Fifoot and Furmston's Law of Contract, 8th edn 1972, to 12th edn 1991; Contractors Guide to ICE Conditions of Contract, 1980; Misrepresentation and Fraud, in Halsbury's Law of England, 1980; Croner's Buying and Selling Law, 1982; (ed jtly) The Effect on English Domestic Law of Membership of the European Communities and Ratification of the European Convention on Human Rights, 1983; (jtly) A Building Contract Casebook, 1984, 2nd edn 1990; (jtly) Cases and Materials on Contract, 1985, 3rd edn 1995; (ed) The Law of Tort: policies and trends in liability for damage to property, 1986; (ed) You and the Law, 1987; Croner's Model Business Contracts, 1988; (jtly) 'A' Level Law, 1988, 2nd edn 1992; Sale and Supply of Goods, 1994. *Recreations:* chess (Member, English team, Postal Olympiads), watching cricket, collecting Austin A35s, dogs. *Address:* The Old Post Office, Shipham, Winscombe, Avon BS25 1TQ. *T:* Winscombe (0193484) 2253; Faculty of Law, University of Bristol, Wills Memorial Building, Queen's Road, Bristol BS8 1RJ. *T:* Bristol (0117) 928 9000, 928 7441. *Clubs:* Reform, Naval and Military.

FURNELL, Very Rev. Raymond; Dean of York, since 1994; *b* 18 May 1935; *s* of Albert George Edward and Hetty Violet Jane Furnell; *m* 1967, Sherril Witcomb; one *s* three *d*. *Educ:* Hinchley Wood School, Surrey; Brasted Place Theological Coll.; Lincoln Theol Coll. Thomas Meadows & Co. Ltd, 1951; RAF, 1953; Lummus Co. Ltd, 1955; Geo. Wimpey & Co. Ltd, 1960; Brasted Place, 1961; Lincoln Theol Coll., 1963; Curate, St Luke's, Cannock, 1965; Vicar, St James the Great, Clayton, 1969; Rector, Hanley Team Ministry and RD, Stoke North, 1975–81; Provost, St Edmundsbury, 1981–94. Member: Gen. Synod of C of E, 1988–; Archbishops' Commn on Cathedrals, 1992–; Chair, Assoc. of English Cathedrals, 1994. *Recreations:* music, drama. *Address:* The Deanery, York YO1 2JD. *T:* York (01904) 623608.

FURNER, Air Vice-Marshal Derek Jack, CBE 1973 (OBE 1963); DFC 1943; AFC 1954; *b* 14 Nov. 1921; *s* of Vivian J. Furner; *m* 1948, Patricia Donnelly; three *s*. *Educ:* Westcliff High Sch., Essex. Joined RAF, 1941; commnd as navigator, 1942; Bomber Comd (2 tours), 1942–44; Transport Comd, Far East, 1945–47; Navigation Instructor, 1948–50; trials flying, Boscombe Down, 1951–53 and Wright-Patterson, Ohio, 1953–56; Air Min., 1957; OC Ops Wing, RAF Waddington, 1958–60; Planning Staff, HQ Bomber Comd, 1961–63 and SHAPE, Paris, 1964–65; Dep. Dir Manning, MoD (Air), 1966–67; OC RAF Scampton, 1968; AOC Central Reconnaissance Estab., 1969–70; Sec., Internat. Mil. Staff, NATO, Brussels, 1970–73; Asst Air Secretary, 1973–75. Gen. Manager, 1976–81, Dir, 1977–81, Harlequin Wallcoverings. FIPD (FIPM 1975); FIMgt (FBIM 1975). Mem., Mensa, 1989. *Recreations:* mathematical problems, music, computing, assisting number of local charities. *Address:* 1D South Cliff Tower, Bolsover Road, Eastbourne, E Sussex BN20 7JN. *T:* Eastbourne (01323) 733447. *Club:* Royal Air Force.

FURNESS, Alan Edwin, CMG 1991; HM Diplomatic Service; Ambassador to Senegal and, concurrently, to Cape Verde, Guinea, Guinea Bissau and Mali, since 1993; *b* 6 June 1937; *s* of late Edwin Furness and Marion Furness (*née* Senton); *m* 1971, Aline Elizabeth Janine Barrett; two *s*. *Educ:* Eltham Coll.; Jesus Coll., Cambridge (BA, MA). Commonwealth Relations Office, 1961; Private Sec. to Parliamentary Under-Secretary of State, 1961–62; Third, later Second Secretary, British High Commn, New Delhi, 1962–66; First Secretary, DSAO (later FCO), 1966–69; First Sec., UK Delegn to European Communities, Brussels, 1969–72; First Sec. and Head of Chancery, Dakar, 1972–75; First Sec., FCO, 1975–78; Counsellor and Head of Chancery, Jakarta, 1978–81; Counsellor and Head of Chancery, Warsaw, 1982–85; Head of S Pacific Dept., FCO, 1985–88; Dep. High Comr, Bombay, 1989–93. *Recreations:* music, literature, gardening. *Address:* c/o Foreign and Commonwealth Office, SW1A 2AH. *Club:* United Oxford & Cambridge University.

FURNESS, Robin; *see* Furness, Sir S. R.

FURNESS, Col Simon John; Vice Lord-Lieutenant of Berwickshire, since 1990; *b* 18 Aug. 1936; 2nd *s* of Sir Christopher Furness, 2nd Bt and Violet Flower Chipchase Furness, OBE (*d* 1988), *d* of Lieut-Col G. C. Roberts, Hollingside, Durham. *Educ:* Charterhouse; RMA Sandhurst; Royal Naval Staff College. Commissioned 2nd Lieut Durham Light Infantry, 1956; served Far East, UK, Germany; active service, Borneo and NI; Comd 5th Bn LI, 1976–78, retired 1978. Dep. Col (Durham), LI, 1989–93. Mem. Exec., Nat. Trust for Scotland. DL Berwickshire, 1984. *Recreations:* gardening, country sports, fine arts. *Address:* The Garden House, Netherbyres, Eyemouth, Berwickshire TD14 5SE. *T:* Eyemouth (018907) 50337. *Clubs:* Army and Navy; Durham County.

FURNESS, Sir Stephen (Roberts), 3rd Bt *cr* 1913; farmer and sporting/landscape artist (as Robin Furness); *b* 10 Oct. 1933; *e s* of Sir Christopher Furness, 2nd Bt, and Flower, Lady Furness, OBE (*d* 1988). *d* of late Col G. C. Roberts; *S* father, 1974; *m* 1961, Mary, *e d* of J. F. Cann, Cullompton, Devon; one *s* one *d*. *Educ:* Charterhouse. Entered RN, 1952; Observer, Fleet Air Arm, 1957; retired list, 1962. NCA, Newton Rigg Farm Inst., 1964. Member: Armed Forces Art Soc.; Darlington Art Soc. *Recreations:* looking at paintings, foxhunting, racing. *Heir:* *s* Michael Fitzroy Roberts Furness, *b* 12 Oct. 1962. *Address:* Otterington Hall, Northallerton, Yorks DL7 9HW. *T:* Northallerton (01609) 772061.

See also S. J. Furness.

FURNISS, Air Vice-Marshal Peter, DFC 1944; TD 1964; Director of Legal Services, RAF, 1978–82; *b* 16 July 1919; *s* of John and Mary Furniss; *m* 1954, Denise Cotet; one *s* two *d*. *Educ:* Sedbergh School. Commissioned 1st Bn The Liverpool Scottish TA, Queen's Own Cameron Highlanders, 1939; seconded to RAF, 1942; Comd No 73 Fighter Sqdn, 1945–46; demobilised 1946; admitted as Solicitor, 1948; commissioned in Legal Branch, RAF, 1950; Director of Legal Services: HQ Air Forces Middle East, Aden, 1961–63; HQ Far East Air Force, Singapore, 1969–71; HQ RAF Germany, 1973–74; Dep. Dir of Legal Services (RAF), 1975–78. *Recreations:* shooting, gardening, fishing. *Address:* 18 Sevington Park, Loose, Maidstone, Kent ME15 9SB. *T:* Maidstone (01622) 744620. *Club:* Royal Air Force.

FURNIVAL JONES, Sir (Edward) Martin, Kt 1967; CBE 1957; *b* 7 May 1912; *s* of Edward Furnival Jones, FCA; *m* 1955, Elizabeth Margaret, *d* of Bartholomew Snowball, BSc, AMIEE; one *d*. *Educ:* Highgate Sch.; Gonville and Caius Coll., Cambridge (exhibitioner). MA 1938. Admitted a Solicitor, 1937. Served War of 1939–45: General Staff Officer at Supreme Headquarters, Allied Expeditionary Force, and War Office (despatches, American Bronze Star Medal). Chm. of Bd, Frensham Heights, 1973–76 (Pres. 1977). *Recreation:* birdwatching.

FURNIVALL, Barony *cr* 1295; in abeyance. *Co-heiresses:* Hon. Rosamond Mary Dent (Sister Ancilla, OSB); *b* 3 June 1933; Hon. Patricia Mary Dent [*b* 4 April 1935; *m* 1st, 1956, Captain Thomas Hornsby (marr. diss., 1963; he *d* 1967); one *s* one *d*; 2nd, 1970, Roger Thomas John Bence; one *s* one *d*].

FURSDON, Maj.-Gen. Francis William Edward, CB 1980; MBE 1958; KStJ 1980; defence consultant and correspondent; Correspondent, Army Quarterly & Defence Journal, since 1985; Contributing Editor Europe, Asia-Pacific Defence Reporter, since 1989; *b* 10 May 1925; *s* of late G. E. S. Fursdon and Mrs Fursdon; *m* 1950, Joan Rosemary (*née* Worssam); one *s* one *d*. *Educ:* Westminster Sch. MLitt (Aberdeen) 1978; DLitt (Leiden) 1979. Passed AMIMechE; FIMgt. Enlisted RE, 1942; RE Course, Birmingham Univ., 1943; in ranks until commnd, 1945; 1945–67: Royal W Afr. Frontier Force, India, Burma and Gold Coast; Student RMCS; staff and regtl duty, UK, Singapore, Canal Zone and Cyprus; Staff Coll.; DAA&QMG 19 Inf. Bde, UK and Port Said; GSO2 RE Sch. of Inf.; JSSC; OC 34 Indep. Fd Sqdn, E Africa and Kuwait; Instr, Staff Coll., Camberley; 2 i/c 38 Engr Regt; Admin. Staff Coll., Henley; CO 25 Engr Regt, BAOR, 1967–69; AA&QMG HQ Land Forces, Gulf, 1970–71; Dep. Comd and COS Land Forces, Gulf, 1971; Col Q (Qtg) HQ BAOR, 1972–73; Service Fellow, Aberdeen Univ., 1974; Dir of Def. Policy (Europe and NATO), MoD, 1974–77; Dir, Military Assistance Office, MoD, 1977–80; Mil. Adv. to Governor of Rhodesia, and later Senior British Officer, Zimbabwe, 1980, retired 1980. Dir of Ceremonies, Order of St John, 1980–94. Defence and Military Correspondent, The Daily Telegraph, 1980–86; Naval Correspondent, Navy Internat., 1991–94. Freeman, City of London, 1987. *Publications:* Grains of Sand, 1971; There are no Frontiers, 1973; The European Defence Community: a History, 1980; Falklands Aftermath: picking up the pieces, 1988. *Recreations:* photography (IAC Internat. Award, 1967), gardening, travel. *Address:* c/o St John House, 50 Eaton Place, SW1 8AP.

FURST, Stephen Andrew; QC 1991; an Assistant Recorder, since 1993; *b* 8 Feb. 1951; *s* of Herbert and Viviane Furst; *m* 1979, Bridget Collins; one *s* one *d*. *Educ:* Edinburgh Academy; St Edmund Hall, Oxford (BA Hons); Leeds Univ. (LLB Hons). Called to the Bar, Middle Temple, 1975. Joint Editor, Construction Law Yearbook. *Address:* Keating Chambers, 10 Essex Street, WC2A 3AA. *T:* 0171–240 6981.

FUSSEY, Dr David Eric; Vice-Chancellor, University of Greenwich, since 1993; *b* 5 Sept. 1943; *s* of Frank Eric Fussey and Edna May Rowntree; *m* 1966, Beryl Kathleen Taylor; two *s*. *Educ:* Hymers College, Hull; Corpus Christi Coll., Cambridge (MA Mech. Scis); Univ. of Warwick (PhD Eng. Sci.). CEng, FIMechE; FInstE; ARCM. Research Officer, CEGB Marchwood Engrg Labs, 1964–69; Lectr in Mech. Eng, Univ. of Nottingham, 1969–78; Prof. and Head of Mech. Eng, Univ. of Technology, PNG, 1978–82; Prof. and Head of Mech. Eng, then Dean of Technology, Plymouth Poly., 1982–89; Dep. Dir, Coventry Poly., later Univ., 1989–93. Former appts with IMechE, CNAA and other professional orgns; Engineering Council: Mem. Council, 1990–; Chm., Standing Cttee for Engrg Profession, 1994–; Science and Engineering Research Council: Mem., Engrg and Technol. Bd, 1992–94; Chm., Educn and Trng Cttee, 1992–94; Mem., Jt Inf. Systems Cttee, 1993–. *Publications:* papers in magnetohydrodynamics, heat transfer, combustion and combustion-generated pollution. *Recreations:* choral and keyboard music, walking. *Address:* Southwood House, Avery Hill Road, Eltham, SE9 2HB. *T:* 0181–331 8880.

FYFE, George Lennox; Chief Executive, Midlands Co-operative Society, since 1995 (Leicestershire Co-operative Society, 1975–95); Chairman, Co-operative Wholesale Society Ltd, since 1989; *b* 10 April 1941; *s* of George L. and Elizabeth S. Fyfe; *m* 1965, Ann Clark Asquith; one *s* one *d*. *Educ:* Alloa Acad.; Co-operative Coll., Loughborough. Gen. Manager, Kirriemuir Co-operative Soc., 1966–68; Regl Manager, Scottish Co-operative Soc., 1968–72; Gp Gen. Manager, CWS, 1972–75. Director: Shoefayre Ltd, 1981– (Chm., 1984–); CWS, 1981– (Vice-Chm., 1986–89); Co-operative Insce Soc. Ltd, 1982–; Central TV-East, 1983–92; Co-operative Bank plc, 1986–. Mem., E Midlands Econ. Planning Council, 1976–79. JP Perthshire, 1972–75. *Recreations:* history, reading, music, classic cars. *Address:* Rooftops, 1 Meadowhill, Great Glen, Leics LE8 0FX.

FYFE, Maria; MP (Lab) Glasgow, Maryhill, since 1987; *b* 25 Nov. 1938; *d* of James O'Neill and Margaret Lacey; *m* 1964, James Joseph Fyfe (decd); two *s*. *Educ:* Strathclyde Univ. (BA Hons. Economic History 1975). Scottish Gas Board, 1959–64; Senior Lecturer, Central College of Commerce, Glasgow Trade Union Studies Unit, 1978–87. Mem., Labour Party, 1960–, Scottish Exec., 1981–88 (Chair, Local Govt Sub-Cttee, 1985–87); Mem., Glasgow District Council, 1980–87 (Vice-Convener, Finance Cttee, 1980–84; Convener, Personnel Cttee, 1984–87). Dep. Shadow Minister for Women, 1988–91; Convener, Scottish Gp of Labour MPs, 1991–92; Scottish front bench spokesperson, 1992–. *Address:* (office) House of Commons, SW1A 0AA. *T:* 0171–219 4430; 1508 Maryhill Road, Glasgow G20 9AB. *T:* 0141–945 1495.

FYFE, Prof. William Sefton, CC (Canada) 1989; FRS 1969; Professor of Geology, University of Western Ontario, since 1972 (Dean of Science, 1986–90); *b* 4 June 1927; *s* of Colin and Isabella Fyfe; *m* 1968; two *s* one *d*. *Educ:* Otago Univ., New Zealand. BSc 1948, MSc 1949, PhD 1952; FRSC 1980. Univ. of California, Berkeley: Lecturer in Chemistry, 1952, Reader, 1958; Prof. of Geology, 1959; Royal Soc. Res. Prof. (Geochemistry), Univ. of Manchester, 1967–72. Guggenheim Fellow, 1983. Pres., IUGS, 1992–. Hon. Fellow, Geological Soc. Amer.; Corresponding Member: Brazilian Acad. of Science; Russian Acad. of Scis; Indian Acad. of Scis. Hon. DSc: Meml Univ. of Newfoundland, 1989; Lisbon, 1990; Lakehead, 1990; Guelph, 1991; Otago, 1995. Mineralogical Soc. of Amer. Award, 1964; Logan Medal, Geolog. Assoc. of Canada, 1982; Willet G. Miller Medal, Royal Soc. of Canada, 1985; Arthur Holmes Medal, European Union of Geoscientists, 1989; Day Medal, Geol Soc. of America, 1990; Canada Gold Medal for Science and Engineering, 1992. Commemoration Medal, New Zealand, 1990, Canada, 1992. *Publications:* Metamorphic Reactions and Metamorphic Facies, 1958; The

Geochemistry of Solids, 1964; Fluids in the Earth's Crust, 1978; also numerous scientific papers. *Address:* Department of Earth Sciences, University of Western Ontario, London, Ontario N6A 5B7, Canada.

FYFE, William Stevenson, CBE 1992 (OBE 1987); FIIM; Chairman, Greater Glasgow Health Board, 1993; *b* Glasgow, 10 June 1935; *s* of Dr Andrew Fyfe and Janet Isabella Fyfe (*née* Soutar), New Cumnock; *m* 1986, Margaret H. H. Auld; one *s* one *d*. *Educ:* Dollar Acad.; Scottish Coll. of Commerce. FIIM 1985. Town Councillor (C), Prestwick, 1963–73; Co. Councillor (C), Ayrshire, 1970–73; Ayrshire and Arran Health Board: Financial Convener, 1973–81; Chm., 1981–93. Chm., Scottish Health Services Adv. Council, 1989–93; Mem., General Whitley Council, 1989–93. *Recreation:* golf. *Address:* Ford House, Pennyglen, by Maybole, Ayrshire KA19 8JW.

FYJIS-WALKER, Richard Alwyne, CMG 1980; CVO 1976; HM Diplomatic Service, retired; Chairman, Commonwealth Institute, 1988–93; *b* 19 June 1927; *s* of Harold and Marion Fyjis-Walker; *m* 1st, 1951, Barbara Graham-Watson (marr. diss.); one *s*; 2nd, 1972, Gabrielle Josefi; one *s*. *Educ:* Bradfield Coll.; Magdalene Coll., Cambridge (BA). Army (KRRC), 1945–48. Joined Foreign (subseq. Diplomatic) Service, 1955; served: Amman, 1956; FO, 1957–61; Paris, 1961–63; Cairo, 1963–65; FCO, 1966–71; Counsellor, 1970; Ankara, 1971–74; Counsellor (Information), Washington, 1974–78; Counsellor, UK Mission to UN, NY, 1978–79; Ambassador to the Sudan, 1979–84; Ambassador to Pakistan, 1984–87. *Address:* 17 Stonefield Street, N1 0HW.

FYSH, Robert Michael; QC 1989; *b* 2 Aug. 1940; *s* of Dr Leslie Fysh and Margaret Fysh, Ashford, Kent; *m* 1971, Mary Bevan; three *s*. *Educ:* Downside Sch.; Exeter Coll., Oxford (MA). Called to the Bar, Inner Temple, 1965; NI, 1974; NSW, 1975; Ireland, 1975; India, 1982; Pakistan, 1987; SC Trinidad and Tobago Bar, 1990; SC Dublin, 1994. Chm., British Law Assoc. for Estonia, Latvia and Lithuania, 1991–. Editor: Reports of Patent Cases, 1975–; Fleet Street Reports, 1975–. *Publications:* Russell-Clarke on Registered Designs, 4th edn, 1974; The Industrial Property Citator, 1982; (ed) The Spycatcher Cases, 1989. *Recreations:* swimming, travel. *Address:* 8 New Square, Lincoln's Inn, WC2A 3QP. *T:* 0171–405 4321. *Clubs:* Royal Over-Seas League; Kildare Street and University (Dublin).

G

GABATHULER, Prof. Erwin, FRS 1990; FInstP; Sir James Chadwick Professor of Physics, Liverpool University, since 1991 (Professor of Experimental Physics, 1983–91); *b* 16 Nov. 1933; *s* of Hans and Lena Gabathuler; *m* 1962, Susan Dorothy Jones, USA; two *s* one *d*. *Educ:* Queen's University Belfast (BSc 1956; MSc 1957); Univ. of Glasgow (PhD 1961). Research Fellow, Cornell Univ., 1961–64; Group Leader, Research, SERC, Daresbury Lab., 1964–73; European Organisation for Nuclear Research: Vis. Scientist, EMC Experiment, 1974–77; Leader, Exp. Physics Div., 1978–80; Dir of Research, 1981–83; Hd of Physics Dept, Liverpool Univ., 1986–91. Chm., Particle Physics Cttee, SERC, 1985–88; Member: Nuclear Physics Bd, 1985–88; NATO Collaborative Research Grants Panels, 1990–93; Educn and Trng Cttee, PPARC, 1994–. Dr *hc* Univ. of Uppsala, 1982. Rutherford Medal, Inst. of Physics, 1992. *Publications:* articles in research jls. *Recreations:* music, ski-ing, walking. *Address:* 3 Danebank Road, Lymm, Cheshire WA13 9DQ. *T:* Lymm (01925) 752753.

GADD, (John) Staffan; Chairman: J. S. Gadd Cie SA, Geneva, since 1989; Saga Securities Ltd, since 1985; Swedish Chamber of Commerce for UK, since 1993; *b* 30 Sept. 1934; *s* of John Gadd and Ulla Olivecrona; *m* 1st, 1958, Margaretha Löfborg (marr. diss.); one *s* one *d*; 2nd, 1990, Kay McGreeghan. *Educ:* Stockholm Sch. of Econs. MBA. Sec., Confedn of Swedish Industries, 1958–61; Skandinaviska Banken, Stockholm, 1961–69 (London Rep., 1964–67); Dep. Man. Dir, Scandinavian Bank Ltd, London, 1969–71, Chief Exec. and Man. Dir, 1971–80; Chief Exec., 1980–84, Chm., 1982–84, Samuel Montagu & Co. Ltd; Chm., Montagu and Co. AB, Sweden, 1982–86; Dir, Guyerzeller Zurmont Bank AG, Switzerland, 1983–84. *Recreations:* shooting, ski-ing, the arts, walking, travel. *Address:* Locks Manor, Hurstpierpoint, West Sussex BN6 9JZ.

GADDES, (John) Gordon; Director General, BEAMA, Federation of British Electrotechnical and Allied Manufacturers' Associations (formerly British Electrical and Allied Manufacturers' Association), since 1982; *b* 22 May 1936; *s* of late James Graham Moscrop Gaddes and of Irene Gaddes (*née* Murray; who married E. O. Kine); *m* 1958, Pamela Jean (*née* Marchbank); one *s* one *d*. *Educ:* Carres Grammar Sch., Sleaford; Selwyn Coll., Cambridge (MA Hons Geography); London Univ. (BScEcon Hons). Joint Services Sch. of Languages, Russian Translator in RAF, 1955–57. Asst Lectr in Business Studies, Peterborough Technical Coll., 1960–64; Lectr in Business Studies, later Head of Business Studies, then Vice-Principal, Dacorum Coll. of Further Educn, Hemel Hempstead, 1964–69; Head of Export Services: British Standards Instn, 1969–72; Quality Assurance Dept, 1972–73; Dir, BSI Hemel Hempstead Centre, 1973–77; Commercial Dir, BSI, 1977–81; Dir, Information, Marketing and Resources, BSI, 1981–82. Secretary, BSI Quality Assurance Council, 1976–80; Member: Council, 1982–, President's Cttee, 1984–86, Production Cttee, 1984–88, CBI; NACCB, 1984–90 (Chm., Assessment Panel, 1985–90); Project Leader for ISO/UNESCO inf. network study, 1974–75; variously, consultant to UNIDO and EC; UK Rep., ORGALIME, 1982– (Chairman: Electrical and Electronic Inds Liaison Cttee, 1982–86; Finance and Admin Cttee, 1986–88; Exec. Cttee, 1988–90); Pres., CENELEC, 1989–91 (Dep. Pres., 1987–89, 1994–95); Chairman: Eur. Electrotechnical Sectoral Cttee for Testing and Certification, 1992–95; ASTA Certification Services, 1994–; UK Ex Forum, 1995–. Freeman, City of London, 1991; Liveryman, Glaziers' Co., 1993. *Recreations:* swimming, fell-walking. *Address:* Federation of British Electrotechnical and Allied Manufacturers' Associations, Leicester House, 8 Leicester Street, WC2H 7BN. *T:* 0171–437 0678. *Club:* Athenæum.

GADSBY, (Gordon) Neville, CB 1972; *b* 29 Jan. 1914; *s* of William George and Margaret Sarah Gadsby; *m* 1938, Jeanne (*née* Harris); two *s* one *d*. *Educ:* King Edward VI Sch., Stratford-upon-Avon; University of Birmingham. BSc 1935, DipEd 1937, Cadbury Prizeman 1937, Birmingham; FRSC, CChem. Princ. Lectr, RMCS, 1946–51; Supt, Army Operational Research Gp, 1951–55; Dep. Sci. Adviser to Army Coun., 1955–59; idc 1960; Dir of Army Operational Science and Research, 1961; Dir, Army Operational Res. Estab., 1961–64; Dir of Biol. and Chem. Defence, MoD, 1965–67; Dep. Chief Scientist (Army), MoD, 1967–68; Dir, Chemical Defence Estabt, Porton, Wilts, 1968–72; Minister, Defence R&D, British Embassy, Washington, 1972–75, retired. *Publications:* Lubrication, 1949; An Introduction to Plastics, 1950. *Recreations:* oil painting, photography. *Address:* Ruan House, Cliff Road, Sidmouth, Devon EX10 8JN. *T:* Sidmouth (01395) 577842.

GADSDEN, Sir Peter (Drury Haggerston), GBE 1979; Hon. AC 1988; MA; FEng; Lord Mayor of London for 1979–80; Company Director; *b* Canada, 28 June 1929; *er s* of late Basil Claude Gadsden, ACT, ThL, and late Mabel Florence Gadsden (*née* Drury); *m* 1955, Belinda Ann, *e d* of late Captain Sir (Hugh) Carnaby de Marie Haggerston, 11th Bt; four *d*. *Educ:* Rockport, Northern Ireland; The Elms, Colwall; Wrekin Coll., Wellington; Jesus Coll., Cambridge (MA; Hon. Fellow, 1988). 2nd Lieut King's Shropshire LI, attached Oxf. and Bucks LI and Durham LI, Germany, 1948–49. Man. Dir, London subsid. of Australian Mineral Sands Producer, 1964–70; Marketing Economist (Mineral Sands) to UN Industrial Development Organisation, 1969; pt-time Mem., Crown Agents for Oversea Govts and Admins, 1981–87. Dep. Chm., W. Canning plc, 1990– (Dir, 1989–); Director: City of London (Arizona) Corp., 1970–88 (Chm., 1985–88); Private Patients Plan Ltd (Chm., 1984–); Wm Jacks PLC, 1984–. Dir, Clothworkers' Foundn, 1978–; Hon. Mem. London Metal Exchange. President: Nat. Assoc. of Charcoal Manufacturers, 1970–86; City of London Rifle & Pistol Club (formerly Embankment Rifle Club), 1975–87; Leukaemia Res. Fund, City of London Br., 1975–86; Metropolitan Soc. for the Blind; Publicity Club of London, 1983–; Council, London World Trade Centre Assoc., 1980–92; St John Ambulance (Eastern Area), 1981–86 (Mem. Council, Shropshire Br.); British-Australasian Heritage Soc., 1986–; Australian British Chamber of Commerce, 1993–. Sheriff London, 1970–71; Common Councilman (Cripplegate Within and Without), 1969–71; Alderman, City of London (Ward of Farringdon Without), 1971–; HM Lieutenant, City of London, 1979–; Founder Master, Engineers' Co., 1983–85; Liveryman: Clothworkers' Co. (Master 1989–90); Plaisterers' Co. (Hon.), 1975–; Marketors Co. (Hon.), 1978–; Hon. Freeman, Actuaries' Co., 1981–; Master, Cripplegate Ward Club, 1982–83; Member: Guild of Freemen, 1963– (Master 1984–85; Hon. Asst, 1995); Company of World Traders (formerly Guild of World Traders in London), 1985– (Master, 1987–88); Royal Soc. of St George (City of London Br.), 1970–; Council, City Univ., 1985–86 (Chancellor, 1979–80); Council, Britain Australia Soc., 1978–92 (Chm., 1989–92; Vice Pres., 1992–); Bermuda Soc., 1987– (Founder Chm., 1987–89). Chairman: Britain Australia Bicentennial Cttee, 1984–88; UK Europe Br., Order of Australia Assoc., 1991–93. Hon. Freeman, Borough of Islwyn, S Wales, 1983. Vice-President: Sir Robert Menzies Meml Trust; Nuffield Nursing Homes Trust, 1984–; Commonwealth Trust, 1988–; Shropshire Soc. in London, 1986–89; Blackwood Little Theatre, 1986–; Governor, Hon. Irish Soc., 1984–87. Fellowship of Engrg Distinction Lectr, 1980; Wm Menelaus Meml Lectr, SW Inst. of Engrs, 1983; paper to MANTECH Symposium, 1983; Royal Instn Lectr, 1991. Trustee: St Bartholomew's and St Mark's Hosps, 1981–88; Britain–Australia Bicentennial Trust, 1986–; Britain–Australia Bicentennial Schooner Trust, 1986–92; Britain-Australia Soc. Educnl Trust, 1990–; Edward King Hse, Lincoln, 1988–; Nat. History Mus. Develt Trust, 1988–; Battle of Britain Meml Trust, 1990–93; Chm., Shropshire Regt Museum Appeal, 1991–; President: Ironbridge Gorge Museum Develt Trust, 1981–; Upper Severn Navigation Trust Ltd, 1992–; Shropshire Horticultural Soc., 1992–93; Life Pres., Freemen of City of London in Islwyn. Member: Management Council, Shakespeare Theatre Trust, 1979–86; Royal Commn for the 1851 Exhibn, 1986–; Chm. and Mem. Council, 1984–88, Vice-Pres., 1988–, Royal Commonwealth Soc.; Patron: Museum of Empire and Commonwealth Trust, 1986–; Guild of Rahere, 1986–; Magic Circle Foundn, 1995–. Chm. of Govs, The Elms, Colwall, 1993–. JP, City of London, 1971 (Inner London Area of Greater London, 1969–71). Hon. FCIM; FIMM 1979; CEng 1979, FEng 1980; Hon. Mem., Instn of Royal Engrs, 1986; Hon. FRSH 1992; Hon. FRCA 1994. Hon. Mem. Court, HAC; Hon. Col 5th (Shropshire and Hereford) Bn LI (Vol.), 1988–93. KStJ 1980 (OStJ 1977). Officier de l'Etoile Equatoriale de la République Gabonaise, 1970. Hon. DSc 1979. *Publications:* articles in: InstMM Transactions, 1971; RSM Jl, 1979; Textile Institute and Industry, 1980; articles on titanium, zirconium, and hafnium in Mining Jl Annual Reviews, 1969–86. *Recreations:* walking, photography, farming, forestry, fishing. *Address:* 606 Gilbert House, Barbican, EC2Y 8BD. *T:* 0171–638 9968. *Clubs:* City Livery (Mem. Council), United Wards, Farringdon Ward (patron), City of London (Hon.), Pilgrims, Light Infantry (Hon.); Royal London Yacht (Hon.).

GAFFNEY; *see* Burke-Gaffney.

GAFFNEY, James Anthony, CBE 1984; FEng; FICE; *b* Bargoed, Glam, 9 Aug. 1928; *s* of James Francis and Violet Mary Gaffney; *m* 1953, Margaret Mary, 2nd *d* of E. and G. J. Evans, Pontypridd; one *s* two *d*. *Educ:* De La Salle Coll.; St Illtyd's Coll., Cardiff; UWIST; UC, Cardiff (Fellow, 1984). BSc (Eng) London. FEng 1979; FICE 1968; FInstHE 1970. Highway Engr, Glam CC, 1948–60; Asst County Surveyor, Somerset CC, 1960–64; Deputy County Surveyor, Notts CC, 1964–69; County Engr and Surveyor, WR Yorks, 1969–74; Dir Engrg Services, W Yorks MCC, 1974–86. President: County Surveyors' Soc., 1977–78; Instn of Highway Engrs, 1978–79; ICE, 1983–84; Vice-Pres., Fellowship of Engrg, 1989–92. Hon. DSc: Wales, 1982; Bradford, 1984. *Recreations:* golf, travel, supporting Rugby. *Address:* Drovers Cottage, 3 Boston Road, Wetherby, W Yorks LS22 5HA. *Clubs:* Royal Automobile; Alwoodley Golf (Leeds).

GAGE, family name of **Viscount Gage.**

GAGE, 8th Viscount *cr* 1720 (Ire.); **Henry Nicholas Gage;** Bt 1622; Baron Gage (Ire.) 1720; Baron Gage (GB) 1790; *b* 9 April 1934; *yr s* of 6th Viscount Gage, KCVO and his 1st wife, Hon. Alexandra Imogen Clare Grenfell (*d* 1969), *yr d* of 1st Baron Desborough, KG, GCVO; *S* brother, 1993; *m* 1974, Lady Diana Adrienne Beatty; two *s*. *Educ:* Eton; Christ Church, Oxford. 2nd Lt Coldstream Guards, 1953. *Recreations:* shooting, riding. *Heir: s* Hon. Henry William Gage, *b* 25 June 1975. *Address:* Firle Place, Lewes, East Sussex BN8 6LP. *T:* Glynde (01273) 858535.

GAGE, Hon. Sir William (Marcus), Kt 1993; **Hon. Mr Justice Gage;** a Judge of the High Court of Justice, Queen's Bench Division, since 1993; *b* 22 April 1938; *s* of late His Honour Conolly Gage; *m* 1962, Penelope Mary Groves; three *s*. *Educ:* Repton; Sidney Sussex Coll., Cambridge. MA. National Service, Irish Guards, 1956–58. Called to the Bar, Inner Temple, 1963, Bencher, 1991; QC 1982; a Recorder, 1985–93. Chancellor, diocese of Coventry, 1980–, of Ely, 1989–. Mem., Criminal Injuries Compensation Bd, 1987–93. *Recreations:* shooting, fishing, travel. *Address:* Royal Courts of Justice, Strand, WC2A 2LL. *Club:* Beefsteak.

GAGGERO, Joseph James, CBE 1989; Chairman, Bland Group of Shipping, Aviation and Travel Companies; *b* 20 Nov. 1927; *s* of Sir George Gaggero, OBE, JP and Mabel Andrews-Speed; *m* 1st, 1958, Marilys Healing (marr. diss. 1987); one *s* one *d*; 2nd, 1994, Christina Russo. *Educ:* Downside Sch. Hon. Consul Gen. for Sweden in Gibraltar and Dir, Gibraltar Chamber of Commerce, 1951–56; Head, Gibraltar Govt Tourist Dept, 1955–59; served on or led other Gibraltar Govt Cttees and Gibraltar Trading Assocs, 1948–. Director: Credit Suisse (Gibraltar) Ltd; Hovertravel; Chairman: GB Airways; Gibraltar Airways; Pres., Rock Hotel. KHS. Order of the North Star (Sweden). *Recreations:* travel, painting. *Address:* Cloister Building, Gibraltar. *T:* 78456. *Clubs:* Travellers'; Royal Gibraltar Yacht.

GAHAGAN, Michael Barclay; Director, Cities and Countryside Policy (formerly Inner Cities) Directorate, Department of the Environment, since 1991; *b* 24 March 1943; *s* of Geoffrey and Doris Gahagan; *m* 1967, Anne Brown; two *s*. *Educ:* St Mary's Coll.,

Southampton; Univ. of Manchester (MA Econ, BA). ARICS. W. H. Robinson & Co., Chartered Surveyors, Manchester, 1964–66; DEA (NW), 1966–69; Min. of Housing and Local Govt (NW), 1969–71; DoE, Central Res. and Inner Cities Directorates, NW, SE and London Regl Offices, 1971–88; seconded to DTI Inner Cities Unit, 1988–91. *Recreations:* soccer, bridge, squash. *Address:* Department of the Environment, 2 Marsham Street, SW1P 3EB. *T:* 0171–276 4473.

GAINFORD, 3rd Baron *cr* 1917; **Joseph Edward Pease;** *b* 25 Dec. 1921; *s* of 2nd Baron Gainford, TD, and of Veronica Margaret, *d* of Sir George Noble, 2nd Bt; *S* father, 1971; *m* 1953, Margaret Theophila Radcliffe, *d* of late Henry Edmund Guise Tyndale; two *d.* *Educ:* Eton and Gordonstoun. FRGS; Member, Society of Surveying Technicians. RAFVR, 1941–46. Hunting Aerosurveys Ltd, 1947–49; Directorate of Colonial Surveys, 1951–53; Soil Mechanics Ltd, 1953–58; London County Council, 1958–65; Greater London Council, 1965–78. UK Delegate to UN, 1973. Mem., Coll. of Guardians, Nat. Shrine of Our Lady of Walsingham, 1979–. Mem., Plaisterers' Co., 1976. *Recreations:* golf, music, veteran and vintage aviation. *Heir: b* Hon. George Pease [*b* 20 April 1926; *m* 1958, Flora Daphne, *d* of late Dr N. A. Dyce Sharp; two *s* two *d*]. *Address:* 1 Dedmere Court, Marlow, Bucks SL7 1PL. *T:* Marlow (01628) 484679. *Clubs:* MCC, Pathfinder.

GAINHAM, Rachel, (Sarah Gainham), (Mrs Kenneth Ames), FRSL 1984; author; *b* 1 Oct. 1922; *d* of Tom Stainer and May Genevieve Gainham; *m* 1964, Kenneth Ames (*d* 1975). *Educ:* Newbury High Sch. for Girls; afterwards largely self educated. From 1947 onwards, travelled extensively in Central and E Europe; Central Europe Correspondent of The Spectator, 1956–66. *Publications:* Time Right Deadly, 1956; Cold Dark Night, 1957; The Mythmaker, 1957; Stone Roses, 1959; Silent Hostage, 1960; Night Falls on the City, 1967 (Book Soc. Choice and US Book of Month Club); A Place in the Country, 1968; Takeover Bid, 1970; Private Worlds, 1971; Maculan's Daughter, 1973; To the Opera Ball, 1975; The Habsburg Twilight, 1979; The Tiger, Life, 1983; contrib. to Encounter, Atlantic Monthly, BBC, etc. *Recreations:* theatre, opera, European history. *Address:* altes Forsthaus, Schlosspark, 2404 Petronell, Austria.

GAINSBOROUGH, 5th Earl of, (2nd) *cr* 1841; **Anthony Gerard Edward Noel,** Bt 1781; Baron Barham, 1805; Viscount Campden, Baron Noel, 1841; JP; *b* 24 Oct. 1923; *s* of 4th Earl and Alice Mary (*d* 1970), *e d* of Edward Eyre, Gloucester House, Park Lane, W1; *S* father 1927; *m* 1947, Mary, *er d* of late Hon. J. J. Stourton, TD and Mrs Kathleen Stourton; four *s* three *d.* *Educ:* Georgetown, Garrett Park, Maryland, USA. Chairman: Oakham RDC, 1952–67; Executive Council RDC's Association of England and Wales, 1963 (Vice-Chairman 1962, Pres., 1965); Pres., Assoc. of District Councils, 1974–80; Vice-Chm. Rutland CC, 1958–70, Chm., 1970–73; Chm., Rutland Dist Council, 1973–76. Chm., Bd of Management, Hosp. of St John and St Elizabeth, NW8, 1970–80. Mem. Court of Assistants, Worshipful Co. of Gardeners of London, 1960 (Upper Warden, 1966; Master, 1967). Hon. FICE (Hon. FIMunE 1969). JP Rutland, 1957, Leics 1974. Knight of Malta, 1948; Bailiff Grand Cross Order of Malta, 1958; Pres. Br. Assoc., SMO, Malta, 1968–74. KStJ 1970. *Recreations:* shooting, sailing. *Heir: s* Viscount Campden, *qv.* *Address:* Horn House, Exton Park, Oakham, Leics LE15 7QU. *T:* (office) Empingham (01780) 460772. *Clubs:* Brooks's, Pratt's; Royal Yacht Squadron (Cowes), Bembridge Sailing.

See also Earl of Liverpool, Hon. G. E. W. Noel.

GAINSBOROUGH, George Fotheringham, CBE 1973; PhD, FIEE; Barrister-at-law; Secretary, Institution of Electrical Engineers, 1962–80; Director, External Relations, International Electrotechnical Commission, Geneva, 1980–83; *b* 28 May 1915; *o s* of late Rev. William Anthony Gainsborough and of Alice Edith (*née* Fennell); *m* 1937, Gwendoline (*d* 1976), *e d* of John and Anne Berry; two *s.* *Educ:* Christ's Hospital; King's Coll., London; Gray's Inn. Scientific Staff, Nat. Physical Laboratory, 1938–46; Radio Physicist, British Commonwealth Scientific Office, Washington, DC, USA, 1944–45; Administrative Civil Service (Ministries of Supply and Aviation), 1946–62. Imperial Defence College, 1960. Secretary, Commonwealth Engineering Conf., 1962–69; Sec.-General, World Fedn of Engineering Organizations, 1968–76. *Publications:* papers in Proc. Instn of Electrical Engineers. *Address:* Moncorbon, 41360 Savigny-sur-Braye, France. *T:* 54239925. *Club:* Athenæum.

See also Michael Gainsborough.

GAINSBOROUGH, Michael; Assistant Secretary, Royal Hospital, Chelsea, since 1994; *b* 13 March 1938; *s* of George Fotheringham Gainsborough, *qv;* *m* 1962, Sally (*née* Hunter); one *s* two *d.* *Educ:* St Paul's Sch.; Trinity Coll., Oxford (MA). Air Ministry, 1959–64; Ministry of Defence, 1964–78, Defence Counsellor, UK Delegn to NATO, Brussels, FCO, 1978–81; Dir, Resources and Programmes (Strategic Systems), MoD, 1981–83; Asst Under-Sec. of State (Naval Staff), 1984, (Programmes), 1985–86, MoD; Center for Internat. Affairs, Harvard Univ., 1986–87; Asst Under-Sec. of State (Adjutant Gen.), 1987–91, (Service Personnel), 1992, MoD. Mem., Royal Patriotic Fund Corp., 1987–. *Recreations:* listening to music, gardening, walking. *Address:* Royal Hospital, Chelsea, SW3 4SL.

GAINSFORD, Sir Ian Derek, Kt 1995; FDSRCS; Dean of King's College School of Medicine and Dentistry, King's College London, since 1988; Vice-Principal, King's College London, since 1994; *b* 24 June 1930; *s* of late Rabbi Morris Ginsberg, MA, PhD, AKC, and Anne Freda; *m* 1957, Carmel Liebster; one *s* two *d.* *Educ:* Thames Valley Grammar Sch., Twickenham; King's Coll. and King's College Hosp. Med. Sch., London (BDS; FKC 1984); Toronto Univ., Canada (DDS Hons). Junior Staff, King's College Hosp., 1955–57; Member staff, Dept of Conservative Dentistry, London Hosp. Med. Sch., 1957–70; Sen. Lectr/Consultant, Dept of Conservative Dentistry, King's College Hosp., 1970–; Dep. Dean of Dental Studies, 1973–77; Dir of Clinical Dental Services, KCH, 1977–87 (Dean of Dental Studies, KCHMS, 1977–83); Dean, Faculty of Clinical Dentistry, KCL, 1983–87. President, British Soc. for Restorative Dentistry, 1973–74; Member: BDA, 1956– (Pres., Metropolitan Br., 1981–82); Internat. Dental Fedn, 1966–; American Dental Soc. of London, 1960– (Pres., 1982); Amer. Dental Soc. of Europe, 1965– (Hon. Treas. 1971–77; Pres., 1982); GDC, 1986–94 (Chm., Educn Cttee, 1990–94). Examiner for Membership in General Dental Surgery, RCS, 1979–84 (Chm., 1982–84); External Examiner: Leeds Univ. Dental Sch., 1985–87; Hong Kong Dental Sch., 1988–90; Fellow, and Mem., 1967–, Pres., 1993–94, Odontological Sect., RSM. Non-Exec. Dir, SE Thames RHA, 1990–93. Hon. Mem., Amer. Dental Assoc., 1983. Hon. Scientific Advr, British Dental Jl, 1982. FICD 1975; MGDS RCS 1979; FACD 1988. *Publication:* Silver Amalgam in Clinical Practice, 1965, 3rd edn 1992. *Recreations:* theatre, canal cruising. *Address:* 31 York Terrace East, NW1 4PT. *T:* 0171–935 8659. *Clubs:* Athenæum, Carlton.

GAIR, Hon. George Frederick, CMG 1994; QSO 1988; High Commissioner for New Zealand in the United Kingdom, 1991–94, and concurrently High Commissioner in Nigeria and Ambassador to the Republic of Ireland; *b* 13 Oct. 1926; *s* of Frederick James Gair and Roemer Elizabeth Elphege (*née* Boecking); *m* 1951, Esther Mary Fay Levy; one *s* two *d.* *Educ:* Wellington Coll.; Wairarapa Coll.; Victoria and Auckland Univ. Colls (BA 1949). Journalist: NZ Herald, 1945–47; BCON, Japan, 1947–48; Sun News Pictorial, 1949–50; Auckland Star, 1950–52; Auckland PRO, 1952–57; Staff Leader of Opposition, NZ, 1958; Press Officer and Personal Asst to Chief Exec., TEAL (later Air NZ), 1960–66. MP (Nat.) North Shore, 1966–90; Parly Under-Sec. to Minister of Educn, 1969–71; Minister of: Customs, and Associate Minister of Finance, 1972; Housing, and Dep. Minister of Finance, 1975–77; Energy, 1977–78; Health, and of Social Welfare, 1978–81; Transport, Railways, and Civil Aviation, 1981–84; Dep. Leader of Opposition, 1986–87; retd 1990. *Recreation:* walking. *Address:* 41 Hauraki Road, Takapuna, Auckland 9, New Zealand.

GAIRY, Rt. Hon. Sir Eric Matthew, Kt 1977; PC 1977; Prime Minister of Grenada, 1974–79; also Minister of External Affairs, Planning and Development Lands and Tourism, Information Service, Public Relations and Natural Resources, 1974–79; *b* 18 Feb. 1922; *m* Cynthia Gairy; two *d.* Member of Legislative Council, 1951–52 and 1954–55; Minister of Trade and Production, 1956–57; Chief Minister and Minister of Finance until 1962; Premier, 1967–74; independence of Grenada, 1974. Leader, Grenada United Labour Party.

GAISFORD, Rt Rev. John Scott; *see* Beverley, Bishop Suffragan of.

GAISMAN, Jonathan Nicholas Crispin; QC 1995; *b* 10 Aug. 1956; *o s* of Peter Gaisman and Beryl Kostoris; *m* 1982, Tessa Jardine Paterson, MBE; one *s* two *d.* *Educ:* Summer Fields; Eton College (King's Scholar); Worcester Coll., Oxford (BCL; MA 1st cl Hons Jurisp.). Called to the Bar, Inner Temple, 1979. Director: English Chamber Orchestra and Music Soc. Ltd, 1992–; Internat. Musicians' Seminar, Prussia Cove, 1994–. *Recreations:* the arts, travel, country pursuits. *Address:* 7 King's Bench Walk, Temple, EC4Y 7DS. *T:* 0171–583 0404. *Clubs:* Brooks's; I Zingari.

GAITSKELL, Robert; QC 1994; CEng, FIEE; FCIArb; *b* 19 April 1948; *s* of late Stanley Gaitskell and late Thelma Phyllis Gaitskell (*née* Holmes); *m* 1974, Dr Deborah Lyndall Bates; one *d.* *Educ:* Hamilton High Sch., Bulawayo, Zimbabwe; Univ. of Cape Town (BSc Eng). CEng 1993; FIEE 1993; FCIArb 1995. Grad. trainee, Reyrolle Parsons, 1971–73; Engr, Electricity Dept, Bulawayo CC, Zimbabwe, 1973–75; Electrical Engr, GEC (South Africa), 1975–76; called to the Bar, Gray's Inn, 1978; in practice at Bar in construction cases; arbitrator; Lectr, Centre of Construction Law and Mgt, KCL, 1993–, and other professional bodies. Institution of Electrical Engineers: Chm., Bd of Mgt and Design Div., 1995; Chm., Professional Gp on Engrg and the Law, 1994. Methodist local preacher. *Publications:* papers and articles on law and engrg. *Recreations:* walking, theatre, travel. *Address:* Keating Chambers, 10 Essex Street, WC2R 3AA.

GAIUS, Rev. Sir Saimon, KBE 1988 (OBE 1975); *b* 6 Aug. 1920; *s* of Peni Tovarur and Miriam Ia Pea; *m* 1941, Margaret Ia Kubak; five *s* one *d* (and one *s* one *d* decd). *Educ:* Mission Sch., East New Britain; theological training, PNG and Sydney, Aust. Ordained 1960; worked as United Church Minister; Principal, Pastors' Training Coll., 1967–68; Bishop of New Guinea Island Region, 1968–77; retired as Minister of Religion, 1983. SBStJ 1976. *Recreation:* reading. *Address:* United Church, PO Box 90, Rabaul, East New Britain, Papua New Guinea.

GAJDUSEK, Daniel Carleton, MD; Director of Program for Study of Child Growth and Development and Disease Patterns in Primitive Cultures, and Laboratory of Slow Latent and Temperate Virus Infections, National Institute of Neurological Disorders (formerly of Neurological and Communicative Disorders and Stroke), National Institutes of Health, Bethesda, Md, since 1958; Chief, Central Nervous System Studies Laboratory, NINDS, since 1970; *b* Yonkers, NY, 9 Sept. 1923; *s* of Karol Gajdusek and Ottilia Dobroczki; fifty-four adopted *s* and *d* (all from New Guinea and Micronesia). *Educ:* Marine Biological Lab., Woods Hole, Mass; Univ. of Rochester (BS *summa cum laude*); Harvard Medical Sch. (MD), California Inst. of Technology (Post-Doctoral Fellow). Residencies: Babies Hosp., NY, 1946–47; Children's Hosp., Cincinatti, Ohio, 1947–48, Children's Hosp., Boston, Mass, 1949–51; Sen. Fellow, Nat. Research Council, Calif Inst. of Tech., 1948–49; Children's Hosp., Boston, Mass, 1949–51; Research Fellow, Harvard Univ. and Sen. Fellow, Nat. Foundn for Infantile Paralysis, 1949–52; Walter Reed Army Medical Center, 1952–53; Institut Pasteur, Tehran, Iran and Univ. of Maryland, 1954–55; Vis. Investigator, Nat. Foundn for Infantile Paralysis and Walter and Eliza Hall Inst., Australia, 1955–57. Member: Nat. Acad. of Sciences, 1974; Amer. Philos. Soc., 1978; Amer. Acad. of Arts and Scis, 1978; Amer. Acad. of Neurol.; Infectious Dis. Soc. of America; Amer. Pediatric Soc.; Amer. Epidemiological Soc.; Amer. Soc. for Virology; Deutsche Akademie der Naturforscher Leopoldina, 1982; Czechoslovak, Portuguese, Australian, Russian and Sakha Acads of Science; Mexican Nat. Acad. of Medicine; Nat. Acad. of Medicine, Colombia; Royal Acad. of Medicine of Belgium. Mem., Scientific Council, Fondn pour l'Etude du Système Nerveux, Geneva. FRCPE 1991. Discovered slow virus infections of man; studied child growth and develt and disease patterns in primitive and isolated populations, virus encephalitides, chronic degenerative brain diseases, cerebral amyloidoses, and aging. E. Meade Johnson Award, Amer. Acad. Pediatrics, 1963; DHEW Superior Service Award, 1970; DHEW Distinguished Service Award, 1975; Lucien Dautrebande Prize, Belgium, 1976; shared with Dr Baruch Blumberg Nobel Prize in Physiology or Medicine, for discoveries concerning new mechanisms for the origin and dissemination of infectious diseases, 1976; George Cotzias Meml Prize, Amer. Acad. of Neurol., 1978; Huxley Medal, RAI, 1988. Hon. Curator, Melanesian Ethnography, Peabody Mus., Salem, Mass. Hon. DSc: Univ. of Rochester, 1977; Med. Coll. of Ohio, 1977; Washington and Jefferson Coll., 1980; Harvard Med. Sch. (Bicentennial), 1982; Hahnemann Univ., 1983; Univ. of Medicine and Dentistry of NJ, 1987; Hon. LHD: Hamilton Coll., 1977; Univ. of Hawaii, 1986; Docteur *hc*: Univ. of Marseille, 1977; Univ. of Lisbon, 1991; Hon. LLD Aberdeen, 1980; Laurea *hc* Univ. of Milan, 1992. *Publications:* Acute Infectious Hemorrhagic Fevers and Mycotoxicoses in the USSR, 1953; (ed with C. J. Gibbs, Jr and M. P. Alpers) Slow, Latent and Temperate Virus Infections, 1965; Journals 1954–91, 51 vols, 1963–87; Smadel-Gajdusek Correspondence 1955–1958; (ed with J. Farquhar) Kuru, 1981; over 1000 papers in major jls of medicine, microbiology, immunology, pediatrics, developmental biology, neurobiology, genetics, evolution and anthropology. *Recreation:* linguistics. *Address:* Laboratory of Central Nervous System Studies, NINDS 36–5B21, National Institutes of Health, Bethesda, MD 20892, USA. *T:* (301) 4963281.

GAJE GHALE, VC 1943; Subedar 2/5 Royal Gurkha Rifles FF; *b* 1 July 1922; *s* of Bikram Ghale; *m* 1939, Dhansuba; no *c.* *Educ:* IA 2nd class certificate of education. Enlisted as a Recruit Boy 2nd Bn 5th Royal Gurkha Rifles FF, Feb. 1935; transferred to the ranks, Aug. 1935; Naik, 1941; Acting Havildar, May 1942; War Subst. Havildar, Nov. 1942; Bn Havildar Major June 1943; Jemadar, Aug. 1943. Waziristan operations, 1936–37 (medal with clasp); Burma, 1942–43 (1939–45 Star, VC). *Recreations:* football, basketball, badminton and draughts.

GALBRAITH, family name of **Baron Strathclyde.**

GALBRAITH, James Hunter, CB 1985; Under Secretary, Department of Employment Industrial Relations Division, 1975–85; *b* 16 July 1925; *o s* of late Prof. V. H. Galbraith, FBA, and Dr G. R. Galbraith; *m* 1954, Isobel Gibson Graham; two *s.* *Educ:* Dragon Sch.; Edinburgh Academy; Balliol Coll., Oxford. 1st Cl. Litt Hum. Fleet Air Arm (pilot),

1944–46. Entered Ministry of Labour, 1950; Private Sec. to Permanent Sec., 1953–55; Jun. Civilian Instructor, IDC, 1958–61; Private Sec. to Minister of Labour, 1962–64; Chm. Central Youth Employment Exec., 1964–67; Sen. Simon Research Fellow, Manchester Univ., 1967–68; Asst Under-Sec. of State, Dept of Employment and Productivity (Research and Planning Div.), 1968–71; Dir, Office of Manpower Economics, 1971–73; Under-Sec., Manpower Gen. Div., Dept of Employment, 1973–74; Sec., Manpower Services Commn, 1974–75. Chm., Bd of Govs. Volunteer Centre UK, 1989–93. *Recreations:* rugby (Oxford Blue), golf, fishing. *Address:* 27 Sandy Lodge Lane, Moor Park, Mddx HA6 2HZ. *T:* Northwood (01923) 822458.

See also G. M. Moore.

GALBRAITH, Prof. John Kenneth; Paul M. Warburg Professor of Economics, Harvard University, 1949–75, now Emeritus Professor; *b* Ontario, Canada, 15 Oct. 1908; *s* of William Archibald and Catherine Galbraith; *m* 1937, Catherine M. Atwater; three *s. Educ:* Univ. of Guelph; California Univ. BS, MS, PhD. Tutor, Harvard Univ., 1934–39; Social Science Research Fellow, Cambridge Univ., 1937; Asst Prof. of Economics, Princeton Univ., 1939; Asst Administrator, Office of Price Administration, 1941; Deputy Administrator, 1942–43; Dir, State Dept Office of Economic Security Policy, 1945; Mem. Bd of Editors, Fortune Magazine, 1943–48. United States Ambassador to India, 1961–63 (on leave from Professorship). Reith Lecturer, 1966; Vis. Fellow, Trinity Coll., Cambridge, 1970–71 (Hon. Fellow, 1987). TV series, The Age of Uncertainty, 1977. Chm., Americans for Democratic Action, 1967–69; President: Amer. Econ. Assoc., 1972; Amer. Acad. of Arts and Letters, 1984 (Mem., 1982–). LLD Bard, 1958; Miami Univ., 1959; University of Toronto, 1961; Brandeis Univ., 1963; University of Mass, 1963; University of Saskatchewan, 1965; Rhode Island Coll., 1966; Boston Coll., 1967; Hobart and William Smith Colls, 1967; Univ. of Paris, 1975; and others. President's Certificate of Merit; Medal of Freedom. *Publications:* American Capitalism, the Concept of Countervailing Power, 1952; The Great Crash, 1929, 1955, new edn 1979; The Affluent Society, 1958, 4th edn, 1985; Journey to Poland and Yugoslavia, 1958; The Liberal Hour, 1960; Made to Last, 1964; The New Industrial State, 1967, rev. edn, 1978; Indian Painting, 1968; Ambassador's Journal, 1969; Economics, Peace and Laughter, 1971; A China Passage, 1973; Economics and the Public Purpose, 1974; Money: whence it came, where it went, 1975; The Age of Uncertainty, 1977; Almost Everyone's Guide to Economics, 1978; Annals of an Abiding Liberal, 1979; The Nature of Mass Poverty, 1979; A Life in Our Times, 1981; The Anatomy of Power, 1983; China Passage, 1983; A View from the Stands, 1987; A History of Economics, 1987; (with S. Menshikov) Capitalism, Communism and Coexistence, 1989; A Tenured Professor (novel), 1990; A Short History of Financial Euphoria, 1990; The Culture of Contentment, 1992; A Journey through Economic Time, 1994; contribs to learned jls. *Address:* 207 Littauer Center, Harvard University, Cambridge, MA 02138, USA; 30 Francis Avenue, Cambridge, MA 02138, USA. *Clubs:* Century (NY); Federal City (Washington).

GALBRAITH, Neil, CBE 1975; QPM 1959; DL; HM Inspector of Constabulary, 1964–76, retired; *b* 25 May 1911; *s* of late Peter and Isabella Galbraith; *m* 1942, Catherine Margaret Thornton; one *s* one *d. Educ:* Kilmarnock Academy. Constable to Inspector, Lancs Constabulary, 1931–46. Chief Supt, Herts Constabulary, 1946–51; Asst Chief Constable, Monmouthshire Constabulary, 1951–55; Chief Constable, Leicester City Police, 1956; Chief Constable, Monmouthshire Constabulary, 1957–64. DL Gwent (formerly Monmouth), 1973. *Recreation:* reading. *Address:* Neath House, Trostrey, Usk, Gwent NP5 1JH. *T:* Usk (01291) 672779.

GALBRAITH, Samuel Laird; MP (Lab) Strathkelvin and Bearsden, since 1987; *b* 18 Oct. 1945. *Educ:* Glasgow Univ. (BSc Hons 1968; MB ChB Hons 1971; MD 1977); FRCSGlas1975. Consultant in Neurosurgery, Gtr Glasgow Health Bd, 1978–87. Opposition spokesman on Scottish affairs and health, 1988–92, on employment, 1992–93. *Publication:* An Introduction to Neurosurgery, 1983. *Address:* c/o House of Commons, SW1A 0AA; (office) 110A Maxwell Avenue, Bearsden, Glasgow G61 1HU.

GALBRAITH, William Campbell; QC 1977; *b* 25 Feb. 1935; *s* of William Campbell Galbraith and Margaret Watson or Galbraith; *m* 1959, Mary Janet Waller; three *s* (and one *s* decd). *Educ:* Merchiston Castle Sch.; Pembroke Coll., Cambridge (BA); Edinburgh Univ. (LLB). Teacher, Turkey, 1959–61; Lectr, Meshed Univ., Iran, 1961–62; admitted to Faculty of Advocates, 1962; in practice at Scottish Bar, 1962–67; Sen. State Counsel, Malaŵi, 1967–70; Parly Draftsman, London, 1970–74; Parly Counsel, Canberra, 1974; returned to practice, 1975; Parly Counsel, Scottish Law Commn, 1975–95. Chm., Nat. Health Tribunal (Scotland), 1987–. *Recreations:* fishing, music, travel.

GALE, Audrey Olga Helen; *see* Sander, A. O. H.

GALE, Prof. Ernest Frederick, FRS 1953; BSc London; BA, PhD, ScD Cantab; Professor of Chemical Microbiology, University of Cambridge, 1960–81, now Emeritus; Fellow of St John's College, Cambridge, 1949–88; *b* 15 July 1914; *s* of Nellie Annie and Ernest Francis Edward Gale; *m* 1937, Eiry Mair Jones; one *s. Educ:* St John's Coll. Cambridge (Scholar). Research in biochemistry, Cambridge, 1936–83; Senior Student, Royal Commn for Exhibition of 1851, 1939; Beit Memorial Fellow, 1941; Scientific Staff of Med. Research Council, 1943; Reader in Chemical Microbiology, University of Cambridge, 1948–60; Dir, Medical Research Council Unit for Chemical Microbiology, 1948–62. Herter Lecturer, Johns Hopkins Hosp., Baltimore, USA, 1948; Commonwealth Travelling Fellow, Hanna Lecturer, Western Reserve Univ., 1951; Harvey Lectr, New York, 1955; Leeuwenhoek Lectr, Royal Society, London, 1956; Malcolm Lectr, Syracuse Univ., 1967; M. Stephenson Meml Lectr, 1971; Linacre Lectr, St John's Coll., Cambridge, 1973; Squibb Lectr, Nottingham Univ., 1986. Visiting Fellow, ANU, 1964–65. Hon. Mem., Society for General Microbiology, 1978 (Meetings Sec., 1954–58; International Representative, 1963–67; Pres., 1967–69); Mem. Food Investigation Board, 1954–58; Mem. International Union of Biochemistry Commission on Enzymes, 1957–61. *Publications:* Chemical Activities of Bacteria, 1947; The Molecular Basis of Antibiotic Action, 1972, 2nd edn 1981; scientific papers in Biochem. Journal, Journal of General Microbiology, Biochimica et Biophysica Acta, etc. *Recreations:* photography, wood carving. *Address:* 7 Hazeldene, Sandhills Road, Salcombe, Devon TQ8 8JP. *T:* Salcombe (01548) 843426.

GALE, Fay; *see* Gale, G. F.

GALE, Hon. George Alexander, CC 1977; Chief Justice of Ontario, 1967–76; Vice-Chairman, Ontario Law Reform Commission, 1977–81; *b* 24 June 1906; *s* of late Robert Henry and Elma Gertrude Gale; *m* 1934, Hilda Georgina Daly; three *s. Educ:* Prince of Wales High Sch., Vancouver; Toronto Univ. (BA); Osgoode Hall Law Sch., Toronto. Called to Ontario Bar, 1932; Partner, Mason, Foulds, Davidson & Gale, 1944; KC (Can.) 1945; Justice, Supreme Court of Ontario, 1946; Justice, Court of Appeal, Ontario, 1963; Chief Justice of High Court of Justice for Ontario, 1964. Formerly Chm. Judicial Council for Provincial Judges; Chm., Cttee on Rules of Practice for Ontario (Mem. 1941–76); former Mem. Canadian Bar Assoc. (formerly Mem. Council); Hon. Mem., Georgia Bar Assoc.; formerly Hon. Lectr, Osgoode Law Sch.; formerly Mem. Exec. Cttee, Canadian Judicial Council. Mem., Ontario Adv. Cttee on Confederation; formerly Chm., Ontario Rhodes Scholarship Selection Cttee; Hon. Mem., Canadian Corps of Commissionaires, 1977. Mem. Bd of Governors: Wycliffe Coll., Toronto Univ.; Ecumenical Foundn of Canada; formerly, Upper Canada Coll., Toronto; Mem. Delta Kappa Epsilon, Phi Delta Phi (Hon.). Anglican; Warden, St John's, York Mills, for 5 years. Hon. Pres., Ontario Curling Assoc. Hon. LLD: McMaster, 1968; York (Toronto), 1969; Windsor, 1980. *Publication:* (ed with Holmested) Practice and Procedure in Ontario, 6th edn. *Recreations:* golf, photography. *Address:* 7700 Bayview Avenue, Thornhill, Ontario L3T 5W1, Canada. *Clubs:* Lawyers, (Hon. Mem.) York (Toronto); Toronto Curling, Chippewa Golf.

GALE, (Gwendoline) Fay, AO 1989; PhD; FASSA; Vice-Chancellor, University of Western Australia, since 1990; *b* 13 June 1932; *d* of Rev. George Jasper Gilding and Kathleen Gertrude Gilding; one *s* one *d. Educ:* Adelaide Univ. (BA 1952, Hons I 1954; PhD 1962). University of Adelaide: Lectr, 1966–71; Sen. Lectr, 1972–74; Reader, 1975–77; Prof., 1978–89; Pro-Vice-Chancellor, 1988–89. Comr, Australian Heritage Commn, 1989–95. Elin Wagner Fellow, 1971; Catherine Helen Spence Fellow, 1972. FASSA 1978. DUniv Adelaide, 1994. British Council Award, 1972. *Publications:* Race Relations in Australia: the Aboriginal situation, 1975; Urban Aborigines, 1972; Poverty among Aboriginal families in Adelaide, 1975; Adelaide Aborigines, a case study of urban life 1966–81, 1982; We are bosses ourselves: the status and role of Aboriginal women today, 1983; Tourists and the National Estate: procedures to protect Australia's heritage, 1987; Aboriginal youth and the criminal justice system: the injustice of justice, 1990; Changing Australia, 1991; Inventing Places: studies in cultural geography, 1992; Juvenile Justice: debating the issues, 1993; Tourism and the Protection of Aboriginal Cultural Sites, 1994. *Recreations:* rock art, bush walking, music, theatre. *Address:* University of Western Australia, Nedlands, Perth, WA 6907, Australia. *T:* (9) 3802801. *Club:* Karrakatta (Perth, WA).

GALE, John, OBE 1987; Director: Lisden Productions Ltd, since 1975; John Gale Productions Ltd, since 1960; Gale Enterprises Ltd, since 1960; West End Managers Ltd, since 1972; *b* 2 Aug. 1929; *s* of Frank Haith Gale and Martha Edith Gale (*née* Evans); *m* 1950, Liselotte Ann (*née* Wratten); two *s. Educ:* Christ's Hospital; Webber Douglas Academy of Dramatic Art. Formerly an actor; presented his first production, Inherit the Wind, London, 1960; has since produced or co-produced, in London, British provinces, USA, Australia, New Zealand and S Africa, over 80 plays, including: Candida, 1960; On the Brighter Side, 1961; Boeing-Boeing, 1962; Devil May Care, 1963; Windfall, 1963; Where Angels Fear to Tread, 1963; The Wings of the Dove, 1963; Amber for Anna, 1964; Present Laughter, 1964, 1981; Maigret and the Lady, 1965; The Platinum Cat, 1965; The Sacred Flame, 1966; An Evening with G. B. S., 1966; A Woman of No Importance, 1967; The Secretary Bird, 1968; Dear Charles, 1968; Highly Confidential, 1969; The Young Churchill, 1969; The Lionel Touch, 1969; Abelard and Héloïse, 1970; No Sex, Please—We're British, 1971; Lloyd George Knew My Father, 1972; The Mating Game, 1972; Parents' Day, 1972; At the End of the Day, 1973; Birds of Paradise, 1974; A Touch of Spring, 1975; Separate Tables, 1977; The Kingfisher, 1977; Sextet, 1977; Cause Célèbre, 1977; Shut Your Eyes and Think of England, 1977; Can You Hear Me at the Back?, 1979; Middle Age Spread, 1979; Private Lives, 1980; A Personal Affair, 1982. The Secretary Bird and No Sex, Please—We're British set records for the longest run at the Savoy and Strand Theatres respectively; No Sex, Please—We're British is the longest running comedy in the history of World Theatre and passed 6,000 performances at the Garrick Theatre in Nov. 1985. Chichester Festival Theatre: Exec. Producer, 1983–84; Director, 1984–89. President, Soc. of West End Theatre Managers, 1972–75; Chm.. Theatres National Cttee, 1979–85. Governor and Almoner, Christ's Hospital, 1976–; Chm. of Govs, Guildford Sch. of Acting, 1989–. Member, Amicable Soc. of Blues, 1981–. Liveryman, Gold and Silver Wyredrawers Company, 1974. FRSA 1990. *Recreations:* travel, Rugby. *Address:* East Dean Cottage, East Dean, near Chichester, W Sussex PO18 0JA. *T:* Chichester (01243) 811407. *Clubs:* Garrick; London Welsh Rugby Football (Richmond) (Chairman, 1979–81).

GALE, Michael; QC 1979; a Recorder of the Crown Court, since 1977; *b* 12 Aug. 1932; *s* of Joseph Gale and Blossom Gale; *m* 1963, Joanna Stephanie Bloom; one *s* two *d. Educ:* Cheltenham Grammar Sch.; Grocers' Sch.; King's Coll., Cambridge (Exhibnr; BA History and Law, 1954, MA 1958). National Service, Royal Fusiliers and Jt Services Sch. for Linguists, 1956–58. Called to the Bar, Middle Temple, 1957, Bencher, 1988; Harmsworth Law Scholar, 1958. Mem., Gen. Council of the Bar, 1987–. *Recreations:* the arts and country pursuits. *Address:* 6 Pump Court, Temple, EC4Y 7AR. *T:* 0171–353 7242. *Clubs:* United Oxford & Cambridge University, MCC.

GALE, Michael Denis, PhD; Research Director, John Innes Centre, Norwich, since 1994; *b* 25 Aug. 1943; *s* of Sydney Ralph Gale and Helen Mary (*née* Johnson); *m* 1979, Susan Heathcote Rosbotham; two *d. Educ:* W Buckland Sch., Barnstaple; Birmingham Univ. (BSc Hons); UCW, Aberystwyth (PhD). Plant Breeding Institute, subseq. AFRC Institute of Plant Science Research, Cambridge: Researcher, 1968–86; Head, Cereals Res. Dept, and Individual Merit SPSO, Cambridge Lab., 1986–92; Head of Cambridge Lab., Norwich, 1992–94. Farrer Meml Bicentennial Fellow, NSW Dept of Agric., 1989; Hon. Res. Prof., Inst. of Crop Germplasm Resources, Acad. Sinica, 1992. Advr, Inst. of Genetics, Beijing, 1992. Res. Medal, RASE, 1994. *Publications:* 200 scientific papers and articles on plant genetics and cytogenetics, esp. dwarfism, quality and genome res. in wheat. *Recreations:* golf, tennis. *Address:* John Innes Centre, Norwich Research Park, Colney, Norwich NR4 7UH. *T:* Norwich (01603) 52571. *Club:* Royal Norwich Golf.

GALE, Michael Sadler, MC 1945; Assistant Under-Secretary of State, Prison Department, Home Office, 1972–79; *b* 5 Feb. 1919; *s* of Rev. John Sadler and Ethel Gale; *m* 1950, Philippa, *d* of Terence and Betty Ennion; two *s* one *d* (and one *s* decd). *Educ:* Tonbridge Sch.; Oriel Coll., Oxford (Scholar, MA). Served War of 1939–45: enlisted 1939, Royal Fusiliers; commnd 1940, Queen's Own Royal W Kent Regt, Major 1944; served N Africa and NW Europe. Housemaster, HM Borstal, Rochester, 1946–48; Dep. Governor, HM Prison, Durham, 1948–49; Staff Course Tutor, Imperial Trng Sch., Wakefield, 1949–50; Principal, 1950–52; Governor, HM Prison: The Verne, 1952–57; Camp Hill, 1957–62; Wandsworth, 1962–66; Asst Dir, Prison Dept, Home Office, 1966–69; Controller, Planning and Develt, 1969–75; Controller, Operational Administration, 1975–79; Mem. Prisons Board, 1969–79. *Recreations:* walking, reading, gardening. *Address:* 5A Christchurch Road, Winchester, Hants SO23 9SR. *T:* Winchester (01962) 853836.

GALE, Roger James; MP (C) North Thanet, since 1983; *b* Poole, Dorset, 20 Aug. 1943; *s* of Richard Byrne Gale and Phyllis Mary (*née* Rowell); *m* 1st, 1964, Wendy Dawn Bowman (marr. diss. 1967); 2nd, 1971, Susan Sampson (marr. diss.); one *d*; 3rd, 1980, Susan Gabrielle Marks; two *s. Educ:* Southbourne Prep. Sch.; Hardye's Sch., Dorchester; Guildhall Sch. of Music and Drama (LGSM). Freelance broadcaster, 1963–72; freelance reporter, BBC Radio, London, 1972–73; Producer, Current Affairs Gp, BBC Radio (progs included Newsbeat and Today), 1973–76; Producer/Dir, BBC Children's Television (progs included Blue Peter and Swap Shop), 1976–79; Producer/Dir, Thames TV, and Editor, teenage unit (progs included White Light, Smith & Goody, CBTV and Crying Out Loud), 1979–83. Joined Conservative Party, 1964; Mem., Cttee, Greater London Young Conservatives, 1964–65. PPS to Minister of State for Armed Forces,

1992–94. Member: Select Cttee on Televising of Proceedings of the House, 1988–91; Home Affairs Select Cttee, 1990–92; All Party Parly Gp, Fund for Replacement of Animals in Med. Experiments; Chairman: All Party Animal Welfare Gp; Backbench Media Cttee; Delegate, Council of Europe, 1987–89. Contested Birmingham, Northfield, Oct. 1982 (Lab. majority, 289). Mem., Gen. Council, BBC, 1992–. Founder Mem., East Kent Development Assoc., 1984–. Fellow: Industry and Parlt Trust; Parlt and Armed Forces Fellowship. *Recreations:* swimming, sailing, canoeing. *Address:* House of Commons, Westminster, SW1A 0AA. *Clubs:* Garrick; Kent County Cricket.

GALE, William Stuart; QC (Scot) 1993; *b* 10 June 1955; *s* of William Grimshaw Gale and Patricia Sheila (*née* Nicol); *m* 1981, Michele Marie Keklak. *Educ:* Univ. of Dundee (LLB Hons 1977); Tulane Univ., New Orleans (LLM 1978). Advocate of Scottish Bar, 1980–93; Standing Jun. Counsel to FCO in Scotland, 1987–93. *Recreation:* modern jazz. *Address:* 41 Heriot Row, Edinburgh EH3 6ES. *T:* 0131–225 8762.

GALES, Kathleen Emily, (Mrs Heinz Spitz); Senior Lecturer in Statistics, London School of Economics, 1966–90, retired; *b* 1927; *d* of Albert Henry and Sarah Thomson Gales; *m* 1970, Heinz Spitz. *Educ:* Gateshead Grammar Sch.; Newnham Coll., Cambridge (Exhibr); Ohio Univ. (Schol.). BA Cantab 1950, MA Ohio, 1951. Asst Statistician, Foster Wheeler Ltd, 1951–53; Statistician, Municipal Statistical Office, Birmingham, 1953–55; Res. Asst and part-time Lectr, LSE, 1955–58; Asst Lectr in Statistics, LSE, 1958–60, Lectr, 1960–66. Vis. Assoc. Prof. in Statistics, Univ. of California, 1964–65. Statistical Consultant: Royal Commn on Doctors' and Dentists' Remuneration, 1959; WHO, 1960; Turkish Min. of Health, 1963. Mem. Performing Rights Tribunal, 1974–80. *Publications:* (with C. A. Moser and P. Morpurgo) Dental Health and the Dental Services, 1962; (with B. Abel-Smith) British Doctors at Home and Abroad, 1964; (with T. Blackstone et al.) Students in Conflict: LSE in 1967, 1970; articles in Jl RSS. *Recreations:* bridge, golf, travel.

GALL, Henderson Alexander, (Sandy), CBE 1988; Foreign Correspondent, Independent Television News, 1963–92 (Newscaster, 1968–90); *b* 1 Oct. 1927; *s* of Henderson Gall and Jean Begg; *m* 1958, Eleanor Mary Patricia Ann Smyth; one *s* three *d*. *Educ:* Glenalmond; Aberdeen Univ. (MA). Foreign Correspondent, Reuters, 1953–63, Germany, E Africa, Hungary, S Africa, Congo; joined ITN, 1963, working in Middle East, Africa, Vietnam, Far East, China, Afghanistan; Newscaster on News at Ten, 1970–90; Producer/Presenter/Writer, documentaries on: King Hussein, 1972; Afghanistan, 1982, 1984, 1986; Cresta Run, 1984; George Adamson, 1989; Richard Leakey, 1995. Rector, Aberdeen Univ., 1978–81 (Hon. LLD, 1981). Sitara-i-Pakistan, 1986; Lawrence of Arabia Medal, RSAA, 1987. *Publications:* Gold Scoop, 1977; Chasing the Dragon, 1981; Don't Worry About the Money Now, 1983; Behind Russian Lines, 1983; Afghanistan: Agony of a Nation, 1988; Salang, 1989; Lord of the Lions, 1991; News from the Front, 1994. *Recreations:* golf, gardening, swimming. *Address:* Doubleton Oast House, Penshurst, Tonbridge, Kent TN11 8JA. *Clubs:* Turf, Special Forces; St Moritz Tobogganing.

GALL, Sandy; *see* Gall, H. A.

GALL, Thomas Mitchell; Hon. Mr Justice Gall; Judge of the High Court, Hong Kong, since 1991; *b* 20 Nov. 1942; *s* of John Berry Gall and Helen Lucy (*née* Mitchell); *m* 1966, Barbara Smart; one *s* one *d*. *Educ:* Univ. of Adelaide (LLB). Admitted barrister and solicitor, 1966; Colin D. Rowe & Co., Barristers and Solicitors, 1966–73; Hong Kong: Crown Counsel, 1973–76; Sen. Crown Counsel, 1976–78; Asst Principal Crown Counsel, 1978–81; Dist Judge, 1981–91. Hon. Sec., Council Early Childhood Educn; Chm., Childsafe Action Gp, 1992–. Vice-Chm., Criminol Soc., Hong Kong, 1992–. Gov., Winchester Internat. Sch., Hong Kong, 1989–. *Address:* 6 Lloyd Path, The Peak, Hong Kong. *T:* 8496166.

GALLACHER, family name of **Baron Gallacher.**

GALLACHER, Baron *cr* 1982 (Life Peer), of Enfield in Greater London; **John Gallacher;** retired; *b* 7 May 1920; *s* of William Gallacher and Janet Stewart; *m* 1947, Freda Vivian Chittenden; one *s*. *Educ:* St Patrick's High School, Dumbarton; Co-operative College, Loughborough. Chartered Secretary. President: Enfield Highway Co-operative Soc., 1954–68; Inst. of Meat, 1983–86; Secretary, International Co-operative Alliance, 1963–67; Parliamentary Sec., Co-operative Union, 1974–83; Mem., Select Cttee on the European Communities, 1983–89. Chief opposition spokesman on agriculture and food, 1989–92. *Publication:* Service on the Board (a handbook for directors of retail co-operatives), 1974, 2nd edn 1976. *Recreation:* gardening. *Address:* House of Lords, SW1A 0PW. *T:* 0171–219 5425.

GALLACHER, Bernard; golf professional, Wentworth Golf Club, since 1975; *b* 9 Feb. 1949; *s* of Bernard and Matilda Gallacher; *m* 1974, Lesley Elizabeth Wearmouth; one *s* two *d*. *Educ:* St Mary's Academy, Bathgate. Golf tournaments won: Scottish Open Amateur Championship, 1967; PGA Schweppes, W. D. & H. O. Wills Open, 1969; Martini Internat., 1971, 1982; Carrolls Internat., 1974; Dunlop Masters, 1974, 1975; Spanish Open, 1977; French Open, 1979; Tournament Players Championship, 1980; Gtr Manchester Open, 1981; Jersey Open, 1982, 1984. Harry Vardon Trophy, 1969. Scottish Professional Champion , 1971, 1973, 1974, 1977, 1984. Ryder Cup Team, 1969, 1971, 1973, 1975, 1977, 1979, 1981, 1983, European Captain, 1991, 1993, 1995. *Publications:* (with Mark Wilson) Teach Yourself Golf, 1988; (with Renton Laidlaw) Captain at Kiawah, 1991. *Recreations:* walking dogs, reading. *Address:* Wentworth Club, Virginia Water, Surrey GU25 4LS. *T:* Wentworth (019904) 3353.

GALLACHER, John; HM Diplomatic Service, retired; Representative (Scotland), Control Risks Group, since 1992; *b* 16 July 1931; *s* of John Gallacher and Catherine Gallacher (*née* Crilly); *m* 1956, Eileen Agnes (*née* McGuire); one *s*. *Educ:* Our Lady's High School, Motherwell. Nat. Service, RAF, 1950–52. Kenya Police, 1953–65 (retired as Supt of Police, 1965); Libyan Govt (attached to Min. of Interior), 1965–67; FCO, 1967–70; Lagos, 1970–73; FCO, 1973–74; Kuwait, 1974–77; FCO 1977; Counsellor, FCO, 1983–84. Gp Security Advr, Gallaher Ltd, 1985–91. *Recreations:* reading, golf, travel, gardening. *Address:* 160 Lochend Road, Gartcosh, Glasgow G69 8BB. *Club:* Royal Over-Seas League.

GALLAGHER, Edward Patrick, CEng, FIEE, FCIWEM; Chief Executive, Environment Agency, since 1995; *b* 4 Aug. 1944; *m* 1969, Helen Wilkinson; two *s*. *Educ:* Univ. of Sheffield (BEng Hons; Diploma in Business Studies; Mappin Medal, 1966; John Brown Award, 1966). MRI 1992. Systems Analyst, Vauxhall Motors, 1963–68; Corporate Planning Manager, Sandoz Products, 1968–70; Computer Services Manager, Robinson Willey, 1970–71; with Black and Decker, 1971–86: Director: Marketing Services, 1978–79; Service and Distribn, 1979–81; Business Analysis, 1981–83; Market and Product Develt, 1983–86; Amersham International: Dir of Corporate Develt, 1986–88; Divl Chief Exec., 1988–90; Mfg Dir, 1990–92; Chief Exec. and Bd Mem., NRA, 1992–95. Vis. Prof., Bus. Sch. and Faculty of Technol., Mem., Faculty of Technol. Adv. Gp, and Gov., Middlesex Univ., 1994–; Mem. Council and Finance Adv. Gp, Bristol Univ., 1994–. Trustee, Living Again Trust, Royal Hosp. for Neurodisability (formerly Royal Hosp. and Home, Putney), 1993–. FRSA 1995. *Recreations:* golf, tennis, theatre, walking, guitar. *Address:* Environment Agency, c/o 2 Marsham Street, SW1P 3EB.

GALLAGHER, (Francis George) Kenna, CMG 1963; HM Diplomatic Service, retired; *b* 25 May 1917; *er s* of late George and Johanna Gallagher. *Educ:* St Joseph's Coll.; King's Coll., University of London (LLB (Hons)). Clerical officer, Min. of Agric., 1935–38; Asst Examr, Estate Duty Office, 1938–44; served in HM Forces, 1941–45; Examr, Estate Duty Office, 1944–45; apptd a Mem., HM Foreign (subseq. Diplomatic) Service, 1945; Vice-Consul Marseilles, 1946–48; Acting Consul-Gen., there, in 1947; HM Embassy, Paris, 1948–50; FO, 1950–53; First Sec., HM Embassy, Damascus, 1953–55; acted as Chargé d'Affaires, 1953, 1954 and 1955; FO, 1955; appointed Counsellor and Head of European Economic Organisations Dept, 1960; Counsellor (Commercial), HM Embassy, Berne, 1963–65; acted as Chargé d'Affaires (Berne) in 1963 and 1964; Head of Western Economic Dept, CO, 1965–67, of Common Market Dept, 1967–68; Asst Under-Sec. of State, FCO, 1968–71; Ambassador and Head of UK Delegn to OECD, 1971–77. Consultant on Internat. Trade Policy, CBI, 1978–80. *Recreations:* music, chess. *Address:* 37 Howard Terrace, Morpeth, Northumberland NE61 1HT. *T:* Morpeth (01670) 504384.

GALLAGHER, Kenna; *see* Gallagher, F. G. K.

GALLAGHER, Sister Maire Teresa, CBE 1992 (OBE 1987); SND; Sister Superior, Convent of Notre Dame, Dumbarton, 1987–94; *b* 27 May 1933; *d* of Owen Gallagher and Annie McVeigh. *Educ:* Notre Dame High Sch., Glasgow; Glasgow Univ. (MA Hons 1965); Notre Dame Coll. of Educn (Dip. 1953). Principal Teacher of History, Notre Dame High Sch., Glasgow, 1965–72; Lectr in Secondary Educn, Notre Dame Coll., 1972–74; Head Teacher, Notre Dame High Sch., Dumbarton, 1974–87. Chair, Scottish Consultative Council (formerly Scottish Consultative Cttee) on the Curriculum, 1987–91 (Mem., 1976–91; Chair: Secondary Cttee, 1983–87; Main Cttee, 1987–90); Mem., Sec. of State's Cttee of Enquiry into Teachers' Pay and Conditions of Service, 1986; Pres., Scottish Br., Secondary Heads Assoc., 1980–82. Fellow, SCOTVEC, 1989. Hon. MEd CNAA, 1992. *Publications:* papers and articles in jls on teaching and management of schools. *Recreations:* homemaking skills, reading. *Address:* Sisters of Notre Dame, 67 Moorpark Avenue, Penilee, Glasgow G52 4ET. *T:* 0141–810 4214.

GALLAGHER, Michael; *b* 1 July 1934; *s* of Michael and Annie Gallagher; *m* 1959, Kathleen Mary Gallagher; two *s* three *d*. *Educ:* Univ. of Nottingham; Univ. of Wales. Dip. General Studies. Branch Official, NUM, 1967–70; day release, Univ. of Nottingham, 1967–69; TUC scholarship, Univ. of Wales, 1970–72; Univ. of Nottingham, 1972–74. Councillor: Mansfield Borough Council, 1970–74; Nottinghamshire CC, 1973–81. Contested (Lab) Rushcliffe, general election, Feb. 1974; Member (Lab) Nottingham, European Parlt, 1979–83, (SDP) 1983–84; contested (SDP) Lancs Central, European elecn, 1984. *Recreations:* leisure, sports.

GALLAGHER, Dame Monica (Josephine), DBE 1976; *m* 1946, Dr John Paul Gallagher, KCSG, KM; two *s* two *d*. Mem. Cttee, Friends of St Mary's Cathedral, Sydney, 1994– (Chm., 1984–87; Dep. Chm., 1988–93); Pres., Flower Festival Cttee, St Mary's Cathedral, 1987–95; Mem. Cttee, Order of British Empire Assoc., NSW, 1995– (Vice-Pres., 1985–89; Pres., 1989–92); Vice-Pres., SCF, NSW, 1992–94; Member: Dr Horace Nowland Travelling Scholarship; Australian Church Women, NSW Div.; Nursing Adv. Cttee, Australian Catholic Univ. (formerly Catholic Coll. of Educn), Sydney; Adv. Bd, Festival of Light. Tour Guide, St Mary's Cathedral. State Pres., NSW, and Gen. Pres., Sydney Archdiocese, Catholic Women's League, Aust., 1972–80 (Nat. Pres., 1972–74); Past President: Catholic Central Cttee for Care of Aged; Catholic Women's Club, Sydney; Associated Catholic Cttee; Austcare; Catholic Inst. of Nursing Studies. Former Member: NSW Div., UNA; UN Status of Women Cttee; Exec. Bd, Mater Misericordiae Hosp., N Sydney; Bd, Gertrude Abbott Nursing Home; Selection Cttee, Queen Elizabeth II Silver Jubilee Trust; former Chm., YWCA Appeal Cttee, Sydney. Good Citizen Award, Festival of Light, 1979; Papal Honour, Augustae Crucis Insigne pro Ecclesia et Pontifice, 1981. *Address:* 1 Robert Street, Willoughby, NSW 2068, Australia.

GALLAGHER, Paul; General Secretary, Electrical, Electronic, Telecommunication and Plumbing Union Section, Amalgamated Engineering and Electrical Union, since 1992; *b* 16 Oct. 1944; *s* of Joe and Annie Gallagher; *m* 1974, Madeleine. *Educ:* St Anne's, Droylesden, Manchester. Electrical, Electronic, Telecommunication and Plumbing Union: full-time officer, 1966–78; Exec. Councillor for Manchester and N Wales, 1978–91; Pres., 1986–91. Mem., HSC, 1990–. *Recreations:* gardening, music, reading. *Address:* (office) Hayes Court, West Common Road, Hayes, Bromley, Kent BR2 7AU. *T:* 0181–462 7755.

GALLEY, Robert Albert Ernest, PhD; FRSC; Director, Shell Research Ltd, Woodstock Agricultural Research Centre, Sittingbourne, Kent, 1960–69; *b* 23 Oct. 1909; *s* of John and Jane A. Galley; *m* 1st 1933, Elsie Marjorie Walton (*d* 1985); one *s* two *d*; 2nd 1988, Ann Louise Grundy (*née* Dale). *Educ:* Colfe's Gram. Sch.; Imperial Coll., London. BSc 1930, PhD 1932, FRIC 1944. Research Chemist, Wool Industries Research Assoc., 1932–34; Chemist, Dept of War Department Chemist, 1934–37; Lectr, Sir John Cass Coll., 1937–39; Prin. Exper. Officer, Min. of Supply, Chemical Inspectorate, 1939–45, Flax Establishment, 1945–46; Sen. Prin. Scientific Officer, Agric. Research Council (Sec. Interdepartmental Insecticides Cttees), 1946–50; seconded to Scientific Secretariat, Office of Lord Pres. of Council, 1950–52; Dir, Tropical Products Institute, Dept of Scientific and Industrial Research (formerly Colonial Products Laboratory), 1953–60. *Publications:* papers in Journal of Chem. Soc., Chemistry and Industry, World Crops, etc. *Recreations:* tennis, gardening, sailing. *Address:* Riversdale, 26 River Reach, Teddington, Middx TW11 9QL.

GALLEY, Roy; Director, Facilities, Royal Mail, London, since 1992; *b* 8 Dec. 1947; *s* of Kenneth Haslam Galley and late Letitia Mary Chapman; *m* 1976, Helen Margaret Butcher; one *s* one *d*. *Educ:* King Edward VII Grammar Sch., Sheffield; Worcester Coll., Oxford. North-East Postal Bd, 1969–83: started as management trainee; Asst Controller, Projects (regional manager), 1980–83; Head of Project Control, London Building and Estates Centre, Royal Mail Letters, 1987–91. Councillor, Calderdale Metropolitan Bor. Council, 1980–83. Chm., Kingston and Richmond (formerly Kingston and Esher) DHA, 1989–. Chm., Yorks Young Conservatives, 1974–76; contested (C): Dewsbury, 1979; Halifax, 1987. MP (C) Halifax, 1983–87. Sec., Cons. Backbench Health Cttee, 1983–87; Mem., Social Services Select Cttee, 1984–87. Chm., Kingston and St George's Coll. of Nursing, 1993–. *Recreations:* history, European literature, theatre, music, gardening, riding. *Address:* 12 Selcroft Road, Purley, Surrey CR8 1AD.

GALLI, Paolo; Italian Ambassador to the Court of St James's, since 1995; *b* 10 Aug. 1934; *s* of Carlo Galli and Bianca Metral-Lambert; *m* 1959, Maria Giuliana Calioni; two *d*. *Educ:* Univ. of Padua (law degree). Entered Italian Diplomatic Service, 1958; Minister of State's Private Office, 1958–61; Vice Consul, Cardiff, 1961–63; Second Sec., Washington, 1963–65; First Sec., Co-ordination Dept, Sec.-Gen's Office, Min. for Foreign Affairs, 1965–68; First Sec., later Counsellor and First Counsellor, London, 1968–72; First Counsellor, Warsaw, 1972–75; Min. for Foreign Affairs, Econ. Affairs Dept, 1975–79; Foreign Minister's Private Office, 1979–80; Minister-Counsellor, Dep. Perm. Rep. to EEC, Brussels, 1980–85; promoted to rank of Minister, 1985; Ambassador to Warsaw, 1986–88; Dir-Gen., Aid and Co-operation Dept, Min. for Foreign Affairs, 1988–89; promoted to rank of Ambassador, 1989; Ambassador to Tokyo, 1992–95. Grande Ufficiale,

Ordine al Merito della Repubblica Italiana, 1981. *Recreations:* classical music, the arts, fencing. *Address:* Italian Embassy, 14 Three Kings Yard, W1Y 2EH. *T:* 0171–312 2200.

GALLIANO, John Charles; Company Director and Couturier for Maison John Galliano, since 1984; Designer of Haute Couture and Prêt-à-Porter for Maison Givenchy, since 1995; *b* 28 Nov. 1960. *Educ:* Wilson's Grammar Sch. for Boys; St Martin's Sch. of Art and Design (BA). Regular seasonal collections, 1985–. British Designer of the Year, British Fashion Council, 1987, 1994; Mejor Creador International, 1995. *Address:* 2 rue de la Roquette, Passage du Cheval Blanc, 75011 Paris, France. *T:* 47002951.

GALLIE, Duncan Ian Dunbar, DPhil; FBA 1995; Official Fellow, Nuffield College, Oxford, since 1985; *b* 16 Feb. 1946; *s* of Ian Gallie and Elsie (*née* Peers); *m* Martine Josephine Jurdant. *Educ:* St Paul's Sch., London (Scholar); Magdalen Coll., Oxford (Demyship; BA 1st Cl. Hons History); LSE (MSc); St Antony's Coll., Oxford (DPhil). Research Fellow, Nuffield Coll., Oxford, 1971–73; Lectr in Sociology, Univ. of Essex, 1973–79; Reader in Sociology, Univ. of Warwick, 1979–85; Dir, ESRC Social Change and Economic Life Initative, 1985–90. Advr, Comité Nat. d'Evaluation de la Recherche, 1991; Member, Scientific Committee: IRESCO, 1989–93; IFRESI, 1993–. FRSA. Dist. Contrib. to Scholarship Award, Amer. Sociol. Assoc., 1985. *Publications:* In Search of the New Working Class, 1978; Social Inequality and Class Radicalism in France and Britain, 1983; (ed jtly) New Approaches to Economic Life, 1985; (ed) Employment in Britain, 1988; (ed jtly) Social Change and the Experience of Unemployment, 1994; articles in learned jls. *Recreations:* travelling, music, museum gazing. *Address:* Nuffield College, Oxford OX1 1NF. *T:* Oxford (01865) 278586; 149 Leam Terrace, Leamington Spa, Warwickshire CV31 1DF. *T:* Leamington Spa (01926) 314941.

GALLIE, Philip Roy; MP (C) Ayr, since 1992; *b* 3 June 1939; *s* of George Albert Gallie and Ivy Edith Gallie (*née* Williams); *m* 1964, Marion Wands Whyte; one *s* one *d*. *Educ:* Dunfermline High Sch.; Kirkcaldy Tech. Coll. MIPlantE; TE. Apprentice elect. fitter, HM Dockyard, Rosyth, 1955–60; Elect. Engineer, Ben Line Steamers, 1960–64; Electricity Supply Industry; Kincardine, Ironbridge and Inverkip Power Stations; SSEB Central Maint. Orgn; Galloway and Lanark Hydros and Inverkip Power Station (Manager, 1989–92). Dist Councillor, Cunninghame, 1980–84. Contested (C): Cunninghame South, 1983, Dunfermline West, 1987. *Recreations:* politics, sports. *Address:* House of Commons, SW1A 0AA. *T:* 0171–219 6251; Ayr Constituency Office, 1 Wellington Square, Ayr. *T:* Ayr (01292) 263991. *Clubs:* Royal Scottish Automobile (Glasgow); Ayr Rugby Football.

GALLIE, Prof. Walter Bryce; Professor of Political Science, and Fellow of Peterhouse, Cambridge University, 1967–78, Professor Emeritus, 1978, Emeritus Fellow 1982; *b* 5 Oct. 1912; 3rd *s* of Walter S. Gallie, structural engineer; *m* 1940, Menna Humphreys (*d* 1990); one *s* one *d*. *Educ:* Sedbergh Sch.; Balliol Coll., Oxford (Classical Exhibitioner). BA (1st Cl. PPE), 1934, BLitt 1937, MA Oxon, 1947. University Coll. of Swansea; Asst Lectr, Philosophy, 1935; Lectr, 1938; Sen. Lectr, 1948; Prof. of Philosophy, University Coll. of North Staffordshire 1950; Prof. of Logic and Metaphysics, Queen's Univ., Belfast, 1954–67. Visiting Prof., New York Univ., 1962–63; Lectures: Lewis Fry Meml, Bristol Univ., 1964; Wiles, QUB, 1976; J. R. Jones Meml, UC Swansea, 1983; E. H. Carr Meml, UC Aberystwyth, 1987. Pres., Aristotelian Soc., 1970–71. Hon. Professorial Fellow, Univ. of Wales, 1980. Served War, 1940–45, ending with rank of Major, Croix de Guerre, 1945. *Publications:* An English School, 1949; Peirce and Pragmatism, 1952; Free Will and Determinism Yet Again (Inaugural Lecture), 1957; A New University: A. D. Lindsay and the Keele Experiment, 1960; Philosophy and the Historical Understanding, 1964; Philosophers of Peace and War, 1978; Understanding War, 1990; articles in Mind, Aristotelian Soc. Proc., Philosophy, Political Studies, etc. *Recreations:* travelling and reading. *Address:* Cilhendre, Upper Saint Mary Street, Newport, Dyfed SA42 0PS. *T:* Newport (Dyfed) (01239) 820574.

GALLIERS-PRATT, Anthony Malcolm, CBE 1977; *b* 31 Jan. 1926; *s* of George Kenneth and Phyllis Galliers-Pratt; *m* 1950, Angela, *d* of Sir Charles Cayzer, 3rd Bt, and of Lady Cayzer, OBE; three *s*. *Educ:* Eton. Entered F. Pratt Engineering Corp. Ltd, 1949; Dir, 1951; subseq. Man. Dir and Chm., to 1981. *Recreations:* yachting, shooting. *Address:* Can Savella, Savella 13, Palma 07001, Mallorca.

GALLIFORD, Rt. Rev. David George; Assistant Bishop, Diocese of York, since 1991; *b* 20 June 1925; *s* of Alfred Edward Bruce and Amy Doris Galliford; *m* 1st, 1954, Enid May Drax (*d* 1983); one *d*; 2nd, 1987, Claire Margaret Phoenix. *Educ:* Bede Coll., Sunderland; Clare Coll., Cambridge (Organ Scholar, 1942, BA 1949, MA 1951); Westcott House, Cambridge. Served 5th Royal Inniskilling Dragoon Guards, 1943–47. Curate of St John Newland, Hull, 1951–54; Minor Canon of Windsor, 1954–56; Vicar of St Oswald, Middlesborough, 1956–61; Rector of Bolton Percy and Diocesan Training Officer, 1961–70; Canon of York Minster, 1969; Canon Residentiary and Treasurer of York Minster, 1970–75; Bishop Suffragan of Hulme, 1975–84; Bishop Suffragan of Bolton, 1984–91. SBStJ 1992. *Publications:* God and Christian Caring, 1973; Pastor's Post, 1975; (ed) Diocese in Mission, 1968. *Recreations:* pottery, music, painting in oils. *Address:* Bishopsgarth, Maltongate, Thornton-le-Dale, N Yorks YO18 7SA. *T:* Pickering (01751) 474605.

GALLIGAN, Prof. Denis James; Professor of Socio-Legal Studies, and Director, Centre for Socio-Legal Studies, University of Oxford, since 1993; *b* 4 June 1947; *s* of John Felix Galligan and Muriel Maud Galligan; *m* 1972, Martha Louise Martinuzzi; one *s* one *d*. *Educ:* Univ. of Queensland (LLB 1970); Univ. of Oxford (BCL 1974; MA 1976). Rhodes Scholar, Magdalen Coll., Oxford, 1971–74; Lectr, Faculty of Law, UCL, 1974–76; Fellow, Jesus Coll., and CUF Lectr, Oxford Univ., 1976–81; Sen. Lectr, Univ. of Melbourne, 1982–84; Prof. of Law, Univ. of Southampton, 1985–92 (Dean, Law Faculty, 1987–90); Prof. of Law, Univ. of Sydney, 1990–92. *Publications:* Essays in Legal Theory, 1984; Law, Rights and the Welfare State, 1986; Discretionary Powers, 1986; Australian Administrative Law, 1993; Socio-Legal Readings in Administrative Law, 1995; Socio-Legal Studies in Context, 1995. *Recreations:* reading, gardening. *Address:* Wolfson College, Linton Road, Oxford OX2 6UD; The Rosery, Beckley, Oxford OX3 9UU. *T:* Oxford (01865) 284220 and 351281.

GALLINER, Peter; Director Emeritus, International Press Institute; Chairman, Peter Galliner Associates, since 1970; *b* 19 Sept. 1920; *s* of Dr Moritz and Hedwig Galliner; *m* 1st, 1948, Edith Marguerite Goldschmidt; one *d*; 2nd, 1990, Helga Stenschke. *Educ:* Berlin and London. Reuters, 1942–47; Foreign Manager, Financial Times, 1947–60; Chm. and Man. Dir, Ullstein Publishing Co., Berlin, 1960–64; Vice-Chm. and Man. Dir, British Printing Corporation Publishing Gp, 1965–70; international publishing consultant, 1965–67 and 1970–75; Dir, Internat. Press Inst., Zürich/London, 1975–93. Order of Merit. 1st cl., 1961, and Comdr's Cross, 1990 (GFR); Ecomienda, Orden de Isabel la Católica (Spain), 1982. *Recreations:* reading, music. *Address:* 27 Walsingham, St John's Wood Park, NW8 6RH. *T:* 0171–722 5502; 8001 Zürich, Untere Zäune 9, Switzerland. *T:* (1) 2518664. *Club:* Reform.

GALLOWAY, 13th Earl of, *cr* 1623; **Randolph Keith Reginald Stewart;** Lord Garlies, 1607; Bt 1627, 1687; Baron Stewart of Garlies (GB), 1796; *b* 14 Oct. 1928; *s* of 12th Earl of Galloway, and Philippa Fendall (*d* 1974), *d* of late Jacob Wendell, New York; *S* father, 1978; *m* 1975, Mrs Lily May Budge, DLJ, *y d* of late Andrew Miller, Duns, Berwickshire. *Educ:* Harrow. KLJ. *Heir: cousin* Andrew Clyde Stewart [*b* 13 March 1949; *m* 1977, Sara, *o d* of Brig. Patrick Pollock; one *s* two *d*]. *Address:* Senwick House, Brighouse Bay, Borgue, Kirkcudbrightshire DG6 4TP.

GALLOWAY, Bishop of, (RC), since 1981; **Rt. Rev. Maurice Taylor,** DD; *b* 5 May 1926; *s* of Maurice Taylor and Lucy Taylor (*née* McLaughlin). *Educ:* St Aloysius Coll., Glasgow; Our Lady's High School, Motherwell; Pontifical Gregorian Univ., Rome (DD). Served RAMC in UK, India, Egypt, 1944–47. Ordained to priesthood, Rome, 1950; lectured in Philosophy, 1955–60, in Theology 1960–65, St Peter's Coll., Cardross; Rector, Royal Scots Coll., Valladolid, Spain, 1965–74; Parish Priest, Our Lady of Lourdes, East Kilbride, 1974–81. Vice-Pres., Catholic Inst. for Internat. Relations, 1985–. *Publications:* The Scots College in Spain, 1971; Guatemala: a bishop's journey, 1991; El Salvador: portrait of a parish, 1992; (with Ellen Hawkes) Opening Our Lives to the Saviour, 1995. *Address:* Candida Casa, 8 Corsehill Road, Ayr KA7 2ST. *T:* Ayr (01292) 266750.

GALLOWAY, Rev. Prof. Allan Douglas; Professor of Divinity, University of Glasgow, 1968–82, now Emeritus Professor; Principal of Trinity College, Glasgow, 1972–82; *b* 30 July 1920; *s* of late William Galloway and Mary Wallace Galloway (*née* Junor); *m* 1948, Sara Louise Phillipp; two *s*. *Educ:* Stirling High Sch.; Univ. of Glasgow; Christ's Coll., Cambridge; Union Theol Seminary, New York. MA, BD, STM, PhD. Ordained, Asst Minister, Clune Park Parish, Port Glasgow, 1948–50; Minister of Auchterhouse, 1950–54; Prof. of Religious Studies, Univ. of Ibadan, Nigeria, 1954–60; Sen. Lectr, Univ. of Glasgow, 1960–66, Reader in Divinity, 1966–68. Hensley Henson Lectr in Theology, Oxford Univ., 1978; Cunningham Lectr, Edinburgh, 1979; Gifford Lectr, Glasgow, 1984. FRSE 1985. *Publications:* The Cosmic Christ, 1951; Basic Readings in Theology, 1964; Faith in a Changing Culture, 1966; Wolfhart Pannenberg, 1973; History of Christian Theology, Vol. 1, Pt III, 1986. *Recreation:* sailing. *Address:* 5 Straid Bheag, Clynder, Helensburgh, Dunbartonshire G84 0QX.

GALLOWAY, Prof. David Malcolm, PhD; FBPsS; Professor of Primary Education, since 1992, Head of School of Education, since 1993, University of Durham; *b* 5 July 1942; *s* of Malcolm Ashby Galloway and Joan Dorah Frances Galloway (*née* Slater); *m* 1971, Christina Mary King; two *s* one *d*. *Educ:* St Edmund Hall, Oxford (BA Psychol., Phil. and Physiol. 1970; MA 1974); UCL (MSc Educnl Psychol. 1972); Sheffield City Poly (PhD 1980). FBPsS 1983. Educnl Psychologist and Sen. Educnl Psychologist, Sheffield LEA, 1972–79; Sen. Lectr, Victoria Univ. of Wellington, NZ, 1980–83; Lectr, UC Cardiff, 1983–87; Lectr and Reader in Educnl Res., Lancaster Univ., 1987–91. *Publications:* books include: Schools and Persistent Absentees, 1985; (with C. Goodwin) The Education of Disturbing Children: pupils with learning and adjustment difficulties, 1987; (with A. Edwards) Primary School Teaching and Educational Psychology, 1991; (jtly) The Assessment of Special Educational Needs: whose problem?, 1994; numerous articles in acad. and professional jls. *Recreations:* bee-keeping, fell search and mountain rescue. *Address:* Leases, Smardale, Kirkby Stephen, Cumbria CA17 4HQ.

GALLOWAY, George; MP (Lab) Glasgow, Hillhead, since 1987; *b* 16 Aug. 1954; *s* of George and Sheila Galloway; *m* 1979, Elaine Fyffe (separated, 1987); one *d*. *Educ:* Charleston Primary Sch.; Harris Acad., Dundee. Engrg worker, 1973; organiser, Labour Party, 1977; Gen. Sec., War on Want, 1983–87. *Publication:* (jtly) Downfall: the Ceausescus and the Romanian revolution, 1991. *Recreations:* boxing, football, films, music. *Address:* House of Commons, SW1A 0AA. *T:* 0171–219 4084.

GALLOWAY, Maj.-Gen. Kenneth Gardiner, CB 1978; OBE 1960; Director Army Dental Service, 1974–March 1978; *b* 3 Nov. 1917; *s* of David and Helen Galloway, Dundee and Oban; *m* 1949, Sheila Frances (*née* Dunsmor); two *d* (one *s* decd). *Educ:* Oban High Sch.; St Andrews Univ. LDS 1939, BDS 1940. Lieut Army Dental Corps, 1940; Captain 1941; Major 1948; Lt-Col 1955; Col 1963; Brig. 1972; Maj.-Gen. 1974. Served in Egypt, Palestine, Syria and Iraq, 1942–46; Chief Instructor and 2nd in comd, Depot and Training Establishment, RADC, 1956–60; Asst Dir Dental Service, MoD, 1967–71; Dep. Dir Dental Service: Southern Comd, 1971–72; BAOR, 1972–74. QHDS 1971–78. Col Comdt, RADC, 1980–83. OStJ 1960. *Recreations:* tennis, golf, gardening. *Address:* Berwyn Court, Avenue Road, Farnborough, Hants GU14 7BH. *T:* Farnborough (01252) 544948.

GALLOWAY, Rev. Dr Peter John; JP; Vicar, Emmanuel Church, West Hampstead, since 1995 (Priest-in-Charge, 1990–95); *b* 19 July 1954; *s* of late Henry John Galloway and of Mary Selina (*née* Beshaw). *Educ:* Westminster City Sch.; Goldsmiths' Coll., Univ. of London (BA); King's Coll., London (PhD); St Stephen's House, Oxford. Ordained deacon, 1983; priest, 1984; Curate: St John's Wood, 1983–86; St Giles-in-the-Fields, 1986–90; Warden of Readers, London Episcopal Area, 1987–92. St John Ambulance: Asst Dir-Gen., 1985–91; Dep. Dir-Gen., 1991–; Chm., Nat. Publications Cttee, 1988–. Mem., Lord Chancellor's Adv. Cttee, 1994–. Mem. Council, Goldsmiths' Coll., London Univ., 1993–. Vice-Chm., Goldsmiths' Soc., 1991–. Trustee, Grant Maintained Schools Charitable Trust (formerly Foundn), 1991–. Gov., Soho Parish Sch., 1989–91; Chm. of Governors, Emmanuel Sch., W Hampstead, 1990–95. FRSA. JP City of London, 1989. ChStJ 1992. *Publications:* The Order of St Patrick 1783–1983, 1983; Henry Falconer Barclay Mackay, 1983; (with Christopher Rawll) Good and Faithful Servants, 1988; The Cathedrals of Ireland, 1992; The Order of the British Empire, 1996. *Recreations:* reading, writing, book collecting, solitude. *Address:* The Vicarage, Lyncroft Gardens, NW6 1JU. *T:* 0171–435 1911. *Club:* Athenæum.

GALLWEY, Sir Philip Frankland P.; *see* Payne-Gallwey.

GALPIN, His Honour Brian John Francis; a Circuit Judge, 1978–93; an Official Referee, Western Circuit, 1986–93; *b* 21 March 1921; *s* of late Christopher John Galpin, DSO and late Gladys Elizabeth Galpin (*née* Souhami); *m* 1st, 1947, Ailsa McConnel (*d* 1959); one *d* decd; 2nd, 1961, Nancy Cecilia Nichols; two adopted *s*. *Educ:* Merchant Taylors' Sch.; Hertford Coll., Oxford. MA 1947. FCIArb. RAF Officer, 1941–45. Editor, Isis, 1946. Called to Bar, 1948; a Recorder of the Crown Court, 1972–78. Councillor, Metropolitan Borough of Fulham, 1950–59; Chm., Galpin Soc. for Study of Musical Instruments, 1954–72, Vice-Pres., 1974–; Pres., Madrigal Soc., 1989–91; Mem. Bach Choir, 1947–93 (Mem. Cttee, 1954–61). Pres., Old Merchant Taylors' Soc., 1988 and 1991. Trustee, Horniman Mus., 1990–. *Publications:* A Manual of International Law, 1950; Maxwell's Interpretation of Statutes, 10th edn 1953 and 11th edn 1962; Every Man's Own Lawyer, 69th edn 1962, 70th edn 1971, 71st edn 1981; contrib. Halsbury's Laws of England, 3rd and 4th edns, Encycl. of Forms and Precedents, Galpin Soc. Jl. *Recreations:* cricket (retired), music, chess. *Clubs:* Travellers', Pratt's; Hampshire (Winchester).

GALPIN, Rodney Desmond; Chairman, Alpha Airports Group PLC, since 1994; *b* 5 Feb. 1932; *s* of Sir Albert James Galpin, KCVO, CBE; *m* 1956, Sylvia Craven; one *s* one *d*. *Educ:* Haileybury and Imperial Service Coll. Joined Bank of England, 1952; Sec. to Governor (Lord Cromer), 1962–66; Dep. Principal, Discount Office, 1970–74; Dep. Chief Cashier, Banking and Money Markets Supervision, 1974–78; Chief of

Establishments, 1978–80; Chief of Corporate Services, 1980–82; Associate Dir, 1982–84; Exec. Dir, Bank of England, 1984–88; Chairman and Group Chief Executive: Standard Chartered plc, 1988–93; Standard Chartered Bank, 1988–93. Director: Cater Allen Holdings PLC, 1993–; Capital Shopping Centres PLC, 1994–; Ascot Holdings PLC, 1995–. Chm., Code of Banking Practice Review Cttee, 1994–. Mem. Council, Foundn for Management Educn, 1984–86. Chm., Look Ahead Housing Assoc. Ltd, 1994–. Life Governor and Council Mem., Haileybury, 1973–; Mem. Council, Scout Assoc., 1972–. CIMgt (FBIM 1979); FCIB. Freeman, City of London, 1981. OStJ. *Recreations:* tennis, gardening, music. *Address:* Alderman's Cottage, Lutmans Haven, Knowl Hill, Reading, Berks RG10 9YN. *Club:* Bankers' (Pres., 1992–93).

GALSWORTHY, Anthony Charles, CMG 1985; HM Diplomatic Service; Chief of Assessments Staff, Cabinet Office, since 1993; *b* 20 Dec. 1944; *s* of Sir Arthur Norman Galsworthy, KCMG, and Margaret Agnes Galsworthy (*née* Hiscocks); *m* 1970, Jan Dawson-Grove; one *s* one *d*. *Educ:* St Paul's Sch.; Corpus Christi Coll., Cambridge (MA). FCO, 1966–67; Hong Kong (language training), 1967–69; Peking, 1970–72; FCO, 1972–77; Rome, 1977–81; Counsellor, Peking, 1981–84; Head of Hong Kong Dept, FCO, 1984–86; Principal Private Sec. to Sec. of State for Foreign and Commonwealth Affairs, 1986–88; seconded to RIIA, 1988–89; Sen. British Rep., Sino-British Jt Liaison Gp, Hong Kong, 1989–93. *Recreations:* bird-watching, wildlife. *Address:* c/o Foreign and Commonwealth Office, King Charles Street, SW1A 2AH. *Club:* United Oxford & Cambridge University.

GALSWORTHY, (Arthur) Michael (Johnstone); DL; Chairman, Trewithen Estates Management Co. Ltd, since 1979; *b* 10 April 1944; *s* of Sir John Galsworthy, KCVO, CMG and Jennifer Ruth Johnstone; *m* 1st, 1972, Charlotte Helena Prudence Roberts (*d* 1989); one *s* two *d*; 2nd, 1991, Sarah Christian Durnford; one *s*. *Educ:* Radley; St Andrews Univ. (MA Hons). International Harvester Corp., 1967–69; English China Clays PLC, 1970–82; Man. Dir, Hawkins Wright Associates, 1982–86. Local Adv. Dir, Barclays Bank, 1987–. Mem., Prince of Wales Council, 1985–; Dir, CoSIRA, 1985–88; a Develt Comr, 1987–92; Trustee, Rural Housing Trust, 1986–92; Chairman: Cornwall Rural Housing Assoc., 1988–; Royal Cornwall Hosps NHS Trust, 1991–93; Devon & Cornwall Develt Co. Ltd, 1991–93; Westcountry Develt Corp., 1993–. Dir, Woodard Corp. (W Region), 1983–88. Chm. Council, Order of St John for Cornwall, 1995. DL Cornwall, 1993; High Sheriff, Cornwall, 1994. *Publication:* In Pursuit of Excellence: testimonial of business in Cornwall, 1994. *Recreations:* gardening, fishing, shooting, walking. *Address:* Trewithen, Grampound Road, near Truro, Cornwall TR2 4DD. *T:* St Austell (01726) 882418; Flat 11, 6/8 Clanricarde Gardens, W2 4NA. *Clubs:* Brooks's, Farmers'.

GALSWORTHY, Michael; *see* Galsworthy, A. M. J.

GALTON, Raymond Percy; author and scriptwriter since 1951; *b* 17 July 1930; *s* of Herbert and Christina Galton; *m* 1956, Tonia Phillips; one *s* two *d*. *Educ:* Garth Sch., Morden. *Television:* with Alan Simpson: Hancock's Half Hour, 1954–61 (adaptation and translation, Fleksnes, Scandinavian TV, film and stage); Comedy Playhouse, 1962–63; Steptoe and Son, 1962–74 (adaptations and translations: Sanford and Son, US TV; Stiefbeen and Zoon, Dutch TV; Albert och Herbert, Scandinavian TV, film and stage); Galton-Simpson Comedy, 1969; Clochemerle, 1971; Casanova '74, 1974; Dawson's Weekly, 1975; The Galton and Simpson Playhouse, 1976–77; with Johnny Speight: Tea Ladies, 1979; Spooner's Patch, 1979–80; with John Antrobus: Room at the Bottom, 1986–87 (Banff TV Fest. Award for Best Comedy, 1987); *films* with Alan Simpson: The Rebel, 1960; The Bargee, 1963; The Spy with a Cold Nose, 1966; Loot, 1969; Steptoe and Son, 1971; Steptoe and Son Ride Again, 1973; Den Siste Fleksnes (Scandinavia), 1974; Die Skraphandlerne (Scandinavia), 1975; with Alan Simpson and John Antrobus: The Wrong Arm of the Law, 1963, with Andrew Galton: Camping (Denmark), 1990; *theatre:* with Alan Simpson. Way Out in Piccadilly, 1966; The Wind in the Sassafras Trees, 1968; Albert och Herbert (Sweden), 1981; Fleksnes (Norway), 1983; Mordet pa Skolgatan 15 (Sweden), 1984; with John Antrobus: When Did You Last See Your Trousers?, 1986, UK tour, 1994. Awards, with Alan Simpson: Scriptwriters of the Year, 1959 (Guild of TV Producers and Directors); Best TV Comedy Series, Steptoe and Son, 1962/3/4/5 (Screenwriters Guild); John Logie Baird Award (for outstanding contribution to Television), 1964; Best Comedy Series (Steptoe and Son, Dutch TV), 1966; Best comedy screenplay, Steptoe and Son, 1972 (Screenwriters Guild). *Publications:* (with Alan Simpson): Hancock, 1961; Steptoe and Son, 1963; The Reunion and Other Plays, 1966; Hancock Scripts, 1974; The Best of Hancock, 1986; The Best of Steptoe and Son, 1988. *Recreations:* reading, worrying. *Address:* The Ivy House, Hampton Court, Mddx KT8 9DD. *T:* 0181–977 1236; Tessa Le Bars Management, 54 Birchwood Road, Petts Wood, Kent BR5 1NZ. *T:* Orpington (01689) 837084.

GALVIN, Bernard Vincent Joseph, CB 1991; Treasurer, Victoria University of Wellington, since 1990; Visiting Fellow, Institute of Policy Studies, since 1989; *b* 15 March 1933; *s* of Eustace Bartholemew Galvin and Margaret Jean (*née* Lenihan); *m* 1st, 1960, Beverly Ann Snook (marr. diss. 1977); three *s* one *d*; 2nd, 1980, Margaret Clark. *Educ:* Univ. of NZ (BSc 1954); Victoria Univ. of Wellington (BA Hons 1959); Harvard Univ. (MPA 1961). Joined Treasury, NZ, 1955; Harkness Fellow, USA, 1960–61; Econ. Counsellor, NZ High Commn, London, 1965–68; Treasury Dir, 1969; Asst Sec., 1972; Dep. Sec., 1974; Perm. Head of PM's Dept, 1975–80; Sec. to Treasury, 1980–86; Chm., Econ. Develt Commn, 1986–89. Alternate Gov., World Bank, 1976–86. Chm., Ministerial Wkg Pty on Disability and Accident Compensation, 1991. Mem. Council, Victoria Univ. of Wellington, 1989–. *Publications:* Policy Co-ordination, Public Sector and Government, 1991; chapters in books on NZ government; articles in public admin jls. *Recreations:* beach house, gardening, reading, walking. *Address:* 10 Jellicoe Towers, 189 The Terrace, Wellington, New Zealand. *T:* (weekdays) (4) 4728143; (weekends) (6) 3643374. *Club:* Wellington (Wellington, NZ).

GALVIN, General John Rogers; General, United States Army, retired; Supreme Allied Commander, Europe, and Commander-in-Chief, US European Command, Stuttgart, 1987–92; Olin Distinguished Professor of National Security, West Point, since 1992; *b* 13 May 1929; *s* of John J. Galvin and Josephine Mary Logan; *m* 1961, Virginia Lee Brennan; four *d*. *Educ:* US Mil. Acad. (BS); Columbia Univ. (MA); US Army Command and General Staff Coll.; Univ. of Pennsylvania; US Army War Coll.; Fletcher Sch. of Law and Diplomacy (US Army War Coll. Fellowship). Platoon Leader, I Co., 65 Inf. Regt, Puerto Rico, 1955–56; Instructor, Ranger Sch., Colombia, 1956–58; Co. Comdr, 501 Airborne Battle Group, 101 Airborne Div., 1958–60; Instructor, US Mil. Acad., 1962–65; DACOS, Plans, 1st Cavalry Div., Vietnam, 1966–67; MA and Aide to Sec. of US Army, 1967–69; Comdr, 1st Bn, 8th Cavalry, 1st Cavalry Div., Vietnam, 1969–70; Dep. Sec., Jt Staff, US European Comd, Stuttgart, 1973–74; MA to SACEUR, 1974–75; Comdr, Div. Support Comd, 1975–77; COS, 3rd Inf. Div. (Mechanized), Würzburg, 1977–78; Asst Div. Comdr, 8th Inf. Div. (Mechanized), Mainz, 1978–80; Asst DCOS for Training, US Army Training and Doctrine Comd, 1980–81; Comdg Gen., 24 Inf. Div. (Mechanized), and Fort Stewart, 1981–83; Comdg Gen., VII Corps, Stuttgart, 1983–85; C-in-C, US Southern Comd, Panama, 1985–87. Defense DSM, Army DSM, Navy DSM, Air Force DSM, Silver Star, Legion of Merit (with 2 Oak Leaf Clusters), DFC, Soldier's Medal, Bronze Star (with 2 Oak Leaf Clusters), Combat Infantryman Badge, Ranger Tab, foreign decorations. *Publications:* The Minute Men, 1967; Air Assault: the development of airmobility, 1969; Three Men of Boston, 1975. *Recreations:* walking, jogging. *Address:* Social Sciences Department, West Point, NY 10996, USA.

GALWAY, 12th Viscount *cr* 1727; **George Rupert Monckton-Arundell;** Baron Killard, 1727; Lieut Comdr RCN, retired; *b* 13 Oct. 1922; *s* of Philip Marmaduke Monckton (*d* 1965) (*g g s* of 5th Viscount) and of Lavender, *d* of W. J. O'Hara; *S* cousin, 1980; *m* 1944, Fiona Margaret, *d* of late Captain P. W. de P. Taylor; one *s* three *d*. *Heir:* *s* Hon. John Philip Monckton [*b* 8 April 1952; *m* 1980, Deborah Holmes (marr. diss.)]. *Address:* 787 Berkshire Drive, London, Ontario N6J 3S5, Canada.

GALWAY AND KILMACDUAGH, Bishop of, (RC), since 1993; **Most Rev. James McLoughlin;** *b* 9 April 1929; *s* of Patrick McLoughlin and Winifred (*née* McDermott). *Educ:* St Patrick's Coll., Maynooth (BA, HDipEd). Ordained priest, 1954; Professor, St Mary's Coll., Galway, 1954–65; Diocesan Secretary, 1965–83; Parish Priest, Galway Cathedral, 1983–93. *Address:* Diocesan Office, The Cathedral, Galway, Ireland. *T:* (91) 63566.

GALWAY, James, OBE 1977; FRCM 1983; fluteplayer; *b* 8 Dec. 1939; *s* of James Galway and Ethel Stewart Clarke; *m* 1st, 1965; one *s*; 2nd, 1972; one *s* twin *d*; 3rd, 1984, Jeanne Cinnante. *Educ:* St Paul's Sch., and Mountcollyer Secondary Modern Sch., Belfast; RCM, and Guildhall Sch. of Music, London; Conservatoire National Supérieur de Musique, Paris. First post in wind band of Royal Shakespeare Theatre, Stratford-upon-Avon; later worked with Sadler's Wells Orch., Royal Opera House Orch. and BBC Symphony Orch.; Principal Flute, London Symphony Orch., 1966, Royal Philharmonic Orch., 1967–69; Principal Solo Flute, Berlin Philharmonic Orch., 1969–75; international soloist, 1975–. Recordings of works by C. P. E. Bach, J. S. Bach, Beethoven, Corigliano, Debussy, Franck, Handel, Khachaturian, Mancini, Mozart, Nielsen, Prokoviev, Reicha, Reincke, Rodrigo, Schubert, Stamitz, Telemann and Vivaldi; also albums of flute showpieces, Australian, Irish and Japanese collections. Grand Prix du Disque, 1976, 1989. Hon. MA Open, 1979; Hon. DMus: QUB, 1979; New England Conservatory of Music, 1980. Officier des Arts et des Lettres, France, 1987. *Publications:* James Galway: an autobiography, 1978; Flute (Menuhin Music Guide), 1982; James Galway's Music in Time, 1983 (TV series, 1983); Masterclass: performance editions of great flute literature, 1987. *Recreations:* music, walking, swimming, films, theatre, TV, chess, backgammon, computing, talking to people. *Address:* c/o Kathryn Enticott, IMG Artists, Media House, 3 Burlington Lane, Chiswick W4 2TH. *T:* 0181–233 5800.

GAM, Rt Rev. Sir Getake, KBE 1995; Head Bishop, Evangelical Lutheran Church of Papua New Guinea, since 1982; *b* 12 August 1943; *s* of Getanuka Gam and Maluave Gam; *m* 1975, Anna Goba; two *s* three *d* and one adopted *s*. *Educ:* Martin Luther Seminary, Lae, PNG (BTh). Pastoral Ministry, Finschhafen and Panguna, Bougainville, 1971–75; teacher, Martin Luther Seminary, 1976–78; Dir, Evangelism Dept, Evangelical Lutheran Ch of PNG, 1978–81. Sec. and Treas., Lae Soccer Referees Assoc. Independence Medal (PNG), 1975. *Recreation:* football (formerly played soccer and Australian rules football). *Address:* Evangelical Lutheran Church of Papua New Guinea, Box 80, Lae, Papua New Guinea. *T:* 423711, *Fax:* 421056.

GAMBLE, Sir David (Hugh Norman), 6th Bt *cr* 1897; *b* 1 July 1966; *s* of Sir David Gamble, 5th Bt and of Dawn Adrienne, *d* of late David Hugh Gittins; *S* father, 1984. *Educ:* Shiplake College, Henley-on-Thames. *Heir:* *cousin* Hugh Robert George Gamble, *b* 3 March 1946. *Address:* Keinton House, Keinton Mandeville, Somerton, Somerset TA11 4DX. *T:* Charlton Mackrell (0145822) 3964.

GAMBLE, Richard Arthur; Group Chief Executive, Royal Insurance Holdings PLC, since 1992; *b* 19 Sept. 1939; *s* of late Arthur Gamble and of Grace Emily Gamble (*née* Little); *m* 1966, Elizabeth Ann, *d* of Edward Godwin-Atkyns; two *s*. *Educ:* Raynes Park Co. Grammar Sch. FCA 1962. Articled clerk, W. J. Gilbert & Co., London, 1957–62; Asst Manager, Turquand Youngs & Co., 1962–66; Dir and Co. Sec., Lee Davy Gp Ltd, 1966–68; Dir and Sec., Hamilton Smith, Lloyd's Brokers, 1968–70; Finance Dir, Lowndes Lambert Internat., Lloyd's Brokers, 1970–76; European Finance Dir, Data100/Northern Telecom Systems, 1976–80; Finance Dir, McDonnell Douglas Inf. Systems and Dir, McDonnell Douglas UK, 1980–84; Dep. Chief Financial Officer, British Airways, 1984–89; Royal Insurance Holdings PLC: Gp Finance Dir, 1989–91; Gp Chief Operating Officer, 1991. Mem. Bd, ABI, 1994–; Chm., Policy Holders Protection Bd, 1994– (Dir, 1993–). Mem., Adv. Cttee on Business in the Envmt and Chm., Financial Services Working Gp, 1993–. *Recreations:* all sport, particularly golf, walking with dogs, theatre. *Address:* Royal Insurance Holdings PLC, 1 Cornhill, EC3V 3QR. *T:* 0171–283 4300, *Fax:* 0171–283 4841; Chart Hall Farm, Green Lane, Chart Sutton, Kent ME17 3ES. *T:* Maidstone (01622) 842526.

GAMBLING, Prof. William Alexander, PhD, DSc; FRS 1983; FEng, Hon. FIEE; Professor of Optical Communication, since 1980, and Director, Optoelectronics Research Centre, since 1989, University of Southampton; industrial consultant and company director; *b* 11 Oct. 1926; *s* of George Alexander Gambling and Muriel Clara Gambling; *m* 1952, Margaret Pooley (marr. diss. 1994); one *s* two *d*; *m* 1994, Barbara Colleen O'Neil. *Educ:* Univ. of Bristol (BSc, DSc); Univ. of Liverpool (PhD). FIERE 1964; CEng, FIEE 1967; FEng 1979. Lectr in Electric Power Engrg, Univ. of Liverpool, 1950–55; National Res. Council Fellow, Univ. of BC, 1955–57; Univ. of Southampton: Lectr, Sen. Lectr, and Reader, 1957–64; Dean of Engrg and Applied Science, 1972–75; Prof. of Electronics, 1964–80, Hd of Dept, 1974–79. Vis. Professor: Univ. of Colo, USA, 1966–67; Bhabha Atomic Res. Centre, India, 1970; Osaka Univ., Japan, 1977; City Univ. of Hong Kong, 1995; Hon. Professor: Huazhong Univ. of Sci. and Technol., Wuhan, China, 1986–; Beijing Inst. of Posts and Telecommunications, Beijing, China, 1987–; Shanghai Univ. of Sci. and Tech., 1991–; Hon. Dir, Beijing Optical Fibre Inst., 1987–. Pres., IERE, 1977–78 (Hon. Fellow 1983). Member: Electronics Res. Council, 1977–80 (Mem., Optics and Infra-Red Cttee, 1965–69 and 1974–80); Board, Council of Engrg Instns, 1974–79; National Electronics Council, 1977–78; 1984–; Technol. Sub-Cttee of UGC, 1973–83; British Nat. Cttee for Radio Science, 1978–87; Nat. Adv. Bd for Local Authority Higher Educn, Engrg Working Gp, 1982–84; Engineering Council, 1983–88; British Nat. Cttee for Internat. Engineering Affairs, 1984–88; Chm., Commn D, Internat. Union of Radio Science, 1984–87 (Vice-Chm., 1981–84). Selby Fellow, Australian Acad. of Science, 1982; For. Mem., Polish Acad. of Scis, 1985. Freeman, City of London, 1988; Liveryman, Worshipful Co. of Engrs, 1988. Dr *hc* Univ. Politècnica de Madrid, 1994. Bulgin Premium, IERE, 1961, Rutherford Premium, IERE, 1964, Electronics Div. Premium, IEE, 1976 and 1978, Oliver Lodge Premium, IEE, 1981, Heinrich Hertz Premium, IERE, 1981, for research papers; J. J. Thomson Medal, IEE, 1982, Faraday Medal, IEE, 1983, Churchill Medal, Soc. of Engineers, 1984 and Simms Medal, Soc. of Engineers, 1989, for research innovation and leadership; Academic Enterprise Award, 1982; Micro-optics Award, Japan, 1989; Dennis Gabor Award, Internat. Soc. for Optical Engrg, USA, 1990; Rank Prize for Optoelectronics, 1991; Medal and Prize, Foundn for Computer and Communications Promotion, Japan, 1993; Mountbatten Medal, Nat. Electronics Council,

1993. *Publications:* papers on electronics and optical fibre communications. *Recreations:* music, reading, walking. *Address:* Optoelectronics Research Centre, University of Southampton, Southampton SO15 7PA. *T:* Southampton (01703) 593373.

GAMBON, Michael John, CBE 1990; actor; *b* 19 Oct. 1940; *s* of Edward and Mary Gambon; *m* 1962, Anne Miller; one *s*. *Educ:* St Aloysius School for Boys, Somers Town, London. Served 7 year apprenticeship in engineering; first appeared on stage with Edwards/MácLiammoir Co., Dublin, 1962; Nat. Theatre, Old Vic, 1963–67; Birmingham Rep. and other provincial theatres, 1967–69 (title rôles incl. Othello, Macbeth, Coriolanus); RSC Aldwych, 1970–71; Norman Conquests, Globe, 1974; Otherwise Engaged, Queen's, 1976; Just Between Ourselves, Queen's 1977; Alice's Boys, Savoy, 1978; King Lear and Antony and Cleopatra (title rôles), RSC Stratford and Barbican, 1982–83; Old Times, Haymarket, 1985; Uncle Vanya, Vaudeville, 1988; Veterans Day, Haymarket, 1989; Man of the Moment, Globe, 1990; Othello and Taking Steps, Scarborough, 1990; National Theatre: Galileo, 1980 (London Theatre Critics' Award, Best Actor); Betrayal, 1980; Tales From Hollywood, 1980; Chorus of Disapproval, 1985 (Olivier Award, Best Comedy Performance); Tons of Money, 1986; A View from the Bridge, 1987 (Best Actor, Evening Standard Awards, Olivier Awards, and Plays and Players London Theatre Critics Awards; Best Stage Actor, Variety Club Awards); A Small Family Business, 1987; Mountain Language, 1988; Skylight, and Volpone, 1995. *Television* includes: The Singing Detective, 1986 (BAFTA Award, Best Actor, 1987); Maigret, 1992, 1993; Faith, 1994. *Films* include: The Cook, The Thief, His Wife and Her Lover, 1989; The Heat of the Day, 1989; Paris by Night, 1989; A Dry White Season, 1990; Mobsters, 1992; Toys, 1992; The Browning Version, 1993; A Man of No Importance, 1994; Mary Reilly, 1994; Two Deaths, 1994; Midnight in Moscow, 1994; The Innocent Sleep, 1995; All Our Fault, 1995. Liveryman, Gunmakers' Co. *Recreations:* flying, gun collecting, clock making. *Address:* c/o Conway Van Gelder Robinson Ltd, 18–21 Jermyn Street, SW1Y 6HP.

GAMES, Abram, OBE 1958; RDI 1959; graphic designer; *b* 29 July 1914; *s* of Joseph and Sarah Games; *m* 1945, Marianne Salfeld; one *s* two *d*. *Educ:* Grocers' Company Sch., Hackney Downs. Studio, 1932–36; freelance designer, 1936–40. Infantry, 1940–41; War Office Poster Designer, 1941–46. Freelance, 1946–; Lecturer Royal College of Art, 1947–53. Postage Stamps for Great Britain and Israel, Festival of Britain, BBC Television, Queen's Award to Industry Emblems. One-man shows of graphic design: London and UK, New York, Chicago, Brussels, Stockholm, Jerusalem, Tel Aviv, São Paulo; Rep. Gt Brit. at Museum of Modern Art, New York. Hon. FRCA 1992. Hon. DLitt Staffordshire Univ., 1994. First prizes, Poster Competitions: Helsinki, 1957; Lisbon, 1959; New York, 1960; Stockholm, 1962; Barcelona, 1964; Design Medal, Soc. of Industrial Artists, 1960; Silver Medal, Royal Society of Arts, 1962; first prize, Internat. Philatelic Competition, Italy, 1976; President's Award, Design and Art Direction, 1991. Inventor of Imagic Copying Processes. *Publication:* Over my Shoulder, 1960. *Recreations:* painting, carpentry. *Address:* 41 The Vale, NW11 8SE. *T:* 0181–458 2811.

GAMMELL, James Gilbert Sydney, MBE 1944; CA; *b* 4 March 1920; *e s* of Lt-Gen. Sir James A. H. Gammell, KCB, DSO, MC; *m* 1944, Susan Patricia Bowring Toms, *d* of late Edward Bowring Toms; five *s* one *d*. *Educ:* Winchester Coll. Chartered Accountant, 1949. Served War, Major Grenadier Guards, 1939–46: France, 1940 and 1944, Russia, 1945. Chm., Ivory & Sime, 1975–85. *Recreation:* farming. *Address:* Foxhall, Kirkliston, West Lothian EH29 9ER. *T:* 0131–333 3275. *Club:* New (Edinburgh).

See also J. F. Gammell.

GAMMELL, John Frederick, MC 1943; MA; *b* 31 Dec. 1921; 2nd *s* of Lieut-Gen. Sir James A. H. Gammell, KCB, DSO, MC; *m* 1947, Margaret Anne, *d* of Ralph Juckes, Fiddington Manor, Tewkesbury; two *s* one *d*. *Educ:* Winchester Coll.; Trinity Coll., Cambridge. MA 1953. Asst Master, Horris Hill, Newbury, 1940–41. War Service with KRRC, 1941–44; wounded, 1943; invalided out, 1944. Trinity Coll., Cambridge, 1946–47 (BA); Asst Master, Winchester Coll., 1944–45 and 1947–68; Exchange with Sen. Classics Master, Geelong Grammar Sch., Australia, 1949–50; Housemaster of Turner's, Winchester Coll., 1958–68; Headmaster, Repton Sch., 1968–78; Asst Sec., Cambridge Univ. Careers Service, 1978–83. *Recreation:* friends. *Address:* The Old School House, Seaton, Uppingham LE15 9HR. *T:* Morcott (01572) 747835.

See also J. G. S. Gammell.

GAMMIE, Gordon Edward, CB 1981; QC 1989; Counsel to the Speaker (European Legislation etc), House of Commons, 1983–93; *b* 9 Feb. 1922; *e s* of Dr Alexander Edward Gammie and Ethel Mary Gammie (*née* Miller); *m* 1949, Joyce Rust; two *s*. *Educ:* St Paul's Sch.; The Queen's Coll., Oxford (MA). War service, 1941–45; Captain, 1st Bn Argyll and Sutherland Highlanders. Called to Bar, Middle Temple, 1948. Entered Govt Legal Service, 1949; Asst Solicitor, Mins of Health and of Housing and Local Govt, 1967; Under-Sec. (Principal Asst Solicitor), Min. of Housing and Local Govt, later DoE, 1969–74; Under-Sec., Cabinet Office, 1975–77; Dep. Treasury Solicitor, 1977–79; Legal Advr and Solicitor to MAFF, 1979–83. Mgt Sec., St Andrew's URC, Cheam. *Recreations:* tennis, listening to music, dog-walking. *Address:* Ty Gwyn, 52 Sutton Lane, Banstead, Surrey SM7 3RB. *T:* Burgh Heath (01737) 355287.

GAMON, Hugh Wynell, CBE 1979; MC 1944; formerly Partner, Winckworth & Pemberton (incorporating Sherwood & Co., 1991); HM Government Agent, since 1970; *b* 31 March 1921; *s* of Judge Hugh R. P. Gamon and E. Margaret Gamon; *m* 1949, June Elizabeth, *d* of William and Florence Temple; one *s* three *d*. *Educ:* St Edward's Sch., Oxford; Exeter Coll., Oxford, 1946–48. MA 1st Cl. Hons Jurisprudence; Law Society Hons; Edmund Thomas Childe Prize. Served War, 1940–46: Royal Corps of Signals, N Africa, Italy and Palestine, with 1st Division. Articled to Clerk of Cumberland CC, 1949–51; joined Sherwood & Co., 1951; Parly Agent, 1954; Sen. Partner, Sherwood & Co., 1972; retd from Winckworth & Pemberton, 1995. *Recreation:* gardening. *Address:* Black Charles, Underriver, Sevenoaks, Kent TN15 0RY. *T:* Hildenborough (01732) 833036. *Club:* St Stephen's Constitutional.

GANDAR, Hon. Leslie Walter; JP; Chairman: Capital Discovery Place, since 1988; Andrews Environmental (NZ) Ltd; Andrews Environmental (Australia) Ltd; *b* 26 Jan. 1919; *s* of Max Gandar and Doris Harper; *m* 1945, M. Justine, *d* of T. A. Smith and Florence Smith; four *s* one *d* (and one *d* decd). *Educ:* Wellington College; Victoria Univ., Wellington (BSc 1940). FNZIAS, FInstP. Served RNZAF and RAF, 1940–44. Farming, 1945–. MP, Ruahine, 1966–78; Minister of Science, Energy Resources, Mines, Electricity, 1972; Minister of Education, Science and Technology, 1975–78; High Comr for NZ in UK, 1979–82. Chairman, Pohangina County Council, 1954–69. Chancellor, Massey Univ., 1970–76. Chairman: NZ Social Adv. Council, 1982–87; NZ SSRC, 1984–89; Queen Elizabeth II Nat. Trust of NZ, 1983–87; NZ Royal Society Prince and Princess of Wales Science Award Liaison Cttee; NZ Cttee, C. A. Baker Trust (UK), 1982–. Mem., Waitangi NT, 1992–. Pres., Friends of Turnbull Library, 1984–91. JP 1958. Hon. DSc Massey, 1977. *Recreations:* music—when not watching cricket; wood-carving; work. *Address:* 34 Palliser Road, Wellington, New Zealand.

GANDHI, Manmohan Purushottam, MA, FREconS, FSS; Editor, Major Industries of India Annual, since 1951 (vol. 34, 1988); Director: Indian Link Chain Manufacturers Ltd; Zenith Ltd; Orient General Industries Ltd; *b* 5 Nov. 1901; *s* of late Purushottam Kahanji Gandhi, of Limbdi (Kathiawad); *m* 1926, Rambhaben, BA (Indian Women's Univ.), *d* of Sukhlal Chhaganlal Shah of Wadhwan. *Educ:* Bahauddin Coll., Junagad; Gujerat Coll., Ahmedabad; Hindu Univ., Benares. BA (History and Econs), Bombay Univ., 1923; MA (Political Econ. and Political Philosophy), Benares Hindu Univ., 1925; Ashburner Prize of Bombay Univ., 1925. Statistical Asst, Govt of Bombay, Labour Office, 1926; Asst Sec., Indian Currency League, Bombay, 1926; Sec., Indian Chamber of Commerce, Calcutta, 1926–36; Sec., Indian Sugar Mills Assoc., 1932–36; Officer-in-Charge, Credit Dept, National City Bank of New York, Calcutta, 1936–37; Chief Commercial Manager, Rohtas Industries Ltd; Dalmia Cement Ltd, 1937–39; Dir, Indian Sugar Syndicate Ltd, 1937–39; Controller of Supplies, Bengal and Bombay, 1941–43; Sec., Indian Nat. Cttee, Internat. Chamber of Commerce, Calcutta, 1929–31; Sec., Fedn of Indian Chambers of Commerce and Industry, 1928–29. Member: East Indian Railway Adv. Cttee, 1939–40; Bihar Labour Enquiry Cttee, 1937–39; UP and Bihar Power Alcohol Cttee, 1938; UP and Bihar Sugar Control Board, 1938; Western Railway Adv. Cttee, Bombay, 1950–52; Small Scale Industries Export Prom. Adv. Cttee; Technical Adviser, Indian Tariff Board, 1947. Hon. Prof., Sydenham Coll. of Commerce, 1943–50. Member: All India Council of Tech. Educn, 1948–73; All India Bd of Studies in Commerce, 1948–70; All India Bd of Management Studies, 1978–84; Indian Merchants Chamber Cttee, 1945–83; Indian Council of Agriculture Res., 1959–66; Senate and Syndicate, Bombay Univ., 1957–69; Dean, Commerce Faculty, Bombay Univ., 1966–67. Director: E India Cotton Assoc., 1953–73 and 1983–84; Bombay Oils & Oilseeds Exchange, 1972–74; Bombay Yarn Exchange, 1972–75. Member: All-India Handloom Bd, 1952–58; Central Silk Bd, 1954–60; Handloom Export Adv. Council, 1965–68; Small-Scale Industries Bd, 1965–69. National FAO Liaison Cttee, 1974–76. Hon. Metropolitan Magistrate, Bombay, 1947–84; JP 1951–68. Swadeshi Prachar Sanuti, 1930–36. *Publications:* (with a foreword by Mahatma Gandhi) How to Compete with Foreign Cloth, 1931; The Indian Sugar Industry: Its Past, Present and Future, 1934; The Indian Cotton Textile Industry-Its Past, Present and Future, 1937; The Indian Sugar Industry (annually, 1935–64); The Indian Cotton Textile Industry, (annually, 1936–60); Centenary Volume of the Indian Cotton Textile Industry, 1851–1950; Problems of Sugar Industry in India, 1946; Monograph on Handloom Weaving in India, 1953; Some Impressions of Japan, 1955; What I learnt from the Mahatma including the Twelve Letters of Mahatma Gandhi to M. P. Gandhi, 1930–32, with reminiscences, 1995. *Recreations:* tennis (name recorded for first time in Limca Book of Records, as oldest tennis player, playing tennis at 91, 1992), badminton, billiards, bridge, cricket. *Address:* Giri Kunj, 3rd Floor, 11 Patkar Marg, Bombay 400007, India. *T:* (home) 3678405; 3624235. *Clubs:* Radio, National Sports, Rotary, Fifty-Five Tennis, Garden (Bombay); Pune (Pune).

GANDY, Christopher Thomas; HM Diplomatic Service, retired; *b* 21 April 1917; *s* of late Dr Thomas H. Gandy and late Mrs Ida Gandy (authoress of A Wiltshire Childhood, Around the Little Steeple, etc); unmarried. *Educ:* Marlborough; King's Coll., Cambridge. On active service with Army and RAF, 1939–45. Entered Foreign Office, Nov. 1945; Tehran, 1948–51; Cairo, 1951–52; FO, 1952–54; Lisbon, 1954–56; Libya, 1956–59; FO, 1960–62; apptd HM Minister to The Yemen, 1962, subsequently Counsellor, Kuwait; Minister (Commercial) Rio de Janeiro, 1966–68. Sen. Common Room Mem., St Antony's Coll., Oxford, 1973–. *Publications:* articles in Asian Affairs, Middle East International, The New Middle East, The Annual Register of World Events, Art International, Arts of Asia, Jl of Royal Asiatic Soc., and Financial Times. *Recreations:* music, photography, gardening. *Address:* 60 Ambleside Drive, Headington, Oxford OX3 0AH. *Club:* Travellers'.

GANDY, David Stewart, CB 1989; OBE 1981; Consultant, Pannone and Partners, solicitors, since 1993; Deputy Director of Public Prosecutions and Chief Executive, Crown Prosecution Service, 1987–93; *b* 19 Sept. 1932; *s* of Percy Gandy and Elizabeth Mary (*née* Fox); *m* 1956, Mabel Sheldon; one *s* one *d*. *Educ:* Manchester Grammar Sch.; Manchester Univ. Nat. Service, Intell. Corps (Germany and Austria), 1954–56. Admitted Solicitor, 1954; Asst Solicitor, Town Clerk, Manchester, 1956–59; Chief Prosecuting Solicitor: Manchester, 1959–68; Manchester and Salford, 1968–74; Gtr Manchester, 1974–85; Head of Field Management, Crown Prosecution Service, 1985–87; Acting DPP, Oct. 1991–May 1992. Lect. tour on English Criminal Justice System, for Amer. Bar Assoc., USA and Canada, 1976. Law Society: Mem., Criminal Law Standing Cttee, 1969–; Mem., Council, 1984–; Prosecuting Solicitors' Society of England and Wales: Mem., Exec. Council, 1966–85; Pres., 1976–78; Chm., Heads of Office, 1982–83; President: Manchester Law Soc., 1980–81; Manchester and Dist Medico-Legal Soc., 1982–84; Manchester Trainee Lawyers Gp, 1982–84. Non-exec. Dir, Mancunian Community Health NHS Trust, 1993–. Mem. Council, Order of St John, 1978–85. *Recreations:* cricket, theatre, bridge, walking. *Address:* c/o Export House, 50 Ludgate Hill, EC4M 7EX. *Clubs:* Royal Automobile; St James's (Manchester).

GANDY, Ronald Herbert; Treasurer to the Greater London Council, 1972–77, retired; *b* 22 Nov. 1917; *s* of Frederick C. H. Gandy and Olive (*née* Wilson) *m* 1942, Patricia M. Turney; two *s* one *d*. *Educ:* Banister Court Sch. and Taunton's Sch. (now Taunton's Coll.), Southampton. Town Clerk's Dept, Civic Centre, Southampton County Borough Council, 1936; LCC: Admin. Officer, Comptroller's (i.e. Treasurer's) Dept, 1937; Asst Comptroller, 1957; Dep. Comptroller, 1964; Dep. Treasurer, GLC, 1965; Dep. Chief Financial Officer, Inner London Educn Authority, 1967. Mem. CIPFA. *Address:* Braemar, 4 Roughwood Close, Watford, Herts WD1 3HN. *T:* Watford (01923) 224215.

GANE, Barrie Charles, CMG 1988; OBE 1978; HM Diplomatic Service, retired; Director Group Research, Group 4 Securitas, since 1993; *b* 19 Sept. 1935; *s* of Charles Ernest Gane and Margaret Gane; *m* 1974, Jennifer Anne Pitt; two *d* of former marriage. *Educ:* King Edward's School, Birmingham; Corpus Christi College, Cambridge. MA. Foreign Office, 1960; served Vientiane, Sarawak, Kuching and Warsaw; First Sec., Kampala, 1967; FCO, 1970; First Sec., later Counsellor, seconded to HQ British Forces, Hong Kong, 1977; Counsellor, FCO, 1982–92. *Recreations:* walking, reading. *Club:* Brooks's.

GANE, Michael, DPhil, MA; economic and environmental consultant; *b* 29 July 1927; *s* of late Rudolf E. Gane and Helen Gane; *m* 1954, Madge Stewart Taylor; one *d*. *Educ:* Colyton Grammar Sch., Devon; Edinburgh Univ. (BSc Forestry 1948); London Univ. (BSc Econ 1963); Oxford Univ. (DPhil, MA 1967). Asst Conservator of Forests, Tanganyika, 1948–62; Sen. Research Officer, Commonwealth Forestry Inst., Oxford, 1963–69; Dir, Project Planning Centre for Developing Countries, Bradford Univ., 1969–74; Dir, England, Nature Conservancy Council, 1974–81. *Publications:* various contribs to scientific and technical jls. *Recreations:* natural history, gardening. *Address:* 8 Rotha Field Road, Oxford OX2 8JJ.

GANELLIN, Charon Robin, PhD, DSc; FRS 1986; CChem, FRSC; Smith Kline and French Professor of Medicinal Chemistry, University College London, since 1986; *b* 25 Jan. 1934; *s* of Leon Ganellin and Beila Cluer; *m* 1956, Tamara Greene; one *s* one *d*. *Educ:* Harrow County Grammar School for Boys; Queen Mary Coll., London Univ. (BSc, PhD, DSc; Fellow, QMW, 1992). Res. Associate, MIT, 1960; Res. Chemist, then Dept Hd in Medicinal Chem., Smith Kline & French Labs Ltd, 1958–59, 1961–75; Smith Kline & French Research Ltd: Dir, Histamine Res., 1975–80; Vice-President: Research,

1980–84; Chem. Res., 1984–86. Hon. Lectr, Dept of Pharmacol., UCL, 1975–; Hon. Prof. of Medicinal Chem., Univ. of Kent at Canterbury, 1979–. Tilden Lectr, RSC, 1982. Chm., Soc. for Drug Res., 1985–87; Hon. Mem., Soc. Española de Quimica Terapeutica, 1982. Hon. DSc Aston, 1995. Medicinal Chem. Award, RSC, 1977; Prix Charles Mentzer, Soc. de Chimie Therap., 1978; Div. of Medicinal Chem. Award, ACS, 1980; Messel Medal, SCI, 1988; Award for Drug Discovery, Soc. for Drug Res., 1989; USA Nat. Inventors' Hall of Fame. 1990. *Publications:* Pharmacology of Histamine Receptors, 1982; Frontiers in Histamine Research, 1985; Dictionary of Drugs, 1990; (jtly) Medicinal Chemistry, 1993; res. papers and reviews in various jls, incl. Jl Med. Chem., Jl Chem. Soc., Brit. Jl Pharmacol. *Recreations:* music, sailing, walking. *Address:* Department of Chemistry, University College London, 20 Gordon Street, WC1H 0AJ.

GANT, John; Director of Personnel, Inland Revenue, since 1992; *b* 25 Feb. 1944; *s* of William and Barbara Gant; *m* 1967, Annette Sonia Cobb; two *s*. *Educ:* Univ. of Newcastle upon Tyne (BA Hons French and German). Inland Revenue: Inspector of Taxes, 1966; Dist Inspector, 1972–74; Head Office Adviser, 1974–77; Dist Inspector, 1977–81; Group Controller, 1981–83; Asst Dir, Ops, 1983–88; Regl Controller, 1988–90; Dep. Dir, Ops, 1990–92. *Recreations:* music, theatre, travel, fell-walking. *Address:* Inland Revenue, Somerset House, Strand, WC2B 1LB.

GANZ, Prof. Peter Felix; Professor of German, University of Oxford, 1972–85, now Emeritus; *b* 3 Nov. 1920; *s* of Dr Hermann and Dr Charlotte Ganz; *m* 1st, 1949, Rosemary (*née* Allen) (*d* 1986); two *s* two *d*; 2nd, 1987, Prof. Nicolette Mout, Univ. of Leiden. *Educ:* Realgymnasium, Mainz; King's Coll., London. MA 1950; PhD 1954; MA Oxon 1960. Army service, 1940–45. Asst Lectr, Royal Holloway Coll., London Univ., 1948–49; Lectr, Westfield Coll., London Univ., 1949–60; Reader in German, 1960–72; Fellow of Hertford Coll., Oxford Univ., 1963–72 (Hon. Fellow, 1977); Fellow of St Edmund Hall, 1972–85, now Emeritus Fellow; Resident Fellow, Herzog August Bibliothek, Wolfenbüttel, W Germany, 1985–88. Vis. Professor: Erlangen-Nürnberg Univ., 1964–65 and 1971 (Hon. Dr 1993); Munich Univ., 1970 and 1974. Comdr, Order of Merit, Germany, 1973. Jt Editor: Beiträge zur Geschichte der deutschen Sprache und Literatur, 1976–90; Oxford German Studies, 1978–90. *Publications:* Der Einfluss des Englischen auf den deutschen Wortschatz 1740–1815, 1957; Geistliche Dichtung des 12. Jahrhunderts, 1960; Graf Rudolf, 1964; (with F. Norman and W. Schwarz) Dukus Horant, 1964; (with W. Schröder) Probleme mittelalterlicher Überlieferung und Textkritik, 1967; Jacob Grimm's Conception of German Studies, 1973; Gottfried von Strassburgs 'Tristan', 1978; Jacob Burckhardt, Über das Studium der Geschichte, 1981; articles on German medieval literature and language in jls. *Recreations:* music, walking, travel. *Address:* Flat 2, 21 Bardwell Road, Oxford OX2 6SU; Oranje Nassaulaan 27, 2361 LB Warmond, Netherlands.

GANZONI, family name of **Baron Belstead.**

GAPES, Michael John; MP (Lab) Ilford South, since 1992; *b* 4 Sept. 1952; *s* of Frank William Gapes and Emily Florence Gapes (*née* Jackson); *m* 1992, Frances Alison Smith. *Educ:* Staples Road Infants' Sch., Loughton; Manford County Primary Sch., Chigwell; Buckhurst Hill County High Sch., Essex; Fitzwilliam Coll., Cambridge (MA Hons Econs 1975); Middlesex Polytechnic (Dip. Indust. Relations and Trade Union Studies 1976). VSO teacher, Swaziland, 1971–72; Sec., Cambridge Students' Union, 1973–74; Chm., Nat. Orgn of Labour Students, 1976–77. Admin. Officer, Middlesex Hosp., 1977; Nat. Student Organiser, Lab. Party, 1977–80; Res. Officer, Internat. Dept, Lab. Party, 1980–88; Sen. Internat. Officer, Lab. Party, 1988–92. Contested (Lab) Ilford North, 1983. Mem., Foreign Affairs Select Cttee, 1992–; Chm., PLP Children and Families' Cttee, 1994–; Vice Chairman: All Party Parly Gp against Anti-Semitism, 1992–; PLP Defence Cttee, 1992–95. *Publications:* co-author of books on defence policy; Labour Party and Fabian Society pamphlets; contribs to Tribune. *Recreations:* blues and jazz music, supporting West Ham United FC. *Address:* House of Commons, SW1A 0AA; (constituency office) 97a Ilford Lane, Ilford, Essex IG1 2RJ. *T:* 0181–514 8261. *Club:* West Ham United Supporters' Association.

GARCIA, Arthur, CBE 1989; JP; Judge of the High Court, Hong Kong, 1979–89; Commissioner for Administrative Complaints, Hong Kong, 1989–94, retired; *b* 3 July 1924; *s* of late F. M. Garcia and of Maria Fung; *m* 1948, Hilda May; two *s*. *Educ:* La Salle Coll., Hong Kong; Inns of Court Sch. of Law. Called to the Bar, Middle Temple, 1957. Jun. Clerk, Hong Kong Govt, 1939–41; Staff Mem., British Consulate, Macao, 1942–45; Clerk to Attorney Gen., Hong Kong, 1946–47; Asst Registrar, 1951–54; Colonial Devel t and Welfare Scholarship, Inns of Court Sch. of Law, 1954–57; Legal Asst, Hong Kong, 1957–59; Magistrate, 1959; Sen. Magistrate, 1968; Principal Magistrate, 1968; Dist Judge, 1971. JP Hong Kong, 1991. *Recreations:* photography, swimming. *Address:* 15 Briar Avenue, Hong Kong. *Club:* Royal Hong Kong Jockey (Hong Kong).

GARCÍA, Arturo; Peruvian Ambassador to the Court of St James's, 1992–95; *b* 3 May 1914; *s* of Arturo and Carmen García; *m* 1989, Rosa (*née* Peña). *Educ:* Universidad Mayor de San Marcos, Lima, Peru; Universidad Católica, Lima. Joined Foreign Service, 1939; served at Peruvian Representation to: French Cttee of Nat. Liberation, Algeria, 1944; France, 1944–48; USA, 1948–51; Cuba, 1949; Switzerland, 1951–54; Portugal, 1955–57; GB, 1957–61; France, 1961; USA, 1962–63; Ambassador: Ecuador, 1964–66; Canada, 1967–68; Chile, 1968–74; Italy and concurrently Greece, 1974–77; Ecuador, 1977–79; Minister of Foreign Affairs, Peru, 1979–80; Mem., Consultative Commn, Min. of Foreign Affairs, 1981–92. Pres., Peruvian Soc. of Internat. Law, 1986–88. Decorations from Peru, Chile, Ecuador, Spain, Italy, France and Venezuela. *Recreation:* golf. *Address:* c/o Embassy of Peru, 52 Sloane Street, SW1X 9SP. *T:* 0171–235 4451. *Clubs:* Nacional, Lima Golf, Regatas, Ecuestre Huachipa (Peru).

GARCÍA MÁRQUEZ, Gabriel; *see* Márquez.

GARCÍA-PARRA, Jaime; Gran Cruz, Orden de San Carlos, Colombia, 1977; Gran Cruz de Boyacá, Colombia, 1981; President, J. García P. y Cía, Consultants, since 1993; *b* 19 Dec. 1931; *s* of Alfredo García-Cadena and Elvira Parra; *m* 1955, Lillian Duperly; three *s*. *Educ:* Gimnasio Moderno, Bogotá, Colombia; Univ. Javeriana, Bogotá; Univ. la Gran Colombia, Bogotá; Syracuse Univ., USA (MA); LSE, London (MSc). Lawyer. Minister (Colombian Delegn) to Internat. Coffee Org., 1963–66; Finance Vice-Pres., Colombian Nat. Airlines AVIANCA, 1966–69; Consultant in private practice, 1969–74; Actg Labour and Social Security Minister and Minister of Communications, 1974–75; Minister of Mines and Energy, 1975–77; Ambassador of Colombia to UK, 1977–78; Minister of Finance, Colombia, 1978–81; Exec. Dir, World Bank, 1981–82; Senator, Colombia, 1982; Pres. and Chief Exec. Officer, Acerías Paz del Río, steel and cement, 1982–90; Ambassador to USA, 1990–93. Mem., several delegns to UNCTAD and FAO Confs at Geneva, 1964, New Delhi, 1968, Rome, 1970, 1971. Hon. Fellow, LSE, 1980. Gran Cruz, Orden del Baron de Rio Branco, Brasil, 1977. *Publications: essays:* La Inflación y el Desarrollo de América Latina (Inflation and Development in Latin America), 1968; La Estrategia del Desarrollo Colombiano (The Strategy of Colombian Development), 1971; El Problema Inflacionario Colombiano (Colombia's Inflationary Problem), 1972; Petróleo un Problema y una Política (Oil—a Problem and a Policy), 1975; El Sector Eléctrico en la Encrucijada (The Electrical Sector at the Cross-Roads), 1975; Una Política para el Carbón (A Policy for Coal), 1976; La Cuestión Cafetera (The Coffee Dilemma), 1977; Política Agraria (Agrarian Policy), 1977. *Recreations:* walking, reading, poetry, tennis, cooking. *Address:* Apartado Aéreo 12025, Bogotá, Colombia. *Clubs:* Jockey, Country (Bogotá).

GARDAM, David Hill, QC 1968; *b* 14 Aug. 1922; *s* of late Harry H. Gardam, Hove, Sussex; *m* 1954, Jane Mary Gardam, *qv;* two *s* one *d*. *Educ:* Oundle Sch.; Christ Church, Oxford. MA 1948. War Service, RNVR, 1941–46 (Temp. Lieut). Called to the Bar, Inner Temple, 1949; Bencher 1977. *Recreations:* painting, etching, printing. *Address:* 1 Atkin Building, Gray's Inn, WC1R 5BQ. *T:* 0171–404 0102; Haven House, Sandwich, Kent CT13 9ES. *Club:* Arts.

GARDAM, Jane Mary; novelist; *d* of William Pearson, Coatham Sch., Redcar and Kathleen Mary Pearson (*née* Helm); *m* 1954, David Hill Gardam, *qv;* two *s* one *d*. *Educ:* Saltburn High Sch. for Girls; Bedford Coll., London Univ. Red Cross Travelling Librarian, Hospital Libraries, 1951; Sub-Editor, Weldon's Ladies Jl, 1952; Asst Literary Editor, Time and Tide, 1952–54. FRSL 1976. *Publications:* A Long Way From Verona, 1971; The Summer After The Funeral, 1973; Bilgewater, 1977; God on the Rocks, 1978 (Prix Baudelaire, 1989; televised, 1992); The Hollow Land (Whitbread Literary Award), 1981; Bridget and William, 1981; Horse, 1982; Kit, 1983; Crusoe's Daughter, 1985; Kit in Boots, 1986; Swan, 1987; Through the Doll's House Door, 1987; The Queen of the Tambourine (Whitbread Novel Award), 1991; Earth Fox, 1995; *non-fiction:* The Iron Coast, 1994; *short stories:* A Few Fair Days, 1971; Black Faces, White Faces (David Highams Award, Winifred Holtby Award), 1975; The Sidmouth Letters, 1980; The Pangs of Love, 1983 (Katherine Mansfield Award, 1984); Showing the Flag, 1989; Going into a Dark House, 1994. *Recreation:* Swaledale. *Address:* Haven House, Sandwich, Kent CT13 9ES. *Clubs:* Academy, Arts, PEN.

GARDEN, Air Marshal Sir Timothy, KCB 1994 (CB 1992); Commandant, Royal College of Defence Studies, since 1994; *b* 23 April 1944; *s* of Joseph Garden and Winifred M. Garden (*née* Mayes); *m* 1965, Susan Elizabeth, *d* of Henry George Button, *qv;* two *d*. *Educ:* King's Sch., Worcester; St Catherine's Coll., Oxford (MA 1967; Hon. Fellow, 1994); Magdalene Coll., Cambridge (MPhil 1982). Joined RAF 1963; Pilot, 3 Sqn, 1967–71; Flying Instructor, 1972–75; Army Staff Coll., 1976; PSO to Air Mem. for Personnel, 1977–79; OC 50 Sqn, 1979–81; Dir Defence Studies RAF, 1982–85; Station Comdr RAF Odiham, 1985–87; Asst Dir, Defence Programmes, 1987–88; Dir Air Force Staff Duties, 1988–90; ACAS, 1991–92; ACDS (Programmes), 1992–94. Mem. Council, RUSI, 1984–87. Mem. Develt Council, St Catherine's Coll., Oxford, 1992–; Gov., King's Sch., Worcester, 1986–. Pres., RAF Rowing, 1992–. Upper Freeman, GAPAN, 1993. *Publications:* Can Deterrence Last?, 1984; The Technology Trap: science and the military, 1989; contribs to books and jls on defence. *Recreations:* writing, bridge, photography, computing. *Address:* (office) Seaford House, 37 Belgrave Square, SW1X 8NS. *T:* 0171–915 4830. *Clubs:* Royal Air Force, National Liberal.

GARDINER, Duncan; *see* Gardiner, J. D. B.

GARDINER, Sir George (Arthur), Kt 1990; MP (C) Reigate, since Feb. 1974; *b* 3 March 1935; *s* of Stanley and Emma Gardiner; *m* 1st, 1961, Juliet Wells (marr. diss. 1980); two *s* one *d*; 2nd, 1980, Helen Hackett. *Educ:* Harvey Grammar Sch., Folkestone; Balliol Coll., Oxford. 1st cl. hons PPE. Sec., Oxford Univ. Conservative Assoc., 1957. Chief Political Corresp., Thomson Regional Newspapers, 1964–74. Member: Select Cttee on Home Affairs and its Sub-Cttee on Race Relations and Immigration, 1979–82; Exec., 1922 Cttee, 1987–93; Sec., Cons. European Affairs Cttee, 1976–79, Vice-Chm., 1979–80, Chm., 1980–87; Vice-Chm., Cons. For. and Commonwealth Affairs Cttee, 1988–. Mem. Council, Cons. Way Forward (Editor, Forward). Contested (C) Coventry South, 1970. *Publications:* The Changing Life of London, 1973; Margaret Thatcher: from childhood to leadership, 1975. *Address:* House of Commons, SW1A 0AA.

GARDINER, Dame Helen (Louisa), DBE 1961 (CBE 1952); MVO 1937; *b* 24 April 1901; *y d* of late Henry Gardiner, Bristol. *Educ:* Clifton High School. Formerly in Private Secretary's Office, Buckingham Palace; Chief Clerk, 1946–61. *Recreations:* reading, gardening. *Address:* Higher Courlands, Lostwithiel, Cornwall PL22 0SA.

GARDINER, (John) Duncan (Broderick); author and broadcaster; Editor, Western Mail, 1974–81; *b* 12 Jan. 1937; *s* of late Frederick Keith Gardiner and Ruth Dixon; *m* 1965, Geraldine Mallen; one *s* one *d*. *Educ:* St Edward's School, Oxford. Various editorial positions in Sheffield, Newcastle, Sunday Times, London (1963–64, 1966–73) and Cardiff. *Recreations:* travel, all sport, wine and food, crosswords. *Address:* 145 Pencisely Road, Llandaff, Cardiff CF5 1DN.

GARDINER, John Eliot, CBE 1990; conductor; Founder and Artistic Director, English Baroque Soloists, Monteverdi Choir, Monteverdi Orchestra, and Orchestre Révolutionnaire et Romantique; Chef fondateur, Opéra de Lyon Orchestra, since 1988 (Musical Director, 1983–88); *b* 20 April 1943; *s* of Rolf Gardiner and late Marabel Gardiner (*née* Hodgkin); *m* 1981, Elizabeth Suzanne Wilcock; three *d*. *Educ:* Bryanston Sch.; King's Coll., Cambridge (MA History); King's Coll., London (Certif. of Advanced Studies in Music, 1966; Hon. FKC 1992). French Govt Scholarship to study in Paris and Fontainebleau with Nadia Boulanger, 1966–68. Founded: Monteverdi Choir, following performance of Monteverdi's Vespers of 1610, King's Coll. Chapel, Cambridge, 1964; Monteverdi Orchestra, 1968; English Baroque Soloists (period instruments), 1978; Orchestre Révolutionnaire et Romantique, 1990; Artistic Dir, Göttingen Handel Fest., 1981–90; Principal Conductor, N German Radio Orch., 1991–94. Youngest conductor of Henry Wood Promenade Concert, Royal Albert Hall, 1968; Début with: Sadler's Wells Opera, London Coliseum, 1969; Royal Opera House, Covent Garden, 1973; Royal Festival Hall, 1972; Guest engagements conducting major European orchestras in Paris, Brussels, Geneva, Frankfurt, Dresden, Leipzig, London and Vienna; US débuts: Dallas Symphony, 1981; San Francisco Symphony, 1982; Carnegie Hall, NY, 1988; Boston Symphony, 1991; Cleveland Orchestra 1992; European Music Festivals: Aix-en-Provence, Aldeburgh, Bath, Berlin, Edinburgh, Flanders, Holland, City of London, etc.; concert revivals in London of major dramatic works of Purcell, Handel and Rameau, including world première (staged) of Rameau's opera Les Boréades, Aix-en-Provence, 1982. Principal Conductor, CBC Vancouver Orchestra, 1980–83; Artistic Dir, Veneto Music Fest., 1986. Has made over 100 records ranging from Monteverdi and Mozart to Massenet, Rodrigo and Central American Percussion Music. Hon. FRAM 1992. Dr *hc* Univ. Lumière de Lyon, 1987. Grand Prix du Disque, 1978, 1979, 1980, 1982, 1984, 1985; Gramophone Awards for early music and choral music records, 1978, 1980, 1986, 1988, 1989, 1990, 1991; Prix Caecilia, 1982, 1983, 1985, 1988, 1991; Edison Award, 1982, 1986, 1987, 1988, 1989; Internat. Record Critics Award, 1982, 1983; Deutscher Schallplattenpreis, 1986; Arturo Toscanini Music Critics Award, 1985, 1986; IRCA Prize, Helsinki, 1987; Best Choir of the Year for Monteverdi Choir, Internat. Classical Music Awards, 1992. Officier, Ordre des Arts et des Lettres (France), 1988. *Publications:* (ed) Claude le Jeune Hélas! Mon Dieu, 1971; contrib. to opera handbook on Gluck's Orfeo, 1980. *Recreations:* forestry, organic farming. *Address:* Gore Farm, Ashmore, Salisbury, Wilts SP5 5AR; 7 Pleydell Avenue, W6 0XX.

GARDINER, Prof. John Graham, PhD; FIEE; FEng; Professor of Electronic Engineering, since 1986, and Head, Department of Electronic and Electrical Engineering, since 1994, University of Bradford; *b* 24 May 1939; *s* of William Clement Gardiner and Ellen (*née* Adey); *m* 1962, Sheila Joyce Andrews; one *s* two *d*. *Educ:* Univ. of Birmingham (BSc 1st Cl. Hons; PhD 1964). FIEE 1988; FEng 1994. Software designer, Racal Res. Ltd, 1966–68; University of Bradford: Lectr, 1968–72; Sen Lectr, 1972–78; Reader, 1978–86. *Publications:* (with J. D. Parsons) Mobile Communication Systems, 1989; (with B. West) Personal Communication Systems and Technologies, 1995. *Recreation:* music. *Address:* 1 Queen's Drive Lane, Ilkley, W Yorks LS29 9QS. *T:* Ilkley (01943) 609581.

GARDINER, John Ralph, QC 1982; *b* 28 Feb. 1946; *s* of late Cyril Ralph Gardiner and of Mary Gardiner; *m* 1976, Pascal Mary Issard-Davies; one *d*. *Educ:* Bancroft's Sch., Woodford; Fitzwilliam Coll., Cambridge (BA (Law Tripos), MA, LLM). Called to the Bar, Middle Temple, 1968 (Harmsworth Entrance Scholar and Harmsworth Law Scholar; Bencher, 1992); practice at the Bar, 1970–; Mem., Senate of Inns of Court and Bar, 1982–86 (Treasurer, 1985–86); Chm., Taxation and Retirement Benefits Cttee, Bar Council, 1982–85. *Publications:* contributor to Pinson on Revenue Law, 6th to 15th (1982) edns. *Recreations:* tennis, cricket, squash. *Address:* 11 New Square, Lincoln's Inn, WC2A 3QB. *T:* 0171–242 3981; Admiral's House, Admiral's Walk, Hampstead, NW3 6RS. *T:* 0171–435 0597. *Club:* Cumberland Lawn Tennis.

GARDINER, Patrick Lancaster, FBA 1985; Fellow and Tutor in Philosophy, Magdalen College, Oxford, 1958–89, now Emeritus Fellow; *b* 17 March 1922; *s* of Clive and Lilian Gardiner; *m* 1955, Kathleen Susan Booth; two *d*. *Educ:* Westminster School; Christ Church, Oxford (MA). Army service (Captain), 1942–45. Lectr, Wadham College, Oxford, 1949–52; Fellow, St Antony's College, Oxford, 1952–58. Vis. Prof., Columbia Univ., NY, 1955. *Publications:* The Nature of Historical Explanation, 1952; (ed) Theories of History, 1959; Schopenhauer, 1963, 2nd edn 1972; (ed) Nineteenth Century Philosophy, 1969; (ed) The Philosophy of History, 1974; Kierkegaard, 1988; articles in philosophical and literary jls, anthologies. *Address:* The Dower House, Wytham, Oxford OX2 8QA. *T:* Oxford (01865) 242205.

GARDINER, Peter Dod Robin; First Deputy Head, Stanborough School, Hertfordshire, 1979–92, retired; *b* 23 Dec. 1927; *s* of late Brig. R. Gardiner, CB, CBE; *m* 1959, Juliet Wright; one *s* one *d*. *Educ:* Radley College; Trinity Coll., Cambridge. Asst Master, Charterhouse, 1952–67, and Housemaster, Charterhouse, 1965–67; Headmaster, St Peter's School, York, 1967–79. *Publications:* (ed) Twentieth-Century Travel, 1963; (with B. W. M. Young) Intelligent Reading, 1964; (with W. A. Gibson) The Design of Prose, 1971. *Recreations:* reading, music, walking, acting. *Address:* Willows, Stream Road, Upton, Didcot, Oxfordshire OX11 9JG.

GARDINER, Robert (Kweku Atta); Commissioner for Economic Planning, Ghana, 1975–78; *b* Kumasi, Ghana, 29 Sept. 1914; *s* of Philip H. D. Gardiner and Nancy Torraine Ferguson; *m* 1943, Linda Charlotte Edwards; one *s* two *d*. *Educ:* Adisadel Coll., Cape Coast, Ghana; Fourah Bay Coll., Sierra Leone; Selwyn Coll., Cambridge (BA); New Coll., Oxford. Lectr in Economics at Fourah Bay Coll., 1943–46; UN Trusteeship Dept, 1947–49; Dir, Extra-Mural Studies, University Coll., Ibadan, 1949–53; Dir, Dept of Social Welfare and Community Development, Gold Coast, 1953–55; Perm. Sec., Min. of Housing, 1955–57; Head of Ghana Civil Service, 1957–59; Dep. Exec. Sec., Economic Commn for Africa, 1959–60; Mem. Mission to the Congo, 1961; Dir Public Admin. Div., UN Dept of Economic and Social Affairs, 1961–62; Officer-in-Charge, UN Operation in the Congo, 1962–63; Exec. Sec., UN Economic Commn for Africa, Addis Ababa, 1962–75. Chm., Commonwealth Foundation, 1970–73. Reith Lectures, 1965; David Livingstone Vis. Prof. of Economics, Strathclyde, 1970–75; Vis. Prof. of Economics, 1974–75, and Consultant, Centre for Development Studies, 1974–77, Univ. of Cape Coast. Lectures: Gilbert Murray Meml, 1969; J. B. Danquah Meml, 1970; Aggrey-Fraser-Guggisberg Meml, 1972. Mem Professional Socs, and activities in internat. affairs. Hon. Fellow: Univ. of Ibadan; Selwyn Coll., Cambridge. Hon. DCL: East Anglia, 1966; Sierra Leone, 1969; Tuskegee Inst., 1969; Liberia, 1972; Hon. LLD: Bristol, 1966; Ibadan, 1967; E Africa, 1968; Haile Sellassie I Univ., 1972; Strathclyde, 1973; Hon. PhD Uppsala, 1966; Hon. DSc: Kumasi, 1968; Bradford, 1969. *Publications:* (with Helen Judd) The Development of Social Administration, 1951, 2nd edn 1959; A World of Peoples (BBC Reith Lectures), 1965. *Recreations:* golf, music, reading, walking. *Address:* PO Box 9274, The Airport, Accra, Ghana.

GARDINER, Victor Alec, OBE 1977; consultant, film and television programme production, facilities and distribution; Director and General Manager, London Weekend Television, 1971–87; *b* 9 Aug. 1929; *m*; one *s* two *d*. *Educ:* Whitgift Middle Sch., Croydon; City and Guilds (radio and telecommunications). Techn. Asst, GPO Engrg, 1947–49; RAF Nat. Service, 1949–51; BBC Sound Radio Engr, 1951–53; BBC TV Cameraman, 1953–55; Rediffusion TV Sen. Cameraman, 1955–61; Malta TV Trng Man., 1961–62; Head of Studio Prodn, Rediffusion TV, 1962–67; Man. Dir, GPA Productions, 1967–69; Production Controller, London Weekend Television, 1969–71; Director: LWT (Hldgs) Ltd, 1976–87; London Weekend Services Ltd, 1976–87; Richard Price Television Associates, 1981–87; Chairman: Dynamic Technology Ltd, 1972–87; Standard Music Ltd, 1972–87; LWT Internat., 1981–87. Mem., Royal Television Soc., 1970– (Vice-Chm. Council, 1974–75; Chm. Papers Cttee, 1975; Chm. Council, 1976–77; Fellow, 1977). *Recreations:* music, building, gardening.

GARDINER-SCOTT, Rev. William, OBE 1974; MA; Emeritus Minister of Scots Memorial Church and Hospice, Jerusalem; *b* 23 February 1906; *o s* of late William Gardiner Scott, Portsoy, Banffshire; *m* 1953, Darinka Milo, *d* of late Milo Glogovac, Oakland, Calif; one *d*. *Educ:* Grange School, Bo'ness, West Lothian; Edinburgh University and New College, Edinburgh. In catering business, 1926–30; graduated in Arts, Edin., 1934; Theological Travel Scholarship to Palestine, 1936; travelled as ship's steward to America and India, 1936; ordained to Ministry of Church of Scotland, 1939; Sub-Warden 1939, Deputy Warden 1940, New College Settlement, Edinburgh; enlisted as Army Chaplain, 1941; served in Egypt, 1942–44 and developed community centre at RA Depot, Cairo and initiated publication of weekly Scots newspaper, The Clachan Crack; founded Montgomery House, Alexandria, as community centre for all ranks of allied troops, 1943; served in Palestine as Church of Scotland Chaplain for Galilee and district, 1944–46; Senior Chaplain at Scottish Command, 1946–47; Warden of Student Movement House, London, 1947–49; Chaplain at Victoria Univ. Coll., Wellington, NZ, 1950–54; locum tenens St John's West Church, Leith, 1955; Minister of Church of Scotland, Jerusalem, 1955–60 and 1966–73; Parish of Abernethy, 1960–66. ChStJ. Distinguished Citizen of Jerusalem. *Recreations:* travel, gardening, cooking, walking. *Address:* Scots Memorial Church and Hospice, PO Box 8619, Jerusalem, Israel.

GARDNER, family name of **Baroness Gardner of Parkes.**

GARDNER OF PARKES, Baroness *cr* 1981 (Life Peer), of Southgate, Greater London, and of Parkes, NSW; **(Rachel) Trixie (Anne) Gardner;** JP; dental surgeon; Chairman: Royal Free Hampstead NHS Trust, since 1994; Plan International (UK) Ltd, since 1990; *b* Parkes, NSW, 17 July 1927; eighth *c* of late Hon. J. J. Gregory McGirr and late Rachel McGirr, OBE, LC; *m* 1956, Kevin Anthony Gardner, *o s* of late George and of Rita Gardner, Sydney, Australia; three *d*. *Educ:* Monte Sant Angelo Coll., N Sydney; East Sydney Technical Coll.; Univ. of Sydney (BDS 1954). Cordon Bleu de Paris, Diplôme 1956. Came to UK, 1955. Member: Westminster City Council, 1968–78 (Lady Mayoress, 1987–88); GLC, for Havering, 1970–73, for Enfield-Southgate, 1977–86. Contested (C) Blackburn, 1970; N Cornwall, Feb. 1974. Chm., Royal Free Hampstead NHS Trust, 1994–; Vice-Chm., NE Thames RHA, 1990–94; Member: Inner London Exec. Council, NHS, 1966–71; Standing Dental Adv. Cttee for England and Wales, 1968–76; Westminster, Kensington and Chelsea Area Health Authority, 1974–82; Industrial Tribunal Panel for London, 1974–; N Thames Gas Consumer Council, 1980–82; Dept of Employment's Adv. Cttee on Women's Employment, 1980–88; Britain–Australia Bicentennial Cttee, 1984–88; London Electricity Bd, 1984–90. British Chm., European Union of Women, 1978–82; UK Rep., UN Status of Women Commn, 1982–88. Director: Gateway Building Soc., 1987–88; Woolwich Building Soc., 1988–93. Chm., Suzy Lamplugh Trust, 1993–. Governor: Eastman Dental Hosp., 1971–80; Nat. Heart Hosp., 1974–90. Hon. Pres., War Widows Assoc. of GB, 1984–87. JP North Westminster, 1971. *Recreations:* gardening, reading, travel, needlework. *Address:* House of Lords, SW1A 0PW.

GARDNER, Antony John; Registrar, Central Council for Education and Training in Social Work, 1988–92 (Principal Registration Officer, 1970–88); *b* 27 Dec. 1927; *s* of David Gardner, head gardener, and Lillian Gardner; *m* 1956, Eveline A. Burden. *Educ:* Elem. school; Co-operative Coll.; Southampton Univ. Pres. Union, Southampton, 1958–59; BSc (Econ) 1959. Apprentice toolmaker, 1941–45; National Service, RASC, 1946–48; building trade, 1948–53. Tutor Organiser, Co-operative Union, 1959–60; Member and Education Officer, Co-operative Union, 1961–66. Contested (Lab): SW Wolverhampton, 1964; Beeston, Feb. and Oct. 1974; MP (Lab) Rushcliffe, 1966–70. Contested (Lab) Dorset and E Devon, Eur. Parly elecns, 1994. *Recreations:* angling, gardening and the countryside generally. *Address:* 118 Ringwood Road, Parkstone, Poole, Dorset BH14 0RW. *T:* Poole (01202) 676683. *Club:* Parkstone Trades and Labour (Poole).

GARDNER, Brigid Catherine Brennan; Principal, St George's English School, Rome, since 1994; *b* 5 May 1941; *d* of John Henthorn Cantrell Brennan and Rosamond Harriet Brennan (*née* Gardner); *m* 1963, Michael Henry Davies (marr. diss. 1980); three *d*. *Educ:* The Alice Ottley Sch., Worcester; Girton Coll., Cambridge (MA). English and History teacher, Harrogate High Sch., 1963–66; part-time English teacher, Hong Kong, 1967–69; English teacher (part-time), Priory Park Comprehensive Sch., 1974; James Allen's Girls' School: Head of History, 1976–83; Dep. Head, 1981–83; Headmistress, 1984–94. Governor: Oundle Sch., 1992–94; Whitgift Foundn, 1992–94. *Recreations:* gardening, travelling, walking, reading, sailing. *Address:* St George's English School, La Storta, Via Cassia, 00123 Roma, Italy.

GARDNER, Christopher James Ellis; QC 1994; a Recorder, since 1993; *b* 6 April 1945; *s* of James Charles Gardner and Phyllis May Gardner (*née* Wilkinson); *m* 1972, Arlene Sellers; one *s* one *d*. *Educ:* Rossall Sch., Lancs; Fitzwilliam Coll., Cambridge (MA). Called to the Bar, Gray's Inn, 1968. Legal Assessor, GMC, 1992–. *Recreations:* theatre, ballet, bell ringing, golf, cooking curries. *Address:* Lamb Chambers, Lamb Building, Temple, EC4Y 7AS. *T:* 0171–797 8300.

GARDNER, Prof. David Pierpont, PhD; President, The William and Flora Hewlett Foundation, since 1993; President, University of California, 1983–92; Professor of Education, University of California at Berkeley, 1983–92; *b* 24 March 1933; *s* of Reed S. Gardner and Margaret (*née* Pierpont); *m* 1958, Elizabeth Fuhriman (*d* 1991); four *d*. *Educ:* Brigham Young Univ. (BS 1955); Univ. of Calif, Berkeley (MA 1959, PhD 1966). Dir, Calif Alumni Foundn and Calif Alumni Assoc., Univ. of Calif, Berkeley, 1962–64. University of California, Santa Barbara: Asst Prof. of Higher Educn, 1964–69; Associate Prof. of Higher Educn, 1969–70; Prof. of Higher Educn (on leave), 1971–73; Asst to the Chancellor, 1964–67; Asst Chancellor, 1967–69; Vice Chancellor and Exec. Asst, 1969–70; Vice Pres., Univ. of Calif, 1971–73; Pres., and Prof. of Higher Educn, Univ. of Utah, 1973–83, Pres. Emeritus, 1985. Vis. Fellow, Clare Hall, Univ. of Cambridge, 1979 (Life Mem. 1979). Member: Nat. Acad. of Public Administration; Council, Hong Kong Univ. of Sci. and Technology; Amer. Philosophical Soc.; Nat. Acad. of Educn. Board of Directors: First Security Corp.; Fluor Corp.; George S. and Delores Dore Eccles Foundn; Nature Conservancy; John Alden Financial Corp.; Getty Trust; Hewlett Foundn. Trustee, Tanner Lectures on Human Values. Fulbright 40th Anniversary Distinguished Fellow, Japan, 1986; Fellow, Amer. Acad. of Arts and Scis, 1986. Hon. LLD: Univ. of The Pacific, 1983; Nevada, Las Vegas, 1984; Westminster Coll., 1987; Brown, 1989; Notre Dame, 1989; Hon. DH Brigham Young, 1981; Hon. DLitt Utah, 1983; Hon. HHD Utah State, 1987; Hon. Dr Bordeaux II, 1988; Hon. DHL Internat. Christian Univ. Benjamin P. Cheney Medal, Eastern Washington Univ., 1984; James Bryant Conant Award, Educn Commn of the States, 1985; Hall of Fame Award, Calif. Sch. Bd Res Foundn, 1988. Chevalier, Légion d'Honneur (France), 1985; Knight Commander, Order of Merit (Germany), 1992. *Publications:* The California Oath Controversy, 1967; contrib. articles to professional jls. *Address:* (office) 525 Middlefield Road, Suite 200, Menlo Park, CA 94025, USA.

GARDNER, Sir Douglas Bruce B.; *see* Bruce-Gardner.

GARDNER, Douglas Frank; Chairman, Brixton Estate plc, since 1993 (Managing Director, 1983–93); *b* 20 Dec. 1943; *s* of late Ernest Frank Gardner and Mary Gardner; *m* 1978, Adèle (*née* Alexander); one *s* two *d*. *Educ:* Woolverstone Hall; College of Estate Management, London Univ. (BSc). FRICS. Chief Exec., Properties Div., Tarmac plc, 1976–83. *Recreations:* tennis, theatre. *Address:* 20 Cottesmore Gardens, Kensington, W8 5PR. *T:* 0171–937 7127.

GARDNER, Sir Edward (Lucas), Kt 1983; QC 1960; a Recorder of the Crown Court, 1972–85; *b* 10 May 1912; *s* of late Edward Walker Gardner, Fulwood, Preston, Lancs; *m* 1st, 1950, Noreen Margaret (marr. diss. 1962), *d* of late John Collins, Moseley, Birmingham; one *s* one *d*; 2nd, 1963, Joan Elizabeth, *d* of late B. B. Belcher, Bedford; one *s* one *d*. *Educ:* Hutton Grammar Sch. Served War of 1939–45: joined RNVR as ordinary seaman, 1940; served in cruisers, Mediterranean; commnd RNVR; Chief of Naval Information, E Indies, 1945. Journalist (free-lance; Lancashire Daily Post, then Daily Mail) prior to 1940; broadcasting and free-lance journalism, 1946–49; called to Bar, Gray's Inn, 1947; Master of the Bench of Gray's Inn, 1968; admitted to Nigerian and British Guianan Bars, 1962; has also appeared in Courts of Goa, High Court of Singapore, and Supreme Court of India. Deputy Chairman of Quarter Sessions: East Kent, 1961–71; County of Kent, 1962–71; Essex, 1968–71. Contested (C) Erith and Crayford, April 1955; MP (C): Billericay Div. of Essex, 1959–66; S Fylde, 1970–83; Fylde, 1983–87. PPS to Attorney-General, 1962–63. Chm., Select Cttee on Home Affairs, 1984–87. Chairman: Justice Working Party on Bail and Remands in Custody, 1966; Bar Council Cttee on Parly Privilege, 1967; Chm., Soc. of Cons. Lawyers, 1975–85 (Chm. Exec. Cttee, 1969–75; Chm., Cttee responsible for pamphlets, Rough Justice, on future of the Law, 1968, Crisis in Crime and Punishment, 1971, The Proper Use of Prisons, 1978, Who Do We Think

We Are?, 1980, on need for new nationality law); Exec. Cttee, Justice, 1968. Member: Departmental Cttee on Jury Service, 1963; Cttee on Appeals in Criminal Cases, 1964; Commonwealth War Graves Commn, 1971–87. A Governor: Thomas Coram Foundn for Children, 1962–; Queenswood Sch., 1975–87. Steward, British Boxing Bd of Control, 1975–84. *Publication:* (part author) A Case for Trial (pamphlet recommending procedural reforms for committal proceedings implemented by Criminal Justice Act, 1967). *Recreation:* walking. *Address:* Sparrows, Hatfield Broad Oak, Bishop's Stortford, Herts CM22 7HN. *T:* Bishop's Stortford (01279) 718265. *Clubs:* Garrick, Pratt's, United and Cecil (Chm. 1970).

GARDNER, Rear-Adm. Herbert, CB 1976; Chartered Engineer; *b* 23 Oct. 1921; *s* of Herbert and Constance Gladys Gardner; *m* 1946, Catherine Mary Roe, Perth, WA. *Educ:* Taunton Sch.; Weymouth Coll. War of 1939–45; joined Dartmouth, 1940; RN Engineering Coll., Keyham, 1940; HMS Nigeria, Cumberland, Adamant, and 4th Submarine Sqdn, 1944; HM S/M Totem, 1945. Dept of Engr-in-Chief, 1947; HM S/M Telemachus, 1949; Admty Develt Establishment, Barrow-in-Furness, 1952; HMS Eagle, 1954; Comdr, 1956; HMS Caledonia, 1956; HMS Blackpool, 1958; Asst to Manager Engrg Dept, Rosyth Dockyard, 1960; HMS Maidstone, 1963; Capt., 1963; Dep. Manager, Engrg Dept, Devonport Dockyard, 1964; Chief Engr and Production Manager, Singapore Dockyard, 1967; Chief Staff Officer (Technical) to Comdr Far East Fleet, 1968; course at Imperial Defence Coll., 1970; Chief of Staff to C-in-C Naval Home Comd, 1971–73; Vice Pres., Ordnance Bd, 1974–76, Pres., 1976–77. *Recreations:* sailing, golf. *Address:* 41 Mayfair Street, Mount Claremont, Perth, WA 6010, Australia. *Club:* Royal Freshwater Bay Yacht (Perth).

GARDNER, James Jesse, CVO 1995; CBE 1986; DL; consultant, since 1986; Chairman, OFWAT National Consumer Council, since 1993; *b* 7 April 1932; *s* of James and Elizabeth Rubina Gardner; *m* 1955, Diana Sotheran; three *s* one *d. Educ:* Kirkham Grammar Sch.; Victoria Univ., Manchester (LLB). Nat. Service, 1955–57. Articled to Town Clerk, Preston, 1952–55; Legal Asst, Preston Co. Borough Council, 1955; Crosby Borough Council: Asst Solicitor, 1957–59; Chief Asst Solicitor, 1959–61; Chief Asst Solicitor, Warrington Co. Borough Council, 1961–65; Stockton-on-Tees Borough Council: Dep. Town Clerk, 1966; Town Clerk, 1966–68; Asst Town Clerk, Teesside Co. Borough Council, 1968; Associate Town Clerk and Solicitor, London Borough of Greenwich, 1968–69; Town Clerk and Chief Exec. Officer, Co. Borough of Sunderland, 1970–73; Chief Exec., Tyne and Wear CC, 1973–86; Chm., Tyne and Wear PTE, 1983–86. Chief Exec., Northern Develt Co. Ltd, 1986–87; Chairman: Sunderland DHA, 1988–90; Northumbrian Water Customer Services Cttee, 1990–; North East Television, 1991–92; Dir, Birtley Enterprise Action Management (BEAM) Ltd, 1989–93; Sec., Northern Region Councils Assoc., 1986. Clerk to Lieutenancy, Tyne and Wear, 1974–91. Dir, Garrod Pitkin (1986) Ltd, 1991–93. Chairman: Prince's Trust Trustees, 1986–94; Prince's Trust and Royal Jubilee Trust Management Bd, 1989–93 (former Chm., Northumbria Cttee, Royal Jubilee and Prince's Trusts); Prince's Trust Events Ltd, 1987–94; Director: Threshold (formerly Prince's Trust Training & Employment Ltd), 1991– (Chm., 1992); NE Civic Trust, 1986–92. Chairman: Radio NE, 1993–; St Benedict's Hospice, Sunderland, 1993–; Trustee: Tyne Tees Telethon Trust, 1988–91; Great North Air Ambulance Service Appeal, 1991–95. DL Tyne and Wear, 1976. FRSA 1976; CIMgt 1987. Hon. Fellow, Sunderland Polytechnic, 1986. *Recreations:* golf, music, theatre, food and drink. *Address:* Wayside, 121 Queen Alexandra Road, Sunderland, Tyne and Wear SR2 9HR. *T:* 0191–528 2525.

GARDNER, (James) Piers; Director, British Institute of International and Comparative Law, since 1989 (Executive Director, 1987–89); *b* 26 March 1954; *s* of Michael Clement Gardner and Brigitte Elsa Gardner (*née* Ekrut); *m* 1978, Penelope Helen Chloros; three *s* one *d. Educ:* Bryanston Sch., Brasenose Coll., Oxford (MA Jurisp. 1st Class). Solicitor of the Supreme Court. Articled and in private practice as solicitor, with Stephenson Harwood, London, 1977–80; Secretariat, European Commn of Human Rights, Council of Europe, Strasbourg, 1980–87. *Recreations:* foreign property, arguing. *Address:* British Institute of International and Comparative Law, Charles Clore House, 17 Russell Square, WC1B 5DR. *T:* 0171–636 5802. *Club:* Athenæum.

GARDNER, John Linton, CBE 1976; composer; *b* 2 March 1917; *s* of late Dr Alfred Gardner, Ilfracombe, and Muriel (*née* Pullein-Thompson); *m* 1955, Jane, *d* of late N. J. Abercrombie; one *s* two *d. Educ:* Eagle House, Sandhurst; Wellington Coll.; Exeter Coll., Oxford (BMus). Served War of 1939–45: RAF, 1940–46. Chief Music Master, Repton Sch., 1939–40. Staff, Covent Garden Opera, 1946–52; Tutor: Morley Coll., 1952–76 (Dir of Music, 1965–69); Bagot Stack Coll., 1955–62; London Univ. (extra-mural) 1959–60; Dir of Music, St Paul's Girls' Sch., 1962–75; Prof. of Harmony and Composition, Royal Acad. of Music, 1956–86. Conductor: Haslemere Musical Soc., 1953–62; Dorian Singers, 1961–62; European Summer Sch. for Young Musicians, 1966–75; Bromley YSO, 1970–76. Brit. Council Lecturer: Levant, 1954; Belgium, 1960; Iberia, 1963; Yugoslavia, 1967. Adjudicator, Canadian Festivals, 1974, 1980. Chm., Composer's Guild, 1963; Member: Arts Council Music Panel, 1958–62; Cttee of Management, Royal Philharmonic Soc., 1965–72; Brit. Council Music Cttee, 1968. Dir, Performing Right Soc., 1965–92 (Dep. Chm., 1983–88). Worshipful Co. of Musicians: Collard Fellow, 1962–64; elected to Freedom and Livery, 1965. Hon. RAM 1959. Bax Society's Prize, 1958. *Works include: orchestral:* Symphony no 1, 1947; Variations on a Waltz of Carl Nielsen, 1952; Piano Concerto no 1, 1957; Sinfonia Piccola (strings), 1960; Occasional Suite, Aldeburgh Festival, 1968; An English Ballad, 1969; Three Ridings, 1970; Sonatina for Strings, 1974; Divertimento, 1977; Symphony no 2, 1984; Symphony no 3, 1989; Concerto for Oboe and Strings, 1990; *chamber:* Concerto da Camera (4 insts), 1968; Partita (solo 'cello), 1968; Chamber Concerto (organ and 11 insts), 1969; English Suite (harpsichord), 1971; Sonata Secolare for organ and brass, 1973; Sonata da Chiesa for two trumpets and organ; String Quartet no 2, 1979; Hebdomade, 1980; Sonatina Lirica for brass, 1983; Triad, 1984; Quartet for Saxes, 1985; Oboe Sonata no 2, French Suite for Sax. 4tet, 1986; String Quartet no 3, 1987; Octad, 1987; Piano Sonata no 3, 1988; Larkin Songs, 1990; Organ Sonata, 1992; *ballet:* Reflection, 1952; *opera:* A Nativity Opera, 1950; The Moon and Sixpence, 1957; The Visitors, 1972; Bel and the Dragon, 1973; The Entertainment of the Senses, 1974; Tobermory, 1976; *musical:* Vile Bodies, 1961; *choral:* Cantiones Sacrae 1973; (sop., chor. and orch.), 1952; Jubilate Deo (unacc. chor.), 1957; The Ballad of the White Horse (bar., chor. and orch.), 1959; Herrick Cantata (ten. solo, chor. and orch.), 1961; A Latter-Day Athenian Speaks, 1962; The Noble Heart (sop., bass, chor, and orch.), Shakespeare Quatercentenary Festival, 1964; Cantor popularis vocis, 18th Schütz Festival Berlin, 1964; Mass in C (unacc. chor.), 1965; Cantata for Christmas (chor. and chamb. orch.), 1966; Proverbs of Hell (unacc. chor.), 1967; Cantata for Easter (soli, chor., organ and percussion), 1970; Open Air (chor. and brass band), 1976; Te Deum for Pigotts, 1981; Mass in D, 1983; Cantata for St Cecilia, 1991; Stabat Mater (sop., chor., organ and timpani), A Burns Sequence (chor. and orch.), 1993; many smaller pieces and music for films, Old Vic and Royal Shakespeare Theatres, BBC. *Publications:* Robert Schumann, the man and his music, 1972; The Musical Companion, 1978; contributor to: Dublin Review, Musical Times, Tempo, Composer, Listener, Music in Education, DNB. *Recreations:* jazz, bore-watching. *Address:* 20 Firswood Avenue, Ewell, Epsom, Surrey KT19 0PR. *T:* 0181–393 7181.

GARDNER, Prof. John William; Miriam and Peter Haas Professor in Public Service, Stanford University, since 1989; *b* 8 Oct. 1912; *s* of William Frederick and Marie (Flora) Gardner; *m* 1934, Aida Marroquin; two *d. Educ:* Stanford Univ. (AB 1935, AM 1936); Univ. of Calif. (PhD 1938). 1st Lt-Captain, US Marine Corps, 1943–46. Teaching Asst in Psychology, Univ. of Calif., 1936–38; Instructor in Psychology, Connecticut Coll., 1938–40; Asst Prof. in Psychology, Mt Holyoke Coll., 1940–42; Head of Latin Amer. Section, Federal Communications Commn, 1942–43. Carnegie Corporation of New York: Staff Mem., 1946–47; Exec. Associate, 1947–49; Vice-Pres., 1949–55; Pres., 1955–67; Pres., Carnegie Foundn for Advancement of Teaching, 1955–67; Sec. of Health, Education and Welfare, 1965–68; Chairman: Urban Coalition, 1968–70; Common Cause, 1970–77; Independent Sector, 1980–83; US Adv. Commn on Internat. Educational and Cultural Affairs, 1962–64; Pres. Johnson's Task Force on Educn, 1964; White House Conf. on Educn, 1965; President's Commn on White House Fellowships, 1977–81. Senior Fellow, Aspen Inst., 1981–. Dir, Amer. Assoc. for Advancement of Science, 1963–65. Director: New York Telephone Co., 1962–65; Shell Oil Co., 1962–65; Time Inc., 1968–71; American Airlines, 1968–71; Rockefeller Brothers Fund, 1968–77; New York Foundn, 1970–76. Trustee: Metropolitan Museum of Art, 1957–65; Stanford Univ., 1968–82; Chm., Nat. Civic League, 1994–. Benjamin Franklin Fellow, RSA, 1964. Holds hon. degrees from various colleges and univs. USAF Exceptional Service Award, 1956; Presidential Medal of Freedom, 1964; Public Welfare Medal, Nat. Acad. of Science, 1967. *Publications:* Excellence, 1961, rev. edn 1984; (ed) Pres. John F. Kennedy's book, To Turn the Tide, 1961; Self-Renewal, 1964, rev. edn 1980; No Easy Victories, 1968; The Recovery of Confidence, 1970; In Common Cause, 1972; Know or Listen to Those who Know, 1975; Morale, 1978; Quotations of Wit and Wisdom, 1980; On Leadership, 1990. *Address:* Graduate School of Business, Stanford University, Stanford, CA 94305–5015, USA.

GARDNER, Norman Keith Ayliffe; *b* 2 July 1925; *s* of late Charles Ayliffe Gardner and Winifred Gardner; *m* 1951, Margaret Patricia Vinson; one *s* one *d. Educ:* Cardiff High Sch.; University Coll., Cardiff (BScEng); College of Aeronautics, Cranfield; Univ. of London Commerce Degree Bureau (BScEcon Hons). CEng. Flight Test Observer, RAE, 1944; Test Observer, Westland Aircraft Ltd, 1946; Development Engr, Handley Page Ltd, 1950; Engr, Min. of Aviation, 1964; Economic Adviser, Min. of Technology, 1970; Asst Dir (Engrg), DTI, 1973; Sen. Economic Adviser, 1974, Under Secretary: DoI, 1977; Dept of Employment, 1979; DTI, 1984–85. *Publications:* Decade of Discontent: the changing British economy, 1987; A Guide to United Kingdom and European Community Competition Policy, 1990, 2nd edn as A Guide to United Kingdom and European Union Competition Policy, 1995; The Economics of Launching Aid, in The Economics of Industrial Subsidies (HMSO), 1976; papers in Jl Instn Prodn Engrs and other engrg jls. *Recreation:* music. *Address:* 15 Chanctonbury Way, N12 7JB. *T:* 0181–445 4162.

GARDNER, Philip John, VC 1941; MC 1941; Chairman and Managing Director, J. Gardner Holdings Ltd, since 1955; *b* 25 Dec. 1914; *s* of Stanley John Gardner and Mable (*née* Puttick); *m* 1939, Renee Sherburn; one *s. Educ:* Dulwich Coll. Westminster Dragoons, TA, 1938–39; served 4th RTR, N Africa, 1939–42, when captured at Tobruk. Dir, J. Gardner Hldgs Ltd. *Club:* Army and Navy.

GARDNER, Piers; *see* Gardner, J. P.

GARDNER, Ralph Bennett, MM 1944; Under Secretary (Legal), Treasury Solicitor's Department, 1976–82, retired; *b* 7 May 1919; *s* of late Ralph Wilson Gardner and Elizabeth Emma (*née* Nevitt-Bennett); *m* 1950, Patricia Joan Ward (*née* Bartlett); one *s* one *d. Educ:* Worksop Coll. Served War, 1939–46, RA. Admitted a solicitor, 1947; Solicitor, private practice, Chester, 1947–48; Legal Asst, Treasury Solicitor's Dept, 1948; Sen. Legal Asst, 1957; Asst Treas. Solicitor, 1972. Lord of the Manor of Shotwick, County of Chester (by inheritance, 1964). *Recreations:* gardening and local history. *Address:* Wychen, St Mary's Road, Leatherhead, Surrey KT22 8HB. *T:* Leatherhead (01372) 373161. *Club:* East India, Devonshire, Sports and Public Schools.

GARDNER, Prof. Richard Lavenham, PhD; FRS 1979; Hon. Director, Imperial Cancer Research Fund's Developmental Biology Unit, since 1986; Royal Society Henry Dale Research Professor, since 1978; Student of Christ Church, Oxford, since 1974; *b* 10 June 1943; *s* of late Allan Constant and Eileen May Gardner; *m* 1968, Wendy Joy Cresswell; one *s. Educ:* St John's Sch., Leatherhead; North East Surrey Coll. of Technology; St Catharine's Coll., Cambridge (BA 1st Cl. Hons Physiol., 1966; MA; PhD 1971). Res. Asst, Physiological Lab., Cambridge, 1970–73; Lectr in Developmental and Reproductive Biology, Dept of Zoology, Oxford Univ., 1973–77; Res. Student, Christ Church, Oxford, 1974–77. Indep. Mem., ABRC, 1990–93. Scientific Medal, Zoological Soc. of London, 1977. *Publications:* contribs to Jl of Embryology and Experimental Morphology, Nature, Jl of Cell Science, and various other jls and symposia. *Recreations:* ornithology, music, sailing, painting, gardening. *Address:* Christ Church, Oxford OX1 1DP.

GARDNER, Robert Dickson Robertson, CBE 1978; Secretary, Greater Glasgow Health Board, 1974–85, retired; *b* 9 May 1924; *s* of Robert Gardner and Isabella McAlonan; *m* 1950, Ada Stewart; two *s* one *d.* Dep. Sec., 1962–66, Sec., 1966–74, Western Regional Hospital Board, Scotland. *Recreations:* swimming, Scottish country dancing, reading. *Address:* 3 Williamwood Drive, Glasgow G44 3TA. *T:* 0141–637 8070.

GARDNER, William Maving; designer, craftsman and writer; *b* 25 May 1914; *s* of Robert Haswell Gardner, MIMarE and Lucy (*née* Maving); *m* 1940, Joan Margaret Pollard (*d* 1982); two *s* one *d.* Trained at Royal College of Art, 1935–39 (ARCA 1938, Design Sch. Trav. Schol., Scandinavia, 1939). Served Army, 1939–45. Mem., Royal Mint Panel of Artists, 1938–. Vis. lectr, Central Sch. of Arts and Crafts, 1959–62, Cambridgeshire Coll. of Art and Technology, 1959–62, Hampstead Garden Suburb Inst., 1959–73; Examr in craft subjects AEB City and Guilds of London Inst., 1957–60; served Typography Jury of RSA, Ind. Design Bursary Scheme. FRSA 1955; FCSD (FSIA 1964); Leverhulme Res. Fellow, 1969–70. Vis. Prof. and Fine Art Program Lectr, Colorado State Univ., 1963; Churchill Meml Trav. Fellow, 1966–67 (USA, Polynesia, NZ, Australia, Nepal). External Examr in Lettering, City & Guilds of London Art Sch., 1987–. Hon. Mem., RNS, NZ, 1966. FSNAD 1991. Work exhib. Fort Collins and Denver, Colo, 1963, Monotype House, London, 1965, Portsmouth Coll. of Art, 1965, Hammond Mus., NY, 1970; (with family) Rye Art Gall., 1977. Awarded the Queen's Silver Jubilee Medal, 1977. *Works include:* HM Privy Council Seal 1955, HM Greater and Lesser Royal Signets 1955, Seal of HM Dependencies, 1955; seals for BMA, 1957, RSA, 1966, Univ. of Aston, Birmingham, 1966; *coinage designs and models:* for Jordan 1950, UK 1953, Cyprus 1955 and 1963, Algeria 1964, New Zealand 1967, Guyana 1967, Dominican Republic 1969, UNFAO (Ceylon 1968, Cyprus 1970, Guyana 1970), Falkland Islands 1974, UK 20p coin 1982; *medallic work:* includes Britannia Commemorative Soc. Shakespeare Medal 1967, Churchill Meml Trust's Foundn Medal 1969, Nat. Commemorative Soc. Audubon Medal 1970, Internat. Iron and Steel Inst. Medal 1971, Inst. of Metals Kroll medal 1972, and thirty-six medallic engravings depicting the history of the Royal Arms, completed 1974; participant in series of Commonwealth Silver Jubilee crown pieces, 1977; *calligraphy:* includes Rolls of Honour for House of Commons 1949, LTE 1954, Household Cavalry, Life Guards, RHG,

Grenadier, Coldstream, Scots, Irish and Welsh Foot Guards, completed 1956, Warrants of Appointment by Queen Elizabeth the Queen Mother as Lord Warden of the Cinque Ports, 1979, Royal Marines Corps Book of Remembrance, MSS for Canterbury Cath., Eton Coll., 1990, RSA 1991 and elsewhere; *work in other media* for Postmaster Gen. (Jersey definitive stamp 1958), Royal Soc. (Tercentenary stained glass window, 1960), King's College, London, 1971, City of London, 1972—and for Univs, schools, presses, libraries, also privately. *Publications:* Chapter VIII of The Calligrapher's Handbook, 1956; Calligraphy for A Wordsworth Treasury, 1978; Alphabet at Work, 1982; New Calligraphy on an Old Theme, 1984; William Gardner's Book of Calligraphy, 1988. *Recreation:* books, books and more books. *Address:* Hollingrove Old Chapel, Brightling, near Robertsbridge, East Sussex TN32 5HU.

GARDOM, Garde Basil; QC (Canada) 1975; Agent General for British Columbia in the United Kingdom and Europe, 1987–92; Director, Crown Life Insurance Co., since 1993; *b* 17 July 1924; *s* of Basil Gardom and Gabrielle Gwladys (*née* Bell); *m* 1956, Theresa Helen Eileen Mackenzie; one *s* four *d*. *Educ:* Univ. of British Columbia (BA, LlB). Called to Bar of British Columbia, 1949; elected to BC Legislature as Mem. for Vancouver-Point Grey, 1966; re-elected, 1969, 1972, 1975, 1979, 1983; Govt House Leader, 1977–86; Attorney Gen. of BC, 1975–79; Minister of Intergovtl Relns, 1979–86; Chairman: Constitution Cttee, 1975–86; Legislation Cttee, 1975–86; Mem., Treasury Bd and Planning and Priorities Cttee, 1983–86; Minister responsible, Official Visits to Expo '86; Policy Cons., Office of the Premier, 1986–87. Member: Canadian Bar Assoc., 1949–; Vancouver Bar Assoc., 1949–; British Columbia Sports Hall of Fame; Phi Delta Theta Fraternity, 1943. *Recreations:* tennis, fishing, ski-ing. *Address:* 1738 Angus Drive, Vancouver, BC V6J 4H5, Canada. *T:* (604) 7360557. *Clubs:* Union Club of BC, Vancouver Lawn Tennis and Badminton (British Columbia).

GAREL-JONES, Rt. Hon. (William Armand Thomas) Tristan, PC 1992; MP (C) Watford, since 1979; *b* 28 Feb. 1941; *s* of Bernard Garel-Jones and Meriel Garel-Jones (*née* Williams); *m* 1966, Catalina (*née* Garrigues); four *s* one *d*. *Educ:* The King's Sch., Canterbury. Principal, Language Sch., Madrid, Spain, 1960–70; Merchant Banker, 1970–74; worked for Cons. Party, 1974–79 (Personal Asst to Party Chm., 1978–79). Contested (C): Caernarvon, Feb. 1974; Watford, Oct. 1974. PPS to Minister of State, CSD, 1981; Asst Govt Whip, 1982–83; a Lord Comr of HM Treasury, 1983–86; Vice-Chamberlain of HM Household, 1986–88; Comptroller of HM Household, 1988–89; Treasurer of HM Household and Dep. Chief Whip, 1989–90; Minister of State, FCO, 1990–93. *Recreation:* collecting books. *Address:* c/o House of Commons, SW1A 0AA. *Club:* Beefsteak.

GARFIELD, Leon, FRSL; author; *b* 14 July 1921; *s* of David Garfield and Rose Garfield; *m* 1949, Vivien Dolores Alcock; one *d*. *Educ:* Brighton Grammar Sch. Served War, RAMC, 1941–46: attained and held rank of Private. Worked in NHS (biochemistry), until 1969; full-time author, 1969–. FRSL 1985. Prix de la Fondation de France, 1984; Swedish Golden Cat, 1985. *Publications:* Jack Holborn, 1964; Devil-in-the-Fog, 1966; Smith, 1967; Black Jack, 1968 (filmed 1979); Mister Corbett's Ghost and Other Stories, 1969; The Boy and the Monkey, 1969; The Drummer Boy, 1970; The Strange Affair of Adelaide Harris, 1971; The Ghost Downstairs, 1972; The Captain's Watch, 1972; Lucifer Wilkins, 1973; Baker's Dozen, 1973; The Sound of Coaches, 1974; The Prisoners of September, 1975; The Pleasure Garden, 1976; The Booklovers, 1976; The House of Hanover, 1976; The Lamplighter's Funeral, 1976; Mirror, Mirror, 1976; Moss and Blister, 1976; The Cloak, 1976; The Valentine, 1977; Labour in Vain, 1977; The Fool, 1977; Rosy Starling, 1977; The Dumb Cake, 1977; Tom Titmarsh's Devil, 1977; The Filthy Beast, 1977; The Enemy, 1977; The Confidence Man, 1978; Bostock & Harris, 1978; John Diamond, 1980 (Whitbread Book of the Year Award, 1980); Mystery of Edwin Drood (completion), 1980; Fair's Fair, 1981; The House of Cards, 1982; King Nimrod's Tower, 1982; The Apprentices, 1982; The Writing on the Wall, 1983; The King in the Garden, 1984; The Wedding Ghost, 1984; Guilt and Gingerbread, 1984; Shakespeare Stories, 1985; The December Rose, 1986; Blewcoat Boy, 1988; The Saracen Maid, 1991; The Animated Shakespeare, 1992; Shakespeare Stories II, 1994; Sabre-Tooth Sandwich, 1994; with Edward Blishen: The God Beneath the Sea, 1970 (Carnegie Medal, (1970); The Golden Shadow, 1973; with David Proctor: Child O'War, 1972. *Recreations:* snooker, collecting pictures and china; also wine, women and song. *Address:* c/o John Johnson (Author's Agent) Ltd, Clerkenwell House, 45/47 Clerkenwell Green, EC1R 0HT. *T:* 0171–251 0125. *Club:* PEN.

GARFITT, His Honour Alan; a Circuit Judge, 1977–92, and Judge, Cambridge County Court and Wisbech County Court, 1978–92; *b* 20 Dec. 1920; *s* of Rush and Florence Garfitt; *m* 1st, 1941, Muriel Ada Jaggers; one *s* one *d*; 2nd, 1973, Ivie Maud Hudson; 3rd, 1978, Rosemary Lazell; one *s* one *d*. *Educ:* King Edward VII Grammar Sch., King's Lynn; Metropolitan Coll. and Inns of Court Sch. of Law. Served War of 1939–45, RAF, 1941–46. LLB London 1947; called to the Bar, Lincoln's Inn, 1948. Hon. Fellow, Faculty of Law, Cambridge, 1978. *Publications:* Law of Contracts in a Nutshell, 4 edns 1949–56; The Book for Police, 5 vols, 1958; jt ed, Roscoe's Criminal Evidence, Practice and Procedure, 16th edn, 1952; contribs to Jl of Planning Law, Solicitors' Jl and other legal pubns. *Recreations:* farming, gardening, DIY activities, horse riding and, as a member since 1961 and President 1978–93 of the Association of British Riding Schools (Fellow, 1989), the provision of good teaching and riding facilities for non-horse owners, dinghy sailing. *Address:* Leap House, Barcham Road, Soham, Ely, Cambs CB7 5TU.

GARING, Air Commodore William Henry, CBE 1943; DFC 1940; *b* Corryong, Victoria, 26 July 1910; *s* of late George Garing, retired grazier, and late Amy Evelyn Garing; *m* 1st, 1940 (marr. diss); one *s* one *d*; 2nd, 1954, Marjorie Irene Smith, Preston, England; two *d*. *Educ:* Corryong Higher Elementary School; Royal Melbourne Inst. of Technol.; Royal Military Coll., Duntroon, ACT. Began career as Electrical and Mechanical Engineer, 1928; entered RMC, Duntroon, 1929, as specially selected RAAF Cadet; Flying Training: Point Cook, Australia, 1931; Sch. of Air Pilotage and Specialist Navigation Sch., UK 1934–35; Seaplane Flying Instructor and Chief Navigation Instructor, Point Cook, Victoria, 1936; commanded Seaplane Squadron, Point Cook; conducted first Specialist Air Navigation Course in Australia, 1938; posted to United Kingdom in 1939; served with No 10 Aust. Sunderland Squadron, RAAF, as Flt Commander in Coastal Command, RAF, 1939; operations in N Atlantic, France and Mediterranean (DFC); flew Lord Lloyd to France for discussions with Pétain Government prior to collapse of France, 1940, and subsequently was pilot to the late Duke of Kent and to Mr Eden (later Earl of Avon), and others (Atlantic Star; despatches); arrived Australia, 1941; Senior Air Staff Officer, HQ Northern Area (extended from Neth. Indies through New Guinea, British Solomons to New Caledonia), 1941; commanded No 9 (Operational) Group RAAF, New Guinea, 1942; Milne Bay Campaign, 1942; Buna Campaign, 1942–43 (American DSC, awarded by Gen. MacArthur); 1943 (CBE, awarded for air operations SW Pacific); commanded No 1 Operational Training Unit, E Sale, Victoria, 1943–44; Director Operational Requirements, 1944; SASO to RAAF Rep., Washington, 1945–46, subseq. RAAF Rep. (1939–45 star); OC Western Area, 1947; JSSC, 1948; ADC to the King, 1951; Commandant School Land/Air Warfare, NSW, 1950; AOC Amberley, Qld, 1951; Imperial Defence Coll., London, 1952; AOC Overseas HQ, and RAAF Rep., London, 1953; AOC RAAF, Richmond, NSW, 1953–55; AOC RAAF and Commandant RAAF Staff Coll., Point Cook, Victoria, 1955–60; Air Officer, South Australia, and OC, RAAF, Edinburgh Field, Salisbury, SA, 1960–64, retired. Exec. Dir, Rothmans Nat. Sport Foundn, Sydney, Australia, 1964; Commercial Relations Manager, Alfred Dunhill Ltd, 1971–75. Holds No 1 1st cl. Air Navigators' Certificate (Australia); Air Master Navigator (RAF). Bd, Royal Freemasons Benevolent Assoc.; Co-ordinator, Masonic Internat. Fest., 1977–79. FAIM 1964. *Recreations:* Alpine ski-ing, water ski-ing, yachting, shooting, flying, carpentry, landscape painting, gardening. *Clubs:* Imperial Service, Royal Automobile, New South Wales Leagues, Tattersall's (Sydney).

GARLAND, Basil; Registrar, Family Division of High Court of Justice (formerly Probate, Divorce and Admiralty Division), 1969–85; *b* 30 May 1920; *o c* of late Herbert George Garland and Grace Alice Mary Martha Garland; *m* 1942, Dora Mary Sudell Hope; one *s*. *Educ:* Dulwich Coll.; Pembroke Coll., Oxford (MA). Served in Royal Artillery, 1940–46: commnd 1941; Staff Officer, HQ RA, Gibraltar, 1943–45; Hon. Major 1946. Called to Bar, Middle Temple, 1948; Treasury Junior Counsel (Probate), 1965; Registrar, Principal Probate Registry, 1969. *Publications:* articles in Law Jl. *Recreations:* sailing, drama. *Address:* Dalethorpe End, Dedham, Essex CO7 6HW. *T:* Colchester (01206) 322263. *Clubs:* Bar Yacht, Royal Harwich Yacht.

GARLAND, (Frederick) Peter (Collison), CVO 1969; QPM 1965; *b* 4 Sept. 1912; *s* of late Percy Frederick Garland, Southsea, Hants; *m* 1945, Gwendolen Mary, *d* of late Henry James Powell, Putney; three *d*. *Educ:* Bradfield Coll. Joined Metropolitan Police, 1934. Served in RAF (Air Crew), 1941–45. Asst Chief Constable of Norfolk, 1952–56, Chief Constable, 1956–75. CStJ 1961. *Address:* 2 Eaton Road, Norwich NR4 6PY. *T:* Norwich (01603) 453043. *Club:* Royal Air Force.

GARLAND, Nicholas Withycombe; Political Cartoonist, The Daily Telegraph, 1966–86 and since 1991; *b* 1 Sept. 1935; *s* of Tom and Peggy Garland; *m*; three *s* one *d*. *Educ:* Slade School of Fine Art. Worked in theatre as stage man. and dir, 1958–64; Political Cartoonist: New Statesman, 1971–78; The Independent, 1986–91; has drawn regularly for The Spectator, 1979–; with Barry Humphries created and drew comic strip, Barry McKenzie, in Private Eye. *Publications:* (illustrated) Horatius, by T. B. Macaulay, 1977; An Indian Journal, 1983; Twenty Years of Cartoons by Garland, 1984; Travels with my Sketchbook, 1987; Not Many Dead, 1990.

GARLAND, Patrick Ewart; director and producer of plays, films, television; writer; Artistic Director, Chichester Festival Theatre, 1980–84 and 1991–94; *b* 10 April 1935; *s* of late Ewart Garland and Rosalind, *d* of Herbert Granville Fell, editor of The Connoisseur; *m* 1980, Alexandra Bastedo. *Educ:* St Mary's Coll., Southampton; St Edmund Hall, Oxford (MA). Actor, Bristol Old Vic, 1959; Age of Kings, BBC TV, 1961; lived in Montparnasse, 1961–62; writing—two plays for ITV, 1962; Research Asst, Monitor, BBC, 1963; Television interviews with: Stevie Smith, Philip Larkin, Sir Noel Coward, Sir John Gielgud, Sir Ralph Richardson, Dame Ninette de Valois, Claire Bloom, Tito Gobbi, Marcel Marceau, 1964–78. Director and Producer, BBC Arts Dept, 1962–74; Stage Director: 40 Years On, 1968, 1984; Brief Lives, 1968; Getting On, 1970; Cyrano, 1971; Hair (Israel), 1972; The Doll's House (New York and London), 1975; Under the Greenwood Tree, 1978; Look After Lulu, 1978; Beecham, 1980 (all West End); York Mystery Plays, 1980; My Fair Lady (US), 1980; Kipling (Mermaid and New York), 1984; Canaries Sometimes Sing, Albery, 1987; The Secret of Sherlock Holmes, Wyndham's, 1988; Victory (adapted from The Dynasts by Thomas Hardy), Chichester, 1989; A Room of One's Own, Hampstead, 1989, New York, 1991; Song in the Night, Lyric, Hammersmith, 1989; The Dressmaker, Windsor and tour, 1990; Tovarich, Piccadilly, 1991; Vita and Virginia, Ambassadors, 1993; co-author, Underneath the Arches, Chichester, and Prince of Wales, 1982–83; Director, Chichester Festival Theatre: The Cherry Orchard, 1981; The Mitford Girls, 1981 (also London, 1981); On the Rocks, 1982; Cavell, 1982; Goodbye, Mr Chips, 1982; As You Like It, 1983; Forty Years On, Merchant of Venice, 1984; Tovarich, 1991; Pickwick, 1993; Pygmalion, 1994; produced: Fanfare for Elizabeth, the Queen's 60th birthday gala, Covent Garden, 1986; Celebration of a Broadcaster, for Richard Dimbleby Cancer Fund at Westminster Abbey, 1986; Thanksgiving service for Lord Olivier, 1989. *Films:* The Snow Goose, 1974; The Doll's House, 1976. Creative Writing Fellowship, Bishop Otter Coll., Chichester, 1984–85. Hon. DLitt Southampton, 1994. *Publications:* Brief Lives, 1967; The Wings of the Morning (novel), 1989; Oswald the Owl (for children), 1990; poetry in: London Magazine, 1954; New Poems, 1956; Poetry West; Encounter; short stories in: Transatlantic Review, 1976; England Erzählt, Gemini, Light Blue Dark Blue. *Recreations:* reading Victorian novels, walking in Corsica. *Club:* Garrick.

GARLAND, Hon. Sir Patrick Neville, Kt 1985; **Hon. Mr Justice Garland;** a Judge of the High Court, Queen's Bench Division, since 1985; *b* 22 July 1929; *s* of Frank Neville Garland and Marjorie Garland; *m* 1955, Jane Elizabeth Bird; two *s* one *d*. *Educ:* Uppingham Sch. (Scholar); Sidney Sussex Coll., Cambridge (Exhibnr and Prizeman; MA, LLM; Hon. Fellow, 1991). Called to Bar, Middle Temple, 1953, Bencher, 1979. Asst Recorder, Norwich, 1971; a Recorder, 1972–85; QC 1972; Dep. High Court Judge, 1981–85; a Judge of the Employment Appeal Tribunal, 1986–95; Presiding Judge, SE Circuit, 1991–94. Mem., Judges' Council, 1993–94. President: Central Council of Probation Cttees, 1986–; Official Referees Bar Assoc.; Mem., Parole Bd, 1988– (Vice-Chm., 1989–91). *Publications:* articles in legal and technical jls. *Recreations:* shooting, gardening, industrial archaeology. *Address:* c/o Royal Courts of Justice, Strand, WC2A 2LL. *Club:* Cumberland Lawn Tennis.

GARLAND, Peter; *see* Garland, F. P. C.

GARLAND, Prof. Peter Bryan, PhD; FRSE; Chief Executive, Institute of Cancer Research, since 1989, and Professor of Biochemistry, British Postgraduate Medical Federation, University of London, since 1992; *b* 1934; *s* of Frederick George Garland and Molly Kate Jones; *m* 1959, Ann Bathurst; one *s* two *d*. *Educ:* Hardye's Sch., Dorchester; Downing Coll., Cambridge (BA 1st Class Hons in Physical Anthropol., 1955; BChir 1958, MB 1959; PhD 1964); King's Coll. Hosp. Med. Sch. (Burney Yeo Schol.). MRC Res. Schol., Chem. Pathol. Dept, KCH Med. Sch., and Biochem. Dept, UCL, 1959–61; British Insulin Manufacturers' Fellow, Biochem. Dept, Cambridge Univ., 1961–64; Lectr, 1964–68, Reader, 1969–70 in Biochem., Bristol Univ.; Prof. of Biochem., Dundee Univ., 1970–84; Principal Scientist and Hd, Biosciences Div., Unilever Research, 1984–87; Dir of Research, Amersham Internat., 1987–89. Vis. Prof., Johnson Res. Foundn, Philadelphia, 1967–69; Vis. Fellow, ANU, 1983. Member: MRC, 1980–84 (Chm., Cell Biol.–Disorders Bd, 1980–82); EMBO, 1981; CRC Scientific Policy Cttee, 1985–92; Chm., CRC Technology Ltd, 1988–91. Dir, CAT Ltd, 1990–. FRSE 1977. Hon. LLD Dundee, 1990. Colworth Medal, Biochem. Soc., 1970. *Publications:* numerous articles in biochemistry and biophysics. *Recreations:* sport (athletics blue, Cambridge, 1954–55), ski-ing, sailing, windsurfing, reading. *Address:* Institute of Cancer Research, 17A Onslow Gardens, SW7 3AL. *Clubs:* Athenæum; Bosham Sailing.

GARLAND, Peter Leslie; Under Secretary and Deputy Director of Finance, NHS Executive, Department of Health, since 1993; *b* 21 Sept. 1946; *s* of Leslie and Stella Garland; *m* 1979, Janet Rosemary Prescott; three *d*. *Educ:* Bristol Cathedral Sch.; Manchester Univ. Joined DHSS, 1974; Asst Sec. 1989. *Recreations:* family, gardening. *Address:* National Health Service Executive, Quarry House, Leeds LS2 7UE.

GARLAND, Hon. Sir (Ransley) Victor, KBE 1982; Chairman, TR Far East Income Trust PLC, since 1990 (Director, since 1984); Company Director: Prudential Corporation plc, 1984–93; Throgmorton Trust plc, since 1985; Nelson Hurst plc, since 1993; Vice Chairman, South Bank Board, since 1985; *b* Perth, 5 May 1934; *m* Lynette Jamieson, BMus (Melb.); two *s* one *d*. *Educ:* Univ. of Western Australia. BA(Econ); FCA. Practised as Chartered Accountant, 1958–70. MP for Curtin, Australian Federal Parliament, 1969–81; Minister for Supply, 1971–72; Executive Councillor, 1971–; Minister Asstg Treasurer, 1972 and 1975–76; Chief Opposition Whip, 1974–75; Minister for Special Trade Representations, also Minister Asstg Minister for Trade and Resources, 1977–79; Minister for Business and Consumer Affairs, 1979–80; High Comr for Australia in UK, 1981–83. Govt Representative Minister: at Commonwealth Ministerial Meeting for Common Fund, London, 1978; at Ministerial Meetings of ESCAP, New Delhi, 1978; Minister representing Treas., at Ministerial Meeting of OECD, Paris, 1978; Leader, Aust. Delegn to UNCTAD V and Chm. Commonwealth Delegns to UNCTAD V, Manila, 1979; attended, with Premier, Commonwealth Heads of Govt meeting, Lusaka, 1979. Parly Adviser, Aust. Mission to UN Gen. Assembly, New York, 1973; Chairman: House of Reps Expenditure Cttee, 1976–77; Govt Members' Treasury Cttee, 1977. Councillor, Royal Commonwealth Society for the Blind, 1988–93. Freeman, City of London, 1982. *Address:* Wilton Place, Knightsbridge, SW1X 8RL. *T:* 0171–235 2729. *Clubs:* White's; Weld (Perth).

GARLICK, Prof. George Frederick John, BSc, PhD, DSc, FInstP; *b* 21 Feb. 1919; *s* of George Robert Henry Garlick and Martha Elizabeth (*née* Davies); *m* 1943, Dorothy Mabel Bowsher; one *d*; *m* 1977, Harriet Herta Forster. *Educ:* Wednesbury High Sch.; Univ. of Birmingham (BSc 1940, PhD 1943, DSc 1955). War service: Scientific Officer (Radar Research). In Charge Luminescence Laboratory, Birmingham Univ., 1946–56 (Research Physicist, 1946–49, Lecturer in Physics, 1949–56); Prof. of Physics, Univ. of Hull, 1956–78; Research Prof., Univ. of Southern California, LA, 1978–79; private scientific consultant, 1979–89. FInstP 1949. Jubilee Medal, 1977. *Publications:* Luminescent Materials, 1949; numerous papers in learned scientific journals. *Recreation:* music (organ). *Address:* 267 South Beloit Avenue, Los Angeles, CA 90049, USA.

GARLICK, Sir John, KCB 1976 (CB 1973); Permanent Secretary, Department of the Environment, 1978–81; *b* 17 May 1921; *m* 1945, Frances Esther Munday (*d* 1992); three *d*. *Educ:* Westcliff High Sch., Essex; University of London. Entered Post Office Engineering Dept, 1937; Ministry of Transport, 1948; Private Secretary to Rt Hon. Ernest Marples, 1959–60; Assistant Secretary, 1960; National Economic Development Office, 1962–64; Under-Sec., Min. of Transport, 1966, later DoE; Dep. Sec., DoE, 1972–73; Dir-Gen., Highways, DoE, 1973–74; Second Permanent Sec., Cabinet Office, 1974–77. Mem., London Docklands Develt Corp., 1981–92. Dir, Abbey National plc (formerly Abbey National Building Soc.), 1981–92. Chm., Alcohol Concern, 1985–. *Address:* 16 Astons Road, Moor Park, Northwood, Mddx. *T:* Northwood (01923) 824628.

GARLICK, Kenneth John; Keeper of Western Art, Ashmolean Museum, Oxford, 1968–84; Professorial Fellow of Balliol College, Oxford, 1968–84, now Emeritus; *b* 1 Oct. 1916; *s* of late D. E. Garlick and Annie Hallifax. *Educ:* Elmhurst Sch., Street; Balliol Coll., Oxford; Courtauld Inst. of Art, London. MA Oxon, PhD Birmingham; FSA, FMA. RAF Signals, 1939–46. Lectr, Bath Academy of Art, 1946–48; Asst Keeper, Dept of Art, City of Birmingham Museum and Art Gallery, 1948–50; Lectr (Sen. Lectr 1960), Barber Inst. of Fine Arts, Univ. of Birmingham, 1951–68. Governor, Royal Shakespeare Theatre, 1978–95. *Publications:* Sir Thomas Lawrence, 1954; Walpole Society Vol. XXXIX (Lawrence Catalogue Raisonné), 1964; Walpole Society Vol. XLV (Catalogue of Pictures at Althorp), 1976; (ed with Angus Macintyre) The Diary of Joseph Farington, Vols I-II, 1978, III-VI, 1979; Sir Thomas Lawrence, 1989; numerous articles and reviews. *Recreations:* travel, music. *Address:* 39 Hawkswell House, Hawkswell Gardens, Oxford OX2 7EX. *Club:* Reform.

GARLING, David John Haldane, ScD; Reader in Mathematical Analysis, since 1978, and Fellow of St John's College, since 1963, Cambridge University; *b* 26 July 1937; *s* of Leslie Ernest Garling and Frances Margaret Garling; *m* 1963, Anthea Mary Eileen Dixon; two *s* one *d*. *Educ:* Highgate Sch.; St John's Coll., Cambridge (BA, MA, PhD, ScD 1978). Cambridge University: Asst Lectr, 1963–64; Lectr, 1964–78; Head of Dept of Pure Maths and Math. Stats, 1984–91; Pro-Proctor, 1995–96, Sen. Proctor, 1996–; Tutor, 1971–78, Pres., 1987–91, St John's Coll. Member: SERC Mathematics Cttee, 1983–86; Council, London Mathematical Soc., 1986–88. *Publications:* A course in Galois Theory, 1987; papers in sci. jls. *Address:* St John's College, Cambridge CB2 1TP. *T:* Cambridge (01223) 338600.

GARMOYLE, Viscount; Hugh Sebastian Frederick Cairns; with Cazenove, stockbrokers, since 1994; *b* 26 March 1965; *s* and *heir* of Earl Cairns, *qv*; *m* 1991, Juliet, *d* of Andrew Palmer; one *s* one *d*. *Educ:* Eton; Edinburgh Univ. (MA Hons); London Coll. of Law. With Freshfields, solicitors, 1990–94. *Heir:* *s* Hon. Oliver David Andrew Cairns, *b* 7 March 1993. *Address:* 11 Lonsdale Road, W11 2BY.

GARNER, Alan; author; *b* 17 Oct. 1934; *s* of Colin and Marjorie Garner; *m* 1st, 1956, Ann Cook; one *s* two *d*; 2nd, 1972, Griselda Greaves; one *s* one *d*. *Educ:* Alderley Edge Council Sch.; Manchester Grammar Sch.; Magdalen Coll., Oxford. Writer and presenter, documentary films: Places and Things, 1978; Images, 1981 (First Prize, Chicago Internat. Film Fest.). Mem. Internat. Editl Bd, Detskaya Literatura Publishers, Moscow, 1991–. *Publications:* The Weirdstone of Brisingamen, 1960 (Lewis Carroll Shelf Award, USA, 1970); The Moon of Gomrath, 1963; Elidor, 1965; Holly from the Bongs, 1966; The Old Man of Mow, 1967; The Owl Service, 1967 (Library Assoc. Carnegie Medal 1967, Guardian Award 1968); The Hamish Hamilton Book of Goblins, 1969; Red Shift, 1973 (with John Mackenzie, filmed 1978); (with Albin Trowski) The Breadhorse, 1975; The Guizer, 1975; The Stone Book, 1976 (Phoenix Award, Children's Lit. Assoc. of Amer., 1996); Tom Fobble's Day, 1977; Granny Reardun, 1977; The Aimer Gate, 1978; Fairy Tales of Gold, 1979; The Lad of the Gad, 1980; Alan Garner's Book of British Fairy Tales, 1984; A Bag of Moonshine, 1986; Jack and the Beanstalk, 1992; Once Upon a Time, 1993; *plays:* Lamaload, 1978; Lurga Lom, 1980; To Kill a King, 1980; Sally Water, 1982; The Keeper, 1983; *dance drama:* The Green Mist, 1970; *libretti:* The Bellybag, 1971 (music by Richard Morris); Potter Thompson, 1972 (music by Gordon Crosse); *screenplay:* Strandloper, 1992. *Recreation:* work. *Address:* Blackden, Cheshire CW4 8BY. *Club:* Portico Library (Manchester).

GARNER, Sir Anthony (Stuart), Kt 1984; parliamentary and public affairs consultant, since 1988; Director of Organisation, Conservative Central Office, 1976–88; *b* 28 Jan. 1927; *s* of Edward Henry Garner, MC, FIAS, and Dorothy May Garner; *m* 1967, Shirley Doris Taylor; two *s*. *Educ:* Liverpool Coll. Grenadier Guards, 1945–48. Young Conservative Organiser, Yorks Area, 1948–51; Conservative Agent, Halifax, 1951–56; Nat. Organising Sec., Young Conservative Org., 1956–61; Conservative Central Office Agent for: London Area, 1961–64; Western Area, 1964–66; North West Area, 1966–76. Chm., Conservative Agents' Examination Bd, 1976–88. Pres., Conservative Agents' Benevolent Assoc., 1976–88. Director: Carroll Anglo-American Corp., 1989–; Clifton Court Residents, 1990–; Farnborough Aerospace Develt Corp., 1994–; Carroll Aircraft Corp., 1994–95. Life Governor, Liverpool Coll., 1980. *Recreations:* sailing, theatre. *Address:* 1 Blomfield Road, W9 1AH. *Clubs:* Carlton, St Stephen's Constitutional.

GARNER, Frederick Leonard; Chairman, Pearl Assurance Company Ltd, 1977–83, President, and President, Pearl Group, 1983–88, retired; *b* 7 April 1920; *s* of Leonard Frank Garner and Florence Emily Garner; *m* 1953, Giovanna Maria Anzani, Italy. *Educ:* Sutton County Sch., Surrey. Served War, RA, 1940–46. Joined Pearl Assurance Co., 1936; rejoined, 1946; sole employment, 1946–83. Director: Schroder Global Trust, 1971–89; Kleinwort Development Fund, 1981–; Age Concern Insurance Services, 1987–. Mem., Finance Cttee, Age Concern England, 1987–. *Address:* 98 Tudor Avenue, Worcester Park, Surrey KT4 8TU. *T:* 0181–337 3313. *Club:* Royal Automobile.

GARNER, John Donald, CMG 1988; CVO 1991 (LVO 1979); HM Diplomatic Service, retired; *b* 15 April 1931; *s* of late Ronald Garner and of Doris Ethel Garner (*née* Norton); *m* Karen Maria Conway; two *d*. *Educ:* Trinity Grammar Sch., N22. Royal Navy, National Service, 1949–51. Foreign Office, 1952–55; Third Secretary: Seoul, 1955; Bangkok, 1957; Foreign Office, 1959–63; Second Secretary: Benghazi and Tripoli, 1963–67; Sydney, 1967–69; First Sec., Tel Aviv, 1969–73; FCO, 1973–76; NDC 1976; Dep. High Commissioner, Lilongwe, 1977–80; Chargé d'affaires, Kabul, 1981–84; High Comr, The Gambia, 1984–87; Consul-Gen., Houston, 1988–91. *Recreation:* golf. *Address:* 30 The Green, N14 6EN. *T:* 0181–882 6808. *Club:* South Herts Golf.

GARNER, Maurice Richard; specialist in the structure and governmental control of public enterprises; *b* 31 May 1915; *o s* of Jesse H. Garner; *m* 1943, Joyce W. Chapman; one *s* one *d*. *Educ:* Glendale County Sch.; London Sch. of Economics and Political Science. Royal Armoured Corps, 1942–45 (despatches). Inland Revenue (Tax Inspectorate), 1938–46; BoT, Asst Principal and Principal, 1947; Commercial Sec. and UK Trade Comr in Ottawa, 1948–55; transf. to Min. of Power, 1957; Asst Sec. 1960; Under-Sec., Electricity Div., Min. of Technology, 1969, later DTI, retired 1973. Vis. Prof., Dept of Govt, LSE, 1981–85. *Recreations:* reading, oenology. *Address:* New Albany, 33 Sand Hill Lane, Leeds LS17 6AJ. *T:* Leeds (0113) 268 5115.

GARNER, Michael Scott; His Honour Judge Garner; a Circuit Judge, since 1988; *b* 10 April 1939; *s* of William Garner and Doris Mary (*née* Scott); *m* 1st, 1964, Sheila Margaret (*d* 1981) (*née* Garland); one *s* one *d*; 2nd, 1982, Margaret Anne (*née* Senior). *Educ:* Huddersfield Coll.; Manchester Univ. (LLB). Admitted Solicitor, 1965. Asst Recorder, 1978–85; a Recorder, 1985–88. *Recreations:* motoring, walking, cooking with wok in Lakeland hideaway. *Address:* 12 Sunningdale Croft, Fixby, Huddersfield HD2 2NX.

GARNETT, Vice-Adm. Ian David Graham; Deputy Supreme Allied Commander Atlantic, since 1995; *b* 27 Sept. 1944; *s* of Capt. Ian Graham Hartt Garnett, DSC, RN and Barbara Anne Langrishe (*née* Hackett); *m* 1973, Charlotte Mary Anderson; one *s* two *d*. *Educ:* Canford Sch.; BRNC, Dartmouth. Entered RN, 1962; Lt 1967; flying trng, 1968–69; HMS Hermes, 814 Sqdn, 1969–70; Loan Service, RAN, 1971–72; HMS Tiger, 826 Sqdn, 1973–74; Warfare Officer, 1974–76; Sen. Pilot, 820 Sqdn, 1977–78; Dep. Dir, JMOTS, 1978–80; in comd, HMS Amazon, 1981–82; RN staff course, 1983; Asst Dir, Operational Requirements, 1983–86; Captain Fourth Frigate Sqnd (HMS Active), 1986–88; RN Presentation Team, 1988–89; Dir Operational Requirements, 1989–92; FO Naval Aviation, 1993–95. *Recreations:* gardening, golf, restoring furniture, walking. *Address:* Box C-01, SACLANT HQ, Naval Party 1964, BFPO 493. *Club:* Royal Navy of 1765 and 1785.

GARNETT, John; *see* Garnett, W. J. P. M.

GARNETT, Julia Charity, (Mrs John Garnett); *see* Cleverdon, J. C.

GARNETT, Kevin Mitchell; QC 1991; *b* 22 June 1950; *s* of Frank Raymond Garnett and Cynthia Ruby Eberstein; *m* 1980, Susan Jane Louise (*née* Diboll); one *s*. *Educ:* Bradfield Coll., Berks; University Coll., Oxford (MA). Called to the Bar, Middle Temple, 1975. Vice-Chm., Cartoon Art Trust. *Publications:* (ed jtly) Williams, Mortimer and Sunnucks on Executors, Administrators and Probate, 16th edn 1982, 17th edn 1993; (ed jtly) Copinger and Skone James on Copyright, 13th edn 1991. *Recreations:* tennis, mountain walking. *Address:* Churchbury House, Windmill Road, SW19 5NQ. *T:* 0181–946 6486; 5 New Square, Lincoln's Inn, WC2A 3RJ. *T:* 0171–404 0404. *Clubs:* Hurlingham; Royal Wimbledon Golf, Woking Golf.

GARNETT, Thomas Ronald, MA; Head Master of Geelong Grammar School, Australia, 1961–73; *b* 1 Jan. 1915; *s* of E. N. Garnett; *m* 1946, Penelope, *d* of Philip Frere; three *s* two *d*. *Educ:* Charterhouse (Scholar); Magdalene Coll., Cambridge (Scholar). BA 1936, MA 1946. Assistant master: Westminster School, 1936–38; Charterhouse, 1938–52; Master of Marlborough College, 1952–61. Served War of 1939–45, RAF, India and Burma, 1941–46, Squadron Leader (despatches). Cricket for Somerset, 1939. *Publications:* Stumbling on Melons, 1984; (ed) A Gardener's Potpourri, 1986; Man of Roses: Alister Clark of Glenara, 1990; The Evolution of a Garden, 1993. *Recreations:* gardening, ornithology. *Address:* Simmons Reef, Blackwood, via Trentham, Vic 3458, Australia. *T:* (53) 686514.

GARNETT, (William) John (Poulton Maxwell), CBE 1970; MA; lecturer on leadership and communication; *b* 6 Aug. 1921; *s* of Dr Maxwell Garnett, CBE, and Margaret Lucy Poulton; *m* 1st, 1943, Barbara Rutherford-Smith (marr. diss.); two *s* two *d*; 2nd, 1986, Julia Cleverdon, *qv*; two *d*. *Educ:* Rugby Sch.; Kent Sch., USA; Trinity Coll., Cambridge. Royal Navy, 1941–46 (commnd, 1942). ICI Ltd, 1947–62; Dir, Industrial Soc., 1962–86; Chm., W Lambeth HA, 1986–90. Dep. Chm. UNA, 1954–56. Mem., Ct of inquiry into miners' strike, 1972; Arbitrator, Lorry Drivers' Strike, 1979. Mem., Royal Dockyard Policy Bd. Chm., Churches Council on Gambling, 1965–71. DUniv Essex, 1977; Hon. DTech Loughborough, 1978; Hon. LLD, CNAA, 1980. *Publications:* The Manager's Responsibility for Communication, 1964; The Work Challenge, 1973, 1985. *Recreation:* timber construction. *Address:* 8 Alwyne Road, Canonbury, N1 2HH. *Club:* Leander (Henley).

See also V. H. B. M. Bottomley.

GARNIER, Edward Henry; MP (C) Harborough, since 1992; barrister; *b* 26 Oct. 1952; *s* of late Col William d'Arcy Garnier and of Hon. Lavender Hyacinth (*née* de Grey); *m* 1982, Anna Caroline Mellows; two *s* one *d*. *Educ:* Wellington Coll.; Jesus Coll., Oxford (BA, MA). Called to the Bar, Middle Temple, 1976. Vice-Pres., Hemsworth Assoc., 1987–. Contested: Wandsworth BC by-election, 1984; Tooting ILEA election, 1986; (C) Hemsworth, Gen. Election, 1987. PPS to Ministers of State, FCO, 1994–. Mem., Home Affairs Select Cttee, 1992–95; Sec., Cons. Foreign Affairs Cttee, 1992–94. *Publications:* (contrib.) Halsbury's Laws of England, 4th edn, 1985; (contrib.) Bearing the Standard,

1991; (contrib.) Facing the Future, 1993. *Recreations:* cricket, shooting, opera. *Address:* House of Commons, SW1A 0AA. *T:* 0171–219 3000.

GARNIER, Rear-Adm. Sir John, KCVO 1990 (LVO 1965); CBE 1982; Private Secretary and Comptroller to HRH Princess Alexandra, since 1991; Extra Equerry to the Queen, since 1988; *b* 10 March 1934; *s* of Rev. Thomas Vernon Garnier and Helen Stenhouse; *m* 1966, Joanna Jane Cadbury; two *s* one *d*. *Educ:* Berkhamsted School; Britannia Royal Naval College. Joined RN 1950; served HM Yacht Britannia, 1956–57; HMS Tyne (Suez Operation) 1956; qualified navigation specialist, 1959; Naval Equerry to HM Queen, 1962–65; Comd HMS Dundas, 1968–69; Directorate of Naval Ops and Trade, 1969–71; Comd HMS Minerva, 1972–73; Defence Policy Staff, 1973–75; HMS Intrepid, 1976; Asst Dir, Naval Manpower Planning, 1976–78; RCDS 1979; Comd HMS London, 1980–81; Dir, Naval Ops and Trade, 1982–84; Commodore Amphibious Warfare, 1985; Flag Officer Royal Yachts, 1985–90. Younger Brother of Trinity House, 1974. Freeman of City of London, 1982. *Recreations:* sailing, golf, gardening, opera. *Address:* Buckingham Palace, SW1A 1AA.

GARNOCK, Viscount; William James Lindesay-Bethune; *b* 30 Dec. 1990; *s* and *heir* of Earl of Lindsay, *qv*.

GARNSEY, Rt. Rev. David Arthur; *b* 31 July 1909; *s* of Canon Arthur Henry Garnsey and Bertha Edith Frances Garnsey (*née* Benn); *m* 1934, Evangeline Eleanor Wood; two *s* two *d*. *Educ:* Trinity and Sydney Grammar Schs; St Paul's Coll., University of Sydney; New Coll., Oxford. University of Sydney, BA (1st cl. Latin and Greek) 1930; Travelling Sec. Australian SCM, 1930–31; NSW Rhodes Scholar, 1931, New Coll. Oxford, BA (2nd cl. Lit. Hum.) 1933, 2nd cl. Theol. 1934, MA 1937; Ripon Hall, Oxford, 1933. Deacon, 1934; Priest, 1935; Curate, St Mary the Virgin (University Church), and Inter-Collegiate Sec. of SCM, Oxford, 1934–38; St Saviour's Cathedral, Goulburn, NSW, 1938–41; Rector of Young, NSW, 1941–45; Gen. Sec. Australian SCM, 1945–48; Exam. Chap. to Bp of Goulburn, 1939–45, 1948–58; Head Master Canberra Grammar Sch., 1948–58; Canon of St Saviour's Cathedral, Goulburn, 1949–58; Bishop of Gippsland, 1959–74. Pres., Australian Council of Churches, 1970–73. Chm., Bd of Delegates, Aust. Coll. of Theology, 1971–77; Hon. ThD, Australian Coll. of Theology, 1955. Coronation Medal, 1953. *Publications:* A. H. Garnsey: a man for truth and freedom, 1985; Songs from a Dry Land (comments on the psalms), 1994; booklets for study. *Recreation:* reading. *Address:* 27/2 Berwick Street, Camberwell, Vic 3124, Australia. *T:* 8822114.

GARRARD, Rt. Rev. Richard; *see* Penrith, Bishop Suffragan of.

GARRELS, John Carlyle; retired; Chairman: Monsanto Chemicals Ltd, 1965–71; Monsanto Textiles Ltd, 1970–71; formerly Director: Forth Chemicals Ltd; Monsanto Australia Ltd; Monsanto Oil Co. of UK, Inc.; British Saccharin Sales Ltd; *b* 5 March 1914; *s* of John C. and Margaret Ann Garrels; *m* 1st, 1938, Valerie Smith; one *s* two *d*; 2nd, 1980, Isabelle Rogers Kehoe. *Educ:* Univ. of Michigan (BS (Chem. Eng.)); Harvard (Advanced Management Programme). Pennsylvania Salt Mfg Co., Production Supervisor, 1936–42; Monsanto Co.: various appts, 1942–54; Asst Gen. Manager, 1955; Monsanto Chemicals Ltd: Dep. Man. Dir, 1960; Man. Dir, 1961; Chm. and Man. Dir, 1965. Pres., British Plastics Fedn, 1970, 1971. Member: National Economic Development Cttee for Chemical Industry, 1971; Council, Chemical Industries Assoc. *Recreations:* golf, shooting, fishing. *Address:* 3111 SE Fairway West, Stuart, FL 34997, USA. *T:* (407) 2836132. *Clubs:* American; Sunningdale Golf; Yacht and Country (Stuart, Fla); Fishing of America (New York).

GARRETT, Anthony David, CBE 1993; Deputy Master and Comptroller, Royal Mint, 1988–92; *b* 26 Aug. 1928; *s* of Sir William Garrett, MBE and Lady Garrett; *m* 1952, Monica Blanche Harris; three *s* one *d*. *Educ:* Ellesmere College; Clare College, Cambridge. MA. National Service, Subaltern IVth QO Hussars, 1946–48; Procter & Gamble Co., 1953–82, Vice-Pres., 1975–82; Bd Mem., 1983–87, and Man. Dir of Parcels, 1986–87, Post Office. Dir, Nat. Provident Instn, 1988–94. FRSA 1991. *Recreations:* golf, bridge, chess, walking. *Address:* Cammock House, Goldsmith Avenue, Crowborough, East Sussex TN6 1RH. *T:* Crowborough (01892) 654557.

GARRETT, Godfrey John, OBE 1982; HM Diplomatic Service; Head of UK Delegation to European Community Monitoring Mission, Zagreb, since 1993; *b* 24 July 1937; *s* of Thomas and May Garrett; *m* 1963, Elisabeth Margaret Hall; four *s* one *d*. *Educ:* Dulwich Coll.; Cambridge Univ. (MA). Joined FO, 1961; Third Sec., Leopoldville (later Kinshasa), 1963; Second Sec. (Commercial), Prague, 1965; FCO, 1968; First Sec., Buenos Aires, 1971; FCO, 1973; First Sec., later Counsellor, Stockholm, 1981; Counsellor: Bonn, 1983; FCO, 1988; E Berlin, 1990; Prague, 1990–92; FCO, 1992–93. Order of the Northern Star, Sweden, 1983. *Recreations:* all outdoor activities, especially skiing; travel, gardening, languages. *Address:* c/o Foreign and Commonwealth Office, SW1A 2AH; White Cottage, Henley, Haslemere, Surrey GU27 3HQ. *T:* Haslemere (01428) 652172.

GARRETT, Maj.-Gen. Henry Edmund Melvill Lennox, CBE 1975; Chairman, Forces Help Society and Lord Roberts Workshops, since 1991; *b* 31 Jan. 1924; *s* of John Edmund Garrett and Mary Garrett; *m* 1973, Rachel Ann Beadon; one step *s* one step *d*. *Educ:* Wellington Coll.; Clare Coll., Cambridge (MA). Commnd 1944; psc 1956; DAAG, HQ BAOR, 1957–60; US Armed Forces Staff Coll., 1960; OC 7 Field Sqdn RE, 1961–63; GSO2 WO, 1963–65; CO 35 Engr Regt, 1965–68; Col GS MoD, 1968–69; Comdr 12 Engr Bde, 1969–71; RCDS, 1972; Chief of Staff HQ N Ireland, 1972–75; Maj.-Gen. i/c Administration, HQ UKLF, 1975–76; Vice Adjutant General, MoD, 1976–78; Dir of Security (Army), MoD, 1978–89. Col Comdt RE, 1982–90. Chm., RE Assoc., 1989–. Chm. Governors, Royal Soldiers' Daughters Sch., 1983–86. *Recreations:* riding, walking. *Address:* c/o National Westminster Bank, 7 Hustlegate, Bradford, W Yorkshire BD1 1PP. *Club:* Army and Navy.

GARRETT, John Laurence; MP (Lab) Norwich South, since 1987; *b* 8 Sept. 1931; *s* of Laurence and Rosina Garrett; *m* 1959, Wendy Ady; two *d*. *Educ:* Selwyn Avenue Primary Sch., London; Sir George Monoux Sch., London; University Coll., Oxford (MA, BLitt); Grad. Business Sch. of Univ. of California at Los Angeles (King George VI Fellow). Labour Officer, chemical industry, 1958–59; Head of Market Research, motor industry, 1959–63; Management Consultant, Dir of Public Services, 1963–74, and Associate Dir, 1983–87, Inbucon Ltd. Consultant to Fulton Cttee on CS, 1966–68. MP (Lab) Norwich South, Feb. 1974–1983; PPS to Minister for Civil Service, 1974, to Minister for Social Security, 1977–79; Opposition Treasury spokesman, 1979–80; spokesman: on industry, 1980–83; on energy, 1987–88; on industry, 1988–89; on civil service, 1993–; Campaigns Coordinator, Southern and Eastern England, 1989–92. Contested (Lab) Norwich South, 1983. *Publications:* Visual Economics, 1966; (with S. D. Walker) Management by Objectives in the Civil Service, 1969; The Management of Government, 1972; Administrative Reform, 1973; Policies Towards People, 1973 (Sir Frederic Hooper Award); Managing the Civil Service, 1980; Westminster, 1992; articles and papers on industry, management and govt. *Recreations:* theatre, dabbling, arguing. *Address:* c/o House of Commons, SW1A 0AA.

GARRETT, Lesley, FRAM; Principal Soprano, English National Opera, since 1984; *b* 10 April 1955; *d* of Derek Arthur Garrett and Margaret Garrett (*née* Wall); *m* 1991; one *s* one *d*. *Educ:* Thorne Grammar Sch.; Royal Acad. of Music (FRAM 1995); Nat. Opera Studio (Post-grad.) Winner, Kathleen Ferrier Meml Competition, 1979. Performed with WNO, Opera North and at Wexford and Buxton Fests and Glyndebourne; joined ENO, 1984; has appeared in opera houses in Geneva, São Paulo, Boboli Gdns, Florence, Bolshoi Theatre, Moscow and Kirov Theatre, St Petersburg; major roles include: Susanna in Marriage of Figaro; Despina in Così Fan Tutte; Musetta in La Bohème; Jenny in The Rise and Fall of The City of Mahaggony; Atalanta in Xerxes; Zerlinda in Don Giovanni; Yum-Yum in The Mikado; Adèle in Die Fledermaus; Oscar in A Masked Ball; Dalinda in Ariodante; Rose in Street Scene; Bella in A Midsummer Marriage and title rôle in The Cunning Little Vixen; concert hall appearances in UK and abroad include: Royal Variety Performance, 1993, Last Night of the Proms, Royal Albert Hall, Royal Fest. Hall, Centre Pompidou, Paris; numerous recordings and TV and radio appearances. Hon. DArts Plymouth, 1995. *Recreation:* watching cricket. *Address:* c/o Allied Artists, 42 Montpelier Square, SW7 1JZ. *T:* 0171–589 6243.

GARRETT, Richard Anthony, CBE 1987; company director; Chairman, National Association of Boys' Clubs, 1980–87, retired; *b* 4 July 1918; 3rd *s* of Charles Victor Garrett and Blanche Michell; *m* 1946, Marie Louise Dalglish; one *s* two *d* (and one *d* decd). *Educ:* King's Sch., Worcester. MInstD; CIMgt (CBIM 1979). Served War, 1939–45 (despatches, 1945). Joined W.D. & H.O. Wills, 1936; Chm., ITL, retd 1979; Chm. and Man. Dir, John Player & Sons, 1968–71; Chm., Dataday Ltd, 1978–83; Director: HTV Gp plc, 1976–89 (Vice-Chm., 1978–83); Standard Commercial (formerly Standard Commercial Tobacco) Corp., 1980–95. Vice Pres., (Founder), Assoc. of Business Sponsorship of the Arts; Mem., National Cttee for Electoral Reform. Chm., Bath Festival, 1986–87; Trustee, Glyndebourne Arts Trust, 1976–88. Liveryman, Worshipful Co. of Tobacco Pipe Makers and Tobacco Blenders. *Recreations:* golf, gardening, music, opera, reading. *Address:* Marlwood Grange, Thornbury, Bristol BS12 2JB. *T:* Thornbury (01454) 412630. *Clubs:* Naval and Military, MCC, XL; Bristol and Clifton Golf.

GARRETT, Terence, CMG 1990; CBE 1967; Assistant Secretary (International Affairs), Royal Society, 1991–94; *b* 27 Sept. 1929; *e s* of late Percy Herbert Garrett and Gladys Annie Garrett (*née* Budd); *m* 1960, Grace Elizabeth Bridgeman Braund, *yr d* of Rev. Basil Kelly Braund; two *s* three *d*. *Educ:* Alleyn's Sch.; Gonville and Caius Coll., Cambridge (Scholar; 1st Cl. Hons, Mathematics). DipMathStat. Instructor Lieut RN, 1952–55. Lecturer, Ewell County Technical Coll., 1955–56; Sen. Lectr, RMCS, Shrivenham, 1957–62; Counsellor (Sci. and Technol.), Moscow, 1962–66 and 1970–74; Programmes Analysis Unit, Min. of Technology, 1967–70; Internat. Technological Collaboration Unit, Dept of Trade, 1974–76; Sec. to Bd of Governors and to Gen. Conf. of Internat. Atomic Energy Agency, Vienna, 1976–78; Counsellor (Science and Technology), Bonn, 1978–82; DCSO, Research and Technology Policy Div., DTI, 1982–87; Counsellor (Sci. and Technol.), Moscow, 1987–91. *Recreation:* travel. *Address:* Lime Tree Farmhouse, Chilton, Didcot, Oxon OX11 0SW.

GARRETT, Thomas John; Member, Independent Commission for Police Complaints (Northern Ireland), since 1990; Principal, Royal Belfast Academical Institution, 1978–90; *b* 13 Sept. 1927; *s* of late Mr and Mrs T. J. Garrett; *m* 1958, Sheenah Agnew (*d* 1991), *o d* of late Mr and Mrs G. Marshall, Drymen, Stirlingshire; one *d*. *Educ:* Royal Belfast Acad. Instn; QUB (BA); Heidelberg Univ. Asst Master: Royal Belfast Acad. Instn, 1951–54; Nottingham High Sch. for Boys, 1954–56; Sen. German Master, Campbell Coll., Belfast, 1956–73, Housemaster, 1968–73; Headmaster, Portora Royal Sch., Enniskillen, 1973–78. Member: Broadcasting Council for N Ireland, 1982–84; Northern Ireland Partnership, 1987–. Mem., Bd of Govs, Bloomfield Collegiate Sch., 1992–. *Publications:* Modern German Humour, 1969; Two Hundred Years at the Top—a dramatised history of Portora Royal School, 1977. *Recreations:* writing, hill-walking, ornithology. *Address:* Carnbeg, 44 Dunmore Road, Spa, Ballynahinch, Co. Down BT24 8PR. *T:* Ballynahinch (01238) 562399. *Club:* East India.

GARRICK, Sir Ronald, Kt 1994; CBE 1986; FEng 1984; FRSE; Managing Director and Chief Executive, Weir Group, since 1982; *b* 21 Aug. 1940; *s* of Thomas Garrick and Anne (*née* McKay); *m* 1965, Janet Elizabeth Taylor Lind; two *s* one *d*. *Educ:* Royal College of Science and Technology, Glasgow; Glasgow University (BSc MechEng, 1st cl. hons). FIMechE; FRSE 1992. Joined G. & J. Weir Ltd, 1962; Weir Pumps: Dir, Industrial Div., 1973; Dir Production Div., 1976; Managing Dir, 1981; Dir, Weir Group, 1981. Vis. Prof., Dept of Mech. Engrg, Univ. of Strathclyde, 1991–. Member: Scottish Council, CBI, 1982–90; Gen. Convocation, 1985–, Court, 1990–, Univ. of Strathclyde; Restrictive Practices Court, 1986–; Scottish Economic Council, 1989–; Offshore Industry Adv. Bd, 1989–; Dep. Chm., Scottish Enterprise Bd, 1991–. Non-Executive Director: Supervisory Bd, NEL, 1989–92; Strathclyde Graduate Business Sch., 1990–; Scottish Power PLC, 1992–; Shell UK Ltd, 1993–. DUniv: Paisley, 1993; Strathclyde, 1994. *Recreations:* golf, reading. *Address:* c/o Weir Group, Cathcart, Glasgow G44 4EX. *T:* 0141–637 7111. *Club:* Caledonian.

GARRIOCH, Sir (William) Henry, Kt 1978; Chief Justice, Mauritius, 1977–78, retired; *b* 4 May 1916; *s* of Alfred Garrioch and Jeanne Marie Madeleine Colin; *m* 1964, Jeanne Louise Marie-Thérèse Desvaux de Marigny. *Educ:* Royal Coll., Mauritius. Called to the Bar, Gray's Inn, 1952. Civil Service (clerical), Mauritius, 1936–48; law student, London, 1949–52; Dist Magistrate, Mauritius, 1955; Crown Counsel, 1958; Sen. Crown Counsel, 1960; Solicitor-Gen., 1964; Dir of Public Prosecutions, 1966; Puisne Judge, 1967; Sen. Puisne Judge, 1970; Actg Governor-Gen., 1977–78. *Recreations:* reading, chess. *Address:* Lees Street, Curepipe, Mauritius. *T:* 6752708.

GARROD, Lt-Gen. Sir (John) Martin (Carruthers), KCB 1988; OBE 1980; DL; Chief of Staff to European Union Administrator of Mostar, since 1994; *b* 29 May 1935; *s* of Rev. William Francis Garrod and Isobel Agnes (*née* Carruthers); *m* 1963, Gillian Mary, *d* of late Lt-Col R. G. Parks-Smith, RM; two *d*. *Educ:* Sherborne School. Joined Royal Marines, 1953; served Malta, Cyprus, DS Officers' Training Wing, RM School of Music, Malaya, Borneo, 1955–66; Staff Coll., Camberley, 1967; HQ 17 Div., Malaya, 1968–69; HQ Farelf, Singapore, 1970–71; 40 Commando RM (Co. Comdr, Plymouth and N Ireland), 1972–73 (despatches); GSO2 Plans, Dept of CGRM, 1973–76; GSO1, HQ Commando Forces RM, 1976–78; CO 40 Commando RM, 1978–79 (OBE operational, NI); Col Ops/Plans, Dept of CGRM, 1980–82; Comdr 3 Commando Bde RM, 1983–84; ADC to the Queen, 1983–84; COS to Comdt Gen. RM, 1984–87; Comdt Gen., RM, 1987–90. Mem., EC Monitor Mission in Bosnia, 1993–94. Special Comr, Duke of York's Royal Mil. Sch., Dover, 1992–. Dep. Dir, Maastricht Referendum Campaign, 1993. Freeman, City of London, 1990; Liveryman, Plaisterers' Co., 1990. DL Kent, 1992. *Recreation:* portrait photography. *Address:* c/o Lloyds Bank, 5 The Square, Petersfield, Hants GU32 3HL. *Club:* East India.

GARSIDE, Charles Roger; QC 1993; a Recorder, since 1994; *b* 13 Aug. 1948; *s* of Richard Murray Garside and Jane Garside (*née* Boby); *m* 1973, Sophie Shem-Tov; two *s* one *d*. *Educ:* Tonbridge Sch. Called to the Bar, Gray's Inn, 1971. *Recreations:* gardening, cricket, Rugby. *Address:* Crown Square Chambers, 1 Deans Court, Crown Square, Manchester M3 3HA. *T:* 0161-833 9801. *Club:* Lancashire County Cricket.

GARSIDE, Prof. John, PhD, DSc(Eng); FEng, FIChemE; Professor of Chemical Engineering, University of Manchester Institute of Science and Technology, since 1982; *b* 9 Oct. 1941; *s* of Eric and Ada Garside; *m* 1965, Patricia Louise Holtom; one *s* one *d*. *Educ:* Christ's Coll., Finchley; University Coll. London (BSc(Eng), PhD, DSc(Eng); Fellow, 1994). FIChemE 1986; FEng 1988. ICI Agricl Div., 1966–69; Lectr, later Reader, UCL, 1969–81; Vice-Principal, UMIST, 1985–87. Vis. Prof., Iowa State Univ., 1976–77. Mem., various cttees and Engrg Bd, SERC, 1989–93. Institution of Chemical Engineers: Mem. Council, 1992–; Pres., 1994–95. *Publications:* (ed) Advances in Industrial Crystallization, 1991; Precipitation: basic principles and industrial application, 1992; papers in Chem. Engrg Sci., Trans IChemE, Amer. Instn Chem. Engrs, Jl Crystal Growth, etc. *Recreations:* music, sailing, gardening. *Address:* Chemical Engineering Department, University of Manchester Institute of Science and Technology, PO Box 88, Manchester M60 1QD. *T:* 0161–200 4360.

GARSIDE, (Pamela) Jane, CBE 1995; JP; Chief Commissioner, The Guide (formerly Girl Guides) Association of the United Kingdom and the Commonwealth, since 1990; *b* 20 Aug. 1936; *d* of Ronald and Nellie Whitwam; *m* 1958, Adrian Fielding Garside; two *s* (two *d* decd). *Educ:* Royds Hall Grammar Sch., Huddersfield; Yorkshire Trng Coll. of Housecraft, Leeds Inst. of Educn (Teaching Dip. 1957). Teacher, Deighton Secondary Sch., 1957–58; Co. Sec. 1959–, Dir 1964–, Highfield Funeral Service Ltd. Girl Guides: Dist Comr, Huddersfield N, 1973–77; County Comr, W Yorks S, 1977–83; Chief Comr, NE England, 1984–89. Vice-Pres., Camping and Caravanning Club. *Recreations:* reading, gardening, music. *Address:* The Guide Association, 17–19 Buckingham Palace Road, SW1W 0PT. *T:* 0171–834 6242.

GARSIDE, Roger Ramsay; Executive Chairman, GMA Capital Markets Ltd (formerly Garside, Miller Associates), advisers to emerging financial markets, since 1990; *b* 29 March 1938; *s* of Captain F. R. Garside and Mrs Peggie Garside; *m* 1969, Evelyne Madeleine Pierrette Guérin; three *d*. *Educ:* Eton; Clare Coll., Cambridge (BA EngLit, MA); Sloan Fellow in Management, Massachusetts Inst. of Technology. 2nd Lieut, 1/6 QEO Gurkha Rifles, 1958–59; entered HM Foreign Service, 1962; served, Rangoon, 1964–65; Mandarin Chinese Lang. Student, Hong Kong, 1965–67; Second Secretary, Peking, 1968–70; FCO, 1970–71, resigned 1971; World Bank, 1972–74; rejoined Foreign Service, 1975; served FCO, 1975; First Sec., Peking, 1976–79; on leave of absence, as Vis. Professor of East Asian Studies, US Naval Postgrad. Sch., Monterey, Calif, 1979–80; Dep. Head, Planning Staff, FCO, 1980–81; seconded, HM Treasury, 1981–82; Financial and Commercial Counsellor, Paris, 1982–87, resigned 1987; Dir, Public Affairs, Internat. Stock Exchange of UK and Rep. of Ireland, 1987–90. *Publication:* Coming Alive: China after Mao, 1981. *Recreations:* writing, tennis, travel. *Address:* 36 Groveway, SW9 0AR. *T:* 0171–582 1577. *Club:* Reform.

GARSON, Greer, Hon. CBE 1993; actress; *b* Northern Ireland, 29 Sept. 1908; *d* of George Garson and Nina Sophia Greer; *m* 1st, Edward A. Snelson (marr. diss.) (*see* Sir E. A. Snelson); 2nd, 1943, Richard Ney (marr. diss.); 3rd, 1949, Col E. E. Fogelson (*d* 1987), Texas. *Educ:* London and Grenoble Univs. BA Hons London. Birmingham Repertory Theatre, 1932 and 1933; London Theatre debut, Whitehall, 1935; lead roles in 13 London plays; entered films in 1939; *films include:* Goodbye Mr Chips, Pride and Prejudice, When Ladies Meet, Blossoms in the Dust, Mrs Miniver (Academy Award), Random Harvest, Madame Curie, Mrs Parkington, Valley of Decision, That Forsyte Woman, Julius Caesar, The Law and the Lady, Her Twelve Men, Sunrise at Campobello (Golden Globe award), Strange Lady in Town, The Singing Nun, The Happiest Millionaire; *stage appearances include:* Auntie Mame, Tonight at 8.30, Captain Brassbound's Conversion. Appeared in pioneer British TV, on American TV. Hon. DHum, Rollins Coll., Florida, 1950, Hon. Dr in Communication Arts, Coll. of Santa Fe, 1970, Hon. DLitt Ulster, 1977; winner of many internat. awards. Current interests include The Greer Garson Theatre and Fogelson Library Center, Coll. of Santa Fe; Mem. Bd, Dallas Theater Center; adjunct prof. in drama, Southern Methodist Univ., Dallas; Mem., State Commn on the arts in Texas and New Mexico; Principal Founding Donor: Fogelson Forum, Dallas Presbyterian Hosp.; Garson Communications Center, Coll. of Santa Fe; Fogelson Pavilion, Meyerson Symphony Center, Dallas; Fogelson Fountain, Dallas Arboretum; Greer Garson Theatre, Southern Methodist Univ., Dallas. Hon. Alumna, St John's Coll., Santa Fe. Operates Forked Lightning Ranch, Pecos, New Mexico, where Pecos Nat. Monument and Visitors Centre located (with Col E. E. Fogelson, received Conservation Service Award, US Dept of Interior, 1981, for this and other civic projects); also involved in breeding and racing thoroughbred horses (stable includes Ack Ack, horse of the year, 1971). *Recreations:* nature study, music, primitive art.

GARSON, Cdre Robin William, CBE 1978; RN retd; Director of Leisure Services, London Borough of Hillingdon, 1975–86; *b* 13 Nov. 1921; *s* of late Peter Garson and Ada Frances (*née* Newton); *m* 1946, Joy Ligertwood Taylor (*née* Hickman); one *s* one *d*. *Educ:* School of Oriental and African Studies. Japanese Interpreter. Entered Royal Navy, 1937; served War of 1939–45, HM Ships: Resolution, Nigeria, Cyclops, and HM Submarines: Seawolf, H.33, Spark; subsequent principal appointments: In Command HM Submarines: Universal, Uther, Seraph, Saga, Sanguine, Springer, Thule, Astute, 1945–54; Chief Staff Officer Intelligence, Far East, 1966–68; Sen. Polaris UK Rep., Washington, 1969–71; Captain 1st Submarine Sqdn, 1971–73; Commodore, HMS Drake, 1973–75; ADC to the Queen, 1974. Adviser to AMA on Arts and Recreation, 1976–86; Adviser to Sports Council, 1985–86; Mem., Library Adv. Council (England), 1977–83. Patron, RN Submarine Mus., 1990–. *Recreations:* golf, ski-ing, tennis. *Address:* Gateways, Hamilton Road West, Old Hunstanton, Norfolk PE36 6JB. *Clubs:* Army and Navy, Royal Navy of 1765 and 1785; Moor Park (Rickmansworth); Hunstanton Golf.

GARTHWAITE, Sir Mark; *see* Garthwaite, Sir W. M. C.

GARTHWAITE, Sir (William) Mark (Charles), 3rd Bt *cr* 1919, of Durham; Director, Steel Burrill Jones Ltd, Lloyds Brokers, since 1992; *b* 4 Nov. 1946; *s* of Sir William Francis Cuthbert Garthwaite, 2nd Bt, DSC and of his 2nd wife, Patricia Beatrice Eden (*née* Neate); *S* father, 1993; *m* 1979, Victoria Lisette Hohler, *e d* of Gen. Sir Harry Tuzo, *qv*; one *s* two *d*. *Educ:* Dragon Sch.; Gordonstoun; Univ. of Pennsylvania (Wharton Sch.; BSc Econ.). Seascope Insurance Services, Lloyds Brokers, 1970–87 (Man. Dir, 1980–87); Brandram and Garthwaite Ltd, 1987–88; Dir, Regis Low Ltd, Lloyds Brokers, 1988–92. *Recreations:* sailing, ski-ing, trekking. *Heir:* *s* William Tuzo Garthwaite, *b* 14 May 1982. *Address:* 3 Hazlewell Road, SW15 6LU. *Clubs:* Turf; Royal Southampton Yacht (Southampton).

GARTON, George Alan, PhD, DSc; FRSE 1966; FRS 1978; Hon. Professorial Fellow, Rowett Research Institute, Bucksburn, Aberdeen, since 1992; Hon. Research Fellow, University of Aberdeen, since 1987; *b* 4 June 1922; *o s* of late William Edgar Garton, DCM, and late Frances Mary Elizabeth Garton (*née* Atkinson), Scarborough, N Yorks; *m* 1951, Gladys Frances Davison, BSc; two *d*. *Educ:* Scarborough High Sch.; Univ. of Liverpool (BSc (War Service) 1944, (Hons Biochem.) 1946; PhD 1949, DSc 1959). Experimental Asst, Chemical Inspection Dept, Min. of Supply, 1942–45; Johnston Research and Teaching Fellow, Dept of Biochem., Univ. of Liverpool, 1949–50; Rowett Research Inst., Bucksburn, Aberdeen: Biochemist, 1950; Dep. Dir, 1968–83; Head of Lipid Biochem. Dept, 1963–83; Hon. Res. Associate, 1983–92; Hon. Res. Associate, Univ. of Aberdeen, 1966–86. Sen. Foreign Fellow of Nat. Science Foundn (USA), and Vis. Prof. of Biochem., Univ. of N Carolina, 1967. Chm., British Nat. Cttee for Nutritional and Food Sciences, 1982–87; Pres., Internat. Confs on Biochem. Lipids, 1982–89. Scientific Gov., British Nutrition Foundn, 1982–. SBStJ 1985. *Publications:* papers, mostly on aspects of lipid biochemistry, in scientific jls. *Recreations:* gardening, golf, foreign travel. *Address:* Ellerburn, 1 St Devenick Crescent, Cults, Aberdeen AB1 9LL. *T:* Aberdeen (01224) 867012. *Clubs:* Farmers'; Deeside Golf (Aberdeen).

GARTON, Rev. Canon John Henry; Principal of Ripon College, Cuddesdon, since 1986; *b* 3 Oct. 1941; *s* of Henry and Dorothy Garton; *m* 1969, Pauline (*née* George); two *s*. *Educ:* RMA Sandhurst; Worcester Coll., Oxford (MA, DipTh); Cuddesdon Coll., Oxford. Commissioned in Royal Tank Regt, 1962. Ordained, 1969; CF, 1969–73; Lectr, Lincoln Theol Coll., 1973–78; Rector of Coventry East Team Ministry, 1978–86. Hon. Canon of Worcester Cathedral, 1988–. *Address:* The Old Vicarage, High Street, Cuddesdon, Oxford OX9 9HP. *T:* Wheatley (018677) 4368.

GARTON, John Leslie, CBE 1974 (MBE (mil.) 1946); President, Henley Royal Regatta, since 1978; *b* 1 April 1916; *er s* of late C. Leslie Garton and Madeline Laurence; *m* 1939, Elizabeth Frances, *d* of late Sir Walter Erskine Crum, OBE; one *s* (and two *s* decd). *Educ:* Eton; Magdalen Coll., Oxford (MA). Commissioned TA, Royal Berkshire Regt, 1938. Served War, in France, 1940; psc 1943; Gen. Staff Ops Br., First Canadian Army HQ, in Europe, 1944–46; transf. to RARO, Scots Guards, 1951. Chm., Coca-Cola Bottling Co. (Oxford) Ltd, 1951–65, Coca-Cola Western Bottlers Ltd, 1966–71. Henley Royal Regatta: Steward, 1960; Mem. Cttee of Management, 1961–77; Chm., 1966–77. Amateur Rowing Association: Exec. Cttee and Council, 1948–77; Pres., 1969–77; Hon. Life Vice-Pres., 1978. Hon. Sec. and Treas., OUBC Trust Fund, 1959–69; Mem., Finance and Gen. Purposes Cttee, British Olympic Assoc., 1969–77; Thames Conservator, 1970–74; Chm., World Rowing Championships, 1975; Pres., Leander Club, 1980–83; Chm., Leander Trust, 1982–. Liveryman, Grocers' Company, 1947–. High Sheriff, Bucks, 1977. *Recreations:* supporting the sport of rowing (rowed in Eton VIII, 1934, 1935, Captain of the Boats, 1935; rowed in the Boat Race for Oxford, 1938, 1939, Pres. OUBC, 1939), shooting (particularly deer-stalking), fishing. *Address:* Mill Green House, Church Street, Wargrave, Berkshire RG10 8EP. *T:* Wargrave (01734) 402944. *Club:* Leander (elected 1936, Life Mem., 1953, Cttee, 1956, Chm. Executive, 1958–59).

GARTON, Prof. William Reginald Stephen, FRS 1969; Professor of Spectroscopy, University of London, Imperial College, 1964–79, now Professor Emeritus; Associate Head, 1970–79, and Senior Research Fellow, since 1979, Department of Physics, Imperial College; *b* Chelsea, SW3, 7 March 1912; *s* of William and Gertrude Emma Caroline Garton; *m* 1st, 1940, Margarita Fraser Callingham (marr. diss. 1976); four *d*; 2nd, 1976, Barbara Lloyd (*née* Jones). *Educ:* Sloane Sch., SW10; Chelsea Polytechnic, SW3; Imperial Coll., (Hon. Fellow 1983). BSc, ARCS 1936; DSc 1958. Demonstrator in Physics, Imperial Coll., 1936–39. Served in RAF, 1939–45. Imperial Coll.: Lectr in Physics, 1946–54; Sen. Lectr, 1954–57; Reader, 1957–64. External Examiner: Univ. of Singapore, 1972–75; Univ. of Malaya, 1986–89. Associate, Harvard Coll. Observatory, 1963–; Nuffield Fellow, Univ. of Western Ontario, 1964; Hertz Fellow, Univ. of Bonn, 1984; Leverhulme Trust Emeritus Fellow, 1987–89. W. F. Meggers Award, 1976, Fellow, 1979, Optical Soc. of America. Hon. DSc York Univ., Toronto, 1972. *Publications:* contrib. on Spectroscopy in Advances in Atomic and Molecular Physics (ed D. R. Bates), 1966 (New York); numerous papers on Spectroscopy and Atomic Physics. *Recreations:* speliology, Oriental history. *Address:* Blackett Laboratory, Imperial College, SW7. *T:* 0171–589 5111; Chart House, Great Chart, Ashford, Kent TN23 3AP. *T:* Ashford (01233) 621657; 9 callé Tico Medina, Mojacar (Almeria), Spain.

GARVAGH, 5th Baron *cr* 1818; **Alexander Leopold Ivor George Canning;** Accredited Representative, Trade and Industry, The Cayman Islands, 1981; *b* 6 Oct. 1920; *s* of 4th Baron and Gladys Dora May (*d* 1982), *d* of William Bayley Parker; *S* father 1956; *m* 1st, 1947, Christine Edith (marr. diss. 1974), *d* of Jack Cooper; one *s* two *d*; 2nd, 1974, Cynthia Valerie Mary, *d* of Eric E. F. Pretty, CMG, Kingswood, Surrey. *Educ:* Eton; Christ Church, Oxford. Commissioned Corps of Guides Cavalry, Indian Army, 1940; served Burma (despatches). Founder Dir, Internat. Business Services Ltd, 1947; Director: Stonehaven Tankers Ltd; Campden Research & Sales Ltd; Independent Chartering Ltd; AODC (UK) Ltd; Camco Machinery Ltd; Telomex (New York) Inc. Founder Mem., Instituto de Proprietarios Extranjeros (Spain), 1985. Mem., Baltic Exchange, 1978. Mem., British Inst. of Exports, 1957; MIMgt (MBIM 1962); FInstD 1964. Past Mem. Court, Painter Stainers Co. Consultant and contributor, Spanish Property Gazette, 1987–88. *Publications:* contrib. to The Manufacturing Optician, 1949. *Recreations:* travel, motoring, and motor sport; writing articles, short stories, etc. *Heir:* *s* Hon. Spencer George Stratford de Redcliffe Canning [*b* 12 Feb. 1953; *m* 1979, Julia Margery Morison Bye, *er d* of Col F. C. E. Bye, Twickenham; one *s* two *d*]. *Address:* c/o Robert Cooles, Abbott Cresswell, 179 Upper Richmond Road West, SW14 8DU.

GARVEY, Thomas, (Tom); Deputy Director General (Environment, Nuclear Safety and Civil Protection), European Commission, since 1992; *b* 27 May 1936; *s* of Thomas and Brigid Garvey; *m* 1961, Ellen Devine; two *s* two *d*. *Educ:* University Coll., Dublin (MA Econ). Fellow, Management Inst. Ireland. Various marketing and internal trade appts, 1958–69; Chief Exec., Irish Export Bd, 1969–76; EEC Delegate, Nigeria, 1977–80; Chief Exec., An Post (Irish Postal Service), 1980–84; Dir, Internal Market and Ind. Affairs, EEC, 1984–89; Dir, DG1 (External Relns), EC, 1990–92. FRSA 1990. *Publications:* various, in industrial, trade and academic jls. *Recreations:* golf, music. *Club:* United Services (Dublin).

GARVIN, Clifton Canter, Jr; Chairman of the Board and Chief Executive Officer, Exxon Corporation, 1975–86, retired; *b* 22 Dec. 1921; *s* of Clifton C. Garvin, Sr, and Esther Ames; *m* 1943, Thelma Volland; one *s* three *d*. *Educ:* Virginia Polytechnic Inst. and State Univ. MS (ChemEng) 1947. Exxon: Process Engr, subseq. Refining Operating Supt, Baton Rouge, Louisiana Refinery, 1947–59; Asst Gen. Manager, Supply Dept, Exxon Corp., 1959–60; Gen. Manager, Supply Dept, Esso Eastern, 1960–61; Manager, Production, Supply & Distribution Dept, Exxon Co., USA, 1961–62, subseq. Vice-Pres., Central Region, 1963–64; Exec. Asst to Pres. and Chm., Exxon Corp., NY, 1964–65; Pres., Exxon Chemical (US), subseq. Pres. Exxon Chemical (Internat.), 1965–68; Dir, subseq. Exec. Vice-Pres., subseq. Pres., Exxon Corp., 1968–75. Director: Citicorp and Citibank; Hosp. Corp. of America; PepsiCo, Inc.; Johnson & Johnson; J. C. Penney Co., Inc.; TRW Inc.; Americas Soc.; Member: Amer. Inst. of Chem. Engrs; Business Roundtable; Council on Foreign Relns; Business Council; Nat. Associate, White Burkett Miller Center of Public Affairs, Univ. of Virginia; Member: Admin Bd, Lab. of Ornithology, Cornell Univ.; Virginia Polytechnic Institute and State University: Cttee of 100—Coll. of Engrg Corporate Develt; Bd of Visitors. *Recreations:* golf, bird watching.

GARY, Lesley; *see* Blanch, L.

GASCH, Pauline Diana, (Mrs F. O. Gasch); *see* Baynes, P. D.

GASCOIGNE, Bamber; author and broadcaster; *b* 24 Jan. 1935; *s* of late Derick Gascoigne and Midi (*née* O'Neill); *m* 1965, Christina Ditchburn. *Educ:* Eton; Magdalene Coll., Cambridge. Commonwealth Fund Fellow, Yale, 1958–59. Theatre Critic, Spectator, 1961–63, and Observer, 1963–64; Co-editor, Theatre Notebook, 1968–74. Founded Saint Helena Press, 1977; Chm., Ackermann Publishing, 1981–85. Trustee: Nat. Gall., 1988–95; Tate Gall., 1993–95; Chm., Friends of Covent Garden, 1991–95; Member: Bd of Dirs, Royal Opera House, Covent Garden, 1988–95; Council, Nat. Trust, 1989–94. Theatre: Share My Lettuce, London, 1957–58; Leda Had a Little Swan, New York, 1968; The Feydeau Farce Festival of Nineteen Nine, Greenwich, 1972; Big in Brazil, Old Vic, 1984. Television: presenter of: University Challenge, (weekly) 1962–87; Cinema, 1964; (also author) The Christians, 1977; Victorian Values, 1987; Man and Music, 1987–89; The Great Moghuls, 1990; Brother Felix and the Virgin Saint, 1992; deviser and presenter of Connoisseur, 1988–89; author of: The Four Freedoms, 1962; Dig This Rhubarb, 1963; The Auction Game, 1968. FRSL 1976. *Publications:* (many with photographs or watercolour illustrations by Christina Gascoigne): Twentieth Century Drama, 1962; World Theatre, 1968; The Great Moghuls, 1971; Murgatreud's Empire, 1972; The Heyday, 1973; The Treasures and Dynasties of China, 1973; Ticker Khan, 1974; The Christians, 1977; Images of Richmond, 1978; Images of Twickenham, 1981; Why the Rope went Tight, 1981; Fearless Freddy's Magic Wish, 1982; Fearless Freddy's Sunken Treasure, 1982; Quest for the Golden Hare, 1983; Cod Streuth, 1986; How to Identify Prints, 1986; Amazing Facts, 1988; Encyclopedia of Britain, 1993. *Address:* Saint Helena Terrace, Richmond, Surrey TW9 1NR.

GASCOIGNE, Stanley, CMG 1976; OBE 1972; Secretary to the Cabinet, Bermuda, 1972–76; Member, Senate, 1976–85, Vice-President, 1980–85; *b* 11 Dec. 1914; *s* of George William Gascoigne and Hilda Elizabeth Gascoigne; *m* 1st, 1941, Sybil Wellspring Outerbridge (*d* 1980); 2nd, 1980, Sandra Alison Lee; two *s*. *Educ:* Mt Allison Univ., Canada (BA 1937): London Univ., England (DipEd 1938): Boston Univ., USA (MEd 1951). Teacher, 1939–51; Inspector of Schools, 1951–59; Director, Marine and Ports Authority, 1959–69; Permanent Sec., Education, 1969–72. Exec. Dir, Inst. of Chartered Accountants of Bermuda, 1976–89. *Recreation:* ornithology. *Address:* #63 Shelly Hall, Shelly Bay, Hamilton Parish CR BX, Bermuda. *T:* 2931304. *Club:* Royal Hamilton Amateur Dinghy (Bermuda).

GASH, Prof. Norman, CBE 1989; FBA 1963; FRSL 1973; FRSE 1977; FRHistS; Professor of History, St Salvator's College, University of St Andrews, 1955–80, now Emeritus; *b* 16 Jan. 1912; *s* of Frederick and Kate Gash; *m* 1935, Ivy Dorothy Whitehorn; two *d*. *Educ:* Reading Sch.; St John's Coll., Oxford (Hon. Fellow 1987). Scholar, St John's Coll.; 1st cl. Hons Mod. Hist., 1933; BLitt, 1934; MA 1938. FRHistS 1953. Temp. Lectr in Modern European History, Edinburgh, 1935–36; Asst Lectr in Modern History, University Coll., London, 1936–40. Served War, 1940–46: Intelligence Corps; Capt. 1942; Major (Gen. Staff), 1945. Lectr in Modern British and American History, St Salvator's Coll., University of St Andrews, 1946–53; Prof. of Modern History, University of Leeds, 1953–55; Vice-Principal, 1967–71, Dean of Faculty of Arts, 1978–80, St Andrews Univ. Hinkley Prof. of English History, Johns Hopkins Univ., 1962; Ford's Lectr in English History, Oxford Univ., 1963–64; Sir John Neale Lectr in English Hist., UCL, 1981; Wellington Lectr, Southampton Univ., 1992. Vice-Pres., Hist. Assoc. of Scotland, 1963–64. Hon. DLitt: Strathclyde, 1984; St Andrews, 1985; Southampton, 1988. *Publications:* Politics in the Age of Peel, 1953; Mr Secretary Peel, 1961; The Age of Peel, 1968; Reaction and Reconstruction in English Politics, 1832–1852, 1966; Sir Robert Peel, 1972; Peel, 1976; (jtly) The Conservatives: a history from their origins to 1965, 1978; Aristocracy and People: England 1815–1865, 1979; Lord Liverpool, 1984; Pillars of Government, 1986; (ed) Wellington: studies in the military and political career of the first Duke of Wellington, 1990; Robert Surtees and Early Victorian Society, 1993; articles and reviews in Eng. Hist. Review, Trans. Royal Historical Society, and other learned jls. *Recreations:* gardening, swimming. *Address:* Old Gatehouse, Portway, Langport, Som TA10 0NQ. *T:* Langport (01458) 250334.

GASK, Daphne Irvine Prideaux, (Mrs John Gask), OBE 1976; JP; Member, Inner London Commission of the Peace, 1982–88; *b* 25 July 1920; *d* of Roger Prideaux Selby and Elizabeth May (*née* Stirling); *m* 1945, John Gask, MA, BM, BCh; one *s* one *d*. *Educ:* St Trinnean's, Edinburgh; Tolmers Park, Herts; Collège Brillantmont, Lausanne, Switzerland. BA Open Univ., 1979. CAB worker, 1985–. Member: Shropshire Probation and After-Care Cttee, 1960–80 (Chm., 1978–80); Exec. Cttee, Central Council of Probation and After-Care Cttees, 1964–80 (Vice-Chm., 1977–80); Royal Commn on Criminal Procedure, 1978–80; Council, Magistrates Assoc., 1968–80 (Mem. Exec. Cttee, 1976–80); Sports Council Adv. Gp, 1978–80; NACRO, 1982–; Asst Sec., L'Association Internationale des Magistrats de la Jeunesse et de la Famille, 1979–86 (Hon. Mem., 1986–; Mem. Gen. Purposes Cttee, 1986–). Served on Salop CC, 1965–77; Chm., Leisure Activities Cttee, 1974–77. Mem., W Midland Reg. Sports Council (Vice-Chm., 1970–77). Member: St Peter's Icthus Soc., Plymouth, 1986– (Chm., Housing Sect., 1987–); Council of Management, Stonham Housing Assoc., 1994–. JP Salop, 1952. Mello Matlos medal, Brazil, 1986. *Recreations:* tennis, skiing, photography. *Address:* 5 The Old School House, Garrett Street, Cawsand, near Torpoint, Cornwall PL10 1PD. *T:* Plymouth (01752) 822136.

GASKELL, Dr Colin Simister, CBE 1988; FEng; Group Managing Director, 600 Group, since 1990; *b* 19 May 1937; *s* of James and Carrie Gaskell; *m* 1961, Jill (*née* Haward); one *s* one *d*. *Educ:* Manchester Grammar Sch.; Manchester Univ. (BSc); St Edmund Hall, Oxford (DPhil). CEng, FEng 1989; FIEE, FIElectIE (Vice-Pres., 1990–). Research Fellow, Oxford Univ., 1960–61; Central Electricity Res. Labs, 1961–62; Microwave Associates, 1962–67; Chief Engineer, Microwave Div., Marconi Instruments, 1967–71; Technical Dir, Herbert Controls, 1971–74; Marconi Instruments: Technical Management, 1974–77; Technical Dir, 1977–79; Man. Dir, 1979–90. Non-executive Director: CODA Gp, 1993–; Telemetrix plc, 1994–. CIMgt; FRSA. *Recreations:* reading, walking, theatre, family pursuits. *Address:* 600 Group plc, Milton Keynes MK9 1EJ. *T:* Milton Keynes (01908) 234600.

GASKELL, (John) Philip (Wellesley), MA, PhD, LittD; Fellow of Trinity College, Cambridge, since 1967 (Librarian, 1967–86; Tutor, 1973–83); *b* 6 Jan. 1926; *s* of John Wellesley Gaskell and Olive Elizabeth, *d* of Philip B. Baker; *m* 1st, 1948, Margaret (marr. diss.), *d* of late H. S. Bennett, FBA, and Joan Bennett; two *s* one *d*; 2nd, 1984, Annette Ursula Beighton; one *d*. *Educ:* Dragon Sch., Oxford; Oundle Sch.; King's Coll., Cambridge. MA, PhD 1956, LittD, 1980. Served War, 1943–47, Lance-Bdr RA: BLA, 1944–45; Radio SEAC, 1946–47. Fellow of King's Coll., Cambridge, 1953–60, Dean, 1954–56, Tutor, 1956–58; Head of English Dept, and Librarian, Oundle Sch., 1960–62; Keeper of Special Collections, Glasgow Univ. Library, 1962–66; Warden of Maclay Hall, 1962–64, of Wolfson Hall, 1964–66, Glasgow Univ. Sandars Reader in Bibliography, Cambridge Univ., 1978–79; Part-time Prof. of Literature, CIT, 1983–88. Editor, The Book Collector, 1952–54. *Publications:* The First Editions of William Mason, 1951; John Baskerville, a bibliography, 1959, rev. edn 1973; Caught!, 1960; A Bibliography of the Foulis Press, 1964, rev. edn 1986; Morvern Transformed, 1968, rev. edn 1980; (with R. Robson) The Library of Trinity College, Cambridge, 1971; A New Introduction to Bibliography, 1972, rev. edns 1974, 1979, 1985; From Writer to Reader, 1978; Trinity College Library, the first 150 years, 1980; (with Clive Hart) Ulysses: a review of three texts, 1989; ed and trans (with P. Bradford) The Orthotypographia of Hieronymus Hornschuch, 1972; contrib. The Library, Jl Printing Historical Soc., etc. *Address:* Primrose Cottage, Mawgan, Helston, Cornwall TR12 6AB. *T:* Mawgan (01326) 221314.

GASKELL, Sir Richard (Kennedy Harvey), Kt 1989; Senior Partner, Lawrence Tucketts, solicitors, since 1989 (Partner, 1963–89); President of the Law Society, 1988–89; *b* 17 Sept. 1936; *o s* of late Dr Kenneth Harvey Gaskell, MRCS, LRCP, DMRD and of Jean Winsome Gaskell; *m* 1965, Judith Poland; one *s* one *d*. *Educ:* Marlborough Coll. Admitted solicitor, 1960. Chm., Nat. Cttee, Young Solicitors' Gp, 1964–65; Law Society: Mem. Council, 1969–92; Dep. Vice-Pres., 1986–87; Vice Pres., 1987–88; President: Bristol Law Soc., 1978–79; Assoc. of South Western Law Socs, 1980–81. Member: Crown Court Rules Cttee, 1977–83; Security Service Tribunal, 1989–; Intelligence Services Tribunal, 1994–; Criminal Justice Consultative Council, 1991–94; Criminal Injuries Compensation Bd, 1992–. Director: Law Society Trustees Ltd, 1974–92; Bristol Waterworks Co., 1989–91; Bristol Water Hldgs plc, 1991–. Dir, Wildfowl Trust (Hldgs) Ltd, 1980–; Mem. Council, Wildfowl and Wetlands (formerly Wildfowl) Trust, 1980–92 (Chm., 1983–87; Vice-Pres., 1992–); Chm., SS Great Britain Project Ltd, 1992– (Chm. Exec. Cttee and Council, SS Great Britain). Trustee: Frenchay and Southmead Med. Trust, 1968–; Laura Ashley Foundn, 1990–; CLIC (UK), 1991–. Mem. Court, 1973–, Convocation, 1989–, Bristol Univ. Hon. LLD Bristol, 1989; Hon. LLM Bristol Polytechnic, 1989. *Address:* Grove Farm, Yatton Keynell, Chippenham, Wilts SN14 7BS. *T:* Castle Combe (01249) 782289; (office) Bush House, 72 Prince Street, Bristol BS99 7JZ. *T:* Bristol (0117) 929 5252. *Club:* Farmers'.

GASKILL, William; freelance stage director; *b* 24 June 1930; *s* of Joseph Linnaeus Gaskill and Maggie Simpson. *Educ:* Salt High Sch., Shipley; Hertford Coll., Oxford. Asst Artistic Dir, English Stage Co., 1957–59; freelance Dir with Royal Shakespeare Co., 1961–62; Assoc. Dir, National Theatre, 1963–65, and 1979; Artistic Director, English Stage Company, 1965–72, Mem. Council, 1978–87; Dir, Joint Stock Theatre Gp, 1973–83. *Publication:* A Sense of Direction: life at the Royal Court (autobiog.), 1988. *Address:* 124A Leighton Road, NW5 2RG.

GASKIN, Catherine; author; *b* Co. Louth, Eire, 2 April 1929; *m* 1955, Sol Cornberg. *Educ:* Holy Cross Coll., Sydney, Australia; Conservatorium of Music, Sydney. Brought up in Australia; lived in London, 1948–55, New York, 1955–65, Virgin Islands, 1965–67, Ireland, 1967–81. *Publications:* This Other Eden, 1946; With Every Year, 1947; Dust In Sunlight, 1950; All Else Is Folly, 1951; Daughter of the House, 1952; Sara Dane, 1955; Blake's Reach, 1958; Corporation Wife, 1960; I Know My Love, 1962; The Tilsit Inheritance, 1963; The File on Devlin, 1965; Edge of Glass, 1967; Fiona, 1970; A Falcon for a Queen, 1972; The Property of a Gentleman, 1974; The Lynmara Legacy, 1975; The Summer of the Spanish Woman, 1977; Family Affairs, 1980; Promises, 1982; The Ambassador's Women, 1985; The Charmed Circle, 1988. *Recreations:* music, reading. *Address:* White Rigg, East Ballaterson, Maughold, Isle of Man IM7 1AR.

GASKIN, Prof. Maxwell, DFC 1944 (and Bar 1945); Jaffrey Professor of Political Economy, Aberdeen University, 1965–85, now Professor Emeritus; *b* 18 Nov. 1921; *s* of late Albert and Beatrice Gaskin; *m* 1952, Brenda Patricia, *yr d* of late Rev. William D. Stewart; one *s* three *d*. *Educ:* Quarry Bank Sch., Liverpool; Liverpool Univ. (MA). Lever Bros Ltd, 1939–41. Served War, RAF Bomber Comd, 1941–46. Economist, Raw Cotton Commn, 1949–50; Asst Lectr, Liverpool Univ., 1950–51; Lectr and Sen. Lectr, Glasgow Univ., 1951–65; Visiting Sen. Lectr, Nairobi Univ., 1964–65. Consultant to Sec. of State for Scotland, 1965–87. Member, Committee of Inquiry: into Bank Interest Rates (N Ire.), 1965–66; into Trawler Safety, 1967–68; Member and Chairman: Wages Councils, 1967–93; Bd of Management for Foresterhill and Associated Hosps, 1971–74; Independent Member: Scottish Agricl Wages Bd, 1972–90; EDC for Civil Engineering, 1978–84; Chm., Industry Strategy Cttee for Scotland (Building and Civil Engrg EDCs), 1974–76. Director: Offshore Med. Support Ltd, 1978–85; Aberdeen Univ. Research & Industrial Services, 1981–85. President: Section F, British Assoc., 1978–79; Scottish Economic Soc., 1981–84. *Publications:* The Scottish Banks, 1965; (co-author and ed) North East Scotland: a survey of its development potential, 1969; (jtly) The Economic Impact of North Sea oil on Scotland, 1978; (ed) The Political Economy of Tolerable Survival, 1981; articles in economic and banking jls; reports on the international coal trade. *Recreations:* music and country life. *Address:* Westfield, Ancrum, Roxburghshire TD8 6XA. *T:* Ancrum (01835) 830237.

GASS, James Ronald, CMG 1989; Consultant, European Economic Commission, since 1989; *b* 25 March 1924; *s* of Harold Amos Gass and Cherry (*née* Taylor); *m* 1950, Colette Alice Jeanne Lejeune; two *s* one *d*. *Educ:* Birkenhead Park High Sch.; Liverpool Univ. (BA Hons); Nuffield and Balliol Colls, Oxford. Flight Lieut Pilot, RAF, service in US, India and Burma, 1942–46. PSO, DSIR Intelligence Div., 1951–57; Special Asst to Chm., Task Force on Western Scientific Co-operation, NATO, Paris, 1957; OEEC, subsequently OECD, Paris: Head of Div., Scientific and Tech. Personnel, 1958–61; Dep. Dir for Scientific Affairs, 1961–68; Director: Centre for Educnl Res. and Innovation, 1968–89; Social Affairs, Manpower and Educn, 1974–89; retired 1989. *Recreations:* restoration of antiques, gymnastics, philosophy. *Address:* 2 avenue du Vert Bois, Ville d'Avray, 92410 Paris, France. *T:* 47095481.

GASSMAN, Lewis, JP; a Recorder of the Crown Court, 1972–83; *b* 28 Oct. 1910; 2nd *s* of late Isaac Gassman and Dora Gassman; *m* 1940, Betty Henrietta, *o c* of late H. Jerrold and Mrs A. F. Annenberg; one *d*. Admitted Solicitor, 1933. Borough of Barnes: Councillor and Chm. of Cttees, 1933–41. Contested (Lab): Richmond, Surrey, 1935; Hastings, 1945. War of 1939–45: Army service, Capt. RAOC. JP Surrey, 1948, also SW London; Chm., Mortlake Magistrates, 1953–56 and 1961–71. Consultant in law firm of Kershaw, Gassman & Matthews. A Dep. Chm. of Surrey Quarter Sessions, 1968–71; Chm. of Magistrates, Richmond-upon-Thames, 1971–74. *Recreations:* music, painting, walking. *Address:* 21 Castelnau, Barnes, SW13 9RP. *T:* 0181–748 7172. *Club:* Reform.

GASSON, (Gordon) Barry, OBE 1985; ARSA; Principal, Barry Gasson, Architects; Member, Royal Fine Art Commission for Scotland; *b* 27 Aug. 1935; *s* of Gladys Godfrey (previously Gasson) and late Stanley Gasson; *m* Rosemary Mulligan; one *s* two *d*. *Educ:* Solihull Sch.; Birmingham Sch. of Architecture (Dip. Arch. 1958); RIBA (Owen Jones Student); Columbia Univ., NY (MS 1961); Q. W. Boese English Speaking Fellowship; MA Cantab 1963. ARIAS, RIBA. Lectr, Univ. of Cambridge, 1963–73; visiting critic: University Coll., Dublin, 1969–72; California State Poly., 1969; Mackintosh Sch. of Arch., 1978–; Edinburgh Coll. of Art, 1986–; Vis. Prof., Univ. of Manchester, 1987–. Assessor, Civic Trust Awards, RIBA student medals, nat. competitions; Chm., RIBA regional awards. Farmer (biodynamic). FRSA. Designed galleries for Burrell Collection, Glasgow (won in open comp., 1972); awards: Stone Fedn, 1983; Arch. Design; RA Premier Arch., 1984; Museum of the Year; British Tourist Trophy; Sotheby Fine Art; Services in Building; Civic Trust; Eternit Internat., 1985; RIBA 1986; RSA Gold Medal,

1983; World Biennale of Arch. Gold Medal, 1987. *Publication:* contrib. to The Burrell Collection, 1983. *Address:* Wardlaw Farm, Auchentiber, Ayrshire KA13 7RP. *Clubs:* Architecture, Arts.

GASSON, John Gustav Haycraft, CB 1990; Head of Policy and Legal Services Group, Lord Chancellor's Department, 1987–91; *b* 2 Aug. 1931; *s* of late Dr and Mrs S. G. H. Gasson; *m* 1964, Lesley, *d* of L. L. Thomas, Nyamandhlovu, Zimbabwe; two *s* one *d*. *Educ:* Diocesan Coll., Rondebosch, Cape Town; Cape Town Univ. (BA); Pembroke Coll., Oxford (Rhodes Schol. Rhodesia 1953; MA, BCL). Called to the Bar, Gray's Inn, 1957; Advocate of High Court of S Rhodesia, 1959; Lord Chancellor's Dept, 1964; Sec., Law Commn, 1982–87. *Recreations:* cycling, gardening. *Address:* 11 Manor Road, Stourpaine, Blandford, Dorset DT11 8TQ. *Club:* Bulawayo (Zimbabwe).

GATEHOUSE, Graham Gould; Director of Social Services, Surrey County Council, 1981–95; *b* 17 July 1935; *s* of G. and G. M. Gatehouse; *m* 1960, Gillian M. Newell; two *s* one *d*; one *d*. *Educ:* Crewkerne Sch., Somerset; Exeter Univ., Devon (DSA); London School of Economics (Dip. Mental Health). Served Royal Artillery, 1954–56. Somerset County Council, 1957–67; Worcestershire CC, 1967–70; Norfolk CC, 1970–73; West Sussex CC, 1973–81. Dir, Hillcrest Homes Ltd, 1994–. Mem. Council, RSAS, 1995– (Mem., Med. Cttee, 1988–). FRSA 1987. *Recreations:* Rugby football, cricket, theatre. *Address:* 8 Orchard Lane, East Molesey, Surrey KT8 0BN.

GATEHOUSE, Sir Robert Alexander, Kt 1985; a Judge of the High Court, Queen's Bench Division, 1985–96; *b* 30 Jan. 1924; *s* of late Major-Gen. A. H. Gatehouse, DSO, MC; *m* 1st, 1951, Henrietta Swann; 2nd, 1966, Pamela Fawcett. *Educ:* Wellington Coll.; Trinity Hall, Cambridge. Served War of 1939–45: commissioned into Royal Dragoons; NW Europe. Called to the Bar, Lincoln's Inn, 1950; Bencher, 1977; QC 1969. Governor, Wellington Coll., 1970–94. *Recreations:* music, wood sculpture. *Address:* Cross Farm, Frimley Green, Surrey GU16 6LS; Flat 9, Elm Quay Court, SW8 5DE.

GATENBY, Michael Richard Brock, FCA; Vice Chairman, Charterhouse Bank Ltd, 1989–95; *b* 5 Oct. 1944; *s* of Arthur Duncan Gatenby and Dora Ethel (*née* Brock); *m* 1990, Lesley Ann Harding; two step *s*. *Educ:* Haileybury; Trinity Hall, Cambridge (BA 1966). ACA 1970. With Peat Marwick Mitchell, 1966–71; Hill Samuel & Co. Ltd, 1971–85 (Dir, 1975–85); Chaterhouse Bank Ltd, 1985–95: Man. Dir, 1986–89; Director: Staveley Industries plc, 1980–; Bridport-Gundry plc, 1980–. *Recreations:* golf, ski-ing. *Address:* 11 Norland Square, W11 4PX. *T:* 0171–221 9420.

GATES, Robert M.; Director of Central Intelligence, USA, 1991–93; *b* Kansas; *m* Becky; two *c*. *Educ:* Coll. of William and Mary (BA 1965); Indiana Univ. (MA History, 1966); Georgetown Univ. (PhD Russian and Soviet History, 1974). Joined CIA, 1966; intelligence analyst; Asst. Nat. Intell. Officer for Strategic Programs; staff, Nat. Security Council, 1974–79; rejoined CIA, 1979: admin. posts; Nat. Intell. Officer for Soviet Union; Dep. Dir for Intell., 1982–86; Chm., Nat. Intell. Council, 1983–86; Dep. Dir of Central Intell., 1986–89 (Actg Dir, 1986–87); Asst to the President, and Dep. for Nat. Security Affairs, Nat. Security Council, 1986–91. Presidential Citizens Medal; Nat. Intell. Distinguished Service Medal; Distinguished Intell. Medal, CIA; Intell. Medal of Merit; Arthur S. Flemming Award. *Address:* c/o Central Intelligence Agency, Washington, DC 20505, USA.

GATES, Emeritus Prof. Ronald Cecil, AO 1978; FASSA; Vice-Chancellor, University of New England, 1977–85; *b* 8 Jan. 1923; *s* of Earle Nelson Gates and Elsie Edith (*née* Tucker); *m* 1953, Barbara Mann; one *s* two *d* (and one *s* decd). *Educ:* East Launceston State Sch., Tas; Launceston C of E Grammar Sch., Tas; Univ. of Tas (BCom Econs and Commercial Law); Oxford Univ. (MA PPE). FASSA 1968. Served War, 1942–45: Private, AIF. Clerk, Aust. Taxation Office, Hobart, 1941–42; Rhodes Scholar (Tas), Oxford, 1946–48; Historian, Aust. Taxation Office, Canberra, 1949–52; Univ. of Sydney: Sen. Lectr in Econs, 1952–64; Associate Prof., 1964–65; Rockefeller Fellow in Social Sciences, 1955, Carnegie Travel Grant, 1960; Prof. of Econs, Univ. of Qld, 1966–77 (Pres., Professorial Bd, 1975–77). Pres., Econ. Soc. of Australia and NZ, 1969–72. Chairman: statutory Consumer Affairs Council of Qld, 1971–73; Aust. Inst. of Urban Studies, 1975–77. Comr, Commonwealth Commn of Inquiry into Poverty, 1973–77. Chairman: Aust. Nat. Commn for Unesco, 1981–83 (Vice-Chm., 1979); Adv. Council for Intergovt Relations, 1979–85; Internat. Relations Cttee, Cttee of Australian Vice-Chancellors, 1981–84; Local Govt Trng Council (formerly Nat. Local Govt Industry Trng Cttee), 1983–92; Armidale-Dumaresq Jt Planning Cttee, 1992–. Hon. FRAPI 1976; Hon. Fellow, Aust. Inst. of Urban Studies, 1979. Hon. DEcon Qld, 1978; Hon. DLitt New England, 1987. *Publications:* (with H. R. Edwards and N. T. Drane) Survey of Consumer Finances, Sydney 1963–65: Vol. 2, 1965; Vols 1, 3 and 4, 1966; Vols 5, 6 and 7, 1967; (jtly) The Price of Land, 1971; (jtly) New Cities for Australia, 1972; (jtly) Land for the Cities, 1973; (with P. A. Cassidy) Simulation, Uncertainty and Public Investment Analysis, 1977; *in Esperanto:* detective novels: La Septaga Murdenigmo, 1991; Kolera Afero, 1993; Morto de Sciencisto, 1994; short stories: Sep Krimnoveloj, 1993; Refoje Krimnoveloj Sep, 1994; chapters in books and articles in learned jls. *Recreations:* music, beef cattle, Esperanto. *Address:* Wangarang, Kelly's Plains Road, Armidale, NSW 2350, Australia.

GATES, William Henry, III; Chairman and Chief Executive Officer, Microsoft Corp.; *b* 28 Oct. 1955; *s* of William Henry and Mary Maxwell Gates; *m* 1994, Melinda French. *Educ:* High Sch., Seattle; Harvard Univ. Co-founder, Microsoft Corp., 1976. *Address:* Microsoft, 1 Microsoft Way, Redmond, WA 98052-6399, USA.

GATFORD, Ven. Ian; Archdeacon of Derby, since 1993; *b* 15 June 1940; *s* of Frederick Ernest and Chrissie Lilian Gatford; *m* 1965, Anne Maire (*née* Whitehead); one *s* three *d*. *Educ:* King's Coll. London (AKC 1965); St Boniface Coll., Warminster. Management Trainee, Taylor Woodrow Gp, 1959–62; Accounts and Admin, Farr's (Construction) Ltd, 1965–66; theolog. trng, 1966–67; ordained deacon 1967, priest 1968; Curate, St Mary, Clifton, Nottingham, 1967–71; Team Vicar, Holy Trinity, Clifton, 1971–75; Vicar, St Martin, Sherwood, 1975–84; Canon Residentiary, Derby Cathedral, 1984–; Sub-Provost, Derby Cathedral, 1990–93. Presenter of weekly help-line programmes, BBC Radio Nottingham, 1972–84; presenter of religious affairs programmes, BBC Radio Derby, 1984–93. *Recreations:* playing the piano, country walking, jazz, classical music, theatre, biographies, reading and speaking German and French. *Address:* Derby Church House, Full Street, Derby DE1 3DR. *T:* Derby (01332) 382233.

GATHERCOLE, Ven. John Robert; Archdeacon of Dudley, since 1987; *b* 23 April 1937; *s* of Robert Gathercole and Winifred Mary Gathercole (*née* Price); *m* 1963, Claire (*née* London); one *s* one *d*. *Educ:* Judd School, Tonbridge; Fitzwilliam Coll., Cambridge (BA 1959, MA 1963); Ridley Hall, Cambridge. Deacon 1962, priest 1963; Curate: St Nicholas, Durham, 1962–66; St Bartholomew, Croxdale, 1966–70; Social and Industrial Adviser to Bishop of Durham, 1967–70; Industrial Chaplain, Redditch, dio. Worcester, 1970–87; RD of Bromsgrove, 1978–85; Team Leader, and Sen. Chaplain, Worcs Industrial Mission, 1985–91. *Recreations:* vintage sports cars, music. *Address:* 15 Worcester Road, Droitwich, Worcs WR9 8AA. *T:* Droitwich (01905) 773301.

GATHORNE-HARDY, family name of **Earl of Cranbrook.**

GATT, Colin, CMG 1993; Director, Managed Projects, Commonwealth Development Corporation, 1991–94; *b* 16 Aug. 1934; *s* of late William John Sim Gatt and Margaret Whyte-Hepburn; *m* 1957, Sheena Carstairs; two *s* one *d*. *Educ:* state schs in Scotland. Engineer, 1955–; asst manager, then manager and consultant for agricl ops in Malaysia, Nigeria, Ghana and Cameroon; Commonwealth Development Corporation, 1971–94: Agricl Exec., 1971–73; Project Manager/Asst Gen. Manager, Savannah Sugar Co., Nigeria, 1973–77; Gen. Manager, Solomon Is Plantations Ltd, 1978–81; Sen. Ops Exec., 1982–83; Dep. Gen. Manager, Cameroon Develt Corp., 1983–85; Manager, Vanuatu, 1986–87; Man. Dir, Sable and Kawalazi Estates, Malaŵi, 1987–88; Dir, Technical Services, 1989–90. Independence Medal (Solomon Is), 1978. *Recreations:* reading, golf, wine, basic survival cookery. *Address:* 30 Maple Road, Thame, Oxon OX9 2BH. *Clubs:* Royal Over-Seas League; Langley Park Golf (Beckenham).

GATTING, Michael William, OBE 1987; cricketer; Captain, Middlesex County Cricket Club, since 1983; *b* 6 June 1957; *s* of William Alfred Gatting and Vera Mavis Gatting; *m* 1980, Elaine Mabbott; two *s*. *Educ:* John Kelly Boys' High Sch. County début, Middlesex, 1975; County Cap, 1977; Test début, 1977; England Captain, 1986–88; overseas tours with England: NZ and Pakistan, 1977–78, 1983–84; W Indies, 1980–81, 1985–86; India and Sri Lanka, 1981–82, 1992–93; India, 1984–85; Australia, 1986–87; Australia and NZ, 1987–88; Australia, 1994–95; also, World Cup, 1987–88, *v* India, Pakistan, Australia and NZ. Highest scores: Middlesex 258, 1984; England 207, 1984–85. *Publications:* Limited Overs, 1986; Triumph in Australia, 1987; Leading from the Front, 1988. *Recreations:* golf, swimming, reading, music. *Address:* Middlesex County Cricket Club, Lord's Cricket Ground, St John's Wood Road, NW8 8QN. *Club:* Wig and Pen.

GATTY, Trevor Thomas, OBE 1974; HM Diplomatic Service, retired; international business consultant, arbitrator and mediator; President, MGT International, since 1989; *b* 8 June 1930; *s* of Thomas Alfred Gatty and Lillian Gatty (*née* Wood); *m* 1st, 1956, Jemima Bowman (marr. diss. 1983); two *s* one *d*; 2nd, 1989, Myrna Saturn; one step *s* one step *d*. *Educ:* King Edward's Sch., Birmingham. Served Army, 1948–50, 2/Lieut Royal Warwickshire Regt, later Lieut Royal Fusiliers (TA), 1950–53. Foreign Office, 1950; Vice-Consul, Leopoldville, 1954; FO, 1958–61; Second (later First) Sec., Bangkok, 1961–64; Consul, San Francisco, 1965–66; Commercial Consul, San Francisco, 1967–68; FCO, 1968–73; Commercial Consul, Zürich, 1973–75; FCO, 1975–76; Counsellor (Diplomatic Service Inspector), 1977–80; Head, Migration and Visa Dept, FCO, 1980–81; Consul-General, Atlanta, 1981–85. Protocol Advr, Atlanta Organising Cttee for 1996 Olympic Games, 1993. Hon. British Consul for N Carolina, 1994–. *Recreations:* reading, physical fitness, English Springer spaniels. *Address:* 229 North Poplar Street (#15), Charlotte, NC 28202, USA. *T:* (704) 3381372.

GATWARD, (Anthony) James; Chief Executive, Complete Media Management Ltd, since 1993; *b* 4 March 1938; *s* of George James Gatward and Lillian Georgina (*née* Strutton); *m* 1969, Isobel Anne Stuart Black, actress; three *d*. *Educ:* George Gascoigne Sch., Walthamstow; South West Essex Technical Coll. and Sch. of Art (drama course). Entered TV industry, 1957; freelance drama producer/director: Canada and USA, 1959–65; BBC and most ITV cos, 1966–70; partner in prodn co., acting as Exec. Prod. and often Dir of many internat. co-prodns in UK, Ceylon, Australia and Germany, 1970–78; instigated and led preparation of application for S and SE England television franchise, 1979–80 (awarded Dec. 1980); Man. Dir, 1979–84, Chief Exec., 1984–91, Television South, subseq. TVS Entertainment PLC; Dep. Chm. and Chief Exec., 1984–90, Chm., 1990–91, TVS Television; Director: Southstar, Scottish and Global TV, 1971–78; Indep. TV Publications Ltd, 1982–88; Oracle Teletext Ltd, 1982–88; Solent Cablevision Ltd, 1983–89; Channel 4 TV Co., 1984–89; Indep. TV News Ltd, 1986–91; Super Channel Ltd, 1986–88; ITV Super Channel Ltd, 1986–89; Chm., TVS Production, 1984–89; Chm. and Chief Exec., TVS N American Hldgs, 1988–91; Pres., Telso Communications Inc., 1987–90; Chairman: Telso Communications Ltd, 1987–91; Telso Overseas Ltd, 1987–91; Midem Orgn SA, 1987–89; MTM Entertainment Inc., 1988–91 (Chief Exec. Officer, 1989–91). Member: Council, Operation Raleigh; Court of the Mary Rose. Pres., SE Agricl Soc., 1992; Governor, S of England Agricl Soc. *Recreations:* farming, sailing, music. *Address:* (office) 22 Suffolk Street, SW1Y 4HS. *Clubs:* Royal Thames Yacht; Porquerolles Yacht (Hyères).

GAU, John Glen Mackay, CBE 1989; independent producer; Joint Chief Executive, John Gau Productions, since 1991 (Managing Director, 1981–88); *b* 25 March 1940; *s* of late Cullis William Gau and Nan Munro; *m* 1966, Susan Tebbs; two *s*. *Educ:* Haileybury and ISC; Trinity Hall, Cambridge; Univ. of Wisconsin. BBC TV: Assistant Film Editor, 1963; Current Affairs Producer, 1965–74; Editor, Nationwide, 1975; Head of Current Affairs Programmes, 1978–81; Dep. Chief Exec. and Dir of Programmes, British Satellite Broadcasting, 1988–90. Dir, Channel 4, 1984–88. Chm., Indep. Programme Producers' Assoc., 1983–86. Chm. Council, RTS, 1986–88. FRTS 1986. *Publication:* (jtly) Soldiers, 1985. *Address:* 4 Queensmere Road, SW19 5NY. *T:* 0181–946 4686.

GAUDRY, Roger, CC (Canada) 1968; DSc; FRSC; President, Jules & Paul-Emile Léger Foundation, since 1983; *b* 15 Dec. 1913; *m* 1941, Madeleine Vallée; two *s* three *d*. *Educ:* Laval Univ. (BA 1933; BSc 1937; DSc 1940); Rhodes Scholar, Oxford Univ., 1937–39. Organic Chemistry, Laval Univ.: Lectr, 1940; Prof., 1945; Full Prof., 1950. Ayerst Laboratories: Asst Dir of Research, 1954; Dir of Research, 1957; Vice-Pres. and Dir of Research, 1963–65; Rector, Univ. of Montreal, 1965–75; Dir, 1975–, Chm., 1984–88, Bio-Research Labs. Chm., Nordic Labs, 1975–91. Director: Corby Distilleries, 1975–89; Bank of Montreal, 1975–84; Alcan Aluminium, 1976–86; Hoechst Canada, 1977–87; SKW Canada, 1978–88; St Lawrence Starch, 1983–89. Chm., Science Council of Canada, 1972–75; President: Internat. Assoc. of Univs, 1975–80; Sci., Technology and Industry Centre of Montreal, 1988–90. Chm. Bd, UN Univ., 1974–76; Dir, Inst. de recherches cliniques, Montreal, 1975–; Chm., Network for Neural Regeneration and Functional Recovery, 1990–94. Hon. FRCP&S (Canada), 1971. Hon. doctorates: (Laws) Univ. of Toronto, 1966; (Science) RMC of Kingston, 1966; (Science) Univ. of BC, 1967; (Laws) McGill Univ., 1967; Univ. of Clermont-Ferrand, France, 1967; (Laws) St Thomas Univ., 1968; (Laws) Brock Univ., 1969; (Civil Laws) Bishop's Univ., 1969; (Science) Univ. of Saskatchewan, 1970; (Science) Univ. of Western Ontario, 1976; (Laws) Concordia Univ., 1980; Parizeau Medal from Assoc. Canadienne Française pour l'Avancement des Sciences, 1958. KM 1976; Silver Jubilee Medal, 1977; Compagnon de Lavoisier, 1985; Grand Officier de l'Ordre du Québec, 1992; Medal of 125th Anniversary of Confederation, 1992. *Publications:* author and co-author of numerous scientific papers in organic and biological chemistry. *Address:* 445 Beverley Avenue, Town of Mount Royal, Montreal, H3P 1L4, Canada.

GAULD, William Wallace; Under-Secretary, Department of Agriculture and Fisheries for Scotland, 1972–79; *b* 12 Oct. 1919; *e s* of late Rev. W. W. Gauld, DD, of Aberdeen, and Charlotte Jane Gauld (*née* Reid); *m* 1943, Jean Inglis Gray; three *d*. *Educ:* Fettes; Aberdeen Univ. MA (1st Cl. Hons Classics). Served Pioneer Corps, 1940–46 (Major 1945). Entered Dept of Agriculture for Scotland, 1947; Private Sec. to Secretary of State for Scotland, 1955–57; Asst Sec., 1958; Scottish Development Dept, 1968–72; Mem. Agricultural

Research Council, 1972–79. Pres., Botanical Soc., Edinburgh, 1978–80. *Recreation:* natural history. *Address:* 1 Banks Crescent, Crieff, Perthshire PH7 3SR.

GAULIN, Jean; Group Chief Executive Officer, Ultramar Group, since 1989; *b* 9 July 1942; *m* 1981, Andrée LeBoeuf; two *s* one *d. Educ:* Univ. of Montreal (degrees in appl. scis and chem. eng.). Vice-Pres., Ultramar Canada, 1977–79; President: Nouveler Inc., 1980–82; Gaz Metropolitan Inc., 1982–85 (and Chief Exec.); Ultramar Canada, 1985–89. *Address:* Ultramar, 141 Moorgate, EC2M 6TX.

GAULT, Charles Alexander, CBE 1959 (OBE 1947); retired from HM Foreign Service, 1959; *b* 15 June 1908; *o s* of Robert Gault, Belfast, and Sophia Ranken Clark; *m* 1947, Madge, *d* of late William Walter Adams, Blundellsands; no *c. Educ:* Harrow; Magdalene Coll., Cambridge. Entered Levant Consular Service, 1931; served in Egypt, Persia, Saudi Arabia, at Foreign Office, India (on secondment to Commonwealth Relations Office), Libya, Israel, Bahrain (HM Political Agent, 1954–59). *Address:* 19 Queens Court, Queens Road, Cheltenham, Glos GL50 2LU.

GAULT, David Hamilton; Executive Chairman, Gallic Management Co. Ltd, 1974–93; *b* 9 April 1928; *s* of Leslie Hamilton Gault and Iris Hilda Gordon Young; *m* 1950, Felicity Jane Gribble; three *s* two *d. Educ:* Fettes Coll., Edinburgh. Nat. Service, commnd in RA, 1946–48; Clerk, C. H. Rugg & Co. Ltd, Shipbrokers, 1948–52; H. Clarkson & Co. Ltd, Shipbrokers: Man. 1952–56; Dir 1956–62; Jt Man. Dir 1962–72; Gp Man. Dir, Shipping Industrial Holdings Ltd, 1972–74; Chm., Jebsen (UK) Ltd, 1962–81; Chm., Seabridge Shipping Ltd, 1965–73. *Recreations:* gardening, walking. *Address:* Telegraph House, North Marden, Chichester, West Sussex PO18 9JX. *T:* Harting (01730) 825206. *Clubs:* Boodle's, City.

GAULT, Rt. Hon. Thomas Munro; PC 1992; **Rt. Hon. Mr Justice Gault;** Judge of Court of Appeal, New Zealand, since 1991; *b* 31 Oct. 1938; *s* of Thomas Gordon Gault and Evelyn Jane Gault (*née* Paulmeir); *m* 1963, Barbara Pauline Stewart; one *s. Educ:* Wellington Coll.; Victoria University Coll. (LLB); Victoria Univ. of Wellington (LLM). Solicitor of Supreme Court of NZ, 1961; A. J. Park & Son, 1961–81; practised at NZ Bar, 1981–87; QC 1984; Judge of High Court of NZ, 1987–91. Mem. of Honour, Internat. Assoc. for Protection of Industrial Property, 1990. *Recreation:* golf. *Address:* PO Box 1606, Wellington, New Zealand; 149A St Helier's Bay Road, Auckland, New Zealand. *T:* (4) 472 7307. *Club:* Wellington (New Zealand).

GAULTER, Derek Vivian, CBE 1978; Chairman, Construction Industry Training Board, 1985–90; *b* 10 Dec. 1924; *s* of late Jack Rudolf Gaulter, MC and Muriel Gaulter (*née* Westworth); *m* 1949, Edith Irene Shackleton; one *s* three *d. Educ:* Denstone College; Peterhouse, Cambridge (MA). RNVR, Sub Lieut MTBs/Minesweepers, 1943–46. Lord Justice Holker Sen. Scholarship, Gray's Inn; called to the Bar, Gray's Inn, 1949; Common Law Bar, Manchester, 1950–55. Federation of Civil Engineering Contractors: Legal Sec., General Sec., Dep. Dir Gen., 1955–86; Dir Gen., 1987. Trustee, Woodland Trust, 1995–. MInstD. *Recreations:* gardening, travel, photography. *Address:* Philips Hill, Old Shire Lane, Chorleywood, Herts WD3 5PW. *T:* Chorleywood (019278) 3004.

GAUNT, Jonathan Robert; QC 1991; *b* 3 Nov. 1947; *s* of Dr Brian Gaunt and Dr Mary Gaunt (*née* Hudson); *m* 1975, Lynn Dennis; one *d. Educ:* St Peter's Coll.; Radley; University Coll., Oxford (BA). Called to the Bar, Lincoln's Inn, 1972. *Publication:* (ed) Halsbury's Laws of England, Vol. 27, 4th edn 1981, rev. 1994. *Recreations:* golf, sailing. *Address:* Falcon Chambers, Falcon Court, EC4Y 1AA. *T:* 0171–353 2484. *Club:* North Middlesex Golf.

GAUSDEN, Ronald, CB 1982; nuclear consultant; *b* 15 June 1921; *s* of Jesse Charles William Gausden and Annie Gausden (*née* Durrant); *m* 1st, 1943, Florence May (*née* Ayres) (*d* 1987); two *s* two *d*; 2nd, 1988, Joan Betty (*née* Simcock). *Educ:* Varndean Grammar Sch., Brighton; Brighton Techn. Coll. and Borough Polytechnic. CEng, FIEE. RN Sci. Service, 1943–47; AERE, Harwell, 1947–50; UKAEA Windscale Works, Cumbria: Instrument Engr, 1950–53; Asst Gp Man., 1953–55; Gp Man., 1955–60; Nuclear Installations Inspectorate: Principal Inspector, 1960–63; Asst Chief Inspector, 1963–73; Dep. Chief Inspector, 1973–75; Chief Inspector, 1976–81; Dir, Hazardous Installations Gp, HSE, 1978–81. *Publications:* contrib. Brit. Nuclear Energy Soc. and Inst. Nuclear Engrs. *Recreations:* golf, fishing. *Address:* Granary Cottage, Itchingfield, near Horsham, W Sussex RH13 7NU. *T:* Slinfold (01403) 790646.

GAUTIER-SMITH, Peter Claudius, FRCP; Physician, National Hospitals for Nervous Diseases, Queen Square and Maida Vale, 1962–89; *b* 1 March 1929; *s* of late Claudius Gautier-Smith and Madeleine (*née* Ferguson); *m* 1960, Nesta Mary Wroth; two *d. Educ:* Cheltenham Coll. (Exhibnr); King's Coll., Cambridge; St Thomas's Hosp. Med. Sch. MA, MD. Casualty Officer, House Physician, St Thomas' Hosp., 1955–56; Medical Registrar, University Coll. Hosp., 1958; Registrar, National Hosp., Queen Square, 1960–62; Consultant Neurologist, St George's Hosp., 1962–75; Dean, Inst. of Neurology, 1975–82. Mem., Bd of Governors, Nat. Hosps for Nervous Diseases, 1975–89. Hon. Neurologist, Dispensaire Français, London, 1983–89. *Publications:* Parasagittal and Falx Meningiomas, 1970; papers in learned jls on neurology. *Recreations:* literary (twenty-three novels published under a pseudonym); French language; squash (played for Cambridge v Oxford, 1951; Captain, London Univ., 1954); tennis. *Clubs:* MCC; Hawks (Cambridge); Jesters.

GAUTREY, Peter, CMG 1972; CVO 1961; DK (Brunei) 1972; HM Diplomatic Service, retired; High Commissioner in Guyana, 1975–78, concurrently Ambassador (non-resident) to Surinam, 1976–78; *b* 17 Sept. 1918; *s* of late Robert Harry Gautrey, Hindhead, Surrey, and Hilda Morris; *m* 1947, Marguerite Etta Uncles; one *s* one *d. Educ:* Abbotsholme Sch., Derbys. Joined Home Office, 1936. Served in Royal Artillery, (Capt.), Sept. 1939–March 1946. Re-joined Home Office; Commonwealth Relations Office, 1948; served in British Embassy, Dublin, 1950–53; UK High Commission, New Delhi, 1955–57 and 1960–63; British Deputy High Commissioner, Bombay, 1963–65; Corps of Diplomatic Service Inspectors, 1965–68; High Commissioner: Swaziland, 1968–71; Brunei, 1972–75. FRSA 1972. *Recreations:* walking, music, art. *Address:* 24 Fort Road, Guildford, Surrey GU1 3TE.

GAVASKAR, Sunil Manohar; Padma Bhushan; cricketer; business executive; *b* 10 July 1949; *s* of Manohar Keshav Gavaskar and Meenal Manohar Gavaskar; *m* 1974, Marshniel Mehrotra; one *s. Educ:* St Xavier's High Sch.; St Xavier's Coll.; Bombay Univ. (BA). Represented India in cricket, 1971–88; Captain, Indian Team, 1978, 1979–80, 1980–82 and 1984–85; passed previous world records: no of runs in Test Matches, 1983; no of Test centuries, 1984; first batsman to score over 10,000 Test runs, 1987. Nominated to Rajya Sabha, 1992. *Publications:* Sunny Days, 1976; Idols, 1983; Runs 'n Ruins, 1984. *Address:* 40-A Sir Bhalchandra Road, Dadar, Bombay 400014, India. *T:* (office) 4931611. *Clubs:* Cricket Club of India, Bombay Gymkhana.

GAVIN, Maj.-Gen. James Merricks Lewis, CB 1967; CBE 1963 (OBE 1953); *b* Antofagasta, Chile, 28 July 1911; *s* of Joseph Merricks Gavin; *m* 1942, Barbara Anne Elizabeth (*d* 1994), *d* of Group Capt. C. G. Murray, CBE; one *s* two *d. Educ:* Uppingham Sch.; Royal Military Academy; Trinity Coll., Cambridge. 2nd Lieut Royal Engineers, 1931. Mem. Mt Everest Expedn, 1936. Instructor, Royal Military Academy, 1938; Capt. 1939; served War of 1939–45 in Far East, Middle East, Italy, France, including special operations; Brit. Jt Services Mission, Washington, 1948–51; Commanding Officer, 1951–53; Col Staff Coll., Camberley, 1953–55; BAOR, 1956–58; Comdt (Brig.) Intelligence Centre, Maresfield, 1958–61; Maj.-Gen. 1964; Asst Chief of Staff (Intelligence), SHAPE, 1964–67. Technical Dir, BSI, 1967–76. Col Comdt, RE, 1968–73. *Recreations:* mountaineering, sailing, ski-ing. *Address:* Slathurst Farm, Milland, near Liphook, Hants GU30 7ND. *Clubs:* Alpine, Royal Cruising, Royal Ocean Racing; Royal Yacht Squadron (Cowes).

GAVRON, Robert, CBE 1990; Chairman and Proprietor, Folio Society Ltd, since 1982; Director, St Ives plc, since 1964 (Chairman, 1964–93); Proprietor, Carcanet Press Ltd, since 1983; *b* 13 Sept. 1930; *s* of Nathaniel and Leah Gavron; *m* 1955, Hannah Fyvel (*d* 1965); two *s*; *m* 1967, Nicolette Coates (marr. diss. 1987); two *d*; *m* 1989, Katharine Gardiner (*née* Macnair). *Educ:* Leighton Park Sch., Reading; St Peter's Coll., Oxford (MA; Hon. Fellow, 1992). Called to the Bar, Middle Temple, 1955. Entered printing industry, 1955; founded St Ives Gp, 1964 (public co., 1985). Director: Octopus Publishing plc, 1975–87; Electra Management Plc, 1981–91; Nat. Gall. Publications Ltd, 1995–. Chm., Open Coll. of the Arts, 1991– (Trustee, 1987–); Director: Royal Opera House, 1992–; Royal Ballet, 1992–; Member: Literature Panel, Arts Council, 1979–83; Council, Book Trust (formerly NBL), 1982–90; Poetry Soc., 1983–86 (Vice Pres., 1986–); Council, Morley Coll., 1975–85. Trustee, Nat. Gall., 1994–; IPPR, 1991– (Treas., 1994–). Hon. Fellow, RCA, 1990. *Address:* Folio Society Ltd, 44 Eagle Street, WC1R 4FS. *T:* 0171–400 4200. *Clubs:* Groucho, MCC.

GAY, Geoffrey Charles Lytton; Consultant, Knight, Frank & Rutley, 1975–85 (Senior Partner, 1969–75); World President, International Real Estate Federation (FIABCI), 1973–75; a General Commissioner for Inland Revenue, 1953–89; *b* 14 March 1914; *s* of late Charles Gay and Ida, *d* of Sir Henry A. Lytton (famous Savoyard); *m* 1947, Dorothy Ann, *d* of Major Eric Rickman; one *s* two *d. Educ:* St Paul's School. FRICS. Joined Knight, Frank & Rutley, 1929. Served War of 1939–45: Durham LI, BEF, 1940; psc; Lt-Col; Chief of Staff, Sind District, India, 1943. Mem. Westminster City Council, 1962–71. Governor: Benenden Sch., 1971–86; Clayesmore Sch. Council; Mem. Council of St John, London, 1971–84; Liveryman, Broderers' Co. Licentiate, RPS, 1983; FRSA 1983. Chevalier de l'Ordre de l'Economie Nationale, 1960. OStJ 1961; KStJ 1979. *Recreations:* photography, fishing, music, theatre. *Address:* Castle View, 122 Newland, Sherborne, Dorset DT9 3DT. *T:* Sherborne (01935) 816676. *Clubs:* Carlton, MCC, Flyfishers'.

GAY, Rear-Adm. George Wilsmore, CB 1969; MBE 1946; DSC 1943; JP; Director-General of Naval Training, 1967–69; retired; *b* 1913; *s* of late Engr Comdr G. M. Gay and late Mrs O. T. Gay (*née* Allen); *m* 1941, Nancy Agnes Clark; two *s* one *d. Educ:* Eastman's Sch., Southsea; Nautical Coll., Pangbourne. Entered RN, 1930; Cadet Trng, 1930–32; RNEC, Keyham, 1932–35; HMS Glorious, 1935–37; Engr. Off., HMS Porpoise, 1939–41, HMS Clyde, 1941–43; HMS Dolphin, 1938 and 1943–46; HM Dockyard, Portsmouth, 1946–47; HMS Euryalus, 1947–49; Sqdn Engr Off., 1st Submarine Sqdn, HMS Forth, 1949–50; Trng Comdr, HMS Raleigh, 1951–53; Admiralty Engr Overseer, Vickers Armstrong Ltd, 1953–55; HMS Dolphin, 1956–58; Senior Officer, War Course, Royal Naval Coll., Greenwich, 1958; HM Dockyard, Malta, 1959–60; CO, HMS Sultan, Gosport, 1960–63; Chief Staff Off. Material to Flag Off. Submarines, 1963–66; Admty Interview Bd, 1966. Comdr 1947; Capt. 1958; Rear-Adm. 1967. FIMechE (MIMechE 1958). JP Plymouth 1970. *Recreations:* fishing, sailing, gardening. *Address:* 29 Whiteford Road, Mannamead, Plymouth, Devon PL3 5LU. *T:* Plymouth (01752) 664486.

GAYDON, Prof. Alfred Gordon, FRS 1953; Warren Research Fellow of Royal Society, 1945–74; Professor of Molecular Spectroscopy, 1961–73, now Emeritus, and Fellow, since 1980, Imperial College of Science and Technology, London; *b* 26 Sept. 1911; *s* of Alfred Bert Gaydon and Rosetta Juliet Gordon; *m* 1940, Phyllis Maude Gaze (*d* 1981); one *s* one *d. Educ:* Kingston Grammar Sch., Kingston-on-Thames; Imperial Coll., London. BSc (Physics) Imperial Coll., 1932; worked on molecular spectra, and on measurement of high temperatures, on spectra and structure of flames, and shock waves; DSc (London) 1942; Hon. Dr (University of Dijon), 1957. Rumford Medal, Royal Society, 1960; Bernard Lewis Gold Medal, Combustion Inst., 1960. *Publications:* Identification of Molecular Spectra (with Dr R. W. B. Pearse), 1941, 1950, 1963, 1965, 1976; Spectroscopy and Combustion Theory, 1942, 1948; Dissociation Energies and Spectra of Diatomic Molecules, 1947, 1953, 1968; Flames, their Structure, Radiation and Temperature (with Dr H. G. Wolfhard), 1953, 1960, 1970, 1979; The Spectroscopy of Flames, 1957, 1974; The Shock Tube in High-temperature Chemical Physics (with Dr I. Hurle), 1963. *Recreations:* wild-life photography; formerly rowing. *Address:* Dale Cottage, Shellbridge Road, Slindon Common, Sussex BN18 0LT. *T:* Slindon (01243) 814277.

GAYRE of Gayre and Nigg, Robert, ERD; Lieutenant-Colonel (late Reserve of Officers); ethnologist and armorist; Editor: The Armorial, 1959–74; The Mankind Quarterly, 1960–78 (Hon. Editor in Chief, since 1979), etc; Director of several companies; *s* of Robert Gayre of Gayre and Nigg, and Clara Hull; *m* 1933, Nina Mary (*d* 1983), *d* of Rev. Louis Thomas Terry, MA and Margaret Nina Hill; one *s. Educ:* University of Edinburgh (MA); Exeter Coll., Oxford. BEF France, 1939; Staff Officer Airborne HQ, 1942; Educnl Adviser, Allied Mil. Govt, Italy, 1943–44; Dir of Educn, Allied Control Commn for Italy, 1944; Chief of Educn and Religious Affairs, German Planning Unit, SHAEF, 1944; Prof. of Anthropology and head of Dept of Anthropo-geography, University of Saugor, India, 1954–56; Falkland Pursuivant Extraord., 1958; Consultore pro lingua Anglica, Coll. of Heralds, Rome, 1954–; Chamberlain to the Prince of Lippe, 1958–; Grand Bailiff and Comr-Gen. of the English Tongue, Order of St Lazarus of Jerusalem, 1961–69; Grand Referendary, 1969–73; Grand Comdr and Grand Almoner, 1973–; Vicar-Gen., 1985–; Sec.-Gen., VIth Internat. Congress of Genealogy, Edinburgh, 1962. Chm., The Seventeen Forty-Five Association, 1964–80. President: Scottish Rhodesia Soc., to 1968; Aberdeenshire and Banffshire Friends of Rhodesia Assoc., 1969; St Andrew Soc. of Malta, 1968; Ethnological Soc. of Malta; Life Pres., Heraldic Soc. of Malta, 1970–; Hon. Pres., Sicilian Anthropological Soc. Sec.-Gen., Internat. Orders' Commn (Chm., 1978–); Mem. Coun. Internat. Inst. of Ethnology and Eugenics, New York. Mem. Cttee of Honour: Inst. Politicos, Madrid; Cercle Internat. Généalogique, Paris, Mem. Nat. Acad. Sci. of India; Fellow: Collegio Araldico, Rome; Nat. Soc., Naples; Peloritana Acad., Messina; Pontaniana Acad., Naples; Royal Academy, Palermo; F Ist Ital di Geneal. e Arald., Rome; FRSH; MInstBE. Hon. or corr. mem. of heraldic and other socs of many countries. Grand Cross of Merit, SMO Malta, 1963 (Kt Comdr, 1957). Holds knighthoods in international and foreign orders, hon. Doctorates from Italian Univs, and heraldic societies' medals, etc. Hon. Lt-Col, ADC to Governor, Georgia, USA, 1969–; Hon. Lt-Col, ADC, State Militia, Alabama; Hon. Lt-Col, Canadian Arctic Air Force. Hon. Citizen, Commune of Gurro, Italy. *Publications:* Teuton and Slav on the Polish Frontier, 1944; Italy in Transition, 1946; Wassail! In Mazers of Mead, 1948, new edn, USA, 1986; The Heraldry of the Knights of St John, 1956; Heraldic Standards and other Ensigns, 1959; The Nature of Arms, 1961; Heraldic Cadency, 1961, Gayre's Booke,

4 vols 1948–59; Who is Who in Clan Gayre, 1962; A Case for Monarchy, 1962; The Armorial Who is Who, 1961–62, 1963–65, 1966–69, 1970–75, 1976–78, 1979–80; Roll of Scottish Arms (Pt I Vol. I, 1964, Pt I Vol. II, 1969); Ethnological Elements of Africa, 1966; More Ethnological Elements of Africa, 1972; The Origin of the Zimbabwean Civilisation, 1972; Miscellaneous Racial Studies, 2 vols, 1972; The Knightly Twilight, 1973; Syro-Mesopotamian Ethnology, 1973; Aspects of British and Continental Heraldry, 1974; The Lost Clan, 1974; The Mackays of the Rhinns of Islay, 1979; Minard Castle, 1980; Minard Castle Collection of Pipe Music, 1986; An Autobiography, 1987; The Power Beyond, 1989; contribs Mankind Quarterly, contrib. Encyc. Brit., etc. *Recreation:* reading. *Address:* Minard Castle, Minard, Argyll PA32 8YB. *Club:* Royal Highland Yacht.

GAZDAR, Prof. Gerald James Michael, FBA 1988; Professor of Computational Linguistics, University of Sussex, since 1985; *b* 24 Feb. 1950; *s* of John and Kathleen Gazdar. *Educ:* Heath Mount; Bradfield Coll.; Univ. of East Anglia (BA Phil with Econ); Reading Univ. (MA Linguistics, PhD). Sussex University: Lectr 1975–80; Reader 1980–85; Dean, Sch. of Cognitive and Computing Scis, 1988–93. Fellow, Center for Advanced Study in the Behavioral Sciences, Stanford Univ., California, 1984–85. *Publications:* (with Klein, Pullum) A Bibliography of Contemporary Linguistic Research, 1978; Pragmatics, 1979; (with Klein, Pullum) Order, Concord, and Constituency, 1983; (with Klein, Pullum, Sag) Generalized Phrase Structure Grammar, 1985; (with Coates, Deuchar, Lyons) New Horizons in Linguistics II, 1987; (with Franz, Osborne, Evans) Natural Language Processing in the 1980s, 1987; (with Mellish): Natural Language Processing in Prolog, An Introduction to Computational Linguistics, 1989; Natural Language Processing in LISP, An Introduction to Computational Linguistics, 1989; Natural Language Processing in POP-11, An Introduction to Computational Linguistics, 1989. *Address:* School of Cognitive and Computing Sciences, University of Sussex, Brighton BN1 9QH. *T:* Brighton (01273) 678029.

GAZE, Dr Raymond Michael, FRS 1972; FRSE 1964; Head, Medical Research Council Neural Development and Regeneration Group, Edinburgh University, 1984–92, Hon. Professor, since 1986; *b* 22 June 1927; *s* of late William Mercer Gaze and Kathleen Grace Gaze (*née* Bowhill); *m* 1957, Robinetta Mary Armfelt; one *s* two *d*. *Educ:* at home; Sch. of Medicine, Royal Colleges, Edinburgh; Oxford Univ. (MA, DPhil). LRCPE, LRCSE, LRFPSG. House Physician, Chelmsford and Essex Hosp., 1949; National Service, RAMC, 1953–55; Lectr, later Reader, Dept of Physiology, Edinburgh Univ., 1955–70; Alan Johnston, Lawrence and Moseley Research Fellow, Royal Soc., 1962–66; Head, Div. of Developmental Biol., 1970–83, Dep. Dir 1977–83, Nat. Inst. for Med. Research. Visiting Professor: of Theoretical Biology, Univ. of Chicago, 1972; of Biology, Middlesex Hosp. Med. Sch., 1972–74. *Publications:* The Formation of Nerve Connections, 1970; Editor, 1975–88, and contrib., Development (formerly Jl Embryology and Exper. Morphology); various papers on neurobiology in Jl Physiology, Qly Jl Exper. Physiology, Proc. Royal Soc., etc. *Recreations:* drawing, hill-walking, music. *Address:* 37 Sciennes Road, Edinburgh EH9 1NS. *T:* 0131–667 6915.

GAZZARD, Roy James Albert (Hon. Major); FRIBA; FRTPI; Pro-Director, 1982–84, Director, 1984–86, Hon. Fellow, 1987, Centre for Middle Eastern and Islamic Studies, Durham University; *b* 19 July 1923; *s* of James Henry Gazzard, MBE, and Ada Gwendoline Gazzard (*née* Willis); *m* 1947, Muriel Joy Morgan; one *s* two *d* (and one *s* decd). *Educ:* Stationers' Company's Sch.; Architectural Assoc. Sch. of Architecture (Dip.); School of Planning and Research for Reg. Develt (Dip.). Commissioned, Mddx Regt, 1943; service Palestine and ME. Acting Govt Town Planner, Uganda, 1950; Staff Architect, Barclays Bank Ltd, 1954; Chief Architect, Peterlee Develt Corp., 1960; Dir of Develt, Northumberland CC, 1962; Chief Professional Adviser to Sec. of State's Environmental Bd, 1976; Under Sec., DoE, 1976–79. Prepared: Jinja (Uganda) Outline Scheme, 1954; Municipality of Sur (Oman) Develt Plan, 1975. Renter Warden, Worshipful Co. of Stationers and Newspaper Makers, 1985–86. Govt medals for Good Design in Housing, Civic Trust awards for Townscape and Conservation. *Publications:* Durham: portrait of a cathedral city, 1983; contribs to HMSO pubns on built environment. *Recreations:* Islamic art and architecture, fortifications, dry-stone walling. *Address:* 13 Dunelm Court, South Street, Durham DH1 4QX. *T:* Durham (0191) 3864067. *Club:* City Livery.

GEACH, Gertrude Elizabeth Margaret; *see* Anscombe, G. E. M.

GEACH, Prof. Peter Thomas, FBA 1965; Professor of Logic, University of Leeds, 1966–81; *b* 29 March 1916; *o s* of Prof. George Hender Geach, IES, and Eleonora Frederyka Adolfina Sgonina; *m* 1941, Gertrude Elizabeth Margaret Anscombe, *qv*; three *s* four *d*. *Educ:* Balliol Coll., Oxford (Domus Schol.; Hon. Fellow, 1979). 2nd cl. Class, Hon. Mods, 1936; 1st cl. Lit. Hum., 1938. Gladstone Research Student, St Deiniol's Library, Hawarden, 1938–39; philosophical research, Cambridge, 1945–51; University of Birmingham: Asst Lectr in Philosophy, 1951; Lectr, 1952; Sen. Lectr, 1959; Reader in Logic, 1961. Vis. Prof., Univ. of Warsaw, 1985. Lectures: Stanton, in the Philosophy of Religion, Cambridge, 1971–74; Hägerström, Univ. of Uppsala, 1975; O'Hara, Univ. of Notre Dame, 1978. Forschungspreis, A. Von Humboldt Stiftung, 1983. *Publications:* Mental Acts, 1957; Reference and Generality, 1962, 3rd rev. edn 1980; (with G. E. M. Anscombe) Three Philosophers, 1961; God and the Soul, 1969; Logic Matters, 1972; Reason and Argument, 1976; Providence and Evil, 1977; The Virtues, 1977; Truth, Love, and Immortality: an introduction to McTaggart's philosophy, 1979; articles in Mind, Philosophical Review, Analysis, Ratio, etc. *Recreations:* reading stories of detection, mystery and horror; collecting and annotating old bad logic texts. *Address:* 3 Richmond Road, Cambridge CB4 3PP. *T:* Cambridge (01223) 353950. *Club:* Union Society (Oxford).

GEAKE, Jonathan Richard Barr; His Honour Judge Geake; a Circuit Judge, Northern Circuit, since 1994; *b* 27 May 1946; *s* of Michael and Margaret Geake; *m* 1978, Sally Louise Dines; three *s*. *Educ:* Sherborne Sch.; Fitzwilliam Coll., Cambridge (BA). Called to the Bar, Inner Temple, 1969; practised on Northern Circuit; a Recorder, 1989; Standing Counsel for Customs & Excise, 1989. *Recreations:* golf and various other sporting activities, gardening. *Address:* Crown Court, Manchester M3 3FL. *Clubs:* Knutsford Golf, St Enodoc Golf; Alderley Edge Cricket.

GEAR, Rt. Rev. Michael Frederick; *see* Doncaster, Bishop Suffragan of.

GEAR, William, DA (Edinburgh) 1936; RA 1995; RBSA 1966; Painter; Head of Department of Fine Art, Birmingham Polytechnic (formerly Birmingham College of Art and Design), 1964–75; Member London Group, 1953; *b* Methil, Fife, 2 Aug. 1915; *s* of Porteous Gordon Gear; *m* 1949, Charlotte Chertok (*d* 1988); two *s*. *Educ:* Buckhaven High Sch.; Edinburgh Coll. of Art; Edinburgh Univ.; Moray House Training Coll.; Edinburgh Coll. of Art: Post-grad. schol., 1936–37; Travelling schol., 1937–38; Académie Fernand Leger, Paris, 1937; study in France, Italy, Balkans; Moray House Trg Coll., 1938–39. War Service with Royal Corps of Signals, 1940–46, in Middle East, Italy and Germany. Staff Officer, Monuments, Fine Arts and Archives Br., CCG, 1946–47; worked in Paris, 1947–50; Curator, Towner Art Gallery, Eastbourne, 1958–64. Guest lecturer, Nat. Gall. of Victoria, Melbourne, and University of Western Australia, 1966. Chairman: Fine Art Panel, Nat. Council for Diplomas in Art and Design, 1972; Fine Art Bd, CNAA, 1974. One-man exhibitions since 1944 in various European cities, N and S America, Japan, etc.; London; Gimpel Fils Gall., 1948–; S London Art Gall. (retrospective), 1954; Edinburgh Fest., 1966; (retrospective) Arts Council, N Ireland, 1969; (retrospective) Scottish Arts Council, 1969; Univ. of Sussex, 1964–75; RBSA Birmingham, 1976 (retrospective); Talbot Rice Art Centre, Univ. of Edinburgh, and Ikon Gall., Birmingham (retrospective), 1982; Kirkcaldy Art Gall., 1985; Netherbow Art Centre, Edinburgh, 1985; Redfern Gall., London, 1987, 1989, 1992; Galerie 1900–2000, Paris, 1988; Karl & Faber, Munich, 1988–89; Galerie Gabriele von Loeper, Hamburg, 1989, 1992; England & Co., London, 1989; Kunsthandel Leeman, Amsterdam, 1990, 1992; Galerie Doris Wullkopf, Darmstadt, 1992; Art Fair, Cologne, 1992. Group exhibitions: with COBRA: Malmö, 1986; Taipeh, Stockholm, 1987; Odense, Oslo, Amsterdam, 1988; Munich, 1989; Berlin, 1990; Liège, 1993; Santiago, Buenos Aires, 1994; Neunenhaus, Antwerp, Amstelveen, 1995; others: Portrait of the Artist, Tate Gall., 1989; 4 Abstract Artists, Redfern Gall., 1989; Scottish Art since 1900, Scottish Nat. Gall. of Modern Art, 1989, Barbican Art Centre, 1990; Scotland's Pictures, Edinburgh Fest., 1990; Avant-Garde British Printmaking 1914–1960, BM, 1990; The Line of Tradition, Edinburgh Fest., 1993; Scottish Arts Club, Emscote Lawn, Warwick, 1994; Redfern Gall., City Art Gall., Birmingham, Scottish Arts Club, 1995; works shown in many exhibitions of contemporary art, also at Royal Acad., 1960, 1961, 1967, 1968, and RSA 1986. Awarded £500 Purchase prize, Fest. of Britain, 1951; David Cargill Award, Royal Glasgow Inst., 1967; Lorne Fellowship, 1976; Herbert Baker Scholarship, 1995. FIAL, 1960; FRSA 1971. DUniv Central England, 1994. *Works in permanent collections:* Tate Gall.; Arts Council; Brit. Council; Contemp. Art Soc.; Scottish National Gall. of Modern Art; Scottish Arts Council; British Museum; Victoria & Albert Museum; Laing Art Gall., Newcastle; Nat. Gall. of Canada; Bishop Suter Art Gall., NZ; Art Gall., Toronto; City Art Gall., Toledo, Ohio; Museum of Art, Tel Aviv; New Coll., Oxford; Cincinnati Art Gall., Ohio; Nat. Gall. of NSW; Bishop Otter Coll., Chichester; City Art Gall., Manchester; Albright Art Gall., Buffalo, NY; Musée des Beaux Arts, Liège; Inst. of Contemp. Art, Lima, Peru; Towner Art Gall., Eastbourne; Brighton Art Gall.; Pembroke Coll., Cambridge; Chelsea Coll. of Physical Educn; Southampton Art Gall.; Univ. of Glasgow; Arts Council of Northern Ireland; Whitworth Art Gall., Manchester; Univ. of Birmingham; City Museum and Art Gall., Birmingham; Museum of Art, Fort Lauderdale, Fla; Nat. Gall. of Aust.; Karel van Stuÿvenberg Collection, Caracas, Venezuela; Birmingham Polytech.; City Art Centre, Edinburgh; Kirkcaldy Art Gall.; Strathclyde Regl Council; Hereford Liby & Mus.; Dept of Educn, Manchester; Rye Art Gall.; Peir Gall., Orkney; Mus. of Modern Art, Amstelveen; Aberdeen, Dundee and Glasgow Art Galleries, and in numerous private collections in GB, USA, Canada, Italy, France, etc. Furnishing textiles designed for various firms. *Recreations:* cricket, music, travel. *Address:* 46 George Road, Edgbaston, Birmingham B15 1PL.

GEDDES, family name of **Baron Geddes.**

GEDDES, 3rd Baron *cr* 1942; **Euan Michael Ross Geddes;** Company Director since 1964; *b* 3 Sept. 1937; *s* of 2nd Baron Geddes, KBE, and of Enid Mary, Lady Geddes, *d* of late Clarance H. Butler; *S* father, 1975; *m* 1966, Gillian, *d* of late William Arthur Butler; one *s* one *d*. *Educ:* Rugby; Gonville and Caius Coll., Cambridge (MA 1964); Harvard Business School. *Recreations:* golf, bridge, music, gardening. *Heir:* *s* Hon. James George Neil Geddes, *b* 10 Sept. 1969. *Address:* House of Lords, SW1A 0PW. *T:* Basingstoke (01256) 862105. *Clubs:* Brooks's; Hong Kong (Hong Kong); Noblemen and Gentlemen's Catch; Aldeburgh Golf, Royal Hong Kong Golf.

GEDDES, Prof. Alexander MacIntosh, (Alasdair), FRCP; FRCPE; Professor of Infection, since 1991, and Deputy Dean, Faculty of Medicine and Dentistry, since 1994, University of Birmingham (Professor of Infectious Diseases, 1982–91); *b* 14 May 1934; *s* of Angus and Isabella Geddes; *m* 1984, Angela Lewis; two *s*. *Educ:* Fortrose Acad.; Univ. of Edinburgh (MB ChB). Served RAMC, Captain, 1958–60. Med. Registrar, Aberdeen Hosps, 1961–63; Sen. Registrar, City Hosp. and Royal Infirmary, Edinburgh, 1963–67; Cons. Phys., E Birmingham Hosp., 1967–91; Hon. Cons. Phys., S Birmingham Health Dist, 1991–. Examiner: MRCP (UK), 1972–; Final MB, Univs of Birmingham, Glasgow, London, Sheffield, 1975–. Forbes Vis. Fellow, Fairfield Hosp., Melbourne, Aust., 1988; Sir Edward Finch Vis. Prof., Univ. of Sheffield, 1989. Chairman: Sub-Cttee on Communicable and Trop. Diseases, Jt Cttee on Higher Med. Trng, 1984–; Isolation Beds Working Party, DoH, 1989–; Member: Birmingham AHA, 1977–81; Health Educn Authority, 1987–; Sub-Cttee on Efficacy and Adverse Reactions, Cttee on Safety of Medicines, 1978–85; DHSS Expert Adv. Gp on AIDS, 1985–92; DoH (formerly DHSS) Jt Cttee on Vaccination and Immunization, 1986–; Trop. Med. Res. Bd, MRC, 1984–88; Ministerial Inquiry into the Public Health Function, 1985–87; DoH Cttee on Safety of Medicines, 1993–; Consultant Advr in Infectious Diseases, DoH, 1990–; Civilian Consultant, Infectious Diseases and Tropical Medicine, RN, 1991–. Chm., Brit. Soc. for Antimicrobial Therapy, 1982–85; Chm., Communicable and Tropical Diseases Cttee, 1983–93, Censor, 1987–89, RCP; Mem., Assoc. of Physicians of GB and Ire., 1976–; Pres., Internat. Soc. for Infectious Diseases, 1994–96. Lectures: Honeyman-Gillespie, Univ. of Edinburgh, 1975; Public, Univ. of Warwick, 1980; Davidson, RCPE, 1981; Watson-Smith, 1988; Lister, RCPE, 1990. Chm., Editorial Bd, Jl of Antimicrobial Therapy, 1975–85. *Publications:* (ed) Control of Hospital Infection, 1975, 4th edn 1992; (ed) Recent Advances in Infection, 1975, 3rd edn 1988; (contrib.) Davidson, Principles and Practice of Medicine, 16th edn 1991, 17th edn 1995; papers on infectious diseases, immunology, antibiotic therapy and epidemiology in learned jls. *Recreations:* gardening, reading. *Address:* 34 The Crescent, Solihull, West Midlands B91 1JR. *T:* 0121–705 8844, *Fax:* 0121–414 6956. *Club:* Athenæum.

GEDDES, Andrew Campbell; His Honour Judge Geddes; a Circuit Judge, since 1994; *b* 10 June 1943; *s* of Hon. Alexander Campbell Geddes, OBE, MC, TD and Hon. Margaret Kathleen Geddes (*née* Addis); *m* 1st, 1974, Jacqueline Tan Bunzl; two *s*; 2nd, 1985, Bridget Bowring; one *s* one *d*. *Educ:* Stowe; Christ Church, Oxford (MA). Founder, Building Products Index, 1965. Called to the Bar, Inner Temple, 1972; a Recorder, 1990. *Publications:* Product and Service Liability in the EEC, 1992; Public Procurement, 1993; The Rights of EU Citizens and their Protection in the National Courts, 1995; contribs to learned jls. *Recreations:* music, walking, reading, writing, gardening. *Address:* 4 Essex Court, Temple, EC4Y 9AJ. *T:* 0171–797 7970. *Club:* Brooks's.

GEDDES, Sir (Anthony) Reay (Mackay), KBE 1968 (OBE 1943); President, Charities Aid Foundation, 1991–93 (Chairman, 1985–90); *b* 7 May 1912; *s* of late Rt Hon. Sir Eric Geddes, PC, GCB, GBE; *m* 1938, Imogen, *d* of late Captain Hay Matthey, Brixham; two *s* three *d*. *Educ:* Rugby; Cambridge. Bank of England, 1932–35; Dunlop Rubber Company Ltd, 1935, Dir 1947, Chm. 1968–78; Dep. Chm., Midland Bank, 1978–84 (Dir, 1967–84). Director: Shell Transport and Trading Co., 1968–82; Rank Orgn, 1975–84. Pres., Soc. of Motor Manufacturers and Traders, 1958–59; Part-time Mem., UKAEA, 1960–65; Mem. Nat. Economic Develt. Council, 1962–65; Chm., Shipbuilding Inquiry Cttee, 1965–66. Pres., Internat. Chamber of Commerce, 1980. Hon. DSc Aston, 1967; Hon LLD Leicester, 1969; Hon. DTech Loughborough, 1970. *Address:* 49 Eaton Place, SW1X 8DE.
See also D. M. Geddes.

GEDDES, Duncan Mackay, MD, FRCP; Consultant Physician, Royal Brompton Hospital, since 1978; *b* 6 Jan. 1942; *s* of Sir Reay Geddes, *qv*, and Lady Imogen Geddes; *m*

1968, Donatella Flaccomio Nardi Dei; two *s* one *d*. *Educ:* Eton Coll.; Magdalene Coll., Cambridge (MA); Westminster Hosp. Med. Sch. (MB, BS 1971; MD 1978). FRCP 1982. Hon. Consultant: Royal London Hosp., 1982–; Royal Marsden Hosp., 1990–; Civilian Consultant in chest disease to the Army and Navy, 1986–. Dir, Finsbury Worldwide Pharmaceutical Trust. *Publications:* Practical Medicine, 1976; Airways Obstruction, 1981; Respiratory Medicine, 1990; Cystic Fibrosis, 1995; numerous papers in med. and scientific jls. *Recreations:* tennis, painting. *Address:* 57 Addison Avenue, W11 4QU. *Club:* Queen's.

GEDDES, Ford Irvine, MBE 1943; *b* 17 Jan. 1913; *e s* of Irvine Campbell Geddes and Dorothy Jefford Geddes (*née* Fowler); *m* 1945, Barbara Gertrude Vere Parry-Okeden; one *s* four *d*. *Educ:* Loretto Sch.; Gonville and Caius Coll., Cambridge (BA). Joined Anderson Green & Co. Ltd, London, 1934. Served War RE, 1939–45 (Major). Director: Bank of NSW (London Adv. Bd), 1950–81; Equitable Life Assce Soc., 1955–76 (Pres. 1963–71); British United Turkeys Ltd, 1962–69, 1976–78 (Chm., 1976–78); Chairman: P&O Steam Navigation Co., 1971–72 (a Dep. Chm., 1968–71; Dir, 1960–72); British Shipping Federation, 1965–68; Pres., Internat. Shipping Fedn, 1967–69. *Address:* 8 Kensington Court Gardens, Kensington Court Place, W8 5QE. *Clubs:* City of London; Union (Sydney).

See also N. L. J. Montagu.

GEDDES, Michael Dawson; Civil Service Commissioner, since 1990; Executive Secretary, Milton Keynes Economic Partnership, since 1995; *b* 9 March 1944; *s* of David and Audrey Geddes; *m* 1966, Leslie Rose Webb; two *s*. *Educ:* Sherborne Sch., Dorset; Univ. of BC (Goldsmith's Exhibitioner) (BA). Cranfield Institute of Technology: Admin. Asst, 1968–71; Planning Officer, 1971–77; Develt and Estates Officer, 1977–83; Financial Controller, RMCS, 1983–84; Sec., Ashridge (Bonar Law Meml) Trust; Dir, Admin, Ashridge Management Coll. and Dir, Ashridge subsids, 1984–90; Chief Exec., Recruitment and Assessment Services Agency, 1990–95. *Publications:* (with W. Briner and C. Hastings) Project Leadership, 1990; papers on resource allocation in univs and on project management. *Recreations:* golf, bridge. *Address:* 11 Main Street, Mursley, Bucks MK17 0RT. *T:* Mursley (01296) 720601.

GEDDES, Sir Reay; *see* Geddes, Sir A. R. M.

GEDLING, Raymond, CB 1969; Deputy Secretary, Department of Health and Social Security, 1971–77; *b* 3 Sept. 1917; *s* of late John and late Mary Gedling; *m* 1956, Joan Evelyn Chapple; one *s*. *Educ:* Grangefield Grammar Sch., Stockton-on-Tees. Entered Civil Service as Executive Officer, Min. of Health, 1936; Asst Principal, 1942, Principal, 1947. Cabinet Office, 1951–52; Principal Private Sec. to Minister of Health, 1952–55; Asst Sec., 1955; Under-Sec., 1961; Asst Under-Sec. of State, Dept of Educn and Science, 1966–68; Dep. Sec., Treasury, 1968–71. *Recreations:* walking, chess. *Address:* 27 Wallace Fields, Epsom, Surrey KT17 3AX. *T:* 0181–393 9060.

GEE, Anthony Hall; QC 1990; a Recorder of the Crown Court, since 1989; *b* 4 Nov. 1948; *s* of late Harold Stephenson Gee and Marjorie Gee (*née* Hall); *m* 1975, Gillian Pauline Glover, St Annes-on-Sea; one *s* two *d*. *Educ:* Cambs High School for Boys; Chester City Grammar Sch.; Inns of Court School of Law. Called to the Bar, Gray's Inn, 1972; Mem., Northern Circuit, 1972–. Mem., Medico-Legal Soc. *Recreations:* golf, skiing, cricket, classic cars. *Address:* (chambers) 28 St John Street, Manchester M3 4DJ. *T:* 0161–834 8418. *Clubs:* Lancashire CC; Bramhall Golf.

GEE, David Charles Laycock; consultant, environmental and occupational risk, since 1992; Partner, WBMG Environmental Communications; *b* 18 April 1947; *s* of Charles Laycock Gee and Theresa Gee (*née* Garrick); *m* 1974, Vivienne Taylor Gee; four *d*. *Educ:* Thomas Linacre and Wigan Grammar Schs; York Univ. (BA Politics). MIOSH 1985. Res. Dept, AUEW, 1970–73; Educn Service, TUC, 1973–78; Nat. Health/Safety Officer, GMB, 1978–88; Occupational/Environmental Cons., 1988–89; Campaign Co-ordinator, 1989–90, Dir, 1990–91, Friends of the Earth. Fellow, Collegium Ramazzini, Italy, 1984; FRSA 1990. *Publications:* (with John Cox and Dave Leon) Cancer and Work, 1982; (with Lesley Doyal et al) Cancer in Britain, 1983; Eco-nomic Tax Reform: a primer, 1994; chapter in Radiation and Health—Biological Effects of Low Level Exposure to Ionising Radiation, 1987. *Recreations:* family, swimming, tennis, running, entertaining, theatre, music. *Address:* 24 Broomwood Road, SW11 6HT. *T:* 0171–223 0595.

GEE, David Stephenson; His Honour Judge David S. Gee; a Circuit Judge, since 1992; *b* 16 Dec. 1944; *s* of William and Marianne Gee; *m* 1972, Susan Margaret Hiley; two *s* two *d*. *Educ:* William Hulme's Grammar Sch., Manchester; Leeds Univ. (LLB Hons). Admitted Solicitor, 1970; Registrar, Manchester County Court and Dist Registry, 1982–90; Dist Judge, 1991–92; a Recorder of the Crown Court, 1991. Chairman: Selcare (Greater Manchester) Trust, 1989–; Rhodes Foundn Scholarship Trust, 1989–. Adv. Editor, Atkins' Court Forms, 1989–; Editor, Butterworth's Family Law Service, 1990–. *Recreations:* music, walking, reading. *Address:* c/o Circuit Administrator, 15 Quay Street, Manchester M60 9FD. *Club:* Commonwealth Trust.

GEE, Prof. Geoffrey, CBE 1958; FRS 1951; Sir Samuel Hall Professor of Chemistry, University of Manchester, 1955–77, now Emeritus Professor; *b* 6 June 1910; *s* of Thomas and Mary Ann Gee; *m* 1934, Marion (*née* Bowden); one *s* two *d*. *Educ:* New Mills Grammar Sch.; Universities of Manchester and Cambridge, BSc 1931, MSc 1932, Manchester; PhD 1936, ScD 1947, Cambridge. ICI (Dyestuffs Group) Research Chemist, 1933–38; British Rubber Producers' Research Association: Research Chemist, 1938–47; Dir, 1947–53. University of Manchester: Prof. of Physical Chemistry, 1953–55; Pro-Vice Chancellor, 1966–68, 1972–77 (full-time, 1975–77). Pres., Faraday Soc., 1969 and 1970. Hon. Fellow, Manchester Polytechnic, 1979. Hon. DSc Manchester, 1983. *Publications:* numerous scientific papers in Transactions of the Faraday Soc., and other journals. *Recreation:* currently interested in relation between science and theology. *Address:* 8 Holmfield Drive, Cheadle Hulme, Cheshire SK8 7DT. *T:* 0161–485 3713.

GEE, Richard; His Honour Judge Gee; a Circuit Judge, since 1991; *b* 25 July 1942; *s* of John and Marie Gee; *m* 1965; three *s*. *Educ:* Kilburn Grammar School; University College London (LLB Hons). Admitted Solicitor, 1966; Assistant Recorder, 1983; Recorder, 1988. Mem., Main Board, Judicial Studies Board, 1988–93 (Mem., Ethnic Minorities Adv. Cttee, 1991–93). *Recreations:* golf, the arts.

GEE, Steven Mark; QC 1993; *b* 24 Aug. 1953; *yr s* of Dr Sidney Gee and Dr Hilda Elman. *Educ:* Tonbridge Sch.; Brasenose Coll., Oxford (Open Scholar; MA 1st Cl. Hons Jurisprudence; Gibbs Prize for Law). Called to the Bar, Middle Temple, 1975 (Inns of Court Prize, Harmsworth Scholar); Standing Jun. Counsel, ECGD, DTI, 1986–93. *Publication:* Mareva Injunctions and Anton Piller Relief, 1995. *Recreations:* marathon running, bridge. *Address:* 1 Essex Court, Temple, EC4Y 9AR. *T:* 0171–583 2000. *Club:* MCC.

GEE, Timothy Hugh; HM Diplomatic Service, retired; Consultant, The Entertainment Corporation, 1987–89; *b* 12 Nov. 1936; *s* of Arthur William Gee and Edith (*née* Ingham); *m* 1964, Gillian Eve St Johnston (marr. diss. 1988); two *s* one *d*. *Educ:* Berkhamsted; Trinity Coll., Oxford. 2 Lieut 3rd Regt RHA, 1959–61. Joined British Council, 1961; New Delhi, 1962–66; entered HM Diplomatic Service, 1966; FO, 1966–68; Brussels, 1968–72; FCO, 1972–74; Kuala Lumpur, 1974–79; Counsellor, on secondment to NI Office, 1979–81; Consul-General, Istanbul, 1981–85; Head of Cultural Relations Dept, FCO, 1985–87. *Club:* Travellers'.

GEELONG, Bishop of; *see* Bayton, Rt Rev. J.

GEERING, Ian Walter; QC 1991; a Recorder, since 1995; *b* 19 July 1947; *s* of late Wilfrid Robert Geering and of Barbara Pearce (*née* James); *m* 1975, (Alison) Diana Burne; two *s* two *d*. *Educ:* Bedford Sch.; Univ. of Edinburgh (BVMS). Called to the Bar, Inner Temple, 1974. *Recreations:* walking, reading, sailing, photography. *Address:* 3 Gray's Inn Place, Gray's Inn, WC1R 5EA.

GEFFEN, Dr Terence John; Medical Adviser, Capsticks Solicitors, since 1990; *b* 17 Sept. 1921; *s* of late Maximilian W. Geffen and Maia Geffen (later Reid); *m* 1965, Judith Anne Steward; two *s*. *Educ:* St Paul's Sch.; University Coll., London; UCH. MD, FRCP. House Phys., UCH, 1943; RAMC, 1944–47; hosp. posts, Edgware Gen. Hosp., Hampstead Gen. Hosp., UCH, 1947–55; Min. of Health (later DHSS), 1956–82, SPMO, 1972–82; Consultant in Public Health Medicine, NW Thames RHA, 1982–90. FRSM 1991. *Publications:* various in BMJ, Lancet, Clinical Science, etc. *Recreations:* music, reading, bridge. *Address:* 2 Stonehill Close, SW14 8RP. *T:* 0181–878 0516.

GEHRELS, Jürgen Carlos; Chief Executive, Siemens plc, since 1986; *b* 24 July 1935; *s* of Hans Gehrels and Ursula (*née* da Rocha); *m* 1963, Sigrid Kausch; one *s* one *d*. *Educ:* Technical Univs, Berlin and Munich (Dipl. Ing.). Siemens AG, Germany, 1965–79; Pres., General Numeric Corp., Chicago, USA, 1979–82; Dir, Factory Automation, Siemens AG, Germany, 1982–86. Chairman: Siemens Communication Systems Ltd, 1986–92; Siemens Financial Services Ltd, 1988–92; Siemens Controls Ltd, 1990–; Siemens–Nixdorf Inf. Systems Ltd, 1990–; Director: AMS/NEVE plc (formerly Neve Electronic International Ltd), 1987–; Siemens Domestic Appliances Ltd, 1987–; Comparex Ltd, 1988–92; Alfred Engelmann Ltd, 1989–; Plessey UK, 1989–; Plessey Overseas, 1989–; Siemens Holdings plc, 1990–. Chm., German–British Chamber of Industry and Commerce in UK, 1992–. FIEE 1991. FRSA 1993. *Recreations:* golf, gardening, architecture. *Address:* Siemens plc, Siemens House, Oldbury, Bracknell, Berks RG12 8FZ. *Clubs:* Reform; Burhill Golf (Surrey).

GELDER, Prof. Michael Graham; W. A. Handley Professor of Psychiatry, University of Oxford, 1969–Oct. 1996; Fellow of Merton College, Oxford, 1969–Oct. 1996 (Subwarden, 1992–94); *b* 2 July 1929; *s* of Philip Graham Gelder and Margaret Gelder (*née* Graham); *m* 1954, Margaret (*née* Anderson); one *s* two *d*. *Educ:* Bradford Grammar Sch.; Queen's Coll., Oxford. Scholar, Theodore Williams Prize 1949 and first class Hons, Physiology finals, 1950; MA, DM Oxon, FRCP, FRCPsych; DPM London (with distinction) 1961. Goldsmit Schol., UCH London, 1951. House Physician, Sen. House Physician, UCH, 1955–57; Registrar, Maudsley Hosp., 1958–61; MRC Fellow in Clinical Research, 1962–63; Sen. Lectr, Inst. of Psychiatry, 1965–67 (Vice-Dean, 1967–68); Physician, Bethlem Royal and Maudsley Hosps, 1967–68. Hon. Consultant Psychiatrist, Oxford RHA, later DHA, 1969–; Mem., Oxford DHA, 1985–92; Dir, Oxford Mental Health Care NHS Trust, 1993–95. Dir, WHO Collaborating Centre, 1994–96. Mem., MRC, 1978–79 (Chm., 1978–79, Mem., 1975–78 and 1987–, Neurosciences Bd). Chm., Wellcome Trust Neuroscience Panel, 1990–95 (Mem., 1984–88). Chairman: Assoc. of Univ. Teachers of Psychiatry, 1979–82; Jt Cttee on Higher Psychiatric Trng, 1981–85. Europ. Vice-Pres., Soc. for Psychotherapy Research, 1977–82. Advisor, WHO, 1992–. Mem., Assoc. of Physicians, 1983–. Mem. Council, RCPsych, 1981–90 (Vice Pres. 1982–83; Sen. Vice-Pres., 1983–84; Chm. Res. Cttee, 1986–). Mayne Guest Prof., Univ. of Queensland, 1990. Lectures: Malcolm Millar, Univ. of Aberdeen, 1984; Yap Meml, Hong Kong, 1987; Guze, Univ. of Washington, 1993. Gold Medal, Royal Medico-Psychol Assoc., 1962. *Publications:* (jtly) Agoraphobia: nature and treatment, 1981; (jtly) The Oxford Textbook of Psychiatry, 1983, 3rd edn 1996; (jtly) Concise Oxford Textbook of Psychiatry, 1994; chapters in books and articles in medical jls. *Recreations:* photography, gardening, real-tennis. *Address:* St Mary's, Jack Straw's Lane, Oxford OX3 0DN.

GELDOF, Bob, Hon. KBE 1986; singer; songwriter; initiator and organiser, Band Aid, Live Aid and Sport Aid fund-raising events; *b* Dublin, 5 Oct. 1954; *m* 1986, Paula Yates; three *d*. *Educ:* Black Rock Coll. Sometime journalist: Georgia Straight, Vancouver; New Musical Express; Melody Maker. Jt Founder, Boomtown Rats, rock band, 1975. Acted in films: Pink Floyd—The Wall, 1982; Number One, 1985. Organised Band Aid, 1984, to record Do They Know It's Christmas, sales from which raised £8 million for famine relief in Ethiopia; organised simultaneous Live Aid concerts in London and Philadelphia to raise £50 million, 1985; organised Sport Aid to raise further £50 million, 1986. Chm., Band Aid Trust, 1985–; Founder, Live Aid Foundn, USA, 1985–. Freeman: Borough of Swale, 1985; Newcastle. Hon. MA Kent, 1985; Hon. DSc(Econ) London, 1987; Hon. DPh Ghent. TV film: The Price of Progress, 1987. Awards include: UN World Hunger Award, FAO Medal; EEC Gold Medal; Irish Peace Prize; music awards include: Ivor Novello (four times); several gold and platinum discs. Order of Two Niles (Sudan); Cavalier, Order of Leopold II (Belgium). *Publication:* Is That It? (autobiog.), 1986.

GELL, Dr Alfred Antony Francis, FBA 1995; Reader in Anthropology, London School of Economics, since 1979; *b* 12 June 1945; *s* of Philip Gell and Susan Gell; *m* 1974, Simeran Man Singh; one *s*. *Educ:* Bryanston Sch.; Trinity Coll., Cambridge (MA 1967); London Sch. of Economics (PhD 1973). Lecturer in Anthropology: Univ. of Sussex, 1972–74; ANU, 1974–79. Anthropological fieldwork in West Sepik, New Guinea, and Bastar district, Madhya Pradesh, India. *Publications:* Metamorphosis of the Cassowaries, 1975; The Anthropology of Time, 1992; Wrapping in Images, 1993. *Recreations:* sketching, music. *Address:* Department of Anthropology, London School of Economics, Houghton Street, Aldwych, WC2 2AE. *T:* 0171–955 7202.

GELL, Prof. Philip George Houthem, FRS 1969; Professor and Head of Department of Experimental Pathology, Birmingham University, 1968–78; retired; *b* 20 Oct. 1914; *s* of late Major P. F. Gell, DSO, and Mrs E. Lewis Hall; *m* 1941, Albinia Susan Roope Gordon; one *s* one *d*. *Educ:* Stowe Sch.; Trinity Coll., Cambridge; University Coll. Hosp. MRCS, LRCP, 1939; MB, BCh, 1940; FRCPath, 1969. Ho. Phys. to Med. Unit, UCH, 1939; Emergency Public Health Laboratory Service, 1940–43. On staff of Nat. Inst. for Med. Research, 1943–48; Reader in Dept of Exptl Pathology, Birmingham Univ., 1948–60; Prof. (Personal) of Immunological Pathology, Dept of Exptl Pathology, 1960–68. *Publications:* (ed with R. R. A. Coombs and P. J. Lachmann) Clinical Aspects of Immunology, 1968, 3rd edn 1974; contribs to Jl of Experimental Med., Immunology, 1960–. *Recreations:* gardening, painting, philosophy of science. *Address:* Wychwood, Cranes Lane, Kingston, Cambridge CB3 7NJ. *T:* Cambridge (01223) 262714.

GELL-MANN, Murray; Robert Andrews Millikan Professor of Theoretical Physics at the California Institute of Technology, 1967–93, now Emeritus; *b* 15 Sept. 1929; *s* of Arthur and Pauline Gell-Mann; *m* 1955, J. Margaret Dow (*d* 1981); one *s* one *d*. *Educ:* Yale Univ.; Massachusetts Inst. of Technology. Mem., Inst. for Advanced Study, Princeton, 1951; Instructor, Asst Prof., and Assoc. Prof., Univ. of Chicago, 1952–55; Assoc. Prof. 1955–56,

Prof. 1956–66, California Inst. of Technology. Vis. Prof., Collège de France and Univ. of Paris, 1959–60. Overseas Fellow, Churchill Coll., Cambridge, 1966. Mem., President's Science Adv. Cttee, 1969–72. Regent, Smithsonian Instn, 1974–88; Chm. of Bd, Aspen Center for Physics, 1973–79; Dir, J. D. and C. T. MacArthur Foundn, 1979–; Vice-Pres. and Chm. of Western Center, Amer. Acad. of Arts and Sciences, 1970–76; Member: Nat. Acad. of Sciences, 1960–; Sci. and Grants Cttee, Leakey Foundn, 1977–. Santa Fe Institute: Founding Trustee, 1982–; Chm., Bd of Trustees, 1982–85; Co–Chm., Sci. Bd, 1985–. Mem. Bd, California Nature Conservancy, 1984–. Foreign Mem., Royal Society, 1978. Hon. ScD: Yale, 1959; Chicago, 1967; Illinois, 1968; Wesleyan, 1968; Utah, 1970; Columbia, 1977; Hon. DSc: Cantab, 1980; Oxon, 1992; Hon. Dr,Turin, 1969. Listed on UN Envmtl Program Roll of Honor for Envmtl Achievement (Global 500), 1988. Dannie Heineman Prize (Amer. Phys. Soc.), 1959; Ernest O. Lawrence Award, 1966; Franklin Medal (Franklin Inst., Philadelphia), 1967; John J. Carty Medal (Nat. Acad. Scis), 1968; Research Corp. Award, 1969; Nobel Prize in Physics, 1969. *Publications:* (with Yuval Ne'eman) The Eightfold Way, 1964; The Quark and the Jaguar, 1994; various articles in learned jls on topics referring to classification and description of elementary particles of physics and their interactions. *Recreations:* walking in wild country, study of natural history, languages. *Address:* Santa Fe Institute, 1660 Old Pecos Trail, Santa Fe, NM 87505, USA. *T:* (505) 9848800. *Clubs:* Cosmos (Washington) Explorers', Century (New York); Athenæum (Pasadena).

GELLHORN, Peter, FGSM; Professor, Guildhall School of Music and Drama, 1981–92; *b* 24 Oct. 1912; *s* of late Dr Alfred Gellhorn, and late Mrs Else Gellhorn; *m* 1943, Olive Shirley (*née* Layton), 3rd *d* of 1st Baron Layton, CH, CBE; two *s* two *d. Educ:* Schiller Realgymnasium, Charlottenburg; University of Berlin; Berlin Music Acad. FGSM 1989. After passing final exams (with dist.) as pianist and conductor, left Germany 1935. Musical Dir, Toynbee Hall, London, E1, 1935–39; Asst Conductor, Sadler's Wells Opera, 1941–43. On industrial war service, 1943–45. Conductor, Royal Carl Rosa Opera (115 perfs), 1945–46; Conductor and Head of Music Staff, Royal Opera House, Covent Garden (over 260 perfs), 1946–53; Conductor and Chorus Master, Glyndebourne Festival Opera, 1954–61, rejoined Glyndebourne Music Staff, 1974 and 1975; Dir, BBC Chorus, 1961–72; Conductor, Elizabethan Singers, 1976–80. Has also worked at National Sch. of Opera, annually at Summer Sch. of Music at Dartington Hall; composes; wrote and arranged music for silhouette and puppet films of Lotte Reiniger (at intervals, 1933–57). Mem., Music Staff, London Opera Centre, 1973–78; Conductor: Morley Coll. Opera Gp, 1974–79; Barnes Choir; Associate Conductor, London Chamber Opera, 1982–; Music Dir, Opera Players Ltd; Mem. Staff, Opera Sch., RCM, 1980–88, conducting its opera perfs, 1981. Lectures on courses arranged by various County Councils and adult colleges; frequently adjudicates at music fests in UK and overseas. Musical Dir, Opera Barga, Italy, from foundn, 1967–69. *Recreations:* reading, walking and going to plays. *Address:* 33 Leinster Avenue, East Sheen, SW14 7JW. *T:* 0181–876 3949. *Club:* BBC.

GELLNER, Prof. Ernest André, FBA 1974; William Wyse Professor of Social Anthropology, Cambridge University, 1984–93; Supernumerary Fellow, King's College, Cambridge, 1992–95 (Professorial Fellow, 1984–92); *b* Paris, 9 Dec. 1925; *s* of Rudolf Gellner and Anna (*née* Fantl), Prague; *m* 1954, Susan Ryan; two *s* two *d. Educ:* Prague English Grammar Sch.; St Albans County (now Verulam) Sch.; Balliol Coll., Oxford (Open schol.; Univ. John Locke Scholar; MA); PhD (Lond). Pte, Czech. Armoured Brig., BLA, 1944–45. On staff of London School of Economics, 1949–84 (Hon. Fellow 1986), Prof. of Philosophy, 1962–84. Res. Prof., and Dir, Centre for Study of Nationalism, Central European Univ., Prague, 1993– (pt-time, 1991–93); Vis. Lectr, Center for European Studies, Harvard, 1994; Erasmus Vis. Prof., Warsaw Univ., 1995; Visiting Fellow: Harvard, 1952–53; Univ. of California, Berkeley, 1968; Centre de Recherches et d'Études sur les Sociétés Méditerranéens, Aix-en-Provence, 1978–79; Vis. Schol., Inst. of Advanced Studies, Tel Aviv Univ., 1982; Guest of Acad. of Scis of USSR, Moscow, 1988–89. Member: Council, SSRC (later ESRC), 1980–86 (Chm., Internat. Activities Cttee, 1982–84); Council, British Acad., 1981–84; Senate, Acad. of Scis of Czech Republic, 1994–. Pres., RAI, 1991–94; First Pres., Soc. for Moroccan Studies, 1990–. Tanner Lectr, Harvard Univ., 1990; Memorial Lectures: Frazer; Radcliffe-Brown; Marett; Myers; M. Stuchlík; H. Arendt; A. Little; H. Enayat; E. Westermarck; Marie Curie; B. Blackwood; L. Schapiro; Munro; E. H. Carr; A. Sakharov; M. Cummings; A. Harriman; J. Monnet. MAE 1989; Member: Amer. Philosophical Soc., 1992; Academia Scientiarum et Artium Europaea, Salzburg, 1993. Hon. For. Mem., Amer. Acad. of Arts and Scis, 1988. FRSA 1992. Hon. DSc Bristol, 1986; Hon. DLit QUB, 1989. Mem., Editorial or Adv. Boards: British Jl of Sociol.; Amer. Jl of Sociol.; Inquiry; Middle Eastern Studies; Jl of Peasant Studies; Society and Theory; Govt and Opposition; Philosophy of the Social Scis; Cambridge Archæological Jl; Jl of Mediterranean Studies; Third World Review; Nations and Nationalism; Anthropology and Archaeology of Eurasia; Sociological Papers; Moderniyzzazio e Sviluppo; Co-Editor: Europ. Jl of Sociol., 1966–84; Govt and Opposition, 1980–. *Publications:* Words and Things, 1959; Thought and Change, 1964; Saints of the Atlas, 1969; (ed with G. Ionescu) Populism, 1969; (ed with C. Micaud) Arabs and Berbers, 1973; Cause and Meaning in the Social Sciences, 1973, 2nd edn, as The Concept of Kinship and other essays, 1986; Contemporary Thought and Politics, 1974; The Devil in Modern Philosophy, 1974; Legitimation of Belief, 1975; (ed with J. Waterbury) Patrons and Clients, 1977; Spectacles and Predicaments, 1979; (ed) Soviet and Western Anthropology, 1980; Muslim Society, 1981; Nations and Nationalism, 1983; (ed) Islamic Dilemmas: reformers, nationalists and industrialisation, 1985; The Psychoanalytic Movement, 1985; Culture, Identity and Politics, 1987; State and Society in Soviet Thought, 1988; Plough, Sword and Book, 1988; (ed jtly) Malinowski between Two Worlds, 1988; Reason and Culture, 1992; Postmodernism, Reason and Religion, 1992; Conditions of Liberty, 1994; Encounters with Nationalism, 1994; Anthropology and Politics, 1995; numerous contributions to learned jls. *Address:* King's College, Cambridge CB2 1ST. *Club:* Reform.

GEM, Dr Richard David Harvey, FSA; Secretary, Cathedrals Fabric Commission for England, since 1991; *b* 10 Jan. 1945. *Educ:* Eastbourne Coll.; Peterhouse, Cambridge (MA, PhD). Inspector of Ancient Monuments, DoE, 1970–80; Res. Officer, Council for Care of Churches, 1981–88; Dep. Sec., then Sec., Cathedrals Adv. Commn for England, 1988–91. Mem., RCHM, 1987–. Pres., British Archaeol Assoc., 1983–89. MIFA. *Publications:* numerous papers on early medieval architecture in British and foreign learned jls. *Recreations:* gardening, theatre, music, foreign travel, philosphy and theology. *Address:* Fielden House, Little College Street, SW1P 3SH. *T:* 0171–222 3793; The Bothy, Mentmore, near Leighton Buzzard, Beds LU7 0QG.

GENDERS, Rt. Rev. Roger Alban Marson, (Father Anselm, CR); *b* 15 Aug. 1919; *yr s* of John Boulton Genders and Florence Alice (*née* Thomas). *Educ:* King Edward VI School, Birmingham; Brasenose College, Oxford (Sen. Scholar 1938, BA Lit. Hum. 1946, MA 1946). Served War, Lieut RNVR, 1940–46. Joined Community of the Resurrection, Mirfield, 1948; professed, 1952; ordained, 1952; Tutor, College of the Resurrection, 1952–55; Vice-Principal 1955, and Principal 1957–65, Codrington Coll., Barbados; Exam. Chaplain to Bishop of Barbados, 1957–65; Treasurer of St Augustine's Mission, Rhodesia, 1966–75; Archdeacon of Manicaland, 1970–75; Asst Bursar, Community of the Resurrection, Mirfield, 1975–77; Bishop of Bermuda, 1977–82; Assistant Bishop of Wakefield, 1983–89. *Publications:* contribs to Theology. *Address:* Community of the Resurrection, House of the Resurrection, Mirfield, W Yorks WF14 0BN.

GENGE, Rt. Rev. Kenneth Lyle; *see* Edmonton (Alberta), Bishop of.

GENGE, Rt. Rev. Mark; Bishop of Central Newfoundland, 1976–90; Pastoral Associate, St John's, Yorkmills, Ontario, 1990–92; *b* 18 March 1927; *s* of Lambert and Lily Genge; *m* 1959, Maxine Clara (*née* Major); five *d. Educ:* Queen's Coll. and Memorial Univ., Newfoundland; Univ. of Durham (MA); BD Gen. Synod of Canada. Deacon, Corner Brook, Newfoundland, 1951; priest, Stephenville, 1952; Durham, 1953–55; Vice-Principal, Queen's Coll., St John's, Newfoundland, 1955–57; Curate, St Mary's Church, St John's, 1957–59; Rector: Foxtrap, 1959–64; Mary's Harbour, 1964–65; Burgeo, 1965–69; Curate, Marbleton, PQ, 1969–71; Rector, South River, Port-de-Grave, 1971–73; District Sec., Canadian Bible Soc., 1973–76. *Recreations:* badminton, swimming. *Address:* 6 Maypark Place, St John's, Newfoundland A1B 2E3, Canada.

GENSCHER, Hans-Dietrich; Member of Bundestag, since 1965; Federal Minister for Foreign Affairs and Deputy Chancellor, Federal Republic of Germany, 1974–92 (in government of Helmut Schmidt, to Oct. 1982, then in government of Helmut Kohl); Chairman of the Free Democratic Party, 1974–85; *b* Reideburg/Saalkreis, 21 March 1927; *m* Barbara; one *d. Educ:* Higher Sch. Certif. (Abitur); studied law and economics in Halle/Saale and Leipzig Univs, 1946–49. Served War, 1943–45. Mem., state-level org. of LDP, 1946. Re-settled in W Germany, 1952: practical legal training in Bremen and Mem. Free Democratic Party (FDP); FDP Asst in Parly Group, 1956; Gen. Sec.: FDP Parly Group, 1959–65; FDP at nat. level, 1962–64. A Parly Sec., FDP Parly Group, 1965–69; Dep. Chm., FDP, 1969–74; Federal Minister of the Interior, Oct. 1969 (Brandt-Scheel Cabinet); re-apptd Federal Minister of the Interior, Dec. 1972. He was instrumental in maintaining pure air and water; gave a modern structure to the Federal Police Authority; Federal Border Guard Act passed; revised weapons laws, etc.; in promoting relations between West and East, prominent role in CSCE, Helsinki, 1975, Madrid, 1980–83, Stockholm, 1984–86 and in setting up conferences on Conventional Armed Forces, Confidence and Security Building Measures, Vienna, 1989; an initiator of reform process that led to the inclusion of the Single European Act 1986. Co-initiator: 'Eureka' initiative; independence process in Namibia. Promotes co-operation between EC and other regional gps, ASEAN, Central Amer. States, (San José Conferences), Golf Co-operation Council. Chm., Bd of Trustees, Franckesche Stiftungen, Halle; Mem., Supervisory Bd, Elf Oil AG, 1993–. Pres., European Movt, Germany, 1992–94. Chm., Assoc. of Friends and Patrons, State Opera, Berlin. Hon. Prof., Free Univ., Berlin, 1994. Hon. Dr: Madras, 1977, Salamanca, 1987, Athens, 1988, Seoul, 1988, Budapest, 1988; Georgetown, Washington, 1990; Kattowitz, 1992; Essex, 1993; Moscow, 1993; Warsaw, 1993; Hon. Master, German Handicrafts 1975; Hon. citizen Costa Rica, 1987; Grand Fed. Cross of Merit 1973, 1975 with star and sash; Wolfgang-Döring Medal 1976; numerous foreign decorations. *Publications:* Umweltschutz: Das Umweltschutzprogramm der Bundesregierung, 1972; Bundestagsreden, 1972; Aussenpolitik im Dienste von Sicherheit und Freiheit, 1975; Deutsche Aussenpolitik, 1977, 3rd edn 1985; Bundestagsreden und Zeitdokumente, 1979; Zukunftsverantwortung, 1990. *Recreations:* reading, walking, swimming. *Address:* c/o Bundestag, 53113 Bonn, Germany.

GENT, (John) David (Wright), FIMI; Director General, Retail Motor Industry Federation (formerly Motor Agents Association), since 1985; *b* 25 April 1935; *s* of late Reginald Philip Gent and Stella Eva Parker; *m* 1970, Anne Elaine Hanson. *Educ:* Lancing Coll. Admitted a Solicitor, 1959. Joined Soc. of Motor Manufacturers as Legal Advr, 1961; Asst Sec., 1964; Sec. 1965; Dep. Dir, 1971–80; joined Lucas Industries as Gen. Man., Lucas Service UK, 1981; Gp PR Man., 1982–83; Dir, British Road Fedn, 1983–84. Mem., Road Transport ITB, 1985–91. Freeman, City of London, 1985, Liveryman, Coach Makers and Coach Harness Makers' Co., 1985. *Recreations:* farming, gardening. *Address:* 44 Ursula Street, SW11 3DW. *T:* 0171–228 8126. *Club:* Royal Automobile.

GENTLEMAN, David (William), RDI 1970; artist and designer; *b* 11 March 1930; *s* of late Tom and Winifred Gentleman; *m* 1st, 1953, Rosalind Dease (marr. diss. 1966); one *d;* 2nd, 1968, Susan, *d* of late George Ewart Evans; two *d* one *s. Educ:* Hertford Grammar Sch.; St Albans Sch. of Art; Royal College of Art. Work includes: painting in watercolour, illustration, graphic design, lithography and wood engraving; commissions include Eleanor Cross mural designs for Charing Cross underground station, 1979; historical panels for East Cloister, Westminster Abbey, 1986; illustrations and designs for many publishers; postage stamps for the Royal Mail, including, 1962–93: Shakespeare, Churchill, Darwin, Ely Cathedral, Abbotsbury Swans; posters for London Transport and the National Trust; symbols for British Steel, Bodleian Library, etc. Solo exhibitions at Mercury Gallery: watercolours of: India, 1970; Carolina, 1973; Africa, 1976; Pacific, 1981; Britain, 1982; London, 1985; British coastline, 1988; Paris, 1991; India, 1994. Editions of lithographs of architecture and landscape, 1967–90. Work in public collections incl. Tate Gall., V&A, BM and Nat. Maritime Mus. and also in private collections. Member: Nat. Trust Properties Cttee; Alliance Graphique Internat.; Council, Artists' Gen. Benevolent Instn. Master of Faculty, RDI, 1989–91. Hon. Fellow, RCA, 1981. Dr *hc* Kingston, 1994. *Publications:* author and illustrator: Design in Miniature, 1972; David Gentleman's Britain, 1982; David Gentleman's London, 1985; A Special Relationship, 1987; David Gentleman's Coastline, 1988; David Gentleman's Paris, 1991; David Gentleman's India, 1994; *for children:* Fenella in Greece, 1967; Fenella in Spain, 1967; Fenella in Ireland, 1967; Fenella in the South of France, 1967; *illustrator:* Plats du Jour, 1957; Bridges on the Backs, 1961; Swiss Family Robinson, 1963 (USA); The Shepherd's Calendar, 1964; Poems of John Keats, 1966 (USA); The Pattern Under the Plough, 1966; covers for New Penguin Shakespeare, 1968–78; The Jungle Book, 1968 (USA); Robin Hood, 1977 (USA); The Dancing Tigers, 1979; Westminster Abbey, 1987; The Illustrated Poems of John Betjeman, 1995; *illustrator and editor:* The Crooked Scythe, 1993. *Address:* 25 Gloucester Crescent, NW1 7DL. *T:* 0171–485 8824.

GEORGALA, Prof. Douglas Lindley, CBE 1986; PhD; FIFST; Director of Food Research, Agricultural and Food Research Council, 1988–94; External Professor, University of Leeds, since 1993; *b* 2 Feb. 1934; *s* of late John Michael Georgala and of Izetta Iris Georgala; *m* 1959, Eulalia Catherina Lochner; one *s* one *d. Educ:* South African College Sch., Cape Town; Univ. of Stellenbosch (BScAgric); Univ. of Aberdeen (PhD). FIFST 1987. Research Officer, Fishing Research Inst., Univ. of Cape Town, 1957–60; Research Microbiologist, 1960–69, Division Manager, 1969–72, Head of Laboratory, 1977–86, Unilever Colworth Laboratory; Technical Member, Unilever Meat Products Co-ordination, 1973–77; Mem., Unilever Res. Div., 1987–88; Indust. Consultant, Biotechnology Unit, DTI, 1987–88. Chairman: Fisheries Res. Bd, 1980–84; Adv. Cttee of Food Science Dept, Leeds Univ., 1984–88; Scientific and Technical Cttee, Food and Drink Fedn, 1986–88; Member: ACARD, 1980–83; Food Cttee, 1984–88, Strategy Bd, 1991–93, AFRC; Co-ordinating Cttee for Marine Science and Technol., 1988–89; Food Adv. Cttee, 1989–; Adv. Cttee on Microbiological Safety of Food, 1991– (Acting Chm., 1994–); Council, Inst. of Food Science and Technology, 1992–. Vis. Prof., UEA, Leeds and Reading Univs, 1988–94. Scientific Governor, British Nutrition Foundn, 1992–.

FRSA 1984. *Publications:* papers in jls of general microbiology, applied bacteriology, hygiene, etc. *Recreations:* gardening, cycling, recorded music.

GEORGE; *see* Lloyd George and Lloyd-George.

GEORGE, Rev. (Alfred) Raymond, MA, BD; Warden, John Wesley's Chapel, Bristol, 1982–95; *b* 26 Nov. 1912; *s* of A. H. and G. M. George. *Educ:* Crypt Sch., Gloucester; Balliol Coll., Oxford (1st cl. Hon. Classical Mods, 1st cl. Lit. Hum., BA 1935, MA 1938, BD 1955); Wesley House, Cambridge (1st cl. Theol Tripos, Pt I Sect. B, BA 1937, MA 1962); Marburg University. Asst Tutor, Handsworth Coll., Birmingham, 1938–40; ordained as Methodist minister, 1940; Asst Tutor, Hartley-Victoria Coll., Manchester, 1940–42; Circuit Minister, Manchester, 1942–46; Tutor, Wesley Coll., Headingley, Leeds, 1946–67, Principal, 1961–67; Associate Lectr, Leeds Univ., 1946–67; Actg Head, Theol. Dept, 1967–68; Principal, Richmond Coll., London Univ., 1968–72; Tutor, Wesley College, Bristol, 1972–81. Select Preacher, Cambridge, 1963; Member, World Council of Churches Commn on Faith and Order, 1961–75; Pres. of Methodist Conf., 1975–76; Moderator, Free Church Federal Council, 1979–80; Chm., Jt Liturgical Group, 1984–89. *Publications:* Communion with God in the New Testament, 1953; chapter in vol. I, A History of the Methodist Church in Great Britain, 1965, ed (jtly), vol. II, 1978, and contrib. chapter, ed (jtly), vol. III, 1983; jt Editor of series: Ecumenical Studies in Worship; also articles in jls. *Address:* 40 Knole Lane, Bristol BS10 6SS. *T:* Bristol (0117) 950 3698.

GEORGE, Rear Adm. Anthony Sanderson, CB 1983; FBIM, CEng, FIIM; Port Manager, Portsmouth, since 1987; *b* 8 Nov. 1928; *s* of Sandys Parker George and Winifred Marie George; *m* 1953, Mary Veronica Frances Bell; two *d. Educ:* Royal Naval Coll., Dartmouth; Royal Naval Engrg Coll., Manadon. MIMechE 1957; FBIM 1977; FIIM 1979. Sea-going appts, 1950–62; warship design, Ship Dept of MoD, 1962–64; RN Staff Coll., 1965; British High Commn, Canberra, 1966–67; MEO, HMS Hampshire, 1968–69; Staff of Flag Officer Sea Trng, 1970–71; Dep. Prodn Manager, HM Dockyard, Portsmouth, 1972–75; RCDS, 1976; CSO (Trng) to C-in-C Naval Home Comd, 1977–78; Prodn Manager, HM Dockyard, Portsmouth, 1979–81; Dir, Dockyard Prodn and Support, 1981–82; Chief Exec., Royal Dockyards, 1983–86. Chief Exec., World Energy Business, 1986. Comdr 1965, Captain 1972, Rear Adm. 1981. *Recreations:* sailing, swimming, walking, painting. *Address:* c/o National Westminster Bank, 5 East Street, Chichester, West Sussex PO19 1HH.

GEORGE, Sir Arthur (Thomas), AO 1987; Kt 1972; solicitor and company director; *b* 17 Jan. 1915; *s* of late Thomas George; *m* 1939, Renee, *d* of Anthony Freeleagus; one *d. Educ:* Sydney High Sch., NSW. Chm., Assoc. for Classical Archæology, of Sydney Univ., 1966–. Chm., Australian Soccer Fedn., 1969–88; Comr, Australian Sports Commn, 1986–; Member: Exec., FIFA, 1981–94; Organising Cttee, 1983 World Youth Championship. Chm. and Founder, The Arthur T. George Foundation Ltd, 1972. Fellow, Confedn of Australian Sport, 1985; Hon. Fellow, Univ. of Sydney, 1985. Gold Order of Merit, FIFA, 1994. Coronation Medal; Silver Jubilee Medal. Grand Commander (Keeper of the Laws), Cross of St Marks, and Gold Cross of Mount Athos, Greek Orthodox Church; Order of Phoenix (Greece). *Recreations:* interested in sport, especially Association football, etc. *Address:* 1 Little Queen's Lane, Vaucluse, NSW 2030, Australia.

GEORGE, Bruce Thomas; MP (Lab) Walsall South since Feb. 1974; *b* 1 June 1942. *Educ:* Mountain Ash Grammar Sch.; UCW Swansea; Univ. of Warwick. BA Politics Wales 1964, MA Warwick 1968. Asst Lectr in Social Studies, Glamorgan Polytechnic, 1964–66; Lectr in Politics, Manchester Polytechnic, 1968–70; Senior Lectr, Birmingham Polytechnic, 1970–74. Vis. Lectr, Univ. of Essex, 1985–86. Member: former Select Cttee on Violence in the Family; Select Cttee on Defence; North Atlantic Assembly, 1982– (Rapporteur Gen., Political Cttee). Member: RIIA; IISS; RUSI. Patron, Nat. Assoc. of Widows; Co-founder, Sec., House of Commons FC. Fellow, Parliament and Industry Trust, 1977–78. Ed., Jane's NATO Handbook. *Publications:* numerous books and articles on defence and foreign affairs. *Recreations:* Association football, snooker, student of American Indians, eating Indian food. *Address:* 42 Wood End Road, Walsall, West Midlands WS5 3BG. *T:* Walsall (01922) 27898.

GEORGE, Charles Richard; QC 1992; an Assistant Recorder, since 1994; *b* 8 June 1945; *s* of Hugh Shaw George, CIE and Joan George (*née* Stokes); *m* 1976, Joyce Tehmina Barnard; two *d. Educ:* Bradfield Coll.; Magdalen Coll., Oxford (MA 1st Cl. Hons Modern History); Corpus Christi Coll., Cambridge. Asst Master, Eton Coll., 1967–72; called to the Bar, Inner Temple, 1974; speciality, Parly, Envmtl and Admin. Law. *Publication:* The Stuarts: an age of experiment, 1973. *Recreations:* tennis, architecture, travel. *Address:* Ashgrove Farm, Ashgrove Road, Sevenoaks, Kent TN13 1SU. *T:* Sevenoaks (01732) 451875; 2 Harcourt Buildings, Temple EC4Y 9DB. *T:* 0171–353 8415.

GEORGE, Prof. Donald William, AO 1979; Vice-Chancellor and Principal, University of Newcastle, New South Wales, 1975–86; *b* 22 Nov. 1926; *s* of late H. W. George, Sydney; *m* 1950, Lorna M. Davey, Parkes, NSW; one *s* one *d. Educ:* Univ. of Sydney. BSc, BE, PhD, FTS, FIEE, FIMechE, FIEAust, FAIP. Lectr, Elec. Engrg, NSW Univ. of Technology, 1949–53; Exper. Officer, UKAEA, Harwell, 1954–55; Res. Officer, Sen. Res. Officer, AAEC, Harwell and Lucas Heights, 1956–59; Sen. Lectr, Elec. Engrg, Univ. of Sydney, 1960–66; Associate Prof., Elec. Engrg, Univ. of Sydney, 1967–68; P. N. Russell Prof. of Mech. Engrg, Univ. of Sydney, 1969–74. Chairman: Australian-American Educational Foundn, 1977–84; Australian Atomic Energy Commn, 1976–83. Trustee, Asian Inst. of Technology, 1978–. Hon. DEng Newcastle, NSW, 1986. *Publications:* numerous sci. papers and techn. reports. *Address:* Shamley Green, Glenning Road, Glenning Valley, NSW 2261, Australia. *T:* (43) 883056.

GEORGE, Edward Alan John; Governor, Bank of England, since 1993; *b* 11 Sept. 1938; *s* of Alan George and Olive Elizabeth George; *m* 1962, Clarice Vanessa Williams; one *s* two *d. Educ:* Dulwich Coll.; Emmanuel Coll., Cambridge (BAEcon 2nd Cl. (i); MA). Joined Bank of England, 1962; worked initially on East European affairs; seconded to Bank for International Settlements, 1966–69, and to International Monetary Fund as Asst to Chairman of Deputies of Committee of Twenty on Internat. Monetary Reform, 1972–74; Adviser on internat. monetary questions, 1974–77; Dep. Chief Cashier, 1977–80; Asst Dir (Gilt Edged Div.), 1980–82; Exec. Dir, 1982–90; Dep. Gov., 1990–93. Hon. DSc (Econ) Hull, 1993; Hon. DLitt Loughborough, 1994. *Recreations:* family, sailing, bridge. *Address:* Bank of England, EC2R 8AH. *T:* 0171–601 4444.

GEORGE, Henry Ridyard, CBE 1979; FInstPet; Director of Petroleum Engineering, Department of Energy, 1973–81; oil and gas exploration and production consultant, retired; *b* 14 May 1921; *s* of Charles Herbert George and Mary Ridyard; *m* 1st, 1948, Irene May Myers (*d* 1981); one *s*; 2nd, 1985, Gwen (*née* Gooderham), *widow* of Prof. E. O'Farrell Walsh. *Educ:* George Dixon's Secondary Sch., Birmingham; Univ. of Birmingham (1st Cl. Hons degree, Oil Engrg and Refining and Petroleum Technol., 1941). Served War, REME/IEME, 1941–46 (2nd Lieut, later Captain). Pet. Engr with Royal Dutch/Shell Gp, 1947–68: service in USA, Holland, Brunei, Nigeria and Venezuela in a variety of positions, incl. Chief Pet. Engr in last 3 countries; Dept of Energy, 1968–81. FRSA 1979. *Recreations:* gardening, golf. *Address:* 39 Lodge Close, Stoke D'Abernon, Cobham, Surrey KT11 2SG. *T:* Cobham (01932) 863878.

GEORGE, Hywel, CMG 1968; OBE 1963; Fellow, Churchill College, Cambridge, since 1971 (Bursar, 1972–90); *b* 10 May 1924; *s* of Rev. W. M. George and Catherine M. George; *m* 1955, Edith Pirchl; three *d. Educ:* Llanelli Gram. Sch.; UCW Aberystwyth; Pembroke Coll., Cambridge; SOAS, London. RAF, 1943–46. Cadet, Colonial Admin. Service, N Borneo, 1949–52; District Officer, 1952–58; Secretariat, 1959–62; Resident, Sabah, Malaysia, 1963–66; Administrator, 1967–69, Governor, 1969–70, St Vincent; Administrator, British Virgin Is, 1971. Panglima Darjah Kinabalu (with title of Datuk), Sabah, 1964; JMN, Malaysia, 1966. CStJ 1969. *Recreation:* walking. *Address:* Churchill College, Cambridge CB3 0DS; Tu Hwnt ir Afon, The Close, Llanfairfechan LL33 0AG.

GEORGE, Most Rev. Ian Gordon Combe; *see* Adelaide, Archbishop of.

GEORGE, Prof. Kenneth Desmond; Professor and Head of Department of Economics, since 1988, and Vice-Principal, 1993–Sept. 1996, University College of Swansea; *b* 11 Jan. 1937; *s* of Horace Avory George and Dorothy Margaret (*née* Hughes); *m* 1959, Elizabeth Vida (*née* Harries); two *s* one *d. Educ:* Ystalyfera Grammar Sch.; University Coll. of Wales, Aberstwyth (MA). Res. Asst, then Lectr in Econs, Univ. of Western Australia, 1959–63; Lectr in Econs, University Coll. of N Wales, Bangor, 1963–64; Univ. Asst Lectr, Univ. of Cambridge, 1964–66, Univ. Lectr, 1966–73; Fellow and Dir of Studies in Econs, Sidney Sussex Coll., Cambridge, 1965–73; Prof. and Head of Dept of Econs, 1973–88, and Dep. Principal, 1980–83, UC, Cardiff; Dean, Faculty of Econ. and Soc. Studies, UC Swansea, 1992–93. Vis. Prof., McMaster Univ., 1970–71. Part-time Mem., Monopolies and Mergers Commn, 1978–86. Editor, Jl of Industrial Economics, 1970–83; Mem. Adv. Bd, Antitrust Law and Econs Rev., 1988–92. *Publications:* Productivity in Distribution, 1966; Productivity and Capital Expenditure in Retailing, 1968; Industrial Organisation, 1971, 4th edn (with C. Joll and E. Lynk), 1992; (with T. S. Ward) The Structure of Industry in the EEC, 1975; (ed with C. Joll) Competition Policy in the UK and EEC, 1975; (with J. Shorey) The Allocation of Resources, 1978; (ed with L. Mainwaring) The Welsh Economy, 1988; articles in Econ. Jl, Oxford Econ. Papers, Aust. Econ. Papers, Jl Indust. Econs, Rev. of Econs and Stats, Oxford Bull., Scottish Jl Polit. Econ., and British Jl Indust. Relations. *Recreations:* walking, music, cricket. *Address:* Ein-Tŷ-Ni, 39 St Fagans Drive, St Fagans, Cardiff CF5 6EF. *T:* Cardiff (01222) 562801.

GEORGE, Llewellyn Norman Havard; a Recorder of the Crown Court, 1980–91; Consultant, V. J. G. Johns & Son, Solicitors, since 1991 (Partner, 1950–91, Senior Partner, 1972–91); *b* 13 Nov. 1925; *s* of Benjamin William George, DSO, RNR, and Annie Jane George; *m* 1950, Mary Patricia Morgan (*née* Davies); one *d. Educ:* Cardiff High Sch.; Fishguard Grammar Sch. HM Coroner, 1965–80; Recorder, Wales and Chester Circuit, 1980–. President: West Wales Law Society, 1973–74; Pembrokeshire Law Society, 1981–83; Chairman: (No 5) South Wales Law Society Legal Aid Cttee, 1979; Agricl Land Tribunal (Wales), 1990– (Dep. Chm., 1985–90). Mem., Farrand Cttee, 1984–85. *Recreations:* golf, reading, chess. *Address:* Four Winds, Tower Hill, Fishguard, Dyfed SA65 9LA. *T:* Fishguard (01348) 873894. *Clubs:* Pembrokeshire County; Newport (Pembs) Golf.

GEORGE, Patrick Herbert; artist; Emeritus Professor of Fine Art, University of London, since 1988; *b* 28 July 1923; *s* of A. H. George and N. George (*née* Richards); *m* 1st, 1953, June Griffith (marr. diss. 1980); four *d*; 2nd, 1981, Susan Ward. *Educ:* Downs Sch.; Bryanston Sch.; Edinburgh Coll. of Art; Camberwell Sch. of Art (NDD). Served War, RNVR, 1942–46. Asst, Slade Sch. of Fine Art, London, 1949–. Head, Dept of Fine Art, Nigerian Coll. of Art, Zaria, 1958–59; Slade School of Fine Art: Lectr, 1962; Reader in Fine Art, 1976; Prof. of Fine Art, Univ. of London, 1983; Slade Prof. of Fine Art, 1985–88. Works in public collections in GB and USA; one-man exhibn, Gainsborough's House, Sudbury, 1975; retrospective exhibn, Serpentine Gall., London, 1980; exhibn, Browse & Darby, 1984, 1989 and 1994; dealer, Browse & Darby. *Recreation:* make do and mend. *Address:* 33 Moreton Terrace, SW1 2NS. *T:* 0171–828 3302; Grandfathers, Great Saxham, Bury St Edmunds, Suffolk IP29 5JW. *T:* Bury St Edmunds (01284) 810997.

GEORGE, Peter John, OBE 1974; HM Diplomatic Service, retired; Counsellor and Consul General, British Embassy, Manila, 1976–79; Chargé d'Affaires *ai*, 1978; *b* 12 Dec. 1919; *s* of late Cecil John George and Mabel George; *m* 1946, Andrée Louise Pernon; one *d. Educ:* Sutton Grammar Sch., Plymouth. Served War, 1939–46: Captain. Home Civil Service, 1936; HM Diplomatic Service, 1966; First Secretary, Commercial: Colombo, 1967–70; Seoul, 1971–73 (Chargé d'Affaires *ai*, 1971 and 1972); Prague, 1973–76. *Recreations:* very rare. *Address:* St Just, Walton Park, Walton-on-Thames, Surrey KT12 3EU.

GEORGE, Rev. Raymond; *see* George, Rev. A. R.

GEORGE, Sir Richard (William), Kt 1995; Director, since 1972, Chairman and Managing Director, since 1982, Weetabix Ltd; Chairman, Whitworths Holdings Ltd, since 1987; *b* 24 April 1944; *m* 1984, Patricia Jane Ogden; two *s* one *d. Educ:* Repton Sch.; Kansas State Univ. (BSc). Joined Weetabix Ltd, 1968: Dep. Man. Dir, 1976–82. Mem. Bd, Envmt Agency, 1995–. Member: Exec. Cttee, Assoc. of Cereal Food Mfrs, 1977– (Chm., 1983–85); Council, Food and Drink Fedn (formerly Food Mfrs Fedn), 1982– (Mem., Exec. Cttee, 1984–; Dep. Pres., 1990–92; Pres., 1993–95); Exec. Cttee, Ceereal (European Breakfast Cereal Assoc.), 1992– (Pres., 1994–March 1996). Chm., Adv. Bd, Inst. of Food Res., 1993–; Mem., Food from Britain Council, 1993–. Mem., Council, Royal Warrant Holders' Assoc., 1983– (Pres., 1993). Prince's Trust: Mem., Mgt Bd, 1993–. Mem., Northants Cttee, 1985–94 (Chm., 1985–88, 1991–94); Vice-Chm., Northants Prince's Youth Business Trust, 1986–. FIGD 1983; CIMgt (CBIM 1985); FInstD 1981; FRSA 1991. Freeman, GAPAN, 1982. *Recreations:* family, golf. *Address:* Weetabix Ltd, Burton Latimer, Kettering, Northants NN15 5JR. *T:* Kettering (01536) 722181. *Clubs:* Saints and Sinners; Royal and Ancient (St Andrews).

GEORGE, Timothy John Burr, CMG 1991; HM Diplomatic Service; Ambassador to Nepal, 1990–95; *b* 14 July 1937; *s* of late Brig. J. B. George, late RAMC and M. Brenda George (*née* Harrison); *m* 1962, Richenda Mary, *d* of late Alan Reed, FRIBA and of Ann Reed (*née* Rowntree); one *s* two *d. Educ:* Aldenham Sch.; Christ's Coll., Cambridge (BA). National Service, 2nd Lieut RA, 1956–58; Cambridge Univ., 1958. FCO, 1961; 3rd Secretary: Hong Kong, 1962; Peking, 1963; 2nd, later 1st Sec., FCO, 1966; 1st Sec. (Economic), New Delhi, 1969; Asst Political Adviser, Hong Kong, 1972; Asst European Integration Dept (Internal), FCO, 1974; Counsellor and Head of Chancery, Peking, 1978–80; Res. Associate, IISS, 1980–81; Counsellor and Hd of Chancery, UK Perm. Delegn to OECD, 1982–86; Hd, Republic of Ireland Dept, FCO, 1986–90. *Publication:* (jtly) Security in Southern Asia, 1984. *Address:* c/o Foreign and Commonwealth Office, SW1A 2AH; Martlets, Ogbourne St George, Marlborough, Wilts SN8 1SL. *T:* Ogbourne St George (01672) 841278.

GEORGE, Prof. William David, FRCS; Professor of Surgery, University of Glasgow, since 1981; *b* 22 March 1943; *s* of William Abel George and Peggy Eileen George; *m* 1st,

1967, Helen Marie (*née* Moran) (*d* 1986); one *s* three *d*; 2nd, 1990, Pauline (*née* Mooney). *Educ:* Reading Bluecoat Sch.; Henley Grammar Sch.; Univ. of London (MB, BS 1966; MS 1977). FRCS 1970. Jun. surgical jobs, 1966–71; Registrar in Surgery, Royal Postgrad. Med. Sch., 1971–73; Lectr in Surg., Univ. of Manchester, 1973–77; Sen. Lectr in Surg., Univ. of Liverpool, 1977–81. *Publications:* articles in BMJ, Lancet, British Jl of Surg. *Recreations:* veteran rowing, fishing, squash. *Address:* 21 Kingsborough Gardens, Glasgow G12 9NH. *T:* 0141–339 9546. *Club:* Clyde Amateur Rowing (Glasgow).

GEORGES, Rt. Hon. (Philip) Telford; PC 1986; Law Reform Commissioner, Bahamas, since 1989; Judge of the Court of Appeal: Cayman Islands, since 1984; Belize, 1975–81 and since 1993; *b* Dominica, 5 Jan. 1923; *s* of John Georges and Milutine Cox; *m* 1954, Grace Glasgow (marr. diss.); *m* 1981, Joyce Cole. *Educ:* Dominica Grammar Sch.; Toronto Univ. (BA). Called to the Bar, 1949; in private practice, Trinidad and Tobago, 1949–62; Judge of the High Court, Trinidad and Tobago, 1962–74; on secondment as Chief Justice of Tanzania, 1965–71; acting Justice of Appeal, Trinidad and Tobago, 1972; Judge of the Courts of Appeal, Bahamas, Turks and Caicos Is, 1975–81, of Bermuda, 1975–81 and 1990–94; Judge of the Supreme Court, 1981–83, Chief Justice, 1983, Zimbabwe; Chief Justice of the Bahamas, 1984–89. Prof. of Law, 1974–81, and Dean of the Faculty of Law, 1977–79, Univ. of WI at Cave Hill. Vice-Chm., Trinidad and Tobago Constitutional Reform Commn, 1971–74; Chm., Crime Commn, Bermuda, 1977–78; Mem., Admin. Tribunal, Inter-American Develt Bank, 1993. Mem., Judicial Cttee, OAS, 1992–95. Hon. LLD: Toronto; Dar-es-Salaam; West Indies, 1985; Dalhousie, 1995. Order of Caribbean Community, 1994. *Recreation:* walking. *Address:* Kilimani, 5A The Mount, St George, Barbados.

GERAINT, Baron *cr* 1992 (Life Peer), of Ponterwyd in the County of Dyfed; **Geraint Wyn Howells;** farmer; *b* 15 April 1925; *s* of David John Howells and Mary Blodwen Howells; *m* 1957, Mary Olwen Hughes Griffiths; two *d*. *Educ:* Ponterwyd Primary Sch.; Ardwyn Grammar School. MP Cardigan, Feb. 1974–1983, Ceredigion and Pembroke North, 1983–92 (L 1983–88, Lib Dem 1988–92). Former Mem., British Wool Marketing Bd (Vice-Chm., 1971–83); Chm., Wool Producers of Wales Ltd, 1977–87. Sec., Ponterwyd Eisteddfod. *Recreations:* walking, sport. *Address:* Glennydd, Ponterwyd, Ceredigion, Dyfed SY23 3LB. *T:* Ponterwyd (0197085) 258.

GERARD, family name of **Baron Gerard.**

GERARD, 5th Baron *cr* 1876; **Anthony Robert Hugo Gerard;** Bt 1611; *b* 3 Dec. 1949; *er s* of Maj. Rupert Charles Frederick Gerard, MBE (*g g s* of 1st Baron), and of Huguette Reiss-Brian; *S* cousin, 1992; *m* 1976, Kathleen, *e d* of Dr Bernard Ryan, New York; two *s*. *Educ:* Harvard. *Heir:* *s* Hon. Rupert Bernard Charles Gerard, *b* 17 Dec. 1981. *Address:* PO Box 2308, East Hampton, NY 11937, USA.

GERARD, Ronald, OBE 1987; *b* 30 Oct. 1925; *s* of Samuel and Caroline Gerard; *m* 1952, Patricia Krieger; one *s* one *d*. *Educ:* Regent Street Polytechnic; College of Estate Management. FSVA; FRSH. Royal Engineers, 1943–47, Italy and Egypt; articled to a City Chartered Surveyor, 1947–50; Principal, R. P. Gerard & Co., Surveyors and Valuers, 1952–59; Jt Man. Dir, 1959–87, Chm., 1982–87, London & Provincial Shop Centres Plc (created regional HQ buildings for many well-known public cos incl. Data General, Midland Bank, National Westminster Bank, Thomas Tilling, EMI, Rank Hovis, Honeywell, Calor Gas, Black & Decker, Chubb, Yellow Pages, Fluor plc etc.). Chm., Ronald Gerard Charitable Trust, 1983–. President: London Community Cricket Assoc., 1992–94; London Cricket Coll., 1992–94; Middlesex Cricket Union, 1992–95; Middlesex Colts Assoc., 1995–; London Community Trust, 1992–94; Vice-Pres., English Schools Cricket Assoc., 1981–; Mem., Middlesex CCC Cttee, 1972– (Chm., Membership Cttee, 1985–89); Life Vice-Pres., Middlesex CCC, 1992; Trustee, Middlesex CCC Centenary Youth Trust, 1984–94; Mem. Council, Lord's Taverners, 1984–90. Patron, Brooklands Club, 1991. Liveryman, Glass Sellers' Co., 1990; Freeman, City of London, 1990. KStJ 1992. FRSA 1985. Granted Arms, 1989. *Clubs:* Athenæum, Arts, Carlton, MCC.

GERARD-PEARSE, Rear-Adm. John Roger Southey, CB 1979; Group Personnel Manager, Jardine Matheson Co. Ltd, Hong Kong, 1980–84; *b* 10 May 1924; *s* of Dr Gerard-Pearse; *m* 1955, Barbara Jean Mercer; two *s* two *d*. *Educ:* Clifton College. Joined RN, 1943; comd HM Ships Tumult, Grafton, Defender, Fearless and Ark Royal; Flag Officer, Sea Training, 1975–76; Asst Chief, Naval Staff (Ops), 1977–79. *Recreations:* sailing, carpentry. *Address:* Enbrook, 170 Offham Road, West Malling, Kent ME19 6RF. *T:* West Malling (01732) 842375.

GERE, Richard; actor; *b* 31 Aug. 1949; *m* 1991, Cindy Crawford. *Educ:* Univ. of Massachusetts. Played trumpet, piano, guitar and bass and composed music with various gps; stage performances: with Provincetown Playhouse, Seattle Rep. Theatre; Richard Farina, Long Time Coming and Long Time Gone, Back Bog Beat Bait, off-Broadway; Soon, Habeus Corpus and Grease on Broadway; A Midsummer Night's Dream, Lincoln Center; Taming of the Shrew, Young Vic, London; Bent, on Broadway (Theatre World Award); *films:* Report to the Commissioner, 1975; Baby Blue Marine, 1976; Looking for Mr Goodbar, 1977; Days of Heaven, 1978; Blood Brothers, 1978; Yanks, 1979; American Gigolo, 1979; An Officer and a Gentleman, 1982; Breathless, 1983; Beyond the Limit, 1983; The Cotton Club, 1984; King David, 1985; Power, 1986; No Mercy, 1986; Miles From Home, 1989; Pretty Woman, 1990; Internal Affairs, 1990; Rhapsody in August, 1991; Final Analysis, 1992; Mr Jones, 1993; Sommersby, 1993; And the Band Played On, 1994; Intersection, 1994; First Knight, 1995. Founding Chm. and Pres., Tibet Hse, NY. *Address:* c/o ICM, 40 West 57th Street, New York, NY 10019, USA.

GERHARD, Dr Derek James, (known as **Jeremy**), CB 1986; Partner, The Dowding Partnership (Planning and Problem Solving for Business), since 1993; Deputy Master and Comptroller, Royal Mint, 1977–88, retired; *b* 16 Dec. 1927; *s* of late F. J. Gerhard, Banstead; *m* 1952, Dr Sheila Cooper, *d* of late Dr G. K. Cooper; three *s* two *d*. *Educ:* Highgate Sch.; Fitzwilliam Coll., Cambridge (MA; Hon. Fellow 1986); Reading Univ. (PhD). Served 3rd Carabiniers (Prince of Wales DG), 1945–48. Dept of Scientific Adviser, Air Ministry, 1952–57; transf. to DSIR, 1957; Sec., British Commonwealth Scientific Cttee, 1959–60; Asst Sci. Attaché, British Embassy, Washington, 1961–64; transf. to Admin. CS, 1964; Board of Trade, latterly leader UK Delgn to Internat. Consultative Shipping Gp, 1964–69; Head of Management Services, BoT, 1969–71; loaned to CSD (Personnel Management), 1971–73; Dept of Industry, leader UK Delgn to Internat. Tin Council, 1973–75; Air Div., DoI, 1975–77. Pres., Mint Dir's Conf., 1982–84. Mem., Welsh Council, CBI, 1984–87. Hon. Treas., Council of Churches for Britain and Ireland, 1993–. *Publications:* various scientific papers. *Recreations:* gardening, woodwork. *Address:* Little Dowding, Dorking Road, Walton Heath, Surrey KT20 7TJ. *T:* Tadworth (01737) 813045.

GERKEN, Ian, LVO 1992; HM Diplomatic Service; Ambassador to El Salvador, since 1995; *b* 1 Dec. 1943; *s* of late Alfred Gerken and Esther Mary (*née* Chesworth); *m* 1976, Susana Drucker; two *s*, and one step *d*. *Educ:* Liverpool Collegiate. Entered Foreign Office, 1962: served in Budepest, 1965; Buenos Aires, 1966–68; FCO, 1968–71; Caracas, 1971–75; FCO, 1975–79; Lima, 1979–84; UN Gen. Assembly, 1984; FCO, 1985–88; Dep. High Comr, Valletta, 1988–92; Counsellor and Dep. Head, Perm. Under Sec's Dept, FCO, 1992–95. *Address:* c/o Foreign and Commonwealth Office, King Charles Street, SW1A 2AH.

GERKEN, Vice-Adm. Sir Robert William Frank, KCB 1986; CBE 1975; DL; Royal Navy, retired 1987; Chairman, Plymouth Development Corporation, since 1993; *b* 11 June 1932; *s* of Francis Sydney and Gladys Gerken; *m* 1st, 1966, Christine Stephenson (*d* 1981); two *d*; 2nd, 1983, Mrs Ann Fermor. *Educ:* Chigwell Sch.; Royal Naval Coll., Dartmouth. Sea service as Lieut and Lt-Comdr, 1953–66; RN Staff Course, 1967; in command HMS Yarmouth, 1968–69; Commander Sea Training, 1970–71; Naval Staff, 1972–73; in command: Sixth Frigate Sqdn, 1974–75; HMS Raleigh, 1976–77; Captain of the Fleet, 1978–81; Flag Officer Second Flotilla, 1981–83; Dir Gen., Naval Manpower and Trng, 1983–85; Flag Officer Plymouth, Port Admiral Devonport, Comdr Central Sub Area Eastern Atlantic, Comdr Plymouth Sub Area Channel, 1985–87. Dir, Corps of Commissionaires, 1988–; Chm., China Fleet Club (UK) Charitable Trust, 1987–. President: British Korean Veterans' Assoc. (Plymouth Br.); Plymouth Lifeboat, RNLI, 1988–. Governor, Chigwell Sch., 1987–. FRSA 1993. DL Devon, 1995. Hon. DSc Plymouth, 1993. *Recreations:* hearth and boat maintenance. *Address:* 22 Custom House Lane, Mill Bay, Plymouth PL1 3TG. *T:* Plymouth (01752) 665104. *Club:* Royal Western Yacht (Cdre, 1993).

GEROSA, Peter Norman; Secretary, Tree Council, 1983–91; *b* 1 Nov. 1928; *s* of late Enrico Cecil and Olive Doris Gerosa; *m* 1955, Dorothy Eleanor Griffin; two *d*. *Educ:* Whitgift Sch.; London Univ. (Birkbeck). BA (Hons) 1st Cl., Classics. Civil Service, 1945–82; Foreign Office, 1945; Home Office, 1949; HM Customs and Excise, 1953; Min. of Transport, 1966; DoE, 1970; Under Secretary: DoE, 1972; Dept of Transport, 1977; Dir of Rural Affairs, DoE, 1981–82. *Recreations:* singing, gardening, walking. *Address:* 17 Friths Drive, Reigate, Surrey RH2 0DS. *T:* Reigate (01737) 243771.

GERRARD, Prof. Alfred Horace; Professor of Sculpture in University of London at University College Slade School of Fine Art, 1948–68, now Emeritus; *b* 7 May 1899; *m* 1933, Katherine Leigh-Pemberton (*d* 1970); *m* 1972, Nancy Sinclair. *Educ:* Hartford County Council Sch.; Manchester Sch. of Art; Slade Sch. of Fine Art, University Coll., London. Head of Dept of Sculpture, Slade Sch., UCL, 1925–48. Served European War, 1914–18, Cameron Highlanders, 1916–17; RFC, 1917–19; War of 1939–45, Staff Captain, War Office, attached Royal Engineers, 1939–43; war artist, 1944–45; temp. Head, Slade Sch. of Fine Art, 1948–49. RBS Silver Medal, 1960. Fellow, University Coll. London, 1969. *Recreation:* gardening. *Address:* Dairy House, Leyswood, Groombridge, Tunbridge Wells, Kent TN3 9PH. *T:* Langton (01892) 864268.

GERRARD, Ven. David Keith Robin; Archdeacon of Wandsworth, since 1989; *b* 15 June 1939; *s* of Eric Henry and Doris Jane Gerrard; *m* 1963, Jennifer Mary Hartley; two *s* two *d*. *Educ:* Royal Grammar School, Guildford; St Edmund Hall, Oxford (BA); Lincoln Theol Coll. Curate: St Olave, Woodberry Down, N16, 1963–66; St Mary, Primrose Hill, NW3, 1966–69; Vicar: St Paul, Lorrimore Square, SE17, 1969–79; St Andrew and St Mark, Surbiton, Surrey, 1979–89; RD of Kingston upon Thames, 1983–88. *Publication:* (co-author) Urban Ghetto, 1976. *Recreations:* embroidery, Proust, Yorkshire, statistics. *Address:* 68 North Side, Wandsworth Common, SW18 2QX. *T:* 0181–874 5766.

GERRARD, John Henry, CBE 1981 (OBE 1972); MC 1944; QPM 1975; Assistant Commissioner, Metropolitan Police, 1978–81; *b* 25 Nov. 1920; *s* of Archie Reginald and Evelyn Gerrard; *m* 1943, Gladys Hefford; two *s*. *Educ:* Cordwainers Technical Coll. Served War, Army, 1939–46: Iceland, 1940–42; commissioned 1st Mddx Regt, 1943; NW Europe, 1944–46 (Captain). Constable to Commander, 1946–65; Comdr, West End Central, 1965–68; Comdr 'A' Dept (Public Order/Operations), 1968–70; Deputy Assistant Commissioner 'A' (Operations), 1970–74; No 1 Area, 1974–78. Chm., Met. Police Museums Adv. Bd, 1975–81. Freeman, City of London, 1978. KStJ 1986; Comr, London Dist, SJAB, 1983–88. *Recreations:* philately, history.

GERRARD, Neil Francis; MP (Lab) Walthamstow, since 1992; *b* 3 July 1942; *m* 1968, Marian Fitzgerald (marr. diss. 1983); two *s*. *Educ:* Manchester Grammar Sch.; Wadham Coll., Oxford (BA Hons); Chelsea Coll., London (MEd). Teacher, Queen Elizabeth's Sch., Barnet, 1965–68; Lectr in Computing, Hackney Coll., 1968–92. Mem. (Lab) Waltham Forest BC, 1973–90 (Leader of Council, 1986–90). Contested (Lab) Chingford, 1979. Member: Bd, Pioneer Theatres; SHAC. *Address:* House of Commons, SW1A 0AA.

GERRARD, Peter Noël, CBE 1991; General Counsel, London Stock Exchange, 1991–94; *b* 19 May 1930; *oc* of Sir Denis Gerrard and of Hilda Goodwin (*née* Jones, who *m* 2nd, Sir Joseph Cantley, OBE); *m* 1957, Prudence Lipson-Ward; one *s* two *d*. *Educ:* Rugby; Christ Church, Oxford (MA). 2nd Lieut, XII Royal Lancers, Malaya, 1953–54. Solicitor, 1959; Partner, Lovell, White & King, 1960, Sen. Partner, 1980–88; Sen. Partner, Lovell White Durrant, 1988–91. Member: Bd of Banking Supervision, 1990–; City Capital Markets Cttee, 1974–91. Member: Council, Law Society, 1972–82; Bd, Inst. of Advanced Legal Studies, 1985–; Council, St George's Hosp. Med. Sch., 1982–94. *Recreations:* music, walking, week-end gardening. *Address:* 40 Canonbury Park North, N1 2JT. *T:* 0171–354 0481; Pightle Cottage, Ashdon, Saffron Walden, Essex CB10 2HG. *T:* Ashdon (01799) 584374. *Clubs:* Athenæum, City of London.

GERRARD, Ronald Tilbrook, FEng, FICE, FIWEM; Senior Partner, Binnie & Partners, Consulting Engineers, 1974–83, retired; *b* 23 April 1918; *s* of Henry Thomas Gerrard and Edith Elizabeth Tilbrook; *m* 1950, Cecilia Margaret Bremner; three *s* one *d*. *Educ:* Imperial Coll. of Science and Technology, Univ. of London. BSc(Eng). FCGI; FEng 1979; FICE 1957; FIWE 1965; MEIC. Served War, RE, 1939–45. Resident Engr, sea defence and hydro-electric works, 1947–50; Asst Engr, design of hydro-power schemes in Scotland and Canada, 1951–54; Binnie & Partners: Sen. Engr, 1954; Partner, 1959; resp. for hydro-power, water supply, river engrg, coast protection and indust. works in UK and overseas. Chm., Assoc. of Cons. Engrs, 1969–70; Mem. Council, ICE, 1974–77. Telford Silver Medal, ICE, 1968. *Publications:* (jtly) 4 papers to ICE. *Address:* 6 Ashdown Road, Epsom, Surrey KT17 3PL. *T:* Epsom (01372) 724834. *Club:* Athenæum.

GERRARD-WRIGHT, Maj.-Gen. Richard Eustace John, CB 1985; CBE 1977 (OBE 1971; MBE 1963); DL; Director, Territorial Army and Cadets, 1982–85, retired; *b* 9 May 1930; *s* of Rev. R. L. Gerrard-Wright; *m* 1960, Susan Kathleen Young; two *s* one *d* (and one *d* decd). *Educ:* Christ's Hospital; RMA, Sandhurst. Commnd Royal Lincolnshire Regt, 1949; served Egypt, Germany and UK, 1950–55; Malaya, 1955–58 (despatches, 1958); Instructor, RMA, Sandhurst, 1958–62 (2nd E Anglian Regt, 1960); Staff Coll., India, 1962–63; served Kenya, Aden, Malta, Malaya, 1963–70 (Royal Anglian Regt, 1964); Bn Comdr, UK, Germany, NI, 1970–73 (despatches 1973); Comdr, 39 Inf. Bde, Belfast, 1975–77; Nat. Defence Coll., Canada, 1977–78; Chief of Staff, 1 (Br) Corps, 1978–79; GOC Eastern District, 1980–82. Dep. Col, Royal Anglian Regt, 1975–80; Col Comdt, Queen's Div., 1981–84. Chief Exec. and Sec., Hurlingham Club, 1985–87. DL Cambs, 1993. *Address:* c/o Lloyds Bank, Minster Place, Ely, Cambs. *Clubs:* MCC; Free Foresters.

GERSHEVITCH, Dr Ilya, FBA 1967; Fellow of Jesus College, Cambridge, since 1962; Reader in Iranian Studies, University of Cambridge, 1965–82, now Emeritus; *b* Zürich, 24 Oct. 1914; *o s* of Arkadi and Mila Gershevitch, Smolensk, Russia; *m* 1951, Lisbeth, *d* of Josef Syfrig, Lucerne; one *d*. *Educ:* Swiss schools at Locarno and Lugano; Univ. of Rome (classics); Univ. of London (Oriental studies). Dottore in Lettere, Univ. of Rome, 1937; PhD, Univ. of London, 1943; MA Cantab 1948. Monitored foreign broadcasts, London, 1942–47; Lecturer in Iranian Studies, Univ. of Cambridge, 1948–65. First European to penetrate into certain areas of Western Makran (dialect field-work), 1956; Vis. Prof. at Columbia Univ., New York, 1960–61 and 1965–66; Univ. Exchange Visitor, USSR, 1965; Ratanbai Katrak Lecturer, Univ. of Oxford, 1968. Pres., Philological Soc., 1980–84. Mem., Danish Acad., 1982; Foreign Fellow: Accademia dei Lincei, Rome, 1987; Acad. of Scis of Russian Fedn, Moscow, 1992. Hon. PhD Berne, 1971. *Publications:* A Grammar of Manichean Sogdian, 1954; The Avestan Hymn to Mithra, 1959; Philologia Iranica, 1985; articles in specialist jls, encyclopaedias and collective books. *Recreation:* music. *Address:* Jesus College, Cambridge CB5 8BL. *T:* Cambridge (01223) 314552; 54 Owlstone Road, Cambridge CB3 9JH. *T:* Cambridge (01223) 357996.

GERSON, John Henry Cary; HM Diplomatic Service; Counsellor, Foreign and Commonwealth Office, since 1992; *b* 25 April 1945; *s* of late Henry and of Benedicta Joan Gerson; *m* 1968, Mary Alison, *d* of late George Ewart Evans; one *s* one *d*. *Educ:* Bradfield; King's Coll., Cambridge (MA). Third Sec., FCO, 1968; language student, Hong Kong, 1969–71; Second Secretary: Singapore, 1971–73; FCO, 1973–74; First Sec. and HM Consul, Peking, 1974–77; First Sec., FCO, 1978; on loan to Home CS, 1978–79; First Sec., later Counsellor, FCO, 1979–87; Counsellor, Hong Kong, 1987–92; Vis. Fellow, Princeton Univ., 1992. Associate Mem., Centre for the Study of Socialist Legal Systems, London Univ., 1986–. *Recreations:* ornithology, sinology, literature. *Address:* c/o Foreign and Commonwealth Office, King Charles Street, SW1A 2AH. *Club:* Athenæum.

GERSTENBERG, Frank Eric, MA; Principal, George Watson's College, Edinburgh, since 1985; *b* 23 Feb. 1941; *s* of late Eric Gustav Gerstenberg and Janie Willis Gerstenberg; *m* 1966, Valerie Myra (*née* MacLellan); one *s* twin *d*. *Educ:* Trinity College, Glenalmond; Clare College, Cambridge (MA); Inst. of Education, Univ. of London (PGCE). Asst History Teacher, Kelly Coll., Tavistock, 1963–67; Housemaster and Head of History, Millfield School, 1967–74; Headmaster, Oswestry School, 1974–85. FRSA 1994. *Recreations:* skiing, golf. *Address:* 27 Merchiston Gardens, Edinburgh EH10 5DD. *T:* 0131–337 6880. *Clubs:* Public Schools; New (Edinburgh).

GERSTENBERG, Richard Charles; *b* Little Falls, NY, 24 Nov. 1909; *s* of Richard Paul Gerstenberg and Mary Julia Booth; *m* 1934, Evelyn Josephine Hitchingham; one *s* one *d*. *Educ:* Univ. of Michigan (AB). General Motors Corporation: Asst Comptroller, 1949–55; Treasurer, 1956–60; Vice-Pres., in charge of financial staff, 1960–67; Exec. Vice-Pres. in charge of Finance, 1967–70; Vice-Chm. Bd and Chm. Finance Cttee, 1970–72; Chm., 1972–74; a Director, 1967–79. *Clubs:* Bloomfield Hills Country; Paradise Valley Country (Scottsdale, Arizona); Mohawk (NY) Fish and Game.

GERSTNER, Louis Vincent, Jr; Chairman and Chief Executive Officer, IBM, since 1993; *b* NY, 1 March 1942. *Educ:* Dartmouth Coll. (BA Engrg 1963); Harvard Business Sch. (MBA 1965). Dir, McKinsey & Co, Inc., 1965–78; Pres., American Express Co., 1978–89; Chm. and Chief Exec. Officer, RJR Nabisco Inc., 1989–93. Director: NY Times Co.; Bristol-Meyers Squibb Co.; RJR Nabisco Inc. Dir, New American Schs Develt Corp. Dir, Japan Soc., 1992–. *Address:* c/o IBM, Old Orchard Road, Armonk, NY 10504, USA.

GERTYCH, Prof. Zbigniew; Professor, Botanical Garden, Polish Academy of Sciences, Warsaw, since 1990; *b* 26 Oct. 1922; *s* of Tadeusz Gertych and Maria Gertych (*née* Marecka); *m* 1st, 1945, Roza (*née* Skrochowska) (decd); one *s* two *d*; 2nd, 1970, Zofia (*née* Dobrzanska). *Educ:* Uniw. Jagiellonski, Krakow. MA eng 1946, DAgric 1950. Joined Army as volunteer and participated in September campaign, 1939; during Nazi occupation took part in clandestine activities, was detained in camps and Gestapo prisons; after escape served Home Army (AK) to 1945 (wounded in partisan combat). Polish Academy of Sciences (PAN), 1946–83: Head of Pomology Dept, Dendrology Research Centre, Kórnik, 1947–53; Dir Exp. Fruit Growing Research Centre, Brzeźna, 1953–64; Dir, Research Centre, Agric. and Forestry Econ. Science, 1964–78; Vice-Dir and Dir, Vegetable Growing Inst., Skierniewice, 1964–82; Vice-Sec. and Sec., Agric. and Forestry Scis Dept, 1964–87; First Dep. Gen. Sec., 1981–83; Mem., PAN, 1976; Mem., Presidium of PAN, 1978–86; Asst Prof., 1963, Associate Prof., 1969, Prof., 1979, Jagiellonian Univ., Cracow and Polish Acad. of Scis. MP, Nowy Sacz, 1957–89; Dep. Speaker, Sejm, 1982–85 (Chm., Budget Commn, Social and Economic Council and Main Cttee, Nat. Action for School Assistance); Dep. Chm., Council of Ministers, 1985–87; Ambassador of Poland to the Court of St James's and to Republic of Ireland, 1987–90. Pres., Homo et Planta Foundn, 1991–; Mem., Supreme Council and Exec. Cttee, Internat. Soc. of Hort. Scis. Hon. Dr, Acad. of Agric. Scis, Berlin, 1974; DAgr *hc* Szczecin Univ., 1989. Cross of Valour, 1944; Comdr's Cross, Order of Polonia Restituta, 1984; other Polish decorations; numerous foreign honours and awards. *Publications:* contribs to sci. jls. *Recreations:* music, art, travels. *Address:* Botanical Garden, Polish Academy of Sciences, vl. Prawdziwka 2, POB 84, 02–973 Warsaw 34, Poland. *Club:* Rotary.

GERVAIS, Most Rev. Marcel; *see* Ottawa, Archbishop of (RC).

GERVIS MEYRICK; *see* Meyrick.

GERY, Sir Robert Lucian W.; *see* Wade-Gery.

GESTETNER, David; President, Gestetner Holdings PLC, since 1987; *b* 1 June 1937; *s* of Sigmund and Henny Gestetner; *m* 1961, Alice Floretta Sebag-Montefiore; one *s* three *d*. *Educ:* Midhurst Grammar Sch.; Bryanston Sch.; University Coll., Oxford (MA). Gestetner Holdings: Jt Chm., 1972–86; Man. Dir, 1982–86; Jt Pres., 1986–87. Dir, Alphameric PLC, 1994. *Recreation:* sailing. *Clubs:* Reform, MCC.
See also J. Gestetner.

GESTETNER, Jonathan; Chairman, Marlborough Rare Books Ltd, since 1990; *b* 11 March 1940; *s* of Sigmund and Henny Gestetner; *m* 1965, Jacqueline Margaret Strasmore; two *s* one *d*. *Educ:* Bryanston Sch.; Massachusetts Institute of Technology (BScMechEngrg). Joined Gestetner Ltd, 1962; Jt Chm., 1972–87, and Jt Pres., 1987–88, Gestetner Hldgs PLC; Director: DRS, USA, 1987–89; Klein Associates, USA, 1987–90. Member: Executive Council, Engineering Employers' London Assoc., 1972–77 (Vice-Pres., 1975–77); Maplin Development Authority, 1973–74; SSRC, 1979–82; Dir, Centre for Policy Studies. Mem., Educnl Council, MIT, 1973–. *Recreation:* the visual arts. *Address:* 7 Oakhill Avenue, NW3 7RD. *T:* 0171–435 0905. *Clubs:* Brooks's, MCC.
See also David Gestetner.

GETHIN, Sir Richard (Joseph St Lawrence), 10th Bt *cr* 1665, of Gethinsgrott, Cork; engineer; *b* 29 Sept. 1949; *s* of Sir Richard Patrick St Lawrence Gethin, 9th Bt and of Fara, *y d* of late J. H. Bartlett; *S* father, 1988; *m* 1974, Jacqueline Torfrida, *d* of Comdr David Cox; three *d*. *Educ:* The Oratory School; RMA Sandhurst; RMCS Shrivenham; Cranfield Inst. of Technology (BSc(Eng), MSc). Joined first unit, 1971; served in Germany and UK. *Recreations:* gardening, tennis, woodwork. *Heir: cousin* Antony Michael Gethin [*b* 10 Jan. 1939; *m* 1965, Vanse, *d* of late Col C. D. Barlow, OBE, KSLI; two *s* one *d*]. *Address:* Trotts Ash, Sole Street, Cobham, Kent DA12 3AY.

GETHING, Air Commodore Richard Templeton, CB 1960; OBE 1945; AFC 1939; *b* 11 Aug. 1911; *s* of George A. Gething, Wilmslow, Cheshire; *m* 1940, Margaret Helen, *d* of late Sir Herbert Gepp, Melbourne, Australia; one *s* one *d*. *Educ:* Malvern; Sydney Sussex Coll., Cambridge. Joined RAF, 1933; navigator and co-pilot of Vickers Wellesley aircraft which set world record for distance in straight line (flying Ismailia, Egypt to Darwin, Australia non-stop), 1938. Served War of 1939–45: Canada; UK; India; Burma. Actg Group Capt., 1943; Group Capt., 1950; Actg Air Commodore, 1956; Dir Operations, Maritime Navigation and Air Traffic, Air Ministry, 1956–60, retired. FRIN (FIN 1956). *Recreation:* gliding. *Address:* Garden Hill, Kangaroo Ground, Victoria 3097, Australia. *Club:* Royal Air Force.

GETTY, Hon. Donald Ross; PC (Can.) 1985; Premier of Alberta, 1985–93; MLA Edmonton Whitemud, 1967–79, 1985–93; *b* 30 Aug. 1933; *s* of Charles Ross Getty and Beatrice Lillian Getty; *m* 1955, Margaret Inez Mitchell; four *s*. *Educ:* Univ. of Western Ontario (Business Administration). MLA Alberta 1967; Minister of Federal and Intergovernmental Affairs, 1971; Minister of Energy and Natural Resources, 1975; resigned 1979; re-elected MLA, 1985. Joined Imperial Oil, 1955; Midwestern Industrial Gas, 1961; formed Baldonnel Oil & Gas, 1964 (Pres. and Man. Dir); Partner, Doherty Roadhouse & McCuaig, 1967; Pres., D. Getty Investments, 1979; Chm., Ipsco, 1981–85; former Chm. and Chief Exec., Nortek Energy Corp.; director of other cos. Played quarterback for Edmonton Eskimos Canadian Football team for 10 years. *Recreations:* horse racing, golf, hunting.

GETTY, J(ohn) Paul, Hon. KBE 1986; philanthropist; *b* 7 Sept, 1932; *s* of J. Paul Getty and Ann (*née* Rork); *m* 1st, 1956, Gail (marr. diss. 1966), *d* of Judge Harris; two *s* two *d*; 2nd, 1966, Talitha (*d* 1971), *d* of William Pol; one *s*; 3rd, 1994, Victoria, *d* of late Comdr Gerald Holdsworth. Worked in Getty Oil, Italia, 1959–70. *Recreations:* watching cricket and old movies, bibliophily. *Address:* PO Box 8799, SW1A 1ZD. *Clubs:* Pratt's, MCC.

GHALE, Subedar Gaje; *see* Gaje Ghale.

GHALI, Boutros B.; *see* Boutros-Ghali.

GHERAIEB, Abdelkrim; Ambassador of Algeria to the Court of St James's, 1989–91; *b* 30 July 1935; *m* Fizia Gheraieb; one *s* three *d*. *Educ:* Univ. of Algiers (LèsL); Inst. of Pol Scis, Univ. of Algiers (Diploma). Hd of Legal Services, First Nat. Assembly, 1962–65; Chm., Assoc. of Algerians in Europe, 1965–79; Ambassador to: Teheran, 1979–82; Peking, 1982–84; Beirut, 1984–86; Saudi Arabia, 1986–89. Member: Assemblée Nationale Populaire, 1977; (nominated) Central Cttee, FLN Party, 1979. Médaille de la Résistance, Algerian war of liberation, 1982. Kt, Order of Cedar (Lebanon), 1986; Order of HM King Abdul Aziz (Saudi Arabia), 1989. *Address:* c/o Ministry of Foreign Affairs, 6 rue 16n-Batran, el-Mouradia, Algiers, Algeria.

GHIZ, Joseph Atallah; QC (Can) 1984; Dean, Faculty of Law, Dalhousie University, since 1993; *b* 27 Jan. 1945; *s* of Atallah J. and Marguerite Farah (McKarris); *m* 1972, Rose Ellen, *d* of Douglas and Elizabeth McGowan; one *s* one *d*. *Educ:* Prince of Wales College; Dalhousie Univ. (BCom 1966, LLB 1969). LLM Harvard, 1981. Senior Partner, Scales, Ghiz, Jenkins & McQuaid, 1970–81; Crown Prosecutor, Queen's Co., 1970–72; Federal Narcotics Drug Prosecutor, 1970–79; private practice, 1981–86; Counsel to Commn of Inquiry into Charlottetown Police Force, 1977. MLA (L) 6th Queens, 1982–93; Pres., Liberal Party of PEI, 1977–78, Leader, 1981–93; Premier, PEI, 1986–93. Chm., Bd of Advrs, Andersen Consulting, Canada, 1993–; Dir, Guardian Insce Co. of Canada, 1994–. Lectr, Univ. of Prince Edward Island, 1970–73. Mem., Canadian Council of Multiculturalism, 1972–75 (Past Regional Chm.); Dir, Canadian Civil Liberties Assoc., 1994–. Member: Bd of Dirs, Canada's Nat. Hist. Soc., 1994–; Bd of Dirs, Canadian Liver Foundn, 1994–. Trustee, McGill Inst. for Study of Canada, 1993–. Hon. LLD Univ. of Prince Edward Island, 1987. *Publications:* Towards a New Canada (jtly), 1978; Constitutional Impasse Over Oil and Gas, 1981. *Address:* Faculty of Law, Dalhousie University, Halifax, NS B3H 4H9, Canada. *T:* (902) 4942114, *Fax:* (902) 4941316. *Club:* The Charlottetown.

GHODSE, Prof. (Abdol) Hamid, MD, PhD; FRCP, FRCPsych; Professor of Psychiatry and Addictive Behaviour, University of London at St George's Hospital Medical School, since 1987; Consultant Psychiatrist, St George's Hospital, since 1978; *b* 30 April 1938; *s* of Abdol Rahim Ghods and Batool Daneshmand; *m* 1973, Barbara Bailin; two *s* one *d*. *Educ:* Esfehan, Tabriz and Tehran; American Univ., Beirut (Schol. 1958); MD Iran 1965; PhD London 1976; DPM 1974. FRCPsych 1985; FRCP 1992. Lieut, Iranian Health Corps, 1965–67. Postgrad. trng, Morgannwg Hosp., Wales, and St Bartholomew's and Maudsley Hosps, London, 1968–74; res. psychiatrist, Inst. of Psychiatry, Univ. of London, 1974–78; Consultant Psychiatrist, St Thomas' Hosp., 1978–88. Director: Regl Drug and Alcohol Team, SW Thames RHA, 1991–; European Collaborating Centre in Addiction Studies, 1992–. Member: WHO Adv. Panel, 1979–; WHO Prog. Planning Wkg Gp, 1986–89; Convenor, Mem., Rapporteur and Chm. of various WHO Expert Cttees and Wkg Gps on Drug Dependence, 1980–. Advr, BNF, 1984–. Editor, Internat. Jl Social Psychiatry, 1982–. Chm., Substance Misuse Section and Mem., Council and Court of Electors, RCPsych, 1980–; President: Assoc. for Prevention of Addiction, 1984–90; Internat. Narcotics Control Bd, 1993– (Mem., 1992–). Hon. Sec., Assoc. of Profs of Psychiatry, 1982–. McLeod Prof., SA, 1990. *Publications:* (jtly) Misuse of Drugs, 1986, 2nd edn 1991, supplement 1993; (jtly) Psychoactive Drugs: improving prescribing practices, 1988 (trans. 8 langs); Drugs and Addictive Behaviour: a guide to treatment, 1989, 2nd edn 1995; (ed jtly) Substance Abuse and Dependence, 1990; (ed jtly) Drug Misuse and Dependence, 1990; numerous articles on self-poisoning, substance misuse and med. educn. *Recreations:* reading, cycling. *Address:* St George's Hospital Medical School, Cranmer Terrace, SW17 0RE. *T:* 0171–672 9944. *Club:* Athenæum.

GHURBURRUN, Sir Rabindrah, Kt 1981; Vice-President, Republic of Mauritius, since 1992; *b* 27 Sept. 1929; *s* of Mrs Sookmeen Ghurburrun; *m* 1959; one *s* one *d*. *Educ:* Keble Coll., Oxford. Called to the Bar, Middle Temple; QC Mauritius, 1991; practised as Lawyer, 1959–68; High Comr for Mauritius in India, 1968–76; MLA 1976; Minister of Justice, 1976; Minister of Economic Planning and Development, 1977–82. Member: Central Board; Bar Council (Chm., 1991–92). Former President: Mauritius Arya Sabha; Mauritius Sugar Cane Planters' Assoc.; Hindu Educn Authority; Nat. Congress of Young Socialists. Patron, Commonwealth ESU in Mauritius. Grand Order of the Star and Key, Mauritius, 1993. *Address:* 18 Dr Lesur Street, Cascadelle, Beau Bassin, Mauritius. *T:* 4546421.

GIACHARDI, Dr David John, FRSC; Executive Director, Courtaulds, since 1987; Member, Engineering and Physical Sciences Research Council, since 1994; *b* 17 May 1948; *o s* of Thomas and Kathleen Giachardi; *m* 1971, Helen Margaret Fraser; one *d*. *Educ:* Watford Boys' Grammar Sch.; Merton Coll., Oxford; St John's Coll., Oxford. MA, DPhil.

Boston Consulting Group, 1975–79; Courtaulds, 1979–: Dir of Research, 1982–94; Human Resources Dir, 1994–. Member: European Science and Technology Assembly, 1994–; Nat. Commn on Educn, 1991–93; Vice-Chm., Industrial R&D Adv. Cttee to Commn for EC, 1991–94. *Publications:* contribs to learned jls. *Recreations:* science, golf. *Address:* Courtaulds plc, 50 George Street, W1A 2BB. *T:* 0171–612 1254.

GIAEVER, Prof. Ivar; Institute Professor, Physics Department, Rensselaer Polytechnic Institute, Troy, New York, since 1988; Professor-at-large, University of Oslo, Norway; *b* 5 April 1929; *s* of John A. Giaever and Gudrun (*née* Skaarud); *m* 1952, Inger Skramstad; one *s* three *d.* *Educ:* Norwegian Inst. of Tech.; Rensselear Polytechnical Inst. ME 1952; PhD 1964. Norwegian Army, 1952–53; Norwegian Patent Office, 1953–54; Canadian General Electric, 1954–56; General Electric, 1956–58; Staff Mem., Gen. Electric R&D Center, 1958–88. Fellow, Amer. Phys. Soc.; Member: Nat. Acad. of Sciences; Nat. Acad. of Engineering; Amer. Acad. of Arts and Scis; Norwegian Acad. of Scis; Norwegian Acad. of Technology; Norwegian Profl Engrs; Swedish Acad. of Engrg. Hon. DSc: RPI, 1974; Union Coll., 1974; Clarkson, Potsdam, NY, 1983; Trondheim, Norway; Hon. DEng, Michigan Tech. Univ., 1976; Hon. DPhys: Oslo, 1976; State Univ. of NY, 1984. Oliver E. Buckley Prize, 1964; Nobel Prize for Physics, 1973; Zworykin Award, 1974. *Publications:* contrib. Physical Review, Jl Immunology. *Recreations:* ski-ing, tennis, camping, hiking. *Address:* Physics Department, Rensselaer Polytechnic Institute, Troy, NY 12180-3590, USA. *T:* (518) 2766429.

GIBB, Andrew Thomas Fotheringham; Partner, Balfour and Manson, Solicitors, Edinburgh, since 1975; President, Law Society of Scotland, 1990–91; *b* 17 Aug. 1947; *s* of Thomas Fotheringham Gibb and Isabel Gow McKenzie or Gibb; *m* 1971, Mrs Patricia Anne Eggo or Gibb; two *s.* *Educ:* Perth Acad.; Edinburgh Univ. (LLB Hons). Temporary Sheriff, 1989–. Member: Lothian and Borders Legal Aid Cttee, 1977–84; Legal Aid Central Cttee, 1984–86; Council, Law Soc. of Scotland, 1981–. Chm. Management Cttee, Lothian Allellon Soc., 1984–. Elder, St Ninian's Church, Corstorphine, Edinburgh. *Recreations:* music, church organist, golf. *Address:* 39 Braehead Road, Edinburgh EH4 6BD. *Clubs:* New (Edinburgh); Bruntsfield Golf.

GIBB, Sir Francis Ross, (Sir Frank Gibb), Kt 1987; CBE 1982; BSc; FEng; FICE; Chairman and Chief Executive, Taylor Woodrow Group, 1985–89 (Joint Managing Director, 1979–85, and a Joint Deputy Chairman, 1983–85); President, Taylor Woodrow Construction, since 1985 (Chairman, 1978–85); *b* 29 June 1927; *s* of Robert Gibb and Violet Mary Gibb; *m* 1950, Wendy Marjorie Fowler; one *s* two *d.* *Educ:* Loughborough Coll. BSc(Eng); CEng. Dir, 1963–70, Man. Dir, then Jt Man. Dir, 1970–84; Taylor Woodrow Construction; Director: Taylor Woodrow Internat., 1969–85; Taylor Woodrow plc, 1972–89; Chm., Taywood Santa Fe, 1975–85. Jt Dep. Chm., Seaforth Maritime Ltd, 1986–89; Director: Seaforth Maritime Hldgs, 1978–89; (non-exec.) Eurotunnel plc, 1986–87; (non-exec.), Babcock Internat. Group, 1989–; (non-exec.), Steetley plc, 1990–92; (non-exec.), Nuclear Electric plc, 1990–94; (indep.) Energy Saving Trust Ltd, 1992–. Member: Construction Industry Adv. Cttee, HSE, 1978–81; Gp of Eight, 1979–81; Board, British Nuclear Associates, 1980–88 (Chm., Agrément Bd, 1980–82); Chm., Nat. Nuclear Corp., 1981–88. Mem. Council, CBI, 1979–80, 1985–90. Dir, Holiday Pay Scheme, 1980–84 and Trustee, Benefits Scheme, 1980–84, Building and Civil Engrg Trustees. Federation of Civil Engineering Contractors: Vice-Chm., 1978–79; Chm., 1979–80; Vice Pres., 1980–84; Pres., 1984–87; Vice-Pres., ICE, 1988–90. Freeman, City of London, 1978. FRSA; CIMgt (CBIM 1983); Hon. FINucE 1984; Hon. FCGI 1990. Hon. DTech Loughborough, 1989. *Recreations:* ornithology, gardening, walking, music. *Address:* Ross Gibb Consultants, 18 Latchmoor Avenue, Gerrards Cross, Bucks SL9 8LJ. *Club:* Arts.

GIBB, Ian Pashley; Director of Public Services, Planning and Administration, British Library (Humanities and Social Sciences), 1985–87; *b* 17 April 1926; *s* of late John Pashley Gibb and of Mary (*née* Owen); *m* 1953, Patricia Mary Butler (*d* 1993); two *s.* *Educ:* Latymer Upper Sch.; UCL (BA). ALA. Sen. Library Asst, Univ. of London, 1951–52; Asst Librarian, UCL, 1952–58; Dep. Librarian, National Central Library, 1958–73; British Library: Dep. Dir, Science Reference Library, 1973–75; Head of Divl Office, Reference Div., 1975–77; Dir and Keeper, Reference Div., 1977–85. Part-time Lectr, UCL, 1967–77, Hon. Research Fellow, 1977–85, Examiner, 1985–87. Hon. Treasurer, Bibliographical Soc., 1961–67; Member Council: Library Assoc., 1980–82; Friends of British Library, 1994– (Dep. Chm., 1989–93). Chm., Dacorum NT Assoc., 1993–. *Publications:* (ed) Newspaper Preservation and Access, 2 vols, 1988; various articles. *Recreations:* music, watching cricket, walking, wine-tasting, travel especially to Austria. *Address:* The Old Cottage, 16 Tile Kiln Lane, Leverstock Green, Hemel Hempstead, Herts HP3 8ND. *T:* Hemel Hempstead (01442) 256352.

GIBB, Walter Frame, DSO 1945; DFC 1943; Chairman, 1980–84, and Managing Director, 1978–84, British Aerospace, Australia, Ltd; retired; *b* 26 March 1919; British; *m* 1944, Pauline Sylvia Reed; three *d.* *Educ:* Clifton Coll. Apprentice, Bristol Aero Engines, 1937. RAF, 1940–46. Test Pilot, Bristol Aircraft Ltd, 1946; Asst Chief Test Pilot, 1953; Chief Test Pilot, Bristol Aeroplane Co. Ltd, 1956–60; Product Support Manager, BAC Filton, 1960–78. World Altitude Height Record 63,668 feet in Olympus-Canberra, 1953, and second record 65,890 ft in same machine, 1955. MRAeS. JP Bristol, 1974. *Recreation:* sailing. *Address:* Merlin Haven Lodge, Wotton-Under-Edge, Glos GL12 7BA. *Clubs:* Royal Air Force; Royal Sydney Yacht Squadron.

GIBBENS, Barnaby John, OBE 1989; Chairman: Enterprise Systems Group Ltd, since 1989; Information Technology Industry Training Organisation, since 1992; *b* 17 April 1935; *s* of late Dr Gerald Gibbens and Deirdre Gibbens; *m* 1st, 1960, Sally Mary Stephenson (marr. diss. 1990); one *s* two *d*; 2nd, 1990, Kristina de Zabala. *Educ:* Winchester College. FCA 1972. Founder, 1962, Dep. Chm., 1962–81, Chm., 1981–90, Computer Analysts & Programmers (later CAP Group, then SEMA Group); Chairman: Computing Services Industry Trng Council, 1984–; IT Industry Lead Body, 1987–; IT Trng Accreditation Council, 1991–; a Director: National Computing Centre, 1987–90; UK Skills, 1990–; Member: Nat. Ctte on Computer Networks, 1978; NCVQ, 1989–92; NCET, 1991–. Pres., Computing Services Assoc., 1975. Chm. Trustees, Skin Treatment and Res. Trust, 1988–. Founding Master, Co. of Information Technologists, 1987. Hon. Mem., C & G, 1993. FRSA 1993. *Publications:* articles in national press and jls on computing. *Recreations:* golf, real tennis, music, gardening. *Address:* 12 Kings Road, Wimbledon, SW19 8QN. *T:* 0181–542 3878.

GIBBERD, Dr Frederick Brian, MD; FRCP, FRCPE; Consultant Physician and Neurologist, Chelsea and Westminster Hospital and Queen Mary's Hospital, Roehampton, since 1965; *b* 7 July 1931; *s* of late George Frederick Gibberd, CBE and Margaret Erica (*née* Taffs); *m* 1960, Margaret Clare Sidey; four *d.* *Educ:* Aldenham Sch. (Schol.); Gonville and Caius Coll., Cambridge (Schol.; BA 1954; MA, MB BChir 1957; MD 1974); Westminster Med. Sch. (Schol.). FRCP 1972; FRCPE 1993. Nat. Service, commnd RA, 1949–51. Jun. doctor posts at Westminster, Addenbrookes, Brompton, Nat. Queen Square and Royal London Hosps, 1957–65. Mem., GMC, 1992–. Chm., Westminster Hosp. Med. Cttee, 1983–86; Mem., Riverside Dist HA, 1987–90. Royal College of Physicians: Censor, 1991–92; Council Mem., 1970–72 and 1990–; Royal Society of Medicine: Pres., Clinical Section, 1972–74; Hon. Librarian, 1975–79. Pres., Harveian Soc., 1995. Society of Apothecaries: Liveryman, 1968; Sen. Warden, 1995–Aug. 1996. Hon. FFOM 1995. *Publications:* (contrib.) Medical Negligence, 1994; MRCP (UK) Examination Book, 1995; articles and papers on epilepsy, Parkinson's Disease, Refsum's Disease, and neurological diseases. *Recreations:* gardening, travelling, history. *Address:* Chelsea and Westminster Hospital, 369 Fulham Road, SW10 9NH. *T:* 0181–746 8316; 7A Alleyn Park, Dulwich, SE21 8AU. *T:* 0181–670 2197.

GIBBINGS, Sir Peter (Walter), Kt 1989; Chairman, Radio Authority, since 1995; *b* 25 March 1929; *s* of late Walter White Gibbings and Margaret Russell Gibbings (*née* Torrance); *m* 1st, Elspeth Felicia Macintosh; two *d*; 2nd, Hon. Louise Barbara, *d* of 2nd Viscount Lambert, TD; one *s.* *Educ:* Rugby; Wadham Coll., Oxford (Scholar). Called to Bar, Middle Temple, 1953 (Garraway Rice Pupillage Prize; Harmsworth Schol.). Served in 9th Queen's Royal Lancers, 1951–52; Dep. Legal Adviser, Trinidad Oil Co. Ltd, 1955–56; Associated Newspapers Ltd, 1956–60; The Observer, 1960–67 (Deputy Manager and Dir, 1965–67); Man. Dir, Guardian Newspapers Ltd, 1967–73; Dir, Manchester Guardian and Evening News Ltd, 1967–73; Chm., Guardian and Manchester Evening News plc, 1973–88; Anglia Television Gp: Dir, 1981–94; Dep. Chm., 1986–88; Chm., 1988–94. Director: Press Assoc. Ltd, 1982–88 (Chm., 1986–87); Reuters Holdings PLC, 1984–88; The Economist, 1987–; Rothschild Trust Corp. Ltd, 1989–; Council, UEA, 1989–. Mem., Press Council, 1970–74; Pres., CPU, 1989–91. *Recreations:* sailing, tennis. *Address:* c/o Radio Authority, Holbrook House, Great Queen Street, WC2B 5DG.

GIBBINS, Rev. Dr Ronald Charles; Methodist Minister; Superintendent Minister, Wesley's Chapel, London, 1978–88; *s* of Charles and Anne Gibbins; *m* 1949, Olive Ruth (*née* Patchett); one *s* two *d.* *Educ:* London Univ. (BScSociol); Wesley Theological Coll., Bristol; Eden Theological Seminary, US (DMin). Methodist Minister: Bradford, 1948–49; Spennymoor, 1949–50; Middlesbrough, 1950–57; Basildon, 1957–64; East End Mission, London, 1964–78. *Publications:* Mission for the Secular City, 1976; The Lumpen Proletariat, 1979; The Stations of the Resurrection, 1987. *Recreations:* travel, journalism. *Address:* 27 Riverside Close, Kingston upon Thames, Surrey KT1 2JG.

GIBBON, Gen. Sir John (Houghton), GCB 1977 (KCB 1972; CB 1970); OBE 1945 (MBE 1944); Master-General of the Ordnance, 1974–77; ADC (General) to the Queen, 1976–77; *b* 21 Sept. 1917; *er s* of Brigadier J. H. Gibbon, DSO, The Manor House, Little Stretton, Salop; *m* 1951, Brigid Rosamund, *d* of late Dr D. A. Bannerman, OBE, ScD, FRSE, and Muriel, *d* of T. R. Morgan; one *s.* *Educ:* Eton; Trinity Coll., Cambridge. Commissioned into Royal Artillery, 1939. Served with 2nd Regt RHA: France, 1939–40; Western Desert, 1940–41; Greece, 1941; on staff of HQ 30 Corps; Western Desert, 1941–43; Sicily, 1943; GSO 1, RA, HQ 21 Army Gp, 1944–45; 6 Airborne Div., Palestine, 1946–47; Instructor and Chief Instructor, RMA Sandhurst, 1947–51; GSO 2, War Office, 1951–53; Battery Comdr, 1953–54; AQMG, War Office, 1955–58; CO Field Regt, BAOR, 1959–60; Bde Comdr, Cyprus, 1962; Dir of Defence Plans, Min. of Def., 1962–64; Sec., Chiefs of Staff Cttee, and Dir, Defence Operations Staff, 1966–69; Dir, Army Staff Duties, MoD, 1969–71; Vice-Chief of the Defence Staff, 1972–74. Col Comdt, RA, 1972–82. Chm., Regular Forces Employment Assoc., 1982–85 (Vice-Chm., 1977–82). *Recreations:* rowing, fishing. *Address:* Beech House, Northbrook Close, Winchester, Hants SO23 0JR. *T:* Winchester (01962) 866155. *Clubs:* Naval and Military; Leander.

GIBBON, Michael, QC 1974; **His Honour Judge Gibbon;** a Senior Circuit Judge, since 1993 (a Circuit Judge, since 1979); *b* 15 Sept. 1930; 2nd *s* of late Frank and Jenny Gibbon; *m* 1956, Malveen Elliot Seager; two *s* one *d.* *Educ:* Brightlands; Charterhouse; Pembroke Coll., Oxford (MA). Commnd in Royal Artillery, 1949. Called to Bar, Lincoln's Inn, 1954. A Recorder of the Crown Court, 1972–79. Hon. Recorder, City of Cardiff, 1986; Resident Judge, Cardiff Crown Court, 1993–. Chairman, Electoral Adv. Cttee to Home Sec., 1972; Local Govt Boundary Commn for Wales, 1978–79 (Dep. Chm., 1974–78); Lord Chancellor's Adv. Cttee for S Glam, 1990–; Criminal Justice Area Liaison Cttee for S and SW Wales, 1992–; Mem., Parole Bd, 1986–88. A Chm., Bar Disciplinary Tribunal, 1988. *Recreations:* music, golf. *Address:* Cardiff Crown Court, The Law Courts, Cathays Park, Cardiff CF1 3PG. *T:* Cardiff (01222) 345931. *Clubs:* Cardiff and County (Cardiff); Royal Porthcawl Golf, Cardiff Golf.

GIBBONS, Hon. Sir David; *see* Gibbons, Hon. Sir J. D.

GIBBONS, Prof. Ian Read, FRS 1983; Professor of Biophysics in the University of Hawaii, since 1967; *b* 30 Oct. 1931; *s* of Arthur Alwyn Gibbons and Hilda Read Cake; *m* 1961, Barbara Ruth Hollingworth; one *s* one *d.* *Educ:* Faversham Grammar School; Cambridge Univ. (BA, PhD). Research Fellow, 1958–63, Asst Prof., 1963–67, Harvard Univ.; Associate Prof., 1967–69, Prof., 1969, Univ. of Hawaii. *Publications:* contribs to learned jls. *Recreations:* gardening, computer programming, music. *Address:* Pacific Biomedical Research Center, Kewalo Marine Laboratory, 41 Ahui Street, Honolulu, HI 96813, USA. *T:* (808) 5397325.

GIBBONS, Jeremy Stewart; QC 1995; a Recorder, since 1993; *b* 15 July 1949; *s* of Geoffrey Gibbons and Rosemary Gibbons (*née* Stewart); *m* 1974, Mary Mercia Bradley; two *s* one *d* (and one *d* decd). *Educ:* Oakmount Sch., Southampton; St Edward's Sch., Oxford. Called to the Bar, Gray's Inn, 1973; Asst Recorder, 1989–93. *Recreations:* cooking, gardening, ski-ing, carpentry. *Address:* 17 Carlton Crescent, Southampton SO15 2XR. *T:* Southampton (01703) 320320; Au Grand Chêne, Chez Perroteau, Champagnolles 17240, Charente Maritime, France. *Club:* Hampshire (Winchester).

GIBBONS, Hon. Sir (John) David, KBE 1985; JP; Chairman: Bank of N. T. Butterfield & Son Ltd, Bermuda, since 1986; Global Asset Management Ltd, since 1986; *b* 15 June 1927; *s* of late Edmund G. Gibbons, CBE, and Winifred G. Gibbons, MBE; *m* 1958, Lully Lorentzen; three *s* (and one *d* by former *m*). *Educ:* Saltus Grammar Sch., Bermuda; Hotchkiss Sch., Lakeville, Conn; Harvard Univ., Cambridge, Mass (BA). CIMgt. Mem. Govt Boards: Social Welfare Bd, 1949–58; Bd of Civil Aviation, 1958–60; Bd of Educn, 1956–59 (Chm., 1973–74); Trade Develt Bd, 1960–74. MP Bermuda, 1972–84; Minister of Health and Welfare, 1974–75, of Finance, 1975–84; Premier of Bermuda, 1977–82. Chairman: Bermuda Monetary Authy, 1984–86; Economic Council, Bermuda, 1984–86. Mem., Law Reform Cttee, 1969–72. Mem. Governing Body, subseq. Chm., Bermuda Technical Inst., 1956–70. Trustee, Massachusetts Financial Services, 1988–. JP Bermuda, 1974. *Recreations:* tennis, golf, skiing, swimming. *Address:* Leeward, 5 Leeside Drive, Pembroke HM 05, Bermuda. *T:* (809) 2952396. *Clubs:* Phoenix (Cambridge, Mass); Harvard (New York); Royal Bermuda Yacht, Royal Hamilton Amateur Dinghy, Mid-Ocean, Riddells Bay Golf, Spanish Point Boat (Bermuda); Lyford Cay (Bahamas).

GIBBONS, Dr John Ernest; Director of Building and Chief Architect, Scottish Office, since 1984; *b* Halesowen, Worcs, 20 April 1940; *s* of late John Howard Gibbons and Lilian Alice Gibbons (*née* Shale); *m* 1963, Patricia Mitchell; one *s* two *d.* *Educ:* Oldbury Grammar Sch.; Birmingham Sch. of Architecture; Edinburgh Univ. PhD; DipArch; DipTP; ARIBA; ARIAS; FSA(Scot). In private practice, 1962–65; Lectr, Birmingham Sch. of Architecture and Univ. of Aston, 1964–66; Res. Fellow, 1967–69, Lectr, 1969–72, Edinburgh Univ.; Scottish Development Department: Prin. Architect, 1972–78; Asst Dir, Building Directorate, 1978–82; Dep. Dir and Dep. Chief Architect, 1982–84. Vis. Res. Scientist, CSIRO, Melbourne, 1974–75. Member, Council: EAA and RIAS, 1977–80; ARCUK, 1984. *Publications:* contribs on architectural and planning matters to professional and technical jls. *Recreations:* reading, photography, music, travel. *Address:* Crichton House, Pathhead, Midlothian EH37 5UX. *T:* Ford (01875) 320085. *Club:* New (Edinburgh).

GIBBONS, Ven. Kenneth Harry; Archdeacon of Lancaster, since 1981; Vicar of St Michael's-on-Wyre, since 1985; *b* 24 Dec. 1931; *s* of Harry and Phyllis Gibbons; *m* 1962, Margaret Ann Tomlinson; two *s*. *Educ:* Blackpool and Chesterfield Grammar Schools; Manchester Univ. (BSc); Cuddesdon Coll., Oxford. RAF, 1952–54. Ordained, 1956; Assistant Curate of Fleetwood, 1956–60; Secretary for Student Christian Movement in Schools, 1960–62; Senior Curate, St Martin-in-the-Fields, Westminster, 1962–65; Vicar of St Edward, New Addington, 1965–70; Vicar of Portsea, 1970–81; RD of Portsmouth, 1973–79; Hon. Canon of Portsmouth, 1974–81; Priest-in-charge of Weeton, 1981–85. Diocesan Dir of Ordinands, 1982–90. Acting Chaplain to HM Forces, 1981–85. *Recreations:* gardening, cinema. *Address:* The Vicarage, St Michael's-on-Wyre, Preston, Lancs PR3 0TQ. *Club:* Reform.

GIBBONS, Sir William Edward Doran, 9th Bt *cr* 1752; JP; Director, Passenger Shipping Association, since 1994; *b* 13 Jan. 1948; *s* of Sir John Edward Gibbons, 8th Bt, and of Mersa Wentworth, *y d* of late Major Edward Baynton Grove Foster; *S* father, 1982; *m* 1972, Patricia Geraldine Archer, *d* of Roland Archer Howse; one *s* one *d*. *Educ:* Pangbourne; RNC Dartmouth; Bristol Univ. (BSc); DipBA. MCIT. Asst Shipping and Port Manager, Sealink UK, Parkeston Quay, 1979–82; Service Manager (Anglo-Dutch), Sealink UK Ltd, 1982–85; Ferry Line Manager (Harwich–Hook), 1985–87, Gen. Manager, IoW Services, 1987–90, Sealink British Ferries. Transport and management consultant, 1990–94. Non-Exec. Mem., IoW DHA, 1990–94. Mem., Manningtree Parish Council, 1981–87 (Chm., 1985–87). JP: Portsmouth, 1990–94; S Westminster Div., Inner London, 1994–. *Heir: s* Charles William Edwin Gibbons, *b* 28 Jan. 1983. *Address:* 5 Yarborough Road, Southsea, Hants PO5 3DZ.

GIBBS, family name of **Barons Aldenham** and **Wraxall.**

GIBBS, Barbara Lynn; Head Teacher, Newstead Wood School for Girls, since 1994; *b* 8 Nov. 1945; *d* of William Newill and Mabel Till; *m* 1967, John Colin Gibbs; two *d*. *Educ:* Bromley Grammar Sch. for Girls; Univ. of Hull (BSc Hons Chem.); Univ. of E Anglia (MA; PGCE). Teaching and lecturing, mainly on chem. and maths, in various educnl estabts in Yorks, Notts, Norfolk and Barnet, 1967–86; Sen. Teacher, Henrietta Barnett Sch., 1986–90; Vice Principal, Havering Sixth Form Coll., 1990–94. FRSA 1994. *Recreations:* music, literature, travel, swimming, Rugby Union. *Address:* Newstead Wood School for Girls, Avebury Road, Orpington, Kent BR6 9SA. *T:* Orpington (01689) 853626.

GIBBS, Air Vice-Marshal Charles Melvin, CB 1976; CBE 1966; DFC 1943; RAF retd; Recruiting Consultant with Selleck Associates, Colchester, 1977–86; *b* 11 June 1921; American father, New Zealand mother; *m* 1947, Emma Pamela Pollard; one *d*. *Educ:* Taumarunui, New Zealand. MECI 1980. Joined RNZAF, 1941; service in Western Desert and Mediterranean, 1942–44; Coastal Comd, 1945; India, 1946–47; commanded Tropical Experimental Unit, 1950–52; RAF Staff Coll., 1953; commanded No 118 Squadron, 1954–55; Directing Staff, RAF Staff Coll., 1956–58; Pakistan, 1958–61; Chief Instructor, RAF Chivenor, 1961–63; CO, Wattisham, 1963–66; idc 1967; Defence Policy Staff, 1968–69; Dir of Quartering, 1970–72; AOA, Germany, 1972–74; Dir-Gen. Personal Services, RAF, 1974–76. *Recreations:* fishing, golf. *Address:* 5 Kew Place, Taupo, New Zealand. *T:* (7) 3771957.

GIBBS, Hon. Sir Eustace Hubert Beilby, KCVO 1986; CMG 1982; HM Diplomatic Service, retired; Vice Marshal of the Diplomatic Corps, 1982–86; *b* 3 July 1929; 2nd surv. *s* of 1st Baron Wraxall, PC; *b* and *heir-pres.* of 2nd Baron Wraxall, *qv*; *m* 1957, Evelyn Veronica Scott; three *s* two *d*. *Educ:* Eton College; Christ Church, Oxford (MA). ARCM 1953. Entered HM Diplomatic Service, 1954; served in Bangkok, Rio de Janeiro, Berlin, Vienna, Caracas, Paris. *Recreations:* music, golf. *Address:* Coddenham House, Coddenham, Ipswich, Suffolk IP6 9TY. *T:* Coddenham (01449) 760332. *Clubs:* Pratt's, Beefsteak.

GIBBS, Rt. Hon. Sir Harry (Talbot), AC 1987; GCMG 1981; KBE 1970; PC 1972; Chief Justice of Australia, 1981–87; *b* 7 Feb. 1917; *s* of late H. V. Gibbs, formerly of Ipswich, Qld; *m* 1944, Muriel Ruth (*née* Dunn); one *s* three *d*. *Educ:* Ipswich Grammar Sch., Qld; Univ. of Queensland (BA, LLM). Served War, Australia and New Guinea, 1939–45, Major (despatches). Admitted as Barrister, Qld, 1939; QC 1957; Judge of Supreme Court of Qld, 1961; Judge of Federal Court of Bankruptcy and of Supreme Court of Australian Capital Territory, 1967; Justice of High Court of Australia, 1970. Hon. Bencher, Lincoln's Inn, 1981. Hon. LLD Queensland, 1980; DUniv Griffith Univ., 1987. *Address:* 30 Lodge Road, Cremorne, NSW 2090, Australia. *T:* (2) 9091844. *Clubs:* Australian (Sydney); Queensland (Brisbane).

GIBBS, Rt. Rev. John; *b* 15 March 1917; *s* of late A. E. Gibbs, Bournemouth; *m* 1943, G. Marion, *d* of late W. J. Bishop, Poole, Dorset; one *s* one *d*. *Educ:* Univ. of Bristol; Western Coll., Bristol; Lincoln Theological Coll. BA (Bristol); BD (London). In the ministry of the Congregational Church, 1943–49. Student Christian Movement: Inter-Collegiate Sec., 1949–51; Study Sec. and Editor of Student Movement, 1951–55. Curate of St Luke's, Brislington, Bristol, 1955–57; Chaplain and Head of Divinity Dept, Coll. of St Matthias, Bristol, 1957–64, Vice-Principal, 1962–64; Principal, Keswick Hall Coll. of Education, Norwich, 1964–73; Examining Chaplain to Bishop of Norwich, Hon. Canon of Norwich Cathedral, 1968–73; Bishop Suffragan of Bradwell, Dio. Chelmsford, 1973–76; Bishop of Coventry, 1976–85. Hon. Asst to Bps of Gloucester and Bristol, 1985–. Member, Durham Commn on Religious Education, 1967–70; Chairman: C of E Children's Council, 1968–71; C of E Bd of Educn Publications Cttee, 1971–79, Education and Community Cttee, 1974–76; Assoc. of Voluntary Colls, 1985–87; Further and Higher Educn Cttee, General Synod Bd of Educn, 1986–91; BCC Wkg Parties: Chm., The Child in the Church, 1973–76; Chm., Understanding Christian Nurture, 1979–81; Anglican Chm., Anglican–Lutheran European Reg. Commn, 1980–82. Chm., Cotswold Care Hospice, 1986–. Introduced H of L, 1982. *Recreations:* music, bird watching. *Address:* Farthingloe, Southfield, Minchinhampton, Stroud, Glos GL6 9DY.

GIBBS, Marion Olive; Headmistress, James Allen's Girls' School, Dulwich, since 1994; *b* 16 Sept. 1951; *d* of Harry Norman Smith and Olive Mabel (*née* Lewis); *m* 1st, 1976, Robert Baldock (marr. diss. 1983); 2nd, 1992, Peter Gibbs. *Educ:* Pate's Grammar Sch. for Girls, Cheltenham; Bristol Univ. (BA 1st cl. Hons Classics 1973; PGCE 1974; MLitt 1981). Assistant Mistress: City of Worcester Girls' Grammar Sch., 1974–76; Chailey Comprehensive Sch., 1977; Hd of Sixth Form, Dir of Studies and Hd of Classics, Burgess Hill Sch. for Girls, 1977–89; Hd of Sixth Form and Classics, Haberdashers' Aske's Girls' Sch., Elstree, 1989–91; HMI of Schools, 1992–94. Tutor, Open Univ., 1979–91. *Publication:* Greek Tragedy: an introduction, 1989. *Recreations:* music, drama, keeping informed about the developing world. *Address:* James Allen's Girls' School, East Dulwich Grove, SE22 8TE. *T:* 0181–693 1181.

GIBBS, Dame Molly (Peel), DBE 1969; (Hon. Lady Gibbs); *b* 13 July 1912; 2nd *d* of John Peel Nelson; *m* 1934, Rt Hon. Sir Humphrey Vicary Gibbs, GCVO, KCMG, OBE, PC (*d* 1990); five *s*. *Educ:* Girls' High School, Barnato Park, Johannesburg. *Address:* 22 Dornie Road, Pomona, PO Borrowdale, Harare, Zimbabwe. *T:* Harare (4) 883281; 6 The Square, High Street, Leigh, Kent TN11 8RJ.

GIBBS, Oswald Moxley, CMG 1976; development and trade consultant, since 1990; High Commissioner for Grenada in London, 1974–78 and 1984–90; Ambassador for Grenada to the European Economic Community, 1985–90; *b* St George's, Grenada, 15 Oct. 1927; *s* of Michael Gibbs and Emelda Mary (*née* Cobb); *m* 1955, Dearest Agatha Mitchell (*d* 1989); two *s* two *d*. *Educ:* Happy Hill RC Sch.; St George's RC Sen. Boys' Sch.; Grenada Boys' Secondary Sch.; Christy Trades Sch., Chicago (Technical Drafting Dip.); City of London Coll. BScEcon London. Solicitors' Clerk, Grenada, 1948–51; petroleum refining, Royal Dutch Shell Co., Curaçao, Netherlands Antilles, 1951–55; Civil Servant, Agricl Rehabilitation Dept, Grenada, 1955–57; Transport Worker, London Transport, and Postman, London, 1957–60; Civil Servant, WI Federal Commn, London, 1961–62; Consular Officer, Commn for Eastern Caribbean Govts, London, 1965–75; Welfare Officer, 1965–67; Trade Sec., 1967–72; Dep. Comr, 1972–73; Actg Comr, 1973–75. Rep. Govt of St Kitts-Nevis-Anguilla on London Cttee of Commonwealth Sugar Producing Countries, 1971–75; Consultant, Centre for Industrial Devalt, Lomé Convention, Brussels, 1979–80 (signed Lomé III Convention for Grenada, 1984); Deleg., 9th Commonwealth Conf. on Devalt and Human Ecology, Univ. of Edinburgh, 1989; Head of Delegn, Commonwealth Heads of Govt Meeting, Kuala Lumpur, 1989; Admin. Dir, N Kensington Family Centre and Unity Assoc., 1980–83; Business Devalt Manager, UK Caribbean Chamber of Commerce, 1983–84. Chairman: Civil Service Salaries Revision Commn, Grenada, 1970; Notting Hill Carnival and Arts Cttee, 1981–84. Member: Exec., Commonwealth Human Ecology Council, 1989–; Governing Council, Internat. Fund for Agricl Devalt (Rome), 1986–90. Mem., delegns to constitutional, Commonwealth and ACP/EEC meetings and confs. Silver Jubilee Medal, 1977. *Publication:* occasional paper on envmtl concerns of small states. *Recreations:* environment, development economics, DIY, photography, gardening. *Address:* 73A Woodside Green, SE25 5HU.

GIBBS, Dr Richard John; Chief Executive, Kingston and Richmond (formerly Kingston and Esher) Health Authority, since 1990; *b* 15 May 1943; *s* of Leslie and Mary Gibbs; *m* 1968, Laura Wanda Olasmi; one *d*. *Educ:* Merchant Taylors' Sch., Northwood; Pembroke Coll., Cambridge (BA 1965); Warwick Univ. (PhD 1974). Teacher, City of London Sch. for Boys, 1965; Scientific Officer, Home Office, 1968; Sen. Scientific Officer, 1970, PSO, 1972, DHSS; Res. Schol., Internat. Inst. for Applied Systems Analysis, Austria, 1977; SPSO, DHSS, 1978; Central Policy Review Staff, 1980; Dir of Operational Res. (DCSO), 1982, CSO, 1985, DHSS; Under Sec. and Dir of Stats and Management, DHSS, then DoH, 1986–90. Vis. Prof., UCL, 1985. *Publications:* contribs to Jl of ORS. *Recreations:* windsurfing, cooking. *Address:* Kingston and Richmond Health Authority, 17 Upper Brighton Road, Surbiton, Surrey KT6 6LH.

GIBBS, Richard John Hedley, QC 1984; **His Honour Judge Gibbs;** a Circuit Judge, since 1990; *b* 2 Sept. 1941; *s* of Brian Conaway Gibbs and Mabel Joan Gibbs; *m* 1965, Janet (*née* Whittall); one *s* two *d* (and one *d* decd). *Educ:* Oundle Sch.; Trinity Hall, Cambridge (MA). Called to the Bar, Inner Temple, 1965; a Recorder, 1981–90. *Address:* Lord Chancellor's Department, Midland and Oxford Circuit, Stafford Group of Courts, Kemley House, 2 Victoria Road, Stafford ST16 2AE.

GIBBS, Sir Roger (Geoffrey), Kt 1994; Chairman, The Wellcome Trust, since 1989 (Governor, since 1983); Director, Gerrard & National Holdings PLC (formerly Gerrard & National Discount Co. Ltd), 1971–94 (Chairman, 1975–89); *b* 13 Oct. 1934; 4th *s* of Hon. Sir Geoffrey Gibbs, KCMG, and Hon. Lady Gibbs, CBE. *Educ:* Eton; Millfield. Jessel Toynbee & Co. Ltd, 1954–64, Dir 1960; de Zoete & Gorton, later de Zoete & Bevan, Stockbrokers, 1964–71, Partner 1966. Chm., London Discount Market Assoc., 1984–86. Director: Arsenal FC, 1980–; Colville Estate Ltd, 1989–; Howard de Walden Estates Ltd, 1989– (Chm., 1993–). Chm., Arundel Castle Cricket Foundn, 1987–. Member: Council, Royal Nat. Pension Fund for Nurses, 1975–; Finance Cttee, 1985–, Council, 1989–92, ICRF. Ct of Advrs, St Paul's Cathedral, 1990–. Governor, London Clinic, 1983–93; Special Trustee, Guy's Hosp., 1983–92. Freeman, City of London; Liveryman, Merchant Taylors' Co. *Publication:* The Cresta Run 1885–1985. *Recreations:* travel, sport. *Address:* The Wellcome Trust, 183 Euston Road, NW1 2BE. *T:* 0171–611 8888. *Clubs:* Boodle's, Pratt's; Queen's, MCC; Swinley Forest Golf (Chm., 1993–); Vanderbilt.

GIBBS, Field Marshal Sir Roland (Christopher), GCB 1976 (KCB 1972); CBE 1968; DSO 1945; MC 1943; Lord-Lieutenant for Wiltshire, since 1989; Chief of the General Staff, 1976–79; ADC General to the Queen, 1976–79; *b* 22 June 1921; *yr s* of late Maj. G. M. Gibbs, Parkleaze, Ewen, Cirencester; *m* 1955, Davina Jean Merry; two *s* one *d*. *Educ:* Eton Coll.; RMC Sandhurst. Commnd into 60th Rifles, 1940; served War of 1939–45 in N Africa, Italy and NW Europe. Comd 3rd Bn Parachute Regt, 1960–62; GSO1, Brit. Army Staff, Washington, 1962–63; Comdr 16 Para. Bde, 1963–66; Chief of Staff, HQ Middle East, 1966–67; IDC 1968; Commander, British Forces, Gulf, 1969–71; GOC 1 (British) Corps, 1972–74; C-in-C, UKLF, 1974–76. Colonel Commandant: 2nd Bn The Royal Green Jackets, 1971–78; Parachute Regt, 1972–77. Constable, HM Tower of London, 1985–90. Salisbury Regional Dir, Lloyds Bank, 1979–91. Chm., Nat. Rifle Assoc., 1984–90. DL, 1980, Vice Lord-Lieutenant, 1982–89, Wilts. KStJ 1990. *Recreation:* out-of-door sports. *Address:* Patney Rectory, Devizes, Wilts SN10 3QZ. *Clubs:* Turf, Cavalry and Guards.

GIBBS, Stephen, CBE 1981; Chairman: Turner & Newall Ltd, 1979–82; Gibbs Associates Ltd (formerly Gibbs Littlewood Associates), since 1984; *b* 12 Feb. 1920; *s* of Arthur Edwin Gibbs and Anne Gibbs; *m* 1941, Louise Pattison; one *s* one *d*. *Educ:* Oldbury Grammar Sch.; Birmingham Univ. (part-time). FIM. British Industrial Plastics Ltd, Oldbury, Warley, W Midlands, 1936–39. Served RASC, 1939–46. British Industrial Plastics Ltd: Technical Dept, 1946–52; General Sales Manager, 1952–56; Director, and Chm. of subsidiary cos, 1956–68; Turner & Newall Ltd, Manchester: Director, 1968–72; Man. Dir, 1972–76; Dep. Chm., 1976–79; Chm., Gascoigne Moody Associates, 1984–87. Dir, Whitford Hall & Dodderhill (formerly Whitford Hall Ltd), 1990–. Chm., Energy Policy Cttee, CBI, 1981–83. *Address:* Corner House, 11 Dodderhill Road, Droitwich, Worcs WR9 8QN.

GIBRALTAR IN EUROPE, Bishop of, since 1993; **Rt. Rev. John William Hind;** *b* 19 June 1945; *s* of Harold Hind and Joan Mary Hind; *m* 1966, Janet Helen McLintock; three *s*. *Educ:* Watford Grammar Sch.; Leeds Univ. (BA 1966). Asst Master, Leeds Modern Sch., 1966–69; Asst Lectr, King Alfred's Coll., Winchester, 1969–70; Cuddesdon Theol Coll.; Deacon 1972, Priest 1973; Asst Curate, St John's, Catford, 1972–76; Vicar, Christ Church, Forest Hill, 1976–82 and Priest-in-Charge, St Paul's, Forest Hill, 1981–82; Principal, Chichester Theol Coll., 1982–91; Area Bishop of Horsham, 1991–93. Canon

Residentiary and Bursalis Preb., Chichester Cathedral, 1982–90. *Recreations:* judo, languages. *Address:* 14 Tufton Street, SW1P 3QZ. *T:* 0171–976 8001.

GIBRALTAR IN EUROPE, Suffragan Bishop of, since 1995; **Rt Rev. Henry William Scriven;** *b* 30 Aug. 1951; *s* of William Hamilton Scriven and Jeanne Mary Edwards; *m* 1975, Catherine Rose Ware; one *s* one *d*. *Educ:* Repton Sch.; Sheffield Univ. (BA Hons); St John's Theol Coll., Nottingham. Ordained deacon, 1975, priest, 1976; Asst Curate, Holy Trinity, Wealdstone, Harrow, 1975–78; Missionary with S American Missionary Soc., N Argentina, 1979–82; Educn Associate Rector, Christ Church, Little Rock, Arkansas, 1982–83; Missionary, S American Missionary Soc., Spain, 1984–90; Chaplain, British Embassy Church of St George, Madrid, 1990–95. *Recreations:* reading, walking, tennis, music. *Address:* Diocese in Europe, 14 Tufton Street, SW1P 3QZ. *T:* 0171–976 8001.

GIBRALTAR IN EUROPE (Diocese), Auxiliary Bishops of; *see* Capper, Rt Rev. E. M. H.; Pina-Cabral, Rt Rev. D. P. dos S. de.

GIBRIL, Hassan Alieu; High Commissioner for The Gambia in London, 1994–95; *b* 10 June 1951; *s* of Alieu Gibril and Haddy Gibril; *m* Zainab; one *d*. *Educ:* Gambia High Sch., Banjul; Univ. of Lovanium, Zaire; Univ. of Nice (BA Hons); Inst. of Public Admin, Paris (MA Diplomacy). Asst Sec., Office of Pres., then Ministry of Ext. Affairs, Banjul, 1978–79; 2nd Sec. and Consul, Dakar, 1979; 1st Sec. and Hd of Chancery, Lagos, 1980–82; 1st Sec. and Hd of Chancery, Lagos, 1980–82; 1st Sec. and Hd of Chancery, then Actg Counsellor, London, 1982–83; Counsellor and Head of Chancery: Dakar, 1983–86; Washington, 1986–87; Actg Dep. Perm. Rep., Mission to UN, NY, 1988–90; Counsellor and Hd of Chancery, Paris, 1991–93; Dep. High Comr, London, 1993–94; Dep. Perm. Delegate to UNIDO, Vienna, 1993–94; Ambassador to: Republic of Ireland, Sweden, Norway, Denmark, Finland, Austria, Israel, The Vatican, UNIDO and Commonwealth Secretariat, 1994–95. *Recreations:* reading, sports. *Address:* c/o Gambia High Commission, 57 Kensington Court, W8 5DG. *T:* 0171–937 6316.

GIBSON, family name of **Barons Ashbourne** and **Gibson.**

GIBSON, Baron *cr* 1975 (Life Peer), of Penn's Rocks; **Richard Patrick Tallentyre Gibson;** Chairman, National Trust, 1977–86; *b* 5 Feb. 1916; *s* of Thornely Carbutt Gibson and Elizabeth Anne Augusta Gibson; *m* 1945, Elisabeth Dione Pearson; four *s*. *Educ:* Eton Coll.; Magdalen Coll., Oxford (Hon. Fellow, 1977). London Stock Exchange, 1937. Served with Mddx Yeo, 1939–46; N Africa, 1940–41; POW, 1941–43; Special Ops Exec., 1943–45; Political Intell. Dept, FO, 1945–46. Westminster Press Ltd, 1947–78 (Dir, 1948); Director: Whitehall Securities Corp. Ltd, 1948–60, 1973–83; Financial Times Ltd, 1957–78 (Chm., 1975–77); Economist Newspaper Ltd, 1957–78; Pearson PLC (formerly S. Pearson & Son Ltd), 1960–88 (Dep. Chm., 1969; Exec. Dep. Chm., 1975; Chm., 1978–83); Royal Exchange Assce, 1961–69; Chm., Pearson Longman Ltd, 1967–79. Hon. Treas. Commonwealth Press Union, 1957–67. Chm., Arts Council, 1972–77. Vice-Pres., RSA, 1986–90; Chm., RSA Environment Cttee, 1986–90. Trustee, Historic Churches Preservation Trust, 1958; Member: Exec. Cttee, National Trust, 1963–72; Council, Nat. Trust, 1966–86; Adv. Council, V&A Museum, 1968–75 (Chm., 1970); UK Arts Adv. Commn, Calouste Gulbenkian Foundn, 1969–72; Redundant Churches Fund, 1970–71; Exec. Cttee, Nat. Art Collections Fund, 1970–91; Bd, Royal Opera House, 1977–87; Treasurer, Sussex Univ., 1983–87; Trustee, Glyndebourne Fest. Opera, 1965–72 and 1977–86. Hon. DLitt: Reading, 1980; Keele, 1992; DUniv Sussex, 1989. *Recreations:* music, gardening, architecture. *Address:* Penn's Rocks, Groombridge, Tunbridge Wells TN3 9PA. *T:* Langton (01892) 864244. *Clubs:* Garrick, Brooks's.

GIBSON, Anne, (Mrs John Bartell); National Officer, (Union for) Manufacturing, Science, Finance, since 1987; Member: TUC General Council, since 1989; Equal Opportunities Commission, since 1991; *b* 10 Dec. 1940; *d* of Harry Tasker and Jessie Tasker (*née* Roberts); *m* 1st, 1962, John Donald Gibson; one *d*; 2nd, 1988, John Bartell. *Educ:* Market Rasen C of E Sch.; Caistor Grammar Sch., Lincs; Chelmsford Coll. of Further Educn, 1970–71, Univ. of Essex, 1972–76 (BA Hons II 1, Govt). Sec., Penney and Porter Engrg Co., Lincoln, 1956; Cashier, Midland Bank, Market Rasen, 1959–62. Organiser, Saffron Walden Labour Party, 1966–70; Asst Sec., Organisation and Industrial Relns Dept, TUC, 1977–87. Mem., Dept of Employment Adv. Gp on Older Workers, 1993–. FRSA 1993. *Recreations:* Francophile, embroidery, reading, politics. *Address:* Park House, 64/66 Wandsworth Common North Side, SW18 2SH. *T:* 0181–871 2100.

GIBSON, Christopher Allen Wood; QC 1995; *b* 5 July 1953; *s* of Rt Hon. Sir Ralph Brian Gibson, *qv*; *m* 1984, Alarys Mary Calvert Eaton; two *d*. *Educ:* St Paul's Sch.; Brasenose Coll., Oxford. FCIArb 1992. Called to the Bar, Middle Temple, 1976. *Recreations:* sailing, motorcycles, family. *Address:* 2 Crown Office Row, Temple, EC4Y 7HJ. *T:* 0171–797 8000. *Clubs:* Vincent's (Oxford); Emsworth Sailing; Whitstable Yacht.

GIBSON, Rev. Sir Christopher (Herbert), 4th Bt *cr* 1931, of Linconia, Argentina, and of Faccombe, Southampton; CP; *b* 17 July 1948; *o s* of Sir Christopher Herbert Gibson, 3rd Bt and of Lilian Lake Young, *d* of Dr George Byron Young; *S* father, 1994. Ordained priest, 1975. *Address:* Passionist Community, 5700 North Harlem Avenue, Chicago, IL 60631, USA.

GIBSON, Rev. Sir David, 4th Bt *cr* 1926; Catholic Priest; retired; *b* 18 July 1922; *s* of Sir Ackroyd Herbert Gibson, 3rd Bt; *S* father, 1975. Founder of Societas Navigatorum Catholica, 1954. *Address:* c/o Hegarty, The Reens, Ross Road, Killarney, Co. Kerry, Ireland.

GIBSON, David; Under Secretary, Department of Economic Development, Northern Ireland, since 1987; *b* 8 Sept. 1939; *s* of Frank Edward Gibson and Nora Jessie Gibson (*née* Gurnhill); *m* 1963, Roberta Alexandra (*née* McMaster); one *s* two *d*. *Educ:* King Edward VI Grammar Sch., Retford. FCCA. GPO, 1958–63; MAFF, 1963–68; Belfast City Council, 1968–72; Dept of Commerce, NI, 1972–82; Dir of Accountancy Services, 1982–85, Asst Sec., 1985–87, Dept of Economic Develt, NI. *Recreations:* reading, music, walking. *Address:* Department of Economic Development, Netherleigh, Massey Avenue, Belfast BT4 2JP. *T:* Belfast (01232) 529900.

GIBSON, Vice-Adm. Sir Donald Cameron Ernest Forbes, KCB 1968 (CB 1965); DSC 1941; JP; *b* 17 March 1916; *s* of late Capt. W. L. D. Gibson, Queen's Own Cameron Highlanders, and of Elizabeth Gibson; *m* 1939, Marjorie Alice, *d* of H. C. Harding, Horley, Surrey; one *s*. *Educ:* Woodbridge Sch., Suffolk. Cadet, Brit. India SN Co. and Midshipman, Royal Naval Reserve, 1933–37; transf. to Royal Navy, 1937; specialised as Pilot, 1938. Served War of 1939–45: HMS Glorious, Ark Royal, Formidable, Audacity; trng Pilots in USA; Empire Central Flying Sch., 1942; Chief Flying Instr, Advanced Flying Sch., 1946–47; HMS Illustrious, 1947–48; Air Gp Comdr, HMS Theseus, 1948–49; Comdr (Air), RNAS Culdrose, 1950–52; RN Staff Course, 1952–53; Comdr (Air) HMS Indomitable and Glory, 1953–54; Capt. RNAS Brawdy, 1954–56, HMS Dainty, 1956–58; Dep. Dir Air Warfare, 1958–60; Canadian Nat. Defence Coll., 1960–61; Capt., HMS Ark Royal, 1961–63; Rear-Adm. 1963; Flag Officer: Aircraft Carriers, 1963–64; Naval Flying Trg, 1964–65; Naval Air Comd, 1965–68; Vice-Adm. 1967. Dir, HMS Belfast Trust, 1971–72; Mem., Gen. Cttee, Devon Community Housing Soc. Ltd, 1983–. JP Barnstaple 1973. *Publication:* Haul Taut and Belay (autobiog.), 1992. *Recreation:* painting. *Address:* Creedy Court Nursing Home, Shobrooke, Crediton, Devon EX17 1AD. *T:* Crediton (01363) 775254.

GIBSON, Prof. Frank William Ernest, FRS 1976; FAA; Emeritus Professor of Biochemistry, and Visiting Fellow, Australian National University, since 1989; *b* 22 July 1923; *s* of John William and Alice Ruby Gibson; *m* 1st, 1949, Margaret Isabel Nancy (marr. diss. 1979); two *d*; 2nd, 1980, Robin Margaret; one *s*. *Educ:* Queensland, Melbourne, and Oxford Univs. BSc, DSc (Melb.), DPhil (Oxon). Research Asst, Melbourne and Queensland Univs, 1938–47; Sen. Demonstrator, Melbourne Univ., 1948–49; ANU Scholar, Oxford, 1950–52. Melbourne University: Sen. Lectr, 1953–58; Reader in Chem. Microbiology, 1959–65; Prof. of Chem. Microbiology, 1965–66; Australian National University: Prof. of Biochem., 1967–88; Hd. of Biochem. Dept, 1967–76, Chm., Div. of Biochemical Scis, 1988, John Curtin Sch. of Medical Res.; Howard Florey Prof. of Medical Res., and Dir, John Curtin Sch. of Med. Res., 1977–79. Newton-Abraham Vis. Prof. and Fellow of Lincoln Coll., Oxford Univ., 1982–83. David Syme Research Prize, Univ. of Melb., 1963. FAA 1971. *Publications:* scientific papers on the biochemistry of bacteria, particularly the biosynthesis of aromatic compounds, energy metabolism. *Recreations:* tennis, skiing. *Address:* John Curtin School of Medical Research, PO Box 334, Canberra City, ACT 2601, Australia.

GIBSON, Ven. (George) Granville; Archdeacon of Auckland, Diocese of Durham, since 1993; *b* 28 May 1936; *s* of late George Henry Gibson and of Jessie Gibson (*née* Farrand); *m* 1958, Edna (*née* Jackson); three *s* one *d*. *Educ:* Queen Elizabeth Grammar Sch., Wakefield; Barnsley Coll. of Technology; Cuddesdon Coll., Oxford. Mining Surveyor, NCB, 1952–62; Field Officer, The Boys' Brigade, 1962–69. Ordained deacon, 1971, priest, 1972; Curate, St Paul, Cullercoats, 1971–73; Team Vicar, Cramlington, 1973–77; Vicar, St Clare, Newton Aycliffe, 1977–85; Rector of Bishopwearmouth and RD of Wearmouth, 1985–93; Hon. Canon of Durham, 1988–. Proctor in Convocation, 1980–; Church Comr, 1991– (Mem., Bd of Govs., 1993–). Trustee, Church Urban Fund, 1991–. *Recreations:* gardening, cactus plants, grandchildren. *Address:* Glebe House, Sunderland Bridge, Durham DH6 5HB. *T:* 0191–378 0273, *Fax:* 0191–378 3885. *Club:* Commonwealth Trust.

GIBSON, John Peter; Chief Executive, Seaforth Maritime, 1986–88 (Deputy Chairman, 1978–83; Chairman, 1983–86); *b* 21 Aug. 1929; *s* of John Leighton Gibson and Norah Gibson; *m* 1954, Patricia Anne Thomas; two *s* three *d*. *Educ:* Caterham Sch.; Imperial Coll., London (BSc (Hons Mech. Engrg), ACGI). Post-grad. apprenticeship Rolls Royce Derby, 1953–55; ICI (Billingham and Petrochemicals Div.), 1955–69; Man. Dir, Lummus Co., 1969–73; Dir Gen. Offshore Supplies Office, Dept of Energy, 1973–76. Dir, Taylor Woodrow Construction Ltd, 1989–90. *Recreations:* work, gardening, handyman. *Address:* Little Stapleton, Haytor, Ilsington, Newton Abbot, Devon TQ13 9RR.

GIBSON, John Sibbald; historian; Under Secretary, Scottish Office, 1973–83, retired; *b* 1 May 1923; *s* of John McDonald Frame Gibson and Marion Watson Sibbald; *m* 1948, Moira Helen Gillespie; one *s* one *d*. *Educ:* Paisley Grammar Sch.; Glasgow Univ. Army, 1942–46, Lieut in No 1 Commando from 1943; Far East. Joined Admin. Grade Home Civil Service, 1947; Asst Principal, Scottish Home Dept, 1947–50; Private Sec. to Parly Under-Sec., 1950–51; Private Sec. to Perm. Under-Sec. of State, Scottish Office, 1952; Principal, Scottish Home Dept, 1953; Asst Sec., Dept of Agriculture and Fisheries for Scotland, 1962; Under Secretary: Scottish Office, 1973; Dept of Agriculture and Fisheries for Scotland, 1979. Mem., Agricl Res. Council, 1979–83. Organiser, Scottish Office Centenary Exhibn, 1985. *Publications:* Ships of the '45: the rescue of the Young Pretender, 1967; Deacon Brodie: Father to Jekyll and Hyde, 1977; The Thistle and the Crown, 1985; Playing the Scottish Card: the Franco-Jacobite invasion of 1708, 1988, (contrib.) The '45: to keep an image whole, 1988; (jtly) The Jacobite Threat: a source book, 1990; (jtly) Summer Hunting a Prince, 1992; Lochiel of the '45, 1994; Edinburgh in the '45, 1995. *Recreation:* historical research. *Address:* 28 Cramond Gardens, Edinburgh EH4 6PU. *T:* 0131–336 2931. *Club:* Scottish Arts (Edinburgh).

GIBSON, John Walter; Chief of Operational Research, SHAPE Technical Centre, 1977–84; *b* 15 Jan. 1922; *s* of late Thomas John Gibson and Catherine Gibson (*née* Gregory), Bamburgh, Northumberland; *m* 1951, Julia, *d* of George Leslie Butler, Buxton, Derbyshire; two *s* one *d*. *Educ:* A. J. Dawson Sch., Durham; Sheffield Univ.; University Coll., London. RNVR, 1942–46. Sheffield Univ., 1940–42, 1946–47 (BSc); University Coll., London, 1947–48; Safety-in Mines Research Estabt, 1948–53; BJSM, Washington, DC, 1953–56; Royal Armament Research and Develt Estabt, 1957–60; Head of Statistics Div., Ordnance Bd, 1961–64; Supt, Assessment Br., Royal Armament Research and Develt Estabt, 1964–66, Prin. Supt, Systems Div., 1966–69; Asst Chief Scientific Adviser (Studies), MoD, 1969–74; Under-Secretary: Cabinet Office, 1974–76; MoD, 1976–77. FSS 1953. *Address:* 7 Links Road, Bamburgh, Northumberland NE69 7AX. *T:* Bamburgh (01668) 214495.

GIBSON, Joseph, CBE 1980; PhD; CChem, FRSC; FEng, FInstE; Coal Science Adviser, National Coal Board, 1981–83 (Member for Science, 1977–81); *b* 10 May 1916; *m* 1944, Lily McFarlane Brown; one *s* one *d*. *Educ:* King's Coll. (now Univ. of Newcastle upon Tyne; MSc, PhD). Res., Northern Coke Res. Lab. 1938; Head of Chemistry Dept, Sunderland Technical Coll., and Lectr, Durham Univ., 1946; Chief Scientist, Northern Div., 1958, and Yorks Div., 1964, NCB; Director: Coal Res. Estab., 1968; Coal Utilisation Res., 1975. President: Inst. of Fuel, 1975–76; BCURA, 1977–81 and 1992– (Chm. 1972–77). Lectures: Cadman Meml, 1980, 1983; Prof. Moore Meml, 1981; Brian H. Morgans Meml, 1983. Coal Science Lecture Medal, 1977; Carbonisation Sci. Medal, 1979. Hon. FIChemE. Hon. DCL Newcastle, 1981. *Publications:* jointly: Carbonisation of Coal, 1971; Coal and Modern Coal Processing, 1979; Coal Utilisation: technology, economics and policy, 1981; papers on coal conversion and utilisation. *Recreations:* bridge, gardening. *Address:* 31 Charlton Close, Charlton Kings, Cheltenham, Glos GL53 8DH. *T:* Cheltenham (01242) 517832.

GIBSON, Joseph David, CBE 1979; Ambassador of Fiji to Japan, 1984–87, retired; *b* 26 Jan. 1928; *s* of late Charles Ivan Gibson and Mamao Lavenia Gibson; *m* Emily Susan Bentley; three *s* two *d*. *Educ:* Levuka Public Sch., Suva; Marist Brothers Secondary Sch.; Auckland Univ., NZ (BA); Auckland Teachers' Coll. (Teachers' Cert.). Asst Teacher, Suva Boys' Grammar Sch., 1952–57; Principal, Suva Educnl Inst., 1957; Principal, Queen Victoria School, Fiji, 1961–62 (Asst Teacher, 1958–59; Sen. Master, 1959; 1st Asst, 1960); Sec. Sch. Inspector, Fiji Educn Dept, 1964–65; Asst Dir of Educn, 1966–69; Dep. Dir of Educn, 1970; Dir of Educn and Permanent Sec. for Educn, 1971–74; Dep. High Comr, London, 1974–76, High Comr, 1976–81; High Comr, New Zealand, 1981–83. Represented Fiji at: Dirs of Educn Conferences, Western Samoa and Pago Pago, 1968, Honolulu, 1970; Commonwealth Ministers of Educn Meeting, Canberra, 1971; Head of Fiji Delegn, Commonwealth Ministers of Educn Meeting, Jamaica, 1974. Member: Fiji Broadcasting Commn, 1971–73; Univ. Council, Univ. of South Pacific, 1971–74.

Recreations: golf, fishing, represented Auckland and Suva, Fiji, in hockey. *Address:* 15 Naimawi Street, Lami, Suva, Fiji.

GIBSON, Air Vice-Marshal Michael John, CB 1994; OBE 1979; FRAeS; Head of Management Support Unit, National Air Traffic Services, since 1994; *b* 2 Jan. 1939; *m* 1961, Dorothy Russell; one *s* one *d. Educ:* Imperial Coll., London (BSc); Selwyn Coll., Cambridge; National Defense Univ., Washington, DC. ACGI; FRAeS. Commnd RAFVR, 1959; commnd RAF, 1961; various appointments as fighter pilot and instructor; Personal Air Sec. to Air Force Minister, 1972–73; Officer Commanding: 45 Sqdn (Hunter), 1974–76; 20 Sqdn (Jaguar), 1976–79; RAF Brawdy, 1982–84; RAF Stanley, 1984–85; Air Officer Plans, HQ Strike Comd, 1987–88; Dir, Airspace Policy, 1988–91, Dir Gen. of Policy and Plans, 1991–94, NATS. *Recreations:* music (singing and church organ playing), boating. *Address:* c/o CAA House, 45–59 Kingsway, WC2B 6TE. *T:* 071–832 5314. *Club:* Royal Air Force.

GIBSON, Paul Alexander; Founder, 1973, and Partner, since 1973, Sidell Gibson Partnership, Architects; *b* 11 Oct. 1941; *s* of Wing-Comdr Leslie Gibson and Betty Gibson (later Betty Stephens); *m* 1969, Julia Atkinson. *Educ:* Kingswood Sch., Bath; King's Coll., London; Canterbury Sch. of Architecture; Regent Street Polytechnic Sch. of Architecture (DipArch 1968). Worked for Farrell Grimshaw Partnership, 1968–69; Lectr, North Dakota State Univ., 1969; worked for Foster Associates, 1970–73. 3 RIBA awards, Good Housing, 1986; won open competition for redevelt of Grand Buildings, Trafalgar Square, 1986; won competition for redevelt of Winchester Barracks, 1988; expansion of Jewel House, HM Tower of London, 1992–94. *Recreations:* struggling pianist, keen gardener. *Address:* Fitzroy Yard, Fitzroy Road, NW1 8TP. *T:* 0171–722 5009.

GIBSON, Rear-Adm. Peter Cecil, CB 1968; *b* 31 May 1913; 2nd *s* of Alexander Horace Cecil Gibson and Phyllis Zeline Cecil Gibson (*née* Baume); *m* 1938, Phyllis Anna Mary Hume, *d* of late Major N. H. Hume, IMS, Brecon; two *s* one *d. Educ:* Ealing Priory; RN Engrg Coll., Keyham. RN, 1931; HMS Norfolk, EI, 1936–38; maintenance test pilot, RN Aircraft Yard, Donibristle, 1940–41; Air Engr Officer, RNAS, St Merryn, 1941–42; Staff of RANAS, Indian Ocean, E Africa, 1942–43, Ceylon, 1943–44; Staff Air Engr. Off., British Pacific Fleet, 1945–46; Aircraft Maintenance and Repair Dept, 1946–49; loan service RAN, 1950–52; Trng Off., RNAS, Arbroath, 1952–54; Engr Off., HMS Gambia, 1954–56 and as Fleet Engr. Off, E Indies, 1955–56; Staff Engr. Off., Flag Off. Flying Trng, 1957–60; Dep. Dir Service Conditions, 1960–61; Dir Engr Officers' Appts, 1961–63; Supt RN Aircraft Yard, Fleetlands, 1963–65; Dep. Controller Aircraft (RN), Min. of Aviation, 1966–67, Min. of Technology, 1967–69, retired, 1969. ADC, 1965–66. Comdr 1946; Capt. 1957; Rear-Adm. 1966. Chm. United Services Catholic Assoc., 1966–69. *Recreations:* vintage cars, bridge. *Address:* Pangmere, Hampstead Norreys, Newbury, Berks RG16 0TR. *Club:* Army and Navy.

GIBSON, Rt. Hon. Sir Peter (Leslie), Kt 1981; PC 1993; **Rt. Hon. Lord Justice Peter Gibson;** a Lord Justice of Appeal, since 1993; *b* 10 June 1934; *s* of late Harold Leslie Gibson and Martha Lucy (*née* Diercking); *m* 1968, Katharine Mary Beatrice Hadow; two *s* one *d. Educ:* Malvern Coll.; Worcester Coll., Oxford (Scholar; Hon. Fellow, 1993). 2nd Lieut RA, 1953–55 (National Service). Called to the Bar, Inner Temple, 1960; Bencher, Lincoln's Inn, 1975. 2nd Jun. Counsel to Inland Revenue (Chancery), 1970–72; Jun. Counsel to the Treasury (Chancery), 1972–81; a Judge of the High Court of Justice, Chancery Div., 1981–93. A Judge of the Employment Appeal Tribunal, 1984–86. Chm., Law Commn, 1990–92. *Address:* Royal Courts of Justice, Strand, WC2A 2LL.

GIBSON, Prof. Quentin Howieson, FRS 1969; Professor of Biochemistry and Molecular Biology, Cornell University, Ithaca, NY, 1966–90, now Emeritus; *b* 9 Dec. 1918; *s* of William Howieson Gibson, OBE, DSc; *m* 1951, Audrey Jane, *yr d* of G. H. S. Pinsent, CB, CMG, and Katharine Kentisbeare, *d* of Sir George Radford, MP; one *s* three *d. Educ:* Repton. MB, ChB, BAO, Belfast, 1941, MD 1944, PhD 1946, DSc 1951. Demonstrator in Physiology, Belfast, 1941–44; Lecturer in Physiology: Belfast, 1944–46; Sheffield Univ., 1946–55; Professor of Biochem., Sheffield Univ., 1955–63; Prof. of Biophys. Chem., Johnson Research Foundn, University of Pennsylvania, 1963–66. Fellow, Amer. Acad. of Arts and Sciences, 1971; MNAS 1982. *Recreation:* sailing. *Address:* 98 Dodge Road, Ithaca, NY 14850, USA.

GIBSON, Rt. Hon. Sir Ralph (Brian), PC 1985; Kt 1977; a Lord Justice of Appeal, 1985–94; *b* 17 Oct. 1922; 2nd *s* of Roy and Emily Gibson; *m* 1949, Ann Chapman Ruether, Chicago; one *s* two *d. Educ:* Charterhouse; Brasenose Coll., Oxford (Hon. Fellow 1986). MA Oxon 1948. Army Service, 1941–45: Lieut, 1st KDG; Captain, TJFF. Called to Bar, Middle Temple, 1948, Bencher 1974; QC 1968. A Recorder of the Crown Court, 1972–77; Judge of the High Court of Justice, Queen's Bench Div., 1977–85. Chm., Law Commn, 1981–85. Bigelow Teaching Fellow, University of Chicago, 1948–49. Member: Council of Legal Educn, 1971–86; Parole Bd, 1979–81; Court of Ecclesiastical Causes Reserved, 1986–; Chm., Fees Adv. Commn, C of E, 1986–. Pres., Central Council of Probation Cttees, 1982–86. Hon. LLD Dalhousie, 1983. *Address:* 8 Ashley Gardens, SW1P 1QD. *T:* 0171–828 9670. *Clubs:* Garrick; Emsworth Sailing.
See also C. D. O. Barrie, C. A. W. Gibson.

GIBSON, Prof. Robert Dennis, PhD, DSc; FTS, FAIM; first Vice-Chancellor, Queensland University of Technology, since 1989; *b* 13 April 1942; *m*; one *s* two *d. Educ:* Hull Univ. (BSc Hons); Newcastle upon Tyne Univ. (MSc, PhD); DSc CNAA. FIMA 1977; FAIM 1982; FTS 1993. Asst Lectr, Maths Dept, Univ. of Newcastle upon Tyne, 1966–67; Scientific Officer, Culham Plasma Lab., UKAEA, 1967–68; Lectr in Maths, Univ. of Newcastle upon Tyne, 1968–69; Sen. Lectr, Maths and Statistics, Teesside Polytechnic, 1969–77; Head, Dept of Maths, Stats and Computing (later Sch. of Maths, Stats and Computing), Newcastle upon Tyne Polytechnic, 1977–82; Queensland Institute of Technology: Dep. Dir then Actg Dir, 1982–83; Dir, 1983–88. Mem., 1988–92, Dep. Chm., 1991–92, Aust. Res. Council. *Publications:* numerous research papers on various aspects of mathematical modelling. *Recreations:* jogging, cricket. *Address:* Queensland University of Technology, GPO Box 2434, Brisbane, Qld 4001, Australia.

GIBSON, Prof. Robert Donald Davidson, PhD; Professor of French, University of Kent at Canterbury, 1965–94, now Emeritus (Master of Rutherford College, 1985–90); *b* Hackney, London, 21 Aug. 1927; *o s* of Nicol and Ann Gibson, Leyton, London; *m* 1953, Sheila Elaine, *o d* of Bertie and Ada Goldsworthy, Exeter, Devon; three *s. Educ:* Leyton County High Sch. for Boys; King's Coll., London; Magdalene Coll., Cambridge; Ecole Normale Supérieure, Paris. BA (First Class Hons. French) London, 1948; PhD Cantab. 1953. Asst Lecturer, St Salvator's Coll., University of St Andrews, 1954–55; Lecturer, Queen's Coll., Dundee, 1955–58; Lecturer, Aberdeen Univ., 1958–61; Prof., Queen's Univ. of Belfast, 1961–65. *Publications:* The Quest of Alain-Fournier, 1953; Modern French Poets on Poetry, 1961; (ed) Le Bestiaire Inattendu, 1961; Roger Martin du Gard, 1961; La Mésentente Cordiale, 1963; (ed) Brouart et le Désordre, 1964; (ed) Provinciales, 1965; (ed) Le Grand Meaulnes, 1968; The Land Without a Name, 1975; Alain-Fournier and Le Grand Meaulnes, 1986; (ed) Studies in French Fiction, 1988; Annals of Ashdon, 1988; The Best of Enemies, 1995; reviews and articles in: French Studies, Modern Language Review, The London Magazine, Times Literary Supplement, Encyclopædia Britannica, Collier's Encyclopædia. *Recreations:* reading, writing, talking. *Address:* Thalassa!, Cliff Road, Sidmouth, Devon EX10 8JN.

GIBSON, Roy; aerospace consultant, since 1980; Director General, British National Space Centre, 1985–87; *b* 4 July 1924; *s* of Fred and Jessie Gibson; *m* 1st, 1946, Jean Fallowes (marr. diss. 1971); one *s* one *d*; 2nd, 1971, Inga Elgerus. *Educ:* Chorlton Grammar Sch.; Wadham College, Oxford; SOAS. Malayan Civil Service, 1948–58; Health and Safety Br., UKAEA, 1958–66; European Space Research Orgn, 1967–75 (Dir of Admin, 1970–75); Dir Gen., European Space Agency, 1975–80. DSC (Kedah, Malaysia), 1953; Das Grosse Silberne Ehrenzeichen mit Stern (Austria), 1977. *Publications:* numerous articles in aerospace technical jls. *Recreations:* music, chess, walking. *Address:* Résidence les Hespérides, 51 Allée J. de Beins, Montpellier 3400, France. *T:* 67648181. *Club:* Naval and Military.

GIBSON, Ven. Terence Allen; Archdeacon of Ipswich, since 1987; *b* 23 Oct. 1937; *s* of Fred William Allen and Joan Hazel Gibson. *Educ:* Jesus Coll., Cambridge (MA); Cuddesdon Coll., Oxford. Curate of St Chad, Kirkby, 1963–66; Warden of Centre 63, Kirkby C of E Youth Centre, 1966–75; Rector of Kirkby, Liverpool, 1975–84; RD of Walton, Liverpool, 1979–84; Archdeacon of Suffolk, 1984–87. *Address:* 99 Valley Road, Ipswich, Suffolk IP1 4NF. *T:* Ipswich (01473) 250333.

GIBSON, Wilford Henry, CBE 1980; QPM 1976; Assistant Commissioner (Administration and Operations), Metropolitan Police, 1977–84, retired; *b* 12 Oct. 1924; *s* of late Ernest Gibson and Frances Mary (*née* Kitching); *m* 1949, Betty Ann Bland; two *d.* Served War, Signaller, RAF, 1943–47. Joined Metropolitan Police as Constable, 1947; Inspector 1960; Supt 1965; Comdr 1971; Dep. Asst Comr, A Dept (Operations), 1974. Chm., Met. Police Flying Club and Met. Police Modern Pentathlon Club, 1976–84. Chm., British Home and Hosp. for Incurables, 1989–. OStJ 1977. *Recreations:* reading, swimming, flying.

GIBSON, Major William David; Chairman, W. J. Tatem Ltd, since 1974 (Director, since 1957); *b* 26 Feb. 1925; *s* of late G. C. Gibson, OBE, Landwade Hall, Exning, Newmarket, Suffolk; *m* 1st, 1959, Charlotte Henrietta (*d* 1973), *d* of N. S. Pryor; three *s* one *d*; 2nd, 1975, Jane Marion, *d* of late Col L. L. Hassell, DSO, MC. *Educ:* St Peter's Court; Harrow; Trinity Coll., Cambridge. Commissioned into Welsh Guards, July 1945; retired as Major, 1957. Dir, West of England Ship Owners Mutual Protection & Indemnity Assoc., 1959–86; Chairman: Atlantic Shipping and Trading Co., 1969–77; Internat. Shipowners Investment Co., SA Luxembourg, 1978–83; Waverley Components and Products, 1990–95; Tatem Industries Ltd, 1990–95. National Hunt Cttee, Oct. 1959– (Sen. Steward, 1966); Jockey Club, 1966– (Dep. Sen. Steward, 1969–71); Tattersalls Cttee, 1963–69 (Chm., 1967–69). Master, Worshipful Co. of Farriers, 1979. *Recreations:* racing (won 4 Grand Military Gold Cups, 1950–52 and 1956); shooting, sailing. *Address:* Bishopswood Grange, Bishopswood, near Ross-on-Wye, Herefordshire HR9 5QX. *T:* Dean (01594) 860444. *Clubs:* Cavalry and Guards, Royal Thames Yacht; Royal Yacht Squadron.

GIBSON-BARBOZA, Mario, Hon. GCMG 1968; Brazilian Ambassador to the Court of St James's, 1982–86; *b* Olinda, Pernambuco, 13 March 1918; *s* of Oscar Bartholomeu Alves Barboza and Evangelina Gibson Barboza; *m* 1975, Julia Blacker Baldassarri Gibson-Barboza. *Educ:* Law School of Recife, Pernambuco (graduated in Law, 1937); Superior War College, 1951. Entered Brazilian Foreign Service, 1940; served: Houston, Washington and Brussels, 1943–54; Minister-Counsellor: Buenos Aires, 1956–59; Brazilian Mission to United Nations, New York, 1959–60; Ambassador: to Vienna, 1962–66; to Asunción, 1967–68; Secretary General for Foreign Affairs, 1968–69; Ambassador to Washington, 1969; Minister of State for External Relations, 1969–74; Ambassador: to Athens, 1974–77; to Rome, 1977–82. Several Grand Crosses of Orders of Brazil and other countries. *Recreations:* riding, reading, theatre. *Address:* c/o Ministry of Foreign Affairs, Palácio do Hamaraty, Esplanada dos Ministérios, 70.170 Brasília, DF, Brazil. *Clubs:* Athenæum, Travellers', White's; Jockey Clube Brasileiro (Rio de Janeiro).

GIBSON-CRAIG-CARMICHAEL, Sir David Peter William, 15th Bt *cr* 1702 (Gibson Carmichael) and 8th Bt *cr* 1831; *b* 21 July 1946; *s* of Sir Archibald Henry William Gibson-Craig-Carmichael, 14th Bt and Rosemary Anita (*d* 1979), *d* of George Duncan Crew, Santiago, Chile; *S* father, 1969; *m* 1973, Patricia, *d* of Marcos Skarnic, Santiago, Chile; one *s* one *d. Educ:* Queen's Univ., Canada (BSc, Hons Geology, 1971). *Heir: s* Peter William Gibson-Craig-Carmichael, *b* 29 Dec. 1975.

GIBSON-WATT, Baron *cr* 1979 (Life Peer), of the Wye in the District of Radnor; **James David Gibson-Watt,** MC 1943 and 2 Bars; PC 1974; DL; a Forestry Commissioner, 1976–86; Chairman, Timber Growers United Kingdom, 1987–90 (Hon. President, since 1993); *b* 11 Sept. 1918; *er s* of late Major James Miller Gibson-Watt, DL, JP; *m* 1942, Diana, 2nd *d* of Sir Charles Hambro; two *s* two *d* (and one *s* decd). *Educ:* Eton; Trinity Coll (BA). Welsh Guards, 1939–46; N African and Italian campaigns. Contested (C) Brecon and Radnor constituency, 1950 and 1951; MP (C) Hereford, Feb. 1956–Sept. 1974; a Lord Commissioner of the Treasury, 1959–61; Minister of State, Welsh Office, 1970–74. FRAgS; Pres., Royal Welsh Agric. Soc., 1976 (Chm. Council, 1976–94). Chm., Council on Tribunals, 1980–86. Mem., Historic Buildings Council, Wales, 1975–79. DL Powys, 1968; JP Rhayader, retd 1989. *Address:* Doldowlod, Llandrindod Wells, Powys. *T:* Newbridge-on-Wye (0159789) 208. *Club:* Boodle's.

GICK, Rear-Adm. Philip David, CB 1963; OBE 1946; DSC and Bar, 1942; Chairman, Emsworth Shipyard Group, 1965–90; *b* 22 Feb. 1913; *s* of late Sir William John Gick, CB, CBE; *m* 1938, Aylmer Rowntree (*d* 1993); one *s* three *d. Educ:* St Lawrence Coll., Ramsgate. Joined RN, 1931; qualified as Pilot, 1936. Capt. 1952; Comd HMS Daring, RNAS, Lossiemouth, HMS Bulwark, 1952–58; Rear-Adm. 1961; Flag Officer, Naval Flying Training, 1961–64, retd. *Recreation:* sailing. *Address:* Furzefield, Bosham Hoe, West Sussex PO18 8ET. *T:* Bosham (01243) 572219. *Clubs:* Royal Yacht Squadron, Royal Ocean Racing; Royal Naval Sailing Association; Bosham Sailing.

GIDDEN, Barry Owen Barton, CMG 1962; *b* Southampton, 4 July 1915; *s* of late Harry William Gidden, MA, PhD. *Educ:* King Edward VI Sch., Southampton; Jesus Coll., Cambridge (Scholar; Class. Tripos Pts 1 and 2; BA). Apptd Asst Principal, HM Office of Works, 1939. Served War of 1939–45: BEF, 1939–40, Major 1943. Principal, Min. of Works, 1946; Private Sec. to Minister of Works, 1946–48; Principal, Colonial Office, 1949, Asst Sec 1951; Counsellor, UK Mission to UN, New York, 1954–58; Establishment Officer, Colonial Office, 1958–65; Asst Sec., DHSS, 1965–75. *Recreation:* golf. *Address:* 15 Chesham Street, SW1X 8ND. *T:* 0171–235 4185. *Club:* Walton Heath.

GIDDENS, Prof. Anthony, PhD; Professor of Sociology, in the Faculty of Economics and Politics, since 1985, and Fellow of King's College, since 1969, University of Cambridge; *b* 18 Jan. 1938; *s* of T. G. Giddens; *m* 1963, Jane M. Ellwood. *Educ:* Hull Univ. (BA); LSE (MA); MA 1970, PhD 1974, Cantab. Lectr in Sociology, subseq. Reader, Cambridge Univ., 1969–85. *Publications:* Capitalism and Modern Social Theory, 1971; (ed) Sociology of Suicide, 1972; Politics and Sociology in the Thought of Max Weber, 1972; (ed and trans) Emile Durkheim: Selected Writings, 1972; (ed) Positivism and Sociology, 1974; New Rules of Sociological Method, 1976; Studies in Social and Political

Theory, 1976; Central Problems in Social Theory, 1979; Class Structure of the Advanced Societies, 2nd edn 1981; Contemporary Critique of Historical Materialism: vol. 1, Power, Property and State, 1981, vol. 2, Nation, State and Violence, 1985; (jtly) Classes, Power and Conflict, 1982; Profiles and Critiques in Social Theory, 1983; (ed jtly) Social Class and the Division of Labour, 1983; Constitution of Society, 1984; Durkheim, 1985; Sociology: a brief but critical introduction, 1986; Social Theory and Modern Sociology, 1987; (ed jtly) Social Theory Today, 1987; Sociology, 1989; The Consequences of Modernity, 1990. *Address:* King's College, Cambridge CB2 1ST.

GIDDINGS, Air Marshal Sir (Kenneth Charles) Michael, KCB 1975; OBE 1953; DFC 1945; AFC 1950 and Bar 1955; *b* 27 Aug. 1920; *s* of Charles Giddings and Grace Giddings (*née* Gregory); *m* 1946, Elizabeth McConnell; two *s* two *d*. *Educ:* Ealing Grammar Sch. Conscripted, RAF, 1940; Comd, 129 Sqdn, 1944; Empire Test Pilots Sch., 1946; Test pilot, RAE, 1947–50; HQ Fighter Command, 1950–52; RAF Staff Coll., 1953; OC, Flying Wing, Waterbeach, 1954–56; CFE, 1956–58; OC, 57 Sqdn, 1958–60; Group Captain Ops, Bomber Command, 1960–62; Supt of Flying, A&AEE, 1962–64; Dir Aircraft Projects, MoD, 1964–66; AOC, Central Reconnaissance Estabt, 1967–68; ACAS (Operational Requirements), 1968–71; Chief of Staff No 18 (M) Group, Strike Command, RAF, 1971–73; Dep. Chief of Defence Staff, Op. Requirements, 1973–76. Dir, Nat. Counties Building Soc., 1982–85. Indep. Panel Inspector, DoE, 1979–91. *Recreations:* golf, gardening, music. *Address:* 159 Long Lane, Tilehurst, Reading, Berks RG3 6YW. *T:* Reading (01734) 423012.

GIELGUD, Sir (Arthur) John, CH 1977; Kt 1953; Hon. LLD St Andrews 1950; Hon. DLitt Oxon 1953; Hon. DLitt London 1977; Actor; *b* 14 April 1904; *s* of late Frank Gielgud and Kate Terry Lewis; unmarried. *Educ:* Westminster. First appearance on stage at Old Vic, 1921; among parts played are Lewis Dodd in Constant Nymph, Inigo Jollifant in The Good Companions, Richard II in Richard of Bordeaux, Hamlet, and Romeo; Valentine in Love for Love, Ernest Worthing in The Importance of Being Earnest, Macbeth and King Lear; directed Macbeth, Piccadilly, 1942; Raskolnikoff in Crime and Punishment, Jason in The Medea, New York, 1947; Eustace in The Return of the Prodigal, Globe, 1948; directed The Heiress, Haymarket, 1949; directed and played Thomas Mendip, The Lady's not for Burning, Globe, 1949; Shakespeare Festival, Stratford-on-Avon, 1950; Angelo in Measure for Measure, Cassius in Julius Caesar, Benedick in Much Ado About Nothing, the name part in King Lear; directed Much Ado About Nothing and King Lear; Shakespeare season at Phoenix, 1951–52; Leontes in The Winter's Tale, Phoenix, 1951, directed Much Ado About Nothing and played Benedick, 1952; season at Lyric, Hammersmith, 1953; directed Richard II and The Way of the World (played Mirabel); played Jaffeir in Venice Preserved; directed A Day by the Sea, and played Julian Anson, Haymarket, Nov. 1953–54; also directed Charley's Aunt, New Theatre, Dec. 1953, and directed The Cherry Orchard, Lyric, May, 1954, and Twelfth Night, Stratford, 1955; played in King Lear and Much Ado About Nothing (also produced Much Ado), for Shakespeare Memorial Theatre Company (London, provinces and continental tour), 1955; directed The Chalk Garden, Haymarket, 1956; produced (with Noel Coward) Nude with Violin, and played Sebastien, Globe, 1956–57; produced The Trojans, Covent Garden, 1957; played Prospero, Stratford, and Drury Lane, 1957; played James Callifer in The Potting Shed, Globe, 1958 and Wolsey in Henry VIII, Old Vic, 1958; directed Variation on A Theme, 1958; produced The Complaisant Lover, Globe, 1959; (Shakespeare's) Ages of Man, Queen's, 1959 (recital, based on Shakespeare anthology of G. Rylands); previous recitals at Edinburgh Fest. and in US, also subseq. in US, at Haymarket, 1960 and tour of Australia and NZ, 1963–64; Gothenburg, Copenhagen, Warsaw, Helsinki, Leningrad, Moscow and Dublin, 1964; produced Much Ado About Nothing, at Cambridge, Mass, Festival, and subseq. in New York, 1959; prod. Five Finger Exercise, Comedy, 1958, NY, 1959; acted in The Last Joke, Phœnix, 1960; prod. Britten's A Midsummer Night's Dream, Royal Opera House, 1961; prod Big Fish Little Fish, New York, 1961; prod Dazzling Prospect, Globe, 1961. Stratford-on-Avon Season, 1961: took part of Othello, also of Gaieff in The Cherry Orchard, Aldwych, 1962; produced The School for Scandal, Haymarket, 1962; prod The School for Scandal, and played Joseph Surface, USA tour, and New York, 1962–63; dir. The Ides of March, and played Julius Caesar, Haymarket, 1963; dir. Hamlet, Canada and USA, 1964; Julian in Tiny Alice, New York, 1965; played Ivanov and directed Ivanov, Phœnix, 1965, United States and Canada, 1966; played Orgon in Tartuffe, Nat. Theatre, 1967; directed Halfway up the Tree, Queen's, 1967; played Oedipus in Oedipus, Nat. Theatre, 1968; produced Don Giovanni, Coliseum, 1968; played Headmaster in 40 Years On, Apollo, 1968; played Sir Gideon in The Battle of Shrivings, Lyric, 1970; Home, Royal Court, 1970, NY 1971 (Evening Standard Best Actor award and Tony award, NY, 1971); dir, All Over, NY, 1971; Caesar and Cleopatra, Chichester Festival, 1971; Veterans, Royal Ct, 1972; dir, Private Lives, Queen's, 1972; dir, The Constant Wife, Albery, 1973; played Prospero, Nat. Theatre, 1974; Bingo, Royal Court, 1974; dir, The Gay Lord Quex, Albery, 1975; No Man's Land, Nat. Theatre, 1975, Toronto, Washington, NY, 1977; Julius Caesar, Volpone, Nat. Theatre, 1977; Half-Life, NT and Duke of York's, 1977; The Best of Friends, Apollo, 1988; *films include:* (GB and US) The Good Companions, 1932; The Secret Agent, 1937; The Prime Minister (Disraeli), 1940; Julius Caesar (Cassius), 1952; Richard III (Duke of Clarence), 1955; The Barretts of Wimpole Street (Mr Moulton Barrett), 1957; St Joan (Warwick), 1957; Becket (Louis VII), 1964; The Loved One, 1965; Chimes at Midnight, 1966; Mister Sebastian, 1967; The Charge of the Light Brigade, 1968; Shoes of the Fisherman, 1968; Oh What a Lovely War!, 1968; Julius Caesar, 1970; Eagle in a Cage, Lost Horizon, 1973; 11 Harrowhouse, 1974; Gold, 1974; Murder on the Orient Express, 1974; Aces High, 1976; Providence, Joseph Andrews, Portrait of a Young Man, Caligula, 1977; The Human Factor, The Elephant Man, 1979; The Conductor, Murder by Decree, Sphinx, Chariots of Fire, The Formula, Arthur (Oscar, 1982), 1980; Lion of the Desert, 1981; Priest of Love, 1982; Wagner, Invitation to the Wedding, Scandalous, The Wicked Lady, 1983; Camille, 1984; The Shooting Party, 1985; Plenty, 1985; Leave All Fair; The Whistle Blower, 1987; Arthur on the Rocks, Getting Things Right, Loser Takes All, 1988; Prospero's Books, Shining Through, Power of One, 1991. Has appeared on *television*, including: The Mayfly and the Frog, 1966; Great Acting, Dorian Gray, 1967; In Good King Charles's Golden Days, 1970; Parson's Pleasure, 1980; Richard Wagner, Brideshead Revisited, 1981; Inside the Third Reich, Neck, The Scarlet and the Black, 1983; presenter of Six Centuries of Verse, 1984; Time After Time, 1986; Marco Polo, Oedipus the King, 1986; War and Remembrance, The Canterville Ghost, 1987; Summer's Lease, 1989; Summer Day's Dream, 1994. President: Shakespeare Reading Soc., 1958–; RADA, 1977–89 (Hon. Fellow, 1989). Fellow, BAFTA, 1992. Special award for services to theatre, Laurence Olivier Awards, 1985. Hon. degree Brandeis Univ. Companion, Legion of Honour, 1960. *Publications:* Early Stages, 1938; Stage Directions, 1963; Distinguished Company, 1972; (jtly) An Actor and His Time (autobiog.), 1979; Backward Glances, 1989; Shakespeare—Hit or Miss, 1991; Notes from the Gods, 1994. *Recreations:* music, painting. *Clubs:* Garrick, Arts; Players' (New York).

GIELGUD, Maina; free-lance ballerina; Artistic Director, Australian Ballet, since 1983; *b* 14 Jan. 1945; *d* of Lewis Gielgud and Elisabeth Grussner. *Educ:* BEPC (French). Ballet du Marquis de Cuevas, 1962–63; Ballet Classique de France, 1965–67; Ballet du XXème Siècle, Maurice Béjart, 1967–72; London Festival Ballet, 1972–77; Royal Ballet, 1977–78; free-lance, 1978–; rehearsal director, London City Ballet, 1981–82. Hon. AO 1991. *Address:* c/o Australian Ballet, 2 Kavanagh Street, South Melbourne, Vic 3205, Australia; Stirling Court, 3 Marshall Street, W1V 1LQ. *T:* 071–734 6612.

GIESKE, Dr Friedhelm; Chairman of Managing Board, RWE AG, since 1989; *b* Schwege/Bohmte, near Osnabrück, 12 Jan. 1928. *Educ:* Göttingen (Dr jur 1954). Joined RWE (Rheinisch-Westfählisches Elektrizitätswerk), 1953; Dep. Mem., 1968, Mem. (Finance), 1972, Bd of Management; Bd spokesman, 1988; Chm., Supervisory Bd of various RWE Gp cos; Member, Supervisory Board: Allianz Lebensversicherungs-AG, Stuttgart; Deutsche Hypothekenbank Frankfurt AG, Frankfurt/Main; Ferrostaal AG, Essen; Karstadt AG, Essen; Metallgesellschaft AG, Frankfurt/Main; National-Bank AG, Essen. Vice-President: Essen Chamber of Industry and Commerce; German Nat. Cttee, World Energy Conf. *Address:* RWE AG, Kruppstrasse 5, 4300 Essen 1, Germany. *T:* (201) 1855101.

GIEVE, (Edward) John (Watson); Assistant Director, Budget and Public Finances, HM Treasury, since 1994; *b* 20 Feb. 1950; *s* of David Watson Gieve and Susan Gieve; *m* 1972, Katherine Vereker; two *s*. *Educ:* Charterhouse; New Coll., Oxford (BA PPE, BPhil). Dept of Employment, 1974–78; HM Treasury: Principal, Industrial Policy Div., 1979–81; Energy Div., 1981–82; Private Sec., 1982–84; Investment Controller, Investors in Industry, 1984–86 (on secondment); HM Treasury: Public Expenditure Survey Div., 1986–88; Press Sec., 1988–89; Principal Private Sec. to Chancellor of the Exchequer, 1989–91; Under Sec., Banking Gp, 1991–94. *Recreations:* golf (playing), football (watching). *Address:* HM Treasury, Parliament Street, SW1P 3AG. *T:* 0171–270 4469.

GIFFARD, family name of **Earl of Halsbury.**

GIFFARD, Adam Edward; *b* 3 June 1934; *o s* of 3rd Earl of Halsbury, *qv* (but does not use courtesy title Viscount Tiverton); *m* 1st, 1963, Ellen, *d* of late Brynjolf Hovde; 2nd, 1976, Joanna Elizabeth, *d* of late Frederick Harry Cole; two *d*.

GIFFARD, Sir (Charles) Sydney (Rycroft), KCMG 1984 (CMG 1976); HM Diplomatic Service, retired; *b* 30 Oct. 1926; *s* of Walter Giffard and Minna Giffard (*née* Cotton); *m* 1st, 1951, Wendy Vidal (marr. diss. 1976); one *s* one *d*; 2nd, 1976, Hazel Roberts, OBE. *Educ:* Repton Sch.; Wadham Coll., Oxford (Hon. Fellow, 1991). Served in Japan, 1952; Foreign Office, 1957; Berne, 1961; Tokyo, 1964; Counsellor, FCO, 1968; Royal Coll. of Defence Studies, 1971; Counsellor, Tel Aviv, 1972; Minister in Tokyo, 1975–80; Ambassador to Switzerland, 1980–82; Dep. Under-Sec. of State, FCO, 1982–84; Ambassador to Japan, 1984–86. Gov., Repton Sch., 1988–94; Mem. Court, Univ. of Southampton, 1993–95. *Publication:* Japan Among the Powers 1890–1990, 1994. *Address:* Winkelbury House, Berwick St John, Wilts, near Shaftesbury, Dorset SP7 0EY. *Club:* Lansdowne.

See also Dr B. J. Greenhill.

GIFFORD, family name of **Baron Gifford.**

GIFFORD, 6th Baron, *cr* 1824; **Anthony Maurice Gifford;** QC 1982; Barrister at Law, practising since 1966; Attorney-at-Law, Jamaica, since 1990; *b* 1 May 1940; *s* of 5th Baron Gifford and Lady Gifford (*née* Margaret Allen) (*d* 1990), Sydney, NSW; *S* father, 1961; *m* 1st, 1965, Katherine Ann (marr. diss. 1988), *o d* of Dr Mundy; one *s* one *d*; 2nd, 1988, Elean Roslyn, *d* of Bishop David Thomas, Kingston, Jamaica; one *d*. *Educ:* Winchester Coll. (scholar); King's Coll., Cambridge (scholar; BA 1961). Student at Middle Temple, 1959–62, called to the Bar, 1962. Chairman: Cttee for Freedom in Mozambique, Angola and Guiné, 1968–75; Mozambique Angola Cttee, 1982–90. Chairman: N Kensington Neighbourhood Law Centre, 1974–77 (Hon. Sec., 1970–74); Legal Action Gp, 1978–83; Vice-Chm., Defence and Aid Fund (UK), 1983–. Pres., Cttee for Human Rights, Grenada, 1987–; Vice-Pres., Haldane Soc. of Socialist Lawyers, 1986–. Chairman: Broadwater Farm Inquiry, 1986; Liverpool 8 Inquiry, 1988–89. *Publication:* Where's the Justice?, 1986. *Heir: s* Hon. Thomas Adam Gifford, *b* 1 Dec. 1967. *Address:* 21 Church Street, Kingston, Jamaica. *T:* 922 6056, *Fax:* 967 0225; 8 King's Bench Walk, Temple, EC4Y 7DU. *T:* 0171–797 8888, *Fax:* 0171–797 8880.

GIFFORD, Prof. (Charles) Henry, FBA 1983; Winterstoke Professor of English, University of Bristol, 1967–75, Professor of English and Comparative Literature, Jan.-July 1976, retired; *b* 17 June 1913; *s* of Walter Stanley Gifford and Constance Lena Gifford (*née* Henry); *m* 1938, Mary Rosamond van Ingen; one *s* one *d*. *Educ:* Harrow Sch.; Christ Church, Oxford. BA 1936, MA 1946. War Service, 1940–46, Royal Armoured Corps; Univ. of Bristol: Asst Lectr, 1946; Sen. Lectr, 1955; Prof. of Modern English Literature, 1963. Clark Lectr, Trinity Coll., Cambridge, 1985. Gen. Editor, Cambridge Studies in Russian Literature, 1980–84. *Publications:* The Hero of his Time, 1950; (with Charles Tomlinson) Castilian Ilexes: versions from Antonio Machado, 1963; The Novel in Russia, 1964; Comparative Literature, 1969; Tolstoy: a critical anthology, 1971; Pasternak: a critical study, 1977; Tolstoy, 1982; Poetry in a Divided World (1985 Clark Lectures), 1986; articles and reviews on English and comparative literature. *Address:* 10 Hyland Grove, Bristol BS9 3NR. *T:* Bristol (0117) 950 2504.

GIFFORD, Michael Brian; Managing Director and Chief Executive, Rank Organisation, since 1983; *b* 9 Jan. 1936; *s* of Kenneth Gifford and Maude Gifford (*née* Palmer); *m* Asa Margareta Lundin; one *s* one *d* (one *s* one *d* by previous marr.). *Educ:* LSE (BSc Econ). Joined Leo Computers (later part of ICL), 1960; Man. Dir, ICL (Pacific), 1973–75; Chief Exec., Cadbury Schweppes Australia, 1975–78; Finance Dir, Cadbury Schweppes plc, 1978–83; Dir, 1983–94, Chm., 1992–94, A. Kershaw and Son; Director: English China Clays PLC, 1992–; Gillette Co., 1993–. *Address:* c/o Rank Organisation plc, 6 Connaught Place, W2 2EZ. *T:* 0171–706 1111.

GIGGALL, Rt. Rev. George Kenneth, OBE 1961; Assistant Bishop, Diocese of Blackburn, since 1982; *b* 15 April 1914; *s* of Arthur William and Matilda Hannah Giggall; unmarried. *Educ:* Manchester Central High Sch.; Univ. of Manchester; St Chad's Coll., Univ. of Durham. BA, DipTheol. Deacon, 1939; Priest, 1940. Curate of St Alban's Cheetwood, Dio. Manchester, 1939–41, St Elisabeth's Reddish, 1941–45; Chaplain, RN, 1945; HMS Braganza, 1945; 34th Amphibious Support Regt, RM, 1945–46; Chaplain, Sch. of Combined Ops, 1946–47; HMS: Norfolk, 1947–49; Ocean, 1949–50; Flotilla Comd Mediterranean and HMS Phoenicia, 1950–52; HMS Campania for Operation Hurricane, 1952; BRNC Dartmouth, 1952–53; HMS: Centaur, 1953–56; Ceylon, 1956–58; Fisgard, 1958–60; Royal Arthur and Lectr RAF Chaplains' Sch., 1960–63; HMS: Eagle, 1963–65; Drake, 1965–69; QHC, 1967–69; Dean of Gibraltar and Officiating Chaplain, HMS Rooke and Flag Officer, Gibraltar, 1969–73; Bishop of St Helena, 1973–79; Chaplain of San Remo with Bordighera, Italy, and Auxiliary Bishop, dio. of Gibraltar, 1979–81. *Recreation:* music. *Address:* Fosbrooke House, 8 Clifton Drive, Lytham, Lancs FY8 5RQ. *T:* Lytham (01253) 735683. *Clubs:* Commonwealth Trust, Sion College; Exiles (Ascension Island).

GILBART, Andrew James; QC 1991; an Assistant Recorder, since 1992; *b* 13 Feb. 1950; *s* of Albert Thomas Gilbart and Carol Christie Gilbart, Vinehall Sch., Robertsbridge; *m* 1979, Morag Williamson; one *s* one *d*. *Educ:* Westminster Sch. (Queen's Scholar); Trinity

Hall, Cambridge (MA). Called to the Bar, Middle Temple, 1972; elected to Northern Circuit, 1973. Mem. Cttee, Local Govt, Planning and Envmtl Bar Assoc., 1988–92. *Publications:* articles in Jl of Planning and Environment Law and Local Govt Chronicle. *Recreations:* history, walking, theatre. *Address:* 40 King Street, Manchester M2 6BA. *T:* 0161–832 9082; 4 Breams Buildings, EC4A 1AQ. *T:* 0171–353 5835. *Club:* Heaton Chapel Reform (Heaton Moor).

GILBART-DENHAM, Lt-Col Seymour Vivian, CVO 1994; Crown Equerry, since 1987; *b* 10 Oct. 1939; *s* of Major Vivian Vandeleur Gilbart-Denham (killed in action, Narvik, 1940), Irish Guards and Diana Mary Beaumont; *m* 1976, Patricia Caroline Brooking; two *d.* Commissioned, Life Guards, 1960; served UK, Germany, Cyprus and Far East; Adjutant, Life Guards, 1965–67; commanded Household Cavalry Regt, 1986–87. Vice-President: Royal Windsor Horse Show, 1988–; Royal Parks Equitation Trust, 1992–; Gtr London Reg., Riding for the Disabled, 1994–. *Recreations:* carriage driving, shooting, ski-ing. *Address:* The Royal Mews, Buckingham Palace, SW1W 0QH. *T:* 0171–930 4832. *Club:* White's.

GILBERD, Rt Rev. Bruce Carlyle; Bishop of Auckland, 1985–94; Priest-in-charge, Albany Greenhithe Mission District, diocese of Auckland, since 1995; *b* 22 April 1938; *s* of Carlyle Bond Gilberd and Dorothy Annie Gilberd; *m* 1963, Patricia Molly Tanton; two *s* one *d. Educ:* King's College, Auckland; Auckland Univ. (BSc); St John's Coll., Auckland (LTh Hons, STh). Deacon 1962, priest 1963, Auckland; Assistant Curate: Devonport, 1962–64; Ponsonby and Grey Lynn, 1965; Panmure, 1965–68; Vicar of Avondale, 1968–71. Trainee Industrial Chaplain, Tees-side Industrial Mission, and Asst Curate of Egglescliffe, 1971–73; visited industrial missions in UK and Europe. Director, Interchurch Trade and Industrial Mission, Wellington, 1973–79; founding Mem., Wellington Industrial Relations Soc.; Hon. Asst Curate, Lower Hutt 1973–77, Waiwhetu 1977–79; Lectr, St John's Coll., Auckland, 1980–85. Mem. Gen. Synod, NZ. Has travelled widely in UK, Europe, China, USA and S Africa. NZ Commemorative Medal, 1990. *Publication:* (ed) Christian Ministry: a definition, 1984. *Recreations:* fishing, surfing, sailing. *Address:* PO Box 67–084, Mt Eden, Auckland, New Zealand.

GILBERT; *see* Johnson-Gilbert.

GILBERT, Prof. Alan David, DPhil; Vice-Chancellor, University of Melbourne, since 1996; *b* 11 Sept. 1944; *s* of Garnet E. Gilbert and Violet Gilbert (*née* Elsey); *m* 1967, Ingrid Sara Griffiths; two *d. Educ:* ANU (BA Hons 1965; MA 1967); Oxford Univ. (DPhil History 1973). Lectr, Univ. of Papua New Guinea, 1967–69; University of New South Wales: Lectr, 1973–77; Sen. Lectr, 1977–79; Associate Prof., 1979–81; Prof. of History, 1981–88; Pro-Vice-Chancellor, 1988–91; Vice-Chancellor, Univ. of Tasmania, 1991–95. Mem., Australian Higher Educn Council, 1991–. FASSA 1990. *Publications:* Religion and Society in Industrial England, 1976; The Making of Post-Christian Britain, 1980; (with R. Currie and L. Horsley) Churches and Churchgoers, 1977; (Gen. Editor) Australians: a historical library, 11 Vols, 1987. *Recreations:* running, golf, chess. *Address:* Vice-Chancellor's Office, University of Melbourne, Parkville, Vic 3052, Australia. *Club:* Tasmanian (Hobart).

GILBERT, Francis Humphrey Shubrick; QC 1992; a Recorder, since 1994; *b* 25 Jan. 1946; *s* of late Comdr Walter Raleigh Gilbert, RN, DL, Compton Castle, Devon and of Joan Mary Boileau Gilbert; *m* 1975, Sarah Marian Kaye, *d* of Col Douglas Kaye, DSO, DL, Brinkley Hall, Newmarket; one *s* two *d. Educ:* Stowe; Trinity Coll., Dublin (MA). Called to the Bar, Lincoln's Inn, 1970. Devon County Councillor, 1977–85. *Recreations:* sailing, shooting. *Address:* (chambers) Walnut House, St David's Hill, Exeter, Devon EX4 4DW. *T:* Exeter (01392) 79751; 4 Pump Court, Temple, EC4Y 7AN. *Club:* Royal Yacht Squadron.

GILBERT, Prof. Geoffrey Alan, FRS 1973; Professor of Biochemistry, University of Birmingham, 1969–85, now Emeritus; *b* 3 Dec. 1917; *s* of A. C. Gilbert and M. M. Gilbert (*née* Cull); *m* 1948, Lilo M. Gilbert (*née* Czigler de Egerszalok); two *s. Educ:* Kingsbury County Sch., Mddx; Emmanuel Coll., Cambridge; Dept of Colloid Science, Cambridge. MA, PhD, ScD (Cantab). Lectr, Chemistry Dept, Univ. of Birmingham, 1943–46. Research Fellow, Medical Sch., Harvard Univ., 1946–47. Univ. of Birmingham: Sen. Lectr, Chemistry Dept, 1947–61, Reader, 1961–69. Chm., British Biophysical Soc., 1974. Mem., Editorial Bd, Jl of Molecular Biol., 1972–87. *Publications:* articles and papers in scientific jls. *Recreations:* photography, gardening, fox-watching. *Address:* 194 Selly Park Road, Birmingham B29 7HY. *T:* 0121–472 0755.

GILBERT, Maj.-Gen. Glyn Charles Anglim, CB 1974; MC 1944; Controller, Airborne Forces Charities Development Trust, since 1990; Director, Fitness for Industry Ltd, since 1980; *b* 15 Aug. 1920; *s* of late C. G. G. Gilbert, OBE, MC, and H. M. Gilbert, MBE; *m* 1943, Heather Mary Jackson; three *s* one *d. Educ:* Eastbourne Coll.; RMC Sandhurst. Commnd 1939; served with 2nd Lincolns, 1940–47, NW Europe and Palestine; Instructor, Sch. of Infantry, 1948–50; 3rd Bn Para. Regt, 1951; Staff Coll., 1952; staff and regimental appts in MoD, Airborne Forces, Royal Lincolns and Para. Regt, 1952–66, Cyprus, Egypt and Malaya; idc 1966; comd Sch. of Infantry, 1967–70; GOC 3rd Div., 1970–72; Comdt, Joint Warfare Estab., 1972–74, retired. *Recreation:* following the sun. *Clubs:* Army and Navy; Royal Bermuda Yacht.

GILBERT, Hugh Campbell; Chairman: Camden and Islington Family Health Service Authority, 1989–92; Price & Pierce Group Limited, 1973–87 (Chief Executive Officer, 1969–87); *b* 25 March 1926; *s* of Hugh Gilbert and Nessie Campbell; *m* 1956, Beti Gwenllian, *d* of Prof. Henry Lewis, CBE. *Educ:* John Neilson High Sch.; Univ. of Glasgow (MA 1st Cl. Hons Pol. Econ.). Mil. Service in Scots Gds, then in Argyll and Sutherland Highlanders, Europe and ME, 1944–48; Territorial Service with 5/6 Argyll and Sutherland Highlanders (Captain), 1948–53. Imperial Chemical Industries, 1951–53; PA Management Consultants Ltd, 1953–62; Dir, Blyth, Greene, Jourdain & Co. Ltd, 1962–81; Dir, Tozer, Kemsley & Millbourn (Holdings) Ltd, 1971–83. Hon. Professorial Fellow, UCNW, Bangor, 1975–79. *Recreations:* racing, opera, travel. *Address:* 59 Wynnstay Gardens, W8 6UU. *T:* 0171–937 3134. *Clubs:* Caledonian, MCC.

GILBERT, Ian Grant; Under Secretary, International Relations Division, Department of Health and Social Security, 1979–85; retired; *b* Kikuyu, Kenya, 18 June 1925; *s* of Captain Alexander Grant Gilbert, DCM, indust. missionary, Lossiemouth and Kenya, and Marion Patrick Cruickshank; *m* 1960, Heather Margaret Donald, PhD (biographer of Lord Mount Stephen), *y d* of Rev. Francis Cantlie and Mary Donald, Lumphanan, Aberdeenshire. *Educ:* Fordyce Acad., Banffshire; Royal High Sch. of Edinburgh; Univ. of Edinburgh (MA 1950). Served HM Forces (Captain Indian Artillery), 1943–47. Entered Home Civil Service as Asst Principal and joined Min. of National Insurance, 1950; Private Sec. to Perm. Sec., 1953, and to Parly Sec., 1955; Principal, Min. of Pensions and Nat. Ins., 1956; seconded to HM Treasury, 1962–66; Asst Sec., Min. of Social Security (later DHSS), 1967; Head of War and Civilian Disabled Branches, DHSS, 1974–79. UK Member: Social Security, Health and Social Affairs Cttees, Council of Europe, Strasbourg, 1979–85; EEC Adv. Cttee on Social Security for Migrant Workers, Brussels, 1979–85; UK Delegate, Governing Body, Internat. Soc. Security Assoc., Geneva, 1979–85; Mem., UK Delegn to World Health Assembly, Geneva, 1979–84; Clerk/Advr to Select Cttee on European Legislation, House of Commons, 1987–90. Hon. Treasurer, Presbytery of England (Church of Scotland), 1965–77; Session Clerk, Crown Court Ch. of Scotland, Covent Garden, 1975–80. A Ch. of Scotland Mem., The Churches Main Cttee, 1986–. Chm., Caledonian Christian Club, 1984–86. *Recreations:* keeping half-an-acre in good heart, local and natural history, choral singing, France. *Address:* Wellpark, Moorside, Sturminster Newton, Dorset DT10 1HJ. *T:* Marnhull (01258) 820306. *Club:* Commonwealth Trust.
See also C. R. C. Donald.

GILBERT, Prof. John Cannon; Professor of Economics in the University of Sheffield, 1957–73, now Emeritus; Dean of Faculty of Economic and Social Studies, 1959–62; *b* 28 Sept. 1908; *s* of James and Elizabeth Louisa Gilbert; *m* 1938, Elizabeth Hadley Crook; two *s. Educ:* Bancroft's Sch.; The London Sch. of Economics and Political Science, University of London. Student of the Handels-Hochschule, Berlin (Sir Ernest Cassel Travelling Schol.), 1927–28; BCom Hons London, 1929. Asst on teaching staff, LSE, 1929–31; Lecturer in Economics, Sch. of Economics, Dundee, 1931–41. Ministry of Supply, 1941–45. Lecturer in Economics, University of Manchester, 1945–48; Senior Lecturer in Economics, University of Sheffield, 1948–56, Reader, 1956–57. Mem. Editorial Bd Bulletin of Economic Research, 1949–73. *Publications:* A History of Investment Trusts in Dundee, 1873–1938, 1939; Keynes's Impact on Monetary Economics, 1982; articles in Economica, Review of Economic Studies, etc. *Recreation:* walking. *Address:* 81 High Storrs Drive, Ecclesall, Sheffield S11 7LN. *T:* Sheffield (0114) 266 3544.

GILBERT, John Orman, CMG 1958; retired; *b* London, 21 Oct. 1907; *s* of Rev. T. H. Gilbert, late of Chedgrave Manor, Norfolk; *m* 1935, Winifred Mary Harris, Dublin; two *s* two *d. Educ:* Felsted Sch., Essex; Pembroke Coll., Oxford. Joined Sarawak Civil Service, 1928; various posts, from Cadet, to District Officer in 1940. During War of 1939–45 served in Bengal Sappers and Miners stationed in India and attained rank of Major. Came back to Sarawak with BM Administration, 1946; Resident, 4th Div., Sarawak, 1946–53; British Resident, Brunei, 1953–58; retd 1959. Coronation Medal, 1953. *Recreations:* conservation of wild life, animal welfare. *Address:* PO Box 100, Somerset West, Cape, South Africa.

GILBERT, Rt. Hon. Dr John (William); PC 1978; MP (Lab) Dudley East, since Feb. 1974 (Dudley, 1970–74); *b* April 1927; *m* 1963, Jean Olive Ross Skinner; two *d* of previous marriage. *Educ:* Merchant Taylors' Sch.; St John's Coll., Oxford; New York Univ. (PhD in Internat. Economics, Graduate Sch. of Business Administration). Chartered Accountant, Canada. Contested (Lab): Ludlow, 1966; Dudley, March 1968. Opposition front-bench spokesman on Treasury affairs, 1972–74; Financial Secretary to the Treasury, 1974–75; Minister for Transport, DoE, 1975–76; Minister of State, MoD, 1976–79. Member: Select Cttee on Expenditure, 1970–74; Select Cttee on Corporation Tax, 1973; Select Cttee on Defence, 1979–87; Select Cttee on Trade and Industry, 1987–92; Cttee on Intelligence and Security, 1994–; Chm., PLP Defence Gp, 1981–83; Vice-Chm., Lab. Finance and Industry Group, 1983–92. Member: Fabian Soc.; RUSI; RIIA; IISS; Amnesty Internat.; GMBATU; WWF. Trustee, Council for Arms Control. Hon. LLD Wake Forest, N Carolina, 1983. *Address:* House of Commons, SW1A 0AA. *Club:* Reform.

GILBERT, Air Chief Marshal Sir Joseph (Alfred), KCB 1985 (CB 1983); CBE 1974; Deputy Commander-in-Chief, Allied Forces Central Europe, 1986–89; retired; *b* 15 June 1931; *s* of late Ernest and Mildred Gilbert; *m* 1955, Betty, *yr d* of late William and of Eva Lishman; two *d. Educ:* William Hulme's Sch., Manchester; Univ. of Leeds (BA Hons, Econ. and Pol Science; Hon. LLD 1989). Commnd into RAF, 1952; Fighter Sqdns, 1953–61; Air Secretary's Dept, 1961–63; RAF Staff Coll., 1964; CO 92 (Lightning) Sqdn, 1965–67; jssc 1968; Sec., Defence Policy Staff, and Asst Dir of Defence Policy, 1968–71; CO, RAF Coltishall, 1971–73; RCDS, 1974; Dir of Forward Policy (RAF), 1975; ACAS (Policy), MoD, 1975–77; AOC 38 Group, 1977–80; ACDS (Policy), 1980–82; Asst Chief of Staff (Policy), SHAPE, 1983–84; Dep. C-in-C, RAF Strike Command, 1984–86. Vice Chm., Commonwealth War Graves Commn, 1993– (Comr, 1991–). Life Vice-Pres., RAFA. *Publications:* articles in defence jls. *Recreations:* grandchildren, fly-fishing, strategic affairs. *Address:* Brook House, Salisbury Road, Shrewton, Salisbury, Wiltshire SP3 4EQ. *T:* Shrewton (01980) 620627. *Club:* Royal Air Force.

GILBERT, Sir Martin (John), Kt 1995; CBE 1990; MA; FRSL; historian; Hon. Fellow of Merton College, Oxford, since 1994 (Fellow, 1962–94); Official Biographer of Sir Winston Churchill since 1968; *b* 25 Oct. 1936; *s* of Peter and Miriam Gilbert; *m* 1st, 1963, Helen Constance, *yr d* of late Joseph Robinson, CBE; one *d*; 2nd, Susan, *d* of late Michael Sacher; two *s. Educ:* Highgate Sch.; Magdalen Coll., Oxford. Nat. Service (Army), 1955–57; Sen. Research Scholar, St Antony's Coll., Oxford, 1960–62; Vis. Lectr, Budapest Univ., 1961; Res. Asst (sometime Sen. Res. Asst) to Hon. Randolph S. Churchill, 1962–67; Vis. Prof., Univ. of S Carolina, 1965; Recent Hist. Corresp t for Sunday Times, 1967; Res. Asst (Brit. Empire) for BBC, 1968; Historical Adviser (Palestine) for Thames Television, 1977–78. Visiting Professor: Tel-Aviv Univ., 1979; Hebrew Univ. of Jerusalem, 1980– (Vis. Lectr 1975); UCL, 1995–; Visiting Lecturer: Univ. of Cape Town (Caplan Centre), 1984; MoD and Acad. of Sciences, Moscow, 1985. Non-Govtl Rep., UN Commn on Human Rights (43rd Session), Geneva, 1987, (44th Session), Geneva, 1988. Mem., Prime Minister's delegn to Israel and Jordan, and to Washington, 1995. Script designer and co-author, Genocide (Acad. Award winner, best doc. feature film), 1981; Historical Consultant to Southern Pictures TV series, Winston Churchill: The Wilderness Years, 1980–81; Historical Adviser, BBC TV, for Auschwitz and the Allies, 1981–82; historical consultant, Yalta 1945, for BBC TV, 1982–83; writer and narrator, Churchill, BBC TV, 1989–91. Governor, Hebrew Univ. of Jerusalem, 1978–. Hon. DLitt: Westminster Coll., Fulton, 1981; Buckingham, 1992. *Publications:* The Appeasers, 1963 (with Richard Gott) (trans. German, Polish, Rumanian); Britain and Germany Between the Wars, 1964; The European Powers, 1900–1945, 1965 (trans. Italian, Spanish); Plough My Own Furrow: The Life of Lord Allen of Hurtwood, 1965; Servant of India: A Study of Imperial Rule 1905–1910, 1966; The Roots of Appeasement, 1966; Recent History Atlas 1860–1960, 1966; Winston Churchill (Clarendon Biogs for young people), 1966; British History Atlas, 1968, 2nd edn 1993; American History Atlas, 1968, 3rd edn 1993; Jewish History Atlas, 1969, 5th edn 1993 (trans. Spanish, Dutch, Hebrew, Russian, Hungarian, Italian); First World War Atlas, 1970, 2nd edn 1994; Winston S. Churchill, vol. iii, 1914–1916, 1971, companion volume (in two parts) 1973; Russian History Atlas, 1972, 2nd edn 1993; Sir Horace Rumbold: portrait of a diplomat, 1973; Churchill: a photographic portrait, 1974, 2nd edn 1988; The Arab-Israeli Conflict: its history in maps, 1974, 6th edn 1993 (trans. Spanish, Hebrew); Churchill and Zionism (pamphlet), 1974; Winston S. Churchill, vol. iv, 1917–1922, 1975, companion volume (in three parts), 1977; The Jews in Arab Lands: their history in maps, 1975, illustr. edn, 1976 (trans. Hebrew, Arabic, French, German); Winston S. Churchill, vol. v, 1922–1939, 1976, companion volume, part one, The Exchequer Years 1922–1929, 1980, part two, The Wilderness Years 1929–1935, 1981, part three, The Coming of War 1936–1939, 1982; The Jews of Russia: Illustrated History Atlas, 1976 (trans. Spanish); Jerusalem Illustrated History Atlas, 1977, 2nd edn 1994 (trans. Hebrew, Spanish); Exile and Return: The Emergence of Jewish Statehood, 1978; Children's Illustrated Bible Atlas, 1979; Final Journey, the Fate of the Jews of Nazi Europe, 1979 (trans. Dutch, Hebrew); Auschwitz and the Allies, 1981 (trans. German, Hebrew); Churchill's Political Philosophy, 1981; The Origin of the 'Iron Curtain' speech, 1981 (pamphlet); Atlas of the Holocaust, 1982, 2nd edn 1993 (trans. German, Hebrew, French, Japanese); Winston S. Churchill, vol. vi, Finest Hour, 1939–41, 1983 (Wolfson Award, 1983); The Jews of Hope: the plight of Soviet Jewry today, 1984 (trans. Hebrew, Japanese); Jerusalem: rebirth of a city, 1985; The Holocaust: the Jewish tragedy, 1986; Winston S. Churchill, vol vii, Road to Victory, 1986; Shcharansky: hero of our time, 1986 (trans. Dutch, Hebrew); Winston S. Churchill, vol viii, 'Never Despair', 1945–65, 1988; Second World War, 1989 (trans. German, Italian, Portuguese, Japanese); Churchill, A Life, 1991 (trans. Italian, Polish, Spanish); Atlas of British Charities, 1993; The Churchill War Papers, vol. 1, At the Admiralty September 1939–May 1940, 1993, vol. 2, Never Surrender, May–December 1940, 1995, vol. 3, The Ever-Widening War, 1941, 1996; In Search of Churchill, 1994; First World War, a History, 1994; The Day the War Ended: VE-Day 1945, 1995; Editor: A Century of Conflict: Essays Presented to A. J. P. Taylor, 1966; Churchill, 1967, and Lloyd George, 1968 (Spectrum Books); compiled Jackdaws: Winston Churchill, 1970; The Coming of War in 1939, 1973; contribs historical articles and reviews to jls (incl. Purnell's History of the Twentieth Century, Reader's Digest). *Recreation:* drawing maps. *Address:* Merton College, Oxford OX1 4JD. *Club:* Athenæum.

GILBERT, Michael Francis, CBE 1980; TD 1950; crime writer; *b* 17 July 1912; *s* of Bernard Samuel Gilbert and Berwyn Minna Cuthbert; *m* 1947, Roberta Mary, *d* of Col R. M. W. Marsden; two *s* five *d*. *Educ:* Blundell's Sch.; London University. LLB 1937. Served War of 1939–45, Hon. Artillery Co., 12th Regt RHA, N Africa and Italy (despatches 1943). Joined Trower Still & Keeling, 1947 (Partner, 1952–83). Legal Adviser to Govt of Bahrain, 1960. Member: Arts Council Cttee on Public Lending Right, 1968; Royal Literary Fund, 1969; Council of Soc. of Authors, 1975; (Founder) Crime Writers' Assoc. (Diamond Dagger, 1994); Mystery Writers of America, Grand Master, 1987. *Publications: novels:* Close Quarters, 1947; They Never Looked Inside, 1948; The Doors Open, 1949; Smallbone Deceased, 1950; Death has Deep Roots, 1951; Death in Captivity, 1952; Fear to Tread, 1953; Sky High, 1955; Be Shot for Sixpence, 1956; The Tichborne Claimant, 1957; Blood and Judgement, 1958; After the Fine Weather, 1963; The Crack in the Tea Cup, 1965; The Dust and the Heat, 1967; The Etruscan Net, 1969; The Body of a Girl, 1972; The Ninety Second Tiger, 1973; Flash Point, 1974; The Night of the Twelfth, 1976; The Empty House, 1978; Death of a Favourite Girl, 1980; The Final Throw, 1983; The Black Seraphim, 1983; The Long Journey Home, 1985; Trouble, 1987; Paint Gold and Blood, 1989; The Queen against Karl Mullen, 1991; Roller Coaster, 1993; Ring of Terror, 1995; *short stories:* Game Without Rules, 1967; Stay of Execution, 1971; Petrella at Q, 1977; Mr Calder and Mr Behrens, 1982; Young Petrella, 1988; Anything for a Quiet Life, 1990; *plays:* A Clean Kill; The Bargain; Windfall; The Shot in Question; *edited:* Crime in Good Company, 1959; The Oxford Book of Legal Anecdotes, 1986; The Fraudsters, 1988; Prep School, 1991; has also written radio and TV scripts. *Recreations:* walking, contract bridge. *Address:* The Old Rectory, Luddesdown, Gravesend, Kent DA13 0XE. *T:* Meopham (01474) 814272. *Club:* Garrick.

GILBERT, Patrick Nigel Geoffrey; General Secretary of the Society for Promoting Christian Knowledge, 1971–92; Consultant: Saga Travel, since 1994; Three Gorges Economic Development Co. (UK), since 1994; *b* 12 May 1934; adopted *s* of late Geoffrey Gilbert and Evelyn (*née* Miller), Devon. *Educ:* Cranleigh Sch.; Merton Coll., Oxford. OUP, 1964–69; Linguaphone Group (Westinghouse), 1969–71 (Man. Dir in Group, 1970). World Assoc. for Christian Communication: Trustee, 1975–87; European Vice-Chm., 1975–82; representative to EEC, 1975–82, to Conf. of Eur. Churches, 1976–82, to Council of Europe, 1976–82, and to Central Cttee, 1979–84. Member: Bd for Mission and Unity of Gen. Synod, 1971–78 (Mem. Exec., 1971–76); Archbishops' Cttee on RC Relations, 1971–81; Church Inf. Cttee, 1978–81; Church Publishing Cttee, 1980–84; Council, Conf. of British Missionary Socs, 1971–78; Council, Christians Abroad, 1974–79; Exec., Anglican Centre, Rome, 1981–91 (Vice Chm. of Friends, 1984–91); British National Cttee, UNESCO World Bank Congress, 1982. Greater London Arts Association: Mem. Exec., 1968–78; Hon. Life Mem., 1978; Chm., 1980–84 (Dep. Chm., 1979–80); Initiator, 1972 Festivals of London. Art Workers' Guild: Hon. Brother, 1971; Chm. Trustees and Hon. Treas., 1976–86 (Trustee, 1975). Chairman: Standing Conf. of London Arts Councils, 1975–78; Embroiderers' Guild, 1977–78 (Hon. Treas., 1974–77); Concord Multicultural Arts Trust, 1980–89; Harold Buxton Trust, 1983–92; Nikaean Club, 1984–92; Vice-President: Camden Arts Council, 1974–89 (Chm., 1970–74); Nat. Assoc. of Local Arts Councils, 1980–89 (Founder Chm., 1976–80); Mem., Arts Adv. Cttee, CRE, 1979; Steward, Artists' Gen. Benevolent Instn, 1971–93. Rep. of Archbishop of Canterbury to Inter-Church Travel, 1987–92. Trustee: Overseas Bishoprics Fund, 1971–92; All Saints Trust, 1978–92 (Chairman: F and GP and Investment Cttees); Schulze Trust, 1980–83; Dancers' Resettlement Fund, 1982–90 (Chm., Finance Cttee); Richards Trust, 1971–92; ACC Res. Fund, 1982–84; Vis. Trustee, Seabury Press, NY, 1978–80; Chm., Dancers' Resettlement Trust, 1987–90. Mem. Executive: GBGSA, 1981–84, 1988–89; Assoc. of Vol. Colls, 1979–87; Mem. Governing Body: SPCK Australia, 1977–92; SPCK (USA), 1984–92; SPCK NZ, 1989–92; Partners for World Mission, 1979–92; Governor: Contemp. Dance Trust, 1981–90; All Saints Coll., Tottenham, 1971–78; St Martin's Sch. for Girls, 1971–92 (Vice Chm., 1978–91; Rep. to Tertiary Educn Council, 1983–89); Ellesmere Coll., 1977–87 (Mem. ISCO Exec., 1984–86); St Michael's Sch., Petworth, 1978–88 (rep. to GBGSA); Roehampton Inst., 1978–92 (rep. to Assoc. of Vol. Colls, 1978–88; Chm., Audit Cttee, 1989–92); Pusey House, 1985–92; Patron, Pusey House Appeal, 1984–88; Fellow, Corp. of SS Mary and Nicholas (Woodard Schs), 1972–92 (Mem. Exec., 1981–92; Chm., S Div. Res. Cttee, 1972–84; Trustee, Endowment Fund; Dir, Corp. Trustee Co.). Member Development Cttee: SPAB, 1985–87; London Symphony Chorus, 1985–87; Bd Mem., Nat. Youth Dance Co., 1988–92; Mem. Council, Publishers Assoc., 1990–92. Cttee, London Europe Soc., 1985–93; Mem. Court, City Univ., 1987–93. Dir, Surrey Building Soc., 1988–93. Dep. Chm. and Chm., Exec. Cttee, Athenæum Club, 1985–89. Hon. Member: Assoc. for Develt in the Arts; Georgia Salzburger Soc., USA, 1986. JP Inner London, 1971–75. Freeman, City of London, 1966; Liveryman, Worshipful Co. of Woolmen (Master, 1985–86; Rep. to City and Guilds); Parish Clerk, All Hallows, Bread Street, 1981–93; Mem., Guild of Freemen (Court, 1991–93); Lord of the Manor of Cantley Netherhall, Norfolk. Hon. Citizen, Savannah, Georgia, 1986. FRSA 1978; FIMgt (FBIM 1982); FInstD 1982. Hon. DLitt Columbia Pacific, 1982. Order of St Vladimir, 1977. *Publications:* articles in various jls. *Recreations:* mountain walking, reading, travel, enjoying the Arts, golf. *Address:* 3 The Mount Square, NW3 6SU. *T:* 0171–794 8893.

GILBERT, Stuart William, CB 1983; Director, Department for National Savings, 1981–86 (Deputy Secretary); *b* 2 Aug. 1926; *s* of Rodney Stuart Gilbert and Ella Edith (*née* Esgate); *m* 1955, Marjorie Laws Vallance; one *s* one *d*. *Educ:* Maidstone Grammar Sch.; Emmanuel Coll., Cambridge (Open Exhibnr and State Scholar; MA). Served RAF, 1944–47. Asst Principal, Min. of Health, 1949; Asst Private Sec.: to Minister of Housing and Local Govt, 1952; to Parly Sec., 1954; Principal, 1955; Sec., Parker Morris Cttee on Housing Standards, 1958–61, Rapporteur to ECE Housing Cttee, 1959–61; Reporter to ILO Conf. on Workers' Housing, 1960; Asst Sec., Local Govt Finance Div., 1964; Under-Sec., DoE, 1970–80 (for New Towns, 1970, Business Rents, 1973, Construction Industries, 1974, Housing, 1974, Planning Land Use, 1977); Dep. Dir, Dept for Nat. Savings, 1980–81. *Recreations:* sailing, music, woodwork. *Address:* 3 Westmoat Close, Beckenham, Kent BR3 2BX. *T:* 0181–650 7213. *Club:* United Oxford & Cambridge University.

GILBERT, Prof. Walter; Carl M. Loeb University Professor, Department of Molecular and Cellular Biology (formerly of Cellular and Developmental Biology), Harvard University, since 1987; Joint Founder, 1978, and Director, Biogen NV (Chairman and Principal Executive Officer, 1981–84); Vice Chairman, Myriad Genetics Inc., since 1992; *b* Boston, 21 March 1932; *s* of Richard V. Gilbert and Emma (*née* Cohen); *m* 1953, Celia Stone; one *s* one *d*. *Educ:* Harvard Coll. (AB *summa cum laude* Chem. and Phys., 1953); Harvard Univ. (AM Phys., 1954); Cambridge Univ. (PhD Maths, 1957). National Science Foundn pre-doctoral Fellow, Harvard Univ. and Cambridge Univ., 1953–57, post-doctoral Fellow in Phys., Harvard, 1957–58; Harvard University: Lectr in Phys., 1958–59; Asst Prof. in Phys., 1959–64; Associate Prof. of Biophys., 1964–68; Prof. of Biochem., 1968–72; Amer. Cancer Soc. Prof. of Molecular Biology, 1972–81; H. H. Timken Prof. of Science, 1986–87. Guggenheim Fellow, Paris, 1968–69. Member: Amer. Acad. of Arts and Sciences, 1968; National Acad. of Sciences, 1976; Amer. Phys. Soc.; Amer. Soc. of Biol Chemists; Foreign Mem., Royal Soc., 1987–. Hon. DSc: Chicago, 1978; Columbia, 1978; Rochester, 1979; Yeshiva, 1981. Many prizes and awards, incl. (jtly) Nobel Prize for Chemistry, 1980. *Publications:* chapters, articles and papers on theoretical physics and molecular biology. *Address:* Biological Laboratories, 16 Divinity Avenue, Cambridge, MA 02138, USA. *T:* (617) 495–0760; 15 Gray Gardens West, Cambridge, MA 02138. *T:* (617) 8648778.

GILBEY, family name of **Baron Vaux of Harrowden.**

GILBEY, Sir Gavin; *see* Gilbey, Sir W. G.

GILBEY, Sir (Walter) Gavin, 4th Bt *cr* 1893, of Elsenham Hall, Essex; *b* 14 April 1949; *s* of Sir (Walter) Derek Gilbey, 3rd Bt and of Elizabeth Mary, *d* of Col K. G. Campbell; *S* father, 1991; *m* 1st, 1980, Mary (marr. diss. 1984), *d* of late William E. E. Pacetti; 2nd, 1984, Anna (marr. diss. 1995), *d* of Edmund Prosser. *Educ:* Eton. *Address:* 8201 SW 115 Street, Miami, FL 33156, USA.

GILCHRIST, Archibald; Managing Director, 1971–79, and Chairman, 1978–79, Govan Shipbuilders; *b* 17 Dec. 1929; *m* 1958, Elizabeth Jean Greenlees; two *s* one *d*. *Educ:* Loretto; Pembroke Coll., Cambridge (MA). Barclay Curle & Co. Ltd, Glasgow, 1954–64, various managerial posts; ultimately Dir, Swan Hunter Group; Brown Bros & Co. Ltd, Edinburgh, 1964–72: Dep. Man. Dir, 1964; Man. Dir, 1969; Man. Dir, Vosper Private, Singapore, 1980–86; Dir, Management Search Internat. Ltd, 1986–89; Pt-time Bd Mem., Scottish Legal Aid Bd, 1986–; non-executive Director: F. J. C. Lilley plc, 1987–93; RMJM Ltd, 1988–; Scottish Friendly Assurance Soc. Ltd (formerly Glasgow Friendly Soc.), 1988–; Caledonian MacBrayne Ltd, 1990–. Vice Chm., Royal Scottish National (formerly Royal Scottish) Orchestra, 1989–94 (Dir, 1987–). Chm. Council, St Leonard's Sch., 1989–95; Gov., Glasgow Polytechnic, 1987–93. *Recreations:* golf, shooting, fishing, music. *Address:* Inchmaholm, 35 Barnton Avenue, Edinburgh EH4 6JJ. *Clubs:* New (Edinburgh); Hon. Company of Edinburgh Golfers.

GILDER, Robert Charles, FIA; Directing Actuary, Government Actuary's Department, 1979–83; *b* 22 April 1923; *s* of Charles Henry Gilder and Elsie May (*née* Sayer); *m* 1954, Norah Mary Hallas; two *s*. *Educ:* Brentwood School. Liverpool Victoria Friendly Soc., 1940–41 and 1946–48. Served War, RAF, 1941–46. Government Actuary's Dept, 1948–83; Actuary, 1959; Principal Actuary, 1973. FIA 1951. *Recreations:* cricket, playing the clarinet, hill-walking, golf.

GILES, Ann, (Mrs Keith Giles); *see* Howard, A.

GILES, Bill; *see* Giles, W. G.

GILES, Frank Thomas Robertson; Editor, The Sunday Times, 1981–83 (Deputy Editor, 1967–81); *b* 31 July 1919; *s* of late Col F. L. N. Giles, DSO, OBE, and Mrs Giles; *m* 1946, Lady Katharine Pamela Sackville, *o d* of 9th Earl De La Warr and Countess De La Warr; one *s* two *d*. *Educ:* Wellington Coll.; Brasenose Coll., Oxford (Open Scholarship in History; MA 1946). ADC to Governor of Bermuda, 1939–42; Directorate of Mil. Ops, WO, 1942–45; temp. mem. of HM Foreign Service, 1945–46 (Private Sec. to Ernest Bevin; Mem. of Sir Archibald Clark Kerr's mission to Java); joined editorial staff of The Times, 1946; Asst Correspondent, Paris, 1947; Chief Corresp., Rome, 1950–53, Paris, 1953–60; Foreign Editor, Sunday Times, 1961–77, Dir, Times Newspapers Ltd, 1981–85. Lectures: tours, USA, 1975, FRG, 1984; Gritti, Venice, 1985. Mem., Exec. Cttee, GB-USSR Assoc., 1966–. Chm., Painshill Park Trust, 1985–; Mem., Governing Body, British Inst. of Florence, 1986–; Governor: Wellington Coll., 1965–89; Sevenoaks Sch., 1967–92. *Publications:* A Prince of Journalists: the life and times of de Blowitz, 1962; Sundry Times (autobiog.), 1986; The Locust Years: the story of the Fourth French Republic 1946–1958, 1991 (Franco-British Soc. award); (ed) Corfu, the Garden Isle, 1994. *Recreations:* going to the opera; collecting, talking about, consuming the vintage wines of Bordeaux and Burgundy. *Address:* 42 Blomfield Road, W9 2PF; Bunns Cottage, Lye Green, Crowborough, East Sussex TN6 1UY. *Clubs:* Brooks's, Beefsteak.

GILES, Rear-Adm. Sir Morgan Charles M.; *see* Morgan-Giles.

GILES, Air Comdt Dame Pauline; *see* Parsons, Air Comdt Dame P.

GILES, Robert Frederick; Senior Clerk, House of Commons, 1979–83; *b* 27 Dec. 1918; *s* of Robert and Edith Giles; *m* 1948, Mabel Florence Gentry; two *d*. *Educ:* Drayton Manor Sch., Hanwell. Min. of Agriculture, 1936–39. Royal Navy, 1939–45: CO, HMS Tango, 1942–44. Various assignments, MAF, from 1945; Regional Controller, Northern Region MAFF, 1963–68; Head, Food Standards/Food Science Div., 1968–74; Under Sec., MAFF, 1975–78; Food Standards and Food Subsidies Gp, 1975; Food Feedingstuffs and Fertilizer Standards Gp, 1977. *Recreations:* walking, theatre. *Address:* 8 The Ridings, Copthill Lane, Kingswood, Surrey KT20 6HJ. *Club:* Civil Service.

GILES, Roy Curtis, MA; Administrator, Busoga Trust, since 1991; Head Master, Highgate School, 1974–89; *b* 6 Dec. 1932; *s* of Herbert Henry Giles and Dorothy Alexandra Potter; *m* 1963, Christine von Alten; two *s* one *d*. *Educ:* Queen Elizabeth's Sch., Barnet; Jesus Coll., Cambridge (Open Scholar). Asst Master, Dean Close Sch., 1956–60; Lektor, Hamburg Univ., 1960–63; Asst Master, Eton Coll., 1963–74, Head of Modern Languages, 1970–74. Educnl Selector, ABM (formerly ACCM), 1979–92; Mem., House of Bishops' Panel on Marriage Educn, 1983–89. Mem., Council of Management, Vernon Educnl Trust (formerly Davies's Educn Services), 1975–; Governor: The Hall, Hampstead, 1976–89; Channing Sch., 1977–89. *Recreations:* music, theatre, Central Europe. *Address:* Wayfield House, Venlake Lane, Uplyme, Lyme Regis, Dorset DT7 3SA. *T:* Lyme Regis (01297) 443065.

GILES, William George, (Bill Giles), OBE 1995; Head of Weather Centre, BBC, since 1983; *b* 18 Nov. 1939; *s* of Albert William George Giles and Florence Ellen Christina

Giles; *m* 1st, 1961, Eileen Myrtle Lake (marr. diss. 1991); one *s* one *d*; 2nd, 1993, Patricia Maureen Stafford. *Educ:* Queen Elizabeth's Sch., Crediton; Bristol Coll. of Sci. and Tech.; Meteorological Office Coll. Meteorological Office, 1959; radio broadcaster, 1972; television broadcaster, 1975. Prix des Scientifiques, Fest. Internat. de Meteo, Paris, 1994. *Publications:* Weather Observations, 1978; The Story of Weather, 1990. *Recreations:* gardening, golf, One Man Weather Show. *Address:* Room 2050, BBC TV Centre, Wood Lane, W12 7RJ. *T:* 0181–576 7873.

GILL, Hon. Lord; Brian Gill; a Senator of the College of Justice in Scotland, since 1994; *b* 25 Feb. 1942; *s* of Thomas and Mary Gill, Glasgow; *m* 1969, Catherine Fox; five *s* one *d*. *Educ:* St Aloysius' Coll., Glasgow; Glasgow Univ. (MA 1962, LLB 1964); Edinburgh Univ. (PhD 1975). Asst Lectr, 1964–65, Lectr, 1965–69 and 1972–77, Faculty of Law, Edinburgh Univ.; Advocate, 1967; Advocate Depute, 1977–79; Standing Junior Counsel: Foreign and Commonwealth Office (Scotland), 1974–77; Home Office (Scotland), 1979–81; Scottish Education Dept, 1979–81; QC (Scot.) 1981; Chm., Industrial Tribunals, 1981–88. Called to the Bar, Lincoln's Inn, 1991. Keeper of the Advocates' Library, 1987–94; Trustee, Nat. Liby of Scotland, 1987–94. Chm., Cttee of Investigation for Scotland (Agricl Marketing), 1985–94 (Mem., Cttees for GB and for England and Wales); Dep. Chm., Copyright Tribunal, 1989–94; Member: Scottish Legal Aid Bd, 1987–90; Scottish Valuation Adv. Council, 1989–94. *Publications:* The Law of Agricultural Holdings in Scotland, 1982, 2nd edn 1990; articles in legal jls. *Recreation:* church music. *Address:* 13 Lauder Road, Edinburgh EH9 2EN. *T:* 0131–667 1888. *Club:* Reform.

GILL, Sir Anthony (Keith), Kt 1991; FEng 1983; FIMechE; Chairman and Chief Executive, Lucas Industries plc, 1987–94; Chairman, Docklands Light Railway, since 1994; *b* 1 April 1930; *s* of Frederick William and Ellen Gill; *m* 1953, Phyllis Cook; one *s* two *d*. *Educ:* High Sch., Colchester; Imperial Coll., London (BScEng Hons). National Service officer, REME, 1954–56. Joined Bryce Berger Ltd, 1956, subseq. Director and Gen. Manager until 1972; Lucas CAV Ltd, 1972, subseq. Director and Gen. Manager until 1978; Divisional Managing Director, Joseph Lucas Ltd, 1978; Jt Gp Man. Dir, 1980–83, Gp Man. Dir, 1984–87 and Dep. Chm., 1986–87, Lucas Industries. Non-exec. Director: Post Office Bd, 1989–91; National Power, 1990–; Tarmac, 1992–. Chm., Teaching Co. Scheme Bd, 1991–; Member: Adv. Council on Science and Technology (formerly Adv. Council for Applied R&D), 1985–91; DTI Technology Requirements Bd, 1986–88; Engineering Council, 1988– (Dep. Chm., 1994–); Nat. Trng Task Force, 1991–93. Pres., IProdE, 1986–87; Mem., Council, IMechE, 1986–92; Vice-Pres., Inst. of Management, 1993–. Mem. Court, Univ. of Warwick, 1986–94; Pro-Chancellor, Cranfield Univ. (formerly Inst of Technology), 1991–. FCGI 1979; Fellow, City of Birmingham Polytechnic, 1989. Hon. FIEE. Hon. DEng Birmingham, 1990. Hon. DSc: Cranfield, 1991; Southampton, 1992; Warwick, 1992; Hon. DTech Coventry, 1992; DUniv Sheffield Hallam, 1993. *Recreations:* boating, music. *Address:* 29 Charles II Place, King's Road, Chelsea, SW3 4NG. *T:* 0171–376 3810. *Club:* Royal Southampton Yacht.

GILL, Arthur Benjamin Norman; Deputy President, National Farmers' Union, since 1992; Chairman, Agricultural Systems Directorate and Member, Biotechnology and Biological Sciences Research Council, since 1994; *b* 1 Jan. 1950; *o s* of William Norman Gill and Annie (Nancy) Gill (*née* Almack); *m* 1973, Carolyn Davis; four *s*. *Educ:* Easingwold Primary Sch.; Barnard Castle Sch.; St John's Coll., Cambridge (MA Agric. 1971). Various posts at Namasagali Coll., Jinja, Uganda, 1972–75; i/c pig unit, Holderness, Humberside, 1975–77; running family farm, Vale of York, 1978–. National Farmers' Union: Mem. Council, 1985–91; Vice-Chm., 1986–87, Chm., 1987–89, Livestock and Wool Cttee; Vice-Pres., 1991–92. Mem., AFRC, 1991–94; Mem. Panel, Agric., Natural Resources and Envmt, Technology Foresight, OST, 1994–95. Dir, FARM Africa, 1991–. *Recreation:* rowing (Founder Mem. and Capt., Guy Fawkes Boat Club, York). *Address:* 22 Long Acre, Covent Garden, WC2E 9LY. *T:* 0171–331 7202; Home Farm, Hawkhills, Easingwold, York YO6 3EG. *T:* Easingwold (01347) 821344, *Fax:* (01347) 823431. *Clubs:* Farmers'; Yorkshire Agricultural Adventurers (York).

GILL, Brian; *see* Gill, Hon. Lord.

GILL, Christopher John Fred, RD 1971; MP (C) Ludlow, since 1987; butcher and farmer; *b* 28 Oct. 1936; *m* 1960, Patricia M. (*née* Greenway); one *s* two *d*. *Educ:* Shrewsbury School. Chm., F. A. Gill Ltd, 1968–. Mem., Agriculture Select Cttee, 1989–. Vice Chairman: Cons. European Affairs Cttee, 1989–91 (Sec., 1988–89); Cons. Agric. Cttee, 1991–94 (Sec., 1990–91); Pres., Midlands W European Cons. Council, 1984–85. Councillor, Wolverhampton BC, 1965–72. *Address:* House of Commons, SW1A 0AA.

GILL, David; television producer; *b* 9 June 1928; *s* of Cecil and Iona Gill; *m* 1953, Pauline Wadsworth; two *d*. *Educ:* Belmont Abbey, Hereford. Dancer with Sadler's Wells Theatre Ballet, 1948–55; joined film-cutting rooms, Associated-Rediffusion TV, 1955; produced Stations of the Cross (mime), BBC, 1957; Film Editor, This Week, Rediffusion TV, 1957–68 (also documentaries); Technical Advisor and Editor, Dave Clark Special, 1968; directed for Thames Television: This Week, 1969–73; Till I End My Song (documentary), 1970; Destination America (documentary series), 1975; with Kevin Brownlow: co-wrote and produced: Hollywood, 1980; Unknown Chaplin, 1983; Buster Keaton: a hard act to follow, 1987; Harold Lloyd—the Third Genius, 1990; D. W. Griffith: Father of Film (3 part documentary), 1993; co-produced: Abel Gance's Napoleon (TV version) 1983; British Cinema—Personal View, 1986; Thames Silents/Live Cinema (also TV versions for Channel 4), 1980–. *Recreations:* cinema, theatre, music, planting trees. *Address:* Photoplay Productions, 21 Princess Road, NW1 8JR.

GILL, (George) Malcolm, FCIB; Head, Banking Department, Bank for International Settlements, since 1995 (Deputy Head, 1991–95); *b* 23 May 1934; *s* of late Thomas Woodman Gill and Alice Muriel Gill (*née* Le Grice); *m* 1966, Monica Kennedy Brooks; one *s* one *d*. *Educ:* Cambridgeshire High Sch.; Sidney Sussex Coll., Cambridge (MA). Entered Bank of England, 1957: seconded to UK Treasury Delegation, Washington DC, 1966–68; Private Sec. to Governor, 1970–72; Asst Chief Cashier, 1975; seconded to HM Treasury, 1977–80; Chief Manager, Banking and Credit Markets, 1980–82; Head of Foreign Exchange Div., 1982–88; Asst Dir, 1987–88; Chief of the Banking Dept and Chief Cashier, 1988–91. *Recreations:* reading, travel, music. *Address:* Bank for International Settlements, Basle, 4002, Switzerland.

GILL, Air Vice-Marshal Harry, CB 1979; OBE 1968; Director-General of Supply, Royal Air Force, 1976–79; *b* 30 Oct. 1922; *s* of John William Gill and Lucy Gill, Newark, Notts; *m* 1951, Diana Patricia, *d* of Colin Wood, Glossop; one *d*. *Educ:* Barnby Road Sch.; Newark Technical Coll. Entered RAF, 1941; pilot trng, 1942; commnd 1943; flying duties, 1943–49; transf. to Equipment Br., 1949; Officer Commanding: Supply Sqdns, RAF Spitalgate and RAF North Coates, 1949–52; HQ Staff No 93 Maintenance Unit Explosives and Fuels Supply Ops, 1952–55; Explosives and Fuels Sch., 1955–58; Staff Officer Logistics Div., HQ Allied Forces Northern Europe, 1958–61; Head of Provision Br., Air Min., 1961–64; Chief Equipment Officer, No 25 Maintenance Unit, RAF Hartlebury, 1964–66; Equipment Staff Officer, HQ Air Forces Middle East, 1966–67; Dep. Dir Supply Systems, MoD Air, 1968–70; RCDS, 1971; Comdt, RAF Supply Control Centre, 1972–73; Dir, Supply Management, MoD Air, 1973–76. Internat. rifle and pistol shot; Silver Medallist, King's Prize, Bisley, 1951. *Recreations:* shooting, fishing, tennis, cricket. *Address:* c/o Lloyds Bank, 37 Castlegate, Newark, Notts NG24 1BD. *Club:* Royal Air Force.

GILL, Maj.-Gen. Ian Gordon, CB 1972; OBE 1959 (MBE 1949); MC 1940, Bar 1945; idc, psc; Colonel, 4/7 Royal Dragoon Guards, 1973–78; *b* Rochester, 9 Nov. 1919; *s* of late Brig. Gordon Harry Gill, CMG, DSO and Mrs Doris Gill, Rochester, Kent; *m* 1963, Elizabeth Vivian Rohr, MD, MRCP (*d* 1990), *o d* of late A. F. Rohr; no *c*. *Educ:* Edinburgh House, Hants; Repton School. Commnd from SRO into 4th/7th Roy. Dragoon Guards, 1938; served with Regt in: BEF, France, 1939–40; BLA, NW Europe, 1944–45 (despatches, 1945); Palestine, 1946–48; Tripolitania, 1951–52; Instructor, Armoured Sch., 1948–50; Staff Coll., Camberley, 1952; Bde Maj., HQ Inf. Bde, 1953–55; comdg 4th/7th RDG, 1957–59; Asst Mil. Sec., HQ, BAOR, 1959–61; Coll. Comdt RMA Sandhurst, 1961–62; Imp. Def. Coll., 1963; Comdr, 7th Armoured Bde, 1964–66; Dep. Mil. Sec. 1, MoD (Army), 1966–68; Head, British Defence Liaison Staff, Dept of Defence, Canberra, 1968–70; Asst Chief of Gen. Staff (Op. Requirements), 1970–72, retired. Hon. Liveryman, Coachmakers' Co., 1974. *Recreations:* equitation, ski-ing, cricket, squash rackets. *Address:* Cheriton House, Thorney, Peterborough PE6 0QD. *Clubs:* Cavalry and Guards, MCC.

GILL, Jack, CB 1984; Chief Executive (formerly Secretary), Export Credits Guarantee Department, 1983–87; Executive Director(part-time), Government Relations, BICC plc, 1987–91; *b* 20 Feb. 1930; *s* of Jack and Elizabeth Gill; *m* 1954, Alma Dorothy; three *d*. *Educ:* Bolton Sch. Export Credits Guarantee Department: Clerical Officer, 1946; Principal, 1962; Asst Sec., 1970; Asst Sec., DTI, 1972–75; Export Credits Guarantee Department: Under Sec., 1975–79; Principal Finance Officer, 1978–79; Sec., Monopolies and Mergers Commn, 1979–81; Dep. Sec., and Dir of Industrial Develt Unit, DoI, 1981–83. Mem., BOTB, 1981–87. Consultant: NEI Power Projects Ltd, 1987–90; British Aerospace plc, 1987–89; CBI Council, 1988–91 (Chm., Public Procurement Contact Gp, 1990–91; Mem., Overseas Cttee, 1990–91). National Service, REME, 1948–50. *Recreations:* music, chess; occasional crossword setter for The Listener. *Address:* 9 Ridley Road, Warlingham, Surrey CR6 9LR. *T:* Upper Warlingham (0188362) 2688.

GILL, (James) Kenneth; President, Saatchi and Saatchi Company PLC, 1989–94; *b* 27 Sept. 1920; *s* of late Alfred Charles and Isabel Gill; *m* 1948, Anne Bridgewater; one *s*. *Educ:* Highgate Sch. Served RAC, 24th Lancers and Intelligence Corps, GSO II, 1939–45. Copywriter, S. T. Garland Advertising Service, 1938–39; Chm., Garland-Compton Ltd, 1970–76; Saatchi and Saatchi Company: Chm., 1976–85; Pres. and Dir, 1985–89. FIPA. *Recreations:* the theatre, the cinema, cricket. *Address:* Davenport House, Duntisbourne Abbots, Cirencester, Glos GL7 7JN. *T:* Cirencester (01285) 821468; (office) 83/89 Whitfield Street, W1A 4XA. *Club:* MCC.

GILL, Kenneth; General Secretary, Manufacturing, Science, Finance, 1989–92; Chairman, Morning Star, since 1984; *b* 30 Aug. 1927; *s* of Ernest Frank Gill and Mary Ethel Gill; *m* 1967, Sara Teresa Paterson; two *s* one *d*. *Educ:* Chippenham Secondary School. Engrg apprentice, 1943–48; Draughtsman Designer, Project Engr, Sales Engr in various cos, 1948–62; District Organiser, Liverpool and Ireland TASS, 1962–68; Editor, TASS Union Jl, 1968–72; Dep. Gen. Sec., 1972–74; Gen. Sec. AUEW (TASS), 1974–86, TASS—the Manufacturing Union, 1986–88; Jt Gen. Sec., MSF, 1988–89. Pres., CSEU, 1987–88. Mem., Gen. Council, TUC, 1974–92 (Chm., 1985–86); Pres. of TUC, 1985–86. Mem., Commn for Racial Equality, 1981–87. *Recreations:* sketching, political caricaturing. *Address:* 164 Ramsden Road, Balham, SW12 8RE. *T:* 0181–675 1489.

GILL, Rt. Rev. Kenneth Edward; Assistant Bishop of Newcastle (full time), since 1980; *b* 22 May 1932; *s* of Fred and Elsie Gill; *m* 1957, Edna Hammond; one *s* two *d*. *Educ:* Harrogate Grammar School; Hartley Victoria Coll., Manchester. Presbyter in Church of South India, Mysore Diocese, 1958–72; Bishop of Karnataka Central Diocese, Church of South India, 1972–80. *Publications:* Meditations on the Holy Spirit, 1979; Count us Equal, 1990. *Recreation:* gardening. *Address:* 83 Kenton Road, Newcastle upon Tyne NE3 4NL. *T:* 0191–285 1502.

GILL, Air Vice-Marshal Leonard William George, DSO 1945; Consultant in personnel planning, since 1973; Director, Merton Associates since 1979 (Chairman, 1984–94); Consultant, Randle Cooke & Associates, since 1994; *b* 31 March 1918; *s* of L. W. Gill, Hornchurch, Essex, and Marguerite Gill; *m* 1st, 1943, Joan Favill Appleyard (marr. diss.); two *s* two *d*; 2nd, Mrs Constance Mary Cull. *Educ:* University Coll. Sch., London. Joined RAF, 1937; served in Far East until 1942; then UK as night fighter pilot; comd No 68 Sqdn for last 6 months of war; subseq. served in various appts incl. comd of Nos 85 and 87 night fighter Sqdns and tour on directing staff at RAF Staff Coll.; Stn Comdr No 1 Flying Trng Sch., Linton-on-Ouse, 1957–60; Dir of Overseas Ops, 1960–62; Nat. Def. Coll. of Canada, 1962–63; Dir of Organisation (Estabs), 1963–66; SASO, RAF Germany, 1966–68; Dir-Gen., Manning (RAF), MoD, 1968–73, retired. Manpower and Planning Advr, P&O Steam Navigation Co., 1973–79. Vice-Pres., RAF Assoc., 1973– (Pres. E Area, 1974–81; Vice-Chm., Central Council, 1984–88). Chm., River Thames Soc., 1994–. FIPD; FIMgt. Order of King George of Bohemia (Czech and Slovak Republic), 1991. *Recreations:* shooting, cricket, boats, amateur woodwork. *Address:* Flat 15, 35 Cranley Gardens, Kensington, SW7 3BD. *T:* 0171–370 2716. *Clubs:* Royal Air Force; Phyllis Court (Henley).

GILL, Malcolm; *see* Gill, G. M.

GILL, Peter, OBE 1980; FWCMD; dramatic author; Associate Director, Royal National Theatre, since 1980; *b* Cardiff, 7 Sept. 1939; *s* of George John Gill and Margaret Mary Browne. *Educ:* St Illtyd's Coll., Cardiff. FWCMD 1992. Associate Dir, Royal Court Theatre, 1970–72; Dir, 1976–80, Associate Dir, 1980, Riverside Studios, Hammersmith; Dir, Royal Nat. Theatre Studio, 1984–90. Productions include: Royal Court: A Collier's Friday Night, 1965; The Local Stigmatic, A Provincial Life, 1966; A Soldier's Fortune, The Daughter-in-law, Crimes of Passion, 1967; The Widowing of Mrs Holroyd, 1968; Life Price, Over Gardens Out, The Sleepers' Den, 1969; The Duchess of Malfi, 1971; Crete & Sergeant Pepper, 1972; The Merry-go-round, 1973; Small Change, The Fool, 1976; Riverside Studios: As You Like It, 1976; Small Change, 1977; The Cherry Orchard (own version), The Changeling, 1978; Measure for Measure, 1979; Julius Caesar, 1980; Scrape off the Black, 1980; Royal National Theatre: A Month in the Country, Don Juan, Scrape off the Black, Much Ado about Nothing, 1981; Danton's Death, Major Barbara, 1982; Kick for Touch, Tales from Hollywood, Antigone (co-dir), 1983; Venice Preserv'd, Fool for Love (transf. Lyric), 1984; The Murderers, As I Lay Dying (also adapted), A Twist of Lemon, In the Blue, Bouncing, Up for None, The Garden of England (co-dir), 1985; Mean Tears, 1987; Mrs Klein, 1988 (transf. Apollo, 1989); Juno and the Paycock, 1989; other London theatres: O'Flaherty VC, Mermaid, 1966; The Way of the World, Lyric, Hammersmith, 1992; New England, Barbican Pit, 1994; Uncle Vanya, Tricycle, 1995; has also produced plays by Shakespeare and modern writers at Stratford-upon-Avon, Nottingham, Edinburgh and in Canada, Germany, Switzerland and USA; Music Theatre and Opera includes: Down By the Green Wood Side (co-dir), Bow Down (co-dir), Queen Elizabeth Hall, 1987; Marriage of Figaro, Opera North, 1987; Television productions include: Grace, 1972; Girl, 1973; A Matter of Taste, Fugitive, 1974; Hitting Town, 1976. *Publications:* plays: The Sleepers' Den, 1965; Over Gardens Out, 1969; Small Change, 1976; Small Change, Kick for Touch, 1985; In the Blue, Mean Tears, 1987; Certain Young Men, 1992. *Address:* c/o Casarotto Ramsay Ltd, 60–66 Wardour Street, W1V 3HP.

GILL, Robin Denys, CVO 1993; Chairman, Organisation and Executive and Founder Trustee, Royal Anniversary Trust, since 1990; Chairman of Executive, The Queen's Anniversary Awards for Higher and Further Education, since 1993; *b* 7 Oct. 1927; *s* of Thomas Henry Gill and Marjorie Mary (*née* Butler); *m* 1st, 1951, Mary Hope Alexander (*d* 1986); three *s*; 2nd, 1991, Denise Spencer Waterhouse. *Educ:* Dulwich Coll.; Brasenose Coll., Oxford (MA). Unilever plc, 1949–54; British Internat. Paper Ltd, 1954–59; Founder and Man. Dir, Border TV Ltd, 1960–64; Man. Dir, ATV Corp. Ltd, 1964–69; Chairman: ITN, 1968–69; 1970 Trust Ltd, 1970–93; Ansvar Insce Co. Ltd, 1975–; Standard Ind. Trust Ltd, 1970–81; Baring Communications Equity Ltd, 1993–; Director: Reed Paper Gp Ltd, 1970–75; Hewlett Packard Ltd, 1975–92; Yarrow Plc, 1979–88; Baring Hambrecht Alpine Ltd, 1986–; SD-Scicon plc, 1988–90. Member: Nat. Adv. Bd for Higher Educn; Oxford Univ. Appts Cttee; Vis. Cttee, RCA; Cttee, Royal Family Film, 1968–70. *Recreations:* golf, sport, travel, art collecting, gardening, new projects. *Address:* PO Box 1, East Horsley, Surrey KT24 6RE. *T:* Guildford (01483) 285290. *Clubs:* Vincent's (Oxford); St George's Hill Golf; Free Foresters Cricket.

GILL, Rev. Prof. Robin Morton, PhD; Michael Ramsey Professor of Modern Theology, University of Kent at Canterbury, since 1992; *b* 18 July 1944; *s* of Alan Morton Gill and Mary Grace (*née* Hammond); *m* 1967, Jennifer Margaret Sheppard; one *s* one *d*. *Educ:* Westminster Sch.; King's Coll., London (BD 1966; PhD 1969); Birmingham Univ. (MSocSc 1972). Deacon, 1968; priest, 1969; Curate, Rugby St Andrews, 1968–71; Lectr, Newton Theol Coll., PNG, 1971–72; Edinburgh University: Lectr in Christian Ethics, 1972–86; Associate Dean, Faculty of Theol., 1985–88; Sen. Lectr, 1986–88; William Leech Res. Prof. in Applied Theol., Newcastle Univ., 1988–92. Priest-in-charge: St Philip, Edinburgh, 1972–75; Ford with Etal, Northumberland, 1975–87; St Mary, Coldstream, 1987–92; Hon. Canon, Canterbury Cathedral, 1992–. *Publications:* The Social Context of Theology, 1975; Theology and Social Structure, 1977; Faith in Christ, 1978; Prophecy and Praxis, 1981; The Cross Against the Bomb, 1984; A Textbook of Christian Ethics, 1985, 2nd edn 1995; Theology and Sociology, 1987; Beyond Decline, 1988; Competing Convictions, 1989; Christian Ethics in Secular Worlds, 1991; Gifts of Love, 1991; Moral Communities, 1992; The Myth of the Empty Church, 1993; A Vision for Growth, 1994; Readings in Modern Theology, 1995; (with Lorna Kendall) Michael Ramsey as Theologian, 1995. *Recreations:* running churches, playing the trumpet. *Address:* Rutherford College, The University, Canterbury, Kent CT2 7NS. *T:* Canterbury (01227) 764000.

GILL, His Honour Stanley Sanderson; a Circuit Judge, 1972–87; *b* Wakefield, 3 Dec. 1923; *s* of Sanderson Henry Briggs Gill, OBE and Dorothy Margaret Gill (*née* Bennett); *m* 1954, Margaret Mary Patricia Grady; one *s* two *d*. *Educ:* Queen Elizabeth Grammar Sch., Wakefield; Magdalene Coll., Cambridge (MA). Served in RAF, 1942–46: 514 and 7 (Pathfinder) Sqdns, Flt Lt 1945. Called to Bar, Middle Temple, 1950; Asst Recorder of Bradford, 1966; Dep. Chm., WR Yorks QS, 1968; County Court Judge, 1971. Mem., County Court Rule Cttee, 1980–84. Chm., Rent Assessment Cttee, 1966–71. *Recreations:* walking, reading, golf, painting. *Club:* Thirsk and Northallerton Golf.

GILLAM, Patrick John; Chairman, Standard Chartered PLC, since 1993 (Director, since 1988); Chairman: Booker Tate Ltd, 1991–93; Asda Group, since 1991; *b* 15 April 1933; *s* of late Cyril B. Gillam and of Mary J. Gillam; *m* 1963, Diana Echlin; one *s* one *d*. *Educ:* London School of Economics (BA Hons History). Foreign Office, 1956–57; British Petroleum Co. Ltd, 1957–91; Vice-Pres., BP North America Inc., 1971–74; General Manager, Supply Dept, 1974–78; Dir, BP International Ltd (formerly BP Trading Ltd), 1978–82; Man. Dir, BP, 1981–91; Chairman: BP Shipping Ltd, 1987–88; BP Minerals Internat. Ltd/Selection Trust Ltd, 1982–89; BP Coal Ltd, 1986–88; BP Coal Inc., 1988–90; BP America Inc., 1989–91; BP Nutrition, 1989–91; BP Oil International, 1990–91; Dep. Chm., Standard Chartered PLC, 1991–93. Chm., ICC UK, 1989–; Mem. Exec. Bd, ICC Worldwide, 1991–; Dir, Commercial Union, 1991–. Mem., Court of Governors, LSE, 1989–; Trustee, Queen Elizabeth's Foundn for Disabled Develt Trust, 1984–. *Recreation:* gardening. *Address:* Standard Chartered PLC, 1 Aldermanbury Square, EC2V 7SB. *T:* 0171–280 7500.

GILLAM, Stanley George, MA, MLitt; Librarian, The London Library, 1956–80; *b* 11 Aug. 1915; *s* of Harry Cosier Gillam, Oxford; *m* 1950, Pauline, *d* of Henry G. Bennett, Oxford; one *s*. *Educ:* Southfield Sch.; Saint Catherine's Coll., Oxford. Bodleian Library, Oxford, 1931–40 and 1946–54. Oxfordshire and Bucks Light Infantry (1st Bucks Bn), 1940–46. Asst Sec. and Sub-Librarian, The London Library, 1954–56. *Publications:* The Building Accounts of the Radcliffe Camera, 1958; The Divinity School and Duke Humfrey's Library at Oxford, 1988; The Radcliffe Camera, 1992; articles in The Bodleian Library Record and other periodicals. *Address:* 18 Forest Side, Kennington, Oxford OX1 5LQ. *T:* Oxford (01865) 730832.

GILLAN, Cheryl Elise Kendall, (Mrs J. C. Leeming); MP (C) Chesham and Amersham, since 1992; Parliamentary Under-Secretary of State, Department of Education and Employment, since 1995; *b* 21 April 1952; *d* of Major Adam Mitchell Gillan and Mona Elsie Gillan (*née* Freeman); *m* 1985, John Coates Leeming, *qv*. *Educ:* Cheltenham Ladies' Coll.; Coll. of Law. MCIM DipM. International Management Group, 1976–84; British Film Year, 1984–86; Ernst & Young, 1986–91; Dir, Kidsons Impey, 1991–93. PPS to Lord Privy Seal, 1994–95. Chm., Bow Group, 1987. Freeman, City of London, 1991; Liveryman, Marketors' Co., 1991. *Recreations:* golf, music, gardening, animals. *Address:* House of Commons, SW1A 0AA. *T:* 0171–219 3000.

GILLANDERS, Prof. Lewis Alexander; Clinical Professor in Radiology, University of Aberdeen, and Consultant in Charge, Radiology Services (Grampian Health Board), 1964–88, now Professor Emeritus in Radiology; *b* 7 Feb. 1925; *s* of Kenneth John Alexander Gillanders and Nellie May Sherris; *m* 1960, Nora Ellen Wild, MB, ChB; one *s* one *d*. *Educ:* Dingwall Academy; Univ. of Glasgow (graduated in medicine, 1947). Commissioned, RAMC, 1948–50; general medical practice, Scottish Highlands, 1950–52; trained in Diagnostic Radiology, Glasgow Royal Infirmary and United Birmingham Hosps, 1953–58; Consultant Radiologist, Aberdeen Teaching Hosps, 1958. Examiner in Radiology for: RCR, 1969–79, and DMRD, Univ. of Aberdeen, 1969–89; Faculty of Radiologists, RCSI, 1975–77; Univ. of Nairobi, 1978–80; Univ. of Wales, 1981–83. Member, GMC, 1979–84; Vice-Pres., RCR, 1981–83. *Publications:* chapter in Pye's Surgical Handicraft (1st edn 1884), 19th edn 1969, 20th edn 1977; papers in general medical and radiological literature, students' magazines, etc. *Recreations:* derivations and meanings; golf, do-it-yourself. *Address:* 11 Kennerty Park, Peterculter, Aberdeen AB1 0LE. *Clubs:* Victory Services; Royal Northern & University (Aberdeen).

GILLARD, Francis George, CBE 1961 (OBE 1946); public broadcasting interests in USA, since 1970; *b* 1 Dec. 1908; *s* of late Francis Henry Gillard and of late Emily Jane Gillard, Stockleigh Lodge, Exford; unmarried. *Educ:* Wellington Sch., Som.; St Luke's Coll., Exeter (BSc London). Schoolmaster, 1932–41; Freelance broadcaster, 1936–; joined BBC as Talks Producer, 1941; BBC War Correspondent, 1941. BBC Head of West Regional Programmes, 1945–55; Chief Asst to Dir of Sound Broadcasting with Controller rank, 1955–56; Controller, West Region, BBC, 1956–63; Dir, Radio, subseq. Man. Dir, and Dir Regions, BBC, 1963–70, retired. Distinguished Fellow, Corp. for Public Broadcasting, Washington, 1970–73. Mem., Council, Educational Foundn for Visual Aids, 1970–87 (Chm., 1977–86). Mem. Finance Cttee, Exeter Univ., 1968–86; Governor, Wellington Sch., Somerset, 1961–91 (Chm., 1974–80). FRSA 1971. Hon. LLD Exeter, 1987. *Address:* Trevor House, Poole, Wellington, Somerset TA21 9HN. *T:* Wellington (01823) 662890.

GILLES, Prof. Dennis Cyril; Professor of Computing Science, University of Glasgow, 1966–90; *b* 7 April 1925; *s* of George Cyril Gilles and Gladys Alice Gilles (*née* Batchelor); *m* 1955, Valerie Mary Gilles; two *s* two *d*. *Educ:* Sidcup Gram. Sch.; Imperial Coll., University of London. Demonstrator, Asst Lectr, Imperial Coll., 1945–47; Asst Lectr, University of Liverpool, 1947–49; Mathematician, Scientific Computing Service, 1949–55; Research Asst, University of Manchester, 1955–57; Dir of Computing Lab., University of Glasgow, 1957–66. *Publications:* contribs to Proc. Royal Society and other scientific jls. *Address:* Ardbeg House, Kilmun, Dunoon, Argyll PA23 8SE. *T:* Kilmun (01369) 840342.

GILLES, Prof. Chevalier Herbert Michael Joseph, MD; FRCP, FFPHM; Alfred Jones and Warrington Yorke Professor of Tropical Medicine, University of Liverpool, 1972–86, now Emeritus; *b* 10 Sept. 1921; *s* of Joseph and Clementine Gilles; *m* 1955, Wilhelmina Caruana (*d* 1972); three *s* one *d*; *m* 1979, Dr Mejra Kačić-Dimitri. *Educ:* St Edward's Coll., Malta; Royal Univ. of Malta (MD). Rhodes Schol. 1942. MSc Oxon; FMCPH (Nig.), DTM&H. Served War of 1939–45 (1939–45 Star, Africa Star, VM). Mem., Scientific Staff, MRC Lab., Gambia, 1954–58; University of Ibadan: Lectr, Tropical Med., 1958–63; Prof. of Preventive and Social Med., 1963–65; Liverpool University: Sen. Lectr, Tropical Med., 1965–70; Prof. of Tropical Med. (Personal Chair), 1970; Dean, Liverpool Sch. of Tropical Medicine, 1978–83. Vis. Prof., Tropical Medicine, Univ. of Lagos, 1965–68; Royal Society Overseas Vis. Prof., Univ. of Khartoum, Sudan, 1979–80; Hon. Prof. of Tropical Medicine, Zhongshan Med. Coll., Guangzhou, People's Republic of China, 1984; Visiting Professor: Public Health, Univ. of Malta, 1989–; Internat. Health, Royal Colls of Physicians and Surgeons, Ireland, 1994–. Consultant Physician in Tropical Medicine, Liverpool AHA(T) and Mersey RHA, 1965–86; Consultant in Malariology to the Army, 1974–86; Consultant in Tropical Medicine to the RAF, 1978–86, to the DHSS, 1980–86. Pres., RSTM&H, 1985–87; Vice President: Internat. Fedn of Tropical Medicine, 1988–92; Liverpool Sch. of Tropical Medicine, 1991–. KStJ 1972. Title of Chevalier awarded for medical work in the tropics. Hon. MD Karolinska Inst., 1979; Hon. DSc Malta, 1984. Darling Foundn Medal and Prize, WHO, 1990; Mary Kingsley Medal, Liverpool Sch. of Tropical Medicine, 1994. *Publications:* Tropical Medicine for Nurses, 1955, 4th edn 1975; Pathology in the Tropics, 1969, 2nd edn 1976; Management and Treatment of Tropical Diseases, 1971; A Short Textbook of Preventive Medicine for the Tropics, 1973, 3rd edn 1990; Atlas of Tropical Medicine and Parasitology, 1976, 4th edn 1995; Recent Advances in Tropical Medicine, 1984; Human Antiparasitic Drugs, Pharmacology and Usage, 1985; The Epidemiology and Control of Tropical Diseases, 1987; Management of Severe and Complicated Malaria, 1991; Hookworm Infections, 1991; (ed) Bruce-Chwatt's Essential Malariology, 3rd edn, 1993. *Recreations:* swimming, music. *Address:* 3 Conyers Avenue, Birkdale, Southport PR8 4SZ. *T:* Southport (01704) 566664.

GILLESPIE, Prof. Iain Erskine, MD, MSc, FRCS; Professor of Surgery, University of Manchester, 1970–92 (Dean of Medical School, 1983–86); *b* 4 Sept. 1931; *s* of John Gillespie and Flora McQuarie; *m* 1957, Mary Muriel McIntyre; one *s* one *d*. *Educ.* Hillhead High Sch., Glasgow; Univ. of Glasgow. MB, ChB, 1953; MD (Hons) 1963, MSc Manchester 1974; FRCSE 1959; FRCS 1963; FRCSGlas 1970. Series of progressive surgical appts in Univs of Glasgow, Sheffield, Glasgow (again), 1953–70. Nat. service, RAMC, 1954–56; MRC grantee, 1956–58; US Postdoctoral Research Fellow, Los Angeles, 1961–62; Titular Prof. of Surgery, Univ. of Glasgow, 1969. Vis. Prof. in USA, Canada, S America, Kenya, S Africa, Australia and New Zealand. Member: Cttee of Surgical Res. Soc. of GB and Ireland, 1975–; Medical Sub-Cttee, UGC, 1975–86; Univs and Polytechnics Grants Cttee, Hong Kong, 1984–89. Non-exec. Mem., Central Manchester HA, 1991–. *Publications:* jt editor and contributor to several surgical and gastroenterological books; numerous articles in various med. jls of GB, USA, Europe. *Recreations:* none. *Address:* 27 Athol Road, Bramhall, Cheshire SK7 1BR. *T:* 0161–439 2811.

GILLESPIE, Ian; Stipendiary Magistrate, West Midlands Area, since 1991; *b* 8 Oct. 1945; *s* of James Alexander and Margaret Cicely Gillespie; *m* 1974, Diana Mary Stevens. *Educ:* King Henry VIII Sch., Coventry. Admitted Solicitor of Supreme Court, 1973; Partner, Brindley Twist Tafft & James, Solicitors, Coventry, 1974–91; Actg Stipendiary Magistrate, Wolverhampton, 1989–91. *Recreations:* ski-ing, sailing, riding, attending concerts and ballet. *Address:* The Law Courts, North Street, Wolverhampton WV1 1RA. *T:* Wolverhampton (01902) 773151.

GILLESPIE, Prof. John Spence; Head of Department of Pharmacology, Glasgow University, 1968–92; *b* 5 Sept. 1926; *s* of Matthew Forsyth Gillespie and Myrtle Murie Spence; *m* 1956, Jemima Simpson Ross; four *s* one *d*. *Educ:* Dumbarton Academy; Glasgow Univ. MB ChB (Commendation), PhD. FRCP; FRSE. Hosp. Residency (Surgery), 1949–50; Nat. Service as RMO, 1950–52; hosp. appts, 1952–53; McCunn Res. Schol. in Physiology, Glasgow Univ., 1953–55; Faulds Fellow then Sharpey Schol. in Physiology Dept, University Coll. London, 1955–57; Glasgow University: Lectr in Physiol., 1957–59; Sophie Fricke Res. Fellow, Royal Soc., in Rockefeller Inst., 1959–60; Sen. Lectr in Physiol., 1961–63; Henry Head Res. Fellow, Royal Soc., 1963–68; Vice-Principal, 1983–87, 1988–91. *Publications:* articles in Jls of Physiol. and Pharmacol. *Recreations:* gardening, painting. *Address:* 5 Boclair Road, Bearsden, Glasgow G61 2AE. *T:* 0141–942 0318.

GILLESPIE, Prof. Ronald James, PhD, DSc; FRS 1977; FRSC; FRSC (UK); FCIC; Professor of Chemistry, McMaster University, Hamilton, Ont, 1960–88, now Emeritus; *b* London, England, 21 Aug. 1924; Canadian citizen; *s* of James A. Gillespie and Miriam G. (*née* Kirk); *m* 1950, Madge Ena Garner; two *d*. *Educ:* London Univ. (BSc 1945, PhD 1949, DSc 1957). FRSC 1965; FCIC 1960; FRIC; Mem., Amer. Chem. Soc. Asst Lectr, Dept of Chemistry, 1948–50, Lectr, 1950–58, UCL; Commonwealth Fund Fellow, Brown Univ., RI, USA, 1953–54; McMaster University: Associate Prof., Dept of Chem., 1958–60; Prof., 1960–62; Chm., Dept of Chem., 1962–65. Professeur Associé, l'Univ. des Sciences et Techniques de Languedoc, Montpellier, 1972–73; Visiting Professor: Univ. of Geneva, 1976; Univ. of Göttingen, 1978. Member: Chem. Soc. (Nyholm Lectr 1979); Faraday Soc. Hon. LLD: Dalhousie Univ., 1988; Concordia Univ., 1988; Dr *hc* Montpellier, 1991; Hon. DSc McMaster, 1993. Medals: Ramsay, UCL, 1949; Harrison Meml, Chem. Soc., 1954; Canadian Centennial, 1967; Chem. Inst. of Canada, 1977; Silver Jubilee, 1978; Henry Marshall Tory, Royal Soc. of Canada, 1983. Awards: Noranda,

Chem. Inst. of Canada, 1966 (for inorganic chem.); Amer. Chem. Soc. N-Eastern Reg., 1971 (in phys. chem.); Manufg Chemists Assoc. Coll. Chem. Teacher, 1972; Amer. Chem. Soc., 1973 (for distinguished service in advancement of inorganic chem.), 1980 (for creative work in fluorine chem.); Chem. Inst. of Canada/Union Carbide, 1976 (for chemical educn); Izaak Walton Killam Meml, Canada Council (for outstanding contrib. to advancement of res. in chemistry), 1987. *Publications:* Molecular Geometry, 1972 (London; German and Russian trans, 1975); (jtly) Chemistry, 1986, 2nd edn, 1989; The VSEPR Model of Molecular Geometry, 1990 (trans. Russian, 1992; Italian, 1994); (jtly) Atoms, Molecules and Reactions: an introduction to chemistry, 1994; papers in Jl Amer. Chem. Soc., Canadian Jl of Chem., and Inorganic Chem. *Recreations:* skiing, sailing. *Address:* Department of Chemistry, McMaster University, Hamilton, Ont L8S 4M1, Canada. *T:* (905) 5259140, ext. 23307, *Fax:* (905) 5222509.

GILLESPIE, William Hewitt, MD, FRCP; FRCPsych; Emeritus Physician, Maudsley Hospital (Physician, 1936–70); Hon. Member, British Psychoanalytical Society, 1975; *b* 6 Aug. 1905; *s* of Rev. W. H. Gillespie, Manchuria and Co. Down, and of Isabella B. Gillespie (*née* Grills), Co. Down, N Ireland; *m* 1st, 1932, Dr Helen Turover (*d* 1975); one *s* one *d*; 2nd, 1975, Sadie Mervis. *Educ:* George Watson's Coll.; Universities of Edinburgh and Vienna. University of Edinburgh: 1st pl. Open Bursary Exam., 1924, MB, ChB (hons), 1929, Dip. in Psychiatry, 1931, MD 1934; MRCP 1936; FRCP 1962; McCosh Travelling Scholarship, in Vienna, 1930–31. LCC Mental Hosps Service, 1931–36; Lecturer, Inst. of Psychiatry, 1944–70; Dir, London Clinic of Psychoanalysis, 1944–47. Freud Meml Vis. Prof. of Psychoanalysis, Univ. Coll. London, 1976–77. Trng Sec., Inst. of Psychoanalysis, 1947–50; Chm., Inst of Psychoanalysis, 1954–56; President: British Psychoanalytical Soc., 1950–53 and 1971–72; Internat. Psychoanalytic Assoc., 1957–61 (Hon. Vice-Pres., 1991). FRSocMed. *Publications:* contrib to: Recent Advances in Psychiatry, 1944; Psychiatrie sociale de l'enfant, 1951; Psychoanalysis and the Occult, 1953; The Sexual Perversions, 1956; The Pathology and Treatment of Sexual Deviation, 1964; Foundations of Child Psychiatry, 1968. Various articles in medical, psychiatric and psychoanalytic jls. *Recreations:* music, reading, walking. *Address:* 4 Eton Villas, NW3 4SX.

GILLETT, Rev. Canon David Keith; Principal, Trinity Theological College, Bristol, since 1988; *b* 25 Jan. 1945; *s* of Norman and Kathleen Gillett; *m* 1988, Valerie Shannon. *Educ:* Leeds Univ. (BA Theol. 1st cl. 1965; MPhil 1968). Curate, St Luke's, Watford, 1968–71; Northern Sec., Pathfinders and Church Youth Fellowship's Assoc., 1971–74; Lectr, St John's Coll., Nottingham, 1974–79; Co-Leader, Christian Renewal Centre for Reconciliation, NI, 1979–82; Vicar of St Hugh's, Luton, 1982–88. Mem., Gen. Synod of C of E, 1985–88, 1990–. Hon. Canon of Bristol Cathedral, 1991–. *Publications:* Learning in the Local Congregation, 1979; The Darkness where God is, 1983; Trust and Obey, 1993; (ed jtly) Treasure in the Field: the Archbishops' Companion to the Decade of Evangelism, 1993; co-author and contributor to various books and reference works. *Recreations:* photography, gardening. *Address:* 16 Ormerod Road, Stoke Bishop, Bristol BS9 1BB. *T:* Bristol (0117) 968 2646.

GILLETT, Sir Robin (Danvers Penrose), 2nd Bt *cr* 1959; GBE 1976; RD 1965; Underwriting Member of Lloyd's; Lord Mayor of London for 1976–77; *b* 9 Nov. 1925; *o s* of Sir (Sydney) Harold Gillett, 1st Bt, MC, and Audrey Isabel Penrose Wardlaw (*d* 1962); *S* father, 1976; *m* 1950, Elizabeth Marion Grace, *e d* of late John Findlay, JP, Busby, Lanarks; two *s*. *Educ:* Nautical Coll., Pangbourne. Served Canadian Pacific Steamships, 1943–60; Master Mariner 1951; Staff Comdr 1957; Hon. Comdr RNR 1971. Elder Brother of Trinity House; Fellow and Founder Mem., Nautical Inst. City of London (Ward of Bassishaw): Common Councilman 1965–69; Alderman 1969; Sheriff 1973; one of HM Lieuts for City of London, 1975; Chm. Civil Defence Cttee, 1967–68; Pres., City of London Civil Defence Instructors Assoc., 1967–78; Vice-Pres., City of London Centre, St John Ambulance Assoc.; Pres., Nat. Waterways Transport Assoc., 1979–83; Dep. Commonwealth Pres., Royal Life Saving Soc. Vice-Chm., PLA, 1979–84. Master, Hon. Co. of Master Mariners, 1979–80. Trustee, Nat. Maritime Mus., 1982–92. Chm. of Governors, Pangbourne Coll., 1978–92. Chancellor, City Univ., 1976–77. FIAM (Pres., 1980–84; Gold Medal, 1982); FRCM 1991. Hon. DSc City, 1976. Gentleman Usher of the Purple Rod, Order of the British Empire, 1985–. KStJ 1977 (OStJ 1974). Gold Medal, Administrative Management Soc., USA, 1983. Officer, Order of Leopard, Zaire, 1973; Comdr, Order of Dannebrog, 1974; Order of Johan Sedia Mahkota (Malaysia), 1974; Grand Cross of Municipal Merit (Lima), 1977. *Recreation:* sailing. *Heir: s* Nicholas Danvers Penrose Gillett, BSc, ARCS [*b* 24 Sept. 1955; *m* 1987, Haylie, *er d* of Dennis Brooks]. *Address:* 4 Fairholt Street, Knightsbridge, SW7 1EQ. *T:* 0171–589 9860. *Clubs:* City Livery, City Livery Yacht (Admiral), Guildhall, Royal Yacht Squadron, Royal London Yacht (Cdre, 1984–85), St Katharine's Yacht (Admiral).

GILLFORD, Lord; Patrick James Meade; Managing Director, Westminster Policy Partnership Ltd, since 1993; *b* 28 Dec. 1960; *s* and *heir* of Earl of Clanwilliam, *qv*; *m* 1989, Serena Emily (marr. diss. 1994), *d* of Lt-Col B. J. Lockhart; one *d*. *Educ:* Eton College. 1 Bn, Coldstream Guards, 1979–83. Exec., Hanson plc, 1983–90, attached Home Office as special advr to Home Sec., 1986–88; with Ian Greer & Associates, 1990–93. Councillor (C) Royal Bor. of Kensington and Chelsea, 1990– (Chm., Traffic and Highways Cttee). *Recreations:* prison reform and prison sentencing policy, free fall parachuting, sub-aqua diving, Palladian architecture. *Address:* 49 Causton Street, SW1P 4AT. *T:* 0171–976 5555. *Clubs:* Turf, Chatham Dining; Mill Reef (Antigua, WI); New Zealand (Weybridge).

GILLIAM, Terry; animator, actor, writer; film director, since 1973; *b* Minneapolis, USA, 22 Nov. 1940; *s* of James H. and Beatrice Gilliam; *m* 1973, Maggie Weston; one *s* two *d*. *Educ:* Occidental Coll., LA, Calif. *Television:* resident cartoonist, We Have Ways of Making You Laugh, 1968; animator: Do Not Adjust Your Set, 1968–69; (also actor and co-writer), Monty Python's Flying Circus, 1969–74 and 1979; The Marty Feldman Comedy Machine, 1971–72; The Do-It-Yourself Film Animation, 1974; *films:* co-writer, actor and animator: And Now For Something Completely Different, 1971; (also co-director) Monty Python and the Holy Grail, 1974; Monty Python's Life of Brian, 1979; Monty Python Live at the Hollywood Bowl, 1982; Monty Python's The Meaning of Life, 1983; (animator, writer) The Miracle of Flight, 1974; (writer, director) Jabberwocky, 1977; (co-writer, producer, director) Time Bandits, 1981; (co-writer, director) Brazil, 1985; (co-writer, director) The Adventures of Baron Münchhausen, 1989; (dir) The Fisher King, 1991; (dir) Twelve Monkeys, 1995. Hon. DFA Occidental Coll., 1987; Hon. Dr RCA, 1989. *Publications:* Animations of Mortality, 1978; contributed to: Monty Python's Big Red Book, 1971; The Brand New Monty Python Book, 1973, Monty Python and the Holy Grail, 1977; Monty Python's Life of Brian, 1979; Time Bandits, 1981; Monty Python's The Meaning of Life, 1983; (jtly) The Adventures of Baron Münchhausen, 1989. *Recreations:* too busy. *Address:* c/o Prominent Studios, 68A Delancey Street, NW1 7RY. *T:* 0171–284 0242.

GILLIBRAND, Sydney, CBE 1991; FEng 1987; FRAeS; Vice Chairman, British Aerospace PLC, since 1991 (Director, since 1987); *b* 2 June 1934; *s* of Sydney and Maud Gillibrand; *m* 1960, Angela Ellen Williams; three *s* (and one *s* decd). *Educ:* Preston Grammar Sch.; Harris Coll., Preston; College of Aeronautics, Cranfield (MSc). FRAeS 1975 (Hon. FRAeS). English Electric: apprentice, Preston, 1950; Chief Stress Engr, 1966; Works Man., Preston, 1974; Special Dir, BAC (Preston) Ltd, 1974; Dir of Manufacturing, Mil. Aircraft Div., 1977; British Aerospace Aircraft Group: Div. Prodn Dir, Warton, 1978; Dep. Man. Dir, Warton Div., and Bd Mem., Aircraft Gp, 1981; Div. Man. Dir, Kingston/Brough Div., 1983, Weybridge Div., 1984; Man. Dir, Civil Aircraft Div., BAe, 1986; Chairman: British Aerospace (Commercial Aircraft) Ltd, 1988; Aerospace Companies, British Aerospace PLC, 1989. Pres., SBAC, 1990–91. CIMgt. Silver Medal, RAeS, 1981. *Recreation:* golf. *Address:* British Aerospace PLC, PO Box 87, Farnborough Aerospace Centre, Farnborough, Hants GU14 6YU. *T:* Farnborough (01252) 383846.

GILLICK, Rev. John, SJ; MA Oxon; Spiritual Director, St Peter's National Seminary, Hammanskraal, S Africa, 1986–90, retired; *b* Wallasey, 27 March 1916; 2nd *s* of Laurence Gillick and Catherine Devine. *Educ:* St Francis Xavier's Coll., Liverpool; Heythrop and Campion Hall, Oxford (1st Cl. Hons Mod. History). Asst Master at Mount St Mary's and Beaumont. Two years writing and photography in Italy and Africa. Headmaster, Beaumont Coll., 1964–67; studied psychology at Loyola Univ., Chicago, 1967–68 (MA); Dir, Laboratories for the Training of Religious Superiors in S Africa, 1969; Dir, Fons Vitae (Pastoral Institute for Religious), 1970–84. *Publications:* Teaching the Mass, 1961; Baptism, 1962; followed by Teaching the Mass: African, 1963; Teaching the Sacraments: African, 1964; Teaching Confirmation: African, 1964, etc; *illustrations for:* The Breaking of Bread, 1950; The Pilgrim Years, 1956; Our Faith, 1956; The Holy Mass, 1958; Christ Our Life, 1960; Catholic Encyclopedia, 1965. *Address:* 8 The Elms, York Road, Rosebank, 7700, South Africa; c/o 114 Mount Street, W1Y 6AH.

GILLIES, (Maurice) Gordon, TD and Bar 1948; QC (Scotland) 1958; Sheriff Principal of South Strathclyde, Dumfries and Galloway, 1982–88; *b* 17 Oct. 1916; *s* of James Brown Gillies, Advocate in Aberdeen, and Rhoda Ledingham; *m* 1954, Anne Bethea McCall-Smith. *Educ:* Aberdeen Grammar Sch.; Merchiston Castle; Edinburgh Univ. Advocate, 1946; Advocate Depute, 1953–58; Sheriff of Lanarkshire, later S Strathclyde, Dumfries and Galloway, 1958–82. *Recreation:* golf. *Address:* 1 The Warren, Gullane, East Lothian EH31 2BE. *T:* Gullane (01620) 842857. *Clubs:* New (Edinburgh); Hon. Company of Edinburgh Golfers.

GILLILAND, David; *see* Gilliland, J. A. D.

GILLILAND, David Jervois Thetford; practising solicitor and farmer; *b* 14 July 1932; *s* of late Major W. H. Gilliland and of Mrs N. H. Gilliland; *m* 1st, 1958, Patricia, *o d* of late J. S. Wilson and late Mrs Wilson (marr. diss. 1976); two *s* three *d*; 2nd, 1976, Jennifer Johnston, *qv*. *Educ:* Rockport Prep. Sch.; Wrekin Coll.; Trinity Coll., Dublin. BA 1954, LLB 1955. Qualified as solicitor, 1957, own practice. Mem. ITA, 1965–70; Chm., N Ireland Adv. Cttee of ITA, 1965–70. Chm., NI Heritage Gardens Cttee, 1991–; Mem. Council, Internat. Dendrology Soc., 1966–75; etc. *Recreations:* gardening, sailing, fishing. *Address:* Brook Hall, 65 Culmore Road, Londonderry, Northern Ireland BT48 8JE. *T:* Londonderry (01504) 351297.

GILLILAND, (James Andrew) David; QC 1984; **His Honour Judge Gilliland;** a Circuit Judge (Official Referee), since 1992; *b* 29 Dec. 1937; *s* of James Albin Gilliland and Mary Gilliland (*née* Gray); *m* 1961, Elsie McCully; two *s*. *Educ:* Campbell College; Queen's University Belfast. LLB (1st Class Hons) 1960. Called to the Bar, Gray's Inn, 1964 (Holt Scholar, Atkin Scholar, Macaskie Scholar); Lectr in Law, Manchester University, 1960–72; a Recorder, 1989–92. *Recreations:* music, opera, stamp collecting, wind surfing, skiing. *Address:* Salford County Court, Prince William House, Peel Cross Road, off Eccles New Road, Salford M5 2RR. *T:* 0161–745 7511. *Club:* Athenæum (Liverpool).

GILLILAND, Jennifer, (Mrs David Gilliland); *see* Johnston, J.

GILLING, Lancelot Cyril Gilbert, OBE 1985; CBiol, FIBiol; FRAgS; Member, Royal Commission on Environmental Pollution, 1984–89; *b* 7 March 1920; *s* of Gilbert Joseph Gilling and Esther Marianne Gilling (*née* Clapp); *m* 1951, Brenda Copp; two *d*. *Educ:* Shebbear Coll., N Devon; Reading Univ. (BSc Agr). Pres. Union, Reading Univ., 1948–49. Lectr, Dorset Coll. of Agric., 1949–51; Head of Agric. Dept, Writtle Coll. of Agric., Essex, 1951–57; Principal, Askham Bryan Coll. of Agric. & Hortic., 1957–84. Member: Technical Develt Cttee and Educn and Gen. Purposes Cttee, Royal Agricl Soc., 1970–85; Northern Regional Panel, MAFF, 1982–88; Adv. Cttee on Agric. and Vet. Sci., British Council, 1972–86; Chm., York Agricl Soc., 1983–92 (Pres., 1981–82). Vice-Chm., Sub-Cttee, Yorkshire Museum, 1985–90; Chm. and Life Vice-Pres., Yorks Philosophical Soc., 1982–88. Chairman: Yorks Wildlife Trust, 1992–94 (Mem. Council and Chm., F and GP Cttee, 1985–92); York Centre, Nat. Trust, 1988–90. Gov., Univ. Coll. of Ripon and York St John, 1976–. Hon. Mem., CGLI. *Publications:* contribs to Agricultural Progress, Jl of Agricl Educn Assoc. and Jl of Royal Agricl Soc. *Recreations:* tennis, badminton, choral music. *Address:* The Spinney, Brandsby, York YO6 4RQ.

GILLINGHAM, (Francis) John, CBE 1982 (MBE 1944); FRSE 1970; Professor of Neurological Surgery, University of Edinburgh, 1963–80, now Emeritus; at Royal Infirmary of Edinburgh and Western General Hospital, Edinburgh, 1963–80; Consultant Neuro-Surgeon to the Army in Scotland, 1966–80; *b* 15 March 1916; *s* of John H. Gillingham, Upwey, Dorset; *m* 1945, Irene Judy Jude; four *s*. *Educ:* Hardye's Sch., Dorset; St Bartholomew's Hosp. Medical Coll., London. Matthews Duncan Gold Medal, 1939, MRCS, LRCP Oct. 1939; MB, BS (London) Nov. 1939; FRCS 1947; FRCSE 1955; FRCPE 1967. Prof. of Surgical Neurol., King Saud Univ., Saudi Arabia, 1983–85, now Emeritus. Advr in Neuro-Surgery, MoD, Kingdom of Saudi Arabia, 1980–83. Hon. Consultant in Neurosurgery, St Bartholomew's Hosp., London, 1981–. Hunterian Prof., RCS, 1957; Morison Lectr, RCP of Edinburgh, 1960; Colles Lectr, College of Surgeons of Ireland, 1962; Elsberg Lectr, College of Physicians and Surgeons, NY, 1967; Penfield Lectr, Middle East Med. Assembly, 1970; Syme Derby Lectr, Univ. of Hong Kong, 1982; Adlington Syme Oration, RACS, 1983. Hon. Mem., Soc. de Neurochirurgie de Langue Française, 1964; Hon. Mem., Soc. of Neurol. Surgeons (USA), 1965; Hon. Mem., Royal Academy of Medicine of Valencia, 1967; Hon. and Corresp. Mem. of a number of foreign neuro-surgical societies; Hon. Pres., World Fedn of Neurosurgical Socs. President: Medico-Chirurgical Soc. of Edinburgh, 1965–67; European Soc. of Stereostatic and Functional Neurosurgery, 1972–76; RCSE, 1979–82 (Vice-Pres., 1974–77; Mem., Court of Regents, 1990–). FRSA 1991. Hon. FRACS 1980; Hon. FCS Sri Lanka 1980; Hon. FRCSI 1981; Hon. FRCSGlas 1982. Hon. MD Thessaloniki, 1973. Jim Clark Foundn Award, 1979; Medal of City of Gdansk, Poland, 1980. *Publications:* Clinical Surgery: Neurological Surgery, 1969; papers on surgical management of cerebral vascular disease, head and spinal injuries, Parkinsonism and the dyskinesias, epilepsy and other neurosurgical subjects. *Recreations:* sailing, travel, gardening (cactus). *Address:* Easter Park House, Barnton Avenue, Edinburgh EH4 6JR. *T:* 0131–336 3528. *Clubs:* Bruntsfield Links Golfing Society; Nautico (Javea, Alicante).

GILLINGHAM, Michael John, FSA; Chairman, Advisory Board for Redundant Churches, since 1989 (Member, since 1979); *b* 26 June 1933; *s* of John Morey Gillingham and Marion Gillingham. *Educ:* Yeovil School; Corpus Christi College, Cambridge (MA, LLB). Director, John Sparks Ltd, 1976–91. Member: London Diocesan Adv. Cttee for Care of

Churches, 1965–; Organs Adv. Cttee, Council for Care of Churches, 1967–91; Westminster Abbey Architectural Adv. Panel, 1990–; Chichester Cathedral Fabric Cttee, 1990–93; Chm., British Inst. of Organ Studies, 1976–83; Organ Consultant: St Michael, Framlingham, 1968; St James, Clerkenwell, 1978; Peterborough Cathedral, 1980; Chichester Cathedral, 1986; St Andrew, Holborn, 1989; St Matthew, Westminster, 1989; for restoration of organ-case, Gloucester Cathedral, 1971; and other historic organs in London and elsewhere. Trustee, Fitzwilliam Mus. Trust, 1990–. Hon. RCO 1986. *Publications:* articles on organ-cases, organ history, Chinese art. *Recreation:* looking at buildings and works of art. *Address:* 4 Fournier Street, Spitalfields, E1 6QE. *T:* 0171–377 1576. *Club:* Athenæum.

GILLINGHAM, Rev. Canon Peter Llewellyn, LVO 1955; MA 1940; Chaplain to the Queen, 1952–84; Hon. Canon of Chichester Cathedral (Wisborough Prebendary), 1969–77, Canon Emeritus since 1977; *b* 3 May 1914; *s* of late Rev. Canon Frank Hay Gillingham; *m* 1947, Diana, *d* of Lieut-Gen. Sir Alexander Hood; two *s* two *d*. *Educ:* Cheam; Marlborough; Oriel Coll., Oxford. Curate, Tonbridge Parish Church, 1937–40; Curate-in-Charge, St George's Church, Oakdale, Poole, 1940–43. Served War of 1939–45, Chaplain, RNVR, 1943–46; Chaplain, Blundell's Sch., Tiverton, 1946–49; Hon. Chaplain to King George VI, 1949–52; Chaplain to Royal Chapel of All Saints, Windsor Great Park, 1949–55; Vicar of St Mildred's, Addiscombe, 1955; Vicar of St Mary the Virgin, Horsham, 1960–77; Rural Dean of Horsham, 1974–77; Asst Chaplain, Sherborne Girls' Sch., 1977–79, Chaplain and Librarian, 1979–82. *Recreations:* golf, sailing. *Address:* Maplestead Cottage, Leiston Road, Aldeburgh, Suffolk IP15 5QD. *T:* Aldeburgh (0172845) 2739.

GILLINGS, Ven. Richard John; Archdeacon of Macclesfield, since 1994; Vicar of Bramhall, since 1993; *b* 17 Sept. 1945; *s* of John Albert Gillings and Constance Ford Gillings; *m* 1972, Kathryn Mary Hill; two *s* one *d*. *Educ:* Sale GS; St Chad's Coll., Durham (BA, Dip Biblical Studies); Lincoln Theol Coll. Ordained deacon, 1970, priest, 1971; Curate, St George's, Altrincham, 1970–75; Priest i/c, then Rector, St Thomas', Stockport, 1975–83, and Priest i/c, St Peter's, Stockport, 1978–83; Rector, Birkenhead Priory, 1983–93; RD, Birkenhead, 1985–93; Hon. Canon, Chester Cathedral, 1992–94. Mem., Gen. Synod, 1980–. *Recreations;* music, cinema, theatre, railways, Rotary. *Address:* The Vicarage, Robins Lane, Bramhall, Stockport, Cheshire SK7 2PE. *T:* 0161-439 2254.

GILLIS, His Honour Bernard Benjamin, QC 1954; MA Cantab; a Circuit Judge (Additional Judge, Central Criminal Court), 1964–80; *m*; one *s*. *Educ:* Downing Coll., Cambridge, Hon. Fellow, 1976. Squadron Leader, RAF, 1940–45. Called to the Bar, Lincoln's Inn, 1927, Bencher 1960, Treasurer 1976; North Eastern Circuit and Central Criminal Court. Commr, Central Criminal Court, 1959; Commissioner of Assize: Lancaster, 1960; Chelmsford, 1961; Bodmin, 1963. Recorder of Bradford, 1958–64. *Address:* 3 Adelaide Crescent, Hove, E Sussex BN3 2JD. *Club:* Royal Air Force.

GILLMAN, Bernard Arthur, (Gerry Gillman); General Secretary, Society of Civil and Public Servants, 1973–85; *b* 14 April 1927; *s* of Elias Gillman and Gladys Gillman; *m* 1951, Catherine Mary Antonia Harvey. *Educ:* Archbishop Tenison's Grammar Sch. Civil Service, 1946–53; Society of Civil Servants, 1953–85. Mem., Police Complaints Authy, 1986–91. *Address:* 2 Burnham Street, Kingston-upon-Thames, Surrey KT2 6QR. *T:* 0181–546 6905. *Clubs:* Royal Over-Seas League, MCC.

GILLMORE, Air Vice-Marshal Alan David, CB 1955; CBE 1944; RAF (retired); *b* 17 Oct. 1905; *s* of late Rev. David Sandeman Gillmore and Allis Emily Widmer; *m* 1931, Kathleen Victoria Morris; three *s*. *Educ:* St Dunstan's Sch., Burnham-on-Sea; King's Sch., Ely. RAF Cadet Coll., Cranwell, Lincs, 1923–25; Commission in RAF, 1925; 13 Sqdn, 1925–27; 208 Sqdn (Egypt), 1927–29; Instr, Sch. of Air Pilotage, 1931–33; O i/c Navigation Flight, 1934–35; 202 Flying Boat Sqdn (Malta), 1935–36; HQ no 6 (Aux.) Gp, 1936–39; RN Staff Coll., 1939; Future Ops Planning Staff, 1940–41; Dep. Dir, Overseas Orgn (Air Min.), 1940–41; Instr, RAF Staff Coll., 1942; OC RAF Station Wick, 1943–44; Dir, Maritime Ops (Air Min.), 1944–45; AOC RAF W Africa, 1945–46; Dir of Postings (Air Min.), 1946–47; IDC, 1948; AOC 64 Gp, 1949–51; Commandant RAF Staff Coll., Bracknell, 1951–53; SASO, FEAF, 1953–56; SASO, Home Command, 1956–59; retired 1959. *Address:* 23 Swallowfield Park, Swallowfield, Reading, Berks RG7 1TG. *Club:* Royal Air Force.
See also Sir D. H. Gillmore.

GILLMORE, Sir David (Howe), GCMG 1994 (KCMG 1990; CMG 1982); HM Diplomatic Service, retired; Senior Adviser to Chairman, BZW Ltd, since 1995; Director, Prudential Corporation, since 1995; *b* 16 Aug. 1934; *s* of Air Vice-Marshal A. D. Gillmore, *qv*; *m* 1964, Lucile Morin; two *s*. *Educ:* Trent Coll.; King's Coll., Cambridge (MA). Reuters Ltd, 1958–60; Asst to Dir-Gen., Polypapier, SA, Paris, 1960–65; Teacher, ILEA, 1965–69; HM Diplomatic Service, 1970; Foreign and Commonwealth Office, 1970–72; First Sec., Moscow, 1972–75; Counsellor, UK Delegn, Vienna, 1975–78; Head of Defence Dept, FCO, 1979–81; Asst Under Sec. of State, FCO, 1981–83; High Comr in Malaysia, 1983–86; Dep. Under-Sec. of State, FCO, 1986–90; Visiting Fellow: Harvard Univ., 1990–91; WEU Inst., Paris, 1990–91; Perm. Under-Sec. of State, FCO, and Head of Diplomatic Service, 1991–94. Chm., LAPADA, 1995–. Governor: Ditchley Foundn, 1992–; Birkbeck Coll., 1994–. *Publication: novel* A Way From Exile, 1967. *Recreations:* books, music, exercise. *Address:* c/o BZW, Ebbgate House, 2 Swan Lane, EC4R 3TS. *Clubs:* Brooks's, Royal Automobile, Special Forces.

GILLON, Dr Raanan Evelyn Zvi, FRCP; part-time general practitioner; Professor of Medical Ethics, St Mary's Hospital Medical School and Imperial College, London, since 1995 (Visiting Professor, 1989–95); Director, Imperial College Health Service, since 1982; Editor, Journal of Medical Ethics, since 1980; *b* Jerusalem, 15 April 1941; *s* of Diana Gillon and late Meir Gillon; *m* 1966, Angela Spear; one *d*. *Educ:* Christ's Hospital; University College London (MB BS 1964); Christ Church, Oxford; Birbeck College London (BA Phil 1st cl. Hons 1979). MRCP 1974, FRCP 1988. Medical journalism, 1964–71 (Ed., Medical Tribune); part-time GP, part-time philosophy student then teacher, 1974–; Dir of Teaching in Medical Ethics (for MA course), KCL, 1986–89. Vis. Prof. in Med. Ethics, KCL, 1988–91. Chm., Imperial Coll. Ethics Cttee, 1984–93. Mem., BMA, 1964; FRSocMed 1966. Hon RCM 1986. *Publications:* Philosophical Medical Ethics, 1986; (ed jtly and contrib.) Principles of Health Care Ethics, 1994; numerous papers on medical ethics. *Recreations:* enjoying the company of wife and daughter; reading moral philosophy and, intermittently, thrillers; playing (own) trumpet, or rather, Uncle Peter's trumpet, kindly lent in 1954; ski-ing, swimming, cooking, winetasting, arguing. *Address:* 42 Brynmaer Road, SW11 4EW. *T:* 0171–622 1450; (office) 14 Prince's Gardens, SW7 1NA. *T:* 0171–584 6301.

GILMORE, Brian Terence, CB 1992; with Towers Perrin, consultants; *b* 25 May 1937; *s* of John Henry Gilmore and Edith Alice Gilmore; *m* 1962, Rosalind Edith Jean Fraser (*see* R. E. J. Gilmore). *Educ:* Wolverhampton Grammar Sch.; Christ Church, Oxford (Passmore-Edwards Prize, 1956; BA Lit. Hum.; MA 1961). CRO and Diplomatic Service Admin Office, 1958–65: Private Sec. to Perm. Sec., 1960–61, to Parly Under Sec., 1961–62; Asst Private Sec. to Sec. of State, 1962–64; British Embassy, Washington, 1965–68; Min. of Technology and DTI, 1968–72: Private Sec. to Minister of State, Industry, 1969–70, and to Lord Privy Seal and Leader of the House of Lords, 1971–72; CSD, 1972–81; Under Sec., 1979; Principal, CS Coll., 1979–81; HM Treasury, 1981–88; Principal Estabt Officer and Principal Finance Officer, 1982–84; Dep. Sec., Office of Minister for CS, Cabinet Office, 1988–92; Dep. Sec., DSS, 1992–94. *Recreations:* reading, music, Greece. *Address:* 3 Clarendon Mews, W2 2NR. *Club:* Athenæum.

GILMORE, Carol Jacqueline; *see* Ellis, C. J.

GILMORE, Rosalind Edith Jean, (Mrs B. T. Gilmore), CB 1995; Director of Regulation, Lloyd's of London, since 1994; *b* 23 March 1937; *o c* of Sir Robert Brown Fraser, OBE, and Betty Fraser; *m* 1962, Brian Terence Gilmore, *qv*. *Educ:* King Alfred Sch.; University Coll. London (BA; Fellow, 1989); Newnham Coll., Cambridge (BA, MA; Associate Fellow, 1986). Asst Principal, HM Treasury, 1960–65; IBRD, 1966–67; Principal, HM Treasury, 1968–73; Prin. Pvte Sec. to Chancellor of Duchy of Lancaster, Cabinet Office, 1974; HM Treasury: Asst Sec., 1975–80; Press Sec. and Hd of Inf., 1980–82; Gen. Man., Corporate Planning, Dunlop Ltd, 1982–83; Dir of Marketing, Nat. Girobank, 1983–86; Directing Fellow, St George's House, Windsor Castle, 1986–89; re-instated, HM Treasury, and seconded to Bldg Socs Commn, 1989; Dep. Chm., 1989–91, Chm. (First Comr), 1991–94, Bldg Socs Commn; Chief Registrar of Friendly Socs, 1991–94; Industrial Assurance Comr, 1991–94. Director: Mercantile Gp plc, 1986–89; London and Manchester Gp plc, 1988–89; Cons. Man., FI Gp plc, 1987–89. Mem., SIB, 1993–. Board Member: Opera North, 1993–; Moorfields Eye Hosp. Trust. FRSA 1985; CIMgt 1992. *Recreations:* swimming (Half Blue, Cambridge Univ.), music, house in Greece. *Address:* 3 Clarendon Mews, W2 2NR.

GILMOUR, family name of **Baron Gilmour of Craigmillar.**

GILMOUR OF CRAIGMILLAR, Baron *cr* 1992 (Life Peer), of Craigmillar in the District of the City of Edinburgh; **Ian Hedworth John Little Gilmour;** Bt 1926; PC 1973; *b* 8 July 1926; *er s* of Lt-Col Sir John Little Gilmour, 2nd Bt, and Hon. Victoria Laura, OBE, TD (*d* 1991), *d* of late Viscount Chelsea (*e s* of 5th Earl Cadogan); *S* father, 1977; *m* 1951, Lady Caroline Margaret Montagu-Douglas-Scott, *yr d* of 8th Duke of Buccleuch and Queensberry, KT, GCVO, PC; four *s* one *d*. *Educ:* Eton; Balliol Coll., Oxford. Served with Grenadier Guards, 1944–47; 2nd Lieut 1945. Called to the Bar, Inner Temple, 1952. Editor, The Spectator, 1954–59. MP (C) Norfolk Central, Nov. 1962–1974, Chesham and Amersham, 1974–92. Parly Under-Sec. of State, MoD, 1970–71; Minister of State: for Defence Procurement, MoD, 1971–72; for Defence, 1972–74; Sec. of State for Defence, 1974; Lord Privy Seal, 1979–81. Chm., Cons. Res. Dept, 1974–75. Pres., Med. Aid for Palestinians, 1993–. *Publications:* The Body Politic, 1969; Inside Right: a study of Conservatism, 1977; Britain Can Work, 1983; Riots, Risings and Revolution: governance and violence in 18th Century England, 1992; Dancing with Dogma: Britain under Thatcherism, 1992. *Heir* (to baronetcy): *s* Hon. David Robert Gilmour [*b* 14 Nov. 1952; *m* 1975, Sarah Anne, *d* of M. H. G. Bradstock; one *s* three *d*]. *Address:* The Ferry House, Old Isleworth, Mddx TW7 6BD. *T:* 0181–560 6769. *Clubs:* Pratt's, White's.
See also A. C. Gilmour.

GILMOUR, Dr Alan Breck, CVO 1990; CBE 1984; FRCGP; Director, National Society for the Prevention of Cruelty to Children, 1979–89, retired; *b* 30 Aug. 1928; *er* surv. *s* of late Andrew Gilmour, CMG and Nelle Twigg; *m* 1957, Elizabeth, *d* of late H. and L. Heath; two *d*. *Educ:* Clayesmore Sch.; King's Coll., London; King's Coll. Hosp. (Raymond Gooch Schol.). MB BS, LMSSA 1956; FRCGP 1974 (MRCGP 1965). General medical practitioner, 1958–67; during this period served as Member: Standing Med. Adv. Cttee, Min. of Health; Working Party on General Practice; Educn Cttee, RCGP; BMA Council, and others. British Medical Association Secretariat, 1967–79: Asst Sec., 1967; Under Sec., 1972, Dep. Sec., 1977; appts included: Overseas Sec. and Med. Dir, Commonwealth Med. Adv. Bureau, 1967–72; Med. Dir, Career Service, 1967–76; Sec., Bd of Sci. and Educn, 1972–76 (Commonwealth Med. Assoc. meetings, Singapore/Malaysia, Jamaica, Ghana; Observer, Commonwealth Med. Conf., Mauritius, 1971); Jt Sec., Med. Sci. meetings, Vancouver, Jamaica, Dublin; Dep. Sec., Jt Consultants Cttee, 1976–79. Chairman: Internat. Alliance on Child Abuse and Neglect, 1983–; Michael Sieff Foundn, 1990–; Mem., Health Educn Authority, 1989–95; Hon. Treas., Assoc. for Study of Med. Educn, 1975–80; Vice-Pres., Sect. Med. Educn, RSM, 1979–82. Pres., Bridport Br., Parkinson's Disease Soc. Trustee: Kidscape, 1991–93 (Chm., 1992–93); Faithfull Foundn, 1992–94 (Patron, 1994–). Gov., Colfox Sch., 1994–; Mem. Council, Clayesmore Sch., 1995– (Chm., Clayesmore Sch. Centenary, 1996). MInstD. Liveryman, Worshipful Soc. of Apothecaries of London, 1973–. *Publications:* Innocent Victims: the question of child abuse, 1988; various articles on child abuse and on med. educn, careers in medicine, gen. practice; ed or ed jtly, Care of the Elderly, Primary Health Care Teams, Competence to Practise, and other reports. *Recreations:* gardening, homecare, walking, music. *Address:* 106 Crock Lane, Bothenhampton, Bridport, Dorset DT6 4DH. *T:* Bridport (01308) 423116. *Club:* Royal Society of Medicine.

GILMOUR, Alexander Clement, CVO 1990; Director, London Wall Capital Group, since 1989; *b* 23 Aug. 1931; *s* of Sir John Little Gilmour, 2nd Bt, and of Lady Mary Gilmour; *m* 1954, Barbara M. L. Constance Berry; two *s* one *d*; *m* 1983, Susan Lady Chetwode. *Educ:* Eton. National Service, commn in Black Watch, 1950–52. With Joseph Sebag & Co. (subseq. Carr, Sebag), 1954–82; Director: Safeguard Industrial Investments, 1974–84; Tide (UK) Ltd, 1986–87; Exec. Dir, Equity Finance Trust Ltd, 1984–86. Consultant, Grieveson Grant, 1982. Chm., Nat. Playing Fields Assoc., 1976–88 (Past-Chm. Appeals Cttee, 10 yrs). Dir, Tate Gallery Foundn, 1986–88. Governor, LSE, 1969–. *Recreations:* tennis, fishing, gardening, golf. *Address:* c/o Drummonds Branch, Royal Bank of Scotland, 49 Charing Cross, SW1A 2DX. *Clubs:* White's; Hon. Company of Edinburgh Golfers.
See also Baron Gilmour of Craigmillar.

GILMOUR, Colonel Sir Allan (Macdonald), KCVO 1990; OBE 1961; MC 1942, and Bar 1943; Lord-Lieutenant of Sutherland, 1972–91; Member, Highland Regional Council, since 1977; Chairman, Highland River Purification Board, since 1994 (Vice-Chairman, 1986–94); *b* 23 Nov. 1916; *o s* of late Captain Allan Gilmour, of Rosehall, Sutherland, and late Mary H. M. Macdonald, of Viewfield, Portree, Skye; *m* 1941, Jean Wood; three *s* one *d*. *Educ:* Winchester Coll. Gazetted, The Seaforth Highlanders, Jan. 1939. Served War, in Middle East, France and Germany (despatches, 1945); DSC (USA) 1945. Staff Coll., 1946; Regimental and Staff Service in: Germany, Middle East, UK, Pakistan and Africa, 1946–67, incl. Instructor, Staff Coll., Quetta, on loan to Pakistan Army, 1952–54. Chief of Gen. Staff, Ghana Armed Forces, 1959–62; service in Congo, 1961–62; retired from Army, 1967. Vice-Pres., Highland TA&VRA, 1972–89, Pres., 1989–91. Chairman: East Sutherland Council of Social Service, 1973–77; Highland Health Bd, 1981–83 (Mem., 1974–81). Mem., Highlands and Is Develt Consultative Council, 1975–87. Member: Sutherland District Council, 1978–86 (Chm., 1974–78); Sutherland CC, 1970–74. DL Sutherland, 1971. *Recreations:* fishing, local government. *Address:* Invernauld, Rosehall, Lairg, Sutherland IV27 4EU. *T:* Rosehall (01549) 402204.

GILMOUR, Col Sir John (Edward), 3rd Bt, *cr* 1897; DSO 1945; TD; JP; Lord-Lieutenant of Fife, 1980–87 (Vice Lord-Lieutenant, 1979–80); Lord High Commissioner, General Assembly of the Church of Scotland, 1982 and 1983; *b* 24 Oct. 1912; *o s* of Col Rt Hon. Sir John Gilmour, 2nd Bt, GCVO, DSO, MP, and Mary Louise (*d* 1919), *e d* of late E. T. Lambert, Telham Court, Battle, Sussex; *S* father, 1940; *m* 1941, Ursula Mabyn, *yr d* of late F. O. Wills; two *s*. *Educ:* Eton; Trinity Hall, Cambridge. Served War of 1939–45 (DSO). Bt Col 1950; Captain, Royal Company of Archers (Queen's Body Guard for Scotland); Hon. Col, The Highland Yeomanry, RAC, T&AVR, 1971–75. MP (C) East Fife, 1961–79. Chm., Cons. and Unionist Party in Scotland, 1965–67. DL Fife, 1953. *Heir: s* John Gilmour [*b* 15 July 1944; *m* 1967, Valerie, *yr d* of late G. W. Russell, and of Mrs William Wilson; two *s* two *d*]. *Address:* Montrave, Leven, Fife KY8 5NZ. *TA:* Leven. *T:* Leven (01333) 426159. *Club:* Royal and Ancient Golf (St Andrews).

See also Dame Anne Bryans, Viscount Younger.

GILMOUR, Nigel Benjamin Douglas; QC 1990; a Recorder, since 1990; *b* 21 Nov. 1947; *s* of late Benjamin Waterfall Gilmour and of Barbara Mary Gilmour (now Mrs E. Harborow); *m* 1972, Isobel Anne, *d* of E. Harborow; two *d*. *Educ:* Tettenhall Coll., Staffordshire; Liverpool Univ. (LLB Hons). Called to the Bar, Inner Temple, 1970; an Asst Recorder, 1984–90. *Recreations:* wine, food. *Address:* Peel House, 5 Harrington Street, Liverpool L2 9QA. *T:* 0151–236 4321.

GILROY BEVAN, David; *see* Bevan, A. D. G.

GILSENAN, Prof. Michael Dermot Cole; Professor of Near Eastern Studies and Anthropology, New York University, since 1995; *b* 6 Feb. 1940; *s* of Michael Eugene Cole Gilsenan and Joyce Russell Horn. *Educ:* Eastbourne Grammar Sch.; Oxford Univ. BA (Oriental Studies), Dip. Anth., MA, DPhil (Soc. Anthropology). Research Fellow, Amer. Univ. in Cairo, 1964–66; Research studentship, St Antony's Coll., Oxford, 1966–67; Research Fellow, Harvard Middle East Center, 1967–68; Asst Prof., Dept of Anthropology, UCLA, 1968–70; Research Lectr, Univ. of Manchester, 1970–73; Associate Fellow, St Antony's Coll., Oxford, 1970–73; Lectr, 1973–78, Reader, 1978–83, Dept of Anthropology, University College London; Mem., Sch. of Social Sci., Inst. for Advanced Study, Princeton, 1979–80; Khalid bin Abdullah al Saud Prof. for study of contemp. Arab world, and Fellow of Magdalen Coll., Oxford Univ., 1984–95, Emeritus Fellow, 1995. Anthrop. field work, Egypt, 1964–66, Lebanon, 1971–72. Mem. Editl Bds, Past and Present, History and Anthropology, and formerly of Man, and Internat. Jl of Middle Eastern Studies; Series Editor, Society and Culture in the Modern Middle East, 1987–. *Publications:* Saint and Sufi in Modern Egypt, 1973; Recognizing Islam, 1982; Lords of the Lebanese Marches, 1996. *Recreations:* music, theatre, being elsewhere. *Address:* Department of Near Eastern Languages and Literature, 50 Washington Square South, New York, NY 10012-1073, USA.

GILSON, Rev. Nigel Langley, DFC 1944; Methodist minister, retired; President of the Methodist Conference, 1986–87; *b* 11 April 1922; *s* of Clifford Edric and Cassandra Jeanette Gilson; *m* 1951, Mary Doreen (*née* Brown); four *d*. *Educ:* Holcombe Methodist Elementary; Midsomer Norton Co. Secondary; St Catherine's Soc., Oxford Univ. (MA Hons); Wesley House and Fitzwilliam House, Cambridge Univ. (BA Hons). Served RAF, 1941–45 (Navigator (Wireless) 107 Sqdn, 1944–45), Flying Officer. Methodist Minister: Tintagel, Cornwall, 1950–52; Newark-upon-Trent, 1952–58; Rhodesia Dist, 1958–67; Chaplain, Hunmanby Hall Sch., Filey, Yorks, 1967–71; Supt Minister of Oxford Methodist Circuit, 1971–75 and 1988–89; Chm., Wolverhampton and Shrewsbury Dist, 1975–88. *Recreations:* gardening, theatre, family, community and multi-cultural activities. *Address:* 30 Spencer Avenue, Yarnton, Kidlington, Oxon OX5 1NG. *T:* Kidlington (01865) 378058.

GIMINGHAM, Prof. Charles Henry, OBE 1990; FRSE 1961; Regius Professor of Botany, University of Aberdeen, 1981–88 (Professor of Botany, since 1969); *b* 28 April 1923; *s* of late Conrad Theodore Gimingham and Muriel Elizabeth (*née* Blake), Harpenden; *m* 1948, Elizabeth Caroline, *o d* of late Rev. J. Wilson Baird, DD, Minister of St Machar's Cathedral, Aberdeen; three *d*. *Educ:* Gresham's Sch., Holt, Norfolk; Emmanuel Coll., Cambridge (Open scholarship; BA 1944; ScD 1977); PhD Aberdeen 1948. FIBiol 1967. Research Asst, Imperial Coll., Univ. of London, 1944–45; University of Aberdeen: Asst, 1946–48, Lectr, 1948–61, Sen. Lectr, 1961–64, Reader, 1964–69, Dept of Botany. Pres., British Ecological Soc., 1986–87. Vice Chairman: NE Regl Bd, NCC for Scot., 1991–92; NE Regl Bd, Scottish Natural Heritage, 1992–; Member: Countryside Commn for Scotland, 1980–92; Bd of Management, Hill Farming Res. Organisation, 1981–87; Council of Management, Macaulay Inst. for Soil Research, 1983–87; Governing Body, Macaulay Land Use Res. Inst., 1987–90. Mem. Governing Body, Aberdeen Coll. of Educn, 1979–87. *Publications:* Ecology of Heathlands, 1972; An Introduction to Heathland Ecology, 1975; The Lowland Heathland Management Handbook, 1992; papers, mainly in botanical and ecological jls. *Recreations:* hill walking, photography, foreign travel, history and culture of Japan. *Address:* 4 Gowanbrae Road, Bieldside, Aberdeen AB1 9AQ.

GIMSON, George Stanley, QC (Scotland) 1961; Sheriff Principal of Grampian, Highland and Islands, 1975–82; Chairman: Pensions Appeals Tribunals, Scotland, since 1971 (President, 1971–75); Medical Appeal Tribunals, 1985–91; *b* 1915. *Educ:* High School of Glasgow; Glasgow Univ. Advocate, 1949; Standing Junior Counsel, Department of Agriculture for Scotland and Forestry Commission, 1956–61; Sheriff Principal of Aberdeen, Kincardine and Banff, 1972–74. Mem., Board of Management: Edinburgh Central Hosps, 1960–70 (Chm., 1964–70); Edinburgh Royal Victoria Hosps, 1970–74 (Vice-Chm.); Dir, Scottish Nat. Orchestra Soc. Ltd, 1962–80; Trustee, Nat. Library of Scotland, 1963–76; Chm., RSSPCC, Edinburgh, 1972–76. Hon. LLD Aberdeen, 1981. *Address:* 11 Royal Circus, Edinburgh EH3 6TL. *T:* 0131–225 8055. *Clubs:* University Staff (Edinburgh); Royal Northern and University (Aberdeen).

GINGELL, Air Chief Marshal Sir John, GBE 1984 (CBE 1973; MBE 1962); KCB 1978; KCVO 1992; RAF, retired; Gentleman Usher of the Black Rod, Serjeant-at-Arms, House of Lords, and Secretary to the Lord Great Chamberlain, 1985–92; *b* 3 Feb. 1925; *e s* of late E. J. Gingell; *m* 1949, Prudence, *d* of late Brig. R. F. Johnson; two *s* one *d*. *Educ:* St Boniface Coll., Plymouth. Entered RAF, 1943; Fleet Air Arm, 1945–46 as Sub-Lt (A) RNVR; returned to RAF, 1951; served with Nos 58 and 542 Sqdns; CFS 1954; psc 1959; jssc 1965; comd No 27 Sqdn, 1963–65; Staff of Chief of Defence Staff, 1966; Dep. Dir Defence Ops Staff (Central Staff), 1966–67; Mil. Asst to Chm. NATO Mil. Cttee, Brussels, 1968–70; AOA, RAF Germany, 1971–72; AOC 23 Group, RAF Trng Comd, 1973–75; Asst Chief of Defence Staff (Policy), 1975–78; Air Member for Personnel, 1978–80; AOC-in-C, RAF Support Comd, 1980–81; Dep. C-in-C, Allied Forces Central Europe, 1981–84. Mem., Commonwealth War Graves Commn, 1986–91. Hon. Bencher, Inner Temple, 1990. *Recreations:* gardening, walking, music. *Address:* c/o Lloyd's Bank, Shaftesbury, Dorset SP7 8JJ. *Club:* Royal Air Force.

GINGELL, Maj.-Gen. Laurie William Albert, CB 1980; OBE 1966 (MBE 1959); General Secretary, Officers' Pensions Society, 1979–90; *b* 29 Oct. 1925; *s* of late Major William George Gingell, MBE, MM, and of Elsie Grace Gingell; *m* 1949, Nancy Margaret Wadsworth; one *s* one *d*. *Educ:* Farnborough Grammar Sch.; Oriel Coll., Oxford. Commissioned into Royal Gloucestershire Hussars, 1945; transf. Royal Tank Regt, 1947; psc 1956; jssc 1961; Commanded: 1st Royal Tank Regt, 1966–67; 7th Armoured Bde, 1970–71; DQMG, HQ BAOR, 1973–76; Maj.-Gen. Admin, HQ UKLF, 1976–79. ADC to the Queen, 1974–76. FIMgt (FBIM 1979). *Recreations:* golf, tennis, swimming, reading. *Address:* 54 Station Road, Thames Ditton, Surrey KT7 0NS. *T:* 0181–224 7023.

GINGER, Phyllis Ethel, (Mrs Leslie Durbin), RWS 1958 (ARWS 1952); freelance artist since 1940; *b* 19 Oct. 1907; *m* 1940, Leslie Durbin, *qv*; one *s* one *d*. *Educ:* Tiffin's Girls' Sch., Kingston on Thames. LCC three years' scholarship at Central School of Arts and Crafts, 1937–39. Water colours for Pilgrim Trust Recording Britain Scheme, 1941–42; Royal Academy Exhibitor; Drawings and Lithographs purchased by: Washington State Library, 1941; Victoria and Albert Museum, 1952; London Museum, 1954; South London Art Gallery, 1960. *Publications:* Alexander the Circus Pony, 1941; book jacket designs; book illustrations include: London by Mrs Robert Henrey, 1948; The Virgin of Aldemanbury, by Mrs Robert Henrey, 1960. *Address:* 298 Kew Road, Kew, Richmond, Surrey TW9 3DU. *T:* 0181–940 2221.

GINGRICH, Newton Leroy, (Newt); Speaker, US House of Representatives, since 1994; *b* 17 June 1943; *s* of Robert Bruce Gingrich and Kathleen (*née* Daugherty); *m* 1st, 1962, Jacqueline Battley (marr. diss. 1981); two *d*; 2nd, 1981, Marianne Ginther. *Educ:* Emory Univ. (BA); Tulane Univ. (MA; PhD 1971). Taught history, W Georgia Coll., Carrollton, 1970–78; Mem. from 6th Dist of Georgia, US Congress, 1979– (Republican Whip, 1989–94). *Publications:* (jtly) Window of Opportunity: a bluprint for the future, 1984; (jtly) 1945, 1995. *Address:* House of Representatives, 2428 Rayburn Office Building, Washington, DC 20515–1006, USA.

GINSBURG, Ruth Bader; Associate Justice of the Supreme Court of the United States, since 1993; *b* 15 March 1933; *d* of Nathan Bader and Celia Amster Bader; *m* 1954, Martin D. Ginsburg; one *s* one *d*. *Educ:* James Madison High Sch., Brooklyn; Cornell Univ. (BA Hons 1954); Harvard Law Sch.; Columbia Law Sch. (Kent Scholar; LLB, JD 1959). Clerk, Southern Dist, NY, 1959–61; Columbia Law Sch. Project on Internat. Procedure, 1961–63; Professor: Rutgers Univ. Sch. of Law, 1963–72; Columbia Law Sch., 1972–80; Circuit Judge, Court of Appeals for Dist of Columbia, 1980–93. American Civil Liberties Union: Gen. Counsel, 1973–80; Nat. Board, 1974–80; Counsel to Women's Rights Project, 1972–80. Fellow: Amer. Bar Foundn, 1978– (Exec. Cttee and Sec., 1979–89); Amer. Acad. of Arts and Scis, 1982– (Mem. Council, Foreign Relations, 1975–). *Publications:* (with A. Bruzelius) Civil Procedure in Sweden, 1965; (with A. Bruzelius) Swedish Code of Judicial Procedure, 1968; (jtly) Text, Cases and Materials on Sex-Based Discrimination, 1974, Supp. 1978; numerous contribs to learned jls. *Address:* Supreme Court, 1 First Street NE, Washington, DC 20543, USA.

GIOLITTI, Dr Antonio; Member, Commission of the European Communities, 1977–85; Senator, Italian Parliament, 1987–92; *b* 12 Feb. 1915; *s* of Giuseppe and Maria Giolitti; *m* 1939, Elena d'Amico; one *s* two *d*. *Educ:* Rome Univ. (Dr Law); Oxford; München. Dep., Italian Parlt, 1946–77; Minister of Budget and Economic Planning, 1964, 1970–72, 1973–74. Member: Italian Communist Party, 1943–57; Italian Socialist Party, 1958–83; Exec., Italian Socialist Party, 1958–83; Sinistra Indipendente, 1987–92. *Publications:* Riforme e rivoluzione, 1957; Il comunismo in Europa, 1960; Un socialismo possibile, 1967; Lettere a Marta, 1992. *Recreations:* music, walking. *Address:* Piazza Cairoli 6, 00186 Rome, Italy.

GIORDANO, Richard Vincent, Hon. KBE 1989; Deputy Chairman, Grand Metropolitan plc, since 1991 (Board Member, since 1985); Chairman, British Gas plc, since 1994; *b* March 1934; *s* of late Vincent Giordano and of Cynthia Giordano (*née* Cardetta); *m* 1956, Barbara Claire Beckett; one *s* two *d*. *Educ:* Harvard Coll., Cambridge, Mass, USA (BA); Columbia Univ. Law Sch. (LLB). Shearman & Sterling, 1959; Airco, Inc., 1963–78: Gp Vice Pres., 1967; Gp Pres., Chief Operating Officer and Mem. Bd, 1971; Chief Exec. Officer, Airco, Inc., 1978; BOC Group: Chief Exec. Officer, 1979–91; Gp Man. Dir, 1979–85; Chm., 1985–92; Non-Exec. Chm., 1994–96. Mem., CEGB, 1982–92; part-time Board Member: RTZ Corp., 1992–; Georgia Pacific Corp., Atlanta, Ga, 1984–; Dir, Lucas Industries, 1993–94. Hon. Dr of Commercial Science, St John's Univ., 1975. *Recreations:* ocean sailing, tennis. *Address:* c/o British Gas plc, The Adelphi, John Adam Street, WC2N 6JT. *Clubs:* The Links, New York Yacht (New York), Edgartown Yacht (Mass); Duquesne (Pittsburgh, Pa).

GIPPS, Dr Jonathan Henry William; Director, London Zoo, since 1993; *b* 7 July 1947; *s* of late Capt. Louis H. F. P. Gipps, RN and Molly Joyce Gipps; *m* 1970, Prof. Caroline Victoria Davis; two *s*. *Educ:* Imperial Coll., Univ. of London (BSc Zool. 1973); Royal Holloway Coll., Univ. of London (PhD 1977). RN, 1966–70. Post-doctoral Research Fellow, Univ. of British Columbia, 1977–79; Lectr in Biology, Univ. of Bath, 1980–81; Res. Fellow, RHBNC, 1981–84; Educn Officer, Computer Centre, Kingston Poly., 1984–87; London Zoo: Curator of Mammals, 1987–91; General Curator, 1991–93. Hon. DSc Kingston, 1993. *Publications:* (ed jtly) The Ecology of Woodland Rodents, 1981; (ed) Beyond Captive Breeding: re-introducing endangered mammals to the wild, 1989. *Recreations:* fishing, making jewellery, ski-ing, cooking, travelling. *Address:* London Zoo, Regent's Park, NW1 4RY. *T:* 0171–722 1802.

GIPPSLAND, Bishop of, since 1994; **Rt Rev. Arthur Lucas Vivian Jones,** ThD; *b* 11 Dec. 1934; *s* of Arthur Edmond Jones and Mona Emily Jones; *m* 1979, Valerie Joan Maxwell; one *s* three *d*. *Educ:* St John's Coll., Morpeth, NSW (ThL); ACT (ThSchol); London Univ. (BD ext); Deakin Univ. (BA); Newcastle Univ., NSW (MA Classics); Adelaide Coll. of Adv. Educn (Grad.Dip.RE); Geneva Theol Coll. (ThD); Lambeth Diploma. Deacon 1966, priest 1967; Curate, Holy Trinity, Orange, NSW, 1966–69; Missionary, Panama, 1970–73 and 1977–80; Rector, St Barnabas, Orange, NSW, 1973–77; Vicar, Corangamite, Vic, 1980–82; Lectr in NT, St John's Coll., Morpeth, 1982–85; Rector, Woy Woy, NSW, 1985–89; Dean, St Paul's Cathedral, Sale, 1989–94; Diocesan Theologian, Gippsland, 1989–94. *Recreations:* golf, writing. *Address:* Bishopscourt, 51 Raglan Street, Sale, Vic 3850, Australia. *T:* (51) 442046; PO Box 28, Sale, Vic 3850, Australia.

GIRDWOOD, Ronald Haxton, CBE 1984; MD, PhD, FRCP, FRCPE, FRCPI, FRCPath; FRSE 1978; Chairman, Scottish National Blood Transfusion Association, 1980–95; President, Royal College of Physicians of Edinburgh, 1982–85; *b* 19 March 1917; *s* of late Thomas Girdwood and Elizabeth Stewart Girdwood (*née* Haxton); *m* 1945, Mary Elizabeth, *d* of late Reginald Williams, Calstock, Cornwall; one *s* one *d*. *Educ:* Daniel Stewart's Coll., Edinburgh; University of Edinburgh; University of Michigan. MB, ChB (Hons) Edinburgh 1939; Ettles Schol., Leslie Gold Medallist, Royal Victoria Hosp.; Tuberculosis Trust Gold Medallist, Wightman, Beaney and Keith Memorial Prize Winner, 1939; MD (Gold Medal for thesis), 1954. Pres. Edinburgh Univ. Church of Scotland Soc., 1938–39. Served RAMC, 1942–46 (mentioned in Orders); Nutrition Research Officer and Officer i/c Med. Div. in India and Burma. Lectr in Medicine, University of Edinburgh, 1946; Rockefeller Research Fellow, University of Michigan, 1948–49; Cons. Phys., Chalmers Hosp., Edinburgh, 1950–51; Sen. Lectr in Med. and Cons. Phys., Royal Infirmary, 1951; Vis. Lectr, Dept of Pharmacology, Yale Univ., 1956; Reader in Med., University of Edinburgh, 1958; Dean of Faculty of Medicine, Edinburgh Univ., 1975–79;

Prof. of Therapeutics and Clinical Pharmacology, Univ. of Edinburgh, 1962–82, Emeritus 1982; Consultant Physician, Royal Infirmary of Edinburgh, 1951–82. Sometime External Examiner for Universities of London, Sheffield, St Andrews, Dundee, Dublin, Glasgow and Hong Kong, and for Med. Colls in Singapore, Dhaka and Karachi. Chm., SE Scotland Blood Transfusion Assoc., 1970–95; Mem. Council, RCPE, 1966–70, 1978–80, Vice-Pres., 1981–82, Pres. 1982–85; Member: South-Eastern Reg. Hosp. Board (Scotland), 1965–69; Board of Management, Royal Infirmary, Edinburgh, 1958–64; Cttee on Safety of Medicines, 1972–83; Exec., Medico-Pharmaceutical Forum, 1972–74 (Vice-Chm., 1983–85; Chm., 1985–87); Chairman: Scottish Group of Hæmophilia Soc., 1954–60; Non-Professorial Medical Teachers and Research Workers Gp Cttee (Scot.) of BMA, 1956–62; Scottish Gp of Nutrition Soc., 1961–62; Consultative Council, Edinburgh Medical Gp, 1977–82; Pres. Brit. Soc. for Hæmatology, 1963–64; Member: Coun. Brit. Soc. of Gastroenterology, 1964–68; Council of Nutrition Soc., 1957–60 and 1961–64; Pres., Univ. of Edinburgh Graduates' Assoc., 1991–93 (Vice-Pres., 1989–91). British Council visitor to W African Hosps, 1963, to Middle East, 1977, to India, 1980; Visiting Prof. and WHO Consultant, India, 1965, Pakistan, 1985. Gov., St Columba's Hospice, 1985–. Former Chm., Bd of Management, Scottish Med. Jl and Mem., Editl Bds, Blood, and British Jl of Haematology; Mem. Editl Bd, Brit. Jl of Nutrition, 1960–65. Awarded Freedom of the township of Sirajgunj, Bangladesh, 1984. Hon. FACP 1983; Hon. FRACP 1985. Cullen Prize, 1970, Lilly Lectr, 1979, RCPE; Suniti Panja gold medal, Calcutta Sch. Trop. Med., 1980; Oliver Meml Award (for services to blood transfusion), 1991. *Publications:* about 350, particularly in relation to nutrition, hæmatology, gastroenterology and medical history; (contrib.) Davidson's Principles and Practice of Medicine, all edns 1952–81; (ed with A. N. Smith) Malabsorption, 1969; (ed with S. Alstead) Textbook of Medical Treatment, 12th edn 1971 to 14th edn 1978, (ed with J. Petrie) 15th edn, 1987 (trans. Spanish, 1992); (ed) Blood Disorders due to Drugs and Other Agents, 1973; (ed) Clinical Pharmacology, 23rd edn 1976 to 25th edn 1984; Travels with a Stethoscope, 1991. *Recreations:* photography, writing. *Address:* 2 Hermitage Drive, Edinburgh EH10 6DD. *T:* (home) 0131–447 5137. *Clubs:* East India, Devonshire, Sports and Public Schools; University Staff (Edinburgh).

GIROLAMI, Sir Paul, Kt 1988; FCA; Chairman, Glaxo Holdings, 1985–94 (Chief Executive, 1980–86); *b* 25 Jan. 1926; *m* 1952, Christabel Mary Gwynne Lewis; two *s* one *d*. *Educ:* London School of Economics (Hon. Fellow, 1989); FREconS; FIMC 1990. Chantrey & Button, Chartered Accountants, 1950–54; Coopers & Lybrand, Chartered Accountants, 1954–65; Glaxo Holdings: Financial Controller, 1965; Finance Director, 1968; Chief Exec., 1980. Director: Inner London Board of National Westminster Bank, 1974–89; Credito Italiano Internat. UK, 1990–93; Forte plc, 1992–; UIS France, 1994–. Member: Bd of Dirs, Amer. Chamber of Commerce (UK), 1983–; CBI Council, 1986–93; Appeal Cttee, ICA, 1987–; Stock Exchange Listed Cos Adv. Cttee, 1987–92. Chm., Senate for Chartered Accountants in Business, 1990–. Hon. President: Accad. Romana di sci. med. e biologiche, 1990–; Accad. Internazionale per l'Unita della Cultura, Rome and St Gallen, 1991–. Chm. Council, Goldsmiths' Coll., Univ. of London, 1994–; Mem. Open Univ. Vis. Cttee, 1987–89. Gov., NIESR, 1992. Freeman, City of London; Liveryman, Goldsmiths' Co., 1980– (Mem., Ct of Assistants, 1986–); Mem., Soc. of Apothecaries, 1993–. Hon. FCGI 1994; FIMgt (FBIM 1986); FRSA 1986. Hon. DSc: Aston, 1990; Trieste, 1991; Sunderland, 1991; Bradford, 1993; Hon. LLD Singapore, 1993; Hon. DBA Strathclyde, 1993. Centenary Medal, UK SCI, 1992; Centenary Award, UK Founding Socs, 1992. Grand Cross, Order of the Holy Sepulchre, 1994. Grande Ufficiale, Ordine al Merito della Repubblica Italiana, 1987; Cavaliere al Merito del Lavoro, Italy, 1991; Insignia of the Order of the Rising Sun, Japan, 1991. *Recreations:* reading, music. *Address:* (office) Newton House, 118 Piccadilly, W1V 9FJ.

GIROUARD, Mark, PhD; writer and architectural historian; Slade Professor of Fine Art, University of Oxford, 1975–76; *b* 7 Oct. 1931; *s* of late Richard D. Girouard and Lady Blanche Girouard; *m* 1970, Dorothy N. Dorf; one *d*. *Educ:* Ampleforth; Christ Church, Oxford (MA); Courtauld Inst. of Art (PhD); Bartlett Sch., UCL (BSc, Dip. Arc). Staff of Country Life, 1958–66; studied architecture, Bartlett Sch., UCL, 1966–71; staff of Architectural Review, 1971–75. George Lurcy Vis. Prof., Columbia Univ., NY, 1987. Member: Council, Victorian Soc., 1979– (Founder Mem. 1958; Mem. Cttee, 1958–66); Royal Fine Art Commn, 1972–; Royal Commn on Historical Monuments (England), 1976–81; Historic Buildings Council (England), 1978–84; Commn for Historic Buildings and Monuments, 1984–90 (Mem., Buildings Adv. Cttee, 1984–86; Mem., Historic Areas Adv. Cttee, 1985–89; Mem., Historic Bldgs Cttee, 1988–90); Chm., Spitalfields Historic Buildings Trust, 1977–83; Trustee, Architecture Foundn, 1992–. Mem., Adv. Council, Paul Mellon Centre for Studies in British Art, 1990–. FSA 1986; Hon. FRIBA, 1980. Hon. DLitt: Leicester, 1982; Buckingham, 1991. *Publications:* Robert Smythson and the Architecture of the Elizabethan Era, 1966, 2nd edn, Robert Smythson and the Elizabethan Country House, 1983; The Victorian Country House, 1971, 2nd edn 1979; Victorian Pubs, 1975, 2nd edn 1984; (jtly) Spirit of the Age, 1975 (based on BBC TV series); Sweetness and Light: the 'Queen Anne' movement 1860–1900, 1977; Life in the English Country House, 1978 (Duff Cooper Meml Prize; W. H. Smith Award, 1979); Historic Houses of Britain, 1979; Alfred Waterhouse and the Natural History Museum, 1981; The Return to Camelot: chivalry and the English gentleman, 1981; Cities and People, 1985; A Country House Companion, 1987; The English Town, 1990; Town and Country, 1992; Windsor: the most romantic castle, 1993; articles in Country Life, Architect. Rev., Listener. *Address:* 35 Colville Road, W11 2BT. *Club:* Beefsteak.

GIRVAN, Hon. Sir (Frederick) Paul, Kt 1995; **Hon. Mr Justice Girvan;** a Justice of the High Court of Northern Ireland, since 1995; *b* 20 Oct. 1948; *s* of Robert Frederick Girvan and Martha Elizabeth (*née* Barron); *m* 1974, Karen Elizabeth Joyce; two *s* one *d*. *Educ:* Belfast Royal Acad.; Clare Coll., Cambridge (BA); Queen's Univ., Belfast; Gray's Inn. Called to the Bar: NI, 1971; Inner Bar (NI), 1982; Jun. Crown Counsel, NI, 1979–82. Mem., Law Reform Adv. Cttee for NI, 1994–. *Recreations:* badminton, walking, swimming, reading, modern languages, gardening, cooking. *Address:* Royal Courts of Justice, Chichester Street, Belfast, Northern Ireland BT1 3JF. *T:* Belfast (01232) 235111.

GISBOROUGH, 3rd Baron, *cr* 1917; **Thomas Richard John Long Chaloner,** JP; Lord-Lieutenant of Cleveland, since 1981; *b* 1 July 1927; *s* of 2nd Baron and Esther Isabella Madeleine (*d* 1970), *yr d* of late Charles O. Hall, Eddlethorpe; *S* father 1951; *m* 1960, Shane, *e d* of late Sidney Newton, London, and *g d* of Sir Louis Newton, 1st Bt; two *s*. *Educ:* Eton; Royal Agricultural Coll. 16th/5th Lancers, 1948–52; Captain Northumberland Hussars, 1955–61; Lt-Col Green Howards (Territorials), 1967–69. Mem., Rural Develt Commn, 1985–89. CC NR Yorks, 1964–74, Cleveland, 1974–77. Hon. Col, Cleveland County Army Cadet Force, 1981–92. Pres., British Ski Fedn, 1985–90. DL N Riding of Yorks and Cleveland, 1973; JP Langbaurgh East, 1981–. KStJ 1981. *Recreations:* field sports, ski-ing, tennis, bridge, piano. *Heir: s* Hon. Thomas Peregrine Long Chaloner [*b* 17 Jan. 1961; *m* 1992, Karen, *o d* of Alan Thomas]. *Address:* Gisborough House, Guisborough, Cleveland TS14 6PT. *T:* Guisborough (01287) 32002. *Club:* White's.

GISCARD d'ESTAING, Valéry; Grand Croix de la Légion d'Honneur; Croix de Guerre (1939–45); President of the French Republic, 1974–81; Deputy for Puy-de-Dôme, since 1993; Chairman, Commission of Foreign Affairs, National Assembly, 1987–89 and since 1993; President: Conseil Régional d'Auvergne, since 1986; Union pour la Démocratie Française, since 1988; European Movement International, since 1989; *b* Coblence, 2 Feb. 1926; *s* of late Edmond Giscard d'Estaing and May Bardoux; *m* 1952, Anne-Aymone de Brantes; two *s* two *d*. *Educ:* Lycée Janson-de-Sailly, Paris; Ecole Polytechnique; Ecole Nationale d'Administration. Inspection of Finances: Deputy, 1952; Inspector, 1954; Dep. Dir, Cabinet of Président du Conseil, June-Dec. 1954. Elected Deputy for Puy-de-Dôme, 1956; re-elected for Clermont N and SW, Nov. 1958, Nov.–Dec. 1962, March 1967, June 1968, March 1973, 1984, 1986 and 1988–89; Sec. of State for Finance, 1959; Minister of Finance, Jan.-April 1962; Minister of Finance and Economic Affairs, April-Nov. 1962 and Dec. 1962–Jan. 1966; Minister of Economy and Finance, 1969–74. Pres., Nat. Fedn of Indep. Republicans, 1966–73 (also a Founder); Pres., comm. des finances de l'économie générale et du plan de l'Assemblée nationale, 1967–68. Mem., Eur. Parlt, 1989–93. Mayor of Chamalières, 1967–74. Deleg. to Assembly of UN, 1956, 1957, 1958. Nansen Medal, 1979. *Publications:* Démocratie Française, 1976 (Towards a New Democracy, 1977); 2 Français sur 3, 1984; Le Pouvoir et la Vie (memoirs), 1988; L'Affrontement, 1991; Le Passage (novel), 1994. *Address:* 11 rue Bénouville, 75116 Paris, France; (office) 19 rue François Ier, 75008 Paris. *Club:* Polo (Paris).

GITTINGS, Harold John; Chairman, Greenfield Group (formerly Greenfield Marketing) Ltd, since 1992; *b* 3 Sept. 1947; *s* of Harold William Gittings and Doris Marjorie Gittings (*née* Whiting); *m* 1988, Andrea (*née* Fisher); two step *c*. *Educ:* Duke of York's Royal Military School, Dover. ACIS. Beecham Group, 1971–73; Peat Marwick Mitchell, Hong Kong, 1973–74; N. M. Rothschild & Sons, 1974–81; Continental Bank, 1981–82; Target Group, 1982–85; Managing Director: Touche Remnant Unit Trust Management, 1985–90; Touche Remnant & Co. 1987–90. *Recreations:* entertaining, travel, collecting, theatre, opera. *Address:* Jacobs Ladder, Froghole, Crockham Hill, Kent TN8 6TD. *T:* Edenbridge (01732) 866267.

GITTUS, John Henry, DSc; FEng 1989; Senior Partner: SPA Consultants, since 1993; NUSYS Consultants, Paris; Director General, British Nuclear Forum, 1990–93; *b* 25 July 1930; *s* of Henry Gittus and Amy Gittus; *m* 1953, Rosemary Ann Geeves; one *s* two *d*. *Educ:* BSc London 1952; DSc Phys London 1976; DTech Metall Stockholm 1975. CEng, FIMechE, FIS, FIM. British Cast Iron Res. Assoc., 1947–55; Mond Nickel Co., R&D Labs, Birmingham, 1955–60 (develt Nimonic series high temp. super alloys for aircraft gas turbine engines); United Kingdom Atomic Energy Authority, 1960–89: Research Manager, Springfields; Head, Water Reactor fuel develt; Head, Atomic Energy Tech. Br., Harwell; Director: Water Reactor Safety Research; Safety and Reliability Directorate, Culcheth; Communication and Information. Consultant: Argonne Nat. Lab., USA, 1968; Oak Ridge Nat. Lab., 1969. Visiting Professor: Ecole Polytechnique Fédérale, Lausanne, 1976; Univ. de Nancy, 1984; Regents' Prof., UCLA, 1990–91. Editor-in-Chief, Res Mechanica, 1980–91. *Publications:* Uranium, 1962; Creep, Viscoelasticity and Creep-fracture in Solids, 1979; Irradiation Effects in Crystalline Solids, 1979; (with W. Crosbie) Medical Response to Effects of Ionizing Radiation, 1989; numerous articles in learned jls. *Recreations:* old houses, old motor cars, old friends. *Address:* (office) 22 Buckingham Gate, SW1E 6LB. *T:* 0171–828 0116. *Clubs:* Royal Society of Medicine, Institute of Directors.

GIULINI, Carlo Maria; conductor; Music Director, Los Angeles Philharmonic Orchestra, 1978–84; *b* 9 May 1914; *m*; three *s*. *Educ:* Accademia Santa Cecilia, Rome. Début as conductor, Rome, 1944; formed Orchestra of Milan Radio, 1950; Principal Conductor, La Scala, Milan, 1953–55; début in Great Britain, conducting Verdi's Falstaff, Edinburgh Festival, 1955; closely associated with Philharmonia Orchestra, 1955–; début at Royal Opera House, Covent Garden, Don Carlos, 1958; Principal Guest Conductor, Chicago Symphony Orch., 1969–78; Music Dir, Vienna Symphony Orch., 1973–76; Music Dir, Los Angeles Philharmonic Orch., 1978–84; conducted new prodn of Falstaff in Los Angeles, at Covent Garden, and at Teatro Comunale, Florence, 1982, after 14 year absence from opera. Hon. Mem., Gesell. der Musikfreunde, Vienna, 1978; Hon. DHL DePaul Univ., Chicago, 1979. Gold Medal: Bruckner Soc., 1978; International Mahler Society; Una Vita Nella Musica. *Recreation:* sailing. *Address:* c/o Signor Francesco Giulini, Via Bonnet 7, 20121 Milan, Italy.

GIVEN, Edward Ferguson, CMG 1968; CVO 1979; HM Diplomatic Service, retired; *b* 13 April 1919; *s* of James K. Given, West Kilbride, Ayrshire; *m* 1st, 1946, Philida Naomi Bullwinkle; one *s*; 2nd, 1954, Kathleen Margaret Helena Kelly. *Educ:* Sutton County Sch.; University Coll., London. Served RA, 1939–46. Entered HM Foreign Service, 1946; served at Paris, Rangoon, Bahrain, Bordeaux, Office of Political Adviser to C-in-C Far East, Singapore, Moscow, Beirut; Ambassador: United Republic of Cameroon and Republic of Equatorial Guinea, 1972–75; Bahrain, 1975–79, retired, 1979. Dir-Gen., Middle East Assoc., 1979–83. *Address:* 10 Clarendon Park, Lymington, Hants SO41 8AX. *Club:* Army and Navy.

GLADSTONE, David Arthur Steuart, CMG 1988; HM Diplomatic Service, retired; *b* 1 April 1935; *s* of late Thomas Steuart Gladstone and Muriel Irene Heron Gladstone; *m* 1961, April (*née* Brunner); one *s* one *d*. *Educ:* Eton; Christ Church, Oxford (MA History). National Service, 1954–56; Oxford Univ., 1956–59. Annan, Dexter & Co. (Chartered Accountants), 1959–60; FO, 1960; MECAS, Lebanon, 1960–62; Bahrain, 1962–63; FO, 1963–65; Bonn, 1965–69; FCO, 1969–72; Cairo, 1972–75; British Mil. Govt, Berlin, 1976–79; Head of Western European Dept, FCO, 1979–82; Consul-Gen., Marseilles, 1983–87; High Comr, Colombo, 1987–91; Chargé d'Affaires *ai*, Kiev, 1992. *Recreations:* squash, tennis, music, theatre, cinema, dreaming, carpentry, gardening. *Address:* 1 Mountfort Terrace, N1 1JJ.

GLADSTONE, Sir (Erskine) William, 7th Bt *cr* 1846; JP; Lord-Lieutenant of Clwyd, since 1985; *b* 29 Oct. 1925; *s* of Charles Andrew Gladstone, (6th Bt), and Isla Margaret (*d* 1987), *d* of late Sir Walter Erskine Crum; *S* father, 1968; *m* 1962, Rosamund Anne, *yr d* of late Major A. Hambro; two *s* one *d*. *Educ:* Eton; Christ Church, Oxford. Served RNVR, 1943–46. Asst Master at Shrewsbury, 1949–50, and at Eton, 1951–61; Head Master of Lancing Coll., 1961–69. Chief Scout of UK and Overseas Branches, 1972–82; Mem., World Scout Cttee, 1977–83 (Chm., 1979–81). DL Flintshire, 1969, Clwyd, 1974, Vice Lord-Lieut, 1984; Alderman, Flintshire CC, 1970–74. Chm., Rep. Body of Church in Wales 1977–92; Chm., Council of Glenalmond Coll. (formerly Trinity Coll., Glenalmond), 1982–86. JP Clwyd 1982. *Publications:* various school textbooks. *Recreations:* reading history, watercolours, shooting, gardening. *Heir: s* Charles Angus Gladstone [*b* 11 April 1964; *m* 1988, Caroline, *o d* of Sir Derek Thomas, *qv*; one *s* three *d*]. *Address:* Hawarden Castle, Clwyd CH5 3PB. *T:* Hawarden (01244) 520210.

GLADWIN, family name of **Baron Gladwin of Clee.**

GLADWIN OF CLEE, Baron *cr* 1994 (Life Peer), of Great Grimsby in the County of Humberside; **Derek Oliver Gladwin,** CBE 1979 (OBE 1977); JP; Regional Secretary (Southern Region), General and Municipal Workers' Union, 1970–90; Member, Post Office Board (formerly Post Office Corporation), 1972–94; *b* 6 June 1930; *s* of Albert Victor Gladwin and Ethel Gladwin (*née* Oliver); *m* 1956, Ruth Ann Pinion; one *s*. *Educ:* Carr Lane Junior Sch., Grimsby; Wintringham Grammar Sch.; Ruskin Coll., Oxford;

London Sch. of Economics. British Railways, Grimsby, 1946–52; fishing industry, Grimsby, 1952–56; Regional Officer 1956–63, Nat. Industrial Officer 1963–70, Gen. and Municipal Workers' Union. Bd Mem., BAe, 1977–91. Chm., Labour Party's Conf. Arrangements Cttee, 1974–90. Mem., Employment Appeal Tribunal, 1992–. Mem. Council, Industrial Soc., 1968 (Mem. Exec. Cttee, 1968–91). Chm., Governing Council, Ruskin Coll., Oxford, 1979–. Vis. Fellow, Nuffield Coll., Oxford, 1978–86. JP Surrey, 1969. *Address:* 2 Friars Rise, Woking, Surrey GU22 7JL. *T:* Woking (01483) 714591; House of Lords, SW1A 0PW.

GLADWIN, Rt. Rev. John Warren; *see* Guildford, Bishop of.

GLADWYN, 1st Baron *cr* 1960; **Hubert Miles Gladwyn Jebb,** GCMG 1954 (KCMG 1949; CMG 1942); GCVO 1957; CB 1947; Grand Croix de la Légion d'Honneur, 1957; Deputy Leader of Liberal Party in House of Lords, and Liberal Spokesman on foreign affairs and defence, 1965–88; *b* 25 April 1900; *s* of late Sydney Jebb, Firbeck Hall, Yorks; *m* 1929, Cynthia (*d* 1990), *d* of Sir Saxton Noble, 3rd Bart; one *s* two *d*. *Educ:* Eton; Magdalen Coll., Oxon. 1st in History, Oxford, 1922. Entered Diplomatic Service, 1924; served in Tehran, Rome, and Foreign Office; Private Sec. to Parliamentary Under-Sec. of State, 1929–31; Private Sec. to Permanent Under-Sec. of State, 1937–40; appointed to Ministry of Economic Warfare with temp. rank of Asst Under-Sec., Aug. 1940; Acting Counsellor in Foreign Office, 1941; Head of Reconstruction Dept, 1942; Counsellor, 1943, in that capacity attended the Conferences of Quebec, Cairo, Tehran, Dunbarton Oaks, Yalta, San Francisco and Potsdam. Executive Sec. of Preparatory Commission of the United Nations (Aug. 1945) with temp. rank of Minister; Acting Sec.-Gen. of UN, Feb. 1946; Deputy to Foreign Sec. on Conference of Foreign Ministers, March 1946; Assistant Under-Sec. of State and United Nations Adviser, 1946–47; UK rep. on Brussels Treaty Permanent Commission with personal rank of Ambassador, April 1948; Dep. Under-Sec., 1949–50; Permanent Representative of the UK to the United Nations, 1950–54; British Ambassador to France, 1954–60, retired. Mem., European Parlt, 1973–76 (Vice Pres., Political Cttee); contested (L) Suffolk, European Parlt, 1979. Pres., European Movement; former Pres., Atlantic Treaty Assoc.; Chm., Campaign for European Political Community; Mem., Parly Delegns to Council of Europe and WEU Assemblies, 1966–73. Hon. DCL: Oxford; Syracuse, NY 1954; Essex 1974; Hon. Fellow Magdalen Coll. *Publications:* Is Tension Necessary?, 1959; Peaceful Co-existence, 1962; The European Idea, 1966; Half-way to 1984, 1967; De Gaulle's Europe, or, Why the General says No, 1969; Europe after de Gaulle, 1970; The Memoirs of Lord Gladwyn, 1972. *Recreations:* gardening, cooking. *Heir: s* Hon. Miles Alvery Gladwyn Jebb [*b* 3 March 1930. *Educ:* Eton and Oxford]. *Address:* Bramfield Hall, Halesworth, Suffolk IP19 9HX. *T:* Bramfield (01986) 784241; 62 Whitehall Court, SW1A 2EL. *T:* 0171–930 3160.
See also Baron Thomas of Swynnerton.

GLAISYER, Ven. Hugh; Archdeacon of Lewes and Hastings, since 1991; *b* 20 Jan. 1930; *s* of Rev. Canon Hugh Glaisyer and Edith Glaisyer; *m* 1962, Alison Marion Heap; one *s* two *d*. *Educ:* Tonbridge Sch.; Oriel Coll., Oxford (MA 2nd cl. Hon. Mods, 2nd Cl. Theol.); St Stephen's House, Oxford. FO, RAF, 1954. Ordained, Manchester, 1956; Curate: St Augustine's, Tonge Moor, Bolton, 1956–62; Sidcup, 1962–64; Vicar, Christ Church, Milton-next-Gravesend, 1964–81; RD, Gravesend, 1974–81; Vicar, Hove, 1981–91; RD, Hove, 1982–91; Canon of Chichester Cathedral, 1982–91. *Recreations:* squash rackets, Shetland sheepdogs. *Address:* 27 The Avenue, Lewes, East Sussex BN7 1QT. *T:* Lewes (01273) 479530.

GLAMANN, Prof. Kristof, OBE 1985; Hon. FBA 1985; author; President, Carlsberg Foundation, 1976–93 (Director, since 1969); Chairman, Carlsberg Ltd, 1977–93 (Director, since 1970); *b* 26 Aug. 1923; *s* of Kai Kristof Glamann, bank manager, and Ebba Henriette Louise (*née* Madsen); *m* 1954, Kirsten Lise (*née* Jantzen), MA, lecturer; two *s*. *Educ:* Odense Katedral-skole; Univ. of Copenhagen (MA Hist. 1948, PhD Econ. Hist., 1958). Univ. of Copenhagen: Research Fellow, 1948–56; Associated Prof., 1956–60; Prof. of History, 1960–80. Visiting Professor: Pennsylvania, 1960; Wisconsin, 1961; LSE 1964; Vis. Overseas Fellow, Churchill Coll., Cambridge, 1971–72; Toho Gakkai, Japan, 1977; Master, 4th May and Hassager Coll., Copenhagen, 1961–81. Chm., Scand. Inst. of Asian Studies, 1967–71; Hon. Pres., Internat. Econ. Hist. Assoc., 1974 (Pres., 1970–74; Vice-Pres., 1968–70). Director: Carlsberg Brewery Ltd, UK, 1977–93; Fredericia Brewery Ltd, 1975–93; Royal Copenhagen (Holmegaard) Ltd, 1975–93; Politiken Foundn, 1990. Chm., Danish State Research Council of Humanities, 1968–70; Mem. Bd, HM Queen Ingrid's Roman Foundn, 1980; Vice-Pres., Scandinavia-Japan Sasakawa Foundn, 1985–; Member: Royal Danish Acad. of Science and Letters, 1969; Royal Danish Hist. Soc., 1961; Swedish Acad., Lund, 1963; Hist. Soc. of Calcutta, 1962; Corresp. FRHistS 1972; Founding Mem., Acad. Europaea, 1988; Fellow, Royal Belgian Acad., 1989. Editor, Scand. Econ. History Review, 1961–70. Hon. LittD Gothenburg, 1974. Comdr (I), Order of the Dannebrog, 1990 (Kt 1984); Comdr, Northern Star of Sweden, 1984; Order of Orange-Nassau, Netherlands, 1984; Comdr, Falcon of Iceland, 1987; Das Grosse Verdienstkreuz, FRG, 1989; Order of Gorkha Dakshina Bahu, 3rd Cl., Nepal, 1989; Grand Comdr, Ordem do Mérito Agricola e Industrial, Portugal, 1992. *Publications:* History of Tobacco Industry in Denmark 1875–1950, 1950; Dutch-Asiatic Trade 1620–1740, 1958, 2nd edn 1981; (with Astrid Friis) A History of Prices and Wages in Denmark 1660–1800, vol. I, 1958; A History of Brewing in Denmark, 1962; Studies in Mercantilism, 1966, 2nd edn 1984; European Trade 1500–1750, 1971; The Carlsberg Foundation, 1976; Cambridge Econ. Hist. of Europe, vol. V, 1977; J. C. Jacobsen of Carlsberg, Brewer and Philanthropist, 1991; The Carlsberg Foundation since 1970, 1993; Carl Jacobsen of New Carlsberg, 1995. *Recreations:* painting, walking. *Address:* Bjerregaardsvej 6, 2500 Valby, Denmark. *T:* 31161347, *Fax:* 36454430.

GLAMIS, Lord; Simon Patrick Bowes Lyon; *b* 18 June 1986; *s* and *heir* of Earl of Strathmore and Kinghorne, *qv*.

GLAMORGAN, Earl of; Robert Somerset; *b* 20 Jan. 1989; *s* and *heir* of Marquess of Worcester, *qv*.

GLANDINE, Viscount; Richard James Graham-Toler; *b* 5 March 1967; *s* and *heir* of 6th Earl of Norbury, *qv*.

GLANUSK, 4th Baron, *cr* 1899; **David Russell Bailey;** Bt, *cr* 1852; Lieutenant-Commander RN (retired); *b* 19 Nov. 1917; *o s* of late Hon. Herbert Crawshay Bailey, 4th *s* of 1st Baron Glanusk and late Kathleen Mary, *d* of Sir Shirley Harris Salt, 3rd Bt; *S* cousin 1948; *m* 1941, Lorna Dorothy, *o d* of late Capt. E. C. H. N. Andrews, MBE, RA; one *s* one *d*. *Educ:* Orley Farm Sch., Harrow; Eton. RN, 1935–51. Managing Dir, Wandel & Goltermann (UK) Ltd, 1966–81; Chm., W&G Instruments Ltd, 1981–87. *Heir: s* Hon. Christopher Russell Bailey [*b* 18 March 1942; *m* 1974, Frances, *d* of Air Chief Marshal Sir Douglas Lowe, *qv*; one *s* one *d*]. *Address:* Apartado 62, La Sort, Pollenca, Mallorca, Spain. *T:* (71) 534673.

GLANVILLE, Alec William; Assistant Under-Secretary of State, Home Office, 1975–81, retired; *b* 20 Jan. 1921; *y s* of Frank Foster and Alice Glanville; *m* 1941, Lilian Kathleen Hetherton; one *s* one *d*. *Educ:* Portsmouth Northern Secondary Sch.; Portsmouth Municipal Coll. War service, RAMC, 1939–46. Exchequer and Audit Dept, 1939–47; General, Criminal, Police and Probation and After-care Depts, Home Office, 1947–81 (seconded to Cabinet Office, 1956–58); Private Sec. to Permanent Under Sec. of State, 1949–50; Principal Private Sec. to Sec. of State, 1960–63; Sec., Interdepartmental Cttee on Mentally Abnormal Offenders, 1972–75.

GLANVILLE, Brian Lester; author and journalist since 1949; *b* 24 Sept. 1931; *s* of James Arthur Glanville and Florence Glanville (*née* Manches); *m* 1959, Elizabeth Pamela de Boer (*née* Manasse), *d* of Fritz Manasse and Grace Manasse (*née* Howden); two *s* two *d*. *Educ:* Newlands Sch.; Charterhouse. Sunday Times (football correspondent), 1958–92; joined The People (sports columnist), 1992. *Publications:* The Reluctant Dictator, 1952; Henry Sows the Wind, 1954; Along the Arno, 1956; The Bankrupts, 1958; After Rome, Africa, 1959; A Bad Streak, 1961; Diamond, 1962; The Director's Wife, 1963; The King of Hackney Marshes, 1965; A Second Home, 1965; A Roman Marriage, 1966; The Artist Type, 1967; The Olympian, 1969; A Cry of Crickets, 1970; The Financiers, 1972; The History of the World Cup, 1973; The Thing He Loves, 1973; The Comic, 1974; The Dying of the Light, 1976; Never Look Back, 1980; (jtly) Underneath The Arches (musical), 1981; A Visit to the Villa (play), 1981; Kissing America, 1985; Love is Not Love, 1985; (ed) The Joy of Football, 1986; The Catacomb, 1988; Champions of Europe, 1991; Story of the World Cup, 1993; *juvenile:* Goalkeepers are Different (novel), 1971; Target Man (novel), 1978; The Puffin Book of Football, 1978; The Puffin Book of Tennis, 1981. *Recreation:* playing football. *Address:* 160 Holland Park Avenue, W11 4UH. *T:* 0171–603 6908. *Club:* Chelsea Casuals.

GLANVILLE-JONES, Thomas; *see* Jones, T. G.

GLASBY, (Alfred) Ian; HM Diplomatic Service, retired; Director: Trust Co. of Australia (UK) Ltd, since 1990; Truco (Australia) Europe Ltd, since 1990; *b* 18 Sept. 1931; *s* of Frederick William Glasby and Harriet Maria Glasby; *m* 1970, Herma Fletcher; one *d*. *Educ:* Doncaster Grammar Sch.; London School of Economics and Political Science (BSc). Served HM Forces, 1950–52. Home Office, 1952–68; Second Sec., CO, later FCO, 1968–71; Second, later First Sec. (Commercial and Energy), Washington, 1971–76; Dep. High Comr, Hd of Chancery and Consul, Kampala, 1976; Hd, British Interests Sect., French Embassy, Kampala, 1976–77; First Sec., Hd of Chancery and Consul, Yaoundé, 1977–81, concurrently non-resident Chargé d'Affaires, Central Afr. Empire, Gabon, and Equatorial Guinea; Asst Hd, Consular Dept, FCO, 1981–84; Dep. Consul Gen., Sydney, 1984–88; Ambassador to People's Republic of the Congo, 1988–90. Hon. Chevalier, Ordre de Mérite (Republique Populaire du Congo). *Recreations:* Rugby, cricket, international affairs, reading, gardening. *Address:* High Pitch, Strande Lane, Cookham, Maidenhead, Berks SL6 9DW. *T:* Bourne End (016285) 28054; 5 rue du Collet, Spéracèdes, near Grasse 06530, France. *Clubs:* Commonwealth Trust; Australasian Pioneers, NSW Rugby (Sydney).

GLASBY, John Hamilton; County Treasurer, Devon County Council, since 1993; Treasurer, Devon and Cornwall Police Authority, since 1993; *b* 29 March 1950; *s* of James Ronald Glasby and Lucie Lillian Glasby (*née* Baxter); *m* 1971, Helen Fielding (marr. diss. 1989); two *s* one *d*. *Educ:* Univ. of Sheffield (BA); Univ. of Birmingham (MSocSc); Liverpool Poly. Mem., CIPFA, 1982. Lectr in Econs, Univ. of E Anglia, 1972–73; Economist: Central Lancs New Town, 1973–76; Shropshire CC, 1976–82; Asst Dir of Finance, Dudley Metropolitan Borough, 1982–84; Dep. Co. Treas., Devon CC, 1984–93. *Recreations:* amateur dramatics, guitar (badly), being with the children. *Address:* Treasurer's Department, Devon County Council, County Hall, Topsham Road, Exeter EX2 4QJ.

GLASER, Prof. Donald Arthur; Professor of Physics and of Molecular and Cell Biology, University of California, since 1960; *b* 21 Sept. 1926; *s* of William Joseph and Lena Glaser. *Educ:* Case Institute of Technology (BS 1946); California Inst. of Technology (PhD 1950). University of Michigan: Instr. of Physics, 1949–53; Asst Prof., 1953–55; Associate Prof., 1955–57; Prof. of Physics, 1957–59; University of California, Berkeley: Vis. Prof., 1959–60; Prof. of Physics, 1960–; Miller Res. Biophysicist, 1962–64; Prof. of Molecular Biol., 1964–89; Prof. of Molecular and Cell Bio., 1989–. National Science Foundation Fellow, 1961; Guggenheim Fellow, 1961–62. Member: National Academy of Sciences (USA), 1962; NY Acad. of Science; Fellow Amer. Physical Soc.; FAAAS. Henry Russel Award, 1955; Charles Vernon Boys Prize, 1958; Amer. Phys. Soc. Prize, 1959; Nobel Prize for Physics, 1960. Hon. ScD Case Inst., 1959. *Publications:* chapters in: Topics in the Biology of Aging, 1965; Biology and the Exploration of Mars, 1966; Frontiers of Pattern Recognition, 1972; New Approaches to the Identification of Microorganisms, 1975; articles in Physical Review, Handbuch der Physik, Jl Molecular Biol., Pattern Recognition and Image Processing, Somatic Cell Genetics, Cell Tissue Kinetics, Computers and Biomed. Res., Proc. Nat. Acad. of Scis (USA), Suppl. to Investigative Ophthalmol & Visual Sci., Jl Opt. Soc. of Amer. A, Vision Res., Visual Neurosci., etc. *Address:* 229 Stanley Hall, Department of Molecular and Cell Biology, University of California, Berkeley, CA 94720, USA; 41 Hill Road, Berkeley, CA 94708, USA.

GLASGOW, 10th Earl of, *cr* 1703; **Patrick Robin Archibald Boyle;** Lord Boyle, 1699; Viscount of Kelburn, 1703; Baron Fairlie (UK), 1897; television director/producer; *b* 30 July 1939; *s* of 9th Earl of Glasgow, CB, DSC, and of Dorothea, *o d* of Sir Archibald Lyle, 2nd Bt; *S* father, 1984; *m* 1975, Isabel Mary James; one *s* one *d*. *Educ:* Eton; Paris Univ. National Service in Navy; Sub-Lt, RNR, 1959–60. Worked in Associated Rediffusion Television, 1961; worked at various times for Woodfall Film Productions; Asst on Film Productions, 1962–64; Asst Dir in film industry, 1962–67; producer/director of documentary films, Yorkshire TV, 1968–70; freelance film producer, 1971–, making network television documentaries for BBC Yorkshire Television, ATV and Scottish Television. Formed Kelburn Country Centre, May 1977, opening Kelburn estate and gardens in Aryshire to the public. *Recreations:* ski-ing, theatre. *Heir: s* Viscount of Kelburn, *qv*. *Address:* Kelburn, Fairlie, Ayrshire KA29 0BE. *T:* Fairlie (01475) 568204; (office) South Offices, Kelburn Estate, Fairlie, Ayrshire KA29 0BE. *T:* Fairlie (01475) 568685.

GLASGOW, Archbishop of, (RC), since 1974; **His Eminence Cardinal Thomas J. Winning,** DCL, STL, DD. Formerly parish priest, St Luke, Braidhurst, Motherwell; Auxiliary Bishop of Glasgow, 1971–74; parish priest, Our Holy Redeemer's, Clydebank, 1972–74. Cardinal, 1994. Member: Sacred Congregation for the Doctrine of the Faith, 1978–83; Pontifical Council for Promoting Christian Unity, 1994–; Pontifical Council for the Family, 1994–. Pres., Bishops' Conf. of Scotland, 1985–. Grand Prior, Scottish Lieutenancy of Equestrian Order of Holy Sepulchre of Jerusalem, 1989–. FEIS 1986. Hon. DD Glasgow, 1983; DUniv Strathclyde, 1992. *Address:* 40 Newlands Road, Glasgow G43 2JD.

GLASGOW, (St Mary's Cathedral), Provost of; *see* Francis, Very Rev. P. B.

GLASGOW, Edwin John; QC 1987; *b* 3 Aug. 1945; *s* of Richard Edwin, (Dick), Glasgow and Diana Geraldine Mary Glasgow (*née* Markby); *m* 1967, Janet Coleman; one *s* one *d*. *Educ:* St Joseph's Coll., Ipswich; University Coll. London (LLB). Called to the Bar, Gray's Inn, 1969, Bencher, 1994. Chm., Financial Reporting Review Panel, 1992–. Trustee: London Opera Players, 1985–; Mary Glasgow Language Trust, 1984– (Chm.). *Recreations:*

family, friends, France, music. *Address:* 39 Essex Street, WC2R 3AT. *T:* 0171–583 1111; Copper Hall, Thames Ditton, Surrey; Entrechaux, Vaucluse, France. *Club:* Royal Automobile (Steward, 1992–).

GLASGOW AND GALLOWAY, Bishop of, since 1991; **Rt. Rev. John Mitchell Taylor;** *b* 23 May 1932; *m* 1959, Edna Elizabeth (*née* Maitland); one *s* one *d*. *Educ:* Banff Acad.; Aberdeen Univ. (MA 1954); Edinburgh Theol Coll. Ordained deacon, 1956, priest, 1957; Asst Curate, St Margaret, Aberdeen, 1956–58; Rector: Holy Cross, Glasgow, 1958–64; St Ninian, Glasgow, 1964–73; St John the Evangelist, Dumfries, 1973–91; Chaplain: Crichton Royal Hospital; Dumfries and Galloway Royal Infirmary, 1973–91; Canon, St Mary's Cathedral, 1979–91. *Recreations:* angling, hill walking, music, ornithology. *Address:* 25 Quadrant Road, Newlands, Glasgow G43 2QP. *T:* 0141–637 5659.

GLASGOW AND GALLOWAY, Dean of; *see* Reid, Very Rev. D. W. J.

GLASHOW, Prof. Sheldon Lee, PhD; Higgins Professor of Physics, Harvard University, since 1979 (Professor of Physics, since 1966); *b* 5 Dec. 1932; *s* of Lewis and Bella Glashow; *m* 1972, Joan (*née* Alexander); three *s* one *d*. *Educ:* Cornell Univ. (AB); Harvard Univ. (AM, PhD). National Science Foundn Fellow, Copenhagen and Geneva, 1958–60; Res. Fellow, Calif Inst. of Technol., 1960–61; Asst Prof., Stanford Univ., 1961–62; Associate Prof., Univ. of Calif at Berkeley, 1962–66. Vis. Professor: CERN, 1968; Marseille, 1971; MIT, 1974 and 1980; Boston Univ., 1983; Univ. Schol., Texas A&M Univ., 1983–. Consultant, Brookhaven Nat. Lab., 1966–; Affiliated Senior Scientist, Univ. of Houston, 1983–. Pres., Sakharov Internat. Cttee, Washington, 1980–. Hon. DSc: Yeshiva, 1978; Aix-Marseille, 1982. Nobel Prize for Physics (jtly), 1979. *Publications:* articles in learned jls. *Recreations:* scuba diving, tennis. *Address:* 30 Prescott Street, Brookline, MA 02146, USA. *T:* (617) 2775446.

GLASS, Anthony Trevor; QC 1986; a Recorder of the Crown Court, since 1985; *b* 6 June 1940. *Educ:* Royal Masonic School; Lincoln College, Oxford (MA). Called to the Bar, Inner Temple, 1965. *Address:* Queen Elizabeth Building, Temple, EC4Y 9BS. *T:* 0171–583 5766. *Club:* Garrick.

GLASS, Norman Jeffrey; Assistant Director (Micro-economics), HM Treasury, since 1995; *b* 31 May 1946; *s* of Philip Harris Glass and Anne (*née* Stein); *m* 1974, Marie-Anne Verger; one *s* one *d*. *Educ:* Trinity Coll., Dublin (BA); Univ. of Amsterdam (Post Grad. Dip.). Shell Mex and BP, 1969–70; Economic Models Ltd, 1970–72; Lectr, Univ. of Newcastle upon Tyne, 1972–74; Res. Scholar, Internat. Inst. for Applied Systems Analysis, Vienna, 1974–75; Economic Adviser: DHSS, 1975–77; HM Treasury, 1977–79; Exchequer and Audit Dept, 1979–81; Sen. Econ. Advr, DHSS, 1981–86; Asst Sec., DoH, 1986–89; Dir, Analytical Services, DSS, 1989–92; Chief Economist, DoE, 1992–95. Mem., ESRC, 1992–. *Publications:* articles on health econs. *Recreations:* music, languages, gardening. *Address:* HM Treasury, Parliament Street, SW1P 3AG.

GLASS, Philip; American composer and performer; *b* 31 Jan. 1937; *s* of Benjamin Glass and Ida Glass (*née* Gouline); *m* 1st, JoAnne Akalaitis; 2nd, Luba Burtyk; one *s* one *d*; 3rd, Candy Jernigan. *Educ:* Peabody Conservatory; Univ. of Chicago; Juilliard Sch. of Music. Has worked as a taxi-driver, plumber and furniture mover. Composer-in-Residence, Pittsburgh Public Schs, 1962–64; studied with Nadia Boulanger, Paris, 1964–66; Musical Dir, Mabou Mines Co., 1965–74; Founder: Philip Glass Ensemble, 1968; record companies; Chatham Square Productions, 1972; Point Music, 1991; music publishers: Dunvagen, Inc., 1982; St Rose Co. Inc., 1991. *Compositions include: operas:* Einstein on the Beach, 1976; Satyagraha, 1980; The Photographer, 1982; The Civil Wars, 1984; Akhnaten, 1984; The Juniper Tree, 1986; The Making of the Representative for Planet 8, 1988; The Fall of the House of Usher, 1988; 1000 Airplanes on the Roof, 1988; The Hydrogen Jukebox, 1990; The Voyage, 1992; Orphee, 1993; *film scores:* Koyaanisqatsi, 1982; Mishima, 1985; Powaqqatsi, 1988; The Thin Blue Line, 1989; Hamburger Hill, 1989; A Brief History of Time, 1991; Anima Mundi, 1991; Mindwalk, 1992; Candyman, 1992; *theatre music:* Endgame, 1984; (with Foday Musa Suso) The Screens, 1989; Cymbelline, 1989; Henry IV, 1992; Woyzeck, 1992; The Mysteries & What's So Funny?, 1992; *instrumental works:* String Quartet no 1, 1966; Strung Out, 1967; Piece in the Shape of a Square, 1968; Music in Similar Motion, 1969; Music in Fifths, 1970; Music in Changing Parts, 1972; Music in Twelve Parts, 1974; Another Look at Harmony, 1974; North Star, 1975; Modern Love Waltz, 1979; Dance nos 1–5, 1979; Company, 1983; String Quartet no 2, 1983; String Quartet no 3, 1985; Songs from Liquid Days, 1986; Violin Concerto, 1987; The Light, 1987; Itaipu, 1988; Canyon, 1988; String Quartet no 4, 1989; Mattogrosso, 1989; Solo Piano, 1989; (with Ravi Shankar) Passages, 1990; String Quartet no 5, 1991; Low Symphony, 1993. Numerous awards and prizes, including: Benjamin Award, 1961; Fulbright Award, 1966–67. *Publication:* Music by Philip Glass, ed R. T. Jones, 1987. *Address:* c/o International Production Associates, 584 Broadway, Suite 1008, New York, NY 10012, USA.

GLASSCOCK, John Lewis, FCIS; aerospace consultant; Director, EH Industries Ltd, since 1989; *b* 12 July 1928; *s* of Edgar Henry and Maude Allison Glasscock; *m* 1959, Anne Doreen Baker; two *s*. *Educ:* Tiffin Sch.; University Coll. London (BA Hons). Served Royal Air Force, 1950–53. Joined Hawker Aircraft Ltd, 1953, Asst Sec., 1956, Commercial Man., 1961; Hawker Siddeley Aviation Ltd: Divl Commercial Man., 1964; Dir and Gen. Man. (Kingston), 1965; Dir and Gen. Man., 1977; British Aerospace Aircraft Group: Admin. Dir, 1978; Commercial Dir, 1979; Man. Dir (Military), 1981; BAe PLC: Dir, 1982–87; Dep. Chief Exec., Aircraft Gp, and Man. Dir, Civil Aircraft Div., 1982–85; Commercial Dir, 1986–87. Mem. Supervisory Bd, Airbus Industrie, 1983–85. Mem. Council, SBAC, 1979–87. *Recreations:* golf, tennis. *Address:* West Meadow, The Wedges, Itchingfield, near Horsham, W Sussex RH13 7TA. *Clubs:* MCC, Royal Air Force, Royal Automobile.

GLASSPOLE, Most Hon. Sir Florizel (Augustus), ON 1973; GCMG 1981; GCVO 1983; CD 1970; Governor-General of Jamaica, 1973–91; *b* Kingston, Jamaica, 25 Sept. 1909; *s* of late Rev. Theophilus A. Glasspole (Methodist Minister) and Florence (*née* Baxter); *m* 1934, Ina Josephine Kinlocke; one *d*. *Educ:* Central British Elementary Sch.; Wolmer's Sch.; Ruskin Coll., Oxford. British TUC Schol., 1946–47. Accountant (practising), 1932–44. Gen. Sec: Jamaica United Clerks Assoc., 1937–48; Jamaica TUC, 1939–52, resigned; Water Commn and Allied Workers Assoc., 1941–48; Municipal and Parochial Gen. Workers Union, 1945–47; First Gen. Sec., Nat. Workers Union, 1952–55; President: Jamaica Printers & Allied Workers Union, 1942–48; Gen. Hosp. and Allied Workers Union, 1944–47; Mental Hosp. Workers Union, 1944–47; Machado Employees Union, 1945–52; etc. Workers rep. on Govt Bds, etc, 1942–. Mem. Bd of Governors Inst. of Jamaica, 1944–57; Mem., Kingston Sch. Bd, 1944–. Founding Mem., PNP, 1938; MHR (PNP) for Kingston Eastern and Port Royal, 1944; Sec., PNP Parly Gp, 1944–73, resigned; Vice-Pres., People's National Party; Minister of Labour, Jamaica, 1955–57; Leader, House of Representatives, 1957–62, 1972–73; Minister of Educn, 1957–62, 1972–73; A Rep. for Jamaica, on Standing Fedn Cttee, West Indies Federation, 1953–58; Mem. House of Reps Cttee which prepared Independence of Jamaica Constitution, 1961; Mem. Delegn to London which completed Constitution document, 1962. Hon. LLD Univ. of the West Indies, 1982. Order of Andres Bello (1st cl.), Venezuela, 1973; Order of the Liberator, Venezuela, 1978. *Recreations:* gardening, sports, reading. *Address:* c/o Kings House, Hope Road, Kingston 10, Jamaica.

GLAUERT, Audrey Marion, ScD; Fellow of Clare Hall, University of Cambridge, since 1966; Head of Electron Microscopy Department, Strangeways Research Laboratory, Cambridge, 1956–89 (Associate Director, 1979–85); *b* 21 Dec. 1925; *d* of late Hermann Glauert, FRS and Muriel Glauert (*née* Barker); *m* 1959, David Franks (marr. diss. 1979). *Educ:* Perse Sch. for Girls, Cambridge; Bedford Coll., Univ. of London. BSc 1946, MSc 1947, London; MA Cantab 1967, ScD Cantab 1970. Asst Lectr in Physics, Royal Holloway Coll., Univ. of London, 1947–50; Mem. Scientific Staff, Strangeways Res. Lab., Cambridge, Sir Halley Stewart Research Fellow, 1950–89. Chairman: British Joint Cttee for Electron Microscopy, 1968–72; Fifth European Congress on Electron Microscopy, 1972; Pres., Royal Microscopical Soc., 1970–72, Hon. Fellow, 1973. Hon. Member: French Soc. for Electron Microscopy, 1967; Microscopy (formerly Electron Microscopy) Soc. of America, 1990 (Dist. Scientist Award for Biol. Scis, 1990). JP Cambridge, 1975–88. Editor: Practical Methods in Electron Microscopy, 1972–; Jl of Microscopy, Royal Microscopial Soc., 1986–88. *Publications:* Fixation Dehydration and Embedding of Biological Specimens, 1974; (ed) The Control of Tissue Damage, 1988; papers on cell and molecular biology in scientific jls. *Recreations:* sailing, gardening. *Address:* 29 Cow Lane, Fulbourn, Cambridge CB1 5HB. *T:* Cambridge (01223) 880463; Clare Hall, Herschel Road, Cambridge CB3 9AL.

GLAVES-SMITH, Frank William, CB 1975; Deputy Director-General of Fair Trading, 1973–79, retired; *b* 27 Sept. 1919; *m* 1st, 1941, Audrey Glaves (*d* 1989); one *s* one *d*; 2nd, 1990, Ursula Mary Murray. *Educ:* Malet Lambert High Sch., Hull. War Service, 1940–46 (Captain, Royal Signals). Called to Bar, Middle Temple, 1947. Board of Trade, 1947; Princ. Private Sec. to Pres. of Bd of Trade, 1952–57; Asst Secretary: HM Treasury, 1957–60; Cabinet Office, 1960–62; Bd of Trade, 1962–65; Under-Sec., BoT, 1965–69, Dept of Employment and Productivity, 1969–70, DTI, 1970–73; Dep. Sec., 1975. Mem., Export Guarantees Adv. Council, 1971–73. *Recreations:* rock-climbing, fell-walking. *Address:* 8 Grange Park, Keswick, Cumbria CA12 4AY.

GLAVIN, William Francis; President, Babson College, Wellesley, Mass, since 1989; *b* 29 March 1932; *m* 1955, Cecily McClatchy; three *s* four *d*. *Educ:* College of the Holy Cross, Worcester, Mass (BS); Wharton Graduate Sch. (MBA). Vice-Pres., Operations, Service Bureau Corp. (subsid. of IBM), 1968–70; Exec. Vice-Pres., Xerox Data Services, 1970; Pres., Xerox Data Systems, 1970–72; Gp Vice-Pres., Xerox Corp., and Pres., Business Development Gp, 1972–74; Rank Xerox Ltd: Man. Dir, 1974–80; Chief Operating Officer, 1974–77; Chief Exec. Officer, 1977–80; Xerox Corp.: Exec. Vice-Pres. Chief Staff Officer, 1980–82; President: Reprographics and Ops, 1982–83; Business Equipment Gps, 1983–89 (Vice Chm., 1985–89). *Recreations:* golf, music, boating, tennis. *Address:* 56 Whiting Road, Wellesley, MA 02181, USA.

GLAZE, Michael John Carlisle, (James), CMG 1988; HM Diplomatic Service, retired; Deputy Secretary-General, Order of St John of Jerusalem, since 1994; *b* 15 Jan. 1935; *s* of late Derek Glaze and of Shirley Gardner (formerly Glaze, *née* Ramsay); *m* 1965, Rosemary Duff; two step-*d*. *Educ:* Repton; St Catharine's Coll., Cambridge (open Exhibitioner, BA 1958); Worcester Coll., Oxford. Colonial Service, Basutoland, 1959–65; HMOCS, Dep. Permanent Sec., Finance, Lesotho, 1966–70; Dept of Trade (ECGD), 1971–73; FCO, 1973–75; Abu Dhabi, 1975–78; Rabat, 1978–80; Consul-Gen., Bordeaux, 1980–84; Ambassador: Republic of Cameroon, 1984–87; Angola, 1987–90; Ethiopia, 1990–94. SBStJ 1995. *Recreations:* golf, grand opera, the garden. *Address:* 32 Doods Park Road, Reigate, Surrey RH1 0QD. *Club:* Athenæum.

GLAZEBROOK, (Reginald) Mark; writer and art dealer; *b* 25 June 1936; *s* of late Reginald Field Glazebrook; *m* 1st, 1965, Elizabeth Lea Claridge (marr. diss. 1969); one *d*; 2nd, 1974, Wanda Barbara O'Neill (*née* Osińska); one *d*. *Educ:* Eton; Pembroke Coll., Cambridge (MA); Slade School of Fine Art. Worked at Arts Council, 1961–64; Lectr at Maidstone Coll. of Art, 1965–67; Art Critic, London Magazine, 1967–68; Dir, Whitechapel Art Gall., 1969–71; Head of Modern English Paintings and Drawings, P. and D. Colnaghi & Co. Ltd, 1973–75; Gallery Director and Art History Lectr, San José State Univ., 1977–79; Dir, Albemarle Gall. Ltd, London, 1986–93. FRSA 1971. *Publications:* (comp.) Artists and Architecture of Bedford Park 1875–1900 (catalogue), 1967; (comp.) David Hockney: paintings, prints and drawings 1960–1970 (catalogue), 1970; Edward Wadsworth 1889–1949: paintings, prints and drawings (catalogue), 1974; (introduction) John Armstrong 1893–1973 (catalogue), 1975; (introduction) John Tunnard (catalogue), 1976; articles in: Studio International, London Magazine. *Recreations:* travelling, theatre, tennis, swimming. *Clubs:* Beefsteak, Lansdowne, Ognisko Polski.

GLEDHILL, Anthony John, GC 1967; Divisional Auditor, NWS plc, since 1993; *b* 10 March 1938; *s* of Harold Victor and Marjorie Edith Gledhill; *m* 1958, Marie Lilian Hughes; one *s* one *d*. *Educ:* Doncaster Technical High Sch., Yorks. Accounts Clerk, Officers' Mess, RAF Bruggen, Germany, 1953–56. Metropolitan Police: Cadet, 1956–57; Police Constable, 1957–75; Detective Sergeant, 1976–87; Investigator, PO Investigation Dept, 1987–88. *Recreations:* football, DIY, philately. *Address:* 98 Pickhurst Lane, Hayes, Bromley, Kent BR2 7JD. *T:* 0181–462 4033. *Club:* No 4 District Metropolitan Police (Hayes, Kent).

GLEDHILL, David Anthony, CBE 1992; JP; Chairman: Modern Terminals, 1981–94 (Director, 1973–81); John Swire & Sons (HK), 1988–92; Swire Pacific, 1988–92; Cathay Pacific Airways, 1988–92; *b* 16 Oct. 1934; *s* of Arnold Grosland Gledhill and Marjorie Yates Johnson; *m* 1968, Kyoko Gledhill. *Educ:* Ellesmere College, Shropshire; Sidney Sussex College, Cambridge. Joined John Swire and Sons (HK), 1958; served Hong Kong, Osaka, Yokohama, Tokyo; China Navigation Co., Hong Kong, 1963–65; Shipping Manager, John Swire & Sons (Japan), 1966–73; Dir, John Swire & Sons (HK), 1973–84, Dep. Chm., 1984–88; Dir, Swire Pacific, 1973–88, Dep. Chm., 1984–88; Chm., Swire Pacific Offshore Services, 1975–88; Director: Hongkong & Shanghai Banking Corp., 1988–92; Lee Gardens Internat. Hotels, 1988–92; Community Chest of Hong Kong, 1988–; Mass Transit Railway Corp., 1990–; Hysan Development Co., 1990–; China Investment & Develt Fund, 1992–; Peregrine Internat. Hldgs, 1993–; Member: IBM World Trade Asia/Pacific Group Bd, 1989–93; IBM Hong Kong/China Bd, 1993–; Adv. Bd, PA Management Consultants, 1993–. Chm., Employers' Fedn of Hong Kong, 1989–91 (Council Mem., 1985–88); Member: Aviation Adv. Bd, 1988–92; Provisional Airport Authy, 1990–; Securities and Futures Commn, 1990–93; Council, Hong Kong Gen. Chamber of Commerce, 1988–92. Chm., Hong Kong Sports Develt Bd, 1992–. Mem. Council, Univ. of Hong Kong. JP Hong Kong, 1988. *Recreations:* swimming, sailing, fishing. *Address:* 9F Headland Road, South Bay, Hong Kong. *T:* 8129216. *Clubs:* Hong Kong, Shek O, Hong Kong Country, China (Hong Kong).

GLEESON, Hon. Anthony Murray, AC 1992 (AO 1986); **Hon. Justice Gleeson;** Chief Justice of New South Wales, since 1988; Lieutenant-Governor of New South Wales, since 1989; *b* 30 Aug. 1938; *s* of Leo John Gleeson and Rachel Alice Gleeson; *m* 1965, Robyn Paterson; one *s* three *d*. *Educ:* St Joseph's Coll., Hunters Hill; Univ. of Sydney (BA, LLB). Called to the NSW Bar, 1963; QC 1974. Tutor in Law, St Paul's

Coll., Sydney Univ., 1963–65; Part-time Lectr in Company Law, Sydney Univ., 1965–74. Pres., Judicial Commn, NSW, 1988–. Mem. Council, NSW Bar Assoc., 1979–85 (Pres., 1984 and 1985). Hon. Bencher, Middle Temple, 1989. *Recreations:* tennis, ski-ing. *Address:* c/o Chief Justice's Chambers, Supreme Court, Queen's Square, Sydney, NSW 2000, Australia. *T:* (2) 2308218. *Club:* Australian (Sydney).

GLEESON, Most Rev. James William, AO 1979; CMG 1958; DD 1957; FACE 1967; Archbishop Emeritus of Adelaide, (RC), since 1985; *b* 24 Dec. 1920; *s* of John Joseph and Margaret Mary Gleeson. *Educ:* St Joseph's Sch., Balaklava, SA; Sacred Heart Coll., Glenelg, SA. Priest, 1945; Inspector of Catholic Schs, 1947–52; Dir of Catholic Education for South Australia, 1952–58; Auxiliary Bishop to the Archbishop of Adelaide and Titular Bishop of Sesta, 1957–64; Coadjutor Archbishop of Adelaide and Titular Archbishop of Aurusuliana, 1964–71; Archbishop of Adelaide, 1971–85. Episcopal Chm., Young Catholic Students Movement of Australia, 1958–65. *Address:* Archbishop's House, 91 West Terrace, Adelaide, SA 5000, Australia. *T:* (8) 2313551.

GLEGG, Maj.-Gen. John B.; *see* Baskervyle-Glegg.

GLEISSNER, Dr Heinrich; Deputy Secretary General for Foreign Affairs, Austria, since 1991; *b* Linz, Upper Austria, 12 Dec. 1927; *s* of Heinrich and Maria Gleissner. *Educ:* Univ. of Vienna (Dr jur 1950); Univ. of Innsbruck; Bowdoin Coll., Brunswick, Maine, USA; Coll. of Europe, Bruges. Entered Austrian Foreign Service, 1951; Austrian Embassy, Paris, and Office of Austrian Observer at Council of Europe, Strasbourg, 1952–53; Min. for Foreign Affairs, Vienna, 1953–55; Austrian Embassy, London, 1955–57; sabbatical, Univ. of Vienna, 1957–59; Min. for For. Affairs, 1959–61; Austrian National Bank, 1961; Min. for For. Affairs, 1961–62; Mission to Office of UN, Geneva, 1962–65; Consulate-General, New York, 1965–66, Consul-Gen., 1966–73; Min. for For. Affairs, 1973–75 (Head, Western Dept, 1974–75); Dir, Security Council and Polit. Cttees Div., UN, New York, 1975–79; Austrian Ambassador to the Court of St James's, 1979–81; Federal Ministry for Foreign Affairs, 1982–. *Recreation:* music. *Address:* Federal Ministry for Foreign Affairs, Ballhausplatz 2, 1010 Vienna, Austria. *Club:* St Johann's (Wien).

GLEN, Sir Alexander (Richard), KBE 1967 (CBE 1964); DSC 1942 (and Bar, 1945); Vice President, British Air Line Pilots' Association, since 1994 (President, 1982–94); *b* 18 April 1912; *s* of late R. Bartlett Glen, Glasgow; *m* 1st, 1936, Nina Nixon (marr. diss. 1945); one *s* decd; 2nd, 1947, Baroness Zora de Collaert. *Educ:* Fettes Coll.; Balliol Coll., Oxford. BA, Hons Geography. Travelled on Arctic Expeditions, 1932–36; Leader, Oxford Univ. Arctic Expedition, 1935–36; Banking, New York and London, 1936–39. RNVR, 1939–59, Capt. 1955. Export Council for Europe: Dep. Chm., 1960–64; Chm., 1964–66; Chairman: H. Clarkson & Co., 1965–73; Anglo World Travel, 1978–81; Dep. Chm., British Transport Hotels, 1978–83; Director: BICC, 1964–70; Gleneagles Hotels, 1980–83. Chm., BTA, 1969–77; Member: BNEC, 1966–72; Board of BEA, 1964–70; Nat. Ports Council, 1966–70; Horserace Totalisator Bd, 1976–84. Chm., Adv. Council, V&A Museum, 1978–84; Mem., Historic Buildings Council, 1976–80. Awarded Cuthbert Peek Grant by RGS, 1933; Bruce Medal by RSE, 1938; Andrée Plaque by Royal Swedish Soc. for Anthropology and Geography, 1939; Patron's Gold Medal by RGS, 1940. Polar Medal (clasp Arctic 1935–36), 1942; Norwegian War Cross, 1943; Chevalier (1st Class), Order of St Olav, 1944; Czechoslovak War Cross, 1946. *Publications:* Young Men in the Arctic, 1935; Under the Pole Star, 1937; Footholds Against a Whirlwind (autobiog.), 1975. *Recreations:* travel, ski-ing, sailing. *Address:* The Dower House, Stanton, Broadway, Worcs WR12 7NE. *Clubs:* City of London; Explorers (NY).

GLEN, Archibald; Solicitor; *b* 3 July 1909; *m* 1938, Phyllis Mary; one *s* two *d. Educ:* Melville Coll., Edinburgh. Admitted Solicitor, 1932. Town Clerk: Burnley, Lancs, 1940–45; Southend-on-Sea, 1945–71. President: Soc. of City and Borough Clerks of the Peace, 1960; Soc. of Town Clerks, 1963–64; Assoc. of Town Clerks of British Commonwealth, 1963–64, etc. Lay Member, Press Council, 1969–75; Mem., Local Govt Staff Commn for England, 1972–76. Hon. Freeman, Southend-on-Sea, 1971. *Recreations:* golf, swimming. *Address:* Harbour House, 2 Drummochy, Lower Largo, Fife KY8 6BZ. *T:* Lundin Links (01333) 320724.

GLEN HAIG, Dame Mary (Alison), DBE 1993 (CBE 1977; MBE 1971); *b* 12 July 1918; *e d* of late Captain William James and Mary (*née* Bannochie); *m* 1943, Andrew Glen Haig (decd). *Educ:* Dame Alice Owen's Girls' School. Mem., Sports Council, 1966–82; Vice Pres., CCPR, 1982– (Chm., 1974–80); Mem., Internat. Olympic Cttee, 1982–93 (Hon. Mem., 1993–); Pres., British Sports Assoc. for the Disabled, 1981–90 (Life Pres., 1991); Vice Pres., Sports Aid Foundn, 1987–. Hon. Pres., Amateur Fencing Assoc., 1986– (Pres., 1974–86). British Ladies' Foil Champion, 1948–50. Olympic Games, 1948, 1952, 1956, 1960; Commonwealth Games Gold Medal, 1950, 1954, Bronze Medal, 1958; Captain, Ladies' Foil Team, 1950–57. Asst Dist Administrator, S Hammersmith Health District, 1975–82. Member: Adv. Council Women's Transport Service (FANY), 1980; Exec. Cttee, Arthritis and Rheumatism Council, 1992–. Chm. of Trustees, HRH The Princess Christian Hosp., Windsor, 1981–94; Trustee, Wishbone Trust, 1991–. *Recreations:* fencing, gardening. *Address:* 66 North End House, Fitzjames Avenue, W14 0RX. *T:* 0171–602 2504; 2 Old Cottages, Holyport Street, Holyport, near Maidenhead, Berks SL6 2JR. *T:* Maidenhead (01628) 33421. *Club:* Lansdowne.

GLENAMARA, Baron *cr* 1977 (Life Peer), of Glenridding, Cumbria; **Edward Watson Short,** PC 1964; CH 1976; Chairman, Cable and Wireless Ltd, 1976–80; *b* 17 Dec. 1912; *s* of Charles and Mary Short, Warcop, Westmorland; *m* 1941, Jennie, *d* of Thomas Sewell, Newcastle upon Tyne; one *s* one *d. Educ:* Bede College, Durham. LLB London. Served War of 1939–45 and became Capt. in DLI. Headmaster of Princess Louise County Secondary School, Blyth, Northumberland, 1947; Leader of Labour Group on Newcastle City Council, 1950; MP (Lab) Newcastle upon Tyne Central, 1951–76; Opposition Whip (Northern Area), 1955–62; Dep. Chief Opposition Whip, 1962–64; Parly Sec. to the Treasury and Govt Chief Whip, 1964–66; Postmaster General, 1966–68; Sec. of State for Educn and Science, 1968–70; Lord Pres. of the Council and Leader, House of Commons, 1974–76. Dep. Leader, Labour Party, 1972–76. Mem. Council, WWF, 1983–92. President: Finchale Abbey Training Coll. for the Disabled (Durham), 1985–; North East People to People, 1989–. Chancellor, Univ. of Northumbria (formerly Polytechnic of Newcastle upon Tyne), 1984–. Hon. FCP, 1965. Hon. DCL Dunelm, 1989; DUniv Open, 1989; Hon. DLitt CNAA, 1990. *Publications:* The Story of The Durham Light Infantry, 1944; The Infantry Instructor, 1946; Education in a Changing World, 1971; Birth to Five, 1974; I Knew My Place, 1983; Whip to Wilson, 1989. *Recreation:* painting. *Address:* 21 Priory Gardens, Corbridge, Northumberland NE45 5HZ. *T:* Corbridge (01434) 632880; Glenridding, Cumbria. *T:* Glenridding (017684) 82273.

GLENAPP, Viscount; Fergus James Kenneth Mackay; *b* 9 July 1979; *s* and *heir* of 4th Earl of Inchcape, *qv*.

GLENARTHUR, 4th Baron *cr* 1918; **Simon Mark Arthur;** Bt 1903; DL; Senior Executive, Hanson PLC, since 1989; Deputy Chairman, Hanson Pacific Ltd, since 1994; *b* 7 Oct. 1944; *s* of 3rd Baron Glenarthur, OBE, and Margaret (*d* 1993), *d* of late Captain H. J. J. Howie; *S* father, 1976; *m* 1969, Susan, *yr d* of Comdr Hubert Wyndham Barry, RN; one *s* one *d. Educ:* Eton. Commissioned 10th Royal Hussars (PWO), 1963; ADC to High Comr, Aden, 1964–65; Captain 1970; Major 1973; retired 1975; Royal Hussars (PWO), TA, 1976–80. British Airways Helicopters Captain, 1976–82. A Lord in Waiting (Govt Whip), 1982–83; Parly Under Sec. of State, DHSS, 1983–85, Home Office, 1985–86; Minister of State: Scottish Office, 1986–87; FCO, 1987–89. Director: Aberdeen and Texas Corporate Finance Ltd, 1977–82; The Lewis Gp, 1993–95; Consultant: BAe PLC, 1989–; Chevron UK Ltd, 1994–. Chairman: St Mary's Hosp., Paddington, NHS Trust, 1991–; British Helicopter Adv. Bd, 1992–. Pres., Nat. Council for Civil Protection, 1991–; Mem. Council, Air League, 1994–. Patron, Butler Trust, 1994–. Brig., Queen's Body Guard for Scotland (Royal Co. of Archers). MCIT 1979; FRAeS 1992. Freeman, GAPAN, 1992. DL Aberdeenshire, 1988. *Recreations:* field sports, flying, gardening, choral singing, photography. *Heir: s* Hon. Edward Alexander Arthur, *b* 9 April 1973. *Address:* House of Lords, SW1A 0PW. *Clubs:* Cavalry and Guards, Pratt's, White's.

GLENCONNER, 3rd Baron *cr* 1911; **Colin Christopher Paget Tennant;** Bt 1885; Governing Director, Tennants Estate Ltd, 1967–91; Chairman, Mustique Co. Ltd, 1969–87; *b* 1 Dec. 1926; *s* of 2nd Baron Glenconner, and Pamela Winefred (*d* 1989), 2nd *d* of Sir Richard Paget, 2nd Bt; *S* father, 1983; *m* 1956, Lady Anne Coke, VO, *e d* of 5th Earl of Leicester, MVO; two *s* twin *d* (and one *s* decd). *Educ:* Eton; New College, Oxford. Director, C. Tennant Sons & Co. Ltd, 1953; Deputy Chairman, 1960–67, resigned 1967. *Heir: s* Hon. Charles Edward Pevensey Tennant [*b* 15 Feb. 1957; *m* 1993, Shelagh, *d* of Matthew Raymond Scott; one *s*].

See also Lady Emma Tennant.

GLENCROSS, David, CBE 1994; Chief Executive, Independent Television Commission, since 1991; *b* 3 March 1936; *s* of John William and Elsie May Glencross; *m* 1965, Elizabeth Louise, *d* of John and Edith Richardson; one *d. Educ:* Salford Grammar School; Trinity College, Cambridge. BBC: general trainee, 1958; talks producer, Midlands, 1959; TV Midlands at Six, 1962; Staff Training section, 1964; Senior Producer, External Services, 1966; Asst Head of Programmes, N Region, 1968; Senior Programme Officer, ITA, 1970; Head of Programme Services, IBA, 1976; Dep. Dir, 1977, Dir, 1983–90, Television, IBA. FRTS 1981; FRSA 1985. Hon. MA Salford, 1993. *Publications:* articles on broadcasting in newspapers and jls. *Recreations:* music, reading, listening to radio, walking. *Address:* Independent Television Commission, 33 Foley Street, W1P 7LB.

GLENDEVON, 1st Baron, *cr* 1964; **John Adrian Hope;** ERD 1988; PC 1959; Director and Deputy Chairman, Ciba-Geigy (UK) Ltd (formerly Geigy (UK) Ltd), 1971–78 (Chairman, 1967–71); Director: ITT (UK) Ltd; Colonial Mutual Life Assurance Society Ltd, 1952–54, 1962–82; British Electric Traction Omnibus Services Ltd, 1947–52, 1962–82; *b* 7 April 1912; *yr* twin *s* of 2nd Marquess of Linlithgow, KG, KT, PC; *m* 1948, Elizabeth Mary, *d* of late (William) Somerset Maugham, CH; two *s. Educ:* Eton; Christ Church, Oxford (MA 1936). Served War of 1939–45 (Scots Guards) at Narvik, Salerno and Anzio (despatches twice); psc†. MP (C) Northern Midlothian and Peebles, 1945–50, Pentlands Div. of Edinburgh, 1950–64; (Joint) Parliamentary Under-Sec. of State for Foreign Affairs, Oct. 1954–Nov. 1956; Parliamentary Under-Sec. of State for Commonwealth Relations, Nov. 1956–Jan. 1957; Jt Parly Under-Sec. of State for Scotland, 1957–Oct. 1959; Minister of Works, Oct. 1959–July 1962. Mem., Departmental Cttee to examine operation of Section 2 of Official Secrets Act, 1971. Chairman: Royal Commonwealth Society, 1963–66; Historic Buildings Council for England, 1973–75. Fellow of Eton, 1956–67. FRSA 1962. *Publication:* The Viceroy at Bay, 1971. *Heir: s* Hon. Julian John Somerset Hope, *b* 6 March 1950. *Address:* Mount Lodge, Mount Row, St Peter Port, Guernsey, Channel Islands.

GLENDINING, Rev. Canon Alan, LVO 1979; Chaplain to the Queen, 1979–94; Hon. Canon of Norwich Cathedral, since 1977; *b* 17 March 1924; *s* of late Vincent Glendining, MS, FRCS and Freda Alice; *m* 1948, Margaret Locke, *d* of Lt-Col C. M. Hawes, DSO and Frances Cooper Richmond; one *s* one *d* (and one *d* decd). *Educ:* Radley; Westcott House, Cambridge. Newspaper publishing, 1945–58. Deacon, 1960; Priest, 1961. Asst Curate, South Ormsby Group of Parishes, 1960–63; Rector of Raveningham Group of Parishes, 1963–70; Rector, Sandringham Group of Parishes, and Domestic Chaplain to the Queen, 1970–79; Rural Dean of Heacham and Rising, 1972–76; Rector of St Margaret's, Lowestoft, and Team Leader of Lowestoft Group, 1979–85; Vicar of Ranworth with Panxworth with Woodbastwick, Bishop's Chaplain for the Broads and Senior Chaplain for Holidaymakers, 1985–89; RD of Blofield, 1987–89. *Recreation:* writing. *Address:* 7 Bellfosters, Kings Staithe Lane, Kings Lynn, Norfolk PE30 1LZ.

GLENDINNING, James Garland, OBE 1973; Chairman, Masterpack Ltd, since 1981; *b* 27 April 1919; *er s* of late George M. Glendinning and Isabella Green; *m* 1st, 1943, Margaret Donald (*d* 1980); one *d*; 2nd, Mrs Anne Ruth Law. *Educ:* Boroughmuir Sch., Edinburgh; Military Coll. of Science. Mil. Service, 1939–46: 2nd Bn London Scottish and REME in UK and NW Europe. HM Inspector of Taxes, 1946–50; various appts with Shell Petroleum Co. Ltd, 1950–58; Dir Anglo Egyptian Oilfields Ltd in Egypt, 1959–61; Gen. Manager in Borneo and East Java for Shell Indonesia, 1961–64; Head of Industrial Studies (Diversification) in Shell Internat. Petroleum Co. Ltd, London, 1964–67; various Shell appts in Japan, 1967–72, incl.: Vice-President: Shell Sekiyu KK; Shell Kosan KK; Dir, various Shell/Showa and Shell/Mitsubishi jt venture cos. Chm., British Chamber of Commerce in Japan, 1970–72; Mem., London Transport Exec., 1972–80; Chairman: London Transport Pension Fund Trustees Ltd, 1974–80; North American Property Unit Trust, 1975–80; Director: Industrial and Commercial Property Unit Trust, 1977–81; The Fine Art Society plc, 1972–89; Man. Dir, Gestam International Realty Ltd, 1981–83. Exec. Sec., Japan Soc., 1985–93. FCIT 1973; FRSA 1977. *Address:* 20 Albion Street, W2 2AS. *Clubs:* Caledonian, Oriental.

GLENDINNING, Hon. Victoria, (Hon. Mrs de Vere White), FRSL; author and journalist, since 1969; *b* 23 April 1937; *d* of Baron Seebohm, TD and Evangeline, *d* of Sir Gerald Hurst, QC; *m* 1st, 1958, Prof. (Oliver) Nigel (Valentine) Glendinning (marr. diss. 1981); four *s*; 2nd, 1982, Terence de Vere White (*d* 1994). *Educ:* St Mary's Sch., Wantage; Millfield Sch.; Somerville Coll., Oxford (MA Mod. Langs); Southampton Univ. (Dip. in Social Admin). FRSL 1982. Part-time teaching, 1960–69; part-time psychiatric social work, 1970–73; Editorial Asst, TLS, 1974–78. Hon. DLitt: Southampton, 1994; Ulster, 1995. *Publications:* A Suppressed Cry, 1969; Elizabeth Bowen: portrait of a writer, 1977; Edith Sitwell: a unicorn among lions, 1981; Vita: a biography of V. Sackville-West, 1983; Rebecca West: a life, 1987; The Grown-Ups (novel), 1989; Hertfordshire, 1989; Trollope, 1992; Electricity (novel), 1995; reviews and articles in newspapers and magazines in Britain, Ireland and USA. *Recreation:* gardening. *Address:* c/o David Higham Associates, 5–8 Lower John Street, Golden Square, W1R 4HA. *Club:* Academy.

GLENDYNE, 3rd Baron, *cr* 1922; **Robert Nivison,** Bt 1914; Chairman, Glenfriars Holdings Ltd, 1977–93, retired; *b* 27 Oct. 1926; *o s* of 2nd Baron and late Ivy May Rose; *S* father, 1967; *m* 1953, Elizabeth, *y d* of late Sir Cecil Armitage, CBE; one *s* two *d. Educ:* Harrow. Grenadier Guards, 1944–47. *Heir: s* Hon. John Nivison, *b* 18 Aug. 1960. *Address:* Craigeassie, by Forfar, Angus DD8 3SE.

See also Maj.-Gen. P. R. Leuchars, Maj.-Gen. D. J. St M. Tabor.

GLENISTER, Prof. Tony William Alphonse, CBE (mil.) 1979; TD; Professor Emeritus, University of London (Professor of Anatomy, at Charing Cross Hospital Medical School, 1970–84, at Charing Cross and Westminster Medical School, 1984–89); Dean, Charing Cross and Westminster Medical School, 1984–89; *b* 19 Dec. 1923; *o s* of late Dudley Stuart Glenister and Maria (*née* Leytens); *m* 1948, Monique Marguerite, *o d* of Emile and Marguerite de Wilde; four *s*. *Educ:* Eastbourne Coll.; St Bartholomew's Hosp. Med. Coll. MRCS, LRCP 1947; MB, BS 1948, PhD 1955, DSc 1963, London. House appts, St Bartholomew's Hosp. and St Andrew's Hosp., Dollis Hill, 1947–48; served in RAMC, 1948–50; Lectr and Reader in Anatomy, Charing Cross Hosp. Med. Sch., 1950–57; Internat. Project Embryological Res., Hubrecht Lab., Utrecht, 1954; Prof. of Embryology, Univ. of London, 1967–70; Dean, Charing Cross Hosp. Med. Sch., 1976–84 (Vice-Dean, 1966–69, 1971–76); Hon. Cons. in Clin. Anatomy and Genetics to Charing Cross Gp of Hosps, 1972–89; Brig. late RAMC, TA, retd (TD, TA 1963 and TAVR 1978). Apothecaries' Soc. Lectr in History of Medicine, 1971–89; Arnott Demonstrator, RCS, 1972, 1986; Pres., Anatomical Soc. GB and Ireland, 1979–81 (Sec., 1974–76). ADMS 44 (Home Counties) Div. TA, 1964–67; CO 217 (London) Gen. Hosp. RAMC(V), 1968–72; QHP 1971–73; Hon. Col 220 (1st Home Counties) Field Amb. RAMC(V), 1973–78; TAVR Advr to DGAMS, 1976–79; Hon. Col 217 (London) Gen. Hosp. RAMC, TAVR, 1981–86. Member: Ealing, Hammersmith and Hounslow AHA(T), 1976–82; Hammersmith and Fulham DHA, 1982–83; North West Thames RHA, 1983–88; GMC, 1979–93; GDC, 1983–93; sometime examiner: Univs of Cambridge, Liverpool, London, St Andrews, Singapore, NUI, Chinese Univ., Hong Kong; RCS; RCSE; RCPGlas. Trustee, Tablet Trust. Master, Soc. of Apothecaries of London, 1991–92; Freeman, City of London. OStJ 1967; KLJ 1993 (OLJ 1989). *Publications:* (with J. R. W. Ross) Anatomy and Physiology for Nurses, 1965, 3rd edn 1980; (contrib.) A Companion to Medical Studies, ed Passmore, 1963, 2nd edn 1976; (contrib.) Methods in Mammalian Embryology, ed Daniel, 1971; (contrib.) Textbook of Human Anatomy, ed Hamilton, 1976; papers and articles mainly on prenatal development. *Recreations:* the countryside, sketching, history. *Club:* Army and Navy.

GLENN, Sir Archibald; *see* Glenn, Sir J. R. A.

GLENN, Senator John H(erschel), Jr; US Senator from Ohio (Democrat), since 1975; *b* Cambridge, Ohio, 18 July 1921; *s* of John H. and Clara Glenn; *m* 1943, Anna Castor; one *s* one *d*. *Educ:* Muskingum Coll., New Concord, Ohio. Joined US Marine Corps, 1943; Served War (2 DFC's, 10 Air Medals); Pacific Theater, 1944; home-based, Capt., 1945–46; Far East, 1947–49; Major, 1952; served Korea (5 DFC's, Air Medal with 18 clusters), 1953. First non-stop supersonic flight, Los Angeles-New York (DFC), 1957; Lieut-Col, 1959. In Jan. 1964, declared candidacy for US Senate from Ohio, but withdrew owing to an injury; recovered and promoted Col USMC, Oct. 1964; retired from USMC, Dec. 1964. Became one of 7 volunteer Astronauts, man-in-space program, 1959; made 3–orbit flight in Mercury capsule, Friendship 7, 20 Feb. 1962 (boosted by rocket; time 4 hrs 56 mins; distance 81,000 miles; altitude 160 miles; recovered by destroyer off Puerto Rico in Atlantic). Vice-Pres. (corporate develt), Royal Crown Cola Co., 1966–68; Pres., Royal Crown Internat., 1967–69. Holds hon. doctorates, US and foreign. Awarded DSM (Nat. Aeronautics and Space Admin.), Astronaut Wings (Navy), Astronaut Medal (Marine Corps), etc, 1962; Galabert Internat. Astronautical Prize (jointly with Lieut-Col Yuri Gagarin), 1963; also many other awards and citations from various countries and organizations.

GLENN, Sir (Joseph Robert) Archibald, Kt 1966; OBE 1965; BCE; FIChemE, FIE (Aust.); Managing Director, 1953–73, Chairman, 1963–73, ICI Australia; *b* 24 May 1911; *s* of late J. R. Glenn, Sale, Vic., Aust.; *m* 1st, 1939, Elizabeth M. M. (*d* 1988), *d* of late J. S. Balderstone; one *s* three *d*; 2nd, 1992, Mrs Sue Debenham (*née* Hennesey). *Educ:* Scotch Coll. (Melbourne); University of Melbourne; Harvard (USA). Joined ICI Australia Ltd, 1935; Design and Construction Engr, 1935–44; Explosives Dept, ICI (UK), 1945–46; Chief Engineer, ICI Australia Ltd, 1947–48; Controller, Nobel Group, 1948–50; General Manager, 1950–52, ICI Australia Ltd; Director: Westpac Banking Corp. (formerly Bank of NSW), 1967–84; ICI, London, 1970–75; Hill Samuel Australia Ltd, 1973–83; Westralian Sands Ltd, 1977–85; Alcoa of Australia Ltd, 1973–86; Tioxide Australia Ltd, 1973–86; Newmont Pty Ltd, 1977–88; Chairman: Fibremakers Ltd, 1963–73; IMI Australia Ltd, 1970–78; Collins Wales Pty Ltd, 1973–84; I. C. Insurance Australia Ltd, 1973–85. Chancellor, La Trobe Univ., 1967–72 (Hon. DUniv 1981); Chairman: Council of Scotch Coll., 1960–81. Ormond Coll. Council, 1976–81; Member: Manufacturing Industry Advisory Council, 1960–77; Industrial Design Council, 1958–70; Australia/Japan Business Co-operation Cttee, 1965–75; Royal Melbourne Hospital Bd of Management, 1960–70; Melbourne Univ. Appointments Bd; Bd of Management, Melbourne Univ. Engrg Sch. Foundn, 1982–88; Council, Inst. of Pacific Affairs, 1976–; Governor, Atlantic Inst. of Internat. Affairs, 1970–88. J. N. Kirby Medal, 1970. *Recreations:* golf, tennis, collecting rare books. *Address:* 8 Freemans Road, Mount Eliza, Vic 3930, Australia. *T:* (3) 7875850. *Clubs:* Australian, Melbourne, Frankston Golf, Melbourne Univ. Boat (all in Melbourne); Australian (Sydney).

GLENNIE, Angus James Scott; QC 1991; barrister and advocate; *b* 3 Dec. 1950; *yr s* of Robert Nigel Forbes Glennie and Barbara Scott (*née* Nicoll); *m* 1981, Patricia Jean Phelan, *er d* of His Honour Judge Phelan, *qv*; three *s* one *d*. *Educ:* Sherborne Sch.; Trinity Hall, Cambridge (MA Hons). Called to the Bar, Lincoln's Inn, 1974; admitted to Faculty of Advocates, 1992. *Recreations:* sailing, real tennis. *Address:* Thamescote, Chiswick Mall, W4 2PR. *T:* 0181–747 8241; Threeburnford Farm, Oxton, Lauder, Berwicks TD2 6PU. *T:* Oxton (01578) 750615. *Clubs:* Queen's; Petworth House Tennis Court; Itchenor Sailing.

GLENNIE, Evelyn Elizabeth Ann, OBE 1993; percussionist; *b* 19 July 1965; *d* of Isobel and Arthur Glennie; *m* 1993, Greg Malcangi. *Educ:* Ellon Acad., Aberdeen; Royal Academy of Music (GRSM Hons, LRAM, ARAM; Queen's Commendation Prize). Shell Gold Medal, 1984; studied in Japan; Leonardo da Vinci Prize, 1987; début, Wigmore Hall, 1986; soloist in Zürich, Paris, Schwetzingen, Holland, Dublin, Norway, Australia; festivals of Aldeburgh, Bath, Edinburgh, Chichester, Salisbury; percussion and timpani concertos specially written; TV and radio presenting; numerous recordings and awards. Hon. DMus Aberdeen, 1991; Hon. DLitt Warwick, 1992. Grammy Award, 1988. *Publication:* Good Vibrations (autobiog.), 1990. *Recreations:* reading, walking, cycling. *Address:* c/o Harrison Parrott, 12 Penzance Place, W11 4PA. *T:* 0171–229 9166.

GLENNY, Misha; freelance journalist, writer and broadcaster, since 1993; *b* 25 April 1958; *s* of late Michael V. G. Glenny and of Juliet Sydenham (*née* Crum); *m* 1987, Snezana Curcic; one *s* one *d*. *Educ:* Bristol Univ. (BA Drama); Charles Univ., Prague. Rights editor, Verso publishing house, London, 1983–86; Central Europe Correspondent (based in Vienna): The Guardian, 1986–89; BBC World Service, 1989–93. Sony Special Award for Broadcasting, 1993; American Overseas Pressclub Award for Best Book on Foreign Affairs, 1993. *Publications:* The Rebirth of History: Eastern Europe in the age of democracy, 1990, 2nd edn 1993; The Fall of Yugoslavia, 1992, 2nd edn 1993. *Address:* Irodotou 8, 546 34 Thessaloniki, Greece. *Fax:* (31) 248402.

GLENNY, Dr Robert Joseph Ervine, CEng, FIM; Consultant to UK Government, industry, and European Economic Community, since 1983; *b* 14 May 1923; *s* of late Robert and Elizabeth Rachel Glenny; *m* 1947, Joan Phillips Reid; one *s* one *d*. *Educ:* Methodist Coll., Belfast; QUB (BSc Chemistry); London Univ. (BSc Metallurgy, PhD). CEng, 1979; FIM 1958. Res. Metallurgist, English Electric Co. Ltd, Stafford, 1943–47; National Gas Turbine Establishment, 1947–70; Materials Dept, 1947–66; Head of Materials Dept, 1966–70; Supt, Div. of Materials Applications, National Physical Lab., 1970–73; Head of Materials Dept, RAE, 1973–79; Group Head of Aerodynamics, Structures and Materials Depts, RAE, 1979–83. *Publications:* research and review papers on materials science and technology, mainly related to gas turbines, in ARC (R&M series) and in Internat. Metallurgical Rev. *Recreations:* reading, gardening, walking. *Address:* 77 Gally Hill Road, Fleet, Hants GU13 0RU. *T:* Fleet (01252) 615877.

GLENTORAN, 3rd Baron *cr* 1939, of Ballyalolly, Co. Down; **Thomas Robin Valerian Dixon;** CBE 1992 (MBE 1969); Bt 1903; Managing Director, Redland (NI) Ltd, since 1971; Chairman, Positively Belfast, since 1987; *b* 21 April 1935; *er s* of 2nd Baron Glentoran, KBE, PC; *S* father, 1995; *m* 1959, Rona, *d* of Captain G. C. Colville; three *s*; *m* 1990, Margaret Rainey. *Educ:* Eton. Mem., Millenium Fund Commn, 1994–. *Recreations:* sailing, golf. *Heir: s* Hon. Daniel George Dixon [*b* 26 July 1959; *m* 1983, Leslie Hope Brooke; two *s*]. *Address:* Drumadarragh House, Ballyclare, Co. Antrim BT39 0TA; The Smithie, Glenieragh Glen, Co. Donegal. *Club:* Royal Cruising.

GLENTWORTH, Viscount; Edmund Christopher Pery; solicitor with Milbank Tweed, since 1994; *b* 10 Feb. 1963; *s* and *heir* of 6th Earl of Limerick, *qv*; *m* 1990, Emily Kate, *o d* of Michael Thomas; two *s*. *Educ:* Eton; New Coll., Oxford (MA); Pushkin Inst., Moscow; City Univ. (Dip. Law). Called to the Bar, Middle Temple, 1987. HM Diplomatic Service, 1987–92: FCO, 1987–88; Ecole Nationale d'Administration, Paris, 1988–89; attachment to Ministère des Affaires Etrangères, Paris, 1990; Second Sec., Senegal, 1990–91, Amman, 1991–92; lawyer: with Clifford Chance, 1992–93; with Freshfields, 1993–94. *Recreations:* skiing, windsurfing. *Heir: s* Hon. Felix Edmund Pery, *b* 16 Nov. 1991. *Address:* 61 Monkton Street, SE11 4TX. *T:* 0171–735 2832.

GLESTER, John William; Chief Executive, Central Manchester Development Corporation, since 1988; *b* 8 Sept. 1946; *o s* of George Ernest Glester and late Maude Emily Glester; *m* 1970, Ann Gleave Taylor; two *s*. *Educ:* Plaistow Grammar Sch.; Reading Univ. (BA Hons). Joined Civil Service 1968; served DEA, DoE and Merseyside Task Force; Regl Controller, NW, DoE, 1985–88. Chm., Castlefield Management Co., 1992–; Dir, Hallogen Ltd, 1995–. Director: Salford Phoenix, 1987–95; Manchester Arts Fest., 1989–93; Manchester Olympic Bid Cttee, 1990–93; Manchester 2000, 1992–94; Manchester 2000 Promotions, 1992–; Manchester City of Drama, 1992–94; Manchester Concert Hall, 1994–; Manchester 2002 Commonwealth Games Management, 1994–. *Recreations:* cricket, football (West Ham United in particular), music, theatre, cooking. *Address:* Central Manchester Development Corporation, 56 Oxford Street, Manchester M1 6EU. *T:* 0161–236 1166. *Club:* St James's (Manchester).

GLICK, Ian Bernard; QC 1987; *b* 18 July 1948; *s* of late Dr Louis Glick and of Phyllis Esty Glick; *m* 1986, Roxane Eban; three *s*. *Educ:* Bradford Grammar School; Balliol College, Oxford (MA, BCL). President, Oxford Union Society, 1968. Called to the Bar, Inner Temple, 1970. Junior Counsel to the Crown, 1985–87; Standing Junior Counsel to DTI in Export Credit Cases, 1985–87. *Address:* 1 Essex Court, Temple, EC4Y 9AR.

GLIDEWELL, Rt. Hon. Sir Iain (Derek Laing), Kt 1980; PC 1985; a Lord Justice of Appeal, 1985–95; *b* 8 June 1924; *s* of late Charles Norman and Nora Glidewell; *m* 1950, Hilary, *d* of late Clinton D. Winant; one *s* two *d*. *Educ:* Bromsgrove Sch.; Worcester Coll., Oxford (Hon. Fellow 1986). Served RAFVR (pilot), 1942–46. Called to the Bar, Gray's Inn, 1949 (Bencher 1977, Treas. 1995). QC 1969; a Recorder of the Crown Court, 1976–80; Judge of Appeal, Isle of Man, 1979–80; a Judge of the High Court of Justice, Queen's Bench Division, 1980–85; Presiding Judge, NE Circuit, 1982–85. Chm., Judicial Studies Bd, 1989–92; Member: Senate of Inns of Court and the Bar, 1976–79; Supreme Court Rule Cttee, 1980–84. Chm., Panels for Examination of Structure Plans: Worcestershire, 1974; W Midlands, 1975; conducted Heathrow Fourth Terminal Inquiry, 1978. Associate, RICS, 1982. *Recreations:* beagling, walking, theatre. *Address:* Rough Heys Farm, Henbury, Macclesfield, Cheshire SK11 9PF. *Club:* Garrick.

GLIN, Knight of; *see* Fitz-Gerald, D. J. V.

GLOAG, Ann Heron; Group Managing Director, Stagecoach Holdings plc, since 1986; *b* 10 Dec. 1942; *d* of Iain and Catherine Souter; *m* 1st, 1965, Robin N. Gloag; one *s* one *d*; 2nd, 1990, David McCleary. *Educ:* Caledonian Road Primary School; Perth High School. Trainee Nurse, Bridge of Earn Hosp., Perth, 1960–65; Ward Sister, Devonshire Royal Hosp., Buxton, 1965–69; Theatre Sister, Bridge of Earn Hosp., 1969–80; Founding Partner, Gloagtrotter, re-named Stagecoach Express Services, 1980–83; Co-Director, Stagecoach Ltd, 1983–86 (acquired parts of National Bus Co., 1987 and 1989 and Scottish Bus Group, 1991). Scottish Marketing Woman of the Year, Scottish Univs, 1989; UK Businesswoman of the Year, Veuve Cliquot and Inst of Dirs, 1989–90. *Recreations:* family, travel, charity support. *Address:* Stagecoach Holdings plc, Charlotte House, 20 Charlotte Street, Perth PH1 5LL. *T:* Perth (01738) 442111.

GLOAK, Graeme Frank, CB 1980; Solicitor for the Customs and Excise, 1978–82; *b* 9 Nov. 1921; *s* of late Frank and of Lilian Gloak; *m* 1944, Mary, *d* of Stanley and Jane Thorne; one *s* one *d* (and one *s* decd). *Educ:* Brentwood School. Royal Navy, 1941–46; Solicitor, 1947; Customs and Excise: Legal Asst, 1947; Sen. Legal Asst, 1953; Asst Solicitor, 1967; Principal Asst Solicitor, 1971. Sec., Civil Service Legal Soc., 1954–62. Member: Dairy Produce Quota Tribunal, 1984–85; Agricl Wages Cttee for Essex and Herts, 1984–90 (Vice-Chm., 1987–90); Chm., Agricl Dwelling House Adv. Cttee, Essex and Herts, 1984–93. Member: Barking and Havering FPC, 1986–90; Barking and Havering FHSA, 1990–. *Publication:* (with G. Krikorian and R. K. F. Hutchings) Customs and Excise, in Halsbury's Laws of England, 4th edn, 1973. *Recreations:* badminton, walking, watching cricket. *Address:* Northwold, 123 Priests Lane, Shenfield, Essex CM15 8HJ. *T:* Brentwood (01277) 212748. *Clubs:* MCC; Essex County Cricket (Chelmsford).

GLOBE, Henry Brian; QC 1994; a Recorder, since 1991; *b* 18 June 1949; *o s* of Theodore Montague Globe and Irene Rita Globe; *m* 1972, Estelle Levin; two *d*. *Educ:* Liverpool Coll.; Birmingham Univ. (LLB). Called to the Bar, Middle Temple, 1972; in practice on Northern Circuit, 1972–; Standing Counsel to: DSS, 1985–94; HM Customs and Excise, 1992–94. Chm. of Govs, King David High Sch., 1990–. *Recreations:* tennis, bridge. *Address:* Exchange Chambers, Pearl Assurance House, Derby Square, Liverpool L2 9XX. *T:* 0151–236 7747.

GLOCK, Sir William (Frederick), Kt 1970; CBE 1964; Controller of Music, BBC, 1959–72; *b* London, 3 May 1908. *Educ:* Christ's Hospital; Caius Coll., Cambridge. Studied pianoforte under Artur Schnabel. Joined The Observer, 1934; chief music critic, 1939–45. Served in RAF, 1941–46. Dir, Summer Sch. of Music, Bryanston, 1948–52, Dartington Hall, 1953–79; Artistic Dir, Bath Fest., 1975–84. Editor of music magazine The Score, 1949–61; adjudicated at Canadian music festivals, 1951; has lectured on music throughout England and Canada. Music Critic, New Statesman, 1958–59. Editor, Eulenburg books on music, 1973–86. Chm., London Orchestral Concerts Bd, 1975–86; Member: Bd of

Dirs, Royal Opera House, 1968–73; Arts Council, 1972–75; South Bank Bd, 1986–91. Pres., Bath Fest. Soc., 1991. Hon. Mem., Royal Philharmonic Soc., 1971. Hon. DMus: Nottingham Univ., 1968; Plymouth Univ., 1993; DUniv York, 1972; Hon. DLitt Bath, 1984. Albert Medal, RSA, 1971. *Publication:* Notes in Advance (autobiog.), 1991. *Address:* Vine House, Brightwell cum Sotwell, Wallingford, Oxon OX10 0RT. *T:* Wallingford (01491) 837144.

GLOSSOP, Peter; Principal Baritone, Royal Opera House, Covent Garden, until 1967, now Guest Artist; *b* 6 July 1928; *s* of Cyril and Violet Elizabeth Glossop; *m* 1st, 1955, Joyce Elizabeth Blackham (marr. diss. 1977); no *c*; 2nd, 1977, Michèle Yvonne Amos; two *d*. *Educ:* High Storrs Grammar Sch., Sheffield. Began singing professionally in chorus of Sadler's Wells Opera, 1952, previously a bank clerk; promoted to principal after one season; Covent Garden Opera, 1962–67. Début in Italy, 1964; La Scala, Milan, début, Rigoletto, 1965. Sang Otello and Rigoletto with Metropolitan Opera Company at Newport USA Festival, Aug. 1967; Rigoletto and Nabucco with Mexican National Opera Company, Sept. 1967. Guest Artist (Falstaff, Rigoletto, Tosca) with American National Opera Company, Oct. 1967. Has sung in opera houses of Bologna, Parma Catania, Vienna, 1967–68, and Berlin and Buenos Aires. Is a recording artist. Hon. DMus, Sheffield, 1970. Winner of 1st Prize and Gold Medal in First International Competition for Young Opera Singers, Sofia, Bulgaria, 1961; Gold Medal for finest performance (in Macbeth) of 1968–69 season, Barcelona. *Films:* Pagliacci, Otello. *Recreations:* New Orleans jazz music, golf. *Address:* c/o S. A. Gorlinsky Ltd, 33 Dover Street, W1X 4NJ; End Cottage, Hawkchurch, Axminster, Devon EX13 5TY. *Club:* Green Room.

GLOSTER, Elizabeth, (Mrs S. E. Brodie); QC 1989; a Judge of the Courts of Appeal of Jersey and Guernsey, since 1993; a Recorder, since 1995; *b* 5 June 1949; *d* of Peter Gloster and Betty Gloster (*née* Read); *m* 1973, Stanley Eric Brodie, *qv*; one *s* one *d*. *Educ:* Roedean Sch., Brighton; Girton Coll., Cambridge (BA Hons). Called to the Bar, Inner Temple, 1971, Bencher 1992. Mem., panel of Counsel who appear for DTI in company matters, 1982–89. Mem. Bd (non-exec.), CAA, 1992–93. *Address:* 1 Essex Court, Temple, EC4Y 9AR. *T:* 0171–583 2000.

GLOSTER, Prof. John, MD; Hon. Consulting Ophthalmologist, Moorfields Eye Hospital; Emeritus Professor of Experimental Opthalmology, University of London; *b* 23 March 1922; *m* 1947, Margery (*née* Williams); two *s*. *Educ:* Jesus Coll., Cambridge; St Bartholomew's Hosp. MB, BChir 1946; MRCS, LRCP 1946; DOMS 1950; MD Cantab 1953; PhD London 1959. Registrar, Research Dept, Birmingham and Midland Eye Hosp., 1950–54; Mem. Staff, Ophth. Research Unit, MRC, 1954–63; Prof. of Experimental Ophthalmology, Inst. of Ophth., Univ. of London, 1975–82; Dean of the Inst. of Ophthalmology, 1975–80. Mem. Ophth. Soc. UK; Hon. Mem., Assoc. for Eye Res. *Publications:* Tonometry and Tonography, 1966; (jtly) Physiology of the Eye, System of Ophthalmology IV, ed Duke-Elder, 1968; contribs to jls. *Address:* Oversley, 24C Ickenham Road, Ruislip, Middlesex HA4 7BX.

GLOUCESTER, Bishop of, since 1993; **Rt. Rev. David Edward Bentley;** *b* 7 Aug. 1935; *s* of William Bentley and Florence (*née* Dalgleish); *m* 1962, Clarice Lahmers; two *s* two *d*. *Educ:* Gt Yarmouth Grammar School; Univ. of Leeds (BA English); Westcott House, Cambridge. Deacon 1960, priest 1961; Curate: St Ambrose, Bristol, 1960–62; Holy Trinity with St Mary, Guildford, 1962–66; Rector: Headley, Bordon, 1966–73; Esher, 1973–86; Suffragan Bishop of Lynn, 1986–93. Hon. Canon of Guildford Cathedral, 1980; RD of Emly, 1977–82. Warden, Community of All Hallows, Ditchingham, 1989–93. Chairman: Guildford dio. House of Clergy, 1977–86; Guildford dio. Council of Social Responsibility, 1980–86; ACCM Candidates Cttee, 1987–91; ABM Recruitment and Selection Cttee, 1991–93. *Recreations:* music; sport, especially cricket; theatre. *Address:* Bishopscourt, Pitt Street, Gloucester GL1 2BQ. *T:* Gloucester (01452) 524598, *Fax:* (01452) 310025. *Clubs:* Royal Commonwealth Trust, MCC.

GLOUCESTER, Dean of; *see* Jennings, Very Rev. K. N.

GLOUCESTER, Archdeacon of; *see* Wagstaff, Ven. C. J. H.

GLOVER, Anthony Richard Haysom; Chief Executive Officer, City Council of Norwich, 1980–88; *b* 29 May 1934; 2nd *s* of late Arthur Herbert Glover and late Marjorie Florence Glover; *m* 1960, Ann Penelope Scupham, *d* of late John Scupham, OBE; two *s* one *d*. *Educ:* Culford Sch., Bury St Edmunds; Emmanuel Coll., Cambridge (BA). HM Customs and Excise: Asst Principal, 1957; Principal, 1961; on secondment to HM Treasury, 1965–68; Asst Sec., 1969; Asst Sec., HM Treasury, 1972–76; Dep. Controller, HM Stationery Office, 1976–80. Sec., Norfolk Historic Bldgs Trust, 1991–95. University of East Anglia: Mem. Council, 1984–88; part-time Tutor, Dept. of Extra-Mural Studies, 1991–. *Recreations:* music, reading, writing, alpine gardening. *Address:* 7 Hillside Road, Thorpe St Andrew, Norwich NR7 0QG. *T:* Norwich (01603) 33508.

GLOVER, Audrey Frances, (Mrs E. C. Glover); HM Diplomatic Service; Director (with rank of Ambassador), Office of Democratic Institutions and Human Rights, Warsaw, since 1994; *d* of Robert John Victor Lush and Frances Lucy de la Roche; *m* 1971, Edward Charles Glover; two *s* two *d* (and one *s* decd). *Educ:* St Anne's Coll., Sanderstead, Surrey; King's Coll. London (LLB Hons). Called to the Bar, Gray's Inn, 1961; LCD, 1965–67; joined Foreign Office, as Asst Legal Advr, 1967; Asst (Temp.), Attorney Gen's Dept, Australia, 1972–73; Advr on British Law, Liby of Congress, Washington, 1974–77; Legal Advr (Asst), FCO, 1978–85; Legal Advr, British Mil. Govt, Berlin, 1985–89; Legal Counsellor, FCO, and UK Agent to EC and Ct of Human Rights, 1990–94. *Recreations:* collecting paintings, sailing, travelling, theatre. *Address:* Office for Democratic Institutions and Human Rights, Krucza 36/Wspólna 6, 00-522 Warsaw 53, Poland; Oak House, Thornham, Norfolk PE36 6LY. *Club:* Brancaster Staithe Sailing (Norfolk).

GLOVER, Eric; Secretary-General, Chartered Institute of Bankers (formerly Institute of Bankers), 1982–94; *b* 28 June 1935; *s* of William and Margaret Glover; *m* 1960, Adele Diane Hilliard; three *s*. *Educ:* Liverpool Institute High Sch.; Oriel Coll., Oxford (MA). Shell International Petroleum (Borneo and Uganda), 1957–63; Institute of Bankers, later Chartered Institute of Bankers, 1963–; Asst Sec., 1964–69; Dir of Studies, 1969–82. Chm., Council for Accreditation of Correspondence Colls, 1993– (Mem., 1983–); Treas., British Accreditation Council for Indep. Further and Higher Educn, 1987– (Mem., 1985–). Hon. Fellow, Sheffield Hallam Univ., 1992. Hon. FCIB. Hon. MBA City of London Polytechnic, 1991. *Publications:* articles on banking education. *Recreations:* mainly sport-golf, squash, tennis. *Address:* 12 Manor Park, Tunbridge Wells, Kent TN4 8XP. *T:* Tunbridge Wells (01892) 531221. *Club:* Bankers'.

GLOVER, Gen. Sir James (Malcolm), KCB 1981; MBE 1964; Director, British Petroleum plc, since 1987; Chairman, Royal Armouries International plc, since 1993; *b* 25 March 1929; *s* of Maj.-Gen. Malcolm Glover, CB, OBE and Jean Catherine Ogilvy (*née* Will); *m* 1958, Janet Diones De Pree; one *s* one *d*. *Educ:* Wellington College; RMA, Sandhurst. Commissioned, 1949; RHA, 1950–54; Instructor RMA Sandhurst, 1955–56; transferred to Rifle Brigade, 1956; Brigade Major, 48 Gurkha Inf. Bde, 1960–62; Directing Staff, Staff Coll., 1966–68; CO, 3rd Bn Royal Green Jackets, 1970–71; Col General Staff, Min. of Defence, 1972–73; Comdr 19 Airportable Bde, 1974–75; Brigadier General Staff (Intelligence), Min. of Defence, 1977–78; Commander Land Forces N Ireland, 1979–80; Dep. Chief of Defence Staff (Intelligence) and Mem., Jt Intelligence Cttee, 1981–83; Vice Chief of General Staff, and Mem., Army Bd, 1983–85; C-in-C, UKLF, 1985–87. Has served in W Germany, Malaya, Singapore, Hong Kong, Cyprus and N Ireland. Col Comdt, RGJ, 1984–88. *Recreations:* reading biographies, shooting, mountain walking. *Address:* c/o Lloyds Bank, Cox's & King's Branch, 7 Pall Mall, SW1Y 5NA. *Club:* Boodle's.

GLOVER, Jane Alison, DPhil; FRCM; conductor; *b* 13 May 1949; *d* of Robert Finlay Glover, *qv*. *Educ:* Monmouth School for Girls; St Hugh's Coll., Oxford (BA, MA, DPhil; Hon. Fellow, 1991). FRCM 1993. Oxford University: Junior Research Fellow, 1973–75, Sen. Res. Fellow, 1982–91, St Hugh's Coll.; Lecturer in Music: St Hugh's Coll., 1976–84; St Anne's Coll., 1976–80; Pembroke Coll., 1979–84; elected to OU Faculty of Music, 1979. Professional conducting début at Wexford Festival, 1975; thereafter, operas and concerts for: BBC; Glyndebourne (Musical Dir, Touring Opera, 1982–85); Royal Op. House, Covent Garden (début, 1988); ENO (début, 1989); Teatro la Fenice, Venice; London Symphony Orch.; London Philharmonic Orch.; Philharmonia Orch.; Royal Philharmonic Orch.; English Chamber Orch.; BBC Symphony Orch.; BBC Welsh Symphony Orch.; Scottish Nat. Orch.; Bournemouth Symphony Orch.; Bournemouth Sinfonietta; and many others in Italy, Holland, Denmark, Canada, Hong Kong, Austria, Yugoslavia, Germany, France, Belgium, Australia, NZ, etc.; Artistic Dir, London Mozart Players, 1984–91; Principal Conductor: London Choral Soc., 1983–; Huddersfield Choral Soc., 1989–96. A Gov., BBC, 1990–95. Member: BBC Central Music Adv. Cttee, 1981–85; Music Adv. Panel, Arts Council, 1986–87. Television documentaries and series, and presentation for BBC and LWT, esp. Orchestra, 1983, Mozart, 1985. Governor, RAM, 1985–90. Hon. DMus: Exeter, 1986; London, 1992; City, 1994; Hon. DLitt: Loughborough, 1988; Bradford, 1992; DUniv Open, 1988; Hon. DMus CNAA, 1991. ABSA/Daily Telegraph Arts Award, 1990. *Publications:* Cavalli, 1978; contribs to: The New Monteverdi Companion, 1986; Monteverdi 'Orfeo' handbook, 1986; articles in Music and Letters, Proc. of Royal Musical Assoc., Musical Times, The Listener, TLS, Early Music, Opera, and others. *Recreations:* The Times crossword puzzle, theatre. *Address:* c/o Lies Askonas Ltd, 6 Henrietta Street, WC2E 8LA. *T:* 0171–379 7700.

GLOVER, Group Capt. John Neville, CMG 1963; *b* 12 July 1913; *s* of John Robert Glover and Sybil Glover (*née* Cureton); *m* 1st, 1940, Margot Burdick; one *s*; 2nd, 1956, June Patricia Bruce Gaskell. *Educ:* Tonbridge Sch. Commissioned 6th Bn Devonshire Regt (TA), 1933; RAF (Gen. Duties Branch), 1934. Served RAF, 1934–46; RAFRO, 1946–59 (retained rank of Group Capt.). Called to Bar, Gray's Inn, 1949. Appointed to Colonial Legal Service, 1951; served: Ghana (Crown Counsel and Senior Crown Counsel), 1951–57; Western Pacific High Commission (Legal Adviser and Attorney-General, British Solomon Islands Protectorate), 1957–63. QC (Western Pacific), 1962. Retired from HM Overseas Civil Service, 1963. Comr to examine Human Rights Laws in the Bahamas, 1964–65. Legal Draftsman in the Bahamas, 1965–66. Law Revision Comr for certain overseas territories, 1967–91. *Recreation:* fishing. *Address:* Clam End, Trebullett, near Launceston, Cornwall PL15 9QQ. *T:* Coad's Green (01566) 782347. *Club:* Royal Air Force.

GLOVER, Prof. Keith, FRS 1993; FIEEE; Professor of Engineering, since 1989, and Fellow of Sidney Sussex College, since 1976, University of Cambridge; *b* 23 April 1946; *s* of William Frank Glover and Helen Ruby Glover (*née* Higgs); *m* 1970, Jean Elizabeth Priestley; one *s* one *d*. *Educ:* Dartford Grammar Sch., Kent; Imperial College London (BScEng); MIT (PhD). Development engineer, Marconi Co., 1967–69; Kennedy Meml Fellow, MIT, 1969–71; Asst Prof. of Electrical Engineering, Univ. of S California, 1973–76; Department of Engineering, University of Cambridge: Lectr, 1976–87; Reader in Control Engineering, 1987–89. *Publications:* (with D. C. McFarlane) Robust Controller Design using Normalized Coprime Factor Plant Descriptions, 1989; (with D. Mustafa) Minimum Entropy H-infinity Control, 1990; contribs to control and systems jls. *Address:* 41 Gough Way, Cambridge CB3 9LN. *T:* Cambridge (01223) 312197.

GLOVER, Kenneth Frank; Assistant Under-Secretary of State (Statistics), Ministry of Defence, 1974–81, retired; *b* 16 Dec. 1920; *s* of Frank Glover and Mabel Glover; *m* 1951, Iris Clare Holmes. *Educ:* Bideford Grammar Sch.; UC of South West, Exeter; LSE (MScEcon). Joined Statistics Div., MoT, 1946; Statistician, 1950; Statistical adviser to Cttee of Inquiry on Major Ports (Rochdale Cttee), 1961–62; Dir of Econs and Statistics at Nat. Ports Council, 1964–68; Chief Statistician, MoT and DoE, 1968–74. *Publications:* various papers; articles in JRSS, Dock and Harbour Authority. *Recreations:* boating, idleness. *Address:* Riverdown, 11 Platway Lane, Shaldon, Teignmouth, South Devon TQ14 0AR. *T:* Shaldon (01626) 872700.

GLOVER, Myles Howard; Secretary, Conference for Independent Further Education, since 1991; *b* 18 Dec. 1928; *yr s* of Cedric Howard Glover and Winifred Mary (*née* Crewdson); *m* 1969, Wendy Gillian, *er d* of C. M. Coleman; one *s* two *d*. *Educ:* Rugby; Balliol Coll., Oxford (MA). Called to the Bar, Lincoln's Inn, 1954. Clerk, Skinners' Co., 1959–90. Chm., Cttee of Clerks to Twelve Chief Livery Cos of City of London, 1975–81. Hon. Sec., GBA, 1967–91. Member: City & Guilds Art Sch. Cttee, 1960–71; Adv. Cttee, Gresham Coll., 1985–86; Governing Council: St Paul's Cathedral Choir Sch., 1986–90; Cambridge Tutors' Coll., 1993–94; Governing Body, St Leonards-Mayfield Sch., 1988–93; Hon. Addtl Mem., GBA Cttee, 1991. Hon. Member: Old Tonbridgian Soc., 1986; Old Skinners' Soc., 1990 (Leopard of the Year Trophy, 1990). Hon. Freeman: Fellmongers' Co., Richmond, N Yorks, 1991; Skinners' Co., 1993. *Recreation:* music. *Address:* Buckhall Farm, Bull Lane, Bethersden, near Ashford, Kent TN26 3HB. *T:* Bethersden (01233) 820634. *Club:* Savile.

GLOVER, Maj.-Gen. Peter James, CB 1966; OBE 1948; *b* 16 Jan. 1913; *s* of late G. H. Glover, CBE, Sheephatch House, Tilford, Surrey, and late Mrs G. H. Glover; *m* 1946, Wendy Archer; one *s* two *d*. *Educ:* Uppingham; Cambridge (MA). 2nd Lieut RA, 1934; served War of 1939–45, BEF France and Far East; Lieut-Col 1956; Brig. 1961; Comdt, Sch. of Artillery, Larkhill, 1960–62; Maj.-Gen. 1962; GOC 49 Infantry Division TA and North Midland District, 1962–63; Head of British Defence Supplies Liaison Staff, Delhi, 1963–66; Director, Royal Artillery, 1966–69, retd. Col Comdt, RA, 1970–78. *Address:* Lukesland, Diptford, Totnes, Devon TQ9 7NW.

GLOVER, Robert Finlay, TD 1954; Headmaster, Monmouth School, 1959–76; *b* 28 June 1917; *yr s* of T. R. Glover, Public Orator in University of Cambridge, and Alice, *d* of H. G. Few; *m* 1941, Jean, *d* of late N. G. Muir, Lincoln; one *s* two *d*. *Educ:* The Leys Sch.; Corpus Christi Coll., Oxford. Served in Royal Artillery (TA), 1939–46; Staff Coll., Camberley, 1944; Major, 1944. Asst Master, Ampleforth Coll., 1946–50; Head of Classics Dept, King's Sch., Canterbury, 1950–53; Headmaster, Adams' Grammar Sch., Newport, Salop, 1953–59; Dep. Sec., Headmasters' Conference and Assoc., 1977–82. Fellow, Woodard Corp., 1982–87. *Publications:* Notes on Latin, 1954; (with R. W. Harris) Latin for Historians, 1954. *Recreations:* normal. *Address:* Brockhill Lodge, West Malvern Road, The Wyche, Malvern, Worcs WR14 4EJ. *T:* Malvern (01684) 564247. *Club:* East India,

Devonshire, Sports and Public Schools.
See also J. A. Glover.

GLOVER, Stephen Charles Morton; journalist; *b* 13 Jan. 1952; *s* of Rev. Prebendary John Morton Glover and Helen Ruth Glover (*née* Jones); *m* 1982, Celia Elizabeth (*née* Montague); two *s*. *Educ:* Shrewsbury Sch.; Mansfield Coll., Oxford (MA). Daily Telegraph, 1978–85: leader writer and feature writer, 1978–85; parly sketch writer, 1979–81; Independent: Foreign Editor, 1986–89; Editor, The Independent on Sunday, 1990–91; Associate Editor, Evening Standard, 1992–. Dir, Newspaper Publishing, 1986–92. Vis. Prof. of Journalism, St Andrews Univ., 1992. *Publication:* Paper Dreams, 1993. *Address:* Evening Standard, 2 Derry Street, W8 5EE. *T:* 0171–938 6000. *Club:* Beefsteak.

GLOVER, Trevor David; UK Managing Director, The Penguin Group, since 1987; Chairman, Penguin Books, Australia, Ltd, since 1987; *b* 19 April 1940; *s* of Frederick Percy and Eileen Frances Glover; *m* 1967, Carol Mary Roberts; one *s* one *d*. *Educ:* Tiffin Sch., Kingston-upon-Thames; Univ. of Hull (BA Hons English Lang. and Lit.). Newspaper reporter, BC, Canada, 1963; began publishing career as college rep. with McGraw-Hill, Sydney, 1964; Coll. Sales Manager, 1966, later Gen. Manager, Professional and Reference Book Div., McGraw-Hill, UK; joined Penguin UK, 1970; UK Sales Manager, later UK Sales and Marketing Dir; Viking Penguin, NY, 1975–76; Man. Dir, Penguin Australia, 1976–87. Pres., Australian Book Publishers Assoc., 1983–85 and 1986–87; Mem. Council, Publishers Assoc., 1992–. *Recreation:* choral singing. *Club:* Groucho.

GLOVER, Hon. Sir Victor (Joseph Patrick), Kt 1989; Chief Justice, Mauritius, 1988–92; *b* 5 Nov. 1932; *s* of Joseph George Harold Glover and Mary Catherine (*née* Reddy); *m* 1960, Marie Cecile Ginette Gauthier; two *s*. *Educ:* Collège du St Esprit; Royal Coll., Mauritius; Jesus Coll., Oxford (BA (Hons) Jurisprudence). Called to the Bar, Middle Temple, 1957. District Magistrate, 1962; Crown Counsel, 1964; Sen. Crown Counsel, 1966; Prin. Crown Counsel, 1970; Parly Counsel, 1972; Puisne Judge, 1976; Sen. Puisne Judge, 1982. Actg Govenor General, July 1988, May 1989, June 1990 and Feb. 1991. Hon. Prof. of Civil Law, Univ. of Mauritius, 1986. Hon. Bencher, Middle Temple, 1991. *Publications:* Abstract of Decisions of Supreme Court of Mauritius 1966–1981, 1982, Supplement 1982–1986, 1987. *Recreations:* reading, swimming, bridge. *Address:* c/o Supreme Court, Port Louis, Mauritius. *Clubs:* Oxford Union Society; Oxford University Boat.

GLOVER, William James, QC 1969; a Recorder of the Crown Court, 1975–91; *b* 8 May 1924; *s* of late H. P. Glover, KC and Martha Glover; *m* 1956, Rosemary D. Long; two *s*. *Educ:* Harrow; Pembroke Coll., Cambridge. Served with Royal West African Frontier Force in West Africa and Burma, 1944–47. Called to Bar, Inner Temple, 1950, Bencher, 1977. Second Junior Counsel to Inland Revenue (Rating Valuation), 1963–69. *Recreation:* golf. *Address:* 1 Mitre Court Buildings, Temple, EC4Y 7BS; Lomea Barn, Stone-cum-Ebony, Kent TN30 7HY.

GLUCKSMANN, Dame Margaret Myfanwy Wood; *see* Booth, Dame Margaret.

GLUE, George Thomas; Director-General of Supplies and Transport (Naval), Ministry of Defence, 1973–77; *b* 3 May 1917; *s* of Percy Albert Glue and Alice Harriet Glue (*née* Stoner); *m* 1947, Eileen Marion Hitchcock; one *d*. *Educ:* Portsmouth Southern Secondary School. Admiralty: Asst Naval Store Officer, 1937; Dep. Naval Store Officer, Mediterranean, 1940; Naval Store Officer, Mediterranean, 1943; Asst Dir of Stores, 1955; Suptg Naval Store Officer, Devonport, 1960; Dep. Dir of Stores, 1963; Dir of Stores, 1970; Dir, Supplies and Transport (Naval), 1971. *Recreations:* gardening, bridge. *Address:* 18 Late Broads, Winsley, near Bradford-on-Avon, Wilts BA15 2NW. *T:* Bath (01225) 722717.

GLYN, family name of **Baron Wolverton.**

GLYN, Sir Alan, Kt 1990; ERD; *b* 26 Sept. 1918; *s* of John Paul Glyn, late Royal Horse Guards (Blues), Barrister-at-Law, Middle Temple, and late Margaret Johnston, Edinburgh; *m* 1962, Lady Rosula Caroline Windsor Clive, OStJ, *y d* of 2nd Earl of Plymouth, PC, GCStJ (*d* 1943), St Fagan's, Cardiff, S Wales; two *d*. *Educ:* Westminster; Caius Coll., Cambridge; St Bartholomew's and St George's Hosps. BA (Hons) Cantab 1939. Qualified medical practitioner, 1948. Served War of 1939–45; Far East, 1942–46; psc 1945; Bde Major, 1946; re-employed Captain (Hon. Major) Royal Horse Guards (ER) until 1967; att. French Foreign Legion, by special permission of French Govt, 1960. Called to Bar, Middle Temple, 1955. Co-opted Mem. LCC Education Cttee, 1956–58. MP (C) Clapham Div. of Wandsworth, 1959–64, Windsor, 1970–74, Windsor and Maidenhead, 1974–92. Member: Chelsea Borough Council, 1959–62; No 1 Divisional Health Cttee (London), 1959–61; Inner London Local Med. Cttee, 1967–92; Governing Body, Brit. Postgrad. Med. Fedn, 1967–82; Greater London Cent. Valuation Panel, 1967–91; Bd of Governors, Nat. Heart and Chest Hosps Special Health Auth., 1982–90. Former Governor, Henry Thornton and Aristotle Schs; Manager, Macaulay C of E Sch., Richard Atkins, Henry Cavendish, Telfescot, Glenbrook and Boneville Primary Schs in Clapham. One of Earl Marshal's Green Staff Officers at Investiture of HRH Prince of Wales, Caernarvon, 1969. Freeman, Worshipful Soc. of the Art and Mystery of Apothecaries of the City of London, 1961. Joined freedom fighters in Hungary during Hungarian Revolution, 1956; Pro-Hungaria Medal of SMO Malta, 1959; War correspondent, Vietnam, 1967. *Publication:* Witness to Viet Nam (the containment of communism in South East Asia), 1968. *Address:* 17 Cadogan Place, Belgrave Square, SW1X 9SA. *T:* 0171–235 2957. *Clubs:* Carlton, Pratt's, Royal Over-Seas League, Special Services.

GLYN, Sir Anthony (Geoffrey Leo Simon), 2nd Bt, *cr* 1927; author; *b* 13 March 1922; *s* of Sir Edward Davson, 1st Bt, and Margot, OBE (*d* 1966), *er d* of late Clayton Glyn and late Mrs Elinor Glyn; *S* father, Sir Edward Rae Davson, KCMG, 1937; assumed by deed poll, 1957, the surname of Glyn in lieu of his patronymic, and the additional forename of Anthony; *m* 1946, Susan Eleanor, barrister-at-law, 1950, *er d* of Sir Rhys Rhys-Williams, 1st Bt, DSO, QC, and Dame Juliet Rhys-Williams, DBE; one *d* (and one *d* decd). *Educ:* Eton. Jnd Welsh Guards, 1941; served Guards Armoured Div., 1942–45; Staff Captain, 1945. Vermeil Medal, City of Paris, 1985. *Publications:* Romanza, 1953; The Jungle of Eden, 1954; Elinor Glyn, a biography, 1955 (Book Society Non-Fiction Choice); The Ram in the Thicket, 1957 (Dollar Book Club Choice); I Can Take it All, 1959 (Book Society Choice); Kick Turn, 1963; The Terminal, 1965; The Seine, 1966; The Dragon Variation, 1969; The Blood of a Britishman, 1970 (US edn, The British; trans. French, Spanish, Japanese); The Companion Guide to Paris, 1985 (trans. Dutch). *Recreations:* skiing, chess. *Heir:* *b* Christopher Michael Edward Davson, ACA, late Capt. Welsh Guards [*b* 26 May 1927; *m* 1962, Evelyn Mary (marr. diss. 1971), *o d* of late James Wardrop; one *s*; 2nd, 1975, Kate, *d* of Ludovic Foster, Greatham Manor, Pulborough]. *Address:* Marina Baie des Anges, Ducal Apt. U-03, 06270 Villeneuve Loubet, Alpes Maritimes, France. *T:* 93736752. *Club:* Pratt's.

GLYN, Sir Richard (Lindsay), 10th Bt *cr* 1759, and 6th Bt *cr* 1800; *b* 3 Aug. 1943; *s* of Sir Richard Hamilton Glyn, 9th and 5th Bt, OBE, TD, and Lyndsay Mary (*d* 1971), *d* of T. H. Baker; *S* father, 1980; *m* 1970, Carolyn Ann Williams (marr. diss. 1979); one *s* one *d*. *Educ:* Eton. Co-Founder, High Lea Sch., 1982; Founder, Gaunts House Centre, 1989. *Recreation:* tennis. *Heir:* *s* Richard Rufus Francis Glyn, *b* 8 Jan. 1971. *Address:* Ashton Farmhouse, Wimborne, Dorset BH21 4JD. *T:* Witchampton (01258) 840585.

GLYNN, Prof. Alan Anthony, MD; FRCP, FRCPath; Director, Central Public Health Laboratory, Colindale, London, 1980–88, retired; Visiting Professor of Bacteriology, London School of Hygiene and Tropical Medicine, 1983–88; *b* 29 May 1923; *s* of late Hyman and Charlotte Glynn; *m* 1962, Nicole Benhamou; two *d*. *Educ:* City of London Sch.; University Coll. London (Fellow, 1982) and UCH Med. Sch., London (MB, BS 1946, MD 1959). MRCP 1954, FRCP 1974; MRCPath 1963, FRCPath 1973. House Physician, UCH, 1946; Asst Lectr in Physiol., Sheffield Univ., 1947–49; National Service, RAMC, 1950–51; Registrar, Canadian Red Cross Meml Hosp., Taplow, 1955–57; St Mary's Hospital Medical School: Lectr in Bacteriology, 1958–61; Sen. Lectr, 1961–67; Reader, 1967–71; Prof., 1971–80; Hon. Consultant Bacteriologist, 1961–83; Visiting Prof. of Bacteriology, St. Mary's Hosp., 1980–83. Examr in Pathol., Univs of Edinburgh, 1974–76, 1983–85, Glasgow, 1975–78, and London, 1979–80. Member: DHSS Jt Cttee on Vaccination and Immunization, 1979–85; Adv. Gp, ARC Inst. for Res. in Animal Diseases. Almroth Wright Lectr, Wright-Fleming Inst., 1972; Erasmus Wilson Demonstrator, RCS, 1973. Mem. Editorial Board: Immunology, 1969–79; Parasite Immunity, 1979–87. *Publications:* papers on bacterial infection and immunity in jls. *Recreations:* theatre, walking, carpentry. *Club:* Athenæum.
See also Prof. I. M. Glynn.

GLYNN, Prof. Ian Michael, MD, PhD, FRS 1970; FRCP; Professor of Physiology, University of Cambridge, 1986–95, now Emeritus; Fellow, Trinity College, since 1955 (Vice-Master, 1980–86); *b* 3 June 1928; 2nd *s* of late Hyman and Charlotte Glynn; *m* 1958, Jenifer Muriel, 2nd *d* of Ellis and Muriel Franklin; one *s* two *d*. *Educ:* City of London Sch.; Trinity Coll., Cambridge; University Coll. Hosp. 1st cl. in Pts I and II of Nat. Sci. Tripos; BA (Cantab) 1949; MB, BChir, 1952; MD 1970; FRCP 1987. House Phys., Central Mddx Hosp., 1952–53; MRC Scholar at Physiol. Lab., Cambridge; PhD 1956. Nat. Service in RAF Med. Br., 1956–57. Cambridge University: Res. Fellow, 1955–59, Staff Fellow and Dir of Med. Studies, 1961–73, Trinity Coll.; Univ. Demonstrator in Physiology, 1958–63; Lecturer, 1963–70; Reader, 1970–75; Prof. Membrane Physiology, 1975–86. Vis. Prof., Yale Univ., 1969. Member: MRC, 1976–80 (Chm., Physiological Systems and Disorders Bd, 1976–78); Council, Royal Soc., 1979–81, 1991–92; AFRC (formerly ARC), 1981–86. Hon. Foreign Mem., Amer. Acad. of Arts and Scis, 1984. Hon. MD Aarhus, 1988. Chm., Editorial Bd, Jl of Physiology, 1968–70. *Publications:* (with J. C. Ellory) The Sodium Pump, 1985; scientific papers dealing with transport of ions across living membranes, mostly in Jl of Physiology. *Address:* Trinity College, Cambridge CB2 1TQ. *T:* Cambridge (01223) 338415.
See also Prof. A. A. Glynn.

GOAD, Sir (Edward) Colin (Viner), KCMG 1974; Director, International Registries Inc., since 1980; *b* 21 Dec. 1914; *s* of Maurice George Viner Goad and Caroline (*née* Masters); *m* 1939, Joan Olive Bradley (*d* 1980); one *s*. *Educ:* Cirencester Grammar Sch.; Gonville and Caius Coll., Cambridge (Scholar, BA). Ministry of Transport: Asst Principal, 1937; Principal, 1942; Asst Sec., 1948; Imperial Defence Coll., 1953; Under-Sec., 1963; Dep. Sec.-Gen., 1963–68, Sec.-Gen., 1968–73, Inter-Govtl Maritime Consultative Orgn. *Address:* The Paddock, Ampney Crucis, Glos GL7 5RY. *T:* Cirencester (01285) 851353.

GOBBO, Hon. Sir James (Augustine), AC 1993; Kt 1982; **Hon. Mr Justice Gobbo;** Judge of the Supreme Court of Victoria, Australia, 1978–94; *b* 22 March 1931; *s* of Antonio Gobbo and Regina Gobbo (*née* Tosetto); *m* 1957, Shirley Lewis; two *s* three *d*. *Educ:* Xavier Coll., Kew, Victoria; Melbourne Univ. (BA Hons); Magdalen Coll., Oxford Univ. (MA; Pres., OUBC, 1955; Mem., Boat Race Crew, 1954, 1955). Called to Bar, Gray's Inn, London, 1956; Barrister and Solicitor, Victoria, Aust., 1956; signed Roll of Counsel, Victorian Bar, 1957; QC 1971. Indep. Lectr in Evidence, Univ. of Melbourne, 1963–68. Comr, Victorian Law Reform Commn, 1985–88. Chairman: Aust. Refugee Council, 1977; Aust. Multicultural Affairs Council, 1987–91; Aust. Bicentennial Multicultural Foundn, 1988–; Palladio Foundn, 1989–; Aust. Banking Industry Ombudsman Council, 1994–; Mercy Private Hosp., Melbourne, 1977–87 (Mem. Bd, Mercy Maternity Hosp., 1972–91); Caritas Christi Hospice, 1986–; Order of Malta Hospice Home Care, 1986–; Italian Historical Soc. of Vic, 1980–; Member: Council, Order of Australia, 1982–92; Exec., Council of Judges, 1986–; Nat. Population Council, 1983–87; Victorian Health Promotion Foundn, 1989–; Victorian Community Foundn, 1992–; Newman Coll. Council, 1970–85; Pres., CO-AS-IT, 1979–84, 1986–. Trustee: Victorian Opera Foundn, 1983–; WWF, Australia, 1991–. Vice-Pres., Aust. Assoc. of SMO Malta, 1984–87, Pres., 1987–; Pres., Scout Assoc. of Victoria, 1987–. Commendatore all'Ordine di Merito, Republic of Italy, 1973; Kt Grand Cross SMO Malta, 1982. *Publications:* (ed) Cross on Evidence (Australian edn), 1970–1978; various papers. *Address:* 6 Florence Avenue, Kew, Victoria 3101, Australia. *T:* (3) 8171669.

GOBLE, John Frederick; Solicitor; Consultant, Herbert Smith, since 1988 (Partner, 1953–88, Senior Partner, 1983–88; Hong Kong office, 1982–83); *b* 1 April 1925; *o s* of late John and Evileen Goble; *m* 1953, Moira Murphy O'Connor; one *s* three *d*. *Educ:* Finchley Catholic GS; Highgate Sch.; Brasenose Coll., Oxford. Sub-Lieut, RNVR, 1944–46. Admitted solicitor, 1951. Crown Agents, 1974–82 (Dep. Chm., 1975–82); Director: British Telecommunications, 1983–91; Wren Underwriting Agencies, 1988–91. A Dep. Chm., City Panel on Takeovers and Mergers, 1989–. Chm., St Barnabas Soc., 1992–95. Governor, Highgate Sch., 1976–. Chm., The Friends of Highgate Sch. Soc., 1978–87; Pres., Old Cholmeleian Soc., 1983–84. KCSG 1994. *Recreations:* music, golf, wine. *Address:* 52 Chelsea Park Gardens, SW3 6AD; Orchard Brae, Thurlestone, Kingsbridge, Devon TQ7 3NX. *Clubs:* Garrick, MCC, Hurlingham; New Zealand Golf (West Byfleet); Hon. Company of Edinburgh Golfers.

GODARD, Jean-Luc; French film director; *b* 3 Dec. 1930; *s* of Paul Godard and Odile Godard (*née* Monad); *m* 1st, 1961, Anna Karina (marr. diss.); 2nd, 1967, Anne Wiazemsky. *Educ:* Collège de Nyon; Lycée Buffon; Faculté de Lettres, Paris. Former journalist and film critic: La Gazette du cinéma; Les Cahiers du cinéma. Mem., Conseil supérieur de la langue française, 1989. *Films include:* A bout de souffle, 1959 (prix Jean Vigo, 1960; Best Dir Award, Berlin Fest., 1960); Le Petit Soldat, 1960; Une femme est une femme, 1961 (Special Prize, Berlin Fest.); Les sept péchés capitaux, 1961; Vivre sa vie, 1962 (Special Prize, Venice Fest.); Les Carabiniers, 1963; Les plus belles escroqueries du Monde, 1963; Le Mépris, 1963; Paris vu par . . ., 1964; Une femme mariée, 1964; Alphaville, 1965; Pierrot le fou, 1965; Masculin-Féminin, 1966; Made in USA, 1966; Deux ou trois choses que je sais d'elle, 1966; La Chinoise, 1967 (Special Prize, Venice Fest.); Week-end, 1967; Loin du Vietnam, 1967; La Contestation, 1970; Ici et ailleurs, 1976; (jtly) Tout va bien, 1972; Moi je, 1974; Comment ça va?, 1975; Sauve qui peut, 1980; Passion, 1982; Prénom Carmen, 1983 (Golden Lion, Venice Fest.); Je vous salue Marie, 1985; Détective, 1985; Soigne ta droite, 1987; Le Roi Lear, 1987; Nouvelle vague, 1990. Chevalier de l'ordre national du Mérite. *Publication:* Introduction à une véritable histoire du cinéma. *Address:* 15 rue du Nord, 1180 Rouille, Switzerland.

GODBER, Geoffrey Chapham, CBE 1961; DL; Chief Executive, West Sussex County Council, 1974–75, retired (Clerk of the Peace and Clerk to the Council, 1966–74); Clerk to the Lieutenancy of West Sussex, 1974–76 (Sussex, 1968–74); *b* 22 Sept. 1912; *s* of late Isaac Godber, Willington Manor, near Bedford; *m* 1937, Norah Enid (*née* Finney); three *s*. *Educ:* Bedford Sch. LLB (London) 1935; Solicitor, 1936. Deputy Clerk of the Peace, Northants, 1938–44; Clerk of the Peace, Clerk of the County Council and Clerk of the Lieutenancy, Salop, 1944–66; Hon. Sec., Soc. of Clerks of the Peace of Counties, 1953–61 (Chm., 1961–64); Chm., Assoc. of County Chief Executives, 1974–75. Member: Probation Adv. and Trg Bd, 1949–55; Child Care Adv. Council, 1953–56; Cttee of Inquiry into Inland Waterways, 1956–58; Redevelopment Adv. Cttee, Inland Waterways, 1959–62; Waterways Sub-Commn, Brit. Transport, 1959–62; Central Adv. Water Cttee, 1961–70; Minister of Health's Long Term Study Group, 1965–69; W Midlands Economic Planning Council, 1965–66; S-E Economic Planning Council, 1969–75; CS Adv. Council, 1971–78; British Waterways Bd, 1975–81; Chichester Harbour Conservancy, 1975–78; Shoreham Port Authority, 1976–82 (Dep. Chm., 1978–82); Chm., 1975–82, Pres., 1988–90, Open Air Museum, Weald and Downland. DL W Sussex 1975. Hon. Freeman, Chichester Harbour, 1994. *Recreation:* sailing. *Address:* Pricklows, Singleton, Chichester, West Sussex PO18 0HA. *T:* Singleton (01243) 811238. *Club:* Naval and Military.

See also Sir G. E. Godber.

GODBER, Sir George (Edward), GCB 1971 (KCB 1962; CB 1958); Chief Medical Officer, Department of Health and Social Security, Department of Education and Science, and Home Office, 1960–73; *b* 4 Aug. 1908; *s* of late I. Godber, Willington Manor, Bedford; *m* 1935, Norma Hathorne Rainey; two *s* one *d* (and two *s* two *d* decd). *Educ:* Bedford Sch.; New Coll., Oxford (Hon. Fellow, 1973); London Hospital; London Sch. of Hygiene. BA 1930, BM 1933, DM 1939, Oxon; MRCP 1935, FRCP 1947; DPH London 1936. Medical Officer, Min. of Health, 1939; Dep. Chief Medical Officer, Min. of Health, 1950–60. Chm., Health Educn Council, 1977–78 (Mem., 1976–78). QHP, 1953–56. Scholar in Residence, NIH Bethesda, 1975. Vice-Pres., RCN, 1973. Fellow: American Hospital Assoc., and American Public Health Assoc., 1961; British Orthopaedic Assoc.; Mem. Dietetic Assoc., 1961; Hon. Member: Faculty of Radiologists, 1958; British Pædiatric Assoc.; Royal Pharmaceut. Soc., 1973. FRCOG *ad eundem*, 1966; FRCPsych 1973; FFCM 1974; Hon. FRCS, 1973; Hon. FRCGP, 1973; Hon. FRSM, 1973. Hon. LLD: Manchester, 1964; Hull, 1970; Nottingham, 1973; Hon. DCL: Newcastle 1972; Oxford 1973; Hon. DSc Bath, 1979. Hon. Fellow, London Sch. of Hygiene and Tropical Medicine, 1976. Bisset Hawkins Medal, RCP, 1965; 150th Anniversary Medal, Swedish Med. Soc., 1966; Leon Bernard Foundn Medal, 1972; Ciba Foundn Gold Medal, 1970; Therapeutics Gold Medal, Soc. of Apothecaries, 1973. Lectures: Thomas and Edith Dixon Belfast, 1962; Bartholomew, Rotunda, Dublin, 1963; Woolmer, Bio-Engineering Soc., 1964; Monkton Copeman, Soc. of Apothecaries, 1968; Michael M. Davis, Chicago, 1969; Harold Diehl, Amer. Public Health Assoc., 1969; Rhys Williams, 1969; W. M. Fletcher Shaw, RCOG, 1970; Henry Floyd, Inst. of Orthopaedics, 1970; First Elizabeth Casson Meml, Assoc. of Occ. Therapists, 1973; Cavendish, W London Med.-Chir. Soc., 1973; Heath Clark, London Univ., 1973; Rock Carling, Nuffield Provincial Hosps Trust, 1975; Thom Bequest, RCSE, 1975; Maurice Bloch, Glasgow, 1975; Ira Hiscock, Yale, 1975; John Sullivan, St Louis, 1975; Fordham, Sheffield, 1976; Lloyd Hughes, Liverpool, 1977; Gale Meml, SW England Faculty RCGP, 1978; Gordon, Birmingham, 1979; Samson Gamgee, Birm. Med. Inst., 1979; W. H. Duncan, Liverpool, 1984; W. Pickles, RCGP, 1985; Green Coll., Oxford, 1988. *Publications:* (with Sir L. Parsons and Clayton Fryers) Survey of Hospitals in the Sheffield Region, 1944; The Health Service: past, present and future (Heath Clark Lectures), 1974; Change in Medicine (Rock Carling monograph), 1975; British National Health Service: Conversations, 1977; papers in Lancet, BMJ, Public Health. *Recreation:* golf. *Address:* 21 Almoners' Avenue, Cambridge CB1 4NZ. *T:* Cambridge (01223) 247491.

See also G. C. Godber.

GODBER, John Harry; playwright, since 1981; *b* 18 May 1956; *s* of Harry Godber and Dorothy (*née* Deakin); *m* 1993, Jane Thornton. *Educ:* Leeds Univ. (CertEd, BEd Hons, MA, MPhil). Sch. teacher, 1979–83; writing for TV, 1981–; Artistic Dir, Hull Truck Theatre Co., 1984–. *Plays:* Up 'N' Under, 1984; Bouncers, 1986; On the Piste, 1993; April in Paris, 1994; Passion Killers, 1994; Shakers: the musical, 1994; Lucky Sods, 1995. Sunday Times Play-writing Award, 1981; Olivier Award for Comedy of Year, 1984. Hon. DLitt Hull, 1988. *Publications:* Up 'N' Under, 1985; Bouncers, 1986; John Godber: 5 plays, 1989; On the Piste, 1991; April in Paris, 1992. *Recreations:* keep fit, reading, theatre, cinema, opera. *Address:* 64 Riverside Avenue, North Ferriby, Humberside HU14 3DT.

GODDARD, Ann Felicity, QC 1982; **Her Honour Judge Goddard;** a Circuit Judge, since 1993; *b* 22 Jan. 1936; *o c* of late Graham Elliott Goddard and Margaret Louise Hambrook Goddard (*née* Clark). *Educ:* Grey Coat Hosp., Westminster; Birmingham Univ. (LLB); Newnham Coll., Cambridge (LLM and Dip. in Comparative Legal Studies). Called to the Bar, Gray's Inn, 1960; Bencher, 1990; a Recorder, 1979–93. Member: Gen. Council of the Bar, 1988–93; Criminal Justice Consultative Council, 1992–93. Freeman, Clockmakers' Co., 1994. *Recreation:* travel. *Address:* 3 Temple Gardens, Temple, EC4Y 9AU. *T:* 0171–353 3102.

GODDARD, David Rodney, MBE 1985; Director, International Sailing Craft Association, since 1966; *b* 16 March 1927; *s* of Air Marshal Sir Victor Goddard, KCB, CBE, and Mildred Catherine Jane, *d* of Alfred Markham Inglis; *m* 1952, Susan Ashton; two *s* one *d*. *Educ:* Bryanston School; Wanganui Collegiate Sch., New Zealand; Peterhouse, Cambridge. MA Hons Geography. Joined Royal Marines, 1944, hostilities only commn, 1946, demob. 1948. Whaling, United Whalers, 1949; Schoolmaster, 1950–52. Joined Somerset Light Infantry, 1952; active service, Malaya (mentioned in despatches, 1954); served: Germany, Kenya (King's African Rifles), Bahrein, N Ireland; retired at own request, as Major, 1968, to found and direct Internat. Sailing Craft Assoc. and Exeter Maritime Museum; Dir, Exeter Maritime Mus., 1968–88, 1991–95. *Recreations:* shooting, fishing, sailing, bird watching, photography. *Address:* The Mill, Lympstone, Exmouth, Devon EX8 5HH. *T:* Exmouth (01395) 265575.

GODDARD, Harold Keith; QC 1979; barrister-at-law; a Recorder of the Crown Court, since 1978; *b* 9 July 1936; *s* of late Harold Goddard and Edith Goddard, Stockport, Cheshire; *m* 1st, 1963, Susan Elizabeth (marr. diss.), *yr d* of late Ronald Stansfield and of Evelyn Stansfield, Wilmslow, Cheshire; two *s*; 2nd, 1983, Alicja Maria, *d* of late Czeslaw Lazuchiewicz and of Eleonora Lazuchiewicz, Lodz, Poland. *Educ:* Manchester Grammar Sch.; Corpus Christi Coll., Cambridge (Scholar; 1st Cl. Law Tripos 1957; MA, LLM). Bacon Scholar, Gray's Inn; called to the Bar, Gray's Inn, 1959. Practised on Northern Circuit, 1959–. Mem., CICB, 1993–. Chm., Disciplinary Appeals Cttee, 1974–80, Mem. Council, 1980–, Mem. Ct of Governors, 1981, UMIST. *Recreation:* golf. *Address:* Deans Court Chambers, Cumberland House, Crown Square, Manchester M3 3HA. *T:* 0161–834 4097. *Club:* Wilmslow Golf.

GODDARD, Prof. John Burgess, OBE 1986; Henry Daysh Professor of Regional Development Studies, University of Newcastle upon Tyne, since 1975; *b* 5 Aug. 1943; *s* of Burgess Goddard and Molly Goddard (*née* Bridge); *m* 1966, Janet Patricia (*née* Peddle); one *s* two *d*. *Educ:* Latymer Upper Sch.; University Coll. London (BA); LSE (PhD). Lectr, LSE, 1968–75; Leverhulme Fellow, Univ. of Lund, 1974; University of Newcastle: Hon. Dir, Centre for Urban and Regional Develt Studies, 1978–; Dean, Faculty of Law, Envmt and Social Scis, 1994–. Dir, ESRC Prog. on Inf. and Communications Technol., 1992–93. Advr, Trade and Industry Select Cttee, H of C, 1994–95. Chm., Assoc. of Dirs of Res. Centres in Social Sciences, 1991–. Member: Northern Economic Planning Council, 1976–79; Human Geography Cttee, SSRC, 1976–80; Bd, Port of Tyne Authority, 1990–93. Governor, University of Northumbria at Newcastle (formerly Newcastle upon Tyne Poly.), 1989–. Editor, Regional Studies, 1980–85. FRSA 1992. Victoria Medal, RGS, 1992. *Publications:* Office Linkages and Location, 1973; Office Location in Urban and Regional Development, 1975; The Urban and Regional Transformation of Britain, 1983; Technological Change, Industrial Restructuring and Regional Development, 1986; Urban Regeneration in a Changing Economy, 1992; articles in professional jls.

GODDARD, Prof. Peter, PhD; FRS 1989; Professor of Theoretical Physics, University of Cambridge, since 1992; Master, St John's College, Cambridge, since 1994; *b* 3 Sept. 1945; *s* of Herbert Charles Goddard and Rosina Sarah Goddard (*née* Waite); *m* 1968, Helen Barbara Ross; one *s* one *d*. *Educ:* Emanuel Sch., London; Trinity Coll., Cambridge (BA, MA, PhD). Res. Fellow, Trinity Coll., Cambridge, 1969–73; Vis. Scientist, CERN, Geneva, 1970–72, 1978; Lectr in Applied Maths, Univ. of Durham, 1972–74; Mem., Inst. for Advanced Study, Princeton, NJ, 1974, 1988; Cambridge University: Asst Lectr 1975–76; Lectr 1976–89; Reader in Mathematical Physics, 1989–92; Dep. Dir, Isaac Newton Inst. for Mathematical Scis, 1991–94 (Sen. Fellow, 1994–); St John's College: Fellow, 1975–94; Lectr in Maths 1975–91; Tutor 1980–87; Sen. Tutor 1983–87. Vis. Prof. of Maths and Physics, Univ. of Virginia, 1983; SERC Vis. Fellow, Imperial Coll., 1987. Mem., Inst. for Theoretical Physics, Univ. of California, Santa Barbara, 1986, 1990. Governor: Berkhamsted Schs, 1985–; Emanuel Sch., 1992–; Shrewsbury Sch., 1994–. *Publications:* articles on elementary particle physics and mathematical physics in sci. jls. *Address:* The Master's Lodge, St John's College, Cambridge CB2 1TP. *T:* Cambridge (01223) 338635.

GODDARD, Air Vice-Marshal Peter John, AFC 1981; Deputy Commander, Interim Combined Air Operations Centre 4, since 1993; *b* 17 Oct. 1943; *s* of John Bernard Goddard and Lily Goddard; *m* 1966, Valerie White; two *s*. *Educ:* Nottingham High Sch. qwi, ndc, aws, rcds. Joined RAF 1963; served 54 and 4 Hunter Sqns, 233 Harrier and 226 Jaguar OCUs; OC, 54 Jaguar Sqn, 1978–80; MoD, 1981–83; OC, Tri-nat. Tornado Trng Estabt, RAF Cottesmore, 1984–86; RCDS 1988; Dir, Air Armament, 1989–93. *Recreations:* golf, gardening, walking. *Address:* c/o Air Secretary, Personnel Management Centre, Innsworth, Glos GL3 1EZ. *Clubs:* Royal Air Force; Felixstowe Ferry Golf.

GODDARD, Roy; independent business consultant, since 1988; Member, Independent Television Commission, since 1990; Chairman, Dyslexia Institute, since 1990; *b* 21 Feb. 1939; *s* of Roy Benjamin Goddard and Emma Annie Coronation (*née* Beckett); *m* 1961, Sally Anne Pain; one *s* one *d*. *Educ:* Henry Thornton Grammar Sch.; Regent Street Polytechnic. Cummins Engine Co., 1964–68; Partner, Alexander Hughes & Associates, executive search consultants, 1968–70; Founder, Goddard Kay Rogers & Associates, 1970–88. Mem., GMC, 1994–. Home Office selection panel appointee, Sussex Police Authy, 1994–. Liveryman, Co. of Glaziers and Painters of Glass. *Recreations:* squash, bad golf, water gardening, reading, eating, debating. *Address:* Newells, Brighton Road, Lower Beeding, West Sussex RH13 6NQ. *T:* Lower Beeding (01403) 891110. *Club:* Royal Automobile.

GODDEN, Charles Henry, CBE 1982; HM Diplomatic Service, retired; Governor (formerly HM Commissioner), Anguilla, 1978–83; *b* 19 Nov. 1922; *s* of late Charles Edward Godden and Catherine Alice Godden (*née* Roe); *m* 1943, Florence Louise Williams; two *d*. *Educ:* Tweeddale Sch., Carshalton; Morley Coll., Westminster. Served Army, 1941–46. Colonial Office, 1950–66 (seconded British Honduras, 1961–64: Perm. Sec., External Affairs; Dep. Chief Sec.; Clerk of Executive Council); FCO, 1966–: First Sec., 1968; Asst Private Sec. to Sec. of State for Colonies; Private Secretary: to Minister of State, FCO, 1967–70; to Parly Under Sec. of State, 1970; First Sec. (Commercial), Helsinki, 1971–75; First Sec., Belize, 1975–76; Dep. High Comr and Head of Chancery, Kingston, 1976–78. *Recreations:* cricket, walking, reading. *Address:* Stoneleigh, Blackboys, Sussex TN22 5JL. *T:* Framfield (01825) 890410. *Clubs:* MCC, Commonwealth Trust.

GODDEN, Prof. Malcolm Reginald, PhD; Rawlinson and Bosworth Professor of Anglo-Saxon, and Fellow of Pembroke College, Oxford, since 1991; *b* 9 Oct. 1945. *Educ:* Devizes Grammar Sch.; Barton Peveril Sch., Eastleigh; Pembroke Coll., Cambridge (BA 1966; MA, PhD 1970). Res. Fellow, Pembroke Coll., Cambridge, 1969–72; Asst Prof., Cornell Univ., 1970–71; Lectr in English, Liverpool Univ., 1972–75; Univ. Lectr in English, and Fellow, Exeter Coll., Oxford, 1976–91. Editor, Anglo-Saxon England, 1989–. *Publications:* (ed) Ælfric's Catholic Homilies, second series, 1979; The Making of Piers Plowman, 1990; The Cambridge Companion to Old English Literature, 1991; contribs to Anglia, English Studies, Anglo-Saxon England, Rev. of English Studies. *Address:* Pembroke College, Oxford OX1 1DW. *T:* Oxford (01865) 276444.

GODDEN, Ven. Max Leon; Archdeacon of Lewes and Hastings, 1975–88 (of Lewes, 1972–75); *b* 25 Nov. 1923; *s* of Richard George Nobel and Lucy Godden; *m* 1945, Anne, *d* of Kenneth and Edith Hucklebridge; four *d*. *Educ:* Sir Andrew Judd Sch., Tonbridge; Worcester Coll., Oxford (MA 1950). Served RAFVR, 1940–47 (despatches). Deacon, 1952; priest, 1953; Assistant Curate: Cuckfield, 1952–53; Brighton, 1953–57; Vicar of Hangleton, 1957–62; Vicar of Glynde, Firle and Beddingham, 1962–82. *Recreations:* life in a country parish, the garden. *Address:* 14 Oak Close, Chichester, W Sussex PO19 3AJ. *T:* Chichester (01243) 531344.

GODDEN, Rumer, (Margaret Rumer Haynes-Dixon), OBE 1993; writer, playwright, poet; *b* 10 Dec. 1907; *d* of late Arthur Leigh Godden, Lydd House, Aldington, Kent, and Katherine Norah Hingley; *m* 1934, Laurence Sinclair Foster (decd), Calcutta; two *d*; *m* 1949, James Haynes Dixon, OBE (*d* 1973). *Educ:* abroad and Moira House, Eastbourne. *Publications: novels:* Chinese Puzzle, 1935; Lady and Unicorn, 1937; Black Narcissus (novel and play), 1938; Gypsy Gypsy, 1940; Breakfast with the Nikolides, 1941; Fugue in Time (novel and play), 1945; The River, 1946 (filmed 1950); Candle for St Jude, 1948; A Breath of Air, 1950; Kingfishers Catch Fire, 1953; An Episode of Sparrows, 1955 (filmed 1957); The Greengage Summer, 1958 (filmed 1961); China Court, 1961; The Battle of the Villa Florita, 1963 (filmed 1964); (with Jon Godden) Two Under the Indian Sun, 1966; In This House of Brede, 1969; (with Jon Godden) Shiva's Pigeons, 1972; The Peacock Spring, 1975; Five for Sorrow, Ten for Joy, 1979; The Dark Horse, 1981; Thursday's Children, 1984; Coromandel Sea Change, 1991; Pippa Passes, 1994; *biography:* Rungli-Rungliot, 1943; Hans Christian Andersen, 1955; The Tale of the Tales, 1971; Gulbadan Begum: portrait of a Rose Princess at the Mughal Court, 1980; *poetry:* In Noah's Ark, 1949; *short stories:* Mooltiki, 1957; Swan and Turtles, 1968; (with Jon Godden) Indian Dust, 1989; *non-fiction:* (comp.) The Raphael Bible, 1970; *autobiography:* A Time to Dance, No Time to Weep, 1987; A House with Four Rooms, 1989; *children's books:* The Doll's House, 1949; The Mousewife, 1951; Impunity Jane, 1954; Fairy Doll, 1956; Mouse House, 1958; The Story of Holly and Ivy, 1958; Candy Floss, 1960; Miss Happiness and

Miss Flower, 1961; Little Plum, 1962; Home is the Sailor, 1964; The Kitchen Madonna, 1967; Operation Sippacik, 1969; The Old Woman Who Lived in a Vinegar Bottle, 1972; The Diddakoi, 1972 (Whitbread Award); The Dragon of Og, 1981; Four Dolls, 1983; Fu-Dog, 1989; A Kindle of Kittens, 1991; Listen to the Nightingale, 1992; Great Grandfather's House, 1992; published internationally (11 languages). *Address:* Macmillan & Co., 4 Little Essex Street, WC2R 3LF.

GODDEN, Tony Richard Hillier, CB 1975; Secretary, Scottish Development Department, 1980–87, retired; *b* 13 Nov. 1927; *o s* of late Richard Godden and Gladys Eleanor Godden; *m* 1953, Marjorie Florence Snell; one *s* two *d. Educ:* Barnstaple Grammar Sch.; London Sch. of Economics (BSc (Econ.) 1st cl.). Commissioned, RAF Education Branch, 1950. Entered Colonial Office as Asst Principal, 1951; Private Sec. to Parly Under-Sec. of State, 1954–55; Principal, 1956; Cabinet Office, 1957–59; transferred to Scottish Home Dept, 1961; Asst Sec., Scottish Development Dept, 1964; Under-Sec., 1969; Sec., Scottish Economic Planning Dept, 1973–80. Member: Council on Tribunals, 1988–94; Ancient Monuments Board for Scotland, 1990–. Sec., Friends of Royal Scottish Acad., 1987–. *Address:* 9 Ross Road, Edinburgh EH16 5QN. *T:* 0131–667 6556. *Club:* New (Edinburgh).

GODFREY, Gerald Michael; Hon. Mr Justice Godfrey; a Justice of Appeal, Supreme Court of Hong Kong, since 1993; *b* 30 July 1933; *s* of late Sidney Godfrey and late Esther (*née* Lewin); *m* 1960, Anne Sheila, *er d* of David Goldstein; three *s* two *d. Educ:* Lower Sch. of John Lyon, Harrow; King's Coll., London Univ. LLB 1952, LLM 1954. FCIArb 1990. Called to the Bar: Lincoln's Inn, 1954 (Bencher 1978); Bahamas, 1972; Hong Kong, 1974; Kenya, 1978; Singapore, 1978; Malaysia, 1979; Brunei, 1979; National Service as 2nd Lt, RASC, 1955; Temp. Captain, 1956. In practice at the Chancery Bar, 1957–86; QC 1971; a Judge of the High Court, Hong Kong, 1986–93. Chm., Justice Cttee on Parental Rights and Duties and Custody Suits (Report, 1975); DoT Inspector into Affairs of Saint Piran Ltd (Report, 1981). Member: Senate of Inns of Court and the Bar, 1974–77, 1981–84 (Chm., Law Reform Cttee, 1981–83); Council of Justice, 1976–81. *Publication:* Editor, Business Law Review, 1958. *Recreations:* walking, travel. *Address:* c/o Supreme Court, Hong Kong.

GODFREY, Rt. Rev. Harold William; *see* Uruguay, Bishop of.

GODFREY, Howard Anthony; QC 1991; a Recorder, since 1992; *b* 17 Aug. 1946; *s* of late Emanuel and of Amy Godfrey; *m* 1972, Barbara Ellinger; two *s. Educ:* William Ellis Sch.; LSE (LLB). Called to the Bar, Middle Temple, 1970; practising on SE Circuit, 1972–. *Recreations:* wine and food, travel, humour. *Address:* 3 Hare Court, Temple, EC4Y 7BJ. *T:* 0171–353 7561, *Fax:* 0171–353 7741; The Red House, Swallowfield Road, Arborfield Cross, Berks RG2 9JZ. *T:* Arborfield Cross (01734) 760657.

GODFREY, Louise Sarah, (Mrs Stanley Bland); QC 1991; a Recorder of the Crown Court, since 1989; *b* 17 April 1950; *d* of Philip Godfrey and Pearl (*née* Goodman); *m* 1977, Stanley Leslie Bland; two *d. Educ:* Tadcaster Grammar Sch.; St Hugh's Coll., Oxford (MA Jurisprudence). Called to the Bar, Middle Temple, 1972. *Recreations:* cooking, walking. *Address:* Park Court Chambers, 40 Park Cross Street, Leeds LS1 2QH. *T:* Leeds (0113) 243 3277.

GODFREY, Dr Malcolm Paul Weston, CBE 1986; Chairman, Public Health Laboratory Service Board, since 1989; *b* 11 Aug. 1926; *s* of late Harry Godfrey and of Rose Godfrey; *m* 1955, Barbara Goldstein; one *s* two *d. Educ:* Hertford Grammar Sch.; King's Coll., London Univ.; KCH Med. Sch. MB, BS (Hons and Univ. Medal) 1950; MRCP 1955, FRCP 1972. Hosp. posts at KCH, Nat. Heart and Brompton Hosps; RAF Med. Br., 1952–54; Fellow in Med. and Asst Physician, Johns Hopkins Hosp., USA, 1957–58; MRC Headquarters Staff, 1960–74: MO, 1960; Sen. MO, 1964; Principal MO, 1970; Sen. Principal MO, 1974; Dean, Royal Postgrad. Med. Sch., 1974–83 (Mem. Council, 1974–83, 1988–; Chm., Audit Cttee, 1995–; Hon. Fellow, 1985); Second Sec., MRC, 1983–88. University of London: Member: Senate, 1980–83; Court, 1981–83; Chm., Jt Med. Adv. Cttee, 1979–82. Mem., Faculty Bd of Clinical Medicine, Univ. of Cambridge, 1988–89. Chm., Brit. Council Med. Adv. Cttee, 1985–90; Member: Sci. Adv. Panel CIBA Foundn, 1974–91; Ealing, Hammersmith and Hounslow AHA(T), 1975–80; NW Thames RHA, 1980–83, 1985–88; Hammersmith SHA, 1982–83; Sec. of States Adv. Gp on London Health Services, 1980–81; GMC, 1979–81. Lay Mem., Professional Standards Dept, Gen. Council of the Bar, 1990–. Consultant Advr, WHO Human Reproduction Programme, 1979–90; Scientific Advr, Foulkes Foundn, 1983–89. Member, Council: Charing Cross Hosp. Med. Sch., 1975–80; St Mary's Hosp. Med. Sch., 1983–88; Royal Free Hosp. Sch. of Medicine, 1991–; Member: Governing Body, British Postgrad. Med. Fedn, 1974–89; Council of Governors, UMDS of Guy's and St Thomas' Hosps, 1990–. Mem. Court of Assts, Worshipful Soc. of Apothecaries, 1979–94 (Master, 1989–90; Assistant Emeritus, 1995). JP Wimbledon, 1972–92 (Chm. of the Bench and of Merton Magistrates' Courts Cttee, 1988–90 (Dep. Chm., 1987); Chm., Juvenile Panel, 1983–87). QHP, 1987–90. FRSA, 1989–92. *Publications:* contrib. med. jls on cardiac and respiratory disorders. *Recreations:* theatre, planning holidays (sometimes taking them), walking. *Address:* 17 Clifton Hill, St John's Wood, NW8 0QE. *T:* 0171–624 6335.

GODFREY, Norman Eric; *b* 16 Aug. 1927; *s* of Cecil and Beatrice Godfrey. *Educ:* Northampton Grammar Sch.; London Sch. of Econs (BScEcon). Career mainly in HM Customs but also served in Min. of Transport/DoE, 1968–71, and Price Commn, 1976–79; Comr, HM Customs and Excise, 1979–86. *Recreations:* music, especially opera, theatre, travel, tennis, walking. *Address:* 2 Belsize Avenue, NW3 4AU. *T:* 0171–435 6085.

GODFREY, Peter, FCA; Senior Partner, Ernst & Whinney, Chartered Accountants, 1980–86, retired; Chairman, Accounting Standards Committee, 1984–Sept. 1986 (Member, 1983–86); *b* 23 March 1924; *m* 1951, Heather Taplin; two *s* one *d. Educ:* West Kensington Central Sch. Served Army, 1942, until released, rank Captain, 1947. Qual. as an Incorporated Accountant, 1949; joined Whinney Smith & Whinney, 1949; admitted to partnership, 1959; Chm., Ernst & Whinney Internat., 1981–83, 1985–86. Appointed: BoT Inspector into Affairs of Pinnock Finance Co. (GB) Ltd, Aug. 1967; DTI Inspector into Affairs of Rolls-Royce Ltd, April 1971; Mem., ODM Cttee of Inquiry on Crown Agents, April 1975. Institute of Chartered Accountants: Mem., Inflation Accounting Sub-Cttee, 1982–84; Mem., Council, 1984–86. *Recreation:* family. *Address:* 2N Maple Lodge, Lythe Hill Park, Haslemere, Surrey GU27 3TE. *T:* Haslemere (01428) 656729.

GODFREY, Rt. Rev. William; *see* Godfrey, Rt Rev. H. W.

GODLEY, family name of **Baron Kilbracken.**

GODLEY, Prof. Hon. Wynne Alexander Hugh; Professor of Applied Economics, University of Cambridge, 1980–93 (Director, 1970–85, Acting Director, 1985–87, Department of Applied Economics); Fellow of King's College, Cambridge, since 1970; *b* 2 Sept. 1926; *yr s* of Hugh John, 2nd Baron Kilbracken, CB, KC and Elizabeth Helen Monteith, *d* of Vereker Monteith Hamilton; *m* 1955, Kathleen Eleonora, *d* of Sir Jacob Epstein, KBE; one *d. Educ:* Rugby; New Coll., Oxford; Conservatoire de Musique, Paris. Professional oboist, 1950. Joined Economic Section, HM Treasury, 1956; Dep. Dir, Economic Sect., HM Treasury, 1967–70. Dir, Investing in Success Equities Ltd, 1970–85. Official Advr, Select Cttee on Public Expenditure, 1971–73; an Economic Consultant, HM Treasury, 1975; Mem., Panel of Indep. Forecasters, 1992–95. Vis. Prof., Aalborg Univ., 1987–88; Distinguished Scholar, Jerome Levy Econs Inst., Annandale-on-Hudson, NY, 1991–92, 1993–95. Director: Royal Opera House, Covent Garden, 1976–87; Kent Opera, 1993–. *Publications:* (with T. F. Cripps) Local Government Finance and its Reform, 1976; The Planning of Telecommunications in the United Kingdom, 1978; (with K. J. Coutts and W. D. Nordhaus) Pricing in the Trade Cycle, 1978; (with T. F. Cripps) Macroeconomics, 1983; articles, in National Institute Review, Economic Jl, London and Cambridge Economic Bulletin, Cambridge Economic Policy Review, Economica, Jl of Policy Modelling, Manchester School, Nationalokonomisk Tidsskrift, Political Qly, New Statesman and Society, Observer, Guardian, London Review of Books, Financial Times. *Address:* Jasmine House, The Green, Cavendish, Suffolk CO10 8BB. *T:* Glemsford (01787) 281166.

GODMAN, Norman Anthony, PhD; MP (Lab) Greenock and Port Glasgow, since 1983; *b* 19 April 1938; *m* Patricia. *Educ:* Westbourne Street Boys' Sch., Hessle Road, Hull; Hull Univ. (BA); Heriot-Watt Univ. (PhD 1982). Nat. Service, Royal Mil. Police, 1958–60. Shipwright to trade teacher in Scottish further and higher educn. Mem., Select Cttee on European Legislation, 1989–. Contested (Lab) Aberdeen South, 1979. *Address:* House of Commons, SW1A 0AA.

GODSELL, Stanley Harry; Regional Director (South West), Departments of Environment and Transport, 1978–80; retired; *b* 19 March 1920; *s* of Thomas Harry Godsell and Gladys Godsell; *m* 1946, Rosemary Blackburn (*d* 1990); one *s* (and one *s* decd). *Educ:* Alsop High Sch., Liverpool. Civil Service: PO, 1937–48; Min. of Town and Country Planning, 1948; Asst Sec., Min. of Housing and Local Govt, 1965. *Recreations:* bridge, swimming, photography. *Address:* 6 Pitch and Pay Park, Sneyd Park, Bristol BS9 1NJ. *T:* Bristol (0117) 968 3791.

GODSIFF, Roger Duncan; MP (Lab) Birmingham, Small Heath, since 1992; *b* 28 June 1946; *s* of late George and of Gladys Godsiff; *m* 1977, Julia Brenda Morris; one *s* one *d. Educ:* Catford Comprehensive Sch. Bank clerk, 1965–70; political officer, APEX, 1970–90; senior research officer, GMB, 1990–92. Mem. (Lab) Lewisham BC, 1971–90 (Mayor, 1977). Contested (Lab) Birmingham, Yardley, 1983. *Recreations:* sport – particularly football and cricket, listening to music, spending time with family. *Address:* House of Commons, SW1A 0AA. *Clubs:* Rowley Regis Labour; Charlton Athletic Supporters.

GODWIN, Peter Raymond, CBE 1992; Managing Director, West Merchant Bank Ltd, since 1989; *b* 16 May 1942; *s* of Percy Raymond Godwin and Ethel Ellen May Godwin (*née* Dowse); *m* 1967, Wendy Dorothy Slater; one *s* one *d. Educ:* Harrow Co. Grammar Sch. ACIB 1965. Joined Lazard Brothers & Co. Ltd, 1958: Exec. Dir, 1979–86; Divl Dir, Standard Chartered Merchant Bank Ltd (later West Merchant Bank Ltd), 1986–89. Non-Executive Director: Korea Merchant Banking Corp., Seoul, 1976–86; Internat. Investment Corp. for Yugoslavia, SA, 1981–86; Standard Chartered Merchant Bank Zimbabwe Ltd, 1986–90; Financial Merchant Bank Nigeria Ltd, 1987–89. Chm., Compton Plough Ltd, 1995–; Dir, Swindon Town FC, 1995–. British Overseas Trade Board: Member: Korea Trade Adv. Gp, 1974–92; Anglo-Taiwan Trade Cttee, 1975–92 (Pres., 1986–92); Tropical Africa Adv. Gp, 1982–95; Chm., Asia Pacific Adv. Gp, 1992–. Chm., Anglo-Ghanaian Business Assoc., 1991–95. Gov., Latymer Foundn at Hammersmith, 1986–92. Organist and choirmaster, St Andrew's Church, Roxbourne, Harrow. Mem., Cinema Organ Soc. *Address:* 16 Newquay Crescent, Harrow, Middx HA2 9LJ. *T:* 0181–422 1801. *Club:* Somerset CC.

GODWIN, William Henry; *b* 29 Nov. 1923; *s* of George Godwin and Dorothy (*née* Purdon); *m* 1961, Lela Milosevic; one *s* one *d. Educ:* Colet Court; Lycée Français de Londres; St John's Coll., Cambridge. Called to the Bar, Middle Temple, 1948. Treasury Solicitor's Office, 1948–90; Under Sec., 1977; UK Agent before Europ. Ct of Justice, 1973–85; Legal Advr to Cabinet Office, European Secretariat, 1982–85. Consultant, 1990–. *Address:* 54 Gerard Road, SW13 9QQ.

GOEHR, Prof. Alexander; composer; Professor of Music, and Fellow of Trinity Hall, University of Cambridge, since 1976; *b* 10 Aug. 1932; *s* of Walter and Laelia Goehr. *Educ:* Berkhamsted; Royal Manchester Coll. of Music; Paris Conservatoire. Lectr, Morley Coll., 1955–57; Music Asst, BBC, 1960–67; Winston Churchill Trust Fellowship, 1968; Composer-in-residence, New England Conservatory, Boston, Mass, 1968–69; Associate Professor of Music, Yale University, 1969–70; West Riding Prof. of Music, Leeds Univ., 1971–76. Artistic Dir, Leeds Festival, 1975; Vis. Prof., Peking Conservatoire of Music, 1980. Reith Lectr, BBC, 1987. Mem., Bd of Dirs, Royal Opera House, 1982–84. Hon. Vice-Pres., SPNM, 1983–. Hon. Mem., Amer. Acad. and Inst. of Arts and Letters. Hon. FRMCM; Hon. FRAM 1975; Hon. FRNCM 1980; Hon. FRCM 1981. Hon. DMus: Southampton, 1973; Manchester, 1990; Nottingham, 1994. *Compositions include:* Songs of Babel, 1951; Fantasia Op. 4, 1954; String Quartet No. 1, 1957; La Belle Dame Sans Merci (ballet), 1958; Suite Op. 11, 1961; Hecuba's Lament, 1961; A Little Cantata of Proverbs, 1962; Concerto Op. 13, 1962; Little Symphony, 1963; Pastorals, 1965; Piano Trio, 1966; String Quartet No. 2, 1967; Romanza, 1968; Paraphrase, 1969; Symphony in One Movement, 1970; Concerto for Eleven, 1970; Concerto Op. 33, 1972; Chaconne for Wind, 1974; Lyric Pieces, 1974; Metamorphosis/Dance, 1974; String Quartet No. 3, 1976; Fugue on the notes of the Fourth Psalm, 1976; Romanza on the notes of the Fourth Psalm, 1977; Chaconne for Organ, 1979; Sinfonia, 1979; Kafka Fragments, 1979; Deux Etudes, 1981; Sonata, 1984; . . . a musical offering (JSB 1985), 1985; Symphony with Chaconne, 1986; . . . in real time, 1989; Still Lands, 1990; Bach Variations, 1990; *Vocal:* The Deluge, 1958; Sutter's Gold, 1960; Virtutes, 1963; Arden Must Die (opera), 1966; Triptych (Naboth's Vineyard, 1968; Shadowplay, 1970; Sonata about Jerusalem, 1970); Psalm IV, 1976; Babylon the Great is Fallen, 1979; The Law of the Quadrille, 1979; Behold the Sun, 1981; Behold the Sun (opera), 1984; Eve Dreams in Paradise, 1988; Sing Ariel, 1990; The Death of Moses, 1992; Colossos or Panic, 1993; Arianna (opera), 1995. *Address:* Trinity Hall, Cambridge CB2 1TJ; University Music School, West Road, Cambridge CB3 9DP; c/o Schott & Co Ltd, 48 Great Marlborough Street, W1V 2BN.

GOFF, family name of **Baron Goff of Chieveley.**

GOFF OF CHIEVELEY, Baron *cr* 1986 (Life Peer), of Chieveley in the Royal County of Berkshire; **Robert Lionel Archibald Goff;** Kt 1975; PC 1982; DCL; FBA 1987; a Lord of Appeal in Ordinary, since 1986; *b* 12 Nov. 1926; *s* of Lt-Col L. T. Goff and Mrs Goff (*née* Denroche-Smith); *m* 1953, Sarah, *er d* of Capt. G. R. Cousins, DSC, RN; one *s* two *d* (and one *s* decd). *Educ:* Eton Coll.; New Coll., Oxford (MA 1953, DCL 1972; Hon. Fellow, 1986). Served in Scots Guards, 1945–48 (commnd 1945). 1st cl hons Jurisprudence, Oxon, 1950. Called to the Bar, Inner Temple, 1951; Bencher, 1975; QC 1967. Fellow and Tutor, Lincoln Coll., Oxford, 1951–55; in practice at the Bar, 1956–75; a Recorder, 1974–75; Judge of the High Ct, QBD, 1975–82; Judge i/c Commercial List, and Chm. Commercial Court Cttee, 1979–81; a Lord Justice of Appeal, 1982–86. Chm., Sub-Cttee E (Law and Instns), H of L Select Cttee on EC, 1986–88. Chairman: Council of Legal Educn, 1976–82 (Vice-Chm., 1972–76; Chm., Bd of Studies, 1970–76); Common

Professional Examination Bd, 1976–78; Court, London Univ., 1986–91; Pegasus Scholarship Trust, 1987–. High Steward, Oxford Univ., 1991–. Hon. Prof. of Legal Ethics, Univ. of Birmingham, 1980–81; Lectures: Maccabean, British Acad., 1983; Lionel Cohen Meml, Hebrew Univ. of Jerusalem, 1987; Cassel, Stockholm Univ., 1993. Member: Gen. Council of the Bar, 1971–74; Senate of Inns of Court and Bar, 1974–82 (Chm., Law Reform and Procedure Cttee, 1974–76). Chm., British Inst. of Internat. and Comparative Law, 1986–. President: CIArb, 1986–91; Bentham Club, 1986; Holdsworth Club, 1986–87. Hon. Fellow: Lincoln Coll., Oxford, 1985; New Coll., Oxford, 1986. Hon. DLitt: City, 1977; Reading, 1990; Hon. LLD: Buckingham, 1990; London, 1990. *Publication:* (with Prof. Gareth Jones) The Law of Restitution, 1966. *Address:* House of Lords, Westminster, SW1A 0PW.

GOFF, Martyn, OBE 1977; Chairman, Book Trust, since 1992 (Deputy Chairman, 1991–92); Executive Chairman, Sotherans, since 1988; *b* 7 June 1923; *s* of Jacob and Janey Goff. *Educ:* Clifton College. Served in Royal Air Force, 1941–46. Film business, 1946–48; bookseller, 1948–70; Dir, NBL, later Chief Exec., Book Trust, 1970–88 (Administrator, Booker Prize, 1970–). Has lectured on: music; English fiction; teenager morality; the book trade, 1946–70; fiction reviewer, 1975–88, non-fiction, 1988–, Daily Telegraph. Founder and Chm., Bedford Square Bookbang, 1971. Member: Arts Council Literature Panel, 1970–78; Arts Council Trng Cttee, 1973–78; Greater London Arts Assoc. Literature Panel, 1973–81; British Nat. Bibliography Res. Fund, 1976–88; British Library Adv. Council, 1977–82; PEN Exec. Cttee, 1978–; Exec. Cttee, Gtr London Arts Council, 1982–88; Library and Information Services Council, 1984–86; Board: British Theatre Assoc., 1983–85; Poetry Book Soc., 1992–; Chairman: Paternosters '73 Library Adv. Council, 1972–74; New Fiction Soc., 1975–88; School Bookshop Assoc., 1977–; Soc. of Bookmen, 1982–84; 1890s Soc., 1990–; Dir, Battersea Arts Centre, 1992– (Trustee, 1981–85); Trustee: Cadmean Trust, 1981–; Nat. Literacy Trust, 1993–. Judge, Glenfiddich Awards, 1993. FIAL 1958, FRSA 1979. *Publications: fiction:* The Plaster Fabric, 1957; A Season with Mammon, 1958; A Sort of Peace, 1960; The Youngest Director, 1961, new edn 1985; Red on the Door, 1962; The Flint Inheritance, 1965; Indecent Assault, 1967; The Liberation of Rupert Bannister, 1978; Tar and Cement, 1988; *non-fiction:* A Short Guide to Long Play, 1957; A Further Guide to Long Play, 1958; LP Collecting, 1960; Why Conform?, 1968; Victorian and Edwardian Surrey, 1972; Record Choice, 1974; Royal Pavilion, 1976; Organising Book Exhibitions, 1982; Publishing, 1988; Prize Writing, 1989. *Recreations:* travel, collecting paintings and sculptures, music. *Address:* 95 Sisters Avenue, SW11 5SW. *Clubs:* Athenæum, Savile, Groucho, Academy.

GOFF, Sir Robert (William Davis-), 4th Bt *cr* 1905; Director, O'Connor & Co., Art Dealers and Property Investment Co., Dublin; *b* 12 Sept. 1955; *s* of Sir Ernest William Davis-Goff, 3rd Bt, and of Alice Cynthia Davis-Goff (*née* Woodhouse); *S* father, 1980; *m* 1978, Nathalie Sheelagh, *d* of Terence Chadwick; three *s* one *d*. *Educ:* Cheltenham College, Glos. *Recreation:* shooting. *Heir:* *s* William Nathaniel Davis-Goff, *b* 20 April 1980.

GOGUEN, Prof. Joseph Amadee; Professor of Computing Science, University of Oxford, since 1988; *b* 28 June 1941; *s* of Joseph Amadee Goguen and Helen Stratton; *m* 1st, 1961, Nancy Hammer; one *s* one *d*; 2nd, 1981, Kathleen Morrow; one *d*. *Educ:* Harvard Univ. (BA); Univ. of California at Berkeley (MA, PhD). Asst Prof., Cttee on Inf. Sciences, Univ. of Chicago, 1968–73; Academic Staff, Naropa Inst., Boulder Colo, 1974–78; Prof., Computer Sci. Dept, UCLA, 1973–79; Man. Dir, Structural Semantics, Palo Alto, 1978–; Sen. Staff Scientist, SRI Internat., Menlo Park, Calif, 1979–88; Sen. Mem., Center for Study of Language and Inf., Stanford Univ., 1984–88. IBM Postdoctoral Fellowship, T. J. Watson Res. Center, 1971; Sen. Vis. Fellow, Univ. of Edinburgh, 1976, 1977, 1983. Exceptional Achievement Award, SRI Internat., 1984. *Publications:* (ed) Theory and Practice of Software Technology, 1983; (ed jtly) Requirements Engineering: social and technical issues, 1994; over 150 articles in professional jls. *Address:* Programming Research Group, University of Oxford, Wolfson Building, Parks Road, Oxford OX1 3QD. *T:* Oxford (01865) 283504, *Fax:* (01865) 273839.

GOH CHOK TONG; Prime Minister of Singapore, since 1990; *b* 20 May 1941; *m* Tan Choo Leng; one *s* one *d* (twins). *Educ:* Raffles Instn; Univ. of Singapore (1st cl. Hons Econs); Williams Coll., USA. Joined Admin. Service, Singapore Govt, 1964, Econ. Planning Unit, Min. of Finance; Planning and Projects Manager, Neptune Orient Lines, 1969–73, Man. Dir, 1973–77. MP for Marine Parade, 1976–; Sen. Minister of State for Finance, 1977–79; Minister: for Trade and Industry, 1979–81; for Health, 1981–85; for Defence, 1981–91; First Dep. Prime Minister, 1985–90. People's Action Party: Mem., Central Exec. Cttee, 1979–; First Organising Sec., 1979; Second Asst Sec. Gen., 1979–84; Asst Sec. Gen., 1984–89; First Asst Sec. Gen., 1989–92; Sec. Gen., 1992–. Formerly Chairman: Singapore Labour Foundn; NTUC Income, NTUC Fairprice. Medal of Honour, NTUC, 1987. *Recreations:* golf, tennis. *Address:* Prime Minister's Office, Istana Annexe, Istana, Singapore 0923.

GOHEEN, Robert Francis; educator; President Emeritus, and Senior Fellow, Public and International Affairs, since 1981, Princeton University; *b* Venguria, India, 15 Aug. 1919; *s* of Dr Robert H. H. Goheen and Anne Ewing; *m* 1941, Margaret M. Skelly; two *s* four *d*. *Educ:* Princeton Univ. AB 1940; PhD 1948. Princeton University: Instructor, Dept of Classics, 1948–50; Asst Prof., 1950–57; Prof., 1957–72; President, 1957–72. Chm., Council on Foundns, 1972–77; US Ambassador to India, 1977–80; Dir, Mellon Fellowships in Humanities, 1982–92. Sen. Fellow in Classics, Amer. Academy in Rome, 1952–53; Dir Nat. Woodrow Wilson Fellowship Program, 1953–56. Member: Adv. Commn on Oceans and Internat. Scientific and Environmental Affairs, US State Dept; Adv. Bd, Nat. Foreign Language Center; Adv. Council, S Asia Inst., Columbia Univ.; Adv. Council, Woodrow Wilson Sch., Princeton Univ.; American Philosophical Soc.; American Academy of Arts and Sciences; Phi Beta Kappa; Trustee: Nat. Humanities Center; Bharatiya Vidya Bhavan (USA). Former Mem. Internat Adv. Bd, Chemical Bank; former Member of Board: Amer. Univ. in Beirut; Carnegie Foundn for Advancement of Teaching; Carnegie Endowment for Internat. Peace; United Bd of Christian Higher Educn in Asia; Rockefeller Foundn; Asia Soc.; Amer. Acad. in Rome; Inst. of Internat. Educn; Equitable Life; Thomson Newspapers Inc.; Dreyfus Third Century Fund; Midlantic Nat. Bank; Reza Shah Kabir Univ., Iran; Univ. Service Cttee, Hong Kong. Hon. degrees: Harvard, Rutgers, Yale, Temple, Brown, Columbia, New York, Madras, Pennsylvania, Hamilton, Middlebury, Saint Mary's (Calif), State of New York, Denver, Notre Dame, N Carolina, Hofstra, Nebraska, Dropsie, Princeton; Tusculum Coll.; Trinity Coll., USA; Coll. of Wooster; Jewish Theological Seminary of America; Ripon Coll.; Rider Coll. *Publications:* The Imagery of Sophocles' Antigone, 1951; The Human Nature of a University, 1969; articles. *Recreations:* books, golf. *Address:* 1 Orchard Circle, Princeton, NJ 08540, USA. *T:* (609) 9242751. *Clubs:* Princeton, University, Century Association (New York); Cosmos (Washington); Nassau (Princeton); Gymkhana, Delhi Golf (Delhi).

GOLD, Sir Arthur (Abraham), Kt 1984; CBE 1974; Chairman, Commonwealth Games Council for England, 1979–90; Honorary Secretary, British Amateur Athletic Board, 1965–77 (Life Vice President, 1977); Vice President, British Olympic Association, since 1992 (Chairman, 1988–92); *b* 10 Jan. 1917; *s* of late Mark and Leah Gold; *m* 1942, Marion Godfrey, *d* of late N. Godfrey; one *s*. *Educ:* Grocers' Company's Sch. Inst. of Motor Industry Wakefield Gold Medallist, 1945. Internat. high jumper, 1937; Athletics Team Leader Olympic Games: Mexico, 1968; Munich, 1972; Montreal, 1976; Commandant, English Commonwealth Games Team: Brisbane, 1982; Edinburgh, 1986; Auckland, 1990; Comdt, British Olympic Team, Albertville and Barcelona, 1992. Chm., Drug Abuse Adv. Cttee, Eur. Sports Conf., 1985–91; Vice-Chm., Cttee on Doping in Sport, Council of Europe, 1983–90; Member: Sports Council, 1980–88 (Chm., Drug Abuse Adv. Gp, 1981–92); Exec. Cttee, CCPR, 1982–90. President: Eur. Athletic Assoc., 1976–87 (Hon. Life Pres., 1988; Mem. Council, 1966–76); Counties Athletic Union, 1978–; UAU, 1984–; AAA of England, 1994–; Past President: London Athletic Club; Middlesex Co. Amateur Athletic Assoc. Hon. FCP 1987. Hon. DTech Loughborough, 1989; Hon. LLD Sheffield, 1991. Olympic Order (Silver), 1991. *Publications:* Ballet Training Exercises for Athletes, 1960; various contribs to technical books on athletics. *Recreations:* walking, talking, reading, weeding. *Address:* 49 Friern Mount Drive, Whetstone, N20 9DJ. *T:* 0181–445 2848. *Clubs:* City Livery, MCC; London Athletic.

GOLD, Jack; film director; *b* 28 June 1930; British; *m* 1957, Denyse (*née* Macpherson); two *s* one *d*. *Educ:* London Univ. (BSc (Econs), LLB). Asst Studio Manager, BBC radio, 1954–55; Editor, Film Dept, BBC, 1955–60; Dir, TV and film documentaries and fiction, 1960–. Desmond Davies Award for services to television, BAFTA, 1976. *TV films:* Tonight; Death in the Morning (BAFTA Award, 1964); Modern Millionairess; Famine; Dispute; 90 Days; Dowager in Hot Pants; World of Coppard (BAFTA Award, 1968); Mad Jack (Grand Prix, Monte Carlo, 1971); Stocker's Copper (BAFTA Award, 1972); Arturo Ui; The Lump; Catholics (Peabody Award, 1974); The Naked Civil Servant (Italia Prize, 1976, Internat. Emmy, and Critics Award, 1976); Thank You Comrades; Marya; Charlie Muffin; A Walk in the Forest; Merchant of Venice; Bavarian Night; A Lot of Happiness (Kenneth Macmillan), 1981 (Internat. Emmy Award); Praying Mantis, Macbeth, L'Elegance, 1982; The Red Monarch, 1983; Good and Bad at Games, 1983; Sakharov, 1984 (Assoc. Cable Enterprises Award); Murrow, 1986 (Assoc. Cable Enterprises Award); Me and the Girls, 1985; Escape from Sobibor, 1987 (Golden Globe Award); Stones for Ibarra, 1988; The Tenth Man, 1989; Masterclass, 1989; Ball-trap on the Côte Sauvage, 1989; The Rose and the Jackal, 1990; She Stood Alone, 1991 (Christopher Award); The Last Romantics, 1992; *cinema:* The Bofors Gun, 1968; The Reckoning, 1969; The National Health, 1973 (Evening News Best Comedy Award); Who?, 1974; Man Friday, 1974; Aces High, 1976 (Evening News Best Film Award); The Medusa Touch, 1977; The Sailor's Return, 1978 (jt winner, Martin Luther King Meml Prize, 1980; Monte Carlo Catholic Award, 1981; Monte Carlo Critics Award, 1981); Little Lord Fauntleroy, 1981 (Christopher Award); The Chain, 1985; The Lucona Affair, 1993; Return of the Native, 1994; Spring Awakening, 1994; *theatre:* The Devil's Disciple, Aldwych, 1976; This Story of Yours, Hampstead, 1987; Danger! Memory, Hampstead, 1988; Three Hotels, Tricycle Th., 1993. *Recreations:* music, reading, tennis. *Address:* 24 Wood Vale, N10 3DP.

GOLD, John (Joseph Manson); Public Relations Consultant, 1979–90, retired; Manager of Public Relations, Hong Kong Mass Transit Railway, 1975–79; *b* 2 Aug. 1925; *m* 1953, Berta Cordeiro; one *d*. *Educ:* Clayesmore Sch., Dorset. Yorkshire Evening News, 1944–47; London Evening News, 1947–52; Australian Associated Press (New York), 1952–55; New York Corresp., London Evening News, 1955–66; Editor, London Evening News, 1967–72; Dir, Harmsworth Publications Ltd, 1967–73. Free-lance writer and lectr, Far East, 1973–75.

GOLD, Sir Joseph, Kt 1980; Senior Consultant, International Monetary Fund, since 1979; *b* 12 July 1912; *m* 1939, Ruth Schechter; one *s* two *d*. *Educ:* Univ. of London (LLB 1935, LLM 1936); Harvard Univ. (SJD). Asst Lectr, University Coll., London, 1937–39; British Mission, Washington, DC, 1942–46; joined IMF, 1946; General Counsel and Dir, Legal Dept, 1960–79. Hon. LLD Southern Methodist Univ., 1985. Silver Medal, Columbia Univ., 1982; Theberge Medal in Internat. Law, Amer. Bar Assoc., 1989. *Publications:* The Fund Agreement in the Courts, vol. I 1962, vol. II 1982, vol. III 1986, vol. IV 1989 (Festschrift); The Stand-by Arrangements of the IMF, 1970; Voting and Decisions in the IMF, 1972; Membership and Nonmembership in the IMF, 1974; Los Acuerdos de Derechos de Giro del Fondo Monetario Internacional, 1976; Legal and Institutional Aspects of the International Monetary System, vol I, 1979, vol II, 1984; Aspectos Legales de La Reforma Monetario Internacional, 1979; Exchange Rates in International Law and Organisation, 1988; Legal Effects of Fluctuating Exchange Rates, 1990; numerous pamphlets and articles on internat. and nat. monetary law in many countries. *Recreations:* collecting first editions 20th century English and American poetry, assemblages of found objects, gardening, defence of English language. *Address:* 7020 Braeburn Place, Bethesda, MD 20817, USA. *T:* (301) 2293278.

GOLD, Stephen Charles, MA, MD, FRCP; Consulting Physician to: the Skin Department, St George's Hospital; St John's Hospital for Diseases of the Skin; King Edward VII Hospital for Officers; Former Hon. Consultant in Dermatology: to the Army; to Royal Hospital, Chelsea; *b* Bishops Stortford, Herts, 10 Aug. 1915; *yr s* of late Philip Gold, Stansted, Essex, and late Amy Frances, *er d* of James and Mary Perry; *m* 1941, Betty Margaret, *o d* of late Dr T. P. Sheedy, OBE; three *s* one *d*. *Educ:* Radley Coll.; Gonville and Caius Coll., Cambridge; St George's Hosp. (Entrance Exhibnr); Zürich and Philadelphia. BA 1937; MRCS, LRCP 1940; MA, MB, BChir 1941; MRCP 1947; MD 1952; FRCP 1958. Served RAMC, 1941–46. Late Med. First Asst to Out-Patients, St George's Hosp., Senior Registrar, Skin Dept, St George's Hosp., Sen. Registrar, St John's Hosp. for Diseases of the Skin; Lectr in Dermatology, Royal Postgraduate Med. Sch., 1949–69. Sec., Brit. Assoc. of Dermatology, 1965–70 (Pres., 1979). FRSM (late Sec. Dermatological Section, Pres., 1972–73); Fellow St John's Hosp. Dermatological Soc. (Pres., 1965–66).

GOLD, Prof. Thomas, FRS 1964; John L. Wetherill Professor of Astronomy, Cornell University, 1971–86, Professor Emeritus of Astronomy, 1987; *b* 22 May 1920; *s* of Max and Josefine Gold; *m* 1st, 1947, Merle E. Gold (*née* Tuberg); three *d*; 2nd, 1972, Carvel B. Gold (*née* Beyer); one *d*. *Educ:* Zuoz Coll., Switzerland; Trinity Coll., Cambridge (Hon. Fellow, 1986). BA Mechanical Sciences (Cambridge), 1942; MA Mechanical Sciences, Cambridge, 1946; ScD, Cambridge, 1969. Fellow Trinity Coll., Cambridge, 1947–51. British Admiralty, 1942–46; Cavendish Laboratory, Cambridge, 1946–47 and 1949–52; Med. Research Council, Zoological Lab., Cambridge, 1947–49; Sen. Principal Scientific Officer (Chief Asst), Royal Greenwich Observatory, 1952–56; Prof. of Astronomy, 1957–58, Robert Wheeler Willson Prof. of Applied Astronomy, 1958–59, Harvard Univ. Dir, Center for Radio-Physics and Space Research, Cornell Univ., 1959–81. Hon. MA (Harvard), 1957. Member: Amer. Philosophical Soc.; Nat. Acad. of Sciences; Fellow, Amer. Acad. of Arts and Sciences. Gold Medal, RAS, 1985. *Publications:* Power from the Earth, 1987; contribs to learned journals on astronomy, physics, biophysics, geophysics. *Recreations:* ski-ing, travelling. *Address:* 7 Pleasant Grove Lane, Ithaca, NY 14850, USA.

GOLDBERG, Prof. Sir Abraham, Kt 1983; Regius Professor of the Practice of Medicine, University of Glasgow, 1978–89, now Emeritus (Regius Professor of Materia Medica, 1970–78); Consultant Physician, Western Infirmary, Glasgow, since 1959; Hon. Senior Research Fellow in Modern History, University of Glasgow, since 1990; *b* 7 Dec. 1923; *s* of late Julius Goldberg and Rachel Goldberg (*née* Varinofsky); *m* 1957, Clarice Cussin; two *s* one *d*. *Educ:* George Heriot's Sch., Edinburgh; Edinburgh University. MB, ChB 1946, MD (Gold Medal for thesis) 1956, Edinburgh; DSc Glasgow 1966; FRCP, FRCPE, FRCPGlas, FRSE. Nat. Service, RAMC, 1947–49. Nuffield Research Fellow, UCH Med. Sch., London, 1952–54; Eli Lilly Trav. Fellow in Medicine (MRC) in Dept of Medicine, Univ. of Utah; Lectr in Medicine 1956, Titular Prof. 1967, Univ. of Glasgow. Mem., Grants Cttee, Clinical Res. Bd, MRC, 1971–77, Chm., Grants Cttee I, Clinical Res. Bd, MRC, 1973–77. Mem., Chief Scientist Cttee, SHHD, 1977–83; Chm., Biomed. Res. Cttee, SHHD Chief Scientist Orgn, 1977–83; Chm., Cttee on Safety of Medicines, 1980–86. Mem., Editorial Bd, Jt Formulary Cttee, British Nat. Formulary, 1972–78. Foundn Pres., Faculty of Pharmaceutical Medicine, RCP, 1989–91. Editor, Scottish Medical Jl, 1962–63. Lectures: Sydney Watson Smith, RCPE, 1964; Henry Cohen, Hebrew Univ., Jerusalem, 1973; Fitzpatrick, RCP, 1988; Archibald Goodall Meml, RCPSG, 1989. Watson Prize, RCPGlas, 1959; Alexander Fleck Award, Univ. of Glasgow, 1967. *Publications:* (jtly) Diseases of Porphyrin Metabolism, 1962; (ed jtly) Recent Advances in Haematology, 1971; (jtly) Disorders of Porphyrin Metabolism, 1987; (ed jtly) Pharmaceutical Medicine and the Law, 1991; papers on clinical and investigative medicine. *Recreations:* walking, swimming, writing. *Address:* 16 Birnam Crescent, Bearsden, Glasgow G61 2AU.

GOLDBERG, David Gerard; QC 1987; *b* 12 Aug. 1947; *s* of late Arthur Goldberg and of Sylvia Goldberg; *m* 1981, Alison Ninette Lunzer; one *s* one *d*. *Educ:* Plymouth Coll.; London School of Economics (LLB, LLM). Called to the Bar, Lincoln's Inn, 1971; practice at Revenue Bar, 1972–. *Publications:* (jtly) Introduction to Company Law, 1971, 4th edn 1987; (jtly) The Law of Partnership Taxation, 1976, 2nd edn 1979; various articles and notes in legal periodicals mainly concerning taxation and company law. *Recreations:* reading, writing letters, working out, thinking. *Address:* Gray's Inn Chambers, Gray's Inn, WC1R 5JA. *T:* 0171–242 2642.

GOLDBERG, Jonathan Jacob; QC 1989; a Recorder, since 1993; *b* 13 Nov. 1947; *s* of late Rabbi Dr and Mrs P. Selvin Goldberg; *m* 1980, Alexis Jane (marr. diss. 1991), *e d* of George Martin, *qv*; one *s* one *d*. *Educ:* Manchester Grammar Sch.; Trinity Hall, Cambridge (MA, LLB). Called to the Bar, Middle Temple, 1971; Member, NY State Bar, 1985. *Recreations:* music, cinema, wine, travel. *Address:* 3 Temple Gardens, Temple, EC4Y 9AU. *T:* 0171–583 1155.

GOLDBERGER, Prof. Marvin Leonard, PhD; Professor of Physics, since 1993, and Dean of Natural Sciences, since 1994, University of California, San Diego; *b* 22 Oct. 1922; *s* of Joseph Goldberger and Mildred (*née* Sedwitz); *m* 1945, Mildred Ginsburg; two *s*. *Educ:* Carnegie Inst. of Technology (BS); Univ. of Chicago (PhD). Asst to Associate Prof., Univ. of Chicago, 1950–55; Prof., Univ. of Chicago, 1955–57; Princeton University: Higgins Prof. of Mathematical Physics, 1957–77; Chm., Dept of Physics, 1970–76; Joseph Henry Prof. of Physics, 1977–78; Pres., California Inst. of Technology, 1978–87; Dir, Inst. for Advanced Study, Princeton, NJ, 1987; Prof. of Physics, UCLA, 1991–93. Hon. ScD: Carnegie-Mellon, 1979; Notre Dame, Indiana, 1979; Hon. DHL: Hebrew Union Coll., 1980; Univ. of Judaism, 1982; Hon. LLD Occidental Coll., 1980. *Publications:* (jtly) Collision Theory, 1964; professional papers in Physical Rev. *Recreations:* jogging, cooking. *Address:* Wrey Hall Annex, University of California, San Diego, 9500 Gilman Drive, La Jolla, CA 92093-0352, USA.

GOLDBLATT, Simon, QC 1972. Called to the Bar, Gray's Inn, 1953 (Bencher, 1982). *Address:* 39 Essex Street, WC2R 3AT.

GOLDBY, Prof. Frank; Professor of Anatomy, London University, St Mary's Hospital Medical School, 1945–70, now Emeritus; *b* Enfield, Middlesex, 25 May 1903; *s* of Frank and Ellen Maud Goldby; *m* 1932, Helen Rosa Tomlin; five *s* one *d*. *Educ:* Mercers' School, Holborn; Gonville and Caius College, Cambridge; King's College Hospital; MRCS, LRCP 1926; MRCP 1928; MD (Cambridge), 1936; FRCP, 1963; Resident appointments King's Coll. Hospital, 1926–28; Asst Clinical Pathologist, King's College Hospital, 1929–30; Senior Demonstrator in Anatomy, University College, London, 1931; Lecturer in charge of Anatomy Dept, Hong Kong, 1932–33; Lecturer in Anatomy, University of Cambridge and Fellow of Queens' College, 1934–37; Prof. of Anatomy, Univ. of Adelaide, 1937–45. *Publications:* papers on Embryology and on the Pathology and Comparative Anatomy of the Nervous System. *Address:* 1 St Mark's Court, Barton Road, Cambridge CB3 9LE.

GOLDEN, Surgeon Rear-Adm. Francis St Clair, OBE 1981; Consultant in Applied Physiology, Robens Institute, Surrey University; *b* 5 June 1936; *s* of Harry Golden and Nora Golden (*née* Murphy); *m* 1964, Jennifer (*née* Beard); two *s* one *d*. *Educ:* Presentation Coll., Cork; University Coll., Cork (MB BCh, BAO); London Univ. (Diploma in Aviation Medicine); Leeds Univ. (PhD Physiol). GP, Kingston on Thames, 1961–63; HMS Jaguar, 1963–64; RNAS Culdrose, 1964–67; RN Air Med. Sch., 1967–73; Inst. of Naval Medicine, 1973–85; MoD, 1985–86; Fleet MO, 1986–88; MO i/c Haslar, 1988–90; Surg. Rear-Adm., Support Med. Services, 1990–93, retd. QHP 1990–93. Chm., Med. and Surg. Cttee, RNLI. Hon. FNI 1982. OStJ. *Publications:* papers in sci. jls and chapters in medical textbooks on immersion, drowning, hypothermia. *Recreations:* born again golfer, armchair Rugby. *Address:* 15 Beech Grove, Gosport, Hants PO12 2JE. *Club:* Royal Society of Medicine.

GOLDHILL, Flora Taylor; Chief Executive, Human Fertilisation and Embryology Authority, since 1991; *b* 13 Feb. 1953; *d* of Thomas Kissock and Flora (*née* McKenzie); *m* 1978, Jonathan Paul Goldhill. *Educ:* Morgan Academy, Dundee; Edinburgh Univ. (MA Hons). Civil Servant, DHSS and DoH, 1976–90. *Recreations:* reading, walking, gardening. *Address:* Human Fertilisation and Embryology Authority, Paxton House, 30 Artillery Lane, E1 7LS. *T:* 0171–377 5077.

GOLDIE, Peter Lawrence; graduate studies in philosophy, Balliol College, Oxford; *b* 5 Nov. 1946; *s* of Kenneth and Norah Goldie; *m* 1990, Sophie Hamilton; two *s* by previous marriage. *Educ:* Felsted Sch., Essex; UCL (BA 1993). Chief Executive: Abaco Investments PLC, 1983–86; British & Commonwealth Hldgs, 1987–89; Dir, Guinness Mahon, 1973–83. *Recreation:* physical and mental exercise.

GOLDING, Dame (Cecilie) Monica, DBE 1958; RRC 1950 (ARRC 1940); *b* 6 Aug. 1902; *o d* of Ben Johnson and Clara (*née* Beames); *m* 1961, Brig. the Rev. Harry Golding, CBE (*d* 1969). *Educ:* Croydon Secondary Sch. Professional training: Royal Surrey County Hospital, Guildford, 1922–25; Louise Margaret Hosp., Aldershot and Queen Victoria's Institute of District Nursing. Joined Army Nursing Services, 1925; India, 1929–34; France, 1939–40; Middle East, 1940–43 and 1948–49; Southern Comd, 1943–44 and 1950–52; WO, 1945–46; India and SE Asia, 1946–48; Far East, 1952–55; Eastern Comd, 1955–56; Matron-in-Chief and Dir of Army Nursing Services, 1956–60, retired (with rank of Brig.), 1960. QHNS 1956–60; Col Commandant, Queen Alexandra's Royal Army Nursing Corps, 1961–66. OStJ 1955. *Recreations:* motoring; amateur bird watching and nature study. *Address:* Retired Nurses' Home, Riverside Avenue, Bournemouth, Dorset BH7 7EE. *T:* Bournemouth (01202) 396418.

GOLDING, Francis Nelson; Secretary, Royal Fine Art Commission, since 1995; *b* 28 Jan. 1944; *s* of late Frank Edwards Golding and Ella Golding (*née* Morris). *Educ:* King's Sch., Macclesfield; Clare Coll., Cambridge (Exhibnr; BA 1966). Min. of Public Building and Works, 1967; DoE, 1972; Royal Commn on the Press, 1975–77; Asst Sec., DoE, 1978; English Heritage: Head of Secretariat, 1984; Head of Properties, 1986–90; Sec., ICOMOS, 1992–94. *Recreations:* Chinese pots and jade, going to India. *Address:* Royal Fine Art Commission, 7 St James's Square, SW1Y 4JU. *T:* 0171–839 6537.

GOLDING, John; General Secretary, National Communications Union, 1986–88; *b* Birmingham, 9 March 1931; *m* 1958, Thelma Gwillym; one *s*; *m* 1980, Llinos Lewis (*see* Llinos Golding). *Educ:* Chester Grammar Sch.; London Univ.; Keele Univ. BA History, Politics, Economics, 1956. Asst Res. Officer, 1960–64, Education Officer, 1964–69, Political and Parly Officer, 1969–86, Post Office Engineering Union. MP (Lab) Newcastle-under-Lyme, 1969–86; PPS to Minister of State, Min. of Technology, Feb.-June 1970; Opposition Whip, July 1970–74; a Lord Comr, HM Treasury, Feb.-Oct. 1974; Parly Under-Sec. of State, Dept of Employment, 1976–79. Chm., Select Cttee on Employment, 1979–82; Former Mem. Select Cttee on Nationalised Industries. Mem., NEC, Lab. Party, 1978–83; Chm., Lab. Party Home Policy Cttee, 1982–83. Governor: University Coll. Hosp., 1970–74; Ruskin Coll., 1970–. *Publications:* co-author Fabian Pamphlets: Productivity Bargaining; Trade Unions—on to 1980. *Address:* 6 Lancaster Avenue, Newcastle-under-Lyme, Staffs ST5 1DR; 31 Westminster Mansions, Great Smith Street, SW1P 3BP.

GOLDING, John, CBE 1992; PhD; FBA 1994; painter; Senior Tutor in the School of Painting, Royal College of Art, 1981–86 (Tutor, 1973); *b* 10 Sept. 1929; *s* of Harold S. Golding and Dorothy Hamer. *Educ:* Ridley Coll. (St Catherine's, Ontario); Univ. of Toronto; Univ. of London. BA; MA; PhD. Lectr, 1962–77, and Reader in History of Art, 1977–81, Courtauld Inst., Univ. of London; Slade Prof. of Fine Art, Cambridge Univ., 1976–77. Trustee, Tate Gallery, 1984–91. Hon. Fellow, RCA, 1987. *Publications:* Cubism 1907–14, 1959, 3rd edn 1988; (with Christopher Green) Leger & Purist Paris, 1970; Duchamp: The Bride Stripped Bare by her Bachelors, Even, 1972; (ed with Roland Penrose) Picasso, 1881–1973, 1973; Visions of the Modern, 1994; (with Elizabeth Cowling) Picasso: sculptor/painter, 1994. *Address:* 24 Ashchurch Park Villas, W12 9SP. *T:* 0181–749 5221.

GOLDING, John Anthony, CVO 1966; Queen's Messenger, 1967–80; *b* 25 July 1920; *s* of George Golding, Plaxtol, Kent; *m* 1950, Patricia May, *d* of Thomas Archibald Bickel; two *s*. *Educ:* Bedford Sch.; King's Coll., Auckland. Served with King's African Rifles and Military Administration, Somalia, 1939–46 (Captain). Entered Colonial Service, 1946; Dep. Provincial Comr, Tanganyika, 1961; Administrator, Turks and Caicos Is, 1965–67. *Publication:* Colonialism: the golden years, 1987. *Recreations:* gardening, fishing. *Address:* c/o Barclays Bank, 11 High Street, Hythe, Kent CT21 5AE.

GOLDING, Hon. Sir John (Simon Rawson), Kt 1986; OJ 1980; CD 1974; OBE 1959; Princess Alice Professor of Orthopaedic Surgery, University of the West Indies, since 1965; *b* 15 April 1921; *s* of Mark Golding and Louise Golding; *m* 1961, Alice Patricia Levy; one *s* one *d*. *Educ:* Marlborough College; Cambridge Univ. MA, MB BChir. FRCS 1948. Middlesex Hosp., 1941–46 and 1948–52; RAMC, 1946–48; Royal Nat. Orthop. Hosp., 1952–53; Univ. of the West Indies, 1953–. ABC Travelling Fellow, Amer., British and Canadian Orthopaedic Assoc., 1956; Hunterian Prof., RCS, 1956; Nuffield Fellow, 1961–62. Hon. LLD Univ. of Toronto, 1984. *Publications:* The Ascent to Mona, 1994; papers in Jl of Bone and Joint Surgery, West Indian Med. Jl, etc. *Recreations:* sailing, walking, bridge. *Address:* 2A Bamboo Avenue, Kingston 6, Jamaica, WI.

GOLDING, Llinos; MP (Lab) Newcastle-under-Lyme, since July 1986; *b* 21 March 1933; *d* of Rt Hon. Ness Edwards, MP and Elina Victoria Edwards; *m* 1st, 1957, Dr John Roland Lewis; one *s* two *d*; 2nd, 1980, John Golding, *qv*. *Educ:* Caerphilly Girls' Grammar Sch.; Cardiff Royal Infirmary Sch. of Radiography. Mem., Soc. of Radiographers. Worked as a radiographer at various times; Assistant to John Golding, MP, 1972–86. An Opposition Whip, 1987–92; opposition spokesman: on social security, 1992–95; on children and the family, 1993–. Vice Chairman: PLP Cttee on Parly Affairs; All Party Parly Gp on Children; Jt Chm., All Party Parly Gp on Homeless, 1989–. Match Sec., Lords and Commons Fly Fishing Club. Member: BBC Gen. Adv. Council, 1988–91; Commonwealth War Graves Commn, 1992–. Former Mem., Dist Manpower Services Cttee; Mem., N Staffs DHA, 1983–. Sec., Newcastle (Dist) Trades Council, 1976–87. *Address:* 6 Lancaster Avenue, Newcastle-under-Lyme, Staffs ST5 1DR. *T:* Newcastle (Staffs) (01782) 636200. *Clubs:* King Street Working Men's (Newcastle-under-Lyme); Halmerend Working Men's (Audley).

GOLDING, Dame Monica; *see* Golding, Dame C. M.

GOLDING, Prof. Raymund Marshall, AO 1994; FNZIC; FRACI; FInstP; Vice-Chancellor, James Cook University of North Queensland, since 1986; *b* 17 June 1935; *s* of Austin E. Golding and Marion H. R. Golding; *m* 1962, Ingeborg Carl; two *d*. *Educ:* Auckland Univ., NZ (BSc 1957, MSc 1958); Cambridge Univ. (PhD 1963). Res. and Sen. Res. Scientist, DSIR, NZ, 1957–68; Prof. of Theoretical and Physical Chemistry, 1968–86, Mem., Bd of Sen. Sch. Studies, 1975–86, Pro-Vice-Chancellor, 1978–86, Univ. of NSW. Dir, St George Hosp., 1982–86. Chm., Aust. Marine Sci. Consortium, 1984–; Dep. Chm., Consultative Gp on Marine Industries Sci. and Technol., 1990–. Hon. Chm., Australian Chapter, Pacific Congress on Marine Sci. and Technol., Internat., 1990–; Dep. Chm., Chiropractors and Osteopaths Bd of Qld, 1991–; Mem., Educn Cttee, NSW Chiropractic Registration Bd, 1983–. Mem. Council, PNG Univ. of Technol., 1987–93. Chm., Aust. Fest. of Chamber Music Pty, 1990–; Dir, Tropic Line Res. Theatre Ltd, 1992–; Mem., Bd, Townsville Enterprise Ltd, 1991–. Hon. DSc Univ. of NSW, 1986. *Publications:* Applied Wave Mechanics, 1969; The Goldings of Oakington, 1992; contribs to books on chem. subjects; numerous research papers and articles. *Recreations:* music, photography, astronomy. *Address:* James Cook University of North Queensland, Townsville, Queensland 4811, Australia. *T:* (77) 814442. *Clubs:* North Queensland (Townsville); Australasian Pioneers' (Sydney).

GOLDING, Terence Edward, OBE 1992; FCA; Chief Executive: National Exhibition Centre, Birmingham, since 1978; International Convention Centre, Birmingham, since 1990; *b* 7 April 1932; *s* of Sydney Richard Golding and Elsie Golding; *m* 1955, Sheila Jean (*née* Francis); one *s* one *d*. *Educ:* Harrow County Grammar Sch. FCA 1967. Earls Court Ltd (Exhibition Hall Proprietors): Chief Accountant, 1960; Co. Sec., 1965; Financial Dir, 1972; Financial Dir, Olympia Ltd, and Earls Court & Olympia Ltd, 1973; Commercial Dir, Earls Court & Olympia Group of Cos, 1975. Member: Exhibition Liaison Cttee, 1979–; Nat. Assoc. of Exhibn Hallowners, 1988–. Director: British Exhibitions Promotion Council, 1981–83; Birmingham Convention and Visitor Bureau, 1981–93; Heart of England Tourist Bd, 1984–91; Central England, TEC, 1990–92; Birmingham Marketing Partnership, 1993–; Mem. Exec. Cttee, Exhibn Industry Fedn, 1988–. Hon. Mem. Council, Birmingham Chamber of Industry and Commerce, 1990–. Midlander of the Year, 1990. *Recreation:* following sport. *Address:* Pinn Cottage, Pinner Hill, Pinner, Mddx HA5 3XX. *T:* 0181–866 2610.

GOLDINGAY, Rev. Dr John; Principal, St John's College, Nottingham, since 1988; *b* 20 June 1942; *s* of Edgar Charles and Ada Irene Goldingay; *m* 1967, Ann Elizabeth Wilson; two *s*. *Educ:* King Edward's School, Birmingham; Keble Coll., Oxford (BA); Nottingham University (PhD). Asst Curate, Christ Church, Finchley, 1966; Tutor, St John's Coll., Nottingham, 1970. *Publications:* Songs from a Strange Land, 1978; Approaches to Old Testament Interpretation, 1981; Theological Diversity and the Authority of the Old Testament, 1987; Daniel, 1989; (ed) Signs, Wonders and Healing, 1989; Models for Scripture, 1994; Models for the Interpretation of Scripture, 1995; (ed) Atonement Today, 1995. *Recreations:* family, Old Testament, France, Israel, rock music. *Address:* 7 Peache Way, Bramcote, Nottingham NG9 3DX. *T:* Nottingham (0115) 925 1114/922 4046, *Fax:* (0115) 943 6438.

GOLDMAN, Antony John, CB 1995; Under Secretary, International Aviation, Department of Transport; *b* 28 Feb. 1940; *s* of Sir Samuel Goldman, *qv*; *m* 1964, Anne Rosemary Lane; three *s*. *Educ:* Marlborough College; Peterhouse, Cambridge (BA). International Computers Ltd, 1961–73; entered Civil Service, DoE, 1973; Private Sec. to Sec. of State for Transport, 1976–78; Asst Sec., 1977; seconded to HM Treasury, 1981–83; Under Sec., 1984. Non. exec. Dir, Hugh Baird & Sons, 1985–86. *Recreations:* music, sailing, writing doggerel.

GOLDMAN, Sir Samuel, KCB 1969 (CB 1964); *b* 10 March 1912; *y s* of late Philip and late Sarah Goldman; *m* 1st, 1933, Pearl Marre (*d* 1941); one *s*; 2nd, 1943, Patricia Rosemary Hodges (*d* 1990). *Educ:* Davenant Foundation Sch.; Raine's Sch.; London Sch. of Economics, London Univ. Inter-Collegiate Scholar. BSc (Econ.), First Class Hons in Economics and Gladstone Memorial Prize, 1931; MSc (Econ.), 1933. Hutchinson Silver Medallist. Moody's Economist Services, 1934–38; Joseph Sebag & Co., 1938–39; Bank of England, 1940–47. Entered Civil Service, 1947, as Statistician in Central Statistical Office; transferred to Treasury, Sept. 1947; Chief Statistician, 1948; Asst Sec., 1952; Under-Sec., 1960–62; Third Sec., 1962–68; Second Perm. Sec., 1968–72. UK Alternate Executive Dir, International Bank, 1961–62. Exec. Dir, 1972–74, Man. Dir, 1974–76, Orion Bank Ltd. Chm., Henry Ansbacher Holdings Ltd and Henry Ansbacher Ltd, 1976–82. Chm., Covent Garden Market Authority, 1976–81. Hon. Fellow LSE. *Publication:* Public Expenditure Management and Control, 1973. *Recreations:* music, gardening. *Address:* 3 Little Tangley, Wonersh, Guildford, Surrey GU5 0PW. *T:* Guildford (01483) 68913. *Club:* Reform.

See also A. J. Goldman.

GOLDREIN, Neville Clive, CBE 1991; Consultant, Deacon Goldrein Green, Solicitors, 1985–92; Senior Partner, Goldrein & Co., 1953–85; *b* 28 Aug.; *s* of Saville and Nina Goldrein; *m* 1949, Dr Sonia Sumner, MB, BS Dunelm; one *s* one *d*. *Educ:* Hymers Coll., Hull; Pembroke Coll., Cambridge (MA). Served Army: commnd E Yorks Regt; served East Africa Comd (Captain). Admitted Solicitor of the Supreme Court, 1949. Mem., Crosby Bor. Council, 1957–71; Mayor of Crosby, 1966–67, Dep. Mayor, 1967–68; Mem., Lancs CC, 1965–74; Merseyside County Council: Mem., 1973–86; Dep. Leader, Cons. Gp, 1974–77; Vice-Chm. of Council, 1977–80; Leader, 1980–81; Leader, Cons. Gp, 1981–86. Chm., Crosby Constituency Cons. Assoc., 1986–89. Area Vice-Pres., Sefton, St John Ambulance, 1980–87 (Chm., S Sefton Div., 1975–87); Member: NW Econ. Planning Council, 1966–72; Bd of Deputies of British Jews, 1966–85, 1992–; Council, Liverpool Univ., 1977–81; Council, Merseyside Chamber of Commerce (Chairman: Envmt and Energy Cttee; Rivers Cttee, 1990–93); Regl Affairs Cttee, British Assoc. of Chambers of Commerce. Director: Merseyside Economic Devélt Co. Ltd, 1981–87; Merseyside Waste Derived Fuels Ltd, 1983–86. Vice-Pres., Crosby Mencap, 1967–; Chm., Crosby Hall Residential Trust Appeal, 1989–91. Governor, Merchant Taylors' Sch., Crosby, 1965–74. *Recreations:* videography, photography, music, grandchildren. *Address:* Torreno, St Andrew's Road, Blundellsands, Merseyside L23 7UR. *T:* and *Fax:* 0151–924 2065. *Club:* Athenæum (Liverpool).

GOLDRING, John Bernard; QC 1987; a Recorder, since 1987; a Deputy Senior Judge, Sovereign Base Areas, Cyprus, since 1991; *b* 9 Nov. 1944; *s* of Joseph and Marianne Goldring; *m* 1970, Wendy Margaret Lancaster Bennett; two *s*. *Educ:* Wyggeston Grammar Sch.; Exeter Univ. (LLB). Called to the Bar, Lincoln's Inn, 1969. Standing Prosecuting Counsel to Inland Revenue, Midland and Oxford Circuit, 1985–87. *Recreation:* gardening. *Address:* 9 Bedford Row, WC1R 4AZ. *T:* 0171–797 7365.

GOLDRING, Mary Sheila, OBE 1987; economist; presenter, Goldring Audit, Channel 4, 1992, 1993, 1994, 1995. *Educ:* Our Lady's Priory, Sussex; Lady Margaret Hall, Oxford (PPE). Air and Science correspondent, 1949–74, Business editor, 1966–74, Economist Newspaper; economist and broadcaster, 1974–; *television:* presenter: Analysis, BBC, 1977–87; Answering Back, Channel 4 interviews, 1989–91. Mem. Selection Cttee, Harkness Fellowships, 1980–86. Trustee, Science Museum, 1987–. Fawley Foundn Lect., 1992. Hon. DLitt UWE, 1994. Blue Circle Award for industrial journalism, 1979; Sony Radio Award for best current affairs programme (Analysis: Post-Recession Britain), 1985; Industrial Journalist Award, Industrial Soc., 1985; Outstanding Personal Contribution to Radio, Broadcasting Press Guild, 1986; Harold Wincott Award for Broadcasting, 1991; Industrial Journalist of the Year, Industrial Soc. and BP, 1991. *Publication:* Economics of Atomic Energy, 1957. *Recreation:* small-scale landscaping. *Address:* 37 Sloane Avenue, SW3 3JB.

GOLDS, Anthony Arthur, CMG 1971; LVO 1961; HM Diplomatic Service, retired; Director, British National Committee, International Chamber of Commerce, 1977–83; *b* 31 Oct. 1919; *s* of late Arthur Oswald Golds and Florence Golds (*née* Massey); *m* 1944, Suzanne Macdonald Young; one *s* one *d*. *Educ:* King's Sch., Macclesfield; New Coll., Oxford (Scholar). HM Forces (Royal Armoured Corps), 1939–46; CRO, 1948; 1st Sec., Calcutta and Delhi, 1951–53; Commonwealth Office, 1953–56; Head of Chancery, British Embassy, Ankara, 1957–59; Karachi, 1959–61; Counsellor in Commonwealth Office and Foreign Office, 1962–65; Head of Joint Malaysia/Indonesia Dept, 1964–65; Counsellor, HM Embassy, Rome, 1965–70; Ambassador to the Republic of Cameroon, the Republic of Gabon and the Republic of Equatorial Guinea, 1970–72; High Comr to Bangladesh, 1972–74; Senior Civilian Instructor, RCDS, 1975–76. *Recreations:* music, cricket, golf, literature. *Address:* 4 Oakfield Gardens, SE19 1HF. *T:* 0181–670 7621. *Club:* Dulwich & Sydenham Hill Golf.

GOLDSACK, Alan Raymond; QC 1990; **His Honour Judge Goldsack;** a Circuit Judge, since 1994; *b* 13 June 1947; *s* of Raymond Frederick Goldsack, MBE and Mildred Agnes Goldsack (*née* Jones); *m* 1971, Christine Marion Clarke; three *s* one *d*. *Educ:* Hastings Grammar School; Leicester Univ. (LLB). Called to the Bar, Gray's Inn, 1970; a Recorder, 1988–94. *Recreations:* gardening, walking. *Address:* Sheffield Crown Court, Castle Street, Sheffield S3 8LW.

GOLDSACK, John Redman, MBE 1971; consultant in tropical agriculture and development, since 1993; *b* 15 Aug. 1932; 2nd *s* of late Bernard Frank and Dorothy Goldsack; *m* 1962, Madeleine Amelia Rowena, *d* of late Stanley and Grace Kibbler; two *s* one *d*. *Educ:* Sutton Grammar Sch., Surrey; Wye Coll., London Univ. (BScAgric); Queens' Coll., Cambridge (DipAgric); Imperial Coll. of Tropical Agric., Trinidad (DTA). Agricl Officer, HMOCS, Kenya, 1956; Hd of Soil Conservation and Planning Officer, Min. of Lands and Settlement, Kenya, 1963–67; Hd of Land Develt Div., Min. of Agriculture, Kenya, 1967–70; Asst Agric. Advr, ODM, 1970–74; Agriculture Adviser: S African Develt Div., 1974–78; ME Develt Div., 1979–81; E. African Develt Div., 1981–83; Sen. Agric. Advr, Asia Div., ODA, 1983–86; Dep. Chief Natural Resources Advr and Prin. Agriculture Advr, ODA, 1986–88; Minister and UK Perm. Rep. to UNFAO, Rome, 1988–93. *Recreations:* cricket, golf, natural history. *Address:* Bradford Peverell Farmhouse, Bradford Peverell, Dorchester, Dorset DT2 9SF. *T:* and *Fax:* Dorchester (01305) 266543. *Clubs:* Farmers', MCC.

GOLDSMITH, Alexander Benedict Hayum; writer; Editor, Geographical Magazine, 1991–94; *b* 10 Dec. 1960; *s* of Edward René David Goldsmith, *qv* and Gillian Marion (*née* Pretty); *m* 1990, Louisa Kate Slack. *Educ:* Westminster Sch.; Jesus Coll., Cambridge (MA Social Anthropol. 1986). Researcher and fundraiser for Survival Internat., 1986; Publisher and Editor, Envmt Digest, 1987–90; Ed., People and Places in Peril series, 1995. FRGS 1993. *Recreation:* walking.

GOLDSMITH, Alexander Kinglake, (Alick); Director-General, Export Group for the Constructional Industries, since 1991; *b* 16 Jan. 1938; *s* of Maj.-Gen. Robert Frederick Kinglake Goldsmith, CB, CBE; *m* 1971, Deirdre Stafford; one *s* one *d*. *Educ:* Sherborne; Trinity Coll., Oxford (MA Modern History). National Service, 1956–58 (DCLI and Queen's Own Nigeria Regt). Asst Principal, CRO, 1961; Hindi student, SOAS, 1962; Third Sec., New Delhi, 1963; FCO, 1967; First Sec. (Inf.), Wellington, NZ, 1971; FCO, 1975; Head of Chancery, E Berlin, 1978; FCO, 1980; Hd of Commonwealth Co-ordination Dept, FCO, 1982; seconded to Hong Kong Govt, 1984; Consul-Gen., Hamburg, 1986–90. *Recreations:* walking, swimming. *Address:* c/o Lloyds Bank, Butler Place, SW1H 0PR. *Club:* Royal Automobile.

GOLDSMITH, Edward René David; author; Publisher and Editor, The Ecologist, since 1970; *b* 8 Nov. 1928; *s* of late Frank B. H. Goldsmith, OBE, TD, MP (C) for Stowmarket, Suffolk, 1910–18, and Marcelle (*née* Mouiller); *m* 1st, 1953, Gillian Marion Pretty; one *s* two *d*; 2nd, 1981, Katherine Victoria James; two *s*. *Educ:* Magdalen Coll., Oxford (MA Hons). Adjunct Associate Prof., Univ. of Michigan, 1975; Vis. Prof., Sangamon State Univ., 1984. Contested (Ecology Party): Eye, Feb. 1974; Cornwall and Plymouth, European parly election, 1979. Hon. Right Livelihood Award, 1991. Chevalier, Légion d'Honneur, 1991. *Publications:* (ed) Can Britain Survive?, 1971; (with R. Prescott-Allen) A Blueprint for Survival, 1972; The Stable Society, 1977; (ed with J. M. Brunetti) La Médecine à la Question, 1981; (with N. Hildyard) The Social and Environmental Effects of Large Dams, vol. I, 1984, vol. II, 1986, vol. III, 1992; (ed with N. Hildyard) Green Britain or Industrial Wasteland?, 1986; (ed with N. Hildyard) The Earth Report, 1988; The Great U-Turn, 1988; (with N. Hildyard and others) 5,000 Days to Save the Planet, 1990; The Way: an ecological world view, 1992. *Address:* 9 Montague Road, Richmond, Surrey TW10 6QW. *Clubs:* Brooks's; Travellers' (Paris).

See also A. B. H. Goldsmith, Sir James Goldsmith.

GOLDSMITH, Sir James (Michael), Kt 1976; Member for France, European Parliament, since 1994; Chief Executive, Goldsmith Foundation, since 1991; *b* 26 Feb. 1933; *s* of Frank Goldsmith, OBE and Marcelle Mouiller; *m* 1st, Maria Isabel Patino (*d* 1954); one *d*; 2nd, Ginette Lery; one *s* one *d*; 3rd, Lady Annabel Vane Tempest Stewart; two *s* one *d*. *Educ:* Eton College. Founder of a number of industrial, commercial and financial enterprises; retired from active business, 1990. Pres., l'Europe des Nations parly gp, EP, 1994–. Chevalier, Légion d'Honneur, 1978. *Publications:* Counterculture, vol. I, 1985, vol. II, 1987, vol. III, 1990, vol. IV, 1991, vol. V, 1993; Pour la Révolution Permanente, 1986; Le Piège, 1993 (The Trap, 1994). *Address:* Casa La Loma, Costa Cuixmala, Jalisco, Mexico. *Club:* Travellers' (Paris).

See also E. R. D. Goldsmith.

GOLDSMITH, John Stuart, CB 1984; Director General Defence Accounts, Ministry of Defence, 1980–84; *b* 2 Nov. 1924; *o s* of R. W. and S. E. Goldsmith; *m* 1948, Brenda; two *s* one *d*. *Educ:* Whitgift Middle Sch.; St Catharine's Coll., Cambridge. Royal Signals, 1943–47 (Captain). War Office, 1948; Principal, 1952; Treasury, 1961–64; Asst Sec., MoD, 1964; RCDS 1971; Asst Under-Sec. of State, MoD, 1973; Chm. Civil Service Selection Bd, 1973. *Recreations:* gardening, jazz, travel. *Address:* Cobthorne House, Church Lane, Rode, Somerset BA3 6PN. *T:* Frome (01373) 830681.

GOLDSMITH, Peter Henry; QC 1987; a Recorder, since 1991; *b* 5 Jan. 1950; *s* of Sydney Elland Goldsmith, solicitor, and Myra Goldsmith; *m* 1974, Joy; three *s* one *d*. *Educ:* Quarry Bank High Sch., Liverpool; Gonville and Caius Coll., Cambridge (Sen. Schol., Tapp Postgrad. Schol., Schuldham Plate, 1968–71; MA); UCL (LLM 1972). Called to the Bar, Gray's Inn (Birkenhead Schol.), 1972; a Jun. Counsel to the Crown, Common Law, 1985–87. Mem., Gen. Council of the Bar, 1992– (Vice Chm., 1994; Chm., 1995; Chm., Legal Services Cttee, 1991–93). *Address:* Fountain Court, Temple, EC4Y 9DH. *T:* 0171–583 3335.

GOLDSMITH, Philip; Director (observation of the Earth and its environment), European Space Agency, Paris, 1985–93; *b* 16 April 1930; *s* of late Stanley Thomas Goldsmith and Ida Goldsmith (*née* Rawlinson); *m* 1st, 1952, Daphne (*d* 1983), *d* of William Webb; two *s* two *d*; 2nd, 1990, Gail Lorraine. *Educ:* Almondbury Grammar Sch.; Pembroke Coll., Oxford (MA). Meteorologist with the Meteorological Office, 1947–54, incl. National Service, RAF, 1948–50; Research Scientist, AERE Harwell, 1957–67; Meteorological Office: Asst Director (Cloud Physics Research), 1967–76; Dep. Director (Physical Research), 1976–82; Dir (Res.), 1982–84. President: Royal Meteorological Society, 1980–82; Internat. Commn on Atmospheric Chem. and Global Pollution, 1979–83. *Publications:* articles in scientific jls mainly on atmospheric physics and chemistry and space research related to associated environmental concerns. *Recreations:* golf, gardening, antiques, old cars. *Address:* Hill House, Broad Lane, Bracknell, Berks RG12 9BY. *Clubs:* East Berks Golf, Woodsome Hall Golf.

GOLDSMITH, Walter Kenneth, FCA; CIMgt; Chairman: Flying Flowers (formerly Trident) Ltd, since 1990; Ansoll Estates Ltd, since 1989; *b* 19 Jan. 1938; *s* of late Lionel and of Phoebe Goldsmith; *m* 1961, Rosemary Adele, *d* of Joseph and Hannah Salter; two *s* two *d*. *Educ:* Merchant Taylors' School. Admitted Inst. of Chartered Accountants, 1960; Manager, Mann Judd & Co., 1964; joined Black & Decker Ltd, 1966: Dir of Investment, Finance and Administration, Europe, 1967; Gen. Man., 1970; Man. Dir, 1974; Chief Executive and European Dir, 1975; Black & Decker USA, 1976–79: Corporate Vice-Pres. and Pres. Pacific Internat. Operations; Dir Gen., Inst. of Dirs, 1979–84; Korn/Ferry International Ltd: Chm., 1984–86; Chief Exec., 1984–85; Chm., Leisure Develt Ltd, 1984–85; Gp Planning and Marketing Dir, Trusthouse Forte plc, 1985–87; Chm., Food from Britain, 1987–90; Dep. Chm., British Food & Farming Ltd, 1990–. Chairman: Nuffield Press, 1994–; Ewart Parsons (Dir, 1992–); Dep. Chm., MICE Gp, 1994–; Director: Bestobell PLC, 1980–85; BUPA Medical Centre, 1980–84; Director Publications Ltd, 1983–84; The Lesser Group, 1983–85; Bank Leumi (UK) plc, 1984–; Trusthouse Forte Inc., 1985–87; The Winning Streak Ltd, 1985–92; The Watts Gp plc, 1987–91; Spong plc, 1987–89; Isys plc (Dep. Chm.), 1987–; Pearson Paul Haworth Nolan Ltd,

1989–92; CLS Group, 1992–; Chambers & Newman, 1994–; Betterware, 1995 (Chm., 1990–94); Mem. Exec. Cttee, Bank Leumi PLC, 1988–. Underwriting Mem., Lloyd's. Member: English Tourist Board, 1982–84; BTA, 1984–86; Vice-Pres., British Overseas Trade Gp for Israel, 1992– (Chm., 1987–91); Chm., Governing Bd, Marketing Quality Assurance, 1990–. Treas., Leo Baeck Coll., 1987–89. Council Member: Co-operation Ireland, 1985–90; RASE, 1988–. Trustee, Israel Diaspora Trust, 1982–92; Chm. of Trustees, Stress Foundation, 1984–88; Chm., Grange Hospice Project, 1994–. FRSA. Liveryman, Worshipful Co. of Chartered Accountants in England and Wales, 1985. Free Enterprise Award, Aims for Industry, 1984. *Publications:* (with D. Clutterbuck): The Winning Streak, 1984; The Winning Streak Workout Book, 1985; (with Berry Ritchie) The New Elite, 1987. *Recreations:* boating, music, painting, property. *Address:* 11 Halland Way, Northwood, Mddx HA6 2AG. *Club:* Carlton.

GOLDSTAUB, Anthony (James); QC 1992; barrister; *b* 26 May 1949; *er s* of late Henry Goldstaub, engineer, and of Hilda (*née* Bendix); *m* 1st, 1982 (marr. diss. 1989); two *s*; 2nd, 1993, Moira Pooley. *Educ:* Highgate Sch.; Nottingham Univ. (LLB 1971). Called to the Bar, Middle Temple, 1972. Common Law litigation, 1972–. *Address:* 24 The Ropewalk, Nottingham NG1 5EF. *T:* Nottingham (0115) 947 2581.

GOLDSTAUB, Jane Hilary, (Mrs T. C. Goldstaub); *see* Procter, J. H.

GOLDSTEIN, Alfred, CBE 1977; FEng; consulting engineer; Senior Partner, Travers Morgan & Partners, 1972–85; Chairman, Travers Morgan Group, 1985–87; *b* 9 Oct. 1926; *s* of late Sigmund and Regina Goldstein; *m* 1959, Anne Milford, *d* of late Col R. A. M. Tweedy and of Maureen Evans, and step *d* of Hubert Evans; two *s*. *Educ:* Rotherham Grammar Sch.; Imperial Coll., Univ. of London. BSc (Eng); ACGI 1946; DIC. FICE 1959; FIStructE 1959; FIHE 1959; MConsE 1959; FEng 1979; FCIT; FCGI 1984. Partner, R. Travers Morgan & Partners, 1951; responsible for planning, design and supervision of construction of major road and bridge projects and for planning and transport studies, incl. M23, Belfast Transportation Plan, Clifton Bridge, Nottingham, Elizabeth Bridge, Cambridge, Itchen Bridge, Southampton. Transport Consultant to Govt SE Jt Planning Team for SE Regional Plan; in charge London Docklands Redevelopment Study; Cost Benefit Study for 2nd Sydney Airport for Govt of Australia; Mem. Cttee on Review of Railway Finances, 1982; UK full mem., EC Article 83 Cttee (Transport), 1982–85; TRRL Visitor on Transport Res. and Safety, 1983–87. Member: Building Research Bd, subseq. Adv. Cttee on Building Research, 1963–66; Civil Engrg EDC on Contracting in Civil Engrg since Banwell, 1965–67; Baroness Sharp's Adv. Cttee on Urban Transport Manpower Study, 1967–69; Commn of Inquiry on Third London Airport, 1968–70; Urban Motorways Cttee, 1969–72; Genesys Bd, 1969–74; Chairman: DoE and Dept of Transport Planning and Tnspt Res. Adv. Council, 1973–79; DoE Environmental Bd, 1975–78; Mem., TRRL Adv. Cttee on Transport, 1974–80; Mem. Bd, Coll. of Estate Management, Reading Univ., 1979–92. *Publications:* papers and lectures (inc. Criteria for the Siting of Major Airports, 4th World Airports Conf., 1973; Highways and Community Response, 9th Rees Jeffreys Triennial Lecture, RTPI, 1975; Environment and the Economic Use of Energy, (Plenary Paper, Hong Kong Transport Conf., 1982); Decision-taking under Uncertainty in the Roads Sector, PIARC Sydney, 1983; Investment in Transport (Keynote address, CIT Conf., 1983); Buses: social enterprise and business (main paper, 9th annual conf., Bus and Coach Council, 1983); Public Road Transport: a time for change (Keynote address, 6th Aust. passenger trans. conf., 1985); Private Enterprise and Highways (Nat. Res. Council conf., Baltimore, 1986); The Expert and the Public: local values and national choice (Florida Univ.), 1987; Travel in London: is chaos inevitable? (LRT), 1989). *Recreations:* carpentry, music, bridge. *Address:* Kent Edge, Crockham Hill, Edenbridge, Kent TN8 6TA. *T:* Edenbridge (01732) 866227. *Club:* Athenæum.

GOLDSTEIN, Joan Delano, (Mrs Julius Goldstein); *see* Aiken, J. D.

GOLDSTEIN, Prof. Joseph Leonard; physician, genetics educator; Paul J. Thomas Professor of Medicine, and Chairman, Department of Molecular Genetics, since 1977, Regental Professor, since 1985, University of Texas Southwestern Medical (formerly Health Science) Center at Dallas (Member of Faculty, since 1972); *b* 18 April 1940; *s* of Isadore E. and Fannie A. Goldstein. *Educ:* Washington and Lee University (BS); Univ. of Texas Health Science Center at Dallas (MD). Intern, then Resident in Medicine, Mass Gen. Hosp., Boston, 1966–88; clinical associate, NIH, 1968–70; Postdoctoral Fellow, Univ. of Washington, Seattle, 1970–72. Harvey Soc. Lecture, Rockefeller Univ., 1977. Member: Sci. Rev. Bd, Howard Hughes Med. Inst., 1978–84, Med. Adv. Bd, 1985–; Bd of Dirs, Passano Foundn, 1985–; Sci. Adv. Bd, Welch Foundn, 1986–; Bd of Trustees, Rockefeller Univ., 1994–. Fellow, Salk Inst., 1983–94. Member, editorial board: Jl Clin. Investigation, 1977–82; Annual Review of Genetics, 1980–85; Arteriosclerosis, 1981–87; Jl Biol Chemistry, 1981–85; Cell, 1983–; Science, 1985–87. Member: Nat. Acad. of Scis (Lounsbery Award, 1979); Amer. Acad. of Arts and Scis, and other bodies; Foreign Mem., Royal Soc., 1991. Hon. DSc: Chicago, 1982; Rensselaer Polytechnic Inst., 1982; Washington and Lee Univ., 1986; Univ. of Paris-Sud, 1988; Univ. of Buenos Aires, 1990. Numerous awards from scientific instns, incl. Pfizer Award in Enzyme Chemistry, Amer. Chem. Soc., 1976; award in biol and med. scis, NY Acad. Scis, 1981; Albert Lasker Award in Basic Science (with Michael Brown), 1985; Nobel Prize (with Michael Brown) for Physiology or Medicine, 1985; US Nat. Medal of Science, 1988. *Publications:* (jtly) The Metabolic Basis of Inherited Diseases, 5th edn 1983; papers on genetics educn and science subjects. *Address:* Department of Molecular Genetics, University of Texas Southwestern Medical Center at Dallas, 5323 Harry Hines Boulevard, Dallas, TX 75235, USA; 3831 Turtle Creek Boulevard, Apt 22-B, TX 75219, USA.

GOLDSTEIN, Dr Michael, FRSC; Vice-Chancellor, Coventry University, since 1992 (Director, Coventry Polytechnic, 1987–92); *b* 1 May 1939; *s* of Sarah and Jacob Goldstein; *m* 1962, Janet Sandra Skevington; one *s*. *Educ:* Hackney Downs Grammar School; Northern Polytechnic, London. BSc, PhD, DSc; CChem. Lectr, sen. lectr, principal lectr, Polytechnic of N London, 1963–73; Head of Dept of Chemistry, 1974–83 and Dean of Faculty of Science, 1979–83, Sheffield City Polytechnic; Dep. Dir, Coventry Lanchester Polytechnic, 1983–87. Mem., cttees and bds, CNAA, 1975–93, incl. Chm., CNAA Chem. Bd, 1978–84; Dep. Chm., Polys and Colls Admissions System, 1989–94; Member: UCAS, 1993–; Univs and Colls Employers Agency, 1994–. Mem. Bd, Coventry and Warwicks TEC, 1992–. Member Committee: Coventry Common Purpose, 1989–; Coventry is making it, 1992–. Member: RSC Council, 1983–86, 1993–; other RSC cttees, 1975– (Pres., Educn Div., 1993–). Hon. FCGI. *Publications:* contribs to sci. jls, chapters in review books. *Recreations:* Coventry City FC, exercise. *Address:* 26 Fairlands Park, Coventry CV4 7DS. *T:* Coventry (01203) 416818.

GOLDSTEIN, Simon Alfred; His Honour Judge Goldstein; a Circuit Judge, since 1987; *b* 6 June 1935; *s* of Harry and Constance Goldstein; *m* 1973, Zoë Philippa, *yr d* of late Basil Gerrard Smith, TD. *Educ:* East Ham Grammar Sch.; Fitzwilliam Coll., Cambridge (BA 1956). Educn Officer, RAF, 1957–60. Called to the Bar, Middle Temple, 1961; Dep. Circuit Judge, 1975; a Recorder, 1980–87. *Recreation:* bridge. *Address:* 1 Albion Close, W2 2AT. *Club:* London Duplicate Bridge.

GOLDSTEIN-JACKSON, Kevin Grierson, JP; writer; company director; *b* 2 Nov. 1946; *s* of H. G. and W. M. E. Jackson; *m* 1975, Jenny Mei Leng, *e d* of Ufong Ng, Malaysia; two *d*. *Educ:* Reading Univ. (BA Phil. and Sociol.); Southampton Univ. (MPhil Law). Staff Relations Dept, London Transport (Railways), 1966; Scottish Widows Pension & Life Assurance Soc., 1967; Prog. Organizer, Southern TV, 1970–73; Asst Prod., HK-TVB, Hong Kong, 1973; freelance writer/TV prod., 1973–75; Head of Film, Dhofar Region TV Service, Sultanate of Oman, 1975–76; Founder and Dir, Thames Valley Radio, 1974–77; Asst to Head of Drama, Anglia TV, 1977–81; Founder, TSW-Television South West: Programme Controller and Dir of Progs, 1981–85; Jt Man. Dir, 1981–82; Chief Exec., 1982–85. Writer of TV scripts. Dir of private cos. Gov., Lilliput First Sch., Poole, 1988–93. FRSA 1978; FIMgt (FBIM 1982); FInstD 1982; FFA 1988; FRGS 1989. JP Poole, 1990. *Publications:* 17 books, including: The Right Joke for the Right Occasion, 1973; Experiments with Everyday Objects, 1976; Things to make with Everyday Objects, 1978; Magic with Everyday Objects, 1979; Dictionary of Essential Quotations, 1983; Jokes for Telling, 1986; Share Millions, 1989; The Public Speaker's Joke Book, 1991; The Astute Private Investor, 1994; contrib. financial and gen. pubns. *Recreations:* writing, TV, films, theatre, travel, music, walking, philosophical and sociological investigation. *Address:* c/o Alcazar, 18 Martello Road, Branksome Park, Poole, Dorset BH13 7DH.

GOLDSTONE, David Joseph; Chairman since 1990, and Chief Executive since 1970, Regalian Properties Plc; *b* 21 Feb. 1929; *s* of Solomon Goldstone and Rebecca Goldstone (*née* Degotts); *m* 1957, Cynthia (*née* Easton); one *s* two *d*. *Educ:* Dynevor Secondary Sch., Swansea; London School of Economics and Political Science (LLB Hons). Admitted Solicitor (Hons), 1955. Legal practice, 1955–66. Dir, Swansea Sound Commercial Radio Ltd, 1974–. Mem., London Forum, 1993–; Vice Pres., London Welsh Trust Ltd, 1990–. Member Council: Football Assoc. of Wales, 1970–72; WNO, 1984–89; Inst. of Jewish Affairs, 1990–. Member: Court of Govs, LSE, 1985–; Council, Atlantic Coll., 1987–; Council, London Univ. *Recreations:* family, reading, sport. *Address:* 44 Grosvenor Hill, W1A 4NR. *T:* 0171–493 9613. *Clubs:* Bath & Racquets, Riverside Racquet Centre.

GOLDSTONE, Prof. Jeffrey, PhD; FRS 1977; Cecil and Ida Green Professor in Physics, Massachusetts Institute of Technology, since 1983 (Director, Center for Theoretical Physics, 1983–89); *b* 3 Sept. 1933; *s* of Hyman Goldstone and Sophia Goldstone; *m* 1980, Roberta Gordon; one *s*. *Educ:* Manchester Grammar Sch.; Trinity Coll., Cambridge (MA 1956, PhD 1958). Trinity Coll., Cambridge: Entrance Scholar, 1951; Res. Fellow, 1956; Staff Fellow, 1962; Cambridge University: Lectr, 1961; Reader in Math. Physics, 1976; Prof. of Physics, MIT, 1977. Vis. appointments: Institut for Teoretisk Fysik, Copenhagen; CERN, Geneva; Harvard Univ.; MIT; Inst. for Theoretical Physics, Santa Barbara; Stanford Linear Accelerator Center; Lab. de Physique Théorique, L'Ecole Normale Supérieure, Paris; Università di Roma I. Smith's Prize, Cambridge Univ., 1955; Dannie Heineman Prize, Amer. Phys. Soc., 1981; Guthrie Medal, Inst. of Physics, 1983; Dirac Medal, Internat. Centre for Theoretical Physics, 1991. *Publications:* articles in learned jls. *Address:* Department of Physics, (6–313) Massachusetts Institute of Technology, Cambridge, MA 02139, USA. *T:* (office) (617) 2536263.

GOLDSTONE, Leonard Clement; QC 1993; a Recorder, since 1992; *b* 20 April 1949; *s* of Maurice and Maree Goldstone; *m* 1972, Vanessa, *yr d* of Donald Forster, *qv*; three *s*. *Educ:* Manchester Grammar Sch.; Churchill Coll., Cambridge (BA). Called to the Bar, Middle Temple, 1971. *Recreations:* golf, bridge, music, theatre. *Address:* 28 St John Street, Manchester M3 4DJ. *T:* 0161–834 8418. *Club:* Dunham Forest Golf and Country (Altrincham).

GOLDSTONE, Peter Walter; His Honour Judge Goldstone; a Circuit Judge, since 1978; *b* 1 Nov. 1926; *y s* of late Adolph Lionel Goldstone and Ivy Gwendoline Goldstone; *m* 1955, Patricia (*née* Alexander), JP; one *s* two *d*. *Educ:* Manchester Grammar Sch.; Manchester Univ. Solicitor, 1951. Fleet Air Arm, 1944–47. Partner in private practice with brother Julian S. Goldstone, 1951–71. Manchester City Councillor (L), 1962–65; Chm., Manchester Rent Assessment Panel, 1967–71; Reserve Chm., Manchester Rent Tribunal, 1969–71; Dep. Chm., Inner London QS, Nov. 1971; a Metropolitan Stipendiary Magistrate, 1971–78; a Recorder of the Crown Court, 1972–78. *Recreations:* walking, gardening, reading. *Address:* c/o Watford County Court, Cassiobury House, 11/19 Station Road, Watford WD1 1EZ. *T:* Watford (01923) 249666. *Club:* MCC.

GOLDSWORTHY, Andrew, (Andy); artist; *b* 25 July 1956; *s* of Frederick Goldsworthy and Muriel Goldsworthy (*née* Stangar); *m* 1982, Judith Gregson; two *s* two *d*. *Educ:* Harrogate Secondary Mod. Sch.; Harrogate High Sch.; Bradford Coll. of Art; Lancashire Poly. Has worked in Yorkshire, Cumbria and Dumfriesshire, 1978–. Hon. MA Bradford, 1993. *Publications:* Touching North, 1989; Leaves, 1989; Hand to Earth, 1990; Andy Goldsworthy, 1990; Snow and Ice Drawings, 1992; Two Autumns, 1993; Stone, 1994; Black Stones–Red Pools, 1995. *Address:* c/o Michael Hue-Williams, Fine Art, 60A Pont Street, SW1X 0AE.

GOLDSWORTHY, Rt. Rev. (Arthur) Stanley; permission to officiate, diocese of The Murray, SA, since 1992; *b* 18 Feb. 1926; *s* of Arthur and Doris Irene Goldsworthy; *m* 1952, Gwen Elizabeth Reeves; one *s* one *d*. *Educ:* Dandenong High School, Vic; St Columb's Theological Coll., Wangaratta. Deacon 1951, priest 1952; Curate of Wodonga, in charge of Bethanga, 1951–52; Priest of Chiltern, 1952; Kensington, Melbourne, 1955; Yarrawonga, Wangaratta, 1959; Shepparton (and Archdeacon), 1972; Parish Priest of Wodonga, and Archdeacon of Diocese of Wangaratta, 1977; Bishop of Bunbury, 1977–83; an Assisting Bishop to Primate of Australia, 1983–84; Parish Priest: St John, Hendra, Brisbane, 1983–84; Tailem Bend, Meningie, SA, 1989–92, retired. Chaplain to Community of the Sisters of the Church, 1956–77. *Recreations:* music, gardening. *Address:* Ikon Lodge, 4 Hall Street, McLaren Vale, SA 5171, Australia. *T:* (8) 3239557.

GOLDSWORTHY, Ian Francis; QC 1992; a Recorder of the Crown Court, since 1991; *b* 7 July 1943; *s* of Francis Charles and Mary Goldsworthy; *m* 1974, Lindsay Mary Steel; three *d*. *Educ:* Clifton Coll.; University Coll., Oxford. Called to the Bar, Inner Temple, 1968. *Recreations:* Master of Ratte-hounds, antiques, music. *Address:* 36 Essex Street, WC2R 3AS. *T:* 0171–413 0353.

GOLDSWORTHY, Rt. Rev. Stanley; *see* Goldsworthy, Rt Rev. A. S.

GOLDTHORPE, John Harry, FBA 1984; Official Fellow, Nuffield College, Oxford, since 1969; *b* 27 May 1935; *s* of Harry Goldthorpe and Lilian Eliza Goldthorpe; *m* 1963, Rhiannon Esyllt (*née* Harry); one *s* one *d*. *Educ:* Wath-upon-Dearne Grammar School; University College London (BA Hons 1st Class Mod. Hist.); LSE. MA Cantab; MA Oxon. Asst Lectr, Dept of Sociology, Univ. of Leicester , 1957–60; Fellow of King's College, Cambridge, 1960–69; Asst Lectr and Lectr, Faculty of Economics and Politics, Cambridge, 1962–69. Lectures: Fuller, Univ. of Essex, 1979; Marshall, Univ. of Southampton, 1989; Aubert, Oslo Univ., 1993. Mem., Academia Europaea, 1988. Hon. FilDr Stockholm Univ., 1990. *Publications:* (with David Lockwood and others): The Affluent Worker: industrial attitudes and behaviour, 1968; The Affluent Worker: political attitudes and behaviour, 1968; The Affluent Worker in the Class Structure, 1969; (with Keith Hope) The Social Grading of Occupations, 1974; (with Fred Hirsch) The Political

Economy of Inflation, 1978; Social Mobility and Class Structure in Modern Britain, 1980, 2nd edn 1987; Order and Conflict in Contemporary Capitalism, 1984; (with Hermann Strasser) Die Analyse Sozialer Ungleichheit, 1985; (contrib.) John H. Goldthorpe: consensus and controversy (ed Clark, Modgil and Modgil), 1990; (with Robert Erikson) The Constant Flux: a study of class mobility in industrial societies, 1992; (with Christopher Whelan) The Development of Industrial Society in Ireland, 1992; papers in Acta Sociologica, American Jl of Sociology, British Jl of Sociology, Sociological Review, Sociology, European Jl of Sociology, European Sociological Rev., Sociologie du Travail, Rev. Française de Sociologie. *Recreations:* lawn tennis, bird watching, computer chess. *Address:* 32 Leckford Road, Oxford OX2 6HX. *T:* Oxford (01865) 56602.

GOLDWATER, Barry M(orris); US Senator from Arizona, 1953–64, and 1969–87; *b* Phoenix, Arizona, 1 Jan. 1909; *s* of late Baron Goldwater and Josephine Williams; *m* 1st, 1934, Margaret Johnson (*d* 1985); two *s* two *d*; 2nd, 1992, Susan McMurray Wechsler. *Educ:* Staunton Mil. Acad., Virginia; University of Arizona. 2nd Lieut, Army Reserve, 1930; transferred to USAAF, 1941; served as ferry-command and fighter pilot instructor, Asia, 1941–45 (Lieut-Col); Chief of Staff, Arizona Nat. Guard, 1945–52 (Col); Maj.-Gen., USAF Reserves. Joined Goldwater's Inc., 1929 (Pres., 1937–53). City Councilman, Phoenix, 1949–52; Republican Candidate for the Presidency of the USA, 1964. Chm., Senate Armed Services Cttee, 1985–; Member: Advisory Cttee on Indian Affairs, Dept of Interior, 1948–50; Commerce, Science and Transportation Cttee; Small Business Cttee; Heard Museum; Museum of Northern Arizona; St Joseph's Hosp.; Vice-Chairman: Amer. Graduate Sch. of Internat. Management; Bd of Regents, Smithsonian Institution; Member: Veterans of Foreign Wars; American Legion; Royal Photographic Society, etc. US Junior Chamber of Commerce Award, 1937; Man of the Year, Phoenix, 1949; Medal of Freedom, 1986. 33° Mason. *Publications:* Arizona Portraits (2 vols), 1940; Journey Down the River of Canyons, 1940; Speeches of Henry Ashurst: The Conscience of a Conservative, 1960; Why Not Victory?, 1962; Where I Stand, 1964; The Face of Arizona, 1964; People and Places, 1967; The Conscience of the Majority, 1970; Delightful Journey, 1970; The Coming Breakpoint, 1976; Barry Goldwater and the Southwest, 1976; With No Apologies, 1979; (with J. Casserly) Goldwater (autobiog.), 1988. *Address:* PO Box 1601, Scottsdale, AZ 85252, USA.

GOLIGHER, Prof. John Cedric, ChM, FRCS; Professor and Chairman, Department of Surgery, Leeds University, 1954–77, now Emeritus; Consulting Surgeon, St Mark's Hospital for Diseases of Rectum and Colon, London, since 1954; *b* Londonderry, N Ireland, 13 March 1912; *s* of John Hunter Goligher; *m* 1952, Gwenllian Nancy, *d* of Norman R. Williams, Melbourne, Aust.; one *s* two *d. Educ:* Foyle Coll., Londonderry; Edinburgh Univ. MB, ChB 1934; ChM 1948, Edinburgh; FRCS, FRCSE 1938. Junior hosp. appts mainly in Edinburgh area; Res. Surg. Officer, St Mark's Hosp., London; served War 1940–46, RAMC, as Surgical Specialist, Major and Lt-Col; then Surgical Registrar, St Mary's Hosp., London; Surg., St Mary's Hosp., and St Mark's Hosp. for Diseases of the Rectum and Colon, 1947–54. Mem. Council, RCS, 1968–80. FRSocMed (Past Pres., Section of Proctology); Fellow, Assoc. Surgeons of Gt Brit. and Ire. (Past Pres.); Mem. Brit. Soc. of Gastroenterology (Past Pres.). Hon. FACS, 1974; Hon. FRCSI, 1977; Hon. FRACS, 1978; Hon. FRSM 1986; Hon. Fellow: Brasilian Coll. of Surgeons; Amer. Surg. Assoc.; Amer. Soc. of Colon and Rectal Surgeons; Soc. for Surgery of the Alimentary Tract; British Soc. of Coloproctology; Internat. Soc. of Univ. Colon and Rectal Surgeons. Corresp. Mem., German Surgical Soc.; Hon. Mem., French, Swiss and Austrian Surg. Socs. Many vis. professorships and named lectures in UK, Europe, N and S America, ME, FE and the Antipodes. Hon. MD: Göteborg, 1976; Belfast, 1981; Uruguay, 1983; Hon. DSc Leeds, 1980. Liston Award, RCSE, 1977; Lister Award, RCS, 1981. *Publications:* Surgery of the Anus, Rectum and Colon, 1961, 5th edn 1984; numerous contribs to books and med. journals, dealing mainly with gastric and colorectal surgery. *Recreations:* reading, tennis, music, gastronomy and oenology, travel. *Address:* Ladywood, Northgate Lane, Linton, Wetherby, West Yorks LS22 4HP.

GOLLANCZ, Livia Ruth; Chairman, Victor Gollancz Ltd, 1983–89 (Governing Director, Joint Managing Director, 1965–85, Consultant, 1990–92); *b* 25 May 1920; *d* of Victor Gollancz and Ruth Lowy. *Educ:* St Paul's Girls' Sch.; Royal Coll. of Music (ARCM, solo horn). Horn player: LSO, 1940–43; Hallé Orch., 1943–45; Scottish Orch., 1945–46; BBC Scottish Orch., 1946–47; Covent Garden, 1947; Sadler's Wells, 1950–53. Joined Victor Gollancz Ltd as editorial asst and typographer, 1953; Dir, 1954. *Publication:* (ed and introd) Victor Gollancz, Reminiscences of Affection, 1968 (posthumous). *Recreations:* singing, hill walking, gardening. *Address:* 26 Cholmeley Crescent, N6 5HA. *Club:* Alpine.

GOLLIN, Prof. Alfred M., DLitt; FRSL; Professor of History, University of California, Santa Barbara, 1967–94, now Professor Emeritus (Chairman, Department of History, 1976–77); *b* 6 Feb. 1926; 2nd *s* of Max and Sue Gollin; *m* 1st, 1951, Gurli Sørensen (marr. diss.); two *d*; 2nd, 1975, Valerie Watkins (*née* Kilner). *Educ:* New York City Public Schs; City College of New York; Harvard Univ.; New Coll., Oxford (BA); St Antony's Coll., Oxford (MA); DPhil Oxon 1957; DLitt Oxon 1968. Served US Army, 1943–46; taught history at New Coll., Oxford, 1951–54; official historian for The Observer, 1952–59; Lectr, City Coll. of New York, 1959; Univ. of California, Los Angeles: Acting Asst Prof., 1959–60; Research Associate, 1960–61; Associate Prof., Univ. of California, Santa Barbara, 1966–67. Dir, Study Center of Univ. of California, UK and Ire., 1971–73; Mem., US-UK Educnl Commn, 1971–72. Fellow: J. S. Guggenheim Foundn, 1962, 1964, 1971; Amer. Council of Learned Socs, 1963, 1975; Nat. Endowment for Humanities, 1989; FRHistS 1976; FRSL 1986. *Publications:* The Observer and J. L. Garvin, 1960; Proconsul in Politics: a study of Lord Milner, 1964; From Omdurman to V. E. Day: the Life Span of Sir Winston Churchill, 1964; Balfour's Burden, 1965; Asquith, a New View, in A Century of Conflict, Essays for A. J. P. Taylor, 1966; Balfour, in The Conservative Leadership (ed D. Southgate), 1974; No Longer an Island, 1984; The Impact of Air Power on the British People and their Government 1909–14, 1989; articles and reviews in various jls. *Recreation:* swimming. *Address:* Department of History, University of California, Santa Barbara, CA 93106, USA. *Club:* Reform.

GOMBRICH, Sir Ernst (Hans Josef), OM 1988; Kt 1972; CBE 1966; FBA 1960; FSA 1961; PhD (Vienna); MA Oxon and Cantab; Director of the Warburg Institute and Professor of the History of the Classical Tradition in the University of London, 1959–76, now Emeritus Professor; *b* Vienna, 30 March 1909; *s* of Dr Karl B. Gombrich, Vice-Pres. of Disciplinary Council of Lawyers' Chamber, Vienna, and Prof. Leonie Gombrich (*née* Hock), pianist; *m* 1936, Ilse Heller; one *s*. *Educ:* Theresianum, Vienna; Vienna Univ. Research Asst, Warburg Inst., 1936–39. Served War of 1939–45 with BBC Monitoring Service. Senior Research Fellow, 1946–48, Lectr, 1948–54, Reader, 1954–56, Special Lectr, 1956–59, Warburg Inst., Univ. of London; Durning-Lawrence Prof. of the History of Art, London Univ., at University Coll., 1956–59; Slade Prof. of Fine Art in the University of Oxford, 1950–53; Visiting Prof. of Fine Art, Harvard Univ., 1959; Slade Prof. of Fine Art, Cambridge Univ., 1961–63; Lethaby Prof., RCA, 1967–68; Andrew D. White Prof.-at-Large, Cornell, 1970–77. A Trustee of the British Museum, 1974–79; Mem., Museums and Galleries Commn (formerly Standing Commn on Museums and Galleries), 1976–82. Hon. Fellow: Jesus Coll., Cambridge, 1963; UCL, 1992. FRSL 1975; Foreign Hon. Mem., American Academy of Arts and Sciences, 1964; For. Mem., Amer. Philosophical Soc., 1968; Hon. Member: American Acad. and Inst. of Arts and Letters, 1985; Akad. der Wissenschaften zu Göttingen, 1986; Modern Lang. Assoc. of America, 1988; Deutsche Akademie für Sprache und Dichtung, 1988; Austrian Acad. of Scis, 1991; Corresponding Member: Accademia delle Scienze di Torino, 1962; Royal Acad. of Arts and Sciences, Uppsala, 1970; Koninklijke Nederlandse Akademie van Wetenschapen, 1973; Bayerische Akad. der Wissenschaften, 1979; Royal Swedish Acad. of Sciences, 1981; European Acad. of Arts, Scis and Humanities, 1980; Accademia Nazionale dei Lincei, 1983; Royal Belgian Acad. of Science, Letters and Fine Arts, 1989. Hon. FRIBA, 1971; Hon. Fellow: Royal Acad. of Arts, 1982; Bezalel Acad. of Arts and Design, 1983. Hon. DLit: Belfast, 1963; London, 1976; Richmond Coll., London, 1993; Hon. LLD St Andrews, 1965; Hon. LittD: Leeds, 1965; Cambridge, 1970; Manchester, 1974; Hon. DLitt: Oxford, 1969; Harvard, 1976; New York, 1986; Urbino, 1992; Hon. Dr Lit. Hum.: Chicago, 1975; Pennsylvania, 1977; DU Essex, 1977; Hon. DHL: Brandeis, 1981; Emory, 1991; Hon. Dr RCA, 1984; Hon. Dr in Geography and History, Universidad Complutense de Madrid, 1992. W. H. Smith Literary Award, 1964; Medal of New York Univ. for Distinguished Visitors, 1970; Erasmus Prize, 1975; Ehrenkreuz für Wissenschaft und Kunst, 1st cl., Austria, 1975; Hegel Prize, 1976; Medal of Collège de France, 1977; Orden Pour le Mérite für Wissenschaften und Künste, 1977; Ehrenzeichen für Wissenschaft und Kunst, Austria 1984; Premio Rosina Viva of Anacapri, 1985; Internat. Balzan Prize, 1985; Kulturpreis der Stadt Wien, 1986; Ludwig Wittgenstein-Preis der Österreichischen Forschungsgemeinschaft, 1988; Britannica Award, Encyclopedia Britannica, 1989; Goethe Medaille, 1989; Austrian Auslands Kulturpreis, 1993; Goethe Prize, Frankfurt, 1994; Golden Medal, Vienna, 1994. *Publications:* Weltgeschichte für Kinder, 1936, rev. and enl. edn 1985; (with E. Kris) Caricature, 1940; The Story of Art, 1950, 15th edn 1989; Art and Illusion (The A. W. Mellon Lectures in the Fine Arts, 1956), 1960; Meditations on a Hobby Horse, 1963; Norm and Form, 1966; Aby Warburg, an intellectual biography, 1970; Symbolic Images, 1972; In Search of Cultural History, 1972; (jtly) Art, Perception and Reality, 1973; (ed jtly) Illusion in Nature and Art, 1973; Art History and the Social Sciences (Romanes Lect.), 1975; The Heritage of Apelles, 1976; Means and Ends (W. Neurath Lect.), 1976; The Sense of Order (Wrightsman Lect.), 1979; Ideals and Idols, 1979; The Image and the Eye, 1982; Tributes, 1984; New Light on Old Masters, 1986; Oskar Kokoschka in his Time, 1986; Reflections on the History of Art (ed R. Woodfield), 1987; Topics of Our Time, 1991; Styles of Art and Styles of Life (Reynolds Lect.), 1991; (with D. Eribon) Ce que l'image nous dit: entretiens sur l'art et la science, 1991; Gastspiele: zur Deutschen Sprache und Germanistik, 1992; Künstler, Kenner, Kunden (Wiener Vorlesungen im Rathaus), 1993; Das forschene Auge, 1994; contributions to learned journals. *Address:* 19 Briardale Gardens, NW3 7PN. *T:* 0171–435 6639.

See also R. F. Gombrich.

GOMBRICH, Prof. Richard Francis, DPhil; Boden Professor of Sanskrit, Oxford University, since 1976; Fellow of Balliol College, Oxford, since 1976; Emeritus Fellow of Wolfson, 1977; *b* 17 July 1937; *s* of Sir Ernst Gombrich, *qv*; *m* 1st, 1964, Dorothea Amanda Friedrich (marr. diss. 1984); one *s* one *d*; 2nd, 1985, Sanjukta Gupta. *Educ:* Magdalen Coll., Oxford (MA, DPhil); Harvard Univ. (AM). Univ. Lectr in Sanskrit and Pali, Oxford Univ., 1965–76; Fellow of Wolfson Coll., 1966–76. Stewart Fellow, Princeton Univ., 1986–87. Pres., Pali Text Soc., 1994– (Hon. Sec., 1982–94). Hon. DLitt Kalyani Univ., West Bengal, 1991. Sri Lanka Ranjana (Sri Lanka), 1994. *Publications:* Precept and Practice: traditional Buddhism in the rural highlands of Ceylon, 1971, 2nd edn, as Buddhist Precept and Practice, 1991; (with Margaret Cone) The Perfect Generosity of Prince Vessantara, 1977; On being Sanskritic, 1978; (ed with Heinz Bechert) The World of Buddhism, 1984; Theravada Buddhism: a social history from ancient Benares to modern Colombo, 1988; (with G. Obeyesekere) Buddhism Transformed, 1988; contribs to oriental and anthropological journals. *Recreations:* singing, walking, photography. *Address:* Balliol College, Oxford OX1 3BJ.

GOMERSALL, Stephen John; HM Diplomatic Service; Deputy Permanent Representative, UK Mission to the United Nations, since 1994; *b* 17 Jan. 1948; *s* of Harry Raymond Gomersall and Helen Gomersall; *m* 1975, Lydia Veronica (*née* Parry); two *s* one *d. Educ:* Forest Sch., Snaresbrook; Queens' Coll., Cambridge (Mod. Langs, MA); Stanford Univ., Calif (MA 1970). Entered HM Diplomatic Service, 1970; Tokyo, 1972–77; Rhodesia Dept, FCO, 1977–79; Private Sec. to Lord Privy Seal, 1979–82; Washington, 1982–85; Econ. Counsellor, Tokyo, 1986–90; Head of Security Policy Dept, FCO, 1990–94. *Recreations:* music, composing silly songs. *Address:* c/o Foreign and Commonwealth Office, King Charles Street, SW1A 2AH.

GOMEZ, Jill; singer; *b* Trinidad, of Spanish and English parents. *Educ:* Royal Academy of Music (FRAM 1986); Guildhall School of Music, London. Operatic début as Adina in L'Elisir d'Amore with Glyndebourne Touring Opera, 1968 (after winning John Christie Award), then Glyndebourne Fest. Opera, 1969, and has subseq. sung leading roles, incl. Mélisande, Calisto, Anne Truelove in The Rake's Progress, Helena in A Midsummer Night's Dream; has appeared with The Royal Opera, English Opera Gp, ENO, WNO and Scottish Opera in roles including Pamina, Ilia, Fiordiligi, The Countess in Figaro, Elizabeth in Elegy for Young Lovers, Tytania, Lauretta in Gianni Schicchi, the Governess in The Turn of the Screw, Jenifer in The Midsummer Marriage, Leila in Les Pêcheurs de Perles; with Kent Opera: Tatiana in Eugene Onegin, 1977; Violetta in La Traviata, 1979; Amyntas in Il Re Pastore, 1987; Donna Anna in Don Giovanni, 1988; created the role of Flora in Tippett's The Knot Garden, 1970, at Covent Garden, and of the Countess in Thea Musgrave's Voice of Ariadne, Aldeburgh, 1974; created title role in William Alwyn's Miss Julie for radio, 1977; title rôle BBC world première, Prokoviev's Maddalena, 1979; Duchess, world première, Adès' Powder Her Face, 1995; other rôles include Donna Elvira, Cinna in Mozart's Lucio Silla, Cleopatra in Giulio Cesare, Teresa in Benvenuto Cellini, title rôle in Massenet's Thaïs, Desdemona in Otello, at Edinburgh, Wexford, and in Austria, France, Germany and Switzerland; première of Eighth Book of Madrigals, Monteverdi Fest., Zürich, 1979. Also recitalist, progs incl. A Spanish Songbook, Songs for the Night, and Night and Day, perf. world-wide; concert repertoire includes Rameau, Bach, Handel (Messiah and cantatas), Haydn's Creation and Seasons, Mozart's Requiem and concert arias, Beethoven's Ninth, Berlioz's Nuits d'Eté, Brahms's Requiem, Fauré's Requiem, Ravel's Shéhérazade, Mahler's Second, Fourth and Eighth Symphonies, Strauss's Four Last Songs, Britten's Les Illuminations, Spring Symphony and War Requiem, Tippett's A Child of Our Time, Messiaen's Poèmes pour Mi, Webern op. 13 and 14 songs, and Schubert songs orch. Webern. Commissioned Cantiga—the song of Iñes de Castro (dramatic scena for soprano and orch.) from David Matthews (world première, BBC Prom., 1988). Regular engagements in France, Belgium, Holland, Germany, Scandinavia, Switzerland, Italy, Spain, Israel, America; festival appearances include Aix-en-Provence, Spoleto, Bergen, Versailles, Flanders, Holland, Prague, Edinburgh, Aldeburgh, and BBC Prom. concerts. Recordings include three solo recitals (French, Spanish, and songs by Mozart), Ravel's Poèmes de Mallarmé, Handel's Admeto, Acis and Galatea, Elvira in Don Giovanni, Fauré's Pelléas et Mélisande, Handel's Ode on St Cecilia's Day, Rameau's La Danse, Britten's Les Illuminations, Canteloube's Songs of the Auvergne, Villa Lobos' Bachianas Brasilieras no 5, Samuel Barber's Knoxville—Summer of 1915, Cabaret Classics (with John Constable), Britten's Blues, Cole Porter Songs, South of the Border, A Spanish Songbook (with John Constable); première recordings: David Matthew's Cantiga, Mahler's Seven Early Songs, and Britten's Quatre Chansons Françaises. *Address:* 16 Milton Park, N6 5QA.

GOMM, Richard Culling C.; *see* Carr-Gomm, R. C.

GOMME, Robert Anthony, CB 1990; Under Secretary, Department of the Environment, 1981–90, retired; *b* 19 Nov. 1930; *s* of Harold Kenelm Gomme and Alice Grace (*née* Jacques); *m* 1960, Helen Perris (*née* Moore); one *s* one *d*. *Educ:* Colfe's Grammar Sch., Lewisham; London School of Economics, Univ. of London (BScEcon 1955). National Service, Korea, with Royal Norfolk Regt, 1951–52; Pirelli Ltd, 1955–66; NEDO, 1966–68; direct entrant Principal, Min. of Public Building and Works, 1968; Asst Sec., DoE, 1972–74; RCDS 1975; Cabinet Office, 1976–79; Department of the Environment: Dir of Defence Services, PSA, 1981–86; Prin. Finance Officer, 1987–90; Chief Exec., Crown Suppliers, 1990. Member: Exec. Cttee, Friends of the National Libraries, 1991–; Cttee, London Library, 1992–. Hon. Treas., Friends of Greenwich Park, 1992–. *Address:* 14 Vanbrugh Fields, Blackheath, SE3 7TZ. *T:* 0181–858 5148.

GOMPERTZ, (Arthur John) Jeremy; QC 1988; *b* 16 Oct. 1937; *s* of late Col Arthur William Bean Gompertz and Muriel Annie Gompertz (*née* Smith). *Educ:* Beaumont Coll.; Trinity Coll., Cambridge (BA). Called to the Bar, Gray's Inn, 1962; in practice, South East Circuit; a Recorder, 1987. *Recreations:* racing and breeding, travel, ski-ing. *Address:* 5 Essex Court, Temple, EC4Y 9AH. *T:* 0171–583 2825.

GÖNCZ, Árpád, Hon. KCMG 1991; President, Republic of Hungary, since 1990; *b* 10 Feb. 1922; *s* of Lajos Göncz and Ilona Heimann; *m* 1946, Mária Zsuzsanna Göntér; two *s* two *d*. *Educ:* Pázmány Péter Univ. (DJ 1944); Univ. of Agric. Scis. Nat. Land Bank, 1942–45; Independent Smallholders' Party: Sec. to Gen. Sec.; Leader, Independent Youth; Editor in Chief, Generation (weekly), 1947–48; jobless from 1948, worked as welder and metalsmith; sentenced to life inprisonment for political activity, 1957; released under general amnesty, 1963; freelance writer and literary translator, esp. of English works, 1963–; Pres., Hungarian Writers' Union, 1989–90; founding mem., Free Initiatives Network, Free Democratic Fedn, Historic Justice Cttee; MP, regional list, 1990; Speaker of Parliament and President *ai*, Republic of Hungary, May–Aug. 1990. József Attila Literary Prize, 1983; Wheatland Prize, 1989; Premio Mediterraneo, 1991. *Publications:* Men of God, 1974; Hungarian Medea, Iron Bars, 1979; Encounters, 1980; Balance, 1990; Homecoming, 1991; Shavings, 1991. *Recreations:* reading, walking. *Address:* Parliament, Kossuth tér 1–3, 1357 Budapest, Hungary. *T:* 269–0367.

GONZÁLEZ MÁRQUEZ, Felipe; Prime Minister of Spain, since 1982; *b* 5 March 1942; *s* of Felipe González and Juana Márquez; *m* 1969, Carmen Romero Lopez; two *s* one *d*. *Educ:* Univ. of Seville (Law degree); Univ. of Louvaine. Opened first labour law office, Seville, 1966; Spanish Socialist Party (PSOE), 1964–: Mem., Seville Provincial Cttee, 1965–69; Mem., Nat. Cttee, 1969–70; Mem., Exec. Bd, 1970; First Sec., 1974–79, resigned; re-elected, 1979; now Sec.-Gen. Pres., Council of Ministers, 1982–; Chm., Socialist Parly Group. Grand Cross, Order of Military Merit, 1984. *Publications:* What is Socialism?, 1976; PSOE, 1977. *Address:* Palacio de la Moncloa, Madrid, Spain. *T:* (1) 2668000.

GOOBEY, Alastair R.; *see* Ross Goobey.

GOOCH, Graham Alan, OBE 1991; cricketer; *b* 23 July 1953; *s* of Alfred and Rose Gooch; *m* 1976, Brenda Daniels; three *d*. *Educ:* Leytonstone. Batsman and bowler; first played for Essex CCC, 1973, Captain, 1986–94; Member, England Test team, 1975–82 and 1986–Jan. 1995 (retired); played in S Africa, 1982; Captain of England, July 1988 and Sept. 1989–1993; 333 against India, highest score by a Test captain, 1990; 20 Test centuries; record no. of runs (8900) in English Test cricket, 1995. *Publications:* Batting, 1980; (with Alan Lee) My Cricket Diary 1981, 1982; (with Alan Lee) Out of the Wilderness, 1985; Testing Times (autobiog.), 1991; (with Frank Keating) Gooch: My Autobiography, 1995. *Address:* c/o Essex County Cricket Club, County Ground, New Writtle Street, Chelmsford, Essex CM2 0PG.

GOOCH, Prof. John, PhD; FRHistS; Professor of International History, Leeds University, since 1992; *b* 25 Aug. 1945; *s* of George Gooch and Doris Evelyn (*née* Mottram); *m* 1967, Catherine Ann Staley; one *s* one *d*. *Educ:* Brockenhurst County High Sch.; King's Coll., Univ. of London (BA Hons History, class 1, 1966; PhD War Studies 1969). FRHistS 1975. Asst Lectr in History, 1966–67, Asst Lectr in War Studies, 1969, KCL; University of Lancaster: Lectr in History, 1969–81; Sen. Lectr, 1981–84; Reader in History, 1984–88; Prof. of History, 1988–92. Sec. of the Navy Sen. Res. Fellow, US Naval War Coll., 1985–86; Vis. Prof. of Military and Naval History, Yale Univ., 1988; Associate Fellow, Davenport Coll., Yale, 1988. Chm. of Council, Army Records Soc., 1983–; Vice-Pres., RHistS, 1990–94. Editor, Jl of Strategic Studies, 1978–; Gen. Editor, Internat. Relations of the Great Powers; Member of Editorial Board: European History Qly; Diplomacy and Statecraft, Terrorism and Small Wars; Security Studies; War in History. Premio Internazionale di Cultura, Città di Anghiari, 1983. Kt, Order of Vila Viçosa (Portugal), 1991. *Publications:* The Plans of War: the general staff and British military strategy *c*. 1900–1916, 1974; Armies in Europe, 1980; The Prospect of War: studies in British defence policy 1847–1942, 1981; Politicians and Defence: studies in the formulation of British defence policy 1847–1970, 1981; Strategy and the Social Sciences, 1981; Military Deception and Strategic Surprise, 1982; Soldati e Borghesi nell' Europa Moderna, 1982; Army, State and Society in Italy 1870–1915, 1989 (Esercito, Stato e Società in Italia 1870–1915, 1994); Decisive Campaigns of the Second World War, 1989; (with Eliot A. Cohen) Military Misfortunes: the anatomy of failure in war, 1990. *Recreations:* Italian food and wine. *Address:* The Coach House, Chapel Lane, Ellel, Lancaster LA2 0PN. *T:* Lancaster (01524) 751525. *Club:* Savile.

GOOCH, Sir Peter; *see* Gooch, Sir T. S.

GOOCH, Sir (Richard) John Sherlock, 12th Bt *cr* 1746; JP; *b* 22 March 1930; *s* of Sir Robert Eric Sherlock Gooch, 11th Bt, KCVO, DSO and Katharine Clervaux (*d* 1974), *d* of late Maj.-Gen. Sir Edward Walter Clervaux Chaytor, KCMG, KCVO, CB; *S* father, 1978. *Educ:* Eton. Captain, The Life Guards; retired, 1963. JP Suffolk, 1970. *Heir:* *b* Major Timothy Robert Sherlock Gooch, MBE [*b* 7 Dec. 1934; *m* 1963, Susan Barbara Christie, *o d* of late Maj.-Gen. Kenneth Christie Cooper, CB, DSO, OBE; two *d*]. *Address:* Benacre Hall, Beccles, Suffolk NR34 7LJ. *T:* Lowestoft (01502) 740333.

GOOCH, Sir Trevor Sherlock, 5th Bt *cr* 1866, of Clewer Park, Berkshire; *b* 15 June 1915; *s* of Charles Trevor Gooch (*d* 1963; *g s* of Sir Daniel Gooch, 1st Bt), and Hester Stratford (*d* 1957), *d* of late Lt-Col Wright Sherlock; *S* kinsman, 1989; *m* 1st, 1956, Denys Anne (*d* 1976), *o d* of late Harold Victor Venables; one *s* four *d*; 2nd, 1978, Jean, *d* of late Joseph Wright. *Educ:* Charterhouse. Flt Lt, RAFVR, 1939–46. *Heir:* *s* Miles Peter Gooch, *b* 3 Feb. 1963. *Address:* Jardin de la Rocque, Mont de la Rocque, St Aubin, Jersey, CI. *T:* Jersey (0534) 42980. *Club:* Royal Channel Islands Yacht (Jersey).

GOOD, Tan Sri Donal Bernard Waters, CMG 1962; JMN (Malaysia), 1965; PSM (Malaysia), 1970; Commissioner of Law Revision, Malaysia, 1963; *b* 13 April 1907; *er s* of William John and Kathleen Mary Good, Dublin; *m* 1930, Kathryn, *er d* of Frank Lucas Stanley and Helena Kathleen Stanley, Dublin; one *s* one *d*. *Educ:* The High Sch., and Trinity Coll., Dublin. Scholar and Moderator in Classics, TCD, 1927–29; MA 1932; LLB 1933; Barrister, King's Inns, Dublin (Benchers' Prizeman), 1935; Barrister, Gray's Inn, 1948. Resident Magistrate, Kenya, 1940–45; Malayan Planning Unit, 1945; Crown Counsel, Malayan Union, 1946–48; Legal Adviser: Negri Sembilan and Malacca, 1948–49; Johore, 1949–50; Legal Draftsman, Sierra Leone, 1951–52; Legal Adviser, Selangor, 1952; Senior Federal Counsel, Federation of Malaya, 1952–55; Actg Solicitor-Gen., 1953 and 1955; Actg Judge of Supreme Court, 1953; Judge of Supreme Court, 1955–59; Judge of the Court of Appeal, Federation of Malaya, 1959–62. Chm. Detainees Review Commn, 1955–60; Pres. Industrial Court, 1956–57; Chm. Detained Persons Advisory Board, 1960. Coronation Medal, 1953. *Address:* Cullum Welch Court, Morden College, SE3 0PW.

GOOD, Sir John K.; *see* Kennedy-Good.

GOOD, Ven. Kenneth Roy; Archdeacon of Richmond, since 1993; *b* 28 Sept. 1941; *s* of Isaac Edward Good and Florence Helen Good (*née* White); *m* 1970, Joan Thérèse Bennett; one *s* one *d*. *Educ:* Stamford Sch.; King's Coll., London (BD 1966; AKC). Ordained deacon 1967, priest 1968; Asst Curate, St Peter, Stockton on Tees, 1967–70; Missions to Seamen: Port Chaplain, Antwerp, 1970–74, Kobe, 1974–79; Asst Gen. Sec., 1979–85; Vicar of Nunthorpe, 1985–93; RD of Stokesley, 1989–93. Hon. Canon, Kobe, 1985. *Recreations:* gardening, caravanning. *Address:* 62 Palace Road, Ripon, Yorks HG4 1HA. *T:* Ripon (01765) 604342.

GOODACRE, Kenneth, TD 1952; DL; Deputy Clerk to GLC, 1964–68; Clerk and Solicitor of Middlesex CC, 1955–65; Clerk of the Peace for Middlesex, 1959–65; *b* 29 Oct. 1910; *s* of Clifford and Florence Goodacre; *m* 1936, Dorothy (*d* 1992), *d* of Harold Kendall, Solicitor, Leeds; one *s*. *Educ:* Doncaster Grammar Sch. Admitted Solicitor, 1934; Asst Solicitor: Doncaster Corp., 1934–35; Barrow-in-Furness Corp., 1935–36; Sen. Solicitor, Blackburn Corp., 1936–39; served War of 1939–45, TA with E Lancs Regt and Staff 53 Div. (Major), and 2nd Army (Lieut-Col); released from Army Service, 1945, and granted hon. rank of Major; Dep. Town Clerk: Blackburn, 1945–49, Leicester, 1949–52; Town Clerk, Leicester, 1952–55. Partner, Gillhams, Solicitors, 1968–71; practised under name of K. Goodacre & Co., Solicitors, 1971–89. DL, Greater London (DL Middlesex, 1960–65), 1965. *Address:* 4 Chartfield Avenue, Putney, SW15 6HD. *T:* 0181–789 0794. *Club:* Hurlingham.

GOODACRE, Peter Eliot, RD 1979, with clasp 1991; Principal, College of Estate Management, Reading, since 1992; *b* 4 Nov. 1945; *s* of Edward Leslie Goodacre and Cicely May (*née* Elliott); *m* 1971, Brita Christina Forsling; two *d*. *Educ:* Kingston Grammar Sch.; Coll. of Estate Management; Loughborough Univ. of Technology (MSc). FRICS 1980. Commnd RNR, 1965; Lt Comdr, 1979. In private practice, 1966–69; Lecturer: Coll. of Estate Mgt, 1970–73; Univ. of Reading, 1973–78, Sen. Lectr 1978–83; Vice-Principal, Coll. of Estate Mgt, 1984–92. Mem., Gen. Council, RICS, 1986–. Freeman, City of London, 1994; Liveryman, Chartered Surveyors' Co., 1995–. *Publications:* Formula Method of Price Adjustment for Building Contracts, 1978, 2nd edn 1987; Cost Factors of Dimensional Co-ordination, 1981; Worked Examples in Quantity Surveying Measurement, 1982. *Recreations:* home and garden, ski-ing, riding. *Address:* College of Estate Management, Whiteknights, Reading, Berks RG6 6AW. *T:* Reading (01734) 861101, *Fax:* (01734) 869878. *Clubs:* Athenæum, MCC; Phyllis Court (Henley).

GOODALL, His Honour Anthony Charles, MC 1942; DL; a Circuit Judge (formerly a Judge of County Courts), 1968–86; *b* 23 July 1916; *er s* of late Charles Henry and Mary Helen Goodall, The Manor House, Sutton Veny, Wilts; *m* 1947, Anne Valerie, *yr d* of late John Reginald Chichester and of Audrey Geraldine Chichester, Lurley Manor, Tiverton, Devon; one *s* two *d*. *Educ:* Eton; King's Coll., Cambridge. Called to Bar, Inner Temple, 1939 (Certif. of Hon.). Served War of 1939–45, 1st Royal Dragoons; taken prisoner (twice), 1944. Practised at Bar, 1946–67. Pres., Plymouth Magistrates' Assoc., 1976–84; Mem., County Court Rule Cttee, 1978–83; Jt Pres., Council of HM Circuit Judges, 1986 (Jt Vice-Pres., 1985). DL Devon 1987. *Publications:* (ed jtly) Faraday on Rating; contrib. to Encycl. Court Forms and Precedents. *Address:* Mardon, Moretonhampstead, Devon TQ13 8LX. *T:* Moretonhampstead (01647) 440239.

See also Baron Clifford of Chudleigh.

GOODALL, Sir (Arthur) David (Saunders), GCMG 1991 (KCMG 1987; CMG 1979); HM Diplomatic Service, retired; Chairman, The Leonard Cheshire Foundation, since 1995 (Chairman, International Committee, 1992–95); *b* 9 Oct. 1931; *o c* of late Arthur William and Maisie Josephine Goodall; *m* 1962, Morwenna, *y d* of late Percival George Beck Peecock; two *s* one *d*. *Educ:* Ampleforth; Trinity Coll., Oxford (1st Cl. Hons Lit. Hum., 1954; MA; Hon. Fellow, 1992). Served 1st Bn KOYLI (2nd Lieut), 1955–56. Entered HM Foreign (subseq. Diplomatic) Service, 1956; served at: Nicosia, 1956; FO, 1957–58; Djakarta, 1958–60; Bonn, 1961–63; FO, 1963–68; Head of Chancery, Nairobi, 1968–70; FCO, 1970–73; UK Delegn, MBFR, Vienna, 1973–75; Head of Western European Dept, FCO, 1975–79; Minister, Bonn, 1979–82; Dep. Sec., Cabinet Office, 1982–84; Dep. Under-Sec. of State, FCO, 1984–87; High Comr to India, 1987–91. Non-Executive Director: Humphreys & Glasgow Internat., 1991–93; Govett India Fund, 1993–; Oryx (India) Fund, 1995–. Chm., Wexford Fest. Opera UK Trust, 1991–; Trustee, Rajiv Gandhi (UK) Foundn, 1993–. Co-Chm., Anglo-Irish Encounter, 1992–; Vice-Chm., British–Irish Assoc., 1994–. Mem. Council, Durham Univ., 1992–; Gov., Westminster Cathedral Choir Sch., 1994–. Hon. LLD Hull, 1994. *Publications:* contribs to: Ampleforth Jl; Tablet; Irish Genealogist; The Past. *Recreation:* painting in watercolours. *Address:* c/o The Leonard Cheshire Foundation, 26–29 Maunsel Street, SW1P 2QN. *Clubs:* Garrick, United Oxford & Cambridge University.

GOODALL, David William, PhD (London); DSc (Melbourne); ARCS, DIC, FLS; FIBiol; Hon. Fellow, CSIRO Division of Wildlife and Ecology (formerly Division of Wildlife and Rangelands Research), since 1983; *b* 4 April 1914; *s* of Henry William Goodall; *m* 1st, 1940, Audrey Veronica Kirwin (marr. diss. 1949); one *s*; 2nd, 1949, Muriel Grace King (marr. diss. 1974); two *s* one *d*; 3rd, 1976, Ivy Nelms (*née* Palmer). *Educ:* St Paul's Sch.; Imperial Coll. of Science and Technology (BSc). Research under Research Inst. of Plant Physiology, on secondment to Cheshunt and East Malling Research Stns, 1935–46; Plant Physiologist, W African Cacao Research Inst., 1946–48; Sen. Lectr in Botany, University of Melbourne, 1948–52; Reader in Botany, University Coll. of the Gold Coast, 1952–54; Prof. of Agricultural Botany, University of Reading, 1954–56; Dir, CSIRO Tobacco Research Institute, Mareeba, Qld, 1956–61; Senior Principal Research Officer, CSIRO Div. of Mathematical Statistics, Perth, Australia, 1961–67; Hon. Reader in Botany, Univ. of Western Australia, 1965–67; Prof. of Biological Science, Univ. of California Irvine, 1966–68; Dir, US/IBP Desert Biome, 1968–73; Prof. of Systems Ecology, Utah State Univ., 1969–74; Sen. Prin. Res. Scientist, 1974–79, Sen. Res. Fellow, 1979–83, Land Resources Management Div., CSIRO. Hon. Dr in Natural Scis, Trieste Univ., 1990. *Publications:* Chemical Composition of Plants as an Index of their Nutritional

Status (with F. G. Gregory), 1947; ed, Evolution of Desert Biota, 1976; editor-in-chief, Ecosystems of the World (series), 1977–; co-editor: Productivity of World Ecosystems, 1975; Simulation Modelling of Environmental Problems, 1977; Arid-land Ecosystems: Structure, Functioning and Management, vol. 1 1979, vol. 2 1981; Mediterranean-type Shrublands, 1981; Hot Deserts, 1985; numerous papers in scientific jls and symposium vols. *Recreations:* acting, reading, walking. *Address:* CSIRO, Locked Bag No 4, PO Midland, WA 6056, Australia.

GOODALL, Rt. Rev. Maurice John, MBE 1974; Bishop of Christchurch, 1984–90; *b* 31 March 1928; *s* of John and Alice Maud Goodall; *m* 1st, 1953, Nathalie Ruth Cummack; two *s* four *d*; 2nd, 1981, Beverley Doreen Moore. *Educ:* Christchurch Technical Coll.; College House, Univ. of NZ (BA 1950); Univ. of Canterbury (LTh 1964); Dip. Social Work (Distinction) 1977; CQSW 1982. Asst Curate, St Albans, Dio. of Christchurch, 1951–54; Vicar of: Waikari, 1954–59; Shirley, 1959–67; Hon. Asst, Christchurch, St John's 1967–69; Chaplain, Kingslea Girls' Training Centre, 1967–69; City Missioner (dio. Christchurch), 1969–76; Nuffield Bursary, 1973; Dir, Community Mental Health Team, 1976–82; Dean of Christchurch Cathedral, 1982–84. *Publications:* (with Colin Clark) Worship for Today, 1967; (contrib.) Christian Responsibility in Society (ed Yule), 1977; contribs to journals. *Recreations:* walking, reading, NZ history. *Address:* Flat 1, 50 Crofton Road, Christchurch 5, New Zealand.

GOODALL, Peter, CBE 1983; TD 1950; Executive Chairman and Chief Executive, 1977–86, and Director, 1970–89, Hepworth Ceramic Holdings PLC; *b* 14 July 1920; *s* of Major Tom Goodall, DSO, MC and Alice (*née* Black); *m* 1948, Sonja Jeanne (*née* Burt); one *s* one *d*. *Educ:* Ashville Coll., Harrogate. Admitted Solicitor, 1948. Served War, Duke of Wellington's Regt and Parachute Regt, 1939–46 (Captain). Practised as Solicitor with family firm, Goodall & Son, and Whitfield Son & Hallam, 1948–67; Dir, Hepworth Iron Co. Ltd, 1967–70; company merged with General Refractories Group Ltd to form Hepworth Ceramic Holdings Ltd, 1970; Man. Dir, 1971–77. Member Council: CBI, 1981–88; British United Industrialists, 1984–89. *Recreations:* shooting, fishing. *Address:* Springfield House, Sicklinghall Road, Wetherby, W Yorks LS22 6AA. *T:* Wetherby (01937) 581297.

GOODALL, Ralph William; DL; Chairman, Manweb plc, since 1994 (Director, since 1993); *b* 15 Oct. 1931; *s* of James Goodall and Evelyn (*née* Hamer); *m* 1958, Marjory Audrey Ellen Flint; three *s* one *d*. *Educ:* Haileybury Coll.; Leeds Univ. (BSc Textile Inds); Pembroke Coll., Cambridge (MA Econs). CText 1967; ATI 1967; CompTI 1983. Flying Officer/Engr, RAF, 1954–56. Joined Scapa Dryers Ltd as Mgt Trainee, 1956; Scapa Group plc: Asst Gp Man. Dir, 1969–76; Gp Man. Dir and Chief Exec., 1976–86; Chm., 1986–93; Volex Group plc: Dir, 1988–; Chm., 1992–; Dir and Chm., Hopkinsons Gp PLC, 1992–; Chm., Inveresk PLC, 1994–. Pres., Textile Inst., 1985–87. Gov., Queen Elizabeth Grammar Sch., Blackburn, 1979– (Chm., 1993–). Freeman, City of London, 1986; Liveryman, Feltmakers' Co., 1986–. DL 1988, High Sheriff, 1995–96, Lancs. Hon. DEng Leeds, 1990. *Recreations:* shooting, golf, music. *Address:* The Old Vicarage, Hoghton, near Preston, Lancs PR5 0SJ. *Clubs:* Farmers', United Oxford & Cambridge University; District & Union, Pleasington Golf (Blackburn).

GOODALL, Air Vice-Marshal Roderick Harvey, CBE 1990; AFC 1981, Bar 1987; Air Officer Commanding No 2 Group, since 1994; *b* 19 Jan. 1947; *s* of Leonard George Harvey Goodall and Muriel Goodall (*née* Cooper); *m* 1973, Elizabeth Susan Haines; two *d*. *Educ:* Elizabeth Coll., Guernsey; RAF Coll., Cranwell. Commissioned 1968; served Bahrain, UK and Germany, to 1981; RAF Staff Coll., 1981; PMC Barnwood, 1982; OC 16 Sqn, Laarbruch, 1983–85; MoD, 1986–87; Station Comdr, RAF Bruggen, 1987–89; RCDS 1990; Station Comdr, RAF Detachment, Bahrain, 1990; Dir, Air Offensive and Air Force Ops, MoD, 1991–93. *Recreations:* golf, photography, family. *Address:* c/o Lloyds Bank, 2 North Gate, Sleaford, Lincs NG34 7BL. *Club:* Royal Air Force.

GOODCHILD, David Hicks, CMG 1992; CBE 1973; Partner of Clifford Chance (formerly Clifford-Turner), Solicitors, 1962–90 (resident in Paris), retired; *b* 3 Sept. 1926; *s* of Harold Hicks Goodchild and Agnes Joyce Wharton Goodchild (*née* Mowbray); *m* 1954, Nicole Marie Jeanne (*née* Delamotte); one *s* one *d*. *Educ:* Felsted School. Lieut, Royal Artillery, 1944–48; articled clerk, Longmores, Hertford; qual. Solicitor, 1952; Mem., Paris Bar, 1992. HAC, 1952–56. Chairman: Hertford British Hosp. Corp., 1976–; Victoria Home, 1982–. Hon. Pres., Franco-British Chamber of Commerce and Industry (formerly British Chamber of Commerce in France), 1982–. *Recreations:* golf, cricket. *Address:* 53 Avenue Montaigne, 75008 Paris, France. *T:* 42254927. *Clubs:* MCC, HAC; Cercle Interallié, Polo (Paris); Golf de Chantilly.

GOODCHILD, David Lionel Napier, CMG 1986; a Director, Directorate-General of External Relations, Commission of the European Communities, 1985–86; *b* 20 July 1935; *s* of Hugh N. Goodchild and Beryl C. M. Goodchild. *Educ:* Eton College; King's College, Cambridge (MA). Joined Foreign Office, 1958; served Tehran, NATO (Paris), and FO, 1959–70; Dep. Political Adviser, British Mil. Govt, Berlin, 1970–72; transferred to EEC, Brussels, 1973; Head of Division, 1973, Principal Counsellor then Director, 1979–86. *Address:* Orchard House, Thorpe Morieux, Bury St Edmunds, Suffolk IP30 0NW. *T:* Cockfield Green (01284) 828181.

GOODCHILD, Marianne, (Mrs Trevor Goodchild); *see* Rigge, M.

GOODCHILD, Peter Robert Edward; Executive Producer, BBC Films, since 1989; *b* 18 Aug. 1939; *s* of Douglas Richard Geoffrey Goodchild and Lottie May Goodchild; *m* 1968, Penelope Jane Pointon-Dick; two *d*. *Educ:* Aldenham Sch., Elstree; St John 's College, Oxford (MA). CChem, FRSC 1979. General trainee, BBC, 1963; BBC TV: Director/Producer, Horizon, 1965–69, Editor, 1969–76; Editor, Special Features, 1977–80; Head, Science Features Dept, 1980–84; Head, Plays Dept, 1984–89. SFTA Mullard Award, 1967, 1968, 1969; BAFTA Awards: best factual series, 1972, 1974; best drama series, 1977–80. *Publication:* J. Robert Oppenheimer: shatterer of worlds, 1980. *Recreations:* tennis, music, painting, environmental action. *Address:* BBC Television Centre, Wood Lane, W12 7RJ. *T:* 0181–743 8000. *Club:* Groucho.

GOODCHILD, Rt. Rev. Ronald Cedric Osbourne; an Assistant Bishop, Diocese of Exeter, since 1983; *b* 17 Oct. 1910; *s* of Sydney Osbourne and Dido May Goodchild; *m* 1947, Jean Helen Mary (*née* Ross); one *s* four *d*. *Educ:* St John's School, Leatherhead; Trinity Coll. (Monk Schol.), Cambridge; Bishops' Coll., Cheshunt. 2nd Cl. Hist. Tripos Parts I and II, 1931, Dealtry Exhibn. 1932, 3rd Class Theol. Tripos, 1932, Asst Master, Bickley Hall Sch., Kent, 1932–34; Curate, Ealing Parish Church, 1934–37; Chap. Oakham Sch., 1937–42. Chap. RAFVR, 1942–46 (despatches), Warden St Michael's House, Hamburg, 1946–49; Gen. Sec., SCM in Schools, 1949–53; Rector of St Helen's Bishopgate with St Martin Outwich, 1951–53; Vicar of Horsham, Sussex, 1953–59; Surrogate and Rural Dean of Horsham, 1954–59; Archdeacon of Northampton and Rector of Ecton, 1959–64; Bishop Suffragan of Kensington, 1964–80. Examiner, Religious Knowledge, Southern Univs Jt Bd, 1954–58; Examining Chaplain to Bishop of Peterborough, 1959. Chairman Christian Aid Dept, British Council of Churches, 1964–74. Mem. of General Synod of C of E, 1974–80. *Publication:* Daily Prayer at Oakham School, 1938. *Recreations:* cabinet making, walking. *Address:* Mead, Welcombe, near Bideford, N Devon EX39 6HH. *Club:* Royal Air Force.

GOODDEN, Robert Yorke, CBE 1956; RDI 1947; Architect and Designer; Professor, School of Silversmithing and Jewellery, 1948–74, and Pro-Rector, 1967–74, Royal College of Art; *b* 7 May 1909; 2nd *s* of late Lieut-Col R. B. Goodden, OBE and Gwendolen Goodden; *m* 1st, 1936, Kathleen Teresa Burrow; 2nd, 1946, Lesley Macbeth Mitchell; two *s* two *d*. *Educ:* Harrow Sch. Trained AA Sch. of Architecture, 1926–31; AA Diploma 1932; ARIBA 1933; private practice as architect and designer, 1932–39; served RAFVR, 1940–41; RNVR, 1941–45; resumed private practice, 1946. Joint architect and designer: Lion and Unicorn Pavilion, South Bank Exhibition, 1951; Western Sculpture Rooms, Print Room Gall. and Gall. of Oriental Art, British Museum, 1969–71; designer of: domestic pressed glassware for Chance Brothers, 1934–48; Asterisk Wallpapers, 1934; sports section, Britain Can Make It Exhbn, 1946; Coronation hangings for Westminster Abbey, 1953; gold and silver plate in collections: Victoria and Albert Museum, Worshipful Co. of Goldsmiths, Royal Society of Arts, Downing Coll. and Sidney Sussex Coll., Cambridge, Royal Coll. of Art; glass for King's Coll., Cambridge, Grosvenor House, Min. of Works, and others; metal foil mural decorations in SS Canberra, 1961. Consulting Architect to Board of Trade for BIF, Olympia, 1947, Earls Ct, 1949, Olympia, 1950 and 1951. Member: Council of Industrial Design, 1955; National Council for Diplomas in Art and Design, 1961; Adv. Council, V&A Museum, 1977; Chm., Crafts Council, 1977–82. Mem. Council, Essex Univ., 1973. FSIA, 1947; Hon. Fellow, Sheffield Polytechnic, 1971. Hon. DesRCA, 1952; Hon. Dr RCA, 1974; Sen. Fellow, RCA, 1981. SIAD Design Medal, 1972. Master of Faculty, RDI, 1959–61. Liveryman, Worshipful Co. of Goldsmiths, Prime Warden 1976. *Publication:* (with P. Popham) Silversmithing, 1972. *Recreation:* daydreaming. *Address:* 16 Hatfield Buildings, Widcombe Hill, Bath, Avon BA2 6AF.

GOODE, (Penelope) Cary (Anne); freelance garden designer, since 1992; *b* 5 Dec. 1947; *d* of Ernest Edgar Spink and Rachel Atcherly Spink; *m* 1987, Richard Nicholas Goode. *Educ:* Westwing Sch. Royal Ascot Enclosure Office, 1971; MoD, 1973; Manager, retail business, 1978; Domestic and Social Sec., RCOG, 1980; Educn Administrator, British Heart Foundn, 1982; Dir, Asthma Res. Council, later Nat. Asthma Campaign, 1988–92. *Recreations:* gardening, vintage cars, dogs. *Address:* 28 Bryanston Square, W1H 7LS. *T:* 0171–262 0490; Thornhill Park, Stalbridge, Dorset DT10 2SH.

GOODE, Prof. Royston Miles, CBE 1994 (OBE 1972); QC 1990; FBA 1988; barrister; Norton Rose Professor of English Law, Oxford University, since 1990; Fellow, St John's College, Oxford, since 1990; *b* 6 April 1933; *s* of Samuel and Bloom Goode; *m* 1964, Catherine Anne Rueff; one *d*. *Educ:* Highgate School. LLB London, 1954; LLD London, 1976. Admitted Solicitor, 1955. Partner, Victor Mishcon & Co., solicitors, 1966–71, Consultant 1971–88. Called to the Bar, Inner Temple, 1988; Hon. Bencher, 1992. Queen Mary College, University of London: Prof. of Law, 1971–73; Head of Dept and Dean of Faculty of Laws, 1976–80; Crowther Prof. of Credit and Commercial Law, 1973–89; Dir and Founder, Centre for Commercial Law Studies, 1980–89. Vis. Prof., Melbourne, 1975; Aust. Commonwealth Vis. Fellow, 1975; Falconbridge Vis. Prof., Osgoode Hall Law Sch., 1987. Chairman: Advertising Adv. Cttee, IBA, 1976–80; Pension Law Rev. Cttee, 1992–93; Member: Cttee on Consumer Credit, 1968–71; Monopolies and Mergers Commn, 1981–86; Departmental Cttee on Arbitration Law, DTI, 1986–; Council of the Banking Ombudsman, 1989–. Justice: Mem. Council, 1975, Chm. Exec. Cttee, 1994– (Vice-Chm., 1988–94); Mem., Council of Management, British Inst. of Internat. and Comparative Law, 1982. Fellow, QMW, 1991. FRSA 1990. *Publications:* Hire-Purchase Law and Practice, 1962, 2nd edn 1970, with Supplement 1975; The Hire-Purchase Act 1964, 1964; (with J. S. Ziegel) Hire-Purchase and Conditional Sale: a Comparative Survey of Commonwealth and American Law, 1965; Introduction to the Consumer Credit Act, 1974; (ed) Consumer Credit Legislation, 1977; Consumer Credit, 1978; Commercial Law, 1982; Legal Problems of Credit and Security, 1982, 2nd edn 1988; Payment Obligations in Commercial and Financial Transactions, 1983; Proprietary Rights and Insolvency in Sales Transactions, 1985, 2nd edn 1989; Principles of Corporate Insolvency Law, 1990; contrib. Halsbury's Laws of England, 4th edn. *Recreations:* chess, reading, walking, browsing in bookshops. *Address:* St John's College, Oxford OX1 3JP; 42 St John Street, Oxford OX1 2LH. *Club:* Reform.

GOODENOUGH, Anthony Michael, CMG 1990; HM Diplomatic Service; Assistant Under-Secretary of State (Africa and Commonwealth), Foreign and Commonwealth Office, since 1992; *b* 5 July 1941; *s* of late Rear-Adm. Michael Grant Goodenough, CBE, DSO, and of Nancy Waterfield (*née* Slater); *m* 1967, Veronica Mary, *d* of Col Peter Pender-Cudlip, MVO; two *s* one *d*. *Educ:* Wellington Coll.; New Coll., Oxford. MA 1980. Voluntary Service Overseas, Sarawak, 1963–64; Foreign Office, 1964; Athens, 1967; Private Secretary to Parliamentary Under Secretary, 1971, and Minister of State, FCO, 1972; Paris, 1974; First Sec., FCO, 1977; Counsellor on secondment to Cabinet Office, 1980; Hd of Chancery, Islamabad, 1982; Counsellor, FCO, 1986–89; High Comr to Ghana and Ambassador (non-resident) to Togo, 1989–92. *Address:* c/o Foreign and Commonwealth Office, SW1A 2AH.

GOODENOUGH, Cecilia Phyllis, MA; STh; DD; *b* 9 Sept. 1905; *d* of late Adm. Sir William Goodenough, GCB, MVO. *Educ:* Rochester Grammar Sch.; Liverpool Coll., Huyton; St Hugh's Coll., Oxford. LCC Care Cttee Sec., 1927–30; Sunday Sch. and Evangelistic work, Diocese of Caledonia, Fort St John, BC, Canada, 1931–36; Head of Talbot Settlement, 14 Bromley Hill, Bromley, Kent, 1937–45; Asst to Diocesan Missioner, Diocese of Southwark, 1954–72. *Address:* 115 Camberwell Grove, Camberwell, SE5 8JH. *T:* 0171–701 0093.

GOODENOUGH, Frederick Roger, DL; FCIB; Director: Barclays PLC, 1985–89; *b* 21 Dec. 1927; *s* of Sir William Macnamara Goodenough, 1st Bt, and late Lady (Dorothea Louisa) Goodenough; *m* 1954, Marguerite June Mackintosh; one *s* two *d*. *Educ:* Eton; Magdalene Coll., Cambridge (MA). MA Oxon; FCIB (FIB 1968). Joined Barclays Bank Ltd, 1950; Local Director: Birmingham, 1958; Reading, 1960; Oxford, 1969–87; Director: Barclays Bank UK Ltd, 1971–87; Barclays Internat. Ltd, 1977–87; Barclays Bank PLC, 1979–89; Adv. Dir, Barclays Bank Thames Valley Region, 1988–89; Mem., London Cttee, Barclays Bank DCO, 1966–71, Barclays Bank Internat. Ltd, 1971–80. Supernumerary Fellow, Wolfson Coll., Oxford, 1989–95 (Hon. Fellow, 1995). Sen. Partner, Broadwell Manor Farm, 1968–; Curator, Oxford Univ. Chest, 1974–93; Trustee: Nuffield Med. Benefaction, 1968– (Chm., 1987–); Nuffield Dominions Trust, 1968– (Chm., 1987–); Nuffield Orthopaedic Trust, 1978– (Chm., 1981–); Oxford and Dist Hosps Improvement and Develt Fund, 1968– (Chm., 1982–88); Radcliffe Med. Foundn, 1987–; Oxford Preservation Trust, 1980–89; Pres., Oxfordshire Rural Community Council, 1993. Governor: Shiplake Coll., 1963–74 (Chm., 1966–70); Wellington Coll., 1968–74; London Hse for Overseas Graduates, 1985–. Patron, Anglo-Ghanian Soc. (UK), 1991–. FLS (Mem. Council, 1968–75; Treasurer, 1970–75); FRSA. High Sheriff, 1987–88, DL 1989, Oxfordshire. *Recreations:* shooting, fishing, photography, ornithology. *Address:* Broadwell Manor, Lechlade, Glos GL7 3QS. *T:* Faringdon (01367) 860326. *Club:* Brooks's.

GOODENOUGH, Prof. John Bannister; Virginia H. Cockrell Centennial Professor of Engineering, University of Texas at Austin, since 1986; *b* 25 July 1922; *s* of Erwin Ramsdell Goodenough and Helen Lewis Goodenough; *m* 1951, Irene Johnston Wiseman. *Educ:* Yale Univ. (AB, Maths); Univ. of Chicago (MS, PhD, Physics). Meteorologist, US Army Air Force, 1942–48; Research Engr, Westinghouse Corp., 1951–52; Research Physicist (Leader, Electronic Materials Gp), Lincoln Laboratory, MIT, 1952–76; Prof. and Hd of Dept of Inorganic Chemistry, Oxford Univ., 1976–86. Raman Prof., Indian Acad. of Science, 1982–83 (Hon. Mem., 1980–). Member: Nat. Acad., of Engrg, 1976–; Presidential Commn on Superconductivity, 1989–90. Foreign Associate, Acad. of Scis, Institut de France, 1992. Dr *hc*, Bordeaux, 1967. Von Hippel Award, Materials Res. Soc., 1989; Sen. Res. Award, Amer. Soc. of Engrg Educn, 1990. Associate Editor: Materials Research Bulletin, 1966–; Jl Solid State Chemistry, 1969–; Structure and Bonding, 1978–; Solid State Ionics, 1980–; Superconductor Science and Technology, 1987–; Jl of Materials Chem., 1990–; Chem. of Materials, 1990–; Co-editor, International Series of Monographs on Chemistry, 1979–86; Member Executive, Editorial Board: Jl of Applied Electrochem., 1983–88; European Jl of Solid State and Inorganic Chem., 1992–. *Publications:* Magnetism and the Chemical Bond, 1963; Les oxydes des métaux de transition, 1973; numerous research papers in learned jls. *Recreations:* walking, travel. *Address:* Center for Materials Science & Engineering, University of Texas at Austin, ETC 5.160, Austin, TX 78712, USA. *T:* (512) 4711646.

GOODENOUGH, Sir Richard (Edmund), 2nd Bt *cr* 1943; *b* 9 June 1925; *e s* of Sir William (Macnamara) Goodenough, 1st Bt, and Dorothea (Louisa) (*d* 1987), *er d* of late Ven. and Hon. K. F. Gibbs, DD; *S* father 1951; *m* 1951, Jane, *d* of late H. S. P. McLernon and of Mrs McLernon, Gisborne, NZ; one *s* two *d*. *Educ:* Eton Coll.; Christ Church, Oxford. Military service, 1943–45, invalided. Christ Church, Oxford, 1945–47. *Heir: s* William McLernon Goodenough [*b* 5 Aug. 1954; *m* 1982, Louise Elizabeth, *d* of Captain Michael Ortmans, MVO, RN and Julia Ortmans; one *d*].

GOODFELLOW, Mark Aubrey; HM Diplomatic Service, retired; Ambassador to Gabon, 1986–90; *b* 7 April 1931; *y s* of Alfred Edward Goodfellow and Lucy Emily (*née* Potter); *m* 1964, Madelyn Susan Scammell; one *s* one *d*. *Educ:* Preston Manor County Grammar Sch. Served RAF, 1949–51. Joined HM Foreign (subseq. Diplomatic) Service, 1949; FO, 1951–54; British Mil. Govt, Berlin, 1954–56; Second Sec., Khartoum, 1956–59; FO, 1959–63; Second Sec., Yaoundé, 1963–66; Asst Comr, later Trade Comr, Hong Kong, 1966–71; FCO, 1971–74; First Sec., Ankara, 1974–78; Consul, Atlanta, 1978–82; Counsellor: Washington (Hong Kong Commercial Affairs), 1982–84; Lagos (Econ. and Comm.), 1984–86. *Recreations:* travelling, photography, visiting historic sites and buildings, gardening.

GOODFELLOW, Prof. Peter Neville, DPhil; FRS 1992; Arthur Balfour Professor of Genetics, Cambridge University, since 1992; *b* 4 Aug. 1951; *s* of Bernard Clifford Roy Goodfellow and Doreen Olga (*née* Berry); *m* 1972, Julia Mary Lansdall; one *s* one *d*. *Educ:* Bristol Univ. (BSc 1st Cl. Hons 1972); Oxford Univ. (DPhil 1975). MRC Postdoctoral Fellow, Oxford Univ., 1975–76; Stanford University: Jane Coffin Childs Postdoctoral Fellow, 1976–78; Amer. Cancer Soc. Sen. Fellow, 1978–79; Imperial Cancer Research Fund: Staff Scientist, 1979–83; Sen. Scientist, 1983–86; Principal Scientist, 1986–92. *Publications:* (ed) Genetic analysis of the cell surface in Receptors and Recognition, Vol. 16, 1984; (ed jtly) The Mammalian Y Chromosome: molecular search for the sex determining gene, 1987; (ed) Cystic Fibrosis, 1989; (ed jtly) Molecular genetics of muscle disease, 1989; (ed jtly) Sex determination and the Y chromosome, 1991; (ed jtly) Mammalian Genetics, 1992; numerous reviews and contribs to learned jls. *Recreations:* soccer, science, sex. *Address:* Department of Genetics, University of Cambridge, Downing Street, Cambridge CB2 3EH. *T:* Cambridge (01223) 333926.

GOODFELLOW, Mrs Rosalind Erica, JP; Moderator of the General Assembly of the United Reformed Church, 1982–83; *b* 3 April 1927; *d* of late Rev. William Griffith-Jones and Kathleen (*née* Speakman); *m* 1949, Keith Frank Goodfellow, QC (*d* 1977); two *s* one *d*. *Educ:* Milton Mount Coll. (now Wentworth Milton Mount); Royal Holloway Coll., London Univ. (BA Hons). Member: British Council of Churches Div. of Community Affairs Bd, 1980–83; Churches' Council for Covenanting, 1981–82; Chm., World Church and Mission Dept, URC, 1983. Chm., Surrey and W Sussex CAB, 1985. JP Surrey (Esher and Walton PSD), 1960. *Recreation:* attending committee meetings. *Address:* Kilverstone House, Gordon Road, Claygate, Surrey. *T:* Esher (01372) 67656.

GOODHART, Hon. Lady; Celia McClare Goodhart; Principal, Queen's College, London, since 1991; *b* 25 July 1939; *d* of 2nd Baron Hemingford and Elizabeth (*née* Clark) (*d* 1979); *m* 1966, Sir William Howard Goodhart, *qv*; one *s* two *d*. *Educ:* St Michael's, Limpsfield; St Hilda's Coll., Oxford (Hon. Fellow 1989). MA Oxon. HM Civil Service, MAFF, seconded to Treasury, 1960–66; Hist. Tutor, Queen's Coll., London and Westminster Tutors, 1966–81. Contested: (SDP) Kettering, 1983; (SDP Liberal Alliance) Kettering, 1987; Northants (for European Parlt), 1984. Chairman: SDP Envmt Policy Gp, 1985–87; Women for Social Democracy, 1986–88; Member: SDP Nat. and Policy Cttees, 1984–88; Liberal Democrats Fed. Exec. Cttee, 1988–90; Pres., E Midlands Liberal Democrats, 1988–91. Member: Elizabeth Nuffield Educnl Fund, 1972–82; St Bartholomew's Hosp. Ethical Cttee, 1974–84; Nat. Gas Consumer Councils, 1978–81 (also Chm., N Thames Gas Consumer Council); Women's Nat. Commn, 1985–88. President: Schoolmistresses and Governesses Benevolent Instn, 1991–; London Marriage Guidance Council, 1991–; Chm., Youth Clubs, UK, 1988–91. Trustee: CPRE, 1987–91; Oxford Univ. Nuffield Medical Benefaction, 1988–. Governor: Godolphin and Latymer, 1976–86; St Michael's, Limpsfield, 1975–83; Isaac Newton Comprehensive, 1977–81. FRSA 1989. *Recreations:* sociability, shopping. *Address:* 11 Clarence Terrace, NW1 4RD. *T:* 0171–262 1319; Youlbury House, Boars Hill, Oxford OX1 5HH. *T:* Oxford (01865) 735477. *Clubs:* Reform; Cosmopolitan (New York).

GOODHART, Charles Albert Eric, PhD; FBA 1990; Norman Sosnow Professor of Banking and Finance, London School of Economics and Political Science, since 1985; *b* 23 Oct. 1936; *s* of late Prof. Arthur Goodhart, Hon. KBE, QC, FBA, and Cecily (*née* Carter); *m* 1960, Margaret (Miffy) Ann Smith; one *s* three *d*. *Educ:* Eton; Trinity Coll., Cambridge (scholar; 1st Cl. Hons Econs Tripos); Harvard Grad. Sch. of Arts and Sciences (PhD 1963). National Service, 1955–57 (2nd Lieut KRRC). Prize Fellowship in Econs, Trinity Coll., Cambridge, 1963; Asst Lectr in Econs, Cambridge Univ., 1963–64; Econ. Adviser, DEA, 1965–67; Lectr in Monetary Econs, LSE, 1967–69; Bank of England: Adviser with particular reference to monetary policy, 1969–80; a Chief Adviser, 1980–85. Mem., Adv. Cttee, Hong Kong Exchange Fund, 1990–. *Publications:* The New York Money Market and the Finance of Trade, 1900–13, 1968; The Business of Banking, 1891–1914, 1972; Money, Information and Uncertainty, 1975, 2nd edn 1989; Monetary Theory and Practice: the UK experience, 1984; The Evolution of Central Banks, 1985, rev. edn 1988; (ed jtly) The Operation and Regulation of Financial Markets, 1987; (ed) EMU and ESCB after Maastricht, 1992; (jtly) The Future of Central Banking, 1994; articles in econ. jls and papers contrib. to econ. books. *Recreation:* keeping sheep. *Address:* London School of Economics and Political Science, Houghton Street, WC2A 2AE. *T:* 0171–955 7555.

See also Sir P. C. Goodhart, Sir W. H. Goodhart.

GOODHART, Rear-Adm. (Hilary Charles) Nicholas, CB 1972; FRAeS; *b* 28 Sept. 1919; *s* of G. C. Goodhart; *m* 1975, Molly Copsey. *Educ:* RNC Dartmouth; RNEC Keyham. Joined RN, 1933; served in Mediterranean in HM Ships Formidable and Dido, 1941–43; trained as pilot, 1944; served as fighter pilot in Burma Campaign, 1945; trained as test pilot, 1946; served on British Naval Staff, Washington, 1953–55; idc 1965; Rear-Adm. 1970; Mil. Dep. to Head of Defence Sales, MoD, 1970–73, retired. British Gliding Champion, 1962, 1967 and 1971. Holder of UK gliding distance record, 360 miles. Freedom of London, 1945; Mem. Ct of Grocers' Co., 1975, Master, 1981. US Legion of Merit, 1958. *Recreation:* computer programming. *Address:* Cable House, Lindridge Park, Teignmouth, Devon TQ14 9TF. *T:* Newton Abbot (01626) 779790.

GOODHART, Sir Philip (Carter), Kt 1981; *b* 3 Nov. 1925; *s* of late Prof. Arthur Goodhart, Hon. KBE, QC, FBA, and Cecily (*née* Carter); *m* 1950, Valerie Winant; three *s* four *d*. *Educ:* Hotchkiss Sch., USA; Trinity Coll., Cambridge. Served KRRC and Parachute Regt, 1943–47. Editorial staff, Daily Telegraph, 1950–54; Editorial staff, Sunday Times, 1955–57. Mem., LCC Educn Cttee, 1956–57. Contested (C) Consett, Co. Durham, Gen. Election, 1950; MP (C) Beckenham, March 1957–1992. Parly Under-Sec. of State, Northern Ireland Office, and Minister responsible for Dept of the Environment (NI), 1979–81; Parly Under Sec. of State, MoD, 1981. Joint Hon. Sec., 1922 Cttee, 1960–79; Mem., Cons. Adv. Cttee on Policy, 1973–79; Chairman: Cons. Parly Defence Cttee, 1972–74 (Vice-Chm., 1974–79); Parly NI Cttee, 1976–79; Parly Select Cttee on Sound Broadcasting, 1983–87; Anglo-Taiwan Parly Gp, 1987–92. Member: British Delegation to Council of Europe and WEU, 1961–63; British Delegation to UN Gen. Assembly, 1963; North Atlantic Assembly, 1964–79 and 1983–92. Member: Council, Consumers' Assoc., 1959–68, 1970–79 (Vice-Pres., 1983–); Adv. Council on Public Records, 1970–79; Exec. Cttee, British Council, 1974–79; Council, RUSI, 1973–76. Chairman: Bd of Sulgrave Manor, 1982–; Warship Preservation Trust, 1988–; Warrior Preservation Trust, 1993–; Dir, Flagship Portsmouth, 1993–. Order of the Brilliant Star (China), 1992. *Publications:* The Hunt for Kimathi (with Ian Henderson, GM), 1958; In the Shadow of the Sword, 1964; Fifty Ships that Saved the World, 1965; (with Christopher Chataway) War without Weapons, 1968; Referendum, 1970; (with Ursula Branston) The 1922: the history of the 1922 Committee, 1973; Full-Hearted Consent, 1975; various pamphlets incl.: Stand on Your Own Four Feet: a study of work sharing and job splitting, 1982; Jobs Ahead, 1984; Skip Ahead, 1985; Colonel George Washington: soldier of the King, 1993. *Recreation:* skiing (Chm., Develt Cttee, Nat. Ski Fedn of GB, 1970–71; Chm., Lords and Commons Ski Club, 1971–73). *Address:* 25 Abbotsbury Road, W14 8EJ. *T:* 0171–602 8237; Whitebarn, Boars Hill, Oxford OX1 5HH. *T:* Oxford (01865) 735294. *Clubs:* Beefsteak, Carlton, Garrick.

See also C. A. E. Goodhart, Sir W. H. Goodhart.

GOODHART, Sir Robert (Anthony Gordon), 4th Bt *cr* 1911; Medical Practitioner, Beaminster, Dorset; *b* 15 Dec. 1948; *s* of Sir John Gordon Goodhart, 3rd Bt, FRCGP, and of Margaret Mary Eileen, *d* of late Morgan Morgan; *S* father, 1979; *m* 1972, Kathleen Ellen, *d* of late Rev. A. D. MacRae; two *s* two *d*. *Educ:* Rugby; Guy's Hospital Medical School, London Univ. MB BS (Lond.), MRCS, LRCP, MRCGP, DObstRCOG. Qualification, 1972; Junior Medical Registrar, Guy's Hosp., 1974; GP, Bromley, 1976–80. *Recreation:* cricket. *Heir: s* Martin Andrew Goodhart, *b* 9 Sept. 1974.

GOODHART, Sir William (Howard), Kt 1989; QC 1979; *b* 18 Jan. 1933; *s* of late Prof. A. L. Goodhart, Hon. KBE, QC, FBA and Cecily (*née* Carter); *m* 1966, Hon. Celia McClare Herbert (*see* Hon. Lady Goodhart); one *s* two *d*. *Educ:* Eton; Trinity Coll., Cambridge (Scholar, MA); Harvard Law Sch. (Commonwealth Fund Fellow, LLM). Nat. Service, 1951–53 (2nd Lt, Oxford and Bucks Light Infantry). Called to Bar, Lincoln's Inn, 1957, Bencher, 1986. Dir, Bar Mutual Indemnity Fund Ltd, 1988–. Member: Council of Legal Educn, 1986–92; Conveyancing Standing Cttee, Law Commn, 1987–89; Tax Law Review Cttee, 1994–; Chm., Cambridge Univ. Court of Discipline, 1993–. Member: Internat. Commn of Jurists, 1993–; Council, Justice, 1972– (Vice Chm., 1978–88, Chm., 1988–94, Exec. Cttee). Contested: Kensington: (SDP) 1983; (SDP/Alliance) 1987; (Lib Dem) July 1988; (Lib Dem) Oxford West and Abingdon, 1992. Chairman: SDP Council Arrangements Cttee, 1982–88; Lib Dem Conf. Cttee, 1988–91; Lib Dem Lawyers Assoc., 1988–91; Mem., Lib Dem Policy Cttee, 1988–. Trustee, Campden Charities, 1975–90. *Publications:* (with Prof. Gareth Jones) Specific Performance, 1986; (jtly) Countdown to 1997 (report of Mission to Hong Kong for Internat. Commn of Jurists), 1992; (jtly) Human Rights in Kashmir, 1995; contribs to Halsbury's Laws of England; articles in legal periodicals. *Recreations:* walking, skiing. *Address:* 11 Clarence Terrace, NW1 4RD. *T:* 0171–262 1319; Youlbury House, Boars Hill, Oxford OX1 5HH. *T:* Oxford (01865) 735477. *Clubs:* Brooks's; Century Association (New York).

See also C. A. E. Goodhart, Sir P. C. Goodhart.

GOODHEW, Most Rev. Richard Henry, (Harry); *see* Sydney, Archbishop of.

GOODHEW, Sir Victor (Henry), Kt 1982; *b* 30 Nov. 1919; *s* of late Rudolph Goodhew, Mannings Heath, Sussex; *m* 1st, 1940, Sylvia Johnson (marr. diss.); one *s* one *d*; 2nd, 1951, Suzanne Gordon-Burge (marr. diss. 1972); 3rd, 1972, Eva Rittinghausen (marr. diss. 1981). *Educ:* King's Coll. Sch. Served War of 1939–45: RAF, 1939–46; comd Airborne Radar Unit, attached 6th Airborne Div.; Sqdn Ldr 1945. Member: Westminster City Council, 1953–59; LCC, 1958–61. Contested (C) Paddington North, 1955; MP (C) St Albans Div., Herts, Oct. 1959–83. PPS to Mr C. I. Orr-Ewing, OBE, MP (when Civil Lord of the Admiralty), May 1962–63; PPS to Hon. Thomas Galbraith, MP (Jt Parly Sec., Min. of Transport), 1963–64; Asst Govt Whip, June–Oct. 1970; a Lord Comr, HM Treasury, 1970–73. Member: Speaker's Panel of Chairmen, 1975–83; Select Cttee, House of Commons Services, 1978–83; House of Commons Commn, 1979–83; Jt Sec. 1922 Cttee, 1979–83; Vice-Chm., Cons. Defence Cttee, 1974–83. Chm., Bd of Management, Inst. of Sports Medicine, 1982– (Mem., 1967–70, 1973–82). *Recreations:* swimming, reading. *Address:* The Coach House, St Leonard's Dale, Winkfield Road, Windsor, Berks SL4 4AQ. *T:* Windsor (01753) 859073. *Clubs:* Buck's, United and Cecil, 1900; Constitutional (Windsor).

GOODING, Anthony James Joseph S.; *see* Simonds-Gooding.

GOODING, Air Vice-Marshal Keith Horace, CB 1966; OBE 1951; *b* 2 Sept. 1913; *s* of late Horace Milford Gooding, Romsey, Hants; *m* 1st, 1943, Peggy Eileen (*d* 1962), *d* of late Albert William Gatfield, Guildford, Surrey; one *s*; 2nd, 1968, Jean, *d* of late Maurice Stanley Underwood, Andover, Hants; two *s* one *d* (of whom one *s* one *d* are twins). *Educ:* King Edward VI Sch., Southampton. Joined RAF 1938; served Aden, Fighter Comd, 1939–45; Germany, 1945–47; NATO, 1953–55; Bomber Comd, 1958–61; AOA Maintenance Comd, 1965–68; Dir-Gen. of Supply (RAF), 1968–71, retired. Dir, Oxley Developments Co. Ltd., 1981–91. Chm., Crohn's in Childhood Res. Assoc. (formerly Appeal), 1986–90. *Recreations:* tennis, bridge. *Club:* Royal Air Force.

GOODISON, Sir Alan (Clowes), KCMG 1985 (CMG 1975); CVO 1980; HM Diplomatic Service, retired; *b* 20 Nov. 1926; *o s* of late Harold and Winifred Goodison (*née* Ludlam); *m* 1956, Anne Rosemary Fitton (*d* 1994); one *s* two *d*. *Educ:* Colfe's Grammar Sch.; Trinity Coll., Cambridge (Scholar, Mod. and Medieval Langs Tripos, first cl.; MA 1951); DipTh London 1995. Army, Lieut, 1947–49. Foreign Office, Third Sec., 1949; Middle East Centre for Arab Studies, 1950; served in Cairo, Tripoli, Khartoum, Lisbon, Amman, and Bonn, with spells in Foreign Office, 1950–68; Counsellor, Kuwait, 1969–71; Head of Trg Dept and Dir, Diplomatic Service Lang. Centre, FCO, 1971–72; Head of S European Dept, FCO, 1973–76; Minister, Rome, 1976–80; Asst Under-Sec. of State, FCO, 1980–83; Ambassador, Dublin, 1983–86. Dir, Wates Foundn, 1988–92. Chm., Charities Evaluation Service, 1993–; Trustee, Hampstead Wells and Campden Trust, 1993–. Pres., Beckenham Chorale, 1972–73. Licensed Reader of Anglican Church, 1959–62, 1966–82, 1988–; a Bishops' Selector for ABM (formerly ACCM), 1989–; Moderator of Reader Training, Edmonton Episcopal Area, 1990–92. Mem. Council: Jerusalem and the East Mission, 1964–65; Anglican Centre, Rome, 1977–80. Grande Ufficiale dell'Ordine al Merito della Repubblica Italiana (Hon.), 1980. *Publications:* articles on devotional subjects and trans. for Encyclopaedia of Islam. *Recreations:* theology, music, acting, reading. *Address:* 12 Gardnor Mansions, Church Row, NW3 6UR.

GOODISON, Sir Nicholas (Proctor), Kt 1982; Chairman, TSB Group plc, since 1989; *b* 16 May 1934; *s* of Edmund Harold Goodison and Eileen Mary Carrington Proctor; *m* 1960, Judith Abel Smith; one *s* two *d*. *Educ:* Marlborough Coll.; King's Coll., Cambridge (Scholar; BA Classics 1958, MA; PhD Architecture and History of Art, 1981). H. E. Goodison & Co., later Quilter Goodison, 1958–88: Partner, 1962; Chm., 1975–88. Mem. Council, Stock Exchange, 1968–88; Chm., Stock Exchange, 1976–88; President: Internat. Fedn of Stock Exchanges, 1985–86; British Bankers' Assoc., 1991–; Vice Chm., Chartered Inst. of Bankers, 1989– (FCIB 1989). Dep. Chm., British Steel, 1993– (Dir, 1989–); Dir, Gen. Accident plc, 1987–95. Member Council: Industrial Soc., 1976–; Securities Inst., 1992–; Chairman: Courtauld Inst. of Art, 1982–; NACF, 1986–; Director: ENO, 1977– (Vice-Chm., 1980–); Burlington Magazine Ltd. Hon. Keeper of Furniture, Fitzwilliam Museum, Cambridge; Pres., Furniture History Soc., 1990– (Hon. Treas., 1970–90). Governor, Marlborough Coll. CIMgt; FInstD 1989; FSA, FRSA, Sen. FRCA; Hon. Fellow RA, 1987; Hon. FRIBA 1992. Hon. DLitt City, 1985; Hon. LLD Exeter, 1989; Hon. DSc Aston, 1994. Chevalier, Légion d'Honneur, 1990. *Publications:* English Barometers 1680–1860, 1968, 2nd edn 1977; Ormolu: The Work of Matthew Boulton, 1974; many papers and articles on history of furniture, clocks and barometers. *Recreations:* history of furniture and decorative arts, opera, walking, fishing. *Address:* 60 Lombard Street, EC3V 9DN. *Clubs:* Athenæum, Beefsteak, Arts.

GOODISON, Robin Reynolds, CB 1964; consultant; Deputy Chairman, 1972–77, Acting Chairman, Jan.-March 1972, Civil Aviation Authority; *b* 13 Aug. 1912; *s* of Arthur Leathley Goodison; *m* 1936, Betty Lydia, *d* of Comdr L. Robinson, OBE, Royal Navy (retired); three *d*. *Educ:* Finchley Grammar Sch.; University Coll., London Univ. (MA). Joined Ministry of Labour, 1935, transferred to Ministry of Transport, 1936; Principal, 1940; Asst Sec., 1946; Imperial Defence Coll., 1950; Under-Sec., Ministry of Transport and Civil Aviation, 1957, Ministry of Aviation, 1959, Board of Trade, 1966; Second Sec., BoT, 1969–70; Dep. Sec., DTI, 1970–72. Assessor, Heathrow Terminal Inquiry, 1978–79; Specialist Adviser, House of Lords Select Cttee, 1979–80, 1984–85. *Recreation:* sailing. *Address:* 37 Coldharbour Lane, Bushey, Herts WD2 3NU. *T:* 0181–950 1911.

GOODLAD, Rt Hon. Alastair (Robertson), PC 1992; MP (C) Eddisbury, since 1983 (Northwich, Feb. 1974–1983); Parliamentary Secretary to HM Treasury and Government Chief Whip, since 1995; *b* 4 July 1943; *y s* of late Dr John Goodlad and late Isabel (*née* Sinclair); *m* 1968, Cecilia Barbara, 2nd *d* of late Col Richard Hurst and Lady Barbara Hurst; two *s*. *Educ:* Marlborough Coll.; King's Coll., Cambridge (MA, LLB). Contested (C) Crewe Div., 1970. An Asst Govt Whip, 1981–82; a Lord Commissioner of HM Treasury, 1982–84; Parly Under-Sec. of State, Dept of Energy, 1984–87; Comptroller of HM Household, 1989–90; Dep. Govt Chief Whip and Treasurer, HM Household, 1990–92; Minister of State, FCO, 1992–95. Member: Select Cttee on Agric., 1979–81; Select Cttee on Televising of Proceedings of the House, 1987–89; Jt Hon. Secretary: Cons. Party Trade Cttee, 1978–81 (Jt Vice-Chm., 1979–81); Cons. NI Cttee, 1979–81; Hon. Sec., All Party Heritage Gp, 1979–81; Chm., All Party Parly Cttee for Refugees, 1987–89. Chm., NW Area Cons. Members, 1987–89. *Address:* House of Commons, SW1A 0AA. *Clubs:* Brooks's, Beefsteak, Pratt's.

GOODLAND, Judith Mary; Headmistress, Wycombe Abbey School, since 1989; *b* 26 May 1938; *d* of Rolf Thornton Ferro and Joan (*née* O'Hanlon); *m* 1961, A. T. Goodland (marr. diss.); one *s* two *d*. *Educ:* Howell's Sch., Denbigh; Bristol Univ. (BA Hons); Charlotte Mason Coll., Ambleside (Cert Ed). Head, Modern Languages Dept, Cartmel Priory C of E Comprehensive Sch., 1968–72; Casterton Sch., Kirkby Lonsdale, 1980–83; Headmistress, St George's Sch., Ascot, 1983–88. FRSA 1994. *Recreations:* fell walking, bridge, golf. *Address:* Wycombe Abbey School, High Wycombe, Bucks HP11 1PE. *T:* High Wycombe (01494) 520381. *Club:* Lansdowne.

GOODMAN, Dame Barbara, DBE 1989; QSO 1981; JP; *b* 5 Oct. 1932; *d* of late Horace Robinson and Lillie Robinson (*née* Shieff); *m* 1954, Harold Goodman (decd); two *s* one *d*. *Educ:* Parnell Sch.; St Cuthbert's Coll. Mayoress, City of Auckland, 1968–80; founding Trustee, HELP Foundn, 1980–85; Chm., Auckland Spastic Soc., 1980–84; Chm., Odyssey House Trust, 1981–92; former Mem. Exec. Cttee, NZ Fedn of Voluntary Welfare Organisations. Mem., Auckland City Council, 1989–. Mem., NZ Internat. Trade Fair Cttee, 1985–89; Chm., Auckland 1990 Trust Board, 1989–91. Guardian, NZ Women's Refuge Foundn; Patron and Mem., Aotearoa NZ Peace Foundn. Member: Cttee, Shalom Court; Women's Internat. Zionist Orgn. Vice Patron, Auckland Cricket Assoc. *Publication:* For Flying Kiwis, 1990. *Recreations:* meeting people, travel, reading, cooking, embroidery. *Address:* 22a Tohunga Crescent, Parnell, Auckland 1001, New Zealand. *T:* (9) 3790650, *Fax:* (9) 3779112. *Clubs:* Athene, Zonta, Rotary (Auckland).

GOODMAN, Maj.-Gen. David; *see* Goodman, Maj.-Gen. J. D. W.

GOODMAN, Elinor Mary; Political Editor, Channel Four News, since 1988; *b* 11 Oct. 1946; *d* of Edward Weston Goodman and Pamela Longbottom; *m* 1985, Derek John Scott. *Educ:* private schools, secretarial college. Financial Times: Consumer Affairs Corresp., 1971–78; Political Corresp., 1978–82; Political Corresp., Channel Four News, 1982–88. *Recreations:* riding, walking. *Address:* Martinscote, Oare, Marlborough, Wilts SN8 4JA.

GOODMAN, Geoffrey George; Editor, British Journalism Review, since 1989; Broadcaster, BBC Current Affairs, and London News Radio (formerly LBC/IRN), since 1986; *b* 2 July 1921; *s* of Michael Goodman and Edythe (*née* Bowman); *m* 1947, Margit (*née* Freudenbergova); one *s* one *d*. *Educ:* elementary schs, Stockport and Manchester; grammar schs, London; LSE (BScEcon). RAF, 1940–46. Manchester Guardian, 1946–47; Daily Mirror, 1947–48; News Chronicle, 1949–59; Daily Herald, 1959–64; The Sun (IPC), 1964–69; Daily Mirror, 1969–86 (Industrial Editor, 1969–86; Asst Editor, 1976–86). Fellow, Nuffield Coll., Oxford, 1974–76. Head of Govt's Counter-inflation Publicity Unit, 1975–76; Member: Labour Party Cttee on Industrial Democracy, 1966–67; Royal Commn on the Press, 1974–77; TGWU; NUJ. Hon. MA Oxon. Gerald Barry Award for Journalism, Granada TV Press Awards, 1984. *Publications:* General Strike of 1926, 1951; Brother Frank, 1969; The Awkward Warrior, 1979; The Miners' Strike, 1985; contrib. London Inst. of World Affairs, 1948. *Recreations:* pottering, poetry, supporting Tottenham Hotspur FC, and climbing—but not social. *Address:* 64 Flower Lane, Mill Hill, NW7 2JL. *Club:* Savile.

GOODMAN, Howard; *see* Goodman, R. H.

GOODMAN, Maj.-Gen. (John) David (Whitlock), CB 1987; Director and defence advisor to ML Holdings plc, since 1989; Consultant, Landair International Defence Services Ltd, since 1987; *b* 20 May 1932; *s* of late Brig. Eric Whitlock Goodman, DSO, MC and Norah Dorothy Goodman (*née* Stacpoole); *m* 1957, Valerie-Ann McDonald; one *s* two *d*. *Educ:* Wellington Coll.; RMA Sandhurst. Commnd RA, 1952; served in UK and Northern Ireland, BAOR, Aden and Hong Kong; Staff Coll. 1962; Battery Comdr, 3rd Regt Royal Horse Artillery, 1966–69; Jt Services Staff Coll., Latimer, 1970; BMRA 2nd Div., 1970–72; Instr, Staff Coll. Camberley and Sudan, 1972–73; CO 26 Field Regt, RA, 1973–76; Comdt, Royal Sch. of Artillery, 1977–79; Royal Coll. of Defence Studies, 1980; Asst Military Secretary, MoD, 1981–82; Dir, Army Air Corps, 1983–87. Hon. Colonel: 26 Field Regt RA, 1985–92; 3 Regt, AAC, 1987–93; 266 (Glos Volunteer Artillery) Observation Post Batt. RA (Vol.), 1990–93. Mem., Regtl Cttee, AAC, 1991–. Chm. Dirs, Mus. of Army Flying, 1992–; Trustee, Kelly Holdsworth Trust, 1990–; LEA Governor: Avenue Sch., Warminster, 1991–; Kingdown Sch., Warminster, 1992–. Chm., Sutton Veny Parish Council, 1992–. FIMgt (FBIM 1980). Freeman, GAPAN, 1987. *Recreations:* the countryside, tennis. *Address:* c/o Lloyds Bank, 37 Market Place, Warminster, Wilts BA12 9BD.

GOODMAN, Prof. John Francis Bradshaw, CBE 1995; PhD; CIPD; Frank Thomas Professor of Industrial Relations, University of Manchester Institute of Science and Technology, since 1975 (Vice-Principal, 1979–81); *b* 2 Aug. 1940; *s* of Edwin and Amy Goodman; *m* 1967, Elizabeth Mary Towns; one *s* one *d*. *Educ:* Chesterfield Grammar Sch.; London Sch. of Economics (BSc Econ; PhD); MSc Manchester. Personnel Officer, Ford Motor Co. Ltd, 1962–64; Lectr in Industrial Econs, Univ. of Nottingham, 1964–69; Industrial Relations Adviser, NBPI, 1969–70; Sen. Lectr in Industrial Relations, Univ. of Manchester, 1970–74; Chm., Manchester Sch. of Management, UMIST, 1977–79, 1987–94. Vis. Professor: Univ. of WA, 1981, 1984; McMaster Univ., 1985. Pres., British Univs Industrial Relations Assoc., 1983–86. Member: Council, ACAS, 1987–; Training Bd, 1991–, Council, 1993–, ESRC. *Publications:* Shop Stewards in British Industry, 1969; Shop Stewards, 1973; Rulemaking and Industrial Peace, 1977; Ideology and Shop-floor Industrial Relations, 1981; Employment Relations in Industrial Society, 1984; Unfair Dismissal Law and Employment Practice, 1985; contribs to British Jl of Industrial Relations, ILR, Industrial Relations Jl, Monthly Labor Rev., Jl of Management Studies, Personnel Management, etc. *Recreations:* fell walking, ornithology, squash, football. *Address:* Lundy Rise, Brookledge Lane, Adlington, Macclesfield, Cheshire SK10 4JX. *T:* Macclesfield (01625) 572480.

GOODMAN, Michael Bradley; His Honour Judge Goodman; a Circuit Judge, since 1983; *b* 3 May 1930; *s* of Marcus Gordon Goodman and Eunice Irene May Goodman (*née* Bradley); *m* 1967, Patricia Mary Gorringe; two *d* (one *s* decd). *Educ:* Aldenham; Sidney Sussex Coll., Cambridge (MA). Called to Bar, Middle Temple, 1953; Western Circuit; a Recorder of the Crown Court, 1972–83. Prosecuting Counsel to DHSS, 1975–83; Pres., Wireless Telegraphy Appeals Tribunal, 1977–88. Chancellor: Dio. Guildford, 1968–; Dio. Lincoln, 1970–; Dio. Rochester, 1971–; Vicar-Gen., Province of Canterbury, 1977–83. Member: Commn on Deployment and Payment of the Clergy, 1965–67; C of E Legal Adv. Commn, 1973– (Chm., 1986–); Faculty Jurisdiction Commn, 1980–83; General Synod, Church of England, 1977–83; Lay Chm., Dulwich Deanery Synod, 1970–73. Chairman: William Temple Assoc., 1963–66; Ecclesiastical Judges Assoc., 1987–. Pres., SE London Magistrates' Assoc., 1989–. Governor: Liddon Hse, London, 1964–; Pusey Hse, Oxford, 1965–88. *Address:* Judge i/c Civil List, Law Courts, Altyre Road, Croydon CR9 5AB.

GOODMAN, Michael Jack, MA, PhD; Social Security Commissioner (formerly National Insurance Commissioner), since 1979; Child Support Commissioner, since 1993; *b* 3 Oct. 1931; *s* of Vivian Roy Goodman and Muriel Olive Goodman; *m* 1958, Susan Kerkham Wherry; two *s* one *d*. *Educ:* Sudbury Grammar Sch., Suffolk; Corpus Christi Coll., Oxford (MA). PhD Manchester. Solicitor. Lectr, Gibson & Weldon, 1957; solicitor, Lincoln, 1958–60; Lectr, Law Society's Sch., 1961–63; Lectr, then Sen. Lectr in Law, Manchester Univ., 1964–70; Prof. of Law, Durham Univ., 1971–76; Perm. Chm. of Indust. Tribunals, Newcastle upon Tyne, 1976–79. Gen. Editor, Encyclopedia of Health and Safety at Work, 1974–. *Publications:* Industrial Tribunals' Procedure, 1976, 4th edn 1987; Health and Safety at Work: law and practice, 1988; contrib. Mod. Law Rev., and Conveyancer. *Recreations:* amateur radio (licence holder), The Times crossword. *Address:* Office of the Social Security Commissioners, Harp House, 83 Farringdon Street, EC4A 4DH. *T:* 0171–353 5145.

GOODMAN, Sir Patrick (Ledger); Kt 1995; CBE 1990; Special Trade Ambassador of New Zealand, 1990; company director; President Emeritus, Goodman Fielder Ltd; *b* 6 April 1929; *s* of Athol Ledger Goodman and Della Marion Goodman; *m* 1960, Hilary Gay Duncan; three *s*. *Educ:* St Patrick's Coll., Silverstream, NZ; Victoria University Coll., Wellington. Chairman: Heinz-Wattie; Tourism Nelson; former Chairman: Quality Bakers of NZ; Goodman Group and subsidiaries. Founder Chm., NZ Business and Parlt Trust; Trustee: Founders of Nelson; Massey Univ. Agric. Foundn; Bishop Suter Art Gall. Foundn Mem., NZ Rugby Foundn. *Recreations:* golf, cricket, Rugby, boating, fishing. *Address:* 52 Tudor Street, Motueka, Nelson, New Zealand. *T:* (3) 5288314.

GOODMAN, Perry; Director (Industry and Regions), The Engineering Council, 1990–92; *b* 26 Nov. 1932; *s* of Cyril Goodman and Anne (*née* Rosen); *m* 1958, Marcia Ann (*née* Morris); one *s* one *d*. *Educ:* Haberdashers' Aske's Hampstead Sch.; University Coll., London (BSc). MIM. 2nd Lieut, Royal Corps of Signals, 1955–57; Jt Head, Chemistry Res. Lab., then Project Leader, Morgan Crucible Co. Ltd, 1957–64; Sen. Scientific Officer, DSIR, 1964–65; Principal Scientific Officer, Process Plant Br., Min. of Technology, 1965–67; 1st Sec. (Scientific), 1968–70, Counsellor (Scientific), 1970–74, British Embassy, Paris; Research Gp, DoI, 1974–79; Hd, Policy and Perspectives Unit, DoI, 1980–81; Department of Trade and Industry: Hd, Design Policy/Technical Adv. Services for Industry, 1981–86; Hd, Electrical Engrg Br., 1986–90. Mem. Bd, Northern Engrg Centre, 1990–92. FRSA 1986. *Recreations:* travel, walking, conversation. *Address:* 118 Westbourne Terrace Mews, W2 6QG. *T:* 0171–262 0925.

GOODMAN, (Robert) Howard, ARIBA; DipArch (Hons); Partner, MPA Health Planners, since 1988; *b* 29 March 1928; *s* of Robert Barnard Goodman and Phyllis Goodman; *m* 1955; two *s*. *Educ:* St George Grammar Sch., Bristol; Northern Polytechnic, London. Articled pupil, 1944–47; Arch. Asst to City of Bristol, 1947–49; Asst Architect to SW Regional Hosp. Bd, 1949–54. Design of various hosp. projects in SW England; with various private architects, 1954–60; design of several hosps in UK, Africa and India.

MOH (now DoH): Main Grade Arch., 1960; Sen. Grade, 1961; Principal Arch., 1963; Asst Chief Arch., 1966; Chief Arch., 1971–78; Dir of Develt, 1978–85; Dir, Health Bldg, 1986–88. Councillor (Lab) Reigate and Banstead BC, 1989–93. Member: Constr. and Housing Res. Adv. Council, 1977–88; BRE Adv. Council, 1977–88; Council of Centre on Environment for the Handicapped, 1978–94; E Surrey CHC, 1992–. Research and develt into health planning, systems building and computer aided design. Hon. FICW, 1984; Hon. FBID, 1985; Hon. FIHopsE, 1988. *Publications:* contribs to: Hospitals Handbook, 1960; Hospital Design, 1963; Hospital Traffic and Supply Problems, 1968; Portfolio for Health, 1971; Technology of the Eighties, 1972; Industrialised Hospital Building, 1972; CAD Systems, 1976; various articles in architectural, medical and general press. *Recreations:* eating, drinking, talking. *Address:* Ion House, 44 Nutley Lane, Reigate, Surrey RH2 9HS.

GOODPASTER, Gen. Andrew Jackson; United States Army, retired; US Medal of Freedom, 1984; DSC (US); DSM (Def.) (Oak Leaf Cluster); DSM (Army) (3 Oak Leaf Clusters); DSM (Navy); DSM (Air Force); Silver Star; Legion of Merit (Oak Leaf Cluster); Purple Heart (Oak Leaf Cluster); Superintendent, United States Military Academy, West Point, New York (in grade of Lt-Gen.), 1977–81; *b* 12 Feb. 1915; *s* of Andrew Jackson Goodpaster and Teresa Mary Goodpaster (*née* Mrovka); *m* 1939, Dorothy Anderson Goodpaster (*née* Anderson); two *d*. *Educ:* McKendree Coll., Lebanon, Ill; US Mil. Academy, 1935–39 (BS); Princeton Univ., 1947–50 (MSE, MA, PhD). 11th Eng. Panama, 1939–42; Ex O, 390th Eng. Gen. Svc Regt, Camp Claiborne, La, 1942–43; Comd and Gen. Staff Sch., Ft Leavenworth, Kansas, Feb.–April 1943; CO, 48th Eng. Combat Bn, II Corps, Fifth Army, 1943–44; Ops Div., Gen. Staff, War Dept (incl. Jt War Plans Cttee, JCS, 1945–46), 1944–47; Student, Civil Eng. Course and Polit. Sc. Grad. Sch., Princeton Univ., 1947–50; Army Mem., Jt Advanced Study Cttee, JCS, 1950–51; Special Asst to Chief of Staff, SHAPE, 1951–54; Dist Eng., San Francisco Dist, Calif, July–Oct. 1954; Def. Liaison Officer and Staff Sec. to President of US, 1954–61; Asst Div. Comdr, 3rd Inf. Div., April–Oct. 1961, and CG, 8th Inf. Div., Oct. 1961–Oct. 1962, USAREUR; Sp. Asst (Policy) to Chm., JCS, Washington, DC, Nov. 1962–Jan. 1964; Asst to Chm., JCS, Washington, DC, Jan. 1964–July 1966; Dir Joint Staff, JCS, Washington, DC, Aug. 1966–Mar. 1967; Dir of Sp. Studies, Office Chief of Staff, USA, Washington, DC, April 1967–July 1967; Senior US Army Mem., Mil. Staff UN, May 1967–July 1968; Comdt, Nat. War Coll., Washington, DC, Aug. 1967–July 1968; Mem. US Delegn for Negotiations with N Vietnam, Paris (addl duty), April 1968–July 1968; Dep. Comdr, US Mil. Assistance Comd, Vietnam, July 1968–April 1969; Supreme Allied Commander Europe, 1969–74; C-in-C, US European Command, 1969–74. Sen. Fellow, Woodrow Wilson Internat. Center for Scholars, Washington DC, 1975–76; Prof. of Govt and Internat. Studies, The Citadel, Charleston, SC, 1976–77. Pres., Inst. for Defence Analyses, Alexandria, Va, 1983–85; Chairman: Atlantic Council of the US, 1985–; George C. Marshall Foundn, 1993–. *Publication:* For the Common Defense, 1977. *Recreations:* golf, fishing, music. *Address:* 409 North Fairfax Street, Alexandria, VA 22314, USA.

GOODRICH, David, CEng, RCNC; Managing Director, since 1985, Chief Executive, since 1986, and Deputy Chairman, since 1995, British Maritime Technology Ltd; Chairman, BMT Group Ltd, since 1995; *b* 15 April 1941; *s* of William B. Goodrich and Florence B. Goodrich; *m* 1965, Margaret R. Riley; one *s* three *d*. MBA. Shipbuilding management apprentice, 1958–63; shipbuilding designer/estimator, 1963–65; Constructor, RCNC, 1965–77; Manager, Shipbuilding Technology, 1977–79, Man. Dir, 1979–85, BSRA. FRINA (Mem. Council). *Publication:* paper to Royal Soc. *Recreations:* squash, walking, family. *Address:* British Maritime Technology Ltd, Orlando House, 1 Waldegrave Road, Teddington, Middx TW11 8LZ.

GOODRICH, Rt. Rev. Philip Harold Ernest; *see* Worcester, Bishop of.

GOODRIDGE, Hon. Noel Herbert Alan; Chief Justice of Court of Appeal and of Newfoundland, since 1986; *b* 18 Dec. 1930; *s* of William Prout Goodridge and Freda Dorothy (*née* Hayward); *m* 1956, Isabelle (*née* Galway); three *s* one *d*. *Educ:* Bishop Field Coll.; King's Collegiate Sch., Windsor, NS; Bishop's College Sch., Lennoxville, PQ; Dalhousie Univ., Halifax, NS (BA, LLB). Practised law, 1953–75; QC (Newfoundland), 1972; originally with Hunt, Emerson, Stirling and Higgins, later Stirling, Ryan and Goodridge; at time of leaving practice, a sen. partner; Puisne Judge, Trial Div. of Supreme Ct of Newfoundland, 1975; Puisne Judge, Ct Martial Appeal Ct, 1981–. Canadian Bar Association: Mem., 1956–; Mem. Nat. Exec., 1975–76; Pres., Nfld Br., 1973–75. Bencher, Law Soc. of Nfld, 1970–75, Sec., 1973–75; Member: Judicial Council estabd under the Provincial Ct Act, 1974–76; Canadian Judicial Council, 1986–; Canadian Judges Conf., 1976–. Exec. positions with Jun. Ch. of Commerce, 1954–57, and Nfld BoT, 1962–64. Vice-Chm., Gen. Hosp. Corp., 1970–75; Chm., St John's Transportation Commn, 1971–75; Mem., Newfoundland Assoc. for the Help of Retarded Children, 1960–62. Life Mem., Assoc. of Kinsmen Clubs of Canada. *Recreations:* golf, tennis, walking, bridge, skiing. *Address:* Supreme Court of Newfoundland, Court of Appeal, PO Box 937, St John's, Newfoundland A1C 5M3, Canada. *T:* (709) 7290066.

GOODRIDGE, Rt. Rev. Sehon Sylvester; *see* Windward Islands, Bishop of.

GOODSMAN, James Melville, CBE 1993; Managing Director, Michael Fraser & Co. Ltd, since 1995; Director, Consensus Ltd; *b* 6 Feb. 1947; *s* of James K. Goodsman and Euphamia Goodsman, Elgin, Moray; *m* 1990, Victoria, *y d* of late Col Philip Smitherman and of Rosemary Smitherman, CBE. *Educ:* Elgin Academy. Joined Cons. Party organisation, 1966; Agent: to Rt Hon. Betty Harvie Anderson, 1970–74; to Rt Hon. Maurice Macmillan, 1974–80; Conservative Central Office: Dep. Agent, NW Area, 1980–84; Asst Dir (Community Affairs), 1984–90; Head, Community and Legal Affairs, May–Sept. 1990; Dir, Cons. Party in Scotland, 1990–93. Hon. Sec., One Nation Forum, 1986–90. *Publications:* contribs to Cons. party and community relations papers. *Recreations:* golf, shooting, church music. *Address:* Michael Fraser & Co. Ltd, Treeton House, Ardersier, Inverness IV1 2QU; The Old Schoolhouse, Collessie, Fife KY15 7UU. *Clubs:* Buck's; Edinburgh Morayshire.

GOODSON, Rear-Adm. Frederick Brian, OBE 1982; Assistant Chief of Defence Staff (Logistics), since 1993; *b* 21 May 1938; *m* 1965, Susan (Sue) Mary Firmin; two *s* two *d*. *Educ:* Campbell Coll. Coastal Forces, 1958–60; HMS Gambia and HMS Lion, 1960–64; Aden, 1964–65; Supply Officer, HMS Diana, 1966–69; Staff, BRNC, Dartmouth, 1970–72; Exchange Service, USN, 1972–74; Comdr 1974; Exchange Service, Royal Naval Supply and Transport Service, 1975–78; Naval Sec's Dept, 1978–79; Supply Officer, HMS Invincible, 1980–81; Fleet Supply Officer, C-in-C Fleet, 1981–82; Capt. 1982; Sec., C-in-C Naval Home Comd, 1983–85; Dir, Naval Logistic Planning, 1985–87; Cdre comdg HMS Centurion, 1988–91; rcds 1992; Rear-Adm. 1993. *Recreations:* offshore sailing, squash, country pursuits. *Address:* c/o Ministry of Defence, Main Building, Whitehall, SW1A 2HB. *Clubs:* Lansdowne; Royal Naval Sailing Association.

GOODSON, Sir Mark (Weston Lassam), 3rd Bt *cr* 1922, of Waddeton Court, Co. Devon; *b* 12 Dec. 1925; *s* of Major Alan Richard Lassam Goodson (*d* 1941) (2nd *s* of 1st Bt) and Clarisse Muriel Weston (*d* 1982), *d* of John Weston Adamson; *S* uncle, 1986; *m* 1949, Barbara Mary Constantine, *d* of Surg.-Capt. Reginald Joseph McAuliffe Andrews, RN; one *s* three *d*. *Educ:* Radley; Jesus College, Cambridge. *Heir: s* Alan Reginald Goodson, *b* 15 May 1960. *Address:* Kilham, Mindrum, Northumberland TD12 4QS. *T:* Mindrum (01890) 850217.

GOODSON, Michael John; Assistant Auditor General, National Audit Office, 1984–93; *b* 4 Aug. 1937; *s* of late Herbert Edward William Goodson and Doris Maud Goodson; *m* 1958, Susan Elizabeth (*née* Higley); one *s* one *d*. *Educ:* King Henry VIII Sch., Coventry. Joined Exchequer and Audit Dept, 1955; Asst Auditor, 1955; Auditor, 1965; Private Sec. to Comptroller and Auditor Gen., 1967–70; Sen. Auditor, 1970; Health Service Ombudsman (on secondment), 1973–76; Chief Auditor, Exchequer and Audit Dept, 1976; Dep. Dir of Audit, 1978; Dir of Audit, 1981. *Recreations:* ornithology, model engineering, caravanning. *Address:* 2 Bayley Mead, St John's Road, Boxmoor, Herts HP1 1NP. *T:* Hemel Hempstead (01442) 242611.

GOODSON-WICKES, Dr Charles; MP (C) Wimbledon, since 1987; *b* 7 Nov. 1945; *s* of late Ian Goodson Wickes, FRCP, Consultant Paediatrician and farmer, of Stock Harvard, Essex and of Monica Goodson-Wickes; *m* 1974, Judith Amanda Hopkinson, *d* of late Comdr John Hopkinson, RN, of Sutton Grange, nr Stamford, Lincs; two *s*. *Educ:* Charterhouse; St Bartholomew's Hosp. (MB BS 1970). Called to the Bar, Inner Temple, 1972. Ho. Physician, Addenbrooke's Hosp., Cambridge, 1972; Surgeon-Capt., The Life Guards, 1973–77 (served BAOR, N Ireland, Cyprus); Silver Stick MO, Hsehold Cavalry, 1977; RARO, 1977–; re-enlisted as Lt-Col, 1991, for Gulf Campaign (served S Arabia, Iraq, Kuwait, with HQ 7 Armoured Bde). Clin. Asst, St Bart's Hosp., 1977–80; Consulting Phys., BUPA, 1977–86; Occupational Phys., 1980–94; Med. advr to Barclays Bank, RTZ, McKinsey, Christie's, British Alcan, Collins, Meat & Livestock Commn etc.; UK Advr, Norwegian Directorate of Health, 1983–, Chm., Appeals Bd, Asbestos Licensing Regulations, 1982–; Member: Med. Adv. Cttee, Industrial Soc., 1981–87; Fitness Adv, Panel, Inst. of Dirs, 1982–84. Dir, Nestor-BNA plc, 1993–, and other internat. cos. Contested (C) Islington Central, 1979. Vice-Pres., Islington South and Finsbury Cons. Assoc., 1982–. PPS to Minister of State for Housing and Planning, DoE, 1992–94, to Financial Sec. to HM Treasury, 1994–. Mem., Select Cttee on Members' Interests, 1992–94; Sec., 1987–90, Vice-Chm., 1990–91, Constitutional Affairs Cttee; Sec., Arts and Heritage Cttee, 1990–92; Sec., 1990–91, Vice Chm., 1991–92, Defence Cttee; Mem., Jt Cttee, Consolidation of Bills, 1987–92; Vice Chm., All Party British-Russian Gp, 1993–; Treas., All Party British Chinese Gp, 1992–. Fellow, Industry and Parlt Trust, 1991. Treas., Dr Ian Goodson Wickes Fund for Handicapped Children, 1979–88; Chm., British Field Sports Soc., 1994– (Mem., Public Affairs Cttee, 1980–93). Governor, Highbury Grove Sch., 1977–85. Pte, The Parachute Regt (TA), 1963–65. Founder Chm., Essex Kit Cat Club, 1965. *Publication:* The New Corruption, 1984. *Recreations:* hunting, shooting, real tennis, gardening, travel, history. *Address:* Watergate House, Bulford, Wilts SP4 9DY. *T:* Stonehenge (01980) 632344; 37 St James's Place, SW1A 1NS. *T:* 0171-629 0981; (consulting rooms) 8 Devonshire Place, W1N 1PB. *T:* 0171-935 5011. *Clubs:* Boodle's, Pratt's, MCC.

GOODWIN, Prof. Albert, MA; Professor of Modern History in the University of Manchester, 1953–69 (Dean of the Faculty of Arts, 1966–68), now Emeritus Professor; *b* 2 Aug. 1906; 3rd *s* of Albert and Edith Ellen Goodwin; *m* 1st, 1935, Mary Ethelwyn (*d* 1981), *e d* of late Capt. W. Millner, Tettenhall, Staffs; two *s* one *d*; 2nd, 1985, Mrs Barbara Mallows (*d* 1990). *Educ:* King Edward VII School, Sheffield; Jesus Coll., Oxford; Sorbonne. Scholar; Gladstone Memorial Prizeman (Oxford), 1926; 1st Cl. Mod. Hist., 1928; Laming Travelling Fellow, The Queen's Coll., Oxford, 1928–29. Asst Lectr in European History, Univ. of Liverpool, 1929–31; Lectr in Mod. Hist. and Economics, 1931, Fellow and Tutor, Jesus Coll., Oxford, 1933; Junior Dean, Librarian and Dean of Degrees, 1931–39; Univ. Lectr in Mod. French Hist., 1938. Staff Officer (Sqdn Ldr) in RAFVR in Air Ministry War Room, 1940–43; Historical Branch, Air Ministry, 1944–45. Senior Tutor, 1947–48, and Vice-Principal of Jesus Coll., Oxford, 1949–51. Examiner in Final Hon. Sch. of Mod. Hist. (Oxford) 1948–49, Chm., 1950; Senior Univ. Lectr in Revolutionary and Napoleonic Period, 1948–53; Vis. Fellow, All Souls Coll., Oxford, 1969–70. Member: Council of Royal Historical Soc. (Vice-Pres.); Royal Commn on Historical MSS, 1966–81; Governor of John Rylands Library, Manchester. Pres., Sherborne Hist. Soc.; Chm., Sherborne Museum Council, 1981–82. *Publications:* The Abbey of St Edmundsbury, 1931; The Battle of Britain (Air Ministry Pamphlet 156), 1943; The French Revolution, 1953; The European Nobility in the Eighteenth Century (contrib. and ed), 1953; A select list of works on Europe and Europe Overseas, 1715–1815 (co-editor contributor), 1956; The Friends of Liberty: the English democratic movement in the age of the French Revolution, 1979; (ed and contrib.) Vol. VIII New Cambridge Modern History; articles in Eng. Hist. Review, History, Encyclopædia Britannica, etc. *Recreations:* golf, antiques. *Address:* Tyndale Nursing Home, 36 Preston Road, Yeovil, Somerset BA21 3AQ.

GOODWIN, Christine, (Mrs Richard Goodwin); *see* Edzard, C.

GOODWIN, Dr Eric Thomson, CBE 1975; retired; *b* 30 July 1913; *s* of John Edward Goodwin and Florence Goodwin; *m* 1st, 1940, Isobel Philip (*d* 1976); two *s*; 2nd, 1977, Avis Mary (*née* Thomson). *Educ:* King Edward VI Sch., Stafford; Harrow County Sch.; Peterhouse, Cambridge. BA 1934, Rayleigh Prize 1936, MA 1937, PhD 1938. Asst Lectr, Sheffield Univ., 1937–39; war service: Mathematical Lab., Cambridge, 1939–43; Admty Signal Estabt, Witley, 1943–44; Admty Computing Service, Bath, 1945; Maths Div., Nat. Physical Lab., 1945–71 (Supt 1951–71); Dep. Dir, Nat. Phys. Lab., 1971–74, retd. *Publications:* papers in learned jls on theoretical physics and numerical analysis. *Recreations:* music, reading, the countryside, philately. *Address:* 32 Castle Mount Crescent, Bakewell, Derbyshire DE45 1AT. *T:* Bakewell (01629) 813647.

GOODWIN, Prof. John Forrest, MD, FRCP; Professor of Clinical Cardiology, Royal Postgraduate Medical School, London, 1963–84, now Emeritus; Consulting Physician, Hammersmith Hospital, since 1949; Hon. Consulting Cardiologist, St George's Hospital, since 1986; *b* 1 Dec. 1918; *s* of late Col William Richard Power Goodwin, DSO, RAMC, and late Myrtle Dale Goodwin (*née* Forrest); *m* 1943, Barbara Cameron Robertson; one *s* one *d*. *Educ:* Cheltenham Coll.; St Mary's Hosp. Medical Sch. (Univ. of London). FRSocMed 1943; MD London 1946; FRCP 1957. Med. Registrar, St Mary's Hosp., 1943–44; Physician, Anglo-Iranian Oil Co., Abadan, 1944–45; Med. 1st Asst, Royal Infirmary, Sheffield, 1946–49; Lectr in Medicine and Cons. Physician, Postgraduate Med. Sch., London, 1949–59; Sen. Lecturer, 1959–63. Visiting Professor: Univ. of California at Los Angeles, 1966; Georgetown Univ. Sch. of Med., Washington, 1973; Mayo Clinic, 1985; Pfizer Vis. Prof., Massachusetts Gen. Hosp., 1987; Lectures: Watson Smith, RCP, 1967; St Cyres, Nat. Heart Hosp., 1970; Lumleian, RCP, 1980. Mem., Expert Cttee on Cardiovascular Diseases, WHO, 1979. Member: Brit. Cardiac Soc., 1950 (Pres., 1972–76); Med. Res. Soc., 1952; Assoc. of Physicians of Great Britain and Ireland, 1953; Council, Brit. Heart Foundation, 1964; Past Pres., Internat. Soc. and Fedn of Cardiology (Pres., 1977–81); Pres., Hypertrophic Cardiomyopathy Assoc., 1991–; 2nd Vice-Pres., RCP, 1979–80; Vice Pres., Coronary Prevention Gp, 1988– (Chm., 1985–88); Chm., Nat. Forum for the Prevention of Coronary Heart Disease, 1987–93. Member: Società Italiana di Cardiologia, 1964; Assoc. of European Pædiatric Cardiologists, 1967; Cardiac Soc. of

Australia and NZ, 1974; Venezuelan Soc. of Cardiology, 1969; Burma Medical Assoc., 1987–; Hon. Member: Swiss Cardiol. Soc.; Cardiac Soc., Ecuador; Hellenic Cardiac Soc., 1974; Cardiac Soc. of Mexico, 1977; Fellow: Amer. Coll. of Cardiology, 1967; Council on Clinical Cardiology, Amer. Heart Assoc., 1970; European Soc. of Cardiology, 1988; Hon. FACP 1985. Dr *hc* Lisbon, 1985. Gifted Teacher Award, Amer. Coll. of Cardiol., 1984. SPk 1968. Commander, Order of Icelandic Falcon, 1972. *Publications:* (jt ed. with R. Daley and R. E. Steiner) Clinical Disorders of the Pulmonary Circulation, 1960; (with W. Cleland, L. McDonald, D. Ross) Medical and Surgical Cardiology, 1969; (ed) Heart Muscle Disease, 1985; (ed with G. Baroldi and F. Camerini) Advances in Cardiomyopathies, 1990; (ed with E. Olsen) Cardiomyopathies—Realisation and Expectation, 1993; (ed with P. Yu) Progress in Cardiology, annually 1973–88; papers on diagnosis and treatment of congenital and acquired heart disease in British and foreign cardiac and other journals. *Recreations:* photography, history, travel. *Address:* 2 Pine Grove, Lake Road, Wimbledon, SW19 7HE. *T:* 0181–947 4851. *Clubs:* Athenæum, Royal Society of Medicine.

GOODWIN, Leonard George, CMG 1977; FRCP; FRS 1976; Director, Nuffield Laboratories of Comparative Medicine, Institute of Zoology, The Zoological Society of London, 1964–80; Director of Science, Zoological Society of London, 1966–80; Consultant, Wellcome Trust, since 1984; *b* 11 July 1915; *s* of Harry George and Lois Goodwin; *m* 1940, Marie Evelyn Coates; no *c. Educ:* William Ellis Sch., London; University Coll. London (Fellow, 1981); School of Pharmacy, London; University Coll. Hospital. BPharm 1935, BSc 1937, MB, BS 1950, (London). MRCP 1966, FRCP 1972. Demonstrator, Sch. of Pharmacy, London, 1935–39; Head of Wellcome Labs of Tropical Medicine, 1958–63 (Protozoologist, 1939–63). Jt Hon. Sec., Royal Soc. of Tropical Medicine and Hygiene, 1968–74, Pres., 1979–81. Chairman: Trypanosomiasis Panel, ODM, 1974–77; Filariasis Steering Cttee, WHO Special Programme, 1978–82. Hon. Dir, Wellcome Museum for Med. Sci., 1984–85. Hon. FPS, 1977; Hon. DSc Brunel, 1986. Soc. of Apothecaries Gold Medal, 1975; Harrison Meml Medal, 1978; Schofield Medal, Guelph Univ., 1979; Silver Medal, Zoological Soc., 1980; Manson Medal, RSTM&H, 1992. Chm. Editorial Bd, Parasitology, 1980–. *Publications:* (pt author) Biological Standardization, 1950; (contrib.) Biochemistry and Physiology of Protozoa, 1955; (jointly) A New Tropical Hygiene, 1960, 2nd edn 1972; (contrib.) Recent Advances in Pharmacology, 1962; many contribs to scientific jls, mainly on pharmacology and chemotherapy of tropical diseases, especially malaria, trypanosomiasis and helminth infections. *Recreations:* Dabbling in arts and crafts especially pottery (slipware), gardening and passive participation in music and opera. *Address:* Shepperlands Farm, Park Lane, Finchampstead, Berks RG11 4QF. *T:* Eversley (01734) 732153.

GOODWIN, Sir Matthew (Dean), Kt 1989; CBE 1981; CA; Chairman, Hewden Stuart PLC, 1979–95 (Executive Director, 1960–79); *b* 12 June 1929; *s* of Matthew Dean Goodwin and Mary Gertrude Barrie; *m* Margaret Eileen Colvil; two *d. Educ:* Hamilton Acad.; Glasgow Acad. FO, RAF, 1952–54. Raeburn & Verel, Shipowners, 1954–56; Partner, Davidson Downe McGowan, CA, 1956–68. Director: Irvine Develt Corp., 1980–90; F/S Assurance, 1980–89; Murray Ventures PLC, 1981–; Easpark Children's Home, 1989–; Chairman: Scotcare Ltd, 1988–; Murray Enterprise plc, 1988–; CrestaCare plc, 1995–. Mem., Scottish Econ. Council, 1991–. Jt Dep. Chm., Scottish Conservative Party, 1991– (Hon. Treas., 1982–90). *Recreations:* bridge, fishing, shooting, farming. *Address:* 87 Kelvin Court, Anniesland, Glasgow G12 0AH. *T:* 0141–221 7331. *Club:* Western (Glasgow).

GOODWIN, Neil, FHSM; Chief Executive, Manchester Health Commission, since 1994; *b* 1 March 1951; *s* of James and Dorothy Goodwin; *m* 1980, Sian Elizabeth Mary Holliday (marr. diss. 1992); two *s. Educ:* North Salford County Secondary Sch.; London Business Sch. (MBA); FHSM 1990. NHS mgt posts, London, Manchester, Liverpool, 1969–85; General Manager, Central Middlesex Hosp., 1985–88; Chief Exec., St Mary's Hosp., subseq. St Mary's Hosp. NHS Trust, 1988–94. Mem., Orgnl Audit Council, King's Fund Coll., 1993–. Hon. Fellow, Health Services Management Unit, Univ. of Manchester, 1994. Mem., Richard III Soc., 1978–. MIMgt (MBIM 1982); FRSA. *Publications:* articles on health service management, incl. customer care in hosps and management develt needs of chief execs. *Recreations:* horse riding, cycling, learning French. *Address:* Gateway House, Piccadilly South, Manchester M60 7LP. *T:* 0161–237 2011, *Fax:* 0161–237 2264. *Clubs:* Carlton, St James's.

GOODWIN, Noël; *see* Goodwin, T. N.

GOODWIN, Peter Austin, CBE 1986; Secretary, Public Works Loan Commission, 1979–87; Comptroller General, National Debt Office, 1980–87; Director, National Investment and Loans Office, 1980–87; *b* 12 Feb. 1929; *s* of late Stanley Goodwin and of Louise Goodwin; *m* 1950, Audrey Vera Webb; one *d. Educ:* Harrow County School. Served Royal Air Force, 1947–49. Executive Officer, Public Works Loan Commn, 1950; Principal, Civil Aviation Authority, 1973–76; Asst Secretary and Establishment Officer, Public Works Loan Commn, 1976–79. UK Mem., Gp of Experts advising on management of Pension Reserve Fund, Europ. Patent Office, 1986–87. *Recreations:* theatre, opera, ballet, country dancing, model railways. *Address:* 87 Woodmansterne Road, Carshalton Beeches, Surrey SM5 4JW. *T:* 0181–643 3530.

GOODWIN, Prof. Richard Murphey; Professor of Economic Science, Siena University, 1980–88, now Emeritus; *b* 24 Feb. 1913; *s* of William Murphey Goodwin and Mary Florea Goodwin; *m* 1937, Jacqueline Wynmalen; no *c. Educ:* Harvard Univ. (AB, PhD); Oxford Univ. (BA, BLitt). Harvard Univ.: Instructor in Econs, 1939–42; Instructor in Physics, 1942–45; Asst Prof. of Econs, 1945–51; Lectr in Econs, 1951–69, Reader in Economics, 1969–80, and Fellow of Peterhouse, 1956–80 (Emeritus Fellow, 1982), Univ. of Cambridge. *Publications:* Elementary Economics from the Higher Standpoint, 1970; Essays in Economic Dynamics, 1982; Essays in Linear Economic Structures, 1983; (with L. F. Punzo) The Dynamics of a Capitalist Economy, 1987; Essays in Nonlinear Economic Dynamics, 1988; Chaotic Economic Dynamics, 1990; contrib. Econ. Jl, Econometrica, Review of Econs and Statistics. *Recreations:* painting, walking. *Address:* Dorvis's, Ashdon, Saffron Walden, Essex CB10 2HP. *T:* Ashdon (01799) 584302.

GOODWIN, (Trevor) Noël; freelance critic, writer and broadcaster, specialising in music and dance; *b* 25 Dec. 1927; *s* of Arthur Daniel Goodwin and Blanche Goodwin (*née* Stephens); *m* 1st, 1954, Gladys Marshall Clapham (marr. diss. 1960); 2nd, Anne Myers (*née* Mason); one step *s. Educ:* mainly in France. BA (London). Assistant Music Critic: News Chronicle, 1952–54; Manchester Guardian, 1954–55; Music and Dance Critic, Daily Express, 1956–78; Exec. Editor, Music and Musicians, 1963–71; regular reviewer for: The Times, 1978–; Internat. Herald Tribune, 1978–84; Opera News, 1975–90; Ballet News, 1979–86; Dance and Dancers, 1957– (Associate Editor, 1972–); Opera, 1984– (Overseas News Editor, 1985–91; Mem. Editl Bd, 1991–). Member: Arts Council of GB, 1979–81 (Mem., 1973–81, Chm., 1979–81, Dance Adv. Panel; Mem., 1974–81, Dep. Chm., 1979–81, Music Adv. Panel; Council's rep. on Visiting Arts Unit of GB, 1979–81); Dance Adv. Panel, UK Branch, Calouste Gulbenkian Foundn, 1972–76; Nat. Enquiry into Dance Educn and Trng in Britain, 1975–80; Drama and Dance Adv. Cttee, British Council, 1973–88; HRH The Duke of Kent's UK Cttee for European Music Year 1985, 1982–84 (Chm., sub-cttee for Writers and Critics); Trustee-dir, Internat. Dance Course for Professional Choreographers and Composers, 1975–. Pres., The Critics' Circle, 1977 (Jt Trustee, 1984–). Planned and presented numerous radio programmes of music and records for BBC Home and World Services, and contributed frequently to music and arts programmes on Radios 3 and 4. *Publications:* London Symphony: portrait of an orchestra, 1954; A Ballet for Scotland, 1979; (with Sir Geraint Evans) A Knight at the Opera, 1984; editor, Royal Opera and Royal Ballet Yearbooks, 1978, 1979, 1980; area editor and writer, New Grove Dictionary of Music and Musicians, 1981; (ed) A Portrait of the Royal Ballet, 1988; contribs to: Encyclopaedia Britannica, 15th edn, 1974; Encyclopaedia of Opera, 1976; Britannica Books of the Year, annually 1980–93; Cambridge Encyclopaedia of Russia and the Soviet Union, 1982, 2nd edn 1994; New Oxford Companion to Music, 1983; Pipers Enzyklopädie des Musiktheaters, 1986; New Grove Dictionary of Opera, 1992; Viking Opera Guide, 1993; International Dictionary of Ballet, 1993; Metropolitan Opera Guide to Recorded Opera, 1993. *Recreation:* travel. *Address:* 76 Skeena Hill, SW18 5PN. *T:* 0181–788 8794.

GOODWIN, Prof. Trevor Walworth, CBE 1975; FRS 1968; Johnston Professor of Biochemistry, University of Liverpool, 1966–83; *b* 22 June 1916; British; *m* 1944, Kathleen Sarah Hill; three *d. Educ:* Birkenhead Inst.; Univ. of Liverpool. Lectr 1944, Sen. Lectr 1949, in Biochemistry, University of Liverpool; Prof. of Biochemistry and Agricultural Biochemistry, UCW, Aberystwyth, 1959. NSF Sen. Foreign Scientist, Univ. of Calif at Davis, 1964. Chairman: British Photobiol. Gp, 1964–66; Phytochemical Soc., 1968–70; MRC Biol Grants Cttee B, 1969–73; Cttee, Biochem. Soc., 1970–73; Brit. Nat. Cttee for Biochem., 1976–82; Royal Soc. Internat. Exchange Cttee (Panel A), 1986–89, 1994–; Member: Council, Royal Society, 1972, 1974, 1985; UGC, 1974–81; SRC Science Bd, 1975–78; ARC Grants Bd, 1975–82; Wirral Educn Cttee, 1974–84; Lawes Agricl Trust Cttee, 1977–91; Exec. Cttee, FEBS, 1975–83 (Chm., Publication Cttee, 1975–83); Vice-Pres., Comité Internat. de Photobiologie, 1967–69. Mem. Court, UCW, Aberystwyth, 1965–; Rep. of Lord Pres. of Council on Court, Univ. of N Wales, Bangor, 1983–; Royal Soc. Rep., Court, Univ. of Liverpool, 1985–92. Gov., Birkenhead Inst., 1976–79; Chm. of Govs, Wirral County Grammar Sch. for Girls, 1980–94. Morton Lectr, Biochem. Soc., 1983. Corresp. Mem., Amer. Soc. Plant Physiologists, 1982; Hon. Member: Phytochemical Soc. of Europe, 1983; Biochem Soc., 1985. Diplôme d'honneur, FEBS, 1984. Ciba Medallist, Biochemical Soc., 1970; Prix Roussel, Societé Roussel Uclaf, 1982. Editor, Protoplasma, 1968–80; Mem., Editl Bd, Phytochemistry, 1966–. *Publications:* Comparative Biochemistry of Carotenoids, 1952 (trans. Russian, 1956), 2nd edn, vol. 1 1980, vol. 2 1983; Recent Advances in Biochemistry, 1960; Biosynthesis of Vitamins, 1964 (trans. Japanese, 1966); (ed) Chemistry and Biochemistry of Plant Pigments, 1965, 3rd edn 1988; (with E. I. Mercer) Introduction to Plant Biochemistry, 1972, 2nd edn 1982 (trans. Russian, 1986); History of the Biochemical Society, 1987; numerous articles in Biochem. Jl, Phytochemistry, etc. *Recreation:* gardening. *Address:* Monzar, 9 Woodlands Close, Parkgate, S Wirral L64 6RU. *T:* 0151–336 4494.

GOODY, Prof. John Rankine, FBA 1976; William Wyse Professor of Social Anthropology, University of Cambridge, 1973–84; Fellow, St John's College, Cambridge, since 1960; *b* 27 July 1919; *m* 1956, Esther Robinson Newcomb; one *s* four *d. Educ:* St Albans Sch.; St John's Coll., Cambridge; Balliol Coll., Oxford. BA 1946, Dip. Anthrop. 1947, PhD 1954, ScD 1969, Cantab; BLitt Oxon 1952. HM Forces, 1939–46. Educnl admin, 1947–49; Cambridge Univ.: Asst Lectr, 1954–59; Lectr, 1959–71; Dir, African Studies Centre, 1966–73; Smuts Reader in Commonwealth Studies, 1972. Mem., Academia Europaea, 1991; Foreign Hon. Mem., Amer. Acad. of Arts and Scis, 1980. International Prize, Fondation Fyssen, 1991. Mem., Ordre des Palmes Académiques, 1993. *Publications:* The Social Organisation of the LoWiili, 1956; (ed) The Developmental Cycle in Domestic Groups, 1958; Death, Property and the Ancestors, 1962; (ed) Succession to High Office, 1966; (with J. A. Braimah) Salaga: the struggle for power, 1967; (ed) Literacy in Traditional Societies, 1968; Comparative Studies in Kinship, 1969; Technology, Tradition and the State in Africa, 1971; The Myth of the Bagre, 1972; (with S. J. Tambiah) Bridewealth and Dowry, 1973; (ed) The Character of Kinship, 1973; (ed) Changing Social Structure in Ghana, 1975; Production and Reproduction, 1977; The Domestication of the Savage Mind, 1977; (with S. W. D. K. Gandah) Une Recitation du Bagré, 1981; Cooking, Cuisine and Class, 1982; The Development of the Family and Marriage in Europe, 1983; The Logic of Writing and the Organization of Society, 1986; The Interface between the Oral and the Written, 1987; The Oriental, the Ancient and the Primitive, 1990; The Culture of Flowers, 1993; contrib. learned jls. *Address:* St John's College, Cambridge CB2 1TP. *T:* Cambridge (01223) 338638.

GOODYER, Prof. Ian Michael, MD; FRCPsych; Foundation Professor of Child and Adolescent Psychiatry, Cambridge University, since 1992; Fellow of Wolfson College, Cambridge, since 1993; *b* 2 Nov. 1949; *s* of Mark and Belle Goodyer; *m* 1979, Jane Elizabeth Akister; one *s* one *d. Educ:* University College London; St George's Hosp.; Oxford Univ.; Newcastle Univ.; Brown Univ. MB BS, MD London; MRCPsych 1976, FRCPsych 1990; DCH 1978. Sen. Lectr, Child/Adolescent Psych. and Consultant, Univ. of Manchester and Salford HA, 1983–87; Cambridge University: Foundn Lectr in Child Psych., 1987–92; Head, Developmental Psych. Section, 1992–. *Publications:* Life Experiences, Development and Child Psychopathology, 1991; The Depressed Child and Adolescent: developmental and clinical perspectives, 1995; contribs to learned jls. *Recreations:* keeping fit, guitar. *Address:* Developmental Psychiatry Section, Douglas House, 18 Trumpington Road, Cambridge CB2 2AH. *T:* Cambridge (01223) 336098.

GOOLD, family name of **Baron Goold**.

GOOLD, Baron *cr* 1987 (Life Peer), of Waterfoot in the District of Eastwood; **James Duncan Goold;** Kt 1983; CA; Lord-Lieutenant of Renfrewshire, since 1994; Chairman, Mactaggart & Mickel Ltd, since 1993 (Director, since 1965); *b* 28 May 1934; *s* of John Goold and Janet Agnes Kirkland; *m* 1959, Sheena Paton (*d* 1992); two *s* one *d. Educ:* Belmont House; Glasgow Acad. CA 1958. W. E. C. Reid & Co., Accts, NZ, 1958–60; Price Waterhouse & Co., Accts, Aust., 1960; Sec., Mactaggart & Mickel Ltd, 1961–65. Director: Gibson & Goold Ltd, 1978–; American Trust plc, 1984–; Edinburgh Oil & Gas PLC, 1986–. President: Scottish Bldg Contractors Assoc., 1971; Scottish Bldg Employers Fedn, 1977; Chm., CBI Scotland, 1981–83. Scottish Conservative Party: Hon. Treas., 1981–83; Chm., 1983–90; Hon. Pres., Eastwood Cons. Assoc., 1978–95. Chm., Royal Scottish Orch., 1991–93. Chm. Court, Univ. of Strathclyde, 1993–. Hon. Gov., Glasgow Acad., 1994 (Gov., 1982–89). DL Renfrewshire, 1985. FRSA 1987; Hon. FCIOB 1979; Hon. FFB 1983. DUniv, 1994. *Recreations:* gardening, the open air, golf. *Address:* Sandyknowe, Waterfoot, Clarkston, Glasgow G76 8RN. *T:* 0141–644 2764. *Clubs:* Carlton; Royal Scottish Automobile (Glasgow); Royal Troon Golf (Troon).

GOOLD, Sir George (Leonard), 7th Bt *cr* 1801; retired engineer; *b* 26 Aug. 1923; *s* of Sir George Ignatius Goold, 6th Bt, and Rhoda Goold; *S* father, 1967; *m* 1945, Joy Cecelia, *d* of William Cutler, Melbourne; one *s* four *d. Educ:* Port Pirie, S Australia. *Heir: s* George William Goold [*b* 25 March 1950; *m* 1973, Julie Ann, *d* of Leonard Crack; two *s*]. *Address:* 60 Canterbury Road, Victor Harbour, SA 5211, Australia. *T:* (85) 522872.

GOONERATNE, Tilak Eranga; Ambassador of Sri Lanka to the Commission of the European Communities, and concurrently to Belgium, 1975–78; *b* 27 March 1919; *m* 1948, Pamela J. Rodrigo (*d* 1978); two *d*; *m* 1986, Ina Heyn. *Educ:* BA (London Univ.); Ceylon Law Coll. Advocate, Supreme Ct of Ceylon. Joined Ceylon Civil Service, 1943; Asst Sec., Min. of External Affairs, 1947–51; Govt Agent: Trincomalee, 1951–54; Matara, 1954–56; Registrar Gen., Marriages, Births and Deaths, 1956–58; Dir-Gen. of Broadcasting and Dir of Information, Ceylon, 1958–60; Comr Co-operative Develt, 1960–63; Dir of Economic Affairs, 1963; Dep. Sec. to Treasury, 1963–65; Pres., Colombo Plan Council for Technical Co-operation in S and SE Asia, 1964–65; Ceylon deleg. to UN Gen. Assembly, 1964–65; Dep. Sec.-Gen., Commonwealth Secretariat, London, 1965–70; High Comr in UK, 1970–75. Commonwealth Fund for Technical Co-operation: Chm., Bd of Representatives, 1975–76; Chm., Review Gp of Experts. *Publications:* An Historical Outline of the Development of the Marriage and Divorce Laws of Ceylon; An Historical Outline of the Development of the Marriage and Divorce Laws Applicable to Muslims in Ceylon; Fifty Years of Co-operative Development in Ceylon. *Address:* 17B Warwick Avenue, W9 2PS. *T:* 0171–286 4675.

GOPAL, Dr Sarvepalli; Professor of Contemporary History, Jawaharlal Nehru University, New Delhi, 1972–83, now Emeritus; Fellow of St Antony's College, Oxford, since 1966; *b* 23 April 1923; *y c* and *o s* of Sir Sarvepalli Radhakrishnan, Hon. OM, Hon. FBA. *Educ:* Mill Hill School; Madras Univ.; Oxford Univ. MA (Madras and Oxon), BL (Madras), DPhil (Oxon), DLitt (Oxon). Lecturer and Reader in History, Andhra Univ., Waltair, 1948–52; Asst Dir, Nat. Archives of India, 1952–54; Dir, Historical Div., Min. of Extl Affairs, New Delhi, 1954–66; Commonwealth Fellow, Trin. Coll., Cambridge, 1963–64; Reader in S Asian History, Oxford Univ., 1966–71. Guest Scholar, Woodrow Wilson Center, Washington, 1992; Vis. Fellow, All Souls Coll., Oxford, 1992. Chairman: Nat. Book Trust, India, 1973–76; Indian Inst. of Advanced Study, 1992–; Madras Inst. of Develt Studies, 1995–; Member: Indian UGC, 1973–79; UNESCO Exec. Bd, 1976–80; Vis. Prof., Leeds, 1977. Pres., Indian History Congress, 1978. Corresp. FRHistS. Hon. Professor: Tirupati, 1971; Hyderabad, 1990. Hon. DLitt: Andhra, 1975; Tirupati, 1979; Banaras, 1984; Hyderabad, 1993. Sahitya Akademi award, 1976. *Publications:* The Permanent Settlement in Bengal, 1949; The Viceroyalty of Lord Ripon, 1953; The Viceroyalty of Lord Irwin, 1957; British Policy in India, 1965; Modern India, 1967; Jawaharlal Nehru, vol. 1, 1975, vol. 2, 1979, vol. 3, 1984; Radhakrishnan, 1989; general editor, Selected Works of Jawaharlal Nehru; contribs articles to historical jls. *Recreations:* good food and travel. *Address:* 97 Radhakrishna Salai, Mylapore, Madras 4, India. *Club:* United Oxford & Cambridge University.

GOPALAN, Coluthur, MD, DSc; FRCP, FRCPE; FRS 1987; President, Nutrition Foundation of India, New Delhi, since 1979; *b* 29 Nov. 1918; *s* of C. Doraiswami Iyengar and Mrs Pattammal; *m* 1940, Seetha Gopalan; one *s* one *d* (and one *s* decd). *Educ:* Univ. of Madras (MD); Univ. of London (PhD, DSc). Fellow, Acad. of Med. Scis, India, 1961; FIASc 1964; FNA 1966. Dir, Nat. Inst. of Nutrition, Hyderabad, 1960–74; Dir-Gen., Indian Council of Med. Res., New Delhi, 1975–79. Hon. DSc. Banares Hindu, 1982. *Publications:* Nutritive Value of Indian Foods, 1966; Nutrition and Health Care, 1984; Use of Growth Charts for Promoting Child Nutrition: a review of global experience, 1985; Combating Undernutrition: basic issues and practical approaches, 1987; Nutrition Problems and Programmes in South East Asia, 1987; Nutrition in Developmental Transition in South East Asia, 1992; Recent Trends in Nutrition, 1993; Towards Better Nutrition: problems and policies, 1993; Nutrition Research in South East Asia: the emerging agenda for the future, 1994; over 200 contribs to sci. jls; chapters on specific topics to several books on nutrition in internat. pubns on nutrition. *Recreation:* music. *Address:* Nutrition Foundation of India, B-37, Gulmohar Park, New Delhi 110049, India. *T:* (11) 669254. *Clubs:* India International Centre (New Delhi); Secunderabad.

GORAI, Rt. Rev. Dinesh Chandra; *see* Calcutta, Bishop of.

GORARD, Anthony John; *b* 15 July 1927; *s* of William James and Rose Mary Gorard; *m* 1954, Barbara Kathleen Hampton; one *s* three *d*. *Educ:* Ealing Grammar School. Chartered Accountant, 1951; Manufacturing Industry, 1952–58; Anglia Television Ltd, 1959–67, Executive Director and Member of Management Cttee; Managing Director, HTV Ltd, 1967–78; Chief Exec., HTV Gp Ltd, 1976–78; Director: Independent Television Publications Ltd, 1967–78; Independent Television News Ltd, 1973–78; Chief Exec., Cardiff Broadcasting Co. Ltd, 1979–81; Consultant, Mitchell Beazley Television, 1982–83; hotel proprietor, 1983–87; restaurant owner, 1987–94. Chm., British Regional Television Association, 1970–71. *Recreations:* tennis, rambling. *Address:* Threbs House, Bull Lane, Maiden Newton, Dorchester, Dorset DT2 0BQ. *T:* Maiden Newton (01300) 321141.

GORBACHEV, Mikhail Sergeyevich; President: International Foundation for Socio-Economic and Political Studies (Gorbachev Foundation), since 1991; Green Cross International, since 1993; Executive President of the Soviet Union, 1990–91; President, Presidium of the Supreme Soviet of USSR, 1989–90 (Member, 1985–90; Chairman, 1988–89); Deputy to Supreme Soviet, 1970–90; *b* 2 March 1931; *m* 1953, Raisa Gorbacheva; one *d*. *Educ:* Moscow State Univ. (law graduate); Stavropol Agric. Inst. Machine operator, 1946; joined CPSU 1952; First Sec., Stavropol Komsomol City Cttee, 1955–58, later Dep. Head of Propaganda; 2nd, later 1st Sec., Komsomol Territorial Cttee; Party Organizer, Stavropol Territorial Production Bd of Collective and State Farms, 1962–66; Head, Dept of party bodies, CPSU Territorial Cttee, 1962–66; 1st Sec., Stavropol City Party Cttee, 1966–68; 2nd Sec., 1968–70, 1st Sec., 1970–78, Stavropol Territorial CPSU Cttee; Central Committee, Communist Party of Soviet Union: Mem., 1971; Sec., with responsibility for agric., 1978–85; Alternate Mem., 1979–80, then Mem., Political Bureau; Gen. Sec., 1985–91. Deputy to Supreme Soviet, RSFSR, 1979; Chm., Foreign Affairs Commn of the Soviet of the Union, 1984–85. Nobel Peace Prize, 1990. Orders of Lenin, of Red Banner of Labour, Badge of Honour. *Publications:* A Time for Peace, 1985; The Coming Century of Peace, 1986; Speeches and Writings, 1986; Peace has no Alternative, 1986; Moratorium, 1986; Perestroika: new thinking for our country and the world, 1987; The August Coup, 1991; December, 1991; My Stand, 1992; The Years of Hard Decisions, 1993; Life and Reforms (memoirs), 1995. *Address:* (office) Leningradsky Prospekt 49, Moscow 125468, Russia. *T:* (095) 9439990, *Fax:* (095) 9439594.

GORDIMER, Nadine; author; *b* 20 Nov. 1923; *d* of Isidore Gordimer; *m* Reinhold Cassirer; one *s* one *d*. *Educ:* Convent Sch.; Witwatersrand Univ. Neil Gunn Fellowship, Scottish Arts Council, 1981. Hon. Member: Amer. Acad. of Art and Literature, 1979; Amer. Acad. of Arts and Sciences, 1980. DLitt *hc* Leuven, Belgium, 1980; DLitt *hc*: City Coll. of NY, 1985; Smith Coll., 1985; Harvard, 1986; Yale, 1986; Columbia, 1987; New Sch. for Social Res., 1987; York, 1987; Oxford, 1994. MLA Award, USA, 1981; Malaparte Prize, Italy, 1985; Nelly Sachs Prize, W Germany, 1985; Bennett Award, USA, 1986; Nobel Prize for Literature, 1991. *Publications: novels:* The Lying Days, 1953; A World of Strangers, 1958; Occasion for Loving, 1963; The Late Bourgeois World, 1966; A Guest of Honour, 1971 (James Tait Black Meml Prize, 1971); The Conservationist, 1974 (jtly, Booker Prize 1974; Grand Aigle d'Or, France, 1975); Burger's Daughter, 1979; July's People, 1981; A Sport of Nature, 1987; My Son's Story, 1990; None to Accompany Me, 1994; *stories:* The Soft Voice of the Serpent, 1953; Six Feet of the Country, 1956; Friday's Footprint, 1960 (W. H. Smith Lit. Award, 1961); Not for Publication, 1965; Livingstone's Companions, 1972; Selected Stories, 1975; Some Monday for Sure, 1976; A Soldier's Embrace, 1980; Something Out There, 1984; Jump, 1991; *non-fiction:* South African Writing Today (jt editor), 1967; The Essential Gesture: writing, politics and places, 1988; Writing and Being (Charles Eliot Norton Lectures), 1995. *Address:* c/o A. P. Watt, 20 John Street, WC1N 2DR.

GORDON, family name of **Marquess of Aberdeen and Temair** and **Marquess of Huntly.**

GORDON, Sir Alexander John, (Sir Alex Gordon), Kt 1988; CBE 1974 (OBE 1967); RIBA; architect; Consultant, Alex Gordon Partnership, since 1983; *b* 25 Feb. 1917; *s* of John Tullis Gordon and Euphemia Baxter Simpson Gordon. *Educ:* Swansea Grammar Sch.; Welsh Sch. of Architecture (Diploma with Special Distinction). ARIBA 1949; FRIBA 1962; FSIAD 1975. Served RE, 1940–46. Partnership with T. Alwyn Lloyd, 1948–60; Sen. Partner, Alex Gordon and Partners, 1960–82. Member: Welsh Arts Council, 1959–73 (Vice-Chm. 1969–73); Central Housing Adv. Cttee, 1959–71; Exec. Bd, BSI, 1971–74 (Chm., Codes of Practice Cttee for Building, 1965–77); UGC Planning, Architecture and Building Studies Sub-Cttee, 1971–74; UGC Technology Sub-Cttee, 1974–79; NAB UGC Review Gp in Architecture, 1983–84; Construction and Housing Res. Adv. Council, 1971–79; ARCUK, 1968–71; Design Council, 1973–77; Council, Architectural Heritage Year (and Welsh Cttee), 1973–76; Royal Fine Art Commn, 1973–91; RCA Visiting Cttee, 1973–82; Council for Sci. and Soc., 1973– (Vice-Chm., 1982–); Bldg Res. Estab. Adv. Council (Chm., 1975–83); Adv. Cttee, York Centre for Continuing Educn, 1975–80; Construction Industry Continuing Professional Develt Gp (Chm. 1981–86); Standing Cttee on Structural Safety, 1976–87; British Council Wales Cttee, 1976–87 (Chm., 1980–87, and Mem. Bd British Council); Pres., Comité de Liaison des Architectes du Marché Commun, 1974–75. Trustee, Civic Trust Board for Wales, 1965–. Pres., Building Centre Trust, 1976–87. Life Mem., Court, UWIST (Mem. Council, 1980–85, Vice-Pres., 1982–85); Vis. Prof., Sch. of Environmental Studies, UCL, 1969, Mem. Bd of Studies, 1970–83, Governor, Centre for Environmental Studies, 1974–77. Vis. Fellow, Clare Hall, Cambridge Univ., 1983. Associate, RICS, 1986. RIBA: Chm., Bd of Educn, 1968–70; Pres., 1971–73; Chm., European Affairs Cttee, 1973–80; Chm., Co-ordinating Cttee for Project Inf., 1979–87. Reg. Dir, Nationwide Bldg Soc., 1972– (Chm., Welsh Bd, 1986–89); Mem., Cardiff Bay Develt Corp., 1987–90. Extraord. Hon. Mem., Bund Deutscher Architekten, 1980; Hon. Mem., Soc. Mexican Architects, 1972; Hon. Corresp. Mem., Fedn of Danish Architects, 1976; Hon. FRAIC; Hon. FAIA, 1974; Hon. FCIBSE 1975; Hon. FISE 1980. Hon. LLD Univ. of Wales, 1972. *Publications:* periodic contribs to professional jls. *Recreations:* skiing, the visual arts. *Address:* River Cottage, Llanblethian, near Cowbridge, S Glam CF7 7JL. *T:* Cowbridge (014463) 3672; 32 Grosvenor Street, W1X 9FF. *T:* 0171–629 7910. *Club:* Cardiff and County.

GORDON, Sir Andrew C. L. D.; *see* Duff Gordon.

GORDON, Rt. Rev. (Archibald) Ronald (McDonald); Canon and Sub-Dean of Christ Church, Oxford, since 1991; Assistant Bishop, diocese of Oxford, since 1991; *b* 19 March 1927; *s* of late Sir Archibald Gordon, CMG, and late Dorothy Katharine Gordon, Bridge House, Gerrards Cross, Bucks. *Educ:* Rugby Sch.; Balliol Coll., Oxford (Organ Schol., MA 1950); Cuddesdon Theol. Coll. Deacon 1952; Priest 1953; Curate of Stepney, 1952–55; Chaplain, Cuddesdon Coll., 1955–59; Vicar of St Peter, Birmingham, 1959–67; Res. Canon, Birmingham Cathedral, 1967–71; Vicar of University Church of St Mary the Virgin with St Cross and St Peter in the East, Oxford, 1971–75; Bishop of Portsmouth, 1975–84; Bishop to the Forces, 1985–90; Bishop at Lambeth (Hd of Archbp's Staff), 1984–91; an Asst Bishop, Dio. of Southwark, 1985–91. Mem., H of L, 1981–84. Fellow of St Cross Coll., Oxford, 1975; Select Preacher, Univ. of Oxford, 1985, 1993. Mem., Church Assembly and General Synod and Proctor in Convocation, 1965–71; Chm., ACCM, 1976–83. Member: Court of Ecclesiastical Causes Reserved, 1991–; Archbishops' Commn on Cathedrals, 1992–94; Adv. Bd for Redundant Churches, 1992–. Chm., Malawi Church Trust, 1993–; Pres., Oxford Mission, 1992–. *Address:* Christ Church, Oxford OX1 1DP. *T:* Oxford (01865) 276278.

GORDON, Aubrey Abraham; a Recorder of the Crown Court, since 1978; *b* 26 July 1925; *s* of Isaac and Fanny Gordon; *m* 1949, Reeva R. Cohen; one *s* one *d*. *Educ:* Bede Collegiate Boys' Sch., Sunderland; King's Coll., Durham Univ., Newcastle upon Tyne (LLB 1945). Admitted solicitor, 1947. President: Houghton le Spring Chamber of Trade, 1955; Hetton le Hole Rotary Club, 1967; Sunderland Law Soc., 1976; NE Joel Intract Meml Home, 1990–93; Chairman: Houghton Round Table, 1959; Sunderland Victims Support Scheme, 1978–80; Sunderland Guild of Help, 1984–92. *Recreations:* local communal and religious interests, photography. *Address:* 1 Acer Court, Sunderland SR2 7EJ. *T:* 0191–565 8993.

GORDON, Boyd; fisheries consultant; Fisheries Secretary, Department of Agriculture and Fisheries for Scotland, 1982–86; *b* 18 Sept. 1926; *er s* of David Gordon and Isabella (*née* Leishman); *m* 1951, Elizabeth Mabel (*née* Smith); two *d*. *Educ:* Musselburgh Grammar School. Following military service with the Royal Scots, joined the Civil Service, initially with Min. of Labour, then Inland Revenue; Department of Agriculture and Fisheries for Scotland: joined, 1953; Principal, Salmon and Freshwater Fisheries Administration and Fisheries R&D, 1962–73; Asst Secretary, Agriculture Economic Policy, EEC Co-ordination and Agriculture Marketing, 1973–82. *Recreations:* family and church affairs, gardening, sport of all kinds, though only golf as participant now, reading, playing and writing Scottish fiddle music. *Address:* 87 Duddingston Road, Edinburgh EH15 1SP. *Club:* Civil Service.

GORDON, Brian William, OBE 1974; HM Diplomatic Service, 1949–81, retired; Commercial Counsellor, Caracas, 1980–81; *b* 24 Oct. 1926; *s* of William and Doris Margaret Gordon; *m* 1951, Sheila Graham Young; two *s* one *d*. *Educ:* Tynemouth Grammar School. HM Forces (Lieut in IA), 1944–47; joined HM Foreign Service (now Diplomatic Service), 1949; served in: Saigon; Libya; Second Sec. in Ethiopia, 1954–58 and in Peru, 1959–61; HM Consul: Leopoldville, Congo, 1962–64; New York, 1965–67; Puerto Rico, 1967–69; Consul-General, Bilbao, 1969–73; Asst Head, Trade Relations and Export Dept, FCO, 1974–77; Dep. Consul-Gen., Los Angeles, 1977–80. *Recreations:* golf, walking. *Address:* Woodlands, Fourstones, Northumberland NE47 5DL.

GORDON, Sir Charles (Addison Somerville Snowden), KCB 1981 (CB 1970); Clerk of the House of Commons, 1979–83; *b* 25 July 1918; *s* of late C. G. S. Gordon, TD, Liverpool, and Mrs E. A. Gordon, Emberton and Wimbledon; *m* 1943, Janet Margaret, (Jane), Beattie (*d* 1995); one *s* one *d*. *Educ:* Winchester; Balliol Coll., Oxford. Served in Fleet Air Arm throughout War of 1939–45. Apptd Asst Clerk in House of Commons, 1946; Senior Clerk, 1947; Fourth Clerk at the Table, 1962; Principal Clerk of the Table Office, 1967; Second Clerk Assistant, 1974; Clerk Asst, 1976. Sec., Soc. of Clerks-at-the-Table in Commonwealth Parliaments, and co-Editor of its journal, The Table, 1952–62. *Publications:* Parliament as an Export (jointly), 1966; Editor, Erskine May's Parliamentary Practice, 20th edn, 1983 (Asst Editor, 19th edn); contribs to: The Table; The

Parliamentarian. *Recreation:* dolce far niente. *Address:* 279 Lonsdale Road, Barnes, SW13 9QB. *T:* 0181–748 6735.

GORDON, (Cosmo) Gerald (Maitland); His Honour Judge Gordon; a Circuit Judge, since 1990; *b* 26 March 1945; *s* of John Kenneth Maitland Gordon and Erica Martia Clayton-East; *m* 1973, Vanessa Maria Juliet Maxine Reilly-Morrison; two *s*. *Educ:* Eton. Called to the Bar, Middle Temple, 1966. Asst Recorder, 1982–86; Recorder, 1986–90. Royal Borough of Kensington and Chelsea: Mem. Council, 1971–90; Chm., Works Cttee, 1978–80; Chm., Town Planning Cttee, 1988; Dep. Leader, 1982–88; Mayor, 1989–90. *Recreations:* planning conservation, cooking, food and wine. *Address:* c/o 36 Essex Street, WC2 3AS. *T:* 0171–413 0353.

GORDON, Prof. Cyrus H.; Director, Center for Ebla Research, New York University, since 1982 (Gottesman Professor of Hebrew, 1973–89, now Emeritus Professor of Hebrew and other Near East Languages and Literatures); *b* 29 June 1908; *s* of Dr Benj. L. and Dorothy Cohen Gordon; *m* 1st, 1946, Joan Elizabeth Kendall (*d* 1985); two *s* three *d*; 2nd, 1986, Constance Victoria Wallace. *Educ:* Univ. of Pennsylvania (AB, MA, PhD). Harrison Schol., Univ. of Pennsylvania 1928–29, and Harrison Fellow, 1929–30; US Army Officer on active duty, 1942–46 (Col, US Air Force Reserve, retired). Instructor of Hebrew and Assyrian, University of Penn., 1930–31; Fellow and Epigrapher, American Schs of Oriental Research in Jerusalem and Baghdad, 1931–35; Fellow, Amer. Coun. of Learned Socs, 1932–33; Teaching Fellow, Oriental Seminary, Johns Hopkins Univ., 1935–38; Lecturer in Hebrew and Ancient History, Smith Coll., 1938–39 and 1940–41; Fellow, Amer.-Scandinavian Foundn, 1939; Mem., Institute for Advanced Study, Princeton, NJ, 1939–40 and 1941–42; Professor of Assyriology and Egyptology, Dropsie Coll., 1946–56; Joseph Foster Prof. of Near Eastern Studies, and Chm., Dept of Mediterranean Studies, Brandeis Univ., 1956–73 (Dean of Graduate Sch. and Associate Dean of Faculty, 1957–58). Mem. Managing Cttee, Amer. Sch. of Classical Studies, Athens, 1958–73; Vis. Fellow in Humanities, Univ. of Colorado, March 1967; Visiting Professor: New York Univ., 1970–73; in History and Archaeology, Univ. of New Mexico at Las Cruces, 1976; in Asian Studies, Dartmouth Coll., 1990; Distinguished Vis. Professor: in Humanities, SW Missouri State Univ., 1977–79; in Archaeology, New Mexico State Univ., 1979; in Maritime Civilizations, Haifa Univ., 1993; Lectures: Gay, Simmons Coll., 1970; Dal Grauer Meml, Univ. of British Columbia, 1988; University, Cornell Univ., 1992; Visitor's Fellowship, Japan Foundn, 1974. Fellow: Amer. Acad. of Arts and Sciences, 1968–; Explorers Club, 1968–; Amer. Acad. of Jewish Res., 1981–; Japan Soc. for Promotion of Science, 1989; Hon. Fellow, Royal Asiatic Soc., 1975–. Member: Amer. Oriental Soc.; Soc. of Biblical Literature; Archæological Inst. of America; Amer. Historical Assoc.; Amer. Philological Assoc.; Amer. Assoc. of Univ. Professors. Corresp. Mem., Inst. for Antiquity and Christianity, Claremont Graduate Sch. and University Center, 1967–. Trustee: Boston Hebrew Coll., 1965–; Internat. Council for Etruscan Studies, Jerusalem, 1970–; Fenster Gallery of Jewish Art, Tulsa, Oklahoma, 1977–. Hon. Dr of Hebrew Letters, Baltimore Hebrew Coll., 1981; Hon. DHL Hebrew Union Coll., 1985; Hon. DLitt Boston Hebrew Coll., 1995. Alumni Award, Gratz Coll., 1961; Directory of Educational Specialists Award, 1970; elected to Soc. of Scholars, Johns Hopkins Univ., 1990. *Publications:* Nouns in the Nuzi Tablets, 1936; Lands of the Cross and Crescent, 1948; Ugaritic Literature, 1949; Smith College Tablets, 1952; Ugaritic Manual, 1955; Adventures in the Nearest East, 1957; Hammurapi's Code, 1957; World of the Old Testament, 1958 (rev. edn: The Ancient Near East, 1965); Before the Bible, 1962 (rev. edn: The Common Background of Greek and Hebrew Civilizations, 1965); Ugaritic Textbook, 1965, rev. edn 1967; Ugarit and Minoan Crete, 1966; Evidence for the Minoan Language, 1966; Forgotten Scripts: How they were deciphered and their Impact on Contemporary Culture, 1968, rev. edn, Forgotten Scripts: their ongoing discovery and decipherment, 1982; Poetic Legends and Myths from Ugarit, 1977; The Pennsylvania Tradition of Semitics, 1986; (ed and contrib.) Publications of the Center for Ebla Research, vol. I, Eblaitica: essays on the Ebla archives and Eblaite Language, 1987, vol. II, 1990, vol. III, 1992; The Background to Jewish Studies in the Bible and in the Ancient East, 1994; some works translated other languages; numerous articles in learned jls dealing with Near East, Mediterranean, OT and Egypto-Semitic philology; *relevant publications:* Orient and Occident: essays presented to Cyrus H. Gordon on the occasion of his Sixty-Fifth Birthday, 1973; The Bible World: essays in honor of Cyrus H. Gordon, 1980. *Address:* (office) Department of Classical Studies, Brandeis University, Rabb 141, Waltham, MA 02254–9110, USA. *T:* (617) 7362180; (home) 130 Dean Road, Brookline, MA 02146. *T:* (617) 7343046.

GORDON, David Sorrell; business adviser; Chief Executive, Independent Television News, 1993–95; *b* 11 Sept. 1941; *s* of late Sholom and Tania Gordon; *m* 1st, 1963, Enid Albagli (marr. diss. 1969); 2nd, 1974, Maggi McCormick; two *s*. *Educ:* Clifton College; Balliol College, Oxford (PPE, BA 1963); LSE; Advanced Management Program, Harvard Business Sch. FCA. Articles with Thomson McLintock, 1965–68; The Economist: editorial staff, 1968–78; Production and Devellt Dir, 1978–81; Gp Man. Dir, then Gp Chief Exec., 1981–93. Dir, Financial Times, 1983–93. Dir, South Bank Bd, 1986–; a Governor, BFI, 1983–91; Dir, Target Gp plc, 1988–91. Chm., Contemporary Art Soc., 1991–; Trustee: Tate Gall., 1993–; Architecture Foundn, 1993–. *Publication:* (with Fred Hirsch) Newspaper Money, 1975. *Recreations:* movies, magic lanterns. *Address:* Greenwood, 56 Duke's Avenue, Chiswick, W4 2AF. *T:* 0181–994 3126. *Clubs:* Garrick; Harvard (New York).

GORDON, Maj.-Gen. Desmond Spencer, CB 1961; CBE 1952; DSO 1943; JP; DL; Commissioner-in-Chief, St John Ambulance Brigade, 1973–78; *b* 25 Dec. 1911; *s* of late Harold Easty Gordon and Gwendoline (*née* Blackett); *m* 1940, Sybil Mary Thompson; one *s* one *d*. *Educ:* Haileybury Coll.; RMC Sandhurst. Commissioned into Green Howards, 1932; India, 1933–38: Adjutant, Regimental Depot, 1938–40; War of 1939–45 (despatches 1944): Norway with Green Howards, 1940; Bde Major, 69 Inf. Bde, 1941–42; Student Staff Coll., Quetta, 1942; Comd 1/7 Queens, 1943; Comd 151 (Durham) Inf. Bde, 146 Inf. Bde, 131 Lorried Inf Bde, 1944–46; Col. GSHQ BAOR, 1946–49; Student Joint Service Staff Coll., 1949; GSO1 Inf. Directorate, War Office, 1950; Dep. Dir Inf., War Office, 1951–52; Comd 16 Indep. Para. Bde Gp, 1952–55; Asst Comd RMA Sandhurst, 1956–57; Student, Imperial Defence Coll., 1958; DA & QMG HQ I (BR) Corps, 1959; GOC 4th Division, 1959–61; Chief Army Instructor, Imperial Defence Coll., 1962–64; Asst Chief of Defence Staff (G), 1964–66: Col The Green Howards, 1965–74. JP Hants, 1966; DL Hants, 1980. KStJ 1973 (CStJ 1972). Knight Commander, Order of Orange Nassau with swords (Holland), 1947. *Recreations:* fishing, gardening. *Address:* Southfields, Greywell, Basingstoke, Hants RG25 1BZ. *T:* Basingstoke (01256) 702088. *Club:* Army and Navy.

GORDON, Douglas; *see* Gordon, R. D.

GORDON, Gerald; *see* Gordon, C. G. M.

GORDON, Gerald Henry, CBE 1995; QC (Scot.) 1972; LLD; Sheriff of Glasgow and Strathkelvin, since 1978; Temporary Judge in Court of Session and High Court of Justiciary, since 1992; *b* 17 June 1929; *er s* of Simon Gordon and Rebecca Gordon (*née* Bulbin), Glasgow; *m* 1957, Marjorie Joseph, *yr d* of Isaac and Aimée Joseph (*née* Strump), Glasgow; one *s* two *d*. *Educ:* Queen's Park Senior Secondary Sch., Glasgow; Univ. of Glasgow (MA (1st cl. Hons Philosophy with English Literature) 1950; LLB (Distinction) 1953; PhD 1960); LLD Edinburgh 1968. National Service, RASC, 1953–55 (Staff-Sgt, Army Legal Aid, BAOR, 1955). Admitted Scottish Bar 1953; practice at Scottish Bar, 1953, 1956–59; Faulds Fellow, Univ. of Glasgow, 1956–59. Procurator Fiscal Depute, Edinburgh, 1960–65. University of Edinburgh: Sen. Lectr, 1965; Personal Prof. of Criminal Law, 1969–72; Head of Dept of Criminal Law and Criminology, 1965–72; Prof. of Scots Law, 1972–76; Dean of Faculty of Law, 1970–73; Sheriff of S Strathclyde, Dumfries and Galloway at Hamilton, 1976–77. Commonwealth Vis. Fellow and Vis. Res. Fellow, Centre of Criminology, Univ. of Toronto, 1974–75. Temporary Sheriff, 1973–76. Member: Interdepartmental Cttee on Scottish Criminal Procedure, 1970–77; Cttee on Appeals Criteria and Alleged Miscarriages of Justice Procedures, 1995–. Hon. LLD Glasgow, 1993. *Publications:* The Criminal Law of Scotland, 1967, 2nd edn 1978; (ed) Renton and Brown's Criminal Procedure, 4th edn 1972, 5th edn 1983; (ed) Scottish Criminal Case Reports, 1981–; various articles. *Recreations:* Jewish studies, coffee conversation, swimming. *Address:* Sheriff Court, PO Box 23, Carlton Place, Glasgow G5 9DA.

GORDON, Giles Alexander Esmé; Literary Agent, Giles Gordon Agency, since 1995; *b* 23 May 1940; *s* of late Alexander Esmé Gordon, RSA, FRIBA, FRIAS and Betsy Gordon (*née* McCurry); *m* 1st, 1964, Margaret Anna Eastoe (*d* 1989); one *s* one *d* (and one *s* decd); 2nd, 1990, Margaret Anne McKernan; two *d*. *Educ:* Edinburgh Academy; (briefly) Edinburgh College of Art. FRSL 1990. Trainee publisher, Oliver & Boyd, Edinburgh, 1959–63; advertising manager, Secker & Warburg, 1963–64; editor, Hutchinson, 1964–66; plays editor, Penguin Books, 1966–67; editl dir, Victor Gollancz, 1967–73; Literary Agent, Anthony Sheil Associates, later Sheil Land Associates, 1973–95. C. Day Lewis Fellow in Writing, KCL, 1974–75. Sec. and Chm., Soc. of Young Publishers; Member: Literature Panel, Arts Council, 1968–72; Cttee of Management, Soc. of Authors; Cttee, Assoc. of Authors' Agents; Council, RSL, 1992–94; Cttee, Authors' Club, 1992–. Lectr, Tufts Univ. in London, 1970–74; Lectr, Hollins Coll. in London, 1983–86. Theatre critic: Spectator; London Daily News; Drama; books columnist, The Times, 1993–95; Editor, Drama. *Publications:* Pictures from an Exhibition, 1970; The Umbrella Man, 1971; About a Marriage, 1972; Girl with Red Hair, 1974; (ed with A. Hamilton) Factions, 1974; (with Margaret Gordon) Walter and the Balloon (for children), 1974; (ed) Beyond the Words, 1975; Farewell, Fond Dreams, 1975; (ed) Prevailing Spirits, 1976; 100 Scenes from Married Life, 1976; (ed with Dulan Barber) Members of the Jury, 1976; (ed jtly) You Always Remember the First Time, 1976; (ed) A Book of Contemporary Nightmares, 1977; Enemies, 1977; The Illusionist, 1978; (ed with Fred Urquhart) Modern Scottish Short Stories, 1978; Ambrose's Vision, 1980; (ed) Shakespeare Stories, 1982; (ed) English Short Stories 1940–1980, 1982; (ed with David Hughes) Best Short Stories (annually), 1986–; (ed) English Short Stories: 1900 to the present, 1988; (ed) The Twentieth Century Short Story in English: a bibliography, 1989; Aren't We Due a Royalty Statement?, 1993; (ed with David Hughes) The Best of Best Short Stories, 1986–1995, 1995. *Recreations:* theatre, opera, walking, travelling, eating, drinking, book collecting. *Address:* 6 Ann Street, Edinburgh EH4 1PJ. *Clubs:* Garrick, PEN.

GORDON, Hannah Cambell Grant; actress; *b* 9 April 1941; *d* of William Munro Gordon and Hannah Grant Gordon; *m* 1970, Norman Warwick; one *s*. *Educ:* St Denis School for Girls, Edinburgh; Glasgow Univ. (Cert. Dramatic Studies); College of Dramatic Art, Glasgow (Dip. in speech and drama). FRSAMD 1980. Hon. DLitt Glasgow, 1993. Winner, James Bridie Gold Medal, Royal Coll. of Music and Dramatic Art, Glasgow, 1962. *Stage:* Dundee Rep., Glasgow Citizens Theatre, Belgrade Theatre, Coventry, Ipswich, Windsor; Can You Hear me at the Back, Piccadilly, 1979; The Killing Game, Apollo, 1980; The Jeweller's Shop, Westminster, 1982; The Country Girl, Apollo, 1983; Light Up the Sky, Old Vic, 1985; Mary Stuart, Edinburgh Fest., 1987; Shirley Valentine, Duke of York's, 1989; Hidden Laughter, Vaudeville, 1991; An Ideal Husband, Globe, 1992; *television:* 1st TV appearance, Johnson Over Jordan, 1965; series: Great Expectations, 1969; Middlemarch, 1969; My Wife Next Door, 1972; Upstairs, Downstairs, 1976; Telford's Change, 1979; Goodbye Mr Kent, 1983; Gardener's Calendar, 1986; My Family and Other Animals, 1987; Joint Account, 1989; *films:* Spring and Port Wine, 1970; The Elephant Man, 1979; numerous radio plays. *Recreations:* tennis, gardening, cooking. *Address:* c/o Hutton Management, 200 Fulham Road, SW10. *Club:* St James's.

GORDON, Prof. Ian Alistair, CBE 1971; MA, PhD; Professor of English Language and Literature, University of Wellington, NZ, 1936–74, now Emeritus; *b* Edinburgh, 1908; *e s* of Alexander and Ann Gordon; *m* 1936, Mary Ann McLean Fullarton, Ayr; one *s* three *d*. *Educ:* Royal High Sch., Edinburgh; University of Edinburgh. Bruce of Grangehill Bursar, Sloan Prizeman, Gray Prizeman, Scott Travelling Scholar (Italy), Dickson Travelling Scholar (Germany), Elliot Prizeman in English Literature, Pitt Scholar in Classical and English Literature; MA (Hons Classics) 1930, (Hons English) 1932; PhD 1936. Asst Lecturer in English language and lit., University of Edinburgh, 1932; Sub-Ed., Scot. Nat. Dictionary, 1930–36; Dean: Faculty of Arts, Victoria Univ. Coll., Wellington, 1944–47, 1952, 1957–61; Faculty of Languages, 1965–68; Vice-Chancellor Univ. of New Zealand, 1947–52; Chm., Academic Bd, 1954–61. Visiting Professor: KCL 1954; Univ. of Edinburgh, 1962; Univ. of South Pacific, Fiji, 1972; France and Belgium, 1976; Univ. of Waikato, 1980; Research Associate, UCL, 1969; Res. Fellow, Auckland Univ., 1993; Vis. Fellow, Edinburgh Univ., 1974–75; Vis. Fellow in Commonwealth Literature, Univ. of Leeds, 1975. Columnist, NZ Listener, 1977–88. Member: Copyright Cttee and Tribunal, 1958; UGC, 1960–70; Chairman: English Language Institute,, 1961–72; NZ Literary Fund, 1951–73; Exec. Council, Assoc. of Univs of Br. Commonwealth, 1949–50. NZ representative at internat. confs: Utrecht, 1948; Bangkok, 1960; Kampala, 1961; Karachi, 1961. Army Educ. Service, 2 NZEF, Hon. Major. Hon. LLD Bristol, 1948; Hon. DLitt NZ, 1961; DUniv Stirling, 1975. *Publications:* John Skelton, Poet Laureate, 1943; New Zealand New Writing, 1943–45; The Teaching of English, a study in secondary education, 1947; English Prose Technique, 1948; Shenstone's Miscellany, 1759–1763, 1952; Katherine Mansfield, 1954; The Movement of English Prose, 1966; John Galt (biog.), 1972; Word (festschrift), 1974; Undiscovered Country, 1974; Katherine Mansfield's Urewera Notebook, 1979; Word Finder, 1979; A Word in Your Ear, 1980; (ed) Collins Concise English Dictionary, NZ edn, 1982; (ed) Collins Compact New Zealand Dictionary, 1985; edited the following works of John Galt: The Entail, 1970; The Provost, 1973; The Member, 1975; The Last of the Lairds, 1976; Short Stories, 1978; part-author: Edinburgh Essays in Scottish Literature, 1933; Essays in Literature, 1934; The University and the Community, 1946; John Galt (bicent. vol.), 1980; Lexicographical and Linguistic Studies, 1988; The Fine Instrument, 1989; articles in research journals and other periodicals. *Address:* 10 Hukanui Crescent, Herne Bay, Auckland, New Zealand. *Club:* Aorangi Ski, New Zealand (former Pres.).

GORDON, Maj.-Gen. James Charles Mellish, CBE 1992; Director General, Association of Train Operating Companies, since 1995; *b* 3 Aug. 1941; *s* of Brig. Leonard Henry Gordon and Joyce Evelyn Mary Gordon (*née* Gurdon); *m* 1964, Rosemary Stella Kincaid; two *s* one *d*. *Educ:* Tonbridge; RMA Sandhurst. Commissioned RA 1961; served in UK, Germany, Singapore; RMCS, Shrivenham, 1972; Staff Coll., Camberley, 1973; MoD,

1974–75; Comdr, D Batt., RHA, UK and BAOR, 1976–78; MA to MGO, MoD, 1978–80; CO 45 Field Regt RA, BAOR, 1980–83; Col, ASD1, MoD, 1983–86; CRA 4th Armoured Div., BAOR, 1986–89; Dir, Mil. Ops, MoD, 1989–91; COS, HQ UKLF, 1991–94. Mem., RYA. FIMgt. *Recreations:* sailing, tennis, music, theatre, travel. *Club:* Royal Artillery Yacht.

GORDON, James Stuart, CBE 1984; Chief Executive, Scottish Radio Holdings (formerly Radio Clyde Holdings), 1991–May 1996; Managing Director, Radio Clyde, since 1973; Vice-Chairman, Melody Radio, since 1991 (Director, since 1990); *b* 17 May 1936; *s* of James Gordon and Elsie (*née* Riach); *m* 1971, Margaret Anne Stevenson; two *s* one *d*. *Educ:* St Aloysius' Coll., Glasgow; Glasgow Univ. (MA Hons). Political Editor, STV, 1965–73. Chm., Scottish Exhibn Centre, 1983–89; Member: Scottish Devlt Agency, 1981–90; Scottish Adv. Bd, BP, 1990–; Dir, Clydeport Hldgs, 1992–. Mem., Cttee of Inquiry into Teachers' Pay and Conditions, 1986. Mem. Court, Univ. of Glasgow, 1984–. DLitt Glasgow Caledonian, 1994. *Recreations:* ski-ing, walking, genealogy, golf. *Address:* Deil's Craig, Strathblane, Glasgow G63 9ET. *T:* Blanefield (01360) 770604. *Clubs:* Caledonian; New (Edinburgh); Glasgow Art (Glasgow); Buchanan Castle Golf, Prestwick Golf.

GORDON, John Keith; international environmentalist; *b* 6 July 1940; *s* of James Gordon and Theodora (*née* Sinker); *m* 1965, Elizabeth Shanks; two *s*. *Educ:* Marlborough Coll.; Cambridge Univ. (1st Cl. Hons History). Henry Fellow, Yale Univ., 1962–63; research in Russian history, LSE, 1963–66; entered FCO, 1966; Budapest, 1968–70; seconded to Civil Service Coll., 1970–72; FCO, 1972–73; UK Mission, Geneva, 1973–74; Head of Chancery and Consul, Yaoundé, 1975–77 (concurrently Chargé d'Affaires, Gabon and Central African Republic); FCO, 1977–80; Cultural Attaché, Moscow, 1980–81; Office of UK Rep. to European Community, Brussels, 1982–83; UK Perm. Deleg. to UNESCO, Paris, 1983–85; Head of Nuclear Energy Dept, FCO, 1986–88; Imperial College, London: Academic Visitor, Centre for Envmtl Technol., 1988–90; Dep. and Policy Dir, Global Envmt Res. Centre, 1990–94. Mem., UK-UNEP Nat. Cttee, 1993–. *Publications:* (with Caroline Fraser) Institutions and Sustainable Development, 1991; (with Tom Bigg) 2020 Vision, 1994; Canadian Round Tables, 1994; reports and articles on internat. envmtl issues. *Recreations:* jogging, sailing, reading. *Address:* 68 Hornsey Lane, N6 5LU.

GORDON, Sir Keith (Lyndell), Kt 1979; CMG 1971; Chairman, Public Service Board of Appeal, St Lucia, 1978–88, retired; Justice of Appeal, West Indies Associated States Supreme Court, 1967–72, retired; *b* 8 April 1906; 3rd *s* of late George S. E. Gordon, Journalist, and Nancy Gordon; *m* 1947, Ethel King; one *d*. *Educ:* St Mary's Coll., St Lucia, WI; Middle Temple, London. Magistrate, Grenada, 1938; Crown Attorney, Dominica, 1942; Trinidad and Tobago: Magistrate, 1943–46 and 1949–53; Exec. Off., Black Market Board, 1946–48; Puisne Judge, Windward Islands and Leeward Islands, 1954–59; Puisne Judge, British Guiana, 1959–62; Chief Justice, West Cameroon, 1963–67. *Recreation:* gardening. *Address:* Vigie, Castries, St Lucia.

GORDON, Sir Lionel Eldred Peter S.; *see* Smith-Gordon.

GORDON, Dr Michael John Caldwell, FRS 1994; Reader in Formal Methods, Computer Laboratory, University of Cambridge, since 1988; *b* 28 Feb. 1948; *m* 1979, Avra Jean Cohn; two *s*. *Educ:* Bedales Sch.; Gonville and Caius Coll., Cambridge (BA Maths); King's Coll., Cambridge (Dip. Linguistics); Edinburgh Univ. (PhD). Research Associate, Stanford Univ., 1974–75; University of Edinburgh: Res. Fellow, 1975–78; SRC Advanced Res. Fellow, 1978–81; Lectr, Univ. of Cambridge, 1981–88; Royal Soc./SERC Industrial Fellow, SRI International, 1987–89. *Publications:* The Denotational Description of Programming Languages, 1979; Programming Language Theory and its Implementation, 1988. *Recreation:* mushroom hunting. *Address:* Computer Laboratory, University of Cambridge, New Museums Site, Pembroke Street, Cambridge CB2 3QG; 4 Bradrushe Fields, Cambridge CB3 0DW. *T:* Cambridge (01223) 62123.

GORDON, Mildred; MP (Lab) Bow and Poplar, since 1987; *b* 24 Aug. 1923; *d* of Dora and Judah Fellerman; *m* 1st, 1948, Sam Gordon (*d* 1982); one *s*; 2nd, 1985, Nils Kaare Dahl. *Educ:* Raines Foundation School; Forest Teacher Training College. Teacher, 1945–85. Mem. Exec., London Labour Party, 1983–86; Jt Chm., Greater London Labour Policy Cttee, 1985–86. Mem., Select Cttee on Educn, Science and Arts, 1991–; Chm., All-Party Parly Child Support Act Monitoring Group; Vice Chm., PLP Educn Cttee and Social Services Cttee, 1990–92. Formerly, Advr, GLC Women's Cttee. School Governor. *Publications:* essays and articles on education. *Recreations:* pottery, designing and making costume jewellery. *Address:* House of Commons, SW1A 0AA. *T:* 0171–219 4125.

GORDON, Nadia, (Mrs Charles Gordon); *see* Nerina, N.

GORDON, Pamela Joan; Chief Executive, City of Sheffield Metropolitan District, since 1989; *b* 13 Feb. 1936; *d* of Frederick Edward Bantick and Violet Elizabeth Bantick; *m* 1959, Wallace Henry Gordon (*d* 1980); two *s*. *Educ:* Richmond (Surrey) Grammar School for Girls: St Hilda's Coll., Oxford (MA). Variety of posts with ILEA, GLC and LCC, 1957–81; Greater London Council: Asst Dir Gen., 1981–83; Dep. Dir of Industry and Employment, 1983–85; Chief Exec., London Bor. of Hackney, 1985–89. Hon. Fellow, Inst. of Local Govt Studies, Birmingham Univ., 1990. *Publications:* articles on management, etc, in local govt jls. *Recreations:* opera, theatre, foreign travel. *Address:* Town Hall, Sheffield S1 2HH. *T:* Sheffield (0114) 273 4000.

GORDON, Patrick W.; *see* Wolrige-Gordon.

GORDON, Peter Macie, CMG 1964; *b* 4 June 1919; *o s* of late Herbert and Gladys Gordon (*née* Simpson); *m* 1945, Marianne, *er d* of Dr Paul Meerwein, Basle; two *d*. *Educ:* Cotham Sch., Bristol; University Coll., Exeter; Merton Coll., Oxford. Served War, 1940–46; commissioned Argyll and Sutherland Highlanders, 1941; Campaign in North-West Europe, 1944–45 (despatches). Entered Colonial Administrative Service as District Officer, 1946; Senior District Commissioner, 1957; Asst Sec., Ministry of Agriculture, 1958; Under-Sec., 1960; Permanent Sec., Ministry of Agriculture and Animal Husbandry, Kenya, 1961; retired, 1964; Asst Sec., Univ. of Exeter, 1964–70. Supervisor, Zimbabwe-Rhodesia Elections, 1980; Mem., Commonwealth Observer Gp, Uganda Elections, 1980. *Address:* Old Poplars Farm House, Chipping Campden, Glos GL55 6EG.

GORDON, Richard, (Dr Gordon Ostlere), MB BChir (Cantab); FRCA; *b* 15 Sept. 1921; *m*; two *s* two *d*. Formerly: anaesthetist at St Bartholomew's Hospital, and Oxford University; assistant editor, British Medical Jl; ship's surgeon. Mem., Punch Table. Author of: Anaesthetics for Medical Students; Doctor in the House, and 14 sequels; 32 other novels and non-fiction (adapted for 8 films and 4 plays, radio and TV); (ed) The Literary Companion to Medicine; TV screenplay, The Good Dr Bodkin Adams; TV series, A Gentlemen's Club; contribs to Punch.

GORDON, Richard John Francis; QC 1994; *b* 26 Nov. 1948; *s* of John Bernard Basil Gordon and Winifred Josephine (*née* Keenan); *m* 1975, Jane Belinda Lucey; two *s*. *Educ:* St Benedict's Sch., Ealing; Christ Church, Oxford (Open Schol.; MA); University Coll. London (LLM). Called to the Bar, Middle Temple, 1972. Sen. Lectr in Admin. Law, KCL, 1991–93. Vis. Prof. of Law, UCL, 1994–. Editor-in-Chief, Crown Office Digest, 1989–. Mem., Exec. Cttee, Admin. Law Bar Assoc., 1991–. *Publications:* The Law Relating to Mobile Homes and Caravans, 1978, 2nd edn 1985; Judicial Review: law and procedure, 1985, 2nd edn 1995; Crown Office Proceedings, 1990; Community Care Assessments, 1993; contrib. to numerous legal jls on admin. law. *Recreations:* reading, writing. *Address:* 39 Essex Street, WC2R 3AT. *T:* 0171–353 4741.

GORDON, Robert Anthony Eagleson, OBE 1983; HM Diplomatic Service; Ambassador to Burma (Union of Myanmar), since 1995; *b* 9 Feb. 1952; *s* of Major Cyril Vivian Eagleson, MC, RE and Clara Renata Romana Gordon (*née* Duse); *m* 1978, Pamela Jane Taylor; two *s* two *d*. *Educ:* King's Sch., Canterbury; Magdalen Coll., Oxford (MA Modern Langs). FCO 1973; Second Sec., Warsaw, 1975–77; First Sec., Santiago, 1978–83; FCO, 1983–87; First Sec., UK Deleg. to OECD, Paris, 1987–92; Counsellor and Dep. Head of Mission, Warsaw, 1992–95. *Recreations:* ski-ing, windsurfing, music. *Address:* c/o Foreign and Commonwealth Office, SW1A 2AH.

GORDON, (Robert) Douglas; HM Diplomatic Service, retired; Ambassador to the Republic of Yemen, 1993–94; *b* 31 July 1936; *s* of Robert Gordon and Helen (*née* MacTaggart); *m* 1st, 1960, Margaret Bruckshaw (marr. diss. 1990); one *s*; 2nd, 1990, Valerie Janet Brownlee, MVO (5th class). *Educ:* Greenock Acad.; Cardiff High Sch. for Boys. FO, 1954. National Service with RM, 1955–57; commnd 2 Lieut Wilts Regt, 1957. FO, 1958; Amman, 1958; MECAS, 1959; Abu Dhabi, 1961; Vienna, 1963; Second Sec. (Commercial), Kuwait, 1966; FCO, 1969; Second, later First Sec., Hd of Chancery and Consul, Doha, 1973; Asst to Dep. Gov., Gibraltar, 1976; FCO, 1979; HM Asst Marshal of the Diplomatic Corps, 1982; First Sec. (Commercial), Washington, 1984; Consul (Commercial), Cleveland, 1986; Ambassador, 1989–90, Consul-General, 1990, Aden; High Comr, Guyana, 1990–93, and Ambassador, Republic of Suriname, 1990–93. Freeman, City of London, 1984. Order of: Gorkha Dakshina Bahu, 5th Cl. (Nepal), 1980; King Abdul Aziz ibn Saud, 4th Cl. (Saudi Arabia), 1982; Officier, l'Ordre Nat. du Mérite (France), 1984. *Recreations:* golf, tennis, walking. *Address:* c/o Foreign and Commonwealth Office, SW1A 2AH. *Clubs:* Royal Over-Seas League; Harewood Downs Golf (Chalfont St Giles).

GORDON, Sir Robert James, 10th Bt *cr* 1706, of Afton and Earlston, Kirkcudbrightshire; farmer since 1958; *b* 17 Aug. 1932; *s* of Sir John Charles Gordon, 9th Bt and of Marion, *d* of late James B. Wright; *S* father, 1982; *m* 1976, Helen Julia Weston Perry. *Educ:* Barker College, Sydney; North Sydney Boys' High School; Wagga Agricultural Coll., Wagga Wagga, NSW (Wagga Dip. of Agric., Hons I and Dux). *Recreations:* tennis, ski-ing, swimming. *Heir:* none. *Address:* Earlstoun, Guyra, NSW 2365, Australia. *T:* (67) 791343.

GORDON, Prof. Robert Patterson, PhD; Regius Professor of Hebrew, Cambridge University, since 1995; Fellow, St Catharine's College, Cambridge, since 1995; *b* 9 Nov. 1945; *s* of Robert Gordon and Eveline (*née* Shilliday); *m* 1970, Helen Ruth Lyttle; two *s* one *d*. *Educ:* Methodist Coll., Belfast; St Catharine's Coll., Cambridge (BA 1st Cl. Hons Oriental Studies 1968; MA 1972; PhD 1973). Asst Lectr in Hebrew and Semitic Langs, 1969–70, Lectr, 1970–79, Glasgow Univ.; Lectr in Divinity, Cambridge Univ., 1979–95; Fellow, St Edmund's Coll., Cambridge, 1985–89 (Tutor, 1986–89). *Publications:* 1 and 2 Samuel, 1984; 1 and 2 Samuel: a commentary, 1986; (ed jtly) The Targum of the Minor Prophets, 1989; Studies in the Targum to the Twelve Prophets, 1994; (ed jtly) Wisdom in Ancient Israel, 1995; contrib. to learned jls incl. Jl Jewish Studies, Jewish Qly Rev., Jl Semitic Studies, Jl for Study of OT, Jl Theol Studies, Revue de Qumran, Vetus Testamentum, and to various composite vols. *Recreations:* jogging, local history (N Ireland). *Address:* 85 Barrons Way, Comberton, Cambridge CB3 7DR. *T:* Cambridge (01223) 263153; Faculty of Oriental Studies, Sidgwick Avenue, Cambridge CB3 9DA.

GORDON, Rt. Rev. Ronald; *see* Gordon, Rt Rev. A. R. McD.

GORDON, Prof. Siamon, PhD; Glaxo Professor of Cellular Pathology, Oxford University, since 1991 (Professor of Cellular Pathology, 1989–91); Fellow, Exeter College, Oxford, since 1976; *b* 29 April 1938; *s* of Jonah and Liebe Gordon; *m* 1963, Lyndall Getz; two *d*. *Educ:* South African Coll. Sch., Cape Town; Univ. of Cape Town (MB ChB 1961); Rockefeller Univ. (PhD 1971). Res. Asst, Wright-Fleming Inst., St Mary's, London, 1964–65; Rockefeller University, NY: Res. Associate, 1965–71; Asst Prof. of Cellular Immunology, 1971–76; Adjunct Associate Prof., 1976–; Reader in Exptl Pathology, Sir Wm Dunn Sch. of Pathology, Univ. of Oxford, 1976–89, Actg Hd of Dept, 1989–90. Chm., Physiol Scis Bd, 1984–86; Member: Lister Scientific Adv. Cttee, 1987–92; General Bd, Univ. of Oxford, 1989–92. Special Fellow and Scholar, Leukaemia Soc. of America, 1971–76; Vis. Scientist, Genetics, Oxford Univ., 1974–75. *Publications:* contribs to jls of exptl medicine, immunology, cell biology, neuroscience. *Recreations:* reading biography, medical history. *Address:* Sir William Dunn School of Pathology, South Parks Road, Oxford OX1 3RE. *T:* Oxford (01865) 275534.

GORDON, Sir Sidney, Kt 1972; CBE 1968 (OBE 1965); CA; JP; Director, Sir Elly Kadoorie & Sons, Ltd; Chairman, China Light & Power Co. Ltd; *b* 20 Aug. 1917; *s* of late P. S. Gordon and late Angusina Gordon; *m* 1950, Olive W. F. Eldon (*d* 1992), *d* of late T. A. Eldon and late Hannah Eldon; two *d*. *Educ:* Hyndland Sch., Glasgow; Glasgow Univ. Sen. Partner, Lowe Bingham & Matthews, Chartered Accountants, Hong Kong, 1956–70. MLC, 1962–66, MEC, Hong Kong, 1965–80. Chairman: Univ. and Polytechnic Grants Cttee, 1974–76; Standing Commn on Civil Service Salaries and Conditions of Service, 1988–. JP Hong Kong, 1961. Hon. LLD The Chinese University of Hong Kong, 1970. *Recreation:* golf. *Address:* 7 Headland Road, Hong Kong. *T:* 28122577. *Clubs:* Oriental; Hong Kong, Royal Hong Kong Jockey (Hon. Steward), Royal Hong Kong Golf (Hon. Life Mem.; formerly, Pres. and Captain), Hong Kong Country, Hong Kong Cricket, Shek O Country, etc.

GORDON, Vera Kate, (Mrs E. W. Gordon); *see* Timms, V. K.

GORDON, Lt-Col William Howat Leslie, CBE 1957 (MBE 1941); MC 1944; Adviser on overseas business to firms, to Ministry of Overseas Development, 1971–75, and to International Finance Corporation; *b* 8 April 1914; *o s* of late Frank Leslie Gordon, ISE, FICE; *m* 1944, Margot Lumb; one *s* three *d*. *Educ:* Rugby; RMA Woolwich. Commnd Royal Signals, 1934; Palestine, Africa, Italy, NW Europe; 1 Armoured, 1 Airborne Divs (despatches); Instructor, Staff Coll., Camberley, 1947–49. Chief Executive, The Uganda Co. Ltd, 1949–60; John Holt & Co. (Liverpool) Ltd and Lonrho Exports Ltd, 1960–71; MLC Uganda, 1952–57; Chm., Rickmansworth Water Co., 1986–88. Chm., St John Council, Bucks, 1974–82; KStJ. *Address:* La Feuilleraie, Ponson Soubiran, Mirande 32300, Le Gers, France.

GORDON, William John, FCIB; Managing Director, UK Banking Services, Barclays Bank plc, since 1992; *b* 24 April 1939; *s* of Sidney Frank Gordon and Grace Louie Gordon; *m* 1963, Patricia Rollason; two *s*. *Educ:* King Edward VI Sch., Fiveways, Birmingham. FCIB 1979. Joined Barclays Bank, 1955: branch and regl appts, 1955–80; Asst Gen. Manager, Barclaycard, 1980–83; Regl Gen. Manager, Central UK, 1983–87; Dir, UK Corporate Services, 1987–90; Gp Personnel Dir, 1990–92. Mem., Herts Bridge Assoc.

Recreations: bridge, golf, chess, music. *Address:* Barclays Bank plc, 54 Lombard Street, EC3P 3AH. *T:* 0171–699 5000. *Club:* Mid Herts Golf (Wheathampstead).

GORDON-BROWN, Alexander Douglas, CB 1984; Receiver for the Metropolitan Police District, 1980–87; *b* 5 Dec. 1927; *s* of late Captain and Mrs D. S. Gordon-Brown; *m* 1959, Mary Hilton; three *s*. *Educ:* Bryanston Sch.; New Coll., Oxford. MA; 1st cl. hons PPE. Entered Home Office, 1951; Sec., Franks Cttee on section 2 of Official Secrets Act 1911, 1971; Asst Under-Sec. of State, Home Office, 1972–75, 1978–80; Under Sec., Cabinet Office, 1975–78. Chm., Home Office Wkg Gp on Costs of Crime, 1988. Mem., Nat. Council, Victim Support, 1991–. *Recreations:* music, golf, walking, gardening.

GORDON-CUMMING, Alexander Roualeyn, CMG 1978; CVO 1969; Director, Invest in Britain Bureau, Department of Industry, 1979–84; *b* 10 Sept. 1924; *s* of late Lt-Comdr R. G. Gordon-Cumming and Mrs M. V. K. Wilkinson; *m* 1st, 1965, Beryl Joyce Macnaughton Dunn (*d* 1973); one *d*; 2nd, 1974, Elizabeth Patricia Blackley (*d* 1983); one *d*. *Educ:* Eton Coll. RAF, 1943; retd with rank of Gp Captain, 1969. Board of Trade, 1969; Dept of Trade and Industry, 1973; seconded HM Diplomatic Service, 1974–78. *Recreations:* gardening, skiing, fell walking, ballet. *Address:* Woodstock, West Way, West Broyle, Chichester, Sussex PO19 3PW. *T:* Chichester (01243) 776413. *Club:* Royal Air Force.

GORDON CUMMING, Sir William Gordon, 6th Bt, *cr* 1804; Royal Scots Greys; *b* 19 June 1928; *s* of Major Sir Alexander Penrose Gordon Cumming, 5th Bt, MC, and of Elizabeth Topham, *d* of J. Topham Richardson, Harps Oak, Merstham; *S* father, 1939; *m* 1953, Elisabeth (marr. diss. 1972), *d* of Maj.-Gen. Sir Robert Hinde, KBE, CB, DSO; one *s* three *d*; *m* 1989, Sheila Bates. *Educ:* Eton; RMC, Sandhurst. Late Royal Scots Greys; retired 1952. *Heir: s* Alexander Penrose Gordon Cumming [*b* 15 April 1954; *m* 1991, Louisa, *e d* of E. G. Clifton-Brown]. *Address:* Altyre, Forres, Morayshire.

GORDON DAVIES, Rev. John; *see* Davies, Rev. John G.

GORDON-DUFF, Col Thomas Robert, MC 1945; JP; Lord-Lieutenant of Banffshire, 1964–87; Convener of County Council, 1962–70; *b* 1911; *er s* of Lachlan Gordon-Duff (killed in action, 1914); *m* 1946, Jean (*d* 1981), *d* of late Leslie G. Moir, Bicester; one *s*. *Educ:* Eton; RMC, Sandhurst. Entered Army, 2nd Lieut, Rifle Brigade, 1932; served War of 1939–45 (MC); retired, 1947. Lt-Col 5/6 Bn Gordon Highlanders (TA), 1947, retiring as Col. DL 1948, JP 1959, Vice-Lieut 1961, Banffshire. *Address:* Drummuir, Keith, Banffshire AB55 3JE. *T:* Drummuir (01542) 810300. *Club:* Army and Navy.

GORDON-FINLAYSON, Maj.-Gen. Robert, OBE 1957 (MBE 1945); DL; *b* 28 Oct. 1916; *yr s* of late Gen. Sir Robert Gordon-Finlayson, KCB, CMG, DSO, DL; *m* 1945, Alexandra, *d* of late John Bartholomew, Rowde Court, Rowde, Wilts; two *s*. *Educ:* Winchester Coll.; RMA, Woolwich. 2 Lt RA, 1936; Major, BEF, 1940; Staff Coll., 1941; Middle East, 1942–43; NW Europe, 1944–45; India and Burma, 1945–47; GSO 1 1945; RHA, 1952–53; JSSC, 1953; Bt Lieut-Col, 1955; AA and QMG, 3 Inf. Div., 1955–57; Near East (Suez Ops), 1956; Middle East, 1958; Lieut-Col 1958; Comdr, 26 Field Regt RA, 1958–59; Col 1959; GSO 1, Staff Coll., 1960–62; Brig. CRA, 49 Div. TA, 1962–64; Brig. DQMG, HQ, BAOR, 1964–66. GOC 49 Inf. Div., TA/N Midland Dist, 1966–67; GOC E Midland District, 1967–70; retd, 1970. Hon. Col, 3rd (Volunteer) Bn The Worcestershire and Sherwood Foresters Regt, TAVR, 1971–78; Chm., Notts Co. Army Benevolent Fund, 1970–85; Mem., Notts Co. and E Midlands TAVR Assocs, 1971–85. Branch Patron, Notts Co. Dunkirk Veterans Assoc., 1990–; Pres., Notts Co. Royal British Legion, 1971–79; Vice-President: Notts Co. SSAFA, 1970–; Notts Co. PDSA, 1970–87; Central Notts Scout Assoc., 1971–80. JP 1972–86. High Sheriff 1974, DL 1974, Notts. *Recreations:* shooting, fishing, ski-ing, gardening, walking. *Address:* South Collingham Manor, near Newark, Notts NG23 7LW. *T:* Newark (01636) 892204; c/o Lloyds Bank, Cox's & King's Branch, 7 Pall Mall, SW1Y 5NA.

GORDON JONES, Air Marshal Sir Edward, KCB 1967 (CB 1960); CBE 1956 (OBE 1945); DSO 1941; DFC 1941; idc; jssc; qs; Air Officer Commanding-in-Chief, Near East Air Force, and Administrator, Sovereign Base Areas, 1966–69; Commander, British Forces Near East, 1967–69; retired 1969; *b* 31 Aug. 1914; *s* of late Lt-Col Dr A. Jones, DSO, MC, MD, DPH; *m* 1938, Margery Thurston Hatfield, BSc; two *s*. Served War of 1939–45 (despatches, DFC, DSO, OBE, Greek DFC). ACOS (Intelligence), Allied Air Forces Central Europe, 1960–61; Air Officer Commanding RAF Germany, 1961–63; Senior RAF Directing Staff, Imperial Defence Coll., 1963–65; AOC, RAF, Malta, and Dep. C-in-C (Air), Allied Forces, Mediterranean, 1965–66. Comdr Order of Orange Nassau. *Recreations:* sport, music. *Address:* 20 Marlborough Court, Grange Road, Cambridge CB3 9BQ. *T:* Cambridge (01223) 363029. *Club:* Royal Air Force.

GORDON-LENNOX, family name of **Duke of Richmond.**

GORDON LENNOX, Maj.-Gen. Bernard Charles, CB 1986; MBE 1968; Regimental Lieutenant-Colonel, Grenadier Guards, 1989–95; *b* 19 Sept. 1932; *s* of Lt-Gen. Sir George Gordon Lennox and Nancy Brenda Darell; *m* 1958, Sally-Rose Warner; three *s*. *Educ:* Eton; Sandhurst. 2nd Lt, Grenadier Guards, 1953; Hong Kong, 1965; HQ Household Div., 1971; Commanding 1st Bn Grenadier Guards, 1974; Army Directing Staff, RAF Staff College, 1976–77; Command, Task Force H, 1978–79; RCDS, 1980; Dep. Commander and Chief of Staff, SE District, 1981–82; GOC Berlin (British Sector), 1983–85; Sen. Army Mem., RCDS, 1986–88, retd. Dir of Regions, Motor Agents Assoc., 1988–89. *Recreations:* field sports, cricket, squash, music. *Address:* c/o Regimental Headquarters, Grenadier Guards, Wellington Barracks, Birdcage Walk, SW1E 6HQ. *Clubs:* Army and Navy, MCC.

GORDON LENNOX, Lord Nicholas Charles, KCMG 1986 (CMG 1978); KCVO 1989 (LVO 1957); HM Diplomatic Service, retired; a Governor, BBC, 1990–95; director of companies; *b* 31 Jan. 1931; *yr s* of 9th Duke of Richmond and Gordon and of Elizabeth Grace, *y d* of late Rev. T. W. Hudson; *m* 1958, Mary, *d* of late Brig. H. N. H. Williamson, DSO, MC; one *s* three *d*. *Educ:* Eton; Worcester Coll., Oxford (Scholar). 2nd Lieut KRRC, 1950–51. Entered HM Foreign Service, 1954; FO, 1954–57; Private Sec. to HM Ambassador to USA, 1957–61; 2nd, later 1st Sec., HM Embassy, Santiago, 1961–63; Private Sec. to Perm. Under-Sec., FO, 1963–66; 1st Sec. and Head of Chancery, HM Embassy, Madrid, 1966–71; seconded to Cabinet Office, 1971–73; Head of News Dept, FCO, 1973–74, Head of N America Dept, 1974–75; Counsellor and Head of Chancery, Paris, 1975–79; Asst Under-Sec. of State, FCO, 1979–84; Ambassador to Spain, 1984–89. Director, 1990–: Foreign and Colonial Investment Trust; Nat West SA (Spain); Sturge Holdings; Sothebys; Commercial Union Vida (Spain); MGM Assurance. Hon. Col, 4th Bn Royal Green Jackets, TA, 1990–. Medal of Honour, Univ. of Madrid, 1988. Grand Cross, Order of Isabel la Católica (Spain), 1986. *Clubs:* Boodle's, Beefsteak.

GORDON-SMITH, David Gerard; CMG 1971; Director-General in Legal Service, Council of Ministers, European Communities, 1976–87; *b* 6 Oct. 1925; *s* of late Frederic Gordon-Smith, QC, and Elsie Gordon-Smith (*née* Foster); *m* 1952, Angela Kirkpatrick Pile; one *d* (and one *s* decd). *Educ:* Rugby Sch.; Trinity Coll., Oxford. Served in RNVR, 1944–46. BA (Oxford) 1948; called to Bar, Inner Temple, 1949; Legal Asst, Colonial Office, 1950; Sen. Legal Asst, 1954; CRO, 1963–65; Asst Legal Adviser, CO, 1965–66; Legal Counsellor, CO, later FCO, 1966–72; Dep. Legal Advr, FCO, 1973–76. *Address:* Kingscote, Westcott, Surrey RH4 3NX.

GORDON-SMITH, Prof. Edward Colin, FRCP, FRCPath; Professor of Haematology, St George's Hospital Medical School, London, since 1987; *b* 26 June 1938; *s* of late Gordon John Gordon-Smith and Valentine (*née* Waddington); *m* 1968, Moira Phelan; two *s*. *Educ:* Oakham Sch.; Epsom Coll.; Exeter Coll., Oxford (MA, BSc, BM BCh); Westminster Med. Sch., London (MSc). FRCP 1978; FRCPath 1987. House Officer, Westminster Hosp., 1964; Sen. House Officer, Nuffield Dept of Medicine, Radcliffe Infirmary, Oxford, 1966; Lectr in Neurology, Churchill Hosp., Oxford, 1966–67; Registrar in Haematology, Hammersmith Hosp., 1968–69; MRC Clinical Trng Fellow, RPMS Metabolic Unit, Oxford, 1970–71; Sen. Lectr 1972–83, Reader 1983–86, RPMS. Editor, Brit. Jl of Haematology, 1983–86. President: European Bone Marrow Transplant Gp, 1980; Internat. Soc. Explt Haematology, 1990–92; British Soc. for Haematology, 1995. Order of Prasidda Prabala Gorkha-Dakshin Bahu, Nepal, 1984. *Publications:* papers on aplastic anaemia, bone marrow transplantation, inherited bone marrow disorders, culture of human bone marrow and drug induced blood disorders. *Recreations:* golf, music, gardening, arguing with the wireless. *Address:* Department of Haematology, St George's Hospital Medical School, Cranmer Terrace, Tooting, SW17 0RE. *T:* 0181–784 2645, *Fax:* 0181–682 4217. *Club:* Royal Society of Medicine.

GORE, family name of **Earl of Arran.**

GORE; *see* Ormsby Gore.

GORE, Albert, Jr; Vice-President of the United States of America, since 1993; *b* 31 March 1948; *s* of Albert and Pauline Gore; *m* 1970, Mary Elizabeth Aitcheson; one *s* three *d*. *Educ:* Harvard and Vanderbilt Univs. Served US Army in Vietnam, 1969–71. Reporter and editorial writer, The Tennessean, 1971–76; livestock and tobacco farmer, 1971–. Mem., US House of Representatives, 1977–85; Mem. for Tennessee, US Senate, 1985–92. Chm., US Senate Delegn to Earth Summit, Rio de Janeiro, 1992. Democrat. *Publication:* Earth in the Balance: ecology and the human spirit, 1992. *Address:* The White House, Washington, DC 20500, USA.

GORE, (Francis) St John (Corbet), CBE 1986; FSA; *b* 8 April 1921; *s* of late Francis Gore and Kirsteen Corbet-Singleton; *m* 1st, 1951, Priscilla (marr. diss. 1975), *d* of Cecil Harmsworth King; one *s* one *d*; 2nd, 1981, Lady Mary Strachey, *d* of 3rd Earl of Selborne, PC, CH. *Educ:* Wellington; Courtauld Inst. of Art. Served War, 1940–45, Captain, Royal Northumberland Fusiliers. Employed Sotheby's, 1950–55; National Trust: Adviser on pictures, 1956–86, Hon. Advr, 1986–; Historic Buildings Sec., 1973–81. Mem., Exec. Cttee, Nat. Art Collections Fund, 1964–; Trustee: Wallace Collection, 1975–89; National Gall., 1986–94. *Publications:* Catalogue, Worcester Art Museum, Mass (British Pictures), 1974; various exhibn catalogues, incl. RA; contribs to Apollo, Country Life, etc. *Recreation:* sight-seeing. *Address:* Grove Farm, Stoke-by-Nayland, Suffolk CO6 4SL. *Clubs:* Brooks's, Beefsteak.

See also Baron O'Hagan.

GORE, Frederick John Pym, CBE 1987; RA 1972 (ARA 1964); Painter; Head of Painting Department, St Martin's School of Art, WC2, 1951–79, and Vice-Principal, 1961–79; *b* 8 Nov. 1913; *s* of Spencer Frederick Gore and Mary Johanna Kerr. *Educ:* Lancing Coll.; Trinity Coll., Oxford; studied art at Ruskin, Westminster and Slade Schs. Taught at: Westminster Sch. of Art, 1937; Chelsea and Epsom, 1947; St Martin's, 1946–79. Chm., RA exhibitions cttee, 1976–87. Trustee, Imperial War Mus., 1967–84 (Chm., Artistic Records Cttee, 1972–1986). *One-man exhibitions:* Gall. Borghèse, Paris, 1938; Redfern Gall., 1937, 1949, 1950, 1953, 1956, 1962; Mayor Gall., 1958, 1960; Juster Gall., NY, 1963; RA (retrospective), 1989. *Paintings in public collections include:* Contemporary Art Soc., Leicester County Council, GLC, Southampton, Plymouth, Rutherston Collection and New Brunswick. Served War of 1939–45: Mx Regt and RA (SO Camouflage). *Publications:* Abstract Art, 1956; Painting, Some Principles, 1965; Piero della Francesca's 'The Baptism', 1969. *Recreation:* Russian folk dancing. *Address:* Flat 3, 35 Elm Park Gardens, SW10 9QF. *T:* 0171–352 4940.

GORE, Michael Edward John, CVO 1994; CBE 1991; HM Diplomatic Service; Governor, Cayman Islands, 1992–95; *b* 20 Sept. 1935; *s* of late John Gore and Elsa Gore (*née* Dillon); *m* 1957, Monica Shellish; three *d*. *Educ:* Xaverian College, Brighton. Reporter, Portsmouth Evening News, 1952–55; Captain, Army Gen. List, 1955–59; Air Ministry, Dep. Comd. Inf. Officer, Cyprus and Aden, 1959–63; CRO, later FCO, 1963; served Jesselton, 1963–66, FCO, 1966–67, Seoul, 1967–71, Montevideo, 1971–74; First Sec., Banjul, 1974–78; FCO, 1978–81; Nairobi, 1981–84; Dep. High Comr, Lilongwe, 1984–87; Ambassador to Liberia, 1988–90; High Comr to the Bahamas, 1991–92. Mem., British Ornithologists' Union; FRPS. Trustee, Trust for Oriental Ornithology, 1992–. *Publications:* The Birds of Korea (with Pyong-Oh Won), 1971; Las Aves del Uruguay (with A. R. M. Gepp), 1978; Birds of the Gambia, 1981, 2nd edn 1991; On Safari in Kenya: a pictorial guide to the national parks and reserves, 1984; papers on birds and conservation; wild-life photographs in books and magazines. *Recreations:* ornithology, wildlife photography, fishing. *Address:* 5 St Mary's Close, Fetcham, Surrey KT22 9HE. *Club:* Army and Navy.

GORE, Sir Nigel (Hugh St George), 14th Bt *cr* 1621 (Ire.), of Magherabegg, Co. Donegal; grazier and farmer, since 1945; *b* 23 Dec. 1922; *yr s* of St George Richard Gore (*d* 1952, *great nephew* of Sir St George Ralph Gore, 9th Bt), and Loo Loo Ruth (*d* 1961), *d* of E. P. Amesbury; *S* nephew, 1993; *m* 1952, Beth Allison (*d* 1976), *d* of R. W. Hooper; one *d*. *Educ:* Church of England Grammar Sch., Brisbane; Gatton Agricl Coll. Served Army, 1940–45. *Heir: cousin* Dundas Corbet Gore [*b* 20 April 1921; *m*]. *Clubs:* Toowoomba Range Probus; Returned Soldiers League.

GORE, Paul Annesley, CMG 1964; CVO 1961; *b* 28 Feb. 1921; *o s* of late Charles Henry Gore, OBE and late Hon. Violet Kathleen (*née* Annesley); *m* 1946, Gillian Mary, *d* of T. E. Allen-Stevens; two *s* (and one *s* decd). *Educ:* Winchester Coll.; Christ Church, Oxford. Military Service, 1941–46: 16/5 Lancers. Colonial Service, 1948–65; Dep. Governor, The Gambia, 1962–65. *Address:* 1 Burkitt Road, Woodbridge, Suffolk IP12 4JJ.

GORE, St John; *see* Gore, F. St J. C.

GORE-BOOTH, Sir Angus (Josslyn), 8th Bt *cr* 1760 (Ire.), of Artarman, Sligo; *b* 25 June 1920; *s* of Sir Josslyn Augustus Richard Gore-Booth, 6th Bt and Mary Sibell (*d* 1968), *d* of Rev. S. L'Estrange-Malone; *S* brother, 1987; *m* 1948, Hon. Rosemary Myra Vane (marr. diss. 1954), *o d* of 10th Baron Barnard; one *s* one *d*. *Educ:* Radley; Worcester Coll., Oxford. Served War of 1939–45, Captain Irish Guards. *Heir: s* Josslyn Henry Robert Gore-Booth [*b* 5 Oct. 1950; *m* 1980, Jane Mary, *o d* of Rt Hon. Sir Roualeyn Hovell-Thurlow-Cumming-Bruce, *qv*; two *d*]. *Address:* Lissadell, Sligo, Irish Republic. *T:* Sligo (71) 63150.

GORE-BOOTH, Hon. David Alwyn, CMG 1990; HM Diplomatic Service; Ambassador to Saudi Arabia, since 1993; *b* 15 May 1943; twin *s* of late Baron Gore-Booth, GCMG, KCVO; *m* 1st, 1964, Jillian Sarah (*née* Valpy) (marr. diss. 1970); one *s*; 2nd, 1977, Mary Elisabeth Janet (*née* Muirhead). *Educ:* Eton Coll.; Christ Church, Oxford (MA Hons). Entered Foreign Office, 1964; Middle East Centre for Arab Studies, 1964; Third Secretary, Baghdad, 1966; Third, later Second Sec., Lusaka, 1967; FCO, 1969; Second Sec., Tripoli, 1969; FCO, 1971; First Sec., UK Permanent Representation to European Communities, Brussels, 1974; Asst Head of Financial Relations Dept, FCO, 1978; Counsellor, Jedda, 1980; Counsellor and Hd of Chancery, UK Mission to UN, NY, 1983; Hd of Policy Planning Staff, FCO, 1987; Asst Under Sec. of State (ME), FCO, 1989. *Recreations:* tennis, squash, the island of Hydra (Greece). *Address:* c/o Foreign and Commonwealth Office, SW1A 2AH. *Clubs:* MCC, Hurlingham, Travellers; Bill's Bar (Hydra).

GORE-LANGTON; *see* Temple-Gore-Langton, family name of Earl Temple of Stowe.

GORELL, 4th Baron *cr* 1909; **Timothy John Radcliffe Barnes;** *b* 2 Aug. 1927; *e s* of 3rd Baron Gorell and Elizabeth Gorell, *d* of Alexander Nelson Radcliffe; *S* father, 1963; *m* 1954, Joan Marion, *y d* of late John Edmund Collins, MC, Sway, Hants; two adopted *d*. *Educ:* Eton Coll.; New Coll., Oxford. Lieut, Rifle Brigade, 1946–48. Barrister, Inner Temple, 1951. Sen. Executive, Royal Dutch/Shell Group, 1959–84. *Heir: b* Hon. Ronald Alexander Henry Barnes [*b* 28 June 1931; *m* 1957, Gillian Picton Hughes-Jones; one *s* one *d*]. *Address:* 4 Roehampton Gate, SW15 5JS. *T:* 0181–876 5522. *Club:* Roehampton.

GORHAM, Robin Stuart; HM Diplomatic Service; Head of Protocol Department and Assistant Marshal of the Diplomatic Corps, Foreign and Commonwealth Office, since 1994; *b* 15 Feb. 1939; *s* of Stuart Gorham and Dorothy Gorham (*née* Stevens); *m* 1st, 1966, Barbara Fechner (marr. diss. 1991); three *d*; 2nd, 1992, Joanna Bradbury. *Educ:* Sutton Manor High Sch.; Oriel Coll., Oxford (MA). CRO, 1961–62; Ottawa, 1962–64; Centre for Econ. Studies, 1964–65; Bonn, 1965–66; Central European Dept, FCO, 1967–69; First Secretary: (External Affairs and Defence) and Dep. Hd of Chancery, Tokyo, 1970–74; (Commercial and Develt), Accra, 1974–77; ME Dept, FCO, 1977–79; Hd of Chancery, Helsinki, 1980–83; Counsellor and Dep. High Comr, Lusaka, 1983–86; rcds, 1987; Hd, W Indian and Atlantic Dept, FCO, 1988–91; Dep. Hd of Mission, Lagos, 1991–94. *Recreations:* riding, swimming, music, theatre. *Address:* c/o Foreign and Commonwealth Office, King Charles Street, SW1A 2AH; 28 Alma Square, St John's Wood, NW8 9PF. *T:* 0171–286 1357.

GORING, Marius, CBE 1991; FRSL; actor, manager, director; *b* Newport, IoW, 23 May 1912; *s* of Dr Charles Buckman Goring, MD, BSc, criminologist, and Katie Winifred (Macdonald), pianist; *m* 1931, Mary Westwood Steel (marr. diss.); one *d*; *m* 1941, Lucie Mannheim (*d* 1976); *m* 1977, Prudence FitzGerald. *Educ:* Perse Sch., Cambridge; Universities of Frankfurt, Munich, Vienna, and Paris. Studying for stage under Harcourt Williams and at Old Vic dramatic school, 1929–32. First stage appearance in Crossings, ADC, Cambridge, 1925; first professional appearance in Jean Sterling Mackinlay's matinées (Rudolph Steiner Hall), 1927; toured in France and Germany with English Classical Players, 1931; stage managed two seasons at Old Vic and Sadler's Wells, playing Romeo, Macbeth, Epihodov and other rôles, 1932–34. First West End appearance as Hugh Voysey, Shaftesbury, 1934; toured France, Belgium, and Holland with Compagnie des Quinze (acting in French), also Hamlet, Old Vic, Noah, New, Hangman, Duke of York's, Sowers of the Hills, Westminster, 1934–35; Mary Tudor, Playhouse, The Happy Hypocrite, His Majesty's, Girl Unknown, New, Wild Duck, Westminster, 1936; rôles in Witch of Edmonton, Hamlet, Twelfth Night and Henry V at Old Vic, Satyr, Shaftesbury, 1937; The Last Straw, Comedy, Surprise Item, Ambassadors, The White Guard, Phoenix, 1938; in management at Duke of York's, 1939: dir, Nora (A Doll's House); Lady Fanny; first player in Hamlet, Lyceum and Elsinore; Pip in Great Expectations (produced with George Devine and Alec Guinness at Rudolph Steiner, first theatre to re-open after war closure); dir (with G. Devine) The Tempest (also played Ariel), Old Vic. Served in Queen's Royal Regiment, 1940; lent to Foreign Office, 1941–45; supervisor of BBC productions broadcast to Germany under name of Charles Richardson. Toured British zone of Germany, 1947 (in German); Rosmersholm, Too True to be Good, Cherry Orchard, Marriage, at Arts Theatre; Daphne Laureola, Berlin (playing in German), 1949; One Hundred Thousand Pounds, Berlin, 1950; The Madwoman of Chaillot, St James's, 1951; Richard III, Antony and Cleopatra, Taming of the Shrew, King Lear, Stratford-upon-Avon, 1953; Marriage, Wuppertal, 1954; toured France, Holland, Finland, and India with own company of English comedians, 1957–58; Tonight at 8.30 (in German), Berlin Fest., 1960; Measure for Measure, Stratford-upon-Avon, 1962; A Penny for a Song, Aldwych, 1962; Ménage à Trois, Lyric, 1963; The Poker Session, Dublin, and Globe, 1964; The Apple Cart, Cambridge, 1965; The Bells, Derby Playhouse and Midlands tour, 1966–67, and Vaudeville, 1968; The Demonstration, Nottingham, 1969; Sleuth, St Martin's, 1970–73; The Wisest Fool, Guildford and tour, 1975; Habeas Corpus, Liverpool Playhouse, 1976; The Concert, Theatre Royal York, 1977; Habeas Corpus, Lyceum, Edinburgh, 1979; Sleuth, Liverpool Playhouse, 1981; Zaïde, Old Vic, 1982; Lloyd George Knew my Father, nat. tour, 1982; Peer Gynt, Nottingham, 1982; Dame of Sark, nat. tour, 1983; The Winslow Boy, nat. tour, 1984; I Have Been Here Before, nat. tour, 1985; God in Mystery plays in Canterbury Cathedral, 1986; The Applecart, Haymarket, 1986; Beyond Reasonable Doubt, Queen's, 1988; Towards Zero, Churchill Theatre, Bromley and nat. tour, 1989; Sunsets and Glories, Playhouse, Leeds, 1990. Co-founder, London Theatre Studio with Michel St Denis and George Devine. *Films include:* Rembrandt; The Case of the Frightened Lady, 1940; A Matter of Life and Death, 1946; The Red Shoes, 1948; Odette, 1950; So Little Time, 1951; Pandora and the Flying Dutchman, 1952; The Barefoot Contessa, 1955; Ill Met by Moonlight, 1956; The Inspector, 1961; La Fille en Robe bleue, 1980; Loser Takes All, 1988. Broadcaster and writer of radio scripts. *Radio:* first performance, Bulldog Drummond; Hitler in the Shadow of the Swastika (first BBC war programme), 1939; for BBC Third Programme, The Divine Comedy, Browning Monologues, Henry Reed's Leopardi, Streets of Pompeii, Tennyson's Maud, 1959; *Television:* first appearance in Tchekov's The Bear, 1938; exec. producer and played lead in Adventures of the Scarlet Pimpernel (series), 1955; The Expert (series), 1968–70, 1974; Fall of Eagles Hindenburg (series), 1977; Edward and Mrs Simpson (series), 1978; The Old Men at the Zoo (series), 1983; Gnostics (series), 1987; War at Woburn, 1987; autobiographical documentary, 1987. FRSL 1976. Founder Mem., British Equity, 1929; Vice-Pres. British Actors' Equity Assoc., 1963–65 and 1975–82. *Recreations:* skating and riding. *Address:* c/o Film Rights Ltd, 483 Southbank House, Black Prince Road, Albert Embankment, SE1 7SJ. *T:* 0171–735 8171. *Club:* Garrick.

GORING, Sir William (Burton Nigel), 13th Bt, *cr* 1627; Member of London Stock Exchange since 1963; *b* 21 June 1933; *s* of Major Frederick Yelverton Goring (*d* 1938) (6th *s* of 11th Bt) and Freda Margaret (*d* 1993), *o d* of N. V. Ainsworth; *S* uncle, Sir Forster Gurney Goring, 12th Bt, 1956; *m* 1st, 1960, Hon. Caroline Thellusson (marr. diss. 1993), *d* of 8th Baron Rendlesham, *qv*, and of Mrs Patrick Barthropp; 2nd, 1993, Mrs Judith Rachel Walton Morison, step *d* of Rev. R. J. W. Morris, OBE. *Educ:* Wellington; RMA Sandhurst, Lieut, The Royal Sussex Regt. *Recreation:* bridge. *Heir: kinsman* Richard Harry Goring [*b* 10 Sept. 1949; *m* 1972, Penelope Ann, *d* of J. K. Broadbent; four *s* two *d*]. *Address:* c/o Quilter Goodison, St Helen's, 1 Undershaft, EC3A 8BB. *Club:* Hurlingham.

GORLEY PUTT, Samuel; *see* Putt.

GORMAN, Christopher Nicoll; Managing Partner, Linklaters & Paines, Solicitors, since 1991; *b* 29 Aug. 1939; *s* of late James Gorman and of Louise Barbara (*née* Rackham); *m* 1967, Anne Beech; one *s* one *d*. *Educ:* Royal Liberty Sch., Romford; St Catharine's Coll., Cambridge (MA, LLM). Admitted Solicitor, 1965; Partner, Linklaters & Paines, 1972–. *Publications:* (ed) Nelson's Tables of Company Procedure, 6th edn 1975 to 8th edn 1983; (ed) Westby Nunn's Company Secretarial Handbook, 7th edn 1977 to 11th edn 1992. *Recreations:* books and bookshops, outdoor activity, unfinished business. *Address:* Linklaters & Paines, Barrington House, 59–67 Gresham Street, EC2V 7JA. *T:* 0171–606 7080. *Clubs:* Royal Automobile; Salcombe Yacht.

GORMAN, John Peter, QC 1974; a Recorder of the Crown Court, since 1972; *b* 29 June 1927; *er s* of James S. Gorman, Edinburgh; *m* 1st, 1955; one *s* three *d*; 2nd, 1979, Patricia (*née* Myatt). *Educ:* Stonyhurst Coll.; Balliol Coll., Oxford (MA). Served with RA, 1945–48. Called to Bar, Inner Temple, 1953, Bencher 1983; Midland and Oxford Circuit. Dep. Chm. 1969, Chm. 1972–79, Agricultural Lands Tribunal (E Midlands); Dep. Chm., Northants QS, 1970–71. *Address:* 9 Gough Square, EC4A 3DE. *Club:* Reform.

GORMAN, John Reginald, CVO 1961; CBE 1974 (MBE 1959); MC 1944; DL; Director, Institute of Directors, Northern Ireland, since 1986; *b* 1 Feb. 1923; *s* of Major J. K. Gorman, MC; *m* 1948, Heather, *d* of George Caruth, solicitor, Ballymena; two *s* two *d*. *Educ:* Rockport, Haileybury and ISC; Portora; Glasgow Univ.; Harvard Business Sch. FCIT, FIPM; MIH. Irish Guards, 1941–46, Normandy, France, Belgium, Holland, Germany (Captain, 1944–46). Royal Ulster Constabulary, 1946–60; Chief of Security, BOAC, 1960–63 (incl. Royal Tour of India, 1961); Personnel Dir and Mem. Bd of Management, BOAC, 1964–69; British Airways: Regional Man., Canada, 1969–75; Regional Man., India, Bangladesh, Sri Lanka, 1975–79; Vice-Chm. and Chief Exec., NI Housing Exec., 1979–85. Dir, NI Airports Bd, 1985–92; Mem., NI Bd, Nationwide Building Soc., 1986–91. Pres., British Canadian Trade Assoc., 1972–74; Vice-Chm., Federated Appeal of Montreal, 1973–74. Chm., Bd of Airline Representatives, India, 1977–79; Chm., Inst. of Housing (NI), 1984. Bd Mem., Co-operation North, 1987–. DL, 1982, High Sheriff, 1987–88, Co. Down. *Recreations:* gardening, bee keeping, country pursuits. *Address:* The Forge, Jericho Road, Killyleagh, Co. Down BT30 9TE. *T:* Killyleagh (01396) 828400. *Clubs:* Cavalry and Guards; Ulster Reform (Belfast); St James (Montreal).

GORMAN, Teresa Ellen; MP (C) Billericay, since 1987; *b* Sept. 1931; *m*. *Educ:* Fulham Co. Sch.; London Univ. (BSc 1st cl. Hons). Founder and manager of own company. Mem., Westminster City Council, 1982–86. Contested (Ind.) Streatham, Oct. 1974. Founder and Chairman: Alliance of Small Firms & Self Employed People Ltd, 1974; Amarant Trust, 1986. Mem., Cons. Women's Nat. Cttee, 1983–. *Publications:* The Bastards: dirty tricks and the challenge to Europe, 1993; The Amarant Book of HRT, 1989; research papers for IEA, Adam Smith Inst., CPS. *Address:* c/o House of Commons, SW1A 0AA.

GORMAN, William Moore, FBA 1978; Emeritus Fellow, Nuffield College, Oxford, since 1990 (Fellow, 1962–67 and 1979–90); *b* 17 June 1923; *s* of late Richard Gorman, Lusaka, Northern Rhodesia, and Sarah Crawford Moore, Kesh, Northern Ireland; *m* 1950, Dorinda Scott. *Educ:* Foyle Coll., Derry; Trinity Coll., Dublin (Hon. Fellow 1990). Asst Lectr, 1949, Lectr, 1951, and Sen. Lectr, 1957, in Econometrics and Social Statistics, University of Birmingham; Prof. of Economics, University of Oxford, 1962–67; Prof. of Economics, London Univ., at LSE, 1967–79. Fellow, 1961, European Chm., 1971–73, Pres. 1972, Econometric Soc. Mem., Academia Europaea, 1990; Hon. Foreign Member: Amer. Acad. of Arts and Scis, 1986; Amer. Economic Assoc., 1987. Hon. DSocSc Birmingham, 1973; Hon. DSc(SocSc) Southampton, 1974; Hon. DEconSc NUI, 1986. *Publications:* articles in various economic journals. *Address:* Nuffield College, Oxford OX1 1NF. *T:* Oxford (01865) 278605; Moorfield, Fountainstown, Myrtleville, Co. Cork, Ireland. *T:* Cork (21) 831174.

GORMANSTON, 17th Viscount *cr* 1478; **Jenico Nicholas Dudley Preston;** Baron Gormanston (Ire.), 1365; Baron Gormanston (UK), 1868; Premier Viscount of Ireland; *b* 19 Nov. 1939; *s* of 16th Viscount and Pamela (who *m* 2nd, 1943, M. B. O'Connor, Irish Guards; he *d* 1961, she *d* 1975), *o d* of late Capt. Dudley Hanly, and Lady Marjorie Heath (by her 1st marriage); *S* father, who was officially presumed killed in action, France, 9 June 1940; *m* 1974, Eva Antoine Landzianowska (*d* 1984); two *s*. *Educ:* Downside. *Heir: s* Hon. Jenico Francis Tara Preston, *b* 30 April 1974. *Address:* 8 Dalmeny House, Thurloe Place, SW7 2RY.

GORMLY, Allan Graham, CBE 1991; Chairman, Royal Insurance Holdings, since 1994 (Deputy Chairman, 1992–94; Director, since 1990); *b* 18 Dec. 1937; *s* of William Gormly and Christina Swinton Flockhart Arnot; *m* 1962, Vera Margaret Grant; one *s* one *d*. *Educ:* Paisley Grammar School. CA. Peat Marwick Mitchell & Co., 1955–61; Rootes Group, 1961–65; John Brown PLC, 1965–68; Brownlee & Co. Ltd, 1968–70; John Brown PLC, 1970: Finance Director, John Brown Engineering Ltd, 1970–77; Director, Planning and Control, John Brown PLC, 1977–80; Dep. Chairman, John Brown Engineers and Constructors Ltd, 1980–83; Gp Man. Dir, John Brown PLC, 1983–92; Chief Exec., Trafalgar House, 1992–94 (Dir, 1986–; Dep. Chm., 1994–); Director: BPB Industries, 1995–; National Grid Co., 1994–; Brixton Estates, 1994–. Chm., Overseas Projects Bd, 1988–91; Dep. Chm., Export Guarantees Adv. Council, 1990–; Member: BOTB, 1988–92; Review Body on Top Salaries, 1990–92. *Recreations:* golf, music. *Address:* 56 North Park, Gerrards Cross, Bucks SL9 8JR.

GORRINGE, Christopher John; Chief Executive, All England Lawn Tennis and Croquet Club, Wimbledon, since 1983; *b* 13 Dec. 1945; *s* of Maurice Sydney William Gorringe and Hilda Joyce Gorringe; *m* 1976, Jennifer Mary Chamberlain; two *d*. *Educ:* Bradfield Coll., Berks; Royal Agricl Coll., Cirencester. ARICS. Asst Land Agent, Iveagh Trustees Ltd (Guinness family), 1968–73; Asst Sec., 1973–79, Sec., 1979–83, All England Lawn Tennis and Croquet Club. *Recreations:* lawn tennis, squash, soccer. *Address:* All England Lawn Tennis Club, Church Road, Wimbledon, SW19 5AE. *T:* 0181–946 2244. *Clubs:* East India, Devonshire, Sports and Public Schools; All England Lawn Tennis and Croquet, International Lawn Tennis of GB, Queen's, St George's Hill Lawn Tennis, Jesters.

GORROD, Prof. John William, CChem, FRSC; FRCPath; Professor of Biopharmacy, King's College London, since 1984; Research Professor, Chelsea Department of Pharmacy, since 1990; *b* 11 Oct. 1931; *s* of Ernest Lionel and Carrie Rebecca Gorrod; *m* 1954, Doreen Mary Collins; two *s* one *d*. *Educ:* Brunel Coll. of Advanced Technology; Chelsea Coll. (DCC, PhD, DSc). Biochem. Asst, Inst. of Cancer Res., 1954–64; Res. Fellow, Univ. of Bari, Italy, 1964; Sen. Student, Royal Commn for Exhibn of 1851, 1965–68; University of London: Lectr 1968–80, then Reader 1980–84, in Biopharmacy, Chelsea Coll.; Hd, Chelsea Dept of Pharmacy, King's Coll., 1984–90; Chm., Univ. Bd of Studies in Pharmacy, 1986–88; Hd of Div. of Health Scis, KCL, 1988–89. Dir, Drug Control and Teaching Centre, Sports Council, 1985–91. Member: Council, Internat. Soc. for Study of Xenobiotics (Chm., Memship Affairs Cttee); Educn Cttee, Pharmaceutical Soc. of GB,

1986–91; Assoc. for Res. in Indoor Air, 1989–; Council, Indoor Air Internat., 1990–; Associates for Res. in Substances of Enjoyment, 1990–92; Air Transport Users Cttee, CAA, 1990–93. Vis. Prof., Univs of Bologna, Bari, and Kebangsan, Malaysia; Canadian MRC Vis. Prof., Univs of Manitoba and Saskatchewan, 1988; Vis. Prof., Chinese Acad. of Preventive Medicine, 1991. Hon. MPS, 1982; Corresp. Mem., German Pharm. Soc., 1985. Hon. Fellow: Greek Pharmaceutical Soc., 1987; Turkish Assoc. of Pharmacists, 1988. Gold Medal, Comenius Univ., Bratislava, 1991. Editorial Board: Xenobiotica; Europ. Jl of Metabolism and Pharmacokinetics; Toxicology Letters; Anti-Cancer Res. *Publications:* Drug Metabolism in Man (ed jtly), 1978; Biological Oxidation of Nitrogen, 1978; Drug Toxicity, 1979; Testing for Toxicity, 1981; (ed jtly) Biological Oxidation of Nitrogen in Organic Molecules, 1985; (ed jtly) Development of Drugs and Modern Medicines, 1986; (ed jtly) Metabolism of Xenobiotics, 1987; (ed jtly) Molecular Aspects of Human Disease, 1989; (ed jtly) Molecular Basis of Neurological Disorders and their Treatment, 1991; (ed jtly) Nicotine and Related Alkaloids, 1993; contribs to Xenobiotica, Europ. Jl Drug Metabolism, Jl Pharm. Pharmacol, Mutation Res., Anti-Cancer Res., Jl Nat. Cancer Inst., Drug Metabolism Revs. *Recreations:* trying to understand government policies on tertiary education, travel, books, running (slowly!), badminton. *Address:* Kingsmead, 13 Park Lane, Hayes, Mddx UB4 8AA; The Rest Orchard, Polstead Heath, Suffolk CO6 5BG. *Clubs:* Athenæum; Hillingdon Athletic (Mddx).

GORST, Sir John (Michael), Kt 1994; MP (C) Hendon North, since 1970; *b* 28 June 1928; *s* of late Derek Charles Gorst and Tatiana (*née* Kolotinsky); *m* 1954, Noël Harington Walker; five *s*. *Educ:* Ardingly Coll.; Corpus Christi Coll., Cambridge (MA). Advertising and Public Relations Manager, Pye Ltd, 1953–63; and Trade Union and Public Affairs Consultant, John Gorst & Associates, 1964–. Public relations adviser to: British Lion Films, 1964–65; Fedn of British Film Makers, 1964–67; Film Production Assoc. of GB, 1967–68; BALPA, 1967–69; Guy's Hosp., 1968–74. Founder: Telephone Users' Assoc., 1964–80 (Sec. 1964–70); Local Radio Assoc. 1964 (Sec., 1964–71). Contested (C) Chester-le-Street, 1964; Bodmin, 1966. Sec., Cons. Consumer Protection Cttee, 1973–74; Member: Employment Select Cttee, 1979–87; Nat. Heritage Select Cttee, 1992–; Vice-Chm., All Party War Crimes Cttee, 1987–; Chm., Cons. Media Cttee, 1987–90. *Recreations:* gardening, photography and video recording, chess. *Address:* House of Commons, SW1A 0AA. *Club:* Garrick.

GORT, 9th Viscount, *cr* 1816 (Ire.); **Foley Robert Standish Prendergast Vereker;** Baron Kiltart 1810; gallery picture framer; *b* 24 Oct. 1951; *er s* of 8th Viscount Gort and of Bettine Mary Mackenzie, *d* of Godfrey Greene; *S* father, 1995; *m* 1st, 1979, Julie Denise Jones (marr. diss. 1984); 2nd, 1991, Sharon Quayle; one *s*. *Educ:* Harrow. *Recreation:* golf. *Heir: s* Robert Foley Prendergast Vereker, *b* 5 April 1993. *Address:* The Coach House, Arbory Street, Castletown, Isle of Man. *T:* Castletown (01624) 822295.

GORTON, Rt. Hon. Sir John (Grey), PC 1968; GCMG 1977; AC 1988; CH 1971; MA; retired; *b* 9 Sept. 1911; *m* 1st, 1935, Bettina (decd), *d* of G. Brown, Bangor, Me, USA; two *s* one *d*; 2nd, 1993, Nancy, *widow* of John Hume. *Educ:* Geelong Gram. Sch.; Brasenose Coll., Oxford (MA, Hon. Fellow, 1968). Orchardist. Enlisted RAAF, Nov. 1940; served in UK, Singapore, Darwin, Milne Bay; severely wounded in air ops; discharged with rank of Flt-Lt, Dec. 1944. Councillor, Kerang Shire, 1947–52 (Pres. of Shire); Mem., Lodden Valley Regional Cttee. Senator for State of Victoria, Parlt of Commonwealth of Australia, 1949–68 (Govt Leader in Senate, 1967–68); Minister for Navy, 1958–63; Minister Assisting the Minister for External Affairs, 1960–63 (Actg Minister during periods of absence overseas of Minister); Minister in Charge of CSIRO, 1962–68; Minister for Works and, under Prime Minister, Minister in Charge of Commonwealth Activities in Educn and Research, 1963–66; Minister for Interior, 1963–64; Minister for Works, 1966–67; Minister for Educn and Science, 1966–68; MHR (L) for Higgins, Vic, 1968–75; Prime Minister of Australia, 1968–71; Minister for Defence, and Dep. Leader of Liberal Party, March-Aug. 1971; Mem. Parly Liberal Party Exec., and Liberal Party Spokesman on Environment and Conservation and Urban and Regional Develt, 1973–75; Dep. Chm., Jt Parly Cttee on Prices, 1973–75. Contested Senate election (Ind.), ACT, Dec. 1975. *Address:* 32 Parsley Road, Vaucluse, NSW 2030, Australia.

GORTVAI, Dame Rosalinde; *see* Hurley, Dame R.

GOSCHEN, family name of **Viscount Goschen**.

GOSCHEN, 4th Viscount *cr* 1900; **Giles John Harry Goschen;** Parliamentary Under-Secretary of State, Department of Transport, since 1994; *b* 16 Nov. 1965; *s* of 3rd Viscount Goschen, KBE, and of Alvin Moyanna Lesley, *yr d* of late Harry England, Durban, Natal; *S* father, 1977; *m* 1991, Sarah Penelope, *d* of late Alan Horsnail. *Educ:* Eton. A Lord in Waiting (Govt Whip), 1992–94. *Address:* Hilton House, Crowthorne, Berks RG11 6AH.

GOSCHEN, Sir Edward (Christian), 3rd Bt, *cr* 1916; DSO 1944; Rifle Brigade; *b* 2 Sept. 1913; *er s* of Sir Edward Henry Goschen, 2nd Bt, and Countess Mary, 7th *d* of Count Danneskiold Samsoe, Denmark; *S* father, 1933; *m* 1946, Cynthia, *d* of late Rt Hon. Sir Alexander Cadogan, PC, OM, GCMG, KCB and Lady Theodosia Cadogan; one *s* one *d*. *Educ:* Eton; Trinity Coll., Oxford. Mem., Stock Exchange Council (Dep. Chm., 1968–71). Commonwealth War Graves Commn, 1977–86. *Heir: s* Edward Alexander Goschen [*b* 13 March 1949; *m* 1976, Louise Annette, *d* of Lt-Col R. F. L. Chance, MC, and Lady Ava Chance; one *d*]. *Address:* Lower Farm House, Hampstead Norreys, Newbury, Berks RG16 0SG. *T:* Hermitage (01635) 201270.

GOSFORD, 7th Earl of, *cr* 1806; **Charles David Nicholas Alexander John Sparrow Acheson;** Bt (NS) 1628; Baron Gosford 1776; Viscount Gosford 1785; Baron Worlingham (UK) 1835; Baron Acheson (UK) 1847; *b* 13 July 1942; *o s* of 6th Earl of Gosford, OBE, and Francesca Augusta, *er d* of Francesco Cagiati, New York; *S* father, 1966; *m* 1983, Lynnette Redmond. *Educ:* Harrow; Byam Shaw Sch. of drawing and painting; Royal Academy Schs. Chm., Artists Union, 1976–80; Mem. Visual Arts Panel, Greater London Arts Assoc., 1976–77; Council Member, British Copyright Council, 1977–80. Represented by: Barry Stern Gall., Sydney; Phillip Bacon Galls, Brisbane; Solander Gall., Canberra; Von Bertouch Gall., Newcastle, NSW. *Heir: u* Hon. Patrick Bernard Victor Montagu Acheson [*b* 4 Feb. 1915; *m* 1946, Judith, *d* of Mrs F. B. Bate, Virginia, USA; three *s* two *d*]. *Address:* c/o House of Lords, SW1A 0PW.

GOSKIRK, (William) Ian (Macdonald), CBE 1986; Partner, Coopers & Lybrand Deloitte, 1990–92; *b* 2 March 1932; *s* of William Goskirk and Flora Macdonald; *m* 1969, Hope Ann Knaizuk; one *d*. *Educ:* Carlisle Grammar Sch.; Queen's Coll., Oxford (MA). Served REME, 1950–52. Shell Internat. Petroleum, 1956–74; Anschutz Corp., 1974–76; BNOC, 1976–85; Man. Dir, BNOC Trading, 1980–82; Chief Exec., BNOC, 1982–85; Dir, Coopers & Lybrand Associates, 1986–90. *Recreation:* gardening. *Address:* c/o 107 Pall Mall, SW1Y 5ER. *Club:* Athenæum.

GOSLING, Allan Gladstone; Sales Director, PSA Projects, Property Services Agency, Department of the Environment, 1991–92, retired (Operational Director, 1990–91); Consultant to TBV Consult, since 1992; *b* 4 July 1933; *s* of late Gladstone Gosling and of Elizabeth Gosling (*née* Ward); *m* 1961, Janet Pamela (*née* Gosling); one *s* one *d*. *Educ:* Kirkham Grammar Sch.; Birmingham Sch. of Architecture. DipArch; RIBA 1961; FRIAS 1988 (RIAS 1984); FFB 1991. Asst Architect, Lancs County Council, 1950–54; Birmingham Sch. of Architecture, 1954–57; Surman Kelly Surman, Architects, 1957–59; Royal Artillery, 1959–61; Army Works Organisation, 1961–63; Min. of Housing R&D Group, 1963–68; Suptg Architect, Birmingham Regional Office, Min. of Housing, 1968–72; Regional Works Officer, NW Region, PSA, 1972–76; Midland Regional Dir, PSA, 1976–83; Dir, Scottish Services, PSA, 1983–90. *Recreations:* walking, gardening, DIY. *Address:* 11 The Moorlands, Four Oaks Park, Sutton Coldfield, West Midlands B74 2RF.

GOSLING, Sir Donald, Kt 1976; Joint Chairman, National Car Parks Ltd, since 1950; Chairman, Palmer & Harvey Ltd, since 1967; *b* 2 March 1929; *m* 1959, Elizabeth Shauna (marr. diss. 1988), *d* of Dr Peter Ingram and Lecky Ingram; three *s*. Joined RN, 1944; served Mediterranean, HMS Leander. Mem., Council of Management, White Ensign Assoc. Ltd, 1970– (Chm., 1978–83; Vice Pres., 1983–93; Pres., 1993–); Mem., Exec. Cttee, Imperial Soc. of Kts Bachelor, 1977–. Chm., Berkeley Square Ball Trust, 1982–; Trustee: Fleet Air Arm Museum, Yeovilton, 1974– (Chm., Mountbatten Meml Hall Appeals Cttee, 1980); RYA Seamanship Foundn, 1981–; Vice Pres., King George's Fund for Sailors, 1993–; Patron: Submarine Meml Appeal, 1978–; HMS Ark Royal Welfare Trust, 1986–. Hon. Capt., RNR, 1993–. *Recreations:* swimming, sailing, shooting. *Address:* National Car Parks Ltd, PO Box 4N1, 21 Bryanston Street, Marble Arch, W1A 4NH. *T:* 0171–499 7050. *Clubs:* Royal Thames Yacht, Royal London Yacht, Royal Naval Sailing Association, Thames Sailing; Saints and Sinners.

GOSLING, Justin Cyril Bertrand; Principal, St Edmund Hall, Oxford, since 1982; *b* 26 April 1930; *s* of Vincent and Dorothy Gosling; *m* 1958, Margaret Clayton; two *s* two *d*. *Educ:* Ampleforth Coll.; Wadham Coll., Oxford (BPhil, MA). Univ. of Oxford: Fereday Fellow, St John's Coll., 1955–58; Lectr in Philosophy, Pembroke Coll. and Wadham Coll., 1958–60; Fellow in Philosophy, St Edmund Hall, 1960–82; Sen. Proctor, 1977–78. Barclay Acheson Prof., Macalester Coll., Minnesota, 1964; Vis. Res. Fellow, ANU, Canberra, 1970 (Pro-Vice-Chancellor, 1989–90, 1991–). *Publications:* Pleasure and Desire, 1969; Plato, 1973; (ed) Plato, Philebus, 1975; (with C. C. W. Taylor) The Greeks on Pleasure, 1982; Weakness of the Will, 1990; articles in Mind, Phil Rev. and Proc. Aristotelian Soc. *Recreations:* gardening, intaglio printing, recorder music. *Address:* St Edmund Hall, Oxford OX1 4AR. *T:* Oxford (01865) 279000.

GOSLING, Prof. Leonard Morris, PhD; CBiol, FIBiol; Director of Science, Zoological Society of London and Director, Institute of Zoology, since 1993; *b* 22 Jan. 1943; *s* of William Richard Gosling and Marian (*née* Morris); *m* 1977, Dr Marion Petrie; two *d*. *Educ:* Wymondham Coll., Norfolk; Queen Mary Coll., London (BSc Zool. 1965); University Coll., Nairobi (PhD 1975). CBiol, FIBiol 1989. Ministry of Agriculture, Fisheries and Food: SSO, Coypu Res. Lab., 1970–73; PSO, Mammal Ecology Gp, 1974–85; SPSO, Central Science Lab., 1986–93. Hon. Lectr, UEA, 1978–81; Vis. Prof., UCL, 1994–. Member, Council: Mammal Soc., 1982–85; Assoc. for Study of Animal Behaviour, 1988–90 (Sec., Ethical Cttee, 1991–94); Royal Vet. Coll., 1994–; Mem., Mgt Cttee, UCL Centre for Ecology and Evolution, 1995–. *Publications:* (ed with M. Dawkins) Ethics in Research on Animal Behaviour, 1992; numerous articles in learned jls and books on population biol. and behavioural ecology. *Recreations:* drawing, ditching, formerly Rugby. *Address:* Institute of Zoology, Zoological Society of London, Regent's Park, NW1 4RY. *T:* 0171–722 4713.

GOSLING, Col Richard Bennett, OBE 1957; TD 1947; DL; *b* 4 Oct. 1914; 2nd *s* of late T. S. Gosling, Dynes Hall, Halstead; *m* 1st, 1950, Marie Terese Ronayne (*d* 1976), Castle Redmond, Co. Cork; one adopted *s* one adopted *d* (one *s* decd); 2nd, 1978, Sybilla Burgers van Oyen, *widow* of Bernard Burgers, 't Kasteel, Nijmegen. *Educ:* Eton; Magdalene Coll., Cambridge (MA). CEng. Served with Essex Yeomanry, RHA, 1939–45; CO, 1953–56; Dep. CRA, East Anglian Div., 1956–58. Dir-Gen., British Agricl Export Council, 1971–73. Chairman: Constructors, 1965–68; Hearne & Co., 1971–82. Director: P-E International, 1956–76; Doulton & Co., 1962–72; Revertex Chemicals, 1974–81; Press Mouldings, 1977–92. DL 1954, High Sheriff 1982, Essex. DUniv Essex, 1993. French Croix de Guerre, 1944. *Recreation:* country pursuits. *Address:* Canterburys Lodge, Margaretting, Essex CM4 0EE. *T:* Ingatestone (01277) 353073. *Clubs:* Naval and Military, MCC; Beefsteak (Chelmsford).

GOSS, Prof. Richard Oliver, PhD; Distinguished Research Professor, University of Wales College of Cardiff, 1995; *b* 4 Oct. 1929; *s* of late Leonard Arthur Goss and Hilda Nellie Goss (*née* Casson); *m* 1st, Lesley Elizabeth Thurbon (marr. diss. 1983); two *s* one *d*; 2nd, 1994, Gillian Mary (*née* Page). *Educ:* Christ's Coll., Finchley; HMS Worcester; King's Coll., Cambridge. Master Mariner 1956; BA 1958; MA 1961; PhD 1979. FCIT 1970; MNI (Founder) 1972; FNI 1977; FRSA 1993. Merchant Navy (apprentice and executive officer), 1947–55; NZ Shipping Co. Ltd, 1958–63; Economic Consultant (Shipping, Shipbuilding and Ports), MoT, 1963–64; Econ. Adviser, BoT (Shipping), 1964–67; Sen. Econ. Adviser (Shipping, Civil Aviation, etc), 1967–74; Econ. Adviser to Cttee of Inquiry into Shipping (Rochdale Cttee), 1967–70; Under-Sec., Depts of Industry and Trade, 1974–80; Prof., Dept of Maritime Studies, UWIST, subseq. Univ. of Wales Coll. of Cardiff, 1980–95. Nuffield/Leverhulme Travelling Fellow, 1977–78. Governor, Plymouth Polytechnic, 1973–84; Mem. Council: RINA, 1969–; Nautical Inst. (from foundn until 1976); Member: CNAA Nautical Studies Bd, 1971–81; CNAA Transport Bd, 1976–78. Pres. (first), Internat. Assoc. of Maritime Economists, 1992–94. Editor and Editor-in-Chief, Maritime Policy and Management, 1985–93. Premio Internazionale delle Comunicazioni Cristoforo Colombo, Genoa, 1991. *Publications:* Studies in Maritime Economics, 1968; (with C. D. Jones) The Economies of Size in Dry Bulk Carriers, 1971; (with M. C. Mann, et al) The Cost of Ships' Time, 1974; Advances in Maritime Economics, 1977; A Comparative Study of Seaport Management and Administration, 1979; Policies for Canadian Seaports, 1984; Port Authorities in Australia, 1987; Collected Papers, 1990; numerous papers in various jls, transactions and to conferences. *Recreations:* cruising inland waterways, local history, travel. *Address:* 1 Weir Gardens, Bridge Street, Pershore, Worcs WR10 1AJ. *T:* Pershore (01386) 561153.

GOSS, Very Rev. Thomas Ashworth; Dean of Jersey, Rector of St Helier, and Hon. Canon of Winchester, 1971–85; *b* 27 July 1912; *s* of George Woolnough Goss and Maud M. (*née* Savage); *m* 1946, Frances Violet Patience Frampton (*d* 1991); one *s* one *d*. *Educ:* Shardlow Hall; Aldenham Sch.; St Andrews Univ. (MA). Deacon, 1937; Priest, 1938; Curate of Frodingham, 1937–41. Chaplain, RAFVR, 1941–47 (PoW Japan, 1942–45). Vicar of Sutton-le-Marsh, 1947–51; Chaplain, RAF, 1951–67; QHC, 1966–67. Rector of St Saviour, Jersey, 1967–71. Canon Emeritus, Winchester, 1985–. *Recreations:* gardening, theatricals. *Address:* Les Pignons, Mont de la Rosière, St Saviour, Jersey JE2 7WD. *Clubs:* Royal Air Force; Victoria (Jersey).

GOSS, Hon. Wayne Keith, MLA; Premier of Queensland, and Minister for Economic and Trade Development, since 1989; *b* 26 Feb. 1951; *s* of Allan James Goss and Norma Josephine Goss; *m* 1981, Roisin Anne Hirschfeld; one *s* one *d*. *Educ:* Univ. of Queensland (LLB). Admitted solicitor, 1973; Partner, Goss and Downey, 1977. MLA (ALP) Logan,

1983–; Opposition Minister for Lands, Forestry and Police, 1983–86, for Justice, 1986–88; Leader of Opposition, 1988–89; Minister for the Arts, 1989–92. *Address:* Premier's Office, 15th Floor, Executive Building, 100 George Street, Brisbane, Qld 4000, Australia.

GOSSCHALK, Joseph Bernard; His Honour Judge Gosschalk; a Circuit Judge, since 1991; *b* 27 Aug. 1936; *s* of late Lionel Samuel Gosschalk and of Johanna (*née* Lion); *m* 1973, Ruth Sandra Jarvis; two *d. Educ:* East Ham Grammar Sch.; Magdalen Coll., Oxford (MA Jurisprudence). Called to the Bar, Gray's Inn, 1961; Asst Recorder, 1983–87; Head of Chambers, Francis Taylor Bldg, Temple, EC4, 1983–91; a Recorder, SE Circuit, 1987–91. *Recreations:* theatre, tennis, foreign travel. *Address:* The Crown Court, Bricket Road, St Albans, Herts AL1 3LB. *T:* St Albans (01727) 834481.

GOSTIN, Larry, DJur; Professor of Law, Georgetown University Law Center, since 1994; Professor of Health Policy, Johns Hopkins School of Hygiene and Public Health, since 1994; Associate Director, Harvard University/World Health Organization Collaborating Center on Health Legislation, since 1988; *b* 19 Oct. 1949; *s* of Joseph and Sylvia Gostin; *m* 1977, Jean Catherine Allison; two *s. Educ:* State Univ. of New York, Brockport (BA Psychology); Duke Univ. (DJur 1974). Dir of Forensics and Debate, Duke Univ., 1973–74; Fulbright Fellow, Social Res. Unit, Univ. of London, 1974–75; Legal Dir, MIND (Nat. Assoc. for Mental Health), 1975–83; Gen. Sec., NCCL, 1983–85; Harvard University: Sen. Fellow of Health Law, 1985–86; Lectr, 1986–87; Adjunct Prof. in Health Law, Sch. of Public Health, 1988–94; Exec. Dir, Amer. Soc. of Law and Medicine, 1986–94. Legal Counsel in series of cases before Eur. Commn and Eur. Court of Human Rights, 1974–. Vis. Prof., Sch. of Social Policy, McMaster Univ., 1978–79; Vis. Fellow in Law and Psychiatry, Centre for Criminological Res., Oxford Univ., 1982–83. Chm., Advocacy Alliance, 1981–83; Member: National Cttee, UN Internat. Year for Disabled People, 1981; Legal Affairs Cttee, Internat. League of Socs for Mentally Handicapped People, 1980–; Cttee of Experts, Internat. Commn of Jurists to draft UN Human Rights Declarations, 1982–; Adv. Council, Interights, 1984–; AE Trust, 1984–85; WHO Expert Cttee on Guidelines on the Treatment of Drug and Alcohol Dependent Persons, 1985; WHO Steering Cttee, Internat. Ethical Guidelines for Human Population Res., 1990–; Nat. Bd of Dirs, Amer. Civil Liberties Union, 1986– (Mem. Exec. Cttee, 1988–). Western European and UK Editor, Internat. Jl of Law and Psychiatry, 1978–81; Exec. Ed., Amer. Jl of Law and Medicine, 1986–; Ed.-in-chief, Jl of Law, Medicine and Health Care, 1986–. Hon. LLD SUNY, 1994. Rosemary Delbridge Meml Award for most outstanding contribution to social policy, 1983. *Publications:* A Human Condition: vol. 1, 1975; vol. 2, 1977; A Practical Guide to Mental Health Law, 1983; The Court of Protection, 1983; (ed) Secure Provision: a review of special services for mentally ill and handicapped people in England and Wales, 1985; Mental Health Services: law and practice, 1986; Human Rights in Mental Health: an international report for the World Federation for Mental Health, 1988; Civil Liberties in Conflict, 1988; Surrogate Motherhood: politics and privacy, 1990; AIDS and the Health Care System, 1990; Implementing the Americans with Disabilities Act: rights and responsibilities of all Americans, 1993; articles in learned jls. *Recreations:* family outings, walking on the mountains and fells of the Lake District. *Address:* Georgetown University Law Center, 600 New Jersey Avenue NW, Washington, DC 20001–2022, USA. *T:* (202) 6629373.

GOSWELL, Sir Brian (Lawrence), Kt 1991; FSVA; Deputy Senior Partner, Healey & Baker, Surveyors, since 1988; *b* 26 Nov. 1935; *s* of late Albert George Goswell and Florence Emily (*née* Barnett); *m* 1961, Deirdre Gillian Stones; two *s.* FSVA 1968; ACIArb 1980. Mil. service, Oxford and Bucks Light Infantry, 1954–57. Joined Healey & Baker, Surveyors, 1957; Partner, 1968; Managing Partner, 1975. Chairman: Healey & Baker Inc., New York, 1976–; Roux Restaurants Ltd, 1988–; Sunley Secure PLC, 1993–; Director: Brent Walker Group PLC, 1993–; New Law Publishing Co. PLC, 1993–; Mem., Adv. Bd, Sir Alexander Gibb & Partners, 1989–. Pres., Amer. Chamber of Commerce in London, 1994– (Dir, 1990). FRSA 1993. *Recreations:* cricket, horse-racing, shooting. *Address:* 27 Austin Friars, EC2N 2AA. *T:* 0171–628 4361. *Clubs:* Carlton, Turf, City of London, City Livery, MCC.

GOTT, Haydn; a Metropolitan Stipendiary Magistrate, since 1992; *b* 29 April 1946; *s* of Alan Gott and Delia Mary Gott (*née* Pugh); *m* 1975, Brigid Mary Kane; one *s* one *d. Educ:* Manchester Grammar Sch.; Oxford Univ. (MA). Admitted solicitor, 1972; Partner, Alexander & Partners, solicitors, 1975–92. Legal Mem., Mental Health Review Tribunal, 1986–. *Recreations:* sport, music. *Address:* Camberwell Magistrates' Court, SE5 7UP. *T:* 0171–703 0909. *Club:* Ronnie Scott's.

GOTT, Richard Willoughby; journalist; Literary Editor, The Guardian, 1992–94; *b* 28 Oct. 1938; *s* of Arthur Gott and Mary Moon; *m* 1st, 1966, Ann Zammit (marr. diss. 1981); one adopted *s* one adopted *d*; 2nd, 1985, Vivien Ashley. *Educ:* Winchester Coll.; Corpus Christi Coll., Oxford (MA). Res. Asst, RIIA, 1962–65; Leader Writer, Guardian, 1964–66; Res. Fellow, Inst. de Estudios Internacionales, Univ. of Chile, 1966–69; Foreign Editor, Tanzanian Standard, Dar es Salaam, 1970–71; Third World corresp., New Statesman, 1971–72; The Guardian: Latin American corresp., 1972–76; Foreign News Editor, 1977–78; Features Editor, 1978–89; Asst Editor, 1988–94. Editor, Pelican Latin American Library, 1969–78; Dir, Latin American Newsletters, 1973–79. Contested (Ind.) North Hull, byelection 1966. *Publications:* The Appeasers (with Martin Gilbert), 1963; Guerrilla Movements in Latin America, 1970; Land Without Evil: Utopian journeys across the South American watershed, 1993. *Recreation:* travelling. *Address:* 88 Ledbury Road, W11 2AH. *T:* 0171–229 5467.

GOTTLIEB, Bernard, CB 1970; retired; *b* 1913; *s* of late James Gottlieb and Pauline (*née* Littaur); *m* 1955, Sybil N. Epstein; one *s* one *d. Educ:* Haberdashers' Hampstead Sch.; Queen Mary Coll., London Univ. BSc First Class Maths, 1932. Entered Civil Service as an Executive Officer in Customs and Excise, 1932. Air Ministry, 1938; Asst Private Sec., 1941, and Private Sec., 1944, to Permanent Under-Sec. of State (late Sir Arthur Street), Control Office for Germany and Austria, 1945; Asst Sec., 1946. Seconded to National Coal Board, 1946; Min. of Power, 1950; Under-Sec., 1961, Dir of Establishments, 1965–69; Under-Sec., Min. of Posts and Telecommunications, 1969–73; Secretariat, Pay Board, 1973–74, Royal Commn for Distribution of Income and Wealth, 1974–78; research with Incomes Data Services, 1978–90. Gwilym Gibbon Research Fellow, Nuffield Coll., Oxford, 1952–53. *Address:* 49 Gresham Gardens, NW11 8PA. *T:* 0181–455 6172. *Club:* Reform.

GOTTLIEB, Robert Adams; Editor-in-Chief, The New Yorker, 1987–92; *b* 29 April 1931; *s* of Charles and Martha Gottlieb; *m* 1st, 1952, Muriel Higgins (marr. diss. 1965); one *s*; 2nd, 1969, Maria Tucci; one *s* one *d. Educ:* Columbia Coll., NY; Cambridge Univ. Simon & Schuster, publishers, 1955–68 (final positions, Editor-in-Chief and Vice-Pres.); Pres. and Editor-in-Chief, Alfred A. Knopf, publishers, 1968–87. *Recreations:* ballet, classic film, shopping.

GOUDIE, Prof. Andrew Shaw; Professor of Geography, University of Oxford, since 1984; Fellow of Hertford College, Oxford, since 1976; *b* 21 Aug. 1945; *s* of late William and Mary Goudie; *m* 1987, Heather (*née* Viles); two *d. Educ:* Dean Close Sch., Cheltenham; Trinity Hall, Cambridge. BA, PhD Cantab; MA Oxon. Oxford University: Departmental Demonstrator, 1970–76; Univ. Lectr, 1976–84; Head, Dept of Geography, 1984–94; Pro-Vice-Chancellor and Head of Develt Prog., 1995–. Hon. Secretary: British Geomorphological Res. Gp, 1977–80 (Chm., 1988–89); RGS, 1981–88; Member: Council, Inst. of British Geographers, 1980–83; British Nat. Cttee for Geography, 1982–87. Dep. Leader: Internat. Karakoram Project, 1980; Kora Project, 1983. President: Geographical Assoc., 1993–94; Section E, BAAS, 1995–96. Cuthbert Peek award, RGS, 1975; Geographic Soc. of Chicago Publication award, 1982; Founder's Medal, RGS, 1991; Mungo Park Medal, RSGS, 1991. *Publications:* Duricrusts of Tropical and Sub-tropical Landscapes, 1973; Environmental Change, 1976, 3rd edn 1992; The Warm Desert Environment, 1977; The Prehistory and Palaeogeography of the Great Indian Desert, 1978; Desert Geomorphology, 1980; The Human Impact, 1981, 4th edn 1993; Geomorphological Techniques, 1981, 3rd edn 1990; The Atlas of Swaziland, 1983; Chemical Sediments and Geomorphology, 1983; The Nature of the Environment, 1984, 3rd edn 1993; (jtly) Discovering Landscape in England and Wales, 1985; The Encyclopædic Dictionary of Physical Geography, 1985, 2nd edn 1994; (jtly) Landshapes, 1989; The Geomorphology of England and Wales, 1990; Techniques for Desert Reclamation, 1990; contribs to learned jls. *Recreations:* bush life, old records, old books. *Address:* Hertford College, Oxford OX1 3BW. *T:* Oxford (01865) 271921. *Clubs:* Geographical; Gilbert (Oxford).

See also T. J. C. Goudie.

GOUDIE, James; *see* Goudie, T. J. C.

GOUDIE, Rev. John Carrick, CBE 1972; Assistant Minister at St John's United Reformed Church, Northwood, 1985–88, retired; *b* 25 Dec. 1919; *s* of late Rev. John Goudie, MA and late Mrs Janet Goudie, step *s* of late Mrs Evelyn Goudie; unmarried. *Educ:* Glasgow Academy; Glasgow Univ. (MA); Trinity Coll., Glasgow. Served in RN: Hostilities Only Ordinary Seaman and later Lieut RNVR, 1941–45; returned to Trinity Coll., Glasgow to complete studies for the Ministry, 1945; Asst Minister at Crown Court Church of Scotland, London and ordained, 1947–50; Minister, The Union Church, Greenock, 1950–53; entered RN as Chaplain, 1953; Principal Chaplain, Church of Scotland and Free Churches (Naval), 1970–73; on staff of St Columba's Church of Scotland, Pont Street, 1973–77; Minister of Christ Church URC, Wallington, 1977–80; on staff of Royal Scottish Corp., London, 1980–84. QHC 1970–73. *Recreations:* tennis, the theatre. *Address:* 309 Howard House, Dolphin Square, SW1V 3PF. *T:* 0171–798 8537. *Club:* Army and Navy.

GOUDIE, (Thomas) James (Cooper), QC 1984; a Recorder, since 1986; *b* 2 June 1942; *s* of late William Cooper Goudie and Mary Isobel Goudie; *m* 1969, Mary Teresa Brick; two *s. Educ:* Dean Close Sch.; London School of Economics (LLB Hons). FCIArb 1991. Solicitor, 1966–70; called to the Bar, Inner Temple, 1970 (Bencher, 1991). Chairman: Law Reform Cttee, Gen. Council of the Bar, 1995–; Administrative Law Bar Assoc., 1994–; Soc. of Labour Lawyers, 1994–. Contested (Lab) Brent North, General Elections, Feb. and Oct. 1974; Leader of Brent Council, 1977–78. *Publication:* (ed jtly and contrib.) Judicial Review, 1992. *Address:* 11 King's Bench Walk, Temple, EC4Y 7EQ. *T:* 0171–583 0610.

See also A. S. Goudie.

GOUDIE, Hon. William Henry, MC 1944; Executive Director and Deputy Chairman, Law Reform Commission of Tasmania, 1974–81; *b* 21 Aug. 1916; *s* of Henry and Florence Goudie; *m* 1948, Mourilyan Isobel Munro (*d* 1981); two *s. Educ:* Bristol Grammar School. Solicitor (England), 1938; called to Bar, Gray's Inn, 1952. War service, 1939–45, London Scottish Regt and Som LI; JAG's Dept, 1945–48; Prosecutor, Dep. JA, Officer i/c branches Italy, Greece, Austria; Officer i/c Legal Section War Crimes Gp, SE Europe; Sen. Resident Magistrate, Acting Judge, Kenya, 1948–63; Puisne Judge, Aden, 1963–66; Puisne Judge, Uganda (Contract), 1967–71; Puisne Judge, Fiji (Contract), 1971–73. Editor, Kenya and Aden Law Reports. *Address:* 24 Nimala Street, Rosny, Hobart, Tasmania 7018, Australia.

GOUGH, family name of **Viscount Gough.**

GOUGH, 5th Viscount (of Goojerat, of the Punjaub, and Limerick), *cr* 1849; **Shane Hugh Maryon Gough;** Irish Guards, 1961–67; *b* 26 Aug. 1941; *o s* of 4th Viscount Gough and Margaretta Elizabeth (*d* 1977), *o d* of Sir Spencer Maryon-Wilson, 11th Bt; *S* father 1951. *Educ:* Abberley Hall, Worcs; Winchester Coll. Mem. Queen's Bodyguard for Scotland, Royal Company of Archers. *Heir:* none. *Address:* Keppoch Estate Office, Strathpeffer, Ross-shire IV14 9AD. *T:* Strathpeffer (01997) 224; 17 Stanhope Gardens, SW7 5RQ. *Clubs:* Pratt's, White's; MCC.

GOUGH, Brandon; *see* Gough, C. B.

GOUGH, Cecil Ernest Freeman, CMG 1956; Director and Secretary, 1974–78, Assistant Director-General, 1978–80, acting Director-General, 1980–81, British Property Federation; *b* 29 Oct. 1911; *s* of Ernest John Gough; *m* 1938, Gwendolen Lily Miriam Longman; one *s* one *d. Educ:* Southend High Sch.; London Sch. of Economics (School of Economics Scholar in Law, 1932). LLB (Hons) 1934. Asst Examiner Estate Duty Office, Board of Inland Revenue, 1930; Air Ministry, 1938; Principal, 1944; Ministry of Defence, 1947; Asst Sec., 1949; on loan to Foreign Office, as Counsellor, United Kingdom Delegation to NATO, Paris, 1952–56; Chm., NATO Infrastructure Cttee, 1952–53; First Chm., Standing Armaments Cttee, Western European Union, 1955; returned Ministry of Defence, 1956; Under-Sec., 1958; Under-Sec. at the Admiralty, 1962–64; Asst Under-Sec. of State, Min. of Defence, 1964–68. Man. Dir, Airwork (Overseas) Ltd, 1968–71; Dir, Airwork Services Ltd and Air Holdings Ltd, 1968–73; Sec., Associated Owners of City Properties, 1975–77. Medal of Freedom (USAF), 1946; Coronation Medal, 1953. *Recreations:* cookery, reading, travel. *Address:* 23 Howbridge Road, Witham, Essex CM8 1BY. *T:* Witham (01376) 518969. *Clubs:* Naval and Military, Civil Service.

GOUGH, (Charles) Brandon, FCA; Chairman, Higher Education Funding Council for England, since 1993; *b* 8 Oct. 1937; *s* of late Charles Richard Gough and of Mary Evaline (*née* Goff); *m* 1961, Sarah Smith; one *s* two *d. Educ:* Douai Sch.; Jesus Coll., Cambridge (MA). FCA 1974. Joined Cooper Brothers & Co. subseq. Coopers & Lybrand, 1964, Partner 1968; Chm., 1983–94; Mem., Exec. Cttee, Coopers & Lybrand (Internat.), 1982–94 (Chm., 1985 and 1991–92); Chm., Coopers & Lybrand Europe, 1989, and 1992–94. Govt Dir, BAe plc, 1987–88; Director: British Invisibles, 1990–94; De La Rue plc, 1994–; S. G. Warburg Gp, 1994–95 (Dep. Chm., 1995); National Power, 1995–. Mem. Council, Inst. of Chartered Accountants in England and Wales, 1981–84; Chm., CCAB Auditing Practices Cttee, 1981–84 (Mem., 1976–84); Member: Accounting Standards Review (Dearing) Cttee, 1987–88; Financial Reporting Council, 1990–. City University Business School: Chm., City Adv. Panel, 1986–91 (Mem., 1980–91); Mem. Council, 1986–93 (Chm., 1992–93); Chm., Finance Cttee, 1988–91; Member: Council of Lloyd's, 1983–86; Cambridge Univ. Careers Service Syndicate, 1983–86; Governing Council, 1984–88, Council, 1988–94, President's Cttee, 1992–, Business in the Community; Council for Industry and Higher Educn, 1985–94; Management Council, GB–Sasakawa Foundn, 1985–; UK Nat. Cttee, Japan-European Community Assoc., 1989–94; CBI Task Force, Vocational Educn and Trng, 1989; CBI Educn & Trng Affairs

Cttee, 1990–94; Council, Foundn for Educn Business Partnerships, 1990–91; Council, City Univ., 1991–93; Council, Prince of Wales Business Leaders Forum of Internat. Business in the Community, 1992–94; Exec. Cttee, Westminster Cathedral 1995 Centenary Trust, 1994–. Chairman: Common Purpose Trust, 1991– (Trustee, 1989–); Nat. Trng Task Force working gp on role of TECs in local econ. develt, 1991–92; Doctors' and Dentists' Pay Review Body, 1993–. Mem., Council of Management, Royal Shakespeare Theatre Trust, 1991–; Trustee, GSMD Foundn, 1990–. CIMgt (CBIM 1985); FRSA 1988. Hon. DSc City, 1994. Lloyd's Silver Medal, 1986. *Recreations:* music, gardening. *Address:* Long Barn, Weald, Sevenoaks, Kent TN14 6NH. *T:* Sevenoaks (01732) 463714.

GOUGH, Prof. Douglas Owen, PhD; Professor of Theoretical Astrophysics, University of Cambridge, since 1993; Fellow, Churchill College, Cambridge, since 1972; *b* 8 Feb. 1941; *s* of Owen Albert John Gough and Doris May Gough (*née* Camera); *m* 1965, Rosanne Penelope Shaw; two *s* two *d. Educ:* Hackney Downs Sch.; St John's Coll., Cambridge (BA 1962; MA 1966; PhD 1966). Res. Associate, Jt Inst. for Lab. Astrophysics, Univ. of Colo, 1966–67; Nat. Acad. of Scis Sen. Postdoctoral Resident Res. Associate, Inst. for Space Studies, NY, 1967–69; University of Cambridge: Mem., Grad. Staff, Inst. of Theoretical Astronomy, 1969–73; Lectr in Astronomy and Applied Maths, 1973–85; Reader in Astrophysics, 1985–93. Astronome Titulaire Associé des Observatoires de France, 1977; SRC Sen. Fellow, 1978–83; Prof. Associé, Univ. of Toulouse, 1984–85; Hon. Prof. of Astronomy, QMW, Univ. of London, 1986–; Fellow Adjoint, Jt Inst. for Lab. Astrophysics, Boulder, Colo, 1986–; Scientific Co-ordinator, Inst. for Theoretical Physics, Univ. of Calif, Santa Barbara, 1990. Lectures: James Arthur, Harvard, 1982; Sir Joseph Larmor, Cambridge Philosophical Soc., 1988; Wernher von Braun, Marshall Space Flight Center, 1991; Morris Loeb, Harvard, 1993. William Hopkins Prize, Cambridge Philosophical Soc., 1984; George Ellery Hale Prize, Amer. Astronomical Soc., 1994. *Publications:* mainly res. papers and reviews in scientific jls. *Recreations:* cooking, listening to music. *Address:* Institute of Astronomy, Madingley Road, Cambridge CB3 0HA. *T:* Cambridge (01223) 337548.

GOUGH, Rt. Rev. Hugh Rowlands, CMG 1965; OBE (mil.) 1945; TD 1950; DD Lambeth; Archbishop of Sydney and Primate of Australia, also Metropolitan of New South Wales, 1959–66; retired; *b* 19 Sept. 1905; *o s* of late Rev. Charles Massey Gough, Rector of St Ebbe's, Oxford; *m* 1929, Hon. Madeline Elizabeth, *d* of 12th Baron Kinnaird, KT, KBE; one *d. Educ:* Weymouth Coll.; Trinity Coll., Cambridge; London Coll. Divinity. BA 1927, MA Cantab 1931. Deacon, 1928; Priest, 1929; Curate of St Mary, Islington, 1928–31; Perpetual Curate of St Paul, Walcot, Bath, 1931–34; Vicar of St James, Carlisle, 1934–39; Chaplain to High Sheriff of Cumberland, 1937; CF (TA), 1937–45; Chaplain to 4th Bn The Border Regt, 1937–39; Vicar of St Matthew, Bayswater 1939–46; Chaplain to 1st Bn London Rifle Bde, 1939–43; served Western Desert and Tunisia (wounded); Senior Chap. to 1st Armd Div., Tunisia, 1943; DACG 10 Corps, Italy, 1943–45 (despatches); DACG, North Midland Dist, 1945. Hon. Chaplain to the Forces (2nd cl.) 1945. Vicar of Islington, Rural Dean of Islington, 1946–48. Preb. St Paul's Cathedral, 1948; Suffragan Bishop of Barking, 1948–59; Archdeacon of West Ham, 1948–58; Rector of Freshford, dio. of Bath and Wells, 1967–72; Vicar of Limpley Stoke, 1970–72. Chaplain and Sub-Prelate, Order of St John of Jerusalem, 1959–72. Formerly Member Council: London Coll. of Divinity, Clifton Theol. Coll. (Chm.), Haileybury Coll., Monkton Combe Sch., St Lawrence Coll. (Ramsgate), Chigwell Sch., Stowe Sch., Kingham Hill Trust. Golden Lectr Haberdashers' Co., 1953 and 1955. Pres. Conference, Educational Assoc., 1956. Mem., Essex County Education Cttee, 1949–59; DL Essex, 1952–59. Hon. DD Wycliffe Coll., Toronto; Hon. ThD, Aust. *Address:* Forge House, Over Wallop, Stockbridge, Hants SO20 8HT. *T:* Andover (01264) 781315. *Club:* National.

GOUGH, Janet, MA; High Mistress, St Paul's Girls' School, since 1993; *b* 1 Aug. 1940; *d* of Clifford Gough and Sarah (*née* Allen). *Educ:* Ludlow High Sch.; Newnham Coll., Cambridge (BA Hons, MA). St Paul's Girls' Sch., 1964–71; Manchester Grammar Sch., 1972; Worcester High Sch. for Girls, 1973; St Paul's Girls' Sch., 1973–. *Recreations:* walking, architecture, opera. *Address:* St Paul's Girls' School, Brook Green, W6 7BS. *T:* 0171–603 2288.

GOUGH, Piers William, RIBA; architect; Partner, CZWG Architects, since 1975; *b* 24 April 1946; *s* of Peter Gough and Daphne Mary Unwin Banks; *m* 1991, Rosemary Elaine Fosbrooke Bates. *Educ:* Uppingham Sch., Rutland; Architectural Assoc. Sch. of Architecture (AA Dip.). Principal works: Phillips West 2, Bayswater, 1976; Lutyens Exhibn, Hayward Gall., 1982; Cochrane Sq., Glasgow, 1987–; China Wharf, 1988, The Circle, 1990, Bermondsey; Craft, Design and Technol. Bldg, 1988, two boarding houses, 1994, Bryanston Sch.; Street-Porter House, 1988, 1–10 Summers St, 1994, Clerkenwell; Crown St Regeneration Proj., Gorbals, 1991–; Westbourne Grove Public Lavatories, 1993; Brindleyplace Café, Birmingham, 1994; 90 Wardour Street, Soho, 1994; Art, Design and Technol. Bldg, Uppingham Sch., 1994. AA Council, 1970–72 (Vice Pres., 1993–). Trustee: Chisenhale Gall., 1993–; Artangel, 1994–. FRSA 1992. *Publication:* English Extremists, 1988. *Recreation:* throwing parties. *Address:* CZWG Architects, 17 Bowling Green Lane, EC1R 0BD. *T:* 0171–253 2523. *Club:* Groucho.

GOUGH-CALTHORPE, family name of **Baron Calthorpe.**

GOULD, family name of **Baroness Gould of Potternewton.**

GOULD OF POTTERNEWTON, Baroness *cr* 1993 (Life Peer), of Leeds in the Metropolitan County of West Yorkshire; **Joyce Brenda Gould;** Director of Organisation, Labour Party, 1985–93; *b* 29 Oct. 1932; *d* of Sydney and Fanny Manson; *m* 1952, Kevin Gould (separated); one *d. Educ:* Cowper Street Primary Sch.; Roundhay High Sch. for Girls; Bradford Technical Coll. Dispenser, 1952–65; Asst Regional Organiser, 1969–75, Asst Nat. Agent and Chief Women's Officer, 1975–85, Labour Party. Sec., National Jt Cttee of Working Women's Orgns, 1975–; Vice-Pres., Socialist Internat. Women, 1978–. *Publications:* (ed) Women and Health, 1979; pamphlets on feminism, socialism and sexism, women's right to work, and on violence in society; articles and reports on women's rights and welfare. *Recreations:* relaxing, sport as a spectator, theatre, cinema, reading. *Address:* 5 Foulser Road, SW17 8UE; House of Lords, SW1A 0PW.

GOULD, Bryan Charles; Vice-Chancellor, Waikato University, New Zealand, since 1994; *b* 11 Feb. 1939; *s* of Charles Terence Gould and Elsie May Driller; *m* 1967, Gillian Anne Harrigan; one *s* one *d. Educ:* Auckland Univ. (BA, LLM); Balliol Coll., Oxford (MA, BCL). HM Diplomatic Service: FO, 1964–66; HM Embassy, Brussels, 1966–68; Fellow and Tutor in Law, Worcester Coll., Oxford, 1968–74. MP (Lab): Southampton Test, Oct. 1974–1979; Dagenham, 1983–94; an opposition spokesman on trade, 1983–86, on economy and party campaigns, 1986–87, on Trade and Industry, 1987–89, on the environment, 1989–92, on national heritage, 1992 (Mem. of Shadow Cabinet, 1986–92). Presenter/Reporter, TV Eye, Thames Television, 1979–83. *Publications:* Monetarism or Prosperity?, 1981; Socialism and Freedom, 1985; A Future for Socialism, 1989; Goodbye to All That (memoirs), 1995. *Recreations:* gardening, food, wine. *Address:* University of Waikato, Private Bag 3105, Hamilton, New Zealand.

GOULD, David John; Assistant Under-Secretary of State, Cabinet Office, since 1993; *b* 9 April 1949; *s* of James McIntosh Gould and Joan Vivienne Gould; *m* 1973, Christiane Clara Krieger; two *s* one *d. Educ:* West Buckland Sch., Barnstaple; Univ. of Sussex (Hons, French and European Studies). Joined MoD Naval Weapons Dept, 1973; Materiel Finance (Air), 1978; NATO Defence College, 1980; MoD (Air), 1981; UK Delegn to NATO, 1983; Asst Sec., Materiel Finance (Air), 1987; Head of Resources and Programmes (Air), 1990; Assistant Under-Secretary of State: (Supply and Orgn) (Air), 1992; Policy, 1993. Silver Jubilee Medal, 1977. *Recreations:* fitness, Rugby union, fly fishing, music, especially opera and lieder. *Address:* Cabinet Office, 70 Whitehall, SW1A 2AS. *T:* 0171-270 0050.

GOULD, Donald (William), BSc (Physiol.), MRCS, DTM&H; writer and broadcaster on medical and scientific affairs; *b* 26 Jan. 1919; *s* of late Rev. Frank J. Gould; *m* 1st, 1940, Edna Forsyth; three *s* four *d*; 2nd, 1969, Jennifer Goodfellow; one *s* one *d. Educ:* Mill Hill Sch.; St Thomas's Hosp. Med. Sch., London. Orthopædic House Surg., Botley's Park Hosp., 1942; Surg. Lieut, RNVR, 1942–46; Med. Off., Hong Kong Govt Med. Dept, 1946–48; Lectr in Physiol., University of Hong Kong, 1948–51, Sen. Lectr, 1951–57; King Edward VII Prof. of Physiol., University of Malaya (Singapore), 1957–60; Lectr in Physiol., St Bartholomew's Hosp. Med. Coll., London, 1960–61, Sen. Lectr, 1961–63; External Examr in Physiol., University of Durham (Newcastle), 1961–63; Dep. Ed., Medical News, 1963–65; Editor: World Medicine, 1965–66; New Scientist, 1966–69; Med. Correspondent, New Statesman, 1966–78. Chm., Med. Journalists' Assoc., 1967–71; Vice-Chm., Assoc. of British Science Writers, 1970–71. *Publications:* The Black & White Medicine Show, 1985; The Medical Mafia, 1987; Nurses, 1988; Examining Doctors, 1991; contributions to: Experimentation with Human Subjects, 1972; Ecology, the Shaping Enquiry, 1972; Better Social Services, 1973; scientific papers in physiological jls; numerous articles on medical politics, ethics and science in lay and professional press. *Recreations:* writing poems nobody will publish, listening, talking, and walking. *Address:* 36 Brookside, Cambridge CB2 1JQ. *T:* Cambridge (01223) 366301.

GOULD, Edward John Humphrey, MA; FRGS; Master, Marlborough College, since 1993; *b* Lewes, Sussex, 31 Oct. 1943; *s* of Roland and Ruth Gould; *m* 1970, Jennifer Jane, *d* of I. H. Lamb; two *d. Educ:* St Edward's Sch., Oxford; St Edmund Hall, Oxford (BA 1966, MA 1970, DipEd 1967). FRGS 1974. Harrow School, 1967–83: Asst Master, 1967–83; Head, Geography Dept, 1974–79; Housemaster, 1979–83; Headmaster, Felsted Sch., 1983–93. Mem., Indep. Schs Curriculum Cttee, 1985–92 (Chm., 1990–92); Chm., ISIS East, 1989–93. FRSA 1993. JP Essex, 1989–93. *Recreations:* Rugby (Oxford Blue, 1963–66), swimming (Half Blue, 1965), rowing (rep. GB, 1967), music. *Address:* The Master's Lodge, Marlborough College, Wilts SN8 1PA. *Clubs:* East India, Devonshire, Sports and Public Schools; Vincent's (Oxford).

GOULD, Prof. Frank William; Vice-Chancellor, University of East London, since 1992 (Pro-Rector, North East London Polytechnic, 1988–92); *b* 12 Aug. 1937; *s* of Frank Gould and Bridget (*née* Tyler); *m* 1963, Lesley Hall; one *s* two *d. Educ:* University Coll. London (BA Hons); Univ. of NSW (MA). Tutor in Econs, Univ. of NSW, 1964–66; Econs Journalist, Beaverbrook Newspapers, 1966–67; Lectr in Econs, Kingston Poly., 1967–73; Principal Lectr in Econs and Dean of Faculty, Poly. of Central London, 1973–85; Asst Dir, Leeds Poly., 1985–88. Vice-Chm., Bd of Dirs, Open Learning Foundn, 1994–; Chairman: Bd of Dirs, Open Learning Foundn Enterprises, 1989–; E London Trng and Consultancy Co., 1994–; Mem. Bd, London East TEC, 1993–. *Publications:* contribs to books and scientific jls in econs, pol sci. and social policy on govt and the economy and develt of public expenditure. *Recreations:* horse-riding, hill-walking, jogging. *Address:* University of East London, Romford Road, Stratford, E15 4LZ. *T:* 0181–849 3630. *Club:* Reform.

GOULD, Gail Ruth, (Mrs Philip Gould); *see* Rebuck, G. R.

GOULD, Patricia, CBE 1978; RRC 1972; Matron-in-Chief, Queen Alexandra's Royal Naval Nursing Service, 1976–80; *b* 27 May 1924; *d* of Arthur Wellesley Gould. *Educ:* Marist Convent, Paignton. Lewisham Gen. Hosp., SRN, 1945; Hackney Hosp., CMB Pt I, 1946; entered QARNNS, as Nursing Sister, 1948; accepted for permanent service, 1954; Matron, 1966; Principal Matron, 1970; Principal Matron Naval Hosps, 1975. QHNS 1976–80. OStJ (Comdr Sister), 1977. *Recreations:* gardening, photography. *Address:* 18 Park Road, Denmead, Waterlooville, Hants PO7 6NE. *T:* Waterlooville (01705) 255499.

GOULD, Robert; JP; Leader: Strathclyde Regional Council, 1992– Apr. 1996; Glasgow City Council, 1995–Apr. 1996; *b* 8 Feb. 1935; *s* of James and Elizabeth Gould; *m* 1953, Helen Wire; two *s* two *d. Educ:* Albert Secondary Sch. Formerly with BR. Entered local government, 1970: Glasgow Corp., 1970–74; Member: Strathclyde Regl Council, 1974–96; City of Glasgow Council, 1995–. JP Glasgow. *Recreations:* all sports (spectator), hill-walking. *Address:* Flat D, 15 Eccles Street, Springburn, Glasgow G22 6BJ. *T:* 0141–558 9586.

GOULD, Thomas William, VC 1942; Lieutenant RNR retired; *b* 28 Dec. 1914; *s* of late Mrs C. E. Cheeseman and late Reuben Gould (killed in action, 1916); *m* 1941, Phyllis Eileen Eldridge (*d* 1985); one *s. Educ:* St James, Dover, Kent. Royal Navy, 1933–37; Submarines, 1937–45 (despatches); invalided Oct. 1945. Business Consultant, 1965–; company director. Pres., Internat. Submarine Assoc. of GB. *Address:* 6 Howland, Orton Goldhay, Peterborough, Cambs PE2 5QY. *T:* Peterborough (01733) 238918.

GOULDEN, (Peter) John, CMG 1989; HM Diplomatic Service; Ambassador and UK Permanent Representative to North Atlantic Council and to Permanent Council of Western European Union, since 1995; *b* 21 Feb. 1941; *s* of George Herbert Goulden and Doris Goulden; *m* 1962, Diana Margaret Elizabeth Waite; one *s* one *d. Educ:* King Edward VII Sch., Sheffield; Queen's Coll., Oxford (BA 1st Cl. Hons History, 1962). FCO, 1962–: Ankara, 1963–67; Manila, 1969–70; Dublin, 1976–79; Head of Personnel Services Dept, 1980–82; Head of News Dept, FCO, 1982–84; Counsellor and Hd of Chancery, Office of the UK Permt Rep. to EEC, Brussels, 1984–87; Asst Under-Sec. of State, FCO, 1988–92; Ambassador to Turkey, 1992–95. *Recreations:* early music, bookbinding, tennis, skiing. *Address:* c/o Foreign and Commonwealth Office, King Charles Street, SW1A 2AH.

GOULDING, Sir (Ernest) Irvine, Kt 1971; Judge of the High Court of Justice, Chancery Division, 1971–85; *b* 1 May 1910; *s* of late Dr Ernest Goulding; *m* 1935, Gladys (*d* 1981), *d* of late Engineer Rear-Adm. Marrack Sennett; one *s* one *d. Educ:* Merchant Taylors' Sch., London; St Catharine's Coll., Cambridge, Hon. Fellow, 1971–. Served as Instructor Officer, Royal Navy, 1931–36 and 1939–45. Called to Bar, Inner Temple, 1936; QC 1961; Bencher, Lincoln's Inn, 1966, Treasurer, 1983. Pres., Internat. Law Assoc., British branch, 1972–81, Hon. Pres., 1983–. President: Omar Khayyâm Club, 1988–89; Selden Soc., 1988–91. *Address:* Penshurst, Wych Hill Way, Woking, Surrey GU22 0AE. *T:* Woking (01483) 761012. *Club:* Travellers'.

See also M. I. Goulding.

GOULDING, Sir Lingard; *see* Goulding, Sir W. L. W.

GOULDING, Marrack Irvine, CMG 1983; Under Secretary-General, Political Affairs, United Nations, New York, since 1993; *b* 2 Sept. 1936; *s* of Sir Irvine Goulding, *qv*; *m* 1961, Susan Rhoda D'Albiac, *d* of Air Marshal Sir John D'Albiac, KCVO, KBE, CB, DSO, and of Lady D'Albiac; two *s* one *d*. *Educ:* St Paul's Sch.; Magdalen Coll., Oxford (1st cl. hons. Lit. Hum. 1959). Joined HM Foreign (later Diplomatic) Service, 1959; MECAS, 1959–61; Kuwait, 1961–64; Foreign Office, 1964–68; Tripoli (Libya), 1968–70; Cairo, 1970–72; Private Sec., Minister of State for Foreign and Commonwealth Affairs, 1972–75; seconded to Cabinet Office (CPRS), 1975–77; Counsellor, Lisbon, 1977–79; Counsellor and Head of Chancery, UK Mission to UN, NY, 1979–83; Ambassador to Angola, and concurrently to São Tomé e Principe, 1983–85; Under Sec.-Gen., Special Political Affairs, later Peace-Keeping Ops, UN, NY, 1986–93. *Recreations:* travel, birdwatching. *Address:* 82 Claverton Street, SW1V 3AX. *T:* 0171–834 3046; 40 East 61st Street, Apt 18, New York, NY 10021, USA. *T:* (212) 8268101. *Club:* Royal Over-Seas League.

GOULDING, Sir (William) Lingard (Walter), 4th Bt *cr* 1904; Headmaster of Headfort School, since 1977; *b* 11 July 1940; *s* of Sir (William) Basil Goulding, 3rd Bt, and of Valerie Hamilton (Senator, Seanad Éireann), *o d* of 1st Viscount Monckton of Brenchley, PC, GCVO, KCMG, MC, QC; *S* father, 1982. *Educ:* Ludgrove; Winchester College; Trinity College, Dublin (BA, HDipEd). Computer studies for Zinc Corporation and Sulphide Corporation, Conzinc Rio Tinto of Australia, 1963–66; Systems Analyst, Goulding Fertilisers Ltd, 1966–67; Manager and European Sales Officer for Rionore, modern Irish jewellery company, 1968–69; Racing Driver, formulae 5000, 3 and 2, 1967–71; Assistant Master: Brook House School, 1970–74; Headfort School (IAPS prep. school), 1974–76. *Recreations:* squash, cricket, running, bicycling, tennis, music, reading, computers. *Heir:* *b* Timothy Adam Goulding [*b* 15 May 1945; *m* 1971, Patricia Mohan]. *Address:* Headfort School, Kells, Co. Meath. *T:* Navan (46) 40065; Dargle Cottage, Enniskerry, Co. Wicklow. *T:* Dublin 862315.

GOULDSBROUGH, Catherine Mary; *see* Newman, C. M.

GOULSTONE, Very Rev. (Thomas Richard) Kerry; Dean of St Asaph Cathedral, since 1993; *b* 5 June 1936; *s* of Thomas Louis and Elizabeth Goulstone; *m* 1963, Lyneth Ann Harris; one *s* one *d*. *Educ:* Llanelli Boys' Grammar Sch.; St David's University Coll., Lampeter (BA); St Michael's Theol Coll., Llandaff. Deacon 1959, priest 1960, St David's; Curate: Llanbadarn Fawr, 1959–61; St Peter's, Carmarthen, 1961–64; Vicar: Whitchurch with Solva, 1964–67; Gorslas, 1967–76; Burry Port with Pwll, 1976–84; St Peter's, Carmarthen, 1984–93; Canon, St David's Cathedral, 1986–91; RD of Carmarthen, 1988–91; Archdeacon of Carmarthen, 1991–93. Chaplain, West Wales Hosp., 1984–93. *Recreations:* music, sport, collecting porcelain. *Address:* The Deanery, St Asaph, Clwyd LL17 0RL. *T:* St Asaph (01745) 583597.

GOULTY, Alan Fletcher; HM Diplomatic Service; Ambassador to Sudan, since 1995; *b* 2 July 1947; *s* of Anthony Edmund Rivers Goulty and Maisie Oliphant Goulty (*née* Stein); *m* 1983, Lillian Craig Harris; one *s* by former marr. *Educ:* Bootham School, York; Corpus Christi College, Oxford (MA 1971). FCO 1968; MECAS, 1969–71; Beirut, 1971–72; Khartoum, 1972–75; FCO, 1975–77; Cabinet Office, 1977–80; Washington, 1981–85; FCO, 1985–90; Counsellor, 1987; Head of Near East and N Africa Dept, 1987–90; Dep. Head of Mission, Cairo, 1990–95. Grand Cordon du Wissam Alaouite (Morocco), 1987. *Recreations:* real tennis, lawn tennis, chess, bird-watching. *Address:* Foreign and Commonwealth Office, SW1A 2AH. *Club:* MCC.

GOUNARIS, Elias; Ambassador of Greece to the Court of St James's, since 1993; *b* 7 Sept. 1941; *s* of Panayotis and Christine Gounaris; *m* 1970, Irene Hadjilias. *Educ:* Univ. of Athens (LLM). Military Service, 1964–66; Attaché, Min. of Foreign Affairs, Athens, 1966–67; 3rd Sec., 1967; Consul, New York, 1969–73; Head, Section for Cyprus Affairs, Min. of Foreign Affairs, 1973–75; Sec., Perm. Mission of Greece to Internat. Orgns, Geneva, 1975–79; Counsellor, 1976; Dep. Chief of Mission, Belgrade, 1979–83; Head, American Desk, Min. of Foreign Affairs, 1983–87; Minister Counsellor, then Minister, Bonn, 1987–89; Minister Plenipotentiary, 1988; Ambassador to Moscow with parallel accreditation to Mongolia, 1989–93. Cross of Prince St Michael of Moscow, Russian Orthodox Church, 1993. Badge of Honour (Austria), 1985; Kt Comdr's Cross with Star, Order of Merit (Germany), 1989. *Recreations:* jogging, classical music, reading, antique hunting. *Address:* Greek Embassy, 1A Holland Park, W11 3TP. *Clubs:* Army and Navy, Travellers; Athenean (Athens).

GOURLAY, Gen. Sir (Basil) Ian (Spencer), KCB 1973; CVO 1990; OBE 1956 (MBE 1948); MC 1944; Vice President, United World Colleges, since 1990 (Director General, 1975–90); *b* 13 Nov. 1920; *er s* of late Brig. K. I. Gourlay, DSO, OBE, MC; *m* 1948, Natasha Zinovieff; one *s* one *d*. *Educ:* Eastbourne Coll. Commissioned, RM, 1940; HMS Formidable, 1941–44; 43 Commando, 1944–45; 45 Commando, 1946–48; Instructor, RNC Greenwich, 1948–50; Adjt RMFVR, City of London, 1950–52; Instructor, RM Officers' Sch., 1952–54; psc 1954; Bde Major, 3rd Commando Bde, 1955–57 (despatches); OC RM Officers' Trng Wing, Infantry Training Centre RM, 1957–59; 2nd in Comd, 42 Commando, 1959–61; GSO1, HQ Plymouth Gp, 1961–63; CO 42 Commando, 1963–65; Col GS, Dept of CGRM, Min. of Defence, 1965–66; Col 1965; Comdr, 3rd Commando Bde, 1966–68; Maj.-Gen. Royal Marines, Portsmouth, 1968–71; Commandant-General, Royal Marines, 1971–75; Lt-Gen., 1971; Gen., 1973. Admiral, Texas Navy. Vice Patron, RM Museum. *Recreations:* do-it-yourself, watching cricket. *Clubs:* Army and Navy, MCC; Royal Navy Cricket (Vice-Pres.).

GOURLAY, Gen. Sir Ian; *see* Gourlay, Gen. Sir B. I. S.

GOURLAY, Dame Janet; *see* Vaughan, Dame Janet.

GOURLAY, Robert Martin; Chairman, Anglian Water plc, since 1994; *b* 21 April 1939; *s* of late Cleland Gourlay and Janice (*née* Martin); *m* 1971, Rosemary Puckle Cooper; one *s* two *d*. *Educ:* Sedbergh Sch.; St Andrews Univ. (BSc). Joined BP, 1958: Gen. Manager, BP of Greece, 1970–74; European Finance and Planning Co-ordinator, 1975–77; Asst Gen. Manager, Corporate Planning, 1978–79; Gen. Manager, Public Affairs, 1979–83; BP Australia: Dir, Refining and Marketing, 1983–86; Chief Exec., 1986–90; Chm., BP PNG, 1986–90; Dir, BP NZ, 1988–90; Chief Exec., BP Nutrition, 1990–94. Non-Exec. Director: Rugby Gp plc, 1994–; Beazer Homes plc, 1994–. Bd Mem., Australia Staff Coll., Mt Eliza, 1986–90; Chm., BITC, Victoria, 1988–90. *Recreations:* music, gardening, tennis. *Address:* c/o Anglian Water plc, Ambury Road, Huntingdon, Cambs PE18 6UZ. *T:* Huntingdon (01480) 433433. *Club:* Melbourne (Melbourne).

GOURLAY, Sir Simon (Alexander), Kt 1989; President, National Farmers' Union, 1986–91; *b* 15 July 1934; *s* of David and Helga Gourlay; *m* 1st, 1956, Sally Garman; one *s*; 2nd, 1967, Caroline Mary Clegg; three *s*. *Educ:* Winchester; Royal Agricultural College. National Service, Commission 16th/5th Lancers, 1954–55. Farm manager, Cheshire, 1956–58; started farming on own account at Knighton, 1958; Man. Dir, Maryvale Farm Construction Ltd, 1977–85; Director: Agricl Mortgage Corp., 1991–; Hertford DHA, 1994–. Chm., Guild of Conservation Grade Producers, 1992–. *Recreations:* gardening, music, hill walking. *Address:* Hill House Farm, Knighton, Powys LD7 1NA. *T:* Knighton (01547) 528542.

GOVAN, Sir Lawrence (Herbert), Kt 1984; President, Lichfield (NZ) Ltd, since 1991 (Director, 1949–79; Deputy Chairman, 1979–91); *b* 13 Oct. 1919; *s* of Herbert Cyril Charles Govan and Janet Armour Govan (*née* Edmiston); *m* 1946, Clara Hiscock; one *s* three *d*. *Educ:* Christchurch Boys' High School. Started in garment industry with Lichfield (NZ) Ltd, 1935, Managing Director, 1950. Pres., NZ Textile and Garment Fedn, 1961–63, Life Mem., 1979. Dir, Superannuation Investments Ltd, 1976–. Pres., Canterbury Med. Res. Foundn, 1987–. *Recreations:* golf, swimming, horticulture. *Address:* 11 Hamilton Avenue, Fendalton, Christchurch 4, New Zealand. *T:* (3) 3519557. *Club:* Rotary (Christchurch) (Pres. 1963–64).

GOVETT, William John Romaine; *b* 11 Aug. 1937; *s* of John Romaine Govett and Angela Mostyn (*née* Pritchard); *m* 1st, Mary Hays (marr. diss. 1970); two *s* one *d*; 2nd, 1970, Penelope Ann Irwin; one *d*. *Educ:* Sandroyd; Gordonstoun. National Service, commnd Royal Scots Greys, 1956–58. Joined John Govett & Co. Ltd, 1961; Chm., 1974–86; Dep. Chm., 1986–90. Director: Legal & General Gp, 1972–; Govett Oriental Investment Trust, 1972–; Govett Strategic Investment Trust, 1975–; Scottish Eastern Investment Trust, 1977–; Govett Atlantic Investment Trust, 1979–; Union Jack Oil Co., 1981–; LEP Gp, 1983–; Investors in Industry, subseq. 3i, 1984–; Coal Investment Nominees NCB Pension Fund, 1985–; Ranger Oil (UK) Ltd, 1988–; Chm., Hungarian Investment Co. Ltd, 1990–. Trustee: Nat. Arts Collection Fund, 1985–; Tate Gall., 1988–. *Recreations:* modern art, fishing. *Address:* 62 Glebe Place, SW3 5JB; Fosbury Manor, Marlborough, Wiltshire SN8 3JN.

GOW, Gen. Sir (James) Michael, GCB 1983 (KCB 1979); DL; Commandant, Royal College of Defence Studies, 1984–86; *b* 3 June 1924; *s* of late J. C. Gow and Mrs Alastair Sanderson; *m* 1946, Jane Emily Scott, *e d* of late Capt. and Hon. Mrs Mason Scott; one *s* four *d*. *Educ:* Winchester College. Enlisted Scots Guards, 1942; commnd 1943; served NW Europe, 1944–45; Mil. Div., Quadripartite Control Commn, Berlin, 1945–46; Malayan Emergency, 1949; Equerry to HRH the Duke of Gloucester, 1952–53; psc 1954; Bde Major 1955–57; Regimental Adjt Scots Guards, 1957–60; Instructor Army Staff Coll., 1962–64; comd 2nd Bn Scots Guards, Kenya and England, 1964–66; GSO1, HQ London District, 1966–67; comd 4th Guards Bde, 1968–69; idc 1970; BGS (Int) HQ BAOR and ACOS G2 HQ Northag, 1971–73; GOC 4th Div. BAOR, 1973–75; Dir of Army Training, 1975–78; GOC Scotland and Governor of Edinburgh Castle, 1979–80; C-in-C BAOR and Comdr, Northern Army Gp, 1980–83 (awarded die Plakette des deutschen Heeres); ADC Gen. to the Queen, 1981–84. Colonel Commandant: Intelligence Corps, 1973–86; Scottish Division, 1979–80. Mem., Queen's Body Guard for Scotland, Royal Company of Archers, 1964– (Brig., 1981). UK Mem., Eurogroup US Tour, 1983. UK Kermit Roosevelt Lectr, USA, 1984. President: Royal British Legion, Scotland, 1986–; Earl Haig Fund (Scotland), 1986–; Nat. Assoc. of Sheltered Employment, 1993–; Chm., Scottish Ex-Services' Charitable Orgn, 1989–; Patron, Disablement Income Group Scotland, 1993–. Vice-Pres., Royal Patriotic Fund Corp., 1983–88. Vice-President: Queen Victoria Sch., Dunblane, 1979–80; Royal Caledonian Schs, Bushey, 1980–. County Comr, British Scouts W Europe, 1980–83 (Silver Acorn). Freeman: City of London, 1980; State of Kansas, USA, 1984; Freeman and Liveryman, Painters' and Stainers' Co., 1980. Elder of Church of Scotland, Canongate Kirk, 1988–; Rep. Elder, Presbytery of Edinburgh, 1993–. FSAScot 1991. DL Edinburgh, 1994. *Publications:* Trooping the Colour: a history of the Sovereign's birthday parade by the Household troops, 1989; Jottings in a General's Notebook, 1989; General Reflections: a military man at large, 1991; articles in mil. and hist. jls. *Recreations:* sailing, music, travel, reading. *Address:* 18 Ann Street, Edinburgh EH4 1PJ. *T:* 0131–332 4752. *Clubs:* Pratt's, Highland Society of London; New (Edinburgh).

See also Lt-Col W. H. M. Ross.

GOW, Dame Jane (Elizabeth), DBE 1990; *b* 14 July 1944; *d* of Major Charles Packe (killed in action, July 1944) and Hon. Margaret Lane Fox; *m* 1st, 1966, Ian Gow, TD, MP (*d* 1990); two *s*; 2nd, 1994, Lt-Col Michael Whiteley. *Educ:* St Mary's School, Wantage. *Recreations:* music, reading, swimming, tennis. *Address:* Lower Lewer, Hatherleigh, Okehampton, Devon EX20 3LF.

GOW, John Stobie, PhD; CChem, FRSC; FRSE 1978; Secretary-General, Royal Society of Chemistry, 1986–93; *b* 12 April 1933; *s* of David Gow and Anne Scott; *m* 1955, Elizabeth Henderson; three *s*. *Educ:* Alloa Acad.; Univ. of St Andrews (BSc, PhD). Res. Chemist, ICI, Billingham, 1958; Prodn Man., Chem. Co. of Malaysia, 1966–68; ICI: Res. Man., Agric. Div., 1968–72; Gen. Man. (Catalysts), Agric. Div., 1972–74; Res. Dir, Organics, 1974–79; Dep. Chm., Organics, 1979–84; Man. Dir, Speciality Chemicals, 1984–86. Assessor, SERC, 1988–94; Treas., CSTI, 1993–. FRSA 1980. *Publications:* papers and patents in Fertilizer Technology and Biotechnology. *Recreations:* choral music, Rugby. *Address:* 19 Longcroft Avenue, Harpenden, Herts AL5 2RD. *T:* Harpenden (01582) 764889.

GOW, Sir Leonard Maxwell H.; *see* Harper Gow.

GOW, Gen. Sir Michael; *see* Gow, Gen. Sir J. M.

GOW, Neil, QC (Scot.) 1970; Sheriff of South Strathclyde, at Ayr, since 1976; *b* 24 April 1932; *s* of Donald Gow, oil merchant, Glasgow; *m* 1959, Joanna, *d* of Comdr S. D. Sutherland, Edinburgh; one *s*. *Educ:* Merchiston Castle Sch., Edinburgh; Glasgow and Edinburgh Univs. MA, LLB. Formerly Captain, Intelligence Corps (BAOR). Carnegie Scholar in History of Scots Law, 1956. Advocate, 1957–76. Standing Counsel to Min. of Social Security (Scot.), 1964–70. Contested (C): Kirkcaldy Burghs, Gen. Elections of 1964 and 1966; Edinburgh East, 1970; Mem. Regional Council, Scottish Conservative Assoc. An Hon. Sheriff of Lanarkshire, 1971. Pres., Auchinleck Boswell Soc. FSA (Scot.). *Publications:* A History of Scottish Statutes, 1959; Jt Editor, An Outline of Estate Duty in Scotland, 1970; A History of Belmont House School, 1979; numerous articles and broadcasts on legal topics and Scottish affairs. *Recreations:* golf, books, antiquities. *Address:* Old Auchenfail Hall, by Mauchline, Ayrshire KA5 5TA. *T:* Mauchline (01290) 550822. *Clubs:* Western (Glasgow); Prestwick Golf.

GOW, Dame Wendy; *see* Hiller, Dame Wendy.

GOW, Very Rev. William Connell; Dean of Moray, Ross and Caithness, 1960–77, retired; Canon of St Andrew's Cathedral, Inverness, 1953–77, Hon. Canon, since 1977; Rector of St James', Dingwall, 1940–77; *b* 6 Jan. 1909; *s* of Alexander Gow, Errol, Perthshire; *m* 1938, Edith Mary, *d* of John William Jarvis, Scarborough; two *s*. *Educ:* Edinburgh Theological Coll.; Durham Univ. (LTh). Deacon, 1936; Priest, 1937; Curate St Mary Magdalene's, Dundee, 1936–39. Awarded Frihetsmedalje (by King Haakon), Norway, 1947. *Recreations:* fishing, bridge. *Address:* 14 Mackenzie Place, Maryburgh, Ross-shire IV7 8DY. *T:* Dingwall (01349) 61832.

GOWANS, Sir James (Learmonth), Kt 1982; CBE 1971; FRCP 1975; FRS 1963; Secretary General, Human Frontier Science Programme, Strasbourg, 1989–93; Secretary,

Medical Research Council, 1977–87; *b* 7 May 1924; *s* of John Gowans and Selma Josefina Ljung; *m* 1956, Moyra Leatham; one *s* two *d*. *Educ:* Trinity Sch., Croydon; King's Coll. Hosp. Med. Sch. (MB BS (Hons) 1947; Fellow, 1979); Lincoln Coll., Oxford (BA (1st cl. Hons Physiology) 1948; MA; DPhil 1953; Hon. Fellow, 1984). MRC Exchange Scholar, Pasteur Institute, Paris, 1952–53; Research Fellow, Exeter Coll., Oxford, 1955–60 (Hon. Fellow, 1983–); Fellow, St Catherine's Coll., Oxford, 1961–87 (Hon. Fellow, 1987); Henry Dale Res. Prof. of Royal Society, 1962–77; Hon. Dir, MRC Cellular Immunology Unit, 1963–77; Dir, 1980–86, Sen. Sci. Advr, 1988–90, Celltech Ltd. Consultant, WHO Global Prog. on AIDS, 1987–88. Member: MRC, 1965–69; Adv. Bd for Res. Councils, 1977–87. Director: Tavistock and Portman NHS Trust, 1994–; European Initiative for Communicators of Science, Munich, 1995–. Royal Society: Mem. Council and a Vice-Pres., 1973–75; Assessor to MRC, 1973–75. Mem. Council, St Christopher's Hospice, 1987–; Chm., Scientific Adv. Cttee, Lister Inst. of Preventive Medicine, 1994–. FRSA 1994. Vis. Prof., NY Univ. Sch. of Med., 1967; Lectures: Harvey, NY, 1968; Dunham, Harvard, 1971; Bayne-Jones, Johns Hopkins, 1973; Harveian Orator, RCP, 1987. Foreign Associate, Nat. Acad. of Scis, USA, 1985. Mem., Academia Europaea, 1991. Hon. Member: Amer. Assoc. of Immunologists; Amer. Soc. of Anatomists. Hon. ScD Yale, 1966; Hon. DSc: Chicago, 1971; Birmingham, 1978; Rochester, 1987; Hon. MD Edinburgh, 1979; Hon. DM Southampton, 1987; Hon. LLD Glasgow, 1988. Gairdner Foundn Award, Toronto, 1968; Paul Ehrlich Ludwig-Darmstaedter Prize, Frankfurt, 1974; Royal Medal, Royal Society, 1976; Feldberg Foundn Award, 1979; Wolf Prize in Medicine, Wolf Foundn, Israel, 1980; Medawar Prize, 1990; Galen Medal, Soc. of Apothecaries, 1991. *Publications:* articles in scientific journals. *Address:* 75 Cumnor Hill, Oxford OX2 9HX. *T:* Oxford (01865) 862304.

GOWANS, James Palmer, JP; DL; Lord Provost of Dundee and Lord-Lieutenant of the City of Dundee, 1980–84; *b* 15 Sept. 1930; *s* of Charles Gowans and Sarah Gowans (*née* Palmer); *m* 1950, Davina Barnett; one *s* three *d* (and one *s* one *d* decd). *Educ:* Rockwell Secondary School, Dundee. With National Cash Register Co., Dundee, 1956–94. Elected to Dundee DC, May 1974; Mem., Dundee City Council, 1975–92. JP 1977; DL Dundee 1984. *Recreations:* golf, motoring. *Address:* 41 Dalmahoy Drive, Dundee DD2 3UT. *T:* Dundee (01382) 84918.

GOWAR, Prof. Norman William; Principal, Royal Holloway and Bedford New College, University of London, since 1990; *b* 7 Dec. 1940; *s* of Harold James and Constance Dawson-Gowar; *m* 1st, 1963, Diane May Parker (marr. diss.); one *s* one *d*; 2nd, 1981, Prof. Judith Margaret Greene, *d* of Lord Gordon-Walker, PC, CH. *Educ:* Sir George Monoux Grammar Sch.; City Univ. (BSc, MPhil). FIMA. English Electric Co., 1963; Lectr in Maths, City Univ., 1963; Open University: Lectr and Sen. Lectr, 1969; Prof. of Mathematics, 1983; Dir, Centre for Maths Educn, 1983; Pro-Vice Chancellor, 1977–81; Dep. Vice-Chancellor, 1985; Dir, Open Coll., 1986. Vis. Fellow, Keble Coll., Oxford, 1972. Member: Council, CNAA, 1979–83; Council, NCET 1986–91 (Chm., Trng Cttee). Chm. and Dir, Open Univ. Educational Enterprises Ltd, 1988–90. Dir, Surrey TEC, 1991–93. Mem., London Math. Soc. Governor: South Bank Univ. (formerly Polytechnic), 1992–; UCS, 1993–; Rugby Sch., 1994–. Mem. Council, IMA, 1993–. FRSA. Hon. DSc City, 1994. *Publications:* Mathematics for Technology: a new approach, 1968; Basic Mathematical Structures, vol. 1, 1973, vol. 2, 1974; Fourier Series, 1974; Invitation to Mathematics, 1980; articles and TV series. *Address:* Royal Holloway, University of London, Egham Hill, Egham, Surrey TW20 0EX.

GOWDY, David Clive; Director of Personnel, Northern Ireland Civil Service, since 1994; *b* 27 Nov. 1946; *s* of Samuel David Gowdy and Eileen Gowdy (*née* Porter); *m* 1973, Linda Doreen Traub; two *d*. *Educ:* Royal Belfast Academical Instn; Queen's Univ. Belfast (BA, MSc). Min. of Finance, NI, 1970; N Ireland Office, 1976; Exec. Dir, Industrial Develt Bd for NI 1985; Under Sec., Dept of Econ. Develt, NI, 1987; Under Sec, Dept of Health and Social Services, NI, 1990. *Recreations:* music, reading, theatre, tennis, archery. *Address:* Department of Finance and Personnel, Rosepark House, Upper Newtownards Road, Belfast BT4 3NR.

GOWENLOCK, Prof. Brian Glover, CBE 1986; PhD, DSc; FRSE; FRSC; Hon. Research Fellow, University of Exeter, since 1992; Professor of Chemistry, 1966–90, Leverhulme Emeritus Fellow, 1990–92, Heriot-Watt University; *b* 9 Feb. 1926; *s* of Harry Hadfield Gowenlock and Hilda (*née* Glover); *m* 1953, Margaret L. Davies; one *s* two *d*. *Educ:* Hulme Grammar Sch., Oldham; Univ. of Manchester (BSc, MSc, PhD). DSc Birmingham. FRIC 1966; FRSE 1969. Asst Lectr in Chemistry 1948, Lectr 1951, University Coll. of Swansea; Lectr 1955, Sen. Lectr 1964, Univ. of Birmingham; Dean, Faculty of Science, Heriot-Watt Univ., 1969–72, 1987–90. Vis. Scientist, National Res. Council, Ottawa, 1963; Erskine Vis. Fellow, Univ. of Canterbury, NZ, 1976. Mem., UGC, 1976–85, Vice-Chm., 1983–85. *Publications:* Experimental Methods in Gas Reactions (with Sir Harry Melville), 1964; First Year at the University (with James C. Blackie), 1964; contribs to scientific jls. *Recreations:* genealogy, foreign travel. *Address:* Riccarton, 5 Roselands, Sidmouth, Devon EX10 8PB. *T:* Sidmouth (01395) 516864.

GOWER; *see* Leveson Gower.

GOWER, David Ivon, OBE 1992; Sunday Express Cricket Correspondent, since 1993; freelance television journalist; *b* 1 April 1957; *s* of Richard Hallam Gower and Sylvia Mary Gower (*née* Ford); *m* 1992, Thorunn Ruth Nash; one *d*. *Educ:* King's Sch., Canterbury; UCL. Professional cricketer, 1975–93; Leicestershire, 1975–89; Hampshire, 1990–93; 117 Test matches for England, 1978–92; 8,231 Test runs (2nd highest for England), incl. 18 centuries; captained England 31 times, 1984–86, 1989; retired from 1st class cricket, Nov. 1993. PR consultant (cricket sponsorship), Nat. Westminister Bank, 1993–. *Publications:* With Time to Spare, 1979; Heroes and Contemporaries, 1983; A Right to Ambition, 1986; On the Rack, 1990; Gower, The Autobiography, 1992. *Recreations:* ski-ing, safari, Cresta Run, tennis. *Address:* 6 George Street, Nottingham NG1 3BE. *Clubs:* East India, MCC; St Moritz Tobogganing.

GOWER, Jim; *see* Gower, L. C. B.

GOWER, John Hugh, QC 1967; **His Honour Judge Gower;** a Circuit Judge, since 1972; *b* 6 Nov. 1925; *s* of Henry John Gower, JP and Edith (*née* Brooks); *m* 1960, Shirley Mameena Darbourne; one *s* one *d*. *Educ:* Skinners' Sch., Tunbridge Wells. RASC, 1945–48 (Staff Sgt). Called to Bar, Inner Temple, 1948, Bencher, 1995; Dep. Chm., Kent QS, 1968–71; Resident and Liaison Judge of Crown Courts in E Sussex, 1986–. Mem., Lord Chancellor's Adv. Cttee on Legal Educn and Conduct, 1991–. Chm., Kent and Sussex Area Criminal Justice Liaison Cttee, 1992–; Vice-Pres., E Sussex Magistrates' Assoc., 1986–. Pres., Tunbridge Wells Council of Voluntary Service, 1974–88. Hon. Vice-Pres., Kent Council of Voluntary Service, 1971–86. Chm., Southdown and Eridge Hunt, 1985–91. Freeman, City of London (by purchase), 1960. *Recreations:* fishing, foxhunting, gardening, tapestry. *Address:* The Crown Court, High Street, Lewes, E Sussex BN7 1YB.

GOWER, Laurence Cecil Bartlett, (Jim), FBA 1965; Solicitor; Professor Emeritus, Southampton University; *b* 29 Dec. 1913; *s* of Henry Lawrence Gower; *m* 1939, Helen Margaret Shepperson, *d* of George Francis Birch; two *s* one *d*. *Educ:* Lindisfarne Coll.; University Coll., London. LLB 1933; LLM 1934. Admitted Solicitor, 1937. Served War of 1939–45, with RA and RAOC. Sir Ernest Cassel Prof. of Commercial Law in University of London, 1948–62, Visiting Prof., Law Sch. of Harvard Univ., 1954–55; Adviser on Legal Educn in Africa to Brit. Inst. of Internat. and Comparative Law and Adviser to Nigerian Council of Legal Educn, 1962–65; Prof. and Dean of Faculty of Law of Univ. of Lagos, 1962–65; Law Comr, 1965–71; Vice-Chancellor, Univ. of Southampton, 1971–79. Holmes Lectr, Harvard Univ., 1966. Fellow of University Coll., London; Comr on Company Law Amendment in Ghana, 1958; Member: Jenkins Cttee on Company Law Amendment, 1959–62; Denning Cttee on Legal Education for Students from Africa, 1960; Ormrod Cttee on Legal Education, 1967–71; Royal Commn on the Press, 1975–77. Trustee, British Museum, 1968–83. For. Hon. Mem., Amer. Acad. of Arts and Scis, 1986; Lee Kuan Yew Distinguished Visitor, Nat. Univ. of Singapore, 1987. Hon. Fellow: LSE, 1970; Portsmouth Polytech., 1981; Hon. LLD: York Univ., Ont; Edinburgh Univ.; Dalhousie Univ.; Warwick Univ.; QUB; Southampton Univ.; Bristol Univ.; London Univ.; Hon. DLitt Hong Kong. Hon. QC 1991. *Publications:* Principles of Modern Company Law, 1954, 5th edn 1992; Independent Africa: The Challenge to the Legal Profession, 1967; Review of Investor Protection, Part 1, 1984, Part 2, 1985; numerous articles in legal periodicals. *Recreation:* travel. *Address:* 26 Willow Road, Hampstead, NW3 1TL. *T:* 0171–435 2507.

GOWER ISAAC, Anthony John; *see* Isaac.

GOWING, Prof. Margaret Mary, CBE 1981; FRS 1988; FBA 1975; FRHistS; Professor of the History of Science, University of Oxford, and Fellow of Linacre College, 1973–86; *b* 26 April 1921; *d* of Ronald and Mabel Elliott; *m* 1944, Donald J. G. Gowing (*d* 1969); two *s*. *Educ:* Christ's Hospital; London Sch. of Economics (BSc(Econ); Hon. Fellow, 1988). Bd of Trade, 1941–45; Historical Section, Cabinet Office, 1945–59; Historian and Archivist, UK Atomic Energy Authority, 1959–66; Reader in Contemporary History, Univ. of Kent, 1966–72. Member: Cttee on Deptl Records (Grigg Cttee), 1952–54; Adv. Council on Public Records, 1974–82; BBC Archives Adv. Cttee, 1976–79; Public Records Inquiry (Wilson Cttee), 1978–80; Trustee: Nat. Portrait Gall., 1978–92; Imperial War Mus., 1986–87. Hon. Dir, Contemporary Scientific Archives Centre, 1973–86. Foundation Mem., Academia Europaea, 1988. Royal Society Wilkins Lectr, 1976; Enid Muir Lectr, Newcastle, 1976; Bernal Lectr, Birkbeck, 1977; Rede Lectr, Cambridge, 1978; Herbert Spencer Lectr, Oxford, 1982; CEGB Lectr, Southampton, 1987. Hon. DLitt: Leeds, 1976; Leicester, 1982; Hon. DSc: Manchester, 1985; Bath, 1987. *Publications:* (with Sir K. Hancock) British War Economy, 1949; (with E. L. Hargreaves) Civil Industry and Trade, 1952; Britain and Atomic Energy, 1964; Dossier Secret des Relations Atomiques, 1965; Independence and Deterrence: vol. I, Policy Making, vol. II, Policy Execution, 1974; Reflections on Atomic Energy History, 1978; (with Lorna Arnold) The Atomic Bomb, 1979; various articles and reviews. *Address:* Linacre College, Oxford OX1 3JA.

GOWING, Prof. Noel Frank Collett; Emeritus Professor of Pathology, University of London; Consultant Pathologist and Director of the Department of Histopathology, The Royal Marsden Hospital, SW3, 1957–82; Professor of Tumour Pathology (formerly Senior Lecturer), Institute of Cancer Research: The Royal Cancer Hospital, 1971–82; *b* 3 Jan. 1917; *s* of Edward Charles Gowing and Annie Elizabeth Gowing; *m* 1942, Rela Griffel; one *d*. *Educ:* Ardingly Coll., Sussex; London Univ. MRCS, LRCP 1941; MB, BS, London, 1947; MD London, 1948. Served RAMC (Capt.), 1942–46, 52nd (Lowland) Div. Lectr in Pathology, St George's Hosp. Med. Sch., 1947–52; Sen. Lectr in Pathology and Hon. Cons. Pathologist, St George's Hosp., 1952–57. Vis. Pathologist, St Vincent's Hosp., Worcester, Mass and Vis. Prof. of Pathology, Univ. of Mass, 1979. Sometime Examiner in Pathology to: Univ. of London; RCPath; Univ. of Newcastle-upon-Tyne; Univ. of Malta; Nat. Univ. of Malaysia. Lectures: Kettle Meml, RCPath, 1968; Whittick Meml, Saskatchewan Cancer Soc., 1974; Symeonidis Meml, Thessaloniki Cancer Inst., Greece, 1977. Pres., Assoc. of Clinical Pathologists, 1982–83. FRCPath (Founder Fellow, Coll. of Pathologists, 1964). *Publications:* A Colour Atlas of Tumour Histopathology, 1980; articles on pathology in medical journals. *Recreations:* gardening, astronomy.

GOWON, Gen. Dr Yakubu, PhD; jssc, psc; Head of the Federal Military Government and C-in-C of Armed Forces of the Federal Republic of Nigeria 1966–75; Visiting Professor in Politics and International Relations, University of Jos, Nigeria; *b* Pankshin Div., Plateau State, Nigeria, 19 Oct. 1934; *s* of Yohanna Gowon (an Angas, a Christian evangelist of CMS) and Saraya Gowon; *m* 1969, Victoria Hansatu Zakari; one *s* two *d*. *Educ:* St Bartholomew's Schs (CMS), Wusasa, and Govt Coll., Zaria, Nigeria; Warwick Univ. (BA Hons 1978; PhD). Regular Officer's Special Trng Sch., Teshie, Ghana; Eaton Hall Officer Cadet Sch., Chester, RMA, Sandhurst, Staff Coll., Camberley and Joint Services Staff Coll., Latimer (all in England). Enlisted, 1954; commissioned, 1956; served in Cameroon, 1960; Adjt, 4th Bn Nigerian Army, 1960 (Independence Oct. 1960); UN Peace-Keeping Forces, Congo, Nov. 1960–June 1961 and Jan.-June 1963 (Bde Major). Lt-Col and Adjt-Gen., Nigerian Army, 1963; Comd, 2nd Bn, Nigerian Army, Ikeja, 1966; Chief of Staff, 1966; Head of State and C-in-C after July 1966 coup; Maj.-Gen. 1967. Maintained territorial integrity of his country by fighting, 1967–70, to preserve unity of Nigeria (after failure of peaceful measures) following on Ojukwu rebellion, and declared secession of the Eastern region of Nigeria, July 1967; created 12 equal and autonomous states in Nigeria, 1967; Biafran surrender, 1970. Promoted Gen., 1971. Chm., Base Development (Nigeria) Ltd (formerly Kanawa Industries (Nigeria) Ltd), Kano, Nigeria, 1987–. Chm. Trustees, Commonwealth Human Ecology Foundn, 1986–. Is a Christian; works for internat. peace and security within the framework of OAU and UNO. Hon. LLD Cambridge, 1975; also hon. doctorates from Univs of Ibadan, Lagos, ABU-Zaria, Nigeria at Nsukka, Benin, Ife, and Shaw Univ., USA, 1973. Holds Grand Cross, etc, of several foreign orders. *Publication:* Faith in Unity, 1970. *Recreations:* squash, lawn tennis, pen-drawing, photography, cinephotography. *Address:* c/o Department of Politics, Warwick University, Coventry CV4 7AL; c/o Department of Developmental Studies, University of Jos, Plateau State, Nigeria. *Clubs:* Army and Navy, Les Ambassadeurs.

GOWRIE, 2nd Earl of, *cr* 1945; **Alexander Patrick Greysteil Hore-Ruthven;** PC 1984; Baron Ruthven of Gowrie, 1919; Baron Gowrie, 1935; Viscount Ruthven of Canberra, 1945; Chairman, Arts Council of England, since 1994; Director, Sotheby's Holdings Inc., since 1985 (Chairman, Sotherby's Europe, 1987–94; Chairman, Sotheby's International, 1985–86); *b* 26 Nov. 1939; *er s* of late Capt. Hon. Alexander Hardinge Patrick Hore-Ruthven, Rifle Bde, and Pamela Margaret (as Viscountess Ruthven of Canberra, she *m* 1952, Major Derek Cooper, MC, The Life Guards), 2nd *d* of late Rev. A. H. Fletcher; *S* grandfather, 1955; *m* 1st, 1962, Xandra (marr. diss. 1973), *yr d* of Col R. A. G. Bingley, CVO, DSO, OBE; one *s*; 2nd, 1974, Adelheid Gräfin von der Schulenburg, *y d* of late Fritz-Dietlof, Graf von der Schulenburg. *Educ:* Eton; Balliol Coll., Oxford. Visiting Lectr, State Univ. of New York at Buffalo, 1963–64; Tutor, Harvard Univ., 1965–68; Lectr in English and American Literature, UCL, 1969–72. Fine Art consultant, 1974–79. Provost, RCA, 1986–95. Chm., The Really Useful Gp, 1985–90. A Conservative Whip, 1971–72; Parly Rep. to UN, 1971; a Lord in Waiting (Govt Whip), 1972–74; Opposition

Spokesman on Economic Affairs, 1974–79; Minister of State: Dept of Employment, 1979–81; NI Office, 1981–83 (Dep. to Sec. of State); Privy Council Office (Management and Personnel), 1983–84; Minister for the Arts, 1983–85; Chancellor, Duchy of Lancaster, 1984–85. *Publications:* A Postcard from Don Giovanni, 1972; (jt) The Genius of British Painting, 1975; (jt) The Conservative Opportunity, 1976; Derek Hill: an appreciation, 1987. *Recreation:* book reviewing. *Heir: s* Viscount Ruthven of Canberra, *qv*. *Address:* Arts Council of England, 14 Great Peter Street, SW1P 3NQ.

GOY, David John Lister; QC 1991; *b* 11 May 1949; *s* of Rev. Leslie Goy and Joan Goy; *m* 1970; Jennifer Anne Symington; three *s*. *Educ:* Haberdashers' Aske's School, Elstree; King's College London. Called to the Bar, Middle Temple, 1973. *Publication:* VAT on Property, 1989, 2nd edn 1993. *Recreations:* running and other sports. *Address:* Gray's Inn Chambers, Gray's Inn, WC1R 5JA. *T:* 0171–242 2642.

GOYDER, Daniel George; solicitor; Consultant to Birkett Westhorp Long (formerly Birketts), Ipswich, since 1983 (Partner, 1968–83); *b* 26 Aug. 1938; *s* of George Armin Goyder, *qv*; *m* 1962, Jean Mary Dohoo; two *s* two *d*. *Educ:* Rugby Sch.; Trinity Coll., Cambridge (MA, LLB); Harvard Law Sch. (Harkness Commonwealth Fund Fellow, LLM). Admitted Solicitor, 1962; Asst Solicitor, Messrs Allen & Overy, 1964–67. Pt-time Lectr in Law, 1981–91, Vis. Prof., 1991–, Univ. of Essex; Vis. Prof., KCL, 1991–. Chm., St Edmundsbury and Ipswich Diocesan Bd of Finance, 1977–85; Hon. Lay Canon, St Edmundsbury Cathedral, 1987–93. Dep. Chm., Monopolies and Mergers Commn, 1991– (Mem., 1980–). Leverhulme Trust Res. Grant, for research into EEC competition law, 1986. FRSA 1991. *Publications:* The Antitrust Laws of the USA (with Sir Alan Neale), 3rd edn 1981; EEC Competition Law, 1988, 2nd edn 1992. *Recreations:* choral singing, table tennis, sport. *Address:* Manor House, Old London Road, Capel St Mary, Ipswich, Suffolk IP9 2JU. *T:* Ipswich (01473) 310583. *Clubs:* Law Society; Ipswich and Suffolk (Ipswich).

GOYDER, George Armin, CBE 1976; Managing Director, British International Paper Ltd, 1935–71; *b* 22 June 1908; *s* of late William Goyder and Lili Julia Kellersberger, Baden, Switzerland; *m* 1937, Rosemary, 4th *d* of Prof. R. C. Bosanquet, Rock, Northumberland; five *s* three *d*. *Educ:* Mill Hill Sch.; London Sch. of Economics; abroad. Gen. Man., Newsprint Supply Co., 1940–47 (responsible for procurement supply and rationing of newsprint to British Press); The Geographical Magazine, 1935–58. Mem., Gen. Synod of C of E (formerly Church Assembly), 1948–75; Chm., Liberal Party Standing Cttee on Industrial Partnership, 1966. Vice-Pres., Centre for Internat. Briefing, Farnham Castle, 1978– (Founding Mem., 1962; Chm., 1969–77); co-Founder and Trustee, William Blake Trust, 1949–82; Governor: Mill Hill Sch., 1943–69; Monkton Combe Sch., 1957–78; Trustee and Hon. Fellow, St Peter's Coll., Oxford; Mem. Council, Wycliffe Hall, 1950–79; Founder Mem. and Hon. Sec., British-North American Cttee, 1960–72. Chm., Suffolk Preservation Soc., 1983–85. *Publications:* The Future of Private Enterprise, 1951, 1954; The Responsible Company, 1961; The People's Church, 1966; The Responsible Worker, 1975; The Just Enterprise, 1987; (with Rosemary Goyder) Signs of Grace, 1994. *Recreations:* music, old books, theology. *Address:* Mansel Hall, Long Melford, Sudbury, Suffolk CO10 9JB. *Club:* Reform.

See also D. G. Goyder.

GOZNEY, Richard Hugh Turton, CMG 1993; HM Diplomatic Service; High Commissioner to Swaziland, since 1993; *b* 21 July 1951; *s* of Thomas Leonard Gozney and Elizabeth Margaret Lilian Gozney (*née* Gardiner); *m* 1982, Diana Edwina Baird; two *s*. *Educ:* Magdalen Coll. Sch., Oxford; St Edmund Hall, Oxford (BA Hons Geol. 1973). Teacher, Tom Mboya Rusinga Secondary Sch., Kenya, 1970; joined FO, 1973; Jakarta, 1974–78; Buenos Aires, 1978–81; FCO, 1981–84; Hd of Chancery, Madrid, 1984–88; Asst Private Sec., later Private Sec., to Foreign Sec., FCO, 1989–93. *Publication:* Gibraltar and the EC, 1993. *Recreations:* bird-watching, walking, wind surfing, learning to fish. *Address:* c/o Foreign and Commonwealth Office, King Charles Street, SW1A 2AH.

GRAAFF, Sir de Villiers, 2nd Bt *cr* 1911; MBE 1946; BA Cape, MA, BCL Oxon; Barrister-at-Law, Inner Temple; Advocate of the Supreme Court of S Africa; MP for Hottentots Holland in Union Parliament 1948–58, for Rondebosch, Cape Town, 1958–77; *b* 8 Dec. 1913; *s* of 1st Bt and Eileen (*d* 1950), *d* of Rev. Dr J. P. Van Heerden, Cape Town; *S* father, 1931; *m* 1939, Helena Le Roux, *d* of F. C. M. Voigt, Provincial Sec. of Cape Province; two *s* one *d*. Served War of 1939–45 (prisoner, MBE). Leader, United Party, S Africa, 1956–77; formerly Leader of Official Opposition. Hon. Col, Cape Garrison Artillery, 1980. Hon. LLD Rhodes, 1969; Hon. DLit South Africa, 1989. Decoration for Meritorious Service (RSA), 1979. *Heir: s* David de Villiers Graaff [*b* 3 May 1940; *m* Sally Williams; three *s* one *d*]. *Address:* De Grendel, Private Bag, GPO, Capetown, South Africa. *Club:* Civil Service (Cape Town).

GRABHAM, Sir Anthony (Herbert), Kt 1988; FRCS; Chairman, BMA Services, since 1982; Director, Private Patients Plan, since 1984; *b* 19 July 1930; *s* of John and Lily Grabham; *m* 1960, Eileen Pamela Rudd; two *s* two *d*. *Educ:* St Cuthbert's Grammar School, Newcastle upon Tyne. MB, BS Durham. RSO, Royal Victoria Infirmary, Newcastle upon Tyne; Consultant Surgeon, Kettering and District Gen. Hosp., 1965–95. Chairman: Jt Consultants Cttee, 1984–90; Central Cttee for Hosp. Med. Services, BMA, 1975–79; Council, BMA, 1979–84; Cttee, BMJ, 1993–; Member: GMC, 1979–; Council, World Med. Assoc., 1979–84; Hon. Sec. and Treasurer, Commonwealth Med. Assoc., 1982–86 (Vice-Pres., 1980–84). *Recreation:* retirement planning. *Address:* Rothesay House, 56 Headlands, Kettering, Northants NN15 6DG. *T:* Kettering (01536) 513299. *Club:* Army and Navy.

GRABINER, Anthony Stephen, QC 1981; a Recorder, since 1990; *b* 21 March 1945; *e s* of late Ralph Grabiner and of Freda Grabiner (*née* Cohen); *m* 1983, Jane, *er d* of Dr Benjamin Portnoy, TD, JP, MD, PhD, FRCP, Hale, Cheshire; three *s* one *d*. *Educ:* Central Foundn Boys' Grammar Sch., London, EC2; LSE, Univ. of London (LLB 1st Cl. Hons 1966, LLM with Distinction 1967). Lincoln's Inn: Hardwicke Scholar, 1966; called to the Bar, 1968; Droop Scholar, 1968; Bencher, 1989. Standing Jun. Counsel to Dept of Trade, Export Credits Guarantee Dept, 1976–81; Jun. Counsel to the Crown, 1978–81. Vice-Chm., Ct of Govs, LSE, 1993– (Mem., 1991–). *Publications:* (ed jtly) Sutton and Shannon on Contracts, 7th edn 1970; contrib. Banking Documents, to Encyclopedia of Forms and Precedents, 5th edn, 1986. *Recreations:* theatre, swimming, golf. *Address:* 1 Essex Court, Temple, EC4Y 9AR. *T:* 0171–583 2000. *Clubs:* Garrick, Royal Automobile, MCC.

GRACE, John Oliver Bowman; QC 1994; *b* 13 June 1948; *s* of Oliver Grace and Marjorie (*née* Bowman); *m* 1973, Carol S. Roundhill; two *s* one *d*. *Educ:* Marlborough; Southampton Univ. (LLB Hons). Called to the Bar, Middle Temple, 1973. *Recreations:* gardening, modern art, reading, music, cricket, church, brick-laying. *Address:* 3 Serjeants' Inn, EC4Y 1BQ. *T:* 0171–353 5537. *Club:* 4W's (Wandsworth).

GRACEY, Howard, FIA, FIAA, FPMI; consulting actuary; Senior Partner, R. Watson and Sons, 1993–95 (Partner, since 1970); *b* 21 Feb. 1935; *s* of late Charles Douglas Gracey and of Margaret Gertrude (*née* Heggie); *m* 1960, Pamela Jean Bradshaw; one *s* two *d*. *Educ:* Birkenhead Sch. FIA 1959; FIAA 1982; FPMI 1977; ASA 1978. National Service, 1960–61 (2nd Lieut). Royal Insurance Co., 1953–69. Church Comr, 1978–; Member: Gen. Synod of C of E, 1970–; C of E Pensions Bd, 1970– (Chm., 1980–); Treasurer, S Amer. Missionary Soc., 1975–93 (Chm., 1994–); Pres., Pensions Management Inst., 1983–85; Chm., Assoc. of Consulting Actuaries, 1991–93. *Recreations:* fell-walking, tennis, photography. *Address:* Timbers, 18 Broadwater Rise, Guildford, Surrey GU1 2LA. *Club:* Army and Navy.

GRACEY, John Halliday, CB 1984; Director General (Deputy Secretary), Board of Inland Revenue, 1981–85; Commissioner of Inland Revenue 1973–85; *b* 20 May 1925; *s* of Halliday Gracey and Florence Jane (*née* Cudlipp); *m* 1950, Margaret Procter; three *s*. *Educ:* City of London Sch.; Brasenose Coll., Oxford (MA). Army, 1943–47. Entered Inland Revenue, 1950; HM Treasury, 1970–73. Hon. Treas., NACRO, 1987–. *Recreations:* walking, bee-keeping. *Address:* 3 Woodberry Down, Epping, Essex CM16 6RJ. *T:* Epping (01992) 572167. *Club:* Reform.

See also T. A. Lloyd Davies.

GRADE, family name of **Baron Grade.**

GRADE, Baron *cr* 1976 (Life Peer), of Elstree, Herts; **Lew Grade,** Kt 1969; Chairman: The Grade Co., since 1985; ITC Entertainment Ltd, since 1995 (Chairman and Managing Director, 1958–82); *b* 25 Dec. 1906; *s* of late Isaac Winogradsky and Olga Winogradsky; *m* 1942, Kathleen Sheila Moody; one *s*. *Educ:* Rochelle Street Sch. Joint Managing Dir of Lew and Leslie Grade Ltd, until Sept. 1955; Chm. and Chief Exec., Associated Communications Corp. Ltd, 1973–82; Pres., ATV Network Ltd, 1977–82; Chairman: Bentray Investments Ltd, 1979–82; ACC Enterprises Inc., 1973–82; Stoll Moss Theatres Ltd, 1969–82; Chm. and Chief Exec., Embassy Communications Internat. Ltd, 1982–85; Dir, Euro Disney SCA, Paris, 1988–. Fellow, BAFTA, 1979. KCSS 1979. *Publication:* (autobiog.) Still Dancing, 1987. *Address:* 8 Queen Street Mayfair, W1X 7PH.

GRADE, Michael Ian; Chief Executive of Channel Four, since 1988; *b* 8 March 1943; *s* of Leslie Grade and *g s* of Olga Winogradski; *m* 1967, Penelope Jane (*née* Levinson) (marr. diss. 1981); one *s* one *d*; 2nd, 1982, Hon. Sarah Lawson (marr. diss. 1991), *y d* of 5th Baron Burnham. *Educ:* St Dunstan's Coll., London. Daily Mirror: Trainee Journalist, 1960; Sports Columnist, 1964–66; Theatrical Agent, Grade Organisation, 1966; joined London Management and Representation, 1969, Jt Man. Dir until 1973; London Weekend Television: Dep. Controller of Programmes (Entertainment), 1973; Dir of Programmes and Mem. Bd, 1977–81; Pres., Embassy Television, 1981–84; Controller, BBC1, 1984–86; Dir of Programmes, BBC TV, 1986–87. Director: ITN, 1989–93; First Leisure, 1991– (Chm., 1995–); Delfont Macintosh Theatres Ltd, 1994–; Chm., VCI plc, 1995–. Member: Council, LAMDA, 1981–93; Council BAFTA, 1981–82, 1986–88; 300 Group; Milton Cttee; British Screen Adv. Council; Council, Cinema and Television Benevolent Fund, 1993–. Chm., Wkg Gp, Fear of Crime, 1989; Mem., Nat. Commn of Inquiry into Prevention of Child Abuse, 1994–. President: TV and Radio Industries Club, 1987–88; Newspaper Press Fund, 1988–89; Entertainment Charities Fund, 1994–; Vice-Pres., Children's Film Unit, 1993–; Director: Open Coll., 1989–; Cities in Schools, 1991–; Gate Theatre, Dublin, 1990–; Internat. Council, Nat. Acad. of Television Arts and Scis, 1991–. Trustee: Band Aid; Healthcare Foundn; Vice-Chm., Stars Organisation for Spastics, 1992– (Hon. Treas., 1986–92). FRTS 1991 (Pres., 1995); Fellow, BAFTA, 1994. Hon. Prof., Thames Valley Univ., 1994. *Recreation:* entertainment. *Address:* Channel Four Television, 124 Horseferry Road, SW1P 2TX. *T:* 0171–396 4444. *Club:* Royal Thames Yacht.

GRADIN, Anita Ingegerd, (Fru Bertil Kersfelt); Member, Commission of the European Communities, since 1995; *b* 12 Aug. 1933; *d* of Ossian Gradin and Alfhild Gradin; *m* Bertil Kersfelt; one *s* one *d*. *Educ:* Grad. Fr. Sch. of Social Work and Public Admin, Stockholm. Journalist in various newspapers, 1950–63, Mem., Social Welfare Planning Cttee, Stockholm, 1963–67; MP, 1968–92; posts include: Chairperson: Council, Cttee on Educn and Financial Affairs; Cttee on Migration, Refugees and Democracy, Council of Europe; Cabinet Minister for Migration and Equality between Women and Men, 1982–86; Minister for Foreign Trade, 1986–91; Ambassador to Austria, 1992–95. Vice-Chairperson, Nat. Fedn of Social Democratic Women, 1975–92; Vice-Pres., Socialist Internat., 1983–92; Pres., Socialist Internat. Women, 1986–92. Women of the Year Award, 1986; Pro Merito Medal, Council of Europe, 1992. Cavalieri di Gran Croce (Italy), 1991. *Recreations:* swimming, walking in the woods. *Address:* European Commission, 200 rue de la Loi, 1049 Brussels, Belgium. *T:* (2) 2959439.

GRADY, Terence, MBE 1967; HM Diplomatic Service, retired; Ambassador at Libreville, 1980–82; *b* 23 March 1924; *s* of Patrick Grady and Catherine (*née* Fowles); *m* 1960, Jean Fischer; one *s* four *d*. *Educ:* St Michael's Coll., Leeds. HM Forces, 1942–47; Foreign Office, 1949; HM Embassy: Baghdad, 1950; Paris, 1951; Asst Private Secretary to Secretary of State for Foreign Affairs, 1952–55; HM Legation, Budapest, 1955–58; HM Embassy, Kabul, 1958–60; FO, 1960–63; Vice Consul, Elisabethville, 1963; Consul, Philadelphia, 1964–69; UK High Commission, Sydney, 1969–72; FCO, 1972–75; Head of Chancery, Dakar, 1975–77; Consul, Istanbul, 1977–80. *Recreations:* tennis, walking. *Address:* 58 The Close, Norwich NR1 4EH. *Club:* Norfolk (Norwich).

GRAEF, Roger Arthur; writer, director and producer of films; *b* NYC, 18 April 1936; *m* 1st, 1971, Karen Bergemann (marr. diss. 1983); one *s* one *d*; 2nd, 1986, Susan Mary Richards. *Educ:* Horace Mann Sch., NYC; Putney Sch., Vermont; Harvard Univ. (BA Hons). Directed, USA, 26 plays and operas; also directed CBS drama; Observer/Dir, Actors Studio, NYC, 1958–62; resident in England, 1962–; Director, London: Period of Adjustment (Royal Court); Afternoon Men; has written, produced and directed more than 80 films; *films for television include:* The Life and Times of John Huston, Esq., 1965; (Exec. Producer) 13-part Who Is series, 1966–67 (wrote/dir. films on Pierre Boulez, Jacques Lipchitz, Walter Gropius, Maurice Béjart); Günter Grass' Berlin, 1965; Why Save Florence?, 1968; In the Name of Allah, 1970; The Space between Words, 1971–72; A Law in the Making, 1973; Inside the Brussels HQ, 1975; Is This the Way to Save our Cities?, 1975; Decision series: British Steel, etc., 1976–77, British Communism, 1978 (Royal Television Soc. Award); Pleasure at Her Majesty's, The Secret Policeman's Ball, 1977–78; Inside Europe, 1977–78; Police series, 1980–82 (BAFTA Award); Police: Operation Carter, 1981–82; Nagging Doubt, 1984; The Fifty-Minute Hour, 1984; Maybe Baby, 1985; Comic Relief, 1986; Stress, 1986; Closing Ranks, 1987; The Secret Life of the Soviet Union, 1990; Turning the Screws, 1993; Look at the State We're In, 1995; In Search of Law and Order, 1995; Series Editor, Signals, 1988–89. Dept of Environment: Mem., Develt Control Review (Dobry Cttee), Chm., Study Gp on Public Participation in Planning, and Mem., Cttee on Control of Demolition, 1974–76. Chm., AIP, 1988–89; Member: Council, ICA, 1970–82; Council, BAFTA, 1976–77; Bd, Channel Four, 1980–85; Governor, BFI, 1974–78. Adviser on broadcasting to Brandt Commn, 1979–80; Media Consultant: Collins Publishing, 1983–88; London Transport (Mem. Bd, LTE, 1976–79; co-designer, new London Bus Map). Pres., Signals Internat. Trust, 1990–. Chairman: Book Aid, 1991; Théâtre de Complicité, 1991–. Member: Collège Analytique de Securité Urbaine, 1993–; British Soc. of Criminology; Sen. Fellow, Mannheim Centre of Criminal Justice, 1993–. *Publications:* Talking Blues, 1989; Living Dangerously, 1992;

In Search of Law and Order, 1994; contrib. Daily Telegraph (columnist, 1992–94), The Times, Sunday Telegraph, Observer, Independent on Sunday, Evening Standard, Police Review, The Independent, Guardian, Sunday Times. *Recreations:* tennis, making music, photography. *Address:* 72 Westbourne Park Villas, W2 5EB. *T:* 0171–727 7868. *Clubs:* Beefsteak, Groucho.

GRAFTON, 11th Duke of, *cr* 1675; **Hugh Denis Charles FitzRoy;** KG 1976; DL; Earl of Euston, Viscount Ipswich; Captain Grenadier Guards; *b* 3 April 1919; *e s* of 10th Duke of Grafton, and Lady Doreen Maria Josepha Sydney Buxton (*d* 1923), *d* of 1st Earl Buxton; *S* father, 1970; *m* 1946, Fortune (*see* Duchess of Grafton); two *s* three *d*. *Educ:* Eton; Magdalene Coll., Cambridge. ADC to the Viceroy of India, 1943–46. Vice-Chm. of Trustees, Nat. Portrait Gall., 1967–92; Mem., Royal Fine Art Commn, 1971–94. Chairman: Architectural Heritage Fund, 1976–94; Cathedrals Adv. Commn, 1981–91; Member: Hist. Bldgs Council for England, 1953–84; Hist. Bldgs Adv. Cttee, 1984–, Cathedrals and Churches Adv. Cttee, 1984–, English Heritage; Properties Cttee, Nat. Trust, 1981–94; President: Suffolk Preservation Soc., 1957–; SPAB, 1989–; Trustee: Sir John Soane's Mus. (Chm., 1975–); Hist. Churches Preservation Trust (Chm., 1980–); Buildings at Risk Trust; Tradescant Trust; Patron, Historic Houses Assoc. President: Internat. Students House, 1972–; East Anglia Tourist Bd, 1973–93; British Soc. of Master Glass Painters. Patron, Hereford Herd Book Soc. DL Suffolk, 1973. Hon. DCL East Anglia, 1990. *Heir: s* Earl of Euston, *qv*. *Address:* Euston Hall, Thetford, Norfolk IP24 2QW. *T:* Thetford (01842) 753282. *Club:* Boodle's.
See also C. D. Mackenzie.

GRAFTON, Duchess of; (Ann) Fortune FitzRoy, GCVO 1980 (DCVO 1970; CVO 1965); Mistress of The Robes to The Queen since 1967; *o d* of Captain Eric Smith, MC, LLD, Lower Ashfold, Slaugham; *m* 1946, Duke of Grafton, *qv*; two *s* three *d*. Lady of the Bedchamber to the Queen, 1953–66. SRCN Great Ormond Street, 1945; Mem. Bd of Governors, The Hospital for Sick Children, Great Ormond Street, 1952–66; Patron, Nurses' League. President: W Suffolk Mission to the Deaf; W Suffolk Decorative and Fine Arts Soc.; Bury St Edmunds Br., BHF; Vice-President: Suffolk Br., Royal British Legion Women's Section; Trinity Hospice, Clapham Common, 1951–. Governor: Felixstowe Coll.; Riddlesworth Hall. Patron: Relate, W Suffolk; Guildhall String Ensemble; Clarence River Historical Soc., Grafton, NSW. JP County of London, 1949, W Suffolk, 1972–90. *Address:* Euston Hall, Thetford, Norfolk IP24 2QW. *T:* Thetford (01842) 753282.
See also Jeremy F. E. Smith, Sir John L. E. Smith.

GRAFTON, NSW, Bishop of, since 1985; **Rt. Rev. Bruce Allan Schultz;** *b* 24 May 1932; *s* of Percival Ferdinand and Elsie Amelia Schultz; *m* 1962, Janet Margaret Gersbach; two *s* two *d* (and one *s* decd). *Educ:* Culcairn High School; St Columb's Hall and St John's Coll., Morpeth. ThL (ACT) 1960. Sheep and wheat property, Manager–Owner, 1950–57. Theolog. student, 1957–60; deacon 1959, priest 1960, dio. Riverina; Asst Priest, Broken Hill, 1961–63; Priest-in-charge, Ariah Park, Ardlethan and Barellan with Weethalle, 1964–67; Rector: Deniliquin, 1967–73; Gladstone, dio. Rockhampton, 1973–79; Archdeacon and Commissary of Rockhampton, 1975–79; Rector of Grafton and Dean of Christ Church Cathedral, 1979–83; Asst Bishop of Brisbane (Bishop for the Northern Region), 1983–85. Nat. Chm., Anglican Boys' Soc. in Australia, 1987–94; Episcopal overseer, Cursillo Movement in Australia, 1987–; Chm., NSW Provincial Commn on Christian Educn, 1989; Bd Mem., Australian Bd of Missions, 1988–. *Recreations:* family, fishing, tennis, water skiing, gardening. *Address:* Bishopsholme, 35 Victoria Street, Grafton, NSW 2460, Australia. *T:* (home) (66) 422070, (office) (66) 424122. *Clubs:* Grafton (Grafton); Carlton (Melbourne).

GRAFTON, Peter Witheridge, CBE 1972; Senior Partner, G. D. Walford & Partners, Chartered Quantity Surveyors, 1978–82 (Partner 1949–78), retired; *b* 19 May 1916; *s* of James Hawkins Grafton and Ethel Marion (*née* Brannan); *m* 1st, 1939, Joan Bleackley (*d* 1969); two *d* (and one *s* one *d* decd); 2nd, 1971, Margaret Ruth Ward; two *s*. *Educ:* Westminster City Sch.; Sutton Valence Sch.; Coll. of Estate Management. FRICS, FCIArb. Served War of 1939–45, Queen's Westminster Rifles, Dorsetshire Regt and RE, UK and Far East (Captain). Pres., RICS, 1978–79 (Vice-Pres., 1974–78); Mem. and Past Chm., Quantity Surveyors Council; Mem. Council, Construction Industries Research and Information Assoc., 1963–69; Member: Research Adv. Council to Minister of Housing and Construction, 1967–71; Nat. Cons. Council for Building and Civil Engrg Industries, 1968–76; British Bd of Agrément, 1973–88; Chm., Nat. Jt Consultative Cttee for Building Industry, 1974–75 (Mem., 1970–77). Master, Worshipful Co. of Chartered Surveyors, 1983–84. Trustee, United Westminster Schs; Governor, Sutton Valence Sch., 1971– (Chm., 1976–91); Past Chm., Old Suttonians Assoc. Contested (L) Bromley, 1959. *Publications:* numerous articles on techn. and other professional subjects. *Recreations:* golf (founder, Chm., 1962–94, Pres., 1994–, Public Schs Old Boys Golf Assoc., Co-donor Grafton Morrish Trophy; past Captain of Chartered Surveyors Golfing Soc.); writing. *Address:* 57 Padbrook, Limpsfield, Oxted, Surrey RH8 0DZ. *T:* Oxted (01883) 716685. *Clubs:* Reform; Rye Golf, Tandridge Golf.

GRAHAM, family name of **Duke of Montrose** and **Baron Graham of Edmonton.**

GRAHAM, Marquis of; James Alexander Norman Graham; *b* 16 Aug. 1973; *s* and heir of Duke of Montrose, *qv*.

GRAHAM OF EDMONTON, Baron *cr* 1983 (Life Peer), of Edmonton in Greater London; **Thomas Edward Graham;** Opposition Chief Whip, House of Lords, since 1990; *b* 26 March 1925; *m* 1950, Margaret, *d* of Frederick Golding; two *s*. *Educ:* elementary sch.; WEA Co-operative College. BA Open Univ., 1976. FIMgt. Newcastle-on-Tyne Co-operative Soc., 1939–52; Organiser, British Fedn of Young Co-operators, 1952–53; Educn Sec., Enfield Highway Co-operative Soc., 1953–62; Sec., Co-operative Union Southern Section, 1962–67; Nat. Sec., Co-operative Party, 1967–74. MP (Lab and Co-op) Enfield, Edmonton, Feb. 1974–1983; PPS to Minister of State, Dept of Prices and Consumer Protection, 1974–76; A Lord Comr of HM Treasury, 1976–79; Opposition spokesman on the environment, 1980–83. Contested (Lab) Edmonton, 1983. Mem. and Leader, Enfield Council, 1961–68. *Address:* 2 Clerks Piece, Loughton, Essex IG10 1NR.

GRAHAM, Prof. Alastair, DSc; FRS 1979; Professor of Zoology, University of Reading, to 1972, now Emeritus Professor; *b* 6 Nov. 1906. *Educ:* Edinburgh Univ. (MA, BSc); London Univ. (DSc). Fellow, Zoological Soc., 1939 (Frink Medal, 1976). *Publications:* British Prosobranch Molluscs (jtly), 1962; Molluscs: prosobranch and pyramidellid gastropods, 1988. *Address:* 207 Wokingham Road, Reading, Berks RG6 2DT. *T:* Reading (01734) 264154.

GRAHAM, Alastair Carew; FRSA; Head Master, Mill Hill School, 1979–92; *b* 23 July 1932; *s* of Col J. A. Graham and Mrs Graham (*née* Carew-Hunt); *m* 1969, Penelope Rachel Beaumont; two *d*. *Educ:* Winchester Coll.; Gonville and Caius Coll., Cambridge (1st Cl. Mod. and Med. Langs). Served 1st Bn Argyll and Sutherland Highlanders, 1951–53. Foy, Morgan & Co. (City), 1956–58; Asst Master, Eton, 1958; House Master, 1970–79. *Recreations:* ball games, walking; theatre and opera; music listening, gardening, educn for the disabled. *Address:* Longbourn, Chawton, Alton, Hants GU34 1SA.
See also Maj.-Gen. J. D. C. Graham.

GRAHAM, Sir Alexander (Michael), GBE 1990; JP; Chairman, FirstCity Insurance Brokers Ltd, since 1993; Lord Mayor of London, 1990–91; *b* 27 Sept. 1938; *s* of Dr Walter Graham and Suzanne Graham (*née* Simon); *m* 1964, Carolyn, *d* of Lt-Col Alan Wolryche Stansfeld, MBE; three *d*. *Educ:* Fyvie Village Sch.; Hall Sch., Hampstead; St Paul's Sch. Joined Norman Frizzell & Partners Ltd, 1957: Dir, 1967–93; Man. Dir, 1973–90; Dep. Chm., 1990–93; Underwriting Member of Lloyd's; Director: Folgate Insce Co. Ltd, 1975– (Chm., 1995–); Employment Conditions Abroad Ltd, 1992– (Chm., 1993–); Chm., Enclidian plc, 1994–. National Service, 1957–59; commnd Gordon Highlanders; TA 1959–67; Chm., Nat. Employers Liaison Cttee for TA and Reserve Forces, 1992–. Mercers' Co.: Liveryman, 1971–; Mem., Ct of Assistants, 1980; Master, 1983–84; Mem., Ct of Common Council, City of London, 1978–79; Alderman for Ward of Queenhithe, 1979–; Pres., Queenhithe Ward Club, 1979–. Sheriff, City of London, 1986–87; HM Lieut, City of London, 1989–. Hon. Liveryman, Co. of Chartered Secretaries and Administrators, 1992; Hon. Freeman: Insurers' Co., 1992; Merchant Adventurers of York, 1983. President: CS Motoring Assoc., 1993–; British Insurance Law Assoc., 1994–; Vice-Pres., Insurance Inst. of London, 1978–. Governor: Hall Sch., Hampstead, 1975–93; Christ's Hosp. Sch., 1979–; King Edward's Sch., Whitley, 1979–; St Paul's Sch., 1980–93; St Paul's Girls' Sch., 1980–93; City of London Boys' Sch., 1983–85; City of London Girls' Sch., 1992–; Mem. Council, Gresham Coll., 1983–93; Trustee, Morden College, 1988– (Chm., 1995–); Chancellor, City Univ., 1990–91. Trustee: United Response, 1988– (Chm., 1993–); Temple Bar Trust, 1992–; Hon. Life Mem., Cancer Relief Macmillan Fund, 1993; Mem., Exec. Cttee, Army Benevolent Fund, 1991–; Chm. Council, Order of St John, Herts, 1993. FCII 1964; FBIIBA 1967; FCIS 1990; FInstD 1975; CIMgt (CBIM 1991); FRSA 1980. Hon. DCL City, 1990. KStJ 1990. Order of Wissam Alouite (Morocco), 1987; Grand Cross Order of Merit (Chile), 1991. *Recreations:* wine, genealogy, music, reading, silver, bridge, golf, swimming, tennis, shooting, getting daughters married. *Address:* Walden Abbotts, Whitwell, Hitchin, Herts SG4 8AJ. *T:* Whitwell (Herts) (01438) 871223. *Clubs:* Carlton, City Livery; Highland Brigade; Royal Worlington and Newmarket Golf.
See also Lt-Gen. Sir P. W. Graham.

GRAHAM, Alistair; *see* Graham, J. A.

GRAHAM, Rt. Rev. Andrew Alexander Kenny; *see* Newcastle, Bishop of.

GRAHAM, Andrew Winston Mawdsley; Fellow, and Tutor in Economics, Balliol College, Oxford, since 1969; *b* 20 June 1942; *s* of Winston Mawdsley Graham, *qv*; *m* 1970, Peggotty Fawssett. *Educ:* Charterhouse; St Edmund Hall, Oxford. MA (PPE). Economic Assistant: NEDO, 1964; Dept of Economic Affairs, 1964–66; Asst to Economic Adviser to the Cabinet, 1966–68; Economic Adviser to Prime Minister, 1968–69; Estates Bursar, 1978, Investment Bursar, 1979–83, Vice Master, 1988 and 1992–94, Balliol Coll., Oxford; Policy Adviser to Prime Minister (on leave of absence from Balliol), 1974–75; Economic Advr to Shadow Chancellor of Exchequer, 1988–92, to Leader of the Opposition, 1992–94. Tutor, Oxford Univ. Business Summer Sch., 1971, 1972, 1973 and 1976. Vis. Researcher, SE Asian Central Banks Res. and Trng Centre, Malaysia, 1984; Vis. Fellow, Griffith Univ., Brisbane, 1984; Vis. Scholar, MIT, and Vis. Fellow, Center for Eur. Studies, Harvard, 1994. Member: Wilson Cttee to Review the Functioning of Financial Institutions, 1977–80; Economics Cttee, SSRC, 1978–80; British Transport Docks Bd, 1979–82; Chm., St James Gp (Economic Forecasting), 1982–84, 1985–92. Mem., ILO/Jobs and Skills Prog. for Africa (JASPA) Mission to Ethiopia, 1982; Hd, Queen Elizabeth House/Food Studies Gp team assisting Govt of Republic of Zambia, 1984; Consultant, BBC, 1989–92. Mem., Media Adv. Cttee, IPPR, 1994–. Mem., Council of Management, Templeton Coll., Oxford, 1990–. Founder Mem. Editorial Bd, Library of Political Economy, 1982–. *Publications:* (ed) Government and Economies in the Postwar Period, 1990; contribs to books on economics and philosophy. *Recreation:* windsurfing on every possible occasion. *Address:* Balliol College, Oxford OX1 3BJ. *T:* Oxford (01865) 277777.

GRAHAM, Anne Silvia, (Lady Graham); Chairman, South Cumbria Health Authority, 1988–94; *b* 1 Aug. 1934; *o d* of late Benjamin Arthur Garcia and Constance Rosa (*née* Journeaux); *m* Sir Peter Graham, *qv*. *Educ:* Francis Holland Sch., SW1; LSE (LLB). Called to the Bar, Inner Temple, 1958; Yarborough-Anderson Scholar, 1959. Joined Min. of Housing and Local Govt, 1960; Dep. Legal Advr, DoE, 1978–86. Mem. Court, Lancaster Univ. *Recreations:* gardening, cookery.

GRAHAM, Antony Richard Malise; management consultant; Director, Clive & Stokes International, since 1985; *b* 15 Oct. 1928; *s* of late Col Patrick Ludovic Graham, MC, and late Barbara Mary Graham (*née* Jury); *m* 1958, Gillian Margaret, *d* of late L. Bradford Cook and of Mrs W. V. Wrigley; two *s* one *d*. *Educ:* Abberley Hall; Nautical Coll., Pangbourne. Merchant Navy, 1945–55 (Master Mariner). Stewarts and Lloyds Ltd, 1955–60; PE Consulting Group Ltd, management consultants, 1960–72 (Regional Dir, 1970–72); Regional Industrial Dir (Under-Sec.), DTI, 1972–76; Dir, Barrow Hepburn Group Ltd, and Maroquinerie Le Tanneur et Tanneries du Bugey SA, 1976–81; Chm., Paton & Sons (Tillicoultry) Ltd, 1981–82. Contested (C) Leeds East, 1966. *Address:* The Gardens, Nun Appleton Hall, York YO5 7BG.

GRAHAM, Billy; *see* Graham, William F.

GRAHAM, Sir Charles (Spencer Richard), 6th Bt *cr* 1783; Lord-Lieutenant of Cumbria, 1983–94; *b* 16 July 1919; *s* of Sir (Frederick) Fergus Graham, 5th Bt, KBE, and of Mary Spencer Revell, CBE (*d* 1985), *d* of late Maj.-Gen. Raymond Reade, CB, CMG; *S* father, 1978; *m* 1944, Isabel Susan Anne, *d* of late Major R. L. Surtees, OBE; two *s* one *d*. *Educ:* Eton. Served with Scots Guards, 1940–50, NW Europe (despatches) and Malaya. President, Country Landowners' Assoc., 1971–73. Mem., Nat. Water Council, 1973–83. Master, Worshipful Co. of Farmers, 1982–83. High Sheriff 1955, DL 1971, Cumbria (formerly Cumberland). KStJ 1984. *Heir: s* James Fergus Surtees Graham [*b* 29 July 1946; *m* 1975, Serena Jane, *yr d* of Ronald Frank Kershaw; one *s* two *d*]. *Address:* Crofthead, Longtown, Cumbria CA6 5PA. *T:* Longtown (01228) 791231. *Clubs:* Brooks's, Pratt's.

GRAHAM, Dr Christopher Forbes, FRS 1981; Professor of Animal Development, and Professorial Fellow, St Catherine's College, University of Oxford, since 1985; *b* 23 Sept. 1940. *Educ:* Oxford Univ. (BA 1963, DPhil 1966). Formerly Junior Beit Memorial Fellow in Med. Research, Sir William Dunn Sch. of Pathology. Lectr, Zoology Dept, Oxford Univ., 1970–85. Member: Brit. Soc. Cell Biology; Brit. Soc. for Developmental Biology; Soc. for Experimental Biology; Genetical Soc. *Publication:* The Developmental Biology of Plants and Animals, 1976, new edn as Developmental Control in Plants and Animals, 1984. *Address:* Department of Zoology, University of Oxford, South Parks Road, Oxford OX1 3PS.

GRAHAM, Colin; Artistic Director: English Music Theatre, since 1975; Aldeburgh Festival, since 1969; Opera Theatre of St Louis, since 1984 (Associate Artistic Director, 1979–84); Director of Productions, English National Opera, 1977–84, Associate Artist, since 1984; stage director, designer, lighting designer, and author; *b* 22 Sept. 1931; *s* of Frederick Eaton Graham-Bonnalie and Alexandra Diana Vivian Findlay. *Educ:* Northaw Prep. Sch.; Stowe Sch.; RADA (Dip.). Dir of Productions, English Opera Gp, 1963–74; Associate Dir of Prodns, Sadler's Wells Opera/English National Opera, 1967–75. Principal productions for: English Music Theatre; Royal Opera, Covent Garden; Scottish Opera; New Opera Co.; Glyndebourne Opera; BBC TV; Brussels National Opera; St Louis Opera Theatre; Santa Fe Opera; Metropolitan Opera, New York; NYC Opera; dir. world premières: of all Benjamin Britten's operas since 1954; of other contemp. composers. Theatre productions for: Old Vic Co.; Bristol Old Vic; Royal Shakespeare Co. Ordained minister, New Covenant Church, St Louis, Mo, 1987. Hon. DA: Webster Univ., 1985; Univ. of Missouri, 1992. Arts and Education Council Award, 1993. Orpheus award (Germany) for best opera production, 1973 (War and Peace, ENO); Opera America award for production, 1988 (Albert Herring, Banff Fest. Opera). *Publications:* A Penny for a Song (libretto for Richard Rodney Bennett), 1969; The Golden Vanity (libretto for opera by Britten), 1970; King Arthur (libretto for new version of Purcell opera), 1971; The Postman Always Rings Twice (libretto for opera by Stephen Paulus), 1981; Jōruri (libretto for opera by Minoru Miki), 1985; The Woodlanders (libretto for opera by Stephen Paulus), 1984; production scores for Britten's: Curlew River, 1969; The Burning Fiery Furnace, 1971; The Prodigal Son, 1973; contrib. Opera. *Recreations:* The Bible, motor cycles, movies, weight training. *Address:* PO Box 191910, Saint Louis, MO 63119, USA.

GRAHAM, David; *see* Graham, S. D.

GRAHAM, Douglas; *see* Graham, M. G. D.

GRAHAM, Duncan Gilmour, CBE 1987; Senior Partner, Duncan Graham Consultants, since 1991; *b* 20 Aug. 1936; *s* of Robert Gilmour Graham and Lilias Turnbull Graham (*née* Watson); *m* 1st, 1962, Margaret Gray Graham (*née* Cairns) (marr diss. 1991); two *s* one *d*; 2nd, 1991, Wendy Margaret Wallace. *Educ:* Hutcheson's, Glasgow; Univ. of Glasgow (MA (Hons) History); Jordanhill Coll. of Education (Teachers' Secondary Cert.). Teacher of History: Whitehill Sec. Sch., Glasgow, 1959–62; Hutcheson's, Glasgow, 1962–65; Lectr in Social Studies, Craigie Coll. of Educn, Ayr, 1965–68; Asst Dir of Educn, Renfrewshire, 1968–70; Sen. Depute Dir of Educn, Renfrewshire, 1970–74, Strathclyde Regl Council, 1974–79; Advr to COSLA and Scottish Teachers' Salaries Cttee, 1974–79; County Educn Officer, Suffolk, 1979–87; Chief Exec., Humberside CC, 1987–88; Chm. and Chief Exec., Nat. Curriculum Council, 1988–91. Advr to ACC, 1982–88; Mem., Burnham Cttee, 1983–87 and of ACAS Indep. Panel, 1986. Sec., Co. Educn Officers Soc., 1985–87; Chm., Assoc. of Educn Officers, 1985; Project Dir, DES Teacher Appraisal Study, 1985–86; Chm., Nat. Steering Gp on Teacher Appraisal, 1987–90. Member: BBC North Adv. Council, 1988–91; Lincs and Humberside Arts Council, 1988–91; Yorks and Humberside Arts, 1991–94; Council of Nat. Foundn for Educnl Res., 1984, and 1989–90; Exec. Council, Industrial Soc., 1988–90; Chm., Nat. Mathematics Wkg Gp, 1988. FRSA 1981. *Publications:* Those Having Torches, 1985; In the Light of Torches, 1986; Sense, Nonsense and the National Curriculum, 1992; A Lesson For Us All, 1992; Sunset on the Clyde, 1993; many articles in nat. press and educn and local govt jls. *Recreations:* amateur radio, fishing. *Address:* Gilmour Mews, Battlebarrow, Appleby, Cumbria CA16 6XT.

GRAHAM, Euan Douglas, CB 1985; Principal Clerk of Private Bills, House of Lords, 1961–84; *b* 29 July 1924; *yr s* of Brig. Lord (Douglas) Malise Graham, CB, DSO, MC, RA; *m* 1st, Pauline Pitt-Rivers (*née* Tennant) (marr. diss. 1972); one adopted *s*; 2nd, Caroline, *d* of K. W. B. Middleton, *qv* and Ruth, Lady Kinross; two *d*. *Educ:* Eton; Christ Church, Oxford (MA). Served RAF, 1943–47. Joined Parliament Office, House of Lords, 1950; Clerk, Judicial Office, 1950–60; Principal Clerk of Private Bills, Examiner of Petitions for Private Bills, Taxing Officer, 1960–85. *Recreations:* deer stalking, mountain bicycling. *Address:* Hill Farm, Heddington, near Calne, Wilts SN11 0PW. *Club:* Beefsteak.

GRAHAM, George Ronald Gibson, CBE 1986; Partner, Maclay, Murray & Spens, Solicitors, Glasgow, Edinburgh and London, since 1968; Director, Scottish Widows' Fund and Life Assurance Society, since 1984; *b* 15 Oct. 1939; *o s* of James Gibson Graham, MD, and Elizabeth Waddell; *m* 1965, Mirren Elizabeth Carnegie; three *s*. *Educ:* Glasgow Academy; Loretto Sch., Musselburgh; Oriel Coll., Oxford (MA); Glasgow Univ. (LLB). Co-ordinator of Diploma in Legal Practice, 1979–83; Clerk to Gen. Council, Glasgow Univ., 1990–. Mem. Council, 1977–89, Pres., 1984–85, Law Soc. of Scotland. Gov., Jordanhill Coll. of Educn, Glasgow, 1991–93. *Recreations:* fishing, swimming, walking. *Address:* 44 Kingsborough Gardens, Glasgow G12 9NL. *T:* 0141–334 2730. *Clubs:* The Western, Western Baths (Glasgow).

GRAHAM, Gordon; *see* Graham, W. G.

GRAHAM, Gordon, CBE 1980; PPRIBA; consultant architect; Director, Foster Associates Ltd, 1984–89; *b* Carlisle, 4 June 1920; *s* of late Stanley Bouch Graham and Isabel Hetherington; *m* 1946, Enid Pennington; three *d*. *Educ:* Creighton Sch.; Nottingham Sch. of Architecture. DipArch, RIBA, 1949; RIBA Arthur Cates Prizeman, 1949; travelling schol., S and Central America, 1953. Served Royal Artillery, N Africa, Italy and NW Europe, 1940–46. Sen. Lectr, Nottingham Sch. of Architecture, 1949–61; Sen. Partner, Architects Design Gp, 1958–84. Pres., Nottingham, Derby and Lincoln Soc. of Architects, 1965–66; RIBA: Chm., E Midlands Region, 1967–69; Mem. Council, 1967–73 and 1974; Vice-Pres., 1969–71; Hon. Sec., 1971–72 and 1975–76; Sen. Vice-Pres., 1976; Pres., 1977–79. Mem., Building EDC, 1978–83. Hon. FRAIC 1978. Hon. MA Nottingham, 1979. *Recreations:* Rugby football, architecture. *Club:* Reform.

GRAHAM, Ian James Alastair, FSA; Director, Maya Corpus Progam, Peabody Museum of Archaeology, Harvard University; *b* 12 Nov. 1923; *s* of Captain Lord Alastair Graham, RN, *y s* of 5th Duke of Montrose, and Lady Meriel Olivia Bathurst (*d* 1936), *d* of 7th Earl Bathurst; unmarried. *Educ:* Winchester Coll.; Trinity Coll., Dublin. RNVR (A), 1942–47; TCD 1947–51; Nuffield Foundn Research Scholar at The National Gallery, 1951–54; independent archaeological explorer in Central America, 1959–68; Res. Fellow, 1968–75, Asst Curator, 1975–93, Peabody Mus. of Archaeol., Harvard Univ. Occasional photographer of architecture. MacArthur Foundn Prize Fellowship, 1981. *Publications:* Splendours of the East, 1965; Great Houses of the Western World, 1968; Archaeological Explorations in El Peten, Guatemala, 1967; Corpus of Maya Hieroglyphic Inscriptions, 15 parts, 1975–; other reports in learned jls. *Address:* Chantry Farm, Campsey Ash, Suffolk IP13 0PZ; c/o Peabody Museum, Harvard University, Cambridge, MA, USA.

GRAHAM, Sir James Bellingham, 11th Bt *cr* 1662; Researcher, Cecil Higgins Museum and Art Gallery, Bedford; *b* 8 Oct. 1940; *e s* of Sir Richard Bellingham Graham, 10th Bt, OBE, and Beatrice, OBE (*d* 1992), *d* of late Michael Hamilton-Spencer-Smith, DSO, MC; *S* father, 1982; *m* 1986, Halina, *d* of Major Wiktor and Eleonora Grubert. *Educ:* Eton College; Christ Church, Oxford (MA). *Publications:* Guide to Norton Conyers, 1976, rewritten 1988; (with Halina Graham) A Guide to the Cecil Higgins Art Gallery, 1987. *Recreations:* travel, visiting historic houses and museums. *Heir: b* William Reginald Graham, *b* 7 July 1942. *Address:* Norton Conyers, Ripon, N Yorks HG4 5EH. *T:* Melmerby (01765) 640333; 3 Glebe Road, Bedford MK40 2PL.

GRAHAM, James Lowery, OBE 1991; Managing Director, Border Television, Carlisle, since 1982, Deputy Chairman, since 1990; *b* 29 Oct. 1932; *s* of William and Elizabeth Graham; *m* 1984, Ann Routledge; two *d* by previous marr. *Educ:* Whitehaven Grammar School. Journalist, North West Evening Mail, Barrow, 1955–62; News Editor, Border Television, 1962–67; Producer, BBC, Leeds, 1967–70; BBC: Regional News Editor, North, 1970–75; Regional Television Manager, North East, 1975–80; Head of Secretariat, Broadcasting House, 1980–82; Sec., Central Music Adv. Council, 1981–82. Jt Sec., Broadcasters' Audience Res. Bd, 1980–82. Dir, Indep. Television Publications, 1982–89. Chm., Independent Television Facilities Centre Ltd, 1987–; Director: Oracle Teletext, 1988–93; Radio Borders, 1989–; Radio SW Scotland, 1989–93 (Chm., 1990–93); Bay Radio Ltd, 1992–94; Central Scotland Radio, 1993–; North East Radio, 1993–. Prix Italia, ITVA rep., 1987–. Dir, Educnl Broadcasting Services Trust, 1992–. Member: BAFTA; European movement; Co-operative Internationale de Recherche et d'Action en Matière de Communication (European Producers). Governor: Newcastle Polytechnic, 1975–80; Cumbria Coll. of Art and Design. FRSA 1987. MInstD; FRTS 1994. News Film Award, RTS, 1975; Beffroi d'Or, Lille (European regional broadcasting award), 1983; RTS Regl Broadcasting Award, 1989. *Recreations:* hill walking, ski-ing. *Address:* Oak House, Great Corby, Carlisle, Cumbria CA4 8NE. *Club:* Groucho.

GRAHAM, Sir James (Thompson), Kt 1990; CMG 1986; farmer, since 1946; Director, 1979–89, Chairman, 1982–89, New Zealand Dairy Board, retired; *b* 6 May 1929; *s* of Harold Graham and Florence Cecily Graham; *m* 1955, Ina Isabelle Low; one *s* two *d*. *Educ:* New Plymouth Boys' High Sch. Dir, NZ Co-op Dairy Co., 1974–89 (Chm., 1979–82). *Recreations:* golf, tennis, bowls. *Address:* 245 Oceanbeach Road, Mount Maunganui, New Zealand. *T:* (75) 754043.

GRAHAM, John, CB 1976; Fisheries Secretary, Ministry of Agriculture, Fisheries and Food, 1967–76; *b* 17 March 1918; *s* of late John Graham; *m* 1940, Betty Ramage Jarvie; two *s* three *d*. *Educ:* Fettes Coll., Edinburgh; Trinity Coll., Cambridge (Schol.). Classical Tripos, MA Cantab. Entered Post Office as Asst Principal, 1939; Min. of Food, 1940.

GRAHAM, Sir John (Alexander Noble), 4th Bt *cr* 1906, of Larbert; GCMG 1986 (KCMG 1979; CMG 1972); HM Diplomatic Service, retired; Registrar, Order of Saint Michael and Saint George, since 1987; Director, Ditchley Foundation, 1987–92; *b* 15 July 1926; *s* of Sir John Reginald Noble Graham, 3rd Bt, VC, OBE and Rachel Septima (*d* 1984), *d* of Col Sir Alexander Sprot, 1st and last Bt; *S* father, 1980; *m* 1st, 1956, Marygold Ellinor Gabrielle Austin (*d* 1991); two *s* one *d*; 2nd, 1992, Jane, *widow* of Christopher Howells. *Educ:* Eton Coll.; Trinity Coll., Cambridge. Army, 1944–47; Cambridge, 1948–50; HM Foreign Service, 1950; Middle East Centre for Arab Studies, 1951; Third Secretary, Bahrain 1951, Kuwait 1952, Amman 1953; Asst Private Sec. to Sec. of State for Foreign Affairs, 1954–57; First Sec., Belgrade, 1957–60, Benghazi, 1960–61; FO 1961–66; Counsellor and Head of Chancery, Kuwait, 1966–69; Principal Private Sec. to Foreign and Commonwealth Sec., 1969–72; Cllr (later Minister) and Head of Chancery, Washington, 1972–74; Ambassador to Iraq, 1974–77; Dep. Under-Sec. of State, FCO, 1977–79; Ambassador to Iran, 1979–80; Deputy Under-Sec. of State, FCO, 1980–82; Ambassador and UK Permanent Representative to NATO, Brussels, 1982–86. *Heir: s* Andrew John Noble Graham, MBE, Lt-Col, Argyll and Sutherland Highlanders [*b* 21 Oct. 1956; *m* 1984, Susie M. B. O'Riordan, *er d* of Rear-Adm. J. P. B. O'Riordan, *qv*; one *s* three *d*]. *Address:* Salisbury Place, Church Street, Shipton under Wychwood, Oxon OX7 6BP. *Club:* Army and Navy.

GRAHAM, (John) Alistair; Chief Executive, Calderdale & Kirklees Training and Enterprise Council, since 1991; *b* 6 Aug. 1942; *s* of late Robert Graham and of Dorothy Graham; *m* 1968, Dorothy Jean Wallace; one *s* one *d*. *Educ:* Royal Grammar Sch., Newcastle upon Tyne. FIPD (FITD 1989; FIPM 1989). Clerical Asst, St George's Hosp., Morpeth, 1961; Admin Trainee, Northern Regional Hosp. Bd, 1963; Higher Clerical Officer, Royal Sussex County Hosp., Brighton, 1964; Legal Dept, TGWU, 1965; The Civil and Public Services Association: Asst Sec., 1966; Asst Gen. Sec., 1975; Dep. Gen. Sec., 1976; Gen. Sec., 1982–86; Dir, Industrial Soc., 1986–91. Chm., Shareholders' Trust FI Group, 1991–. Vis. Fellow, Nuffield Coll., Oxford, 1984–92; Vis. Prof., Management Sch., Imperial Coll., London Univ., 1989–91. External assessor, teacher trng courses, Univ. of Huddersfield, 1993–. Chairman: BBC S and E Regl Adv. Council, 1987–90; Training and Develt Lead Body, 1989–94; Member: Personnel Lead Body, 1991–94; BBC Educn Broadcasting Council, 1991–; Restrictive Practices Court, 1993–; Bd, Univ. of Huddersfield Trng and Quality Services Certification Div., 1993–. Mem., TUC Gen. Council, 1982–84, 1985–86. Mem., 1988–, Chm., Staff Cttee, 1991–, OU Council. Trustee, Duke of Edinburgh Study Conf., 1989–92. Bd Mem., Opera North, 1989–; Mem. Management Cttee, Huddersfield Contemporary Music Fest., 1992–. Assessor, Guildford and Woolwich Inquiry, 1990–94. Contested (Lab), Brighton Pavilion, 1966. FRSA 1989. *Recreations:* music, theatre. *Address:* Parkview House, Woodvale Road, Brighouse, W Yorks HD6 4AB.

GRAHAM, Maj.-Gen. John David Carew, CB 1978; CBE 1973 (OBE 1966); Secretary to the Administrative Trustees of the Chevening Estate, 1978–86; *b* 18 Jan. 1923; *s* of late Col J. A. Graham, late RE, and Constance Mary Graham (*née* Carew-Hunt); *m* 1956, Rosemary Elaine Adamson; one *s* one *d*. *Educ:* Cheltenham Coll. psc 1955; jssc 1962. Commissioned into Argyll and Sutherland Highlanders, 1942 (despatches, 1945); served with 5th (Scottish) Bn, The Parachute Regt, 1946–49; British Embassy, Prague, 1949–50; HQ Scottish Comd, 1956–58; Mil. Asst to CINCENT, Fontainebleau, 1960–62; comd 1st Bn, The Parachute Regt, 1964–66; Instr at Staff Coll., Camberley, 1967; Regtl Col, The Parachute Regt, 1968–69; Comdr, Sultan's Armed Forces, Oman, 1970–72; Indian Nat. Defence Coll., New Delhi, 1973; Asst Chief of Staff, HQ AFCENT, 1974–76; GOC Wales, 1976–78. Hon. Col, Kent ACF, 1981–88 (Chm. Kent ACF Cttee, 1979–86); Hon. Col, 203 (Welsh) Gen. Hosp., RAMC, TA, 1983–88. Freeman, City of London, 1992. OStJ 1978, and Chm., St John Council for Kent, 1978–86; CStJ 1983. Order of Oman, 1972. *Address:* Fintry, 6 Sheraton Park, Christ Church, Barbados, WI.

See also A. C. Graham.

GRAHAM, Sir John (Moodie), 2nd Bt *cr* 1964; Director, Kinnegar Inns Ltd, since 1981; Chairman, John Graham (Dromore) Ltd, 1966–83; *b* 3 April 1938; *s* of Sir Clarence Graham, 1st Bt, MICE, and Margaret Christina Moodie (*d* 1954); *S* father, 1966; *m* 1970, Valerie Rosemary (marr. diss. 1983), *d* of late Frank Gill, Belfast; three *d*. *Educ:* Trinity Coll., Glenalmond; Queen's Univ., Belfast. BSc, Civil Engineering, 1961. Joined family firm of John Graham (Dromore) Ltd, Building and Civil Engineering Contractors, on graduating from University. Director: Electrical Supplies Ltd, 1967–83; Concrete (NI) Ltd, 1967–83; Ulster Quarries Ltd; Graham (Contracts) Ltd, 1971–83; Fieldhouse Plant (NI) Ltd, 1976–83. Chm., Concrete Soc., NI, 1972–74; Senior Vice-Pres., Concrete Soc., 1980; Pres., Northern Ireland Leukaemia Research Fund, 1967. *Recreations:* sailing, ski-ing, photography. *Address:* Les Bordes d'Arinsal, Andorra. *T:* 837863; 77 South Birch Road 11D, Fort Lauderdale, FL 33316, USA. *T:* (305) 7288720.

GRAHAM, John Strathie; Under Secretary (Local Government), Scottish Office Environment Department, since 1991; *b* 27 May 1950; *s* of Sir Norman Graham, *qv*; *m*

1979, Anne Janet Stenhouse; two *s* one *d*. *Educ:* Edinburgh Academy; Corpus Christi College, Oxford (BA Lit Hum). Joined Scottish Office, 1972; Private Sec. to Minister of State, 1975–76; Industrial Develt and Electricity Divs, 1976–82; Private Sec. to Sec. of State, 1983–85; Asst Sec., Planning and Finance Divs, 1985–91. *Recreations:* music, hillwalking. *Address:* Scottish Office, New St Andrew's House, Edinburgh EH1 3TG. *T:* 0131–244 4722.

GRAHAM, Kathleen Mary, CBE 1958 (MBE 1945); *d* of late Col R. B. Graham, CBE, and Mrs M. G. Graham, London; unmarried. *Educ:* Cheltenham Ladies' Coll.; Univ. of London (Courtauld Inst. of Art). Courtauld Inst., Dept of Technology War-time Laboratory, 1940–41; Political Warfare Executive, 1942–45; entered HM Foreign Service, 1945; served in FO, 1946–49; Consul (Information) at San Francisco, Calif, 1949–53; served in FO, 1953–55; made Counsellor in HM Foreign Service in 1955 and appointed Dep. Consul-Gen. in New York, 1955–59; HM Consul-Gen. at Amsterdam, 1960–63; in FO, 1964–69, retired. Exec. Dir, 1970–73, a Governor, 1973–80, E-SU. *Recreations:* music, history of art. *Address:* 16 Graham Terrace, SW1W 8JH. *T:* 0171–730 4611.

GRAHAM, Kenneth, CBE 1987 (OBE 1971); Deputy General Secretary, Trades Union Congress, 1985–87 (Assistant General Secretary, 1977–85); Member: Board, The Open College, since 1987; Professional Conduct Committee, General Council of the Bar, since 1990; *b* 18 July 1922; *er s* of late Ernest Graham and Ivy (*née* Hutchinson), Cleator, Cumbria; *m* 1945, Ann Winifred Muriel Taylor. *Educ:* Workington Techn. Sch.; Leyton Techn. Coll.; Univ. of London (external). Engrg apprentice, 1938–42; Wartime Radar Research Unit, 1942–45; Air Trng Sch., qual. licensed engr, Air Registration Bd, 1947; employed in private industry, Mins of Aircraft Prodn and Supply, BOAC, and RN Scientific Service. Joined AEU, 1938: Mem. Final Appeal Court, Nat. Cttee, Divisional Chm., District Pres., etc, 1947–61; Tutor (part-time) in Trade Union Studies, Univ. of Southampton and WEA, 1958–61; joined TUC Organisation Dept, 1961, Head of TUC Organisation and Industrial Relations Dept, 1966–77. Comr, MSC, 1974–87; Member: Council, Inst. for Employment Studies (formerly Inst. of Manpower Studies), 1975–; Bd, European Foundn for Improvement of Living and Working Conditions, 1976–87; Adv. Cttee, European Social Fund, 1976–87; Council, Templeton Coll. (Oxford Centre for Management Studies), 1984–; NCVQ, 1986–92; Interim Adv. Cttee to Sec. of State for Educn and Sci., on Teachers' Pay and Conditions, 1987–89; Employment Appeal Tribunal, 1989–93; Management Bd, Univs' Staff Develt and Trng Unit, subseq. Univs' Staff Develt Unit, 1989–93. Mem. Bd, Remploy Ltd, 1987–92. A Vice-Pres., Airborne Forces Charities Appeal, 1990–. FRSA, 1987. Hon. LLD CNAA, 1986. Special Award of Merit, AEU, 1981; TUC Trades Councils Silver Badge for Merit, 1987; TUC Congress Gold Badge, 1987. *Publication:* contrib. Job Satisfaction: Challenge and Response in Modern Britain, 1976. *Recreations:* music, military history. *Address:* 90 Springfield Drive, Ilford, Essex IG2 6QS. *T:* 0181–554 0839.

GRAHAM, Prof. Lawrence Gordon, PhD; Regius Professor of Moral Philosophy, University of Aberdeen, since 1996; *b* 15 July 1949; *s* of William Moore Graham and Hyacinth Elizabeth (*née* Donald); *m* 1971; one *s* one *d*. *Educ:* Univ. of St Andrews (MA); Univ. of Durham (MA; PhD 1975). University of St Andrews: Lectr in Moral Philosophy, 1975–88; Reader, 1988–95; Dir of Music, 1991–95. *Publications:* Historical Explanation Reconsidered, 1983; Politics in its Place, 1986; Contemporary Social Philosophy, 1988, 4th edn 1995; The Idea of Christian Charity, 1990; Living the Good Life, 1990, 2nd edn 1994; The Shape of the Past, 1996. *Recreations:* music, walking, poetry. *Address:* Department of Philosophy, University of Aberdeen, Old Aberdeen AB9 2UB. *T:* Aberdeen (01224) 272367.

GRAHAM, (Malcolm Gray) Douglas; Chairman: The Midland News Association Ltd, since 1984 (Deputy Chairman, 1978–84); Claverley Co., since 1993; Stars News Shops Ltd, since 1994; *b* 18 Feb. 1930; *s* of late Malcolm Graham and Annie Jeanette Robinson; *m* 1980, Sara Anne Elwell (*née* Anderson). *Educ:* Shrewsbury Sch. National Service, RM, 1948–50. Newspaper trng, UK and Australia, 1950–53; Dir, Express & Star (Wolverhampton) Ltd, 1957. President: Young Newspapermen's Assoc., 1969; W Midlands Newspaper Soc., 1973–74; Chm., Evening Newspaper Advertising Bureau, 1978–79. *Recreation:* shooting. *Address:* Roughton Manor, Bridgnorth, Shropshire WV15 5HE. *T:* Worfield (017464) 209.

GRAHAM, Martin, QC 1976; **His Honour Judge Graham;** a Circuit Judge, since 1986; *b* 10 Feb. 1929; *m* 1962, Jane Filby; one *d*. *Educ:* Emanuel School; Trinity College, Oxford (Scholar; MA, PPE). Called to Bar, Middle Temple, 1952; a Recorder, 1986. Nat. Service, Officer BAOR, 1953–55. *Recreations:* swimming, tennis. *Address:* 1 Garden Court, Temple, EC4Y 9BJ. *Clubs:* Reform, Royal Automobile, Hurlingham.

GRAHAM, Sir Norman (William), Kt 1971; CB 1961; FRSE; Secretary, Scottish Education Department, 1964–73, retired; *b* 11 Oct. 1913; *s* of William and Margaret Graham; *m* 1949, Catherine Mary Strathie; two *s* one *d*. *Educ:* High Sch. of Glasgow; Glasgow Univ. Dept of Health for Scotland, 1936; Private Sec. to Permanent Under-Sec. of State, 1939–40; Ministry of Aircraft Production, 1940; Principal Private Sec. to Minister, 1944–45; Asst Sec., Dept of Health for Scotland, 1945; Under-Sec., Scottish Home and Health Dept, 1956–63. Hon. DLitt Heriot-Watt, 1971; DUniv Stirling, 1974. *Recreations:* golf, gardening. *Address:* 6 The Steading, Chesterhall, Longniddry, East Lothian EH32 0PQ. *T:* Longniddry (01875) 852130. *Club:* New (Edinburgh).
See also J. S. Graham.

GRAHAM, Sir Peter, KCB 1993 (CB 1982); QC 1990; First Parliamentary Counsel, 1991–94; *b* 7 Jan. 1934; *o s* of late Alderman Douglas Graham, CBE, Huddersfield, and Ena May (*née* Jackson); *m* 1st, Judith Mary Dunbar; two *s*; 2nd, Anne Silvia Garcia (*see* A. S. Graham). *Educ:* St Bees Sch., Cumberland (scholar); St John's Coll., Cambridge (scholar, 1st cl. Law Tripos, MA, LLM, McMahon Law Studentship). Served as pilot in Fleet Air Arm, 1952–55, Lieut, RNR. Called to Bar, Gray's Inn, 1958 (Holker Exhbn; H. C. Richards Prize, Ecclesiastical Law; Bencher, 1992), Lincoln's Inn, 1982; joined Parliamentary Counsel Office, 1959; Parly Counsel, 1972–86; Second Parly Counsel, 1987–91. External Examr (Legislation), Univ. of Edinburgh, 1977–81; with Law Commn, 1979–81. Hon. Legal Adviser, Historic Vehicle Clubs Cttee, 1967–86. *Recreations:* motoring, gardening. *Address:* La Vallette, 87190 Magnac Laval, France. *Club:* Sette of Odd Volumes.

GRAHAM, Sir Peter (Alfred), Kt 1987; OBE 1969; FCIB, CIMgt; Chairman, Crown Agents for Oversea Governments and Administrations, 1983–90; *b* 25 May 1922; *s* of Alfred Graham and Margaret (*née* Winder); *m* 1953, Luned Mary (*née* Kenealy-Jones); two *s* two *d*. *Educ:* St Joseph's Coll., Beulah Hill. FCIB (FIB 1975); CIMgt (CBIM 1981). Served War, RNVR: Pilot, FAA. Joined The Chartered Bank of India, Australia and China, 1947; 24 yrs overseas banking career, incl. appts in Japan, India and Hong Kong; i/c The Chartered Bank, Hong Kong, 1962–70; Chm. (1st), Hong Kong Export Credit Insurance Corp., 1965–70; General Manager 1970, Dep. Man. Dir 1975, Gp Man. Dir, 1977–83, Sen. Dep. Chm., 1983–87, Chm., 1987–88, Standard Chartered Bank, London. Director: Standard Chartered Finance Ltd, Sydney (formerly Mutual Acceptance Corp.), 1974–87; First Bank Nigeria, Lagos, 1976–87; Union Bank Inc., Los Angeles, 1979–88; Singapore Land Ltd, 1988–89; Employment Conditions Abroad Ltd, 1988–94; Chairman: Standard Chartered Merchant Bank Ltd, 1977–83; Mocatta Commercial Ltd, 1983–87; Mocatta & Goldsmid Ltd, 1983–87; Equatorial Bank, 1989–93; Deputy Chairman: Chartered Trust plc, 1983–85; Governing Body, ICC UK, 1985–92; Mem., Bd of Banking Supervision, 1986–87; Pres., Inst. of Bankers, 1981–83. City University: Chm., Adv. Cttee, 1981–86, Council, 1986–92, Business Sch.; Chm., Council, 1986–92. Formerly Chm., Exchange Banks' Assoc., Hong Kong; Mem., Govt cttees connected with trade and industry, Hong Kong. FRSA 1983. Hon. DSc City Univ., 1985. *Recreations:* golf, tennis, ski-ing. *Address:* Heron Lea, Hobbs Lane, Beckley, near Rye, Sussex TN31 6TT. *Clubs:* Naval, Royal Automobile; Hong Kong (Hong Kong); Rye Golf.

GRAHAM, Lt.-Gen. Sir Peter (Walter), KCB 1991; CBE 1981 (OBE 1978; MBE 1972); GOC Scotland and Governor of Edinburgh Castle, 1991–93, retired; *b* 14 March 1937; *s* of Dr Walter Graham and Suzanne Graham (*née* Simon); *m* 1963, Alison Mary, MB ChB, MRCGP, *d* of D. B. Morren, TD; three *s*. *Educ:* Fyvie Village School, Aberdeenshire; Hall Sch., Hampstead; St Paul's Sch.; RMA Sandhurst; ocds (Can), psc (Aust). Commissioned, The Gordon Highlanders, 1956; regtl appts, Dover, BAOR, Scotland, Kenya, 1957–62; HQ Highland Bde, 1962–63; Adjt, 1 Gordons, Kenya, Scotland, Borneo (despatches), 1963–66; Staff Capt., HQ (1 Br) Corps, 1966–67; Aust. Staff Coll., 1968; Co. Comdr, 1 Gordons, BAOR, 1969–70; Bde Maj., 39 Inf. Bde, 1970–72; 2nd i/c 1 Gordons, Scotland, Ulster, Singapore, 1972–74; MA to Adjt-Gen., 1974–75; CO, 1 Gordons, Scotland, Ulster, 1976–78; COS, HQ 3rd Armd Div., BAOR, 1978–82; Comdr UDR, 1982–84 (despatches); Nat. Defence Coll., Canada, 1984–85; Dep. Mil. Sec., MoD, 1985–87; GOC Eastern Dist, 1987–89; Comdt, RMA, Sandhurst, 1989–91. Col, The Gordon Highlanders, 1986–94; Col Comdt, The Scottish Div., 1991–93. Mem., Royal Company of Archers, Queen's Body Guard for Scotland, 1986. *Publications:* (with Pipe Major B. MacRae) The Gordon Highlanders Pipe Music Collection, Vol. 1, 1983, 3rd edn 1986, Vol. 2, 1985; (contrib.) John Baynes, Soldiers of Scotland, 1988; contrib. to Jl of RUSI. *Recreations:* stalking, hill walking, fishing, shooting, reading, pipe music, gardening under wife's directions. *Address:* RHQ The Highlanders, Viewfield Road, Aberdeen AB1 7XH. *Club:* Caledonian.
See also Sir A. M. Graham.

GRAHAM, Prof. Philip Jeremy; Lecturer, Department of Developmental Psychiatry, University of Cambridge, since 1994; Professor of Child Psychiatry, University of Oslo, since 1993; *b* 3 Sept. 1932; *s* of Jacob Rackham Graham and Pauline Graham; *m* 1960, Nori (*née* Burawoy); two *s* one *d*. *Educ:* Perse Sch., Cambridge; Cambridge Univ. (MA); University Coll. Hosp., London. FRCP 1973; FRCPsych 1972. Consultant Psychiatrist: Maudsley Hosp., London, 1966–68; Hosp. for Sick Children, Great Ormond Street, London, 1968–74; Prof. of Child Psychiatry, 1975–94 and Dean, 1985–90, Inst. of Child Health, London Univ. President: European Soc. for Child and Adolescent Psychiatry, 1987–91; Psychiatry Section, RSM, 1994–95. Chm., Nat. Children's Bureau, 1994– (Chm., Child Policy Rev. Gp, 1987–89). Sen. Mem., Wolfson Coll., Cambridge, 1994–. *Publications:* A Neuropsychiatric Study in Childhood (jtly), 1970; (ed) Epidemiological Approaches to Child Psychiatry, 1977; Child Psychiatry: a developmental approach, 1986, 2nd edn 1991; various publications on child and adolescent psychiatry. *Recreations:* reading, play-going, tennis. *Address:* 27 St Alban's Road, NW5 1RG.

GRAHAM, Sir Ralph Stuart, 14th Bt *cr* 1629 (NS), of Esk, Cumberland; *b* 5 Nov. 1950; *s* of Sir Ralph Wolfe Graham, 13th Bt and of Geraldine, *d* of Austin Velour; *S* father, 1988; *m* 1st, 1972, Roxanne (*d* 1978), *d* of Mrs Lovette Gurzan; 2nd, 1979, Deena Vandergrift; one adopted *s*. *Heir: b* Robert Bruce Graham [*b* 14 Nov. 1953; *m* 1974, Denise, *d* of T. Juranich; two *s*].

GRAHAM, Robert Martin; Chief Executive, British United Provident Association, 1984–91; *b* 20 Sept. 1930; *s* of Francis P. Graham and Margaret M. Graham (*née* Broderick); *m* 1959, Eileen (*née* Hoey); two *s* two *d*. *Educ:* Dublin; ACII. Hibernian Fire and General Insurance Co. Ltd, 1948–57; Voluntary Health Insurance Board, 1957–82 (to Chief Exec.); Dep. Chief Exec., BUPA 1982. Chm., Board of Management, Meath Hosp., 1972–82; Pres., Internat. Fedn of Voluntary Health Service Funds, 1988–90 (Dep. Pres., 1986–88); Vice-Pres., Assoc. Internationale de la Mutualité, 1990– (Mem. Bd of Govs, 1978–91); Mem., Central Council, Federated Voluntary Hosps, Ireland, 1978–82. *Address:* 20 Hampton Grove, Ewell, Epsom, Surrey KT17 1LA. *T:* 0181–393 2837. *Clubs:* Royal Automobile, Rotary Club of London.

GRAHAM, Dr Ronald Cairns, CBE 1992; General Manager, Tayside Health Board, 1985–93 (Chief Administrative Medical Officer, 1973–85); *b* 8 Oct. 1931; *s* of Thomas Graham and Helen Cairns; *m* 1959, Christine Fraser Osborne; two *s* one *d*. *Educ:* Airdrie Acad.; Glasgow Univ. MB, ChB Glasgow 1956; DipSocMed Edin. 1968; FFCM 1973; FRCPE 1983. West of Scotland; house jobs, gen. practice and geriatric med., 1956–62; Dep. Med. Supt, Edin. Royal Infirmary, 1962–65; Asst Sen. Admin. MO, SE Regional Hosp. Bd, 1965–69; Dep. and then Sen. Admin. MO, Eastern Regional Hosp. Bd, 1969–73. *Recreation:* fishing. *Address:* 34 Dalgleish Road, Dundee DD4 7JT. *T:* Dundee (01382) 455426.

GRAHAM, Sir Samuel Horatio, Kt 1988; CMG 1965; OBE 1962; **Mr Justice Graham;** Chief Justice of Grenada, since 1987; *b* Trinidad, 3 May 1912; *o s* of late Rev. Benjamin Graham and Mrs Graham, Trinidad; *m* 1943, Oris Gloria (*née* Teka); two *s* four *d*. *Educ:* Barbados; External Student, London Univ. BA (London) 1945; LLB (London) 1949. Teacher and journalist until called to Bar, Gray's Inn, 1949. Private practice as Barrister in Grenada, 1949–53; Magistrate, St Lucia, 1953–57; Crown Attorney, St Kitts, 1957–59; Attorney-General, St Kitts, 1960–62; Administrator of St Vincent, 1962–66; Puisne Judge, British Honduras, 1966–69; Pres., Industrial Court of Antigua, 1969–70, Associate Pres., 1981–84; Puisne Judge, Supreme Court of the Commonwealth of the Bahamas, 1973–78. Acted Chief Justice: British Honduras, Feb.-May 1968; Bahamas, Oct. 1977; Temp. Judge, Belize Court of Appeal, 1980. Judicial Mem., Bermuda Constituencies Boundaries Commn, 1979. Chairman: Grenada Develt Bank, 1985–87; Grenada Industrial Develt Corp., 1985–87. Mem., Council of Legal Educn, WI, 1971–. Chairman Inquiries into: Income Tax Reliefs; Coconut Industry, St Lucia, 1955; Legislators' Salaries, St Kitts, 1962. Acted Administrator of St Lucia, St Kitts and Dominica on various occasions. CStJ 1964. *Recreations:* bridge, swimming. *Address:* PO Box 99, St George's, Grenada, West Indies.

GRAHAM, (Stewart) David, QC 1977; Partner, Cork Gully, 1985–92; *b* 27 Feb. 1934; *s* of late Lewis Graham and of Gertrude Graham; *m* 1959, Corinne Carmona; two *d*. *Educ:* Leeds Grammar Sch.; St Edmund Hall, Oxford (MA, BCL). Called to the Bar, Middle Temple, 1957; Harmsworth Law Scholar, 1958. Mem. Council, Justice, 1976– (Chm., Cttee on Protection of Small Investor, 1989–92; Chm., Cttee on Insolvency, 1993–94); Mem., Insolvency Rules Adv. Cttee, 1984–86; Chm., Law, Parly and Gen. Purposes Cttee, Bd of Deputies of British Jews, 1983–88. Indep. Mem. Council, The Insurance Ombudsman Bureau, 1993–; Associate Mem., UK Ombudsman Assoc., 1994–. Vis. Fellow, Centre for Commercial Law, QMW, London, 1992–95. Chm. Editorial Bd, Insolvency Intelligence, 1988–94. FRSA 1995. *Publications:* (ed jtly) Williams and Muir Hunter on Bankruptcy, 18th edn 1968, 19th edn 1979; (contrib.) Longman's Insolvency,

1986; (ed) legal textbooks. *Recreations:* biography, music, travel. *Address:* 133 London Road, Stanmore, Mddx HA7 4PQ. *T:* 0181–954 3783.

GRAHAM, Stuart Twentyman, CBE 1981; DFC 1943; FCIS, FCIB; Chairman, Aitken Hume Bank (formerly Aitken Hume) Ltd, 1985–93; *b* 26 Aug. 1921; *s* of late Twentyman Graham; *m* 1948, Betty June Cox; one *s*. *Educ:* Kilburn Grammar Sch. Served War, 1940–46: commissioned, RAF, 1942. Entered Midland Bank, 1938; Jt Gen. Manager, 1966–70; Asst Chief Gen. Manager, 1970–74; Chief Gen. Manager, 1974–81; Gp Chief Exec., 1981–82; Dir, 1974–85. Chairman: Northern Bank Ltd, 1982–85; International Commodities Clearing House Ltd, 1982–86; Director: Allied Lyons plc, 1981–92; Sheffield Forgemasters Holdings, 1983–85; Aitken Hume International, 1985–93; Scotia (formerly Efamol) Hldgs, 1985–95. *Recreations:* music, reading. *Club:* Royal Air Force.

GRAHAM, Thomas; MP (Lab) Renfrew West and Inverclyde, since 1987; *b* 1944; *m* Joan Graham; two *s*. Former engineer with Rolls-Royce; manager, solicitors' office. Mem., Strathclyde Reg. Council, 1978. *Address:* c/o House of Commons, SW1A 0AA; 265 Gilmartin Road, Linwood, Paisley PA3 3SU.

GRAHAM, Rear-Adm. Wilfred Jackson, CB 1979; *b* 17 June 1925; *s* of William Bryce Graham and Jean Hill Graham (*née* Jackson); *m* 1951, Gillian Mary Finlayson; three *s* one *d*. *Educ:* Rossall Sch., Fleetwood, Lancs. Served War of 1939–45, Royal Navy: Cadet, 1943; specialised in gunnery, 1951; Comdr 1960; Captain 1967; IDC, 1970; Captain, HMS Ark Royal, 1975–76; Flag Officer, Portsmouth, 1976–79, retired. Dir and Sec., RNLI, 1979–87. Mem. Council, Rossall Sch., 1988–95. FNI 1987. *Recreations:* sailing, walking. *Address:* Yarnfield Cottage, Maiden Bradley, Warminster, Wilts BA12 7HY. *Clubs:* Royal Naval Sailing Association, Royal Yacht Squadron, Royal Lymington Yacht.

GRAHAM, William Franklin, (Billy Graham); Evangelist; *b* Charlotte, NC, 7 Nov. 1918; *s* of late William Franklin Graham and Morrow (*née* Coffey); *m* 1943, Ruth McCue Bell; two *s* three *d*. *Educ:* Florida Bible Institute, Tampa (ThB); Wheaton Coll., Ill (AB). Ordained to Baptist ministry, 1940; first Vice-Pres., Youth for Christ Internat., 1946–48; Pres., Northwestern Coll., Minneapolis, 1947–52; Evangelistic campaigns, 1946–; world-wide weekly broadcast, 1950–; many evangelistic tours of Great Britain, Europe, the Far East, South America, Australia and Russia. Chairman, Board of World Wide Pictures Inc. FRGS. Holds numerous honorary degrees in Divinity, Laws, Literature and the Humanities, from American universities and colleges; also varied awards from organisations, 1954–, inc. Templeton Foundn Prize, 1982; President's Medal of Freedom Award, 1983. *Publications include:* Peace with God, 1954; World Aflame, 1965; Jesus Generation, 1971; Angels—God's Secret Agents, 1975; How to be Born Again, 1977; The Holy Spirit, 1978; Till Armageddon, 1981; Approaching Hoofbeats: the four horsemen of the Apocalypse, 1983; A Biblical Standard for Evangelists, 1984; Unto the Hills, 1986; Facing Death and the Life After, 1987; Answers to Life's Problems, 1988; Hope for the Troubled Heart, 1991; Storm Warning, 1992. *Recreations:* swimming, walking. *Address:* (office) 1300 Harmon Place, Minneapolis, MN 55403, USA. *T:* (612) 3380500.

GRAHAM, (William) Gordon, MC 1944 (Bar 1945); FRSA; Editor, LOGOS, since 1990; Group Chairman, Butterworth Publishers, 1975–90 (Chief Executive, 1974–87); *b* 17 July 1920; *s* of Thomas Graham and Marion Hutcheson; *m* 1st, 1943, Margaret Milne, Bombay (*d* 1946); one *d*; 2nd, 1948, Friedel Gramm (*d* 1992), Zürich; one *d*; 3rd, 1994, Betty Cottrell, USA. *Educ:* Hutchesons' Grammar Sch.; Glasgow Univ. (MA 1940). Commissioned, Queen's Own Cameron Highlanders, 1941; served in India and Burma, 1942–46: Captain 1944, Major 1945; GSO II India Office, 1946. Newspaper correspondent and publishers' representative in India, 1946–55; Internat. Sales Manager, 1956–63, Vice-Pres., 1961, McGraw-Hill Book Co., New York; US citizen, 1963; Man. Dir, McGraw-Hill Publishing Co., UK, 1963–74; Director: W & R Chambers, Edinburgh, 1974–83; International Publishing Corp., 1975–82; Reed Publishing Gp, 1982–90; Chairman: Internat. Electronic Publishing Res. Centre Ltd, 1981–84; Publishers Database Ltd, 1982–84; Bd, R. R. Bowker Co., 1986–90; Mem. Bd, Polish Scientific Publishers, 1993–. Chm., Soc. of Bookmen, 1972–75; Publishers Association: Mem. Council, 1972–87; Chm., Electronic Publishing Panel, 1980–83; Vice Pres., 1984–85, 1987–88; Pres., 1985–87. Chm., Bd of Trustees, Kraszna-Krausz Foundn, 1990–95; Member Board: British Liby, 1980–86; Eur. Foundn for Liby Co-operation, 1991–. Correspondent, Christian Science Monitor, 1946–56. FRSA 1978. DUniv Stirling, 1993. *Publications:* As I Was Saying: essays on the international book business, 1994; articles in US and British trade press. *Recreations:* ski-ing, writing, fostering transatlantic understanding, landscape gardening. *Address:* White Lodge, Beechwood Drive, Marlow, Bucks SL7 2DH. *T:* Marlow (01628) 483371; Juniper Acres, East Hill, Keene, New York State, USA.

GRAHAM, Winston Mawdsley, OBE 1983; FRSL; *b* Victoria Park, Manchester; *m* 1939, Jean Mary Williamson (*d* 1992); one *s* one *d*. Chm., Soc. of Authors, 1967–69. Books trans. into 17 languages. *Publications:* some early novels (designedly) out of print, and: Night Journey, 1941 (rev. edn 1966); The Merciless Ladies, 1944 (rev. edn 1979); The Forgotten Story, 1945 (ITV prodn, 1983); Ross Poldark, 1945; Demelza, 1946; Take My Life, 1947 (filmed 1947); Cordelia, 1949; Night Without Stars, 1950 (filmed 1950); Jeremy Poldark, 1950; Fortune is a Woman, 1953 (filmed 1956); Warleggan, 1953; The Little Walls, 1955; The Sleeping Partner, 1956 (filmed 1958; ITV prodn, 1967); Greek Fire, 1957; The Tumbled House, 1959; Marnie, 1961 (filmed 1963); The Grove of Eagles, 1963 (Book Society Choice); After the Act, 1965; The Walking Stick, 1967 (filmed 1970); Angell, Pearl and Little God, 1970; The Japanese Girl (short stories), 1971; The Spanish Armadas, 1972; The Black Moon, 1973; Woman in the Mirror, 1975; The Four Swans, 1976; The Angry Tide, 1977; The Stranger from the Sea, 1981; The Miller's Dance, 1982; Poldark's Cornwall, 1983; The Loving Cup, 1984; The Green Flash, 1986; Cameo, 1988; The Twisted Sword, 1990; Stephanie, 1992; Tremor, 1995. BBC TV Series Poldark (the first four Poldark novels), 1975–76, second series (the next three Poldark novels), 1977, Circumstantial Evidence (play), 1979. *Recreations:* golf, gardening. *Address:* Abbotswood House, Buxted, East Sussex TN22 4PB. *Clubs:* Savile, Beefsteak, Pratt's.

See also A. W. M. Graham.

GRAHAM-BRYCE, Ian James, DPhil; Principal and Vice-Chancellor, University of Dundee, since 1994; *b* 20 March 1937; *s* of late Alexander Graham-Bryce, FRCS, and of Dame Isabel Graham-Bryce, *qv*; *m* 1959, Anne Elisabeth Metcalf; one *s* three *d*. *Educ:* William Hulme's Grammar Sch., Manchester; University Coll., Oxford (Exhibnr). BA, MA, BSc, DPhil (Oxon); FRSC, CChem 1981. Research Asst, Univ. of Oxford, 1958–61; Lectr, Dept of Biochemistry and Soil Sci., UCNW, Bangor, 1961–64; Sen. Scientific Officer, Rothamsted Exper. Station, 1964–70; Sen. Res. Officer, ICI Plant Protection Div., Jealott's Hill Res. Station, Bracknell, Berks, 1970–72; Special Lectr in Pesticide Chemistry, Dept of Zoology and Applied Entomology, Imperial Coll. of Science and Technology, 1970–72 (Vis. Prof., 1976–79); Rothamsted Experimental Station: Head, Dept of Insecticides and Fungicides, 1972–79; Dep. Director, 1975–79; Dir, East Malling Res. Stn, Maidstone, Kent, 1979–86 (Trustee, Develt and Endowment Fund, 1986–); Cons. Dir, Commonwealth Bureau of Horticulture and Plantation Crops, 1979–86; Hon. Lectr, Dept of Biology, Univ. of Strathclyde, 1977–80; Hd of Envmtl Affairs Div., Shell Internat. Petroleum Maatschappij BV, 1986–94. Society of Chemical Industry, London: Pres., 1982–84; Mem. Council, 1969–72 and 1974–89; Hon. Sec., Home Affairs, 1977–80; Chm., Pesticides Gp, 1978–80; Sec., Physico-Chemical and Biophysical Panel, 1968–70, Chm., 1973–75; Mem., British Nat. Cttee for Chemistry, 1982–84. Pres., Assoc. of Applied Biologists, 1988 (Vice-Pres., 1985–87). Chm., Agrochemical Planning Gp, IOCD, 1985–88; Mem., Scientific Cttee, Eur. Chemical Industry Ecol. and Toxicol. Centre, 1988–94; Vice-Chm., Environmental Res. Wkg Gp, Industrial R&D Adv. Cttee to EC, 1988–91; Mem., NERC, 1989–. Governor: Wye Coll., 1979–86, Imperial Coll., 1985–, Univ. of London. Member, Editorial Board: Chemico-Biological Interactions, 1973–77; Pesticide Science, 1978–80; Agriculture, Ecosystems and Environment, 1978–87. *Publications:* Physical Principles of Pesticide Behaviour, 1980; papers on soil science, plant nutrition and crop protection in sci. jls. *Recreations:* music (espec. opera), fly fishing, windsurfing. *Address:* The University, Dundee DD1 4HN. *Clubs:* Athenæum, Caledonian.

GRAHAM-BRYCE, Dame Isabel, DBE 1968; Chairman: Oxford Regional Hospital Board, 1963–72; National Nursing Staff Committee, 1967–75; National Staff Committee, 1969–75; Consultant, British Transport Hotels, 1979–81 (Board Member, 1962–79); Vice-President, Princess Christian College, Manchester, since 1953; *b* 30 April 1902; *d* of late Prof. James Lorrain Smith, FRS; *m* 1934, Alexander Graham-Bryce, FRCS (*d* 1968); two *s*. *Educ:* St Leonards Sch., St Andrews; Edinburgh Univ. (MA). Investigator, Industrial Fatigue Research Board, 1926–27; HM Inspector of Factories, 1928–34; Centre Organiser, WVS, Manchester, 1938–39; Dir of Organization, Ontario Div., Canadian WVS, 1941–42; Tech. Adviser, American WVS, 1942–43; Res. Fellow Fatigue Lab. Harvard Univ., 1943–44; Nat. Council of Women: Chm., Manchester Br., 1947–50; Vice-Chm., Education Cttee, 1950–51; Mem., Oxford Assoc., 1987–. JP and Mem. Juvenile Court Panel, Manchester City, 1949–55; Vice-Chairman: Assoc. of HMC's, 1953–55; Bd of Visitors, Grendon Prison, 1962–67. Member: Nurses and Midwives Whitley Council, 1953–57; General Nursing Council, 1956–61; Bd of Governors, Eastman Dental Hosp., 1957–63; Maternity and Midwifery Standing Cttee, 1957–72; Public Health Insp., Education Bd, 1958–64; Independent Television Authority, 1960–65 (Chm., General Advisory Council, 1964–65); Bd, ATV Network Ltd, 1968–72; Ancillary Dental Workers Cttee, 1956–68; Experimental Scheme for Dental Auxiliaries, 1958–69. Pres., Goring and Dist Day Centre for the Elderly, 1980–89; Vice Pres., League of Friends, Radcliffe Infirmary, Oxford, 1993– (Pres., 1988–93); Patron, Oxford Br., Motor Neurone Disease Assoc., 1990–. Life Mem., British Fedn Univ. Women. Hon. Member: Oxford Br., Zouta International; Edinburgh Univ. Club of Oxford. *Publications:* (joint) reports on research into industrial psychological problems. *Address:* 1 Quinton House, 98 Woodstock Road, Oxford OX2 7NE.

See also I. J. Graham-Bryce.

GRAHAM-DIXON, Anthony Philip, QC 1973; *b* 5 Nov. 1929; *s* of late Leslie Charles Graham-Dixon, QC; *m* 1956, Margaret Suzanne Villar; one *s* one *d*. *Educ:* Westminster School; Christ Church, Oxford. MA (1st Cl. Hon. Mods, 1st Cl. Lit. Hum.). RNVR, 1953–55, Lieut (SP). Called to the Bar, Inner Temple, 1956, Bencher 1982; Member of Gray's Inn, 1965–. Mem. Council, Charing Cross Hosp. Medical School, 1976–83. Chm., London Concertino Ltd, 1982–. Dep. Chm., PHLS, 1988– (Bd Mem., 1987–). Gov., Bedales Sch., 1988–. Trustee, SPNM, 1988– (Chm. Trustees, 1994). *Publication:* (mem. adv. bd) Competition Law in Western Europe and the USA, 1976. *Recreations:* music (especially opera), gardening, tennis. *Address:* 31 Hereford Square, SW7 4NB. *T:* 0171–370 1902; Masketts Manor, Nutley, Uckfield, East Sussex TN22 3HD. *T:* Nutley (0182571) 2719.

GRAHAM HALL, Jean; *see* Hall, J. G.

GRAHAM-HARRISON, Francis Laurence Theodore, CB 1962; Deputy Under-Secretary of State, Home Office, 1963–74; *b* 30 Oct. 1914; *s* of late Sir William Montagu Graham-Harrison, KCB, KC, and Lady Graham-Harrison, *d* of Sir Cyril Graham, 5th and last Bt, CMG; *m* 1941, Carol Mary St John, 3rd *d* of late Sir Francis Stewart, CIE; one *s* three *d*. *Educ:* Eton; Magdalen Coll., Oxford. Entered Home Office, 1938. Private Secretary to Parliamentary Under-Secretary of State, 1941–43; Asst Private Secretary to Prime Minister, 1946–49; Secretary, Royal Commission on Capital Punishment, 1949–53; Asst Secretary, Home Office, 1953–57; Asst Under-Secretary of State, Home Office, 1957–63. Chm., Nat. Sound Archive Adv. Cttee, British Library, 1984–88; Trustee: Tate Gallery, 1975–82; Nat. Gallery, 1981–82. Gov., Thomas Coram Foundn, 1975–95. Chm., Exec. Finance Cttee, Dr Barnardo's, 1978–81. *Address:* 32 Parliament Hill, NW3 2TN. *T:* 0171–435 6316.

See also R. M. Graham-Harrison.

GRAHAM-HARRISON, Robert Montagu; UK Executive Director, European Bank for Reconstruction and Development, since 1992; *b* 16 Feb. 1943; *s* of Francis Laurence Theodore Graham-Harrison, *qv*; *m* 1977, Kathleen Patricia Maher; two *d*. *Educ:* Eton Coll.; Magdalen Coll., Oxford. VSO India, 1965; GLC, 1966; Min. of Overseas Development (later Overseas Development Administration), 1967; World Bank, Washington, 1971–73; Private Sec. to Minister for Overseas Development, 1978; Asst Sec., ODA, 1979; Hd, British Develt Div. in E Africa, Nairobi, 1982–86; Hd, E Asia Dept, ODA, 1986–89; Alternate Exec. Dir, World Bank, Washington, 1989–92. *Address:* c/o European Bank for Reconstruction and Development, 1 Exchange Square, EC2A 2EH.

GRAHAM-MOON, Sir Peter Wilfred Giles; *see* Moon.

GRAHAM-SMITH, Sir Francis; *see* Smith.

GRAHAM-TOLER, family name of the **Earl of Norbury.**

GRAHAME-SMITH, Prof. David Grahame, CBE 1993; Rhodes Professor of Clinical Pharmacology, University of Oxford, since 1972; Hon. Director, Smith Kline Beecham Centre of Applied Neuropsychobiology, Oxford University, since 1990; Fellow of Corpus Christi College, Oxford, since 1972; *b* 10 May 1933; *s* of George E. and C. A. Smith; *m* 1957, Kathryn Frances, *d* of Dr F. R. Beetham; two *s*. *Educ:* Wyggeston Grammar Sch., Leicester; St Mary's Hosp. Medical Sch., Univ. of London. MB, BS (London) 1956; MRCS, LRCP 1956; MRCP 1958; PhD (London) 1966; FRCP 1972. House Phys., Paddington Gen. Hosp., London, 1956; House Surg., Battle Hosp., Reading, 1956–57. Captain, RAMC, 1957–60. Registrar and Sen. Registrar in Medicine, St Mary's Hosp., Paddington, 1960–61; H. A. M. Thompson Research Scholar, RCP, 1961–62; Saltwell Research Scholar, RCP, 1962–65; Wellcome Trust Research Fellow, 1965–66; Hon. Med. Registrar to Med. Unit, St Mary's Hosp., 1961–66; MRC Travelling Fellow, Dept of Endocrinology, Vanderbilt Univ., Nashville, Tennessee, USA, 1966–67; Sen. Lectr in Clinical Pharmacology and Therapeutics, St Mary's Hosp. Med. Sch., Univ. of London, 1967–71; Hon. Cons. Physician, St Mary's Hosp., Paddington, 1967–71; Hon. Dir, MRC Unit of Clin. Pharm., Radcliffe Infirmary, Oxford, 1972–93. Vis. Prof., Peking Union Medical Coll., Beijing, China, 1985–. Member: Cttee on Safety of Medicines, 1975–86; Jt Cttee on Vaccination and Immunisation, 1987–89; Chairman: Adv. Gp on Hepatitis, 1987–89; Adv. Council on Misuse of Drugs, 1988–. *Publications:* (with J. K. Aronson) Oxford Textbook of Clinical Pharmacology and Drug Therapy, 1984, 2nd edn 1992;

papers on biochemical, therapeutic and med. matters in scientific jls. *Recreations:* horse riding, jazz. *Address:* University Department of Clinical Pharmacology, Radcliffe Infirmary, Woodstock Road, Oxford OX2 6HE. *T:* Oxford (01865) 241091.

GRAHAMSTOWN, Bishop of, since 1987; **Rt. Rev. David Hamilton Russell;** *b* 6 Nov. 1938; *s* of James Hamilton Russell and Kathleen Mary Russell; *m* 1980, Dorothea Madden; two *s*. *Educ:* Diocesan College, Rondebosch; Univ. of Cape Town (BA, PhD); Univ. of Oxford (MA). Assistant Priest, 1965–75; Chaplain to migrant workers, 1975–86; banned and house arrested by SA Government, 1977–82; Suffragan Bishop, Diocese of St John's, 1986. *Address:* 17 Durban Street, Grahamstown, South Africa; PO Box 162, Grahamstown, CP, 6140, South Africa. *T:* (home) (461) 22500, (office) (461) 311996.

GRAINGER, Leslie, CBE 1976; BSc; FEng; MInstF; Chairman, Mountain Petroleum PLC, 1984–88; *b* 8 August 1917. Mem. for Science, NCB, 1966–77; Chairman: NCB (Coal Products) Ltd, 1975–78; NCB (IEA Services) Ltd, 1975–79; Man. Dir, Branon PLC, 1981–83; Dir, Cavendish Petroleum Plc, 1982–85 (Chm., 1982–84). *Publication:* Coal Utilisation: Technology, Economics and Policy (with J. G. Gibson), 1981. *Address:* 16 Blackamoor Lane, Maidenhead, Berks SL6 8RD. *T:* Maidenhead (01628) 23923.

GRANADO, Donald Casimir, TC 1970; *b* 4 March 1915; *m* 1959, Anne-Marie Faustin Lombard; one *s* two *d*. *Educ:* Trinidad. Gen. Sec., Union of Commercial and Industrial Workers, 1951–53; Sec./Treas., Fedn of Trade Unions, 1952–53; Elected MP for Laventille, Trinidad, 1956 and 1961; Minister of: Labour and Social Services, 1956–61; Health and Housing, and Dep. Leader House of Representatives, 1961–63. Ambassador to Venezuela, 1963–64; High Comr to Canada, 1964–69; Ambassador to Argentina and to Brazil, 1965–69; High Comr to London, 1969–71, and Ambassador to France, Germany, Belgium, Switzerland, Italy, Holland, Luxembourg and European Common Market, 1969–71. Led Trinidad and Tobago delegations to: India, Ceylon, Pakistan, 1958; CPA in Nigeria, Israel, Uganda, 1962; UN, 1965; St Lucia, 1966; attended Heads of Commonwealth Govts Conf., Singapore, 1971; rep. Trinidad and Tobago at missions to Grenada, Jamaica, France, and inaugurations of heads of govt of Chile and Brazil. First Gen. Sec., People's National Movement. Formerly: Vice-Chm., West India Cttee, London; Governor, Commonwealth Inst; Vice-Pres., Trinidad & Tobago Contract Bridge League. President: Fidelis Youth Club; National Golf Club; Vice-Pres., Trinidad & Tobago Golf Assoc.; Pres., Potentials Sports Club (also Manager, soccer team). National Father of the Year 1981. Speaks, reads and writes French and Spanish. *Recreations:* cricket, soccer, bridge and golf; music (tape-recording), writing. *Address:* 20 Grove Road, Valsayn North, Trinidad, West Indies. *T:* 6625905.

GRANARD, 10th Earl of, *cr* 1684 (Ire.); **Peter Arthur Edward Hastings Forbes;** Bt (NS) 1628; Viscount Granard, Baron Clanehugh (Ire.), 1675; Baron Granard (UK), 1806; *b* 15 March 1957; *s* of Hon. John Forbes (*d* 1982), *yr s* of 8th Earl, and of Joan, *d* of A. Edward Smith; *S* uncle, 1992; *m* 1980, Noreen Mitchell; three *s* one *d*. *Heir: s* Viscount Forbes, *qv*. *Address:* Strathallan Cliff House, Strathallan Road, Onchan, Isle of Man.

GRANBY, Marquis of; David Charles Robert Manners; *b* 8 May 1959; *s* and *heir* of 10th Duke of Rutland, *qv*; *m* 1992, Emma, *d* of John Watkins; one *d*. Dealer in antique and modern sporting weapons. Mem. Civilian cttee, ATC Sqdn, Grantham. Member: CLA Cttee for Leicestershire/Rutland; Successor Cttee, HHA (Vice-Chm., E Midlands Area); Salmon and Trout Assoc.; Game Conservancy. President: Notts Rifle Assoc.; Ex-Aircrew Assoc., Grantham and Dist Br. Freeman, City of London; Liveryman, Gunsmiths' Co. Governor, RNLI, 1985–. *Recreations:* shooting, fishing. *Address:* Knipton Lodge, Knipton, near Grantham, Lincs NG32 1RE. *T:* Grantham (01476) 870798. *Clubs:* Turf; Annabel's.

GRANDY, Marshal of the Royal Air Force Sir John, GCB 1967 (KCB 1964; CB 1956); GCVO 1988; KBE 1961; DSO 1945; RAF; Constable and Governor of Windsor Castle, 1978–88; *b* Northwood, Middlesex, 8 Feb. 1913; *s* of late Francis Grandy and Nellie Grandy (*née* Lines); *m* 1937, Cecile Elizabeth Florence Rankin, CStJ (*d* 1993), *yr d* of Sir Robert Rankin, 1st and last Bt; two *s*. *Educ:* University College Sch., London. Joined RAF 1931. No 54 (Fighter) Sqdn, 1932–35; 604 (Middx) Sqdn., RAuxAF, 1935–36; Adjt and Flying Instructor, London Univ. Air Sqdn, 1937–39; Comd No 249 (Fighter) Sqdn during Battle of Britain; Staff Duties, HQ Fighter Comd, and Wing Comdr Flying RAF Coltishall, 1941; commanded: RAF Duxford, 1942 (First Typhoon Wing); HQ No 210 Group, No 73 Op Training Unit, and Fighter Conversion Unit at Abu Sueir, 1943–44; No 341 Wing (Dakotas), SE Asia Comd, 1944–45; DSO 1945, despatches 1943 and 1945. SASO No 232 Gp, 1945; *psc* 1946; Dep. Dir Operational Training, Air Min., 1946; Air Attaché, Brussels, 1949; Comd Northern Sector, Fighter Comd, 1950; Air Staff HQ Fighter Comd, 1952–54; Comdt, Central Fighter Estab., 1954–57; *idc* 1957; Comdr, Task Force Grapple (British Nuclear Weapon Test Force), Christmas Is., 1957–58; Assistant CAS (Ops), 1958–61; Commander-in-Chief, RAF, Germany and Comdr, Second Allied TAF, 1961–63; AOC-in-C, Bomber Command, 1963–65; C-in-C, British Forces, Far East, and UK Mil. Adviser to SEATO, 1965–67; Chief of the Air Staff, 1967–71; Governor and C-in-C, Gibraltar, 1973–78. Dir, Brixton Estate Ltd, 1971–73, 1978–83; Trustee, Imperial War Museum, 1971–78 (Chm., 1978–89); Dep. Chm. Council, RAF Benevolent Fund, 1980–; Trustee: Burma Star Assoc., 1979– (Vice-Pres.); Shuttleworth Remembrance Trust, 1978–88 (Chm., Aerodrome Cttee, 1980–88); RAF Church, St Clement Danes, 1971–; Prince Philip Trust Fund, Windsor and Maidenhead, 1982–92; Past President: Officers' Assoc.; Air League; Vice-President: Officers' Pension Soc., 1971–; Nat. Assoc. of Boys' Clubs, 1971–; Life Vice-Pres., RNLI, 1988– (Vice-Pres., 1986–88, Mem. Management Cttee, 1971–); Friends of Gibraltar Heritage Soc., 1986–; Mem. Cttee, Royal Humane Soc., 1978–; Patron, Polish Air Force Assoc. in GB, 1979–. PMN 1967. Hon. Liveryman, Haberdashers' Co., 1968. Freeman, City of London, 1968. KStJ 1974. *Clubs:* White's, Pratt's, Royal Air Force; Royal Yacht Squadron (Cowes); Swinley Forest Golf.

GRANGE, Kenneth Henry, CBE 1984; RDI, FCSD; industrial designer; in private practice since 1958; Founder Partner, Pentagram Design, since 1972; *b* 17 July 1929; *s* of Harry Alfred Grange and Hilda Gladys (*née* Long). *Educ:* London. Technical Illustrator, RE, 1948–50; Design Asst, Arcon Chartered Architects, 1948; Bronek Katz & Vaughn, 1950–51; Gordon Bowyer & Partners, 1951–54; Jack Howe & Partners, 1954–58. Pres., CSD, 1987–88; Master of Faculty, RDI, 1985–87. RDI 1969; FCSD (FSIAD 1959). Hon. Prof., Heriot-Watt, 1987. Hon. Dr RCA, 1985; DUniv Heriot-Watt, 1986. 10 Design Council Awards; Duke of Edinburgh Award for Elegant Design, 1963. *Recreations:* tennis, ski-ing. *Address:* Pentagram, 11 Needham Road, W11 2RP.

GRANT, family name of **Baron Strathspey.**

GRANT, Alexander (Marshall), CBE 1965; Artistic Director, National Ballet of Canada, 1976–83; *b* Wellington, New Zealand, 22 Feb. 1925; *s* of Alexander and Eleather Grant. *Educ:* Wellington Coll., NZ. Arrived in London, Feb. 1946, to study with Sadler's Wells School on Scholarship given in New Zealand by Royal Academy of Dancing, London; Sadler's Wells Ballet (later Royal Ballet Company), Aug. 1946–76. Dir, Ballet for All (touring ballet company), 1971–76 (Co-director, 1970–71). Senior Principal, London Fest. Ballet, later English National Ballet, 1985–91; Guest Artist: Royal Ballet, 1985–89; Joffrey Ballet, USA, 1987–89. Frequent judge at internat. ballet competitions, notably Varna (Bulgaria), Paris, Budapest, Jackson, Mississippi and Moscow. Danced leading rôles in following: Mam'zelle Angot, Clock Symphony, Boutique Fantasque, Donald of the Burthens, Rake's Progress, Job, Three Cornered Hat, Ballabile, Cinderella, Sylvia, Madame Chrysanthème, Façade, Daphnis and Chloé, Coppélia, Petrushka, Ondine, La Fille Mal Gardée, Jabez and the Devil, Perséphone, The Dream, Jazz Calendar, Enigma Variations, Sleeping Beauty (Carabosse), A Month in the Country, La Sylphide, The Nutcracker, Napoli, Schéhérazade, Variations on a Theme of Purcell, Don Quixote; *films:* Tales of Beatrix Potter (Peter Rabbit and Pigling Bland); Steps of the Ballet. *Recreations:* gardening, cinema going, cuisine.

GRANT, Alistair; *see* Grant, D. A. A.

GRANT, Sir Alistair; *see* Grant, Sir M. A.

GRANT, Allan Wallace, OBE 1974; MC 1941; TD 1947; President, Ecclesiastical Insurance Office Ltd, 1981–87 (Managing Director, 1971–77; Chairman, 1975–81); retired; *b* 2 Feb. 1911; *s* of late Henry Grant and late Rose Margaret Sheppard; *m* 1st, 1939, Kathleen Rachel Bamford (marr. diss. 1990); one *d*; 2nd, 1990, Mary Wyles. *Educ:* Dulwich Coll. LLB Hons (London). FCII. Eccles. Insurance Office, 1929; Chief Officer, 1952; Dir, 1966. Served War of 1939–45: Major, 2 i/c, 3rd Co. of London Yeomanry (Sharpshooters), N Africa, Sicily, Italy, NW Europe. Pres., Sharpshooters Assoc. Called to Bar, Gray's Inn, 1948. President: Insurance Inst. of London, 1966–67; Chartered Insce Inst., 1970–71; Insce Charities, 1973–74; Insce Orchestral Soc., 1973–74; Chairman: Insce Industry Training Council, 1973–75; Clergy Orphan Corp., 1967–80 (Vice-Pres., 1980); Coll. of All Saints, Tottenham, 1967–76; Chm., Allchurches Trust Ltd, 1975–85; Governor: St Edmund's Sch., Canterbury, 1967–; St Margaret's Sch., Bushey, 1967–; Mem., Policyholders Protection Bd, 1975–81; Treasurer: Historic Churches Preservation Trust, 1977–85; Soc. for Advancing Christian Faith, 1977–87. Master, Coopers' Co., 1984–85; Asst, Insurers' Co., 1979–86. Hon. DCanL Lexington, 1975. *Recreations:* golf, travel. *Address:* 5 Queens Court, Queens Road, Richmond, Surrey TW10 6LA. *T:* 0181–940 2626. *Clubs:* City Livery; Richmond Golf (Captain 1977).

GRANT, Andrew Young; Principal, Grant Leisure Group, since 1982; *b* 8 April 1946; *s* of Marshall Grant and Marilyn Greene (*née* Phillips); *m* 1st, 1969, Dietra (marr. diss.); one *d*; 2nd, 1973, Lindy Lange; one *d*. *Educ:* Univ. of Oregon (BSc). Personnel Manager, Universal Studios Tour, Universal City, Calif., 1967–69; Dir of Personnel, Busch Gardens, LA, 1969–71, Ops Dir, 1971–73; Gen. Manager, Squaw Valley Ski Resort, 1973–74; Gen. Manager, Busch Gardens, 1974–76; Dir, Economic Research Associates, LA, 1976–79; Dep. Dir, Zoological Soc., San Diego, 1979–83; Dir, Leeds Castle Enterprises, 1983–88; Director: Granada Studios Tour, 1987–90; Grant Leisure Developments, 1987–; Grant fforde Developments Ltd, 1994–; Man. Dir, Zoo Operations Ltd, Zoological Soc., 1988–91. Member: Tourism Soc., 1988–; Tourism and Leisure Industries Sector Gp, NEDC, 1990–. *Recreations:* running, fishing, golf, tennis. *Address:* Grant Leisure Group, 12 Adeline Place, WC1B 3AJ. *T:* 0171–436 9592.

GRANT, Sir Anthony, Kt 1983; MP (C) Cambridgeshire South-West, since 1983 (Harrow Central, 1964–83); Solicitor and Company Director; *b* May 1925; *m* Sonia Isobel; one *s* one *d*. *Educ:* St Paul's Sch.; Brasenose Coll., Oxford. Admitted a Solicitor, 1952; Liveryman, Worshipful Company of Solicitors; Freeman, City of London; Master, Guild of Freemen, 1979. Army 1943–48, Third Dragoon Guards (Capt.). Opposition Whip, 1966–70; Parly Sec., Board of Trade, June–Oct. 1970; Parliamentary Under-Secretary of State: Trade, DTI, 1970–72; Industrial Develt, DTI, 1972–74; Chm., Cons. back bench Trade Cttee, 1979–83; Mem., Foreign Affairs Select Cttee, 1980–83; a Vice-Chm., Conservative Party Organisation, 1974–76. Mem. Exec., 1992 Cttee, 1978–. Member: Council of Europe (Chm., Econ. Cttee, 1980–87); WEU. Pres., Guild of Experienced Motorists. *Recreations:* watching Rugby and cricket, playing golf; Napoleonic history. *Address:* House of Commons, SW1A 0AA. *Clubs:* Walton Heath Golf, Gog Magog Golf.

GRANT of Monymusk, Sir Archibald, 13th Bt, *cr* 1705; *b* 2 Sept. 1954; *e s* of Captain Sir Francis Cullen Grant, 12th Bt, and of Lady Grant (Jean Margherita, *d* of Captain Humphrey Douglas Tollemache, RN), who *m* 2nd, Baron Tweedsmuir, *qv*; *S* father, 1966; *m* 1982, Barbara Elizabeth, *e d* of A. G. D. Forbes, Druminnor Castle, Rhynie, Aberdeenshire; two *d*. *Heir: b* Francis Tollemache Grant [*b* 18 Dec. 1955; *m* 1993, Virginia, *d* of R. Scott Russell; one *d*]. *Address:* House of Monymusk, Aberdeenshire AB51 7HL. *T:* Monymusk (01467) 651220.

GRANT, Bernard Alexander Montgomery; MP (Lab) Tottenham, since 1987; *b* 17 Feb. 1944; *s* of Eric and late Lily Grant; *m* (marr. diss.); three *s*. *Educ:* St Stanislaus College, Georgetown, Guyana; Tottenham Technical College. Analyst, Demerara Bauxite Co., Guyana, 1961–63; Clerk, British Rail, 1963–65; Telephonist, Internat. Telephones, GPO, 1969–78; Area Officer, NUPE, 1978–83; Develt Worker, Black Trade Unionists Solidarity Movement, 1983–84; Local Govt Officer, London Borough of Newham, 1985–87. Councillor, London Borough of Haringey, 1978–88 (Council Leader, 1985–87). Chm. and Founder Mem., Parly Black Caucus, 1988; Chm., Campaign Gp of Labour MPs, 1990–92; Mem., NEC, Anti-Apartheid Movement, 1989–91; Chairman: Standing Conf. on Race Equality in Europe, 1990–; African Reparations Movement (UK), 1993–. Mem., Gp of Eminant Persons on Reparations for Africa, OAU, 1994–. Editor, Black Parliamentarian Magazine, 1990–92. Hon. LLD Pace Univ., NY, 1993. *Recreations:* cooking, cricket. *Address:* House of Commons, SW1A 0AA.

GRANT, His Honour Brian; *see* Grant, His Honour H. B.

GRANT, Sir Clifford (Harry), Kt 1977; Chief Stipendiary Magistrate, Western Australia, 1982–90; *b* England, 12 April 1929; *m* 1962, Karen Ann Ferguson. *Educ:* Montclair, NJ, USA; Harrison Coll., Barbados; Liverpool Coll.; Liverpool Univ. (LLB (Hons) 1949). Solicitor, Supreme Court of Judicature, 1951; Comr for Oaths, 1958; in private practice, London; apptd to HM Overseas Judiciary, 1958; Magistrate, Kenya, 1958, Sen. Magistrate, 1962; transf. to Hong Kong, Crown Solicitor, 1963, Principal Magistrate, 1965; transf. to Fiji, Sen. Magistrate, 1967; admitted Barrister and Solicitor, Supreme Court of Fiji, 1969; Chief Magistrate, 1971; Judge of Supreme Court, 1972; Chief Justice of Fiji, 1974–80. Pres., Fiji Court of Appeal, and Chm., Judicial and Legal Services Commn, 1974–80; sole Comr, Royal Commn on Crime, 1975 (report published 1976). Sometime Actg Governor-General, 1973–79. Fellow, Flinders Univ. Foundn, 1992. Fiji Independence Medal, 1970. *Publications:* articles for legal jls. *Recreations:* sociobiology, photography, literature, music. *Address:* c/o Under Secretary for Law, PO Box F317, Perth, WA 6001, Australia.

GRANT, David James, CBE 1980; JP; Lord-Lieutenant and Custos Rotulorum of County Durham, since 1988; *b* 18 Jan. 1922; *s* of late Frederick Grant, MC, QC and Grace Winifred Grant (*née* McLaren); *m* 1949, Jean Margaret, *d* of Gp Capt. T. E. H. Birley, OBE; two *s* one *d*. *Educ:* Fettes Coll., Edinburgh; Oriel Coll., Oxford (Open Schol.; MA). Served RAFVR, Bomber Command and overseas 1940–45 (Flight Lieut). Chm., Darchem Ltd, 1963–92 (Chief Exec., 1959–88); Dep. Chm., William Baird plc, 1981–92.

Chairman: Teesside Productivity Assoc., 1965–68; Northern Regl Council, CBI, 1973–75; Northern Regl Council, BIM, 1982–87; Member: Northern Econ. Planning Council, 1968–79; NE Industrial Develt Bd, 1975–84. President: N of England TA & VRA, 1990–; N of England Anglo-Japanese Soc., 1990–. Chm., Council, Univ. of Durham, 1985–92 (Hon. DCL, 1988). Hon. DCL Newcastle upon Tyne, 1989. Co. Durham: DL 1982; High Sheriff, 1985–86; Vice Lord-Lieut, 1987–88; JP Durham, 1988. KStJ 1988. CIMgt. *Recreations:* lawn tennis, golf. *Address:* Aden Cottage, Durham DH1 4HJ. *T:* Durham (0191) 3867161. *Club:* Naval and Military.

GRANT, His Honour Derek Aldwin, DSO 1944; QC 1962; a Circuit Judge (formerly an Additional Judge of the Central Criminal Court), 1969–84; *b* 22 Jan. 1915; *s* of late Charles Frederick Grant, CSI, ICS; *m* 1954, Phoebe Louise Wavell-Paxton; one *s* three *d*. *Educ:* Winchester Coll.; Oriel Coll., Oxford. Called to Bar 1938. Served in RAF, 1940–46 (King's Commendation, DSO). Master of the Bench, Inner Temple, 1969. Deputy Chairman, East Sussex County Sessions, 1962–71; Recorder of Salisbury, 1962–67, of Portsmouth, 1967–69. *Address:* Carters Lodge, Handcross, West Sussex RH17 6AA.

GRANT, Donald Blane, CBE 1989; TD 1964; Partner, KMG Thomson McLintock, CA (formerly Moody Stuart & Robertson, then Thomson McLintock & Co.), 1950–86; *b* 8 Oct. 1921; *s* of Quintin Blane Grant and Euphemia Phyllis Grant; *m* 1944, Lavinia Margaret Ruth Ritchie; three *d*. *Educ:* High Sch. of Dundee. CA 1948. Served War, RA, 1939–46: TA Officer, retd as Major. Director: Dundee & London Investment Trust PLC, 1969–93; HAT Group PLC, 1969–86; Don Brothers Buist PLC, 1984–87. Inst. of Chartered Accountants of Scotland: Mem. Council, 1971–76; Vice Pres., 1977–79, Pres., 1979–80. Chairman: Tayside Health Bd, 1984–91; Scottish Legal Aid Bd, 1986–91. Hon. LLD Dundee, 1989. *Recreations:* shooting, fishing, golf, bridge, gardening. *Address:* Summerfield, 24 Albany Road, West Ferry, Dundee DD5 1NT. *T:* Dundee (01382) 737804. *Clubs:* Institute of Directors; New (Edinburgh); Royal and Ancient Golf (St Andrews); Panmure Golf (Carnoustie); Blairgowrie Golf (Rosemount).

GRANT, Donald David, CB 1985; Director General, Central Office of Information, 1982–85; *b* 1 Aug. 1924; *s* of Donald Herbert Grant and Florence Emily Grant; *m* 1954, Beatrice Mary Varney; two *d*. *Educ:* Wandsworth Sch. Served War, RNVR, Sub-Lt (A), 1942–46. Journalist, Evening Standard, Reuters, 1946–51; Dir, Sidney Barton Ltd, PR Consultants, 1951–61; Chief Information Officer, Min. of Aviation and Technology, 1961–67; Dir, Public Relations, STC Ltd, 1967–70; Director of Information: GLC, 1971–72; DTI, 1972–74; Home Office, 1974–82. Vis. Prof., Graduate Centre for Journalism, City Univ., 1986–90. *Recreation:* sailing. *Address:* Ferry View, Castle House, Southtown, Dartmouth, Devon TQ6 9BU. *T:* Dartmouth (01803) 833095. *Club:* Dartmouth Yacht.

GRANT, Prof. (Duncan) Alistair (Antoine), RBA, RE, ARCA; Professor of Printmaking, 1984–90, Head of Printmaking Department, 1970–90, Royal College of Art; Professor Emeritus, 1990; Chairman, Faculty of Printmaking, British School at Rome, since 1978; *b* London, 3 June 1925; *s* of Duncan and Germaine Grant; *m* 1st, 1949, Phyllis Fricker (*d* 1988); one *d*; 2nd, 1991, Joan Strickland. *Educ:* Froebel, Whitehill, Glasgow; Birmingham Sch. of Art; Royal Coll. of Art. Joined staff of RCA, 1955. *One Man Shows* at the following galleries: Zwemmer; Piccadilly; AIA; Ashgate; Bear Lane, Oxford; Midland Group, Nottingham; Balclutha; Ware, London; 46, Edinburgh; Editions Alecto; Redfern; Scottish; Le Touquet Museum, France. *Works in the collections of:* V&A Museum; Tate Gallery; Min. of Works; DoE; LCC (later GLC); Arts Council; Carlisle Art Gall.; Ferens Art Gall., Hull; The King of Sweden; Dallas Museum; Dallas Art Gall.; Cincinnati; Boston; Museum of Modern Art, New York; Public Library, NY; Chicago Art Inst.; Lessing J. Rosenwald Collection; Beaverbrook Foundn, Fredericton, NB; Vancouver Art Gall.; Victoria Art Gall; Tel Aviv Museum; Cairo Art Gall.; Nat. Gall. of S Australia; Nat. Museum of Stockholm; IBM; Mobil Oil; Unilever; BP International; BM; Hunterian Mus., Glasgow; Le Touquet Mus., France. *Group Exhibitions* in Bahamas, Canada, Europe, S America, USA and UK. FRSA. Awarded Silver Medal, Internat. Festival of Youth, Moscow, 1957. *Address:* 13 Redcliffe Gardens, SW10 9BG. *T:* 0171–352 4312.

GRANT, Edward; Lord Mayor, City of Manchester, May 1972–May 1973; *b* 10 Aug. 1915; *s* of Edward and Ada Grant; *m* 1942, Winifred Mitchell. *Educ:* Moston Lane Sch.; Manchester High Sch. of Commerce. City Councillor, Manchester, 1950–84 (Alderman, 1970–74); Hosp. Administrator, Manchester AHA (T) North Dist (formerly NE Manchester HMC), 1948–75, now retired. *Recreations:* swimming, reading, gardening. *Address:* 4 Hudson Court, Sherwell Road, Blackley, Manchester M9 8DJ. *T:* 0161–720 8312.

GRANT, His Honour (Hubert) Brian; a Circuit Judge of Sussex and Kent (formerly Judge of County Courts), 1965–82; *b* Berlin, 5 Aug. 1917; *m* 1946, Jeanette Mary Carroll; one *s* three *d*. *Educ:* Trinity Coll., Cambridge (Sen. Schol.). 1st cl. hons, Law Tripos, 1939; MA. War service, 1940–44: Commandos, 1942–44. Called to Bar, Gray's Inn, 1945 (Lord Justice Holker Senior Scholar). Mem., Law Reform Cttee, 1970–73. Vice-Chm., Nat. Marriage Guidance Council, 1970–72; Founder Pres., Parenthood, 1979. FRSA 1991. *Publications:* Marriage, Separation and Divorce, 1946; Family Law, 1970; Conciliation and Divorce, 1981; The Quiet Ear, 1987; The Deaf Advance, 1990; Not Guilty, 1994. *Address:* Eden Hill, Armathwaite, Carlisle CA4 9PQ. *Club:* Penrith Golf.

GRANT, Ian David, CBE 1988; Chairman, Scottish Tourist Board, since 1990 (Board Member, 1988–90); Board Member, British Tourist Authority, since 1990; *b* Dundee, 28 July 1943; *s* of late Alan H. B. Grant and of Florence O. Grant; *m* 1968, Eileen May Louisa Yule; three *d*. *Educ:* Strathallan Sch.; East of Scotland College of Agriculture (Dip.). Vice Pres. 1981–84, Pres. 1984–90, National Farmers' Union of Scotland; Mem., Scottish Council, CBI, 1984–. Director: Clydesdale Bank PLC, 1989–; NFU Mutual Insce Soc. Ltd, 1990–; Scottish Hydro Electric PLC, 1992–. FRAgS 1988. *Recreations:* travel, swimming, shooting, reading, music. *Address:* Leal House, Alyth PH11 8JQ.

GRANT, Maj.-Gen. Ian Hallam L.; *see* Lyall Grant.

GRANT, (Ian) Nicholas; Managing Director, Mediatrack Ltd, since 1992; Chairman, Pearson Grant Associates, since 1989; Director, Kaleidoscope Television Production Co. Ltd, since 1991; *b* 24 March 1948; *s* of late Hugo and of Cara Grant; *m* 1977, Rosalind Louise Pipe; one *s* one *d*. *Educ:* Univ. of London (LLB); Univ. of Warwick (MA, Industrial Relns). Confederation of Health Service Employees: Research Officer, 1972–74; Head of Research and Public Relations, 1974–82; Dir of Information, Labour Party, 1982–85; Public Affairs Advr, Mirror Group Newspapers and Maxwell Communication Corp., 1985–89. Member: Council London Borough of Lambeth, 1978–84; Lambeth, Southwark and Lewisham AHA, 1978–82; W Lambeth DHA, 1982–83. Contested (Lab) Reigate, 1979. *Publications:* contrib. to: Economics of Prosperity, ed D. Blake and P. Ormerod, 1980; Political Communications: the general election campaign of 1983, ed I. Crewe and M. Harrop, 1985. *Recreations:* walking, reading, photography. *Address:* 9 Lincoln's Inn Fields, WC2A 3BP. *T:* 0171–430 0699. *Club:* Reform.

GRANT, Prof. Ian Philip, DPhil; FRS 1992; CMath; Professor of Mathematical Physics, University of Oxford, since 1992; Tutorial Fellow in Mathematics, Pembroke College, Oxford, since 1969; *b* 15 Dec. 1930; *er s* of Harold Hyman Grant and Isabella Henrietta Ornstien; *m* 1958, Beryl Cohen; two *s*. *Educ:* St Albans Sch., Herts; Wadham Coll., Oxford (Open Scholar; MA; DPhil 1954). CMath 1992. SSO, 1957–61, PSO, 1961–64, UKAEA, Aldermaston; Res. Fellow, Atlas Computer Lab., SRC, 1964–69; Lectr in Maths, 1969–90, Reader in Mathematical Physics, 1990–92, Oxford Univ.; Res. Fellow in Maths, 1964–69, Actg Master, 1984–85, Pembroke Coll., Oxford. Visiting Professor: McGill Univ., 1976; Åbo Akademi, Finland, 1977; Inst. de Fisica, Univ. Nacional Autónoma de México, 1981. Governor: Royal Grammar Sch., High Wycombe, 1981–; St Paul's Schs, 1993–. *Publications:* papers in learned jls on relativistic quantum theory in atomic and molecular physics, and on radiative transfer theory in astrophysics and atmospheric science. *Recreations:* walking, music, theatre-going, gardening, travel. *Address:* Pembroke College, Oxford OX1 1DW. *T:* Oxford (01865) 276444; Mathematical Institute, 24–29 St Giles', Oxford OX1 3LB. *T:* Oxford (01865) 273525.

GRANT, Rt. Rev. James Alexander, AM 1994; Assistant Bishop, Diocese of Melbourne, since 1985; Dean of St Paul's Cathedral, Melbourne, since 1985; *b* 30 Aug. 1931; *s* of late V. G. Grant, Geelong; *m* 1983, Rowena Margaret Armstrong. *Educ:* Trinity College, Univ. of Melbourne (BA Hons); Melbourne College of Divinity (BD). Deacon 1959 (Curate, St Peter's, Murrumbeena), Priest 1960; Curate, West Heidelberg 1960, Broadmeadows 1961; Leader Diocesan Task Force, Broadmeadows, 1962; Domestic and Examining Chaplain to Archbishop of Melbourne, 1966–70; Bishop Coadjutor, dio. of Melbourne, 1970–85; Chairman, Brotherhood of St Laurence, 1971–87 (Director, 1969); Chaplain, Trinity Coll., Univ. of Melbourne, 1970–75, Fellow, 1975; Pres., Diocesan Mission to Streets and Lanes, 1987–. *Publications:* (with Geoffrey Serle) The Melbourne Scene, 1957; Perspective of a Century-Trinity College, 1872–1972, 1972. *Recreation:* historical research. *Address:* Cathedral Buildings, 209 Flinders Lane, Melbourne, Vic 3000, Australia. *Club:* Melbourne (Melbourne).

GRANT, James Shaw, CBE 1968 (OBE 1956); Member, Highlands and Islands Development Board, 1970–82; *b* 22 May 1910; *s* of William Grant and Johanna Morison Grant, Stornoway; *m* 1951, Catherine Mary Stewart (*d* 1988); no *c*. *Educ:* Nicolson Inst.; Glasgow Univ. Editor, Stornoway Gazette, 1932–63; Mem., Crofters' Commn, 1955–63, Chm., 1963–78. Dir, Grampian Television, 1969–80. Mem. Scottish Adv. Cttee, British Council, 1972–94. Governor, Pitlochry Festival Theatre, 1954–84, Chairman, 1971–83; Chm., Harris Tweed Assoc. Ltd, 1972–84. Mem. Council, Nat. Trust for Scotland, 1979–84. FRAgS 1973; FRSE 1982. Hon. LLD Aberdeen, 1979. *Publications:* Highland Villages, 1977; Their Children Will See, 1979; The Hub of My Universe, 1983; Surprise Island, 1983; The Gaelic Vikings, 1984; Stornoway and the Lews, 1985; Discovering Lewis and Harris, 1987; Enchanted Island, 1989; A Shilling for your Scowl, 1992; several plays. *Recreations:* golf, photography. *Address:* Ardgrianach, Inshes, Inverness IV1 2BQ. *T:* Inverness (01463) 231476. *Clubs:* Royal Over-Seas League; Highland (Inverness).

GRANT, Rear-Adm. John, CB 1960; DSO 1942; *b* 13 Oct. 1908; *s* of late Maj.-Gen. Sir Philip Grant, KCB, CMG, and Annette, *d* of John Coventry, JP, Burgate Manor, Fordingbridge; *m* 1935, Ruth Hayward Slade; two *s* two *d*. *Educ:* St Anthony's, Eastbourne; RN Colls, Dartmouth and Greenwich. Midshipman, HMS Queen Elizabeth, 1926; Sub-Lieut, HMS Revenge, 1930; Lieut, HMS Kent, China Station, 1932; specialised in anti-submarine warfare, 1933–39; Staff Officer Convoys, Rosyth, 1940; in comd HMS Beverley, 1941–42 (DSO); Trng Comdr, HMS Osprey, 1942, and subseq. in HMS Western Isles; in comd HMS Philante, 1943; Trng Comdr, HMS Osprey, 1944; in comd HMS Opportune, Fame and Crispin, 1945–47; Joint Staff Coll., 1947; Executive Officer, HMS Vernon; Capt. 1949; Dep. Dir Torpedo Anti-Submarine and Mine Warfare Div., Naval Staff, Admiralty, 1949–51; in comd HMS Cleopatra, 1952–53; Imperial Defence Coll., 1954; in comd HMS Vernon, 1955–57; on staff of Chief of Defence Staff, Min. of Defence, 1957–59; Rear-Adm., 1959; Flag Officer Commanding Reserve Fleet (HMS Vanguard), 1959–60; retired list, 1961. Rank Organisation, 1961–65; Director, Conference of the Electronics Industry, 1965–71. *Address:* 9 Rivermead Court, Ranelagh Gardens, SW6 3RT.

See also B. V. M. Strickland.

GRANT, Sir (John) Anthony; *see* Grant, Sir A.

GRANT, John Donald; Consultant, Grant & Fairgrieve, since 1988; Director, Cadogan Management Ltd, 1991–95; *b* 31 Oct. 1926; *s* of Ian and Eleanor Grant; *m* 1951, Helen Bain Fairgrieve Wilson, *d* of late James Wilson and of Clara Wilson; two *s*. *Educ:* various schs; King's Coll., Cambridge (Exhibnr; MA Nat. Sciences). National Service, REME, 1947–49; TA, London Rifle Bde, 1949–56. N Thames Gas Bd, 1949–60; Imperial Chemical Industries: Plastics Div., 1960–71; Head Office, 1971–82; Chief Exec., FIMBRA (formerly NASDIM), 1983–88. Chairman: Strategic Planning Soc., 1989–91; Fedn of Software Systems, 1989–91. Mem., Money Management Council, 1989–. *Recreations:* opera, music, travel (particularly to islands). *Address:* 6 Bailey Mews, Auckland Road, Cambridge CB5 8DR; also in Westmorland. *Club:* United Oxford & Cambridge University.

GRANT, John Douglas; writer, media and public affairs consultant; Head of Communications, Electrical, Electronic, Telecommunication and Plumbing Union, 1984–89; Member, Radio Authority, 1990–94; *b* 16 Oct. 1932; *m* 1955, Patricia Julia Ann; two *s* one *d*. *Educ:* Stationers' Company's Sch., Hornsey. Reporter on various provincial newspapers until 1955; Daily Express, 1955–70 (Chief Industrial Correspondent, 1967–70). Contested: (Lab) Beckenham, 1966; (SDP) Islington N, 1983; (SDP/Alliance) Carshalton and Wallington, 1987. MP Islington East, 1970–74, Islington Central, 1974–83 (Lab, 1970–81, SDP, 1981–83). Opposition Front Bench Spokesman for policy on broadcasting and the press, 1973–74, on employment, 1979–81; Parly Sec., CSD, March–Oct. 1974; Parliamentary Under-Secretary of State: ODM, 1974–76; Dept of Employment, 1976–79; SDP employment spokesman, 1981–83; SDP industry spokesman, 1982–83. Chm., Bromley Constituency Labour Party, 1966–70. Chm., Labour and Industrial Correspondents' Group, 1967. *Publications:* Member of Parliament, 1974; Blood Brothers, 1992; articles in national newspapers and periodicals. *Recreations:* tennis, golf, barbershop singing, watching soccer. *Address:* Branscombe, Upper Street, Kingsdown, near Deal, Kent CT14 8BJ. *T:* Deal (01304) 363991.

GRANT, John James, CBE 1960; Director, University of Durham Institute of Education, 1963–77; *b* 19 Oct. 1914; *s* of John and Mary Grant; *m* 1945, Jean Graham Stewart; two *s*. *Educ:* Shawlands Academy, Glasgow; Univ. of Glasgow (MA, EdB). Supply teaching, Glasgow, 1939–40. Served War: UK, India, Burma, 1940–46. Mod. Lang. Master, High Sch. of Glasgow, 1946–48; Lectr in Educn, Univ. of Durham, 1948–52; Vice-Principal, Fourah Bay Coll., Sierra Leone, 1953–55, Principal, 1955–60; Principal, St Cuthbert's Soc., Univ. of Durham, 1960–63. Hon. DCL Durham, 1960. *Recreations:* theatre, gardening. *Address:* 1 Marklands, Julian Road, Sneyd Park, Bristol BS9 1JY.

GRANT, Keith Wallace; Dean, Faculty of Design, Kingston University (formerly Polytechnic), since 1988; *b* 30 June 1934; *s* of Randolph and Sylvia Grant; *m* 1968, Deanne (*née* Bergsma); one *s* one *d*. *Educ:* Trinity Coll., Glenalmond; Clare Coll., Cambridge (MA). Account Exec., W. S. Crawford Ltd, 1958–62; General Manager: Covent Garden

Opera Co., later Royal Opera, 1962–73; English Opera Group, 1962–73; Sec., Royal Soc. of Arts, 1973–77; Dir, Design Council, 1977–88. Member: Adv. Council, V&A Mus., 1977–83; PO Stamp Adv. Cttee, 1978–89; Exec. Bd, Internat. Council of Socs of Industrial Design, 1983–87; Chm., Nat. Lead Body for Design, 1995–. Chm., English Music Theatre Co., 1979–92; Mem., Management Cttee, Park Lane Gp, 1988–; Sec., Peter Pears Award for Singers, 1988–. Governor: Central Sch. of Art and Design, 1974–77; Birmingham Polytechnic, 1981–86; Edinburgh Coll. of Art, 1982–86; Mem., Ct, Brunel Univ., 1985–89. Hon. Prof., Heriot-Watt Univ., 1987. Hon. Fellow, Birmingham Polytechnic, 1988. Hon. FCSD (Hon. FSIAD, 1983). *Address:* c/o Kingston University, Knights Park, Kingston upon Thames, KT1 2QJ. *Clubs:* Garrick, Arts.

GRANT, Very Rev. Malcolm Etheridge; Provost and Rector of St Andrew's Cathedral, Inverness, since 1991; Rector of St Paul's, Strathnairn, and Priest-in-charge of St Mary's-in-the-Fields, Culloden, since 1991; *b* 6 Aug. 1944; *s* of Donald Etheridge Grant and Nellie Florence May Grant (*née* Tuffey); *m* 1984, Katrina Russell Nuttall (*née* Dunnett); one *s* one *d*. *Educ:* Dunfermline High School; Univ. of Edinburgh (Bruce of Grangehill Bursar, 1962; BSc (Hons Chemistry); BD (Hons New Testament); Divinity Fellowship, 1969); Edinburgh Theological College. Deacon 1969, priest 1970; Assistant Curate: St Mary's Cathedral, Glasgow, 1969; St Wulfram's, Grantham (in charge of Church of the Epiphany, Earlesfield), 1972; Team Vicar of Earlesfield, Grantham, 1972; Priest-in-charge, St Ninian's, Invergordon, 1978; Examining Chaplain to Bishop of Moray, Ross and Caithness, 1979; Provost and Rector, St Mary's Cathedral, Glasgow, 1981. Member, Highland Regional Council Education Cttee, 1979–81. *Address:* 15 Ardross Street, Inverness IV3 5NS. *T:* Inverness (01463) 233535.

GRANT, Prof. Malcolm John, LLD; Professor of Land Economy, University of Cambridge, since 1991; Fellow of Clare College, Cambridge, since 1991; *b* 29 Nov. 1947; *s* of Francis William Grant and Vera Jessica Grant; *m* 1974, Christine (*née* Endersbee); two *s* one *d*. *Educ:* Waitaki Boys' High Sch., NZ; Univ. of Otago (LLB 1970; LLM 1973; LLD 1986). Lectr, subseq. Sen. Lectr in Law, Southampton Univ., 1972–86; University College London: Sen. Lectr in Law, 1986–88; Prof. of Law, and Vice-Dean, Faculty of Laws, 1988–91. Local Govt Comr for England, 1992– (Acting Chm., 1995). Hon. MRTPI 1993; Hon. ARICS 1995. Gen. Editor, Encyclopedia of Planning Law and Practice, 1981–; Co-Editor, Encyclopedia of Environmental Law, 1993–. *Publications:* Planning Law Handbook, 1981; Urban Planning Law, 1982, 2nd Suppl. 1990; Rate Capping and the Law, 1985, 2nd edn 1986; Permitted Development, 1989; (ed jtly) Concise Lexicon of Environmental Terms, 1995. *Recreations:* reading, music. *Address:* Clare College, Cambridge CB2 1TL. *T:* Cambridge (01223) 337134; Department of Land Economy, 19 Silver Street, Cambridge CB3 9EP.

GRANT, Sir (Matthew) Alistair, Kt 1992; Chairman: Argyll Group, since 1988 (Deputy Chairman, 1986–88; Chief Executive, 1986–93); Biotechnology and Biological Sciences Research Council (formerly Agricultural and Food Research Council), since 1990; *b* 6 March 1937; *s* of John and Jessie Grant; *m* 1963, Judith Mary Dent; two *s* one *d*. *Educ:* Woodhouse Grove School, Yorks. 2nd Lieut Royal Signals, 1955–57. Unilever, 1958–63; J. Lyons, 1963–65; Connell May & Steavenson, 1965–68; Dir, Fine Fare, 1968–72; Managing Dir, Oriel Foods, 1973–77; Argyll Group, 1977–. Director: Bank of Scotland, 1992–; Scottish & Newcastle plc, 1994–. Visiting Professor: Retail, Stirling Univ., 1984–91; Marketing, Strathclyde Univ., 1991–. Chm., Food Policy Cttee, Retail Consortium, 1986–89. President: Nat. Grocers' Benevolent Fund, 1987–89; Inst. of Grocery Distribution, 1992–94; Advertising Assoc., 1989–93; RASE, 1993–94. Member: Listed Companies Adv. Cttee, 1990–93; Council, Scottish Council Develt and Industry, 1994–; Conseil de Surveillance, Casino, Guichard-Perrachon SA (France), 1994–. Mem. Bd of Trustees, Nat. Museums of Scotland, 1991–. Regent, RCSE, 1994. FRSA 1988; FRAgS 1993. Hon. DBA: Strathclyde, 1992; Napier, 1994; Hon. DSc Cranfield, 1993; Dr *hc* Edinburgh, 1993. KStJ 1993. *Recreations:* books, paintings, horses, friends. *Address:* c/o Argyll Group PLC, 6 Millington Road, Hayes, Middlesex UB3 4AY. *Club:* Caledonian.

GRANT, Michael, CBE 1958 (OBE 1946); MA, LittD (Cambridge); *b* 21 Nov. 1914; *s* of late Col Maurice Harold Grant and Muriel, *d* of C. Jörgensen; *m* 1944, Anne Sophie Beskow, Norrköping, Sweden; two *s*. *Educ:* Harrow Sch.; Trinity Coll., Cambridge. Porson Prizeman, First Chancellor's Classical Medallist, Craven Student; Fellow Trinity Coll., Cambridge, 1938–49. Served War of 1939–45, Army, War Office, 1939–40, Actg Capt.; first British Council Rep. in Turkey, 1940–45; Prof. of Humanity at Edinburgh Univ., 1948–59; first Vice-Chancellor, Univ. of Khartoum, 1956–58; Pres. and Vice-Chancellor of the Queen's Univ. of Belfast, 1959–66; Pres., 1953–56, Medallist, 1962, and Hon. Fellow, 1984, Royal Numismatic Soc.; Huntington Medalist, American Numismatic Soc., 1965. J. H. Gray Lectr, Cambridge, 1955; FSA. Chairman, National Council for the Supply of Teachers Overseas, 1963–66. President: Virgil Soc., 1963–66; Classical Assoc., 1977–78. Chm., Commonwealth Conf. on Teaching of English as 2nd Language at Makerere, Uganda, 1961. Hon. LittD Dublin, 1961; Hon. LLD QUB, 1967. Gold Medal for Educn, Sudan, 1977; Premio Internazionale Le Muse, Florence, 1989. *Publications:* From Imperium to Auctoritas, 1946; Aspects of the Principate of Tiberius, 1950; Roman Anniversary Issues, 1950; Ancient History, 1952; The Six Main Aes Coinages of Augustus, 1953; Roman Imperial Money, 1954; Roman Literature, 1954; translations of Tacitus and Cicero; Roman History from Coins, 1958; The World of Rome, 1960; Myths of the Greeks and Romans, 1962; (ed) Birth of Western Civilization, 1964 (new edn as Greece and Rome, 1986); The Civilizations of Europe, 1965; The Gladiators, 1967; The Climax of Rome, 1968; The Ancient Mediterranean, 1969 (Premio del Mediterraneo, Mazara del Vallo, 1983, for Italian edn); Julius Caesar, 1969; The Ancient Historians, 1970; The Roman Forum, 1970; Nero, 1970; Cities of Vesuvius, 1971; Herod the Great, 1971; Roman Myths, 1971; Cleopatra, 1972; The Jews in the Roman World, 1973; (with J. Hazel) Who's Who in Classical Mythology, 1973 (Premio Latina for Italian edition, 1986); The Army of the Caesars, 1974; The Twelve Caesars, 1975; (ed) Greek Literature, 1976; The Fall of the Roman Empire, 1976; Saint Paul, 1976; Jesus, 1977; History of Rome, 1978; (ed) Latin Literature, 1978; The Etruscans, 1980; Greek and Latin Authors 800 BC–AD 1000, 1980; The Dawn of the Middle Ages, 1981; From Alexander to Cleopatra, 1982; History of Ancient Israel, 1984; The Roman Emperors, 1985; A Guide to the Ancient World, 1986; The Rise of the Greeks, 1987; (ed with R. Kitzinger) Civilization of the Ancient Mediterranean, 1988; The Classical Greeks, 1989; The Visible Past, 1990; Short History of Classical Civilization, 1991 (US edn, The Founders of the Western World); Greeks and Romans: a social history, 1992; Readings in the Classical Historians, 1992; The Emperor Constantine, 1993; (ed) Sayings of the Bible, 1994; Saint Peter, 1994; My First Eighty Years, 1994. *Address:* Le Pitturacce, Gattaiola, Lucca 55050, Italy. *Club:* Athenæum.

GRANT, Nicholas; *see* Grant, I. N.

GRANT of Dalvey, Sir Patrick Alexander Benedict, 14th Bt *cr* 1688 (NS); Chieftain of Clan Donnachy; (Donnachaidh); Managing Director, Grant's of Dalvey Ltd, since 1988; *b* 5 Feb. 1953; *e s* of Sir Duncan Alexander Grant, 13th Bt, and Joan Penelope (*d* 1991), *o d* of Captain Sir Denzil Cope, 14th Bt; *S* father, 1961; *m* 1981, Dr Carolyn Elizabeth Highet, MB, ChB, DRCOG, MRCGP, *d* of Dr John Highet, Glasgow; two *s*. *Educ:* St Conleth's Coll., Dublin; The Abbey Sch., Fort Angustus; Univ of Glasgow (LLB 1981). FSAScot. Former deer-stalker, inshore fisherman. *Recreations:* professional competing piper, deerstalking, shooting. *Heir: s* Duncan Archibald Ludovic Grant, *b* 19 April 1982. *Address:* Tomintoul House, Flichity, Inverness-shire IV1 2XD. *Club:* New (Edinburgh).

GRANT, Peter James; Chairman, Sun Life Assurance Society plc, since 1983 (Director, since 1973, Vice-Chairman, 1976); *b* 5 Dec. 1929; 2nd *s* of late Lt-Col P. C. H. Grant, Scots Guards, and Mrs Grant (*née* Gooch); *m* 1st, Ann, *d* of late Christopher Pleydell-Bouverie; one *s* one *d*; 2nd, Paula, *d* of late E. J. P. Eugster; one *s* two *d*. *Educ:* Winchester; Magdalen Coll., Oxford. Lieut, Queen's Own Cameron Highlanders. Edward de Stein & Co., 1952, merged with Lazard Brothers & Co. Ltd, 1960; Vice-Chm., 1983–85, Dep. Chm., 1985–88, Lazard Bros & Co. Chm., Highlands and Islands Airports, 1993–; Director: Walter Runciman plc, 1973–90; Standard Industrial Gp, 1966–72; Charrington, Gardner, Lockett & Co. Ltd, 1970–74; London Merchant Securities, 1985– (Dep. Chm., 1994–); Scottish Hydro, 1990–94; Union des Assurances de Paris International, 1989–91 (Internat. Adv. Bd, 1991–95); BNP (UK) plc, 1991–; Transatlantic Hldgs, 1992–. Member: Industrial Develt Adv. Bd, 1985–92; CAA, 1993–95; Cromarty Firth Port Authority, 1994–. Mem. Council and Chm., Finance Cttee, British Red Cross Soc., 1972–85; Mem., Council, Inst. of Dirs, 1989–. *Recreations:* shooting, golf, gardening. *Address:* Mountgerald, near Dingwall, Ross-shire IV15 9TT. *T:* Dingwall (01349) 62244; 14 Eaton Row, SW1W 0JA. *T:* 0171–235 2092. *Clubs:* Boodle's, Caledonian.

GRANT, Prof. Peter John, MA, PhD; MIMechE, FINucE; FInstP; Professor of Nuclear Power, Imperial College of Science, Technology and Medicine, 1966–91, now Emeritus; Deputy Vice-Chancellor, University of London, 1990–92; *b* London, 2 July 1926; *s* of Herbert James Grant; *m* Audrey, *d* of Joseph Whitham; one *s*. *Educ:* Merchant Taylors' Sch.; Sidney Sussex Coll., Cambridge. BA 1947, MA, PhD 1951. Research in Nuclear Physics at Cavendish Laboratory, 1947–50; Lectr in Natural Philosophy, Univ. of Glasgow, 1950–55; Chief Physicist, Atomic Energy Div., GEC Ltd, 1956–59; Reader in Engineering Science, Imperial Coll. of Science and Technology, 1959–66; Mem. Governing Body, Imperial Coll., 1985–89; London University: Dean of Engrg, 1984–86; Chm. of Academic Council, 1986–89; Mem. Court, 1988–93. Mem., Adv. Cttee on Safety of Nuclear Installation, 1983–94. Pres., Instn of Nuclear Engrs, 1994–95. Gov., Hampton Sch., 1984–. *Publications:* Elementary Reactor Physics, 1966; Nuclear Science, 1971; papers on radioactivity, nuclear reactions, physics of nuclear reactors. *Address:* 49 Manor Road South, Esher, Surrey KT10 0QA.

GRANT, Prof. Peter Raymond, FRS 1987; Class of 1877 Professor of Zoology, Princeton University, since 1989; *b* 26 Oct. 1936; *s* of Frederick Thomas Charles and Mavis Irene Grant (now Reading); *m* 1962, Barbara Rosemary Matchett; two *d*. *Educ:* Whitgift Sch.; Cambridge Univ. (BA Hons); Univ. of British Columbia (PhD). Seessel-Anonymous Postdoctoral Fellow in Biology Dept of Yale Univ., 1964–65; Asst Prof. 1965–68, Associate Prof. 1968–73, Prof. 1973–78, McGill Univ.; Prof., Univ. of Michigan, 1977–85; Prof. of Biology, Princeton Univ., 1985–89. FLS 1986. Hon. PhD Uppsala, 1986. *Publications:* Ecology and Evolution of Darwin's Finches, 1986; (with B. R. Grant) Evolutionary Dynamics of a Natural Population, 1989 (Wildlife Soc. Publication Award, 1991); contribs to Science, Nature, Proc. Royal Society, Proc. Nat. Acad. of Scis (USA), etc. *Recreations:* walking, tennis, music. *Address:* Department of Ecology and Evolutionary Biology, Princeton University, Princeton, NJ 08544-1003, USA. *T:* (609) 2585156.

GRANT, Rodney Arandall; His Honour Judge Grant; a Circuit Judge, since 1995; *b* 8 May 1944; *s* of Thomas and Olive Grant; *m* 1988, Elaine Illingworth. *Educ:* Leeds Grammar Sch.; Trinity Coll., Oxford (Minor Scholar; MA Mod. Langs). Called to the Bar, Inner Temple, 1970; NE Circuit, 1970–95; Head of Chambers, 1992–95; a Recorder, 1993–95. *Recreations:* fell walking, golf, carpentry, gardening, reading, music. *Address:* c/o Circuit Administrator, 17th Floor, West Riding House, Albion Street, Leeds LS1 5AA. *Club:* Bradford Golf.

GRANT, Lt-Gen. Scott Carnegie, CB 1995; Commandant, Royal College of Defence Studies, since 1996; *b* 28 Sept. 1944; *s* of Maurice and Margaret Wotherspoon Gibb Grant; *m* 1973, Catharine Susan Pawsey; one *s* one *d*. *Educ:* King's Sch., Pontefract; RMA Sandhurst; Clare Coll., Cambridge (MA). Commissioned Royal Engineers, 1965; Regtl duty Aden, Sharjah, BAOR and UK, 1965–73; Instructor, RMA, 1973–74; student, Staff Coll., 1975–76; MoD, 1977–78; Sqn Comdr, BAOR, 1979–80; Instructor, Staff Coll., 1981–82; CO 26 Engineer Regt, 1982–84; MoD, 1985; SHAPE, 1986–87; Comdr, 33 Armoured Brigade, 1988–89; RCDS 1990; Army Member, Prospect Team, 1991; Dir Gen. of Army Trng, 1991–93; GOC, Support Comd (Germany), 1994–95. Team Leader, Army Command Structure Review, 1993–. Col, The Queen's Lancashire Regt, 1993–. *Recreations:* 20th Century art and literature. *Address:* c/o Midland Bank, 11 Ropergate, Pontefract, Yorks WF8 1LJ. *Clubs:* Army and Navy; Hawks (Cambridge).

GRANT-FERRIS, family name of **Baron Harvington.**

GRANT-SUTTIE, Sir (George) Philip; *see* Suttie, Sir G. P. G.

GRANTCHESTER, 3rd Baron, *cr* 1953; **Christopher John Suenson-Taylor;** *b* 8 April 1951; *e s* (twin) of 2nd Baron Grantchester, CBE, QC and of Betty, *er d* of Sir John Moores, CBE; *S* father, 1995; *m* 1973, Jacqueline, *d* of Dr Leo Jaffé; two *s* two *d*. *Educ:* Winchester; LSE (MA). *Heir: s* Hon. Jesse David Suenson-Taylor, *b* 6 June 1977. *Address:* Lower House Farm, Back Coole Lane, Audlem, Crewe, Cheshire CW3 0ER.

GRANTHAM, Bishop Suffragan of, since 1987; **Rt. Rev. William Ind;** Dean of Stamford, since 1988; *b* 26 March 1942; *s* of William Robert and Florence Emily Ind; *m* 1967, Frances Isobel Bramald; three *s*. *Educ:* Univ. of Leeds (BA); College of the Resurrection, Mirfield. Asst Curate, St Dunstan's, Feltham, 1966–71; Priest in charge, St Joseph the Worker, Northolt, 1971–74; Team Vicar, Basingstoke, 1974–87; Diocesan Director of Ordinands, 1982–87; Hon. Canon of Winchester, 1985–87. *Recreations:* bird watching, cricket watching, orchid finding. *Address:* Fairacre, 243 Barrowby Road, Grantham, Lincs NG31 8NP. *T:* Grantham (01476) 64722.

GRANTHAM, Roy Aubrey, CBE 1990; National Secretary, APEX Partnership (white collar section of GMB), 1989–91; *b* 12 Dec. 1926; *m* 1964 (marr. diss. 1988); two *d*. *Educ:* King Edward Grammar Sch., Aston, Birmingham. Association of Professional, Executive, Clerical & Computer Staff: Midland area Organiser, 1949; Midland area Sec., 1959; Asst Sec., 1963; Gen. Sec., 1970–89, when APEX merged with GMB. Mem., TUC Gen. Council, 1983–92. Exec. Mem., Labour Cttee for Europe. Member: Royal Commn on Environmental Pollution, 1976–79; CNAA, 1976–79; IBA, 1984–90; former Mem., MSC, subseq. Training Commn. Director: Chrysler UK Ltd, 1977–79, Talbot UK Ltd, 1979–81; Ansvar Insce Co. Ltd, 1990–. Governor, Henley Management Coll., 1979–91; Mem., Ditchley Foundn, 1982–. Chm., UK Temperance Alliance, 1989–. *Publication:* Guide to Grading of Clerical and Administrative Work, 1968. *Recreations:* walking, reading, chess. *Address:* 16 Owendale, 359 Grange Road, SE19 3BN.

GRANTLEY, 8th Baron *cr* 1782; **Richard William Brinsley Norton;** Baron of Markenfield 1782; Director, Morgan Grenfell International Ltd, since 1994; *b* 30 Jan. 1956; *er s* of 7th Baron Grantley, MC and of Lady Deirdre Freda Mary Hare, *e d* of Earl of Listowel, *qv*; *S* father, 1995. *Educ:* Ampleforth Coll.; New Coll., Oxford (Open Schol. in Maths; BA (Law), MA). Pres., Oxford Union Soc., 1976. Cons. Res. Dept, 1977–81; Morgan Grenfell & Co. Ltd, 1981–. Contested (C) Wentworth, 1983. Councillor, RBK&C, 1982–86. Kt SMO Malta, 1981. *Recreation:* bridge. *Heir: b* Hon. Francis John Hilary Norton, *b* 30 Sept. 1960. *Address:* 8 Halsey Street, SW3 2QH. *T:* (home) 0171–589 7531; (office) 0171–588 4545. *Clubs:* White's, Pratt's.

GRANVILLE, family name of **Baron Granville of Eye.**

GRANVILLE, 5th Earl, *cr* 1833; **Granville James Leveson Gower,** MC 1945; Viscount Granville, 1815; Baron Leveson, 1833; Major Coldstream Guards (Supplementary Reserve); Lord-Lieutenant, Islands Area of the Western Isles, 1983–93 (Vice Lord-Lieutenant, 1976–83); *b* 6 Dec. 1918; *s* of 4th Earl Granville, KG, KCVO, CB, DSO, and Countess Granville, GCVO; *S* father, 1953; *m* 1958, Doon Aileen, *d* of late Hon. Brinsley Plunket and of Mrs V. Stux-Rybar, Luttrellstown Castle, Co. Dublin; two *s* one *d*. *Educ:* Eton. Served throughout War, 1939–45, Tunisia and Italy (twice wounded, despatches, MC). DL Inverness, 1974. *Heir: s* Lord Leveson, *qv*. *Address:* 51 Lyall Mews, SW1X 8DJ. *T:* 0171–235 5114; Callernish, Sollas, North Uist, Outer Hebrides, Inverness-shire PA51 3JH.

GRANVILLE OF EYE, Baron *cr* 1967, of Eye (Life Peer); **Edgar Louis Granville;** *s* of Reginald and Margaret Granville; *b* Reading, 12 Feb. 1899; *m* 1943, Elizabeth *d* of late Rev. W. C. Hunter; one *d*. *Educ:* High Wycombe, London and Australia. Served as officer in AIF, Gallipoli, Egypt and France. Capt. RA, 1939–40. MP (L) Eye Div. of Suffolk, 1929–51; Hon. Sec., Liberal Agricultural Group, House of Commons, 1929–31; Hon. Sec. Foreign Affairs Group, Vice-Pres. National League of Young Liberals; Chm., Young Liberals Manifesto Group; Parliamentary Private Sec. to Sir Herbert Samuel, first National Government, 1931; Parliamentary Private Sec. to Sir John Simon, National Government, 1931–36; Mem. of Inter-Departmental Cttee for the World Economic Conference, 1933. Sits in House of Lords as an Independent. *Recreations:* cricket, football, ski-ing. *Address:* 112 Charlton Lane, Cheltenham, Glos GL53 9EA.

GRANVILLE-CHAPMAN, Maj.-Gen. Timothy John, CBE 1991; Assistant Chief of the General Staff, Ministry of Defence, since 1994; *b* 5 Jan. 1947; *s* of Guy Granville-Chapman and Elsa Granville-Chapman (*née* Campbell); *m* 1971, Elizabeth Stevens; one *s* one *d*. *Educ:* Charterhouse; Christ's Coll., Cambridge (BA Law 1968). Commissioned RA, 1968; regtl duties, 1968–77; Staff Coll., 1978–79; MA to Comdr, 1st BR Corps, 1980–82; CO 1st Regt RHA, 1985–88; Higher Command and Staff Course, 1988; Mil. Doctrine Author, 1988; Policy Staff, MoD, 1989–90; Comdr 12th Armd Bde, 1990–93; Dir, Army Staff Duties, MoD, 1994. *Recreations:* sailing, some country pursuits, architecture, clocks. *Address:* c/o Cox's & King's, 7 Pall Mall, SW1Y 5NA.

GRANVILLE SLACK, George; *see* Slack, G. G.

GRAPPELLI, Stéphane; musician; *b* 26 Jan. 1908; *s* of Prof. Ernest Grappelli and Anna Grappelli (*née* Hanocke); one *d*. Placed in orphanage, 1911; 6 months training in dance with Isadora Duncan, 1914; orphanage to 1918; learnt to play violin together with father; studied for short period at Paris Conservatoire; musical accompanist for silent films, 1923–25; played at social functions, incl. Ambassadeurs Club, 1927–29; joined Grégor and Grégorians, Nice, 1929 (piano and violin, later saxophone and accordion); returned to Paris, 1931; played several instruments at La Croix du Sud, informally with Django Reinhardt, later founding Quintette de Hot Club de France; specialized in jazz improvisations; numerous recordings, 1935–39; spent war years, 1939–45, in London; teamed occasionally with Reinhardt, 1946–53; clubs in London and Paris (incl. Paris Hilton house band, 1967–71); concerts and recordings with fellow musicians, incl. Jean-Luc Ponty, George Shearing, Diz Disley, Oscar Peterson, Baden Powell, Barney Kessel, Earl Hines, Teddy Wilson, Martial Solal, Michel Legrand, Benny Goodman, Subramaniam, Yehudi Menuhin, Yo-Yo Ma, Juillard String Quartet; US début, Newport Jazz Festival, 1969, début Carnegie Hall, 1974. Has homes in Paris and Cannes. Officier, Légion d'honneur; Commandeur, Ordre Nat. du Mérite; Commandeur des Arts et des Lettres; Médaille de Vermeil, Paris. *Address:* 87 rue de Dunkerque, 75009 Paris, France.

GRASS, Günter Wilhelm; German writer and artist; *b* Danzig, 16 Oct. 1927; *m* 1st 1954, Anna Schwarz; three *s* (inc. twin *s*) one *d*; 2nd, 1979, Ute Grunert. *Educ:* Volksschule and Gymnasium, Danzig; Düsseldorf Kunstakademie; Hochschule für Bildende Künste. Lecture Tour of US, 1964, and many other foreign tours. Member: Akademie der Künste, Berlin; Deutscher PEN, Zentrum der Bundesrepublik; Verband Deutscher Schriftsteller; Amer. Academy of Arts and Sciences. Prizes: Lyric, Süddeutscher Rundfunk, 1955; Gruppe 47, 1959; Bremen Literary, 1959 (prize money withheld); Literary, Assoc. of German Critics, 1960; Meilleur livre étranger, 1962; Georg-Büchner, 1965; Fontane, Berlin, 1968; Theodor-Heuss, 1969; Internat. Literatur, 1978; Antonio-Feltrinelli, 1982. *Publications: novels:* Die Blechtrommel, 1959 (The Tin Drum, 1962; filmed 1979); Katz und Maus, 1961 (Cat and Mouse, 1963); Hundejahre, 1963 (Dog Years, 1965); Örtlich Betäubt, 1969 (Local Anaesthetic, 1970); Der Butt, 1977 (The Flounder, 1978); Das Treffen in Telgte, 1979 (The Meeting at Telgte, 1981); Kopfgeburten, 1980 (Headbirths, 1982); Unkenrufe (The Call of the Toad), 1992; Ein weites Feld (A Wide Field), 1995; *poetry:* Die Vorzüge der Windhühner, 1956; Gleisdreieck, 1960; Ausgefragt, 1967; Ach Butt, dein Märchen geht böse aus, 1983; *poetry in translation:* Selected Poems, 1966; Poems of Günter Grass, 1969; In the Egg and other poems, 1978; *drama:* Hochwasser, 1957 (Flood, 1968); Noch zehn Minuten bis Buffalo, 1958 (Only Ten Minutes to Buffalo, 1968); Onkel, Onkel, 1958 (Onkel, Onkel, 1968); Die bösen Köche, 1961 (The Wicked Cooks, 1968); Die Plebejer proben den Aufstand, 1966 (The Plebeians rehearse the Uprising, 1967); Davor, 1969; *prose:* Über das Selbstverständlische, 1968 (Speak Out!, 1969); Aus dem Tagebuch einer Schnecke, 1972 (From the Diary of a Snail, 1974); Dokumente zur politischen Wirkung, 1972; Der Bürger und seine Stimme, 1974; Denkzettel, 1978; Aufsätze zur Literatur, 1980; Zeichnen und Schreiben, Band I, 1982, Band II, 1984; Widerstand lernen, 1984; On Writing and Politics 1967–83, 1985; Die Rättin, 1986 (The Rat, 1987); Zünge Zeigen, 1988 (Show Your Tongue, 1989); Two States—One Nation?, 1990. *Address:* Niedstrasse 13, 1 Berlin 41, Germany.

GRATTAN, Donald Henry, CBE 1989; Chairman: Adult Continuing Education Development Unit, 1984–91; National Council for Educational Technology (formerly Council for Educational Technology), 1985–91 (Member, 1973–84); *b* St Osyth, Essex, 7 Aug. 1926; *s* of Arthur Henry Grattan and Edith Caroline Saltmarsh; *m* 1950, Valmai Dorothy Morgan; one *s* one *d*. *Educ:* Harrow Boys Grammar Sch.; King's Coll., Univ. of London. BSc 1st Cl. Hons, Mathematics Dip. in Radio-Physics. Jun. Scientific Officer, TRE, Gt Malvern, 1945–46; Mathematics Teacher, Chiswick Grammar Sch., 1946–50; Sen. Master, Downer Grammar Sch., Mddx, 1950–56. BBC: Sch. Television Producer, 1956–60; Asst Head, Sch. Television, 1960–64; Head of Further Educn, Television, 1964–70; Asst Controller, Educnl Broadcasting, 1970–72, Controller, 1972–84. Member: Open Univ. Council, 1972–84 and Univ. Delegacy for Continuing Educn, 1978–84; Vis. Cttee, Open Univ., 1987–92; Adv. Council for Adult and Continuing Educn, 1978–83; European Broadcasting Union Working Party on Educn, 1972–84; Venables' Cttee on Continuing Educn, 1976–78. Chm., Adult Literacy Support Services Fund, 1975–80. Mem., Royal TV Soc., 1982–. Chm., Marlow Soc., 1993–. FRSA 1988. DUniv Open, 1985. Burnham Medal of BIM for services to Management Educn, 1969. *Publications:* Science and the Builder, 1963; Mathematics Miscellany (jt, BBC), 1966; numerous articles. *Recreations:* education (formal and informal), planning and organizing, people. *Address:* Delabole, Gossmore Close, Marlow, Bucks SL7 1QG. *T:* Marlow (01628) 473571.

GRATTAN-BELLEW, Sir Henry Charles, 5th Bt, *cr* 1838; *b* 12 May 1933; *s* of Lt-Col Sir Charles Christopher Grattan-Bellew, 4th Bt, MC, KRRC and Maureen Peyton, *niece* and adopted *d* of late Sir Thomas Segrave, Shenfield, Essex; *S* father, 1948; *m* 1st, 1956, Naomi Ellis (marr. diss. 1966); 2nd, 1967, Gillian Hulley (marr. diss. 1973); one *s* one *d*; 3rd, 1978, Elzabé Amy (*née* Body), *widow* of John Westerveld, Pretoria, Tvl, SA. *Educ:* St Gerard's, Bray, Co. Wicklow; Ampleforth Coll., York. Publisher: Horse and Hound, SA, and Sustagen Supersport, 1977. Sports administrator, leading radio and TV commentator, hotelier, thoroughbred breeder and owner. *Heir: s* Patrick Charles Grattan-Bellew, *b* 7 Dec. 1971.

GRATTAN-COOPER, Rear Admiral Sidney, CB 1966; OBE 1946; *b* 3 Dec. 1911; *s* of Sidney Cooper; *m* 1940, Felicity Joan Pitt; two *s*. *Educ:* privately. Entered RN 1936; served in war of 1939–45; Chief of Staff Flag Officer (Air) Home, 1957–59; Staff of Supreme Allied Cdr Atlantic (NATO), 1961–63; Dep. Controller (Aircraft) RN, Min. of Aviation, 1964–66; retired 1966. *Recreations:* golf, swimming. *Address:* Hursley, St James, Cape 7951, S Africa. *Club:* Army and Navy.

GRATWICK, John, OBE 1979; Chairman, Empire Stores Group plc (formerly Empire Stores (Bradford)), 1978–90 (Director, 1973–90); Director, New Law Publishing Co. plc, since 1993; *b* 23 April 1918; *s* of Percival John and Kathleen Mary Gratwick; *m* 1944, Ellen Violet Wright; two *s* two *d*. *Educ:* Cranbrook Sch., Kent; Imperial Coll., Univ. of London. Asst Production Manager, Armstrong Siddeley, 1941–45; Director, Urwick, Orr & Partners Ltd, 1959, Man. Dir, 1968, Vice-Chm., 1971. Chm., EDC for the Clothing Industry, 1985–90 (Mem., 1967–85); Member: Monopolies and Mergers Commn, 1969–76; CAA, 1972–74. Chm., Management Consultants Assoc., 1971–72. University of London: Member: Careers Adv. Bd, 1962–78; Senate, 1967–94; Court, 1987–94; Governor, Cranbrook Sch., Kent, 1972–85. Mem., Bd of Finance, dio. of Guildford, 1989–. Trustee, Foundn for Business Responsibilities. Liveryman, Worshipful Co. of Glovers (Master, 1993–94). *Recreations:* golf, sailing, photography, philately. *Address:* Silver Howe, Nuns Walk, Virginia Water, Surrey GU25 4RT. *T:* Wentworth (01344) 843121. *Clubs:* City Livery; Wentworth (Surrey).

See also Stephen Gratwick.

GRATWICK, Stephen, QC 1968; *b* 19 Aug. 1924; *s* of late Percival John Gratwick, Fawkham, Kent; *m* 1954, Jocelyn Chaplin, Horton Kirby, Kent; four *d*. *Educ:* Charterhouse, Balliol Coll., Oxford. Oxford 1942–44; Signals Research and Develt Estab., 1944–47. BA (Physics) 1946; MA 1950. Called to Bar, Lincoln's Inn, 1949, Bencher, 1976. *Recreations:* tennis, swimming, making and mending things. *Address:* 11 South Square, Gray's Inn, WC1R 5EU.

See also John Gratwick.

GRAVE, Walter Wyatt, CMG 1958; MA (Cambridge); Hon. LLD (Cambridge and McMaster); Hon. Fellow of Fitzwilliam College, Cambridge; *b* 16 Oct. 1901; *o s* of late Walter and Annie Grave; *m* 1932, Kathleen Margaret, *d* of late Stewart Macpherson; two *d*. *Educ:* King Edward VII Sch., King's Lynn; Emmanuel Coll., Cambridge (Scholar); Fellow of Emmanuel Coll., 1926–66, 1972–; Tutor, 1936–40; University Lecturer in Spanish, 1936–40; Registrary of Cambridge Univ., 1943–52; Principal of the University Coll., of the West Indies, Jamaica, 1953–58; Censor of Fitzwilliam House, Cambridge, 1959–66; Master of Fitzwilliam Coll., Cambridge, 1966–71. Temporary Administrative Officer, Ministry of Labour and National Service, 1940–43. *Publication:* Fitzwilliam College Cambridge 1869–1969, 1983. *Address:* 16 Kingsdale Court, Peacocks, Great Shelford, Cambridge CB2 5AT. *T:* Cambridge (01223) 840722.

GRAVES, family name of **Baron Graves.**

GRAVES, 9th Baron *cr* 1794 (Ire.); **Evelyn Paget Graves;** farmer, retired; *b* 17 May 1926; *s* of Alweyn Montague Graves (*d* 1956), and Kathleen Eleanor Cowle Priest (*d* 1974), and *g g s* of 2nd Baron Graves; *S* kinsman, 1994; *m* 1957, Marjorie Ann (OAM 1992), *d* of late Dr Sidney Ernest Holder; two *s* two *d*. *Heir: s* Hon. Timothy Evelyn Graves, 27 March 1960. *Address:* Woodlands, RSD 846, Deloraine, Tas 7304, Australia. *T:* (03) 622009. *Club:* Launceston (Tasmania).

GRAY, family name of **Baron Gray of Contin.**

GRAY, 22nd Lord, *cr* 1445; **Angus Diarmid Ian Campbell-Gray;** *b* 3 July 1931; *s* of Major Hon. Lindsay Stuart Campbell-Gray, Master of Gray, MC (*d* 1945), and Doreen (*d* 1948), *d* of late Cyril Tubbs, Thedden Grange, Alton, Hants; *S* grandmother 1946; *m* 1959, Patricia Margaret (*d* 1987), *o d* of late Capt. Philip Alexander, Kilmorna, Lismore, Co. Waterford; one *s* three *d*; *m* 1994, Mrs Cecilia Williams. *Heir: s* Master of Gray, *qv*. *Address:* Airds Bay House, Taynuilt, Argyll PA35 1JR. *Clubs:* Carlton, MCC.

GRAY, Master of; Hon. Andrew Godfrey Diarmid Stuart Campbell-Gray; *b* 3 Sept. 1964; *s* and *heir* of 22nd Lord Gray, *qv*; *m* 1993, Hon. Lucy, *y d* of 2nd Baron Elton, *qv*.

GRAY OF CONTIN, Baron *cr* 1983 (Life Peer), of Contin in the District of Ross and Cromarty; **James, (Hamish), Hector Northey Gray;** PC 1982; Vice Lord-Lieutenant, Lochaber, Inverness, Badenoch and Strathspey, since 1994; parliamentary and business consultant, since 1986; *b* 28 June 1927; *s* of late J. Northey Gray, Inverness, and Mrs E. M. Gray; *m* 1953, Judith Waite Brydon, BSc, Helenburgh; two *s* one *d*. *Educ:* Inverness Royal Academy. Served in Queen's Own Cameron Hldrs, 1945–48. A director of private and family companies, 1950–70. MP (C) Ross and Cromarty, 1970–83; an Asst Govt Whip, 1971–73; a Lord Comr, HM Treasury, 1973–74; an Opposition Whip, 1974–Feb. 1975; Opposition spokesman on Energy, 1975–79; Minister of State: Dept of Energy, 1979–83; Scottish Office, 1983–86; Govt spokesman on Energy, H of L, 1983–86. Contested (C) Ross, Cromarty and Skye, 1983. Member, Inverness Town Council, 1965–70. DL Inverness, Nairn and Lochaber, 1989. *Recreations:* golf, cricket, walking, family life. *Address:* Achneim House, Flichity, Inverness-shire IV1 2XE.

GRAY, Alasdair James; self-employed verbal and pictorial artist; *b* 28 Dec. 1934; *s* of Alexander Gray and Amy (*née* Fleming); *m* 1st, 1961, Inge Sørensen (marr. diss.); one *s*; 2nd, 1991, Morag McAlpine. *Educ:* Glasgow Sch. of Art (Scottish Educn Dept Dip. in mural painting and design); Jordanhill Teachers' Trng Coll. (CertEd). Part-time teacher and painter, 1958–62; theatrical scene painter, 1962–63; social security scrounger, 1963–64; painter and playwright, 1965–76 (8 one-man exhibns, one retrospective; 17 TV and radio plays broadcast; 4 plays staged); Glasgow's official artist-recorder for People's Palace local history mus., 1977; Writer-in-Residence, Glasgow Univ., 1977–79. Collections of paintings owned by Collins Gall., Strathclyde Univ. and People's Palace local history mus., Glasgow Green. *Publications: novels:* Lanark, 1981; Janine, 1984; The Fall of Kelvin Walker, 1985; Something Leather, 1990; McGrotty and Ludmilla, 1990; Poor Things, 1992; A History Maker, 1994; *short story collections:* Unlikely Stories Mostly, 1983; (with J. Kelman and A. Owens) Lean Tales, 1985; Ten Tales Tall and True, 1993; Teachers, 1995; Mavis Belfrage, 1996; Old Negatives (poetry), 1989; Saltire Self-Portrait no 4 (autobiog.), 1989; Why Scots Should Rule Scotland (polemic), 1992. *Address:* c/o McAlpine, 2 Marchmont Terrace, Glasgow G12 9LT. *T:* 0141–339 0093.

GRAY, Alexander Stuart, FRIBA; Consultant to Watkins, Gray, Woodgate International, 1968–75, retired; *b* 15 July 1905; *s* of Alexander and Mary Gray; *m* 1932, Avis (*d* 1980), *d* of John Radmore, Truro; one *s* two *d*. *Educ:* Mill Hill Sch. Articled to R. S. Balgarnie Wyld, ARIBA; studied at Central Sch. of Arts and Crafts; Royal Academy Schools (Bronze Medal, 1928; Silver Medal and Travelling Studentship, 1932; Gold Medal and Edward Stott Trav. Studentship (Italy), 1933); Brit. Instn Schol., 1929. Lectr on Arch. subjects at Central Sch. of Arts and Crafts, Brixton Sch. of Bldg, and Hammersmith Sch. of Bldg, 1936–39; Lectr on Hosp. Planning at King Edward VII Hosp. Fund Colleges, 1950–. In partnership with W. H. Watkins won architectural comp. for new St George's Hosp., Hyde Park Corner, London (partnership 1939–68); before retirement Architect with partners to: Radcliffe Infirmary, Oxford, United Bristol Hospitals, Royal Free Hospital, Guy's Hospital, London Hospital, Eastman Dental Hospital, St Mary's, Manchester, and other hosps in London and the provinces; also in West Indies, where they were responsible for banks, and commercial buildings as well; hospitals for Comptroller of Development and Welfare in BWI, 1941–46; rebuilding of centre of Georgetown, British Guiana, after the fire of 1945, including new GPO, Telecommunications Building, etc. In Nigeria, University Coll. Hosp., Ibadan, and other works, also in Qatar (Persian Gulf), etc. *Publications:* Edwardian Architecture: a biographical dictionary, 1985; (jtly) Fanlights, 1990; (jtly) Hampstead Garden Suburb, 1992; various papers read at confs on Hosp. Planning with special ref. to designing for the tropics, and contrib. Tech. Jls. *Address:* 1 Temple Fortune Hill, NW11 7XL. *T:* 0181–458 5741. *Clubs:* Arts, Old Millhillians.

GRAY, Andrew Aitken, MC 1945; Chairman, Wellcome Foundation Ltd, 1971–77; *b* 11 Jan. 1912; *s* of John Gray and Margaret Eckford Gray (*née* Crozier); *m* 1st, 1939, Eileen Mary Haines (*d* 1980); three *s*; 2nd, 1984, Jess, *widow* of C. M. Carr. *Educ:* Wyggeston School, Leicester; Christ Church, Oxford. Served Royal Engineers, 1939–46 (MC, despatches). Unilever Ltd, 1935–52. Dir, Wellcome Foundation Ltd, 1954, Dep. Chm., 1967; Chm. and Man. Dir, Cooper, McDougall & Robertson, 1963–70. Chm., Herts AHA, 1974–77. Comdr, Orden del Mérito Agricola; Comdr, Order of Merit, Italy. *Recreations:* fishing, gardening, theatre. *Address:* Rainhill Spring, Stoney Lane, Bovingdon, Herts HP3 0DP. *T:* Hemel Hempstead (01442) 833277. *Club:* East India, Devonshire, Sports and Public Schools.

GRAY, Anthony James; *b* 12 Feb. 1936; *o s* of Sir James Gray, CBE, MC, FRS; *m* 1963, Lady Lana Mary Gabrielle Baring (*d* 1974), *d* of Earl of Cromer, *qv*; one *s* one *d*; *m* 1980, Mrs Maxine Redmayne, *er d* of Captain and Mrs George Brodrick. *Educ:* Marlborough Coll.; New Coll., Oxford. C. T. Bowring & Co. (Insurance) Ltd, 1959–64; Sen. Investment Analyst, de Zoete & Gorton, 1965–67; Head of Investment Research and Partner, James Capel & Co., 1967–73. Member, London Stock Exchange, 1971–73. Dep. Dir, Industrial Development Unit, Dept of Trade and Industry, 1973–75; Special Industrial Advr, Dept of Industry, 1975–76; Assoc., PA Management Consultants Ltd, 1977–81; Chief Exec., Cogent (Hldgs), 1982–88. Chairman: Bioscot Ltd, 1986–88; Scotgen Ltd, 1986–90. Member: Foundries EDC (NEDO), 1977–79; Hammersmith and Fulham DHA, 1982–85; Research and Manufacturing Cttee, CBI, 1988–90; Science and Industry Cttee, BAAS, 1989–91. Member Council: Charing Cross Hosp. Med. Sch., 1982–84; ERA Technology Ltd (formerly Electrical Res. Assoc.), 1986–89. Director: Apollo Soc., 1966–73; Nat. Trust Concert Soc., 1966–73; PEC Concerts, 1979–81. *Recreations:* golf, fishing, music. *Address:* 5 Ranelagh Avenue, SW6 3PJ. *Club:* Garrick.

GRAY, Charles Antony St John, QC 1984; a Recorder, since 1990; *b* 6 July 1942; *s* of late Charles Herbert Gray and Catherine Margaret Gray; *m* 1968, Rosalind Macleod Whinney (marr. diss. 1990); one *s* one *d*. *Educ:* Winchester; Trinity College, Oxford (scholar). Called to Bar, Lincoln's Inn, 1966, Bencher, 1991. *Recreations:* ski-ing, travel, walking. *Address:* 4 Priory Walk, SW10 9SP. *Club:* Brooks's.

GRAY, Charles Horace, MD (London), DSc, FRCP, FRSC, FRCPath; Emeritus Professor of Chemical Pathology in the University of London (Professor, at King's College Hospital Medical School, 1948–76); Consulting Chemical Pathologist, King's College Hospital District, 1976–81 (Consultant, 1938–76); *b* 30 June 1911; *s* of Charles H. Gray and Ethel Hider, Erith, Kent; *m* 1938, Florence Jessie Widdup, ARCA, *d* of Frank Widdup, JP, Barnoldswick, Yorks; two *s*. *Educ:* Imperial Coll. and University Coll., London (Fellow, UCL, 1979); University Coll. Hospital Medical Sch. Demonstrator in Biochemistry, University Coll., London, 1931–36; Bayliss-Starling Scholar in Physiology and Biochemistry, 1932–33; Visiting Teacher in Biochemistry, Chelsea Polytechnic, 1933–36; Demonstrator and Lecturer in Physiology, University Coll., 1935–36; Graham Scholar in Pathology, UCH Medical Sch., 1936–38; Pathologist in Charge Sector Biochemical Laboratory, Sector 9, Emergency Health Service, 1939–44; Hon. Consultant, Miles Laboratories Ltd, 1953–76. Acting Head, Dept of Chem. Pathol., Hosp. for Sick Children, Gt Ormond St, Jan.-Dec. 1979. Vis. Prof., Div. of Clinical Chem., MRC Clinical Res. Centre, Harrow, 1976–83. Member: Clinical Res. Bd of Med. Res. Council, 1964–68; Arthritis and Rheumatism Council Res. Cttee, 1960–68 (Chm., 1963–66); Chairman: MCB Exams Cttee, 1971–73; Steroid Reference Collection and Radioactive Steroid Synthesis Steering Cttee, MRC, 1973–76; Regional Scientific Cttee, SE Thames RHA, 1974–76 (Mem. Regional Research Cttee, 1974–82). Sec., Soc. for Endocrinology, 1950–53; Chm. Cttee of Management, Jl of Endocrinology Ltd, 1970–74; Member: Cttee of Management, Inst. of Psychiatry, 1966–73; Council and Chm., Specialist Adv. Cttee in Chemical Pathology, RCPath, 1972–75; Assoc. of Clinical Biochemists, 1961– (Pres. 1969–71, Emeritus Mem., 1980–). Mem. Livery, Worshipful Soc. of Apothecaries of London, 1951–. Mem., Editorial Bd, Biochemical Jl, 1955–60. *Publications:* The Bile Pigments, 1953; Clinical Chemical Pathology, 1953, 10th edn (jtly), 1985; The Bile Pigments in Health and Disease, 1961; (ed) Laboratory Handbook of Toxic Agents; (ed jtly) Hormones in Blood, 1961, 3rd edn vols 1–3, 1979, vols 4–5, 1983; (ed jtly) High Pressure Liquid Chromatography in Clinical Chemistry, 1976; contributions to medical and scientific journals. *Recreations:* music and travel. *Address:* Barn Cottage, Linden Road, Leatherhead, Surrey KT22 7JF. *T:* Leatherhead (01372) 372415; 34 Cleaver Square, SE11 4EA. *T:* 0171–735 9652. *Clubs:* Athenæum, Royal Over-Seas League.

GRAY, Charles Ireland, CBE 1994; JP; Leader of Strathclyde Regional Council, 1986–92; *b* 25 Jan. 1929; *s* of Timothy Gray and Janet (*née* Brown); *m* 1952, Catherine Creighton Gray; three *s* two *d*. *Educ:* Coatbridge. Dept of Public Affairs, Scotrail, 1946; Mem. (later Chm.), Lanark DC, 1958–64; Mem., Lanark CC, 1964–75; founder Mem., 1975–, and first Vice-Convener, Strathclyde Regl Council. Leader, UK delegn to Euro Cttee of the Regions, 1994–. Pres., Convention of Scottish Local Authorities, 1992–94. Member: Scottish Exhibn and Conf. Centre, 1986–91; Scottish Enterprise Bd, 1990–93. FRSA 1991. JP Strathclyde, 1970. *Recreations:* music, reading, politics. *Address:* 9 Moray Place, Chryston G69 9LZ. *T:* 0141–779 2962, *Fax:* 0141–779 3142.

GRAY, David, CBE 1977 (OBE 1964); QPM 1960; HM Chief Inspector of Constabulary for Scotland, 1970–79; retired; *b* 18 Nov. 1914; *s* of William Gray and Janet Borland Gray; *m* 1st, 1944, Mary Stewart Scott (*d* 1985); two *d*; 2nd, 1989, Laura Margaret Mackinnon. *Educ:* Preston Grammar Sch. Chief Constable: Greenock, 1955–58; Stirling and Clackmannan, 1958–69. Hon. Sec., Chief Constables' (Scotland) Assoc., 1958–69. English-Speaking Union Thyne Scholar, 1969. *Recreations:* fishing, shooting, golf. *Address:* Kingarth, 42 East Barnton Avenue, Edinburgh EH4 6AQ. *T:* 0131–312 6342; Ganavan, The Bay, Strachur, Argyll PA27 8DE. *T:* Strachur (01369) 860466. *Club:* Bruntsfield (Edinburgh).

GRAY, Dr Denis Everett, CBE 1983 (MBE 1972); JP; Resident Staff Tutor since 1957, and Senior Lecturer, 1967–84, Department of Extramural Studies, University of Birmingham; *b* 25 June 1926; *s* of Charles Norman Gray and Kathleen Alexandra (*née* Roberts); *m* 1949, Barbara Joyce, *d* of Edgar Kesterton. *Educ:* Bablake Sch., Coventry; Univ. of Birmingham (BA); Univ. of London; Univ. of Manchester (PhD). Tutor-organiser, WEA, S Staffs, 1953–57. Chairman: Jt Negotiating Cttees for Justices' Clerks and Justices' Clerks' Assts, 1978–86; Central Council of Magistrates' Courts Cttees, 1980–86 (Dep. Chm., 1978–80); Member: Magistrates' Courts Rule Cttee, 1982–86; Lord Chancellor's Adv. Cttee on Trng of Magistrates, 1974–84. JP Solihull, 1962; Dep. Chm., 1968–71 and 1978–82, Chm., 1971–75, Solihull Magistrates; Chm., Licensing Cttee, 1972–76. *Publication:* Spencer Perceval: the evangelical Prime Minister, 1963. *Recreations:* travel, church architecture, reading. *Address:* 11 Brueton Avenue, Solihull, West Midlands B91 3EN. *T:* 0121–705 2935.

GRAY, Prof. Denis John Pereira, OBE 1981; FRCGP; General Medical Practitioner, since 1962; Professor of General Practice, since 1986, Director of Postgraduate Medical School, since 1987, University of Exeter; *b* 2 Oct. 1935; *s* of late Dr Sydney Joseph Pereira Gray and of Alice Evelyn Gray; *m* 1962, Jill Margaret Hoyte; one *s* three *d*. *Educ:* Exeter Sch.; St John's Coll., Cambridge (MA); St Bartholomew's Hosp. Med. Sch. MB BChir. Sen. Lectr in Charge, Univ. of Exeter, 1973–86. Regional Adviser in Gen. Practice, 1975–, Associate Medical Postgrad. Dean, 1992–, Univ. of Bristol; Consultant Adviser in Gen. Practice to Chief MO, DHSS, 1984–87. Mem., GMC, 1994–; Chm., Jt Cttee of Postgrad. Trng for Gen. Practice, 1994–. Trustee, Nuffield Provincial Hosps Trust, 1994–. Chm. Council, RCGP, 1987–90 (Hon. Editor, Journal, 1972–80, Publications, 1976–). Editor, Medical Annual, 1983–87. Lectures: James Mackenzie, RCGP, 1977; Pfizer, N England Faculty, RCGP, Gale Meml, SW England Faculty, RCGP, 1979; Eli Lilly, Haliburton Hume Meml, Newcastle upon Tyne and Northern Counties Med. Soc., Northcott Meml, Harvard Davis, McConaghey Meml, 1988; Murray Scott Meml, 1990; Harben Meml, 1994. Gold Medal, Hunterian Soc., 1966, 1969; Sir Charles Hastings Prize, BMA, 1967, 1970; George Abercrombie Award, RCGP, 1978; Foundn Council Award, RCGP, 1980; Sir Harry Platt Prize, Modern Medicine Jl, 1981; Silver Medal, SIMG, 1989. *Publications:* Running a Practice (jtly), 1978, 3rd edn 1981; Training for General Practice, 1981; Forty Years On: the story of the first forty years of the RCGP, 1992; articles in Lancet, BMJ, Jl RCGP. *Recreation:* reading. *Address:* Alford House, 9 Marlborough Road, Exeter EX2 4TJ. *T:* Exeter (01392) 55235.

GRAY, Rev. Canon Dr Donald Clifford, TD 1970; Canon of Westminster and Rector of St Margaret's, Westminster Abbey, since 1987; Chaplain to HM The Queen, since 1982; Chaplain to the Speaker, House of Commons, since 1987; *b* 21 July 1930; *s* of Henry Hackett Gray and Constance Muriel Gray; *m* 1955, Joyce (*née* Jackson); one *s* two *d*. *Educ:* Newton Heath Technical High Sch.; King's Coll., London and Warminster (AKC); Univ. of Liverpool (MPhil); Univ. of Manchester (PhD) FRHistS. Curate, Leigh Parish Church, 1956–60; Vicar: St Peter's, Westleigh, 1960–67; All Saints', Elton Bury, 1967–74; Rector of Liverpool, 1974–87; RD of Liverpool, 1975–81; Canon Diocesan of Liverpool, 1982–87. Proctor-in-Convocation for Manchester, 1964–74; Mem., Gen. Synod, 1980–87. Chm., Soc. for Liturgical Study, 1978–84; President, Societas Liturgica, 1987–89 (Treas. 1981–87); Mem., Liturgical Commn, 1968–86; Chm., Jt Liturgical Gp, 1989–94 (Mem., 1969–; Sec., 1980–89); Mem., Cathedrals Fabric Commn, 1991–. Chm., Alcuin Club, 1987–. CF (TA), 1958–67; CF (T&AVR), 1967–77; QHC, 1974–77; Chaplain, Order of St John of Jerusalem, 1990 (Sub Chaplain, 1982). *Publications:* (contrib.) Worship and the Child, 1975; (contrib.) Getting the Liturgy Right, 1982; (contrib.) Liturgy Reshaped, 1982; (ed) Holy Week Services, 1983; Earth and Altar, 1986; (ed) The Word in Season, 1988; (contrib.) Towards Liturgy 2000, 1989; (contrib.) Liturgy for a New Century, 1990; Chaplain to Mr Speaker, 1991. *Recreations:* watching cricket, reading modern poetry. *Address:* 1 Little Cloister, Westminster Abbey, SW1P 3PL. *T:* 0171–222 4027; 3 Bara Hill Mews, Stamford, Lincs PE9 2GN. *T:* Stamford (01780) 65024. *Club:* Artists' (Liverpool).

GRAY, Prof. Douglas, FBA 1989; J. R. R. Tolkien Professor of English Literature and Language, University of Oxford, since 1980; *b* 17 Feb. 1930; *s* of Emmerson and Daisy Gray; *m* 1959, Judith Claire Campbell; one *s*. *Educ:* Wellington College, NZ; Victoria Univ. of Wellington (MA 1952); Merton Coll., Oxford (BA 1954, MA 1960). Asst Lecturer, Victoria Univ. of Wellington, 1952–54; Lectr, Pembroke and Lincoln Colls, Oxford, 1956–61; Fellow, Pembroke Coll., 1961–80, now Emeritus; University Lectr in English Language, 1976–80; Professorial Fellow, Lady Margaret Hall, Oxford, 1980–. Mem. Council, EETS, 1981–; Pres., Soc. for Study of Mediæval Langs and Lit., 1982–86. De Carle Lectr, Univ. of Otago, 1989; M. M. Bhattacharya Lectr, Calcutta Univ., 1991. Hon. LittD Victoria Univ. of Wellington, 1995. *Publications:* (ed) Spenser, The Faerie Queene, Book 1, 1969; Themes and Images in the Medieval English Religious Lyric, 1972; (ed) A Selection of Religious Lyrics, 1975; (part of) A Chaucer Glossary, 1979; Robert Henryson, 1979; (ed with E. G. Stanley): Middle English Studies presented to Norman Davis, 1983; Five Hundred Years of Words and Sounds for E. J. Dobson, 1983; (ed) The Oxford Book of Late Medieval Verse and Prose, 1985; (ed) J. A. W. Bennett, Middle English Literature, 1986; (ed jtly) From Anglo-Saxon to Early Middle English: studies presented to E. G. Stanley, 1994; articles on medieval literature. *Address:* Lady Margaret Hall, Oxford OX2 6QA.

GRAY, Dulcie; *see* Denison, D. W. C.

GRAY, Dr Edward George, FRS 1976; Head of the Laboratory of Ultrastructure, National Institute for Medical Research, Mill Hill, 1977–83; *b* 11 Jan. 1924; *s* of Will and Charlotte Gray; *m* 1953, May Eine Kyllikki Rautiainen; two *s*. *Educ:* University Coll. of Wales, Aberystwyth (BSc, PhD). Anatomy Dept, University Coll., London: Lectr, 1958; Reader, 1962; Prof. (Cytology), 1968–77. *Recreations:* violin playing, water colouring, gardening. *Address:* 58 New Park Road, Newgate Street, Hertford SG13 8RF. *T:* Cuffley (01707) 872891.

GRAY, George Thomas Alexander; Second Legislative Counsel for Northern Ireland, since 1988; *b* 20 Jan. 1949; *s* of George Gray and Eveline Gray; *m* 1985, Mary Louise Gray; one *s*. *Educ:* Annadale Grammar Sch., Belfast; The Queen's University of Belfast (LLB 1st Cl. Hons). Called to the Bar of N Ireland; Draftsman, Office of the Legislative

Counsel, 1971–88. *Recreation:* cricket. *Address:* Office of the Legislative Counsel, Parliament Buildings, Stormont, Belfast BT4 3SW. *T:* Belfast (01232) 63210.

GRAY, Prof. George William, CBE 1991; PhD; FRS 1983; FRSE; CChem, FRSC; Research Consultant; Visiting Professor, Southampton, since 1990; *b* 4 Sept. 1926; *s* of John William Gray and Jessie Colville (*née* Hunter); *m* 1953, Marjorie Mary (*née* Canavan); three *d. Educ:* Univ. of Glasgow (BSc); Univ. of London (PhD). CChem, FRSC 1972; FRSE 1989. Staff of Chem. Dept, Univ. of Hull, 1946–: Sen. Lectr, 1960; Reader, 1964; Prof. of Organic Chem., 1978; G. F. Grant Prof. of Chem., 1984–90; Emeritus Prof., 1992. Res. Co-ordinator, Merck Ltd (formerly BDH Ltd), 1990–93. Hon. DSc: Hull, 1991; Nottingham Trent, 1994. Clifford Paterson Prize Lectr, Royal Soc., 1985. Queen's Award for Technol Achievement, 1979; Rank Prize for Optoelectronics, 1980; Leverhulme Medal, Royal Soc., 1987; SCI Medallist, 1993. Editor, Liquid Crystals, 1992–. *Publications:* Molecular Structure and the Properties of Liquid Crystals, 1962; (ed and jtly with P. A. Winsor) Liquid Crystals and Plastic Crystals, 1974; (ed jtly with G. R. Luckhurst) The Molecular Physics of Liquid Crystals, 1979; (with J. W. Goodby) Smectic Liquid Crystals – textures and structures, 1984; (ed) Thermotropic Liquid Crystals, 1987; 300 pubns on liquid crystals in Jl Chem. Soc., Trans Faraday Soc., Phys. Rev., Molecular Cryst. and Liquid Cryst., Jl Chem. Phys., and Proc. IEEE. *Recreations:* gardening, philately. *Address:* Merck Ltd, Merck House, West Quay Road, Poole, Dorset BH15 1TD. *T:* Poole (01202) 669700; Juniper House, Furzehill, Wimborne, Dorset BH21 4HD. *T:* Poole (01202) 880164.

GRAY, Gilbert, QC 1971; a Recorder of the Crown Court, since 1972; *b* 25 April 1928; *s* of late Robert Gray, JP, Scarborough, and of Mrs Elizabeth Gray; *m* 1954, Olga Dilys Gray (*née* Thomas), BA, JP; two *s* two *d. Educ:* Scarborough Boys' High Sch.; Leeds Univ. (LLB). Pres., Leeds Univ. Union. Called to the Bar, Gray's Inn, 1953; Bencher, 1979. Leader of NE Circuit, 1984–87. *Recreation:* sailing. *Address:* 3 Raymond Buildings, Gray's Inn, WC1R 5BH; Park Court Chambers, 40 Park Cross Street, Leeds LS1 2QH; Lingholm Farm, Lebberston, Scarborough.

GRAY, Rear-Adm. Gordon Thomas Seccombe, CB 1964; DSC 1940; *b* 20 Dec. 1911; *s* of late Rev. Thomas Seccombe Gray and Edith Gray; *m* 1939, Sonia Moore-Gwyn; one *s* one *d. Educ:* Nautical Coll., Pangbourne. Entered RN, 1929; Sub-Lieut and Lieut, Mediterranean Fleet, 1934–36, ashore Arab revolt in Palestine (despatches); 1st Lieut, HMS Stork, 1939, Norwegian campaign (despatches, DSC); Comd HMS Badsworth, 1942–43 (despatches); Comd HMS Lamerton, 1943–45 (despatches). After the War comd destroyers Consort, Contest and St Kitts; JSSC, 1948; Comdr 1949; Directing Staff, RN Staff Coll., Greenwich, 1950; Exec. Officer, cruiser HMS Glasgow, 1951–53; Capt. 1953; Naval Deputy to UK Nat. Military Representative, at SHAPE; Capt. of 5th Frigate Sqdn, and Comd HMS Wakeful and HMS Torquay, 1956–59; Asst Chief of Staff to C-in-C Eastern Atlantic Command, 1959–61; in comd of Naval Air Anti-Submarine Sch. at Portland and Chief Staff Officer to Flag Officer Sea Trng, 1961–62; Senior Naval Instructor, Imperial Defence Coll., 1963–65, retd. *Recreation:* yachting. *Address:* c/o Lloyds Bank, Liphook, Hants GU30 7AE.

GRAY, (Hamish) Martin (Vincent); Main Board Director, since 1993, Chief Executive, NatWest UK (formerly UK Branch Business), since 1992, National Westminster Bank; *b* 8 June 1946; *s* of Kenneth Dunwell Gray and Helen McGeorge Gray; *m*; two *s*; *m* 2nd, 1992, Alison Margaret Wells. *Educ:* Cockburn High Sch., Leeds. FCIB. Appts with National Westminster Bank, 1963–; Head of Group Planning, Business Develt Div., 1986–88; Asst Gen. Manager, Group Develt, 1988–89; Dep. Gen. Manager, UK Branch Business, 1990–92. *Recreations:* fell-walking, fishing. *Address:* Drapers Gardens, 12 Throgmorton Avenue, EC2N 2DL. *T:* 0171–920 5555.

GRAY, Prof. Hanna Holborn, PhD; Harry Pratt Judson Distinguished Service Professor of History, University of Chicago, since 1993 (President, 1978–93, now President Emeritus); *b* 25 Oct. 1930; *d* of Hajo and Annemarie Holborn; *m* 1954, Charles Montgomery Gray. *Educ:* Bryn Mawr Coll., Pa (BA); Univ. of Oxford (Fulbright Schol.); Univ. of Harvard (PhD). Instructor, Bryn Mawr Coll., 1953–54; Harvard University: Teaching Fellow, 1955–57, Instr, 1957–59, Asst Prof., 1959–60, Vis. Lectr, 1963–64; Asst Prof., Univ. of Chicago, 1961–64, Associate Prof., 1964–72; Dean and Prof., Northwestern, Evanston, Ill, 1972–74; Provost, and Prof. of History, Yale Univ., 1974–78, Acting Pres., 1977–78. Hon. degrees include: LHD: Duke, 1982; Brandeis, 1983; Amer. Coll. of Greece, 1986; LLD: Dartmouth Coll., Yale, 1978; Brown, 1979; Rochester, Notre Dame, 1980; Michigan, 1981; Princeton, 1982; Georgetown, 1983; Columbia, 1987; Toronto, 1991; DLitt: Oxford, 1979; Washington, 1985. *Publications:* ed (with Charles M. Gray) Jl Modern History, 1965–70; articles in professional jls. *Address:* (office) 1126 E 59th Street, Chicago, IL 60637, USA. *T:* (312) 7027799. *Clubs:* Commercial, Economic, Quadrangle, Chicago (Chicago); Cosmopolitan (New York City).

GRAY, Harold James, CMG 1956; retired, 1972; *b* 17 Oct. 1907; 2nd *s* of late John William Gray and of Amelia Frances (*née* Miller); *m* 1928, Katherine Gray (*née* Starling) (*d* 1985); one *d. Educ:* Alleyn's Sch.; Dover County Sch.; Queen Mary Coll., London Univ. (MSc, LLB); Gray's Inn; Harvard University, USA (MPA). MInstP, CPhys; FRSA. Customs and Excise Dept, 1927; Asst Examiner, Patent Office, 1930, Examiner, 1935; Industries and Manufactures Dept, Board of Trade, 1938; Ministry of Supply, 1939; Asst Sec., Min. of Supply, 1942. transf. to Bd of Trade, 1946; Commercial Relations and Exports Dept, Board of Trade, 1950; Under-Sec., 1954; UK Senior Trade Comr and Economic and Commercial Adviser to High Comr in Australia, 1954–58; UK Senior Trade Comr and Economic Adviser to the High Comr in Union of South Africa, 1958–60; Dir, Nat. Assoc. of British Manufacturers, 1961–65; Dir, Legal Affairs, CBI, 1965–72. Commonwealth Fund Fellowship, 1949–50. Chm., NUMAS (Management Services) Ltd. *Publications:* Electricity in the Service of Man, 1949; Economic Survey of Australia, 1955; Dictionary of Physics, 1958; (jtly) New Dictionary of Physics, 1975. *Recreations:* golf, swimming, riding. *Address:* Copper Beeches, 58 Tudor Avenue, Maidstone, Kent ME14 5HJ.

GRAY, Hugh, BSc(Soc), PhD; former International Secretary, Theosophical Society; *b* 19 April 1916; *s* of William Marshall Kemp Gray; *m* 1954, Edith Esther (*née* Rudinger); no *c. Educ:* Battersea Grammar Sch.; London Sch. of Economics. Army Service, Intelligence Corps. UNRRA and Internat. Refugee Organisation, 1945–52; Social Worker; Lectr at SOAS, University of London, 1962–66 and 1970–81; Chm., Centre for S Asian Studies, 1980–81; Gen. Sec., Theosophical Soc. in England, 1983–89. MP (Lab) Yarmouth, 1966–70. *Publications:* various articles on Indian politics and philosophy. *Address:* 22 Bridstow Place, W2 5AE; Castello 1852, Venice.

GRAY, Prof. Jeffrey Alan, PhD; Professor and Head of Department of Psychology, Institute of Psychiatry, University of London, since 1983; *b* 26 May 1934; *s* of Maurice and Dora Gray; *m* 1961; two *s* two *d. Educ:* Magdalen Coll., Oxford (BA Hons Mod Langs 1957; BA Hons Psychology 1959); Univ. of London (DipPsych 1960; PhD 1964). Research Worker, Inst. of Psychiatry, 1960–64; Lectr in Psychol., Dept of Exp. Psych., Oxford, 1964–83; Fellow, University Coll., Oxford, 1965–83; Travelling Fellow, MRC, and Guest Investigator, Rockefeller Univ., NY, 1968–69; Soc. Sci. Res. Fellow, Nuffield Foundn, 1975–76; Associate Prof., Univ. of Paris VI, 1979–80. Dir, Psychology at Work Ltd, 1989–. President's Award, BPsS, 1983; Kenneth Craik Award, St John's Coll., Cambridge, 1995. *Publications:* Pavlov's Typology, 1964; The Psychology of Fear and Stress, 1971; The Biological Bases of Individual Behaviour, 1972; Elements of a Two-Process Theory of Learning, 1975; Pavlov, 1979; The Neuropsychology of Anxiety, 1982, and other works. *Recreation:* ski-ing. *Address:* Department of Psychology, Institute of Psychiatry, De Crespigny Park, Denmark Hill, SE5 8AF. *T:* 0171–919 3245.

GRAY, Rev. Prof. John; Professor of Hebrew, University of Aberdeen, 1962–80, now Professor Emeritus; *b* 9 June 1913; *s* of James Telfer Gray; *m* Janet J. Gibson; five *c. Educ:* Kelso High Sch.; Edinburgh Univ. (MA, BD, PhD). Colonial Chaplain and Chaplain to Palestine Police, 1939–41; Minister of the Church of Scotland, Kilmory, Isle of Arran, 1942–47; Lectr in Semitic Languages and Literatures, Manchester Univ., 1947–53; Lectr in Hebrew and Biblical Criticism, University of Aberdeen, 1953–62. Mem., Soc. for Old Testament Study. Hon. DD St Andrews, 1977. *Publications:* The Krt Text in the Literature of Ras Shamra, 1955 (2nd edn 1964); The Legacy of Canaan, 1957 (2nd edn 1965); Archæology and the Old Testament World, 1962; The Canaanites, 1964; Kings I and II: a Commentary, 1964, 3rd edn 1977; Joshua, Judges and Ruth, 1967, 3rd edn 1986; A History of Jerusalem, 1969; Near Eastern Mythology, 1969, 2nd edn 1982; The Biblical Doctrine of the Reign of God, 1979; contribs to various Bible Dictionaries, memorial volumes and learned journals. *Recreations:* beekeeping, gardening, trout-fishing. *Address:* Tanlaw Cottage, Hendersyde, Kelso, Roxburgh TD5 7ST. *T:* Kelso (01573) 24374.

GRAY, Sir John (Archibald Browne), Kt 1973; MA, MB, ScD; FRS 1972; Member, External Scientific Staff, MRC, 1977–83: working at Marine Biological Association Laboratory, Plymouth, 1977–93; *b* 30 March 1918; *s* of late Sir Archibald Gray, KCVO, CBE; *m* 1946, Vera Kathleen Mares; one *s* one *d. Educ:* Cheltenham Coll.; Clare Coll., Cambridge (Hon. Fellow, 1976); University Coll. Hospital. BA 1939; MA 1942; MB, BChir 1942; ScD 1962. Service Research for MRC, 1943–45; Surg. Lieut, RNVR, 1945–46; Scientific Staff of MRC at Nat. Inst. for Med. Research, 1946–52; Reader in Physiology, University Coll., London, 1952–58; Prof. of Physiology, University Coll., London, 1959–66; Medical Research Council: Second Sec., 1966–68; Sec., 1968–77; Dep. Chm., 1975–77; Mem., EC Cttee for Medical Res., 1972–76; Member of Council: Marine Biol Assoc., 1969–88 (Vice-Pres., 1988–); Freshwater Biol Assoc., 1981–88 (Pres., 1983–88; Chm. of Council, 1985–88; Vice-Pres., 1988–). QHP 1968–71. FIBiol; FRCP 1974. Hon. DSc Exeter, 1985. *Publications:* papers, mostly on sensory receptors and sensory nervous system, in Jl of Physiology, Procs of Royal Soc. series B, Jl of Marine Biol Assoc., etc. *Recreations:* painting, sailing, tennis. *Address:* Seaways, Kingsway, Kingsand, near Plymouth PL10 1NG. *T:* Plymouth (01752) 822745.

GRAY, John Malcolm; Chairman and Chief Executive Officer, Hongkong and Shanghai Banking Corporation Ltd, since 1993; *b* 28 July 1934; *s* of Samuel Gray and Christina (*née* Mackay-Sim); *m* 1984, Ursula Siong Koon; three *d. Educ:* Strathallan Sch., Scotland. With Hongkong and Shanghai Banking Corp. Ltd, 1952–. MEC, Hong Kong, 1993–. Chm., Hong Kong Port Develt Bd, 1990–93. Mem., Governor's Business Council, Hong Kong, 1993–. *Recreations:* reading, golf. *Address:* (office) Level 34, 1 Queen's Road, Central, Hong Kong. *T:* 8221134. *Club:* Hong Kong (Hong Kong).

GRAY, Vice Adm. Sir John (Michael Dudgeon), KBE 1967 (OBE 1950); CB 1964; *b* Dublin, 13 June 1913; British; *m* 1939, Margaret Helen Purvis (*d* 1994); one *s* one *d. Educ:* RNC, Dartmouth. HMS Nelson, 1931; Midshipman, HMS Enterprise, 1932–33; Sub-Lieut, HMS Devonshire, 1934; specialised in Gunnery, 1938. Served War of 1939–45; HMS Hermes; HMS Spartan; with US in Anzio; 8th Army in Italy; French Army in France (despatches). HMS Duke of York, 1945, Comdr 1947; Naval Adviser, UK Mission, Japan, 1947–50 (OBE Korean War); HMS Swiftsure, 1950, Capt. 1952; HMS Lynx, 1956; HMS Victorious, 1961; Rear Adm. 1962; Dir-Gen. of Naval Trng, Min. of Def., 1964–65 (Admiralty, 1962–64); Vice Adm. 1965; C-in-C, S Atlantic and S America Station, 1965–67. Sec., 1973–91, Consultant, 1991–92, Oriental Ceramic Soc. *Recreations:* squash, tennis, athletics (represented RN in 220 and 440 yds). *Club:* Naval and Military.

GRAY, Prof. John Richard; Professor of African History, University of London, 1972–89, now Emeritus; *b* 7 July 1929; *s* of Captain Alfred William Gray, RN and of Christobel Margaret Gray (*née* Raikes); *m* 1957, Gabriella, *d* of Dr Camillo Cattaneo; one *s* one *d. Educ:* Charterhouse; Downing Coll., Cambridge (Richmond Scholar). BA Cantab 1951; PhD London 1957. Lectr, Univ. of Khartoum, 1959–61; Res. Fellow, Sch. of Oriental and African Studies, London, 1961–63, Reader, 1963–72. Vis. Prof., UCLA, 1967. Editor, Jl African History, 1968–71; Chairman: Africa Centre, Covent Garden, 1967–72; Britain-Zimbabwe Soc., 1981–84. Mem., Pontifical Cttee of Historical Sciences, 1982–. Order of St Silvester, 1966. *Publications:* The Two Nations: aspects of the development of race relations in the Rhodesias and Nyasaland, 1960; A History of the Southern Sudan, 1839–1889, 1961; (with D. Chambers) Materials for West African History in Italian Archives, 1965; (ed, with D. Birmingham) Pre-Colonial African Trade, 1970; (ed) The Cambridge History of Africa, vol. 4, 1975; (ed, with E. Fasholé-Luke and others) Christianity in Independent Africa, 1978; Black Christians and White Missionaries, 1990. *Recreation:* things Italian. *Address:* 39 Rotherwick Road, NW11 7DD. *T:* 0181–458 3676.

GRAY, Sir John Walton David, KBE 1995; CMG 1986; HM Diplomatic Service; Ambassador to Belgium, since 1992; *b* Burry Port, Carmarthenshire, 1 Oct. 1936; *s* of Myrddin Gray and Elsie Irene (*née* Jones), Llanelli, Carms; *m* 1957, Anthoula, *e d* of Nicolas Yerasimou, Nicosia, Cyprus; one *s* two *d. Educ:* Blundell's Sch.; Christ's Coll., Cambridge (MA; Scholar and Tancred Student); ME Centre, Oxford; Amer. Univ., Cairo. National Service, 1954–56. Joined Foreign Service, 1962; served: Mecas, 1962; Bahrain Agency, 1964; FO, 1967; Geneva, 1970; Sofia, 1974; Counsellor (Commercial), 1978, Counsellor and Hd of Chancery, 1980, Jedda; Hd of Maritime, Aviation and Environment Dept, FCO, 1982–85; Ambassador to Lebanon, 1985–88; Ambassador and UK Perm. Rep. to OECD, Paris, 1988–92. Chm., OECD Information Policy Wkg Gp, 1980–82; Rapporteur, Study Team on Performance of OECD's Centre for Co-operation with Eur. Econs in Transition, 1994. Member: RIIA; Welsh Centre for Internat. Affairs (Vice-Chm.); Inst. of Welsh Affairs (Hon. Pres., Paris Chapter); British-Lebanese Assoc.; Crawshays Welsh Rugby Club (Vice Pres.). *Recreations:* most spectator sports, amateur dramatics, light history, things Welsh, public speaking (Internat. Toastmasters' After Dinner Speaker of the Year, 1993). *Address:* c/o Foreign and Commonwealth Office, SW1A 2AH. *T:* 0171–270 3000. *Clubs:* Athenæum, Commonwealth Trust, Royal Anglo-Belgian (Hon.); Cardiff and County (Cardiff); (Hon. Mem.) Cercle Royal Gaullois, (Hon. Mem.) Cercle des Nations (Brussels).

GRAY, Rt. Rev. Joseph; *see* Shrewsbury, Bishop of, (RC).

GRAY, Kenneth Walter, CBE 1992; PhD; FInstP, FIEE; Technical Director, THORN EMI plc, since 1986 (Director of Research, 1984–86); Managing Director, Thorn Transaction, since 1993; *b* 20 March 1939; *s* of late Robert W. Gray and Ruby M. Gray; *m* 1962, Jill Henderson; two *s* one *d. Educ:* Blue Coat Sch.; Univ. of Wales (BSc, PhD). FInstP 1991; FIEE 1992. Research on magnetic resonance, as Nat. Res. Council of Canada post-doctoral Fellow, Univ. of British Columbia, Vancouver, 1963–65; research on semiconductor devices and on radiometry, N American Rockwell Science Center, Thousand Oaks, Calif, 1965–70; research on devices and systems at Royal Signals and Radar Estabt, 1971; Supt Solid State Physics and Devices Div., 1976; Head of Physics Group, 1979; RCDS 1981. Royal Signals and Radar Establishment: CSO, MoD, Dep. Dir (Applied Physics), 1982–84; Under Sec., Dep. Dir (Information Systems), 1984. Exec. Chm., Thorn Software, 1987–89; Technical Dir, Thorn Security and Electronics, 1991–93. Visiting Research Fellow: Univ. of Newcastle, 1972–74; Univ. of Leeds, 1976–; Vis. Prof., Univ. of Nottingham, 1986–. Member: DTI Innovation Adv. Bd, 1988–93; SERC, 1991–94; Cabinet Office, OST, Technology Foresight Steering Cttee, 1993–. *Publications:* over 30 scientific and technical papers in various learned jls. *Recreations:* running, tennis, bridge. *Address:* Broadgates, Manor Road, Penn, Buckinghamshire HP10 8JA.

GRAY, Prof. Kevin John, PhD, LLD, DCL; Professor of Law, University of Cambridge, since 1993; Fellow, Trinity College, Cambridge, 1981–90 and since 1993; *b* 23 July 1951; *s* of Bryce Holmes Gray and Priscilla Margaret Gray (*née* McCullough). *Educ:* Trinity Hall, Cambridge (BA 1972 (1st Cl. Law Tripos Parts I and II); MA, PhD 1976; Yorke Prize, 1977; LLD 1991); DCL Oxford, 1994). Called to the Bar, Middle Temple, 1993. University of Cambridge: Fellow, Queens' Coll., 1975–81; Asst Lectr and Lectr in Law, 1978–90; Univ. Advocate, 1986–88; Res. Fellow, ANU, 1990, 1996; Drapers' Prof. of Law, QMW, Univ. of London, 1991–93. Sen. Vis. Res. Fellow, St John's Coll., Oxford, 1993–94; Associate Mem., Acad. Internat. de Droit Comparé, 1995. *Publications:* Reallocation of Property on Divorce, 1977; Elements of Land Law, 1987, 2nd edn 1993; other books and articles on law. *Recreations:* mountaineering, rock climbing. *Address:* Trinity College, Cambridge CB2 1TQ. *T:* Cambridge (01223) 338497. *Club:* Roof-climbers (Cambridge).

GRAY, Linda Esther, (Mrs Peter McCrorie); retired as opera singer, now teaching; *b* 29 May 1948; *d* of James and Esther Gray; *m* 1971, Peter McCrorie; one *d*. *Educ:* Greenock Academy; Royal Scottish Academy of Music and Drama. Cinzano Scholarship, 1969; Goldsmith Schol., 1970; James Caird Schol., 1971; Kathleen Ferrier Award, 1972; Christie Award, 1972. London Opera Centre, 1969–71; Glyndebourne Festival Opera, 1972–75; Scottish Opera, 1974–79; Welsh Opera, 1980; English National Opera, 1979; American début, 1981; Royal Opera House: Sieglinde, 1982; Fidelio, 1983. Records: Tristan und Isolde, 1981; Wagner's Die Feen, 1983. Principal rôles: Isolde, Sieglinde, Kundry (Wagner); Tosca (Puccini); Fidelio (Beethoven). *Recreations:* cooking, swimming. *Address:* 35 Green Lane, New Malden, Surrey KT3 5BX.

GRAY, Margaret Caroline, MA Cantab; Headmistress, Godolphin and Latymer School, 1963–73; *b* 25 June 1913; *d* of Rev. A. Herbert Gray, DD, and Mrs Gray (Mary C. Dods, *d* of Principal Marcus Dods of New Coll., Edinburgh). *Educ:* St Mary's Hall, Brighton; Newnham Coll., Cambridge. Post graduate fellowship to Smith Coll., Mass, USA, 1935–36. Asst History mistress, Westcliff High Sch. for Girls, 1937–38; Head of History Dept, Mary Datchelor Girls' Sch., Camberwell, 1939–52; Headmistress, Skinners' Company's Sch., Stamford Hill, 1952–63. Chm., Nat. Advisory Centre on Careers for Women, 1970–91. Governor: Francis Holland Schs, 1974–; Hampton Sch., 1976–88; West Heath Sch., Sevenoaks, 1974–89; Unicorn Sch., Kew, 1974–89; Chm. of Trustees, Godolphin and Latymer Bursary Fund, 1976–. Hon. Sec., RUKBA, Kingston-upon-Thames, 1973–. Elder, St John's Wood URC, 1960–. *Recreations:* gardening, motoring, walking. *Address:* 15 Fitzwilliam Avenue, Kew, Richmond, Surrey TW9 2DQ. *T:* 0181–940 4439.

GRAY, Martin; *see* Gray, H. M. V.

GRAY, Lt-Gen. Sir Michael Stuart, KCB 1986; OBE 1970; Lieutenant of the Tower of London, since 1995; General Officer Commanding, South East District, and Commander Joint Force Headquarters, 1985–88, retired; Defence Industries Adviser, Wardle Storeys plc, since 1989; Chief Executive, Rainford Developments Ltd, since 1992; *b* Beverley, E Yorkshire, 3 May 1932; *e s* of late Lieut Frank Gray, RNVR, and Joan Gray (*née* Gibson); *m* 1958, Juliette Antonia Noon, Northampton; two *s* one *d*. *Educ:* Beverley Grammar Sch.; Christ's Hosp., Horsham; RMA, Sandhurst. FIMgt; FInstD; FICFM. Enlisted RA, 1950; commissioned E Yorkshire Regt, 1952; served Malaya; transf. to Parachute Regt, 1955; served Cyprus, Suez, Jordan, Greece, Bahrein, Aden, N Ireland; sc Camberley, 1963; commanded 1st Bn Parachute Regt, 1969–71; DS Staff Coll., Camberley, 1971–73; Col GS 1 Div. BAOR, 1973–75; RCDS 1976; last Comdr 16 Para Bde, 1977; Comdr 6 Field Force and COMUKMF, 1977–79; Comdr British Army Staff and Mil. Attaché, Washington, 1979–81, and Head of British Def. Staff and Def. Attaché, Washington, 1981; GOC SW District, and Maj.-Gen., UKMF(L), 1981–83; COS, HQ BAOR, 1984–85. Dep. Col Comdt, Parachute Regt, 1986–90, Col Comdt, 1990–93. Hon. Colonel: 10 Para (V), 1984–88; 250 (Hull) Field Amb. RAMC (V), 1991–. Consultant, Brittany Ferries (writing Battlefield Tours), 1988. Chm., Airborne Assault Normandy Trust (AAN), to preserve the history of 6 AB Division in Normandy, 1978–; Trustee, AB Forces Museum, 1976– (Chm., 1985–93); Chm., Military Aerospace Museums Trust, Aldershot, 1989–; Trustee, AB Forces Charities Develt Trust (Chm., 1990–94); Pres., York Br., Parachute Regt Assoc.; Trustee, AB Forces Security Fund, 1986–; Vice Pres., Army Parachute Assoc., 1987– (Pres., 1981–87); Normandy Veterans Association: Vice-Pres., Goole Br., 1988–; Pres., Leeds Br., 1991–; Chm., E Yorks Cttee, King George's Fund for Sailors, 1988–; Mem., Amicable Soc. of Blues, 1989–; Patron, Combined Ex-Service Assoc., Bridlington, 1988–. Freeman, City of London, 1983. Officier, Légion d'Honneur (France), 1994. *Recreations:* military history, travelling, DIY, photography, painting. *Address:* c/o National Westminster Bank, 60 Market Place, Beverley, North Humberside HU17 8AH.

GRAY, Milner Connorton, CBE 1963; RDI 1938; FCSD; AGI; FInstPack; Founder Partner and Senior Consultant, Design Research Unit; Past Master, Faculty of Royal Designers for Industry; Past President, Society of Industrial Artists and Designers (now Chartered Society of Designers); Past Master Art Workers' Guild; *b* 8 Oct. 1899; *s* of late Archibald Campbell Gray and Katherine May Hart, Eynsford, Kent; *m* 1934, Gnade Osborne-Pratt; no *c*. *Educ:* studied painting and design, London Univ., Goldsmiths' Coll. Sch. of Art. Head of Exhibitions Branch, Ministry of Information, 1940–41, and Adviser on Exhibitions, 1941–44; Senior Partner in Industrial Design Partnership, 1934–40; Principal, Sir John Cass Coll. of Art, 1937–40; on Visiting Staff: Goldsmiths' Coll. Sch. of Art, London Univ., 1930–40; Chelsea Sch. of Art, 1934–37; Royal Coll. of Art, 1940; Founder Mem., Soc. of Industrial Artists, 1930, Hon. Sec., 1932–40, Pres., 1943–48 and 1968; Member of Council: Design and Industries Assoc., 1935–38; RSA, 1959–65; Artists Gen. Benevolent Instn, 1959– (Vice Pres., 1986); Adviser to BBC "Looking at Things" Schs Broadcasts, 1949–55. Member: Min. of Education Nat. Adv. Cttee on Art Examinations, 1949–52; Nat. Adv. Council on Art Education, 1959–69; Royal Mint Adv. Cttee, 1952–86. Mem. Council, RCA, 1963–67, Mem. Court 1967–, Senior Fellow, 1971. British Pres., Alliance Graphique Internationale, 1963–71. Consultant Designer: BR Bd for BR Corporate Design Prog., 1963–67; (jointly) to Orient Line, SS Oriana, 1957–61; Ilford Ltd, 1946–66; Internat. Distillers and Vintners, 1954–69; Watney Mann Group, 1956–70; British Aluminium Co., 1965–72; ICI, 1966–70; Min. of Technology, 1970–. Governor: Central Sch. of Art and Design, 1944–46; Hornsey Coll. of Art and Design, 1959–65. Hon. Fellow, Soc. of Typographic Designers, 1979. Hon. Des. RCA, 1963, Hon. Dr RCA, 1979; Hon. DA Manchester, 1964. Freeman City of London, 1987. Served in 19th London Regt, and Royal Engineers, attached Camouflage Sch., 1917–19; admitted HAC, 1923. Gold Medal, Soc. of Ind. Artists and Designers, 1955. *Publications:* The Practice of Design (jointly), 1946; Package Design, 1955; (jtly) Lettering for Architects and Designers, 1962; articles, lectures and broadcasts on various aspects of design. *Address:* Felix Hall, Kelvedon, Essex CO5 9DG. *T:* Kelvedon (01376) 570485. *Club:* Arts.

GRAY, Monique Sylvaine, (Mrs P. F. Gray); *see* Viner, M. S.

GRAY, Paul Edward, ScD; Chairman of the Corporation, Massachusetts Institute of Technology, since 1990; *b* 7 Feb. 1932; *s* of Kenneth Frank Gray and Florence (*née* Gilleo); *m* 1955, Priscilla Wilson King; one *s* three *d*. *Educ:* Massachusetts Inst. of Technol. (SB 1954, SM 1955, ScD 1960). Served Army, 1955–57 (1st Lieut). Massachusetts Inst. of Technology: Mem., Faculty of Engrg, 1960–71, 1990–; Class of 1922 Prof. of Electrical Engrg, 1968–71; Dean, Sch. of Engrg, 1970–71; Chancellor, 1971–80; Pres., 1980–90; Mem. of Corp., 1971–. Director: A. D. Little Inc., Cambridge; The New England, Boston; Boeing Co., Seattle; Eastman Kodak, Rochester. Trustee and Mem. of Corporation, Museum of Science, Boston; Trustee, Wheaton Coll., Mass. Fellow, Amer. Acad. of Arts and Sciences; Member: National Acad. of Engrg; Mexican National Acad. of Engrg; AAAS; Fellow, IEEE. *Address:* Massachusetts Institute of Technology, 77 Massachusetts Avenue, Cambridge, MA 02139, USA; 100 Memorial Drive, Cambridge, MA 02142.

GRAY, Paul Richard Charles; Director, Personnel and Support Services, HM Treasury, since 1994; *b* 2 Aug. 1948; *s* of Rev. Sidney Gray and Ina (*née* Maxey); *m* 1972, Lynda Elsie Braby; two *s*. *Educ:* Wyggeston Boys' Sch., Leicester; LSE (BSc Econ 1969). Dept of Econ. Affairs, 1969; HM Treasury, 1969–77; with Booker McConnell Ltd, 1977–79; HM Treasury: Principal, 1979–83; Asst Sec., 1984–87; Econ. Affairs Private Sec. to Prime Minister, 1988–90; Under Sec., Monetary Gp, 1990–93. Dir (non-exec.), Laing Management Ltd, 1993–95. *Recreations:* family, walking, Wensleydale sheep. *Address:* HM Treasury, Allington Towers, Allington Street, SW1E 5EB. *T:* 0171–270 5000.

GRAY, Paul Shapter, FRSC; Director, Environment and Climate and Marine Science and Technology Programme, European Commission, since 1992; *b* 18 Sept. 1932; *s* of Frederick Archibald and Vera Emma Gray; *m* 1958, Diane Lillian Platt; one *s* one *d* (and one *s* decd). *Educ:* St Chad's Coll., Wolverhampton; Birmingham Univ. (BSc Hons; MSc). FRSC (FRIC 1967). Chief Chemist, Midland Tar Distillers, 1954–57; Sen. Research Fellow, Ministry of Power, 1957–59; Head of Div., Reactor Chemistry, UKAEA, Winfrith, 1959–63; Ops Controller, OECD DRAGON (high temp. gas cooled reactor expt), 1963–73; European Commission, 1973–: Dep. Head of Div., Elimination of Technical Barriers to Trade, 1977–81; Head of Service, Wood, Paper and Construction Industries, 1981–83; Head of Div., Food Law and Food Trade, 1983–91; Advr for industrial aspects of biotechnology, 1991–92. *Publications:* numerous in scientific and economic jls. *Recreations:* music, singing, sailing, gardening. *Address:* Commission of the European Communities, 200 rue de la Loi, 1049 Brussels, Belgium. *T:* (2) 2951815.

GRAY, Prof. Peter, MA, PhD, ScD (Cantab); FRS 1977; CChem, FRSC; Master of Gonville and Caius College, Cambridge, since 1988; *b* Newport, 25 Aug. 1926; *er s* of late Ivor Hicks Gray and Rose Ethel Gray; *m* 1952, Barbara Joan Hume, PhD (*d* 1992), 2nd *d* of J. B. Hume, London; two *s* two *d*. *Educ:* Newport, High Sch.; Gonville and Caius Coll., Cambridge. Major Schol., 1943; Prizeman, 1944, 1945 and 1946; BA 1st cl hons Nat. Sci. Tripos, 1946; Dunlop Res. Student, 1946; Ramsay Mem. Fellow, 1949–51; PhD 1949; Fellow, Gonville and Caius Coll., 1949–53; ICI Fellow, 1951; ScD 1963. University Demonstrator in Chem. Engrg, University of Cambridge, 1951–55; Physical Chemistry Dept, University of Leeds: Lectr, 1955; Reader, 1959; Prof., 1962; Head of Dept, 1965–88; Chm., Bd of Combined Faculties of Science and Applied Science, 1972–74; Hon. Vis. Prof., 1988–; University of Cambridge: Chm., Faculty of Engrg, 1989–94; Mem., Council of Senate, 1990–; Mem., Financial Bd, 1991–94. Visiting Professor: Univ. of BC, 1958–59; Univ. of W Ont., 1969; Univ. of Göttingen, 1979, 1986; Macquarie Univ., 1980; Univ. of Paris, 1986; H. C. Hottel Lectr, Orléans, 1990; Pierre Bruylants Lectr, Louvain, 1994; Visitor, Fire Res. Organisation, 1984–90. Mem. Council: Faraday Soc., 1965 (Vice-Pres., 1970; Treasurer, 1973; Pres., 1983–85); Chemical Soc., 1969. Pres., Cambridge Phil Soc., 1992–93. Meldola Medal, Royal Inst. Chem., 1956; Marlow Medal, Faraday Soc., 1959; Gold Medal, Combustion Inst., 1978; Award for Combustion, Royal Soc. of Chemistry, 1986; Italgas Prize for Chemistry, 1988. Associate Editor, Royal Society, 1983–; Member, Editorial Board: Combustion and Flame, 1976–82; Dynamics and Stability of Systems, 1986–. *Publications:* (with S. K. Scott) Chemical Oscillations and Instabilities, 1990; numerous papers on phys. chem. subjects in scientific jls. *Recreation:* hill walking. *Address:* The Master's Lodge, Gonville and Caius College, Cambridge CB2 ITA. *T:* Cambridge (01223) 332404. *Club:* United Oxford & Cambridge University.

GRAY, Peter Francis; Chairman: Exmoor Dual Investment Trust, since 1988; Abtrust Lloyd's Insurance Trust, since 1993; Contra-Cyclical Investment Trust, since 1994 (Director, since 1991); *b* 7 Jan. 1937; *s* of Revd George Francis Selby Gray; *m* 1978, Fiona Bristol; two *s*. *Educ:* Marlborough; Trinity College, Cambridge. MA; FCA. Served Royal Fusiliers, attached 4th Kings African Rifles, Uganda, 1956–58. Coopers & Lybrand, 1967–69; Samuel Montagu & Co., 1970–77; Head of Investment Div., Crown Agents for Oversea Govts & Admins, 1977–83; Man. Dir, Touche Remnant Hldgs Ltd, 1983–87; Director: TR Industrial & General Trust, 1984–88; NZ Investment Trust, 1988–; Gartmore Value Investments, 1989–; Second Consolidated Trust, 1992–; Gartmore Shared Equity Trust, 1993–; Foreign & Colonial Private Equity Trust, 1994–. Dep. Chm., Assoc. of Investment Trust Cos, 1985–87. Trustee, John Hancock Global Trust, 1985–87. *Address:* 1 Bradbourne Street, SW6 3TF. *Club:* Brooks's.

GRAY, Richard Dennis; Director, Manchester City Art Galleries, since 1989; *b* 19 Sept. 1951; *s* of John Dennis and Betty Gray; *m* 1976, Cherry Elizabeth Allen; two *s*. *Educ:* Carre's Grammar Sch.; Bristol Univ. (BA History and History of Art); Manchester Univ. AMA. Asst Keeper and Keeper, Manchester City Art Galls, 1974–89. Member: English Ceramic Circle, 1976–; Glass Circle, 1981–; Cttee, Glass Assoc., 1983–87; Cttee, Northern Ceramic Soc., 1986–89; NW Museums Service Adv. Panel, 1988–; Bd of Management, 1994–; Indep. Assessor, Reviewing Cttee on Export of Works of Art; Ext. Examnr, Manchester Polytechnic, 1989–92. Trustee, Rekonstruktsiya Trust, 1991–. *Publications:* The History of Porcelain, Chapter 1, 1982; catalogues and inventories, Manchester City Art Galleries; articles and book reviews for arts jls. *Recreations:* music, fishing, walking. *Address:* Manchester City Art Galleries, Mosley Street, Manchester M2 3JL.

GRAY, Prof. Richard John, PhD; FBA 1993; Professor of Literature, University of Essex, since 1990; *b* 5 Jan. 1944; *s* of George Ernest Gray and Helen Gray; *m* 1st, 1965, Joyce Mary Gray (marr. diss. 1991); one *s* one *d*; 2nd, 1991, Sheona Catherine Binnie; one *s* one *d*. *Educ:* St Catharine's Coll., Cambridge (BA, MA, PhD). Sen. Res. Schol., St Catharine's Coll., Cambridge, 1966–67; Harkness Fellow, for res. in US Univs, 1967–69; Lectr, Sen.

Lectr and Reader in Literature, Univ. of Essex, 1969–90. Robert E. McNair Vis. Prof. in Southern Studies, Univ. of South Carolina, 1993. Res. awards. Amer. Philos. Soc., 1979; Internat. Communications Agency, 1981. *Publications:* American Verse of the Nineteenth Century, 1973; American Poetry of the Twentieth Century, 1976; The Literature of Memory: modern writers of the American South, 1977; Robert Penn Warren: essays, 1980; American Fiction: new readings, 1983; Writing the South: ideas of an American region (C. Hugh Holman Award, Soc. for Study of Southern Lit.), 1986; American Poetry of the Twentieth Century, 1990; The Complete Poems of Edgar Allan Poe, 1993; The Life of William Faulkner: a critical biography, 1994. *Recreations:* running, tennis, wine tasting, cinema. *Address:* Department of Literature, University of Essex, Wivenhoe Park, Colchester, Essex CO4 3SQ. *T:* Colchester (01206) 872590.

GRAY, Richard Paul; QC 1993; *b* 1 Nov. 1945; *s* of John Montgomery Gray and Margaret Elizabeth Gray (*née* Welsh); *m* 1977, Emma Serena Halpin; one *s*. *Educ:* Tonbridge Sch.; St Andrew's Univ. (LLB). Called to the Bar, Inner Temple, 1970. *Recreations:* family, gardens, games.

GRAY, Robert, CBE 1988; JP; building consultant and clerk of works; Vice Lord-Lieutenant, City of Glasgow, since 1992; *b* 3 March 1928; *s* of John Gray and Mary (*née* McManus); *m* 1955, Mary (*née* McCartney); one *d*. *Educ:* St Mungo's Acad., Glasgow. LIOB 1970. Lecturer: Glasgow Coll. of Building, 1964–65; Anniesland Coll., 1965–70; Sen. Lectr, Cardonald Coll., 1970–84. Mem. (Lab) City of Glasgow (formerly Glasgow Dist, then Glasgow City) Council, 1974–; Lord Provost and Lord-Lieutenant of Glasgow, 1984–88. DL City of Glasgow, 1988. OStJ. Fellow, Glasgow Coll. of Technol., 1987. Hon. LLD Strathclyde, 1987. *Recreations:* walking, reading, music. *Address:* 106 Churchill Drive, Glasgow G11 7EZ. *T:* 0141–357 3328. *Clubs:* Royal Scottish Automobile, Art (Glasgow).

GRAY, Hon. Sir Robert McDowall, (Sir Robin), Kt 1994; MP (National) Clutha, since 1978; Minister of State, Associate Minister of Foreign Affairs and Trade, New Zealand, since 1993; *b* 2 July 1931; *s* of Adam Gray and Elsie McDowall; *m* 1957, Mary Thomson (*d* 1981); one *s* two *d*. *Educ:* George Watson's Boys' Coll., Edinburgh. Served 4th/7th Royal Dragoon Guards, 1949–51; immigrated to NZ, as farm labourer, 1952; purchased farm, 1956; entered politics, 1978; Whip, 1985, Sen. Whip, 1987; Speaker, NZ House of Reps, 1990–93. Chm., Parly Service Commn, 1990–93. *Address:* Parliament House, Wellington, New Zealand. *T:* (4) 4719908.

GRAY, Robert Michael Ker, QC 1983; QC (NI) 1984; a Recorder, since 1985. *Educ:* Radley (Scholar); Humboldt Gymnasium, Düsseldorf (Exchange Scholar); Balliol College, Oxford (Scholar) (MA 1963); St John's College, Cambridge (LLM (LLB 1967), Russian Tripos 1968). Articled to Sir Anthony Lousada, Messrs Stephenson, Harwood and Tatham; Solicitor, 1962. Called to the Bar, Lincoln's Inn (Bencher, 1991), Gray's Inn, and Inner Temple, 1969, King's Inns, Dublin, 1989; MacMahon Studentship, St John's College, Cambridge, 1969–73. European Office, UN, Geneva, 1962–64; Dept of Slavonic Studies, Cambridge, 1964. A Dep. High Court Judge, Family Div., 1983–, Chancery Div., 1993–, QBD, 1994–. Chancellor, dio. of Southwark, 1990–. Mem., Gen. Council of the Bar, 1972–74; Mem., Senate of the Bar, 1974–79, 1980–87 (Chm., Young Barristers, 1978–79); Examr, Bar Finals, 1970–79. Gen. Comr of Income Tax, 1992–; a Legal Assessor, GMC and GDC, 1995–. Chm., Harrison Homes (formerly Homes for the Aged Poor), 1980–; Sec., London Friends of St George's Cathedral, Cape Town, 1983–; Mem., Cttee, Nat. Aural Gp, 1988–; Trustee, Holy Cross Centre Trust, 1988–. Freeman, City of London, 1994. *Recreations:* walking, swimming. *Address:* 2 Mitre Court Buildings, Temple, EC4Y 7BX. *T:* 0171–583 1380. *Clubs:* Garrick, Royal Automobile; Budleigh Salterton; Pangbourne Working Men's; Stewards (Henley-on-Thames); Hampshire CC; City and Civil Service (Cape Town).

GRAY, Robert Walker; *see* Gray, Robin.

GRAY, Robin; Business Development Director, PSA Projects Ltd, 1992–93; *b* 16 April 1944; *s* of Robert George and Jeannie Gray; *m* 1971, Kathleen Rosemary Kuhn; two *d*. *Educ:* Woking County Grammar Sch. for Boys; Birkbeck Coll., London Univ. (BA Hons). UKAEA, 1962–64; HM Treasury, 1964–70; Asst Sec. to Crowther Cttee on Consumer Credit, 1968–70; Min. of Housing and Local Govt, subseq. DoE, 1970–93; seconded to Water Resources Bd/Central Water Planning Unit, 1973–75, to W Sussex CC, 1982–83; Sec., London and Metropolitan Govt Staff Commn, 1984–86; PSA, 1986–92; Under Sec., 1988–92; Dir of Civil Accommodation, 1988; Dir, Civil Projects and Head, Projects Business Policy Unit, 1989; Dir, Marketing and Planning, 1990–92, Internat. Dir, 1991–92, PSA Projects. *Recreations:* cricket, walking and other outdoor activities, talking.

GRAY, Robin, (Robert Walker Gray), CB 1977; Deputy Secretary, Department of Trade, 1975–84; retired; part-time consultant on international trade relations; *b* 29 July 1924; *s* of Robert Walker Gray and Dorothy (*née* Lane); *m* 1955, Shirley Matilda (*née* Taylor); two *s* one *d*. *Educ:* John Lyon Sch., Harrow; London Sch. of Economics. BScEcons 1946; Farr Medal in Statistics. Air Warfare Analysis Section of Air Min., 1940–45; BoT, 1947; UK Delegn to OEEC, 1950–51; BoT, 1952–66; Commercial Counsellor, British High Commn, Ottawa, 1966–70; Under-Secretary: DTI, 1971–74; Dept of Prices and Consumer Protection, 1974–75; Dep. Sec., DoI, 1975. Sec. and Governor, INFORM. *Address:* Tansy, Brook Road, Wormley, Godalming, Surrey GU8 5UA. *T:* Wormley (01428) 682486.

GRAY, Hon. Robin (Trevor), BAgrSc; MHA (L) for Lyons, Tasmania, since 1985 (for Wilmot, 1976–85); Premier of Tasmania and Treasurer, 1982–89; Minister for Primary Industry, Fisheries and Energy, since 1992; Minister for the TT-Line, since 1993; *b* 1 March 1940; *s* of late Rev. W. J. Gray; *m* 1965, Judith, *d* of late A. G. Boyd; two *s* one *d*. *Educ:* Box Hill High Sch.; Dookie Agricl Coll., Melbourne Univ. (Dookie Dip. of Agric.). Teacher, 1961–65 (in UK, 1964); agricl consultant, Colac, Vic, 1965, Launceston, Tas, 1965–76; pt-time Lectr in Agricl Econs, Univ. of Tasmania, 1970–76. Dep. Leader of the Opposition, Tasmania, 1979–81; Leader of the Opposition, 1981–82 and 1989–91; Minister: for Racing and Gaming, 1982–84; for Energy, 1982–88; for Forests, 1984–86; for State Develt, 1984–89; for Small Business, 1986–89; for Status of Women, 1989; for Antarctic Affairs, 1989; for Science and Technology, 1989. *Recreations:* gardening, golf. *Address:* House of Assembly, Parliament House, Hobart, Tas 7000, Australia; 11 Beech Road, Launceston, Tas 7250, Australia.

GRAY, Simon James Holliday; writer; *b* 21 Oct. 1936; *s* of Dr James Davidson Gray and Barbara Cecelia Mary Holliday; *m* 1965, Beryl Mary Kevern; one *s* one *d*. *Educ:* Westminster; Dalhousie Univ.; Trinity Coll., Cambridge (MA). Trinity Coll., Cambridge: Sen. Schol., Research Student and Harper-Wood Trav. Student, 1960; Supervisor in English, 1960–63; Sen. Instructor in English, Univ. of British Columbia, 1963–64; Lectr in English, QMC, London Univ., 1965–85 (Hon. Fellow, 1985). Co-dir, The Common Pursuit, Promenade Theatre, NY, 1986, and dir, Phoenix Theatre, 1988. Screenplay: A Month in the Country, 1987. *Publications: novels:* Colmain, 1963; Simple People, 1965; Little Portia, 1967, repr. 1986; (as Hamish Reade) A Comeback for Stark, 1968; *plays:* Wise Child, 1968; Sleeping Dog, 1968; Dutch Uncle, 1969; The Idiot, 1971; Spoiled, 1971; Butley, 1971; Otherwise Engaged, 1975 (voted Best Play, 1976–77, by NY Drama Critics Circle); Plaintiffs and Defendants, 1975; Two Sundays, 1975; Dog Days, 1976; Molly, 1977; The Rear Column, 1978; Close of Play, 1979; Stage Struck, 1979; Quartermaine's Terms, 1981 (televised 1987); adap. Tartuffe (for Washington, DC; unpublished), 1982; The Common Pursuit, 1984 (televised 1992); Plays One, 1986; Melon, 1987; The Holy Terror and Tartuffe, 1990; Hidden Laughter, 1990; Cell Mates, 1995; *television plays:* After Pilkington, 1987; Old Flames, 1990; They Never Slept, 1991; Running Late, 1992; Unnatural Pursuits, 1993; Femme Fatale, 1993; *radio plays:* The Rector's Daughter, 1992; Suffer the Little Children, 1993; With a Nod and a Bow, 1993; *non-fiction:* An Unnatural Pursuit and Other Pieces, 1985; How's That for Telling 'Em, Fat Lady?, 1988; Fat Chance, 1995. *Recreations:* watching cricket and soccer, tennis, swimming. *Address:* c/o Judy Daish Associates, 2 St Charles Place, W10 6EG.

GRAY, Prof. Thomas Cecil, CBE 1976; KCSG 1982; JP; MD, FRCS, FRCP, FRCA; FFARCS; FFARACS (Hon.); FFARCSI (Hon.); Professor of Anæsthesia, The University of Liverpool, 1959–76, now Emeritus; Dean of Postgraduate Medical Studies, 1966–70, of Faculty of Medicine, 1970–76; *b* 11 March 1913; *s* of Thomas and Ethel Gray; *m* 1st, 1937, Marjorie Kathleen (*née* Hely) (*d* 1978); one *s* one *d*; 2nd, 1979, Pamela Mary (*née* Corning); one *s*. *Educ:* Ampleforth Coll.; University of Liverpool. General Practice, 1937–41; Hon. Anaesthetist to various hospitals, 1940–47. Active Service, Royal Army Medical Corps, 1942–44. Demonstrator in Anæsthesia, University of Liverpool, 1942, 1944–46; Reader in Anæsthesia, University of Liverpool, 1947–59; Hon. Cons Anæsthetist: United Liverpool Hosps, Royal Infirmary Branch; Liverpool Thoracic Surgical Centre, Broadgreen Hosp.; Mem. Bd, Faculty of Anæsthetists, RCSEng, 1948–69 (Vice-Dean, 1952–54; Dean, 1964–67). Member Council: RCS, 1964–67; Assoc. of Anæsthetists of Great Brit. and Ire., 1948–67 (Hon. Treas. 1950–56; Pres. 1957–59); ASME, 1972–76; FRSocMed (Mem. Council, 1958–61; Pres. Anæsthetic Section, 1955–56; Mem. Council, Sect. of Med. Educn, 1969–72); Chm. BMA Anæsthetic Group, 1957–62; Mem., Liverpool Regional Hosp. Board, 1968–74 (Chm., Anæsthetic Adv. Cttee, 1948–70; Chm., Med. Adv. Council, 1970–74); Mem., Merseyside RHA, 1974–77; Mem., Bd of Governors, United Liverpool Hosp., 1969–74; Mem. Clinical Res. Bd, Med. Res. Council, 1965–69; Hon. Civilian Consultant in Anæsthetics to the Army at Home, 1964–78 (Guthrie Medal 1977), Emeritus Consultant to the Army, 1979. Hon. Consultant to St John's Ambulance; Member Council, Order of St John for Merseyside; Asst Dir-Gen., St John Ambulance, 1977–82; Vice-Pres., Med. Defence Union, 1954–88 (Treasurer, 1977–82); Chm., Bd of Governors, Linacre Center for Study of Ethics of Health Care, 1973–83. Examiner in FFARCS, 1953–70; FFARCSI 1967–70: Dip. Vet. Anæsth., RCVS, 1968–76. Hon. FRSocMed, 1979; Hon. Member: Sheffield and East Midlands Soc. of Anæsthetists; Yorks Soc. of Anæsthetists; SW Regl Soc. of Anæsthetists; Austrian Soc. of Anæesthetists; Soc. Belge d'Anesthesie et de Reanimation; Argentinian and Brazilian Socs of Anesthesiologists; Australian and Malaysian Socs of Anæsthetists; Assoc. of Veterinary Anæsthetists. Hon. Corresp. Member: Sociedade das Ciencias Medical di Lisboa; W African Assoc. of Surgeons. Clover Lectr and Medallist, RCS, 1953; Lectures: Simpson-Smith Meml, W London Sch. of Med., 1956; Jenny Hartmann Meml, Univ. of Basle, 1958; Eastman, Univ. of Rochester, NY, 1958; Sir James Young Simpson Meml, RCSE, 1967; Torsten Gordh, Swedish Soc. of Anaesthetists, 1978; Kirkpatrick, Faculty of Anaesthetists, RCSI, 1981; John Gillies, Scottish Soc. of Anaesthetists, 1982; Mitchiner Meml, RAMC, 1983; Florence Elliott, Royal Victoria Hosp., Belfast, 1984. Sims Commonwealth Travelling Prof., 1961. JP City of Liverpool, 1966 (retd list). Freeman, City of London, 1984; Liveryman, Soc. of Apothecaries, 1956. OStJ 1979. Medallist, Univ. of Liège, 1947; Henry Hill Hickman Medal, 1972; Hon. Gold Medal, RCS, 1978; Ralph M. Waters medal and award, Illinois Soc. of Anesthesiologists, 1978; Silver Medal, Assoc. of Anaesthetists, 1982. *Publications:* Modern Trends in Anæsthesia (ed jtly), 1958, 3rd edn 1967; (ed jtly) General Anæsthesia, 1959, 4th edn 1980 (Spanish edns, 1971, 1983);(ed jtly) Paediatric Anæsthesia, 1981; many contribs to gen. med. press and specialist jls. *Recreations:* music, golf, amateur dramatics. *Address:* 6 Raven Meols Lane, Formby, Liverpool L37 4DF.

GRAY, Sir William (Hume), 3rd Bt *cr* 1917; Director: Hartlepool Water plc; William Gray Associates; *b* 26 July 1955; *s* of William Talbot Gray (*d* 1971) (*er s* of 2nd Bt), and of Rosemarie Hume Gray, *d* of Air Cdre Charles Hume Elliott-Smith; *S* grandfather, 1978; *m* 1984, Catherine Victoria Willoughby, *y d* of late John Naylor and of Mrs Jerram, Wadebridge, Cornwall; one *s* two *d*. *Educ:* Aysgarth School, Bedale, Yorks; Eton College; Polytechnic of Central London BA (Hons) Architecture; DipArch; RIBA. *Recreation:* sport. *Heir: s* William John Cresswell Gray, *b* 24 Aug. 1986. *Address:* Eggleston Hall, Barnard Castle, Co. Durham DL12 0AG. *T:* Teesdale (01833) 650553.

GRAY, Sir William (Stevenson), Kt 1974; JP; DL; solicitor and notary public; Lord Provost, City of Glasgow and Lord Lieutenant, County of the City of Glasgow, 1972–75; *b* 3 May 1928; *o s* of William Stevenson Gray and Mary Johnstone Dickson; *m* 1958, Mary Rodger; one *s* one *d*. *Educ:* Hillhead High Sch.; Glasgow Univ. Admitted solicitor, 1958; notary public, 1960. Chairman: Scottish Special Housing Assoc., 1966–72; WPHT Scotland Ltd (formerly World of Property Housing Trust Scottish Housing Assoc. Ltd), 1974–; Irvine New Town Develt Corp., 1974–76; Scotland W Industrial Promotion Gp, 1972–75; Scottish Develt Agency, 1975–79; The Oil Club, 1975–; Barrell Selection Ltd, 1987–; Gap Housing Assoc. Ltd, 1988–; Gap Housing Assoc. (Ownership) Ltd, 1988–; Norcity Homes plc, 1988–; Norcity II plc, 1990–; Clan Homes plc, 1988–; Manchester Village Homes plc, 1989–; Norhomes plc, 1989–; First to Sixth Tax Homes Plc (Paragon), 1990–; Home Partners Plus 01 & 02 Plc, 1991–; Peppa Plc, 1992–; Paragon Protected Growth plc, 1993–; Norcity III and IV plc (Glasgow Student Village Cos), 1993–. Member: Exec., Scottish Council (Develt and Industry), 1971–75; Scottish Econ. Council, 1975–83; Lower Clyde Water Bd, 1971–72; Clyde Port Authority, 1972–75; Adv. Council for Energy Conservation, 1974–84; Convention of Royal Burghs, 1971–75; Central Adv. Cttee on JPs, 1975–; Glasgow Adv. Cttee on JPs, 1975–; Third Eye Centre Ltd, Glasgow, 1984–90 (Chm., 1975–84); Hodgson Martin Ltd Adv. Bd, 1988–. Chairman: Glasgow Independent Hosp. Ltd (Ross Hall Hosp.), 1982–89; Clyde Tourist Assoc., 1972–75; Res. Trust for Inst. of Neurol Scis, 1978–94. Member: Nat. Trust for Scotland, 1971–72; Scottish Opera Bd, 1971–72; Scottish Nat. Orch. Soc., 1972–75; Vice-President: Glasgow Citizens' Theatre, 1975– (Mem., Bd of Dirs, 1970–75); Strathclyde Theatre Gp, 1975–86; Charles Rennie Mackintosh Soc., 1974–; Scottish Assoc. for Care and Resettlement of Offenders, 1982–86 (Chm., 1975–82); Governor, Glasgow Sch. of Art, 1961–75; Patron: Scottish Youth Theatre, 1978–86; Scottish Pakistani Soc., 1984–. Member: Court, Glasgow Univ., 1972–75; Council, Strathclyde Univ. Business Sch., 1978–88. FRSA 1991. Hon. LLD: Strathclyde, 1974; Glasgow, 1980. Mem., Glasgow Corp., 1958–75 (Chm., Property Management Cttee, 1964–67); Treasurer, City of Glasgow, 1971–72. JP City of Glasgow, 1961–64, Co. of City of Glasgow 1965; DL Co. of City of Glasgow, 1971, City of Glasgow 1976. *Recreations:* sailing, theatre. *Address:* 13 Royal Terrace, Glasgow G3 7NY. *T:* 0141–332 8877, *Fax:* 0141–332 2809.

GRAY DEBROS, Winifred Marjorie, (Mrs E. Gray Debros); *see* Fox, W. M.

GRAYDON, Air Chief Marshal Sir Michael (James), GCB 1993 (KCB 1989); CBE 1984; FRAeS; Chief of the Air Staff, since 1992; Air ADC to the Queen, since 1992; *b* 24

Oct. 1938; *s* of James Julian Graydon and Rita Mary Alkan; *m* 1963, Margaret Elizabeth Clark. *Educ:* Wycliffe Coll.; RAF Coll., Cranwell. Qualified Flying Instructor No 1 FTS, Linton-on-Ouse, 1960–62; No 56 Sqn, 1962–64; No 226 OCU, 1965–67 (Queen's Commendation); Flight Comd, No 56 Sqn, 1967–69; RAF Staff Coll., Bracknell, 1970; PSO to Dep. C-in-C Allied Forces Central Region, Brunssum, 1971–73; Operations, Joint Warfare, MoD, 1973–75; NDC, Latimer, 1976; OC No 11 Sqn, Binbrook, 1977–79; MA to CDS, MoD, 1979–81; OC RAF Leuchars, 1981–83; OC RAF Stanley, Falkland Is, 1983; RCDS, 1984; SASO 11 Gp, Bentley Priory, 1985–86; ACOS Policy, SHAPE, 1986–89; AOC-in-C, RAF Support Comd, 1989–91; AOC-in-C, RAF Strike Comd, and C-in-C, UK Air Forces, 1991–92. Gov., Wycliffe Coll., 1986–. FRAeS 1993. Freeman, City of London, 1995; GAPAN, 1993. *Publications:* contrib. to professional jls. *Recreations:* golf, birdwatching, reading. *Address:* c/o Lloyds Bank, Cox and King's Branch, PO Box 1190, 7 Pall Mall, SW1Y 5NA. *Clubs:* Royal Air Force; Royal & Ancient Golf (St Andrews).

GRAYSON, Prof. Cecil, CBE 1992; MA; FBA 1979; Serena Professor of Italian Studies in the University of Oxford, and Fellow of Magdalen College, 1958–87 (Emeritus Fellow, 1987); *b* 5 Feb. 1920; *s* of John M. Grayson and Dora Hartley; *m* 1947, Margaret Jordan; one *s* three *d*. *Educ:* Batley Grammar Sch.; St Edmund Hall, Oxford (Hon. Fellow, 1986). Army service (UK and India), 1940–46 (Major); First Class Hons (Mod. Langs), 1947; Univ. Lectr in Italian, Oxford, 1948; Lectr at St Edmund Hall, 1948; Lectr at New Coll., 1954. Corresp. Fellow, Commissione per i Testi di Lingua, Bologna, 1957; Mem., Accademia Letteraria Ital. dell' Arcadia, 1958; Corresp. Mem., Accademia della Crusca, 1960; Accademia delle Scienze, Bologna, 1964; Accademia dei Lincei, 1967; Istituto Veneto di Scienze, Lettere ed Arti, 1977; Barlow Lecturer, University Coll., London, 1963; Resident Fellow, Newberry Library, Chicago, 1965; Visiting Professor: Yale Univ., 1966; Berkeley, Calif, 1969, 1973; UCLA, 1980, 1984, 1989, 1994; Perth, WA, 1973, 1980; Cape Town, 1980, 1983; NY Univ., 1992–93. Pres., Modern Humanities Res. Assoc., 1988. Premio Internazionale Galileo (storia della lingua italiana), 1974; Serena Medal for Italian Studies, British Academy, 1976. Comdr, Order of Merit, Italy, 1975. *Publications:* Early Italian Texts (with Prof. C. Dionisotti), 1949; Opuscoli inediti di L. B. Alberti, 1954; Alberti and the Tempio Malatestiano, 1957; Vincenzo Calmeta, Prose e Lettere edite e inedite, 1959; A Renaissance Controversy: Latin or Italian?, 1960; L. B. Alberti, Opere volgari, I, 1960, II, 1966, III, 1973; L. B. Alberti e la prima grammatica volgare, 1964; Cinque saggi su Dante, 1972; (trans.) The Lives of Savonarola, Machiavelli and Guicciardini by Roberto Ridolfi, 1959, 1963, 1967; (ed) selected works of Guicciardini, 1964; (ed and trans.) L. B. Alberti, De pictura, De statua, 1972; (ed) The World of Dante, 1980; (ed jtly) Piero della Francesca, Libellus de 5 corp. regul., 1995; articles in Bibliofilia, Burlington Mag., English Misc., Giorn. Stor. d. Lett. Ital., Ital. Studies, Lettere Italiane, Lingua Nostra, Rassegna d. Lett. Ital., Rinascimento, The Year's Work in Mod. Languages. *Recreation:* music. *Address:* 11 Norham Road, Oxford OX2 6SF. *T:* Oxford (01865) 57045.

GRAYSON, Sir Jeremy (Brian Vincent), 5th Bt *cr* 1922, of Ravenspoint, Co. Angelsey; photographer; *b* 30 Jan. 1933; *s* of Brian Harrington Grayson (*d* 1989), 3rd *s* of 1st Bt and of Sofia Maria (*née* Buchanan); *S* uncle, 1991; *m* 1958, Sara Mary, *d* of C. F. Upton; three *s* three *d* (and one *d* decd). *Educ:* Downside. *Heir: s* Simon Jeremy Grayson, *b* 12 July 1959. *Address:* 54 Bucharest Road, SW18 3AR. *T:* 0181–871 0678.

GRAYSTON, Rev. Prof. Kenneth, MA, DLitt; Professor of Theology, Bristol University, 1965–79, now Emeritus Professor; Pro-Vice-Chancellor, Bristol University, 1976–79; *b* Sheffield, 8 July 1914; *s* of Ernest Edward and Jessie Grayston; *m* 1942, Elizabeth Alison, *d* of Rev. Walter Mayo and Beatrice Aste, Elsfield, Oxon.; no *c*. *Educ:* Colfe's Grammar Sch., Lewisham; Universities of Oxford and Cambridge; DLitt Bristol 1991. Ordained Methodist Minister, 1942; Ordnance Factory Chaplain, 1942–44; Asst Head of Religious Broadcasting, BBC, 1944–49; Tutor in New Testament Language and Literature, Didsbury Coll., 1949–64; Bristol University: Special Lecturer in Hellenistic Greek, 1950–64; Dean, Faculty of Arts, 1972–74; Hon. Fellow, 1992. Select Preacher to Univ. of Cambridge, 1952, 1962, to Univ. of Oxford, 1971; Sec. Studiorum Novi Testamenti Societas, 1955–65; Chairman: Theolog. Adv. Gp, British Council of Churches, 1969–72; Christian Aid Scholarships Cttee, 1973–78. *Publications:* The Epistles to the Galatians and to the Philippians, 1957; The Letters of Paul to the Philippians and the Thessalonians, 1967; The Johannine Epistles, 1984; Dying, We Live, 1990; The Gospel of John, 1990; (contrib. in): A Theological Word Book of the Bible, 1950; The Teacher's Commentary, 1955; The Interpreter's Dictionary of the Bible, 1962; A New Dictionary of Christian Theology, 1983, etc; contrib. to Expository Times, New Testament Studies, Theology, Scottish Jl Theology, Epworth Review, etc. *Recreation:* music. *Address:* 11 Rockleaze Avenue, Bristol BS9 1NG. *T:* Bristol (0117) 968 3872.

GREATHEAD, Dr David John; Director, International Institute of Biological Control, 1985–91; Hon. Senior Research Fellow, Centre for Population Biology, Imperial College of Science, Technology and Medicine at Silwood Park; *b* 12 Dec. 1931; *s* of Harold Merriman Greathead and Kathleen May (*née* Collett); *m* 1958, Annette Helen Blankley; one *s* two *d*. *Educ:* Merchant Taylors' Sch., Middx; Imperial Coll., London Univ. (BSc, PhD, DSc). ARCS; CBiol; FIBiol. Anti-Locust Res. Centre, 1953–59; research on desert locust in Ethiopia, Somalia, Kenya, Aden Protectorates, Desert Locust Survey, 1959–61; Commonwealth (later Internat.) Institute of Biological Control: set up and managed East African Station in Uganda, res. on crop pests and weeds, 1962–73; based in UK, 1973–91; Asst Dir, 1976–85. *Publications:* A Review of Biological Control in the Ethiopian Region, 1971; A Review of Biological Control in Western and Southern Europe, 1976; (with J. K. Waage) Insect Parasitoids, 1986; numerous publications in learned jls. *Recreations:* natural history, walking, travelling. *Address:* Centre for Population Biology, Imperial College at Silwood Park, Ascot, Berks SL5 7PY. *T:* Bracknell (01344) 294494; 6 The Walled Garden, Wargrave, Reading, Berks RG10 8LL.

GREATREX, Neil; National President and General Secretary, Union of Democratic Mineworkers, since 1993; *b* 1 April 1951; *s* of John Edward and Joyce Irene Greatrex; *m* 1972, Sheila Waterhouse; two *d*. *Educ:* Greenwood Drive Jun. Sch.; Mowlands Intermediate Sch.; Ashfield Comprehensive Sch. Bentinck Colliery, 1965–85. National Union of Mineworkers: Cttee Mem., 1970–74; Branch Treas., 1974–80; Branch Pres., 1980–85; full-time Area Official, 1985–86; Union of Democratic Mineworkers: Area Pres., 1986–88; Nat. Vice-Pres., 1988–93. *Recreations:* Do It Yourself, shooting, following Beaufort Youth Football Club. *Address:* Miners' Offices, Berry Hill Lane, Mansfield, Notts NG18 4JU. *T:* Mansfield (01623) 26094; The Sycamores, Moor Road, Bestwood, Nottingham NG6 8UE. *T:* Nottingham (0115) 976 3468; 2 Chestnut Avenue, Kirkby in Ashfield, Notts NG17 8BB. *T:* Mansfield (01623) 758346.

GREAVES, Jeffrey; HM Diplomatic Service, retired; Consul General, Alexandria, 1978–81; *b* 10 Dec. 1926; *s* of Willie Greaves and Emily Verity; *m* 1949, Joyce Mary Farrer; one *s* one *d*. *Educ:* Pudsey Grammar Sch. Served RN, 1945–48. Joined HM Foreign Service, 1948; FO, 1948; Benghazi, 1951; Vice Consul, Tehran, 1953; ME Centre for Arab Studies, 1955; Second Sec. and Vice Consul, Paris, 1960; Vice Consul, Muscat, 1962; Second Sec. and Consul, Athens, 1965; Second Sec. (Commercial), Cairo, 1968; First Sec. and Consul, Muscat, 1970; First Sec. (Com.), Bangkok, 1972; FCO, 1976. *Address:* 38A Alexandra Road, Pudsey, West Yorks LS28 8BY. *T:* Leeds (0113) 257 7238.

GREAVES, Prof. Malcolm Watson, MD; FRCP; Dean, St John's Institute of Dermatology, United Medical and Dental Schools of Guy's and St Thomas' Hospitals, since 1989; Professor of Dermatology, University of London, since 1975; *b* 11 Nov. 1933; *s* of Donald Watson Greaves and Kathleen Evelyn Greaves; *m* 1964, Evelyn Yeo, JP; one *s* one *d*. *Educ:* Epsom College; Charing Cross Med. Sch. MD, PhD London. MRC Clinical Res. Fellow, UCL, 1963–66; Reader in Dermatology, Univ. of Newcastle upon Tyne, 1966–75. Vis. Consultant, Maadi Armed Forces Hosp., Cairo, 1984–94. Pres., European Soc. for Dermatological Research, 1984; Vice-Pres., Psoriasis Assoc. of GB, 1991–; Chm., Scientific Cttee and Trustee, Skin Disease Res. Fund, 1980–; Member: Internat. Adv. Panel, Cutaneous Biol. Res., Harvard Univ., 1989–; Pharmacopoeia Commn, 1982–; Cttee on Safety of Medicines, DHSS, 1982–89; British Nat. Formulary expert adv. cttee, 1990–. Internat. Hon. Mem., Amer. Dermatol. Assoc., 1987; Hon. Mem., Amer. Soc. for Investigative Dermatol., 1989. Mem. Management Exec., UMDS; Member of Governing Body: Sch. of Pharmacy, Univ. of London, 1990–; Epsom Coll. Alvin J. Cox Award for dist. research in psoriasis, 1984; Egyptian Armed Forces Award for Distinguished Med. Services, 1990. *Publications:* Pharmacology of the Skin, Vol. I, Pharmacology of Skin Systems and Autocoids in Normal and Inflamed Skin, 1989; Vol. II, Methods, Absorption, Metabolism, Toxicity, Drugs and Diseases, 1989. *Recreation:* equestrian activities. *Address:* Dovecote House, Church Street, Guilden Morden, Royston, Herts SG8 0JD. *Club:* Athenæum.

GREAVES, Prof. Melvyn Francis; Director, Leukaemia Research Fund Centre, Institute of Cancer Research, London, since 1984; *b* 12 Sept. 1941; *s* of Edward and Violet Greaves; *m* 1966, Josephine Pank; one *s* one *d*. *Educ:* City of Norwich Grammar Sch.; University Coll. London; Middlesex Hosp. Med. Sch. BSc, PhD London. MRCPath. Vis Scientist, Karolinska Inst., Stockholm, 1968–69; Res. Fellow, Nat. Inst. for Med. Res., London, 1969–72; Res. Scientist, Dept of Zoology, UCL, 1972–76; Hd, Membrane Immunology Dept, Imperial Cancer Res. Fund, 1976–84. Hon. MRCP 1987. Paul Martini Prize (Germany), 1977; Peter Debye Prize (Holland), 1981; King Faisal Internat. Prize for Medicine, 1988. *Publications:* T and B Lymphocytes, 1973; Cellular Recognition, 1975; Atlas of Blood Cells, 1981, 2nd edn 1988; Monoclonal Antibodies to Receptors, 1984; contribs to bio-med. jls. *Recreations:* music, cooking, photography, natural history. *Address:* 24 Newhouse Park, St Albans, Herts AL1 1UQ. *T:* St Albans (01727) 63713.

GREBENIK, Eugene, CB 1976; MSc (Economics); Managing Editor, Population Studies; Consultant, Office of Population Censuses and Surveys, 1977–84; *b* 20 July 1919; *s* of S. Grebenik; *m* 1946, Virginia, *d* of James D. Barker; two *s* one *d*. *Educ:* abroad; London Sch. of Economics. Statistician, Dept of Economics, Univ. of Bristol, 1939–40; London Sch. of Economics: Asst. 1940–44 and Lecturer, 1944–49, in Statistics (on leave, 1944–46; served in RN, 1944; Temp. Statistical Officer, Admiralty, 1944–45; Secretariat, Royal Commn on Population, 1945–46); Reader in Demography, Univ. of London, 1949–54; Research Sec., Population Investigation Cttee, 1947–54; Prof. of Social Studies, Univ. of Leeds, 1954–69. Principal, Civil Service Coll., 1970–76 and Dep. Sec., Civil Service Dept, 1972–76. Mem., Impact of Rates Cttee, Ministry of Housing, 1963–64. Social Science Research Council: Statistics Cttee, 1966–69; Cttee on Social Science and Government, 1968–72; Population Panel, 1971–73; Member: Cttee on Governance of London Univ., 1970–72; Council, RHBNC (formerly RHC), Univ. of London, 1971–90. Pres., British Soc. for Population Studies, 1979–81. Sec.-Treasurer, Internat. Union for Scientific Study of Population, 1963–73. Hon. Fellow, LSE, 1969; Vis. Fellow, ANU, 1982–83; Hon. Vis. Prof., City Univ., 1986–89. *Publications:* (with H. A. Shannon) The Population of Bristol, 1943; (with D. V. Glass) The Trend and Pattern of Fertility in Great Britain; A Report on the Family Census of 1946, 1954; various articles in statistical and economic journals. *Address:* 16 Spindlers, Kidlington, Oxon OX5 2YP. *T:* Kidlington (01865) 842697.

GREEN, Albert A.; *see* Aynsley-Green.

GREEN, Prof. Albert Edward, FRS 1958; MA, PhD, ScD (Cambridge); Sedleian Professor of Natural Philosophy, University of Oxford, 1968–77, now Emeritus Professor; Supernumerary Fellow, The Queen's College, Oxford, since 1977 (Fellow, 1968–77); *b* 11 Nov. 1912; *m* 1939, Gwendoline May Rudston. *Educ:* Jesus Coll., Cambridge Univ. (Scholar). PhD 1937; MA 1938; ScD 1943. Fellow, Jesus Coll., Cambridge, 1936–39; Lecturer in Mathematics, Durham Colls, University of Durham, 1939–48; Prof. of Applied Mathematics, University of Newcastle upon Tyne, 1948–68. Hon. DSc: Durham, 1969; NUI, 1977; Hon. LLD Glasgow, 1975. Timoshenko Medal, ASME, 1974; Theodore von Karmen Medal, ASCE, 1983. *Address:* 25 Ritchie Court, 380 Banbury Road, Oxford OX2 7PW.

GREEN, Sir Allan (David), KCB 1991; QC 1987; *b* 1 March 1935; *s* of late Lionel and Irene Green; *m* 1967, Eva (*d* 1993), *yr d* of Prof. Artur Attman and Elsa Attman, Gothenburg, Sweden; one *s* one *d*. *Educ:* Charterhouse; St Catharine's Coll., Cambridge (Open Exhibnr, MA). Served RN, 1953–55. Called to the Bar, Inner Temple, 1959, Bencher, 1985; Jun. Prosecuting Counsel to the Crown, Central Criminal Court, 1977, Sen. Prosecuting Counsel, 1979, First Senior Prosecuting Counsel, 1985; a Recorder, 1979–87; DPP and Hd of Crown Prosecution Service, 1987–91. Mem., Gen. Council of the Bar, 1992. *Publications:* trans. with wife several Swedish books. *Recreation:* music. *Address:* 1 Hare Court, Temple, EC4Y 7BE. *Club:* Athenæum.

GREEN, Andrew Curtis; farmer and horticulturist, since 1960; *b* 28 March 1936; *s* of Christopher Green and Marjorie (*née* Bennett); *m* 1966, Julia Margaret (*née* Davidson); two *s*. *Educ:* Charterhouse; Magdalene Coll., Cambridge. MA (Nat. Scis), Dip. of Agriculture. Commnd RNVR, 1954–56. Farm management, 1960–67; founded Greens of Soham farming and horticultural business, 1967; Dir, Elsoms Spalding Seed Co., 1982–; Chm., Hassy Ltd, 1983–89. Mem., AFRC, 1984–88. FLS 1978; Hon. FIHort 1986 (Industrial Mem. Council, 1988–94); FRAgS. Extra Mem., Court of Skinners' Co., 1994–. *Recreations:* sailing, fishing, shooting, ski-ing. *Address:* Kingfishers Bridge, Wicken, Ely, Cambs CB7 5XL. *T:* Ely (01353) 721112. *Clubs:* Army and Navy, Farmers'; Hawks (Cambridge); Royal Thames Yacht.

GREEN, Andrew Fleming, CMG 1991; HM Diplomatic Service; Assistant Under-Secretary of State (Middle East), Foreign and Commonwealth Office, since 1994; *b* 6 Aug. 1941; *s* of late Gp Captain J. H. Green, RAF, and Beatrice Mary (*née* Bowditch); *m* 1968, C. Jane Churchill; one *s* one *d*. *Educ:* Haileybury and ISC; Magdalene Coll., Cambridge (MA). Served Army, 1962–65; joined HM Diplomatic Service, 1965; Middle East Centre for Arab Studies, 1966–68; Aden, 1968–69; Asst Political Agent, Abu Dhabi, 1970–71; First Secretary, FCO, 1972–74; Private Sec. to Minister of State, FCO, 1975, and to Parliamentary Under Sec. of State, 1976; First Secretary, UK Delegn to OECD, Paris, 1977–79; First Sec., FCO, 1980–81; Counsellor, Washington, 1982–85; Counsellor, Hd of Chancery and Consul Gen., Riyadh, 1985–88; Counsellor, FCO, 1988–90; Ambassador to Syria, 1991–94. *Recreations:* tennis, sailing, bridge. *Address:* c/o Foreign and Commonwealth Office, SW1A 2AH.

GREEN, Anthony Eric Sandall, RA 1977 (ARA 1971); Member, London Group, 1964; Artist (Painter); *b* 30 Sept. 1939; *s* of late Frederick Sandall Green and Marie Madeleine (*née* Dupont); *m* 1961, Mary Louise Cozens-Walker; two *d.* *Educ:* Highgate Sch., London; Slade Sch. of Fine Art, University Coll. London (Fellow, UCL, 1991). Henry Tonks Prize for drawing, Slade Sch., 1960; French Govt Schol., Paris, 1960; Gulbenkian Purchase Award, 1963; Harkness Fellowship, in USA, 1967–69. Has exhibited in: London, New York, Haarlem, Rotterdam, Stuttgart, Hanover, Helsingborg, Malmö, Tokyo, Brussels, W Berlin, Chicago and Sydney. Paintings in various public collections, including: Tate Gallery; Metropolitan Mus. of Art, N York; Olinda Museum, Brazil; Baltimore Mus. of Art, USA; Nat. Mus. of Wales; Gulbenkian Foundn; Arts Council of Gt Brit.; British Council; Victoria and Albert Mus.; Contemporary Art Soc.; Frans Hals Mus., Holland; Boymans-van Bevningen Mus., Holland; Ulster Mus., Belfast; Ikeda and Niigata Mus., Setagaya Art Mus., Metropolitan, Tokyo; Hiroshima; Fukuoka. Exhibit of the Year award, RA, 1977. *Publication:* A Green Part of the World, 1984. *Recreations:* travelling, family life. *Address:* 17 Lissenden Mansions, Highgate Road, NW5 1PP. *T:* 0171–485 1226.

GREEN, Arthur; Senior Partner, Grant Thornton, 1986–88, retired; President, Institute of Chartered Accountants in England and Wales, 1987–88; *b* 15 June 1928; *s* of Arthur Henry and Elizabeth Burns Green; *m* 1952, Sylvia Myatt; one *s* one *d.* *Educ:* Liverpool Collegiate. FCA. Qualified Chartered Accountant, 1950; Partner, Bryce Hanmer & Co., Liverpool, 1954 (merged Thornton Baker; later Grant Thornton); Nat. Managing Partner, Thornton Baker, 1975–84; Chm. and Man. Dir, Grant Thornton International, 1984–85. Vice-Pres., 1985–86, Dep. Pres., 1986–87, ICA. *Recreations:* golf, tennis, theatre. *Address:* Up Yonder, Herbert Road, Salcombe, Devon TQ8 8HP. *T:* Salcombe (0154884) 2075.

GREEN, Arthur Edward Chase, MBE (mil.) 1955; TD (and Bar) 1950; DL; FRICS; Chartered Surveyor; Chief Estates Surveyor, Legal and General Assurance Society, 1946–71 (Surveyor, 1934–46); *b* 5 Nov. 1911; *s* of Harry Catling and Sarah Jane Green, Winchmore Hill, London; *m* 1941, Margaret Grace (*d* 1991), *yr d* of John Lancelot and Winifred Churchill, Wallington, Surrey; one *s* one *d* (and one *d* decd). *Educ:* Merchant Taylors' Sch.; Coll. of Estate Management. HAC, 1932–: commnd, 1939; Adjt 11 (HAC) Regt RHA, 1941–42; Western Desert, ME; PoW 1942; despatches, Germany, 1945; Territorial Efficiency Medal and bar; Court of Assistants, HAC, 1946–76, Treasurer, 1966–69, Vice-Pres., 1970–72; Metropolitan Special Constabulary, HAC Div., 1937–39 and 1946–74 (Long Service Medal and bar); Hon. Mem., Transvaal Horse Artillery. Property Advr, J. H. Schroder Wagg & Co., 1972–82; Advr, Schroder Property Fund for Pension Funds and Charities, 1972–82; Dir, Schroder Properties Ltd, 1974–82; Member: Cttee of Management, Pension Fund Property Unit Trust, 1972–82; Transcontinental Property Unit Trust, 1974–82; Advr on Policy, Post Office Staff Superannuation Fund, until 1977, Dir, Mereacre Ltd, and Mereacre Farms Ltd (PO Staff Superann. Fund), 1977–83; Member: Chancellor of the Exchequer's Property Adv. Panel, 1975–80; Govt Cttee of Inquiry into Agriculture in GB, 1977–79 (Northfield Cttee). Chm., Elecrent Properties Ltd (Electronic Rentals Gp), 1974–83; Director: Marlborough Property Hldgs plc, 1978–86; Studley Farms Ltd, 1980–82. Mem., TA&VR Assocs for City of London, 1970–77, and for Greater London, 1970–81. President: Camden and Islington Corps, 1974–75, No 7 Corps, City of London and Hackney, 1976–77, St John Ambulance; City of London, St John Ambulance Brigade, 1978–. Governor: Bridewell Royal Hosp., 1962–88; City of London Sch., 1976–81; Queenswood Sch., 1966–78; Corp. of Sons of the Clergy, 1966– (Mem. Court of Assistants, 1966–86); Vice-Pres., Brunswick Boys' Club Trust, 1978– (Founder-Trustee, 1945–78, elected while POW, Oflag 79, Germany). City of London Court of Common Council (Bread Street Ward), 1971–81. Freedom of the City of London, 1939; Liveryman: Merchant Taylors' Co., 1946; Gunmakers' Co., 1954. DL Greater London, 1967 (Representative DL for London Borough of Islington, 1967–81). CStJ 1988. *Recreations:* various. *Address:* The Coach House, High Street, Cranleigh, Surrey GU6 8AS. *T:* Cranleigh (01483) 267372. *Clubs:* HAC, Guildhall, Bread Street Ward, Cordwainer Ward.

GREEN, Arthur Jackson; Under Secretary, Department of Education for Northern Ireland, 1983–87, retired; *b* 12 Nov. 1928; *s* of F. Harvey Green and Sylvia Green (*née* Marsh), MB; *m* 1957, Rosemary Bradley, MA; two *s.* *Educ:* Friends Sch., Lisburn, Co. Antrim; Leighton Park Sch., Reading; Lincoln Coll., Oxford (BA Mod. Hist.); Haverford Coll., Philadelphia (MA Philosophy). Asst Principal, NICS, 1952; Secretary: Cameron Commn, 1969; Scarman Tribunal, 1969–72; Asst Sec., NI Dept of Finance, 1972–78; Under Sec., NI Office, 1978–79; Dir, NI Court Service (Lord Chancellor's Dept), 1979–82; Fellow, Center for Internat. Affairs, Harvard Univ., 1982–83. Mem. Bd, British Council, 1992–. First Chm., S Down Conservative Assoc., 1990–94. *Publications:* articles on Anglo-Irish topics. *Address:* 36 St Patrick's Road, Saul, Downpatrick, N Ireland BT30 7JQ. *T:* Downpatrick (01396) 614360. *Club:* Reform.

GREEN, Barry Spencer; QC 1981; **His Honour Judge Green;** a Circuit Judge, since 1993; *b* 16 March 1932; *s* of Lionel Maurice Green, FRCS and Juliette Green; *m* 1st, 1960, Marilyn Braverman (marr. diss. 1987); two *s*; 2nd, 1988, Muriel Coplan. *Educ:* Westminster Sch.; Christ Church, Oxford (MA, BCL). Called to the Bar, Inner Temple, 1954, Bencher, 1987; a Recorder, 1979–93. Legal Mem., Mental Health Review Tribunal, 1983–93; Mem., Criminal Injuries Compensation Bd, 1988–93. *Recreation:* tennis. *Clubs:* Garrick, Roehampton.

GREEN, Father Benedict; *see* Green, Rev. H. C.

GREEN, Benny; free-lance writer; *b* 9 Dec. 1927; *s* of David Green and Fanny Trayer; *m* 1962, Antoinette Kanal; three *s* one *d.* *Educ:* Clipstone Street Junior Mixed; subsequently uneducated at St Marylebone Grammar Sch. Mem., West Central Jewish Lads Club (now extinct). Saxophonist, 1947–60 (Most Promising New Jazz Musician, 1953), Jazz Critic, Observer, 1958–77; Literary Critic, Spectator, 1970–80; Film Critic, Punch, 1972–77, TV Critic, 1977–87; frequent radio and TV appearances, 1955–. Artistic Dir, New Shakespeare Co., 1973–; Mem., BBC Archives Cttee, 1976. Book and lyrics, Boots with Strawberry Jam, Nottingham Playhouse, 1968; revised libretto, Showboat, Adelphi Theatre, London, 1972; co-deviser: Cole, Mermaid, 1974; Oh, Mr Porter, Mermaid, 1977; lyrics, Bashville, Open Air Theatre, 1983–84. Sony Radio Award for best popular music series, 1984. *Publications:* The Reluctant Art, 1962; Blame it on my Youth, 1967; 58 Minutes to London, 1969; Drums in my Ears, 1973; I've Lost my little Willie, 1976; Swingtime in Tottenham, 1976; (ed) Cricket Addict's Archive, 1977; Shaw's Champions, 1978; Fred Astaire, 1979; (ed) Wisden Anthology, vol. I 1864–1900, 1979, vol. II 1900–1940, 1980, vol. III 1940–1963, 1982, vol. IV 1963–1982, 1983; P. G. Wodehouse: a literary biography, 1981; Wisden Book of Obituaries, 1986; (ed) The Last Empires, 1986; (ed) The Lord's Companion, 1987; (ed) A Hymn to Him, 1987; A History of Cricket, 1988; Let's Face the Music, 1989; (ed) The Wisden Papers 1888–1946, 1989; The Concise Wisden: an illustrated anthology of 125 years, 1990; Valentine's Day, 1992. *Recreation:* cricket. *Address:* c/o New Shakespeare Company, Regent's Park, NW1; c/o BBC, Broadcasting House, Portland Place, W1A 1AA.

GREEN, Rev. Bernard; General Secretary, Baptist Union of Great Britain, 1982–91; Moderator of the Free Church Federal Council, 1988–89; *b* 11 Nov. 1925; *s* of George Samuel Green and Laura Annie Agnes (*née* Holliday); *m* 1952, Joan Viccars; two *s* one *d.* *Educ:* Wellingborough Sch.; Bristol Baptist Coll.; Bristol Univ. (BA); Regent's Park Coll., Oxford, and St Catherine's Coll., Oxford (MA); London Univ. BD taken externally. Served War as coal-miner, 1944–47. Ordained as Baptist Minister, 1952; pastorates at: Yardley, Birmingham, 1952–61; Mansfield Road, Nottingham, 1961–76; Horfield, Bristol, 1976–82. Dir, Baptist Insce Co., 1982–93. Vice Pres., Churches' Council for Health and Healing, 1988–. Regular broadcaster on BBC Radio Nottingham until 1976 and on BBC Radio Bristol until 1982. *Publications:* (jtly) Patterns and Prayers for Christian Worship, 1991; (ed jtly) Baptist Praise and Worship, 1991. *Recreations:* reading, music (listening), gardening. *Address:* 34 Mill Road, Abingdon, Oxon OX14 5NS. *T:* Abingdon (01235) 521092.

GREEN, Prof. Brynmor Hugh, OBE 1995; Sir Cyril Kleinwort Professor of Countryside Management, University of London, Wye College, since 1987; *b* 14 Jan. 1941; *s* of Albert Walter Green and Margaret Afona Green (*née* Griffiths); *m* 1965, Jean Armstrong; two *s.* *Educ:* Dartford Grammar Sch.; Univ. of Nottingham (BSc 1st Cl. Hons Botany, PhD Plant Ecol.). Lectr in Plant Ecology, Dept of Botany, Univ. of Manchester, 1965–68; Dep. Regl Officer (SE) 1968–69, Regl Officer (SE) 1969–75, Nature Conservancy Council; Lectr and Sen. Lectr, Wye Coll., 1975–87. A Countryside Comr, 1984–93. *Publications:* Countryside Conservation: the protection and management of amenity ecosystems, 1981, 2nd edn 1985; (jtly) The Diversion of Land: conservation in a period of farming contraction, 1990; (jtly) The Changing Role of the Common Agricultural Policy: the future of farming in Europe, 1991; numerous chapters in books, conf. reports, sci. jls. *Recreations:* golf, watercolour sketching, bird-watching. *Address:* Selsfield, Oxenturn Road, Wye, Ashford, Kent TN25 5AZ. *T:* Wye (Kent) (01233) 812575.

GREEN, Candida L.; *see* Lycett Green.

GREEN, Charles Frederick; Director, 1982–89, and Deputy Group Chief Executive, 1986–89, National Westminster Bank; *b* 20 Oct. 1930; *m* 1956, Rev. Pauline (*née* Jackson); two *s* one *d.* *Educ:* Harrow County School. FCIB (FIB 1971); FIMgt (FBIM 1982). Joined National Provincial Bank, 1946, Secretary, 1967–70; Head of Planning, National Westminster Bank, 1970; Manager, Lombard Street, 1972; Managing Dir, Centre-file, 1974; General Manager: Business Develt Div., 1977; Financial Control Div., 1982. Chairman: CBI/ICC Multinational Affairs Panel, 1982–87; Overseas Cttee, CBI, 1987–89; Dir, Business in the Community, 1981–91 (Vice-Chm., 1985–89); Mem. Council, PSI, 1984– (Treas., 1984–93). Mem., General Synod, 1980–90; Vice-Chm., C of E Bd for Social Responsibility, 1983–91; Chm., Industrial and Econ. Affairs Cttee, 1986–93; Mem., Central Stewardship Cttee, Central Bd of Finance, 1991– (Chm., 1993–); Trustee, Church Urban Fund, 1987–89. Chm., Co. of Glos Community Foundn, 1991–; Vice-Chm., Dio. of Gloucester Bd of Finance, 1991–; Mem., Council for Charitable Support, 1989–93; Trustee: Small Business Res. Trust, 1986–; Monteverdi Choir, 1986–; Charities Aid Foundn, 1989–. Governor: Westonbirt Sch., 1990–; Monkton Combe Sch., 1990–; Mem. Council, 1993–, Vice Chm., 1994, Cheltenham & Gloucester Coll. of Higher Educn (Fellow, 1990). FRSA 1994. Hon. FLCM 1988. Freeman, City of London, 1990. *Recreations:* opera, concert music, drama. *Address:* The Old House, Parks Farm, Old Sodbury, Bristol BS17 6PX. *Clubs:* Athenæum, National, Langbourn Ward.

GREEN, Christopher Edward Wastie, MA; FCIT; Chief Executive, English Heritage, since 1995; *b* 7 Sept. 1943; *s* of James Wastie Green and Margarita Mensing; *m* 1966, Mitzie Petzold; one *s* one *d.* *Educ:* St Paul's School, London; Oriel College, Oxford. MA Mod. Hist. British Rail: Management Trainee, 1965–67; served Birmingham, Nottingham, Hull, Wimbledon; Passenger Operating Manager, HQ, 1979–80; Chief Operating Manager, Scotland, 1980–83; Dep. Gen. Manager, Scotland, 1983–84; Gen. Manager, Scottish Region, 1984–86; Dir, Network SouthEast, 1986–91; Managing Director: InterCity, 1992–94; ScotRail, 1994–95. Mem., Regl Council, CBI, 1986. Pres., Railway Study Assoc., 1989–90; Vice Pres., CIT, 1988. *Recreations:* music, reading, walking, canals, architecture. *Address:* English Heritage, 23 Savile Row, W1X 1AB. *T:* 0171–973 3000.

GREEN, Colin Raymond; Secretary and Chief Legal Adviser, British Telecommunications, since 1994; *b* 16 April 1949; *s* of Gerald and Maisie Green; *m* 1975, Hazel Ruth Lateman; one *s* one *d.* *Educ:* Hampton Grammar Sch.; LSE (LLB Hons); Coll. of Law; WUJS Post-grad. Inst., Israel. Solicitor, 1973; Paisner & Co., 1971–74; Partner, Clintons, 1975–77; Solicitor's Office, Post Office, 1977; BT Solicitor's Office, 1981: Head, Privatisation Div., 1982–84; Head, M&A Div., 1984–85; Dir, Commercial Dept, 1985–89; Solicitor and Chief Legal Adviser, BT, 1989–94. Dir, BT Property Ltd; Trustee, BT Pension Scheme. Member: LSE Lawyers' Steering Gp, 1992–; Faculty, Univ. of Nottingham Centre for Legal Studies, 1992–; Chm., Kingston Jt Israel Appeal Cttee, 1986–. *Recreations:* music (playing and composing), walking, go-karting. *Address:* BT Centre, 81 Newgate Street, EC1A 7AJ. *T:* 0171–356 5237.

GREEN, David; *see* Green, G. D.

GREEN, Prof. David Headley, FRS 1991; FAA; Director, Research School of Earth Sciences, Australian National University, since 1994; *b* 29 Feb. 1936; *s* of Ronald Horace Green and Josephine May Headley; *m* 1959, Helen Mary McIntyre; three *s* three *d.* *Educ:* Univ. of Tasmania (BSc Hons 1957; MSc 1959; DSc 1988); Univ. of Cambridge (PhD 1962). FAA 1974; Fellow, Aust. Inst. of Mining and Metallurgy, 1987. Geologist, Bureau of Mineral Resources, Geology and Geophysics, Canberra, 1957–59; Postgrad. Scholarship, Royal Commn for Exhibn of 1851, 1959–62; Research School of Earth Sciences, Australian National University: Res. Fellow, 1962–65; Fellow, 1965–68; Sen. Fellow, 1968–74; Professorial Fellow, 1974–76; Prof. of Geology, Univ. of Tasmania, 1977–93. Chief Science Advr, Dept of Arts, Sport, Envmt, Tourism and Territories, 1991–93. Hallimond Lect., Mineralogical Soc., 1996. Hon. Fellow: Eur. Union of Geoscis, 1985; Geolog. Soc. of America, 1986. Hon DLitt Tasmania, 1994. Edgeworth David Medal, Royal Soc., NSW, 1968; Stilwell Medal, Geol Soc. of Australia, 1977; Mawson Medal, 1982, Jaeger Medal, 1990, Aust. Acad. of Sci. *Publications:* numerous articles in fields of experimental petrology and geochemistry, in learned jls. *Recreations:* tennis, music. *Address:* Research School of Earth Sciences, Australian National University, Canberra, ACT 0200, Australia. *T:* (6) 2492487, *Fax:* (6) 2490756.

GREEN, Prof. Dennis Howard, FBA 1992; Schröder Professor of German, University of Cambridge, 1979–89; Fellow of Trinity College, Cambridge, since 1949; *b* 26 June 1922; *s* of Herbert Maurice Green and Agnes Edith Green (*née* Fleming); *m* 1972, Margaret Parry. *Educ:* Latymer Upper Sch., London; Trinity Coll., Cambridge; Univ. of Basle. Univ. of Cambridge, 1940–41 and 1945–47; Univ. of Basle (Dr Phil.), 1947–49; Military service (RAC), 1941–45; Univ. Lecturer in German, St Andrews, 1949–50; Research Fellowship, Trinity Coll., Cambridge (first year held *in absentia*), 1949–52; Univ. Asst Lectr in German, Cambridge, 1950–54; Teaching Fellowship, Trinity Coll., Cambridge, 1952–66; Head of Dept of Other Languages, 1956–79, and Prof. of Modern Languages, Cambridge, 1966–79; Visiting Professor: Cornell Univ., 1965–66; Auckland Univ., 1966; Yale Univ., 1969; ANU, Canberra, 1971; UCLA, 1975; Univ. of Pennsylvania, 1975;

Univ. of WA, 1976; Univ. of Freiburg, 1990; Vis. Fellow, Humanities Res. Centre, Canberra, 1978. *Publications:* The Carolingian Lord, 1965; The Millstätter Exodus: a crusading epic, 1966; (with Dr L. P. Johnson) Approaches to Wolfram von Eschenbach, 1978; Irony in the Medieval Romance, 1979; The Art of Recognition in Wolfram's Parzival, 1982; Medieval Listening and Reading, 1994; reviews and articles in learned journals. *Recreations:* walking and foreign travel. *Address:* Trinity College, Cambridge CB3 9LW; 7 Archway Court, Barton Road, Cambridge CB3 9LW. *T:* Cambridge (01223) 514386.

GREEN, Rev. Canon (Edward) Michael (Bankes); Archbishops' Adviser in Evangelism, since 1992; *b* 20 Aug. 1930; British; *m* 1957, Rosemary Wake (*née* Storr); two *s* two *d*. *Educ:* Clifton Coll.; Oxford and Cambridge Univs. BD Cantab 1966. Exeter Coll., Oxford, 1949–53 (1st cl. Lit. Hum.); Royal Artillery (Lieut, A/Adjt), 1953–55; Queens' Coll., Cambridge, 1955–57 (1st cl. Theol. Tripos Pt III; Carus Greek Testament Prize; Fencing Blue), and Ridley Hall Theol Coll., 1955–57; Curate, Holy Trinity, Eastbourne, 1957–60; Lectr, London Coll. of Divinity, 1960–69; Principal, St John's Coll., Nottingham (until July 1970, London Coll. of Divinity), 1969–75; Canon Theologian of Coventry, 1970–76, Canon Theologian Emeritus, 1978–; Rector of St Aldate's, Oxford, 1975–87 (with Holy Trinity, Oxford, 1975–82 and with St Matthew, 1982–87); Prof. of Evangelism at Regent Coll., Vancouver, Univ. of BC, 1987–92. Member: Doctrine Commission of the Church, 1968–77; Church Unity Commn, 1974–. Leader of missions, overseas and in UK. Hon. DD Toronto, 1992. *Publications:* Called to Serve, 1964; Choose Freedom, 1965; The Meaning of Salvation, 1965; Man Alive, 1967; Runaway World, 1968; Commentary on 2 Peter and Jude, 1968; Evangelism in the Early Church, 1970; Jesus Spells Freedom, 1972; New Life, New Lifestyle, 1973; I Believe in the Holy Spirit, 1975, new edn 1985; You Must Be Joking, 1976; (ed) The Truth of God Incarnate, 1977; Why Bother With Jesus?, 1979; Evangelism—Now and Then, 1979; What is Christianity?, 1981; I Believe in Satan's Downfall, 1981; The Day Death Died, 1982; To Corinth with Love, 1982; World on the Run, 1983; Freed to Serve, 1983; The Empty Cross of Jesus, 1984; Come Follow Me, 1984; Lift Off to Faith, 1985; Baptism, 1987; Matthew for Today, 1988; Ten Myths about Christianity, 1988; Evangelism Through the Local Church, 1990; Reflections from the Lions Den, 1990; Who is this Jesus?, 1991; My God, 1992; Acts for Today, 1993; (with Alister McGrath) Springboard for Faith, 1993; (with Paul Stevens) New Testament Spirituality, 1994; contribs to various jls. *Recreations:* family, countryside pursuits, squash, fly fishing. *Address:* 7 The Green, Chilwell, Nottingham NG9 5BE. *T:* Nottingham (0115) 943 1738, *Fax:* (0115) 943 1737.

GREEN, Sir (Edward) Stephen (Lycett), 4th Bt, *cr* 1886; CBE 1964; JP; Chairman, East Anglian Regional Hospital Board, 1959–74; *b* 18 April 1910; *s* of Sir E. A. Lycett Green, 3rd Bt, and Elizabeth Williams; *S* father, 1941; *m* 1935, Constance Mary, *d* of late Ven. H. S. Radcliffe; one *d*. *Educ:* Eton; Magdalene Coll., Cambridge. Called to Bar, Lincoln's Inn, 1933. Served War of 1939–45 (Major, RA). CC 1946–49, JP 1946, DL 1963–88, High Sheriff 1973, Norfolk; Dep. Chairman Norfolk QS, 1948–71. Chairman: King's Lynn Hospital Management Cttee, 1948–59; Assoc. of Hosp. Management Cttees, 1956–58; Cttee of Inquiry into Recruitment, Training and Promotion of Administrative and Clerical Staff in Hospital Service, 1962–63; Docking RDC, 1950–57. *Recreations:* shooting, watching TV, reading. *Heir: b* Lt-Col Simon Lycett Green, TD, Yorks Dragoons Yeomanry [*b* 11 July 1912; *m* 1st, 1935, Gladys (marr. diss. 1971; she *d* 1980), *d* of late Arthur Ranicar, JP, Springfield, Wigan; one *d*; 2nd, 1971, Mary, *d* of late George Ramsden]. *Address:* Ken Hill, Snettisham, King's Lynn PE31 7PG. *TA:* Snettisham, Norfolk. *T:* Heacham (01485) 570001. *Clubs:* White's, Pratt's; Norfolk (Norwich); Allsorts (Norfolk).

GREEN, Dr Frank Alan, CEng; FIM, FIMgt; Principal, Charing Green Associates, since 1983; Managing Director, Charing Green Ltd, since 1990; Senior Consultant, Europa Consultancy Ltd, since 1994; *b* 29 Oct. 1931; *s* of Frank Green and Winifred Hilda (*née* Payne); *m* 1957, Pauline Eleanor Tayler; one *s* two *d*. *Educ:* Mercers Sch., London; Univ. of London (BScEng, PhD). CEng 1980; FIM 1978; FIMgt (FBIM 1979). UKAEA, 1956–57; various appts, Glacier Metal Co. Ltd (Associated Engrg Gp), 1957–65; Technical Dir, Alta Friccion SA, Mexico City, 1965–68; Manufg Dir, Stewart Warner Corp., 1968–72; Marketing Develt Manager, Calor Gp, 1972–74; Manufg Dir, 1974–77, Man. Dir, 1977–81, British Twin Disc Ltd, Rochester; Industrial Advr (Under-Sec.), DTI, 1981–84. Director: Gen. Technology Systems (Scandinavia), 1989–91; Gen. Technology Systems (Portuguesa), 1989–91; Principal Consultant, General Technology Systems Ltd, 1984–90; Sen. Consultant, Centre for Consultancy, 1990–93. Dir, Anglo-Mexican Chamber of Commerce, Mexico City, 1966–68. Member of Council: Inst. of Metals, 1990–91; Inst. of Materials, 1992–94. *Publications:* contrib. technical, historical and managerial jls in UK and Mexico. *Recreations:* photography, military history, rough walking, wine. *Address:* Courtwood House, Burleigh Road, Charing, Kent TN27 0JB. *T:* Charing (0123371) 3152. *Club:* Old Mercers.

GREEN, Geoffrey Hugh, CB 1977; Deputy Under-Secretary of State (Policy), Procurement Executive, Ministry of Defence, 1975–80; *b* 24 Sept. 1920; *o s* of late Duncan M. and Kate Green, Bristol; *m* 1948, Ruth Hazel Mercy; two *d*. *Educ:* Bristol Grammar Sch.; Worcester Coll., Oxford (Exhibr), 1939–41, 1945–47 (MA). Served with Royal Artillery (Ayrshire Yeomanry): N Africa and Italy, 1942–45 (Captain). Entered Min. of Defence, Oct. 1947; Principal, 1949; Asst Sec., 1960; Asst Under-Sec. of State, 1969; Dep. Under-Sec. of State, 1974. *Recreations:* travel, music, walking. *Address:* 47 Kent Avenue, Ealing, W13 8BE.

GREEN, Gerard Nicholas Valentine; Chief Executive, St Bartholomew's, Royal London, London Chest Hospitals NHS Trust, since 1994; *b* 6 Aug. 1950; *s* of James Arnold Green and Margarathe Ella Green; *m* 1977, Maralyn Ann Ranger; one *s* one *d*. *Educ:* Highgate Sch.; University Coll., London (BA); Univ. of Warwick (MA); Birkbeck Coll., London (MA). AHSM. Nat. admin. trainee, 1974–75; Dep. Hosp. Sec., St George's Hosp., SW17, 1975–77; Asst Sector Administrator, Cane Hill Hosp., Surrey, 1977–79; Sector Administrator, Farnborough Hosp., Kent, 1979–82; Administrator, KCH, 1982–84; Chief Exec. Officer, Tabuk Military Hosp., Saudi Arabia, 1984–87; Dist Gen. Man., Bromley HA, 1987–89; Regl Gen. Man., SE Thames RHA, 1989–94. Mem., UKCC, 1993–. FRSA 1989. *Recreations:* travel, reading. *Address:* Royal London Hospital, Alexandra House, E1. *Club:* Reform.

GREEN, (Gregory) David; Director of Voluntary Service Overseas, since 1990; *b* 2 Dec. 1948; *s* of Thomas Dixon Green and Mary Mabella Green (*née* Walley); *m* 1977, Corinne Butler; three *d*. *Educ:* Leys Sch., Cambridge; Keswick Hall Coll. of Educn, Norwich (Cert Ed); Trinity Hall, Cambridge (BEd). Volunteer, VSO, Pakistan, 1967–68; teaching, Conisborough and Rotherham, 1972–76; Dir, Children's Relief Internat., 1976–79; Save the Children Fund: Staff Develt and Trng Officer, 1979; Dep. Dir of Personnel, 1982; Dir of Personnel, 1983; Dir of Personnel and Admin., 1988–90. Dir and Council Mem., Council for Colony Holidays for School-children, 1970–80; Mem. Council, Assoc. of Active Learning, 1990–92. Mem., Laurence Olivier Awards Panel, 1984–85. FRGS 1991; FRSA 1990. *Publication:* Chorus, 1977. *Recreations:* theatre, music, painting, woodworking. *Address:* c/o VSO, 317 Putney Bridge Road, SW15 2PN. *T:* 0181–780 2266.

GREEN, Hon. Sir Guy (Stephen Montague), AC 1994; KBE 1982; Chief Justice of Tasmania, since 1973; Lieutenant-Governor of Tasmania, since 1982; Chancellor, University of Tasmania, since 1985; *b* 26 July 1937; *s* of Clement Francis Montague Green and Beryl Margaret Jenour Green; *m* 1963, Rosslyn Mary Marshall; two *s* two *d*. *Educ:* Launceston Church Grammar Sch.; Univ. of Tasmania. Alfred Houston Schol. (Philosophy) 1958; LLB (Hons) 1960. Admitted to Bar of Tasmania, 1960; Partner, Ritchie & Parker Alfred Green & Co. (Launceston), 1963–71; Mem., Faculty of Law, Univ. of Tas, 1974–85. Pres., Tasmanian Bar Assoc., 1968–70; Magistrate 1971–73. Chm., Council of Law Reporting, 1978–85. Dep. Chm., Australian Inst. of Judicial Admin, 1986–88. Chm., Tasmanian Cttee, Duke of Edinburgh's Award Scheme in Australia, 1975–80; Dir, Winston Churchill Meml Trust, 1975–85 (Dep. Nat. Chm., 1980–85; Chm. Tasmanian Regional Cttee, 1975–80). St John Ambulance, Australia: Pres., Tasmanian Council, 1984–92; Priory Exec. Officer, 1984–91; Chancellor, 1991–. KStJ 1984. *Address:* Judges' Chambers, Supreme Court, Salamanca Place, Hobart, Tasmania 7000. *Club:* Tasmanian (Hobart).

GREEN, Rev. Humphrey Christian, (Father Benedict Green, CR); formerly Principal, College of the Resurrection, Mirfield; *b* 9 Jan. 1924; *s* of late Rev. Canon Frederick Wastie Green and Marjorie Susan Beltt Green (*née* Gosling). *Educ:* Dragon Sch., Oxford; Eton (King's Scholar); Merton Coll., Oxford (Postmaster). BA 1949, MA 1952. Served War, RNVR, 1943–46. Deacon 1951, priest 1952; Asst Curate of Northolt, 1951–56; Lectr in Theology, King's Coll., London, 1956–60. Professed in Community of the Resurrection (taking additional name of Benedict), 1962; Vice-Principal, Coll. of the Resurrection, 1965–75; Principal, 1975–84. Associate Lectr in Dept of Theology and Religious Studies, Univ. of Leeds, 1967–87. Mem., SNTS, 1989–. *Publications:* The Gospel according to Matthew (New Clarendon Bible), 1975; Lay Presidency at the Eucharist, 1994; contrib.: Towards a Church Architecture (ed P. Hammond), 1962; The Anglican Synthesis (ed W. R. F. Browning), 1964; Synoptic Studies (ed C. M. Tuckett), 1984; The Making of Orthodoxy (ed R. Williams), 1989; The Synoptic Gospels: source criticism and the new literary criticism (ed C. Focant), 1993; theological jls. *Recreations:* walking, music, synoptic criticism. *Address:* House of the Resurrection, Mirfield, W Yorks WF14 0BN. *T:* Mirfield (01924) 494318.

GREEN, John Dennis Fowler; *b* 9 May 1909; *s* of late Capt. Henry and Amy Gertrude Green, Chedworth, Glos; *m* 1946, Diana Judith, JP, *y d* of late Lt-Col H. C. Elwes, DSO, MVO, Colesbourne, Glos. *Educ:* Cheltenham Coll.; Peterhouse, Cambridge. President of the Union. Called to the Bar, Inner Temple, 1933 (Entrance Scholar); BBC, 1934–62 (Controller, Talks Div., 1956–61); established agricultural broadcasting, 1935. Special Agric. Mission to Aust. and NZ (MAFF), 1945–47; Pres. National Pig Breeders Assoc., 1955–56; Chm., Agricultural Adv. Council, 1963–68; Exec. Mem., Land Settlement Assoc., 1965–80; Trustee, RASE, 1984– (Dep. Pres., 1983–84); Council for the Protection of Rural England: Mem., Nat. Exec., 1967–80; Pres., Glos. Br., 1985– (Chm., 1964–85). Chm., Cirencester and Tewkesbury Conservative Assoc., 1964–78. FRASE 1990; Fellow, Royal Agricl Soc. of the Commonwealth, 1991. *Publications:* Mr Baldwin: A Study in Post War Conservatism, 1933; articles and broadcasts on historical and agricultural subjects. *Recreations:* livestock breeding, forestry, shooting. *Address:* The Manor, Chedworth, Cheltenham GL54 4AA. *T:* Cirencester (01285) 720233. *Clubs:* Oriental, Naval and Military, Buck's, Farmers'.

GREEN, John Edward, PhD; FEng 1994; FRAeS; Chief Executive, Aircraft Research Association Ltd, since 1988; *b* 26 Aug. 1937; *s* of John Green and Ellen O'Dowd; *m* 1959, Gillian (*née* Jackson); one *s* one *d*. *Educ:* Birkenhead Inst. Grammar Sch.; St John's Coll., Cambridge (Scholar). BA 1959; MA 1963; PhD 1966. Student Apprentice, Bristol Aircraft Ltd, 1956; De Havilland Engine Co., 1959–61; Royal Aircraft Establishment, 1964–81: Head of Transonic/Supersonic Wind Tunnel Div., 1971; Head of Propulsion Div., 1973; Head of Noise Div., 1974; Head of Aerodynamics Dept., 1978–81; Dir, Project Time and Cost Analysis, MoD (PE), 1981–84; Minister–Counsellor Defence Equipment, and Dep. Head of British Defence Staff, Washington, 1984–85; Dep. Dir (Aircraft), RAE, 1985–87. Mem., Internat. Council of the Aeronautical Scis, 1986–. Member Council: RAeS, 1986– (Vice Pres., 1992–95, Pres.-elect, 1995–96; Hon. Treas., 1992–96); AIRTO, 1988–; Court, Cranfield Univ. (formerly Cranfield Inst. of Technol.), 1988–. Goldstein Lectr, 1991, Busk Prize, 1992, RAeS. *Publications:* contribs to books and learned jls, chiefly on fluid mechanics and aerodynamics. *Recreations:* music, mountain walking (Munroist, 1994). *Address:* Aircraft Research Association Ltd, Manton Lane, Bedford, Beds MK41 7PF. *T:* Bedford (01234) 350681.

GREEN, John Michael, CB 1976; Commissioner, 1971–85, Deputy Chairman, 1973–85, Board of Inland Revenue; *b* 5 Dec. 1924; *s* of late George Green and of Faith Green; *m* 1951, Sylvia (*née* Crabb); one *s* one *d*. *Educ:* Merchant Taylors' Sch., Rickmansworth; Jesus Coll., Oxford (MA (Hons)). Served War, Army, RAC, 1943–46. Entered Inland Revenue as Asst Principal, 1948; served in HM Treasury, as Principal, 1956–57; Asst Sec., 1962; Under Sec., Bd of Inland Revenue, 1971. Mem., NW Surrey HA, 1989–95. *Recreation:* gardening. *Address:* 5 Bylands, White Rose Lane, Woking, Surrey GU22 7LA. *T:* Woking (01483) 772599. *Club:* Reform.

GREEN, Dr John Timothy; Chief Executive, Royal Society of Medicine, since 1993; *b* 1 Jan. 1944; *s* of Thomas Albert Green and Joan (*née* Chamberlain); *m* 1985, Susan Mary Shattock; one *s*. *Educ:* King Edward's Five Ways Sch., Birmingham; Queens' Coll., Cambridge (BA 1966; MA 1970; PhD Maths 1970). Queens' College, Cambridge: Bye Fellow, 1970–72; Fellow, 1972–93; Lectr in Maths, 1972–93; Dean of Coll., 1972–77; Tutor, 1977–80; Sen. Tutor, 1980–93; Life Fellow, 1993. Director: S Leics Garages Ltd, 1985–; Pennant Hotels Ltd, 1987–; RSM Press Ltd, 1993–. Recruitment Advr, FCO, 1992–. Trustee, Harpur Trust, Bedford, 1984–87. Gov., Hills Rd Sixth Form Coll., Cambridge, 1993–. *Publications:* contrib. Jl Fluid Mechanics and others. *Recreations:* opera, music, fell-walking. *Address:* 40 Newton Road, Cambridge CB2 2AL. *T:* Cambridge (01223) 353756.

GREEN, Julian Hartridge; American and French writer; *b* Paris, France, 6 Sept. 1900; one *s*. *Educ:* Lycée Janson, Paris; Univ. of Virginia. Member: Raven Club, 1922; Phi Beta Kappa, 1948. *Publications: fiction:* The Apprentice Psychiatrist, 1920; Le voyageur sur la terre, 1924, new enl. edn 1979; Mont-Cinère, 1926; Adrienne Mesurat, 1927; Les clés de la mort, 1928; Léviathan, 1929; L'autre sommeil, 1930; Epaves, 1932; Le visionnaire, 1934; Minuit, 1936; Varouna, 1940; Si j'étais vous ...., 1947; Moira, 1950; Le malfaiteur, 1956, new enl. edn 1974; Chaque homme dans sa nuit, 1960; L'autre, 1971; La nuit des fantômes, 1976; Le Mauvais Lieu, 1977; Histoires de Vertige, 1984; Les Pays Lointains, 1987; Les Etoiles du Sud, 1989; Merveilles et Démons (trans. of Lord Dunsany's Tales), 1991; Ralph et la quatrième dimension, 1991; Dixie, 1995; *plays:* Sud, 1953; L'ennemi, 1954; L'ombre, 1956; Demain n'existe pas, 1979; L'automate, 1980; L'étudiant roux, 1993; *autobiography and journals:* Memories of Happy Days, 1942; Jeunes Années: i, Partir avant le jour, 1963; ii, Mille chemins ouverts, 1964; iii, Terre lointaine, 1966; iv, Jeunesse, 1974; Ce qu'il faut d'amour à l'homme, 1978; On est si sérieux quand on a 19 ans, Journal 1919–24, 1993; Journal: i, Les années faciles, 1928–34, 1938; ii, Derniers beaux jours, 1935–39, 1939; La fin d'un monde: Juin 1940, 1992; iii, Devant la porte sombre, 1940–43,

1946; iv, L'œil de l'ouragan, 1943–45, 1949; v, Le revenant, 1946–50, 1952; vi, Le miroir intérieur, 1950–54, 1955; vii, Le bel aujourd'hui, 1955–58, 1958; viii, Vers l'invisible, 1958–66, 1967; ix, Ce qui reste de jour, 1967–72, 1972; x, La bouteille à la mer, 1972–76, 1976; xi, La Terre est si belle, 1976–78, 1982; xii, La lumière du monde, 1978–81, 1983; xiii, L'arc-en-ciel, 1981–84, 1988; xiv, L'expatrié, 1984–90, 1990; xv, L'avenir n'est à personne, 1990–92, 1993; Dans la gueule du temps (illust. jl), 1979–; Journal du Voyageur (illust. jl), 1985; Œuvres complètes (La Pléïade), vol. I, 1972; vols II and III, 1973; vols IV and V, 1974; vol. VI, 1990; vol. VII, 1994; *history:* Suite Anglaise, 1925; Frère François, 1983; *essays:* Pamphlet contre les catholiques de France, 1924; Liberté Chérie, 1974; Qui sommes-nous?, 1971; Une grande amitié: correspondance avec Jacques Maritain, 1982; Paris, 1983; *bilingual essays:* Le Langage et son double, 1985; L'homme et son ombre, 1991; Les statues parlent, 1991; The Apprentice Writer, 1992; *poem:* Dionysos et la chasse aventureuse, 1994. *Address:* Editions de la Pléïade, 5 rue Sébastien-Bottin, 75007 Paris, France.

GREEN, Sir Kenneth, Kt 1988; MA; Vice-Chancellor (formerly Director), Manchester Metropolitan University (formerly Manchester Polytechnic), since 1981; *b* 7 March 1934; *s* of James William and Elsie May Green; *m* 1961, Glenda (*née* Williams); one *d*. *Educ:* Helsby Grammar Sch.; Univ. of Wales, Bangor (BA 1st Cl. Hons); Univ. of London (MA). 2nd Lieut, S Wales Borderers, 1955–57. Management Trainee, Dunlop Rubber Co., 1957–58; Teacher, Liverpool, 1958–60; Lecturer: Widnes Technical Coll., 1961–62; Stockport College of Technology, 1962–64; Sen. Lectr, Bolton College of Education, 1964–68; Head of Educn, City of Birmingham College of Education, 1968–72; Dean of Faculty, Manchester Polytechnic, 1973–81. Vice-Chm., Manchester TEC, 1989–93 (Mem. Bd, 1989–93); Member: Council, CNAA, 1985–93; UFC, 1989–93. Chm., Council of Mgt, Rathbone Soc., 1993–; Member: Governing Body, The Heath Comprehensive Sch., Runcorn, 1988–92; Governing Body, Victoria Rd Co. Primary Sch., Runcorn, 1990– (Chm., 1993–). Hon. Mem., Manchester Literary & Philosophical Soc. Hon. MRNCM. Hon. LLD Manchester, 1992. *Recreations:* Rugby football, beer tasting. *Address:* 40 Royden Avenue, Runcorn, Cheshire WA7 4SP. *T:* Runcorn (019285) 75201.

GREEN, Rt Rev. Laurence Alexander; *see* Bradwell, Area Bishop of.

GREEN, Prof. Leslie Leonard, CBE 1989; PhD; FInstP; Professor of Experimental Physics, University of Liverpool, 1964–86, now Emeritus; Director, Daresbury Laboratory, 1981–88; *b* 30 March 1925; *s* of Leonard and Victoria Green; *m* 1952, Dr Helen Therese Morgan; one *s* one *d*. *Educ:* Alderman Newton's Sch., Leicester; King's Coll., Cambridge (MA, PhD). FInstP 1966. British Atomic Energy Proj., 1944–46; Univ. of Liverpool: Lectr, 1948–57; Sen. Lectr, 1957–62; Reader, 1962–64; Dean, Faculty of Sciences, 1969–72; Pro-Vice-Chancellor, 1978–81. Mem., SRC Nuclear Physics Bd, 1972–75 and 1979–82. *Publications:* articles on nuclear physics in scientific jls. *Address:* Seafield Cottage, De Grouchy Street, West Kirby, Merseyside L48 5DX.

GREEN, Lucinda Jane, MBE 1978; three-day event rider; *b* 7 Nov. 1953; *d* of late Maj.-Gen. George Erroll Prior-Palmer, CB, DSO, and of Lady Doreen Hersey Winifred Prior-Palmer; *m* 1981, David (marr. diss. 1992), *s* of Burrington Green, Brisbane; one *s* one *d*. *Educ:* St Mary's, Wantage; Idbury Manor, Oxon. Member of winning Junior European Team, 1971; Winner, 3 Day Events: Badminton Horse Trials Championships, 1973, 1976, 1977, 1979, 1983, 1984; Burghley, 1977, 1981; Individual European Championships, 1975, 1977; World Championship, 1982; Member: Olympic Team, Montreal, 1976, Los Angeles, 1984; European Championship Team: Luhmühlen, W Germany, 1975 (team Silver Medallist and individual Gold Medallist); Burghley, 1977 (team Gold Medallist), 1985 (team Gold Medallist), 1987 (team Gold Medallist); European Team, 1979, 1983 (team and individual Silver Medallist); Alternative Olympic Team, 1980; World Championship Team: Kentucky, 1978; Luhmühlen, W Germany, 1982 (team and individual Gold Medallist). Co-presenter, Horses, Channel 4, 1987; Commentator: BBC, Badminton, 1987–94; BBC, Olympic Games, 1988; Channel 7, Australia, Olympic Games, 1992. Editorial Consultant, Eventing, 1989–92. *Publications:* Up, Up and Away, 1978; Four Square, 1980; Regal Realm, 1983; Cross-Country Riding, 1986, 2nd edn 1995; The Young Rider, 1993. *Recreations:* driving, ski-ing, scuba diving, travelling abroad. *Address:* The Tree House, Appleshaw, Andover, Hants SP11 9BS.

GREEN, Dr Malcolm, FRCP; Consultant Physician, Brompton Hospital, since 1975; Director, British Postgraduate Medical Federation, since 1991; *b* 25 Jan. 1942; *s* of James Bisdee Malcolm Green and Frances Marjorie Lois Green; *m* 1971, Julieta Caroline Preston; two *s* two *d* (and one *d* decd). *Educ:* Charterhouse Sch. (Foundn Scholar); Trinity Coll., Oxford (Exhibnr; BA 1963; BSc 1965; MA, BM, BCh 1967; DM 1978); St Thomas's Hosp. Med. Sch. (Scholar). FRCP 1980 (MRCP 1970). Jun. appts, St Thomas' and Brompton Hosps, 1968–71; Lectr, Dept of Medicine, St Thomas' Hosp., 1971–74; Radcliffe Travelling Fellow, Harvard University Med. Sch., 1971–73; Sen. Registrar, Westminster and Brompton Hosps, 1974–75; Consultant Physician and Physician i/c Chest Dept, St Bartholomew's Hosp. 1975–86; Dean, Nat. Heart and Lung Inst., 1988–90 (Mem., Cttee of Management, 1988–). Member: Supraregl Services Adv. Cttee, 1991–; NHS Taskforce on Res., 1993–94; Health of the Nation Wider Health Wkg Gp, 1991–. Chm., Exec. Cttee and Nat. Council, British Lung Foundn, 1984–94 (Pres. and Chm., Council, 1994–); Chm. Acad. Steering Gp, BPMF, 1989–90; Member, Committees of Management, Institutes of Child Health, Psychiatry, Neurology, Ophthalmology, Cancer Research, Dental Surgery, and RPMS, 1991–. Mem. Bd of Govs, Nat. Heart and Chest Hosps, 1988–90. Trustee, Heart Disease and Diabetes Res. Trust, 1988–. Treasurer, 1977–85, Pres., 1992–, United Hosps Sailing Club. *Publications:* chapters and articles in med, books and jls on gen. medicine, respiratory medicine and respiratory physiology. *Recreations:* sailing, ski-ing. *Address:* 38 Lansdowne Gardens, SW8 2EF. *T:* 0171–622 8286. *Clubs:* Royal Thames Yacht; Itchenor Sailing; Imperial Poona Yacht (Hon. Sec.).

GREEN, Prof. Malcolm Leslie Hodder, PhD; FRS 1985; CChem, FRSC; Professor of Inorganic Chemistry, since 1989, and Head of Department, Inorganic Chemistry Laboratory, since 1988, University of Oxford; Fellow of St Catherine's College, Oxford, since 1988; *b* 16 April 1936; *s* of late Leslie Ernest Green, MD and Sheila Ethel (*née* Hodder); *m* 1965, Jennifer Clare Bilham; two *s* one *d*. *Educ:* Denstone Coll.; Acton Technical Coll. (BSc); Imperial Coll. of Science and Technol., London Univ. (DIC, PhD 1958); MA Cantab. CChem, FRSC 1981. Asst Lectr in Inorganic Chem., Univ. of Cambridge, 1960–63; Fellow of Corpus Christi Coll., Cambridge, 1961–63; University of Oxford: Septcentenary Fellow and Tutor in Inorganic Chem., Balliol Coll., 1963–88; Deptl Demonstrator, 1963; Lectr, 1965–88; British Gas Royal Soc. Sen Res. Fellow, 1979–86. A. P. Sloan Vis. Prof., Harvard Univ., 1973; Sherman Fairchild Vis. Scholar, CIT, 1981. Tilden Lectr and Prize, RSC, 1982; Debye Lectr, Cornell Univ., 1985; Sir Edward Frankland Prize Lectr, 1988. Corday–Morgan Medal and Prize in Inorganic Chem., Chemical Soc., 1974; Medal for Transition Metal Chem., Chemical Soc., 1978; Award for Inorganic Chem., Amer. Chemical Soc., 1984; RSC Award for Organometallic Chem., 1986; Karl-Ziegler Prize, Ges. Deutscher Chemiker, 1992. *Publications:* Organometallic Compounds: Vol. II, The Transition Elements, 1968; (with G. E. Coates, P. Powell and K. Wade) Principles of Organometallic Chemistry, 1968. *Address:* St Catherine's College, Oxford OX1 3UJ.

GREEN, Malcolm Robert, DPhil; Lecturer, University of Glasgow, since 1967; *b* 4 Jan. 1943; *m* 1971; one *s* two *d*. *Educ:* Wyggeston Boys' School, Leicester; Magdalen College, Oxford. MA, DPhil. Member: Glasgow Corp., 1973–75; Strathclyde Regional Council, 1975–; Chairman: Educn Cttee, 1982–90, Envmt Sub-Cttee, 1990–, Strathclyde Regional Council; Educn Cttee, Convention of Scottish Local Authorities, 1978–90; Management Side, Scottish Jt Negotiating Cttees for Teaching Staff in Sch. and Further Educn, 1977–90; Nat. Cttee for In-Service Training of Teachers, 1977–86; Scottish Cttee for Staff Develt in Educn, 1987–91. Commissioner, Manpower Services Commn, 1983–85. *Recreation:* talking politics. *Address:* 46 Victoria Crescent Road, Glasgow G12 9DE. *T:* 0141–339 2007.

GREEN, Rt. Rev. Mark, MC 1945; an Assistant Bishop, Diocese of Chichester, since 1982; Hon. Assistant, St Mary, Eastbourne, since 1994; *b* 28 March 1917; *s* of late Rev. Ernest William Green, OBE, and Miranda Mary Green; unmarried. *Educ:* Rossall Sch.; Lincoln Coll., Oxford (MA). Curate, St Catherine's Gloucester, 1940; Royal Army Chaplains' Dept, 1943–46 (despatches, 1945); Dir of Service Ordination Candidates, 1947–48; Vicar of St John, Newland, Hull, 1948–53; Short Service Commn, Royal Army Chaplains' Dept, 1953–56; Vicar of South Bank, Teesside, 1956–58; Rector of Cottingham, Yorks, 1958–64; Vicar of Bishopthorpe and Acaster Malbis, York, 1964–72; Hon. Chaplain to Archbp of York, 1964–72; Rural Dean of Ainsty, 1964–68; Canon and Prebendary of York Minster, 1963–72; Bishop Suffragan of Aston, 1972–82; Hon. Asst, Christ Church, St Leonards-on-Sea, 1982–94. Chm. of Governing Body, Aston Training Scheme, 1977–83; Provost, Woodard Schs Southern Div., 1982–89. Hon. DSc Aston, 1980. *Publication:* Diary of Doubt and Faith, 1974. *Address:* 27 Selwyn House, Selwyn Road, Eastbourne, E Sussex BN21 2LF. *T:* Eastbourne (01323) 642707.

GREEN, Dame Mary Georgina, DBE 1968; BA; Head Mistress, Kidbrooke School, SE3, 1954–73; Chairman, BBC London Local Radio Council, 1973–78; Chairman, General Optical Council, 1979–85 (Member, 1977–79); *b* 27 July 1913; *er d* of late Edwin George Green and Rose Margaret Green (*née* Gibbs). *Educ:* Wellingborough High Sch.; Westfield Coll., University of London (Hon. Fellow, 1976, Fellow, QMW, 1989). Assistant Mistress: Clapham High Sch., 1936–38; Streatham Hill and Clapham High Sch., 1938–40; William Hulme's Sch., Manchester, 1940–45; Head Mistress, Colston's Girls' Sch., Bristol, 1946–53. Member: Central Advisory Council for Education (Eng.), 1956–63; Church of England Board of Education, 1958–65; Council King George's Jubilee Trust, 1963–68; Court of Governors, London Sch. of Economics and Political Science, 1964–83; Royal Commission on Trade Unions and Employers' Assocs, 1965–68; Council, City University, 1969–78; Cttee of Inquiry into Nurses' Pay, 1974; Press Council, 1976–79; Review Body on Doctors' and Dentists' Remuneration, 1976–79. Dep. Chm., E-SU, 1976–82 (Governor, 1974–82); a Governor: BBC, 1968–73; Royal Ballet Sch., 1969–72; Centre for Educnl Develt Overseas, 1970–74; Rachel McMillan Coll. of Educn, 1970–73; Ditchley Foundn, 1978–. Hon. DSc: City, 1981; Bradford, 1986. Hon. MADO 1985; Hon. FBCO 1985. *Address:* 45 Winn Road, SE12 9EX. *T:* 0181–857 1514.

GREEN, Michael; *see* Green, N. M.

GREEN, Rev. Canon Michael; *see* Green, Rev. Canon E. M. B.

GREEN, Prof. Michael Boris, FRS 1989; John Humphrey Plummer Professor of Theoretical Physics and Fellow of Clare College, University of Cambridge, since 1993; *b* 22 May 1946; *s* of Absalom and Genia Green. *Educ:* Cambridge Univ. (BA, PhD; Rayleigh Prize 1969). Res. Fellow, Inst. for Advanced Study, Princeton, NJ, 1970–72; Fellowships in Cambridge, 1972–77; SERC Advanced Fellow, Oxford, 1977–79; Lectr, Queen Mary Coll., London Univ., 1979–85; Prof. of Physics, QMC, later QMW, 1985–93. Vis. Associate, Caltech, Pasadena, for periods during 1981–85; Nuffield Science Fellowship, 1984–86; SERC Sen. Fellowship, 1986–91. Maxwell Medal and Prize, Inst. of Physics, 1987; Hopkins Prize, Cambridge Philosophical Soc., 1987; Dirac Medal, Internat. Centre for Theoretical Physics, Trieste, 1989. *Publications:* Superstring Theory, vols I and II (with J. H. Schwarz and E. Witten), 1987; many contribs to physics and mathematics jls. *Address:* Department of Applied Mathematics and Theoretical Physics, University of Cambridge, Cambridge CB2 1TN.

GREEN, Dr Michael Frederick; Consultant Physician, Department of Geriatric Medicine, Board of Health, Guernsey, since 1984; *b* 29 Aug. 1939; *s* of Frederick and Kathleen Green; *m* 1977, Janet Mary; seven *s* one *d*. *Educ:* Dulwich Coll.; Jesus Coll., Cambridge (MA); St Thomas' Hosp. (MB, BChir). FRCP 1980. Consultant, N Middlesex and St Ann's Hosps, 1969–71; Consultant Physician, Dept of Geriatric Medicine, Royal Free Hospital, 1972–84. Mem., GMC, 1973–79. Medical Adviser, Royal Life Saving Soc., 1970–84. Member various bodies mainly involved with the elderly, including: British Geriatrics Soc.; Age Concern; Cruse (Nat. Assoc. for Widows); London Medical Gp; British Soc. for Research on Ageing. Governor: Queen Elizabeth Schs, Barnet, 1973–79; Christchurch Sch., Hampstead, 1980–83. Mem. Bd, Jl of Medical Ethics, 1980–84; Chm., Editl Bd, Geriatric Medicine, 1983–. *Publications:* Health in Middle Age, 1978; co-author books on medical admin; articles on geriatric medicine, heating, lifesaving, hypothermia, endocrinology, medical records, psychiatry in old age, pressure sores. *Recreations:* family, magic, swimming and lifesaving, writing, lecturing and teaching, gardening, boating. *Address:* Glenview, Les Effards Road, St Sampson's, Guernsey.

GREEN, Michael John; Controller, BBC Radio 4, since 1986; Deputy Managing Director, BBC Network Radio, since 1993; *b* 28 May 1941; *s* of David Green and Kathleen (*née* Swann); *m* 1965, Christine Margaret Constance Gibson; one *s* one *d*. *Educ:* Repton Sch.; Barnsley Grammar Sch.; New Coll., Oxford (BA Modern Langs). Swiss Broadcasting Corp., 1964–65; Sheffield Star, 1965–67; Producer, BBC Radio Sheffield, 1967–70; Documentary Producer, BBC Manchester, 1970–77; Editor, File on Four, 1977; Head of Network Radio, Manchester, 1978–86. Chm., Radio Acad., 1990–95. *Recreations:* France, canals, cinema, collecting glass. *Address:* BBC, Broadcasting House, W1A 1AA.

GREEN, Michael Philip; Chairman: Carlton Communications Plc, since 1983 (Chief Executive, 1983–91); Independent Television News Ltd, since 1993; *b* 2 Dec. 1947; *s* of Cyril and Irene Green; *m* 1st, 1972, Hon. Janet Frances (marr. diss. 1989), *d* of Lord Wolfson, *qv*; two *d*; 2nd, 1990, Theresa Buckmaster; two *s*. *Educ:* Haberdashers' Aske's School. Director and Co-Founder, Tangent Industries, 1968. Founder, Tangent Charitable Trust, 1984; Chm., Carlton Television Ltd, 1991–94; Director: Central Independent Television plc, 1991–; GMTV Ltd, 1992–; Reuters Holdings PLC, 1992–. Mem. Council, Royal Holloway, Univ. of London, 1992–. Gov., Theale Green Sch., 1992–. *Recreations:* reading, bridge, television. *Address:* Carlton Communcations Plc, 15 St George Street, W1R 9DE. *T:* 0171–499 8050. *Club:* Portland.

GREEN, Prof. Mino, FIEE; Professor of Electrical Device Science, Electrical Engineering, 1983–92, now Emeritus, Senior Research Fellow, since 1992, Imperial College of Science and Technology; *b* 10 March 1927; *s* of Alexander and Elizabeth Green; *m* 1951, Diana Mary Allen; one *s* one *d*. *Educ:* Dulwich Coll.; University Coll., Durham Univ. (BSc,

PhD, DSc). Group Leader: Solid State Res., Lincoln Laboratory, MIT, 1951–55; Res., Zenith Radio Corp., USA, 1956–60; Associate Dir, Electrochemistry Lab., Univ. of Pennsylvania, 1960–62; Man. Dir, Zenith Radio Research Corp. (UK) Ltd, 1962–72; Lectr, then Reader, Elec. Engrg Dept, Imperial Coll. of Science and Technology, 1972–83. *Publications:* Solid State Surface Science, vols I, II and III (ed), 1969–73; many pubns (and some patents) on various aspects of semiconductor and optical device science. *Recreations:* walking, art appreciation. *Address:* 55 Gerard Road, SW13 9QH. *T:* 0181–748 8689. *Club:* Hurlingham.

GREEN, Dr (Norman) Michael, FRS 1981; affiliated to Department of Mathematical Biology, National Institute for Medical Research, since 1992; *b* 6 April 1926; *s* of Ernest Green and Hilda Margaret Carter; *m* 1953, Iro Paulina Moschouti; two *s* one *d*. *Educ:* Dragon Sch., Oxford; Clifton Coll., Bristol; Magdalen Coll., Oxford (BA; Athletics Blue, Cross Country Blue); UCH Med. Sch., London (PhD). Res. Student, Univ. of Washington, Seattle, 1951–53; Lectr in Biochemistry, Univ. of Sheffield, 1953–55; Res. Fellow and Lectr in Chem. Pathol., St Mary's Hosp. Med. Sch., London, 1956–62; Vis. Scientist, NIH, Maryland, 1962–64; Res. Staff, Divs of Biochem. and Protein Structure, NIMR, 1964–91. *Publications:* research papers on the structure of proteins and of membranes, in scientific jls. *Recreations:* mountain climbing, pyrotechnics. *Address:* 57 Hale Lane, Mill Hill, NW7 3PS.

GREEN, Sir Owen (Whitley), Kt 1984; Chairman, BTR plc, 1984–93 (Managing Director, 1967–86); *b* Stockton-on-Tees, 14 May 1925; *m* 1948, Doreen Margaret Spark; one *s* two *d*. FCA 1950. Served RNVR, 1942–46. With Charles Wakeling & Co., accountants, 1947–56; BTR, 1956; Asst Man. Dir, 1966. Dir, The Spectator, 1988–93. Trustee, Natural History Mus., 1986–. Businessman of the Year, 1982; BIM Gold Medal, 1984; Founding Societies' Centenary Award, ICA, 1985. *Recreation:* golf. *Address:* Edgehill, Succombs Hill, Warlingham, Surrey CR6 9JG.

GREEN, Pauline; Member (Lab) London North, European Parliament, since 1989; Leader of the Group of the Party of European Socialists, since 1994; *b* 8 Dec. 1948; *d* of late Bertram Wiltshire and of Lucy Wiltshire; *m* 1971, Paul Adam Green; one *s* one *d*. *Educ:* John Kelly Secondary Modern Sch. for Girls, Brent; Kilburn Poly.; Open Univ. (BA); London School of Economics (MSc). Sec., 1981, Chair, 1983, Chipping Barnet Labour Party; Leader, European PLP, 1993–94. Contested (Lab) Arkley ward, Barnet Council elecns, 1986. Lobbyist on European Affairs for Co-operative Movement, 1986–89. *Recreations:* music, swimming. *Address:* (office) Broad House, 205 Fore Street, Edmonton, N18 2TZ. *T:* 0181–803 7635.

GREEN, Brig. Percy William Powlett, CBE 1960 (OBE 1956); DSO 1946; *b* 10 Sept. 1912; *er s* of late Brig.-Gen. W. G. K. Green, CB, CMG, DSO, Indian Army; *m* 1943, Phyllis Margery Fitz Gerald May (*d* 1995), *d* of late Lieut-Col A. H. May, OBE; one *s* one *d*. *Educ:* Wellington Coll.; RMC. Commnd Northamptonshire Regt, 1932; Op. NW Frontier, India, 1936–37; BEF 1939–40; Lt-Col Comdg 2nd W Yorks Regt, 1945–46; Burma, 1944–45; Lt-Col Comdg 1 Malay Regt, 1946–47; Comd 4th King's African Rifles, 1954–56; Op. against Mau Mau; Col, Gen. Staff, War Office, 1956–57; Chief of Staff (Brig.) E Africa Comd, 1957–60; DDMI, War Office, 1961–63; Chief of Staff, N Ireland Command, 1963–65; Dep. Comdr, Aldershot District, 1965–67; retired, 1967. ADC to the Queen, 1965–67. Dep. Colonel, Royal Anglian Regt, 1966–76. *Recreations:* field sports. *Address:* Grudds, South Warnborough, Basingstoke, Hants RG25 1RW. *T:* Basingstoke (01256) 862472. *Club:* Army and Navy.

GREEN, Sir Peter (James Frederick), Kt 1982; Chairman, Janson Green Holdings Ltd, 1986–89 (Chairman, Janson Green Ltd, 1966–86); Chairman, Lloyd's, 1980, 1981, 1982, 1983; *b* 28 July 1924; *s* of J. E. Green and M. B. Holford; *m* 1st, 1950, A. P. Ryan (*d* 1985); 2nd, 1986, Jennifer Whitehead. *Educ:* Harrow Sch.; Christ Church, Oxford. Lloyd's: Underwriter, 1947; Mem. Cttee, 1974–77; Dep. Chm., 1979; Gold Medal, 1983. *Recreations:* shooting, fishing, sailing, farming. *Clubs:* City of London, Royal Ocean Racing, Pratt's; Royal Yacht Squadron (Cowes); Cruising of America (New York); Mount Royal (Montreal).

GREEN, Prof. Peter Morris; author and translator since 1953; Professor of Classics, University of Texas at Austin, since 1972 (James R. Dougherty Jr Centennial Professor of Classics, 1982–84 and since 1985); *b* 22 Dec. 1924; *o c* of late Arthur Green, CBE, MC, LLB, and Olive Slaughter; *m* 1st, 1951, Lalage Isobel Pulvertaft (marr. diss.); two *s* one *d*; 2nd, 1975, Carin Margreta, *y d* of late G. N. Christensen, Saratoga, USA. *Educ:* Charterhouse; Trinity Coll., Cambridge. Served in RAFVR, 1943–47: overseas tour in Burma Comd, 1944–46. 1st Cl. Hons, Pts I and II, Classical Tripos, 1949–50; MA and PhD Cantab 1954; Craven Schol. and Student, 1950; Dir of Studies in Classics, 1951–52; Fiction Critic, London Daily Telegraph, 1953–63; Literary Adviser, The Bodley Head, 1957–58; Cons. Editor, Hodder and Stoughton, 1960–63; Television Critic, The Listener, 1961–63; Film Critic, John o'London's, 1961–63; Mem. Book Soc. Cttee, 1959–63. Former Mem. of selection cttees for literary prizes: Heinemann Award, John Llewellyn Rhys, W. H. Smith £1000 Award for Literature. Translator of numerous works from French and Italian, including books by Simone de Beauvoir, Fosco Maraini, Joseph Kessel. FRSL 1956; Mem. Council, Royal Society of Literature, 1958–63 (resigned on emigration). In 1963 resigned all positions and emigrated to Greece as full-time writer (1963–71). Vis. Prof. of Classics: Univ. of Texas, 1971–72; UCLA, 1976; Mellon Prof. of Humanities, Tulane Univ., 1986; Sen. Fellow for independent study and res., National Endowment for the Humanities, 1983–84. *Publications:* The Expanding Eye, 1953; Achilles His Armour, 1955; Cat in Gloves (pseud. Denis Delaney), 1956; The Sword of Pleasure (W. H. Heinemann Award for Literature), 1957; Kenneth Grahame, 1859–1932: A Study of his Life, Work and Times, 1959; Essays in Antiquity, 1960; Habeas Corpus and other stories, 1962; Look at the Romans, 1963; The Laughter of Aphrodite, 1965, repr. 1993; Juvenal: The Sixteen Satires (trans.), 1967; Armada from Athens: The Failure of the Sicilian Expedition, 415–413 BC, 1970; Alexander the Great: a biography, 1970; The Year of Salamis, 480–479 BC, 1971; The Shadow of the Parthenon, 1972; The Parthenon, 1973; A Concise History of Ancient Greece, 1973; Alexander of Macedon 356–323 BC: a historical biography, 1974; Ovid: The Erotic Poems (trans.), 1982; Beyond the Wild Wood: the world of Kenneth Grahame, 1982; Medium and Message Reconsidered: the changing functions of classical translation, 1986; Classical Bearings: interpreting ancient history and culture, 1989; Alexander to Actium: the historical evolution of the Hellenistic Age, 1990; (ed) Hellenistic History and Culture, 1993; Yannis Ritsos: The Fourth Dimension (trans.), 1993; Ovid: The Poems of Exile (trans.), 1994. *Recreations:* travel, swimming, spear-fishing, lawn tennis, table-tennis, squash racquets, amateur archæology, avoiding urban life. *Address:* c/o Department of Classics, University of Texas, Waggener Hall 123, Austin, TX 78712, USA. *T:* (512) 4718502 or 4715742. *Club:* Savile.

GREEN, Robert James; Member (Lib Dem): Berkshire County Council, since 1995; Reading Borough Council, since 1995; *b* 27 Jan. 1937; *er s* of Ronald Percy Green and Doris Rose (*née* Warman); *m* 1960, Jill Marianne Small; one *d* (one *s* decd). *Educ:* Kent College, Canterbury. Executive Officer, Board of Trade, 1957; Asst Principal, 1963, Principal, 1967, Min. of Housing and Local Govt; Secretary, Water Resources Board, 1972–74; Asst Secretary: Dept of the Environment, 1974; Dept of Transport, 1980; Under Sec., 1982; Regl Dir, Northern Reg., 1982–83, and Yorks and Humberside Reg., 1982–86; Dir of Rural Affairs, DoE, 1988–91; Dir, Local Govt, 1991–92; Prin. Estabt and Finance Officer, Office of the Rail Regulator, 1993–94. Non-exec. Dir, Butterley Bricks Ltd, 1988–90. *Recreation:* theatre, including amateur dramatics. *Address:* Runge's Cottage, 11 St Andrews Road, Caversham, Reading RG4 7PH.

GREEN, Maj.-Gen. Robert Leslie Stuart; Chairman, Care for the Mentally Handicapped, since 1991 (Executive Governor, 1980); *b* 1 July 1925; *s* of Leslie Stuart Green and Eliza Dorothea Andrew; *m* 1952, Nancy Isobel Collier; two *d*. *Educ:* Chorlton Sch. 2nd Bn Black Watch, India, 1944–46; 6 Airborne Div., Palestine, 1946; 2 Parachute Bde, UK and Germany, 1946–47; 1st Bn HLI, UK, ME and Cyprus, 1947–56; ptsc 1959; jssc 1962; 1st Bn Royal Highland Fusiliers, UK, Germany and Gibraltar, 1959–69, Comd 1967–69; staff apptmt 1970; Military Dir of Studies, RMCS, 1970–72; Sen. Military Officer, Royal Armament Res. and Develt Estabt, 1973–75; Vice-Pres., Ordnance Bd, 1976–78, Pres., March–June 1978. Col, The Royal Highland Fusiliers, 1979–91. Freeman, City of London, 1983. FBIM. *Recreations:* fishing, music. *Address:* Royal Bank of Scotland, 43 Curzon Street, Mayfair, W1Y 7RF. *Club:* Naval and Military.

GREEN, Sam, CBE 1960; Chairman: Dula (ISMA) Ltd, since 1969; Green & Associates Ltd, since 1970; Spear Bros Ltd, since 1970; Vice Chairman, Royal British Legion Poppy Factory, Richmond (Director since 1964); Director, Royal British Legion Industries, since 1967; *b* Oldham, Lancs, 6 Feb. 1907; *s* of Fred Green; *m* 1942, Dr Lilly (*née* Pollak); one *d*. *Educ:* Manchester Coll. of Technology. Apprentice, Platt Bros, Oldham, 1920–34; Designer and Development Engr, British Northrop Automatic Loom Co., Blackburn, 1934–39 (invented 4-colour loom); Chief Engr, Betts & Co., London, 1939–42; Works Manager, Morphy-Richards Ltd, St Mary Cray, Kent, 1942–44; General Works Manager, Holoplast Ltd, New Hythe, near Maidstone, 1944–47; Industrial Adviser, Industrial and Commercial Finance Corp., London, 1947–52; Managing Dir of Remploy Ltd, 1952–64; Chm. and Man. Dir, Ralli Bros (Industries) Ltd, 1964–69; Chm., Industrial Advisers to the Blind, 1964–74; Director: J. E. Lesser Group Ltd, 1969–74; New Day Holdings Ltd, 1972–74. Chm., Inst. of Patentees and Inventors, 1975 (Vice-Chm., 1961); Vice Pres., Internat. Fed. of Inventors' Assocs, 1984–. FRSA 1962. CEng; FIEE. Gold Medal, World Intellectual Property Orgn, 1984. *Recreations:* reading, gardening, cycling, walking, golf. *Address:* Holly Lodge, 39 Westmoreland Road, Bromley, Kent BR2 0TF. *T:* 0181–460 3306. *Clubs:* Reform, Directors', Pickwick (oldest Bicycle Club).

GREEN, Sir Stephen; *see* Green, Sir E. S. L.

GREEN, Terence Arthur; Director and Deputy Group Chief Executive, National Westminster Bank, 1987–89; *b* 19 May 1934; *m* 1956, Leeta (*née* Beales); two *s* one *d*. *Educ:* South East Essex County Technical College; Harvard Business School (AMP 1980). ACIB. Joined Westminster Bank, 1950; Dep. Gen. Manager, Internat. Banking Div., Nat. Westminster Bank, 1982; Gen. Manager, Business Development Div., 1985. *Recreations:* golf, cricket.

GREEN, Thomas Charles, CB 1971; Chief Charity Commissioner, 1966–75; *b* 13 Oct. 1915; *s* of late Charles Harold Green and late Hilda Emma Green (*née* Thomas); *m* 1945, Beryl Eva Barber, *widow* of Lieut N. Barber; one *d* (and one step *d*). *Educ:* Eltham Coll.; Oriel Coll., Oxford. Entered Home Office, 1938. Served with RAF, 1940–45. Asst Secretary: Home Office, 1950–64; Charity Commn, 1964–65. UK representative on UN Commn on Narcotic Drugs, 1957–64. Nuffield Travelling Fellowship, 1959–60. *Recreations:* gardening, photography. *Address:* Coombe Bungalow, Coombe Lane, Compton Bishop, Somerset BS26 2HE.

GREEN, Rev. Vivian Hubert Howard, DD, FRHistS; Fellow and Tutor in History, 1951–83, Rector, 1983–87, Hon. Fellow, 1987, Lincoln College, Oxford; *b* 18 Nov. 1915; *s* of Hubert James and Edith Eleanor Playle Green; unmarried. *Educ:* Bradfield Coll., Berks; Trinity Hall, Cambridge (Scholar). Goldsmiths' Exhibnr; 1st Cl. Hist. Tripos, Parts I and II; Lightfoot Schol. in Ecclesiastical Hist.; Thirlwall Medal and Prize, 1941; MA 1941; MA Oxon by incorp., 1951; DD Cambridge, 1958; DD Oxon by incorp., 1958. Gladstone Research Studentship, St Deiniol's Library, Hawarden, 1937–38; Fellow of St Augustine's Coll., Canterbury, 1939–48; Chaplain, Exeter Sch. and St Luke's Training Coll., Exeter, 1940–42; Chaplain and Asst Master, Sherborne Sch., Dorset, 1942–51; Lincoln College, Oxford: Chaplain, 1951–69; Sen. Tutor, 1953–62 and 1974–77; Sub-Rector, 1970–83; acting Rector, 1972–73. Deacon, 1939; Priest, 1940. Select Preacher, Oxford, 1959–60, 1992. Vis. Prof. of History, Univ. of S Carolina, 1982. *Publications:* Bishop Reginald Pecock, 1945; The Hanoverians, 1948; From St Augustine to William Temple, 1948; Renaissance and Reformation, 1952; The Later Plantagenets, 1955; Oxford Common Room, 1957; The Young Mr Wesley, 1961; The Swiss Alps, 1961; Martin Luther and the Reformation, 1964; John Wesley, 1964; Religion at Oxford and Cambridge (historical survey), 1964; The Universities, 1969; Medieval Civilization in Western Europe, 1971; A History of Oxford University, 1974; The Commonwealth of Lincoln College 1427–1977, 1979; Love in a Cool Climate: the letters of Mark Pattison and Meta Bradley 1879–1884, 1985; (ed) Memoirs of an Oxford Don: Mark Pattison, 1988; (with William Scoular) A Question of Guilt: the murder of Nancy Eaton, 1988; The Madness of Kings, 1993; contributor to: Dictionary of English Church History (ed Ollard, Crosse and Bond); The Oxford Dictionary of the Christian Church (ed Cross); European Writers, The Middle Ages and Renaissance (ed W. T. H. Jackson and G. Stade), vols I and II, 1983; The History of the University of Oxford, vol. V, The Eighteenth Century (ed L. S. Sutherland and L. G. Mitchell), 1986. *Address:* Lincoln College, Oxford OX1 3DR. *T:* Oxford (01865) 279830; Calendars, Burford, Oxford OX8 4LS. *T:* Burford (0199382) 3214.

GREEN-PRICE, Sir Robert (John), 5th Bt, *cr* 1874; Assistant Professor of English, Chiba University of Commerce, since 1982; *b* 22 Oct. 1940; *o s* of Sir John Green-Price, 4th Bt, and Irene Marion (*d* 1954), *d* of Major Sir (Ernest) Guy Lloyd, 1st Bt, DSO; *S* father, 1964. *Educ:* Shrewsbury. Army Officer, 1961–69; Captain, RCT, retd. ADC to Governor of Bermuda, 1969–72. Lectr in English, Teikyo Univ., 1975–82. Part-time Lecturer: Keio Univ., 1977–; Waseda Univ., 1986–; Guest Lectr, NHK Radio, 1978–83. *Heir:* uncle Powell Norman Dansey Green-Price [*b* 22 July 1926; *m* 1963, Ann Stella, *d* of late Brig. Harold George Howson, CBE, MC, TD; one *s* one *d*]. *Address:* 4–A Shoto Mansions, 5–4–20 Shinden, Ichikawa-shi, Chiba-ken, Japan 272; Villa De Avellanos, Poblacion 1 Currimao, Ilocos Norte, Philippines.

GREENALL, family name of **Baron Daresbury.**

GREENALL, Hon. Peter Gilbert; Managing Director, The Greenalls Group plc, since 1992 (Director, since 1982); *b* 18 July 1953; *e s* and *heir* of 3rd Baron Daresbury, *qv*; *m* 1982, Clare Alison, *d* of Christopher Weatherby; four *s*. *Educ:* Eton; Univ. of Cambridge (MA); London Business Sch. (Sloan Fellowship). Dir, First Leisure PLC; Chm., Aintree Racecourse Co. Ltd. DL Cheshire, 1993. *Address:* Hall Lane Farm, Daresbury, Warrington, Cheshire WA4 4AF. *T:* Warrington (01925) 740212; The Greenalls Group plc,

Wilderspool House, Greenalls Avenue, Warrington, Cheshire WA4 4RH. *T:* Warrington (01925) 651234. *Clubs:* Jockey, MCC; Royal & Ancient Golf (St Andrews).

GREENAWAY, Frank, MA, PhD; CChem, FRSC, FSA, FMA; Research Fellow, The Science Museum, 1980–91 (Hon. Fellow, 1992); Reader in the History of Science, Davy-Faraday Research Laboratory of the Royal Institution, 1970–85; *b* 9 July 1917; 3rd *s* of late Henry James Greenaway; *m* 1942, Margaret (Miranda), 2nd *d* of late R. G. Heegaard Warner and *widow* of John Raymond Brumfit; one *s* three *d*, and one step *s*. *Educ:* Cardiff High Sch.; Jesus Coll., Oxford (Meyricke Exhibitioner); University Coll. London. MA Oxon, PhD London. Served War of 1939–45, RAOC, as Inspecting Ordnance Officer, 1940–41 (invalided). Science Master: Bournemouth Sch., 1941–42; Epsom Gram. Sch., 1942–43; Passport Control, 1943–44; Research Labs, Kodak Ltd, 1944–49; Asst Keeper, Science Museum, 1949; Dep. Keeper, 1959; Keeper, Dept of Chemistry, 1967–80. Regents' Fellow, Smithsonian Instn, Washington, DC, 1985. Member Council: Brit. Soc. for the Hist. of Science, 1958–68, 1974–78 (Vice-Pres. 1962–65); Museums Assoc., 1961–70, 1973–76 (Hon. Editor, 1965–70); Royal Instn, 1990–93 (Vice-Pres., 1992–93; Chm., Cttee of Visitors, 1964–65); Mem. Brit. Nat. Cttee of Internat. Council of Museums, 1956–58, 1962–71, 1977–83; Membre Correspondant de l'Académie Internationale d'Histoire des Sciences, 1963. Member: Council, Soc. for History of Alchemy and Chemistry, 1967– (Sec., 1967–74); History of Medicine Adv. Panel, The Wellcome Trust, 1968–74; Higher Educn Adv. Cttee, The Open Univ., 1970–73; British Nat. Cttee for Hist. of Sci., 1972–81; British Nat. Cttee, ICSU, 1972–77; Council, Internat. Union of the Hist. and Philos. of Science, 1972–81 (Sec., 1972–77); Council of Management, Royal Philharmonic Soc., 1980–84, 1986–89; Pres., Commonwealth Assoc. of Museums, 1979–83. Boerhaave Medal, Leyden Univ., 1968. *Publications:* Science Museums in Developing Countries, 1962; John Dalton and the Atom, 1966; (ed) Lavoisier's Essays Physical and Chemical, 1971; (ed) Science in the Early Roman Empire, 1986; Editor, Royal Institution Archives, 1971–; Official Publications of the Science Museum; Papers on history of chemistry and on museology. *Recreations:* music, travel. *Address:* 135 London Road, Ewell, Epsom, Surrey KT17 2BS. *T:* 0181–393 1330. *Club:* Athenæum.

See also C. J. Brumfit.

GREENAWAY, Sir John (Michael Burdick), 3rd Bt *cr* 1933, of Coombe, Surrey; farmer, since 1980; *b* 9 Aug. 1944; *o s* of Sir Derek Burdick Greenaway, 2nd Bt, CBE, and of Sheila Beatrice Greenaway (*née* Lockett); *S* father, 1994; *m* 1982, Susan Margaret (*née* Birch); one *s* one *d*. *Educ:* Harrow Sch.; Grenoble Univ. The Life Guards, 1965–70. Dir, Daniel Greenaway & Sons Ltd, 1970–79. *Recreations:* ski-ing, tennis, riding. *Heir:* *s* Thomas Edward Burdick Greenaway, *b* 3 April 1985. *Address:* Lois Weedon House, Weedon Lois, Towcester, Northants NN12 8PJ. *T:* Blakesley (01327) 860472.

GREENAWAY, Peter; film director, painter and writer; *b* April 1942; *m*; two *d*. *Educ:* Forest Sch.; Walthamstow Coll. of Art. Film Editor, Central Office of Information, 1965–76. Maker of short films, 1966–, of feature length films, 1978–. Exhibitions: Lord's Gall., 1964; The Physical Self, Rotterdam, 1991; 100 Objects to Represent the World, Acad. of Fine Arts, Vienna, 1992; Flying Out of this World, Louvre, 1992; Watching Water, Venice, 1993; The Audience of Macon, Cardiff, 1993; *one-man shows:* Canterbury, 1989; Carcassone, Paris, 1989; NY, Melbourne, Liège, Tokyo, Fukoa, Munich, Copenhagen, Oddense, Brussels, 1990; Brentford, Dublin, 1991; Bremen, NY, 1992. *Films:* (writer and director): Train, 1966; Tree, 1966; Five Postcards from Capital Cities, 1967; Revolution, 1967; Intervals, 1969; Erosion, 1971; H is for House, 1973; Windows, 1975; Water Wrackets, 1975; Goole by Numbers, 1976; Dear Phone, 1977; 1–1Co, 1978; A Walk Through H, 1978; Vertical Features Remake, 1978; The Falls, 1980 (Special Award, BFI); Act of God, 1981 (Best short film, Melbourne Film Fest.); Zandra Rhodes, 1981; The Draughtsman's Contract, 1982; Four American Composers, 1983; Making a Splash, 1984; (jtly) A TV Dante-Canto V, 1984; Inside Rooms – The Bathroom, 1985; A Zed and Two Noughts, 1985; The Belly of an Architect, 1986; Fear of Drowning, 1988; Drowning by Numbers, 1988 (Prize for Best Artistic Contribution, Cannes Film Fest.); The Cook, the Thief, his Wife and her Lover, 1989; Prospero's Books, 1990; M is for Man, Music, Mozart, 1991; Rosa, 1992; Darwin, 1992; The Baby of Macon, 1993, The Stairs, Geneva, 1994; *opera:* Rosa: a Horse Drama, 1994. Chevalier de l'Ordre des Arts et des Lettres (France), 1990. *Publications:* Prospero's Subjects, 1992; Watching Water, 1993; The Falls, 1993; filmscripts and exhibn catalogues. *Address:* c/o Allarts Ltd, 387b King Street, W6 9NJ.

GREENBAUM, Prof. Sidney; Director of the Survey of English Usage, since 1983, and Visiting Professor, since 1991, University College London; *b* 31 Dec. 1929; *s* of Lewis and Nelly Greenbaum. *Educ:* Univ. of London (BA Hons and MA Hebrew and Aramaic; Postgrad. Cert. in Educn; BA Hons English; PhD Mod. English Grammar). Teacher at London primary sch., 1954–57; Head of English Dept at London grammar sch., 1957–64; Research asst, Survey of English Usage, UCL, 1965–68; Vis. Asst Prof., English Dept, Univ. of Oregon, 1968–69; Associate Prof., English Dept, Univ. of Wisconsin-Milwaukee, 1969–72; Vis. Prof., English Dept, Hebrew Univ., Jerusalem, 1972–73; Prof., English Dept, Univ. of Wisconsin-Milwaukee, 1972–83; Quain Prof. of English Lang. and Lit., 1983–90, Dean of the Faculty of Arts, 1988–90, UCL; Dean, Faculty of Arts, London University, 1986–88. Hon. DH Wisconsin-Milwaukee, 1989. Editor of series: (with C. Cooper) Written Communication Annual, 1984–91; Studies in English Language, 1987–. *Publications:* Studies in English Adverbial Usage, 1969; Verb-Intensifier Collocations in English: an experimental approach, 1970; (with R. Quirk) Elicitation Experiments in English: linguistic studies in use and attitude, 1970; (jtly) A Grammar of Contemporary English, 1972; (with R. Quirk) A University Grammar of English (Amer. edn A Concise Grammar of Contemporary English), 1973; Acceptability in Language, 1977; (jtly) Studies in English Linguistics: for Randolph Quirk, 1980; The English Language Today, 1985; (jtly) A Comprehensive Grammar of the English Language, 1985; (with C. Cooper) Studying Writing: linguistic approaches, 1986; (with J. Whitcut) rev. edn of Gower's Complete Plain Words, 1986; Good English and the Grammarian, 1988; (with J. Whitcut) Longman Guide to English Usage, 1988; A College Grammar of English, 1989; (with R. Quirk) A Student's Grammar of the English Language, 1990; An Introduction to English Grammar, 1991; (associate editor and contrib.) The Oxford Companion to the English Language, 1992; The Oxford English Grammar, 1996; numerous articles in learned jls. *Address:* Department of English, University College London, Gower Street, WC1E 6BT. *T:* 0171–387 7050. *Club:* Reform.

GREENBERG, Joanna Elishever Gabrielle; QC 1994; a Recorder, since 1995; *b* 28 Nov. 1950; *d* of Ivan Marion Greenberg and Doris Rosalie Greenberg (*née* Sandground). *Educ:* Brondesbury and Kilburn High Sch. for Girls; King's Coll. London (LLB, AKC). Called to the Bar, Gray's Inn, 1972. An Asst Recorder, 1992–95. *Address:* 3 Temple Gardens, Temple, EC4Y 9AU. *T:* 0171–583 1155.

GREENBOROUGH, Sir John Hedley, KBE 1979 (CBE 1975); Chairman, Newarthill, 1980–93; Deputy Chairman: Bowater Industries (formerly Bowater Corporation), 1984–87 (Director, since 1979); Lloyds Bank, 1985–92 (Director, since 1980); *b* 7 July 1922; *s* of William Greenborough and Elizabeth Marie Greenborough (*née* Wilson); *m* 1951, Gerta Ebel; one step *s*. *Educ:* Wandsworth School. War service: Pilot, RAF, later Fleet Air Arm, 1942–45; graduated Pensacola; Naval Aviator, USN, 1944. Joined Asiatic Petroleum Co., London, 1939; served with Shell Oil, Calif, 1946–47; Shell Brazil Ltd, 1948–57; Commercial Dir, later Exec. Vice-Pres., Shell Argentina Ltd, Buenos Aires, 1960–66; Area Coordinator, East and Australasia, Shell Internat., London, 1967–68; Man. Dir (Marketing), Shell-Mex and BP Ltd, 1969–71, Man. Dir and Chief Exec., 1971–75; Chm., UK Oil Pipelines Ltd, 1971–77; Dep. Chm., 1976–80, Man. Dir, 1976–78, Shell UK Ltd. Director: Laporte Industries (Hldgs), 1983–86; Hogg Robinson, subseq. Hogg Gp, 1980–91. President of Confederation of British Industry, 1978–80 (Mem. Council, 1971–). Chairman: UK Oil Ind. Emergency Cttee, 1971–80; UK Petroleum Ind. Adv. Cttee, 1971–77; Member: British Productivity Council, 1969–72; Clean Air Council, 1971–75; Bd of Fellows, BIM, 1973–78 (Chm., 1976–78); NEDC, 1977–80; Vice-Chairman: British Chamber of Commerce in Argentina, 1962–66; British Road Fedn, 1969–75. President: Nat. Soc. for Clean Air, 1973–75; Incorporated Soc. of British Advertisers (ISBA), 1976–78; Inst. of Petroleum, 1976–78; Nat. Council for Voluntary Orgns, 1980–86; Strategic Planning Soc., 1986–. Chm., Review Body for Nursing and Midwifery Staff and Professions Allied to Medicine, 1983–86. Fellow, Inst. Petroleum; CBIM; FCIM (Vice-Pres., 1982–91). Mem., Management Bd, Adam Smith Inst., 1989–. Governor, Ashridge Management Coll., 1972– (Chm., 1977–92; Pres., 1992–); Chm. Governing Council, UMDS of Guy's and St Thomas' Hosps, 1982–89. Liveryman, Co. of Distillers, 1975–. Freeman, City of London. Hon. LLD Birmingham, 1983. *Recreations:* golf, travel, music. *Clubs:* Carlton, MCC; Royal and Ancient Golf; Royal Wimbledon Golf.

GREENBURY, Sir Richard, Kt 1992; Chairman, since 1991, and Chief Executive, since 1988, Marks & Spencer plc; *b* 31 July 1936; *s* of Richard Oswald Greenbury and Dorothy (*née* Lewis); *m* 1st, 1959, Sian Eames Hughes; two *s* two *d*; 2nd, 1985, Gabrielle Mary McManus. *Educ:* Ealing County Grammar Sch. Joined Marks & Spencer Ltd as Jun. Management Trainee, 1952; Alternate Dir, 1970; Full Dir, 1972; Jt Man. Dir, 1978–85; Chief Operating Officer, 1986–88. Non-exec. Director: British Gas, 1976–87; MB Group (formerly Metal Box), 1985–89; ICI, 1992–; Lloyds Bank, 1992–; Zeneca, 1993–. *Recreations:* tennis (Member Mddx County Team for 12 years, has also played for International Tennis Club of GB), reading, music. *Address:* c/o 57 Baker Street, W1A 1DN. *Clubs:* All England Lawn Tennis and Croquet, International Tennis Club of GB.

GREENE, family name of **Baron Greene of Harrow Weald.**

GREENE OF HARROW WEALD, Baron *cr* 1974 (Life Peer), of Harrow; **Sidney Francis Greene,** Kt 1970; CBE 1966; Director: Trades Union Unit Trust, 1970–80; RTZ Corporation, 1975–80; Times Newspapers Holdings Ltd, 1980–82 (Times Newspapers Ltd, 1975–80); *b* 12 Feb. 1910; *s* of Frank James Greene and Alice (*née* Kerrod); *m* 1936, Masel Elizabeth Carter; three *d*. *Educ:* elementary. Joined Railway Service, 1924; appointed Union Organiser, 1944, Asst Gen. Sec., 1954, Gen. Sec., Nat. Union of Railwaymen, 1957–75. Mem., TUC Gen. Council, 1957–75 (Chm., 1969–70); Chm., TUC Economic Cttee, 1968–75. Member: National Economic Development Council, 1962–75; Advisory Council, ECGD, 1967–70; part-time Member: Southern Electricity Board, 1964–77; Nat. Freight Corp., 1973–77; a Dir, Bank of England, 1970–78. JP London, 1941–65. FCIT. *Recreations:* reading, gardening. *Address:* 26 Kynaston Wood, Boxtree Road, Harrow Weald, Mddx HA3 6UA.

GREENE, Graham Carleton, CBE 1986; publisher; Chairman, Museums and Galleries Commission, since 1991; *b* 10 June 1936; *s* of Sir Hugh Carleton Greene, KCMG, OBE and Helga Mary Connolly; *m* 1957, Judith Margaret (marr. diss.), *d* of Rt Hon. Lord Gordon-Walker, CH, PC; *m* 1976, Sally Georgina Horton, *d* of Sidney Wilfred Eaton; one *s*, and one step *s* one step *d*. *Educ:* Eton; University Coll., Oxford (MA). Merchant Banking, Dublin, New York and London, 1957–58; Secker & Warburg Ltd, 1958–62; Jonathan Cape, 1962–90 (Man. Dir, 1966–88). Director: Chatto, Virago, Bodley Head & Jonathan Cape Ltd, 1969–88 (Chm., 1970–88); Jackdaw Publications Ltd (Chm. 1964–88); Cape Goliard Press Ltd, 1967–88; Guinness Mahon Holdings Ltd, 1968–79; Australasian Publishing Co. Pty Ltd, 1969–88 (Chm., 1978–88); Sprint Productions Ltd, 1971–80; Book Reps (New Zealand) Ltd, 1971–88 (Chm., 1984–88); CVBC Services Ltd (Chm. 1972–88); Guinness Peat Group PLC, 1973–87; Grantham Book Storage Ltd (Chm. 1974–88); Triad Paperbacks Ltd, 1975–88; Chatto, Virago, Bodley Head & Jonathan Cape Australia Pty Ltd (Chm., 1977–88); Greene, King PLC, 1979–; Statesman & Nation Publishing Co. Ltd, 1980–85 (Chm., 1981–85); Statesman Publishing Co. Ltd, 1980–85 (Chm., 1981–85); Nation Pty Co. Ltd (Chm., 1981–87); New Society Ltd (Chm., 1984–87); Random House Inc., 1987–88; Random House UK Ltd, 1988–90; Chm., British Museum Co. (formerly British Museum Publications) Ltd, 1988–; Merlin Internat. Green, subseq. Jupiter Internat. Green Investment Trust plc, 1989–; Henry Sotheran Ltd, 1990–; Ed Victor Ltd, 1991–; Rosemary Sandberg Ltd, 1991–; Libra KFT (Budapest), 1991–. Pres., Publishers Assoc., 1977–79 (Mem. Council, 1969–88); Member: Book Develt Council, 1970–79 (Dep. Chm., 1972–73); Internat. Cttee, Internat. Publishers Assoc., 1977–88 (Exec. Cttee, 1981–88); Groupe des Editeurs de Livres de la CEE, (Fedn of European Publishers), 1977–86 (Pres., 1984–86); Arts Council Working Party Sub-Cttee on Public Lending Right, 1970; Paymaster General's Working Party on Public Lending Right, 1970–72; Board, British Council, 1977–88; Chm., Nat. Book League, 1974–76 (Dep. Chm., 1971–74); Mem. Gen. Cttee, Royal Literary Fund, 1975. Chm., Friends of Musica nel Chiostro, 1993–; Member: Garsington Opera Adv. Cttee, 1990–; Adv. Bd, Mus. of Modern Art, Oxford, 1992–. Trustee: British Museum, 1978–; George Bernard Shaw Estate, 1986–; Han Suyin Fund for Scientific Exchange between China and the West, 1989–; Open Coll. of the Arts, 1990–; Chm., BM Develt Trust, 1986–93 (Vice Chm., 1993–); Pres., BM Foundn Inc., 1989–90; Dir, American Friends of BM, 1990–. Chm., GB-China Centre, 1986–. Freeman, City of London, 1960; Liveryman, Fishmongers' Co., 1960–. Chevalier de l'Ordre des Arts et des Lettres, France, 1985. *Address:* 6 Bayley Street, Bedford Square, WC1B 3HB. *T:* 0171–304 4101. *Clubs:* Garrick, Groucho.

GREENE, Jenny, (Mrs Michael Boys-Greene); Editor, Country Life, 1986–93, retired; *b* 9 Feb. 1937; *d* of James Wilson Greene and Mary Emily Greene; *m* 1971, John Gilbert (marr. diss. 1987); *m* 1994, Michael Boys-Greene. *Educ:* Rochelle Sch., Cork; Trinity Coll., Dublin; Univ. of Montpellier, France. Researcher, Campbell-Johnson Ltd, 1963–64; Account-Exec., Central News, 1964–65; Account-Exec., Pemberton Advertising, 1965–66; Publicity Exec., Revlon, 1966–71; Beauty Editor, Woman's Own, 1971–75; Features Writer and Theatre Critic, Manchester Evening News, 1975–77; Asst Editor, Woman's Own, 1977–78; Editor: Homes and Gardens, 1978–86; A La Carte, 1984–85; food columnist, Today, 1985–87. *Recreations:* gardening, cooking. *Address:* En Chau, 71520 Trivy, France.

GREENE, Sir (John) Brian M.; *see* Massy-Greene.

GREENER, Anthony Armitage, FCMA; Chief Executive, since 1992, Chairman, since 1993, Guinness PLC (Joint Managing Director, 1989–91); *b* 26 May 1940; *s* of William and Diana Marianne Greener; *m* 1974, Min Ogilvie; one *s* one *d*. *Educ:* Marlborough

Coll. Marketing Manager, Thames Board Mills, 1969; Retail Controller 1972, Dir 1974, Alfred Dunhill Ltd; Man. Dir, Alfred Dunhill Ltd, subseq. Dunhill Holdings plc, 1975; Man. Dir, United Distillers, 1987–92; Director: Guinness PLC, 1986–; Louis Vuitton Moet Hennessy, 1989–; Reed International, 1990–; Reed Elsevier, 1993–. *Recreations:* ski-ing, sailing. *Address:* Guinness, 39 Portman Square, W1H 0EE. *T:* 0171–486 0288. *Clubs:* Royal Ocean Racing; Royal Yacht Squadron (Cowes).

GREENFIELD, Prof. (Archibald) David (Mant), CBE 1977; FRCP; Foundation Dean of the Medical School, 1966–81 and Professor of Physiology, 1966–82 in the University of Nottingham; now Professor Emeritus; *b* 31 May 1917; *s* of late A. W. M. Greenfield, MA, and Winifred (*née* Peck), Parkstone, Dorset; *m* 1943, Margaret (*née* Duane); one *s* one *d. Educ:* Poole Grammar Sch.; St Mary's Hospital Medical Sch. BSc London, 1st class hons Physiology, 1937; MB, BS, 1940, MSc 1947, DSc 1953, London; FRCP, 1973. Dunville Prof. of Physiology in the Queen's Univ. of Belfast, 1948–64; Prof. of Physiology in the Univ. of London, at St Mary's Hosp. Med. Sch., 1964–67. WHO Visiting Prof., India, 1960; Visiting Prof., Univ. of California, San Francisco Medical Centre, 1962–63. Sometime Examr, Oxford, Cambridge and 21 other Univs, RCS and RCSI; Chm., Special Trustees, Nottingham Univ. Hosps, 1984–90. Member: Physiol. Systems Bd, MRC, 1976–77; UGC, 1977–82 (Chm. Med. and Dental Sub-Cttees, Assessor to MRC); UPGC, Hong Kong, 1984–89 (Mem. 1981–89 and Chm. 1985–89, Med. Sub-Cttee); GMC and GMC Educn Cttee, 1979–82; Med. Acad. Adv. Cttee, Chinese Univ., Hong Kong, 1976–80; Foundn Cttee, Sultan Qaboos Univ., Oman, 1981–86; Councils for Postgrad. Med. Educn, for England and Wales, and Scottish Council, 1977–82; DHSS Adv. Cttee on Artificial Limbs, 1971–75; DHSS Med. Manpower and Educn Liaison Cttee, 1974–78; DHSS Academic Forum, 1980–82; Sheffield RHB, 1968–74; Nottingham Univ. HMC, 1969–74; Notts AHA(T), 1974–79. Pres., Sect. of Biomed. Scis, British Assoc. for Advancement of Sci., 1972; Mem., Biochemical and Medical Research Societies. Hon. Mem., Physiological Soc., 1987. Chm., Editorial Bd, Monographs of the Physiological Soc., 1975–79; Member, Editorial Board: Amer. Heart Jl, 1959–66; Clinical Science, 1960–65; Cardiovascular Research, 1966–79; Circulation Res., 1967–73. OStJ 1978. Hon. LLD Nottingham, 1977; Hon DSc QUB, 1978. Order of Sultan Qaboos of Oman, 2nd Class, 1986. *Publications:* papers on control of circulation of the blood, mainly in Lancet, Journal of Physiology, Clinical Science, and Journal of Applied Physiology. *Recreations:* sketching, bird watching, travel. *Address:* 25 Sutton Passeys Crescent, Nottingham NG8 1BX. *T:* Nottingham (0115) 978 2424.

GREENFIELD, Edward Harry, OBE 1994; Chief Music Critic, The Guardian, 1977–93; *b* 30 July 1928; *s* of Percy Greenfield and Mabel (*née* Hall). *Educ:* Westcliff High Sch.; Trinity Hall, Univ. of Cambridge (MA). Joined staff of Manchester Guardian, 1953: Record Critic, 1955; Music Critic, 1964; succeeded Sir Neville Cardus as Chief Music Critic, 1977. Broadcaster on music and records for BBC radio, 1957–. Mem., critics' panel, Gramophone, 1960–. Hon. GSM 1991. Goldener Verdienstzeichen, Salzburg, 1981. *Publications:* Puccini: keeper of the seal, 1958; monographs on Joan Sutherland, 1972, and André Previn, 1973; (with Robert Layton, Ivan March and initially Denis Stevens) Stereo Record Guide, 9 vols, 1960–74; Penguin Stereo Record Guide, 5th edn 1986; (jtly) Penguin Guide to Compact Discs, Cassettes and LPs, 1986, 4th edn as Penguin Guide to Compact Discs, 1992, 5th edn 1994; Penguin Guide to Opera on Compact Discs, 1993. *Recreations:* work, living in Spitalfields. *Address:* 16 Folgate Street, E1 6BX. *T:* 0171–377 7555. *Club:* Critics' Circle.

GREENFIELD, Howard; *see* Greenfield, R. H.

GREENFIELD, Dr Peter Rex; Senior Principal Medical Officer, Department of Health (formerly of Health and Social Security), 1983–91, retired; *b* 1 Dec. 1931; *s* of late Rex Youhill Greenfield and Elsie Mary Greenfield (*née* Douthwaite); *m* 1954, Faith Stella, *d* of George and Stella Gigg; eight *s* two *d. Educ:* Cheltenham College; Pembroke College, Cambridge (BA 1954; MB, BChir 1957; MA 1985); St George's Hosp. Med. Sch., London. DObst RCOG 1960. 2nd Lieut, R Signals, 1950–51; House appts, St George's Hosp., 1958; Gen. Med. Pract., Robertsbridge, Sussex, 1959–69; MO, Vinehall Sch., Robertsbridge, 1964–69; MO, Battle Hosp., 1964–69; joined DHSS, 1969; Chief Med. Advr (Social Security), 1983–86. Mem., Jt Formulary Cttee, British Nat. Formulary, 1978–82; Chm., Informal Working Gp on Effective Prescribing, 1981–82; Chm. of Trustees, Chaseley Home for Disabled Ex-Servicemen, Eastbourne, 1995– (Trustee, 1983–); First Aid at Work Examr, St John Ambulance, 1965–. QHP 1987–90. Hon. Mem., BPA, 1991. *Publications:* contribs to med. jls on geriatric day care, hypothermia and DHSS Regional Med. Service. *Recreations:* golf, swimming, walking, music, pinball. *Address:* Lorne House, Robertsbridge, East Sussex TN32 5DW. *T:* Robertsbridge (01580) 880209.

GREENFIELD, (Robert) Howard, FCA; CIGasE; Project Director, Regional Organisation Review, British Gas plc, 1990, retired; *b* 4 Feb. 1927; *s* of James Oswald Greenfield and Doris Burt Greenfield; *m* 1951, Joyce Hedley Wells; one *s* one *d. Educ:* Rutherford Coll., Newcastle upon Tyne. FCA 1953; CIGasE 1982. Northern Gas Board: Chief Accountancy Asst, 1956; Dep. Divl Manager, Tees Area, 1961; Divl Manager, Cumberland Div., 1963; Regional Service Manager, 1968; Northern Gas: Dir of Customer Service, 1974; Dir of Marketing, 1976; Dep. Chm., 1977; Chm., N Eastern Reg., 1982–85; Regl Chm., British Gas, N Western, 1985–89. OStJ 1988. *Recreations:* salmon fishing, photography. *Address:* Manor Top, Chestnut Hill, Keswick, Cumbria CA12 4LT.

GREENGROSS, Sir Alan (David), Kt 1986; DL; Managing Director, Indusmond (Diamond Tools) Ltd; Director, Blazy & Clement Ltd and associated companies; *b* 1929; *m* (*see* Sally Greengross); one *s* three *d. Educ:* University Coll. Sch.; Trinity Coll., Cambridge (Sen. Schol.; MA). Formerly Member Council, London Borough of Camden (past Alderman). Dep. Traffic Comr, 1968–70. GLC: Member (C), 1977–84; Leader, Planning and Communications Policy, 1979–81; Leader of the Opposition, 1983–84. Director: Port of London Authority, 1979–83; London First Centre; Mem., London Regl Passenger Cttee, 1988–. Chm., Bloomsbury and Islington HA, 1990–93. Vis Prof., City of London Polytechnic, 1988–. Dir, The Roundhouse Black Arts Centre, 1988–89. Chairman: Steering Gp, Inst. for Metropolitan Studies, 1989–; Bartlett Sch. of the Built Envmt, UCL, 1993–. Member, Governing Council: UCS, 1987–; UCL, 1991–. DL Greater London, 1986. *Address:* 9 Dawson Place, W2 4TD. *Club:* Hurlingham.

GREENGROSS, Sally, (Lady Greengross), OBE 1993; Director General (formerly Director), Age Concern England, since 1987; Vice-President (Europe), International Federation on Ageing, since 1987 (Secretary General, 1982–87); Secretary General, Eurolink Age, since 1989; *b* 29 June 1935; *m* Sir Alan Greengross, *qv*; one *s* three *d. Educ:* Brighton and Hove High Sch.; LSE. Formerly linguist, executive in industry, lectr and researcher; Asst Dir, 1977–82, Dep. Dir, 1982–87, Age Concern England. Jt Chm. Bd, Age Concern Inst. of Gerontology, KCL, 1987–; Co-ordinator, Prog. for Elderly People within Second EEC Prog. to Combat Poverty, 1985–89; Vice Pres., Res. Inst. for Care of Elderly, 1987–; Member: Standing Adv. Cttee on Transport for Disabled and Elderly People, 1986–88; Adv. Cttee, Carnegie Inquiry into Third Age, 1992–93; Adv. Cttee on European Year of Older People, 1992–93; Adv. Council of European Movement, 1992–; Adv. Panel, Centre for Voluntary Orgns, LSE, 1991–; Adv. Cttee to the Sec. of State, Dept of Employment, on Older Workers, 1993–; Adv. Gp to Sec. of State, DoH, on Health of the Nation, 1991–; Bd, World Orgn for Care in Home and Hospice, 1993–. Pres., Action on Elder Abuse. Independent Member: UN Network on Ageing, 1983–; WHO Network on Ageing, 1983–. Former Member: Inner London Juvenile Court Panel; Management Bd, Hanover Housing Gp. Trustee: British Assoc. of Domiciliary Care Officers, 1989–; Telethon, 1992–; Patron, Home Concern, 1993–. Consultant, Jl of Educnl Gerontology, 1987–; Editl Advr, Home Care, 1993–. FRSH 1994. Hon. DLitt Ulster, 1994. UK Woman of Europe Award, EC, 1990. *Publications:* (ed) Ageing: an adventure in living, 1985; (ed) The Law and Vulnerable Elderly People, 1986; (jtly) Living, Loving and Ageing, 1989; and others on ageing issues and social policy. *Recreations:* countryside, music. *Address:* 9 Dawson Place, W2 4TD. *T:* 0171–229 1939. *Clubs:* Reform, Hurlingham.

GREENHALGH, Colin Ayton, MA; Principal, Hills Road Sixth Form College, Cambridge, since 1984; *b* 11 Aug. 1941; *s* of Robert Ayton Greenhalgh and Ethel Mary Henderson (*née* Cattermole); *m* 1966, Vivienne Christine Grocock; one *s* two *d. Educ:* Gateway Sch., Leicester; St John's Coll., Cambridge (MA); Univ. of Nottingham (PGCE). Teacher of Hist., Bradford Grammar Sch., 1964–70; Hd of Hist., Hd of Upper Sch. and Dep. Hd, Bulmershe Sch., Reading, 1970–76; Dep. Hd and Second Master, St Bartholomew's Sch., Newbury, 1976–84. Member: Cambs LEA Inspectorate, 1991–92; Eastern Regl Cttee, FEFC, 1993–. Cambridgeshire Association of Secondary Heads: Sec., 1988–89; Chm., 1989–90. Hon. Sen. Mem., Wolfson Coll., Cambridge, 1990–. Sec., Johnian Soc., St John's Coll., Cambridge, 1992–. *Recreations:* churches and country houses, cinema, collecting books, sport, travel. *Address:* Hills Road Sixth Form College, Cambridge CB2 2PE. *T:* Cambridge (01223) 247251. *Clubs:* MCC; Hawks (Cambridge); Cambridge University Cricket, Leicestershire County Cricket.

GREENHALGH, Jack; Vice-Chairman, Cavenham Ltd, 1974–81; retired; *b* 25 July 1926; *s* of Herbert Greenhalgh and Alice May (*née* Clayton); *m* 1951, Kathleen Mary Hammond (*d* 1983); two *s* two *d. Educ:* Manchester Grammar Sch.; Trinity Coll., Cambridge (MA Hons). FIMgt. Marketing Dept, Procter & Gamble Ltd, Newcastle upon Tyne, 1950–59; Marketing Dir, Eskimo Foods Ltd, Cleethorpes, 1959–64; Dir of Continental Ops, Compton Advertising Inc., NY, 1964–65; Cavenham Ltd, 1965–81: Man. Dir, 1968–79. *Recreations:* golf, sailing.

GREENHALGH, Prof. Roger Malcolm, FRCS; Professor of Surgery, Chairman, Department of Surgery, and Dean, Charing Cross and Westminster Medical School; Hon. Consultant Surgeon, Charing Cross Hospital, since 1976; Chairman, Directorate of Surgery, Hammersmith Hospitals NHS Trust; *b* 6 Feb. 1941; *s* of John Greenhalgh and Phyllis Poynton; *m* 1964, Karin Maria Gross; one *s* one *d. Educ:* Clare Coll., Cambridge; St Thomas' Hosp., London. BA 1963, BChir 1966, MB, MA 1967, MChir 1974, MD 1983 (Cantab); FRCS 1971. Ho. Surg., 1967, Casualty Officer, 1968, St Thomas' Hosp.; Sen. Ho. Officer, Hammersmith Hosp., 1969; Registrar in Surgery, Essex County Hosp., Colchester, 1970–72; Lectr and Sen. Registrar in Surgery, St Bartholomew's Hosp., 1972–76; Sen. Lectr in Surgery, Charing Cross Hosp., 1976–81; Head of Dept of Surgery, 1981, Prof. of Surgery, 1982–, Chm. of Dept of Surgery, 1989–, Dean, 1993–, Charing Cross Hosp. Med. Sch., later Charing Cross and Westminster Med. Sch. Sometime examiner, Univs of Cambridge, London, Bristol, Leicester, UCD, Southampton, Birmingham, Hong Kong. Chairman: Liaison Cttee, Bioengrg Centre, Roehampton, London, 1985–88; Riverside Med. Council, 1992–93; Member: Ind. Scientific Enquiry into Smoking and Health, 1979–. Vice-Pres., Section of Surgery, RSM, 1986–89; Sec. Gen. and Chm. Exec. Cttee, Assoc. of Internat. Vascular Surgeons, 1982–; Mem. Council: European Soc. for Vascular Surgery, 1987–93; Assoc. of Surgeons of GB and Ireland, 1993–; Corresponding Mem., Soc. for Vascular Surgery, 1991; Hon. Member: Canadian Vascular Soc., 1991; Polish Surgical Soc., 1991; German Vascular Soc., 1992; Hellenic Surgical Soc., 1992. Moynihan Fellow of Assoc. of Surgeons, 1974; Hunterian Prof., RCS, 1980. Chm. Editl Bd, European Jl of Vascular Surgery, 1987–93. *Publications:* Progress in Stroke Research, 1, 1979; Smoking and Arterial Disease, 1981; Hormones and Vascular Disease, 1981; Femoro-distal bypass, 1981; Extra-Anatomic and Secondary Arterial Reconstruction, 1982; Progress in Stroke Research, 2, 1983; Vascular Surgical Techniques, 1984, 2nd edn 1989, 3rd edn as Vascular and Endovascular Surgical Techniques, 1994; Diagnostic Techniques and Assessment Procedures in Vascular Surgery, 1985; Vascular Surgery: issues in current practice, 1986; Indications in Vascular Surgery, 1988; Limb Salvage and Amputations for Vascular Disease, 1988; The Cause and Management of Aneurysms, 1990; The Maintenance of Arterial Reconstruction, 1991; Vascular Surgical Emergencies, 1992; Surgery for Stroke, 1993; Vascular Imaging for Surgeons, 1995. *Recreations:* tennis, skiing, swimming, music. *Address:* 271 Sheen Lane, East Sheen, SW14 8RN. *T:* 0181–878 1110. *Club:* Athenæum.

GREENHILL, family name of **Barons Greenhill** and **Greenhill of Harrow.**

GREENHILL, 3rd Baron *cr* 1950, of Townhead; **Malcolm Greenhill;** retired from Ministry of Defence; *b* 5 May 1924; *s* of 1st Baron Greenhill, OBE and Ida (*d* 1985), *d* of late Mark Goodman; *S* brother, 1989. *Educ:* Kelvinside Acad., Glasgow; Glasgow Univ. (BSc). CPA. Ministries of Aircraft Production and Supply, 1944–54; UK Scientific Mission, Washington DC, USA, 1950–51; UKAEA, 1954–73; MoD, 1973–89. *Recreation:* gardening. *Address:* 28 Gorselands, Newbury, Berks RG14 6PX. *T:* Newbury (01635) 45651. *Club:* Civil Service.

GREENHILL OF HARROW, Baron *cr* 1974 (Life Peer), of the Royal Borough of Kensington and Chelsea; **Denis Arthur Greenhill,** GCMG 1972 (KCMG 1967; CMG 1960); OBE (mil.) 1941; HM Government Director, British Petroleum Co. Ltd, 1973–78; Member, Security Commission, 1973–82; *b* 7 Nov. 1913; *s* of James and Susie Greenhill, Loughton; *m* 1941, Angela McCulloch; one *s* (and one *s* decd). *Educ:* Bishop's Stortford Coll.; Christ Church, Oxford (Hon. Student 1977). Served War of 1939–45 (despatches twice): Royal Engineers; in Egypt, N Africa, Italy, India and SE Asia; demobilised with rank of Col. Entered Foreign Service, 1946; served: Sofia, 1947–49; Washington, 1949–52; Foreign Office, 1952–54. Imperial Defence Coll., 1954; UK Delegation to NATO, Paris, 1955–57; Singapore, 1957–59; Counsellor, 1959–62; Minister, 1962–64, Washington DC; Asst Under-Sec. of State, FO, 1964–66; Dep. Under-Sec. of State, FO, 1966–69; Perm. Under-Sec. of State, FCO, and Head of the Diplomatic Service, 1969–73. Director: S. G. Warburg & Co., 1974–87 (Adviser, 1987–95); Clerical Medical and General Assce Soc., 1974–86; Wellcome Foundn Ltd, 1974–85; BAT Industries Ltd, 1974–83; Hawker Siddeley Group, 1974–84; Leyland International, 1977–82; Mem., Internat. Adv. Cttee, First Chicago Ltd, 1976–81. A Governor of the BBC, 1973–78. Mem., several H of L Select Cttees on European Communities, 1985–. Governor, BUPA, 1978–84, Dep. Chm., 1979–84. President: Royal Soc. for Asian Affairs, 1976–84; Anglo-Finnish Soc., 1981–84. Chm., KCH Med. Sch. Council, 1977–83; Fellow, King's Coll., London, 1984. Trustee, Rayne Foundn, 1974; Governor, Wellington Coll., 1974–83; Chm. of Governors, SOAS, 1978–85. Grand Cross, Order of the Finnish Lion, 1984. *Publication:* More By Accident, 1992. *Address:* 25 Hamilton House, Vicarage Gate, W8 4HL. *T:* 0171–937 8362. *Club:* Travellers'.

GREENHILL, Dr Basil Jack, CB 1981; CMG 1967; FRHistS; FSA; author; Vice President, SS Great Britain Project, since 1992 (Chairman, 1982–92); Chairman, Centre for Maritime Historical Studies, University of Exeter, since 1991; Consultant, Conway Maritime Press, since 1990; *b* 26 Feb. 1920; *o c* of B. J. and Edith Greenhill; *m* 1st, 1950, Gillian (*d* 1959), *e d* of Capt. Ralph Tyacke Stratton, MC; one *s*; 2nd, 1961, Ann, *d* of Walter Ernest Giffard; one *s*. *Educ:* Bristol Grammar Sch.; Bristol Univ. (T. H. Green Scholar; PhD 1980). Served War of 1939–45: Lieut RNVR (Air Br.). Diplomatic Service, 1946–66; served: Pakistan; UK Delegn, New York; Tokyo; UK Delegate to Conf. on Law of the Sea, Geneva; British Dep. High Comr in E Pakistan; Ottawa. Dir, Nat. Maritime Mus., Greenwich, 1967–83, Caird Res. Fellow, 1983–86. Member: Ancient Monuments Bd for England, 1972–84; Council, Maritime Trust, 1977–83 (Hon. Vice-Pres., 1984–); Finnish Exhibn 1985 Cttee, 1983–85; Vice Chm. Bd, Trustees of the Royal Armouries, 1984–88; Vice Pres., Soc. for Nautical Res., 1975–; First Pres., Internat. Congress of Maritime Museums, 1975–81 (Hon. Life Mem., 1981); President: Devonshire Assoc., 1984; Devon Hist. Soc., 1993–; Trustee: Royal Naval Museum, Portsmouth, 1973–83; Mary Rose Trust, 1979–83; RAF Museum, 1987–. Governor, Dulwich Coll., 1974–88; Chairman: Dulwich Picture Gall., 1977–88; Nat. Museums' Directors' Conf., 1980–83; Govt Adv. Cttee on Historic Wreck Sites, 1986–. Principal Advisor: BBC TV series: The Commanding Sea, 1980–82; Trade Winds, 1984–85; BBC Radio series: The British Seafarer, 1980–82; The Sea, The Sea, 1991. Hon. Fellow, Univ. of Exeter, 1985. Kt Comdr, Order of White Rose, Finland, 1980. *Publications:* The Merchant Schooners, Vol. I, 1951, Vol. II, 1957, rev. edns 1968, 1978, 1988; (ed and prefaced) W. J. Slade's Out of Appledore, 1959, rev. edns 1972, 1974, 1980; Sailing For A Living, 1962; (with Ann Giffard) Westcountrymen in Prince Edward's Isle, 1967, 3rd edn 1990 (Amer. Assoc. Award) (filmed 1975); (with Ann Giffard) The Merchant Sailing Ship: A Photographic History, 1970; (with Ann Giffard) Women under Sail, 1970; Captain Cook, 1970; Boats and Boatmen of Pakistan, 1971; (with Ann Giffard) Travelling by Sea in the Nineteenth Century, 1972; (with Rear-Adm. P. W. Brock) Sail and Steam, 1973; (with W. J. Slade) West Country Coasting Ketches, 1974; A Victorian Maritime Album, 1974; A Quayside Camera, 1975; (with L. Willis) The Coastal Trade: Sailing Craft of British Waters 900–1900, 1975; Archaeology of the Boat, 1976; (with Ann Giffard) Victorian and Edwardian Sailing Ships, 1976, rev. edns 1981, 1982, 1987; (with Ann Giffard) Victorian and Edwardian Ships and Harbours, 1978; (ed and prefaced) Georg Kåhrés The Last Tall Ships, 1978; (with Ann Giffard) Victorian and Edwardian Merchant Steamships, 1979; Schooners, 1980; The Life and Death of the Sailing Ship, 1980; (with Michael Mason) The British Seafarer, 1980; (with Denis Stonham) Seafaring Under Sail, 1981; Karlsson, 1982; The Woodshipbuilders, 1986; The Grain Races, 1986; (with Ann Giffard) The British Assault on Finland 1854–55, 1988; The Evolution of the Wooden Ship, 1988; (ed and prefaced) Edmund Eglinton's The Mary Fletcher, 1990; (with John Hackman) The Herzogin Cecilie, 1991 (trans. Swedish, 1991, German, 1993); (ed jtly and contrib.) The New Maritime History of Devon, vol. 1, 1993, vol. 2, 1994; (ed and contrib.) The Advent of Steam, 1993; (ed and contrib.) The Last Century of Sail, 1993; (with Owain Roberts) The Årby Boat, 1993; (with Ann Giffard) Steam, Politics and Patronage, 1994; The Bertha L. Downs, 1995; The New Archaeology of the Boat, 1995; numerous articles, reviews and broadcasts. *Recreations:* boating, travel, coarse gardening. *Address:* West Boetheric Farmhouse, St Dominic, Saltash, Cornwall PL12 6SZ. *Clubs:* Arts (Hon. Mem.); Royal Western Yacht (Plymouth); Karachi Yacht (Karachi); Åland Nautical (Mariehamn).

See also Sir C. S. R. Giffard.

GREENING, Rear-Adm. Sir Paul (Woollven), GCVO 1992 (KCVO 1985); Master of HM's Household, 1986–92; an Extra Equerry to the Queen, since 1983; *b* 4 June 1928; *s* of late Captain Charles W. Greening, DSO, DSC, RN, and Mrs Molly K. Greening (*née* Flowers); *m* 1951, Monica, *d* of late Mr and Mrs W. E. West, East Farndon, Market Harborough; one *s* one *d*. *Educ:* Mowden Sch., Brighton; Nautical Coll., Pangbourne. Entered RN, 1946; Midshipman, HMS Theseus, 1947–48; Sub-Lt and Lieut, HM Ships Zodiac, Neptune, Rifleman, Asheldham (CO), and Gamecock, 1950–58; Lt-Comdr, HM Ships Messina (CO), Loch Killisport, Urchin, and Collingwood, 1958–63; Comdr 1963; CO HMS Lewiston, and SO 2nd Minesweeping Sqdn, 1963–64; jssc 1964; Naval Plans, MoD (Navy), 1965–67; CO HMS Jaguar, 1967–68; Fleet Plans Officer, Far East Fleet, 1969; Captain 1969; CO HMS Aurora, 1970–71; Captain Naval Drafting, 1971–74; Sen. Officers War Course, 1974, Dir of Officers Appts (Seamen), MoD (Navy), 1974–76; Captain BRNC Dartmouth, 1976–78; Naval Secretary, 1978–80; Flag Officer, Royal Yachts, 1981–85; retired 1985. ADC to the Queen, 1978. Council, Missions to Seamen, 1994–. Younger Brother of Trinity House, 1984. *Recreations:* golf, gardening, following cricket. *Club:* Army and Navy.

GREENING, Wilfrid Peter, FRCS; Consultant Surgeon to Royal Marsden Hospital, 1952–79; Consulting Surgeon, Charing Cross Hospital since 1975; Lecturer in Surgery to Charing Cross Hospital Medical School; *s* of Rev. W. Greening and M. M. Waller, Saxlingham, Norfolk; *m* 1st, 1939, Hilary Berryman (marr. diss., 1961); one *d*; 2nd, 1962, Susan Ann Clair Huber (marr. diss. 1977); 3rd, 1978, Touba Ghazinoor. *Educ:* St Edmund's Sch., Canterbury; King's Coll.; Charing Cross Hospital Medical Sch. MRCS 1937; LRCP 1937; FRCS 1939. Houseman and Surgical Registrar, Charing Cross Hosp., 1938. Served War of 1939–45 (despatches); Wing Comdr i/c Surgical Div., RAFVR, 1943. Surgical Registrar, Gordon Hospital, 1946; Consultant Surgeon: Woolwich Hospital, 1948; Bromley and District Hospital, 1947–66. *Publications:* contributions to medical literature. *Recreations:* fishing, golf. *Address:* 67 Harley Street, W1N 1DE. *Club:* Garrick.

GREENLAND, Dennis James, DPhil; FRS 1994; FIBiol; Chairman, Scientific Advisory Panel, Commonwealth Development Corporation, since 1992; Visiting Professor, University of Reading, since 1987; *b* 13 June 1930; *s* of James John and Lily Florence Greenland; *m* 1955, Edith Mary Johnston; one *s* two *d*. *Educ:* Portsmouth Grammar Sch.; Christ Church, Oxford (MA, DPhil). Lecturer: Univ. of Ghana, 1955–59; Waite Agricl Res. Inst., Adelaide, 1959–63; Reader and Head of Soil Science, Waite Agricl Res. Inst., 1963–70; Professor and Head of Dept of Soil Science, Univ. of Reading, 1970–79; Director of Research, Internat. Inst. of Tropical Agriculture, Nigeria, 1974–76 (on secondment from Univ. of Reading); Dep. Dir Gen., Internat. Rice Res. Inst., Los Baños, Philippines, 1979–87; Scientific Dir, CAB Internat., 1987–92. FIBiol 1974; FWA 1987. Hon. Member: Amer. Soc. of Soil Science, 1993; Amer. Soc. of Agronomy, 1993. Hon. DrAgSci Ghent, 1982. *Publications:* contributions: (jtly) The Soil Under Shifting Cultivation, 1960; (ed jtly) Soil Conservation and Management in the Humid Tropics, 1977; (ed jtly) Chemistry of Soil Constituents, 1978; (ed jtly) Soil Physical Properties and Crop Production in the Tropics, 1979; (ed) Characterisation of Soils in Relation to Their Classification and Management for Crop Production: some examples from the humid tropics, 1981; (ed jtly) The Chemistry of Soil Processes, 1981; (ed jtly) Soil Resilience and Sustainable Land Use, 1994; numerous scientific articles in learned jls. *Recreations:* golf, bridge, watching cricket. *Address:* Low Wood, The Street, South Stoke, Oxon RG8 0JS.

GREENOAK, Francesca; Gardens Editor, Good Housekeeping, since 1993; Environmental Columnist, Times Educational Supplement, since 1993; *b* 6 Sept. 1946; *d* of Francis Buchanan Greenoak and Alice Lavinia (*née* Marston); *m* 1981, John Kilpatrick; one *s* one *d*. *Educ:* St Mary's Convent Grammar Sch., Woodford Green; Univ. of Essex (BA Hons). Book Club Associates, 1968; Editor: George Harrap, 1970; Penguin Educn, Penguin Books, 1972; Chameleon Publishing Co-operative, 1974; Gardening Correspondent: She mag., 1978–80; The Times, 1986–94. Natural Hist. Advr, Sunday Times Countryside Project, 1978. *Publications:* Guide to Wildflowers, 1977; All The Birds of the Air, 1979; Forgotten Fruit, 1983; (with R. Mabey) Back to the Roots, 1983; God's Acre, 1985, 2nd edn 1993; (ed) Journals of Gilbert White, 3 vols, 1989; Glorious Gardens, 1989; Fruit and Vegetable Gardens, 1990. *Recreations:* literature, gardening, botany, music, education and science. *Address:* Good Housekeeping, 72 Broadwick Street, W1V 2BP. *T:* 0171–439 5000.

GREENOCK, Lord; Charles Alan Andrew Cathcart, ACA; Director, Murray Lawrence Members Agencies; *b* 30 Nov. 1952; *s* and *heir* of 6th Earl Cathcart, *qv*; *m* 1981, Vivien Clare, *o d* of F. D. McInnes Skinner; one *s* one *d*. *Educ:* Eton. Commnd Scots Guards, 1972–75. Whinney Murray, 1976–79; Ernst & Whinney, 1979–83; Gardner Mountain and Capel-Cure Agencies Ltd, 1983–94. Mem., Queen's Bodyguard for Scotland, Royal Co. of Archers. Liveryman, Merchant Taylors' Co. *Recreations:* ski-ing, sailing, country pursuits. *Heir:* *s* Hon. Alan George Cathcart, *b* 16 March 1986. *Address:* 18 Smith Terrace, SW3 4DL; Gateley Hall, Norfolk.. *Clubs:* Pratt's, City of London.

GREENOUGH, Beverly, (Mrs P. B. Greenough); *see* Sills, B.

GREENSHIELDS, Robert McLaren; HM Diplomatic Service, retired; Counsellor, Foreign and Commonwealth Office, 1985–88; *b* 27 July 1933; *s* of late Brig. James Greenshields, MC, TD, and of Mrs J. J. Greenshields; *m* 1960, Jean Alison Anderson; one *s* two *d*. *Educ:* Edinburgh Academy; Lincoln Coll., Oxford (MA Hons). National Service, 2nd Lieut Highland Light Infantry, 1952–54. District Officer, Tanganyika, HMOCS, 1958–61; Asst Master and Housemaster, Gordonstoun Sch., 1962–68; HM Diplomatic Service, 1969–88. *Recreations:* ornithology, conservation, farming.

GREENSLADE, Roy; freelance journalist, broadcaster and author, since 1992; *b* 31 Dec. 1946; *s* of Ernest Frederick William Greenslade and Joan Olive (*née* Stocking); *m* 1984, Noreen Anna Taylor (*née* McElhone); one step *s* one step *d*. *Educ:* Dagenham County High Sch.; Sussex Univ. (BA (Hons) Politics, 1979). Trainee journalist, Barking Advertiser, 1962–66; Sub-Editor: Lancashire Evening Telegraph, 1966–67; Daily Mail, 1967–69; The Sun, 1969–71; researching and writing book, 1973–75; Daily Star, 1979–80; Daily Express, 1980–81; Daily Star, 1981; Asst Editor, The Sun, 1981–87; Man. Editor, Sunday Times, 1987–90; Editor, Daily Mirror, 1990–91; Consultant Editor, Today and Sunday Times, 1991. *Publications:* Goodbye to the Working Class, 1975; Maxwell's Fall, 1992; The Penguin Book of Columnists, 1996. *Recreations:* tennis, reading. *Address:* Ballyarr House, Ramelton, Co. Donegal, Ireland.

GREENSMITH, Edwin Lloydd, CMG 1962; *b* 23 Jan. 1900; *s* of Edwin Greensmith; *m* 1932, Winifred Bryce; two *s* two *d*. *Educ:* Victoria Univ., Wellington, NZ. MCom (Hons), 1930. Accountant; Solicitor. Chief Accountant, Ministry of Works, New Zealand, to 1935; then Treasury (Secretary, 1955–65). Chm., NZ Wool Commn, 1965–72. *Recreation:* gardening. *Address:* Unit 42, Crestwood Village, Titirangi, Auckland, New Zealand. *Club:* Wellington (Wellington NZ).

GREENSPAN, Alan; Chairman, Board of Governors of the Federal Reserve System, since 1987; *b* 6 March 1926; *o s* of Herbert Greenspan and Rose (*née* Goldsmith). *Educ:* New York Univ. (BS 1948; MA 1950; PhD 1977). Vice-Pres., 1954–58, Pres., 1958–74 and 1977–87, Townsend-Greenspan & Co., NY; co-founder, Greenspan O'Neil Associates, NY, 1985–87. Adjunct Prof., Graduate Sch. of Business Management, NY Univ., 1977–87. Director: Trans World Financial Co., 1962–74; Dreyfus Fund, 1970–74; Gen. Cable Corp., 1973–74, 1977–78; Sun Chemical Corp., 1973–74; Gen. Foods Corp., 1977–85; J. P. Morgan & Co., 1977–87; Mobil Corp., 1977–87; ALCOA, 1978–87. Consultant to Council of Economic Advisers, 1970–74, to US Treasury, 1971–74, to Fed. Reserve Board, 1971–74; Chairman: Council of Economic Advisers, 1974–77; Nat. Commn on Social Security Reform, 1981–83; Dir, Council on Foreign Relations; Member: President's Econ. Policy Adv. Board, 1981–87; President's Foreign Intell. Adv. Board, 1983–85. Jefferson Award, 1976; William Butler Meml Award, 1977. *Address:* Federal Reserve System, 20th Street & Constitution Avenue NW, Washington, DC 20551, USA.

GREENSTOCK, Jeremy Quentin, CMG 1991; HM Diplomatic Service; Deputy Under Secretary of State, Foreign and Commonwealth Office, since 1995; *b* 27 July 1943; *s* of late John Wilfrid Greenstock and Ruth Margaret Logan; *m* 1969, Anne Derryn Ashford Hodges; one *s* two *d*. *Educ:* Harrow Sch.; Worcester Coll., Oxford (MA Lit. Hum.). Asst Master, Eton Coll., 1966–69; entered HM Diplomatic Service, 1969; MECAS, 1970–72; Dubai, 1972–74; Private Sec. to the Ambassador, Washington, 1974–78; FCO, 1978–83 (Planning Staff, Personnel Ops Dept, N East and N African Dept); Counsellor (Commercial), Jedda, 1983–85, Riyadh, 1985–86; Hd of Chancery, Paris, 1987–90; Asst Under-Sec. of State, FCO, 1990–93; Minister, Washington, 1994–95. *Recreations:* travel, photography, golf, ski-ing. *Address:* Foreign and Commonwealth Office, Whitehall, SW1A 2AH.

GREENTREE, (William Wayne) Chris, FInstPet; Chairman (non-executive), Xxtra Oil Inc., since 1993; *b* 6 April 1935; *s* of J. Murray and Grace M. Greentree; *m* 1st, 1956, Patricia Ann Hugo (marr. diss. 1990); four *d* (and one *d* decd); 2nd, 1990, Hilary J. Wilson. *Educ:* Moose Jaw Technical High Sch., Saskatoon; Univ. of Alberta (BSc Hons, PEng). Joined Shell Canada, 1957: technical and managerial appts, onshore and offshore exploration; Ranger Oil London, 1972–79: Man. Dir, 1976; Mapco Inc. USA: Sen. Vice Pres. Exploration and Production, 1979–82; Chief Exec., LASMO Gp, 1982–93. Ordre National du Mérite (Gabon), 1987. *Recreations:* golf, ski-ing. *Address:* Quinta do Lago, Almancil, Portugal.

GREENWAY, family name of **Baron Greenway.**

GREENWAY, 4th Baron *cr* 1927; **Ambrose Charles Drexel Greenway;** Bt 1919; photographer and author; *b* 21 May 1941; *s* of 3rd Baron Greenway and of Cordelia Mary, *d* of late Major Humfrey Campbell Stephen; *S* father, 1975; *m* 1985, Mrs Rosalynne Schenk. *Educ:* Winchester. Chm., Marine Soc., 1994. *Publications:* Soviet Merchant Ships, 1976; Comecon Merchant Ships, 1978; A Century of Cross Channel Passenger Ferries, 1980; A Century of North Sea Passenger Steamers, 1986. *Recreations:* ocean racing and cruising, swimming. *Heir:* *b* Hon. Mervyn Stephen Kelvynge Greenway, *b* 19 Aug. 1942. *Address:* c/o House of Lords, SW1A 0PW. *Club:* House of Lords Yacht.

GREENWAY, Harry; MP (C) Ealing North, since 1979; *b* 4 Oct. 1934; *s* of John Kenneth Greenway and Violet Adelaide (*née* Bell); *m* 1969, Carol Elizabeth Helena, *e d* of late Major John Robert Thomas Hooper, barrister at law and Metropolitan Stipendiary Magistrate; one *s* two *d*. *Educ:* Warwick Sch.; College of St Mark and St John, London; Univ. of Caen, Normandy. Assistant Master, Millbank Sch., 1957–60; successively, Head of English Dept, Sen. Housemaster, Sen. Master, Acting Dep. Head, Sir William Collins Sch., 1960–72; Dep. Headmaster, Sedgehill Sch. (Comprehensive for 2,000 plus pupils), 1972–79. Vice-Chm., Greater London Cons. Members, 1981–; Chairman: All Party

Adult Educn Cttee, 1979–; All Party Parly Friends of Cycling, 1987–95; Member: Parly Select Cttee on Educn, Science and the Arts, 1979–92; Parly Select Cttee on Employment, 1992–; Vice-Chairman: Cons. Parly Educn Cttee, 1983–87 (Sec., 1981); Cons. Parly Sports Cttee, 1986–; Parly Sec., Cons. National Adv. Cttee on Educn, 1981–94; Sec., Cons. Parly Arts and Heritage Cttee, 1986–87. Parly Sec., Cons. Nat. Educn Soc., 1995–. Led All Party Parly Delegn to Sri Lanka, 1985, to Gibraltar, 1989. Pres., Cons. Trade Unionist Teachers, 1982–83; Chm., Atlantic Educn Cttee, 1981–85; Member: Educn Cttee, NACRO, 1985–88; Council, Open Univ., 1982–. Freeman, City of London, 1986; Liveryman, Farriers' Co., 1986–. British Horse Soc. Award of Merit, 1980. *Publications:* Adventure in the Saddle, 1971; regular contributor to educnl and equestrian jls. *Recreations:* riding (Asst Instructor, BHS, 1966), ski-ing, choral music, hockey (Vice-Pres., England Schoolboys' Hockey Assoc.; Founder, Lords and Commons Hockey Club), cricket, parliamentary parachutist. *Address:* House of Commons, SW1A 0AA. *Clubs:* St Stephen's Constitutional, Ski Club of Gt Britain.

GREENWAY, John Robert; MP (C) Ryedale, since 1987; *b* 15 Feb. 1946; *s* of Thomas William and Kathleen Greenway; *m* 1974, Sylvia Ann Gant; two *s* one *d*. *Educ:* Sir John Deane's Grammar School, Northwich; London College of Law. Midland Bank, 1964; Metropolitan Police, 1965–69; Equitable Life Assurance Soc., 1970–71; National Provident Instn, 1971–72; own firm of insurance brokers, J. R. Greenway, subseq. Greenway Middleton, & Co. Ltd, York, 1972–. Treasurer, Ryedale Cons. Assoc., 1984–86; Mem., North Yorks CC, 1985–87; Vice-Chm., N Yorks Police Authy., 1986–87. PPS to Minister of State, MAFF, 1991–92; Mem., Home Affairs Select Cttee, 1987–. Sec., Cons. back bench Health Cttee, 1988–91; Vice-Chairman: Cons. back bench Agricl Cttee, 1989–; All Party Football Cttee, 1989–; Chairman: All Party Racing and Bloodstock Cttee; All Party Insce and Financial Services Gp, 1992– (Sec., 1991–92); Jt Chm., All Party Opera Gp. Mem., Insce Brokers Registration Council, 1991–. *Recreations:* opera, football (Pres., York City FC), wine, travel, gardening. *Address:* 11 Oak Tree Close, Strensall, York YO3 5TE. *T:* York (01904) 490535.

GREENWELL, (Arthur) Jeffrey, CBE 1991; Chief Executive, Northamptonshire County Council, since 1973; *b* 1 Aug. 1931; *s* of late George Greenwell and of Kate Mary Greenwell (*née* Fleming), Durham, *m* 1958, Margaret Rosemary, *d* of late Sidney David Barnard; one *s* two *d*. *Educ:* Durham Sch.; University Coll., Oxford (MA). FCIS. Solicitor (Hons). Nat. Service, RHA, 1950–51. Articled to Town Clerk, Newcastle upon Tyne, 1955–58; law tutor, Gibson & Weldon, 1958–59; Asst Solicitor, Birmingham Corp., 1959–61; Hants County Council: Asst Solicitor, 1961–64; Asst Clerk, 1964–67; Dep. Clerk of Council, Dep. Clerk of the Peace and Dep. Clerk, Hants River Authy, 1967–73; Clerk of Northants Lieutenancy, 1977–. Chm., Assoc. of Co. Chief Execs, 1993–94 (Hon. Sec., 1980–84); Hon. Sec., SOLACE, 1984–88 (Pres., 1991–92); President: CIS, 1989; Northants Assoc. of Local Councils. Chm., Home Office Gp on Juvenile Crime, 1987; Dir and Treas., Crime Concern. Vice-Pres., Internat. City Management Assoc., 1990–92. Mem., Peterborough Dio. Synod. Trustee, Central Festival Opera. Gov., Nene Coll. *Recreations:* bridge, travel, local history, going to meetings. *Address:* County Hall, Northampton NN1 1DN. *T:* Northampton (01604) 236050, *Fax:* Northampton (01604) 236223.

GREENWELL, Sir Edward (Bernard), 4th Bt *cr* 1906; DL; farmer, since 1975; *b* 10 June 1948; *s* of Sir Peter McClintock Greenwell, 3rd Bt, TD, and of Henrietta (who *m* 1985, Hugh Kenneth Haig), 2nd *d* of late Peter and Lady Alexandra Haig-Thomas; *S* father, 1978; *m* 1974, Sarah Louise Gore-Anley; one *s* three *d*. *Educ:* Eton; Nottingham University (BSc); Cranfield Institute of Technology (MBA). DL Suffolk, 1988. *Heir:* *s* Alexander Bernard Peter Greenwell, *b* 11 May 1987. *Address:* Gedgrave Hall, Woodbridge, Suffolk IP12 2BX. *T:* Orford (01394) 450440. *Club:* Turf.

GREENWELL, Jeffrey; *see* Greenwell, A. J.

GREENWOOD, family name of **Viscount Greenwood.**

GREENWOOD, 2nd Viscount, *cr* 1937; **David Henry Hamar Greenwood;** Baron, *cr* 1929; Bt, *cr* 1915; *b* 30 Oct. 1914; *e s* of 1st Viscount Greenwood, PC, KC, LLD, BA, and Margery (*d* 1968), 2nd *d* of Rev. Walter Spencer, BA; *S* father 1948; unmarried. *Educ:* privately and at Bowers Gifford. Agriculture and Farming. *Heir:* *b* Hon. Michael George Hamar Greenwood, *b* 5 May 1923. *Recreations:* shooting and reading.

GREENWOOD, Allen Harold Claude, CBE 1974; JP; Deputy Chairman, British Aerospace, 1977–83 (Member, Organizing Committee, 1976–77); Chairman, British Aircraft Corporation, 1976 (Deputy Chairman, 1972–75); *b* 4 June 1917; *s* of Lt-Col Thomas Claude Greenwood and Hilda Letitia Greenwood (*née* Knight). *Educ:* Cheltenham Coll. Coll. of Aeronautical Engineering. Pilot's Licence, 1939. Joined Vickers-Armstrongs Ltd, 1940; served RNVR (Fleet Air Arm), 1942–52 (Lt-Cmdr); rejoined Vickers-Armstrongs Ltd, 1946, Dir, 1960; British Aircraft Corp., 1962, Dep. Man. Dir, 1969; Director: British Aircraft Corp. (Holdings), 1972; BAe Australia Ltd, 1977–83; Chm., BAe Inc., 1977–80. Director: SEPECAT SA, 1964; Europlane Ltd, 1974–83; Chairman: Panavia GmbH, 1969–72; Remploy Ltd, 1976–79 (Vice-Chm., 1973). Pres., Assoc. Européenne des Constructeurs de Material Aerospatial, 1974–76; Pres., 1970–72, Dep. Pres., 1981–82, SBAC; Vice-Pres., Engineering Employers' Fedn, 1982–83; Mem., National Def. Industry Council, 1970–72. Pres., Cheltenham Coll. Council, 1980–85; Member: Council, Cranfield Inst. of Technology, 1970–79; Council, CBI, 1970–77; Assoc. of Governing Bodies of Public Schools, 1982–85; Council, St John's Sch., Leatherhead, 1970–85 (Chm., 1979–85). JP Surrey 1962, Hampshire, 1975. Freeman, City of London. Liveryman, Company of Coachmakers, Guild of Air Pilots. General Comr for Income Tax, 1970–74. *Address:* 2 Rookcliff, Park Lane, Milford-on-Sea, Hants SO41 0SD. *T:* Lymington (01590) 642893. *Clubs:* White's, Royal Automobile; Royal Lymington Yacht.

GREENWOOD, David Ernest; Director, Centre for Defence Studies, University of Aberdeen, since 1976; *b* 6 Feb. 1937; *s* of Ernest Greenwood and Doris (*née* Cowsill); *m* 1st, 1960, Helen Ramshaw (marr. diss.); two *s*; 2nd, 1986, Margaret McRobb (*née* Cruickshank). *Educ:* Manchester Grammar Sch.; Liverpool Univ. (BA, MA). Educn Officer, RAF, 1959–66; Economic Advr, MoD, 1966–67; Lectr 1967, Sen. Lectr 1970, Reader 1975, in Higher Defence Studies, Univ. of Aberdeen. Vis. Fellow, IISS, 1974–75; Vis. Prof., Nat. Defense Acad., Yokosuka, 1981–82; Olin Prof., USAF Acad., Colorado Springs, 1991–92. Member: FCO Adv. Panel on Arms Control and Disarmament, 1974–; Honeywell Adv. Council, 1981–85; ACOST Study Gp on Defence R&D, 1987–88; Council, Internat. Inst. for Defence Procurement Studies, 1989–. Cons., EEC, 1980–85 and 1987–. Dir, IIDPS Ltd, 1989–. *Publications:* Budgeting for Defence, 1972; (jtly) British Security Policy and the Atlantic Alliance: prospects for the 1990s, 1987; The European Defence Market, 1991; numerous monographs, res. reports, contribs to symposia, jl and newspaper articles. *Recreations:* cooking, gardening, reading, walking, watching television. *Address:* 7 Westhill Grange, Westhill, Skene AB32 6QJ. *T:* Aberdeen (01224) 741508. *Club:* Royal Air Force.

GREENWOOD, Duncan Joseph, CBE 1993; PhD, DSc; FRS 1985; CChem, FRSC; FIHort; Head of Soils and Crop Nutrition, 1966–92, Emeritus Research Fellow, since 1992, Horticulture Research International (formerly National Vegetable Research Station, then AFRC Institute of Horticultural Research), Wellesbourne, Warwick; Visiting Professor of Plant Sciences, Leeds University, since 1985; Hon. Professor of Agricultural Chemistry, Birmingham University, since 1986; *b* 16 Oct. 1932; *s* of Herbert James Greenwood and Alison Fairgrieve Greenwood. *Educ:* Hutton Grammar Sch., near Preston; Liverpool Univ. (BSc 1954); Aberdeen Univ. (PhD 1957; DSc 1972). CChem, FRSC 1977; FIHort 1986. Res. Fellow, Aberdeen Univ., 1957–59; Res. Leader, National Vegetable Res. Station, 1959–66. Chm., Agriculture Gp, Soc. of Chemical Industry, 1975–77; President: Internat. Cttee of Plant Nutrition, 1978–82; British Soc. of Soil Science, 1991–92. Lectures: Blackman, Univ. of Oxford, 1982; Distinguished Scholars, QUB, 1982; Hannaford, Univ. of Adelaide, 1985; Shell, Univ. of Kent, 1988; Amos, Wye Coll., 1989. Sir Gilbert Morgan Medal, Soc. of Chemical Industry, 1962; Res. Medal, RASE, 1979. *Publications:* over 150 scientific papers on soil science, crop nutrition and fertilizers. *Address:* 23 Shelley Road, Stratford-upon-Avon, Warwicks CV37 7JR. *T:* Stratford-upon-Avon (01789) 204735.

GREENWOOD, Prof. Geoffrey Wilson, PhD, DMet; FRS 1992; FInstP; FIM; FEng; Professor of Metallurgy, University of Sheffield, 1966–94, now Emeritus; *b* 3 Feb. 1929; *s* of Richard Albert Greenwood and Martha Alice (*née* Wilson); *m* 1954, Nancy Cole; two *s* one *d*. *Educ:* Grange Grammar Sch., Bradford; Univ. of Sheffield (BSc, PhD, DMet). FInstP 1966; FIM 1966; FEng 1990. SO and SSO, UKAEA, Harwell, 1953–60; Head, Fuel Materials Section, Berkeley Nuclear Labs, CEGB, 1960–65; Res. Manager, Scis Div., Electricity Council Res. Centre, 1965–66. Pro-Vice-Chancellor, Univ. of Sheffield, 1979–83. L. B. Pfeil Prize, Inst. Metals and Iron and Steel Inst., 1972; Rosenhain Medal, Metals Soc., 1975. *Publications:* contribs to Metallurgy, Materials Science, Physics and Engrg. *Recreations:* music (oboe and piano playing), travel, variety of outdoor activities. *Address:* Department of Engineering Materials, University of Sheffield, PO Box 600, Sir Robert Hadfield Building, Mappin Street, Sheffield S1 4DU. *T:* Sheffield (0114) 276 8555; 26 Stumperlowe Hall Road, Sheffield S10 3QS. *T:* Sheffield (0114) 230 3565. *Club:* Hallam Rotary (Sheffield).

GREENWOOD, Jeffrey Michael; Senior Partner, Nabarro Nathanson, 1987–95, now Consultant; *b* 21 April 1935; *s* of Arthur Greenwood and Ada Greenwood (*née* Gordon); *m* 1964, Naomi Grahame; three *s* one *d*. *Educ:* Raine's Foundation Sch.; LSE; Downing Coll., Cambridge (MA, LLM). Admitted solicitor 1960; Partner, Nabarro Nathanson, 1963; Head of Property Dept, 1972–87. Chm., Central Council for Education and Training in Social Work, 1993–. Dir, Bank Leumi (UK), 1990–; Dep. Chm., Jewish Chronicle, 1994–. Chairman: Jewish Welfare Bd, 1986–90; Jewish Care, 1990; Council Member: Business in the Community; Hampstead Garden Suburb Trust (Law Soc. Appointee, 1984–87). Liveryman, Glovers' Co. *Publications:* articles in learned jls. *Recreations:* running, swimming, ski-ing, literature, travel. *Address:* (office) 50 Stratton Street, W1X 5FL. *T:* 0171–493 9933.

GREENWOOD, Dr Jeremy John Denis; Director, British Trust for Ornithology, since 1988; *b* 7 Sept. 1942; *s* of Denis Greenwood and Phyllis Marjorie Greenwood (*née* Leat); *m* 1971, Cynthia Anne Jones; two *d*. *Educ:* Royal Grammar Sch., Worcester; St Catherine's Coll., Oxford (BA 1964); Univ. of Manchester (PhD 1972). MIBiol 1990; MIEEM 1991. Dundee University: Asst Lectr in Zoology, 1967–70; Lectr in Biol. Scis, 1970–87; Hon. Lectr, 1988–. Vis. Prof. in Animal Ecology, Univ. of Khartoum, 1976. Hon. Lectr, UEA, 1994–. Natural Environment Research Council: Workshop on Grey Seal Population Biol., 1979–84; Special Cttee on Seals, 1986–; Terrestrial Life Scis Cttee, 1988–91; Chm. Exec. Cttee, European Bird Census Council, 1992–; Member: Council, RSPB, 1983–88; Adv. Cttee on Birds, NCC, 1988–91; Envtl Res. Cttee, British Agrochem. Assoc., 1988–93; Grants Cttee, Internat. Council for Bird Preservation, British Section, 1988–92; Council, British Ornith. Union, 1989–93; Sci. Adv. Cttee, Wildfowl & Wetlands Trust, 1989–92; Inst. of Ecology and Envmtl Management, 1991–. Dir, West Palaearctic Birds Ltd, 1990–. Pres., Scottish Ornithologists' Club, 1987. Editor, Bird Study, 1984–87; Mem., Editl Bd, Heredity, 1988–92. *Publications:* (ed jtly) Joint Biological Expedition to North East Greenland 1974, 1978; (ed jtly) Birds as Monitors of Environmental Change, 1993; papers in learned jls; chapters in books. *Recreations:* birdwatching, walking, gardening. *Address:* National Centre for Ornithology, Thetford, Norfolk IP24 2PU. *T:* Thetford (01842) 750050.

GREENWOOD, Prof. Norman Neill, DSc Melbourne; PhD, ScD Cambridge; FRS 1987; CChem, FRSC; Professor of Inorganic and Structural Chemistry, University of Leeds, 1971–90, now Emeritus; *b* Melbourne, Vic., 19 Jan. 1925; *er s* of Prof. J. Neill Greenwood, DSc and Gladys, *d* of late Moritz and Bertha Uhland; *m* 1951, Kirsten Marie Rydland, Bergen, Norway; three *d*. *Educ:* University High School, Melbourne; University of Melbourne; Sidney Sussex Coll., Cambridge. Laboratory Cadet, CSIRO Div. of Tribophysics, Melbourne, 1942–44; BSc Melbourne 1945, MSc Melbourne 1948; DSc Melbourne 1966. Masson Memorial Medal, Royal Australian Chem. Institute, 1945. Resident Tutor and Lecturer in Chemistry, Trinity Coll., Melbourne, 1946–48. Exhibn of 1851, Overseas Student, 1948–51; PhD Cambridge 1951; ScD Cambridge 1961. Senior Harwell Research Fellow, 1951–53; Lectr, 1953–60 Senior Lectr, 1960–61, in Inorganic Chemistry, Univ. of Nottingham; Prof. of Inorganic Chemistry, Univ. of Newcastle upon Tyne, 1961–71. Visiting Professor: Univ. of Melbourne, 1966; Univ. of Western Australia, 1969; Univ. of Western Ontario, 1973; Univ. of Copenhagen, 1979; La Trobe Univ., Melbourne, 1985; Wuhan Univ., People's Republic of China, 1985; Toho Univ., Tokyo, 1991–93; National Science Foundation Distinguished Vis. Prof., Michigan State Univ., USA, 1967. International Union of Pure and Applied Chemistry: Mem., 1963–83; Vice-Pres., 1975–77, Pres., 1977–81, Inorganic Chemistry Div.; Chm., Internat. Commn on Atomic Weights, 1969–75. Chemical Society: Vice Pres., 1979–80; Pres., Dalton Div., 1979–81; Award in Main Group Chemistry, 1975. Vice-Pres., 1989–90, Pres., 1990–91, Section B, Chemistry, BAAS. Lectures: Tilden, Chemical Soc., 1966–67; Hofmann, Ges. Deutscher Chemiker, 1983; Liversidge , RSC, 1983; first Egon Wiberg, Munich Univ., 1989; Ludwig Mond, RSC, 1991. For. Associate, Académie des Sciences, Institut de France, 1992. Dr *hc* de l'Université de Nancy I, 1977. *Publications:* Principles of Atomic Orbitals, 1964 (rev. edns 1968, 1973, 1980); Ionic Crystals, Lattice Defects, and Nonstoichiometry, 1968; (jointly) Spectroscopic Properties of Inorganic and Organometallic Compounds, vols I-IX, 1968–76; (with W. A. Campbell) Contemporary British Chemists, 1971; (with T. C. Gibb) Mössbauer Spectroscopy, 1971; Periodicity and Atomic Structure, 1971; (with B. P. Straughan and E. J. F. Ross) Index of Vibrational Spectra, vol. I, 1972, (with E. J. F. Ross) vol. II, 1975, vol. III, 1977; The Chemistry of Boron, 1973 (rev. edn 1975); (with A. Earnshaw) Chemistry of the Elements, 1984; numerous original papers and reviews in chemical jls and chapters in scientific monographs. *Recreations:* ski-ing, music. *Address:* School of Chemistry, University of Leeds, Leeds LS2 9JT.

GREENWOOD, Peter Bryan; His Honour Judge Greenwood; a Circuit Judge, since 1972. Called to the Bar, Gray's Inn, 1955. Dep. Chm., Essex QS, 1968–71.

GREENWOOD, Ronald, CBE 1981; Manager, England Association Football Team, 1977–82, retired; *b* 11 Nov. 1921; *s* of Sam and Margaret Greenwood; *m* Lucy Joan Greenwood; one *s* one *d*. *Educ:* Alperton School. Apprenticed signwriter, 1937; joined Chelsea FC, 1940; served RAF, 1940–45; Bradford Park Avenue FC, 1945 (Captain); Brentford FC, 1949 (over 300 matches); rejoined Chelsea FC, 1952 (League Champions, 1954–55); Fulham FC, Feb. 1955; coached Oxford Univ. team, 3 years, Walthamstow Avenue FC, 2 years; Manager, Eastbourne United FC and England Youth team; Asst Manager, Arsenal FC, 1958; Team Manager, England Under-23, 1958–61; Manager and Coach, later Gen. Manager, West Ham United FC, 1961–77 (FA Cup, 1964 and 1975; European Cup Winners' Cup, 1965); a FIFA technical adviser, World Cup series, 1966 and 1970. *Publication:* Yours Sincerely, 1984. *Address:* 8 Kestrel Close, Upper Drive, Hove, Sussex BN3 6NS.

GREER, Prof. David Clive; Professor of Music, University of Durham, since 1986 (Chairman, Music Department, 1986–94); *b* 8 May 1937; *s* of William Mackay Greer and Barbara (*née* Avery); *m* 1961, Patricia Margaret Regan; two *s* one *d*. *Educ:* Dulwich Coll.; Queen's Coll., Oxford (BA 1960; MA 1964). MusD TCD, 1991. Lectr in Music, Birmingham Univ., 1963–72; Hamilton Harty Prof. of Music, QUB, 1972–84; Prof. of Music, Univ. of Newcastle upon Tyne, 1984–86. Mellon Vis. Fellow, 1989, Mayers Foundn Fellow, 1991, Huntington Liby, Calif; Folger Vis. Fellow, Folger Shakespeare Liby, Washington, 1994. FRSA 1986. Editor, Proceedings, subseq. Jl, of Royal Musical Assoc, 1977–90. *Publications:* (ed) English Madrigal Verse, 1967; Hamilton Harty: his life and music, 1979, 2nd edn 1980; Hamilton Harty: early memories, 1979; (ed) Collected English Lutenist Partsongs, 2 vols, 1987–89, and other editions of 16th and 17th century music; articles in Music and Letters, Music Review, Musical Times, Shakespeare Qly, English Studies, Notes & Queries, Lute Soc. Jl. *Recreations:* reading, cinema, walking. *Address:* The Music School, Palace Green, Durham DH1 3RL. *T:* Durham (0191) 3743220. *Club:* Athenæum.

GREER, Germaine, PhD; author and lecturer; Special Lecturer and Unofficial Fellow, Newnham College, Cambridge, since 1989; *b* 29 Jan. 1939. *Educ:* Star of the Sea Convent, Gardenvale, Vic; Melbourne Univ. (BA 1959); Sydney Univ. (MA 1962); Cambridge Univ. (PhD 1967). Sen. Tutor in English, Sydney Univ., 1963–64; Asst Lectr, then Lectr in English, Warwick Univ., 1967–72; Founder Dir, Tulsa Centre for the Study of Women's Literature, 1979–82; Prof. of Modern Letters, Univ. of Tulsa, 1980–83. Vis. Prof., Univ. of Tulsa, 1979. Dir, Stump Cross Books, 1988–. *Publications:* The Female Eunuch, 1970; The Obstacle Race: the fortunes of women painters and their work, 1979; Sex and Destiny: the politics of human fertility, 1984; (contrib.) Women: a world report, 1985; Shakespeare, 1986; The Madwoman's Underclothes: essays and occasional writings 1968–85, 1986; (ed jtly) Kissing the Rod: an anthology of 17th century women's verse, 1988; Daddy, We Hardly Knew You, 1989 (J. R. Ackerly Prize; Premio Internazionale Mondello); (ed) The Uncollected Verse of Aphra Benn, 1989; The Change: women, ageing and the menopause, 1991; contribs: articles to Listener, Spectator, Esquire, Harpers Magazine, Playboy, Private Eye (as Rose Blight). *Address:* c/o Aitken and Stone, 29 Fernshaw Road, SW10 0TG.

GREER, Ian Bramwell; Chairman, Ian Greer Associates, since 1982; *b* 5 June 1933; *s* of Bramwell and Janet Greer. *Educ:* Cranbrook Coll., Essex; Victoria Sch., Glasgow. Conservative Central Office and Party Agent, 1956–67; Nat. Dir, Mental Health Trust, 1967–70; Man. Dir, Russell Greer & Associates, 1970–82. *Publication:* Right to be Heard, 1985. *Recreations:* antiques, walking, gardening, dogs. *Address:* Medley, Kingston Hill, Kingston-upon-Thames, Surrey KT12 7LN. *T:* 0181–546 5119. *Club:* Royal Automobile.

GREET, Rev. Dr Kenneth Gerald; Secretary of the Methodist Conference, 1971–84; President of the Methodist Conference, 1980–81; Moderator, Free Church Federal Council, 1982–83; President, World Disarmament Campaign, since 1989 (Co-Chairman, 1983–86; Vice-Pres., 1986–89); *b* 17 Nov. 1918; *e s* of Walter and Renée Greet, Bristol; *m* 1947, Mary Eileen Edbrooke; one *s* two *d*. *Educ:* Cotham Grammar Sch., Bristol; Handsworth Coll., Birmingham. Minister: Cwm and Kingstone Methodist Church, 1940–42; Ogmore Vale Methodist Church, 1942–45; Tonypandy Central Hall, 1947–54; Sec. Dept of Christian Citizenship of Methodist Church, 1954–71; Member: BCC, 1955–84 (Chm. of Exec., 1977–81); World Methodist Council, 1957– (Chm., Exec. Cttee, 1976–81); Chairman: Exec., Temperance Council of Christian Churches, 1961–71; World Christian Temperance Fedn, 1962–72. Rep. to Central Cttee, World Council of Churches, Addis Ababa, 1971, Nairobi, 1975; Beckly Lectr, 1962; Willson Lectr, Kansas City, 1966; Cato Lectr, Sydney, 1975. Chm. Govs, Southlands Coll., Wimbledon, 1987–. Hon. DD Ohio, USA. *Publications:* The Mutual Society, 1962; Man and Wife Together, 1962; Large Petitions, 1964; Guide to Loving, 1965; The Debate about Drink, 1969; The Sunday Question, 1970; The Art of Moral Judgement, 1970; When the Spirit Moves, 1975; A Lion from a Thicket, 1978; The Big Sin: Christianity and the arms race, 1983; What Shall I Cry?, 1986; Life of Jabez Bunting, 1995. *Recreations:* tennis, photography. *Address:* 89 Broadmark Lane, Rustington, Sussex BN16 2JA. *T:* Rustington (01903) 773326.

GREETHAM, (George) Colin; Headmaster, Bishop's Stortford College, 1971–84; *b* 22 April 1929; *s* of late George Cecil Greetham and of Gertrude Greetham (*née* Heavyside); *m* 1963, Rosemary (*née* Gardner); two *s* one *d*. *Educ:* York Minster Song Sch.; St Peter's Sch., York; (Choral Scholar) King's Coll., Cambridge. BA (Hons) History Tripos Cantab, Class II, Div. I, 1952; Certif. of Educn (Cantab), 1953. Chm., Strathisla and Grange Community Councils, Banffs. *Recreations:* music, choral training, horticulture, bowls. *Address:* Chapelhead Farm, Crossroads, Keith, Banffshire AB5 3LQ.

GREETHAM, John Francis, CBE 1994; Chairman, Whitewater Leisure Group, since 1993; Chairman, Northern and Yorkshire Regional Health Authority, since 1994; *b* 17 July 1939; *s* of Francis Greetham and Marjorie Greetham (*née* Seal); *m* 1977, Jill Herring; three *s* one *d*. *Educ:* Nunthorpe Grammar Sch., York. Served RE, 1957–59. Dental equipt mfr and designer, 1959–77; dairy farmer, 1977–87; Chief Exec., Whitewater Leisure Gp, 1987–93. N Yorkshire County Council: Member (Independent), 1978–82; (C), 1982–86; Vice-Chm., Children and Young Persons Cttee, 1978–82; Mem., N Yorks Moors Cttee, 1978–86; Mem., Social Services Cttee, 1978–86. Mem., N Yorks Family Practitioners Cttee, 1979–83; Member: Scarborough DHA, 1980–84; Yorks RHA, 1984–90 (Vice-Chm., 1987–90); York DHA, 1990–91; Chm., St James's Univ. Teaching Hosp. NHS Trust, 1991–94. Founder Chm., NHS Trust Fedn, 1991–93; Council Mem., NAHAT, 1992–94; Member: NHS Audit Cttee, 1993–94; Private Sector Finance Gp, NHS, 1994; Bd, NHS Estates, 1994–; NHS Policy Bd, 1994–. Mem. Court Leeds Univ., 1991–; Gov., Leeds Metropolitan Univ., 1991–. *Recreations:* golf, swimming, walking, horse-riding, shooting, music. *Address:* The Old Rectory, Lockton, Pickering, York YO18 7PZ. *T:* Pickering (01751) 460253.

GREGG, Hubert Robert Harry; actor, composer, lyric writer, author, playwright and director; *b* London, 19 July 1914; *s* of Robert Joseph Gregg and Alice Maud (*née* Bessant); *m* 1st, 1943, Zoe Gail (marr. diss. 1950); one *d*; 2nd, 1956, Pat Kirkwood (marr. diss. 1979); 3rd, 1980, Carmel Lytton; one *s* one *d*. *Educ:* St Dunstan's Coll.; Webber-Douglas Sch. of Singing and Dramatic Art. Served War, 1939–44: private, Lincs Regt, 1939; commnd 60th Rifles, 1940; transf. Intell.; with Polit. Warfare Exec., 1942 (duties included broadcasting in German). *Stage:* 1st London appearance, Julien in Martine, Ambassadors', 1933; Birmingham Rep., 1933–34; Shakespearean roles, Open Air Theatre, Regent's Park and at Old Vic, 1934, 1935; 1st New York appearance, Kit Neilan in French without Tears, 1937 (and London, 1938–39); London appearances include: Pip in The Convict, 1935; roles in classics (Orlando, Henry V, Hamlet), 1935–36; Frederick Hackett in Great Possessions, 1937; Peter Scott-Fowler in After the Dance, 1939; Polly in Men in Shadow, 1942; Michael Caraway in Acacia Avenue, 1944; Earl of Harpenden in While the Sun Shines, 1945, 1946; Tom D'Arcy in Off the Record, 1947; Gabriel Hathaway in Western Wind, 1949; (1st musical), John Blessington-Briggs in Chrysanthemum, 1958; Lionel Toope in Pools Paradise, 1961. *Chichester Festival Theatre:* Alexander MacColgie Gibbs in The Cocktail Party, Antonio in The Tempest, and Announcer in The Skin of our Teeth, 1968; Sir Lucius O'Trigger in The Rivals, Britannus in Caesar and Cleopatra, and Marcellin in Dear Antoine (also London), 1971. *Directed, London:* The Hollow (Agatha Christie's 1st stage success), 1951; re-staged To Dorothy - a Son, 1952 (subseq. toured in play, 1952–53); The Mousetrap (for 7 yrs from 1953); Speaking of Murder, 1958; The Unexpected Guest, 1958; From the French, 1959; Go Back for Murder, 1960; Rule of Three, 1962; re-staged The Secretary Bird, 1969 (subseq. toured in play, 1969–70). 1st solo performance, Leicester, 1970; subseq. performances in Britain and America (subjects include Shakespeare, Shaw, Jerome K. Jerome, the London Theatre, and the 20s, 30s and 40s); solo perf., Words by Elgar, Music by Shaw, Malvern Fest., 1978, Edinburgh Fest., 1979. *Films include:* In Which We Serve; Flying Fortress; Acacia Avenue (USA as The Facts of Love); The Root of all Evil; Vote for Huggett; Once upon a Dream; Robin Hood (Walt Disney); The Maggie (USA as High and Dry); Svengali; Doctor at Sea (also wrote music and lyrics); Simon and Laura; Speaking of Murder; The Third Visitor; Final Appointment; Room in the House; Stars in Your Eyes (also co-dir. and wrote music and lyrics). *Author of plays:* We Have Company (played in tour, 1953); Cheque Mate (dir. and appeared in); Villa Sleep Four (played in tour, 1965); From the French (written under pseudonym of Jean-Paul Marotte); Who's Been Sleeping . . . ? (also appeared in); The Rumpus (played in tour, 1967); Dear Somebody (perf. Germany as Geliebtes Traumbild, 1984); (screenplay) After the Ball (adapted from own television biog. of Vesta Tilley). *Songs:* Author of over 200, including: I'm going to get lit up; Maybe it's because I'm a Londoner. BBC broadcasts in drama, revue, poetry, etc, 1933–; announcer, BBC Empire Service, 1934–35; radio musical of Three Men in a Boat, 1962 (adapted, wrote music and words, and appeared in); weekly radio progs with accent on nostalgia, 1965– (A Square Deal, I Remember it Well, Now and Then, Thanks for the Memory); Chairman: BBC TV Brains Trust, 1955; Youth Wants to Know, ITV, 1957; 40 week radio series on London theatres, 1974–75; biog. series: I Call it Genius, 1980–81; I Call it Style, 1981–; Hubert Gregg Remembers, ITV solo series, 1982–; 50 Years of Broadcasting, BBC celebration prog. Maybe It's Because . . .), 1984 (Sony Radio Award, 1985); Hubert Gregg Remembers (series for BBC World Service), 1985–; (wrote book, music and lyrics, and appeared in) Sweet Liza (radio musical play), 1985; (wrote script, music and lyrics for, and presented) My London (radio), 1986; (wrote and presented) Sounds and Sweet Airs (celebration of 60 yrs at the microphone), 1993; (wrote music and lyrics for) Sherry, 1993; (wrote and presented) Hubert Gregg and the Forties (commemorating 50th anniversary of D-Day), 1994; (wrote and presented) Hubert Gregg and the Twenties, Hubert Gregg and the Thirties, (radio), 1995. Has dir., lectured and adjudicated at Webber-Douglas Sch., Central Sch. of Speech Trng and RADA. Patron, Cinema Theatre Assoc., 1973–; President: Northern Boys' Book Club, 1975– (succeeded P. G. Wodehouse); Concert Artists Assoc., 1979–80. Freedom of City of London, 1981. Gold Badge of Merit, British Acad. of Composers, Authors and Song Writers, 1982. *Publications:* April Gentleman (novel), 1951; We Have Company (play), 1953; A Day's Loving (novel), 1974; Agatha Christie and all that Mousetrap, 1980; Thanks for the Memory (biographies collected from radio series I Call it Genius and I Call it Style), 1983; Geliebtes Traumbild (play), 1984; music and lyrics. *Recreation:* cinematography. *Address:* c/o Broadcasting House, W1A 1AA. *Club:* Garrick.

GREGORIOUS, His Eminence The Most Rev. the Archbishop of Thyateira and Great Britain; *see* Theocharus, Archbishop Gregorios.

GREGORY, Alan Thomas, CBE 1984; Director, Willis Corroon (formerly Willis Faber) plc, 1987–95; *b* 13 Oct. 1925; *s* of Lloyd Thomas Gregory and Florence Abbott; *m* 1st, 1952, Pamela Douglas Scott (*d* 1986); one *s* two *d*; 2nd, 1988, Mrs Marion Newth (*née* Nash), JP. *Educ:* Dulwich Coll.; St John's Coll., Cambridge (Classics). Directed into coal mining, coal face worker, 1944; Min. of Power, 1948; JSSC 1957; Chm., NATO Petroleum Planning Cttee, 1967–70; joined British Petroleum, 1971; Gen. Manager, BP Italiana, 1972–73; Dir, Govt and Public Affairs, 1975–85, and Dir, UK and Ireland Region, 1980–85, British Petroleum Co.; Chm., BP Oil Ltd, 1981–85; Director: BP Chemicals International Ltd, 1981–85; National Home Loans Corp., 1985–91. Governor, Queen Mary Coll., London Univ., 1981–87. President, Inst. of Petroleum, 1982–84. Univ. Comr, 1988–95. *Recreations:* books, gardening, theatre. *Address:* Red Oak, 31 Fairmile Avenue, Cobham, Surrey KT11 2JA. *T:* Cobham (01932) 864457. *Club:* Travellers'.

GREGORY, Clifford; Chief Scientific Officer, Department of Health and Social Security, 1979–84, retired; *b* 16 Dec. 1924; *s* of Norman and Grace Gregory; *m* 1948, Wyn Aveyard; one *d* (one *s* decd). *Educ:* Royal Coll. of Science, London Univ. (2nd Cl. Hons Physics; ARCS). Served War, RN, 1943–46. Lectr, Mddx Hosp. Med. Sch., 1949; Sen. Physicist, Mount Vernon Hosp., 1954; Dep. Reg. Physicist, Sheffield, 1960; Sen. Principal Scientific Officer, Min. of Health, 1966; Dep. Chief Scientific Officer, DHSS, 1972. *Publications:* scientific papers in med. and scientific jls. *Recreations:* outdoor pursuits, natural history. *Address:* 53 Roundwood Park, Harpenden, Herts AL5 3AG. *T:* Harpenden (01582) 712047.

GREGORY, Conal Robert; company director, wine consultant and lecturer; *b* 11 March 1947; *s* of Patrick George Murray Gregory and Marjorie Rose Gregory; *m* 1971, Helen Jennifer Craggs; one *s* one *d*. *Educ:* King's College Sch., Wimbledon; Univ. of Sheffield (BA Hons Mod. Hist. and Pol Theory and Instns, 1968). Master of Wine by examination, Vintners' Co., 1979. Manager, Saccone & Speed Vintage Cellar Club, 1971–73; Wine Buyer, Reckitt & Colman, 1973–77; Editor, Internat. Wine and Food Soc's Jl, 1980–83; Dir, Standard Fireworks Ltd, 1987–92. Contested Lakenham, Norwich City election, 1976; Norfolk County Councillor, Thorpe Div., 1977–81; Vice-Pres., Norwich Jun. Chamber of Commerce, 1975–76; Mem., E Anglia Tourist Bd, 1979–81. Chairman: Norwich N Cons. Assoc., 1980–82; Norwich CPC, 1978–81; Vice-Chm., Eastern Area CPC, 1980–83; Member: Cons. Eastern Area Agric. Cttee, 1975–79; Norfolk Cons. Eur. Constituency Council, 1981–82; Cons. Provincial Council, Eastern Area, 1978–82; Chm. and Founder, Bow Gp of E Anglia, 1975–82; Nat. Vice-Chm., Bow Gp, 1976–77. MP (C) York, 1983–92. Hon. Treas., British/Cyprus CPA Gp, 1987–92; Sec., UK-Manx Parly Gp, 1987–92; Chm., Cons. Parly Food and Drinks Industries Cttee, 1989–92 (Vice-Chm., 1985–89); Vice-Chairman: Cons. Parly Tourism Cttee, 1985–92; Cons. Parly Transport Cttee, 1987–89 and 1990–92 (Sec., 1983–87); All Party Parly Hospice Gp,

1990–92; All Party Parly Tourism Cttee, 1991–92 (Sec., 1983–91); Mem., Cttee, British Atlantic Gp of Young Politicians, 1983–92 (Chm., 1988–89; Pres., 1989–92); Pres., York Young Conservatives, 1982–93; Vice-President: Nat. Soc. of Cons. and Unionist Agents, Yorks Br., 1983–92; York Br., UNA, 1983–92. Parly Consultant: The Market Res. Soc., 1984–91; Consort Hotels Ltd, 1984–91; Consultant: Andry Montgomery Ltd, 1979–; Smith & Taylor Ltd, 1992–; CC&C Research, 1993–. Fellow, Industry and Parlt Trust, 1984–87. Private Member's Bills on consumer safety, 1985, on smoke alarms, 1991, on cheque fraud, 1992. Patron, Nat. Trust for Welfare of the Elderly, 1983–; Founder Mem., Wymondham Br., CEMS, 1979; Member: Wymondham Abbey PCC, 1982–83; Humbleyard Deanery Synod, 1982–83; High Steward's Cttee, York Minster Fund, 1983–89; York Archaeol Trust, 1983–; York Georgian Soc., 1982–92; York Civic Trust, 1982–92; 20th Century British Art Fair Council, 1992–; ESU, 1994–. Governor, Heartsease Sch., Norwich, 1977–83; Mem., Court of Governors: Univ. of Sheffield, 1977–; Univ. of York, 1983–92; Univ. of Hull, 1983–92. Wine Corresp., Catering Times, 1979–83. *Publications:* (with W. Knock) Beers of Britain, 1975; (with R. A. Adley) A Policy for Tourism?, 1977; A Caterer's Guide to Drinks, 1979; (with M. Shersby and A. McCurley) Food for a Healthy Britain, 1987; contribs to The Times, Scotsman, Wine and Spirit, etc. *Address:* c/o Smith & Taylor Ltd, 1 Broughton Street, SW8 3QJ.

GREGORY, John Peter, JP; CEng, FIMechE; Director, ASL Ltd, 1986–91; *b* 5 June 1925; *s* of Mr and Mrs P. Gregory; *m* 1949, Lilian Mary (*née* Jarvis); one *s* one *d*. *Educ:* Ernest Bailey Sch., Matlock; Trinity Hall, Cambridge (Scholar, MA). CEng, FIMechE 1970. Served War, RAF Pilot, 1943–47. Joined Cadbury Bros Ltd, 1949, Dir 1962; Vice Chm., Cadbury Ltd, 1969–70, Dir, Cadbury Schweppes, 1971–82 (Chm., Overseas Gp and Internat. Tech. Dir, 1973–80); Director: National Vulcan Engrg Ins. Group Ltd, 1970–79; Amalgamated Power Engrg Ltd, 1973–81; Chm., Data Recording Instruments Ltd, 1982–84. Gen. Comr of Income Tax, 1978–82. Chm. Trustees, Middlemore Homes, 1970–82. Liveryman, Worshipful Co. of Needlemakers. JP Birmingham, 1979. *Recreations:* music, bridge, country pursuits, sailing. *Address:* Moorgreen Hall, Weatheroak, Alvechurch, Worcs B48 7DZ. *T:* Wythall (01564) 822303. *Clubs:* Carlton; Royal Fowey Yacht.

GREGORY, Prof. Kenneth John; Warden, Goldsmiths' College, University of London, since 1992; *b* 23 March 1938; *s* of Frederick Arthur Gregory and Marion Gregory; *m* Margaret Christine Wilmot; one *s* two *d*. *Educ:* University College London (BSc Special 1959; PhD 1962; DSc 1982). University of Exeter: Lectr in Geography, 1962–72; Reader in Physical Geography, 1972–76; University of Southampton: Prof. of Geography, 1976–92; Head of Geography Dept, 1978–83; Dean of Science, 1984–87; Dep. Vice-Chancellor, 1988–92. Hon. Res. Fellow, UCL, 1993–. Vis. Lectr, Univ. of New England, NSW, 1975; Distinguished Visiting Professor, 1987: Univ. Kebangsaan; Arizona State Univ.; Snyder Lectr, Univ. of Toronto, 1990. Vice Pres., Commn on Global Continental Palaeohydrology, Internat. Assoc. on Union for Quaternary Res., 1992. Mem., Higher Educn Quality Steering Council. Back Award, 1980, Founder's Medal, 1993, RGS. *Publications:* (with A. H. Shorter and W. L. D. Ravenhill) Southwest England, 1969; (with D. E. Walling) Drainage Basin Form and Process, 1973; (jtly) An Advanced Geography of the British Isles, 1974; (with E. Derbyshire and J. R. Hails) Geomorphological Processes, 1979; The Yellow River, 1980; The Nature of Physical Geography, 1985 (trans. Russian and Portuguese); (ed jtly) The Encyclopedic Dictionary of Physical Geography, 1985; (ed) Energetics of Physical Environment, 1987; (ed jtly) Human Activity and Environmental Processes, 1987; (ed jtly) Palaeohydrology in Practice, 1987; (ed jtly) Horizons in Physical Geography, 1988; (ed) The Earth's Natural Forces, 1990; (ed) The Guinness Guide to the Restless Earth, 1991; (ed jtly) Temperate Palaeohydrology, 1991; (ed jtly) Global Continental Palaeohydrology, 1995; (ed) Geological Conservation Review Fluvial Geomorphology of Great Britain, 1995. *Recreations:* travel, gardening, reading. *Address:* Goldsmiths' College, University of London, New Cross, SE14 6NW. *T:* 0181–692 7171. *Club:* Athenæum.

GREGORY, Leslie Howard James; former National Officer of EETPU; *b* 18 Jan. 1915; *s* of J. F. and R. E. Gregory; *m* 1949, D. M. Reynolds; one *s* one *d*. *Educ:* Junior Section, Ealing College (formerly Acton Coll.) and state schools. Mem. Exec. Council, ETU, 1938–54; full-time Nat. Officer, 1954–79, retired. Member: CSEU Nat. Sub-Cttees, for Shipbuilding, 1966–79, for Railway Workshops, 1968–78; Craft Training Cttees of Shipbuilding ITB, 1965–77, and Engineering ITB, 1965–68; EDC for Elec. Engrg, 1967–74; EDC for Shipbuilding, 1974–76; Org. Cttee, British Shipbuilders, 1976–77; Bd, British Shipbuilders (part-time), 1977–80. *Address:* 3 Addington Court, Keats Avenue, Milford-on-Sea, Hants SO41 0WN. *T:* Lymington (01590) 645883.

GREGORY, Michael Anthony, OBE 1990; freelance journalist and author; Chief Legal Adviser, Country Landowners' Association, 1977–90; *b* 8 June 1925; *s* of late Wallace James Ignatius Gregory, FRIBA, FRICS, AMIMechE, and Dorothy Gregory; *m* 1951, Patricia Ann, *d* of late Frank Hodges and late Gwendoline Hodges; three *s* four *d* (and one *d* decd). *Educ:* Douai Sch.; University Coll. London (LLB). Served RAF, Air Navigator, 1943–47; called to the Bar, Middle Temple, 1952; practised at Bar, 1952–60; Legal Dept, Country Landowners' Assoc., 1960–90. Member: BSI Cttee on Installation of Pipelines in Land, 1965–83; Thames Water Authority (now NRA (Thames)) Reg. Fisheries Adv. Cttee, 1974–; Inland Waterways Amenity Adv. Council, 1982–92; Council, John Eastwood Water Protection Trust, 1984–. Hon. Legal Advr, Nat. Anglers' Council, 1968–91; Pres., Basingstoke Canal Angling Assoc., 1991–; Member Council: Salmon and Trout Assoc., 1980–90; Anglers' Co-op. Assoc., 1980–. Founder Mem., Agricl Law Assoc., 1975; Trustee, CLA Charitable Trust, 1980–. Hon. Sec., Soc. of Our Lady of Good Counsel, 1953–58; Mem., Management Cttee, Bourne Trust (formerly Catholic Social Services for Prisoners), 1952–93 (Chm., 1960–71 and 1974–85; Hon. Sec., 1953–60); Pres., Douai Soc., 1984–86. Chairman: Internat. Help for Children, Fleet and Dist Br., 1967–77; Fleet United Bowling Club, 1992–; Mem. Cttee, 1981–, and Trustee, 1987–, Fedn for Promotion of Horticulture for Disabled People. Papal medal *pro ecclesia et pontifice*, 1988. *Publications:* Organisational Possibilities in Farming, 1968; (with C. Townsend) Joint Enterprises in Farming, 1968, 2nd edn 1973; Angling and the Law, 1967, 2nd edn 1974, supp. 1976; Title, Pipelines, for Encycl. of Forms and Precedents, 1970; (with Richard Seymour) All for Fishing, 1970; contributor to Walmsley's Rural Estate Management, 6th edn, 1978; (with G. R. Williams) Farm Partnerships, 1979; (with Margaret Parrish) Essential Law for Landowners and Farmers, 1980, 3rd edn (with Angela Sydenham), 1990; (with Richard Stratton and G. R. Williams) Share Farming, 1983, 2nd edn 1985; (contrib.) Agriculture, Conservation and Land Use, ed Howarth and Rodgers, 1992; Conservation Law in the Countryside, 1994; numerous articles, booklets, short stories. *Recreations:* fishing, ball and saloon games, music, playing saxophones. *Address:* Beam Ends, Dipley Common, Hartley Wintney, Hook, Hampshire RG27 8JS. *T:* Hartley Wintney (01252) 842559.

GREGORY, Peter Roland; Director, Welsh Office Health Department, Welsh Office, since 1994; *b* 7 Oct. 1946; *s* of Tom and Ruby Gregory; *m* 1978, Frances Margaret Hogan. *Educ:* Sexeys Grammar Sch., Blackford, Som.; University College Swansea (BA Hons 1968); Manchester Univ. (PhD 1972). Joined Welsh Office, 1971; Private Sec. to Perm. Sec., 1974–75; Principal, 1976; Asst Sec., 1982; Under Sec, Transport, Planning and Envmt Gp, 1990–94. *Recreations:* walking, theatre, music. *Address:* Welsh Office, Cathays Park, Cardiff CF1 3NQ.

GREGORY, Prof. Richard Langton, CBE 1989; DSc; FRS 1992; FRSE 1969; Professor of Neuropsychology and Director of Brain and Perception Laboratory, University of Bristol, 1970–88, now Emeritus; *b* 24 July 1923; *s* of C. C. L. Gregory, astronomer, and Patricia (*née* Gibson); *m* 1st, 1953, Margaret Hope Pattison Muir (marr. diss. 1966); one *s* one *d*; 2nd, 1967, Freja Mary Balchin (marr. diss. 1976). *Educ:* King Alfred Sch., Hampstead; Downing Coll., Cambridge, 1947–50. DSc Bristol, 1983. Served in RAF (Signals), 1941–46; Research, MRC Applied Psychology Research Unit, Cambridge, 1950–53; Univ. Demonstrator, then Lecturer, Dept of Psychology, Cambridge, 1953–67; Fellow, Corpus Christi Coll., Cambridge, 1962–67; Professor of Bionics, Dept of Machine Intelligence and Perception, Univ. of Edinburgh, 1967–70 (Chm. of Dept, 1968–70). Visiting Prof.: UCLA, 1963; MIT, 1964; New York Univ., 1966. Founder and Chm. Trustees, 1983–91, Pres., 1991–, The Exploratory Hands-on Science Centre. President: Section J, British Assoc. for Advancement of Science, 1975, Section X, 1986, and Section Q, 1989 and 1990; Experimental Psychol. Soc., 1981–82. Member: Royal Soc. Cttee for Public Understanding of Sci., 1986–; BBC Sci. Consultative Gp, 1988–. Royal Institution: Manager, 1971–74; Mem. Council and Vice-Pres., 1991–94; Christmas Lectr, 1967–68. FRSA 1973. DUniv: Open, 1990; Stirling, 1990; Hon. LLD Bristol, 1993. CIBA Foundn Research Prize, 1956; Craik Prize for Physiological Psychology, St John's Coll., Cambridge, 1958; Waverley Gold Medal, 1960; Capire Internat. Prize, Internat. Cttee for Promotion of Advanced Educnl Res., Italy; Primo Rovis Prize, Trieste Internat. Foundn for Scientific Progress and Freedom, Italy; Michael Faraday Medal, Royal Soc., 1993. Founder Editor, Perception, 1972. *Publications:* Recovery from Early Blindness (with Jean Wallace), 1963; Eye and Brain, 1966, 4th edn 1990; The Intelligent Eye, 1970; Concepts and Mechanisms of Perception, 1974; (ed jtly) Illusion in Nature and Art, 1973; Mind in Science, 1981; Odd Perceptions (essays), 1986; (ed) Oxford Companion to the Mind, 1987; (ed jtly) Evolution of the Eye and Visual System, vol. 2 of Vision and Visual Dysfunction, 1991; Even Odder Perceptions (essays), 1994; articles in various scientific jls and patents for optical and recording instruments and a hearing aid; radio and television appearances. *Recreations:* punning and pondering. *Address:* 23 Royal York Crescent, Clifton, Bristol BS8 4JX. *Clubs:* Athenæum, Savile.

GREGORY, Roger Michael; Deputy Receiver for the Metropolitan Police, 1989–94, retired; *b* 1 June 1939; *s* of Walter James Gregory and Catherine Emma Gregory (*née* Regan); *m* 1961, Johanna Margaret O'Rourke; five *s* two *d*. *Educ:* Gillingham (Kent) Grammar Sch. Joined Metropolitan Police Civil Staff, 1957; Hd of Operations, Police National Computer Unit, 1976; Dep. Dir of Finance, Metropolitan Police, 1981; Dir of Computing, Metropolitan Police, 1983. *Recreations:* cricket, bridge, gentle gardening. *Address:* 29 Milton Road, Harpenden, Herts AL5 5LA.

GREGORY, Roland Charles Leslie; *see* Gregory, Roy.

GREGORY, Ronald, CBE 1980; QPM 1971; DL; Chief Constable of West Yorkshire Metropolitan Police, 1974–83, retired; *b* 23 Oct. 1921; *s* of Charles Henry Gregory and Mary Gregory; *m* 1942, Grace Miller Ellison; two *s*. *Educ:* Harris College. Joined Police Service, Preston, 1941. RAF (Pilot), 1942–44; RN (Pilot), 1944–46. Dep. Chief Constable, Blackpool, 1962–65; Chief Constable, Plymouth, 1965–68; Dep. Chief Constable, Devon and Cornwall, 1968–69; Chief Constable, West Yorkshire Constabulary, 1969–74. DL West Yorks, 1977. *Recreations:* golf, sailing, ski-ing.

GREGORY, Roy, (Roland Charles Leslie Gregory), CBE 1973; QC 1982; *b* 16 Jan. 1916; *s* of Charles James Alfred and Lilian Eugenie Gregory; *m* 1st, 1949, Olive Elizabeth (*d* 1973), *d* of late Andrew Gay; one *s*; 2nd, 1974, Charlotte, *d* of late Lt-Col Peter Goddard, MBE. *Educ:* Strand Sch.; London Univ (LLB Hons). Served in Army, 1941–42. Called to Bar, Gray's Inn, 1950. First entered Civil Service, 1933; Head of Civil Procedure Br., Lord Chancellor's Office, 1966–79, retired; Consultant, 1979–82. Secretary: Austin Jones Cttee on County Court Procedure, 1947–49; Evershed Cttee on Supreme Court Practice and Procedure, 1949–53; County Court Rule Cttee, 1962–79; Matrimonial Causes Rule Cttee, 1967–79; Asst Sec., Supreme Court Rule Cttee, 1968–79; Chm., Working Party on Revision of County Court Rules, 1979–81; Mem., Expert Cttees of Council of Europe, 1978–82. *Publications:* County Court Manual, 1st edn 1946 to 4th edn 1962; editor, County Court Practice, annually, 1950–; contribs to legal publications on civil procedure. *Recreations:* music, travel. *Address:* 36 Howard Avenue, Ewell, Surrey KT17 2QJ. *T:* 0181–393 8933.

GREGSON, family name of **Baron Gregson.**

GREGSON, Baron *cr* 1975 (Life Peer), of Stockport in Greater Manchester; **John Gregson,** AMCT, CIMgt; DL; Non-Executive Director, Fairey Group plc (formerly Fairey Holdings Ltd), 1989–94; with British Steel plc (formerly British Steel Corporation), 1976–94; *b* 29 Jan. 1924. Joined Stockport Base Subsidiary, 1939; Fairey R&D team working on science of nuclear power, 1946; appointed to Board, 1966. Non-executive Dir, Otto-Simon Carves Ltd; Mem., Electra Corporate Ventures Ltd, 1989–; Mem. Bd, NRA, 1992–. Mem., Hse of Lords Select Cttee on Sci. & Technol., 1980–; Pres., Parly and Scientific Cttee, 1986–89; Chm., Finance and Industry Gp of Labour Party, 1978–; Vice Pres., Assoc. of Metropolitan Authorities, 1984–. Pres., Defence Manufacturers Assoc., 1984–. Mem. Court Univ. of Manchester Inst. of Science and Technology, 1976–. Hon. Fellow, Manchester Polytechnic, 1983; Hon. FIProdE 1982; Hon. FEng 1986; Hon FICE 1987; DUniv Open, 1986; Hon. DSc Aston, 1987; Hon. DTech Brunel, 1989; Hon. DSc RMCS, 1990. Pres., Stockport Youth Orch.; Vice-Pres., Fedn of British Police Motor Clubs. DL Greater Manchester, 1979. *Recreations:* mountaineering, skiing. *Address:* 12 Rosemont Road, Richmond-upon-Thames, Surrey TW10 6QL. *T:* 0181–948 2244, *Fax:* 0181–948 3388; The Spinney, Cragg Vale, Mytholmroyd, Hebden Bridge, West Yorks HX7 5SR; 407 Hawkins House, Dolphin Square, SW1V 3XL.

GREGSON, Sir Peter (Lewis), KCB 1988; (CB 1983); Permanent Secretary, Department of Trade and Industry, since 1989; *b* 28 June 1936; *s* of late Walter Henry Gregson and of Lillian Margaret Gregson. *Educ:* Nottingham High Sch.; Balliol Coll., Oxford. Classical Hon. Mods, class I; Lit. Hum. class I; BA 1959; MA 1962. Nat Service, 1959–61; 2nd Lieut RAEC, attached to Sherwood Foresters. Board of Trade: Asst Principal, 1961; Private Sec. to Minister of State, 1963–65; Principal, 1965; Resident Observer, CS Selection Bd, 1966; London Business Sch., 1967; Private Sec. to the Prime Minister, 1968–72 (Parly Affairs, 1968–70; Econ. and Home Affairs, 1970–72); Asst Sec., DTI, and Sec., Industrial Development Adv. Bd, 1972–74; Under Sec., DoI, and Sec., NEB, 1975–77; Under Sec., Dept of Trade, 1977–80, Dep. Sec. (Civil Aviation and Shipping), 1980–81; Dep. Sec., Cabinet Office, 1981–85; Perm. Under-Sec. of State, Dept of Energy, 1985–89. Council Mem., Industrial Soc., 1990. CIMgt (CBIM 1988). *Recreations:* gardening, listening to music. *Address:* Department of Trade and Industry, 1–19 Victoria Street, SW1H 0ET.

GREGSON, William Derek Hadfield, CBE 1970; DL; company director; Deputy Chairman, British Airports Authority, 1975–85; *b* 27 Jan. 1920; *s* of William Gregson; *m*

1944, Rosalind Helen Reeves; three *s* one *d*. *Educ:* King William's Coll., IoM; Alpine Coll., Villars; Faraday House Engrg College. DFH, CEng, FIEE, CIMgt, FIIM. Served with RAF, NW Europe, 1941–45 (Sqdn Ldr); Techn. Sales Man., Ferranti Ltd, Edinburgh, 1946–51, London Man., 1951–59; Asst Gen. Man., Ferranti (Scotland) Ltd, 1959–83; Director: Ferranti EI, New York, 1969–83; Ferranti Hldgs, 1983–85. Director: British Telecom Scotland (formerly Scottish Telecommunications Bd), 1977–85; Anderson Strathclyde plc, 1978–86; Brammer plc, 1983–88; East of Scotland Industrial Investments plc, 1980–; Consultant to ICI, 1984–88. Chm., Scottish Gen. Practitioners Res. Support Unit, 1971–79; Dep. Chm., Scottish Council (Develt and Industry), 1982–88 (Dir, 1974–88); Mem. Council: Electronic Engrg Assoc. 1959–83 (Pres. 1963–64); Soc. of British Aerospace Companies, 1966–83 (Chm. Equipment Gp Cttee 1967); BIM, 1975–80. BEAMA: Chm. Industrial Control and Electronics Bd 1964; Mem. Council, 1970–; Chm., Measurement, Control and Automation Conference Bd, 1973; Dep. Pres., 1982–83; Pres., 1983–85. Member: BIM Adv. Bd for Scotland, 1969–85 (Chm., 1970–75); Electronics EDC, 1965–75; Bd of Livingston New Town, 1968–76; Jt BIM/NEDO Prof. Management Adv. Cttee on Indust. Strategy, 1976–78; Management Assoc. of SE Scotland, 1977– (Chm., 1980–81); Scottish Econ. Planning Council, 1965–71; Machine Tool Expert Cttee, 1969–70; Scottish Design Council, 1974–81; Design Council, 1980–85; CBI (Mem., Scottish Council, 1977–81); Bd, BSI, 1985–87; Edinburgh Chamber of Commerce, 1975–83. Commissioner, Northern Lighthouse Bd, 1975–90 (Chm., 1979). Dir, Scottish Nat. Orch., 1977–85 (Vice-Chm., 1981–84; Chm., 1984–85). DL City of Edinburgh, 1984–. FRSA. *Recreations:* reading, cabinet-making, automation in the home. *Address:* Murrayfield House, 66 Murrayfield Avenue, Edinburgh EH12 6AY. *T:* 0131–337 3858. *Clubs:* Royal Air Force; New (Edinburgh).

GREIG, Sir (Henry Louis) Carron, KCVO 1995 (CVO 1973); CBE 1986; DL; Chairman, Horace Clarkson PLC (formerly H. Clarkson (Holdings) plc), 1976–93; Director, James Purdey & Sons Ltd, since 1972; an Extra Gentleman Usher to the Queen, since 1995 (Gentleman Usher, 1961–95); *b* 21 Feb. 1925; *s* of late Group Captain Sir Louis Greig, KBE, CVO, DL; *m* 1955, Monica Kathleen, *d* of late Hon. J. J. Stourton, TD; three *s* one *d*. *Educ:* Eton. Scots Guards, 1943–47, Captain. Joined H. Clarkson & Co. Ltd, 1948; Dir, 1954; Man. Dir, 1962; Chairman: H. Clarkson & Co. Ltd, 1973–85; Baltic Exchange (formerly Baltic Mercantile and Shipping Exchange), 1983–85 (Dir, 1978–85); Director: Williams & Glyn's Bank, 1983–85; Royal Bank of Scotland, 1985–95; Charterhouse, 1990–93. Vice-Chm., Not Forgotten Assoc., 1979–. Chm., Schoolmistresses and Governesses Benevolent Instn, 1992– (Dep. Chm., 1966–92). Governor, United World Coll. of the Atlantic, 1985–. DL Hants, 1992. *Address:* Brook House, Fleet, Hants GU13 8RF; Binsness, Forres, Moray. *Clubs:* White's; Royal Findhorn Yacht.

GREIG of Eccles, James Dennis, CMG 1967; *b* 1926; *o s* of late Dennis George Greig of Eccles and Florence Aileen Marjoribanks; *m* 1st, 1952, Pamela Marguerite Stock (marr. diss., 1960); one *s* one *d*; 2nd, 1960 (marr. diss., 1967); one *s*; 3rd, 1968, Paula Mary Sterling. *Educ:* Winchester Coll.; Clare Coll., Cambridge; London Sch. of Economics. Military Service (Lieut, The Black Watch, seconded to Nigeria Regt), 1944–47. HMOCS: Administrative Officer, Northern Nigeria, 1949–55; Fedn of Nigeria, 1955–59; Dep. Financial Sec. (Economics), Mauritius, 1960–64; Financial Secretary, Mauritius, 1964–67; retired voluntarily on Mauritius achieving internal self-government, 1967. With Booker Bros. (Liverpool) Ltd, 1967–68; Head of Africa and Middle East Bureau, IPPF, 1968–76; Dir, Population Bureau, ODA, 1976–80; retired. *Recreations:* rough shooting, bowls, gardening, national hunt racing. *Address:* 6 Beverley Close, Barnes, SW13 0EH. *T:* 0181–876 5354; The Braw Bothy, Eccles, Kelso, RoxburghshireTD5 7QS. *T:* Leitholm (01890) 840544. *Clubs:* Hurlingham, Annabel's.

GREINER, Hon. Nicholas Frank, (Nick), AC 1994; Deputy Chairman, Stockland Trust Property Group, since 1992; *b* 27 April 1947; *s* of Nicholas and Clare Greiner; *m* 1970, Kathryn Callaghan; one *s* one *d*. *Educ:* St Ignatius Coll., Riverview; Sydney Univ. (BEc Hons); Harvard Univ. (MBA High Dist.). Asst Vice-Pres., Boise Cascade Corp., USA, 1970–71; NSW Dir and Chief Exec., White River Corp., 1972–80; Chm., Harper & Row (Australasia), 1977–83. Chairman: Baulderstone Hornibrook, 1993–; North West Water (Australasia), 1993–; Natwest Markets, 1994– (Dir, 1992–); SBS–IAMA Ltd, 1994–. Director: Coles Myer, 1992–; Defiance Mills, 1992–; Brian McGuigan Wines, 1992–; QBE Insce Gp, 1992–. Prof., Macquarie Sch. of Management, 1992–. MP (L) Ku-ring-gai, NSW, 1980–92; Shadow Minister for Urban Affairs, June 1981; Shadow Treasurer, and Shadow Minister for Housing and Co-operatives, Oct. 1981; Leader of State Opposition, 1983; Shadow Treasurer, and Shadow Minister for Ethnic Affairs, 1983; Premier, Treasurer, and Minister for Ethnic and Aboriginal Affairs, NSW Coalition Govt, 1988–92. Dir, Sydney Organising Cttee for Olympic Games, 1993. *Recreations:* squash, ski-ing, theatre, opera, spectator sports. *Address:* Level 10, 139 Macquarie Street, Sydney, NSW 2000, Australia.

GRENFELL, family name of **Baron Grenfell.**

GRENFELL, 3rd Baron *cr* 1902; **Julian Pascoe Francis St Leger Grenfell;** Senior Adviser, European Office, World Bank, since 1995; *b* 23 May 1935; *o s* of 2nd Baron Grenfell, CBE, TD, and of Elizabeth Sarah Polk, *o d* of late Captain Hon. Alfred Shaughnessy, Montreal, Canada; *S* father, 1976; *m* 1st, 1961, Loretta Maria (marr. diss. 1970), *e d* of Alfredo Reali, Florence, Italy; one *d*; 2nd, 1970, Gabrielle Katharina (marr. diss. 1987), *o d* of late Dr Ernst Raab, Berlin, Germany; two *d*; 3rd, 1987, Mrs Elisabeth Porter (*née* Scott) (marr. diss. 1992), Washington, DC; 4th, 1993, Mrs Dagmar Langbehn Debreil. *Educ:* Eton; King's Coll., Cambridge. BA (Hons), President of the Union, Cambridge, 1959. 2 Lieut, KRRC (60th Rifles), 1954–56; Captain, Queen's Royal Rifles, TA, 1963; Programme Asst, ATV Ltd, 1960–61; frequent appearances and occasional scripts, for ATV religious broadcasting and current affairs series, 1960–64. Film and TV adviser, Encyclopaedia Britannica Ltd, 1961–64. Joined World Bank, Washington, DC, 1965; Chief of Information and Public Affairs for World Bank Group in Europe, 1970; Dep. Dir, European Office, 1973; Special rep. of World Bank to UN, 1974–81; Special Advr, 1983–87, Sen. Advr, 1987–90; Head of Ext. Affairs, European Office, 1990–95. *Publication:* (novel) Margot, 1984. *Recreations:* walking, diplomatic history. *Heir: cousin* Francis Pascoe John Grenfell [*b* 28 Feb. 1938; *m* 1977, Elizabeth Katharine, *d* of Hugh Kenyon]. *Address:* c/o World Bank, 66 avenue d'Iéna, 75116 Paris, France. *T:* 40693012. *Clubs:* Travellers', Royal Green Jackets.

GRENFELL, Andrée, (Mrs David Milman); Director, Milman International Australia, since 1990; *b* 14 Jan. 1940; *d* of Stephen Grenfell (writer) and Sybil Grenfell; *m* 1972, Roy Warden; two step *s*; *m* 1984, David Milman; two step *s*. *Educ:* privately. Graduate Diploma in Agric., 1989. Man. Dir, Elizabeth Arden Ltd, UK, 1974–76; Pres., Glemby Internat., UK and Europe, 1976–80; Sen. Vice Pres., Glemby Internat., USA, 1976–80. Chm., Kelly Burrell & Jones, 1988–91; Director: Harvey Nichols Knightsbridge, 1972–74; Peter Robinson Ltd, 1968–72; Non-executive Director: NAAFI, 1981–83; Prince of Wales Res. Inst., Sydney, 1994–. Mem. Council, Inst. of Dirs, 1976; FIMgt (FBIM 1977). Mem., Cercle des Amis de la Veuve. Business Woman of the Year, FT, 1979. *Recreations:* riding, dressage, swimming, yoga. *Address:* Jacaranda, 24 Cranbrook Road, Rose Bay, Sydney, NSW 2029, Australia. *Fax:* (2) 3262289.

GRENFELL, (Jeremy) Gibson; QC 1994; a Recorder, since 1992; *b* 13 Dec. 1945; *s* of Edward Gerald James Grenfell and June (*née* Hunkin). *Educ:* Falmouth Grammar Sch.; Fitzwilliam Coll., Cambridge (Open Exhibnr, MA). Called to the Bar, Middle Temple, 1969 (Harmsworth Schol.). *Address:* 2 Pump Court, Temple, EC4Y 7AH. *T:* 0171–353 5597.

GRENFELL, Simon Pascoe; His Honour Judge Grenfell; a Circuit Judge, since 1992; *b* 10 July 1942; *s* of Osborne Pascoe Grenfell and Margaret Grenfell; *m* 1974, Ruth De Jersey Harvard; one *s* three *d*. *Educ:* Fettes College; Emmanuel College, Cambridge (MA). Called to the Bar, Gray's Inn, 1965; practice on NE Circuit; a Recorder, 1985–92. Chancellor, dio. of Ripon, 1992–. *Recreations:* music, sailing, coarse gardening.

GRENFELL-BAINES, Prof. Sir George, Kt 1978; OBE 1960; DL; FRIBA; FRTPI; consultant architect-planner; consultant to Building Design Partnership; *b* Preston, 30 April 1908; *s* of Ernest Charles Baines and Sarah Elizabeth (*née* Grenfell); *m* 1st, 1939, Dorothy Hodson (marr. diss. 1952); two *d*; 2nd, 1954, Milena Ruth Fleischmann; one *s* one *d*. *Educ:* Roebuck Street Council Sch.; Harris Coll., Preston; Manchester Univ. (DipTP). RIBA Dist Town Planning, 1963. Commenced architectural practice, 1937; founded: Grenfell Baines Gp, 1940; Building Design Partnership, a multi-disciplinary practice covering all aspects of built environment, 1959 (Partner/Chm.), retired 1974; The Design Teaching Practice, 1974, retired 1979. Prof. and Head of Dept of Architecture, Univ. of Sheffield, 1972–75, Emeritus, 1976. Lectr/Critic, 14 USA and Canadian univs, 1966; initiated own lecture tour USSR, visiting 19 cities, 1971; expert adviser: UNESCO Conf. Bldgs; Higher Educn, Chile, 1968; Conescal, Mexico City, 1973. RIBA: Mem. Council (nationally elected), 1952–70; Vice-Pres., 1967–69; Ext. Examr, 12 Schs of Architecture, 1953–70. Chm. of Cttees on Professional Practice, Town Planning, Gp Practice and Consortia; Architectural Competition Assessor 8 times; competition entrant, several awards: first place in 7 (one internat.); 18 premiums (four internat.). Hon. Fellow: Metrop. Univ. of Manchester (formerly Manchester Poly.), 1974; Univ. of Central Lancs (formerly Lancashire Poly.), 1985; Hon. Vice-Pres., N Lancs Soc. Architects, 1977. Hon. Fellow, Amer. Inst. of Architects, 1982. Broadcaster, UK and Canada. Hon. DLitt Sheffield, 1981. DL Lancs, 1982. *Publications:* contribs to tech. jls. *Recreations:* brooding: on economics and alternative medicine; walking: on hills and by sea-shore. *Address:* 56 & 60 West Cliff, Preston, Lancs PR1 8HU. *T:* Preston (01772) 52131, 555824.

GRENIER, Rear-Adm. Peter Francis, (Frank), CB 1989; self-employed artist; Defence Advisor, House of Commons Defence Committee, since 1991; *b* 27 Aug. 1934; *s* of late Dr F. W. H. Grenier and Mrs M. Grenier; *m* 1957, Jane Susan Bradshaw; two *s* one *d* (and one *s* decd). *Educ:* Montpelier School, Paignton; Blundell's School, Tiverton. Entered RN (Special Entry), 1952; Midshipman, Mediterranean Fleet, 1953; commissioned, 1955; joined Submarine service, 1956; 1st command (HMS Ambush), 1965; final command (HMS Liverpool), 1982; Chief of Staff to C-in-C Naval Home Command, 1985–87; FO Submarines, and Comdr Submarine Forces E Atlantic, 1987–89. Vice-Pres., Royal Naval FA, 1988–. Liveryman: Painter-Stainers' Co., 1984; Glass Sellers' Co., 1987. Chm. of Govs, Blundell's Sch., 1991– (Gov., 1986–). *Recreations:* family, sketching and painting, glass engraving, golf. *Clubs:* Army and Navy; West Wilts Golf.

GRENSIDE, Sir John (Peter), Kt 1983; CBE 1974; Senior Partner, Peat, Marwick, Mitchell & Co., Chartered Accountants, 1977–86; *b* 23 Jan. 1921; *s* of late Harold Cutcliffe Grenside and late Muriel Grenside; *m* 1946, Yvonne Thérèse Grau; one *s* one *d*. *Educ:* Rugby School. ACA 1948, FCA 1960. War Service, Royal Artillery, 1941–46 (Captain). Joined Peat, Marwick, Mitchell & Co., 1948, Partner, 1960, Senior Partner, 1977; Chm., Peat Marwick Internat., 1980–83. Inst. Chartered Accountants: Mem Council, 1966–83; Chm. of Parliamentary and Law Cttee, 1972–73; Vice-Pres., 1973–74; Dep. Pres., 1974–75; Pres., 1975–76; Chm., Overseas Relations Cttee, 1976–78; UK Rep. on Internat. Accounting Standards Cttee, 1976–80. Jt Vice-Pres., Groupe d'Etudes des Experts Comptables de la CEE, 1972–75; Chm., Review Bd for Govt Contracts, 1983–86; Mem. Panel of Judges for Accountants' Award for Company Accounts, 1973–77. Director: Allied-Lyons plc, 1986–93; Nomura Bank Internat. plc, 1987–. Master, Worshipful Co. of Chartered Accountants in England and Wales, 1987–88. *Publications:* various articles for UK and US accountancy jls. *Recreations:* tennis, bridge. *Address:* 51 Cadogan Lane, SW1X 9DT. *T:* 0171–235 3372. *Clubs:* Pilgrims, MCC, All England Lawn Tennis, Hurlingham.

GRENVILLE; *see* Freeman-Grenville, family name of Lady Kinloss.

GRENVILLE, Prof. John Ashley Soames; Professor of Modern History, 1969–94, Professorial Research Fellow, Institute of German Studies, since 1994, University of Birmingham; *b* Berlin, 11 Jan. 1928; *m* 1st, 1960, Betty Anne Rosenberg (*d* 1974), New York; three *s*; 2nd, 1975, Patricia Carnie; one *d* one step *d*. *Educ:* Mistley Place and Orwell Park Prep. Sch.; Cambridge Techn. Sch.; corresp. courses; Birkbeck Coll.; LSE; Yale Univ. BA, PhD London; FRHistS. Postgrad. Schol., London Univ., 1951–53; Asst Lectr, subseq. Lectr, Nottingham Univ., 1953–64; Commonwealth Fund Fellow, 1958–59; Postdoctoral Fellow, Yale Univ., 1960–63; Reader in Modern History, Nottingham Univ., 1964–65; Prof. of Internat. History, Leeds Univ., 1965–69. Vis. Prof., Queen's Coll., NY City Univ., 1964, etc; Guest Professor, Univ. of Hamburg, 1980, 1994. Chm., British Univs History Film Consortium, 1968–71; Mem. Council: RHistS, 1971–73; List and Index Soc., 1966–71; Baeck Inst., London, 1981–. Consultant, American and European Bibliographical Centre, Oxford and California and Clio Press, 1960–88; Dir of Film for the Historical Assoc., 1975–78; Historical Adviser, World History, ZDF, German Television, 1982–. Editor: Fontana History of War and Society, 1969–78; Leo Baeck Year Book, 1992–. *Publications:* (with J. G. Fuller) The Coming of the Europeans, 1962; Lord Salisbury and Foreign Policy, 1964 (2nd edn 1970); (with G. B. Young) Politics, Strategy and American Diplomacy: studies in foreign policy 1873–1917, 1966 (2nd edn 1971); Documentary Films (with N. Pronay), The Munich Crisis, 1968; The End of Illusions: from Munich to Dunkirk, 1970; The Major International Treaties 1914–1973: a history and guide, 1974, enlarged edn in 2 vols, 1987; Europe Reshaped 1848–78, 1975; Nazi Germany, 1976; World History of the Twentieth Century I, 1900–1945, 1980; Collins World History of the Twentieth Century, 1994; contrib. various learned jls. *Recreation:* listening to music. *Address:* University of Birmingham, School of History, PO Box 363, Birmingham B15 2TT. *Club:* Athenæum.

GRENVILLE-GREY, Wilfrid Ernest; journalist at United Nations, New York, since 1990; *b* 27 May 1930; *s* of late Col Cecil Grenville-Grey, CBE and of Monica Grenville-Grey (*née* Morrison-Bell); *m* 1963, Edith Sibongile Dlamini (marr. diss. 1989), *d* of Rev. Jonathan Dlamini, Johannesburg; two *s* one *d*. *Educ:* Eton; Worcester College, Oxford (scholar; MA); Yale University (Henry Fellow, 1953–54). 2nd Lieut, KRRC, 1949–50. Overseas Civil Service, Nyasaland, 1956–59; Booker McConnell Ltd, 1960–63; Mindolo Ecumenical Foundn, Zambia, 1963–71 (Dir, 1966–71); Sec., Univ. Study Project on Foreign Investments in S Africa, 1971–72; Dir, Centre for Internat. Briefing, Farnham Castle, 1973–77; Internat. Defence and Aid Fund for Southern Africa, London and UN, 1978–83; Sec. for Public Affairs to Archbishop of Canterbury, 1984–87; British Dir,

Global Forum of Spiritual and Parly Leaders on Human Survival, 1987–88; Internat. Develt Dir, Icewalk, 1988–89. *Publications:* All in an African Lifetime, 1969; Sixty Marker Buoys for a Sixtieth Birthday (anthology), 1990; Sixty-Five Marker Buoys for a Sixty-Fifth Birthday (aphorisms), 1995. *Recreations:* gardening, apophthegms. *Address:* Apartment 4A, 30 Eastchester Road, New Rochelle, NY 10801, USA. *Club:* Travellers'.

GRENYER, Herbert Charles, FRICS; Vice-President, London Rent Assessment Panel, 1973–79; Deputy Chief Valuer, Board of Inland Revenue, 1968–73; *b* 22 Jan. 1913; *s* of Harry John and Daisy Elizabeth Grenyer (*née* De Maid); *m* 1940, Jean Gladwell Francis; one *s* one *d*. *Recreations:* golf, gardening, listening to music. *Address:* Old Rickford, Worplesdon, Surrey GU3 3PJ. *T:* Worplesdon (01483) 232173.

GRESHAM, Prof. (Geoffrey) Austin, TD 1966; FRCPath, FRCPE; Professor of Morbid Anatomy and Histopathology, Cambridge, 1973–92; Fellow and President, Jesus College, Cambridge, since 1964; Home Office Pathologist, since 1968; *b* 1 Nov. 1924; *s* of Thomas Michael and Harriet Anne Gresham; *m* 1950, Gweneth Margery Leigh; three *s* two *d*. *Educ:* Grove Park Sch., Wrexham; Caius Coll., Cambridge (Tancred Student and Schol.; MA; ScD); King's Coll. Hosp., London (Burney Yeo Schol., Todd and Jelf Medallist; MB BChir, MD). FRCPE 1994. Served RAMC, 1950–52, Lt-Col RAMC V, 1961. Cambridge University: Demonstrator and Lectr in Pathology, 1953–62; Univ. Morbid Anatomist, 1962–73; Sec., Faculty Bd of Medicine, 1956–61; Chm., MD Cttee, 1991–; Dep. to Regius Prof. of Physics, 1991–; Dep. to Vice Chancellor, 1993–. Consultant Mem., Cambridge Dist Management Team, 1974–84; Chairman: Cambridge Dist Medical Cttee, 1974–84; Medical Staff Leave Cttee, 1974–84; Cambridge Dist Ethical Cttee, 1974–84; Member: European Atherosclerosis Soc., 1959–; British Atherosclerosis Discussion Gp, 1965–. Roy Cameron Meml Lectr, RC Path, 1983. Mem. Bd of Governors, United Cambridge Hosps, 1972–74. Scientific Medal, Univ. of Tokyo, 1985. *Publications:* Introduction to Comparative Pathology, 1962; Biological Aspects of Occlusive Vascular Disease, 1964; Colour Atlas of General Pathology, 1971, 2nd edn 1993; Primate Atherosclerosis, 1976; Colour Atlas of Forensic Pathology, 1977; Post Mortem Procedures, 1979; Reversing Atherosclerosis, 1980; Arterial Pollution, 1981; Wounds and Wounding, 1987; contrib. chapters, and papers in many jls, about pathology. *Recreations:* gardening, playing organ, wine, silver, talking. *Address:* 18 Rutherford Road, Cambridge CB2 2HH. *T:* Cambridge (01223) 841326.

GRESWELL, Air Cdre Jeaffreson Herbert, CB 1967; CBE 1962 (OBE 1946); DSO 1944; DFC 1942; RAF, retired; *b* 28 July 1916; *s* of William Territt Greswell; *m* 1939, Gwyneth Alice Hayes; one *s* three *d*. *Educ:* Repton. Joined RAF, 1935, Pilot. Served War of 1939–45, in Coastal Command, Anti-Submarine No. 217 Sqdn, 1937–41; No. 172 Sqdn, 1942; OC No. 179 Sqdn, Gibraltar, 1943–44. Air Liaison Officer, Pacific Fleet, 1946–47; Staff of Joint Anti-Submarine Sch., 1949–52; Staff of Flying Coll., Manby, 1952–54; Planning Staff, Min. of Defence, 1954–57; OC, RAF Station Kinloss, 1957–59; Plans HQ, Coastal Comd, 1959–61; Standing Group Rep. to NATO Council, Paris, 1961–64; Commandant, Royal Observer Corps, 1964–68. Sqdn Ldr 1941; Wing Comdr 1942; Gp Capt. 1955; Air Cdre 1961. *Recreation:* croquet. *Address:* Red Cedars, Oddley Lane, Saunderton, Princes Risborough, Bucks HP27 9NQ.

GRETTON, family name of **Baron Gretton.**

GRETTON, 4th Baron *cr* 1944, of Stapleford; **John Lysander Gretton;** *b* 17 April 1975; *s* of 3rd Baron Gretton and of Jennifer Ann, *o d* of Edmund Moore; *S* father, 1989. *Educ:* Shrewsbury. *Heir:* none. *Address:* Somerby House, Somerby, Melton Mowbray, Leics LE14 2PZ. *T:* Somerby (01664) 454607.

GRETTON, Vice Adm. Michael Peter; Representive of Supreme Allied Commander Atlantic in Europe, since 1994; *b* 14 March 1946; *s* of Vice Adm. Sir Peter Gretton, KCB, DSO, OBE, DSC, MA and of Dorothy (*née* Du Vivier); *m* 1973, Stephanie O'Neill; one *s* three *d*. *Educ:* Ampleforth Coll.; BRNC Dartmouth; Trinity Coll., Oxford (BA PPE; MA). Joined RN, 1963; served HMS Torquay, Tiger, Rothesay, Ark Royal and Bacchante; commanded: HMS Bossington, 1972–73; HMS Ambuscade, 1977–80; RCDS, 1987; commanded: HMS Invincible, 1988–90; NATO Standing Naval Force Atlantic, 1990–91; Dir of Naval Staff Duties, MoD, 1991–93; comd UK Task Force and NATO Anti-Submarine Warfare Striking Force, 1993–94. Governor: St Edward's Sch., Oxford, 1985–; Farleigh Sch., Red Rice, 1992–. Pres., RN RFU, 1993–. FNI 1994. *Recreations:* sport, sightseeing, listening to music. *Address:* c/o Naval Secretary, Victory Building, Portsmouth, Hants PO1 3LS. *Clubs:* Naval; I Zingari.

GREVE, Prof. John; Hon. Senior Research Fellow, University of York, since 1988; Professor of Social Policy and Administration, University of Leeds, 1974–87, now Emeritus; *b* 23 Nov. 1927; *s* of Steffen A. and Ellen C. Greve; *m* (marr. diss. 1986); one *s* one *d*. *Educ:* elementary and secondary Schs in Cardiff; London Sch. of Economics (BSc(Econ)). Various jobs, incl. Merchant Navy, Youth Employment Service, and insurance, 1946–55; student, 1955–58; research work, then Univ. teaching, 1958–. Has worked in Norway at research institutes. Community Programmes Dept, Home Office, 1969–74; Prof. of Social Admin, Univ. of Southampton, 1969–74. Hon. Vis. Prof., Univ. of York, 1987–88. Mem., Royal Commn on Distribution of Income and Wealth, 1974–79; directed GLC Enquiry into Homelessness in London, 1985–86; Mem., Management Cttee E London Housing Assoc., 1988–. *Publications:* The Housing Problem, 1961 (and 1969); London's Homeless, 1964; Private Landlords in England, 1965; (with others) Comparative Social Administration, 1969, 2nd edn 1972; Housing, Planning and Change in Norway, 1970; Voluntary Housing in Scandinavia, 1971; (with others) Homelessness in London, 1971; Low Incomes in Sweden, 1978; (jtly) Sheltered Housing for the Elderly, 1983; Homelessness in Britain, 1990, rev. edn 1991; Poland—the reform of housing, 1994; various articles and papers, mainly on social problems, policies and administration, a few short stories. *Recreations:* walking, painting, listening to music, writing, good company. *Address:* 9 Westfield Close, Wigginton, York YO3 3JG.

GREVILLE, family name of **Earl of Warwick.**

GREVILLE, Brig. Phillip Jamieson, CBE 1972; freelance writer on defence, foreign affairs and Australian history; Australian Director, International Institute for Prisoners of War, since 1992; *b* 12 Sept. 1925; *s* of Col S. J. Greville, OBE and Mrs D. M. Greville; *m* 1948, June Patricia Anne Martin; two *s* one *d* (and one *s* one *d* decd). *Educ:* RMC Duntroon; Sydney Univ. (BEng). 2/8 Field Co., 2nd AIF, New Guinea, 1945; 1 RAR Korea (POW), 1951–53; Senior Instructor SME Casula, 1953–55; CRE, RMC Duntroon, 1955–58; Staff Coll., Camberley and Transportation Trng UK, 1959–61; Dir of Transportation AHQ, 1962–65; GSO1 1st Div., 1966; CE Eastern Comd, 1969–71; Comdr 1st Australian Logistic Support Group, Vietnam, 1971; Actg Comdr 1st Australian Task Force, Vietnam, 1971–72 (CBE); Dir of Transport, 1973–74; Dir Gen., Logistics, 1975–76; Comdr, Fourth Mil. District, 1977–80, retired. Adelaide Advertiser: Defence Writer, 1980–86; Pacific Defence Reporter, 1987–. Dir, Dominant Australia Pty, 1982–86. Nat. Pres., RUSI of Aust., 1983–. FIE(Aust), FCIT. *Publications:* A Short History of Victoria Barracks Paddington, 1969; The Central Organisation for War and its Application to Movements, 1975, Sapper series (RE Officers in Australia); The Army Portion of the National Estate, 1977; Why Australia Should Not Ratify the New Law of War, 1989. *Recreation:* golf. *Address:* 3 River Downs Crescent, River Downs, Qld 4210, Australia. *Club:* United Services (Brisbane).

GREWAL, Harnam Singh, CBE 1990; ED 1976; Secretary for the Civil Service, Government Secretariat, Hong Kong, 1987–90, retired; *b* 5 Dec. 1937; *s* of late Joginder Singh Grewal and Ajaib Kaur; *m* 1973, Shiv Pal Kaur Chima; one *s* one *d*. *Educ:* Sir Ellis Kadoorie Sch.; King's Coll., Univ. of Hong Kong (BA Hons 1959; DipEd 1960); Pembroke Coll., Cambridge Univ. (BA 1962; MA 1974). Asst Educn Officer, Hong Kong, 1962; Admin Officer, 1964; Dist Officer, Tai Po, 1970; Dep. Dir of Urban Services, Hong Kong, 1976; Dep. Sec. for CS, 1980; Comr of Customs and Excise, 1984; Sec. for Transport, 1986. Royal Hong Kong Regt (The Volunteers), 1963–84, Major (retd); Hon. Col, 1987–90. *Recreations:* hockey, squash. *Address:* 3495 Cadboro Bay Road, Victoria, BC V8R 5K7, Canada. *Club:* Royal Hong Kong Jockey (Hong Kong).

GREY, family name of **Earl Grey,** and of **Baron Grey of Naunton.**

GREY; *see* De Grey.

GREY, 6th Earl, *cr* 1806; **Richard Fleming George Charles Grey;** Bt 1746; Baron Grey, 1801; Viscount Howick, 1806; *b* 5 March 1939; *s* of late Albert Harry George Campbell Grey (Trooper, Canadian Army Tanks, who *d* on active service, 1942) and Vera Helen Louise Harding; *S* cousin, 1963; *m* 1st, 1966, Margaret Ann (marr. diss. 1974), *e d* of Henry Bradford, Ashburton; 2nd, 1974, Stephanie Caroline, *o d* of Donald Gaskell-Brown and formerly wife of Surg.-Comdr Neil Leicester Denham, RN. *Educ:* Hounslow Coll.; Hammersmith Coll. of Bldg (Quantity Surveying). Public relations consultant. Chairman: Academy Beverage Co. Ltd, 1990–; London Cremation Co., 1992–; Roper Catering Events, 1993–; Director: Countess Grey Collection, 1993–; Covent Garden Quality, 1993–. President: Assoc. of Cost and Executive Accountants, 1978; Cremation Soc. of GB, 1992–. Mem., Liberal Party. *Recreations:* golf, sailing. *Heir:* *b* Philip Kent Grey [*b* 11 May 1940; *m* 1968, Ann Catherine, *y d* of Cecil Applegate, Kingsbridge, Devon; one *s* one *d*]. *Address:* House of Lords, SW1A 0PW.

GREY OF CODNOR, 5th Baron *cr* 1397 (in abeyance 1496–1989); **Charles Legh Shuldham Cornwall-Legh,** CBE 1977 (OBE 1971); AE 1946; DL; *b* 10 Feb. 1903; *er s* of late Charles Henry George Cornwall Legh, of High Legh Hall, Cheshire, and late Geraldine Maud, *d* of Lt-Col Arthur James Shuldham, Royal Inniskilling Fusiliers; *S* to barony on termination of abeyance, 1989; *m* 1930, Dorothy (*d* 1993), *er d* of late J. W. Scott, Seal, Sevenoaks; one *s* two *d*. Served 1939–45 with AAF and RAF. JP Cheshire, 1938–73; High Sheriff, 1939; DL, 1949; CC 1949–77. Chm., Cheshire Police Authority, 1957–74; Chm., New Cheshire CC, 1974–76 (Shadow Chm., 1973); Hon. Alderman, 1977. *Heir:* *s* Hon. Richard Henry Cornwall-Legh [*b* 14 May 1936; *m* 1974, Joanna Storm, *y d* of Sir Kenelm Cayley, 10th Bt; three *s* one *d*]. *Address:* High Legh House, Knutsford, Cheshire WA16 0QR. *T:* Lymm (01925) 752303. *Clubs:* Carlton, MCC.

GREY OF NAUNTON, Baron, *cr* 1968 (Life Peer); **Ralph Francis Alnwick Grey,** GCMG 1964 (KCMG 1959, CMG 1955); GCVO 1973 (KCVO 1956); OBE 1951; Chancellor, University of Ulster, 1984–93 (New University of Ulster, 1980–84); Lord Prior of the Order of St John, 1988–91; *b* 15 April 1910; *o s* of late Francis Arthur Grey and Mary Wilkie Grey (*née* Spence); *m* 1944, Esmé, DStJ, *widow* of Pilot Officer Kenneth Kirkcaldie, RAFVR, and *d* of late A. V. Burcher and Florence Burcher, Remuera, Auckland, New Zealand; two *s* one *d*. *Educ:* Scots Coll.; Wellington Coll., NZ; Auckland Univ. Coll.; Pembroke Coll., Cambridge. LLB (NZ). Barrister and Solicitor of Supreme Court of New Zealand, 1932; Associate to Hon. Mr Justice Smith, 1932–36; Probationer, Colonial Administrative Service, 1936; Administrative Service, Nigeria: Cadet, 1937; Asst Financial Sec., 1949; Administrative Officer, Class I, 1951; Development Sec., 1952; Sec. to Governor-Gen. and Council of Ministers, 1954; Chief Sec. of the Federation, 1955–57; Dep. Gov.-Gen., 1957–59; Gov. and C-in-C, British Guiana, 1959–64; Governor and C-in-C of The Bahamas, 1964–68, and of the Turks and Caicos Islands, 1965–68; Governor of N Ireland, 1968–73. Dep. Chm., Commonwealth Development Corp., 1973–79, Chm. 1979–80. Pres., Chartered Inst. of Secretaries, NI, 1970–; Hon. Life Mem., NI Chamber of Commerce and Industry, 1970; Hon. Pres., Lisburn Chamber of Commerce, 1972–. Mem., Bristol Regional Bd, Lloyds Bank Ltd, 1973–81. Grand Pres., Royal Over-Seas League, 1993 (Pres., 1981–93; Chm. Central Council, 1976–81); President: Scout Council, NI, 1968–93; Britain–Nigeria Assoc., 1983–89; Overseas Service Pensioners' Assoc., 1983–. Mem. Council, Cheltenham Ladies' College, 1975–87. Hon. Bencher: Inn of Court of N Ireland, 1970; Gray's Inn, 1991. Hon. Freeman: City of Belfast, 1972; Lisburn, 1975; Freeman, City of London, 1980. Hon. LLD: QUB, 1971; NUI, 1985; Hon. DLitt NUU, 1980; Hon. DSc Ulster, 1985. GCStJ (Bailiff of Egle, 1975–87, Chancellor of the Order, 1987–88); Kt Comdr, Commandery of Ards, 1968–76. GC Merito Melitense, 1989. *Recreation:* golf. *Address:* Overbrook, Naunton, near Cheltenham, Glos GL54 3AX. *T:* Guiting Power (01451) 850263. *Club:* Travellers'.

GREY, Alan Hartley; HM Diplomatic Service, retired; Judge, Council of Europe Administrative Tribunal (formerly Member, Council of Europe Appeals Board), since 1993; *b* 26 June 1925; *s* of William Hartley Grey and Gladys Grey; *m* 1950, Joan Robinson (*d* 1985); one *s* one *d*. *Educ:* Bootle Secondary Sch. for Boys. RAF, 1943–48; Foreign Service (Br. B), 1948; Tel Aviv, 1949; Tabriz and Beaumshahr, 1950–52; 3rd Sec., Belgrade, 1952–54; Vice-Consul, Dakar, 1954–57; Second Sec. (Commercial), Helsinki, 1958–61; FO, 1961–64; Second Sec. (Econ.), Paris, 1964–66; FO (later FCO), 1966–70; Consul (Commercial), Lille, 1970–74; FCO, 1974–82; Ambassador at Libreville, 1982–84; re-employed in FCO (as Staff Assessor), 1985–90. *Recreations:* gardening, bamboo pipe making and playing.

GREY, Sir Anthony (Dysart), 7th Bt *cr* 1814; former Inspector, Department of Industrial Affairs, Government of Western Australia; *b* 19 Oct. 1949; *s* of Edward Elton Grey (*d* 1962) (*o s* of 6th Bt) and of Nancy, *d* of late Francis John Meagher, Perth, WA; *S* grandfather, 1974; *m* 1970 (marr. diss.). *Educ:* Guildford Grammar School, WA. *Recreations:* fishing, painting. *Address:* 86 Ringsway Gardens, 38 Rings Park Road, W Perth, WA 6005, Australia.

GREY, Dame Beryl, DBE 1988 (CBE 1973); Prima Ballerina, Sadler's Wells Ballet, now Royal Ballet, 1942–57; Artistic Director, London Festival Ballet, 1968–79; *b* London, 11 June 1927; *d* of late Arthur Ernest Groom; *m* 1950, Dr Sven Gustav Svenson; one *s*. *Educ:* Dame Alice Owens Girls' Sch., London. Professional training: Madeline Sharp Sch., Sadler's Wells Sch. (Schol.), de Vos Sch. Début Sadler's Wells Co., 1941, with Ballerina rôles following same year in Les Sylphides, The Gods Go A'Begging, Le Lac des Cygnes, Act II, Comus. First full-length ballet, Le Lac des Cygnes on 15th birthday, 1942. Has appeared since in leading rôles of many ballets including: Sleeping Beauty, Giselle, Sylvia, Checkmate, Ballet Imperial, Donald of the Burthens, Homage, Birthday Offering, The Lady and the Fool. Film: The Black Swan (3 Dimensional Ballet Film), 1952. Left Royal Ballet, Covent Garden, Spring 1957, to become free-lance ballerina. Regular guest appearances with Royal Ballet at Covent Garden and on European, African, American and Far Eastern Tours. Guest Artist, London's Festival Ballet in London and abroad,

1958–64. First Western ballerina to appear with Bolshoi Ballet: Moscow, Leningrad, Kiev, Tiflis, 1957–58; First Western ballerina to dance with Chinese Ballet Co. in Peking and Shanghai, 1964. Engagements and tours abroad include: Central and S America, Mexico, Rhodesia and S Africa, Canada, NZ, Lebanon, Germany, Norway, Sweden, Denmark, Finland, Belgium, Holland, France, Switzerland, Italy, Portugal, Austria, Czechoslovakia, Poland, Rumania; Producer: Sleeping Beauty, 1967; Swan Lake, 1972, London Fest. Ballet; Giselle, Western Australia Ballet, 1984; Sleeping Beauty, Royal Swedish Co., Stockholm, 1985. Regular television and broadcasts in England and abroad; concert narrator. Dir-Gen., Arts Educational Trust, 1966–68. President: Dance Council of Wales, 1981–; ISTD, 1991– (Mem. Council, 1966–91; Chm., 1984–91); Vice-Pres., Royal Acad. of Dancing, 1980– (Exec. Mem., 1982–89); Trustee: London City Ballet, 1978–92; Adeline Genée Theatre, 1982–90; Royal Ballet Benevolent Fund, 1982– (Chm. Trustees, 1992–); Vice Chm., Dance Teachers Benevolent Fund, 1985– (Trustee, 1981–); Pres., Keep Fit Assoc., 1992–; Vice-Pres., British Fedn of Music Festivals, 1985. Governor: Dame Alice Owens Girls' Sch., London, 1960–77; Frances Mary Buss Foundn, 1963–72; Royal Ballet, 1993–. FISTD 1960; FRSA 1989. Hon. DMus Leicester, 1970; Hon. DLitt: City, 1974; Buckingham, 1993; Hon. DEd CNAA, 1989. *Publications:* Red Curtain Up, 1958; Through the Bamboo Curtain, 1965; My Favourite Ballet Stories, 1981. *Relevant publications:* biographical studies (by Gordon Anthony), 1952, (by Pigeon Crowle), 1952; Beryl Grey, Dancers of Today (by Hugh Fisher), 1955; Beryl Grey, a biography (by David Gillard), 1977. *Recreations:* music, painting, reading, swimming. *Address:* Fernhill, Priory Road, Forest Row, Sussex RH18 5JE. *T:* Forest Row (0134282) 2539.

GREY, John Egerton, CB 1980; Clerk Assistant and Clerk of Public Bills, House of Lords, 1974–88; *b* 8 Feb. 1929; *s* of late John and Nancy Grey; *m* 1961, Patricia Hanna; two adopted *s*. *Educ:* Dragon Sch., Oxford; Blundell's; Brasenose Coll., Oxford. MA, BCL. Called to Bar, Inner Temple, 1954; practised at Chancery Bar, 1954–59. Clerk in Parliament Office, House of Lords, 1959–88. Adviser, Colchester CAB, 1989–. *Recreations:* gardening, boating. *Address:* 51 St Peters Road, West Mersea, Colchester, Essex CO5 8LL. *T:* West Mersea (01206) 383007. *Clubs:* Arts; West Mersea Yacht.

GREY, Maj.-Gen. John St John, CB 1987; Clerk, Worshipful Company of Pewterers, 1988–March 1996; *b* 6 June 1934; *s* of late Major Donald John Grey, RM and Doris Mary Grey (*née* Beavan); *m* 1958, Elisabeth Ann (*née* Langley); one *s* one *d*. *Educ:* Christ's Hospital. rcds, ndc, psc(M), osc(US). Commissioned 2/Lt 1952; Commando service, Malta, Egypt, Cyprus, 1955–64; Cruiser HMS Lion as OC RM, 1964–65; Instructor, Army Sch. of Infantry, 1967–69; US Marine Corps, 1970–71; Commanded 45 Cdo Gp (incl. tours in N Ireland and Arctic Norway), 1976–78; Mil. Sec. and Col Ops/Plans, MoD, 1979–84; Maj.-Gen. RM Commando Forces, 1984–87; RM COS, 1987–88, retired. Col Comdt RM, 1993–. Member: HAC, 1991–; Council, Officers' Pension Soc., 1991–. Pres., SSAFA, Devon, 1993. *Recreation:* sailing. *Address:* c/o Lloyds Bank, 4 Regent Street, Teignmouth, S Devon TQ14 8SL. *Clubs:* Army and Navy; Royal Naval Sailing Association (Portsmouth); Royal Marines Sailing.

GREY, Robin Douglas, QC 1979; a Recorder of the Crown Court, since 1979; *b* 23 May 1931; *s* of Dr Francis Temple Grey, MA, MB, and Eglantine Grey; *m* 1st, 1972, Berenice Anna Wheatley (marr. diss.); one *s* one *d*; 2nd, 1993, Mrs Annick Regnault. *Educ:* Summer Fields Prep. Sch., Oxford; Eastbourne Coll.; London Univ. (LLB Hons). Called to the Bar, Gray's Inn, 1957. Crown Counsel, Colonial Legal Service, Aden, 1959–63 (Actg Registrar Gen. and Actg Attorney Gen. for short periods); practising barrister, 1963–; Dep. Circuit Judge, 1977. FCO Consultant to Govt of Russian Fedn, 1993–94; led FCO team to Moscow on Jury Trials, 1993. Chm., Home Office Police Appeals Tribunals, 1990–. Member: Internat. Bar Assoc., 1994; Cttee, Criminal Bar Assoc., 1990–93 (Chm., Internat. Sub-Cttee, 1993); British Acad. of Forensic Sciences. *Recreations:* tennis, golf, fishing. *Address:* Queen Elizabeth Building, Temple, EC4Y 9BS. *T:* 0171–583 5766; Dun Cottage, The Marsh, Hungerford, Berks RG17 0SN. *T:* Hungerford (01488) 683578. *Club:* Hurlingham.

GREY, Wilfrid Ernest G.; *see* Grenville-Grey.

GREY EGERTON, Sir (Philip) John (Caledon), 15th Bt, *cr* 1617; *b* 19 Oct. 1920; *er s* of Sir Philip Grey Egerton, 14th Bt; *S* father, 1962; *m* 1st, 1952, Margaret Voase (*d* 1971) (who *m* 1941, Sqdn Ldr Robert A. Ullman, *d* 1943), *er d* of late Rowland Rank; 2nd, 1986, Frances Mary (who *m* 1941 Sqdn Ldr William Dudley Williams, DFC, *d* 1976), *y d* of late Col R. M. Rainey-Robinson. *Educ:* Eton. Served Welsh Guards, 1939–45. *Recreation:* fishing. *Heir:* *b* Brian Balguy Le Belward Egerton, *b* 5 Feb. 1925. *Address:* Meadow House, West Stafford, Dorchester, Dorset DT2 8AQ.

GRIBBLE, Rev. Canon Arthur Stanley, MA; Canon Residentiary and Chancellor of Peterborough Cathedral, 1967–79; Canon Emeritus since 1979; *b* 18 Aug. 1904; *er s* of J. B. Gribble; *m* 1938, Edith Anne, *er d* of late Laurence Bailey; one *s*. *Educ:* Queens' Coll. and Westcott House, Cambridge (Burney Student, Univ. of Cambridge); Univ. of Heidelberg. Curate: St Mary, Windermere, 1930–33, Almondbury, 1933–36; Chaplain Sarum Theological Coll., 1936–38; Rector of Shepton Mallet, 1938–54. Examining Chaplain to Bp of Bath and Wells, 1947–54; Proctor in Convocation, diocese Bath and Wells, 1947–54; Rural Dean of Shepton Mallet, 1949–54; Prebendary of Wiveliscombe in Wells Cathedral, 1949–54; Principal, Queen's Coll., Birmingham, 1954–67; Recognised Lectr, Univ. of Birmingham, 1954–67. Hon. Canon, Birmingham Cathedral, 1954–67. Commissary for the Bishop of Kimberley and Kuruman, 1964–66. Examng Chaplain to Bishop of Peterborough, 1968–84. Visiting Lectr, Graduate Theological Union, Berkeley, USA, 1970. *Recreation:* mountaineering. *Address:* 2 Princes Road, Stamford, Lincs PE9 1QT. *T:* Stamford (01780) 55838.

GRIBBON, Edward John; Under Secretary, Board of Inland Revenue, since 1991; Director, Business Profits Division, since 1991; *b* 10 July 1943; *s* of Henry Derwent Gribbon and late Dorothy Gribbon (*née*Boyd); *m* 1968, Margaret Nanette Flanagan; one *s* two *d*. *Educ:* Coleraine Academical Instn; Univ. of London (LLB). FCA. Qualified as Chartered Accountant, 1965; joined Inland Revenue as HM Inspector of Taxes, 1966; HM Principal Inspector of Taxes, 1981; Dep. Dir of Operations, Compliance, 1989. *Recreations:* family, photography, local church. *Address:* Board of Inland Revenue, Somerset House, Strand, WC2R 1LB. *T:* 0171–438 6774.

GRIBBON, Maj.-Gen. Nigel St George, OBE 1960; Director, Chancellor Insurance Co. Ltd, 1986–93; Consultant, Chancellor Group Ltd, 1987–92; *b* Feb. 1917; *s* of late Brig. W. H. Gribbon, CMG, CBE; *m* 1943, Rowan Mary MacLiesh; two *s* one *d*. *Educ:* Rugby Sch.; Sandhurst. King's Own, 1937–42; active service, Iraq (Habbaniya), 1941 (wounded), Western Desert, 1942; GSO3 10th Indian Div., 1942; Staff Coll. Quetta, 1943; Bde Major, 1st Parachute Bde, 1946; served Palestine, 1946, Trieste, 1947–48, Malaysia, 1948–50; RAF Staff Coll., 1947; OC 5 King's Own, 1958–60; AMS WO, 1960–62; Comdr 161 Bde, 1963–65; Canadian Nat. Defence Coll., 1965–66; DMC MoD, 1966–67; BGS (I) BAOR, 1967–69; ACOS (Intelligence), SHAPE, 1970–72. Managing Director: Partnerplan Public Affairs Ltd, 1973–75; Sallingbury Ltd, 1977–85 (Chm., 1975–77 and 1984–85); Sallingbury Casey Ltd, 1986–87; Dir, Gatewood Engineers Ltd, 1976–83. Operational Planning Consultant, Venice-Simplon Orient Express, 1980–84. Canada-UK Chamber of Commerce: Mem. Council, 1979–; Chm., Trade Cttee, 1980; Pres., 1981; Chm., Jt Cttee, Canadian Chamber of Commerce, 1982–91. Hd of Secretariat, European Channel Tunnel Gp and Public Affairs Cttee, 1980–85; Chairman: UK Falkland Islands Trust, 1982–; Forces Financial Services, 1983–85; SHAPE Assoc. (UK Chapter), 1984–; Adv. Cttee, Shackleton Meml Fund, 1995–. Member: Council, British Atlantic Cttee, 1975–93 (Mem. Exec. Cttee, 1983–88); Cttee, Amer. European Atlantic Cttee, 1985–92; Eur. Atlantic Gp, 1974–87; Council, Mouvement Européen Français (Londres), 1979–87; Council, Wyndham Place Trust, 1979–82; Canadian War Meml Foundn, 1988–. Vice-Pres., King's Own Affairs, 1974–88. Radio commentator and lectr on public affairs. Freeman, City of London; Liveryman, Worshipful Co. of Shipwrights. *Recreations:* sailing, ski-ing, swimming, watercolour sketching. *Address:* 99 Pump Street, Orford, Woodbridge, Suffolk IP12 2IX. *T:* Orford (01394) 450413. *Clubs:* Army and Navy (Mem., Gen. and Finance Cttees, 1989–92); Little Ship (Rear Commodore Training, 1978–80); Royal Yachting Association.

GRIDLEY, family name of **Baron Gridley.**

GRIDLEY, 2nd Baron, *cr* 1955; **Arnold Hudson Gridley;** *b* 26 May 1906; *er* surv. *s* of 1st Baron Gridley, KBE, Culwood, Lye Green, Chesham, Bucks; *S* father, 1965; *m* 1948, Edna Lesley, *d* of late Richard Wheen of Shanghai, China; one *s* three *d*. *Educ:* Oundle. Colonial Civil Service, Malaya, 1928–57; interned during Japanese occupation in Changi Gaol, Singapore, 1941–45; returned to duty, 1946; Dep.-Comptroller of Customs and Excise, Malaya, 1956, retired 1957. Mem. Council and Exec. Cttee, Overseas Service Pensioners Assoc., 1961–; Govt Trustee, Far East (POW and Internee) Fund, 1971–; with Parly Delegn to BAOR, 1976; visited and toured Rhodesia during Lancaster House Conf., speaking to local civil servants on the future of their pensions, 1979; special duty in Singapore and Malaya (incl. commemoration of those who gave their lives, 1941–45), during visit of HRH the Duke of Kent, 1985. Dir, New Homes Bldg Soc., 1963 (incorp. into Britannia Bldg Soc., 1970); Chm., Centralised Audio Systems Ltd, 1971–86, Life Pres., 1987. Mem., Somerset CC Rating Appeals Tribunal, 1970–73; Political Adviser to Peoples' Trust for Endangered Species, 1979–. Pres., Gillingham (Dorset) Civic Trust, 1992–. Chm., Board of Governors, Hall Sch., Bratton Seymour, Som, 1970–76. *Heir:* *s* Hon. Richard David Arnold Gridley [*b* 22 Aug. 1956; *m* 1983, Suzanne Elizabeth Ripper; one *s* one *d*]. *Address:* Coneygore, Stoke Trister, Wincanton, Somerset BA9 9PG. *T:* Wincanton (01963) 32209. *Club:* Royal Over-Seas League.

GRIER, Patrick Arthur, OBE 1963; HM Diplomatic Service, retired; *b* 2 Dec. 1918; *s* of late Very Rev. R. M. Grier, Provost of St Ninian's Cath., Perth, and Mrs E. M. Grier; *m* 1946, Anna Fraembs, *y d* of Hüttendirektor H. Fraembs, Rasselstein, Neuwied, Germany; one *d*. *Educ:* Lancing; King's Coll., Cambridge (MA 1946). Served War of 1939–45 with RA and Indian Mountain Artillery, NW Frontier of India and Burma (Major). Kreis Resident Officer of Mönchen-Gladbach, 1946–47; Colonial Administrative Service, N Nigeria, 1947, later HMOCS; Clerk to Exec. Council, Kaduna, 1953–55; W African Inter-territorial Secretariat, Accra, 1955–57; Principal Asst Sec. to Governor of N Nigeria, 1957–59; Dep. Sec. to Premier, 1959–63; retired from HMOCS, 1963. CRO, 1963–64; First Sec., Canberra, 1964–66; Head of Chancery, Port of Spain, 1966–69; Dep. UK Permanent Rep. to Council of Europe, Strasbourg, 1969–74; Counsellor and Head of Chancery, Berne, 1974–78. *Recreations:* tennis, ski-ing. *Address:* Buffalo Cottage, Wootton, New Milton, Hants BH25 5TT. *T:* New Milton (01425) 618398. *Club:* Commonwealth Trust.

GRIERSON, Sir Michael (John Bewes), 12th Bt *cr* 1685 (NS), of Lag, Dumfriesshire; retired; *b* 24 July 1921; *s* of Lt-Col Alexander George William Grierson, RM retd (*d* 1951) (2nd *s* of 9th Bt) and Violet Ethel (*d* 1980), *d* of Lt-Col Arthur Edward Bewes, CMG; *S* cousin, 1987; *m* 1971, Valerie Anne, *d* of late Russell Wright, Gidea Park, Essex, one *d*. *Educ:* Warden House School, Deal; St Edmund's School, Canterbury. Served War, RAF, 1941–46; subsequent career in civil engineering and local government; retired, 1986. *Recreations:* gardening, motoring, plane spotting, woodwork, photography. *Heir:* none. *Address:* 40c Palace Road, Streatham Hill, SW2 3NJ.

GRIERSON, Prof. Philip, MA, LittD; FBA 1958; FSA; Fellow, since 1935, Librarian, 1944–69, and President, 1966–76, Gonville and Caius College, Cambridge; Professor of Numismatics, University of Cambridge, 1971–78, now Emeritus; Professor of Numismatics and the History of Coinage, University of Brussels, 1948–81; Hon. Keeper of the Coins, Fitzwilliam Museum, Cambridge, since 1949; Adviser in Byzantine Numismatics to the Dumbarton Oaks Library and Collections, Harvard University, at Washington, USA, since 1955; *b* 15 Nov. 1910; *s* of Philip Henry Grierson and Roberta Ellen Jane Pope. *Educ:* Marlborough Coll.; Gonville and Caius Coll., Cambridge (MA 1936, LittD 1971). University Lectr in History, Cambridge, 1945–59; Reader in Medieval Numismatics, Cambridge, 1959–71. Literary Dir of Royal Historical Society, 1945–55; Ford's Lectr in History, University of Oxford, 1956–57. Pres. Royal Numismatic Society, 1961–66. Corresp. Fellow, Mediaeval Acad. of America, 1972; Corresp. Mem., Koninklijke Vlaamse Acad., 1955; Assoc. Mem., Acad. Royale de Belgique, 1968. Hon. LittD: Ghent, 1958; Leeds, 1978; Hon. LLD Cambridge, 1993. *Publications:* Les Annales de Saint-Pierre de Gand, 1937; Books on Soviet Russia, 1917–42, 1943; Sylloge of Coins of the British Isles, Vol. I (Fitzwilliam Museum: Early British and Anglo-Saxon Coins), 1958; Bibliographie numismatique, 1966, 2nd edn 1979; English Linear Measures: a study in origins, 1973; (with A. R. Bellinger) Catalogue of the Byzantine Coins in the Dumbarton Oaks Collection and in the Whittemore Collection, vols 1, 2, 3, 1966–73; Numismatics, 1975; Monnaies du Moyen Age, 1976; The Origins of Money, 1977; Les monnaies, 1977; Dark Age Numismatics, 1979; Later Medieval Numismatics, 1979; Byzantine Coins, 1982; (with M. Blackburn) Medieval European Coinage, vol. 1 The Early Middle Ages, 1986; The Coins of Medieval Europe, 1991; Tarì, Follari e Denari, 1991; (with M. Mays) Catalogue of Late Roman Coins in the Dumbarton Oaks Collection and in the Whittemore Collection, 1992; trans. F. L. Ganshof, Feudalism, 1952; editor: C. W. Previté-Orton, The Shorter Cambridge Medieval History, 1952; H. E. Ives, The Venetian Gold Ducat and its Imitations, 1954; Studies in Italian History presented to Miss E. M. Jamison, 1956; (with U. Westermark) O. Mørkholm, Early Hellenistic Coins, 1991; Studies in Numismatic Method, presented to Philip Grierson (Festschrift), 1983. *Recreation:* science fiction. *Address:* Gonville and Caius College, Cambridge CB2 1TA. *T:* Cambridge (01223) 332450.

GRIERSON, Sir Ronald (Hugh), Kt 1990; Chairman: GEC International, since 1992; GEC Inc., since 1984; Advisory Board, Blackstone Group, since 1989; Bain & Co. International, since 1988; Daily Mail & General Trust, since 1993; Director of other cos; *b* Nürnberg, Bavaria, 1921; *s* of Mr and Mrs E. J. Griessmann (name changed by Deed Poll in 1943); *m* 1966, (Elizabeth) Heather, Viscountess Bearsted (*d* 1993), *er d* of Mr and Mrs G. Firmston-Williams; one *s*. *Educ:* Realgymnasium, Nürnberg; Lycée Pasteur, Paris; Highgate Sch., London; Balliol Coll., Oxford. Served War 1939–45 (despatches). Staff Mem., The Economist, 1947–48; S. G. Warburg & Co., 1948–86 (Dir, 1958–68 and 1980–86); Dep. Chm. and Man. Dir, IRC, 1966–67; Vice-Chm., General Electric Co., 1968–91; Chm., Orion Bank, 1971–73; Dir-Gen., Industrial and Technological Affairs, EEC, 1973–74; Sen. Partner, Panmure Gordon & Co., 1974–76. Board Member: BAC,

1970–71; Internat. Computers, 1974–76; Davy Internat., 1969–73; Nat. Bus Co., 1984–86; RJR Nabisco Inc. (formerly R. J. Reynolds), 1977–89; Chrysler Corp., 1983–91; W. R. Grace & Co., 1987–94. Chairman: European Orgn for Cancer Treatment Res., 1976–; South Bank Bd, 1984–90. Mem., Bd of Trustees, Phillips Collection, Washington, 1980–. Member: Atlantic Coll. Council, 1960–70; Harvard Coll. Faculty, 1964–65; CNAA, 1978–84; Arts Council of GB, 1984–88; Ernst von Siemens Foundn, 1977–; Bd of Visitors, N Carolina Sch. of the Arts, 1984–90; European Arts Foundn, 1987–88; Trustee: Prince of Liechtenstein Foundn, 1991–; European Studies Foundn, Oxford Univ., 1991–. Hon. Dr of Law, Grove City Coll., USA, 1986. Comdr, Order of Merit of the Republic of Italy, 1980; Comdr's Cross, Order of Merit (Germany), 1993; Officier, Légion d'honneur (France), 1994. *Address:* c/o General Electric Company, 1 Stanhope Gate, W1A 1EH.

GRIESE, Sister Carol, CHN; Religious Sister since 1970; *b* 26 Sept. 1945; *d* of Gwendoline and Donald Griese. *Educ:* Merrywood Grammar School, Bristol; King's College London (BA Hons English 1968); Clare Hall, Cambridge (Cert. Theol. 1970). Member, Community of the Holy Name, 1970–; Lay Rep. of Religious in General Synod, 1980–95. Mem., Crown Appointments Commn, 1990–92. *Recreations:* reading, walking. *Address:* Convent of the Holy Name, Morley Road, Oakwood, Derby DE2 4QZ. *T:* Derby (01332) 671716.

GRIEVE, Hon. Lord; William Robertson Grieve, VRD 1958; a Senator of the College of Justice in Scotland, 1972–88; *b* 21 Oct. 1917; *o s* of late William Robertson Grieve (killed in action 1917) and late Mrs Grieve; *m* 1947, Lorna St John (*d* 1989), *y d* of late Engineer Rear-Adm. E. P. St J. Benn, CB; one *s* one *d*. *Educ:* Glasgow Academy; Sedbergh; Glasgow Univ. MA 1939, LLB 1946 (Glasgow); Pres. Glasgow Univ. Union, 1938–39. John Clark (Mile-end) Scholar, 1939. RNVR: Sub-Lt 1939; Lieut 1942; Lt-Comdr 1950; served with RN, 1939–46. Admitted Mem. of Faculty of Advocates, 1947; QC (Scot.) 1957. Junior Counsel in Scotland to Bd of Inland Revenue, 1952–57. Advocate-Depute (Home), 1962–64; Sheriff-Principal of Renfrew and Argyll, 1964–72; Procurator of the Church of Scotland, 1969–72; a Judge of the Courts of Appeal of Jersey and Guernsey, 1971. Independent Chm., Fish Farming Adv. Cttee, 1989. Chm. of Governors, Fettes Trust, 1978–86. *Recreations:* golf, painting. *Address:* 20 Belgrave Crescent, Edinburgh EH4 3AJ. *T:* 0131–332 7500. *Clubs:* New (Edinburgh); Hon. Company of Edinburgh Golfers; West Sussex Golf; Queen's Park Rangers Football.

GRIEVE, Alan Thomas; Chairman, Jerwood Foundation, since 1991; *b* 22 Jan. 1928; *s* of late Lewis Miller Grieve and Doris Lilian (*née* Amner); *m* 1st, 1957, Anne, *d* of Dr Lawrence Dulake (marr. diss. 1971); two *s* one *d*; 2nd, 1971, Karen Louis, *d* of Michael de Sirvac Dunn; one *s* one *d*. *Educ:* Aldenham; Trinity Hall, Cambridge (MA, LLM). Nat. Service, 2nd Lieut, 14/20 King's Hussars; Capt., City of London Yeo., TA. Admitted solicitor, 1953; Senior Partner: Taylor & Humbert, 1979–82; Taylor Garrett, 1982–88; Cons., Taylor Joynson Garrett, 1988–. Director: Baggeridge Brick plc, 1964; Wilson Bowden plc, 1993–, and other cos; Chm., Reliance Resources Ltd, 1978–. Royal College of Physicians: Member: F and GP Bd, 1986–92; Educnl Assets Bd, 1988–90. Chm., Racehorse Owners Award, 1978–. Patron, Brendoncare for the Elderly, 1993–. Trustee, Med. Insce Agency Charity, 1992–. *Publication:* Purchase Tax, 1958. *Recreations:* ski-ing, horse-racing, country life. *Address:* (office) 22 Fitzroy Square, W1P 5HJ. *T:* 0171–388 6287, *Fax:* 0171–388 6289; Stoke Lodge, Clee Downton, Ludlow, Salop SY8 3EG. *T:* Ludlow (01584) 75212, *Fax:* (01584) 75419. *Clubs:* Boodle's; Baur au Lac (Zurich).

See also Baron Harlech.

GRIEVE, Percy; *see* Grieve, W. P.

GRIEVE, Prof. Sir Robert, Kt 1969; MA, FRSE, FRTPI, MICE; Professor Emeritus, University of Glasgow; Hon. Professor, Heriot-Watt University, since 1986; *b* 11 Dec. 1910; *s* of Peter Grieve and Catherine Boyle; *m* 1933, Mary Lavinia Broughton Blackburn; two *s* two *d*. *Educ:* N. Kelvinside Sch., Glasgow; Royal Coll. of Science and Technology (now Univ. of Strathclyde), Glasgow. Trng and qual. as Civil Engr, eventually Planner. Local Govt posts, 1927–44; preparation of Clyde Valley Regional Plan, 1944–46; Civil Service, 1946–54; Chief Planner, Scottish Office, 1960–64. Prof. of Town and Regional Planning, Glasgow Univ., 1964–74; retired from Chair, 1974. Chairman: Highlands and Islands Develt Bd, 1965–70; Highlands and Islands Development Consultative Council, 1978–86; Royal Fine Art Commn for Scotland, 1978–83; President: Scottish Countryside Rangers Assoc.; Saltire Soc., 1991–; Hon. President: Scottish Rights of Way Soc.; New Glasgow Soc.; Inverness Civic Trust; Stewartry Mountaineering Club; Scottish Branch, RTPI (Vice Pres., 1971–73); Friends of Loch Lomond. Former President: Scottish Mountaineering Council; Scottish Mountaineering Club; Former Vice-Pres., Internat. Soc. of Town and Regional Planners. Hon. Vice-Pres., Scottish Youth Hostels Assoc. Gold Medal, RTPI, 1974. Hon. DLitt Heriot-Watt; Hon. LLD Strathclyde, 1984; Dr *hc* Edinburgh, 1985. Hon. FRIAS; Hon. FRSGS 1989. Lord Provost's Award, Glasgow, 1989. *Publications:* part-author and collaborator in several major professional reports and books; many papers and articles in professional and technical jls. *Recreations:* mountains, poetry. *Address:* 5 Rothesay Terrace, Edinburgh EH3 7RY. *Club:* Scottish Arts (Edinburgh).

GRIEVE, William Percival, (W. Percy Grieve), QC 1962; a Recorder, 1972–87 (Recorder of Northampton, 1965–71); *b* 25 March 1915; *o s* of 2nd Lieut W. P. Grieve, the Middlesex Regt (killed in action, Ypres, Feb. 1915), Rockcliffe, Dalbeattie, and Dorothy Marie Hartley (she *m* 2nd, 1925, Dr W. Cunningham, Monkseaton); *m* 1949, Evelyn Raymonde Louise (*d* 1991), *y d* of late Comdt Hubert Mijouain, Paris, and of Liliane, *e d* of late Sir George Roberts, 1st and last Bt; one *s* (and one *s* one *d* decd). *Educ:* privately; Trinity Hall, Cambridge (Exhibitioner, 1933); Lord Kitchener Nat. Memorial Schol., 1934; MA 1940. Called to Bar, Middle Temple, 1938 (Harmsworth Law Schol., 1937); Bencher, 1969; Master Reader, 1985. Joined Midland Circuit, 1939. Called to the Hong Kong Bar, 1960. Commissioned the Middlesex Regt, 1939; Liaison Officer, French Mil. Censorship, Paris, 1939–40; Min. of Information, 1940–41; HQ Fighting France, 1941–43; Staff Capt. and Exec. Officer, SHAEF Mission to Luxembourg, 1944; Major and GSO2 Brit. Mil. Mission to Luxembourg, 1945; DAAG, BAOR, 1946. Asst Recorder of Leicester, 1956–65; Dep. Chm., Co. of Lincoln (Parts of Holland) QS, 1962–71. Mem. Mental Health Review Tribunal, Sheffield Region, 1960–64. Has served on Gen. Council of the Bar. Contested (C) Lincoln By-election, 1962; MP (C) Solihull Div., Warks, 1964–83. Member: House of Commons Select Cttees on Race Relations and Immigration, 1968–70, on Members' Interests, 1979–83; UK Delegn, Council of Europe (Chm., Legal Affairs Cttee) and WEU (Chm. Procedure Cttee), 1969–83; Hon. Vice-Pres., Franco-British Parly Relations Cttee, 1975–83 (Chm., 1970–75); Chm., Luxembourg Soc., 1975; Chm., Parly Anglo Benelux Group, 1979–83; Hon. Associate: Council of Europe, 1989; WEU, 1990. Pres., Fulham Cons. Assoc., 1982–. Member: Council, Officers' Assoc., 1969–88; Council of Justice, 1971–; Council, Franco-British Soc., 1970; Council, Alliance Française, 1974. Officier avec Couronne, Order of Adolphe of Nassau; Chevalier, Order of Couronne de Chêne and Croix de Guerre avec Palmes (Luxembourg), 1945–46; Bronze Star (USA), 1945; Chevalier de la Légion d'Honneur, 1974; Commandeur de l'Ordre de Mérite (Luxembourg), 1976; Officer de l'ordre de la Couronne (Belgium), 1980; Silver Medal, Council of Europe, 1983; Commandeur de l'Ordre de la Couronne de Chêne (Luxembourg), 1990. *Recreations:* swimming, travel, the theatre. *Address:* 32 Gunterstone Road, W14 9BU. *T:* 0171–603 0376. *Clubs:* Carlton, Hurlingham, Special Forces.

GRIEVE, William Robertson; *see* Grieve, Hon. Lord.

GRIEVES, David, CBE 1988; Vice Chairman, British Steel plc, 1991–94; Chairman, Avesta Sheffield, 1992–94; *b* 10 Jan. 1933; *s* of Joseph and Isabel Grieves; *m* 1960, Evelyn Muriel Attwater; two *s*. *Educ:* Durham Univ. BSc. PhD. Graduate apprentice, United Steel cos, 1957; Labour Manager, Appleby Frodingham Steel Co., 1962; British Steel Corporation: Manager, Industrial Relations, S Wales Group, 1967; Gen. Man., Stocksbridge and Tinsley Park Works, 1971; Personnel Dir, Special Steels Div., 1973; Dir, Indust. Relations, 1975; Man. Dir, Personnel and Social Policy, 1977; Dep. Chm. BSC Industry plc, 1980; Dir, BSC, later British Steel plc, 1983. Mem. (non-exec), Post Office, 1990–. Mem., Employment Appeal Tribunal, 1983.

GRIEVES, John Kerr; Senior Partner, Freshfields, since 1990; *b* 7 Nov. 1935; *s* of Thomas and Nancy Grieves; *m* 1961, Ann Gorrell (*née* Harris); one *s* one *d*. *Educ:* King's Sch., Worcester; Keble Coll., Oxford (MA Law); Harvard Business Sch. (AMP). Articled clerk and asst solicitor, Pinsent & Co., Birmingham, 1958–61; joined Freshfields, 1963; Partner, 1964–; Deptl Man. Partner, Company Dept, 1974–78; Man. Partner, 1979–85; Head, Corporate Finance Group, 1985–89. Dir, British Invisibles, 1992–. Officer, Order of the Crown (Belgium), 1993. *Recreations:* the arts (especially music), running. *Address:* 7 Putney Park Avenue, SW15 5QN. *T:* 0181–876 1207. *Clubs:* Athenæum, Roehampton.

GRIEW, Prof. Stephen, PhD; President, Senior University, Toronto, since 1993; Adjunct Professor of Psychology, Curtin University of Technology, Perth, Western Australia, since 1993; *b* 13 Sept. 1928; *e s* of late Harry and Sylvia Griew, London, England; *m* 1st, 1955, Jane le Geyt Johnson (marr. diss.); one *s* two *d* (and one *s* decd); 2nd, 1977, Eva Margareta Ursula, *d* of late Dr and Fru Johannes Ramberg, Stockholm, Sweden; one *d* and one step *s*. *Educ:* Univ. of London (BSc, Dip Psych); Univ. of Bristol (PhD). Vocational Officer, Min. of Labour, 1951–55; Univ. of Bristol: Research Worker, 1955–59; Lectr, 1959–63; Kenneth Craik Research Award, St John's Coll., Cambridge, 1960; Prof. of Psychology: Univ. of Otago, Dunedin, NZ, 1964–68 (Dean, Faculty of Science, 1967–68); Univ. of Dundee, 1968–72; Vice-Chancellor, Murdoch Univ., Perth, WA, 1972–77; Chm., Dept of Behavioural Science, Faculty of Medicine, Univ. of Toronto, 1977–80; Pres., 1980–85, University Prof., 1986–87, Athabasca Univ.; Dean, 1987–90, Prof. of Admin. Studies, 1990–93, Sen. Scholar, 1993–, Atkinson Coll., York Univ., Toronto. Consultant, OECD, Paris, 1963–64; Expert, ILO, Geneva, 1966–67; Mem., Social Commn of Rehabilitation Internat., 1967–75; Consultant, Dept of Employment, 1970–72; Vis. Prof., Univ. of Western Ont., London, Canada, 1970 and 1971; Vis. Fellow, Wolfson Coll., Cambridge, 1985–86; Vis. Professorial Fellow, Curtin Univ. of Technol., Perth, 1993. Vice-Pres., Australian Council on the Ageing, 1975–76. FBPsS 1960; Fellow, Gerontological Soc. (USA), 1969. *Publications:* Beyond Permissiveness, 1992; handbooks and monographs on ageing and vocational rehabilitation, and articles in Jl of Gerontology and various psychological jls. *Recreations:* music, travel, writing. *Address:* Atkinson College, York University, 4700 Keele Street, North York, Ont M3J 1P3, Canada.

GRIFFIN, Adm. Sir Anthony (Templer Frederick Griffith), GCB 1975 (KCB 1971; CB 1967); President, Royal Institution of Naval Architects, 1981–84; Chairman, British Shipbuilders, 1977–80 (Chairman-designate, Dec. 1975); *b* Peshawar, 24 Nov. 1920; *s* of late Col F. M. G. Griffin, MC, and B. A. B. Griffin (*née* Down); *m* 1943, Rosemary Ann Hickling; two *s* one *d*. *Educ:* RN Coll., Dartmouth. Joined RN, 1934; to sea as Midshipman, 1939; War Service in E Indies, Mediterranean, Atlantic, N Russia and Far East; specialised in navigation, 1944; Staff Coll., 1952; Imp. Defence Coll., 1963; comd HMS Ark Royal, 1964–65; Naval Secretary, 1966; Asst Chief of Naval Staff (Warfare), 1966–68; Flag Officer, Second-in-Command, Far East Fleet, 1968–69; Flag Officer, Plymouth, Comdr Central Sub Area, Eastern Atlantic, and Comdr Plymouth Sub Area, Channel, 1969–71; Adm. Supt Devonport, 1970–71; Controller of the Navy, 1971–75. Rear-Adm. of the UK, 1986–88, Vice-Adm., 1988–90. Comdr 1951; Capt. 1956; Rear-Adm. 1966; Vice-Adm. 1968; Adm., 1971. Vice-Pres., Wellington College, 1980–90; Chm., British Maritime League, 1982–87. Hon. FRINA 1984. *Recreation:* sailing. *Address:* Moat Cottage, The Drive, Bosham, West Sussex PO18 8JG. *T:* Bosham (01243) 573373. *Clubs:* Army and Navy, Pratt's.

See also S. C. Finch.

GRIFFIN, Major Sir (Arthur) John (Stewart), KCVO 1990 (CVO 1974; MVO 1967); Press Secretary to HM Queen Elizabeth the Queen Mother, 1956–91; *b* 1924; *s* of Arthur Wilfrid Michael Stewart Griffin and Florence May Griffin; *m* 1962, Henrietta Montagu-Douglas-Scott; two *s*. *Educ:* Harrow School. Regular Army Officer, The Queen's Bays, later The Queen's Dragoon Guards, 1942–58. *Recreations:* cricket, fishing, shooting. *Address:* Barton's Cottage, Bushy Park, Teddington, Middx TW11 0EA. *Club:* MCC.

GRIFFIN, Avril; *see* MacRory, A.

GRIFFIN, Sir (Charles) David, Kt 1974; CBE 1972; Chairman, Monte Paschi Australia (formerly Icle Finance Corporation) Ltd, since 1986; *b* 8 July 1915; *s* of Eric Furnival Griffin and Nellie Clarendon Griffin (*née* Devenish-Meares); *m* 1941, Jean Falconer Whyte; two *s*. *Educ:* Cranbrook Sch., Sydney; Univ. of Sydney (LLB and Golf Blue). 8th Aust. Div. 2nd AIF, 1940–45; POW Changi, Singapore, 1942–45. Associate to Sir Dudley Williams and Mem. Bar NSW, 1946–49; Solicitor, Sydney, 1949–64. Alderman, Sydney City Council, 1962–74, Chm. Finance Cttee, 1969–72; Lord Mayor of Sydney, 1972–73. Hon. Chm., Nabalco Pty Ltd, 1980–; Dir, OTC/Lawpoint, 1988–. Mem. Council, Royal Agricl Soc.; Mem. Nat. Council, Scout Assoc. of Australia (Life Councillor, NSW Br.); Dir, Nat. Seniors' Assoc. of Aust., 1991–. *Publications:* The Happiness Box (for children); The Will of the People; sundry speeches and short stories. *Recreations:* golf, fly-fishing. *Address:* c/o Lawpoint Pty, Suite 1501, 15 Castlereagh Street, Sydney, NSW 2000, Australia. *Clubs:* Union (Sydney); Royal Sydney Golf, Pine Valley Golf (NJ, USA).

GRIFFIN, Col Edgar Allen, CMG 1965; OBE (mil.) 1943; ED 1945; Regional Director, Northern Region (Arras, France), Commonwealth War Graves Commission, 1969–72; *b* 18 Jan. 1907; 3rd *s* of Gerald Francis and Isabella Margaret Griffin; *m* 1936, Alethea Mary Byrne; two *s* two *d*. Asst Adjt and QMG, 3 Aust. Div., 1942–44; 5 Aust. Div., 1944–45; Grad., Sen. Wing, Aust. Mil. Staff Coll., 1944; Asst Adjt Gen. (Dir of PoWs and internees), Army HQ, Melbourne; retired from AMF, 1947; Australian Govt Nominee to Staff of War Graves Commn, 1947; Chief Admin. Officer, Eastern Dist (Cairo), 1947–54; UK Dist (London), 1954–58; Regional Dir, Southern Region (Rome), 1958–69. Chairman: Anglo-Amer. Hosp. Benevolent Fund, 1958–75; Commonwealth Club, Rome, 1968–69; Govs, English Sch., Rome, 1970–75. *Address:* 9 Arley Close, Plas Newton, Chester CH2 1NW.

GRIFFIN, Prof. George Edward, PhD; FRCP, FRCPE; Chairman, Division of Infectious Diseases, and Professor of Infectious Diseases and Medicine, since 1992, and Chairman, Department of Internal Medicine, since 1994, St George's Hospital Medical

School; *b* 27 Feb. 1947; *s* of Herbert Griffin and Enid Mary Griffin (*née* Borril); *m* 1972, Daphne Joan Haylor, Romford; two *s* one *d*. *Educ:* Malet Lambert Grammar Sch., Kingston upon Hull; King's Coll., London (BSc); St George's Hosp. Med. Sch. (MB, BS); Univ. of Hull (PhD 1974); Harvard Univ. (Harkness Fellow). MRCP 1979, FRCP 1988; FRCPE 1994. Registrar and Tutor in Medicine, RPMS, 1977–78; St George's Hospital Medical School: Lectr in Medicine, 1978–82; Wellcome Trust Sen. Lectr, 1982–90; Dir, Wellcome Trust Clinical Tropical Unit, 1994–; Hon. Cons. Physician, St George's Hosp., 1988–. Vis. Prof. of Medicine, Univ. of Michigan, 1992–. Mem., Adv. Cttee on Dangerous Pathogens, DoH, 1994–. Wellcome Trust: Member: Infection and Immunity Panel, 1989–94; Tropical Interest Gp, 1991–94; Internat. Interest Gp, 1991–; Medical Research Council: Chm., Cttee for Develt and Implementation of Vaccines, 1994–; Member: Physiological Medicine and Infection Bd, 1994–; AIDS Vaccine Cttee, 1995–; HIV Virucidal Cttee, 1995–. *Publications:* scientific and clinical papers relating to pathogenesis of infection, vaccines. *Recreations:* walking, gardening, music. *Address:* 8 Buxton Drive, New Malden, Surrey KT3 3UZ. *T:* 0181–949 4953. *Club:* Royal Automobile.

GRIFFIN, Prof. Jasper, FBA 1986; Professor of Classical Literature, since 1992, and Public Orator, since 1993, Oxford University; Fellow and Tutor in Classics, Balliol College, Oxford, since 1963; *b* 29 May 1937; *s* of Frederick William Griffin and Constance Irene Griffin (*née* Cordwell); *m* 1960, Miriam Tamara Dressler; three *d*. *Educ:* Christ's Hospital; Balliol College, Oxford (1st Cl. Hon. Mods 1958; 1st Cl. Lit. Hum. 1960; Hertford Scholar 1958; Ireland Scholar 1958). Jackson Fellow, Harvard Univ., 1960–61; Oxford University: Dyson Research Fellow, Balliol Coll., 1961–63; Reader in Classical Lit., 1990–92. T. S. Eliot Meml Lectr, Univ. of Kent at Canterbury, 1984. *Publications:* Homer on Life and Death, 1980; Homer, 1980; Snobs, 1982; Latin Poets and Roman Life, 1985; The Mirror of Myth, 1986; (ed with J. Boardman and O. Murray) The Oxford History of the Classical World, 1986; Virgil, 1986; Homer, The Odyssey, 1987; Homer, Iliad ix, 1995. *Address:* Balliol College, Oxford OX1 3BJ. *T:* Oxford (01865) 77782.

GRIFFIN, Sir John; *see* Griffin, Sir A. J. S.

GRIFFIN, Dr John Parry, BSc, PhD, MB, BS; FRCP, FRCPath; Director, John Griffin Associates Ltd; Hon. Consultant, Lister Hospital, Stevenage; *b* 21 May 1938; *o s* of late David J. Griffin and Phyllis M. Griffin; *m* 1962, Margaret, *o d* of late Frank Cooper and Catherine Cooper; one *s* two *d*. *Educ:* Howardian High Sch., Cardiff; London Hosp. Medical Coll. Lethby and Buxton Prizes, 1958; BSc (1st Cl. Hons) 1959; PhD 1961; George Riddoch Prize in Neurology, 1962; MB, BS 1964; LRCP, MRCS 1964; MRCP 1980, FRCP 1990; FRCPath 1986 (MRCPath 1982). Ho. Phys., London Hosp. Med. Unit, and Ho. Surg., London Hosp. Accident and Orthopaedic Dept, 1964–65; Lectr in Physiology, King's Coll., London, 1965–67; Head of Clinical Research, Riker Laboratories, 1967–71; SMO, Medicines Div., 1971–76; PMO, Medicines Div., and Medical Assessor, Cttee on Safety of Medicines, 1976–77; SPMO and Professional Head of Medicines Div., DHSS, 1977–84; Med. Assessor, Medicines Commn, 1977–84. Dir, Assoc. of the British Pharmaceutical Industry, 1984–94. Mem., Jt Formulary Cttee for British Nat. Formulary, 1978–84; UK Rep., EEC Cttee on Proprietary Med. Products; Chm., Cttee on Prop. Med. Products Working Party on Safety Requirements, 1977–84. FRSM. *Publications:* (jtly) Iatrogenic Diseases, 1972, 3rd edn 1985; (jtly) Manual of Adverse Drug Interactions, 1975, 4th edn 1988; (jtly) Drug Induced Emergencies, 1980; Medicines: research, regulation and risk, 1989, 2nd edn 1992; (jtly) International Medicines Regulations, 1989; (jtly) Textbook of Pharmaceutical Medicine, 1993, 2nd edn 1994; numerous articles in sci. and med. jls, mainly on aspects of neurophysiology, clinical pharmacology, toxicology and pharmacoeconomics. *Recreations:* gardening, local history. *Address:* Quartermans, Digswell Lane, Digswell, Herts AL7 1SP.

GRIFFIN, Keith Broadwell, DPhil; Professor of Economics, University of California, Riverside, since 1988 (Chairman, Department of Economics, 1988–93); *b* 6 Nov. 1938; *s* of Marcus Samuel Griffin and Elaine Ann Broadwell; *m* 1956, Dixie Beth Griffin; two *d*. *Educ:* Williams Coll., Williamstown, Mass (BA; Hon DLitt, 1980); Balliol Coll., Oxford (BPhil, DPhil). Fellow and Tutor in Econs, Magdalen Coll., Oxford, 1965–76, Fellow by special election, 1977–79; Warden, Queen Elizabeth House, Oxford, 1978–79 (Actg Warden, 1973 and 1977–78); Dir, Inst. of Commonwealth Studies, Oxford, 1978–79 (Actg Dir, 1973 and 1977–78); Pres., Magdalen Coll., Oxford, 1979–88. Chief, Rural and Urban Employment Policies Br., ILO, 1975–76; Vis. Prof., Inst. of Econs and Planning, Univ. of Chile, 1962–63 and 1964–65. Consultant: ILO, 1974, 1982, 1994; Internat. Bank for Reconstruction and Develt, 1973; UN Res. Inst. for Social Develt, 1971–72; FAO, 1963–64, 1967, 1978; Inter-Amer. Cttee for Alliance for Progress, 1968; US Agency for Internat. Develt, 1966; UNDP, 1989, 1991–95. Res. Adviser, Pakistan Inst. of Develt Econs, 1965, 1970; Sen. Adviser, OECD Develt Centre, Paris, 1986–88; Economic Advr, Govt of Bolivia, 1989–91. Member: Council, UN Univ., 1986–92; UN Cttee for Develt Planning, 1987–94; Chm., UN Res. Inst. for Social Develt, 1988–. Mem., World Commn on Culture and Develt, 1994–95. Pres., Develt Studies Assoc., 1978–80. *Publications:* (with Ricardo ffrench-Davis) Comercio Internacional y Politicas de Desarrollo Economico, 1967; Underdevelopment in Spanish America, 1969; (with John Enos) Planning Development, 1970; (ed) Financing Development in Latin America, 1971; (ed with Azizur Rahman Khan) Growth and Inequality in Pakistan, 1972; The Political Economy of Agrarian Change, 1974, 2nd edn 1979; (ed with E. A. G. Robinson) The Economic Development of Bangladesh, 1974; Land Concentration and Rural Poverty, 1976, 2nd edn 1981; International Inequality and National Poverty, 1978; (with Ashwani Saith) Growth and Equality in Rural China, 1981; (with Jeffrey James) The Transition to Egalitarian Development, 1981; (ed) Institutional Reform and Economic Development in the Chinese Countryside, 1984; World Hunger and the World Economy, 1987; Alternative Strategies for Economic Development, 1989; (ed with John Knight) Human Development and the International Development Strategy for the 1990s, 1990; (ed) The Economy of Ethiopia, 1992; (ed with Zhao Renwei) The Distribution of Income in China, 1993; (with Terry McKinley) Implementing a Human Development Strategy, 1994; (ed) Poverty and the Transition to a Market Economy in Mongolia, 1995. *Recreation:* travel. *Address:* Department of Economics, University of California, Riverside, CA 92521, USA. *Clubs:* Athenæum, United Oxford & Cambridge University.

GRIFFIN, Kenneth James, OBE 1970; Deputy Chairman, Ugland International, since 1993; *b* 1 Aug. 1928; *s* of late Albert Griffin and late Catherine (*née* Sullivan); *m* 1951, Doreen Cicely Simon (*d* 1992); one *s* one *d* (and one *s* decd). *Educ:* Dynevor Grammar Sch., Swansea; Swansea Technical College. Area Sec., ETU, 1960; Dist Sec., Confedn of Ship Building Engrg Unions, 1961; Sec., Craftsmen Cttee (Steel), 1961; Mem., Welsh Council, 1968; Mem., Crowther Commn on Constitution (Wales), 1969; Joint Sec., No 8 Joint Industrial Council Electrical Supply Industry, 1969; Industrial Adviser, DTI, 1971–72; Co-ordinator of Industrial Advisers, DTI, 1972–74; Special Adviser, Sec. of State for Industry, 1974; part-time Mem., NCB, 1973–82; a Dep. Chm., British Shipbuilders, 1977–83; Chm., Blackwall Engrg, 1983–85; Member: Suppl. Benefits Commn, 1968–80; Solicitors Disciplinary Tribunal, 1982–. Chairman: Castleton Retirement Homes, 1989–90; Network Housing Assoc., 1991–; Vice-Chm., UK Housing Trust, 1989–; Mem., Bd of Management, N British Housing Assoc., 1991–; Exec. Advr, Mobile Training, 1989–90. *Recreations:* golf, music, reading. *Address:* 214 Cyncoed Road, Cyncoed, Cardiff CF2 6RS. *T:* Cardiff (01222) 752184. *Club:* Reform.

GRIFFIN, Rear-Adm. Michael Harold, CB 1973; antiquarian horologist; *b* 28 Jan. 1921; *s* of late Henry William Griffin and Blanche Celia Griffin (*née* Michael); *m* 1947, Barbara Mary Brewer; two *d*. *Educ:* Plymouth Junior Techn. Coll. CEng, FIMechE, FIMarE. MBHI. Commnd, 1941; HMS Kent, 1942; HM Submarines Trusty, Tactician, Tally Ho, Alderney, 1944–50; Admty, 1950–52; HMS Eagle, 1952–54; staff C-in-C Portsmouth, 1954–57; HM Dockyard, Rosyth, 1957–60; Third Submarine Sqdn, 1960–62; Captain, 1962; HM Dockyard, Chatham, 1963–65; HMS St Vincent, 1966–69; Cdre Supt, Singapore, 1969–71; Dir of Dockyard Production and Support, MoD, 1972–77, retired. Naval Adviser to Vosper Shiprepairers Ltd, 1977–81. *Recreations:* horology, motoring, grandchildren. *Address:* 48 Little Green, Alverstoke, Gosport, Hants PO12 2EX. *T:* Gosport (01705) 646481.

GRIFFIN, Paul, MBE 1961; MA Cantab; writer; *b* 2 March 1922; *s* of late John Edwin Herman Griffin; *m* 1946, Felicity Grace, *d* of late Canon Howard Dobson; one *s* one *d*. *Educ:* Framlingham Coll.; St Catharine's Coll., Cambridge. Served War in Gurkhas, India, Burma, Malaya, 1940–46; North-West Frontier, 1941–43; Chindits, 1943–44. Asst Master and Senior English Master, Uppingham Sch., 1949–55; Principal, English Sch. in Cyprus, 1956–60; Headmaster, Aldenham Sch., 1962–74; Principal, Anglo-World Language Centre, Cambridge, 1976–82; Treasurer, Corp. of Sons of the Clergy, 1978–86. *Publications:* collaborated in: How to Become Ridiculously Well-Read in One Evening, 1985; How to Become Absurdly Well-Informed about the Famous and Infamous, 1987; The Dogsbody Papers, 1988; How to Be Tremendously Tuned-in to Opera, 1989; How to Be Well-Versed in Poetry, 1990; How to Be European, 1991; poems, humour, articles, broadcasts. *Recreations:* sea angling, literary competitions. *Address:* 1 Crombie House, The Common, Southwold, Suffolk IP18 6AL. *T:* Southwold (01502) 723709. *Club:* Army and Navy.

GRIFFIN, Very Rev. Victor Gilbert Benjamin; Dean of St Patrick's Cathedral, Dublin, 1969–91; *b* 24 May 1924; *s* of Gilbert B. and Violet M. Griffin, Carnew, Co. Wicklow; *m* 1958, Daphne E. Mitchell; two *s*. *Educ:* Kilkenny Coll.; Mountjoy Sch., and Trinity Coll., Dublin. MA, 1st class Hons in Philosophy. Ordained, 1947; Curacy, St Augustine's, Londonderry, 1947–51; Curacy, Christ Church, Londonderry, 1951–57; Rector of Christ Church, Londonderry, 1957–69. Lecturer in Philosophy, Magee Univ. Coll., Londonderry, 1950–69. Hon. MRIAI 1992. Hon. DD TCD, 1992. *Publications:* Trends in Theology, 1870–1970, 1970; Anglican and Irish, 1976; Pluralism and Ecumenism, 1983; The Mark of Protest: experience of a Southern Protestant in Northern Ireland and the Republic, 1993; contrib. to New Divinity. *Recreations:* music, golf. *Address:* 7 Tyler Road, Limavady, N Ireland BT49 0DW. *Club:* Friendly Brothers of St Patrick (Dublin).

GRIFFITH, Rev. (Arthur) Leonard; Lecturer in Homiletics, Wycliffe College, Toronto, 1977–87, retired; *b* 20 March 1920; *s* of Thomas Griffiths and Sarah Jane Taylor; *m* 1947, Anne Merelie Cayford; two *d*. *Educ:* Public and High Schs, Brockville, Ont; McGill Univ., Montreal (BA, McGill, 1942); United Theological Coll., Montreal (BD 1945; Hon. DD 1962); Mansfield Coll., Oxford, England, 1957–58. Ordained in The United Church of Canada, 1945; Minister: United Church, Arden, Ont, 1945–47; Trinity United Church, Grimsby, Ont, 1947–50; Chalmers United Church, Ottawa, Ont, 1950–60; The City Temple, London, 1960–66; Deer Park United Church, Toronto, 1966–75; ordained in Anglican Church 1976; Minister, St Paul's Church, Bloor St, Toronto, 1975–85. Hon. DD Wycliffe Coll., Toronto, 1985. *Publications:* The Roman Letter Today, 1959; God and His People, 1960; Beneath The Cross of Jesus, 1961; What is a Christian?, 1962; Barriers to Christian Belief, 1962; A Pilgrimage to the Holy Land, 1962; The Eternal Legacy, 1963; Pathways to Happiness, 1964; God's Time and Ours, 1964; The Crucial Encounter, 1965; This is Living!, 1966; God in Man's Experience, 1968; Illusions of our Culture, 1969; The Need to Preach, 1971; Hang on to the Lord's Prayer, 1973; We Have This Ministry, 1973; Ephesians: a positive affirmation, 1975; Gospel Characters, 1976; Reactions to God, 1979; Take Hold of the Treasure, 1980; From Sunday to Sunday, 1987. *Recreations:* music, drama, travelling, adult education. *Address:* 91 Old Mill Road, Etobicoke, Ont M8X 1G9, Canada.

GRIFFITH, (Edward) Michael (Wynne), CBE 1986; Vice Lord-Lieutenant for the County of Clwyd, since 1986; Chairman, Countryside Council for Wales, since 1991; *b* 29 Aug. 1933; *e s* of Major H. W. Griffith, MBE; *m* Jill Grange, *d* of Major D. P. G. Moseley, Dorfold Cottage, Nantwich; one *s* (and two *s* decd). *Educ:* Eton; Royal Agricultural College. Regional Dir, National Westminster Bank Ltd, 1974–92; Mem. Welsh Bd, Nationwide Anglia Bldg Soc., 1986–89. High Sheriff of Denbighshire, 1969. Chairman: Clwyd HA, 1980–90; National Trust Cttee for Wales, 1984–91 (Mem., National Trust Exec. and Council, 1989–); Glan Clwyd Hosp. Trust, 1993–; Dir, Land Authority Wales, 1989–90. Member: Countryside Commn Cttee for Wales, 1972–78; Min. of Agriculture Regional Panel, 1972–77; ARC, 1973–82; UFC (Wales), 1989–92; HEFCW, 1992–95; British Library Bd, 1992–. FRSA 1993; FLS 1995. DL Clwyd, 1985. *Address:* Greenfield, Trefnant, Clwyd. LL16 5UE. *T:* Trefnant (0174) 574633. *Club:* Boodle's.

GRIFFITH, Prof. John Aneurin Grey, LLB London, LLM London; Hon. LLD Edinburgh 1982, York, Toronto, 1982, Manchester 1987; FBA 1977; Barrister-at-law; Chancellor of Manchester University, 1986–93; Emeritus Professor of Public Law, University of London; *b* 14 Oct. 1918; *s* of Rev. B. Grey Griffith and Bertha Griffith; *m* 1941, Barbara Eirene Garnet, *d* of W. Garnet Williams; two *s* one *d*. *Educ:* Taunton Sch.; LSE. British and Indian armies, 1940–46. Lectr in Law, UCW, Aberystwyth, 1946–48; Lectr in Law and Reader, LSE, 1948–59, Prof. of English Law, 1959–70, Prof. of Public Law, 1970–84. Vis. Professor of Law: Univ. of California at Berkeley, 1966; York Univ., 1985. Mem., Marlow UDC, 1950–55, and Bucks CC, 1955–61. Editor, Public Law, 1956–81. *Publications:* (with H. Street) A Casebook of Administrative Law, 1964; Central Departments and Local Authorities, 1966; (with H. Street) Principles of Administrative Law, 5th edn, 1973; Parliamentary Scrutiny of Government Bills, 1974; (with T. C. Hartley) Government and Law, 1975, 2nd edn 1981; (ed) From Policy to Administration, 1976; The Politics of the Judiciary, 1977, 4th edn 1991; Public Rights and Private Interests, 1981; (with M. T. Ryle) Parliament, 1989; Judicial Politics, since 1920: a chronicle, 1993; articles in English, Commonwealth and American jls of law, public administration and politics. *Recreations:* drinking beer and writing bad verse. *Address:* 25 Bedford Row, WC1R 4HE.

GRIFFITH, Kenneth; actor, writer and documentary film-maker; formed own film company, Breakaway Productions Ltd, 1982; *b* 12 Oct. 1921; *g s* of Ernest and Emily Griffith; three marriages dissolved; three *s* two *d*. *Educ:* council and grammar schs, Tenby, Pembrokeshire, SW Wales. Became a professional actor at Festival Theatre, Cambridge, 1937; films and television; served War, RAF; post war, associated with Tyrone Guthrie at Old Vic; unknown number of films, partic. for Boulting brothers; unknown number of television plays; rarely theatre; made first documentary film at invitation of David

Attenborough and Huw Wheldon, 1964; best documentaries include: Life of Cecil Rhodes; Hang Up Your Brightest Colours (life of Michael Collins; suppressed by Lew Grade at behest of IBA for twenty years, until broadcast in 1993); The Public's Right to Know; The Sun's Bright Child (life of Edmund Kean); Black as Hell, Thick as Grass (the 24th Regt in Zulu War); The Most Valuable Englishman Ever (life of Thomas Paine for BBC TV); Clive of India (Channel Four); The Light (life of David Ben Gurion for Channel Four); But I Have Promises to Keep (life of Jawaharlal Nehru for Indian Govt), 1987; The Girl Who Didn't Run (on Zola Budd for BBC TV), 1989; Roger Casement, the Heart of Darkness (for BBC TV), 1992; *film:* The Englishman Who Went Up a Hill but Came Down a Mountain, 1995; *relevant film:* The Tenby Poisoner (film biography, BBC TV), 1993. *Publications:* Thank God we kept the Flag Flying, 1974; (with Timothy O'Grady) Curious Journey, 1981 (based on unshown TV documentary); The Discovery of Nehru, 1989; The Fool's Pardon (autobiog.), 1994. *Recreations:* talking; collecting British Empire military postal history (envelopes, post-cards), also ephemera connected with southern Africa. *Address:* 110 Englefield Road, Islington, N1 3LQ. *T:* 0171–226 9013.

GRIFFITH, Rev. Leonard; *see* Griffith, Rev. A. L.

GRIFFITH, Michael; *see* Griffith, E. M. W.

GRIFFITH, Owen Glyn, CBE 1980 (OBE 1969); MVO 1954; HM Diplomatic Service, retired; High Commissioner in Lesotho, 1978–81; *b* 19 Jan. 1922; *s* of late William Glyn Griffith and Gladys Glyn Griffith (*née* Picton Davies); *m* 1949, Rosemary Elizabeth Cecil Earl; two *s*. *Educ:* Oundle Sch.; Trinity Hall, Cambridge. Commnd in Welsh Guards (twice wounded in N Africa), 1941–43; Colonial Service (later HMOCS), Uganda, 1944–63: District Officer, 1944–51; Private Sec. to Governor, 1952–54; Dist Comr, 1954–61; Perm. Sec., Min. of Commerce and Industry, 1961–63; Principal, CRO, 1963; 1st Sec. and Head of Chancery, British Embassy, Khartoum, 1965; 1st Sec. (Commercial), British Embassy, Stockholm, 1969; Dep. British High Comr, Malaŵi, 1973; Inspector, 1976–78. *Recreations:* golf, fishing. *Address:* The Sundial, Marsham Way, Gerrards Cross, Bucks SL9 8AD. *Club:* Denham Golf.

GRIFFITH EDWARDS, James; *see* Edwards, J. G.

GRIFFITH WILLIAMS, John; *see* Williams.

GRIFFITHS, family name of **Barons Griffiths** and **Griffiths of Fforestfach.**

GRIFFITHS, Baron *cr* 1985 (Life Peer), of Govilon in the County of Gwent; **William Hugh Griffiths;** Kt 1971; MC 1944; PC 1980; a Lord of Appeal in Ordinary, 1985–93; *b* 26 Sept. 1923; *s* of late Sir Hugh Griffiths, CBE, MS, FRCS; *m* 1949, Evelyn, *d* of Col K. A. Krefting; one *s* three *d*. *Educ:* Charterhouse; St John's Coll., Cambridge (Hon. Fellow, 1985). Commissioned in Welsh Guards, 1942; demobilised after war service, 1946. Cambridge, 1946–48. BA 1948. Called to the Bar, Inner Temple, 1949, Bencher, 1971; QC 1964; Treasurer of the Bar Council, 1968–69. Recorder of Margate, 1962–64, of Cambridge, 1964–70; a Judge of the High Court of Justice, Queen's Bench Division, 1971–80; a Lord Justice of Appeal, 1980–85. A Judge, National Industrial Relations Court, 1973–74. Chm., Security Commn, 1985–92; Mem., Adv. Council on Penal Reform, 1967–70; Chm., Tribunal of Inquiry on Ronan Point, 1968; Vice-Chm., Parole Bd, 1976–77; Mem., Chancellor's Law Reform Cttee, 1976–93; Pres., Senate of the Inns of Court and the Bar, 1982–84; Chm., Lord Chancellor's Adv. Cttee on Legal Educn and Conduct, 1991–93. Hon. Mem., Canadian Bar Assoc., 1981; Hon. Fellow: Amer. Inst. of Judicial Admin, 1985; Amer. Coll. of Trial Lawyers, 1988. Hon. LLD: Wales, 1987; De Montfort, 1993. *Recreations:* cricket, golf, fishing. *Address:* c/o House of Lords, SW1A 0PW. *Clubs:* Garrick, MCC (Pres., 1990–91); Hawks (Cambridge); Royal and Ancient (St Andrews) (Captain, 1993–94); Sunningdale Golf.

GRIFFITHS OF FFORESTFACH, Baron *cr* 1991 (Life Peer), of Fforestfach in the county of West Glamorgan; **Brian Griffiths;** International Adviser, Goldman Sachs, since 1991; Director: Thorn-EMI, since 1991; Hermann Miller, since 1991; Times Newspapers Ltd, since 1991; Servicemaster, since 1992; Telewest, 1994; *b* 27 Dec. 1941; *s* of Ivor Winston Griffiths and Phyllis Mary Griffiths (*née* Morgan); *m* 1965, Rachel Jane Jones; one *s* two *d*. *Educ:* Dynevor Grammar School; London School of Economics, Univ. of London. BSc (Econ), MSc (Econ). Assistant Lecturer in Economics, LSE, 1965–68, Lecturer in Economics, 1968–76; City University: Prof. of Banking and Internat. Finance, 1977–85; Dir, Centre for Banking and Internat. Finance, 1977–82; Dean, Business Sch., 1982–85; Head of Prime Minister's Policy Unit, 1985–90. Vis. Prof., Univ. of Rochester, USA, 1972–73; Prof. of Ethics, Gresham Coll., 1984–87; Dir, Bank of England, 1984–86 (Mem., Panel of Academic Consultants, 1977–86). Chairman: Centre for Policy Studies, 1991–; Sch. Exams and Assessment Council, 1991–93. *Publications:* Is Revolution Change? (ed and contrib.) 1972; Mexican Monetary Policy and Economic Development, 1972; Invisible Barriers to Invisible Trade, 1975; Inflation: The Price of Prosperity, 1976; (ed with G. E. Wood) Monetary Targets, 1980; The Creation of Wealth, 1984; (ed with G. E. Wood) Monetarism in the United Kingdom, 1984; Morality and the Market Place, 1989. *Recreations:* the family and reading. *Address:* c/o House of Lords, SW1A 0PW. *Club:* Garrick.

GRIFFITHS, Prof. Allen Phillips; Professor of Philosophy, University of Warwick, 1964–92, now Emeritus; Director, Royal Institute of Philosophy, 1979–94; *b* 11 June 1927; *s* of John Phillips Griffiths and Elsie Maud (*née* Jones); *m* 1st, 1948, Margaret Lock (*d* 1974); one *s* one *d*; 2nd, 1984, Vera Clare (marr. diss. 1990). *Educ:* University Coll., Cardiff (BA; Hon. Fellow 1984); University Coll., Oxford (BPhil). Sgt, Intell. Corps, 1945–48 (despatches). Asst Lectr, Univ. of Wales, 1955–57; Lectr, Birkbeck Coll., Univ. of London, 1957–64. Pro-Vice-Chancellor, Univ. of Warwick, 1970–77. Vis. Professor: Swarthmore Coll., Pa, 1963; Univ. of Calif, 1967; Univ. of Wisconsin, 1965 and 1970; Carleton Coll., Minnesota, 1985. Silver Jubilee Medal, 1977. *Publications:* (ed) Knowledge & Belief, 1967; (ed) Of Liberty, 1983; (ed) Philosophy and Literature, 1984; Philosophy and Practice, 1985; (ed) Contemporary French Philosophy, 1988; (ed) Key Themes in Philosophy, 1989; (ed) Wittgenstein Centenary Essays, 1990; (ed) A. J. Ayer Memorial Essays, 1992; (ed) The Impulse to Philosophise, 1993; articles in learned philosophical jls. *Address:* 6 Brockley Road, West Bridgford, Nottingham NG2 5JY. *T:* Nottingham (0115) 981 0319.

GRIFFITHS, Rt. Rev. Ambrose; *see* Griffiths, Rt Rev. M. A.

GRIFFITHS, Antony Vaughan; Keeper, Department of Prints and Drawings, British Museum, since 1991; *b* 28 July 1951; *s* of Richard Cerdin Griffiths and Pamela de Grave Griffiths (*née* Hetherington). *Educ:* Highgate Sch.; Christ Church, Oxford (BA); Courtauld Inst. of Art, London Univ. (MA). Joined Dept of Prints and Drawings, BM, 1976, as Asst Keeper; Dep. Keeper, 1981–91. *Publications:* Prints and Printmaking, 1980; (with Reginald Williams) The Department of Prints and Drawings in the British Museum: a user's guide, 1987; British Museum exhibn catalogues; contribs to learned jls, esp. Print Qly. *Address:* 1 Highbury Hill, N5 1SU.

GRIFFITHS, Air Vice-Marshal Arthur, CB 1972; AFC 1964; Director, Trident Safeguards Ltd; *b* 22 Aug. 1922; *s* of late Edward and Elizabeth Griffiths; *m* 1950, Nancy Maud Sumpter; one *d*. *Educ:* Hawarden Grammar School. Joined RAF, 1940; war service with No 26 Fighter Reconnaissance Sqdn; post-war years as Flying Instructor mainly at CFS and Empire Flying Sch.; pfc 1954; comd No 94 Fighter Sqdn Germany, 1955–56; Dirg Staff, RCAF Staff Coll., Toronto, 1956–59; HQ Bomber Comd, 1959–61; comd No 101 Bomber Sqdn, 1962–64; Gp Captain Ops, Bomber Comd, 1964–67; comd RAF Waddington, 1967–69; AOA and later Chief of Staff, Far East Air Force, 1969–71; Head of British Defence Liaison Staff, Canberra, 1972–74; Dir Gen., Security (RAF), 1976–77, and Comdt-Gen. RAF Regt, 1975–77. *Address:* Water Lane House, Castor, Peterborough PE5 7BJ. *T:* Peterborough (01733) 380742. *Club:* Royal Air Force.

GRIFFITHS, His Honour Bruce (Fletcher); QC 1970; a Circuit Judge, 1972–86; *b* 28 April 1924; *s* of Edward Griffiths and Nancy Olga (*née* Fuell); *m* 1952, Mary Kirkhouse Jenkins, *y d* of late Judge George Kirkhouse Jenkins, QC; two *s* one *d*. *Educ:* Whitchurch Grammar Sch., Cardiff; King's Coll., London. LLB (Hons) London, 1951 (Jelf Medallist); Cert. Theol. St David's UC, 1988. RAF, 1942–47. Chm., Local Appeals Tribunal (Cardiff), Min. of Social Security, 1964–70; an Asst Recorder of Cardiff, Swansea and Merthyr Tydfil, 1966–71; Vice-Chm., Mental Health Review Tribunal for Wales, 1968–72; Dep. Chm., Glamorgan QS, 1971; Comr of Assize, Royal Cts of Justice, London, 1971; Mem., Parole Bd, 1983–85; Chancellor, Dio. of Monmouth, 1977–92; President of Provincial Court, and Mem. Governing Body (Panel of Chairmen), Church in Wales, 1979–92. Chm., Welsh Sculpture Trust; former Mem., Welsh Arts Council, and Chm., Art Cttee; Chm., Contemp. Art Soc. for Wales, 1987–92 (Purchaser, 1975–76; Vice-Chm., 1977–87). *Address:* 15 Heol Don, Whitchurch, Cardiff CF4 2AR. *T:* Cardiff (01222) 625001; 15 Carrer Alaró, Es Traves, Port de Soller, Mallorca, Spain. *T:* (71) 63380. *Clubs:* Naval and Military; Cardiff and County (Cardiff).

GRIFFITHS, David Howard, OBE 1982; Chairman, Eastern Region, British Gas Corporation, 1981–87; *b* 30 Oct. 1922; *s* of David Griffiths and Margaret (*née* Jones); *m* 1949, Dilys Watford John; two *d*. *Educ:* Monmouth Sch.; Sidney Sussex Coll., Cambridge (Exhibnr; BA 1941, MA 1946, LLB 1946). Admitted Solicitor of the Supreme Court, 1948. Asst Solicitor, Newport Corp., 1948; Wales Gas Board: Solicitor, 1949; Management Develt Officer, 1965; Dir of Develt, 1967; Wales Gas: Dir of Conversion, 1970; Sec., 1973; Dep. Chm., Eastern Gas, 1977. Vice Pres., Contemporary Arts Soc., Wales, 1977. *Recreations:* reading, golf, music. *Address:* 12 Fallows Green, Harpenden, Herts AL5 4HD. *Club:* Salcombe Yacht.

GRIFFITHS, David Hubert; Head of Arable Crops and Horticulture Group, Ministry of Agriculture, Fisheries and Food, since 1995; *b* 24 Dec. 1940; *s* of Hubert Griffiths and Margaret Joan Waldron; *m* Mary Abbott; one *s* one *d*. *Educ:* Kingswood School, Bath; St Catharine's College, Cambridge (MA). Joined Ministry of Agriculture, Fisheries and Food as Asst Principal, 1963; Principal, 1968; Asst Secretary, 1975; Hd, European Communities Gp, 1982–83; Fisheries Sec., 1983–87; Hd, Food, Drink and Marketing Policy Gp, 1987–90; Dir of Establishments, 1990–94. Non-exec. Dir, ICI (Paints Div.), 1985–87. *Recreations:* golf, cooking, music. *Address:* c/o Ministry of Agriculture, Fisheries and Food, Whitehall Place, SW1A 2AH. *Club:* Richmond Golf.

GRIFFITHS, David John; His Honour Judge David Griffiths; a Circuit Judge, since 1984; *b* 18 Feb. 1931; *m* Anita; three *s* one *d*. *Educ:* St Dunstan's Coll., Catford, SE6. Admitted to Roll of Solicitors, 1957; apptd Notary Public, 1969; Principal: D. J. Griffiths & Co., Bromley, 1960–84; Harveys, Lewisham, 1970–84. A Recorder, 1980–84. Mem., Scriveners Co., 1983. *Recreations:* riding, music (male voice choir). *Address:* Crosswell, Fosten Green, Biddenden, Kent TN27 8ER.

GRIFFITHS, David Laurence; His Honour Judge Griffiths; a Circuit Judge, since 1989; *b* 3 Aug. 1944; *s* of late Edward Laurence Griffiths and of Mary Middleton Pudge; *m* 1971, Sally Hollis; four *d*. *Educ:* Christ's Hospital; Jesus College, Oxford (MA). Called to the Bar, Lincoln's Inn, 1967; an Asst Recorder, 1981; Recorder, 1985. *Recreations:* gardening, hash running, sailing, walking, cycling, watching Rugby and cricket, opera, history, classical music. *Address:* Lord Chancellor's Department, Trevelyan House, Great Peter Street, SW1P 2BY. *T:* 0171–210 8500.

GRIFFITHS, Ven. Dr David Nigel, FSA; Archdeacon of Berkshire, 1987–92, now Emeritus; Chaplain to The Queen, since 1977; *b* 29 Oct. 1927; *o s* of late William Cross Griffiths, LDS, and Doris May (*née* Rhodes); *m* 1953, Joan Fillingham; two *s* one *d*. *Educ:* King Edward's Sch., Bath; Cranbrook; Worcester Coll., Oxford (MA; Gladstone Meml Prize, Arnold Historical Essay Prize); Lincoln Theol Coll.; PhD Reading, 1991. An economist before ordination; Consultant at FAO, Rome, 1952–53. Curate, St Matthew, Northampton, 1958–61; Headquarters Staff, SPCK, 1961–67; Rector of Minster Parishes, Lincoln, 1967–73; Vice-Chancellor and Librarian, Lincoln Cathedral, 1967–73; Rector of Windsor, 1973–87; Rural Dean of Maidenhead, 1977–82 and 1985–87; Hon. Canon of Christ Church, Oxford, 1983–88, now Emeritus. Warden, St Anne's Bede Houses, Lincoln, 1993–. Served TARO and RMFVR, 1946–50; Chaplain, RNR, 1963–77 (Reserve Decoration, 1977); OCF, Household Cavalry, 1973–87, 1st Bn Irish Guards, 1977–80. FSA 1973. *Publications:* articles on bibliography and church history. *Recreations:* walking, bibliomania. *Address:* 2 Middleton's Field, Lincoln LN2 1QP. *T:* Lincoln (01522) 525753.

GRIFFITHS, Edward; *b* 7 March 1929; Welsh; *m* 1954, Ella Constance Griffiths; one *s* one *d*. *Educ:* University Coll. of N Wales, Bangor. Industrial Chemist, 1951. Mem., Flintshire CC, 1964. MP (Lab) Brightside Div. of Sheffield, June 1968–Sept. 1974; contested (Ind Lab) Sheffield Brightside, Oct. 1974. *Recreation:* sport.

GRIFFITHS, Sir Eldon (Wylie), Kt 1985; MA Cantab, MA Yale; *b* 25 May 1925; *s* of Thomas H. W. Griffiths and Edith May; *m*; one *s* one *d*. *Educ:* Ashton Grammar Sch.; Emmanuel Coll., Cambridge. Fellow, Saybrook Coll., Yale, 1948–49; Correspondent, Time and Life magazines, 1949–55; Foreign Editor, Newsweek, 1956–63; Columnist, Washington Post, 1962–63; Conservative Research Department, 1963–64. MP(C) Bury St Edmunds, May 1964–1992; Parly Sec., Min. of Housing and Local Govt, June-Oct. 1970; Parly Under-Sec. of State, DoE, and Minister for Sport, 1970–74; opposition spokesman on trade and industry, and Europe, 1974–76. Former Chairman: Anglo-Iranian Parly Gp; Anglo-Polish Parly Gp. Pres., Special Olympics (UK). Consultant/Adviser, Nat. Police Federation, to 1988; President: Assoc. of Public Health Inspectors, 1969–70; Friends of Gibraltar; World Affairs Council, Orange County, California. Regents' Prof., Univ. of California, Irvine. Dir, Center for Internat. Business, Chapman Univ., Orange, Calif. Dir, US and UK cos. Hon. Freeman, City of London; Hon. Citizen, Orange County, California. Medal of Honour, Republic of China, Taiwan. *Recreations:* reading, swimming, cricket. *Address:* The Wallow, Great Barton, Bury St Edmunds, Suffolk IP31 2QK; 29091 Ridgeview, Laguna Niguel, CA 92691, USA. *Clubs:* Carlton; Dutch Treat (New York).

GRIFFITHS, Harold Morris; Assistant Secretary, HM Treasury, 1978–86; *b* 17 March 1926; *s* of Rt Hon. James Griffiths, CH; *m* 1st, 1951, Gwyneth Lethby (*d* 1966); three *s* one *d*; 2nd, 1966, Elaine Burge (*née* Walsh); two *s*. *Educ:* Llanelly Grammar Sch.; London

Sch. of Economics. Editorial Staff: Glasgow Herald, 1949–55; Guardian, 1955–67; Information Division, HM Treasury: Deputy Head, 1967–68, Head, 1968–72; Asst Sec., HM Treasury, 1972–75; Counsellor (Economic), Washington, 1975–78. *Address:* 32 Teddington Park, Teddington, Mddx TW11 8DA. *T:* 0181–977 2464.

GRIFFITHS, Howard; Command Secretary, RAF Logistics Command, since 1994; *b* 20 Sept. 1938; *s* of Bernard and Olive Griffiths; *m* 1963, Dorothy Foster (*née* Todd); one *s* one *d*. *Educ:* London School of Economics (BScEcon, MScEcon). Ministry of Defence: Research Officer, 1963–69; Principal, Army Dept, 1970–72; Central Staffs, 1972–76; Asst Secretary, Head of Civilian Faculty, National Defence Coll., 1976–78; Procurement Executive, 1978–80; Deputy and Counsellor (Defence), UK Delegn, Mutual and Balanced Force Reductions (Negotiations), Vienna, 1980–84; Asst Sec., Office of Management and Budget, 1984–86; Asst Sec. and Head of Defence Arms Control Unit, 1986–88; Asst Under Sec. of State (Policy), 1988–91; Fellow, Center for Internat. Affairs, Harvard Univ., 1991–92; Assistant Under Secretary of State: (Ordnance), 1992; (Supply and Orgn) (Air), 1993–94. *Address:* RAF Brampton, Huntingdon, Cambs PE18 8QL.
See also L. Griffiths.

GRIFFITHS, Howard; Editor, Pulse, since 1979; Group Editor: Financial Pulse, since 1987; The Practitioner, since 1994 (Editor, 1988–94); *b* 6 Aug. 1947; *m* 1977, Lynda Smith; three *d*. *Educ:* Cowbridge Grammar School; Merton College, Oxford (BA). Feature writer, Pulse, 1973. *Recreation:* family. *Address:* Morgan-Grampian House, Calderwood Street, SE18 6QH. *T:* 0181–316 3577.

GRIFFITHS, Islwyn Owen, QC 1973; a Recorder of the Crown Court, 1972–84; *b* 24 Jan. 1924; *m* 1951, Pamela Norah Blizard. *Educ:* Swansea Grammar Sch.; Christ Church, Oxford (MA, BCL). Army (Royal Artillery), 1942–47; TA (RA), 1947–51; TARO, 1951. Called to Bar, Lincoln's Inn, 1953; Dep. Chm., Bucks QS, 1967–71. Comr, 1979–84, Chief Comr, 1981–84, National Insurance, later Social Security, Commn. *Recreation:* sailing. *Address:* Kings Farm House, Wimland Road, Faygate, near Horsham, Sussex RH12 4SS. *Club:* Garrick.

GRIFFITHS, John Calvert, CMG 1983; QC 1972; a Recorder of the Crown Court, since 1972; *b* 16 Jan. 1931; *s* of Oswald Hardy Griffiths and Christina Flora Griffiths; *m* 1958, Jessamy, *er d* of Prof. G. P. Crowden and Jean Crowden; three *d*. *Educ:* St Peter's Sch., York (scholar); Emmanuel Coll., Cambridge (sen. exhibnr) (BA 1st Cl. Hons 1955; MA 1960). Called to Bar, Middle Temple, 1956 (Bencher, 1983). Attorney-General of Hong Kong, Mem. Exec. and Legislative Councils, and Chm. Hong Kong Law Reform Commn, 1979–83. Member: Exec. Cttee, General Council of the Bar, 1967–71 (Treas., 1987); Senate of Inns of Court and the Bar, 1983– (Mem., Exec. Cttee, 1973–77); Council of Legal Educn, 1983–; Nat. Council of Social Service, 1974–; Greater London CAB Exec. Cttee, 1978–79; (co-opted) Develt and Special Projects Cttee, 1977–79; Court, Hong Kong Univ., 1980–; Exec. Cttee, Prince Philip Cambridge Scholarships, 1980–. Lieutenant, RE, 1949–50 (Nat. Service). *Recreations:* fishing reading, gardening. *Address:* Des Voeux Chambers, 10F Bank of East Asia Building, 10 Des Vœux Road, Central, Hong Kong. *T:* 25263071; 1 Brick Court, Temple, EC4Y 9BY. *T:* 0171–583 0777. *Clubs:* Flyfishers', Hurlingham; Hong Kong, Royal Hong Kong Jockey (Hong Kong).

GRIFFITHS, John Charles, JP; Chairman: Minerva Arts Channel, since 1989; Minerva Vision, since 1989; *b* 19 April 1934; *s* of Sir Percival Griffiths, KBE, CIE; *m* 1st, 1956, Ann Timms (marr. diss.); four *s*; 2nd, 1983, Carole Jane Mellor (marr. diss.); one *d*. *Educ:* Uppingham; Peterhouse, Cambridge (MA). Dep. General Manager, Press Association, 1968–70; PR adviser, British Gas, 1970–74; Chm., MSG Public Relations, 1974–78; Chm. and founder, The Arts Channel, 1983–89. Chairman: National League of Young Liberals, 1962–64 (Mem., Nat. Exec., 1964–66); Assoc. of Liberals in Small Business and Self Employed, 1980; Pres., Liberal Party, 1982–83. Contested (L): Ludlow, 1964; Wanstead and Woodford, 1966; Bedford, Feb. 1974, Oct. 1974. Develt Dir, Bardsey Island Trust, 1992–. Chm. Govs, Llangynidr Sch., 1993–. JP Cardiff, 1960. *Publications:* The Survivors, 1964; Afghanistan, 1967; Modern Iceland, 1969; Three Tomorrows, 1980; The Science of Winning Squash, 1981; Afghanistan: key to a Continent, 1981; The Queen of Spades, 1983; Flashpoint Afghanistan, 1986; The Third Man: the life and times of William Murdoch, 1992; Nimbus, 1994. *Recreations:* conversation, reading, music. *Address:* The Grove, Gosbury Lane, Medbrook, Monmouth, Gwent NP5 4LX. *Club:* Royal Automobile.

GRIFFITHS, Sir John N.; *see* Norton-Griffiths.

GRIFFITHS, John Pankhurst, RIBA; Vice-President, Upkeep, since 1993; *b* 27 Sept. 1930; *s* of late William Bramwell Griffiths and Ethel Doris Griffiths (*née* Pankhurst); *m* 1959, Helen Elizabeth (*née* Tasker); two *s* one *d*. *Educ:* Torquay Grammar School; King George V School, Southport; School of Architecture, Manchester Univ. Dip Arch. Resident architect, Northern Nigeria, for Maxwell Fry, 1956–58; staff architect, Granada Television, 1959; Founder and first Dir, Manchester Building Centre, 1959–65; Head of Tech. Inf., Min. of Public Buildings and Works, later DoE, 1965–77; formed Building Conservation Assoc. later Building Conservation Trust, subseq. Upkeep, 1977, Dir, 1979–93. Trustee, Tylers and Bricklayers Craft Trust, 1993–. *Publications:* articles in tech. and prof. jls. *Recreations:* looking at buildings, writing, speaking, cooking. *Address:* 28 Palace Road, East Molesey, Surrey KT8 9DL. *T:* 0181–979 4065.

GRIFFITHS, (John) Peter (Gwynne); QC 1995; a Recorder, since 1991; *b* 9 Dec. 1945; *s* of Arwyn Griffiths and late Vera Griffiths; *m* (marr. diss.); four *c*. *Educ:* Hereford Cathedral Sch.; Bristol Univ. (Civil Engrg); UWIST (LLB Hons). Work in oil exploration industry, 1968–70; called to the Bar, Gray's Inn, 1970; Asst Recorder, 1987–91. Mem., Arts Council of Wales (formerly Welsh Arts Council), 1992–. Chm., Visual Arts Bd for Wales; Vice Pres., Cywaith Cymru (formerly Welsh Sculpture Trust). *Publication:* (ed jtly) Injuries at Work, 1996. *Recreations:* angling, sailing, ski-ing, golf, the arts. *Address:* 30 Park Place, Cardiff CF1 3BA. *T:* Cardiff (01222) 398421. *Club:* Cardiff and County (Cardiff).

GRIFFITHS, Prof. John William Roger, FEng; Professor of Electronics, Department of Electronic and Electrical Engineering, Loughborough University of Technology, 1967–84, now Emeritus; *b* 27 Nov. 1921; *s* of Samuel William Henry Griffiths and Alice Griffiths; *m* 1945, Pauline Edyth Griffiths (*née* Marston); one *s*. *Educ:* Waterloo Grammar Sch.; Bristol Univ. BSc 1949, PhD 1958. FEng 1991, FIEE; FIOA. Served War, HM Forces, 1939–46. Scientific Civil Service, 1949–55; Lectr, then Sen. Lectr, Birmingham Univ., 1955–67; Loughborough Univ. of Technology: Head of Dept, 1968–80; Dean of Engineering, 1972–75; Sen. Pro-Vice-Chancellor, 1978–80. Vis. Prof., Inst. of Radio Physics, Calcutta, 1963–65. Mem., Govt Adv. Panel on Satellite TV Standards, 1983. *Publications:* Signal Processing in Underwater Acoustics, 1972; many papers in learned jls. *Recreations:* sport, gardening. *Address:* 80 Rectory Road, Wanlip, Leicestershire LE7 4PL. *T:* Leicester (0116) 267 6336.

GRIFFITHS, Lawrence; a Recorder of the Crown Court, 1972–93; *b* 16 Aug. 1933; *s* of Bernard Griffiths and Olive Emily Griffiths (*née* Stokes); *m* 1959, Josephine Ann (*née* Cook); one *s* two *d*. *Educ:* Gowerton Grammar Sch.; Christ's Coll., Cambridge (MA). Called to Bar, Inner Temple, 1957; practised Swansea, 1958–; Mem. Wales and Chester Circuit; Prosecuting Counsel to Inland Revenue for Wales and Chester Circuit, 1969–93. Standing Counsel to HM Customs and Excise for Wales and Chester Circuit, 1989–93. Mem., Mental Health Review Tribunal for Wales, 1970–91. *Recreations:* wine, walking, travel by sea, snooker. *Address:* 26 Hillside Crescent, Uplands, Swansea SA2 0RD. *T:* Swansea (01792) 473513; (chambers) Iscoed Chambers, 86 St Helens Road, Swansea SA1 4BQ. *T:* Swansea (01792) 652988. *Club:* Bristol Channel Yacht (Swansea).
See also H. Griffiths.

GRIFFITHS, Rev. Dr Leslie John; President of the Methodist Conference, 1994–95; Superintendent Minister, Finchley and Hendon Circuit, Methodist Church, since 1991; *b* 15 Feb. 1942; *s* of late Sidney and Olwen Griffiths; *m* 1969, Margaret, *d* of Alfred and Kathleen Rhodes; two *s* one *d*. *Educ:* Llanelli Grammar Sch.; Univ. of Wales (BA); Univ. of Cambridge (MA); Univ. of London (PhD). Junior Res. Fellow, University Coll. of S Wales and Monmouthshire, Cardiff, 1963; Asst Lectr in English, St David's Coll., Lampeter, 1964–67; trained for Methodist Ministry, Wesley Ho., Cambridge, 1967–70; Asst Minister, Wesley Church, Cambridge, 1969–70; Petit Goâve Circuit, Haïti, 1970–71; Port-au-Prince Circuit and Asst Headmaster, Nouveau Collège Bird, 1971–74; Minister, Reading Circuit, 1974–77; Superintendent Minister: Cap Haïtien Circuit, Haïti, 1977–80; Wanstead and Woodford Circuit, 1980–86; W London Mission, 1986–91. Mem., British–S African Conf., 1991–. Trustee, Addiction Recovery Foundn, 1989–. Dir, Birnbeck Housing Assoc., 1992–. Governor: Kingswood Sch., Bath, 1982–90; Central London YMCA, 1987–89; Bd of Christian Aid, 1990– (Chm., Africa and ME Cttee, 1991–95); Chm., Methodist Church's Caribbean and Latin America Adv. Group, 1982–89. *Publication:* A History of Haïtian Methodism, 1991. *Recreations:* fun and fellowship spiced with occasional moments of solitude. *Address:* 24 Monkville Avenue, NW11 0AH. *T:* 0181–455 8063. *Club:* Graduate Centre (Cambridge).

GRIFFITHS, Rt. Rev. (Michael) Ambrose; *see* Hexham and Newcastle, Bishop of, (RC).

GRIFFITHS, Nigel, JP; MP (Lab) Edinburgh South, since 1987; *b* 20 May 1955; *s* of late Lionel and Elizabeth Griffiths; *m* 1979, Sally, *d* of Hugh and Sally McLaughlin. *Educ:* Hawick High Sch.; Edinburgh Univ. (MA 1977); Moray House Coll. of Education. Joined Labour Party, 1970; Pres., EU Labour Club, 1976–77; Sec., Lothian Devolution Campaign, 1978; Rights Adviser to Mental Handicap Pressure Group, 1979–87. City of Edinburgh: District Councillor, 1980–87 (Chm., 1986–87; Chm., Housing Cttee; Chm., Decentralisation Cttee); Member: Edinburgh Festival Council, 1984–87; Edinburgh Health Council, 1982–87; Exec., Edinburgh Council of Social Service, 1984–87; Wester Hailes Sch. Council, 1981. Opposition Whip, 1987–89; Opposition frontbench spokesman on consumer affairs, 1989–. Exec. Mem. and Convenor, Finance Cttee, Scottish Constitutional Convention. Member: War on Want, SEAD, Amnesty Internat., Anti-apartheid, Friends of the Earth, Nat. Trust, Ramblers' Assoc. *Publications:* Guide to Council Housing in Edinburgh, 1981; Council Housing on the Point of Collapse, 1982; Welfare Rights Survey, 1981; Welfare Rights Guide, 1982; A Guide to DHSS Claims and Appeals, 1983; Welfare Rights Advice for Doctors, Health Visitors and Social Workers, 1983; Claiming Attendance Allowance, 1982. *Recreations:* squash, travel, live entertainment, badminton, hill walking and rock climbing, architecture, reading, politics. *Address:* 30 McLaren Road, Edinburgh EH9 2BN. *T:* 0131–667 1947; (office) 93 Causewayside, Edinburgh. *T:* 0131–662 4520; House of Commons, SW1A 0AA. *T:* 0171–219 3442.

GRIFFITHS, Paul Anthony; Music Critic of The New Yorker, since 1992; *b* 24 Nov. 1947; *s* of Fred Griffiths and Jeanne Veronica (*née* George); *m* 1977, Rachel Isabel Reader (*née* Cullen); two *s*. *Educ:* King Edward's Sch., Birmingham; Lincoln Coll., Oxford (BA, MSc). Area Editor for Grove's Dictionary of Music and Musicians, 6th edn, 1973–76; Asst Music Critic, 1979–82, Music Critic, 1982–92, The Times. *Publications:* A Concise History of Modern Music, 1978; Boulez, 1978; A Guide to Electronic Music, 1979; Modern Music, 1980; Cage, 1981; Igor Stravinsky: The Rake's Progress, 1982; Peter Maxwell Davies, 1982; The String Quartet, 1983; György Ligeti, 1983; Bartók, 1984; Olivier Messiaen, 1985; New Sounds, New Personalities, 1985; The Thames & Hudson Encyclopaedia of 20th-Century Music, 1986; Myself and Marco Polo (novel), 1989; The Lay of Sir Tristram (novel), 1991; The Jewel Box (libretto), 1991; Stravinsky, 1992; Modern Music and After, 1995. *Recreation:* swimming. *Address:* The Old Bakery, Lower Heyford, Oxford OX6 3NS. *T:* Steeple Aston (01869) 340584.

GRIFFITHS, Prof. Paul David, MD; Professor of Virology, since 1989, and Chairman of University Division of Pathology and Communicable Diseases, since 1991, Royal Free Hospital School of Medicine; *b* 30 Jan. 1953; *s* of George Griffiths and Jean Beckett (formerly Griffiths, *née* Pring); *m* 1979, Brenda Louise Attenborough; three *s*. *Educ:* St Bartholomew's Hosp. Med. Coll., Univ. of London (BSc 1974; MB BS Hons 1977; MD 1982); DSc (Med) 1995. MRCPath 1985. Lawrence Postgrad. Res. Schol., 1979; Lectr, Bart's Med. Coll., 1979–82; Fogarty Internat. Scholar, NIH, USA, 1980–81; Royal Free Hospital School of Medicine: Sen. Lectr in Virology, 1982–86; Reader, 1986–87. William Julius Mickle Fellow, London Univ., 1991. Member: UK med. socs; Amer. Soc. for Microbiol.; Internat. AIDS Soc. Editor, Reviews in Medical Virology, 1990–. Ian Howat Prize in Med. Microbiol., 1975, Wheelwright Prize for Paediatrics, 1977, St Bartholomew's Hosp. Med. Coll.; Wellcome Award, European Gp for Rapid Viral Diagnosis, 1988. *Publications:* papers on viruses, HIV/AIDS, herpes viruses and cytomegalovirus. *Recreations:* family, music, viruses, bridge. *Address:* Royal Free Hospital School of Medicine, Department of Virology, Rowland Hill Street, Hampsted NW3 2PF. *T:* 0171–794 0500.

GRIFFITHS, Peter; *see* Griffiths, J. P. G.

GRIFFITHS, Peter Anthony; Director, King's Fund College, and Deputy Chief Executive of King's Fund, since 1994; *b* 19 May 1945; *m* 1966, Margaret Harris; two *s*. *Educ:* Swansea Technical Coll. Regl admin. trainee, Welsh Hosp. Bd, Cardiff Royal Inf., 1963–66; nat. admin. trainee, Birmingham Reg./Nuffield Centre, Leeds, 1966–69; Dep. Hosp. Sec., E Birmingham HMC, 1969–71; Dep. Dist Administrator, Hosp. Sec., Southampton and SW Hampshire Health Dist (Teaching), 1971–76; Dist Administrator, Medway Health Dist, 1976–81; Actg Area Administrator, Kent AHA, 1981–82; Dist Administrator 1982–84, Dist Gen. Man. 1984–88, Lewisham and N Southwark HA; Regl Gen. Manager, SE Thames RHA, 1988–89; Dep. Chief Exec., NHS Management Exec., 1990–91; Chief Exec., Guy's and Lewisham NHS Trust, 1991–94. *Recreation:* golf.

GRIFFITHS, Prof. Peter Denham, CBE 1990; MD, FRCPath; Professor of Biochemical Medicine 1968–89, and Dean, Faculty of Medicine and Dentistry, 1985–89, University of Dundee (Vice-Principal, 1979–85); Hon. Consultant Clinical Chemist, Tayside Health Board, 1966–89; *b* 16 June 1927; *s* of Bernard Millar Griffiths and Florence Marion Fletcher; *m* 1949, Joy Burgess; three *s* one *d*. *Educ:* King Edward VI Sch., Southampton; Guy's Hosp. Med. Sch., Univ. of London (BSc 1st Cl. Hons, MD). LRCP, MRCS; FRCPath 1978. Served RN, 1946–49. Jun. Lectr in Physiol., Guy's Hosp. Med. Sch., 1957–58; Registrar, then Sen. Registrar in Clin. Path., Guy's and Lewisham Hosps, London, 1958–64; Consultant Pathologist, Harlow Gp of Hosps, Essex, 1964–66; Sen. Lectr in Clin. Chemistry, Univ. of St Andrews and subseq. Univ. of Dundee, 1966–68. Pres., Assoc. of Clin. Biochemists, UK, 1987–89 (Chm. Council, 1973–76); Member:

Tayside Health Bd, 1977–85; GMC, 1986–93; various cttees of SHHD and DHSS, 1969–. Dir, Drug Development (Scotland), 1982–89. Dir, Dundee Rep. Theatre, 1977–90. FIMgt; FRSA. Consulting Editor, Clinica Chimica Acta, 1986– (Mem. Editl Bd, 1976; Jt Editor-in-Chief, 1979–85). *Publications:* contrib. scientific and med. jls (pathology, clin. chemistry, computing). *Recreations:* music, gardening, walking. *Address:* 52 Albany Road, West Ferry, Dundee DD5 1NW. *T:* Dundee (01382) 776772.

GRIFFITHS, Peter Harry Steve; MP (C) Portsmouth North, since 1979; *b* 24 May 1928; *s* of W. L. Griffiths, West Bromwich; *m* 1962, Jeannette Christine (*née* Rubery); one *s* one *d. Educ:* City of Leeds Training Coll. BSc (Econ.) Hons London, 1956; MEd Birmingham, 1963. Headmaster, Hall Green Road Sch., West Bromwich, 1962–64. Senior Lectr in Economic Hist., The Polytechnic, Portsmouth (formerly Portsmouth Coll. of Technology), 1967–79. Fulbright Exchange Prof. of Economics, Pierce Coll., Los Angeles, Calif, 1968–69. Chm., Smethwick Education Cttee; Leader, Conservative Group of Councillors in Smethwick, 1960–64. MP (C) Smethwick, 1964–66; Contested (C) Portsmouth N, Feb. 1974. *Publication:* A Question of Colour?, 1966. *Recreations:* motoring, writing, camping. *Address:* c/o House of Commons, SW1A 0AA. *Clubs:* Sloane; Conservative (Smethwick and Portsmouth).

GRIFFITHS, Peter John; Secretary and Chief Administrative Officer, Charing Cross and Westminster Medical School, University of London, since 1993; *b* 19 April 1944; *s* of Ronald Hugh Griffiths and Emily Vera (*née* Cockshutt); *m* 1968, Lesley Florence (*née* Palmer) (marr. diss. 1993); two *d. Educ:* Battersea Grammar Sch.; Univ. of Leicester (BA Classics); McMaster Univ. (MA Classics). University of London: Asst to Principal, 1968–70; Asst Sec. to Cttee of Enquiry into governance of the university, 1970–72; Special Duties Officer, Vice-Chancellor's and Principal's Office, 1972–78; Dep. Head, Legal and Gen. Div., Court Dept, 1978–82; Asst Clerk of the Court, 1982–85; Dep. Clerk of the Court, 1985–87; Clerk of the Court, 1987–91; Dir of Resources and Planning, 1991–93. *Recreation:* choral singing (Pro Musica chorus). *Address:* Upland House, Upland Road, Sutton, Surrey SM2 5HW. *T:* 0181–643 3599.

GRIFFITHS, Phillip A., PhD; Director, Institute for Advanced Study, Princeton, since 1991; *b* 18 Oct. 1938; *s* of Phillip Griffiths and Jeanette (*née* Field); *m* 1st, 1958, Ann Lane Crittenden-Witt (marr. diss.); one *s* one *d*; 2nd, 1968, Marian Folsom Jones; two *d. Educ:* Wake Forest Univ. (BS 1959); Princeton Univ. (PhD 1962). University of California, Berkeley: Miller Fellow, 1962–64, 1975–76; Faculty Mem., 1964–67; Princeton University: Vis. Prof., 1967–68; Prof., 1968–72; Mem., Inst. for Advanced Study, 1968–70; Harvard University: Prof., 1972–83; Dwight Parker Robinson Prof. of Maths, 1983; Provost and James B. Duke Prof. of Maths, Duke Univ., 1983–91. Hon. DSc Wake Forest, 1973; De *hc* Angers, France, 1979; Hon. degree Peking, 1983. Leroy P. Steele Prize, Amer. Math. Soc., 1971; Dannie Heineman Prize, Acad. of Scis, Göttingen, 1979. *Publications:* (with J. Adams) Topics in Algebraic and Analytic Geometry, 1974; Entire Holomorphic Mappings in One and Several Complex Variables, 1976; (with J. Harris) Principles of Algebraic Geometry, 1978; An Introduction to the Theory of Special Divisors on Algebraic Curves, 1980; (jtly) Exterior Differential Systems, 1980; (jtly) Geometry of Algebraic Curves, Vol. I, 1985; Algebraic Curves, 1985; (with G. R. Jensen) Differential Systems and Isometric Embeddings, 1987; contrib. Annals of Math. Studies, Progress in Maths. *Recreation:* sailing. *Address:* Institute for Advanced Study, Olden Lane, Princeton, NJ 08540, USA. *T:* (609) 7348200.

GRIFFITHS, Prof. Ralph Alan, PhD; DLitt; FRHistS; Professor of Medieval History, University of Wales, Swansea, since 1982; *b* 4 Nov. 1937; *er s* of Thomas Rowland Griffiths and Marion Lovin Griffiths (*née* Jones). *Educ:* Lewis School, Pengam, Gwent; Univ. of Bristol (BA 1959; PhD 1963; DLitt 1983). FRHistS 1966. Research Asst, Bd of Celtic Studies, Univ. of Wales, 1961–64; University of Wales, Swansea: Asst Lectr, 1964–66; Lectr, 1966–71; Sen. Lectr, 1971–78; Reader, 1978–82; Dean of Admissions, 1990–. Visiting Professor: Dalhousie Univ., Canada, 1964; Ohio Univ., 1977, 1981; Haverford Coll., USA, 1977, 1981; James Ford Lectr in English Hist., Univ. of Oxford, 1993. Member: Royal Commn on Ancient and Historical Monuments (Wales), 1990–; Hist. and Archaeol Panel, Humanities Res. Bd, 1994–; Adv. Council on Public Records, 1996–. Mem. Council, RHistS, 1987–91 (Vice-Pres., 1992–96). Hon. Sec., Glamorgan Co. History Trust, 1974–; Trustee, Glamorgan-Gwent Archaeol Trust, 1985–. *Publications:* The Principality of Wales in the Later Middle Ages, I: South Wales 1277–1536, 1972; The Reign of King Henry VI, 1981; (with R. S. Thomas) The Making of the Tudor Dynasty, 1985, 2nd edn 1990; (with J. Cannon) The Oxford Illustrated History of the British Monarchy, 1988; King and Country: England and Wales in the Fifteenth Century, 1990; Sir Rhys ap Thomas and his Family, 1993; Conquerors and Conquered in Medieval Wales, 1994; contrib. to books and learned jls. *Recreations:* music, travel, American writing, Shakespeare. *Address:* Department of History, University of Wales, Swansea SA2 8PP. *T:* Swansea (01792) 295226.

GRIFFITHS, Robert; *see* Griffiths, W. R.

GRIFFITHS, Prof. Roderic Keith; Professor of Public Health, University of Birmingham, since 1990 and Director of Public Health, West Midlands Regional Health Authority, since 1993; *b* 12 April 1945; *s* of Tom and Olwen Griffiths; *m* 1967, Margaret Ash (separated 1983); one *s* two *d*; partner, 1985, Lois Parker. *Educ:* Birmingham Univ. (BSc, MB ChB 1969). Lectr in Anatomy, 1970, in Social Medicine, 1978, Birmingham Univ; GP in Birmingham, 1975; Dir of Public Health, Central Birmingham HA, 1982. Mem., Birmingham Lunar Soc., 1992–. *Publications:* articles on stress in bones, and public health in UK. *Recreations:* ski-ing, pottery, sailing very occasionally. *Address:* The University, Edgbaston, Birmingham B15 2TT. *T:* 0121–414 6774.

GRIFFITHS, Roger Noel Price, MA Cantab; Membership Secretary, The Headmasters' Conference, since 1990 (Deputy Secretary, The Headmasters' Conference and Secondary Heads' Association, 1986–89); *b* 25 Dec. 1931; *er s* of late William Thomas and of Annie Evelyn Griffiths; *m* 1966, Diana, *y d* of late Capt. J. F. B. Brown, RN; three *d. Educ:* Lancing Coll.; King's Coll., Cambridge. Asst Master at Charterhouse, 1956–64; Headmaster, Hurstpierpoint Coll., 1964–86. Governor: Mill Hill Sch., 1987–92; Tormead Sch., 1987–94; Prebendal Sch., Chichester, 1987–; Worth Sch., 1990–. Mem., Management Cttee, Pallant House Trust, Chichester, 1987–92. Asst to Court of Worshipful Co. of Wax Chandlers, 1985, Master, 1990. MA Oxon, by incorporation, 1960. JP Mid Sussex, 1976–86. *Recreations:* music, theatre, bowls. *Address:* Hanbury Cottage, Cocking, near Midhurst, West Sussex GU29 0HF. *T:* Midhurst (01730) 813503. *Clubs:* East India, Devonshire, Sports and Public Schools; Sussex (Sussex).

GRIFFITHS, Siân Meryl, (Mrs Ian Wylie), FFPHM; Director of Public Health/Health Policy, Oxfordshire Health (Oxfordshire Health Authority and Oxfordshire Family Health Services Association, 1994–March 1996); *b* 20 March 1952; *d* of John Daniel Griffiths and Rosemary Marjorie Griffiths (*née* Quick); *m* 1st, 1978, Anthony Chu; two *d*; 2nd, 1987, Ian Wylie; one *s. Educ:* Felixstowe College; N London Collegiate Sch.; New Hall, Cambridge (MB BChir 1977; MA). MSc London, 1981. DRCOG 1979; FFPHM 1991. Clinical MO, KCH, 1979–80; Res. Fellow, NY, 1981; Dist. MO, City and Hackney HA, 1985–87; Consultant in Public Health Medicine, Oxford RHA, 1988–90; Regl Dir of Public Health and Health Policy, SW Thames RHA, 1990–93. Treas., FPHM, 1995–; Co-Chair, Assoc. of Public Health, 1995–; Mem. Bd, NAHAT, 1995–. *Publications:* Indicators for Mental Health, 1990; Creating a Common Profile, 1990; (ed jtly) Prevention of Suicide, 1993; contribs to med. jls. *Recreations:* spending time with family, films, theatre. *Address:* 39 Leckford Road, Oxford OX2 6HY. *T:* Oxford (01865) 514855.

GRIFFITHS, Trevor; playwright; *b* 4 April 1935; *s* of Ernest Griffiths and Anne Connor. *Educ:* Manchester Univ. BA (Hons) Eng. Lang. and Lit. Teaching, 1957–65; Educn Officer, BBC, 1965–72. Writer's Award, BAFTA, 1981. *Publications:* Occupations, 1972, 3rd edn 1980; Sam Sam, 1972; The Party, 1974, 2nd edn 1978; Comedians, 1976, 2nd edn 1979; All Good Men, and Absolute Beginners, 1977; Through the Night, and Such Impossibilities, 1977; Thermidor and Apricots, 1977; (jtly) Deeds, 1978; (trans.) The Cherry Orchard, 1978; Country, 1981; Oi for England, 1982; Sons and Lovers (television version), 1982; Judgement Over the Dead (television screenplays of The Last Place on Earth), 1986; Fatherland (screenplay), and Real Dreams, 1987; Collected Plays for Television, 1988; Piano, 1990; The Gulf Between Us, 1992; Hope in the Year Two, 1994; Thatcher's Children, 1994. *Address:* c/o Peters, Fraser & Dunlop, 503/4 The Chambers, Chelsea Harbour, Lots Road, SW10 0XF. *T:* 0171–344 1000.

GRIFFITHS, William Arthur; management consultant, Griffiths Seckerson, since 1986; *b* 25 May 1940; *s* of Glyndwr and Alice Rose Griffiths; *m* 1963, Margaret Joan Dodd; two *s* one *d. Educ:* Owen's Sch., London; Queens' Coll., Cambridge; Univ. of Manchester. Probation Officer, Southampton, 1965–71; Home Office, 1971–76; Chief Probation Officer, N Ireland, 1977–84; Dir, NCVO, 1985–86. Member Executive Committee: NI Council for Voluntary Action, 1985; Wales Council for Voluntary Action, 1985; Scottish Council for Community and Voluntary Organisations, 1985; Trustee, Charities Aid Foundn, 1985. Chm. Finance, Westminster CC, 1990–94. *Recreation:* literature.

GRIFFITHS, (William) Robert; QC 1993; *b* 24 Sept. 1948; *s* of late (William) John Griffiths and of Megan Marjorie Griffiths (*née* Green); *m* 1984, Angela May Crawford; one *s* two *d. Educ:* Haverfordwest Grammar Sch.; St Edmund Hall, Oxford (Open Schol.; BCL, MA). Called to the Bar, Middle Temple, 1974; Jun. Counsel to the Crown (Common Law), 1989–93. *Recreations:* reading, collecting modern first editions, cricket (Schoolboy Cricket Internt., Wales, 1966–68; rep. Glamorgan CCC, 1967–68), tennis. *Address:* 4/5 Gray's Inn Square, Gray's Inn, WC1R 5AY. *T:* 0171–404 5252. *Clubs:* MCC, Lord's Taverners.

GRIFFITHS, Winston James; MP (Lab) Bridgend, since 1987; *b* 11 Feb. 1943; *s* of (Rachel) Elizabeth Griffiths and (Evan) George Griffiths; *m* 1966, (Elizabeth) Ceri Griffiths; one *s* one *d. Educ:* State schools in Brecon; University College of South Wales and Monmouthshire, Cardiff. BA, DipEd. Taught in Tanzania, Birmingham, Barry, Cowbridge. MEP (Lab) Wales South, 1979–89; a Vice Pres., 1984–87; formerly Chm., Parliamentarians Global Action for Disarmament, Develt and World Reform (formerly Parliamentarians for World Order); formerly Mem., delegn to S Asia; Hon. Mem., European Parlt, 1989. Opposition frontbench spokesman on: envmtl protection, 1990–92, on education, 1992–. Member: World Development Movement; Christian Socialist Movement; Amnesty International; Fabian Society; Anti-Apartheid Movement; VSO; Socialist Educn Assoc., 1986–. Vice Pres., Wales Aid to Poland. President: Kenfig Hill and Dist Male Voice Choir, 1986–; Porthcawl Choral Soc., 1993–. Methodist local preacher, 1966–. FRSA 1991. *Address:* Tŷ Llon, John Street, Y Graig, Cefn Cribwr, Mid Glamorgan CF32 0AB. *T:* Kenfig Hill (01656) 740526.

GRIGG, John (Edward Poynder), FRSL; writer; *b* 15 April 1924; *s* of late 1st Baron Altrincham and Joan Dickson-Poynder; *m* 1958, Patricia, *d* of late H. E. Campbell and of Marion Wheeler; two *s. Educ:* Eton; New Coll., Oxford (Exhibitioner). MA, Modern History; Gladstone Memorial Prize. Grenadier Guards, 1943–45. Editor, National and English Review, 1954–60; Columnist for The Guardian, 1960–70; with The Times, 1986–93. Chm., The London Library, 1985–91. Pres., Blackheath Soc.; Gov., Nehru Meml Trust. Contested (C) Oldham West, 1951 and 1955. *Publications:* Two Anglican Essays, 1958; The Young Lloyd George, 1973; Lloyd George: the People's Champion, 1978 (Whitbread Award); 1943: The Victory That Never Was, 1980; Nancy Astor: Portrait of a Pioneer, 1980; Lloyd George: From Peace to War 1912–1916, 1985 (Wolfson Literary Prize); The History of The Times, Vol. 6: the Thomson Years, 1993; contribs to other books, incl. DNB; articles and reviews. *Address:* 32 Dartmouth Row, SE10 8AW. *T:* 0181–692 4973. *Clubs:* Garrick, Beefsteak.
See also Sir W. A. Campbell.

GRIGGS, Rt Rev. Ian Macdonald; Bishop Suffragan of Ludlow, 1987–94; Hon. Assistant Bishop, Diocese of Carlisle, since 1994; *b* 17 May 1928; *s* of late Donald Nicholson Griggs and of Agnes Elizabeth Griggs; *m* 1953, Patricia Margaret Vernon-Browne; two *s* three *d* (and one *s* decd). *Educ:* Brentwood School; Trinity Hall, Cambridge (MA); Westcott House, Cambridge. Curate, St Cuthbert, Copnor, dio. Portsmouth, 1954–59; Domestic Chaplain to Bishop of Sheffield, 1959–64; Diocesan Youth Chaplain (part-time), 1959–64; Vicar of St Cuthbert, Fir Vale, dio. Sheffield, 1964–71; Vicar of Kidderminster, 1971–83; Hon. Canon of Worcester Cathedral, 1977–83; Archdeacon of Ludlow, 1984–87; Priest-in-Charge, St Michael, Tenbury, 1984–88. Chm., Churches' Council for Health and Healing, 1990–. Gov., Atlantic Coll., 1991–. *Recreations:* mountaineering, hill-walking. *Address:* Rookings, Patterdale, Penrith, Cumbria CA11 0NP. *T:* Glenridding (017684) 82064.

GRIGGS, Jeremy David; His Honour Judge Griggs; a Circuit Judge, since 1995; *b* 5 Feb. 1945; *s* of Celadon Augustine Griggs and Ethel Mary Griggs (*née* Anderson); *m* 1st, 1971, Wendy Anne Russell (*née* Culham) (marr. diss. 1982); two *s* one *d*; 2nd, 1985, Patricia Maynard; two step *d. Educ:* St Edward's Sch., Oxford; Magdalene Coll., Cambridge (MA). Called to the Bar, Inner Temple, 1968; Mem., Western Circuit, 1968–; a Recorder, 1990–95. Bar Rep., CCBE, 1990–94. Chm., London Choral Soc., 1986–90. *Recreations:* playing the piano, sailing on Norfolk Broads. *Address:* Exeter Combined Court Centre, The Castle, Exeter EX9 3TH. *Club:* Hickling Sailing.

GRIGGS, Norman Edward, CBE 1976; Vice-President, The Building Societies Association, since 1981 (Secretary-General, 1963–81); *b* 27 May 1916; *s* of late Archibald Griggs and late Maud Griggs (*née* Hewing); *m* 1947, Livia Lavinia Jandolo; one *s* one step *s. Educ:* Newport Grammar Sch.; London Sch. of Econs and Polit. Science (BScEcon). FCIS. Accountancy Dept, County of London Electric Supply Co. Ltd, 1933–40; service in RE and RAPC, Middle East, 1940–46; Asst Sec., Glass Manufrs' Fedn, 1946–52; Sec., Plastics Inst., 1952–56; Asst Sec., Building Socs Assoc., 1956–61, Dep. Sec. 1961–63. Sec.-Gen., Internat. Union of Building Socs and Savings Assocs, 1972–77; Vice-Pres., Metropolitan Assoc. of Building Socs, 1981–89. *Publications:* poetry: Life in the Withered Shell, 1990; Sharp-Eyed and Wary, 1991. *Recreation:* print addict. *Address:* 5 Gledhow Gardens, SW5 0BL. *T:* 0171–373 5128.

GRIGSON, Geoffrey Douglas; His Honour Judge Grigson; a Circuit Judge, since 1989; *b* 28 Oct. 1944; *s* of Frederic Walter Grigson and Nora Marion Grigson; *m* 1967, Jay Sibbring; two *s* one *d. Educ:* Denstone Coll.; Selwyn Coll., Cambridge (MA). Called to the Bar, Gray's Inn, 1968; Midland and Oxford Circuit; a Recorder, 1985–89. *Recreation:* reading newspapers. *Address:* Central Criminal Court, Old Bailey, EC4M 7EH. *Club:* Achilles.

GRIGSON, Sophie; freelance food writer and broadcaster, since 1983; *b* 19 June 1959; *d* of late Geoffrey Edward Harvey Grigson and Jane Grigson; *m* 1992, William Black; one *d*. *Educ:* UMIST (BSc Hons Maths). Cookery Correspondent: Evening Standard, 1986–93; Independent, 1993–94; Sunday Times Magazine, 1994–. Presenter: Grow Your Greens, and, Eat Your Greens, Channel 4, 1993; Travels à la Carte, 1994; Sophie's Meat Course, Channel 4, 1995; Curious Cooks, Radio 4. Chm., Jane Grigson Trust, 1991–. Food Writer of the Year, Restaurateurs' Assoc. of GB, 1992. *Publications:* Food For Friends, 1987; (with J. Molyneux) The Carved Angel Cookbook, 1990; Sophie's Table, 1990; Sophie Grigson's Ingredients Book, 1991; The Students' Cookbook, 1992; Eat Your Greens, 1993; (with William Black) Travels à la Carte, 1994; Sophie's Meat Course, 1995. *Recreations:* travel, reading, eating. *Address:* c/o David Higham Associates, 5–7 Lower John Street, W1R 4HA. *T:* 0171–437 7888.

GRILLET, Alain R.; *see* Robbe-Grillet.

GRILLS, Michael Geoffrey; a Recorder of the Crown Court, since 1982; a District Judge, since 1991; *b* 23 Feb. 1937; *s* of Frank and Bessie Grills; *m* 1969, Ann Margaret Irene (*née* Pyle); two *d*. *Educ:* Lancaster Royal Grammar Sch.; Merton Coll., Oxford (MA). Admitted Solicitor, 1961; Partner with Crombie Wilkinson & Robinson, York, 1965; County Court and District Registrar, York and Harrogate District Registries, 1973–90. *Recreations:* music, tennis, ski-ing. *Address:* Cobblestones, Skelton, York YO3 6XX. *T:* York (01904) 470 246.

GRIMA, Andrew Peter; Jeweller by appointment to HM the Queen; Managing Director, Andrew Grima Ltd, since 1966; *b* 31 May 1921; *s* of late John Grima and Leopolda Farnese; *m* 1st, 1947, Helène Marianne Haller (marr. diss. 1977); one *s* two *d*; 2nd, 1977, Joanne Jill, (Jojo), Maughan-Brown, *d* of late Captain Nigel Maughan-Brown, MC and of Mrs Graham Rawdon; one *d*. *Educ:* St Joseph's Coll., Beulah Hill; Nottingham Univ. Served War of 1939–45, REME, India and Burma, 1942–46 (despatches, 1945); commanded div. workshop. Director and jewellery designer. Exhibitions worldwide, designed and made prestige watch collection for Omega, "About Time", 1971; 40 year retrospective exhibn, Goldsmiths' Hall, 1991. Opened shops in Jermyn Street, 1966; Sydney and New York, 1970; Zürich, 1971; Tokyo, 1973; Lugano, 1987; Gstaad, 1992. Duke of Edinburgh Prize for Elegant Design, 1966; Queen's Award to Industry, 1966; 12 Diamond Internat. New York Awards, 1963–67. Freeman, City of London, 1964; Liveryman, Worshipful Co. of Goldsmiths, 1968. *Publications:* contribs to: International Diamond Annual, S Africa, 1970; 6 Meister Juweliere unserer Zeit, 1971; *relevant publication:* Grima 1951–1991, by Johann Willsberger, 1991. *Recreations:* paintings, sculpture, food and wine. *Address:* Vieux Gstaad, 3780 Gstaad, Switzerland; Albany, Piccadilly, W1V 9RR.

GRIME, Mark Stephen Eastburn; QC 1987; a Recorder, since 1990; *b* 16 March 1948; *s* of R. T. Grime, ChM, FRCS and late M. D. Grime; *m* 1973, Christine Emck; two *d*. *Educ:* Wrekin College; Trinity College, Oxford (Scholar; MA). Called to the Bar, Middle Temple, 1970; practising Northern Circuit, 1970–; Asst Recorder, 1988–90. Chairman: Disciplinary Appeal Tribunal, UMIST, 1980–; Northern Arbitration Assoc., 1994– (Mem. Council, 1990–94). *Recreations:* antiquarian horology, sailing. *Address:* Deans Court Chambers, Cumberland House, Crown Square, Manchester M3 3HA. *T:* 0161–834 4097.

GRIMLEY EVANS, Prof. John, FRCP; Professor of Geriatric Medicine, University of Oxford, since 1985; Fellow of Green College, Oxford, since 1985; *b* 17 Sept. 1936; *s* of Harry Walter Grimley Evans and Violet Prenter Walker; *m* 1966, Corinne Jane Cavender; two *s* one *d*. *Educ:* King Edward's Sch., Birmingham (Foundn Scholar); St John's Coll., Cambridge (Rolleston Scholar; MA, MD); Balliol Coll., Oxford (DM); FFPHM. Res. Asst, Nuffield Dept of Clin. Med., Oxford, 1963–65; Vis. Scientist, Sch. of Public Health, Univ. of Michigan, 1966; Res. Fellow, Med. Unit, Wellington Hosp., NZ, 1966–69; Lectr in Epidemiology, LSHTM, 1970–71; Consultant Physician, Newcastle Gen. Hosp., 1971–73; Prof. of Medicine (Geriatrics), Univ. of Newcastle upon Tyne, 1973–84. Chairman: Specialist Adv. Cttee on Geriatric Medicine, Jt Cttee for Higher Med. Trng, 1979–86; RCP Geriatric Medicine Cttee, 1989–94; Member: WHO Expert Panel on Care of Elderly, 1984– (Rapporteur, 1987); MRC, 1992–95 (Chm., Health Services Res. Cttee, 1989–92; Chm., Health Service and Public Health Res. Bd, 1992–94); Cttee on Med. Aspects of Food Policy, DoH, 1992–; GMC, 1994–. Chm., Examining Bd, Dip. in Geriatric Medicine, 1985–90. Pro-censor, 1990–91, Censor, 1991–92, Vice-Pres., 1993–95, RCP. Editor, Age and Ageing, 1988–. *Publications:* Care of the Elderly, 1977; (jtly) Advanced Geriatric Medicine (series), 1981–; (jtly) Improving the Health of Older People: a world view, 1990; (jtly) The Oxford Textbook of Geriatric Medicine, 1992; papers on geriatric medicine and epidemiology of chronic disease. *Recreations:* photography, fly-fishing, literature. *Address:* Donnington Farmhouse, Meadow Lane, Iffley, Oxford OX4 4ED. *Club:* Royal Society of Medicine.

GRIMMETT, Prof. Geoffrey Richard, DPhil; Professor of Mathematical Statistics, Cambridge University, since 1992; *b* 20 Dec. 1950; *s* of Benjamin and Patricia Grimmett; *m* 1986, Rosine Bonay; one *s*. *Educ:* King Edward's Sch., Birmingham; Merton Coll., Oxford (BA 1971; MSc 1972; MA, DPhil 1974). Jun. Res. Fellow, New Coll., and IBM Res. Fellow, Oxford Univ., 1974–76; Bristol University: Lectr, 1976–85; Reader, 1985–89; Prof. of Maths, 1989–92. Vis. appts at Cornell Univ., Univ. of Arizona, Univ. of Rome II, Univ. of Utah, etc. *Publications:* (with D. R. Stirzaker) Probability and Random Processes, 1982, 2nd edn 1992; (with D. J. A. Welsh) Probability: an introduction, 1986; Percolation, 1989; contrib. to learned jls. *Recreations:* mountaineering, music. *Address:* Statistical Laboratory, University of Cambridge, 16 Mill Lane, Cambridge CB2 1SB. *T:* Cambridge (01223) 337957. *Clubs:* Alpine; Climbers'.

GRIMSBY, Bishop Suffragan of, since 1979; **Rt. Rev. David Tustin;** *b* 12 Jan. 1935; *s* of John Trevelyan Tustin and Janet Reynolds; *m* 1964, Mary Elizabeth (*née* Glover); one *s* one *d*. *Educ:* Solihull School; Magdalene Coll., Cambridge (MA Hons); Geneva Univ. (Cert. in Ecumenical Studies); Cuddesdon Coll., Oxford Philip Usher Memorial Scholar (in Greece), 1957–58; Deacon 1960, priest 1961; Curate of Stafford, 1960–63; Asst Gen. Sec., C of E Council on Foreign Relations and Curate of St Dunstan-in-the-West, Fleet St, 1963–67; Vicar of S Paul's, Wednesbury, 1967–71; Vicar of Tettenhall Regis, 1971–79; RD of Trysull, 1977–79. Canon and Prebendary of Lincoln Cathedral, 1979–. Co-Chm., Anglican/Lutheran Internat. Commn, 1986–; Pres., Anglican/Lutheran Soc., 1987–; Mem., Gen. Synod of C of E, 1990– (Chm., Council for Christian Unity, 1993–). *Recreations:* music, family life, languages, travel. *Address:* Bishop's House, Church Lane, Irby-upon-Humber, Grimsby DN37 7JR. *T:* Swallow (01472) 371715, *Fax:* (01472) 371716.

GRIMSEY, Colin Robert; Under Secretary, Railways, Department of Transport, since 1993; *b* Manchester, 24 Dec. 1943; *yr s* of Arthur and Joan Grimsey; *m* 1976, Elizabeth Sermon; one *s* one *d*. *Educ:* Dartford Grammar Sch.; King's Coll., London (BSc Hons Physics 1964). Asst Principal, MoT, 1968–72; Principal, DoE, 1972–75; CSSB, 1975; DoE, 1976–79; Asst Sec., Dept of Transport, 1979–89; Under Sec., seconded to LRT, 1989–91; Dir of Finance, Dept of Transport, 1991–93. *Recreations:* family, choral singing, opera and theatre going, walking. *Address:* Department of Transport, 2 Marsham Street, SW1P 3EB. *T:* 0171–276 3000.

GRIMSHAW, Maj.-Gen. Ewing Henry Wrigley, CB 1965; CBE 1957 (OBE 1954); DSO 1945; *b* 30 June 1911; *s* of Col E. W. Grimshaw; *m* 1943, Hilda Florence Agnes Allison (*d* 1993); two *s* one *d*. *Educ:* Brighton Coll. Joined Indian Army, 1931. Served War of 1939–45, Western Desert and Burma (despatches twice). Transferred to Royal Inniskilling Fusiliers, 1947; Active Service in Malaya, 1948 and 1950, Kenya, 1954, Suez, 1956 and Cyprus, 1958. GOC 44th Div. (TA) and Home Counties Dist, 1962–65. Col, The Royal Inniskilling Fusiliers, 1966–68; Dep. Col, The Royal Irish Rangers, 1968–73.

GRIMSHAW, Nicholas Thomas, CBE 1993; RA 1994; Chairman, Nicholas Grimshaw & Partners Ltd, architects, planners and industrial designers, since 1980; *b* 9 Oct. 1939; *s* of Thomas Cecil Grimshaw and Hannah Joan Dearsley; *m* 1972, Lavinia, *d* of John Russell, *qv*; two *d*. *Educ:* Wellington College, Edinburgh College of Art; Architectural Assoc. Sch. AA Dip. Hons 1965; RIBA 1967; FCSD (FSIAD 1969); numerous prizes and scholarships. Major projects include: Channel Tunnel terminal, Waterloo (Mies van der Rohe Pavilion Award, 1994, RIBA Building of the Year Award, 1994); British Pavilion for Expo '92, Seville, Spain; Financial Times Printing Plant (Royal Fine Art Commn/Sunday Times Building of the Year Award, 1989); New Satellite and Piers, Heathrow Airport; Research Centre for Rank Xerox; BMW headquarters, Bracknell; Herman Miller Factory, Bath; Oxford Ice Rink; Gillingham Business Park; J. Sainsbury Superstore, Camden; Head Office and Printing Press for Western Morning News; Berlin Stock Exchange and Communications Centre; British Airways Combined Operations Centre, Heathrow; Headquarters for Igus GmbH, Cologne; RAC Rescue Services HQ. Vice Pres., AA, 1993–. Assessor for: British Construction Industry Awards; DoE; British Gas; Scottish Develt Agency. Hon. FAIA 1995. Hon. DLitt South Bank, 1993. Awards and Commendations include: RIBA, 1975, 1978, 1980, 1983, 1986, 1989, 1990, 1991, 1994; Financial Times (for Industrial Architecture), 1977, 1980; Structural Steel Design, 1969, 1977, 1980, 1989, 1993, 1994; Civic Trust, 1978, 1982, 1989, 1990, 1991; British Construction Industry Awards, 1988, 1989, 1992, 1993; Constructa Preis for Industrial Architecture in Europe, 1990; Quaternario Foundn Internat. Award for Innovative Technol. in Architecture, 1993. *Publications:* Nicholas Grimshaw & Partners: product and process, 1988; (jtly) Architecture, Industry and Innovation: the work of Nicholas Grimshaw & Partners 1966–88, 1995; (jtly) Structure, Space & Skin: the work of Nicholas Grimshaw & Partners 1988–93, 1993; articles for RSA Jl. *Recreations:* sailing, tennis. *Address:* 1 Conway Street, Fitzroy Square, W1P 6LR. *T:* 0171–631 0869.

GRIMSTON, family name of **Baron Grimston of Westbury** and of **Earl of Verulam.**

GRIMSTON, Viscount; James Walter Grimston; *b* 6 Jan. 1978; *s* and *heir* of Earl of Verulam, *qv*.

GRIMSTON OF WESTBURY, 2nd Baron *cr* 1964; **Robert Walter Sigismund Grimston;** Bt 1952; Director, Gray's Inn (Underwriting Agencies) Ltd, 1965–90, retired (Chairman, 1970–88); Director, River Clyde Holdings, 1986–88; *b* 14 June 1925; *s* of 1st Baron Grimston of Westbury and Sybil Edith Muriel Rose (*d* 1977), *d* of Sir Sigismund Neumann, 1st Bt; *S* father, 1979; *m* 1949, Hon. June Mary Ponsonby, *d* of 5th Baron de Mauley; two *s* one *d*. *Educ:* Eton. Served as Lt Scots Guards, 1943–47; NW Europe, 1944–45. Oil Industry, 1948–53; Sales Director, Ditchling Press, 1953–61; Dir, Hinton Hill & Coles Ltd, 1962–83. Freeman, City of London, 1981; Liveryman, Worshipful Co. of Gold and Silver Wyre Drawers, 1981. *Recreations:* tennis, shooting, golf, walking. *Heir:* *s* Hon. Robert John Sylvester Grimston [*b* 30 April 1951; *m* 1984, Emily Margaret, *d* of Major John Shirley; one *d*. *Educ:* Eton; Reading Univ. (BSc). Chartered Accountant. Commnd The Royal Hussars (PWO), 1970–81, Captain 1976]. *Address:* The Old Rectory, Westwell, near Burford, Oxon OX18 4JT. *Clubs:* Boodle's, City of London.

GRIMTHORPE, 4th Baron, *cr* 1886; **Christopher John Beckett,** Bt 1813; OBE 1958; DL; Deputy Commander, Malta and Libya, 1964–67; *b* 16 Sept. 1915; *e s* of 3rd Baron Grimthorpe, TD, and Mary Lady Grimthorpe (*d* 1962); *S* father, 1963; *m* 1954, Lady Elizabeth Lumley (*see* Lady Grimthorpe); two *s* one *d*. *Educ:* Eton. 2nd Lieut, 9 Lancers, 1936; Lt-Col, 9 Lancers, 1955–58; AAG, War Office, 1958–61; Brigadier, Royal Armoured Corps, HQ, Western Command, 1961–64. Col, 9/12 Royal Lancers, 1973–77. ADC to the Queen, 1964–67. Director: Standard Broadcasting Corp. of Canada (UK), 1972–86; Thirsk Racecourse Ltd, 1972–; Yorkshire Post Newspapers, 1973–86; Pres., London Metropolitan Region YMCA, 1972–86. Mem., Jockey Club. DL North Yorkshire, 1969. *Recreations:* travel, horse sports. *Heir:* *s* Hon. Edward John Beckett [*b* 20 Nov. 1954; *m* 1992, Mrs Carey Elisabeth McEwen, *d* of Robin Graham; one *s*]. *Address:* 87 Dorset House, Gloucester Place, NW1 5AF. *T:* 0171–486 4374; Westow Hall, York YO6 7NE. *T:* Whitwell-on-the-Hill (01653) 618225. *Clubs:* Cavalry and Guards, Portland.

GRIMTHORPE, Lady; Elizabeth Beckett, DCVO 1995 (CVO 1983); Lady of the Bedchamber to HM Queen Elizabeth The Queen Mother, since 1973; *b* 22 July 1925; 2nd *d* of 11th Earl of Scarbrough, KG, GCVO, PC and Katharine Isabel, Countess of Scarbrough, DCVO, K-i-H Gold Medal; *m* 1954, 4th Baron Grimthorpe, *qv*; two *s* one *d*. *Address:* Westow Hall, York YO6 7NE. *T:* Whitwell-on-the-Hill (01653) 618225.

GRIMWADE, Sir Andrew (Sheppard), Kt 1980; CBE 1977; Australian industrialist, *b* 26 Nov. 1930; *s* of late Frederick and Gwendolen Grimwade; *m* 1959, Barbara (*d* 1990), *d* of J. B. D. Kater; one *s*. *Educ:* Melbourne C of E Grammar Sch.; Trinity Coll., Melbourne Univ. (Exhib. Eng.; BSc); Oriel Coll., Oxford (swimming blue; MA). FRACI, FAIM. Vice-Chm., Nat. Mutual Life Assoc., 1988– (Dir, 1970–); Dep. Chm., NZ Ski Fields Ltd; Director: IBM (Aust.); Sony (Aust.) Pty Ltd; Nat. Aust. Bank, 1965–85; Commonwealth Ind. Gases, 1960–90. Mem., first Aust. Govt Trade Mission to China, 1973. Mem., Australian Govt Remuneration Tribunal, 1974–82. Pres., Walter and Eliza Hall Inst. of Med. Research, 1978– (Mem. Bd, 1963–). Chairman: Australian Art Exhibn Corp. (Chinese Exhibn), 1976–77; Australian Govt Official Estabts Trust, 1976–82; Trustee, Victorian Arts Centre, 1980–90; Emeritus Trustee, Nat. Gallery of Vic, 1990– (Trustee, 1964–90; Pres., 1976–90). Member: Council for Order of Australia, 1975–82; Felton Bequests' Cttee, 1973–. *Publication:* Involvement: The Portraits of Clifton Pugh and Mark Strizic, 1969. *Recreations:* skiing, cattle breeding, Australian art. *Address:* PO Box 134, E Melbourne, Vic 3002, Australia. *T:* (3) 98225990. *Clubs:* Melbourne, Australian (Melbourne).

GRIMWADE, Rev. Canon John Girling; Chaplain to the Queen, 1980–90; permission to officiate, dioceses of Gloucester and Oxford, since 1989; *b* 13 March 1920; *s* of Herbert Alfred and Edith Grimwade; *m* 1951, Adini Anne Carus-Wilson; one *s* one *d*. *Educ:* Colet Court; St Paul's Sch.; Keble Coll., Oxford; Cuddesdon Coll. MA Oxon. Friends' Ambulance Unit, 1940–45. Curate of Kingston-upon-Thames, 1950–53; Curate, University Church of St Mary-the-Virgin, Oxford, and Secretary of Oxford Univ. Student

Christian Movement, 1953–56; Vicar of St Mark's, Smethwick, 1956–62; Rector of Caversham, 1962–81, and Priest-in-Charge of Mapledurham, 1968–81; Rector of Caversham and Mapledurham, 1981–83; Priest-in-Charge, Stonesfield, Oxford, 1983–89. Chm., House of Clergy, Oxford Diocesan Synod, 1976–82; Agenda Sec., Oxford Dio. Synod, 1983–88; Diocesan Press Officer, Oxford, 1983–89. Hon. Canon of Christ Church, Oxford, 1974–90, Hon. Canon Emeritus, 1990–. *Recreations:* gardening, walking. *Address:* 88 Alexander Drive, Cirencester, Glos GL7 1UJ.

GRINDEA, Miron, OBE 1986 (MBE 1977); Editor: ADAM International Review (Anglo-French literary magazine), since 1941; ADAM Poets, since 1960; *b* 31 Jan. 1909; *m* 1936, Carola Rabinovici, concert pianist; one *d. Educ:* Bucharest Univ.; Sorbonne. Literary and music critic, 1928–39; settled in England, Sept. 1939; together with Benjamin Britten, Stephen Spender and Henry Moore founded the International Arts Guild, 1943; war-time work with BBC European Service and Min. of Information; coast to coast lecture tours, USA. Visiting Lecturer: Univs of Paris, Aix-en-Provence, Athens, Karachi, Kyoto, Montreal, Toronto, Rejkiavik, Jerusalem, etc. Hon. DLitt Kent, 1983. Prix de l'Académie Française, 1955; Lundquist Literary Prize, Sweden, 1965. Chevalier de la Légion d'Honneur, 1974; Comdr, Order of Arts and Letters, France, 1985. *Publications:* Malta Calling, 1943; Henry Wood (a symposium), 1944; Jerusalem, a literary chronicle of 3000 years, 1968, 2nd edn, Jerusalem, the Holy City in literature, preface by Graham Greene, 1982; Natalie Clifford Barney, 1963; The London Library (a symposium), 1978; contrib. The Listener, TLS, Figaro, Les Nouvelles Littéraires, New Statesman, The Times, Independent, Guardian, Sunday Times, Observer, Spectator, Books and Bookmen. *Recreations:* Mozart, lazing in the sun. *Address:* 28 Emperor's Gate, SW7 4HS. *T:* 0171–373 7307.

GRINDON, John Evelyn, CVO 1957; DSO 1945; AFC 1948; Group Captain, RAF retired; *b* 30 Sept. 1917; *s* of Thomas Edward Grindon (killed in action, Ypres, Oct. 1917), and Dora (*née* Eastlake), Corisande, East Pentire, Cornwall. *Educ:* Dulwich College. Flight Cadet at RAF College, Cranwell, 1935–37; served in Advanced Air Striking Force, BEF, France, 1939–40 (No 150 Sqdn) and in No 5 Group Bomber Command (Nos 106, 630 and 617 Sqdns) during War of 1939–45, as Flight and Sqdn Comdr; Chief Instructor, Long Range Transport Force, 1946–49; Commanded The Queen's Flight, 1953–56; V-bomber captain and Station Comdr, 1956–57; retired at own request 1959. Dir/Gen. Manager in printing/publishing, 1961–71; Metropolitan Police, New Scotland Yard, 1976–81. *Recreations:* opera, ocean surf, racing. *Club:* Royal Air Force.

GRINDROD, Helen Marjorie, QC 1982; a Recorder of the Crown Court, 1981–95; *b* 28 Feb. 1936; *d* of late Joseph and Marjorie Pritchard; *m* 1958, Robert Michael Grindrod; one *s. Educ:* Liverpool Inst. High Sch. for Girls; St Hilda's Coll., Oxford. MA. Teacher, 1957–59. Called to the Bar, Lincoln's Inn, 1966, Bencher, 1990; Northern Circuit, 1966–. *Address:* Globe House, 4 Temple Place, WC2R 3HP; 18 St John Street, Manchester M3 4EA.

GRINDROD, Most Rev. John Basil Rowland, KBE 1983; Archbishop of Brisbane and Metropolitan of Queensland, 1980–89; Primate of Australia, 1982–89; *b* 14 Dec. 1919; *s* of Edward Basil and Dorothy Gladys Grindrod; *m* 1949, Ailsa W. (*d* 1981), *d* of G. Newman; two *d*; *m* 1983, Mrs Dell Cornish, *d* of S. J. Caswell. *Educ:* Repton School; Queen's College, Oxford; Lincoln Theological College. BA 1949; MA 1954. Deacon, 1951; Priest, 1952, Manchester. Curate: St Michael's, Hulme, 1951–54; Bundaberg, Qld, 1954–56; Rector: All Souls, Ancoats, Manchester, 1956–60; Emerald, Qld, 1960–61; St Barnabas, N Rockhampton, Qld, 1961–65; Archdeacon of Rockhampton, Qld, 1960–65; Vicar, Christ Church, S Yarra, Vic, 1965–66; Bishop of Riverina, NSW, 1966–71; Bishop of Rockhampton, 1971–80. Hon. ThD, 1985. *Address:* 14B Thomas Street, Murwillumbah, NSW 2484, Australia.

GRINLING, Jasper Gibbons, CBE 1978; Chairman, London Jazz Radio plc, 1989–91, retired; *b* 29 Jan. 1924; *s* of late Lt-Col Antony Gibbons Grinling, MBE, MC, and Jean Dorothy Turing Grinling; *m* 1950, Jane Moulsdale; one *s* two *d. Educ:* Harrow (Scholar); King's Coll., Cambridge (Exhibnr, BA). CIMgt (FBIM 1969). Served War, 12th Lancers, 1942–46 (Captain). Joined W. & A. Gilbey Ltd, 1947, Dir 1952; Man. Dir, Gilbeys Ltd, 1964; Man. Dir, International Distillers & Vintners Ltd, 1967; Dir, North British Distillery Co. Ltd, 1968–86; Dir of Corporate Affairs, Grand Metropolitan, 1981–85, Dir of Trade Relations, 1985–86; Chm., The Apple & Pear Develt Council, 1986–89. Pres., EEC Confedn des Industries Agricoles et Alimentaires, 1976–80; Mem. Council, Scotch Whisky Assoc., 1968–86. Chevalier, Ordre National du Mérite, France, 1983. *Publication:* The Annual Report, 1986. *Recreations:* gardening, jazz drumming, painting, vineyard proprietor. *Address:* The Old Vicarage, Helions Bumpstead, near Haverhill, Suffolk CB9 7AS. *T:* Steeple Bumpstead (01440) 730316.

GRINSTEAD, Sir Stanley (Gordon), Kt 1986; FCA; CIMgt; Chairman and Director, Harmony Leisure Group, 1989–92; *b* 17 June 1924; *s* of Ephraim Grinstead and Lucy Grinstead (*née* Taylor); *m* 1955, Joyce Preston; two *d. Educ:* Strodes, Egham. Served Royal Navy, 1943–46 (Pilot, FAA). Franklin, Wild & Co., Chartered Accountants, 1946–56; Hotel York Ltd, 1957; Grand Metropolitan Ltd, 1957–62; Union Properties (London) Ltd, 1958–66; Grand Metropolitan Ltd, 1964–87: Dep. Chm. and Group Man. Dir, 1980–82; Gp Chief Exec., 1982–86; Chm., 1982–87; Chm., Reed Internat., 1988–89 (Dir, 1981–90). Trustee, FAA Museum. Vice-Pres., CGLI, 1986–90. Master, Brewers' Co., 1983–84. *Recreations:* gardening, cricket, racing, breeding of thoroughbred horses. *Clubs:* Army and Navy, MCC; Surrey County Cricket (Hon. Treas., 1987–94).

GRINT, Edmund Thomas Charles, CBE 1960; *b* 14 Feb. 1904; *e s* of Edmund Albert Grint; *m* 1930, Olive Maria (*d* 1991), *d* of Albert Cheyne Sherras; one *s* two *d. Educ:* London Univ. (Dip. Econs). Joined ICI 1929; Commercial Dir, Nobel Div., 1946; Director: Billingham Div., 1952–61; Alkali Div., 1961–63; Mond Div., 1964. Dep. Chief Labour Officer, 1951; Chief Labour Officer, 1952–63; Gen. Manager Personnel, 1963–65. Chm., Nat. Dock Labour Board, 1966–69; Pres., Midland Iron and Steel Wages Bd, 1971–79. *Recreations:* golf, gardening. *Address:* Old Walls, Seal, Sevenoaks, Kent TN15 0JB. *T:* Sevenoaks (01732) 61364.

GRINYER, Prof. Peter Hugh; Honorary and Emeritus Professor, University of St Andrews, since 1993; *b* 3 March 1935; *s* of Sidney George and Grace Elizabeth Grinyer; *m* 1958, Sylvia Joyce Boraston; two *s. Educ:* Balliol Coll., Oxford (BA, subseq. MA, PPE); LSE (PhD in Applied Economics). Unilever Sen. Managerial Trainee, 1957–59; PA to Man. Dir, E. R. Holloway Ltd, 1959–61; Lectr and Sen. Lectr, Hendon Coll. of Tech., 1961–64; Lectr, 1965–69, Sen. Lectr, 1969–72, City Univ.; Reader, 1972–74, Prof. of Business Strategy, 1974–79, City Univ. Business School; Esmée Fairbairn Prof. of Econs (Finance and Investment), Univ. of St Andrews, 1979–93 (Vice-Principal, 1985–87, Actg Principal). Chairman: St Andrews Management Inst., 1989–; St Andrews Strategic Management Ltd, 1989–. Vis. Prof., Stern Sch. of Business, New York Univ., 1992; Erskine Fellow, Univ. of Canterbury, NZ, 1994. Member: Business and Management Studies Sub-Cttee, UGC, 1979–85; Scottish Legal Aid Bd, 1992–. Founding Dir, Glenrothes Enterprise Trust, 1983–86; Director: John Brown PLC, 1984–86; Don and Low (Hldgs) Ltd (formerly Don Bros Buist), 1985–91; Ellis and Goldstein (Hldgs) PLC, 1987–88; Chm., McIlroy Coates, 1991–. *Publications:* Corporate Models Today (with J. Wooller), 1975, 2nd edn 1979; (with G. D. Vaughan and S. Birley) From Private to Public, 1977; (with J.-C. Spender) Turnaround: the fall and rise of Newton Chambers, 1979; (with D. G. Mayes and P. McKiernan) Sharpbenders, 1988; (with Dr Foo Check Teck) Organzing for Strategy: Sun Tzu business warcraft, 1994; some 50 papers in academic jls. *Recreations:* hill walking, golf. *Address:* 60 Buchanan Gardens, St Andrews, Fife KY16 9LX. *Club:* Royal & Ancient Golf (St Andrews).

GRISEWOOD, Harman Joseph Gerard, CBE 1960; Chief Assistant to the Director-General, BBC, 1955–64, retired; *b* 8 Feb. 1906; *e s* of late Lieut-Col Harman Grisewood and Lucille Cardozo; *m* 1940, Clotilde Margaret Bailey; one *d. Educ:* Ampleforth Coll., York; Worcester Coll., Oxford. BBC Repertory Co., 1929–33; Announcer, 1933–36; Asst to Programme Organiser, 1936–39; Asst Dir Programme Planning, 1939–41; Asst Controller, European Div., 1941–45; Actg Controller, European Div., 1945–46; Dir of Talks, 1946–47; Planner, Third Programme, 1947–48; Controller of the Third Programme, BBC, 1948–52; Dir of the Spoken Word, BBC, 1952–55. Member: Younger Cttee on Privacy, 1970–72; Lord Chancellor's Cttee on Defamation, 1971; Res. Officer, Royal Commn on Civil Liberty, 1973–75. Vice-President: European Broadcasting Union, 1953–54; Royal Literary Fund. Chm., The Latin Mass Soc., 1969. King Christian X Freedom Medal, 1946. Mem. Hon. Soc. of Cymmrodorion, 1956. Knight of Grace and Devotion, SMO Malta, 1960. *Publications:* Broadcasting and Society, 1949; The Recess, 1963 (novel); The Last Cab on the Rank, 1964 (novel); David Jones: Welsh National Lecture, 1966; One Thing at a Time (autobiography), 1968; The Painted Kipper, 1970; Stratagem, 1987. *Address:* The Old School House, Castle Hill, Eye, Suffolk IP23 7AP.

GRIST, Ian; Chairman, South Glamorgan Health Authority, since 1992; *b* 5 Dec. 1938; *s* of late Basil William Grist, MBE and Leila Helen Grist; *m* 1966, Wendy Anne (*née* White), JP, BSc; two *s. Educ:* Repton Sch.; Jesus Coll., Oxford (Schol.). Plebiscite Officer, Southern Cameroons, 1960–61; Stores Manager, United Africa Co., Nigeria, 1961–63; Wales Information Officer, Conservative Central Office, 1963–74; Conservative Research Dept, 1970–74. MP (C) Cardiff North, Feb. 1974–1983, Cardiff Central, 1983–92; contested (C) Cardiff Central, 1992. PPS to Secretary of State for Wales, 1979–81; Parly Under Sec. of State, Welsh Office, 1987–90. Mem., Select Cttee on: Violence in the Family, 1977–79; Welsh Affairs, 1981–83 and 1986–87; Register of Members' Interests, 1983–87. Chm., Cons. W African Cttee, 1977–87 and 1991–92. Vice-Chm., Assoc. of Conservative Clubs, 1978–82. FRSA 1984. *Recreations:* reading, listening to music. *Address:* 29 Oakfield Street, Roath, Cardiff CF2 3RE.

GRIST, John Frank; broadcasting consultant; Supervisor of Parliamentary Broadcasting, 1991–93 (Supervisor of Broadcasting, House of Commons, 1989–91); *b* 10 May 1924; *s* of Austin Grist, OBE, MC, and Ada Mary Grist (*née* Ball); *m* Gilian, *d* of Roger Cranage and Helen Marjorie Rollett; one *s* two *d. Educ:* Ryde Sch., IoW; London Sch. of Economics and Political Science (BSc Econ); Univ. of Chicago. RAF Pilot, 1942–46. BBC External Services, 1951–53; Nigerian Broadcasting Service, 1953–56: Talks Producer; Programme Organiser, Northern Region; Controller, Nat. Programmes; BBC TV Talks and Current Affairs at Lime Grove, 1957–72, producer of political programmes and Editor of Gallery and of Panorama; Hd of Current Affairs Gp, 1967–72; Controller, English Regions BBC, 1972–77; US Rep., BBC, 1978–81; Man. Dir, Services Sound and Vision Corp., 1982–88. Specialist Advr to Select Cttee on Televising of Proceedings of H of C, 1988–89. Observer, Russian Election, 1993; Advr, Indep. Media Commn, S African Elections, 1994. Founder and first Man. Dir, NY World Television Fest., 1978. BP Press Fellow, Wolfson Coll., Cambridge, 1988. Chm., Howard Steele Foundn for Training in Television, Film and Video, 1985–88. Gov., Royal Star and Garter Home, 1986–94. FRTS 1986 (Mem. Council, 1984–88). *Address:* 4 Burlington House, Kings Road, Richmond, Surrey TW10 6NW. *T:* 0181–940 6351. *Club:* Reform.

GRIST, Prof. Norman Roy, FRCPEd; Professor of Infectious Diseases, University of Glasgow, 1965–83, now Emeritus; *b* 9 March 1918; *s* of Walter Reginald Grist and Florence Goodwin Grist (*née* Nadin); *m* 1943, Mary Stewart McAlister. *Educ:* Shawlands Acad., Glasgow; University of Glasgow. Postgrad. studies at Dept of Bacteriology, University of Liverpool, 1948–49; Virus Reference Lab., Colindale, London, 1951–52; Dept of Epidemiology, University of Michigan, 1956–57. BSc 1939; MB, ChB (Commendation), 1942; Mem. 1950, Fellow 1958, RCP, Edinburgh; Founder Mem., 1963, FRCPath 1967; Mem. 1980, Fellow 1983, RCPGlas. Ho. Phys. Gartloch Hosp., 1942–43; RAMC, GDO 223 Fd Amb. and RMO 2/KSLI, 1943–46; Ho. Surg. Victoria Inf., Glasgow, 1946–47; Res. Phys, Ruchill Hosp., Glasgow, 1947–48; Research Asst, Glasgow Univ. Dept of Infectious Diseases, 1948–52; Lectr in Virus Disease, Glasgow Univ., 1952–62, and Regional Adviser in Virology to Scottish Western Reg. Hosp. Bd, 1960–74; Reader in Viral Epidemiology, Glasgow Univ., 1962–65. Mem., Expert Adv. Panel on Virus Diseases to WHO, 1967–. Pres., Glasgow Natural History Soc., 1993–. Hon. Mem., Assoc. of Clin. Pathology, 1989. Bronze Medal, Helsinki Univ., 1973; Orden Civil de Sanidad, cat. Encomienda, Spain, 1974. *Publications:* Diagnostic Methods in Clinical Virology, 1966, 3rd edn, 1979; (with D. Reid and I. W. Pinkerton) Infections in Current Medical Practice, 1986; (with D. O. Ho-Yen, E. Walker and G. R. Williams) Diseases of Infection, 1987, 2nd edn 1993; numerous contribs. to British and international med. jls. *Recreations:* gardener's mate, natural history. *Address:* 5A Hyndland Court, 6A Sydenham Road, Glasgow G12 9NR. *T:* 0141–339 5242. *Clubs:* Royal Automobile; Royal Scottish Automobile (Glasgow).

GRIST, Maj.-Gen. Robin Digby, CB 1994; OBE 1979; DL; Regional Co-ordinator, South West, Training and Enterprise Councils, since 1994; *b* 21 Oct. 1940; *s* of late Lt-Col and Mrs Digby Grist; *m* 1971, Louise Littlejohn; one *s* two *d. Educ:* Hazlegrove House; Radley Coll.; Royal Military Acad., Sandhurst. Commnd, Gloucestershire Regt, 1960; service in UK and Cyprus, 1961–65; seconded to Army Air Corps, 1965–69; active service, Aden and S Arabia, 1966–67 (despatches); service with 1 Glosters, incl. active service in NI, 1969–70; Army Staff course, 1971–72; Staff Officer, MoD, 1973–74 and 1977–79; service with 1 Glosters, Germany, UK and Belize, 1975–76; CO 1st Bn Gloucestershire Regt, 1979–82; Mil. Dir of Studies, RMCS, 1982–84; Comdr 6 Airmobile Bde, 1985–86; RCDS 1987; Mil. Attaché and Comdr Brit. Army Staff, Washington, USA, 1988–89; Dir, AAC, 1989–92; Dir Gen., AGC, 1992–94. Col, The Gloucestershire Regt, 1990–94, The Royal Gloucestershire, Berkshire and Wiltshire Regt, 1994–. Chairman: Mus. of Army Flying, 1989–92; Middle Wallop Air Show Ltd, 1989–92; Regts of Gloucestershire Mus., 1990–. Gov., Royal Sch., Bath, 1989–. DL Gloucestershire, 1995. *Publications:* articles in mil. jls, particularly on airmobility. *Recreations:* fishing, gardening. *Address:* Regimental Headquarters, Royal Gloucestershire, Berkshire and Wiltshire Regiment, Custom House, Gloucester GL1 2HE. *Club:* Army and Navy.

GROBLER, Richard Victor; Deputy Secretary of Commissions, since 1984; *b* Umtali, S Rhodesia, 27 May 1936; *m* 1961, Julienne Nora de la Cour (*née* Sheath); one *s* three *d. Educ:* Bishop's, Capetown; Univ. of Cape Town (BA). Called to the Bar, Gray's Inn, 1961; joined staff of Clerk of the Court, Central Criminal Court, 1961; Dep. Clerk of the Court, 1970; Dep. Courts Administrator, 1972; Courts Administrator, Inner London Crown Court, 1974; Sec., Lord Chancellor's Adv. Cttee on Justices of the Peace for Inner

London and Jt Hon. Sec., Inner London Br. of Magistrates' Assoc., 1974–77; Courts Administrator, Central Criminal Court, and Co-ordinator, Crown Courts Taxations, SE Circuit, 1977–79; Dep. Circuit Administrator, S Eastern Circuit, 1979–83. Liveryman, Worshipful Company of Gold and Silver Wyre Drawers. *Recreations:* gardening, swimming, golf. *Address:* Commissions Office, Southside, 105 Victoria Street, SW1E 6QT. *T:* 0171–210 3479.

GROCOTT, Bruce Joseph; MP (Lab) The Wrekin, since 1987; *b* 1 Nov. 1940; *s* of Reginald Grocott and Helen Grocott (*née* Stewart); *m* 1965, Sally Barbara Kay Ridgway; two *s*. *Educ:* Hemel Hempstead Grammar Sch.; Leicester and Manchester Univs. BA(Pol), MA(Econ). Admin. Officer, LCC, 1963–64; Lectr in Politics, Manchester Univ., Birmingham Polytechnic, and N Staffs Polytechnic, 1964–74. Television presenter and producer, 1979–87. Chm., Finance Cttee, Bromsgrove UDC, 1972–74. MP (Lab) Lichfield and Tamworth, Oct. 1974–1979; PPS to: Minister for Local Govt and Planning, 1975–76; Minister of Agriculture, 1976–78; Dep. Shadow Leader, H of C, 1987–92; Leader of the Opposition, H of C, 1994–; Opposition front bench spokesman on foreign affairs, 1992–93; Mem., Select Cttee on Nat. Heritage, 1994–95. Contested (Lab): Lichfield and Tamworth, 1979; The Wrekin, 1983. *Recreations:* cricket, snooker, fiction writing, steam railways. *Address:* House of Commons, SW1A 0AA. *Club:* Trench Labour.

GRONHAUG, Arnold Conrad; *b* 26 March 1921; *s* of James Gronhaug, MBE, and Beatrice May Gronhaug; *m* 1945, Patricia Grace Smith; two *d*. *Educ:* Barry Grammar Sch.; Cardiff Technical Coll. CEng, FIEE; Hon. FCIBSE. Electrical Officer, RNVR, 1941–46. Air Ministry Works Directorate, 1946–63: Area Mech. and Elec. Engr, AMWD Malaya, 1951–52; Air Min. Headquarters, 1952–60; Dep. Chief Engr, AMWD, RAF Germany, 1960–63; Sen. Mech. and Elec. Engr, Portsmouth Area MPBW, 1963–67; Jt Services Staff Coll., 1964–65; Suptg Engr, MPBW, 1967–71; Dir Defence Works (Overseas), MPBW, 1971–73; Dir of Social and Research Services, DoE, 1973–75; Under Sec., and Dir of Engrng Services Develt, 1975–76; Dir of Mechanical and Electrical Engineering Services, 1976–81. Member: Engrg Council Nominations Cttee, 1983–; IEE Memship Cttee, 1975–82 (Chm., 1979–82); CIBSE Qualifications Bd, 1981–87; IEE Memship Advr, Surrey, 1984–90. Freeman, City of London, 1979; Liveryman, Engineers Co., 1984. *Recreations:* music, photography. *Address:* 6 Pine Hill, Epsom, Surrey KT18 7BG. *T:* Epsom (01372) 721888.

GRONOW, David Gwilym Colin, MSc, PhD; Member, Electricity Council, 1985–90, retired; *b* Leigh-on-Sea, 13 Jan. 1929; *s* of David Morgan Gronow and Harriet Hannah Gronow; *m* 1st, 1953, Joan Andrew Bowen Jones (marr. diss. 1970); one *s* one *d*; 2nd, 1970, Rosemary Freda Iris Keys. *Educ:* North Street Elem. Sch., Leigh-on-Sea; Grammar Sch., Swansea; University Coll. London (MSc, PhD). Institute of Aviation Medicine, RAF Farnborough, Hants: Jun. Technician, 1951–53; Sci. Officer, then Sen. Sci. Officer, 1953–57; Sen. Sci. Officer, UKAEA, Capenhurst, Cheshire, 1957; Second Asst Engr, then Sen. Asst Engr, CEGB, HQ Operations Dept, London, 1957–64; Asst Commercial Officer/Asst Chief Commercial Officer/Chief Commercial Officer, SSEB, Glasgow, 1964–78; Marketing Advr, 1978–80, Commercial Advr, 1980–85, Electricity Council, London. *Recreations:* travel, bird watching, theatre, clarinet. *Address:* 8 Arundel Way, Highcliffe, Christchurch, Dorset BH23 5DX.

GROOM, Brian William Alfred; Editor, Scotland on Sunday, since 1994; *b* 26 April 1955; *s* of Fred and Muriel Groom; *m* 1980, Carola May Withington; one s one *d*. *Educ:* Manchester Grammar Sch.; Balliol Coll., Oxford (BA Hons). Journalist: Goole Times, 1976–78; Financial Times, 1978–88; Dep. Editor, Scotland on Sunday, 1988–94. *Recreations:* reading, cinema, cricket, walking. *Address:* Scotland on Sunday, 20 North Bridge, Edinburgh EH1 1YT. *T:* 0131–243 3475.

GROOM, Maj.-Gen. John Patrick, CB 1984; CBE 1975 (MBE 1963); Director General, Guide Dogs for the Blind Association, 1983–89; *b* Hagley, Worcs, 9 March 1929; *s* of Samuel Douglas Groom and Gertrude Groom (*née* Clinton); *m* 1951, Jane Mary Miskelly; three *d*. *Educ:* King Charles I Sch., Kidderminster; Royal Military Academy, Sandhurst. Enlisted as Sapper, Dec. 1946; commnd into RE, 1949; regimental service, N Africa, Egypt, Singapore, Malaya, UK, 1949–59; sc Camberley, 1960; War Office, 1961–63; regimental service, UK, Aden, 1963–65 (despatches); Directing Staff, Staff Coll., 1965–68; Regimental Comdr, BAOR, 1968–70; MoD, Military Operations, 1970–71; Dep. Sec., Chiefs of Staff Cttee, 1971–73; HQ Near East Land Forces, Cyprus, 1973–75; RCDS 1976, Comdr, Corps of Royal Engineers, BAOR (Brig.), 1976–79; Chief Engineer, HQ BAOR, 1979–82; Head of Army Trng Rev. Team, MoD (Army), 1982–83. Col Comdt, 1983–91, Rep. Col Comdt, 1986, RE. Chairman: GDBA (Trading Co.) Ltd, 1984–89; GDBA (Recreational Services) Co. Ltd, 1986–89; (non-exec.) BKP Services Ltd, 1992–; Dir, GDBA (Pension Fund Trustees) Ltd, 1985–89; Hon Vice-Pres., Internat. Fedn of Guide Dog Schs, 1989–. Chm., Reach Foundn, 1993–; Member: Adv. Bd, Talking Newspapers, 1988; Council, Oakhaven Hospice, 1992. Governor: Gordon's Sch., Woking, 1982–88; Sandle Manor Sch., Fordingbridge, 1984–88. Member: RYA, 1982; ASA, 1982–. FIMgt (FBIM 1979); FIPlantE 1976; Fellow, RSPB 1975. Freeman, City of London, 1978; Liveryman, Worshipful Co. of Plumbers, 1978–92. *Recreations:* ocean sailing, country pursuits, the environment. *Address:* Bridge End Cottage, Walhampton, Lymington, Hants SO41 5RD. *T:* Lymington (01590) 675710. *Clubs:* Royal Ocean Racing; Royal Engineer Yacht; Royal Lymington Yacht; British Kiel Yacht (Germany) (Life Mem.); Kieler Yacht (Germany) (Hon. Mem.).

GROOM, Hon. Raymond John; MHA (Lib) for Denison, Tasmania, since 1986; Premier of Tasmania, since 1992; Minister for State Development and Resources, for Forests, and for Mines, since 1993; *b* 3 Sept. 1944; *s* of Raymond James Groom and Eileen Margaret (*née* Walters); *m* 1967, Gillian M. Crisp; four *s* two *d*. *Educ:* Burnie High Sch., Tasmania; Univ. of Melbourne (LLB 1967). Barrister and Solicitor, Supreme Court, Victoria, 1968, Tasmania, 1970; practised: Melbourne, 1968–69; Burnie, 1969–76; Partner, Hudson and Mann, Tasmania, 1969–76. Sec., Law Liby Cttee, NW Tasmania Law Soc., 1969–75; Mem. Council, Bar Assoc., Tasmania, 1974–75. MHR, Braddon, Tasmania, 1975–84; Federal Minister for: Envmt, Housing, Community Develt, 1977–78; Housing and Construction, 1978–80; Mem., Parly Delegn to Bangladesh, India, Sri Lanka, 1978; Leader, Australian Delegn to ESCAP UN Meeting, Manila (Chm., First Session), 1979; Chm., S Pacific Commonwealth and State Housing Ministers Conf., NZ, 1980; Minister for Forests, Sea Fisheries and Mines, and Minister Assisting the Premier, 1986–89; Dep. Premier, 1988; Dep. Leader, Liberal Party, 1986–91; Shadow Attorney-General and Shadow Minister for Deregulation, 1989–91; Leader of Opposition, Shadow Treas. and Shadow Minister for Commonwealth and State Relns, 1991–92; Treas. and Minister for Economic Develt, 1992–93. Chm., Australian Construction Industry Council, 1979–80. *Recreations:* family, painting, golf, football. *Address:* 25 Cromwell Street, Battery Point, Tas 7004, Australia. *T:* (02) 248181; Level 11, 15 Murray Street, Hobart, Tas 7000, Australia. *Clubs:* Melbourne Cricket; Royal Hobart Golf.

GROOTENHUIS, Prof. Peter, FEng 1982, FIMechE; Professor of Mechanical Engineering Science, Imperial College of Science, Technology and Medicine, 1972–89, now Emeritus Professor and Senior Research Fellow; *b* 31 July 1924; *yr s* of Johannes C. Grootenhuis and Anna C. (*née* van den Bergh); *m* 1954, Sara J. Winchester, *o c* of late Major Charles C. Winchester, MC, The Royal Scots (The Royal Regt), and Margaret I. (*née* de Havilland); one *d* one *s*. *Educ:* Nederlands Lyceum, The Hague; City and Guilds College. BSc MechEng 1944, PhD, DIC, DSc London Univ.; FCGI 1976, Mem., Inst. of Acoustics; Fellow, Soc. of Environmental Engineers (Pres., 1964–67). Apprenticeship and Design Office, Bristol Aero Engine Co., 1944–46; Lectr 1949, Reader 1959, Mech. Eng. Dept, Imperial College, research in heat transfer and in dynamics; Dir, Derritron Electronics, 1969–82; Partner, Grootenhuis Allaway Associates, consultants in noise and vibration, 1970–93; Associate Mem., Ordnance Board, 1965–70; Mem. Governing Body, Imperial College, 1974–79. *Publications:* technical papers to learned jls, and patents. *Recreations:* sailing, gardening. *Club:* Athenæum.

GROSBERG, Prof. Percy, PhD; CEng, MIMechE, FTI; Research Professor of Textile Engineering, 1961–90, and Head of Department of Textile Industries, 1975–83 and 1987–89, University of Leeds, now Emeritus Professor; Hon. Consultant, Shenkar College of Textile Technology and Fashion, Ramat Gan, Israel, since 1991; *b* 5 April 1925; *s* of late Rev. and Mrs Gershon Grosberg, Tel-Aviv; *m* 1951, Queenie Fisch; one *s* one *d* (and one *s* decd). *Educ:* Parktown Boys' High Sch., Johannesburg; Univ. of the Witwatersrand; University of Leeds. BScEng, MScEng, PhD Witwatersrand; CEng, MIMechE 1965; FTI 1966 (Hon. FTI 1988). Sen. Res. Officer S African Wool Textile Res. Inst., 1949–55; University of Leeds: ICI Res. Fellow, 1955; Lectr in Textile Engrg, 1955–61. Hon. Fellow, Shenkar Coll. of Textile Technology and Fashion, Israel, 1993. FRSA 1990. Warner Memorial Medal, 1968; Textile Inst. Medal, 1972; Distinguished Service Award, Indian Inst. of Technol., Delhi, 1985. *Publications:* An Introduction to Textile Mechanisms, 1968; Structural Mechanics of Fibres, Yarns and Fabrics, 1969; papers on rheology of fibrous assemblies, mechan. processing of fibres, and other res. topics in Jl of Textile Inst., Textile Res. Jl, and other sci. jls. *Recreations:* music, gardening, travel. *Address:* Apartment 25, 55 Shlomo Hamelech Street, Netanya 42267, Israel. *T:* (9) 628652.

GROSE, Vice-Adm. Sir Alan, KBE 1989; Flag Officer Plymouth, Naval Base Commander Devonport, Commander Central Sub Area Eastern Atlantic, and Commander Plymouth Sub Area Channel, 1990–92, retired; *b* 24 Sept. 1937; *s* of George William Stanley Grose and Ann May Grose (*née* Stanford); *m* 1961, Gillian Ann (*née* Dryden-Dymond); two *s* one *d*. *Educ:* Strodes School; Britannia Royal Naval College, Dartmouth. Served: Mediterranean and S Atlantic, 1957–63; sub-specialised in Navigation, 1964; RAN, 1964–66; Home, W Indies, Med., 1966–72; Comd, HMS Eskimo, 1973–75; Staff of C-in-C, Naval Home Command, 1975–77; MoD, 1977–79; RCDS 1980; Comd, HMS Bristol, 1981–82; RN Presentation Team, 1983–84; Comd, HMS Illustrious, 1984–86; Flag Officer, Sept. 1986; ACDS, Operational Requirements (Sea Systems), MoD, 1986–88; Flag Officer Flotilla Three and Comdr, Anti-Submarine Warfare Striking Force, 1988–90. *Recreations:* tennis, walking, reading. *Address:* c/o Barclays Bank, Princes Street, Plymouth PL1 2HA. *Club:* Royal Naval Reserve.

GROSS, John Jacob; writer and editor; theatre critic, Sunday Telegraph, since 1989; *b* 12 March 1935; *s* of late Abraham Gross and Muriel Gross; *m* 1965, Miriam May (*see* M. M. Gross) (marr. diss. 1988); one *s* one *d*. *Educ:* City of London Sch.; Wadham Coll., Oxford. Editor, Victor Gollancz Ltd, 1956–58; Asst Lectr, Queen Mary Coll., Univ. of London, 1959–62; Fellow, King's Coll., Cambridge, 1962–65; Literary Editor, New Statesman, 1973; Editor, TLS, 1974–81; editorial consultant, Weidenfeld (Publishers) Ltd, 1982; on staff of New York Times, 1983–88; Dir, Times Newspapers Holdings, 1982. A Trustee, National Portrait Gall., 1977–84. Hon. DHL Adelphi Univ., 1995. *Publications:* The Rise and Fall of the Man of Letters (1969 Duff Cooper Memorial Prize), 1969; Joyce, 1971; (ed) The Oxford Book of Aphorisms, 1983; (ed) The Oxford Book of Essays, 1991; Shylock, 1992; (ed) The Modern Movement, 1992; (ed) The Oxford Book of Comic Verse, 1994. *Address:* 74 Princess Court, Queensway, W2 4RE. *Club:* Beefsteak.

GROSS, Miriam Marianna, (Lady Owen); Literary Editor, Sunday Telegraph, since 1991; *b* 12 May 1939, *d* of late Kurt May and of Wera May; *m* 1st, 1965, John Gross (marr. diss. 1988); one *s* one *d*; 2nd, 1993, Sir Geoffrey Owen, *qv*. *Educ:* Dartington Hall Sch.; St Anne's Coll., Oxford (MA). Observer: Dep. Lit. Editor, 1969–81; Woman's Editor, 1981–84; Arts Editor, Daily Telegraph, 1986–91. Editor, Book Choice, Channel Four TV, 1986–91. *Publications:* (ed) The World of George Orwell, 1971; (ed) The World of Raymond Chandler, 1976. *Recreations:* painting, upholstering. *Address:* 24A St Petersburgh Place, W2 4LB. *T:* 0171–538 7191.

GROSS, Peter Henry; QC 1992; a Recorder, since 1995; *b* 13 Feb. 1952; *s* of Samuel Lewis Gross and Fanny Alice Gross; *m* 1985, Ruth Mary Cullen; two *s*. *Educ:* Herzlia Sch., Cape Town; Univ. of Cape Town (BBusSc, MBusSc); Oriel Coll., Oxford (Rhodes Scholar, MA, BCL, Eldon Scholar). Called to the Bar, Gray's Inn, 1977; admitted to the Bar of NSW, 1986. *Publication:* Legal Aid and its Management, 1976. *Recreations:* jogging, cricket, sailing. *Address:* 20 Essex Street, WC2R 3AL. *Club:* United Oxford & Cambridge University.

GROSS, Solomon Joseph, CMG 1966; Chairman, Barnes Court (New Barnet) Ltd, since 1995; *b* 3 Sept. 1920; *s* of late Abraham Gross; *m* 1948, Doris Evelyn (*née* Barker); two *d*. *Educ:* Hackney Downs Sch.; University Coll., London. RAF, Burma, India. Ministry of Supply, 1947; OEEC, Paris, 1948–51; British Embassy, Washington, 1951–53; Board of Trade, 1954–57; British Trade Commr, Pretoria, SA, 1958–62; Principal British Trade Commr, Ghana, 1963–66; British Deputy High Commr, Ghana, 1966–67; Board of Trade, 1967–69; Minister, British Embassy, Pretoria, 1969–73; Chargé d'Affaires at various times in Ghana and S Africa; Under-Sec., Dept of Industry, 1974–80; Dir for Regional Affairs, British Technology Gp, 1983–84. Bd Mem., BSC, later British Steel plc, 1978–90; Dir, Technical Audit Group Ltd, 1986–90. Mem., Overseas Cttee, CBI, 1987–90; Mem., External Relations Cttee and Chm., USA Wkg Pty, UNICE, Brussels, 1987–90. *Recreations:* gardening, history, do-it-yourself. *Address:* 38 Barnes Court, Station Road, New Barnet, Herts EN5 1QY. *T:* 0181–449 2710. *Club:* Royal Automobile.

GROSSART, Angus McFarlane McLeod, CBE 1990; Managing Director, since 1969, and Chairman, Noble Grossart Ltd, Merchant Bankers, Edinburgh, since 1990; Chairman, Scottish Investment Trust PLC, since 1975; director of companies; *b* 6 April 1937; 3rd *s* of William John White Grossart and Mary Hay Gardiner; *m* 1978, Mrs Gay Thomson; one *d*. *Educ:* Glasgow Acad.; Glasgow Univ. (MA 1958, LLB 1960). CA 1962; Mem., Faculty of Advocates, 1963. Practised at Scottish Bar, 1963–69. Major directorships include: American Trust PLC, 1973–; Alexander & Alexander, USA, 1985–; Royal Bank of Scotland plc, 1982–; Scottish Financial Enterprise, 1987–; Hewden Stuart PLC, 1988–; Scottish TV plc, 1989–. British Petroleum Scottish Bd, 1990–; Dep. Chm., Edinburgh Fund Managers PLC, 1991– (Chm., 1983–91). Mem., Scottish Develt Agency, 1974–78; Dir, St Andrews Management Inst., 1990– (Chm. Adv. Council, 1994–). Chm., Bd of Trustees, National Galleries of Scotland, 1988– (Trustee, 1986–); Vice Pres., Scottish Opera, 1986–93; Director: Edinburgh Internat. Film Festival, 1994–; Friends of Royal Scottish Acad., 1989–. Formerly: Trustee, Scottish Civic Trust; Dir, Scottish Nat. Orch.; Mem., Scottish Industrial Develt Adv. Bd. Livingstone Captain of Industry Award, 1990. Hon. LLD Glasgow, 1985. Lord Provost of Glasgow Award for public service, 1994.

Formerly, Scottish Editor, British Tax Encyc., and British Tax Rev. *Recreations:* golfing (runner-up, British Youths' Golf Championship, 1957; Captain, Scottish Youths Internat., 1956 and 1957), the applied and decorative arts, Scottish castle restoration. *Address:* 48 Queen Street, Edinburgh EH2 3NR. *T:* 0131–226 7011. *Clubs:* New, Honourable Company of Edinburgh Golfers (Edinburgh); Royal and Ancient (St Andrews).

GROSVELD, Franklin Gerardus, (Frank), PhD; FRS 1991; Senior Scientist, National Institute for Medical Research, since 1982; *b* 18 Aug. 1948; *m* Ernie De Boer; two *s*. *Educ:* Univ. of Amsterdam (MSc); McGill Univ. (PhD). *Publications:* papers on human globin genes. *Address:* National Institute for Medical Research, The Ridgeway, Mill Hill, NW7 1AA. *T:* 0181–959 3666.

GROSVENOR, family name of **Baron Ebury,** and of **Duke of Westminster.**

GROSVENOR, Earl; Hugh Richard Louis Grosvenor; *b* 29 Jan. 1991; *o s* and *heir* of Duke of Westminster, *qv*.

GROTRIAN, Sir Philip Christian Brent, 3rd Bt *cr* 1934; *b* 26 March 1935; *s* of Robert Philip Brent Grotrian (*d* on active service, 1945) (*y s* of 1st Bt), and Elizabeth Mary, *d* of Major Herbert Hardy-Wrigley; *S* uncle, 1984; *m* 1st, 1960, Anne Isabel, *d* of Robert Sieger Whyte, Toronto; one *s*; 2nd, 1979, Sarah Frances, *d* of Reginald Harry Gale, Montreal; one *s* one *d*. *Educ:* Eton; Trinity Coll., Toronto. *Heir:* *s* Philip Timothy Adam Brent Grotrian, *b* 9 April 1962. *Address:* RR3, Mansfield, Ontario LON 1MO, Canada; Calle Ample 2, Regencós, Gerona, Spain.

GROUES, Henri Antoine; *see* Pierre, Abbé.

GROUND, (Reginald) Patrick; QC 1981; *b* 9 Aug. 1932; *s* of late Reginald Ground and Ivy Elizabeth Grace (*née* Irving); *m* 1964, Caroline Dugdale; three *s* one *d*. *Educ:* Beckenham and Penge County Grammar Sch.; Lycée Gay Lussac, Limoges, France; Selwyn Coll., Cambridge (Open Exhibnr; MA Mod. Langs, French and Spanish); Magdalen Coll., Oxford (MLitt, Mod. History). Inner Temple Studentship and Foster Boulton Prize, 1958; called to the Bar, Inner Temple, 1960, Bencher, 1987. National Service, RN, 1954–56: Sub-Lt RNVR; served in Mediterranean Fleet and on staff of C-in-C Mediterranean; rep. RN at hockey and lawn tennis; Lt-Comdr RNR. Worked for FO on staff of Wilton Park European Conf. Centre, 1958–60. Councillor, London Bor. of Hammersmith, 1968–71 (Chm., Cttees responsible for health and social services, 1969–71). Contested (C): Hounslow, Feltham and Heston, Feb. and Oct. 1974, and 1979; Feltham and Heston, 1992; MP (C) Feltham and Heston, 1983–92. PPS to the Solicitor General, 1987–92. Treasurer and Pres., Oxford Univ. Cons. Assoc., 1958; Chm., Fulham Soc., 1975–. *Publications:* articles on housing, security of tenure and the Rent Acts in jls and periodicals. *Recreations:* lawn tennis, theatre, sailing, travel. *Address:* 13 Ranelagh Avenue, SW6 3PJ. *T:* 0171–736 0131. *Clubs:* Brooks's, Carlton.

GROUNDS, Stanley Paterson, CBE 1968; Charity Commissioner, 1960–69; *b* 25 Oct. 1904; 2nd *s* of late Thomas Grounds and Olivia Henrietta (*née* Anear), Melbourne, Australia; *m* 1932, Freda Mary Gale Ransford (*d* 1994); twin *s* and *d*. *Educ:* Melbourne High Sch.; Queen's Coll., Melbourne Univ. (1st Cl. hons, MA). With Melbourne Herald, 1926–28; British Empire Producers' Organisation, London, 1928–33. Called to Bar, Middle Temple, 1933; at Chancery Bar, 1934–40. Served Royal Air Force, 1940–45 (Squadron Leader). Asst Charity Commissioner, 1946–58; Sec., Charity Commission, 1958–60. *Publications:* contrib. Encyclopædia of Forms and Precedents, Encyclopædia of Court Forms (on Charities), Halsbury's Laws of England, 3rd edn (on Charities). Articles in law jls. *Recreation:* other men's flowers. *Address:* St Helena, 19 Bell Road, Haslemere, Surrey GU27 3DQ. *T:* Haslemere (01428) 651230.

GROVE, Dr Andrew S.; President since 1979, and Chief Executive Officer since 1987, Intel Corporation; *b* 2 Sept. 1936; *m*; two *d*. *Educ:* City Coll. of NY (BSc Chem. Engrg); Univ. of Calif, Berkeley (PhD Chem. Engrg). FIEEE. Asst Dir of R&D, Fairchild Semiconductor, 1967–. Mem., Nat. Acad. of Engrg. Fellow, Amer. Acad. of Arts & Scis, 1994. Hon. DEng Worcester. Engrg Leadership Recognition Award, 1987; Heinz Foundn Award for Technol. and the Econ., 1995. *Publications:* Physics and Technology of Semiconductor Devices, 1967; High Output Management, 1983; One-on-One With Andy Grove, 1987. *Address:* Intel Corporation, 2200 Mission College Boulevard, Santa Clara, CA 95052–8119, USA.

GROVE, Sir Charles Gerald, 5th Bt *cr* 1874; *b* 10 Dec. 1929; *s* of Walter Peel Grove (*d* 1944) (3rd *s* of 2nd Bt) and Elena Rebecca, *d* of late Felipe Crosthwaite; *S* brother, 1974. *Heir:* *b* Harold Thomas Grove, *b* 6 Dec. 1930.

GROVE, Maj.-Gen. David Anthony, OBE 1985; retired, 1993; *b* 26 Aug. 1941; *s* of Lancelot Townley Grove and Joan Blanche Grove (*née* Hill); *m* 1971, Olivia Mary Crook; one *s* one *d*. *Educ:* Charterhouse Sch.; Univ. of Alberta (BSc Hons Physics). psc† 1974, RCDS 1988. Commissioned Royal Engineers, 1965; served BAOR, 1965–68; UKLF, 1969–70; Instructor, RSME, 1971–72; Staff College; DAA&QMG, 24 Airportable Bde, 1975–76; BAOR, 1977–78; Instructor, Staff College, 1983; MA to VCGS, 1983–84; ASD, 1985; Comdt, RSME, 1986–87; Dep. Mil. Sec. (A), 1989–90; DGPS (Army), 1991–92; led Study into Future Career Structures for Army Officers and Soldiers, 1992–93. Col Comdt, RE, 1995–. *Recreations:* golf, gardening, ski-ing. *Address:* c/o Lloyds Bank, Cox's & King's Branch, 7 Pall Mall, SW1Y 5NA. *Club:* Army and Navy.

GROVE, Dennis; *see* Grove, W. D.

GROVE, Sir Edmund (Frank), KCVO 1982 (CVO 1974; LVO 1963; MVO 1953); Chief Accountant of the Privy Purse, 1967–82, and Serjeant-at-Arms, 1975–82, retired; *b* 20 July 1920; *s* of Edmund Grove and Sarah Caroline (*née* Hunt); *m* 1945, Grete Elisabet, *d* of Martinus Skou, Denmark; two *d*. Served War, RASC, ME, 1940–46. Entered the Household of King George VI, 1946 and of Queen Elizabeth II, 1952. Chevalier: Order of the Dannebrog, Denmark, 1974; Légion d'Honneur, France, 1976; Officer, Order of the Polar Star, Sweden, 1975. *Recreation:* gardening. *Address:* Chapel Cottage, West Newton, King's Lynn, Norfolk PE31 6AU.

GROVE, Rear-Adm. John Scott, CB 1984; OBE 1964; RN retired, 1985; Director, Devonport Management Ltd, Devonport Royal Dockyard, 1987–91; engineering consultant, since 1991; *b* 7 July 1927; *s* of late William George Grove and Frances Margaret Scott Grove; *m* 1950, Betty Anne (*née* Robinson); one *s* (one *d* decd). *Educ:* Dundee High Sch.; St Andrews Univ. University Coll., 1944–47 (BScEng 1st Cl. Hons). National Service, Royal Engineers, 1947–48; Instructor Br., Royal Navy, 1948–50; Electrical Engrg Br., RN, 1950, qualified in Submarines, 1953; post graduate trng in Nuclear Engrg, Imperial Coll., London, 1958–59; sea service in HMS Forth and HM Submarines Tally-Ho, Turpin, Porpoise, Dreadnought; service in Ship Dept, 1964–67; staff of Flag Officer Submarines, 1967–70; Naval Asst to Controller of the Navy, 1970–73; staff of Flag Officer Submarines, 1975–77; commanded HMS Fisgard, 1977–79; Chief Strategic Systems Exec. (formerly Chief Polaris Exec.), 1980–85; Chief Naval Engr Officer, 1983–85. Comdr 1963; Captain 1970; Rear-Adm. 1980. Gov., British Maritime Technol. (Quality Assurance), 1990–. Master, Engineers' Co., 1994–95 (Sen. Warden, 1993–94). *Recreations:* walking, gardening. *Address:* Maryfield, South Close, Wade Court, Havant, Hants PO9 2TD. *T:* Havant (01705) 475116. *Club:* Army and Navy.

GROVE, Trevor Charles; editorial consultant and writer; *b* 1 Jan. 1945; *s* of Ronald and Lesley Grove; *m* 1975, Valerie Jenkins (*née* Smith); one *s* three *d*. *Educ:* St George's, Buenos Aires; Radley; St Edmund Hall, Oxford. Editorial Staff, Spectator, 1967–70; Leader Writer, then Features Editor, Evening Standard, 1970–78; Asst Editor, Sunday Telegraph, 1978–80; Sen. Asst Editor, Observer, 1980–83; Editor, Observer Magazine, 1983–86; Asst Editor, Daily Telegraph, 1986–89; Editor, Sunday Telegraph, 1989–92; Gp Exec. Ed. and Dep. Ed., Daily Telegraph, 1992–94. Launch Editor, El Periódico de Tucumán, Argentina, 1994. *Publications:* (co-ed) Singlehanded, 1984; (ed) The Queen Observed, 1986. *Recreations:* family life, tennis, cooking. *Address:* 14 Avenue Road, Highgate, N6 5DW. *T:* 0181–348 2621.

GROVE, (William) Dennis; Chairman, North West Water Group, 1989–93; *b* 23 July 1927; *s* of late William Grove and Elizabeth Charlotte Grove (*née* Bradley); *m* 1953, Audrey Irma Saxel; one *s* one *d*. *Educ:* Gowerton School; King's College, London (BSc). Joined Dunlop Group, 1951, subseq. Overseas Gen. Manager, to 1970; Chm. and Chief Exec., TPT, 1970–85; Vice-Pres., Sonoco International, 1978–85; Chm., NW Water Authy, 1985–89. *Recreations:* sports bystander, travel, golf. *Address:* Alderley Edge, Cheshire SK9 7XD. *Clubs:* Bramall Park Golf; Mottram Hall Golf.

GROVE-WHITE, Robin Bernard; Director, Centre for Study of Environmental Change, Lancaster University, since 1991; *b* 17 Feb. 1941; *s* of Charles William Grove-White and Cecile Mary Rabbidge; *m* 1st, 1970, Virginia Harriet Ironside (marr. diss.); one *s*; 2nd, 1979, Helen Elizabeth Smith; two *s* one *d*. *Educ:* Uppingham Sch.; Worcester Coll., Oxford (BA). Freelance writer for TV, radio, press and advertising in UK, Canada and US, 1963–70; McCann-Erickson Ltd, London, 1970; Asst Secretary, 1972–80, Dir, 1981–87, CPRE; Res. Fellow, Centre for Envmtl Technol., Imperial Coll., London, 1987–89; Sen. Res. Fellow, Lancaster Univ., 1989–. Mem., Forestry Commn, 1991–. *Publications:* (contrib.) Politics of Physical Resources, 1975; (contrib.) Future Landscapes, 1976; (with Michael Flood) Nuclear Prospects, 1976; contribs to New Scientist, Nature, Times, Independent, etc. *Recreations:* walking, cricket. *Address:* Conder Mill Cottage, Quernmore, Lancaster LA2 9EE. *T:* Lancaster (01524) 382501.

GROVER, Derek James Langlands; Senior Director of Operations (formerly Deputy Chief Executive), Employment Service, since 1994; *b* 26 Jan. 1949; *s* of Donald James Grover and late Mary Barbara Grover; *m* 1972, Mary Katherine Morgan; one *s*. *Educ:* Hove County Grammar Sch. for Boys; Clare Coll., Cambridge (Foundn Schol. 1970; BA Eng. Lit. 1971, MA 1975; Grene Prize 1971). Various positions, Dept. of Employment, 1971–78; Cabinet Office, 1978–80; MSC, 1980–87; Head of Personnel, Training Agency, 1987–89; Dir of Youth Training, 1989; Dir of Systems and Strategy, 1989; Dir of Trng Strategy and Standards, later of Trng Stretegy and Infrastructure, 1990–94. FRSA 1991. MIPD (MIPM 1993). *Recreations:* music, reading, walking, watching cricket. *Address:* c/o Employment Service, Steel City House, West Street, Sheffield S1 2GQ. *T:* Sheffield (0114) 259 5004.

GROVES, John Dudley, CB 1981; OBE 1964; Director-General, Central Office of Information, 1979–82; Head of Profession for Government Information Officer Group, 1981–82; *b* 12 Aug. 1922; *y s* of late Walter Groves; *m* 1943, Pamela Joy Holliday; one *s* two *d*. *Educ:* St Paul's Sch. Reporter, Richmond Herald, 1940–41; Queen's Royal Regt, 1941–42; commnd in 43rd Reconnaissance Regt, 1942; served in NW Europe, 1944–45 (despatches); Observer Officer, Berlin, 1945; Press Association (Press Gallery), 1947–51; Times (Press Gallery and Lobby), 1951–58; Head of Press Sect., Treasury, 1958–62; Dep. Public Relations Adviser to Prime Minister, 1962–64 (Actg Adviser, 1964); Chief Information Officer, DEA, 1964–68; Chief of Public Relations, MoD, 1968–77; Dir of Information, DHSS, 1977–78. Mem., Working Party on Censorship, 1983. *Publication:* (with R. Gill) Club Route, 1945. *Recreations:* walking, painting. *Address:* Mortimers, Manningford Bohune, Pewsey, Wilts SN9 5PG.

GROVES, Richard Bebb, TD 1966; RD 1979; **His Honour Judge Groves;** a Circuit Judge, since 1985; *b* 4 Oct. 1933; *s* of George Thomas Groves and Margaret Anne (*née* Bebb); *m* 1958, Eileen Patricia (*née* Farley); one *s* one *d*. *Educ:* Bancroft's Sch., Woodford Green, Essex. Admitted Solicitor of the Supreme Court, 1960. Partner, H. J. Smith & Co. and Richard Groves & Co., 1962–85. Dep. Circuit Judge, 1978–80; a Recorder, 1980–85. Nijmegen Medal, Royal Netherlands League for Physical Culture, 1965 and 1966. *Recreations:* Royal Naval Reserve, tennis, philately, walking, reading. *Clubs:* Royal Automobile; Colchester Garrison Officers (Colchester); Chelmsford (Chelmsford).

GROVES, Ronald Edward, CBE 1972; Chairman, 1982–87, and Managing Director, 1984–86, Meyer International plc (following merger of International Timber with Montague L. Meyer in 1982); *b* 2 March 1920; *s* of Joseph Rupert and Eva Lilian Groves; *m* 1940, Beryl Doris Lydia Collins; two *s* one *d*. *Educ:* Watford Grammar School. Joined J. Gliksten & Son Ltd; served War of 1939–45, Flt-Lt RAF, subseq. Captain with BOAC; re-joined J. Gliksten & Son Ltd, 1946: Gen. Works Man. 1947; Dir 1954; Jt Man. Dir 1964; Vice-Chm. 1967; Dir, Gliksten (West Africa) Ltd, 1949; Vice-Chm., International Timber Corp. Ltd, 1970 (name of J. Gliksten & Son Ltd changed to International Timber Corp. Ltd, 1970 following merger with Horsley Smith & Jewson Ltd); Chief Exec., 1973, Chm., 1976, Internat. Timber. Dir, Nat. Building Agency, 1978–82; Mem., EDC for Building, 1982–86; President: National Council of Building Material Producers, 1987–90 (Mem., Cttee of Management, 1982–94); Timber Trade Fedn of UK, 1969–71; London and District Sawmill Owners Assoc., 1954–56; Timber Res. and Develt Assoc., 1990–; Chm., Nat. Sawmilling Assoc., 1966–67; Mem., London and Regional Affairs Cttee, 1980–95, and Mem. Council, 1982–95, London Chamber of Commerce and Industry; Mem., London Regl Council, CBI, 1983–87; Dir, Business in the Community, 1984–87. Chairman: Rickmansworth UDC, 1957–58, 1964–65 and 1971–72; W Herts Main Drainage Authority, 1970–74; Three Rivers District Council, 1977–78; Mem., Herts CC, 1964–74. Chairman of Governors: Watford Grammar Sch. for Girls, 1980–; Watford Grammar Sch. for Boys, 1980–. *Recreations:* visiting theatre and opera; local community work. *Address:* 8 Pembroke Road, Moor Park, Northwood, Mddx HA6 2HR. *T:* Northwood (01923) 823187.

GRUBB, Dr Peter John; Reader in Ecology, Cambridge University, since 1992; President, Magdalene College, Cambridge, since 1991; *b* 9 Aug. 1935; *s* of Harold Amos Grubb and Phyllis Gertrude (*née* Hook); *m* 1965, Elizabeth Adelaide Anne, *d* of Charles Edward and Adelaide Gertrude Hall; one *s* one *d*. *Educ:* Royal Liberty Sch.; Magdalene Coll., Cambridge (Schol.; BA 1957; PhD 1962; ScD 1995). Magdalene College, Cambridge: John Stothert Bye Fellow, 1958–60; Res. Fellow, 1960; Official Fellow, 1961–; Tutor, 1963–74; Jt Dir of Studies in Natural Scis, 1980–; Cambridge University: Demonstrator in Botany, 1961–64; Lectr, 1964–92. Nuffield-Royal Soc. Bursar, Univ. of Adelaide, 1963; Hon. Res. Fellow, ANU, 1970–71; Vis. Prof., Cornell Univ., 1982, 1987; Sen. Vis. Researcher, CSIRO Tropical Forest Res. Centre, Atherton, 1992–. Editor: Jl of Ecology, 1972–77; Biol Flora of British Isles, 1978–87. Jt Leader, Cambridge Expedn to Colombian Cordillera Oriental, 1957; Leader, Oxford Univ. Expedn to Ecuador, 1960. President:

Brit. Ecol Soc., 1990–91; Cambridge Philosophical Soc., 1990–91. Frank Smart Prize in Botany, Cambridge Univ., 1956; Rolleston Meml Essay Prize, Oxford Univ., 1963. *Publications:* (with P. F. Stevens) Forests of Mt Kerigomna, Papua New Guinea, 1985; (ed with J. B. Whittaker) Toward a More Exact Ecology, 1989; papers in ecol and botanical jls. *Recreations:* history of buildings and landscape, biographies. *Address:* Magdalene College, Cambridge CB3 0AG. *T:* Cambridge (01223) 332109.

GRUENBERG, Prof. Karl Walter; Professor of Pure Mathematics in the University of London, at Queen Mary and Westfield (formerly Queen Mary) College, 1967–93, Emeritus since 1993; *b* 3 June 1928; *s* of late Paul Gruenberg and Anna Gruenberg; *m* 1973, Margaret Semple; one *s* one *d. Educ:* Shaftesbury Grammar Sch.; Kilburn Grammar Sch.; Cambridge Univ. BA 1950, PhD 1954. Asst Lectr, Queen Mary Coll., 1953–55; Commonwealth Fund Fellowship, 1955–57 (at Harvard Univ., 1955–56; at Inst. for Advanced Studies, Princeton, 1956–57). Queen Mary College: Lectr, 1957–61; Reader, 1961–67. Visiting Professor: Univ. of Michigan, 1961–62, 1978; Cornell Univ., 1966–67; Univ. of Illinois, 1972; Australian Nat. Univ., 1979 and 1987. Mem., Maths Cttee, SERC, 1983–86. *Publications:* Cohomological Topics in Group Theory, 1970; Relation Modules of Finite Groups, 1976; Linear Geometry (jtly with A. J. Weir), 2nd edn 1977; articles on algebra in various learned jls. *Address:* Department of Pure Mathematics, Queen Mary and Westfield College (University of London), Mile End Road, E1 4NS. *T:* 0181–980 4811.

GRUFFYDD, Prof. (Robert) Geraint, FBA 1991; Director, University of Wales Centre for Advanced Welsh and Celtic Studies, Aberystwyth, 1985–93; *b* 9 June 1928; *s* of Moses and Ceridwen Griffith; *m* 1953, Elizabeth Eluned Roberts; two *s* one *d. Educ:* University Coll. of N Wales, Bangor (BA; Hon. Fellow, 1993); Jesus Coll., Oxford (DPhil; Hon. Fellow, 1992). Asst Editor, Geiriadur Prifysgol Cymru, 1953–55; Lectr, Dept of Welsh, UCNW, 1955–70; Prof. of Welsh Language and Literature, UCW, Aberystwyth, 1970–79; Librarian, Nat. Library of Wales, 1980–85. Chairman: Welsh Books Council, 1980–85; Welsh Language Section, Welsh Acad., 1986–90; Bd of Celtic Studies, Univ. of Wales, 1991–93. Pres., Cambrian Archæol Assoc., 1991–92. *Publications:* (ed) Meistri'r Canrifoedd, 1973; (ed) Cerddi '73, 1973; (ed) Bardos, 1982; (ed) Cerddi Saunders Lewis, 1986; Dafydd ap Gwilym, 1987; (ed) Y Gair ar Waith, 1988; Llenyddiaeth y Cymry, ii, 1989; articles, etc, on Welsh literary and religious history in various collaborative vols and learned jls. *Recreations:* reading, walking, travel. *Address:* Eirianfa, Caradog Road, Aberystwyth, Dyfed SY23 2JY. *T:* Aberystwyth (01970) 623396.

GRUFFYDD JONES, Daniel; *see* Jones, D. G.

GRUGEON, Sir John (Drury), Kt 1980; DL; Chairman, Kent Police Authority, since 1992; *b* 20 Sept. 1928; *s* of Drury Grugeon and Sophie (*née* Pratt); *m* 1st, 1955, Mary Patricia (*née* Rickards) (marr. diss. 1986); one *s* one *d*; 2nd, 1989, Pauline Lois, *widow* of Dr Roland Phillips. *Educ:* Epsom Grammar Sch.; RMA, Sandhurst. Commissioned, The Buffs, Dec. 1948; served 1st Bn in Middle and Far East and Germany; Regimental Adjt, 1953–55; Adjt 5th Bn, 1956–58; left Army, 1960. Joined Save and Prosper Group, 1960. Kent County Council: Mem., 1967–; Leader, 1973–82; Vice-Chm., 1987–89; Chm., 1989–91; Chairman: Superannuation Fund, 1982–87; Fire and Public Protection Cttee, 1984–87. Chm., Policy Cttee, Assoc. of County Councils, 1978–81 (Chm., Finance Cttee, 1976–79). Dir, Internat. Garden Fest. '84, Liverpool, 1982–83. Chm., Tunbridge Wells HA, 1984–92. Member: SE Economic Planning Council, 1971–74; Cons. Nat. Cttee on Local Govt, 1975–82; Medway Ports Authority, 1977–93; Dep. Chm., Medway (Chatham) Dock Co., 1983–92. FRSA 1991. Liveryman, Ironmongers' Co., 1977–. DL Kent, 1986. *Recreations:* cricket, shooting, local govt. *Address:* 3 Eastgate Road, Tenterden, Kent TN30 7AH. *T:* Tenterden (01580) 763494. *Clubs:* Carlton, MCC; Kent County CC.

GRUNDY, David Stanley; Commissioner for Policy and Resources, Forestry Commission, since 1992; *b* 10 April 1943; *s* of Walter Grundy and Anne Grundy (*née* Pomfret); *m* 1965, Elizabeth Jenny Schadla Hall; one *s. Educ:* De La Salle Coll., Manchester; Jesus Coll., Cambridge (MA); Jesus Coll., Oxford (MPhil). Asst Principal, MOP, 1967–70; Asst Private Sec. to Minister, Min. of Technology, 1970–71; Principal, DTI, 1971–73; Economic Adviser: FCO, 1976–78; DoE, 1978–79; Chief Economic Advr, Govt of Vanuatu, 1979–81, Forestry Commission: Chief Economist, 1982–90; Comr for Finance and Admin, 1990–92. Mem., Scottish Ornithological Club. *Recreations:* angling, bird watching, gardening, tennis. *Address:* Forestry Commission, 231 Corstorphine Road, Edinburgh EH12 7AT. *T:* 0131–334 0303. *Club:* Dean Tennis (Edinburgh).

GRUNDY, (James) Milton; Founder and Chairman of the Warwick Arts Trust, since 1978; *b* 13 June 1926. *Educ:* Sedbergh Sch.; Gonville and Caius Coll., Cambridge (MA). Called to the Bar, Inner Temple, 1954. Founder and Chm., Gemini Trust for the Arts, 1959–66; Founder Mem. and Pres., Internat. Tax Planning Assoc., 1975–; Charter Mem., Peggy Guggenheim Collection, 1980–89; Chm., Internat. Management Trust, 1986–; Trustee: Nat. Museums and Galls of Merseyside, 1987–; New End Theatre, Hampstead, 1994–. *Publications:* Tax and the Family Company, 1956, 3rd edn 1966; Tax Havens, 1968, 6th edn 1993; Venice, 1971, 4th edn 1985; The World of International Tax Planning, 1984; (jtly) Asset Protection Trusts, 1990, 2nd edn 1993; (with V. I. Atroshenko) Mediterranean Vernacular, 1991. *Recreation:* conversation. *Address:* Gray's Inn Chambers, Gray's Inn, WC1R 5JA. *T:* 0171–242 2642.

GRUNDY, Ven. Malcolm Leslie; Archdeacon of Craven, since 1994; *b* 22 March 1944; *s* of Arthur James Grundy and Gertrude Alice Grundy; *m* 1972, Wendy Elizabeth Gibson; one *s. Educ:* Sandye Place Sch., Beds; Mander Coll., Bedford; King's Coll., London (AKC 1968); Open Univ. (BA 1976). Ordained deacon, 1969, priest, 1970; Curate, St George's, Doncaster, 1969–72; Chaplain and Sen. Chaplain, Sheffield Industrial Mission, 1972–80; Dir of Educn, dio. of London, 1980–86; Team Rector of Huntingdon, 1986–91; Dir, Avec, 1991–94; Hon. Canon of Ely, 1988–94. *Publications:* Light in the City, 1990; An Unholy Conspiracy, 1992; Community Work: a handbook for volunteer groups and local churches, 1995; (ed) The Parchmore Partnership, 1995. *Recreations:* classic cars, gardening, writing. *Address:* The Vicarage, Gisburn, Clitheroe, Lancs BB7 4HR; Peace Cottage, 38 The Leys, Langford, Beds SG18 9RS.

GRUNDY, Stephanie Christine; Legal Adviser, Treasury Solicitor's Department, since 1992; *b* 11 Dec. 1958; *d* of Harry Grundy and June (*née* Hazell). *Educ:* Grange Sch., Oldham; Hertford Coll., Oxford (Schol.; Gibbs Prize; MA, BCL). Called to the Bar, Middle Temple, 1983. Research Asst, Law Commn, 1985; Asst Parly Counsel, 1985–92; on secondment to Law Commn, 1988–90. *Recreations:* running, mountaineering, ballooning, singing. *Address:* Office of Treasury Solicitor, Queen Anne's Chambers, 28 Broadway, SW1H 9JS.

GRUNFELD, Prof. Cyril; Professor of Law, London School of Economics, 1966–82, now Emeritus; *b* 26 Sept. 1922; *o s* of Samuel and Sarah Grunfeld; *m* 1945, Phyllis Levin; one *s* two *d. Educ:* Canton High Sch., Cardiff; Trinity Hall, Cambridge (MA, LLB). Called to Bar, Inner Temple. British Army, 1942–45; Trinity Hall (Studentship), 1946–48; LSE: Asst, 1946–47; Asst Lectr, 1947–49; Lectr, 1949–56; Reader in Law, 1956–66; Pro-Dir, 1973–76; Convener, Law Dept, 1976–79; Dean, Faculty of Law, Univ. of London, 1978–80. Part-time Lectr in Trade Union Law, Ruskin Coll., Oxford, 1954–64. Vis. Research Fellow, ANU, 1970–71; Legal Adviser: to Commn on Industrial Relations, 1971–74; to Industrial Soc., 1982–87; to Nat. Assoc. of Port Employers, 1988–89. Mem., Trade Union Reform Cttee, Centre for Policy Studies, 1982–85. *Publications:* Modern Trade Union Law, 1966; The Law of Redundancy, 1971, 3rd edn, 1989; contrib. to books and learned jls. *Recreations:* reading, walking. *Address:* c/o London School of Economics and Political Science, Houghton Street, WC2A 2AE.

GRUNFELD, Henry; President, 1987–June 1995, Senior Adviser, from June 1995, S. G. Warburg Group plc (Chairman, 1969–74, President, 1974–87, S. G. Warburg & Co. Ltd); *b* 1 June 1904; *m* 1931, Berta Lotte Oliven (*d* 1993); one *s* (one *d* decd). *Address:* 2 Finsbury Avenue, EC2M 2PA. *T:* 0171–606 1066.

GRUNSELL, Prof. Charles Stuart Grant, CBE 1976; PhD; Professor of Veterinary Medicine, University of Bristol, 1957–80, now Emeritus; *b* 6 Jan. 1915; *s* of Stuart and Edith Grunsell; *m* 1939, Marjorie Prunella Wright; one *s* two *d. Educ:* Shanghai Public Sch.; Bristol Grammar Sch. Qualified as MRCVS at The Royal (Dick) Veterinary Coll., Edinburgh, 1937; FRCVS 1971. In general practice at Glastonbury, Som., 1939–48. PhD Edinburgh, 1952. Senior Lecturer in Veterinary Hygiene and Preventive Medicine, University of Edinburgh, 1952. Pro-Vice-Chancellor, Univ. of Bristol, 1974–77. Chm., Veterinary Products Cttee, 1970–80. Mem., General Synod of C of E, 1980–85; a Diocesan Reader. Defence Medal 1946. *Publications:* papers on the Erythron of Ruminants, on Vital Statistics in Veterinary Medicine, on Preventive Medicine, and on veterinary education. *Recreation:* gardening. *Address:* Greenleaves, Mead Lane, Sandford, Bristol BS19 5RG. *T:* Banwell (01934) 822461.

GRYLLS, Sir (William) Michael (John), Kt 1992; MP (C) North West Surrey, since 1974 (Chertsey, 1970–74); *b* 21 Feb. 1934; *s* of late Brig. W. E. H. Grylls, OBE; *m* 1965, Sarah Smiles Justice, *d* of Captain N. M. Ford and Lady (Patricia) Fisher; one *s* one *d. Educ:* RN College, Dartmouth; Univ. of Paris. Lieut, Royal Marines, 1952–55. Mem., St Pancras Borough Council, 1959–62. Contested (C) Fulham, Gen. Elecs, 1964 and 1966; Mem., Select Cttee on Overseas Develt, 1970–78; Chairman: Cons. Trade and Industry Cttee, 1981– (Vice-Chm., Cons. Industry Cttee, 1975–81); Small Business Bureau, 1979–. Mem. GLC, 1967–70; Dep. Leader, Inner London Educn Authority, 1969–70; Chm., Further and Higher Educn, 1968–70. Chm., Millennium Club. *Recreations:* sailing, riding, gardening, reading. *Address:* c/o House of Commons, SW1A 0AA. *Club:* Royal Yacht Squadron (Cowes).

GRYN, Rabbi Hugo Gabriel, CBE 1992; Senior Rabbi, West London Synagogue, since 1964; *b* 25 June 1930; adopted British nationality, 1993; *s* of Bella and Geza Gryn; *m* 1957, Jacqueline Selby; one *s* three *d. Educ:* Univs of Cambridge, London and Cincinnati (BA, MA); Hebrew Union Coll., Cincinnati (BHL, MHL, DHL). Ordained rabbi, 1957; Rabbi, Jewish Religious Union, Bombay, 1957–60; Exec. Dir, World Union for Progressive Judaism, 1960–62; Senior Exec., American Jewish Jt Distrib. Cttee, 1962–64; Vice-Pres. and Lectr, Leo Baeck Coll., 1964–. Chairman: European Bd, World Union for Progressive Judaism, 1980–91; Standing Cttee for Interfaith Dialogue in Educn, 1972–; Joint Chairman: Interfaith Network (UK), 1987–94; London Rainbow Group, 1975–91; Pres., Reform Synagogues of GB, 1990–; Mem., numerous educnl and Jewish organisations. Hon. DD Hebrew Union Coll., 1982. *Publications:* Forms of Prayer, 1977; contribs to publications of Standing Conf. on Interfaith Dialogue in Educn, British Jl of Religious Educn, Jl of Central Conf. of Amer. Rabbis, Jewish Chronicle. *Recreations:* swimming, travel, biblical archaeology. *Address:* 33 Seymour Place, W1H 6AT. *T:* 0171–723 4404.

GUAY, Richard; Agent General for Quebec in London, since 1995; *b* Montreal, 15 Nov. 1943; *s* of late Maurice Guay and Irène (*née* Brassard); *m* 1980, Marie-France Fortier; one *s* one *d. Educ:* Coll. Jean de Brébeuf, Montreal; Univ. of Montreal (law degree). Radio Canada: journalist, Montreal, 1966–69; Corresp., UN and NY, 1969–71; Lectr, Sch. of Journalism, Dakar Univ., 1971–73; Co-ordinator of Intergovtl Relns, Min. of Communications, Quebec, 1973–75; Counsellor to Dep. Minister, Min. of Culture, 1975–76. National Assembly, Quebec: Mem. for Taschereau, 1976–85; Parly Asst, Min. of Communications, 1976–79, Min. of Housing, 1979–82; Dep. Leader of Govt, 1982–83; Speaker, 1983–85. Mem. Bd, Internat. Assoc. of French-speaking Parliamentarians, 1983–85 (Grand Officier, Ordre de la Pléiade, 1991); Canadian Rep., Internat. Exec., CPA, 1983–85. Lawyer, specialising in arbitration, Montreal, 1986–95. *Recreations:* music, reading, ski-ing. *Address:* Quebec Government Office, 59 Pall Mall, SW1Y 5JH. *T:* 0171–930 8314.

GUAZZELLI, Rt. Rev. Victor; Auxiliary Bishop of Westminster (Bishop in East London) (RC), and Titular Bishop of Lindisfarne since 1970; *b* 19 March 1920; *s* of Cesare Guazzelli and Maria (*née* Frepoli). *Educ:* Parochial Schools, Tower Hamlets; English Coll., Lisbon. Priest, 1945. Asst, St Patrick's, Soho Square, 1945–48; Bursar and Prof. at English Coll., Lisbon, 1948–58; Westminster Cathedral: Chaplain, 1958–64; Hon. Canon, 1964; Sub-Administrator, 1964–67; Parish Priest of St Thomas', Fulham, 1967–70; Vicar General of Westminster, 1970. President: Pax Christi; Handicapped Children's Pilgrimage Trust. *Address:* The Lodge, Pope John House, Hale Street, E14 0BT. *T:* 0171–987 4663.

GUBBAY, Hon. Anthony Roy; Chief Justice of Zimbabwe, since 1990; *b* 26 April 1932; *s* of Henry and Gracia Gubbay; *m* 1962, Alice Wilma Sanger; two *s. Educ:* Univ. of Witwatersrand, SA (BA); Jesus Coll., Cambridge Univ. (MA, LLM; Hon. Fellow, 1992). Admitted to practice, 1957; emigrated to S Rhodesia, 1958; in private practice as advocate, Bulawayo; SC 1974; Judge: of the High Court, 1977–83; of the Supreme Court, 1983–90. Pres., Valuations Bd, 1974–77; National President: Special Court for Income Tax Appeals, 1974–77; Fiscal Court, 1974–77; Patents Tribunal, 1974–77. Chairman: Legal Practitioners' Disciplinary Tribunal, 1981–87; Law Develt Commn; Judicial Service Commn, 1990–. Mem., Perm. Court of Arbitration. Patron, Commonwealth Magistrates' and Judges' Assoc. Pres., Oxford and Cambridge Soc. of Zimbabwe. DU Essex, 1994. *Recreations:* classical music, philately, tennis. *Address:* Supreme Court of Zimbabwe, PO Box CY870, Causeway, Harare, Zimbabwe. *T:* (4) 736951. *Club:* Harare.

GUBBAY, Raymond Jonathan; Managing Director, Raymond Gubbay Ltd, since 1966; *b* 2 April 1946; *s* of David and Ida Gubbay; *m* 1972, Johanna Quirke (marr. diss. 1988); two *d. Educ:* University Coll. Sch., Hampstead. Concert promoter, 1966–: regular series of concerts at major London concert halls, including: Royal Festival Hall; Royal Albert Hall; The Barbican (*c* 1,000 concerts, 1982–); also major regl arenas and concert venues; has presented many of the world's greatest artists in concert; The Ratepayers Iolanthe, South Bank and Phoenix Theatre, 1984; The Metropolitan Mikado, South Bank, 1985; also Royal Opera prodn of Turandot, Wembley Arena, 1991. Founder, City of London Antiques and Fine Art Fair, Barbican Exhibn Halls, 1987–92. Hon. FRAM 1988. *Recreations:* gardening, going to the opera. *Address:* 176A High Street, Barnet, Herts EN5 5SZ. *T:* 0181–441 8940.

GUCKIAN, Dr Noel Joseph; HM Diplomatic Service; Counsellor and Deputy Head of Mission, Muscat, since 1994; *b* 6 March 1955; *s* of William Joseph Guckian and Mary Patricia Joan Guckian (*née* Kelly); *m* 1990, Lorna Ruth Warren; two *d. Educ:* Notre Dame

Internat. Sch., Rome; New Univ. of Ulster (BA Hons History 1976); UCW, Aberystwyth (MSc Econ, Internat. Politics 1977; PhD Internat. Politics 1985). FCO 1980; Arabic at SOAS, 1983–84; Jedda, 1984–87; 1st Sec., Financial, Paris, 1988; Head, British Interest Section, Tripoli, 1990; Head, Political Section, Kuwait, 1991–92. *Recreations:* fly-fishing, diving, sailing, sports. *Address:* c/o Foreign and Commonwealth Office, SW1A 2AH. *Clubs:* Commonwealth Trust, Royal Over-Seas League; Salisbury and District Angling.

GUDERLEY, Daisy Deborah, (Mrs C. Guderley); *see* Hyams, D. D.

GUÉGUINOU, Jean; Chevalier de la Légion d'Honneur, 1991; Chevalier de l'Ordre du Mérite, 1979; Ambassador of France to the Court of St James's, since 1993; *b* 17 Oct. 1941. *Educ:* Ecole Nationale d'Administration. Press and Inf. Dept, Min. of Foreign Affairs, Paris, 1967–69; Second Sec., London, 1969–71; Chargé de Mission, Private Office of Ministre d'Etat, Minister of Nat. Defence, 1971–73; Asst Private Sec., then Special Advr to Minister of Foreign Affairs, 1973–76; Principal Private Sec. to Minister of State resp. to Prime Minister, 1976–77; Head of Southern Africa and Indian Ocean Dept, Min. of Foreign Affairs, 1977–82; Consul Gen., Jerusalem, 1982–86; Dir of Press and Inf. Dept, Min. of Foreign Affairs, and Ministry Spokesman, 1986–90; French Ambassador in Prague, 1990–93 (Czechoslavakia, 1990–92; Czech Republic, 1993). Mem. Governing Body, Agence France Presse, 1986–90. KSG 1976. *Address:* French Embassy, 58 Knightsbridge, SW1X 7JT. *T:* 0171–201 1006; 11 Kensington Palace Gardens, W8 4QP. *Clubs:* Brooks's, Travellers'; Cercle Foch (Paris); Golf de St Germain en Laye.

GUERITZ, Rear-Adm. Edward Findlay, CB 1971; OBE 1957; DSC 1942, and Bar, 1944; defence consultant, writer and broadcaster; *b* 8 Sept. 1919; *s* of Elton and Valentine Gueritz; *m* 1947, Pamela Amanda Bernhardina Britton, *d* of Commander L. H. Jeans, and *widow* of Lt-Comdr E. M. Britton, RN; one *s* one *d*. *Educ:* Cheltenham Coll. Entered Navy, 1937; Midshipman, 1938; served War of 1939–45 (wounded; DSC and Bar): HMS Jersey, 5th Flotilla, 1940–41; Combined Ops (Indian Ocean, Normandy), 1941–44; HMS Saumarez (Corfu Channel incident), 1946; Army Staff Coll., Camberley, 1948; Staff of C-in-C S Atlantic and Junior Naval Liaison Officer to UK High Comr, S Africa, 1954–56; Near East Operations, 1956 (OBE); Dep. Dir, RN Staff Coll., 1959–61; Naval Staff, Admty, 1961–63; idc 1964; Captain of Fleet, Far East Fleet, 1965–66; Dir of Defence Plans (Navy), 1967; Dir, Jt Warfare Staff, MoD, 1968; Admiral-President, Royal Naval Coll., 1968–70 (concurrently first Pres., RN Staff Coll.); Comdt, Jt Warfare Estabt, 1970–72. Lt-Comdr 1949; Comdr 1953; Captain 1959; Rear-Adm. 1969; retd 1973. Dep. Dir and Editor, 1976–79, Dir and Editor-in-Chief, 1979–81, RUSI. Specialist Adviser, House of Commons Select Cttee on Defence, 1975–. Chief Hon. Steward, Westminster Abbey, 1975–85. President: Soc. for Nautical Res., 1974–90 (Hon. Vice Pres., 1990); J and K Class Destroyer Assoc., 1990–; Vice-Pres., RN Commando Assoc., 1993–; Vice Chairman: Council for Christian Approaches to Defence and Disarmament, 1974–80; Victoria League, 1985–88; Marine Soc., 1988–93 (Vice Pres., 1991); Member Council: Fairbridge-Drake Soc., 1981–90; British Atlantic Cttee, 1977–89; HOST (Hosting for Overseas Students Trust), 1987–90 (founding Governor). Mem., Bd of War Studies, Univ. of London, 1969–85. *Publications:* (jtly) The Third World War, 1978; (ed jtly) Ten Years of Terrorism, 1979; (ed jtly) Will the Wells Run Dry, 1979; (ed jtly) Nuclear Attack: Civil Defence, 1982; editor, RUSI Brassey's Defence Year Book, 1977–78, 1978–79, 1980, 1981. *Recreations:* history, reading. *Address:* Hemyngsby, 56 The Close, Salisbury, Wilts SP1 2EL. *Club:* Army and Navy.

GUERNSEY, Lord; Charles Heneage Finch-Knightley; Vice Lord-Lieutenant for West Midlands, since 1990; *b* 27 March 1947; *s* and *heir* of 11th Earl of Aylesford, *qv*; *m* 1971, Penelope Anstice, *y d* of Kenneth A. G. Crawley; one *s* four *d* (incl. twin *d*). *Educ:* Oundle, Trinity Coll., Cambridge. DL West Midlands, 1986. *Recreations:* shooting, fishing, Real tennis, cricket. *Heir: s* Hon. Heneage James Daniel Finch-Knightley, *b* 29 April 1985. *Address:* Packington Hall, Meriden, Coventry CV7 7HF. *T:* Meriden (01676) 522274.

GUERNSEY, Dean of; *see* Trickey, Very Rev. F. M.

GUEST, family name of **Viscount Wimborne.**

GUEST; *see* Haden-Guest.

GUEST, Prof. Anthony Gordon, CBE 1989; QC 1987; FBA 1993; FCIArb; Barrister-at-Law; Professor of English Law, King's College, University of London, 1966–95; *b* 8 Feb. 1930; *o s* of late Gordon Walter Leslie Guest and Marjorie (*née* Hooper), Maidencombe, Devon; unmarried. *Educ:* Colston's Sch., Bristol; St John's Coll., Oxford (MA). Exhibr and Casberd Schol., Oxford, 1950–54; 1st cl. Final Hon. Sch. of Jurisprudence, 1954. Bacon Schol., Gray's Inn, 1955; Barstow Law Schol., 1955; called to Bar, Gray's Inn, 1956, Bencher, 1978. University Coll., Oxford: Lectr, 1954–55; Fellow and Prælector in Jurisprudence, 1955–65; Dean, 1963–64; Reader in Common Law to Council of Legal Educn (Inns of Court), 1967–80. Travelling Fellowship to S Africa, 1957; Mem., Lord Chancellor's Law Reform Cttee, 1963–84; Mem., Adv. Cttee on establishment of Law Faculty in University of Hong Kong, 1965; UK Deleg. to UN Commn on Internat. Trade Law, NY, Geneva and Vienna, 1968–84 and 1986–87, to UN Conf. on Limitation of Actions, 1974; Mem., Board of Athlone Press, 1968–73; Mem. Governing Body, Rugby Sch., 1968–88. FKC 1982; FCIArb 1984. Served Army and TA, 1948–50 (Lieut RA). *Publications:* (ed) Anson's Principles of the Law of Contract, 21st to 26th edns, 1959–84; Chitty on Contracts: (Asst Editor) 22nd edn, 1961, (Gen. Editor) 23rd to 27th edns, 1968–94; (ed) Oxford Essays in Jurisprudence, 1961; The Law of Hire-Purchase, 1966; (Gen. Editor) Benjamin's Sale of Goods, 1st to 4th edns, 1974–92; (ed jtly) Encylopedia of Consumer Credit, 1975; (jtly) Introduction to the Law of Credit and Security, 1978; (ed) Chalmers and Guest on Bills of Exchange, 14th edn, 1991; Only Remember Me (anthology), 1993; articles in legal jls. *Address:* 16 Trevor Place, SW7 1LB. *T:* 0171–584 9260. *Club:* Garrick.

GUEST, Douglas Albert, CVO 1975; MA Cantab and Oxon; MusB Cantab; MusD Cantuar; FRCM, Hon. RAM, FRCO, FRSCM; Organist Emeritus, Westminster Abbey, since 1981; *b* 9 May 1916; 2nd *s* of late Harold Guest, Henley-on-Thames, Oxon; *m* 1941, Peggie Florentia, *d* of late Thomas Falconer, FRIBA, Amberley, Gloucestershire; two *d*. *Educ:* Reading Sch.; Royal College of Music, London; King's Coll., Cambridge. Organ Scholar, King's Coll., Cambridge, 1935–39; John Stewart of Rannoch Scholar in Sacred Music, Cambridge Univ., 1936–39. Served War of 1939–45, Major (Battery Comdr), Royal Artillery (HAC) (despatches, Normandy, 1944). Gazetted Hon. Major, RA, April 1945. Dir of Music, Uppingham Sch., 1945–50; Organist and Master of the Choristers, Salisbury Cathedral, 1950–57; Conductor of Salisbury Musical Soc., 1950–57; Dir of Music St Mary's Sch., Calne, 1950–57; Master of the Choristers and Organist, Worcester Cathedral, 1957–63; Conductor Worcester Festival Chorus and Three Choirs Festival, 1957–63; Organist and Master of the Choristers, Westminster Abbey, 1963–81. Examiner, Associated Bd of Royal Schs of Music, 1948–81; Prof., RCM, 1963–81. First Vice-Pres., National Youth Orchestra of Great Britain, 1984– (Chm. Council, 1953–84); Member Council: RCO, 1966–; Musicians' Benevolent Fund, 1968–. Hon. Mem., Royal Soc. of Musicians, 1963–. *Recreations:* fly fishing, golf. *Address:* The Gables, Minchinhampton, Glos GL6 9JE. *T:* Brimscombe 883191. *Club:* Flyfishers'.

GUEST, Eric Ronald; Metropolitan Magistrate (West London), 1946–68; Barrister-at-Law; *b* 7 June 1904; *s* of late William Guest; *m* 1932, Sybil Blakelock; one *d*. *Educ:* Berkhamsted Sch.; Oriel Coll., Oxford. BA 1925 (1st Class Hons Sch. of Jurisprudence); BCL 1926; called to Bar, 1927; practised in London and on Oxford Circuit. Recorder of Worcester, 1941–46; served as Sqdn Leader with RAFVR, 1940–45.

GUEST, George Howell, CBE 1987; MA, MusB (Cantab); MusD (Lambeth), 1977; FRCO 1942; FRSCM 1973; Hon. RAM 1984; Organist of St John's College, Cambridge, 1951–91 (Fellow, 1956); University Organist, Cambridge University, 1974–91; Special Commissioner, Royal School of Church Music, since 1953; *b* 9 Feb. 1924; *s* of late Ernest Joseph Guest and late Gwendolen (*née* Brown); *m* 1959, Nancy Mary, *o d* of late W. P. Talbot; one *s* one *d*. *Educ:* Friars Sch., Bangor; King's Sch., Chester; St John's Coll., Cambridge. Chorister: Bangor Cath., 1933–35; Chester Cath., 1935–39. Served in RAF, 1942–46. Sub-Organist, Chester Cath., 1946–47; Organ Student, St John's Coll., Cambridge, 1947–51; John Stewart of Rannoch Scholar in Sacred Music, 1948; University Asst Lectr in Music, Cambridge, 1953–56, Univ. Lectr, 1956–82; Prof. of Harmony and Counterpoint, RAM, London, 1960–61. Director: Berkshire Boy Choir, USA, 1967, 1970; Arts Theatre, Cambridge, 1977–90. Concerts with St John's Coll. Choir in USA, Canada, Japan, Aust., Brazil, Hong Kong, most countries in W Europe; concerts and choral seminars in the Philippines and in S Africa; concerts with Community of Jesus Choir, USA, in Hungary, Yugoslavia and USSR. Mem. Council: RCO, 1964– (Pres., 1978–80); RSCM, 1983–. Examiner to Associated Bd of Royal Schs of Music, 1959–92. Aelod er Anrhydedd, Gorsedd y Beirdd, Eisteddfod Genedlaethol Cymru, 1977; Dir, Côr Cenedlaethol Ieuenctid Cymru, 1984; Artistic Dir, Llandaf Festival, 1985. President: Cathedral Organists' Assoc., 1980–82; IAO, 1987–89. Hon. FRCCO 1991; Hon. Fellow, UCNW, 1989; Hon. FWCMD, 1992. Hon. DMus Wales, 1989. John Edwards Meml Award, Guild for Promotion of Welsh Music, 1986. *Publication:* A Guest at Cambridge, 1994. *Recreation:* the Welsh language. *Address:* 9 Gurney Way, Cambridge CB4 2ED. *T:* Cambridge (01223) 354932. *Club:* United Oxford & Cambridge University.

GUEST, Henry Alan, MBE 1990; Chairman, Rhodes Foods Ltd, since 1980; *b* 29 Feb. 1920; *m* 1947, Helen Mary Price; one *s* one *d*. *Educ:* Lindisfarne College. FHCIMA. War Service, 1940–46, France, India, Malaya; Captain RA. Supplies Man., J. Lyons & Co. Ltd, Catering Div., 1955; Rank Organisation, Theatre Div.: Dep. Controller, Catering, 1963; Controller, 1965; Group Catering Adviser, Associated British Foods, 1966; Chief Exec., Civil Service Catering Organisation, 1972–80. Mem. Royal Instn of Great Britain. *Publications:* papers on marketing and organisation in techn. jls and financial press. *Recreation:* swimming. *Address:* 14 Pensford Avenue, Kew, Surrey TW9 4HP.

GUEST, Ivor Forbes, FRAD 1982; Chairman, 1969–93, Member, 1965–93, Executive Committee, a Vice-President, since 1993, Royal Academy of Dancing; Solicitor; *b* 14 April 1920; *s* of Cecil Marmaduke Guest and Christian Forbes Guest (*née* Tweedie); *m* 1962, Ann Hutchinson; no *c*. *Educ:* Lancing Coll.; Trinity Coll., Cambridge (MA). Admitted a Solicitor, 1949; Partner, A. F. & R. W. Tweedie, 1951–83, Tweedie & Prideaux, 1983–85. Organised National Book League exhibn of books on ballet, 1957–58; Mem. Cttee, Soc. for Theatre Research, 1955–72; Chm., Exec. Cttee, Soc. for Dance Research, 1982–; Jt Pres., Dolmetsch Early Dance Soc., 1990–; Member: Exec. Cttee, British Theatre Museum, 1957–77 (Vice-Chm., 1966–77); Cttee, The Theatre Museum, 1984–89 (Mem., Adv. Council, 1974–83). Editorial Adviser to the Dancing Times, 1963–; Sec., Radcliffe Trust, 1966–; Trustee: Calvert Trust, 1976–; Cecchetti Soc. Trust, 1978–. Queen Elizabeth II Coronation Award for services to ballet, 1992. *Publications:* Napoleon III in England, 1952; The Ballet of the Second Empire, 1953–55; The Romantic Ballet in England, 1954; Fanny Cerrito, 1956; Victorian Ballet Girl, 1957; Adeline Genée, 1958; The Alhambra Ballet, 1959; La Fille mal gardée, 1960; The Dancer's Heritage, 1960; The Empire Ballet, 1962; A Gallery of Romantic Ballet, 1963; The Romantic Ballet in Paris, 1966; Carlotta Zambelli, 1969; Dandies and Dancers, 1969; Two Coppélias, 1970; Fanny Elssler, 1970; The Pas de Quatre, 1970; Le Ballet de l'Opéra de Paris, 1976; The Divine Virginia, 1977; Adeline Genée: a pictorial record, 1978; Lettres d'un Maître de ballet, 1978; contrib. Costume and the 19th Century Dancer, in Designing for the Dancer, 1981; Adventures of a Ballet Historian, 1982; Jules Perrot, 1984; Gautier on Dance, 1986; Gautier on Spanish Dancing, 1987; Dr John Radcliffe and his Trust, 1991; Ballet in Leicester Square, 1992. *Address:* 17 Holland Park, W11 3TD. *T:* 0171–229 3780. *Clubs:* Garrick, MCC.

GUEST, Prof. John Rodney, FRS 1986; Professor of Microbiology, Sheffield University, since 1981; *b* 27 Dec. 1935; *s* of Sidney Ramsey Guest and Dorothy Kathleen Guest (*née* Walker); *m* 1962, Barbara Margaret (*née* Dearsley); one *s* two *d*. *Educ:* Campbell College, Belfast; Leeds Univ. (BSc); Trinity Coll., Oxford Univ. (DPhil). Guinness Fellow, Oxford, 1960–62, 1965; Fulbright Scholar and Research Associate, Stanford, 1963, 1964; Sheffield University: Lectr, Sen. Lectr, Reader in Microbiology, 1965–81. SERC Special Res. Fellow, 1981–86. Marjory Stephenson Prize Lectr, Soc. Gen. Microbiol., 1992. *Publications:* contribs to Jl of Gen. Microbiol., Biochem. Jl, Molec. Microbiol. *Recreations:* walking in the Peak District, squash, beekeeping, polyfilling. *Address:* Department of Molecular Biology and Biotechnology, Sheffield University, Western Bank, Sheffield S10 2UH. *T:* Sheffield (0114) 276 8555.

GUEST, Melville Richard John; HM Diplomatic Service; Head, South East Asian Department, Foreign and Commonwealth Office, since 1994; *b* 18 Nov. 1943; *s* of late Ernest Melville Charles Guest and of Katherine Mary Guest; *m* 1970, Beatriz Eugenia, (Jenny), Lopez Colombres de Velasco; four *s*. *Educ:* Rugby Sch.; Magdalen Coll., Oxford (MA Jurisprudence). Entered HM Diplomatic Service, 1966; Third, later Second, Sec., Tokyo, 1967–72; Pvte Sec. to Parly Under-Sec. of State, FCO, 1973–75; First Sec., Paris, 1975–79; FCO, 1979–80; Prés.-Dir Gén., Soc. Française des Industries Lucas, 1980–85; Dir, Thomson-Lucas SA, 1980–85; Bd of Govs, British Sch. of Paris, 1981–85; Director: Franco-British Chamber of Commerce, 1980–85; Channel Tunnel Gp, 1985–86; Counsellor (Commercial), Tokyo, 1986–89; Counsellor (Political) and Consul General, Stockholm, 1990–93; Hd, S Pacific Dept, FCO, 1993–94. *Recreations:* family, music, ball-games, ski-ing. *Address:* c/o Foreign and Commonwealth Office, SW1A 2AH. *Clubs:* United Oxford & Cambridge University, MCC, Hurlingham.

GUEST, Trevor George; a District Judge (formerly Registrar of the Principal Registry), Family Division of the High Court of Justice, 1972–93; Barrister-at-Law; *b* 30 Jan. 1928; *m* 1951, Patricia Mary (*née* Morrison) (*d* 1983); two *d*; *m* 1988, Diane Constance (*née* Platts). *Educ:* Denstone Coll., Uttoxeter, Staffs; Birmingham Univ. (LLB (Hons)). Called to the Bar, Middle Temple, 1953. *Recreations:* dogs, Church affairs, gardening. *Address:* The Old Rectory, Purleigh, Essex CM3 6QH. *T:* Maldon (01621) 828375.

GUETERBOCK, family name of **Baron Berkeley.**

GUILD, Ivor Reginald, CBE 1985; FRSE; Partner in Shepherd and Wedderburn, WS, 1951–94; *b* 2 April 1924; 2nd *s* of Col Arthur Marjoribanks Guild, DSO, TD, DL, and Phyllis Eliza Cox. *Educ:* Cargilfield; Rugby; New Coll., Oxford (MA); Edinburgh Univ. (LLB). FRSE 1990. WS 1950. Procurator Fiscal of the Lyon Court, 1960–94; Bailie of Holyrood House, 1980–95; Registrar, Episcopal Synod of Episc. Church in Scotland,

1967–; Chancellor, dioceses of Edinburgh and St Andrews, 1985–95. Chairman: Edinburgh Investment Trust Ltd, 1974–94 (Dir, 1972–94); Dunedin Income Growth Investment Trust plc (formerly First Scottish American Investment Trust plc), 1973–94 (Dir, 1964–94); Dunedin Worldwide Investment Trust plc (formerly Northern American Investment Trust plc), 1973–94 (Dir, 1964–94); Dir, Fulcrum Investment Trust, 1986–. Member: Council on Tribunals, 1976–85; Interception of Communications Tribunal, 1985–; Immigration Appeal Adjudicator, 1988–95. Chm., Nat. Mus. of Antiquities of Scotland, 1981–85. Editor, Scottish Genealogist, 1959–94. *Recreations:* genealogy, golf. *Club:* New (Edinburgh).

GUILDFORD, Bishop of, since 1994; **Rt. Rev. John Warren Gladwin;** *b* 30 May 1942; *s* of Thomas Valentine and Muriel Joan Gladwin; *m* 1981, Lydia Elizabeth Adam. *Educ:* Hertford Grammar School; Churchill Coll., Cambridge (BA History and Theology, MA 1969); St John's Coll., Durham (Dip. Theol). Asst Curate, St John the Baptist Parish Church, Kirkheaton, Huddersfield, 1967–71; Tutor, St John's Coll., Durham and Hon. Chaplain to Students, St Nicholas Church, Durham, 1971–77; Director, Shaftesbury Project on Christian Involvement in Society, 1977–82; Secretary, Gen. Synod Board for Social Responsibility, 1982–88; Prebendary, St Paul's Cathedral, 1984–88; Provost of Sheffield, 1988–94. Mem., Gen Synod of C of E, 1990–. *Publications:* God's People in God's World, 1979; The Good of the People, 1988. *Recreations:* gardening, travel. *Address:* Willow Grange, Woking Road, Guildford GU4 7QS. *T:* Guildford (01483) 573922.

GUILDFORD, Dean of; *see* Wedderspoon, Very Rev. A. G.

GUILFORD, 9th Earl of *cr* 1752; **Edward Francis North;** Baron Guilford, 1683; DL; *b* 22 Sept. 1933; *s* of Major Lord North (*d* 1940) and Joan Louise (she *m* 2nd, 1947, Charles Harman Hunt, and *d* 1993), *er d* of late Sir Merrik Burrell, 7th Bt, CBE; *S* grandfather, 1949; *m* 1956, Osyth Vere Napier (*d* 1992), *d* of Cyril Napier Leeston Smith; one *s*. *Educ:* Eton. FRSA 1976. DL Kent 1976. *Heir: s* Lord North, *qv*. *Address:* Waldershare Park, Dover, Kent CT15 5BA. *T:* Dover (01304) 820244.

See also Major Hon. Sir Clive Bossom, Bt, Sir Jonathan North, Bt.

GUILFOYLE, Dame Margaret (Georgina Constance), DBE 1980; Senator for Victoria, 1971–87; *b* 15 May 1926; *d* of William and Elizabeth McCartney; *m* 1952, Stanley M. L. Guilfoyle; one *s* two *d*. *Educ:* ANU (LLB 1990). Accountant, 1947–. Minister: for Education, Commonwealth of Australia, 1975; for Social Security, 1975–80; for Finance, 1980–83. FCIS; FCPA. *Recreations:* reading, gardening. *Address:* 21 Howard Street, Kew, Vic 3101, Australia. *Club:* Lyceum (Melbourne).

GUILLEBAUD, (Jette) Margaret; JP; Chairman, South West Arts, since 1991; Member, Arts Council of England, since 1994; *b* 24 March 1948; *d* of Justin Brooke and Kirsten (*née* Møller-Larsen); *m* 1st, 1971, Robin Simon, *qv* (marr. diss. 1978); one *s* one *d*; 2nd, 1984, Hugh Guillebaud. *Educ:* Wycombe Abbey Sch.; Exeter Univ. (BA Hons Eng.). Tutor, Oxford Sch. of English, Verona, Italy, 1971–72; Examr, Oxford Exams Bd, 1972–75; Tutor, Open Univ., 1973–75; Man. Dir, Jobline Employment Agency, 1989–91; Chm., English Regl Arts Bds, 1993–94. Chm., Glos Ambulance NHS Trust, 1991–93. Dir, Cheltenham Festivals Ltd, 1991–. JP S Glos, 1988. FRSA 1992. *Recreations:* opera, theatre, visual arts, fishing, travel. *Address:* Wellington Lodge, Wellington Square, Cheltenham, Glos GL50 4JU. *T:* Cheltenham (01242) 244408.

GUILLEM, Sylvie; ballet dancer; *b* Paris, 23 Feb. 1965. *Educ:* Ecole de Danse, Paris Opera. With Paris Opera, 1981–89, Etoile, 1984; with Royal Ballet Co., 1989–; guest artist with other cos, 1989–. Lead roles in: Giselle; Swan Lake; La Bayadère; Cinderella; Sleeping Beauty; Romeo and Juliet; Raymonda; Manon; Don Quixote. Title role created for her in Sissi, Rudra Béjart Co.; other created roles in: In the Middle, somewhat Elevated; Le Martyre de Saint-Sebastien; Firstext. Comdr des Arts et des Lettres (France), 1988. *Address:* c/o Royal Ballet Company, Royal Opera House, Covent Garden, WC2E 9DD.

GUILLEMIN, Prof. Roger Charles Louis, MD, PhD; Distinguished Scientist, since 1989, and Director, since 1993, Whittier Institute for Diabetes and Endocrinology, La Jolla, California; Adjunct Professor of Medicine, University of California, San Diego, since 1970; *b* Dijon, France, 11 Jan. 1924 (naturalized US Citizen, 1963); *s* of Raymond Guillemin and Blanche (*née* Rigollot); *m* 1951, Lucienne Jeanne Billard; one *s* five *d*. *Educ:* Univ. of Dijon (BA 1941, BSc 1942); Faculty of Medicine, Lyons (MD 1949); Univ. of Montreal (PhD 1953). Resident Intern, univ. hosps, Dijon, 1949–51; Associate Dir, then Asst Prof., Inst. of Exper. Medicine and Surgery, Univ. of Montreal, 1951–53; Associate Dir, Dept of Exper. Endocrinol., Coll. de France, Paris, 1960–63; Prof. of Physiol., Baylor Coll. of Med., Houston, 1953–70; Adjunct Prof. of Physiol., Baylor Coll. of Med., 1970–; Resident Fellow and Res. Prof., Salk Inst. for Biol Studies, 1970–89. Chm., Labs for Endocrinology, Salk Inst., 1970–89. Member: Nat. Acad. of Sciences, USA; Amer. Acad. Arts and Scis; Amer. Physiol Soc.; Endocrine Soc. (Pres., 1986); Soc. of Exptl Biol. and Medicine; Internat. Brain Res. Orgn; Internat. Soc. Res. Biol Reprodn. Foreign Associate: Acad. des Sciences, France; Acad. Nat. de Médecine, Paris; Hon. Mem., Swedish Soc. of Med. Scis; Foreign Mem., Acad. Royale de Médecine de Belgique. Mem. Club of Rome. Hon. DSc: Rochester, NY, 1976; Chicago, 1977; Manitoba, 1984; Kyung Hee Univ., Seoul, Korea, 1986; Univ. de Paris VII, 1986; Madrid, 1988. Hon. MD: Ulm, 1978; Montreal, 1979; Univ. Libre de Bruxelles, Belgium, 1979; Turin, 1985; Barcelona, 1988; Univ. Claude Bernard, Lyon I, 1989; Hon. LMed Baylor Coll. of Med., 1978. Gairdner Internat. Award, 1974; Lasker Award, USA, 1975; Dickson Prize in Medicine, Univ. of Pittsburgh, 1976; Passano Award in Med. Sci., Passano Foundn, Inc., 1976; Schmitt Medal in Neuroscience, Neurosciences Res. Prog., MIT, 1977; National Medal of Science, USA, 1977; (jtly) Nobel Prize in Physiology or Medicine, 1977; Barren Gold Medal, USA, 1979; Dale Medal (Soc. for Endocrinology), UK, 1980; Ellen Browning Scripps Soc. Medal, Scripps Meml Hosps Foundn, San Diego, 1988. Légion d'Honneur, France, 1974. *Publications:* scientific pubns in learned jls. *Address:* Whittier Institute for Diabetes and Endocrinology, 9894 Genesee Avenue, La Jolla, CA 92037, USA.

GUILLERY, Prof. Rainer Walter, PhD; FRS 1983; Dr Lee's Professor of Anatomy, and Fellow of Hertford College, University of Oxford, 1984–Sept. 1996; *b* 28 Aug. 1929; *s* of Hermann Guillery and Eva (*née* Hackel); *m* 1954, Margot Cunningham Pepper; three *s* one *d*. *Educ:* University Coll. London (BSc, PhD; Fellow, 1987). Asst Lectr, subseq. Reader, Anatomy Dept, UCL, 1953–64; Associate Prof., subseq. Prof., Anatomy Dept, Univ. of Wisconsin, Madison, USA, 1964–77; Prof., Dept of Pharmacol and Physiol Sciences, Univ. of Chicago, 1977–84. Pres., Anatomical Soc. of GB&I, 1994–96. Editor-in-chief, European Jl of Neuroscience, 1988–92. *Publications:* contrib. Jl of Anat., Jl of Comp. Neurol., Jl of Neuroscience, and Brain Res. *Address:* Department of Human Anatomy, South Parks Road, Oxford OX1 3QX.

GUILLOU, Prof. Pierre John, MD; FRCS; Professor of Surgery, St James's University Hospital, Leeds, since 1993; *b* 30 Oct. 1945; *s* of Sarah Anne Guillou (*née* Greenfield) and Yves Guillou; *m* 1974, Elizabeth Anne Sowden; one *s* one *d*. *Educ:* Normanton Grammar Sch.; Univ. of Leeds (BSc; MB ChB 1970; MD 1975). Leeds Gen. Infirmary and St James's Univ. Hosp., 1970–73; S Manchester Univ. Hosp., 1973–74; Surgical Registrar, Leeds Gen. Infirmary, 1974–76; Lectr in Surgery, Univ. of Leeds, 1976–79; MRC Fellow in Immunology, Hôpital Necker, Paris, 1979–80; Sen. Lectr in Surgery, Univ. of Leeds, 1980–88; Prof. of Surgery, Imperial Coll. of Sci., Technology and Medicine and Dir, Academic Surgical Unit, St Mary's Hosp., London, 1988–93. Visiting Professor: Aust. Surgical Res. Soc., 1989, 1992; Univ. of Richmond, Va, 1992; S African Surgical Res. Soc., 1993; Ethicon, Malaysia, 1995; Lectures: Crookshank, Royal Soc. of Radiologists, 1990; Smith, Univ. of WA, 1991; A. B. Mitchell, QUB, 1991; jt meeting of Royal Colls of Surgeons of India and Glasgow, Madras, 1992; G. B. Ong, also Wilson T. S. Wang Internat. Surgical Symposium on Surgical Oncology, Chinese Univ. of Hong Kong, 1992, 1994; Annual Scientific Meeting of the Royal Coll. of Surgeons of Thailand, 1993; Stanford Cade, RCS, 1994; Marjorie Budd, Univ. of Bristol, 1995; 12th Asia Pacific Cancer Conf., Singapore, 1995. Member: James VI Assoc. of Surgeons, 1992–; Eur. Surgical Assoc., 1994–. Mem. Bd, British Jl of Surgery, 1994–. *Publications:* (ed) Surgical Oncology, 1991; Clinical Surgery, 1992; numerous papers on immunology, cell biology and surgery in treatment of cancer. *Recreations:* work, golf, fishing, work. *Address:* Academic Surgical Unit, Clinical Sciences Building, St James's University Hospital, Beckett Street, Leeds LS9 7TF. *T:* and *Fax:* Leeds (0113) 244 9618. *Club:* Royal Society of Medicine.

GUILLY, Rt. Rev. Richard Lester, SJ; OBE 1945; *b* 6 July 1905; *s* of late Richard Guilly. *Educ:* Stonyhurst Coll.; Campion Hall, Oxford (Hons Mod. Hist.; BA, MA); Heythrop Coll. Entered Soc. of Jesus, 1924; Asst Master, Beaumont Coll., 1933–35; ordained 1938. Served War of 1939–45, Chaplain to the Forces: BEF (France), 1939–40; CF 3rd Cl. 1940; Senior RC Chaplain, N Ireland, 1 Corps District, AA Cmd, 2nd Army, 1940–45 (OBE, despatches). Superior of Soc. of Jesus in British Guiana and Barbados, 1946–54; Titular Bishop of Adraa and Vicar Apostolic of British Guiana and Barbados, 1954–56; Bishop of Georgetown, 1956–72; Parish Priest in Barbados, 1972–77 and 1981–93; Apostolic Administrator, Archdiocese of Castries, 1977–81. *Publications:* various articles on Church History, Christian Social Doctrine and Church in Guyana. *Address:* St Francis Catholic Church, St James, Barbados, West Indies.

GUINNESS, family name of **Earl of Iveagh** and **Baron Moyne.**

GUINNESS, Sir Alec, CH 1994; Kt 1959; CBE 1955; actor; *b* Marylebone, 2 April 1914; *m* 1938, Merula Salaman; one *s*. *Educ:* Pembroke Lodge, Southbourne; Roborough, Eastbourne. On leaving school went into Arks Publicity, Advertising Agents, as copywriter. First professional appearance walking on in Libel at King's Theatre, Hammersmith, 1933; played Hamlet in modern dress, Old Vic, 1938; toured the Continent, 1939. Served War of 1939–45; joined Royal Navy as a rating, 1941; commissioned 1942. Rejoined Old Vic, 1946–47. Fellow, BAFTA, 1989. Hon. DFA Boston Coll., 1962; Hon. DLitt Oxon, 1977; Hon. LittD Cantab, 1991. Special Oscar, for contribution to film, 1979; Olivier Award for Services to the Theatre, SWET, 1989; Evening Standard Film Award for lifetime achievement, 1995. *Films include:* Oliver Twist; Kind Hearts and Coronets; The Bridge on the River Kwai (Oscar for best actor of the year, 1957); Lawrence of Arabia; Star Wars; Little Dorrit; A Handful of Dust. *Plays include:* The Cocktail Party (New York); Dylan (New York) (Antoinette Perry Award); A Voyage Round My Father; Habeas Corpus; The Old Country, 1977; A Walk in the Woods, 1989; *television:* Tinker, Tailor, Soldier, Spy, 1979 (BAFTA Award, 1980); Smiley's People, 1981–82 (BAFTA Award, 1983); Tales from Hollywood, 1991; A Foreign Field, 1993. *Publication:* Blessings in Disguise (autobiog.), 1985. *Address:* c/o McReddie, 91 Regent Street, W1R 7TB. *Clubs:* Athenæum, Garrick.

GUINNESS, Hon. Desmond (Walter); writer; *b* 8 Sept. 1931; *yr s* of 2nd Baron Moyne and of Hon. Diana Mitford (now Hon. Lady Mosley); *m* 1st, 1954, Marie-Gabrielle von Urach (marr. diss. 1981; she *d* 1989); one *s* one *d*; 2nd, Penelope, *d* of Graham and Teresa Cuthbertson. *Educ:* Gordonstoun; Christ Church, Oxford (MA). Founder, 1958, Irish Georgian Society to work for the study of, and protection of, buildings of architectural merit in Ireland, particularly of the Georgian period. Hon. LLD TCD, 1980. *Publications:* Portrait of Dublin, 1967; Irish Houses and Castles, 1971; Mr Jefferson, Architect, 1973; Palladio, 1976; Georgian Dublin, 1980; The White House: an architectural history, 1981; Newport Preserv'd, 1982; (with Jacqueline O'Brien) Great Irish Houses and Castles, 1992; (with Jacqueline O'Brien) Dublin: a Grand Tour, 1994. *Clubs:* White's, Chelsea Arts; Kildare Street and University, Friendly Brothers of St Patrick (Dublin).

GUINNESS, Sir Howard (Christian Sheldon), Kt 1981; VRD 1953; *b* 3 June 1932; *s* of late Edward Douglas Guinness, CBE and Martha Letière (*née* Sheldon); *m* 1958, Evadne Jane Gibbs; two *s* one *d*. *Educ:* King's Mead, Seaford, Sussex; Eton Coll. National Service, RN (midshipman); Lt-Comdr RNR. Union Discount Co. of London Ltd, 1953; Guinness Mahon & Co. Ltd, 1953–55; S. G. Warburg & Co. Ltd, 1955–85 (Exec. Dir, 1970–85). Dir, Harris & Sheldon Gp Ltd, 1960–81; Dir and Dep. Chm., Youghal Carpets (Holdings) Ltd, 1972–80. Director: Quality Milk Producers Ltd, 1988–; Riyad Bank Europe, 1993–. Chm., N Hampshire Conservative Assoc., 1971–74; Vice-Chm. 1974, Chm. 1975–78, and Treasurer 1978–81, Wessex Area, Cons. Assoc. Mem. Council, English Guernsey Cattle Soc., 1963–72. *Recreations:* skiing, tennis. *Address:* The Manor House, Glanvilles Wootton, Sherborne, Dorset DT9 5QF. *T:* Holnest (01963) 210217. *Club:* White's.

See also J. R. S. Guinness.

GUINNESS, James Edward Alexander Rundell, CBE 1986; Director, Guinness Peat Group, 1973–87 (Joint Chairman, 1973–77; Deputy Chairman, 1977–84); Deputy Chairman, Provident Mutual Life Assurance Association, 1983–89; *b* 23 Sept. 1924; *s* of late Sir Arthur Guinness, KCMG and Frances Patience Guinness, MBE (*née* Wright); *m* 1953, Pauline Mander; one *s* four *d*. *Educ:* Eton; Oxford. Served in RNVR, 1943–46. Joined family banking firm of Guinness Mahon & Co., 1946, Partner 1953; Chm., Guinness Mahon Hldgs Ltd, 1968–72. Chm., Public Works Loan Bd, 1979–90 (Comr, 1960–90). *Recreations:* shooting, fishing. *Address:* Coldpiece Farm, Mattingley, Basingstoke RG27 8LQ. *T:* Heckfield (01734) 326292. *Clubs:* Brooks's, Pratt's; Royal Yacht Squadron (Cowes).

GUINNESS, John Ralph Sidney, CB 1985; Chairman, British Nuclear Fuels PLC, since 1992; *b* 23 Dec. 1935; *s* of late Edward Douglas Guinness and Martha Letière (*née* Sheldon); *m* 1967, Valerie Susan North; one *s* one *d* (and one *s* decd). *Educ:* Rugby Sch.; Trinity Hall, Cambridge (BA Hons History, MA Hons). Union Discount Co. Ltd, 1960–61; Overseas Develt Inst., 1961–62; joined FO, 1962; Econ. Relations Dept, 1962–63; Third Sec., UK Mission to UN, New York, 1963–64; seconded to UN Secretariat as Special Asst to Dep. Under-Sec. and later Under-Sec. for Econ. and Social Affairs, 1964–66; FCO, 1967–69; First Sec. (Econ.), Brit. High Commn, Ottawa, 1969–72; seconded to Central Policy Rev. Staff, Cabinet Office, 1972–75; Counsellor, 1974; Alternate UK Rep. to Law of the Sea Conf., 1975–77; seconded to CPRS, 1977–79; transferred to Home Civil Service, 1980; Under-Sec., 1980–83, Dep. Sec., 1983–91, Permanent Sec., 1991–92, Dept of Energy. Director: Guinness Mahon Hldgs, 1993–; Ocean Gp, 1993–; Mithras Investment Trust, 1994–. Governor, Oxford Energy Inst., 1984–92. Member: E Anglia Regl Cttee, NT, 1989–94; Develt Cttee, Nat. Portrait Gall.; Council: BITC, 1992–; CBI, 1993–; Dir, UK-Japan 2000 Gp; Trustee, Prince's Youth Business Trust, 1992–. *Recreation:* iconography. *Address:* c/o BNFL, 65 Buckingham Gate,

SW1E 6AP. *T:* 0171–222 9717. *Clubs:* Brooks's, Beefsteak.
See also Sir H. C. S. Guinness.

GUINNESS, Sir Kenelm (Ernest Lee), 4th Bt, *cr* 1867; independent engineering consultant; *b* 13 Dec. 1928; *s* of late Kenelm Edward Lee Guinness and Mrs Josephine Lee Guinness; *S* uncle 1954; *m* 1961, Mrs Jane Nevin Dickson; two *s*. *Educ:* Eton Coll.; Massachusetts Institute of Technology, USA. Late Lieut, Royal Horse Guards. With IBRD, Washington, 1954–75. *Heir:* *s* Kenelm Edward Lee Guinness, *b* 30 Jan. 1962. *Address:* (home) Rich Neck, Claiborne, MD 21624, USA. *T:* (410) 7455079. *Clubs:* Cavalry and Guards; Household Division Yacht.

GUISE, Sir John (Grant), 7th Bt *cr* 1783; Jockey Club Official, 1968; *b* 15 Dec. 1927; *s* of Sir Anselm William Edward Guise, 6th Bt and Nina Margaret Sophie (*d* 1991), *d* of Sir James Augustus Grant, 1st Bt; *S* father, 1970; *m* 1992, Sally, *d* of late Cdre H. G. C. Stevens, RN. *Educ:* Winchester; RMA, Sandhurst. Regular officer, 3rd The King's Own Hussars, 1948–61. *Recreations:* hunting, shooting. *Heir:* *b* Christopher James Guise [*b* 10 July 1930; *m* 1969, Mrs Carole Hoskins Benson, *e d* of Jack Master; one *s* one *d*]. *Address:* Elmore Court, Gloucester GL2 6NT. *T:* Gloucester (01452) 720293.

GUJADHUR, Hon. Sir Radhamohun, Kt 1976; CMG 1973; solicitor; Chairman, Consortium Cinematographique Maurice Ltée; Director, Trianon Estates Ltd; Managing Director of Companies; *b* Curepipe Road, Mauritius, 1909; *m*; eight *c*. *Educ:* Church of England Aided Sch., Curepipe; Curepipe De la Salle Sch., Port Louis; Royal Coll., Curepipe; St Xavier Coll., Calcutta. Mem. Municipal Council, 1943–47; Dep. Mayor, Port Louis, 1947; Mem. (nominated) Town Council, Curepipe, 1957–60 (Chm., 1963). MLA, Bon-Accord/Flacq, 1967–82; Dep. Speaker of Legislative Assembly, Mauritius, 1968–69, 1974–82. *Address:* Port Louis, Mauritius. *Club:* Mauritius Turf (Steward, 1970; Chm. 1974).

GULL, Sir Rupert (William Cameron), 5th Bt *cr* 1872, of Brook Street; company director; *b* 14 July 1954; *s* of Sir Michael Swinnerton Cameron Gull, 4th Bt and Yvonne (*d* 1975), *o d* of Dr Albert Oliver Macarius Heslop, Cape Town; *S* father, 1989; *m* 1980, Gillian Lee, *d* of Robert MacFarlaine; three *d*. *Educ:* Diocesan Coll., Cape Town; Cape Town Univ. *Heir:* *great-uncle* John Evelyn Gull, MC [*b* 26 March 1914; *m* 1957, Margaret Colquhoun, *d* of late Capel Berger; one *s*, and one adopted *s* one adopted *d*]. *Address:* 2 Harcourt Road, Claremont, Cape Town, South Africa.

GULLIVER, James Gerald, FRSE; Chairman, James Gulliver Associates Ltd, since 1977; *b* 17 Aug. 1930; *s* of William Frederick and Mary Gulliver; *m* 1st, 1958, Margaret Joan (*née* Cormack) (marr. diss.); three *s* two *d*; 2nd, 1977, Joanne (*née* Sims) (marr. diss.); 3rd, 1985, Marjorie H. Moncrieff (marr. diss. 1991); 4th, 1993, Melanie (*née* Crossley). *Educ:* Campbeltown Grammar Sch.; Univ of Glasgow; Georgia Inst. of Technol., USA. Royal Navy (Short Service Commn), 1956–59; Dir, Concrete (Scotland) Ltd, 1960–61; Management Consultant, Urwick, Orr & Partners Ltd, 1961–65; Man. Dir, 1965–72, Chm., 1967–72, Fine Fare (Holdings) Ltd; Dir, Associated British Foods Ltd, 1967–72; Founder and Chm., James Gulliver Associates Ltd, subseq. Argyll Gp PLC, 1977–88; Argyll Foods PLC, 1980–88; Amalgamated Distilled Products PLC, 1981–88; Country House Hotels Ltd, 1983–88; Broad Street Gp, 1987–90; Lowndes Queensway, 1988–90; non-executive Chairman: Select Country Hotels, 1986–89; Waverley Cameron, 1987–90; Jackson's of Bourne End, 1988–89; City Gate Estates, 1988–90; Ancasta Marine Hldgs, 1988–91. Vis. Prof., Glasgow Univ., 1985–. Mem. Council, Inst. of Directors, 1972–92; Vice-Pres., Marketing Soc. Chm., Prime Minister's Enquiry into Beef Prices, 1973; Member: Scottish Economic Council, 1985–93; Governing Council, Scottish Business in the Community, 1983–; Dir, Scottish Investment Trust, 1986–; Chm., Scottish Business Gp, 1988–92. Vice-Pres., Manchester United FC, 1984– (Dir, 1979–84); Vice Chm., Heart of Midlothian FC, 1991–93. Trustee: Duke of Edinburgh's Award, 1988–; Glasgow Univ. Trust, 1986–. Mem. Council, Buckingham Univ., 1984–. FRSE 1990; FInstD; FRSA; FIMgt. Freedom and Livery, Worshipful Co. of Gardeners. DUniv Glasgow, 1989. Guardian Young Businessman of the Year, 1972. *Recreations:* ski-ing, sailing, music, motoring. *Address:* 22 Godfrey Street, SW3 3TA. *Club:* Royal Thames Yacht.

GULLY, family name of **Viscount Selby.**

GUMBS, Hon. Sir Emile (Rudolph), Kt 1994; Chief Minister, Anguilla, 1977–80 and 1984–94; *b* 18 March 1928; *s* of Johnson Emile Gumbs and Inez Beatrice Gumbs (*née* Carty); *m* 1st, 1964, Janice Anne Bradley; one *s* one *d*; 2nd, 1993, Louisa Josephine DeRoche. *Educ:* St Kitts/Nevis Grammar Sch. Captain, Schooner Warspite, 1955–64; Manager, Anguilla Road Salt Co., 1964–77 and 1980–84. Elected Rep., Road N Anguilla, 1968–94; Minister of Govt, 1976–80 and 1984–94. *Recreations:* sailing, fishing, bird watching. *Address:* Sandy Ground, PO Box 70, Anguilla, British West Indies. *T:* 8094972711; 170 W 23rd Street, Apt 6F, NY 10011, USA. *T:* (212) 6912177.

GUMLEY, Frances Jane, (Mrs A. S. Mason), MA; television and radio producer, broadcaster and journalist; *b* 28 Jan. 1955; *o d* of late Franc Stewart Gumley and Helen Teresa (*née* McNicholas); *m* 1988, Andrew Samuel Mason; one *s* one *d*. *Educ:* St Augustine's Priory, Ealing; St Benedict's Sch., Ealing (Greek only); Newnham Coll., Cambridge (MA). Parly research, 1974; Braille transcriber, 1975; Catholic Herald: Editorial Assistant and Assistant Literary Editor, Dec. 1975; Literary Editor and Staff Reporter, 1976–79; Editor, 1979–81; RC Asst to Head of Religious Broadcasting, and sen. producer, religious progs, radio, and producer, religious television, 1981–88; Series Editor, Religious Programmes, C4, 1988–89; guest producer, scriptwriter and presenter, BBC World Service and Radio 4, 1989–94. Mistress of The Keys, Guild of Catholic Writers, 1983–88. *Publications:* (with Brian Redhead): The Good Book, 1987; The Christian Centuries, 1989; The Pillars of Islam, 1990; Protestors for Paradise, 1993. *Recreations:* deep-sea diving, petit point.

GUMMER, Ellis Norman, CBE 1974 (OBE 1960); Assistant Director-General (Administration), British Council, 1972–75; *b* 18 June 1915; *o s* of late Robert Henry Gummer, engr, and of Mabel Thorpe, Beckenham, Kent; *m* 1949, Dorothy Paton Shepherd; one *s* (and one *s* decd). *Educ:* St Dunstan's Coll.; St Catherine's Society, Oxford. BLitt, MA. Library service: Nottingham Univ., 1939; Queen's Coll., Oxford, 1940–42; served War of 1939–45, Admty, 1942–45; British Council: East Europe Dept, 1945–50; Personnel Dept, 1950–52; Student Welfare Dept, 1952–59; Literature Group, 1959–61; Controller, Arts and Science Div., 1961–66; Controller, Finance Div., 1966–71. *Publication:* Dickens' Works in Germany, 1940. *Recreations:* books, topography, archaeology. *Address:* 9 Campden Street, W8 7EP. *T:* 0171–727 4823.

GUMMER, Rt. Hon. John Selwyn, PC 1985; MP (C) Suffolk Coastal, since 1983 (Eye, Suffolk, 1979–83); Secretary of State for the Environment, since 1993; *b* 26 Nov. 1939; *s* of Canon Selwyn Gummer and late Sybille (*née* Mason); *m* 1977, Penelope Jane, *yr d* of John P. Gardner; two *s* two *d*. *Educ:* King's Sch., Rochester; Selwyn Coll., Cambridge (Exhibr). BA Hons History 1961; MA 1971; Chm., Cambridge Univ. Conservative Assoc., 1961; Pres., Cambridge Union, 1962; Chm., Fedn of Conservative Students, 1962. Editor, Business Publications, 1962–64; Editor-in-Chief, Max Parrish & Oldbourne Press, 1964–66; BPC Publishing: Special Asst to Chm., 1967; Publisher, Special Projects, 1967–69; Editorial Coordinator, 1969–70. Mem., ILEA Educn Cttee, 1967–70; Dir, Shandwick Publishing Co., 1966–81; Man. Dir, EP Gp of Cos, 1975–81; Chairman: Selwyn Shandwick Internat., 1976–81, Siemssen Hunter Ltd, 1979–80 (Dir, 1973–80). Contested (C) Greenwich, 1964 and 1966; MP (C) Lewisham W, 1970–Feb. 1974; PPS to Minister of Agriculture, 1972; an additional Vice-Chm., Conservative Party, 1972–74; an Asst Govt Whip, 1981; a Lord Comr of HM Treasury, 1981–83; Parly Under-Sec. of State for Employment, Jan.–Oct. 1983; Minister of State, Dept of Employment, 1983–84; Paymaster-Gen., 1984–85; Chm., Cons. Party, 1983–85; Minister of State: MAFF, 1985–88; DoE, 1988–89; Minister of Agric., Fisheries and Food, 1989–93. Mem., Gen. Synod of the Church of England, 1979–92. *Publications:* (jtly) When the Coloured People Come, 1966; The Permissive Society, 1971; (with L. W. Cowie) The Christian Calendar, 1974; (contrib.) To Church with Enthusiasm, 1969; (contrib.) Faith In Politics, 1987; Christianity and Conservatism, 1990. *Address:* House of Commons, SW1A 0AA.
See also P. S. Gummer.

GUMMER, Peter Selwyn; Chairman, Shandwick plc, since 1974; *b* 24 Aug. 1942; *s* of Canon Selwyn Gummer and late Sybille (*née* Mason); *m* 1982, Lucy Rachel, *er d* of A. Ponsonby Dudley-Hill; one *s* three *d*. *Educ:* King's Sch., Rochester, Kent; Selwyn Coll., Cambridge (BA, MA). Portsmouth and Sunderland Newspaper Gp, 1964–65; Viyella International, 1965–66; Hodgkinson & Partners, 1966–67; Industrial & Commercial Finance Corp., 1967–74. Non-executive Director: CIA Group PLC, 1990–94; Halifax Building Soc., 1994– (non-exec. Mem., London Bd, 1990–94). Member: NHS Policy Bd, 1991–; Arts Council of England (formerly of GB), 1991–; Chm., Nat. Lottery Adv. Bd for Arts and Film, 1994–. Chm., Understanding Industry Trust, 1991. FRSA. *Publications:* various articles and booklets on public relations and marketing. *Recreations:* opera, rugby, cricket. *Address:* 61 Grosvenor Street, W1X 9DA. *T:* 0171–408 2232. *Clubs:* Garrick, MCC, Hurlingham.
See also Rt Hon. J. S. Gummer.

GÜMRÜKÇÜOGLU, Rahmi Kamil, Hon. GCVO 1988; Co-Chairman, Euro Turkish Corporation, since 1990; *b* 18 May 1927; *m* Elçin; one *s* one *d*. *Educ:* Haydar Pasha Lycée, Istanbul; Faculty of Political Sciences, Ankara Univ. Master's degree in Pol. Economy and Govt, Harvard Univ. Second Secretary, 1952–55, First Sec., 1955, Turkish Embassy, London; Head of Section dealing with Internat. Economic Affairs, Min. of Foreign Affairs, Ankara, 1958–60; Counsellor, Turkish Embassy, Cairo, 1960–63; Dep. Director General, Dept of Internat. Economic Affairs, Ankara, 1963–65; Head of Special Bureau dealing with Economic Co-operation between Turkey and the Soviet Union, 1965–67; Dir Gen., Dept of Internat. Economic Affairs, 1967–71; Turkish Ambassador: to Council of Europe, Strasbourg, 1971–75; to Iran, 1975–78; Sen. Advr to Min. of Foreign Affairs, 1978; Pres., Defence Industry Co-ordination Board, Ankara, 1978–79; Dep. Sec. Gen. for Economic Affairs, Min. of Foreign Affairs, 1979–81; Amb. to UK, 1981–88; Inspector, Min. of Foreign Affairs, 1989–90; Dep. Ldr for For. Affairs, Democratic Center Party, 1990–92. Actg Chm., Taturos Co., 1992–; Board Member: Turkish Airlines, 1992–; Degere Enterprises, 1992–; Kent Bank, 1992–; Petro-Chemical Industries. *Publications:* various articles and booklets on foreign investment, questions of economic develt, Soviet economic develt, economic integration amongst developing countries. *Address:* Köybasi Caddesi 191, Yeniköy, Istanbul, Turkey.

GUN-MUNRO, Sir Sydney Douglas, GCMG 1979; Kt 1977; MBE 1957; FRCS; Governor-General of St Vincent and the Grenadines, 1979–85, retired (Governor, 1977–79); *b* 29 Nov. 1916; *s* of Barclay Justin Gun-Munro and Marie Josephine Gun-Munro; *m* 1943, Joan Estelle Benjamin; two *s* one *d*. *Educ:* Grenada Boys' Secondary Sch.; King's Coll. Hosp., London (MB, BS Hons 1943); Moorfields Hosp., London (DO 1952). MRCS, LRCP 1943; FRCS 1985. House Surg., EMS Hosp., Horton, 1943; MO, Lewisham Hosp., 1943–46; Dist MO, Grenada, 1946–49; Surg., Gen. Hosp., St Vincent, 1949–71; Dist MO, Bequia, St Vincent, 1972–76. *Recreations:* tennis, boating. *Address:* PO Box 51, Bequia, St Vincent and the Grenadines, West Indies. *T:* St Vincent 83261.

GUNN, (Alan) Richard, CBE 1991; High Commissioner for Eastern Caribbean States in London, 1987–94; *b* 19 Jan. 1936; *s* of Alan Leslie Gunn and Violet Gunn; *m* 1962, Flora Beryl (*née* Richardson); one *s* two *d*. *Educ:* Boys' Grammar Sch., St Vincent; Portsmouth College of Architecture; Regent Street Polytechnic, London. Marketing Dir, Hazells Ltd, St Vincent, 1968–74; Chm./Man. Dir, Property Investments Ltd, St Vincent, 1974–87. Director: Vincentian Newspaper Ltd, 1970–; Caribbean Assoc. of Industry and Commerce, 1985–87; Chairman: St Vincent Chamber of Commerce, 1984–85; Nat. Shipping Corp., St Vincent, 1987; Nat. Broadcasting Corp., 1986–87; Sec.-Gen., Caribbean Assoc. of Industry and Commerce/EEC 'Europe-Caribbean Contact II', 1987. *Recreations:* yachting, fishing, reading. *Address:* Fairhall, PO Box 126, St Vincent and the Grenadines. *Clubs:* Royal Over-Seas League, Commonwealth Trust; St Vincent Yacht.

GUNN, Mrs Bunty Moffat, CBE 1993 (OBE 1981); JP; Chairman, Lanarkshire Health Board, 1981–93; *b* 4 Sept. 1923; *d* of William M. and Dolina Johnston; *m* 1946, Hugh McVane Houston Gunn; three *s* one *d*. *Educ:* Grange School for Girls; Grangemouth High School. DSCHE 1980. Councillor: Lanark CC, 1970–73; Strathclyde Regional Council, 1973–82; Chairman, Scottish Council for Health Education, 1974–80; Member, Lanarkshire Health Board, 1973–81. Vice-Pres., Royal British Legion, CS&W Branch, 1978–. JP City of Glasgow 1972. *Recreations:* grandchildren, golf, theatre, music. *Address:* 198 Dukes Road, Burnside, Rutherglen, Glasgow G73 5AA. *T:* 0141–647 8258. *Club:* Cathkin Braes Golf (Strathclyde).

GUNN, John Angus Livingston; Head of Heritage and Tourism Group, Department of National Heritage, 1992; *b* 20 Nov. 1934; *s* of late Alistair L. Gunn, FRCOG, and Mrs Sybil Gunn, JP; *m* 1959, Jane, *d* of Robert Cameron; one *s* one *d*. *Educ:* Fettes Coll., Edinburgh (Foundationer); Christ Church, Oxford (Scholar). MA Oxford, 1st Cl. Hons in Classical Hon. Mod., 1955, and in final sch. of Psychology, Philosophy and Physiology, 1957; Passmore-Edwards Prizeman, 1956. National Service, commnd in S Wales Borderers (24th Regt), 1957–59. Entered Min. of Transport, 1959; Principal Private Sec. to Ministers of Transport, 1967–68; Asst Sec., MoT, DoE and Civil Service Dept, 1969–75; Under-Sec., DoE, 1976–92; Greater London Housing and Planning Directorate, 1976; Water Directorate, 1981; Water Privatisation Directorate, 1987; Heritage and Royal Estate Directorate, 1990. *Address:* 108 Westcombe Park Road, SE3 7RX.

GUNN, Prof. John Charles, CBE 1994; MD; FRCPsych; Professor of Forensic Psychiatry, Institute of Psychiatry, since 1978; *b* 6 June 1937; *s* of Albert Charles Gunn and late Lily Hilda Edwards; *m* 1st, 1959, Celia Willis (marr. diss. 1986, she *d* 1989); one *s* one *d*; 2nd, 1989, Pamela Taylor. *Educ:* Brighton, Hove and Sussex Grammar Sch.; Reigate Grammar Sch.; Birmingham Univ. (MB ChB 1961; Acad. DPM 1966; MD 1969). MRCPsych 1971, FRCPsych 1980. Queen Elizabeth Hosp., Birmingham, 1961–63; Maudsley Hosp., 1963–67; Institute of Psychiatry: Res. Worker, 1967–69; Lectr, 1969–71; Sen. Lectr, 1971–75; Dir, Special Hosps Res. Unit, 1975–78. H. B. Williams Vis. Prof. to Aust. and NZ, 1985. Chm., Res. Cttee, 1976–80, Dep. Chief Examr, 1993–95, RCPsych. Advisor, H of C Select Cttees on Violence in Marriage, 1975, on Prison Med. Service, 1986; Member: Home Sec's Adv. Bd on Restricted Patients, 1982–91; Royal Commn on

Criminal Justice, 1991–93. WHO Specialist Advisor in Forensic Psychiatry to China, 1987; Consultant, Eur. Cttee for Prevention of Torture, 1993. Editor, Criminal Behaviour and Mental Health, 1991–. *Publications:* Epileptics in Prison, 1977; Psychiatric Aspects of Imprisonment, 1978; Current Research in Forensic Psychiatry and Psychology, vols 1–3, 1982–85; Violence in Human Society, 1983; Forensic Psychiatry: clinical, legal and ethical issues, 1993. *Recreations:* theatre, opera, cinema, photography, walking, living with Pamela. *Address:* Department of Forensic Psychiatry, Institute of Psychiatry, De Crespigny Park, Denmark Hill, SE5 8AF. *T:* 0171–701 7063. *Clubs:* Athenæum, Royal Society of Medicine.

GUNN, Prof. Sir John (Currie), Kt 1982; CBE 1976; MA (Glasgow and Cambridge); FRSE, FIMA; FInstP; Cargill Professor of Natural Philosophy, 1949–82 and Head of Department, 1973–82, Dean of Faculties, 1989–91, University of Glasgow; *b* 13 Sept. 1916; *s* of Richard Robertson Gunn and Jane Blair Currie; *m* 1944, Betty Russum (OBE 1984); one *s*. *Educ:* Glasgow Acad.; Glasgow Univ.; St John's Coll., Cambridge. Engaged in Admiralty scientific service, first at Admiralty Research Laboratory, later at Mine Design Dept, 1939–45; Research Fellow of St John's Coll., Cambridge, 1944; Lecturer in Applied Mathematics: Manchester Univ., 1945–46; University Coll., London, 1946–49. Member: SRC, 1968–72; UGC, 1974–81. Hon. DSc: Heriot-Watt, 1981; Loughborough, 1983; DUniv Open, 1989. *Publications:* papers on mathematical physics in various scientific journals. *Recreations:* golf, music, chess. *Address:* 32 Beaconsfield Road, Glasgow G12 0NY. *T:* 0141–357 2001.

GUNN, John Humphrey; company director and corporate development adviser; Director, John Duncan & Co. Ltd (formerly Edgar Hamilton Consultants Ltd), since 1992; *b* 15 Jan. 1942; *s* of Francis (Bob) Gunn and Doris Gunn; *m* 1965, Renate Sigrid (*née* Boehme); three *d*. *Educ:* Sir John Deane's Grammar School, Northwich; Univ. of Nottingham (BA Hons 1964). Barclays Bank, 1964–68; Astley & Pearce, 1968–85; Chief Executive: Exco International, 1979–85; British & Commonwealth Holdings, 1986–87 and 1990 (Chm., 1987–90). Hon. LLD Nottingham, 1989. *Recreations:* golf, ski-ing, mountain walking, classical music, opera. *Address:* Midland and Scottish Resources PLC, 36/37 King Street, EC2. *Club:* MCC.

GUNN, Marion Ballantyne; Head of Fire Service and Emergency Planning Division, Scottish Office Home and Health Department, since 1992; *b* 31 Oct. 1947; *d* of Dr Allan Christie Tait and Jean Ballantyne Hay; *m* 1985, Donald Hugh Gunn; one step *s*. *Educ:* Jordanhill College School; Dumfries Academy; Univ. of Edinburgh (MA Hons 1969); Open Univ. (BA 1975). Management trainee, Lewis's, Bristol, 1969–70; joined Scottish Office, 1970; posts in Scottish Educn Dept and Scottish Develt Dept, 1970–90; Asst Sec., 1984; Head of Roads Policy and Programme Div., 1987; Head of Water Policy Div., Scottish Office Envmt Dept, 1990. Research Fellow, Univ. of Glasgow, 1983–84. *Recreations:* gardening, Scottish country dancing. *Address:* 32 Warriston Avenue, Edinburgh EH3 5NB. *T:* 0131–552 4476.

GUNN, Peter Nicholson; author; *b* 15 Aug. 1914; 2nd *s* of Frank Lindsay Gunn, CBE, and Adèle Margaret (*née* Dunphy); *m* 1953, Diana Maureen James; one *s*. *Educ:* Melbourne; Trinity Coll., Cambridge (MA). Served War 1939–45: Rifle Bde; POW 1942. Sen. Lectr, RMA, Sandhurst, 1949–54. *Publications:* Naples: a Palimpsest, 1961 (German trans. 1964, Italian trans. 1971); Vernon Lee: a Study, 1964; The Companion Guide to Southern Italy, 1969; My Dearest Augusta: a Biography of Augusta Leigh, Byron's half-sister, 1969; A Concise History of Italy, 1971; (ed) Byron's Prose, 1972; Normandy: Landscape with figures, 1975; Burgundy: Landscape with figures, 1976; The Actons, 1978; Napoleon's Little Pest: The Duchess of Abrantès, 1979; (with R. Beny) Churches of Rome, 1981 (trans. German, Italian and Danish, 1982); Yorkshire Dales: Landscape with figures, 1984; (ed) Lord Byron: Selected Letters and Journals, 1984. *Address:* Gruchet-sur-Arques, Arques-la-Bataille, 76880, France. *T:* 35045710.

GUNN, Richard; *see* Gunn, A. R.

GUNN, Sir Robert (Norman), Kt 1995; DL; Chairman, 1985–90, Chief Executive, 1983–87 and Director, 1976–90, The Boots Company PLC; *b* 16 Dec. 1925; *s* of late Donald Macfie Gunn and Margaret (*née* Pallister); *m* 1956, Joan Parry, JP; one *d*. *Educ:* Royal High Sch., Edinburgh; Worcester Coll., Oxford (MA). Served RAC, 1944–47 (Lieut). Joined Boots, 1951; Merchandise Buyer, 1962–70; Head of Warehousing and Distribn, 1971–73; Dir of Property, 1973–78; Dir, Industrial Div., 1979–83 (Man. Dir 1980–83); Vice-Chm., 1983–85. Chm., FEFCE, 1992–. Director: Foseco plc (formerly Foseco Minsep), 1984–91; East Midlands Electricity, 1990–95; Nottingham Building Soc., 1990–. Member: Bd of Management, Assoc. of British Pharmaceutical Industry, 1981–84 (Vice-Pres., 1983–84); Council, CBI, 1985–90; PCFC, 1989–93; HEFCE, 1992–94. CIMgt (CBIM 1983); FInstD 1985; FRSA. DL Notts, 1995. Hon. LLD Nottingham, 1993. *Recreations:* gardening, theatre. *Address:* Tor House, Pinfold Lane, Elston, near Newark, Notts NG23 5PD.

GUNN, Thomson William, (Thom Gunn); poet; Senior Lecturer, English Department, University of California (Berkeley), since 1990; *b* 29 Aug. 1929; *s* of Herbert Smith Gunn, and Ann Charlotte Gunn (*née* Thomson); unmarried. *Educ:* University Coll. Sch., Hampstead; Trinity Coll., Cambridge. British Army (National Service), 1948–50; lived in Paris six months, 1950; Cambridge, 1950–53; lived in Rome, 1953–54; has lived in California since 1954. Lectr, later Associate Prof., English Dept, University of Calif (Berkeley), 1958–66, Vis. Lectr, 1975–90. *Publications:* Poetry from Cambridge, 1953; Fighting Terms, 1954; The Sense of Movement, 1957; My Sad Captains, 1961; Selected Poems (with Ted Hughes), 1962; Five American Poets (ed with Ted Hughes), 1962; Positives (with Ander Gunn), 1966; Touch, 1967; Poems 1950–1966: a selection, 1969; Moly, 1971; Jack Straw's Castle and other poems, 1976; Selected Poems, 1979; The Passages of Joy, 1982; The Occasions of Poetry (ed Clive Wilmer), 1982; The Man with Night Sweats, 1992; Collected Poems, 1993; Shelf Life, 1993. *Recreations:* cheap thrills. *Address:* 1216 Cole Street, San Francisco, CA 94117, USA.

GUNN, Sir William (Archer), AC 1990; KBE 1961; CMG 1955; JP; Australian grazier and company director; Chairman, International Wool Secretariat, 1961–73; *b* Goondiwindi, Qld, 1 Feb. 1914; *s* of late Walter and Doris Isabel Gunn, Goondiwindi; *m* 1939, Mary (Phillipa), *d* of F. B. Haydon, Murrurundi, NSW; one *s* two *d*. *Educ:* The King's Sch., Parramatta, NSW. Director: Rothmans of Pall Mall (Australia) Ltd; Grazcos Co-op. Ltd; Clausen Steamship Co. (Australia) Pty Ltd; Walter Reid and Co. Ltd; Gunn Rural Management Pty Ltd; Chairman and Managing Director: Moline Pastoral Co. Pty Ltd; Roper Valley Pty Ltd; Coolibah Pty Ltd; Mataranba Pty Ltd; Unibeef Australia Pty Ltd; Gunn Development Pty Ltd; Chairman: Australian Wool Bd, 1963–72; Qld Adv. Bd, Develt Finance Corp., 1962–72; Member: Commonwealth Bank Bd, 1952–59; Qld Bd, Nat. Mutual Life Assoc., 1955–67; Reserve Bank Bd, 1959–; Aust. Meat Bd, 1953–66; Aust. Wool Bureau, 1951–63 (Chm. 1958–63); Aust. Wool Growers Council, 1947–60 (Chm. 1955–58); Graziers Federal Council of Aust., 1950–60 (Pres. 1951–54); Aust. Wool Growers and Graziers Council, 1960–65; Export Develt Council, 1962–65; Australian Wool Corp., 1973; Faculty of Veterinary Science, University of Qld, 1953–; Exec. Council, United Graziers Assoc. of Qld, 1944–69 (Pres., 1951–59; Vice-Pres., 1947–51); Aust. Wool Testing Authority, 1958–63; Council, NFU of Aust., 1951–54; CSIRO State Cttee, 1951–68; Chairman: The Wool Bureau Inc., New York, 1962–69; Trustee: Qld Cancer Fund; Australian Pastoral Research Trust, 1959–71. Coronation Medal, 1953; Golden Fleece Achievement Award (Bd of Dirs of Nat. Assoc. of Wool Manufrs of America), 1962; Award of Golden Ram (Natal Woolgrowers Assoc. of SA), 1973. *Address:* Unit 15, 145 Moray Street, New Farm, Qld 4005, Australia. *Clubs:* Queensland, Tattersalls, Queensland Turf (Brisbane); Union (Sydney); Australian (Melbourne).

GUNNELL, Sally, MBE 1993; athlete; *b* 29 July 1966; *m* 1992, Jonathan Bigg. *Educ:* Chigwell High School. Member, Essex Ladies' Club, 1978–; GB Team Captain, 1992–; 400 m hurdles wins include: Olympic Champion, 1992; World Champion, 1993; World Record Holder, 1993; European Champion, 1994; Commonwealth Champion, 1994; also Commonwealth Champion, 100 m hurdles, 1986, 1990. *Publication:* Running Tall, 1994. *Address:* 18 Shepherds Croft, Brighton, East Sussex BN1 5JF.

GUNNELL, (William) John; MP (Lab) Leeds South and Morley, since 1992; *b* 1 Oct. 1933; *s* of late William Henry and Norah Gunnell; *m* 1955, Jean Louise, *d* of late Frank and Harriet Louise Lacey; three *s* one *d*. *Educ:* King Edward's Sch., Birmingham; Univ. of Leeds (BSc Hons). Hospital porter, St Bartholomew's, London, 1955–57; Teacher, Leeds Modern Sch., 1959–62; Head of Science, United Nations International Sch., New York, 1962–70; Lectr, Centre for Studies in Science and Mathematics Education, Univ. of Leeds, 1970–88. County Councillor for Hunslet, 1977–86; Leader of Opposition, 1979–81, Leader, 1981–86, W Yorks MCC; Mem. for Hunslet, Leeds MDC, 1986–92 (Chm., Social Services Cttee, 1990–92). Chm., Crown Point Foods, 1988–90. Chairman: Yorkshire Enterprise Ltd (formerly W Yorks Enterprise Bd), 1982–90 and 1994– (Vice-Chm., 1990–94); Chm., Yorkshire Fund Management Ltd, 1989–. Chairman: Yorks and Humberside Develt Assoc., 1981–93; Leeds/Bradford Airport jt cttee, 1981–83; N of England Regional Consortium, 1984–92; Member: Audit Commn, 1983–90; Leeds Develt Corp., 1988–92; Leeds Eastern AHA, later Leeds Health Care, 1990–92. Advr to Conseil des Régions d'Europe, subseq. Assembly of Regions of Europe, 1986– (Mem. Bureau, 1985–86). Hon. Pres., RETI, 1985–87. Spokesman for MCCs in their campaign against abolition, 1983–85. Mem., Fabian Soc., 1972–. Director: Opera North, 1982–; Leeds Theatre Trust, 1986–93; Belle Isle North Estate Management, 1990–92. *Publications:* Selected Experiments in Advanced Level Chemistry, 1975, and other texts (all with E. W. Jenkins); (contrib.) Local Economic Policy, 1990. *Recreations:* music, opera, watching cricket and soccer. *Address:* 6 Arthington View, Hunslet, Leeds LS10 2ND. *T:* Leeds (0113) 277 0592, (constituency) Leeds (0113) 247 7138; House of Commons, SW1A 0AA. *T:* 0171–219 4549. *Clubs:* East Hunslet Labour (Leeds); Warwickshire CC; Yorkshire CC.

GUNNING, Prof. Brian Edgar Scourse, FRS 1980; FAA 1979; Professor of Plant Cell Biology, Australian National University, since 1974; *b* 29 Nov. 1934; *s* of William Gunning and Margaret Gunning (*née* Scourse); *m* 1964, Marion Sylvia Forsyth; two *s*. *Educ:* Methodist Coll., Belfast; Queen's Univ., Belfast (BSc (Hons), MSc, PhD); DSc ANU. Lecturer in Botany, 1957, Reader in Botany, 1965, Queen's Univ., Belfast. *Publications:* Ultrastructure and the Biology of Plant Cells (with Dr M. Steer), 1975; Intercellular Communication in Plants: studies on plasmodesmata (with Dr A. Robards), 1976; contribs to research jls. *Recreations:* hill walking, photography. *Address:* 29 Millen Street, Hughes, ACT 2605, Australia. *T:* (6) 2812879.

GUNNING, Sir Charles Theodore, 9th Bt *cr* 1778, of Eltham, Kent; CD 1964; RCN retired; *b* 19 June 1935; *s* of Sir Robert Gunning, 8th Bt and of Helen Nancy, *d* of Vice-Adm. Sir Theodore John Hallett, KBE, CB; *S* father, 1989; *m* 1st, 1969, Sarah (marr. diss. 1982), *d* of Col Patrick Arthur Easton; one *d*; 2nd, 1989, Linda Martin (*née* Kachmar). *Educ:* Canadian Mil. Coll.; RNEC Plymouth; Tech. Univ. of NS. PEng, AMIMechE; AMIMarE. Chm., Nat. Council in Canada, Royal Commonwealth Soc., 1990–93 (Pres., Ottawa Br.; a Nat. Vice-Chm.). Silver Jubilee Medal, 1977. *Heir: b* John Robert Gunning [*b* 17 Sept. 1944; *m* 1969, Alina Tylicki; two *s* one *d*]. *Address:* 2940 McCarthy Road, Ottawa, Ont K1V 8K6, Canada.

GUNSTON, Sir John (Wellesley), 3rd Bt *cr* 1938, of Wickwar, Co. Gloucester; freelance photojournalist; *b* 25 July 1962; *s* of Sir Richard Gunston, 2nd Bt and of Mrs Joan Elizabeth Marie Gunston; *S* father, 1991; *m* 1990, Rosalind (publisher, co. director), *y d* of Edward Gordon Eliott; one *s*. *Educ:* Harrow; RMA Sandhurst. BSAP Reserve, Rhodesia, 1979–80. Commnd 1st Bn Irish Guards, 1981. Since 1983 has covered wars, revolutions and foreign travel assignments in: Afghanistan, Albania, Brazil, Burma, Colombia, Egypt, Eritrea, Israel (West Bank and Gaza), Lebanon, Liberia, South Africa, Sudan, Uganda, Ulster and also in North America, Eastern Europe and South East Asia. FRGS 1988. *Recreations:* books, biking, ballistics. *Heir: s* Richard St George Gunston, *b* 3 July 1992. *Address:* c/o 127 Piccadilly, W1E 6YZ. *Clubs:* Cavalry and Guards, Special Forces.

GUNTER, John Forsyth; freelance designer; Associate Designer, Royal National Theatre, since 1991 (Head of Design, 1989–91); *b* 31 Oct. 1938; *s* of Herbert and Charlotte Gunter; *m* 1969, Micheline McKnight; two *d*. *Educ:* Bryanston Public Sch.; Central Sch. of Art and Design (Dip. with distinction). Started career in rep. theatre in GB; Resident Designer: English Stage Co., 1965–66 (subseq. designed 28 prodns for co.); Zürich Schauspielhaus, 1970–73; freelance design work for West End, NT, RSC and for Broadway, New York, 1973–; designer of operas: for cos in GB, Italy, Germany, Austria, Australia and USA; Glyndebourne Fest. Op., 1985–; La Scala, Milan, 1988. Head, Theatre Dept, Central Sch. of Art and Design, 1974–82. FRSA 1982. Many awards for design of Guys and Dolls, NT, 1982, incl. SWET Award for Best Design 1982, Drama Magazine Best Design Award 1982, Plays and Players Award for Best Design 1983; Plays and Players and Olivier Awards for Best Design 1984, for design of Wild Honey, NT, 1984; Emmy Award, 1994, for Porgy and Bess. *Recreations:* getting out into the countryside, tennis. *Address:* c/o Peter Murphy, Curtis Brown, 4th Floor, Haymarket House, 28–29 Haymarket, SW1Y 4SP.

GUNTON, Rev. Prof. Colin Ewart, DPhil, DD; Professor of Christian Doctrine, King's College, University of London, since 1984; *b* 19 Jan. 1941; *s* of Herbert Ewart Gunton and Mabel Priscilla Gunton; *m* 1964, Jennifer Mary Osgathorpe; two *s* two *d*. *Educ:* Nottingham High Sch.; Hertford Coll., Oxford (Schol; BA Lit. Hum. 1964); Mansfield Coll., Oxford (BA Theol. 1966; MA 1967; DPhil 1973); DD London 1993. Ordained Minister, United Reform Ch., 1972; Associate Minister, Brentwood URC, 1975–. King's College, London: Lectr in Philosophy of Religion, 1969–80; Lectr in Systematic Theol., 1980–83; Sen. Lectr, 1983–84; Dean, Faculty of Theol. and Religious Studies, 1988–90; Head, Dept of Theol. and Religious Studies, 1994–. Bampton Lectr, Univ. of Oxford, 1992; Warfield Lectr, Princeton Theol Seminary, 1993. Pres., Soc. for Study of Theol., 1993–94. *Publications:* Becoming and Being: the doctrine of God in Charles Hartshorne and Karl Barth, 1978; Yesterday and Today: a study of continuities in Christology, 1983; Enlightenment and Alienation: an essay towards a Trinitarian Theology, 1985; The Actuality of Atonement: a study of metaphor, rationality and the Christian Tradition, 1989; (ed with D. W. Hardy) On Being the Church: essays on the Christian Community, 1989; The Promise of Trinitarian Theology, 1991; (ed with C. Schwoebel) Persons,

Divine and Human: King's College essays in theological anthropology, 1992; Christ and Creation: the 1990 Didsbury Lectures, 1993; The One, the Three and the Many: God, Creation and the Culture of Modernity (Bampton Lectures), 1993; A Brief Theology of Revelation (Warfield Lectures), 1995; (ed) God and Freedom: essays in historical and systematic theology, 1995; contrib. to Scottish Jl of Theol., Jl of Theol Studies, Religious Studies, Mod. Theol., Theol., Expository Times, Theol. Today. *Recreations:* music, gardening, walking. *Address:* Department of Theology and Religious Studies, King's College, Strand, WC2R 2LS. *T:* 0171–873 2459; 33 South Drive, Brentwood, Essex CM14 5DL. *T:* Brentwood (01277) 221585.

GURDON, family name of **Baron Cranworth.**

GURDON, Sir John Bertrand, Kt 1995; DPhil; FRS 1971; Master, Magdalene College, Cambridge, since 1995; John Humphrey Plummer Professor of Cell Biology, University of Cambridge, since 1983; Chairman, Wellcome Cancer Research Campaign Institute, Cambridge, since 1991; *b* 2 Oct. 1933; *s* of late W. N. Gurdon, DCM, formerly of Assington, Suffolk, and of late Elsie Marjorie (*née* Byass); *m* 1964, Jean Elizabeth Margaret Curtis; one *s* one *d. Educ:* Edgeborough; Eton (Fellow, 1978); Christ Church, Oxford; BA 1956; DPhil 1960. Beit Memorial Fellow, 1958–61; Gosney Research Fellow, Calif. Inst. Technol., 1962; Departmental Demonstrator, Dept of Zool., Oxford, 1963–64; Vis. Research Fellow, Carnegie Instn, Baltimore, 1965; Lectr, Dept of Zoology, Oxford, 1965–72; Research Student, Christ Church, 1962–72; Mem. Staff, MRC Lab. of Molecular Biology, Cambridge, 1972–83 (Hd, Cell Biology Div., 1979–83); Fellow, Churchill Coll., Cambridge, 1973–94. Fullerian Prof. of Physiology and Comparative Anatomy, Royal Instn, 1985–91. Lectures: Harvey Soc., NY, 1973; Dunham, Harvard, 1974; Croonian, Royal Soc., 1976; Carter-Wallace, Princeton, 1978; Woodhull, Royal Instn, 1980; Florey, Aust., 1988. Pres., Internat. Soc. Develt Biol., 1989–93. Gov., The Wellcome Trust, 1995–. Hon. Foreign Mem., Amer. Acad. of Arts and Scis, 1978; Foreign Associate: Nat. Acad. of Sciences, USA, 1980; Belgian Royal Acad. of Scis, Letters and Fine Arts, 1984; Foreign Mem., Amer. Philos. Soc., 1983. Hon. Student, Christ Church, Oxford, 1985. Hon. DSc: Chicago, 1978; René Descartes, Paris, 1982; Oxford, 1988. Albert Brachet Prize (Belgian Royal Academy), 1968; Scientific Medal of Zoological Soc., 1968; Feldberg Foundn Award, 1975; Paul Ehrlich Award, 1977; Nessim Habif Prize, Univ. of Geneva, 1979; CIBA Medal, Biochem. Soc., 1980; Comfort Crookshank Award for Cancer Research, 1983; William Bate Hardy Prize, Cambridge Philos. Soc., 1984; Prix Charles Léopold Mayer, Acad. des Scis, France, 1984; Ross Harrison Prize, Internat. Soc. Develt Biol., 1985; Royal Medal, Royal Soc., 1985; Emperor Hirohito Internat. Prize for Biology, Japan Acad., 1987; Wolf Prize in Medicine, Israel, 1989. *Publications:* Control of Gene Expression in Animal Development, 1974; articles in scientific jls, especially on nuclear transplantation. *Recreations:* skiing, tennis, horticulture, Lepidoptera. *Address:* The Master's Lodge, Magdalene College, Cambridge CB3 0AG. *Club:* Eagle Ski.

GURNEY, Nicholas Bruce Jonathan; City Manager, Portsmouth City Council, since 1994; *b* 20 Jan. 1945; *s* of Bruce William George Gurney and Cynthia Joan Watkins Mason (*née* Winn); *m* 1st, 1970, Patricia Wendy Tulip (marr. diss. 1987); two *s* one *d*; 2nd, 1989, Caroline Mary (*née* Bentley). *Educ:* Wimbledon College; Christ's College, Cambridge. BA 1966, MA 1969. Lectr in English, Belize Teachers' Training College, Belize, as part of British Volunteer Programme, 1966–67; MoD 1967; Asst Private Sec., Minister of State for Defence, 1970–72; Civil Service Dept, 1972–74; Private Sec. to Lord Privy Seal and Leader of House of Lords, 1974–77; Civil Service Dept and Management Personnel Office, 1978–83; Grade 3, Cabinet Office, and CS Comr, 1983–88; Dept of Health, 1988–90; Chief Exec., Wokingham DC, 1990–93. *Address:* Civic Offices, Guildhall Square, Portsmouth PO1 2AL.

GURNEY, Oliver Robert, MA, DPhil Oxon; FBA 1959; Shillito Reader in Assyriology, Oxford University, 1945–78; Professor, 1965; Fellow of Magdalen College, 1963–78, now Emeritus; *b* 28 Jan. 1911; *s* of Robert Gurney, DSc, and Sarah Gamzu, MBE, *d* of Walter Garstang, MD, MRCP; *m* 1957, Mrs Diane Hope Grazebrook (*née* Esencourt); no *c. Educ:* Eton Coll.; New Coll., Oxford. Served War of 1939–45, in Royal Artillery and Sudan Defence Force. Freeman of City of Norwich. For. Mem., Royal Danish Acad. of Sciences and Letters, 1976. Pres., British Institute of Archaeology at Ankara, 1983–. Hon. DHL Chicago, 1991. *Publications:* The Hittites (Penguin), 1952; (with J. J. Finkelstein and P. Hulin) The Sultantepe Tablets, 1957, 1964; (with John Garstang) The Geography of the Hittite Empire, 1959; Ur Excavations, Texts, VII, 1974; Oxford Editions of Cuneiform Texts V (with S. N. Kramer), 1976, XI, 1989; Some Aspects of Hittite Religion (Schweich Lectures, 1976), 1977; The Middle Babylonian Legal and Economic Texts from Ur, 1983; Oxford Editions of Cuneiform Texts XI, 1989; articles in Annals of Archæology and Anthropology (Liverpool), Anatolian Studies, etc. *Recreation:* golf. *Address:* Fir Tree House, 10 Milton Lane, Steventon, Abingdon, Oxon OX13 6SA. *T:* Abingdon (01235) 831212.

GURR, Prof. Michael Ian; Maypole Scientific Services, private nutrition consultancy, since 1990; Visiting Professor: University of Reading, since 1986; Oxford Brookes University (formerly Oxford Polytechnic), since 1990; *b* 10 April 1939; *s* of Henry Ormonde Gurr and Hilda Ruth Gurr; *m* 1963, Elizabeth Anne Mayers; two *s* one *d. Educ:* Dunstable Grammar Sch.; Univ. of Birmingham (BSc, PhD). Postdoctoral Fellowship, Harvard Univ., 1964–66; Unilever European Fellowship of Biochem. Soc., State Univ. of Utrecht, 1966–67; Res. Scientist, Unilever Res. Lab., Sharnbrook, Bedford, 1967–78; Hd, Department of Nutrition, Nat. Inst. for Res. in Dairying, Shinfield, Reading, 1978–85; Dir, Reading Lab. of AFRC Inst. of Food Res., 1985–86; Nutrition Consultant and Hd of Nutrition Dept, MMB, 1986–90. Chairman: Editl Bd, British Jl of Nutrition, 1988–90; Editl Adv. Bd, British Nutrition Foundn, 1994–; Man. Ed., Nutrition Research Reviews, 1991–. *Publications:* Lipid Biochemistry: an introduction (jtly), 1971, 4th edn 1991; Role of Fats in Food and Nutrition, 1984, 2nd edn 1992; numerous original pubns and reviews. *Recreations:* sailing, walking, photography, piano playing. *Address:* Vale View Cottage, Maypole, St Mary's, Isles of Scilly TR21 0NU. *T:* Scillonia (01720) 422224.

GUTFREUND, Prof. Herbert, FRS 1981; Professor of Physical Biochemistry, University of Bristol, 1972–86, now Emeritus; Scientific Member (external), Max-Planck-Institut für medizinische Forschung, Heidelberg, since 1987; *b* 21 Oct. 1921; *s* of late Paul Peter Gutfreund and Clara Angela (*née* Pisko); *m* 1958, Mary Kathelen, *er d* of late Mr and Mrs L. J. Davies, Rugby; two *s* one *d. Educ:* Vienna; Univ. of Cambridge (PhD). Research appts at Cambridge Univ., 1947–57; Rockefeller Fellow, Yale Univ., 1951–52; part-time Research Associate, Yale Univ., 1953–58; Principal Scientific Officer, National Inst. for Research in Dairying, Univ. of Reading, 1957–65; Visiting Professor: Univ. of California, 1965; Max Planck Inst., Göttingen, 1966–67; Reader in Biochemistry and Director of Molecular Enzymology Laboratory, Univ. of Bristol, 1967–72. Visiting appointments: Univ. of Leuven, 1972; Univ. of Adelaide, 1979; Univ. of Alberta, 1983. Part-time Scholar in Residence, NIH, Bethesda, 1986–89. Hon. Mem., Amer. Soc. for Biochem. and Molecular Biol., 1993. *Publications:* An Introduction to the Study of Enzymes, 1966; Enzymes: Physical Principles, 1972; (ed) Chemistry of Macromolecules, 1974; (ed) Biochemical Evolution, 1981; Biothermodynamics, 1983; Kinetics for the Life Sciences, 1995; papers and reviews on many aspects of physical biochemistry. *Recreations:* mountain walking in Austria, gardening, reading general literature and philosophy of science, listening to music and all other good things in life. *Address:* University of Bristol Medical School, University Walk, Bristol BS8 1TD. *T:* Bristol (0117) 930 3910; 12a The Avenue, Bristol BS9 1PA. *T:* Bristol (0117) 968 4453. *Club:* United Oxford & Cambridge University.

GUTFREUND, John Halle; Chairman, President and Chief Executive, Salomon Inc, 1986–91; Chairman and Chief Executive, Salomon Brothers Inc, 1981–91; *b* 14 Sept. 1929; *s* of B. Manuel Gutfreund and Mary Halle Gutfreund; *m* 1st, 1958, Joyce L. Gutfreund; three *s*; 2nd, 1981, Susan K. Gutfreund; one *s. Educ:* Oberlin College, Ohio (BA 1951). Served in Army, 1951–53; Salomon Brothers, 1953–91: Exec. Partner, 1966; Managing Partner, 1978; Chief Exec., 1981–91, Chm. and Pres., 1986–91, Salomon Inc. Vice-Chm., NY Stock Exchange, 1985–87; formerly: Mem., Bd of Dirs, Securities Industry Assoc.; Mem., Bd of Govs and Pres., Bond Club of NY; Chm., Downtown-Lower Manhattan Assoc.; Chm., Wall Street Cttee for Lincoln Center's 1986–87 Corporate Fund Campaign. Mem., Council on Foreign Relations and Tri-Lateral Commn. Dir, Montefiore Medical Center Corp. (Mem. Exec. Cttee, Bd of Trustees; Mem., Financial and Real Estate Cttees); Mem., Bd of Trustees and Finance Cttee, NY Public Library (Vice-Chm., Corporate Congress); Hon. Trustee, Oberlin Coll. Hon. DH Oberlin Coll., 1987. *Address:* 712 Fifth Avenue, 38th Floor, New York, NY 10019, USA. *T:* (212) 9561190.

GUTHARDT, Rev. Dame Phyllis (Myra), DBE 1993; PhD; retired Methodist minister; *b* 1 Aug. 1929; *d* of Johan Detlef Guthardt and Amelia Guthardt. *Educ:* Auckland Univ. (BA 1957); Canterbury Univ. (MA 1959); Newnham Coll., Cambridge (PhD 1963). Primary school teacher, 1950–53; Methodist theol trng, 1954–56; ordained, 1959 (first woman ordained in NZ); active ministry in Methodist and Presbyterian parishes, incl. hosp. and univ. chaplaincy, 1957–90. Pres., Methodist Ch. of NZ, 1985–86; Mem. Praesidium, World Methodist Council, 1986–91. Pro-Chancellor, Univ. of Canterbury, 1992– (Mem. Council, 1981–). Hon. Dr Waikato, 1986. *Publications:* contrib. theol jls. *Recreations:* music, reading, restoring house, gardening. *Address:* 29 Merlincote Crescent, Governors Bay, RD1 Lyttelton, New Zealand. *T:* (3) 3299675.

GUTHRIE, Gen. Sir Charles (Ronald Llewelyn), GCB 1994 (KCB 1990); LVO 1977; OBE 1980; Chief of the General Staff, since 1994; Aide-de-Camp General to the Queen, since 1993; *b* 17 Nov. 1938; *s* of late Ronald Guthrie and Nina (*née* Llewelyn); *m* 1971, Catherine, *er d* of late Lt Col Claude Worrall, MVO, OBE, Coldstream Guards; two *s. Educ:* Harrow; RMA Sandhurst. Commnd Welsh Guards, 1959; served: BAOR, Aden; 22 SAS Regt, 1965–69; psc 1972; MA (GSO2) to CGS, MoD, 1973–74; Brigade Major, Household Div., 1976–77; Comdg 1st Bn Welsh Guards, Berlin and N Ireland, 1977–80; Col GS Military Ops, MoD, 1980–82; Commander: British Forces New Hebrides, 1980; 4th Armoured Brigade, 1982–84; Chief of Staff 1st (BR) Corps, 1984–86; GOC NE Dist and Comdr 2nd Infantry Div., 1986–87; ACGS, MoD, 1987–89; Comdr 1 (BR) Corps, 1989–91; Comdr Northern Army Gp, 1992–93; C-in-C BAOR, 1992–94. Col Comdt, Intelligence Corps, 1986–. President: Army Saddle Club, 1991–; Army LTA, 1991–. Freeman, City of London, 1988; Liveryman, Painter Stainers' Co., 1989. *Recreations:* tennis, ski-ing, travel. *Address:* c/o Lloyds Bank, Knightsbridge Branch, 79 Brompton Road, SW3 1DD. *Clubs:* White's, Beefsteak.

See also J. D. Guthrie.

GUTHRIE, Rev. Donald Angus; Rector, Holy Spirit Episcopal Church, Missoula, Montana, 1979–93; *b* 18 Jan. 1931; *s* of Frederick Charles and Alison Guthrie; *m* 1st, 1959, Joyce Adeline Blunsden (*d* 1976); two *s* one *d*; 2nd, 1977, Lesley Josephine Boardman (marr. diss. 1983); 3rd, 1984, Carolyn Wallop Alderson. *Educ:* Marlborough Coll.; Trinity Coll., Oxford (MA). Rector, St John's Church, Selkirk, 1963–69; Vice-Principal, Episcopal Theological Coll., Edinburgh, 1969–74; Priest-in-Charge, Whitburn Parish Church, Tyne and Wear, 1974–76; Provost, St Paul's Cathedral, Dundee, 1976–77; Episcopal Chaplain to Univ. of Montana, 1977–79. *Recreations:* walking, reading. *Address:* 655 West Mountain View Drive, Missoula, MT 59802, USA.

GUTHRIE, (Garth) Michael; Founder Director, 1990, Chairman and Chief Executive, since 1991, BrightReasons Group plc; *b* 30 April 1941; *s* of Harry and Ann Guthrie; *m* 1963, Joyce Fox; one *s* two *d. Educ:* Blackpool Catering Coll. (FHCIMA). Joined Mecca Leisure, 1961; Man. Dir, 1980; Chm., 1981–90; Chief Exec., 1985–90. Non-exec. Chm., Cascade Clubs Hldgs, 1992. *Recreations:* ski-ing, swimming, gardening. *Address:* BrightReasons Group plc, Bakers House, 25 Bakers Road, Uxbridge, Mddx UB8 1RG. *T:* Uxbridge (01895) 811911.

GUTHRIE, James Dalglish; QC 1993; *b* 21 Feb. 1950; *s* of late Ronald Guthrie and Nina Guthrie (*née* Llewelyn); *m* 1981, Lucille Gay Page-Roberts; one *s* one *d. Educ:* Harrow; Worcester Coll., Oxford (BA Modern History). Called to the Bar, Inner Temple, 1975. *Recreations:* fishing, painting, travel. *Address:* 1 Crown Office Row, Temple, EC4Y 7HH. *T:* 0171–583 9292. *Club:* Turf.

See also Gen. Sir C. R. L. Guthrie.

GUTHRIE, Sir Malcolm (Connop), 3rd Bt *cr* 1936; *b* 16 Dec. 1942; *s* of Sir Giles Connop McEacharn Guthrie, 2nd Bt, OBE, DSC, and of Rhona, *d* of late Frederic Stileman; *S* father, 1979; *m* 1967, Victoria, *o d* of late Brian Willcock; one *s* one *d. Educ:* Millfield. *Heir: s* Giles Malcolm Welcome Guthrie, *b* 16 Oct. 1972. *Address:* Brent Eleigh, Belbroughton, Stourbridge, Worcestershire DY9 0DW.

GUTHRIE, Michael; *see* Guthrie, G. M.

GUTHRIE, Robert Isles Loftus, (Robin); Director of Social and Economic Affairs, Council of Europe, since 1992; *b* 27 June 1937; *s* of late Prof. W. K. C. Guthrie, FBA and of Adele Marion Ogilvy, MA; *m* 1963, Sarah Julia Weltman; two *s* one *d. Educ:* Clifton Coll.; Trinity Coll., Cambridge (MA); Liverpool Univ. (CertEd); LSE (MScEcon). Head of Cambridge House (Univ. settlement in S London), 1962–69; teacher, ILEA, 1964–66; Social Develt Officer, Peterborough Develt Corp., 1969–75; Asst Dir, Social Work Service, DHSS, 1975–79; Dir, Joseph Rowntree Meml Trust, 1979–88; Chief Charity Comr for England and Wales, 1988–92. Mem., expedns in Anatolia, British Inst. of Archaeol. at Ankara, 1958–62. Member: Arts Council of GB, 1979–81 and 1987–88 (Regional Cttee, 1976–81); Council, Policy Studies Institute, 1979–88; Council, York Univ., 1982–; Chairman: Yorkshire Arts Assoc., 1984–88; Council of Regional Arts Assocs, 1985–88. FRSA. Hon. DLitt Bradford, 1991. *Publications:* (ed) Outlook, 1963; (ed) Outlook Two, 1965; articles, esp. in New Society. *Recreations:* music, mountains, travel, sheep. *Address:* Braeside, Acomb, York YO2 4EZ.

GUTHRIE, Roy David, (Gus), PhD, DSc; CChem, FRSC, FRACI; FAIM; Vice-Chancellor and President, University of Technology, Sydney, 1988–March 1996. (President, NSW Institute of Technology, 1986–87); *b* 29 March 1934; *s* of David Ephraim Guthrie and Ethel (*née* Kimmins); *m* 1st, 1956, Ann Hoad (marr. diss. 1981); three *s*; 2nd, 1982, Lyn Fielding. *Educ:* Dorking Grammar Sch.; King's Coll., Univ. of London (BSc, PhD, DSc). Shirley Inst., Manchester, 1958–60; Asst Lectr, then Lectr, Univ. of Leicester, 1960–63; Lectr, then Reader, Univ. of Sussex, 1963–73; Griffith University, Brisbane: Foundation Prof. of Chemistry, 1973–81; Inaugural Chm., School of Science, 1973–78; Pro-Vice-Chancellor, 1980–81; Professor Emeritus, 1982; Sec. Gen., Royal Soc. of Chemistry, 1982–85. Hon. DUniv Griffith, 1981. *Publications:* An Introduction to the Chemistry of Carbohydrates (with J. Honeyman), 2nd edn 1964, 3rd edn 1968, 4th edn 1974; over 130 scientific papers. *Recreations:* theatre, music, antique maps, croquet. *Address:* University of Technology, Sydney, Broadway, NSW 2007, Australia. *T:* (2) 3301330.

GUTTERIDGE, Prof. William Frank, MBE (mil.) 1946; Director, Research Institute for the Study of Conflict and Terrorism, since 1994; *b* 21 Sept. 1919; *s* of Frank Leonard Gutteridge and Nora Conwy (*née* Tighe); *m* 1944, Margaret McCallum Parker; three *d*. *Educ:* Stamford Sch., Lincs; Hertford Coll., Oxford (MA Mod. Hist., DipEd). Served War, 1939–46: commnd Manchester Regt; India/Burma, 1942/45: Staff Officer, 33 Indian Corps, finally DAAG 2nd British Div. Sen. Lectr in Commonwealth Hist. and Govt, RMA Sandhurst, 1949–63; Nuffield Foundn/Home CS Travelling Fellow studying rôle of Armed Forces in Commonwealth Africa, 1960–61; Hd, Langs and Mod. Studies Dept, Lanchester Poly., Coventry, 1963–71; Aston University: Dir, Complementary Studies, 1971–80; Prof. of Internat. Studies, 1976–82; Hd, Pol and Econ. Studies Dept, 1980–82; Prof. Emeritus, 1982; Editl Cons., Inst. for Study of Conflict, 1982–89; Exec. and Editl Dir, Res. Inst. for Study of Conflict and Terrorism, 1989–94. Sec., Brit. Pugwash Gp for Sci. and World Affairs, 1965–86. Chm., CNAA Cttee for Arts and Social Studies, 1978–84. *Publications:* Armed Forces in New States, 1962; Military Institutions and Power in New States, 1965; The Military in African Politics, 1969; Military Regimes in Africa, 1975; The New Terrorism, 1986; South Africa from Apartheid to National Unity 1981–94, 1995; South Africa's Defence and Security Forces into the 21st Century, 1995. *Recreations:* research, writing. *Address:* 26 St Mark's Road, Leamington Spa, Warwickshire CV32 6DL. *T:* Leamington Spa (01926) 425276.

GUY, Geoffrey Colin, CMG 1964; CVO 1966; OBE 1962 (MBE 1957); Governor and Commander in Chief, St Helena and its Dependencies, 1976–81, retired; first elected Speaker of the Legislative Council, St Helena, 1989; *b* 4 Nov. 1921; *s* of late E. Guy, 14 Woodland Park Road, Headingley, Leeds, and of Constance Reed Guy (*née* Taylor); *m* 1946, Joan Elfreda Smith; one *s*. *Educ:* Chatham House Sch., Ramsgate; Brasenose Coll., Oxford. Served RAF, 1941–46: reconnaissance pilot Spitfires and Hurricanes, Middle East and Burma, 1943–45; Special Force 136, 1945 (Flight Lieut). Asst Ed., Courtaulds Works Mag., 1948; management staff, Scribbans-Kemp Ltd, 1948–51; Colonial Administrative Service, Sierra Leone: Cadet, 1951; Asst Sec. Chief Comr Protectorate, 1953–54; District Comr, Tonkolili Dist, 1955; Administrator, Turks and Caicos Islands, and Chm. and Man. Dir, Turks Island Salt Co., 1958–65; Administrator, Dominica, 1965–67, Governor, March-Nov. 1967; Asst Sec., Soil Assoc., 1968; Sec., Forces Help Soc. and Lord Roberts' Workshops, 1970–73; Administrator, Ascension Island, 1973–76. *Recreations:* reading, walking, swimming. *Address:* Tamarisk Cottage, Kirk Hammerton, York YO5 8DA. *Clubs:* Commonwealth Trust, Royal Air Force, Victory Services.

GUY, John Westgarth, OBE 1986; HM Diplomatic Service; Consul General, St Petersburg, since 1995; *b* 17 July 1941; *s* of late John Westgarth Guy and Stella (*née* Sanderson); *m* 1961, Sylvia Kathleen Stokes; one *s* one *d*. *Educ:* Queen Mary's Sch. for Boys, Basingstoke. CRO, 1960; Karachi, 1961–63; Calcutta, 1964–67; Vice Consul, New York, 1968–70; FCO, 1970–72; Third Secretary: Moscow, 1972–73; Jakarta, 1974; Second Sec., São Paulo, 1975–77; FCO, 1977–79; DTI, 1979–80; First Secretary: Yaoundé, 1981–84; Maputo, 1984–87; FCO, 1987–91; High Comr, PNG, 1991–94; RCDS, 1995. *Recreations:* squash, golf, sailing. *Address:* c/o Foreign and Commonwealth Office, King Charles Street, SW1A 2AH.

GUY, (Leslie) George; Assistant Secretary, Craft Sector, Amalgamated Union of Engineering Workers/Technical Administrative and Supervisory Section, 1983–84, retired; *b* 1 Sept. 1918; *s* of Albert and Annie Guy; *m* 1940, Audrey Doreen (*née* Symonds); two *d*. *Educ:* secondary modern school. National Union of Sheet Metal Workers: shop steward; Member: Branch and District Cttees; Nat. Executive Cttee; National President, June 1972–74; Asst General Secretary, 1974–77; Gen. Sec., Nat. Union of Sheet Metal Workers, Coppersmiths, Heating and Domestic Engrs, 1977–83, when Union transferred its engagements to AEUW/TASS. Member: General Council, TUC, 1977–83; Exec., CSEU, 1977–84; Engrg Industry Trng Bd, 1979–84; Council, Marine Training Assoc., 1983–. *Recreations:* work and politics.

GUY, Captain Robert Lincoln, LVO 1980; RN; *b* 4 Sept. 1947; *s* of late John Guy and Susan Guy; *m* 1981, Rosemary Ann Walker. *Educ:* Radley Coll. Entered BRNC Dartmouth, 1966; ADC to Governor and Commander-in-Chief, Gibraltar, 1973; commanded: HMS Ashton, 1974; HMS Kedleston, 1975; HMS Sirius, 1984–85. Equerry to the Queen, 1977–80; First Lieut, HMS Antelope, 1981–82. Lieut 1971; Lt-Comdr 1979; Comdr 1983; Captain 1991. *Recreations:* polo, skiing, shooting. *Address:* Stable House, South Warnborough, Basingstoke, Hants RG25 1RQ. *T:* Basingstoke (01256) 862254. *Club:* White's.

GUY, Gen. Sir Roland (Kelvin), GCB 1987 (KCB 1981); CBE 1978 (MBE 1955); DSO 1972; Governor, Royal Hospital, Chelsea, 1987–93; *b* 25 June 1928; *s* of Lt-Col Norman Greenwood Guy and Mrs Edna Guy; *m* 1957, Dierdre, *d* of Brig. P. H. Graves Morris, DSO, MC, and Mrs Auriol Graves-Morris; two *d*. *Educ:* Wellington Coll.; RMA Sandhurst. Commnd KRRC, 1948; 1950–71: Signals Officer, Germany; Adjt Kenya Regt, and 2 KRRC; Weapon Trng Officer 1 KRRC; Staff Coll., Camberley; MoD; Co. Comdr 2 RGJ; DS Staff Coll.; Bn 2 i/c; Mil. Asst to Adjt Gen.; CO 1 RGJ; Col GS HQ Near East Land Forces, 1971; Comd 24 Airportable Bde, 1972; RCDS, 1975; Principal SO to CDS, 1976–78; Chief of Staff, HQ BAOR, 1978–80; Mil. Sec., 1980–83; Adjt Gen., 1984–86; ADC Gen. to the Queen, 1984–87; served in Kenya, Libya, British Guiana, Cyprus, Malaysia, W Germany and Berlin. Col Comdt: 1st Bn Royal Green Jackets, 1981–86 (Rep. Col Comdt, 1985–86); Small Arms School Corps, 1981–87. Chairman: Army Benevolent Fund, 1987–93; Royal Cambridge Home for Soldiers' Widows, 1987–93; Council of Management, PDSA, 1994–. Governor: Wellington Coll., 1987– (Vice Pres., 1990–); Milton Abbey Sch., 1987–. *Recreations:* music, travel, gardening. *Address:* c/o Grindlays Bank, 13 St James's Square, SW1Y 4LF. *Clubs:* Army and Navy, MCC.

GUYATT, Richard Gerald Talbot, CBE 1969; Rector, Royal College of Art, 1978–81 (Pro-Rector, 1974–78; Professor of Graphic Arts, 1948–78); *b* 8 May 1914; *s* of Thomas Guyatt, sometime HM Consul, Vigo, Spain and Cecil Guyatt; *m* 1941, Elizabeth Mary Corsellis; one step *d*. *Educ:* Charterhouse. Freelance designer: posters for Shell-Mex and BP, 1935. War Service: Regional Camouflage Officer for Scotland, Min. of Home Security. Dir and Chief Designer, Cockade Ltd, 1946–48; Co-designer of Lion and Unicorn Pavilion, Festival of Britain, 1951; Consultant Designer to: Josiah Wedgwood & Sons, 1952–55, 1967–70; Central Electricity Generating Bd, 1964–68; British Sugar Bureau, 1965–68; W. H. Smith, 1970–87. Vis. Prof., Yale Univ., 1955 and 1962. Ceramic Designs for Min. of Works (for British Embassies), King's Coll. Cambridge, Goldsmiths' Co. and Wedgwood commem. mugs for Coronation, 1953, Investiture, 1969 and Royal Silver Wedding, 1973. Designed: silver medal for Royal Mint, Mint Dirs Conf., 1972; 700th Anniv. of Parlt stamp, 1965; Postal Order forms, 1964 for Post Office; Silver Jubilee stamps, 1977; commem. crown piece for 80th birthday of HM Queen Elizabeth The Queen Mother, 1980. Member: Stamp Adv. Cttee, 1963–74; Internat. Jury, Warsaw Poster Biennale, 1968; Bank of England Design Adv. Cttee, 1968–75; Adv. Council, Victoria and Albert Mus., 1978–81. Chm., Guyatt/Jenkins Design Group. Governor, Imperial Coll. of Sci. and Technol., 1979–81. FSIA; Hon. ARCA. *Address:* Forge Cottage, Ham, Marlborough, Wilts SN8 3RB. *T:* Inkpen (01488) 668270.

GUYTON, Marjorie A.; *see* Allthorpe-Guyton.

GUZ, Prof. Abraham, MD; FRCP; Professor of Medicine, Charing Cross and Westminster Medical School, University of London, 1981–94, now Emeritus; *b* 12 Aug. 1929; *s* of Akiwa Guz and Esther Guz; *m* 1957, Nita (*née* Florenz); three *d*. *Educ:* Grocers' Co. Sch.; Charing Cross Hosp. Med. Sch., Univ. of London (MB BS 1952; MD 1967). MRCP 1954, FRCP 1969. Hosp. appts, Charing Cross Hosp., 1952–53; Asst Lectr in Pharmacol., Charing Cross Hosp. Med. Sch., 1953–54; RAMC 1954–56; Hosp. appts, RPMS, Hammersmith Hosp., 1956–57; Research Fellow: Harvard Med. Sch., 1957–59; Cardiovascular Res. Inst., Univ. of California, 1959–61; Lectr in Medicine, 1961, later Sen. Lectr and Reader, Charing Cross Hosp. Med Sch. Pro-Censor and Censor, RCP, 1979–87. *Publications:* Dyspnoea, 1984; articles on mechanisms underlying breathlessness, mechanisms resp. for ventilatory response to exercise, measurement of performance of left ventricle. *Recreations:* family, violin in quartet, Jewish culture study. *Address:* 3 Littleton Road, Harrow, Middx HA1 3SY. *T:* 0181–422 2786.

GWANDU, Emir of; Alhaji Haruna, (Muhammadu Basharu), CFR 1965; CMG 1961; CBE 1955; 18th Emir of Gwandu, 1954; Member, North Western State House of Chiefs, and Council of Chiefs; Member, and Chairman, Executive Council, State Self-Development Funds Council; President, former Northern Nigeria House of Chiefs, since 1957 (Deputy President 1956); *b* Batoranke, 1913; *m* 1933; fifteen *c*. *Educ:* Birnin Kebbi Primary Sch.; Katsina Training Coll. Teacher: Katsina Teachers Coll., 1933–35; Sokoto Middle Sch., 1935–37; Gusau Local Authority Sub-Treasurer, 1937–43; Gwandu Local Authority Treasurer, 1943–45; District Head, Kalgo, 1945–54. Member former N Reg. Marketing Board. *Recreations:* hunting, shooting. *Address:* Emir's Palace, PO Box 1, Birnin Kebbi, North Western State, Nigeria.

GWILLIAM, John Albert, MA Cantab; Headmaster of Birkenhead School, 1963–88; *b* 28 Feb. 1923; *s* of Thomas Albert and Adela Audrey Gwilliam; *m* 1949, Pegi Lloyd George; three *s* two *d*. *Educ:* Monmouth Sch.; Trinity Coll., Cambridge. Assistant Master: Trinity Coll., Glenalmond, 1949–52; Bromsgrove Sch., 1952–56; Head of Lower Sch., Dulwich Coll., 1956–63. *Address:* Araulfan, 13 The Close, Llanfairfechan, Gwynedd LL33 0AG.

GWILLIAM, Prof. Kenneth Mason; with World Bank, Washington; *b* 27 June 1937; *s* of John and Marjorie Gwilliam; *m* 1987, Sandra Wilson; two *s* by former *m*. *Educ:* Magdalen Coll., Oxford (BA 1st Cl. Hons PPE). Res. Asst, Fisons Ltd, 1960–61; Lecturer: Univ. of Nottingham, 1961–65; Univ. of E Anglia, 1965–67; Prof. of Transport Economics, Univ. of Leeds, 1967–89; Prof. of Econs of Transport and Logistics, Erasmus Univ., Rotterdam, 1989. Director: Nat. Bus Co., 1978–82; Yorkshire Rider, 1986–88. Editor, Jl of Transport Economics and Policy, 1977–87. *Publications:* Transport and Public Policy, 1964; Economics and Transport Policy, 1975; (jtly) Deregulating the Bus Industry, 1984. *Recreations:* badminton, walking, golf. *Address:* World Bank, 1818 H Street NW, Washington, DC 20433, USA. *T:* (202) 4733743, *Fax:* (202) 5223223.

GWILLIAM, Robert John; Senior Associate Solicitor, British Telecommunications PLC, since 1990; *b* 6 Jan. 1943; *s* of Benjamin Harold Gwilliam and Dora Gwilliam; *m* 1966, Linda Mary Ellway; two *s*. *Educ:* Lydney Grammar Sch.; Nottingham Univ. (BA Hons Law); Cambridge Univ. (Dip. Criminology); College of Law. Admitted Solicitor, 1969, practised in Local Govt Prosecuting Depts, 1969–83; Chief Prosecuting Solicitor for Hampshire, 1983–86; Chief Crown Prosecutor, Crown Prosecution Service: London South/Surrey Area, 1986; Inner London Area, 1987; London and SE Regl Dir, Grade 3, 1987–89. *Recreations:* listening to all types of music, amateur music making, supporting Rugby, walking in Purbeck. *Address:* Group Legal Services, British Telecommunications PLC, Group Headquarters, 81 Newgate Street, EC1A 7AJ.

GWILT, George David, FFA; General Manager, 1979–84, Managing Director and Actuary, 1984–88, Standard Life Assurance Company; *b* 11 Nov. 1927; *s* of Richard Lloyd Gwilt and Marjory Gwilt (*née* Mair); *m* 1956, Ann Dalton Sylvester; three *s*. *Educ:* Sedbergh Sch.; St John's Coll., Cambridge (MA). FFA 1952; FBCS. Joined Standard Life Assurance Co., 1949: Asst Official, 1956; Asst Actuary, 1957; Statistician, 1962; Mechanisation Manager, 1964; Systems Manager, 1969; Dep. Pensions Manager, 1972; Pensions Actuary, 1973; Asst General Manager and Pensions Manager, 1977; Asst Gen. Man. (Finance), 1978. Dep. Chm., Associated Scottish Life Offices, 1986–88. Special Advr in Scotland, Citicorp, 1989–91; Director: Hammerson Property Investment and Devel Corp., 1979–94; Scottish Mortgage and Trust, 1983–; European Assets Trust NV, 1979–; Hodgson Martin, 1989–. Trustee, TSB of South of Scotland, 1966–83. Member: Younger Cttee on Privacy, 1970–72; Monopolies and Mergers Commn, 1983–87. Pres., Faculty of Actuaries, 1981–83. Convenor, Scottish Poetry Library Assoc., 1988–. *Recreation:* flute playing. *Address:* 39 Oxgangs Road, Edinburgh EH10 7BE. *T:* 0131–445 1266. *Clubs:* Royal Air Force; New (Edinburgh).

GWYNEDD, Viscount; David Richard Owen Lloyd George; *b* 22 Jan. 1951; *s* and *heir* of 3rd Earl Lloyd George of Dwyfor, *qv*; *m* 1985, Pamela, *o d* of late Alexander Kleyff; two *s*. *Educ:* Eton. *Heir:* *s* Hon. William Alexander Lloyd George, *b* 16 May 1986.

GWYNN, Edward Harold, CB 1961; Deputy Under-Secretary of State, Ministry of Defence, 1966–72; retired 1972; *b* 23 Aug. 1912; *y s* of late Dr E. J. Gwynn, Provost of Trinity Coll., Dublin, and late Olive Ponsonby; *m* 1937, Dorothy, *d* of late Geoffrey S. Phillpotts, Foxrock, Co. Dublin; one *s* three *d* (and one *d* decd). *Educ:* Sedbergh School; TCD. Entered Home Office, 1936; Assistant Secretary, 1947; Assistant Under-Secretary of State, 1956; Principal Finance Officer (Under-Secretary), Ministry of Agriculture, 1961–62; Deputy Under-Secretary of State, Home Office, 1963–66. *Recreations:* gardening, the countryside. *Address:* The Chestnuts, Minchinhampton, Glos GL6 9AR. *T:* Stroud (01453) 832863.

GWYNN-JONES, Peter Llewellyn, LVO 1994; Garter Principal King of Arms, since 1995; *b* 12 March 1940; *s* of late Major Jack Llewellyn Gwynn-Jones, Cape Town, and late Mary Muriel Daphne, *d* of Col Arthur Patrick Bird Harrison, and step *s* of late Lt-Col Gavin David Young, Long Burton, Dorset. *Educ:* Wellington Coll.; Trinity Coll., Cambridge (MA). Assistant to Garter King of Arms, 1970; Bluemantle Pursuivant of Arms, 1973; Secretary, Harleian Society, 1981–94; House Comptroller of College of Arms, 1982; Lancaster Herald of Arms, 1982–95. *Publication:* Heraldry, 1993. *Recreations:* tropical forests, wild life conservation, fishing. *Address:* College of Arms, Queen Victoria Street, EC4V 4BT. *T:* 0171–248 0911; 79 Harcourt Terrace, SW10. *T:* 0171–373 5859.

GWYNNE JONES, family name of **Baron Chalfont.**

GYLLENHAMMAR, Dr Pehr Gustaf; Chairman, MC European Capital (Holdings), SA; Executive Chairman, Board of Directors, Volvo, 1990–93 (Chairman and Chief Executive Officer, 1983–90); *b* 28 April 1935; *s* of Pehr Gustaf Victor Gyllenhammar and Aina Dagny Kaplan; *m* 1959, Eva Christina, *d* of Gunnar Ludvig Engellau; one *s* three *d*. *Educ:* University of Lund. LLB. Mannheimer & Zetterlöf, solicitors, 1959; Haight, Gardner, Poor & Havens, NY, 1960; Amphion Insurance Co., Gothenburg, 1961–64; Skandia Insurance Co., 1965, Exec. Vice-Pres., 1968, Pres. and Chief Exec. Officer, 1970; AB Volvo, Gothenburg, 1970, Man. Dir and Chief Exec. Officer, 1971; Dir of companies in Sweden, Netherlands, UK and USA. Member: Internat. Adv. Cttee, Chase Manhattan Bank, NA, NY, 1972–; Bd, Cttee of Common Market Automobile Constructors, 1977–91; Bd, Assoc. des Constructeurs Européens d'Automobiles, 1991–93; Bd, Fedn of Swedish Industries, 1979–; Roundtable of European Industrialists, 1982–; Bd Trustees, Rockefeller Univ., NY, 1991–. Lethaby Prof., Royal Coll. of Art, London, 1977; Mem., Royal Swedish Acad. of Engineering Scis, 1974. Hon. DM Gothenburg Univ., 1981; Hon. DTech Brunel, 1987; Hon. DEng Technical Univ., NS, 1988; Hon. DSocSc Helsinki, 1990. Golden Award, City of Gothenburg, 1981. Officer, Royal Order of Vasa, 1973; King's Medal, with Ribbon of Order of Seraphim, 1981; Commander: Order of Lion of Finland, 1977 (Comdr 1st Class 1986); Ordre National du Mérite, France, 1980; St Olav's Order, Norway, 1984; Légion d'honneur, France, 1987; Order of Leopold, Belgium, 1989; Kt Grand Officer, Order of Merit, Italy, 1987. *Publications:* Mot sekelskiftet på måfå (Toward the Turn of the Century, at Random), 1970; Jag tror på Sverige (I Believe in Sweden), 1973; People at Work (US), 1977; En industripolitik för människan (Industrial policy for human beings), 1979. *Recreations:* tennis, sailing, skiing, riding. *Address:* Commercial Union Tower, One Undershaft, EC3A 8LH.

H

HAAN, Christopher Francis; Partner, Hammond Suddards, solicitors, since 1995. LLB. Admitted solicitor, 1968. Sen. Partner, S. J. Berwin & Co., 1988–92. *Address:* Moor House, 119 London Wall, EC2Y 5PT. *T:* 0171–628 4767.

HAAVELMO, Prof. Trygve; Norwegian economist; Professor of Economics, University of Oslo, since 1948; *b* 13 Dec. 1911. Leading pioneer in modern econometrics (quantitative economics). Res. Asst, Cowles Comm. Univ. of Chicago, 1945–56. Member: Amer. Econ. Assoc.; Amer. Acad. of Arts and Letters. Nobel Prize for Economics, 1989. *Publications include:* Study in the Theory of Economic Evolution, 1954; Investment Decision, 1960. *Address:* Department of Economics, University of Oslo, POB 1095 Blindern, 0317 Oslo 3, Norway.

HAAVISTO, Heikki Johannes; Minister of Foreign Affairs, Finland, 1993–95; *b* Turku, Finland, 20 Aug. 1935; *s* of Johan Svensson and Alli Haavisto; *m* 1964, Maija Rihko; three *s*. *Educ:* Univ. of Helsinki (MSc, LLM). Hd of Dept, Oy Vehnä Ab, 1963–66; Sec.-Gen., Central Union of Agricl Producers and Forest Owners, 1966–75 (Pres., 1976–94); Member, Administrative Council: Osuuskunta Metsäliitto, Helsinki, 1976–93 (Vice-Chm. and Pres., 1976–93); Central Union Co-op. Banks, Helsinki, 1985–93. Mem., Internat. Policy Council on Agric. and Trade, Washington, 1988–. Mem., Centre Party, Finland. Hon. PhD Turku; Hon. Dr Agr. & For., Hon. DVM Helsinki, 1995. *Address:* Hintsa, 21200 Raisio, Finland.

HABAKKUK, Sir John (Hrothgar), Kt 1976; FBA 1965; FRHistS; Fellow, All Souls College, Oxford, 1950–67 and since 1988; Principal of Jesus College, Oxford, 1967–84, Hon. Fellow, 1984; *b* 13 May 1915; *s* of Evan Guest and Anne Habakkuk; *m* 1948, Mary Richards; one *s* three *d*. *Educ:* Barry County Sch.; St John's Coll., Cambridge (scholar and Strathcona student), Hon. Fellow 1971. Historical Tripos: Part I, First Class, 1935; Part II, First Class (with distinction), 1936. Fellow, Pembroke Coll., Cambridge, 1938–50, Hon. Fellow 1973; Director of Studies in History and Librarian, 1946–50; Temporary Civil Servant: Foreign Office, 1940–42, Board of Trade, 1942–46; University Lecturer in Faculty of Economics, Cambridge, 1946–50; Chichele Prof. of Economic History, Oxford, 1950–67; Vice-Chancellor, Oxford Univ., 1973–77, a Pro Vice-Chancellor, 1977–83; Pres, UC Swansea, 1975–84 (Hon. Fellow, 1991). Visiting Lecturer, Harvard University, 1954–55; Ford Research Professor, University of California, Berkeley, 1962–63; Ford Lecturer, 1984–85. Member: Grigg Cttee on Departmental Records, 1952–54; Advisory Council on Public Records, 1958–70; SSRC, 1967–71; Nat. Libraries Cttee, 1968–69; Royal Commn on Historic Manuscripts, 1978–90; Admin. Bd, Internat. Assoc. of Univs, 1975–85. Chairman: Cttee of Vice Chancellors and Principals of Univs of UK, 1976–77, Adv. Gp on London Health Servs, 1980–81; Oxfordshire DHA, 1981–84. Pres., RHistS, 1976–80. Foreign Member: Amer. Phil. Soc.; Amer. Acad. of Arts and Sciences. Hon. DLitt: Wales, 1971; Cambridge, 1973; Pennsylvania, 1975; Kent, 1978; Ulster, 1988. *Publications:* American and British Technology in the Nineteenth Century, 1962; Population Growth and Economic Development since 1750, 1971; Landowners: marriage, debt and the estates system 1650–1950, 1994; articles and reviews. *Address:* 28 Cunliffe Close, Oxford OX2 7BL. *T:* Oxford (01865) 56583.

HABERFELD, Dame Gwyneth; *see* Jones, Dame Gwyneth.

HABGOOD, family name of **Baron Habgood.**

HABGOOD, Baron *cr* 1995 (Life Peer), of Calverton in the county of Buckinghamshire; **Rt Rev. and Rt Hon. John Stapylton Habgood,** PC 1983; MA, PhD; Archbishop of York, 1983–95; *b* 23 June 1927; *s* of Arthur Henry Habgood, DSO, MB, BCh, and Vera (*née* Chetwynd-Stapylton); *m* 1961, Rosalie Mary Anne Boston; two *s* two *d*. *Educ:* Eton; King's Coll., Cambridge (Hon. Fellow, 1986); Cuddesdon Coll., Oxford. Univ. Demonstrator in Pharmacology, Cambridge, 1950–53; Fellow of King's Coll., Cambridge, 1952–55; Curate of St Mary Abbots, Kensington, 1954–56; Vice-Principal of Westcott House, Cambridge, 1956–62; Rector of St John's Church, Jedburgh, 1962–67; Principal of Queen's College, Birmingham, 1967–73; Bishop of Durham, 1973–83. Hulsean Preacher, Cambridge Univ., 1987–88. Moderator, Church and Society Sub-Unit, WCC, 1983–91. Pro-Chancellor, Univ. of York, 1985–90. Hon. DD: Durham, 1975; Cambridge, 1984; Aberdeen, 1988; Huron, 1990; Hull, 1991. *Publications:* Religion and Science, 1964; A Working Faith, 1980; Church and Nation in a Secular Age, 1983; Confessions of a Conservative Liberal, 1988; Making Sense, 1993. *Recreations:* painting, DIY. *Address:* 18 The Mount, Malton, N Yorks YO17 0ND. *Club:* Athenæum.

HABGOOD, Anthony John; Chief Executive, Bunzl plc, since 1991; *b* 8 Nov. 1946; *s* of John Michael Habgood and Margaret Diana Middleton Habgood (*née* Dalby); *m* 1974, Nancy Atkinson; two *s* one *d*. *Educ:* Gonville and Caius Coll., Cambridge (MA Econ 1971); Carnegie Mellon Univ., Pittsburgh (MS Indust. Admin 1970). Boston Consulting Gp, 1970–86: Director, 1976; Management Cttee, 1979; Exec. Cttee, 1981; Tootal Group, 1986–91: Director, 1986; Chief Exec., 1991. Director: Geest, 1988–93; Power Gen, 1993–. *Recreations:* country pursuits. *Address:* Bunzl plc, 110 Park Street, W1Y 3RB. *Club:* Royal Norfolk and Suffolk Yacht.

HACAULT, Most Rev. Antoine; *see* St Boniface, Archbishop of, (RC).

HACKER, Alan Ray, OBE 1988; clarinettist and conductor; *b* 30 Sept. 1938; *s* of Kenneth and Sybil Hacker; *m* 1st, 1959, Anna Maria Sroka; two *d*; 2nd, 1977, Karen Evans (marr. diss.); one *s*. *Educ:* Dulwich Coll.; Royal Academy of Music. FRAM. Joined LPO, 1958; Prof., RAM, 1960–76; Lectr, 1976–84, Sen. Lectr in Music, 1984–87, Univ of York. Founded: Pierrot Players (with S. Pruslin and H. Birtwistle), 1965; Matrix, 1971; Music Party for authentic performance of classical music, 1972; Classical Orch., 1977; Guest Cond., Orchestra la Fenice, Venice, 1981–; operatic cond. début, Den Bergtagna, Sweden, 1986, York Fest., 1988; conducted 1st major British prodn of Mozart's La Finta Giardiniera, 1989; German operatic début, Don Giovanni, Così fan Tutte, Stuttgart, 1991, Julius Caesar, Halle, Ulisse, Stuttgart, 1992. Orchestral work with Südwestfunk and Berlin Radio Orch., 1992. First modern "authentic" perfs, 1977–, incl: Mozart's Symphonies 39, 40; Beethoven's Symphonies 2, 3, 7, 9 and Egmont; Haydn's Harmonie and Creation Masses, Symphony 104 and Trumpet Concerto. Revived basset clarinet and restored orig. text, Mozart's concerto and quintet, 1967; revived baroque clarinet (hitherto unplayed), 1975. Premieres of music by Birtwistle, Boulez, Morton Feldman, Goehr, Maxwell Davies, Stockhausen, Blake, Mellers, Salvatore Sciarrino and Judith Weir; cond 5 staged perfs of Bach's St John Passion for European Music Year, 1984. Sir Robert Mayer Lectr, Leeds Univ., 1972–73. Mem. Fires of London, 1970–76; Dir, York Early Music Festival. Teacher, lectr and conductor, Bauff Centre, Canada, 1986–. Many recordings. *Publications:* Scores of Mozart Concerto and Quintet, 1972; 1st edn of reconstructed Mozart Concerto, 1973; Schumann's Soiréestucke, 1985. *Recreation:* cookery. *Address:* Hindlea, Broughton, Malton, N Yorks YO17 0QJ.

HACKER, Rt. Rev. George Lanyon; Bishop Suffragan of Penrith, 1979–94; *b* 27 Dec. 1928; *s* of Edward Sidney Hacker and Carla Lanyon; *m* 1969, June Margaret Erica Smart; one *s* one *d*. *Educ:* Kelly College, Tavistock; Exeter College, Oxford (BA 1952, MA 1956); Cuddesdon College, Oxford. Deacon 1954, priest 1955, Bristol; Curate of St Mary Redcliffe, Bristol, 1954–59; Chaplain, King's College London at St Boniface Coll., Warminster, 1959–64; Perpetual Curate, Church of the Good Shepherd, Bishopwearmouth, 1964–71; Rector of Tilehurst, Reading, 1971–79. Pres., Rural Theol. Assoc., 1989–94; Pres., Age Concern Cumbria, 1991– (Chm., 1987–91); Chm., Age Concern Eden, 1994–; Episcopal Advr, Anglican Young People's Assoc., 1987–94. *Recreations:* gardening, book binding, writing poetry. *Address:* Keld House, Milburn, Penrith, Cumbria CA10 1TW. *T:* Kirkby Thore (017683) 61506.

HACKETT, Prof. Brian; Professor of Landscape Architecture, University of Newcastle upon Tyne, 1967–77, now Emeritus Professor; *b* 3 Nov. 1911; *s* of Henry and Ida Adeline Mary Hackett; *m* 1st, 1942, Frederica Claire Grundy (*d* 1979); one *s* two *d*; 2nd, 1980, Dr Elizabeth Ratcliff. *Educ:* Grammar Sch., Burton-on-Trent; Birmingham Sch. of Architecture; Sch. of Planning for Regional Development, London. MA Dunelm, PPILA, RIBA, MRTPI. Professional experience, 1930–40; Flt-Lt, RAFVR, 1941–45; Lectr, Sch. of Planning for Regional Develt, London, 1945–47; Univ. of Durham: Lectr in Town and Country Planning, 1947; Lectr in Landscape Architecture, 1948, Sen. Lectr, 1949–59; Vis. Prof. of Landscape Architecture, Univ. of Illinois, 1960–61; Reader in Landscape Arch., Univ. of Newcastle upon Tyne, 1962–66. Member: N England Regl Adv. Cttee, Forestry Commn, 1983–90; Water Space Amenity Commn, 1973–80. Chairman: Northumberland and Newcastle Soc., 1968–77; Northumbria Historic Churches Trust, 1987–94. Pres., Inst. of Landscape Architects, 1967–68; Hon. Vice Pres., Landscape Inst., 1991; Hon. Corresp. Mem., Amer. Soc. of Landscape Architects, 1962. European Prize for Nature Conservation and Landscape Develt, 1975. *Publications:* Man, Society and Environment, 1950; (jtly) Landscape Techniques, 1967; Landscape Planning, 1971; Steep Slopes Landscape, 1971; (jtly) Landscape Reclamation, 1971–72; (jtly) Landscape Reclamation Practice, 1977; Planting Design, 1979; Landscape Conservation, 1980; numerous papers in internat. jls. *Recreation:* musical performance. *Address:* 27 Larkspur Terrace, Jesmond, Newcastle upon Tyne NE2 2DT. *T:* 0191–281 0747. *Club:* Commonwealth Trust.

HACKETT, Prof. Cecil Arthur, MA Cantab, Docteur de l'Université de Paris; Professor of French, University of Southampton, 1952–70, now Professor Emeritus; *b* 19 Jan. 1908; *s* of Henry Hackett and Alice Setchell; *m* 1942, Mary Hazel Armstrong. *Educ:* King's Norton Grammar Sch., Birmingham; University of Birmingham; Emmanuel Coll., Cambridge (Scholar and Prizeman; Hon. Fellow, 1988). Assistant d'Anglais, Lycée Louis-le-Grand, Paris, 1934–36; Lecturer in French and English, Borough Road Coll., Isleworth, 1936–39. Served War of 1939–45: enlisted 1/8th Bn Middlesex Regt, 1939. Education Representative, British Council, Paris, 1945–46; Lecturer in French, University of Glasgow, 1947–52. Hon. DLitt Southampton 1984. Chevalier de la Légion d'Honneur. *Publications:* Le Lyrisme de Rimbaud, 1938; Rimbaud l'Enfant, 1948; An Anthology of Modern French Poetry, 1952, 4th edn 1976; Rimbaud, 1957; Autour de Rimbaud, 1967; (ed and introd) New French Poetry: an anthology, 1973; Rimbaud, a critical introduction, 1981; Rimbaud, Œuvres Poétiques, a critical edition, 1986, The Writer and his other Self, 1995; contributions to English and French Reviews. *Address:* Shawford Close, Shawford, Winchester, Hants SO21 2BL. *T:* Twyford (01962) 713506.

HACKETT, Dennis William; journalist; publishing and communications consultant; Director, Media Search & Selection Ltd, since 1988; *b* 5 Feb. 1929; *s* of James Joseph Hackett and Sarah Ellen Hackett (*née* Bedford); *m* 1st, 1953, Agnes Mary Collins; two *s* one *d*; 2nd, 1974, Jacqueline Margaret Totterdell; one *d*. *Educ:* De La Salle College, Sheffield. Served with RN, 1947–49. Sheffield Telegraph, 1945–47 and 1949–54; Daily Herald, 1954; Odhams Press, 1954; Deputy Editor, Illustrated, 1955–58; Daily Express, 1958–60; Daily Mail, 1960; Art Editor, Observer, 1961–62; Deputy Editor, 1962, Editor, 1964–65, Queen; Editor, Nova, 1965–69; Publisher, Twentieth Century Magazine, 1965–72; Editorial Dir, George Newnes Ltd, 1966–69; Dir, IPC Newspapers, 1969–71; Associate Editor, Daily Express, 1973–74; TV critic: The Times, 1981–85; Tablet, 1984–92; Editorial Consultant, You, The Mail on Sunday magazine, 1982–86; Exec. Editor, 1986–87, Editor-in-chief, 1987, Today; Editor-in-Chief, M, The Observer Magazine, 1987–88; Editor, Management Today, 1992–94. Chm., Design and Art Directors' Assoc., 1967–68. *Publications:* The History of the Future: Bemrose Corporation 1826–1976, 1976; The Big Idea: the story of Ford in Europe, 1978. *Recreations:* reading, walking. *Address:* 4 East Heath Road, NW3 1BN. *Club:* Royal Automobile.

HACKETT, John Charles Thomas, FIMgt; Director General, Federation of Civil Engineering Contractors, since 1992; *b* 4 Feb. 1939; *s* of Thomas John Hackett and late Doris Hackett; *m* 1958, Patricia Margaret, *d* of late Eric Ronald Clifford and Margaret Tubb. *Educ:* Glyn Grammar Sch., Epsom, Surrey; London Univ. (LLB Hons, external). FBIM 1981. Prodn Planning Manager, Rowntree Gp, 1960–64; Prodn Controller, Johnson's Wax, 1964; Commercial Sec., Heating and Ventilating Contractors' Assoc., 1964–70; Sec., Cttee of Assocs of Specialist Engrg Contractors, 1968–79; Dep. Dir, 1970–79, Dir, 1980–84, British Constructional Steelwork Assoc.; Dir Gen., BIBA, subseq. BIIBA, 1985–91. Member: Council, CBI, 1980–88 and 1992–; CBI Gp of Chief Execs of Major Sector Assocs, 1980–84 and 1992–. MInstD. FRSA. *Publication:* BCSA Members' Contractual Handbook, 1972, 2nd edn 1979. *Recreations:* music, reading, walking, motoring. *Address:* 15 Downsway Close, Tadworth, Surrey KT20 5DR. *T:* Tadworth (01737) 813024.

HACKETT, John Wilkings, CMG 1989; Director, Financial, Fiscal and Enterprise Affairs, Organisation for Economic Co-operation and Development, Paris, 1979–89; *b* 21 Jan. 1924; *s* of Albert and Bertha Hackett; *m* 1952, Anne-Marie Le Brun. *Educ:* LSE (BSc(Econ) 1950); Institut d'Etudes Politiques, Paris (Diplôme 1952); Univ. of Paris (Dr d'état ès sciences economiques 1957). Served RN, 1942–46. Economic research, 1952–57; OECD, 1958–89. FRSA 1986. *Publications:* Economic Planning in France (with A.-M. Hackett), 1963; L'Economie Britannique—problèmes et perspectives, 1966; (with A.-M. Hackett) The British Economy, 1967; articles on economic subjects in British and French economic jls. *Recreations:* music, painting, reading. *Address:* 48 rue de la Bienfaisance, 75008 Paris, France. *Club:* Cercle de l'Union Interalliée (Paris).

HACKETT, Gen. Sir John Winthrop, GCB 1967 (KCB 1962; CB 1958); CBE 1953 (MBE 1938); DSO 1942 and Bar 1945; MC 1941; DL; BLitt, MA Oxon; FRSL 1982; Principal of King's College, London, 1968–July 1975; *b* 5 Nov. 1910; *s* of late Sir John Winthrop Hackett, KCMG, LLD, Perth, WA; *m* 1942, Margaret, *d* of Joseph Frena, Graz, Austria; one *d* decd, and two adopted step *d*. *Educ:* Geelong Grammar Sch., Australia; New Coll., Oxford, Hon. Fellow 1972. Regular Army, commissioned 8th KRI Hussars, 1931; Palestine, 1936 (despatches); seconded to Transjordan Frontier Force, 1937–41 (despatches twice); Syria, 1941 (wounded); Sec. Commn of Control Syria and Lebanon; GSO2 9th Army; Western Desert, 1942 (wounded); GSO1 Raiding Forces GHQ, MELF; Comdr 4th Parachute Brigade, 1943; Italy, 1943 (despatches); Arnhem, 1944 (wounded); BGS (1) Austria, 1946–47; Comdr Transjordan Frontier Force, 1947–48; Sen. Army Instr, RNC, Greenwich, 1950; idc 1951; DQMG, BAOR, 1952; Comdr 20th Armoured Bde, 1954; GOC 7th Armoured Div., 1956–58; Comdt, Royal Mil. Coll. of Science, 1958–61; GOC-in-C, Northern Ireland Command, 1961–63; Dep. Chief of Imperial Gen. Staff, 1963–64; Dep. Chief of the Gen. Staff, Ministry of Defence, 1964–66. Comdr-in-Chief, British Army of the Rhine, and Comdr Northern Army Gp in NATO, 1966–68. ADC (Gen.), 1967–68. Col. Commandant, REME, 1961–66; Hon. Colonel: 10th Bn The Parachute Regt, TA, 1965–67; 10th Volunteer Bn, The Parachute Regt, 1967–73; Oxford Univ. Officers Training Corps, 1967–78; Col, Queen's Royal Irish Hussars, 1969–75. Mem., Lord Chancellor's Cttee on Reform of Law of Contempt, 1971–74; Mem., Disciplinary Tribunal, Inns of Court and Bar, 1972–83. Vis. Prof. in Classics, KCL, 1977–. Lectures: Lees Knowles, Cambridge, 1961; Basil Henriques Meml, 1970; Harmon Meml, USAF Acad., 1970; Jubilee, Imperial Coll., 1979. President: UK Classical Assoc., 1971; English Assoc., 1973. Hon. Liveryman, Worshipful Company of Dyers, 1975; Freeman of City of London, 1976. DL Glos 1982. Hon. LLD: Queen's Univ. Belfast; Perth, WA, 1963; Exeter, 1977; Buckingham, 1987. FKC, 1968; Hon. Fellow St George's Coll., University of Western Australia, 1965. Chesney Gold Medal, RUSI, 1985. *Publications:* I Was a Stranger, 1977; (jtly) The Third World War, 1978; (jtly) The Untold Story, 1982; The Profession of Arms, 1983; (ed) Warfare in the Ancient World, 1989; articles and reviews. *Recreations:* fishing, wine, music; the pursuit of exactitude, called by some pedantry. *Address:* Coberley Mill, Cheltenham, Glos GL53 9NH. *T:* Coberley (01242) 870207. *Clubs:* Cavalry and Guards, Carlton, United Oxford & Cambridge University, White's.

HACKETT, Peter, OBE 1990; DL; PhD; FEng 1983; Director, 1993–94, and Principal, 1970–94, Camborne School of Mines (first Fellow, 1990); Adviser on Cornwall, Exeter University, since 1994; *b* 1 Nov. 1933; *s* of Christopher and Evelyn Hackett; *m* 1958, Esmé Doreen (*née* Lloyd); one *s* one *d*. *Educ:* Mundella Grammar Sch.; Nottingham Univ. (BSc 1st Cl. Hons Mining Engrg; PhD). FIMM 1971, Hon. FIMM 1993. Lecturer, Nottingham Univ., 1958–70; Vis. Lectr, Univ. of Minnesota, 1969; Vis. Professor, Univ. of California at Berkeley, 1979. Pres., IMM, 1989–90. DL Cornwall, 1993. *Publications:* contribs to learned jls on geotechnical subjects and mining engrg educn. *Recreations:* sailing, vintage vehicles, shooting. *Club:* Royal Cornwall Yacht (Falmouth).

HACKING, family name of **Baron Hacking.**

HACKING, 3rd Baron *cr* 1945, of Chorley; **Douglas David Hacking;** Bt 1938; Solicitor of Supreme Court of England and Wales, since 1977; Managing Partner (London), Sonnescheins; Attorney and Counselor-at-Law of State of New York, since 1975; *b* 17 April 1938; *er s* of 2nd Baron Hacking, and of Daphne Violet, *e d* of late R. L. Finnis; *S* father, 1971; *m* 1982, Dr Tessa M. Hunt, MB, MRCP, FRCA, *er d* of Roland C. C. Hunt, *qv*; three *s* (two *s* one *d* by former marriage). *Educ:* Aldro School, Shackleford; Charterhouse School; Clare College, Cambridge (BA 1961, MA 1968). Called to the Bar, Middle Temple, Nov. 1963 (Astbury and Harmsworth Scholarships). Served in RN, 1956–58; Ordinary Seaman, 1956; Midshipman, 1957; served in HMS Ark Royal (N Atlantic), 1957; HMS Hardy (Portland) and HMS Brocklesby (Portland and Gibraltar), 1958; transferred RNR as Sub-Lt, 1958, on completion of National Service; transf. List 3 RNR, HMS President, 1961; Lieut 1962; retired RNR, 1964. Barrister-at-Law, 1963–76; in practice, Midland and Oxford Circuits, 1964–75. With Simpson, Thacher and Bartlett, NYC, 1975–76; with Lovell, White and King, 1976–79; with Richards Butler, 1981–94. Mem., H of L Select Cttee on the European Community. Member: Amer. Bar Assoc.; NY State Bar Assoc.; Bar Assoc. of City of New York. Pres., Assoc. of Lancastrians in London, 1971–72. Apprenticed to Merchant Taylors' Co., 1955, admitted to Freedom, 1962; Freedom, City of London, 1962. FCIArb 1979. *Recreations:* running, walking. *Heir:* *s* Hon. Douglas Francis Hacking, *b* 8 Aug. 1968. *Address:* 27 West Square, Kennington, SE11 4SP. *Clubs:* MCC; Century (NY).

HACKING, Anthony Stephen; QC 1983; a Recorder, since 1985; *b* 12 Jan. 1941; *s* of John Kenneth and Joan Horton Hacking, Warwick; *m* 1969, Carin, *d* of Dr Svante and Brita Holmdahl, Gothenburg; one *d* three *s*. *Educ:* Warwick Sch.; Lincoln Coll., Oxford (MA). Called to the Bar, Inner Temple, 1965, Bencher, 1993. *Address:* 1 King's Bench Walk, Temple, EC4Y 7DB. *T:* 0171–583 6266, *Fax:* 0171–583 2068.

HACKLAND, Sarah Ann; *see* Spencer, S. A.

HACKNEY, Archdeacon of; *see* Young, Ven. C.

HACKNEY, Arthur, RWS 1957 (VPRWS 1974–77); RE 1960 (Hon. RE 1982); ARCA 1949; artist; Principal Lecturer (formerly Deputy Head), Fine Art Department, West Surrey College of Art and Design (Farnham Centre) (formerly Farnham School of Art), 1979–85, retired; *b* 13 March 1925; *s* of late J. T. Hackney; *m* 1955, Mary Baker, ARCA; two *d*. *Educ:* Burslem Sch. of Art; Royal Coll. of Art, London. Served in Royal Navy, 1942–46. Travelling scholarship, Royal College of Art, 1949; part-time Painting Instructor, Farnham Sch. of Art, 1950, Lecturer, 1962; Head of Dept: Graphic, 1963–68; Printmaking, 1968–79. Work represented in Public Collections, including Bradford City Art Gallery, Victoria and Albert Museum, Ashmolean Museum, Wellington Art Gallery (NZ), Nottingham Art Gallery, Keighley Art Gallery (Yorks), Wakefield City Art Gallery, Graves Art Gallery, Sheffield, GLC, Preston Art Gallery, City of Stoke-on-Trent Art Gall., Kent Educn Cttee, Staffordshire Educn Cttee. Mem., Fine Art Bd, CNAA, 1975–78. Work reproduced in 20th Century Painters and Sculptors, by Francis Spalding, 1990. *Address:* Woodhatches, Spoil Lane, Tongham, Farnham, Surrey GU10 1BP. *T:* Aldershot (01252) 23919. *Club:* Chelsea Arts.

HACKNEY, Roderick Peter, PhD; PPRIBA; Managing Director, Rod Hackney & Associates, since 1972; *b* 3 March 1942; *s* of William Hackney and Rose (*née* Morris); *m* 1964, Christine Thornton; one *s*. *Educ:* John Bright's Grammar School, Llandudno; Sch. of Architecture, Manchester Univ. (BAArch 1966, MA, PhD 1979). ARIBA 1969; FCIArb 1977; ASAI; FFB 1987; MCIOB 1987. Job Architect, EXPO '67, Montreal, for Monorail Stations; Housing Architect, Libyan Govt, Tripoli, 1967–68; Asst to Arne Jacobsen, Copenhagen, working on Kuwait Central Bank, 1968–71. Established Castward Ltd, building and develt firm, 1983 (Sec., 1983–92). Pres., RIBA, 1987–89 (Mem. Council, 1978–84 (Vice-Pres., Public Affairs, and Overseas Affairs, 1981–83), and 1991– (Vice-Pres., Internat. Affairs, 1992–94)); Mem. Council, Internat. Union of Architects, 1981–85, and 1991–, First Vice-Pres., 1985–87, Pres., 1987–90. Vis. Prof., Paris, 1984; Special Prof., Nottingham Univ., 1987–90; has lectured in Europe, India, Sri Lanka, Argentina, China, Russia, Australia, Japan, Kenya, USA, Chile and Pakistan. Chm., Times/RIBA Community Enterprise Scheme, 1985–89; Mem. Council, Nat. Historical Bldg Crafts Inst., 1989–; Advr on regeneration and inner city problems in Sweden, Italy and USA, 1990–; Internat. Advr, Centre for Internat. Archl Studies, Univ. of Manchester Sch. of Architecture, 1992–; Jury Mem., overseas housing develts; Juror for internat. competitions in Netherlands and China, 1992–; deleg., UK and overseas confs. Chm. of Trustees, Inner City Trust, 1986–; President: Snowdonia Nat. Park Soc., 1987–; N Wales Centre, NT, 1990–. Patron, Llandudno Mus. and Art Gall, 1988–. Hon. FAIA 1988; Hon. FRAIC 1990; Hon. Fellow: United Architects of Philippines, 1988; Fed. de Colegios de Arquitectos, Mexico, 1988; Indian Inst. of Architecture, 1990. Hon. DLitt Keele, 1989. Awards and prizes include: DoE Award for Good Design in Housing (1st Prize), 1975; 1st Prize, St Ann's Hospice Arch. Comp., 1976; PA Award for Innovation in Bldg Design and Construction (for Colquhoun St, Stirling); Award for work and leader of Community Arch. Movt, Charleston, USA. *Television:* Build Yourself a House, 1974; Community Architecture, 1977; BBC Omnibus, 1987; consultant, Europe by Design, BBC, 1991; *radio:* The Listener, 1986; Third Ear, 1990; Call to Account, 1992; Woman's Hour, 1992. Consultant, World Architecture Review Agency, China, 1992; Advr, Habitat Center News Jl, India, 1992–. *Publications:* Highfield Hall: a community project, 1982; The Good the Bad and the Ugly, 1990; Good Golly Miss Molly (music play), 1991; articles in UK and foreign architectural jls. *Recreations:* outdoor pursuits, walking, butterflies, photography, travelling, looking at buildings, speaking at conferences. *Address:* St Peter's House, Windmill Street, Macclesfield, Cheshire SK11 7HS. *T:* Macclesfield (01625) 431792. *Club:* Commonwealth Trust.

HADDACKS, Rear-Adm. Paul Kenneth; Assistant Chief of Staff (Policy) to Supreme Allied Commander Europe, since 1994; *b* 27 Oct. 1946; *s* of Kenneth Alexander Haddacks and Edith Lillian Haddacks (*née* Peardon); *m* 1970, Penny Anne Robertson; one *s*. *Educ:* Plymouth Coll.; Kingswood Sch., Bath; BRNC; RN Staff Coll., RCDS. Joined RN 1964; commanded HM Ships: Scimitar, 1971–72; Cleopatra, 1981–82; Naiad, 1982–83; Intrepid, 1986–88; US Naval Acad., 1979–80; Asst Dir, Navy Plans, 1984–86; Dep. Dir, Naval Warfare, 1988–89; Comdr, RN Task Force, Gulf, 1990; Captain of the Fleet, 1991–94. *Recreations:* family, travel. *Address:* c/o Naval Secretary, Victory Building, HM Naval Base, Portsmouth PO1 3LR. *Clubs:* Naval and Military; Royal Naval Sailing Association.

HADDAOUI, Khalil; Moroccan Ambassador to the Court of St James's, since 1991; *b* 21 April 1937; *m*; three *c*. *Educ:* School of Higher Business Studies, Paris; Inst. of Internat. Relations, Paris. Joined Ministry of Foreign Affairs, 1966; served Rome, London, Algiers, Madrid; Adviser to Moroccan Minister for Foreign Affairs, 1976; Ambassador to Liberia and Sierra Leone, 1982, to UN, 1985; Dir of Internat. Orgn, 1986, of European and American Affairs, 1990, Min. for Foreign Affairs. *Address:* Moroccan Embassy, 49 Queen's Gate Garden, SW7 5NE.

HADDINGTON, 13th Earl of, *cr* 1619; **John George Baillie-Hamilton;** Lord Binning, 1613; Lord Binning and Byres, 1619; *b* 21 Dec. 1941; *o s* of 12th Earl of Haddington, KT, MC, TD, and of Sarah, *y d* of G. W. Cook, Montreal; *S* father, 1986; *m* 1st, 1975, Prudence Elizabeth (marr. diss. 1981), *d* of A. Rutherford Hayles; 2nd, 1984, Susan Jane Antonia, 2nd *d* of John Heyworth; one *s* two *d*. *Educ:* Ampleforth. *Heir:* *s* Lord Binning, *qv*. *Address:* Mellerstain, Gordon, Berwickshire TD3 6LG; Tyninghame, Dunbar, East Lothian. *Clubs:* Turf, Chelsea Arts; New (Edinburgh).

HADDO, Earl of; Alexander George Gordon; ARICS; *b* 31 March 1955; *s* and *heir* of 6th Marquess of Aberdeen and Temair, *qv*; *m* 1981, Joanna Clodagh Houldsworth; three *s* one *d*. *Educ:* Cothill House, Abingdon; Harrow School; Polytechnic of Central London (DipBE). ARICS 1979. With Gardiner and Theobald, Chartered Quantity Surveyors, 1976–82; Speyhawk plc, Property Developers, 1982–86; London & Edinburgh Trust plc, Property Developers, 1986–94; Man. Dir, Letinvest, 1989–94. *Recreations:* golf, music, theatre. *Heir:* *s* Viscount Formartine, *qv*. *Address:* House of Formartine, Methlick, Ellon, Aberdeenshire AB41 0EQ. *T:* Methlick (01651) 806897. *Clubs:* MCC; Huntercombe Golf; Royal Aberdeen Golf.

HADDON-CAVE, Sir (Charles) Philip, KBE 1980; CMG 1973; Director, Kleinwort Benson Group, since 1986; Chairman, Fleming Overseas Investment Trust, since 1988 (Director, since 1986); *b* 6 July 1925; *m* 1948, Elizabeth Alice May Simpson; two *s* one *d*. *Educ:* Univ. Tasmania; King's Coll., Cambridge. Entered Colonial Administrative Service, 1952: East Africa High Commn, 1952; Kenya, 1953–62; Seychelles, 1961–62; Hong Kong, 1962–85; Financial Secretary, 1971–81, Chief Sec., 1981–85, Hong Kong. *Publication:* (with D. M. Hocking) Air Transport in Australia, 1951. *Address:* The Old Farmhouse, Nethercote Road, Tackley, Oxon OX5 3AW. *Clubs:* Oriental; Hong Kong, Royal Hong Kong Golf.

HADEN, William Demmery, TD, MA; Headmaster, Royal Grammar School, Newcastle upon Tyne, 1960–72, retired; *b* 14 March 1909; *s* of Reverend William Henry and Gertrude Haden, Little Aston; *m* 1939, Elizabeth Marjorie, *d* of R. S. Tewson, Chorley Wood; one *s* two *d*. *Educ:* Nottingham High Sch.; Wadham Coll., Oxford (2nd Class Lit. Hum.; MA 1934). English Master, Merchant Taylors' Sch., 1938–46; Headmaster, Mercers' Sch., 1946–59. War Service, 1940–45: served as Battery Comdr RA with

Fourteenth Army in Burma Campaign (despatches twice); Administrative Commandant, Hmawbi Area, S Burma District, 1945. *Recreations:* games, gardening, listening to music. *Address:* 11 Pensham Hill, Pershore, Worcs WR10 3HA.

HADEN-GUEST, family name of **Baron Haden-Guest.**

HADEN-GUEST, 4th Baron *cr* 1950, of Saling, Essex; **Peter Haden Haden-Guest;** *b* 29 Aug. 1913; *s* of 1st Baron Haden-Guest, MC and Muriel Carmel (*d* 1943), *d* of Colonel Albert Goldsmid, MVO; *S* half-brother, 1987; *m* 1945, Jean, *d* of late Dr Albert George Hindes, NY; two *s* one *d*. *Educ:* City of London School; New Coll., Oxford (MA). Editorial and theatrical work, 1934–42. Served War of 1939–45, Lieut RCNVR. UN official 1946–72. Took seat in House of Lords as cross-bencher, 1989. *Recreations:* grandchildren, walking, reading, theatre. *Heir: s* Hon. Christopher Haden-Guest [*b* 5 Feb. 1948; *m* 1984, Jamie Lee, *d* of Tony Curtis and Janet Leigh; one *d*]. *Address:* 198 Old Stone Highway, East Hampton, NY 11937, USA.

HADFIELD, Antony; Chief Executive, Northern Electric plc, since 1994 (Managing Director, 1991–94); *b* 9 Sept. 1936; *s* of Thomas Henry Hadfield and Edna (*née* Cooke); *m* 1959, Dorothy Fay Osman; one *s*. *Educ:* Sheffield; Brighton; Middx Poly. (BA). Design engr, Plessey, 1958–62; design and project engr, Metal Industries Gp, 1962–65; design engr, CEGB, 1965–67; Sen. Engr and Manager, Eastern Electricity, 1967–77; Area Manager, Yorks Electricity, 1977–79; Dir of Engrg, Midlands Electricity, 1979–85; Chief Exec. and Dep. Chm., NI Electricity, 1985–91. Dir, Teesside Power Ltd, 1991–. Chm., BITC, Tyneside, 1993–. *Recreations:* mountaineering, sailing. *Address:* Northern Electric plc, Carliol House, Market Street, Newcastle upon Tyne NE1 6NE. *T:* 0191–235 2103.

HADFIELD, (Ellis) Charles (Raymond), CMG 1954; *b* 5 Aug. 1909; *s* of Alexander Charles Hadfield, Transvaal Colony Magistracy; *m* 1945, Alice Mary Miller (*d* 1989), *d* of Lt-Col Henry Smyth, DSO; one *s* one *d* (and one *s* decd). *Educ:* Blundell's Sch.; St Edmund Hall, Oxford. Joined Oxford University Press, 1936; Dir of Publications, Central Office of Information, 1946–48; Controller (Overseas), 1948–62. Dir, David and Charles (Publishers) Ltd, 1960–64. Mem., British Waterways Bd, 1962–66. *Publications:* The Young Collector's Handbook (with C. Hamilton Ellis), 1940; Civilian Fire Fighter, 1941; (with Alexander d'Agapayeff) Maps, 1942; (with Frank Eyre) The Fire Service Today, 1944; (with Frank Eyre) English Rivers and Canals, 1945; (with J. E. MacColl) Pilot Guide to Political London, 1945; (with J. E. MacColl) British Local Government, 1948; (as Charles Alexander) The Church's Year, 1950; British Canals, 1950, 8th edn 1994; The Canals of Southern England, 1955; Introducing Canals, 1955; The Canals of South Wales and the Border, 1960; (with John Norris) Waterways to Stratford, 1962; Canals of the World, 1964; Canals and Waterways, 1966; (with Alice Mary Hadfield) The Cotswolds, 1966; The Canals of the East Midlands, 1966; The Canals of the West Midlands, 1966; The Canals of South West England, 1967; Atmospheric Railways, 1967; (with Michael Streat) Holiday Cruising on Inland Waterways, 1968; The Canal Age, 1968; The Canals of South and South East England, 1969; (with Gordon Biddle) The Canals of North West England, 1970; The Canals of Yorkshire and North East England, 1972; Introducing Inland Waterways, 1973; (with Alice Mary Hadfield) Introducing the Cotswolds, 1976; Waterways Sights to See, 1976; Inland Waterways, 1978; (with A. W. Skempton) William Jessop, Engineer, 1979; (with Alice Mary Hadfield) Afloat in America, 1979; World Canals, 1986; Thomas Telford's Temptation, 1993; *festschrift:* Canals: a new look; studies in honour of Charles Hadfield (ed M. Baldwin and A. Burton), 1984. *Recreations:* writing; exploring canals. *Address:* 13 Meadow Way, South Cerney, Cirencester, Glos GL7 6HY. *T:* Cirencester (01285) 860422.

HADFIELD, (Geoffrey) John, CBE 1980; TD 1963; MS, FRCS; Surgeon, Stoke Mandeville Hospital, 1960–88, retired; Hon. Tutor in Surgery, University College Hospital Medical School, since 1968; *b* 19 April 1923; *s* of late Prof. Geoffrey Hadfield, MD, and Eileen D'Arcy Irvine; *m* 1960, Beryl, *d* of late Hubert Sleigh, Manchester; three *d*. *Educ:* Merchant Taylors' Sch.; St Bartholomew's Hosp., London Univ. MB BS 1947, MS 1954, London; MRCS LRCP 1946, FRCS 1948. Hon. Officer Appts, Demonstr. of Anatomy, Registrar and Sen. Lectr in Surgery, St Bart's Hosp.; Fellow in Surgery, Memorial Hosp., New York; served RAMC, Far East, 1948–50; TAVR, 1950–73; Bt-Col, RAMC RARO, Hon. Col 219 Gen. Hosp., TAVR. Royal College of Surgeons of England: Arris and Gale Lectr, 1954; Hunterian Prof., 1959; Erasmus Wilson Demonstr., 1969; Arnott Demonstr., 1972; Stamford Cade Meml Lectr, 1978; Mem., Council, 1971–83, Vice-Pres., 1982–83; Mem., Court of Examiners, Final FRCS, 1972–78 (Chm., 1977–78); Mem., Ct of Examiners, Primary FRCS, 1982–85. Examiner in Surgery for Univs of Liverpool, Bristol and Leeds, and Vis. Examiner to univs in Middle and Far East. Fellow, 1955, Sen. Fellow, 1988, Assoc. of Surgs of GB and Ireland; Senior Member: Brit. Assoc. of Urol Surgs (Mem. Council, 1979–82); Brit. Assoc. of Surg. Oncology (Mem., Nat. Cttee, 1972–75); Brit. Assoc. of Clin. Anatomists (Mem. Council, 1976–80). Hon. FCPS (Pak) (Liaison Officer), 1991. *Publications:* (with M. Hobsley) Current Surgical Practice, vol. 1, 1976, vol. 2, 1978, vol. 3, 1981, vol. 4, 1986, vol. 5, 1990; (with M. Hobsley and B. C. Morson) Pathology in Surgical Practice, 1985; (jtly) Imaging in Surgical Practice, 1989; articles in jls and chapters in books on diseases of the breast, cancer, urology, trauma, varicose veins and med. educn. *Recreations:* ocean racing and cruising, travel, walking, golf. *Address:* Milverton House, 6 St John's Close, Bishopsteignton, near Teignmouth, Devon TQ14 9RT. *T:* Teignmouth (016267) 79537. *Clubs:* Army and Navy; Teign Corinthian Yacht.

See also J. I. H. Hadfield.

HADFIELD, James Irvine Havelock, FRCS, FRCSE; Consultant Surgeon (Urologist), Bedford General Hospital, since 1965; Medical Director, Bedford Hospital NHS Trust, since 1992; *b* 12 July 1930; *s* of Prof. G. Hadfield and S. V. E. Hadfield (*née* Irvine); *m* 1957, Ann Pickernell Milner; one *s* two *d*. *Educ:* Radley College; Brasenose College, Oxford (MA, BM, BCh 1955, MCh Pt I 1960); St Thomas's Hosp. Med. Sch. FRCS 1960, FRCSE 1960; FICS 1990. House Surgeon, St Thomas' Hosp., 1955; Lectr in Anatomy, St Thomas's Hosp. Med. Sch., 1956–57; RSO, Leicester Royal Inf., 1960–62; Surgical Tutor, Oxford Univ., 1962–66; Arris and Gale Lectr, RCS, 1967; Examnr in Surgery, Univ. of Cambridge, 1976–82; Examnr in MRCS, LRCP, 1974–80; Examnr, FRCSE, 1989–. *Publications:* articles in surgical jls on Metabolic Response to Trauma, Urology, and Surgical Anatomy of the Veins of the Legs. *Recreations:* watching rowing, shooting, unwilling gardener, trying to catch unwilling salmon in South West Wales. *Address:* Baker's Barn, Stagsden West End, near Bedford MK43 8SZ. *T:* Oakley (012302) 4514. *Clubs:* Vincent's (Oxford); Leander, London Rowing.

See also G. J. Hadfield.

HADFIELD, John; *see* Hadfield, G. J.

HADFIELD, John Charles Heywood; author; Proprietor, The Cupid Press, since 1949; Director, Rainbird Publishing Group, 1965–82; *b* 16 June 1907; 2nd *s* of H. G. Hadfield, Birmingham; *m* 1st, 1931, Phyllis Anna McMullen (*d* 1973); one *s* decd; 2nd, 1975, Joy Westendarp. *Educ:* Bradfield. Editor, J. M. Dent & Sons, Ltd, 1935–42; Books Officer for British Council in the Middle East, 1942–44; Dir of the National Book League, 1944–50; Organiser, Festival of Britain Exhibition of Books, 1951; Editor, The Saturday Book, 1952–73. *Publications:* The Christmas Companion, 1939; Georgian Love Songs, 1949; Restoration Love Songs, 1950; A Book of Beauty, 1952, rev. edn 1976; A Book of Delights, 1954, rev. edn 1977; Elizabethan Love Songs, 1955; A Book of Britain, 1956; A Book of Love, 1958, revd edn 1978; Love on a Branch Line, 1959; A Book of Pleasures, 1960; A Book of Joy, 1962; A Chamber of Horrors, 1965; (ed) The Shell Guide to England, 1970, rev. edn 1981; (ed) Cowardy Custard, 1973; (ed) The Shell Book of English Villages, 1980; (ed) Everyman's Book of English Love Poems, 1980; The Best of The Saturday Book, 1981; Every Picture Tells a Story, 1985; Victorian Delights, 1987; (with Miles Hadfield): The Twelve Days of Christmas, 1961; Gardens of Delight, 1964. *Recreations:* books, pictures, gardens. *Address:* 2 Quay Street, Woodbridge, Suffolk IP12 1BX. *T:* Woodbridge (01394) 387414. *Club:* Savile.

HADFIELD, Sir Ronald, Kt 1995; QPM 1989; DL; Chief Constable, West Midlands, since 1990; *b* 15 July 1939; *s* of George and Phyllis Marjorie Hadfield; *m* 1961, Anne Phyllisia Worrall; one *s* one *d*. *Educ:* Chadderton Grammar School. Joined Oldham Borough Police Force, 1958; served in Lancashire and Greater Manchester Police Forces; Asst Chief Constable, Derbyshire Constabulary, 1981; Dep. Chief Constable, 1986, Chief Constable, 1987, Nottinghamshire Constabulary. DL W Midlands, 1994. *Recreations:* golf, fishing, Police Athletic Association. *Address:* West Midlands Police, Lloyd House, Colmore Circus, Queensway, Birmingham B4 6NQ.

HADINGHAM, Reginald Edward Hawke, CBE 1988 (OBE 1971); MC 1943 and Bar 1943; TD 1946; Life President, Sparks, the sportsman's charity, 1995 (Chairman, 1968–94); Deputy Chairman, Action Research for the Crippled Child, since 1976; *b* 6 Dec. 1915; *s* of Edward Wallace Hadingham and Ethel Irene Penelope Gwynne-Evans; *m* 1940, Lois Pope, *d* of Edward and Nora Pope; two *d*. *Educ:* Rokeby Preparatory, Wimbledon; St Paul's. Joined Slazengers, 1933, European Sales Manager, 1936. Joined TA, 57th Anti-Tank Regt, 1938, commnd into 67th Anti-Tank Regt 1938; served War of 1939–45 with 67th Anti-Tank Regt, RA; commanded 302 Battery, 1942–45 (MC Salerno 1943 ar Bar, Garigliano 1943); CO 67 Regt, 1945 until disbanded, Oct. 1945. Returned t Slazengers as Asst Export Manager, Jan. 1946; Export Manager, 1949; Gen. Sales Manage 1951; Sales Dir, 1952; Man. Dir, 1969; Chm. and Man. Dir, 1973; Chm. (Non-Exec. 1976–83. All England Lawn Tennis Club: Mem. Cttee, 1976–84; Chm. of Club, and Cttee of Management, The Championships, Wimbledon, 1984–89; Vice-Pres., 199 Pres., Internat. Lawn Tennis Club of GB, 1991–. Vice-Pres., PHAB, 1978–; Twice Pr Sette of Odd Volumes, Treasurer, 1953–. *Recreations:* lawn tennis and writing ve *Address:* 15 Harroldene Court, 6 Belvedere Drive, Wimbledon, SW19 7BY. *T:* 0181- 9611. *Clubs:* Queen's, All England Lawn Tennis, Hurlingham, International Lawn Te of GB.

HADLEE, Sir Richard (John), Kt 1990; MBE 1980; New Zealand cricketer, retired July 1951; *s* of Walter Hadlee; *m* 1973, Karen Ann; two *s*. *Educ:* Christchurch Boys' I Sch. Played for: Canterbury, 1972–89; Nottinghamshire (UK), 1978–87 (made 1000 and took 100 wickets in English season, 1984); Tasmania, 1979–80; Test début for NZ, 1973; toured: Australia, 1972–73, 1973–74, 1980–81, 1985–86; England, 1973, 1978, 1983, 1986, 1990; India, 1976, 1988; Pakistan, 1976; Sri Lanka, 1983–84, 1987; West Indies, 1984–85. Holder of world record of 431 Test wickets, 1990 (passed previous record of 373 in 1988). *Publication:* Rhythm and Swing (autobiog.), 1989. *Address:* Box 29186, Christchurch, New Zealand.

HADLEY, David Allen, CB 1991; Deputy Secretary (Agricultural Commodities, Trade and Food Production), Ministry of Agriculture, Fisheries and Food, since 1993; *b* 18 Feb. 1936; *s* of Sydney and Gwendoline Hadley; *m* 1965, Veronica Ann Hopkins; one *s*. *Educ:* Wyggeston Grammar Sch., Leicester; Merton Coll., Oxford. MA. Joined MAFF, 1959; Asst Sec., 1971; HM Treas., 1975–78; Under Sec., 1981–87, Dep. Sec., 1987–89, MAFF; Dep. Sec., Cabinet Office, 1989–93. *Recreations:* gardening, music. *Address:* c/o Ministry of Agriculture, Fisheries and Food, Whitehall Place, SW1A 2HH.

HADLEY, Graham Hunter, FRSA; Executive Director, since 1990, and Managing Director, International Business Development, since 1993, National Power; *b* 12 April 1944; *s* of Dr A. L. Hadley and Mrs L.E. Hadley; *m* 1971, Lesley Ann Smith; one *s*. *Educ:* Eltham Coll., London; Jesus Coll., Cambridge (BA Hons Mod. Hist.). Entered Civil Service (Min. of Aviation), 1966; Dept of Energy, 1974; seconded to: Civil Service Commn, 1976–77; British Aerospace, 1980–81; Under-Sec., Dept of Energy, 1983; Sec., CEGB, 1983–90. FRSA 1986. *Recreations:* include cricket, running, golf, theatre, architecture, aviation. *Address:* The Coach House, 14 Genoa Avenue, SW15 6DY. *T:* 0181–788 2698.

HADLEY, Sir Leonard Albert, Kt 1975; JP; Union Secretary, Wellington, NZ, retired 1984; *b* Wellington, 8 Sept. 1911; *s* of Albert A. Hadley, JP; *m* 1st, 1939, Jean Lyell (*d* 1965), *d* of E. S. Innes; one *s* one *d*; 2nd, 1978, Amelia Townsend. Mem., Nat. Exec., NZ Fedn of Labour, 1946–76; Dir, Reserve Bank of NZ, 1959–85; Mem., Bd of Trustees since formation, 1964–87, Pres., 1976–79, Wellington Trustee Savings Bank. Relieving Mem., Industrial Commn and Industrial Court, 1974 (Arbitration Court, 1960–84); Mem., Waterfront Industry Tribunal, 1981–83. Member: NZ Immigration Adv. Council; Industrial Relations Council, 1953–75; Periodic Detention Work Centre Adv. Cttee (Juvenile), and Adult Centre, 1962–84 (both since formation); Absolute Liability Enquiry Cttee, 1963–, and Govt Cttees to review Exempted Goods, 1959 and 1962. Rep., NZ Fedn of Labour Delegns to ILO, Geneva, 1949 and 1966; Internat. Confedn of Free Trade Unions Inaugural Conf., 1949; Social Security Conf., Moscow, 1971; SE Asian Trade Union Conf., Tokyo, 1973; OECD Conf., Paris, 1974. Member: Terawhiti Licensing Trust, 1975–80; Witako Regl Prison Adv. Cttee, 1983–88. Life Member: Vogelmorn Tennis Club, 1961; Wellington Working Men's Club and Literary Inst., 1979; NZ Plumbers' Union, 1978; Wellington Clerical Union, 1983. Patron, Vogelmorn Bowling Club, 1982–. Awarded Smith-Mundt Ldr Study Grant in USA, 1953. JP 1967. *Recreations:* reading, music, outdoor bowls, Rugby, tennis, and sport generally. *Address:* (private) 3 Cheesman Street, Brooklyn, Wellington, New Zealand.

HADRILL, Andrew Frederic W.; *see* Wallace-Hadrill.

HAENDEL, Ida, CBE 1991; violinist; *b* Poland, 15 Dec. 1928; Polish parentage. Began to play at age of 3½; amazing gift discovered when she picked up her sister's violin and started to play. Her father, a great connoisseur of music, recognised her unusual talent and abandoned his own career as an artist (painter) to devote himself to his daughter; studied at Warsaw Conservatoire and gained gold medal at age of seven; also studied with such masters as Carl Flesch and Georges Enesco. British début, Queen's Hall, with Sir Henry Wood, playing Brahms' Violin Concerto. Gave concerts for British and US troops and in factories, War of 1939–45; after War, career developed to take in North and South America, USSR and Far East, as well as Europe; has accompanied British orchestras such as London Philharmonic, BBC Symphony and English Chamber on foreign tours including Hong Kong, China, Australia and Mexico; performs with major orchestras worldwide, incl. Berlin Philharmonic, Boston Symphony, and Concertgebouw. Has performed with conductors such as Beecham, Klemperer, Szell, Barenboim, Mata, Pritchard, Rattle, Haitink, Ashkenazy; performances include appearances at BBC Prom. Concerts, Edinburgh

Fest., masterclasses. Sibelius Medal, Sibelius Soc. of Finland, 1982. *Publication:* Woman with Violin (autobiog.), 1970. *Address:* c/o Harold Holt, 31 Sinclair Road, W14 0NS.

HAFFNER, Albert Edward, PhD; Chairman, North Eastern Gas Board, 1971–72 (Deputy Chairman, 1966–71); *b* 17 Feb. 1907; 4th *s* of late George Christian and late Caroline Haffner, Holme, near Burnley, Lancs; *m* 1934, Elizabeth Ellen Crossley (*d* 1989), Cheadle Heath, Stockport; one *s* one *d*. *Educ:* Burnley Grammar Sch.; Royal College of Science; Imperial Coll., London; Technische Hochschule, Karlsruhe. BSc (1st Cl. Hons), ARCS, PhD, DIC, London. Burnley Gas Works, 1924–26; Gas Light & Coke Co, 1932–56; Research Chemist and North Thames Gas Bd; Gp Engr, Chief Engineer and later Bd Member, Southern Gas Bd, 1956–66. Past Pres., Instn Gas Engineers (Centenary Pres., 1962–63); Past Vice-Pres., Internat. Gas Union. CEng, MIChemE. *Publications:* Contributor to: Proc. Roy. Soc., Jl Instn Gas Engrs, Instn Chem. Engrs, Inst. of Fuel, New Scientist; papers presented to Canadian Gas Assoc., French Chem. Soc., Japanese Gas Industry and at IGU Confs in USA, USSR and Germany, etc. *Recreations:* photography, travel, gardening, cabinetmaking. *Address:* Burnthwaite, Iwerne Courtney, near Blandford Forum, Dorset DT11 8QL. *T:* Child Okeford (01258) 860749. *Club:* New Cavendish.

HAGARD, Dr Spencer, FFPHM; public health consultant, London Health Economics Consortium, London School of Hygiene and Tropical Medicine; *b* 25 Oct. 1942; *s* of Maurice (Bozzie) Markham (killed in action, 11 June 1944) and Eva Markham (*née* Mearns, subseq. Hagard) and, by adoption, of late Noel Hagard; *m* 1968, Michele Dominique, *d* of Stanislas and late Madeleine Aquarone; two *s* one *d*. *Educ:* Varndean Grammar Sch., Brighton; Univ. of St Andrews (MB ChB 1968); Univ. of Glasgow (PhD 1977); MA Cantab 1977. DPH 1972; FFPHM (FFCM 1981). Jun. med. appts, Arbroath, ndon and Dorking; MO and Med. Supt, Kawolo Hosp., Lugazi, Uganda, 1971–72;), Health Dept, Glasgow, 1972–74; Trainee in Community Med., Greater Glasgow lth Bd, 1974–77; Specialist in Comm. Med., Cambs AHA, 1977–82; Dist MO, bridge HA, 1982–87; Chief Exec., HEA, 1987–94. Associate Lectr, Univ. of ridge Sch. of Clinical Med., 1977–87; Vis. Prof., LSHTM, 1993–95. Hon. ltant, N Thames Health Reg., 1995–; Consultant, WHO, 1991–. *Publications:* , Society and Medicine (with Roy Acheson), 1984; papers in BMJ and other learned *reations:* marriage, family, studying human beings, politics, gardening, reading, aphy, appreciation of art, music, sporting lost causes (Brighton & Hove Albion, CC). *Address:* 396 Milton Road, Cambridge CB4 1SU. *T:* Cambridge (01223) *Fax:* (01223) 423970.

ALEXANDER, Sir Claud; *see* Alexander.

ctor W. Von; *see* Von Hagen.

William John Gell; writer and broadcaster; Theatre Critic, since 1993, Film 1994, Today; Consultant Editor, Tribune, since 1993; *b* 23 April 1939; *s* of ...eve) Hagerty and Doris Hagerty (*née* Gell); *m* 1st, 1965, Lynda Beresford (marr. diss. 1990); one *s* one *d* (and one *d* decd); 2nd, 1991, Elizabeth Vercoe (*née* Latta); one *s*. *Educ:* Beal Grammar Sch., Ilford. Local newspapers, East London, 1955–58; RAF Nat. Service, 1958–60; local newspapers, Sunday Citizen, Daily Sketch, 1960–67; Daily Mirror, 1967–81; Sunday Mirror and Sunday People, 1981–85; Managing Editor (Features), Today, 1986; Editor, Sunday Today, 1987; Deputy Editor: Sunday Mirror, 1988–90; Daily Mirror, 1990–91; Editor, The People, 1991–92. Press Guy, Variety Club of GB, 1994–. *Publication:* Flash, Bang, Wallop! (with Kent Gavin), 1978. *Recreations:* musical theatre, watching cricket, lunch with Keith Waterhouse. *Address:* Bull Cottage, 10/11 Strand-on-the-Green, Chiswick, W4 3PQ. *Club:* Royal Automobile.

HAGESTADT, John Valentine; Director, Invest in Britain Bureau, Department of Trade and Industry, since 1995; *b* 11 Oct. 1938; *s* of late Leonard and Constance Hagestadt; *m* 1963, Betty Tebbs; three *d*. *Educ:* Dulwich Coll.; Worcester Coll., Oxford (BA). Asst Principal, Min. of Aviation, 1963; Principal, BoT, 1967; Nuffield Travelling Fellow, 1973–74; Asst Sec., Vehicles Div., Dept of Industry, 1976; Asst Sec., Overseas Trade Div. (Middle East and Latin America), Dept of Trade, 1980; Dir, British Trade Develt Office, NY 1982; Dir, Invest in Britain Bureau, NY, 1984–87; Head, N Amer. Br., DTI, 1987–93; Dir, Govt Office for London, 1994. *Address:* 14 Carlisle Mansions, Carlisle Place, SW1P 1HX. *T:* 0171–828 0042.

HAGGARD, Prof. Mark Peregrine, PhD; founder Director, Medical Research Council Institute of Hearing Research, since 1977; *b* 26 Dec. 1942; *m* 1962, Liz (*née* Houston); two *s*. *Educ:* Edinburgh Univ. (MA Psych, 1st cl. hons); Corpus Christi Coll., Cambridge (PhD Psych 1967). Univ. Demonstrator in Experimental Psychology, Univ. of Cambridge, 1967–71; Prof. of Psychology and Head of Dept, QUB, 1971–76; sabbatical, 1975–76; Special Prof. in Audiological Scis, Nottingham Univ., 1980–. *Publications:* Screening Children's Hearing, 1991; Research in the Development of Effective Services for Hearing-impaired People, 1993; contribs to learned jls. *Recreations:* ski-ing, choral music. *Address:* MRC Institute of Hearing Research, University Park, Nottingham NG7 2RD. *T:* Nottingham (0115) 922 3431. *Club:* Royal Society of Medicine.

HAGGART, Rt. Rev. Alastair Iain Macdonald; *b* 10 Oct. 1915; *s* of Alexander Macdonald Haggart and Jessie Mackay; *m* 1st, 1945, Margaret Agnes Trundle (*d* 1979); two *d*; 2nd, 1983, Mary Elizabeth Scholes, *qv*. *Educ:* Hatfield Coll. (Exhibnr); Durham Univ. (Exhibnr); Edinburgh Theol College. LTh 1941; BA 1942; MA 1945. Deacon, 1941, Priest 1942. Curate: St Mary's Cath., Glasgow, 1941–45; St Mary's, Hendon, 1945–48; Precentor, St Ninian's Cath., Perth, 1948–51; Rector, St Oswald's, King's Park, Glasgow, 1951, and Acting Priest-in-Charge, St Martin's, Glasgow, 1953–58; Synod Clerk of Glasgow Dio. and Canon of St Mary's Cath., Glasgow, 1958–59; Provost, St Paul's Cathedral, Dundee, 1959–71; Principal and Pantonian Prof., Episcopal Theological Coll., Edinburgh, 1971–75; Canon, St Mary's Cathedral, Edinburgh, 1971–75; Bishop of Edinburgh, 1975–85; Primus of the Episcopal Church in Scotland, 1977–85. Exam. Chap. to Bp of Brechin, 1964. Hon. LLD Dundee, 1970. *Recreations:* walking, reading, listening to music, asking questions. *Address:* 19 Eglinton Crescent, Edinburgh EH12 5BY. *T:* 0131–337 8948.

HAGGART, Mary Elizabeth; *see* Scholes, M. E.

HAGGERSTON GADSDEN, Sir Peter Drury; *see* Gadsden.

HAGGETT, Prof. Peter, CBE 1993; FBA 1992; Professor of Urban and Regional Geography, University of Bristol, since 1966, Vice-Chancellor (Acting), 1984–85; *b* 24 Jan. 1933; *s* of Charles and Elizabeth Haggett, Pawlett, Somerset; *m* 1956, Brenda Woodley; two *s* two *d*. *Educ:* Dr Morgan's Sch., Bridgwater; St Catharine's Coll., Cambridge (Exhib. and Scholar; MA 1958; PhD 1970; ScD 1985). Asst Lectr, University Coll. London, 1955; Demonstrator and University Lectr, Cambridge, 1957; Fellow, Fitzwilliam Coll., 1963 (Hon. Fellow, 1994); Leverhulme Research Fellow (Brazil), 1959; Canada Council Fellow, 1977; Erskine Fellow (NZ), 1979; Res. Fellow, Res. Sch. of Pacific Studies, ANU, 1983. Visiting Professor: Berkeley; Monash; Pennsylvania State; Toronto; Western Ontario; Wisconsin; Hill Prof., Minnesota, 1994. Member, SW Economic Planning Council, 1967–72. Governor, Centre for Environmental Studies, 1975–78; Member: Council, RGS, 1972–73, 1977–80; UGC, 1985–89; Nat. Radiological Protection Bd, 1986–93; Chm., Hist. of Med. Grants Panel, Wellcome Trust., 1994–. Hon. DSc: York, Canada, 1983; Durham, 1989; Hon LLD Bristol, 1986. Cullum Medal of American Geographical Soc., 1969; Meritorious Contribution Award, Assoc. of American Geographers, 1973; Patron's Medal, RGS, 1986; Prix Internationale de Géographie, 1991; Lauréat d'Honneur, IGU, 1992; Scottish Medal, RSGS, 1993; Anders Retzius Gold Medal, Sweden, 1994. *Publications:* Locational Analysis in Human Geography, 1965; (ed jtly) Frontiers in Geographical Teaching, 1965; Models in Geography, 1967; (with R. J. Chorley) Network Analysis in Geography, 1969; Progress in Geography, vols 1–9, 1969–77; Regional Forecasting, 1971; Geography: a modern synthesis, 1972, 4th edn, 1983; (with A. D. Cliff and others) Elements of Spatial Structure, 1975; Processes in Physical and Human Geography: Bristol Essays, 1975; Spatial Diffusion, 1981; Spatial Aspects of Epidemics, 1986; Atlas of Disease Distributions, 1988; The Geographer's Art, 1990; Atlas of AIDS, 1992; Measles: an historical geography, 1993; research papers. *Recreations:* natural history, cricket. *Address:* 5 Tun Bridge Close, Chew Magna, Somerset BS18 8SU. *Club:* United Oxford & Cambridge University.

HAGGETT, Stuart John, MA; Headmaster, Birkenhead School, since 1988; *b* 11 April 1947; *s* of William Francis and Doreen Ada Haggett; *m* 1971, Hilary Joy Hammond; two *d*. *Educ:* Dauntsey's Sch., West Lavington, Wilts; Downing Coll., Cambridge (MA 1972); PGCE London (ext.), 1970. Canford Sch., Wimborne, Dorset, 1970–83: Head of Modern Languages, 1973–83; Housemaster, 1975–83; Second Master, King's Sch., Rochester, 1983–88. *Recreations:* France (travel and culture), sport, theatre, architecture, cooking. *Address:* Birkenhead School, 58 Beresford Road, Birkenhead, Merseyside L43 2JD. *T:* 0151–652 4014.

HÄGGLÖF, Gunnar, GCVO (Hon.), 1954; Swedish Diplomat; *b* 15 Dec. 1904; *s* of Richard Hägglöf and Sigrid Ryding, Stockholm, Sweden; *m* Anna, *d* of Count Folchi-Vici, Rome. *Educ:* Upsala Univ., Sweden. Entered Swedish Diplomatic Service, 1926; Minister without Portfolio, 1939. During War of 1939–45, led various Swedish delegns to Berlin, London, and Washington; Envoy to Belgian and Dutch Govts, 1944; Envoy in Moscow, 1946; permanent delegate to UN, 1947; Ambassador to Court of St James's, 1948–67; Ambassador to France, 1967–71. Delegate to Conf. for Constitution, European Council, 1949; delegate to Suez Confs, 1956; Mem. of Menzies Cttee to Cairo, 1956. Hon. DCL Birmingham, 1960. *Publications:* Diplomat, 1972; several books and essays in economics, politics and history. *Recreations:* ski-ing, swimming, reading, writing. *Address:* Vigna Orsini, Bracciano, Rome, Italy.

HAGUE, Prof. Sir Douglas (Chalmers), Kt 1982; CBE 1978; Chairman: Oxford Strategy Network, since 1984; Associate Fellow, Templeton College, Oxford, since 1983; *b* Leeds, 20 Oct. 1926; *s* of Laurence and Marion Hague; *m* 1947, Brenda Elizabeth Fereday (marr. diss. 1986); two *d*; *m* 1986, Janet Mary Leach. *Educ:* Moseley Grammar Sch.; King Edward VI High Sch., Birmingham; University of Birmingham. Assistant Tutor, Faculty of Commerce, Birmingham Univ., 1946; Assistant Lecturer, University College, London, 1947, Lecturer, 1950; Reader in Political Economy in University of London, 1957; Newton Chambers Professor of Economics, University of Sheffield, 1957–63. Visiting Professor of Economics, Duke Univ., USA, 1960–61; Head of Department of Business Studies, University of Sheffield, 1962–63; Professor of Applied Economics, University of Manchester, 1963–65; Prof. of Managerial Economics, Manchester Business Sch., 1965–81, Dep. Dir, 1978–81, Vis. Prof., 1981–; Vis. Prof., Imperial Coll. of Science and Technol., London, 1988–92. Chairman: Metapraxis Ltd, 1984–90; Doctus Consulting Europe, 1991–94; Director: Economic Models Ltd, 1970–78; The Laird Gp, 1976–79; CRT Gp, 1990– (Chm., 1992–93). Rapporteur to International Economic Association, 1953–78, Editor General, 1981–86; Chm., ESRC, 1983–87; Member Working Party of National Advisory Council on Education for Industry and Commerce, 1962–63; Consultant to Secretariat of NEDC, 1962–63; Member: Treasury Working Party on Management Training in the Civil Service, 1965–67; EDC for Paper and Board, 1967–70; (part-time) N Western Gas Board, 1966–72; Working Party, Local Govt Training Bd, 1969–70; Price Commn, 1973–78 (Dep. Chm., 1977); Director: Manchester School of Management and Administration, 1964–65; Centre for Business Research, Manchester, 1964–66. Member Council, Manchester Business School, 1964–81; Chairman, Manchester Industrial Relations Society, 1964–66; President, NW Operational Research Group, 1967–69; British Chm., Carnegie Project on Accountability, 1968–72; Jt Chm., Conf. of Univ. Management Schools, 1971–73; Chairman: DoI Working Party, Kirkby Manufacturing and Engineering Co., 1978; Professional Develt Cttee, Inst. of Dirs, 1993–. Economic adviser to Mrs Thatcher, Gen. Election campaign, 1979; Adviser to PM's Policy Unit, 10 Downing St, 1979–83. Industrial Consultant. Hon. LittD Sheffield, 1987. *Publications:* Costs in Alternative Locations: The Clothing Industry (with P. K. Newman), 1952; (with A. W. Stonier) A Textbook of Economic Theory, 1953, 4th edn 1973; (with A. W. Stonier) The Essentials of Economics, 1955; The Economics of Man-Made Fibres, 1957; (ed) Stability and Progress in the World Economy, 1958; (ed) The Theory of Capital, 1961; (ed) Inflation, 1962; (ed with Sir Roy Harrod) International Trade Theory in a Developing World, 1965; (ed) Price Formation in Various Economies, 1967; Managerial Economics, 1969; (ed with Bruce L. R. Smith) The Dilemma of Accountability in Modern Government, 1970; Pricing in Business, 1971; (with M. E. Beesley) Britain in the Common Market: a new business opportunity, 1973; (with W. E. F. Oakeshott and A. A. Strain) Devaluation and Pricing Decisions: a case study approach, 1974; (with W. J. M. Mackenzie and A. Barker) Public Policy and Private Interests: the institutions of compromise, 1975; (with Geoffrey Wilkinson) The IRC: an experiment in industrial intervention, 1983; (with Peter Hennessy) How Adolf Hitler reformed Whitehall, 1985; (ed) The Management of Science, 1991; Beyond Universities: a new republic of the intellect, 1991; Transforming the Dinosaurs, 1993; articles in economic, financial and management journals. *Recreations:* church organs, watching Manchester United. *Address:* Templeton College, Oxford OX1 5NY. *T:* Oxford (01865) 735422. *Club:* Athenæum.

HAGUE, Rt Hon. William (Jefferson); PC 1995; MP (C) Richmond, Yorks, since Feb. 1989; Secretary of State for Wales, since 1995; *b* 26 March 1961; *s* of Timothy Nigel Hague and Stella Hague. *Educ:* Wath-upon-Dearne Comprehensive School; Magdalen College, Oxford (MA); Insead (MBA). Pres., Oxford Union, 1981; Pres., Oxford Univ. Cons. Assoc., 1981. Management Consultant, McKinsey & Co., 1983–88. Political Adviser, HM Treasury, 1983. Contested (C) Wentworth, S Yorks, 1987. PPS to Chancellor of the Exchequer, 1990–93; Parly Under-Sec. of State, DSS, 1993–94; Minister for Social Security and Disabled People, DSS, 1994–95. *Address:* House of Commons, SW1A 0AA. *T:* Northallerton (01609) 779093. *Club:* Carlton.

HAHN, Dr Carl Horst; Chairman, Board of Management, Volkswagen AG, Wolfsburg, 1981–92; *b* 1 July 1926; *m* 1960, Marisa Traina; three *s* one *d*. Formerly: Chairman, Supervisory Board: Audi AG; Gerling-Konzern Speziale Kreditversicherungs-AG, Cologne; Deputy Chairman, Supervisory Board, Aktiengesellschaft für Industrie und Verkehrswesen, Frankfurt (Main); Member, Supervisory Board: Gerling-Konzern Allgemeine Versicherungs-AG, Cologne; Gerling Konzern Versicherungs Beteiligung

AG; Wilhelm Karmann GmbH, Osnabrück; Deutsche Messe- und Ausstellungs-AG, Hanover; Deutsche BP AG; Erste Allgemeine Versicherungs AG, Vienna; Thyssen AG; Commerzbank AG; Mem., Admin. Council, Deutsche Automobilges. Member: Bd of Dirs, Cttee of Common Market Automobile Constructors; Foreign Trade Adv. Council, Fed. Economics Min.; Internat. Adv. Council, Salk Inst., La Jolla, Calif; Bd of Management, Founders' Adv. Council of German Science; Presidium, Confedn of German Industry (also Vice-Pres.); Assoc. of German Automotive Industry; Bd of Trustees, Volkswagenwerk Foundn. *Address:* c/o Volkswagen AG, Postfach, 3180 Wolfsburg 1, Germany.

HAHN, Prof. Frank Horace, FBA 1975; Professor of Economics, University of Cambridge, 1972–92, now Emeritus; Fellow of Churchill College, Cambridge, since 1960; *b* 26 April 1925; *s* of Dr Arnold Hahn and Maria Hahn; *m* 1946, Dorothy Salter; no *c. Educ:* Bournemouth Grammar School; London School of Economics (Hon. Fellow, 1989). PhD London, MA Cantab. Univ. of Birmingham, 1948–60, Reader in Mathematical Economics, 1958–60; Univ. Lectr in Econs, Cambridge, 1960–67; Prof. of Economics, LSE, 1967–72; Frank W. Taussig Res. Prof., Harvard, 1975–76. Visiting Professor: MIT, 1956–57; Univ. of California, Berkeley, 1959–60; Schumpeter Prof., Vienna Univ. of Econs and Business Admin, 1984; Prof. Ordinario, Univ. of Siena, 1992–. Fellow, Inst. of Advanced Studies in Behavioural Sciences, Stanford, 1966–67. Mem. Council for Scientific Policy, later Adv. Bd of Res. Councils, 1972–75. Fellow, Econometric Soc., 1962; Vice-Pres., 1967–68; Pres., 1968–69; Pres., Royal Economic Soc., 1986–89. Managing Editor, Review of Economic Studies, 1965–68. Foreign Hon. Mem., Amer. Acad. of Arts and Sciences, 1974; Hon. Mem., Amer. Economic Assoc., 1986; For. Associate, US Nat. Acad. of Scis, 1988; Mem., Academia Europaea, 1989. Hon. DSocSci Birmingham, 1981; Hon DLitt: East Anglia, 1984; Leicester, 1993; Dr Econ *hc* Strasbourg, 1984; Hon. DSc(Econ) London, 1985; DUniv York, 1991; Hon. PhD Athens, 1993. Palacky Gold Medal, Czechoslovak Acad. of Scis, 1991. *Publications:* (with K. J. Arrow) General Competitive Analysis, 1971; The Share of Wages in the National Income, 1972; Money and Inflation, 1982; Equilibrium and Macro-Economics, 1984; Money, Growth and Stability, 1985; (ed and contrib.) The Economics of Missing Markets, Information and Games, 1989; (with Robert Solow) A Critical Essay on Modern Macroeconomic Theory, 1995; articles in learned journals. *Address:* 16 Adams Road, Cambridge CB3 9AD. *T:* Cambridge (01223) 352560; 30 Tavistock Court, Tavistock Square, WC1H 9HE. *T:* 0171–387 4293.

HAIG, family name of **Earl Haig.**

HAIG, 2nd Earl, *cr* 1919; **George Alexander Eugene Douglas Haig,** OBE 1966; DL; ARSA 1988; Viscount Dawick, *cr* 1919; Baron Haig and 30th Laird of Bemersyde; is a painter; Member, Queen's Body Guard for Scotland; *b* March 1918; *o s* of 1st Earl and Hon. Dorothy Vivian (*d* 1939) (Author of A Scottish Tour, 1935), *d* of 3rd Lord Vivian; *S* father, 1928; *m* 1st, 1956, Adrienne Thérèse, *d* of Derrick Morley; one *s* two *d*; 2nd, 1981, Donna Geroloma Lopez y Royo di Taurisano. *Educ:* Stowe; Christ Church, Oxford. MA Oxon. 2nd Lieut Royal Scots Greys, 1938; retired on account of disability, 1951, rank of Captain; Hon. Major on disbandment of HG 1958; studied painting Camberwell School of Art; paintings in collections of Arts Council and Scottish Nat. Gallery of Modern Art. War of 1939–45 (prisoner). Member: Royal Fine Art Commission for Scotland, 1958–61; Council and Executive Cttee, Earl Haig Fund, Scotland, 1950–65 and 1966– (Pres., 1980–86); Scottish Arts Council, 1969–75; President, Scottish Craft Centre, 1950–75. Member Council, Commonwealth Ex-Services League; Pres., Officers' Association (Scottish Branch), 1987– (Chm., 1977–87); Vice-President: Scottish National Institution for War Blinded; Royal Blind Asylum and School; President Border Area British Legion, 1955–61; Chairman SE Scotland Disablement Advisory Cttee, 1960–73; Vice-Chairman, British Legion, Scotland, 1960, Chairman, 1962–65, Pres., 1980–86; Chm., Bd of Trustees, Scottish National War Memorial, 1983– (Trustee, 1961–); Trustee, National Gallery of Scotland, 1962–72; Chairman: Berwickshire Civic Soc., 1971–73; Friends of DeMarco Gall., 1968–71. Berwickshire: DL 1953; Vice-Lieutenant, 1967–70; DL Ettrick and Lauderdale (and Roxburghshire), 1977–. KStJ 1977. FRSA 1951. *Heir: s* Viscount Dawick, *qv. Address:* Bemersyde, Melrose, Scotland TD6 9DP. *T:* St Boswells (01835) 22762. *Clubs:* Cavalry and Guards, Beefsteak; New (Edinburgh).
See also Baron Astor of Hever, Baron Dacre of Glanton.

HAIG, General Alexander Meigs, Jr; Chairman and President, Worldwide Associates, Inc., since 1984; Chairman, Atlantic and Pacific Advisory Councils, United Technologies, since 1982; *b* 2 Dec. 1924; *m* 1950, Patricia Fox; two *s* one *d. Educ:* schs in Pennsylvania; Univ. of Notre Dame; US Mil. Acad., West Point (BS); Univs of Columbia and Georgetown (MA); Ground Gen. Sch., Fort Riley; Armor Sch., Fort Knox; Naval and Army War Colls. 2nd Lieut 1947; Far East and Korea, 1948–51; Europe, 1956–59; Vietnam, 1966–67; CO 3rd Regt, subseq. Dep. Comdt, West Point, 1967–69; Sen. Mil. Adviser to Asst to Pres. for Nat. Security Affairs, 1969–70; Dep. Asst to Pres. for Nat. Security Affairs, 1970–73; Vice-Chief of Staff, US Army, Jan.-July 1973, retd; Chief of White House Staff, 1973–74 when recalled to active duty; Supreme Allied Commander Europe, 1974–79, and Commander-in-Chief, US European Command, 1974–79. President and Chief Operating Officer, United Technologies, 1979–81. Secretary of State, USA, 1981–82. Sen. Fellow, Hudson Inst. for Policy Research, 1982–84. Director: Commodore Internat. Ltd; Gen. Atomics; America Online Inc.; Interneuron Pharmaceuticals, Inc. Member: Presidential Cttee on Strategic Forces, 1983–; Presidential Commn on Chemical Warfare Review, 1985; Bd of Special Advisers, President's Commn on Physical Fitness and Sports, 1984–. Hon. LLD: Niagara; Utah; hon. degrees: Syracuse, Fairfield, Hillsdale Coll., 1981. Awarded numerous US medals, badges and decorations; also Vietnamese orders and Cross of Gallantry; Medal of King Abd el-Aziz (Saudi Arabia). *Publications:* Caveat: realism, Reagan and foreign policy, 1984; Inner Circles, 1992. *Recreations:* tennis, golf, squash, equitation. *Address:* 1155 15th Street NW (Suite 800), Washington, DC 20005, USA.

HAIG, Ian Maurice, AM 1988; Chief Executive, Monash-ANZ Centre for International Briefing, since 1990; *b* 13 Dec. 1936; *s* of P. K. Haig; *m* 1959, Beverley, *d* of J. A. Dunning, OBE; two *s* one *d. Educ:* Pulteney Grammar School, Adelaide; University of Adelaide. Private Sec. to Pres. of Senate, Canberra, 1958–59; Asst Sec., Commonwealth Parly Conf., London, 1960; Public Relations Officer, Shell Co. of Australia, 1962; British Foreign Office School of Middle East Studies, 1963; Asst Trade Comr and Trade Comr, Los Angeles, 1966–68; Trade Comr, Beirut, 1969–73; Ambassador at large, Middle East, 1973; Ambassador to Saudi Arabia, Kuwait and United Arab Emirates, 1974–76; Australian Comr, Hong Kong, 1976–79; Dir of Administration, A.C.I. Ltd, 1979–81; Man. Dir, A.C.I. Fibreglass (Aust.), 1982; Agent Gen. for Victoria in London, 1983–85 and 1988–90; Chm., Immigration Panel, 1987; Dir, Aust. Wheat Bd, 1985–88. *Publications:* Arab Oil Politics, 1978; Oil and Alternative Sources of Energy, 1978; Australia and the Middle East, 1983. *Recreations:* cricket, golf. *Address:* 3 Chastleton Avenue, Toorak, Vic 3142, Australia. *Clubs:* MCC; Melbourne, Australian (Melbourne); Royal Melbourne Golf.

HAIG, Dame Mary Alison G.; *see* Glen Haig.

HAIGH, Brian Roger; Lecturer for Hawksmere plc, since 1993; *b* 19 Feb. 1931; *s* of Herbert Haigh and Ruth Haigh (*née* Lockwood); *m* 1953, Sheila Carter; one *s* one *d. Educ:* Hillhouse Central School, Huddersfield. Min. of Supply, 1949; National Service, RAF, 1949–51. Min. of Supply/Min. of Aviation, 1951–62; NATO Bullpup Production Orgn, 1962–67 (Head of Contracts, Finance and Admin, 1965–67); Min. of Technology, Aviation Supply, Defence (Defence Sales Orgn), 1968–73 (Asst Dir, Sales, 1971–73); Nat. Defence Coll., 1973–74; Ministry of Defence: Asst Dir, Contracts, 1974; Dir of Contracts (Weapons), Dec. 1974; Principal Dir of Navy Contracts, 1978; Under Secretary, 1980; Dir-Gen., Defence Contracts, 1980–86. Dir of Professional Educn and Trng, Lion Worldwide Div., Keiser Enterprises Inc., 1986–91. *Recreations:* family, music, opera, bridge. *Address:* c/o Barclays Bank plc, Surbiton Branch, 9 Clarence Road, Kingston-upon-Thames KT1 1NY.

HAIGH, Clement Percy, PhD; CPhys, FInstP; scientific and engineering consultant; *b* 11 Jan. 1920; *m* 1945, Ruby Patricia Hobdey; three *s. Educ:* Univ. of Leeds (BSc); King's Coll., London (PhD). Radiochemical Centre, Thorium Ltd, 1943–49; Medical Physicist, Barrow Hosp., Bristol, 1949–56; joined CEGB, 1956: Director, Berkeley Nuclear Laboratories, 1959–73; Dep. Director-General, Design and Construction Div., Gloucester, 1973–78; Dir of Research, BNOC, 1978–81. Dir, South Western Industrial Res., 1981–86. Distinguished Lectr, American Nuclear Soc., San Francisco, 1965; Assessor, Nuclear Safety Adv. Cttee, 1972–76; Member: BBC West Adv. Council, 1972–76; Mechanical Engrg and Machine Tools Requirements Bd, 1973–76; Off-Shore Energy Technology Bd, 1978–81; Board, National Maritime Inst., 1981–82; UK Chm., Joint UK/USSR Working Gp on Problems of Electricity Supply, 1974–78; Chm., Programme Steering Cttee, UK Offshore Steels Res. Project, 1981–87. FRSA. *Publications:* various papers on applied nuclear physics and on nuclear energy. *Recreations:* music; study of magnificent failures in technology. *Address:* Painswick, Old Sneed Park, Bristol, Avon BS9 1RG. *T:* Bristol (0117) 968 2065. *Club:* Savile.

HAIGH, Clifford; Editor, The Friend, 1966–73; *b* 5 Feb. 1906; *yr s* of Leonard and Isabel Haigh, Bradford, Yorks; *m* 1st, 1934, Dora Winifred Fowler (*d* 1959); one *s* one *d*; 2nd, 1970, Grace Elizabeth Cross. Editorial Staff: Yorkshire Observer, 1924–27; Birmingham Post, 1928–46; The Times, 1947–61; Assistant Editor, The Friend, 1961–65. *Recreation:* walking. *Address:* 4 Chichester Road, Sandgate, Kent CT20 3BN. *T:* Folkestone (01303) 248212.

HAIGH, Edward; Assistant General Secretary, Transport and General Workers' Union, since 1985; *b* 7 Nov. 1935; *s* of Edward and Sarah Ellen Haigh; *m* 1st, 1958, Patricia (marr. diss. 1982); one *s* two *d*; 2nd, 1982, Margaret; two step *d. Educ:* St Patrick's RC Sch., Birstall; St Mary's RC Sch., Batley, W Yorks. Carpet weaver, 1956–69; shop steward, 1960–69; National Union of Dyers, Bleachers and Textile Workers: Dist Organiser, 1969–73; Dist Sec., 1973–77; Nat. Organiser/Negotiator, 1977–79; Asst Gen. Sec., 1979–82; Nat. Sec., Textile Gp, TGWU, 1982–85. Mem., Labour Party NEC, 1982–. JP Batley, W Yorks, 1971–85. *Address:* (office) Transport House, Smith Square, SW1P 3JB. *Recreations:* politics (Labour Party), Rugby League football, cricket. *Club:* Birstall Irish Democratic League (W Yorks).

HAIGH, Maurice Francis; Barrister; a Recorder of the Crown Court, since 1981; a Chairman, Medical Appeal Tribunals, since 1984; *b* 6 Sept. 1929; *s* of William and Ceridwen Francis Haigh. *Educ:* Repton. Asst cameraman in film production; worked for Leslie Laurence Productions Ltd, London, Manchester Film Studios, and finally for Anglo-Scottish Pictures Ltd at London Film Studios, Shepperton, 1946–49; in commerce, 1950–52. Called to the Bar, Gray's Inn, 1955. *Recreations:* reading, cycling, fell and mountain walking. *Address:* Kenworthy's Buildings, 83 Bridge Street, Manchester M3 2RF. *T:* 0161–832 4036. *Club:* English-Speaking Union.

HAILEY, Arthur, author; *b* 5 April 1920; *s* of George Wellington Hailey and Elsie Mary Wright; *m* 1st, 1944, Joan Fishwick (marr. diss. 1950); three *s*; 2nd, 1951, Sheila Dunlop; one *s* two *d. Educ:* English elem. schs. Pilot, RAF, 1939–47 (Flt-Lt; AE); RCAF (R) (Flt-Lt 1951). Emigrated to Canada, 1947; became Canadian citizen, with dual nationality, 1952; various positions in industry and sales until becoming free-lance writer, 1956. Member: Authors League of America; (Life), Writers Guild of America; (Hon. Life), Alliance of Canadian Cinema, Television and Radio Artists. *Films:* Zero Hour, 1956; Time Lock, 1957; The Young Doctors, 1961; Hotel, 1966; Airport, 1970; The Moneychangers, 1976; Wheels, 1978; Strong Medicine, 1986. *Publications:* (in 38 languages): Runway-Zero Eight (with John Castle), 1958; The Final Diagnosis, 1959; Close-Up (collected plays), 1960; In High Places, 1962; Hotel, 1965; Airport, 1968; Wheels, 1971; The Moneychangers, 1975; Overload, 1979; Strong Medicine, 1984; The Evening News, 1990. *Address:* (home) Lyford Cay, PO Box N7776, Nassau, Bahamas; (office) Nancy Stauffer Associates, 171 Newbury Street, Boston, MA 02116, USA. *Club:* Lyford Cay (Bahamas).

HAILSHAM, 2nd Viscount, *cr* 1929, of Hailsham; Baron, *cr* 1928 [disclaimed his peerages for life, 20 Nov. 1963]; *see under* Baron Hailsham of St Marylebone.

HAILSHAM OF SAINT MARYLEBONE, Baron *cr* 1970 (Life Peer), of Herstmonceux; **Quintin McGarel Hogg,** PC 1956; KG 1988; CH 1974; FRS 1973; Editor, Halsbury's Laws of England, 4th edition, since 1972; *b* 9 Oct. 1907; *er s* of 1st Viscount Hailsham, PC, KC, and Elizabeth (*d* 1925), *d* of Judge Trimble Brown, Nashville, Tennessee, USA, and *widow* of Hon. A. J. Marjoribanks; *S* father, 1950, as 2nd Viscount Hailsham, but disclaimed his peerages for life, 20 Nov. 1963 (Baron *cr* 1928, Viscount *cr* 1929); *m* 1944, Mary Evelyn (*d* 1978), *d* of late Richard Martin of Ross; two *s* three *d*; *m* 1986, Deirdre Shannon. *Educ:* Eton (Schol., Newcastle Schol.); Christ Church, Oxford (Scholar). First Class Hon. Mods, 1928; First Class Lit. Hum., 1930, Pres., Oxford Union Soc., 1929. Served War of 1939–45: commissioned Rifle Bde Sept. 1939; served Middle East Forces, Western Desert, 1941 (wounded); Egypt, Palestine, Syria, 1942; Temp. Major, 1942. Fellow of All Souls Coll., Oxford, 1931–38, 1961–; Barrister, Lincoln's Inn, 1932; a Bencher of Lincoln's Inn, 1956, Treasurer, 1975; QC 1953. MP (C) Oxford City, 1938–50, St Marylebone, (Dec.) 1963–70; Jt Parly Under-Sec. of State for Air, 1945; First Lord of the Admiralty, 1956–57; Minister of Education, 1957; Dep. Leader of the House of Lords, 1957–60; Leader of the House of Lords, 1960–63; Lord Privy Seal, 1959–60; Lord Pres. of the Council, 1957–59 and 1960–64; Minister for Science and Technology, 1959–64; Minister with special responsibility for: Sport, 1962–64; dealing with unemployment in the North-East, 1963–64; higher education, Dec. 1963–Feb. 1964; Sec. of State for Education and Science, April-Oct. 1964; Lord High Chancellor of GB, 1970–74 and 1979–87. Chm. of the Conservative Party Organization, Sept. 1957–Oct. 1959. Rector of Glasgow Univ., 1959–62; Chancellor, Univ. of Buckingham, 1983–92. Pres. Classical Assoc., 1960–61. Lectures: John Findley Green Foundation, 1960; Richard Dimbleby, 1976; Hamlyn, 1983; Granada, 1987; Warburton, 1987, F. A. Mann, 1988, Lincoln's Inn. Hon. Student of Christ Church, Oxford, 1962; Hon. Bencher, Inn of Court of NI, 1981; Hon. FICE 1963; Hon. FIEE 1972; Hon. FIStructE 1960. Hon. Freeman, Merchant Taylors' Co., 1971. Hon. DCL: Westminster Coll., Fulton, Missouri, USA, 1960; Newcastle, 1964; Oxon, 1974; Hon. LLD: Cambridge, 1963; Delhi, 1972; St

Andrews, 1979; Leeds, 1982; Hon. DLitt Ulster, 1988. *Publications:* The Law of Arbitration, 1935; One Year's Work, 1944; The Law and Employers' Liability, 1944; The Times We Live In, 1944; Making Peace, 1945; The Left was never Right, 1945; The Purpose of Parliament, 1946; Case for Conservatism, 1947; The Law of Monopolies, Restrictive Practices and Resale Price Maintenance, 1956; The Conservative Case, 1959; Interdependence, 1961; Science and Politics, 1963; The Devil's Own Song, 1968; The Door Wherein I Went, 1975; Elective Dictatorship, 1976; The Dilemma of Democracy, 1978; Hamlyn Revisited: the British legal system (Hamlyn Lectures), 1983; A Sparrow's Flight (autobiog.), 1990; On The Constitution, 1992; Values: collapse and cure, 1994. *Heir: (to disclaimed viscountcy): s* Rt Hon. Douglas Martin Hogg, *qv. Address:* House of Lords, SW1A 0PW. *Clubs:* Carlton, Alpine, MCC.

See also Baroness Hogg and Hon. Dame M. C. Hogg.

HAIN, Peter Gerald; MP (Lab) Neath, since April 1991; *b* 16 Feb. 1950; *s* of Walter and Adelaine Hain; *m* 1975, Patricia Western; two *s. Educ:* Queen Mary College, London (BSc Econ 1st cl. hons); Univ. of Sussex (MPhil). Brought up in S Africa, until family forced to leave in 1966, due to anti-apartheid activity, since when lived in UK. Union of Communication Workers: Asst Research Officer, 1976–87; Head of Research, 1987–91. Chm., Stop the Seventy Tour campaign, 1969–70; Nat. Chm., Young Liberals, 1971–73; Press Officer, Anti-Nazi League, 1977–80. Contested (Lab) Putney, 1983, 1987. *Publications:* Don't Play with Apartheid, 1971; Community Politics, 1976; Mistaken Identity, 1976; (ed) Policing the Police, vol. I, 1978, vol. II, 1980; Neighbourhood Participation, 1980; Crisis and Future of the Left, 1980; Political Trials in Britain, 1984; Political Strikes, 1986; A Putney Plot?, 1987; The Peking Connection (novel), 1995; Ages to the Left, 1995. *Recreations:* soccer, cricket, Rugby player, fan of Chelsea FC and Neath RFC, rock and folk music fan. *Address:* House of Commons, SW1A 0AA. *T:* 0171–219 3000; 14 The Parade, Neath SA11 1RA. *T:* Neath (01639) 630152. *Clubs:* Neath Workingmen's; Resolven Rugby, Resolven Royal British Legion Institute.

HAINES, Christopher John Minton; Director, Yorkshire Foods, since 1989; *b* 14 April 1939; *m* 1967, Christine Cobbold; two *s* two *d. Educ:* Stowe. The Rifle Brigade, 1959–68; sugar trade, 1968–89; Chm., James Budgett & Son, 1984–89. Chief Exec., The Jockey Club, 1989–93. *Recreations:* music, gardening, racing. *Club:* Turf.

HAINES, Joseph Thomas William; Assistant Editor, The Daily Mirror, 1984–90; Group Political Editor, Mirror Group Newspapers, 1984–90; *b* 29 Jan. 1928; *s* of Joseph and Elizabeth Haines; *m* 1955, Irene Betty Lambert; no *c. Educ:* Elementary Schools, Rotherhithe, SE16. Parly Correspondent, The Bulletin (Glasgow) 1954–58, Political Correspondent, 1958–60; Political Correspondent: Scottish Daily Mail, 1960–64; The Sun, 1964–68; Dep. Press Sec. to Prime Minister, Jan.-June 1969; Chief Press Sec. to Prime Minister, 1969–70 and 1974–76, and to Leader of the Opposition, 1970–74; Feature Writer, 1977–78, Chief Leader Writer, 1978–90, The Daily Mirror. Director: Mirror Gp Newspapers (1986) Ltd, 1986–92; Scottish Daily Record & Sunday Mail Ltd, 1986–92. Mem. Tonbridge UDC, 1963–69, 1971–74. Mem., Royal Commn on Legal Services, 1976–79. *Publications:* The Politics of Power, 1977; (co-editor) Malice In Wonderland, 1986; Maxwell, 1988. *Recreations:* heresy and watching football. *Address:* 1 South Frith, London Road, Southborough, Tunbridge Wells, Kent TN4 0UQ. *T:* Tonbridge (01732) 365919.

HAINING, Thomas Nivison, CMG 1983; HM Diplomatic Service, retired; writer and lecturer on international affairs and Mongolian history; Hon. Research Fellow, Department of History, University of Aberdeen, since 1991 (Hon. Research Associate, 1988–90); *b* 15 March 1927; *m* 1955, Dorothy Patricia Robson; one *s. Educ:* Edinburgh Univ.; Göttingen Univ. Foreign Office, 1952; served Vienna, Moscow, Rome and New York; Counsellor, FCO, 1972–79; Ambassador and Consul-Gen. to the Mongolian People's Republic, 1979–82. Hon. Pres., Chinese Studies Gp, Aberdeen Univ, 1989–. FRAS 1993. *Publications:* (contrib.) Mongolia Today, 1989; (trans. and ed) Ratchnevsky, Genghis Khan: his life and legacy, 1991; (contrib.) Legacy of the Mongol Empire, 1993; (contrib.) The Mongols of the 13th century through the eyes of early European travellers, 1995. *Address:* Carseview, 7 The Banks, Brechin, Angus DD9 6JD. *T:* Brechin (01356) 622584. *Clubs:* Royal Automobile; Royal Northern and University (Aberdeen).

HAINSWORTH, Gordon, MA; public sector consultant, since 1992; Chief Executive, Manchester, 1988–92; *b* 4 Nov. 1934; *s* of Harry and Constance Hainsworth; *m* 1962, Diane (*née* Thubron); one *s* one *d. Educ:* Leeds Modern Sch.; Trinity Coll., Cambridge (MA). Teaching, Leeds, Birmingham and West Riding, 1958–65; Admin. Assistant, Leeds, 1965–69; Asst Education Officer, Manchester, 1969–74; Under-Secretary (Education), Assoc. of Metropolitan Authorities, 1974–76; Dep. Educn Officer, Manchester, 1976–80; Director of Education, Gateshead, 1980–83; Chief Educn Officer, Manchester, 1983–88. Mem., NW Arts Bd, 1991–. *Recreations:* family, books, golf, bridge, walking. *Address:* 14 Oldham Road, Denshaw, Oldham OL3 5SL. *T:* Saddleworth (01457) 820398.

HAINWORTH, Henry Charles, CMG 1961; HM Diplomatic Service, retired; *b* 12 Sept. 1914; *o s* of late Charles S. and Emily G. I. Hainworth; *m* 1944, Mary, *yr d* of late Felix B. and Lilian Ady; two *d. Educ:* Blundell's Sch.; Sidney Sussex Coll., Cambridge. Entered HM Consular Service, 1939; HM Embassy, Tokyo, 1940–42; seconded to Ministry of Information (Far Eastern Bureau, New Delhi), 1942–46; HM Embassy, Tokyo, 1946–51; Foreign Office, 1951–53; HM Legation, Bucharest, 1953–55; NATO Defence Coll., Paris, 1956; Political Office, Middle East Forces (Nicosia), 1956; Foreign Office, 1957–61 (Head of Atomic Energy and Disarmament Dept, 1958–61); Counsellor, United Kingdom Delegation to the Brussels Conference, 1961–63; HM Minister and Consul-Gen. at British Embassy, Vienna, 1963–68; Ambassador to Indonesia, 1968–70; Ambassador and Perm. UK Rep. to Disarm. Conf., Geneva, 1971–74. Chm., Anglo-Indonesian Soc., 1992–. *Publication:* A Collector's Dictionary, 1980. *Recreations:* reading, fishing. *Address:* 23 Rivermead Court, Ranelagh Gardens, SW6 3RU.

HAITINK, Bernard, Hon. KBE 1977; Commander, Order of Orange Nassau, 1988; Music Director: Royal Opera House, Covent Garden, since 1987; European Union Youth Orchestra, since 1994; *b* Amsterdam, 4 March 1929. *Educ:* Amsterdam Conservatory. Studied conducting under Felix Hupke, but started his career as a violinist with the Netherlands Radio Philharmonic; in 1954 and 1955 attended annual conductors' course (org. by Netherlands Radio Union) under Ferdinand Leitner; became 2nd Conductor with Radio Union at Hilversum with co-responsibility for 4 radio orchs and conducted the Radio Philharmonic in public during the Holland Fest., in The Hague, 1956; conducted the Concertgebouw Orch., Oct. 1956; then followed guest engagements with this and other orchs in the Netherlands and elsewhere. Debut in USA, with Los Angeles Symph. Orch., 1958; 5 week season with Concertgebouw Orch., 1958–59, and toured Britain with it, 1959; apptd (with Eugen Jochum) as the Orchestra's permanent conductor, Sept. 1961; sole artistic dir and permanent conductor of the orch., 1964–88; toured Japan, USSR, USA and Europe; 1974; début at Royal Opera House, Covent Garden, 1977. London Philharmonic Orchestra: Principal Conductor, Artistic Dir, 1967–79, Pres., 1990; toured: Japan, 1969; USA, 1970, 1971, 1976; Berlin, 1972; Holland, Germany, Austria, 1973; USSR, 1975. Musical Dir, Glyndebourne Opera, 1978–88; conducted Figaro for rebuilt opera house of Glyndebourne (60th anniversary), 1994. Appearances at BBC Promenade Concerts and at Tanglewood, Salzburg and Edinburgh Festivals. Hon. RAM 1973; Hon. FRCM 1984. Hon. DMus: Oxford, 1988; Leeds, 1988. Bruckner Medal of Honour, 1970; Gold Medal, Internat. Gustav Mahler Soc., 1971; Erasmus Prize, Netherlands, 1991. Chevalier de L'Ordre des Arts et des Lettres, 1972; Officer, Order of the Crown (Belgium), 1977. *Address:* c/o Harold Holt Ltd, 31 Sinclair Road, W14 0NS.

HAJNAL, John, FBA 1966; Professor of Statistics, London School of Economics, 1975–86 (Reader, 1966–75); *b* 26 Nov. 1924; *s* of late Kálmán and Eva Hajnal-Kónyi; *m* 1950, Nina Lande; one *s* three *d. Educ:* University Coll. Sch., London; Balliol Coll., Oxford. Employed by: Royal Commission on Population, 1944–48; UN, New York, 1948–51; Office of Population Research, Princeton Univ., 1951–53; Manchester Univ., 1953–57; London Sch. of Economics, 1957–. Vis. Fellow Commoner, Trinity Coll., Cambridge, 1974–75; Vis. Prof., Rockefeller Univ., NY, 1981. Mem. Internat. Statistical Institute. *Publications:* The Student Trap, 1972; papers on demography, statistics, mathematics, etc. *Address:* 95 Hodford Road, NW11 8EH. *T:* 0181–455 7044.

HALABY, Najeeb Elias; President, Halaby International Corporation; Chairman: Dulles Access Rapid Transit Inc.; National Center for Atmospheric Research Foundation; *b* 19 Nov. 1915; *s* of late Najeeb Elias Halaby and of Laura Wilkins Halaby; *m* 1st, 1946, Doris Carlquist (marr. diss. 1976); one *s* two *d*; 2nd, 1980, Jane Allison Coates. *Educ:* Stanford Univ. (AB); Yale Univ. (LLB); Bonar Law Coll., Ashridge, (Summer) 1939. Called to the Bar: California, 1940; District of Columbia, 1948; NY, 1973. Practised law in Los Angeles, Calif, 1940–42, 1958–61; Air Corps Flight Instructor, 1940; Test pilot for Lockheed Aircraft Corp., 1942–43; Naval aviator, established Navy Test Pilot Sch., 1943; formerly Chief of Intelligence Coordination Div., State Dept; Foreign Affairs Advisor to Sec. of Defense; Chm., NATO Military Production and Supply Board, 1950; Asst Administrator, Mutual Security Economic Cooperation Administration, 1950–51; Asst Sec. of Defense for Internat. Security, 1952–54; Vice-Chm., White House Advisory Group whose report led to formation of Federal Aviation Agency, 1955–56, Administrator of the Agency, 1961–65; Pan American World Airways: Director, 1966–72; President, 1968–71; Chief Executive, 1969–72; Chairman, 1970–72; Associate of Laurance and Nelson Rockefeller, 1954–57; Past Exec. Vice-Pres. and Dir, Servomechanisms Inc.; Sec.-Treas., Aerospace Corp., 1959–61; Pres., American Technology Corp. Founder-Chm., US-Japan Econ. Council, 1971–73; Trustee: Aspen Inst., Aspen, Colo.; Eisenhower Exchange Fellowships, Inc.; Wolf Trap Foundn; Amer. Univ. of Beirut; Coll. of William and Mary; Governor, Flight Safety Foundn. Member: Smithson Soc.; Brookings Council; Madison Council. Chm., SCF, 1992–. Fellow, Amer. Inst. of Aeronautics and Astronautics. Hon. LLB: Allegheny Coll., Pa, 1967; Loyola Coll., LA, 1968. Monsanto Safety Award; FAA Exceptional Service Medal; G. L. Cabot Medal, Aero Club of New England, 1964; Gilbert Award, Air Traffic Controllers' Assoc., 1989. *Publications:* Crosswinds (memoir), 1979; First Forty Years of Jet Aviation, 1979. *Recreations:* golf, skiing, flying. *Address:* (office) PO Drawer Y, McLean, VA 22101, USA; (residence) 175 Chain Bridge Road, McLean, Va 22101–1907, USA. *Clubs:* Alibi, Metropolitan, Chevy Chase (Washington); Bohemian (California); Tower (Virginia).

HALBERG, Sir Murray (Gordon), Kt 1988; MBE 1961; *b* 7 July 1933; *s* of Raymond Halberg; *m* 1959, Phyllis, *d* of Alex Korff; two *s* one *d. Educ:* Avondale College. Started internat. distance running, Commonwealth Games, 1954; Commonwealth Gold Medals, 3 miles, 1958, 1962; Olympic Gold Medal, 5,000 metres, Rome, 1960; world records at 2 miles and 3 miles, 1961, participant in 4×1 mile record. Founder, Halberg Trust (to honour sporting excellence and to support children with disabilities).

HALBERT, Derek Rowland; His Honour Judge Halbert; a Circuit Judge, since 1995; *b* 25 March 1948; *s* of Ronald Halbert and Freda Mabel Halbert (*née* Impett); *m* 1972, Heather Rose Ashe; two *d. Educ:* King's Sch., Chester; Selwyn Coll., Cambridge (MA Law 1974); Open Univ. (BA Technol. 1984). Called to the Bar, Inner Temple, 1971; Mem., Wales and Chester Circuit, 1971–; a Recorder, 1991–95. *Recreations:* walking, ice skating, tennis. *Address:* The Crown Court, The Castle, Chester CH1 2AN. *Club:* Leander (Henley).

HALE, Hon. Dame Brenda (Marjorie), DBE 1994; **Hon. Mrs Justice Hale;** a Judge of the High Court of Justice, Family Division, since 1994; *b* 31 Jan. 1945; *d* of Cecil Frederick Hale and Marjorie Hale (*née* Godfrey); *m* 1st, 1968, Anthony John Christopher Hoggett, *qv* (marr. diss. 1992); one *d*; 2nd, 1992, Julian Thomas Farrand, *qv. Educ:* Richmond High School for Girls, Yorks; Girton College, Cambridge. MA. Called to the Bar, Gray's Inn, 1969; University of Manchester: Asst Lectr in Law, 1966; Lectr, 1968; Sen. Lectr, 1976; Reader, 1981; Prof., 1986–89. Vis. Prof., KCL, 1990–94. Barrister, Northern Circuit, 1969–72; Law Comr, 1984–93. QC 1989; a Recorder, 1989–94. Legal Mem., Mental Health Review Tribunal for NW Region, 1979–80; Member: Council on Tribunals, 1980–84; Civil and Family Cttee, Judicial Studies Bd, 1990–94; Human Fertilisation and Embryology Authy, 1990–93. Man. Trustee, Nuffield Foundn, 1987–; Governor, Centre for Policy on Ageing, 1990–93. Pres., Nat. Family Mediation, 1994– (Chm., Nat. Family Conciliation Council, then Nat. Assoc. of Family Mediation and Conciliation Services, 1989–93). Editor, Jl of Social Welfare Law, 1978–84. Hon. LLD Sheffield, 1989. *Publications:* Mental Health Law, 1976, 3rd edn 1990; Parents and Children, 1977, 4th edn 1993; (with D. S. Pearl) The Family Law and Society: Cases and Materials, 1983, 3rd edn 1991; (with S. Atkins) Women and the Law, 1984; (contrib.) Mental Health Law, Halsbury's Laws of England, 4th edn 1992; contribs to legal periodicals and other texts. *Recreations:* domesticity, drama, duplicate bridge. *Address:* Royal Courts of Justice, Strand, WC2A 2LL.

HALE, John Hampton; Director: Pearson plc, 1983–93 (Managing Director, 1983–86); Pearson Inc. (USA), 1983–93 (Chairman, 1983–86); *b* 8 July 1924; *s* of Dr John Hale and Elsie (Coles) Hale; *m* 2nd, 1980, Nancy Ryrie Birks; one *s* two *d* by former marriage. *Educ:* Eton College (King's Scholar); Magdalene Coll., Cambridge (Mech. Scis Tripos, BA, MA); Harvard Grad. Sch. of Business Admin (Henry Fellow, 1948). RAF and Fleet Air Arm Pilot, 1943–46. Alcan Aluminium Ltd, Montreal, NY and London, 1949–83; Exec. Vice-Pres., Finance, 1970–82, Dir, Alcan Aluminium, 1970–85; Dir, Aluminium Co. of Canada, 1970–85 (Chm., 1979–83). Director: Nippon Light Metal Co., Japan, Indian Aluminium Co. and Alcan Australia, 1970–83; Canadian Adv. Bd, Allendale Mutual Insurance Co., 1977–83; Scovill Inc. (USA), 1978–85; Ritz-Carlton Hotel, Montreal, 1981–83; Concordia Univ. Business Sch., 1981–83; Bank of Montreal, 1985– (Mem., Internat Adv. Council, 1986–89); The Economist Newspaper, 1984–; SSMC Inc. (USA), 1986–89; Chm., Fairey Holdings, 1983–87. Member: Lloyds, 1960–91; Exec. Cttee, British-North American Cttee, 1980–90; Council, Industry for Management Educn, 1983–87; Lay Mem., Stock Exchange Council, London, 1987–91. Chairman: Chambly County Protestant Central Sch. Bd, 1957–60; Business Graduates Assoc., 1967–70; Mem., Accounting Research Adv. Bd, Canadian Inst. of Chartered Accountants, 1975–81 (Chm., 1978–81). Director: Mont St Hilaire Nature Conservation Assoc., 1977–83 (Pres., 1980–83); Foundn for Canadian Studies, 1988–; Governor, Stratford Festival, Ontario, 1981–83. Trustee, Royal Armouries, 1992–. Mem., Court of Assts, Armourers' & Brasiers' Co., 1985– (Master, 1990). *Recreations:* ski-ing, sailing, fishing, shooting, old Canadian books. *Address:* 71 Eaton Terrace, SW1W 8TN. *T:* 0171–730 2929. *Clubs:* Royal Thames Yacht; Mount Royal (Montreal); Toronto.

HALE, Prof. Sir John (Rigby), Kt 1984; FBA 1977; Professor of Italian History, 1981–83, and Professor of Italian, 1985–88, University College London, now Professor Emeritus; Public Orator, University of London, 1981–83; *b* 17 Sept. 1923; *s* of E. R. S. Hale, FRCP, MD, and Hilda Birks; *m* 1st, 1952, Rosalind Williams; one *s* two *d*; 2nd, 1965, Sheila Haynes MacIvor; one *s*. *Educ:* Neville Holt Preparatory Sch.; Eastbourne Coll.; Jesus Coll., Oxford. BA first cl. hons Mod. Hist., 1948; MA (Oxon) 1950; DLitt (Oxon) 1986. Served War, Radio Operator in Merchant Service, 1942–45. Commonwealth Fellow, Johns Hopkins and Harvard Univs, 1948–49; Fellow and Tutor in Modern History, Jesus Coll., Oxford, 1949–64, Hon. Fellow, 1986; Prof. of History, Univ. of Warwick, 1964–69. Editor, Oxford Magazine, 1958–59; Visiting Prof., Cornell Univ., 1959–60; Vis. Fellow, Harvard Centre for Renaissance Studies, I Tatti, 1963; Vis. Prof., Univ. of California, Berkeley, 1969–70; Folger Library Washington, Fellowship, 1970. Fellow, Davis Center, Univ. of Princeton, 1982; Mem., Princeton Inst. for Adv. Study, 1984–85. Chm. of Trustees, Nat. Gallery, 1974–80 (Trustee, 1973–80); Trustee: V&A Museum, 1984–88 (Chm., Theatre Museum Cttee, 1984–87); BM, 1985–92; Member: Royal Mint Adv. Cttee, 1979–92; Museums and Galleries Commn, 1983–93 (Chm., Working Party on Museum Professional Trng and Career Structure, report pubd 1987); Royal Commn for Exhibn of 1851, 1983–88. Chairman: British Soc. for Renaissance Studies, 1973–76; Advisory Cttee, Govt Art Collection, 1983–92; Pres., British Assoc. of Friends of Museums, 1988–94. FSA 1962; FRHistS 1968; FRSA 1974. Socio Straniero: Accademia Arcadia, 1972; Ateneo Veneto, 1987. Academicus ex Classe (Bronze Plaque Award), Academia Medicea, 1980; Commendatore, Ordine al Merito della Repubblica Italiana, 1981; Premio Bolla (services to Venice), 1982; Serena Medal, British Acad., 1986. *Publications:* England and the Italian Renaissance, 1954; The Italian Journal of Samuel Rogers, 1956; Machiavelli and Renaissance Italy, 1961; (trans. and ed) The Literary Works of Machiavelli, 1961; (ed) Certain Discourses Military by Sir John Smythe, 1964; The Evolution of British Historiography, 1964; (co-ed) Europe in the Late Middle Ages, 1965; Renaissance Exploration, 1968; Renaissance Europe 1480–1520, 1971; (ed) Renaissance Venice, 1973; Italian Renaissance Painting, 1977; Renaissance Fortification: art or engineering?, 1978; Florence and the Medici: the pattern of control, 1977; The Travel Journal of Antonio de Beatis, 1979; (ed) A Concise Encyclopaedia of the Italian Renaissance, 1981; Renaissance War Studies, 1983; (with M. E. Mallett) The Military Organisation of a Renaissance State: Venice *c* 1400–1617, 1984; War and Society in Renaissance Europe 1450–1620, 1985 (Edmund Gardner Prize, London Univ., 1983–87); Artists and Warfare in the Renaissance, 1990; The Civilisation of Europe in the Renaissance, 1993 (RSL Award; Time-Life Silver Pen Award); contributor: New Cambridge Modern History, vols 1, 2, 3; The History of the King's Works vol. 4; Past and Present; Studi Veneziani, Italian Studies, etc. *Recreation:* Venice. *Address:* 26 Montpelier Row, Twickenham, Mddx TW1 2NQ. *T:* 0181–892 9636.

HALE, Kathleen, (Mrs Douglas McClean), OBE 1976; artist; illustrator and author of books for children; *b* 24 May 1898; *d* of Charles Edward Hale and Ethel Alice Aylmer Hughes; *m* 1926, Dr Douglas McClean (*d* 1967); two *s*. *Educ:* Manchester High Sch. for Girls; Manchester Sch. of Art; Art Dept (scholar) of University Coll., Reading; Central Sch. of Art; East Anglian Sch. of Painting and Drawing. Has exhibited paintings at: New English Art Club, Whitechapel Art Gallery, London Group, Grosvenor Galleries, Vermont Gallery, Warwick Public Library Gallery; Gallery Edward Harvane, New Grafton Gallery, Parkin Gallery; metal groups and pictures at: Lefèvre Galleries; Leicester Galleries; Oxford Arts Council, Arts Centre; Mural for South Bank (Festival) Schs Section, 1951; Orlando Ballet for Festival Gardens, 1951; contrib. ballet exhibn and exhibited Orlando Ballet costume and scenery designs, V & A Museum. TV and radio programmes. *Publications:* The Orlando The Marmalade Cat Series, since 1938: Camping Holiday; Trip Abroad; Buys a Farm; Becomes a Doctor; Silver Wedding; Keeps a Dog; A Seaside Holiday; The Frisky Housewife; Evening Out; Home Life; Invisible Pyjamas; The Judge; Zoo; Magic Carpet; Country Peep-Show; Buys a Cottage; and The Three Graces; Goes to the Moon; and the Water Cats; Henrietta, the Faithful Hen, 1946; Puss-in-Boots Peep-Show, 1950; Manda, 1952; Henrietta's Magic Egg, 1973; A Slender Reputation (autobiog.), 1994. *Recreation:* painting. *Address:* c/o Frederick Warne & Co., Penguin Books Ltd, 27 Wrights Lane, W8 5TZ.

HALE, Norman Morgan, CB 1992; Under Secretary, Department of Health (formerly of Health and Social Security), 1975–93; *b* 28 June 1933; *s* of late Thomas Norman Hale and Ada Emily Hale, Evesham, Worcs; *m* 1965, Sybil Jean (*née* Maton); one *s* one *d*. *Educ:* Prince Henry's Grammar Sch., Evesham; St John's Coll., Oxford (MA). Min. of Pensions and National Insurance, 1955; Asst Sec., Nat. Assistance Bd, 1966; Min. of Social Security, 1966; CSD, 1970–72. Consultant: MoD, 1994; Medicines Control Agency, 1994–; National Trust, 1995—. *Recreations:* gardening, historical geography. *Address:* 64 Castle Avenue, Ewell, Epsom, Surrey KT17 2PH. *T:* 0181–393 3507. *Club:* United Oxford & Cambridge University.

HALE, Raymond, IPFA; County Treasurer, Leicestershire County Council, since 1977; *b* 4 July 1936; *s* of Tom Raymond Hale and Mary Jane (*née* Higgin); *m* 1959, Ann Elvidge; one *s*. *Educ:* Baines Grammar Sch., Poulton-le-Fylde. Lancashire CC, 1952–54; served Royal Air Force, 1954–56; Lancashire CC, 1956–61; Nottinghamshire CC, 1961–65; Leicestershire CC, 1965–. Treasurer: Leics Police Authy, 1977–; Leicester Univ. Med. Sch. and Associated Leics Teaching Hosps Jt Trust (Medisearch), 1988–; Chm., Hind Sisters Homes Charity, 1993–; Vice-Chm., Leics Guild of Disabled, 1990–. *Recreations:* Rugby, cricket, gardening. *Address:* The Stables, Main Street, Nailstone, Nuneaton, Warwicks CV13 0QB.

HALES, Antony John; Director, since 1989, Chief Executive, since 1991, Allied Domecq (formerly Allied-Lyons) PLC; *b* 25 May 1948; *s* of Sidney Alfred Hales and Margaret Joan (*née* Wood); *m* 1975, Linda Churchlow; three *s* one *d*. *Educ:* Repton; Bristol Univ. (BSc Chem). With Cadbury Schweppes, 1969–77; Foods Mkting Manager, Cadbury Typhoo, 1977–79; Mkting Dir, Joshua Tetley & Son, 1979–83; Managing Director: Halls Oxford & West Brewery Co., 1983–85; Ind Coope-Taylor Walker, 1985–87; Retail Dir, Allied Breweries, 1987; Man. Dir, Ansells, 1987–89; Chief Exec., J. Lyons & Co., 1989–91; Chairman: Hiram Walker Gp, 1992– (Dir, 1991–); J. Lyons & Co., 1992–; Allied Domecq (formerly Allied Lyons) Retail, 1992–. Director: Welsh Water, 1993–; Midland Bank, 1994–. Chm., Nat. Manufg Council, CBI, 1993–. *Address:* Allied Domecq PLC, 24 Portland Place, W1N 4BB. *T:* 0171–323 9000.

HALES, Prof. (Charles) Nicholas, PhD, MD; FRCPath; FRCP; FRS 1992; Professor of Clinical Biochemistry, University of Cambridge, since 1977; *b* 25 April 1935; *s* of late Walter Bryan Hales and Phyllis Marjory Hales; *m* 1st, 1959, Janet May Moss; two *s*; 2nd, 1978, Margaret Griffiths; one *d*. *Educ:* King Edward VI Grammar Sch., Stafford; Univ. of Cambridge (BA 1956, MB, BChir, MA 1959, PhD 1964, MD 1971). MRCPath 1971, FRCPath 1980; MRCP 1971, FRCP 1976. House Surgeon, UCH, 1959, House Physician, 1960; Stothert Res. Fellow, Royal Soc., 1963–64; Lectr, Dept of Biochem., Univ. of Cambridge, 1964–70; Clinical Asst, Addenbrooke's Hosp., Cambridge, 1961–68, Hon. Consultant in Clin. Biochem, 1968–70; Prof. of Med. Biochem., Welsh National Sch. of Medicine, Cardiff, and Hon. Consultant in Med. Biochem., University Hosp. of Wales, Cardiff, 1970–77. Consultant in Med. Biochem., South Glam Health Authority (T). Mem., MRC, 1988–90. Lectures: Banting Meml, British Diabetic Assoc., 1991; Croonian, RCP, 1992; Kroc, Center for Diabetes Res., Univ. of Uppsala, 1992; Dale, Nat. Inst. for Biol Standards & Control, 1992; Kettle, RCPath, 1993; W. H. S. George Meml, 1993. Medal, Soc., for Endocrinology, 1981; Foundn Award, Assoc. of Clin. Biochemists, 1991. *Recreations:* music, fishing. *Address:* Department of Clinical Biochemistry, Addenbrooke's Hospital, Hills Road, Cambridge CB2 2QR. *T:* Cambridge (01223) 336787.

HALES, Prof. Frederick David, FEng 1990; FIMechE, FIMA; Professor of Surface Transport, Loughborough University of Technology, 1968–93, now Professor Emeritus; *b* 19 Dec. 1930; *s* of Christina Frances and Frederick David Hales; *m* 1955, Pamela Hilary Warner; one *s* one *d* (and one *d* decd). *Educ:* Kingswood Grammar Sch.; Bristol Univ. (BSc Hons Maths, PhD). MBCS, Sigma Xi. Asst Chief Aerodynamicist, Bristol Aircraft, 1953–60; Group Research Head, MIRA, 1960–67; Vis. Scientist, Stevens Inst., Hoboken, 1967–68; Loughborough University: Hd of Dept of Transport Technology, 1982–89; Pro-Vice-Chancellor, 1984–85, Sen. Pro-Vice-Chancellor, 1985–87; acting Vice-Chancellor, 1987–88; Dean of Engrng, 1989–92. Mem., Tech. Adv. Council to Ford Motor Co., 1985–93; Scientific Visitor to Dept of Transport, 1986–90. *Publications:* papers on dynamics and vehicle control and stability. *Recreations:* sailing, bridge, wine, wood carving. *Address:* 14 Kenilworth Avenue, Loughborough, Leics LE11 0SL. *T:* Loughborough (01509) 261767. *Clubs:* Rutland Sailing, Clyde Cruising.

HALES, Prof. Nicholas; *see* Hales, Prof. C. N.

HALEY, Prof. Keith Brian, PhD; CMath, FIMA; CEng, FIEE, FOR; Professor of Operational Research since 1968, and Director, Centre of Applied Gerontology, since 1991, Birmingham University; *b* 17 Nov. 1933; *s* of Arthur Leslie Haley and Gladys Mary Haley; *m* 1960, Diana Elizabeth Mason; one *s*. *Educ:* King Edward VI, Five Ways, Birmingham; Birmingham Univ. (BSc, PhD). FIMA 1970; FOR 1976. OR Scientist, NCB, 1957–59; Birmingham University: Lectr, 1959–63; Sen. Lectr, 1963–68; Head, Dept of Engrg Prodn, 1981–89; Head, Centre for Ergonomics and OR, 1990–91. President: ORS, 1982–83; IFORS, 1992–94 (Vice-Pres., 1983–86); Editor, Jl of ORS, 1972–80. Governor, Bromsgrove Sch., 1968–. *Publications:* Mathematical Programming for Business and Industry, 1966; Operational Research '75, 1976; Operational Research '78, 1979; Search Theory and Applications, 1980; Applied Operations Research in Fishing, 1981; many articles. *Recreations:* squash, bridge. *Address:* 22 Eymore Close, Selly Oak, Birmingham B29 4LB. *T:* 0121–475 3331. *Club:* Royal Over-Seas League.

HALEY, Prof. Kenneth Harold Dobson, FBA 1987; Professor of Modern History, Sheffield University, 1962–82, now Emeritus Professor; *b* 19 April 1920; *s* of Alfred Harold Dobson Haley and Winifred Hetty Haley (*née* Beale); *m* 1948, Iris (*née* Houghton); one *s* two *d*. *Educ:* Huddersfield College; Balliol College, Oxford (MA, BLitt). University of Sheffield: Asst Lectr in Modern History, 1947, later Lectr, Sen. Lectr and Prof.; Dean, Faculty of Arts, 1979–81. Member: Anglo-Netherlands Mixed Cultural Commn, 1976–82; William and Mary Tercentenary Trust, 1985–89. Hon. Vice-Pres., Historical Assoc., 1994–. *Publications:* William of Orange and the English Opposition 1672–1674, 1953, repr. 1975; The First Earl of Shaftesbury, 1968; The Dutch in the Seventeenth Century, 1972 (Dutch trans. 1979); Politics in the Reign of Charles II, 1985; An English Diplomat in the Low Countries: Sir William Temple and John de Witt 1665–1672, 1986; The British and the Dutch, 1988; articles in historical jls. *Recreation:* computer chess. *Address:* 15 Haugh Lane, Sheffield S11 9SA. *T:* Sheffield (0114) 236 1316.

HALFORD, Maj.-Gen. Michael Charles Kirkpatrick, DSO 1946; OBE 1957 (MBE 1944); DL; *b* 28 Oct. 1914; *s* of Lieut-Col M. F. Halford, OBE, and Violet Halford (*née* Kirkpatrick); *m* 1945, Pamela Joy (*née* Wright); three *s*. *Educ:* Wellington Coll., Trinity Coll., Cambridge. Commissioned Royal Guernsey Militia, 1932; 2nd Lieut York and Lancaster Regt, 1935; served Egypt and Palestine, 1936; France 1940; N Africa, Italy, France and Germany; comd Hallamshire Bn, York and Lancaster Regt, 1945, 1st Bn, 1954; GSOI (Intelligence), Hong Kong, 1953; Asst Army Instr, Imperial Defence Coll., 1957, comd 147 Inf. Bde (TA), 1960; COS HQ Western Comd, 1963; GOC 43 (Wessex) Div./District, 1964–67; retd, 1967. Representative Col The York and Lancaster Regt, 1966–79. DL Hants 1975. *Recreations:* fishing, golf. *Club:* Army and Navy.

HALFORD-MacLEOD, Aubrey Seymour, CMG 1958; CVO 1965; HM Diplomatic Service, retired; *b* 15 Dec. 1914; *o s* of late Joseph and Clara Halford; changed name by deed poll from Halford to Halford-MacLeod, 1964; *m* 1939, Giovanna Mary, *o d* of late W. H. Durst; three *s* one *d*. *Educ:* King Edward's Sch., Birmingham; Magdalen Coll., Oxford. Entered HM Diplomatic (subseq. Foreign, now again Diplomatic) Service as Third Sec., 1937; Bagdad, 1939; Second Sec., 1942; transferred to Office of Minister Resident in N Africa, 1943; First Sec., 1943; British mem. of Secretariat of Advisory Council for Italy, 1944; British High Commission in Italy, 1944; Asst Political Adviser to Allied Commission in Italy, Sept, 1944, Political Adviser, 1945; transferred to HM Foreign Office, 1946, Principal Private Sec. to Permanent Under-Sec.; Dep. Exec. Sec. to Preparatory Commission for Council of Europe, May 1949, and promoted Counsellor; Dep. Sec. Gen. of the Council of Europe, 1949–52; Counsellor, HM Embassy, Tokyo, 1953–55; in charge of HM Legation, Seoul, 1954; Counsellor at HM Embassy in Libya, 1955–57; HM Political Agent at Kuwait, 1957–59; HM Consul-Gen., Munich, 1959–65; HM Ambassador to Iceland, 1966–70. Foreign Affairs Adviser, Scottish Council (Devlt and Ind.), 1971–78. Dir, Scottish Opera, 1971–78. Pres., Scottish Soc. for Northern Studies, 1973–76. Vice-Pres., Clan MacLeod Soc. of Scotland, 1976–79. *Publication:* (with G. M. Halford) The Kabuki Handbook, 1956. *Recreations:* fishing, shooting, ornithology. *Address:* Mulag House, Ardvourlie, N Harris PA85 3AB. *T:* Harris (01859) 502054.

HALFPENNY, Rev. Brian Norman, CB 1990; Team Rector of the Parish of the Ridge, Redditch, since 1991; *b* 7 June 1936; *s* of Alfred Ernest Halfpenny and Fanny Doris Halfpenny (*née* Harman); *m* 1961, Hazel Beatrice Cross; three *d*. *Educ:* George Dixon Grammar Sch., Birmingham; St John's Coll., Oxford (BA 1960; MA 1964); Wells Theol Coll. Curate, Melksham, 1962–65; Chaplain, RAF, 1965–91; served RAF Stations Cosford, Wildenrath, Leeming, Hong Kong, Brize Norton, Halton, Akrotiri; RAF Coll., Cranwell, 1982–83; Asst Chaplain-in-Chief, Support Comd, 1983–85, Strike Comd, 1985–88; QHC 1985–91; Chaplain-in-Chief and Archdeacon, RAF, 1988–91. Canon and Prebendary, Lincoln Cathedral, 1989–91. *Recreations:* music, theatre, running. *Address:* St Luke's Rectory, 69 Evesham Road, Redditch B97 4JX. *T:* Redditch (01527) 545521. *Clubs:* Royal Air Force; Oxford Union Society.

HALIFAX, 3rd Earl of, *cr* 1944; **Charles Edward Peter Neil Wood;** Bt 1784; Viscount Halifax, 1866; Baron Irwin, 1925; JP, DL; *b* 14 March 1944; *s* of 2nd Earl of Halifax and Ruth (*d* 1989), *d* of late Captain Rt Hon. Neil James Archibald Primrose, MC, sometime MP; *S* father, 1980; *m* 1976, Camilla, *d* of late C. F. J. Younger, DSO, TD; one *s* one *d*. *Educ:* Eton; Christ Church, Oxford. Contested (C) Dearne Valley, Feb. and Oct. 1974. Director: Hambros Bank, 1978–; Yorkshire Post Newspapers, 1985–. High Steward of

York Minster, 1988–. JP Wilton Beacon, 1986, DL Humberside, 1983. *Heir:* s Lord Irwin, *qv. Address:* Garrowby, York YO4 1QD. *Clubs:* White's, Pratt's.

HALIFAX (NS), Archbishop of, (RC), since 1991; **Most Rev. Austin-Emile Burke;** *b* 1922. Ordained priest, 1950; Suffragan Bishop of Yarmouth, 1968–91. *Address:* Chancery Office, PO Box 1527, 1531 Grafton Street, Halifax, NS B3J 2Y3, Canada. *Fax:* 423–5201.

HALIFAX, Archdeacon of; *see* Inwood, Ven. R. N.

HALL, Adam; *see* Trevor, Elleston.

HALL, Rt. Rev. Albert Peter; *see* Woolwich, Bishop Suffragan of.

HALL, Alfred Charles, CBE 1977 (OBE 1966); HM Diplomatic Service, retired; *b* 2 Aug. 1917; *s* of Alfred Hall and Florence Mary Hall; *m* 1945, Clara Georgievna Strunina, Moscow; five *s* one *d*. *Educ:* Oratory Sch.; Open Univ. (BA); Univ. of Kent. Served War, RA and Intell. Corps, 1939–43. LCC, 1934–39 and 1946–49; FO, with service in Saudi Arabia, Algeria, Egypt, Iran and USSR, 1943–46; FCO (formerly CRO and CO), with service in Pakistan, India, Nigeria, Canada and Australia, 1949–75; Dep. High Comr in Southern India, 1975–77. Grants Officer, SCF, 1979–82. *Publications:* freelance journalism and technical papers. *Recreations:* music, reading, politics. *Address:* White Cliff, St Margaret's Bay, Kent CT15 6HR. *T:* Dover (01304) 852230. *Club:* Commonwealth Trust.

HALL, Prof. Alfred Rupert, LittD; FBA 1978; Professor of the History of Science and Technology, Imperial College of Science and Technology, University of London, 1963–80; *b* 26 July 1920; *s* of Alfred Dawson Hall and Margaret Ritchie; *m* 1st, 1942, Annie Shore Hughes; two *d*; 2nd, 1959, Marie Boas (*see* M. B. Hall). *Educ:* Alderman Newton's Boy's Sch., Leicester; Christ's Coll., Cambridge (scholar). LittD Cantab 1975. Served in Royal Corps of Signals, 1940–45. 1st cl. Historical Tripos Part II, 1946; Allen Scholar, 1948; Fellow, Christ's Coll., 1949–59, Steward, 1955–59; Curator, Whipple Science Mus., Cambridge and University Lectr, 1950–59. Medical Research Historian, University of Calif, Los Angeles, 1959–60, Prof. of Philosophy, 1960–61; Prof. of History and Logic of Science, Indiana Univ., 1961–63. Royal Society Lectures: Wilkins, 1973; Leeuwenhoek, 1988. FRHistS. Pres., British Soc. for History of Science, 1966–68; Pres., Internat. Acad. of the History of Science, 1977–81; Wellcome Trust: Chm., Adv. Panel on History of Medicine, 1974–80; Co-ordinator, History of Medicine, 1981–85. Co-editor, A History of Technology, 1951–58. Corresp. Mem., Soc. for the History of Technology, 1970. Silver Medal, RSA, 1974; (jtly) Sarton Medal, History of Science Soc., 1981. *Publications:* Ballistics in the Seventeenth Century, 1952; The Scientific Revolution, 1954; From Galileo to Newton, 1963; The Cambridge Philosophical Society: a history, 1819–1969, 1969; Philosophers at War, 1980; Short History of the Imperial College, 1982; The Revolution in Science 1500–1750, 1983; Henry More: Magic, Religion and Experiment, 1990; with Marie Boas Hall: Unpublished Scientific Papers of Isaac Newton, 1962; Correspondence of Henry Oldenburg, 1965–86; (with Laura Tilling) Correspondence of Isaac Newton, vols 5–7, 1974–77; (ed with Norman Smith) History of Technology, 1976–83; (with B. A. Bembridge) Physic and Philanthropy: a history of the Wellcome Trust, 1986; Isaac Newton: Adventurer in Thought, 1992; Newton, his Friends and his Foes, 1993; All was Light, 1993; Essays on the History of Science and Technology, 1994; contributor to Isis, Annals of Science, etc. *Address:* 14 Ball Lane, Tackley, Oxford OX5 3AG. *T:* Tackley (0186983) 257.

HALL, Anthony Stewart, (Tony); Director, Central Council for Education and Training in Social Work, since 1986; *b* 26 Oct. 1945; *s* of Dora Rose Ellen Hall (*née* Rundle) and Albert Hall; *m* 1968, Phoebe Katharine Souster; one *s* one *d*. *Educ:* Gillingham Grammar School; London Sch. of Economics (BScSoc). Research Student, LSE, 1968–71; Lectr in Management and Organisation Studies, Nat. Inst. for Social Work, 1971–73; Lectr in Social Admin, Univ. of Bristol, 1973–78; Dir, Assoc. of British Adoption and Fostering Agencies, 1978–80; Dir and Sec., British Agencies for Adoption and Fostering, 1980–86. *Publications:* A Management Game for the Social Service (with J. Algie), 1974; The Point of Entry: a study of client reception in the social services, 1975; (ed) Access to Birth Records: the impact of S.26 of the Children Act 1975, 1980; (with Phoebe Hall) Part-time Social Work, 1980; (series editor) Child Care Policy and Practice, 1982–86; chapters in books and articles in professional and learned jls. *Recreations:* photography, genealogy, watching sport and old films. *Address:* 115 Babington Road, Streatham, SW16 6AN. *T:* 0181–769 1504.

HALL, Anthony William, (Tony); Managing Director, News and Current Affairs, BBC, since 1993 (Director, 1990–93); *b* 3 March 1951; *s* of Donald William Hall and Mary Joyce Hall; *m* 1977, Cynthia Lesley Hall (*née* Davis); one *s* one *d*. *Educ:* King Edward's Sch., Birmingham; Birkenhead Sch., Merseyside; Keble Coll., Oxford (Exhibnr; MA). Joined BBC as News trainee, 1973; Producer: World Tonight, 1976; New York (Radio), 1977; Sen. Producer, World at One, 1978; Output Editor, Newsnight, 1980; Sen. Producer, Six O'Clock News, 1984; Asst Editor, Nine O'Clock News, 1985; Editor: News and Election '87, 1987; News and Current Affairs, BBC TV, 1988–90. Liveryman, Painter Stainers' Co., 1989–. FRTS 1994. *Publications:* King Coal: a history of the miners, 1981; Nuclear Politics, 1984; articles in various periodicals. *Recreations:* reading and writing books, church architecture, opera, walking in Dorset. *Address:* c/o BBC TV Centre, Wood Lane, W12 7RJ. *T:* 0181–743 8000.

HALL, Sir Arnold (Alexander), Kt 1954; FRS 1953; MA; FEng; Chairman, Hawker Siddeley Group plc, 1967–86 (Director, 1955, Vice-Chairman, 1963–67, Managing Director, 1963–81; Executive Chairman, 1967–84); Managing Director, Bristol Siddeley Engines, 1959–63; former Chairman: Hawker Siddeley Diesels Ltd; Hawker Siddeley Electric Ltd; Hawker Siddeley Canada Inc.; Hawker Siddeley Rail Ltd; *b* 23 April 1915. *Educ:* Clare Coll., Cambridge (Rex Moir Prize in Engineering, John Bernard Seely Prize in Aeronautics, Ricardo Prize in Thermodynamics). Res. Fellow in Aeronautics of the Company of Armourers and Brasiers (held at University of Cambridge), 1936–38; Principal Scientific Officer, Royal Aircraft Establishment, Farnborough, Hants, 1938–45; Zaharoff Prof. of Aviation, University of London, and Head of Dept of Aeronautics, Imperial Coll. of Science and Technology, 1945–51; Dir of the Royal Aircraft Establishment, Farnborough, 1951–55. Chm., Fasco Industries Inc., 1980–81. Pres., Royal Aeronautical Society, 1958–59, Hon. Fellow, 1965; Dep. Pres., BEAMA, 1966–67, Pres., 1967–68; Vice-Pres., Engineering Employers' Fedn, 1968–80, 1984–86; President: Locomotive and Allied Manufacturers Assoc. of GB, 1968–69, 1969–70; SBAC, 1972–73. Member: Advisory Council on Scientific Policy, 1962–64; Air Registration Board, 1963–73; Electricity Supply Research Council, 1963–72; Advisory Council on Technology (Min. of Technology), 1964–67; Defence Industries Council, 1969–77; Industrial Develt Adv. Bd, 1973–75; Dep. Chm., Engineering Industries Council, 1975–86. Director: Lloyds Bank, 1966–85; Lloyds Bank UK Management Ltd, 1979–84; Phoenix Assurance, 1969–85; ICI, 1970–85; Onan Corp., 1976–80; Rolls-Royce Ltd, 1983–88; Royal Ordnance, 1984–86. Pro-Chancellor, Warwick Univ., 1965–70; Chancellor, Loughborough Univ. of Technology, 1980–89. Chm. Bd of Trustees, Science Museum, 1983–85. Freeman, City of London, 1988. Fellow, Imperial Coll. of Science and Technology, 1963–; Founder Fellow, Fellowship of Engineering, 1976 (Vice-Pres., 1977); For. Associate, US Nat. Acad. of Engrg, 1976–; Hon. Fellow, Clare Coll., Cambridge, 1966; Hon. ACGI; Hon. FRAeS; Hon. FAIAA; Hon. MIMechE, 1968; Hon. FIEE, 1975; Hon. DTech Loughborough 1976; Hon. DSc: London, 1980; Cambridge, 1986. Gold Medal, RAeS, 1962; Hambro Award (Business Man of the Year), 1975; Gold Medal, BIM, 1981; Albert Medal, RSA, 1983. *Address:* Wakehams, Dorney, near Windsor, Berks SL4 6QD.

HALL, Arthur Herbert; Librarian and Curator, Guildhall Library and Museum, and Director of Guildhall Art Gallery, 1956–66; retired; *b* 30 Aug. 1901; *y s* of Henry and Eliza Jane Hall, Islington, London; *m* 1927, Dorothy Maud (*née* Barton); two *s* one *d*. *Educ:* Mercers' Sch., Holborn, London. Entered Guildhall Library as junior asst, 1918; Dep. Librarian, 1943–56. Hon. Librarian, Clockmakers' and Gardeners' Companies, 1956–66. Served with RAOC, 1942–46. Chm. Council, London and Middlesex Archæological Soc., 1957–64, Vice-Pres., 1962–; Member: Council of London Topographical Soc., 1960–67; Exec. Cttee, Friends of Nat. Libraries, 1965–69. Hon. Sec., Middlesex Victoria County History Council, 1966–78; Enfield Archaeological Soc. (Hon. Sec., 1966–71); Master, 1974–75, Hon. Clerk, 1965–74, Asst Hon. Clerk, 1975–86, Civic Guild of Old Mercers. Liveryman of the Clockmakers Co. Pres., Upper Norwood Athenæum, 1993–. FLA 1930; FSA 1963.

HALL, Sir Basil (Brodribb), KCB 1977 (CB 1974); MC 1945; TD 1952; Member, European Commission of Human Rights, 1985–93; Legal Adviser, Broadcasting Complaints Commission, 1981–93; *b* 2 Jan. 1918; *s* of late Alfred Brodribb Hall and of Elsie Hilda Hall, Woking, Surrey; *m* 1955, Jean Stafford Gowland; two *s* one *d*. *Educ:* Merchant Taylors' Sch. Articled Clerk with Gibson & Weldon, Solicitors, 1935–39; admitted Solicitor, 1942. Served War of 1939–45: Trooper, Inns of Court Regt, 1939; 2nd Lieut, 12th Royal Lancers, 1940; Captain, 27th Lancers, 1941; Major, 27th Lancers, 1942. Legal Asst, Treasury Solicitor's Dept, 1946; Sen. Legal Asst, 1951; Asst Treasury Solicitor, 1958; Principal Asst Solicitor, 1968; Dep. Treasury Solicitor, 1972; HM Procurator Gen. and Treasury Solicitor, 1975–80. Chm., Civil Service Appeal Bd, 1981–84 (Dep. Chm., 1980–81). Mem. Council, Nat. Army Museum, 1981–92. *Recreations:* military history, travel. *Address:* Woodlands, 16 Danes Way, Oxshott, Surrey KT22 0LX. *T:* Oxshott (01372) 842032. *Club:* Athenæum.

HALL, Very Rev. Bernard, SJ; Superior, Jesuit House of Writers, Rome, since 1994; *b* 17 Oct. 1921. *Educ:* St Michael's Coll., Leeds; Heythrop Coll., Oxford. LicPhil, STL. Captain RA, 1941–46. Entered Society of Jesus, 1946; ordained priest, 1955; Provincial of the English Province, Society of Jesus, 1970–76; Rector, Collegio San Roberto Bellarmino, Rome, 1976–82 and 1989–94; English Asst to Father General, SJ, Rome, 1982–88. *Address:* Casa degli Scrittori, via dei Penitenzieri 20, 00193 Rome, Italy.

HALL, Betty, CBE 1977; Regional Nursing Officer, West Midlands Regional Health Authority, 1974–81; *b* 6 June 1921; *d* of John Hall and Jane (*née* Massey), Eagley, Lancs. *Educ:* Bolton Sch.; Royal Infirm., Edinburgh (RGN); Radcliffe Infirm., Oxford and St Mary's Hosp., Manchester (SCM); Royal Coll. of Nursing (RNT). Nursed tuberculous patients from concentration camps, Rollier Clinic, Leysin, 1948–49; Ward Sister, Salford Royal Hosp., 1949–51; Sister Tutor, Royal Masonic Hosp., London, 1952–54; Principal Tutor, St Luke's Hosp., Bradford, 1954–61 (Mem. Leeds Area Nurse Trng Cttee); King Edward's Hosp. Fund Admin. Staff Coll., 1961–62; Work Study Officer to United Bristol Hosps, 1961–64; Asst Nursing Officer to Birmingham Regional Hosp. Bd, 1964–65, Regional Nursing Officer, 1966–81. Mem., Exec. Cttee, Grange-over-Sands Abbeyfield Soc., 1982–93. Hon. Sec., Grange-over-Sands RUKBA, 1987–. *Recreations:* reading, tapestry making, cricket. *Address:* Chailey, Ash Mount Road, Grange-over-Sands, Cumbria LA11 6BX. *Club:* Naval and Military.

HALL, Dame Catherine (Mary), DBE 1982 (CBE 1967); FRCN; General Secretary, Royal College of Nursing of the United Kingdom, 1957–82; *b* 19 Dec. 1922; *d* of late Robert Hall, OBE and late Florence Irene Hall (*née* Turner). *Educ:* Hunmanby Hall Sch. for Girls, Filey, Yorks. Gen. Infirmary, Leeds: nursing trng, 1941–44 (SRN); Ward Sister, 1945–47; sen. nursing appts, 1949–53; midwifery trng, Leeds and Rotherham, 1948 (SCM); travelling fellowship, US and Canada, 1950–51; student in nursing administration, Royal College of Nursing, 1953–54; Asst Matron, Middlesex Hosp., London, 1954–56. Part-time Member: CIR, 1971–74; British Railways Regional Bd for London and the South East, 1975–77; Mem. GMC, 1979–89; Chm., UK Central Council for Nursing, Midwifery and Health Visiting, 1980–85. Hon. Mem., Florida Nurses Assoc., 1973. FRCN 1976. OStJ 1977. Hon. DLitt City, 1975. *Address:* Barnsfield, Barnsfield Lane, Buckfastleigh, Devon TQ11 0NP. *T:* Buckfastleigh (01364) 642504.

HALL, Christopher Myles; Editor of The Countryman, since 1981; *b* 21 July 1932; *s* of Gilbert and Muriel Hall; *m* 1957, Jennifer Bevan Keech (marr. diss. 1980); one *s* one *d*. *Educ:* New Coll., Oxford. 2nd cl. Hons PPE. Reporter and Feature-writer, Daily Express, 1955–58; Sub-editor and Leader-writer, Daily Mirror, 1958–61; Feature-writer and Leader-writer, Daily Herald/Sun, 1961–65; Special Asst (Information): to Minister of Overseas Develt, 1965–66; to Minister of Transport, 1966–68; Chief Information Officer, MoT, 1968; Ramblers' Association: Sec., 1969–74; Mem. Exec. Cttee, 1982–84; Vice-Chm., 1984–87; Chm., 1987–90; Pres., 1990–93; Vice-Pres., 1993–; Chm., Oxfordshire Area, 1984–87, 1994–; Dir, Council for Protection of Rural England, 1974–80. Pres., The Holiday Fellowship, 1974–77; Vice-Chm., S Reg. Council of Sport and Recreation, 1976–82; Member: DoT Cttee of Inquiry into Operators' Licensing, 1977–79; Common Land Forum, 1984–86; Hon. Sec., Chiltern Soc., 1965–68. Columnist, Rambling Today, 1993–. *Publications:* How to Run a Pressure Group, 1974; (jtly) The Countryside We Want, 1988; The Countryman's Yesterday, 1989; Scenes from The Countryman, 1992; contributions to: Motorways in London, 1969; No Through Road, 1975; The Countryman's Britain, 1976; Book of British Villages, 1980; Sunday Times Book of the Countryside, 1981; Walker's Britain, 1982; Britain on Backroads, 1985; Making Tracks, 1985; (with John Tookey) The Cotswolds, 1990; pamphlets; contrib. to Vole, The Countryman, New Statesman, New Scientist, The Geographical Magazine, Country Living, The Guardian and various jls. *Recreation:* walking in the countryside. *Address:* c/o The Countryman, Sheep Street, Burford, Oxon OX18 4LH.

HALL, David, CBE 1983; QPM 1977; consultant in security and personnel management; Chief Constable of Humberside Police, 1976–91; *b* 29 Dec. 1930; *s* of Arthur Thomas Hall and Dorothy May Charman; *m* 1952, Molly Patricia Knight; two *s*. *Educ:* Richmond and East Sheen Grammar School for Boys. Joined Metropolitan Police and rose through ranks from PC to Chief Supt, 1950–68; Staff Officer to Chief Inspector of Constabulary, Col Sir Eric St Johnson, 1968; Asst Chief Constable, 1970, Dep. Chief Constable, 1976, Staffordshire Police. Vice-Pres., Assoc. of Chief Police Officers of England, Wales and NI, 1982–83, Pres. 1983–84. CIMgt (CBIM 1988). Freeman, City of London, 1987. OStJ 1980. *Recreations:* gardening, walking, playing the piano. *Address:* Fairlands, 1 Copper Beech Close, West Leys Park, Kemp Road, Swanland, North Humberside HU14 3LR.

HALL, David John; Head of Projects Export Promotion (formerly Projects and Export Policy) Division, Department of Trade and Industry, since 1991; *b* 15 July 1942; *s* of late Alexander G. Hall and Molly Hall, Aberdeen; *m* 1965, Elizabeth Adams; one *s* two *d*.

Educ: Trinity Coll., Glenalmond; Pembroke Coll., Oxford (BA Mod. Langs). FO, 1964–67; Bahrain, 1967–69; Dubai, 1969–70; FCO, 1970–74; Bonn, 1974–76; joined Dept of Trade, later DTI, 1976; Asst Sec., 1982; Counsellor (Trade and Envmt), Washington, 1988; Under-Sec., 1991. *Recreations:* music, gardening, dogs. *Address:* c/o Department of Trade and Industry, Ashdown House, 123 Victoria Street, SW1E 6RB. *T:* 0171–215 5462.

HALL, Prof. David Oakley, PhD; Professor of Biology, King's College London, since 1974; *b* 14 Nov. 1935; *s* of Charles Edward Hall and Ethel Marion Oakley; *m* 1981, Peta Jacqueline Smyth; two *d. Educ:* Kearsney Coll., S Africa (matric. 1952); Univ. of Natal, SA (BSc 1957); Univ. of California, Berkeley (PhD 1962). Fellow, Johns Hopkins Med. Sch., Baltimore, USA (Post-doctoral Fellow, 1963–64); Lectr, 1964–68, Reader, 1968–74, KCL. Vis. Sen. Res. Scientist, Princeton Univ., 1990–91. Chm., UK SCOPE Cttee, Royal Soc. *Publications:* Photosynthesis, 1972, 5th edn 1994; Biomass, 1987; Plants as solar collectors, 1983; numerous articles in jls on photosynthesis, biomass for energy, bioproductivity and biotechnology. *Recreations:* swimming, reading, theatre. *Address:* King's College London, Campden Hill Road, W8 7AH. *T:* 0171–333 4317. *Club:* Athenæum.

HALL, Denis C.; *see* Clarke Hall.

HALL, Denis Whitfield, CMG 1962; late Provincial Commissioner, Kenya; *b* 26 Aug. 1913; *s* of late H. R. Hall, Haslemere, Surrey; *m* 1940, Barbara Carman; two *s. Educ:* Dover College; Wadham Coll., Oxford. Dist Officer, Kenya, 1936; Personal Asst to Chief Native Comr, 1948; Senior Dist Comr, 1955; Provincial Comr, Coast Province, 1959. Dep. Chm., Sussex Church Campaign, 1964–73. *Recreations:* sailing, tennis, walking, motoring. *Address:* Martins, Priory Close, Boxgrove, West Sussex PO18 0AE. *Clubs:* Oxford Union; Oxford University Yacht.

HALL, Air Marshal Sir Donald (Percy), KCB 1984 (CB 1981); CBE 1975; AFC 1963; Deputy Chairman, GEC-Marconi, since 1990; *b* 11 Nov. 1930; *s* of William Reckerby Hall and Elsie Hall; *m* 1953, Joyce (*née* Warburton); two *d. Educ:* Hull Grammar Sch. Royal Air Force Coll., 1949; flying appts until 1963; staff and command appointments, 1964–86, including: OC, No 111 Sqdn, Empire Test Pilots Sch., and RAF Akrotiri; AOC No 11 Gp; ACAS (Operational Requirements); AOC No 38 Gp; Dep. Chief, Defence Staff. Chm., Marconi Defence Systems, 1987–89. *Recreations:* walking, swimming, planting trees. *Address:* c/o Lloyds Bank, Cox's and King's Branch, 7 Pall Mall, SW1Y 5NA. *Clubs:* Royal Air Force; Colonels.

HALL, Sir Douglas (Basil), 14th Bt *cr* 1687; KCMG 1959 (CMG 1958); *b* 1 Feb. 1909; *s* of late Capt. Lionel Erskine Hall and late Jane Augusta Hall (*née* Reynolds); *S* brother, Sir Neville Hall, 13th Bt, 1978; *m* 1933, Rachel Marion Gartside-Tippinge (*d* 1990); one *s* two *d* (and one *s* decd). *Educ:* Radley Coll.; Keble Coll., Oxford (MA). Joined Colonial Admin. Service, 1930; posted to N Rhodesia as Cadet; District Officer, 1932; Senior District Officer, 1950; Provincial Commr, 1953; Administrative Sec., 1954; Sec. for Native Affairs to Government of Northern Rhodesia, 1956–59, Acting Chief Sec. for a period during 1958; Governor and C-in-C, Somaliland Protectorate, 1959–60. JP Co. Devon, 1964, Chm., Kingsbridge Petty Sessional Div., 1971–79. *Publications:* various technical articles. *Recreation:* vintage cars. *Heir: s* John Douglas Hoste Hall [*b* 7 Jan. 1945; *m* 1972, Angela Margaret, *d* of George Keys; two *s*]. *Address:* Barnford, Ringmore, near Kingsbridge, Devon TQ7 4HL. *T:* Bigbury-on-Sea (01548) 810401.

HALL, Duncan; Chief Executive, Teesside Development Corporation, since 1987; *b* 2 Sept. 1947; *s* of Leslie and Joan Elizabeth Hall; *m* 1970, Jane Elizabeth Menzies; two *s* one *d. Educ:* Acklam Hall Grammar Sch. LLB Hons. Articled Clerk and Senior Legal Assistant, Wellingborough UDC, 1970–74; Corby District Council: PA to Chief Exec., 1974–75; Asst Chief Exec., 1975–78; Housing and Property Controller, 1978–79; Chief Exec., 1980–87. CIMgt; FRSA. *Recreations:* reading, travel, music, theatre, shooting. *Address:* Teesside Development Corporation, Dunedin House, Riverside Quay, Stockton-on-Tees, Cleveland TS17 6BJ. *T:* Stockton (01642) 677123.

HALL, Prof. Edward Thomas, CBE 1988; Professor, Research Laboratory for Archaeology and the History of Art, Oxford University, 1975–89, now Emeritus Professor of Archaeological Sciences (Director 1954–89); Fellow of Worcester College, Oxford, 1969–89, now Emeritus; *b* 10 May 1924; *s* of late Lt-Col Walter D'Arcy Hall, MC, and of Ann Madelaine Hall; *m* 1957, Jennifer (Jeffie) Louise de la Harpe; two *s. Educ:* Eton; New Coll., Oxford (BA 1948, MA 1953, DPhil 1953; Hon. Fellow, 1994). FPhysS. Served RNVR, 1942–45. Dir, GEC plc, 1988–90. Designer and manufacturer of scientific apparatus, Littlemore, Oxford, 1952–. Vis. Prof., UCL, 1995. Member: Science Mus. Adv. Council, 1979–84; Ancient Monuments Adv. Cttee, 1984–90; Hon. Scientific Cttee, Nat. Gall., 1970– (Chm., 1978–84); Council, Internat. Inst. of Conservation, 1971–94 (Pres., 1989–92); Trustee: British Mus., 1973–; Nat. Gall., 1977–84; Science Mus., 1984–92. Mem. Court, Goldsmiths' Co., 1976, Prime Warden, 1985–86; Chm., Goldsmiths' Antique Plate Cttee, 1987–. FSA. Hon. FBA 1984. *Publications:* contrib. Archaeometry, various jls concerning science applied to archaeology. *Address:* Beenhams, Railway Lane, Littlemore, Oxford OX4 4PY. *T:* Oxford (01865) 777800; Lawnfield, Holbeton, Devon PL8 1JL. *T:* Holbeton (0175530) 226.

HALL, Sir Ernest, Kt 1993; OBE 1986; DL; pianist and composer, since 1954; property developer, since 1971; Chairman, Dean Clough Business, Arts and Education Centre, since 1983; *b* 19 March 1930; *s* of Ernest and Mary Elizabeth Hall; *m* 1st, 1951, June (*née* Annable) (*d* 1994); two *s* two *d*; *m* 2nd, 1975, Sarah (*née* Wellby); one *s. Educ:* Bolton County Grammar Sch.; Royal Manchester Coll. of Music (ARMCM (teacher and performer) 1950–51; Royal Patron's Fund Prize for Composition, 1951). Textile manufr, 1961–71. Mem., TEC, Calderdale and Kirklees, 1990–. Dep. Chm., Eureka! Children's Museum, 1989–; Member: President's Cttee, Business in the Community, 1988–; Arts Council of England (formerly of GB), 1990–; Chm., Yorks and Humberside Arts Bd, 1991–; Pres., Yorks Business in the Arts, 1990–. Chm., Northern Ballet Theatre, 1994–. Trustee, Yorkshire Sculpture Park, 1989–. DL W Yorks, 1991. Hon. Fellow: Huddersfield Polytechnic, 1989; Leeds Polytechnic, 1991; Bolton Inst., 1994. DUniv York, 1986; Hon. DLitt Bradford, 1990; Hon. DArt Bristol Poly, 1991. Envmt Award, Business and Industry Panel, RSA, 1988; Guildhall Helping Hand, Nat. Fedn of Self-Employed and Small Businesses, 1989; Special Free Enterprise Award, Aims of Industry, 1989; Best Practice Award, BURA, 1992; Lifetime Achievement Award, Inst. for Social Inventions, 1992; Albert Medal, RSA, 1994. *Recreations:* equestrianism, gardening, art collecting, theatre, languages. *Address:* Dean Clough, Halifax HX3 5AX. *T:* Halifax (01422) 344555.

HALL, Francis Woodall; HM Diplomatic Service, retired 1978; *b* 10 May 1918; *s* of Francis Hall and Florence Adelaide Woodall; *m* 1951, Phyllis Anne Amelia Andrews; one *s* one *d. Educ:* Taunton School. Inland Revenue, 1936–40; Admty (Alexandria, Port Said, Haifa, Freetown), 1940–46; FO, 1946; Bahrain and Baghdad, 1949; Vice-Consul, Malaga, 1950; FO, 1952; 2nd Sec., Cairo, 1955; Consul: Madrid, 1957; Zagreb, 1960; FO 1962; Consul, Stockholm, 1964; Head of Mombasa Office of British High Commn to Kenya, 1969; Consul-Gen., Alexandria, 1971–78; Hon. Consul, Seville, 1979–83. *Recreations:* music, walking. *Address:* Ed. Torre de la Roca, Piso 1002, 29620 Torremolinos, Málaga, Spain. *T:* (95) 2389590.

HALL, Sir (Frederick) John (Frank), 3rd Bt, *cr* 1923; *b* 14 Aug. 1931; *er s* of Sir Frederick Henry Hall, 2nd Bt, and Olwen Irene (*d* 1993), *yr d* of late Alderman Frank Collis, Stokeville, Stoke-on-Trent, and Deganwy, Llandudno; *S* father, 1949; *m* 1st, 1956, Felicity Anne (marr. diss. 1960), *d* of late Edward Rivers-Fletcher, Norwich, and of Mrs L. R. Galloway; 2nd, 1961, Patricia Ann Atkinson (marr. diss. 1967); two *d*; re-married, 1967, 1st wife, Felicity Anne Hall; two *d. Educ:* Bryanston Sch. Personnel Manager, Universal Pattern & Precision Engineering Co. Ltd, 1955–59; Personnel Officer, The Nestlé Co. Ltd, 1959–63; Personnel Man., Johnson Wax Ltd, 1963–65; UK Head Office Trng and Mgt Develt Man., The Nestlé Co. Ltd, 1965–67; Gp Personnel Man., Findus Ltd, 1967–69; Sen. Man., McLintock Mann & Whinney Murray, 1969–76; Dir, Thomson McLintock Associates, 1976–87; founder Chm., KPMG Career Consultancy Services, 1983–93; Partner, KPMG Peat Marwick, 1987–93, retd. Dir, Roffey Park Inst., 1978–90 (Vice Chm., 1983–85; Chm., 1985–87). *Recreations:* music, collecting antique gramophone records, magic (Mem., Magic Circle). *Heir: b* David Christopher Hall [*b* 30 Dec. 1937; *m* 1st, 1962, Irene (marr. diss. 1987), *d* of William Duncan, Aberdeen; one *s* one *d*; 2nd, 1991, Annie Madelaine Renée Olivier, adopted *d* of late Bottemanne Raould]. *Address:* Carradale, 29 Embercourt Road, Thames Ditton, Surrey KT7 0LH. *T:* 0181–398 2801.

HALL, Rear-Adm. Geoffrey Penrose Dickinson, CB 1973; DSC 1943; DL; Hydrographer of the Navy 1971–75; retired; *b* 19 July 1916; *er s* of late Major A. K. D. Hall and late Mrs P. M. Hall; *m* 1945, Mary Ogilvie Carlisle; two *s* one *d. Educ:* Haileybury. Served in American waters, 1935–37 and on Nyon Patrol during Spanish Civil War; joined surveying service, 1938, served in Indian Ocean until 1939 when transf. to minesweeping in Far East; hydrographic duties, home waters, Iceland, W Africa; navigational and minesweeping duties, Icelandic waters; transf. to Combined Ops, SE Asia; subseq. comd frigate, British Pacific Fleet; from 1947, hydrographic work: with RNZN, 1949–51; subseq. five comds i/c surveys at home and abroad; served ashore and in Atlantic, Indian Ocean, Antarctic waters (Cuthbert Peek Grant, RGS, for work in furtherance of oceanographical exploration); twice Asst Hydrographer; surveyed between S Africa and Iceland, 1965–67; Asst Dir (Naval), Hydrographic Dept, Taunton, 1970. Cadet 1934; Midshipman 1935; Sub-Lt 1938; Lieut 1939; Lt-Comdr 1945; Comdr 1953; Captain 1961; Rear-Adm. 1971. Pres., Hydrographic Soc., 1975. DL Lincs, 1982. *Publications:* contribs to Nature, Deep Sea Research, Internat. Hydrographic Review, Navy International. *Recreation:* country pursuits. *Address:* Manby House, Manby, Louth, Lincs LN11 8UF. *T:* South Cockerington (01507) 327777. *Clubs:* Naval and Military, Royal Navy; Louth (Louth).

HALL, Prof. Geoffrey Ronald, CBE 1985; FEng, CChem, FRSC, SFInstE; Director, 1970–90, and Professor, 1986–90, Brighton Polytechnic, now Professor Emeritus and Hon. Fellow, University of Brighton; *b* 18 May 1928; *er s* of late Thomas Harold Hall, JP, and late Muriel Frances Hall, Douglas, IoM; *m* 1950, Elizabeth Day Sheldon; two *s* one *d. Educ:* Douglas High Sch., IoM; Univ. of Manchester (BSc). Research in Nuclear Science and Engineering at AERE, Harwell, 1949–56; sabbatical at Oxford Univ., 1955; Colombo Plan Expert to Indian Atomic Energy Commn, 1956–58; Reader in Nuclear Technology, Imperial Coll., London, 1958–63; Prof. of Nuclear Technology, Imperial Coll., 1963–70. Member: CNAA, 1977–82; Engineering Council, 1981–86 (Vice-Chm., 1984–85); SERC, 1982–86 (Mem., Engrg Bd, SRC, later SERC, 1978–83); NCVQ, 1986–89; Chm., Engrg Working Gp, Nat. Adv. Body for Local Authority Higher Educn, 1982–84. Mem., Educnl Counselling Service, British Council, 1988–91 (Chm., 1989–91). Dir, Macmillan Intek, 1985–89. President: British Nuclear Energy Soc., 1970–71; Inst. of Fuel, 1976–77; Chm., Lewis Cohen Urban Studies Centre Support Trust, 1993; Founder Fellow, Fellowship of Engineering, now Royal Acad. of Engrg, 1976. *Publications:* papers related to nuclear science, fuels and engineering. *Recreations:* travel, caravanning, golf. *Address:* 23 Firsdown Road, Worthing BN13 3DG.

HALL, His Honour George; *see* Hall, H. G.

HALL, Rev. Canon George Rumney; Rector of the Sandringham Group of Parishes, since 1987; Domestic Chaplain, since 1987, Chaplain to The Queen, since 1989; *b* 7 Nov. 1937; *s* of John Hall; *m* 1965, Diana Lesley Brunning; one *s* one *d. Educ:* Brasted Place, Kent; Westcott House, Cambridge. Deacon 1962, priest 1963; Assistant Curate: St Philip's, Camberwell, 1962–65; Holy Trinity, Waltham Cross, 1965–67; Rector of Buckenham, Hassingham, Strumpshaw, dio. Norwich, 1967–74; Chaplain: St Andrew's Psychiatric Hosp., Norwich, 1967–72; HM Prison, Norwich, 1972–74; Vicar of Wymondham, 1974–87; RD of Humbleyard, 1986–87; Hon. Canon, Norwich Cathedral, 1987–; RD of Heacham and Rising, 1989–. Founder Mem., Wymondham Branch of Mind Day Centre; Mem. Bd, Cotman Housing Assoc., Norwich. *Recreations:* walking, reading, theatre, music. *Address:* The Rectory, Sandringham, Norfolk PE35 6EH. *T:* Dersingham (01485) 540587.

HALL, His Honour (Harold) George; a Circuit Judge, 1975–91; *b* 20 Sept. 1920; *s* of late Albert Hall and Violet Maud Hall (*née* Etherington); *m* 1950, Patricia Delaney; four *s* one *d. Educ:* Archbishop Holgate's Grammar Sch., York. RAF, 1940–46 (Flt-Lt). Called to Bar, Middle Temple, 1958; practised NE Circuit; Dep. Chm., WR Yorks QS, 1970; a Recorder, 1972–75.

HALL, Harold Percival, CMG 1963; MBE 1947; Director of Studies, Royal Institute of Public Administration, 1974–85; *b* 9 Sept. 1913; *s* of late Major George Charles Hall; *m* 1939, Margery Hall, *d* of late Joseph Dickson; three *s* (including twin *s*). *Educ:* Portsmouth Grammar Sch.; Royal Military College, Sandhurst (Prize Cadet; King's India Cadet; Hockey Blue Cricket Cap). Commissioned Indian Army, 1933. Indian Political Service, 1937–47. Private Sec. to Resident, Central India States, 1937; Magistrate and Collector, Meerut, 1938–39. Military Service, 1938–43 (Major). Staff Coll., Quetta, 1941. Asst Political Agent, Loralai, 1943, Nasirabad, 1944; Dir, Food and Civil Supplies, and Dep. Sec., Revenue, Baluchistan, 1945–46; Principal, Colonial Office, 1947; Asst Sec. (Head of Pacific and Indian Ocean Dept), Colonial Office, 1955–62; Sec., Commonwealth Royal Comn on Fedn of Malaya's independence, 1956; Seconded to Office of UK Comr-Gen. for SE Asia, 1962–63; British Dep. High Comr for Eastern Malaysia, Kuching, Sarawak, 1963–64; Asst Sec., Colonial Office, 1965–66; Assistant Under-Secretary of State: Commonwealth Office, 1966–68; MoD, 1968–73. Mem. Governing Body, Sch. of Oriental and African Studies, 1971–74. *Recreation:* gardening. *Address:* Robina, The Chase, Ringwood, Dorset BH24 2AN. *T:* Ringwood (01425) 479880.

HALL, Prof. Henry Edgar, FRS 1982; Emeritus Professor of Physics, University of Manchester, since 1995; *b* 1928; *s* of John Ainger Hall; *m* 1962, Patricia Anne Broadbent; two *s* one *d. Educ:* Latymer Upper Sch., Hammersmith; Emmanuel Coll., Cambridge. BA 1952; PhD 1956. At Royal Society Mond Laboratory, Cambridge, 1952–58; Senior Student, Royal Commission for the Exhibition of 1851, 1955–57; Research Fellow of Emmanuel Coll., 1955–58; Lecturer in Physics, 1958–61, Prof. of Physics, 1961–95, Univ. of Manchester. Simon Memorial Prize (with W. F. Vinen), 1963. Visiting Professor: Univ. of Western Australia, 1964; Univ. of Oregon, 1967–68; Cornell Univ., 1974, 1982–83;

Univ. of Tokyo, 1985. *Publications:* Solid State Physics, 1974; papers in scientific journals. *Recreation:* mountain walking. *Address:* The Schuster Laboratory, The University, Manchester M13 9PL.

HALL, Air Vice-Marshal Hubert Desmond, CB 1979; CBE 1972; AFC 1963; FRAeS; RAF retd; *b* 3 June 1925; *s* of Charles William and Violet Victoria Kate Hall; *m* 1951, Mavis Dorothea (*née* Hopkins). *Educ:* Portsmouth Municipal Coll. Commissioned RAF, 1945; RAF Coll., Cranwell QFI, 1951–55; Flt Comdr, 9 Sqdn, 1955–56; 232 OCU Gaydon, Sqdn Ldr, Medium Bomber Force; Instructor, Wing Comdr 1962; 3 Group Headquarters (Training), 1963–65; Air Warfare Coll., 1965; commanded No 57 Sqdn (Victors), 1966–68; Gp Captain Nuclear Operations SHAPE HQ, 1968–71; comd RAF Waddington, 1971–73; Overseas Coll. of Defence Studies India, 1974; MoD: Director (Air Cdre) of Establishments, RAF, 1975–77; Air Comdr Malta, 1977–79; Air Vice-Marshal 1979; Defence Advr, Canberra, 1980–82. Pres., ACT, Australian-Britain Soc., 1994–. Mem., St John Council, ACT, 1983– (Chm., 1996). KStJ 1991. Queen's Commendation, 1957. *Recreations:* shooting, gardening, reading. *Address:* 7 Richardson Street, Garran, ACT 2605, Australia; c/o Lloyds Bank, 115 Commercial Road, Portsmouth, Hants PO1 1BY. *Clubs:* Royal Air Force, Commonwealth Trust; Commonwealth (Canberra); Lord's Taverners (ACT).

HALL, Prof. James Snowdon, CBE 1976; Professor of Agriculture, Glasgow University, and Principal, West of Scotland Agricultural College, 1966–80; *b* 28 Jan. 1919; *s* of Thomas Blackburn Hall and Mary Milburn Hall; *m* 1942, Mary Smith; one *s* one *d*. *Educ:* Univ. of Durham (BSc Hons). FRAgS, FIBiol. Asst Technical Adviser, Northumberland War Agric. Exec. Commn, 1941–44; Lectr in Agriculture, Univ. of Newcastle upon Tyne, 1944–54; Principal, Cumbria Coll. of Agriculture and Forestry, 1954–66. *Address:* 26 Earls Way, Doonfoot, Ayr KA7 4HE. *T:* Alloway (01292) 441162. *Club:* Farmers'.

HALL, Her Honour Jean Graham, LLM (London); a Circuit Judge (formerly Deputy Chairman, South-East London Quarter Sessions), 1971–89; *b* 26 March 1917; *d* of Robert Hall and Alison (*née* Graham). *Educ:* Inverkeithing Sch., Fife; St Anne's Coll., Sanderstead; London Sch. of Economics. Gold Medal (Elocution and Dramatic Art), Incorporated London Acad. of Music, 1935; Teacher's Dipl., Guildhall Sch. of Music, 1937; Social Science Cert., London Sch. of Economics, 1937; LLB (Hons), London, 1950. FCIArb 1990. Club Leader and subseq. Sub-Warden, Birmingham Univ. Settlement, 1937–41; Sec., Eighteen Plus (an experiment in youth work), 1941–44; Probation Officer, Hants, subseq. Croydon, 1945–51. Called to Bar, Gray's Inn, 1951. Metropolitan Stipendiary Magistrate, 1965–71. Pres., Gray's Inn Debating Soc., 1953; Hon. Sec., Soc. of Labour Lawyers, 1954–64; Pres., British Soc. of Criminology, 1971–74. Chm. Departmental Cttee on Statutory Maintenance Limits, 1966–68. Contested (Lab) East Surrey, 1955. Pres., Edridge Benevolent Trust, 1984. FRSA. Hon. LLD Lincoln, USA, 1979. *Publications:* Towards a Family Court, 1971; (jtly) Child Abuse: procedure and evidence, 1978, 3rd edn 1993; (jtly) The Expert Witness, 1992; (jtly) Crimes Against Children, 1992. *Recreations:* travel, congenial debate, writing. *Address:* 9 Gough Square, EC4A 3DE. *Club:* University Women's.

HALL, Jean Morag; *see* Rankine, J. M.

HALL, Joan Valerie, CBE 1990; Member, Central Transport Consultative Committee, 1981–86; *b* 31 Aug. 1935; *d* of late Robert Percy Hall and Winifred Emily Umbers. *Educ:* Queen Margaret's Sch., Escrick, York; Ashridge House of Citizenship. Contested (C) Barnsley, 1964 and 1966. MP (C) Keighley, 1970–Feb. 1974; PPS to Minister of State for Agriculture, Fisheries and Food, 1972–74. Vice-Chm., Greater London Young Conservatives, 1964. Chm., Sudan Studies Soc. of UK, 1989–92. Mem. Council, Univ. of Buckingham (formerly University Coll. Buckingham), 1977–. *Address:* Mayfields, Darton Road, Cawthorne, Barnsley, South Yorks S75 4HY. *T:* Barnsley (01226) 790230.

HALL, Sir John; *see* Hall, Sir F. J. F.

HALL, John; *see* Hall, W. J.

HALL, Sir John, Kt 1991; Chairman: Cameron Hall Developments Ltd, 1973–93; Newcastle United Football Club, since 1992; *b* 21 March 1933; *m* Mae; one *s* one *d*. *Educ:* Bedlington Grammar Sch. Chartered surveyor. Developed MetroCentre (shopping and leisure complex), Gateshead, 1985. Mem., Millennium Fund Commn, 1994–. Gordon Grand Fellow, Yale Univ., 1991. Hon. DCL Newcastle upon Tyne, 1988. NE Business Man of the Year, 1987. *Address:* Wynyard Hall, Billingham, Cleveland TS22 5NF.

HALL, John Anthony Sanderson, DFC 1943; QC 1967; FCIArb 1982; *b* 25 Dec. 1921; *s* of late Rt Hon. W. Glenvil Hall, PC, MP, and late Rachel Ida Hall (*née* Sanderson); *m* 1st, Nora Ella Hall (*née* Crowe) (marr. diss. 1974); one *s* two *d*; 2nd, Elizabeth Mary, widow of Alan Riley Maynard. *Educ:* Leighton Park Sch.; Trinity Hall, Cambridge (MA). Served RAF, 1940–46, 85 Squadron and 488 (NZ) Squadron (Squadron Leader; DFC and Bar). Called to Bar, Inner Temple, 1948, Master of the Bench, 1975; Western Circuit; Dep. Chm., Hants Quarter Sessions, 1967; Recorder of Swindon, 1971; a Recorder of the Crown Court, 1972–78. Member: Gen. Council of the Bar, 1964–68, 1970–74; Senate of the Four Inns of Court, 1966–68, 1970–74; Council of Legal Educn, 1970–74. Mem., 1972–79, Chm., 1978–79, UK Deleg. to Consultative Cttee, Bars and Law Socs of EEC; Mem., Foreign Compensation Commn, 1983–. Dir Gen., Internat. Fedn of Producers of Phonograms and Videograms, 1979–81. Governor, St Catherine's Sch., Bramley. *Recreation:* fly fishing. *Address:* 2 Dr Johnson's Buildings, Temple, EC4Y 7AY; Swallows, Blewbury, Oxon. *Club:* Royal Air Force.

HALL, Sir John (Bernard), 3rd Bt *cr* 1919; Chairman, The Nikko Bank (UK) plc, 1992–95 (Managing Director, 1990–92); *b* 20 March 1932; *s* of Lieut-Col Sir Douglas Montgomery Bernard Hall, DSO, 2nd Bt, and Ina Nancie Walton (Nancie Lady Hall), *d* of late Col John Edward Mellor, CB (she *m* 2nd, 1962, Col Peter J. Bradford, DSO, MC, TD, who *d* 1990); *S* father, 1962; *m* 1957, Delia Mary, *d* of late Lieut-Col J. A. Innes, DSO; one *s* two *d*. *Educ:* Eton; Trinity Coll., Oxford (MA). FCIB 1976. Lieut, Royal Fusiliers (RARO). J. Henry Schroder Wagg & Co. Ltd, formerly J. Henry Schröder & Co., 1955–73 (Dir, 1967–73); Director: The Antofagasta (Chili) and Bolivia Rly Co. Ltd, 1967–73; Bank of America International, 1974–82; Man. Dir, European Brazilian Bank, subseq. Eurobraz, 1983–89 (Dir, 1976–89); a Vice-Pres., Bank of America NT & SA, 1982–90; Chm., Assoc. of British Consortium Banks, 1985–86. Chm., Anglo-Colombian Soc., 1978–81. Member: St Alban's Diocesan Synod and Bd of Finance, 1992–; Bishop's Stortford Deanery Synod, 1991–; Albury PCC, 1990–. FRGS 1988; FRSA 1989. Liveryman, Clothworkers' Co., 1957 (Mem., Court of Assts, 1987–). *Recreations:* travel, fishing. *Heir: s* David Bernard Hall, *b* 12 May 1961. *Address:* Penrose House, Patmore Heath, Albury, Ware, Herts SG11 2LT. *T:* Albury (01279) 771255. *Clubs:* Boodle's, Lansdowne, Bankers'.

HALL, Dr John Tristan Dalton; University Librarian, University of Durham, since 1989; *b* 28 Oct. 1945; *m* 1970, Inge Lise Lindqvist; one *s* two *d*. *Educ:* Lady Lumley's Sch., Pickering; Univ. of Manchester (BA 1968; PhD 1977); MA Cantab 1989. Asst Librarian, John Rylands Univ. Library of Manchester, 1971–78; Sub-Librarian (Special Collections), Edinburgh Univ. Library, 1978–86; Dep. Librarian, Cambridge Univ. Library, 1986–89; Fellow, Darwin Coll., Cambridge, 1987–89. *Publications:* Manuscript Treasures in Edinburgh University Library: an album of illustrations, 1980; The Tounis College: an anthology of Edinburgh University student journals 1823–1923, 1985; articles and reviews in learned jls. *Recreations:* music, pottery, gardening. *Address:* 8 Springfield Park, Durham DH1 4LS. *T:* 0191–383 1032.

HALL, Jonathan David D.; *see* Durham Hall.

HALL, Maj.-Gen. Jonathan Michael Francis Cooper, OBE 1987; General Officer Commanding Scotland, and Governor of Edinburgh Castle, since 1995; *b* 10 Aug. 1944; *s* of Charles Richard Hall and Rosemary Hall (*née* Beckwith); *m* 1968, Sarah Linda Hudson; two *d*. *Educ:* Taunton Sch.; RMA Sandhurst. Commissioned 3rd Carabiniers, 1965; Staff Coll., 1977; commanded Royal Scots Dragoon Guards, 1984–86 and 12th Armd Bde, 1988–90; Higher Command and Staff Course, 1988; RCDS, 1991; Dep. Mil. Sec., MoD(A), 1992–93; DRAC, 1994. Col Comdt, RAVC, 1995–. Trustee, Royal Scots Draoon Guards. *Recreations:* country, music, tennis, ski-ing, travel. *Address:* Home HQ, Royal Scots Dragoon Guards, The Castle, Edinburgh EH1 2YT. *T:* 0131–310 5100/5101. *Club:* Cavalry and Guards (Mem., Gen. Cttee).

HALL, Julian; His Honour Judge Julian Hall; a Circuit Judge, since 1986; *b* 13 Jan. 1939; *s* of late Dr Stephen Hall, FRCP and Dr Mary Hall, Boarstall Tower, Bucks; *m* 1st, 1968, M. Rosalind Perry (marr. diss. 1988); one *s* one *d*; 2nd, 1989, Ingrid Cecilia, *er d* of late Rev. Canon Ronald Lunt, MC. *Educ:* Eton (Scholar); Christ Church, Oxford (Scholar; MA); Trinity Coll., Dublin (LLB). ARCM (flute). Industrial Chemist, Shell Internat. Chemical Co., 1961–63. Called to the Bar, Gray's Inn, 1966; in practice in Common Law Chambers on Northern Circuit, Manchester, 1966–86; Standing Prosecuting Counsel to Inland Revenue, Northern Circuit, 1985–86; a Recorder, 1982–86. Tutor judge, Judicial Studies Bd, 1989–93. *Recreation:* making music, in orchestras, choirs and at home. *Address:* c/o Crown and County Courts, 85–87 Ladys Lane, Northampton NN1 3HQ. *T:* Northampton (01604) 250131.

See also C. E. Henderson.

HALL, (Laura) Margaret; *see* MacDougall, Laura Margaret.

HALL, Prof. Laurance David, PhD; FRS(Can) 1982; CChem, FRSC, FCIC; Herchel Smith Professor of Medicinal Chemistry, University of Cambridge, since 1984, and Professorial Fellow, Emmanuel College, since 1987; *b* 18 March 1938; *s* of Daniel William Hall and Elsie Ivy Hall; *m* 1962, Winifred Margaret (*née* Golding); two *s* two *d*. *Educ:* Leyton County High Sch.; Bristol Univ. (BSc 1959; PhD 1962); MA Cantab 1990. FCIC 1973; FRSC 1985. Post-doctoral Fellow, Ottawa Univ., 1962–63; Dept of Chemistry, Univ. of British Columbia: Instr II, 1963–64; Asst Prof., 1964–69; Associate Prof., 1969–73; Prof., 1973–84. Alfred P. Sloan Foundn Res. Fellow, 1971–73; Canada Council Killam Res. Fellow, 1982–84. Lederle Prof., RSM, 1984; Vis. Professor: Univ. of NSW, 1967; Univ. of Cape Town, 1974; Northwestern Univ., Evanston, Ill, 1982. Lectures: Van Cleave, Univ. of Saskatchewan, Regina, 1983; Cecil Green, Galveston Univ., Texas, 1983; Brotherton, Leeds Univ., 1985; Philip Morris, Richmond Univ., Va, 1985; Scott, Cambridge Univ., 1986; Larmor, Cambridge Philosophical Soc., 1986; C. B. Purves, McGill Univ., 1987; Eduard Faber Med. Physics, Univ. of Chicago, 1990. Fellow, Cambridge Philosophical Soc. Jacob Bielly Faculty Res. Prize, Univ. of BC, 1974; Tate and Lyle Award for Carbohydrate Chemistry, Chemical Soc., 1974; Merck, Sharpe and Dohme Lecture Award, Chemical Inst. of Canada, 1975; Corday Morgan Medal and Prize, Chemical Soc., 1976; Barringer Award, Spectroscopy Soc. of Canada, 1981; Interdisciplinary Award, RSC, 1988; Chemical Analysis and Instrumentation Award, RSC, 1990. *Publications:* over 400 research pubns. *Recreations:* sailing, skiing, wine-making, music, travel, research. *Address:* Herchel Smith Laboratory for Medicinal Chemistry, Robinson Way, Cambridge CB2 2PZ. *T:* Cambridge (01223) 336805, *Fax:* (01223) 336748.

HALL, Sir Laurence Charles B.; *see* Brodie-Hall.

HALL, Margaret Dorothy, OBE 1973; RDI 1974; Head of Design, British Museum, since 1964; *b* 22 Jan. 1936; *d* of Thomas Robson Hall and Millicent (*née* Britton). *Educ:* Bromley County Grammar Sch.; Bromley College of Art; Royal College of Art (DesRCA). Design Assistant: Casson, Condor & Partners, 1960–61; Westwood Piet & Partners, 1961–63; Dennis Lennon & Partners, 1963–64; British Museum, 1964–: exhibitions designed include: Masterpieces of Glass, 1968; Museum of Mankind, 1970; Treasures of Tutankhamun, 1972; Nomad and City, 1976; Captain Cook in the South Seas, 1979. Designer, Manuscripts and Men, National Portrait Gallery, 1969. Chm., Gp of Designers/Interpreters in Museums, 1978–81; Mem. Council, RSA, 1984–89. FCSD (FSIAD 1975–90; MSIAD 1968) (Chm., SIAD Salaried Designers Cttee, 1979–81). Chm., Wynkyn de Worde Soc., 1982. Governor, Ravensbourne College of Art, 1973–78. FRSA 1974; FMA 1983. *Publication:* On Display: a grammar of museum exhibition design, 1987. *Address:* The British Museum, WC1B 3DG. *T:* 0171–323 8514. *Club:* Double Crown.

HALL, Dr Marie Boas, FBA 1994; Reader in History of Science and Technology, University of London, 1964–80, Reader Emeritus, since 1980; *b* 18 Oct. 1919; *d* of Ralph Philip Boas and Louise (*née* Schutz); *m* 1959, Alfred Rupert Hall, *qv*. *Educ:* Radcliffe Coll. (AB 1940; MA 1942); Cornell Univ. (PhD 1949). Assistant Professor of History: Univ. of Mass, 1949–52; Brandeis Univ., 1952–57; Associate Prof., UCLA, 1957–61; Prof. of Hist. and Logic of Sci., Indiana Univ., 1961–63; Sen. Lectr, Imperial Coll., Univ. of London, 1963–64. Guggenheim Fellow, 1955–56. Mem., Liby Cttee, Royal Soc., 1983–93. Fellow, Amer. Acad. of Arts and Scis, 1955–63. Mem., Académie internat. d'histoire des sciences, 1960; Sec., Hist. of Science Soc., 1953–57. Pfizer Award, 1959, (jtly) Sarton Medal, 1981, Hist. of Science Soc. *Publications:* The Establishment of the Mechanical Philosophy, 1952, 2nd edn 1981; Robert Boyle and Seventeenth Century Chemistry, 1958; The Scientific Renaissance 1450–1630, 1962; Robert Boyle on Natural Philosophy, 1965; All Scientists Now: the Royal Society in the Nineteenth Century, 1984; Promoting Experimental Learning: experiment and the Royal Society 1660–1727, 1991; The Library and Archives of the Royal Society, 1992; with A. R. Hall: Unpublished Scientific Papers of Isaac Newton, 1962; A Brief History of Science, 1962, 2nd edn 1988; The Correspondence of Henry Oldenburg, 13 vols, 1965–86; contribs to major history of science jls. *Address:* 14 Ball Lane, Tackley, via Kidlington, Oxon OX5 3AG.

HALL, Dr Michael George, FRS 1993; scientific consultant, since 1991; *b* 16 Oct. 1931; *s* of George Albert Victor Hall and Mabel Hall (*née* Gittins); *m* 1964, Merete Blatz; one *s* one *d*. *Educ:* Sydney Grammar Sch.; Univ. of Sydney (BSc, BE, MEngSc, PhD). Research in Fluid Dynamics at Aerodynamics Dept, RAE, 1958–91, retired 1991; sabbatical at Dept of Mechanics, Johns Hopkins Univ., 1966–67. Founder-Director, Hall C. F. D. Ltd, 1991–. *Publications:* contribs on fluid dynamics to sci. and tech. jls. *Recreations:* ski-ing, walking, do-it-yourself, squash. *Address:* 8 Dene Lane, Farnham, Surrey GU10 3PW. *T:* Farnham (01252) 793283.

HALL, Michael Kilgour H.; *see* Harrison-Hall.

HALL, Prof. Michael Robert Pritchard, FRCP, FRCPE; Professor of Geriatric Medicine, University of Southampton, 1970–87, now Emeritus; Hon. Consultant Physician, Southampton University Hospitals, 1970–87; *b* 13 May 1922; *s* of Augustus Henry Hall, MC and Elizabeth Jane Lord; *m* 1947, Joan Jardine, (Eileen), *d* of Dr John McCartney; two *d*. *Educ:* Shrewsbury Sch.; Worcester Coll., Oxford (MA, BM, BCh). FRCP 1970; FRCPE 1971. Served War, Indian Army, 1941–46 (Temp. Captain). Consultant Physician, Newcastle-upon-Tyne Gen. Hosp., 1962–70; Hon. Lecturer in Medicine: Univ. of Durham, 1962–63; Univ. of Newcastle upon Tyne, 1963–70. Auckland Savings Bank Vis. Prof., Univ. of Auckland, NZ, 1974; Vis. Lecturer: Dalhousie Univ., NS, 1979; (Tayside Health Bd), Univ. of Dundee, 1981; Examr, Dip. of Geriatric Medicine, RCP, 1985–91. Chairman: British Soc. for Res. on Ageing, 1976–79; Assoc. of Professors of Geriatric Medicine, 1985–86; European Cttee, Sandoz Foundn of Gerontological Research, 1986–90 (Mem., 1990–92); Member: DHSS Cttee for Review of Medicines, 1976–82; Fitness and Health Adv. Gp to Sports Council, 1977–90; Governing Body and Exec. Cttee, Age Concern (England), 1975–77 and 1980–83; Council, Internat. Assoc. of Gerontology, 1981–85; President: Tissue Viability Soc., 1983–84; Bath Res. Inst. for Care of the Elderly, 1987–94; Chm., Age Concern (Hants), 1992–95; Life Vice-Pres., Northumberland Cheshire Home, 1970; Trustee and Governor, British Foundn for Age Res., 1979–; Vice-Chm., Brendoncare Foundn, 1986–; Member: NEC, Abbeyfield Soc., 1989–93 (Chm., Extra Care Cttee, 1989–90; Chm., Care and Develt Cttee, 1990–93); Council, RSAD, 1989–; Trustee, McCarthy Foundn, 1987–. FRSocMed 1991. *Publications:* Medical Care of the Elderly, 1978, 3rd edn 1993; chapters and contribs to various books on aspects of ageing and geriatric medicine; articles and papers in med. jls. *Recreations:* fly-fishing, golf, gardening. *Address:* Peartree Cottage, Emery Down, Lyndhurst, Hants SO43 7FH. *T:* Lyndhurst (01703) 282541. *Club:* MCC.

HALL, Michael Thomas; MP (Lab) Warrington South, since 1992; *b* 20 Sept. 1952; *s* of Thomas and Veronica Hall; *m* 1975, Lesley Evelyn Gosling; one *s*. *Educ:* Padgate Coll. of Higher Educn (Teachers' Cert. 1977); N Cheshire Coll., Victoria Univ., Manchester (BEd Hons 1987). Scientific Asst, ICI Ltd, 1969–73; teaching history and physical educn, Bolton, 1977–85; support teacher, Halton Community Assessment Team, 1985–92. Councillor, Warrington Borough Council, 1979–93: Chairman: Envmtl Health Cttee, 1981–84; Finance Sub-Cttee, 1984–85; Policy and Resources Cttee, 1985–92; Dep. Leader of Council, 1984–85, Leader 1985–92. Member, Parish Council: Great Sankey, 1979–83; Birchwood and Croft, 1983–87; Poulton with Fearnhead, 1987–93. *Recreations:* tennis, camping, reading. *Address:* House of Commons, SW1A 0AA.

HALL, Rt. Rev. Peter; *see* Woolwich, Bishop Suffragan of.

HALL, Peter Dalton, CB 1986; Under Secretary, Solicitor's Office, Board of Inland Revenue, 1979–86; *b* 1 Aug. 1924; *s* of Edward and Kathleen Hall; *m* 1952, Stella Iris Breen; four *s* two *d*. *Educ:* Rishworth Sch.; St Catharine's Coll., Cambridge (exhibnr; MA, LLB). Served War of 1939–45, Intelligence Corps; seconded to AIF and served with US Forces in New Guinea and Philippines; GOC Commendation; Major. Called to the Bar, Middle Temple, 1951; entered Inland Revenue Solicitor's Office, 1952. Mem., Bar Council 1967–70; Clerk to City of London Comrs, 1988–. Parish Councillor, 1967–. Non-exec. Dir, Milton Keynes HA, 1992–93. Freeman, City of London, 1993. *Publications:* contrib.: Simon's Taxes; Foster's Capital Taxes Encyclopaedia. *Recreations:* gardening, music, conservation. *Address:* Apple Tree Cottage, Woughton-on-the-Green, Bucks MK6 3BE. *T:* (day) 0171–353 2618.

HALL, Sir Peter (Edward), KBE 1993; CMG 1987; HM Diplomatic Service; Ambassador to Argentina, since 1993; *b* 26 July 1938; *s* of late Bernard Hall and Monica Hall (*née* Blackbourn); *m* 1972, Marnie Kay; one *s* one *d*. *Educ:* Portsmouth Grammar Sch.; HM Services (Jt Services Sch. for Linguists); Pembroke Coll., Cambridge (Scholar; 1st Cl. parts I and II, Mediaeval and Modern Langs Tripos). Foreign Office, 1961–63; 3rd Sec., Warsaw, 1963–66; 2nd Sec., New Delhi, 1966–69; FCO (European Integration Dept), 1969–72; 1st Sec., UK Permanent Representation to EEC, 1972–76; Asst Head, Financial Relations Dept, FCO, 1976–77; Counsellor, Caracas, 1977–78; Hd of British Information Services, NY, 1978–83 and Counsellor, British Embassy, Washington, 1981–83; Dir of Res., FCO, 1983–86; Under Sec., Cabinet Office, 1986–88; Vis. Schol., Stanford Univ., 1988–89; Ambassador to Yugoslavia, 1989–92; Advr to Lord Carrington, 1992, Lord Owen, 1992–93, Peace Conf. on Yugoslavia. *Recreations:* reading (A. Powell, Byron), music (Rolling Stones, Mozart). *Address:* c/o Foreign and Commonwealth Office, King Charles Street, SW1A 2AH.

HALL, Prof. Peter Geoffrey, FBA 1983; Professor of Planning, University College London, since 1992; *b* 19 March 1932; *s* of Arthur Vickers Hall and Bertha Hall (*née* Keefe); *m* 1st, 1962, Carla Maria Wartenberg (marr. diss. 1966); 2nd, 1967, Magdalena Mróz; no *c*. *Educ:* Blackpool Grammar Sch.; St Catharine's Coll., Cambridge Univ. (MA, PhD; Hon. Fellow, 1988). Asst Lectr, 1957, Lectr, 1960, Birkbeck Coll., Univ. of London; Reader in Geography with ref. to Regional Planning, London Sch. of Economics and Political Science, 1966; University of Reading: Prof. of Geography, 1968–89, now Prof. Emeritus; Head, Dept of Geog., 1968–80; Chm., Sch. of Planning Studies, 1971–77 and 1983–86; Dean of Urban and Regional Studies, 1975–78; Prof. of City and Regl Planning, 1980–92, and Dir, Inst. of Urban and Regl Develt, 1989–92, Univ. of Calif, Berkeley, now Prof. Emeritus. Member: SE Regional Planning Council, 1966–79; Nature Conservancy, 1968–72; Transport and Road Research Laboratory Adv. Cttee on Transport, 1973–78; Environmental Bd, 1975–79; SSRC, 1975–80 (Chm., Planning Cttee); EEC Expert Gp on New Tendencies of Social and Economic Develt, 1975–77; Standing Adv. Cttee on Trunk Road Assessment, 1978–80; Exec. Cttee, Regional Studies Assoc., 1967– (Hon. Jl Editor, 1967–78); Exec. Cttee, Fabian Soc., 1964–80 (Chm. 1971–72). Special Advr, Sec. of State for Environment, 1991–94. Governor, Centre for Environmental Studies, 1975–80. Chm., Tawney Soc., 1983–85 (Vice-Chm., 1982–83). FRGS; Hon. RTPI, 1975. Editor, Built Environment, 1977–. *Publications:* The Industries of London, 1962; London 2000, 1963 (reprint, 1969); Labour's New Frontiers, 1964; (ed) Land Values, 1965; The World Cities, 1966, 3rd edn 1984; Containment of Urban England, 1973; Urban and Regional Planning, 1974, 2nd edn 1982; Europe 2000, 1977; Great Planning Disasters, 1980; Growth Centres in the European Urban System, 1980; The Inner City in Context, 1981; Silicon Landscapes, 1985; Can Rail Save the City?, 1985; High Tech America, 1986; Cities of Tomorrow, 1988; London 2001, 1989; The Rise of the Gunbelt, 1991; Technoples of the World, 1994. *Recreations:* writing, reading, talking. *Address:* Bartlett School, University College London, Wates House, 22 Gordon Street, WC1H 0QB; 14 Blandford Road, W4 1DU. *Club:* Athenæum.

HALL, Peter George; (part-time) Chairman, Snamprogetti Ltd, since 1988; *b* 10 Dec. 1924; *s* of Charles and Rosina Hall; *m* 1949, Margaret Gladys (*née* Adams); two *s* two *d*. *Educ:* Sandown, IoW, Grammar Sch.; Southampton Univ. (BScEng). FInstPet. Anglo-Iranian Oil Co., 1946–51; Esso Petroleum Co. Ltd: various positions at Fawley Refinery, 1951–63; Manager, Milford Haven Refinery, 1963–66; Employee Relations Manager, 1966–70; Vice-Pres., General Sekiyu Seisei, Tokyo, 1971–74; Asst Gen. Man., Refining, Imperial Oil Ltd, Toronto, 1974–76; Refining Man., Exxon Corp., New York, 1976–77; Director, Esso Petroleum Co. Ltd, London, 1977–78; Vice-Pres., Esso Europe Inc. London, 1979–81; Man. Dir, Esso Petroleum Co., 1982–84; Pres., Esso Norge, 1984–87. *Recreations:* opera, classical music, walking, gardening. *Address:* Oakley, Mill Lawn, Burley, Ringwood, Hants BH24 4HP.

HALL, Sir Peter (Reginald Frederick), Kt 1977; CBE 1963; director of plays, films and operas; own producing company, Peter Hall Co., formed 1988; Director, National Theatre, 1973–88; *b* Bury St Edmunds, Suffolk, 22 Nov. 1930; *s* of late Reginald Edward Arthur Hall and Grace Pamment; *m* 1956, Leslie Caron (marr. diss. 1965); one *s* one *d*; *m* 1965, Jacqueline Taylor (marr. diss. 1981); one *s* one *d*; *m* 1982, Maria Ewing, *qv* (marr. diss. 1990); one *d*; *m* 1990, Nicola Frei; one *d*. *Educ:* Perse Sch., Cambridge; St Catharine's Coll., Cambridge (MA Hons; Hon. Fellow, 1964). Dir, Arts Theatre, London, 1955–56 (directed several plays incl. first productions of Waiting for Godot, South, Waltz of the Toreadors); formed own producing company, International Playwrights' Theatre, 1957, and directed their first production, Camino Real; at Sadler's Wells, directed his first opera, The Moon and Sixpence, 1957. First productions at Stratford: Love's Labour's Lost, 1956; Cymbeline, 1957; first prod. on Broadway, The Rope Dancers, Nov. 1957. Plays in London, 1956–58: Summertime, Gigi, Cat on a Hot Tin Roof, Brouhaha, Shadow of Heroes; Madame de . . ., Traveller Without Luggage, A Midsummer Night's Dream and Coriolanus (Stratford), The Wrong Side of the Park, 1959; apptd Dir of Royal Shakespeare Theatre, Jan. 1960, responsible for founding RSC as a permanent ensemble, and its move to Aldwych Theatre, 1960; Man. Dir at Stratford-on-Avon and Aldwych Theatre, London, 1960–68; Co-Dir, RSC, 1968–73; Artistic Dir, Glyndebourne Fest., 1984–90. Plays produced/directed for *Royal Shakespeare Company:* Two Gentlemen of Verona, Twelfth Night, Troilus and Cressida, 1960; Ondine, Becket, Romeo and Juliet, 1961; The Collection, Troilus and Cressida, A Midsummer Night's Dream, 1962; The Wars of the Roses (adaptation of Henry VI Parts 1, 2 and 3, and Richard III), 1963 (televised for BBC, 1965); Sequence of Shakespeare's histories for Shakespeare's 400th anniversary at Stratford: Richard II, Henry IV Parts 1 & 2, Henry V, Henry VI, Edward IV, Richard III, 1964; The Homecoming, Hamlet, 1965; The Government Inspector, Staircase, 1966; The Homecoming (NY), Macbeth, 1967; A Delicate Balance, Silence and Landscape, 1969; The Battle of the Shrivings, 1970; Old Times, 1971 (NY, 1971, Vienna, 1972); All Over, Via Galactica (NY), 1972; Julius Caesar, 1995; plays produced/directed for *National Theatre:* The Tempest, 1974; John Gabriel Borkman, 1975; No Man's Land, Happy Days, Hamlet, 1975; Tamburlaine the Great, 1976; No Man's Land (NY), Volpone, Bedroom Farce, The Country Wife, 1977; The Cherry Orchard, Macbeth, Betrayal, 1978; Amadeus, 1979, NY 1981 (Tony Award for Best Director); Othello, 1980; Family Voices, The Oresteia, 1981, 1986; Importance of Being Earnest, 1982; Other Places, 1982; Jean Seberg, 1983; Animal Farm, Coriolanus, 1984; Martine, Yonadab, 1985; The Petition, 1986; Coming into Land, Antony and Cleopatra, Entertaining Strangers, 1987; The Tempest, Cymbeline, Winter's Tale, 1988; plays produced/directed for *Peter Hall Company:* Orpheus Descending, NY, 1988; Merchant of Venice, 1989; The Wild Duck, Phoenix, 1990; The Homecoming, Comedy, 1991; Twelfth Night, The Rose Tattoo, Tartuffe, Playhouse, 1991; Four Baboons Adoring the Sun, NY, 1992; Sienna Red, 1992; All's Well That Ends Well, RSC, 1992; An Ideal Husband, Globe, 1992; The Gift of the Gorgon, Wyndham's, 1993; Separate Tables, Albery, 1993; Lysistrata, Old Vic and Wyndhams, 1993; She Stoops to Conquer, Queen's, 1993; Piaf, Piccadilly, 1993; An Absolute Turkey, Globe, 1994; On Approval, Playhouse, 1994; Hamlet, Gielgud, 1994. *Films:* Work is a Four Letter Word, 1968; A Midsummer Night's Dream, Three into Two Won't Go, 1969; Perfect Friday, 1971; The Homecoming, 1973; Akenfield, 1974; She's Been Away, 1989; Orpheus Descending, 1991. *Opera:* at Covent Garden: Moses and Aaron, 1965; The Magic Flute, 1966; The Knot Garden, 1970; Eugene Onegin, Tristan and Isolde, 1971; Salome, 1988; Albert Herring, 1989; at Glyndebourne: La Calisto, 1970; Il Ritorno d'Ulisse in Patria, 1972; The Marriage of Figaro, 1973, 1989; Don Giovanni, Così Fan Tutte, 1978, 1984; Fidelio, 1979; A Midsummer Night's Dream, 1981, 1989; Orfeo ed Euridice, 1982; L'Incoronazione di Poppea, 1984, 1986; Carmen, 1985; Albert Herring, 1985, 1986; Simon Boccanegra, 1986; La Traviata, 1987, 1988; Falstaff, 1988; at Metropolitan Opera, NY: Macbeth, 1982; Carmen, 1986; at Bayreuth: The Ring, 1983; at Geneva: Figaro, 1983; at Los Angeles: Salome, 1986; Così Fan Tutte, 1988; The Magic Flute, 1992; at Chicago: Figaro, 1987; Salome, 1988; at Houston: New Year (world première), 1989. *Television:* Presenter, Aquarius (LWT), 1975–77; Carmen, 1985; Oresteia (C4), L'Incoronazione di Poppea, Albert Herring, 1986; La Traviata, 1987; The Marriage of Figaro, 1989; (series) The Camomile Lawn (C4), 1992. Associate Prof. of Drama, Warwick Univ., 1966–. Mem., Arts Council, 1969–73; Founder Mem., Theatre Dirs' Guild of GB, 1983–. DUniv York, 1966; Hon. DLitt Reading, 1973; Hon. LittD: Liverpool, 1974; Leicester, 1977. Tony Award (NY) for best director, 1966; Hamburg Univ. Shakespeare Prize, 1967; Standard Special Award, 1979; Standard Award Best Director, 1981, 1987; Standard Award for outstanding achievement in Opera, 1981. Chevalier de l'Ordre des Arts et des Lettres, 1965. *Publications:* (with John Barton) The Wars of the Roses, 1970; (with Inga-Stina Ewbank) John Gabriel Borkman, an English version, 1975; Peter Hall's Diaries (ed John Goodwin), 1983; Animal Farm, a stage adaptation, 1986; (with Inga-Stina Ewbank) The Wild Duck, an English adaptation, 1990; Making an Exhibition of Myself (autobiog.), 1993; (with Nicki Frei) trans. Feydeau, An Absolute Turkey, 1994. *Recreation:* music. *Address:* Peter Hall Company Ltd, Albery Theatre, St Martin's Lane, WC2N 4AH. *Clubs:* Garrick, Royal Automobile.

HALL, Sir Robert de Zouche, KCMG 1953 (CMG 1952); MA; resident in New Zealand; *b* 27 April 1904; *s* of late Arthur William Hall, Liverpool; *m* 1932, Lorna Dorothy (*née* Markham); one *s* one *d*. *Educ:* Willaston Sch.; Gonville and Caius Coll., Cambridge. MA, 1932. Colonial Administrative Service, Tanganyika, 1926; Provincial Comr, 1947; Senior Provincial Comr, 1950; Mem. for Local Government, Tanganyika, 1950–53. Governor, Comdr-in-Chief, and Vice-Adm., Sierra Leone, 1953–56. Hon. Sec. Vernacular Architecture Group, 1959–72, Pres., 1972–73; Chm. Governing Body, Somerset County Museum, 1961–73; Mem. Gisborne Museum Staff, NZ, 1974–80. *Publication:* (ed) A Bibliography on Vernacular Architecture, 1973.

HALL, Simon Robert Dawson, MA; Warden of Glenalmond College, 1987–91; *b* 24 April 1938; *s* of late Wilfrid Dawson Hall and Elizabeth Helen Hall (*née* Wheeler); *m* 1961, Jennifer Harverson; two *s*. *Educ:* Tonbridge School; University College, Oxford. 2nd Lieut, 7th Royal Tank Regt, 1956–58. Asst Master, Gordonstoun School, 1961–65; Joint Headmaster, Dunrobin School, 1965–68; Haileybury: Asst Master, 1969–79; Senior Modern Languages Master, 1970–76; Housemaster, Lawrence, 1972–79; Second Master, 1976–79; Headmaster, Milton Abbey School, 1979–87. 21st SAS Regt (TA), 1958–61; Intelligence Corps (V), 1968–71. FRSA 1983. *Recreations:* reading, music, motoring, sailing, hill-walking. *Address:* High Green House, Temple Sowerby, Penrith CA10 1SB.

HALL, Prof. the Rev. Stuart George; Priest-in-Charge, St Michael's, Elie, and St John's, Pittenweem, since 1990; Professor of Ecclesiastical History, King's College, University of London, 1978–90; *b* 7 June 1928; *s* of George Edward Hall and May Catherine Hall; *m* 1953, Brenda Mary Henderson; two *s* two *d*. *Educ:* University Coll. Sch., Hampstead; New Coll., and Ripon Hall, Oxford (BA 1952, MA 1955, BD 1973). National Service, Army, 1947–48. Deacon 1954, priest 1955; Asst Curate, Newark-on-Trent Parish Church, 1954–58; Tutor, Queen's Coll., Birmingham, 1958–62; Lectr in Theology, Univ. of

Nottingham, 1962–73, Sen. Lectr, 1973–78. Editor for early church material, Theologische Realenzyklopädie. *Publications:* Melito of Sardis On Pascha and fragments: (ed) texts and translations, 1979; Doctrine and Practice in the Early Church, 1991; (ed) Gregory of Nyssa, Homilies on Ecclesiastes, 1993; contrib. to Expository Times, Heythrop Jl, Jl of Eccles. History, Jl of Theol Studies, Religious Studies, Studia Evangelica, Studia Patristica, Theology and Theologische Realenzyklopädie. *Recreations:* gardening, choral music. *Address:* 15 High Street, Elie, Leven, Fife KY9 1BY. *T:* Elie (01333) 330216.

HALL, Prof. Stuart McPhail; Professor of Sociology, The Open University, since 1979; *b* 3 Feb. 1932; *s* of Herman and Jessie Hall; *m* 1964, Catherine Mary Barrett; one *s* one *d. Educ:* Jamaica Coll.; Merton Coll., Oxford (MA; Rhodes Scholar, 1951). Editor, New Left Review, 1957–61; Lectr, Film and Mass Media Studies, Chelsea Coll., London Univ., 1961–64; Centre for Cultural Studies, Univ. of Birmingham: Res. Fellow, 1964–68; Actg Dir, 1968–72; Dir, 1972–79. Hon. Fellow, Portsmouth Polytechnic, 1988; Centenary Fellow, Thames Polytechnic, 1990. Hon DLitt: Massachusetts, 1989; City, Kingston, Oxford Brookes, 1993; Sussex, 1994. *Publications:* The Popular Arts, 1964; Resistance Through Rituals, 1974; Policing The Crisis, 1978; Culture, Media, Language, 1980; The Politics of Thatcherism, 1983; State and Society in Contemporary Britain, 1984; Politics and Ideology, 1986; The Hard Road to Renewal, 1988. *Address:* 5 Mowbray Road, Kilburn, NW6 7QX.

HALL, Col Thomas Armitage, OBE 1966; Lieutenant, HM Body Guard of Honourable Corps of Gentlemen at Arms, since 1994; *b* 13 April 1928; *s* of Athelstan Argyle Hall and Nancy Armitage Hall (*née* Dyson); *m* 1954, Mariette Hornby; two *s* four *d. Educ:* Heatherdown Sch.; Eton Coll. Commissioned, 11th Hussars, 1947, Berlin; ADC to CIGS, 1952–53; Adjutant, 11 H Malayan Emergency, 1953–56 (despatches); Army Staff Coll., 1960–61; Sqdn Leader 11 H, Aden, Gulf, Kenya, Kuwait, 1961–62; Instr, RN Staff Coll., Greenwich, 1962–64; CO 11 H, Germany, 1965–66; Equerry to King of Thailand, 1966; Regtl Col, Royal Hussars, 1974–83; Advr to Crown Prince of Japan, 1983–85. Regl Dir, Lloyds Bank, 1983–85. Chm., Internat. Lang. Centres, 1971–88. High Sheriff, Oxon, 1981–82. FRSA. *Recreations:* ski-ing, shooting, travel, architecture. *Address:* Marylands Farm, Chiselhampton, Oxford OX44 7XD. *T:* Oxford (01865) 890350. *Club:* Cavalry and Guards (Chm.).

HALL, Thomas William; Under-Secretary, Department of Transport, 1976–79 and 1981–87; retired; *b* 8 April 1931; *s* of Thomas William and Euphemia Jane Hall; *m* 1961, Anne Rosemary Hellier Davis; two *d. Educ:* Hitchin Grammar Sch.; St John's Coll., Oxford (MA); King's Coll., London (MA). Asst Principal, Min. of Supply, 1954; Principal: War Office, Min. of Public Building and Works, Cabinet Office, 1958–68; Asst Sec., Min. of Public Building and Works, later DoE, 1968–76; Under Sec., Depts of Environment and Transport, 1979–81. Member: Road Traffic Law Review, 1985–88; Transport Tribunal, 1990–. *Recreations:* music, literature, gardening, walking. *Address:* 43 Bridge Road, Epsom, Surrey KT17 4AN. *T:* Epsom (01372) 725900.

HALL, Vernon F., CVO 1960; Anæsthetist, King's College Hospital, 1931–69, retired; *b* 25 Aug. 1904; *s* of Cecil S. and M. M. Hall; *m* 1935, C. Marcia Cavell; one *s* two *d. Educ:* Haberdashers' Sch.; King's Coll. Hosp., London. MRCS, LRCP, 1927; DA, 1938; FFARCS, 1948. Served War of 1939–45 in Army (Emergency Commission), 1942–46; Consultant Anæsthetist, India Command (Local Brig.), 1945; Dean, King's Coll. Hosp. Medical Sch., 1951–65. Chm., London Univ. Bd of Advanced Med. Studies, 1952–62; former Member: Senate, Univ. of London; Faculty of Medicine, Univ. of London. FKC 1958; Hon. FFARCS 1975. *Publications:* History of King's College Hospital Dental School, 1973; A Scrapbook of Snowdonia, 1982; (jtly) The Story of King's College Hospital and its Medical School 1839–1990, part II, 1991; chapters on Anaesthesia in Rose & Carless, Surgery, etc. *Recreations:* riding, walking, reading and music. *Address:* 83A Foxgrove Road, Beckenham, Kent BR3 2DA. *T:* 0181–650 2212.

HALL, Victor Edwin; His Honour Judge Victor Hall; a Circuit Judge, since 1994; *b* 2 March 1948; *s* of Robert Arthur Victor James Hall and Gwladys (*née* Fukes); *m* 1974, Rosemarie Berdina Jenkinson; two *s. Educ:* Univ. of Hull (LLB 1969). Lectr in Law, Kettering Tech. Coll., 1969–71; called to the Bar, Inner Temple, 1971; an Asst Recorder, 1983–88; a Recorder, 1988. Asst Parly Boundary Comr, 1991–93. Deacon in Free Church. *Recreations:* walking, ski-ing, cookery. *Address:* Leicester Crown and County Courts, Wellington Street, Leicester LE1 6HG.

HALL, (Wallace) John; Regional Director, DTI East (Cambridge), Department of Trade and Industry, 1989–94; *b* 5 Oct. 1934; *s* of Claude Corbett Hall and Dulcie Hall (*née* Brinkworth); *m* 1962, Janet Bowen; three *d. Educ:* Crypt Sch., Gloucester; Hertford Grammar Sch.; Downing Coll., Cambridge (MA Classics). National Service, RAF, 1953–55. Pirelli-General Cable Works Ltd, 1958–62; Sales Manager, D. Meredew Ltd, 1962–67; Principal, Min. of Technology, 1967–70; Dept of Trade and Industry, Civil Aviation Policy, 1970–72; Consul (Commercial), São Paulo, Brazil, 1972–76; Asst Secretary, Dept of Trade, Shipping Policy, 1976–79; Counsellor (Economic), Brasilia, 1979–81; Consul-Gen., São Paulo, 1981–83; Assistant Secretary, DTI: Internat. Trade Policy, 1983–85; Overseas Trade (E Asia), 1985–89. *Recreations:* bridge, tennis and other sports, daughters. *Address:* 27 Wilbury Road, Letchworth, Herts SG6 4JW.

HALL, William, CBE 1991; DFC 1944, FRICS; Member of the Lands Tribunal for Scotland, 1971–91, and for England and Wales, 1979–91; *b* 25 July 1919; *s* of Archibald and Helen Hall; *m* 1945, Margaret Semple (*née* Gibson); one *s* three *d. Educ:* Paisley Grammar Sch. FRICS 1948. Served War, RAF (pilot) 1939–45 (despatches, 1944). Sen. Partner, R. & W. Hall, Chartered Surveyors, 1949–79. Chm., Scottish Br., RICS, 1971; Member: Valuation Adv. Council, 1970–80; Erskine Hosp. Exec., 1976–. Hon. Sheriff, Paisley, 1974–. *Recreation:* golf. *Address:* Windyridge, Brediland Road, Paisley, Renfrewshire PA2 9HF. *T:* Brediland (0150581) 3614. *Club:* Royal Air Force.

HALL, Prof. William Bateman, FEng 1986; Professor of Nuclear Engineering, University of Manchester, 1959–86, now Emeritus; *b* 28 May 1923; *s* of Sidney Bateman Hall and Doris Hall; *m* 1950, Helen Mary Dennis; four *d. Educ:* Urmston Grammar Sch.; College of Technology, Manchester. Engineering apprenticeship, 1939–44; Royal Aircraft Establishment, 1944–46; United Kingdom Atomic Energy Authority (formerly Dept of Atomic Energy, Min. of Supply), 1946–59: Technical Engineer, 1946–52; Principal Scientific Officer, 1952–56; Senior Principal Scientific Officer, 1956–58; Dep. Chief Scientific Officer, 1958. Mem., Adv. Cttee on Safety of Nuclear Installations, 1972–83. Pro-Vice-Chancellor, Univ. of Manchester, 1979–82. *Publications:* Reactor Heat Transfer, 1958; papers to scientific and professional institutions. *Recreations:* music, designing and making steam engines. *Address:* High Raise, Eskdale, Holmrook, Cumbria CA19 1UA. *T:* Eskdale (019467) 23275.

HALL, Brig. Sir William (Henry), KBE 1979 (CBE 1962); Kt 1968; DSO 1942; ED; Comptroller of Stores, State Electricity Commission of Victoria, 1956–70; Colonel Commandant, RAA Southern Command, since 1967; *b* 5 Jan. 1906; *s* of William Henry Hall, Edinburgh, Scotland; *m* 1930, Irene Mary, *d* of William Hayes; one *s* four *d. Educ:* Morgan Acad., Dundee; Melbourne Univ. Joined Staff of State Electricity Commn of Vic, 1924. Enlisted AIF, 1939: Capt. Royal Aust. Artillery, Palestine, Egypt; Syria, Papua, New Guinea, 1941 (Major); Aust. Dir of Armaments at AHQ, 1942 (Lt-Col); Dir of Armament at AHQ, 1945 (Col); CRA 3 Div. Artillery CMF, 1955–59 (Brig.). Director: Royal Humane Society of Vic.; Multiple Sclerosis Soc.; Chairman: War Widows and Widowed Mothers' Trust; RSL War Veterans' Trust; State Pres. Victorian Br., RSL, 1964–74 (now Chm. Trustees); Nat. Pres., Aust. RSL, 1974–78; Aust. Councillor, World Veterans' Foundn; Patron: Aust.-Free China Economic Assoc.; Royal Artillery Assoc. (Vic.); Carry On, Vic.; Vic. Blinded Soldiers Assoc.; Trustee, Victorian Overseas Foundn. Associate Fellow, Aust. Inst. Management; Mem., Inst. of Purchasing and Supply (London). *Recreation:* golf. *Address:* Rosemont, 112 Kooyong Road, Caulfield, Vic 3162, Australia; Montrose, Flinders, Victoria 3929. *Clubs:* Naval and Military (Melbourne); Victoria Racing; Melbourne Cricket, Peninsula Country Golf, Flinders Golf.

HALL, Willis; writer; *b* 6 April 1929; *s* of Walter and Gladys Hall; *m* 1973, Valerie Shute; one *s* (and three *s* by previous marriages). *Educ:* Cockburn High Sch., Leeds. Member: Internat. Brotherhood of Magicians; Northern Magic Circle; Soc. of Amer. Magicians; Malta Magicians Soc. TV plays include: The Villa Maroc; They Don't all Open Men's Boutiques; Song at Twilight; The Road to 1984; TV series: The Fuzz, 1977; The Danedyke Mystery, 1979; Stan's Last Game, 1983; The Bright Side, 1985; The Return of the Antelope, 1986; The Reluctant Dragon, 1988; (with Keith Waterhouse): The Upper Crusts, 1973; Billy Liar, 1974; Worzel Gummidge, 1979 (adapted as stage musical, 1981). *Publications:* (with Michael Parkinson) The A-Z of Soccer, 1970; Football Report, 1973; Football Classified, 1974; My Sporting Life, Football Final, 1975; *children's books:* The Royal Astrologer, 1960; The Gentle Knight, 1967; The Incredible Kidnapping, 1975; The Summer of the Dinosaur, 1977; The Last Vampire, 1982; The Inflatable Shop, 1984; The Return of the Antelope, 1985; Spooky Rhymes, 1987; The Antelope Company at Large, 1987; Dr Jekyll and Mr Hollins, 1988; Henry Hollins and the Dinosaur, 1988; The Vampire's Holiday, 1991; The Vampire's Revenge, 1993; The Vampire's Christmas, 1994; The Vampire Vanishes, 1995; *plays:* The Long and the Short and the Tall, 1959; A Glimpse of the Sea, 1969; Kidnapped at Christmas, 1975; Walk on, Walk on, 1975; Stag Night, 1976; Christmas Crackers, 1976; A Right Christmas Caper, 1977; (with Keith Waterhouse): Billy Liar, 1960; Celebration, 1961; All Things Bright and Beautiful, 1962; England Our England, 1962; Squat Betty and The Sponge Room, 1963; Say Who You Are, 1965; Whoops-a-Daisy, 1968; Children's Day, 1969; Who's Who, 1972; *adaptations:* (with Keith Waterhouse) de Filippo, Saturday, Sunday, Monday, 1973; (with Keith Waterhouse) de Filippo, Filumena, 1977; (with Denis King) A. A. Milne, The Wind in the Willows (musical), 1985; (with John Cooper) Charles Kingsley, The Water Babies (musical), 1987; Charlotte Brontë, Jane Eyre, 1992; Jane Austen, Mansfield Park, 1993; Alexandre Dumas, The Three Musketeers, 1994; *musicals:* (with Keith Waterhouse): The Card, 1973; Budgie, 1989; (with Denis King) Treasure Island, 1985. *Recreation:* magic. *Address:* c/o Alexandra Cann representation, 337 Fulham Road, SW10 5TW. *Clubs:* Garrick, Savage, Lansdowne.

HALL-MATTHEWS, Rt Rev. Anthony Francis Berners; Bishop of Carpentaria, 1984–Feb. 1996; *b* 14 Nov. 1940; *s* of Rev. Cecil Berners Hall and Barbara (who *m* 1944, Rt Rev. Seering John Matthews); *m* 1966, Valerie Joan Cecil; two *s* three *d. Educ:* Sanctuary School, Walsingham, Norfolk; Southport School, Queensland; St Francis Theol Coll., Milton, Brisbane. ThL Aust. Coll. of Theology, 1962. Curate of Darwin, 1963–66; Chaplain, Aerial Mission, and Rector of Normanton with Croydon, 1966–76; Hon. Canon of Carpentaria, 1970–76; Archdeacon of Cape York Peninsula, 1976–84; Priest-in-charge of Cooktown, Dio. Carpentaria, 1976–84. *Recreations:* flying, reading, sailing. *Address:* Bishop's House, Thursday Island, Queensland 4875, Australia. *T:* (70) 691455.

HALL WILLIAMS; *see* Williams.

HALLADAY, Eric, MA; Principal, St Chad's College, University of Durham, 1991–94; *b* 9 July 1930; *s* of Rev. A. R. Halladay and Helena Renton; *m* 1956, Margaret Baister; one *s* two *d. Educ:* Durham Sch.; St John's Coll., Cambridge (BA 1953; MA 1957); Ripon Hall, Oxford. National Service, commnd 5th Regt, RHA, 1948–50. Exeter Sch., 1954–60, Sen. History Master, 1956–60; Sen. Lectr in History, RMA, Sandhurst, 1960–64; Grey College, University of Durham: Sen. Tutor, and part-time Lectr in History, 1964–80; Vice-Master, 1967–80; Master, 1980–89; Rector, 1989–91; Rector, St Aidan's Coll., Univ. of Durham, 1990–91. Chm., Northumbrian Univs Military Educn Cttee, 1981–94; Mem. Exec. Cttee, Council of Military Educn Cttees of Univs of UK, 1982–87. Mem., TA&VRA, N of England, 1980–; Sec., Durham Br., SSAFA, 1977–89. Chm., Durham Regatta, 1982–88; Steward, Henley Royal Regatta, 1993. *Publications:* The Building of Modern Africa (with D. D. Rooney), 1966, 2nd edn 1968; The Emergent Continent: Africa in the Nineteenth Century, 1972; Rowing in England—a Social History, 1990. *Recreations:* gardening, rowing. *Address:* The Coign, Corbridge, Northumberland NE45 5LE. *T:* Hexham (01434) 632838. *Club:* Leander (Henley-on-Thames).

HALLAM, Bishop of, (RC), since 1980; **Rt. Rev. Gerald Moverley,** JCD; *b* 9 April 1922; *s* of William Joseph Moverley and Irene Mary Moverley (*née* Dewhirst). *Educ:* St Bede's Grammar Sch., Bradford; Ushaw Coll., Durham; Angelicum Univ., Rome. Priest, 1946; Sec. to Bishop Poskitt, Leeds, 1946–51; Angelicum Univ., 1951–54; Chancellor, Dio. Leeds, 1958–68; Domestic Prelate to HH Pope Paul VI, 1965; apptd Bishop, Dec. 1967; Titular Bishop of Tinisa in Proconsulari and Bishop Auxiliary of Leeds, 1968–80; translated to new diocese of Hallam, established May 1980. *Address:* Quarters, Carsick Hill Way, Sheffield S10 3LT. *T:* Sheffield (0114) 230 9101.

HALLAM, David John Alfred; Member (Lab) Hereford and Shropshire, European Parliament, since 1994; *b* 13 June 1948; *s* of Arthur Ernest Hallam and Marjorie Ethel Hallam (*née* Gibbs); *m* 1988, Claire Vanstone; two *s* one *d. Educ:* Upton House Secondary Modern Sch., London; Univ. of Sussex (BA). Res. Asst, Sussex CC, 1971–73; Information Officer, Birmingham Social Services Dept, 1973–80; Public Relations Officer, Nat. Children's Home, 1984–89. Mem., Sandwell BC, W Midlands, 1976–79. Mem., Agricl and Rural Affairs Cttee, Europ. Parlt, 1994–. Contested (Lab) Shropshire and Staffordshire, European parly elections, 1984, 1989. MCIM. Methodist local preacher. Editor, The Potter, newspaper, 1982–94. *Address:* European Parliament, 97 Rue Belliard, 1040 Brussels, Belgium.

HALLAM HIPWELL, H.; *see* Vivenot, Baroness Raoul de.

HALLATT, Rt. Rev. David Marrison; *see* Shrewsbury, Bishop Suffragan of.

HALLCHURCH, David Thomas, TD 1965; barrister-at-law; a Recorder of the Crown Court, since 1980; *b* 4 April 1929; *s* of Walter William Hallchurch and Marjorie Pretoria Mary Hallchurch (*née* Cooper); *m* 1st, 1954, Gillian Mary Jagger (marr. diss. 1972); three *s*; 2nd, 1972, Susan Kathryn Mather Brennan; one step *s* one step *d. Educ:* Bromsgrove Sch.; Trinity Coll., Oxford (MA Hons). Called to the Bar, Gray's Inn, 1953; Whitehead Travelling Scholarship, Canada and USA, 1953–54; practised as barrister-at-law on Midland and Oxford Circuit, 1954–60 and 1964–. Puisne Judge, Botswana, 1986–88; Actg Chief Justice, Turks and Caicos Is, 1993. Pt-time Immigration Adjudicator, 1990–; Asst Comr, Parly Boundary Commn for England, 1992–. Legal Mem., Mental Health

Review Tribunal for the West Midlands, 1979–86. Major, Staffs Yeomanry (Queen's Own Royal Regiment), TA, 1953–66. *Recreations:* cricket, drawing (cartoons). *Address:* Neachley House, Tong, near Shifnal, Shropshire TF11 8PH. *T:* Albrighton (0190722) 3542. *Club:* Vincent's (Oxford).

HALLETT, Captain Anthony Philip, RN; Secretary, Rugby Football Union, since 1995; *b* 11 Feb. 1945; *s* of Maurice George Hallett and Ann Halliwell Bailey; *m* 1972, Faith Mary Holland-Martin; three *s*. *Educ:* Ipswich Sch.; Britannia RN Coll. Joined RN 1963; served in HM Ships Victorious and Hermes; Flag Lieut, Hong Kong; HMS Eskimo; RNC Greenwich; BRNC, 1975–77; MoD, 1978–79; HMS Invincible, 1979–81; served C-in-C Fleet, 1982–83; HMS Illustrious, 1983–85; MoD, 1986–90; RNSC Greenwich, 1990–91; Sec. to Chief of Fleet Support, 1992–94. Rugby Football: Navy Captain, 1969; 11 caps; played for US Portsmouth, Blackheath, Richmond, Oxfordshire, S Counties, Combined Services, Hong Kong v England 1971; Selector and Chm., RNRU, 1985–94; Chm., Richmond, 1991–95; RFU 1979–; Chm., Redevelopment of Twickenham, 1991–95. *Recreations:* plantsman and garden design (Mem., Nat. Gardens Scheme), paintings, golf, ski-ing, shooting, cricket. *Address:* Rugby Football Union, Twickenham TW1 1DZ. *T:* 0181–892 8161. *Clubs:* Army and Navy, East India, British Sportsman's.

HALLETT, Prof. George Edward Maurice, MDS; Child Dental Health Professor, University of Newcastle upon Tyne (formerly King's College, University of Durham), 1951–77, now Emeritus; Dean, Sutherland Dental School, 1960–77, and Hospital, 1970–77; retired; *b* 30 July 1912; *s* of Edward Henry and Berthe Hallett; *m* 1936, Annetta Eva Grant Napier; three *d*. *Educ:* Birkenhead Institute; Liverpool Univ. (LDS, Gilmour Medal and other prizes). HDD RCSE 1939; FDS RCS 1948; MDS Durham, 1952; DOrth RCS, 1954; FDS RCSE 1960; FFD RCSI 1964. House Surgeon, Liverpool Dental Hosp., 1934–35; School Dental Officer, Doncaster CB, 1935–36, Notts, 1936–40; served War, 1940–46: Army Dental Corps, Major, despatches. University of Durham: Lecturer in Children's Dentistry, 1946, Reader, 1948; Lectr in Orthodontics, 1946. Examiner in Dental subjects, Universities of Dundee, Durham, Edinburgh and Glasgow; RCS of Eng., 1954–77; Consultant, United Teaching Hosps Newcastle upon Tyne; Head of Dept of Child Dental Health, Dental Hosp., Newcastle upon Tyne, 1948. Mem. Dental Council, RCSE; Past President: Société Française d'Orthopedie Dento-Faciale; European Orthodontic Soc. (also former Editor; Hon. Life Mem.); North of England Odontological Soc.; Brit. Soc. for the study of Orthodontics (Hon. Life Mem.); Newcastle Medico-Legal Soc.; former Mem., Newcastle RHB; former Mem., Newcastle AHA (T). Hon. Life Mem., British Dental Assoc. Past Pres., British Med. Pilots' Assoc. Hon. FDSRCPS Glas 1979. Silver Medal, Ville de Paris, 1980. *Publications:* contribs to scientific and dental jls. *Recreations:* dilettantism in the glyptic arts, flying. *Address:* 63 Runnymede Road, Darras Hall, Ponteland, Newcastle upon Tyne NE20 9HJ. *T:* Ponteland (01661) 22646. *Club:* Newcastle Aero.

HALLETT, Heather Carol; QC 1989; a Recorder, since 1989; *b* 16 Dec. 1949; *d* of late Hugh Hallett, QPM and of Doris Hallett; *m* 1974, Nigel Wilkinson, *qv*; two *s*. *Educ:* St Hugh's Coll., Oxford (MA). Called to the Bar, Inner Temple, 1972, Bencher, 1993. *Recreations:* theatre, music, games. *Address:* 6 Pump Court, Temple, EC4Y 7AR. *T:* 0171–797 8400.

HALLETT, Victor George Henry; Deputy Social Security Commissioner and Deputy Child Support Commissioner, 1993–95; *b* 11 Feb. 1921; *s* of Dr Denys Bouhier Imbert Hallett; *m* 1947, Margaret Hamlyn. *Educ:* Westminster; Queen's Coll., Oxford (MA). Served War, 1939–45 (despatches 1946). Called to Bar, Inner Temple, 1949. Mem., Land Registration Rules Cttee, 1971–76; Conveyancing Counsel of the Court, 1971–76; Nat. Insce, subseq. Social Security, Comr, 1976–93. *Publications:* Key and Elphinstone's Conveyancing Precedents (ed jtly), 15th edn, 1952; Prideaux's Precedents in Conveyancing (ed jtly), 25th edn, 1953; Hallett's Conveyancing Precedents, 1965; (with Nicholas Warren) Settlements, Wills and Capital Transfer Tax, 1979. *Address:* c/o Office of the Social Security and Child Support Commissioners, Harp House, 83/86 Farringdon Street, EC4A 4BL.

HALLEY, Laurence; *see* O'Keeffe, P. L.

HALLGARTEN, Anthony Bernard Richard; QC 1978; **His Honour Judge Hallgarten;** a Circuit Judge, since 1993; *b* 16 June 1937; *s* of late Fritz and Friedel Hallgarten; *m* 1962, Katherine Borchard; one *s* three *d*. *Educ:* Merchant Taylors' Sch., Northwood; Downing Coll., Cambridge (BA). Called to the Bar, Middle Temple, 1961 (Barstow Scholar, Inns of Court, 1961); Bencher, 1987; a Recorder, 1990–93. Chm., Bar/Inns' Councils Jt Regulations Cttee, 1990–. Chair, Management Cttee, Camden Victim Support, 1989–. *Recreations:* cricket, canals, cycling. *Clubs:* Garrick, MCC.

HALLIBURTON, Rev. Canon Robert John; Canon Residentiary and Chancellor of St Paul's Cathedral, since 1989; *b* 23 March 1935; *s* of Robert Halliburton and Katherine Margery Halliburton (*née* Robinson); *m* 1968, Jennifer Ormsby Turner; one *s* three *d* (and one *s* decd). *Educ:* Tonbridge Sch.; Selwyn Coll., Cambridge (MA); Keble Coll., Oxford (DPhil); St Stephen's House, Oxford. Curate, St Dunstan and All Saints, Stepney, 1961; Tutor, St Stephen's House, Oxford, 1967; Vice-Principal, St Stephen's House, 1971; Lectr, Lincoln Coll., Oxford, 1973; Principal of Chichester Theol Coll., 1975–82, Canon and Prebend of Chichester Cathedral, 1976–82, Canon Emeritus, 1982–88, Canon and Preb. of Wightring and Theol Lectr, 1988–90; Priest in Charge, All Souls, St Margaret's-on-Thames, 1982–89. Lecturer: Southwark Ordination Course, 1984–89; Missionary Inst., Mill Hill, 1984–89. Select Preacher, Oxford Univ., 1976–77. Consultant, Anglican-Roman Catholic Internat. Commn, 1971–81; Mem., Doctrinal Commn of C of E, 1978–86. Examining Chaplain to Bishop of Kensington, 1983–. *Publications:* The Authority of a Bishop, 1986; Educating Rachel, 1987; contribs to: The Eucharist Today, ed R. C. D. Jasper, 1974, The Study of Liturgy, ed C. P. M. Jones, 1978; Confession and Absolution, ed G. Rowell and M. Dudley, 1990; The Oil of Gladness, ed G. Rowell and M. Dudley, 1992; reports of C of E Doctrinal Commission, Believing in the Church, 1982, We believe in God, 1987; articles in Studia Patristica, La Revue des Etudes Augustiniennes, Faith and Unity. *Recreations:* music, gardening. *Address:* 1 Amen Court, EC4M 7BU. *T:* 0171–248 1817. *Club:* Athenæum.

HALLIDAY, Prof. Fred; Professor of International Relations, London School of Economics and Political Science, since 1985; *b* 22 Feb. 1946; *s* of Arthur Halliday and Rita (*née* Finigan); *m* Dr Maxine Molyneux; one *s*. *Educ:* Univ. of Oxford (BA 1st Cl.); School of Oriental and African Studies (MSc); London School of Economics (PhD 1985). Freelance writer, 1967; Dept. of Internat. Relations, LSE, 1983–. Associate Fellow, Inst. for Policy Studies, Washington. Mem., Internat. Cttee, Gilbert Murray Trust, 1985–; Sen. Fellow, 21st Century Trust; Gov., LSE, 1994–. Contributing Ed., Middle East Reports, 1978–. *Publications:* Arabia without Sultans, 1974; Iran: dictatorship and development, 1978; (with Maxine Molyneux) The Ethiopian Revolution, 1981; Threat from the East?, 1982; The Making of the Second Cold War, 1983, 2nd edn 1986; Cold War, Third World, 1989; Revolution and Foreign Policy: the case of South Yemen 1967–1987, 1990; Arabs in Exile: the Yemen communities in Britain, 1992; Rethinking International Relations, 1994. *Recreations:* languages, travel, lunch, Le Monde. *Address:* A136, London School of Economics and Political Science, Houghton Street, WC2A 2AE. *T:* 0171–955 7389, *Fax:* 0171–955 7446.

HALLIDAY, Ian Francis, FCA; Finance Director, Lowndes Lambert Group Ltd, 1981–87; *b* 16 Nov. 1927; *s* of Michael and Jean Halliday; *m* 1952, Mary Busfield; one *s* two *d*. *Educ:* Wintringham Grammar Sch., Grimsby; Lincoln Coll., Oxford (MA Mathematics). Armitage & Norton, Chartered Accountants, 1951–69; qual. as Chartered Accountant, 1954; Partner, 1957; Finance Dir, Allied Textile Co. Ltd, 1970–74; on secondment as Dep. Director of Industrial Development Unit, Dept of Industry, 1974–77; Finance Dir, Leslie & Godwin (Holdings) Ltd, internat. insce and re-insce Lloyd's Brokers, 1977–80; Chief Exec., NEB, 1980. Mem., PLA, 1984–. *Recreation:* gardening. *Address:* 84 Benomley Road, Huddersfield HD5 8LS.

HALLIDAY, Prof. Ian Gibson, PhD; Professor of Physics, Head of Department and Dean of Graduate School, University College, Swansea, since 1992; *b* 5 Feb. 1940; *s* of John Alexander Halliday and Gladys (*née* Taylor); *m* 1965, Ellenor Gardiner Hervey Wilson; one *s* one *d*. *Educ:* Kelso High Sch.; Perth Acad.; Edinburgh Univ. (MA 1961; MSc 1962); Clare Coll., Cambridge (PhD 1964). Instructor, Princeton Univ., 1964–66; Fellow, Christ's Coll., Cambridge, 1966–67; Imperial College, University of London: Lectr, 1967–75; Reader, 1975–90; Prof., 1990–92. Mem., PPARC, 1994–. *Publications:* numerous papers on theoretical particle physics in Nuclear Physics, Physics Letters. *Recreations:* sewin fishing, golf, tennis. *Address:* 65 Owls Lodge Lane, Mayals, Swansea SA3 5DP. *T:* (office) Swansea (01792) 295372.

HALLIDAY, John Frederick, CB 1994; Deputy Under Secretary of State, Home Office, since 1990; *b* 19 Sept. 1942; *s* of E. Halliday; *m* 1970, Alison Burgess; four *s*. *Educ:* Whitgift School, Croydon; St John's College, Cambridge (MA). Teacher, under VSO, Aitchison College, Lahore, 1964–66; Home Office, 1966; Principal Private Sec. to Home Sec., 1980; Asst Under-Sec. of State, Home Office, 1983–87; Under Sec., DHSS, then Dept of Health, 1987–90, on secondment. *Recreations:* music, squash, theatre.

HALLIDAY, Prof. Michael Alexander Kirkwood; Professor of Linguistics in the University of Sydney, 1976–87, Emeritus Professor since 1988; *b* 13 April 1925; *s* of late Wilfrid J. Halliday and Winifred Halliday (*née* Kirkwood). *Educ:* Rugby School; University of London. BA London; MA, PhD, Cambridge. Served Army, 1944–47. Asst Lectr in Chinese, Cambridge Univ., 1954–58; Lectr in General Linguistics, Edinburgh Univ., 1958–60; Reader in General Linguistics, Edinburgh Univ., 1960–63; Dir, Communication Res. Centre, UCL, 1963–65; Linguistic Soc. of America Prof., Indiana Univ., 1964; Prof. of General Linguistics, UCL, 1965–71; Fellow, Center for Advanced Study in the Behavioral Sciences, Stanford, Calif., 1972–73; Prof. of Linguistics, Univ. of Illinois, 1973–74; Prof. of Language and Linguistics, Essex Univ., 1974–75. Visiting Professor of Linguistics: Yale, 1967; Brown, 1971; Nairobi, 1972; Nat. Univ. of Singapore, 1990–91; Internat. Christian Univ., Tokyo, 1992; Lee Kuan Yew Distinguished Visitor, Nat. Univ. of Singapore, 1986; Hon. Sen. Res. Fellow, Birmingham Univ., 1991. FAHA 1979. Corresp. FBA 1989; For. Mem., Academia Europaea, 1994. Guest Prof., Peking Univ., 1995; Dr *hc* Nancy; Hon. DLitt: Birmingham, 1987; York (Canada), 1988. *Publications:* The Language of the Chinese 'Secret History of the Mongols', 1959; (with A. McIntosh and P. Strevens) The Linguistic Sciences and Language Teaching, 1964; (with A. McIntosh) Patterns of Language, 1966; Intonation and Grammar in British English, 1967; A Course in Spoken English: Intonation, 1970; Explorations in the Functions of Language, 1973; Learning How To Mean, 1975; (with R. Hasan) Cohesion in English, 1976; System and Function in Language, ed G. Kress, 1976; Language as Social Semiotic, 1978; An Introduction to Functional Grammar, 1985; Spoken and Written Language, 1985; (with J. Martin) Writing Science, 1993; articles in Jl of Linguistics, Word, Trans of Philological Soc., etc. *Address:* 5 Laing Avenue, Killara, NSW 2071, Australia.

HALLIDAY, Norman Pryde; General Manager, European Dialysis and Transplant Association, since 1994; Hon. Deputy Medical Director, Children Nationwide medical research fund, since 1992; *b* 28 March 1932; *s* of late James and Jessie Thomson Hunter Halliday; *m* 1953, Eleanor Smith; three *s* one *d*. *Educ:* Woodside, Glasgow; King's Coll., London; King's Coll. Hosp. Med. Sch. SRN 1955; MB, BS, MRCS, LRCP 1964; DCH RCPGlas 1969; MBA: Warwick, 1991; Open Univ., 1992. Various posts in clinical medicine, incl. Registrar (Paediatrics), KCH, London; SMO, DHSS, 1972; SPMO (Under Sec.), DHSS, later DoH, 1977–92. Tutor: Open Univ., 1992–; Warwick Univ., 1992–. QHP 1990–93. *Publications:* articles on medical subjects in professional journals. *Recreations:* photography, sub aqua diving, fashion, DIY, cross-bow shooting. *Address:* Gurrs Farm, Crowborough Hill, Crowborough, E Sussex TN6 2SD. *T:* Crowborough (01892) 669132.

HALLIDAY, Rt. Rev. Robert Taylor; *see* Brechin, Bishop of.

HALLIDAY, Vice-Adm. Sir Roy (William), KBE 1980; DSC 1944; company director; Director General of Intelligence, Ministry of Defence, 1981–84; *b* 27 June 1923; *m* 1945, Dorothy Joan Meech. *Educ:* William Ellis Sch.; University College Sch. Joined Royal Navy, 1941; served in Fleet Air Arm (fighter pilot) in World War II, in HMS Chaser, HMSs Victorious and Illustrious; test pilot, Boscombe Down, 1947–48; Comdg Officer 813 Sqdn (Wyverns, HMS Eagle), 1954; Army Staff Coll., Camberley; Comdr, 1958; Exec. Officer Coastal Forces Base (HMS Diligence), 1959; Sen. Officer 104th Minesweeping Sqdn, Far East Flt, in comd (HMS Houghton), 1961–62; Naval Asst to Chief of Naval Information, 1962–64; comdr (Air) HMS Albion, 1964–66; Captain, 1966; Dep. Dir Naval Air Warfare, 1966–70; HMS Euryalus in comd and as Captain D3 Far East Fleet and D6 Western Fleet, 1970–71; Commodore, 1971; Cdre Amphibious Warfare, 1971–73; Cdre Intelligence, Defence Intelligence Staff, 1973–75; Comdr British Navy Staff, Washington, Naval Attaché, and UK Nat. Liaison Rep. to SACLANT, 1975–78; Dep. Chief of Defence Staff (Intelligence), 1978–81. ADC to the Queen, 1975. *Recreations:* gardening, walking. *Address:* c/o Barclays Bank, Lyndhurst Branch, PO Box 55, Lymington SO41 9WF. *Club:* Naval.

HALLIDAY, S. F. P.; *see* Halliday, F.

HALLINAN, Sir (Adrian) Lincoln, Kt 1971; DL; Barrister-at-law; Stipendiary Magistrate, South Glamorgan (Cardiff), 1976–93; a Recorder of the Crown Court, 1972–82; *b* 13 Nov. 1922; *e s* of late Sir Charles Hallinan, CBE and late Theresa Doris Hallinan, JP (*née* Holman); *m* 1955, Mary Parry Evans, *qv*; two *s* two *d*. *Educ:* Downside. Lieut, Rifle Bde, 1942–47; TA, 1950–52 (Captain). Called to Bar, Lincoln's Inn, 1950; Wales and Chester Circuit. A Legal Mem., Mental Health Review Tribunal for Wales, 1966–76; Chm., Med. Appeals Tribunal, 1970–76. Cardiff CC, 1949–74 (serving on several educational and cultural cttees); Alderman, 1961–74; Lord Mayor of Cardiff, 1969–70. Contested (C), Aberdare, 1946, Cardiff West, 1951, 1959. Chm., Cardiff Educn Cttee, 1961–63 and 1965–70; Chm., Governing Body, Cardiff Coll. of Art, and Cardiff Coll. of Music and Drama, 1961–73; First Chm., Nat. Court of Governors, Welsh Coll. of Music and Drama, 1970. Chm., Commemorative Collectors Soc.; Pres., S Wales Gp, Victorian Soc.; Founder and Chm., Cardiff 2000–Cardiff Civic Trust, 1964–73, 1st Pres. 1973; Chm., Cardiff-Nantes Fellowship, 1961–68. Chevalier, Ordre des Palmes Académiques, 1965; Chevalier de la Légion d'Honneur, 1973. OStJ 1969 (Pres., Newport Br., 1993–). DL Glamorgan, 1969. *Recreations:* music, the arts. *Address:* Cotham Lodge, Newport, Pembrokeshire SA42 0TD.

HALLINAN, Sir Lincoln; *see* Hallinan, Sir A. L.

HALLINAN, Mary Alethea, (Lady Hallinan); *see* Parry Evans, M.A.

HALLIWELL, Brian; VAT Consultant, KPMG (formerly Peat, Marwick, Mitchell & Co.), since 1985; *b* 17 Dec. 1930; *s* of late Norman and Emma Halliwell; *m* 1957, Agnes Lee. *Educ:* Preston Grammar Sch. DMS 1968. Joined HM Customs and Excise as Clerical Officer, 1947; Principal, 1969; Asst Sec., 1973; Dep. Accountant General, 1976; Accountant and Comptroller Gen., 1980–85; Hd of VAT Services, Peat, Marwick, Mitchell & Co., subseq. KPMG Peat Marwick McLintock, 1989–93. FIMgt. *Recreations:* chess, reading, sport. *Address:* Waverlee, Great Heads Road, Grange-over-Sands, Cumbria LA11 7EA. *T:* Grange-over-Sands (015395) 34335.

HALLIWELL, Prof. Richard Edward Winter; William Dick Professor of Veterinary Clinical Studies, Royal (Dick) School of Veterinary Studies, University of Edinburgh, since 1988 (Dean, Faculty of Veterinary Medicine, 1990–94); *b* 16 June 1937; *s* of Arthur Clare Halliwell and Winifred Dorothea Goode; *m* 1963, Jenifer Helen Roper; two *d*. *Educ:* St Edward's Sch., Oxford; Gonville and Caius Coll., Cambridge (MA, VetMB, PhD); MRCVS. Jun. Fellow in Vet. Surgery, Univ. of Bristol, 1961–63; private vet. practice, London, 1963–68; Vis. Fellow in Dermatology, Univ. of Pennsylvania Sch. of Vet. Med., 1968–70; Wellcome Vet. Fellowship Univ. of Cambridge, 1970–73; Asst Prof. of Dermatology, Univ. of Pennsylvania Sch. of Vet. Med., 1973–77; Prof. and Chm., Dept of Med. Scis, Univ. of Florida Coll. of Vet. Med., 1977–88; Prof., Dept of Med. Microbiol., Univ. of Florida Coll. of Med., 1977–88. UK Rep., Adv. Cttee on Vet. Educn of EU. President: Amer. Acad. of Veterinary Allergy, 1978–80; Amer. Assoc. of Veterinary Immunologists, 1984; Amer. Coll. of Veterinary Dermatology, 1984–86; Eur. Assoc. of Estabs for Vet. Educn, 1994–. *Publications:* (with N. T. Gorman) Veterinary Clinical Immunology, 1989; (with C. von Tscharner) Advances in Veterinary Dermatology, 1990; numerous pubns in area of clin. immunology and vet. dermatology. *Recreations:* hill walking, surfing. *Address:* 2A Ainslie Place, Edinburgh EH3 6AR. *T:* 0131–225 8765. *Club:* St John's House.

HALLON, Gayle, (Mrs J. A. Hodgson); Her Honour Judge Hallon; a Circuit Judge, South Eastern Circuit, since 1992; *b* 10 Aug. 1946; *d* of late Douglas Hallon, VRD, FRCS and Enid (*née* Bailey); *m* 1971, John Arnold Hodgson. *Educ:* Cheltenham Ladies' Coll.; St Hugh's Coll., Oxford (MA). Called to the Bar, Inner Temple, 1968; practised at the Bar, 1969–92; Recorder, 1987–92. *Recreations:* gardening, acting. *Address:* The Court House, College Road, Bromley, Kent BR1 3PX. *T:* 0181–464 9727.

HALLSWORTH, Prof. Ernest Gordon, DSc, FRSC, FTS; Scientific Consultant and Chairman of Directors, Hallsworth and Associates; *b* 1913; *s* of Ernest and Beatrice Hallsworth, Ashton-under-Lyne, Lancs; *m* 1st, 1943, Elaine Gertrude Seddon (*d* 1970), *d* of R. C. Weatherill, Waverley, NSW; two *s* one *d* and one step *s*; 2nd, 1976, Merrily Ramly; one step *d*. *Educ:* Ashton Grammar Sch., Ashton-under-Lyne, Lancs; Univ. of Leeds. University of Leeds: First Cl. Hons in Agric. Chem., Sir Swire Smith Fellow, 1936; Asst Lectr in Agric. Chem., 1936; PhD 1939; DSc 1964. Lectr in Agric. Chem., Univ. of Sydney, 1940–51; Prof. of Soil Science, Univ. of West Australia, 1960–61; Prof. of Agric. Chem. and Head Dept Agric. Sci., Univ. Nottingham, 1951–64 (Dean, Faculty of Agric. and Hort., 1951–60); Chief of Div. of Soils, CSIRO, 1964–73; Chm., Land Resources Labs, CSIRO, 1973–78; Hon. Professorial Fellow, Science Policy Res. Unit, Sussex Univ., 1979–85. Pres. Lecturers' Assoc., Sydney Univ., 1946–49. Treas., Aust. Assoc. of Scientific Workers, 1943; Member: Science Advisory Panel, Australian Broadcasting Commn, 1949–51; Pasture Improvement Cttee, Australian Dairy Produce Bd (NSW), 1948–51; Chm. Insecticides and Fungicides Cttee, Australian Standards Inst., 1949–51. President: Internat. Soc. of Soil Science, 1964–68; Sect. 13, Aust. and NZ Assoc. for the Advancement of Science, 1976. Mem. Council, Flinders Univ., 1967–79; Chief Scientific Liaison Officer (Aust.), London, 1971. Fellow: Aust. Acad. of Technol Scis and Engrg, 1976–; World Acad. of Art and Science, 1989–; Mem., Académie d'Agriculture de France, 1983–; Hon. Mem., Internat. Soc. of Soil Sci., 1990–. Prescott Medal, Aust. Soc. Soil Science, 1984; Dokuchaev Medal, All-Union Soc. of Soil Sci., 1990. *Publications:* (Ed) Nutrition of the Legumes, 1958; (ed with D. V. Crawford) Experimental Pedology, 1964; (with others) Handbook of Australian Soils, 1968; (with others) Principles of a Balanced Land Use Policy for Australia, 1976; Where Shall We Build Our New Cities?, 1978; Land and Water Resources of Australia, 1979; Socio-economic Effects and Restraints in Tropical Forest Management, 1982; The Anatomy, Physiology and Psychology of Erosion, 1987; contributions to: Aust. Jl Science, Jl Soc. Chem. Indust., Experimental Agric., Jl Agric. Science, Aust. Medical Jl, Jl Soil Science. *Recreations:* talking, pedology. *Address:* 8 Old Belair Road, Mitcham, SA 5062, Australia. *T:* (8) 2716423; 1 Bellevue Cottages, Blackboys, near Uckfield, Sussex. *T:* Framfield (01825) 890606. *Club:* Farmers'.

HALLWARD, Bertrand Leslie, MA; *b* 24 May 1901; *er s* of late N. L. Hallward, Indian Educational Service, and Evelyn A. Gurdon; *m* 1926, Catherine Margaret (*d* 1991), 2nd *d* of late Canon A. J. Tait, DD; four *d*. *Educ:* Haileybury Coll. (Scholar); King's Coll., Cambridge (Scholar). Fellow of Peterhouse, 1923–39. Hon. Fellow 1956. Headmaster of Clifton Coll., 1939–48; Vice-Chancellor, Nottingham Univ., 1948–65 (Hallward Library named at Nottingham Univ., 1989). Hon. LLD: Chattanooga, USA, 1958; Sheffield, 1964; Nottingham, 1965. *Publications:* Chapters II, III, IV, and part of VII (the Second and Third Punic Wars) in Cambridge Ancient History, Vol. VIII, 1930; Editor of the Classical Quarterly, 1935–39. *Address:* Flat 4, Gretton Court, Girton, Cambridge CB3 0QN. *T:* Cambridge (01223) 277327.

See also W. O. Chadwick, G. C. H. Spafford.

HALNAN, Patrick John; His Honour Judge Halnan; a Circuit Judge, since 1986; *b* 7 March 1925; *s* of E. T. and A. B. Halnan; *m* 1955, Judith Mary (*née* Humberstone); four *c*. *Educ:* Perse Sch., Cambridge; Trinity Coll., Cambridge (MA). Army, 1943–47; TA, 1951–58. Solicitor. Asst Solicitor, Hants CC, 1954–58; Clerk to the Justices, Cambs, 1958–78; Metropolitan Stipendary Magistrate, 1978–86; a Recorder, 1983–86; SE Circuit. Sec., Justices' Clerks' Soc., 1972–76, Pres., 1978. Chm., Road Traffic Cttee, Magistrates' Assoc., 1981–87. *Publications:* (ed with Prof. R. M. Jackson) Leo Page, Justice of the Peace, 3rd edn 1967; (ed) Wilkinson's Road Traffic Offences, 7th edn 1973 to 14th edn 1989; (with David Latham) Drink/Driving Offences, 1979; Road Traffic, 1981; Drink/Drive: the new law, 1984. *Recreations:* travelling, sailing (as idle crew), village bridge, stamp collecting. *Club:* United Oxford & Cambridge University.

HALPERN, Prof. Jack, FRS 1974; Louis Block Distinguished Service Professor of Chemistry, University of Chicago, since 1984; *b* Poland, 19 Jan. 1925 (moved to Canada, 1929; USA 1962); *s* of Philip Halpern and Anna Sass; *m* 1949, Helen Peritz; two *d*. *Educ:* McGill Univ., Montreal. BSc 1946, PhD 1949. NRC Postdoc. Fellow, Univ. of Manchester, 1949–50; Prof. of Chem., Univ. of Brit. Columbia, 1950–62 (Nuffield Foundn Travelling Fellow, Cambridge Univ., 1959–60); Prof. of Chem., Univ. of Chicago, 1962–71, Louis Block Prof., 1971–84. Visiting Prof.: Univ. of Minnesota, 1962; Harvard Univ., 1966–67; California Inst. of Techn., 1969; Princeton Univ., 1970–71; Copenhagen Univ., 1978; Firth Vis. Prof., Sheffield, 1982; Sherman Fairchild Dist. Scholar, California Inst. of Technology, 1979; Guest Scholar, Kyoto Univ., 1981; Phi Beta Kappa Vis. Scholar, 1990; R. B. Woodward Vis. Prof., Harvard Univ., 1991; External Sci. Mem., Max Planck Institut für Kohlenforschung, Mulheim, 1983–; Lectureships: 3M, Univ. of Minnesota, 1968; FMC, Princeton Univ., 1969; Du Pont, Univ. of Calif., Berkeley, 1970; Frontier of Chemistry, Case Western Reserve Univ., 1971, 1989; Venable, Univ. of N Carolina, 1973; Ritter Meml, Miami Univ., 1980; University, Univ. of Western Ontario, 1981; F. J. Toole, Univ. of New Brunswick, 1981; Werner, Univ. of Kansas, 1982; Lansdowne, Univ. of Victoria, 1982; Welch, Univ. of Texas, 1983; Kilpatrick, Illinois Inst. of Tech., 1984; Dow, Univ. of Ottawa, 1985; Boomer, Univ. of Alberta, 1985; Bailar, Univ. of Illinois, 1986; Priestley, Penn State Univ., 1987; Taube, Stanford Univ., 1988; Res. Schol., Drew Univ., 1989; Liebig. Univ. of Colorado, 1989; Kennedy, Washington Univ., 1992; Karcher, Univ. of Oklahoma, 1992; Nieuland, Notre Dame, 1992; Swift, CIT, 1992. Associate Editor: Jl of Amer. Chem. Soc.; Inorganica Chimica Acta; Mem. Editorial Bds: Accounts of Chemical Research; Jl of Catalysis; Catalysis Reviews; Jl of Coordination Chem.; Inorganic Syntheses; Jl of Molecular Catalysis; Jl of Organometallic Chemistry; Amer. Chem. Soc. Advances in Chemistry series; Gazzetta Chimica Italiana; Organometallics; Catalysis Letters; Reaction Kinetics and Catalysis Letters; Co-editor, OUP International Series of Monographs in Chemistry; Sen. Contributing Editor, Proceedings of Nat. Acad. of Scis. Member: Nat. Sci. Foundn Chemistry Adv. Panel, 1967–70; MIT Chemistry Vis. Cttee, 1968–70; Argonne Nat. Lab. Chemistry Vis. Cttee, 1970–73; Amer. Chem. Soc. Petroleum Res. Fund Adv. Bd, 1972–74; NIH Medicinal Chem. Study Sect., 1975–78 (Chm., 1976–78); Princeton Univ. Chem. Adv. Council, 1982–; Chemistry Adv. Cttee, CIT, 1991–; Encyclopaedia Britannica Univ. Adv. Cttee, 1985–. Mem., Bd of Trustees and Council, Gordon Research Confs, 1968–70; Chm., Gordon Conf. on Inorganic Chem., 1969; Chm., Amer. Chemical Soc. Div. of Inorganic Chem., 1971; Mem., 1985–, Mem., Council, 1990–, Chm., Chem. Sect., Vice-Pres., 1993–, Nat. Acad. of Scis (For. Mem., 1984–85). Chm., German–Amer. Acad. Council, 1993–. Member: Bd of Dirs, Renaissance Soc., 1984–; Bd of Govs, Smart Mus., Univ. of Chicago, 1988–; Adv. Bd, Court Theatre, Univ. of Chicago, 1989–. Fellow, Amer. Acad. of Arts and Sciences, 1967; Sci. Mem., Max Planck Soc., 1983. Hon. FRSC 1987. Hon. DSc Univ. of British Columbia, 1986. Holds numerous honours and awards, including: Amer. Chem. Soc. Award in Inorganic Chem., 1968; Chem. Soc. Award, 1976; Humboldt Award, 1977; Kokes Award, Johns Hopkins Univ., 1978; Amer. Chem. Soc. Award for Distinguished Service in the Advancement of Inorganic Chemistry, 1985; Willard Gibbs Medal, 1986; Bailar Medal, Univ. of Illinois, 1986; Hoffman Medal, German Chem. Soc., 1988; Chemical Pioneer Award, Amer. Inst. of Chemists, 1991; Paracelsus Prize, Swiss Chem. Soc., 1992; Robert A. Welch Award in Chemistry, 1994; Amer. Chem. Soc. Award in Organometallic Chemistry, 1995. *Publications:* Editor (with F. Basolo and J. Bunnett) Collected Accounts of Transition Metal Chemistry, vol. I, 1973, vol. II, 1977; contrib. articles on Catalysis and on Coordination Compounds to Encyclopaedia Britannica; numerous articles to Jl of Amer. Chemical Soc. and other scientific jls. *Recreations:* art, music, theatre. *Address:* Department of Chemistry, University of Chicago, 5735 South Ellis Avenue, Chicago, IL 60637, USA. *T:* (312) 7027095. *Clubs:* Quadrangle (Chicago); Chemists (New York).

HALPERN, Sir Ralph (Mark), Kt 1986; Chairman, 1981–90, and Chief Executive, 1978–90, Burton Group plc (Managing Director, 1978); *b* 1938; *m* Joan Halpern, JP; one *d*. *Educ:* St Christopher School, Letchworth. Started career as trainee, Selfridges; joined Burton Group, 1961; co-Founder, Top Shop, 1970. Member: President's Cttee, CBI, 1984–90; President's Cttee, Business in the Community, 1991–92; Adv. Council, Prince's Youth Business Trust, 1991–. Chm., British Fashion Council, 1990–94. FInstD; CIMgt. *Club:* Reform.

HALPIN, Miss Kathleen Mary, CBE 1953 (OBE 1941); Chief Administrator, Regions, WRVS (formerly WVS), 1945–73; *b* 19 Nov. 1903; unmarried. *Educ:* Sydenham High Sch. (GPDST). Organising Sec., Women's Gas Council, 1935, and represented Gas Industry at International Management Congress, Washington, USA, 1938, Sweden, 1947. Appointed Chief of Metropolitan Dept, WVS, 1939; lent to Min. of Health and went to Washington as UK representative on Standing Technical Cttee on Welfare, UNRRA; Comr, Trainer, and Camp Adviser, Girl Guides Assoc., 1924–48; Comdt, BRCS, 1937–39; Mem. Council, London Hostels Assoc., 1941–91; Chm. Women's Gas Fedn, 1945–49, Pres., 1949–60. A Governor of St Bartholomew's Hospital, 1948–73. Chm., Soroptomist (London) Housing Assoc., 1963–89; President Fedn of Soroptomist Clubs of Gt Britain and Ireland, 1959–60; Vice-Pres., Fawcett Soc., 1978– (Chm., 1967–71); Trustee, Women's Service Trust, 1964–89. OStJ. *Recreations:* motoring, reading, theatre. *Address:* 3 Chagford House, Chagford Street, NW1 6EG. *T:* 0171–262 6226.

HALSBURY, 3rd Earl of, *cr* 1898; **John Anthony Hardinge Giffard,** FRS 1969; FEng 1976; Baron Halsbury, 1885; Viscount Tiverton, 1898; Chancellor of Brunel University, since 1966; *b* 4 June 1908; *o s* of 2nd Earl and Esmé Stewart (*d* 1973), *d* of late James Stewart Wallace; *S* father, 1943; *m* 1st, 1930, Ismay Catherine, *er d* of late Lord Ninian Crichton-Stuart and Hon. Mrs Archibald Maule Ramsay; one *s*; 2nd, 1936, Elizabeth Adeline Faith (*d* 1983), *o d* of late Major Harry Crewe Godley, DSO, Northamptonshire Regt and of late Mrs Godley, of Claremont Lodge, Cheltenham; two *d*. *Educ:* Eton. BSc (1st Cl. Hons Chem. and Maths) London (External), 1935; FRIC 1947, Hon. FRSC 1983; FInstP 1946; CEng, FIProdE 1956, Hon. FIProdE 1979. Employed by Lever Bros, 1935–42; Brown-Firth Res. Labs, 1942–47; Dir of Res., Decca Record Co., 1947–49; Man. Dir, Nat. Research Development Corporation, 1949–59; Consultant and Director: Joseph Lucas Industries, 1959–74; Distillers Co. Ltd, 1959–78; Head-Wrightson Ltd, 1959–78. External Examiner, OECD, on mission to Japan, 1965. Chairman: Science Museum Advisory Council, 1951–65; Cttee on Decimal Currency, 1961–63; Cttee of Management, Inst. of Cancer Research, Royal Marsden Hosp., 1962–77; Review Body on Doctors' and Dentists' Pay, 1971–74; Deptl Cttee of Enquiry into pay of Nurses, Midwives, Speech Therapists and Professions Supplementary to Medicine, 1974–75; Meteorological Cttee, 1970–82; President: Institution of Production Engineers, 1957–59; Royal Inst. of Philosophy, 1961–90; Parly and Scientific Cttee, 1963–66; Instn of Nuclear Engineers, 1963–65; Nat. Inst. of Industrial Psychol., 1963–75; Machine Tool Industry Res. Assoc., 1964–77; Coll. of Speech Therapists, 1983–87; Nat. Council for Christian Standards in Society, 1986–; Chm., Atlas Computing Lab., 1965–69; Member: Adv. Council to Cttee of Privy Council for Scientific and Industrial Research, 1949–54; SRC, 1965–69; Computer Bd for Univs and Research Councils, 1966–69; Decimal Currency Bd, 1966–71; Nationalised Transport Advisory Council, 1963–67; Standing Commn on Museums and Galleries, 1960–76; MRC, 1973–77; Cttee of Managers, Royal Institution, 1976–79. A Governor: BBC, 1960–62; LSE, 1959–90; UMIST, 1966– (formerly Mem. Council, Manchester Coll. of Sci. and Technol., 1956–65). Hon. FICE 1975; Hon. ARCVS 1984; Hon. FIBiol 1989. Hon. DTech Brunel Univ., 1966; DUniv Essex, 1968. *Heir:* *s* Adam Edward Giffard, *qv*. *Address:* 4 Campden House, 29 Sheffield Terrace, W8 7NE. *T:* 0171–727 3125. *Clubs:* Athenæum, Royal Automobile (a Steward, 1966–).

HALSEY, Prof. Albert Henry, FBA 1995; Professor of Social and Administrative Studies, University of Oxford, 1978–90, now Emeritus; Professorial Fellow of Nuffield College, Oxford, 1962–90, now Emeritus; *b* 13 April 1923; *m* 1949, Gertrude Margaret Littler; three *s* two *d*. *Educ:* Kettering Grammar Sch.; London Sch. of Econs (BSc (Econ); PhD; Hon. Fellow, 1993); MA Oxon. RAF, 1942–47; student LSE, 1947–52; Research Worker, Liverpool Univ., 1952–54; Lectr in Sociology, Birmingham Univ., 1954–62; Dir, Dept of Social and Admin. Studies, Oxford Univ., 1962–78. Fellow, Center for Advanced Study of Behavioral Sciences, Palo Alto, Calif, 1956–57; Vis. Prof. of Sociology, Univ. of Chicago, 1959–60. Adviser to Sec. of State for Educn, 1965–68; Chm. of CERI at OECD, Paris, 1968–70. Reith Lectr, 1977. MAE 1992; Foreign Associate, Amer. Acad. of Educn.; Foreign Mem., Amer. Acad. of Arts and Scis, 1988. Hon. Fellow, Goldsmiths' Coll., 1992. Hon. DSocSc Birmingham, 1987; DUniv Open, 1990; Hon. DLitt: Glamorgan, 1994; Leicester, 1995; Warwick, 1995. *Publications:* (jtly) Social Class and Educational Opportunity, 1956; (jtly) Technical Change and Industrial Relations, 1956; (with J. E. Floud) The Sociology of Education, Current Sociology VII, 1958; (jtly) Education, Economy and Society, 1961; Ability and Educational Opportunity, 1962; (with G. N. Ostergaard) Power in Co-operatives, 1965; (with Ivor Crewe) Social Survey of the Civil Service, 1969; (with Martin Trow) The British Academics, 1971; (ed) Trends in British Society since 1900, 1972; (ed) Educational Priority, 1972; Traditions of Social Policy, 1976; Heredity and Environment, 1977; Change in British Society, 1978, 4th edn 1995; (jtly) Origins and Destinations, 1980; (with Norman Dennis) English Ethical Socialism, 1988; Decline of Donnish Dominion, 1992, 2nd edn 1995; numerous articles and reviews. *Address:* 28 Upland Park Road, Oxford OX2 7RU. *T:* Oxford (01865) 58625.

HALSEY, Rt. Rev. (Henry) David; Bishop of Carlisle, 1972–89; *b* 27 Jan. 1919; *s* of George Halsey, MBE and Gladys W. Halsey, DSc; *m* 1947, Rachel Margaret Neil Smith; four *d*. *Educ:* King's Coll. Sch., Wimbledon; King's Coll., London (BA); Wells Theol College. Curate, Petersfield, 1942–45; Chaplain, RNVR, 1946–47; Curate, St Andrew, Plymouth, 1947–50; Vicar of: Netheravon, 1950–53; St Stephen, Chatham, 1953–62; Bromley, and Chaplain, Bromley Hosp., 1962–68; Rural Dean of Bromley, 1965–66; Archdeacon of Bromley, 1966–68; Bishop Suffragan of Tonbridge, 1968–72. Entered House of Lords, 1976. *Recreations:* cricket, sailing, reading, gardening, walking. *Address:* Bramblecross, Gully Road, Seaview, Isle of Wight PO34 5BY.

See also D. French.

HALSEY, Rev. John Walter Brooke, 4th Bt *cr* 1920 (but uses designation Brother John Halsey); *b* 26 Dec. 1933; *s* of Sir Thomas Edgar Halsey, 3rd Bt, DSO, and of Jean Margaret Palmer, *d* of late Bertram Willes Dayrell Brooke; *S* father, 1970. *Educ:* Eton; Magdalene College, Cambridge (BA 1957). Deacon, 1961, priest, 1962, Diocese of York; Curate of Stocksbridge, 1961–65; Brother in Community of the Transfiguration, 1965–. *Heir: cousin* Nicholas Guy Halsey, TD [*b* 14 June 1948; *m* 1976, Viola Georgina Juliet, *d* of Maj. George Thorne, MC, DL; one *s*]. *Address:* Community of the Transfiguration, 23 Manse Road, Roslin, Midlothian EH25 9LF.

HALSEY, Philip Hugh, CB 1986; LVO 1972; Member, School Teachers' Review Body, since 1991; Deputy Secretary, Department of Education and Science, 1982–88; *b* 9 May 1928; *s* of Sidney Robert Halsey and Edith Mary Halsey; *m* 1956, Hilda Mary Biggerstaff; two *s*. *Educ:* University Coll. London (BSc; Fellow, 1992). Headmaster, Hampstead Sch., 1961; Principal, DES, 1966; Under-Sec., 1977. Chm. and Chief Exec., Sch. Exams and Assessment Council, 1988–91.

HALSTEAD, Sir Ronald, Kt 1985; CBE 1976; Deputy Chairman, British Steel plc (formerly British Steel Corporation), 1986–94; *b* 17 May 1927; *s* of Richard and Bessie Harrison Halstead; *m* 1968, Yvonne Cecile de Monchaux (*d* 1978); two *s*. *Educ:* Lancaster Royal Grammar Sch.; Queens' Coll., Cambridge (Hon. Fellow, 1985). MA, FRSC. Research Chemist, H. P. Bulmer & Co, 1948–53; Manufg Manager, Macleans Ltd, 1954–55; Factory Manager, Beecham Products Inc. (USA), 1955–60; Asst Managing Dir, Beecham Research Labs, 1960–62; Vice-Pres. (Marketing), Beecham Products Inc. (USA), 1962–64; Pres., Beecham Research Labs Inc. (USA), 1962–64; Chairman: Food and Drink Div., Beecham Group Ltd, 1964–67; Beecham Products, 1967–84; Man. Dir (Consumer Products) Beecham Gp, 1973–84; Chm. and Chief Exec., Beecham Gp, 1984–85. Dir, Otis Elevator Co. Ltd (UK), 1978–83; Non-Exec. Director: BSC, later British Steel, 1979–94; The Burmah Oil PLC, 1983–89; Amer. Cyanamid Co. (USA), 1986–94; Davy Corp. plc, 1986–91; Gestetner Holdings PLC, 1986–; Laurentian Financial Gp, 1991–. Mem. Egg Re-organisation Commn, 1967–68; Pres., Incorp. Soc. of Brit. Advertisers, 1971–73; Chairman: British Nutrition Foundn, 1970–73; Knitting Sector Gp (formerly Knitting Sector Working Party), NEDO, 1978–90; Bd for Food Studies, Reading Univ., 1983–86; Garment and Textile Sector Gp, NEDO, 1991–93; CAB Internat., 1995–. Vice-Chairman: Proprietary Assoc. of GB, 1968–77; Advertising Assoc., 1973–81; Food and Drink Industries Council, 1973–76; Member: Council and Exec. Cttee, Food Manufrs' Fedn Inc., 1966–85 (Pres., 1974–76); Council, British Nutrition Foundn, 1967–79; Cambridge Univ. Appts Bd, 1969–73; Council, CBI, 1970–86; Council, BIM, 1972–77; Council, Univ. of Buckingham (formerly University Coll. at Buckingham), 1973–; Council, Nat. Coll. of Food Technol., 1977–78 (Chm. Bd, 1978–83); Council, Univ. of Reading, 1978–; AFRC, 1978–84; Council, Trade Policy Res. Centre, 1985–89; Monopolies and Mergers Commn, 1993– (Mem., Newspaper Panel, 1980–92); Industrial Develt Adv. Bd, 1984–93 (Chm., 1985–93); Council and Exec. Cttee, Imperial Soc. of Knights Bachelor, 1986–. Dir and Hon. Treas., Centre for Policy Studies, 1984–93. Trustee, Inst. of Economic Affairs, 1980–93. Governor, Ashridge Management Coll., 1970– (Vice-Chm., 1977–); President: Nat. Advertising Benevolent Soc., 1978–80; Inst. of Packaging, 1981–82 (a Vice-Pres., 1979–81). Fellow, Marketing Soc., 1981; FIMgt; FInstM; FIGD; FRSA; FRSC. Hon. Fellow, Inst. of Food Sci. and Technol., 1983–84. Hon. DSc Reading, 1982; Hon. DSc Lancaster, 1987. *Recreations:* sailing, squash racquets, ski-ing. *Address:* 37 Edwardes Square, W8 6HH. *T:* 0171–603 9010. *Clubs:* Athenæum, Brooks's, Hurlingham, Carlton, Lansdowne, Royal Thames Yacht.

HAM, David Kenneth R.; *see* Rowe-Ham.

HAM, Prof. James Milton, OC 1980; ScD; FIEEE; President, Canadian Academy of Engineering, 1990–91; President and Professor Emeritus, University of Toronto; *b* 21 Sept. 1920; *s* of James Arthur Ham and Harriet Boomer Gandier; *m* Mary Caroline, *d* of Albert William Augustine; one *s* two *d*. *Educ:* Runnymede Coll. Inst., Toronto, 1936–39; Univ. of Toronto (BASc 1943); MIT (SM, ScD). Served with RCNVR as Elect. Lt, 1944–45. Lectr and Housemaster, Univ. of Toronto, 1945–46; Mass Inst. of Technology: Res. Associate, 1949–51; Res. Fellow in Electronics, 1950; Asst Prof. of Elect. Engrg, 1951–52; University of Toronto: Associate Prof., 1952–59; Prof., 1959–88; Prof. of Science, Technology and Public Policy, 1983–88; Pres., 1978–83; Fellow, New Coll., 1963; Head, Dept of Elect. Engrg, 1964–66; Dean, Fac. of Applied Science and Engrg, 1966–73; Chm., Research Bd, 1974–76; Dean, Sch. of Graduate Studies, 1976–78. Vis. Scientist, Cambridge Univ. and USSR, 1960–61. Dir, Shell Canada, 1981–91. Mem., Nat. Res. Council, 1969–74 (Chm., Associate Cttee on Automatic Control, 1959–65); Governor, Ont. Res. Foundn, 1971–86; Chairman: Cttee on Engrg Educn of World Fed. of Engrg Orgs, 1970; Res. and Technol. Review Bd, Noranda Inc., 1985; Industrial Disease Standards Panel, Ont., 1986–88. Member: Assoc. Prof. Engrs, Ont., 1943–; Internat. Fed. Automatic Control (Exec. Council), 1966–72; Fellow: Engrg Inst. Canada; Canadian Academy of Engrg, 1987. Hon. DèsScA Montreal, 1973; Hon. DSc: Queen's, 1974; New Brunswick, 1979; McGill, 1979; McMaster, 1980; Guelph, 1992; Hon. LLD: Manitoba, 1980; Hanyang (Korea), 1981; Concordia Univ., 1983; Hon. DEng: Tech. Univ. of Nova Scotia, 1980; Memorial Univ., 1981; Toronto, 1991; Hon. DSacLet Wycliffe Coll., 1983. British Assoc. for Advancement of Science Medal, 1943; Centennial Medal, 1967, Engrg Medal, 1974, Gold Medal, 1984, Assoc. Professional Engrs, Ontario; Engrg Alumni Medal, 1973; McNaughton Medal, IEEE, 1977; Sir John Kennedy Medal, Engrg Inst. Canada, 1983. Silver Jubilee Medal, 1977; Order of Ontario, 1989; Confederation Medal, 1992. *Publications:* Scientific Basis of Electrical Engineering (with G. R. Slemon), 1961; Report of Royal Commission on Health and Safety of Workers in Mines, 1976; papers for scientific jls on automatic control. *Recreations:* sailing, fractals, photography. *Address:* 135 Glencairn Avenue, Toronto, Ontario M4R 1N1, Canada.

HAMANN, Paul; Head of Documentaries, since 1992, and Deputy Head of Factual Programmes, since 1994, BBC TV; *b* 9 Nov. 1948; *s* of Leonard Hamann and Anita Davies; *m* 1st, 1971, Kay Allen (marr. diss. 1981); one *d*; 2nd, 1981, Marilyn Wheatcroft; one *s* one *d*. Over 50 documentaries for BBC TV, 1976–88; Editor, BBC 1 Documentaries, 1988–92. Awards include: Best Factual Series Award, BAFTA, for The Duty Men, 1987; Grierson Award, BFI, for Fourteen Days in May, 1988. *Publication:* (with Peter Gillman) The Duty Men, 1987. *Recreations:* contemporary art, reading, music, wine, ski-ing. *Address:* c/o BBC TV Centre, W12 7RJ. *T:* 0181–743 8000.

HAMBIDGE, Most Rev. Douglas Walter, DD; Principal, St Mark's Theological College, Dar es Salaam, since 1993; *b* London, England, 6 March 1927; *s* of Douglas Hambidge and Florence (*née* Driscoll); *m* 1956, Denise Colvill Lown; two *s* one *d*. *Educ:* London Univ.; London Coll. of Divinity. BD, ALCD; DD, Anglican Theol. Coll. of BC, 1970. Asst Curate, St Mark's, Dalston, 1953–56; Rector: All Saints, Cassiar, BC, 1956–58; St James, Smithers, BC, 1958–64; Vicar, St Martin, Fort St John, BC, 1964–69; Canon, St Andrew's Cathedral, Caledonia, 1965–69; Bishop of Caledonia, 1969–80; Bishop of New Westminster, 1980; Archbishop of New Westminster and Metropolitan of Province of BC, 1981–93. Mem., ACC, 1990–93 (Mem., Standing Cttee, 1990–93). Pres., Missions to Seamen, 1980–93; Mem. Bd of Governors, Vancouver Sch. of Theology, 1980–85. *Address:* St Mark's Theological College, PO Box 25017, Dar es Salaam, Tanzania.

HAMBLEDEN, 4th Viscount, *cr* 1891; **William Herbert Smith;** *b* 2 April 1930; *e s* of 3rd Viscount and Patricia, GCVO (*d* 1994), *d* of 15th Earl of Pembroke, MVO; *S* father 1948; *m* 1st, 1955, Donna Maria Carmela Attolico di Adelfia (marr. diss. 1988), *d* of late Count Bernardo Attolico and of Contessa Eleonora Attolico di Adelfia, Via Porta Latina, Rome; five *s*; 2nd, 1988, Mrs Lesley Watson. *Educ:* Eton. *Heir: s* Hon. William Henry Bernard Smith [*b* 18 Nov. 1955; *m* 1983, Sarah Suzanne, *d* of Joseph F. Anlauf and Mrs Suzanne K. Anlauf; two *d*]. *Address:* The Estate Office, Hambleden, Henley-on-Thames, Oxon. *T:* Henley-on-Thames (01491) 571252.

See also Baron Margadale.

HAMBLEN, Derek Ivens Archibald, CB 1978; OBE 1956; *b* 28 Oct. 1917; *s* of Leonard Tom Hamblen and late Ruth Mary Hamblen, *d* of Sir William Frederick Alphonse Archibald; *m* 1950, Pauline Alison, *d* of late Gen. Sir William Morgan, GCB, DSO, MC; one *s* one *d*. *Educ:* St Lawrence Coll., Ramsgate; St John's Coll., Oxford (Casberd Exhibn); Portuguese Essay Prize, 1938; BA Hons (Mod. Langs) 1940, MA 1949. Served War, 1940–46: 1st Army, N Africa, 1942–43; Major, GS, AFHQ, N Africa and Italy, and Adv. Mission to British Mil. HQ, Greece, 1944–45; GSO1, Allied Commn for Austria, 1945–46; Lt-Col, 1946. War Office, later Ministry of Defence, 1946–77: seconded HQ British Troops, Egypt, 1946–47; Asst Sec., Office of UK High Commn in Australia, 1951–55; seconded Foreign Office, 1957–60; Asst Sec., 1964–68; a Special Advr to NATO and SHAPE, 1968–74; Under Sec., 1974–77, retired. Mem. Bd of Governors, St Lawrence Coll., 1977–91 (Vice-Pres., 1991–). FRSA 1987. Medal of Merit, 1st cl. (Czechoslovakia), 1946. *Recreations:* cricket, hockey (represented Oxford v Cambridge, 1940), golf, music, reading. *Address:* c/o Lloyds Bank, East Grinstead, West Sussex RH19 1AH. *Clubs:* MCC; Vincent's (Oxford).

HAMBLETON, Prof. Kenneth George, FEng 1994; Professor of Defence Engineering, University College London, since 1991; *b* 15 Jan. 1937; *s* of George William Hambleton and Gertrude Nellie Hambleton (*née* Brighouse); *m* 1959, Glenys Patricia Smith; one *s* one *d*. *Educ:* Chesterfield Grammar Sch.; Queens' Coll., Cambridge (MA). CEng, FIEE; FRAeS. Services Electronics Res. Lab., Baldock, 1958–73; ASWE, Portsdown, 1973–81; a Dep. Dir, ASWE, 1981–82; Dir, Strategic Electronics-Radar, MoD PE, 1982–85; Asst Chief Scientific Advr (Projects and Res.), MoD, 1985–86; Dir Gen., Air Weapons and Electronic Systems, 1986–90, Air 3, 1990–91, MoD. *Publications:* numerous articles and letters in nat. and internat. physics and electronic jls. *Recreations:* chess, bridge, golf, music—especially jazz. *Address:* c/o University College London, Torrington Place, WC1E 7JE. *Club:* City Livery.

HAMBLING, Sir (Herbert) Hugh, 3rd Bt, *cr* 1924; *b* 3 Aug. 1919; *s* of Sir (Herbert) Guy (Musgrave) Hambling, 2nd Bt; *S* father, 1966; *m* 1st, 1950, Anne Page Oswald (*d* 1990), Spokane, Washington, USA; one *s*; 2nd, 1991, Helen, *widow* of David Gavin. Educ: Wixenford Preparatory Sch.; Eton Coll. British Airways Ltd, 1937–39. RAF Training and Atlantic Ferry Command, 1939–46. British Overseas Airways: Montreal, 1948; Seattle, 1950; Manager, Sir Guy Hambling & Son, 1956; BOAC Representative, Douglas, Los Angeles, and Boeing Co., Seattle, 1957–75; Royal Brunei Airlines Rep., Boeing Co., Seattle, 1975. *Heir: s* (Herbert) Peter Hugh Hambling [*b* 6 Sept. 1953; *m* 1991, Lorayn Louise, *d* of late Frank Koson; two *s*]. *Address:* 1219 Evergreen Point Road, Bellevue, WA 98004, USA. *T:* (206) 4540905; Rookery Park, Yoxford, Suffolk IP17 3LQ, England. *T:* Yoxford (01728) 668310.

HAMBLING, Maggi, OBE 1995; artist; *b* 23 Oct. 1945; *d* of Harry Hambling and Marjorie Hambling (*née* Harris). *Educ:* Hadleigh Hall Sch., Suffolk; Amberfield Sch., Suffolk; Ipswich Sch. of Art; Camberwell Sch. of Art (DipAD 1967); Slade Sch. of Fine Art (HDFA 1969). Boise Travel Award, NY, 1969; first Artist in Residence, Nat. Gall., London, 1980–81; Tutor in Painting and Drawing, Morley Coll. *One-man exhibitions include:* Paintings and Drawings, Morley Gall., London, 1973; New Oil Paintings, Warehouse Gall., London, 1977; Drawings and Paintings on View, Nat. Gall., 1981; Pictures of Max Wall, Nat. Portrait Gall., 1983 (and tour); Maggi Hambling, Serpentine Gall., 1987 (and tour); An Eye Through a Decade, Yale Center for British Art, Newhaven, Conn, 1991; Towards Laughter, Northern Centre for Contemporary Art, 1993–94 (and tour); Maggi Hambling, Malborough Fine Art, London, 1996; *public collections include:* Arts Council; Australian Nat. Gall.; Birmingham City Art Gall.; British Council; BM; Contemporary Art Soc.; Gulbenkian Foundn, Lisbon; Harris Mus. and Art Gall., Preston; Imperial War Mus.; Nat. Gall.; Nat. Portrait Gall.; Rugby Collection; Scottish Nat. Gall. of Modern Art, Edinburgh; Scottish Nat. Portrait Gall., Edinburgh; Southampton Art

Gall.; Swindon Art Gall.; Tate Gall.; V&A Mus.; Wakefield Art Gall.; Whitworth Art Gall.; Yale Center for British Art. *Recreation:* tennis. *Address:* Morley College, Westminster Bridge Road, SE1 7HT. *Clubs:* Chelsea Arts, Green Street.

HAMBRO, family name of **Baron Hambro.**

HAMBRO, Baron *cr* 1994 (Life Peer), of Dixton and Dumbleton, in the County of Gloucester; **Charles Eric Alexander Hambro;** Chairman: Hambros PLC, since 1983; Guardian Royal Exchange Assurance, since 1988 (Director, since 1968; Deputy Chairman, 1974–88); *b* 24 July 1930; *s* of late Sir Charles Hambro, KBE, MC, and Pamela Cobbold; *m* 1st, 1954, Rose Evelyn (marr. diss. 1976), *d* of Sir Richard Cotterell, 5th Bt, CBE; two *s* one *d*; 2nd, 1976, Cherry Felicity, *d* of Sir John Huggins, GCMG, MC. *Educ:* Eton. Served Coldstream Guards, 1949–51; joined Hambros Bank Ltd, 1952: Man. Dir, 1957; Dep. Chm., 1965; Chm., 1972–83; Director: P&OSN Co., 1987–; Taylor Woodrow, 1962–; General Oriental Investments; San Paolo Bank Hldgs (formerly Istituto Bancario San Paolo di Torino), 1989–. Chm., Royal National Pension Fund for Nurses, 1968. Trustee, British Museum, 1984–94. *Recreations:* shooting, farming, forestry. *Address:* Dixton Manor, Gotherington, Cheltenham, Glos GL52 4RB. *T:* Bishops Cleeve (0124267) 2011. *Clubs:* White's, Carlton, MCC.

HAMBRO, James Daryl; Managing Director, J. O. Hambro & Co., since 1994; *b* 22 March 1949; *s* of late Jocelyn Hambro, MC and Ann Silvia Hambro (*née* Muir); *m* 1981, Diana Cherry; three *d*. *Educ:* Eton College; Harvard Business Sch. Hambros Bank, 1970–85 (Exec. Dir, 1982–85); J. O. Hambro & Co., 1986–. Gov., Peabody Trust; Trustee, Henry Smith's Charity; Chm., Internat. Students' Trust. *Recreations:* shooting, golf. *Address:* 15 Elm Park Road, SW3 6BP. *T:* 0171–352 0526; Manor Farm, Kimberley, Wymondham, Norfolk NR9 4DT. *T:* Norwich (01603) 759329. *Clubs:* White's, Pratt's; Royal West Norfolk.
See also R. A. Hambro, R. N. Hambro.

HAMBRO, Richard Alexander; Chairman, J. O. Hambro Investment Management Co., since 1986; *b* 1 Oct. 1946; 2nd *s* of late Jocelyn Olaf Hambro, MC; *m* 1st, 1973, Hon. Charlotte Soames (marr. diss. 1982); one *d*; 2nd, 1984, Juliet Mary Elizabeth Grana (*née* Harvey) (marr. diss. 1992); 3rd, 1993, Mary James (*née* Briggs). *Educ:* Eton; Univ. of Munich. Joined Hambros Bank, 1966, Director, 1979; Pres., Hambro America Inc., 1977–82; Chairman: I. Hennig & Co., 1982–; Lynton Group Inc., 1986–; Hattron, 1992–; Director: Wilton's (St James's), 1982–; J. O. Hambro & Co., 1986–; Chm., Cancer Relief Macmillan Fund, 1991–. *Recreations:* golf, shooting, horse breeding. *Address:* Waverton House, Sezincote, Moreton-in-Marsh, Glos GL56 9TB. *T:* Blockley (01386) 700700; 4 Egerton Place, SW3 2EF. *T:* 0171–589 7483. *Clubs:* Pratt's, Turf, White's; The Brook (New York) (Gov.).
See also J. D. Hambro, R. N. Hambro.

HAMBRO, Rupert Nicholas; Chairman, J. O. Hambro & Co., since 1994 (Group Managing Director, 1986–94); *b* 27 June 1943; *s* of late Jocelyn Olaf Hambro, MC and Ann Silvia (*née* Muir); *m* 1970, Mary Robinson Boyer; one *s* one *d*. *Educ:* Eton; Aix-en-Provence. Joined Hambros Bank, 1964, Director, 1969, Chm., 1983–86; Director: Anglo American Corporation of South Africa, 1981–; Racecourse Hldgs Trust Ltd, 1985–94; The Telegraph (formerly Daily Telegraph) PLC, 1986–; Sedgwick Group plc, 1987–92; Triton Europe plc, 1987–90; Pioneer Concrete Hldgs PLC, 1989–; Hamleys plc, 1988–; Chairman: Wilton's (St James's) Ltd, 1987–; J. O. Hambro Magan Irby Hldgs (formerly J. O. Hambro Magan Group) Ltd, 1988–; Mayflower Corp. Plc, 1988–; Internat. Adv. Bd, Montana AG, Vienna, 1988–; Fenchurch plc, 1993–; CTR Group PLC, 1990–. Chm., Assoc. of International Bond Dealers, 1979–82; Member: SE Econ. Planning Council, 1971–74; Internat. Council, US Information Agency, 1988–. Vice-Chm., NABC, 1991–; Chairman: Trustees, Boys' Club Trust; Silver Trust; Trustee, Partners of the World, 1990–. Dep. Pres., Anglo-Danish Soc., 1987–. Liveryman: Fishmongers' Co, 1969–; Goldsmiths' Co., 1994–. Knight of the Falcon (Iceland), 1986. *Recreations:* racing, shooting, walking. *Address:* 30 Queen Anne's Gate, SW1H 9AL. *T:* 0171–222 2020, *Fax:* 0171–222 1993. *Clubs:* White's, Pratt's, Portland; Jupiter Island (Florida).

HAMBURGER, Michael Peter Leopold, OBE 1992; MA (Oxon); *b* Berlin, 22 March 1924; *e s* of late Prof. Richard Hamburger and Mrs L. Hamburger (*née* Hamburg); *m* 1951, Anne Ellen File; one *s* two *d*. *Educ:* Westminster Sch.; Christ Church, Oxford. Army Service, 1943–47; Freelance Writer, 1948–52; Asst Lectr in German, UCL, 1952–55; Lectr, then Reader in German, Univ. of Reading, 1955–64. Florence Purington Lectr, Mount Holyoke Coll., Mass, 1966–67; Visiting Professor, State Univ. of NY: at Buffalo, 1969; at Stony Brook, 1971; Vis. Fellow, Center for Humanities, Wesleyan Univ., Conn, 1970; Vis. Prof. Univ. of S Carolina, 1973; Regent's Lectr, Univ. of California, San Diego, 1973; Vis. Prof., Boston Univ., 1975–77; part-time Prof., Univ. of Essex, 1978. Bollingen Foundn Fellow, 1959–61, 1965–66. FRSL 1972–86. Corresp. Mem., Deutsche Akademie für Sprache und Dichtung, Darmstadt, 1973. Hon. LittD UEA, 1988. Translation Prizes: Deutsche Akademie für Sprache und Dichtung, Darmstadt, 1964; Arts Council, 1969; Arts Prize, Inter Nationes, Bonn, 1976; Medal, Inst. of Linguists, 1977; Schlegel-Tieck Prize, London, 1978, 1981; Wilhelm-Heinse Prize (medallion), Mainz, 1978; Goethe Medal, 1986; Austrian State Prize for Literary Translation, 1988. *Publications: poetry:* Flowering Cactus, 1950; Poems 1950–1951, 1952; The Dual Site, 1958; Weather and Season, 1963; Feeding the Chickadees, 1968; Penguin Modern Poets (with A. Brownjohn and C. Tomlinson), 1969; Travelling, 1969; Travelling, I-V, 1973; Ownerless Earth, 1973; Travelling VI, 1975; Real Estate, 1977; Moralities, 1977; Variations, 1981; Collected Poems, 1984; Trees, 1988; Selected Poems, 1988; Roots in the Air, 1991; Collected Poems 1941–1994, 1995; *translations:* Poems of Hölderlin, 1943, rev. edn as Hölderlin: Poems, 1952; C. Baudelaire, Twenty Prose Poems, 1946, repr. 1968 and 1988; L. van Beethoven, Letters, Journals and Conversations, 1951, repr. 1967 and 1984; J. C. F. Hölderlin, Selected Verse, 1961, repr. 1986; G. Trakl, Decline, 1952; A. Goes, The Burnt Offering, 1956; (with others) H. von Hofmannsthal, Poems and Verse Plays, 1961; B. Brecht, Tales from the Calendar, 1961; (with C. Middleton) Modern German Poetry 1910–1960, 1962; (with others) H. von Hofmannsthal, Selected Plays and Libretti, 1964; G. Büchner, Lenz, 1966; H. M. Enzensberger, Poems, 1966; (with C. Middleton) G. Grass, Selected Poems, 1966; J. C. F. Hölderlin, Poems and Fragments, 1967, new enlarged edn 1994; (with J. Rothenberg and the author) H. M. Enzensberger, The Poems of Hans Magnus Enzensberger, 1968; H. M. Enzensberger, Poems For People Who Don't Read Poems, 1968; (with C. Middleton), G. Grass, The Poems of Günter Grass, 1969; P. Bichsel, And Really Frau Blum Would Very Much Like To Meet The Milkman, 1968; G. Eich, Journeys, 1968; N. Sachs, Selected Poems, 1968; Peter Bichsel, Stories for Children, 1971; Paul Celan, Poems, 1972, new enlarged edn, as Poems of Paul Celan, 1988 (European Translation Prize, 1990), 3rd edn 1995; (ed) East German Poetry, 1972; Peter Huchel, Selected Poems, 1974; German Poetry 1910–1975, 1977; Helmut Heissenbüttel, Texts, 1977; Franco Fortini, Poems, 1978; An Unofficial Rilke, 1981; Peter Huchel, The Garden of Theophrastus, 1983; Goethe, Poems and Epigrams, 1983; Günter Eich, Pigeons and Moles, 1991; H. M. Enzensberger, Selected Poems, 1994; *prose:* Testimonies, selected shorter prose 1950–1987, 1989; *criticism:* Reason and Energy, 1957; From Prophecy to Exorcism, 1965; The Truth of Poetry, 1970, new edn 1982; Hugo von Hofmannsthal, 1973; Art as Second Nature, 1975; A Proliferation of Prophets, 1983; After the Second Flood: essays in modern German Literature, 1986; *memoirs:* A Mug's Game, 1973, rev. edn as String of Beginnings, 1991. *Recreations:* gardening, walking. *Address:* c/o John Johnson Ltd, Clerkenwell House, 45/47 Clerkenwell Green, EC1R 0HT.
See also P. B. Hamlyn.

HAMBURGER, Sir Sidney (Cyril), Kt 1981; CBE 1966; JP; DL; Chairman, North Western Regional Health Authority, 1973–82; *b* 14 July 1914; *s* of Isidore and Hedwig Hamburger; *m* 1940; three *s*. *Educ:* Salford Grammar Sch. Served in Army, 1940–46, Capt. Salford City Council: Mem., 1946–70; Alderman, 1961–70; Mayor of Salford, 1968–69. Pres., Gtr Manchester Area CAB, 1990– (Chm., 1985–90); Chairman: NE Manchester Hosp. Management Cttee, 1970–74; NW ASH, 1977–; Age Concern, Salford, 1984–; Manchester Cttee for Soviet Jewry, 1984–; Member: NW Electricity Bd Consultative Council, 1953–59 (Chm. Manchester Cttee, 1963–68); Manchester Regional Hosp. Bd, 1966–74 (Chm. Finance Cttee); Supplementary Benefits Commn, 1967–77; BBC NW Adv. Cttee, 1970–73; Manchester Univ. Court, 1973–84. President: Council, Manchester-Salford Jews, 1962–65; Jt Israel Appeal, Manchester, 1984–; Life-President: Manchester Jewish Homes for the Aged, 1965–; Zionist Central Council of Greater Manchester; Vice-Pres., Friends of Israel Assoc., Manchester; Nat. Pres., Trades Advisory Council, 1984–; Pres., Motability NW, 1989–; Vice-Pres., British Lung Foundn, 1987–. Governor, Ben Gurion Univ., Israel, 1979–. Hon. Fellow, Bar-Ilan Univ., Israel, 1979; Hon. MA Salford, 1979; Hon. LLD Manchester, 1983. Pro Ecclesia, Papal Award, 1982. JP Salford, 1957; DL Greater Manchester, 1981. *Recreation:* football. *Address:* 26 New Hall Road, Salford M7 0JU.

HAMEED, Hon. A. C. Shahul; MP Harispattuwa, Sri Lanka, since 1960; Minister of Foreign Affairs, Sri Lanka, 1977–89 and since 1993; *b* 10 April 1929; *m*; two *s* one *d*. Mem., United National Party; former Dep. Chm., Public Accounts Cttee; has been concerned with foreign affairs, public finance and higher education; Minister of Higher Educn, Science and Technology, 1989–90; Minister of Justice and of Higher Educn, 1990–93. Leader of delegns to internat. confs, incl. UN; Chm., Ministerial Conf. of Non-Aligned Countries, 1977–79; Mem., Conf. of UN Cttee on Disarmament, 1989–93. Governor, Univ. of Sri Lanka. *Publications:* In Pursuit of Peace: on non-alignment and regional cooperation, 1983; Owl and the Lotus, 1986; Disarmament—a multilateral approach, 1988; Foreign Policy Perspectives of Sri Lanka, 1988; short stories and poems. *Address:* Ministry of Foreign Affairs, Republic Building, Colombo 1, Sri Lanka.

HAMER, Hon. Sir Rupert (James), AC 1992; KCMG 1982; ED; LLM (Melb.); FAIM; Premier of Victoria, Australia, and Treasurer, 1972–81; *b* 29 July 1916; *s* of H. R. Hamer; *m* 1944, April F., *d* of N. R. Mackintosh; two *s* two *d*. *Educ:* Melbourne Grammar and Geelong Grammar Schs; Trinity Coll., Univ. of Melbourne (LLM; Fellow, 1982). Solicitor, admitted 1940. Served War of 1939–45: 5½ years, AIF, Tobruk, Alamein, NG, Normandy. MLA (Lib.) E Yarra, 1958–71, Kew, Vic., 1971–81; Minister for: Immigration, 1962–64; Local Govt, 1964–71; Chief Sec. and Dep. Premier, Victoria, 1971–72; Minister for: the Arts, 1972–79; State Develt, Decentralization and Tourism, 1979–81. Chairman: Vic. State Opera; Friends of Royal Botanic Gdns, Melbourne, 1992–. Vice-Chm., Cttee of Management, Werribee Park; Nat. Pres., Save the Children Fund (Australia), 1989–; President: Vic. Coll. of the Arts, 1982–; Greenhouse Action, Australia, 1989–; Consultative Council on Cancer & Heart Disease, 1994–; Mem., Melbourne Scots Council, 1981–. Chieftain, Vic. Pipe Bands Assoc., 1976–; Trustee: Yarra Bend Park, 1974–; Melbourne Cricket Ground, 1976–. CO, Vic. Scottish Regt, CMF, 1954–58. Hon. LLD Univ. of Melbourne, 1982; DUniv Swinburne, 1995. *Recreations:* tennis, Australian Rules football, walking, music. *Address:* 35 Heather Grove, Kew, Victoria 3101, Australia. *Club:* Naval and Military.

HAMILL, Sir Patrick, Kt 1984; QPM 1979; Chief Constable, Strathclyde Police, 1977–85; *b* 29 April 1930; *s* of Hugh Hamill and Elizabeth McGowan; *m* 1954, Nell Gillespie; four *s* one *d*. *Educ:* St Patrick's High Sch., Dumbarton; Open Univ. (BA). Joined Dunbartonshire Constabulary, 1950; transf. to City of Glasgow Police, 1972; apptd Assistant Chief Constable: Glasgow, 1974; Strathclyde Police, 1975; attended Royal Coll. of Defence Studies Course, 1976. Assoc. of Chief Police Officers (Scotland): Rep. to Interpol, 1977–81; Pres., 1982–83; Hon. Sec., 1983–85. Chm., Management Bd, St Margaret's Hospice, Clydebank, 1986–; Member Board of Governors: Scottish Police Coll., 1977–85; St Aloysius' Coll., Glasgow, 1983–90 (Vice-Chm., 1986–90); St Andrew's Coll. of Educn, Bearsden, 1987–88; Mem., Gen. Convocation, Univ. of Strathclyde, 1984–87. OStJ 1978. *Recreations:* walking, reading history, golf.

HAMILTON, family name of **Duke of Abercorn,** of **Lord Belhaven,** and of **Barons Hamilton of Dalzell** and **HolmPatrick.**

HAMILTON; *see* Baillie-Hamilton, family name of Earl of Haddington.

HAMILTON; *see* Douglas-Hamilton.

HAMILTON, 15th Duke of, *cr* 1643, Scotland, **AND BRANDON,** 12th Duke of, *cr* 1711, Great Britain; **Angus Alan Douglas Douglas-Hamilton;** Premier Peer of Scotland; Hereditary Keeper of Palace of Holyroodhouse; *b* 13 Sept. 1938; *e s* of 14th Duke of Hamilton and Brandon, PC, KT, GCVO, AFC, and of Lady Elizabeth Percy, OBE, DL, *er d* of 8th Duke of Northumberland, KG; *S* father, 1973; *m* 1st, 1972, Sarah (marr. diss. 1987; she *d* 1994), *d* of Sir Walter Scott, 4th Bt; two *s* two *d*; 2nd, 1988, Jillian, *d* of late Noel Robertson, Sydney, Australia. *Educ:* Eton; Balliol Coll., Oxford (MAEngrg). Flt Lieut RAF; invalided, 1967. Flying Instructor, 1965; Sen. Commercial Pilot's Licence, 1967; Test Pilot, Scottish Aviation, 1971–72. Mem. Council, CRC, 1978–. Mem., Queen's Body Guard for Scotland, 1975–. Hon. Mem., Royal Scottish Pipers Soc., 1977; Patron, British Airways Pipe Band, 1977–. Hon. Air Cdre, No 2 (City of Edinburgh) Maritime HQ Unit, RAuxAF, 1982–. KStJ 1975 (Prior, Order of St John in Scotland, 1975–82). *Publication:* Maria R, 1991. *Heir:* *s* Marquess of Douglas and Clydesdale, *qv*. *Address:* Lennoxlove, Haddington, E Lothian EH41 4NZ. *T:* Haddington (0162082) 3720. *Clubs:* Royal Air Force; New (Edinburgh).
See also Lord James Douglas-Hamilton.

HAMILTON, Marquess of; James Harold Charles Hamilton; *b* 19 Aug. 1969; *s* and *heir* of Duke of Abercorn, *qv*. A Page of Honour to the Queen, 1982–84. *Address:* Barons Court, Omagh, Co. Tyrone BT78 4EZ.

HAMILTON OF DALZELL, 4th Baron *cr* 1886; **James Leslie Hamilton;** DL; *b* 11 Feb. 1938; *s* of 3rd Baron Hamilton of Dalzell, GCVO, MC and Rosemary Olive (*d* 1993), *d* of Maj. Hon. Sir John Coke, KCVO; *S* father, 1990; *m* 1967, Corinna, *yr d* of Sir Pierson Dixon, GCMG, CB; four *s* (incl. twins). *Educ:* Eton. Served Coldstream Guards, 1956–58. Mem., Stock Exchange, 1967–80. Dir, Rowton Hotels plc, 1978–84; Chm., Queen Elizabeth's Foundn for the Disabled, 1989–. DL Surrey, 1993. *Heir:* *s* Hon. Gavin Goulburn Hamilton, *b* 8 Oct. 1968. *Address:* Stockton House, Stockton, Norton Shifnal, Salop TF11 9EF; Betchworth House, Betchworth, Surrey RH3 7AE.
See also Rt Hon. Sir A. G. Hamilton.

HAMILTON, Hon. Lord; Arthur Campbell Hamilton; a Senator of the College of Justice in Scotland, since 1995; *b* 10 June 1942; *s* of James Whitehead Hamilton and Isobel Walker Hamilton (*née* McConnell); *m* 1970, Christine Ann Croll; one *d*. *Educ:* The High School of Glasgow; Glasgow Univ.; Worcester Coll., Oxford (BA); Edinburgh Univ. (LLB). Admitted member, Faculty of Advocates, 1968; QC (Scot.) 1982; Standing Junior Counsel: to Scottish Development Dept, 1975–78; to Board of Inland Revenue (Scotland), 1978–82; Advocate Depute, 1982–85; Judge, Courts of Appeal, Jersey and Guernsey, 1988–95; Pres., Pensions Appeal Tribunals for Scotland, 1992–95. *Recreations:* hill walking, fishing, music, history. *Address:* 8 Heriot Row, Edinburgh EH3 6HU. *T:* 0131–556 4663. *Club:* New (Edinburgh).

HAMILTON (NZ), Bishop of, (RC), since 1994; **Rt Rev. Denis George Browne;** *b* 21 Sept. 1937; *s* of Neville John Browne and Catherine Anne Browne (*née* Moroney). *Educ:* Holy Name Seminary, Christchurch, NZ; Holy Cross College, Mosgiel, NZ. Assistant Priest: Gisborne, 1963–67; Papatoetoe, 1968–71; Remuera, 1972–74; Missionary in Tonga, 1975–77; Bishop of Rarotonga, 1977–83; Bishop of Auckland, 1983–94. Hon. DD. *Recreation:* golf. *Address:* Chanel Park, PO Box 4353, Hamilton East, New Zealand.

HAMILTON, Adrian Walter, QC 1973; a Recorder of the Crown Court, since 1974; *b* 11 March 1923; *er s* of late W. G. M. Hamilton, banker, Fletching, Sussex and of late Mrs S. E. Hamilton; *m* 1966, Jill, *d* of S. R. Brimblecombe, Eastbourne; two *d*. *Educ:* Highgate Sch.; Balliol Coll., Oxford. BA 1st cl. Jurisprudence 1948, MA 1954. Served with RN, 1942–46: Ord. Seaman, 1942; Sub-Lt RNVR, 1943, Lieut 1946. Balliol Coll., 1946–48: Jenkyns Law Prize; Paton Mem. Student, 1948–49; Cassel Scholar, Lincoln's Inn, 1949; called to Bar, Lincoln's Inn, 1949 (Bencher 1979), Middle Temple and Inner Temple; Mem., Senate of Inns of Court and the Bar, 1976–82, Treas., 1979–82; Mem. Council, Inns of Court, 1987–91. Mem., Council of Legal Educn, 1977–87. Inspector, Peek Foods Ltd, 1977. *Recreations:* family, golf, sailing, gardening. *Address:* 7 King's Bench Walk, Temple, EC4Y 7DS. *T:* 0171–583 0404. *Clubs:* Garrick, Roehampton; Piltdown Golf.

HAMILTON, Adrianne Pauline U.; *see* Uziell-Hamilton.

HAMILTON, Rt. Rev. Alexander Kenneth, MA; Hon. Assistant Bishop, Diocese of Bath and Wells, since 1988; *b* 11 May 1915; *s* of Cuthbert Arthur Hamilton and Agnes Maud Hamilton; unmarried. *Educ:* Malvern Coll.; Trinity Hall, Cambridge; Westcott House, Cambridge. MA 1941. Asst Curate of Birstall, Leicester, 1939–41; Asst Curate of Whitworth with Spennymoor, 1941–45. Chaplain, RNVR, 1945–47. Vicar of S Francis, Ashton Gate, Bristol, 1947–58; Vicar of S John the Baptist, Newcastle upon Tyne, 1958–65; Rural Dean of Central Newcastle, 1962–65; Bishop Suffragan of Jarrow, 1965–80. *Publication:* Personal Prayers, 1963. *Recreations:* golf, trout fishing. *Address:* 3 Ash Tree Road, Burnham-on-Sea, Somerset TA8 2LB. *Clubs:* Naval; Burnham and Berrow Golf.

HAMILTON, Alexander Macdonald, CBE 1979; Senior Partner, 1977–90, Consultant, 1990–94, McGrigor Donald, Solicitors, Glasgow; *b* 11 May 1925; *s* of John Archibald Hamilton and Thomasina Macdonald or Hamilton; *m* 1953, Catherine Gray; two *s* one *d*. *Educ:* Hamilton Acad. (Dux, 1943); Glasgow Univ. (MA 1948, LLB 1951). Solicitor. Served War, RNVR, 1943–46. Dir, Royal Bank of Scotland, 1978– (Vice Chm., 1990–). Law Soc. of Scotland: Mem. Council, 1970–82; Vice-Pres., 1975–76; Pres., 1977–78. Pres., Glasgow Juridical Soc., 1955–56. Vice-Pres. and Chm., Greater Glasgow Scout Council, 1978–85; Cttee Chm., Scottish Council, Scout Assoc., 1986–92. Sec., Cambuslang Old Parish Church, 1991– (Session Clerk, 1969–91); Vice-Chm., Cambuslang Community Council, 1978–94. *Recreations:* golf, sailing. *Address:* 30 Wellshot Drive, Cambuslang, Glasgow G72 8BT. *T:* 0141–641 1445. *Clubs:* Royal Scottish Automobile (Glasgow); Royal Northern & Clyde Yacht.

HAMILTON, Rt. Hon. Sir Archibald (Gavin), Kt 1994; PC 1991; MP (C) Epsom and Ewell, since April 1978; Minister of State, Ministry of Defence, 1988–93; *b* 30 Dec. 1941; *yr s* of 3rd Baron Hamilton of Dalzell, GCVO, MC; *m* 1968, Anne Catharine Napier; three *d*. *Educ:* Eton Coll. Borough Councillor, Kensington and Chelsea, 1968–71. Contested (C) Dagenham, Feb. and Oct., 1974. PPS to Sec. of State for Energy, 1979–81, to Sec. of State for Transport, 1981–82; an Asst Govt Whip, 1982–84; a Lord Comr of HM Treasury (Govt Whip), 1984–86; Parly Under-Sec. of State for Defence Procurement, MoD, 1986–87; PPS to Prime Minister, 1987–88. Mem., Intelligence and Security Cttee, 1994–. Gov., Westminster Foundn for Democracy, 1993–. *Address:* House of Commons, SW1A 0AA.

HAMILTON, Arthur Campbell; *see* Hamilton, Hon. Lord.

HAMILTON, Arthur Richard C.; *see* Cole-Hamilton.

HAMILTON, Donald Rankin Douglas; His Honour Judge Donald Hamilton; a Circuit Judge, since 1994; *b* 15 June 1946; *s* of Allister McNicoll Hamilton and Mary Glen Hamilton (*née* Rankin); *m* 1974, (Margaret) Ruth Peuens; one *s* one *d*. *Educ:* Rugby Sch.; Balliol Coll., Oxford (BA). Called to the Bar, Gray's Inn, 1969 (Atkin Schol.); pupillage in Birmingham, 1970–71; practised in Birmingham, 1971–74. Mem., Council of Mgt, CBSO, 1974–80; Dir, CBSO Soc. Ltd, 1984–; Trustee, City of Birmingham Orchestral Endowment Fund. *Recreation:* music. *Address:* c/o Circuit Administrator, Lord Chancellor's Department, 2 Newton Street, Birmingham B4 7LU.

HAMILTON, Douglas Owens; Senior Partner, Norton Rose (formerly Norton, Rose, Botterell & Roche), 1982–94; *b* 20 April 1931; *s* of Oswald Hamilton and Edith Florence Hamilton; *m* 1962, Judith Mary Wood; three *s*. *Educ:* John Fisher Sch., Purley, Surrey; Univ. of London (LLB). Admitted Solicitor, 1953; joined Botterell & Roche, 1955, Partner, 1959; Exec. Partner, Norton, Rose, Botterell & Roche, 1976–82. Mem., Chancellor's Court of Benefactors, Oxford Univ., 1990–94, Vice-Chm., Marine Soc., 1993–; Hon. Treasurer: British Maritime Charitable Foundn, 1987–; British Polish Legal Assoc., 1989–93. *Recreation:* travelling. *Address:* Boarsney, Salehurst, near Robertsbridge, East Sussex TN32 5SR.

HAMILTON, Dundas; *see* Hamilton, J. D.

HAMILTON, Eben William; QC 1981; *b* 12 June 1937; *s* of late Rev. John Edmund Hamilton, MC and Hon. Lilias Hamilton (*née* Maclay); *m* 1st, 1973, Catherine Harvey (marr. diss. 1977); 2nd, 1985, Themy Rusi Bilimoria, *y d* of late Brig. Rusi Bilimoria. *Educ:* Winchester; Trinity Coll., Cambridge. Nat. Service: 4/7 Royal Dragoon Guards, 1955–57; Fife and Forfar Yeomanry/Scottish Horse, TA, 1958–66. Called to the Bar, Inner Temple, 1962, Bencher, 1985. Jt DTI Inspector, Atlantic Computers plc, 1990–94. FRSA 1988. *Address:* 1 New Square, Lincoln's Inn, WC2A 3SA. *T:* 0171–405 0884. *Club:* Garrick.
See also Martha Hamilton.

HAMILTON, Sir Edward (Sydney), 7th and 5th Bt, *cr* 1776 and 1819; *b* 14 April 1925; *s* of Sir (Thomas) Sydney (Percival) Hamilton, 6th and 4th Bt, and Bertha Muriel, *d* of James Russell King, Singleton Park, Kendal; *S* father, 1966. *Educ:* Canford Sch. Served Royal Engineers, 1943–47; 1st Royal Sussex Home Guard, 1953–56. *Recreations:* Spiritual matters, music. *Heir:* none. *Address:* The Cottage, East Lavant, near Chichester, West Sussex PO18 0AL. *T:* Chichester (01243) 527414.

HAMILTON, Prof. George Heard; Director, Sterling and Francine Clark Art Institute, 1966–77, now Emeritus; Professor of Art, Williams College, Williamstown, Massachusetts, 1966–75, now Emeritus; Director of Graduate Studies in Art History, Williams College, 1971–75; *b* 23 June 1910; *s* of Frank A. Hamilton and Georgia Neale Heard; *m* 1945, Polly Wiggin; one *s* one *d*. *Educ:* Yale Univ. BA 1932; MA 1934; PhD 1942. Research Asst, Walters Art Gallery, Baltimore, 1934–36; Mem. Art History Faculty, Yale Univ., 1936–66 (Prof., 1956–66); Robert Sterling Clark Prof. of Art, Williams Coll., 1963–64. Slade Prof. of Fine Art, Cambridge Univ., 1971–72; Kress Prof. in Residence, Nat. Gall of Art, Washington, DC, 1978–79. FRSA 1973; Fellow, Amer. Acad. of Arts and Science, 1979. Hon. LittD Williams Coll., 1977; Wilbur Lucius Cross Medal, Yale Grad. Sch., 1977; Amer. Art Dealers' Assoc. award for excellence in art hist., 1978. *Publications:* (with D. V. Thompson, Jr) De Arte Illuminandi, 1933; Manet and His Critics, 1954; The Art and Architecture of Russia, 1954; Monet's Paintings of Rouen Cathedral, 1960; European Painting and Sculpture, 1880–1940, 1967; (with W. C. Agee) Raymond Duchamp-Villon, 1967; 19th and 20th Century Art: Painting, Sculpture, Architecture, 1970; Articles in Burlington Magazine, Gazette des Beaux-Arts, Art Bulletin, etc. *Recreations:* music, gardening. *Address:* 121 Gale Road, Williamstown, MA 01267, USA. *T:* (413) 4588626. *Clubs:* Century Association (New York); Elizabethan (New Haven); Edgartown Yacht (Mass).

HAMILTON, Graeme Montagu, TD; QC 1978; a Recorder of the Crown Court, since 1974; *b* 1 June 1934; *s* of late Leslie Montagu Hamilton and of Joan Lady Burbidge (Joan Elizabeth Burbidge, *née* Moxey); *m* 1978, Mrs Deirdre Lynn. *Educ:* Eton; Magdalene Coll., Cambridge (MA). National Service, 4/7 Royal Dragoon Guards, 1953–55. Called to Bar, Gray's Inn, 1959, Bencher, 1987; Mem., Senate of Inns of Court and Bar, 1975–78. Mem., Criminal Injuries Compensation Bd, 1987–. Gen. Comr of Income Tax, 1989–. TA City of London Yeomanry, Inns of Court and City Yeomanry, 1955–70. *Recreations:* sailing, shooting, gardening. *Address:* 2 Crown Office Row, Temple, EC4Y 7HJ. *Clubs:* Cavalry and Guards, Royal Thames Yacht, Royal Automobile; Western (Glasgow); Royal Hong Kong Jockey.

HAMILTON, Brig. Hugh Gray Wybrants, CBE 1964 (MBE 1945); DL; Chairman, Forces Help Society and Lord Roberts Workshops, 1976–91; *b* 16 May 1918; *s* of Lt-Col H. W. Hamilton, late 5th Dragoon Guards; *m* 1944, Claire Buxton; two *d*. *Educ:* Wellington Coll., Berks; Peterhouse, Cambridge; Royal Mil. Academy. Commissioned with Royal Engineers, 1938. War Service in BEF, BNAF, BLA, 1939–45. Post War Service in Australia, BAOR, France and UK. Instructor, Army Staff Coll., Camberley, 1954–56; Student, IDC, 1965; retired, 1968. Gen. Manager, Corby Develt Corp., 1968–80. DL Northants, 1977. *Recreations:* riding, sailing, DIY. *Address:* Cherwell House, Hogg End, Chipping Warden, Banbury OX17 1LY. *T:* Chipping Warden (01295) 660656.

HAMILTON, Iain Ellis, BMus, FRAM; composer; pianist; Mary Duke Biddle Professor of Music, Duke University, North Carolina, USA, 1962–78 (Chairman of the Department, 1966); *b* Glasgow, 6 June 1922; *s* of James and Catherine Hamilton. *Educ:* Mill Hill; Royal Academy of Music. Engineer (Handley Page Ltd), 1939–46; RAM (Scholar) 1947–51; BMus (London University), 1951. Lecturer at Morley Coll., 1952–58; Lecturer, London Univ., 1956–60. Prizes and awards include: Prize of Royal Philharmonic Society, 1951; Prize of Koussevitsky Foundation (America), 1951; Butterworth Award, 1954; Arnold Bax Gold Medal, 1956; Ralph Vaughan Williams Award, Composers' Guild of GB, 1975. FRAM, 1960. Chm. Composers' Guild, 1958; Chm. ICA Music Cttee, 1958–60. *Works: orchestral works:* Symphonies; Sinfonia for two orchestras (Edinburgh Festival Commission); Concertos, for piano, clarinet, organ, violin and harp; The Bermudas, for baritone, chorus and orchestra (BBC Commission); Symphonic Variations for string orchestra; Overture, Bartholomew Fair; Overture, 1912; Ecossaise; Concerto for jazz trumpet and orchestra (BBC Commn); Scottish Dances; 5 Love Songs for tenor and orchestra; Jubilee; Arias for small orchestra; Vers Apollinaire, for orch.; Epitaph for this World and Time: 3 choruses and 2 organs; Vespers, for chorus, 2 pianos, harp and percussion; Voyage for horn and orchestra; Alastor; Amphion for violin and orchestra; Commedia; Threnos for solo organ; Aubade and Paraphrase for solo organ; Clerk Saunders, a ballet; BBC Commissions: Cantos; Circus; The Transit of Jupiter; *chamber works include:* four String Quartets; String Octet; Sonatas for piano, viola, clarinet, flute and oboe; Sonata for chamber orchestra; Flute Quartet; Clarinet Quintet; 3 Nocturnes for clarinet and piano; 5 Scenes for trumpet and piano; Sextet; Sonatas and Variants for 10 winds; Antigone for Winds; Octet for Winds; Dialogues for soprano and 5 instruments; Nocturnes with Cadenzas for solo piano; 4 Border Songs, The Fray of Suport, a Requiem and a Mass for unaccompanied voices; St Mark Passion for 4 soloists, chorus and orchestra; Cleopatra for soprano and orchestra; Sextet for Strings; Prometheus, for soloists, chorus and orch.; La Mort de Phèdre, for mezzo-soprano and orch.; *opera:* Agamemnon; Royal Hunt of the Sun; Pharsalia; The Catiline Conspiracy; Tamburlaine; Anna Karenina; Lancelot; Raleigh's Dream; The Tragedy of Macbeth; London's Fair. Music for theatre and films. Hon. DMus Glasgow, 1970. *Publications:* articles for many journals. *Address:* Flat 4, 85 Cornwall Gardens, SW7 4XY.

HAMILTON, Ian; poet; *b* 24 March 1938; *s* of Robert Tough Hamilton and Daisy McKay; *m* 1st, 1963, Gisela Dietzel; one *s*; 2nd, 1981, Ahdaf Soueif; two *s*. *Educ:* Darlington Grammar Sch.; Keble Coll., Oxford (BA Hons). Editor, Review, 1962–72; Poetry and Fiction Editor, Times Literary Supplement, 1965–73; Lectr in Poetry, Univ. of Hull, 1972–73; Editor, The New Review, 1974–79. Presenter, Bookmark (BBC TV series), 1984–87. E. C. Gregory Award, 1963; Malta Cultural Award, 1974. *Publications:* (ed) The Poetry of War 1939–45, 1965; (ed) Alun Lewis: poetry and prose, 1966; (ed) The Modern Poet, 1968; The Visit (poems), 1970; A Poetry Chronicle, 1973; (ed) Robert Frost: selected poems, 1973; The Little Magazines, 1976; Returning (poems), 1976; Robert Lowell: a biography, 1983; (ed) Yorkshire in Verse, 1984; (ed) The New Review Anthology, 1985; Fifty Poems, 1988; In Search of J. D. Salinger, 1988; (ed) Soho Square, 1989; Writers in Hollywood, 1990; (ed) The Faber Book of Soccer, 1992; Keepers of the Flame: literary estates and the rise of biography, 1992; (ed) The Oxford Companion to Twentieth Century Poetry in English, 1994; Walking Possession: essays and reviews, 1994; Gazza Italia, 1994. *Address:* 54 Queen's Road, SW19 8LR. *T:* 0181–946 0291.

HAMILTON, Ian Robertson; QC (Scot.) 1980; *b* Paisley, Scotland, 13 Sept. 1925; *s* of John Harris Hamilton and Martha Robertson; *m* 1974, Jeannette Patricia Mari Stewart, Connel, Argyll; one *s* (one *s* two *d* by former *m*). *Educ:* John Neilson Sch., Paisley; Allan Glens Sch., Glasgow; Glasgow and Edinburgh Univs (BL). Served RAFVR, 1944–48. Called to the Scottish Bar, 1954 and to the Albertan Bar, 1982. Advocate Depute, 1962; Dir of Civil Litigation, Republic of Zambia, 1964–66; Hon. Sheriff of Lanarks, 1967; retd from practice to work for National Trust for Scotland and later to farm in Argyll, 1969; returned to practice, 1974; Sheriff of Glasgow and Strathkelvin, May–Dec. 1984; resigned commn Dec. 1984; returned to practice. Founder, Castle Wynd Printers, Edinburgh, 1955 (published four paper-back vols of Hugh MacDiarmid's poetry, 1955–56). Founder and first Chm., The Whichway Trust, to provide adventure training for young offenders, 1988. Chief Pilot, Scottish Parachute Club, 1978–80. Student Pres., Heriot-Watt Univ., 1990–Oct. 1996. Rector, Aberdeen Univ., 1994–. *Publications:* No Stone Unturned, 1952 (also New York); The Tinkers of the World, 1957 (Foyle award-winning play); The Taking of the Stone of Destiny, 1991; *autobiography:* A Touch of Treason, 1990; A Touch More Treason, 1994; contrib. various jls. *Recreation:* motor biking. *Address:* Advocates' Library, Parliament House, Edinburgh EH1 1RF.

HAMILTON, James, CBE 1979; *b* 11 March 1918; *s* of George Hamilton and Margaret Carey; *m* 1945, Agnes McGhee; one *s* three *d* (and one *s* decd). *Educ:* St Bridget's, Baillieston; St Mary's, High Whifflet. District Councillor, 6th Lanarks, 1955–58; Lanarks County Council, 1958–64. National Executive Mem., Constructional Engrg Union, 1958–71, Pres., 1968–69; Chm., Trade Union Group, Parly Labour Party, 1969–70. MP (Lab): Bothwell, 1964–83; Motherwell N, 1983–87. Asst Govt Whip, 1969–70; an Opposition Whip, 1970–74; a Lord Comr of the Treasury and Vice-Chamberlain of the Household, 1974–78; Comptroller of HM Household, 1978–79. *Recreations:* tennis, badminton, golf. *Address:* 12 Rosegreen Crescent, North Road, Bellshill, Lanarks ML4 1NT. *T:* Bellshill (01698) 842071.

HAMILTON, Prof. James; Professor of Physics, Nordic Institute for Theoretical Atomic Physics, 1964–86; *b* 29 Jan. 1918; *s* of Joseph Hamilton, Killybegs, Co. Donegal and Jessie Mackay, Keiss, Caithness; *m* 1945, Glen, *d* of Charles Dobbs, London; one *s* one *d* (and one *s* decd). *Educ:* Royal Academical Institution, Belfast; Queen's Univ., Belfast; Institute for Advanced Study, Dublin, 1941–43; Manchester Univ. Scientific Officer (Ops Research), Admiralty, London, and South East Asia Command, 1943–45; ICI Fellow, Manchester Univ., 1945–48; Lectr in Theoretical Physics, Manchester Univ., 1948–49; University Lectr in Mathematics, Cambridge Univ., 1950–60. Fellow of Christ's Coll., Cambridge, 1953–60; Research Associate in Nuclear Physics, Cornell Univ., NY, 1957–58; Prof. of Physics, University Coll., London, 1960–64. Donegall Lectr, TCD, 1969. Dir, Nordita, 1984–85. Foreign Mem., Royal Danish Acad., 1967. Dr *hc* Trondheim, 1982; DrPhil *hc* Lund, 1986. *Publications:* The Theory of Elementary Particles, 1959; (with B. Tromborg) Partial Wave Amplitudes and Resonance Poles, 1972; Admty report (1944), on first use of radar in marine navigation, Normandy; papers and articles on interaction of radiation with atoms, elementary particle physics, causality, and related topics. *Address:* 4 Almoners Avenue, Cambridge CB1 4PA. *T:* Cambridge (01223) 244175.

HAMILTON, Sir James (Arnot), KCB 1978 (CB 1972); MBE 1952; FRSE; FEng 1981; Permanent Under-Secretary of State, Department of Education and Science, 1976–83; *b* 2 May 1923; *m* 1947, Christine Mary McKean (marr. diss.); three *s*. *Educ:* University of Edinburgh (BSc). Marine Aircraft Experimental Estab., 1943: Head of Flight Research, 1948; Royal Aircraft Estab., 1952; Head of Projects Div., 1964; Dir, Anglo-French Combat Aircraft, Min. of Aviation, 1965; Dir-Gen. Concorde, Min. of Technology, 1966–70; Deputy Secretary: (Aerospace), DTI, 1971–73; Cabinet Office, 1973–76. Dir, Hawker Siddeley Gp, 1983–91; Mem. Adv. Bd, Brown and Root (UK) Ltd, 1983–; Director: Smiths Industries plc, 1984–93; Devonport Royal Dockyard, 1987–. Trustee, British Museum (Natural Hist.), 1984–88. President: Assoc. for Science Educn, 1984–85; NFER in England and Wales, 1984–. Vice-Pres., Council, Reading Univ., 1983–; Vice-Chm. Council, UCL, 1985–. DUniv Heriot-Watt, 1983; Hon. LLD CNAA, 1983. *Publications:* papers in Reports and Memoranda series of Aeronautical Research Council, Jl RAeS, and technical press. *Address:* Pentlands, 9 Cedar Road, Farnborough, Hants GU14 7AF. *T:* Farnborough (01252) 543254. *Club:* Athenæum.

HAMILTON, (James) Dundas, CBE 1985; Chairman: Wates City of London Properties plc, 1984–94; LWT Pension Trustees Ltd, 1992–94; *b* 11 June 1919; *o s* of late Arthur Douglas Hamilton and Jean Scott Hamilton; *m* 1954, Linda Jean, *d* of late Sinclair Frank Ditcham and Helen Fraser Ditcham; two *d*. *Educ:* Rugby; Clare Coll., Cambridge. Served War, Army (Lt-Col RA), 1939–46. Member, Stock Exchange, 1948, Mem. Council, 1972–78 (Dep. Chm., 1973–76). Partner, 1951–86, Sen. Partner, 1977–85, Fielding, Newson-Smith & Co. Chairman: TSB Commercial Holdings (formerly UDT Holdings), 1985–90 (Dir, 1983–90); United Dominions Trust Ltd, 1985–89; Director: Richard Clay plc, 1971–84 (Vice-Chm., 1981–84); LWT (Holdings) plc, 1981–91; Datastream Hldgs Ltd, 1982–86; TSB Gp plc, 1985–90; TSB Investment Management Ltd, 1986–88; Archival Facsimiles Ltd, 1986–89; WIB Publications Ltd, 1987–; Camp Hopson & Co., 1991–. Dep. Chm., British Invisible Exports Council, 1976–86; Member: Exec. Cttee, City Communications Centre, 1976–88; City and Industrial Liaison Council, 1987– (Chm., 1970–73 and 1991–). Governor, Pasold Res. Fund, 1976–90 (Chm., 1978–86). Member: Council of Industrial Soc., 1959–78 (Exec. Cttee, 1963–68; Life Mem., 1978); Adv. Bd, RCDS, 1980–87. Contested (C) East Ham North, 1951. FRSA 1988. *Publications:* The Erl King (radio play), 1949; Lorenzo Smiles on Fortune (novel), 1953; Three on a Honeymoon (TV series), 1956; Six Months Grace (play, jointly with Robert Morley), 1957; Stockbroking Today, 1968, 2nd edn 1979; Stockbroking Tomorrow, 1986; 21 Years to Christmas (short stories and verse), 1994. *Recreations:* writing, swimming, golf, watching tennis. *Address:* 45 Melbury Court, W8 6NH. *T:* 0171–602 3157. *Clubs:* City of London, Hurlingham, All England Lawn Tennis and Croquet; Royal and Ancient Golf (St Andrews); Hankley Common; Worplesdon (Life Mem.); Kandahar Ski.

HAMILTON, John; His Honour Judge John Hamilton; a Circuit Judge, since 1987; *b* 27 Jan. 1941; *s* of John Ian Hamilton and of late Mrs Margaret Walker; *m* 1965, Patricia Ann Hamilton (*née* Henman); two *s* one *d*. *Educ:* Durlston Court Prep. Sch., New Milton, Hants; Harrow (schol.); Hertford Coll., Oxford (schol.). MA Jurisp. Oxon. Called to Bar, Gray's Inn, 1965; a Recorder, 1985. KStJ 1982. *Recreations:* jogging, golf, bridge. *Address:* Red Stack, Anstey, near Buntingford, Herts SG9 0BN. *T:* Barkway (01763) 848536.

HAMILTON, Loudon Pearson, CB 1987; Chairman: Scottish Agricultural and Rural Development Centre, since 1992; Scottish Food Quality Certification Co., since 1995; *b* 12 Jan. 1932; *s* of Vernon Hamilton and Jean Mair Hood; *m* 1956, Anna Mackinnon Young (*d* 1993); two *s*. *Educ:* Hutchesons' Grammar Sch., Glasgow; Glasgow Univ. (MA Hons Hist.). National Service, 2nd Lieut RA, 1953–55. Inspector of Taxes, Inland Revenue, 1956–60; Asst Principal, Dept of Agriculture and Fisheries for Scotland, 1960; Private Sec. to Parly Under-Secretary of State for Scotland, 1963–64; First Secretary, Agriculture, British Embassy, Copenhagen and The Hague, 1966–70; Asst Secretary, Dept of Agriculture and Fisheries for Scotland, 1973–79; Principal Estabt Officer, Scottish Office, 1979–84; Sec., Scottish Office Agric. and Fisheries Dept, 1984–92. Mem., AFRC, 1984–92. Chm., Corstorphine Trust, 1990–95. *Address:* 5 Belgrave Road, Edinburgh EH12 6NG. *T:* 0131–334 5398.

HAMILTON, Sir Malcolm William Bruce S.; *see* Stirling-Hamilton.

HAMILTON, Martha, (Mrs R. R. Steedman),OBE 1988; Headmistress, St Leonards School, St Andrews, 1970–88; *d* of Rev. John Edmund Hamilton and Hon. Lilias Maclay; *m* 1977, Robert Russell Steedman, *qv*. *Educ:* Roedean Sch.; St Andrews Univ. (MA Hons Hist.); Cambridge Univ. (DipEd); Edinburgh Univ. (Dip. Adult Educn). Principal, Paljor Namgyal Girls' High School, Gangtok, Sikkim, 1959–66. Member: Assoc. for Protection of Rural Scotland Award Panel, 1989–92; Fife Health Bd, 1991– (Vice Chm., 1994–); Court of Dirs, Edinburgh Acad., 1992–. Convenor, Assoc. for Applied Arts, 1992–. Awarded Pema Dorji (for services to education), Sikkim, 1966. *Recreations:* ski-ing, photography. *Address:* Muir of Blebo, Blebo Craigs, by Cupar, Fife KY15 5TZ.
See also E. W. Hamilton.

HAMILTON, Mary Margaret; *see* Kaye, M. M.

HAMILTON, Sir Michael Aubrey, Kt 1983; *b* 5 July 1918; *s* of late Rt Rev. E. K. C. Hamilton, KCVO; *m* 1947, Lavinia, 3rd *d* of late Col Sir Charles Ponsonby, 1st Bt, TD; one *s* three *d*. *Educ:* Radley; Oxford. Served War of 1939–45, with 1st Bn, Coldstream Guards. MP (C): Wellingborough Div. Northants, 1959–64; Salisbury, Feb. 1965–1983; Asst Govt Whip, 1961–62; a Lord Comr of the Treasury, 1962–64; PPS to Sec. of State for Foreign and Commonwealth Affairs, 1982–83. Former Director: Army & Navy Stores; Hops Marketing Board; Royal Exchange Assurance. UK Representative: UN Gen. Assembly, 1970; US Bicentennial Celebrations, 1976. *Address:* Lordington House, Chichester, Sussex PO18 9DX. *T:* Emsworth (01243) 371717.

HAMILTON, (Mostyn) Neil; MP (C) Tatton, since 1983; *b* 9 March 1949; *s* of Ronald and Norma Hamilton; *m* 1983, (Mary) Christine Holman. *Educ:* Amman Valley Grammar School; University College of Wales, Aberystwyth (BSc Econ, MSc Econ); Corpus Christi College, Cambridge (LLB). Called to the Bar, Middle Temple, 1979. PPS to Minister of State for Transport, 1986–87; an Asst Govt Whip, 1990–92; Parly Under-Sec. of State, DTI, 1992–94. Mem., Select Cttee on Treasury and Civil Service, 1987–90; Vice-Chm., Conservative backbench Trade and Industry Cttee, 1984–90 (Sec., 1983); Secretary: Cons. backbench Finance Cttee, 1987–90; UK–ANZAC Parly Gp, 1984–; Chm., All Party Anglo-Togo Parly Gp, 1988–; Vice-Pres., Small Business Bureau, 1985–. Vice-Pres., Cheshire Agricl Soc., 1986–. *Publications:* UK/US Double Taxation, 1980; The European Community—a Policy for Reform, 1983; (ed) Land Development Encyclopaedia, 1981–; (jtly) No Turning Back, 1985; pamphlets on state industry, schools and the NHS. *Recreations:* gardening, book collecting, the arts, architecture and conservation, country pursuits, silence. *Address:* House of Commons, SW1A 0AA. *T:* 0171–219 4157.

HAMILTON, Myer Alan Barry K.; *see* King-Hamilton.

HAMILTON, Neil; *see* Hamilton, M. N.

HAMILTON, Nigel John Mawdesley, QC 1981; *b* 13 Jan. 1938; *s* of Archibald Dearman Hamilton and Joan Worsley Mawdesley; *m* 1963, Leone Morag Elizabeth Gordon; two *s*. *Educ:* St Edward's Sch., Oxford; Queens' Coll., Cambridge. Nat. Service, 2nd Lieut, RE, Survey Dept, 1956–58. Assistant Master: St Edward's Sch., Oxford, 1962–63; King's Sch., Canterbury, 1963–65. Called to the Bar, Inner Temple, 1965, Bencher, 1989. Mem., Gen. Council of the Bar, 1989–. Mem. (C) for Chew Valley, Avon CC, 1989–93. *Recreation:* fishing. *Address:* St John's Chambers, Small Street, Bristol BS1 1DW. *Club:* Flyfishers'.

HAMILTON, North Edward Frederick D.; *see* Dalrymple Hamilton.

HAMILTON, Richard; painter; *b* 24 Feb. 1922; *s* of Peter and Constance Hamilton; *m* 1st, 1947, Terry O'Reilly (*d* 1962); one *s* one *d*; 2nd, 1991, Rita Donagh. *Educ:* elementary; Royal Academy Schs; Slade Sch. of Art. Jig and Tool draughtsman, 1940–45. Lectr, Fine Art Dept, King's Coll., Univ. of Durham (later Univ. of Newcastle upon Tyne), 1953–66. *Devised exhibitions:* Growth and Form, 1951; Man, Machine and Motion, 1955. *Collaborated on:* This is Tomorrow, 1956; 'an Exhibit', 1957; exhibn with D. Roth, ICA New Gall., 1977. *One man art exhibitions:* Gimpel Fils, 1951; Hanover Gall., 1955, 1964; Robert Fraser Gall., 1966, 1967, 1969; Whitworth Gall, 1972; Nigel Greenwood Inc., 1972; Serpentine Gall., 1975; Stedelijk Mus., Amsterdam, 1976; Waddington Gall., 1980, 1982, 1984; Anthony d'Offay Gall., 1980, 1991; Charles Cowles Gall., NY, 1980; Galérie Maeght, Paris, 1981; Tate Gall., 1983–84; Thorden and Wetterling, Stockholm, 1984; DAAD Gall., Berlin, 1985; Fruitmarket Gall., Edinburgh, 1988; Moderna Museet, Stockholm, 1989; Venice Bienale, 1993; other exhibitions abroad include: Kassel, 1967, New York, 1967; Milan, 1967, 1968, 1969, 1971, 1972, 1974, 1990; Hamburg, 1969; Berlin, 1970, 1971, 1973; *retrospective exhibitions:* Tate Gallery, 1970 (also shown in Eindhoven and Bern), 1992; Guggenheim Museum, New York, 1973 (also shown in Cincinnati, Munich, Tübingen, Berlin); Musée Grenoble, 1977; Kunsthalle Bielefeld, 1978; Kunstmus., Winterthur, 1990 (also shown in Hannover and Valencia); Tate Gall., 1992; Irish Mus. of Modern Art, Dublin, 1992. William and Noma Copley award, 1960; John Moores prize, 1969; Talens Prize International, 1970; Golden Lion of Venice, 1993. *Publication:* Collected Words 1953–1982, 1982. *Address:* c/o Tate Gallery, Millbank, SW1P 4RG.

HAMILTON, Sir Richard Caradoc; *see* Hamilton, Sir Robert C. R. C.

HAMILTON, Richard Graham; His Honour Judge Hamilton; a Circuit Judge, since 1986; Chancellor, Diocese of Liverpool, since 1976; *b* 26 Aug. 1932; *s* of late Henry Augustus Rupert Hamilton and Frances Mary Graham Hamilton; *m* 1960, Patricia Craghill Hamilton (*née* Ashburner); one *s* one *d*. *Educ:* Charterhouse; University Coll., Oxford (MA). Called to Bar, Middle Temple, 1956; a Recorder, 1974–86. Regular broadcasting work for Radio Merseyside, inc. scripts: Van Gogh in England, 1981; Voices from Babylon, 1983; A Longing for Dynamite, 1984; Dark Night, 1988 (winner of first prize for a short religious play, RADIUS); Murder Court productions (dramatised trials), Liverpool: The Maybrick Case, 1989; The Veronica Mutiny, 1990. *Publications:* Foul Bills and Dagger Money, 1979; All Jangle and Riot, 1986; A Good Wigging, 1988. *Recreations:* reading, walking, films. *Club:* Athenæum (Liverpool).

HAMILTON, Sir (Robert Charles) Richard (Caradoc), 9th Bt, *cr* 1647; *b* 8 Sept. 1911; *s* of Sir Robert Caradoc Hamilton, 8th Bt, and Irene Lady Hamilton (*née* Mordaunt) (*d* 1969); *S* father, 1959; *m* 1952, Elizabeth Vidal Barton; one *s* three *d*. *Educ:* Charterhouse; St Peter's Coll., Oxford (MA). Served in the Intelligence Corps, 1940–45. Schoolmaster at Ardingly Coll., Sussex, 1946–60. Owner, Walton Estate, Warwick; Mem., Warwickshire Br., CLA, 1962– (Chm., 1979–83). *Publications:* (trans.) de Luze, A History of the Royal Game of Tennis, 1979; (trans.) Pierre Barcellon, Rules and Principles of Tennis, 1987. *Recreations:* dramatist; Real tennis. *Heir: s* Andrew Caradoc Hamilton, *b* 23 Sept. 1953. *Address:* Walton, Warwick CV35 9HX. *T:* Stratford-on-Avon (01789) 840460.

HAMILTON, Robert William, FBA 1960; *b* 26 Nov. 1905; *s* of William Stirling Hamilton and Kathleen Hamilton (*née* Elsmie); *heir-pres.* to Sir Malcolm Stirling-Hamilton, Bt, *qv*; *m* 1935, Eileen Hetty Lowick; three *s* two *d*. *Educ:* Winchester Coll.; Magdalen Coll., Oxford. Chief Insp. of Antiquities, Palestine, 1931–38; Dir of Antiquities, Palestine, 1938–48; Sec.-Librarian, British Sch. of Archæology, Iraq, 1948–49; Senior Lecturer in Near Eastern Archæology, Oxford, 1949–56; Keeper of Dept of Antiquities, 1956–72, Keeper, 1962–72, Ashmolean Museum, Oxford. Fellow Magdalen Coll., Oxford, 1959–72. *Publications:* Samaria-Sebaste, 1944; The Church of the Nativity, Bethlehem, 1947; Structural History of the Aqsa Mosque, 1949; Khirbat al Mafjar, 1959; (with others) Oxford Bible Atlas, 1974; Walid and his Friends: an Umayyad tragedy, 1988; Letters from

1982; Cornell Prof., Swarthmore Coll., Pennsylvania, 1983; Trinity Coll., Hartford, 1984; Adelaide Univ., 1984; Nat. Hellenic Res. Foundn, Athens, 1985; Nat. Humanities Center, N Carolina, 1986; Newcastle Univ., NSW, 1988, 1990, 1992. Chm., Managing Cttee, British Sch. at Athens, 1972–75. Served War of 1939–45, as Lt-Col, campaigns in Greece, Crete, Syria, and Mem. Allied Mil. Mission, Greece, 1943–44 (despatches twice, DSO). Pres., Hellenic Soc., 1965–68. For. Mem., Acad. of Athens, 1993. DL: Bristol, 1965; Cambridge, 1974. Hon. DLett: Wisconsin, 1981; St Olaf Coll., 1982; Carleton Coll., 1988. Steven Runciman Award, Anglo-Hellenic League, 1989. Officer, Order of the Phœnix, Greece, 1946; Companion, Soc. of Friends of the Greek People, 1992. *Publications:* Memoir of Sir John Edwin Sandys, 1933; History of Greece, 1959, 3rd edn 1986; Epirus, 1967; A History of Macedonia, Vol. 1, Historical Geography and Prehistory, 1972, Vol. 2 (with G. T. Griffith) 550–336 BC, 1974, Vol. 3 (with F. W. Walbank) 336–167 BC, 1988; Studies in Greek History, 1973; The Classical Age of Greece, 1976; Migrations and Invasions in Greece, 1976; Alexander the Great: King Commander and Statesman, 1981, 2nd edn 1989; Venture into Greece: with the guerillas, 1943–44, 1983 (Greek trans., 1986); Three Historians of Alexander the Great, 1983; The Macedonian State, 1989; The Miracle that was Macedonia, 1991; West Macedonia: Resistance and Allied Military Mission 1943–44, 1993 (Greek edn 1992); Sources for Alexander the Great, 1993; Collected Studies, Vol. 1, 1993, Vol. 2, 1994, Vol. 3, 1994; Philip of Macedon, 1994; The Genius of Alexander the Great, 1995; Editor: Clifton Coll. Centenary Essays, 1962; Cambridge Ancient History, 3rd edn, vols I, II, III and IV; Oxford Classical Dictionary, 2nd edn, 1970; Atlas of the Greek and Roman World in Antiquity, 1981; articles and reviews in learned jls. *Address:* 3 Belvoir Terrace, Trumpington Road, Cambridge CB2 2AA. *T:* Cambridge (01223) 357151.

See also C. P. Bammel.

HAMMOND, Prof. Norman David Curle, FSA, FRAS; Archaeology Correspondent, The Times, since 1967; Professor of Archaeology, Boston University, and Associate in Maya Archaeology, Peabody Museum, Harvard University, since 1988; *b* 10 July 1944; *er s* of William Hammond and Kathleen Jessie Hammond (*née* Howes); *m* 1972, Jean, *er d* of late A. H. Wilson and Beryl Wilson; one *s* one *d.* *Educ:* Varndean GS; Peterhouse, Cambridge (Trevelyan Schol.; BA 1966; Dip. Classical Archaeol. 1967; MA 1970; PhD 1972; ScD 1987). Centre of Latin American Studies, Cambridge: Res. Fellow, 1967–71; Leverhulme Res. Fellow, 1972–75; Res. Fellow, Fitzwilliam Coll., Cambridge, 1973–75; Sen. Lectr, Univ. of Bradford, 1975–77; Rutgers University: Vis. Prof., 1977–78; Associate Prof., 1978–84; Prof. of Archaeol., 1984–88. Visiting appointments: Univ. of California, Berkeley, 1977; Jilin Univ., Changchun, 1981; Irvine Chair of Anthropol., Calif. Acad. of Scis, 1984–85; Univ. of Paris, Sorbonne, 1987; Univ. of Bonn, 1994; Fellow: Dumbarton Oaks, Washington, 1988; Worcester Coll., Oxford, 1989; Peterhouse, Cambridge, 1991. Curl Lectr, RAI, 1985. Acad. Trustee, Archaeol. Inst. of America, 1990–93. Hon. Mem., Phi Beta Kappa, 1989. Mem. editl bds, archaeol. jls, USA, UK, 1984–; editor, Afghan Studies, 1976–79; Consulting Editor, Liby of Congress, 1977–89; archaeol. consultant, Scientific American, 1979–95. Excavations and surveys: Libya and Tunisia, 1964; Afghanistan, 1966; Belize, 1970–94 (Lubaantun, Nohmul, Cuello, La Milpa); Ecuador, 1972–84. Press Award, British Archaeol Awards, 1994. *Publications:* (ed) South Asian Archaeology, 1973; (ed) Mesoamerican Archaeology, 1974; Lubaantun: a classic Maya realm, 1975; (ed) Social Process in Maya Prehistory, 1977; (ed with F. R. Allchin) The Archaeology of Afghanistan, 1978; (ed with G. R. Willey) Maya Archaeology and Ethnohistory, 1979; (ed jtly) Pattern of the Past, 1981; Ancient Maya Civilisation, 1982, 5th edn 1994; (gen. editor) Archaeology Procs, 44th Congress of Americanists, 1982–84; Nohmul: excavations 1973–83, 1985; Cuello: an early Maya community in Belize, 1991; contribs to learned and unlearned jls. *Recreations:* fine wine, intelligent women, opera. *Address:* Wholeway, Harlton, Cambridge CB3 7ET. *T:* Cambridge (01223) 262376; 83 Ivy Street, Apt 32, Brookline, MA 02146, USA. *T:* (617) 7399077. *Clubs:* Athenæum; Cosmos (Washington).

HAMMOND, Roy John William; Director, City of Birmingham Polytechnic, 1979–84; *b* 3 Oct. 1928; *s* of John James Hammond and Edith May Hammond; *m* 1st, 1949, Audrey Cecilia Dagmar Avello (*d* 1988); three *d*; 2nd, 1990, Dorothy Forder. *Educ:* East Ham Grammar Sch.; University College of the South West, Exeter; Sorbonne, Paris. BA Hons, 1st Cl. French and Latin, London. Royal Air Force Education Branch, 1952–56; Asst Lectr, Blackburn Municipal Technical Coll. and School of Art, 1956–59; Head of Department: Herefordshire Technical Coll., 1960–66; Leeds Polytechnic, 1966–71; Asst Dir, City of Birmingham Polytechnic, 1971–79. Hon. Fellow, Univ. of Central England in Birmingham (formerly City of Birmingham Poly.), 1985. FRSA. *Recreations:* cricket, theatre, music, walking, flying.

HAMMOND, Simon Tristram; His Honour Judge Simon Hammond; a Circuit Judge, since 1993; *b* 5 Jan. 1944; *s* of Philip J. Hammond and Sylvia D. (*née* Sillem); *m* 1976, Louise (*née* Weir); one *s* two *d.* *Educ:* Eastbourne Coll.; Coll. of Law. Articled to Philip J. Hammond, Leicester; admitted Solicitor, 1967; Solicitor, later Partner, Victor J. Lissack, London, 1968–76; Partner, Philip J. Hammond & Sons, Leicester, 1977–93. An Asst Recorder, 1985–90; a Recorder, 1990–93. Asst Comr to Parly Boundary Commn for England, 1992. Member: Law Soc's Standing Cttee on Criminal Law, 1982–91; Crown Court Rules Cttee, 1988–93; Enforcement Sub-cttee, Home Office Rev. of Magistrates Court Procedure, 1989–90. Churchwarden, 1990–. *Recreations:* horses, hunting, ski-ing, vegetable gardening. *Address:* c/o Circuit Administrator's Office, Midland and Oxford Circuit, 2 Newton Street, Birmingham B4 6NE.

HAMMOND-CHAMBERS, (Robert) Alexander; Chairman, Ivory & Sime, 1985–91; Chairman, Edinburgh Green Belt Trust, since 1991; *b* 20 Oct. 1942; *s* of late Robert Rupert Hammond-Chambers and of Leonie Elise Noble (*née* Andrews); *m* 1968, Sarah Louisa Madeline (*née* Fanshawe); two *s* one *d.* *Educ:* Wellington College; Magdalene College, Cambridge (Hons Economics). Ivory & Sime: joined 1964; Partner, 1969; Director, 1975, upon incorporation; Dep. Chm., 1982. First Overseas Governor, Nat. Assoc. of Securities Dealers Inc., 1984–87; Dir GBC North America Growth Fund Inc.; Chairman: Covey Advertising Ltd, 1991–, and other cos. Governor, Fettes College. *Recreations:* tennis, sailing, photography, golf. *Address:* Grange Dell, Penicuik, Midlothian EH26 9LE. *T:* Penicuik (01968) 76686. *Club:* New (Edinburgh).

HAMMOND INNES, Ralph, CBE 1978; author and traveller; *b* 15 July 1913; *s* of late William Hammond and Dora Beatrice Innes; *m* 1937, Dorothy Mary Lang (*d* 1989). Staff of Financial News, 1934–40. Served Artillery, 1940–46. Member: various cttees, Soc. of Authors, sailing foundns; Vice President: Assoc. of Sea Training Orgns; World Ship Trust. Hon. DLitt Bristol, 1985. Works regularly translated into numerous languages; many book club and paperback edns throughout the world. *Publications include:* Wreckers Must Breathe, 1940; The Trojan Horse, 1940; Attack Alarm, 1941; Dead and Alive, 1946; The Lonely Skier, 1947; The Killer Mine, 1947; Maddon's Rock, 1948; The Blue Ice, 1948; The White South (Book Society Choice), 1949; The Angry Mountain, 1950; Air Bridge, 1951; Campbell's Kingdom (Book Society Choice), 1952; The Strange Land, 1954; The Mary Deare (chosen by Literary Guild of America, Book Soc. Choice), 1956; The Land God Gave to Cain, 1958; Harvest of Journeys (Book Soc. Choice), 1959; The Doomed Oasis (chosen by Literary Guild of America, Book Soc. Choice), 1960; Atlantic Fury (Book Society Choice), 1962; Scandinavia, 1963; The Strode Venturer, 1965; Sea and Islands (Book Society Choice), 1967; The Conquistadors (Book of the Month and Literary Guild), 1969; Levkas Man, 1971; Golden Soak, 1973; North Star, 1974; The Big Footprints, 1977; The Last Voyage (Cook), 1978; Solomons Seal, 1980; The Black Tide, 1982; High Stand, 1985; Hammond Innes' East Anglia, 1986; Medusa, 1988; Isvik, 1991; Target Antarctica, 1993; Delta Connection, 1996; *films:* Snowbound, Hell Below Zero, Campbell's Kingdom, The Wreck of the Mary Deare; *TV:* Explorers (Cook), 1975; Golden Soak, 1979; Levkas Man, 1981. *Recreations:* cruising and ocean racing, forestry. *Address:* Ayres End, Kersey, Suffolk IP7 6EB. *T:* Hadleigh (01473) 823294. *Clubs:* Royal Ocean Racing, Royal Cruising; Royal Yacht Squadron.

HAMMOND-STROUD, Derek, OBE 1987; concert and opera baritone; Professor of Singing, Royal Academy of Music, 1974–90; *b* 10 Jan. 1926; *s* of Herbert William Stroud and Ethel Louise Elliott. *Educ:* Salvatorian Coll., Harrow, Mddx; Trinity Coll. of Music, London; in Vienna and Munich with Elena Gerhardt and Gerhard Hüsch. Glyndebourne Festival Opera, 1959; Sadler's Wells Opera (later ENO), 1961; Royal Opera, Covent Garden, 1971; Houston Grand Opera, USA, 1975; Netherlands Opera, 1976; Metropolitan Opera, NY, 1977; Teatro Colón, Buenos Aires, 1981; Munich State Opera, 1983. Concerts and Lieder recitals at Edinburgh, Aldeburgh, Munich and Vienna Festivals, and in Spain, Iceland and Denmark. BBC Promenade Concerts, 1968–. Pres., Univ. of London Opera Gp, 1971. Freeman, City of London, 1952; Hon. RAM 1976; Hon. FTCL, 1982. Sir Charles Santley Meml Gift, Worshipful Co. of Musicians, 1988. Recordings include: The Ring (Goodall); Der Rosenkavalier (de Waart). *Recreations:* chess, study of philosophy. *Address:* 18 Sutton Road, Muswell Hill, N10 1HE. *T:* 0181–883 2120.

HAMNETT, Thomas Orlando; Chairman, Greater Manchester Council, 1975–1976, Vice-Chairman, 1976; *b* 28 Sept. 1930; *s* of John and Elizabeth Hamnett; *m* 1954, Kathleen Ridgway; one *s* five *d.* *Educ:* Stockport Jun. Techn. Sch. Sheetmetal craftsman, 1946. Member, Manchester City Council, 1963 until re-organisation (Vice-Chm., Health Cttee, Chm. sub cttee on Staff on Cleansing Cttee, Mem. Policy and Finance Cttees), and 1978–92 (Member: Direct works, Markets, and Personnel Cttees; Transportation, Education, and Recreation and Arts Cttees, Greater Manchester Council; Chm., Environmental Services Cttee, City Council, Manchester, 1982). *Recreations:* football, cricket, table tennis. *Address:* 199 Chapman Street, Gorton, Manchester M18 8WP. *T:* 0161–223 3098. *Club:* Gorton Trades and Labour (Chm.).

HAMPDEN; *see* Hobart-Hampden.

HAMPDEN, 6th Viscount *cr* 1884; **Anthony David Brand,** DL; land agent; *b* 7 May 1937; *s* of 5th Viscount Hampden and of Imogen Alice Rhys, *d* of 7th Baron Dynevor; *S* father, 1975; *m* 1969, Cara Fiona (marr. diss. 1988), *e d* of Claud Proby; two *s* one *d*; *m* 1993, Mrs Sally Snow, *d* of Sir Charles Hambro, KBE, MC. *Educ:* Eton. Chairman: Sussex CLA, 1985–88; Governing Body, Emanuel Sch., 1985–. DL E Sussex, 1986. *Publication:* Henry and Eliza, 1980. *Heir:* *s* Hon. Francis Anthony Brand, *b* 17 Sept. 1970. *Address:* Glynde Place, Glynde, Lewes, Sussex BN8 6SX. *Club:* White's.

HAMPEL, Sir Ronald Claus, Kt 1995; Chairman, ICI plc, since 1995; *b* 31 May 1932; *s* of Karl Victor Hugo Hampel and Rutgard Emil Klothilde Hauck; *m* 1957, Jane Bristed Hewson; three *s* one *d.* *Educ:* Canford Sch., Wimborne; Corpus Christi Coll., Cambridge (MA Mod. Lang. and Law). Nat. service, 2nd Lt, 3rd RHA, 1951–52. Joined ICI, 1955; Vice-Pres., ICI US, 1973–77; Dir, ICI Plant Protection, 1973–77; Gen. Manager, Commercial, 1977–80; Chairman: ICI Paints, 1980–83; ICI Agrochemicals, 1983–85; Dir, ICI, 1985–; Chief Operating Officer, 1991–93, Dep. Chm. and Chief Exec., 1993–95, ICI plc. Non-executive Director: Powell Duffryn, 1984–88; Commercial Union, 1988–; British Aerospace, 1989–. Dir, Amer. Chamber of Commerce, 1986–91; Mem. Exec. Cttee, British North America Cttee, 1989–. CIMgt (CBIM 1985); FRSA 1992. *Recreations:* tennis, golf, ski-ing, music (opera/ballet). *Address:* ICI plc, 9 Millbank, SW1P 3JF. *T:* 0171–834 4444. *Clubs:* MCC, All England Lawn Tennis; Royal & Ancient; Sunningdale Golf, West Sussex Golf (Pulborough); Pine Valley Golf (USA).

HAMPSHIRE, Margaret Grace, MA; JP; Principal of Cheltenham Ladies' College, 1964–79; *b* 7 Sept. 1918; *o d* of Dr C. H. Hampshire, CMG, MB, BS, BSc, sometime Sec. of British Pharmacopœia Commission, and Grace Mary Hampshire. *Educ:* Malvern Girls' Coll.; Girton Coll., Cambridge. BA 1941; MA 1945. Entered Civil Service, Board of Trade, 1941. Joined Staff of Courtaulds, 1951. Head of Government Relations Department, 1959–64. Member: Board of Governors, University Coll. Hosp., 1961–64; Marylebone Borough Council, 1962–64; SW Regional Hosp. Board, 1967–70; Midlands Electricity Consultative Council, 1973–80; Vice-Pres., Intensive Care Trust, Cheltenham Hosp., 1985– (Chm., 1982–85). Reader, Painswick and Sheepscombe Parishes, dio. of Gloucester, 1987–. County Sec., Gloucestershire Girl Guides, 1980–85; Governor, Alice Ottley Sch., Worcester, 1979–92. JP Cheltenham, 1970. *Recreations:* music, reading, foreign travel. *Address:* Ringwood, 9 The Croft, Painswick, Glos GL6 6QP.

HAMPSHIRE, Prof. Michael John, CBE 1987; CPhys, CEng; Professor of Electronic Information Technology, University of Salford, since 1985; Assistant Managing Director, Salford University Business Services Ltd, since 1989; *b* 13 Oct. 1939; *s* of Jack and Hilda May Hampshire; *m* 1962, Mavis (*née* Oakes); one *d.* *Educ:* Heckmondwike Grammar Sch.; Univ. of Birmingham (BSc Physics, PhD Elec. Engrg). FIEE, FInstP. University of Salford: Lectr, 1964; Sen. Lectr, 1972; Prof. of Solid State Electronics, 1977; Chm., Dept of Electronic and Electrical Engrg, 1981–89. Consultant: Ferranti, 1970–74; Volex Gp, 1977– (Chm., R&D Cttee, 1987–92); Thorn EMI Flow Measurement, 1980–88. Founder and Chm., Vertec (Electronics), 1982–92 (Dir, 1992–). Commendation EPIC Award, 1982; Academic Enterprise Award, 1982; Techmart Technology Transfer Trophy, 1984. Hon. MIED 1982. *Publications:* Electron Physics and Devices, 1969; 80 pubns and patents on solid state electronics and electronic systems, vehicle multiplexing, innovation. *Recreations:* music, golf. *Address:* 3 Brookfield, Upper Hopton, Mirfield, West Yorks WF14 8HL.

HAMPSHIRE, Sir Stuart (Newton), Kt 1979; FBA 1960; Warden of Wadham College, Oxford University, 1970–84; *b* 1 Oct. 1914; *s* of G. N. Hampshire and Marie West; *m* 1st, 1961, Renee Ayer (*d* 1980); 2nd, 1985, Nancy Cartwright; two *d.* *Educ:* Repton; Balliol Coll., Oxford. 1st Cl. Lit Hum, Oxford, 1936. Fellow of All Souls Coll., and Lectr in Philosophy, Oxford, 1936–40. Service in Army, 1940–45. Personal Asst to Minister of State, Foreign Office, 1945; Lectr in Philosophy, University Coll., London, 1947–50; Fellow of New Coll., Oxford, 1950–55; Domestic Bursar and Research Fellow, All Souls Coll., 1955–60; Grote Prof. of Philosophy of Mind and Logic, Univ. of London, 1960–63; Prof. of Philosophy, Princeton Univ., 1963–70; Prof., Stanford Univ., 1985–91. Fellow, Amer. Acad. of Arts and Sciences, 1968. Hon. DLitt Glasgow, 1973. *Publications:* Spinoza, 1951; Thought and Action, 1959; Freedom of the Individual, 1965; Modern Writers and other essays, 1969; Freedom of Mind and other essays, 1971; (ed jtly) The Socialist Idea, 1975; Two Theories of Morality, 1977; (ed) Public and Private Morality, 1978; Morality and Conflict, 1983; Innocence and Experience, 1989; articles in philosophical journals.

Address: 7 Beaumont Road, The Quarry, Headington, Oxford OX3 8JN. *T:* Oxford (01865) 41688.

HAMPSHIRE, Susan, OBE 1995; actress; *b* 12 May 1942; *d* of George Kenneth Hampshire and June Hampshire; *m* 1st, 1967, Pierre Granier-Deferre (marr. diss. 1974); one *s* (one *d* decd); 2nd, 1981, Sir Eddie Kulukundis, *qv*. *Educ:* Hampshire Sch., Knightsbridge. *Stage:* Expresso Bongo, Saville, tour, 1959; 'that girl' in Follow That Girl, Vaudeville, 1960; Fairy Tales of New York, Comedy, 1961; Marion Dangerfield in Ginger Man, Royal Court, 1963; Past Imperfect, St Martin's and Savoy, 1964; Kate Hardcastle in She Stoops to Conquer, tour, 1966; On Approval, tour, 1966; Mary in The Sleeping Prince, St Martin's, tour, 1968; Nora in A Doll's House, Greenwich, 1972; Katharina in The Taming of the Shrew, Shaw, 1974; Peter in Peter Pan, Coliseum, 1974; Jeannette in Romeo and Jeannette, tour, 1975; Rosalind in As You Like It, Shaw, 1975; title rôle in Miss Julie, Greenwich, 1975; Elizabeth in The Circle, Haymarket, 1976; Ann Whitefield in Man and Superman, Savoy, 1978; Siri Von Essen in Tribades, Hampstead, 1978; Victorine in An Audience Called Edouard, Greenwich, 1978; Irene in The Crucifer of Blood, Haymarket, 1979; Ruth Carson in Night and Day, Phoenix, 1979; Elizabeth in The Revolt, New End, 1980; Stella Drury in House Guest, Savoy, 1981; Elvira in Blithe Spirit, Vaudeville, 1986; Marie Stopes in Married Love, Wyndhams, 1988; Countess in A Little Night Music, Piccadilly, 1989; Mrs Anna in The King and I, Sadler's Wells, 1990; Gertrude Lawrence in Noel and Gertie, Duke of York's, 1991; Dowager Countess of Marshwood in Relative Values, Savoy, 1993; *TV Serials:* Katy in What Katy Did; Andromeda (title rôle), Fleur Forsyte in The Forsyte Saga (Emmy Award for Best Actress, 1970), Becky Sharp in Vanity Fair (Emmy Award for Best Actress, 1973), Sarah Churchill, Duchess of Marlborough, in The First Churchills (Emmy Award for Best Actress, 1971), Glencora Palliser in The Pallisers; Lady Melfont in Dick Turpin; Signora Neroni in The Barchester Chronicles; Martha in Leaving, 2 series; Going to Pot, 3 series; Don't tell Father. *Films include:* During One Night, The Three Lives of Thomasina, Night Must Fall, Wonderful Life, Paris in August, The Fighting Prince of Donegal, Monte Carlo or Bust, Rogan, David Copperfield, Living Free, A Time for Loving, Malpertius (E. Poe Prizes du Film Fantastique, Best Actress, 1972), Neither the Sea Nor the Sand, Roses and Green Peppers, Bang. Dir, Conservation Foundn; Mem. Exec. Cttee, Population Concern; Pres., Dyslexia Inst. Hon. DLitt: London, 1981; City, 1984; St Andrews, 1986; Hon. DEd Kingston, 1994; Hon. DArts Pine Manor Coll., Boston, USA, 1994. *Publications:* Susan's Story, 1981; The Maternal Instinct, 1984; Lucy Jane at the Ballet, 1989; Lucy Jane on Television, 1989; Trouble Free Gardening, 1989; Every Letter Counts, 1990; Lucy Jane and the Dancing Competition, 1991; Easy Gardening, 1991; Lucy Jane and the Russian Ballet, 1993. *Recreations:* gardening, music, the study of antique furniture. *Address:* c/o Chatto & Linnit Ltd, Prince of Wales Theatre, Coventry Street, W1V 7FE. *T:* 0171–930 6677, *Fax:* 0171–930 0091.

HAMPSON, Christopher, CBE 1994; Chairman, Yorkshire Electricity Group, since 1994; *b* 6 Sept. 1931; *s* of Harold Ralph Hampson and Geraldine Mary Hampson; *m* 1954 Joan Margaret Cassils Evans; two *s* three *d*. *Educ:* McGill Univ. (BEng Chem 1952). Vice-Pres., 1956–78 and Sen. Vice-Pres., 1982–84, Canadian Industries, Canada; Imperial Chemical Industries: Gen. Manager, Planning, 1978–82; Man. Dir and Chief Exec. Officer, ICI Australia, 1984–87; Exec. Dir, ICI, 1987–94. Non-executive Director: Costain Group, 1988–; SNC-Lavelin Group, 1992–; TransAlfa Corp., 1993–. *Recreations:* tennis, ski-ing. *Address:* 77 Kensington Court, W8 5DT. *Clubs:* Hurlingham; York (Toronto).

HAMPSON, Prof. Elwyn Lloyd, MDS, FDSRCS; HDD RCSE; Professor of Restorative Dentistry, University of Sheffield, 1960–81, now Emeritus; Hon. Consultant Dental Surgeon to Sheffield Area Health Authority, since 1981; *b* 31 Jan. 1916; *s* of John and Mary Hampson; *m* 1940, Anne Cottrell; one *s* one *d*. *Educ:* Calday Grange Grammar Sch., W Kirby, Cheshire; Univ. of Liverpool. BDS with 1st Class Hons 1939; HDD RCSE 1944; FDSRCS 1949; MDS 1954; FDSE 1964. House surg., Liverpool Dental Hosp., 1939; Royal Army Dental Corps, 1941–45; Lecturer in Operative Dental Surgery, Edinburgh Dental Sch., 1945–47; Lecturer and later Senior Lecturer in Operative Dental Surgery, Univ. of Sheffield, 1947–60, Dean of Sch. of Clinical Dentistry, 1968–72. Mem., GDC, 1968–73. *Publications:* Hampson's Textbook of Operative Dental Surgery, 1961, 4th edn 1980; many papers in scientific jls. *Recreations:* water colour painting, golf. *Address:* 8 Milborne Close, Chester CH2 1HH.

HAMPSON, Dr Keith; MP (C) Leeds North-West, since 1983 (Ripon, Feb. 1974–1983); *b* 14 Aug. 1943; *s* of Bertie Hampson and Mary Elizabeth Noble; *m* 1st, 1975, Frances Pauline (*d* 1975), *d* of Mr and Mrs Mathieu Donald Einhorn; 2nd, 1979, Susan, *d* of Mr and Mrs John Wilkie Cameron. *Educ:* King James I Grammar Sch., Bishop Auckland, Co. Durham; Univ. of Bristol; Harvard Univ. BA, CertEd, PhD. Personal Asst to Edward Heath, 1966 and 1970 Gen. Elections and in his House of Commons office, 1968; Lectr in American History, Edinburgh Univ., 1968–74. Mem., Gen. Adv. Council, IBA, 1980–88. PPS: to Minister for Local Govt, 1979–83; to Sec. of State for Environment, 1983; to Sec. of State for Defence, 1983–84. Member: Select Cttee on Trade and Industry, 1987–; Public Accounts Commn, 1992–; Vice Chairman: Cons. Parly Educn Cttee, 1975–79; Cons. Parly Defence Cttee, 1988–89 (Sec., 1984–88). Mem., Educn Adv. Cttee of UK Commn for UNESCO, 1980–84. Vice President: WEA, 1978–; Assoc. of Business Executives, 1979–; Vice-Chm., Youthaid, 1979–83. *Recreations:* DIY, music. *Address:* House of Commons, SW1A 0AA. *T:* 0171–219 4463. *Club:* Carlton.

HAMPSON, Prof. Norman, FBA 1980; Professor of History, University of York, 1974–89; *b* 8 April 1922; *s* of Frank Hampson and Elizabeth Jane Fazackerley; *m* 1948, Jacqueline Gardin; two *d*. *Educ:* Manchester Grammar Sch.; University Coll., Oxford (MA); Dr de l'Univ. Paris. Service in Royal Navy, 1941–45. Manchester Univ., 1948–67: Lectr and Sen. Lectr; Prof. of Modern History, Univ. of Newcastle, 1967–74. Hon. DLitt Edinburgh, 1989. *Publications:* La Marine de l'an II, 1959; A Social History of the French Revolution, 1963; The Enlightenment, 1968; The First European Revolution, 1969; The Life and Opinions of Maximilien Robespierre, 1974; A Concise History of the French Revolution, 1975; Danton, 1978; Will and Circumstance: Montesquieu, Rousseau and the French Revolution, 1983; Prelude to Terror, 1988; Saint-Just, 1991. *Address:* 305 Hull Road, York YO1 3LB. *T:* York (01904) 412661.

HAMPSON, Stephen Fazackerley; Under Secretary, Scottish Office, since 1993; *b* 27 Oct. 1945; *s* of Frank Hampson and Helen (*née* Ellis); *m* 1970, Gunilla Brunk; one *s* one *d*. *Educ:* University Coll., Oxford (BPhil; MA). Lectr, Aberdeen Univ., 1969–71; Economist, NEDO, 1971–75; various posts, Scottish Office, 1975–78 and 1981–; First Sec., FCO, New Delhi, 1978–81. *Address:* Glenelg, Park Road, Kilmacolm PA13 4EE. *T:* Kilmacolm (01505) 872615.

HAMPSON, Stuart; Chairman, John Lewis Partnership, since 1993; *b* 7 Jan. 1947; *s* of Kenneth and Mary Hampson; *m* 1973, Angela McLaren; one *s* one *d*. *Educ:* Royal Masonic Sch., Bushey; St John's Coll., Oxford (BA Mod. Langs, MA). Board of Trade, 1969–72; FCO UKMIS to UN, Geneva, 1972–74; Dept of Prices and Consumer Protection, 1974–79; Dept of Trade, 1979–82; John Lewis Partnership, 1982–: Dir of Research and Expansion, 1986; Dep. Chm., 1989. *Address:* John Lewis Partnership, 171 Victoria Street, SW1E 5NN. *T:* 0171–828 1000.

HAMPSTEAD, Archdeacon of; *see* Wheatley, Ven. P. W.

HAMPTON, 6th Baron *cr* 1874; **Richard Humphrey Russell Pakington;** Bt 1846; *b* 25 May 1925; *s* of 5th Baron Hampton, OBE, and Grace Dykes (*d* 1959), 3rd *d* of Rt Hon. Sir Albert Spicer, 1st Bt; *S* father, 1974; *m* 1958, Jane Elizabeth Farquharson, *d* of late T. F. Arnott, OBE, TD, MB, ChB; one *s* two *d*. *Educ:* Eton; Balliol Coll., Oxford. Observer in Fleet Air Arm, RNVR, 1944–47. Varied employment, mainly with advertising agencies, 1949–58; Worcestershire Branch Council for the Protection of Rural England, 1958–71; Tansley Witt & Co., Chartered Accts, Birmingham, 1971–73. Liberal Party Spokesman on NI, 1977–87. President: S Worcs Liberal Assoc., 1978–88; Upton-on-Severn Civic Soc., 1986–. A Liberal Democrat. *Publication:* (written with his father, Humphrey Pakington) The Pakingtons of Westwood, 1975. *Heir: s* Hon. John Humphrey Arnott Pakington, *b* 24 Dec. 1964.

HAMPTON, Antony Barmore, TD 1954; DL; President, Record Marples Tools Ltd (formerly Bahco Record Tools), since 1981 (Chairman, 1958–81); President, Engineering Employers Federation, 1980–82; *b* 6 March 1919; *s* of Charles William Hampton and Winifred Elizabeth Hampton; *m* 1948, Helen Patricia Lockwood; five *s*. *Educ:* Rydal Sch.; Christ's Coll., Cambridge, 1938–40 (MA). Indian Army 1941–46 (despatches). C. and J. Hampton Ltd, 1947, until merger with Ridgway, 1972 (Chm. of both, 1958–81); Lloyds Bank Ltd: Chm., Yorkshire Board, 1972–84 (Mem., 1961–85); Director, UK Board, 1972–85. Dir, Black Horse Agencies Ltd, 1983–85; Mem., Engrg Industry Trng Bd, 1979–82; Master Cutler of Hallamshire, 1966–67. Chm., Crucible Theatre Trust, Sheffield, 1970–82. DL S Yorkshire (previously W Riding) 1972. *Recreations:* sailing, fishing. *Address:* Tideway, 20 Wittering Road, Hayling Island, Hants PO11 9SP. *T:* Hayling Island (01705) 464361. *Club:* Little Ship.

HAMPTON, Bryan; Head of Exports to the Americas (formerly Latin American, Caribbean and Australasian) Branch, Department of Trade and Industry, since 1992; *b* 4 Dec. 1938; *s* of William Douglas Hampton and Elizabeth Cardwell; *m* 1964, Marilyn Joseph; five *d*. *Educ:* Harrow County Grammar Sch. for Boys. Board of Trade: Exec. Officer, 1957; Asst Private Sec. to Parly Sec., 1961; Private Sec. to Minister of State (Lords), 1963; Asst Principal, 1965; Second Sec., UK Delegn to EFTA/GATT, Geneva, 1966; Principal, DTI, 1969; Asst Sec., Dept of Energy, 1974; Counsellor (Energy), Washington, 1981–86; Head, Br. 1, Atomic Energy Div., 1986–89, Dir, Personnel, 1989–92, Dept of Energy. *Recreations:* music, golf. *Address:* Orchard House, Berks Hill, Chorleywood, Herts WD3 5AG. *T:* Chorleywood (01923) 282311. *Club:* Northwood Golf.

HAMPTON, Christopher James, FRSL 1976; playwright; *b* 26 Jan. 1946; *s* of Bernard Patrick Hampton and Dorothy Patience Hampton (*née* Herrington); *m* 1971, Laura Margaret de Holesch; two *d*. *Educ:* Lancing Coll.; New Coll., Oxford (MA). First play: When Did You Last See My Mother?, 1964 (perf. Royal Court Theatre, 1966; transf. Comedy Theatre; prod. at Sheridan Square Playhouse, New York, 1967). Resident Dramatist, Royal Court Theatre, Aug. 1968–70. Mem. Council, RSL, 1984–90. *Plays:* Total Eclipse, Prod. Royal Court, 1968; The Philanthropist, Royal Court and Mayfair, 1970 (Evening Standard Best Comedy Award, 1970; Plays & Players London Theatre Critics Best Play, 1970), Ethel Barrymore Theatre, New York, 1971, Chichester, 1985; Savages, Royal Court, 1973, Comedy, 1973, Mark Taper Forum Theatre, Los Angeles, 1974 (Plays & Players London Theatre Critics Best Play, Jt Winner, 1973; Los Angeles Drama Critics Circle Award for Distinguished Playwriting, 1974); Treats, Royal Court, 1976, Mayfair, 1976; Able's Will, BBC TV, 1977; After Mercer, Nat. Theatre, 1980; The History Man (from Malcolm Bradbury) BBC TV, 1981; Total Eclipse (rev. version) Lyric, Hammersmith, 1981; The Portage to San Cristobal of A. H. (from George Steiner), Mermaid, 1982; Tales from Hollywood, Mark Taper Forum Theatre, Los Angeles, 1982, NT 1983 (Standard Best Comedy Award, 1983); Les Liaisons Dangereuses (from Laclos), RSC, 1985, transf. Ambassadors Th., 1986, NY, 1987 (Plays & Players London Theatre Critics Best Play, Jt Winner, 1985; Time Out Best Production Award, 1986; London Standard Best Play Award, 1986; Laurence Olivier Best Play Award, 1986; NY Drama Critics' Circle Best For. Play Award, 1987); Hotel du Lac (from Anita Brookner), BBC TV, 1986 (BAFTA Best TV Film Award, 1987); The Ginger Tree (from Oswald Wynd), BBC TV, 1989; White Chameleon, Nat. Theatre, 1991; Alice's Adventures Under Ground, Nat. Theatre, 1994; *musical:* Sunset Boulevard (book and lyrics with Don Black), Adelphi, and Shubert Theatre, LA, 1993, Minskoff Theatre, NY, 1994; *translations:* Marya, by Isaac Babel, Royal Court, 1967; Uncle Vanya, by Chekhov, Royal Court, 1970; Hedda Gabler, by Ibsen, Fest. Theatre, Stratford, Ont, 1970, Almeida, Islington, 1984, rev. version, NT, 1989; A Doll's House, by Ibsen, Playhouse Theatre, New York, 1971, Criterion, London, 1973, Vivian Beaumont Theatre, New York, 1975; Don Juan, by Molière, Bristol Old Vic, 1972; Tales from the Vienna Woods, by Horváth, National Theatre, 1977; Don Juan Comes Back from the War, by Horváth, Nat. Theatre, 1978; Ghosts, by Ibsen, Actors' Co., 1978; The Wild Duck, by Ibsen, Nat. Theatre, 1979; The Prague Trial, by Chereau and Mnouchkine, Paris Studio, 1980; Tartuffe, by Molière, RSC, 1983; Faith, Hope and Charity, by Horváth, Lyric, Hammersmith, 1989; *screenplays:* A Doll's House, 1973; Tales From the Vienna Woods, 1979; The Honorary Consul, 1983; The Good Father, 1986 (Prix Italia 1988); Wolf at the Door, 1986; Dangerous Liaisons, 1988 (Academy Award, and Writers Guild of America Award, for best adapted screenplay; Critics' Circle Award for best screenplay, 1989; BAFTA best screenplay award, 1990); Total Eclipse, 1995; Mary Reilly, 1995; (also dir.) Carrington, 1995. *Publications:* When Did You Last See My Mother?, 1967; Total Eclipse, 1969, rev. version, 1981; The Philanthropist, 1970, 2nd edn 1985, The Philanthropist and other plays, 1991; Savages, 1974; Treats, 1976; Able's Will, 1979; Tales from Hollywood, 1983; The Portage to San Cristobal of A. H. (George Steiner), 1983; Les Liaisons Dangereuses, 1985; Dangerous Liaisons: the film, 1989; The Ginger Tree, 1989; White Chameleon, 1991; Alice's Adventures Under Ground, 1995; Carrington, 1995; *translations:* Isaac Babel, Marya, 1969; Chekhov, Uncle Vanya, 1971; Ibsen, Hedda Gabler, 1972, rev. version 1989; Ibsen, A Doll's House, 1972, 2nd edn 1989; Molière, Don Juan, 1972; Horváth, Tales from the Vienna Woods, 1977; Horváth, Don Juan Comes Back from the War, 1978; Ibsen, The Wild Duck, 1980; Ibsen, Ghosts, 1983; Molière, Tartuffe, 1984, 2nd edn 1991; Horváth, Faith, Hope and Charity, 1989. *Recreations:* travel, cinema. *Address:* 2 Kensington Park Gardens, W11 3HB. *Club:* Dramatists'.

HAMPTON, John; a Recorder of the Crown Court, since 1983; *b* 13 Nov. 1926; *e s* of late Thomas Victor Hampton and Alice Maud (*née* Sturgeon), Oulton Broad; *m* 1954, Laura Jessie, *d* of Ronald Mylne Ford and Margaret Jessie Ford (*née* Coghill), Newcastle-under-Lyme; three *d*. *Educ:* Bradford Grammar School; University College London (LLB). Served Royal Navy, 1945–47. Called to the Bar, Inner Temple, 1952; NE Circuit; Solicitor General and Attorney General; Dep. Circuit Judge, 1975–82. Dep. Chm., Agricultural Land Tribunal, Yorks and Lancs Area, 1980–82, Yorks and Humberside Area, 1982–; Dep. Traffic Comr, NE Traffic Area, 1988–94. *Recreations:* mountaineering, sailing. *Address:* 37 Park Square, Leeds LS1 2NY. *T:* Leeds (0113) 243 9422.

HAMPTON, Surgeon Rear-Adm. Trevor Richard Walker, CB 1988; FRCPE; Surgeon Rear-Admiral (Operational Medical Services), 1987–89; *b* 6 June 1930; *s* of Violet and Percy Hampton; *m* 1st, 1952, Rosemary (*née* Day); three *d*; 2nd, 1976, Jennifer (*née* Bootle). *Educ:* King Edward VII Grammar School, King's Lynn; Edinburgh University. MB, ChB 1954; MRCPE 1964. Resident House Officer, Edinburgh Royal Infirmary, 1954–55; joined RN as Surgeon Lieut, 1955; served in HM Ships Ganges, Harrier and Victorious, 1955–62; Clinical Asst, Dept of Medicine, Edinburgh Univ., 1964; RN Hosp., Gibraltar, 1965–68; Consultant Physician, RN Hospitals, Plymouth, 1969–74, Haslar, 1975–79; MO i/c, RN Hosp., Gibraltar, 1980–82, RN Hosp., Plymouth, 1982–84; Surgeon Rear-Adm., Support Medical Services, 1984–87. QHP 1983–89. OStJ 1983. *Publications:* contribs to Jl of RN Med. Service. *Recreations:* reading, writing, resting.

HAMWEE, Baroness *cr* 1991 (Life Peer), of Richmond upon Thames; **Sally Rachel Hamwee;** Partner, Clintons, solicitors; *b* 12 Jan. 1947; *d* of late Alec Hamwee and of Dorothy Hamwee (*née* Saunders). *Educ:* Manchester High Sch. for Girls; Girton Coll., Cambridge (MA). Admitted as solicitor, 1972. Councillor, London Borough of Richmond upon Thames, 1978– (Chm., Planning Cttee, 1983–87; Vice Chm., Policy and Resources Cttee, 1987–92); Chair, London Planning Adv. Cttee, 1986–94; Chm., Members' Policy Gp, London and SE Regl Planning Conf., 1989–91. Vice Chm., Assoc. of Liberal Democrat Councillors, 1988–; Member: Nat. Exec., Liberal Party, 1987–88; Federal Exec., Liberal Democrats, 1989–91; Lib Dem spokesman on envmt (local govt, 1991–, planning and housing, 1993–), H of L. Dir, London First, 1993–. Member: Council, Parents for Children, 1977–86; Joseph Rowntree Foundn Inquiry, Planning for Housing, 1992–94; Council, Family Policies Study Centre, 1994–. Legal Advr, Simon Community, 1980–; Co-Chair, Refuge (formerly Chiswick Family Rescue), 1991–; Dir, In Harmony, 1994–. *Address:* 101A Mortlake High Street, SW14 8HQ. *T:* 0181–878 1380.

HAMYLTON JONES, Keith, CMG 1979; HM Diplomatic Service, retired; HM Ambassador, to Costa Rica, 1974–79, to Honduras, 1975–78, and to Nicaragua, 1976–79; *b* 12 Oct. 1924; *m* 1953, Eira Morgan; one *d*. *Educ:* St Paul's Sch.; Balliol Coll., Oxford (Domus Scholar in Classics, 1943); BA 1948; MA 1950. Welsh Guards, 1943; Italy, 1944 (Lieut); S France, 1946 (Staff Captain). HM Foreign Service, 1949; 3rd Sec., Warsaw, 1950; 2nd Sec., Lisbon, 1953; 1st Sec., Manila, 1957; Head of Chancery and HM Consul, Montevideo, 1962; Head of Chancery, Rangoon, 1967; Asst Head of SE Asia Dept, FCO, 1968; Consul-General, Lubumbashi, 1970–72; Counsellor, FCO, 1973–74. Operation Raleigh: Chm. for Devon and Cornwall, 1983–85; led internat. expedn to Costa Rica, Feb–May 1985. Chairman: Anglo-Costa Rican Soc., 1983–88; Anglo-Central American Soc., 1988–91. *Publication:* (as Peter Myllent) The Ideal World, 1972. *Recreations:* reading, writing, walking. *Address:* Morval House, Morval, near Looe, Cornwall PL13 1PN.

HAN Suyin, (Dr Elizabeth Comber); doctor and author; (*née* Elizabeth Kuanghu Chow); *b* 12 Sept. 1917; *d* of Y. T. Chow (Zhou) (Chinese) and M. Denis (Belgian); *m* 1st, 1938, General P. H. Tang (*d* 1947); one *d*; 2nd, 1952, L. F. Comber (marr. diss. 1968); 3rd, 1971, Vincent Ruthnaswamy. *Educ:* Yenching Univ., Peking, China; Brussels Univ., Brussels, Belgium; London Univ., London, England. Graduated MB, BS, London (Hons) in 1948, a practising doctor until 1964. *Publications: as Han Suyin:* Destination Chungking, 1942; A Many Splendoured Thing, 1952; And the Rain My Drink, 1956; The Mountain Is Young, 1958; Cast but One Shadow and Winter Love, 1962; The Four Faces, 1963; China in the Year 2001, 1967; The Morning Deluge, 1972; Wind in the Tower, 1976; Lhasa, the Open City, 1977; Les Cent Fleurs: La Peinture Chinoise, 1978; La Chine aux Mille Visages, 1980; Chine: Terre Eau et Hommes, 1981; Till Morning Comes, 1982; The Enchantress, 1985; A Share of Loving, 1987; Han Suyin's China, 1988; Fleur de Soleil, 1988; Tigers and Butterflies, 1990; Les Yeux de Demain, 1992; Eldest Son: Zhou Enlai and the making of modern China (1898–1976), 1994; *autobiography:* China: autobiography, biography, history (6 vols): The Crippled Tree, 1965; A Mortal Flower, 1966; Birdless Summer, 1968; My House Has Two Doors, 1980; Phoenix Harvest, 1980; Wind in my Sleeve, 1992. *Recreations:* economics studies, lecturing, founding exchanges in science. *Address:* 37 Montoie, Lausanne 1007, Switzerland.

HANBURY-TENISON, (Airling) Robin, OBE 1981; MA, FLS, FRGS; farmer; President, Survival International (Chairman since 1969); *b* 7 May 1936; *s* of late Major Gerald Evan Farquhar Tenison, Lough Bawn, Co. Monaghan, Ireland, and Ruth, *o* surv. *c* of late John Capel Hanbury, JP, DL, Pontypool Park, Monmouthshire; *m* 1st, 1959, Marika Hopkinson (*d* 1982); one *s* one *d*; 2nd, 1983, Mrs Louella Edwards, *d* of Lt Col G. T. G. Williams, DL, and Mrs Williams, Menkee, St Mabyn, Cornwall; one *s*. *Educ:* Eton; Magdalen Coll., Oxford (MA). Made first land crossing of South America at its widest point, 1958 (Mrs Patrick Ness Award, RGS, 1961); explored Tassili N'Ajjer, Tibesti and Aïr mountains in Southern Sahara, 1962–66; crossed S America in a small boat from the Orinoco to Buenos Aires, 1964–65; Geographical Magazine Amazonas Expedn, by Hovercraft, 1968; Trans-African Hovercraft Expedn (Dep. Leader), 1969; visited 33 Indian tribes as guest of Brazilian Govt, 1971; Winston Churchill Memorial Fellow, 1971; British Trans Americas Expedn, 1972; explored Outer Islands of Indonesia, 1973; Eastern Sulawesi, 1974; Sabah, Brunei, Sarawak, 1976; RGS Mulu (Sarawak) Expedn (Leader), 1977–78; expedns to Ecuador, Brazil and Venezuela, 1980–81; rode across France, 1984; rode along Great Wall of China, 1986; rode through New Zealand, 1988; led mission for IUCN, Friends of the Earth and Survival Internat. to Malaysia to investigate imprisonment of envmtl protesters, 1988; rode as pilgrim to Santiago de Compostela, 1989; rode across Spain driving 300 cattle on Trans Lumance, 1991; visited tribal peoples of E Siberia for Survival Internat., 1992 and 1994; rode route of proposed Pennine Bridleway, 1994; visited tribal people of Arunachal Pradesh, NE India, 1995. Comr of Income Tax, 1965–; Mem., SW Regl Panel, MAFF, 1993–; Mem. of Lloyd's, 1976–. Mem., Invest in Britain (formerly Think British) Campaign, 1987–; Trustee, Ecological Foundn, 1988–; Pres., Cornwall Trust for Nature Conservation, 1988–. Mem. Council, RGS, 1968–70, 1971–76, 1979–82, Vice-Pres., 1982–86; Patron's Medal, RGS, 1979; Krug Award of Excellence, 1980. Dr *hc* Mons-Hainaut, 1992. *Publications:* The Rough and the Smooth, 1969; Report of a Visit to the Indians of Brazil, 1971; A Question of Survival, 1973; A Pattern of Peoples, 1975; Mulu: the rain forest, 1980; Aborigines of the Amazon Rain Forest: the Yanomami, 1982; Worlds Apart (autobiog.), 1984; White Horses Over France, 1985; A Ride along the Great Wall, 1987; Fragile Eden: a ride through New Zealand, 1989; Spanish Pilgrimage: a canter to St James, 1990; (ed) The Oxford Book of Exploration, 1993; articles in: The Times, Spectator, etc; articles and reviews in Geographical Magazine (numerous), Geographical Jl, Ecologist, Traveller, etc. *Recreations:* travelling, riding across countries. *Address:* Cabilla Manor, Cardinham, Bodmin, Cornwall PL30 4DW. *T:* Cardinham (01208) 821224. *Clubs:* Groucho, Geographical; Kildare Street and University (Dublin).

See also Sir R. Hanbury-Tenison.

HANBURY-TENISON, Sir Richard, KCVO 1995; JP; Lord-Lieutenant of Gwent, since 1979; *b* 3 Jan. 1925; *e s* of late Major G. E. F. Tenison, Lough Bawn, Co. Monaghan, Ireland, and Ruth, *o* surv. *c* of late J. C. Hanbury, JP, DL, Pontypool Park, Monmouthshire; *m* 1955, Euphan Mary, *er d* of late Major A. B. Wardlaw-Ramsay, 21st of Whitehill, Midlothian; three *s* two *d*. *Educ:* Eton; Magdalen Coll., Oxford. Served Irish Guards, 1943–47 (Captain, wounded). Entered HM Foreign Service, 1949: 1st Sec., Vienna, 1956–58; 1st Sec. (and sometime Chargé d'Affaires), Phnom Penh, 1961–63, and Bucharest, 1966–68; Counsellor, Bonn, 1968–70; Head of Aviation and Telecommunications Dept, FCO, 1970–71; Counsellor, Brussels, 1971–75; retired from Diplomatic Service, 1975. South Wales Regional Dir, Lloyds Bank, 1980–91 (Chm., 1987–91). Dir, Gwent TEC, 1991–. Mem. Council, Nat. Museum of Wales, 1980– (Chm., Art Cttee, 1986–90). President: Monmouthshire Rural Community Council, 1959–75; Gwent Local Hist. Council; Gwent County Scout Council; Gwent Community Services Council, 1985– (Chm., 1975–85). President: TA&VRA for Wales, 1985–90; S Wales Regl Cttee, TA&VRA, 1990–. Hon. Col, 3rd (V) Bn, The Royal Regt of Wales, 1982–90. DL 1973, High Sheriff 1977, JP 1979, Gwent. KStJ 1990 (CStJ 1980). Award for Forestry and Woodland Management, Timber Growers (UK), 1990. *Recreations:* shooting, fishing, conservation. *Address:* Clytha Park, Abergavenny, Gwent NP7 9BW. *T:* Abergavenny (01873) 840300; Lough Bawn, Co. Monaghan. *Clubs:* Boodle's; Kildare Street and University (Dublin).

See also A. R. Hanbury-Tenison.

HANBURY-TENISON, Robin; *see* Hanbury-Tenison, A. R.

HANBURY-TRACY, family name of **Baron Sudeley.**

HANCOCK, Christine; General Secretary, Royal College of Nursing, since 1989. *Educ:* London School of Economics (BScEcons). RGN. Formerly: Chief Nursing Officer, Bloomsbury Health Authority; General Manager, Waltham Forest Health Authority. *Address:* Royal College of Nursing, 20 Cavendish Square, W1M 0AB. *T:* 0171–409 3333.

HANCOCK, Sir David (John Stowell), KCB 1985; Executive Director, Hambros Bank Ltd, since 1989; Director, Hambros PLC, since 1989; *b* 27 March 1934; *s* of late Alfred George Hancock and Florence Hancock (*née* Barrow); *m* 1966, Sheila Gillian Finlay; one *s* one *d*. *Educ:* Whitgift Sch.; Balliol Coll., Oxford. 2nd Lieut, RTR, 1953–54. Asst Principal, Bd of Trade, 1957; transf. to HM Treasury, 1959; Principal, 1962; Harkness Fellow, 1965–66; Private Sec. to Chancellor of the Exchequer, 1968–70; Asst Sec., 1970; Financial and Economic Counsellor, Office of UK Permanent Rep. to European Communities, 1972–74; Under Sec., 1975–80; Dep. Sec., 1980–82; Dep. Sec., Cabinet Office, 1982–83; Perm. Sec., DES, 1983–89. Dir, European Investment Bank, 1980–82. Chairman: Dyvell (Hldgs), 1990–94; MRC Pension Trust Ltd, 1991–; Combined Landfill Projects Ltd, 1993–; Dir, AXA Equity & Law, 1992–. NFHA Inquiry into Governance of Housing Assocs, 1994–95. Chairman: British Selection Cttee of Harkness Fellowships, 1988–92 (Mem., 1984–92); Foundn for Young Musicians, 1990–; Mem., E London Partnership, 1991–; Trustee, St Catharine's Foundn, Cumberland Lodge, 1989–; Chm., St Katharine and Shadwell Trust, 1990–.Freeman, City of London, 1989. FRSA 1986; CIMgt (CBIM 1987). Hon. LLD Poly. of E London, 1990. *Recreations:* walking, reading, gardening, theatre, opera. *Address:* c/o Hambros Bank Ltd, 41 Tower Hill, EC3N 4HA. *Clubs:* Athenæum, Civil Service.

HANCOCK, Elisabeth Joy; Head, Bromley High School (GPDST), since 1989; *b* 2 Dec. 1947; *d* of Reginald Arthur Lord and Evelyn Maud Mary Lord; *m* 1970, Barry Steuart Hancock; one *d*. *Educ:* Queen's Coll., Harley Street; Nottingham Univ. (BA Hons); Univ. of Sussex (PGCE). GB East Europe Centre, 1969; Nevill Sch., Hove, 1969–72; Brighton and Hove High Sch. (GPDST), 1972–89, Dep. Hd, 1986–89. FRSA 1988. *Publication:* Teaching History, 1970. *Recreations:* playing tennis, theatre, opera, watching cricket. *Address:* Bromley High School (GPDST), Blackbrook Lane, Bickley, Bromley, Kent BR1 2TW. *T:* 0181–468 7981. *Clubs:* Royal Over-Seas League, St James'.

HANCOCK, Group Captain Ethnea Mary, RRC 1990; Director and Matron-in-Chief, Princess Mary's Royal Air Force Nursing Service, and Deputy Director, Defence Nursing Services (Organisation), 1991–94; *b* 5 April 1937; *d* of late Sydney Ludwig Hancock and Catherine Teresa Hancock (*née* O'Dea). *Educ:* Convent of the Cross, Boscombe; University Coll. Hosp., London; RGN 1958; Southlands Hosp., Shoreham; Whittington Hosp., London; RM 1960. Joined PMRAFNS, 1961–65; Columbia Presbyterian Medical Center, NY, 1966–67; rejoined PMRAFNS, 1967; served RAF Hosps and Units, UK, N Africa, Cyprus, Singapore, Germany; appts include Sen. Matron, RAF Hosp., Ely, 1985–87; MoD, 1987–88; Principal Nursing Officer, PMRAFNS, 1988–91. QHNS, 1991–94. *Recreations:* home and garden, music, travelling, ski-ing. *Address:* First Direct, PO Box HK16, Millshaw Park Lane, Leeds LS11 0YF. *Club:* Royal Air Force.

HANCOCK, Geoffrey Francis, CMG 1977; HM Diplomatic Service, retired; Foreign and Commonwealth Office, 1979–82; *b* 20 June 1926; *s* of Lt-Col Sir Cyril Hancock, KCIE, OBE, MC; *m* 1960, Amelia Juana Aragon; one *s* one *d*. *Educ:* Wellington; Trinity Coll., Oxford. MA 1951. Third Sec., Mexico City, 1953; Second Sec., Montevideo, 1956; Foreign Office, 1958; Madrid, 1958; FO, 1960; MECAS, 1962; First Sec., Baghdad, 1964–67 and 1968–69; FCO, 1969–73; Counsellor, Beirut, 1973–78. Founder, Middle East Consultants, 1983. *Recreations:* music, sailing. *Address:* c/o Lloyds Bank, 8/10 Waterloo Place, SW1Y 4BE. *Clubs:* Athenæum, Royal Air Force.

HANCOCK, Prof. Keith Jackson, AO 1987; Vice-Chancellor, The Flinders University of South Australia, 1980–87; Senior Deputy President, Australian Industrial Relations Commission (formerly Australian Conciliation and Arbitration Commission), since 1992 (Deputy President, 1987–92); *b* 4 Jan. 1935; *s* of late A. S. Hancock and Mrs R. D. Hancock; three *s* one *d*. *Educ:* Univ. of Melbourne (BA); Univ. of London (PhD). Tutor in Economic History, Univ. of Melbourne, 1956–57; Lectr in Economics, Univ. of Adelaide, 1959–63; Professor of Economics, 1964–87, now Emeritus, Pro-Vice-Chancellor, 1975–79, Flinders Univ. of SA. Pres., Acad. of Social Sciences in Australia, 1981–84. FASSA 1968. Hon. Fellow, LSE, 1982. Hon. DLitt Flinders, 1987. *Publications:* (with P. A. Samuelson and R. H. Wallace) Economics (Australian edn), 1969, 2nd edn 1975; articles in Economic Jl, Economica, Amer. Econ. Rev. and other jls. *Recreations:* bridge, sailing, music. *Address:* 6 Maturin Road, Glenelg, SA 5045, Australia. *T:* (8) 2948667. *Clubs:* Adelaide (Adelaide); Royal South Australian Yacht Squadron.

HANCOCK, Maj.-Gen. Michael Stephen, CB 1972; MBE 1953; retired 1972; Planning Inspector, Department of the Environment, 1972–87; *b* 19 July 1917; *s* of late Rev. W. H. M. Hancock and late Mrs C. C. Hancock (*née* Sherbrooke); *m* 1941, Constance Geraldine Margaret Ovens, *y d* of late Brig.-Gen. R. M. Ovens, CMG; one *s* one *d*. *Educ:* Marlborough Coll.; RMA, Woolwich. Commnd into Royal Signals, 1937; Comdr, Corps Royal Signals, 1st British Corps, 1963–66; Sec., Mil. Cttee, NATO, 1967–68; Chief of Staff, FARELF, 1968–70; VQMG, MoD, 1970–72. Col Comdt, Royal Signals, 1970–77. Chm., CCF Assoc., 1972–82, Vice Pres., 1982–; Chm., NE Surrey Dist Scouts, 1979–82, Pres., 1982–. CEng; FIEE. *Recreations:* DIY, chess.

HANCOCK, Michael Thomas, CBE 1992; District Officer for Hampshire, Isle of Wight and Channel Islands, Royal Society for Mentally Handicapped Children and Adults, since 1989; Leader, Hampshire County Council, since 1993; *b* 9 April 1946; *m* 1967, Jacqueline, *d* of Sidney and Gwen Elliott; one *s* one *d*. *Educ:* well. Member: Portsmouth City Council, 1971– (for Fratton Ward, 1973–; Leader, LibDem Gp, 1989–; Chm., Planning and Econ. Develt Cttee, 1991–); Hampshire County Council, 1973– (Leader of the Opposition,

1977–81, 1989–93; Leader, LibDem Gp, 1989–). Joined SDP, 1981 (Mem., Nat. Cttee, 1984); contested Portsmouth S (SDP) 1983, (SDP/Alliance) 1987. MP (SDP) Portsmouth S, June 1984–87. Contested (Lib Dem) Wight and Hampshire South, Eur. Parly elecns, 1994. Vice Chairman: Portsmouth Operating Co., 1992–; Portsmouth Docks, 1992–. Dir, Daytime Club, BBC, 1987–90. Bd of Dirs, Drug Rehabilitation Unit, Alpha Drug Clinic, Alpha House, Droxford, 1971–; Chm., Southern Br., NSPCC, 1989–. Trustee, Royal Marine Museum, 1993. Hon. award for contrib. to Anglo-German relations, Homborn, W Germany, 1981. *Publications:* contribs to various jls. *Recreations:* people, living life to the full. *Address:* (office) Somerstown Health Centre, Blackfriars Close, Southsea, Hants PO5 4NJ. *T:* Portsmouth (01705) 830530; (political office) Portsmouth (01705) 834172; (home) Fareham (01329) 287340. *Clubs:* too many to mention.

HANCOCK, Norman, CB 1976; CEng, FRINA; RCNC; Director of Warship Design, and Project Director, Invincible and Broadsword, Ministry of Defence, 1969–76; *b* 6 March 1916; *o s* of Louis Everard Hancock, Plymouth; *m* 1940, Marie E., *d* of William E. Bow; two *s*. *Educ:* Plymouth Grammar Sch.; RNC Greenwich. Asst Constructor, AEW, Haslar, 1940; Constructor, Naval Construction Dept, 1944; British Services Observer (Constructor Comdr), Bikini, 1946. HM Dockyard, Singapore, 1949; Frigate design, Naval Construction Dept, 1952; Chief Constructor in charge of R&D, 1954; Prof. of Naval Architecture, RNC, Greenwich, 1957–62; Asst Dir of Naval Construction, in charge of Submarine Design and Construction, 1963–69. Liveryman, Worshipful Co. of Shipwrights; past Mem. Council, RINA. *Recreations:* organ music, cabinet making, travel. *Address:* 41 Cranwells Park, Bath, Avon BA1 2YE. *T:* Bath (01225) 426045.

HANCOCK, P(ercy) E(llis) Thompson, FRCP; Former Hon. Consultant Physician: The Royal Free Hospital; The Royal Marsden Hospital; Potters Bar and District Hospital; National Temperance Hospital; Bishop's Stortford and District Hospital; *b* 4 Feb. 1904; *s* of Frank Hancock; *m* 1932, Dorothy Barnes (*d* 1953); two *d*; *m* 1955, Laurie Newton Sharp. *Educ:* Wellington Coll., Berks; Caius Coll., Cambridge; St Bartholomew's Hospital. MB 1937, BCh 1930, Cantab; FRCP 1944. Formerly: Senior Examiner in Medicine, Univ. of London; Dir of Dept of Clinical Res., Royal Marsden Hosp. and Inst. of Cancer Res. Member: Council, Imperial Cancer Res. Fund; Grand Council, Cancer Research Campaign; Mem. Exec. Cttee, Action on Smoking and Health; Sen. Mem., Assoc. of Physicians, GB and Ireland. Hosp. Visitor, King Edward's Hosp. Fund for London. FRSocMed (Pres., Section of Oncology, 1974–75); Fellow, Assoc. Européene de Médecine Interne d'Ensemble. Corresp. Mem., Società Italiana de Cancerologia. Hon. Member: American Gastroscopic Soc., 1958; Sociedad Chilena de Cancerología; Sociedad Chilena de Hematología; Sociedad Médica de Valparaíso; Medal, Societa Medica Chirurgica di Bologna, 1964. *Publications:* (joint) Cancer in General Practice; The Use of Bone Marrow Transfusion with massive Chemotherapy, 1960; (joint) Treatment of Early Hodgkin's Disease, 1967. *Recreations:* dining and wining. *Address:* 23 Wigmore Place, W1H 9DD. *T:* 0171–631 4679.

HANCOCK, Ronald John; business consultant; Director: Insituform Ltd, 1987–94; Travelines, 1991–94; Permaline, 1991–94; *b* 11 Feb. 1934; *s* of George and Elsie Hancock; *m* 1970, Valerie Hancock; two *d*. *Educ:* Dudley Grammar Sch., Dudley. FCMA. Served HM Forces, 1952–61. Schweppes Ltd, 1962–63; Mullard Ltd, 1963–66; Valor Group, 1966–68; BL Ltd, 1968–85. Chairman: Leyland Vehicles, 1981–85; Leyland Vehicles Exports Ltd, 1981–85; Bus Manufacturers Limited, 1981–85; Bus Manufacturers (Holdings) Ltd, 1981–85; Eastern Coachworks Ltd, 1981–85; Bristol Commercial Vehicles Ltd, 1981–85; Self-Changing Gears Ltd, 1981–85; Bedfordshire Chamber of Training Ltd, 1990–; Director: BL Staff Trustees Ltd, 1981–85; Leyland Nigeria Ltd, 1981–85; BL International Ltd, 1981–85; Land Rover-Leyland International Holdings Ltd (formerly BLIH), 1982–85; Land Rover-Leyland Ltd, 1983–85; Chloride Gp plc, 1985–87; Man. Dir, AWD Ltd, 1987–90. *Recreations:* travel, reading. *Address:* 5 Shardeloes, Amersham, Bucks HP7 0RL.

HANCOCK, Sheila, OBE 1974; actress and director; *d* of late Enrico Hancock and late Ivy Woodward; *m* 1st, 1955, Alexander Ross (*d* 1971); one *d*; 2nd, 1973, John Thaw, *qv*; one *d*. *Educ:* Dartford County Grammar Sch.; Royal Academy of Dramatic Art. Acted in Repertory, Theatre Workshop, Stratford East, for 8 years. Associate Dir, Cambridge Theatre Co., 1980–82; Artistic Dir, RSC Regional Tour, 1983–84; acted and directed, NT, 1985–86. Dir, The Actors Centre, 1978–. West End starring roles in: Rattle of a Simple Man, 1962; The Anniversary, 1966; A Delicate Balance (RSC), 1969; So What About Love?, 1969; Absurd Person Singular, 1973; Déjà Revue, 1974; The Bed Before Yesterday, 1976; Annie, 1978; Sweeney Todd, 1980; The Winter's Tale, RSC, Stratford 1981, Barbican 1982; Peter Pan, Barbican, 1982–83; The Cherry Orchard, The Duchess of Malfi, National, 1985–86; Greenland, Royal Court, 1988; Prin, Lyric, Hammersmith, 1989, Lyric, Shaftesbury Avenue, 1990; A Judgement in Stone, The Way of the World, Lyric, Hammersmith, 1992. Has starred in several successful revues; appeared on Broadway in Entertaining Mr Sloane. Directed: The Soldier's Fortune, Lyric, Hammersmith, 1981; A Midsummer Night's Dream, RSC, 1983; The Critic, National, 1986. *Films:* The Love Child, 1987; Making Waves, 1987; Hawks, 1988; Buster, 1988; Three Men and a Little Lady, 1990. *Television:* many successes, including Jumping the Queue, The Rivals, and several comedy series, incl. Gone to the Dogs, 1991, Gone to Seed, 1992, Brighton Belles, 1993; other appearances include: The Buccaneers, 1994; Dangerous Lady, 1994; wrote and acted in Royal Enclosure, 1990. Awards: Variety Club, London Critics, Whitbread Trophy (for best Actress on Broadway). *Publication:* Ramblings of an Actress, 1987. *Recreations:* reading, music. *Address:* c/o John Wood, London Management, 2–4 Noel Street, W1V 3RB.

HANCOCK, Air Marshal Sir Valston Eldridge, KBE 1962 (CBE 1953; OBE 1942); CB 1958; DFC 1945; retired; grazier; *b* 31 May 1907; *s* of R. J. Hancock, Perth, W Australia; *m* 1932, Joan E. G., *d* of Col A. G. Butler, DSO, VD; two *s* one *d*. *Educ:* Hale Sch., Perth; RMC, Duntroon; psa; idc. Joined Royal Military College, Duntroon, 1925; transferred RAAF, 1929; Dir of Plans, 1940–41; commanded 71 (Beaufort) Wing, New Guinea, 1945; Commandant RAAF Academy, 1947–49; Deputy Chief of Air Staff, 1951–53; Air Mem. for Personnel, Air Board, 1953–54; Head of Australian Joint Services Staff, UK, 1955–57; Extra Gentleman Usher to the Royal Household, 1955–57; AOC 224 Group, RAF, Malaya, 1957–59; Air Officer Commanding Operational Command, 1959–61; Chief of Air Staff, Royal Australian Air Force, 1961–65. Commissioner-Gen., Australian Exhibit Organization, Expo 1967. Foundation Chm., Australian Defence Assoc., 1975–81, Life Patron, 1982–. Life Mem., Royal Commonwealth Soc. (WA) (Pres., 1976–81). *Recreations:* literature and sport. *Address:* 108a Victoria Avenue, Dalkeith, WA 6009, Australia. *Club:* Weld (Perth).

HAND, Rt. Rev. Geoffrey David, KBE 1984 (CBE 1975); *b* 11 May 1918; *s* of Rev. W. T. Hand. *Educ:* Oriel College, Oxford; Cuddesdon Theological Coll., BA 1941, MA 1946. Deacon, 1942; Priest, 1943. Curate of Heckmondwike, 1942–46; Missioner, Diocese of New Guinea, 1946–50; Priest in charge: Sefoa, 1947–48; Sangara, 1948–50; Archdeacon, North New Guinea, 1950–65; Bishop Coadjutor of New Guinea, 1950–63; Bishop of New Guinea (later Papua New Guinea), 1963–77; Archbishop of Papua New Guinea, 1977–83; Bishop of Port Moresby, 1977–83; Priest-in-charge, East with West Rudham, Houghton next Harpley, Syderstone, Tatterford and Tattersett, dio. Norwich, 1983–85. *Address:* PO Box 49, Gerehu, NCD, Papua New Guinea. *T:* Papua New Guinea 260317.

HAND, Prof. Geoffrey Joseph Philip, DPhil; Barber Professor of Jurisprudence in the University of Birmingham, 1980–92, now Professor Emeritus; *b* 25 June 1931; *s* of Joseph and Mary Macaulay Hand. *Educ:* Blackrock Coll.; University Coll., Dublin (MA); New Coll., Oxford (DPhil); King's Inns, Dublin. Called to Irish Bar, 1961. Lecturer: Univ. of Edinburgh, 1960; Univ. of Southampton, 1961; University Coll., Dublin, 1965; Professor: University Coll., Dublin, 1972–76; European University Inst., Fiesole, 1976–80; Dean of Faculty of Law, University Coll., Dublin, 1970–75. Chairman, Arts Council of Ireland, 1974–75. Mem. Council, RIA, 1994–. *Publications:* English Law in Ireland 1290–1324, 1967; Report of the Irish Boundary Commission 1925, 1969; (with Lord Cross of Chelsea) Radcliffe and Cross's English Legal System, 5th edn 1971, 6th edn 1977; (with J. Georgel, C. Sasse) European Election Systems Handbook, 1979; Towards a Uniform System of Direct Elections, 1981; (ed with J. McBride) Droit sans Frontières, 1991; numerous periodicals. *Recreations:* listening to classical music, playing chess. *Address:* 72 Granitefield, Dun Laoghaire, Republic of Ireland. *Clubs:* United Oxford & Cambridge University; Royal Irish Yacht (Dun Laoghaire); Kildare Street and University (Dublin).

HAND, Graham Stewart; HM Diplomatic Service; Deputy High Commissioner, Nigeria, since 1994; *b* 3 Nov. 1948; *s* of Ronald Charles Hand and Mary Fraser Hand (*née* Stewart); *m* 1973, Anne Mary Seton Campbell; one *s* one *d* (and one *s* decd). *Educ:* RMA Sandhurst; St John's Coll., Cambridge (MA 1979). Regular Army, 1969–80; FCO, 1980; served UN Dept, 1980–82; Dakar, 1982–84; News Dept, FCO, 1984–87; Head of Chancery, Helsinki, 1987–90; Aid Policy Dept, ODA, 1991–92; Head of Human Rights Policy Dept, FCO, 1992–94. *Recreations:* opera, choral singing, sailing, golf, cooking. *Address:* c/o Foreign and Commonwealth Office, SW1A 2AH.

HAND, John Lester; QC 1988; a Recorder, since 1991; *b* 16 June 1947; *s* of John James and Violet Hand; *m* 1st, 1972, Helen Andrea McWatt (marr. diss.); 2nd, 1990, Lynda Ray Ferrigno; one *d*. *Educ:* Huddersfield New College; Univ. of Nottingham (LLB 1969). Called to the Bar, Gray's Inn, 1972; Northern Circuit, 1972. Legal Assessor, GMC and GDC, 1990–. *Recreations:* sailing, travel. *Address:* 9 St John Street, Manchester M3 4DN. *T:* 0161–833 9801; 15 Old Square, Lincoln's Inn, WC2A 3UH. *T:* 0171–831 0801.

HANDCOCK, family name of **Baron Castlemaine.**

HANDFORD, Ven. (George) Clive; *see* Warwick, Bishop Suffragan of.

HANDLEY, Ven. Anthony Michael; Archdeacon of Norfolk, since 1993; *b* 3 June 1936; *s* of Eric Harvey Handley and Janet Handley; *m* 1962, Christine May Adlington; two *s* one *d*. *Educ:* Spalding Grammar School; Selwyn Coll., Cambridge (MA Hons); Chichester Theological Coll. Asst Curate, Thorpe St Andrew, 1962–66; Anglican Priest on Fairstead Estate, 1966–72; Vicar of Hellesdon, 1972–81; RD of Norwich North, 1979–81; Archdeacon of Norwich, 1981–93. Proctor in Convocation, 1980–85; Mem., General Synod, 1990–. Research Project, The Use of Colour, Shape, and Line Drawings as Experiential Training Resources, 1976. County Scout Chaplain for Norfolk. *Publication:* A Parish Prayer Card, 1980. *Recreations:* climbing mountains, painting, bird watching. *Address:* 40 Heigham Road, Norwich NR2 3AU. *T:* Norwich (01603) 611808.

HANDLEY, Mrs Carol Margaret; Headmistress, Camden School for Girls, 1971–85; *b* 17 Oct. 1929; *d* of Claude Hilary Taylor and Margaret Eleanor Taylor (*née* Peebles); *m* 1952, Eric Walter Handley, *qv*. *Educ:* St Paul's Girls' Sch.; University Coll., London (BA), Fellow 1977. Asst Classics Mistress: North Foreland Lodge Sch., 1952; Queen's Gate Sch., 1952; Head of Classics Dept, Camden Sch. for Girls, 1956; Deputy Headmistress, Camden Sch. for Girls, 1964. Sen. Mem., Wolfson Coll., Cambridge, 1989–. Member Council: RHC, then RHBNC, 1977–; Middx Hosp. Med. Sch., 1980–84; Mem. Governors and Council, Bedford Coll., 1981–85. *Publications:* articles and book reviews for classical jls. *Recreation:* gardening. *Address:* Colt House, High Street, Little Eversden, Cambs CB3 7HE.

HANDLEY, Sir David John D.; *see* Davenport-Handley.

HANDLEY, Prof. Eric Walter, CBE 1983; FBA 1969; Professor of Ancient Literature, Royal Academy, since 1990; Fellow, Trinity College, Cambridge, since 1984; *b* 12 Nov. 1926; *s* of late Alfred W. Handley and A. Doris Cox; *m* 1952, Carol Margaret Taylor (*see* C. M. Handley). *Educ:* King Edward's Sch., Birmingham; Trinity Coll., Cambridge. Stewart of Rannoch Schol. and Browne Medal, 1945. University College London: Asst Lectr in Latin and Greek, 1946; Lectr, 1949; Reader, 1961; Prof. of Latin and Greek, 1967–68; Prof. and Head of Dept of Greek, 1968–84; Hon. Fellow, 1989; Dir, Inst. of Classical Studies, Univ. of London, 1967–84; Regius Prof. of Greek, Cambridge Univ., 1984–94. Vis. Lectr on the Classics, Harvard, 1966; Vis. Mem., Inst. for Advanced Study, Princeton, 1971; Visiting Professor: Stanford Univ., 1977; Melbourne Univ., 1978; Vis. Senior Fellow, Council of the Humanities, Princeton, 1981. Sec. Council Univ. Classical Depts, 1969–70, Chm., 1975–78. President: Classical Assoc., 1984–85; Hellenic Soc., 1993–; Foreign Sec., British Academy, 1979–88; Member: Comité Scientifique, Fondation Hardt, Geneva, 1978–; Commn des Affaires Internes, Union Académique Internationale, 1984– (Mem. du Bureau, 1991–); Academia Europaea, 1988–. Foreign Mem., Societas Scientiarum Fennica, 1984; Hon. Mem., Hungarian Acad. of Scis, 1993. Chm., Gilbert Murray Trust, 1988–. Hon. RA 1990. (Jtly) Cromer Greek Prize, 1958. *Publications:* (with John Rea) The Telephus of Euripides, 1957; The Dyskolos of Menander, 1965; (contrib.) Cambridge History of Classical Literature, 1985; (with André Hurst) Relire Ménandre, 1990; (with J.-M. Bremer) Aristophane, 1993; (with J. R. Green) Images of the Greek Theatre, 1994; Greek literary papyri, papers in class. jls, etc. *Recreations:* walking, travel. *Address:* Trinity College, Cambridge CB2 1TQ. *Club:* United Oxford & Cambridge University.

HANDLEY, Paul; Editor, Church Times, since 1995; *b* 29 May 1958; *s* of Arnold Terence Handley and Margaret Hardy; *m* 1980, Terence MacMath; one *s* one *d*. *Educ:* Colchester Royal Grammar Sch.; Goldsmiths Coll., Univ. of London (BA English 1980). News Editor, Church of England Newspaper, 1981–85; freelance publisher, writer, 1986–88; Reporter, Church Times, 1988–90; Press Sec. to Archbishop of Canterbury, 1990–92; freelance writer, 1992–94; News Editor, Church Times, 1994. *Address:* c/o Church Times, 33 Upper Street, N1 0PN. *T:* 0171–359 4570.

HANDLEY, Vernon George, FRCM 1972; Principal Guest Conductor, Royal Liverpool Philharmonic Orchestra, since 1989; Associate Conductor, London Philharmonic Orchestra, 1983–86 (Guest Conductor, 1961–83); *b* 11 Nov. 1930; 2nd *s* of Vernon Douglas Handley and Claudia Lilian Handley, Enfield; *m* 1st, 1954, Barbara (marr. diss.), *e d* of Kilner Newman Black and Joan Elfriede Black, Stoke Gabriel, Devon; one *s* one *d* (and one *s* decd); 2nd, 1977, Victoria (marr. diss.), *d* of Vaughan and Nona Parry-Jones, Guildford, Surrey; one *s* one *d*; 3rd, 1987, Catherine, *e d* of Kenneth and Joan Newby, Harrogate, Yorks; one *s*. *Educ:* Enfield Sch.; Balliol Coll., Oxford (BA); Guildhall Sch. of Music. Conductor: Oxford Univ. Musical Club and Union, 1953–54; OUDS, 1953–54; Tonbridge Philharmonic Soc., 1958–61; Hatfield Sch. of Music and Drama, 1959–61;

Proteus Choir, 1962–81; Musical Dir and Conductor, Guildford Corp., and Conductor, Guildford Philharmonic Orch. and Choir, 1962–83; Prof. at RCM: for Orchestra and Conducting, 1966–72; for Choral Class, 1969–72. Principal Conductor: Ulster Orch., 1985–89; Malmö SO, 1985–88. Guest Conductor from 1961: Bournemouth Symph. Orch.; Birmingham Symph. Orch.; Royal Philharmonic Orch.; BBC Welsh Orch.; BBC Northern Symph. Orch.; Royal Liverpool Philharmonic Orch.; Ulster Orch.; Scottish Nat. Orch.; Philharmonia Orch.; Strasbourg Philharmonic Orch., 1982–; Helsinki Philharmonic, 1984–; Amsterdam Philharmonic, 1985; Guest Conductor, 1961–83, Principal Guest Conductor, 1983–85, BBC Scottish Symphony Orch.; conducted London Symphony Orch. in internat. series, London, 1971; toured: Germany, 1966, 1980; S Africa, 1974; Holland, 1980; Sweden, 1980, 1981; Germany, Sweden, Holland and France, 1982–83; Australia, 1986; Japan, 1988; Australia, 1989; Artistic Dir, Norwich and Norfolk Triennial Fest., 1985. Regular broadcaster and has made many records. Pres., Nat. Federation of Gramophone Socs, 1984–; Vice-President: Delius Soc., 1983–; Elgar Soc., 1984–; Fellow Goldsmiths' Coll. 1987; Hon. Mem., Royal Philharmonic Soc., 1989. Hon. RCM, 1970; FRCM 1972. Arnold Bax Meml Medal for Conducting, 1962; Conductor of the Year, British Composers' Guild, 1974; Hi-Fi News Audio Award, 1982; BPI Classical Award, 1986, 1988; Gramophone Record of the Year, 1986, 1989. DUniv Surrey, 1980. *Recreations:* bird photography, old-fashioned roses. *Address:* Hen Gerrig, Pen-y-Fan, near Monmouth, Gwent NP5 4RA. *T:* Trelleck (01600) 860318.

HANDLEY-TAYLOR, Geoffrey, FRSL 1950; author; Hon. Home and Overseas Information Correspondent, John Masefield Research and Studies, 1958–93; *b* 25 April 1920; 2nd *s* of Walter Edward Taylor and Nellie Hadwin (*née* Taylor), Horsforth. *Educ:* widely. Served War of 1939–45: Duke of Wellington's Regt and War Office. Literary and ballet lecture tours, UK and overseas, 1946–57. Chairman, British Poetry-Drama Guild, 1948–52; Vice-Pres., Leeds Univ. Tudor Players, 1948–50; Publisher, Leeds University Poetry, 1949; featured in NBC-TV (USA) People series, 1955; Founder, Winifred Holtby Meml Collection, Fisk Univ., Nashville, 1955; Hon. Gen. Sec., Dumas Assoc., 1955–57; Founder, Sir Ralph Perring City of London Collection, Fisk Univ., 1962; Pres., St Paul's Literary Soc., Covent Garden, 1966–68; Chm., General Council, Poetry Society, 1967–68; served on PCC, St Paul's, Covent Garden, 1967–68; Mem. Gen. Council, National Book League, 1968; Pres., Lancashire Authors' Assoc., 1969–72; a Trustee, Gladstone Meml Library, London, 1974–78; Jt Literary Trustee, Estate of Vera Brittain, 1979–90; (with Corliss Lamont) Hon. Founder Mem., John Masefield Soc., 1993. Several Foreign decorations and awards. *Publications:* Mona Inglesby, Ballerina and Choreographer, 1947; Italian Ballet Today, 1949; (foreword to) Stars of the Opera, ed Frank Granville Barker, 1949; New Hyperion, 1950; Literary, Debating and Dialect Societies of GB, Ireland and France, 5 pts, 1950–54; A Selected Bibliography of Literature Relating to Nursery Rhyme Reform, 1952; Winifred Holtby Bibliography and Letters, 1955; (with Frank Granville Barker) John Gay and the Ballad Opera, 1956; (with Thomas Rae) The Book of the Private Press, 1958; John Masefield, OM, The Queen's Poet Laureate, 1960; (with Vera Brittain) Selected Letters of Winifred Holtby and Vera Brittain 1920–1935, 1961, 2nd edn 1970; Bibliography of Monaco, 1961, 2nd edn 1968; Bibliography of Iran, 1964, 5th edn 1969; (with Timothy d'Arch Smith) C. Day Lewis, Poet Laureate, 1968; ed, County Authors Today Series, 9 vols, 1971–1973; Pogg (a satire), 1980; (with John Malcolm Dockeray) Vera Brittain, Occasional Papers, 1983; also contribs to: Encycl. Britannica, Hinrichsen Music Book, 1949–1958; Airs from The Beggar's Opera, arr. Edith Bathurst, 1953; The Beggar's Opera, ed Edward J. Dent, 1954; Kathleen: the life of Kathleen Ferrier 1912–1953, ed Maurice Leonard, 1988; (foreword to) John Masefield: a bibliographical description of his first, limited, signed and special editions, ed Crocker Wight, 1992.

HANDLIN, Prof. Oscar; Carl M. Loeb University Professor, Harvard University, since 1984; Director, Harvard University Library, 1979–84; *b* 29 Sept. 1915; *m* 1st, 1937, Mary Flug; one *s* two *d*; 2nd, 1977, Lilian Bombach. *Educ:* Brooklyn Coll. (AB); Harvard (MA, PhD). Instructor, Brooklyn Coll., 1938–39; Harvard Univ.: Instructor, 1939–44; Asst Prof., 1944–48; Associate Prof., 1948–54; Prof. of History, 1954–65; Charles Warren Prof. of Amer. Hist., and Dir, Charles Warren Center for Studies in Amer. Hist., 1965–72; Carl H. Pforzheimer Univ. Prof., 1972–84; Harmsworth Prof. of Amer. History, Oxford Univ., 1972–73. Dir, Center for Study of History of Liberty in America, 1958–67; Chm., US Bd of Foreign Scholarships, 1965–66 (Vice-Chm. 1962–65). Hon. Fellow, Brandeis Univ., 1965. Hon. LLD: Colby Coll., 1962; Harvard, 1993; Hon. LHD: Hebrew Union Coll., 1967; Northern Michigan, 1969; Seton Hall Univ., 1972; Hon. HumD Oakland, 1968; Hon. LittD Brooklyn Coll., 1972; Hon. DHL: Boston Coll., 1975; Lowell, 1980; Cincinnati, 1981; Massachusetts, 1982; Clark Univ., Mass, 1989. *Publications:* Boston's Immigrants, 1790–1865, 1941; (with M. F. Handlin) Commonwealth, 1947; Danger in Discord, 1948; (ed) This Was America, 1949; Uprooted, 1951, 2nd edn 1972; Adventure in Freedom, 1954; American People in the Twentieth Century, 1954 (rev. edn 1963); (ed jtly) Harvard Guide to American History, 1954; Chance or Destiny, 1955; (ed) Readings in American History, 1957; Race and Nationality in American Life, 1957; Al Smith and his America, 1958; (ed) Immigration as a Factor in American History, 1959; John Dewey's Challenge to Education, 1959; (ed) G. M. Capers, Stephen A. Douglas, Defender of the Union, 1959; Newcomers, 1960; (ed jtly) G. Mittleberger, Journey to Pennsylvania, 1960; (ed) American Principles and Issues, 1961; (with M. F. Handlin) The Dimensions of Liberty, 1961; The Americans, 1963; (with J. E. Burchard) The Historian and the City, 1963; Firebell in the Night, 1964; A Continuing Task, 1964; (ed) Children of the Uprooted, 1966; The History of the United States, vol. 1, 1967, vol. 2, 1968; America: a History, 1968; (with M. F. Handlin) The Popular Sources of Political Authority, 1967; The American College and American Culture, 1970; Facing Life: Youth and the Family in American History, 1971; A Pictorial History of Immigration, 1972; (with M. F. Handlin) The Wealth of the American People, 1975; Truth in History, 1979; The Distortion of America, 1981; with L. Handlin: Abraham Lincoln and the Union, 1980; A Restless People, 1982; Liberty and Power, 1986; Liberty in Expansion, 1989; Liberty in Peril, 1992; Liberty and Equality, 1994. *Address:* 18 Agassiz Street, Cambridge, MA 02140, USA. *Clubs:* St Botolph (Boston); Harvard (NY); Faculty (Cambridge, Mass).

HANDS, David Richard Granville; QC 1988; *b* 23 Dec. 1943; *s* of late Leonard Frederick Horace Hands and Nancye Wilkes (*née* Kenyon); *m* 1982, Penelope Ann Jervis. *Educ:* Radley. Called to the Bar, Inner Temple, 1965. *Recreations:* gardening, trees, looking after dogs and cats. *Address:* 4 Breams Buildings, Temple, EC4A 1AQ. *T:* 0171–353 5835. *Club:* Travellers'.

HANDS, Terence David, (Terry Hands); theatre and opera director; *b* 9 Jan. 1941; *s* of Joseph Ronald Hands and Luise Berthe Kohler; *m* 1st, 1964, Josephine Barstow (marr. diss. 1967); 2nd, 1974, Ludmila Mikael (marr. diss. 1980); one *d*; 3rd, 1988, Julia Lintott; two *s*. *Educ:* Woking Grammar Sch.; Birmingham Univ. (BA Hons Eng. Lang. and Lit.); RADA (Hons Dip.). Founder-Artistic Dir, Liverpool Everyman Theatre, 1964–66; Artistic Dir, RSC Theatregoround, 1966–67; Associate Dir, 1967–77, Jt Artistic Dir, 1978–86, Chief Exec. and Artistic Dir, 1986–91, Director Emeritus, 1991, RSC; Consultant Dir, Comédie Française, 1975–80. Associate Mem., RADA; Hon. Fellow, Shakespeare Inst. Hon. DLitt Birmingham, 1988. Chevalier des Arts et des Lettres, 1973. *Director* (for Liverpool Everyman Theatre, 1964–66): The Importance of Being Earnest; Look Back in Anger; Richard III; The Four Seasons; Fando and Lis; *Artistic Director* (for RSC Theatregoround): The Proposal, 1966; The Second Shepherds' Play, 1966; The Dumb Waiter, 1967; Under Milk Wood, 1967; *directed for RSC:* The Criminals, 1967; Pleasure and Repentance, 1967; The Latent Heterosexual, 1968; The Merry Wives of Windsor, 1968, Japan tour, 1970; Bartholomew Fair, 1969; Pericles, 1969; Women Beware Women, 1969; Richard III, 1970, 1980; Balcony, 1971, 1987; Man of Mode, 1971; The Merchant of Venice, 1971; Murder in the Cathedral, 1972; Cries from Casement, 1973; Romeo and Juliet, 1973, 1989; The Bewitched, 1974; The Actor, 1974; Henry IV, Parts 1 and 2, 1975; Henry V, 1975, USA and European Tour, 1976; Old World, 1976; Henry VI parts 1, 2 and 3 (SWET Award, Dir of the Year, Plays and Players, Best Production, 1978), Coriolanus, 1977, European tour, 1979; The Changeling, 1978; Twelfth Night, The Children of the Sun, 1979; As You Like It, Richard II, 1980; Troilus and Cressida, 1981; Arden of Faversham, Much Ado About Nothing, 1982 (European tour and Broadway, 1984), Poppy, 1982; Cyrano de Bergerac, 1983 (SWET Best Dir award), Broadway, 1984 (televised, 1984); Red Noses, 1985; Othello, 1985; The Winter's Tale, 1986; Scenes from a Marriage, 1986; Julius Caesar, 1987; Carrie (Stratford and Broadway), 1988; (with John Barton) Coriolanus, 1989; Romeo and Juliet, 1989; Singer, 1989; Love's Labours Lost, 1990; The Seagull, 1990; Tamburlaine the Great, 1992 (Evening Standard Award, London Drama Critics Award, 1993); *directed for Royal Nat. Theatre:* The Merry Wives of Windsor, 1995; *directed for Chichester Festival Theatre:* Hadrian VII, 1995; *directed for Birmingham Rep.:* The Importance of Being Earnest, 1995 (transf. Old Vic, 1995); *directed for Comédie Française:* Richard III, 1972 (Meilleur Spectacle de l'Année award); Pericles, 1974; Twelfth Night, 1976 (Meilleur Spectacle de l'Année award); Le Cid, 1977; Murder in the Cathedral, 1978; *directed for Paris Opéra:* Verdi's Otello, 1976 (televised 1978); *directed for Burg Theatre, Vienna:* Troilus and Cressida, 1977; As You Like It, 1979; *directed for Royal Opera:* Parsifal, 1979; *directed for Teatro Stabile di Genova, Italy:* Women Beware Women, 1981; *directed for Schauspielhaus, Zürich:* Arden of Faversham, 1992; *directed for Recklinghausen:* Buffalo Bill, 1992; *directed for Bremen:* Simon Boccanegra, 1992; Hamlet, Marigny Theatre, Paris, 1994; *recording:* Murder in the Cathedral, 1976; *television:* Cyrano de Bergerac, 1984. *Publications:* trans. (with Barbara Wright) Genet, The Balcony, 1971; Pleasure and Repentance, 1976; (ed Sally Beauman) Henry V, 1976; Hamlet (French trans.), 1994; contribs to Theatre 72, Playback. *Address:* c/o Royal Shakespeare Theatre, Stratford-upon-Avon, Warwicks CV37 6BB. *T:* Stratford-upon-Avon (01789) 296655.

HANDY, Charles Brian; author; *b* 25 July 1932; *s* of Archdeacon Brian Leslie Handy and Joan Kathleen Herbert Handy (*née* Scott); *m* 1962, Elizabeth Ann Hill; one *s* one *d*. *Educ:* Oriel Coll., Oxford (BA 1956; MA 1966); MIT (SM 1967). Shell Internat. Petroleum Co., 1956–65; Charter Consolidated Ltd, 1965–66; Sloan Sch. of Management, MIT (Internat. Faculty Fellow), 1967–68; London Business School, 1968–: Prof., 1972–77; Vis. Prof., 1977–94; Fellow, 1994; Warden, St George's House, Windsor Castle, 1977–81. Chm., Royal Soc. for Encouragement of Arts, Manufactures and Commerce, 1987–89. Hon. DLitt: Bristol Poly., 1988; Open Univ., 1989; UEA, 1993. *Publications:* Understanding Organizations, 1976, 4th edn 1993; Gods of Management, 1978, 2nd edn 1991; Future of Work, 1982; Understanding Schools as Organizations, 1986; Understanding Voluntary Organizations, 1988; The Age of Unreason, 1989; Inside Organizations, 1990; Waiting for the Mountain to Move, 1991; The Empty Raincoat, 1994; Beyond Certainty, 1995. *Address:* 1 Fairhaven, 73 Putney Hill, SW15 3NT. *T:* 0181–788 1610; Old Hall Cottages, Bressingham, Diss, Norfolk IP22 2AG. *T:* Diss (01379) 687546.

HANDY, Prof. Nicholas Charles, PhD; FRS 1990; Professor of Quantum Chemistry, Cambridge University, since 1991; Fellow, since 1965, President, since 1994, St Catharine's College, Cambridge; *b* 17 June 1941; *s* of Kenneth George Edwards Handy and Ada Mary Handy (*née* Rumming); *m* 1967, Elizabeth Carole Gates; two *s*. *Educ:* Clayesmore Sch., Dorset; St Catharine's College, Cambridge (MA, PhD). Cambridge University: Salters' Fellow, 1967–68; Demonstrator, 1972–77; Lectr, 1977–89; Reader in Quantum Chemistry, 1989–91; Steward, St Catharine's Coll., 1971–88; Harkness Fellow, Johns Hopkins Univ., 1968–69. Vis. Prof., Berkeley, Bologna, Sydney, Georgia. Lennard-Jones Lectr, RSC, 1983. Mem., Internat. Acad. of Quantum Molecular Science, 1988–. Prize in Theoretical Chem., RSC, 1987. *Publications:* papers in learned jls of chem. phys. *Recreations:* gardening, bridge, philately, travel. *Address:* University Chemical Laboratory, Lensfield Road, Cambridge CB2 1EW. *T:* Cambridge (01223) 336373.

HANFF, Helene; writer and broadcaster; *b* 15 April 1916; *d* of Arthur and Miriam Levy Hanff. *Educ:* none beyond secondary sch. Won a playwriting fellowship from The Theatre Guild, 1939; wrote: unproduced plays through '40s; dramatic TV scripts in '50s; American history books for children in '60s; books in '70s and '80s. Monthly radio broadcasts, Woman's Hour, BBC, 1978–85. *Publications:* Underfoot in Show Business, 1961, repr. 1980; 84 Charing Cross Road, 1970; Duchess of Bloomsbury Street, 1973; Apple of My Eye, 1978; Q's Legacy, 1985; Letter from New York, 1992 (BBC scripts); Helene Hanff Omnibus, 1995. *Recreations:* classical music lover, (Mets) baseball fan; also addicted to Guardian (Weekly) crossword puzzles. *Address:* 305 East 72nd Street, New York, NY 10021, USA. *T:* (212) 8794952.

HANGARTNER, John Robert Wilfred; Senior Principal Medical Officer, Department of Health, since 1993; *b* 5 Feb. 1955; *s* of John Hangartner and Ita Patricia (*née* Brett); *m* 1980, Jillian Mary Ansell; one *s* one *d*. *Educ:* Merchant Taylors' Sch., Northwood; Guy's Hosp. Med. Sch., Univ. of London (BSc Hons 1976; MB, BS 1979). MRCS, LRCP 1979; MRCPath 1988. Dip. in Management, Open Univ., 1991. Clin. Lectr in Histopathology, St George's Hosp. Med. Sch., 1983–88; Department of Health: SMO, 1988–91; Temp. PMO, 1991–93; PMO, 1993; Under Sec., 1993. Chm., Hosp. Jun. Staff Cttee, BMA, 1984–85. FRSocMed; FRSA. *Recreations:* photography, singing. *Address:* Department of Health, Medical Education Training and Staffing Division, Room 2W59, Quarry House, Quarry Hill, Leeds LS2 7UE. *T:* Leeds (0113) 254 5000.

HANHAM, Prof. Harold John; Vice-Chancellor, University of Lancaster, 1985–95; *b* Auckland, New Zealand, 16 June 1928; *s* of John Newman Hanham and Ellie Malone; *m* 1973, Ruth Soulé Arnon, *d* of Prof. Daniel I. Arnon, Univ. of Calif, Berkeley. *Educ:* Mount Albert Grammar Sch.; Auckland UC (now Univ. of Auckland); Univ. of New Zealand (BA 1948, MA 1950); Selwyn Coll, Cambridge (PhD 1954). FRHistS 1960; FAAAS 1974. Asst Lectr to Sen. Lectr, in Govt, Univ. of Manchester, 1954–63; Prof. and Head of Dept of Politics, Univ. of Edinburgh, 1963–68; Prof. of History, 1968–73 and Fellow of Lowell House, 1970–73, Harvard Univ.; Prof. of History and Political Science, 1972–85 and Dean, Sch. of Humanities and Social Sci., 1973–84, MIT; Hon. Prof. of History, Univ. of Lancaster, 1985–. Mem., ESRC, 1986. Guggenheim Fellow, 1972–73. Hon. AM Harvard, 1968. John H. Jenkins Prize for Bibliography, Union Coll., 1978. *Publications:* Elections and Party Management, 1969, 2nd edn 1978; The Nineteenth-Century Constitution, 1969; Scottish Nationalism, 1969; Bibliography of British History 1851–1914, 1976. *Recreations:* discovering Canada, squash. *Address:* c/o Vice-Chancellor's Office, University of Lancaster, University House, Lancaster LA1 4YW. *Clubs:* United Oxford & Cambridge University, Commonwealth Trust; St Botolph (Boston).

HANHAM, Joan Brownlow, (Mrs I. W. F. Hanham); JP; Leader of the Council, Royal Borough of Kensington and Chelsea, since 1989; *b* 23 Sept. 1939; *d* of Alfred Spark and Mary (*née* Mitchell); *m* 1964, Dr Iain William Ferguson Hanham; one *s* one *d*. *Educ:* Hillcourt Sch., Dublin. Royal Borough of Kensington and Chelsea: Mem., 1970–; Mayor, 1983–84; Chairman: Town Planning Cttee, 1984–86; Social Services Cttee, 1987–89; Policy and Resources Cttee, 1989–. Chm., Policy Cttee, London Boroughs Assoc., 1991–. Mem., Mental Health Act Commn, 1983–90; Non-Exec. Mem., NW Thames RHA, 1983–94; non-exec. Dir, Chelsea and Westminster Health Care NHS Trust, 1994–. Trustee, Commonwealth Inst., 1991–. JP City of London Commn 1984, and Inner London Family Proceedings Court, 1992. Freeman, City of London, 1984. *Recreations:* music, travel, tennis. *Address:* c/o The Town Hall, Hornton Street, W8 7NX. *Club:* Hurlingham.

HANHAM, Leonard Edward; HM Diplomatic Service, retired; Consul-General, Amsterdam, 1978–80; *b* 23 April 1921; *m* 1945, Joyce Wrenn; two *s* two *d*. Served War, RN, 1939–48. Foreign Office, 1948; Vice-Consul: Rouen, 1949; Basra, 1950; Ponta Delgada, 1952; Foreign Office, 1955; 1st Sec. and Consul: Rangoon, 1957; Tegucigalpa, 1961; Foreign Office, 1963; Consul: Durban, 1965; Medan, 1969; FCO, 1972; Counsellor and Consul-Gen., Lisbon, 1975–78. *Address:* 26 First Avenue, Gillingham, Kent ME7 2LG.

HANHAM, Sir Michael (William), 12th Bt *cr* 1667; DFC 1945; RAFVR; *b* 31 Oct. 1922; *s* of Patrick John Hanham (*d* 1965) and Dulcie (*d* 1979), *yr d* of William George Daffarn and *widow* of Lynn Hartley; *S* kinsman, Sir Henry Phelips Hanham, 11th Bt, 1973; *m* 1954, Margaret Jane, *d* of W/Cdr Harold Thomas, RAF retd, and Joy (*née* MacGeorge); one *s* one *d*. *Educ:* Winchester. Joined RAF 1942, as Aircrew Cadet; served No 8 (Pathfinder) Gp, Bomber Command, 1944–45; FO 1945. At end of war, retrained as Flying Control Officer; served UK and India, 1945–46; demobilised, 1946. Joined BOAC, 1947, Traffic Branch; qualified as Flight Operations Officer, 1954; served in Africa until 1961; resigned, 1961. Settled at Trillinghurst Farmhouse, Kent and started garden and cottage furniture making business, 1963; moved to Wimborne, 1974; now engaged with upkeep of family house and estate. Governor of Minster and of Dumpton School. *Recreations:* conservation (Vice-Chm. Weald of Kent Preservation Soc., 1972–74 and Wimborne Civic Soc., 1977–); preservation of steam railways; sailing, gardening. *Heir:* *s* William John Edward Hanham [*b* 4 Sept. 1957; *m* 1982, Elizabeth Anne Keyworth (marr. diss. 1988), *yr d* of Paul Keyworth, Farnham and Mrs Keith Thomas, Petersfield]. *Address:* Deans Court, Wimborne, Dorset BH21 1EE. *Club:* Royal Air Force.

HANKES-DRIELSMA, Claude Dunbar; strategist and financial adviser; *b* 8 March 1949. *Educ:* Grey. With Manufacturers Hanover, 1968–72; Robert Fleming & Co. Ltd, 1972–77, Director 1974–77; Chairman: Export Finance Co. Ltd, 1982–89; Management Cttee, Price Waterhouse and Partners, 1983–89; Action Resource Centre, 1986–91 (Mem., 1983–86); Mem., Governing Council, 1986–91, Pres's Cttee, 1988–91, Business in the Community (Chm., Target Team on Voluntary Sector Initiatives, 1987–90). Advr to Bd, (Corange) Boehringer Mannheim, 1988–; Dep. Chm., Leutwiler and Partners Ltd, 1992–. Assisted Dr Fritz Leutwiler in his role as independent mediator between South African govt and foreign banks, 1985–86; initiated attempt to secure Thyssen Collection for Britain, 1988; Chm., Adv. Cttee to Kingdom of Jordan on Strategic Economic Policy Issues, 1993–. Mem., Deanery Synod, 1984–93. Hon. Fellow, Corpus Christi Coll., Oxford. *Publications:* The Dangers of the Banking System: funding country deficits, 1975; Nobel Industrier indep. report, Stockholm, 1991. *Recreations:* gardening, walking, ski-ing, reading, ancient art. *Address:* Stanford Place, Faringdon, Oxon SN7 8EX. *T:* Faringdon (01367) 240547, *Fax:* Faringdon (01367) 242853. *Club:* Turf.

HANKEY, family name of **Baron Hankey.**

HANKEY, 2nd Baron *cr* 1939, of The Chart; **Robert Maurice Alers Hankey,** KCMG 1955 (CMG 1947); KCVO 1956; *b* 4 July 1905; *s* of 1st Baron Hankey, PC, GCB, GCMG, GCVO, FRS, and Adeline (*d* 1979), *d* of A. de Smidt; *S* father, 1963; *m* 1st, 1930, Frances Bevyl Stuart-Menteth (*d* 1957); two *s* two *d*; 2nd, 1962, Joanna Riddall Wright (*d* 1991), *d* of late Rev. James Johnstone Wright; 3rd, 1992, Mrs Stephanie Langley, *yr d* of late Brig. Percy Paulet King. *Educ:* Rugby Sch.; New Coll., Oxford. Diplomatic Service, 1927; served Berlin, Paris, London, Warsaw, Bucharest, Cairo, Teheran, Madrid, Budapest. HM Ambassador at Stockholm, 1954–60. Permanent UK Delegate to OEEC and OECD, and Chm., Economic Policy Cttee, 1960–65; Vice-Pres., European Inst. of Business Administration, Fontainebleau, 1966–82. Dir, Alliance Bldg Soc., 1970–83. Member: Internat. Council of United World Colleges, 1966–78; Council, Internat. Baccalaureat Foundn, Geneva, 1967–76. Pres., Anglo-Swedish Soc., 1969–75. Grand Cross of Order of the North Star (Sweden), 1954. *Recreations:* reading, tennis, ski-ing, music. *Heir:* *s* Hon. Donald Robin Alers Hankey [*b* 12 June 1938; *m* 1st, 1963, Margaretha (marr. diss. 1974), *yr d* of H. Thorndahl, Copenhagen; 2nd, 1974, Eileen Désirée (marr. diss. 1994), *yr d* of late Maj.-Gen. Stuart Battye, CB; two *d*; 3rd, 1994, June, *d* of late Dr Leonard Taboroff.]. *Address:* Hethe House, Cowden, Edenbridge, Kent TN8 7DZ. *T:* Cowden (01342) 850538.

See also Sir Jonathan Benn, Hon. H. A. A. Hankey.

HANKEY, Hon. Henry Arthur Alers, CMG 1960; CVO 1959; HM Diplomatic Service, retired; *b* 1 Sept. 1914; *y s* of 1st Baron Hankey, PC, GCB, GCMG, GCVO, FRS; *m* 1941, Vronwy Mary Fisher; three *s* one *d*. *Educ:* Rugby Sch.; New Coll., Oxford. Entered HM Diplomatic Service, 1937; Third Sec., HM Embassy, Paris, 1939; Second Sec., Madrid, 1942; First Sec., Rome, 1946; Consul, San Francisco, 1950; First Sec., Santiago, 1953; promoted Counsellor and apptd Head of American Dept, Foreign Office, Sept. 1956; Counsellor, HM Embassy, Beirut, 1962–66; Ambassador, Panama, 1966–69; Asst Under-Sec. of State, FCO, 1969–74. Director: Lloyds Bank International, 1975–80; Antofagasta (Chile) & Bolivia Railway Co. Ltd, 1975–82. Sec., British North American Cttee, 1981–85. *Publication:* Archaeology: artifacts and artification, 1985. *Recreations:* ski-ing, tennis, music, painting. *Address:* Hosey Croft, Hosey Hill, Westerham, Kent TN16 1TA. *T:* Westerham (01959) 62309. *Club:* United Oxford & Cambridge University.

HANKINS, (Frederick) Geoffrey; Chairman, Fitch Lovell plc, 1983–90 (Chief Executive, 1982–89); Director, Booker plc, since 1990; *b* 9 Dec. 1926; *s* of Frederick Aubrey Hankins and Elizabeth (*née* Stockton); *m* 1951, Iris Esther Perkins; two *d*. *Educ:* St Dunstan's College. Commissioned Army, 1946–48; J. Sainsbury management trainee, 1949–51, manufacturing management, 1951–55; Production/Gen. Manager, Allied Suppliers, 1955–62; Production Dir, Brains Food Products, 1962–69; Kraft Foods, 1966–69; Gen. Man., Millers, Poole, 1970–72, Man. Dir, 1972–82, Chm., 1975–86; Fitch Lovell: Dir, 1975–90; Chief Exec., 1982; Chm., Manufacturing Div., 1975–84; Chairman: Robirch, 1975–84; Jus Rol, 1976–85; Blue Cap Frozen Food Services, 1975–84; Newforge Foods, 1979–84; Bells Bacon (Evesham), 1980–83; L. Noel, 1982–84; Dir, Salaison Le Vexin, 1980–90. FRSA. Liveryman, Poulters' Co., 1982–. *Recreations:* genealogy, antiques, practical pursuits. *Address:* 51 Elms Avenue, Parkstone, Poole, Dorset BH14 8EE. *T:* (01202) 745874.

HANKINS, Prof. Harold Charles Arthur, PhD; FEng 1993; FIEE; Principal and Vice-Chancellor, University of Manchester Institute of Science and Technology, 1984–95; *b* 18 Oct. 1930; *s* of Harold Arthur Hankins and Hilda Hankins; *m* 1955, Kathleen Higginbottom; three *s* one *d*. *Educ:* Crewe Grammar Sch.; Univ. of Manchester Inst. of Science and Technol. (BSc Tech, 1st Cl. Hons Elec. Engrg, 1955; PhD 1971). CEng, FIEE 1975; AMCT 1952. Engrg Apprentice, British Rail, 1947–52; Electronic Engr, subseq. Asst Chief Engr, Metropolitan Vickers Electrical Co. Ltd, 1955–68; Univ. of Manchester Inst. of Science and Technology: Lectr in Elec. Engrg, 1968–71; Sen. Lectr in Elec. Engrg, 1971–74; Prof. of Communication Engrg, and Dir of Med. Engrg Unit, 1974–84; Vice Principal, 1979–81; Dep. Principal, 1981–82; Actg Principal, 1982–84. Non-Executive Director: THORN EMI Lighting Ltd, 1979–85; Bodycote International, 1992–; Dir, Inward, 1992–. Instn of Electrical Engineers: Mem., NW Centre Cttee, 1969–77, Chm. 1977–78; Chm., M2 Exec. Cttee, 1979–82; Mem., Management and Design Div. Bd, 1980–82. Chm., Chemical Engrg, Instrumentation, Systems Engrg Bd, CNAA, 1975–81; Member: Cttee for Science and Technol., CNAA, 1975–81; Cttee of Vice-Chancellors and Principals, 1984–95; Parly Scientific Cttee, 1985–; Engrg Council, 1993–95; Bd of Govs, Manchester Polytechnic, 1989– (Hon. Fellow, 1984); Bd of Govs, South Cheshire Coll., 1990–. Hon. DSc Manchester, 1995. Reginald Mitchell Gold Medal, Assoc. of Engrs, 1990. *Publications:* 55 papers in learned jls; 10 patents for research into computer visual display systems. *Recreations:* hill walking, music, choral work. *Address:* Rosebank, Kidd Road, Glossop, Derbyshire SK13 9PN. *T:* Glossop (014574) 3895. *Club:* Athenæum.

HANKS, Patrick Wyndham; Chief Editor, Current English Dictionaries, Oxford University Press, since 1990; *b* 24 March 1940; *s* of Wyndham George Hanks and Elizabeth Mary (*née* Rudd): *m* 1st, 1961, Helga Gertrud Ingeborg Lietz (marr. diss. 1968); one *s* one *d*; 2nd, 1979, Julie Eyre; two *d*. *Educ:* Ardingly Coll., Sussex; University Coll., Oxford (BA, MA). Editor, Dictionaries and Reference Books, Hamlyn Group, 1964–70; Man. Dir, Laurence Urdang Associates, 1970–79; Dir, Surnames Res. Project, Univ. of Essex, 1980–83; Project Manager, Cobuild, Univ. of Birmingham, 1983–87; Chief Editor, Collins English Dictionaries, 1987–90. *Publications:* (ed) Hamlyn World Dictionary, 1971; (ed) Collins English Dictionary, 1979, 2nd edn 1986; (with J. Corbett) Business Listening Tasks, 1986; (managing editor) Collins Cobuild English Learners' Dictionary, 1987; (with F. Hodges) Dictionary of Surnames, 1988; (with F. Hodges) Dictionary of First Names, 1990; articles in Computational Linguistics, Onoma and other jls. *Recreations:* onomastics, hiking, punting. *Address:* Oxford University Press, Walton Street, Oxford OX2 6DP. *T:* Oxford (01865) 56767.

HANLEY, Howard Granville, CBE 1975; MD, FRCS; Consulting Urologist, King Edward VII's Hospital for Officers, London; Dean, 1968–72, Chairman, 1972–80, President, 1980–88, Institute of Urology, University of London; *b* 27 July 1909; *s* of F. T. Hanley; *m* 1939, Margaret Jeffrey; two *s*. *Educ:* St Bees Sch., Cumberland. MB 1932; MD 1934; FRCS 1937. Urologist: St Peter's Hosps Gp, 1947–75; Royal Masonic Hosp., London, 1960–77; Urol Consultant to Army, 1951–75; Hon. Consulting Urologist, Royal Hosp., Chelsea, 1951–75. Visiting Prof. of Urology: University of Calif, Los Angeles, 1958; Ohio State Univ., Columbus, 1961; University of Texas Southwestern Medical Sch., 1963; Tulane University, New Orleans, 1967. Royal College of Surgeons: Hunterian Prof., 1955; Dean, Inst. of Basic Med. Scis, 1972–76; Mem. Council, 1969–81; Vice-Pres., 1979–81; Royal Society of Medicine: Pres., Urol Sect., 1969–81; Hon. Librarian. Trustee, St Peter's Research Trust for the Cure of Kidney Disease, 1970–86. Fellow, Assoc. of Surgeons of GB and Ireland; Past Pres. (formerly Sec. and Treasurer), British Assoc. Urological Surgeons; Past Sec., Hunterian Soc.; Past Pres., Chelsea Clinical Soc. Member: Internat. Soc. Urology; German Urol. Soc.; Soc. Française d'Urologie; European Assoc. of Urology. Corresponding Member: Amer. Assoc. Genito-urinary Surgeons; Western Sect. Amer. Urological Assoc. Liveryman, Worshipful Soc. of Apothecaries of London. Hon. FACS; Hon. FRSM 1991; Hon. FRSocMed 1991. *Publications:* chapters in: British Surgical Practice, 1957; Recent Advances in Urology, 1960; contribs to: A Textbook of Urology, 1960; Modern Trends in Urology, 1960; contribs to jls on surgery and urology. *Recreation:* gardening. *Address:* Brandon House, North End Avenue, NW3 7HP. *T:* 0181–458 2035. *Club:* Athenæum.

HANLEY, Rt Hon. Jeremy (James), PC 1994; MP (C) Richmond and Barnes, since 1983; Minister of State, Foreign and Commonwealth Office, since 1995; chartered accountant, certified accountant, chartered secretary, lecturer and broadcaster; *b* 17 Nov. 1945; *s* of late Jimmy Hanley and of Dinah Sheridan; *m* 1973, Verna, Viscountess Villiers (*née* Stott); one *s*, one step *d*, and one *s* by previous marriage. *Educ:* Rugby. FCA 1969; FCCA 1980; FCIS 1980. Peat Marwick Mitchell & Co., 1963–66; Lectr in law, taxation and accountancy, Anderson Thomas Frankel, 1969, Dir 1969; Man. Dir, ATF (Jersey and Ireland), 1970–73; Dep. Chm., The Financial Training Co. Ltd, 1973–90; Sec., Park Place PLC, 1977–83; Chm., Fraser Green Ltd, 1986–90. Parly Advr to ICA, 1986–90. Contested (C) Lambeth Central, April 1978, 1979. PPS to Minister of State, Privy Council Office (Minister for CS and the Arts), 1987–90, to Sec. of State for Envmt, 1990; Parly Under-Sec. of State, NI Office, 1990–93 (Minister for Health, Social Security and Agric., 1990–92, for Pol Develt, Community Relns and Educn, 1992–93); Minister of State for the Armed Forces, MoD, 1993–94; Chm. of Cons. Party and Minister without Portfolio, 1994–95. Mem., H of C Select Cttee on Home Affairs, 1983–87 (Mem., Subcttee on Race Relns and Immigration, 1983–87); Jt Vice-Chm., Cons. Back-bench Trade and Industry Cttee, 1983–87. Member: British-American Parly Gp, 1983–; Anglo-French Parly Gp, 1983–; CPA, 1983–; IPU, 1983–; British-Irish Interparly Body, 1990; Chm., Cons Candidates Assoc., 1982–83. Member: Bow Gp, 1974– (Chm., Home Affairs Cttee); European Movt, 1974–; Mensa, 1968–. Freeman, City of London, 1989; Liveryman, Chartered Accountants' Co., 1993–. *Recreations:* cookery, chess, cricket, languages, theatre, cinema, music, golf. *Address:* House of Commons, SW1A 0AA. *T:* 0171–219 4099. *Clubs:* Garrick, Pilgrims, Lord's Taverners.

HANLEY, Sir Michael (Bowen), KCB 1974; *b* 24 Feb. 1918; *s* of late Prof. J. A. Hanley, PhD, ARCS; *m* 1957, Hon. Lorna Margaret Dorothy, *d* of late Hon. Claude Hope-Morley. *Educ:* Sedbergh School; Queen's Coll., Oxford (MA). Served War of 1939–45. *Address:* c/o Ministry of Defence, SW1.

HANMER, Sir John (Wyndham Edward), 8th Bt *cr* 1774; JP; DL; *b* 27 Sept. 1928; *s* of Sir (Griffin Wyndham) Edward Hanmer, 7th Bt, and Aileen Mary (*d* 1967), *er d* of Captain J. E. Rogerson; *S* father, 1977; *m* 1954, Audrey Melissa, *d* of Major A. C. J. Congreve; two *s*. *Educ:* Eton. Captain (retired), The Royal Dragoons. JP Flintshire, 1971; High Sheriff of Clwyd, 1977; DL Clwyd, 1978. *Recreations:* horseracing, shooting. *Heir:* *s* (Wyndham Richard) Guy Hanmer [*b* 27 Nov. 1955; *m* 1986, Elizabeth A., *yr d* of Neil Taylor; two *s* one *d*]. *Address:* The Mere House, Hanmer, Whitchurch, Salop SY13 3DG. *T:* Hanmer (01948) 830383. *Club:* Army and Navy.

See also Sir James Wilson, Bt.

HANN, Air Vice-Marshal Derek William; Director-General RAF Personal Services, Ministry of Defence, 1987–89, retired; *b* 22 Aug. 1935; *s* of Claude and Ernestine Hann; *m* 1st, 1958, Jill Symonds (marr. diss. 1987); one *s* one *d*; 2nd, 1987, Sylvia Jean Holder.

Educ: Dauntsey's Sch., Devizes. Joined RAF, 1954; served in Fighter (65 Sqdn) and Coastal (201 and 203 Sqdns) Commands and at HQ Far East Air Force, 1956–68; MoD, 1969–72 and 1975–77; Comd No 42 Sqdn, RAF St Mawgan, 1972–74; Comd RAF St Mawgan, 1977–79; RCDS 1980; Dir of Operational Requirements 2, MoD, 1981–84; C of S, HQ No 18 Gp, 1984–87. Membership Sec., Hawk and Owl Trust. *Recreations:* theatre, music, horology, campanology. *Address:* 41B Dartmouth Road, NW2 4ET. *T:* and *Fax:* 0181–450 0662.

HANN, James, CBE 1977; Chairman: Scottish Nuclear, since 1990; Hickson International, since 1994; *b* 18 Jan. 1933; *s* of Harry Frank and Bessie Gladys Hann; *m* 1958, Jill Margaret Howe; one *s* one *d. Educ:* Peter Symonds Sch., Winchester; IMEDE, Lausanne, Switzerland. FCIM, FInstPet, CIMgt. James Hann & Sons, 1950–52; Royal Artillery, 1952–54; United Dairies, 1954–65; IMEDE, 1965–66; Managing Director: Hanson Dairies, Liverpool, 1966–72; Seaforth Maritime, Aberdeen, 1972–86; Chairman: Bauteil Engineering, Glasgow, 1986–88; Exacta Holdings, Selkirk, 1986–90; Associated Fresh Foods, Leeds 1987–89; Strathclyde Inst., Glasgow, 1987–90; Dep. Chm., Scottish Transport Gp, 1987–90. Director: William Baird, 1991–; NFU Mutual and Avon Gp, 1993–. Comr, Northern Lighthouse Bd, 1990– (Chm., 1993–94). Member: Offshore Energy Technology Bd, 1982–85; Offshore Tech. Adv. Gp, 1983–86; Nationalised Industries Chairman's Gp, 1990–. Life Mem., Beaver Club, Montreal, 1981 (for services to Canadian offshore industry). Burgess of Guild, Aberdeen, 1982–. Hon. FINucE 1993; Hon. Fellow European Nuclear Soc., 1994. *Recreations:* sailing, reading, music. *Address:* Scottish Nuclear, 3 Redwood Crescent, Peel Park, East Kilbride, Glasgow G74 5PR.

HANNAH, Prof. Leslie; Professor, London School of Economics, since 1982; Dir, London Economics Ltd, since 1991; *b* 15 June 1947; *s* of Arthur Hannah and Marie (*née* Lancashire); *m* 1984, Nuala Barbara Zahedieh (*née* Hockton), *e d* of Thomas and Deirdre Hockton; one *s* two step *d. Educ:* Manchester Grammar Sch.; St John's and Nuffield Colleges, Oxford. MA, PhD, DPhil. Research Fellow, St John's Coll., Oxford, 1969–73; Lectr in economics, Univ. of Essex, 1973–75; Lectr in recent British economic and social history, Univ. of Cambridge, and Fellow and Financial Tutor, Emmanuel Coll., Cambridge, 1976–78; Dir, Business History Unit, LSE, 1978–88. Vis. Prof., Harvard Univ., 1984–85. Dir, NRG London Reinsurance, 1986–93. *Publications:* Rise of the Corporate Economy, 1976, 2nd edn 1983; (ed) Management Strategy and Business Development, 1976; (with J. A. Kay) Concentration in Modern Industry, 1977; Electricity before Nationalisation, 1979; Engineers, Managers and Politicians, 1982; Entrepreneurs and the Social Sciences, 1983; Inventing Retirement, 1986; contribs to jls. *Recreation:* Scotland. *Address:* London School of Economics, Houghton Street, WC2A 2AE. *T:* 0171–955 7110. *Club:* Institute of Directors.

HANNAH, William; His Honour Judge Hannah; a Circuit Judge, since 1988; *b* 31 March 1929; *s* of William Bond Hannah and Elizabeth Alexandra Hannah; *m* 1950, Alma June Marshall; one *s* one *d. Educ:* Everton School, Notts. Called to the Bar, Gray's Inn, 1970. RAF 1947–52; Police Officer, 1952–77. *Recreations:* golf, swimming, walking, theatre. *Address:* c/o Newcastle Crown Court, Quayside, Newcastle upon Tyne NE1 3LA. *Club:* South Shields Golf.

HANNAM, Sir John (Gordon), Kt 1992; MP (C) Exeter, since 1970; *b* 2 Aug. 1929; *s* of Thomas William and Selina Hannam; *m* 1st, 1956, Wendy Macartney; two *d*; 2nd, 1983, Mrs Vanessa Wauchope (*née* Anson). *Educ:* Yeovil Grammar Sch. Studied Agriculture, 1945–46. Served in: Royal Tank Regt (commissioned), 1947–48; Somerset LI (TA), 1949–51. Studied Hotel industry, 1950–52; Managing Dir, Hotels and Restaurant Co., 1952–61; Developed Motels, 1961–70; Chm., British Motels Fedn, 1967–74, Pres. 1974–80; Mem. Council, BTA, 1968–69; Mem. Economic Research Council, 1967–85. PPS to: Minister for Industry, 1972–74; Chief Sec., Treasury, 1974. Mem., Select Cttee on Procedure, 1993–; Secretary: Cons. Parly Trade Cttee, 1971–72; All-Party Disablement Gp, 1974–92 (Co-Chm., 1992–); 1922 Cttee, 1987–; Mem., Govt Adv. Cttee on Transport for Disabled, 1983–, Chairman: Anglo-Swiss Parly Gp, 1987–; West Country Cons. Cttee, 1973–74, 1979–81; Cons. Party Energy Cttee, 1979–92; Arts and Leisure Standing Cttee, Bow Group, 1975–84; Vice-Chairman: Arts and Heritage Cttee, 1974–79; British Cttee of Internat. Rehabilitation, 1979–92. Captain: Lords and Commons Tennis Club, 1975–; Lords and Commons Ski Club, 1977–82; Cdre, House of Commons Yacht Club, 1975. Mem., Snowdon Working Party on the Disabled, 1975–76. Vice-President: Disablement Income Gp; Royal Assoc. for Disability and Rehabilitation; Council, Action Research for Crippling Diseases; Disabled Motorists Gp; Alzheimer's Disease Soc.; Bd, Nat. Theatre, 1979–92. Member: Glyndebourne Festival Soc.; Council, British Youth Opera, 1989–. Hon. MA Open, 1986. *Recreations:* music (opera), theatre, sailing (anything), skiing (fast), Cresta tobogganing (foolish), gardening; county tennis and hockey (Somerset tennis champion, 1953). *Address:* House of Commons, SW1A 0AA; Orchard House, Plymtree, near Cullompton, Devon. *Clubs:* Royal Yacht Squadron, All England Lawn Tennis, International Lawn Tennis.

HANNAM, Michael Patrick Vivian, CBE 1980; HM Diplomatic Service, retired; Consul General, Jerusalem, 1976–80; *b* 13 Feb. 1920; *s* of Rev. Wilfrid L. Hannam, BD, and Dorothy (*née* Parker); *m* 1947, Sybil Huggins; one *s* one *d. Educ:* Westminster Sch. LMS Railway, 1937–40. Served in Army, 1940–46 (Major, RE). LMS Railway, 1946–50; Malayan Railway, 1950–60. FO, 1960–62; First Sec., British Embassy, Cairo, 1962–65; Principal British Trade Comr, Hong Kong, 1965–69 (and Consul, Macao, 1968–69); Counsellor, Tripoli, 1969–72; Counsellor (Economic and Commercial), Nairobi, 1972–73, Dep. High Commissioner, Nairobi, 1973–76. Mem. Exec. Cttee, Palestine Exploration Fund, 1982–92 (Keeper of Written Archive, 1989–92). Chm. Governors, Rose Hill Sch., Tunbridge Wells, 1980–85; Chm. Council, British Sch. of Archaeology in Jerusalem, 1983–90. *Recreations:* music, research into 19th century Jerusalem, translating Homer. *Address:* Little Oaklands, Langton Green, Kent TN3 0HP. *T:* Langton (01892) 862163. *Club:* Army and Navy.

HANNAY, Sir David (Hugh Alexander), GCMG 1995 (KCMG 1986; CMG 1981); HM Diplomatic Service, retired; British Permanent Representative to the United Nations, 1990–94; *b* 28 Sept. 1935; *s* of late Julian Hannay; *m* 1961, Gillian Rex; four *s. Educ:* Winchester; New Coll., Oxford. Foreign Office, 1959–60; Tehran, 1960–61; 3rd Sec., Kabul, 1961–63; 2nd Sec., FO, 1963–65; 2nd, later 1st Sec., UK Delegn to European Communities, Brussels, 1965–70; 1st Sec., UK Negotiating Team with European Communities, 1970–72; Chef de Cabinet to Sir Christopher Soames, Vice President of EEC, 1973–77; Head of Energy, Science and Space Dept, FCO, 1977–79; Head of Middle East Dept, FCO, 1979; Asst Under-Sec. of State (European Community), FCO, 1979–84; Minister, Washington, 1984–85; Ambassador and UK Permanent Rep. to Eur. Communities, Brussels, 1985–90. *Recreations:* travel, gardening, photography. *Address:* c/o Foreign and Commonwealth Office, SW1A 2AH. *Club:* Travellers'.

HANNAY, Elizabeth Anne Scott, MA; Head Mistress, Godolphin School, Salisbury, 1980–89; *b* 28 Dec. 1942; *d* of Thomas Scott Hannay and Doreen Hewitt Hannay. *Educ:* Heathfield Sch., Ascot; St Hugh's Coll., Oxford (MA). Assistant Mistress: St Mary's Sch., Calne, 1966–70; Moreton Hall Sch., Shropshire, 1970–72; S Michael's, Burton Park, Petworth, 1973–75; Dep. Headmistress, St George's Sch., Ascot, 1975–80. *Address:* Downend Cottage, Tichborne, near Alresford, Hants SO24 0NA.

HANNEN, Rt. Rev. John Edward; *see* Caledonia, Bishop of.

HANNIGAN, James Edgar, CB 1981; Deputy Secretary, Department of Transport, 1980–88; *b* 12 March 1928; *s* of late James Henry and of Kathleen Hannigan; *m* 1955, Shirley Jean Bell; two *d. Educ:* Eastbourne Grammar Sch.; Sidney Sussex Coll., Cambridge (BA). Civil Service, 1951; Asst Sec., Housing Div., Min. of Housing and Local Govt, 1966–70; Asst Sec., Local Govt Div., DoE, 1970–72. Under Sec. 1972; Regional Dir for West Midlands, DoE, 1972–75; Chm., West Midlands Economic Planning Bd, 1972–75; Dir of Housing 'B', DoE, 1975–78; Dep. Sec., 1978. Mem., Internat. Exec. Cttee, PIARC, 1985–90. Trustee, Clapham Junction Disaster Fund, 1989–90.

HANNING, Hugh Peter James; Vice-President, Atlantic Council of the United Kingdom, since 1991; Chairman, Fontmell Group on Disaster Relief, since 1990; *b* 5 Feb. 1925; *s* of John Rowland Hanning and Valentine Mary (*née* Bradshaw); *m* 1954, Caragh McClure Williams; one *s. Educ:* Winchester Coll. (Schol.); University Coll., Oxford (BA Hons 1949). Served War, RNVR (rocketships). Leader-writer, Westminster Press, 1951–60; Defence Corresp., ITN, 1961; Consultant, IISS, 1964–70; Defence Corresp., Observer, 1963–; Defence Consultant, Guardian, 1967–69. Advr to MoD, NATO and US Govt. Dep. Dir, RUSI, 1967–70. Dir, Brit. Atlantic Cttee, 1975–82. Founder Member: ITDG, 1967; Internat. Peace Acad., NY, 1970. Mission to Biafra with Leonard Cheshire, 1969. Internat. Sec., C of E, 1972–80. Lectures to Chatham Hse, RUSI, IISS and sen. officers courses. *Publications:* Bow Group pamphlets on the UN, 1963–64; The Peaceful Uses of Military Forces, 1968; NATO: our guarantee of peace, 1985; Peace: the plain man's guide, 1988; reports for Fontmell Gp on military and disaster relief. *Recreations:* piano, golf, painting, Weltverbesserungswahn. *Address:* 18 Montpelier Row, Blackheath, SE3 0RL. *T:* 0181–852 4101. *Club:* Army and Navy.

HANNON, Rt. Rev. Brian Desmond Anthony; *see* Clogher, Bishop of.

HANNON, Richard Michael; racehorse trainer; *b* 30 May 1945; *m* 1966, Josephine Ann McCarthy; two *s* four *d* (of whom two *s* one *d* are triplets). First trainer's licence, 1970; wins include: 2000 Guineas, 1973 (Mon Fils), 1987 (Don't Forget Me), 1990 (Tirol); Irish 2000 Guineas, 1987 (Don' Forget Me), 1990 (Tirol); leading trainer, 1992; trained record number of winners (182), 1993 season. *Address:* East Everleigh Stables, Marlborough, Wilts SN8 3EY.

HANON, Bernard; Officier, Ordre National du Mérite, 1980; Managing Director, Hanon Associés, since 1986; *b* 7 Jan. 1932; *s* of Max Hanon and Anne Smulevicz; *m* 1965, Ghislaine de Bragelongne; two *s. Educ:* HEC 1955; Columbia Univ. (MBA 1956; PhD 1962). Dir of Marketing, Renault Inc., USA, 1959–63; Asst Prof. of Management Sci., Grad. Sch. of Business, NY Univ., 1963–66; Head, Dept of Economic Studies and Programming, 1966–69, Dir of Corporate Planning and Inf. Systems, 1970–75, Régie Nat. des Usines Renault; Dir, Renault Automotive Ops, 1976; Executive Vice President: i/c Automobile Div., 1976–81; Renault Gp, 1981; Chm. and Pres., Régie Nationale des Usines Renault, 1981–85. *Address:* Hanon Associés, 8 avenue de Montaigne, 75008 Paris, France. *Clubs:* Racing Club de France, Automobile Club de France (Paris); Golf de St Germain.

HANRAHAN, Brian; Diplomatic Affairs correspondent, BBC Television, since 1989; *b* 22 March 1949; *s* of Thomas Hanrahan and Kathleen McInerney; *m* 1986, Honor Wilson; one *d. Educ:* Essex University (BA). BBC, 1971–: Far East correspondent, 1983–85; Moscow correspondent, 1986–89. DU Essex, 1990. *Publication:* (with Robert Fox) I Counted Them All Out and I Counted Them All Back, 1982. *Address:* c/o Foreign News Department, BBC TV Centre, Wood Lane, W12 7SB.

HANROTT, Francis George Vivian, CBE 1981; Chief Officer, Technician Education Council, 1973–82; *b* 1 July 1921; *s* of late Howard Granville Hanrott and Phyllis Sarah Hanrott; *m* 1953, Eileen Winifred Appleton; three *d. Educ:* Westminster Sch.; King's Coll., Univ. of London (BA Hons). Served War, RN (Air Br.), 1940–45; Lieut (A) RNVR. Asst Master, St Marylebone Grammar Sch., 1948–50; Lectr, E Berks Coll. of Further Educn, 1950–53; Asst Educn Officer, Wilts, 1953–56; Staff Manager, GEC Applied Electronics Labs, 1956–59; Asst Educn Officer, Herts, 1959–66; Registrar and Sec., CNAA, 1966–73. Hon. MA Open Univ., 1977. *Recreations:* music, angling. *Address:* Coombe Down House, Salcombe Road, Malborough, Kingsbridge, Devon TQ7 3BX. *T:* Salcombe (0154884) 2721.

HÄNSCH, Dr Klaus; Member (SPD), since 1979, and President, since 1994, European Parliament; *b* Sprottau, Silesia, 15 Dec. 1938; *s* of Willi Hänsch and Erna (*née* Sander); *m* 1969, Ilse Hoof. *Educ:* Univ. of Cologne (degree in Pol Sci. 1965); Univ. of Paris; Univ. of Berlin (PhD 1969). Escaped from Silesia to Schleswig-Holstein, 1945. Mil. Service, 1959–60. Res. Asst, Otto Suhr Inst., Free Univ. of Berlin, 1966–68; Ed., Dokumente, 1968–69; Advr to Rep. of FRG under Franco-German Treaty, 1969–70; Press Officer, 1970–79 and expert advr, 1977–79, to Minister for Sci. and Res., N Rhine/Westphalia; Lectr, Duisburg Univ., 1976– (Hon. Prof., 1994). European Parliament: Mem., Foreign Affairs and Security and other cttees, 1979–94; Adv. Mem., Bundestag Cttee on EC issues, 1985–95; Chm., Delgn for relns with US, 1987–89. Member: SPD, 1964–; ÖTV (Union of Tspt and Public Service Workers). *Publications:* pamphlets, contribs to books, and many articles on politics and society in France and on issues relating to unification of Europe and European security policy. *Address:* European Parliament, 97–113 rue Belliard, 1047 Brussels, Belgium; Europabüro, Kavelleriestrasse 22/V, 40213 Düsseldorf, Germany. *T:* (211) 132912.

HANSENNE, Michel; Director-General, International Labour Office, since 1989; *b* 23 March 1940; *s* of Henri and Charlier Georgette Hansenne; *m* 1978, Mme Gabrielle Vanlandschoot; one *s* one *d. Educ:* Liège Univ. (Dr Law 1962; degree in Econs and Finance, 1967). Research work, Univ. of Liège, 1962–72. Mem. Belgian Parliament, 1974–89; Minister: for French Culture, 1979–81; for Employment and Labour, 1981–88; for Civil Service, 1988–89. *Publications:* Emploi, les scénarios du possible, 1985; articles in national and international jls. *Address:* International Labour Office, 1211 Geneva 22, Switzerland. *T:* 22/799.60.20.

HANSFORD, John Edgar, CB 1982; Under-Secretary, Defence Policy and Matériel Group, HM Treasury, 1976–82, retired; *b* 1 May 1922; *s* of Samuel George Hansford, ISO, MBE, and Winifred Louise Hansford; *m* 1947, Evelyn Agnes Whitehorn; one *s. Educ:* Whitgift Middle Sch., Croydon. Clerical Officer, Treasury, 1939. Served War of 1939–45: Private, Royal Sussex Regt, 1940; Lieutenant, Royal Fusiliers, 1943; served in: Africa, Mauritius, Ceylon, India, Burma, on secondment to King's African Rifles; demobilised, 1946. Exec. Officer, Treasury, 1946–50; Higher Exec. Officer, Regional Bd for Industry, Leeds, 1950–52; Exchange Control, Treasury, 1952–54; Agricultural Policy, Treasury, 1954–57; Sen. Exec. Officer, and Principal, Defence Div., Treasury, 1957–61; Principal, Social Security Div., Treasury, 1961–66; Public Enterprises Div., 1966–67;

Overseas Develt Div., 1967–70; Asst Sec., Defence Policy and Matériel Div., Treasury, 1970–76; Under-Sec. in charge of Gp, 1976. *Recreations:* gardening, motoring.

HANSON, family name of **Baron Hanson.**

HANSON, Baron *cr* 1983 (Life Peer), of Edgerton in the County of West Yorkshire; **James Edward Hanson;** Kt 1976; Chairman: Hanson PLC, since 1965; Hanson Transport Group Ltd, since 1965; *b* 20 Jan. 1922; *s* of late Robert Hanson, CBE and late Louisa Ann (Cis) (*née* Rodgers); *m* 1959, Geraldine (*née* Kaelin); two *s*, and one step *d*. War Service 1939–46. Mem., Ct of Patrons, RCS, 1991–; Trustee, Hanson Fellowship of Surgery, Oxford; Fellow, Cancer Res. Campaign. Life Mem., Royal Dublin Soc., 1948. Freeman, City of London, 1964; Hon. Liveryman, Worshipful Co. of Saddlers. Hon. LLD Leeds, 1984; Hon. DBA Huddersfield, 1991. FRSA; CIMgt. *Address:* 1 Grosvenor Place, SW1X 7JH. *T:* 0171–245 1245. *Clubs:* Brooks's; Huddersfield Borough; The Brook (NY); Toronto.

HANSON, Sir Anthony (Leslie Oswald), 4th Bt, *cr* 1887; *b* 27 Nov. 1934; *s* of Sir Gerald Stanhope Hanson, 2nd Bt, and Flora Liebe (*d* 1956), *e d* of late Lieut-Col W. A. R. Blennerhassett; *S* half-brother, 1951; *m* 1964, Denise Jane (Tuppence), *e d* of Richard Rolph; one *d*. *Educ:* Hawtrey's; Gordonstoun, Elgin, Morayshire. Career in Royal Navy until 1955; farming, 1956–67. St Luke's College, Exeter Univ. (BEd Hons 1974). Teacher, 1974–83; took very early retirement due to severe road accident. Conservation Officer, MSC, 1984. Supported by wife who teaches at St Luke's, Teignmouth. Member: Greenpeace; Amnesty International. *Recreations:* sailing, talking. *Address:* Woodland Cottage, Woodland, Ashburton, Devon TQ13 7HJ. *T:* Ashburton (01364) 652711.

HANSON, Dr Bertram Speakman, CMG 1963; DSO 1942; OBE 1941; ED; *b* 6 Jan. 1905; *s* of William Speakman Hanson and Maggie Aitken Hanson; *m* 1932, Mayne, *d* of T. J. Gilpin; three *s* one *d*. *Educ:* St Peter's Coll., Adelaide; University of Adelaide (MB, BS). War Service: Comd 2/8 Aust. Field Amb., 1940–43; ADMS, 9 Aust. Div., 1943–44. Pres., SA Branch of BMA, 1952–53; Pres. College of Radiologists of Australasia, 1961–62 (Gold Medal, 1990); Mem., Radiation Health Cttee of Nat. Health and Med. Research Coun., 1963–67; Hon. Radiotherapist, Royal Adelaide Hospital, 1952–64; Pres., The Australian Cancer Soc., 1964–67 (Gold Medal, 1979); Chairman: Exec. Board, Anti-Cancer Foundation, University of Adelaide, 1955–74; Anti-Cancer Foundation, Universities of South Aust., 1980–86; Mem. Council, International Union Against Cancer, 1962–74. Pres., Nat. Trust of South Aust., 1979–82. FFR (Hon.) 1964; FAMA 1967; FRCR (Hon.) 1975. DUniv Adelaide, 1985. *Publications:* sundry addresses and papers in Med. Jl of Australia. *Recreation:* gardening. *Address:* 10 Rugby Street, Kingswood, SA 5062, Australia. *Club:* Adelaide.

HANSON, Brian John Taylor; Registrar and Legal Adviser to General Synod of Church of England, since 1975; Joint Principal Registrar, Provinces of Canterbury and York, since 1980; Registrar, Convocation of Canterbury, since 1982; *b* 23 Jan. 1939; *o s* of Benjamin John Hanson and Gwendoline Ada Hanson (*née* Taylor); *m* 1972, Deborah Mary Hazel, *yr d* of Lt-Col R. S. P. Dawson, OBE; two *s* three *d*. *Educ:* Hounslow Coll.; Law Society's Coll. of Law; Univ. of Wales (LLM 1994). Solicitor (admitted 1963) and ecclesiastical notary; in private practice, Wilson Houlder & Co., 1963–65; Solicitor with Church Comrs, 1965–; Asst Legal Advr to General Synod, 1970–75. Member: Legal Adv. Commn of General Synod, 1980– (Sec., 1970–86); Gen. Council, Ecclesiastical Law Soc., 1987–. Guardian, Nat. Shrine of Our Lady of Walsingham, 1984–; Fellow, Corp. of SS Mary and Nicholas (Woodard Schools), 1987–; Mem. Council, St Luke's Hosp. for the Clergy, 1985–; Governor: St Michael's Sch., Burton Park, 1987–94; Pusey House, Oxford, 1993–; Quainton Hall Sch., 1994–. Freeman, City of London, 1991; Liveryman, Co. of Glaziers and Painters of Glass, 1992–. *Publications:* (ed) The Canons of the Church of England, 2nd edn 1975, 5th edn 1993; (ed) The Opinions of the Legal Advisory Commission, 6th edn 1985; (adv. ed.) Atkin's Court Forms, ecclesiastical vol., 1992; (jtly) Moore's Introduction to English Canon Law, 3rd edn 1992. *Recreations:* the family, gardening, genealogy. *Address:* Dalton's Farm, Bolney, West Sussex RH17 5PG. *T:* Bolney (01444) 881890. *Club:* Commonwealth Trust.

HANSON, Sir (Charles) John, 3rd Bt *cr* 1918; *b* 28 Feb. 1919; *o s* of Major Sir Charles Edwin Bourne Hanson, 2nd Bt, and Violet Sybil (*d* 1966), 3rd *d* of late John B. Johnstone, Coombe Cottage, Kingston Hill, Surrey; *S* father 1958; *m* 1st, 1944, Patricia Helen (marr. diss. 1968), *o c* of late Adm. Sir (Eric James) Patrick Brind, GBE, KCB; one *s* one *d*; 2nd, 1968, Mrs Helen Yorke, *d* of late Charles Ormonde Trew. *Educ:* Eton; Clare Coll., Cambridge. Late Captain, The Duke of Cornwall's Light Infantry; served War of 1939–45. *Heir: s* Charles Rupert Patrick Hanson [*b* 25 June 1945; *m* 1977, Wanda, *d* of Don Arturo Larrain, Santiago, Chile; one *s*]. *Address:* Gunn House, Shelfanger, near Diss, Norfolk IP22 2DP. *T:* Diss (01379) 643207. *Clubs:* Army and Navy, MCC.

HANSON, David George; MP (Lab) Delyn, since 1992; *b* 5 July 1957; *s* of Brian George Hanson and Glenda Doreen (*née* Jones); *m* 1986, Margaret Rose Mitchell; one *s* two *d*. *Educ:* Verdin Comprehensive, Winsford, Ches.; Hull Univ. (BA Hons, PGCE). Vice-Pres., Hull Univ. Students' Union, 1978–79. Management trainee, Co-op. Union/Plymouth Co-op. Soc., 1980–82; with Spastics Soc., 1982–89; Dir, RE-SOLV (Soc. for Prevention of Solvent Abuse), 1989–92. Councillor: Vale Royal BC, 1983–91 (Leader, Lab Gp, 1989–91); Northwich Town Council, 1987–91. Contested (Lab): Eddisbury, 1983; Delyn, 1987; Cheshire W (European Parlt), 1984. *Recreations:* football, family, cinema. *Address:* House of Commons, SW1A 0AA. *T:* 0171–219 5064; (constituency office) 64 Chester Street, Flint, Clwyd CH6 5DH. *T:* Flint (01352) 763159.

HANSON, Derrick George; financial consultant; writer, director of companies; Chairman: Moneyguide Ltd, since 1978; A. C. Morrell Employees' Trust, since 1983; Director: Albany Investment Trust plc, since 1980; James Beattie PLC, since 1984; Barrister; *b* 9 Feb. 1927; *s* of late John Henry Hanson and of Frances Elsie Hanson; *m* 1st, 1951, Daphne Elizabeth (*née* Marks) (*d* 1971); one *s* two *d*; 2nd, 1974, Hazel Mary (*née* Buckley) (*d* 1984); 3rd, 1986, Patricia (*née* Skillicorn). *Educ:* Waterloo Grammar Sch.; London Univ. (LLB (Hons)); Liverpool Univ. (LLM). Called to Bar, Lincoln's Inn, 1952. Joined Martins Bank Ltd, 1943; Chief Trustee Manager, Martins Bank Ltd, 1963; Dir and Gen. Manager, Martins Bank Trust Co. Ltd, 1968; Dir and Gen. Manager, Barclays Bank Trust Co. Ltd, 1969–76; Chairman: Barclays Unicorn Ltd, 1972–76; Barclays Life Assce Co. Ltd, 1972–76; City of London & European Property Co. Ltd, 1980–86; Key Fund Managers Ltd, 1984–87; Birmingham Midshires Bldg Soc., 1988–90 (Dir, 1982–90); Director: Barclaytrust Property Management Ltd, 1971–76; Barclays Bank plc, Manchester Bd, 1976–77; Toye & Co. plc, 1981–92; British Leather Co. Ltd, 1983–94; Sen. Adviser (UK), Manufacturers Hanover Trust Co., 1977–79; Adviser, Phillips Gp, Fine Art Auctioneers, 1977–82. Assessor, Cameron Tribunal, 1962; Dir, Oxford Univ. Business Summer Sch., 1971. Chm., Southport and Formby DHA, 1986–89; Member: NW Industrialists' Council, 1977–83; South Sefton Health Authority, 1979–82; Mersey RHA, 1982–86. Pres., Assoc. of Banking Teachers, 1979–88. Mem. Council, Liverpool Univ., 1980–84; Chm., Christian Arts Trust, 1980–86. Mem., NW Regl Cttee, NT, 1990–. Hon. FCIB 1987. Hon. Fellow, City Univ., 1977–86. *Publications:* Within These Walls: a century of Methodism in Formby, 1974; Service Banking, 1979; Moneyguide: The Handbook of Personal Finance, 1981; Dictionary of Banking and Finance, 1985. *Recreations:* golf, gardening, hill-walking. *Address:* Bridgend, Brook Bridge, Patterdale, Cumbria CA11 0NS; Grasshopper House, Freshfield Road, Formby, Merseyside L37 7BJ. *Clubs:* Royal Automobile; Formby Golf (Formby, Lancs).

HANSON, James Donald; Managing Partner, Strategic Affairs and Communications, Arthur Andersen & Co. Worldwide, since 1989; *b* 4 Jan. 1935; *s* of late Mary and Leslie Hanson; *m* 1st, 1959, Patricia Margaret Talent (marr. diss. 1977); two *s*; 2nd, 1978, Anne Barbara Asquith. *Educ:* Heath Grammar School, Halifax. ACA 1956, FCA 1966. Joined Arthur Andersen & Co., Chartered Accountants, 1958; established north west practice, 1966, Managing Partner, North West, 1968–82, Sen. Partner, UK, 1982–89. Member: Internat. Operating Cttee, 1982–; Internat. Board of Partners, 1985–; Manchester Soc. of Chartered Accountants, 1967–81 (Pres., 1979); Council, CBI, 1982–. Mem., Council and Court, Manchester Univ., 1982–. *Recreations:* ski-ing, tennis. *Address:* Arthur Andersen & Co., 1 Surrey Street, WC2R 2PS. *T:* 0171–438 3000.

HANSON, Sir John; *see* Hanson, Sir Charles John.

HANSON, Sir John (Gilbert), KCMG 1995; CBE 1979; Director-General, British Council, since 1992; *b* 16 Nov. 1938; *s* of Gilbert Fretwell Hanson and Gladys Margaret (*née* Kay); *m* 1962, Margaret Clark; three *s*. *Educ:* Manchester Grammar Sch.; Wadham Coll., Oxford (BA Lit. Hum. 1961, MA 1964). Asst Principal, WO, 1961–63; British Council: Madras, India, 1963–66; ME Centre for Arab Studies, Lebanon, 1966–68; Rep., Bahrain, 1968–72; Dep. Controller, Educn and Science Div., 1972–75; Representative, Iran, and Counsellor (Cultural) British Embassy, Tehran, 1975–79; Controller, Finance Div., 1979–82; RCDS, 1983; Head, British Council Div. and Minister (Cultural Affairs), British High Commn, New Delhi, 1984–88; Dep. Dir-Gen., 1988–92. Patron, GAP, 1989–. Member: Franco-British Council, 1992–; UK-Japan 2000 Gp, 1993–; Council, VSO, 1993–. Member Governing Council: Soc. for S Asian Studies, 1989–93; SOAS, 1991–. FRSA 1993; CIMgt 1993. *Recreations:* books, music, sport, travel. *Address:* c/o The British Council, 10 Spring Gardens, SW1A 2BN. *T:* 0171–930 8466. *Clubs:* Athenæum, MCC; Gymkhana (Madras).

HANSON, Neil; Under Secretary, and Controller, Newcastle upon Tyne Central Office, Department of Health and Social Security, 1981–83; *b* 21 March 1923; *s* of late Reginald William Hanson and Lillian Hanson (*née* Benson); *m* 1st, 1950, Eileen Ashworth (*d* 1976); two *s*; 2nd, 1977, Margaret Brown-Smelt. *Educ:* City of Leeds Sch. Served War, 1942–46, N Africa, Sicily, Italy. Jun. Clerk, Leeds Social Welfare Cttee, 1939; Clerical Officer, 1948–50, Exec. Officer, 1950–56, Nat. Assistance Bd; Manager, Suez and Hungarian Refugee Hostels, 1956–59; Higher Exec. Officer, 1959–62, Sen. Exec. Officer, 1963–66, Nat. Assistance Bd; Principal, Min. of Social Security, 1967–73; Sen. Principal, 1973–76, Asst Sec., 1976–80, DHSS. *Recreations:* bridge, cricket, music, walking. *Address:* 4 Woodbourne, Park Avenue, Leeds LS8 2JW. *T:* Leeds (0113) 265 3452.

HANTON, Alastair Kydd, OBE 1986; Chairman, Ethical Investment Research Service; Deputy Managing Director, Girobank (formerly National Girobank, Post Office), 1982–86; *b* 10 Oct. 1926; *er s* of late Peter Hanton and Maude Hanton; *m* 1956, Margaret Mary (*née* Lumsden); two *s* one *d*. *Educ:* Mill Hill Sch.; Pembroke Coll., Cambridge. Commonwealth Develt Corp., 1948–54; ICFC, 1954–57; Unilever, 1957–66; Rio Tinto-Zinc, 1966–68; Post Office, 1968–86. Chm., Envmtl Transport Assoc., 1990–; Vice-Chm., Christian Aid. *Recreation:* forestry. *Address:* 8 Gilkes Crescent, Dulwich Village, SE21 7BS. *T:* 0181–693 2618.

HANWORTH, 2nd Viscount, *cr* 1936, of Hanworth; **David Bertram Pollock,** CEng, MIMechE, FIEE, FRPS, FIQA; Baron, *cr* 1926; Bt, *cr* 1922; Lt-Col Royal Engineers, retired; Barrister-at-Law (Inner Temple), 1958; *b* 1 Aug. 1916; *s* of Charles Thomas Anderson Pollock and Alice Joyce Becher; *S* grandfather, 1936; *m* 1940, Isolda Rosamond, *yr d* of Geoffrey Parker, of Cairo; two *s* one *d*. *Educ:* Wellington Coll.; Trinity Coll., Cambridge. (Mechanical Science Tripos, 1939). Joined Social Democratic Party, 1981, Soc & Lib Dem, 1989. *Publications:* Amateur Carbro Colour Prints, 1950; Amateur Dye Transfer Colour Prints, 1956. *Heir: s* Hon. David Stephen Geoffrey Pollock [*b* 16 Feb. 1946; *m* 1968, Elizabeth Liberty, *e d* of Lawrence Vambe; two *d*]. *Address:* Quoin Cottage, Shamley Green, Guildford, Surrey GU5 0UJ.

HAPGOOD, Mark Bernard; QC 1994; *b* 2 April 1951; *m* 1978, Linda Fieldsend; two *d*. *Educ:* Nottingham Univ. (LLB). Called to the Bar, Gray's Inn, 1979. *Publications:* (ed) Paget's Law of Banking, 10th edn, 1989; (contrib.) Halsbury's Laws of England, vol. 3 (1): Banking, reissue, 1989; Bills of Exchange, vol. 4 (1), reissue, 1992. *Recreations:* running, roller-skating, 16th/17th century financial documents. *Address:* Brick Court Chambers, 15–19 Devereux Court, WC2R 3JJ. *Clubs:* St Enedoc Golf; Rock Sailing.

HAPPOLD, Prof. Sir Edmund, Kt 1994; RDI 1983; FEng 1983; Professor of Building Engineering, University of Bath, since 1976; Senior Partner, Buro Happold, consulting engineers, since 1976; *b* 8 Nov. 1930; *s* of late Prof. Frank Charles Happold, PhD, DSc and A. Margaret M. Smith, MA; *m* 1967, Evelyn Claire Matthews, MSc; two *s*. *Educ:* Leeds Grammar Sch.; Bootham Sch., York; Leeds Univ. BSc, FICE, FIStructE, FCIOB, FIEHK. Site Engineer, Sir Robert McAlpine & Sons, 1952–54; Engineer, Ove Arup & Partners, 1956–58, Severud Elstad & Kruger, NY, 1958–60; Senior Engineer then Associate, later Exec. Partner, Ove Arup & Partners, 1960–76; assisted Tom Hancock in winning 2nd prize, Houses of Parlt competition, 1972; won jtly with 4 others Centre Pompidou, Plateau Beaubourg competition, 1971; won jtly with 2 others Vauxhall Cross competition, 1982; jtly with 4 others won High Wycombe Cultural Centre Competition, 1987; won, with Sir Norman Foster, competition for Faisal Foundn Complex, Saudi Arabia, 1994. Chm., Construction Industry Council, 1988–91. Institution of Structural Engineers: Mem. Council, 1974–77, 1979–93; Chm., Educn Cttee, 1979–82; Vice-Pres., 1982–86; Pres., 1986–87; Guthrie Brown Medal, 1970; Oscar Faber Medal, 1974, 1977; Henry Adams Award, 1976; Gold Medal, 1992; Mem., Standing Cttee on Structural Safety, 1976–86; International Association of Bridge and Structural Engineers: Mem., Nat. Council, 1977–; Mem., Internat. Tech. Cttee, 1978–83; Chm., Commn V, 1978–83. Member: Board, Property Services Agency, 1979–81, Adv. Bd, 1981–86; Design Council, 1988–94; Building Regulations Adv. Cttee, 1988–. Master, RDI, 1991–93; Vice-Pres., RSA, 1991–. Chm., Theatre Royal, Bath, 1988–94. Murray Leslie Medal, CIOB, 1982. Sen. FRCA 1993; Hon. FRIBA 1983; Hon. FCIBSE 1988; Hon. FBIAT 1991; Hon. FASI 1991; Hon. FABE 1994. Hon. DSc City Univ., 1988; Hon. DEng Braunschweig, 1995. *Publications:* papers in learned journals. *Recreations:* engineering and family activities. *Address:* 4 Widcombe Terrace, Bath, Avon BA2 6AJ. *T:* Bath (01225) 337510; Flat 18, 32 Grosvenor Street, W1X 9FF. *Club:* Athenæum.

HARARE (formerly SALISBURY), Archbishop of, (RC), since 1976; **Most Rev. Patrick Chakaipa;** *b* 25 June 1932; *s* of Chakaipa and Chokutaura. *Educ:* Chishawasha Minor and Regional Major Seminary, nr Harare; Kutama Teachers' Coll. Ecclesiastic qualifications in Philosophy and Theology; Teacher Training Cert. Asst priest, Makumbi Mission, 1967–69; Priest-in-Charge, All Souls Mission, Mutoko, 1969–73; Episcopal Vicar, Mutoko-Mrewa Area, 1970–73; Auxiliary Bishop of Salisbury, 1973–76. Pres.,

Inter-Regl Meeting of Bishops of Southern Africa, 1992. *Publications:* Karikoga, 1958; Pfumo reRopa, 1961; Rudo Ibofu, 1961; Garandichauya, 1963; Dzasukwa, 1967. *Recreation:* chess. *Address:* PO Box Cy 330, Causeway, Harare, Zimbabwe. *T:* 792125.

HARBERTON, 10th Viscount *cr* 1791; **Thomas de Vautort Pomeroy;** Baron Harberton 1783; *b* 19 Oct. 1910; *s* of 8th Viscount Harberton, OBE, and Mary Katherine (*d* 1971), *d* of A. W. Leatham; *S* brother, 1980; *m* 1978, Vilma, *widow* of Sir Alfred Butt, 1st Bt. *Educ:* Eton. Joined Welsh Guards, 1932; transferred to RAOC, 1939; served BEF, then in India; retired, 1952. *Heir: b* Hon. Robert William Pomeroy [*b* 29 Feb. 1916; *m* 1953, Winifred Anne, *d* of late Sir Arthur Colegate, MP; two *s*]. *Address:* 2 Hazely Manor, Rohais, Guernsey, CI. *Club:* Cavalry and Guards.

HARBISON, Dr Samuel Alexander; HM Chief Inspector of Nuclear Installations, Health and Safety Executive, since 1991; *b* 9 May 1941; *s* of Adam Harbison and Maude Harbison (*née* Adams); *m* 1st, 1964, Joyce Margaret Buick (marr. diss. 1991); three *d*; 2nd, 1991, Margaret Gail (*née* Vale). *Educ:* Queen's Univ., Belfast (Hons BSc); Univ. of California, Los Angeles (MSc); Univ. of London (PhD). Reactor Physicist, UKAEA, Windscale, 1962–64; Research and Teaching Asst, UCLA, 1964–66; Research at Rutherford High Energy Lab., Harwell, 1966–69; Sen. Lectr, Royal Naval Coll., Greenwich, 1969–74; Nuclear Installations Inspectorate, HSE, 1974–. *Publications:* An Introduction to Radiation Protection (with A. Martin), 1972, 4th edn 1995; numerous sci. and tech. papers in learned jls. *Recreations:* tennis, gardening, folk music. *Address:* Health and Safety Executive, Rose Court, 2 Southwark Bridge, SE1 9HS. *T:* 0171–717 6850.

HARBISON, Air Vice-Marshal William, CB 1977; CBE 1965; AFC 1956; RAF, retired; Vice-President, British Aerospace Inc., Washington, DC, 1979–92; *b* 11 April 1922; *s* of W. Harbison; *m* 1950, Helen, *d* of late William B. Geneva, Bloomington, Illinois; two *s*. *Educ:* Ballymena Academy, N Ireland. Joined RAF, 1941; 118 Sqdn Fighter Comd, 1943–46; 263, 257 and 64 Sqdns, 1946–48; Exchange Officer with 1st Fighter Group USAF, 1948–50; Central Fighter Estabt, 1950–51; 4th Fighter Group USAF, Korea, 1952; 2nd ATAF Germany: comd No 67 Sqdn, 1952–55; HQ No 2 Group, 1955; psc 1956; Air Min. and All Weather OCU, 1957; comd No 29 All Weather Sqdn Fighter Comd, Acklington and Leuchars, 1958–59; British Defence Staffs, Washington, 1959–62; jssc 1962; comd RAF Leuchars Fighter Comd, 1963–65; ndc 1965–66; Gp Capt. Ops: HQ Fighter Comd, 1967–68; No 11 Group Strike Comd, 1968; Dir of Control (Ops), NATCS, 1968–72; Comdr RAF Staff, and Air Attaché, Washington, 1972–75; AOC 11 Group, RAF, 1975–77. *Recreations:* flying, motoring. *Address:* c/o Lloyds Bank, Cox's & King's Branch, 7 Pall Mall, SW1Y 5NA. *Club:* Royal Air Force.

HARBORD-HAMOND, family name of **Baron Suffield.**

HARBORNE, Prof. Jeffrey Barry, PhD, DSc; FRS 1995; Emeritus Professor of Botany, University of Reading, since 1993; *b* 1 Sept. 1928; *s* of late Frank Percy Harborne, Bristol, and Phyllis Maud (*née* Sherriff); *m* 1953, Jean Charlotte, *d* of late Dr John Buchanan; two *s*. *Educ:* Wycliffe Coll., Stonehouse, Glos; Univ. of Bristol (BSc; PhD 1953; DSc 1966). Biochemist, John Innes Inst., 1955–65; Res. Fellow, Univ. of Liverpool, 1965–68; University of Reading: Reader, 1968–76; Prof. of Botany, 1976–93. Visiting Professor: Univ. of Texas, 1976; Univ. of Calif, 1977; Plenary Lectr, IUPAC Nat. Prods Symposium, 1976. Editor-in-Chief, Jl Phytochemistry, 1972–. Member: RSC, 1956; Biochemical Soc., 1957. FLS 1986. Gold Medal in Botany, Linnean Soc., 1985; Silver Medal, Phytochemical Soc. of Europe, 1986. *Publications:* Biochemistry of Phenolic Compounds, 1964; Comparative Biochemistry of the Flavonoids, 1967; Phytochemical Phylogeny, 1970; Phytochemical Ecology, 1972; Phytochemical Methods, 1973, 2nd edn 1984; Introduction to Ecological Biochemistry, 1977, 4th edn 1993; Phytochemical Aspects of Plant and Animal Coevolution, 1978; Plant Chemosystematics, 1984; Phytochemical Dictionary, 1993; The Flavonoids: advances in research since 1986, 1994. *Recreations:* rambling, classical music. *Address:* Department of Botany, Plant Science Laboratories, University of Reading, Reading RG6 2AS. *T:* Reading (01734) 318162.

HARBORNE, Peter Gale; HM Diplomatic Service; Ambassador to the Slovak Republic, since 1995; *b* 29 June 1945; *s* of late Leslie Herbert and Marie Mildred Edith Harborne; *m* 1976, Tessa Elizabeth Henri; two *s*. *Educ:* King Edward's Sch., Birmingham; Birmingham Univ. (BCom). Dept of Health, 1966–72; FCO, 1972–74; 1st Sec., Ottawa, 1974–75; 1st Sec. Commercial, Mexico City, 1975–78; Lloyd's Bank Internat., 1979–81; FCO, 1981–83; Head of Chancery, Helsinki, 1983–87; Dep. Head of Mission, Budapest, 1988–91; Counsellor, FCO, 1991–95. *Recreations:* watching cricket, playing bad tennis, music, cross-country ski-ing. *Address:* c/o Foreign and Commonwealth Office, King Charles Street, SW1A 2AH. *Club:* MCC.

HARBOTTLE, Rev. Anthony Hall Harrison, LVO 1979; Rector of East Dean with Friston and Jevington, since 1981; Chaplain to the Queen, 1968–95; *b* 3 Sept. 1925; *y s* of Alfred Charles Harbottle, ARIBA, and Ellen Muriel, *o d* of William Popham Harrison; *m* 1955, Gillian Mary, *o d* of Hugh Goodenough; three *s* one *d*. *Educ:* Sherborne Sch.; Christ's Coll., Cambridge (MA); Wycliffe Hall, Oxford. Served War in Royal Marines, 1944–46. Deacon 1952, priest 1953; Asst Curacies: Boxley, 1952–54; St Peter-in-Thanet, 1954–60; Rector of Sandhurst with Newenden, 1960–68; Chaplain of the Royal Chapel, Windsor Great Park, 1968–81. Founder Mem., Kent Trust for Nature Conservation, 1954; Mem., Green Alliance, 1984. County Chaplain, Royal British Legion (Sussex), 1982–. FRES 1971. *Publications:* contribs to entomological jls, on lepidoptera. *Recreations:* butterflies and moths, nature conservancy, entomology, ornithology, philately, coins, Treasury and bank notes, painting, cooking, lobstering. *Address:* East Dean Rectory, Eastbourne, East Sussex BN20 0DL. *T:* East Dean (01323) 423266.

HARBOTTLE, (George) Laurence; Senior Partner, Harbottle & Lewis, Solicitors, since 1956; *b* 11 April 1924; *s* of George Harbottle and Winifred Ellen Benson Harbottle. *Educ:* The Leys Sch., Cambridge; Emmanuel Coll., Cambridge (MA). Solicitor 1952. Served War: commnd RA, 1942; Burma and India; Temp. Captain; Adjt 9th Fd Regt, 1945–47. Theatre Companies: Chairman: Theatre Centre, 1959–88; Prospect, 1966–77; Royal Exchange (69), 1968–83; Cambridge, 1969–92 (Pres., 1992); Director: The Watermill, 1970–75; The Bush (Alternative), 1975–77. Arts Council: Mem., 1976–77–78; Mem., Drama Panel, 1974–78; Chairman: Housing the Arts, 1977–78; Trng Cttee, 1977–78; Chairman: Central Sch. of Speech and Drama, 1982– (Vice Chm., 1977–82); ICA, 1986–90 (Dep. Chm., 1977–86). Pres., Theatrical Management Assoc., 1979–85; Vice-President: Music Users Council, 1985–; Theatres Adv. Council, 1986–88; Theatres Nat. Cttee, 1986–91. Member: Justice Cttee on Privacy, 1970; Theatres Trust, 1980– (Chm., 1992–). Gov., City Literary Inst., 1990–; Trustee, Equity Trust Fund, 1989–. *Recreations:* works of art, gardening, tennis. *Address:* Hanover House, 14 Hanover Square, W1R 0BE. *Club:* Savile.

HARBOTTLE, Brig. Michael Neale, OBE 1959; PhD; Director, Centre for International Peacebuilding, since 1983; *b* 7 Feb. 1917; *s* of Thomas Benfield Cecil and Kathleen Millicent Harbottle; *m* 1st, 1940, Alison Jean Humfress; one *s* one *d*; 2nd, 1972, Eirwen Helen Simonds. *Educ:* Marlborough Coll.; Royal Military Coll., Sandhurst; Open Internat. Univ. for Complementary Medicine, Sri Lanka (PhD 1993). Commissioned Oxfordshire and Buckinghamshire Light Infantry, 1937 (despatches 1944); commanded 1st Royal Green Jackets, 1959–62; Security Commander, Aden, 1962–64; Comd 129 Inf. Bde, TA, 1964–66; Chief of Staff, UN Peacekeeping Force Cyprus, 1966–68; retired, 1968. Vice-Pres., Internat. Peace Academy, 1971–73, Consultant, 1973–; Vis. Sen. Lectr (Peace Studies), Bradford Univ., 1974–79; Vice-Pres., UNA (UK), 1974–; Cons., United World College of Atlantic, 1974–81; Member: Management Cttee, Council for Educn in World Citizenship, 1978–89; Generals (Retd) for Peace and Disarmament, 1981–90; Internat. Council, Inst. of Conflict Analysis and Resolution, USA, 1992–; Educn Planning Dir, British Council for Aid to Refugees (Vietnamese Sec.), 1979–80; Gen. Sec., World Disarmament Campaign, 1980–82; Co-ordinator, Worldwide Consultative Assoc. of Retd Generals and Admirals, 1991–. Cons/Advr, Internat. Inst. for Peaceful Change. *Publications:* The Impartial Soldier, 1970; The Blue Berets, 1971, 2nd edn 1975; (jtly) The Thin Blue Line: International Peacekeeping and its Future, 1974; The Knaves of Diamonds, 1976; (collator) Peacekeeper's Handbook, 1978; (jtly) 10 Questions Answered, 1983; (jtly) Reflections on Security in the Nuclear Age, 1988; What is Proper Soldiering, 1991; contributor to: Unofficial Diplomats, 1977 (USA); The Arab-Israel Conflict, Readings and Documents, 1977 (USA). *Recreations:* cricket, golf, crossword puzzles. *Address:* 9 West Street, Chipping Norton, Oxon OX7 5LH. *T:* Chipping Norton (01608) 642335.

HARCOURT, Prof. Geoffrey Colin, AO 1994; PhD, LittD; FASSA; Fellow and College Lecturer in Economics, since 1982, President, 1988–89 and 1990–92, Jesus College, Cambridge; Reader (*ad hominem*) in the History of Economic Theory, Cambridge University, since 1990; *b* 27 June 1931; *s* of Kenneth Kopel Harcourt and Marjorie Rahel (*neé* Gans); *m* 1955, Joan Margaret Bartrop; two *s* two *d*. *Educ:* Malvern Grammar Sch.; Wesley Coll., Melbourne; Queen's Coll., Univ. of Melbourne (BCom (Hons) 1954; MCom 1956); King's Coll., Cambridge. PhD 1960, LittD 1988, Cantab. University of Adelaide: Lectr in Econs, 1958–62; Sen. Lectr, 1963–65; Reader, 1965–67; Prof. of Econs (Personal Chair), 1967–85, Prof. Emeritus 1988; Cambridge University: Lectr in Econs and Politics, 1963–66, 1982–90; Fellow and Dir of Studies in Econs, Trinity Hall, 1964–66. Leverhulme Exchange Fellow, Keio Univ., Tokyo, 1969–70; Vis. Fellow, Clare Hall, Cambridge, 1972–73; Vis. Prof., Scarborough Coll., Univ. of Toronto, 1977, 1980. Howard League for Penal Reform, SA Branch: Sec., 1959–63; Vice-Pres., 1967–74; Pres., 1974–80. Mem., Exec. Cttee, Campaign for Peace in Vietnam, 1967–75 (Chm., 1970–72). Mem., Aust. Labor Party Nat. Cttee of Enquiry, 1978–79. Pres., Econ. Soc. of Aust. and NZ, 1974–77; Mem. Council, Roy. Econ. Soc., 1990–. FASSA 1971 (Exec. Cttee Mem., 1974–77). Lectures: Wellington–Burnham, Tufts Univ., USA, 1975; Edward Shann Meml, Univ. of WA, 1975; Newcastle, in Pol Economy, Univ. of Newcastle, NSW, 1977; Academy, Acad. of Social Scis in Aust., 1978; G. L. Wood Meml, Univ. of Melbourne, 1982; John Curtin Meml, ANU, 1982; Special Lectr in Econs, Manchester Univ., 1983–84; Nobel Conf., Minnesota, USA, 1986; Laws, Univ. of Tennessee at Knoxville, USA, 1991; Second Donald Horne Address, Melbourne, 1992. *Publications:* (with P. H. Karmel and R. H. Wallace) Economic Activity, 1967 (trans. Italian, 1969); (ed jtly) Readings in the Concept and Measurement of Income, 1969, 2nd edn 1986; (ed with N. F. Laing) Capital and Growth: Selected Readings, 1971 (trans. Spanish, 1977); Some Cambridge Controversies in the Theory of Capital, 1972 (trans. Italian, 1973, Polish and Spanish, 1975, Japanese 1980); Theoretical Controversy and Social Significance: an evaluation of the Cambridge controversies (Edward Shann Meml Lecture), 1975; (ed) The Microeconomic Foundations of Macroeconomics, 1977; The Social Science Imperialists: selected essays (ed Prue Kerr), 1982; (ed) Keynes and his Contemporaries, 1985; (ed with Jon Cohen) International Monetary Problems and Supply-Side Economics: Essays in Honour of Lorie Tarshis, 1986; Controversies in Political Economy (selected essays, ed O. F. Hamouda), 1986; Post-Keynesian Essays in Biography: portraits of Twentieth Century political economists, 1993; On Political Economists and Modern Political Economy (selected essays, ed C. Sardoni), 1992; Markets, Madness and a Middle Way (Second Annual Donald Horne Address), 1992; (ed jtly) The Dynamics of the Wealth of Nations, Growth, Distribution and Structural Change: essays in honour of Luigi Ludovico Pasinetti, 1993; (ed jtly) Income and Employment in Theory and Practice, 1994; Capitalism, Socialism and Post-Keynesianism: selected essays, 1995; many articles in learned jls and chapters in edited books. *Recreations:* cricket, Australian rules football, running (not jogging), bike riding, reading, politics. *Address:* P3, Jesus College, Cambridge CB5 8BL. *T:* Cambridge (01223)339436; Faculty of Economics and Politics, Austin Robinson Building, University of Cambridge, Sidgwick Avenue, Cambridge CB3 9DD. *T:* Cambridge (01223) 335231; 43 New Square, Cambridge CB1 1EZ. *T:* Cambridge (01223) 60833. *Clubs:* Melbourne Cricket, South Australian Cricket Association.

HARCOURT, Geoffrey David, JP; RDI 1978; DesRCA, FCSD; freelance designer, since 1962; Consultant to Artifort, Dutch furniture manufacturer, since 1963; *b* 9 Aug. 1935; *s* of William and Barbara Harcourt; *m* 1965, Jean Mary Vaughan Pryce-Jones; one *s* one *d*. *Educ:* High Wycombe Sch. of Art; Royal Coll. of Art; DesRCA, Silver Medal 1960. FSIAD 1968. Designer: Latham, Tyler, Jensen, Chicago, 1960–61; Jacob Jensen, Copenhagen, 1961; Andrew Pegram Ltd, London, 1961–62. Vis. Lecturer: High Wycombe Coll. of Art and Design, 1963–74; Leicester Polytechnic, 1982–93; Ext. Assessor for BA Hons degrees, Kingston Polytechnic, 1974–77, Loughborough Coll. of Art and Design, 1978–81, Belfast Polytechnic, 1977–81 and Buckinghamshire Coll. of Higher Educn, 1982–85. Chair design for Artifort awarded first prize for creativity, Brussels, 1978; Member: Design Awards Cttee, Design Council, 1979–80; Furniture Design Wkg Party, EDC, 1986–87; Chm., RSA Bursaries Cttee (Furniture Design Section, 1982–86, Ceramics Section, 1989–91, Woven Textiles, 1992–94); approved consultant, Design Council 'Support for Design' initiative. Work exhibited: Steidlijk Mus., Amsterdam, 1967; Prague Mus. of Decorative Arts, 1972; Science Mus., London, 1972; Design Council, London and Glasgow, 1976 and 1981; Eye for Industry Exhibn, V&A, 1987; Nederlands Textielmuseum, 1988; Manchester Prize exhibn, City Art Gall., 1988; St George's Hall, Windsor Exhibn, Architecture Foundn, London, 1993. FRSA 1979. Freeman, City of London; Liveryman, Worshipful Co. of Furniture Makers (Chm., Design Awards Cttee, 1994 and 1995). JP Thame and Henley, 1981; Chm., Youth Court Panel, 1993–95. *Recreations:* making things, cooking, golf. *Address:* The Old Vicarage, Benson, Oxfordshire OX10 6SF. *Club:* Goring and Streatley Golf.

HARCOURT, Hon. Michael Franklin; MLA (New Democrats) Vancouver-Mount Pleasant, since 1991 (Vancouver Centre, 1986–91); Premier of British Columbia, since 1991; *b* Edmonton, Alta, 6 Jan. 1943; *e s* of Frank and Stella Louise Harcourt; *m* 1971, Beckie Salo; one *s*. *Educ:* Sir Winston Churchill High Sch., Vancouver; University of British Columbia (LLB 1968). Lawyer, Vancouver, 1968–72. Alderman, 1972–80, Mayor, 1980–86, City of Vancouver. Leader of the Opposition, BC, 1987–92. *Recreations:* tennis, golf, ski-ing, watching basketball and football. *Address:* Parliament Buildings, Victoria, BC V8V 1X4, Canada.

HARCOURT-SMITH, Air Chief Marshal Sir David, GBE 1989; KCB 1984; DFC 1957; aviation consultant; Chairman, Chelworth Defence Ltd, since 1991; Controller Aircraft, Ministry of Defence, Procurement Executive, 1986–89, retired; *b* 14 Oct. 1931; *s* of late Air Vice-Marshal G. Harcourt-Smith, CB, CBE, MVO, and of M. Harcourt-

Smith; *m* 1957, Mary (*née* Entwistle); two *s* one *d*. *Educ:* Felsted Sch.; RAF College. Commnd 1952; flying appts with Nos 11, 8 and 54 Squadrons; Staff Coll., 1962; OC No 54 Squadron, 1963–65; PSO to AOC-in-C, Tech. Training Comd, 1965–67; Defence Planning Staff, 1967–68; OC No 6 Squadron, 1969–70; Central Tactics and Trials Organisation, 1970–72; OC RAF Brüggen, 1972–74; Dir of Op. Requirements, 1974–76; RCDS, 1977; Comdt, RAF Coll., Cranwell, 1978–80; Asst Chief of Air Staff (Op. Reqs), 1980–84; AOC-in-C, RAF Support Command, 1984–85. Dir, DESC, 1991–. Gov., Downe House. *Recreations:* walking, golf. *Address:* c/o Barclays Bank, 13 High Street, Shaftesbury, Dorset SP7 8JD. *Club:* Royal Air Force.

HARDAKER, Rev. Canon Ian Alexander; Clergy Appointments Adviser, since 1985; Chaplain to the Queen, since 1994; *b* 14 May 1932; *s* of Joseph Alexander Hardaker and Edna Mary (*née* Theede); *m* 1963, Susan Mary Wade Bottom; two *s* two *d*. *Educ:* Kingston Grammar Sch.; Royal Military Acad., Sandhurst; King's Coll., London (BD, AKC). Commnd East Surrey Regt, 1952. Curate, Beckenham Parish Ch., 1960–65; Vicar of Eynsford and Rector of Lullingstone, 1965–70; Vicar of St Stephen's, Chatham, 1970–85; Rural Dean of Rochester, 1978–85. *Recreations:* walking, photography, family. *Address:* Church House, Shipbourne, Tonbridge, Kent TN11 9PE. *Club:* Commonwealth Trust.

HARDCASTLE, Sir Alan (John), Kt 1992; FCA; Chief Accountancy Adviser to HM Treasury and Head of Government Accountancy Service, 1989–93; *b* 10 Aug. 1933; *s* of late William and of Catherine Hardcastle; *m* 1st, 1958, Dinah (*née* Beattie) (marr. diss. 1983); two *s*; 2nd, 1983, Ione Marguerite (*née* Cooney); two step *d*. *Educ:* Haileybury Coll. Articled to B. W. Brixey, 1951–56; qualified, 1956; Nat. Service as Sub-Lieut RNVR, 1956–58. Joined Peat, Marwick, Mitchell & Co. (later Peat Marwick McLintock, then KPMG Peat Marwick), 1958; Partner 1967; Gen. Partner 1972–88. DoT Inspector into affairs of Saint Piran Ltd (reported 1981). Non-Exec. Dir, Chelsfield. Inst. of Chartered Accountants in England and Wales: Mem. Council, 1974–94; Pres., 1983–85; Chairman: London and District Soc. of Chartered Accountants, 1973–74; Consultative Cttee of Accountancy Bodies, 1983–85; Pres., Chartered Accountants Students' Soc. of London, 1976–80. Chm., Regulatory Bd and Dep. Chm. of Council, Lloyd's, 1993– (Mem. Council, 1987–88); Mem., Bd of Banking Supervision, 1986–. Master, Co. of Chartered Accountants in England and Wales, 1978–79. Mem., Council of Management, The White Ensign Assoc.; Hon. Treas., Berkeley Square Charitable Trust. Speaker and author of papers on accountancy topics. *Recreations:* music, theatre, fishing, the company of family and friends. *Clubs:* Athenæum, City Livery, Naval.

HARDCASTLE, Prof. Jack Donald, MChir (Cantab); FRCP, FRCS; Professor of Surgery, University of Nottingham, since 1970; *b* 3 April 1933; *s* of Albert Hardcastle and Bertha (*née* Ellison); *m* 1965, Rosemary Hay-Shunker; one *s* one *d*. *Educ:* St Bartholomew's Grammar Sch., Newbury; Emmanuel Coll., Cambridge (Senior Scholar 1954; BA, MA; Windsor Postgrad. Schol.); London Hospital (Open Scholarship 1955; MB, BChir, MChir (Distinction)). MRCP 1961; FRCS 1962; FRCP 1984. House Phys./Surg., Resident Accoucheur, London Hosp., 1959–60; Ho. Surg. to Prof. Aird, Hammersmith Postgraduate Hosp., 1961–62; London Hospital: Research Asst, 1962; Lectr in Surgery, 1963; Registrar in Surgery, 1964; Registrar in Surgery, Thoracic Unit, 1965; Sen. Registrar in Surgery, 1965; Sen. Registrar, St Mark's Hosp., London, 1968; Sen. Lectr in Surgery, London Hosp., 1968. Sir Arthur Sims Commonwealth Travelling Prof., RCS, 1985; Mayne Vis. Prof., Univ. of Brisbane, 1987. Mem. Council, RCS, 1987– (Dir, Raven Dept of Educn, 1994–). *Publications:* Isolated Organ Perfusion (with H. D. Ritchie), 1973; various scientific papers. *Recreation:* field sports. *Address:* Goverton Heights, Goverton, Bleasby, Nottingham NG14 7FN. *T:* Newark (01636) 830316.

HARDCASTLE, (Jesse) Leslie, OBE 1974; exhibition and museum consultant; *b* 8 Dec. 1926; *s* of Francis Ernest Hardcastle and Dorothy Schofield; *m* 1968, Vivienne Mansel Richards; two *s*. *Educ:* St Joseph's College, Croydon. British Lion Film Productions, 1943–44; Royal Navy, 1944–47. British Film Inst., 1947–94; Telekinema Festival of Britain, 1951; London Film Fest. admin, 1958–91; Controller, NFT, 1968–91; Museum of the Moving Image: co-author, 1981–88; Curator, 1988–94; Consultant, 1995. Pres., The Soho Soc.; Dep. Chm., Soho Housing Assoc. *Recreations:* community work, theatre, music, cinema. *Address:* 37c Great Pulteney Street, W1R 3DE.

HARDEN, Major James Richard Edwards, OBE 1983; DSO; MC; farmer; *b* 12 Dec. 1916; *s* of late Major J. E. Harden, DL, JP, Royal Irish Fusiliers, and L. G. C. Harden; *m* 1948, Ursula Joyce, *y d* of G. M. Strutt, Newhouse, Terling, Chelmsford, Essex; one *s* two *d*. *Educ:* Oriel House, St Asaph; Bedford Sch.; Sandhurst. Commissioned into Royal Tank Regt 1937; retired on agricultural release, 1947; MP (UU) for County Armagh, 1948–54. JP County Armagh, 1956, Cærnarvonshire, later Gwynedd, 1971–82; DL, Co. Armagh, 1946, Cærnarvonshire, later Gwynedd, 1968; High Sheriff, Cærnarvonshire, 1971–72. *Recreations:* shooting, fishing. *Address:* Hendy, Nanhoran, Pwllheli, Gwynedd LL53 8DL. *T:* Botwnnog (01758) 730432.

HARDENBERGER, (Ulf) Håkan; musician; international trumpet soloist; *b* 27 Oct. 1961; *s* of Åke and Mona Hardenberger; *m* 1986, Heidi Thomassen; one *s*. *Educ:* Paris Conservatory. Hon. RAM 1992. *Address:* c/o Clarion/Seven Muses, 64 Whitehall Park, N19 3TN.

HARDERS, Sir Clarence Waldemar, Kt 1977; OBE 1969; Partner and Consultant, Freehill, Hollingdale and Page, Canberra, ACT, 1980–92; *b* Murtoa, 1 March 1915; *s* of E. W. Harders, Dimboola, Vic; *m* 1947, Gladys, *d* of E. Treasure; one *s* two *d*. *Educ:* Concordia Coll., Unley, S Australia; Adelaide Univ. (LLB). Joined Dept of the Attorney-General, 1947; Dep. Sec., 1965–70; Sec., 1970–79; Legal Adviser, Dept of Foreign Affairs, 1979–80. *Address:* 43 Stonehaven Crescent, Deakin, ACT 2600, Australia. *Clubs:* Commonwealth, National Press, Canberra Bowling (Canberra); Royal Canberra Golf.

HARDIE, Dr Alexander, OBE 1990; HM Diplomatic Service; Counsellor, Pretoria, since 1993; *b* 5 March 1947; *s* of Alexander Merrie Hardie and Phyllis A. I. Hardie; *m* 1971, Jillian Hester Rowlands; one *s* two *d*. *Educ:* Aberdeen Grammar Sch.; Bristol Grammar Sch.; Univ. of Edinburgh (MA); Corpus Christi Coll., Oxford (DPhil). Jun. Research Fellow, Univ. of Bristol, 1972–73; joined HM Diplomatic Service, 1973; FCO, 1973–77; First Secretary: Budapest, 1977–78; Bucharest, 1979–81; FCO, 1981–86; Lusaka, 1986–90; FCO, 1990–93. *Publication:* Statius and the Silvae, 1983. *Recreations:* classical studies, golf. *Address:* c/o Foreign and Commonwealth Office, King Charles Street, SW1A 2AH.

HARDIE, Andrew Rutherford; QC (Scot.) 1985; Dean, Faculty of Advocates, since 1994 (Treasurer, 1989–94); *b* 8 Jan. 1946; *s* of Andrew Rutherford Hardie and Elizabeth Currie Lowe; *m* 1971, Catherine Storrar Elgin; two *s* one *d*. *Educ:* St Mungo's Primary Sch., Alloa; St Modan's High Sch., Stirling; Edinburgh Univ. (MA, LLB Hons). Enrolled Solicitor, 1971; Mem., Faculty of Advocates, 1973; Advocate Depute, 1979–83. *Address:* 4 Oswald Road, Edinburgh EH9 2HF. *T:* 0131–667 7942. *Clubs:* Caledonian, Murrayfield Golf (Edinburgh).

HARDIE, Ven. Archibald George; Archdeacon of West Cumberland and Hon. Canon of Carlisle Cathedral, 1971–79; also Vicar of Haile, 1970–79; *b* 19 Dec. 1908; *s* of late Archbishop Hardie and late Mrs Hardie; *m* 1936, Rosalie Sheelagh Hamilton (*née* Jacob); three *s* one *d*. *Educ:* St Lawrence Coll., Ramsgate; Trinity Coll., Cambridge (MA); Westcott House, Cambridge. Hockey Blue, Cambridge, 1931–32. Curate of All Hallows, Lombard St, EC, and London Sec. of Student Christian Movement, 1934–36; Chaplain, Repton Sch., 1936–38; Vicar of St Alban, Golders Green, London, NW11, 1938–44; OCF. Rector of Hexham Abbey, 1944–63; Vicar and Rural Dean of Halifax, 1963–71, and Hon. Canon of Wakefield Cathedral. *Recreations:* tilling the soil and chewing the cud. *Address:* Westcliffe, Pondicherry, Rothbury, Northumberland NE65 7YP.

HARDIE, Sir Charles (Edgar Mathewes), Kt 1970; CBE 1963 (OBE 1943); chartered accountant; Partner in Dixon, Wilson, 1934–81, Senior Partner, 1975–81; *b* 10 March 1910; *s* of Dr C. F. and Mrs R. F. Hardie (*née* Moore), Barnet, Herts; *m* 1st, 1937, Dorothy Jean (*née* Hobson) (*d* 1965); one *s* three *d*; 2nd, 1966, Mrs Angela Richli, *widow* of Raymond Paul Richli; 3rd, 1975, Rosemary Margaret Harwood. *Educ:* Aldenham Sch. Qualified as Chartered Accountant, 1932; practised in London, 1934–81. War Service, 1939–45, Col (GS). Chairman: BOAC, 1969–70 (Dir, 1964–70); Metropolitan Estate & Property Corp., 1964–71; White Fish Authority, 1967–73; Fitch Lovell plc, 1970–77; Director: British American and General Trust plc, 1961–85; British Printing Corp. plc, 1965–82 (Chm., 1969–76); Royal Bank of Canada, 1969–81; Mann Egerton & Co. Ltd, 1959–80; Forte plc (formerly Trusthouse Forte plc), 1970–95 (Dep. Chm., 1983–93); Hill Samuel Group plc, 1970–77; William Cook Ltd, 1953–93; Dep. Chm., NAAFI, 1953–72; Mem., BEA Board, 1968–70. Mem. Council, Inst. of Directors, 1966–80 (Hon. Life Fellow, 1991). Liveryman, Fishmongers' Co., 1968. Legion of Merit, USA, 1944. *Recreation:* bridge. *Address:* Pitt House, 25 New Street, Henley-on-Thames, Oxon RG9 2BP. *T:* Henley-on-Thames (01491) 577944.

See also C. J. M. Hardie.

HARDIE, (Charles) Jeremy (Mawdesley), CBE 1983; Chairman, W. H. Smith Group, since 1994 (Director, since 1988; Deputy Chairman, 1992–94); Director, John Swire & Sons Ltd, since 1982; *b* 9 June 1938; *s* of Sir Charles Hardie, *qv*; *m* 1st, 1962, Susan Chamberlain (marr. diss. 1976); two *d* two *s*; 2nd, 1978, Xandra, Countess of Gowrie, *d* of late Col R. A. G. Bingley, CVO, DSO, OBE; one *d*. *Educ:* Winchester Coll.; New Coll., Oxford (2nd Cl. Hon. Mods, 1st Cl. Lit. Hum.); Nuffield Coll., Oxford (BPhil Econs). ACA 1965, Peat, Marwick, Mitchell & Co.; Nuffield Coll., Oxford, 1966–67; Jun. Res. Fellow, Trinity Coll., Oxford, 1967–68; Fellow and Tutor in Econs, Keble Coll., Oxford, 1968–75. Partner, Dixon Wilson & Co., 1975–82. Chairman: Nat. Provident Instn, 1980–89 (Dir, 1972–89, Dep. Chm., 1977); Alexander Syndicate Management Ltd, 1982–; Radio Broadland Ltd, 1983–85 (Dir, 1983–90); D. P. Mann Underwriting Agency Ltd, 1983–; Director: Alexanders Discount Co. Ltd, 1978–87 (Dep. Chm., 1981–84; Chm., 1984–86); Amdahl (UK) Ltd, 1983–86; Mercantile House Holdings Ltd, 1984–87; Additional Underwriting Agencies (No 3) Ltd, 1985–90; Alexanders Laing & Cruickshank Gilts Ltd, 1986–87 (Chm., 1986); Northdoor Hldgs, 1989–. Chm., Centre for Economic Policy Res., 1984–89; Treas., REconS, 1987–93; Dep. Chm., NAAFI, 1986–92 (Dir, 1981–). Member: Monopolies and Mergers Commn, 1976–83 (Dep. Chm., 1980–83); Council, Oxford Centre for Management Studies, 1978–85; Hammersmith Health Authority, 1982–83; Arts Council of GB, 1984–86; Peacock Cttee on Financing of BBC, 1985–86. Contested Norwich South, (SDP) 1983, (SDP/Alliance) 1987. Trustee: Esmée Fairbairn Charitable Trust, 1972–; Butler Trust, 1985–87. *Recreations:* sailing, skiing. *Address:* 13 Ainger Road, NW3 3AR. *T:* 0171–722 6916.

HARDIE, Colin Graham; Official Fellow and Tutor in Classics, Magdalen College, Oxford, 1936–73; Public Orator of Oxford University, 1967–73; *b* 16 Feb. 1906; 3rd *s* of William Ross Hardie, Fellow of Balliol Coll. and Prof. of Humanity in Edinburgh Univ., and Isabella Watt Stevenson; *m* 1940, Christian Viola Mary Lucas; two *s*. *Educ:* Edinburgh Acad.; Balliol Coll., Oxford (Warner Exhibitioner and Hon. Scholar); 1st class Classical Moderations, 1926, and Lit Hum BA, 1928; MA, 1931; Craven Scholar, 1925; Ireland Scholar, 1925; Hertford Scholar, 1926; Gaisford Prize for Greek Prose, 1927; Junior Research Fellow of Balliol, 1928–29; Fellow and Classical Tutor, 1930–33; Dir of the British Sch. at Rome, 1933–36. Hon. Prof. of Ancient Lit., RA, 1971–90. *Publications:* Vitae Vergilianae antiquae, 1954; papers on Virgil and Dante. *Recreation:* gardening. *Address:* Rackham Cottage, Greatham Lane, Pulborough, Sussex RH20 2ES. *T:* Pulborough (01798) 873170.

HARDIE, Brig. Donald David Graeme, TD 1968; JP; FPRI; Lord-Lieutenant, Strathclyde Region (Districts of Dumbarton, Clydebank, Bearsden and Milngavie, Strathkelvin, Cumbernauld and Kilsyth), since 1990; Director: Hardie Polymers, since 1976; Hardie Polymers (England), since 1989; Ronaash, since 1988; *b* 23 Jan. 1936; *m* 1961, Rosalind Allan Ker; two *s*. *Educ:* Larchfield, Blairmore and Merchiston Castle Schools. U.T.R. Management Trainee, 1956–59; F. W. Allen & Ker, 1960–61; J. & G. Hardie & Co., 1961–81; Gilbert Plastics, 1973–76. Mem., Erskine Hosp. Exec. Cttee. Commissioned 41st Field Regt RA, 1955; Battery Comdr, 277 (Argyll & Sutherland Highlanders) Regt, RA TA, 1966; CO GSV OTC, 1973; TA Colonel: Lowlands, 1976; DES, 1980; Scotland, 1985; Hon. Colonel: Glasgow and Lanarks Bn, ACF, 1990–; 105 Air Defence Regt, RA(V), 1992–; ACF Brig. Scotland, 1987; Vice-Chm., RA Council for Scotland; Vice-Pres., ACFA Scotland. Dir, Scottish Tooling Ltd, 1993–. JP Dumbarton, 1990. *Recreations:* ski-ing, sailing, shooting, fishing. *Address:* Dun Ruadh Farm, Gartocharn, Dunbartonshire G83 8SB. *T:* Gartocharn (01389) 830241. *Club:* Royal Northern and Clyde Yacht.

HARDIE, Sir Douglas (Fleming), Kt 1990; CBE 1979; JP; Chairman, Edward Parker & Co. Ltd, since 1960 (Managing Director, 1960–90); *b* 26 May 1923; *s* of late James Dunbar Hardie, JP, and of Frances Mary (*née* Fleming); *m* 1945, Dorothy Alice Warner; two *s* one *d*. *Educ:* Arnhall & Seafield House Prep. Schs; Trinity Coll., Glenalmond, Perthshire. Trooper, 58 Trng Regt, RAC, Bovington, 1941; commnd RMA, Sandhurst, 1942; 1st Fife and Forfar Yeomanry, NW Europe, 1942–46 (despatches); demobilised rank of Major. Dir 1964–84, Chm. 1984–85, H. & A. Scott (Holdings) Ltd; Chairman: A. G. Scott (Textiles) Ltd, 1985–88; Grampian TV, 1989–93 (Dir, 1984–93); Director: Dayco Rubber (UK) Ltd, 1956–86; Clydesdale Bank, 1981–92; Alliance Trust, 1982–93; Second Alliance Trust, 1982–93. Dep. Chm., SDA, 1978–91. Chm., CBI Scotland, 1976–78; Bd Mem., N of Scotland Hydro Elec. Bd, 1977–83; Mem., Scottish Econ. Council, 1977–91; Dir, Prince's Scottish Youth Business Trust, 1988–. Mem. Council, Winston Churchill Meml Trust, 1985–. Deacon Convener, Nine Incorporated Trades (Dundee), 1951–54. FRSA 1988; CBIM 1990. JP Dundee, 1970. Hon. LLD Dundee, 1992. *Recreations:* golf, fishing. *Address:* 6 Norwood Terrace, Dundee DD2 1PB. *T:* Dundee (01382) 669107. *Clubs:* Caledonian; Royal & Ancient Golf (St Andrews); Blairgowrie Golf; Panmure Golf (Barry).

HARDIE, Jeremy; *see* Hardie, C. J. M.

HARDIE, Michael John, OBE 1989; HM Diplomatic Service, retired; *b* 14 July 1938; *s* of John Thomas Hardie and Annie Smethurst; *m* 1st, 1967, Patricia Louisa Hulme; two *s* one *d*; 2nd, 1990, Jean Fish; one step *s* one step *d*. *Educ:* St Ambrose Coll., Hale Barns, Cheshire; De La Salle Coll., Salford. HM Forces (Intelligence Corps), 1957–59; FO 1959;

served Bahrain, Elisabethville, Bathurst, Sofia, Vienna, Munich and Cape Town, to 1979; First Secretary, 1979; BMG Berlin, 1979–81; Malta, 1981–83; FCO, 1983–86; Lagos, 1986–89; Counsellor, 1988; New Delhi, 1990–93; High Comr, Gambia, 1994–95. *Recreations:* golf, music. *Address:* c/o Foreign and Commonwealth Office, SW1A 2AH. *Club:* Commonwealth Trust.

HARDIE, Miles Clayton, OBE 1988; Director General, International Hospital Federation, 1975–87; *b* 27 Feb. 1924; *s* of late Frederick Hardie and Estelle (*née* Clarke); *m* 1st, 1949, Pauline (marr. diss. 1974), *d* of late Sir Wilfrid Le Gros Clark, FRS; two *s*; 2nd, 1974, Melissa (marr. diss. 1984), *d* of late James Witcher, Houston, Texas; 3rd, 1985, Elizabeth, *d* of late Dudley Ash, *widow* of H. Spencer Smith. *Educ:* Charterhouse; Oriel Coll., Oxford (MA). Served War, RAF, 1943–46. Admin. Asst, Hosp. for Sick Children, London, 1949–51; Sec., Victoria Hosp. for Children, 1951–55; Sec., Bahrain Govt Med. Dept, 1956–58; joined staff of King Edward's Hosp. Fund for London, 1958, Dep. Dir, King's Fund Centre, 1963–66, Dir, 1966–75. Hon. Sec., British Hosps Export Council, later Assoc. of British Health-Care Industries, 1964–67, Mem. Council, 1967–75, 1987–; Mem. Council, Nat. Assoc. of Leagues of Hosp. Friends, 1970–75; Member: Adv. Council, Nat. Corp. Care of Old People, 1973–76; Council of Management, MIND/Nat. Assoc. for Mental Health, 1967–86; Man. Cttee of Spinal Injuries Assoc., 1975–79; Bd of Governors, Volunteer Centre, 1977–80; Council, Appropriate Health Resources and Technologies Action Gp, 1977–89. Adviser to WHO, 1978– (WHO Health for All by the year 2000 Medal, 1987). Hon. Member: Amer. Hosp. Assoc., 1983–; Polish Hosp. Assoc., 1985–. Mem., Ct of Assistants, Salters' Co., 1969–79. *Recreations:* gardening, walking. *Address:* Tallow Cottage, Fishers Lane, Charlbury, Oxford OX7 3RX. *T:* Charlbury (01608) 810088.

HARDIE BOYS, Rt Hon. Michael; PC 1989; Judge of the Court of Appeal, New Zealand, (desig. Rt Hon. Mr Justice Michael Hardie Boys), 1989–Feb. 1996; Governor General of New Zealand, from March 1996; *b* Wellington, 6 Oct. 1931; *s* of Hon. Mr Justice Reginald Hardie Boys and Edith May (*née* Bennett); *m* 1957; Edith Mary Zohrab; two *s* two *d*. *Educ:* Wellington Coll.; Victoria Univ. (BA, LLB). Admitted Barrister and Solicitor, 1954; Partner, Scott Hardie Boys & Morrison, 1955–80; Chm., Legal Aid Bd, 1978–80; Judge of NZ High Court, 1980–89. Pres., Wellington Dist Law Soc., 1979; Treas., NZ Law Soc., 1980. *Address:* (until March 1996) Judge's Chambers, Court of Appeal, PO Box 1606, Wellington, New Zealand; (from March 1996) Government House, Wellington, New Zealand.

HARDING, family name of **Baron Harding of Petherton.**

HARDING OF PETHERTON, 2nd Baron *cr* 1958, of Nether Compton; **John Charles Harding;** farmer, 1969–90; *b* 12 Feb. 1928; *s* of Field Marshal 1st Baron Harding of Petherton, GCB, CBE, DSO, MC, and Mary Gertrude Mabel (*d* 1983), *er d* of late Joseph Wilson Rooke, JP; *S* father, 1989; *m* 1966, Harriet, *d* of Maj.-Gen. James Francis Hare, CB, DSO; two *s* one *d*. *Educ:* Marlborough College; Worcester Coll., Oxford (BA). National Service, 1945–48; 2nd Lieut, 11th Hussars (PAO), 1947; demobilised, 1948; Oxford Univ., 1948–51; Regular Commn, 11th Hussars (PAO), 1953; retired from Army, 1968. *Recreations:* hunting, racing. *Heir:* *s* Hon. William Allan John Harding, *b* 5 July 1969. *Address:* Barrymore Farm House, Pict's Hill, Langport, Somerset TA10 9EZ *T:* Langport (01458) 250416.

HARDING, Sir Christopher (George Francis), Kt 1991; Chairman and Director, BET plc, since 1992; Chairman, Legal & General plc, since 1994 (Director, since 1993); *b* 17 Oct. 1939; *s* of Frank Harding and Phyllis (*née* Wise); *m* 1st, 1963, Susan Berry (marr. diss. 1977); one *s* one *d*; 2nd, 1978 (marr. diss. 1988); 3rd, 1994, Anne Skelley. *Educ:* Merchant Taylors' School; Corpus Christi College, Oxford (MA Hons). Imperial Chemical Industries, 1961–69; Hanson PLC, 1969–, Non-Exec. Dir, 1979–; Man. Dir, 1974–, Vice Chm., 1991–, Hanson Transport Gp. Dir, 1984–92, Chm., 1986–92, British Nuclear Fuels plc. Director: ProShare (UK), 1992–93; English China Clays, 1992–94; Slough Estates, 1992–94; Newarthill, 1992– (Chm., 1993–); General Electric Co., 1992–; Post Office Bd, 1993–. Council Member: CBI, 1986–; Business in the Community, 1986–; Member: Adv. Bd, Univ. of Bradford Management Centre, 1981–93; Exec. Cttee, British Energy Assoc., 1986– (Chm., 1989–92); UK–Japan 2000 GP, 1987– (Dir, 1995–); Court, UMIST, 1987–92; Adv. Bd, Prince's Youth Business Trust, 1988– (Chm. of Trustees, 1994–); Science & Industry Cttee, BAAS, 1989–93; NACETT, 1993–. Dir, Foyer Fedn for Youth, 1992–. FRSA 1987; CIMgt (CBIM 1988). Freeman, City of London, 1965; Member, 1965, Liveryman, 1986, Merchant Taylors' Co. Hon. Fellow: Huddersfield Univ. (formerly Poly.), 1990; Linacre Coll., Oxford, 1993; Hon. FCGI 1990; Hon. FIChemE 1992; Hon. FINucE 1992. *Recreations:* theatre, music, travel, tennis, pocillovy. *Address:* BET plc, Stratton House, Stratton Street, Piccadilly, W1X 6AS. *T:* 0171–629 8886. *Club:* Brooks's.

HARDING, Prof. Dennis William, MA, DPhil; FRSE; Abercromby Professor of Archaeology, University of Edinburgh, since 1977; *b* 11 April 1940; *s* of Charles Royston Harding and Marjorie Doris Harding. *Educ:* Keble Coll., Oxford (BA, MA, DPhil). Assistant Keeper, Dept of Antiquities, Ashmolean Museum, Oxford, 1965–66; Lecturer in Celtic Archaeology, 1966, Sen. Lectr, 1975–77, Univ. of Durham; University of Edinburgh: Dean, Faculty of Arts, 1983–86; Vice-Principal, 1988–91. Member: Board of Trustees, National Museum of Antiquities of Scotland, 1977–85; Ancient Monuments Board for Scotland, 1979–83. FRSE 1986. *Publications:* The Iron Age in the Upper Thames Basin, 1972; The Iron Age in Lowland Britain, 1974; (with A. J. Challis) Later Prehistory from the Trent to the Tyne, 1975; ed and contrib., Archaeology in the North: Report of the Northern Archaeological Survey, 1976; ed and contrib., Hillforts: later prehistoric earthworks in Britain and Ireland, 1976; Prehistoric Europe, 1978; (with I. M. Blake and P. J. Reynolds) An Iron Age Settlement in Dorset: excavation and reconstruction, 1993. *Recreation:* private flying. *Address:* Department of Archaeology, The Old High School, Infirmary Street, Edinburgh EH1 1LT. *T:* 0131–667 1011. *Club:* Athenæum.

HARDING, Derek William; Executive Secretary, Royal Statistical Society, 1986–95; *b* 16 Dec. 1930; *o s* of late William Arthur Harding; *m* 1954, Daphne Sheila, *yr d* of late Reginald Ernest Cooke; one *s* one *d*. *Educ:* Glendale Grammar Sch., London; Univ. of Bristol (BSc). FInstP, CPhys, FIM, CEng. Develt Engr, Pye Ltd, 1954–56; Sen. Physics Master, Thornbury Grammar Sch., Bristol, 1956–60; Sen. Lectr in Physical Science, St Paul's Coll., Cheltenham, 1960–64; Asst Organiser, Nuffield Foundn Science Teaching Project, 1964–67; joined staff of Instn Metallurgists, 1967, Registrar-Sec., 1969–76. Sec.-Gen., British Computer Soc., 1976–86. *Recreation:* off-shore sailing. *Address:* 16 Exeter Road, N14 5JY. *T:* 0181–368 1463. *Clubs:* Athenæum, Cruising Association.

HARDING, Sir (George) William, KCMG 1983 (CMG 1977); CVO 1972; HM Diplomatic Service, retired; *b* 18 Jan. 1927; *o s* of late Lt Col G. R. Harding, DSO, MBE, and Grace Henley (*née* Darby); *m* 1955, Sheila Margaret Ormond Riddel; four *s*. *Educ:* Aldenham; St John's College, Cambridge. Royal Marines, 1945–48. Entered HM Foreign Service, 1950; served (other than in London) in Singapore, 1951–52; Burma, 1952–55; Paris, 1956–59; Santo Domingo, 1960–63; Mexico City, 1967–70; Paris, 1970–74; Ambassador to Peru, 1977–79; Asst Under-Sec. of State, FCO, 1979–81; Ambassador to Brazil, 1981–84; Dep. Under-Sec. of State, FCO, 1984–86. Chairman: First Spanish Investment Trust, 1987–; Thai-Euro Fund, 1988–; British Thai Business Gp, 1995–; Dir, Lloyds Bank Plc, 1988–93. Chairman: Margaret Mee Amazon Trust, 1988–94; Anglo-Peruvian Soc., 1987–89; Brazilian Chamber of Commerce in Britain, 1988–91. Vice-Pres., RGS, 1991–93; Mem. Council, RIIA, 1988–94. *Address:* La Dreyrie, 24510 Pezuls, France. *Clubs:* Beefsteak; Leander.

HARDING, Hugh Alastair, CMG 1958; Under-Secretary, Department of Education and Science, 1967–77; *b* 4 May 1917; 2nd *s* of late Roland Charles Harding, Norton-le-Moors, Staffordshire; *m* 1943, Florence Esnouf; one *s* one *d*. *Educ:* Rugby; Trinity Coll., Cambridge. Colonial Office, 1939; Asst Sec., 1950; Asst Sec., Treasury, 1961; Under-Sec., Treasury, 1962–64; Minister, UK Delegation to OECD, 1964–67. Served War of 1939–45, Army (Captain RA). *Address:* c/o National Westminster Bank, 130 High Street, Tunstall, Stoke-on-Trent, Staffs.

HARDING, John Philip, PhD; Keeper of Zoology, British Museum (Natural History), 1954–71, retired; *b* 12 Nov. 1911; *s* of Philip William and Eleanor Harding, Rondebosch, Cape Town; *m* 1937, Sidnie Manton, PhD, ScD, FRS (*d* 1979); one *s* one *d*. *Educ:* Torquay; University Coll., Exeter; University of Cincinnati; King's Coll., Cambridge. Ministry of Agriculture and Fisheries, 1936–37; British Museum (Natural History), 1937–71. Vis. Prof., Westfield Coll., Univ. of London, 1971–77. *Publications:* scientific papers on Crustacea. *Recreations:* photomicrography, mechanical devices, handicap aids. *Address:* 7 Ashcroft Close, Ringmer, Lewes, East Sussex BN8 5QY. *T:* Ringmer (01273) 812385.

HARDING, Rt. Rev. Malcolm Alfred Warden; *see* Brandon, Bishop of.

HARDING, Air Vice-Marshal Peter John, CB 1993; CBE 1985; AFC 1974; Defence Services Secretary, and Assistant Chief of Defence Staff (Personnel and Reserves), since 1994; *b* 1 June 1940; *s* of John Fitz Harding and Marjorie Clare; *m* 1966, Morwenna Jacquiline St John Grey; two *s*. *Educ:* Solihull School. Joined RAF, 1960; Pilot, 249 Sqn, Cyprus, 1962–65; RAF Coll., 1965–70; Cyprus, 1971–72; Waddington, 1972–74; RNC, 1974; RAF Germany, 1974–76; OC Pilot Buccaneers Sqns, 1977–80; Directing Staff, RAF Staff Coll., 1981; Station Comdr, Honington, 1982–84; RCDS 1985; Dir Nuclear Systems, MoD, 1986–88; Dep. C-in-C, RAF Germany, 1989–91; Dep. COS (Ops), HQ AAFCE, 1991–94. ADC to the Queen, 1982–84. *Recreations:* cricket, golf, tennis, gardening, family, philately. *Address:* c/o Lloyds Bank, 7 Pall Mall, SW1Y 5NA. *Clubs:* Royal Air Force, Innominate; Royal Cinque Ports (Deal).

HARDING, Marshal of the Royal Air Force Sir Peter (Robin), GCB 1988 (KCB 1983; CB 1980); FRAeS; CIMgt; Deputy Chairman, GEC Marconi Ltd, since 1995; Director, Double Sky Co. Ltd, since 1995; *b* 2 Dec. 1933; *s* of late Peter Harding and Elizabeth Clear; *m* 1955, Sheila Rosemary May; three *s* one *d*. *Educ:* Chingford High Sch. Joined RAF, 1952; Pilot, 12 Sqdn, 1954–57; QFI and Flt Comdr, RAF Coll., Cranwell, 1957–60; Pilot, 1 Sqdn, RAAF, 1960–62; sc 1963; Air Secretary's Dept, MoD, 1964–66; OC, 18 Sqdn, Gutersloh and Acklington, 1966–69; jssc, Latimer, 1969–70; Defence Policy Staff, MoD, 1970–71; Director, Air Staff, Briefing, MoD, 1971–74; Station Comdr, RAF Brüggen, 1974–76; ADC to the Queen, 1975; Dir of Defence Policy, MoD, 1976–78; Asst Chief of Staff (Plans and Policy), SHAPE, 1978–80; AOC No 11 Group, 1981–82; VCAS, 1982–84; VCDS, 1985; AOC-in-C, RAF Strike Comd, and C-in-C, UK Air Forces, 1985–88; Chief of Air Staff, 1988–92; Chief of the Defence Staff, 1992–94. FRAeS 1983, Hon. CRAeS 1989; CIMgt (CBIM 1984); FRSA 1988. Liveryman, GAPAN, 1989. Mem. Council, Winston Churchill Meml Trust, 1990–. Vice Pres., Guild of Aviation Artists, 1994–. Hon. DSc Cranfield, 1990. Legion of Merit (USA), 1992. *Publications:* articles for professional jls, magazines and books. *Recreations:* tennis, pianoforte, bridge, birdwatching and shooting.

HARDING, Peter Thomas, Director General, Petroleum Engineering Division, Department of Energy, 1989–91; *b* 5 Dec. 1930; *s* of late James Alfred Harding and Catherine Frances Harding; *m* 1954, Joyce Holmes; two *s* two *d*. *Educ:* Ealing Grammar School. Exec. Officer, Min. of Supply, 1949; Principal, Min. of Technology, 1967; Asst Sec., DTI, 1973, Dept of Energy, 1974, Under Sec. (Grade 3), 1989. *Recreations:* music, watching cricket, gardening. *Address:* Pookwell, Ridgway, Pyrford, Woking, Surrey GU22 8PW. *T:* Byfleet (01932) 346766.

HARDING, Roger John, CMG 1986; Chairman: Sujanara Ltd, since 1991; Sonatest plc, since 1995; Director, ITT Defence Ltd, since 1993; *b* 7 April 1935; *s* of Charles William Harding and Lilian Mabel (*née* Trowbridge); *m* 1960, June Elizabeth Tidy; four *d*. *Educ:* Price's Sch., Fareham, Hants; Southern Grammar Sch., Portsmouth, Hants. Board of Trade, 1954–74; War Office, then Min. of Defence, 1974–91: Head of Defence Secretariat 8, 1979–82; Counsellor, Defence Supply, 1982–86, Minister, Defence Material, 1986–88, Washington; Dir Gen., Marketing, MoD, 1988–91. *Recreations:* soccer, cricket, golf, following fortunes of Portsmouth FC. *Club:* St John's Village (Woking).

HARDING, Air Vice-Marshal Ross Philip, CBE 1968; RAF retired; *b* 22 Jan. 1921; *s* of P. J. Harding, Salisbury; *m* 1948, Laurie Joy Gardner; three *s*. *Educ:* Bishop Wordsworth Sch., Salisbury; St Edmund Hall, Oxford (MA). No 41 Sqdn Fighter Comd and 2 TAF, 1943–45; RAF Staff Coll., Andover, 1951; Air Min. (ACAS Ops), 1952–54; CO No 96 Sqdn, Germany, 1955–58; Directing Staff, RAF Staff Coll., Andover, 1958–60; CO Oxford Univ. Air Sqdn, 1960–62; Dep. Chief, British Mil. Mission, Berlin, 1963–65; CO RAF Valley, 1965–68; Senior Directing Staff (Air), Jt Services Staff Coll., 1968–69; Defence and Air Attaché, Moscow, 1970–72; Dir of Personal Services 1, MoD (Air), 1973; Senior RAF Member, RCDS, 1974–76. Hd of Airwork Services Ltd, Oman, 1976–78. Chm., MoD Selection Bd, 1979–. Specialist Advr to H of C Defence Cttee, 1979–84. *Recreations:* ski-ing, shooting. *Address:* Tally-Ho, 8 Hadrian's Close, Lower Bemerton, Salisbury, Wilts SP2 9NN. *Club:* Royal Air Force.

HARDING, Sir Roy (Pollard), Kt 1985; CBE 1978; education consultant; *b* 3 Jan. 1924; *s* of W. F. N. Harding, BEM and P. E. Harding; *m* 1948, Audrey Beryl Larkin, JP; two *s* one *d*. *Educ:* Liskeard Grammar Sch.; King's Coll., Univ. of London (BSc; AKC; DPA). CMath, FIMA; FZS. Ballistics research, schools and college teaching, to 1950; Educn Admin, Wilts, Bucks, Herts, Leics, to 1960; Dep. Chief Educn Officer, 1960–66, Chief Educn Officer, 1966–84, Bucks. Adviser: County Councils Assoc., 1972–74; Assoc. of County Councils, 1973–84 (incl. Finance, 1978–81, Policy, 1981–84); Council of Local Educn Authorities, 1975–84. Member: Printing and Publishing Ind. Trng Bd, 1970–72; BBC Further Educn Adv. Council, 1970–75; Burnham Cttee, 1972–77; Sec. of State's Vis. Cttee, Cranfield Inst. of Technology, 1976–81; DES/Local Authority Expenditure Steering Gp, Educn, 1976–84; Councils and Educnl Press (Longmans) Editorial Adv. Panel, 1977–86; Teaching of Mathematics in Schools (Cockcroft) Cttee, 1978–82; Educn Management Inf. Exchange, 1981–89; Board, Nat. Adv. Body for Higher Educn, 1982–84; A Level (Higginson) Cttee, 1987–88; Assoc. of Educn Cttees Trust, 1989–; CBI Educn Foundn, 1990–94; Educn Cttee, Royal Soc., 1991– (Vice-Chm., 1995–); various univ. cttees, incl. Open Univ. Council, 1985–; Chairman: County Educn Officers' Soc., 1978–79 (Sec., 1973–76); Educn Policy Interchange Cttee, 1979–89; Open Univ. INSET

Sector Programme Bd, 1983–87; Governing Body, Staff Coll. (formerly Further Educn Staff Coll.), 1986–; FEFCE Tariff Adv. Cttee, 1993–; Vice-Chm., Secondary Exams Council, 1983–86. President: Soc. of Educn Officers, 1977–78 (Mem. Exec., 1974–79; Chm. Internat. Cttee, 1980–83; Gen. Sec., 1984–89); British Educnl Equipment Assoc., 1980–83; Educn Sect., BAAS, 1986–87; Nat. Inst. Adult Continuing Educn, 1988–94; IMA, 1990, 1991 (Council, 1983–88, 1990–; Vice-Pres., 1986–88). Chm., EMIS Ltd, 1988–91. Centenary Fellow, Thames Polytechnic, 1990. FRSA. DUniv Open, 1985; Hon. LLD Leicester, 1995. Wappenteller, Rheinland/Pfalz, Germany, 1978. Gold Cross of Merit, Polish Govt in Exile, 1984. *Recreations:* travel, music. *Address:* 27 King Edward Avenue, Aylesbury, Bucks HP21 7JE. *T:* Aylesbury (01296) 23006. *Clubs:* Royal Over-Seas League; Rotary.

HARDING, Wilfrid Gerald, CBE 1978; FRCP, FFCM, DPH; Area Medical Officer, Camden and Islington Area Health Authority (Teaching), 1974–79; Hon. Consultant in Community Medicine, University College Hospital, London, 1971–79; *b* 17 March 1915; *s* of late Dr *hc* Ludwig Ernst Emil Hoffmann and Marie Minna Eugenie (*née* Weisbach); *m* 1st, 1938, Britta Charlotta Haraldsdotter, Malmberg (marr. diss. 1970); three *s*; 2nd, 1973, Hilary Maxwell. *Educ:* Französisches Gymnasium, Berlin; Süddeutsches Landerziehungsheim, Schondorf, Bavaria; Woodbrooke Coll., Selly Oak, Birmingham; University Coll. London; University Coll. Hosp. Med. Sch. (interned twice in 1939 and 1940). MRCS, LRCP 1941; DPH London 1949; MRCP 1968; FFCM 1972; Hon. FFCM 1986; FRCP 1972. Ho. Phys. and Ho. Surg., UCH, 1941–42; Asst MOH, City of Oxford, 1942–43; RAMC, 1943–47, Field Units in NW Europe, 1 Corps Staff and Mil. Govt, Lt-Col (Hygiene Specialist). In charge of health services, Ruhr Dist of Germany, CCG, 1947–48; LSHTM, 1948–49; career posts in London public health service, 1949–64; MOH, London Bor. of Camden, and Principal Sch. MO, ILEA, 1965–74. Hon. Lectr, Dept of Sociol., Bedford Coll., London Univ., 1969–77; Civil Consultant in Community Medicine to RAF, 1974–78. Chm. of Council, Soc. of MOH, 1966–71 (Pres. 1971–72); Chm., Prov. Bd of FCM, Royal Colls of Physicians of UK, 1971–72 (Vice-Pres., 1972–75, Pres., 1975–78). Member: Central Health Services Council and Standing Med. Adv. Cttee, 1966–71 and 1975–78; Standing Mental Health Adv. Cttee, 1966–71; Bd of Studies in Preventive Med. and Public Health, Univ. of London, 1963–79; Council, UCH Med. Sch., 1965–78; Bd of Management, LSHTM, 1968–82; Council for Educn and Trng of Health Visitors, 1965–77; Council, ASH, 1970–73 and 1978–82; Public Health Laboratory Service Bd, 1972–83. Armed Services Med. Adv. Bd, 1975–78; GMC, 1979–84; Vice-Chm., Dartford and Gravesham CHC, 1984–89. Chm., DHSS Working Gp on Primary Health Team, 1978–80 (reported 1981). Hon. Advr, Office of Health Econs, 1977–. Councillor, Sevenoaks DC, 1979–; Chm., Farningham Parish Council, 1983–89. Chm., Farningham Woods Nature Reserve, 1983–. Broadcasts on public health and community medicine. *Publications:* papers on public health and community med. in medical books and jls; Parkes Centenary Meml Lecture (Community, Health and Service), 1976. *Recreations:* watching river birds, music, wine. *Address:* Bridge Cottage, High Street, Farningham, Dartford DA4 0DW. *T:* Farningham (01322) 862733. *Club:* Athenæum.

HARDING, Sir William; *see* Harding, Sir G. W.

HARDINGE, family name of **Viscount Hardinge** and **Baron Hardinge of Penshurst.**

HARDINGE, 6th Viscount *cr* 1846, of Lahore and of King's Newton, Derbyshire; **Charles Henry Nicholas Hardinge;** Bt 1801; Manager, Private Banking, for Royal Bank of Canada in London; *b* 25 Aug. 1956; *s* of 5th Viscount Hardinge and of Zoë Anne, *d* of Hon. Hartland de Montarville Molson, OBE, Montreal; *S* father, 1984; *m* 1985, Julie Therese Sillett, *d* of Joan Sillett of Sydney, Australia; two *d* one step *s*. *Heir: b* Hon. Andrew Hartland Hardinge [*b* 7 Jan. 1960; *m* 1990, Sophia Mary, *e d* of Capt. W. D. A. Bagnell; one *s*]. *Address:* Broadmere House, Broadmere, Farleigh Wallop, Basingstoke, Hants RG25 2JA.

HARDINGE OF PENSHURST, 3rd Baron *cr* 1910; **George Edward Charles Hardinge;** *b* 31 Oct. 1921; *o s* of 2nd Baron Hardinge of Penshurst, PC, GCB, GCVO, MC, and Helen Mary Cecil (*d* 1979); *S* father, 1960; *m* 1st, 1944, Janet Christine Goschen (marr. diss. 1962, she *d* 1970), *d* of late Lt-Col F. C. C. Balfour, CIE, CVO, CBE, MC; three *s*; 2nd, 1966, Margaret Trezise; one *s*, and one step-*s*, now adopted. *Educ:* Eton; Royal Naval College, Dartmouth. RN 1940–47; subsequently in publishing; Sen. Editor: Collins; Longmans; Macmillan (London) Ltd, 1968–86 (also dir); Founder and Editor, Winter's Crime series. *Publication:* An Incompleat Angler, 1976. *Recreations:* reading, fishing, bridge. *Heir: s* Hon. Julian Alexander Hardinge, *b* 23 Aug. 1945. *Address:* Bracken Hill, 10 Penland Road, Bexhill-on-Sea, East Sussex TN40 2JG. *T:* Bexhill (01424) 211866. *Club:* Brooks's.

See also Lt-Col Sir J. F. D. Johnston, Sir J. A. J. Murray.

HARDMAN, Sir Henry, KCB 1962 (CB 1956); *b* 15 Dec. 1905; *s* of late Harry Hardman and Bertha Hardman; *m* 1937, Helen Diana, *d* of late Robert Carr Bosanquet and Ellen Sophia Bosanquet; one *s* two *d*. *Educ:* Manchester Central High Sch.; University of Manchester. Lecturer for Workers' Educational Association, 1929–34; Economics Tutor, University of Leeds, 1934–45; joined Ministry of Food, 1940; Deputy Head, British Food Mission to N America, 1946–48; Under-Sec., Ministry of Food, 1948–53; Minister, UK Permanent Delegation, Paris, 1953–54; Dep. Sec., Ministry of Agriculture, Fisheries and Food, 1955–60; Dep. Sec., Ministry of Aviation, 1960; Permanent Sec., 1961–63: Permanent Sec., Ministry of Defence, 1963–64; Permanent Under Sec. of State, Min. of Defence, 1964–66. Mem., Monopolies Commn, 1967–70 (Dep. Chm., 1967–68); Chm., Cttee of enquiry into the Post Office pay dispute, 1971; Consultant to CSD on dispersal of govt work from London, 1971–73 (report published, 1973). Chairman: Covent Garden Mkt Authority, 1967–75; Home-Grown Cereals Authority, 1968–77. Governor and Trustee, Reserve Bank of Rhodesia, 1967–79. Hon. LLD Manchester, 1965. *Address:* 9 Sussex Square, Brighton BN2 1FJ. *T:* Brighton (01273) 688904.

HARDMAN, James Arthur, MBE 1968; HM Diplomatic Service, retired; *b* 12 Sept. 1929; *er s* of late James Sidney Hardman and Rachel Hardman; *m* 1953, Enid Mary Hunter; two *s*. *Educ:* Manchester Grammar Sch.; Manchester Univ. (BA Hons 1950). FCIS (FCCS 1964). Served in Intelligence Corps, 1951–53; Admiralty, 1953–54. HM Foreign Service, 1954; served: Tehran, 1955; FO, 2nd Sec., 1960; Bonn, 2nd, later 1st, Sec. (Comm.), 1962; Atlanta, Consul, 1967; New York, Consul (Comm.), 1970; FCO, Dep. Dir Diplomatic Service Language Centre, 1972; Consul-Gen., Strasbourg, 1975–79; Consul (Commercial), Düsseldorf, 1979–83; FCO, 1983–85; First Sec. (Commercial), Algiers, 1985–88. Mem., Secretariat, Internat. Primary Aluminium Inst., 1988–94. *Address:* Gulestan, Apers Avenue, Westfield, Woking, Surrey GU22 9NB. *Club:* Civil Service.

HARDMAN, John Nimrod, FCA; Chairman, ASDA Group PLC (formerly ASDA-MFI), 1988–91 (Deputy Chairman, 1986–87; Director, 1984–91); *b* 8 Oct. 1939; *s* of late Harry John Hardman and of Florence Gladys Sybil Anne Hardman (*née* Dolby); *m* 1966, Joan McHugh; one *s* one *d*. *Educ:* Quarry Bank High Sch., Liverpool; Liverpool Univ. (BComm Hons). FIGD. Duncan Watson & Short, Chartered Accts, 1962–66; RCA Corp., 1967–69; Finance Dir, Thorn Colour Tubes Ltd, 1969–75; Dir, Europe, Africa and Far East, RCA Corp. Picture Tube Div., 1976–80; Finance Director: Oriel Foods, 1981; ASDA Stores, 1981–84 (Man. Dir, 1984–89); Director: Maples Stores plc; Adderley and Featherstone plc. Director: Leeds Develt Corp, 1988–; Yorks Electricity Bd, 1989–. CIMgt. *Recreations:* golf, tennis, shooting, cricket. *Address:* Hillside, Spofforth Hill, Wetherby, Yorks LS22 4SF. *Clubs:* Lord's Taverners'; Liverpool Artists, Royal Liverpool Golf, Liverpool Racquets (Liverpool); Pannal Golf (Harrogate).

HARDSTAFF, Veronica Mary; Member (Lab) Lincolnshire and Humberside South, European Parliament, since 1994; *b* 23 Oct. 1941; *d* of Rev. Ernest Tutt and Mary Tutt; *m* 1964 (marr. diss. 1977); one *s* one *d*. *Educ:* Manchester Univ. (BA Hons German); Cologne Univ. Teacher of German and French, Sheffield, 1963–66 and 1969–70; Mem. (Lab), Sheffield CC, 1971–78; teacher of German and French: High Storrs Girls' GS, 1963–66; St Peter's Sec. Mod. Sch., 1969–70; Knottingley High Sch., 1977–79; Frecheville Sch., 1979–86; Birley Sch., 1986–94. *Recreations:* reading, walking, classical music, playing flute. *Address:* 64 Linaker Road, Sheffield S6 5DT. *T:* Sheffield (0114) 233 5414; European Office, 397 High Street, Lincoln LN5 7SS. *T:* Lincoln (01522) 511612, *Fax:* (01522) 535522. *Clubs:* Sheffield Trades and Labour, Lincoln Labour.

HARDWICK, Christopher, MD, FRCP; Physician Emeritus, Guy's Hospital, since 1976; *b* 13 Jan. 1911; *s* of Thomas Mold Hardwick and Harriet Taylor; *m* 1938, Joan Dorothy Plummer; two *s*. *Educ:* Berkhamsted Sch.; Trinity Hall, Cambridge; Middlesex Hospital. MRCS, LRCP 1935; MA (Cambridge) 1937; MD (Cambridge) 1940; FRCP 1947. House Physician, House Surgeon and Med. Registrar, Middlesex Hosp., 1935 and 1938–41; House physician and Registrar, Hosp. for Sick Children, Gt Ormond Street, 1936–38. Wing Comdr, Medical Specialist, RAF Med. Service, 1941–46. Physician, Guy's Hosp., 1946–76. Hon. Vis. Phys., Johns Hopkins Hosp., Baltimore, 1954. Mem. Council, RCP, 1965–68; Mem. Board of Governors, Guy's Hospital, 1967–74. Chm., British Diabetic Assoc., 1974–80. *Publications:* contribs to medical literature. *Recreations:* gardening, reading. *Address:* 8 Sondes Farm, Glebe Road, Dorking, Surrey RH4 3EF.

HARDWICK, Donald, CBE 1980; PhD; Director, Johnson & Firth Brown plc, 1973–89 (Chairman, Steel Division, 1975–85); *b* 1926; *m* 1950, Dorothy Mary Hardwick; two *s*. *Educ:* Tadcaster Grammar Sch.; Sheffield Univ. (BMet 1st Cl. Hons 1947, Mappin Medal; PhD 1954). FIM. After appointments with English Electric Co., BISRA, and BSA Gp Research Centre, became first C. H. Desch Res. Fellow, Sheffield Univ. Joined Brown Firth Res. Laboratories, 1959; Man. Dir, Firth Brown Ltd, 1974–78; Mem. Bd, Johnson & Firth Brown, on amalgamation with Richard Johnson & Nephew, 1973. Director: Mitchell Somers Gp, 1974–89; Eagle Trust plc, 1987–89. Pres., BISPA, 1977–79. *Recreations:* fell walking, gardening. *Address:* 43 Dore Road, Dore, Sheffield S17 3NA.

HARDWICK, Prof. James Leslie, MSc, PhD, DDS; FDSRCS; Professor of Preventive Dentistry, University of Manchester, 1960–78, now Emeritus; *b* 27 March 1913; *o s* of George Hardwicke and Mary Ann Hardwick; *m* 1954, Eileen Margaret Isobel Gibson; two *s* two *d*. *Educ:* Rugby Sch.; Birmingham Univ. MDS 1948, PhD 1950, DDS 1984, Birmingham; FDSRCS 1954; MSc 1964. Private and hospital dental practice, 1935–39. Served War of 1939–45, Army Dental Corps. University of Birmingham: Lecturer, 1945–48, Sen. Lecturer in Operative Dental Surgery, 1948–52; Reader in Dental Surgery, 1952–60. *Publications:* editor of and contributor to dental and other scientific journals and textbooks. *Address:* 167 Stanley Road, Cheadle Hulme, Cheshire SK8 6RF. *T:* 0161–437 3555.

HARDWICK, Mollie; author; *b* Manchester; *d* of Joseph Greenhalgh and Anne Frances Atkinson; *m* 1961, Michael John Drinkrow Hardwick (*d* 1991); one *s*. *Educ:* Manchester High Sch. for Girls. Announcer, BBC (Radio) N Region, 1940–45; BBC (Radio) Drama Dept, 1946–62; freelance, 1963–. FRSA 1966. *Publications:* Stories from Dickens, 1968; Emma, Lady Hamilton, 1969; Mrs Dizzy, 1972; Upstairs Downstairs: Sarah's Story, 1973, The Years of Change, 1974, The War to end Wars, 1975, Mrs Bridges' Story, 1975, The World of Upstairs Downstairs, 1976; Alice in Wonderland (play), 1975; Beauty's Daughter, 1976 (Elizabeth Goudge Award for best historical romantic novel of year); The Duchess of Duke Street: The Way Up, 1976, The Golden Years, 1976, The World Keeps Turning, 1977; Charlie is my Darling, 1977; The Atkinson Heritage, 1978; Thomas and Sarah, 1978; Thomas and Sarah: Two for a Spin, 1979; Lovers Meeting, 1979; Sisters in Love, 1979; Dove's Nest, 1980; Willowwood, 1980; Juliet Bravo 1, 1980; Juliet Bravo 2, 1980; Monday's Child, 1981; Calling Juliet Bravo: New Arrivals, 1981; I Remember Love, 1982; The Shakespeare Girl, 1983; By the Sword Divided, 1983; The Merrymaid, 1984; Girl with a Crystal Dove, 1985; Malice Domestic, 1986; Parson's Pleasure, 1987; Uneaseful Death, 1988; Blood Royal, 1988; The Bandersnatch, 1989; Perish in July, 1989; The Dreaming Damozel, 1990; *with Michael Hardwick:* The Jolly Toper, 1961; The Sherlock Holmes Companion, 1962; Sherlock Holmes Investigates, 1963; The Man Who Was Sherlock Holmes, 1964; Four Sherlock Holmes plays, 1964; The Charles Dickens Companion, 1965; The World's Greatest Sea Mysteries, 1967; Writers' Houses: a literary journey in England, 1968; Alfred Deller: A Singularity of Voice, 1968, rev. edn 1980; Charles Dickens As They Saw Him, 1969; The Game's Afoot (Sherlock Holmes Plays), 1969; Plays from Dickens, 1970; Dickens's England, 1970; The Private Life of Sherlock Holmes, 1970; Four More Sherlock Holmes Plays, 1973; The Charles Dickens Encyclopedia, 1973; The Bernard Shaw Companion, 1973; The Charles Dickens Quiz Book, 1974; The Upstairs Downstairs Omnibus, 1975; The Gaslight Boy, 1976; The Hound of the Baskervilles and Other Sherlock Holmes Plays, 1982; numerous plays and scripts for radio and TV; contribs to women's magazines.

HARDWICKE, 10th Earl of, *cr* 1754; **Joseph Philip Sebastian Yorke;** Baron Hardwicke 1733; Viscount Royston 1754; *b* 3 Feb. 1971; *s* of Philip Simon Prospero Rupert Lindley, Viscount Royston (*d* 1973) and Virginia Anne (*d* 1988), *d* of Geoffrey Lyon; *S* grandfather, 1974. *Heir: cousin* David John Napier Edward Yorke [*b* 17 Oct. 1919; *m* 1st, 1950, Anne Margaret (*d* 1984), *d* of D. G. Mackail; two *s*; 2nd, 1990 June Rose Charlotte Rachel Fyfe (*née* Gurney)]. *Address:* 12 Lansdowne Road, W11 3LW.

HARDY; *see* Gathorne-Hardy, family name of Earl of Cranbrook.

HARDY, Alan; Member (C) for Brent North, Greater London Council, 1967–86 (Chairman, Finance and Establishment Committee, 1977–81); *b* 24 March 1932; *s* of late John Robert Hardy and Emily Hardy; *m* 1972, Betty Howe, *d* of late Walter and Hilda Howe. *Educ:* Hookergate Grammar Sch.; Univ. of Manchester; Inst. of Historical Res., Univ. of London (MA). Res. Asst to Sir Lewis Namier, History of Parliament Trust, 1955–56; Res. Officer and Dep. Dir, London Municipal Soc., 1956–63; Mem. British Secretariat, Council of European Municipalities, 1963–64. Lectures on British Monarchy. Member: Local Authorities' Conditions of Service Adv. Bd, 1977–81; Nat. Jt Council for Local Authorities' Services (Manual Workers), 1977–81. Mem. Bd, Harlow Develt Corp., 1968–80. Hon. Life Pres., Brent North Conservative Assoc., 1986. Contested (C) Islington SW, 1966. *Publications:* Queen Victoria Was Amused, 1976; The Kings' Mistresses, 1980. *Recreation:* admiring old things. *Address:* 20 Meadowside, Cambridge Park, Twickenham, Middx TW1 2JQ. *T:* 0181–892 7968. *Clubs:* Guards' Polo, Exiles.

HARDY, Anna Gwenllian; *see* Somers Cocks, A. G.

HARDY, Prof. Barbara Gladys; Professor of English Literature, Birkbeck College, University of London, 1970–89, now Emeritus; teacher and author; *b* 27 June 1924; *d* of Maurice and Gladys Nathan; *m* Ernest Dawson Hardy (decd); two *d*. *Educ:* Swansea High Sch. for Girls; University Coll. London. BA, MA. Subsequently on staff of English Dept of Birkbeck Coll., London; Prof. of English, Royal Holloway Coll., Univ. of London, 1965–70. Dir, Yeats Summer School, 1990–91. Pres., Dickens Soc., 1987–88; Vice-President: Thomas Hardy Soc., 1991–; George Eliot Fellowship, 1992–. Mem. Welsh Acad. Hon. Mem., MLA. Hon. Prof. of English, UC Swansea, 1991. Hon. Fellow: Birkbeck Coll., London, 1991; RHBNC, 1992. DUniv Open, 1981. *Publications:* The Novels of George Eliot, 1959; The Appropriate Form, 1964; (ed) George Eliot: Daniel Deronda, 1967; (ed) Middlemarch: Critical Approaches to the Novel, 1967; The Moral Art of Dickens, 1970; (ed) Critical Essays on George Eliot, 1970; The Exposure of Luxury: radical themes in Thackeray, 1972; (ed) Thomas Hardy: The Trumpet-Major, 1974; Tellers and Listeners: the narrative imagination, 1975; (ed) Thomas Hardy: A Laodicean, 1975; A Reading of Jane Austen, 1975; The Advantage of Lyric, 1977; Particularities: readings in George Eliot, 1982; Forms of Feeling in Victorian Fiction, 1985; Narrators and Novelists: collected essays, vol. 1, 1987; Swansea Girl, 1993. *Address:* c/o Birkbeck College, Malet Street, WC1E 7HX.

HARDY, Rev. Canon Brian Albert; Rector, All Saints, St Andrews, 1991–July 1996; *b* 3 July 1931; *s* of Albert Charles Hardy and Edith Maude Sarah Mabe. *Educ:* City Boys' School, Leicester; St John's Coll., Oxford (MA, DipTheol); Westcott House, Cambridge. Curate, Rugeley, Staffs, 1957–62; Chaplain, Downing Coll., Cambridge, 1962–66; Livingston (West Lothian) Ecumenical Team Ministry, 1966–74; Churches' Planning Officer for Telford, Salop, 1974–78; Chaplain, Coates Hall Theological Coll., Edinburgh, 1978–82; Rector, St Columba's by the Castle Episcopal Church, Edinburgh, 1982–91; Episcopalian Chaplain, Royal Infirmary of Edinburgh and Royal Edinburgh Hosp., 1982–86; Dean of the dio. of Edinburgh, 1986–91. Hon. Canon, Edinburgh Cathedral, 1991. *Recreations:* music, especially choral and piano; cycling. *Address:* (until Aug. 1996) All Saints Rectory, North Street, St Andrews, Fife KY16 9AQ. *T:* St Andrews (01334) 473193.

HARDY, Rev. Prof. Daniel Wayne; Director, Center of Theological Inquiry, Princeton, New Jersey, since 1990; *b* 9 Nov. 1930; *s* of John Alexander Hardy and Barbara Wyndham Harrison; *m* 1958, Kate Perrin Enyart; two *s* two *d*. *Educ:* Phillips Exeter Acad., Exeter, NH; Haverford Coll., Haverford, Penn (BA); Gen. Theological Seminary, NY (STB, STM); St John's Coll., Univ. of Oxford. Deacon 1955, Priest 1956. Asst Minister, Christ Ch., Greenwich, Conn, 1955–59; Vicar, St Barnabas Ch., Greenwich, 1956–59; Instr, Rosemary Hall, Greenwich, 1957–59; Fellow and Tutor, Gen. Theol Seminary, NY, 1959–61; Lectr in Modern Theol Thought, 1965–76, Sen. Lectr, 1976–86, Univ. of Birmingham; Van Mildert Prof. of Divinity, Univ. of Durham, and Residentiary Canon, Durham Cathedral, 1986–90 (Hon. Fellow, Durham Univ., 1991). Moderator, Gen. Ministerial Exam., C of E, 1983–89. Pres., Soc. for the Study of Theology, 1987–88. Editor, Cambridge Studies in Christian Doctrine, 1991–. *Publications:* (with D. F. Ford) Jubilate: theology in praise, 1984; (with D. F. Ford) Praising and Knowing God, 1985; Education for the Church's Ministry, 1986; (contrib.) Schleiermacher and Barth: beyond the impasse, ed R. Streetman, 1987; (contrib.) Keeping the Faith, ed G. Wainwright, 1987; (contrib.) The Modern Theologians, ed D. F. Ford, 1989; (contrib. and ed jtly) On Being the Church, 1989; (contrib. and ed jtly) The Weight of Glory: essays in honour of Peter Baelz, 1991; articles in Theology, Expository Times, Anglican Theol Rev., etc. *Recreations:* tennis, swimming, ski-ing, music, photography. *Address:* 210 Ross Stevenson Circle, Princeton, NJ 08540, USA.

See also D. F. Ford.

HARDY, David Ian Brooker; Chief Executive, Open Learning Foundation (formerly Open Polytechnic), since 1990; *b* 28 Sept. 1950; *s* of Leslie Hardy and Ruth Eveline Hardy (*née* Brooker); *m* 1979, Christine Mary Wilson; two *d*. *Educ:* Bradford Grammar Sch.; Univ. of London (BSc Hons); Univ. of Leeds (Grad. Cert Ed). FIPD. Dept of Educn, Leeds City Council, 1979–85; Department of Education and Science: Yorks and Humberside, 1985–86; Nat. Manager, Post Experience Vocational Educn, 1986–90; Asst Sec., 1990. Moderator, BTEC, 1982–85; Member: CNAA, 1991–92; Board, Eur. Assoc. Distance Teaching Univs, 1993–. Mem. Council, Bradford Chamber of Commerce, 1982–86. *Publications:* (jtly) Onchocerciasis in Zaire, 1977; articles in learned jls. *Recreations:* swimming, fell walking, squash. *Address:* Open Learning Foundation, 3 Devonshire Street, W1N 2BA. *T:* 0171–636 4186.

HARDY, David Malcolm; Chief Executive, The London Clearing House, since 1987; *b* 16 July 1955; *s* of Roy Hardy and Mary (*née* Ebsworth); *m* 1981, Maureen Petherick (marr. diss. 1995); one *s* one *d*. *Educ:* Westcliff High Sch. ACIB; FCT. Barclays Bank, 1973–81; Barclays Merchant Bank, 1981–85; London Clearing House, 1985–. Freeman, City of London, 1994. *Recreations:* golf, photography. *Address:* London Clearing House, Roman Wall House, 1–2 Crutched Friars, EC3N 2AN. *T:* 0171–265 2040. *Clubs:* Nizels Golf; Westcliff Hockey.

HARDY, Sir David (William), Kt 1992; Chairman: MGM Assurance, since 1986 (Deputy Chairman and Director, since 1985); Buckingham (formerly Leisuretime International) PLC, since 1988; Burmine Ltd, since 1992; Y. J. Lovell, since 1994; *b* 14 July 1930; 3rd *s* of late Brig. John H. Hardy, CBE, MC; *m* 1957, Rosemary, *d* of late Sir Godfrey F. S. Collins, KCIE, CSI, OBE; one *s* one *d*. *Educ:* Wellington Coll.; Harvard Business School (AMP). Chartered Accountant. Served 2nd RHA, 2/Lt, 1953–54. With Funch Edye Inc., and Imperial Tobacco, USA, 1954–70; HM Govt Co-ordinator of Industrial Advrs, 1970–72; Gp Finance Dir, Tate & Lyle Ltd, 1972–77; Dir, Ocean Transport & Trading PLC, 1977–83; Chairman: Ocean Inchcape, 1980–83; London Park Hotels, 1983–87; Globe Investment Trust, 1983–90 (Dir, 1976–90); Docklands Light Railway, 1984–87; Swan Hunter, 1986–88; Europa Minerals, 1991–94; Bankers Trust Investment Management, 1992–94; 100 Group Chartered Accountants, 1986–88; LDDC, 1988–92 (Dep. Chm., 1988); Deputy Chairman: LRT, 1984–87; Agricultural Mortgage Corp., 1985–92 (Dir, 1973–); Director: Sturge Holdings PLC, 1985–95; Waterford Wedgwood plc (formerly Waterford Glass), 1984–90; Paragon Group, 1985–88; Aberfoyle Holdings, 1986–91; Chelsea Harbour Ltd, 1986–90; Electra Kingsway Managers Hldgs Ltd, 1990–91; Tootal Gp, 1990–91; CIBA-GEIGY, 1991–; Hanson, 1991–; J. A. Devenish, 1991–93; Stirling-Lloyd Holdings, 1992–; James Fisher & Sons, 1993–; Adv. Dir, Samuel Montagu, 1995–. Chm., Engrg Marketing Adv. Cttee, DTI, 1989–90; Member: NEDC Cttee for Agriculture, 1970–72; Export Credit Guarantees Adv. Council, 1973–78; Industrial Develt Adv. Bd, DTI, 1992–; Co-opted Council of Inst. of Chartered Accountants, 1974–78; Economic and Fiscal Policy Cttee, CBI, 1981–88; Council, BIM, 1974–78; CIMgt (CBIM 1975). Mem., Develt Cttee, NACF, 1988–. Mem., St Katherine and Shadwell Trust, 1990–; Founder Mem., Royal Albert Dock Trust, 1992–; Trustee, Nat. Maritime Mus., Greenwich, 1992– (Chm. Trustees, 1995–). President: Poplar, Blackwall and Dist Rowing Club, 1992–; Pitlochry Angling Club, 1994–. Gov., Chelsea Open Air Nursery Sch., 1992– (Dep. Chm., 1994–). Hon. British Consul, Norfolk, Va, 1960–62. Member: Co. of Chartered Accountants, 1976; Co. of Shipwrights, 1990. FCIT 1988. *Address:* 10 Lower Thames Street, EC3R 6AE. *Clubs:* Brooks's, MCC, Flyfishers', HAC.

HARDY, Herbert Charles; Chief Executive, The European, since 1995; Director: Channel 4 Television Corporation, since 1992; Channel One Television, since 1994; Teletext Holdings, since 1995; *b* 13 Dec. 1928; *s* of Charles John Hardy and Margaret Elizabeth (*née* Burniston); *m* 1959, Irene Burrows; one *d*. *Educ:* RMA, Sandhurst. Man. Dir, Associated Newspapers Ltd, 1989–94. *Recreations:* golf, horse racing. *Address:* The European, 200 Gray's Inn Road, WC1X 8NE. *T:* 0171–418 7777. *Club:* Thirty.

HARDY, Sir James (Gilbert), Kt 1981; OBE 1975; Director, BRL Hardy Ltd, since 1992; Chairman of Directors: Thomas Hardy & Sons Pty Ltd, since 1981; Houghton Wines Pty Ltd, since 1981; Rural Resorts of Australia, since 1993; *b* 20 Nov. 1932; *s* of Tom Mayfield Hardy and Eileen C. Hardy; *m* 1st, 1956, Anne Christine Jackson (marr. diss. 1991); two *s*; 2nd, 1991, Joan Margaret McInnes. *Educ:* St Peter's Coll., Adelaide, SA; S Australian Sch. of Mines; S Australian Inst. of Technol. (Dip. in Accountancy). FCPA. National Service, 13th Field Artillery Regt, Adelaide, 1951. Elder Smith & Co. Ltd, 1951; J. C. Correll & Co., 1952; Thomas Hardy & Sons Pty Ltd, Winemakers, Adelaide, 1953–: Shipping Clerk, Sales Rep., Sales Supervisor and Lab. Asst, 1953–62; Dir and Manager, Sydney Br., 1962–77; Regional Dir, Eastern Australia, 1977–81. Director: S Australian Film Corp., 1981–87; America's Cup Challenge 1983 Ltd, 1981–85; Advertiser Newspapers Ltd, 1983–88; Lorna Hodgkinson Sunshine Home Ltd, 1993–. Dep. Chm., Racing Rules Cttee, Yachting Fedn, 1969–81; Dir of Sailing/Captain, S Australian Challenge for the Defence of America's Cup 1984–87. Vice Pres., Internat. 12 Metre Assoc., 1986–. Treasurer, Liquor Trade Supervisory Council of NSW, 1965–70; Fellow, Catering Inst. of Australia, 1972; Pres., Wine and Brandy Assoc. of NSW, 1980–83. NSW Chm., Aust. National Travel Assoc., 1976; Vice Pres., Royal Blind Soc. of NSW, 1980–88 (Mem. Council, 1967–91); Pres., NSW Aust. Football League and Sydney Football League, 1982–83; Pres., "One and All" Sailing Ship Assoc. of SA Inc., 1981–90; Chm., Adelaide 1998 Commonwealth Games Bid, 1990–92; Mem., Bd of Advice, Rothmans Nat. Sport Foundn, 1985–87; Trustee: Rothmans Foundn, 1987–93; Sydney Cricket and Sports Ground Trust, 1990–95; Mem., Council, Australian Nat. Maritime Mus., 1992–. Chairman: Adv. Cttee, Life Educn Centre of SA, 1988–91; Landcare Australia Ltd Foundn, 1994–. Member: Exec. Cttee, Neurosurgical Res. Foundn of SA, 1988–; Adv. Bd, John Curtin Sch. of Medical Res., ANU, Canberra, 1982–87. Dep. Grand Master, United Grand Lodge of NSW, 1977–80. Australian Yachtsman of the Year, 1981. *Recreation:* yachting (skipper or helmsman in America's Cup and Admiral's Cup races). *Address:* BRL Hardy Wine Co., 27 Myrtle Street, Pagewood, NSW 2019, Australia. *T:* (2) 6665855, *Fax:* (2) 3169738. *Clubs:* Royal Ocean Racing; Australian, Tattersalls, Royal Sydney Yacht Squadron (Sydney); Cruising Yacht of Australia (NSW); Royal Perth Yacht; Fort Worth Boat (Texas, USA); New York Yacht.

HARDY, Maj.-Gen. John Campbell, CB 1985; LVO 1978; Administrator, Sion College, since 1993; *b* 13 Oct. 1933; *s* of late General Sir Campbell Hardy, KCB, CBE, DSO; *m* 1961, Jennifer Mary Kempton; one *s* one *d*. *Educ:* Sherborne School. Joined Royal Marines, 1952; 45 Commando, 1954; HMS Superb, 1956; Instructor, NCOs' School, Plymouth, 1957; 42 Commando, 1959; 43 Commando, 1962; Adjt, Jt Service Amphibious Warfare Centre, 1964; Company Comdr, 45 Commando, 1965; sc Bracknell, 1966; Instr, RNC Greenwich, 1967; Extra Equerry to Prince Philip, 1968–69; SO, Dept of CGRM, 1969; Rifle Company Comdr, 41 Commando, 1971; ndc Latimer, 1972; Staff of Chief of Defence Staff, 1973; Staff Officer HQ Commando Forces, 1975; CO RM Poole, 1977; CofS and Asst Defence Attaché, British Defence Staff Washington, 1979; ADC to the Queen, 1981–82; Chief of Staff to Comdt Gen. RM, 1982–84; DCS (Support) to C-in-C Allied Forces N Europe, 1984–87. Col Comdt, RM, 1990–. Dir, British Digestive Foundn, 1987–92. *Recreations:* sailing, tennis. *Address:* c/o National Westminster Bank plc, 51 The Strand, Walmer, Deal, Kent CT14 7DR. *Club:* Army and Navy.

HARDY, Michael James Langley; Director for Telecommunications Policy and Postal Services, Directorate General for Information Technologies and Industries, and Telecommunications, Commission of the European Communities, 1992–93; *b* 30 Jan. 1933; *s* of James Hardy and Rosina (*née* Langley); *m* 1959, Dr Swana Metger; one *s* two *d*. *Educ:* Beckenham Grammar Sch.; Magdalen Coll., Oxford (Exhibnr; BA 1956; MA 1959); Magdalene Coll., Cambridge (LLB 1957; LLM 1963). Called to the Bar, Gray's Inn, 1957. Asst Lecturer, Law Faculty: Manchester Univ., 1958–59; KCL, 1959–60; Legal Officer, later Sen. Legal Officer, Legal Service, UN, 1960–73; Legal Adviser, Govt of Nepal, 1968–69 (on leave of absence from UN); Commn of the European Communities, 1973–: Legal Adviser, Legal Service, 1973–77; Head of Div., Japan, Australia and NZ, Directorate-General for External Relations, 1978–82; Head of Commn Delegn, New York, 1982–87; Dir for Gen. Affairs, Directorate-Gen. for Telecommunications, Information Industries and Innovation, 1987–92. *Publications:* Blood Feuds and the Payment of Blood Money in the Middle East, 1963; Modern Diplomatic Law, 1968; articles in legal and political science jls. *Recreations:* walking, talking. *Address:* Castle House, Gidleigh, Devon TQ13 8HR. *T:* Chagford (01647) 433567.

HARDY, Peter; MP (Lab) Wentworth, since 1983 (Rother Valley, 1970–83); *b* 17 July 1931; *s* of Lawrence Hardy and of Mrs I. Hardy, Wath upon Dearne; *m* 1954, Margaret Anne Brookes; two *s*. *Educ:* Wath upon Dearne Grammar Sch.; Westminster Coll., London; Sheffield Univ. Schoolmaster in S Yorkshire, 1953–70. Member: Wath upon Dearne UDC, 1960–70 (Chm. Council, 1968–69); Governing Body of Wath Grammar Sch. (Chm. of Governors, 1969–70). Pres., Wath upon Dearne Labour Party, 1960–68; contested (Lab): Scarborough and Whitby, 1964; Sheffield, Hallam, 1966. PPS to Sec. of State for the Environment, 1974–76; PPS to Foreign Sec., 1976–79. Hon. Sec., All-Party Gp for Energy Studies, 1992–; Chm., PLP Energy Cttee, 1974–92; Parly attachment to RAF, 1992–93. Member: UK delegn to Council of Europe, 1976–; CSCE Asssembly, 1992–; Leader, Lab. delegn to Council of Europe and WEU, 1983–; Chm., Cttee on Environment, Council of Europe, 1986–89 (Chm., Sub Cttee on Natural Envmt, 1978–86 and 1990–94; Vice-Chm., Socialist Gp, 1983–). Member: Council, RSPB, 1984–89; Central Exec. Cttee, NSPCC, 1985–92. Vice-Pres., S Yorks Foundn, 1993; Patron, Yorkshire Wildlife Trust. Hon. Mem., Kennel Club. *Publications:* A Lifetime of Badgers, 1975; various articles on educational and other subjects. *Recreation:* watching wild life, exhibiting and judging dogs. *Address:* 53 Sandygate, Wath upon Dearne, Rotherham, South Yorkshire S63 7LU. *T:* Rotherham (01709) 874590. *Club:* Rawmarsh Trades and Labour.

HARDY, Robert; *see* Hardy, T. S. R.

HARDY, His Honour Robert James; a Circuit Judge, 1979–94; *b* 12 July 1924; *s* of James Frederick and Ann Hardy; *m* 1951, Maureen Scott; one *s* one *d*. *Educ:* Mostyn House Sch.; Wrekin Coll.; University Coll., London (LLB). Served, 1942–46, Royal Navy, as Pilot, Fleet Air Arm. Called to Bar, 1950; a Recorder of the Crown Court, 1972–79. *Recreation:* sailing. *Address:* Smithy House, Sandlebridge, Little Warford, Cheshire SK9 7TY. *T:* Mobberley (01565) 872535; Betlem, Mallorca.

HARDY, Rt. Rev. Robert Maynard; *see* Lincoln, Bishop of.

HARDY, Sir Rupert (John), 4th Bt, *cr* 1876; Lieutenant-Colonel Life Guards, retired; *b* 24 Oct. 1902; *s* of 3rd Bt and Violet Agnes Evelyn (*d* 1972), *d* of Hon. Sir Edward

Chandos Leigh, KCB, KC; *S* father 1953; *m* 1930, Hon. Diana Joan Allsopp, *er d* of 3rd Baron Hindlip; one *s* one *d*. *Educ:* Eton; Trinity Hall, Cambridge. BA 1925. Joined The Life Guards, 1925; Major, 1940; retired, 1948, and rejoined as RARO, 1952; Lieut-Col comdg Household Cavalry Regt, 1952–56; ceased to belong to R of O, Dec. 1956; granted hon. rank of Lieut-Col. *Recreations:* hunting and shooting. *Heir: s* Richard Charles Chandos Hardy [*b* 6 Feb. 1945; *m* 1972, Venetia, *d* of Simon Wingfield Digby, *qv*; four *d*]. *Address:* Gullivers Lodge, Guilsborough, Northampton NN6 8RB. *Club:* Turf.

HARDY, (Timothy Sydney) Robert, CBE 1981; actor and writer; *b* 29 Oct. 1925; *s* of late Major Henry Harrison Hardy, CBE, and Edith Jocelyn Dugdale; *m* 1st, 1952, Elizabeth (marr. diss.), *d* of late Sir Lionel Fox and Lady Fox; one *s*; 2nd, 1961, Sally (marr. diss. 1986), *d* of Sir Neville Pearson, 2nd Bt, and Dame Gladys Cooper, DBE; two *d*. *Educ:* Rugby Sch.; Magdalen Coll., Oxford (Hons degree, Eng. Lit.). *Stage:* Shakespeare Meml Theatre, 1949–51; London, West End, 1951–53; Old Vic Theatre, 1953–54; USA, 1954 and 1956–58 (plays incl. Hamlet and Henry V); Shakespeare Meml 1959 Centenary Season; Rosmersholm, Comedy, 1960; The Rehearsal, Globe, 1961; A Severed Head, Criterion, 1963; The Constant Couple, New, 1967; I've Seen You Cut Lemons, Fortune, 1969; Habeas Corpus, Lyric, 1974; Dear Liar, Mermaid, 1982; Winnie, Victoria Palace, 1988; Body and Soul, Albery, 1992; *films include:* The Far Pavilions, 1983; The Shooting Party, 1985; Jenny's War, 1985; Paris by Night, 1988; War and Remembrance, 1988; Mary Shelley's Frankenstein, 1994; A Feast at Midnight, 1995; *television:* David Copperfield; Age of Kings, 1960; Trouble-shooters, 1966–67; Elizabeth R, 1970; Manhunt, 1970; Edward VII, 1973; All Creatures Great and Small, 1978–80, 1983, 1985, 1987–90; Speed King; Fothergill; Winston Churchill—The Wilderness Years, 1981; Paying Guests, 1986; Make and Break, 1986; Churchill in the USA, 1986; Hot Metal, 1987, 1988; Northanger Abbey, 1987; Marcus Welby in Paris (film), 1988; Sherlock Holmes, 1991; Inspector Morse, 1992; Middlemarch, 1993. Author of TV documentaries: Picardy Affair, 1962; The Longbow, 1972; Horses in our Blood, 1977; Gordon of Khartoum, 1982. Consultant, Mary Rose Trust, 1979– (Trustee, 1991–); Trustee, WWF (UK), 1983–89; Mem., Bd of Trustees of the Royal Armouries, 1984–; Chm., Berkshire, Buckinghamshire and Oxfordshire Naturalists' Trust Appeal, 1984–90. Master, Court of Worshipful Co. of Bowyers, 1988–90. Hon. DLitt Reading, 1990. *Publication:* Longbow, 1976, 2nd edn 1992. *Recreations:* archery, horsemanship, bowyery. *Address:* c/o Chatto & Linnit, Prince of Wales Theatre, Coventry Street, SW1V 8AS. *Clubs:* Buck's, Royal Toxophilite, British Longbow.

HARDY-ROBERTS, Brig. Sir Geoffrey (Paul), KCVO 1972; CB 1945; CBE 1944 (OBE 1941); JP; DL; Master of HM's Household, 1967–73; Extra Equerry to the Queen, since 1967; Secretary-Superintendent of Middlesex Hospital, 1946–67; *b* 1907; *s* of A. W. Roberts; *m* 1945, Eldred (*d* 1987), *widow* of Col J. R. Macdonell, DSO. *Educ:* Eton; RMC Sandhurst. Regular Commission, 9th Lancers, 1926–37. Served War of 1939–45 (OBE, CBE, CB). Mem., West Sussex AHA, 1974–82; Dep. Chm., King Edward VII Hospital, Midhurst, 1972–82. JP 1960, DL 1964, West Sussex (formerly Sussex), High Sheriff, 1965, Sussex. Officer, Legion of Merit, 1945. *Address:* The Lodge, Bury Gate House, Pulborough, West Sussex RH20 1HA. *T:* Fittleworth (01798) 831921.

HARDYMAN, Norman Trenchard, CB 1984; Secretary, Universities Funding Council, 1988–90 (University Grants Committee, 1982–89); *b* 5 Jan. 1930; *s* of late Rev. Arnold Victor Hardyman and late Laura Hardyman; *m* 1961, Carol Rebecca Turner; one *s* one *d*. *Educ:* Clifton Coll.; Christ Church, Oxford. Asst Principal, Min. of Educn, 1955; Principal 1960; Private Sec. to Sec. of State for Educn and Science, 1966–68; Asst Sec. 1968–75, Under-Sec., 1975–79, DES; Under-Sec., DHSS, 1979–81. Mem., UGC for Univ. of S Pacific, 1990–. Treasurer, Univ. of Exeter, 1991–. *Recreations:* walking, gardening, reading, photography. *Address:* Sherwell, The Drive, Dawlish, Devon EX7 9JB. *T:* Dawlish (01626) 866091.

HARE, family name of **Viscount Blakenham** and **Earl of Listowel.**

HARE, David, FRSL 1985; playwright; *b* 5 June 1947; *s* of Clifford Theodore Rippon Hare and Agnes Cockburn Hare; *m* 1st, 1970, Margaret Matheson (marr. diss. 1980); two *s* one *d*; 2nd, 1992, Nicole Farhi, *qv*. *Educ:* Lancing Coll.; Jesus Coll., Cambridge (MA Hons). Founded Portable Theatre, 1968; Literary Manager and Resident Dramatist, Royal Court, 1969–71; Resident Dramatist, Nottingham Playhouse, 1973; founded Joint Stock Theatre Group, 1975; US/UK Bicentennial Fellowship, 1977; founded Greenpoint Films, 1982; Associate Dir, Nat. Theatre, 1984–88, 1989–. Author of plays: Slag, Hampstead, 1970, Royal Court, 1971 (Evening Standard Drama Award, 1970); The Great Exhibition, Hampstead, 1972; Knuckle (televised, 1989), Comedy, 1974 (John Llewellyn Rhys Award, 1974); Fanshen, Joint Stock, 1975; The Secret Rapture, NT, 1988 (Drama Award, best play of the year; London Critics Poll, Best Play), NY, 1989 (dir, NY only); Racing Demon, NT, 1990 (Olivier Award, Plays and Players Award, for best play of the year; Critics' Circle Best Play of the Year; Time Out Award, 1990); Murmuring Judges, NT, 1991; The Absence of War, NT, 1993; Skylight, NT, 1995; *author and director of plays:* Brassneck (with Howard Brenton), Nottingham Playhouse, 1973; Teeth 'n' Smiles, Royal Court, 1975, Wyndhams, 1976; Plenty, NT, 1978, NY, 1983 (NY Critics' Circle Award); A Map of the World, Adelaide Fest., 1982, NT, 1983, NY 1985 (Dramalogue Award); (with Howard Brenton) Pravda, NT, 1985 (London Standard Award; Plays and Players Award; City Limits Award); The Bay at Nice, and Wrecked Eggs, NT, 1986; opera libretto, The Knife, NY Shakespeare Fest., 1987 (also directed); *TV plays:* Man Above Men, 1973; Licking Hitler, 1978 (BAFTA award, 1978) (also directed); Dreams of Leaving, 1980 (also directed); Saigon—Year of the Cat, 1983; Heading Home, 1991; The Rules of the Game, 1994; The Absence of War, 1995. *Directed:* The Party, NT, 1974; Weapons of Happiness, NT, 1976; Total Eclipse, Lyric, Hammersmith, 1981; King Lear, NT, 1986. *Adapted:* Pirandello, The Rules of the Game, NT, 1971, Almeida, 1992; Brecht, Life of Galileo, Almeida, 1994; Brecht, Mother Courage and her Children, NT, 1995. *Films:* wrote and directed: Wetherby, 1985 (Golden Bear award, 1985); Paris by Night, 1988; Strapless, 1989; (screenplay) Plenty, 1985; The Secret Rapture, 1994; Damage (adapted from novel by Josephine Hart), 1992; The Secret Rapture, 1994. *Publications:* Slag, 1970; The Great Exhibition, 1972; Knuckle, 1974; Brassneck, 1974; Fanshen, 1976; Teeth 'n' Smiles, 1976; Plenty, 1978; Licking Hitler, 1978; Dreams of Leaving, 1980; A Map of the World, 1982; Saigon, 1983; The History Plays, 1984; Pravda, 1985; Wetherby, 1985; The Asian Plays, 1986; The Bay at Nice and Wrecked Eggs, 1986; The Secret Rapture, 1988; Paris By Night, 1989; Strapless, 1990; Racing Demon, 1990; Writing Lefthanded, 1991; Heading Home, 1991; The Early Plays, 1991; Murmuring Judges, 1991; The Absence of War, 1993; Asking Around, 1993; Skylight, 1995; Mother Courage, 1995.

HARE, Ewan Nigel Christian, (Nick); Deputy Secretary-General (Development Co-operation) of the Commonwealth, since 1993; *b* 11 May 1939; *m* 1985, Raina Ho; one *s* two *d*. *Educ:* Earlham Coll. (BA); Carleton Univ. (DPA). First Sec., Canadian High Commn, Accra, 1969–72; Canadian International Development Agency: Regl Dir, Asia SE, 1972–76; Regl Dir, Central and S Africa, 1976–78; Dir-Gen., Resources Br., 1978–80; Dir-Gen., UN Progs, 1980–84; Ambassador of Canada to Zaire, 1984–87; Dept of External Affairs, Ottawa, 1987–88; Dir-Gen., Industrial Co-operation Prog., Canadian Internat. Develt Agency, 1988–91; High Comr to Nigeria, 1991–93. *Recreations:* ski-ing, canoeing, squash, jogging. *Address:* Commonwealth Secretariat, Marlborough House, Pall Mall, SW1Y 5HX. *Club:* Royal Over-Seas League.

HARE, Prof. Frederick Kenneth, CC 1987 (OC 1978); PhD; FRSC 1968; Professor of Geography and Physics, 1969–84, and Director, Institute for Environmental Studies, 1974–79, now University Professor Emeritus in Geography, University of Toronto; Chancellor, Trent University, since 1988; Provost, Trinity College, Toronto, 1979–86; Chairman, Advisory Board on International Programmes, University of Toronto, 1990–94; *b* Wylye, Wilts, 5 Feb. 1919; *s* of Frederick Eli Hare and Irene Smith; *m* 1st, 1941, Suzanne Alice Bates (marr. diss. 1952); one *s*; 2nd, 1953, Helen Neilson Morrill; one *s* one *d*. *Educ:* Windsor Grammar Sch.; King's Coll., University of London (BSc); Univ. of Montreal (PhD). Lectr in Geography, Univ. of Manchester, 1940–41; War service in Air Min., Meteorological Office, 1941–45; McGill University: Asst and Assoc. Prof. of Geography, 1945–52; Prof. of Geography and Meteorology, 1952–64; Chm. of Dept, 1950–62; Dean of Faculty of Arts and Science, 1962–64; Prof. of Geography, Univ. of London (King's Coll.), 1964–66; Master of Birkbeck Coll., Univ. of London, 1966–68; Pres., Univ. of British Columbia, 1968–69. Vis. Centenary Prof., Univ. of Adelaide, 1974. FKC 1967. Sci. Advr, Dept of the Environment, Canada, 1972–74. Mem. Nat. Research Council of Canada, 1962–64; Chm. of Bd, Arctic Inst. of N America, 1963; Mem., NERC, 1965–68; Dir, Resources for the Future, 1968–80; Member: SSRC, Canada, 1974–76; Adv. Council, Electric Power Res. Inst., 1978–80. Chairman: Adv. Cttee on Canadian Demonstration Projects, 1974–75, for 1976 UN Conf. on Human Settlements; Special Prog. Panel on Ecoscis, NATO, 1975; Federal Study Gp on Nuclear Waste Disposal, 1977; Climate Programme Planning Bd, Govt of Canada, 1979–90; Commn on Lead in the Environment, RSC, 1984–86; Section W, AAAS, 1985–86; Comr, Ontario Nuclear Safety Review, 1987–88. President: Canadian Assoc. of Geographers, 1963–64; RMetS, 1967–68 (Vice-Pres., 1968–70); Sigma Xi, 1986–87; Fellow, Amer. Meteorological Soc., 1969 (Emeritus Fellow, 1994); Hon. Fellow, Amer. Geographical Soc., 1963; Hon. Pres., Assoc. of Amer. Geographers, 1964. Hon. Life Mem., Birkbeck Coll., 1969; Hon. Fellow, Trinity Coll., Toronto, 1990. Hon. LLD: Queen's (Canada) Univ., 1964; Univ. of W Ontario, 1968; Trent Univ., 1979; Memorial Univ., 1985; Toronto, 1987; Hon. DSc: McGill, 1969; York (Canada), 1978; Windsor, 1988; DSc *ad eund.* Adelaide, 1974; Hon. DSLitt Thorneloe Coll., Sudbury (Canada), 1984. Hon. Cert. Graduation, Nat. Defence Coll., Kingston, Canada, 1986. Meritorious Achievement Citation, Assoc. Amer. Geographers, 1961; President's Prize, RMetS (Can.), 1961, 1962; Patterson Medal, Can. Met. Service, 1973; Massey Medal, Royal Can. Geographical Soc., 1974; Patron's Medal, RGS, 1977; Award for Scholarly Distinction, Canadian Assoc. of Geographers, 1979; Univ. of Toronto Alumni Assoc. Faculty Award, 1982; Sir William Dawson Award, RSC, 1987; Cullum Medal, Amer. Geographical Soc., 1987; Internat. Meteorol Orgn Prize, 1988. Order of Ontario, 1989. *Publications:* The Restless Atmosphere, 1953; On University Freedom, 1968; (with M. K. Thomas) Climate Canada, 1974, 2nd edn 1979; numerous articles in Quarterly Jl Royal Meteorological Soc., Geography, and other learned jls. *Recreation:* music. *Address:* 301 Lakeshore Road West, Oakville, Ont L6K 1G2, Canada. *Clubs:* McGill Faculty (Montreal) (Hon. Life Mem.); Toronto Faculty, York (Toronto).

HARE, Nick; *see* Hare, E. N. C.

HARE, Nicole; *see* Farhi, N.

HARE, Sir Philip (Leigh), 6th Bt *cr* 1818, of Stow Hall, Norfolk; antique dealer, since 1969; *b* 13 Oct. 1922; *s* of Captain Edward Philip Leigh Hare (*d* 1954), *y s* of Sir Thomas Hare, 2nd Bt, and his 3rd wife, Lady Kathleen Florence Mary Hare (*d* 1971), *d* of 9th Earl of Harrington; *S* cousin, 1993; *m* 1950, Anne Lisle, *d* of Major Geoffrey Nicholson, CBE, MC; one *s* one *d* (twins). *Educ:* private crammers; RAC Cirencester. Military service, 1941–46 (Trooper, 7th Queen's Own Hussars). Farming, 1947–69. *Recreations:* gardening, field sports, furniture and picture restoration. *Heir: s* Nicholas Patrick Hare [*b* 27 Aug. 1955; *m* 1982, Caroline Keith, *d* of T. P. K. Allan; two *s*]. *Address:* The Nettings, Hook Norton, near Banbury, Oxon OX15 5NP. *T:* Hook Norton (01608) 737964. *Club:* Universal Skint.

HARE, Kenneth; *see* Hare, F. K.

HARE, Rt. Rev. Richard; *see* Hare, Rt Rev. Thomas Richard.

HARE, Prof. Richard Mervyn, FBA 1964; White's Professor of Moral Philosophy, University of Oxford, and Fellow of Corpus Christi College, Oxford, 1966–83 (Hon. Fellow, 1983); *b* 21 March 1919; *s* of late Charles Francis Aubone Hare and late Louise Kathleen (*née* Simonds); *m* 1947, Catherine, *d* of Sir Harry Verney, 4th Bt, DSO; one *s* three *d*. *Educ:* Rugby (Schol.); Balliol Coll., Oxford (Schol.). Commissioned Royal Artillery, 1940; Lieut, Indian Mountain Artillery, 1941; Prisoner of War, Singapore and Siam, 1942–45. 1st Lit. Hum. 1947. Fellow and Tutor in Philosophy, Balliol Coll., Oxford, 1947–66, Hon. Fellow, 1974; Wilde Lectr in Natural Religion, Oxford, 1963–66. Graduate Res. Prof. of Phil., Univ. of Florida at Gainesville, 1983–94. Visiting Fellow: Princeton, 1957; ANU, 1966; Center for Advanced Study in Behavioral Sciences, Stanford, 1980; Visiting Professor: Univ. of Michigan, 1968; Univ. of Delaware, 1974. Pres., Aristotelian Soc., 1972–73. Member: Nat. Road Safety Advisory Council, 1966–68; C of E Working Parties on Medical Questions, 1964–75. Hon. Fellow, Inst. of Life Scis, Hastings Center, 1974; For. Hon. Mem., American Acad. of Arts and Sciences, 1975. Hon. PhD Lund, 1991. Tanner Award, 1979. *Publications:* The Language of Morals, 1952; Freedom and Reason, 1963; Essays on Philosophical Method, 1971; Practical Inferences, 1971; Essays on the Moral Concepts, 1972; Applications of Moral Philosophy, 1972; Moral Thinking, 1981; Plato, 1982; Hare and Critics, 1988; Essays in Ethical Theory, 1989; Essays on Political Morality, 1989; Essays on Religion and Education, 1992; Essays on Bioethics, 1993; Zum Moralischen Denken, 1994. *Recreations:* music, gardening. *Address:* Saffron House, Ewelme, near Wallingford, Oxon OX10 6HP.

HARE, Rt. Rev. (Thomas) Richard; Suffragan Bishop of Pontefract, 1971–92; *b* 1922; *m* 1963, Sara, *d* of Lt-Col J. E. Spedding, OBE; one *s* two *d*. *Educ:* Marlborough; Trinity Coll., Oxford; Westcott House, Cambridge. RAF, 1942–45, Curate of Haltwhistle, 1950–52; Domestic Chaplain to Bishop of Manchester, 1952–59; Canon Residentiary of Carlisle Cathedral, 1959–65; Archdeacon of Westmorland and Furness, 1965–71; Vicar of St George with St Luke, Barrow-in-Furness, 1965–69; Vicar of Winster, 1969–71. *Address:* Wood Cottage, Mirehouse, Underskiddaw, Keswick, Cumbria CA12 4QE. *T:* Keswick (017687) 72996.

HARE DUKE, Rt. Rev. Michael Geoffrey; Bishop of St Andrews, Dunkeld and Dunblane, 1969–94; *b* 28 Nov. 1925; *s* of late A. R. A. Hare Duke, Civil Engineer; *m* 1949, Grace Lydia Frances McKean Dodd; one *s* three *d*. *Educ:* Bradfield Coll.; Trinity Coll., Oxford. BA 1949, MA 1951. Sub-Lt, RNVR, 1944–46. Deacon, 1952; Priest, 1953; Curate, St John's Wood Church, 1952–56; Vicar, St Mark's, Bury, 1956–62; Pastoral Dir, Clin. Theol. Assoc., 1962–64; Vicar, St Paul's, Daybrook, and Pastoral Consultant to Clin. Theol. Assoc., 1964–69; OCF, E Midland Dist HQ, 1968–69. Chm., Scottish Assoc. for Mental Health, 1978–85. Mem. Editorial Bd, Contact Magazine,

1962–79. Hon. DD St Andrews, 1994. *Publications:* (jtly) The Caring Church, 1963; (jtly) First Aid in Counselling, 1968; Understanding the Adolescent, 1969; The Break of Glory, 1970; Freud, 1972; Good News, 1976; Stories, Signs and Sacraments in the Emerging Church, 1982; (ed) Praying for Peace, 1991; Hearing the Stranger, 1994; contributor to: Expository Times, Blackfriars, New Christian, Church Quarterly Review, Church Times, Contact. *Address:* 2 Balhousie Avenue, Perth PH1 5HN. *T:* Perth (01738) 622642.

HARES, Phillip Douglas George, CBE 1985; Chairman and Chief Executive, 1986–87, and Board Member for Finance, 1981–86, British Shipbuilders (Deputy Chief Executive, 1983–86); *b* 31 Dec. 1926; *s* of Edgar Sidney George and Edith Winifred Frances Hares; *m* 1955, Violet May Myers; one *s* one *d*. *Educ:* Richmond and East Sheen Grammar Sch. Involved with management sciences and computing in various commercial, industrial, and consulting organisations, 1952–69, dating from early application of computers in 1952 with J. Lyons & Co. Ltd; Asst Man. Dir (Ops), British Mail Order Corp. Ltd (Great Universal Stores), 1969–77; Man. Dir (Finance), British Shipbuilders, 1978–81, Corporate Man. Dir, 1982–83; Chairman: Falmouth Shiprepair Ltd, 1983–85; Vosper Shiprepairers Ltd, 1983–85; Dir, Iron Trades Insce Gp, 1985–. Member Council: CBI, 1983–87 (Mem., Economic Situation Cttee, 1983–87); Amer. Bureau of Shipping, 1986–87. FRSA 1987–91. Freeman, City of London, 1983; Liveryman, Worshipful Co. of Shipwrights, 1984–94. *Recreations:* reading, music, genealogy. *Address:* Honeywood, Lower Sea Lane, Charmouth, Dorset DT6 6LR. *T:* Charmouth (01297) 560042.

HAREWOOD, 7th Earl of, *cr* 1812; **George Henry Hubert Lascelles,** KBE 1986; Baron Harewood, 1796; Viscount Lascelles, 1812; President, British Board of Film Classification, since 1985; *b* 7 Feb. 1923; *er s* of 6th Earl of Harewood, KG, GCVO, DSO, and HRH Princess Mary (Princess Royal; who *d* 28 March 1965); *S* father, 1947; *m* 1st, 1949, Maria Donata (marr. diss. 1967; she *m* 1973, Rt Hon. (John) Jeremy Thorpe), *d* of late Erwin Stein; three *s*; 2nd, 1967, Patricia Elizabeth, *d* of Charles Tuckwell, Australia; one *s* and one step *s*. *Educ:* Eton; King's Coll., Cambridge (MA; Hon. Fellow, 1984). Served War of 1939–45, Capt. Grenadier Guards (wounded and prisoner, 1944, released May 1945); ADC to Earl of Athlone, 1945–46, Canada. Editor of magazine "Opera" 1950–53; Royal Opera House, Covent Garden: a Dir, 1951–53; on staff, 1953–60; a Dir, 1969–72; Chm. Bd, ENO (formerly Sadler's Wells Opera), 1986–95 (Man. Dir, 1972–85); Artistic Director: Edinburgh Internat. Festival, 1961–65; Leeds Festival, 1958–74; Adelaide Festival 1988; Artistic Adviser: New Philharmonia Orch., London, 1966–76; Buxton Fest., 1993–; Man. Dir, English Nat. Opera North, 1978–81. Governor of BBC, 1985–87. Chm., Music Advisory Cttee of British Council, 1956–66; Chancellor of the Univ. of York, 1963–67; Member: Arts Council, 1966–72; Gen. Adv. Council of BBC, 1969–77. President: English Football Assoc., 1963–72; Leeds United Football Club, 1962–. Hon. RAM, 1983; Hon. LLD: Leeds, 1959; Aberdeen, 1966; Hon. DMus Hull, 1962; DUniv York, 1982. Janáček Medal, 1978. *Publications:* (ed) Kobbé's Complete Opera Book, 1953, 3rd edn 1987; The Tongs and the Bones (autobiog.), 1981; Kobbés Illustrated Opera Book, 1989; Pocket Kobbé, 1994. *Heir:* *s* Viscount Lascelles, *qv*. *Address:* Harewood House, Leeds LS17 9LG.

See also Barry Tuckwell.

HARFORD, Sir (John) Timothy, 3rd Bt *cr* 1934; Chairman, Wesleyan (formerly Wesleyan and General) Assurance Society, since 1993 (Vice-Chairman, 1985–87; Deputy Chairman, 1987–93); Deputy Chairman: Wolseley Group plc (formerly Wolseley-Hughes Group plc), since 1983; Wagon Industrial Holdings, since 1991; Kwik Save Group plc, since 1994 (Chairman, 1990–94); *b* 6 July 1932; *s* of Sir George Arthur Harford, 2nd Bt and Anstice Marion (*d* 1993), *d* of Sir Alfred Tritton, 2nd Bt; *S* father, 1967; *m* 1962, Carolyn Jane Mullens; two *s* one *d*. *Educ:* Harrow Sch.; Oxford Univ.; Harvard Business Sch. Philip Hill Higginson Erlangers Ltd, 1960–63; Director: Birmingham Industrial Trust Ltd, 1963–67; Singer & Friedlander Ltd, 1970–88 (Local Dir, 1967–69). *Recreations:* wine and food, travel. *Heir:* *s* Mark John Harford, *b* 6 Aug. 1964. *Address:* South House, South Littleton, Evesham, Worcs WR11 5TJ. *T:* Evesham (01386) 830478. *Club:* Boodle's.

HARGREAVES, Andrew Raikes; MP (C) Birmingham, Hall Green, since 1987; *b* 15 May 1955; *s* of Col and Mrs D. W. Hargreaves; *m* 1978, Fiona Susan, *o d* of G. W. Dottridge; two *s*. *Educ:* Eton; St Edmund Hall, Oxford (MA Hons). Auctioneer and valuation expert, Christies, 1977–81; executive, Hill Samuel & Co. Ltd, 1981–83; Asst Dir, Sanwa Internat. Ltd, 1983–85; Asst Dir J. Henry Schroder Wagg & Co. Ltd, 1985–87. Contested (C) Blyth Valley, 1983. Mem., Select Cttee on Information, 1992–; Secretary: back bench Urban and Inner Cities Cttee, 1987–91 (Chm., 1992–94); back bench Defence Cttee, 1992–94. Mem., Bow Gp. *Recreations:* fishing, gardening, walking, antiques, art. *Address:* House of Commons, SW1A 0AA. *T:* 0171–219 3000; (office) 0121–471 3909. *Club:* Boodle's.

HARGREAVES, Prof. David Harold, PhD; Professor of Education, and Fellow of Wolfson College, University of Cambridge, since 1988; *b* 31 Aug. 1939; *s* of Clifford and Marion Hargreaves. *Educ:* Bolton School; Christ's College, Cambridge. MA, PhD. Asst Master, Hull Grammar Sch., 1961–64; Research Associate, Dept. of Sociology and Social Anthropology, Univ. of Manchester, 1964–65; Lectr, Senior Lectr then Reader, Dept. of Education, Univ. of Manchester, 1965–79; Reader in Education and Fellow of Jesus College, Oxford, 1979–84; Chief Inspector, ILEA, 1984–88. University of Cambridge: Member: Gen. Bd of the Faculties, 1989–92; Local Exams Syndicate, 1990–92; Bd of Grad. Studies, 1990–92; Chairman: Council, Sch. of Humanities and Soc. Scis, 1990–92; Cttee on the Training and Develt of Univ. Teachers, 1990–92; Needs Cttee, 1991–92. Member: Educn Res. Bd, SSRC, 1979–82; Educn Adv. Council, Royal Opera House, Covent Garden, 1985–90; Educn Adv. Council, IBA, 1988–90; ESRC, 1991–95; Res. Cttee, Teacher Trng Agency, 1995–. Chairman: Eastern Arts Bd, 1991–94; Res. Centres Bd, 1992–94; Internat. Adv. Council on Quality of Educn, NSW, 1993–. FRSA 1984. *Publications:* Social Relations in a Secondary School, 1967; Interpersonal Relations and Education, 1972; (jtly) Deviance in Classrooms, 1975; The Challenge for the Comprehensive School, 1982; (jtly) Planning for School Development, 1990; (jtly) The Empowered School, 1991; The Mosaic of Learning, 1994. *Recreation:* the arts. *Address:* Department of Education, 17 Trumpington Street, Cambridge CB2 1QA. *Club:* Athenæum.

HARGREAVES, Ian Richard; Editor, Independent, since 1994; *b* 18 June 1951; *s* of Ronald and Edna Hargreaves; *m* 1st, 1972, Elizabeth Anne Crago (marr. diss. 1991); one *s* one *d*; 2nd, 1993, Adele Esther Blakebrough, *d* of Rev. E. and M. Blakebrough. *Educ:* Burnley Grammar Sch.; Altrincham Grammar Sch.; Queens' Coll., Cambridge (MA). Community worker, Kaleidescope Project, 1972–73; Reporter, Keighley News, 1973–74; Journalist, Bradford Telegraph & Argus, 1974–76; Financial Times, 1976–87: Industrial Corresp.; Transport Corresp.; New York Corresp.; Social Affairs Ed.; Resources Ed.; Features Ed.; Man. Ed., 1987–88, Controller, 1988–89, Dir, 1989–90, News and Current Affairs, BBC; Dep. Editor, The Financial Times, 1990–94. Member: Adv. Council, Demos; Supervisory Council, Bromley-by-Bow Centre. *Recreations:* football, fell-walking, tennis. *Address:* 2 Admirals Court, 30 Horselydown Lane, Tower Bridge, SE1 2LN. *T:* 0171–403 1693.

HARGREAVES, Prof. John Desmond; Professor of History, University of Aberdeen, 1962–85; *b* 25 Jan. 1924; *s* of Arthur Swire Hargreaves and Margaret Hilda (*née* Duckworth); *m* 1950, Sheila Elizabeth (*née* Wilks); one *s* two *d*. *Educ:* Skipton Grammar Sch.; Bootham; Manchester Univ. War service, 1943–46. Asst Princ., War Office, 1948; Lectr in History: Manchester Univ., 1948–52; Fourah Bay Coll., Sierra Leone, 1952–54; Aberdeen Univ., 1954–62. Vis. Prof., Union Coll. Schenectady, New York, 1960–61; Univ. of Ibadan, 1970–71. Mem., Kidd Cttee on Sheriff Court Records, 1966. Pres., African Studies Assoc. (UK), 1972–73. Hon. DLitt Sierra Leone, 1984. *Publications:* Life of Sir Samuel Lewis, 1958; Prelude to the Partition of West Africa, 1963; West Africa: the Former French States, 1967; France and West Africa, 1969; West Africa Partitioned: Vol. I, The Loaded Pause, 1974, Vol. II, The Elephants and the Grass, 1985; The End of Colonial Rule in West Africa, 1979; Aberdeenshire to Africa, 1981; Decolonization in Africa, 1988; (ed) Aberdeen University 1945–81, 1989; Tensions and Trust (Crathes Castle Community Play), 1992; Academe and Empire, 1994. *Recreations:* hill-walking, theatre, lawn tennis. *Address:* Balcluain, Raemoir Road, Banchory, Kincardine AB31 3UJ. *T:* Banchory (01330) 822655.

HARGREAVES, (Joseph) Kenneth; Secretary, Association of Conservative Clubs, since 1995; *b* 1 March 1939; *s* of James and Mary Hargreaves. *Educ:* St Mary's Coll., Blackburn; Manchester Coll. of Commerce. ACIS. Standard Cost/Wages Clerk, NCB, 1957–61; Audit Asst, Treasurer's Dept, Lancs CC, 1961–63; Office Manager, Shopfitters (Lancashire) Ltd, Oswaldtwistle, 1963–83. MP (C) Hyndburn, 1983–92; contested (C) Hyndburn, 1992. ACIS, 1962; FFA, 1989. Fellow, Inst. of Financial Accountants. *Recreations:* Gilbert and Sullivan, classical music, travel. *Address:* 31 Park Lane, Oswaldtwistle, Accrington, Lancs BB5 3AF. *T:* Accrington (01254) 396184.

HARGROVES, Brig. Sir (Robert) Louis, Kt 1987; CBE 1965; DL; *b* 10 Dec. 1917; *s* of William Robert and Mabel Mary Hargroves; *m* 1940, Eileen Elizabeth Anderson; four *d*. *Educ:* St John's College, Southsea. Commissioned South Staffordshire Regt, 1938; served War of 1939–45; CO 1 Staffords, 1959–61; GSO1, RMA Sandhurst, 1962–63; Brig. 1964; comd Aden Bde, 1964–66; MoD, 1966–69; N Command, 1969–72; retired, 1972. Col. Staffordshire Regt, 1971–77. DL Staffs 1974. *Recreations:* field sports. *Address:* Hyde Cottage, Temple Guiting, Cheltenham, Glos GL54 5RT. *T:* Guiting Power (01451) 850242.

HARINGTON, Gen. Sir Charles (Henry Pepys), GCB 1969 (KCB 1964; CB 1961); CBE 1957 (OBE 1953); DSO 1944; MC 1940; ADC (General) to the Queen, 1969–71; *b* 5 May 1910; *s* of Lt-Col H. H. Harington and Dorothy Pepys; *m* 1942, Victoire Marion Williams-Freeman; one *s* two *d*. *Educ:* Malvern; Sandhurst. Commissioned into 22nd (Cheshire) Regt, 1930. Served War of 1939–45: France and Belgium, 2nd Bn Cheshire Regt, 1939–40; CO, 1st Bn Manchester Regt and GSO1, 53 (Welch) Div., NW Europe, 1944–45. DS Staff Coll., 1946; GSO1 Mil. Mission Greece, 1948; CO 1st Bn The Parachute Regt, 1949; Mil. Asst to CIGS, 1951; SHAPE, 1953; Comdr 49 Inf. Bde in Kenya, 1955; idc 1957; Comdt Sch. of Infantry, 1958; GOC 3rd Div., 1959; Comdt, Staff Coll., Camberley, 1961; C-in-C Middle East, 1963; DCGS, 1966; Chief of Personnel and Logistics, to the three Services, 1968–71, retired; Col The Cheshire Regt, 1962–68. Col Comdt, Small Arms Sch. Corps, 1964–70; Col Comdt, The Prince of Wales Div., 1968–71. President: Combined Cadet Force Assoc., 1971–80; Milocarian (Tri-Service) Athletic Club. Chm. Governors, Royal Star and Garter Home, 1972–80. Commissioner: Royal Hosp., Chelsea, 1970–79; Duke of York's Royal Military Sch., 1971–89. Vice-Pres., Dogs' Home, Battersea, 1993–. Knight Officer with swords, Order of Orange Nassau (Netherlands), 1945. *Clubs:* Army and Navy, Hurlingham (Pres.).

HARINGTON, (Edward Henry) Vernon; *b* 13 Sept. 1907; *er s* of late His Honour Edward Harington; *m* 1st, 1937, Mary Elizabeth (marr. diss. 1949), *d* of late Louis Egerton; one *d* (and one *d* decd); 2nd, 1950, Mary Johanna Jean, JP, *d* of late Lt Col R. G. S. Cox, MC; two *d*. *Educ:* Eton. Called to Bar, Inner Temple, 1930. Private Sec. to Lord Chancellor and Dep. Serjeant-at-Arms, House of Lords, 1934–40; served with HM Forces, 1940–45 (Major, Coldstream Guards); WO, 1944–45; Austrian Control Commn, Legal Div., 1945; Asst Sec. to Lord Chancellor for Commns of the Peace, 1945; Dep. Judge Advocate, 1946; Asst Judge Advocate Gen., 1954–73. Dep. Chm., Herefordshire QS, 1969–71; a Recorder of the Crown Court, 1972–75. Chm., Hereford, Worcester, Warwicks and W Midlands Regional Agricl Wages Cttee, 1976–82. Councillor, Malvern Hill DC, 1979–87. JP Herefordshire, 1969–71. *Recreations:* shooting, fishing. *Address:* 16 Lower Mill Lane, Ludlow, Shropshire SY8 1BH. *T:* Ludlow (01584) 878103.

HARINGTON, Kenneth Douglas Evelyn Herbert; Metropolitan Magistrate, 1967–84; *b* 30 Sept. 1911; *yr s* of late His Honour Edward Harington; *m* 1st, 1939, Lady Cecilia Bowes-Lyon (*d* 1947), *er d* of 15th Earl of Strathmore; 2nd, 1950, Maureen Helen McCalmont (*d* 1992), *d* of Brig.-Gen. Sir Robert McCalmont, KCVO, CBE, DSO; two *s*. *Educ:* Stowe. War of 1939–45: Served NW Europe (Major, Coldstream Guards). Hon. Attaché, British Legation, Stockholm, 1930–32; Barrister, Inner Temple, 1952; Acting Deputy Chm., Inner London and NE London Quarter Sessions, 1966–67. *Recreations:* shooting, fishing. *Address:* Orchard End, Upper Oddington, Moreton-in-Marsh, Glos GL56 0AH. *T:* Cotswold (01451) 830989.

HARINGTON, Sir Nicholas (John), 14th Bt *cr* 1611; Legal Adviser, Export Credits Guarantee Department, since 1988; *b* 14 May 1942; *s* of His Honour John Charles Dundas Harington, QC (*d* 1980) (*yr s* of 12th Bt) and Lavender Cecilia Harington (*d* 1982), *d* of late Major E. W. Denny, Garboldisham Manor, Diss; *S* uncle, 1981. *Educ:* Eton; Christ Church, Oxford (MA Jurisprudence). Called to the Bar, 1969. Employed in Persian Gulf, 1971–72. Joined Civil Service, 1972. *Recreations:* numerous. *Heir:* *b* David Richard Harington [*b* 27 June 1944; *m* 1983, Deborah (*née* Catesby); two *s*]. *Address:* The Ring o'Bells, Whitbourne, Worcester WR6 5RT. *T:* Knightwick (01886) 21819.

HARINGTON, Vernon; *see* Harington, E. H. V.

HARKIN, Brendan; Chairman, Industry Matters (Northern Ireland) Ltd, 1987–90; *b* 21 April 1920; *s* of Francis and Catherine Harkin; *m* 1949, Maureen Gee; one *s* two *d*. *Educ:* St Mary's Christian Brothers' Primary and Grammar Schs, Belfast. Apprentice Electrician, 1936. Asst Sec. 1953, Gen. Sec. 1955–76, NI Civil Service Assoc. (which after amalgamations became Public Service Alliance, 1971). Chm. and Chief Exec., Labour Relations Agency, 1976–85. Chm., Strathearn Audio Ltd, 1974–76; Deputy Chairman: NI Finance Corp., 1972–76; NI Development Agency, 1976. Mem., EEC Economic and Social Cttee, 1973–76. Chm., Industry Year. Pres., Irish Congress of Trade Unions, 1976. Member: Council, NUU, now Univ. of Ulster, 1982– (Chm., Staffing Cttee, 1993–); Council, Co-operation North, 1984–. Pres., NI Hospice, 1985–. MUniv Open, 1986. *Publications:* contrib. on industrial relations. *Recreations:* theatre, music, reading. *Address:* 113 Somerton Road, Belfast, Northern Ireland BT15 4DH. *T:* Belfast (01232) 774979.

HARKINS, Gerard Francis Robert; His Honour Judge Harkins; a Circuit Judge, since 1986; *b* 13 July 1936; *o s* of Francis Murphy Harkins and Katherine Harkins (*née* Hunt). *Educ:* Mount St Mary's College, Spinkhill, near Sheffield; King's College in University of Durham (now Univ. of Newcastle upon Tyne). LDS Dunelm 1961. Dental surgeon in general practice, Yorks, 1961–70; called to the Bar, Middle Temple, 1969; practised NE Circuit, 1970–86. Mem., Northumbria Probation Cttee, 1993–. Pres., Mount Assoc., 1991–92. Governor, Mount St Mary's, 1990–93. *Address:* c/o The Law Courts, Quayside, Newcastle upon Tyne NE1 2LA. *Club:* Lansdowne.

HARKNESS, Lt-Col Hon. Douglas Scott, OC 1978; GM 1943; ED 1944; PC (Canada) 1957; Minister of National Defence, Canada, 1960–63; *b* 29 March 1903; *s* of William Keefer and Janet Douglas Harkness (*née* Scott); *m* 1932, Frances Elisabeth, *d* of James Blair McMillan, Charlottetown and Calgary; one *s*. *Educ:* Central Collegiate, Calgary; University of Alberta (BA). Served overseas in War (Italy and NW Europe), 1940–45; Major and Lt-Col, Royal Canadian Artillery; with Reserve Army, CO 41st Anti-Tank Regt (SP), Royal Canadian Artillery. MP (Calgary E) gen. elecs, 1945, 1949; Re-elected: (Calgary N) gen. elecs, 1953, 1957, 1958, 1962, 1963, 1965, (Calgary Centre) 1968, retired 1972; Min. for Northern Affairs and Nat. Resources and Actg Minister of Agric., June 1957; Minister of Agric., Aug. 1957; relinquished portfolios of Northern Affairs and Nat. Resources, Aug. 1957, of Agriculture, Oct. 1960. Mem. Alta Military Institute. Hon. LLD Calgary, 1975. *Address:* 716 Imperial Way SW, Calgary, Alta T2S 1N7, Canada. *T:* Calgary (403) 243–0825. *Clubs:* Ranchmen's, Calgary Petroleum (Calgary).

HARKNESS, Rt Rev. James, CB 1993; OBE 1978; Moderator of the General Assemby of The Church of Scotland, 1995–May 1996 (designation subseq. Very Rev.); an Extra Chaplain to the Queen in Scotland, since 1995; *b* 20 Oct. 1935; *s* of James and Jane Harkness; *m* 1960, Elizabeth Anne Tolmie; one *s* one *d*. *Educ:* Univ. of Edinburgh (MA). Asst Minister, North Morningside Parish Church, Edinburgh, 1959–61; joined RAChD, 1961: Chaplain: 1 KOSB, 1961–65; 1 Queen's Own Highlanders, 1965–69; Singapore, 1969–70; Dep. Warden, RAChD Centre, 1970–74; Senior Chaplain: N Ireland, 1974–75; 4th Div., 1975–78; Asst Chaplain Gen., Scotland, 1980–81; Senior Chaplain: 1st British Corps, 1981–82; BAOR, 1982–84; Dep. Chaplain Gen. to the Forces, 1985–86, Chaplain Gen., 1987–95. QHC 1982–95. FRSA 1992. OStJ 1988. *Recreations:* general pursuits. *Address:* 13 Saxe Coburg Place, Edinburgh EH3 5BR. *Club:* New (Edinburgh) (Hon. Mem.).

HARKNESS, Rear-Adm. James Percy Knowles, CB 1971; *b* 28 Nov. 1916; *s* of Captain P. Y. Harkness, West Yorkshire Regt, and Gladys Dundas Harkness (*née* Knowles); *m* 1949, Joan, *d* of late Vice-Adm. N. A. Sulivan, CVO; two *d*. Dir-Gen., Naval Manpower, 1970; retired 1972. *Recreation:* sailing.

HARLAND, Bryce; *see* Harland, W. B.

HARLAND, Rt. Rev. Ian; *see* Carlisle, Bishop of.

HARLAND, Air Marshal Sir Reginald (Edward Wynyard), KBE 1974; CB 1972; AE 1945; engineering and management consultant; *b* 30 May 1920; *s* of Charles Cecil Harland and Ida Maud (*née* Bellhouse); *m* 1942, Doreen Rosalind, *d* of late W. H. C. Romanis; two *s* two *d* (and one *s* decd). *Educ:* Summer Fields, Oxford; Stowe; Trinity Coll., Cambridge (MA). Served War of 1939–45: RAE Farnborough, 1941–42; N Africa, Italy and S France, 1942–45. Techn. trng, techn. plans and manning depts, Air Min., 1946–49; pilot trng, 1949–50; Chief Engrg Instructor, RAF Coll., Cranwell, 1950–52; Guided Weapon trng, RMCS Shrivenham, 1952–53; Thunderbird Project Officer: RAE Farnborough, 1953–55; Min. of Supply, 1955–56; psa 1957; Ballistic Missile Liaison Officer, (BJSM) Los Angeles, 1958–60; CO, Central Servicing Develt Estab., Swanton Morley, 1960–62; STSO, HQ No 3 (Bomber) Gp, Mildenhall, 1962–64; AO i/c Engrg, HQ Far East Air Force, Singapore, 1964–66; Harrier Project Dir, HQ Min. of Technology, 1967–68; idc 1969; AOC No 24 Group, RAF, 1970–72; AO Engineering, Air Support Command, 1972; AOC-in-C, RAF Support Command, 1973–77. Technical Dir, W. S. Atkins & Partners, 1977–82; Consultant to Short Brothers Ltd, 1983–88. Mem. Council, IMgt (formerly BIM), 1973–78, 1980–86, 1987–90, 1992–; Pres., Soc. Environmental Engrs, 1974–78; Vice-Chm., CEI, 1983–84. Chairman: Suffolk Preservation Soc., 1988–91; Suffolk Professional Engrs, 1991–; Gov., ESU, 1993–; Pres., East Reg., ESU, 1992–. Contested Bury St Edmunds, (SDP) 1983, (SDP/Alliance) 1987. Sen. Academic Fellow, Leicester Poly. (now De Montfort Univ.), 1989. CEng 1966; FIMechE 1967; FIEE 1964; FRAeS 1967; CIMgt (FBIM 1974; Verulam Medal, 1991). FRSA 1993. *Publications:* occasional articles in engrg and management jls. *Recreations:* better management, better government. *Address:* 49 Crown Street, Bury St Edmunds, Suffolk IP33 1QX. *T:* Bury St Edmunds (01284) 763078. *Club:* Royal Air Force.

HARLAND, (William) Bryce, QSO 1992; High Commissioner for New Zealand in the United Kingdom 1985–91; *b* 11 Dec. 1931; *s* of Edward Dugard Harland and Annie McDonald Harland (*née* Gordon); *m* 1st, 1957, Rosemary Anne Gordon (marr. diss. 1977); two *s* (and one *s* decd); 2nd, 1979, (Margaret) Anne Blackburn; one *s*. *Educ:* Victoria Univ., Wellington, NZ (MA Hons); Fletcher School of Law and Diplomacy, Boston, Mass, USA (AM). Joined NZ Dept of External Affairs, 1953; diplomatic postings: Singapore, 1956; Bangkok, 1957; NY, 1959; Wellington, 1962; Washington, 1965; Wellington, 1969; First NZ Ambassador to China, 1973–75; Ministry of Foreign Affairs, Wellington: Head of African and European Divs, 1976–77; Asst Sec., 1977–82; Perm. Rep. of NZ to the UN, NY, 1982–85 (Chm., Economic and Financial Cttee, Gen. Assembly, 1984). Vis. Fellow, All Souls Coll., Oxford, 1991. KStJ 1985. Hon. Freeman, City of London, 1987. *Publications:* On Our Own: New Zealand in the emerging tripolar world, 1992; Asia—What Next?, 1992; sundry articles. *Recreations:* reading history, walking. *Address:* 15 Selwyn Avenue, Richmond TW9 2HB. *Club:* Brooks's.

HARLE, James Coffin, DPhil, DLitt; Keeper, Department of Eastern Art, Ashmolean Museum, Oxford, 1967–87; Student of Christ Church, Oxford, 1970–87, now Emeritus; *b* 5 April 1920; *s* of James Wyly Harle and Elfrieda Frances (*née* Baumann); *m* 1st, 1949, Jacqueline Thérèse Ruch (marr. diss. 1966, she *d* 1968); 2nd, 1967, Mrs Carola Sybil Mary Fleming (*d* 1971); 3rd, 1973, Lady (Betty) Hulbert. *Educ:* St George's Sch., Newport, RI; Princeton Univ. (BA 1942, Phi Beta Kappa); Oxford Univ. (BA 1st cl. Sanskrit and Pali, 1956; DPhil 1959; DLitt 1989). Served War, 1942–46, USNR (Aviation Br.), retd as Lieut; DFC (US). Asst to Dean of the College, Princeton, 1947; Part-time instructor in English, Princeton, 1948–49; Fulbright Lectr, Philippines, 1953–54; Ashmolean Museum: Asst Keeper, 1960; Sen. Asst Keeper, 1962. Pres., Soc. for S Asian Studies (British Acad.), 1990–95. *Publications:* Tower Gateways in South India, 1963; Gupta Sculpture, 1974; The Art and Architecture of the Indian Subcontinent, 1986; articles in periodicals on Indian Art. *Address:* Hawkswell, 34 Portland Road, Oxford OX2 7EY. *T:* Oxford (01865) 515236. *Club:* Princeton (New York).

HARLE, John Crofton, FGSM; saxophonist, composer, arranger, conductor; *b* 20 Sept. 1956; *s* of Jack Harle and Joyce Harle (*née* Crofton); *m* 1985, Julia Jane Eisner; two *s*. *Educ:* Newcastle Royal Grammar Sch.; Royal Coll. of Music (Foundn Schol.; ARCM (Hons) 1978); private study in Paris, 1981–82. FGSM 1990. Leader of Myrha Saxophone Quartet, 1977–82; formed duo with pianist John Lenehan, 1979; saxophone soloist, 1980–, with major internat. orchs, incl. LSO, English Chamber Orch., LPO, Amsterdam Concertgebouw, New World Symphony; Principal Saxophone, London Sinfonietta, 1987–; Prof. of Saxophone, GSMD, 1988–. Formed: Berliner Band, 1983; John Harle Band, 1988. Compositions for several ensembles, 1983–, incl. London Brass and LSO. Frequent composer and soloist on TV and feature films; regular broadcaster on BBC Radio; featured in One Man and his Sax, BBC2 TV, 1988. Has made many recordings. Major works written for him by Dominic Muldowney, Ned Rorem, Richard Rodney Bennett, Luciano Berio, Michael Nyman, Gavin Bryars, Mike Westbrook, Stanley Myers, Harrison Birtwistle and Michael Torke. Dannreuther Concerto Prize, Royal Coll. of Music, 1980; GLAA Young Musician, 1979, 1980. *Publication:* John Harle's Saxophone Album, 1986. *Recreations:* family life, cooking. *Address:* c/o Clarion/7 Muses, 47 Whitehall Park, N19 3TW. *T:* 0171–272 4413.

HARLECH, 6th Baron *cr* 1876; **Francis David Ormsby Gore;** *b* 13 March 1954; *s* of 5th Baron Harlech, KCMG, PC, and Sylvia (*d* 1967), *d* of Hugh Lloyd Thomas, CMG, CVO; *S* father, 1985; *m* 1986, Amanda Jane, *d* of Alan T. Grieve, *qv*; one *s* one *d*. *Educ:* Worth. *Heir: s* Hon. Jasset David Cody Ormsby Gore, *b* 1 July 1986. *Address:* The Mount, Racecourse Road, Oswestry, Shropshire SY10 7PH; House of Lords, SW1A 0PW. *Club:* Brooks's.

HARLECH, Pamela, Lady; journalist and producer; *b* 18 Dec. 1934; *d* of Ralph Frederick Colin and Georgia Talmey; *m* 1969, 5th Baron Harlech, PC, KCMG (*d* 1985); one *d*. *Educ:* Smith Coll., Northampton, Mass; Finch Coll. (BA). London Editor, (American) Vogue, 1964–69; Food Editor, (British) Vogue, 1971–82; freelance journalist, 1972–; prodn work for special events, 1986–87; Commissioning Editor, Thames and Hudson, Publishers, 1987–89. Chairman: Women's Playhouse Trust, 1984–94; V & A Enterprises, 1987–94; English Nat. Ballet, 1990–; Council, British Amer. Arts Assoc., 1990–92; Member: Welsh Arts Council, 1981–85; Arts Council of GB, 1986–90; South Bank Bd, 1986–94; Council, Managing Bd, Cruisaid, 1987–; Council, Assoc. of Business Sponsorship for the Arts, 1988–95 (Chm., Judging Panel for Awards, 1989–90). Trustee, V&A Mus., 1986–94. *Publications:* Feast without Fuss, 1976; Pamela Harlech's Complete Guide to Cooking, Entertainment and Household Management, 1981; Vogue Book of Menus, 1985. *Recreations:* music, cooking, laughing. *Address:* English National Ballet, 39 Jay Mews, SW7. *T:* 0171–581 1245.

HARLEY, Lt-Gen. Alexander George Hamilton, CB 1991; OBE 1981; Deputy Chief of Defence Staff (Commitments), Ministry of Defence, since 1995; *b* India, 3 May 1941; *s* of Lt-Col William Hamilton Coughtrie Harley, 1st Punjab Regt and later Royal Indian Engineers, and Eleanor Blanche (*née* Jarvis); *m* 1967, Christina Valentine, *d* of Edmund Noel Butler-Cole and Kathleen Mary (*née* Thompson); two *s*. *Educ:* Caterham Sch.; RMA Sandhurst. Commissioned RA 1962; various appointments, 1962–73: 7 Para Regt RHA; Staff Capt. MoD; Adjutant; Canadian Staff Coll.; Mil. Asst, MoD, 1974–75; Battery Comdr, 1975–78 (despatches); Directing Staff, Staff Coll., 1978–79; CO 19 Field Regt RA, 1979–82; Col Defence Staff, MoD, 1983–85; Comdr 33 Armd Brigade, 1985–87; Asst Chief of Staff (Ops), Northern Army Group, 1988–90; ACDS (Overseas), 1990–93; Administrator, Sovereign Base Areas, and Comdr British Forces Cyprus, 1993–95. Hon. Regtl Col, 19 Field Regt RA. Pres., Army Hockey Assoc. Patron, United All Services Hockey Club (The Nordics). FIMgt (FBIM 1982). *Recreations:* country pursuits, hockey, clocks. *Address:* Ministry of Defence, Main Building, Whitehall, SW1A 2HB. *Club:* Commonwealth Trust.

HARLOW, Archdeacon of; *see* Fox, Ven. M. J.

HARMAN, Harriet; MP (Lab) Peckham, since Oct. 1982; *b* 30 July 1950; *d* of late John Bishop Harman, FRCS, FRCP, and of Anna Charlotte Harman; *m* 1982, Jack Dromey; two *s* one *d*. *Educ:* St Paul's Girls' Sch.; York Univ. Brent Community Law Centre, 1975–78; Legal Officer, NCCL, 1978–82. Opposition Chief Sec. to the Treasury, 1992–. Mem., NEC, Labour Party, 1993–. *Publications:* Sex Discrimination in Schools, 1977; Justice Deserted: the subversion of the jury, 1979; The Century Gap, 1993. *Address:* House of Commons, SW1A 0AA.

HARMAN, Gen. Sir Jack (Wentworth), GCB 1978 (KCB 1974); OBE 1962; MC 1943; Deputy Supreme Allied Commander, Europe, 1978–81, retired; *b* 20 July 1920; *s* of late Lt-Gen. Sir Wentworth Harman, KCB, DSO, and late Dorothy Harman; *m* 1947, Gwladys May Murphy (*widow* of Lt-Col R. J. Murphy), *d* of Sir Idwal Lloyd; one *d* and two step *d*. *Educ:* Wellington Coll.; RMC Sandhurst. Commissioned into The Queen's Bays, 1940, Bt Lt-Col, 1958; Commanding Officer, 1st The Queen's Dragoon Guards, 1960–62; commanded 11 Infantry Bde, 1965–66; attended IDC, 1967; BGS, HQ Army Strategic Command, 1968–69; GOC, 1st Div., 1970–72; Commandant, RMA, Sandhurst, 1972–73; GOC 1 (British) Corps, 1974–76; Adjutant-General, 1976–78. ADC Gen. to the Queen, 1977–80. Col, 1st The Queen's Dragoon Guards, 1975–80; Col Comdt, RAC, 1977–80. Dir, Wilsons Hogg Robinson (formerly Wilsons (Insurance Brokers)), 1982–88. Vice-Chairman: Nat. Army Museum, 1980–87; AA, 1986–89 (Mem. Cttee, 1981–85). *Address:* Sandhills House, Dinton, near Salisbury, Wilts SP3 5ER. *T:* Teffont (01722) 716288. *Club:* Cavalry and Guards.

HARMAN, Hon. Sir Jeremiah (LeRoy), Kt 1982; **Hon. Mr Justice Harman;** a Justice of the High Court, Chancery Division, since 1982; *b* 13 April 1930; *er s* of late Rt Hon. Sir Charles Eustace Harman; *m* 1960, Erica Jane (marr diss. 1986), *e d* of late Hon. Sir Maurice Richard Bridgeman, KBE; two *s* one *d*; *m* 1987, Katharine Frances Goddard, *d* of late Rt Hon. Sir Eric Sachs and *widow* of George Pulay. *Educ:* Horris Hill Sch.; Eton Coll. Served Coldstream Guards and Parachute Regt, 1948–51; Parachute Regt (TA), 1951–55. Called to the Bar, Lincoln's Inn, 1954, Bencher, 1977; QC 1968; called to Hong Kong Bar, 1978, Singapore Bar, 1980; Mem., Bar Council, 1963–67. Dir, Dunford & Elliott Ltd, 1972–79. *Recreations:* fishing, stalking, watching birds. *Address:* Royal Courts of Justice, The Strand, WC2A 2LL.

HARMAN, Robert Donald, QC 1974; a Recorder of the Crown Court, since 1972; a Judge of the Courts of Appeal of Jersey and Guernsey, since 1986; *b* 26 Sept. 1928; *o s* of late Herbert Donald Harman, MC; *m* 1st, 1960, Sarah Elizabeth (*d* 1965), *o d* of late G. C. Cleverly; two *s*; 2nd, 1968, Rosamond Geraldine, JP, 2nd *d* of late Cmdr G. T. A. Scott, RN; two *d*. *Educ:* privately; St Paul's Sch.; Magdalen Coll., Oxford. Called to Bar, Gray's Inn, 1954, Bencher, 1984; South-Eastern Circuit; a Junior Prosecuting Counsel to the Crown at Central Criminal Court, 1967–72; a Senior Treasury Counsel, 1972–74. Mem., Senate of the Inns of Court and the Bar, 1985–87. Jt Hon. Sec., Barristers' Benevolent Assoc. Appeal Steward, BBB of C. Liveryman, Goldsmiths' Co. *Address:* 2 Harcourt Buildings, Temple, EC4. *T:* 0171–353 2112; 17 Pelham Crescent, SW7 2NR. *T:* 0171–584 4304. *Clubs:* Garrick, Beefsteak, Pratt's; Swinley Forest Golf.

HARMAR-NICHOLLS, family name of **Baron Harmar-Nicholls.**

HARMAR-NICHOLLS, Baron *cr* 1974 (Life Peer), of Peterborough, Cambs; **Harmar Harmar-Nicholls,** JP; Bt 1960; Member (C) Greater Manchester South, European Parliament, 1979–84; *b* 1 Nov. 1912; 3rd *s* of Charles E. C. Nicholls and Sarah Anne Nicholls, Walsall; *m* 1940, Dorothy Elsie, *e d* of James Edwards, Tipton; two *d*. *Educ:* Dorsett Road Sch., Darlaston; Queen Mary's Gram. Sch., Walsall. Mem. Middle Temple Inn of Court. Chairman: Nicholls and Hennessy (Hotels) Ltd; Malvern Festival Theatre Trust Ltd; Radio Luxembourg (London) Ltd, 1983– (Dir, 1963–); Dir, J. & H. Nicholls

& Co., Paints, etc, 1945–. Mem. of Syndicate at Lloyd's. Mem. Darlaston UDC at age of 26 (Chm., 1949–50); County Magistrate, 1946. Vice-Chm. W Midland Fedn, Junior Imperial League, 1937; contested (C): Nelson and Colne, 1945; Preston by-election, 1946; MP (C) Peterborough Div. of Northants, 1950–Sept. 1974; PPS to Asst Postmaster-Gen., 1951–April 1955; Parly Sec., Min. of Agriculture, Fisheries and Food, April 1955–Jan. 1957; Parliamentary Sec., Min. of Works, 1957–60; Mem. Conservative Housing Cttee; Sec. of Parly Road Safety Cttee (Conservative); Jt Sec. All party Parly Group Empire Migration; Mem. Govt Overseas Settlement Board on migration to Commonwealth. War of 1939–45: volunteered as sapper, commnd Royal Engineers; served India and Burma. *Recreations:* gardening, reading, walking, theatre. *Address:* Abbeylands, Weston, Stafford ST18 0HX. *T:* Weston (01889) 252. *Clubs:* St Stephen's Constitutional; (Pres.) Unionist, City and Counties (Peterborough); Conservative (Darlaston); Unionist (Walsall).

HARMER, Michael Hedley, MA, MB Cantab, FRCS; Consulting Surgeon, Royal Marsden Hospital and Paddington Green Children's Hospital (St Mary's Hospital); *b* 6 July 1912; *y s* of late Douglas Harmer, MC, FRCS, and May (*née* Hedley); *m* 1939, Bridget Jean, *d* of late James Higgs-Walker, MA, and of Muriel Jessie, *e d* of Rev. Harold Smith; one *s* one *d*. *Educ:* Marlborough; King's Coll., Cambridge; St Bartholomew's Hosp., London. Surgical Specialist, RAFVR, 1943–46. Bellman Snark Club, Cambridge, 1934–. Freeman of Norwich by Patrimony, 1935; Freeman, City of London, 1936. *Publications:* A Handbook of Surgery, 1951; Aids to Surgery, 1962; (Jt Editor) Rose and Carless's Manual of Surgery, 19th edn, 1959; The Forgotten Hospital, 1982; Look Back in Happiness, 1992; papers on the surgery and classification of malignant disease. *Recreations:* music, the country. *Address:* Perrot Wood, Graffham, Petworth, Sussex GU28 0NZ. *T:* Graffham (01798) 867307.

HARMSWORTH, family name of **Viscount Rothermere** and **Baron Harmsworth.**

HARMSWORTH, 3rd Baron, *cr* 1939, of Egham; **Thomas Harold Raymond Harmsworth;** publisher; *b* 20 July 1939; *s* of Hon. Eric Beauchamp Northcliffe Harmsworth (*d* 1988) and Hélène Marie (*d* 1962), *d* of Col Jules Raymond Dehove; *S* uncle, 1990; *m* 1971, Patricia Palmer, *d* of late M. P. Horsley; two *s* three *d*. *Educ:* Eton; Christ Church, Oxford (MA). Nat. Service, Royal Horse Guards (The Blues), 1957–59 (2nd Lieut). Stockbroker, 1962–74; DHSS, 1974–88. Chm., Dr Johnson's House Trust. *Recreations:* sundry, including music. *Heir:* *s* Hon. Dominic Michael Eric Harmsworth, *b* 18 Sept. 1973. *Address:* The Old Rectory, Stoke Abbott, Beaminster, Dorset DT8 3JT. *T:* Broadwindsor (01308) 868139.

HARMSWORTH, Sir Hildebrand Harold, 3rd Bt *cr* 1922; *b* 5 June 1931; *s* of Sir Hildebrand Alfred Beresford Harmsworth, 2nd Bt, and Elen, *d* of Nicolaj Billenstein, Randers, Denmark; *S* father, 1977; *m* 1960, Gillian Andrea, *o d* of William John Lewis; one *s* two *d*. *Educ:* Harrow; Trinity College, Dublin. *Heir:* *s* Hildebrand Esmond Miles Harmsworth [*b* 1 Sept. 1964; *m* 1988, Ruth Denise, *d* of Dennis Miles; two *d*]. *Address:* Ewlyn Villa, 42 Leckhampton Road, Cheltenham GL53 0BB.

HARNDEN, Arthur Baker, CB 1969; BSc, CEng, FIEE; FIMgt; Chairman, Appeals Tribunals, Supplementary Benefits Commission, 1970–82; *b* 6 Jan. 1909; *s* of Cecil Henry Harnden and Susan (*née* Baker); *m* 1st, 1935, Maisie Elizabeth Annie (*d* 1970), *d* of A. H. Winterburn, LRIBA; one *s*; 2nd, 1971, Jean Kathleen, *d* of H. F. Wheeler and *widow* of Eric J. Dedman; one step *s*. *Educ:* various state schools. Exec. Engr, GPO, 1933; Royal Corps of Signals, 1939–45; Lt-Col GSO1, WO, 1942; DCSO Antwerp, 1944, Hamburg 1945. Dir, London Telecommunications Region, GPO, 1962; Senior Dir, Operations, PO (Telecommunications), 1967–69. Principal, Comrie House Sch., Finchley, 1971–72. *Recreations:* painting and potting. *Address:* Comrie, Park Street, Fairford, Glos GL7 4JL. *T:* Cirencester (01285) 712805.

HARNDEN, Prof. David Gilbert, PhD, FRSE 1982, FIBiol, FRCPath; Director, Paterson Institute for Cancer Research, Christie Hospital NHS Trust, Manchester; *b* 22 June 1932; *s* of William Alfred Harnden and Anne McKenzie Wilson; *m* 1955, Thora Margaret Seatter; three *s*. *Educ:* George Heriot's School, Edinburgh; University of Edinburgh. BSc. Lectr, Univ. of Edinburgh, 1956–57; Sci. Mem., Radiobiology Unit, MRC, Harwell, 1957–59; Sci. Mem., Clinical and Population Cytogenetics Unit, MRC, Edinburgh, 1959–69; Prof. of Cancer Studies, Univ. of Birmingham, 1969–83; Dir, Paterson Labs, now Paterson Inst. for Cancer Res., Christie Hosp. and Holt Radium Inst., now Christie Hosp. NHS Trust, 1983–; Hon. Prof. of Experimental Oncology, Univ. of Manchester, 1983–. Chairman: Educn Cttee, Cancer Res. Campaign, 1987–92; NW Regl Adv. Cttee on Oncology Services, 1991–. Dir, Christie Hosp. (NHS) Trust, 1991–. Hon. MRCP 1987. Chm., Editorial Bd, British Jl of Cancer, 1983–. *Publications:* papers on cancer research and human genetics in learned jls. *Recreation:* sketching people and places. *Address:* Paterson Institute for Cancer Research, Christie Hospital NHS Trust, Wilmslow Road, Manchester M20 9BX. *T:* 0161–446 3101.

HARNIMAN, John Phillip, OBE 1984; Director, British Council (Counsellor, Cultural Affairs), Canada, since 1992; *b* 7 May 1939; *s* of William Thomas Harniman and Maud Kate Florence (*née* Dyrenfurth); *m* 1961, Avryl (*née* Hartley); one *s* one *d*. *Educ:* Leyton County High School; Culham College, Oxon (DipEd); London University (BA Hons); Université de la Sorbonne. William Morris School, Walthamstow, 1960–62; Ecole Normale Supérieure de Saint-Cloud, 1962–67; British Council: Algeria, 1967–70; Specialist Careers Officer, Personnel, 1970–73; Head, Overseas Careers, Personnel, 1973–76; Representative, Singapore, 1976–81; Cultural Attaché, Romania, 1981–84; Rep. and Cultural Counsellor, Belgium and Luxembourg, 1984–87; Asst Controller, Personnel Div., 1987–92. *Recreations:* reading, listening to music, letter-writing, cats. *Address:* c/o British Defence Liaison Staff (Ottawa), Naval Party 1010, BFPO Ships; 68 Church Street, Lavenham, Suffolk CO10 9QT.

HARPER, Alan Henry; Chairman, Baltic Exchange Ltd, 1994–June 1996; Managing Director, Jackson Son & Co (London), since 1989; *b* 27 Jan. 1943; *s* of Frank Dennis Luker and Patricia May (*née* Harper); *m* 1965, Nicol Susan Reid; three *d*. *Educ:* Southend Grammar Sch. General office, Louis Dreyfus and Co., London, 1958–62; worked in: jute industry, Louis Dreyfus and Co., Calcutta, 1963; animal feeds, India, 1964, and grain trade, London, 1965–73, European Grain & Shipping Ltd, commodity futures, Coley & Harper Ltd, 1974–89. Dir, Baltic Exchange Ltd, 1982–87 and 1989–94. *Recreations:* dinghy sailing, tennis. *Address:* Hillersdon, Hervines Road, Amersham, Bucks HP6 5HS. *T:* Amersham (01494) 724861.

HARPER, Alfred Alexander, MA, MD; Professor of Physiology, University of Newcastle upon Tyne, 1963–72; *b* 19 June 1907; *er s* of James and Elizabeth Harper. *Educ:* Aberdeen Grammar Sch.; Aberdeen Univ. Lecturer in Physiology, University of Leeds, 1935–36; Demonstrator in Physiology, St Thomas's Hosp., London, 1936–39; Lectr, later Reader, in Human Physiology, Univ. of Manchester, 1939–49; Prof. of Physiology, Univ. of Durham, 1949–63. *Publications:* papers in Jl of Physiology mostly on physiology of digestion. *Address:* Wellburn House, Benwell Lane, Newcastle upon Tyne NE15 6LX. *T:* 0191–274 8178.

HARPER, Donald John; Aerospace Systems and Defence Procurement consultant; *b* 6 Aug. 1923; *s* of Harry Tonkin and Caroline Irene Harper; *m* 1947, Joyce Beryl Kite-Powell; two *d*. *Educ:* Purley County Grammar Sch. for Boys; Queen Mary Coll., London. 1st cl. BSc (Eng) 1943; CEng, FRAeS. Joined Aero Dept, RAE Farnborough, 1943; Scientific Officer, Spinning Tunnel, 1947–49; High Speed and Transonic Tunnel, 1950–59; Sen. Scientific Officer; Principal Scientific Officer, 1955; Dep. Head of Tunnel, 1958–59; Space Dept RAE, Satellite Launching Vehicles, 1960–62; Senior Principal Scientific Officer, MoD, Central Staff, 1963–65; Head of Assessment Div., Weapons Dept RAE, 1966–68; Dir of Project Time and Cost Analysis, MoD (PE), 1968–71; Dir-Gen., Performance and Cost Analysis, MoD (PE), 1972–77; Dir-Gen. Research C, MoD (PE), 1978–83, and Chief Scientist, RAF, 1980–83. Mem. Council, RAeS, 1990–92. *Publications:* contrib. Aeronautical Res. Council reports and memoranda and techn. press. *Recreations:* music, especially choral singing; gardening; home improvement. *Address:* Beech Cottage, Beech Gardens, Woking, Surrey GU21 4QT. *T:* Woking (01483) 760541.

HARPER, Dame Elizabeth (Margaret Way), DBE 1995; farmer and house-wife; New Zealand President, Save the Children, 1990–93; *b* 20 June 1937; *d* of Jack Horsford Horrell and Margaret Faith Horrell (*née* Rickard); *m* 1956, Charles John Harper; two *s* (one *d* decd). *Educ:* Lagmhor Sch., Mid-Canterbury, NZ; Ashburton High Sch.; Craighead Diocesan Sch., Timaru. Save the Children: Br. Sec., 1970–84; Pres., Ashburton Br., 1984–87; S Island Vice-Pres., 1987–89. Red Cross volunteer, Dist Nursing Service, 1984–; night sitter volunteer for terminally ill, 1987–. Save the Children Award for Dist. and Meritorious Service, 1994. *Recreations:* golf, sewing, knitting, breeding coloured sheep. *Address:* Stratfield, No 1 RD, Ashburton, New Zealand. *T:* (3) 3025831.

HARPER, Prof. Fred, PhD; Dean, Seale-Hayne Faculty of Agriculture, Food and Land Use, University of Plymouth (formerly Plymouth Polytechnic), since 1989; *b* 7 June 1947; *s* of Frederick and Queenie Elizabeth Harper; *m* 1971, Moyna Carole Hunter; one *d*. *Educ:* Univ. of Nottingham (BSc Hons Agric., PhD). Lecturer: Writtle Agricl Coll., Chelmsford, 1971–75; and Dir of Studies, Univ. of Edinburgh, 1975–82; Vice-Principal and Dir of Studies, Harper Adams Agricl Coll., Shropshire, 1983–88; Principal, Seale-Hayne Coll., Devon, 1988–89. ARAgS, 1993. *Publications:* The Principles of Arable Crop Production, 1983; numerous pubns on crop physiology and production, agricl educn and overseas agriculture. *Recreations:* walking, travel, observing wildlife, watching sport. *Address:* Dean's House, Seale-Hayne, Newton Abbot, Devon TQ12 6NQ. *T:* Newton Abbot (01626) 54638.

HARPER, Heather (Mary), (Mrs E. J. Benarroch), CBE 1965; soprano; Professor of Singing and Consultant, Royal College of Music, 1985–93; Director of Singing Studies, Britten-Pears School, Aldeburgh, since 1986; *b* 8 May 1930; *d* of late Hugh Harper, Belfast; *m* 1973, Eduardo J. Benarroch. *Educ:* Trinity Coll. of Music, London. Has sung many principal roles incl. Arabella, Ariadne, Marschallin, Chrysothemis, Elsa and Kaiserin, at Covent Garden, Glyndebourne, Sadler's Wells, Bayreuth, Teatro Colon (Buenos Aires), Edinburgh Fest., La Scala, NY Met, San Francisco, Deutsche Oper (Berlin), Frankfurt, Netherlands Opera, Canadian Opera Co., Toronto, and sang at every Promenade Concert season 1957–90; created the soprano role in Benjamin Britten's War Requiem in Coventry Cathedral in 1962; soloist at opening concerts: Maltings, Snape, 1967; Queen Elizabeth Hall, 1967. Toured USA, 1965, and USSR, 1967, with BBC SO; has toured USA annually, 1967–, and appeared regularly at European music fests; toured: Japan and S Korea as Principal Soloist Soprano with Royal Opera Co., 1979; Australia and Hong Kong with BBC Symph. Orch., 1982; has also sung in Asia, Middle East, Australia and S America; Principal Soloist Soprano with Royal Opera House Co., visit to Los Angeles Olympic Games, 1984; Principal Soloist with BBC Philharmonic Orch's first South American tour, 1989. Has made many recordings, incl. works of Britten, Beethoven, Berg, Mahler, Mozart, Strauss and Verdi; broadcasts frequently throughout the world, and appears frequently on TV; Masterclasses for advanced students and young professionals, Britten-Pears Sch.; retired from operatic stage, 1984, from concert stage, 1991. Member: BBC Music Panel, 1989; RSA Music Panel, 1989. FTCL; FRCM 1988; Hon. RAM, 1972. Hon. DMus Queen's Univ., Belfast, 1966; Hon. DLitt Ulster, 1992. Edison Award, 1971; Grammy Nomination, 1973; Grammy Award, 1979, 1984, 1991; Best vocal performance for Ravel's Scheherezade; Grand Prix du Disque, 1979. *Recreations:* gardening, cooking.

HARPER, James Norman; barrister; a Recorder of the Crown Court, 1980–84; *b* 30 Dec. 1932; *s* of late His Honour Judge Norman Harper and Iris Irene Harper; *m* 1956, Blanka Miroslava Eva Sigmund; one *s* one *d*. *Educ:* Marlborough Coll.; Magdalen Coll., Oxford (BA Hons). Called to the Bar, Gray's Inn, 1957; Attorney Gen. of NE Circuit, 1992–95. Pres., Northumberland County Hockey Assoc., 1982–. *Recreations:* cricket, hockey, painting. *Address:* 33 Broad Chare, Newcastle upon Tyne NE1 3DQ. *T:* 0191–232 0541. *Club:* MCC.

HARPER, Prof. John Lander, CBE 1989; DPhil; FRS 1978; Emeritus Professor of Botany, University of Wales, since 1982: Head, Unit of Plant Population Biology, School of Plant Biology, Bangor, 1982–90; *b* 27 May 1925; *s* of John Hindley Harper and Harriett Mary (*née* Archer); *m* 1954, Borgny Lerø; one *s* two *d*. *Educ:* Lawrence Sheriff Sch., Rugby; Magdalen Coll., Oxford (BA, MA, DPhil). Demonstr, Dept of Agriculture, Univ. of Oxford, 1951, Lectr 1953; Rockefeller Foundn Fellow, Univ. of Calif, 1960–61; Prof. of Agricultural Botany, 1960, Prof. of Botany, 1977–82 and Head of Sch. of Plant Biology, 1967–82, University Coll. of North Wales, Bangor. Member: NERC, 1971–81; AFRC, 1980–90; Jt Nature Conservation Cttee, 1991–94. Trustee, Natural Hist. Mus., 1993–. For. Assoc., US Nat. Acad. of Sciences, 1984. Hon. DSc Sussex, 1984. *Publications:* Biology of Weeds, 1960; Population Biology of Plants, 1977; (with M. Begon and C. Townsend) Ecology: organisms, populations and communities, 1985; papers in Jl of Ecol., New Phytologist, Annals of Applied Biol., Evolution, and Proc. Royal Soc. (Editor, Series B, 1993–). *Recreation:* gardening. *Address:* Cae Groes, Glan y Coed Park, Dwygyfylchi, near Penmaenmawr, N Wales LL34 6TL. *T:* Penmaenmawr (01492) 622362. *Club:* Farmers'.

HARPER, John Mansfield; Senior Partner, The Lullington Group, since 1993; Director, International Information Exchange Ltd, since 1990; *b* 17 July 1930; *s* of late T. J. Harper and May (*née* Charlton); *m* 1956, Berenice Honorine, *d* of Harold Haydon; one *s* one *d*. *Educ:* Merchant Taylors' Sch.; St John's Coll., Oxford. 2nd Lieut Royal Corps of Signals, 1948–49. Asst Principal, Post Office, 1953; Private Sec. to Dir-Gen., 1956–58; Principal, 1958–66; Asst Sec., Reorganization Dept, 1966–69; Dir, North-Eastern Telecommunications Region, 1969–71; Dir, Purchasing and Supply, 1972–75; Sen. Dir, Planning and Provisioning, 1975–77; Asst Man. Dir, Telecommunications, 1978–79; Dep. Man. Dir, British Telecommunications (Post Office), 1979–81; Man. Dir, Inland Division, BT, 1981–83, retired. Advr to Bd, NEC (UK) Ltd, 1985–92; Specialist Advr, Parly Select Cttee on Trade and Industry, 1994. Vis. Fellow, Sci. Policy Res. Unit, Univ. of Sussex, 1992–93. Chm., Infrastructure Policy Gp, Electronic Engrg Assoc., 1989–90. Comp IEE; CIMgt. *Publications:* Telecommunications and Computing: the uncompleted revolution, 1986; Telecommunications Policy and Management, 1989; The Third Way: telecommunications and the environment, 1990; A 21st Century Structure for UK

Telecoms, 1991. *Recreations:* music, gardening, amateur radio. *Address:* 11 Lullington Close, Seaford, E Sussex BN25 4JH. *Club:* National Liberal.

HARPER, Prof. John Martin, FRCO (CHM); Professor of Music, University of Wales, Bangor (formerly University College of North Wales, Bangor), since 1991; *b* 11 July 1947; *s* of Geoffrey Martin and Kathleen Harper; *m* 1970, Cynthia Margaret Dean (marr. diss.); three *s*; *m* 1991, Sally Elizabeth Roper. *Educ:* King's Coll. Sch., Cambridge (Chorister); Clifton Coll., Bristol (Music Scholar); Selwyn Coll., Cambridge (Organ Scholar; MA); Birmingham Univ. (PhD); MA Oxon. Music Tutor, West Bromwich Residential Arts Centre, 1970–71; Dir, Edington Music Fest., 1971–78; Dir of Music, St Chad's Cathedral, Birmingham, 1972–78; Lectr in Music, Birmingham Univ., 1974–75, 1976–81; Asst Dir of Music, King Edward's Sch., Birmingham, 1975–76; Fellow, Organist, Informator Choristarum and Tutor in Music, Magdalen Coll., and Univ. Lectr in Music, Oxford, 1981–90. Member Council: UCNW, 1991–; Plainsong and Medieval Music Soc., 1994–. Advr, Panel of Monastic Musicians, 1976–. Recordings, 1974–, incl. The English Anthem (5 vols), with Magdalen Coll. Choir. Benemerenti Papal award, 1978. *Publications:* choral compositions, 1974–; (ed) Orlando Gibbons: consort music, 1982; The Forms and Orders of Western Liturgy, 1991; contribs to: New Grove Dictionary of Music and Musicians, 1980; Frescobaldi Studies, 1987; Die Musik in Geschichte und Gegenwart, 1994; Blackwell History of Music in Britain, Vol. 2, 1995; articles and reviews in music jls and papers. *Recreations:* walking, church architecture. *Address:* Department of Music, University of Wales, Bangor, Gwynedd LL57 2DG. *T:* Bangor (01248) 382181.

HARPER, Prof. (John) Ross, CBE 1986; Senior Partner: Ross Harper & Murphy, Solicitors, since 1961; Harper Macleod, since 1991; Professor of Law, Strathclyde University, since 1986; *b* 20 March 1935; *s* of late Rev. Thomas Harper, BD, STM, PhD and Margaret Simpson Harper (later Clarkson); *m* 1963, Ursula Helga Renate Gathman; two *s* one *d*. *Educ:* Hutchesons' Boys' Grammar School; Glasgow Univ. (MA, LLB), Pres., Students Rep. Council, 1955. Pres., Scottish Union of Students, 1956–58; Chm.,, Internat. Students' Conf., 1958. Asst Solicitor, McGettigan & Co., Glasgow, 1959; founded Ross Harper & Murphy, 1961, as two Partner firm (now 23 Partners), specialised in Criminal Law, later developing into Commercial Law. Temp. Sheriff, 1979–89; a Parly Comr, 1992–. Pres., Law Soc. of Scotland, 1988–89 (Vice-Pres., 1987–88). Pres., Glasgow Bar Assoc., 1975–78; International Bar Association: Chm., Criminal Law Div., 1983–87; Chm., Gen. Practice Section, 1990–92 (Sec. and Treas., 1988–90); Vice-Pres., 1992–94; Pres., 1994–Oct. 1996. Jt Chm., Mining (Scotland), 1993–; Chairman: Scotia Environmental Services, 1993–; Promenade Productions Ltd, 1994–. Chm., Finance Cttee, Greater Glasgow Health Board, 1984–87; Non-Exec. Dir, Scottish Prison Service, 1993–. Contested (C): Hamilton, 1970; W Renfrewshire, Feb. and Oct. 1974. Founder Chm., Soc. of Scottish Cons. Lawyers, 1982–86; Pres., Scottish Cons. & Unionist Assoc., 1989 (Hon. Sec., 1986–89). *Publications:* A Practitioner's Guide to Criminal Procedure, 1981; My Client, My Lord, 1981; A Practitioner's Guide to the Criminal Courts, 1985; Glasgow Rape Case, 1985; Fingertip Criminal Law, 1986; Rates Re-Valuation: the great myth, 1986; Devolution, 1988; New Unionism, 1992. *Recreations:* bridge, angling. *Address:* 23 Clabon Mews, Cadogan Square, SW1X 0EG. *Club:* Western (Glasgow).

HARPER, Joseph Charles; QC 1992; *b* 21 March 1939; *e s* of Frederick Charles Harper and Kitty (*née* Judah); *m* 1984, Sylvia Helen Turner (marr. diss. 1994); two *d*. *Educ:* Charterhouse; LSE (BA, LLB, LLM). ARCM 1960. Lectr, later Hd, Dept of Law, Kingston Poly., 1965–70; called to the Bar: Gray's Inn, 1970; Antigua, 1985. Mem. Council, Justice, 1979–91. *Publications:* (Specialist Editor) Hill and Redman, Law of Landlord and Tenant, 17th edn 1982, 18th edn 1988. *Recreations:* music (especially playing the French horn), bibliomania. *Address:* 4 Breams Buildings, EC4A 1AQ. *T:* 0171–353 5835. *Club:* Garrick.

HARPER, William Ronald; Divisional Director, Products and Services, Thames Water plc, since 1994; *b* 5 June 1944; *s* of William and Dorothy Harper; *m* 1969, Susan Penelope (*née* Rider); two *s* two *d*. *Educ:* Barton Peveril Grammar Sch., Eastleigh, Hants. IPFA 1965. Hampshire CC, 1960–64; Eastbourne CBC, 1964–68; Chartered Inst. of Public Finance and Accountancy, 1968–70; Greenwich London BC, 1970–74; Thames Water Authority: joined 1974; Dir of Finance, 1982; Dir of Corporate Strategy, 1984; Man. Dir, 1986; Dep. Chm., Thames Water Utilities, 1989; Bd Mem., Thames Water PLC, 1989; Gp Dir, Corporate Activities, 1992. Chm., Foundn for Water Res., 1989–94. Member: Council, Water Services Assoc., 1990–94; Bd of Management, Water Training, 1991– (Chm., 1993–). *Address:* Nugent House, Vastern Road, Reading, Berks RG1 8DB. *T:* Reading (01734) 399377.

HARPER GOW, Sir (Leonard) Maxwell, Kt 1985; MBE 1944; CIMgt; Director, 1952–87, Chairman, 1964–81, Vice-Chairman, 1981–87, Christian Salvesen PLC; *b* 13 June 1918; *s* of late Leonard Harper Gow and Eleanor Amalie (*née* Salvesen); *m* 1944, Lillan Margaret Kiaer; two *s* one *d*. *Educ:* Cargilfield; Rugby; Corpus Christi Coll., Cambridge Univ. (BA). CIMgt (FBIM 1976). Served War, 1939–46: Major RA 1st Commando Bde. 3 seasons with Antarctic Whaling Fleet, 1946–47, 1948–49 and 1952–53. Director: Scottish Widows' Fund and Life Assurance Soc., 1964–85 (Chm., 1972–75); Royal Bank of Scotland plc, 1965–87; Royal Bank of Scotland Group plc, 1978–87; DFM Holdings Ltd, 1985–89 (Chm., 1985–89); Radio Forth Ltd, 1973–89 (Chm., 1977–87). Member Council: Inst. of Directors, 1983–88; Scottish Council of Develt and Industry, 1972– (Vice Pres., 1985–88; elected Founder Fellow, 1987). Member, Queen's Body Guard for Scotland, the Royal Co. of Archers. Liveryman, Royal Co. of Shipwrights. Hon. Consul for Norway in Edinburgh/Leith, 1949–88. Comdr, Order of St Olav, Norway. *Recreations:* hill farming, fishing. *Address:* Eventyr, Lyars Road, Longniddry, East Lothian EH32 0PT. *T:* Longniddry (01875) 52142. *Club:* New (Edinburgh).

HARPHAM, Sir William, KBE 1966 (OBE 1948); CMG 1953; HM Diplomatic Service, retired; Director, Great Britain-East Europe Centre, 1967–80; *b* 3 Dec. 1906; *o s* of W. Harpham and N. Harpham (*née* Stout); *m* 1943, Isabelle Marie Sophie Droz; one *s* one *d*. *Educ:* Wintringham Secondary Sch., Grimsby; Christ's Coll., Cambridge. Entered Dept of Overseas Trade, 1929; transferred to Embassy, Brussels, 1931, Rome, 1934; Private Sec. to Parliamentary Sec. for Overseas Trade, 1936; seconded to League of Nations, 1937; reverted to Dept of Overseas Trade, 1939; served: Cairo, 1940–44; Beirut, 1944–47; appointed Counsellor (Commercial) at Berne, 1947; Head of Gen. Dept, Foreign Office, 1950–53; Dep. to UK Delegate to OEEC, 1953–56; Minister, British Embassy, Tokyo, 1956–59; Minister (Economic), Paris, 1959–63; Ambassador to Bulgaria, 1964–66; retd 1967. Order of Madara Horseman, Bulgaria, 1969; Order of Stara Planina, Bulgaria, 1976. *Address:* 9 Kings Keep, Putney Hill, SW15 6RA. *T:* 0181–788 1383. *Club:* Royal Automobile.

HARPUM, Charles; a Law Commissioner, since 1994; Fellow, Downing College, since 1977, and Lecturer in Law, since 1984, Cambridge University; *b* 29 March 1953; *s* of Dr John Richard Harpum and Beatrice Doreen Harpum (*née* Harper). *Educ:* Queen Elizabeth Grammar Sch., Penrith; Cheltenham Grammar Sch.; Downing Coll., Cambridge (BA 1st Cl. Hons with Dist. 1975; LLB 1st Cl. Hons with Dist. 1977; Chancellor's Medal; MA 1979). Called to the Bar, Lincoln's Inn, 1976; Asst Lectr in Law, Cambridge Univ., 1979–84. Vis. Schol., Sch. of Law, Univ. of Va, Charlottesville, USA, 1991. *Publications:* numerous articles on property law in learned jls. *Recreations:* travelling, listening to classical music, designing gardens, drinking single island malts. *Address:* Downing College, Cambridge CB2 1DQ; Law Commission, Conquest House, 37/38 John Street, Theobalds Road, WC1N 2BQ. *T:* 0171–453 1240.

HARRELL, Lynn Morris; 'cellist; Principal, Royal Academy of Music, 1993–95; *b* 30 Jan. 1944; *s* of Mack Harrell, Metropolitan Opera baritone and Marjorie Harrell (*née* Fulton), violinist; *m* 1976, Linda Blandford; one *s* one *d* (twins). *Educ:* Julliard Sch. of Music; Curtis Inst. of Music. Principal 'Cellist, Cleveland Orch., 1963–71; Professor: College Conservatory of Music, Cincinatti, 1971–77; Juilliard Sch. of Music, 1977–86; International Chair of 'Cello Studies, RAM, 1987–93; Piatigorsky Chair, Sch. of Music, USC, 1987–93; Artistic Dir, Los Angeles Philharmonic Inst., 1988–92. Numerous recording awards. *Recreations:* fishing, music. *Address:* c/o IMG Europe, 3 Burlington Lane, Chiswick, W4 2TH.

HARRER, Prof. Heinrich; author and explorer; awarded title of Professor by President of Austrian Republic, 1964; *b* Hüttenberg, 6 July 1912; *m*; one *s*; *m* 1953, Margaretha Truxa (marr. diss. 1958); *m* 1962, Katharina Haarhaus. *Educ:* University of Graz, Austria (graduated in Geography, 1938). First ascent, Eiger North Wall, 1938; Himalayan Expedition, 1939; interned in India, 1939–44; Tibet, 1944–51; Himalayan Expedition, 1951; expeditions: to the Andes, 1953; to Alaska, 1954; to Ruwenzori (Mountains of the Moon), Africa, 1957; to West New Guinea, 1961–62; to Nepal, 1965; to Xingu Red Indians in Mato Grosso, Brazil; to Bush Negroes of Surinam (Surinam Expedn with King Leopold of Belgium), 1966; to the Sudan, 1970; to North Borneo (Sabah) (with King Leopold of Belgium), 1971; N-S crossing of Borneo, 1972; Valley of Flowers (Alaknanda), 1974; Andaman Islands, 1975; Zangkar-Ladakh, 1976. Inauguration of Heinrich Harrer Mus., Hüttenberg, 1992. 35 short films on expeditions. Prize for best documentary book, Donanland, 1982; Orders from Germany, Austria, Carinthia, Styria, 70th birthday, 1982; highest orders from Carinthia, Styria, 80th birthday, 1992; Golden medal, Humboldt Soc., 1985; Medal, Explorers' Club, NY, 1991. Hon. Citizen, Hüttenberg, 1983. Austrian National Amateur Golf Champion, 1958; Austrian National Seniors Golf Champion, 1970. Hon. Pres., Austrian Golf Association, 1964 (Pres., 1949–64). *Publications:* Seven Years in Tibet, 1953 (Great Britain, and numerous other countries); Meine Tibet-Bilder, 1953 (Germany); The White Spider, History of the North Face of the Eiger, 1958; Tibet is My Country: Biography of Thubten Jigme Norbu, *e b* of Dalai Lama, 1960 (Eng.); I Come from the Stone Age, 1964 (London); The Last 500, 1975; The Last Caravan, 1976; Return to Tibet, 1984; Meine Forschungsreisen, 1986; Das Buch vom Eiger, 1988; Borneo, 1988; Bhutan, 1989; Lost Lhasa, 1992. *Address:* Neudorf 577, 9493–Mauren, Liechtenstein. *Clubs:* Explorers' (New York) (Hon. Mem.), Royal and Ancient (St Andrews); PEN (Liechtenstein).

HARRHY, Eiddwen Mair; soprano; *b* 14 April 1949; *d* of David and Emily Harrhy; *m* Greg Strange, journalist and broadcaster; one *d*. *Educ:* St Winefride's Convent, Swansea; Royal Manchester College of Music (Gold Medal Opera Prize); Paris (Miriam Licette Prize). Welsh Nat. Opera Chorus, 1970–71; Glyndebourne Festival Opera Chorus, 1971–73; début at Royal Opera House, Covent Garden, Wagner Ring Cycle, 1974; début, ENO, 1975; performances: Welsh Nat. Opera; La Scala Milan; Teatro Colon Buenos Aires; ENO; Glyndebourne; Opera North; Scottish Opera; UK and overseas orchestras; BBC promenade concerts; Australia, NZ, Hong Kong, S America, Europe, Scandinavia, USA; numerous recordings. Founder: Trust for Young Musicians, 1992; Crisis Messiah, 1992. *Recreations:* chamber music, ski-ing, enjoying Radios 3 and 4. *Address:* c/o The Broadcasting Company, 71 High Street, Cowbridge, S Glam CF7 7AF. *T:* Cowbridge (01446) 773344, *Fax:* (01446) 772261.

HARRIES, Rt. Rev. Richard Douglas; *see* Oxford, Bishop of.

HARRIMAN, Pamela; Ambassador of the United States of America to France, since 1994; *b* 20 March 1920; *e d* of 11th Baron Digby, KG, DSO, MC, TD; *m* 1st, 1939, Hon. Randolph Frederick Edward Spencer Churchill, MBE (marr. diss 1946; he *d* 1968); one *s*; 2nd, 1960, Leland Hayward (*d* 1971); 3rd, 1971, William Averell Harriman (*d* 1986). *Educ:* Downham Sch., Suffolk; Sorbonne. Mem., Democratic Nat. Cttee, 1988–93; Chm., Qly Policy Issues Forum, Democratic Govs Assoc., 1990–92; Nat. Co-Chm., Clinton-Gore campaign, 1990–92. Mem., Council on Foreign Relns; former Vice-Chm., Atlantic Council. Formerly: Vice-Pres., ESU of US; Trustee: Rockefeller Univ. Winston Churchill Foundn of US; Mem., Trustees Council, Nat. Gall. of Art; Hon. Trustee and Hon. Mem., Exec. Cttee, Brookings Instn. Former Member: Adv. Council, W. Averell Harriman Inst., Columbia Univ.; Bd of Dirs, Franklin and Eleanor Roosevelt Inst. Hon. LLD Columbia. *Address:* American Embassy, 2 avenue Gabriel, 75382 Paris, France. *T:* 43122755,

HARRINGTON, 11th Earl of, *cr* 1742; **William Henry Leicester Stanhope;** Viscount Stanhope of Mahon and Baron Stanhope of Elvaston, Co. Derby, 1717; Baron Harrington, 1729; Viscount Petersham, 1742; late Captain 15th/19th Hussars; *b* 24 Aug. 1922; *o s* of 10th Earl and Margaret Trelawney (Susan) (*d* 1952), *d* of Major H. H. D. Seaton; *S* father, 1929; *m* 1st, 1942, Eileen (from whom he obtained a divorce, 1946), *o d* of late Sir John Grey, Enville Hall, Stourbridge; one *s* one *d* (and one *d* decd); 2nd, 1947, Anne Theodora (from whom he obtained a divorce, 1962), *o d* of late Major Richard Arenbourg Blennerhassett Chute; one *s* two *d*; 3rd, 1964, Priscilla Margaret, *d* of Hon. A. E. Cubitt and Mrs Ronald Dawnay; one *s* one *d*. *Educ:* Eton; RMC, Sandhurst. Served War of 1939–45, demobilised 1946. Owns about 700 acres. Became Irish Citizen, 1965. *Heir:* *s* Viscount Petersham, *qv*. *Address:* Greenmount Stud, Patrickswell, Co. Limerick, Eire.

See also Baron Ashcombe, Earl Cawdor.

HARRINGTON, Dr Albert Blair, CB 1979; Head of Civil Service Department Medical Advisory Service, 1976–79; *b* 26 April 1914; *s* of late Albert Timothy Harrington and Lily Harrington; *m* 1939, Valerie White; one *d*. *Educ:* Brisbane Grammar Sch., Qld; Aberdeen Univ. MB, ChB 1938, MD 1944. House Phys., Woodend Hosp., Aberdeen, 1938–39; service in RAMC (Field Amb., Blood Transfusion Phys., Neurologist), 1940–45; MO (Head Injuries) and Dep. Supt, Stoke Mandeville Hosp., 1946–48; Med. Supt, Dunston Hill Hosp., Gateshead, 1948–50; SMO (Pensions), Cleveleys, 1950–53; Med. Supt, Queen Mary's Hosp., Roehampton, 1954–56; SMO, Dept of Health (Hosp. Bldg and later Regional Liaison Duties), 1956–68; PMO (Hosp. Bldg), 1968–73; SPMO (Under-Sec.), DHSS, 1973–76. Chm., CS Med. Appts Bds, 1979–86. FFCM (Foundn Fellow) 1972. *Publications:* articles on Sjögren's Disease, paralytic poliomyelitis, and hospital planning, medical care and the work of the Medical Advisory Service. *Recreations:* gardening, country life; formerly tennis. *Address:* 59 Lauderdale Drive, Petersham, Richmond, Surrey TW10 7BS. *T:* 0181–940 1345. *Club:* Athenæum.

HARRINGTON, Illtyd, JP; DL; *b* 14 July 1931; *s* of Timothy Harrington and Sarah (*née* Burchell); unmarried. *Educ:* St Illtyd's RC Sch., Dowlais; Merthyr County Sch.; Trinity Coll., Caermarthen. Member: Paddington Borough Council, 1959–64; Westminster City Council, 1964–68 and 1971–78, Leader, Lab. Gp, 1972–74; GLC, 1964–67 and for Brent S, 1973–86: Alderman, 1970–73; Chairman, Policy and Resources Cttee, 1973–77, Special Cttee, 1985–86; Dep. Leader, 1973–77, 1981–84; Dep. Leader of the Opposition,

1977–81; Chm. of the Council, 1984–85. Special Advr to Chm. and Leader of ILEA, 1988–90. JP Willesden 1968. First Chairman, Inland Waterways Amenity Adv. Council, 1968–71; Chm., London Canals Consultative Cttee, 1965–67, 1981–; Vice Pres., IWA, 1990–; Member: British Waterways Bd, 1974–82; BTA, 1976–80. Member: Bd, Theatre Royal, Stratford E, 1978–; Bd, Wiltons Music Hall, 1979–; Nat. Theatre Bd, 1975–77; Bd, National Youth Theatre, 1976–; Globe Theatre Trust, 1986–; Chm., Half Moon Theatre, 1978–90; Director: Soho Poly Theatre, 1981–; The Young Vic, 1981–. President: Grand Union Canal Soc., 1974–; Islington Boat Club, 1985–; SE Region, IWA, 1986–; Immunity (Legal aid facility for AIDS victims), 1986–; Chairman: Kilburn Skills, 1977–; Battersea Park Peace Pagoda, 1984–; Limehouse Basin Users Gp, 1986–; Vice Pres., Coventry Canal Soc., 1970–. Patron, Westminster Cathedral Appeal, 1977–. Gov., London Marathon, 1980–91. Trustee: Kew Bridge Pumping Mus., 1976–; Chiswick Family Rescue, 1978–; Queen's Jubilee Walkway, 1986–; Arthur Koestler Awards for Prisoners, 1987–; CARE, 1987–; Dominica Overseas Student Fund, 1987–; Mem., Montgomery Canal Trust, 1988–; Managing Trustee, Mutual Municipal Insurance Co., 1985–. Governor, Brunel Univ., 1981–87. DL Greater London, 1986. Contributor, The Guardian, 1982–. *Recreations:* a slave to local government; laughing, singing and incredulity. *Address:* 16 Lea House, Salisbury Street, NW8 8BJ. *T:* 0171–402 6356. *Club:* Savile.

HARRINGTON, Prof. (John) Malcolm, CBE 1992; MD; FRCP, FFOM, FFOMI; Foundation Professor of Occupational Health, University of Birmingham, since 1981; *b* 6 April 1942; *s* of John Roy Harrington and Veda Naomi Harrington; *m* 1967, Madeline Mary Davies; one *d*. *Educ:* King's Coll., London (BSc, MSc); Westminster Hosp. Med. Sch. MD 1976; FFOM 1981; FRCP 1982. Hospital appointments, 1966–69; Lectr in Occupational Medicine, LSHTM, 1969–75; Vis. Scientist, Centers for Disease Control, Atlanta, US Public Health Service, 1975–77; Sen. Lectr in Occupational Medicine, LSHTM, 1977–80. Chm., Ind. Injuries Adv. Council, 1982–. *Publications:* (ed jtly) Occupational Hygiene, 1980, 2nd edn 1995; (with F. S. Gill) Occupational Health, 1983, 3rd edn 1992; (ed) Recent Advances in Occupational Health, Vol. 2 1984, Vol. 3 1987; papers in scientific professional jls. *Recreations:* music, gardening, cricket, reading biographies, theatre. *Address:* Institute of Occupational Health, University of Birmingham, Edgbaston, Birmingham B15 2TT. *T:* 0121–414 6022. *Club:* Royal Society of Medicine.

HARRINGTON, Patrick John; QC 1993; a Recorder, since 1991; *b* 23 June 1949; *s* of late Murtagh Joseph Harrington and of Eileen Mary Harrington (*née* Kelly); *m* 1975, Susan Jane, *d* of Captain K. W. Bradley, RN retd; one *s* one *d*. *Educ:* Ebbw Vale Grammar Sch.; Birmingham Coll. of Commerce. LLB Hons London. Called to the Bar, Gray's Inn, 1973. Chm., Gwent Health Research Ethics Cttee, 1993–. *Recreations:* music, sport, especially ski-ing, classic motoring. *Address:* 30 Park Place, Cardiff CF1 3BA. *T:* Cardiff (01222) 398421. *Club:* Cardiff and County.

HARRIS, family name of **Barons Harris, Harris of Greenwich, Harris of High Cross** and of **Earl of Malmesbury.**

HARRIS, 6th Baron *cr* 1815, of Seringapatam and Mysore, and of Belmont, Kent; **George Robert John Harris;** Captain RA, retired; *b* 17 April 1920; *s* of 5th Baron Harris, CBE, MC, and Dorothy Mary (*d* 1981), *d* of Rev. W. J. Crookes; *S* father, 1984. *Educ:* Eton; Christ Church, Oxford. *Heir: cousin* Derek Marshall Harris [*b* 23 July 1916; *m* 1938, Laura Cecilia, *e d* of late Major Edmund Thomas William McCausland, Gurkha Rifles; one *s* one *d*]. *Address:* Huntingfield, Eastling, near Faversham, Kent.

HARRIS OF GREENWICH, Baron *cr* 1974 (Life Peer), of Greenwich; **John Henry Harris;** director of companies; *b* Harrow, Middlesex, 5 April 1930; *s* of late Alfred George and May Harris; *m* 1st, 1952, Patricia Margaret Alstrom (marr. diss. 1982); one *s* one *d*; 2nd, 1983, Angela Smith. *Educ:* Pinner County Grammar Sch., Middlesex. Journalist on newspapers in Bournemouth, Leicester, Glasgow and London. National Service with Directorate of Army Legal Services, WO. Personal assistant to Rt Hon. Hugh Gaitskell when Leader of the Opposition, 1959–62; Director of Publicity, Labour Party, 1962–64, Special Assistant: to Foreign Secretary, 1964–65; to Rt Hon. Roy Jenkins as Home Secretary, 1965–Nov. 1967, and as Chancellor, Nov. 1967–1970. Staff of Economist newspaper, 1970–74. Minister of State, Home Office, 1974–79. Spokesman on home affairs, Lib Dem, House of Lords, 1988–94; Lib Dem Chief Whip, H of L, 1994–. Mem., H of L Select Cttee on Murder and Life Imprisonment, 1988–89. Chm., Parole Bd for England and Wales, 1979–82; Pres., Nat. Assoc. of Senior Probation Officers, 1983–92; Trustee, Police Foundn (Chm., Exec. Cttee), 1980–. Eisenhower Exchange Fellow from UK, 1972. Mem. Council, Harlow, Essex, 1957–63, Chm. Council 1960–61, Leader of Labour Gp, 1961–63. Mem. Exec. Cttee, Britain in Europe, referendum campaign, 1975 (Jt Chm., Publicity Cttee). *Address:* House of Lords, SW1A 0PW. *Clubs:* Reform, MCC.

HARRIS OF HIGH CROSS, Baron *cr* 1979 (Life Peer), of Tottenham in Greater London; **Ralph Harris;** Founder President, Institute of Economic Affairs, since 1990 (General Director, 1957–87, Chairman, 1987–89); *b* 10 Dec. 1924; *m* 1949, Jose Pauline Jeffery; one *s* one *d* (and one *s* decd). *Educ:* Tottenham Grammar Sch.; Queens' Coll., Cambridge (Exhibr, Foundn Schol.). 1st Cl. Hons Econs, MA Cantab. Lectr in Polit. Economy, St Andrews Univ., 1949–56. Contested (C): Kirkcaldy, 1951; Edinburgh Central, 1955. Leader-writer, Glasgow Herald, 1956. Trustee, Wincott Foundn; Trustee and Hon. Treasurer, Ross McWhirter Foundn. Chairman: Council, FARM Africa, 1988–91; Bruges Gp, 1989–91; FOREST, 1989–; Jt Chm., Internat. Centre for Res. into Economic Transformation, Moscow, 1990–. Mem. Council, Univ. of Buckingham; Dir, (Independent National) Times Newspapers Hldgs Ltd, 1988–. Free Enterprise Award, 1976. Hon. DSc Buckingham, 1984. *Publications:* Politics without Prejudice, a biography of R. A. Butler, 1956; Hire Purchase in a Free Society, 1958, 3rd edn 1961; (with Arthur Seldon) Advertising in a Free Society, 1959; Advertising in Action, 1962; Advertising and the Public, 1962; (with A. P. Herbert) Libraries: Free for All?, 1962; Choice in Welfare, 1963; Essays in Rebirth of Britain, 1964; Choice in Welfare, 1965; Right Turn, 1970; Choice in Welfare, 1970; Down with the Poor, 1971; (with Brendan Sewill) British Economic Policy 1970–74, 1975; Crisis '75, 1975; Catch '76, 1976; Freedom of Choice: consumers or conscripts, 1976; (with Arthur Seldon) Pricing or Taxing, 1976; Not from Benevolence, 1977; (ed, with Arthur Seldon) The Coming Confrontation, 1978; (with Arthur Seldon) Over-ruled on Welfare, 1979; End of Government, 1980; Challenge of a Radical Reactionary, 1981; No, Minister!, 1985; What Price Democracy?, 1985; The Enemies of Progress, 1986; (with Arthur Seldon) Welfare Without the State, 1987; Beyond the Welfare State, 1988; columnist in Truth, Statist, etc. *Recreations:* conjuring and devising spells against over-government. *Address:* 4 Walmar Close, Beech Hill, Hadley Wood, Barnet, Herts EN4 0LA. *Clubs:* Political Economy, Mont Pelerin Society.

HARRIS, Prof. Adrian Llewellyn, FRCP; Imperial Cancer Research Fund Professor of Clinical Oncology, Oxford University, since 1988; *b* 10 Aug. 1950; *s* of Luke and Julia Harris; *m* 1975, Margaret Susan Denman; one *s* one *d*. *Educ:* Univ. of Liverpool (BSc Hons Biochem. 1970; MB ChB Hons 1973); DPhil Oxon 1978. MRCP 1975, FRCP 1985. Hosp. appts, Liverpool, 1973–74; Clinical Scientist, MRC Clinical Pharmacology Unit, Radcliffe Infirmary, Oxford and Nuffield Dept of Medicine, 1975–78; Registrar in Academic Unit, Royal Free Hosp., 1978–80; Lectr and Sen. Registrar, Inst. for Cancer Res., Royal Marsden Hosp., 1980–82; Vis. Researcher, Imp. Cancer Res. Fund Mutagenesis Lab., London, 1982–83; Prof. of Clinical Oncology, Newcastle upon Tyne Univ., 1983–88. *Publications:* papers on growth factors in cancer, mechanisms by which cancers become resistant to treatment, hormone and drug treatment of cancer. *Recreations:* swimming, modern dance, science fiction. *Address:* Imperial Cancer Research Fund Clinical Oncology Unit, Churchill Hospital, Headington, Oxford OX3 7LJ. *T:* Oxford (01865) 64841.

HARRIS, Prof. Sir Alan (James), Kt 1980; CBE 1968; BScEng, FEng, FICE, FIStructE; Senior Partner, Harris & Sutherland, Consulting Engineers, 1955–81, consultant since 1981; Professor of Concrete Structures, Imperial College, London, 1973–81, now Emeritus; *b* 8 July 1916; *s* of Walter Herbert Harris and Ethel Roach, Plymouth; *m* 1948, Marie Thérèse, *d* of Prof. Paul Delcourt, Paris; two *s*. *Educ:* Owen's Sch., Islington; Northampton Polytechnic (London Univ.). Local Government engineer, 1933–40; served Royal Engineers (Mulberry, Rhine Bridges) (despatches), 1940–46; with Eugène Freyssinet in Paris studying prestressing, 1946–49; Director, Prestressed Concrete Co. Ltd, 1949–55; in private practice, 1955–81. Member: Council, Agrément Board, 1968–81; Engrg Council, 1981–84; part-time Board Mem., Property Services Agency, 1974–78; Pres., Hydraulics Research Station, 1989– (Chm., 1982–89). President, Instn of Structural Engineers, 1978–79 (Gold Medal, 1984). Trustee, Imperial War Museum, 1983–90. Hon. DSc: City, 1982; Aston, 1982; Exeter, 1984. Croix de Guerre (France) 1945; Ordre du Mérite (France) 1975. *Publications:* numerous papers in learned jls. *Recreation:* sailing. *Address:* 128 Ashley Gardens, Thirleby Road, SW1P 1HL. *T:* 0171–834 6924.

HARRIS, Anne Macintosh, (Mrs H. J. L. Harris), CBE 1985; National Chairman, National Federation of Women's Institutes, 1981–85; *b* 17 April 1925; *d* of Montague Macintosh Williams and Marguerite Anne Williams (*née* Barrington); *m* 1950, Henry John Leshley Harris; one *s* three *d*. *Educ:* Battle Abbey Sch.; Swanley Horticultural Coll. and Wye Coll. (Swanley Dip. in Horticulture, 1946). Owned and ran nursery/market garden and shop, 1946–53. Mem., WI, 1947–; Mem., NFWI Exec. Cttee, 1973–85 (Vice-Chm., 1979–81); Chm., NFWI Markets Sub-Cttee, 1972–79; WI representative: on Women's National Commn, 1982–85; on Advertising Adv. Cttee, IBA, 1984–87. Mem. Council Nat. Trust, 1981–85. Trustee, Help the Aged, 1985–. Chm., Tunbridge Wells East District Local Assoc. Girl Guides, 1963–79; Vice-Chm., Brenchley PCC, 1978–82. FRSA 1986. *Recreations:* gardening, walking, reading, music. *Club:* Agricola Club and Swanley Guild (Wye).

HARRIS, Anthony David, CMG 1995; LVO 1979; HM Diplomatic Service; Ambassador to the United Arab Emirates, since 1994; *b* 13 Oct. 1941; *s* of Reginald William Harris and Kathleen Mary Harris (*née* Daw); *m* 1st, 1970, Patricia Ann Over (marr. diss. 1988); one *s*; 2nd, 1988, Sophie Kisling; two *s* one *d*. *Educ:* Plymouth College; Exeter College, Oxford (BA, 2nd cl. Hons Lit. Hum.). Third Sec., Commonwealth Relations Office, 1964; Middle East Centre for Arab Studies, Lebanon, 1965; Third, later Second Sec., and Vice-Consul, Jedda, 1967; Second Sec. (Inf.), Khartoum, 1969; First Sec., FCO, 1972; First Sec., Head of Chancery and Consul, Abu Dhabi, 1975; First Sec., UK Mission to UN, Geneva, 1979; Counsellor, FCO, 1982; seconded to MoD as Regl Marketing Dir 1 (Arabian Peninsula and Pakistan), 1983; Dep. Head of Mission, Cairo, 1986; Head of Information Dept, FCO, 1990–93; Scrutiny of Security in FCO, 1993–94. *Recreations:* shooting (HM the Queen's Prize, Bisley, 1964; British team to Canada, 1974), skiing, climbing, diving. *Address:* c/o Foreign and Commonwealth Office, SW1A 2AH. *Clubs:* Reform; North London Rifle, Commonwealth Rifle (Bisley).

HARRIS, Anthony Geoffrey S.; *see* Stoughton-Harris.

HARRIS, Anthony George, OBE 1991; Principal, Harper Adams Agricultural College, 1977–94, retired; *b* 29 July 1929; *s* of John and Emily Kate Harris; *m* 1955, Sylvia Pyle; two *s* one *d* (and one *s* decd). *Educ:* Seale-Hayne Agricl Coll. (NDA, CDA Hons). FIBiol, FRAgS. Lectr in Agric., Dorset Coll. of Agric., 1953–55, Lectr in Crop Production, Harper Adams Agricl Coll., 1955–58; Vice-Principal, Walford Coll. of Agric., 1958–66; Principal, Merrist Wood Agric. Coll., 1967–77. *Publications:* Crop Husbandry, 1961; Farm Machinery, 1965, 2nd edn 1974. *Recreations:* walking, reading. *Club:* Farmers'.

HARRIS, Rt. Rev. Mgr. Anthony John, SCA; priest, Our Lady of the Visitation, Greenford, since 1994; *b* 6 May 1940; *s* of Philip John Harris and Eileen (*née* Kelly). *Educ:* St Patrick's Seminary, Thurles, Co. Tipperary (graduated in Phil. and Theol.). Ordained as Pallottine Priest, 1965; Dean of Discipline, 1965; Assistant Priest: Clerkenwell, 1965–68; Hastings, 1968–73; joined Chaplains' Br., RAF, 1973; served in UK, Germany, Cyprus and Ascension Island; Asst Principal Chaplain, 1986–92; Prin. RC Chaplain to RAF, 1992–94. VG. *Recreations:* walking, swimming. *Address:* Our Lady of the Visitation, Greenford Road, Greenford, Middx UB6 9AN. *Club:* Royal Air Force.

HARRIS, Prof. Anthony Leonard, CGeol; FRSE, FGS; Professor of Geology, since 1987, and Dean, Faculty of Science, since 1994, University of Liverpool; *b* 11 May 1935; *s* of Thomas Haydn Harris and Dora Harris (*née* Wilkinson); *m* 1959, Noreen Jones; one *s* one *d*. *Educ:* Cardiff High Sch.; University College of Wales, Aberystwyth (BSc, PhD). Geologist and Principal Geologist, British Geol. Survey, 1959–71; Liverpool University: Lectr, Sen. Lectr, then Reader, 1971–87; Head, Dept of Earth Scis, 1987–94. Pres., Geolog. Soc., 1990–92. Major John Coke Medal, Geolog. Soc., 1985; C. T. Clough Meml Medal, Geolog. Soc. of Edinburgh, 1989. *Publications:* (ed and contrib.) Caledonides of the British Isles, 1979; The Caledonian-Appalachian Orogen, 1988; papers in learned jls. *Recreations:* music, ornithology. *Address:* Department of Earth Sciences, University of Liverpool, PO Box 147, Liverpool L69 3BX; 12 Aigburth Hall Road, Liverpool L19 9DQ.

HARRIS, Sir Anthony (Travers Kyrle), 2nd Bt *cr* 1953; retired; *b* 18 March 1918; *s* of Marshal of the RAF Sir Arthur Travers Harris, 1st Bt, GCB, OBE, AFC, and Barbara Kyrle, *d* of Lt-Col E. W. K. Money, 85th KSLI; *S* father, 1984. *Educ:* Oundle. Served European War, 1939–45 with Queen Victoria's Rifles and Wiltshire Regt; Auxiliary Units, 1941; ADC to GOC-in-C Eastern Command, 1944. Reader for MGM, 1951–52; subsequently work with antiques and objets d'art. *Recreations:* music, horology. *Heir:* none. *Address:* 33 Cheyne Court, Flood Street, SW3 5TR.

See also R.J. Harris.

HARRIS, Rt. Rev. Augustine; Bishop (RC) of Middlesbrough, 1978–92, retired; *b* 27 Oct. 1917; *s* of Augustine Harris and Louisa Beatrice (*née* Rycroft). *Educ:* St Francis Xavier's Coll., Liverpool; Upholland Coll., Lancs. Ordained, 1942; Curate at: St Oswald's, Liverpool, 1942–43; St Elizabeth's, Litherland, Lancs, 1943–52; Prison Chaplain, HM Prison, Liverpool, 1952–65; Sen. RC Priest, Prison Dept, 1957–66; English Rep. to Internat. Coun. of Sen. Prison Chaplains (RC), 1957–66; Titular Bishop of Socia and Auxiliary Bishop of Liverpool, 1965–78. Mem. Vatican Delegn to UN Quinquennial Congress on Crime, London, 1960 and Stockholm, 1965; Liaison between English and Welsh Hierarchy (RC) and Home Office, 1966–; Episcopal Moderator to Fédération Internationale des Associations Médicales Catholiques, 1967–76; Episcopal Pres., Commn for Social Welfare (England and Wales), 1972–83; Chm., Dept for Social Responsibility,

Bishops Conf. of Eng. and Wales, 1984–92. Mem. Central Religious Advisory Council to BBC and IBA, 1974–78. *Publications:* articles for criminological works. *Address:* 17 Old Town Lane, Formby, Merseyside L37 3HJ.

HARRIS, Basil Vivian, CEng, MIEE; Chief Engineer, Communications Division, Foreign and Commonwealth Office, 1979–81, retired; *b* 11 July 1921; *s* of late Henry William and Sarah May Harris; *m* 1943, Myra Winifred Mildred Newport. *Educ:* Watford Grammar School. GPO Engineering Dept (Research), 1939; served RAF, 1943–46; GPO Engineering Dept (Radio Branch), 1946; Diplomatic Wireless Service, FCO, 1963; Dep. Chief Engineer, Communications Division, FCO, 1971. *Publications:* contribs to technical jls on communications. *Recreations:* golf, photography, travel. *Address:* 13 Decoy Drive, Eastbourne, Sussex BN22 0AB. *T:* Eastbourne (01323) 505819. *Club:* Royal Eastbourne Golf.

HARRIS, Ven. Brian; *see* Harris, Ven. R. B.

HARRIS, Brian Nicholas, FRICS; a Senior Partner, Richard Ellis, Chartered Surveyors and International Property Consultants (Chairman of Partnership, 1984–93; Partner, since 1961); *b* 12 Dec. 1931; *s* of Claude Harris and Dorothy (*née* Harris); *m* 1961, Rosalyn Marion Caines; two *d*. *Educ:* King Alfred's Sch., Wantage; College of Estate Management. Chartered Surveyor. Chm., City of London Br. of RICS, 1984–85; Member of Council: London Chamber of Commerce, 1985– (Dep. Chm., 1990–92; Pres., 1992–94; Bd Mem., 1989–); ABCC, 1992– (Mem. Bd, 1994–; Chm., Southern Reg., 1994–); Australian British Chamber of Commerce (UK), 1986–; Mem., Aust. and NZ Trade Adv. Cttee, 1991–. Chm., Heathrow Airport Support Gp, 1993–; Bd Mem., London First, 1993–94. Gov., Woldingham Sch., 1986–93 (Dep. Chm., 1991–93). FRSA 1987. Liveryman, 1975, Mem., Ct of Assistants, 1990, Co. of Glaziers and Painters of Glass. *Recreations:* flyfishing, gardening, golf. *Address:* Grants Paddock, Grants Lane, Limpsfield, Surrey RH8 0RQ. *T:* Oxted (01883) 723215. *Clubs:* Carlton, City of London, Flyfishers'.

HARRIS, Brian Thomas, OBE 1983; QC 1982; *b* 14 Aug. 1932; *s* of Thomas and Eleanor Harris; *m* 1957, Janet Rosina Harris (*née* Hodgson); one *s* one *d*. *Educ:* Henry Thornton Grammar Sch.; King's Coll., Univ. of London. LLB (Hons). Called to the Bar, Gray's Inn, 1960; joined London Magistrates' Courts, 1963; Clerk to the Justices, Poole, 1967–85; Dir, Professional Conduct Dept, 1985–94, Sec., Exec. Cttee, Jt Disciplinary Scheme, 1986–94, ICAEW. Member: Juvenile Courts Committee, Magistrates' Assoc., 1973–85; NACRO Juvenile Crime Adv. Cttee, 1982–85; former member: CCETSW working party on legal trng of social workers (report, 1974); NACRO cttee on diversion (Zander report, 1975); HO/DHSS working party on operation of Children and Young Persons' Act 1969 (report, 1978); ABAFA working party on care proceedings (report, 1979). Pres., Justices' Clerks Soc., 1981–82. Editor, Justice of the Peace Review, 1982–85 (Legal Editor, 1973; Jt Editor, 1978). *Publications:* Criminal Jurisdiction of Magistrates, 1969, 11th edn 1988; Warrants of Search and Entry, 1973; The Courts, the Press and the Public, 1976; The Rehabilitation of Offenders Act 1974, 1976, 2nd edn 1988; New Law of Family Proceedings in Magistrates' Courts, 1979; (ed jtly) Clarke Hall and Morrison on Children, 1985; The Law and Practice of Disciplinary and Regulatory Proceedings, 1995; The Tribunal Member, 1995; (ed) entry on Magistrates in Halsbury's Laws of England, 4th edn 1979. *Recreation:* the contemplation of verse. *Address:* Church Barn, High Street, Yardley Hastings, Northants NN7 1ER. *T:* Yardley Hastings (01604) 696387.

HARRIS, Cecil Rhodes, FCIS, FSCA; Deputy Chairman, Trade Indemnity PLC, 1986–93; Chief Executive, Commercial Union Assurance Company Ltd, 1982–85; *b* 4 May 1923; *s* of Frederick William Harris and Dorothy Violet Plum; *m* 1946, Gwenyth Evans; one *s* two *d*. *Educ:* private schools. FCIS 1950; FSCA 1951. Joined Employers Liability Assurance, 1949, Asst Sec., 1961–64, Overseas Manager, Northern & Employers, 1965–68; Commercial Union Assurance Co. Ltd: Asst Gen. Man., 1969–73; Dep. Gen. Man., 1974; Dir and Sec., 1975–78; Exec. Dir, 1979; Dep. Chief Gen. Man., 1980–82. *Recreations:* tennis, study of the Scriptures. *Address:* Ashley, 35a Plough Lane, Purley, Surrey CR8 3QJ. *T:* 0181–668 2820.

HARRIS, Charles; *see* Harris, G. C. W.

HARRIS, Sir Charles Herbert S.; *see* Stuart-Harris.

HARRIS, Prof. Christopher John, DPhil; Professor of Mathematical Economics, University of Cambridge and Fellow, King's College, Cambridge, since 1995; *b* 22 Sept. 1960; *s* of Colin Christopher Harris and Barbara Kay (*née* Hall); *m* 1993, Qun Li. *Educ:* Oundle Sch.; Corpus Christi Coll., Oxford (BA Maths 1981); Nuffield Coll., Oxford (MPhil Econ 1983; DPhil Econ 1984). Prize Research Fellow, Nuffield Coll., Oxford, 1983–84; Univ. Lectr in Econs, Univ. of Oxford and Fellow of Nuffield Coll., 1984–94. Vis. Prof., MIT, 1990–91. *Publications:* articles on dynamic games and theory of industrial organisation in Econometrica, Rev. of Econ. Studies, Jl of Econ. Theory, etc. *Recreations:* walking, running, swimming. *Address:* Faculty of Economics and Politics, Austin Robinson Building, Sidgwick Avenue, Cambridge CB3 9DD.

HARRIS, David; Director, Commission of the European Communities, Directorate for Social and Demographic Statistics, 1973–87; *b* 28 Dec. 1922; *s* of David and Margaret Jane Harris; *m* 1946, Mildred Alice Watson; two *d*. *Educ:* Bootle Grammar Sch.; LSE (BScEcon). FSS. Statistician, BoT, 1960; Statistician 1966 and Chief Statistician 1968, HM Treasury; Chief Statistician, Central Statistical Office, Cabinet Office, 1969. *Recreations:* tennis, swimming, economics. *Address:* 64 Rue de Rodenbourg, 6950 Olingen, Luxembourg.

HARRIS, David Anthony; MP (C) St Ives, since 1983; *b* 1 Nov. 1937; *s* of late E. C. Harris and Betty Harris; *m* 1962, Diana Joan Hansford; one *s* one *d*. *Educ:* Mount Radford Sch., Exeter. Jun. Reporter, Express and Echo, Exeter, 1954–58. Nat. Service, commnd Devonshire and Dorset Regt, 1958; Staff Captain (Public Relns) GHQ, MELF, 1959. Reporter, Western Morning News, 1960–61; joined Daily Telegraph, Westminster Staff, 1961; Political Correspondent, Daily Telegraph, 1976–79; MEP (C) Cornwall and Plymouth, 1979–84. Chm., Parly Lobby Journalists, 1977–78. Mem. (C) Bromley, and Bromley, Ravensbourne, GLC, 1968–77; Chm. Thamesmead Cttee, 1971–73. Contested (C), Mitcham and Morden, Feb. 1974. PPS to Minister of State for Foreign and Commonwealth Affairs, 1987–88, to Sec. of State for Foreign and Commonwealth Affairs, 1988–89, to Dep. Prime Minister and Leader of Commons, 1989–90. Member, Select Committee: on Agriculture, 1983–87; on Broadcasting, 1988–; on Foreign Affairs, 1991–; on Social Security, 1991–92. Chairman: Cons. Fisheries Cttee, 1987–; W Country Cons. MPs, 1991–92. President: Sea Safety Gp UK, 1992–; Lizard Lifeboat, 1990–. *Recreations:* gardening, walking the dog. *Address:* House of Commons, SW1A 0AA. *Club:* Farmers'.

HARRIS, (David) Kenneth, CBE 1992; journalist, author and broadcaster; Chairman, George Outram & Co. Ltd, later Caledonian Newspaper Publishing, 1981–92; Director, The Observer Ltd, since 1978; *b* 11 Nov. 1919; *s* of David and Kathleen Harris; *m* 1st, 1949, Doris Young-Smith (*d* 1970); 2nd, 1987, Jocelyn Rymer. *Educ:* Trowbridge High Sch.; Wadham Coll., Oxford. Served War, RA, 1940–45. Sheffield Telegraph, 1948–50; The Observer: Washington Corresp., 1950–53; Editl Staff, 1953–76; Associate Editor, 1976–84. Freelance TV and radio broadcaster, BBC and ITV, 1957–85. Debating tour for Oxford Union, USA, 1947; Founder, Observer Mace Debating Tournaments, 1953; Chm., ESU Overseas Debating Selection Cttee, 1960–. *Publications:* Travelling Tongues, 1949; Conversations, 1967; Talking To - - -, 1971; Attlee (authorised biog.), 1982; David Owen Personally Speaking, 1987; Thatcher, 1988; The Queen, 1993. *Recreations:* walking, horse racing, fishing, reading. *Address:* 45 Molyneux Street, W1H 5HW. *T:* 0171–262 6172. *Club:* Athenæum.

HARRIS, David Michael; QC 1989; a Recorder, since 1988; *b* 7 Feb. 1943; *s* of Maurice and Doris Harris; *m* 1970, Emma Lucia Calma; two *s* one *d*. *Educ:* Liverpool Institute High School for Boys; Lincoln Coll., Oxford (BA 1964; MA 1967); Trinity Hall, Cambridge (PhD 1969). Asst Lectr in Law, Manchester Univ., 1967–69. Called to the Bar, Middle Temple, 1969; Asst Recorder, 1984–88; a Dep. High Ct Judge, 1993–. *Publications:* (ed jtly) Winfield and Jolowicz on Tort, 9th edn, 1971; (ed jtly) Supplement to Bingham's Modern Cases on Negligence, 3rd edn, 1985. *Recreations:* the Arts, travel, sport. *Address:* Peel House (Third Floor), 5–7 Harrington Street, Liverpool L2 9XN. *T:* 0151–236 0718.

HARRIS, Prof. David Russell, FSA; Professor of Human Environment, since 1979, and Director, since 1989, Institute of Archaeology, University College London; *b* 14 Dec. 1930; *s* of Dr Herbert Melville Harris and Norah Mary Harris; *m* 1957, Helen Margaret Wilson; four *d*. *Educ:* St Christopher Sch., Letchworth; Oxford Univ. (MA, BLitt); Univ. of California, Berkeley (PhD). Nat. Service, RAF, 1949–50. Teaching Asst and Instructor, Univ. of California, 1956–58; Lectr, QMC, London, 1958–64; Lectr and Reader, UCL, 1964–79. Member: Mus. of London Archaeol. Cttee, 1984–; English Heritage Sci. and Conservation Panel, 1985–; Chm., Sci.-based Archaeol. Cttee, SERC, 1989–92. President: Prehistoric Soc., 1990–94; UK Chapter, Soc. for Economic Botany, 1995–. *Publications:* Plants, Animals and Man in the Outer Leeward Islands, 1965; (with B. W. Hodder) Africa in Transition, 1967; Human Ecology in Savanna Environments, 1980; (with G. C. Hillman) Foraging and Farming, 1989; Settling Down and Breaking Ground: rethinking the neolithic revolution, 1990; (with K. D. Thomas) Modelling Ecological Change, 1991; The Archaeology of V. Gordon Childe, 1994; The Origins and Spread of Agriculture and Pastoralism in Eurasia, 1996. *Recreations:* mountain walking, archaeological-ecological travel. *Address:* Institute of Archaeology, University College London, 31–34 Gordon Square, WC1H 0PY. *T:* 0171–380 7483. *Club:* Athenæum.

HARRIS, Dame Diana R.; *see* Reader Harris.

HARRIS, Rev. Donald Bertram; Vicar of St Paul's, Knightsbridge, 1955–78; *b* 4 Aug. 1904; unmarried. *Educ:* King's Coll. Choir Sch., Cambridge; Haileybury Coll.; King's Coll., Cambridge; Cuddesdon Coll., Oxford. Chorister, King's Coll. Choir, 1915–19; Choral Scholar, King's Coll., Cambridge, 1923–26; BA 1925; MA 1929; Ordained Deacon, 1927; Priest, 1928; Curate of Chesterfield Parish Church, 1927–31; St Mary the Less, Cambridge, 1931–36. Chaplain of King's Coll., Cambridge, 1932–33; Examg Chaplain to Bishop of Wakefield, 1932–36; Rector of Great Greenford, Middx, 1936–45; Archdeacon of Bedford 1946–55, and Rector of St Mary's Bedford, 1945–55, Life Governor, Haileybury and Imperial Service Coll., 1946–. Pres., Assoc. for Promoting Retreats, 1968–71. *Address:* 105 Marsham Court, Marsham Street, SW1P 4LA. *T:* 0171–828 1132. *Club:* Royal Thames Yacht.

HARRIS, Dr Edmund Leslie, CB 1981; FRCP, FRCPE, FFPHM, FFPM; Director of Medical Services, Disablement Services Authority, 1988–91, retired; *b* 11 April 1928; *s* of late M. H. and S. Harris; *m* 1959, Robina Semple (*née* Potter). *Educ:* Univ. of Witwatersrand. MB, BCh 1952; MRCPE 1959, FRCPE 1971, MRCP 1959, FRCP 1975; MFCM 1978; FFPHM (FFCM 1980); FFPM 1989. Gen. practice, Benoni, S Africa, 1954; various NHS posts, 1955–61; Medical Dir, pharmaceutical industry, 1962–68; SMO, DHSS, 1969–72; PMO, Cttee on Safety of Medicines and Medicines Commn, 1973; SPMO, Under-Sec., and Head of Medicines Div., DHSS, 1974–77; Dep. Chief Med. Officer, Dept of Health (formerly DHSS), 1977–89. Examiner for Dip. Pharm. Med., Royal Colls of Physicians, 1976–84. Chairman: Assoc. of Med. Advisers in Pharmaceutical Industry, 1966; Adv. Cttee on Nat. Blood Transfusion Service, 1980–89; Expert Gp on Viral Haemorrhagic Fevers, 1984–89; Adv. Cttee, NHS Drugs, 1985–89. Member: Nat. Biol. Bd, 1975–77; Bd, Public Health Lab. Service, 1977–91; Central Blood Products Authority, 1982–85; Adviser to WHO, 1970–90. Rep. Governor, Imperial Cancer Res. Fund, 1977–89. Mem., Court of Govs and Bd of Management, LSHTM, 1986–89. *Publications:* various, mainly on aspects of clinical pharmacology and control of medicines. *Recreations:* walking, photography. *Address:* 5 Ashcroft Court, 10 Oaklands Road, Bromley, Kent BR1 3TX. *T:* 0181–460 3665.

HARRIS, Frank; *see* Harris, W. F.

HARRIS, Prof. Frank, MD; FRCP, FRCPE; Dean, Faculty of Medicine and Professor of Paediatrics, University of Leicester, since 1990; Hon. Consultant Paediatrician, Leicester Royal Infirmary, since 1990; *b* 6 Oct. 1934; *s* of David and Miriam Harris; *m* 1963, Brenda van Embden; two *s*. *Educ:* Univ. of Cape Town (MB ChB 1957; MMed (Paed), MD). Groote Schuur and Red Cross War Memorial Children's Hosp., Cape Town; CSIR Res. Fellow, Dept of Medicine, Univ. of Cape Town; Lectr and Sen. Lectr in Child Health, Univ. of Sheffield, 1965–74; University of Liverpool: Prof. of Child Health and Dir, Inst. of Child Health, 1974–89; Pro-Vice-Chancellor, 1981–84; Dean, Faculty of Medicine, 1985–89; Hon. Cons. Paediatrician to Royal Liverpool Children's Hosps at Myrtle Street and Alderhey. Exec. Sec., Council of Deans of UK Med. Schs and Faculties, 1992–. Member: Liverpool AHA and DHA, 1977–84; Mersey RHA, 1983–89; Trent RHA, 1990; Vice-Chm., Leics HA, 1993– (non-exec. Dir, 1990–). Member: Cttee on Review of Medicines, 1981–90; Cttee on Safety of Medicines, 1990–92; Joint Planning Adv. Cttee, DoH, 1990–94; GMC, 1990– (Overseas Review Bd, 1992–; Educn Cttee, 1994–; Preliminary Proceedings Cttee); NAHAT Wkg Gp on Teaching, Res. and Audit, 1992–93. Exec., Univ. Hosps Assoc., 1991–; Exec. Cttee, Assoc. of Med. Schs in Europe, 1993–; Adv. Cttee on Med. Trng, EC, 1994–. Examr for RCP and Univs, UK and overseas. *Publications:* Paediatric Fluid Therapy, 1973; chapters in med. books; contribs to med. jls. *Recreations:* golf, reading, travel. *Address:* School of Medicine, University of Leicester, PO Box 138, Leicester LE1 9HN. *T:* Leicester (0116) 252 2962.

HARRIS, (Geoffrey) Charles (Wesson); QC 1989; **His Honour Judge Charles Harris;** a Circuit Judge, since 1993; *b* 17 Jan. 1945; *s* of late G. Hardy Harris and M. J. P. Harris (*née* Wesson); *m* 1970, Carol Ann Alston; two *s* one *d*. *Educ:* Repton; Univ. of Birmingham (LLB). Called to the Bar, Inner Temple, 1967; a Recorder, 1990–93. Practice on Midland and Oxford Circuit and in London. Contested (C) Penistone, Yorks, Oct. 1974. *Publications:* contrib. to Halsbury's Laws of England, 4th edn 1976, and other legal publications; magazine articles on stalking and ballooning. *Recreations:* history, architecture, fireworks, shooting, stalking, ski-ing. *Address:* 1 Harcourt Buildings, Temple, EC4. *T:* 0171–353 0375; Westcote Barton Manor, Oxfordshire. *Club:* Carlton.

HARRIS, Geoffrey (Herbert); Member, Transport Users' Consultative Committee for London, 1961–77 (Chairman, 1972–77, Deputy Chairman, 1971–72); Chairman, London

Transport Passengers' Committee, 1972–74; *b* 31 Jan. 1914; *s* of late W. Leonard Harris and late Sybil M. Harris; *m* 1945, Eve J. Orton; two *d*. *Educ:* Colchester Royal Grammar School. FCIS. Commercial Union Gp of Cos, 1932–37; Shell Gp of Cos, 1937–73; Manager Office Administration, London, 1963–73. Royal Artillery, 1937–45. *Recreations:* music, architecture, travel. *Address:* Fyfield Cottage, West Street, Marlow, Bucks SL7 2BU. *T:* Marlow (01628) 472550. *Club:* Phyllis Court (Henley-on-Thames).

HARRIS, Sir Henry, Kt 1993; FRCP; FRCPath; FRS 1968; Regius Professor of Medicine, University of Oxford, 1979–92; Head of the Sir William Dunn School of Pathology, 1963–94; Hon. Director, Cancer Research Campaign, Cell Biology Unit, 1963–92; Fellow of Lincoln College, 1963–79, Hon. Fellow 1980; Student of Christ Church, 1979–92, Emeritus Student, 1992; *b* 28 Jan. 1925; *s* of late Sam and late Ann Harris; *m* 1950, Alexandra Fanny Brodsky; one *s* two *d*. *Educ:* Sydney Boys' High Sch. and University of Sydney, Australia; Lincoln Coll., Oxford. Public Exhibnr, University of Sydney, 1942; BA Mod. Langs, 1944; MB BS 1950; Travelling Schol. of Austr. Nat. Univ. at Univ. of Oxford, 1952; MA; DPhil (Oxon.), 1954, DM 1979. Dir of Research, Brit. Empire Cancer Campaign, at Sir William Dunn Sch. of Pathology, Oxford, 1954–59; Visiting Scientist, Nat. Institutes of Health, USA, 1959–60; Head of Dept of Cell Biology, John Innes Inst., 1960–63; Prof. of Pathology, Univ. of Oxford, 1963–79. Vis. Prof., Vanderbilt Univ., 1968; Walker-Ames Prof., University of Washington, 1968; Foreign Prof., Collège de France, 1974. Non-Exec. Mem., Oxford RHA, 1990–92; Hon. Consulting Pathologist, Oxford HA, 1992. Member: ARC, 1968–78 (Chm., Animals Res. Bd, 1976–78); Council, European Molecular Biology Organization, 1974–76; Council, Royal Society, 1971–72; Scientific Adv. Cttee, CRC, 1961–85; Governor, European Cell Biology Organization, 1973–75. Lectures: Almroth Wright, 1968; Harvey, Harvey Soc. NY, 1969; Dunham, Harvard, 1969; Jenner Meml, 1970; Croonian, Royal Soc., 1971; Nat. Insts of Health, USA, 1971; Foundation, RCPath, 1973; Woodhull, Royal Instn, 1975; Rotherham, Lincoln Coll., Oxford, 1979; Herbert Spencer, Oxford Univ., 1979, 1992; Opening Plenary, Internat. Congress of Cell Biology, 1980; First Distinguished, in Experimental Pathology, Pittsburgh Univ., 1982; Louis Gross Meml, NY, 1983; Claude Bernard, Acad. des Sciences, Paris, 1984; Jean Brachet Meml, Vancouver, 1990; Kettle, RCPath, 1991; Romanes, Oxford Univ., 1993. Foreign Hon. Mem., Amer. Acad. Arts and Sciences; Foreign Mem., Max-Planck Soc.; Hon. Member: Amer. Assoc. of Pathologists; German Soc. of Cell Biology; Corresp. Member: Amer. Assoc. for Cancer Res.; Aust. Acad. of Science. Foreign Correspondent, Waterford Striped Bass Derby Assoc.; Hon. Fellow, Cambridge Philosophical Soc. Hon. FRCPath Aust. Hon. DSc Edinburgh, 1976; Hon. MD: Geneva, 1982; Sydney, 1983. Feldberg Foundn Award, Ivison Macadam Meml Prize, RCSE; Prix de la Fondation Isabelle Decazes de Noüe for cancer research; Madonnina Prize for medical scis (City of Milan), 1979; Royal Medal, Royal Soc., 1980; Osler Medal, RCP, 1984; Katherine Berkan Judd Award, Sloan-Kettering Inst., NY, 1991. *Publications:* Nucleus and Cytoplasm, 1968, 3rd edn, 1974; Cell Fusion, 1970; La Fusion cellulaire, 1974; The Balance of Improbabilities, 1987; papers on cellular physiology and biochemistry, in scientific books and jls, and some fiction. *Recreation:* history. *Address:* c/o Sir William Dunn School of Pathology, South Parks Road, Oxford OX1 3RE. *T:* Oxford (01865) 275501.

HARRIS, Hugh Christopher Emlyn; Associate Director, Bank of England, since 1988; *b* 25 March 1936; *s* of Thomas Emlyn Harris and Martha Anne (*née* Davies); *m* 1968, Pamela Susan Woollard; one *s* one *d*. *Educ:* The Leys Sch., Cambridge; Trinity Coll., Cambridge (BA 1959; MA). ACIB 1963; FIPM 1990. Bank of England, 1959–: Chief of Corporate Services, 1984–88. Director: BE Services Ltd, 1984–; BE Museum Ltd, 1989–; BE Property Holdings Ltd, 1989–; Securities Management Trust Ltd, 1987–; Solefield School Educational Trust Ltd, Sevenoaks, 1986–. Member: Governing Council, Business in the Community, 1986–; Windsor Fellowship Adv. Council, 1988–. FRSA. *Recreations:* tennis, watching Rugby, theatre, opera. *Address:* Bank of England, Threadneedle Street, EC2R 8AH. *T:* 0171–601 3131.

HARRIS, Lt-Gen. Sir Ian (Cecil), KBE 1967 (CBE 1958); CB 1962; DSO 1945; Chairman, 1977–79, President, 1984–88, Irish Bloodstock Breeders Association; *b* 7 July 1910; *y s* of late J. W. A. Harris, Victor Stud, Golden, Tipperary; *m* 1945, Anne-Marie Desmotreux; one *s* (and one *s* decd). *Educ:* Portora Royal Sch., Enniskillen, Northern Ireland; RMC, Sandhurst. 2nd Lt Royal Ulster Rifles, 1930; served War of 1939–45, NW Frontier of India, 1939 (despatches); comd 2nd Bn Royal Ulster Rifles, 1943–45; GSO1, 25 Ind. Div. and 7 Div. in Burma and Malaya, 1945–46 (despatches), India and Pakistan, 1946–47; AQMG Scottish Comd, 1949–51; comd 6th Bn Royal Ulster Rifles (TA), 1951–52; Chief of Staff, Northern Ireland, 1952–54; Comdr 1 Federal Infantry Bde, Malaya, 1954–57 (despatches); Dep. Dir of Staff Duties (A), WO, 1957–60; GOC Singapore Base District, 1960–62; Chief of Staff, Contingencies Planning, Supreme HQ, Allied Powers, Europe, 1963–66; GOC-in-C, then GOC, N Ireland, 1966–69. Colonel: Royal Ulster Rifles, 1962–68; Royal Irish Rangers, 1968–72. Chm., British Support Cttee for Meml Museum of Caen, 1988–. Hon. Citizen of Caen, 1984. *Address:* 24 Belgrave Square, Monkstown, Co. Dublin, Ireland. *T:* 280 7312. *Club:* Army and Navy.

HARRIS, Air Cdre Irene Joyce, (Joy), CB 1984; RRC 1976; SRN, SCM; Director, Nursing Services (RAF), and Matron-in-Chief, Princess Mary's Royal Air Force Nursing Service, 1981–84; *b* 26 Sept. 1926; *d* of late Robert John Harris and Annie Martha Harris (*née* Breed). *Educ:* Southgate County Sch.; Charing Cross Hosp.; The London Hosp.; Queen Mary's Maternity Home, Hampstead. SRN 1947, SCM 1950. Joined Princess Mary's RAF Nursing Service, 1950; gen. nursing and midwifery duties in UK, Singapore, Germany and Cyprus; Dep. Matron, 1970; Sen. Matron, 1975; Principal Matron, 1978; Dep. Dir, Nursing Services (RAF), 1981. QHNS 1981–84. *Recreations:* travel, ornithology, music, archaeology, gardening. *Address:* 51 Station Road, Haddenham, Ely, Cambs CB6 3XD. *Club:* Royal Air Force.

HARRIS, Sir Jack Wolfred Ashford, 2nd Bt, *cr* 1932; Chairman, Bing Harris & Co. Ltd, Wellington, NZ, 1935–78 (Director until 1982), retired; *b* 23 July 1906; *er s* of Rt Hon. Sir Percy Harris, 1st Bt, PC, and Frieda Bloxam (*d* 1962); *S* father 1952; *m* 1933, Patricia, *o d* of A. P. Penman, Wahroonga, Sydney, NSW; two *s* one *d*. *Educ:* Shrewsbury Sch.; Trinity Hall, Cambridge. BA (Cantab) History; then one year's study in Europe. Joined family business in New Zealand, 1929, and became director shortly afterwards. Past Pres. Wellington Chamber of Commerce. Served during War of 1939–45, for three years in NZ Home Forces. *Recreations:* gardening, fishing, swimming. *Heir:* *s* Christopher John Ashford Harris [*b* 26 Aug. 1934; *m* 1957, Anna, *d* of F. de Malmanche, Auckland, NZ; one *s* two *d*]. *Address:* Te Rama, Waikanae, near Wellington, NZ. *Club:* Wellington (Wellington).

HARRIS, Jeffery Francis, FCA; Chief Executive, UniChem plc, since 1992; *b* 8 April 1948; *s* of Ernest and Kathleen Veronica Harris; *m* 1976, Elizabeth Helen Hancock; two *s*. *Educ:* Rendcomb Coll., Cirencester; Southampton Univ. (BSc Hons 1970). FCA 1979. Trainee chartered accountant, 1970; with Barton Mayhew & Co, later Ernst & Young, 1980–85; joined UniChem, 1985; Gp Chief Accountant, 1985–86; Finance Dir, 1986–91; Dep. Chief Exec., 1991–92. *Recreations:* walking, ski-ing, cycling, gardening, opera. *Address:* UniChem House, Cox Lane, Chessington, Surrey KT9 1SN. *T:* 0181–391 2323.

HARRIS, Very Rev. John; Dean of Brecon, and Vicar of Brecon St Mary with Battle and Llanddew, since 1993; *b* 12 March 1932; *s* of Richard and Ivy Harris; *m* 1956, Beryl June Roberts; two *s* one *d*. *Educ:* St David's Coll., Lampeter (BA 1955); Salisbury Theol Coll. Ordained deacon, 1957, priest, 1958; Curate: Pontnewynydd, 1957–60; Bassaleg, 1960–63; Vicar: Penmaen, 1963–69; St Paul, Newport, 1969–84; Maindee, 1984–93; RD of Newport, 1977–93. Canon, St Woolos Cath., 1984–. *Recreations:* classical archæology, music, ballet, natural history. *Address:* Blackstone, 25 Pendre, Brecon LD3 9EA. *T:* Brecon (01874) 624876.

HARRIS, John Charles; solicitor; Management and Legal Consultant, John Harris Consultancy, since 1986; Executive Director, Solace International Ltd, since 1992; Administrator, English Camerata, since 1988; *b* 25 April 1936; *s* of Sir Charles Joseph William Harris, KBE; *m* 1961, Alison Beryl Sturley; one *s* one *d*. *Educ:* Dulwich College; Clare College, Cambridge. MA, LLM. 2nd Lieut, Intelligence Corps, 1954–56. UKAEA (seconded to OECD), 1959–63; articled to Town Clerk, Poole, 1963–66; Asst Sol., then Senior Asst Sol., Poole BC, 1966–67; Asst Sol., then Principal Asst to Chief Exec. and Town Clerk, 1967–71, Dep. Town Clerk, 1972–73, County Borough of Bournemouth; County Sec., 1973–83, Chief Exec. and County Clerk, 1983–86, S Yorks CC; Dir, S Yorks Passenger Transport Exec., 1984–86; Sec. to Yorkshire and Humberside County Councils Assoc., 1984–86; Advr and Dir, S Yorks Residuary Body, 1985–86; Clerk to Lord Lieutenant of S Yorks, 1984–86; Public Sector Adviser/Associate Consultant: PA Consulting Gp, 1986–91; Daniel Bates Partnership, 1991–95. Adviser to AMA Police and Fire Cttee, 1976–86; Member: Home Office Tripartite Working Party on Police Act 1964, 1983–86; Rampton SHSA Cttee, 1989–; Arts Council Touring Bd, 1989–92; Pontefract HA, 1990–93; Bd, Northern Counties Housing Assoc., 1990– (Chm., 1994–); Council, Local Govt Internat. Bureau, 1993–. Chm., Soc. of County Secretaries, 1983–84; Mem. Exec. Council, Solace, 1984–86; Mem., Law Society. Independent Member: W Yorks Police Authy, 1994–; Police Cttee, AMA, 1995–. Hon. PR Officer, S Yorks and Humberside Region, Riding for Disabled Assoc. (Mem., Publications Cttee, 1987–90); Trustee: S Yorks Charity Inf. Service, 1977–87; Housing Assocs Charitable Trust, 1994–; Founder Mem./Sec., Barnsley Rockley Rotary Club, 1976–79; Vice-Chm. and Sec., Friends of Opera North, 1979–86; Member: Council/Co., and Develt Cttee, Opera North, 1980–; Guild of Freemen, City of London, 1967; Justice; European Movement. DL S Yorks, 1986. FRSA 1984. *Publications:* correspondent on public affairs. *Recreations:* being with family and friends; competitive trail riding; riding Welsh cobs; opera, foreign travel. *Address:* Long Lane Close, High Ackworth, Pontefract, Yorks WF7 7EY. *T:* Pontefract (01977) 795450; *Fax:* (01977) 707409. *Club:* Leeds (Leeds).

HARRIS, Dr John Edwin, MBE 1981; FEng 1987; FRS 1988; independent consultant on materials, and freelance writer and lecturer, since 1990; *b* 2 June 1932; *s* of late John Frederick Harris and Emily Margaret (*née* Prosser); *m* 1956, Ann Foote; two *s* two *d*. *Educ:* Larkfield Grammar Sch., Chepstow; Dept of Metallurgy, Univ. of Birmingham (BSc 1953, PhD 1956, DSc 1973). FIM 1974; FInstP 1992. Joined Associated Electrical Industries, 1956; CEGB, 1959–89; seconded to Sheffield Univ., 1959–61; Berkeley Nuclear Labs, 1961–89, Sect. Head, 1966–89; Univ. Liaison Manager, Nuclear Electric plc, 1989–90. Visiting Professor: Nuclear Engrg, Manchester Univ., 1991–; Corrosion Sci., UMIST, 1992–; Materials and Manufacture, Univ. of Plymouth (formerly Plymouth Poly.), 1992–. Member: Metal Science Cttee, Metals Soc., 1974; Bd, British Nuclear Energy Soc., 1974–88; Watt Cttee Wkg Party on Atmospheric Attack on Inorganic Materials, 1987; Home Office Wkg Party on Adjudications in HM Prisons, 1974; Chm., Leyhill Prison Bd of Visitors, 1973–74. Mem., Assoc. of British Science Writers. Public Lectr, Tate Gall., 1984; Molecule Club Lectr, 1985 and 1987. FRSA 1989. Internat. Metallographic Soc. Award, 1976; Esso Gold Medal, Royal Soc., 1979; Interdisciplinary Award, RSC, 1987. *Publications:* (ed) Physical Metallurgy of Reactor Fuel Elements, 1975; Vacancies '76, 1977; scientific papers on nuclear metallurgy, deformation and corrosion; articles in New Scientist and The Guardian. *Recreations:* writing popular science articles, studying decay of buildings. *Address:* Church Farm House, 28 Hopton Road, Upper Cam, Dursley, Glos GL11 5PB. *T:* Dursley (01453) 543165. *Club:* Cam Bowling (non-playing member).

HARRIS, John Frederick, OBE 1986; FSA; Curator, British Architectural Library's Drawing Collection and Heinz Gallery, 1960–86; Consultant: to Collection, Canadian Centre for Architecture, 1986–88 (Member Advisory Board, 1983–88); Heinz Architectural Center, Carnegie, 1991–94; *b* 13 Aug. 1931; *s* of Frederick Harris and Maud (*née* Sellwood); *m* 1960, Eileen Spiegel, New York; one *s* one *d*. *Educ:* Cowley C of E School. Itinerant before 1956; Library of Royal Inst. of Architects, 1956. Mem., Mr Paul Mellon's Adv. Bd, 1966–78; Trustee, Amer. Mus. in Britain, 1974–88; Chm., Colnaghi & Co., 1982–92. President: Internat. Confedn on Architectural Museums, 1981–84 (Chm., 1979–81; Hon. Life Pres., 1984); Marylebone Soc., 1978–80; Twentieth Century Soc. (formerly Thirties Soc.), 1986– (Mem. Cttee, 1979–); Member: Council, Drawing Soc. of America, 1962–68; Council, Victorian Soc., 1974–; Nat. Council, Internat. Council of Monuments and Sites, 1976–83; Soc. of Dilettanti, 1977–; Member Committee: Soc. of Architectural Historians of GB, 1958–66; Georgian Gp, 1970–74, 1986–89; Save Britain's Heritage, 1970–; Stowe Landscape, 1980– (Patron, Stowe Gardens Buildings Trust, 1986–92); Bldg Museum Proj., 1980–86; Garden History, 1980–84; Jl of Garden History, 1980–89. Member: Adv. Council, Drawings Center, NY, 1983–89; Management Cttee, Courtauld Inst. of Art, 1983–87; Somerset House Building Cttee, 1986–89; Council, Royal Archaeol. Inst., 1984–86; Adv. Cttees, Historic Bldgs and Monuments Commn, 1984–88; Ashton Meml Steering Gp, 1984–86; GLC Historic Buildings Panel, 1984–86; Ambrose Congreve Award, 1980–82; Ashmole Archive Cttee, 1985–87; Adv. Bd, Irish Architectural Archive, 1988–91; Appeal Cttee, Painshill Park Trust, 1988–89; Spencer House Restoration Cttee, 1986–; Trustee, Architecture Foundn, 1991–94. Andrew W. Mellon Lectr in Fine Arts, Nat. Gall., Washington, 1981; Slade Prof. of Fine Art, Univ. of Oxford, 1982–83. Exhibitions Organizer: The King's Arcadia, 1973; The Destruction of the Country House (with Marcus Binney), 1974; The Garden, 1979; Dir, British Country House Exhibn, Nat. Gall., Washington, 1982–83; many exhibns in Heinz Gall.; travelling exhibns and catalogues: Italian Architectural Drawings, 1966; Sir Christopher Wren, 1970; Designs of the British Country House, 1985. FSA 1968; FRSA 1975; Hon. FRIBA 1972; Hon. MA Oxon, 1982; Hon. Brother Art Workers' Guild, 1972. Editor, Studies in Architecture, 1976–. *Publications:* English Decorative Ironwork, 1960; Regency Furniture Designs, 1961; ed, The Prideaux Collection of Topographical Drawings, 1963; (jtly) Lincolnshire, 1964; contrib. The Making of Stamford, 1965; (jtly) Illustrated Glossary of Architecture, 1966, 2nd edn 1969; (jtly) Buckingham Palace, 1968; Georgian Country Houses, 1968; contrib., Concerning Architecture, 1968; Sir William Chambers, Knight of the Polar Star, 1970 (Hitchcock Medallion 1971); ed, The Rise and Progress of the Present State of Planting, 1970; ed (jtly) The Country Seat, 1970; Catalogue of British Drawings for Architecture, Decoration, Sculpture and Landscape Gardening in American Collections, 1971; A Country House Index, 1971, 2nd edn 1979; Catalogue of the Drawings Collection RIBA: Inigo Jones and John Webb, 1972; contrib., Guide to Vitruvius Britannicus, 1972; (jtly) The King's Arcadia: Inigo Jones and The Stuart Court, 1973; Catalogue of the Drawings Collection RIBA: Colin Campbell, 1973; Headfort House and Robert Adam, 1973; (jtly) The Destruction of the Country House, 1974;

Gardens of Delight, The Art of Thomas Robins, 1976; Gardens of Delight, The Rococo English Landscape of Thomas Robins, 1978; (jtly) Catalogue of Drawings by Inigo Jones, John Webb and Isaac de Caus in Worcester College, Oxford, 1979; A Garden Alphabet, 1979; ed, The Garden Show, 1979; The Artist and the Country House, 1979 (Sir Banister Fletcher prize, 1979), 2nd edn 1986; contrib., Village England, 1980; (contrib.) Lost Houses of Scotland, 1980; The English Garden 1530–1840: a contemporary view, 1981; contrib., John Claudius Loudon and the Early Nineteenth Century in Great Britain, Washington, 1980; (jtly) Interiors, 1981; The Palladians, 1981; Die Hauser der Lords und Gentlemen, 1982; William Talman, Maverick Architect, 1982; (contrib.) SAVE Gibraltar's Heritage, 1982; Architectural Drawings in the Cooper Hewitt Museum, New York, 1982; (contrib.) Vanishing Houses of England, 1982; (contrib.) Macmillan Encyclopedia of Architecture, 1982; (contrib.) Great Drawings from the Collection of Royal Institute of British Architects, 1983; (jtly) Britannia Illustrata Knyff & Kip, 1984; The Design of the British Country House, 1985; (jtly) Inigo Jones—Complete Architectural Drawings, 1989; (contrib.) In Honor of Paul Mellon, Collector and Benefactor, 1986; (contrib.) Canadian Centre for Architecture Building and Gardens, 1989; (contrib.) The Fashioning and Functioning of the British Country House, 1989; (jtly) Jamaica's Heritage: an untapped resource, 1991; (contrib.) Writers and their Houses, 1993; The Palladian Revival: Lord Burlington, his villa and garden at Chiswick, 1994; articles in Country Life, Apollo, and other jls. *Recreations:* grand hotels, history of World War I and flinting.

HARRIS, John Frederick, CEng, FIEE; Chairman, East Midlands Electricity plc (formerly East Midlands Electricity Board), 1982–94; *b* 9 Dec. 1938; *s* of Jack Harris and Lily Harris; *m* 1960, Diana Joyce Brown; one *s* two *d*. *Educ:* Central Grammar School, Birmingham. Technical posts, Midlands Electricity, 1955–70; managerial posts, Southern Electricity, 1970–78; Chief Engineer, NW Electricity Board, 1978–79, Dep. Chm., 1979–82; Dir, Nottingham Develt Enterprise, 1992–. Gov., Nottingham Trent Univ., 1993–; Trustee, Djanogly City Tech. Coll., 1990–. Pres., Nottingham VSO, 1984–. CIMgt. Hon. DTech. *Recreation:* golf. *Address:* 57 Sheepwalk Lane, Ravenshead, Nottingham NG15 9FD. *Club:* Reform.

HARRIS, Air Marshal Sir John (Hulme), (Win), KCB 1992 (CB 1991); CBE 1982; Air Officer Commanding No 18 Group (RAF Strike Command) and Commander Maritime Air Eastern Atlantic and Allied Forces Northwestern Europe (formerly Channel), since 1992; *b* 3 June 1938; *s* of late George W. H. Harris and Dorothy Harris (*née* Hulme); *m* 1962, Williamina (*née* Murray); two *s*. *Educ:* English Sch., Cairo; King Edward VII Sch., King's Lynn. No. 224 Sqn, RAF, 1960–62; RAF Leeming, Flying Instructor, 1963–67; Exchange Officer, US Navy Air Test and Evaluation Sqn, Florida, 1968–70; Central Tactics and Trials Organisation, 1970–73; OC No 201 Sqn, 1973–75; Nat. Defence Coll., 1975–76; OPCON (CCIS) Project Team, Northwood, 1976–78; SASO, RAF Pitreavie Castle, 1979; OC RAF Kinloss, 1979–81; Internat. Mil. Staff, Brussels, 1982–83; RCDS, 1984; Dir Training (Flying), RAF, 1985–87; Comdt Gen., RAF Regiment and Dir. Gen. of Security (RAF), 1987–89; ACDS (Logistics), 1990–91; COS, HQ No 18 Gp (RAF Strike Comd), 1991–92. ADC to the Queen, 1979–81. *Recreations:* fly fishing for salmon, trout and navigators, gardening, travel. *Address:* c/o Lloyds Bank, Cox's and King's Branch, 7 Pall Mall, SW1Y 5NA. *Club:* Royal Air Force.

HARRIS, His Honour John Percival, DSC 1945; QC 1974; a Circuit Judge, 1980–95; *b* 16 Feb. 1925; *o s* of late Thomas Percival Harris and Nora May Harris; *m* 1959, Janet Valerie Douglas; one *s* two *d*. *Educ:* Wells Cathedral Sch.; Pembroke Coll., Cambridge. BA 1947. Served in RN, 1943–46: Midshipman, RNVR, 1944, Sub-Lt 1945. Called to Bar, Middle Temple, 1949, Bencher 1970. A Recorder of the Crown Court, 1972–80; Dep. Sen. Judge, Sovereign Base Areas, Cyprus, 1983–95. *Recreations:* golf, reading, Victorian pictures. *Address:* Tudor Court, Fairmile Park Road, Cobham, Surrey KT11 2PP. *T:* Cobham (01932) 864756. *Clubs:* Royal St George's Golf (Sandwich); Woking Golf, Rye Golf.

HARRIS, John Robert, FRIBA; architect; Founder and Senior Partner, John R. Harris Architects, London, since 1949 (also Founder and Senior Partner of associated firms in Brunei, Oman, Qatar, Dubai, Hong Kong and Boston); Partner, CDH Architectes, Paris, since 1978; *b* 5 June 1919; *s* of late Major Alfred Harris, CBE, DSO and Rosa Alfreda Alderson; *m* 1950, Gillian, *d* of Col C. W. D. Rowe, CB, MBE, TD, DL, JP; one *s* one *d*. *Educ:* Harrow Sch.; Architectural Assoc. Sch. of Architecture (AA Dipl. Hons). FRIBA 1949; HKIA 1982; Membre de l'Ordre des Architectes Français, 1978. Served War, TA and Active Service, 1939–45 (TEM 1945); Lieut RE, Hong Kong, 1940–41; POW of Japanese, 1941–45; Mem., British Army Aid Gp, China, 1943–45; Hong Kong Resistance, 1942–45. Projects won in internat. competition: State Hosp., Qatar, 1953; New Dubai Hosp., 1976; Corniche Develt and Traffic Intersection, Dubai, 1978; HQ for Min. of Social Affairs and Labour, Oman, 1979; Tuen Mun Hosp., Hong Kong, 1981 (internat. assessment); Ruler's Office develt, Dubai, 1985. Architects and planners for Zhuhai New Town, Economic Zone, People's Republic of China, 1984; Q-Tel HQ, Qatar, 1991; Deira Sea Corniche masterplan, Dubai, 1993. Major works in UK include: hospitals: Royal Northern, London, 1973; Ealing, 1976; RAF Upper Heyford, 1982; RAF Bentwaters, 1982; Stoke Mandeville, 1983; Wellesley House and St Peter's Court school re-develt, 1975; apartments, Hyde Park, 1983; dept stores in Barnstaple, Basildon, Cwmbran, Eltham, Harlow, Hammersmith, Sutton Coldfield and Worthing; refurbishment, Natural Hist. Mus., 1982–89; redevelt, Dorchester Hotel, 1989; develt, Gloucester Road Station site; redevelt, Sheraton Grand Hotel, Edinburgh, 1993. Major works overseas include: National Bank of Dubai HQ Bldg, 1968; Sulaibikhat Hosp., Kuwait, 1968; Grindlay's Bank, Muscat, 1969; Rashid Hosp., Dubai, 1973; dept stores in Antwerp, Brussels, Lille, Paris and Strasbourg, 1973–83; shopping centres, Oman, 1978 and 1984; Internat. Trade Centre, Dubai, 1979; British Embassy, Chancery Offices and Ambassador's Residence, Abu Dhabi, 1982; University Teaching Hosp., Maiduguri, Nigeria, 1982; Caritas Hosp., Hong Kong, 1983; Women's Hosp., Doha, 1984; Shell Recreation Centre, Brunei, 1984; Wafi Shopping Mall, Dubai, 1991; British Bank of ME HQ, Dubai, 1993. FRSA 1982. Cert., Internat. Hosp. Fedn, 1993; Structural Steel Design Award, London Docklands, 1993. Silver Jubilee Medal, 1977. *Publications:* (jtly) John R. Harris Architects, 1984; contrib. to books and architectural and technical jls. *Recreations:* architecture, sailing, travel. *Address:* 24 Devonshire Place, W1N 2BX. *T:* 0171–935 9353. *Clubs:* Athenæum, Royal Thames Yacht.

See also R. M. Harris.

HARRIS, (Jonathan) Toby; Director, Association of Community Health Councils for England and Wales, since 1987; Leader, Haringey Borough Council, since 1987; Chair, Association of London Government, since 1995; *b* 11 Oct. 1953; *s* of Prof. Harry Harris, FRS and of Muriel Hargest; *m* 1979, Ann Sarah Herbert; two *s*. *Educ:* Haberdashers' Aske's Sch., Elstree; Trinity Coll., Cambridge (BA Hons NatScis and Econ). Chair, Cambridge Univ. Labour Club, 1973; Pres., Cambridge Union Soc., 1974. Economics Div., Bank of England, 1975–79; Electricity Consumers' Council, 1979–86, Dep. Dir, 1983. Mem., Haringey BC, 1978– (Chair, Social Services Cttee, 1982–87); Dep. Chair, AMA, 1991– (Chair, Social Services Cttee, 1986–93); Chair: Assoc. of London Authorities, 1993–95 (Dep. Chair, 1990–93; Chair, Social Services Cttee, 1984–88); LBTC-Training for Care, 1986–94; Local Govt Anti-Poverty Unit, 1994–. Nat. Chair, Young Fabian Gp, 1976–77; Chair, Hornsey Labour Party, 1978, 1979, 1980; Mem., Labour Party Nat. Policy Forum, 1992–; Co-opted Mem., Lab. Party Domestic and Internat. Policy Cttee, 1993–. Dep. Chair, Nat. Fuel Poverty Forum, 1981–86; Mem., London Drug Policy Forum, 1990–. Jt Chair, London Pride Partnership, 1995–; Member: King's Fund Orgnl Audit Adv. Council, 1991–; Exec. Cttee, RADAR, 1991–93; Nat. Nursery Exam. Bd, 1992–94; Home Office Adv. Council on Race Relations, 1992–; Bd, London First, 1993–; Exec. Council, RNIB, 1993–94; Cttee of Regns of EU, 1994–. Trustee: Evening Standard Blitz Meml Appeal, 1995–; Help for Health Trust, 1995–. Governor: Nat. Inst. for Social Work, 1986–94; Sch. of St David and St Katherine, 1978–; St Mary's Schs, Hornsey, 1978–. FRSA 1993. *Publications:* (with Nick Butler and Neil Kinnock) Why Vote Labour?, 1979; (contrib.) Economics of Prosperity, 1980; (ed with Jonathan Bradshaw) Energy and Social Policy, 1983; (contrib.) Rationing in Action, 1993; (contrib.) Whistleblowing in the Health Service: accountability, law, and professional practice, 1994. *Recreations:* reading, walking. *Address:* c/o Association of Community Health Councils for England and Wales, 30 Drayton Park, N5 1PB.

HARRIS, Dr Jose Ferial, FBA 1993; Fellow, St Catherine's College, Oxford, since 1978; Reader in Modern History, University of Oxford, since 1990; *d* of Leonard Cecil Chambers and Freda Ellen Chambers (*née* Brown); *m* 1968, James Harris; one *s*. *Educ:* Dame Alice Harpur Sch., Bedford; Newnham Coll., Cambridge (MA, PhD). Res. Fellow, Nuffield Coll., Oxford, 1966–69; Lectr, 1969–74, Sen. Lectr, 1974–78, Dept of Social Sci. and Admin, LSE. Vis. Res. Fellow, Princeton, 1985–86. *Publications:* Unemployment and Politics: a study in English social policy, 1972, 2nd edn 1984; William Beveridge: a biography, 1977; Private Lives, Public Spirit: a social history of Britain 1870–1914, 1993. *Recreations:* the lesser arts, walking, solitude, family life. *Address:* 5 Belbroughton Road, Oxford OX2 6UZ.

HARRIS, Joseph Hugh; JP; Vice Lord-Lieutenant of Cumbria, since 1994; *b* 1932; *s* of late John Frederick Harris and of Gwendolen Arden Harris; *m* 1957, Anne, *d* of Brig. Leslie Harrison McRobert, CBE. *Educ:* Aysgarth Sch.; Harrow; Royal Agric. Coll. (MRAC). Lieut, 11th Hussars, PAO. Chairman: Cumbrian Newspapers Ltd, 1987–; Grasmere Sports (Dir, 1977). Member: Northern Regl Panel, MAFF, 1977–83; Rural Develt Commn, 1989–. Royal Agricultural Society: Sen. Steward, 1960–77; Dep. Pres., 1987; Trustee, 1992–; Hon. Dir, Royal Show, 1978–82. High Sheriff of Cumbria, 1976–77; DL 1984, JP 1971, Cumbria. Chm., Penrith and Alston Bench, 1991–. Chm. of Govs, Aysgarth Sch., 1975–78. *Recreations:* shooting, country sports, conservation. *Address:* Brackenburgh, Calthwaite, Penrith, Cumbria CA11 9PW. *T:* Penrith (01768) 885253, *Fax:* (01768) 885020.

HARRIS, Air Cdre Joy; *see* Harris, I. J.

HARRIS, Dr Keith Murray, CBiol, FIBiol, FRES; Director, International (formerly Commonwealth) Institute of Entomology, 1985–92; *b* 26 Nov. 1932; *s* of Clifford Murray Harris and Doris (*née* Cottam); *m* 1957, Elizabeth Harrison; one *s* one *d*. *Educ:* Lewis Sch., Pengam; Univ. of Wales, Aberystwyth (BSc, DSc); Selwyn Coll., Cambridge (DipAgricSci); Imperial Coll. of Tropical Agric., Trinidad (DipTA). FRES 1960; FIBiol 1985. Entomologist, then Sen. Entomologist, Federal Dept of Agricl Res., Nigeria, 1955–62; Sen. Res. Fellow, BM (Natural History), 1962–66; Entomologist and Sen. Scientist, RHS, Wisley, 1966–74; Principal Taxonomist, Commonwealth Inst. of Entomology, 1974–85. *Publications:* (jtly) Collins Guide to the Pests, Diseases and Disorders of Garden Plants, 1981; scientific research papers and articles on pests of cultivated plants, esp. pests of African cereal crops, and on taxonomy and biol. of gall midges. *Recreations:* walking, cycling, gardening, music. *Address:* 81 Linden Way, Ripley, Woking, Surrey GU23 6LP. *T:* Guildford (01483) 224963.

HARRIS, Kenneth; *see* Harris, D. K.

HARRIS, Leonard John; Commissioner, and Director, VAT Policy (formerly Internal Taxes), Customs and Excise, since 1991; *b* 4 July 1941; *s* of Leonard and May Harris; *m* 1st, 1965, Jill Christine Tompkins (marr. diss.); one *s* two *d*; 2nd, 1986, Jennifer Dilys Biddiscombe (*née* Barker). *Educ:* Westminster City Sch.; St John's Coll., Cambridge. BA 1964 (Eng. Lit.), MA 1967. HM Customs and Excise: Asst Principal, 1964; Private Sec. to Chairman, 1966–68; Principal, 1969; CS Selection Bd, 1970; HM Customs and Excise, 1971; Cabinet Office, 1971–74; First Sec., UK Rep. to EEC, 1974–76, Counsellor, 1976–77; Asst Sec., HM Customs and Excise, 1977–80, Cabinet Office, 1980–83; Under Sec., 1983; Comr of Customs and Excise, 1983–87; Under Sec., MPO, 1987; Under Sec., HM Treasury, 1987–91. *Recreations:* cooking, music, naturism. *Address:* c/o HM Customs and Excise, New King's Beam House, 22 Upper Ground, SE1 9PJ. *Clubs:* Oxford Naturist (Oxford).

HARRIS, Brigadier Lewis John, CBE 1961 (OBE 1949; MBE 1943); consultant, surveys and mapping; *b* 19 Dec. 1910; *e s* of David Rees Harris and Cecilia Harris; *m* 1975, Thelma Opal, *d* of James Marshall Carr and Zettie Lou Witt, and *widow* of Lt-Col A. L. Nowicki, US Corps of Engineers. *Educ:* Christ Coll., Brecon; RMA, Woolwich; Pembroke Coll., Cambridge (Exhibitioner), Mech. Sci. Tripos, MA. Commissioned RE 1930; Triangulation of Jamaica, 1937–39; served War of 1939–45: British Expeditionary Force, 1939–40 (despatches); First Army in North Africa, 1942–43, AFHQ and American Seventh Army, Italy, 1944; Land Forces SE Asia, India, Burma and Malaya, 1944–46; Chief Instructor, Sch. of Mil. Survey, 1946–49; War Office, Geog. Section GS, 1949–52; Ordnance Survey, 1952–53; Dir, Survey GHQ, Middle East, and GHQ, E Africa, 1953–55; Land Survey Adviser, Allied Forces, Mediterranean, 1954–55; Ordnance Survey of Great Britain, 1955–61; Brig. 1956; Dir, Map Production and Publication, 1956–59; Dir, Field Surveys, 1959–61; Dir of Mil. Survey, MoD and Chief of Geographical Section Gen. Staff, 1961–65. Consultant, Federal Surveys and Mapping, Canada, 1967–85. Hon. Col 135 Survey Engineer Regt, TA, 1965–67. Chm., Nat. Cttee for Cartography, Royal Society, 1961–67. Hon. Foreign Sec., Royal Geographical Soc., 1964–67; Vice-Pres., Internat. Cartographic Assoc., 1958–61. Hon. Vice-Pres., Army Rugby Union. FRAS, FRGS, FRICS. *Publications:* various papers on cartography in learned jls. *Recreations:* music, outdoor sports, travelling. *Address:* 12410 Hound Ears Point, Fox Den, PO Box 22129, Knoxville, TN 37933, USA. *Clubs:* Naval and Military, MCC; Hawks (Cambridge); Royal Ottawa Golf; IZ, FF, BB.

HARRIS, Lyndon Goodwin, RI 1958; RSW 1952; RWA 1947; artist in oil, water-colour, stained glass, and etching; *b* 25 July 1928; *s* of late S. E. Harris, ACIS and late Mary Elsie Harris. *Educ:* Halesowen Grammar Sch. Studied Art at: Birmingham Coll. of Art; Slade Sch. of Fine Art, 1946–50; University of London Inst. of Education, 1950–51; Courtauld Inst.; Central Sch. of Art and Crafts, London. Leverhulme Schol., Pilkington Schol., Slade Schol., and Slade Anatomy Prizeman; Dip. Fine Art (London) 1949; Courtauld Certificate, 1950; ATD 1951. *Works exhibited:* Paris Salon (Gold Medal, Oil Painting; Honourable Mention, Etching); RA (first exhibited at age of 13), RSA, RI, RSW, NEAC, RBA, RGI, RWA, and principal provincial galleries. *Works in permanent collections:* Govt Art Collection; University Coll., London; Birmingham and Midland Inst.;

City of Worcester; (stained glass) Gorsty Hill Methodist Church, Halesowen. *Recreation:* music (organ and pianoforte).

HARRIS, Margaret Frances, OBE 1975; Co-Director, Motley Theatre Design Course, Covent Garden, since 1992; *b* 28 May 1904; *d* of late William Birkbeck Harris and of Kathleen Marion Carey. *Educ:* Downe House. In partnership with Elizabeth Montgomery and late Sophie Devine as firm of Motley, 1931–; Co-Dir, former Theatre Design Course, at RNT Studio, Almeida, Riverside Studios, ENO, and Sadler's Wells. Has designed many productions in London and New York of drama, opera and ballet: first notable production, Richard of Bordeaux, for John Gielgud, 1932; sets and costumes for: Prokofiev's War and Peace, Coliseum, 1972; (with Elizabeth Montgomery) Unknown Soldier and His Wife, New London, 1973; A Family and a Fortune, 1975; Tosca, English Nat. Opera, 1976; Paul Bunyan, English Music Theatre, 1976; The Consul, Coliseum, 1978. *Publications:* Designing and Making Costume, by Motley, 1965; Theatre Props, by Motley, 1976. *Address:* 36 Rocks Lane, Barnes, SW13 0DA. *T:* 0181–878 3705; Motley Theatre Design Course, 67 Drury Lane, WC2.

HARRIS, Mark; Assistant Treasury Solicitor, Department for Education (formerly Education and Science), 1988–94; *b* 23 Feb. 1943; *s* of late Solomon Harris and Eva (*née* Lazarus); *m* 1972, Sharon Frances Colin; one *d*. *Educ:* Central Foundation Boys' Grammar Sch., London; London School of Economics and Political Science, London Univ. (LLB Hons). Solicitor of the Supreme Court, 1967. Entered Solicitor's Office, Dept of Employment, as Legal Asst, 1968; Sen. Legal Asst, 1973; Asst Solicitor, 1978; Legal Advr, 1987–88. *Recreations:* travel, walking, short-story writing, painting, London Jewish Male Choir (first tenor). *Address:* 17 Marlands Road, Clayhall, Ilford, Essex IG5 0JL.

HARRIS, Prof. Martin Best, CBE 1992; Vice-Chancellor, Manchester University, since 1992; *b* 28 June 1944; *s* of William Best Harris and Betty Evelyn (*née* Martin); *m* 1966, Barbara Mary (*née* Daniels); two *s*. *Educ:* Devonport High Sch. for Boys, Plymouth; Queens' Coll., Cambridge (BA, MA; Hon. Fellow, 1992); Sch. of Oriental and African Studies, London (PhD). Lecturer in French Linguistics, Univ. of Leicester, 1967; University of Salford: Sen. Lectr in Fr. Ling., 1974; Prof of Romance Ling., 1976–87; Dean of Social Sciences and Arts, 1978–81; Pro-Vice-Chancellor, 1981–87; Vice-Chancellor, Essex Univ., 1987–92. Member: Internat. Cttee for Historical Linguistics, 1979–86; UGC, 1984–87; HEFCE Review of Univ. Libraries, 1992–93; Chairman: NI Sub Cttee, UFC (formerly UGC), 1985–91; Nat. Curriculum Wkg Gp for Modern Foreign Langs, 1989–90. Mem. Council, Philological Soc., 1979–86, 1988–92. Chm. of Govs, Centre for Inf. on Lang. Teaching, 1990–; Vice Chm. of Governors, Parrs Wood High Sch., 1982–86; Gov., Colchester Sixth Form Coll., 1988–92; Member Governing Body: Anglia Polytechnic Univ. (formerly Anglia Poly.), 1989–93; SOAS, London Univ., 1990–93. Mem., Academia Europaea, 1991. Mem. Editorial Board: Journal Linguistics, 1982–91; Diachronica, 1983–92; French Studies, 1987–93; Jt Gen. Editor, Longman Linguistics Library, 1982–. Hon. LLD QUB, 1992; DUniv Essex, 1993. *Publications:* (ed) Romance Syntax: synchronic and diachronic perspectives, 1976; The Evolution of French Syntax: a comparative approach, 1978; (ed with N. Vincent) Studies in the Romance Verb, 1982; (ed with P. Ramat) Historical Development of Auxiliaries, 1987; (ed with N. Vincent) The Romance Languages, 1988; about 35 articles in appropriate jls and collections. *Recreations:* gardening, travel, wine. *Address:* University of Manchester, Oxford Road, Manchester M13 9PL. *T:* 0161–275 2010.

HARRIS, Martin Richard; Director, National Westminster Bank PLC, 1977–93; *b* 30 Aug. 1922; *m* 1952, Diana Moira (*née* Gandar Dower) JP, Mayor of Merton, 1985–86; four *s*. *Educ:* Wellington Coll. FCA. Captain, RE, ME and Italy, 1941–46. Joined Price Waterhouse & Co., 1946, Partner, 1956–74; Dir Gen., Panel on Take-Overs and Mergers, 1974–77; Director: Reckitt and Colman, 1977–82 (Dep. Chm., 1979–82); County Bank, then NatWest Investment Bank, 1977–92; Inmos International, 1980–84; Equity & Law Life Assce Soc., 1981–87 (Dep. Chm., 1983–87), Westland plc, 1981–85, De La Rue Co. plc, 1981–93; TR Industrial & General Trust plc, 1983–86; Chm. and Dir, Nineteen Twenty-Eight Investment Trust plc, 1984–86; Dir, NatWest Smaller Cos Investment Trust, 1991–. Inst. of Chartered Accountants in England and Wales: Mem. Council, 1971–79; Chm., Parly and Law Cttee, 1973–74; Chm., Prof. Standards Cttee, 1977–79; Mem., Accountants Internat. Study Gp, 1972–74. Mem., DTI's Company Law Consultative Gp, 1972–74. Member: Court, Drapers' Co., 1978– (Master, 1987); Court, Co. of Chartered Accountants, 1977–90 (Master, 1983). Mem. Council, RCM, 1985– (Chm. Development Fund, 1984–92); Governor, QMC, London Univ., 1979–89; Chm. Council, Queen Mary & Westfield Coll., London Univ., 1989–. FRCM 1988. US Silver Star 1945. *Recreations:* music and opera, philately, antique furniture and china, keeping busy. *Address:* 29 Belvedere Grove, Wimbledon, SW19 7RQ. *T:* 0181–946 0951. *Clubs:* Carlton, MCC.

HARRIS, Maurice Kingston, CB 1976; formerly Secretary, Northern Ireland Ministry of Home Affairs, Jan. 1973, seconded to Northern Ireland Office, 1974–76; *b* 5 Oct. 1916; *s* of Albert Kingston Harris and Annie Rebecca Harris; *m* 1948, Margaret, *d* of Roderick Fraser and Gertrude McGregor; one *s* three *d*. *Educ:* The Perse Sch.; London Univ. 1st cl. Hons Mod. Langs, 1939. Served in Indian Army, 8th Punjab Regt, 1942–46. Colonial Office, 1946–47. Entered Northern Ireland Civil Service, 1947, and served in various Ministries; retired 1976. *Recreations:* music, walking. *Address:* 27 Strangford Avenue, Belfast BT9 6PG. *T:* Belfast (01232) 681409.

HARRIS, Mervyn Leslie Richard; Stipendiary Magistrate, Nottinghamshire, since 1991; *b* 9 Aug. 1942; *s* of Albert Leslie Harris and Gladys Mary (*née* Plummer); *m* 1967, Marcia Jane Tomblin; one *s* one *d*. *Educ:* King Henry VIII Sch., Coventry; University Coll. London (LLB 1964). Admitted solicitor, 1969; Partner, Hughes & Masser, solicitors, Coventry, 1969–91. Chm. (part-time), Social Security Appeals Tribunal, 1985–91; Actg Stipendiary Magistrate, 1987–91. Clerk to local charities in Coventry and Atherstone. *Recreations:* walking, railways, railway history, watching football, Rugby and cricket.

HARRIS, Michael Frank; His Honour Judge Michael Harris; a Circuit Judge, since 1992; *b* 11 Jan. 1942; *s* of Joseph Frank Harris and Edna Harris; *m* 1969, Veronica Brend; one *s* one *d*. *Educ:* St Bartholomew's Grammar Sch., Newbury; Merton Coll., Oxford (BA). Called to the Bar, Middle Temple, 1965; a Recorder, 1990–92. *Recreations:* piano playing, amateur dramatics, walking, music, theatre, travel, reading. *Address:* c/o South Eastern Circuit Office, New Cavendish House, 18 Maltravers Street, WC2R 3EU.

HARRIS, Rear-Adm. Michael George Temple; Clerk to the Clothworkers' Co. of the City of London and Secretary to the Clothworkers' Foundation, since 1992; *b* 5 July 1941; *s* of Cdr Antony John Temple Harris, OBE, RN and Doris Drake Harris; *m* 1970, Katrina Chichester; three *d*. *Educ:* Pangbourne Coll.; RNC, Dartmouth. FRGS 1978; FNI 1988. Qualified Submarines, 1963, TAS 1968; commanded HM Submarines: Osiris, 1970–72; Sovereign, 1975–77 (N Pole, 1976); 3rd Submarine Sqn, 1982–85; commanded HM Ships: Cardiff, 1980–82 (Falkland Is, 1982); Ark Royal, 1987–89; ACDS (NATO/UK), 1989–92. Exchange service with USN, 3rd Fleet Staff, 1972–75. Younger Brother of Trinity House, 1989–. Liveryman, Shipwrights' Co., 1991–. *Recreations:* riding, fishing, bell-ringing, monumental brasses, reading. *Address:* Clothworkers' Hall, Dunster Court, Mincing Lane, EC3R 7AH. *Club:* Naval and Military.

HARRIS, Miriam Janine; Executive Director, Clore Foundation, since 1988; *b* 22 June 1945; *d* of late Frank Lesser and Mira Lesser; *m* 1968, John Harris. *Educ:* Liverpool Univ. (BA Hons Psychol.). Res. assistant, Tavistock Inst. of Human Relns, 1966–69; SO, then SSO, SSRC, 1969–78; Social Science Grants Officer, Nuffield Foundn, 1979–80; Sen. Res. Fellow, Goldsmiths' Coll., Univ. of London, 1980–82; Sec., Nuffield Foundn Pharmacy Inquiry, 1983–85; Res. Advr, ABRC, 1986–87. *Address:* c/o Clore Foundation, 3 Chelsea Manor Studios, Flood Street, SW3 5SR. *T:* 0171–351 6061.

HARRIS, Nigel John; General Secretary, Engineering Section, since 1995, and Member, Executive Council, since 1980, Amalgamated Engineering and Electrical Union; *b* 20 March 1943; *s* of Frederick and Irene Harris; *m* 1964, Cynthia; two *s*. *Educ:* C of E Sch., Dawley, Shropshire; Pool Hill Sec. Modern. Worked at Kemberton Colliery to 1962; ironfounding, John Maddocks & Co., 1963–65; Union representative, Glynwed Foundries, 1965–80; full time Officer, 1980, rep. foundry workers for AEW and on health and safety matters; Nat. Sec., Foundry Sect., AEU, then AEEU, 1980–95; Pro-tem. Pres., AEEU, Feb.–Nov. 1995. Member: Exec. Cttee, CSEU, 1985–; NEC, Lab. Party, 1991–. Former Editor, The Foundry Worker. Mem., Royal British Legion. *Recreations:* swimming, driving. *Address:* 18 Merlin Avenue, Knutsford, Cheshire WA16 8HJ. *T:* Knutsford (01565) 652094.

HARRIS, Patricia Ann, (Mrs J. N. K. Harris); Central President, The Mothers' Union, 1989–94 (Vice-President, 1986–88); *b* 29 May 1939; *m* 1963, Rev. James Nigel Kingsley Harris, BA; one *s* one *d*. *Educ:* Trinity Coll., Carmarthen. Teaching Dip. Teacher, 1959–63; pt-time special needs teacher, 1963–88; vol. teacher, Gloucester Prison, 1978–85. Member: Glos Dio. Synod, 1980–; C of E General Synod, 1985– (Mem., Bd of Mission Exec., 1991–); Women's Nat. Commn, 1994; USPG Council, 1994–; Cttee, Black Anglican Concerns, 1995–. Mothers' Union: Young Wives Leader, 1963–65; Enrolling Mem., 1967–76; Presiding Mem., 1969–74; Diocesan Social Concern Chm., 1974–80; Pres., Glos dio., 1980–85. *Recreations:* swimming, watching Rugby, cooking, craft work. *Address:* The Vicarage, Elm Road, Stonehouse, Glos GL10 2NP. *T:* Stonehouse (01453) 822332.

HARRIS, Rt. Rev. Patrick Burnet; *see* Southwell, Bishop of.

HARRIS, Prof. Peter Charles, MD, PhD, FRCP; Editor, Cardioscience, since 1990; Simon Marks Professor of Cardiology, University of London, 1966–88, now Emeritus; Consultant Physician, National Heart and Chest Hospitals; *b* 26 May 1923; *s* of late David Jonathan Valentine and Nellie Dean Harris; *m* 1st, 1952, Felicity Margaret Hartridge (marr. diss. 1982); two *d*; 2nd, 1989, Frances Monkarsh. *Educ:* St Olave's Grammar Sch.; Univ. of London. MB, BS (London) 1946; MRCP 1950; MD (Univ. medal) 1951; PhD 1955; FRCP 1965. House appts at King's Coll. Hospital, and elsewhere, 1946–55. Nuffield Fellow, Columbia Univ., New York, 1955–57; Lectr, Sen. Lectr and Reader in Medicine, Univ. of Birmingham, 1957–66; Dir, Inst. of Cardiology, Univ. of London, 1966–73. Pres., Internat. Soc. for Heart Research, 1981–83. Mem., Instituto Veneto, 1994. Hon. FACC, 1976. *Publications:* The Human Pulmonary Circulation (with D. Heath), 1962, 3rd edn 1986; articles to jls, etc, on cardio-pulmonary physiology and biochemistry. *Recreation:* chamber music. *Address:* 42 Great Percy Street, WC1X 9QR. *T:* 0171–278 2911; Cannaregio 3698A, Venice, Italy. *T:* (41) 5289001; 2089 Gulf of Mexico Drive #209, Longboat Key, FL 34228, USA. *T:* (813) 3831067.

HARRIS, Group Captain Peter Langridge, CBE 1988; AE 1961 (Clasp 1971); CEng, FIEE; DL; ADC to the Queen, 1984–88; Inspector, Royal Auxiliary Air Force, 1983–88; *b* 6 Sept. 1929; *s* of Arthur Langridge Harris and Doris Mabel (*née* Offen); *m* 1955, (Yvonne) Patricia Stone; two *d*. *Educ:* St Edward's Sch., Oxford; Univ. of Birmingham (BSc). CEng, FIEE 1976. Served: RAF, 1947–49; RAFVR, 1949–60; RAuxAF, 1960–78 and 1982–88; commanded 1 (Co. Hertford) Maritime HQ Unit, 1973–77; Air Force Mem., 1978–94, Vice-Chm. (Air), 1988–94, TA&VRA for Greater London; Gp Captain 1983. Elliott Bros (London) Ltd, 1952–55; Decca Navigator Co. Ltd, 1955–59; GEC plc, 1959–89; retired. Mem. Bd, Milton Keynes Business Venture, 1983–89. Mem. Bd of Management, Princess Marina House, Rustington, 1990–. Chm., Hatfield Dist IEE, 1979–80. Mem., Council, Reserve Forces Assoc., 1989–. Freeman, GAPAN, 1987–. DL Greater London, 1986. Chevalier, SMO of Temple of Jerusalem, 1994. *Recreation:* travel. *Address:* 10 Dolphin Court, St Helens Parade, Southsea, Hants PO4 0QL. *T:* Portsmouth (01705) 817602; 29 Davenham Avenue, Northwood, Mddx HA6 3HW. *T:* Northwood (019274) 24291. *Clubs:* Royal Air Force; Royal Naval and Royal Albert Yacht (Portsmouth).

HARRIS, Peter Michael; Official Solicitor to the Supreme Court, since 1993; *b* 13 April 1937; *s* of Benjamin Warren Harris and Ethel Evelyn Harris (*née* Mabbutt); *m* 1963, Bridget Burke; one *s* two *d*. *Educ:* Cirencester Grammar School; Britannia Royal Naval College, Dartmouth. Cadet, RN, 1953; Lieut Comdr 1967; retired from RN 1972. Called to the Bar, Gray's Inn, 1971; Lord Chancellor's Department: Legal Asst, 1974; Dep. Circuit Administrator, Midland and Oxford Circuit, 1980; Head of Property and Family Law Div., 1982; Head of Civil Courts Div., 1985; Circuit Administrator, Northern Circuit, 1986–93. Asst Editor, County Court Practice, 1985–. *Publication:* The Children Act 1989: a procedural handbook, 1991. *Recreations:* reading, walking, swimming, gardening. *Address:* 81 Chancery Lane, WC2A 1DD. *T:* 0171–911 7116.

HARRIS, Philip; Principal, Monopolies and Mergers Commission, 1977–85, retired; *b* Manchester, 15 Dec. 1915; *er s* of S. D. Harris and Sarah Chazan; *m* 1939, Sarah Henriques Valentine; three *d*. *Educ:* Manchester Grammar Sch.; Trinity Hall, Cambridge (Open Scholarship, BA 1st Cl (with dist.), Historical Tripos, MA 1970). Asst Principal, Board of Trade, 1938–40. Served War, 1940–45; Anti-Aircraft Command and Western Europe; 2nd Lieut RA, 1941; Lieut, 2/8th Lancs Fusiliers, 1944; Capt., 6th Royal Welch Fusiliers, 1945. Principal, Board of Trade, 1946; Asst Sec., Board of Trade, 1948–64; Asst Registrar, Office of the Registrar of Restrictive Trading Agreements, 1964–66, Principal Asst Registrar, 1966–73; Principal Asst Registrar, Fair Trading Div. I, DTI, 1973; Dir, Restrictive Trade Practices Div., Office of Fair Trading, 1973–76. Nuffield Travelling Fellowship, 1956–57 (study of Indian Industrial Development). UK Mem., EEC Adv. Cttee on Cartels and Monopolies, 1973–76; Mem., Labour Finance and Industry Gp, 1990–. Leader, UK Delgn to Internat. Cotton Advisory Cttee, 1960, 1963. Lectr, Univ. of the Third Age, London, 1995–. *Publications:* various articles on monopolies and restrictive trade practices policy and current developments in UK competition law and administration. *Recreation:* history. *Address:* 23 Court House Gardens, Finchley, N3 1PU. *T:* 0181–346 3138.

HARRIS, Sir Philip (Charles), Kt 1985; Chairman: Carpetright of London, since 1993; Harris Ventures Ltd, since 1988; C. W. Harris Properties, since 1988; *b* 15 Sept. 1942; *s* of Charles William Harris and Ruth Ellen (*née* Ward); *m* 1960, Pauline Norma (*née* Chumley); three *s* one *d*. *Educ:* Streatham Grammar School. Chm., 1964–88, Chief Exec., 1987–88, Harris Queensway Plc. Dir, Harveys Hldgs, 1986–; non-executive Director:

Great Universal Stores, 1986–; Fisons Plc, 1986–94; Molyneux Estates, 1990–. Mem., British Show Jumping Assoc., 1974. Chm., Guy's and Lewisham NHS Trust, 1991–; Member: Council of Governors, UMDS of Guy's and St Thomas's Hosps, 1984– (Hon. Fellow, 1992); Court of Patrons, RCOG, 1984–; Chm., Generation Trust, 1984–. Dep. Chm., Cons. Party Treasurers, 1993. Freeman, City of London, 1992. Hon. Fellow, Oriel Coll., Oxford, 1989; Hon. FRCR 1993. Hambro Business Man of the Year, 1983. *Recreations:* football, cricket, show jumping, tennis. *Address:* Harris Ventures Ltd, 187/189 Sevenoaks Way, Orpington, Kent BR5 3AQ.

HARRIS, Phillip, FRCSE, FRCPE, FRCSGlas; FRSE; Consultant Neurosurgeon; formerly Deputy Director, Department of Surgical Neurology, Royal Infirmary and Western General Hospital, Edinburgh; Senior Lecturer, Edinburgh University, 1955–87; Member, MRC Brain Metabolism Unit, University of Edinburgh, 1952–80; Editor, Paraplegia, since 1980; *b* Edinburgh, 28 March 1922; *s* of late Simon Harris, Edinburgh; *m* 1949, Sheelagh Shèna (*née* Coutts); one *s* one *d.* *Educ:* Royal High Sch., Edinburgh; Edinburgh Univ.; Sch. of Med. of Royal Colls, Edinburgh. Medallist in Anatomy, Physiol., Physics, Materia Medica and Therapeutics, Med., Midwifery and Gynaec., and Surgery. LRCP and LRCSE, LRCP and SG 1944; FRCSE 1948; MRCPE 1954; FRCPE 1959; FRCS(Glas) 1964 (*ad eundem*). Capt., RAMC, 1945–48. Past Chm., Sch. of Occupational Therapy, Edinburgh. Sometime Vis. Prof./Guest Chief in Neurosurg., USA, Canada, Europe, S America, Far East and Middle East; Lectures: Sydney Watson-Smith, RCPE, 1967; Honeymoon-Gillespie, Edinburgh Univ., 1968. Mem., WHO Cttee for Prevention of Neurotrauma, 1985. Past Chm., Professional and Linguistics Assessments Bd, GMC. World Federation of Neurosurgical Societies: Sen. UK Deleg. in Neurosurg. and Hon. Vice-Pres., 1977–; Dep. Chm., Neurotraumatol. Cttee; Founder, Internat. Conf. of Recent Advances in Neurotraumatol.; Founder and Past Chairman: Epilepsy Soc., SE Scotland; Scottish Assoc. of Neurol Scis; Scottish Sports Assoc. for Disabled (Hon. Pres.); Past Member of Council: Soc. of British Neurolog. Surgs; Neurol Sect., RSocMed; Past Pres., British Cervical Spine Soc. Past Director, Epilepsy Internat.; Dir and Trustee, Scottish Trust for Physically Disabled; Mem. Council, Thistle Foundn. President: Royal High Sch. FP Club, 1978; Edinburgh Rotary Club, 1991–92. Inventor of neurosurg. instruments and apparatus. Medal, Internat. Med. Soc. of Paraplegia, 1985; Dr A. S. Lakshumpathi Medal and Prize, Madras, 1986. *Publications:* (ed jtly) Epilepsy, 1971; (ed jtly) Head Injuries, 1971; chapters in books on neurological surgery; over 100 papers in scientific jls on various neurosurgical topics. *Recreations:* sport, music, travel. *Address:* 4/5 Fettes Rise, Edinburgh EH4 1QH. *T:* 0131–552 8900. *Clubs:* New (Edinburgh); Royal Scottish Automobile (Glasgow).

HARRIS, Ven. (Reginald) Brian; Archdeacon of Manchester, since 1980; a Residentiary Canon of Manchester Cathedral, since 1980, Sub-Dean since 1986; *b* 14 Aug. 1934; *s* of Reginald and Ruby Harris; *m* 1959, Anne Patricia Hughes; one *s* one *d.* *Educ:* Eltham College; Christ's College Cambridge (MA); Ridley Hall, Cambridge. Curate of Wednesbury, 1959–61; Curate of Uttoxeter, 1961–64; Vicar of St Peter, Bury, 1964–70; Vicar of Walmsley, Bolton, 1970–80; RD of Walmsley, 1970–80. *Recreations:* walking, painting, music. *Address:* 4 Victoria Avenue, Eccles, Manchester M30 9HA. *T:* 0161–707 6444.

HARRIS, Richard Reader; *b* 4 June 1913; *s* of Richard Reader Harris; *m* 1940, Pamela Rosemary Merrick Stephens; three *d.* *Educ:* St Lawrence Coll., Ramsgate. Called to the Bar, 1941. Fire Service, 1939–45. MP (C) Heston and Isleworth, 1950–70. *Recreations:* squash, tennis.

HARRIS, Richard Travis; Director, Burton Group plc, 1984–92; *b* 15 April 1919; 2nd *s* of Douglas Harris and Emmeline Harris (*née* Travis); *m* 1st, 1941, June Constance Rundle (marr. diss. 1953); two *d*; 2nd, 1953, Margaret Sophia Nye (*née* Aron); one *s* one *d.* *Educ:* Charterhouse; RMA Woolwich. Served War of 1939–45, France, Western Desert, Tunisia, Italy (despatches twice); BAOR, 1945–46; Sudan Defence Force Signal Regt, 1947–50 (CO, 1948–50); retired from Royal Signals, 1950, Lt-Col. Man. Dir, Rediffusion (Nigeria) Ltd and Gen. Manager, Rediffusion in Africa, 1951–54; Dep. Gen. Manager, Associated-Rediffusion Ltd, 1954–57; Man. Dir, Coates & Co. (Plymouth) Ltd, 1957–64 (Dir, 1957–68); Man. Dir, 1964–78, Chm., 1970–78, Dollond & Aitchison Ltd; Chm., Dollond & Aitchison Group Ltd (formerly TWW Enterprises Ltd), 1970–78 (Dir, 1968–85); Director: Gallaher Ltd, 1970–87 (Dep. Chm., 1978–84); Dollond International Ltd, 1973–83; Filotechnica Salmoiraghi SpA, 1974–83; Istituto Ottico Vigano SpA, 1974–83; Saunders Valve Co. Ltd, 1978–84; Mono Pumps Ltd, 1978–84; Formatura Iniezione Polimeri SpA, 1978–84; Tobacco Kiosks Ltd, 1978–84; Gallaher Pensions Ltd, 1975–84. Chairman: Fedn of Optical Corporate Bodies, 1970–82; Fedn of Ophthalmic & Dispensing Opticians, 1985–87; Vice-Pres., Inst. of Dirs, 1985–89 (Chm. Council, 1982–85); Mem. Exec. Cttee, Wider Share Ownership Council, 1987–91; Mem. Council, Univ. of Birmingham, 1978–93, Life Mem., Court, 1981. Governor, Royal Shakespeare Theatre, 1980–94; Master, Coachmakers and Coach Harness Makers, 1963–64. *Recreations:* fishing, theatre. *Address:* 21 Lucy's Mill, Stratford-upon-Avon, Warwickshire CV37 6DE. *T:* Stratford-upon-Avon (01789) 266016.

HARRIS, Robert Dennis; author and journalist; *b* 7 March 1957; *s* of Dennis Harris and Audrey (*née* Hardy); *m* 1988, Gillian Hornby; one *s* one *d.* *Educ:* King Edward VII Sch., Melton Mowbray; Selwyn Coll., Cambridge (BA Hons English). Chm., Cambridge Fabian Soc., 1977; Pres., Cambridge Union, 1978. Joined BBC TV Current Affairs Dept, 1978; Researcher and Film Dir, Tonight, Nationwide and Panorama, 1978–81; Reporter, Newsnight, 1981–85, Panorama, 1985–87; Political Editor, Observer, 1987–89; Political Reporter, This Week, Thames TV, 1988–89; Political Columnist, Sunday Times, 1989–92. *Publications:* (with Jeremy Paxman) A Higher Form of Killing: the history of gas and germ warfare, 1982; Gotcha! the media, the government and the Falklands crisis, 1983; The Making of Neil Kinnock, 1984; Selling Hitler: the story of the Hitler diaries, 1986 (televised, 1991); Good and Faithful Servant: the unauthorized biography of Bernard Ingham, 1990; Fatherland (novel), 1992 (filmed, 1994); The Media Trilogy, 1994; Enigma (novel), 1995. *Recreations:* collecting books, walking, fishing, snooker. *Address:* The Old Vicarage, Kintbury, Berks RG17 9TR. *T:* Kintbury (01488) 658073.

HARRIS, Robin (David Ronald), CBE 1988; Assistant to Baroness Thatcher, since 1990; *b* 22 June 1952; *s* of Ronald Desmond Harris and Isabella Jamieson Harris. *Educ:* Canford Sch.; Exeter Coll., Oxford (Stapeldon Schol., MA History, DPhil). Desk Officer, Conservative Res. Dept, 1978–81; Special Adviser: to Financial Sec. to the Treasury, 1981–83; to Home Secretary, 1983–85; Dir, Conservative Res. Dept, 1985–89; Mem., Prime Minister's Policy Unit, 1989–90. *Recreations:* reading, travel. *Club:* United Oxford & Cambridge University.

HARRIS, Rosemary Jeanne; author; *b* 1923; *yr d* of Marshal of the RAF Sir Arthur Harris, 1st Bt, GCB, OBE, AFC, LLD, and of Barbara Kyrle Money. *Educ:* privately; Thorneloe Sch., Weymouth; St Martin's, Central and Chelsea Schs of Art. Red Cross Nursing Auxiliary, London, Westminster Div., from 1941. Student, 1945–48; picture restorer, 1949; student at Courtauld Inst. (Dept of Technology), 1950; Reader, MGM, 1951–52; subseq. full-time writer. Reviewer of children's books for The Times, 1970–73. Television plays: Peronik, 1976; The Unknown Enchantment, 1981. *Publications:* The Summer-House, 1956; Voyage to Cythera, 1958; Venus with Sparrows, 1961; All My Enemies, 1967; The Nice Girl's Story, 1968; A Wicked Pack of Cards, 1969; The Double Snare, 1975; Three Candles for the Dark, 1976; *for children:* The Moon in the Cloud, 1968 (Carnegie Medal); The Shadow on the Sun, 1970; The Seal-Singing, 1971; The Child in the Bamboo Grove, 1971; The Bright and Morning Star, 1972; The King's White Elephant, 1973; The Lotus and the Grail, 1974; The Flying Ship, 1974; The Little Dog of Fo, 1976; I Want to be a Fish, 1977; A Quest for Orion, 1978; Beauty and the Beast, 1979; Greenfinger House, 1979; Tower of the Stars, 1980; The Enchanted Horse, 1981; Janni's Stork, 1982; Zed, 1982; (adapted) Heidi, by Johanna Spyri, 1983; Summers of the Wild Rose, 1987; (ed) Poetry Anthology: Love and the Merry-Go-Round, 1988; Colm of the Islands, 1989; Ticket to Freedom, 1991; The Wildcat Strike, 1995. *Recreations:* music, theatre, gardening. *Address:* c/o A P Watt, 20 John Street, WC1N 2DR.

See also Sir A. T. K. Harris, Bt.

HARRIS, Rosina Mary; Consultant, Taylor Joynson Garrett, since 1989; Partner, Joynson-Hicks, Solicitors, 1954–89 (Senior Partner, 1977–86); *b* 30 May 1921; *d* of late Alfred Harris, CBE, DSO, and Rosa Alfreda Harris. *Educ:* St Swithun's Sch., Winchester; Oxford Univ. (BA 1946, MA; BCL). Joined American Ambulance of Gt Britain, 1940. Member, Whitford Committee (a Cttee set up under the Chairmanship of Hon. Mr Justice Whitford to enquire into and report as to copyright law), 1973. The Queen's Silver Jubilee Medal, 1977. *Recreations:* theatre, riding. *Address:* 23 Devonshire Place, W1N 1PD. *T:* (office) 0171–353 1234.

See also J. R. Harris.

HARRIS, Prof. Roy, MA, DPhil, PhD; FRSA; Professor of General Linguistics, University of Oxford, 1978–88, now Emeritus; Fellow of Worcester College, Oxford, 1978–88; *b* 24 Feb. 1931; *s* of Harry and Emmie J. Harris; *m* 1955, Rita Doreen Shulman; one *d.* *Educ:* Queen Elizabeth's Hospital, Bristol; St Edmund Hall, Oxford (MA, DPhil; Hon. Fellow 1987); SOAS, London (PhD). Lecteur, Ecole Normale Supérieure, Paris, 1956–57; Asst Lectr, 1957–58, Lectr, 1958–60, Univ. of Leicester; Exeter Coll., Oxford, 1960–76; Keble Coll., Oxford, 1960–67; Magdalen Coll., Oxford, 1960–76; New Coll., Oxford, 1960–67; Faculty of Medieval and Modern Languages, Oxford, 1961–76; Fellow and Tutor in Romance Philology, Keble Coll., Oxford, 1967–76; Prof. of the Romance Langs, Oxford Univ., and Fellow of Trinity Coll., 1976–77; Prof. of English Language, Univ. of Hong Kong, 1988–91; Dir d'études associé, Ecole Pratique des Hautes Etudes, Paris, 1991–92; Fellow, Univ. Professors, Boston, 1993–95. Visiting Professor: Jawaharlal Nehru Univ., New Delhi, 1986; State Univ. of NY, 1987. Council Member, Philological Soc., 1978–82. Editor, Language & Communication, 1980–. Scott Moncrieff prize, Translators' Assoc. (Soc. of Authors), 1984. *Publications:* Synonymy and Linguistic Analysis, 1973; Communication and Language, 1978; The Language-Makers, 1980; The Language Myth, 1981; (trans.) F. de Saussure: Course in General Linguistics, 1983; (ed) Approaches to Language, 1983; (ed) Developmental Mechanisms of Language, 1985; The Origin of Writing, 1986; Reading Saussure, 1987; Language, Saussure and Wittgenstein, 1988; (ed) Linguistic Thought in England 1914–1945, 1988; (with T. J. Taylor) Landmarks in Linguistic Thought: the Western tradition from Socrates to Saussure, 1989; La sémiologie de l'écriture, 1994; contribs to Analysis, Behavioral and Brain Sciences, Encounter, Essays in Criticism, French Studies, History and Philosophy of Logic, International Jl of Moral and Social Studies, Jl of Linguistics, Language Sciences, Linguistics, Medium Ævum, Mind, Revue de linguistique romane, Semiotica, Studies in Eighteenth-Century Culture, Theoria, TLS, Zeitschrift für romanische Philologie. *Recreations:* cricket, modern art and design. *Address:* 2 Paddox Close, Oxford OX2 7LR. *T:* Oxford (01865) 54256.

HARRIS, (Theodore) Wilson, CCH 1991; *b* 24 March 1921; *m* 1st, 1945, Cecily Carew; 2nd, 1959, Margaret Whitaker (*née* Burns). *Educ:* Queen's Coll., Georgetown, British Guiana. Studied land surveying, British Guiana, 1939, and subseq. qualified to practise; led many survey parties (mapping and geomorphological research) in the interior; Senior Surveyor, Projects, for Govt of British Guiana, 1955–58. Came to live in London, 1959. Writer in Residence, Univ. of West Indies and Univ. of Toronto, 1970; Commonwealth Fellow, Leeds Univ., 1971; Vis. Prof., Univ. of Texas at Austin, 1972; Guggenheim Fellow, 1973; Henfield Fellow, UEA, 1974; Southern Arts Writer's Fellowship, 1976; Guest Lectr, Univ. of Mysore, 1978; Vis. Lectr, Yale Univ., 1979; Writer in Residence: Univ. of Newcastle, Australia, 1979; Univ. of Qld, Australia, 1986; Vis. Prof., Univ. of Texas at Austin, 1981–82; Regents' Lectr, Univ. of California, 1983. Hon. DLit Univ. of West Indies, 1984; Hon. DLitt Kent at Canterbury, 1988. Guyana Prize for Fiction, 1985–87; Premio Mondello dei Cinque Continenti, 1992. *Publications:* Eternity to Season (poems, privately printed), 1954; Palace of the Peacock, 1960; The Far Journey of Oudin, 1961; The Whole Armour, 1962; The Secret Ladder, 1963; Heartland, 1964; The Eye of the Scarecrow, 1965; The Waiting Room, 1967; Tradition, the Writer and Society: Critical Essays, 1967; Tumatumari, 1968; Ascent to Omai, 1970; The Sleepers of Roraima (a Carib Trilogy), 1970; The Age of the Rainmakers, 1971; Black Marsden, 1972; Companions of the Day and Night, 1975; Da Silva da Silva's Cultivated Wilderness (filmed, 1987), and Genesis of the Clowns, 1977; The Tree of the Sun, 1978; Explorations (essays), 1981; The Angel at the Gate, 1982; The Womb of Space: the cross-cultural imagination, 1983; Carnival, 1985; The Infinite Rehearsal, 1987; The Four Banks of the River of Space, 1990; The Radical Imagination (essays), 1992; Resurrection at Sorrow Hill, 1993. *Address:* c/o Faber and Faber, 3 Queen Square, WC1N 3AU.

HARRIS, Thomas George, CMG 1995; HM Diplomatic Service; Ambassador to the Republic of Korea, since 1994; *b* 6 Feb. 1945; *s* of Kenneth James Harris and Dorothy Harris; *m* 1967, Mei-Ling Hwang; three *s.* *Educ:* Haberdashers' Aske's School; Gonville and Caius College, Cambridge. MA. Board of Trade, 1966–69; British Embassy, Tokyo, 1969–71; Asst Private Sec. to Minister for Aerospace, 1971–72; Dept. of Trade, 1972–76; Cabinet Office, 1976–78; Principal Private Sec. to Sec. of State for Trade and Industry, 1978–79; Asst Sec., Dept of Trade, 1979–83; Counsellor (Commercial), British Embassy, Washington, 1983–88; Head of Chancery, Lagos, 1988–90; Dep. High Comr, Nigeria, 1990–91; Head, East African Dept, 1991–92, African Dept (Equatorial), 1992–94, FCO. *Address:* c/o Foreign and Commonwealth Office, King Charles Street, SW1A 2AH. *Club:* United Oxford & Cambridge University.

HARRIS, Toby; *see* Harris, J. T.

HARRIS, Hon. Walter Edward, PC (Canada); QC (Canada); DCL; *b* 14 Jan. 1904; *s* of Melvin Harris and Helen (*née* Carruthers); *m* 1933, Grace Elma Morrison; one *s* two *d.* *Educ:* Osgoode Hall, Toronto. Served War of 1939–45. First elected to House of Commons, Canada, 1940 (re-elected 1945, 1949, 1953), MP (Canada) until 1957. Parliamentary Asst to Sec of State for External Affairs, 1947; Parly Asst to Prime Minister, 1948; Minister of Citizenship and Immigration, 1950; of Finance, 1954–57. Mem. of the firm of Harris, Willis, Barristers, Markdale. *Address:* Markdale, Ontario N0L 1H0, Canada.

HARRIS, (Walter) Frank; retired 1982; *b* 19 May 1920; *m* Esther Blanche Hill; two *s* two *d.* *Educ:* King Edward's Sch., Birmingham; University of Nottingham, BCom (Hons) 1949; BSc (1st cl. Hons) Open Univ., 1994. Served Royal Air Force, 1939–46. University,

1946–49. Ford Motor Company, 1950–65; Principal City Officer and Town Clerk, Newcastle upon Tyne, 1965–69. Comptroller and Dir, Admin, Massey-Ferguson (UK), 1969–71; Finance Dir, Dunlop SA Ltd, 1972–79; Business Planning Exec., Dunlop Ltd (UK Tyre Gp), 1979–81. *Recreations:* astrophysics, fell walking, DIY, gardening. *Address:* Acomb High House, Northumberland NE46 4PH. *T:* Hexham (01434) 602844.

HARRIS, William Barclay, QC 1961; *b* 25 Nov. 1911; *s* of W. Cecil Harris, Moatlands, E Grinstead, Sussex; *m* 1937, Elizabeth, 2nd *d* of Capt. Sir Clive Milnes-Coates, 2nd Bt, and of Lady Celia Milnes-Coates, JP; one *s* two *d. Educ:* Harrow; Trinity Coll., Cambridge (MA). Served 1940–45: with Coldstream Guards, N Africa, Italy, Germany (despatches), Major. Barrister, Inner Temple, 1937 (Bencher, 1991). Chm., Rowton Hotels, 1965–83. A Church Commissioner, 1966–82 (Chm., Redundant Churches Cttee, 1972–82; Mem., Bd of Governors, 1972–82). Pres., Georgian Group, 1990– (Chm., 1985–90). Liveryman, Worshipful Co. of Merchant Taylors. *Address:* Moatlands, East Grinstead, West Sussex RH19 4LL. *T:* Sharpthorne (01342) 810228; 29 Barkston Gardens, SW5 0ER. *T:* 0171–373 8793. *Clubs:* Athenæum, MCC, Brooks's, Nikaean.

HARRIS, Sir William (Gordon), KBE 1969; CB 1963; MA (Cantab); FEng; FICE; Director-General, Highways, Ministry of Transport, later Department of the Environment, 1965–73; *b* 10 June 1912; *s* of late Capt. James Whyte Harris, Royal Naval Reserve, and Margaret Roberta Buchanan Forsyth; *m* 1st, 1938, Margaret Emily Harvie (*d* 1991); three *s* one *d*; 2nd, 1992, Mrs Rachel Bishop (*née* Goucher). *Educ:* Liverpool Coll.; Sidney Sussex Coll., Cambridge. Mechanical Sciences Tripos and BA 1932, MA 1937. London Midland & Scottish Railway, 1932–35; Sudan Irrigation Dept, 1935–37; Joined Civil Engineer in Chief's Dept, Admiralty, 1937; Asst Civil Engineer in Chief, 1950; Deputy Civil Engineer in Chief, 1955; Civil Engineer in Chief, 1959; Dir-Gen., Navy Works, 1960–63; Dir-Gen. of Works, MPBW, 1963–65. Partner, Peter Fraenkel & Partners, 1973–78; Chm., B & CE Holiday Management Co. & Benefit Trust Co., 1978–87. Dir, British Sch. of Osteopathy, 1982–92 (Chm., 1990–92). Chief British Delegate to: Perm. Internat. Assoc. of Navigation Congresses, 1969–June 1985 (Vice-Pres., 1976–79); Perm. Internat. Assoc. of Road Congresses, 1970–73; Mem., Dover Harbour Bd, 1959–82 (Dep. Chm., 1975–79; Chm., 1980–82); Chm., Construction Industry Manpower Bd, 1976–79. Commonwealth Fund (of New York) Fellowship, 1950–51. A Vice-Pres., Instn Civil Engineers, 1971–74, Pres. 1974–75. FEng 1977. Mem., Smeatonian Soc. of Civil Engineers, 1966– (Pres., 1984). Hon. DSc City, 1977. Hon. Seabee, US Navy, 1961. Decoration for Distinguished Civilian Service to US Army, 1985. *Recreations:* gardening, 14 grand-children. *Address:* Ninesprings, 10 Church Lane, East Carlton, Market Harborough, Leics LE16 8YA. *T:* Rockingham (01536) 771307.

HARRIS, Wilson; *see* Harris, T. W.

HARRISON; *see* Graham-Harrison.

HARRISON, (Alastair) Brian (Clarke); DL; farmer; *b* 3 Oct. 1921; *s* of late Brig. E. F. Harrison, Melbourne; *m* 1952, Elizabeth Hood Hardie, Oaklands, NSW, Aust.; one *s* one *d. Educ:* Geelong Grammar Sch.; Trinity Coll., Cambridge. Capt. AIF. MP (C) Maldon, Essex, 1955–Feb. 1974; Parliamentary Private Secretary to: Min. of State, Colonial Office, 1955–56; Sec. of State for War, 1956–58; Min. of Agriculture, Fisheries and Food, 1958–60. Mem. Victoria Promotion Cttee (London); Mem. One Nation Gp which published The Responsible Society, and One Europe; toured USA on E-SU Ford Foundation Fellowship, 1959; Commonwealth Parliamentary Assoc. Delegations: Kenya and Horn of Africa, 1960; Gilbert and Ellice Islands, New Hebrides and British Solomon Islands Protectorate. Chm., Standing Conf. of Eastern Sport and Physical Recreation, 1974–. Organizer (with Univ. of WA), expedns to Nepal studying human physiol., 1979–87. High Sheriff, 1979, DL 1980, Essex. *Publications:* (jtly) The cumulative effect of High Altitude on Motor Performance: a comparison between caucasian visitors and native highlanders, 1985; (jtly) Entrainment of respiratory frequency to exercise rhythm during hypoxia, 1987. *Recreations:* photography, gardening. *Address:* Green Farm House, Coptord, Colchester, Essex CO6 1DA; 4/14 Cook Street, Crawley, Perth, WA 6009, Australia. *Clubs:* Pratt's; Melbourne (Melbourne); Weld (Perth).

HARRISON, Air Vice-Marshal Anthony John, CBE 1992 (OBE 1986); Assistant Chief of Defence Staff (Operations), Ministry of Defence, since 1994; *b* 9 Nov. 1943; *s* of Jack and Jean Harrison; *m* 1965, Glynn Dene Hyland-Smith; one *s* one *d. Educ:* Woodbridge Sch., Suffolk. Commnd RAF, 1963; Commanding Officer: 617 Sqdn (The Dambusters), 1982–85; RAF Bruggen, 1989–92; Dir, Jt Warfare, MoD, 1992–94. Upper Freeman, GAPAN, 1985. Pres., Woodbridge RAF Assoc., 1994. *Recreations:* golf, tennis, aviation history. *Address:* Ministry of Defence, Main Building, Whitehall, SW1A 2HB. *Club:* Royal Air Force.

HARRISON, Brian; *see* Harrison, A. B. C.

HARRISON, Brian Howard, DPhil; FRHistS; Fellow and Tutor in Modern History and Politics, Corpus Christi College, since 1967, and Reader in Modern British History, since 1990, Oxford University; *b* 9 July 1937; *s* of Howard Harrison and Mary Elizabeth (*née* Savill); *m* 1967, Anne Victoria Greggain. *Educ:* Merchant Taylors' Sch., Northwood; St John's Coll., Oxford (BA 1st Cl. Hons Mod. Hist. 1961; MA 1966; DPhil 1966). FRHistS 1973. Nat. Service, 2nd Lieut, Malta Signal Sqdn, 1956–58. Sen. Schol., St Antony's Coll., Oxford, 1961–64; Jun. Res. Fellow, Nuffield Coll., Oxford, 1964–67. Visiting Professor: Univ. of Michigan (Ann Arbor), 1970–71; Harvard Univ., 1973–74; Visiting Fellow: Melbourne Univ., 1975; ANU, 1995. *Publications:* Drink and the Victorians, 1971, 2nd edn 1994; Separate Spheres: the opposition to women's suffrage in Britain, 1978; (ed with P. Hollis) Robert Lowery: Chartist and lecturer, 1979; Peaceable Kingdom: stability and change in modern Britain, 1982; (with C. Ford) A Hundred Years Ago: Britain in the 1880s in words and photographs, 1983; Prudent Revolutionaries: portraits of British feminists between the wars, 1987; (ed and contrib.) The History of the University of Oxford, Vol. 8: The Twentieth Century, 1994; (ed) Corpuscles: a history of Corpus Christi College, Oxford, 1994. *Recreations:* looking at architecture, listening to classical music. *Address:* Corpus Christi College, Oxford OX1 4JF. *T:* Oxford (01865) 276700.

HARRISON, Prof. Bryan Desmond, CBE 1990; PhD; FRS 1987; FRSE; Professor of Plant Virology, University of Dundee, since 1991; *b* 16 June 1931; *s* of John William and Norah Harrison; *m* 1968, Elizabeth Ann Latham-Warde; two *s* one *d. Educ:* Whitgift Sch., Croydon; Reading Univ. (BSc Hons Agric. Bot. 1952); London Univ. (PhD 1955). FRSE 1979. Postgraduate student, ARC, 1952; Scottish Hort. Res. Inst., Dundee, 1954; Rothamsted Exp. Station, 1957; Head, Virology Section, 1966, Dep. Dir, 1979, Scottish Hort. Res. Inst.; Head, Virology Dept, Scottish Crop Res. Inst., 1981–91. Visiting Professor: Japan Soc. for Promotion of Science, 1970; Organization of American States, Venezuela, 1973; Hon. Prof., Univ. of St Andrews, 1986–; Hon. Vis. Prof., Univ. of Dundee, 1988–91. Pres., Assoc. of Applied Biologists, 1980–81. Hon. Member: Assoc. of Applied Biologists, 1989; Soc. for Gen. Microbiol., 1990; Phytopathological Soc. of Japan, 1992. Hon. DAgr For Univ. of Helsinki, 1990. *Publications:* Plant Virology: the principles (with A. J. Gibbs), 1976 (trans Russian and Chinese); research papers and reviews on plant viruses and virus diseases. *Recreations:* growing garden crops, foreign travel. *Address:* Department of Biological Sciences, University of Dundee, Dundee DD1 4HN; Scottish Crop Research Institute, Invergowrie, Dundee DD2 5DA. *T:* Dundee (01382) 562731, *Fax:* (01382) 562426.

HARRISON, Bryan James; Chief Executive, Forest Healthcare Trust, since 1995; *b* 30 Oct. 1947; *s* of late James Harrison and of Doris (*née* Burnham); *m* 1st, 1973 (marr. diss. 1988); two *d*; 2nd, 1990, Valerie Mayo; one *d. Educ:* Southmoor Sch., Sunderland; Exeter Univ. (BA Politics). DHSS, 1971–81; seconded to Camden and Islington AHA, 1981–82; Dist Administrator, Islington HA, 1982–84; District General Manager: Islington HA, 1984–88; Bloomsbury HA, 1988–90; Bloomsbury and Islington HA, 1990–92; Regl Gen. Manager, NE Thames RHA, 1992–94. *Recreations:* reading, music, history, soccer. *Address:* PO Box 13, Claybury Hall, Woodford Green, Essex IG8 8DB. *T:* 0181–504 4411.

HARRISON, Cameron Elias; Chief Executive, Scottish Consultative Council on the Curriculum, since 1991; *b* 27 Aug. 1945; *s* of Elias Harrison and Herries Harrison; *m* 1968, Pearl Leimon; one *s* one *d. Educ:* Cumnock Acad.; Strathclyde Univ. (BSc Hons Physics); Stirling Univ. (MEd). Physics Teacher, Greenock Acad., 1968–71; Head of Physics, Graeme High Sch., 1971–79; Depute Rector, Kirkcudbright Acad., 1979–82; Rector, The Gordon Schools, 1982–91. Sec.-Gen., Consortium of Instns for Develt & Res. in Educn in Europe, 1993–. *Publication:* Managing Change, 1989. *Recreations:* Rugby, walking, singing, talking, listening, teaching, learning. *Address:* Scottish Consultative Council on the Curriculum, Gardyne Road, Broughty Ferry, Dundee DD5 1NY. *T:* Dundee (01382) 455053; Woodfield, Priormuir, St Andrews, Fife KY16 8LP.

HARRISON, Prof. Charles Victor; retired; Professor of Pathology, University of Ife, Nigeria, 1972–75; *b* Newport, Mon, 1907; *s* of Charles Henry Harrison, LDS, and Violet Harrison (*née* Witchell); *m* 1937, Olga Beatrice Cochrane; one *s* one *d. Educ:* Dean Close Sch., Cheltenham; University Coll., Cardiff; University Coll. Hosp., London. MB, BCh, BSc (Wales), 1929; MB, BS (London), 1929; MD (London), 1937; FRCPath 1965; FRCP 1967. Demonstrator in Pathology, Welsh National School of Medicine, 1930; Asst Morbid Anatomist, British Postgraduate Medical Sch., 1935; Senior Lecturer, Liverpool Univ., 1939; Reader in Morbid Anatomy, Postgraduate Medical Sch. of London, 1946; Prof., Royal Postgrad. Med. Sch., Univ. of London, 1955–72. Hon. DSc Wales, 1972. Willie Seager Gold Medal in Pathology, 1927. *Publications:* (ed) Recent Advances in Pathology, 1973; various scientific papers in Jl of Pathology and Bacteriology, British Heart Journal, Jl Clin. Pathology, etc. *Recreations:* carpentry and gardening. *Address:* 8 Wattleton Road, Beaconsfield, Bucks HP9 1TS. *T:* Beaconsfield (01494) 672046.

HARRISON, Claude William, RP 1961; Artist; portrait painter and painter of conversation pieces, imaginative landscapes and murals, etc; *b* Leyland, Lancs, 31 March 1922; *s* of Harold Harrison and Florence Mildred Ireton; *m* 1947, Audrey Johnson; one *s. Educ:* Hutton Grammar Sch., Lancs. Served in RAF, 1942–46. Royal Coll. of Art, 1947–49; Studio in Ambleside, 1949–52. Exhibited since 1950 at: RA; RSA; Royal Society Portrait Painters; New English Art Club, etc. *Publication:* The Portrait Painter's handbook, 1968. *Recreation:* painting. *Address:* Barrow Wife, Cartmel Fell, near Grange over Sands, Cumbria LA11 6NZ. *T:* Newby Bridge (015395) 31323.

HARRISON, Sir Colin; *see* Harrison, Sir R. C.

HARRISON, Dr David, CBE 1990; FEng 1987; Fellow, since 1957, and Master, since 1994, Selwyn College, Cambridge; *b* 3 May 1930; *s* of Harold David Harrison and Lavinia Wilson; *m* 1962, Sheila Rachel Debes; one *s* one *d* (and one *s* decd). *Educ:* Bede Sch., Sunderland; Clacton County High Sch.; Selwyn Coll., Cambridge (1st Cl. Pts I and II Natural Sciences Tripos, BA 1953, PhD 1956, MA 1957, ScD 1979). CEng; FRSC (FRIC 1961), FIChemE 1968. 2nd Lieut, REME, 1949. Cambridge University: Research student, Dept of Physical Chemistry, 1953–56; Univ. Asst Lectr in Chem. Engrg, 1956–61; Univ. Lectr, 1961–79; Sen. Tutor, Selwyn Coll., 1967–79; Mem. Council, Senate, 1967–75; Chm., Faculty Bd of Educn, 1976–78, of Engrg, 1994–; Vice-Chancellor: Univ. of Keele, 1979–84; Univ. of Exeter, 1984–94. Visiting Professor of Chemical Engineering: Univ. of Delaware, USA, 1967; Univ. of Sydney, 1976. Chm., Adv. Cttee on Safety in Nuclear Installations, 1993–. Mem., Engineering Council, 1994–. Member Council: Lancing Coll., 1970–82; Haileybury, 1974–84; St Edward's, Oxford, 1977–89; Bolton Girls' Sch., 1981–84; Shrewsbury Sch., 1983– (Chm., 1989–); Taunton Sch., 1986–89; Fellow, Woodard Corporation of Schools, 1972–94; Chairman: Bd of Trustees, Homerton Coll., Cambridge, 1979–; UCCA, 1984–91; Voluntary Sector Consultative Council, 1984–88; Southern Univs Jt Bd, 1986–88; Church and Associated Colls Adv. Cttee, PCFC, 1988–91; CVCP, 1991–93; Bd of Management, Northcott Theatre, 1984–94; Eastern Arts Bd, 1994–. Pres., IChemE, 1991–92 (Vice-Pres., 1989–91); Dir, Salters' Inst. of Industrial Chemistry, 1993–. Mem., Marshall Aid Commemoration Commn, 1982–89. FRSA 1985; CIMgt (CBIM 1990). DUniv Keele, 1992. Hon. Editor, Trans Instn of Chemical Engrs, 1972–78. *Publications:* (with J. F. Davidson) Fluidised Particles, 1963; (also with J. F. Davidson) Fluidization, 1971, rev. edn (with J. F. Davidson and R. Clift) 1985; numerous articles in scientific and technological jls. *Recreations:* music, tennis, hill walking, good food. *Address:* The Master's Lodge, Selwyn College, Cambridge CB3 9DQ. *T:* Cambridge (01223) 335889. *Clubs:* Athenæum; Federation House (Stoke-on-Trent).

HARRISON, Denis Byrne; Town Clerk and Chief Executive Officer, Sheffield, 1966–74; *b* 11 July 1917; *y s* of late Arthur and Priscilla Harrison; *m* 1956, Alice Marion Vickers (*d* 1989), *e d* of late Hedley Vickers. *Educ:* Birkenhead Sch.; Liverpool Univ. (LLM). Articled to late E. W. Tame, OBE (Town Clerk of Birkenhead). Admitted Solicitor, 1939; Asst Solicitor to Birkenhead Corp., 1939. Legal Associate Mem. RTPI, 1949. Served War, 1939–46: 75th Shropshire Yeo. (Medium Regt) RA, Combined Ops Bombardment Unit; Staff Captain at HQ of OC, Cyprus. First Asst Solicitor, Wolverhampton Co. Borough, 1946–49; Dep. Town Clerk of Co. Boroughs: Warrington, 1949–57; Bolton, 1957–63; Sheffield, 1963–66; Local Govt Ombudsman, 1974–81, and Vice-Chm., Commn for Local Admin, 1975–81. Member: Advisory Council on Noise, 1970–79; Cttee on the use of valuers in the public service, 1972–73. Mem. Council, 1975–82, Pro-Chancellor, 1980–82, Univ. of Sheffield. JP City of London, 1976–86. *Recreations:* reading, walking. *Address:* 2 Leicester Close, Henley-on-Thames, Oxon RG9 2LD. *T:* Henley-on-Thames (01491) 572782.

HARRISON, (Desmond) Roger (Wingate); Deputy Chairman, Capital Radio, since 1991 (Director, since 1975); *b* 9 April 1933; *s* of late Maj.-Gen. Desmond Harrison, CB, DSO and of Kathleen Harrison (*née* Hazley); *m* 1965, Victoria Lee-Barber, MVO, *d* of Rear-Adm. John Lee-Barber, *qv*; four *d* (and one *s* decd). *Educ:* Rugby School; Worcester College, Oxford (MA); Harvard Univ. Business Sch. Writing freelance, principally for The Times, 1951–57; joined staff of The Times, 1957–67; The Observer: joined 1967; Dir, 1970–92; Jt Managing Dir, 1977–84; Chief Exec., 1984–87. Dir, The Oak Foundn, 1987–89. Chairman: Greater Manchester Cablevision, 1990–93; Sterling Publishing, 1993–95; Director: LWT and LWT (Holdings), 1976–94; Sableknight, 1981–; Trinity International Holdings, 1991–. Mem. Council, NPA, 1967–87. Chairman: Toynbee Hall, 1990–; Asylum Aid, 1991–; Royal Acad. of Dancing, 1993–. Governor, Sadler's Wells,

1984–. *Recreations:* theatre, country pursuits, tennis. *Address:* 35 Argyll Road, W8 7DA. *Clubs:* Beefsteak, Flyfishers', Queen's.

HARRISON, Sir Donald (Frederick Norris), Kt 1990; MD, MS, PhD; FRCS; Professor of Laryngology and Otology (University of London), 1963–90, and Dean, 1989–90, Institute of Laryngology and Otology, Gray's Inn Road, WC1, Emeritus Professor, 1990; Emeritus Surgeon, Moorfields Eye Hospital, 1991; Surgeon, Royal National Throat, Nose and Ear Hospital; Civilian Consultant on ENT to RN; *b* 9 March 1925; *s* of Frederick William Rees Harrison, OBE, JP, and Florence, *d* of Robert Norris, Portsmouth, Hants; *m* 1949, Audrey, *o d* of Percival Clubb, Penarth, Glam.; two *d. Educ:* Newport High Sch., Mon.; Guy's Hosp. MD (London) 1960; MS (London) 1959; PhD (London) 1983; FRCS 1955. Ho. Surg., Guy's Hosp. and Royal Gwent Hospital, Newport; Surg. Registrar, Shrewsbury Eye and Ear Hosp.; Senior Registrar, Throat and Ear Dept, Guy's Hosp.; University Reader in Laryngology, Inst. of Laryngol. and Otol. Hunterian Prof., RCS, 1962; Eramus Wilson Demonstrator, RCS, 1971. Lectures: Chevalier Jackson, 1964; Yearsley, 1972; Wilde, 1972; Litchfield, 1973; Semon, 1974; Colles, RCSI, 1977; Jobson Horne, BMA, 1979; Conacher, Toronto, 1978; Harris, USA, 1984; Putney, USA, 1985; Baker, USA, 1986; Bryce, Toronto, 1987; McBride, Edinburgh, 1987; Douglas J. Guthrie, Edinburgh, 1988; Bob Owen (first), Cardiff, 1988; Ogura, USA, 1990; Som, USA, 1991; Stirk Adams, Birmingham, 1992; Watson-Williams, Bristol, 1994. Wellcome Prof., S Africa, 1988. Master, British Acad. Conf. on ENT, 1991. W. J. Harrison Prize, RSM, 1978; Medal of Paris, 1988; Gold medal, Internat. Fedn of Oto Rhino Laryngological Socs, 1985; Gold Medal, NY Eye & Ear Alumni Assoc., 1988; Gold Medal, Joshi Meml Lecture, Indian ENT Soc., 1990; Holmgren Medal, Sweden, 1993. Mem. of Court of Examiners, RCS; Examr, NUI; External Examr, Univs of Melbourne, Southampton, Sydney, Manchester, Liverpool, Glasgow, Hong Kong, Belfast, Oxford and Cambridge; Scientific Fellow, Royal Zoological Soc. of London; FRSM (Pres., 1994; Pres., Sect. of Laryngology, 1984 (former Vice-Pres.); Mem. Council, Sect. of Oncology; Hon. Sec., 1987–93). Mem. Council: Brit. Assoc. of Otolaryngologists; Brit. Assoc. of Head and Neck Oncologists (Pres.). Former Chairman: Special Adv. Cttee on Human Communication; Bd Postgrad. Med. Studies, London Univ.; Pres., World Congress Laryngeal Cancer, 1994; Chm., Centennial Conf., Laryngeal Cancer, 1974; Asst Sec., Collegium Oto-Rhino-Laryngologium; Sen. Mem., Anatomical Soc. of Great Britain; Member: Cttee of Management, Institute of Cancer Research; Internat. Cttee for Cancer of Larynx; Chm., NE Thames Region Postgrad. Cttee. Editorial Board: Acta Otolaryngologica; Practica Oto-Rhino-Laryngologica; Annals of Oto-Rhino-Laryngology; Excerpta Medica (Sect. II); Otolaryngological Digest. Hon. Fellow: Acad. ENT, America, 1976; Triol. Soc., USA, 1977; Amer. Laryngol Assoc., 1979; Hon. FRACS 1977; Hon. FRCSE 1981; Hon. FCSSA 1988; Hon. FACS 1990; Hon. FRSM 1991; Hon. FRCSI 1991; FRCOphth 1993. Hon. Member: NZ ENT Soc.; Jamaican ENT Soc.; Polish ENT Soc.; Egyptian ENT Soc.; Otolaryngological Soc., Australia; Yugoslavian ENT Soc.; Spanish ENT Soc.; Philippine ENT Soc.; Hong Kong ENT Soc.; For. Mem., Internat. Broncho-œsophagological Soc.; Corresp. Member: Amer. Head and Neck Soc.; Soc. Française d'Otorhinolaryngologie; Otolaryngological Soc., Denmark; Amer. Acad. of Facial Plastic Reconstr. Surgery; Pacific Coast Oto-Ophthalmological Soc.; Amer. Laryngological Soc.; Yeoman, Soc. of Apothecaries. *Publications:* (ed jtly) Scientific Basis of Otolaryngology, 1976; Dilemmas in ENT, 1990; Neoplasms of the Upper Jaw, 1993; Comparative Anatomy of Mammalian Larynx, 1995; articles on familial hæmorrhagic telangiectases, meatal oseomata, cancer chemotherapy, head and neck surgery in learned jls; chapters in Text Books on Ent. and Gen. Surgery. *Recreations:* heraldry, radio control models. *Address:* Springfield, Fisher's Farm, Horley, Surrey RH6 9DQ. *T:* Horley (01293) 4307.

HARRISON, Douglas Creese, DSc London, PhD Cantab; CChem; Professor of Biochemistry, Queen's University, Belfast, 1935–67, now Professor Emeritus; *b* 29 April, 1901; *s* of Lovell and Lillian E. Harrison, MBE, JP; *m* 1926, Sylva Thurlow, MA, PhD, Philadelphia, USA; one *s. Educ:* Highgate Sch.; King's Coll., London; Emmanuel Coll., Cambridge. MRSC. Keddey Fletcher-Warr Research Studentship, 1925–28; Lecturer at Sheffield Univ., 1926–35. Hon. DSc Belfast, 1987. *Publications:* various papers in the Biochemical Journal, Proc. Royal Society, Lancet, etc. *Address:* 4 Broomhill Park Central, Belfast BT9 5JD. *T:* Belfast (01232) 665685.

HARRISON, Edward Peter Graham, (Ted); broadcaster, writer and cartoonist; *b* 14 April 1948; *s* of Rev. Peter Harrison and Joan Harrison; *m* 1968, Helen Grace Waters; one *s* one *d. Educ:* Grenville Coll., Bideford, Devon; University of Kent at Canterbury. Graduate trainee, Kent Messenger, 1968–72; Reporter: Morgan-Grampian Magazines, 1972; Southern Television, 1970–73; BBC World Service, Radio 4 You and Yours, 1972–80; BBC Radio 4 Sunday, 1972–; BBC TV Scotland Current Account, 1981–83; Presenter and Reporter, BBC Radio Scotland News and Current Affairs, 1980–85; Reporter: BBC Radio 4 World Tonight, 1981–83; BBC Radio 4 World at One and PM, 1983–87; Presenter: Radio 4 Opinions, 1986–87; Radio 4 Sunday, 1986–88 and Soundings, 1985–88; ITV series The Human Factor, 1986–92; Channel 4 series on Lambeth Conf., 1988; BBC Religious Affairs Corresp., 1988–89; presenter, Does He Take Sugar?, Radio 4, 1991–95. Dir, Pilgrim Productions, 1992–. Contested (L) gen. elections: Bexley, 1970; Maidstone, Feb. 1974. London exhibition of caricatures, 1977; exhibition of watercolours, Oxford, Canterbury, 1981. *Publications:* Modern Elizabethans, 1977; (jtly) McIndoe's Army, 1978; Marks of the Cross, 1981; Commissioner Catherine, 1983; Much Beloved Daughter, 1984; The Durham Phenomenon, 1985; Living with kidney failure, 1990; Kriss Akabusi — on track, 1991; The Elvis People, 1992; Members Only, 1994; Stigmata: a medieval mystery for a modern age, 1994; Letters to a friend I never knew, 1995. *Recreations:* drawing caricatures, painting in watercolour.

HARRISON, Sir Ernest (Thomas), Kt 1981; OBE 1972; FCA; Chairman: Racal Electronics Plc, since 1966 (Chief Executive, 1966–92); Vodafone Group Plc (formerly Racal Telecom Plc), since 1988; Chubb Security Plc, since 1992; Director, Camelot Group plc, since 1993; *b* 11 May 1926; *s* of Ernest Horace Harrison and Gertrude Rebecca Gibbons Harrison; *m* 1960, Phyllis Brenda Knight (Janie); three *s* two *d. Educ:* Trinity Grammar Sch., Wood Green, London. Qualified as Chartered Accountant, 1950; served Articles with Harker Holloway & Co.; joined Racal Electronics as Secretary and Chief Accountant, when company commenced manufacturing, 1951; Director, 1958, Dep. Man. Dir, 1961. Active in National Savings movement, 1964–76, for which services awarded OBE. Chm., Ronald Raven Chair in Clinical Oncology Trust, 1991–. Mem., Jockey Club, 1990–. Mem., RSA. Liveryman, Scriveners' Co. CompIERE 1975; CIMgt (CBIM 1976); CompIEE 1978. Hon. FCGI 1990. Hon. DSc: Cranfield, 1981; City, 1982; DUniv: Surrey, 1981; Edinburgh, 1983. Businessman of the Year, 1981; Founding Society's Centenary Award, ICA, 1990; Mountbatten Medal, Nat. Electronic Council, 1992. *Recreations:* horse racing (owner and breeder), gardening, wild life, sport, espec. soccer. *Address:* Racal Electronics Plc, Western Road, Bracknell, Berkshire RG12 1RG.

HARRISON, Sir Francis Alexander Lyle, (Sir Frank Harrison), Kt 1974; MBE 1943; QC (NI); DL; President, Lands Tribunal for Northern Ireland, 1964–83; District Electoral Areas Commissioner, 1984; *b* 19 March 1910; *s* of Rev. Alexander Lyle Harrison and Mary Luise (*née* Henderson), Rostrevor, Co. Down; *m* 1940, Norah Patricia (*née* Rea); two *d. Educ:* Campbell Coll., Belfast; Trinity Coll., Dublin. BA (Moderator in Legal Sci.), LLB (Hons). Called to Bar of NI, 1937. Served War: commissioned Gen. List, Oct. 1939; ADC to GOC, NI, 1939–40; Major, Dep. Asst Adjt-Gen., HQ, NI, 1941–45 (MBE). Apptd to determine Industrial Assurance disputes in NI, 1946–62; Counsel to Attorney-Gen., NI, 1946–48; KC 1948. Legal Adviser to Min. of Home Affairs, 1949–64; Sen. Crown Prosecutor, Co. Fermanagh, 1948–54; subseq. for Counties Tyrone, Londonderry and Antrim, 1954–64; Chm., Mental Health Review Tribunal, 1948–64; Counsel to the Speakers of House of Commons and Senate of NI, 1953–64; Mem. Statute Law Cttee, NI, 1953–64; Chm., Advisory Cttee under Civil Authorities Special Powers Acts (NI), 1957–62; Bencher, Inn of Court of NI, 1961; Chm., Shaftesbury Sq. Hosp. Management Cttee, 1964–73; Founder Mem., NI Assoc. of Mental Health, 1959. Boundary Comr under Local Govt (Boundaries) Act (NI), 1971 and 1982–84. DL Co. Down, 1973. *Publications:* Report of Working Party on Drug Dependence, 1968; Recommendations as to Local Government Boundaries and Wards in Northern Ireland, 1972, 1984; Recommendations as to District Electoral Areas in Northern Ireland, 1985. *Recreations:* hybridisation of narcissi, country pursuits, social service. *Address:* Ballydorn Hill, Killinchy, Newtownards, Co. Down, Northern Ireland BT23 6QB. *T:* Killinchy (01238) 541 250.

HARRISON, Francis Anthony Kitchener; *b* 28 Aug. 1914; *s* of late Fred Harrison, Headmaster of Newcastle High Sch., Staffs, and Mrs M. M. Harrison (*née* Mitchell); *m* 1955, Sheila Noëlle, *d* of late Lt-Col N. D. Stevenson and of Lady Nye; three *s* one *d. Educ:* Winchester; New Coll., Oxford. Asst Principal, India Office, Nov. 1937; 1st Sec., UK High Commn, New Delhi, 1949–51; Commonwealth Relations Office, 1951–56; Asst Sec., 1954; Dep. High Comr for the UK at Peshawar, 1956–59; Asst Sec., CRO, 1959–61; British Dep. High Comr, New Zealand, 1961–64; Asst Sec., Cabinet Office, 1965–67; Asst Dir, Civil Service Selection Bd, 1967–79. *Recreations:* reading, writing. *Address:* Lea Farm, Bramley, near Guildford, Surrey GU5 0LR. *T:* Guildford (01483) 893138.

HARRISON, Sir Frank; *see* Harrison, Sir Francis A. L.

HARRISON, Fred Brian, CBE 1982; FCA; *b* 6 March 1927; *s* of Fred Harrison and Annie Harrison; *m* 1950, Margaret Owen; two *s. Educ:* Burnley Grammar Sch. FCA 1960 (ACA 1950). East Midlands Div., NCB, 1953–67 (Chief Accountant, No 1 Area, 1962–67); Chief Accountant, N Derbyshire Area, NCB, 1967–68; Finance Dir, Coal Products Div., NCB, 1968–71; Dep. Chief Exec., NCB (Coal Products) Ltd, 1971–76, Chm., 1978–83. Mem., NCB, 1976–85. Chm., British Investment Trust, 1978–85. Master, Chartered Accountants' Co., 1994–95. *Recreations:* music, theatre. *Address:* 11 Hillcrest, King Harry Lane, St Albans, Herts AL3 4AT. *T:* St Albans (01727) 46938.

HARRISON, (George) Michael (Antony), CBE 1980; education systems consultant; Chief Education Officer, City of Sheffield, 1967–85; *b* 7 April 1925; *s* of George and Kathleen Harrison; *m* 1951, Pauline (*née* Roberts); two *s* one *d. Educ:* Manchester Grammar Sch.; Brasenose Coll., Oxford. MA (LitHum); DipEd. Military service, Lieut, Parachute Regt, 1947. Asst Master, Bedford Modern Sch., 1951–53; Admin. Asst, W Riding CC, Education Dept, 1953–55; Asst Educn Officer, Cumberland CC Educn Dept, 1955–64; Dep. Educn Officer, Sheffield, 1965–67. Advr, Educn and NVQ Programmes, Dept of Employment, 1985–. Hon. Research Fellow, Leeds Univ., 1985–89; Associate Prof., Sheffield Univ., 1991–95. Member various cttees, incl.: Taylor Cttee of Enquiry on Govt in Schools, 1975–77; UK Nat. Commn for Unesco Educn Adv. Cttee, 1977–83; Yorkshire and Humberside Econ. Planning Council, 1978–79; Technician Educn Council, 1979–83; Engineering Council, 1982–87; Board, Nat. Adv. Body on Local Authority Higher Educn, 1981–83. Pres., Soc. of Educn Officers, 1976; Vice-Pres., Standing Conf. on Schools' Science and Technology, 1980– (Chm. 1975–79). Chm., St William's Foundn, York, 1992–95. Hon. LLD Sheffield, 1988. *Recreation:* foreign travel. *Address:* 20 Robin Hood Chase, Stannington, Sheffield S6 6FH. *T:* Sheffield (0114) 231 2805.

HARRISON, Maj.-Gen. Ian Stewart, CB 1970; Captain of Deal Castle, since 1980; *b* 25 May 1919; *s* of Leslie George Harrison and Evelyn Simpson Christie; *m* 1942, Winifred Raikes Stavert; one *s* one *d. Educ:* St Albans Sch. Commissioned, Royal Marines, 1937; service at sea, in Norway, Middle East, Sicily, BAOR, 1939–45; Staff Coll., Camberley (student), 1948; HQ 3rd Commando Bde, 1949–51 (despatches); Staff of Comdt-Gen., RM, 1951–52; Staff Coll., Camberley (Directing Staff), 1953–55; Commandant, RM Signal Sch., 1956–58; Joint Services Staff Coll. (Student), 1958; CO 40 Commando, RM, 1959–61; Dir, Royal Marines Reserves, 1962; Staff of Comdt-Gen., RM, 1963–64; Joint Warfare Estabt, 1965–67; British Defence Staff, Washington, DC, 1967–68; Chief of Staff to Comdt-Gen., RM, 1968–70, retired. ADC to HM the Queen, 1967–68. Representative Col Comdt, Royal Marines, 1981–82. Dir-Gen. British Food Export Council, 1970–77; Dir, British Consultants Bureau, 1977–87. Chm., Chichester Festivities, 1979–89. *Recreations:* sailing, real tennis, golf. *Address:* Manor Cottage, Runcton, Chichester, W Sussex PO20 6PU. *T:* Chichester (01243) 785480. *Clubs:* Army and Navy; Royal Yacht Squadron, Royal Naval Sailing Association, Royal Marines Sailing (Commodore, 1968–70), Itchenor Sailing; Royal St George's Golf.

HARRISON, Jessel Anidjah; President, Slimma Group Holdings Ltd, retired 1989; *b* 28 May 1923; *s* of Samuel Harrison and Esta (*née* Romain); *m* 1st, 1943, Irene (*née* Olsberg) (marr. diss. 1956); one *s* one *d*; 2nd, 1961, Doreen Leigh. *Educ:* Vernon House Preparatory Sch.; Brondesbury Coll.; Macauley Coll., Cuckfield, Sussex. Chairman: Slimma Ltd, 1964; Slimma (Wales) Ltd, 1971; Emu Wool Industries, later Slimma Gp Hldgs, 1973; Dir, Tootals Clothing Div., 1977–89. Member: European Trade Cttee, 1975–; Clothing Industry Productivity Resources Agency, 1978–85; British Overseas Trade Adv. Council, 1978–85. Vice Pres., Clothing Export Council of Great Britain, 1977 (Chm., 1973); Chm., British Overseas Trade Group for Israel, 1978–83, Vice-Pres., 1987–. Pres., Clothing Institute, 1978. *Recreations:* golf, walking. *Address:* 113 Abbotsbury Road, W14 8EP. *T:* 0171–603 7468. *Club:* Royal Automobile.

HARRISON, Surgeon Vice-Adm. Sir John (Albert Bews), KBE 1982; FRCP, FRCR; Medical Director General (Naval), 1980–83; *b* 20 May 1921; *s* of late Albert William Harrison and Lilian Eda Bews, Dover, Kent; *m* 1943, Jane (*née* Harris) (*d* 1988); two *s. Educ:* Queens' Coll., Cambridge; St Bartholomew's Hosp. RN 1947–83: served: RM Infirmary, Deal, 1948; HMS Sparrow, Amer. WI stn, 1949; RN Hosp., Plymouth, 1951; HMS Ganges, 1952; Admiralty Med. Bd and St Bartholomew's Hosp., 1953; RN Hosps, Hong Kong, 1955, Chatham, 1958, Haslar, 1959; St Bart's and Middlesex Hosps, 1961; RN Hosps Malta, 1962, Haslar, 1964–75; Adviser in Radiol., 1967–79; Dep. Med. Dir Gen. and Dir Med. Personnel and Logistics, 1975–77; Dean of Naval Medicine and Surgeon Rear-Adm., Inst. of Naval Medicine, 1977–80. Mem., Council for Med. Postgrad. Educn of Eng. and Wales, 1977–79. Pres., Section of Radiology, RSM, 1984–85. Fellow: RSM; MedSocLond (Pres. 1985–86). CStJ 1983. QHP 1976–83. *Publications:* Hyperbaric Osteonecrosis et al, 1975; articles in med. press on sarcoidosis, tomography, middle ear disease, and dysbaric osteonecrosis. *Recreations:* fishing, cricket, countryman. *Address:* Alexandra Cottage, Swanmore, Hampshire SO3 2PB. *Club:* MCC.

HARRISON, John Clive, LVO 1971; HM Diplomatic Service; High Commissioner, Mauritius, since 1993; *b* 12 July 1937; *s* of Sir Geoffrey Harrison, GCMG, KCVO; *m* 1967, Jennifer Heather Burston; one *s* two *d*. *Educ:* Winchester Coll.; Jesus Coll., Oxford. BA. Entered Foreign Office, 1960; Rangoon, 1961; Vientiane, 1964; FO, 1964; Second, later First, Sec. (Information), Addis Ababa, 1967; Ankara, 1971; seconded to Cabinet Office, 1973; First Sec., FCO, 1976; First Sec., Head of Chancery and Consul, Luxembourg, 1978; Counsellor and Head of Chancery, Lagos, 1981–84; Counsellor, attached to Protocol Dept, FCO, 1984; Hd of Consular Dept, FCO, 1985–89; Dep. High Comr, Islamabad, 1989–93. *Recreations:* gardening, tennis, golf, family holidays. *Address:* c/o Foreign and Commonwealth Office, King Charles Street, SW1A 2AH. *Club:* Mannings Heath Golf (Sussex).

HARRISON, Prof. John Fletcher Clews, PhD; Emeritus Professor of History, University of Sussex, since 1985 (Professor of History, 1970–82; Hon. Professor of History, 1982–85); *b* 28 Feb. 1921; *s* of William Harrison and Mary (*née* Fletcher); *m* 1945, Margaret Ruth Marsh; one *s* one *d*. *Educ:* City Boys' Sch., Leicester; Selwyn Coll., Cambridge (Schol. and Prizeman; Goldsmiths' Open Exhibnr in History, BA 1st Cl. Hons 1942, MA 1946); PhD Leeds. Served Army, 1941–45 (overseas 1942–45): commnd, Leics Regt and seconded to KAR, 1942; Captain and Adjt, 17th Bn, KAR, 1943–44; Staff Captain, GSOIII, E Africa Comd, 1944–45. Lectr, Dept of Adult Educn and Extra-Mural Studies, Univ. of Leeds, 1947–58; Dep. Dir, Extra-Mural Studies and Dep. Head of Dept, Univ. of Leeds, 1958–61; Prof. of History, Univ. of Wisconsin, USA, 1961–70. Research and teaching (Fulbright Award), Univ. of Wisconsin, 1957–58; Faculty Res. Fellow, SSRC, USA, 1963–64; Vis. Professorial Res. Fellow, ANU, 1968–69 and 1977; Res. Fellow, Harvard Univ., 1972–73; Social Sci. Res. Fellow, Nuffield Foundn, 1975; Vice-Chancellor's Cttee Visitor, NZ, 1977; Herbert F. Johnson Res. Prof., Univ. of Wisconsin, 1977–78; Hon. Prof. of History, Warwick Univ., 1987–92. Vice-Pres., Soc. for Study of Labour History, 1984– (Sec., 1960–61; Chm., 1974–81); Mem., Adv. and Editorial Bds, Victorian Studies, 1963–. Hon. Mem., Phi Beta Kappa, Wisconsin, 1978. *Publications:* A History of the Working Men's College 1854–1954, 1954; Social Reform in Victorian Leeds: The Work of James Hole 1820–1895, 1954; Learning and Living 1790–1960: A Study in the History of the English Adult Education Movement, 1961, Toronto 1961; ed, Society and Politics in England 1780–1960, NY 1965; ed, Utopianism and Education: Robert Owen and the Owenites, NY 1968; Quest for the New Moral World: Robert Owen and the Owenites in Britain and America, 1969, NY 1969 (Walter D. Love Meml Prize, USA, 1969); The Early Victorians 1832–1851, 1971, NY 1971; The Birth and Growth of Industrial England 1714–1867, 1973; ed, Eminently Victorian, BBC 1974; (with Dorothy Thompson) Bibliography of the Chartist Movement 1837–1976, 1978; The Second Coming: Popular Millenarianism 1780–1850, 1979, NJ 1979; The Common People, 1984; Late Victorian Britain 1875–1901, 1990; Scholarship Boy: a personal history of the mid-twentieth century, 1995; *festschrift:* New Views of Co-operation, ed S. Yeo, 1988; articles and reviews in Victorian Studies, TLS and usual academic history jls. *Recreations:* walking, gardening, book collecting. *Address:* Mill Cottage, Sandford Mill Close, Cheltenham, Glos GL53 7QZ. *T:* Cheltenham (01242) 510205.

HARRISON, John H.; *see* Heslop-Harrison.

HARRISON, Hon. Sir (John) Richard, Kt 1980; ED; grape grower; *b* 23 May 1921; *s* of William Harrison and Jean (*née* Bell); *m* 1948, Margaret Kelly; three *s* one *d*. *Educ:* Wanganui Collegiate Sch.; Canterbury University Coll. (BA). CO, Hawke's Bay Regt, 1956–59. MP (Nat) for Hawke's Bay, 1963–84; Govt Whip, 1970–71; Opposition Whip, 1974–75; Chm. of Cttees, 1972, 1976–77; Speaker, House of Representatives, 1978–84. Pres., Commonwealth Parly Assoc., 1978–79. Pres., Nat. Soc. on Alcoholism and Drug Dependence, 1986–89; Patron, Prison Fellowship, NZ, 1988–. *Recreations:* gardening, Rotary. *Address:* Springfield, RD2, Takapau, New Zealand. *Club:* Hastings.

HARRISON, Kathleen, (Mrs J. H. Back); leading character actress, stage and films; *b* Blackburn, Lancs, 23 Feb. 1892; *d* of Arthur Harrison, MICE, Civil Engineer, and Alice Maud Harrison (*née* Parker); *m* 1916, John Henry Back, Western Telegraph Co. (*d* 1960); one *s* one *d* (and one *s* decd). *Educ:* St Saviour's and St Olave's Grammar Sch,; Clapham High Sch. RADA, 1914–15 (Du Maurier Bronze Medal). *Notable plays include:* The Cage, Savoy, 1927; Aren't Women Wonderful, Royal Court, 1928; Happy Families, Garrick, 1929; Badger's Green, Prince of Wales Theatre, 1930; Jane's Legacy, Duchess, 1930; Lovers' Meeting, Prince of Wales, 1931; Can the Leopard, Theatre Royal, Haymarket, 1931; The Private Room, Westminster, 1934; Night Must Fall, Duchess, 1935; I Killed the Count, Whitehall, 1937; Comedienne, Theatre Royal, Haymarket, 1938; The Corn is Green, Duchess, 1938; Flare Path, Apollo, 1942; The Winslow Boy, Lyric, 1946; A Woman's Place, Vaudeville, 1949; Flowers for the Living, Duchess, 1950; The Silver Box (revival), Lyric, Hammersmith, 1951; Waters of the Moon, Theatre Royal, Haymarket, 1951; All for Mary, Duke of York's, 1954; Nude with Violin, Globe, 1956; How Say You?, Aldwych, 1959; Watch It, Sailor!, Aldwych, 1960; The Chances, Chichester Festival, 1962; Norman, Duchess, 1963; title rôle in Goodnight Mrs Puffin, New Theatre, Bromley; Harvey, Richmond Theatre, 1971; She Stoops to Conquer, Young Vic, 1972; toured N Africa and Italy with Emlyn William's ENSA Co., 1944; Chichester Festival Theatre Co., 1962; toured in All for Mary and Goodnight Mrs Puffin, 1970. *Films include:* Our Boys, 1915; Hobson's Choice, 1931; Happy Ever After, 1932; The Man from Toronto, 1932; The Ghoul, 1933; Line Engaged, 1935; Broken Blossoms, 1936; Night Must Fall, 1937; Bank Holiday, 1938; Almost a Gentleman, 1938; A Girl Must Live, 1939; They Came By Night, 1940; Tilly of Bloomsbury, 1940; The Girl in the News, 1940; The Ghost Train, 1941; One a Crook, 1941; I Thank You, 1941; Much Too Shy, 1942; In Which We Serve, 1942; Temptation Harbour, 1947; Holiday Camp, 1947; The Huggett series, from 1948; Oliver Twist, 1948; The Winslow Boy, 1948; Waterfront, 1950; Trio, 1950; Scrooge, 1951; The Pickwick Papers, 1952; Turn the Key Softly, 1953; Lilacs in the Spring, 1954; Cast a Dark Shadow, 1955; All for Mary, 1956; Seven Thunders, 1957; Alive and Kicking, 1958. *TV includes:* title role in Mrs Thursday series, 1966; Martin Chuzzlewit and Our Mutual Friend serials. *Address:* c/o T. Plunket Greene, 4 Ovington Gardens, SW3. *T:* 071–584 0688.

HARRISON, Kenneth Cecil, OBE 1980 (MBE mil. 1946); FLA; City Librarian, Westminster, 1961–80, retired; Consultant Librarian, Ranfurly Library Service, 1983–90; *b* 29 April 1915; *s* of Thomas and Annie Harrison; *m* 1941, Doris Taylor; two *s*. *Educ:* Grammar Sch., Hyde. Asst, Hyde Public Library, 1931–37; Branch Librarian, Coulsdon and Purley Public Libraries, 1937–39; Borough Librarian: Hyde, 1939–47; Hove (also Curator), 1947–50; Eastbourne, 1950–58; Hendon, 1958–61. HM Forces, 1940–46; Commnd RMC Sandhurst, 1942; served with E Yorks Regt in Middle East, Sicily and NW Europe (wounded, 1944; Major 1944–46). President: Library Assoc., 1973; Commonwealth Library Assoc., 1972–75, Exec. Sec., 1980–83; Vice-President: Internat. Assoc. Metropolitan Libraries; Westminster Arts Council (Hon. Sec. 1965–80). Member: IFLA Public Libraries Cttee, 1969–81; Central Music Library Council, 1961–80; Library Assoc. Council, 1953–79; MCC Arts and Library Cttee, 1973–89; Chm. Jt Organising Cttee for Nat. Library Week, 1964–69. British Council: Cultural Exchange Scholar to Romania, 1971; Mem., Library Adv. Panel, 1974–80; Consultant to Sri Lanka, 1974, to India, 1981. UNESCO Consultant to the Seychelles and Mauritius, 1977–78; Commonwealth Relations Trust Consultant to Ghana, Sierra Leone and The Gambia, 1979; Library Consultant, Bermuda, 1983. Commonwealth Foundn Scholar, E and Central Africa, 1975. C. C. Williamson Meml Lectr, Nashville, Tenn, 1969. Governor, Westminster College, 1962–80. Editor, The Library World, 1961–71. Knight, First Class, Order of the Lion (Finland), 1976. *Publications:* First Steps in Librarianship, 1950, 5th edn 1980; Libraries in Scandinavia, 1961, 2nd edn 1969; The Library and the Community, 1963, 3rd edn 1977; Public Libraries Today, 1963; Facts at your Fingertips, 1964, 2nd edn 1966; British Public Library Buildings (with S. G. Berriman), 1966; Libraries in Britain, 1968; Public Relations for Librarians, 1973, 2nd edn 1982; (ed) Prospects for British Librarianship, 1976; Public Library Policy, 1981; Public Library Buildings 1975–83, 1987; International Librarianship, 1989; Library Buildings 1984–89, 1990; contribs to many British and foreign jls and encyclopædias. *Recreations:* reading, writing, travel, wine, cricket, crosswords. *Address:* 5 Tavistock, Devonshire Place, Eastbourne, E Sussex BN21 4AG. *T:* Eastbourne (01323) 726747. *Clubs:* Commonwealth Trust, MCC; Surrey CC, Sussex CC.

HARRISON, Lyndon Henry Arthur; Member (Lab) European Parliament, Cheshire West and Wirral, since 1994 (Cheshire West, 1989–94); *b* 28 Sept. 1947; *s* of Charles William Harrison and late Edith (*née* Johnson); *m* 1980, Hilary Anne Plank; one *s* one *d*. *Educ:* Oxford Sch.; Univ. of Warwick (BA Hons 1970); Univ. of Sussex (MA 1971); Univ. of Keele (MA 1978). Part time Lectr, N Staffs Polytechnic, 1973–75; Research Officer, Students' Union, UMIST, 1975–78; Union Manager, NE Wales Inst. of Higher Educn, Wrexham, 1978–89. Cheshire County Councillor, 1981–90 (Chairman: Libraries and Countryside Cttee, 1982, 1984–89; Further Educn, 1984–89; Tourism, 1985–89). Dep. Chm., NW Tourist Bd, 1987–89. Vice Chm., ACC, 1990–. Socialist spokesman on monetary union, EP. *Recreations:* chess, the arts, sport. *Address:* Watergate Building, Crane Wharf, Chester CH1 4JW. *T:* Chester (01244) 320623.

HARRISON, Michael; *see* Harrison, G. M. A.

HARRISON, Dr Michael; JP; Director, Archadia Associates, since 1994; *b* 1 March 1939; *s* of Frank Harrison and Ruby Wilhelmina (*née* Proctor); *m* 1962, Ann Haiser; two *d*. *Educ:* Leamington Coll.; Univ. of London (St Mary's Hosp.) (MB BS, BA). LRCP, MRCS, DPH, FFPHM, MHSM, FRSH. Hosp. med. appts, 1964–66; health MO appts, 1966–70; Birmingham RHB, 1971–74; specialist in community medicine, W Midlands RHA, 1974–76; Area MO, Sandwell AHA, 1976–83; Dist MO, 1983–88, Dist Gen. Manager, 1985–88, Sandwell HA; Sen. Clinical Lectr, Univ. of Birmingham, 1988; Regl Dir of Public Health and Regl MO, 1988–93, Exec. Dir, 1990–94, Dep. Chief Exec., 1993–94, West Midlands RHA. Cons. Advr, WHO, 1989. FIMgt. SBStJ. JP Birmingham, 1980. *Recreations:* sailing, photography, industrial archaeology. *Address:* 6 Moor Green Lane, Moseley, Birmingham B13 8ND. *T:* 0121–449 1739. *Clubs:* Reform, Royal Society of Medicine.

HARRISON, Hon. Sir Michael (Guy Vicat), Kt 1993; **Hon. Mr Justice Harrison;** a Judge of the High Court of Justice, Queen's Bench Division, since 1993; *b* 28 Sept. 1939; *s* of Hugh Francis Guy Harrison and Elizabeth Alban Harrison (*née* Jones); *m* 1966, Judith (*née* Gist); one *s* one *d*. *Educ:* Charterhouse; Trinity Hall, Cambridge (MA). Called to the Bar, Gray's Inn, 1965, Bencher, 1993; QC 1983; a Recorder, 1989–93. Asst Comr, Parly Boundary Commn for England, 1981–93. Chm., Panel for Examination of Structure Plans, Somerset, 1981, Isles of Scilly, 1982, W Sussex, 1986. *Recreations:* tennis, sailing, fishing. *Address:* Royal Courts of Justice, Strand, WC2A 2LL.

HARRISON, Prof. Michael Jackson; Vice-Chancellor, University of Wolverhampton, since 1992 (Director, Wolverhampton Polytechnic (formerly The Polytechnic, Wolverhampton), 1985–92); *b* 18 Dec. 1941; *s* of Jackson Harrison and Norah (*née* Lees); *m* 1974, Marie Ghislaine Félix. *Educ:* Guildford Tech. Coll.; Univ. of Leicester (BA, MA). Lecturer in Sociology: Enfield Coll. of Technol., 1966–67; Univ. of Leeds, 1967–68, Sen. Lectr, Enfield Coll. of Technol., 1968–72; Principal Lectr, Sheffield City Polytechnic, 1972–76; Head of Dept, Hull Coll. of Higher Educn, 1976–81; Asst Dir, 1982–84, Dep. Dir, 1985, The Polytechnic, Wolverhampton. Vis. Lectr, Univ. of Oregon, 1971. Governor: Bilston Community Coll.; Thomas Telford CTC. FIMgt (FBIM 1983). *Publications:* (jtly) A Sociology of Industrialisation, 1978; contribs to learned jls. *Recreations:* cinema, travelling, music. *Address:* 34 Mount Road, Penn, Wolverhampton WV4 5SW. *T:* Wolverhampton (01902) 338807; University of Wolverhampton, Wulfrana Street, Wolverhampton WV1 1SB.

HARRISON, Sir Michael James Harwood, 2nd Bt *cr* 1961, of Bugbrooke; JP; Director of private companies; *b* 28 March 1936; *s* of Sir (James) Harwood Harrison, 1st Bt, TD, MP (C) Eye, Suffolk 1951–79, and Peggy Alberta Mary (*d* 1993), *d* of late Lt-Col V. D. Stenhouse, TD; *S* father, 1980; *m* 1967, Rosamund Louise, *d* of Edward Clive; two *s* two *d*. *Educ:* Rugby. Served with 17th/21st Lancers, 1955–56. Member of Lloyd's. Mem. Council, Sail Training Assoc.; Vice-Pres., Assoc. of Combined Youth Clubs. Patron and Lord of the Manor, Bugbrooke, Northampton, 1980–. Master, Mercers' Co., 1986–87; Freeman of the City of London. JP London, 1993. *Recreations:* sailing, ski-ing, riding (horse and bicycle), Daily Telegraph crossword. *Heir:* *s* Edwin Michael Harwood Harrison, *b* 29 May 1981. *Address:* 35 Paultons Square, SW3 5DT. *T:* 0171–352 1760. *Clubs:* Boodle's, MCC; Aldeburgh Yacht.

HARRISON, Mrs Molly, MBE 1967; Curator, Geffrye Museum, 1941–69; *b* Stevenage, 1909; *d* of late Ethel and late Ernest Charles Hodgett; *m* 1940, Gordon Frederick Harrison; three *d*. *Educ:* Friends Sch., Saffron Walden; Convent in Belgium; Sorbonne. Teaching in various Schs, 1934–39; Asst to Curator, Geffrye Museum, 1939–41. FMA 1952; Member: Council Museums Assoc., 1953–56; Council of Industrial Design, 1958–61; Cttee of Management, Society of Authors, 1967. Lectr on varied educational topics. FRSA 1968. Editor, Local Search Series, 1969–77. *Publications:* Museum Adventure, 1950; Picture Source Books for Social History, 1951, 1953, 1955, 1957, 1958, 1960 and 1966; Furniture 1953; Learning out of School, 1954; Food, 1954; Homes, 1960; Children in History, 1958, 1959, 1960, 1961; Your Book of Furniture, 1960; Shops and Shopping, 1963; How They Lived, 1963; Changing Museums, 1967; Hairstyles and Hairdressing, 1968; The English Home, 1969; People and Furniture, 1971; The Kitchen in History, 1972; Homes, 1973; Museums and Galleries, 1973; On Location: Museums, 1974; People and Shopping, 1975; Home Inventions, 1975; Homes in Britain, 1975; Markets and Shops, 1979; Growing Up in Victorian Times, 1980; Homes in History, 1983; The Story of Travelling (4 vols), 1983, 1984; numerous articles and reviews. *Recreations:* reading, gardening. *Address:* New Place, High Street, Whitchurch-on-Thames, Oxon RG8 7ET. *T:* Pangbourne (01734) 843736.

HARRISON, Patrick Kennard, CBE 1982; Director, Building Museum Project, since 1990 (Project Secretary, 1988–89); *b* 8 July 1928; *e s* of late Richard Harrison and Sheila Griffin; *m* 1955, Mary Wilson, *y d* of late Captain G. C. C. Damant, CBE, RN; one *d*. *Educ:* Lord Williams's Sch., Thame; Downing Coll., Cambridge (Exhbnr in English). Asst Principal, Dept of Health for Scotland, 1953; Private Sec. to Deptl Sec. and to Parly Secs, Scottish Office, 1958–60; Principal, Scottish Develt Dept and Regional Develt Div.,

Scottish Office, 1960–68; Sec., RIBA, 1968–87. Hon. Mem., Amer. Inst. of Architects, 1978. Hon. FRIAS, 1987; Hon. FRIBA, 1988. *Publication:* (ed) Civilising the City: quality or chaos in historic towns, 1991. *Address:* 63 Princess Road, NW1 8JS. *T:* 0171–722 8508; Upper Stewarton, Eddleston, Peebles EH45 8PP. *T:* Eddleston (01721) 730602. *Clubs:* Reform; New (Edinburgh).

HARRISON, Hon. Sir Richard; *see* Harrison, Hon. Sir J. R.

HARRISON, Prof. Sir Richard (John), Kt 1984; MD, DSc; FRS 1973; Professor of Anatomy, Cambridge University, 1968–82, now Emeritus; Fellow of Downing College, Cambridge, 1968–82, Hon. Fellow, 1982; *b* 8 Oct. 1920; *er s* of late Geoffrey Arthur Harrison, MD, and Theodora Beatrice Mary West; *m* 1st, 1943, Joanna Gillies (marr. diss. 1967); two *s* one *d*; 2nd, 1967, Barbara Fuller (*d* 1988); 3rd, 1990, Gianetta Drake, *d* of late Capt. C. K. Lloyd, CBE, RN retd and Phyllis Lloyd. *Educ:* Oundle; Gonville and Caius Coll., Cambridge (Scholar); St Bartholomew's Hosp. Medical Coll. LRCP, MRCS, 1944. House Surgeon, St Bartholomew's Hosp., 1944. MB, BChir, 1944; MA 1946; MD Cantab 1954. Demonstrator in Anatomy, St Bartholomew's Hosp. Medical Coll., 1944; Lectr in Anatomy, Glasgow Univ., 1946, DSc Glasgow 1948; Sen. Lectr, 1947, and Reader in Anatomy, 1950, Charing Cross Hosp. Medical Sch. (Symington Prize for research in Anatomy); Reader in charge of Anatomy Dept, London Hosp. Medical Coll., 1951–54; Prof. of Anatomy, University of London, at London Hosp. Medical Coll., 1954–68; Fullerian Prof. of Physiology, Royal Institution, 1961–67. Wooldridge Lectr, BVA, 1983. Chairman: Farm Animal Welfare Adv. Cttee, MAFF, 1974–79; Farm Animal Welfare Council, 1979–88. President: European Assoc. for Aquatic Mammals, 1974–76; Anat. Soc. of GB and Ireland, 1978–79. XIIth Internat. Congress of Anatomists, London, 1985; Internat. Fedn of Assocs of Anatomists, 1985–87. A Trustee, British Museum (Natural History), 1978–88 (Chm. Trustees, 1984–88); Member Council: Royal Soc., 1981–82; Zool. Soc., 1974–78, 1980–83; Nat. Trust, 1984–85; Internat. Monachus Cttee, Ministère de l'Environnement, Paris, 1987–90. Hon. Member: American Assoc. of Anatomists; Società Italiana Anatomia. *Publications:* Man the Peculiar Animal, 1958; (with J. E. King) Marine Mammals, 1965, 2nd edn 1979; Reproduction and Man, 1967; (with W. Montagna) Man, 2nd edn 1972; Functional Anatomy of Marine Mammals, vol. I, 1972, vol. II, 1974, vol. III, 1977; (with S. H. Ridgway) Handbook of Marine Mammals, vols I and II, 1981, vol. III, 1985, vol. IV, 1989, vol. V, 1994; (with M. M. Bryden): Research on Dolphins, 1986; Whales, Dolphins and Porpoises, 1988; numerous papers on embryology, comparative and human anatomy. *Recreations:* marine biology, painting. *Address:* Milestone House, 58A High Street, Barkway, Royston, Herts SG8 8EE. *T:* Barkway (01763) 8974. *Club:* Garrick.

HARRISON, Sir (Robert) Colin, 4th Bt, *cr* 1922; *b* 25 May 1938; *s* of Sir John Fowler Harrison, 2nd Bt, and Kathleen (*d* 1993), *yr d* of late Robert Livingston, The Gables, Eaglescliffe, Co. Durham; *S* brother, 1955; *m* 1963, Maureen, *er d* of late E. Leonard Chiverton, Garth Corner, Kirkbymoorside, York; one *s* two *d*. *Educ:* St Peter's Coll., Radley; St John's Coll., Cambridge. Commissioned with Fifth Royal Northumberland Fusiliers (National Service), 1957–59. Chm., John Harrison (Stockton) Ltd; Vice Chm., Darlington Bldg Soc. Chm., Young Master Printers Nat. Cttee, 1972–73. *Heir: s* John Wyndham Fowler Harrison, *b* 14 Dec. 1972. *Address:* Stearsby Hall, Stearsby, York YO6 4SA. *T:* Easingwold (01347) 888226.

HARRISON, Robert Michael; QC 1987; a Recorder, since 1985; *b* 3 Nov. 1945; *s* of Robert William and Bertha Harrison; *m* 1974, Jennifer Armstrong; one *s*. *Educ:* Heckmondwike Grammar School; Hull Univ. (LLB). Called to the Bar, Gray's Inn, 1969. *Recreations:* history, music, walking, swimming. *Address:* 22 Park Drive, Mirfield, West Yorks. *T:* Mirfield (01924) 492863.

HARRISON, Roger; *see* Harrison, D. R. W.

HARRISON, Prof. Roy Michael, PhD, DSc; FRSC, FRMetS, FRSH; Queen Elizabeth II Birmingham Centenary Professor of Environmental Health, since 1991, and Director, Institute of Public and Environmental Health, since 1994, University of Birmingham; *b* 14 Oct. 1948; *s* of Wilfred Harrison and Rosa (*née* Cotton); *m* 1st, 1981, Angela Copeman (marr. diss.); one *s* one *d*; 2nd, 1989, Susan Sturt; one *s*. *Educ:* Henley Grammar Sch.; Univ. of Birmingham (BSc; PhD 1972; DSc 1988). FRMetS 1982; FRSC 1988; FRSH 1991. Res. Asst, Imperial Coll., Univ. of London, 1972–74; Lectr, Lancaster Univ., 1974–84; Reader, Univ. of Essex, 1984–91. Margary Lectr, RMetS, 1994; John Jeyes Lectr, RSC, 1995. Department of the Environment: Mem., Photochem. Oxidants Rev. Gp, 1986–; Chm., Quality of Urban Air Rev. Gp, 1991–; Mem., Expert Panel on Air Quality Standards, 1992–; Department of Health: Member: Cttee on Med. Effects of Air Pollution, 1993–; Health Adv. Gp on Chem. Contamination Incidents, 1994–. Hon. Consulting Envmtl Toxicologist, Nat. Poisons Inf. Service, Birmingham Centre and W Midlands Poisons Unit, 1994–. Chm., Envmt Gp, RSC, 1990–91. *Publications:* (with D. P. H. Laxen) Lead Pollution: causes and control, 1981; Pollution: causes, effects and control, 1983, 2nd edn 1990; (with R. Perry) Handbook of Air Pollution Analysis, 2nd edn 1986; (jtly) Acid Rain: scientific and technical advances, 1987; (with S. Rapsomanikis) Environmental Analysis using Chromatography Interfaced with Atomic Spectroscopy, 1989; (jtly) Introductory Chemistry for the Environmental Sciences, 1991; (with R. S. Hamilton) Highway Pollution, 1991; (jtly) Handbook for Urban Air Improvement, 1992; Understanding Our Environment: an introduction to environmental chemistry and pollution, 1992 (with M. Radojevic) Atmospheric Acidity: sources, consequences and abatement, 1992; (with F. E. Warner) Radioecology after Chernobyl: biogeochemical pathways of artificial radionuclides, SCOPE 50, 1993; (jtly) Urban Air Quality in the United Kingdom, 1993; (jtly) Diesel Vehicle Emissions and Urban Air Quality, 1993; many papers to learned jls. *Recreations:* mowing and other outdoor pursuits. *Address:* Institute of Public and Environmental Health, School of Chemistry, University of Birmingham, Edgbaston, Birmingham B15 2TT. *T:* 0121–414 3494.

HARRISON, Ted; *see* Harrison, E. P. G.

HARRISON, Sir Terence, Kt 1995; DL; FEng 1988; FIMechE; FIMarE; Chief Executive, Rolls-Royce PLC, since 1992 (Director, since 1989); *b* 7 April 1933; *s* of late Roland Harrison and of Doris (*née* Wardle); *m* 1956, June (*née* Forster); two *s*. *Educ:* A. J. Dawson Grammar Sch., Co. Durham; West Hartlepool and Sunderland Tech. Colls. BSc(Eng) Durham. CEng 1964; FIMechE 1984; FIMarE 1973. Marine engrg apprenticeship, Richardson's Westgarth, Hartlepool, 1949–53; commnd REME, service in Nigeria, 1955–57; Clarke Chapman, Gateshead (Marine Division): Res. Engr, 1957; Chief Mechanical Engr, 1967; Man. Dir, 1969; Man. Dir, Clarke Chapman Ltd, Gateshead, 1976; Northern Engineering Industries plc: Dir, 1977; Man. Dir, UK Ops, 1980–83; Chief Exec., 1983–86; Exec. Chm., 1986–93. Director: Barclays Bank (Regl Bd), 1986; Northumbria Water Authority, 1988. Member: ACOST, 1987; Engrg Council, 1990–. Pres., BEAMA, 1989–90. Pres., NEC Inst., 1988. DL Tyne and Wear, 1989. Hon. DEng Newcastle, 1991. *Publications:* technical papers to mechanical, marine and mining societies. *Recreations:* golf, fell walking. *Address:* 2 The Garden Houses, Whalton, Northumberland NE61 3HB. *T:* Morpeth (01670) 775400; (office) Rolls-Royce PLC, 65 Buckingham Gate, SW1E 6AT.

HARRISON, Theophilus George, OBE 1971; JP; Member, Greater Manchester Council, 1973–77 (Chairman, 1973–1974 and 1974–1975, Deputy Chairman, 1975–76); General Secretary, National Association of Powerloom Overlookers, 1947–76, now Life Member; Member Executive, General Union of Associations of Loom Overlookers, 1947–76, now Life Member (President, 1964–66); *b* 30 Jan. 1907; *s* of Alfred and Emma Harrison; *m* 1935, Clarissa Plevin; one *s* one *d*. Swinton and Pendlebury Borough Council: Mem., 1941–56; Alderman, 1956–74; Mayor, 1954–55; Chairman: Housing Cttee; Highways and Lighting Cttee; Mem., Div. Planning Cttee; Lancs CC: Mem. Educn Cttee, 1946–74 (Vice-Chm. 1951–53, Chm. 1953–74); Chm., Road Safety Cttee; Vice-Chairman: Public Health and Housing Cttee; Greater Manchester Transport Cons. Cttee; Pres., Lancs Non-County Boroughs Assoc., 1960–62; Chairman: Swinton and Pendlebury Youth Employment Cttee; Youth Adv. Cttee and Youth Centres; Mem., Div. Exec., Educn Cttee; Member: Gen. Council, Lancs and Merseyside Ind. Develt Corp.; N Counties Textile Trades Fedn Central Board; Life Member: Salford Trades Council (formerly Mem., Swinton and Pendlebury Trades Council); Swinton Labour Club. Member: Manchester Reg. Hosp. Bd, 1961–74; Mental Health Review Tribunals, 1961–70; W Manchester HMC, 1957–74 (Chm. 1963–74); Wrightington HMC, 1957–74; Salford Community Health Council, 1973–83 (former Vice-Chm. and Chm., Develt Cttee); Assoc. of Community Health Councils, 1973–83 (former Vice-Chm., NW Region). Hon. Vice-Pres., Greater Manchester Council for Voluntary Service. Past Chm. or Mem. many other Co. or local organizations and cttees. Former Pres., SE Lancs and Cheshire Accident Prevention Fedn; Dir, RoSPA; Freeman of Swinton and Pendlebury, 1973 (now Salford BC). JP 1949. *Recreations:* reading, Rugby League football (spectator); much of his political and public activities.

HARRISON, Tony, FRSL; poet; *b* 30 April 1937; *s* of Harry Ashton Harrison and Florrie (*née* Wilkinson-Horner); *m* 1st, 1960, Rosemarie Crossfield (*née* Dietzsch); one *s* one *d*; 2nd, 1984, Teresa Stratas. *Educ:* Cross Flatts County Primary Sch.; Leeds Grammar Sch.; Univ. of Leeds (BA, Dip.Linguistics). Lecturer in English: Ahmadu Bello Univ., Zaria, N Nigeria, 1962–66; Charles Univ., Prague, 1966–67; Northern Arts Fellow in Poetry, Univs of Newcastle and Durham, 1967–68 and 1976–77; UNESCO Fellow in Poetry, Cuba, Brazil, Senegal, Gambia, 1969; Gregynog Arts Fellow, Univ. of Wales, 1973–74; Resident Dramatist, National Th., 1977–79; UK/US Bi-Centennial Fellow, New York, 1979–80. Pres., Classical Assoc., 1987–88. FRSL 1984. *Publications:* Earthworks, 1964; Aikin Mata, 1966; Newcastle is Peru, 1969; The Loiners (Geoffrey Faber Meml Prize), 1970; The Misanthrope, 1973; Phaedra Britannica, 1975; Palladas: poems, 1975; The Passion, 1977; Bow Down, 1977; From The School of Eloquence and other poems, 1978; The Bartered Bride, 1978; Continuous, 1981; A Kumquat for John Keats, 1981; US Martial, 1981; The Oresteia, 1981; Selected Poems, 1984, expanded edn 1987; The Mysteries, 1985; Dramatic Verse 1973–85, 1985; v., 1985; The Fire-Gap, 1985; Theatre Works 1973–85, 1986; The Trackers of Oxyrhynchus, 1990; v. and other poems, 1990; A Cold Coming: Gulf War poems, 1991; The Common Chorus, 1992; The Gaze of the Gorgon (Whitbread Award for Poetry), 1992; Square Rounds, 1992; Black Daisies for the Bride, 1993; Poetry or Bust, 1993; A Maybe Day in Kazakhstan, 1994; The Shadow of Hiroshima, 1995; Permanently Bard, 1995. *Address:* c/o Peters, Fraser & Dunlop, 5th Floor, The Chambers, Chelsea Harbour, Lots Road, SW10 0XF.

HARRISON, Valerie, (Mrs D. M. Harrison); *see* Caton, V.

HARRISON, Rt. Hon. Walter, PC 1977; JP; public affairs consultant, since 1987; *b* 2 Jan. 1921; *s* of Henry and Ada Harrison; *m* 1948, Enid Mary (*née* Coleman) (*d* 1990); one *s* one *d*; *m* 1991, Jane Marguerite Richards. *Educ:* Dewsbury Technical and Art Coll. Served RAF, 1940–45. Electrical Inspector and Electrical Foreman, Electricity Supply Industry, 1937–64; Welfare Personnel Officer, Civil and Engrg Industry, 1945–48. MP (Lab) Wakefield, 1964–87. Asst Govt Whip, 1966–68; a Lord Comr of the Treasury, 1968–70; Dep. Chief Opposition Whip, 1970–74 and 1979–83; Treasurer of HM Household and Dep. Chief Govt Whip, 1974–79. Held several positions in the Trade Union and Labour movements. West Riding CC, 1958–64; Alderman, Castleford Borough Council, 1959–66 (Councillor, 1952–59); JP West Riding Yorks, 1962. *Address:* 1 Milnthorpe Drive, Sandal, Wakefield WF2 7HU. *T:* Wakefield (01924) 255550.

HARRISON-CHURCH, Prof. Ronald James; Professor of Geography, University of London, at London School of Economics, 1964–77; *b* 26 July 1915; *s* of late James Walter Church and late Jessie May Church; *m* 1944, Dorothy Violet, *d* of late Robert Colchester Harrison and late Rose Harrison; one *s* one *d*. *Educ:* Westminster City Sch.; Universities of London and Paris. BSc (Econ) 1936, PhD 1943, London. LSE: Asst Lectr, 1944–47; Lectr, 1947–58; Reader, 1958–64. Consultant to UN Economic Commn for Africa on large scale irrigation schemes, 1962. Geographical Dir, Trans-African Hovercraft Expedition, 1969. Visiting Professor: University of Wisconsin, 1956; Indiana Univ., 1965; Tel Aviv and Haifa Univs, 1972–73. Has lectured in many other univs in Brazil, US, Canada, West Africa, Belgium, France, Germany, Poland and Sweden. Member: French Embassy Scholarships Cttee, 1946–68; British Cttee, Coll. of Europe, 1951–72; Cttee for Staff Fulbright Awards, US-UK Educnl Commn, 1958–61 and 1972–75; Cttee, British Fulbright Schols Assoc., 1981–83; Africa Field Cttee, Oxfam, 1974–80. Chm., Firbank Housing Soc., 1977–83. Hon. Vice-Pres., Royal Afr. Soc., 1992– (Vice-Pres., 1977–92; Mem. Council, 1973–92; Mem., Speakers and Publics Cttee, 1972–85). Hon. Mem., Société Géographique de Liège, 1977. Back Award, RGS, 1957; Regl Conf. IGU Award, 1978. *Publications:* Modern Colonization, 1951; West Africa, 1957, 8th edn, 1980; Environment and Policies in West Africa, 1963, 2nd edn 1976; Looking at France, 1970, rev. repr. 1976, French edn 1969, US edn 1970, Spanish edn 1973; (jtly) Africa and the Islands, 1964, 4th edn, 1979; (jtly) An Advanced Geography of Northern and Western Europe, 1967, 3rd edn 1980; contribs to Geograph. Jl, W Africa, etc. *Recreations:* lecturing on cruises, private travel. *Address:* 40 Handside Lane, Welwyn Garden City, Herts AL8 6SJ. *T:* Welwyn Garden (01707) 323293.

HARRISON-HALL, Michael Kilgour; DL; **His Honour Judge Harrison-Hall;** a Circuit Judge, since 1972; *b* 20 Dec. 1925; *s* of late Arthur Harrison-Hall, Oxford; *m* 1951, Jessie Margaret, *d* of late Rev. Arthur William Brown, Collingbourne Ducis, Wilts; two *s* two *d*. *Educ:* Rugby; Trinity College, Oxford. Called to Bar, Inner Temple, 1949. Dep. Chm., Warwickshire QS, 1968–71; a Recorder of the Crown Court, 1972. DL Warwicks, 1985. *Address:* Ivy House, Church Street, Barford, Warwick CV35 8EN. *T:* Barford (01926) 624272. *Clubs:* United Oxford & Cambridge University; Leander.

HARRISS, Gerald Leslie, DPhil; FBA 1986; Fellow and Tutor, Magdalen College, Oxford, 1967–92, Emeritus Fellow, since 1992; Reader in Modern History, Oxford University, 1990–92; *b* 22 May 1925; *s* of Walter and Mabel Harriss; *m* 1959, Margaret Anne Sidaway; two *s* three *d*. *Educ:* Chigwell Sch.; Magdalen Coll., Oxford (BA 1st Cl. History, MA, DPhil). Service in RNVR, 1944–46. Research Fellow, Durham Univ., 1953–55; Asst Lectr, Manchester Univ., 1955–56; Lectr 1956, Sen. Lectr 1965, Reader 1965–67, Durham Univ. *Publications:* King, Parliament and Public Finance in Medieval England, 1975; (ed) Henry V: the practice of kingship, 1985; Cardinal Beaufort, 1988; numerous articles on late medieval English history. *Address:* Fairings, 2 Queen Street, Yetminster, Dorset DT9 6LL.

HARROD, Dominick Roy; journalist and broadcaster; Programme Director, St George's House, Windsor Castle, since 1994; President, Institute of Journalists, 1994–95; *b* 21 Aug. 1940; *s* of Sir Roy Forbes Harrod, FBA and of Wilhelmine Harrod (*née* Cresswell), OBE; *m* 1974, Christina Hobhouse; one *s*. *Educ:* Westminster School; Christ Church, Oxford (MA Modern Greats). Sunday Telegraph, 1962–66; Daily Telegraph: Washington corresp., 1966–69; Economics corresp., 1969–71; BBC Economics corresp., 1971–78; Dir of Information, Dunlop Ltd, 1979; Economics Editor, BBC Radio, 1979–93; City Editor, The Yorkshire Post, 1993–94. Mem. Council, SCF, 1988–. FJI 1990; FRSA 1992. *Publications:* The Politics of Economics, 1978; Making Sense of the Economy, 1983. *Recreations:* reading, sailing. *Address:* 4 Duke's Avenue, W4 2AE. *Clubs:* Garrick, Beefsteak.

HARROLD, Roy Mealham; farmer, 1947–91; *b* 13 Aug. 1928; *s* of John Frederick Harrold and Ellen Selena Harrold (*née* Mealham); *m* 1968, Barbara Mary, *yr d* of William and Florence Andrews; one *s* one *d*. *Educ:* Stoke Holy Cross Primary Sch.; Bracondale Sch., Norwich. County Chm., Norfolk Fedn of Young Farmers' Clubs, 1956–57; Mem., Nat. Council of Young Farmers, 1957–60; Mem. Council, Royal Norfolk Agric. Assoc., 1972–75, 1980–83, 1987–89; Mem., Press Council, 1976–83. Lay Chm., Norwich East Deanery Synod, 1970–79; Member: Norwich Dio. Synod, 1970–; Norwich Dio. Bd of Patronage, 1970–82; Norwich Dio. Bd of Finance, 1983–; Pastoral Asst, St Peter Mancroft, Norwich, 1991– (Church Warden, 1978–82, 1988–92). *Recreations:* music, opera, ballet. *Address:* Salamanca Farm, Stoke Holy Cross, Norwich NR14 8QJ. *T:* Framingham Earl (01508) 492322.

HARROP, Sir Peter (John), KCB 1984 (CB 1980); Second Permanent Secretary, Department of the Environment, 1981–86; *b* 18 March 1926; *s* of late Gilbert Harrop, OBE; *m* 1975, Margaret Joan, *d* of E. U. E. Elliott-Binns, CB; two *s*. *Educ:* King Edward VII Sch., Lytham, Lancs; Peterhouse, Cambridge. MA (Hist. Tripos). Served RNVR, 1945–47 (Sub-Lt). Min. of Town and Country Planning, 1949; Min. of Housing and Local Govt, 1951; Dept of the Environment, 1970 (Chm., Yorks and Humberside Economic Planning Bd, and Regional Dir, 1971–73); Under Sec., HM Treasury, 1973–76; Deputy Secretary: DoE, 1977–79, 1980–81; Cabinet Office, 1979–80. Mem. Bd, 1987–91, Chm., 1988–91, National Bus Co.; non-executive Director: Nat. Home Loans Hldgs (formerly Corp.) plc, 1987–92; Thames Water plc, 1989– (Mem., Thames Water Authority, 1986–89); Managing Trustee, Municipal Mutual Insurance Ltd, 1988–. Chm., UK Cttee, European Year of the Environment, 1987–88. Chm. of Govs., Richmond upon Thames Coll., 1993–. Hon. Trustee, British Mus., 1987–. *Recreations:* golf, sailing. *Address:* 19 Berwyn Road, Richmond, Surrey TW10 5BP. *Clubs:* United Oxford & Cambridge University, Roehampton; Ski Club of Great Britain; Island Cruising (Salcombe).

HARROWBY, 7th Earl of, *cr* 1809; **Dudley Danvers Granville Coutts Ryder,** TD; Baron Harrowby, 1776; Viscount Sandon, 1809; Chairman, Private Financial Holdings Ltd, since 1992; *b* 20 Dec. 1922; *er s* of 6th Earl of Harrowby and Lady Helena Blanche Coventry (*d* 1974), *e d* of late Viscount Deerhurst; *S* father, 1987; *m* 1949, Jeannette Rosalthé, *yr d* of late Captain Peter Johnston-Saint; one *s* one *d*. *Educ:* Eton. Lt-Col RA; OC 254 (City of London) Field Regt, RA (TA), 56 Armoured Div., 1962–64. Served War of 1939–45: 59 Inf. Div., in NW Europe (wounded); 5 Para. Bde, India and Java (political offr), 1941–45. Man. Dir, 1949–89, Dep. Chm., 1970–89, Coutts & Co.; Director: Dinorwic Slate Quarries Co., 1951–69; United Kingdom Provident Institution, 1955–86 (Dep. Chm., 1956–64); National Provincial Bank, 1964–69; National Westminster Bank Plc, 1968–87 (Dep. Chm., 1971–87); Olympia Group, 1968–73 (Chm., 1971–73); Sheepbridge Engrg Ltd, 1977–79; Saudi Internat. Bank, 1980–82, 1985–87; Powell Duffryn Trustees Ltd, 1981–86; Orion Pacific Ltd, 1980–81; Orion Pension Trustee Co. Ltd, 1980–81; Chairman: International Westminster Bank Plc, 1977–87; Powell Duffryn Gp, 1981–86 (Dir, 1976–86); National Westminster Unit Trust Managers, 1979–83; Orion Bank Ltd, 1979–81; Bentley Engineering Co. Ltd, 1983–86; NatWest Investment Bank, 1986–87, Dowty Group, 1986–91 (Dir, 1986–91), The Private Bank & Trust Co., 1989–92. Chm., Nat. Biol Standards Bd, 1973–88. Mem. Kensington Borough Council, 1950–65 (Chm., Gen. Purposes Cttee, 1957–59), Kensington and Chelsea BC, 1965–71 (Chm., Finance Cttee, 1968–71); Mem. Exec. Cttee, London area Cons. Assoc., 1949–50; Hon. Treasurer, S Kensington Cons. Assoc., 1953–56; Pres., Wolverhampton SW Cons. Assoc., 1959–68. Pres., Historical and Civic Soc. Hon. Treasurer: Family Welfare Assoc., 1951–65; Central Council for the Care of Cripples, 1953–60. General Commissioner for Income Tax, 1954–71; Member: Lord Chancellor's Adv. Investment Cttees, for Court of Protection, 1965–77, for Public Trustee, 1974–77; Inst. Internat. d'Etudes Bancaires, 1977–87; Trilateral Commn, 1980–94. Manager, Fulham and Kensington Hosp. Group, 1953–56; Member: Cttee of Management, Inst. of Psychiatry, 1953–73 (Chm. 1965–73); Board of Governors, Bethlem Royal and Maudsley (Postgraduate Teaching) Hosps, 1955–73 (Chm. 1965–73); Dep. Chm., London Postgraduate Cttee, Teaching Hosps Assoc., 1968–69; Trustee, Psychiatry Research Trust, 1982–; Mem. Bd of Govs, Univ. of Keele, 1956–68. Pres., Staffordshire Soc., 1957–59 (Hon. Treas., 1947–51). Dep. Pres., Staffs Army Cadet League. Mem., Ct of Assts, Goldsmiths Co., 1972–77. Governor, Atlantic Inst. for Internat. Affairs. MRIIA; CIMgt; Hon. FRCPsych 1983–88. *Heir:* *s* Viscount Sandon, *qv*. *Address:* 5 Tregunter Road, SW10 9LS. *T:* 0171–373 9276; Sandon Hall, Stafford ST18 0BY. *T:* Sandon (01889) 508338; Burnt Norton, Chipping Campden, Glos GL55 6PR. *T:* Evesham (01386) 840358.

HARSANYI, Prof. John Charles, PhD; Professor of Business Administration and Economics, University of California, Berkeley, 1964–90, now Emeritus; *b* 29 May 1920; *s* of Charles and Alice Harsanyi; *m* 1951, Anne Klauber; one *s*. *Educ:* Univ. of Budapest, Hungary (Dr Phil 1947); Sydney Univ., Australia (MA 1953); Stanford Univ. (PhD 1959). Asst, Univ. of Budapest, 1947–48; Lectr in Econs, Univ. of Qld, 1954–56; Sen. Fellow, ANU, 1959–61; Prof. of Econs, Wayne State Univ., 1961–63. Hon. DSc Northwestern, 1989; Hon. *Dr* Buenos Aires, 1995. (Jtly) Nobel Prize in Econs, 1994. *Publications:* Essays on Ethics, Social Behaviour and Scientific Explanation, 1976; Rational Behaviour and Bargaining Equilibrium in Games and Social Situations, 1977; Papers in Game Theory, 1982; (with R. Selten) A General Theory of Equilibrium Selection in Games, 1988; numerous articles in learned jls. *Address:* Haas School of Business, University of California, Berkeley, CA 94720–1900, USA. *T:* (510) 6425588.

HARSCH, Joseph Close, CBE (Hon.) 1965; writer; *b* Toledo, Ohio, 25 May 1905; *s* of Paul Arthur Harsch and Leila Katherine Close; *m* 1932, Anne Elizabeth Wood; three *s*. *Educ:* Williams Coll., Williamstown, Mass (MA); Corpus Christi Coll., Cambridge (MA). Joined staff Christian Science Monitor, 1929; Washington corresp., then foreign corresp.; Asst Dir, Intergovt Cttee, London, 1939; Monitor Corresp. in Berlin, 1940, SW Pacific area, 1941 and 1942. Began radio broadcasting, 1943; Senior European Correspondent, NBC, 1957–65; Diplomatic Correspondent, NBC, 1965–67; Commentator, American Broadcasting Co., 1967–71; Chief Editorial Writer, Christian Science Monitor, 1971–74. Edward Weintal award for writing on foreign affairs, 1979. *Publications:* Pattern of Conquest, 1941; The Curtain Isn't Iron, 1950; At the Hinge of History, 1993. *Address:* PO Box 457, Jamestown, RI 02835, USA. *Clubs:* Garrick; Metropolitan, Cosmos (Washington, DC); Century (New York); St Botolph (Boston).

HARSTON, Julian John Robert Clive; HM Diplomatic Service; Counsellor, UK Mission, Geneva, since 1991; *b* 20 Oct. 1942; *s* of late Col Clive Harston, ERD, and of Kathleen Harston; *m* 1966, Karen Howard Oake (*née* Longfield); one *s*. *Educ:* King's Sch., Canterbury; Univ. of London (BSc). British Tourist Authority, 1965–70; FCO, 1970; Consul, Hanoi, 1973; 1st Secretary: Blantyre, 1975; Lisbon, 1982; Counsellor, Harare, 1984–88; FCO, 1988–91. *Recreations:* photography, travel. *T:* (home) Godalming (01483) 417393. *Clubs:* East India, Royal Automobile; Gremio Literario (Lisbon); Harare (Zimbabwe).

HART, Alan; broadcasting consultant, since 1991; Director: Eurosport, since 1991 (Chairman, 1989–91); Global AMG, since 1995; *b* 17 April 1935; *s* of Reginald Thomas Hart and Lillian Hart; *m* 1961, Celia Mary Vine; two *s* one *d*. *Educ:* Pinnerwood Primary Sch.; University College Sch., Hampstead. Reporter: Willesden Chronicle and Kilburn Times, 1952–58; Newcastle Evening Chronicle, 1958; London Evening News, 1958–59; Editorial Asst, BBC Sportsview, 1959–61; Television Sports Producer, BBC Manchester, 1962–64; Asst Editor, Sportsview, 1964–65; Editor, Sportsview, 1965–68; Editor, Grandstand, 1968–77; Head of Sport, BBC Television, 1977–81; Controller, BBC1 Television, 1981–84; Special Asst to Dir Gen., BBC, 1985; Controller, Internat. Relations, BBC, 1986–91. Advr on management of E European broadcasting services, EBU, 1991–93. FRTS 1983. *Recreations:* sport, music, walking. *Address:* Cutwellwalls, Avonwick, near South Brent, Devon TQ10 9HA.

HART, Alan Edward; Chief Executive, Equal Opportunities Commission, 1985–89; *b* 28 July 1935; *m* 1961, Ann Derbyshire; one *s* one *d*. *Educ:* Varndean County Grammar Sch., Brighton; Lincoln Coll., Univ. of Oxford (MA). Solicitor. Dep. Town Clerk, City of Salford, 1970–73; Dir of Admin, 1973–75, Chief Exec., 1975–85, Wigan MBC.

HART, Alexander Hendry, QC (Canada) 1969; Agent General for British Columbia in the United Kingdom and Europe, 1981–87; *b* Regina, Sask., 17 July 1916; *s* of Alexander Hart and Mary (*née* Davidson); *m* 1948, Janet MacMillan Mackay; three *s* one *d*. *Educ:* Dalhousie Law School (LLB). Served War, Royal Canadian Artillery, 1939–45; retired with rank of Major. Read law with McInnis, Mcquarrie and Cooper; called to Bar of Nova Scotia, 1947. Vice-Pres., Marketing, 1967–71; Sen. Vice-Pres., Canadian Nat. Rlwys, 1971–81. Dep. Internat. Pres., Pacific Basin Economic Council, 1980–81; Pres., Canada-UK Chamber of Commerce, 1983; Past Pres., Vancouver Board of Trade; Past Chm., Western Transportation Adv. Council; Past Mem., University Council of British Columbia; Past Pres., Canada Japan Soc. of Vancouver. *Recreation:* golf. *Address:* 1515 Dorcas Point Road, Nanoose Bay, BC V0R 2R0, Canada. *Clubs:* Royal & Ancient Golf (St Andrews); Vancouver, Men's Canadian, Shaughnessy Golf and Country (Vancouver).

HART, Anelay Colton Wright; Partner in Appleby, Hope & Matthews, since 1963; *b* 6 March 1934; *s* of Anelay Thomas Bayston Hart and Phyllis Marian Hart; *m* 1979, Margaret Gardner (*née* Dewing). *Educ:* Stamford Sch.; King's Coll., London (LLB). Solicitor. Advisory Director, World Society for the Protection of Animals, 1982–; RSPCA: Mem. Council, 1969–95; Hon. Treasurer, 1974–81; Chm. of Council, 1981–83, 1985–86, 1988–90; Vice-Chm. Council, 1983–84, 1986–88; Queen Victoria Silver Medal, 1984. President, Rotary Club of South Bank and Eston, 1972–73. *Recreation:* walking. *Address:* Village Farm, Moulton, Richmond, N Yorks DL10 6QQ. *T:* (office) Eston Grange (01642) 440444. *Club:* Royal Over-Seas League.

HART, Anthony; *see* Hart, T. A. A.

HART, Anthony Bernard, PhD; Co-Chairman, World Disarmament Campaign, since 1986; Head of Chemistry Division, Research Division of Central Electricity Generating Board, 1976–82; *b* 7 July 1917; *s* of late Oliver and Jessie Hart; *m* 1946, Judith Ridehalgh (later Baroness Hart of South Lanark, DBE, PC) (*d* 1991); two *s*. *Educ:* Enfield Grammar Sch.; Queen Mary Coll., London. BSc, PhD; CEng, CChem, FRSC, FInstE. RN Cordite Factories, 1940–46; RN Scientific Service, 1946–50; Lectr in Physical Chem., Royal Coll. of Sci. and Technol., Glasgow (now Strathclyde Univ.), 1950–60; Res. Div., CEGB, 1960–82. Exec. Mem., later Chm., Glasgow Trades Council, 1952–60; Nat. Exec. Mem., AUT, 1954–59. Mem., Barnes BC, 1962–64; Mem. and Leader of Opposition, Richmond upon Thames Council, 1964–68 and 1971–74; Chm., Richmond upon Thames Local Govt Cttee, 1968–77; Mem. for Hornsey, GLC, 1981–86 (Chm., F & GP Cttee, 1981–82, Dep. Chief Whip, 1983–86). *Publications:* (with G. J. Womack) Fuel Cells, 1967; (with A. J. B. Cutler) Deposition and Corrosion in Gas Turbines, 1973; contribs to scientific jls. *Recreation:* campaigning for peace and socialism. *Address:* 3 Ennerdale Road, Kew, Richmond, Surrey TW9 3PG. *T:* 0181–948 1989.

HART, Anthony John, OBE 1995; DSC 1945; JP; Chairman, Cunningham Hart & Co. Ltd, 1985–87 (Senior Partner, 1972–85), retired; *b* 27 Dec. 1923; *s* of Cecil Victor Hart and Kate Winifred Hart (*née* Boncey); *m* 1947, E. Penelope Morris; one *s* one *d*. *Educ:* King's College Sch., Wimbledon; Dauntsey's Sch. ACII, FCILA. RN 1942–46 (Ordinary Seaman to Lieut). Joined Hart & Co., 1946, Partner 1952, Senior Partner 1969; on merger name changed to Cunningham Hart & Co. Mem. Council, CILA, 1964, Pres., 1970–71. Chm., Medic Alert Foundn in UK, 1971–83; Governor, Dauntsey's Sch., 1982–93; Mem. Council, Mansfield House University Settlement, 1975–90. Liveryman, 1960, Master, 1976–77, Broderers' Co.; Liveryman, 1979, Mem. Court, 1986, Insurers' Co. Alderman, Ward of Cheap, City of London, 1977–84. FRSA. JP City of London, 1977 (Vice-Chm. of Bench, 1991–93). *Recreation:* golf. *Address:* Merrington Place, Rolvenden, Cranbrook, Kent TN17 4PJ. *T:* Cranbrook (01580) 241428. *Clubs:* City Livery; Littlestone Golf.

HART, Anthony Ronald; QC (NI) 1983; **His Honour Judge Hart;** a County Court Judge, Northern Ireland, since 1985 (for the Division of Ards, since 1995); Chancellor, Diocese of Clogher, Church of Ireland, since 1990; *b* 30 April 1946; *s* of Basil and Hazel Hart; *m* 1971, Mary Morehan; two *s* two *d*. *Educ:* Portora Royal Sch., Enniskillen; Trinity Coll., Dublin (BA Mod.); Queen's Univ., Belfast. Called to the Bar of NI, 1969; called to the Bar, Gray's Inn, 1975. Jun. Crown Counsel for Co. Londonderry, 1973–75 and for Co. Down, 1975–79; Asst Boundary Comr, 1980–81; part-time Chm. of Industrial Tribunals, 1980–83; Dep. County Court Judge, 1983–85; Recorder of Londonderry, 1985–90. Member: Council of Legal Educn (NI), 1977–83; Review Cttee on Professional Legal Educn in NI, 1984–85; Standing Adv. Commn on Human Rights, 1984–85; Judicial Studies Bd for NI, 1993–; Criminal Justice Consultative Gp for NI, 1993–; Hon. Sec., Council of HM Co. Court Judges in NI, 1989–. Pres., Irish Legal History Soc., 1991–94. *Publications:* (Consultant Ed) Valentine on Criminal Procedure in Northern Ireland, 1989; (contrib.) Brehons, Serjeants and Attorneys: studies in the history of the Irish legal profession, 1990; (contrib.) Irish Legal History Society Discourses 1989–1994, 1995. *Recreations:* gardening, reading. *Address:* c/o Northern Ireland Court Service, Windsor House, Bedford Street, Belfast BT2 7LT.

HART, David Michael, OBE 1988; General Secretary, National Association of Head Teachers, since 1978; *b* 27 Aug. 1940; *s* of Edwin Henry Hart and Freda Muriel Hart; *m* (marr. diss.); two *s*. *Educ:* Hurstpierpoint Coll., Sussex. Solicitor 1963, Herbert Ruse Prizeman. Editor, Heads' Legal Guide, 1984. Hon. FCollP 1986; FRSA 1990. *Recreations:* tennis, walking, riding. *Address:* 1 Heath Square, Boltro Road, Haywards Heath, W Sussex

RH16 1BL. *T:* Haywards Heath (01444) 416708. *Clubs:* Commonwealth Trust, Wig and Pen, Civil Service, MCC.

HART, Donald; QC 1978; **His Honour Judge Donald Hart;** a Circuit Judge, since 1989; President, Mental Health Review Tribunals (restricted patients), since 1983; Designated Family Judge for Liverpool, since 1992; *b* 6 Jan. 1933; *s* of Frank and Frances Hart; *m* 1st, 1958, Glenys Thomas (marr. diss. 1990); two *s* two *d*; 2nd, 1990, Joan Turton. *Educ:* Altrincham Grammar Sch.; Magdalen Coll., Oxford. MA. Macaskie Scholar, Arden and Atkin Prize, Lee Essay Prize (Gray's Inn), 1956. Called to the Bar, Gray's Inn, 1956; Northern Circuit, 1956; a Recorder, 1978–89. *Recreations:* garden, travel, opera, cuisine. *Address:* 217 Knutsford Road, Grappenhall, Cheshire WA4 2TX. *T:* Warrington (01925) 604228; Queen Elizabeth II Law Courts, Derby Square, Liverpool L2 1XA. *T:* 0151–473 7373.

HART, Dr (Everard) Peter, CChem, FRSC; Rector, Sunderland Polytechnic, 1981–90; *b* 16 Sept. 1925; *s* of Robert Daniel Hart and Margaret Stokes; *m* Enid Mary Scott; three *s* one *d*. *Educ:* Wyggeston Grammar Sch., Leicester; Loughborough Coll.; London Univ. (BSc, PhD). Asst Lectr, Lectr and Sen. Lectr, Nottingham and Dist Technical Coll., 1951–57; Sunderland Technical College, later Sunderland Polytechnic: Head of Dept of Chemistry and Biology, 1958–69; Vice-Principal, 1963–69; Dep. Rector, 1969–80. Member: Cttee for Sci. and Technol., CNAA, 1974–77; Gen. Council, Northern Arts, 1982–90. Royal Institute of Chemistry: Mem. Council, 1963–65, 1970–73; Vice-Pres., 1973–75. FRSA 1985. Hon. DCL Sunderland, 1994. *Recreations:* music, opera, theatre, travel. *Address:* Redesdale, The Oval, North End, Durham City DH1 4NE. *T:* Durham (0191) 384 8305. *Club:* National Liberal.

HART, F(rancis) Dudley, FRCP; Physician, and Physician-in-charge Rheumatism Unit, Westminster Hospital, SW1, 1946–74; Emeritus Physician: Hospital of St John and St Elizabeth, London; Westminster Hospital; lately Consulting Rheumatologist, The Star and Garter Home for Disabled Sailors, Soldiers and Airmen, Richmond; lately Hon. Consulting Physician (Civilian) to the Army; *b* 4 Oct. 1909; *s* of Canon C. Dudley Hart and Kate Evelyn Bowden; *m* 1944, Mary Josephine, *d* of late Luke Tully, Carrigaline, Co. Cork; one *s* two *d*. *Educ:* Grosvenor Sch., Nottingham; Edinburgh Univ. MB, ChB Edinburgh 1933, MD 1939; MRCP 1937, FRCP 1949. House physician and clinical asst, Brompton Hosp., 1937; Med. Registrar, Royal Northern Hosp., 1935–37; Med. Registrar, Westminster Hosp., 1939–42; Med. Specialist and Officer i/c Med. Div., RAMC, 1942–46. Mem., Cttee on Review of Medicines, 1975–82. Ex-Pres. Heberden Soc.; Member: BMA; Med. Soc. of London. Arris and Gale Lectr, RCS, 1955; Ellman Lectr, RCP, 1969; Stanley Davidson Lectr, Univ. of Aberdeen, 1970; Bradshaw Lectr, RCP, 1975; Alexander Brown Meml Lectr, Univ. of Ibadan, Nigeria, 1979; Bernadine Becker Lectr, NY, 1984. Exec. Mem. and Vice-Chm., Arthritis and Rheumatism Council (formerly Empire Rheumatism Council); Hon. FRSM. Hon. Member: British Soc. for Rheumatology; Ligue Française contre le Rheumatisme; La Societa di Rheumatologia Italia; American Rheumatism Association; Australian Rheumatism Association. *Publications:* (co-author) Drugs: actions, uses and dosage, 1963; (ed) French's Differential Diagnosis, 10th edn, 1973, 12th edn, 1985; (ed) The Treatment of Chronic Pain, 1974; Joint Disease: all the arthropathies, 1975, 4th edn 1987; (ed) Drug Treatment of the Rheumatic Diseases, 1978, 3rd edn 1987; (ed) Clinical Rheumatology Illustrated, 1987; (ed) Diagnostic Features of Disease, 1987; Colour Atlas of Rheumatology, 1987; (jtly) Clinical Problems in Rheumatology, 1993; contributions to: Pye's Surgical Handicraft, 1939–72; Cortisone and ACTH, 1953; Miller's Modern Medical Treatment, 1962; Copeman's Textbook of the Rheumatic Diseases (ed J. T. Scott), 3rd edn 1964, 5th edn 1978; Encyclopedia of General Practice, 1964; Chambers's Encyclopædia, 1964; Drug Treatment, 1976; Butterworth's Medical Dictionary (all rheumatological sections), 1978; Overcoming Arthritis, 1981; articles and broadcasts on general medicine and rheumatism. *Recreations:* multi-track recording, travelling. *Address:* 24 Harmont House, 20 Harley Street, W1N 1AN. *T:* 0171–935 4252; (private) 19 Ranulf Road, Hampstead, NW2. *T:* 0171–794 2525.

HART, (Frank) Donald; *see* Hart, Donald.

HART, Frank Thomas, BA; JP; *b* London, 9 Nov. 1911; *s* of late Samuel Black and Ada Frances Laura Hart; *m* 1938, Eveline Brenda Deakin (*d* 1993), Leek, Staffs; three *s*. *Educ:* Gravesend and Sheerness Junior Technical Schs. DPA (London); Diploma of Economics (London); BA Open, 1982. Asst Sec., Buchanan Hospital, St Leonards-on-Sea, 1931–34; Sec., 1934–42; Sec., Central London Eye Hospital, 1942–44; Sec.-Superintendent, Princess Louise Hospital, 1944–48; Superintendent, Royal Infirmary, Sheffield, 1948–52; House Governor and Sec. to the Bd, Charing Cross Hospital, 1952–73; Hospital Manager, Zambia Medical Aid Soc., 1973–75. Mem. Tribunal set up by President of Zambia to hear applications for release from political detainees. Life Pres., League of Friends, Charing Cross Hosp., 1985–; Past Pres., Assoc. of Hosp. Secretaries; Past Pres. of the Hospital Officers' Club. JP: Co. Mddx, 1955–65; Co. Surrey, 1965–77, East Sussex, 1978–81. Freeman, City of London, 1959; Mem., Worshipful Soc. of Apothecaries. *Publications:* (jointly) A Study of Hospital Administration, 1948; Roots of Service (A History of Charing Cross Hospital), 1985. *Recreations:* all games, walking, reading. *Address:* 124 Marine Court, St Leonards on Sea, East Sussex TN38 0DY.

HART, George Vaughan; retired; Consultant, Law Reform Division, Department of Justice, Dublin, 1972–92; *b* 9 Sept. 1911; *e s* of George Vaughan Hart and Maude (*née* Curran); *m* 1949, Norah Marie, *d* of Major D. L. J. Babington; one *s* one *d*. *Educ:* Rossall; Corpus Christi Coll., Oxford. Called to Bar, Middle Temple, 1937. Served Royal Irish Fusiliers, 1940–45. Entered Home Office as Legal Asst, 1946; Principal Asst Legal Advr, 1967–72. Sec., Criminal Law Revision Cttee, 1959–72. *Recreations:* walking, bird-watching. *Address:* 1 Mount Salus, Knocknacree Road, Dalkey, Co. Dublin. *T:* Dublin 2850420. *Clubs:* Athenæum; Kildare Street and University (Dublin).

HART, Graham Allan, CB 1987; Permanent Secretary, Department of Health, since 1992; *b* 13 March 1940; *s* of Frederick and Winifred Hart; *m* 1964, Margaret Aline Powell; two *s*. *Educ:* Brentwood Sch.; Pembroke Coll., Oxford. Assistant Principal, 1962, Principal, 1967, Ministry of Health; Asst Registrar, General Medical Council, 1969–71; Principal Private Sec. to Secretary of State for Social Services, 1972–74; Asst Sec., 1974, Under Sec., 1979, DHSS; Under Sec., Central Policy Review Staff, 1982–83; Dep. Sec., DHSS, then DoH, 1984–89; Sec., Home and Health Dept, Scottish Office, 1990–92. *Address:* Richmond House, 79 Whitehall, SW1A 2NS.

HART, Guy William Pulbrook, OBE 1985; HM Diplomatic Service, retired; *b* 24 Dec. 1931; *s* of late Ernest Guy Hart and Muriel Hart (*née* Walkington); *m* 1954, Elizabeth Marjorie (*née* Bennett); one *s* two *d*. *Educ:* Cranleigh School. Commissioned, Intelligence Corps, 1951–60. British Cellophane Ltd, 1960–62; CRO, 1962; Consular Officer, Kuala Lumpur, 1963–67; Hungarian Language Course, 1967; Second Sec. (Inf.), Budapest, 1968–71; News Dept, FCO, 1971–74; Second Sec. (Econ.), later First Sec. (Inf.), British Mil. Govt, Berlin, 1974–78; First Sec. (Comm.), Port of Spain, 1978–82, Budapest, 1982–85; Asst Head, Inf. Dept, FCO, 1986; Ambassador to the Mongolian People's Republic, 1987–89; High Comr to Seychelles, 1989–91; Head of British delegn, EC monitor mission, Zagreb, 1993–94; Mem., UN Observer mission, SA election; CSCE observer, election in former Yugoslav republic of Macedonia, 1994. *Publication:* White Month's Return: Mongolia comes of age, 1993. *Recreations:* Alpine sports, shooting, painting. *Address:* 1 Marsh Mill, Wargrave Road, Henley on Thames, Oxon RG9 3JD. *Club:* Austrian Alpine.

HART, Michael, CBE 1990; MA; FRSA; Education Consultant, European Commission, 1990–93; *b* 1 May 1928; *yr s* of late Dr F. C. Hardt; *m* 1956, Lida Dabney Adams, PhD (Wisconsin Univ.). *Educ:* Collège Français, Berlin; Landerziehungsheim Schondorf; Keble Coll., Oxford (Exhib.). 1st Cl. Hons History, 1951. Administrative Asst, UNRRA, 1945–47; Asst Master and Head of History, Sherborne Sch., 1951–56; Head of History, 1956–61, and Housemaster of School House, 1961–67, Shrewsbury Sch.; Headmaster of Mill Hill Sch., 1967–74; HM Inspector of Schs, DES, 1974–76; Headmaster, European Sch., Mol, Belgium, 1976–80; Headmaster, European Sch., Luxembourg, 1980–89; Dir, European Classes, Alden Biesen, Belgium, 1989–92. Commandeur de l'Ordre de Mérite (Luxembourg), 1989. *Publications:* The EEC and Secondary Education in the UK, 1974; The European Dimension in Primary and Secondary Education, 1992; contrib. to Reader's Digest World Atlas and Atlas of British Isles. *Recreations:* travel, music, bridge. *Address:* 49 Chesterfield Road, Eastbourne BN20 7NU.

HART, Prof. Michael, CBE 1993; FRS 1982; CPhys, FInstP; Professor of Physics, University of Manchester, 1984–93, now Emeritus; *b* 4 Nov. 1938; *s* of Reuben Harold Victor Hart and Phyllis Mary (*née* White); *m* 1963, Susan Margaret (*née* Powell); three *d*. *Educ:* Cotham Grammar Sch., Bristol; Bristol Univ. (BSc, PhD, DSc). FInstP 1971. Research Associate: Dept of Materials Science and Engrg, Cornell Univ., 1963–65; Dept of Physics, Bristol Univ., 1965–67; Lectr in Physics, 1967–72, Reader in Physics, 1972–76, Bristol Univ.; Sen. Resident Res. Associate of Nat. Research Council, Nat. Aeronautics and Space Admin Electronics Research Center, Boston, Mass, 1969–70; Special Advisor, Central Policy Review Staff, Cabinet Office, 1975–77; Wheatstone Prof. of Physics and Head of Physics Dept, KCL, 1976–84; Science Pogramme Co-ordinator (part-time, on secondment), Daresbury Lab., SERC, 1985–88. Prof. of Applied Physics, De Montfort Univ., 1993–; Hon. Prof. in Engrg, Warwick Univ., 1993–. Amer. Crystallographic Assoc.'s Bertram Eugene Warren Award for Diffraction Physics (jtly with Dr U. Bonse), 1970; Charles Vernon Boys Prize of Inst. of Physics, 1971. *Publications:* numerous contribs to learned jls on x-ray optics, defects in crystals and synchrotron radiation. *Recreations:* weaving, flying kites. *Address:* 54 Manor Park South, Knutsford, Cheshire WA16 8AN. *T:* Knutsford (01565) 632893. *Club:* Athenæum.

HART, Michael Christopher Campbell; QC 1987; *b* 7 May 1948; *s* of Raymond David Campbell Hart and Penelope Mary Hart (*née* Ellis); *m* 1972, Melanie Jane Sandiford; two *d*. *Educ:* Winchester College; Magdalen College, Oxford (MA, BCL). Called to the Bar, Gray's Inn, 1970; Bencher, 1995. QC (NI) 1994. Fellow, All Souls College, Oxford, 1970–77, 1979–86, 1993–. *Address:* 5 Stone Buildings, Lincoln's Inn, WC2A 3XT. *T:* 0171–242 6201.

HART, Prof. Oliver Simon D'Arcy, PhD; Professor of Economics, Harvard University, since 1993; *b* 9 Oct. 1948; *s* of Philip Montagu D'Arcy Hart, *qv* and Ruth Hart; *m* 1974, Rita Goldberg (who retains maiden name); two *s*. *Educ:* University Coll. Sch.; Univ. of Cambridge (BA 1969); Univ. of Warwick (MA 1972); Princeton Univ. (PhD 1974). Lectr in Econs, Univ. of Essex, 1974–75; Asst Lectr in Econs, subseq. Lectr, Univ. of Cambridge, 1975–81; Fellow of Churchill Coll., Cambridge, 1975–81; Prof. of Economics, LSE, 1982–85; Prog. Dir, Centre for Economic Policy Res., 1983–84; Prof. of Economics, MIT, 1985–93. Fellow: Econometric Soc., 1979 (Mem. Council, 1982–); Amer. Acad. of Arts and Scis, 1988. Editor, Review of Economic Studies, 1979–83. Dr *hc* Free Univ. of Brussels, 1992; Univ. of Basel, 1994. *Publications:* articles on economic theory in Econometrica, Rev. of Econ. Studies, Jl of Pol Economy. *Recreations:* playing and watching tennis. *Address:* Department of Economics, Harvard University, Cambridge, MA 02138, USA.

HART, Peter; *see* Hart, E. P.

HART, P(hilip) M(ontagu) D'Arcy, CBE 1956; MA, MD (Cambridge), FRCP; Medical Research Council grant holder, National Institute for Medical Research, 1965–93 (Director, Tuberculosis Research Unit, Medical Research Council, 1948–65); *b* 25 June 1900; *s* of late Henry D'Arcy Hart and late Hon. Ethel Montagu; *m* 1941, Ruth, *d* of late Herbert Meyer and late Grete Meyer-Larsen; one *s*. *Educ:* Clifton Coll.; Gonville and Caius Coll., Cambridge; University Coll. Hospital. Dorothy Temple Cross Fellowship to USA, 1934–35; Consultant Physician, UCH, 1934–37; Mem. Scientific Staff, MRC, 1937–48; Mem. Expert Cttee on Tuberculosis, WHO, 1947–64. Goldsmith Entrance Exhibnr, Filliter Exhibnr, Magrath Scholarship, Tuke Medals, UCH Medical Sch., 1922–25; Horton Smith MD Prize, Cambridge, 1930; Royal College of Physicians: Milroy Lecture, 1937; Mitchell Lecture, 1946; Weber-Parkes Prize, 1951; Marc Daniels Lecture, 1967; Stewart Prize, BMA, 1964. *Publications:* scientific papers on respiratory disease, epidemiology and cell biology. *Address:* 37 Belsize Court, NW3 5QN. *T:* 0171–435 4048. *Club:* Athenæum.

See also O. S. D'A. Hart.

HART, Captain Raymond, CBE 1963; DSO 1945; DSC 1941, Bar 1943; Royal Navy; *b* 24 June 1913; *o s* of late H. H. Hart, Bassett, Southampton; *m* 1945, Margaret Evanson, *o d* of Capt. S. B. Duffin, Danesfort, Belfast; two *s* one *d*. *Educ:* Oakmount Preparatory Sch.; King Edward VI Sch. Joined Merchant Navy, 1929; Joined Royal Navy, 1937; HMS Hasty, 2nd Destroyer Flotilla, 1939–42; in command: HMS Vidette, 1942–44 (despatches); HMS Havelock, 1944; Sen. Officer, 21st Escort Gp, 1944–45; served in HMS Vanguard during Royal Tour of S Africa, 1947. RN Staff Course, 1949–52; in command, HMS Relentless, 1952–53; Joint Services Staff Course, 1953–54; Staff C-in-C Allied Forces Mediterranean, as Liaison Officer to C-in-C Allied Forces Southern Europe, HQ Naples, Italy, 1954–56; in command, HMS Undine, and Capt. 6th Frigate Sqdn, 1957–58; Cdre Naval Drafting, 1960–62; retd from RN, 1963. Nautical Advr, British & Commonwealth Shipping Co., 1963–72; Fleet Manager, Cayzer, Irvine & Co. Ltd, 1972–76; Director: Union-Castle Mail Steamship Co. Ltd; Clan Line Steamers Ltd, 1964–76; Cayzer, Irvine & Co. Ltd, 1966–76; British & Commonwealth Shipping Co. Ltd, 1966–76. Vice President: Seamen's Hosp. Soc., 1983; Marine Soc., 1989. FNI 1966; FRIN 1970. Officer Order of Merit of Republic of Italy, 1958. *Recreations:* swimming, golf, gardening.

HART, Roger Dudley; HM Diplomatic Service; Ambassador to Angola, since 1995; *b* 29 Dec. 1943; *s* of Alfred John Hart and Emma Jane Hart; *m* 1968, Maria de Los Angeles (Angela) de Santiago Jimenez; two *s*. *Educ:* St Olave's Grammar Sch., London; Univ. of Birmingham (BA 1965). FO 1965; served British Mil. Govt W Berlin, Bahrain and FCO, to 1975; First Sec. (Aid), Nairobi, 1975–78; First Sec. (Commercial), Lisbon, 1978–83; FCO, 1983–85; RCDS 1985; BNSC, 1986; Consul-Gen., Rio de Janeiro, 1986–90; Dep. Hd of Mission, Mexico City, 1990–93; Head of Nationality, Treaty and Claims Dept, FCO, 1993–95. Citizen, 1989, Pedro Ernesto Medal, 1990, Rio de Janeiro. *Recreations:*

travel, classical music, watching football and cricket. *Address:* 7 Rosscourt Mansions, 4 Palace Street, SW1E 5HZ. *T:* 0171–834 6032. *Club:* Royal Over-Seas League.

HART, (Thomas) Anthony (Alfred), MA; Headmaster, Cranleigh School, since 1984; *b* 4 March 1940; *er s* of Rev. Arthur Reginald Hart and Florence Ivy Hart; *m* 1971, Daintre Margaret Withiel (*née* Thomas); one *s* one *d*. *Educ:* City of Bath Sch.; New Coll., Oxford (2nd Cl. Hons PPE; MA); Pres., Oxford Union, 1963. Served with VSO, Mzuzu Secondary Sch., Nyasaland, 1959–60. Asst Principal and Principal, Min. of Transport, 1964–69; seconded to Govt of Malaŵi as Transport Adviser, 1969–70; Principal, DoE and CSD, 1970–73; Head, Voluntary Services Unit, Home Office, 1973–75; Asst Sec., CSD and HM Treasury, 1975–84. Gov., Danes Hill Prep. Sch., 1994–. *Recreations:* reading, travel, listening to music, dining out. *Address:* The Headmaster's House, Cranleigh School, Cranleigh, Surrey GU6 8QQ. *T:* Cranleigh (01483) 276377. *Club:* Travellers'.

HART, Thomas Mure, CMG 1957; *b* 1 March 1909; *s* of late Maxwell M. Hart and of Elizabeth Watson, Aiknut, West Kilbride; *m* 1936, Eileen Stewart Lawson; one *s* one *d*. *Educ:* Strathallan; Glasgow Univ.; Brasenose Coll., Oxford. Colonial Administrative Service, 1933; seconded Colonial Office, 1933–36; Malayan Civil Service, 1936; Dir of Commerce and Industry, Singapore, 1953; Financial Sec., Singapore, 1954; retired, 1959. Bursar, Loretto Sch., Musselburgh, 1959–69. *Recreation:* golf. *Address:* Charlton Down Cottage, Charlton Down, Andover, Hants SP11 0HZ. *T:* Andover (01264) 735590. *Club:* Honourable Company of Edinburgh Golfers.

HART, Maj.-Gen. Trevor Stuart, CB 1982; MRCS, LRCP; FFPHM; Hospital and Medical Director, National Guard King Khalid Hospital, Jeddah, 1983–84; *b* 19 Feb. 1926; *s* of R. J. Hart and C. G. Hart (*née* Blyfield); *m* 1954, P. G. Lloyd; two *s* one *d*. *Educ:* Dulwich Coll.; Guy's Hosp. MB, BS; FFPHM (FFCM); DPH, DTM&H. DDMS HQ 1 (BR) Corps, 1975–78; DMS: UKLF, 1978–81; BAOR, 1981–83. QHP 1978–83. Col Comdt, RAMC, 1984–90. Mem., Wessex RHA, 1984–88. OStJ 1973. *Recreations:* gardening, growing orchids (more leaves than blooms). *Address:* c/o Barclays Bank, Atlas House, 1–7 King Street, EC2V 8AU.

HART-DAVIS, Sir Rupert (Charles), Kt 1967; author, editor and former publisher; Director of Rupert Hart-Davis, Ltd, Publishers, 1946–68; Vice-President, Committee of the London Library, since 1971 (Chairman 1957–69); *b* 28 Aug. 1907; *o s* of Richard Vaughan Hart-Davis and Sybil Mary Cooper, *er sister* of 1st Viscount Norwich; *m* 1st, 1929, Peggy Ashcroft (later Dame Peggy Ashcroft) (marr. diss.; she *d* 1991); 2nd, 1933, Catherine Comfort Borden-Turner (marr. diss.), *d* of Mary Borden and George Douglas Turner; two *s* one *d*; 3rd, 1964, Winifred Ruth (*d* 1967), *d* of C. H. Ware, Bromyard, and *widow* of Oliver Simon; 4th, 1968, June (*née* Clifford), *widow* of David Williams. *Educ:* Eton; Balliol Coll., Oxford. Student at Old Vic, 1927–28; Actor at Lyric Theatre, Hammersmith, 1928–29; office boy at William Heinemann Ltd, 1929–31; Manager of Book Soc., 1932; Dir of Jonathan Cape Ltd, 1933–40. Served in Coldstream Guards, 1940–45. Founded Rupert Hart-Davis Ltd, 1946. Hon. DLitt: Reading, 1964; Durham, 1981. *Publications:* Hugh Walpole: a biography, 1952; The Arms of Time: a memoir, 1979; The Power of Chance: a table of memory, 1991; *edited:* The Essential Neville Cardus, 1949; E. V. Lucas: Cricket all his Life, 1950; George Moore: Letters to Lady Cunard, 1957; The Letters of Oscar Wilde, 1962; Max Beerbohm: Letters to Reggie Turner, 1964; Max Beerbohm: More Theatres, 1969; Max Beerbohm: Last Theatres, 1970; Max Beerbohm: A Peep into the Past, 1972; A Catalogue of the Caricatures of Max Beerbohm, 1972; The Autobiography of Arthur Ransome, 1976; William Plomer: Electric Delights, 1978; The Lyttelton Hart-Davis Letters, vol. I, 1978, vol. II, 1979, vol. III, 1981, vol. IV, 1982, vol. V, 1983, vol. VI, 1984; Selected Letters of Oscar Wilde, 1979; Two Men of Letters, 1979; Siegfried Sassoon Diaries: 1920–1922, 1981, 1915–1918, 1983, 1923–25, 1985; The War Poems of Siegfried Sassoon, 1983; A Beggar in Purple: commonplace book, 1983; More Letters of Oscar Wilde, 1985; Siegfried Sassoon: Letters to Max Beerbohm, 1986; Letters of Max Beerbohm 1892–1956, 1989. *Recreations:* reading, book-collecting, watching cricket. *Address:* The Old Rectory, Marske-in-Swaledale, Richmond, N Yorks DL11 7NA.
See also Baron Silsoe.

HART DYKE, Captain David, CBE 1990; LVO 1980; RN; Clerk to Worshipful Company of Skinners, since 1990; *b* 3 Oct. 1938; *s* of Comdr Rev. Eric Hart Dyke and Mary Hart Dyke; *m* 1967, Diana Margaret, *d* of Sir William Luce, GBE, KCMG; two *d*. *Educ:* St Lawrence College, Ramsgate; BRNC Dartmouth. RN 1958; served Far East and Middle East; navigation specialist; Exec. Officer, HMS Hampshire, 1974–76; Staff, RN Staff Coll., 1976–78; Comdr, HM Yacht Britannia, 1978–80; Captain HMS Coventry; action in Falklands, 1982; ACOS to C-in-C Fleet, 1982–84; Asst Naval Attaché, Washington, 1985–87; Dir, Naval Recruiting, 1987–89. ADC to the Queen, 1988–89. *Publications:* articles on Falklands campaign for professional jls, incl. Naval Review. *Recreations:* painting, music, reading, military history. *Address:* Hambledon House, Hambledon, Hants PO7 4RU. *T:* Hambledon (01705) 632380. *Club:* Naval and Military.

HART DYKE, Sir David (William), 10th Bt *cr* 1677, of Horeham, Sussex; journalist; *b* 5 Jan. 1955; *s* of Sir Derek William Hart Dyke, 9th Bt and Dorothy Moses; *S* father, 1987. *Educ:* Ryerson Polytechnical Institute (BA). *Recreations:* portage camping, ice hockey, reading. *Heir: uncle* (Oliver) Guy Hart Dyke [*b* 9 Feb. 1928; *m* 1974, Sarah Alexander, *d* of late Rev. Eric Hart Dyke; one *s* one *d*]. *Address:* 28 King Street West, Apt 14B, Stoney Creek, Ontario L8G 1H4, Canada.

HART-LEVERTON, Colin Allen; QC 1979; a Recorder of the Crown Court, since 1979; *b* 10 May 1936; *s* of Monty Hart-Leverton and Betty (*née* Simmonds). *Educ:* Stowe; self-taught thereafter. Mem., Inst. of Taxation, 1957 (youngest to have ever qualified); called to the Bar, Middle Temple, 1957 (youngest to have ever qual.). Contested (L): Bristol West, 1959 (youngest cand.); Walthamstow West, 1964. Prosecuting Counsel, Central Criminal Court, 1974–79; Dep. Circuit Judge, 1975; Attorney-at-Law, Turks and Caicos Islands, Caribbean, 1976. Occasional television and radio broadcasts. *Recreations:* table-tennis, jazz. *Address:* 1 Dr Johnson's Buildings, EC4Y 7AX. *T:* 0171–353 9328.

HARTE, Julia Kathleen; *see* McKenzie, J. K.

HARTE, Dr Michael John; consultant in information technology, since 1995; Director General Information Technology Systems, Ministry of Defence, 1994–95; *b* 15 Aug. 1936; *s* of Harold Edward Harte and Marjorie Irene Harte; *m* 1st, 1962, Diana Hayes (marr. diss. 1971); 2nd, 1975, Mary Claire Preston; four step *d*. *Educ:* Charterhouse; Trinity Coll., Cambridge (BA); University Coll., London (PhD; Dip. in Biochem. Engrg). Sen. Scientific Officer, Micro-biol Res. Estab., MoD, 1963; Principal, MoD, 1967; Private Sec. to Minister of State for Def., 1972; Asst Sec., Central Policy Rev. Staff, 1973; Asst Sec., MoD, 1975–77; Counsellor, Budget and Infrastructure, UK Delegn to NATO, 1977–81; Chm., NATO Civil and Mil. Budget Cttees, 1981–83; Asst Sec., MoD, 1983–85; Assistant Under Secretary of State: (Dockyard Planning Team), MoD, 1985–87; (Personnel) (Air), MoD, 1987–90; (Resources), MoD, 1990–93. Non-exec. Dir, GlaxoChem., 1988–91. FRSA. *Recreation:* growing and cooking vegetables. *Address:* Greenman Farm, Wadhurst, E Sussex TN5 6LE. *T:* Wadhurst (01892) 783292. *Club:* Army and Navy.

HARTER, Caryl, (Mrs David Harter); *see* Churchill, Caryl.

HARTHAN, John Plant, MA, FLA; Keeper of the Library, Victoria and Albert Museum, 1962–76; *b* 15 April 1916; *y s* of late Dr George Ezra Harthan, Evesham, Worcs, and Winifred May Slater. *Educ:* Bryanston; Jesus Coll., Cambridge; University Coll., London. Asst-Librarian, Southampton Univ., 1940–43; Royal Society of Medicine Library, 1943–44; Asst Under-Librarian, Cambridge Univ. Library, 1944–48; Asst-Keeper of the Library, Victoria and Albert Museum, 1948. FLA 1939. *Publications:* Bookbindings in the Victoria and Albert Museum, 1950, 3rd edn 1985; co-editor, F.D. Klingender, Animals in Art and Thought, 1971; Books of Hours, 1977, 3rd edn 1988; The History of the Illustrated Book, 1981; Introduction to Illuminated Manuscripts, 1983. *Recreations:* history of religion, royalty, music, botany, writing. *Address:* Ludshott Manor, Bramshott, Hants GU30 7RD.

HARTILL, Edward Theodore, FRICS; City Surveyor, Corporation of London, since 1985; *b* 23 Jan. 1943; *s* of Clement Augustus Hartill and late Florence Margarita Hartill; *m* 1975, Gillian Ruth (*née* Todd); two *s*, and two *s* from previous marr. *Educ:* Priory Sch. for Boys, Shrewsbury; Coll. of Estate Management, London Univ. BSc (Estate Management); FRICS 1978. Joined Messrs Burd and Evans, Land Agents, Shrewsbury, 1963; Estates Dept, Legal and Gen. Assce Soc., 1964–73; Property Investment Dept, Guardian Royal Exchange Assce Gp, 1973–85. Vis. Lectr in Law of Town Planning and Compulsory Purchase, Hammersmith and W London Coll. of Advanced Business Studies, 1968–78. Royal Institution of Chartered Surveyors: Mem., City Br. Cttee, 1986–; Mem., Gen. Practice Divl Council, 1989– (Pres., 1992–93); Mem., Quantity Surveyors Divl Council, 1993–; Mem., Gen. Council, 1990–. Member: Nat. Exec. Cttee, Local Authority Valuers Assoc., 1988–; Construction Industry Standing Conf. Steering Gp, 1992–. Hon. Associate, Czech Chamber of Appraisers, 1992–. Mem., British Schs Exploring Soc. FRSA 1993. Liveryman, Worshipful Co. of Chartered Surveyors, 1985– (Mem., Court of Assistants, 1991–). *Publications:* occasional lectures and articles on professional topics. *Recreations:* travel, hill walking, cinema, family. *Address:* 215 Sheen Lane, East Sheen, SW14 8LE. *T:* 0181–878 4494.
See also R. J. Hartill.

HARTILL, Rosemary Jane; broadcaster and writer; Religious Affairs Correspondent, BBC, 1982–88; *b* 11 Aug. 1949; *d* of Clement Augustus Hartill and late Florence Margarita Ford. *Educ:* Wellington Girls' High Sch., Salop; Bristol Univ. (BA (Hons) English). Editor: Tom Stacey (Publishing) Ltd, 1970–73; David and Charles Ltd, 1973–75; Sen. Non-Fiction Editor, Hamish Hamilton Children's Books Ltd, 1975–76; freelance journalist and broadcaster, 1976–82; freelance book and ballet reviewer, TES, 1976–80; Religious Affairs Reporter, BBC, 1979–82; Reporter: BBC Everyman Prog., 1987; ITV Human Factor series, 1989–92; Presenter: BBC Woman's Hour (NE edns), 1989–90; Meridian Books (BBC World Service), 1988–92 and 1994–. Sandford St Martin Trust personal award for outstanding contrib. to religious broadcasting, 1994. *Publications:* (ed) Emily Brontë: poems, 1973; Wild Animals, 1978; In Perspective, 1988; Writers Revealed, 1989; Were You There?, 1995. *Recreations:* wildlife, walking, laughing and being in Northumberland. *Address:* Old Post Office, Eglingham, Alnwick, Northumberland NE66 2TX.
See also E. T. Hartill.

HARTING, Henry Maria Robert Egmont M.; *see* Mayr-Harting.

HARTINGTON, Marquess of; Peregrine Andrew Morny Cavendish; Chairman, British Horseracing Board, since 1993; *b* 27 April 1944; *s* of 11th Duke of Devonshire, *qv*; *m* 1967, Amanda Carmen, *d* of late Comdr E. G. Heywood-Lonsdale, RN, and of Mrs Heywood-Lonsdale; one *s* two *d*. *Educ:* Eton; Exeter Coll., Oxford. Sen. Steward, Jockey Club, 1989–94. Dir, Sotheby's Holdings Inc., 1994–. *Heir:* *s* Earl of Burlington, *qv*. *Address:* Beamsley Hall, Skipton, N Yorks BD23 6HD.

HARTLAND, Michael; *see* James, M. L.

HARTLAND-SWANN, Julian Dana Nimmo, CMG 1992; HM Diplomatic Service, retired; Ambassador to Burma (Myanmar), 1990–95; *b* 18 Feb. 1936; *s* of late Prof. J. J. Hartland-Swann and of Mrs Kenlis Hartland-Swann (*née* Taylour); *m* 1960, Ann Deirdre Green; one *s* one *d*. *Educ:* Stowe; Lincoln Coll., Oxford (History). HM Forces, 1955–57. Entered HM Diplomatic Service, 1960; 3rd Sec., Brit. Embassy, Bangkok, 1961–65; 2nd, later 1st Sec., FO, 1965–68; 1st Sec., Berlin, 1968–71; 1st Sec. and Head of Chancery, Vienna, 1971–74; FCO, 1975–77; Counsellor, 1977; Ambassador to Mongolian People's Republic, 1977–79; Counsellor and Head of Chancery, Brussels, 1979–83; Head of SE Asian Dept, FCO, 1983–85; Consul Gen., Frankfurt, 1986–90. *Recreations:* French food, sailing, restoring ruins. *Address:* c/o Foreign and Commonwealth Office, SW1A 2AH.

HARTLEY, Brian Joseph, CMG 1950; OBE 1945 (MBE 1934); *b* 1907; *s* of late John Joseph Hartley, Tring, Herts; *m* 1951, Doreen Mary, *d* of Col R. G. Sanders; three *s* one *d*. *Educ:* Loughborough; Midland Agricultural Coll.; Wadham Coll., Oxford; Imperial Coll. of Tropical Agriculture, Trinidad. Entered Colonial Service; Agricultural Officer, Tanganyika, 1929; Aden Protectorate: Agricultural Officer, 1938; Asst Comdt, Govt Guards Auxiliaries (Camel Corps, Subeihi), 1940; Agricultural Adviser, 1944; Dir of Agriculture, 1946–54; retd 1954; Chief, FAO(UN), mission in Iraq, 1955; Mem., Tanganyika Agricultural Corporation, 1956–62; Trustee, Tanganyika Nat. Parks, 1957–64; Mem., Ngorongoro Conservation Authority Advisory Board, 1963–64. UN (Special Fund) Consultant Team Leader, Kafue Basin Survey, N Rhodesia, 1960; Team Leader, Livestock Develt Survey, Somalia, 1966; Chief Livestock Adviser, FAO, Somalia, 1967–70; Project Manager, UNSF Survey of Northern Rangelands Project, Somalia, 1970–72; Consultant, FAO-IBRD Project, Anatolia, Turkey, 1972–73; Consultant, ODA, Wadi Rima and Montane Plains, Yemen Arab Republic, 1975; Consultant, 1973–76, Technical Manager, 1976–79, World Bank Nomadic Rangelands Project, Ethiopia; Consultant: Oxfam Karamoja Relief Prog. in Uganda, 1980; Oxfam E Africa, 1981–85; Oxfam Red Sea Province, Relief Project, Sudan, Jan./Feb. 1988. Estabd Tanganyika Camel Co., 1987. Consultant: Food and Agricl Res. Management; Africa Camel Project, Oman, 1989. *Publications:* Camels in the Horn of Africa, 1979; (contrib.) The Camelid, 1985; Scientific report, Camelus dromedarius in N Tanzania, 1987 (following the introduction of camels to Tanzania by the author). *Address:* Box 337, Malindi, Kenya.

HARTLEY, Prof. Brian Selby, PhD; FRS 1971; Chairman, Agrol Ltd, since 1993; Professor of Biochemistry, Imperial College, University of London, 1974–91, Emeritus Professor, 1991; Senior Research Fellow, Centre for Biotechnology, 1991–94 (Director, 1982–91); *b* 16 April 1926; *s* of Norman and Hilda Hartley; *m* 1949, Kathleen Maude Vaughan; three *s* one *d*. *Educ:* Queens' Coll., Cambridge; Univ. of Leeds. BA 1947, MA 1952, Cantab; PhD 1952, Leeds. ICI Fellow, Univ. of Cambridge, 1952; Helen Hay Whitney Fellow, Univ. of Washington, Seattle, USA, 1958; Fellow and Lectr in Biochemistry, Trinity Coll., Cambridge, 1964; Scientific Staff, MRC Laboratory of Molecular Biology, 1961–74. Mem. Council: EMBO (European Centre for Molecular Biology), 1978–84; Royal Soc., 1982–84. Hon. Mem., Amer. Soc. of Biological Chemists, 1977. British Drug Houses Medal for Analytical Biochemistry, 1969. *Publications:* papers and articles in scientific jls and books. *Recreations:* fishing, gardening. *Address:* Grove Cottage, Smith Street, Elsworth, Cambridge CB3 8HY.

HARTLEY, Air Marshal Sir Christopher (Harold), KCB 1963 (CB 1961); CBE 1957 (OBE 1949); DFC 1945; AFC 1944; BA Oxon; *b* 31 Jan. 1913; *s* of late Brig.-Gen. Sir Harold Hartley, GCVO, CH, CBE, MC, FRS; *m* 1st, 1937, Anne Sitwell (marr. diss., 1943); 2nd, 1944, Margaret Watson; two *s*. *Educ:* Eton; Balliol Coll., Oxford (Williams Exhibnr); King's Coll., Cambridge. Zoologist on Oxford Univ. expeditions: to Sarawak, 1932; Spitsbergen, 1933; Greenland, 1937. Asst Master at Eton Coll., 1937–39. Joined RAFVR, 1938. Served War of 1939–45: 604 Sqdn, 256 Sqdn, Fighter Interception Unit, Central Fighter Establishment. Permanent Commission, 1945; AOC 12 Group, Fighter Command, 1959; ACAS (Operational Requirements), Air Min., 1961; DCAS, 1963–66; Controller of Aircraft, Min. of Aviation and Min. of Technology, 1966–70, retired. Dep. Chm., British Hovercraft Corporation, 1979– (Chm., 1974–78); Dir, Westland Aircraft Ltd, 1971–83. *Recreation:* fishing. *Address:* c/o Barclays Bank, PO Box 36, Bank Plain, Norwich NR2 4SP. *Club:* Travellers'.

HARTLEY, David Fielding, PhD; CEng; FBCS; Chief Executive, United Kingdom Education and Research Networking Association, since 1994; Fellow of Clare College, Cambridge, since 1987; *b* 14 Sept. 1937; *s* of late Robert M. Hartley and late Sheila E. Hartley, LRAM; *m* 1960, Joanna Mary, *d* of late Stanley and of Constance Bolton; one *s* two *d*. *Educ:* Rydal Sch.; Clare Coll., Cambridge (MA, PhD). University of Cambridge: Sen. Asst in Research, Mathematical Lab., 1964–65; Asst Dir of Research, 1966–67; Univ. Lectr, 1967–70; Dir, Univ. Computing Service, 1970–94; Jun. Research Fellow, Churchill Coll., Cambridge, 1964–67; Fellow, Darwin Coll., Cambridge, 1969–86. British Computer Society: Mem. Council, 1970–73, 1977–80, 1985–90; Vice Pres. (Technical), 1985–87, (External Relns), 1987–90. Chm., Inter-University Cttee on Computing, 1972–74; Mem., Computer Board for Univs and Research Councils, 1979–83; Mem. Council of Management, Numerical Algorithms Gp Ltd, 1979– (Chm., 1986–); adviser to Prime Minister, Information Technology Adv. Panel, 1981–86; DTI Hon. Adviser in Information Technology (on sabbatical leave), 1983; Mem. various Govt, Res. Council and Industry cttees and consultancies. Mem., BBC Science Consultative Gp, 1984–87. Dir, CADCentre Ltd, 1983–94. Governor, Rydal Sch., 1982–88. Medal of Merits, Nicholas Copernicus Univ., Poland, 1984. *Publications:* papers in scientific jls on operating systems, programming languages, computing service management. *Address:* 26 Girton Road, Cambridge CB3 0LL. *T:* Cambridge (01223) 571717.

HARTLEY, Sir Frank, Kt 1977; CBE 1970; PhD London, CChem, FRPharmS, FRSC; Vice-Chancellor, University of London, 1976–78; Dean of the School of Pharmacy, University of London, 1962–76; *b* 5 Jan. 1911; *s* of late Robinson King Hartley and Mary Hartley (*née* Holt); *m* 1937, Lydia May England; two *s*. *Educ:* Municipal Secondary (later Grammar) Sch., Nelson, Lancs; Sch. of Pharmacy (Fellow, 1977), University Coll. (Fellow, 1972), and Birkbeck Coll. (Fellow, 1970), University of London. Jacob Bell Schol., 1930, Silver Medallist in Pharmaceutics, Pharmaceut. Chem. and Pharmacognosy, 1932. Pharmacy apprenticeship with J. Hayhurst, MPS, Nelson, Lancs, 1927–30; Pharmaceutical Chemist, 1932, Demonstrator and Lectr, 1932–40, at Sch. of Pharmacy; 1st cl. hons BSc (Chem.), University of London, 1936, and PhD, 1941; Chief Chemist, Organon Laboratories Ltd, 1940–43; Sec., Therapeutic Research Corp., 1943–46; Sec., Gen. Penicillin Cttee (Min. of Supply), 1943–46; Dir of Research and Sci. Services, The British Drug Houses, Ltd, 1946–62; Chm. Brit. Pharmaceut. Conf., 1957, and of Sci. Adv. Cttee of Pharmaceut. Soc. of Great Britain, 1964–66; Mem. Council, 1955–58, 1961–64, Vice-Pres., 1958–60, 1964–65, 1967–69, Pres., 1965–67, of Royal Institute of Chemistry; Hon. Treasurer, 1956–61, Chm. 1964–68 of Chem. Council; Mem. 1953–80, Vice-Chm. 1963–68, Chm. 1970–80, of British Pharmacopoeia Commn (Mem., Nomenclature Cttee, 1946–), and a UK Deleg., 1964–80, to European Pharmacopoeia Commn; Mem., 1970–84, Vice-Chm., 1977–84, Medicines Commn; Member: Poisons Bd (Home Office), 1958–66; Cttee on Safety of Drugs (Min. of Health), 1963–70; Cttee on Prevention of Microbiol Contamination of Medicinal Products, 1972–73; Nat. Biological Standards Bd, 1975–83; Cttee of Enquiry on Contaminated Infusion Fluids, 1972; NW Thames RHA Univ. Liaison Cttee, 1984–89; Chairman: Bd of Studies in Pharmacy, Univ. of London, 1964–68; Pharmacy Bd, CNAA, 1965–77; Collegiate Council, 1969–73; Panel on Grading of Chief Pharmacists in Teaching Hosps, 1972–74, Qualified Person Adv. Cttee, DHSS, 1979; Comrs for Lambeth, Southwark and Lewisham Health Area, 1979–80; Pharmacy Working Gp, Nat. Adv. Bd for Higher Educn, Local Authorities, 1982–84; Health Care Sci. Adv. Cttee, Council of Science and Technol. Insts, 1982–86; Working Gp on Cardiothoracic Surgery Options, 1986–87; Member: Academic Council, 1969–73; British Council for Prevention of Blindness, 1975– (Chm., 1988–). Co-opted Mem. Senate, 1968–76, 1978–88, ex officio Mem., 1976–78, Senate Mem. of Court, 1970–76, 1978–88, ex officio Mem., 1976–78, Dep. Vice-Chancellor, 1973–76, University of London; Member Council: St Thomas's Hosp. Medical Sch., University of London, 1968–80; Royal Free Hosp. Med. Sch., 1970–88; Mem., Consultative Bd of Regents, Univ. of Qatar, 1978–; Member Bd of Governors: Royal Free Hosp. Gp, 1970–74; Kingston Polytechnic, 1970–75; British Postgrad. Med. Fedn, London Univ., 1972–89; Royal Postgrad. Med. Sch., 1972–91 (Vice-Chm., 1989–91); Inst. of Basic Med. Sci, 1973–86, subseq. Hunterian Inst., RCS, 1986–91. Chm., Consortium of Charing Cross and Westminster Med. Schs, London Univ., 1981–84. Lectures: Sir William Pope Meml, RSA, 1962; Wilkinson, Inst. of Dental Surg., 1978; Astor, Middlesex Hosp. Med. Sch., 1980; Bernal, Birkbeck Coll., 1982; Association, Hosp. Physicists Assoc., 1986. Hon. FRCP 1979; Hon. FRCS 1980 (Mem. Finance Bd, RCS, 1985–91); Hon. FRSC 1981; Hon. Fellow: Hosp. Physicists Assoc., 1986; Imperial Coll. of Science, Technol. and Medicine, 1990. Liveryman, Worshipful Soc. of Apothecaries of London, 1958. Freeman, City of London, 1959. Hon. DSc Warwick, 1978; Hon. LLD: Strathclyde, 1980; London, 1987. Charter Gold Medal, Pharm. Soc. of GB, 1974. *Publications:* papers on chem. and pharmaceut. research in Quarterly Jl of Pharmacy, Jl of Pharmacy and Pharmacology and Jl of Chem. Soc. Reviews and articles in sci. and tech. jls. *Recreations:* reading, watching sport. *Address:* 16 Town Thorns, Easenhall, Rugby, Warwickshire CV23 0JE. *T:* Rugby (01788) 833483. *Club:* Athenæum.

See also F. R. Hartley.

HARTLEY, Prof. Frank Robinson, CChem, FRSC; Vice-Chancellor, Cranfield University (formerly Cranfield Institute of Technology), since 1989; *b* 29 Jan. 1942; *s* of Sir Frank Hartley, *qv*; *m* 1964, Valerie Peel; three *d*. *Educ:* King's College Sch., Wimbledon (Sambrooke Schol.); Magdalen Coll., Oxford (Demy; BA, MA, DPhil, DSc). Post-doctoral Fellow, Commonwealth Scientific and Industrial Research Organisation, Div. of Protein Chemistry, Melbourne, Aust., 1966–69; Imperial Chemical Industries Research Fellow and Tutor in Physical Chemistry, University Coll. London, 1969–70; Lectr in Inorganic Chemistry, Univ. of Southampton, 1970–75; Professor of Chemistry and Head of Dept of Chemistry and Metallurgy, 1975–82, Acting Dean, 1982–84, Principal and Dean, 1984–89, RMCS, Shrivenham. Chm., Cranfield IT Inst., 1989–90 (Dir, 1986–89); Man. Dir, CIT (Holdings) Ltd, 1993– (Dir, 1989–93); Chm., CIM Inst., 1990–; Dir, Cranfield Ventures Ltd, 1990–; Non-Executive Director: T & N, 1989–; Eastern Regl Adv. Bd, National Westminster Bank, 1990–92; Kalon, 1994–. Sen. Travelling Fellow, ACU, 1986. Special Advr to Prime Minister on defence systems, 1988–91; Special Advr to H of L Select Cttee on Sci. and Technol., 1994–; Mem., Parly Scientific Cttee, 1986– (Mem. Council and Gen. Purposes Cttee, 1992–). Member: Internat. Adv. Bd, Kanagawa Acad. of Sci. and Technol., Japan, 1989–; Bd, Internat. Foundn for Artificial Intelligence, 1990–. Gov., Welbeck Coll., 1984–89; Mem. Court, Bath Univ., 1982–89. Mem., Oxford Union. FRSA. Editor-in-Chief, Brassey's New Battlefield Weapons Systems and Technology series, 1988–. *Publications:* The Chemistry of Platinum and Palladium (Applied Science), 1973; Elements of Organometallic Chemistry (Chemical Soc.), 1974, Japanese edn 1981, Chinese edn 1989; (with C. Burgess and R. M. Alcock) Solution Equilibria, 1980, Russian edn 1983; (with S. Patai) The Chemistry of the Metal—Carbon Bond, vol. 1 1983, vol. 2 1984, vol. 3 1985, vol. 4 1987, vol. 5 1989; Supported Metal Complexes, 1985, Russian edn 1987; The Chemistry of Organophosphorus Compounds, vol. 1, 1990, vol. 2, 1992, vol. 3, 1994; Chemistry of the Platinum Group Metals, 1991; papers in inorganic, coordination and organometallic chemistry in major English, Amer. and Aust. chemical jls. *Recreations:* Rugby refereeing, swimming, gardening, cliff walking, reading. *Address:* Cayley Lodge, Prince Philip Avenue, Wharley End, Cranfield, Bedford MK43 0SX. *Clubs:* Institute of Directors; Shrivenham.

HARTLEY, His Honour Gilbert Hillard; retired; a Circuit Judge (formerly Judge of County Courts), 1967–82; *b* 11 Aug. 1917; *s* of late Percy Neave Hartley and late Nellie Bond Hartley (*née* Hillard); *m* 1948, Jeanne, *d* of late C. W. Gall, Leeds; one *s* two *d*. *Educ:* Ashville, Harrogate; Exeter Coll. Oxford. Called to Bar, Middle Temple, 1939. Served with Army, 1940–46. Recorder of Rotherham, 1965–67; Dep. Chm., WR of Yorkshire QS, 1965–71. *Address:* Nidd Rise, Main Street, Moor Monkton, York YO5 8JA.

HARTLEY, Prof. Keith, PhD; Professor of Economics, since 1987, and Director, Centre for Defence Economics, since 1990, University of York; *b* 14 July 1940; *s* of Walter and Ivy Hartley; *m* 1966, Winifred Keally; one *s* two *d*. *Educ:* Univ. of Hull (BSc Econs; PhD 1974). Dir, Inst. for Res. in Social Scis, Univ. of York, 1982–94. NATO Res. Fellow, 1977–79 and 1986–87. *Publications:* Economics of Defence Policy, 1991; (with T. Sandler) Economics of Defense, 1995. *Recreations:* walking, angling, football, reading. *Address:* Centre for Defence Economics, University of York, York YO1 5DD. *T:* York (01904) 433680.

HARTLEY, Richard Leslie Clifford, QC 1976; *b* 31 May 1932; *s* of late Arthur Clifford Hartley, CBE and late Nina Hartley. *Educ:* Marlborough Coll.; Sidney Sussex Coll., Cambridge (MA). Called to the Bar, Gray's Inn, 1956, Bencher, 1986. *Recreations:* golf, tennis, horse racing. *Address:* 15 Chesham Street, SW1X 8ND. *T:* 0171–235 2420. *Clubs:* Garrick, MCC; Woking Golf, Rye Golf, St Enodoc Golf.

HARTLING, Poul; Grand Cross of Dannebrog; United Nations High Commissioner for Refugees, 1978–85; Member of Folketing, Denmark, 1957–60 and 1964–78; *b* 14 Aug. 1914; *s* of Mads Hartling and Mathilde (*née* Nielsen); *m* 1940, Elsebeth Kirkemann; three *s* one *d*. *Educ:* Univ. of Copenhagen (Master of Divinity 1939). Curate, Frederiksberg Church, 1941–45; Chaplain, St Luke Foundn, 1945–50; Principal, Zahle's Teachers' Trng Coll., 1950–68. Chm., Liberal Party Parly Group, 1965–68; Mem., Nordic Council, 1964–68 (Pres., 1966–68); Minister of Foreign Affairs, 1968–71; Prime Minister, 1973–75; Chm., Liberal Party, 1964–78. Secretary: Christian Academic Soc., 1934–35; Christian Movement of Sen. Secondary Students, 1939–43. Dr *hc* Valparaiso Univ., Indiana, 1981. Grand-Croix: l'Ordre de la Couronne, Belgique; l'Ordre de Mennlik II, Ethiopie; Grosskreuz des Verdienstordens der Bundesrep, Deutschland; Royal Order of St Olav, Norway; Falcon of Iceland; Merit of Luxembourg; Yugoslovenske Zvezde. *Publications:* Sursum Corda, 1942; Growth of church idea in the missionary field, 1945; (ed) Church, School, Culture, 1963; The Danish Church, 1964 (2nd edn 1967); From 17 Years in Danish Politics, 1974; Autobiography vol. I, 1980, vol. II, 1981, vol. III, 1983, vol. IV, 1985; Erik Eriksen (biog.), 1990. *Recreation:* music. *Address:* Emilievej 6 E, 2920 Charlottenlund, Denmark.

HARTMANN, Dr Peter, Hon. KBE 1992; State Secretary, Foreign Ministry, Germany, since 1995; *b* 9 Oct. 1935; *m* Baroness Lonny von Blomberg-Hartmann. *Educ:* Frankfurt; Papal Univ., Rome (LPH); Cologne; Fribourg Univ. (DPhil). Foreign Service, 1965; Washington, 1966; Karachi, 1968; EC Brussels, 1971; Buenos Aires, 1978; Head, Foreign Relations Office, CDU, 1981–84; Federal Chancellery: Head, European Policy, 1984–87; Asst Under-Sec., Foreign, Security and Develt Policy, 1987–90; Dep Under-Sec., Foreign Security Policy, and Advr to Federal Chancellor, 1991–93; Ambassador to UK, 1993–95. *Address:* Auswärtiges Amt, Postfach 1148, 53001 Bonn, Germany.

HARTNACK, Paul Richard Samuel; Comptroller General and Chief Executive, The Patent Office, since 1990: *b* 17 Nov. 1942; *s* of Carl Samuel and Maud Godden Hartnack; *m* 1966, Marion Quirk; two *s*. *Educ:* Hastings Grammar Sch. Clerical and Exec. posts, BoT, 1961–67; Asst Sec., Cttee of Enquiry into Civil Air Transport, 1967–68; Second Sec., British Embassy, Paris, 1969–71; Exec. posts, DTI, 1972–78; Asst Sec., NEB, 1978–80; Sec., Brit. Technology Gp, 1981–85; Asst Sec., Finance and Resource Management Div., DTI, 1985–89. *Recreation:* gardening. *Address:* The Patent Office, Cardiff Road, Newport, Gwent NP9 1RH. *T:* Newport (Gwent) (01633) 814502.

HARTNOLL, Mary Charmian, CBE 1990; Director of Social Work, Glasgow City Council, since 1995; *b* 31 May 1939; *d* of Rev. Sydney W. Hartnoll and Margaret Hartnoll. *Educ:* Colston's Girls' Grammar Sch., Bristol; Bedford Coll., Univ. of London (BA Hons); Univ. of Liverpool (HO Cert. in Child Care). Child Care Officer, Dorset CC, 1961–63; various posts, County Borough of Reading, 1963–74; Asst Dir, Berks CC, 1974–75; Divl Officer, Reading, 1975–77; Dir of Social Work: Grampian Regl Council, 1978–93; Strathclyde Regl Council, 1993–95. Hon. LLD Robert Gordon Univ., 1993. *Recreations:* natural history, walking, music, theatre going. *Address:* Social Work Department, Strathclyde House, 20 India Street, Glasgow G2 4PF.

HARTOG, Harold Samuel Arnold; Knight, Order of the Netherlands Lion; KBE (Hon.) 1970; Advisory Director, Unilever NV, 1971–75; *b* Nijmegen, Holland, 21 Dec. 1910; *m* 1963, Ingeborg Luise Krahn. *Educ:* Wiedemann Coll., Geneva. Joined Unilever, 1931. After service with Dutch forces during War of 1939–45 he joined management of Unilever interests in France, and subseq. took charge of Unilever cos in the Netherlands; elected to Bds of Unilever, 1948; Mem. Rotterdam Group Management and responsible for Unilever activities in Germany, Austria and Belgium, 1952–60; subseq. Mem. Cttee for Unilever's overseas interests, in London; became, there, one of the two world co-ordinators of Unilever's foods interests, 1962; Chm., Unilever NV, 1966–71. *Recreations:* history of art; collecting Chinese pottery and porcelain. *Address:* Kösterbergstrasse 40B, 22587 Hamburg, Germany. *Clubs:* Dutch; Ubersee (Hamburg); Golf (Falkenstein).

HARTOP, Barry; Chief Executive, Welsh Development Agency, since 1994; *b* 15 Aug. 1942; *s* of Philip William Hartop and Constance Winifred (*née* Drew); *m* 1966, Sandra; one *s* one *d*. *Educ:* Durham Univ. (BSc Hons Chem. Engrg). Prodn and technical mgt, Lever Bros Ltd, 1965–72; Unilever PLC: Chm., Cost Reduction and R&D, 1972–80; Man. Dir, European Business Centre, 1980–83; Chm. and Man. Dir, Lever Industrial Ltd, 1983–89; Man. Dir, Gestetner Hldgs, 1989–92; Chm., Hammicks Bookshops Ltd, 1994–.

Gov., Royal Grammar Sch., Guildford, 1991–. *Recreations:* squash, tennis, keep fit, sitting in the sun, gardening. *Address:* Welsh Development Agency, Pearl House, Greyfriars Road, Cardiff CF1 3XX. *T:* Cardiff (01222) 222666.

HARTOPP, Sir John Edmund Cradock-, 9th Bt, *cr* 1796; TD; *b* 8 April 1912; *s* of late Francis Gerald Cradock-Hartopp, Barbrook, Chatsworth, Bakewell, Derbyshire (kinsman of 8th Bt) and Elizabeth Ada Mary (*née* Stuart); *S* kinsman, Sir George Francis Fleetwood Cradock-Hartopp, 1949; *m* 1953, Prudence, 2nd *d* of Sir Frederick Leith-Ross, GCMG, KCB; three *d. Educ:* Summer Fields, Oxford; Uppingham Sch. Travelled in United States of America before joining at age of 18, Staff of Research Laboratories, Messrs Thos Firth & John Brown Ltd, Steel Makers, Sheffield, 1930; travelled in India and the Far East, 1948–49; Dir, Firth Brown Tools Ltd, 1961–76. War of 1939–45 (despatches twice); joined TA and served with Royal Engineers in UK; Norway, 1940; North Africa (1st Army), 1943; Italy, 1943–45; released, 1945, with rank of Major. Mem. Council: Machine Tool Research Assoc., 1965–70; Machine Tool Trades Assoc., 1970–73. *Recreations:* golf (semi-finalist English Golf Champ., 1935; first reserve, Eng. *v* France, 1935); cricket, tennis, motoring. *Heir: cousin* Lt-Comdr Kenneth Alston Cradock-Hartopp, MBE, DSC, RN [*b* 26 Feb. 1918; *m* 1942, Gwendolyn Amy Lilian Upton; one *d*]. *Address:* The Cottage, 27 Wool Road, Wimbledon Common, SW20 0HN. *Clubs:* East India, MCC; Royal and Ancient (St Andrews).

HARTWELL, Baron, *cr* 1968 (Life Peer), of Peterborough Court in the City of London; **(William) Michael Berry,** MBE 1944; TD; Chairman and Editor-in-Chief: The Daily Telegraph, 1954–87; Sunday Telegraph, 1961–87; *b* 18 May 1911; 2nd *s* of 1st Viscount Camrose and Mary Agnes, *e d* of late Thomas Corns, London; *S* brother, 1995 as 3rd Viscount Camrose but disclaimed his peerages for life (Viscount *cr* 1941, Baron *cr* 1929, Bt 1921); *m* 1936, Lady Pamela Margaret Elizabeth Smith (*d* 1982), *yr d* of 1st Earl of Birkenhead, PC, GCSI, KC; two *s* two *d. Educ:* Eton (Captain of Oppidans; Editor of Chronicle); Christ Church, Oxford (MA). 2nd Lieut 11th (City of London Yeo.) Light AA Bde, RA (TA), 1938; served War of 1939–45; Capt. and Major, 1940; Lieut-Col 1944 (despatches twice, MBE). Editor, Sunday Mail, Glasgow, 1934–35; Managing Editor, Financial Times, 1937–39; Chm. Amalgamated Press Ltd, 1954–59. Dir, and subseq. Dep. Chm., LWT, 1968–81. Trustee, Reuters, 1962–89. *Publications:* Party Choice, 1948; William Camrose, Giant of Fleet Street, 1992. *Heir: (to disclaimed Viscountcy) s* Hon. Adrian Michael Berry [*b* 15 June 1937; *m* 1967, Marina Beatrice, *d* of Cyrus Sulzberger; one *s* one *d*]. *Address:* 18 Cowley Street, Westminster, SW1P 3LZ. *T:* 0171–222 4673; Oving House, Whitchurch, near Aylesbury, Bucks HP22 4HN. *T:* Aylesbury (01296) 641307; (office) 36 Broadway, SW1 0BH. *T:* 0171–222 2345. *Clubs:* White's, Beefsteak; Royal Yacht Squadron.

See also Hon. N. W. Berry.

HARTWELL, Sir Anthony; *see* Hartwell, Sir F. A. C. P.

HARTWELL, Benjamin James, OBE 1959; Clerk to Southport Borough Justices, 1943–73; *b* Southport, 24 June 1908; *s* of late Joseph Hartwell, Bucks, and late Margaret Ann Hartwell; *m* 1937, Mary (*née* Binns) (*d* 1986), Southport; one *s* one *d. Educ:* Kirkcudbright Acad.; King George V Sch., Southport; London Univ. (LLM). Admitted a Solicitor of the Supreme Court, 1936; Hon. Sec. Justices' Clerks' Soc., 1947–59; Pres. Lancs and Cheshire Dist of Boys' Brigade, 1950–63; Chm. Council, Congregational Union of England and Wales, 1952–58; Chm. Congregational Union of England and Wales 1959–60. Member: Central Cttee, World Council of Churches, 1954–61; Home Secretary's Advisory Council on the Treatment of Offenders, 1955–63. *Address:* Willow Cottage, New Road, Pamber Green, near Basingstoke, Hants RG26 6AG.

HARTWELL, Eric, CBE 1983; Vice-Chairman, Forte plc (formerly Trusthouse Forte plc), 1972–93 (Chief Executive, 1979–82, Joint Chief Executive, 1982–83); *b* 10 Aug. 1915; *m* 1st, 1937, Gladys Rose Bennett (marr. diss.); one *s* one *d*; 2nd, 1952, Dorothy Maud Mowbray; one *s* one *d. Educ:* Mall Sch., Twickenham, Worthing High School. FHCIMA; CIMgt; FBHA. Electrical industry, 1932–37; Dir, Fortes & Co. Ltd, 1938; HM Forces, 1940–45; Jt Man. Dir, Forte Holdings Ltd, 1962; Dep. Man. Dir, Trust Houses Forte Ltd, 1970; Dep. Chief Exec., Trust Houses Forte Ltd, 1972–75, Jt Chief Exec., 1975–78. Chm., BHRCA, 1981–85. Mem. Nat. Council, CBI, 1971–86 (Chm., Finance Sub-Cttee, 1981–86). Mem. Council, Thames Heritage Trust Ltd, 1981– (Vice-Chm., 1983–87); Mem. Cttee, Nuffield Hosp., Enfield, 1984–87; Dir, LV Catering Educn Trust Ltd, 1965–87. Liveryman, Upholders' Co., 1952–. FRSA 1984. *Recreations:* yachting, painting, photography, golf. *Address:* Tall Trees, 129 Totteridge Lane, N20 8NS. *T:* 0181–445 2321. *Clubs:* National Sporting, River Emergency Service Association, Inner Magic Circle; Thames Motor Yacht; South Herts Golf.

HARTWELL, Sir (Francis) Anthony (Charles Peter), 6th Bt *cr* 1805, of Dale Hall, Essex; marine consultant; *b* 1 June 1940; *o s* of Sir Brodrick William Charles Elwin Hartwell, 5th Bt and of his 1st wife, Marie Josephine Hartwell, *d* of S. P. Mullins; *S* father, 1993; *m* 1968, Barbara Phyllis Rae (marr. diss. 1989), *d* of H. Rae Green; one *s. Educ:* Thames Nautical Coll., HMS Worcester. Cadet, RNR. Master's Foreign Going (Cl. 1) Cert. MNI, MRIN. Captain (Master Mariner), 1972. Sea Service Navigating Officer, Asst Nautical Inspector, then Cargo Supt (Overseas Containers Ltd) London, P&O Group, 1958–71; Chief Officer/Master, North Sea ops, Ocean Inchcape Ltd, 1972–73; P&O Cadet Trng Officer, 1973–75; overseas port management, Nigeria, Papua New Guinea and Saudia Arabia, 1975–87; Branch Manager, Lloyds Agency, Dammam, Saudi Arabia, 1987–89; marine surveyor and nautical consultant, Saudi Arabia, The Maldives, Nigeria, Cyprus, 1989–93. *Recreations:* ocean sailing, scuba diving, photography. *Heir: s* Timothy Peter Michael Charles Hartwell, *b* 8 July 1970. *Clubs:* Cachalots-Southampton Master Mariners'; Old Worcester's Association.

HARTY, Bernard Peter; Chamberlain, City of London Corporation, since 1983; Managing Director, Barbican Centre, 1994–95; *b* 1 May 1943; *s* of William Harty and Eileen Nora (*née* Canavan); *m* 1965, Glenys Elaine Simpson; one *d. Educ:* St Richards Coll., Droitwich; Ullathorne Grammar Sch., Coventry. CIPFA 1966; MBCS 1983. Accountant, Coventry CBC, 1961–69; Forward Budget Planning Officer, Derbyshire CC, 1969–72; Chief Accountant, Bradford CBC, 1972–74; Chief Finance Officer, Bradford MDC, 1973–76; County Treasurer, Oxfordshire CC, 1976–83. Dir, CLF Municipal Bank. Mem. Nat. Cttee, Information Technol. Year 1982 (IT82); Chm., IT82 Local Govt Cttee, 1982. Chm., Foundn for IT in Local Govt, 1988–91. Chm., Treasury Management Panel, 1991–94, Superannuation Investments Panel, 1994–, CIPFA; Member: Local Govt Sub Gp, Financial Law Panel, 1993–; HM Treasury Cttee on Local Authy Borrowing, 1994–. Freeman, City of London, 1983; Liveryman, Worshipful Co. of Tallow Chandlers, 1984; Founder Mem., Co. of Information Technologists. *Publications:* papers in professional jls. *Recreations:* theatre, music, National Trust, cricket. *Address:* Chamber of London, PO Box 270, Guildhall, EC2P 2EJ. *T:* 0171–606 3030.

HARTY, Most Rev. Michael; *see* Killaloe, Bishop of, (RC).

HARUNA, Alhaji; *see* Gwandu, Emir of.

HARVEY, family name of **Baron Harvey of Tasburgh.**

HARVEY OF TASBURGH, 2nd Baron, *cr* 1954, of Tasburgh, Norfolk; **Peter Charles Oliver Harvey;** Bt 1868; FCA; *b* 28 Jan. 1921; *er s* of 1st Baron Harvey of Tasburgh, GCMG, GCVO, CB, and Maud Annora (*d* 1970), *d* of late Arthur Watkin Williams-Wynn; *S* father, 1968; *m* 1957, Penelope Anne (*d* 1995), *d* of Lt-Col Sir William Makins, 3rd Bt; two *d. Educ:* Eton; Trinity College, Cambridge. Served 1941–46 with Royal Artillery, Tunisia, Italy. Bank of England, 1948–56; Binder Hamlyn & Co., 1956–61; Lloyds Bank International Ltd (formerly Bank of London and South America), 1961–75; English Transcontinental Ltd, 1975–78; Brown, Shipley & Co., 1978–81. *Recreations:* sailing, music. *Heir: nephew* Charles John Giuseppe Harvey, *b* 4 Feb. 1951. *Address:* Crownick Woods, Restronguet, Mylor, Falmouth, Cornwall TR11 5ST. *Clubs:* Brooks's; Royal Cornwall Yacht.

HARVEY, Alan Frederick Ronald, OBE 1970; HM Diplomatic Service, retired; *b* 15 Dec. 1919; *s* of Edward Frederick and Alice Sophia Harvey; *m* 1946, Joan Barbara (*née* Tuckey); one *s. Educ:* Tottenham Grammar Sch. Air Ministry, 1936–40 (Civil Service appt). Served War, RAF, 1940–46. Air Min., 1946–49; Foreign Office, 1949–52 (on transfer to Diplomatic Service); HM Vice-Consul, Turin, 1953–55; Second Sec.: Rome, 1956; Tokyo, 1957–59; HM Consul (Information): Chicago, 1959–62; FO, 1963–65; First Sec. (Commercial): Belgrade, 1965–67; Tokyo, 1967–72; Commercial Counsellor: Milan, 1973–74; Rome, 1975–76; Consul-General in Perth, 1976–78. *Recreations:* tennis, golf. *Address:* Tresibbett, Altarnun, near Launceston, Cornwall PL15 7RF. *Clubs:* Commonwealth Trust, Civil Service.

HARVEY, Prof. Andrew Charles; Professor of Econometrics, London School of Economics, since 1984; *b* 10 Sept. 1947; *s* of Richard Arthur Harvey and Margaret Frances Harvey (*née* Clark); *m* 1969, Lavinia Mary Young; one *s* one *d. Educ:* Leeds Modern Sch.; Univ. of York (BA); LSE (MSc). Economist and statistician, Central Bureau of Stats, Nairobi, 1969–71; Lectr, Univ. of Kent at Canterbury, 1971–77; Vis. Prof., Univ. of British Columbia, 1977–78; London School of Economics: Sen. Lectr, 1978–81; Reader, 1981–84. Fellow, Econometric Soc., 1990. *Publications:* The Econometric Analysis of Time Series, 1981, 2nd edn 1990; Time Series Models, 1981, 2nd edn 1993; Forecasting, Structural Time Series Models and the Kalman Filter, 1989. *Recreation:* football. *Address:* Department of Statistics, London School of Economics, Houghton Street, WC2A 2AE. *T:* 0171–955 7633.

HARVEY, Anne Caroline Ballingall, (Mrs John Harvey); *see* McIntosh, A. C. B.

HARVEY, Rev. Canon Anthony Ernest, DD; Canon of Westminster since 1982, Librarian since 1983, and Sub-Dean since 1987; *b* 1 May 1930; *s* of Cyril Harvey, QC, and Nina (*née* Darley); *m* 1957, Julian Elizabeth McMaster; four *d. Educ:* Dragon Sch., Oxford; Eton Coll.; Worcester Coll., Oxford (BA, MA, DD 1983); Westcott House, Cambridge. Curate, Christ Church, Chelsea, 1958; Research Student, Christ Church, Oxford, 1962; Warden, St Augustine's Coll., Canterbury, 1969; Univ. Lectr in Theology and Fellow of Wolfson Coll., Oxford, 1976; Chaplain, The Queen's Coll., 1977. Examining Chaplain to Archbishop of Canterbury, 1975; Six Preacher, Canterbury Cathedral, 1977; Bampton Lectr, 1980. Member: Gen. Synod Doctrine Commn, 1977–86; Archbishop's Commn on Urban Priority Areas, 1983–85. *Publications:* Companion to the New Testament (New English Bible), 1970, 2nd edn 1980; Priest or President?, 1975; Jesus on Trial, 1976; Something Overheard, 1977; (ed) God Incarnate: story and belief, 1981; Jesus and the Constraints of History, 1982; Believing and Belonging, 1984; (ed) Alternative Approaches to New Testament Study, 1985; (ed) Theology in the City, 1989; Strenuous Commands, 1990; Retaliation, 1992; Promise or Pretence?: a Christian's guide to sexual morals, 1994; (ed) The Funeral Effigies of Westminster Abbey, 1994; Renewal through Suffering: a study of 2 Corinthians, 1995; articles in classical and theological jls. *Recreations:* music, walking. *Address:* 3 Little Cloister, Westminster Abbey, SW1P 3PL. *T:* 0171–222 4174

HARVEY, Anthony Peter; Chairman, The Broad Oak Consultancy, since 1991; Director, L & R European Museum Consultancy, since 1991; Director, Bo'ness Development Trust, since 1994; *b* 21 May 1940; *s* of Frederick William Henry Harvey and late Fanny Evelyn Harvey (*née* Dixon); *m* 1963, Margaret Hayward; three *s* one *d. Educ:* Hertford Grammar Sch. MIInfS. Dept of Oriental Printed Books, British Museum, 1958–60; British Museum (Natural History): Dept of Palaeontology, 1960–75; Librarian, 1963–75; Head, Dept of Library Services, 1981–88; Co-ordinator of Planning and Development, 1985–88; Head of Marketing and Develt, 1988–91. Dir, Natural History Mus. Develt Trust, 1990–91. Chm., Geology Inf. Gp, 1975–78, Liby Cttee, 1981–84, Geolog. Soc.; Member: Printing Hist. Soc., 1965–; Garden Hist. Soc., 1988–; Soc. for Hist. of Natural Hist., 1963– (Treas., 1964–); London Cttee, Ironbridge Gorge Mus. Develt Trust, 1991–. Mem., Edward King House Britain-Australia Cttee, Lincoln Cathedral, 1992–. Trustee, Britain Australia Bicentennial Trust, 1988–. Freeman, City of London, 1985; Liveryman, Co. of Marketors, 1991. *Publications:* (ed) Secrets of the Earth, 1967; (ed) Directory of Scientific Directories, 1969, 4th edn 1986; Prehistoric Man, 1972; Guide to World Science, vol. 1, 1974; (ed) Encyclopedia of Prehistoric Life, 1979; European sources of scientific and technical information, 1981, 7th edn 1986; numerous contribs to learned jls, ref. works and periodicals. *Recreations:* music, books, gardens and gardening, the countryside. *Address:* L & R European Museum Consultancy, Pellingbridge House, Scaynes Hill, West Sussex RH17 7NG. *T:* Haywards Heath (01444) 831711; Ragstones, Broad Oak, Heathfield, East Sussex TN21 8UD. *T:* Heathfield (01435) 862012.

HARVEY, Arthur Douglas; Assistant Under-Secretary of State, Ministry of Defence, 1969–76; *b* 16 July 1916; *o s* of late William Arthur Harvey and Edith Alice; *m* 1940, Doris Irene Lodge; one *s* (and one *s* decd). *Educ:* Westcliff High Sch.; St Catharine's Coll., Cambridge. Wrangler, Maths Tripos, 1938. Entered War Office, 1938; served in Army, 1940–45; Princ. 1945; Registrar, Royal Military College of Science, 1951–54; Asst Sec. 1954; Under-Sec. 1969. *Address:* 36b Lovelace Road, Long Ditton, Surrey KT6 6ND. *T:* 0181–399 0587.

HARVEY, Barbara Fitzgerald, FSA 1964; FBA 1982; Fellow of Somerville College, Oxford, 1956–93, now Emeritus Fellow; Reader (*ad hominem*) in Medieval History, Oxford University, 1990–93; *b* 21 Jan. 1928; *d* of Richard Henry Harvey and Anne Fitzgerald (*née* Julian). *Educ:* Teignmouth Grammar Sch.; Bishop Blackall Sch., Exeter; Somerville Coll., Oxford (Schol.). First Cl. Final Honour Sch. of Modern History, Oxford, 1949; Bryce Student, Oxford Univ., 1950–51; BLitt Oxon 1953. Assistant, Dept of Scottish History, Edinburgh Univ., 1951–52; Asst Lectr, subseq. Lectr, Queen Mary Coll., London Univ., 1952–55; Tutor, Somerville Coll., Oxford, 1955–93; Vice-Principal, 1976–79, 1981–83. Assessor, Oxford Univ., 1968–69. Ford's Lectr, Oxford, 1989. Mem., Royal Commn on Historical MSS, 1991–; A Vice-Pres., RHistS, 1986–. Gen. Editor, Oxford Medieval Texts, 1987–. *Publications:* Documents Illustrating the Rule of Walter de Wenlok, Abbot of Westminster 1283–1307, 1965; Westminster Abbey and its Estates in the Middle Ages, 1977; (ed, with L. C. Hector) The Westminster Chronicle 1381–94, 1982; Living and Dying in England 1100–1540: the monastic experience, 1993 (jtly, Wolfson Foundn History Prize, 1993); contribs to Economic History Rev., Trans Royal

Historical Soc., Bulletin of Inst. of Historical Research, etc. *Address:* 66 Cranham Street, Oxford OX2 6DD. *T:* Oxford (01865) 54766.

HARVEY, Benjamin Hyde, OBE 1968; FCA; IPFA; DPA; General Manager, Harlow Development Corporation, 1955–73; *b* 29 Sept. 1908; *s* of Benjamin Harvey and Elizabeth (*née* Hyde); *m* 1938, Heather Frances Broome; one *d.* *Educ:* Stationers' Company's Sch. Local Govt, 1924–40; Treas., Borough of Leyton, 1940–47; Comptroller, Harlow Develt Corp., 1947–55. Hon. LLD Newfoundland, 1985. *Publication:* (jtly) Harlow: the story of a new town, 1980. *Recreations:* books, sport. *Address:* Brick House, Broxted, Essex CM6 2BU. *T:* Bishops Stortford (01279) 850233.

HARVEY, Prof. Brian Wilberforce; Professor of Property Law, University of Birmingham, since 1973; *b* 17 March 1936; *s* of Gerald and Noelle Harvey. *Educ:* Clifton Coll., Bristol; St John's Coll., Cambridge (Choral Schol., MA, LLM). Solicitor, 1961. Lectr, Birmingham Univ., 1962–63; Sen. Lectr, Nigerian Law Sch., 1965–67; Lectr, Sen. Lectr and Prof. of Law, QUB, 1967–73; University of Birmingham: Dir, Legal Studies, 1973–76; Dean, Faculty of Law, 1982–85; Pro-Vice-Chancellor, 1986–91; Founding Dir, Legal Office, 1990–. Vis. Prof., Univ. of Singapore, 1985–86. Chairman: Gtr Birmingham Social Security Appeal Tribunals, 1982–; Medical Appeals Tribunals, 1985–; Disability Appeal Tribunals, 1992–. Member: Statute Law Cttee (NI), 1972–73; Cttee on Legal Educn (NI), 1972–73; Adviser, Council of Legal Educn, NI, 1976–79. Mem., British Hallmarking Council, 1989–91. *Publications:* Law of Probate Wills and Succession in Nigeria, 1968; (jtly) Survey of Northern Ireland Land Law, 1970; Settlements of Land, 1973; (ed) Vocational Legal Training in UK and Commonwealth, 1975; (ed) The Lawyer and Justice, 1978; The Law of Consumer Protection and Fair Trading, 1978, 4th edn 1992; (jtly) Consumer and Trading Law Cases and Materials, 1985; (jtly) Law and Practice of Auctions, 1985, 2nd edn 1995; (jtly) The Law and Practice of Marketing Goods and Services, 1990; Violin Fraud: deception, forgery, theft and the law, 1992; The Violin Family and its Makers in the British Isles: an illustrated history and directory, 1995. *Recreations:* performing and listening to music. *Address:* c/o Faculty of Law, The University, Birmingham B15 2TT.

See also J. D. Harvey.

HARVEY, Bryan Hugh, CBE 1978; Adviser, Ministry of Defence, 1985–94; Chairman, Advisory Committee on Major Hazards, 1974–83; *b* 17 Oct. 1914; *y s* of late Oliver Harvey and Ellen Harvey (*née* Munn); *m* 1st, 1941, Margaret (*d* 1986), 2nd *d* of late E. G. Palmer; one *d*; 2nd, 1989, Christiane, *widow* of Maj. John Walton. *Educ:* KES Birmingham; Bristol Grammar Sch.; Corpus Christi Coll., Oxford; Harvard Univ. BA 1936; MA 1945; MSc 1953 (Industrial Hygiene). RAFVR, 1943–45. Printing industry until 1938, when joined Inspectorate of Factories; Dep. Chief Inspector, 1965; Chief Inspector, 1971–74; Dep. Dir Gen. (Dep. Sec.), Health and Safety Exec., 1975–76. Advr to Employment Cttee, H of C, 1980–83. Rockefeller Foundn Fellow, 1952–53; Hon. Lectr, Dept of Occupational Health, Univ. of Manchester, 1954–59; Vis. Prof., Univ. of Aston in Birmingham, 1972–79; External Examiner, Loughborough Univ. of Technology, 1984–89. Hon. Mem., British Occupational Hygiene Soc. (Pres. 1976–77). FSA 1964; Hon. Fellow, Instn of Occupational Safety and Health. *Publications:* (with R. Murray) Industrial Health Technology, 1958; (ed) Handbook of Occupational Hygiene, 1980; many articles in jls on industrial safety and hygiene, and industrial archaeology. *Recreations:* industrial archaeology, Georgian architecture, steam engines. *Address:* 2 Surley Row, Caversham, Reading, Berks RG4 8LY. *T:* Reading (01734) 479453. *Club:* Leander.

HARVEY, Caroline; *see* Trollope, Joanna.

HARVEY, Prof. Charles Richard Musgrave; (3rd Bt *cr* 1933, but does not use the title); *b* 7 April 1937; *s* of Sir Richard Musgrave Harvey, 2nd Bt, and Frances Estelle (*d* 1986), *er d* of late Lindsay Crompton Lawford, Montreal; *S* father, 1978; *m* 1967, Celia Vivien, *d* of late George Henry Hodson; one *s* one *d.* *Educ:* Marlborough; Pembroke Coll., Cambridge (BA 1960, MA 1964). Professorial Fellow, Institute of Development Studies, Sussex. *Heir: s* Paul Richard Harvey, *b* 1971.

HARVEY, Colin Stanley, MBE 1964; TD 1962; DL; a Recorder of the Crown Court, Western Circuit, since 1975; a Solicitor of the Supreme Court; *b* 22 Oct. 1924; *s* of Harold Stanley and Lilian May Harvey; *m* 1949, Marion Elizabeth (*née* Walker); one *s* one *d.* *Educ:* Bristol Grammar Sch.; University Coll., Oxford (BA). Served 1939–45 war in Queen's Regt and RA, India, Burma, Malaya, Java. In private practice as a solicitor. Bt Lt-Col TAVR, 1973. DL Avon, 1977. *Recreations:* TAVR, riding, beagling. *Address:* 12 Southfield Road, Westbury-on-Trym, Bristol BS9 3BH. *T:* Bristol (0117) 962 0404. *Clubs:* Commonwealth Trust; Clifton (Bristol); Royal Western Yacht (Plymouth).

HARVEY, Prof. David William; Professor of Geography and Environmental Engineering, Department of Geography and Environmental Engineering, Johns Hopkins University, since 1993; *b* 31 Oct. 1935; *s* of Frederick and Doris Harvey. *Educ:* St John's Coll., Cambridge (BA (Hons), MA, PhD). Lectr, Univ. of Bristol, 1961–69; Prof. of Geography, Johns Hopkins Univ., 1969–86; Halford Mackinder Prof. of Geography, 1987–93, and Fellow, St Peter's Coll., 1987–93, Sen. Res. Fellow, 1993–, Oxford Univ. Guggenheim Meml Fellow, 1976–77. Outstanding Contributor Award, Assoc. of Amer. Geographers, 1980; Gill Meml Award, RGS, 1982; Anders Retzius Gold Medal, Swedish Soc. for Anthropology and Geography, 1989. *Publications:* Explanation in Geography, 1969, 4th edn 1978; Social Justice and the City, 1973, 3rd edn 1989; The Limits to Capital, 1982, 2nd edn 1984; The Urbanisation of Capital, 1985; Consciousness and the Urban Experience, 1985; The Urban Experience, 1989; The Condition of Postmodernity, 1989. *Address:* Department of Geography and Environmental Engineering, Johns Hopkins University, Baltimore, MD 21218, USA.

HARVEY, Rt Rev. Donald Frederick; *see* Newfoundland, Eastern, and Labrador, Bishop of.

HARVEY, Estella Jacqueline, (Mrs J. G. Harvey); *see* Hindley, E. J.

HARVEY, John Edgar, CBE 1994; Director, Burmah Oil Trading Ltd and subsidiary companies in Burmah Oil Group, 1974–80; *b* 24 April 1920; *s* of John Watt Harvey and Charlotte Elizabeth Harvey; *m* 1945, Mary Joyce Lane, BA, JP; one *s.* *Educ:* Xaverian Coll., Bruges, Belgium; Lyme Regis Grammar Sch. Radio Officer, in the Merchant Navy, 1939–45. Contested (C): St Pancras North, 1950; Walthamstow East, 1951; Mem. Nat. Exec. Cttee., Conservative Party, 1950–55; Chm., Woodford Conservative Assoc., 1954–56. MP (C) Walthamstow East, 1955–66. Pres., Wanstead & Woodford Conservative Assoc., 1986–93. Mem., NSPCC Central Executive Cttee, 1963–68. Governor, Forest Sch., 1966–78. Verderer of Epping Forest, 1970–. Past Master, Guild of Freemen of City of London. *Recreations:* various in moderation. *Address:* 43 Traps Hill, Loughton, Essex IG10 1TB. *T:* 0181–508 8753. *Clubs:* City of London, City Livery.

HARVEY, Prof. Jonathan Dean; composer; Professor of Music, University of Sussex, since 1980; *b* 3 May 1939; *s* of Gerald and Noelle Harvey; *m* 1960, Rosaleen Marie Barry; one *s* one *d.* *Educ:* St Michael's Coll., Tenbury; Repton; St John's Coll., Cambridge (MA, DMus); Glasgow Univ. (PhD). Lectr, Southampton Univ., 1964–77; Reader, Sussex Univ., 1977–80. Harkness Fellow, Princeton Univ., 1969–70. Works performed at many festivals and international centres. Mem., Academia Europaea, 1989. Hon. DMus: Southampton, 1990; Bristol, 1994. *Publications:* The Music of Stockhausen, 1975; compositions: Persephone Dream, for orch., 1972; Inner Light (trilogy), for performers and tape, 1973–77; Smiling Immortal, for chamber orch., 1977; String Quartet, 1977; Magnificat and Nunc Dimittis, for choir and organ, 1978; Album, for wind quintet, 1978; Hymn, for choir and orch., 1979; Be(com)ing, for clarinet and piano, 1979; Concelebration, instrumental, 1979, rev. 1981; Mortuos Plango, Vivos Voco, for tape, 1980; Passion and Resurrection, church opera, 1981; Resurrection, for double chorus and organ, 1981; Whom Ye Adore, for orch., 1981; Bhakti, for 15 insts and tape, 1982; Easter Orisons, for chamber orch., 1983; The Path of Devotion, for choir and orch., 1983; Nachtlied, for soprano, piano and tape, 1984; Gong-Ring, for ensemble with electronics, 1984; Song Offerings, for soprano and players, 1985 (Britten Award for Composition, 1993); Madonna of Winter and Spring, for orch., synthesizers and electronics, 1986; Lightness and Weight, for tuba and orch., 1986; Forms of Emptiness, for choir, 1986; Tendril, for ensemble, 1987; Timepieces, for orch., 1987; From Silence for soprano and players with electronics, 1988; Valley of Aosta for 13 players, 1988; String Quartet No 2, 1989; Ritual Melodies for tape, 1990; Cello Concerto, 1990; Serenade in Homage to Mozart, for wind, 1991; Inquest of Love (opera), 1992; Lotuses, 1992; Scena, 1992; The Riot, for trio, 1993; One Evening, for 2 singers, instruments and electronics, 1994. *Recreations:* tennis, walking, meditation. *Address:* c/o Faber Music, 3 Queen Square, WC1N 3AU. *T:* 0171–278 7436.

See also B. W. Harvey.

HARVEY, Kenneth George, CEng, FIEE; Chairman, NORWEB plc (formerly North Western Electricity Board), since 1989; *b* 22 July 1940; *s* of George Harvey and Nellie Harvey (*née* Gilmore); *m* 1st, 1963, Wendy Youldon (*d* 1982); one *s* one *d*; 2nd, 1990, Anne Model. *Educ:* Urmston Grammar Sch., Manchester; City Univ. (BSc, 1st Cl. Hons Elec. Eng). Student Apprentice, Westinghouse, 1958–63; Southern and London Electricity Boards, 1963–81; London Electricity Board: Engineering Dir, 1981–84; Dep. Chm., 1984–89. Pres., Electricity Assoc., 1992–93. Chm., Royal Exchange Theatre Co., Manchester, 1994–. CIMgt. *Recreations:* sport, gardening, DIY. *Address:* c/o NORWEB, Talbot Road, Manchester M16 0HQ. *T:* 0161–873 8000.

HARVEY, Prof. Leonard Patrick; Fellow, Oxford Centre for Islamic Studies, since 1994; Cervantes Professor of Spanish, King's College, University of London, 1973–84, now Professor Emeritus; *b* 25 Feb. 1929; *s* of Francis Thomas Harvey and Eva Harvey; *m* 1954, June Rawcliffe; two *s.* *Educ:* Alleyn's Sch., Dulwich; Magdalen Coll., Oxford. 1st cl. hons BA Mod. Langs 1952; 2nd cl. Oriental Studies 1954; MA 1956; DPhil 1958. Lectr in Spanish, Univ. of Oxford, 1957–58; Univ. of Southampton, 1958–60; Queen Mary Coll., Univ. of London: Lectr, 1960–63; Reader and Head of Dept, 1963; Prof. of Spanish, 1967–73; Dean of Faculty of Arts, 1970–73; Dean of Faculty of Arts, KCL, 1979–81; FKC 1992. Vis. Prof., Univ. of Victoria, BC, 1966; Vis. Fellow, Oxford Centre for Islamic Studies, 1993–94. Mem. UGC, 1979–83. Chm., Educn Cttee, Hispanic and Luso-Brazilian Council, 1984–87. *Publications:* Islamic Spain 1250–1500, 1990; articles in Al-Andalus, Bulletin of Hispanic Studies, Nueva Revista de Filología Española, Al-Masāq, Al-Qantara, etc. *Address:* Oxford Centre for Islamic Studies, St Cross College, Oxford OX1 3LZ. *T:* Oxford (01865) 278730.

HARVEY, Mary Frances Clare, (Mrs D. R. Feaver), MA; Headmistress, St Mary's Hall, Brighton, 1981–88; *b* 24 Aug. 1927; *d* of Rev. Oliver Douglas Harvey, Maidstone, Kent; *m* 1988, Rt Rev. Douglas Russell Feaver, *qv.* *Educ:* St Mary's Sch., Colchester; St Hugh's Coll., Oxford (BA, Final Honour Sch. of Mod. Hist., 1950; Diploma in Educn, 1951; MA 1954). History Mistress, St Albans High Sch., 1951; Head of History Dept, Portsmouth High Sch., GPDST, 1956; Headmistress: Sch. of St Clare, Penzance, 1962–69; Badminton Sch., Westbury on Trym, Bristol, 1969–81. Governor, Bristol Cathedral Sch., 1978–81; Foundn Gov. and Trustee, Sexey's Sch., Bruton, 1994–. *Recreations:* music, travel, reading, needlework. *Address:* 6 Mill Lane, Bruton, Somerset BA10 0AT.

HARVEY, Michael Llewellyn Tucker, QC 1982; a Recorder, since 1986; *b* 22 May 1943; *s* of Rev. Victor Llewellyn Tucker Harvey and Pauline Harvey (*née* Wybrow); *m* 1972, Denise Madeleine Neary; one *s* one *d.* *Educ:* St John's Sch., Leatherhead; Christ's Coll., Cambridge (BA Hons Law, LLB, MA). Called to the Bar, Gray's Inn, 1966 (Uthwatt Schol. 1965, James Mould Schol. 1966; Bencher, 1991). *Publication:* joint contributor of title 'Damages' in Halsbury's Laws of England, 4th edn 1975. *Recreations:* shooting, golf. *Address:* 2 Crown Office Row, Temple, EC4Y 7HJ. *T:* 0171–797 8100. *Clubs:* Athenæum; Hawks (Cambridge).

HARVEY, Neil; Head of Business Statistics Division, Central Statistical Office, 1989–93; *b* 10 Feb. 1938; *s* of Edward Felters and Lucy Felters (*née* Graves; she *m* 2nd, Frederick Harvey); *m* 1963, Clare Elizabeth Joscelyne; two *s.* *Educ:* Eton House Sch., Essex; LSE. BSc(Econ). Economist/Statistician, Kuwait Oil Co., 1959–62; Statistician, Midland Bank Economics Dept, 1962–65; Asst Statistician/Statistician, DEA, 1965–69; Statistician, HM Treasury, 1969–73; Chief Statistician, Inland Revenue, 1973–77; Controller, Statistical Office, HM Customs and Excise, 1977–84; Under Sec., Statistics Div. 1, DTI, 1984–89. *Recreation:* reading.

HARVEY, Nicholas Barton; MP (Lib Dem) North Devon, since 1992; *b* 3 Aug. 1961; *s* of Frederick Barton Harvey and Christine Diana Rosalind (*née* Gildea). *Educ:* Queen's Coll., Taunton; Middlesex Poly. (BA Hons). Public Relations Consultant: Profile Public Relns, 1984–86; Dewe Rogerson Ltd, 1986–91; Westminster Consortium, 1991–92. Lib Dem spokesman: on transport, 1992–; on trade and industry, 1994–; Chair, Campaigns and Communications, 1994–. *Recreations:* travelling, walking, playing piano, soccer enthusiast. *Address:* House of Commons, SW1A 0AA. *T:* 0171–219 6232. *Club:* National Liberal.

HARVEY, Prof. Paul Dean Adshead, FSA, FRHistS; Emeritus Professor, University of Durham, since 1985; *b* 7 May 1930; *s* of John Dean Monroe Harvey and Gwendolen Mabel Darlington (*née* Adshead); *m* 1968, Yvonne Crossman. *Educ:* Bishop Feild Coll., St John's, Newfoundland; Warwick Sch.; St John's Coll., Oxford (BA 1953; MA; DPhil 1960); FRHistS 1961, FSA 1963. Asst Archivist, Warwick County Record Office, 1954–56; Asst Keeper, Dept of Manuscripts, British Museum, 1957–66; Lectr, 1966–70, Sen. Lectr, 1970–78, Dept of History, Univ. of Southampton; Prof. of Mediaeval Hist., Univ. of Durham, 1978–85. Mem., Adv. Council on Public Records, 1984–89. Vice-Pres., Surtees Soc., 1978–. Hon. Fellow, Portsmouth Polytechnic, 1987. Jt Gen. Editor, Southampton Records Series, 1966–78; Gen. Editor, Portsmouth Record Series, 1969–. *Publications:* The printed maps of Warwickshire 1576–1900 (with H. Thorpe), 1959; A Medieval Oxfordshire Village: Cuxham 1240–1400, 1965; (ed with W. Albert) Portsmouth and Sheet Turnpike Commissioners' minute book 1711–1754, 1973; Manorial records of Cuxham, Oxfordshire, circa 1200–1359, 1976; The history of topographical maps: symbols, pictures and surveys, 1980; (ed) The peasant land market in medieval England, 1984; Manorial records, 1984; (ed with R. A. Skelton) Local maps and plans from medieval England, 1986; Medieval Maps, 1991; Maps in Tudor England, 1993; contribs to: The Victoria History of the County of Oxford, vol. 10, 1972; History of Cartography, vol. 1,

Coll., London. BSc, ARCS, PhD. Asst Lectr, Zoology Dept, Imperial Coll., London, 1951–53; Lectr, 1953–55; Sen. Sci. Officer, Anti-Locust Research Centre, Colonial Office, 1955–57; Principal Sci. Officer, 1957–59; Dep. Dir, 1959–62; Dir, Anti-Locust Research Centre, ODM, 1962–71; Dir, Centre for Overseas Pest Res. and Chief Advr on Pest Control, ODA, 1971–83; Dir, Cleppa Park Field Res. Stn, UC Cardiff, later Univ. of Wales Coll. of Cardiff, 1984–91. Consultant: FAO, UN, 1962–; UNDP, 1970–; WHO, 1973–91; OECD, 1975–; UNEP, 1976–91; Agricl and Vet. Adv. Cttee, British Council, 1976–90; Plants and Soils Res. Cttee, AFRC, later Plants and Envnt Res. Cttee, 1988–91; Mem., UNDP/FAO Special Adv. Cttee on Desert Locust, 1990–. Vice-Pres., Inst. of Biology, 1982. Professorial Res. Fellow, University Coll., Cardiff, 1971–83. Mem., Bd of Governors, Internat. Centre for Insect Physiology and Ecology, Kenya, 1972– (Vice-Chm., 1978; Chm., 1979–). Vis. Prof., Univ. of Newcastle, 1977. Thamisk Lectr, Royal Swedish Acad. of Scis, 1979. Van Den Brande Internat. Prize, 1982. Chief Editor, Tropical Pest Management, 1985–92; Mem., Editorial Bd, Review of Applied Entomol., 1988–91. *Publications:* Insect Sounds, 1962; The Language of Insects, 1962; Pesticide Application: principles and practice, 1985; many papers and articles in scientific and literary jls. *Recreations:* gardening, reading. *Address:* 7 The Tudors, Melrose Avenue, Cardiff CF3 7BA.

HASKINS, Christopher Robin; Chairman, Northern Foods, since 1986; *b* 30 May 1937; *s* of Robin and Margaret Haskins; *m* 1959, Gilda Horsley; three *s* two *d*. *Educ:* Trinity Coll., Dublin (BA Mod). Ford Motor Co., Dagenham, 1960–62; Northern Foods, formerly Northern Dairies, 1962–. Mem., Commn for Social Justice, 1992–94. Trustee, Runnymede Trust, 1989–. *Recreations:* farming, cricket, writing, politics. *Address:* Quarryside Farm, Skidby, near Cottingham, East Yorks HU16 5TG. *T:* Hull (01482) 842692.

HASKINS, Sam, (Samuel Joseph); photographic designer; *b* 11 Nov. 1926; *s* of Benjamin G. Haskins and Anna E. Oelofse; *m* 1952, Alida Elzabé van Heerden; two *s*. *Educ:* Helpmekaar Sch.; Witwatersrand Technical Coll.; Bolt Court Sch. of Photography. Freelance work: Johannesburg, 1953–68; London, 1968–. One-man Exhibitions: Johannesburg, 1953, 1960; Tokyo, 1970, 1973, 1976, 1981, 1985, 1987–88, 1990, 1992, 1993; London, 1972, 1976, 1978, 1980, 1987; Paris, 1973; Amsterdam, 1974; NY, 1981; San Francisco, 1982; Toronto, 1982; Bologna, 1982; Auckland, 1991; Sydney, 1991; Hong Kong, 1991; Taipei, 1991; Singapore, 1991; Osaka, 1990, 1992, 1993; Prague, 1993; Palermo, 1993. *Publications:* Five Girls, 1962; Cowboy Kate and other stories, 1964 (Prix Nadar, France, 1964); November Girl, 1966; African Image, 1967 (Silver Award, Internat. Art Book Contest, 1969); Haskins Posters, 1972 (Gold Medal, New York Art Directors Club, 1974); Photo-Graphics, 1980 (Kodak Book Award); portfolios in most major internat. photographic magazines. *Recreations:* sculpting, books, music. *Address:* 9A Calonne Road, SW19 5HH. *T:* 0181–946 9660.

HASLAM, family name of **Baron Haslam**.

HASLAM, Baron *cr* 1990 (Life Peer), of Bolton in the County of Greater Manchester; **Robert Haslam,** Kt 1985; CEng, FInstME; Chairman, Wasserstein Perella & Co. Ltd, since 1991; *b* 4 Feb. 1923; *s* of Percy and Mary Haslam; *m* 1947, Joyce Quin (*d* 1995); two *s*. *Educ:* Bolton Sch.; Birmingham Univ. (BSc Coal Mining, 1st Cl.). Joined Manchester Collieries Ltd, 1944; National Coal Board, Jan. 1947; Mining Engr, Oct. 1947, Personnel Director, 1960, ICI Nobel Division; Director, 1963, Dep. Chm., 1966, ICI Plastics Div.; Dep. Chm., 1969, Chm., 1971, ICI Fibres Div.; Director, ICI Ltd, 1974; Chairman: ICI Americas Inc., 1978–81; Dep. Chm., ICI plc, 1980–83; Chairman: British Steel Corporation, 1983–86; Tate & Lyle plc, 1983–86 (non-exec. Dep. Chm., 1982; Dir, 1978–86); British Coal, 1986–90 (Non-exec. Dep. Chm., 1985–86; Dep. Chm., 1986); Bechtel Ltd, 1991–94; Director: Fibre Industries, Inc., 1971–75; Imperial Metal Industries, 1975–77; AECI Ltd, 1978–79; Carrington Viyella, 1982–83; Cable and Wireless, 1982–83; Bank of England, 1985–93; Adv. Dir, Unilever, 1986–93. Chairman: Man-Made Fibres Producers Cttee, 1972–74; Nationalized Industries Chairmen's Group, 1985–86 (Mem., 1983–90); British Occupl Health Res. Foundn, 1991–; Member: BOTB, 1981–85 (Chm., N America Adv. Gp, 1982–85); NEDC, 1985–89. Pres., IMinE, 1989–90. Chairman: Council, Manchester Business Sch., 1985–90; Governors, Bolton Sch., 1990–. Freeman, City of London, 1985. Hon. FIMinE 1987. Hon. DTech Brunel, 1987; Hon. DEng Birmingham, 1987. *Recreations:* golf, travel. *Address:* c/o House of Lords, SW1A 0PW. *Clubs:* Brooks's; Wentworth.

HASLAM, Hon. Sir Alec (Leslie), Kt 1974; Judge of the Supreme Court of New Zealand, 1957–76, Senior Puisne Judge, 1973–76; *b* 10 Feb. 1904; *s* of Charles Nelson Haslam and Adeline Elsie Haslam; *m* 1933, Kathleen Valerie Tennent (*d* 1985); two *s* two *d*. *Educ:* Waitaki Boys' High Sch.; Canterbury UC; Oriel Coll., Oxford. Rhodes Scholar 1927; 1st cl. hons LLM NZ; DPhil, BCL Oxon. Served with 10th Reinf. 2 NZEF, ME and Italy, 1943–46. Barrister and Solicitor, 1925; in private practice, 1936–57. Lectr in Law, Canterbury Univ., 1936–50 (except while overseas). Chm. Council of Legal Educn, 1962–75 (Mem. 1952); Mem., Rhodes Scholarship Selection Cttee, 1936–74; NZ Sec. to Rhodes Scholarships, 1961–74; Mem., Scholarships (Univ. Grants) Cttee, 1962–80; Pres., Canterbury District Law Soc., 1952–53; Vice-Pres., NZ Law Soc., 1954–57; Mem., Waimairi County Council, 1950–56; Mem., NZ Univ. Senate, 1956–61. Sen. Teaching Fellow, Univ. of Canterbury, 1977–81. Hon. LLD Canterbury, 1973. *Publication:* Law Relating to Trade Combinations, 1931. *Recreations:* reading; formerly athletics (rep. Canterbury Univ. and Oriel Coll.) and rowing (rep. Oriel Coll.). *Address:* 22 Brackendale Place, Burnside, Christchurch 4, NZ. *T:* (3) 588589.

HASLAM, Rear Adm. Sir David William, KBE 1984 (OBE 1964); CB 1979; President, Directing Committee, International Hydrographic Bureau, Monaco, 1987–92; *b* 26 June 1923; *s* of Gerald Haigh Haslam and Gladys Haslam (*née* Finley). *Educ:* Ashe Prep. Sch., Etwall; Bromsgrove Sch., Worcs. FRGS, FRIN, FRICS. Special Entry Cadet, RN, 1941; HMS Birmingham, HMAS Quickmatch, HMS Resolution (in Indian Ocean), 1942–43; specialised in hydrographic surveying, 1944; HMS White Bear (surveying in Burma and Malaya), 1944–46; comd Survey Motor Launch 325, 1947; RAN, 1947–49; HMS Scott, 1949–51; HMS Dalrymple, 1951–53; i/c RN Survey Trng Unit, Chatham, 1953–56; HMS Vidal, 1956–57; comd, HMS Dalrymple, 1958; comd, HMS Dampier, 1958–60; Admty, 1960–62; comd, HMS Owen, 1962–64; Exec. Officer, RN Barracks, Chatham, 1964–65; Hydrographer, RAN, 1965–67; comd, HMS Hecla, 1968–70; Asst Hydrographer, MoD, 1970–72; comd, HMS Hydra, 1972–73; Asst Dir (Naval) to Hydrographer, 1974–75; sowc 1975; Hydrographer of the Navy, 1975–85. Acting Conservator, River Mersey, 1985–87; Advr on Port Appts, Dept of Transport, 1986–87. Underwriting Mem., Lloyd's, 1986–93. Pres., Hydrographic Soc., 1977–79. Governor, Bromsgrove Sch., 1977– (Chm., Govs and Trustees, 1991–). President: English Schs Basketball Assoc., 1973–; Derbyshire CCC, 1991–92. Liveryman, Chartered Surveyors' Co., 1983–. FRSA. *Address:* 146 Worcester Road, Bromsgrove, Worcs B61 7AS. *T:* Bromsgrove (01527) 574068.

HASLAM, Geoffrey; *see* Haslam, W. G.

HASLAM, Rev. John Gordon; Regional Chairman of Industrial Tribunals, since 1992; non-stipendiary Church of England priest; a Chaplain to the Queen, since 1989; *b* 15 July 1932; *s* of Ernest Henry Haslam and Constance Mabel (*née* Moore); *m* 1st, 1957, Margaret Anne Couse (*d* 1985); two *s* one *d*; 2nd, 1987, Marian Kidson Clarke. *Educ:* King Edward's Sch., Birmingham; Birmingham Univ. (LLB); Queen's Coll., Birmingham. National Service, RA, 1956–58 (2nd Lieut). Solicitor's Articled Clerk, Johnson & Co., Birmingham, 1953–56; Asst Solicitor, 1958–62, Partner, 1962–75, Pinsent & Co., Solicitors, Birmingham; a Chm. of Industrial Tribunals, 1976–92. Ordained deacon and priest, Birmingham dio., 1977; Hon. Curate: St Michael's, Bartley Green, Birmingham, 1977–79; St Mary's, Moseley, Birmingham, 1980–; Hon. Hosp. Chaplain, 1980–88; temp. service as priest in many Birmingham parishes, 1983–. *Recreations:* gardening, steam railways, fell walking. *Address:* 34 Amesbury Road, Moseley, Birmingham B13 8LE. *T:* 0121–449 3394.

HASLAM, Dr Michael Trevor, FRCPG, FRCPsych; Medical Director, South West Durham Mental Health Trust, since 1993; Consultant in Psychological Medicine, Harrogate Clinic, since 1989; *b* 7 Feb. 1934; *s* of Gerald Haslam and Edna Beatrice Haslam (*née* Oldfield); *m* 1959, Shirley Dunstan Jefferies; one *s* two *d*. *Educ:* Sedbergh Sch.; St John's Coll., Cambridge (MA, MD); St Bartholomew's Hosp. Captain, RAMC, 1960–62; hosp. posts, York, 1962–64, Newcastle upon Tyne, 1964–67; Consultant Psychiatrist: Doncaster, 1967–70; York, 1970–89; Medical Dir, Harrogate Clinic, 1989–91. Chm., Soc. of Clinical Psychiatrists; former Cttee Chm., RCP. Warden of North Guild of Freemen; Freeman, City of London, 1973; Liveryman, Soc. of Apothecaries, 1973. *Publications:* Psychiatric Illness in Adolescence, 1975; Sexual Disorders, 1978 (trans. Spanish, 1980); Psychosexual Disorders, 1979; Psychiatry Made Simple, 1982, 2nd edn 1990; Transvestism, 1993; articles in learned jls. *Recreations:* writing, music, fives, squash, croquet, travel. *Address:* Chapel Garth, Crayke, York YO6 4TE. *T:* Easingwold (01347) 823042. *Club:* Authors'.

HASLAM, (William) Geoffrey, OBE 1985; DFC 1944; Director, Prudential Corporation PLC, 1980–87 (Deputy Chairman, 1980–84); *b* 11 Oct. 1914; *yr s* of late William John Haslam and late Hilda Irene Haslam; *m* 1941, Valda Patricia Adamson; two *s* one *d*. *Educ:* New Coll. and Ashville Coll., Harrogate. War Service with RAF, No 25 Sqdn (night fighters), 1940–46. Joined Prudential Assurance Co. Ltd, 1933: Dep. Gen. Manager, 1963; Gen. Manager, 1969; Chief Gen. Manager, 1974–78; Chief Exec., 1979; Dep. Chm., 1980–84. Chairman: Industrial Life Offices Assoc., 1972–74; British Insurance Assoc., 1977–78. Chm., St Teresa's Hospital, Wimbledon, 1983–87; Vice Pres., NABC, 1983–. *Recreation:* golf. *Address:* 6 Ashbourne Road, W5 3ED. *T:* 0181–997 8164. *Clubs:* Royal Air Force, MCC.

HASLEGRAVE, Herbert Leslie, WhSch (Sen.), MA Cantab, PhD London, MSc (Eng), CEng, FIMechE, FIEE; FIMgt; Vice-Chancellor, Loughborough University of Technology, 1966–67; *b* 16 May 1902; *s* of late George Herbert Haslegrave and Annie (*née* Tottey), Wakefield; *m* 1938, Agnes Mary, *er d* of Leo Sweeney, Bradford; one *d*. *Educ:* Wakefield Gram. Sch.; Bradford Technical Coll.; Trinity Hall Cambridge (Scholar). Rex Moir Prizeman, John Bernard Seeley Prizeman, Ricardo Prizeman, 1928; 1st Cl. Mechanical Sciences Tripos, 1928. English Electric Co. Ltd: Engineering Apprentice, 1918–23; Asst Designer, Stafford, 1928–30; Lecturer: Wolverhampton and Staffs Technical Coll., 1931; Bradford Technical Coll., 1931–35; Head of Continuative Education Dept, Loughborough Coll., 1935–38; Principal: St Helens Municipal Technical Coll., 1938–43; Barnsley Mining and Technical Coll., 1943–46; Leicester Coll. of Technology, 1947–53; Loughborough Coll. of Technology, 1953–66. Bernard Price Lectr, SA Inst. of Electrical Engrs, 1971. Member of: Productivity Team on Training of Supervisors, visiting USA, 1951; Delegation on Education and Training of Engineers visiting USSR, 1956; Council, IMechE, 1965–66; Council, IEE, 1956–58. Chairman: Council, Assoc. of Technical Institutions, 1963–64; Cttee on Technician Courses and Examinations, 1967–69; Pres., Whitworth Soc., 1972–73. FRSA. Hon. FIMGTechE. Hon. DTech Loughborough Univ. of Technology. *Publications:* various on engineering, education and management in proceedings of professional engineering bodies and educational press; chapter in Management, Labour and Community. *Recreations:* motoring, swimming, music. *Address:* 1 Woodland View, Southwell, Nottinghamshire NG25 0AG. *T:* Southwell (01636) 814018.

HASLEGRAVE, Neville Crompton; Town Clerk, 1965–74, and Chief Executive Officer, 1969–74, Leeds; Solicitor; *b* 2 Aug. 1914; *o s* of late Joe Haslegrave, Clerk of Council, and late Olive May Haslegrave; *m* 1943, Vera May, *o d* of late Waldemar Julius Pedersen, MBE, and Eva Pedersen; two *d*. *Educ:* Exeter Cathedral Choristers School; Leeds Univ. Asst Examr, Estate Duty Office, Bd of Inland Revenue, 1940–44; Asst Solicitor, Co. Borough of Leeds, 1944–46. Chief Prosecuting Solicitor, Leeds, 1946–51; Principal Asst Solicitor, Leeds, 1951–60; Dep. Town Clerk, Leeds, 1960–65. Pres., Leeds Law Soc., 1972–73. Mem., IBA Adv. Council, 1969–73. *Recreations:* cricket, music, walking. *Address:* 37 West Court, Roundhay, Leeds LS8 2JP. *Club:* Headingley Taverners'.

HASSALL, Prof. Cedric Herbert, FRS 1985; CChem; Hon. Visiting Professor: University of Warwick, since 1985; University College, Cardiff, 1985–92; Imperial College, London, since 1989; *b* 6 Dec. 1919; *s* of late H. Hassall, Auckland, NZ; *m* 1st, 1946, H. E. Cotti (marr. diss. 1982); one *d* (and one *s* decd); 2nd, 1984, J. A. Mitchelmore. *Educ:* Auckland Grammar Sch., NZ; Auckland Univ. (MSc); Univ. of Cambridge (PhD, ScD). Lectr, Univ. of Otago, NZ, 1943–45; Sen. studentship, Royal Commn for 1851, Cambridge, 1946–48; Foundn Prof. of Chem., Univ. of WI, 1948–56; Carnegie and Rockefeller Fellowships in USA, 1950, 1956; Head, Dept of Chemistry, Univ. Coll., of Swansea, UCW, 1957–71; Dir of Research, Roche Products Ltd, 1971–84. Comr, Royal Univ. of Malta, 1964–71; Planning Adviser: Univ. of Jordan, 1965–71; Univ. of Aleppo, 1965; Abdul Aziz Univ., Jedda, 1966, 1968. Vis. Professor: Univ. of Kuwait, 1969, 1979; Aligarh Univ., India (Royal Soc.), 1969–70; Univ. of Liverpool, 1971–79. Pres., Chem. Section of British Assoc., 1987; Member: various cttees of Royal Soc. Chem., 1959– (Pres., Perkin Div., 1985–87); Council, British Technol. Gp, 1986–92; various Govt cttees relating to sci. affairs; Co-ordinator, Molecular Recognition Initiative, SERC, 1987–90; ODA Advr on science, technology and educn in India, China and Indonesia, 1989–. Chm., Steering Cttee, Oxford Centre for Molecular Scis, 1988–92; Hon. Fellow, UC of Swansea, 1986; Hon. DSc West Indies, 1975. *Publications:* papers on aspects of organic chemistry, largely in Jl of Chemical Soc. *Recreation:* travel. *Address:* 2 Chestnut Close, Westoning, Beds MK45 5LR. *T* and *Fax:* Flitwick (01525) 712909.

HASSALL, Tom Grafton, FSA 1971; MIFA; Secretary, Royal Commission on Historical Monuments of England, since 1986; Fellow, St Cross College, Oxford, since 1974; *b* 3 Dec. 1943; *s* of late William Owen Hassall and of Averil Grafton Beaves; *m* 1967, Angela Rosaleen Goldsmith; three *s*. *Educ:* Dragon Sch., Oxford; Lord Williams's Grammar Sch., Thame; Corpus Christi Coll., Oxford (BA History). Assistant local editor, Victoria County History of Oxford, 1966–67; Director, Oxford Archaeological Excavation Cttee, 1967–73; Dir, Oxfordshire (now Oxford) Archaeological Unit, 1973–85; Associate Staff Tutor, Oxford Univ. Dept for External Studies, 1978–85. Trustee, Oxford Preservation Trust, 1973–; Chairman: Standing Conf. of Archaeol Unit Managers, 1980–83; British

Archaeological Awards, 1983–88; President: Council for British Archaeology, 1983–86; Oxfordshire Architectural and Historical Soc., 1984–92; Mem., Ancient Monuments Adv. Cttee, Historic Buildings and Monuments Commn, 1984–93. Crew mem., Athenian Trireme, 1987. *Publications:* Oxford: the city beneath your feet, 1972; specialist articles on archaeology. *Recreations:* manic weeding, Norfolk Cottage. *Address:* The Manor House, Wheatley, Oxford OX33 1XX. *T:* Wheatley (01865) 874428. *Club:* Athenæum.

HASSAN, Hon. Sir Joshua (Abraham), GBE 1988 (CBE 1957); KCMG 1986; Kt 1963; LVO 1954; QC (Gibraltar) 1961; JP; Chief Minister of Gibraltar, 1964–69, and 1972–87; *b* 1915; *s* of late Abraham M. Hassan, Gibraltar; *m* 1945, Daniela (marr. diss. 1969), *d* of late José Salazar; two *d*; *m* 1969, Marcelle, *d* of late Joseph Bensimon; two *d*. *Educ:* Line Wall Coll., Gibraltar. Called to Bar, Middle Temple, 1939; Hon. Bencher, 1983. HM Deputy Coroner, Gibraltar, 1941–64; Mayor of Gibraltar, 1945–50 and 1953–69; Mem. Executive Council, Chief Mem. Legislative Council, Gibraltar, 1950–64; Leader of the Opposition, Gibraltar House of Assembly, 1969–72. Chm., Gibraltar Bar Council, 1992–. Chairman: Cttee of Management, Gibraltar Museum, 1952–65; Gibraltar Govt Lottery Cttee, 1955–70; Central Planning Commn, 1947–70. Hon. LLD Hull Univ., 1985. *Address:* 11/18 Europa Road, Gibraltar. *T:* 77295. *Clubs:* United Oxford & Cambridge University; Royal Gibraltar Yacht.

HASSAN, Mamoun Hamid; independent producer/director; *b* Jedda, 12 Dec. 1937; *s* of late Dr Hamid Hassan and of Fatma Hassan (*née* Sadat); *m* 1966, Moya Jacqueline Gillespie, MA Oxon; two *s*. Formerly script writer, editor and director; Head of Production Board, British Film Inst., 1971–74; Head of Films Branch, UNRWA, Lebanon, 1974–76; Bd Mem., 1978–84, Man. Dir, 1979–84, Nat. Film Finance Corp. Member: Cinematograph Films Council, 1977–78; Scottish Film Production Fund, 1983–87; Advr, European Script Fund, 1989–; Sen. Consultant for UNESCO, Harare, Zimbabwe, 1991–; Governor, Nat. Film and Television Sch., 1983–92. Films produced include: No Surrender, 1985. Producer and presenter, Movie Masterclass, C4 series, 1988, 2nd series, 1990. *Address:* High Ridge, 9 High Street, Deddington, Oxford OX15 0SJ.

HASSELL, Barry Frank; Chief Executive, Independent Healthcare Association, since 1992; *b* 26 Sept. 1944; *s* of late Edgar Frank Hassell and of Rosetta Ethel Hassell (*née* Townsend); *m* 1971, Sylvia Booth; two step *s*. *Educ:* Swanscombe County Secondary Sch. (Head Boy); London Business Sch. (London Exec. Prog.). FIM. Accounting, marketing and directors appts, UK, Scandinavia, Africa, 1959–73; Management Consultant, 1973–85; Special Projects Exec., Spastics Soc., 1980–85; Chief Exec., Tadworth Court Trust, 1983–92. Dir, Project Bombay, 1983–88. Hon. Sec., Union of European Private Hosps, 1993–. *Publications:* articles on health care issues. *Recreations:* travel, photography, ski-ing. *Address:* Independent Health Care Association, 22 Little Russell Street, WC1A 2HT. *T:* 0171–430 0537, *Fax:* 0171–242 2681.

HASSELL, Prof. Michael Patrick, FRS 1987; Professor of Insect Ecology, since 1979, and Head of Department of Biology, since 1993, Imperial College of Science, Technology and Medicine; Director, Silwood Park, since 1988; *b* 2 Aug. 1942; *s* of Albert Marmaduke Hassell and Gertrude Hassell (*née* Loeser); *m* 1st, 1966, Glynis Mary Everett (marr. diss. 1981); two *s*; 2nd, 1982, Victoria Anne Taylor; one *s* one *d*. *Educ:* Whitgift School; Clare College, Cambridge (BA 1964, MA); Oriel College, Oxford (DPhil 1967); DSc Oxford 1980. NERC Research Fellow, Hope Dept of Entomology, Oxford, 1968–70; Imperial College, London: Lectr, 1970–75, Reader, 1975–79, Dept of Zoology and Applied Entomology; Dep. Head, 1984–92, Head, 1993–, Dept of Biology. Vis. Lectr, Univ. of California, Berkeley, 1967–68; Storer Life Sciences Lectr, Univ. of California, Davis, 1985. Mem., NERC, 1991–94. Scientific Medal, Zoological Soc., 1981; Gold Medal, British Ecol Soc., 1994; Wheldon Prize, Oxford Univ., 1995. *Publications:* Insect Population Ecology (with G. C. Varley and G. R. Gradwell), 1973; The Dynamics of Competition and Predation, 1975; The Dynamics of Arthropod Predator-Prey Systems, 1978; research papers and review articles on dynamics of animal populations, esp. insects. *Recreations:* natural history, hill walking, croquet. *Address:* Silwood Lodge, Silwood Park, Ascot, Berks SL5 7PZ.

HASSETT, Gen. Sir Francis (George), AC 1975; KBE 1976 (CBE 1966; OBE 1945); CB 1970; DSO 1951; LVO 1954; Chief of the Defence Force Staff, 1975–77, retired; *b* 11 April 1918; *s* of John Francis Hassett, Sydney, Australia; *m* 1946, Margaret Hallie Roberts, *d* of Dr Edwin Spencer Roberts, Toowoomba, Qld; one *s* two *d* (and one *s* decd). *Educ:* RMC, Duntroon, Australia. Graduated RMC, 1938. Served War of 1939–45, Middle East and South West Pacific Area (Lt-Col; wounded; despatches twice); CO 3 Bn Royal Australian Regt, Korea, 1951–52; Marshal for ACT Royal Tour, 1954; Comd 28 Commonwealth Bde, 1961–62; idc, 1963; DCGS, 1964–65; Head of Aust. Jt Services Staff, Australia House, 1966–67; GOC Northern Comd, Australia, 1968–70; Chm., Army Rev. Cttee, 1969–70; Vice Chief of Gen. Staff, Australia, 1971–73; CGS, Australia, 1973–75. Extra Gentleman Usher to the Queen, 1966–68. *Recreations:* gardening, writing. *Address:* 42 Mugga Way, Red Hill, Canberra, ACT 2603, Australia. *Club:* Commonwealth.

HASSETT, Maj.-Gen. Ronald Douglas Patrick, CB 1978; CBE 1975; Executive Director, Orient New Zealand Trading Co. Ltd, 1979–85; *b* 27 May 1923; *s* of Edmond Hassett and Elinor Douglas; *m* 1953, Lilian Ivy Gilmore; two *s* one *d*. *Educ:* St Patrick's Coll., Wellington; RMC Duntroon. psc, G, rcds. 2nd NZ Expeditionary Force, Italy, 1944–46; NZ Army Liaison Staff, London, 1948–50; served Korea, NZ and Malaya, 1952–62; NZ Instructor, Australian Staff Coll., 1963–65; Dir of Equipment, NZ Army, 1966–67; DQMG, 1967–69; Comdr NZ Inf. Brigade Group, 1969; DCGS, 1970; RCDS, 1971; ACDS (Policy), 1972–74; Dep. Chief of Defence Staff, 1974–76; Chief of General Staff, NZ Army, 1976–78. *Recreations:* gardening, golf. *Address:* 130 Cheviot Road, Lowry Bay, Eastbourne, Wellington, New Zealand.

HASTERT, Roger Joseph Leon; Grand Cross, Order of Adolphe de Nassau, Luxembourg; Hon. CMG 1972; Dr-en-Droit; Hon. Maréchal de la Cour, Luxembourg, since 1986; *b* Luxembourg City, 10 July 1929; *m* Eléonore Heijmerink; one *s* one *d*. Barrister-at-law, Luxembourg, 1956–59; joined Diplomatic Service, 1959 (Political Affairs); First Sec. and Consul Gen., Brussels, 1963–69; Dir of Protocol and Juridical Affairs, Min. of Foreign Affairs; Pres., Commn Internationale de la Moselle; and Mem., Commn de Contrôle des Comptes des Communautés Européennes, 1969–73; Ambassador to The Netherlands, 1973–1978; Ambassador to UK and Perm. Rep. to Council of WEU, 1978–85, concurrently Ambassador to Ireland and Iceland. *Address:* 44 rue de Mersch, 8181 Kopstal, Luxembourg.

HASTIE, Robert Cameron, CBE 1983; RD 1968 (Bar 1978); JP; Chairman: Bernard Hastie & Co. Ltd, UK and Australia, since 1973; Lord-Lieutenant, West Glamorgan, since 1995 (Vice Lord-Lieutenant, 1991–95); *b* Swansea, 24 May 1933; *s* of B. H. C. Hastie and M. H. Hastie; *m* 1961, Mary Griffiths; two *s* one *d*. *Educ:* Bromsgrove School. Joined RN, National Service, 1951; Midshipman 1953; qual. RNR Ocean comd, 1963; progressive ranks to Captain RNR, 1974, in comd HMS Cambria, 1974–77; Aide-de-Camp to the Queen, 1977; Commodore RNR 1979. Pres., Swansea Unit Sea Cadet Corps, 1982–. Chairman: Mumbles Lifeboat Station Cttee, 1987–95; Milford Haven Port Authy, 1994–. Member: Inst. of Directors, 1960–; W Wales Cttee, CBI, 1982–; Cttee of Management, RNLI, 1991–. DL West Glamorgan, 1974; JP Swansea, 1989; High Sheriff of W Glamorgan County, 1977–78. *Recreations:* farming, sailing, shooting. *Address:* Upper Hareslade Farm, Bishopston, Swansea SA3 3BU. *T:* Swansea (01792) 232957; (day) Swansea (01792) 651541. *Clubs:* Naval; Cardiff and County (Cardiff); Royal Naval Sailing Association (Portsmouth); Bristol Channel Yacht (Swansea); Royal Sydney Yacht Squadron (Sydney, Aust.).

HASTIE-SMITH, Richard Maybury, CB 1984; FIPM 1986; Chairman: Incorporated Froebel Educational Institute, since 1993; Council, Cranleigh and Bramley Schools, since 1993; Member, Council, Roehampton Institute of Higher Education, since 1993; *b* 13 Oct. 1931; *s* of Engr-Comdr D. Hastie-Smith and H. I. Hastie-Smith; *m* 1956, Bridget Noel Cox; one *s* two *d*. *Educ:* Cranleigh Sch. (Schol.); Magdalene Coll., Cambridge (Schol.; MA). HM Forces, commnd Queen's Royal Regt, 1950–51. Entered Administrative Class, Home CS, War Office, 1955; Private Sec. to Permanent Under-Sec., 1957; Asst Private Sec. to Sec. of State, 1958; Principal, 1960; Asst Private Sec. to Sec. of State for Defence, 1965; Private Sec. to Minister of Defence (Equipment), 1968; Asst Sec., 1969; RCDS, 1974; Under-Sec., MoD, 1975, Cabinet Office, 1979–81; Dep. Under-Sec. of State, MoD, 1981–91. Mem., Civil Service Appeal Bd, 1992–; Non-Service Mem., Home Office Assessment Consultancy Unit for police, prison and fire services, 1992–. Chm., 1983–94, Vice-Pres., 1994–, Magdalene Coll. Assoc. *Address:* 18 York Avenue, East Sheen, SW14 7LG. *T:* 0181–876 4597.

HASTILOW, Michael Alexander; Director, Glynwed Ltd, 1969–81; *b* 21 Sept. 1923; *s* of late Cyril Alexander Frederick Hastilow, CBE, MSc, BCom, FRIC, and Doreen Madge, MA; *m* 1953, Sheila Mary Tipper (*née* Barker); one *s* two *d*. *Educ:* Mill Hill Sch.; Birmingham Univ. (Pres., Guild of Undergrads; BSc Civil Engrg, BCom). Served in Fleet Air Arm, RNVR, 1944–46. Commercial Manager, J. H. Lavender & Co. Ltd, 1948–54; Birmid Industries Ltd, 1954–57: Asst Gen. Man., Birmidal Developments Ltd, 1956–57; Commercial Man., Birmetals Ltd, 1957; Commercial and Gen. Sales Man., Bilston Foundries Ltd, 1957–63; Dir, Cotswold Buildings Ltd, 1963–64; Glynwed Ltd, 1964–81: Dir, The Wednesbury Tube Co. Ltd, 1966–81 (Man. Dir, 1968–74; Chm., 1973–76); dir or chm. of various Glynwed divs and subsids. British Non-Ferrous Metals Federation: Mem. Council, 1973–81; Vice Pres., 1975–79; Pres., 1979–80; Chm., Tube Gp, 1975–77. National Home Improvement Council: Mem. Council, 1975–84; Mem. Bd, 1975–84; Vice Chm., 1979–80; Chm., 1980–81. Member: Commn for New Towns, 1978–86; Construction Exports Adv. Bd, 1975–78; Exec. Cttee, 1973–84, and Council, 1974–84, Nat. Council for Bldg Material Producers; EDC for Building, 1980–82. Hon. Treasurer, Midlands Club Cricket Conf., 1970–81, Pres., 1981–82. *Recreations:* cricket, railways. *Address:* The Mount, 3 Kendal End Road, Rednal, Birmingham B45 8PX. *T:* 0121–445 2007. *Clubs:* MCC, Old Millhillians.

See also N. G. Hastilow.

HASTILOW, Nigel Graham; Editor, Birmingham Post, since 1993; *b* 22 Feb. 1956; *s* of Michael Alexander Hastilow, *qv*; *m* 1980, Fiona Mary Findlay. *Educ:* Mill Hill Sch.; Birmingham Univ. (BA 2nd Cl. Hons Eng. Lang. and Lit.). Reporter: Solihull News, 1978–80; Evening Mail, Birmingham, 1980–85; Mktg Manager, Birmingham Post & Mail Ltd, 1985–87; Birmingham Post: Political Editor, 1987–90; Asst Editor, 1990–91; Dep. Editor, 1991–92; Exec. Editor, 1992–93. *Recreations:* usual sporting and cultural interests. *Address:* Hill Barn, Danzey Green, Tanworth-in-Arden, Warwickshire B94 5BJ.

HASTINGS; *see* Abney-Hastings, family name of Countess of Loudoun.

HASTINGS, 22nd Baron, *cr* 1290; **Edward Delaval Henry Astley,** Bt 1660; *b* 14 April 1912; *s* of 21st Baron and Lady Marguerite Nevill (*d* 1975), *d* of 3rd Marquess of Abergavenny; *S* father 1956; *m* 1954, Catherine Rosaline Ratcliffe Coats, 2nd *d* of late Capt. H. V. Hinton; two *s* one *d*. *Educ:* Eton and abroad. Supplementary Reserve, Coldstream Guards, 1934; served War of 1939–45, Major 1945; farming in Southern Rhodesia, 1951–57. Mem. of Parliamentary delegation to the West Indies, 1958; a Lord in Waiting, 1961–62; Jt Parly Sec., Min. of Housing and Local Govt, 1962–64. Chairman: British-Italian Soc., 1957–62 (Pres., 1972–); Italian People's Flood Appeal, 1966–67; Governor: Brit. Inst. of Florence, 1959–; Royal Ballet, 1971–93; Chairman: Royal Ballet Benevolent Fund, 1966–84; Dance Teachers Benevolent Fund, 1982–; Pres., British Epilepsy Assoc., 1965–93. Grand Officer, Order of Merit (Italy), 1968. *Recreations:* riding, ballet, foreign travel. *Heir:* *s* Hon. Delaval Thomas Harold Astley [*b* 25 April 1960; *m* 1987, Veronica, *er d* of Richard Smart; one *s* one *d*]. *Address:* Seaton Delaval Hall, Whitley Bay, Northumberland NE26 4QR. *T:* 0191–237 0786. *Clubs:* Brooks's, Army and Navy; Northern Counties (Newcastle); Norfolk (Norwich).

HASTINGS, Rev. Prof. Adrian Christopher; Professor of Theology, University of Leeds, 1985–94, now Emeritus; *b* 23 June 1929; *s* of late William George Warren Hastings and Mary Hazel Hastings (*née* Daunais); *m* 1979, Elizabeth Ann Spence. *Educ:* Worcester Coll., Oxford (MA 1953); Christ's Coll., Cambridge (PGCE 1958); Urban Univ., Rome (DTheol 1958). Ordained 1955; Diocesan Priest, Masaka, Uganda, 1958–66; Editor, Post-Vatican II, Tanzania, 1966–68; Mindolo Ecumenical Foundn, Zambia, 1968–70; Res. Officer, SOAS, 1973–76; Fellow, St Edmund's House, Cambridge, 1974–76; Lectr and Reader in Religious Studies, Univ. of Aberdeen, 1976– 82; Prof. of Religious Studies, Univ. of Zimbabwe, 1982–85. Editor, Jl of Religion in Africa, 1985–. Hon. DD Edinburgh Univ., 1992. *Publications:* Prophet and Witness in Jerusalem, 1958; (ed) The Church and the Nations, 1959; One and Apostolic, 1963; Church and Mission in Modern Africa, 1967; A Concise Guide to the Documents of the Second Vatican Council, 2 vols, 1968–69; Mission and Ministry, 1971; Christian Marriage in Africa, 1973; Wiriyamu, 1974; The Faces of God, 1975; African Christianity, 1976; (ed) Bishops and Writers, 1977; In Filial Disobedience, 1978; A History of African Christianity 1950–1975, 1979; In the Hurricane, 1986; A History of English Christianity 1920–1985, 1986, 2nd edn 1991; African Catholicism, 1989; The Theology of a Protestant Catholic, 1990; Robert Runcie, 1991; (ed) Modern Catholicism, 1991; Church and State: the English Experience, 1991; SOS Bosnia, 1993; The Church in Africa 1450–1950, 1994; The Shaping of Prophecy, 1995. *Recreations:* walking, visiting historic buildings, cutting hedges. *Address:* c/o Department of Theology and Religious Studies, The University, Leeds LS2 9JT. *T:* Leeds (0113) 233 3640; 3 Hollin Hill House, 219 Oakwood Lane, Leeds LS8 2PE. *T:* Leeds (0113) 240 0154.

HASTINGS, Alfred James; Clerk of the Journals, House of Commons, since 1991; *b* 10 Feb. 1938; *s* of William Hastings and Letitia (*née* Loveridge); *m* 1972, Susan Edge; three *s*. *Educ:* Leamington College; New College, Oxford (MA). A Clerk of the House of Commons, 1960–: Registrar of Members' Interests, 1987–91. *Recreations:* music, high fidelity sound reproduction. *Address:* Journal Office, House of Commons, SW1A 0AA.

HASTINGS, Max Macdonald; Editor, The Daily Telegraph, since 1986; Director, since 1989, Editor-in-Chief, since 1990, The Daily Telegraph plc; *b* 28 Dec. 1945; *s* of Macdonald Hastings and Anne Scott-James, *qv*; *m* 1972, Patricia Mary Edmondson (marr. diss. 1994); two *s* one *d*. *Educ:* Charterhouse (Scholar); University Coll., Oxford (Exhibnr). Served TA Parachute Regt, 1963. Researcher, BBC TV Great War series, 1963–64; Reporter, Evening Standard, 1965–67; Fellow, US World Press Inst., 1967–68; Roving

Correspondent, Evening Standard, 1968–70; Reporter, BBC TV Current Affairs, 1970–73; freelance journalist and broadcaster, 1973–; Editor, Evening Standard Londoner's Diary, 1976–77; Columnist, Daily Express, 1981–83; contributor, Sunday Times, 1985–86. As War Correspondent, covered Middle East, Indochina, Angola, India-Pakistan, Cyprus, Rhodesia and S Atlantic. Mem., Press Complaints Commn, 1991–92. TV documentaries for BBC and Central TV, 1970–: Ping-Pong in Peking, 1971; The War about Peace, 1983; Alarums and Exercursions, 1984; Cold Comfort Farm, 1985; The War in Korea (series), 1988; We Are All Green Now, 1990. Trustee: Liddell Hart Archive, KCL, 1988–; Nat. Portrait Gall., 1995–. FRHistS 1988. Hon. DLitt Leicester, 1992. Journalist of the Year, British Press Awards, 1982 (cited 1973 and 1980); What The Papers Say, Granada TV: Reporter of the Year, 1982; Editor of the Year, 1988. *Publications:* America 1968: the fire this time, 1968; Ulster 1969: the struggle for civil rights in Northern Ireland, 1970; Montrose: the King's champion, 1977; Yoni: the hero of Entebbe, 1979; Bomber Command, 1979 (Somerset Maugham Prize for Non-Fiction, 1980); (with Len Deighton) The Battle of Britain, 1980; Das Reich, 1981; (with Simon Jenkins) The Battle for The Falklands, 1983 (Yorkshire Post Book of the Year Award); Overlord: D-Day and the battle for Normandy, 1984, 2nd edn 1989 (Yorkshire Post Book of the Year Award); Victory in Europe, 1985; (ed) Oxford Book of Military Anecdotes, 1985; The Korean War, 1987 (NCR Prize shortlist); Outside Days, 1989; contrib. DNB, Country Life, The Field. *Recreations:* shooting, fishing. *Address:* The Daily Telegraph, 1 Canada Square, E14 5DT. *T:* 0171–538 5000. *Clubs:* Brooks's, Pratt's.

HASTINGS, Michael; playwright; *b* 2 Sept. 1938; *s* of Max Emmanuel Gerald and Marie Katherine Hastings; *m* 1975, Victoria Hardie; two *s*; one *d* by previous *m*. *Educ:* various South London schools. Bespoke tailoring apprenticeship, London, 1953–56. FRGS. *Plays:* Don't Destroy Me, 1956; Yes and After, 1957; The World's Baby, 1962; Lee Harvey Oswald: 'a far mean streak of indepence brought on by negleck', 1966; The Cutting of the Cloth (unperformed autobiographical play), 1969; The Silence of Saint-Just, 1971; For the West (Uganda), 1977; Gloo Joo, 1978; Full Frontal, 1979; Carnival War a Go Hot, 1980; Midnite at the Starlite, 1980; Molière's The Miser (adaptation), 1982; Tom and Viv, 1984; Stars of the Roller State Disco (community play), 1985; The Emperor (adapted with Jonathan Miller), 1987; A Dream of People, 1990; Roberto Cossa's La Nona (adaptation), 1991; Unfinished Business, 1994; *for film and television:* For the West (Congo), 1963; Blue as his Eyes the Tin Helmet He Wore, 1966; The Search for the Nile, 1972; The Nightcomers, 1972; Auntie Kathleen's Old Clothes, 1977; Murder Rap, 1980; Midnight at the Starlight, 1980; Michael Hastings in Brixton, 1980; Stars of the Roller State Disco, 1984; The Emperor (dir. by Jonathan Miller), 1988; Tom and Viv, 1994; adaptations for television: La Nona (also trans.)., 1992; Six Characters in Search of an Author (also trans.), 1993; The Changeling, 1994. *Publications: plays include:* Don't Destroy Me, 1956; Yes and After, 1959; Three Plays, 1965; Lee Harvey Oswald: 'a far mean streak of indepence brought on by negleck', 1968; Three Plays, 1978; Carnival War/Midnite at the Starlite, 1979; Tom and Viv, 1985; Three Political Plays, 1990; A Dream of People, 1991; Unfinished Business and Other Plays, 1994; *novels:* The Game, 1957; The Frauds, 1960; Tussy is Me, 1968; The Nightcomers, 1971; And in the Forest the Indians, 1975; *poems:* Love me Lambeth, 1959; *stories:* Bart's Mornings and other Tales of Modern Brazil, 1975; *criticism:* Rupert Brooke, The Handsomest Young Man in England, 1967; Sir Richard Burton: a biography, 1978. *Address:* 2 Helix Gardens, Brixton Hill, SW2 2JP.

HASTINGS, Sir Stephen (Lewis Edmonstone), Kt 1983; MC 1944; *b* 4 May 1921; *s* of late Lewis Aloysius MacDonald Hastings, MC, and of Edith Meriel Edmonstone; *m* 1st, 1948, Harriet Mary Elisabeth (marr. diss. 1971), *d* of Col Julian Latham Tomlin, CBE, DSO; one *s* one *d*; 2nd, 1975, Hon. Elisabeth Anne Lady Naylor-Leyland, *yr d* of late Viscount FitzAlan of Derwent and of Countess Fitzwilliam. *Educ:* Eton, RMC, Sandhurst. Gazetted Ensign, Scots Guards, 1939; served 2nd Bn, Western Desert, 1941–43 (despatches); SAS Regt, 1943. Joined Foreign Office, 1948. British Legation, Helsinki, 1950–52; British Embassy, Paris, 1953–58; First Sec., Political Office, Middle East Forces, 1959–60. MP (C) Mid-Bedfordshire, Nov. 1960–1983. Director: BMSS Ltd, 1978–; Fitzwilliam Estates Co., 1980–; Partner and Manager, Milton Park Stud, 1985–. Chm., British Field Sports Soc., 1982–88; Mem. Council, Thoroughbred Breeders Assoc., 1989–91. Jt Master, Fitzwilliam Hounds. *Publications:* The Murder of TSR2, 1966; The Drums of Memory: an autobiography, 1995. *Recreations:* fieldsports, skiing, painting. *Address:* Milton, Peterborough PE6 7AA; 12A Ennismore Gardens, SW7. *Clubs:* White's, Pratt's, Buck's.

See also Sir P. V. Naylor-Leyland, Bt.

HASTINGS BASS, family name of **Earl of Huntingdon**.

HASWELL, (Anthony) James (Darley), OBE 1985; Insurance Ombudsman, 1981–89; Chairman, Appeals Tribunals, Financial Intermediaries, Managers and Brokers Regulatory Association, 1989; *b* 4 Aug. 1922; *s* of Brig. Chetwynd Henry Haswell, CIE, and Dorothy Edith (*née* Berry); *m* 1957, Angela Mary (*née* Murphy); three *s* one *d*. *Educ:* Winchester Coll.; St John's Coll., Cambridge (MA). Solicitor of the Supreme Court. Admitted Solicitor, 1949; RAC Legal Dept, 1949; private practice, London and Cornwall, 1950–51; commnd, Army Legal Services Staff List (Captain), 1952; Temp. Major 1956; Lt-Col 1967; retired from Army Legal Corps, 1981. *Publications:* Insurance Ombudsman Bureau annual reports for years 1981–88; miscellaneous articles in industry jls. *Recreations:* chamber music, theatre, painting, woodwork, Insurance Orchestra (Chm. and playing member). *Address:* 31 Chipstead Street, SW6 3SR. *T:* 0171–736 1163.

HASZELDINE, Dr Robert Neville, ScD; FRS 1968; CChem, FRSC; scientific consultant; Professor of Chemistry, 1957–82, Head of Department of Chemistry, 1957–76, and Principal, 1976–82, University of Manchester Institute of Science and Technology (Faculty of Technology, The University of Manchester); *b* Manchester, 3 May 1925; *s* of late Walter Haszeldine and late Hilda Haszeldine (*née* Webster); *m* 1954, Pauline Elvina Goodwin (*d* 1987); two *s* two *d*. *Educ:* Stockport Grammar Sch.; University of Birmingham (John Watt Meml Schol., 1942; PhD 1947; DSc 1955); Sidney Sussex Coll., Cambridge (MA, PhD 1949); Queens' Coll., Cambridge (ScD 1957). University of Cambridge: Asst in Research in Organic Chemistry, 1949; University Demonstrator in Organic and Inorganic Chemistry, 1951; Asst Dir of Research, 1956; Fellow and Dir of Studies, Queens' Coll., 1954–57, Hon. Fellow, 1976. Mem. various Govt Cttees, 1957–89. Tilden Lectr, 1968; Vis. Lectr at universities and laboratories in the USA, Russia, Switzerland, Austria, Germany, Japan, China, Israel, S America and France. Chm., Langdales Soc., 1987–93; Lord of the Manor of Langdale, 1988. Meldola Medal, 1953; Corday-Morgan Medal and Prize, 1960; Prix Henri Moissan, 1994. *Publications:* numerous scientific publications in chemical jls. *Recreations:* mountaineering, gardening, natural history, good food, wine, wilderness travel. *Address:* Copt Howe, Chapel Stile, Great Langdale, Cumbria LA22 9JR. *T:* Langdale (015394) 37685.

HATCH, David Edwin, CBE 1994; JP; Adviser to Director-General, BBC, 1993–95; *b* 7 May 1939; *s* of Rev. Raymond Harold Hatch and Winifred Edith May (*née* Brookes); *m* 1964, Ann Elizabeth Martin; two *s* one *d*. *Educ:* St John's Sch., Leatherhead; Queens' Coll., Cambridge (MA, DipEd). Actor, Cambridge Circus, 1963; BBC: I'm Sorry I'll Read That Again, 1964; Producer, Light Entertainment Radio, 1964, Executive Producer, 1972; Network Editor Radio, Manchester, 1974; Head of Light Entertainment Radio, 1978; Controller: Radio Two, 1980–83; Radio 4, 1983–86; Dir of Programmes, Radio, 1986–87; Man. Dir, Network Radio BBC (formerly BBC Radio), 1987–93; Vice-Chm., BBC Enterprises, 1987–93. Dir, The Listener, 1988–90. Vice-Chairman: Sound and Vision Corp., 1991– (Mem., Bd of Management Services, 1981–90); EBU Radio Prog. Cttee, 1987–94; Pres., TRIC, 1990. CIMgt; FRSA. JP Aylesbury, 1993. *Recreations:* laughing, family. *Address:* The Windmill, Ray's Hill, Cholesbury, near Chesham, Bucks HP5 2UJ. *T:* Cholesbury (01494) 758542. *Clubs:* Garrick, Rugby, Lord's Taverners'.

HATCH, Dr Marshall Davidson, AM 1981; FRS 1980; FAA 1975; Chief Research Scientist, Division of Plant Industry, CSIRO, Canberra, since 1970; *b* 24 Dec. 1932; *s* of Lloyd Davidson Hatch and Alice Endesby Hatch (*née* Dalziel); *m* 1st (marr. diss.); two *s*; 2nd, 1983, Lyndall P. Clarke. *Educ:* Newington Coll., Sydney; Univ. of Sydney (BSc, PhD). FAA 1975. Res. Scientist, Div. of Food Res., CSIRO, 1955–59; Post Doctoral Res. Fellow, Univ. of Calif., Davis, 1959–61; Res. Scientist, Colonial Sugar Refining Co. Ltd, Brisbane, 1961–66 and 1968–69 (Reader in Plant Biochemistry, Univ. of Queensland, Brisbane, 1967). Foreign Associate, Nat. Acad. of Sciences, USA, 1990. Rank Prize, Rank Foundn, UK, 1981; Internat. Prize for Biology, Japan Soc. for Promotion of Science, 1991. *Publications:* 155 papers, reviews and chaps in scientific jls and text books in field of photosynthesis and other areas of plant biochemistry. *Recreations:* skiing, running. *Address:* (office) Division of Plant Industry, CSIRO, PO Box 1600, Canberra City, ACT 2601, Australia. *T:* (6) 2465264.

HATCH, Tasmin; *see* Little, T.

HATCHARD, Frederick Henry; Stipendiary Magistrate for Metropolitan County of West Midlands (Birmingham), 1981–91, retired; *b* 22 April 1923; *s* of Francis and May Hatchard; *m* 1955, Patricia Egerton; two *s*. *Educ:* Yardley Grammar Sch., Birmingham. Justices Clerk: Sutton Coldfield and Coleshill, 1963–67; Walsall, 1967–81. *Recreations:* walking, gardening. *Address:* 3(B) Manor Road, Streetly, Sutton Coldfield B74 3NQ.

HATENDI, Rt Rev. Ralph Peter; Bishop of Harare, 1981–95; *b* 9 April 1927; *s* of Fabian and Amelia Hatendi; *m* 1954, Jane Mary Chikumbu; two *s* three *d*. *Educ:* St Peter's Coll., Rosettenville, S Africa (LTh); King's Coll. London (DD; AKC). School teacher, 1952–; clergyman, 1957–; Seminary Tutor, 1968–72; Executive Secretary, 1973–75; Distribution Consultant, 1976–78; Suffragan Bishop of Mashonaland, 1979–80. *Publications:* Sex and Society, 1971; Shona Marriage and the Christian Churches, in Christianity South of the Zambezi, 1973. *Recreation:* poultry. *Address:* c/o PO Box 3585, Harare, Zimbabwe, S Africa. *Club:* Harare (Zimbabwe).

HATFIELD, Rt. Rev. Leonard Fraser; Bishop of Nova Scotia, 1980–84, retired; *b* 1 Oct. 1919; *s* of Otto Albert Hatfield and Ada Hatfield (*née* Tower). *Educ:* Port Greville and Amherst High School; King's and Dalhousie Univ., Halifax (BA 1940, MA 1943, Sociology). Deacon 1942, priest 1943; Priest Assistant, All Saints Cathedral, Halifax, NS, 1942–46; Rector of Antigonish, NS, 1946–51; Asst. Sec., Council for Social Service of Anglican Church of Canada, 1951–54; Gen. Sec., 1955–61; Rector: Christ Church, Dartmouth, NS, 1961–71; St John's, Truro, NS, 1971–76. Canon of All Saints Cathedral, Halifax, 1969; Bishop Suffragan, Dio. NS, 1976. Has served: Dio. Council, NS Synod; Corpn of Anglican Dio. Centre; Dean and Chapter, All Saints Cathedral; Bd of Governors, King's Coll.; Program Cttee and Unit of Public Social Responsibility, Gen. Synod; Council of Churches on Justice and Corrections; Anglican Cons. Council, and various cttees of WCC; Organizing Sec., Primate's World Relief and Develt Fund; founding mem., Vanier Inst. of the Family, Ottawa; convened Primate's Task Force on Ordination of Women to the Priesthood; rep. Anglican Church of Canada at Internat. Bishops' Seminar, Anglican Centre in Rome, 1980. Hon. DD: Univ. of King's Coll., Halifax, NS, 1956; Atlantic Sch. of Theology, Halifax, NS, 1985. *Publications:* He Cares, 1958; Simon Gibbons (First Eskimo Priest), 1987; Sammy the Prince, 1990; Great Fun with Organists, 1995. *Recreations:* fishing, gardening, travelling, and playing bridge. *Address:* Port Greville, Site 31, Box O, RR#3, Parrsboro, Nova Scotia B0M 1S0, Canada.

HATFIELD, Richard Paul, CBE 1991; Director General, Management and Organisation, Ministry of Defence, since 1993; *b* 8 Feb. 1953; *m* 1982, Penelope Charlotte Bratton. *Educ:* Whitgift Sch., Croydon; University Coll., Oxford (MA). Admin. trainee, MoD, 1974; Private Secretary to: Under Sec. of State (Army), 1978–80; Cabinet Sec., 1982–85; Asst Private Sec. to Defence Sec., 1986; Head: Defence Lands, 1986–88; Overseas Div., MoD, 1988–91; Programme and Policy Div., MoD, 1991–93. *Address:* c/o Ministry of Defence, Northumberland House, Northumberland Avenue, WC2N 5BP.

HATFULL, Alan Frederick; Counsellor (Labour), Bonn, 1981–87; *b* 12 June 1927; *s* of Frederick George Hatfull and Florence May Hatfull (*née* Dickinson); *m* 1951, Terttu Kaarina Wahlroos; one *s* one *d*. *Educ:* St Olave's and St Saviour's Grammar School; London School of Economics. BSc (Econ) 1951. Assistant Principal, Min. of Labour, 1951, Principal 1957, Assistant Sec., 1965; Director, Commn on Industrial Relations, 1970–73; Counsellor (Labour), Paris, 1977–81. *Address:* 75 Darwin Court, Gloucester Avenue, NW1 7BQ.

HATHERTON, 8th Baron *cr* 1835; **Edward Charles Littleton;** agronomist; *b* 24 May 1950; *s* of Mervyn Cecil Littleton (*d* 1970) (*g s* of 3rd Baron) and of Margaret Ann, *d* of Frank Sheehy; *S* cousin, 1985; *m* 1974, Hilda Maria, *d* of Rodolfo Robert; one *s* two *d*. *Heir:* *s* Hon. Thomas Edward Littleton, *b* 7 March 1977. *Address:* PO Box 3358, San José, Costa Rica.

HATTERSLEY, Edith Mary, (Molly Hattersley); educational consultant, since 1990; Visiting Fellow, Institute of Education, University of London (Management Development Centre), since 1990; *b* 5 Feb. 1931; *d* of Michael and Sally Loughran; *m* 1956, Rt Hon. Roy Sydney George Hattersley, *qv*. *Educ:* Consett Grammar Sch.; University College of Hull. BA Hons English (London), CertEd (Hull). Assistant Mistress at schools in Surrey and Yorkshire, 1953–61; Sen. Mistress, Myers Grove Sch., Sheffield, 1961–64; Dep. Headmistress, Kidbrooke Sch., SE3, 1965–69; Headmistress, Hurlingham Sch., SW6, 1969–74; Headmistress, Creighton Sch., N10, 1974–82; Asst Educn Officer, then Dep. Dir of Educn, ILEA, 1983–90. Advr on educnl matters to Trustees of BM, 1978–86. Chairman of Cttee, Assoc. of Head Mistresses, 1975–77; Pres., Secondary Heads Assoc., 1980–81; Chm., Soc. of Educn Consultants, 1994–. Mem. Ct of Governors, LSE, 1970–. FRSA 1982. *Recreation:* reading.

HATTERSLEY, Rt. Hon. Roy Sydney George, PC 1975; BSc (Econ.); MP (Lab) Sparkbrook Division of Birmingham since 1964; Deputy Leader of the Labour Party, 1983–92; *b* 28 Dec. 1932; *s* of Frederick Roy Hattersley, Sheffield; *m* 1956, Molly Hattersley, *qv*. *Educ:* Sheffield City Grammar Sch.; Univ. of Hull. Journalist and Health Service Executive, 1956–64; Mem. Sheffield City Council, 1957–65 (Chm. Housing Cttee and Public Works Cttee). PPS to Minister of Pensions and National Insurance, 1964–67; Jt Parly Sec., DEP (formerly Min. of Labour), 1967–69; Minister of Defence for Administration, 1969–70; Labour Party spokesman: on Defence, 1972; on Educn and Sci., 1972–74; Minister of State, FCO, 1974–76; Sec. of State for Prices and Consumer Protection, 1976–79; principal opposition spokesman on environment, 1979–80, on home affairs, 1980–83, on Treasury and economic affairs, 1983–87, on home affairs, 1987–92. Visiting Fellow: Inst. of Politics, Univ. of Harvard, 1971, 1972; Nuffield Coll., Oxford, 1984–. Dir, Campaign for a European Political Community 1966–67. Columnist: Punch; The Guardian; The Listener, 1979–82; Columnist of the Year, Granada, 1982. Hon. DSc Sheffield Hallam; Hon. DLitt Hull; Hon. DLit West Midlands. *Publications:* Nelson, 1974; Goodbye to Yorkshire (essays), 1976; Politics Apart, 1982; Press Gang, 1983; A Yorkshire Boyhood, 1983; Choose Freedom: the future for Democratic Socialism, 1987; Economic Priorities for a Labour Government, 1987; *novels:* The Maker's Mark, 1990; In That Quiet Earth, 1991; Skylark Song, 1994; Between Ourselves, 1994. *Address:* House of Commons, SW1A 0AA. *Clubs:* Reform, Garrick, Pratt's.

HATTO, Prof. Arthur Thomas, MA; FBA 1991; Head of the Department of German, Queen Mary College, University of London, 1938–77; *b* 11 Feb. 1910; *s* of Thomas Hatto, LLB and Alice Walters; *m* 1935, Margot Feibelmann; one *d*. *Educ:* Dulwich Coll.; King's Coll., London (Fellow, 1971); University Coll., London. BA (London) 1931; MA (with Distinction), 1934. Lektor für Englisch, University of Berne, 1932–34; Asst Lectr in German, KCL, 1934–38; Queen Mary Coll., University of London, 1938 (Head of Dept of German). Temp. Sen. Asst, Foreign Office, 1939–45; part-time Lectr in German, University Coll., London, 1944–45; returned to Queen Mary Coll., 1945; Reader in German Language and Literature, 1946, Prof. of German Language and Literature, 1953, University of London. Governor: SOAS, Univ. of London, 1960 (Foundn Day Lecture, 1970; Hon. Fellow, 1981); QMC, Univ. of London, 1968–70 (Hon. Fellow, QMW, 1992). Chairman: London Seminar on Epic; Cttee 'A' (Theol. and Arts), Central Research Fund, Univ. of London, 1969. Fellow: Royal Anthropological Institute; Royal Asiatic Society (lecture: Plot and character in Kirghiz epic poetry of the mid 19th cent., 1976); Leverhulme Emeritus Fellow (heroic poetry in Central Asia and Siberia), 1977–. Lectr, Rheinisch-Westfälische Akad. der Wissenschaften, Düsseldorf, 1990. Corresp. Mem., Finno-Ugrian Soc., 1978; Associate Mem., Seminar für Sprach-und Kulturwissenschaft Zentralasiens, Univ. of Bonn, 1984. *Publications:* (with R. J. Taylor) The Songs of Neidhart von Reuental, 1958; Gottfried von Strassburg, Tristan (trans. entire for first time) with Tristran of Thomas (newly trans.) with an Introduction, 1960; The Niblungenlied: a new translation, with Introduction and Notes, 1964; editor of Eos, an enquiry by fifty scholars into the theme of the alba in world literature, 1965; (ed for first time with translation and commentary) The Memorial Feast for Kökötöy-khan: a Kirghiz epic poem, 1977; Essays on Medieval German and Other Poetry, 1980; Parzival, Wolfram von Eschenbach, a new translation, 1980; gen. editor, Traditions of Heroic and Epic Poetry, vol. I 1980, vol. II 1989; (re-ed with trans. and commentary) The Manas of Wilhelm Radloff, 1990; articles in learned periodicals. *Recreations:* reading, gardening, walking.

HATTON; *see* Finch Hatton, family name of Earl of Winchilsea.

HATTY, Hon. Sir Cyril (James), Kt 1963; Minister of Finance, Bophuthatswana, 1979–82; *b* 22 Dec. 1908; *o s* of James Hatty and Edith (*née* Russen); *m* 1937, Doris Evelyn, *o d* of James Lane Stewart and Mable Grace Stewart; two *s*. *Educ:* Westminster City Sch. Deputy Dir, O and M Division, UK Treasury, until Jan. 1947; emigrated to S Africa, in industry, Feb. 1947; moved to Bulawayo, Southern Rhodesia, in industry, Jan. 1948. MP for Bulawayo North, Sept. 1950–Dec. 1962; Minister of Treasury, Jan. 1954–Sept. 1962, also Minister of Mines, Feb. 1956–Dec. 1962. FCIS; Fellow, Inst. of Chartered Management Accountants; FIMgt. *Publications:* Digest of SR Company Law, 1952; There's Peace in Baobabwe, 1989. *Recreations:* painting, music. *Address:* Merton Park, Norton, Zimbabwe. *Clubs:* Harare, New (Harare, Zimbabwe).

HAUGHEY, Charles James; Taoiseach (Prime Minister of Ireland), 1979–81, March–Dec. 1982 and 1987–92; *b* 16 Sept. 1925; *s* of Seán Haughey and late Sarah Ann (*née* McWilliams); *m* 1951, Maureen Lemass; three *s* one *d*. *Educ:* Scoil Mhuire, Marino, Dublin; St Joseph's Christian Brothers' Sch., Fairview, Dublin; University College Dublin (BCom); King's Inns, Dublin. Called to Irish Bar, 1949. Member, Dublin Corporation, 1953–55; Member (FF) Dail Eireann for a Dublin constituency, 1957–92 (Dublin NE, 1957–77, then Dublin Artane, later Dublin N Central); Parliamentary Secretary to Minister for Justice, 1960–61; Minister: for Justice, 1961–64; for Agriculture, 1964–66; for Finance, 1966–70; Chairman, Jt Cttee on the Secondary Legislation of the European Communities, 1973–77; Minister for Health and Social Welfare, 1977–79; Leader of the Opposition, 1982–87. President: Fianna Fail Party, 1979–92; European Council, Jan.–June 1990. Hon. Fellow, RHA. Hon. doctorates: Dublin City Univ.; UC Dublin; Univ. of Clermont-Ferrand; Univ. of Notre Dame, USA. *Recreations:* music, art, sailing, riding, swimming. *Address:* Abbeville, Kinsaley, Co. Dublin, Ireland. *T:* (1) 8450111. *Clubs:* Ward Union Hunt (Dublin); Howth Yacht; Royal Cork Yacht.

HAUPTMAN, Prof. Herbert Aaron, PhD; President, Hauptman Woodward Medical Research Institute, Inc. (formerly Medical Foundation of Buffalo), since 1986; *b* 14 Feb. 1917; *s* of Israel Hauptman and Leah Hauptman (*née* Rosenfeld); *m* Edith Citrynell; two *d*. *Educ:* City Coll., NY (BS 1937); Columbia Univ. (MA 1939); Univ. of Maryland (PhD 1955). Census Bureau, 1940–42; Electronics Instructor, USAF, 1942–43, 1946–47; Aerology Officer, USNR, 1943–46; Naval Research Laboratory: Physicist-Mathematician, 1947–70; Rep. of Univ. of Maryland Math. Dept, 1956–70, and part-time Prof., Univ. of Maryland; Head, Mathematical Physics Br., 1965–67; Acting Supt, Math. and Inf. Scis. Div., 1967–68; Head, Applied Math. Br., Math. Div., 1968–69; Head, Math. Staff, Optical Scis Div., 1969–70; Medical Foundation of Buffalo: Head, Math. Biophysics Lab., 1970–72; Dep. Res. Dir, 1972; Exec. Vice-Pres., and Res. Dir, 1972–85; Res. Prof. of Biophysical Scis, State Univ. of NY at Buffalo, 1970–. Mem., US scientific instns. Holder of numerous honours and awards; Hon. DSc: Maryland, 1985; City Coll. of NY, 1986; D'Youville Coll., 1989; Bar-Ilan Univ., Israel, and Columbia Univ., NY, 1990; Technical Univ. of Lodz, Poland, 1992; Queen's Univ., Kingston, Ont, 1993; Hon. Dr Chem., Univ. of Parma, 1989. Nobel Prize in Chemistry (with Jerome Karle), 1985. *Publications:* Solution of the Phase Problem (with J. Karle), 1953; Crystal Structure Determination, 1972; (ed) Direct Methods in Crystallography (procs 1976 Intercongress Symposium), 1978; numerous articles on crystallography in learned jls. *Recreations:* stained glass art, swimming, hiking. *Address:* Hauptman Woodward Medical Research Institute, 73 High Street, Buffalo, NY 14203–1196, USA. *Clubs:* Cosmos (Washington); Saturn (Buffalo).

HAUSER, Frank Ivor, CBE 1968; free-lance director; *b* 1 Aug. 1922; *s* of late Abraham and of Sarah Hauser; unmarried. *Educ:* Cardiff High Sch.; Christ Church, Oxford. Oxford, 1941–42; RA, 1942–45; Oxford, 1946–48. BBC Drama Producer, 1948–51; Director: Salisbury Arts Theatre, 1952–53; Midland Theatre Co., 1945–55. Formed Meadow Players Ltd, which re-opened the Oxford Playhouse, 1956, Dir of Productions, 1956–73; took Oxford Playhouse Co. on tour of India, Pakistan and Ceylon, 1959–60. Produced at Sadler's Wells Opera: La Traviata, 1961; Iolanthe, 1962; Orfeo, 1965; produced: at Oxford Playhouse: Antony and Cleopatra, 1965; Phèdre, 1966; The Promise, 1966; The Silent Woman, 1968; Pippa Passes, 1968; Uncle Vanya, 1969; Curtain Up, 1969; The Merchant of Venice, 1973; also: Il Matrimonio Segreto, Glyndebourne, 1965; A Heritage and its History, Phoenix, 1965; The Promise, Fortune, 1967; Volpone, Garrick, 1967; The Magic Flute, Sadler's Wells, 1967; Kean, Globe, 1971; The Wolf, Apollo, 1973; Cinderella, Casino, 1974; On Approval, Haymarket, 1975; All for Love, Old Vic, 1977; The Importance of Being Earnest, Old Vic, 1980; Captain Brassbound's Conversion, Haymarket, 1982; An Enemy of the People, NY, 1985; Thursday's Ladies, Apollo, 1987; Candida, Arts, 1988; Getting Married, Chichester, 1993; Hobson's Choice, Chichester, 1995. *Recreation:* piano. *Address:* 5 Stirling Mansions, Canfield Gardens, NW6 3JT. *T:* 0171–624 4690.

HAVARD, John David Jayne, CBE 1989; MD; Secretary, British Medical Association, 1980–89; Hon. Secretary, Commonwealth Medical Association, since 1986; *b* 5 May 1924; *s* of late Dr Arthur William Havard and Ursula Jayne Vernon Humphrey; *m* 1st, 1950, Margaret Lucy Lumsden Collis (marr. diss. 1982); two *s* one *d*; 2nd, 1982, Audrey Anne Boutwood, FRCOG, *d* of Rear Adm. L. A. Boutwood, CB, OBE. *Educ:* Malvern Coll.; Jesus Coll., Cambridge (MA, MD, LLM); Middlesex Hosp. Med. Sch. FRCP 1994. Called to the Bar, Middle Temple, 1953. Professorial Med. Unit, Middlesex Hosp., 1950; National Service, RAF, 1950–52; general practice, Lowestoft, 1952–58 (Sec., E Suffolk LMC, 1956–58). British Medical Assoc.: Asst Sec., 1958–64; Under-Sec., 1964–76; Dep. Sec., 1976–79. Short-term Cons., Council of Europe, 1964–67, OECD 1964–69, WHO 1967–, on Road Accident Prevention. Dep. Chm., Staff Side, Gen. Whitley Council for the Health Services, 1975–89; Sec., Managerial, Professional and Staffs Liaison Gp, 1978–89; Member: various Govt Working Parties on Coroners' Rules, Visual Standards for Driving, Licensing of Professional Drivers, etc. Chm., Internat. Driver Behaviour Res. Assoc., 1971–94. Pres., British Acad. of Forensic Scis, 1984–85. Mem., GMC, 1989–94 (Mem., Professional Conduct and Standards Cttee, 1989–94). Lectr, Green Coll., Oxford, 1989. Governor, Malvern Coll., 1984. Gold Medal, Inter-Scandinavian Union for Non-Alcoholic Traffic, 1962; Stevens Lectr and Gold Medallist, 1989; Widmark Award, Internat. Cttee on Alcohol, Drugs and Traffic Safety, 1989; BMA Gold Medal for Dist. Merit, 1990. Pres., CUAC, 1945–46; Captain United Hosps AC, 1946–47; London Univ. Record for 100 yards, 1947. Member, Editorial Board: Blutalkohol, 1968–; Forensic Science Rev. 1989–. *Publications:* Detection of Secret Homicide (Cambridge Studies in Criminology), 1960; Research on Effects of Alcohol and Drugs on Driving Behaviour (OECD), 1968; chapters in textbooks on legal medicine, research advances on alcohol and drugs, etc; many articles in med., legal and sci. periodical lit.; several WHO reports. *Recreations:* history, English countryside. *Address:* 1 Wilton Square, N1 3DL. *T:* 0171–359 2802, *Fax:* 0171–354 9690. *Clubs:* United Oxford & Cambridge University; Achilles.

HAVEL, Václav; writer; President of Czech Republic, since 1993; *b* Prague, 5 Oct. 1936; *s* of Václav M. Havel and Božena Havel (*née* Vavrečková); *m* 1964, Olga Šplíchalová. *Educ:* Faculty of Economy, 1955–57 (unfinished); Drama Dept, Acad. of Arts, Prague, 1966. Chemical Lab. Technician, 1951–55; in Czechoslovak army, 1957–59; stagehand, ABC Theatre, Prague, 1959–60; Theatre on the Balustrade, Prague: stagehand, 1960–61; Asst to Artistic Dir, 1961–63; Literary Manager, 1963–68 (play, Zahradní slavnost (The Garden Party), 1963); Resident Playwright, 1968; Editl Bd, Tvář, 1965; freelance work, 1969–74; labourer, Trutnov Brewery, N Bohemia, 1974; freelance work, 1975–89; Co-Founder, Charter 77 (human rights movement), 1977, and one of its first three spokesmen; Co-Founder, Cttee for Defence of Unjustly Prosecuted (VONS), 1978; under house arrest, 1978–79; imprisoned, Oct. 1979–March 1983; Editl Bd and regular contributor, Lidové noviny, 1987–89; imprisoned, Jan.–May 1989; Co-Founder, Civic Forum, 1989; Pres. of Czech and Slovak Federal Republic, 1989–92. Chm., Young Writers, Czechoslovak Writers Assoc., 1965–69; Member: Czechoslovak Helsinki Cttee, 1989–; Czech Pen Club, 1989–. Holds hon. degrees from many institutions. Awards received include: Austrian State Prize for European Literature, 1969; Erasmus Prize, 1986; Olof Palme Prize, 1989; Simon Bolivar Prize, UNESCO, 1990. *Publications: plays in translation:* The Garden Party, 1969; The Increased Difficulty of Concentration, 1972; The Memorandum, 1980; Selected Plays by Václav Havel, 1991; *others in translation:* Letters to Olga, 1988; Disturbing the Peace, 1990; Open Letters: selected writings 1965–1990, 1991; Summer Meditations, 1992; Toward a Civil Society, 1994; essays in New York Rev. of Books, Granta, Index on Censorship, Independent, etc. *Address:* 11908 Prague 1-Hrad, Czech Republic.

HAVELANGE, Dr Jean Marie Faustin Godefroid, (João); President, Fédération Internationale de Football Association, since 1974; Member, International Olympic Committee, since 1963; *b* 8 May 1916; *m* Anna Maria; one *d*. *Educ:* Univ. of Rio de Janeiro (Dr jur). Has practised law, 1936–. Pres., COMETA SA, Brazil; Man. Dir, several cos in Brazil. Olympic Games participant, swimming, 1936, and water polo, 1952. Hon. Citizen, Chicago, 1994. Order of Special Merit in Sports (Brazil), 1973; Kt, Order of Vasa (Sweden), 1959; Commandeur de l'Ordre du Lion (Senegal), 1973; Gran Cruz de Isabel la Católica (Spain), 1982; Commendatore dell' Ordine dell Repubblica Italiana (Italy), 1980; Commandeur de la Légion d'Honneur (France), 1991. *Recreation:* swimming. *Address:* FIFA, FIFA House, Hitzigweg 11, 8030 Zurich, Switzerland. *T:* (1) 3849595.

HAVELOCK, Sir Wilfrid (Bowen), Kt 1963; *b* 14 April 1912; *s* of late Rev. E. W. Havelock and Helen (*née* Bowen); *m* 1st, 1938, Mrs M. E. Pershouse (*née* Vincent) (marr. diss. 1967); one *s*; 2nd, 1972, Mrs Patricia Mumford, *widow* of Major Philip S. Mumford. *Educ:* Imperial Service Coll., Windsor, Berks. Elected to Kenya Legislative Council, 1948; Chairman, European Elected Members, 1952; Mem., Kenya Executive Council, 1952; Minister for Local Government, Kenya, 1954; Minister for Agriculture, Kenya, 1962–63. Chm., Kenya Assoc. of Hotelkeepers and Caterers, 1974, 1975, 1976. Dep. Chm., Agricl Finance Corp., Kenya, 1964–84; Member: Nat. Irrigation Bd, 1974–79; Hotels and Restaurant Authority, 1975–81. Dir, Baobab Farm Ltd, 1980–. Chm. Trustees, Gertrude's Children's Hosp., 1984–. Badge of Honour and Hon. Vice-Pres., BRCS, 1961. *Address:* PO Box 30181, Nairobi, Kenya. *T:* Nairobi 762835. *Clubs:* Commonwealth Trust; Mombasa, Muthaiga Country, Nairobi, Mount Kenya Safari (Kenya).

HAVELOCK-ALLAN, Sir Anthony James Allan, 4th Bt *cr* 1858; film producer; *b* 28 Feb. 1904; *s* of Allan (2nd *s* of Sir Henry Havelock-Allan, 1st Bt, VC, GCB, MP), and Annie Julia, *d* of Sir William Chaytor, 3rd Bt; *S* brother, 1975; *m* 1st, 1939, Valerie Louise Hobson, *qv* (marr. diss. 1952), *d* of late Comdr Robert Gordon Hobson, RN; one *s* (and one *s* decd); 2nd, 1979, Maria Theresa Consuela (Sara) Ruiz de Villafranca, *d* of late Don Carlos Ruiz de Villafranca (formerly Ambassador to Chile and to Brazil), and Doña Julia Ruiz de Villafranca y Osuña, Villafranca, prov. Madrid. *Educ:* Charterhouse; Switzerland. Artists and Recording Manager, Brunswick Gramophone Co., London and Vox AG, Berlin, 1924–29; entered films as Casting Dir and Producer's Asst, 1933; produced quota films for Paramount; produced for Pinebrook Ltd and Two Cities Films, 1938–40; Assoc. Producer to Noel Coward, 1941; with David Lean and Ronald Neame, formed Cineguild, 1942; Producer, Assoc. Producer or in charge of production for Cineguild, 1942–47; formed Constellation Films, independent co. producing for Rank Org. and British Lion, 1949; Mem. Cinematographic Films Council and Nat. Film Production Council, 1948–51; Mem. Home Office Cttee on Employment of Children in Entertainment; Chm. British Film Academy, 1952; formed with Lord Brabourne and Major Daniel Angel British Home Entertainment to introduce Pay TV, 1958; Chm. Council of Soc. of Film and Television Arts (now BAFTA), 1962, 1963; Mem. Nat. Film Archive Cttee; a Gov. British Film Inst. and Mem. Institute's Production Cttee, 1958–65; Mem. US Academy of Motion Pictures Arts and Sciences, 1970. Films include: This Man is News, This Man in Paris, Lambeth

Walk, Unpublished Story, From the Four Corners (documentary prod and dir), Brief Encounter (shared Academy script nomination), Great Expectations (shared Academy script nomination), Take my Life, Blanche Fury, Shadow of the Eagle, Never Take No for an Answer, Interrupted Journey, Young Lovers (dir Anthony Asquith), Orders to Kill (dir Anthony Asquith), Meet Me Tonight, The Quare Fellow, An Evening with the Royal Ballet (directed two ballets); (for television): National Theatre's Uncle Vanya, Olivier's Othello, Zeffirelli's Romeo and Juliet, David Lean's Ryan's Daughter. *Heir: s* (Anthony) Mark David Havelock-Allan, *qv*. *Address:* c/o Lloyds Bank, Berkeley Square, W1.

HAVELOCK-ALLAN, (Anthony) Mark (David), QC 1993; *b* 4 April 1951; *s* and *heir* of Sir Anthony James Allan Havelock-Allan, Bt, *qv* and Valerie Babette Louise Hobson, *qv*; *m* 1st, 1976, Lucy Clare (marr. diss. 1984), *y d* of late Alexander Plantagenet Mitchell-Innes; 2nd, 1986, Alison Lee Caroline, *o d* of late Leslie Francis Foster; one *s* one *d*. *Educ:* Eton; Durham Univ. (BA Hons Law 1972); Trinity Coll., Cambridge (LLB 1974; Dip. in Internat. Law, 1976). FCIArb 1991. Called to the Bar, Inner Temple, 1974, Bencher, 1995; Asst Recorder, 1993–. *Recreations:* salmon fishing, foreign travel (preferably combined). *Address:* 38 West Square, SE11 4SP. *T:* 0171–582 9009. *Club:* Royal Automobile.

HAVERS, Hon. Philip Nigel; QC 1995; *b* 16 June 1950; *s* of Lord Havers, PC and of Carol Elizabeth (*née* Lay) (who *m* 1993, C. F. Hughesdon, *qv*); *m* 1976, Patricia Frances Searle; one *s* one *d*. *Educ:* Eton Coll.; Corpus Christi Coll., Cambridge. Called to the Bar, Inner Temple, 1974. *Recreations:* tennis, music, wine, gardening, travel. *Address:* 1 Crown Office Row, Temple, EC4Y 7HH. *T:* 0171–797 7500. *Club:* Garrick.

HAVERY, Richard Orbell; QC 1980; **His Honour Judge Havery;** a Circuit Judge and Official Referee, since 1993; *b* 7 Feb. 1934; *s* of late Joseph Horton Havery and Constance Eleanor (*née* Orbell). *Educ:* St Paul's; Magdalen Coll., Oxford (MA 1961). Called to the Bar, Middle Temple, 1962, Bencher, 1989; an Asst Recorder, 1982–86; a Recorder, 1986–93. *Publication:* (with D. A. McI. Kemp and M. S. Kemp) The Quantum of Damages: personal injury claims, 3rd edn, 1967. *Recreations:* music, croquet, steam locomotives. *Address:* St Dunstan's House, 133–137 Fetter Lane, EC4A 1HD. *T:* 0171–936 6022. *Clubs:* Athenæum, Garrick, Hurlingham.

HAVILAND, Denis William Garstin Latimer, CB 1957; MA; CIMgt; FIIM; FRSA; idc; Director, Organised Office Designs Ltd, since 1972; *b* 15 Aug. 1910; *s* of late William Alexander Haviland and of Edyth Louise Latimer. *Educ:* Rugby Sch., St John's Coll., Cambridge (MA, exam. of AMInstT). LMS Rly, 1934–39. Army, RE (Col), 1940–46. Prin., Control Office for Germany and Austria, 1946; Asst Sec., 1947; transf. FO (GS), 1947; seconded to IDC, 1950; transf. Min. of Supply, 1951; Under Sec., 1953; Dep. Sec., 1959; trans. Min. of Aviation, 1959, Deputy Sec., 1959–64. Chm., Preparatory Commn European Launcher Develt Organisation, 1962–64. Jt Man. Dir and Dep. Chm., 1964, Chm. and Man. Dir, 1965–69, Staveley Industries Ltd; Dir, Short Bros Ltd, 1964–81; consultant. Mem. Council, BIM, 1967–83 (Vice-Chm., 1973–74; Chm., Professional Standards Cttee, 1975–82). Member: Management Studies Bd, CNAA, 1974–79; Business and Management Cttee and Academic Cttee, CNAA, 1979–83; Ct, Cranfield Inst. of Technology, 1970–83. Chairman: Confedn of Healing Organisations, 1981–90; Holistic Cancer Council, 1984–86; Mem. Council and Exec. Cttee, British Complementary Medicine Assoc., 1990–. Liveryman, Coachmakers' Co. Verulam Gold Medal, BIM, 1984. *Address:* 113 Hampstead Way, NW11 1JN. *T:* 0181–455 2638. *Club:* Naval and Military.

HAVILLAND; *see* de Havilland.

HAWARDEN, 9th Viscount (Ire.), *cr* 1793; **Robert Connan Wyndham Leslie Maude;** Bt 1705, Baron de Montalt 1785; *b* 23 May 1961; *s* of 8th Viscount and of Susannah Caroline Hyde, *d* of late Maj. Charles Phillips Gardner; *S* father, 1991; *m* 1995, Judith Anne, *yd* of John Bates. *Educ:* St Edmund's Sch., Canterbury; RAC Cirencester. *Heir: b* Hon. Thomas Patrick Cornwallis Maude, *b* 1 Oct. 1964.

HAWES, Ven. Arthur John; Archdeacon of Lincoln, since 1995; *b* 31 Aug. 1943; *s* of John and Sylvia Hawes; *m* 1969, Melanie Harris; one *s* one *d*. *Educ:* City of Oxford High Sch. for Boys; Univ. of E Anglia (BA Hons); Univ. of Birmingham (Dip. in Pastoral Studies; Dip. in Liturgy and Architecture). Ordained deacon, 1968, priest, 1969; Asst Curate, St John the Baptist, Kidderminster, 1968–72; Priest-in-charge, St Richard's, Droitwich, 1972–76; Rector: Alderford with Attlebridge and Swannington, 1976–92; St Faith's, Gaywood, King's Lynn, 1992–95. Chaplain, Hellesdon and David Rice Hosps, Yare Clinic, 1976–92; Rural Dean of Sparham, 1981–91; Hon. Canon of Norwich Cathedral, 1988–. Chm., Norwich Diocesan Bd for Social Responsibility, 1990–95. Comr, NHS Mental Health Act, 1986–94. *Publications:* contribs to theol jls. *Recreations:* golf, theatre, music. *Address:* Archdeacon's House, Northfield Road, Quarrington, Lincs NG34 8RT. *T:* Sleaford (01529) 304348, *Fax:* (01529) 304354. *Club:* Royal Norwich Golf.

HAWKE, family name of **Baron Hawke.**

HAWKE, 11th Baron *cr* 1776, of Towton; **Edward George Hawke,** TD; FRICS; *b* 25 Jan. 1950; *s* of 10th Baron and of his 2nd wife, Georgette Margaret, *d* of George S. Davidson; *S* father, 1992; *m* 1993, Bronwen, *d* of William James, MRCVS. *Educ:* Eton. 2nd Lt, 1st Bn Coldstream Guards, 1970–73; Territorial Army, Queen's Own Yeomanry, 1973–93 (Major).

HAWKE, Hon. Robert James Lee, AC 1979; Adjunct Professor, Research School of Pacific Studies and Social Sciences, Australian National University, since 1992; Prime Minister of Australia, 1983–91; *b* 9 Dec. 1929; *m* 1956, Hazel Masterson (marr. diss.); one *s* two *d* (and one *s* decd); *m* 1995, Blanche d'Alpuget. *Educ:* Univ. of Western Australia (LLB, BA(Econ)); Oxford Univ. (BLitt; Hon. Fellow, University Coll., 1984). Research Officer and Advocate for Aust. Council of Trade Unions, 1958–69. Pres., ACTU, 1970–80. MP (Lab) Wills, Melbourne, 1980–92; Australian Labor Party: Mem., Nat. Exec., 1971–91; Pres., 1973–78; Leader, 1983–91. Leader of the Opposition, Feb.–March 1983. Member: Governing Body of Internat. Labour Office, 1972–80; Board, Reserve Bank of Australia, 1973–80; Aust. Population and Immigration Council, 1976–80; Aust. Manufacturing Council, 1977–80. Chm., Cttee of Experts on Membership of Educn Internat., 1993–. Vis. Prof., Univ. of Sydney, 1992. Hon. DLitt W Australia, 1984; Hon. Dr Nanjing, 1986; Hon. DPhil Hebrew Univ. of Jerusalem, 1987; Hon. LLD Univ. of NSW, 1987. *Publication:* The Hawke Memoirs, 1994. *Recreations:* tennis, cricket, reading, golf, horse racing, snooker. *Address:* c/o GPO Box 36, Sydney, NSW 2001, Australia.

HAWKEN, Lewis Dudley, CB 1983; a Deputy Chairman of the Board of Customs and Excise, 1980–87; *b* 23 Aug. 1931; *s* of late Richard and Doris May Evelyn Hawken; *m* 1954, Bridget Mary Gamble (*d* 1989); two *s* one *d*. *Educ:* Harrow County Sch. for Boys; Lincoln Coll., Oxford (MA). Comr of Customs and Excise, 1975. *Recreations:* collecting Victorian books, tennis. *Address:* 19 Eastcote Road, Ruislip, Mddx HA4 8BE. *T:* Ruislip (01895) 32405. *Clubs:* United Oxford & Cambridge University, MCC.

HAWKER, Rt. Rev. Dennis Gascoyne; Hon. Assistant Bishop, diocese of Norwich, since 1993; *b* 8 Feb. 1921; *o s* of late Robert Stephen and Amelia Caroline Hawker; *m* 1944, Margaret Hamilton, *d* of late Robert and Daisy Henderson; one *s* one *d*. *Educ:* Addey and Stanhope Grammar Sch.; Queens' Coll., Cambridge (MA); Cuddesdon Theological Coll., Oxford. Lloyds Bank, 1939–40. Served War, Commissioned Officer, Royal Marines, 1940–46 (War Substantive Major). Deacon, 1950; Priest, 1951; Asst Curate, St Mary and St Eanswythe, Folkestone, 1950–55; Vicar, St Mark, South Norwood, 1955–60; St Hugh's Missioner, Dio. Lincoln, 1960–65; Vicar, St Mary and St James, Gt Grimsby, 1965–72; Bishop Suffragan of Grantham, 1972–87. Canon and Prebendary of Clifton, in Lincoln Cath., 1964–87; Proctor in Convocation, 1964–74. Hon. Chaplain, RNR, 1979–. *Address:* Pickwick Cottage, Hall Close, Heacham, Kings Lynn, Norfolk PE31 7JT. *T:* Heacham (01485) 570450. *Club:* Army and Navy.

HAWKER, Graham Alfred; Chief Executive, Welsh Water PLC, since 1993; *b* 12 May 1947; *s* of Alfred Hawker and Sarah Rebecca (*née* Bowen); *m* 1967, Sandra Ann Evans; one *s* one *d*. *Educ:* Bedwelty Grammar Sch. CIPFA 1969; FCCA 1981. Trainee Acctnt, Caerphilly DC, 1964–66; Abercarn District Council: Acctnt, 1966–67; Chief Acctnt, 1967–68; Dep. Treas., 1968–70; Chief Auditor, Taf Fechan Water Bd, 1970–74; Welsh Water Authority: Audit Manager, 1974–78; Div. Finance Manager, 1978–84; Chief Acctnt, 1984–86; Dir, Planning and Develt, 1986–87; Dir, Finance, 1987–89; Welsh Water PLC: Dir, Finance, 1989–91; Gp Man. Dir, 1991–93. Dir, Queen Anne's Gate Ltd, 1991–; Chm., Dwr Cymru Ltd, 1993–. CIMgt. *Recreations:* family, walking, wine, career. *Address:* Welsh Water PLC, Plas-y-Ffynnon, Cambrian Way, Brecon, Powys LD3 7HP. *T:* Brecon (01874) 623181; St Teilo House, Llantilio Pertholey, Abergavenny, Gwent NP7 6NY. *Club:* Cardiff and County (Cardiff).

HAWKES, David, MA, DPhil; Research Fellow, All Souls College, Oxford, 1973–83, now Emeritus; *b* 6 July 1923; *s* of Ewart Hawkes and Dorothy May Hawkes (*née* Davis); *m* 1950, Sylvia Jean Perkins; one *s* three *d*. *Educ:* Bancroft's Sch. Open Scholarship in Classics, Christ Church, Oxford, 1941; Chinese Hons Sch., Oxford, 1945–47; Research Student, National Peking Univ., 1948–51. Formerly University Lecturer in Chinese, Oxford; Prof. of Chinese, Oxford Univ., 1959–71. *Publications:* Ch'u Tz'ŭ, Songs of the South, 1959, rev. edn as The Songs of the South: an Ancient Chinese Anthology of Poems by Qu Yuan and Other Poets, 1985; A Little Primer of Tu Fu, 1967, repr. 1987; The Story of the Stone, vol. 1, 1973, vol. 2, 1977, vol. 3, 1980; Classical, Modern and Humane: essays in Chinese Literature (ed J. Minford and Siu-kit Wong), 1989.

HAWKES, Jacquetta, OBE 1952; author and archaeologist; *b* 1910; *yr d* of Sir Frederick Gowland Hopkins, OM and Jessie Anne Stephens; *m* 1st, 1933, Christopher Hawkes, FBA (marr. diss. 1953; he *d* 1992); one *s*; 2nd, 1953, J. B. Priestley, OM (*d* 1984). *Educ:* Perse Sch.; Newnham Coll., Cambridge. MA. Associate, Newnham Coll., 1951. Research and excavation in Great Britain, Eire, France and Palestine, 1931–40; FSA, 1940. Asst Principal, Post-War Reconstruction Secretariat, 1941–43; Ministry of Education, becoming established Principal and Sec. of UK National Commn for UNESCO, 1943–49; retired from Civil Service to write, 1949. John Danz Vis. Prof., Univ. of Washington, 1971. Vice-Pres. Council for Brit. Archæology, 1949–52; Governor, Brit. Film Inst., 1950–55. Archæological adviser, Festival of Britain, 1949–51. Mem., UNESCO Culture Advisory Cttee, 1966–79. Pres., Warwicks, CPRE, 1989–. Life Trustee, Shakespeare Birthplace Trust, 1985. Hon. DLitt Warwick, 1986. *Publications:* Archæology of Jersey, 1939; Prehistoric Britain (with Christopher Hawkes), 1944; Early Britain, 1945; Symbols and Speculations (poems), 1949, A Land, 1951 (£100 Kemsley Award), Guide to Prehistoric and Roman Monuments in England and Wales, 1951, Dragon's Mouth, (play) (with J. B. Priestley); Fables, 1953; Man on Earth, 1954; Journey Down a Rainbow (with J. B. Priestley), 1955; Providence Island, 1959; Man and the Sun, 1962; Unesco History of Mankind, Vol. I, Part 1, 1963; The World of the Past, 1963; King of the Two Lands, 1966; The Dawn of the Gods, 1968; The First Great Civilizations, 1973; (ed) Atlas of Ancient Archaeology, 1975; The Atlas of Early Man, 1976; A Quest of Love, 1980; Mortimer Wheeler: Adventurer in Archaeology, 1982; Shell Guide to British Archaeology, 1986; contrib. learned jls and national periodicals. *Recreation:* natural history. *Address:* Littlecote, Leysbourne, Chipping Campden, Glos GL55 6HL.

HAWKES, Prof. John Gregory, OBE 1994; Mason Professor of Botany and Head of Plant Biology Department, University of Birmingham, 1967–82, now Emeritus; *b* 27 June 1915; *s* of C. W. and G. M. Hawkes; *m* 1941, Ellen Barbara Leather; two *s* two *d*. *Educ:* Univ. of Cambridge. BA, MA, PhD, ScD. Botanist, Potato Res. Station of Commonwealth Agricultural Bureaux, 1939–48, 1951–52; Dir of Potato Research Project, Min. of Ag., Colombia, S America, 1948–51; Lectr and Sen. Lectr in Taxonomic Botany, 1952–61; Prof. of Taxonomic Botany (Personal Chair), 1961–67. Pres., Linnean Soc. of London, 1991–94. Linnean Soc. Gold Medal, 1984. *Publications:* (with J. P. Hjerting) The Potatoes of Argentina, Brazil, Paraguay, and Uruguay, 1969; (with D. A. Cadbury and R. C. Readett) A Computer-Mapped Flora, 1971; (with O. H. Frankel) Crop Genetic Resources for Today and Tomorrow, 1975; Conservation and Agriculture, 1978; (with R. N. Lester and A. D. Skelding) The Biology and Taxonomy of the Solanaceae, 1979; The Diversity of Crop Plants, 1983; (with J. P. Hjerting) The Potatoes of Bolivia, 1989; The Potato: evolution, biodiversity and genetic resources, 1990; (with J. M. M. Engels and M. Worede) Plant Genetic Resources of Ethiopia, 1991; Genetic Conservation of World Crop Plants, 1991; (jtly) Solanaceae III – taxonomy, chemistry, evolution, 1991; contribs to various botanical and plant breeding jls. *Recreations:* walking, gardening, travel, art, archaeology. *Address:* 66 Lordswood Road, Birmingham B17 9BY. *T:* 0121–427 2944. *Club:* Athenæum.

HAWKES, Michael John; Deputy Chairman, Kleinwort, Benson Group plc, 1988–90; *b* 7 May 1929; *s* of Wilfred Arthur Hawkes and Anne Maria Hawkes; *m* 1st, 1957, Gillian Mary Watts; two *s* two *d*; 2nd, 1973, Elizabeth Anne Gurton. *Educ:* Bedford School; New College, Oxford (Exhibnr; MA); Gray's Inn. Kleinwort Sons & Co. Ltd, 1954; Kleinwort, Benson Ltd: Director, 1967; Vice Chm., 1974; Dep. Chm., 1982; Chm., 1983–87; Director, Kleinwort, Benson, Lonsdale plc, 1974–88; Chairman: Sharps Pixley Ltd, 1971–89; Kleinwort Benson Investment Trust, 1984–89. Mem., Management Bd, Sovereign (formerly W Berks) Housing Assoc., 1988–. Gov., The Willink Sch., 1988–. *Recreations:* long distance walking, golf, gardening. *Address:* Brookfield House, Burghfield Common, Berks RG7 3BD. *T:* Burghfield Common (01734) 832912; White Bays, Daymer Lane, Trebetherick, N Cornwall PL27 6SA. *T:* Trebetherick (01208) 862280. *Club:* Leander (Henley on Thames).

HAWKES, Raymond; Deputy Director, Naval Ship Production, 1977–78, retired; *b* 28 April 1920; *s* of Ernest Hawkes; *m* 1951, Joyce Barbara King; one *s* one *d*. *Educ:* RNC Greenwich. 1st cl. Naval Architecture, RCNC; CEng; FRINA. Ship design, Bath, 1942–45 and 1954–56; aircraft carrier research at RAE Farnborough, 1945–49; hydrodynamic research at A.E.W. (Admiralty Experiment Works) Haslar, 1949–54; Principal Admty Overseer, Birkenhead, 1956–58; ship prodn, Bath, 1958–62; Chief Cons. Design, assault ships, survey fleet, small ships and auxiliaries, 1962–69; Senior Officers War Course 1966; Asst Dir Warship Design and Project Man. for Through Deck Cruiser,

1969–72; Dep. Dir, Warship Design, 1972–77. *Recreation:* golf. *Address:* Wood Meadow, Beechwood Road, Combe Down, Bath BA2 5JS. *T:* Combe Down (01225) 832885.

HAWKESBURY, Viscount; Luke Marmaduke Peter Savile Foljambe; *b* 25 March 1972; *s* and *heir* of 5th Earl of Liverpool, *qv*. *Educ:* Ampleforth; Roehampton Inst. *Recreations:* golf, field sports, sailing, sub-aqua. *Address:* Barham Court, Exton, Oakham, Rutland LE15 8AP. *Club:* Bembridge Sailing.

HAWKESWORTH, John Stanley; film and television producer and dramatist; *b* 7 Dec. 1920; *s* of Lt-Gen. Sir John Hawkesworth, KBE, CB, DSO, and Lady (Helen Jane) Hawkesworth; *m* 1943, Hyacinthe Gregson-Ellis; one *s*. *Educ:* Rugby Sch.; Oxford Univ. (BA war degree). Joined Grenadier Guards, 1940; commnd 1941; demobilised 1946 (Captain). Entered film industry as Designer: The Third Man, The Man Who Never Was, The Prisoner, Father Brown; became Producer/Dramatist, Tiger Bay; TV creations include: Upstairs, Downstairs; The Duchess of Duke Street; Danger UXB; The Flame Trees of Thika; The Tale of Beatrix Potter; By the Sword Divided; Oscar; Sherlock Holmes, The Return of Sherlock Holmes and The Sign of Four; Campion; Chelworth; screenplay: Mrs 'Arris Goes to Paris, 1992. One man show (paintings), The Studio, Glebe Place, London, 1989; exhibn, film designs, Austin/Desmond Fine Art, London, 1991; exhibn, paintings of Pembrokeshire, Newport, 1994. Many television awards, incl. Peabody Award, Univ. of Georgia, 1977. *Publications:* Upstairs, Downstairs, 1972; In My Lady's Chamber, 1973. *Recreations:* tennis, hunting, gardening. *Address:* Fishponds House, Knossington, Oakham, Rutland LE15 8LX. *T:* Somerby (01664) 454339.

HAWKESWORTH, (Thomas) Simon (Ashwell); QC 1982; a Recorder of the Crown Court, since 1982; *b* 15 Nov. 1943; *s* of late Charles Peter Elmhirst Hawkesworth and of Felicity Hawkesworth; *m* 1st, 1970, Jennifer Lewis (marr. diss. 1989); two *s*; 2nd, 1990, Dr May Bamber, MD, MRCP; twin *s*. *Educ:* Rugby Sch.; The Queen's Coll., Oxford. MA. Called to the Bar, Gray's Inn, 1967, Bencher 1990; Head of Chambers at York Chambers, 14 Toft Green, York; Asst Recorder, 1980–82. *Address:* Kirby Hill House, Boroughbridge, N Yorks.

HAWKING, Prof. Stephen William, CH 1989; CBE 1982; FRS 1974; Fellow of Gonville and Caius College, Cambridge; Lucasian Professor of Mathematics, Cambridge University, since 1979; *b* 8 Jan. 1942; *s* of Dr F. and Mrs E. I. Hawking; *m* 1965, Jane Wilde (marr. diss.); two *s* one *d*. *Educ:* St Albans Sch.; University Coll., Oxford (BA), Hon. Fellow 1977; Trinity Hall, Cambridge (PhD), Hon. Fellow 1984. Research Fellow, Gonville and Caius Coll., 1965–69; Fellow for distinction in science, 1969–; Mem. Inst. of Theoretical Astronomy, Cambridge, 1968–72; Research Asst, Inst. of Astronomy, Cambridge, 1972–73; Cambridge University: Research Asst, Dept of Applied Maths and Theoretical Physics, 1973–75; Reader in Gravitational Physics, 1975–77, Professor, 1977–79. Fairchild Distinguished Schol., Calif Inst. of Technol., 1974–75. Mem., Pontifical Acad. of Scis, 1986–; Foreign Member: Amer. Acad. of Arts and Scis, 1984; Amer. Philosophical Soc., 1985. Hon. Mem., RAS (Can), 1985. Hon. DSc: Oxon, 1978; Newcastle, Leeds, 1987; Cambridge, 1989; hon. degrees: Chicago, 1981; Leicester, New York, Notre Dame, Princeton, 1982. (Jtly) Eddington Medal, RAS, 1975; Pius XI Gold Medal, Pontifical Acad. of Scis, 1975; Dannie Heinemann Prize for Math. Phys., Amer. Phys. Soc. and Amer. Inst. of Physics, 1976; William Hopkins Prize, Cambridge Philosoph. Soc., 1976; Maxwell Medal, Inst. of Physics, 1976; Hughes Medal, Royal Soc., 1976; Albert Einstein Award, 1978; Albert Einstein Medal, Albert Einstein Soc., Berne, 1979; Franklin Medal, Franklin Inst., USA, 1981; Gold Medal, RAS, 1985; Paul Dirac Medal and Prize, Inst. of Physics, 1987; (jtly) Wolf Foundn Prize for Physics, 1988; Britannica Award, 1989. *Publications:* (with G. F. R. Ellis) The Large Scale Structure of Space-Time, 1973; (ed W. W. Israel) General Relativity: an Einstein centenary survey, 1979; (ed with M. Roček) Superspace and Supergravity, 1981; (ed jtly) The Very Early Universe, 1983; (with W. Israel) 300 Years of Gravitation, 1987; A Brief History of Time, 1988; Black Holes and Baby Universes, 1993. *Address:* Department of Applied Mathematics and Theoretical Physics, Silver Street, Cambridge CB3 9EW. *T:* Cambridge (01223) 337843.

HAWKINS, Prof. Anthony Donald, PhD; FRSE; Director of Fisheries Research, Scottish Office Agriculture and Fisheries Department, since 1987; Hon. Research Professor, Aberdeen University, since 1987; *b* 25 March 1942; *s* of Kenneth St David Hawkins and Marjorie Lillian Hawkins; *m* 1966, Susan Mary Fulker; one *s*. *Educ:* Poole Grammar Sch.; Bristol Univ. (BSc 1st Cl. Hons Zoology, 1963; PhD 1968). Dept of Agriculture and Fisheries for Scotland: Scientific Officer, Marine Lab., Aberdeen, 1965, Chief Scientific Officer, 1987. Consultant to FAO, Peru, 1975; Hon. Lectr, Univ. of St Andrews, 1983. FRSE 1988. A. B. Wood Medal and Prize, Inst. of Acoustics, 1978. *Publications:* (ed and contrib.) Sound Reception in Fish, 1976; (ed and contrib.) Aquarium Systems, 1981; pubns on marine science, fish physiology and salmon biology. *Recreations:* angling, riding, whippet breeding. *Address:* Kincraig, Blairs, by Aberdeen AB1 5YT. *T:* Aberdeen (01224) 868984.

HAWKINS, Sir Arthur (Ernest), Kt 1976; BSc (Eng); CEng, FIMechE, FIEE, FInstE; Chairman 1972–77, Member, 1970–77, Central Electricity Generating Board; *b* 10 June 1913; *s* of Rev. H. R. and Louisa Hawkins; *m* 1939, Laura Judith Tallent Draper; one *s* two *d*. *Educ:* The Grammar Sch., Gt Yarmouth; City of Norwich Technical Coll. Served (prior to nationalisation) with Gt Yarmouth Electricity Dept, Central Electricity Bd and Islington Electricity Dept (Dep. Engr and Gen. Manager); Croydon Dist Manager of SE Elec. Bd, 1948; joined Brit. Electricity Authority as Chief Asst Engr in System Operation Br., 1951; Personal Engrg Asst to Chief Engr, 1954. With the CEGB since its formation in 1957, at first as System Planning Engr and then as Chief Ops Engr, 1959–64; Midlands Regional Dir, 1964–70. Mem., Nuclear Power Adv. Bd, 1973. Chm., F International Ltd, 1978–79. *Publications:* contrib. Jl of Management Studies; various papers to technical instns. *Recreations:* walking, swimming. *Address:* 61 Rowan Road, W6 7DT. *Club:* Hurlingham.

HAWKINS, Catherine Eileen, CBE 1992; World Health Organisation Consultant to Middle Eastern Sector, since 1993; *b* 16 Jan. 1939; *d* of Stanley Richard Hawkins and Mary-Kate Hawkins. *Educ:* La Retraite High Sch., Clifton. SRN, CMB (Pt 1), HVCert, DN London, Queen's Inst. of Nursing Cert, IRCert. General nursing, student, 1956–59; Staff Nursing, Charing Cross Hosp., SRN, 1960–61; Pt 1 midwifery, St Thomas' Hosp., 1961; Health Visitor Student, LCC, RCN, 1961–62; LCC Health Visitor, 1962–63; Bristol CC HV, 1963–64; Project Leader, Bahrain Public Health Service, 1964–66; Field Work Teacher, HV, 1966–68; Health Centre Administrator, 1968–71; Administrator, Res. Div., Health Educn Council, 1971–72; Sen. Nursing Officer, Community Services, 1972–74; Area Nurse Service Capital Planning, Avon AHA, 1974–79; Dist Nursing Officer, Bristol and Weston DHA, 1979–82; Chief Nursing Officer, Southmead DHA, 1982–84; Regional Nursing Officer, 1984, Regl Gen. Manager, 1984–93, SW RHA. *Address:* 20 Gordano Gardens, Easton-in-Gordano, Bristol BS20 0PD.

HAWKINS, Christopher James; Deputy Chairman, Black Country Development Corporation, since 1992; non-executive chairman of a number of cos; *b* 26 Nov. 1937; *s* of Alec Desmond Hawkins and Christina Barbara; *m* Susan Ann Hawkins; two *d*. *Educ:* Bristol Grammar Sch.; Bristol Univ. BA (Hons) Economics. Joined Courtaulds Ltd, Head Office Economics Dept, 1959; seconded to UK aid financed industrial and economic survey of Northern Nigeria, 1960; similar mission to Tunisia to work on 5 year plan, 1961; Research Div. Economist, Courtaulds Ltd, 1961–66, Building Develt Manager, 1965–66; Lectr in Economics, 1966, Sen. Lectr, 1973–83, Univ. of Southampton. MP (C) High Peak, 1983–92. *Publications:* Capital Investment Appraisal, 1971; Theory of the Firm, 1973; The British Economy: what will our children think?, 1982; Britain's Economic Future: an immediate programme for revival, 1983; articles in Jl of Industrial Economics, Amer. Economic Review. *Recreations:* reading, music, sailing. *Address:* 38 Cumberland Drive, Hinchley Wood, Esher, Surrey KT10 0BB.

HAWKINS, Air Vice-Marshal David Richard, CB 1992; MBE 1975; DL; Yeoman Usher of the Black Rod and Deputy Serjeant-at-Arms, House of Lords, since 1994; Gentleman Usher to the Queen, since 1994; *b* 5 April 1937; 2nd *s* of Gp Capt. Charles Richard John Hawkins, OBE, AFC and Norah (*née* Terry); *m* 1st, 1965, Wendy Elizabeth Harris (marr. diss. 1981); one *s* one *d*.; 2nd, 1982, Elaine Kay, *d* of Dr Henry and Mrs Fay Nelson, Dallas, Texas. *Educ:* Worth; Downside Sch.; RMA Sandhurst. Commnd RAF Regt, 1959; Flt Comdr Cyprus and Singapore, 1960–62; ADC to CAS, Air Chief Marshal Sir Charles Elworthy, 1963–65; jun. RAF Regt instructor, RAF Coll., Cranwell, 1965–68; 2nd i/c 63 Sqdn, Singapore, 1968–69; Sqdn Ldr, 1969; Jt Thai/US Mil. R&D Centre as airfield defence specialist, Bangkok, 1969–71; CO, 37 Sqdn, UK, NI and Belize, 1971–74; CO, Queen's Colour Sqdn of RAF, 1974–76; Wing Comdr, on staff of Comdt-Gen., RAF Regt, MoD, 1976–79; Chief, Survivability Br., HQ AAFCE, 1979–82; Sen. Comd RAF Regt Officer, HQ Strike Comd/HQ UK Air, 1982–86; Gp Capt., 1982; CO, RAF Catterick, RAF Regt Depot, 1986–88; NATO Defence Coll., Rome, 1988–89; Dir, RAF Personal Services 1, MoD, 1989–90; Air Cdre, 1989; Dir, RAF Regt, MoD, 1990–91; Comdt-Gen., RAF Regt, and Dir-Gen., RAF Security, 1991–93. Parachute Wings: UK, 1969; Thai Army (Master), 1970; Thai Police (Master), 1970; US Army (1st class), 1971. Vice-Chm. (Air), TA&VRA, Gtr London, 1994–. Freeman, City of London. FIMgt; FITD. DL Gtr London, 1994. *Recreations:* golf, ski-ing, walking, shooting, acting as unpaid groom to wife's horse. *Address:* c/o Barclays Bank, 8/12 Church Street, Walton-on-Thames, Surrey KT12 2YW. *Clubs:* Royal Air Force; Sherborne Golf.

HAWKINS, Desmond, OBE 1963; BBC Controller, South and West, 1967–69; *b* 1908; *m* Barbara Hawkins (*née* Skidmore); two *s* two *d*. Novelist, critic and broadcaster, 1935–45; Literary Editor of New English Weekly and Purpose Quarterly; Fiction Chronicler of The Criterion; Features Producer, BBC West Region, 1946; Head of Programmes, 1955; founded BBC Natural History Unit, 1957. FRSL 1977. Hon. LLD Bristol, 1974. Silver Medal, RSPB, 1959; Imperial Tobacco Radio Award for best dramatisation, 1976 and 1978. *Publications:* Poetry and Prose of John Donne, 1938; Hawk among the Sparrows, 1939; Stories, Essays and Poems of D. H. Lawrence, 1939; Lighter than Day, 1940; War Report, 1946 rev. edn (as BBC War Report), 1985; Sedgemoor and Avalon, 1954; The BBC Naturalist, 1957; Hardy the Novelist, 1965; Wild Life in the New Forest, 1972; Avalon and Sedgemoor, 1973; Hardy, Novelist and Poet, 1976; preface to Richard Jefferies' Wild Life in a Southern County, 1978; Cranborne Chase, 1980; Concerning Agnes, 1982; Hardy's Wessex, 1983; (ed and introd) Wake Smart's Chronicle of Cranborne, 1983; The Tess Opera, 1984; (introd.) Thomas Hardy's Collected Short Stories, 1988; When I Was (autobiog.), 1989; Hardy at Home, 1989; Thomas Hardy: his life and landscape, 1990; Wessex: an anthology, 1991; (ed and introd) William Chafin, Anecdotes and History of Cranborne Chase, 1991; Shelley's First Love, 1992; The Grove Diaries, 1995; Dorset Bedside Book, 1995. *Address:* 2 Stanton Close, Blandford Forum, Dorset DT11 7RT. *T:* Blandford (01258) 454954. *Clubs:* BBC, Royal Over-Seas League.

HAWKINS, Air Vice-Marshal Desmond Ernest, CB 1971; CBE 1967; DFC and Bar, 1942; *b* 27 Dec. 1919; *s* of Ernest and Lilian Hawkins; *m* 1947, Joan Audrey (*née* Munro); one *s*, and one step *s*. *Educ:* Bancroft Sch. Commissioned in RAF, 1938. Served War of 1939–45: Coastal Command and Far East, commanding 36, 230 and 240 Sqdns, 1940–46 (despatches). Commanded RAF Pembroke Dock, 1946–47 (despatches). Staff appts, 1947–50; RAF Staff Coll., 1950; Staff appts, 1951–55; commanded 38 Sqdn, OC Flg, RAF Luqa, 1955–57; jssc, 1957; Staff appts, 1958–61; SASO 19 Gp, 1961–63; commanded RAF Tengah, 1963–66; idc 1967; commanded RAF Lyneham, 1968; SASO, HQ, RAF Strike Command, 1969–71; Dir-Gen., Personal Services (RAF), MoD, 1971–74; Dep. Man. Dir, Services Kinema Corp., 1974–80. *Recreation:* sailing. *Clubs:* Royal Air Force, Cruising Association, Royal Cruising; Royal Lymington Yacht.

HAWKINS, Prof. Eric William, CBE 1973; Director, Language Teaching Centre, University of York, 1965–79, now Professor Emeritus; *b* 8 Jan. 1915; *s* of James Edward Hawkins and Agnes Thompson (*née* Clarie); *m* 1938, Ellen Marie Thygesen, Copenhagen; one *s* one *d*. *Educ:* Liverpool Inst. High Sch.; Trinity Hall, Cambridge (Open Exhibn). MA, CertEd, FIL. War Service, 1st Bn The Loyal Regt, 1940–46 (despatches 1945); wounded N Africa, 1943; Major 1945. Asst Master, Liverpool Coll., 1946–49; Headmaster: Oldershaw Grammar Sch., Wallasey, 1949–53; Calday Grange Grammar Sch., Ches, 1953–65. Member: Central Adv. Council for Educn (England) (Plowden Cttee), 1963–66; Rampton Cttee (educn of ethnic minorities), 1979–81. Hon. Prof., University Coll. of Wales, Aberystwyth, 1979–89. Gold Medal, Inst. Linguists, 1971. Comdr, Ordre des Palmes Académiques (France), 1986. *Publications:* (ed) Modern Languages in the Grammar School, 1961; (ed) New Patterns in Sixth Form Modern Language Studies, 1970; A Time for Growing, 1971; Le français pour tout le monde, vols 1–5, 1974–79; Modern Languages in the Curriculum, 1981; Awareness of Language: an Introduction, 1984; (ed) Intensive Language Teaching and Learning, 1988. *Recreations:* walking, cello.

See also M. R. Jackson.

HAWKINS, Frank Ernest; Chairman, 1959–73, and Managing Director, 1956–73, International Stores Ltd, Mitre Square, EC3, retired; *b* 12 Aug. 1904; 2nd *s* of late George William and Sophie Hawkins; *m* 1933, Muriel, *d* of late Joseph and Isabella Sinclair; two *s* one *d*. *Educ:* Leyton County High Sch. Joined staff of International Stores Ltd as boy clerk, 1919; apptd: Asst Sec., 1934; Sec., 1935; Director, 1949; Managing Dir, 1956; Vice-Chm., 1958; Chairman, 1959.

HAWKINS, Sir Howard Caesar, 8th Bt *cr* 1778, of Kelston, Somersetshire; *b* 17 Nov. 1956; *e s* of Sir Humphry Hawkins, 7th Bt and of Anita, *d* of C. H. Funkey, Johannesburg; *S* father, 1993. *Educ:* Hilton Coll.; S African Air Force, 1975. *Heir:* *b* Richard Caesar Hawkins, *b* 29 Dec. 1958.

HAWKINS, Prof. John David, FBA 1993; Professor of Ancient Anatolian Languages, School of Oriental and African Studies, University of London, since 1993; *b* 11 Sept. 1940; *s* of John and Audrey Hawkins. *Educ:* Bradfield Coll.; University Coll., Oxford (BA 1962; MA 1965); Inst. of Archaeol., Univ. of London (Postgrad. Dip. 1964). School of Oriental and African Studies, University of London: Res. Fellow, 1964–67; Lectr, then Sen. Lectr, 1967–93. *Publications:* The Hieroglyphic Inscription of the Sacred Pool Complex at Boğazköy-Hattusa, 1994; Corpus of Hieroglyphic Luwian Inscriptions, 1995. *Recreation:* gardening. *Address:* School of Oriental and African Studies, University of London, Thornhaugh Street, WC1H 0XG. *T:* 0171-323 6291.

HAWKINS, Nicholas John; MP (C) Blackpool South, since 1992; *b* 27 March 1957; *s* of Arthur Ernest Hawkins, PhD, FInstP, CPhys and Patricia Jean Hawkins, BSc (*née* Papworth); *m* 1979, Angela Margaret Turner, MA Oxon, IPFA; two *s* one *d*. *Educ:* Bedford Modern Sch.; Lincoln Coll., Oxford (MA). ACIArb. Called to the Bar, Middle Temple, 1979 (Harmsworth Sen. Scholar). Practised from chambers in Birmingham and Northampton, 1979–86. Mem., Bar Council, 1988–95. Company Legal Advr, Access, 1987–89; Gp Legal Advr, Lloyds Abbey Life, 1989–92. Contested (C) Huddersfield, 1987. Sec., Cons. Back bench Educn Cttee, 1993–; Chm., Cons. Back bench Sports Cttee, 1994–; Vice-Chm., All-Party Gp on Insurance and Financial Services, 1995–. Chm., W Lancs Br., Marie Curie Cancer Care. *Publications:* (jtly) 1992: The Single Market in Insurance, 1990; Competitive Sport in Schools, 1994; articles on transport hist. *Recreations:* cricket, music, theatre, transport history, Rugby, soccer, swimming. *Address:* House of Commons, SW1A 0AA. *T:* 0171–219 6329. *Club:* Carlton.

HAWKINS, Sir Paul (Lancelot), Kt 1982; TD 1945; FRICS; *b* 7 Aug. 1912; *s* of L. G. Hawkins and of Mrs Hawkins (*née* Peile); *m* 1st, 1937, E. Joan Snow (*d* 1984); two *s* one *d*; 2nd, 1985, Tina Daniels. *Educ:* Cheltenham Coll. Joined Family Firm, 1930; Chartered Surveyor, 1933. Served in TA, Royal Norfolk Regt, 1933–45; POW Germany, 1940–45. MP (C) SW Norfolk, 1964–87. An Asst Govt Whip, 1970–71; a Lord Comr of the Treasury, 1971–73; Vice-Chamberlain of HM Household, 1973–74. Mem., H of C (Services) Select Cttee, 1976–87. Mem., Delegn to Council of Europe and WEU, 1976–87; Chm., Agricl Cttee, Council of Europe, 1985–87. Dir (non-exec.), Gorham Bateson (Agriculture) Seed Specialists, 1989–. CC Norfolk, 1949–70, Alderman, 1968–70. *Recreations:* walking, gardening, travel. *Address:* Stables, Downham Market, Norfolk PE38 9NL.

HAWKINS, Richard Graeme; QC 1984; **His Honour Judge Hawkins;** a Circuit Judge, since 1989; *b* 23 Feb 1941; *s* of late Denis William Hawkins and Norah Mary (*née* Beckingsale); *m* 1969, Anne Elizabeth, *d* of Dr and Mrs Glyn Edwards, The Boltons, Bournemouth; one *s* one *d*. *Educ:* Hendon County Sch.; University College London (LLB Hons 1962). Called to the Bar, Gray's Inn, 1963. A Recorder, 1985–89. Mem., Hon. Soc. of Gray's Inn, 1959–. *Recreation:* sailing. *Address:* Central Criminal Court, EC4M 7EH. *T:* 0171–248 3277. *Club:* Royal Thames Yacht.

HAWKINS, Rt. Rev. Richard Stephen; *see* Plymouth, Bishop Suffragan of.

HAWKSLEY, (Philip) Warren; MP (C) Halesowen and Stourbridge, since 1992; Director, Edderton Hall, since 1989; *b* 10 March 1943; *s* of late Bradshaw Warren Hawksley and Monica Augusta Hawksley. *Educ:* Denstone Coll., Uttoxeter. Employed by Lloyd's Bank after leaving school. Member: Salop County Council, 1970–81; West Mercia Police Authority, 1977–81. Contested (C) The Wrekin, 1987; MP (C) The Wrekin, 1979–87. Mem., Select Cttee on Employment, 1986–87 and 1994–; Jt Sec., Cons. Back bench Cttee for New Town and Urban Affairs, 1984–87; Sec., W Midlands Cons. Parly Gp, 1992–. Hon. Pres., Catering Industries Liaison Council, 1992–. *Recreations:* collecting political memorabilia, shooting, good food and wines. *Address:* Edderton Hall, Forden, near Welshpool, Powys SY21 8RZ.

HAWKSWORTH, Prof. David Leslie, DSc; FIBiol, FLS; Director, International Mycological Institute, CAB International, since 1983; *b* Sheffield, 5 June 1946; *e s* of late Leslie Hawksworth and Freda Mary (*née* Dolamore); *m* 1968, Madeleine Una Ford; one *s* one *d*. *Educ:* Herbert Strutt Grammar Sch., Belper; Univ. of Leicester (BSc 1967; PhD 1970; DSc 1980). FIBiol 1982; FLS 1969. Mycologist, Commonwealth Mycological Inst., Kew, 1969–81; sci. asst to Exec. Dir, CAB, 1981–83. Visiting Professor: Univ. of Riyadh, 1978; Univ. of Reading, 1984–; Univ. of Assiut, 1985; Univ. of Kent 1990–; Univ. of London, 1992–. President: British Lichen Soc., 1986–87; Eur. Congress of Mycologists, 1989; Br. Mycol Soc., 1990; Internat. Mycol Assoc., 1990–94 (Hon. Pres., 1994–); Internat. Union Biol Sci., 1994–; Vice-Pres., Linnean Soc., 1985–88; Treasurer and Editor-in-Chief, Systematics Assoc., 1972–86; Treas., Internat. Congress of Systematic and Evolutionary Biol., 1989–; Sec.-Gen., Internat. Mycol Assoc., 1977–90; Chairman: Internat Commn on Taxonomy of Fungi, 1982–; Ruislip-Northwood Woods Adv. Working Party, 1979–82; Chief Rapp., CAB Internat. Review Confs, 1985, 1990, 1993. Hon. Member: Soc. Lichenologica Italiana, 1989; Ukranian Bot. Soc., 1992; Mycol. Soc. of America, 1994. First Bicent. Medal, Linnean Soc., 1978. Editor: The Lichenologist, 1970–90; Systema Ascomycetum, 1986–; Mycosystema, 1987–. *Publications:* (jtly) Dictionary of the Fungi, 6th edn 1971 to 8th edn 1995; (ed jtly) Air Pollution and Lichens, 1973; Mycologist's Handbook, 1974; (ed) The Changing Flora and Fauna of Britain, 1974; (jtly) Lichens as Pollution Monitors, 1976; (ed jtly) Lichenology: progress and problems, 1976; (jtly) Lichenology in the British Isles 1568–1975, 1977; (jtly) Key Works to the Fauna and Flora of the British Isles and Northwestern Europe, 4th edn 1978, 5th edn 1988; (ed) Advancing Agricultural Production in Africa, 1984; (jtly) The Lichen-Forming Fungi, 1984; (jtly) The British Ascomycotina, 1985; (ed jtly) Coevolution and Systematics, 1986; (ed jtly) Coevolution of Fungi with Plants and Animals, 1988; (ed jtly) Living Resources for Biotechnology, 1988; (ed) Prospects in Systematics, 1988; (jtly) International Mycological Directory, 1990; (ed) Frontiers in Mycology, 1991; (ed) Improving the Stability of Names, 1991; (ed) The Biodiversity of Microorganisms and Invertebrates: their role in sustainable agriculture, 1991; (jtly) Lichen Flora of Great Britain and Ireland, 1992; (jtly) Biodiversity and Biosystematic Priorities: microorganisms and invertebrates, 1993; (jtly) IMI: retrospect and prospect, 1993; (ed) Identification and Characterization of Pest Organisms, 1994; (ed) Ascomycete Systematics: problems and perspectives in the nineties, 1994; (jtly) The Biodiversity of Micro-organisms and the Role of Microbial Resource Centres, 1994; numerous papers on biodiversity, botanical nomenclature, fungi (including lichens). *Recreations:* lichenology, natural history, bionomenclature, second-hand books, swimming. *Address:* International Mycological Institute, Bakeham Lane, Egham, Surrey TW20 9TY.

HAWLEY, Sir Donald (Frederick), KCMG 1978 (CMG 1970); MBE 1955; HM Diplomatic Service, retired; British High Commissioner in Malaysia, 1977–81; Barrister-at-law; consultant in Middle Eastern and South East Asian affairs; *b* 22 May 1921; *s* of late Mr and Mrs F. G. Hawley, Little Gaddesden, Herts; *m* 1964, Ruth Morwenna Graham Howes, *d* of late Rev. P. G. Howes and of Mrs Howes, Charmouth, Dorset; one *s* three *d*. *Educ:* Radley; New Coll., Oxford (MA). Served in HM Forces, 1941. Sudan Political Service, 1944; joined Sudan Judiciary, 1947. Called to Bar, Inner Temple, 1951. Chief Registrar, Sudan Judiciary, and Registrar-Gen. of Marriages, 1951; resigned from Sudan Service, 1955; joined HM Foreign Service, 1955; FO, 1956: Political Agent, Trucial States, in Dubai, 1958; Head of Chancery, British Embassy, Cairo, 1962; Counsellor and Head of Chancery, British High Commission, Lagos, 1965; Vis. Fellow, Dept of Geography, Durham Univ., 1967; Counsellor (Commercial), Baghdad, 1968; HM Consul-General, Muscat, 1971; HM Ambassador to Oman, 1971–75; Asst Under Sec. of State, FCO, 1975–77. Mem., London Adv. Cttee, Hongkong and Shanghai Banking Corp.; Chairman: Ewbank Preece Gp, 1982–86, Special Advr, 1986–; Centre for British Teachers, 1987–91. Pres. Council, Reading Univ., 1987–94; Vice-Pres., Anglo-Omani Soc., 1981–; Chairman: British Malaysian Soc., 1983–95 (Vice Pres., 1993–); Confedn of British and SE Asia Socs., 1988–; Sudan Pensioners Assoc., 1992–; Royal Soc. for Asian Affairs, 1994. Gov., ESU, 1989–. Pres., Sudan Defence Force Dinner Club. Hon. DLitt Reading, 1994. *Publications:* Handbook for Registrars of Marriage and Ministers of Religion, 1963 (Sudan Govt pubn); Courtesies in the Trucial States, 1965; The Trucial States, 1971; Oman and its Renaissance, 1977; Courtesies in the Gulf Area, 1978; Manners and Correct Form in the Middle East, 1984; Sandtracks in the Sudan, 1995. *Recreations:* tennis, travel, gardening; Hon. Sec., Sudan Football Assoc., 1952–55. *Address:* Little Cheverell House, near Devizes, Wilts SN10 4JJ. *T:* Devizes (01380) 813322. *Clubs:* Travellers, Beefsteak.

HAWLEY, Henry Nicholas, (8th Bt *cr* 1795). *S* father, 1988, but does not use the title and his name is not on the Official Roll of Baronets.

HAWLEY, James Appleton, TD 1969; Lord-Lieutenant for Staffordshire, since 1993; Chairman and Managing Director, John James Hawley (Speciality Works) Ltd; *b* 28 March 1937; *s* of late John J. Hawley and of Mary Hawley, JP, Walsall; *m* 1961, Susan, *d* of Alan Stott, JP, DL, Armitage; one *s* two *d*. *Educ:* Uppingham; St Edmund Hall, Oxford (MA). Called to the Bar, Middle Temple, 1961. Nat. Service, 2nd Lieut South Staffs Regt, Cyprus; Lieut to Major, Staffs Yeomanry Regt (QORR). Chm., J. W. Wilkinson & Co.; Dir, Stafford Railway Building Soc. Past Pres., Made-Up Textiles Assoc.; Past Chm., Camping Trade Assoc. Vice-Pres., Walsall Soc. for the Blind (Chm., 1977–92); Pres., Vice-Pres., and Patron, many organisations and charities, Staffs. Freeman, City of London; Liveryman, Saddlers' Co. JP Staffs 1969; High Sheriff, Staffs, 1976–77; DL Staffs 1978. KStJ 1993. *Recreations:* family, Staffordshire, outdoor pursuits. *Address:* Lieutenancy Office, Martin Street, Stafford ST16 2LH. *T:* Stafford (01785) 223121.

HAWLEY, Dr Robert, FEng 1979; FIEE, FIMechE, FInstP; Chief Executive, Nuclear Electric plc, since 1992; *b* 23 July 1936; *s* of William and Eva Hawley; *m* 1962, Valerie (*née* Clarke); one *s* one *d*. *Educ:* Wallasey Grammar Sch.; Wallasey Technical Coll.; Birkenhead Technical Coll.; Durham Univ. (BSc 1959; PhD 1963); Newcastle upon Tyne Univ. (DSc 1976). FIEE 1970; FIMechE 1987; FInstP 1971 (MInstP 1959). Student apprentice, BICC, Prescot, 1952–55; C. A. Parsons & Co. Ltd: Head of Res. Team, 1961–64; electrical designer, 1964–66; Dep. Chief Generator Engr, 1966–70; Chief Elec. Engr, 1970–74; Dir of Prodn and Engrg, 1974–76; Man. Dir, NEI Parsons Ltd, 1976–84; NEI plc: Man. Dir, Power Engrg Gp, 1984–89; Man. Dir, 1989–92; Chm., NEI ABB Gas Turbines Ltd, 1990–92. Dir of various subsid. cos, C. A. Parsons Ltd, NEI Parsons Ltd and NEI plc, 1973–92; Mem. Bd, Rolls-Royce plc, 1989–92. Non-Executive Director: ABB Transportation Hldgs Ltd, 1993–; W. S. Atkins Ltd, 1994–. Member: NE Indust. Develt Bd, DTI, 1989–92; Bd, Northern Develt Co., 1989–92; Industrial Develt Adv. Bd, DTI, 1994–. Chairman: Internat. Cttee on Rotating Machines, 1974–77; Hawley Cttee on Corporate Governance Information Management, 1993–. Mem., British Nat. Cttee, 1979, CIGRE; Mem., Annual Review Sub-group, and Chm., Energy Wkg Pty, 1986–87, ACARD. Institution of Electrical Engineers: Mem., NE Students Cttee, 1956–62 (sometime Chm.); Mem. Cttee, NE Centre, 1964–79 (Chm., 1978–79); Mem. Council, 1965–68 and 1978–80; Mem. Exec., 1978; Chm., Engrg Policy Bd, 1979–80; Vice Pres., 1991–; Dep. Pres., 1994–; Chm., Internat. Bd, 1992–94. Mem. Council, Fellowship of Engrg, 1981–84. Pres., Energy Industries Club, 1989–91. Mem., Boat and Shoreworks Cttee, RNLI, 1992–. Lectures include: C. A. Parsons Meml, IEE and Royal Soc., 1977; Hunter Meml, IEE, 1990; Blackadder, NEC Inst., 1992; Wilson Campbell Meml, Univ. of Newcastle upon Tyne, 1994; Bowden, UMIST, 1994. Member: Court, Univ. of Newcastle upon Tyne, 1979–; Bd of Advrs, Elec. Engrg, Univ. of London, 1982–. Trustee, Power Aid Logistics, 1993–. Freeman, City of London, 1985. Hon. FINucE 1994, Waverley Gold Medal, RSA, 1960, Achievement Medal, for outstanding contribn to power engrg, IEE, 1989. *Publications:* (with A. Maitland) Vacuum as an Insulator, 1967; (with A. A. Zaky): Dielectric Solids, 1970; Conduction and Breakdown in Mineral Oil, 1973; Fundamentals of Electromagnetic Field Theory, 1974; technical papers on electrical breakdown in vacuum, liquids and solids, electrical machine design and power generation. *Recreations:* gardening, philately, community affairs. *Address:* Nuclear Electric plc, Barnett Way, Barnwood, Gloucester GL4 7RS. *T:* Gloucester (01452) 654270. *Club:* Athenæum.

HAWORTH, Rev. Betsy Ellen; Non-Stipendiary Minister, St Paul, Astley Bridge, Bolton, Diocese of Manchester, since 1989; *b* 23 July 1924; *d* of Ambrose and Annie Kenyon; *m* 1953, Rev. Fred Haworth (*d* 1981); one *s* two *d*. *Educ:* William Temple Coll. IDC (C of E). Licensed as lay worker, dio. Manchester, 1952, dio. Blackburn, 1965; elected Mem., Church Assembly, 1965–70, Gen. Synod, 1970–75, 1975–80, 1980–85, Ex-officio Mem., 1985–88. Advr for Women's Ministry, dio. Manchester, 1971–81. Third Church Estates Comr, 1981–88. Deaconess 1980; ordained Deacon, 1989. Examining Chaplain to Bishop of Manchester, 1981–94. *Address:* 14 Sharples Hall Fold, Sharples, Bolton, Lancs BL1 7EH.

HAWORTH, John Liegh W.; *see* Walker-Haworth.

HAWORTH, Lionel, OBE 1958; FRS 1971; RDI 1976; FEng; Senior Partner, Lionel Haworth and Associates; *b* 4 Aug. 1912; *s* of John Bertram Haworth and Anna Sophia Ackerman; *m* 1956, Joan Irene Bradbury; one *s* one *d*. *Educ:* Rondebosch Boys' High Sch.; Univ. of Cape Town. Cape Town Corp's Gold Medal and schol. tenable abroad. BSc (Eng); FIMechE; FRAeS. Graduate Apprentice, Associated Equipment Co., 1934; Rolls-Royce Ltd, Derby: Designer, 1936; Asst Chief Designer, 1944; Dep. Chief Designer, 1951; Chief Designer (Civil Engines), 1954; Chief Engr (Prop. Turbines), 1962; Bristol Siddeley Engines Ltd: Chief Design Consultant, 1963; Chief Designer, 1964; Dir of Design, Aero Div., 1965, Dir of Design, Aero Div., Rolls-Royce Ltd, 1968–77. Brit. Gold Medal for Aeronautics, 1971; Founder Fellow, Fellowship of Engineering, 1976. *Recreation:* sailing. *Address:* 10 Hazelwood Road, Sneyd Park, Bristol BS9 1PX. *T:* Bristol (0117) 968 3032.

HAWORTH, Sir Philip, 3rdBt *cr* 1911, of Dunham Massey, Co. Chester; farmer; *b* 17 Jan. 1927; *s* of Sir Arthur Geoffrey Haworth, 2nd Bt, and Emily Dorothea, (Dorothy) (*d* 1980), *er d* of H. E. Gaddum; *S* father, 1987; *m* 1951, Joan Helen, *d* of late S. P. Clark, Ipswich; four *s* one *d*. *Educ:* Dauntsey's; Reading Univ. BSc (Agric.) 1948. *Recreations:* music, art, ornithology. *Heir:* *s* Christopher Haworth [*b* 6 Nov. 1951; *m* 1994, Susan Rachel, *d* of David Ives and *widow* of Jonathan Dent]. *Address:* Free Green Farm, Over Peover, Knutsford, Cheshire WA16 9QX. *Club:* Farmers'.

HAWORTH, Richard James; His Honour Judge Haworth; a Circuit Judge, since 1993; *b* 1 Dec. 1943; *s* of late Richard Arthur Haworth and Lily Haworth; *m* 1974, Jane Seren, *y d* of His Honour John Glyn Burrell, QC and of Dorothy Burrell. *Educ:* Ampleforth. Called to the Bar, Inner Temple, 1970; practised on SE Circuit, 1970–93; a Recorder, 1990–93. Mem., Inner Temple Bar Liaison Cttee, 1987–93. *Recreations:* music, English naive paintings, carpentry, walking.

HAWTHORN, Ven. Christopher John; Archdeacon of Cleveland, since 1991; *b* 29 April 1936; *s* of late Rev. John Christopher Hawthorn and Susan Mary Hawthorn; *m* 1964, Elizabeth Margaret Lowe; three *s* one *d*. *Educ:* Marlborough Coll.; Queens' Coll., Cambridge (MA Hons); Ripon Hall, Oxford. Deacon 1962, priest 1963; Asst Curate,

Sutton-in-Holderness, 1962–66; Vicar: St Nicholas, Hull, 1966–72; Christ Church, Coatham, 1972–79; St Martin's-on-the-Hill, Scarborough, 1979–91; Proctor in Convocation, 1987–90; Canon of York, 1987–. *Recreations:* gardening, fell walking, sport. *Address:* Park House, Rosehill, Great Ayton, Middlesbrough TS9 6BH. *T:* Middlesbrough (01642) 723221.

HAWTHORNE, James Burns, CBE 1982; media consultant; Partner, James Hawthorne Associates; *b* 27 March 1930; *s* of Thomas Hawthorne and Florence Hawthorne (*née* Burns); *m* 1958, Patricia King; one *s* two *d*. *Educ:* Queen's Univ., Belfast (BA); Stranmillis Coll. of Educn. Master at Sullivan Upper Sch., Holywood, 1951–60; joined Educn Dept, BBC, 1960; Schools Producer in charge, N Ireland, 1967; Chief Asst, N Ireland, 1969–70; seconded to Hong Kong Govt, as Controller Television, 1970; Dir of Broadcasting, Hong Kong, 1972–77 (resigned from BBC staff, 1976, *ie* seconded status ended; rejoined BBC, Jan. 1978); Controller, BBC NI, 1978–87. Member: NI Council for Educn Develt, 1980–85; Fair Employment Agency, 1988–89; Accreditation Panel, Hong Kong Acad. for the Performing Arts, 1988. Chairman: Ulster History Circle, 1987–89; NI Health Promotion Agency (formerly Unit), 1988–; Cultural Traditions Gp, 1989–90; NI Community Relations Council, 1990–. Vis. Prof., Media Studies, Univ. of Ulster, 1993–. JP Hong Kong, 1972–77. Queen's Univ. New Ireland Soc. award for community relations work, 1967; Winston Churchill Fellowship, 1968; FRTS 1988 (Cyril Bennett Award, 1986). Hon. LLD QUB, 1988. *Publications:* (ed) Two Centuries of Irish History, 1966, repr. 1967, 1969, rev. edn 1974; Reporting Violence: lessons from Northern Ireland, 1981. *Recreations:* angling, music. *Address:* The Long Mill, Lissara, 67 Kilmore Road, Crossgar, N Ireland BT30 9HJ. *Club:* BBC.

HAWTHORNE, Nigel Barnard, CBE 1987; self-employed actor and writer; *b* Coventry, 5 April 1929; *s* of Charles Barnard Hawthorne and Agnes Rosemary (*née* Rice). *Educ:* Christian Brothers' Coll., Cape Town, S Africa. Entered theatre professionally, 1950; returned to England, 1951, where he has worked ever since, with the exception of a small number of engagements abroad. *Stage:* Otherwise Engaged, 1976; Privates on Parade, 1978 (Best Supporting Actor, SWET and Clarence Derwent awards); Peer Gynt, and Tartuffe, with RSC, 1983–84 (Tartuffe televised 1985); Across from the Garden of Allah, 1986; Jacobowski and the Colonel, NT, 1986; The Magistrate, NT, 1986; Hapgood, Aldwych, 1988; Shadowlands, Queen's, 1989, Broadway, 1990–91 (Tony Award for Best Actor, 1991); The Madness of George III, NT, 1992 (Olivier Award for Best Actor, 1992; Evening Standard Best Actor Award, 1992), American tour, 1993, European tour, 1994; The Clandestine Marriage (also dir), Queen's, 1994; *television:* Marie Curie, 1977; Destiny, 1978; Edward and Mrs Simpson, 1978; The Knowledge, 1979; Yes Minister (series), annually 1980–83, 1985–86, Yes, Prime Minister (series), 1986, 1987 (Broadcasting Press Guild Award, 1980; BAFTA Best Light Entertainment Performance, 1981, 1982, 1986, 1987); The Critic, 1982; The Barchester Chronicles, 1982; Mapp and Lucia, 1984–86; The Miser, 1988; The Shawl, 1989; Relatively Speaking, 1989; The Trials of Oz, 1991; Flea-Bites, 1992; Late-Flowering Lust, 1994; *films:* Firefox, 1981; Gandhi, 1981; Golda, 1981; John Paul II, 1983; The House, 1984; The Chain, 1985; Demolition Man, 1993; The Madness of King George, 1994. Hon. MA: Sheffield, 1987; Leicester, 1994; Hon. DLitt Hertfordshire, 1992. *Recreations:* swimming, gardening, painting.

HAWTHORNE, Prof. Sir William (Rede), Kt 1970; CBE 1959; MA; ScD; FRS 1955; FEng; FIMechE; Master of Churchill College, Cambridge, 1968–83; Hopkinson and ICI Professor of Applied Thermodynamics, University of Cambridge, 1951–80; Head of Department of Engineering, 1968–73; *b* 22 May 1913; *s* of William Hawthorne, MInstCE, and Elizabeth C. Hawthorne; *m* 1939, Barbara Runkle (*d* 1992), Cambridge, Massachusetts, USA; one *s* two *d*. *Educ:* Westminster Sch.; Trinity Coll., Cambridge; Massachusetts Institute of Technology, USA. Development Engineer, Babcock & Wilcox Ltd, 1937–39; Scientific Officer, Royal Aircraft Establishment, 1940–44; seconded to Sir Frank Whittle, 1940–41; British Air Commission, Washington, 1944; Dep. Dir Engine Research, Min. of Supply, 1945; Massachusetts Institute of Technology: Associate Prof. of Mechanical Engineering, 1946; George Westinghouse Prof. of Mechanical Engineering, 1948–51; Jerome C. Hunsaker Prof. of Aeronautical Engineering, 1955–56; Vis. Inst. Prof., 1962–63; Mem. Corporation, 1969–74. Chairman: Home Office Scientific Adv. Council, 1967–76; Defence Scientific Adv. Council, 1969–71; Adv. Council for Energy Conservation, 1974–79; Member: Energy Commn, 1977–79; Standing Commn on Energy and the Environment, 1978–81. Director: Dracone Developments Ltd, 1958–87; Cummins Engine Co. Inc., 1974–86. Governor, Westminster Sch., 1956–76. A Vice-Pres., Royal Soc., 1969–70 and 1979–81; Mem. Council, 1968–70, 1979–81 (Royal Medal, 1982). Foreign Associate: US Nat. Acad. of Sciences, 1965; US Nat. Acad. of Engrg, 1976. Fellow, Imperial Coll., London Univ., 1983. Hon. FAIAA; Hon. FRAeS; Hon. FASME; Hon. FRSE 1983. Hon. DEng: Sheffield, 1976; Liverpool 1982; Hon. DSc: Salford, 1980; Strathclyde, 1981; Bath, 1981; Oxon, 1982; Sussex, 1984. Medal of Freedom (US), 1947. *Publications:* papers in mechanical and aeronautical journals. *Address:* Churchill College, Cambridge CB3 0DS. *Club:* Athenæum.

See also J. O'Beirne Ranelagh.

HAWTIN, Brian Richard; Assistant Under Secretary of State (Programmes), Ministry of Defence, since 1992; *b* 31 May 1946; *s* of Dick Hawtin and late Jean (*née* Middleton); *m* 1969, Anthea Fry; two *d*. *Educ:* Portsmouth Grammar Sch.; Christ Church, Oxford (MA). MoD 1967; Asst Private Sec. to Permt Under Sec. of State, 1970; on loan to FCO as First Sec., UK Delegn to NATO, Brussels, 1978–80; Asst Sec., 1981; RCDS 1987; Private Sec. to Sec. of State for Defence, 1987–89; Asst Under Sec. of State (material/naval), 1989–92. *Recreations:* walking, ceramics, squash. *Address:* c/o Ministry of Defence, Main Building, Whitehall, SW1A 2HB.

HAWTIN, Ven. David Christopher; Archdeacon of Newark, since 1992; *b* 7 June 1943; *m* 1968, Elizabeth Ann (*née* Uden); one *s* two *d*. *Educ:* King Edward VII Sch., Lytham St Annes; Keble Coll., Oxford (BA 1965; MA 1970); William Temple Coll., Rugby; Cuddesdon Coll., Oxford. Ordained: deacon, 1967, priest 1968; Curate: St Thomas, Pennywell, Sunderland, 1967–71; St Peter's, Stockton, 1971–74; Priest in charge, St Andrew's, Leam Lane, Gateshead, 1974–79; Rector, Washington, 1979–88; Diocesan Ecumenical Officer, Durham, 1988–91. Member: Gen. Synod, 1983– (Mem., Bd for Mission and Unity, 1986–91); BCC, 1987–90; Churches Together in England, 1990– (Enabling Gp, 1991–); Council of Churches for Britain and Ireland, 1990–; Chm., Diocesan Bd of Educn, Southwell, 1993. Churches Project Co-ordinator, Nat. Garden Fest., Gateshead, 1988–91. Consultant, Council for Christian Unity, 1991–; Local Unity Advr, Durham Ecumenical Relations Gp, 1991. *Address:* 4 The Woodwards, New Balderton, Newark, Notts. NG24 3GG. *T:* (office) Newark (01636) 814490, *Fax:* (01636) 815882.

HAWTIN, Michael Victor; Director, Underwriting Group, Export Credits Guarantee Department, since 1992; *b* 7 Sept. 1942; *s* of Guy and Constance Hawtin; *m* 1966, Judith Mary Eeley; one *s* one *d*. *Educ:* Bournemouth Sch.; St John's Coll., Cambridge (MA); Univ. of Calif, Berkeley (MA). Asst Principal, 1964–69, Principal, 1969–77, HM Treasury; seconded to Barclays Bank, 1969–71; Asst Sec., HM Treasury, 1977–83, Under Sec. (Principal Finance Officer), PSA, 1983–86; Under Sec., HM Treasury, 1986–88; Dir, Resource Management Gp and Principal Establishment and Finance Officer, ECGD, 1988–92. *Recreations:* music, travel. *Address:* Export Credits Guarantee Department, 2 Exchange Tower, Harbour Exchange Square, E14 9GS. *T:* 0171–512 7008.

HAWTREY, John Havilland Procter, CBE 1958; FICE; *b* 16 Feb. 1905; *e s* of late Edmond Charles Hawtrey and late Helen Mary Hawtrey (*née* Durand); *m* 1947, Kathleen Mary (*d* 1992), *d* of late Captain M. T. Daniel, RN, Henley-on-Thames; one *s* one *d*. *Educ:* Eton; City and Guilds Engineering Coll., London (BSc 1927). Asst Engineer, later Dist Engineer, Burma Railways, 1927–47. Served War of 1939–45: with RE, 1940–46; Major 1942, in India and Burma, 1942–46 (despatches). Entered office of Crown Agents for Oversea Govts and Administrations, 1948: Chief Civil Engineer, 1956; Crown Agent and Engineer-in-Chief, 1965; retired, 1969. *Address:* 76 Makins Road, Henley-on-Thames, Oxon RG9 1PR. *T:* Henley-on-Thames (01491) 574896.

HAXBY, Donald Leslie, CBE 1988; principal of veterinary practice, Southwell, 1979–93; *b* 4 Aug. 1928; *s* of Leslie Norman Haxby and Ruth Blount; *m* 1953, Barbara Mary Smith (marr. diss. 1986); one *s* two *d*. *Educ:* Queen Elizabeth Grammar Sch., Barnet; Royal Veterinary Coll., London. MRCVS 1953. Army Service, Queen's Royal Regt, RAEC, Sudan Defence Force, 1946–48 (Warrant Officer I). Practice in Leics and Shropshire, 1953–55; research, Boots Pure Drug Co., 1955–57 (clinical pathologist); vet. practice, Southwell, 1957–93. Lecturer: Animal Husbandry, Nottingham Coll. of Agriculture, 1969–93; Poultry Production and Public Health, London and Glasgow Univs, 1978–93; External Examiner: Vet. Medicine, Glasgow Univ., 1980–85; Animal Husbandry, Bristol Univ., 1987–93. Official Vet. Surgeon, Newark DC, 1979–85; Consultant to: W. & J. B. Eastwood, 1972–78; Hillsdown Holdings, 1982–90; Smith Kline Beecham Animal Health, 1982–; Cyanamid GB, 1982–85; Duphar-Philips Solvay, 1982–; I. M. C. & Cambridge-Naremco Products, USA, 1985–90. Mem., Parly and Sci. Cttee, H of C, 1979–86; Sci. Advr to Agric. Select Cttee, H of C, 1989–93. Mem. Council, 1983–84, Hon. Lectr, 1984–91, Royal Vet. Coll.; President: E Midlands Vet. Assoc. (and Treasurer), 1973–; BVA, 1977–78 (Mem. Council, 1983–84); RCVS, 1983–84 (Mem. Council, 1971–); Mem., Animal Health and Tech. Cttee, British Poultry Fedn, 1974–90; Chm., World Vet. Poultry Assoc., 1985–89. Mem., Farm Animal Welfare Council, 1981–92; Trustee and Treasurer, Gordon Meml Trust, 1982–93; Governor, Houghton Poultry Res. Station, 1983–90. Man. Dir, Don Haxby Associates, 1993–. *Recreations:* work, reading, golf, gardening, cycling. *Address:* Candant House, Main Street, Upton, Newark, Notts NG23 5ST. *T and Fax:* Southwell (01636) 812020. *Clubs:* Farmers', Savile.

HAY, family name of **Earls of Erroll** and **Kinnoull,** and of **Marquis of Tweeddale.**

HAY, Lord; Harry Thomas William Hay; *b* 8 Aug. 1984; *s* and *heir* of Earl of Erroll, *qv*.

HAY, Prof. Allan Stuart, PhD; FRS 1981; Professor of Polymer Chemistry, McGill University, Montreal, since 1987; *b* 23 July 1929; *s* of Stuart Lumsden and Verna Emila Hay; *m* 1956, Janet Mary Keck; two *s* two *d*. *Educ:* Univ. of Alberta (BSc Hon, MSc); Univ. of Illinois (PhD). General Electric Research and Development Center, Schenectady, NY: Research Associate, 1955; Manager, Chemical Laboratory, 1968; Research and Develt Manager, Chemical Labs, 1980–87. Adjunct Professor, Polymer Science and Engineering Dept, Univ. of Massachusetts, 1975. Hon. DSc Alberta, 1987. Soc. of Plastics Engrs Internat. award in Plastics Science and Engineering, 1975; Achievement award, Industrial Res. Inst., 1984. *Publications:* numerous papers and contribs to learned jls. *Recreations:* philately, reading, swimming. *Address:* 5015 Glencairn Avenue, Montreal, Quebec H3W 2B3, Canada.

HAY, Barbara Logan, MBE 1991; HM Diplomatic Service; Ambassador to Republic of Uzbekistan and (non-resident) to Republic of Tajikistan, since 1995; *b* 20 Jan 1953; *d* of late Alfred Hay and of Isa Hay (*née* Burgon). *Educ:* Boroughmuir Sen. Secondary Sch., Edinburgh. Joined Diplomatic Service, 1971; Russian language training, 1974–75; served Moscow and Johannesburg; Asst Private Sec. to Perm. Under-Sec. and Head of Diplomatic Service, 1981–83; FCO and Montreal; First Sec. (Inf.), Moscow, 1988–91; Consul-Gen., St Petersburg, 1991–92; Jt Assistance Unit (Central Europe), FCO, 1992–94. FRSA. *Recreations:* theatre, travel, Scottish country dancing, music, keeping in touch with friends. *Address:* c/o Foreign and Commonwealth Office, SW1A 2AH. *Club:* University Women's.

HAY, Sir David (Osborne), Kt 1979; CBE 1962; DSO 1945; retired public servant; *b* 29 Nov. 1916; 2nd *s* of late H. A. Hay, Barwon Heads, Victoria; *m* 1944, Alison Marion Parker Adams; two *s*. *Educ:* Geelong Grammar Sch.; Brasenose Coll., Oxford; Melbourne Univ. Joined Commonwealth Public Service, 1939. Australian Imperial Force, 1940–46: Major, 2nd Sixth Infantry Bn; served in Western Desert, Greece, New Guinea. Rejoined External Affairs Dept, 1947; Imp. Def. Coll., 1954; Minister (later Ambassador) to Thailand, 1955–57; High Comr in Canada, 1961–64; Ambassador to UN, New York, 1964–65; First Asst Secretary, External Affairs, 1966; Administrator of Papua and New Guinea, 1967–70; Sec., Dept of External Territories, Canberra, 1970–73; Defence Force Ombudsman, 1974–76; Sec., Dept of Aboriginal Affairs, 1977–79. *Publications:* The Delivery of Services financed by the Department of Aboriginal Affairs, 1976; Nothing Over Us: the story of the 2nd Sixth Australian Infantry Battalion, 1985; The Life and Times of William Hay of Boomanoomana 1816–1908, 1990. *Address:* Boomanoomana Homestead, via Mulwala, NSW 2647, Australia. *Clubs:* Australian, Melbourne (Melbourne).

HAY, Sir David (Russell), Kt 1991; CBE 1981; FRCP; FRACP; (first) Medical Director, National Heart Foundation of New Zealand, 1977–92; Cardiologist, Canterbury Hospital (formerly North Canterbury Hospital) Board, 1964–89; Hon. Consulting Physician, Canterbury Area Health Board, since 1990; *b* 8 Dec. 1927; twin *s* of Sir James Lawrence Hay, OBE, and Lady (Davidina Mertel) Hay; *m* 1958, Dr Jocelyn Valerie Bell; two *d*. *Educ:* St Andrew's Coll., Christchurch; Otago Univ., Univ. of New Zealand (MB, ChB; MD). FRACP 1965; FRCP 1971. Resident appts, Christchurch, Royal South Hants, Hammersmith, Brompton and National Heart Hosps, 1951–55; Sen. Registrar, Dunedin and Christchurch Hosps, 1956–59; Physician, N Canterbury Hosp. Bd, 1959–64; Head of Dept of Cardiology, 1969–78; Chm. of Medical Services and Hd of Dept of Medicine, 1978–84. Chm., Christchurch Hosps Med. Staff Assoc., 1983–85; Clin. Lectr, Christchurch Clinical Sch., Univ. of Otago, 1973–80; Clin. Reader, 1980–88; Foundn Councillor, Nat. Heart Foundn of NZ, 1968–92 (Mem. Scientific Cttee, 1968–92; Sec., 1974–77); Vice-Pres., RACP, 1988–92 (Councillor, 1964–66, 1987–88; Examiner, 1974–75; Censor, 1975–79, and 1990–92); Mem. Specialist Adv. Cttee on Cardiology, 1980–90; Chm., Central Specialists Cttee of BMA, 1967–68; Pres., Canterbury Div. of BMA, 1972. Chm., NZ Region of Cardiac Soc. of Australia and NZ, and Councillor, 1977–81. Overseas Regl Advr, RCP, 1987–. Member: Resuscitation Cttee of Nat. Cttee on Emergency Care, 1979–87; Health Promotion Forum of NZ, 1984–91; NZ Govt Adv. Cttee on Prevention of Cardiovascular Disease, 1985–86; NZ Govt Adv. Cttee on Smoking and Health, 1974–88; Ethics Cttee, Southern Regl HA, Canterbury, 1994–; WHO Expert Adv. Panel on Tobacco or Health, 1977–; WHO Working Gp on Tobacco and Health in Western Pacific Reg., Manila, 1994; Hypertension Task Force, 1988–89; Life Member: Nat. Heart Foundn, 1992; ANZ Cardiac Soc., 1992. Speaker: World Conf. on Smoking and Health, Stockholm, 1979; Internat. Soc. and Fedn of Cardiology

Workshop, Jakarta, 1982; Internat. Congress on Preventive Cardiology, Washington, 1989; World Congress of Cardiology, Manila, 1990. Nat. Heart Foundn Lecture, 1992; Charles Burns Oration, 1992. Trustee: J. L. Hay Charitable Trust; W. H. Nicholls Charitable Trust; Edna and Winifred White-Parsons Charitable Trust; Keith Langesen Charitable Trust. College Medal, RACP, 1993; WHO Tobacco or Health Medal, 1995. Commemoration Medal, NZ, 1990. *Publications:* (ed) Coronary Heart Disease: prevention and control in NZ, 1983; over ninety sci. papers in various med. jls, mostly on smoking and health and preventive cardiology. *Recreations:* golf, writing. *Address:* 20 Greers Road, Christchurch 4, New Zealand. *T:* 3585482. *Club:* Christchurch Golf.

See also Sir Hamish Hay, Dame M. L. Salas.

HAY, Rt. Rev. Mgr George Adam; Parish Priest, Parish of St Boniface, Okehampton, and Holy Family, Chagford, since 1991; *b* 14 Nov. 1930; *s* of late Sir William Rupert Hay, KCMG, KCIE, CSI, and late Sybil Ethel, *d* of Sir Stewart Abram. *Educ:* Ampleforth College, York; New Coll., Oxford (BA History, MA); Venerable English Coll., Rome (STL). National Service as Midshipman RNVR, 1949–50; student, Oxford, 1950–53; Venerable English Coll., Rome, 1953–60. Ordained priest at Rome, 1959; Curate, Sacred Heart Church, Exeter, and part-time RC Chaplain to students at Exeter Univ., 1960; Chaplain to students at Exeter Univ. and Priest-in-charge, Crediton, 1966–78; Rector, Venerable English Coll., Rome, 1978–84; Parish Priest: St John the Baptist, Dartmouth, 1984; Sacred Heart and St Teresa, Paignton, 1984–91. *Recreations:* fly fishing, squash, mountain walking. *Address:* 95 Station Road, Okehampton EX20 1ED.

HAY, Sir Hamish (Grenfell), Kt 1982; JP; Mayor of Christchurch, New Zealand, 1974–89; Director: Canterbury Development Corporation, since 1983; Christchurch International Airport Ltd, since 1988; *b* 8 Dec. 1927; twin *s* of Sir James Lawrence Hay, OBE, and Lady (Davidina) Hay; *m* 1955, Judith Leicester Gill (QSO 1987); one *s* four *d*. *Educ:* St Andrew's Coll., Christchurch; Univ. of Canterbury, NZ (BCom). FCA(NZ). Councillor, Christchurch City Council, 1959–74. Member: Victory Park Bd, 1974–89; Lyttelton Harbour Bd, 1983–89. Chairman: Christchurch Town Hall Board of Management, 1962–92; Canterbury Museum Trust Bd, 1981–84; Canterbury United Council, 1983–86; Museum of New Zealand, Wellington, 1992– (Chm., 1992–94). President: Christchurch Aged People's Welfare Council, 1974–89; Christchurch Civic Music Council, 1974–89; Christchurch Symphony Orchestra, 1982–88; Chm., Christchurch Arts Festival, 1965–74; past Mem., Queen Elizabeth II Arts Council. Chm., New Zealand Soc. of Accountants (Canterbury Br.), 1958; Dep. Man. Dir, Haywrights Ltd, 1962–74. Mem. Council, Univ. of Canterbury, 1974–89; Chm. of Governors, McLean Inst., 1974–89; Governor, St Andrew's Coll., 1986–92. Vice-Pres., Municipal Assoc. of NZ, 1974–88. Trustee, Canterbury Savings Bank, 1962–88 (Pres., 1974–75); Dir, Trust Bank Canterbury Ltd, 1988–. Mem., Charles Upham Trust, 1986–; Trustee: Trust Bank Canterbury Community Trust, 1988–; J. L. Hay Charitable Trust, 1959–. JP New Zealand, 1990. Silver Jubilee Medal, 1977; Commemoration Medal, NZ, 1990; Order of the Rising Sun (with Gold Rays), Japan, 1990. *Publication:* Hay Days (autobiog.), 1989. *Recreations:* gardening, listening to good music. *Address:* 70 Heaton Street, Merivale, Christchurch 5, New Zealand. *T:* 3557244; Rue Balguerie, Akaroa, New Zealand. *Clubs:* Christchurch, Christchurch Rotary (New Zealand).

See also Sir D. R. Hay, Dame M. L. Salas.

HAY, Lady (Helen) Olga; *see* Maitland, Lady H. O.

HAY, Sir James B. D.; *see* Dalrymple-Hay.

HAY, John Albert; Managing Director, Walport Group, 1968–81; *b* 21 Nov. 1919, *o s* of Alderman J. E. Hay; *m* 1st, 1947, Beryl Joan (marr. diss. 1973), *o d* of Comdr H. C. Found, RN (retired); one *s* one *d*; 2nd, 1974, Janet May, *y d* of A. C. Spruce. *Educ:* Brighton, Hove and Sussex Grammar Sch. Solicitor admitted May 1945. Chairman: Brighton and Hove Young Conservatives, 1945–47; Sussex Federation of Young Conservatives, 1945–47; Young Conservative and Unionist Central Cttee, 1947–49; Conservative Party Housing and Local Govt Cttee, 1956–59; formerly Dir London Municipal Soc.; formerly Vice-Pres. Urban District Councils Assoc.; Hon. Sec. UK Council of the European Movement, 1965–66; Mem. of Exec. Cttee, Nat. Union of Conservative and Unionist Assoc., 1947–49 and 1950–51. Served War of 1939–45, in RNVR; temp. Sub-Lieut, RNVR, 1940–44; temp. Lieut, RNVR, 1944; invalided 1944. Member: British Delegn, Congress of Europe, 1948, and 1973; UK Delegns, Council of Europe and Western European Union, 1956–59. MP (C) Henley, Oxon, 1950–Feb. 1974; PPS to Pres. of BoT, 1951–56; Parly Sec., MoT, 1959–63; Civil Lord of the Admiralty, 1963–64; Parly Under-Sec. of State for Defence for the Royal Navy, April–Oct. 1964. Chm., British Section, Council of European Municipalities, 1971–76, Vice-Chm., 1976–77, Pres., 1977–81, Vice-Pres., 1981–87. *Recreations:* writing, music, historical study. *Address:* 1134 Hillside, West Vancouver, BC V7S 2G4, Canada. *T:* (604) 9251623.

HAY, John Anthony; Vice-Chancellor, Deakin University, since 1992; *b* 21 Sept. 1942; *s* of J. E. Hay; *m* 1965, Barbara McKenna; three *s* one *d*. *Educ:* Perth Modern Sch.; Univ. Western Australia (BA Hons 1964; PhD 1976); Pembroke Coll., Cambridge (BA 1966; MA 1969). University of Western Australia: Lectr, Sen. Lectr and Prof. of English, 1967–87; Dep. Chm., Acad. Bd, 1985; Monash University: Dean, Faculty of Arts, 1987–89; Dep. Vice-Chancellor, 1989–91. Editor, Aumla, Jl of Australasian Univs Lang. and Lit. Assoc., 1985–92. *Publications:* Spectrum I, II & III, 1971–79; Directions in Australian Secondary English, 1975; Western Australian Literature: a bibliography, 1975; Testing English Comprehension, 1979; K. S. Pritchard, 1984; European Relations, 1985; The Early Imprints at New Norcia, 1986; Australian Studies in Tertiary Institutions, 1987; Western Australian Writing, 1989; Narrative Issues, 1990. *Recreations:* swimming, cinema. *Address:* The Chancellery, Deakin University, Geelong, Vic 3217, Australia. *T:* (52) 271147.

HAY, Prof. John Duncan, MA, MD, FRCP; Professor of Child Health, University of Liverpool, 1957–74, now Professor Emeritus; *b* 6 Feb. 1909; *s* of late Prof. John Hay; *m* 1936, Jannett Ceridwen Evans; one *s* two *d*. *Educ:* Liverpool Coll.; Sidney Sussex Coll., Cambridge; Liverpool Univ. MB, ChB, 1st Cl. Hons, Liverpool, 1933; MA 1934, MB 1935, Cambridge; MD Liverpool, 1936; DCH London, MRCP 1939; FRCP 1951. Holt Fellowship in Pathology, Liverpool, 1935; Cons. Pædiatrician to: Royal Liverpool Children's Hospital, 1939–74; Royal Liverpool Babies' Hospital, 1939–61; Birkenhead Children's Hosp., 1937–54; Liverpool Maternity Hosp. 1946–74; Lancashire County Hosp., Whiston, 1942–51; Liverpool Open-Air Hospital, Leasowe, and Mill Road Maternity Hosp., 1947–74; Alder Hey Children's Hosp., 1957–74; Liverpool Education Cttee, 1951–72. Demonstrator in Pathology, University of Liverpool, 1935 and 1938; Asst Lectr in Clinical Pædiatrics, University of Liverpool, 1948–57. Brit. Paediatric Association: Treasurer, 1964–71; Pres., 1972–73; Hon. Mem., 1973; President: Liverpool Med. Instn, 1972–73; Liverpool Paediatric Club, 1975–; Hon. Mem. Assoc. European Paediatric Cardiologists, 1975–. RAMC (Major and Lieut-Col), 1942–46. *Publications:* contribs to Archives of Disease in Childhood, British Heart Journal, BMJ, Lancet, Practitioner, Brit. Encyclopædia of Medical Practice, Medical Progress, 1957, Cardiovascular Diseases in Childhood. *Recreations:* music, fell walking.

HAY, Sir John (Erroll Audley), 11th Bt *cr* 1663 (NS) of Park, Wigtownshire; *b* 3 Dec. 1935; *o s* of Sir Arthur Thomas Erroll Hay, 10th Bt, ISO, ARIBA and his 1st wife, Hertha Hedwig Paula Louise (decd), *d* of Ludwig Stölzle, Nagelberg, Austria; *S* father, 1993. *Educ:* Gordonstoun; St Andrews Univ. (MA). *Heir:* none. *Address:* c/o National Westminster Bank, Fitzroy Square, W1P 6DX.

HAY, Richard, CMG 1992; training for ordination, Cranmer Hall, Durham, since 1994; *b* 4 May 1942; *s* of Prof. Denys Hay, FBA, FRSE and of Sarah Gwyneth Morley; *m* 1969, Miriam Marguerite Alvin England; two *s*. *Educ:* George Watson's Coll., Edinburgh; Edinburgh Univ.; Balliol Coll., Oxford (BA Hons, Mod. Hist.). Assistant Principal, HM Treasury, 1963–68; Secretary, West Midlands Economic Planning Council, 1966–67; Private Sec. to Financial Sec., Treasury, 1967–68; Principal, Treasury, 1968–73; European Commission: Member, Cabinet of Sir Christopher (now Lord) Soames, Vice-Pres., 1973–75; Dep. Chef de Cabinet, 1975–77; Chef de Cabinet to Mr Christopher Tugendhat, Member, 1977–79; Dir, Economic Structures and Community Interventions, Directorate-Gen. for Economic and Financial Affairs, 1979–81; Dep. Dir-Gen., 1981–86, Dir-Gen., 1986–91, Directorate-General for Personnel and Admin, EC; Special Advr, EC, 1991. Consultant, Sharing of Ministries Abroad, 1992–94. *Address:* 31 Briardene, Durham DH1 4QU. *Club:* United Oxford & Cambridge University.

HAY, Maj.-Gen. Robert Arthur, CB 1970; MBE 1946; Australian Army Officer, retired 1977; *b* 9 April 1920; *s* of Eric Alexander Hay and Vera Eileen Hay (*née* Whitehead); *m* 1944, Endrée Patricia Hay (*née* McGovern); two *s* one *d*. *Educ:* Brighton Grammar Sch., Melbourne, Victoria; RMC Duntroon, ACT (graduated Dec. 1939); Australian Staff Coll., 1944; USA Staff Coll., Fort Leavenworth, 1944. Lt-Col, 1945; Col, 1955; Col GS HQ Eastern Comd; Military Attaché, Washington, DC, 1956; Dir Administrative Planning, AHQ, 1959; Defence Representative, Singapore and Malaya, 1962; Brig., 1964; IDC London, 1965; Dir Military Ops and Plans, AHQ, 1966; Maj.-Gen., 1967; Dep. Chief of the General Staff, AHQ; Comdr, Australian Forces, Vietnam, 1969; Comdr, First Australian Div., 1970; Chief, Mil. Planning Office, SEATO, 1971–73; Comdt, Royal Military Coll., Duntroon, 1973–77. Sec., Australian Council of Professions, 1978–86; Exec. Officer, Australian Centre for Publications acquired for Develt, 1982–87. Pres., Veterans Tennis Assoc. of Australia, 1981–92. *Recreations:* tennis, golf. *Address:* Unit 6, Kingston Tower, 9 Jardine Street, Kingston, ACT 2604, Australia. *Clubs:* Melbourne Cricket; Commonwealth, Royal Canberra Golf (Canberra); Tanglin (Singapore).

HAY, Robert Colquhoun, CBE 1988; WS; Sheriff Principal of North Strathclyde, since 1989; *b* 22 Sept. 1933; *s* of late J. B. Hay, dental surgeon, Stirling and Mrs J. Y. Hay; *m* 1958, Olive Black; two *s* two *d*. *Educ:* Univ. of Edinburgh (MA, LLB). Legal practice, 1957–63, 1968–76; Depute Procurator Fiscal, Edinburgh, 1963–68; Temp. Sheriff, 1984–89; Chm., 1976–81, Pres., 1981–89, Industrial Tribunals for Scotland. Mem., Sheriff Court Rules Council, 1989– (Chm., 1993–). Comr, Northern Lighthouse Bd, 1989– (Vice-Chm., 1991–92; Chm., 1992–93). Consultant for the Clan Hay, 1995–. *Publication:* contrib. Laws of Scotland: Stair Memorial Encyclopedia, 1988. *Recreations:* walking, sailing. *Address:* Sheriff Principal's Chambers, Sheriff Court House, Paisley PA3 2HW. *T:* 0141–887 5291. *Clubs:* Royal Highland Yacht (Oban); Royal Northern and Clyde Yacht (Rhu).

HAY, Robin William Patrick Hamilton; Recorder, since 1985; barrister; *b* 1 Nov. 1939; *s* of William R. Hay and Dora Hay; *m* 1969, Lady Olga Maitland, *qv*; two *s* one *d*. *Educ:* Eltham; Selwyn Coll., Cambridge (MA, LLB). Called to the Bar, Inner Temple, 1964. Chm., Young Musicians Symphony Orchestra, 1990–. *Recreations:* church tasting, gastronomy, choral singing. *Address:* Goldsmith Building, Temple EC4Y 7BL. *Club:* Garrick.

HAY, Sir Ronald Frederick Hamilton, 12th Bt *cr* 1703, of Alderston; *b* 1941; *s* of Sir Ronald Nelson Hay, 11th Bt and of Rita, *d* of John Munyard; *S* father, 1988; *m* 1978, Kathleen, *d* of John Thake; two *s* one *d*. *Heir:* *s* Alexander James Hay, *b* 1979. *Address:* Aspendale, Vic 3195, Australia.

HAY DAVISON, Ian Frederic; *see* Davison, I. F. H.

HAYBALL, Frederick Ronald, CMG 1969; *b* 23 April 1914; *s* of late Frederick Reuben Hayball and late Rebecca Hayball; *m* 1938, Lavinia Violet Palmer; one *s* one *d*. *Educ:* Alleyn's Sch., Dulwich. Accountant, Myers, Gondouin & Co. Ltd, 1932–39. Flying Officer, RAF, 1939–45. Foreign and Commonwealth Office, 1945–69 (Counsellor, retired); Asst Sec., Longman Gp Ltd, 1969–81. *Recreations:* cricket, angling, motoring, bowls. *Address:* 50 Theydon Park Road, Theydon Bois, Essex CM16 7LP. *T:* Theydon Bois (01992) 812195.

HAYCRAFT, Anna Margaret; writer; *b* 9 Sept. 1932; *d* of John and Alexandra Lindholm; *m* 1956, Colin Haycraft (*d* 1994); four *s* one *d* (and one *s* one *d* decd). *Educ:* Bangor County Grammar School for Girls; Liverpool School of Art. Fiction editor, Gerald Duckworth & Co., 1970; Columnist: The Spectator, 1985–89; The Universe, 1989–91; The Catholic Herald, 1991–. *Publications: as Anna Haycraft:* Natural Baby Food, 1977; (with Caroline Blackwood) Darling, You Shouldn't Have Gone to So Much Trouble, 1980; *as Alice Thomas Ellis:* The Sin Eater, 1977; The Birds of the Air, 1980; The Twenty-Seventh Kingdom, 1982; The Other Side of the Fire, 1983; Unexplained Laughter, 1985 (Yorkshire Post Novel of the Year, 1985); (with Tom Pitt-Aikens) Secrets of Strangers, 1986; Home Life, 1986; More Home Life, 1987; The Clothes in the Wardrobe, 1987, The Skeleton in the Cupboard, 1988, The Fly in the Ointment, 1989, trilogy; Home Life Three, 1988; (with Tom Pitt-Aikens) The Loss of the Good Authority, 1989; (ed) Wales: an anthology, 1989; Home Life Four, 1989; A Welsh Childhood (autobiog.), 1990; The Inn at the Edge of the World, 1990 (Writers' Guild Award, 1990); Pillars of Gold, 1992; The Serpent on the Rock, 1994; The Evening of Adam, 1994; Cat Among the Pigeons: collection of 'Catholic Herald' essays, 1994. *Address:* 22 Gloucester Crescent, NW1 7DS. *T:* 0171–485 7408.

HAYCRAFT, John Stacpoole, CBE 1982; Director General, International House (formerly English International (International House)), 1975–90 (Consultant, 1990–91); *b* 11 Dec. 1926; *s* of late Major W. C. S. Haycraft and Olive Haycraft; *m* 1953, Brita Elisabeth Langenfelt; two *s* one *d*. *Educ:* Wellington Coll.; Jesus Coll., Oxford (Open Exhibnr; MA). E-SU Fellowship. Yale Univ., 1951–52. Founder and Dir, Academia Britanica, Córdoba, 1953; Founder and Principal: International Language Centre, London, 1960; International Teacher Trng Inst., 1963; Founder and Director: International House, London, 1964–90; International House, Rome, 1967–68; Director: International House, Paris, 1971–72; Soros English Lang. Prog., 1991–94; Founder: English Teaching Theatre, 1970; English Language Schools in Tinnisoara and Kiev, 1992, Vilnius and Tallinn, 1993. Mem., English Teaching Adv. Cttee, British Council, 1974–80. *Publications:* Babel in Spain, 1958, 2nd edn 1958; Getting on in English, 1964, 7th edn 1982 (trans. 9 langs); Babel in London, 1965; George and Elvira, 1970; Choosing Your English, 1972, 8th edn 1982; Action, 1977; Introduction to English Language Teaching, 1978; Think, Then Speak, 1984; Italian Labyrinth, 1985; In Search of the French Revolution, 1989; contrib. Guardian, Independent, The Times, Observer (Spanish correspondent, 1958–59), Modern

English Teacher, etc. *Recreations:* tennis, swimming, chess, cinema, theatre, history, travel. *Address:* 79 Lee Road, SE3 9EN. *T:* 0181–852 5495. *Club:* Canning.

HAYDAR, Dr Loutof Allah; Syrian Ambassador to the People's Republic of China, since 1990; *b* 22 March 1940; *s* of Haydar and Mary; *m* 1968, Hayat Hassan; one *s* three *d.* *Educ:* Damascus Univ. (BA English Literature 1964); Moscow State Univ. (PhD 1976). Joined Foreign Office, 1965; served at Syrian Embassy: London, 1965–67; Bonn, 1967–68; Moscow, 1970–75; served with Syrian Delegation to UN, New York, 1978–82. *Publication:* The Ancient History of Palestine and the Middle East (PhD Thesis), 1976. *Address:* Syrian Embassy, 6 Dong Si Jie, San Li Tun, Beijing 100600, China.

HAYDAY, Anthony Victor; HM Diplomatic Service, retired; Ambassador to Madagascar, 1987–90; *b* 1 June 1930; *s* of Charles Leslie Victor Hayday and Catherine (*née* McCarthy); *m* 1966, Anne Heather Moffat (*d* 1995); one *s* one *d.* *Educ:* Beckenham and Penge Grammar School. Royal Air Force, 1949–50; HM Foreign (later Diplomatic) Service, 1950; Brazzaville, 1953; British Information Services, New York, 1955; FO, 1958; Vice Consul, Houston, 1961; 2nd Secretary, Algiers, 1962; FO (later FCO), 1966; 1st Secretary, New Delhi, 1969; Head of Chancery, Freetown, 1973; on secondment to Commonwealth Secretariat, 1976–80; Dep. High Comr, Calcutta, 1981–85; Consul-Gen., Cleveland, 1985–87. *Recreations:* birdwatching, athletics. *Address:* Meadow Cottage, Swillbrook, Minety, Malmesbury, Wilts SN16 9QA. *Clubs:* Blackheath Harriers, Mensa; Bengal (Calcutta).

HAYDEN, Hon. William George, AC 1989; Governor-General of Australia, 1989–Feb. 1996; *b* Brisbane, 23 Jan. 1933; *s* of G. Hayden, Oakland, Calif, USA; *m* 1960, Dallas, *d* of W. Broadfoot; one *s* two *d.* *Educ:* Brisbane State High Sch. BEcon, Univ. of Qld. Public Service, Qld, 1950–52; Police Constable in Queensland, 1953–61. MHR (Lab) for Oxley, Qld, 1961–88. Parly Spokesman on Health and Welfare, 1969–72; Minister for Social Security, Australian Commonwealth Govt, 1972–75; Federal Treasurer, June-Nov. 1975; Leader of Australian Labor Party and the Opposition, 1977–83; spokesman on defence, 1976–83 and on economic management, 1977–83; Minister for Foreign Affairs, 1983–88, and for Trade, 1987–88. Chancellor, Order of Australia, 1989–; Prior, Order of St John in Australia, 1989–. Hon. Dr Griffith Univ., 1990; Hon. LLD Univ. of Qld, 1990. Gwangha Medal, Order of Diplomatic Merit, Korea. *Recreations:* reading, music, golf, horse riding, fly-fishing, cross-country skiing, bushwalking. *Address:* (until Feb. 1996) Government House, Canberra, ACT, Australia; (home) PO Box 33, Ipswich, Queensland 4305, Australia.

HAYDEN, William Joseph, CBE 1976; Chairman and Chief Executive, Jaguar plc, 1990–92; *b* 19 Jan. 1929; *s* of George Hayden and Mary Ann Hayden (*née* Overhead); *m* 1954, Mavis Ballard; two *s* two *d.* *Educ:* Romford Tech. College. Served Army, 1947–49. Ford Motor Co.: Briggs Motor Bodies, Dagenham, 1950–57; financial staff, Dagenham, 1957–63; Div. Controller, Ford Chassis, Transmission and Engine Div., Dagenham, 1963–67; Gen. Ops Manager, Transmission, Chassis and Truck Mfg Ops, 1967–71; Vice-President: Truck Mfg Ops, 1971; Power Train Ops, 1972; Mfg Ford of Europe, Inc., 1974–90. Director (non-executive): Hawtell Whiting, 1992–; Trans Tec. 1993–. *Recreations:* golf, gardening, soccer. *Address:* Buckley Green Farm, Buckley Green, Henley in Arden, Warwickshire B95 5QF. *Clubs:* Thorndon Park Golf; Royal Porthcawl Golf; Stratford on Avon Golf.

HAYDON, Francis Edmund Walter; HM Diplomatic Service, retired; *b* 23 Dec. 1928; *s* of late Surgeon Captain Walter T. Haydon, RN and Maria Christina Haydon (*née* Delahoyde); *m* 1959, Isabel Dorothy Kitchin; two *s* two *d.* *Educ:* Downside School; Magdalen College, Oxford. BA (1st cl. Modern History) 1949. Asst London correspondent, Agence France-Presse, 1951–52; Asst diplomatic correspondent, Reuters, 1952–55; joined Foreign Office, 1955; Second Sec., Benghazi, 1959, Beirut, 1962; First Sec., Blantyre, 1969, Ankara, 1978; Counsellor, FCO, 1981–87. *Recreations:* lawn tennis, cricket, bridge, travel, enjoying the countryside. *Address:* Le Picachon, La Rue des Bouillons, Trinity, Jersey JE3 5BB. *T:* Jersey (01534) 863155.

HAYDON, Sir Walter Robert, (Sir Robin Haydon), KCMG 1980 (CMG 1970); HM Diplomatic Service, retired; *b* 29 May 1920; *s* of Walter Haydon and Evelyn Louise Thom; *m* 1943, Joan Elizabeth Tewson (*d* 1988); one *d* (and one *s* one *d* decd). *Educ:* Dover Grammar Sch. Served in Army in France, India and Burma, 1939–46. Entered Foreign Service, 1946; served at London, Berne, Turin, Sofia, Bangkok, London, Khartoum, UK Mission to UN (New York), Washington; FO spokesman and Head of News Dept, FCO, 1967–71; High Comr, Malaŵi, 1971–73; Chief Press Sec., 10 Downing Street, 1973–74; High Comr, Malta, 1974–76; Ambassador to Republic of Ireland, 1976–80. Dir of Gp Public Affairs, Imperial Gp, 1981–84; Dir, Imperial Tobacco Ltd, 1984–87. Member: Reviewing Cttee on Export of Works of Art, 1984–87; Tobacco Adv. Council, 1984–88. Governor: E-SU, 1980–86, 1987–93; Dover Grammar Sch., 1982–89. *Recreations:* walking, swimming, tennis. *Address:* c/o Lloyds Bank, Cox's & King's Branch, 7 Pall Mall, SW1Y 5NA. *Clubs:* Travellers', Special Forces.

HAYE, Colvyn Hugh, CBE 1983; Commissioner for Hong Kong, 1984–87; *b* 7 Dec. 1925; 3rd *s* of Colvyn Hugh Haye and Avis Rose Kelly; *m* 1949, Gloria Mary Stansbury; two *d.* *Educ:* Sherwood Coll.; Univ. of Melbourne (BA, Teachers' Cert.); Christchurch Coll., Oxford (Overseas Service Trng Course). Served War, RNVR, Midshipman and Sub-Lt, 1944–46. Victorian State Educn Service, 1947–52; joined Colonial Service, now HMOCS, Hong Kong Government: Educn Officer, 1953; Sen. Educn Officer, 1962 (world tour, educnl estabs, and trng at Centre for Educnl Television Overseas, London, 1964); Asst Dir and Head of Educnl Television Service, 1969; Dep. Dir, 1975; Dir of Educn and Official Mem., Legislative Council, 1980; Sec., Administrative Service and Comr, London Office, 1984. Jardine Educn Foundn Visitor, Univs of Oxford and Cambridge, 1990–. Mem. Council, Overseas Service Pensioners' Assoc., 1988–. JP Hong Kong, 1971–87. *Recreations:* reading, writing, talking, walking. *Address:* Wymering, Sheet Common, near Petersfield, Hants GU31 5AT. *T:* Petersfield (01730) 268480. *Clubs:* Hong Kong, Tripehounds, Toastmasters (Hong Kong).

HAYES, Brian, CBE 1992; QPM 1985; Deputy Commissioner of Metropolitan Police, since 1995; *b* 25 Jan. 1940; 2nd *s* of James and Jessie Hayes; *m* 1960, Priscilla Rose Bishop; one *s* three *d.* *Educ:* Plaistow County Grammar Sch.; Sheffield Univ. (BA Hons 1st Cl. Mod. Langs). Metropolitan Police, 1959–77; seconded Northern Ireland, 1971–72; Police Adviser, Mexico, 1975 and 1976, Colombia, 1977 and 1993; British Police representative, EEC, 1976–77; Asst Chief Constable, Surrey Constabulary, 1977–81; Dep. Chief Constable, Wiltshire Constabulary, 1981–82; Chief Constable, Surrey Constabulary, 1982–91; Inspector of Constabulary for SE England, 1991–95. Vice-Pres., ACPO, 1990–91. Chm., Police Athletic Assoc., 1989–91 (Nat. Sec., 1984–88); Pres., Union Sportive des Polices d'Europe, 1990–92. OStJ 1987. Police Long Service and Good Conduct Medal, 1981. *Recreations:* martial arts, running, sailing, golf. *Address:* New Scotland Yard, Broadway, SW1H 0BG. *T:* 0171–230 1212, *Telex:* 893421 Metpol Ldn.

HAYES, Sir Brian (David), GCB 1988 (KCB 1980; CB 1976); Permanent Secretary, Department of Trade and Industry, 1985–89, retired (Joint Permanent Secretary, 1983–85); *b* 5 May 1929; *s* of late Charles and Flora Hayes, Bramerton, Norfolk; *m* 1958, Audrey Jenkins; one *s* one *d.* *Educ:* Norwich Sch.; Corpus Christi Coll., Cambridge. BA (Hist.) 1952, PhD (Cambridge) 1956. RASC, 1947–49. Joined Min. of Agriculture, Fisheries and Food, 1956; Asst Private Sec. to the Minister, 1958; Asst Sec., 1967; Under-Sec., Milk and Poultry Gp, 1970–73; Dep. Sec., 1973–78; Permanent Sec., 1979–83. Director: Guardian Royal Exchange, 1989–; Tate & Lyle, 1989–; Adv. Director: Unilever plc, 1990–; Hay Management Consultants, 1992–. Chm., CBI Educn Foundn, 1991–. Dir, SANE, 1990–. Lloyd's Members' Ombudsman, 1994–. *Recreations:* reading, watching cricket.

HAYES, Sir Claude (James), KCMG 1974 (CMG 1969); MA, MLitt; Chairman, Crown Agents for Oversea Governments and Administrations, 1968–74; *b* 23 March 1912; *er s* of late J. B. F. Hayes, West Hoathly, Sussex; *m* 1940, Joan McCarthy (*d* 1984), *yr d* of Edward McCarthy Fitt, Civil Engineer; two *s* one *d.* *Educ:* Ardingly Coll.; St Edmund Hall, Oxford (Scholar); Sorbonne; New Coll., Oxford (Sen. Scholar). Heath Harrison Travelling Scholarship; Zaharoff Travelling Fellowship; Paget Toynbee Prize; MA, MLitt. Asst Dir of Examinations, Civil Service Commn, 1938. Captain RASC 1st Inf. Div. BEF, 1939; Major 1940, Combined Ops; Lieut-Col, 1942–45 (N Africa, Sicily, Italy, NW Europe). Dep. Dir of Examinations, Civil Service Commn, 1945; Dir and Comr, 1949, also Sec., 1955; Nuffield Foundn Fellowship, 1953–54, toured Commonwealth studying public service recruitment and management. Asst Sec., HM Treasury, 1957; British Govt Mem., Cttee on Dissolution of Central African Fedn, 1963; Under-Sec., HM Treasury, 1964–65; Prin. Finance Officer, Min. of Overseas Development, 1965–68. *Recreations:* music; unaided gardening; antique furniture; 18th century bourgeois chattels; getting value for money from shops. *Address:* Prinkham, Chiddingstone Hoath, Kent TN8 7DN. *T:* Cowden (01342) 850335.

HAYES, Colin Graham Frederick, MA; RA 1970 (ARA 1963); painter; *b* 17 Nov. 1919; *s* of Gerald Hayes and Winifred (*née* Yule); *m* 1st, 1949, Jean Westbrook Law (*d* 1988); three *d*; 2nd, 1992, Marjorie Christensen. *Educ:* Westminster Sch.; Christ Church, Oxford. Served Royal Engineers, 1940–45 (Middle East) (Capt.). Ruskin Sch. of Drawing, 1946–47. Tutor, Sen. Tutor and Reader, Royal College of Art, 1949–84; Hon. ARCA, 1960; Fellow, RCA, 1960–84 (Hon. Fellow, 1984). Work in Collections: Arts Council; British Council; Carlisle Museum, etc. *Publications include:* Renoir, 1961; Stanley Spencer, 1963; Rembrandt, 1969; many articles on painting in jls. *Address:* 26 Cleveland Avenue, W4 1SN. *T:* 0181–994 8762.

HAYES, Most Rev. James Martin; Archbishop (RC) of Halifax (NS), 1967–90, now Archbishop Emeritus; *b* 27 May 1924; *s* of late L. J. Hayes. *Educ:* St Mary's Univ., Halifax; Holy Heart Seminary, Halifax; Angelicum Univ., Rome. Asst, St Mary's Basilica, 1947–54; Chancellor and Sec. of Archdiocese of Halifax, 1957–65; Rector, St Mary's Basilica, 1963–65; Auxil. Bp of Halifax, 1965–66; Apostolic Administrator of Archdiocese of Halifax, 1966–67. Pres., Canadian Conf. of Catholic Bishops, 1987–89. Hon. DLitt St Anne's Coll., Church Point, NS, 1966; Hon. DTh King's Coll., Halifax, NS, 1967; Hon. DHL Mount St Vincent Univ., Halifax, 1985; Hon. LLD: St Mary's Univ., Halifax, 1985; St Thomas Univ., 1989; Hon. DD Atlantic Sch. of Theol., Halifax, 1986. *Address:* Catholic Pastoral Centre, Archdiocese of Halifax, PO Box 1527, 1531 Grafton Street, Halifax, NS B3J 2Y3, Canada.

HAYES, Jeremy Joseph James; MP (C) Harlow, since 1983; barrister; *b* 20 April 1953; *s* of Peter and Daye Hayes; *m* 1979, Alison Gail Mansfield; one *s* one *d.* *Educ:* Oratory Sch.; Chelmer Inst. LLB London. Called to the Bar, Middle Temple, 1977. PPS to Minister of State, NI Office, 1992–94, DoE, 1994–. Member: Select Cttee on Social Services, 1987–90; Select Cttee on Health, 1990–91; All Party Parly Gp on Human Rights; All Party Parly Gp on Race Relations; Vice Chm., All Party AIDS Cttee; Chm., All Party ASH Gp. Promoter: Parents' Aid (No 2) Bill; Sexual Offences Bill; Sponsor: Video Recordings Act; Protection of Children against Tobacco Act; Freedom of Information (Medical Records) Act. Vice-Pres., Epping Forest YCs. Member: FRAME; Amnesty Internat. Fellow, Industry and Parliament Trust. Hon. Dir, State Legislative Leaders Foundn, USA. Gov., Oratory Sch.; Vice Pres., Wendens Ambo Cricket Club. Freeman, City of London; Liveryman, Fletchers' Co.; Freeman, Co. of Watermen and Lightermen. *Recreations:* playing biffing games with my son, practising the violin with my daughter, and slumping in front of the TV with my wife. *Address:* House of Commons, SW1A 0AA. *T:* 0171–219 5205. *Clubs:* Carlton; Essex.

HAYES, Vice-Admiral Sir John (Osler Chattock), KCB 1967 (CB 1964); OBE 1945; Lord-Lieutenant of Ross and Cromarty, Skye and Lochalsh, 1977–88; *b* 9 May 1913; *er s* of late Major L. C. Hayes, RAMC and Mrs Hayes; *m* 1939, Hon. Rosalind Mary Finlay, *o d* of 2nd and last Viscount Finlay of Nairn; two *s* one *d.* *Educ:* RN Coll., Dartmouth. Entered RN, 1927. Served War of 1939–45; Atlantic, HMS Repulse, Singapore, Russian Convoys, Malta. The Naval Sec., 1962–64; Flag Officer: Flotillas, Home Fleet, 1964–66; Scotland and NI, 1966–68; retd. Comdr 1948; Capt. 1953; Rear-Adm. 1962; Vice-Adm. 1965. Chm., Cromarty Firth Port Authority, 1974–77. Pres., Scottish Council, King George's Fund for Sailors, 1968–78. King Gustav V of Sweden Jubilee Medal, 1948. *Publication:* Face the Music: a sailor's story, 1991. *Recreations:* walking, music, writing. *Address:* Wemyss House, Nigg, by Tain, Ross and Cromarty IV19 1QW. *T:* Nigg (0186285) 212.

HAYES, John Philip, CB 1984; Assistant Under-Secretary of State (Economics), Foreign and Commonwealth Office, 1975–84, retired; *b* 1924; *s* of late Harry Hayes and late Mrs G. E. Hayes (*née* Hallsworth); *m* 1956, Susan Elizabeth, *d* of Sir Percivale Liesching, GCMG, KCB, KCVO; one *s* one *d.* *Educ:* Cranleigh Sch.; Corpus Christi Coll., Oxford. RAFVR, 1943–46. Barnett Memorial Fellowship, 1948–49; Political and Economic Planning, 1950–53; OEEC, 1953–58; Internat. Bank for Reconstruction and Develt, 1958–64; Head, Economic Develt Div., OECD, 1964–67; Dir, World Economy Div., Economic Planning Staff, ODM, 1967–69; Dep. Dir Gen. of Economic Planning, ODM, later ODA, 1969–71; Dir, Econ. Program Dept, later Econ. Analysis and Projections Dept, IBRD, 1971–73; Dir, Trade and Finance Div., Commonwealth Secretariat, 1973–75. Sen. Fellow, Trade Policy Res. Centre, 1984–89. *Publications:* Economic Effects of Sanctions on Southern Africa, 1987; Making Trade Policy in the European Community, 1993. *Recreations:* music, travel. *Address:* 51 Enfield Road, Brentford, Mddx TW8 9PA. *T:* 0181–568 7590.

HAYES, John Trevor, CBE 1986; MA Oxon, PhD London; FSA; Director of the National Portrait Gallery, London, 1974–94; *b* 21 Jan. 1929; *er s* of late Leslie Thomas Hayes and late Gwendoline (*née* Griffiths), London. *Educ:* Ardingly; Keble Coll. Oxford (Open Exhibr; Hon. Fellow, 1984); Courtauld Inst. of Art, London; Inst. of Fine Arts, New York. Asst Keeper, London Museum, 1954–70, Dir, 1970–74; Commonwealth Fund Fellow, 1958–59 (NY Univ.); Vis. Prof. in History of Art, Yale Univ., 1969. Chm., Walpole Soc., 1981–. *Publications:* London: a pictorial history, 1969; The Drawings of Thomas Gainsborough, 1970; Catalogue of Oil Paintings in the London Museum, 1970; Gainsborough as Printmaker, 1971; Rowlandson: Watercolours and Drawings, 1972; Gainsborough: Paintings and Drawings, 1975; The Art of Graham Sutherland, 1980; The

several of its Cttees, throughout war period). Contested (Lab) Barkston Ash Parliamentary Division, 1945 and 1950 Gen. Elections; MP (Lab) North Norfolk, 1964–70. Chairman: E and W Ridings Regional Bd for Industry, 1954–64; N Yorks AHA, 1974–82; York DHA, 1981–84; Vice-Chm., Agricultural, Horticultural and Forestry Trng Bd, 1972–74; Member: E Riding Co. Agricultural Exec. Cttee, 1946–64; Agricultural Wages Board, 1946–78; Leeds Regional Hosp. Board, 1948–74 (Chm. Works and Buildings Cttee); Potato Marketing Bd, 1970–79. Magistrate, City of York, 1950–; Chairman: York and District Employment Cttee, 1963–74; N Yorks District Manpower Cttee, 1975–80; Vice-Chm., Leeds Regional Hosp. Bd, 1967–74. Mem. Council, Univ. of E Anglia. MUniv York, 1984. *Recreation:* gardening. *Address:* 42 Fellbrook Avenue, Beckfield Lane, Acomb, York YO2 5PS. *T:* York (01904) 798443.

HAZELL, Ven. Frederick Roy; Priest-in-charge, Chard Furnham with Chaffcombe, Knowle St Giles and Cricket Malherbie, since 1995; Adviser in Pastoral Care and Counselling, Diocese of Bath and Wells, since 1994; Archdeacon of Croydon, 1978–93; *b* 12 Aug. 1930; *s* of John Murdoch and Ruth Hazell; *m* 1956, Gwendoline Edna Armstrong (*née* Vare) (*d* 1993), *widow* of Major J. W. D. Armstrong; one step *s* decd; *m* 1994, Norma Irene Palmer (*née* Gardner). *Educ:* Hutton Grammar School, near Preston; Fitzwilliam Coll., Cambridge (MA); Cuddesdon Coll., Oxford. HM Forces, 1948–50. Asst Master, Kingham Hill School, 1953–54; Asst Curate, Ilkeston Parish Church, 1956–59; Priest-in-Charge, All Saints', Marlpool, 1959–62; First Vicar of Marlpool, 1962–63; Chaplain, Univ. of the West Indies, 1963–66; Asst Priest, St Martin-in-the-Fields, 1966–68; Vicar of Holy Saviour, Croydon, 1968–84; Rural Dean of Croydon, 1972–78. Hon. Canon of Canterbury, 1973–84. *Recreations:* music, history. *Address:* Furnham Rectory, Furnham Road, Chard, Som TA20 1AE. *T:* Chard (01460) 63167.

HAZELL, Sir Quinton, Kt 1995; CBE 1978 (MBE 1961); DL; Director, Foreign and Colonial Investment Trust, 1978–90; *b* 14 Dec. 1920; *s* of late Thomas Arthur Hazell and Ada Kathleen Hazell; *m* 1942, Morwenna Parry-Jones; one *s*. *Educ:* Manchester Grammar School. FIMI 1964. Management Trainee, Braid Bros Ltd, Colwyn Bay, 1936–39; Royal Artillery, 1939–46; formed Quinton Hazell Ltd, 1946; Chm., 1946–73; Chairman: Edward Jones (Contractors) Ltd, 1973–74; Supra Group plc, 1973–82 (Pres., 1983–85); Humberside Electronic Controls, 1987–89; Aerospace Engineering PLC, 1987–90 (Dir, 1986–90). Chm., W Midlands Econ. Planning Council, 1971–77. Mem., Welsh Adv. Cttee for Civil Aviation, 1961–67; Director: Wales Gas Bd, 1961–65; Phoenix Assce Co., 1965–85; Winterbottom Energy Trust, 1978–82; Hawker-Siddeley Gp, 1979–91; Banro Industries plc, 1985–89; British Law Executor and Trustee Co., 1986–87; Wagon Industries plc, 1989–; Non-Exec. Chm., F&C Enterprise Trust plc, 1981–86; Dep. Chm., Warwickshire Private Hosp., Leamington Spa, 1981–94; Chm., WPH Charitable Trust, 1994–; Governor, Lord Leycester Hosp., Warwick, 1971–. Member Council: UC Bangor, 1966–68; Univ. of Birmingham. Freeman, City of London, 1960; Liveryman, Coachmakers' and Coach Harness Makers' Co., 1960. DL Warwicks, 1982. *Recreations:* antiques, horology. *Address:* Wootton Paddox, Leek Wootton, Warwick CV35 7QX. *T:* Kenilworth (01926) 50704.

HAZELL, Robert John Davidge; Director, Constitution Unit, Law Faculty, University College London, since 1995; *b* 30 April 1948; *s* of Peter Hazell and Elizabeth Complin Fowler; *m* 1981, Alison Sophia Mordaunt Richards; two *s*. *Educ:* Eton (King's Schol.); Wadham Coll., Oxford (Minor Schol.; BA Hons). Called to the Bar, Middle Temple, 1973; Barrister, 1973–75. Home Office, 1975–89, working in Immigration Dept, Policy Planning Unit, Gaming Bd, Race Relns, Broadcasting, Police and Prison Depts; CS travelling fellowship to investigate freedom of inf. in Australia, Canada, NZ, 1986–87; Dir, Nuffield Foundn, 1989–95. Haldane Medal, RIPA, 1978. *Publications:* Conspiracy and Civil Liberties, 1974; (ed) The Bar on Trial, 1978; articles in legal and govt jls. *Recreations:* bird-watching, badgers, opera, canoeing. *Address:* 94 Constantine Road, NW3 2LS. *T:* 0171–267 4881; (office) The Constitution Unit, 4 Tavistock Place, WC1H 9RA.

HÁZI, Dr Vencel; Hungarian Ambassador to United States of America, 1983–89; *b* 3 Sept. 1925; *m* 1952, Judit Zell; one *d*. *Educ:* Technical Univ. and Univ. of Economics, Budapest. Entered Diplomatic Service, 1950; served in Min. of Foreign Affairs, Budapest, 1950; Press Attaché, Hungarian Legation, London, 1951–53; Counsellor, Legation, Stockholm, 1957–58; Ambassador: to Iraq, and to Afghanistan, 1958–61; to Greece, and to Cyprus, 1962–64; Head of Western Dept, Min. of For. Affairs, Budapest, 1964–68; Dep. For. Minister, Budapest, 1968–70, 1976–83; Ambassador to Court of St James's, 1970–76. Golden Grade of Order of Merit for Labour, 1962, and of Medal of Merit of Hungarian People's Republic, 1953; Grand Cordon of Order of Omayoum, 1st Class, Iran. *Recreations:* reading, music, swimming, chess. *Address:* 1025 Budapest, II Kulpa utca 8, Hungary. *Club:* Opera Fans (Budapest).

HAZLERIGG, family name of **Baron Hazlerigg.**

HAZLERIGG, 2nd Baron, *cr* 1945, of Noseley; **Arthur Grey Hazlerigg,** Bt, *cr* 1622; MC 1945; TD 1948; DL, JP; *b* 24 Feb. 1910; *e s* of 1st Baron and Dorothy Rachel (*d* 1972), *e d* of John Henry Buxton, Easneye, Ware, Herts; *S* father 1949; *m* 1945, Patricia (*d* 1972), *e d* of late John Pullar, High Seat, Fields Hill, Kloof, Natal, SA; one *s* two *d*. *Educ:* Eton; Trinity Coll., Cambridge. BA 1932. FRICS 1946. Served War of 1939–45, Leics Yeomanry (MC); Major, 1941; served in Italy. DL Leics 1946; JP 1946. *Recreation:* golf. *Heir:* *s* Hon. Arthur Grey Hazlerigg [*b* 5 May 1951; *m* 1986, Laura, *e d* of Sir William Dugdale, Bt, *qv*; one *s* three *d* incl. twin *d*]. *Address:* Noseley Hall, Leicester LE7 9EH. *Clubs:* Army and Navy, MCC.

HAZLEWOOD, Prof. Arthur Dennis; Research Professor in Commonwealth Studies, Oxford University, 1986–88, now Emeritus; Professorial Fellow, Pembroke College, Oxford, 1979–88, now Emeritus; *b* 24 April 1921; *s* of Harry Arthur Sinclair Hazlewood and Miriam Esther Maltby; *m* 1954, Tamara Oszpicyn; one *d*. *Educ:* Finchley County Sch.; LSE (BSc Econ 1948); The Queen's Coll., Oxford (BPhil 1950; MA 1954). Post Office engineer, 1938–48 (RAF radar stations, 1940–44); Oxford University, 1950–: Tutor to Colonial Service courses, 1950–56; research staff, Inst. of Economics and Statistics, 1956–79; Pembroke College: tutorial fellow, 1961–79; Domestic Bursar, 1970–79; Vicegerent, 1978–79; Warden, Queen Elizabeth House, Dir, Inst. of Commonwealth Studies, 1979–86. Adviser, Nyasaland Govt on Central African Fedn, 1962; Dir, Common Market Secretariat, President's Office, Kenya, 1965–66; Dir, Trade and Finance Div., Commonwealth Secretariat and Special Adviser, Commonwealth Fund for Technical Co-operation, 1975–76. *Publications:* (jtly) Nyasaland: the economics of federation, 1960; The Economy of Africa, 1961; (jtly) An Econometric Model of the UK, 1961; Rail and Road in East Africa, 1964; (ed) African Integration and Disintegration, 1967; Economic Integration: the East African experience, 1975; (jtly) Aid and Inequality in Kenya, 1976; The Economy of Kenya, 1979; (jtly) Irrigation Economics in Poor Countries, 1982; Education, Work, and Pay in East Africa, 1989; articles in jls and symposia. *Address:* 14 Fyfield Road, Oxford OX2 6QE. *T:* Oxford (01865) 59119.

HAZLEWOOD, Air Vice-Marshal Frederick Samuel, CB 1970; CBE 1967 (OBE 1960); AFC 1951 (Bar to AFC, 1954); retired; *b* 13 May 1921; *s* of Samuel Henry and Lilian Hazlewood; *m* 1943, Isabelle Mary (*née* Hunt); one *s*. *Educ:* Kimbolton Sch. Served War of 1939–45: joined RAF, 1939; ops with Bomber Command, 1941; MEAF and UK Coastal Command, 1940–45. Lancaster Units, 1948–53; Comdg Officer, No 90 Valiant Sqdn, 1958–61; HQ, Bomber Comd, 1961–63; HQ, RAF, Germany, 1963–64; OC RAF Lyneham, 1965–67; HQ, RAF, Germany, 1968–69; AOC and Commandant, Central Flying School, 1970–72; AOC 38 Gp, RAF, 1972–74; Comdt, Jt Warfare Estab., 1974–76. *Recreations:* golf, tennis, rough shooting. *Club:* Royal Air Force.

HAZLEWOOD, Rt. Rev. John, SSC; Bishop of Ballarat, 1975–93; *b* 19 May 1924; *s* of George Harold Egerton Hazlewood and Anne Winnifred Edeson; *m* 1961, Dr Shirley Shevill; two *s*. *Educ:* Nelson Coll., New Zealand; King's Coll., Cambridge (BA 1948, MA 1952); Cuddesdon Coll., Oxford. Deacon 1949, priest 1950, Southwark; Asst Curate: SS Michael and All Angels, Camberwell, 1949–50, 1953–55; St Jude, Randwick, Sydney, 1950–51; Holy Trinity, Dubbo, NSW, 1951–53; Vice-Principal, St Francis Coll., Brisbane, 1955–60; Asst Lectr in Ecclesiastical History, Univ. of Queensland, 1959–60; Dean of Rockhampton, Qld, 1960–68; Dean of Perth, WA, 1968–75. Chaplain to Victorian Br., Order of St Lazarus of Jerusalem, 1984–. Mem., Australian Anglican Nat. Doctrine Commn, 1978–89. Mem., Soc. of Holy Cross (SSC), 1985–. *Recreations:* travelling, music, gardening, reading, theatre, art. *Address:* 1409 Gregory Street, Ballarat, Vic 3350, Australia. *Clubs:* Melbourne, Royal Automobile of Victoria (Melbourne).

HEAD, family name of **Viscount Head.**

HEAD, 2nd Viscount *cr* 1960, of Throope; **Richard Antony Head;** *b* 27 Feb. 1937; *s* of 1st Viscount Head, GCMG, CBE, MC, PC, and Dorothea, Viscountess Head (*d* 1987), *d* of 9th Earl of Shaftesbury, KP, GCVO, CBE, PC; *S* father, 1983; *m* 1974, Alicia Brigid, *er d* of Julian Salmond; two *s* one *d*. *Educ:* Eton; RMA Sandhurst. The Life Guards, 1957–66 (Captain), retd. Trainer of racehorses, 1968–83. *Recreations:* shooting, sailing, golf. *Heir:* *s* Hon. Henry Julian Head, *b* 30 March 1980. *Address:* Throope Manor, Bishopstone, Salisbury, Wilts SP5 4BA. *T:* Coombe Bissett (0172277) 318. *Club:* White's.

HEAD, Adrian Herbert; His Honour Judge Head; a Circuit Judge since 1972; *b* 4 Dec. 1923; *s* of late Judge Head and late Mrs Geraldine Head (*née* Pipon); *m* 1947, Ann Pamela, *d* of late John Stanning and late Mrs A. C. Lewin, of Leyland and Njoro, Kenya; three *s*. *Educ:* RNC Dartmouth (invalided, polio); privately; Magdalen Coll., Oxford (MA). Arden Scholar, Gray's Inn, 1947. Called to Bar, Gray's Inn, 1947 (subseq. ad eundem Inner Temple). Chm., Agricultural Land Tribunals (SE Region), 1971; Dep. Chm., Middlesex QS, 1971. Dir, later Chm., Norfolk Lavender Ltd, 1953–71. Tredegar Memorial Lectr, RSL, 1948. Licensed Reader, C of E, 1961. Co-founder and subseq. Sen. Trustee, Norfolk Family Conciliation Service, 1983–; Pres., W Norfolk and Fenland, Marriage Guidance Council, now Relate, 1984–. Hon. DCL East Anglia, 1987. *Publications:* (contrib.) Oxford Poetry 1942–1943, 1943; The Seven Words and The Civilian, 1946; contrib. Essays by Divers Hands, 1953; Safety Afloat (trans. from Dutch of W. Zantvoort), 1965; Consumer Credit Act Supplement to McCleary's County Court Precedents, 1979; Poems in Praise, 1982, 2nd edn 1987; (devised and general ed., 1985–87, consulting ed., 1987–, and contrib.) Butterworths County Court Precedents and Pleadings, 1985, thereafter frequent supplements. *Recreations:* painting, sailing, writing, trees. *Address:* Overy Staithe, Kings Lynn, Norfolk PE31 8TG. *T:* Fakenham (01328) 738312; 5 Raymond Buildings, Gray's Inn, WC1R 5BP. *T:* 0171–405 7146. *Clubs:* Jersey Soc.; Norfolk (Norwich); Royal Naval Sailing Association, Cruising Association.

HEAD, Alan Kenneth, AO 1992; PhD, DSc; FAA 1971; FRS 1988; Hon. Research Fellow, Commonwealth Scientific and Industrial Research Organization, Australia, since 1990 (Chief Research Scientist, 1969–90); *b* 10 Aug. 1925; *s* of Rowland Henry John Head and Elsie May (*née* Burrell); *m* 1951, Gwenneth Nancy Barlow. *Educ:* Ballarat Grammar Sch.; Scotch Coll.; Univ. of Melbourne (BA, BSc, DSc); Univ. of Bristol (PhD). Research Scientist: CSIR Div. of Aeronautics, 1947–50; Aeronautical Res. Labs, 1953–57; CSIRO Division: of Tribo Physics, 1957–81; of Chemical Physics, 1981–86; of Materials Science, 1987. Visiting Professor: Brown Univ., 1961–62; Univ. of Florida, 1971; Christensen Fellow, 1986, Vis. Fellow, 1990–, St Catherine's Coll., Oxford. *Publications:* Computed Electron Micrographs and Defect Identification, 1973, Chinese edn 1979; numerous contribs to sci. jls. *Address:* 10 Ellesmore Court, Kew, Vic 3101, Australia. *T:* (office) (3) 95422861; (home) (3) 98530673, *Fax:* (office) (3) 95441128.

HEAD, Audrey May; Member, Monopolies and Mergers Commission, 1986–89; Director, 1973–85, Managing Director, 1976–85, Hill Samuel Unit Trust Managers Ltd; *b* 21 Jan. 1924; *d* of Eric Burton Head and Kathleen Irene Head. *Educ:* St Catherine's Sch., Bramley, Surrey. Chartered Auctioneers' and Estate Agents' Institute, 1949–58; Hill Samuel Group, 1958–85, a Manager, 1968; Director: Hill Samuel Investment Management, 1974–86; Hill Samuel Life Assurance, 1983–86; Trade Union Unit Trust Managers Ltd, 1983–85. Chm., Unit Trust Assoc., 1983–85. Non-exec. Mem., Royal Surrey and St Luke's NHS Trust, 1991–93. Chm., Governing Body, St Catherine's Sch., Bramley, Surrey, 1988– (Gov. 1979–); Gov., Cranleigh Sch., Surrey, 1988–. Nominated as Business Woman of the Year, 1976. Silver Jubilee Medal, 1977. *Recreations:* golf, gardening. *Address:* West Chantry, 4 Clifford Manor Road, Guildford, Surrey GU4 8AG. *T:* Guildford (01483) 61047.

HEAD, Dennis Alec, CBE 1979; CEng, FRAeS; Divisional Director (Northern Ireland), STC, 1986–91; *b* 8 Nov. 1925; *s* of late Alec Head and Florence Head; *m* 1966, Julia Rosser-Owen, BA; one *s*. *Educ:* Whitgift Sch.; Peterhouse, Cambridge (Mech. Sciences Tripos, MA); Royal Naval Engrg Coll., Manadon. Served FAA, RN, 1943–47: Sub-Lt (A) RNVR, 1945; Air Engr Officer. Rolls-Royce Ltd: grad. apprentice, 1949; Manager, Design Services, Aero Engine Div., 1962, Dir of Personnel and Admin, 1967; Dir and Gen. Man., subseq. Man. Dir, Derby Engine Div., 1973; Man. Dir Aero Div., 1976; Man. Dir Operations, 1980–82; Member Board: Rolls-Royce Ltd, 1973–82; Rolls-Royce Turbomeca, 1973–82 (Chm., 1981–82); Turbo-Union, 1979–82; Chm., Rolls-Royce & Associates, 1981–82; Mem. Bd and Dir Operations, Short Brothers, 1982–86. Member: Reg. Adv. Council for Further Educn, 1968–73; Engrg Employers' Fedn Policy Cttee, 1978–82. *Recreations:* photography, history, music. *Address:* Bodmans, 48D High Street, Marshfield, Wilts SN14 8LP; Well House, 27 Cultra Avenue, Holywood, Co. Down BT18 0AZ. *T:* Holywood (01232) 425583.

HEAD, Major Sir Francis (David Somerville), 5th Bt, *cr* 1838; late Queen's Own Cameron Highlanders; *b* 17 Oct. 1916; *s* of 4th Bt and Grace Margaret (*d* 1967), *d* of late David Robertson; *S* father, 1924; *m* 1st, 1950, Susan Patricia (marr. diss. 1965), *o d* of A. D. Ramsay, OBE; one *s* one *d*; 2nd, 1967, Penelope, *d* of late Wilfred Alexander. *Educ:* Eton; Peterhouse, Cambridge, BA 1937. Served War of 1939–45 (wounded and prisoner); retired 1951. *Heir:* *s* Richard Douglas Somerville Head [*b* 16 Jan. 1951; *m* 1991, Edwina, *d* of late Edward Mansell. *Educ:* Eton; Magdalene Coll., Cambridge]. *Address:* 63 Chantry View Road, Guildford, Surrey GU1 3XU. *Club:* Naval and Military.

HEAD, Michael Edward, CVO 1991; Assistant Under Secretary of State and Head of Equal Opportunities and General Department, Home Office, since 1991; *b* 17 March 1936; *s* of Alexander Edward Head and Wilhelmina Head; *m* 1963, Wendy Elizabeth, *d* of R. J. Davies; two *s* two *d*. *Educ:* Leeds, Kingston, and Woking Grammar Schools;

University College London (BA; Pollard Prize for History); Univ. of Michigan (MA). 2nd Lieut, Royal Artillery (Nat. Service), 1958–60. Home Office, 1960; Private Sec. to Parly Under Secs of State, 1964–66; Sec., Deptl Cttee on Liquor Licensing (Erroll), 1971–72; Asst Sec., 1974–84: Probation and After Care Dept; Community Programmes and Equal Opportunities Dept; Criminal Dept; Asst Under Sec. of State, General Dept, 1984, Criminal Justice and Constitutional Dept (Registrar of the Baronetage), 1986, Broadcasting Dept, 1991. FRSA. *Recreations:* theatre, reading. *Address:* Byways, The Ridge, Woking, Surrey GU22 7EE. *T:* Woking (01483) 772929. *Clubs:* Reform; Rotary (Woking Dist).

HEAD, Mildred Eileen, OBE 1971; owner, director and partner in several furniture and drapery shops, 1950–83; *b* 13 June 1911; *d* of Philip Strudwick Head and Katie Head. *Educ:* Sudbury Girls' Secondary Sch.; Chelsea Coll. of Physical Educn (Dipl.). MCSP. Teacher, Lectr and Organiser of Physical Educn, 1933–50. Pres., Nat. Fedn of Business and Professional Women of Gt Britain and N Ireland, 1966–69; Pres., Nat. Chamber of Trade, 1977–79 (Chm. Bd of Management, 1971–77). Mayor of Borough of Sudbury, 1970–71; Member: Price Commn, 1973–77; Nat. Economic Cttee for Distributive Trades, 1974–84; Retail Consortium, 1971–83; Davignon/Narjes Cttee for Commerce and Distribution (EEC), 1979–86; Discip. Cttee of Assoc. of Certified Accountants, 1980–83; Assessor, Auld Cttee of Inquiry into Shops Hours, 1984–85. Comr of Inland Revenue, 1959–86. Pres., Internat. Fedn of Business and Professional Women, 1977–80 (First Vice-Pres., 1974–77). Chm., Management Cttee, Quay Theatre, Sudbury, 1982–87. *Recreations:* theatre, gardening, bridge. *Address:* Rosebank, Ingrams Well Road, Sudbury, Suffolk CO10 6RT. *T:* Sudbury (01787) 72185.

HEAD, Philip John, FRICS; Head of Property Services, since 1994, and private finance unit, since 1995, Further Education Funding Council for England; *b* 24 Nov. 1951; *s* of Dennis George Head and Marjorie Head; *m* 1974, Barbara Fox; two *s*. *Educ:* Surbiton Grammar Sch.; Univ. of Reading (BSc Hons Estate Management). FRICS 1985. Estates Surveyor, 1973–77, Sen. Commercial Surveyor, 1977–78, Milton Keynes Develt Corp.; Welsh Development Agency, 1978–93: Develt and Funding Manager, 1981–83; Dep. Commercial Dir, 1983–84; Commercial Dir, 1984–87; Exec. Dir, Property and Regional Services, 1987–91; Chief Exec., 1991–93. Mem., Urban Regeneration Panel, 1992–, Facilities Management Skill Panel, 1995–, RICS. Hon. Treas., Coventry Phoenix Rotary Club, 1995–. *Recreations:* Llantrisant 41 Club, swimming, gardening, golf, family. *Address:* Further Education Funding Council, Cheylesmore House, Quinton Road, Coventry CV1 2WT. *T:* Coventry (01203) 863119.

HEADFORT, 6th Marquis of, *cr* 1800; **Thomas Geoffrey Charles Michael Taylour,** FRICS; Bt 1704; Baron Headfort, 1760; Viscount Headfort, 1762; Earl of Bective, 1766; Baron Kenlis (UK), 1831; *b* 20 Jan. 1932; *o s* of 5th Marquis and Elsie Florence (*d* 1972), *d* of J. Partridge Tucker, Sydney, NSW, and *widow* of Sir Rupert Clarke, 2nd Bt of Rupertswood; *S* father, 1960; *m* 1st, 1958, Hon. Elizabeth Nall-Cain (from whom he obtained a divorce, 1969), *d* of 2nd Baron Brocket; one *s* two *d*; 2nd, 1972, Virginia, *d* of late Mr Justice Nable, Manila. *Educ:* Stowe; Christ's Coll., Cambridge (MA; Cert. of Proficiency in Rural Estate Management). 2nd Lieut Life Guards, 1950; acting Pilot Officer, RAFVR, 1952. Dir, Bective Electrical Co. Ltd, 1953; Sales Manager and Chief Pilot, Lancashire Aircraft Co. Ltd, 1959. Freeman, Guild of Air Pilots and Air Navigators, 1958. Piloted Prospector aircraft around Africa, 1960, etc. FRICS; FCIArb; Mem., Irish Auctioneers and Valuers Inst. Council, Royal Agricultural Society of England, 1961. Inspector, Royal Hong Kong Police, 1977. Commercial Pilot's Licence, 1967. Underwriting Mem. of Lloyds. *Heir: s* Earl of Bective, *qv*. *Address:* 1425 Figueroa Street, Paco, Manila, Philippines. *T:* (632) 8174819, *Fax:* (632) 8191757; Affix Ltd, Rooms 1603–4, New Victory House, 93–103 Wing Lok Street, Hong Kong. *T:* Hong Kong 5452977; *Fax:* 8541229. *Clubs:* Cavalry and Guards, Lansdowne, Little Ship, Lloyds Yacht, House of Lords Yacht, Kildare Street and University (Dublin); Ellan Vannin (Isle of Man); Manila, Manila Polo, Manila Yacht (Philippines); Hong Kong, Foreign Correspondents, Aberdeen Boat (Hong Kong).

HEADLY, Derek, CMG 1957; lately Malayan Civil Service; Midlands Secretary, Independent Schools Careers Organisation, 1966–77; *b* 1908; *s* of L. C. Headly, The House-on-the-Hill, Woodhouse Eaves, Leics; *m* 1946, Joyce Catherine (marr. diss. 1975), *d* of C. F. Freeman; one *s* one *d*. *Educ:* Repton Sch.; Corpus Christi Coll., Cambridge (BA). Military Service, 1944–46, Lieut-Col, Special Ops Exec., Force 136 (despatches), and British Mil. Admin. Malayan CS, 1931; served Trengganu, Muar, Pekan etc.; seconded to Palestine Mandate, 1938–44; Resident N Borneo, 1949–53; British Adviser, Kelantan, 1953–57. Dir, Vipan & Headly Ltd, 1957–66. Mem. Melton and Belvoir RDC, 1958–67. Officer (Brother) Order of St John. *Publication:* From Learning to Earning (Independent Schools Careers Organisation Careers Guide), 1977. *Recreations:* hill walking, gardening. *Address:* Rooftree Cottage, Hoby, Melton Mowbray, Leics LE14 3DT. *T:* Melton Mowbray (01664) 434214. *Club:* Special Forces.

HEAF, Peter Julius Denison, MD; FRCP; Chairman, Medical Sickness Annuity and Life Insurance Society Ltd, 1988–93; *b* 1922; *s* of late Prof. F. R. G. Heaf, CMG; *m* 1947, Rosemary Cartledge; two *s* two *d*. *Educ:* Stamford Sch., Lincs; University Coll., London, Fellow 1973. MB, BS 1946; MD London 1952; MRCP 1954; FRCP 1965. House Physician and Surg., also RMO, University Coll. Hosp., and Capt. RAMC, 1946–51; Research Asst, Brompton Hosp., 1953–54; Sen. Registrar, St Thomas' Hosp., 1955–58; Consultant Physician, UCH, 1958–86, retired. *Publications:* papers on chest disease and pulmonary physiology, in Lancet, etc. *Recreations:* painting, gardening. *Address:* Ferrybrook House, Chalmore Gardens, Wallingford, Oxon OX10 9EP. *T:* Wallingford (01491) 839176.

HEAL, Oliver Standerwick; Commercial Director, Faïenceries de Quimper, France, since 1992; *b* 18 April 1949; *s* of late Anthony Standerwick Heal; *m* 1990, Annik Coatalen; one *s*. *Educ:* Leighton Park Sch., Reading. Joined Heal's, 1970; Dir, Heal & Son Ltd, 1974–83, Chm., 1977–83; Chm., Heal & Son Holdings PLC, 1981–83 (Dir, 1975–83); Dir, Staples & Co. Ltd, 1981–84; Chm., Heal Textil GmbH, 1984–90; VRP multi-carte, France, 1990–91. *Recreation:* vintage cars. *Address:* 4 rue de la Gare, 29120 Pont l'Abbé, France. *Club:* Vintage Sports Car (Newbury).

HEAL, Sylvia Lloyd; JP; National Officer, Carers National Association, since 1992; *b* 20 July 1942; *d* of John Lloyd Fox and Ruby Fox; *m* 1965, Keith Heal; one *s* one *d*. *Educ:* Elfed Secondary Modern School, Buckley, N Wales; Coleg Harlech; University College Swansea (BSc Econ 1968). Medical Records Clerk, Chester Royal Infirmary, 1957–63; social worker, health service and Dept of Employment, 1968–70 and 1980–90. MP (Lab) Mid Staffordshire, March 1990–1992; contested (Lab) Mid Staffordshire, 1992. Mem., Select Cttee on Educn, Sci. and Arts, 1990–92; opposition spokesperson on health and women's issues, 1991–92. Mem. Council, ASA, 1992–; Mem., Exec. Council, SSAFA, 1990–91. JP Surrey, 1973. *Recreations:* walking, theatre, listening to male voice choirs. *Address:* Meadlake, 15 Vicarage Avenue, Egham, Surrey TW20 8NW.

HEALD, Mervyn; QC 1970; a Social Security Commissioner, since 1988; a Child Support Commissioner, since 1993; *b* 12 April 1930; *s* of Rt Hon. Sir Lionel Heald, QC, and of Daphne Constance, CBE 1976, *d* of late Montague Price; *m* 1954, Clarissa Bowen; one *s* three *d*. *Educ:* Eton College; Magdalene College, Cambridge. Called to the Bar, Middle Temple, 1954; Bencher, 1978. A Recorder, 1985–88. *Recreations:* country pursuits. *Address:* (office) 83 Faringdon Street, EC4A 4DH. *T:* 0171–353 5145.

HEALD, Oliver; MP (C) North Hertfordshire, since 1992; Parliamentary Under-Secretary of State, Department of Social Security, since 1995; *b* 15 Dec. 1954; *s* of John Anthony and Joyce Heald; *m* 1979, Christine Whittle; one *s* two *d*. *Educ:* Reading Sch.; Pembroke Coll., Cambridge (MA Hons Law). Called to the Bar, Middle Temple, 1977; practice in E Anglia and London, 1979–. Contested (C) Southwark and Bermondsey, 1987. PPS to Minister of Agric., Fisheries and Food, 1994–95. Mem., Employment Select Cttee, 1992–94; Vice-Chm., Cons. Back bench Employment Cttee, 1992–94. *Recreations:* sports, family. *Address:* House of Commons, SW1A 0AA; Fenners Chambers, Madingley Road, Cambridge CB3 0EE. *T:* Cambridge (01223) 68761. *Clubs:* Carlton, St Stephen's Constitutional; Cambridgeshire Farmers' (Cambridge).

HEALD, His Honour Thomas Routledge; a Circuit Judge (formerly County Court Judge), 1970–95; *b* 19 Aug. 1923; *s* of late John Arthur Heald and Nora Marion Heald; *m* 1950, Jean, *d* of James Campbell Henderson; two *s* two *d*. *Educ:* Merchant Taylors' Sch.; St John's Coll., Oxford. Fish Schol., St John's Coll., Oxford, 1941; Lieut, RAC, 1943–45; BA (Jurisprudence) 1947; MA 1949. Called to Bar, Middle Temple, 1948; Midland Circuit; Prosecuting Counsel to Inland Revenue (Midland Circuit), 1965–70; Deputy Chairman, QS: Lindsey, 1965–71; Notts, 1969–71; Notts designated Family Judge, 1991–. Council of HM Circuit Judges: Asst Sec., 1980–83; Sec., 1984–85; Vice-Pres., 1986–87; Pres., 1988–89; Member: Matrimonial Rules Cttee, 1980–83; President's Cttee on Adoption, 1983–95; President's Family Cttee, 1984–93. Mem., Senate of Inns of Court, 1984–86. Mem. Council, Nottingham Univ., 1974–93 (Chm., Physical Recreation Adv. Cttee, 1979–85; Chm., Law Adv. Cttee, 1976–84; Chm., Estates and Buildings Cttee, 1985–89); Chm., Law Adv. Cttee, Trent Polytechnic, 1979–84. *Recreations:* golf, local history, family history. *Address:* Rebbur House, Nicker Hill, Keyworth, Nottingham NG12 5ED. *T:* Nottingham (0115) 937 2676. *Clubs:* United Services (Nottingham); Notts Golf, Woking Golf.

HEALEY, family name of **Baron Healey.**

HEALEY, Baron *cr* 1992 (Life Peer), of Riddlesden in the County of West Yorkshire; **Denis Winston Healey,** CH 1979; MBE 1945; PC 1964; *b* 30 Aug. 1917; *s* of late William Healey, Keighley, Yorks; *m* 1945, Edna May Edmunds (*see* Lady Healey); one *s* two *d*. *Educ:* Bradford Grammar Sch.; Balliol Coll., Oxford (Hon. Fellow, 1979). First Cl. Hons Mods 1938; Jenkyns Exhib. 1939; Harmsworth Sen. Schol., First Cl. Lit. Hum., BA 1940; MA 1945. War of 1939–45; entered Army, 1940; served N Africa, Italy. Major RE 1944 (despatches). Contested (Lab) Pudsey and Otley Div., 1945; Sec., International Dept, Labour Party, 1945–52. MP (Lab) SE Leeds, Feb. 1952–1955, Leeds E, 1955–92; Shadow Cabinet, 1959–64, 1970–74, 1979–87; Secretary of State for Defence, 1964–70; Chancellor of the Exchequer, 1974–79; opposition spokesman on Foreign and Commonwealth Affairs, 1980–87; Dep. Leader of Labour Party, 1980–83. Mem. Brit. Delegn to Commonwealth Relations Conf., Canada, 1949; British Delegate to: Consultative Assembly, Council of Europe, 1952–54; Inter Parly Union Conf., Washington, 1953; Western European Union and Council of Europe, 1953–55. Chm., IMF Interim Cttee, 1977–79. Mem. Exec. Fabian Soc., 1954–61. Mem., Labour Party Nat. Exec. Cttee, 1970–75. Councillor: RIIA, 1948–60; Inst. of Strategic Studies, 1958–61. Pres., Birkbeck Coll., 1993. Freeman, City of Leeds, 1992. FRSL 1993. Hon. Fellow, Leeds Polytechnic, 1987. Hon. DLitt Bradford, 1983; Hon. LLD Sussex, 1991. Grand Cross of Order of Merit, Germany, 1979. *Publications:* The Curtain Falls, 1951; New Fabian Essays, 1952; Neutralism, 1955; Fabian International Essays, 1956; A Neutral Belt in Europe, 1958; NATO and American Security, 1959; The Race Against the H Bomb, 1960; Labour Britain and the World, 1963; Healey's Eye, 1980; Labour and a World Society, 1985; Beyond Nuclear Deterrence, 1986; The Time of My Life (autobiog.), 1989; When Shrimps Learn to Whistle (essays), 1990; My Secret Planet, 1992. *Recreations:* travel, photography, music, painting. *Address:* Pingles Place, Alfriston, East Sussex BN26 5TT.

HEALEY, Lady; Edna May Healey; writer; *b* 14 June 1918; *d* of Rose and Edward Edmunds; *m* 1945, Baron Healey, *qv*: one *s* two *d*. *Educ:* Bell's Grammar School, Coleford, Glos; St Hugh's College, Oxford (BA, Dip Ed). Taught English and History: Keighley Girls' Grammar School, 1940–44; Bromley Girls' High Sch., 1944–47; freelance lecturer, England and America; television writer and presenter; radio writer and broadcaster. *Publications:* Lady Unknown: life of Angela Burdett-Coutts, 1978; Wives of Fame, 1986; Coutts & Co. 1692–1992: the portrait of a private bank, 1992. *Recreations:* gardening, listening to music. *Address:* Pingles Place, Alfriston, East Sussex BN26 5TT.

HEALEY, Sir Charles Edward C.; *see* Chadwyck-Healey.

HEALEY, Deryck John; FRSA 1978; FCSD; artist, sculptor; *b* 30 Jan. 1937; *s* of Leonard Melvon Healey and Irene Isabella Healey (*née* Ferguson); *m* 1962, Mary Elizabeth Pitt Booth (decd); two *s*. *Educ:* Northlands High Sch., Natal, SA (Victoria League Empire Scholar; DipAD, SA, 1955; Golden Jubilee Cert. of Merit, 1957); Manchester Polytechnic (DipAd 1958, Textile Design Prize, 1957, 1958; Design Travel Bursary, 1958; Royal Manch. Inst. Cert. of Merit, 1958; Calico Printers' Assoc. Fellow, 1961–62). Design Man., Good Hope Textiles, SA, 1959–66; Chairman: Deryck Healey Associates, London, 1966–85; Deryck Healey International, 1969–85; Dreamshire, 1985–87; Design Man., WPM London (Wallpaper mfrs), 1966–68; ICI Design Studio Manager, Asst to Elsbeth Juda, 1968–80; Consultant, D. H. I. Interiors Ltd, 1983–85; Design Consultant, Wedgwood, 1984–88. Chm., CNAA Textile and Fashion Bd, 1971–81; Member: CNAA Art and Design Cttee, 1971–81; Design Council Textile Design Selection Cttee, 1978–87; Craft Council Bd, 1983–85 (Textile Panel, 1980; Finance and Gen. Purposes Cttee, 1983–85; Chairman: Textile Develt Group, 1982–84; Projects and Organisations Cttee, 1983–85). RSA: Annual Sponsor, D. Healey Fashion and Colour Bursaries, 1978–85; Mem. Bursary Bd, 1982–88. Patron, New Art Tate Gall., 1983–. Member: Contemp. Art Soc., 1982–; ICA, 1970–; Chelsea Arts Club, 1982–88; Friend of RA, 1980–. SIAD: Mem., British Design Export Gp, 1980; Chm., Textile and Fashion Gp, 1966–67. External Examiner, Textile and Fashion courses: CNAA BA and MA; Liverpool, BA, 1978–80; Manchester, MA, 1976–79; Kingston, BA, 1978–80; St Martin's, BA, 1978–80; Glasgow, BA, 1979–82; RCA, Textiles, 1980; Adviser and External Examiner, Middx Polytechnic, BA, 1982–86; External Examiner: London Coll. of Furniture, BTEC, 1985–86; BA Fashion, St Martin's Sch. of Art, 1985–87. Exhibitions: Salama-Caro Gall., London, 1990, 1991, 1994; Frankfurt Internat. Art Fair, 1990; Venice, 1990; Internat. Art Fairs, Cologne and Chicago, 1990; Phoenix Univ., Arizona, 1991; Fosbury, UK, 1991; Santa Fé, Mexico, 1992; Galerie Langer Fain, Paris, 1992; Koplin Gall., LA, 1993; Art of Concern, Base, London, 1994. Installation, Seamen's Mission, Glasgow, 1992; special commn sculpture, Manchester Internat. Concert Hall, 1996. FCSD (FSIAD 1964). CoID Design Award, 1964; Queen's Award to Industry for Export, 1974; RSA Bicentenary Medal, 1981; Textile Institute Design Medal, 1982. *Publications:* Colour, 1980 (Mem. Editorial Bd and contrib.); Living with Colour, 1982; The New Art of Flower Design, 1986; Big Names,

1991; Open Studio, 1994; Our Island Garden Project, 1995. *Address:* Box 476, 2 Old Brompton Road, SW7 3DQ. *Clubs:* various.

HEALEY, Edna May; *see* Lady Healey.

HEALY, Bernadine P., (Mrs F. Loop), MD; Director, National Institutes of Health, Bethesda, Maryland, 1991–93; *b* 2 Aug. 1944; *d* of Michael J. Healy and Violet (*née* McGrath); *m* 1985, Floyd Loop; two *d. Educ:* Vassar Coll. (AB *summa cum laude* 1965); Harvard Med. Sch. (MD *cum laude* 1970). Intern in medicine, 1970–71, asst resident, 1971–72, Johns Hopkins Hosp., Balt.; Staff Fellow, Sect. Pathology, Nat. Heart, Lung and Blood Inst., NIH, 1972–74; Johns Hopkins University School of Medicine: Fellow, Cardiovascular Div., Dept of Medicine, 1974–76; Fellow, Dept of Pathology, 1975–76; Asst Prof. of Medicine and Pathology, 1976–81; Associate Prof. of Medicine, 1977–82; Asst Dean for Postdoctoral Programs and Faculty Develt, 1979–84; Associate Prof. of Pathology, 1981–84; Prof. of Medicine, 1982–84; Active Staff, Medicine and Pathology, 1976, Dir, Coronary Care Unit, 1977–84, Johns Hopkins Hosp.; Dep. Dir, Office of Sci. and Technol. Policy, Exec. Office of Pres., White House, Washington, 1984–85; Chm., Res. Inst., Cleveland Clinic Foundn, 1985–91.

HEALY, Prof. John Francis, MA, PhD; Professor of Classics, London University, 1966–90, now Professor Emeritus; Chairman of Department, Royal Holloway and Bedford New College, 1985–88 (Head of Department, Royal Holloway College, 1966–85); *b* 27 Aug. 1926; *s* of late John Healy and Iris Maud (*née* Cutland); *m* 1st, 1957, Carol Ann McEvoy; one *s*; 2nd, 1985, Barbara Edith Henshall. *Educ:* Trinity Coll., Cambridge (Open Exhbn in Classics 1943; Classical Prelim. Cl. 1 1944; Classical Tripos: 1st Cl. Pt I 1949, 1st Cl. Pt II 1950 (dist. Cl. Archaeol.); Sen. Schol. 1950; BA 1950, MA 1952, PhD 1955). War service, 1944–48; Captain, Intelligence Corps, 1946–48. Walston student, Brit. Sch. of Archaeol., Athens, 1950; G. C. Winter Warr Schol., Cambridge, 1951; Manchester University: Asst Lectr in Classics, 1953–56; Lectr in Classics and Class. Archaeol., 1956–61; London University: Reader in Greek, Bedford Coll., 1961–66; Chm., Bd of Studies in Classics, 1979–81; Dean of Faculty of Arts, Royal Holloway Coll., 1978–81. Chm. Finance Cttee, Inst. of Classical Studies, London, 1967–88. FRNS 1950; FRSA 1971; MRI 1979. *Publications:* contrib. (A. Rowe) Cyrenaican Expeditions of the University of Manchester, 1955–57; Mining and Metallurgy in the Greek and Roman World, 1978, rev. and trans. edn, Miniere e Metallurgia nel Mondo Greco e Romano, 1993; Sylloge Nummorum Graecorum, vol. VII, The Raby and Güterbock collections in Manchester University Museum, 1986; Pliny the Elder, Natural History, 1991; articles and reviews in Jl of Hellenic St., Numismatic Chron., Nature, Amer. Num. Soc.'s Mus. Notes, Jl of Metals, Class. Rev., Gnomon. *Recreations:* travel, music, creative gardening. *Club:* Cambridge Union Society.

HEALY, Maurice Eugene; Director, National Consumer Council, 1987–91; *b* 27 Nov. 1933; *s* of late Thomas Healy and Emily Healy (*née* O'Mahoney); *m* 1958, Jose Barbara Speller Dewdney; two *d* (and one *d* decd). *Educ:* Downside School; Peterhouse, Cambridge (BA Classics). Nat. service, Royal Artillery, 1954–56. BoT, 1956–60; Consumers' Assoc., working on Which?, 1960–76; Head of Editl Dept and Editor of Which?, 1973–76; Nat. Consumer Council, 1977–91. Member: Council, Bureau Européen des Unions de Consommateurs, 1977–91; Council, Insurance Ombudsman Bureau, 1991–; Code of Banking Practice Review Cttee, 1991–; Indep. Management Cttee, Optical Consumer Complaints Service, 1992–; Bd, Jazz Services Ltd, 1992–; Chm., Consumer Policy Cttee, BSI, 1993–; Mem., Consumer Panel, PIA, 1993–; Assessor to Auld Cttee on reform of shop hours, 1984. Chm., Patients' Assoc., 1991–93. Trustee, European Res. Inst. for Consumer Affairs, 1990–. Hon. Vice Pres., NFCG. Chm. of Governors, Highgate Wood School, 1983–86. FRSA. Hon. Mem., Inst. of Consumer Affairs; Assoc. Mem., UK Ombudsman Assoc. *Publications:* contribs to Which? and Nat. Consumer Council and other jls and conf. papers. *Recreations:* jazz, Irish music, Shona sculpture. *Address:* 15 Onslow Gardens, Muswell Hill, N10 3JT. *T:* 0181–883 8955. *Clubs:* Ronnie Scott's, Burmese Cat.

HEALY, Tim T.; *see* Traverse-Healy.

HEANEY, Henry Joseph, FRSE; FLA; University Librarian and Keeper of the Hunterian Books and Manuscripts, Glasgow, since 1978; *b* 2 Jan. 1935; *s* of late Michael Heaney and Sarah (*née* Fox); *m* 1976, Mary Elizabeth Moloney. *Educ:* Abbey Grammar Sch., Newry; Queen's Univ. of Belfast (MA). FLA 1967; FRSE 1992. Asst Librarian, QUB, 1959–62; Libr., Magee University Coll., Londonderry, 1962–67; Dep. Libr., New Univ. of Ulster, 1967–69; Asst Sec., Standing Conf. of National and Univ. Libraries, 1969–72; Librarian: QUB, 1972–74; University Coll., Dublin, 1975–78. Member: Adv. Cttee on Public Lib. Service, NI, 1965; Standing Cttee, Univ. Libraries Sect. IFLA, 1985–91; British Liby Bd, 1989–95; Jt Funding Councils' Libraries Review Gp, 1992–93; Chm., Consortium of Univ. Res. Libraries, 1995–. Dir, Co. of Biologists, 1993–. Chm., NI Branch, Lib. Assoc., 1966, 1973; Pres., Scottish Liby Assoc., 1990. Trustee: Nat. Lib. of Scotland, 1980–91; Nat. Manuscripts Conservation Trust, 1990–95. *Publications:* (ed) IFLA Annual, 1971; (ed) World Guide to Abbreviations of Organisations, 8th edn, 1988 to 10th edn, 1993. *Address:* Glasgow University Library, Glasgow G12 8QE. *T:* 0141–330 5633.

HEANEY, Leonard Martin, CMG 1959; Overseas Civil Service, retired; *b* 28 Nov. 1906; *s* of Alexander John and Lilian Heaney; *m* 1947, Kathleen Edith Mary Chapman; no *c. Educ:* Bristol Grammar Sch.; Oriel Coll., Oxford. Joined Colonial Service on leaving Oxford, 1929; served in Tanganyika, retiring as a Senior Provincial Commissioner, 1959. Military service with East African Forces in Abyssinia, Madagascar, Ceylon, Burma, 1940–45. *Recreation:* reading. *Address:* Flat No 9, Salcombe Court, Salcombe Hill Road, Sidmouth, Devon EX10 8JR.

HEANEY, Seamus Justin; Member of Irish Academy of Letters; Professor of Poetry, Oxford University, 1989–94; Boylston Professor of Rhetoric and Oratory at Harvard University (formerly Visiting Professor), since 1985; *b* 13 April 1939; *s* of Patrick and Margaret Heaney; *m* 1965, Marie Devlin; two *s* one *d. Educ:* St Columb's College, Derry; Queen's University, Belfast. BA first cl. 1961. Teacher, St Thomas's Secondary Sch., Belfast, 1962–63; Lectr, St Joseph's Coll. of Educn, Belfast, 1963–66; Lectr, Queen's Univ., Belfast, 1966–72; free-lance writer, 1972–75; Lectr, Carysfort Coll., 1975–81. Bennett Award, 1982. *Publications:* Preoccupations: Selected Prose 1968–1978, 1980; The Government of the Tongue, 1988; The Cure at Troy (a version of Sophocles' Philoctetes), 1990; The Redress of Poetry, 1995; *poetry:* Eleven Poems, 1965; Death of a Naturalist, 1966 (Somerset Maugham Award, 1967; Cholmondeley Award, 1968); Door into the Dark, 1969; Wintering Out, 1972; North, 1975 (W. H. Smith Award; Duff Cooper Prize); Field Work, 1979; Selected Poems, 1965–1975, 1980; (ed with Ted Hughes) The Rattle Bag, 1982; Sweeney Astray, 1984, rev. edn as Sweeney's Flight, (with photographs by Rachel Giese), 1992; Station Island, 1984; The Haw Lantern, 1987 (Whitbread Award, 1987); New Selected Poems 1966–1987, 1990; Seeing Things, 1991; (ed) The May Anthology of Oxford and Cambridge Poetry, 1993. *Address:* c/o Faber & Faber, 3 Queen Square, WC1N 3RU.

HEANLEY, Charles Laurence, TD 1950; FRCS; Consulting Surgeon; *b* 28 Feb. 1907; *e s* of Dr C. M. Heanley; *m* 1935; three *s. Educ:* Epsom Coll.; Downing Coll., Cambridge (Exhib., Schol.); London Hosp. BA Cambridge (Nat. Sci. Tripos) 1929, MA 1934; MRCS, LRCP 1932; MB, BCh Cambridge 1934; FRCS 1933; MRCP 1935. London Hosp., 1929; Surg. First Asst, 1936. Served War of 1939–45; France, Surgical Specialist, 17th Gen. Hosp., 1939–40; Surgeon Specialist, RAMC Park Prewitt Plastic Unit, 1941–42; India, OC No 3 British Maxillo-Facial Surgical Unit and Lieut-Col OC Surgical Div., 1942–45; Surg. in charge of Dept of Plastic Surg., London Hosp., 1946–64. Cons. Surg. Worthing Hosp., Bethnal Green Hosp., and Plastic Unit Queen Victoria Hosp., East Grinstead, 1945; Plastic Surg. London Hosp.; Hon. Cons. Plastic Surg. Royal National and Golden Square Hosps, 1969. *Publications:* varied medical articles. *Recreations:* swimming, archæology. *Address:* Vainona, St George, Woodmancote, Henfield, West Sussex BN5 9ST. *T:* Brighton (01273) 492947.

HEAP, Brian; *see* Heap, R. B.

HEAP, Sir Desmond, Kt 1970; LLM, Hon. LLD, PPRTPI; solicitor; *b* 17 Sept. 1907; *o s* of William Heap, Architect, Burnley, Lancs, and Minnie Heap; *m* 1945, Adelene Mai, *o d* of Frederick Lacey, Harrogate, and Mrs F. N. Hornby; one *s* two *d. Educ:* The Grammar Sch., Burnley; Victoria University of Manchester. LLB Hons 1929; LLM 1936; Hon. LLD 1973; admitted Solicitor, 1933; Hons Final Law Examination. Lecturer in the Law of Town and Country Planning and Housing, Leeds Sch. of Architecture, 1935–47; Prosecuting Solicitor, 1935–38 and Chief Asst Solicitor for City of Leeds, 1938–40; Dep. Town Clerk of Leeds, 1940–47; Comptroller and City Solicitor to the Corporation of London, 1947–73. Consultant: Coward Chance, London, 1974–87; Hammond Suddards, Leeds and Bradford, 1974–91; Sugden & Spencer, Bradford, 1974–94. Pres., Law Soc., 1972–73 (Mem. Council, 1954–78, Chm. Law Reform Cttee, 1955–60, and Chm., Town Planning Cttee, 1964–70). Legal Mem., RTPI (formerly TPI), 1935–, Mem. of Council, 1947–77, Pres., 1955–56; Mem. of Editorial Board of Journal of Planning and Environment Law, 1948–; Mem. of Colonial Office Housing and Town Planning Adv. Panel, 1953–65; Mem., Council on Tribunals, 1971–77; Vice-Pres., Statute Law Soc., 1982–94. Dep. Pres., City of London Branch, British Red Cross Soc., 1956–76. Chm. of Governors, Hurstpierpoint Coll., 1975–82. Senior Past Master, Worshipful Company of Solicitors (Hon. Associate, 1987); Liveryman of Worshipful Company of Carpenters (Hon. Mem. of Ct, 1993); Hon. Mem., Court of Worshipful Co. of Chartered Surveyors. ARICS 1953 (Mem. Council, 1957–84); FRSA (Mem. Council, 1974–78). Hon. Member: Amer. Bar Foundn, 1971–; Hawaii Chapter, Phi Beta Kappa; Hon. Fellow, Inc. Soc. of Valuers and Auctioneers, 1979–. Gold Medal, RTPI, 1983; Gold Medal, Lincoln Inst. of Land Policy, Cambridge, Mass, 1983. *Publications:* Planning Law for Town and Country, 1937; Planning and the Law of Interim Development, 1944; The Town and Country Planning Act, 1944, 1945; An Outline of Planning Law, 1943 to 1945, 1945; The New Towns Act, 1946, 1947; Introducing the Town and Country Planning Act, 1947, 1947; Encyclopædia of Planning, Compulsory Purchase and Compensation, Vol. 1, 1949; An Outline of Planning Law, 1949, 10th edn 1991; Heap on the Town and Country Planning Act, 1954, 1955; Encyclopædia of Planning Law and Practice, 5 vols, 1960; Introducing the Land Commission Act 1967, 1967; Encyclopædia of Betterment Levy, 1967; The New Town Planning Procedures, 1969; How to Control Land Development, 1974, 2nd edn 1981; The Land and the Development; or, the Turmoil and the Torment (Hamlyn Lectures), 1975; Lectures on tape: The Community Land Act, 1975; The Marvellous Years: pages from a scrapbook, 1993; articles in legal jls. *Recreations:* formerly swimming, pedal biking, stage and theatre; now, taking things gently and observing the injunction to "consider the lilies of the field" because, though they neither toil nor spin, Solomon in *all* his glory "was not arrayed like one of those". *Clubs:* Athenæum, City Livery, Guildhall.

HEAP, Dr John Arnfield, CMG 1991; Director, Scott Polar Research Institute, Cambridge University, since 1992; *b* 5 Feb. 1932; *s* of late David and Ann Heap; *m* 1960, Margaret Grace Gillespie (*née* Spicer); one *s* two *d. Educ:* Leighton Park Sch.; Edinburgh Univ. (MA 1955); Clare Coll., Cambridge (PhD 1962). Falkland Islands Dependencies Survey, 1955–62; Res. Fellow, Dept of Geology, 1962–63, Great Lakes Res. Div., 1963–64, Univ. of Michigan; Polar Regions Section, FCO, 1964–92: Head of Section, 1975–92; Adminr, British Antarctic Territory, 1989–92. Mem., UK Delegns to Antarctic Treaty Consultative Meetings, 1966–92. Editor, Handbook of the Antarctic Treaty System, 1977–. *Publication:* Sea Ice in the Antarctic, 1963. *Address:* The Old House, 25 High Street, Harston, Cambridge CB2 5PX. *T:* Cambridge (01223) 870288; Acharonich, Ulva Ferry, Isle of Mull PA73 6LY. *T:* Ulva Ferry (01688) 500219.

HEAP, Sir Peter William, KCMG 1995 (CMG 1987); HM Diplomatic Service, retired; Ambassador to Brazil, 1992–95; *b* 13 April 1935; *s* of Roger and Dora Heap; *m* 1st, Helen Wilmerding; two *s* two *d*; 2nd, Dorrit Breitenstein; 3rd, 1986, Ann Johnson; one step *s* one step *d. Educ:* Bristol Cathedral Sch.; Merton Coll., Oxford. 2nd Lt Glos Regt and RWAFF, 1954–56. CRO, 1959; Third Sec., Dublin, 1960; Third and Second Sec., Ottawa, 1960; First Sec., Colombo, 1963–66; seconded to MoD, 1966–68; FO, 1968–71; Dep. Dir-Gen., British Information Services, New York, 1971–76; Counsellor (Political and Economic), 1976–78, Counsellor (Commercial), 1978–80, Caracas; Head of Energy, Science and Space Dept, FCO, 1980–83; High Comr to the Bahamas, 1983–86; Minister and Dep. High Comr, Lagos, 1986–89; British Sen. Trade Comr, Hong Kong, 1989–92. *Address:* 6 Carlisle Mansions, Carlisle Place, SW1P 1HX.

HEAP, Prof. (Robert) Brian, CBE 1994; FRS 1989; FRSC; FIBiol; Visiting Senior Fellow, School of Clinical Medicine, since 1994, Babraham Institute, since 1995, University of Cambridge; *b* 27 Feb. 1935; *s* of late Bertram Heap and Eva Mary Heap (*née* Melling); *m* 1961, Marion Patricia Grant; two *s* one *d. Educ:* New Mills Grammar Sch.; Univ. of Nottingham (Chm. Students' Union, Sch. of Agric., 1958; BSc, PhD); King's Coll., Cambridge (MA, ScD). Univ. Demonstrator, Cambridge, 1960; Lalor Res. Fellow, ARC Babraham, Cambridge, 1963; Staff Mem., AFRC Babraham, 1964–95: Hd, Dept of Physiology, 1976; Hd, Cambridge Res. Station, 1986; Dir, Inst. of Animal Physiol. and Genetics Res., Cambridge and Edinburgh, 1989–93; Dir of Science, AFRC, 1991–94; Dir, AFRC Babraham Inst., 1993–94. Vis. Prof., Univ. of Nairobi, 1974; Vis. Res. Fellow, Murdoch Univ., 1976; Special Prof., Univ. of Nottingham, 1988; Vis. Prof., Univ. of Guelph, 1990. Scientific Advr, Merck, Sharp and Dohme, 1990–. Mem. Exec. Cttee, ESF, 1994; Mem. Council, Royal Soc., 1994–; Member Committee: Soc. for Study of Fertility, 1967–72 (Treas. 1968–71); Jls of Reproduction and Fertility Ltd (Associate Ed., 1964–72; Council of Management, 1965–73, 1986–91; Exec., 1988–93); Bibliography of Reproduction, 1967–70; Soc. and Jl of Endocrinology, 1980–84 (Sci. Ed., 1977–82); Placenta (Associate Ed., 1980–); Oxford Reviews of Reproductive Biology, 1981–94. Consultant: WHO, Geneva, 1975–82; China, 1981–85. Chairman: Ciba Foundn Symposium, 1978; Harden Conf., 1984. Fellow, Internat. Inst. of Biotechnology, 1994. Lectures: Hammond, Soc. for Study of Fertility, 1986; Linacre, Oxford Univ., 1993; Annual, RASE, 1995. Hon. DSc Nottingham, 1994. Research Medallist, RASE, 1976; Inventor's Award, AFRC, 1980. *Publications:* sci. papers on reproductive biology, endocrinology, growth and lactation, and biotechnology, in various biol and med. jls.

Recreations: music, walking, travel. *Address:* Lincoln House, 8 Fendon Road, Cambridge CB1 4RT. *T:* Cambridge (01223) 248509.

HEAPS, Jeremy David P.; *see* Pickett-Heaps.

HEAPS, John Edward; Chief Executive, Britannia Building Society, since 1993; *b* 24 Feb. 1939; *m* 1985, Shirley (*née* Jones); two *d*; one *s* one *d* from previous marr. *Educ:* Caldy Grange Grammar Sch., W Kirby; Oldershaw Grammar Sch., Wallasey. FCIB. Colne Building Society: Sec., 1972; Chief Exec., 1972–80; Chief Exec. and Dir, 1980–83; Britannia Building Society: Dep. Gen. Manager, 1983–87; Gen. Manager, 1987–91; Inf. Systems Dir, 1991; Dep. Man. Dir, 1991–93. Member: Council, BSA, 1994–; Court, Univ. of Keele, 1994–95. MIMgt. *Recreations:* family pursuits. *Address:* Britannia House, Leek, Staffs ST13 5RG.

HEARD, Peter Graham, CB 1987; FRICS; IRRV; Deputy Chief Valuer, Valuation Office, Board of Inland Revenue, 1983–89; *b* 22 Dec. 1929; *s* of late Sidney Horwood Heard and Doris Winifred Heard, MBE; *m* 1953, Ethne Jean Thomas; two *d*. *Educ:* Exmouth Grammar School. Articled to W. W. Needham, 1946; joined Valuation Office, 1950; served in Exeter, Kidderminster, Dudley, Leeds; District Valuer, Croydon, 1971; Superintending Valuer, Chief Valuer's Office, 1973; Asst Sec., Bd of Inland Revenue, 1975; Superintending Valuer, Midlands, 1977; Asst Chief Valuer, 1978. *Recreations:* cricket, golf, countryside, walking the dog, theatre. *Address:* Romany Cottage, High Street, Lindfield, Sussex RH16 2HR. *T:* Lindfield (01444) 482095. *Clubs:* MCC, Civil Service.

HEARN, Barry Maurice William, FCA; Chairman, Matchroom Ltd, since 1982; *b* 19 June 1948; *s* of George Sydney and Barbara Winifred Hearn; *m* 1970, Susan Clark; one *s* one *d*. *Educ:* Buckhurst Hill Grammar School. *Publication:* The Business, 1990. *Recreations:* cricket, marathons, fishing, snooker. *Address:* Matchroom Ltd, 10 Western Road, Romford, Essex RM1 3JT. *T:* Romford (01708) 730480.

HEARN, David Anthony; General Secretary, Broadcasting Entertainment Cinematograph Theatre Union, 1991–93 (General Secretary, 1987–90, Joint General Secretary, 1984–87, Broadcasting and Entertainment Trades Alliance); *b* 4 March 1929; *s* of James Wilfrid Laurier Hearn and Clara (*née* Barlow); *m* 1952, Anne Beveridge; two *s*. *Educ:* Trinity Coll., Oxford (MA). Asst to Gen. Sec., Assoc. of Broadcasting Staff, 1955; subseq. Asst Gen. Sec., then Dep. Gen. Sec.; Gen. Sec., Assoc. of Broadcasting and Allied Staffs, 1972–84. Dir, Nat. Campaign for the Arts Ltd, 1986–93. Chm., Film and Electronic Media Cttee, Fedn of Entertainment Unions, 1991–93; Mem., British Screen Adv. Council, 1987; President: Internat. Fedn of Audio Visual Unions, 1991–93 (Gen. Sec., W European Sect., 1984–91); Eur. Cttee of Trade Unions in Arts, Mass Media and Entertainment, 1992–93. Sen. Res. Fellow, Nuffield Coll., Oxford, 1970–71. *Address:* 4 Stocks Tree Close, Yarnton, Kidlington, Oxon OX5 1LU. *T:* Oxford (01865) 374613.

HEARN, Donald Peter; Secretary, since 1989, Finance Director, since 1986, Royal Horticultural Society; *b* 2 Nov. 1947; *s* of Peter James Hearn and Anita Margaret Hearn; *m* 1973, Rachel Mary Arnold; two *d*. *Educ:* Clifton College; Selwyn College, Cambridge (MA). FCA. Ernst & Whinney, 1969–79; Group Financial Controller, Saga Holidays, 1979–83; Chief Financial Officer, Lee Valley Water Co., 1983–86. Gen. Comr for Taxes, 1990–. Mem., F and GP Cttee, RPMS, Univ. of London, 1991–. Governor, Woldingham Sch., 1990–93. *Recreations:* gardening, running. *Address:* Royal Horticultural Society, Vincent Square, SW1P 2PE. *T:* 0171–821 3034.

HEARN, Rt. Rev. George Arthur; *see* Rockhampton, Bishop of.

HEARN, Prof. John Patrick; Director, Wisconsin Regional Primate Research Center and Professor in Physiology, Medical School, University of Wisconsin-Madison, since 1989; *b* Limbdi, India, 24 Feb. 1943; *s* of Lt-Col Hugh Patrick Hearn, Barrister, and Cynthia Ellen (*née* Nicholson); *m* 1967, Margaret Ruth Patricia McNair; four *s* one *d*. *Educ:* Crusaders' Sch., Headley, Hants; St Mary's Sch., Nairobi, Kenya; University Coll., Dublin (BSc, MSc); ANU, Canberra (PhD). Sen. Demonstrator in Zool., University Coll., Dublin, 1966–67; Lectr in Zool., 1967–69, and Dean of Science, 1968–69, Strathmore Coll., Nairobi; Res. Scholar, ANU, 1969–72; Staff Mem., MRC Reproductive Biology Unit, Edinburgh, 1972–79; Hon. Fellow, Univ. of Edinburgh, 1974–79; Consultant Scientist, WHO Special Prog. of Res. in Human Reproduction, Geneva, 1978–79; Zoological Society of London: Dir, Wellcome Labs of Comparative Physiology, 1979–80; Dir of Science and Dir, Inst. of Zool., 1980–87; Hon. Research Fellow, 1987–; Dep. Sec., AFRC, 1987–90; Dir, MRC/AFRC Comparative Physiology Res. Gp, 1983–89. Vis. Prof. in Biology (formerly in Zoology), UCL, 1979–; Vis. Prof., New England Primate Res. Center, Harvard Univ. Med. Sch., 1989–91. Pres., Internat. Primatological Soc., 1984–88. Scientific Medal, Zool Soc. London, 1983; Osman Hill Medal, Primate Soc. of GB, 1986. *Publications:* (ed with H. Rothe and H. Wolters) The Biology and Behaviour of Marmosets, 1978; (ed) Immunological Aspects of Reproduction and Fertility Control, 1980; (ed) Reproduction in New World Primates, 1982; (ed) Advances in Animal Conservation, 1985; (ed) Reproduction and Disease in Captive and Wild Animals, 1988; (ed) Conservation of Primate Species studied in Biomedical Research, 1994; papers on develtl and reproductive physiol. in scientific jls. *Recreations:* music, travel, wildlife, squash, running, swimming. *Address:* Wisconsin Regional Primate Research Center, 1223 Capitol Court, Madison, WI 53715–1299, USA. *T:* (608) 2633500, *Fax:* 2634031. *Club:* Athenæum.

HEARNE, Graham James, CBE 1990; Chief Executive, since 1984, and Chairman, since 1991, Enterprise Oil plc; *b* 23 Nov. 1937; *s* of Frank Hearne and Emily (*née* Shakespeare); *m* 1961, Carol Jean (*née* Brown); one *s* two *d* (and one *d* decd). *Educ:* George Dixon Grammar Sch., Birmingham. Admitted solicitor, 1959: Pinsent & Co., Solicitors, 1959–63; Fried, Frank, Harris, Shriver & Jacobson, Attorneys, NYC, 1963–66; Herbert Smith & Co., Solicitors, 1966–67; IRC, 1967–68; N. M. Rothschild & Sons Ltd, 1968–77; Finance Dir, Courtaulds Ltd, 1977–81; Chief Exec., Tricentrol, 1981–83; Gp Man. Dir, Carless, Capel and Leonard, 1983–84. Non-exec. Director: N. M. Rothschild & Sons Ltd, 1970–; Northern Foods, Ltd, 1976–82; BPB Industries, 1982–91; Reckitt & Colman, 1990–; Courtaulds, 1991–; Wellcome, 1991–; The Wellcome Foundn, 1991–; part-time Member: British National Oil Corp., 1975–78; Dover Harbour Bd, 1976–78. Chm., Brindex (Assoc. of British Indep. Oil Exploration Cos), 1986–88. Trustee: Philharmonia Orch. Trust, 1982–; Chichester Fest. Theatre Trust, 1988–. High Sheriff, Greater London, 1995. *Address:* 5 Crescent Place, SW3 2EA. *T:* 0171–460 0296. *Clubs:* Reform, MCC.

HEARNE, Peter Ambrose; FEng 1984; Chairman, GEC Avionics, 1992–94; *b* 14 Nov. 1927; *e s* of late Arthur Ambrose Hearne, MD, and Helen Mackay Hearne; *m* 1952, Georgina Gordon Guthrie; three *s*. *Educ:* Sherborne Sch., Dorset; Loughborough Coll. of Technol. (DLC); Cranfield Inst. of Technol. (MSc); MIT. Design Engr, Saunders Roe, 1946–47; Ops Develt Engr, BOAC, 1949–54; Helicopter Proj. Engr, BEA, 1954–58; Marketing Manager, British Oxygen, 1958–59; Divl Man., Guided Weapons, Elliott Flt Automation, 1959; Asst Gen. Man., 1960; Dir and Gen. Man., 1965–70; Dir and Gen. Manager, 1970–87, Marconi (later GEC) Avionics; Asst Man. Dir, 1987–90, Pres., US Ops, 1990–92, GEC Marconi. Vis. Prof., Cranfield Inst. of Technol., 1981–82. Chm., Cranfield Soc., 1965–67, Pres., 1981–88; Pres., Royal Aeronautical Society, 1980–81 (Vice-Pres., 1976–79); Hon FRAeS 1990; Wright Bros Lectr, 1991). John Curtis Sword, Aviation Week, 1982; Diamond C badge, 1988. *Publications:* papers in Jl of RAeS and NATO Agard series. *Recreations:* flying with and without engines, sailing, model railways. *Address:* The Limes, Wateringbury, Kent ME18 5NY. *Clubs:* Surrey and Hants Gliding; Southwold Sailing; Aero Alpin (Gap).

HEARST, Stephen, CBE 1980; FRSA; independent television producer, since 1986; *b* Vienna, Austria, 6 Oct. 1919; *m* 1948, Lisbeth Edith Neumann; one *s* one *d*. *Educ:* Vienna Univ.; Reading Univ. (Dip. Hort.); Brasenose Coll., Oxford (MA). Free lance writer, 1949–52; joined BBC as producer trainee, 1952; Documentary television: script writer, 1953–55; writer producer, 1955–65; Exec. Producer, Arts Programmes Television, 1965–67; Head of Arts Features, Television, 1967–71; Controller, Radio 3, 1972–78; Controller, Future Policy Gp, 1978–82; Special Adviser to Dir-Gen., BBC, 1982–86. Vis. Fellow, Inst. for Advanced Studies, Edinburgh Univ., 1988. FRSA 1980. *Publications:* Two Thousand Million Poor, 1965; Artistic Heritage and its Treatment by Television, 1982; (contrib.) The Third Age of Broadcasting (ed Wenham), 1982; (contrib.) Television and the Public Interest (ed Jay G. Blumler), 1991. *Recreations:* gardening, swimming, reading, listening to music. *Address:* c/o British Academy of Film and Television Arts, 195 Piccadilly, W1V 9LG.

HEARTH, John Dennis Miles, CBE 1983; Chief Executive, Royal Agricultural Society of England, 1972–89 and 1991–92; *b* 8 April 1929; *s* of late Cyril Howard Hearth, MC, and Dr Pauline Kathleen Hearth, MB, BSc; *m* 1959, Pamela Anne (*née* Bryant); two *s* (one *d* decd). *Educ:* The King's Sch., Canterbury; Brasenose Coll., Oxford (MA). Called to the Bar, Gray's Inn, 1962. Administrative Officer, HM Overseas Civil Service, 1953–61; Editor, Fairplay Shipping Journal, Fairplay Publications Ltd, 1961–66; Cunard Steam-Ship Co. Ltd, 1966–71 (various appts and Main Board Joint Ventures Director, 1969–71). Mem., Gen. Adv. Council, BBC, 1990–; Chairman: Rural and Agricl Affairs Cttee, BBC, 1990–March 1996; Nat. Rural Enterprise Centre, RASE, 1988–94; British Food and Farming Ltd, 1989–; Management Cttee, Nat. Fedn of Young Farmers' Clubs, 1989–95. Pres., British Pig Assoc., 1990–93. Mem. Council, Conservation Foundn, 1987–94; Dep. Chm., Rural Housing Trust (formerly NAC Rural Trust), 1992– (Trustee, 1987–); Mem., and Chm., Finance Cttee, English Villages Housing Assoc., 1990–; Cttee, English Rural Housing Assoc., 1993–. Governor, RAC, Cirencester, 1975–92; Mem., 1985–, Treasurer, 1989–, Warwick Univ. Council. CIMgt (CBIM 1980); FRSA 1989. Hon. FRASE 1989. *Recreations:* travel, history, theatre, golf. *Address:* Bayard's, Fenny Compton, near Leamington Spa, Warwicks CV33 0XY. *T:* Fenny Compton (01295) 770849. *Club:* Farmers'.

HEASLIP, Rear-Adm. Richard George, CB 1987; Director-General, English-Speaking Union, 1987–90; *b* 30 April 1932; *s* of Eric Arthur Heaslip and Vera Margaret (*née* Bailey); *m* 1959, Lorna Jean Grayston, Halifax, NS, Canada; three *s* one *d* (incl. twin *s* and *d*). *Educ:* Royal Naval Coll., Dartmouth. CO HMS Sea Devil, 1961–62; Exec. Officer, HMS Dreadnought (1st British nuclear submarine), 1965–66; CO HMS Conqueror (nuclear submarine), 1971–72; CO Second Submarine Sqdn, 1975–77; Staff, SACLANT, 1980–82; Staff, CDS, 1982–84; Dep. Asst COS (Ops), Staff of SACEUR, 1984; Flag Officer Submarines, and Comdr Submarine Forces Eastern Atlantic, 1984–87. ADC 1984–85. Member: European Atlantic Gp Cttee, 1988–89; Bureau, Standing Conf. of Atlantic Orgns, 1988–89. Chm., RN Football Assoc., 1976–84. *Recreations:* walking, music, gardening. *Address:* South Winds, Wallis Road, Waterlooville, Hants PO7 7RX. *T:* Portsmouth (01705) 241679.

HEATH, Andrew; HM Diplomatic Service; Deputy High Commissioner to New Zealand, since 1993; *b* 17 April 1953; *s* of Eric Loveland Heath and Marjorie Irene Heath (*née* Pollard); *m* 1982, Christina Friday; two *s*. *Educ:* Christ's Hospital; Corpus Christi Coll., Cambridge (BA Hons 1975). FCO 1975; language trng, 1976; MECAS, 1977–78; Amman, 1978–81; on loan to Cabinet Office, 1981–83; FCO, 1983–85; Kuwait, 1985–88; Washington, 1988–92; FCO, 1992–93. *Recreations:* reading, squash. *Address:* c/o Foreign and Commonwealth Office, SW1A 2AH.

HEATH, Angela; *see* Heath, L. A.

HEATH, Dr Anthony Francis, FBA 1992; Official Fellow in Sociology, Nuffield College, Oxford, since 1987; *b* 15 Dec. 1942; *s* of Ronald John Heath and Cicely Florence (*née* Roberts); *m* 1983, Dr Mary-Jane Pearce, MRCGP, MRCPsych; two *s* one *d*. *Educ:* Merchant Taylors', Crosby; Trinity Coll., Cambridge (BA 1st cl. Classics pt I, 1st cl. Econs pt II; PhD 1971). Asst Principal, HM Treasury, 1965–66; Fellow of Churchill Coll., 1967–70, Asst Lectr, Faculty of Econs, 1968–70, Cambridge Univ.; Univ. Lectr and Fellow of Jesus Coll., Oxford, 1970–86. Dir, 1983, 1987 and 1992 British Election Studies, and Co-Dir, Jt Unit for Study of Social Trends, 1989–, ESRC. *Publications:* Rational Choice and Social Change, 1976; (jtly) Origins and Destinations, 1980; Social Mobility, 1981; (jtly) How Britain Votes, 1985; (jtly) Understanding Political Change, 1991; (jtly) Labour's Last Chance, 1994; contribs to Jl of Royal Stat. Soc., Eur. Sociol Rev., Eur. Jl of Sociol., Eur. Jl of Pol Res., Sociology, British Jl of Pol. Sci.; Electoral Studies, Acta Sociologica, Oxford Rev. of Educn. *Recreations:* piano playing, cross-country running. *Address:* 72 Lonsdale Road, Oxford OX2 7EP. *T:* Oxford (01865) 53512. *Club:* Achilles.

HEATH, Bernard Oliver, OBE 1980; CEng, FRAeS; Professor of Aeronautical Engineering (British Aerospace Integrated Chair), Salford University, 1983–89; *b* 8 March 1925; *s* of Bernard Ernest Heath and Ethel May Heath; *m* 1948, Ethel Riley; one *s*. *Educ:* Derby Sch.; Bemrose Sch., Derby; University Coll. of Nottingham (BSc Univ. of London 1944); Imperial Coll. of Science and Technology (DIC 1945). CEng 1966; FRAeS 1978; HMIED 1975. English Electric Co.: Stressman (loading and stressing of Canberra), 1945; Aerodynamicist, Lightning, 1948; Aerostructures Gp Leader, 1951; Chief Proj. Engr, 1957; Asst Chief Engr, Canberra and TSR2, 1959; British Aircraft Corporation: TSR2 Proj. Manager (Develt), 1963; Special Dir, 1965; Leader, Jaguar Technical Team, 1965; Proj. Manager, AFVG, 1966; Panavia: Dir, Systems Engrg (Warton), 1969–81; Dir, MRCA, 1970; Dir of Engrg, 1974; British Aerospace: Technical Dir, Warton Div., 1978–81; Divisional Dir of Advanced Engrg, 1981–84. Chm., SBAC Technical Bd, 1980–82. RAeS Silver Medal (for outstanding work over many yrs on design and develt of mil. aircraft), 1977; (jtly) Internat. Council of Aeronautical Sciences Von Karman Award (for successful internat. co-operation on Tornado), 1982; Corresp. Mem., Deutsche Ges. für Luft und Raumfahrt, 1993. *Publications:* papers to AGARD, Internat. Council of Aeronautical Sciences Congresses; contrib. RAeS Jl, Flight, The Times, R & D Mgt and Aircraft Engrg. *Recreation:* history of transport. *Address:* c/o Company Secretary, British Aerospace, Warton Aerodrome, Preston, Lancs PR4 1AX.

HEATH, Edward Peter, OBE 1946; *b* 6 June 1914; a Deputy Chairman, Inchcape & Co. Ltd, 1976–79; *m* 1953, Eleanor Christian Peck; one *s* three *d*. *Educ:* St Lawrence Coll., Ramsgate. Joined Borneo Co. Ltd, 1934; interned in Thailand, 1941–45. Gen. Manager, Borneo Co. Ltd, 1953–63; a Man. Dir, 1963–67; a Man. Dir, Inchcape & Co. Ltd, 1967–75. Director: Mann Egerton & Co. Ltd, 1973–79; Dodwell & Co. Ltd, 1974–79; Inchcape Far East Ltd, 1972–79; Chairman: Toyota GB and Pride & Clark, 1978–79;

Anglo-Thai Corp. Ltd, 1978–79; Dep. Chm., Bewac Motor Corp., 1970–79. Consultant, Matheson & Co. Ltd, 1980–83; Director: Matheson Motor Hldgs, 1981–83; Lancaster Gp Hldgs, 1981–83. Dep. Chairman: Hong Kong Assoc., 1975–79; Anglo Thai Soc., 1975–85. Order of White Elephant (5th Cl.) (Thailand); Officer, Order of Orange Nassau (Netherlands). *Recreations:* hunting, gardening, motoring. *Address:* Cooks Place, Albury, Guildford, Surrey GU5 9BJ. *T:* Guildford (01483) 202698.

HEATH, Rt. Hon. Sir Edward (Richard George), KG 1992; MBE 1946; PC 1955; MP (C) Old Bexley and Sidcup, since 1983 (Bexley, 1950–74; Bexley, Sidcup, 1974–83); Member, Public Review Board, Arthur Andersen & Co., since 1978; *b* Broadstairs, Kent, 9 July 1916; *s* of late William George and Edith Anne Heath. *Educ:* Chatham House Sch., Ramsgate; Balliol Coll., Oxford (Scholar; Hon. Fellow, 1969). Scholar, Gray's Inn, 1938 (Hon. Bencher, 1972). Pres. Oxford Univ. Conservative Assoc., 1937; Chm. Federation of Univ. Conservative Assocs, 1938; Pres. Oxford Union, 1939; Oxford Union debating tour of American Univs, 1939–40; Pres. Federation of University Conservative and Unionist Associations, 1959–77, Hon. Life Patron, 1977. Served War of 1939–45 (despatches, MBE); in Army, 1940–46, in France, Belgium, Holland and Germany; gunner in RA, 1940; Major 1945. Lieut-Col comdg 2nd Regt HAC, TA, April 1947–Aug. 1951; Master Gunner within the Tower of London, 1951–54. Administrative Civil Service, 1946–47 resigning to become prospective candidate for Bexley. Asst Conservative Whip, Feb. 1951; Lord Commissioner of the Treasury, Nov. 1951, and Joint Deputy Govt Chief Whip, 1952, and Dep. Govt Chief Whip, 1953–55; Parliamentary Sec. to the Treasury, and Government Chief Whip, Dec. 1955–Oct. 1959; Minister of Labour, Oct. 1959–July 1960; Lord Privy Seal, with Foreign Office responsibilities, 1960–63; Sec. of State for Industry, Trade, Regional Development and Pres. of the Board of Trade, Oct. 1963–Oct. 1964; Leader of the Opposition, 1965–70; Prime Minister and First Lord of the Treasury, 1970–74; Leader of the Opposition, 1974–75. Chm., Commonwealth Parly Assoc., 1970–74. Mem., Indep. Commn on Internat. Development Issues, 1977–79. Mem. Council, Royal College of Music, 1961–70; Chm., London Symphony Orchestra Trust, 1963–70; Vice-Pres., Bach Choir, 1970–; Pres., European Community Youth Orchestra, 1977–80; Hon. Mem., LSO, 1974–. Smith-Mundt Fellowship, USA, 1953; Vis. Fellow, Nuffield Coll., Oxford, 1962–70, Hon. Fellow, 1970; Chubb Fellow, Yale, 1975; Montgomery Fellow, Dartmouth Coll., 1980. Lectures: Cyril Foster Meml, Oxford, 1965; Godkin, Harvard, 1966; Montagu Burton, Leeds, 1976; Edge, Princeton, 1976; Romanes, Oxford, 1976; Ishizaka, Japan, 1979; Felix Neubergh, Gothenburg, 1979, 10th STC Communication, London, 1980, Noel Buxton, Univ. of Essex, 1980; Alastair Buchan Meml, London, 1980; Hoover, Univ. of Strathclyde, 1980; Stanton Griffis Disting., Cornell Univ., 1981; Edwin Stevens, RSM, 1981; William Temple, York, 1981; City of London, Chartered Insce Inst., 1982; John Findley Green, Westminster Coll., Missouri, 1982; Mizuno, Tokyo, 1982; ITT European, Brussels, 1982; Bruce Meml, Keele Univ., 1982; Gaitskell, Univ. of Nottingham, 1983; Trinity Univ., San Antonio, 1983; lect. to mark opening Michael Fowler Centre, Wellington, NZ, 1983; Bridge Meml, Guildhall, 1984; David R. Calhoun Jr Meml, Washington Univ., St Louis, 1984; Corbishley Meml, RSA, 1984; John Rogers Meml, Llandudno, 1985; George Woodcock, Univ. of Leicester, 1985; RIIA, 1985; John F. Kennedy Meml, Oxford, 1986; Edward Boyle Meml, RSA, 1988. Deroy Prof., Univ. of Michigan, 1990. Liveryman, Goldsmiths' Co., 1966; Hon. Freeman, Musicians' Co., 1973. Hon. FRCM; Hon. FRCO; Hon. Fellow, Royal Canadian Coll. of Organists. Hon. DCL: Oxon, 1971; Kent, 1985; Hon. DTech Bradford, 1971; Hon. LLD Westminster Coll., Salt Lake City, 1975; Dr *hc* Univ. of Paris, Sorbonne, 1976; Hon. Dr of Public Admin, Wesleyan Coll., Macon, Ga, 1981; Hon. DL Westminster Coll., Fulton, Missouri, 1982; Hon. HLD Bellarmine Coll., Kentucky, 1994. Charlemagne Prize, 1963; Estes J. Kefauver Prize 1971; Stresemann Gold Medal, 1971; Freiherr Von Stein Foundn Prize, 1972; Gold Medal of City of Paris, 1978; World Humanity Award, 1980; Gold Medal, European Parlt, 1981; Gold Medal, Fondation du Mérite Européen, 1994. Grand Cross, Order of Merit (Germany), 1993; Grand Cross, Order of Liberty and Unity (Latin America), 1994; Order of the Aztec Eagle (Mexico), 1994. Winner, Sydney to Hobart Ocean Race, 1969; Captain: Britain's Admiral's Cup Team, 1971, 1979; Britain's Sardinia Cup Team, 1980. *Publications:* (joint) One Nation—a Tory approach to social problems, 1950; Old World, New Horizons (Godkin Lectures), 1970; Sailing: a course of my life, 1975; Music: a joy for life, 1976; Travels: people and places in my life, 1977; Carols: the joy of Christmas, 1977. *Recreations:* sailing, music. *Address:* House of Commons, SW1A 0AA. *Clubs:* Buck's, Carlton, St Stephen's Constitutional (Jt Pres., 1979–88); Royal Yacht Squadron.

HEATH, Henry Wylde Edwards, CMG 1963; QPM; Commissioner of Police, Hong Kong, 1959–67, retired; *b* 18 March 1912; *s* of late Dr W. G. Heath and late Mrs L. B. Heath; *m* Joan Mildred Crichett; two *s* one *d. Educ:* Dean Close Sch.; HMS Conway. Probationer Sub-Inspector of Police, Leeward Islands, 1931; Asst Supt, Hong Kong, 1934; Superintendent, 1944; Asst Commissioner, 1950. Colonial Police Medal, 1953; QPM, 1957. *Recreations:* golf, ski-ing. *Address:* Quintynes Cottage, 4 Firle Drive, Seaford, Sussex BN25 2HT. *Clubs:* Seaford Golf; Kandahar Ski.

HEATH, Prof. John Baldwin; management consultant; Director, Health Policy Unit, since 1994; *b* 25 Sept. 1924; *s* of late Thomas Arthur Heath and late Dorothy Meallin; *m* 1953, Wendy Julia Betts; two *s* one *d. Educ:* Merchant Taylors' Sch.; St Andrews Univ.; Cambridge Univ. RNVR, 1942–46. Spicers Ltd, 1946–50; Lecturer in Economics, Univ. of Manchester, 1956–64; Rockefeller Foundation Fellowship, 1961–62; Dir, Economic Research Unit, Bd of Trade, 1964–67; Dir, Economic Services Div., BoT, 1967–70; Prof. of Economics, London Business Sch., 1970–86; Dir, London Sloan Fellowship Programme, 1983–86. Chm., EXE Ltd, 1982–93. Member: Mechanical Engrg EDC, 1971–76; British Airports Authy, 1980–86; Economic Adviser, CAA, 1972–78. *Publications:* Public Enterprise at the Crossroads, 1990; Revitalizing Socialist Enterprise, 1993; articles in many learned jls on competition and monopoly, productivity, cost-benefit analysis. *Recreations:* music, walking. *Address:* 27 Chalcot Square, NW1 8YA. *T:* 0171–722 4301, *Fax:* 0171–483 0369.

HEATH, John Moore, CMG 1976; HM Diplomatic Service, retired; *b* 9 May 1922; *s* of late Philip George and Olga Heath; *m* 1952, Patricia Mary Bibby; one *s* one *d. Educ:* Shrewsbury Sch.; Merton Coll., Oxford (MA). Served War of 1939–45, France, Belgium and Germany: commnd Inns of Court Regt, 1942; Capt. GSO3 11th Armoured Div., 1944–45 (despatches). Merton Coll., 1940–42, 1946–47. Entered Foreign Service, 1950; 2nd Sec., Comr-Gen.'s Office, Singapore, 1950–52; 1st Sec. (Commercial), Jedda, 1952–56; 1st Sec., FO, 1956–58; Nat. Def. Coll., Kingston, Ont., 1958–59; Head of Chancery and HM Consul, Brit. Embassy, Mexico City, 1959–62; Head of Chancery, Brit. Embassy, Kabul, Afghanistan, 1963–65; Counsellor and Head of Establishment and Organisation Dept, FCO (formerly DSAO), 1966–69; Counsellor (Commercial), Brit. Embassy, Bonn, 1969–74; Overseas Trade Advr, Assoc. of British Chambers of Commerce, on secondment, 1974; Consul-Gen., Chicago, 1975–79; Ambassador to Chile, 1980–82. Dir Gen., Canning House (Hispanic and Luso-Brazilian Council), 1982–87. Chm., Anglo-Chilean Soc., 1987–89. Orden al Merito por Servicios Distinguidos, Peru, 1984; Orden al Merito, Gran Oficial, Chile, 1991. *Publications:* The British Postal Agencies in Mexico 1825–1876, 1969; The Heath family engravers 1779–1878, 1993. *Recreations:* book collecting, Mexican philately, walking. *Address:* 6 Cavendish Crescent, Bath, Avon BA1 2UG. *Club:* Naval and Military.

HEATH, (Lettyce) Angela; Regional Director for London, Department of the Environment, since 1992; *b* 27 May 1944; *d* of late Frank Buchanan Ryde and Emily Rose Ryde (*née* Davies); *m* 1st, 1966, Gareth Thomas (marr. diss. 1975); 2nd, 1985, Roger Heath; two step *d. Educ:* Birmingham Univ. (BA 1966; MA 1968). Admin. Trainee, DoE, 1971; Private Sec. to Minister of Housing, 1979; Asst Sec., 1983; Central Policy Planning Unit, DoE, 1983–85; Local Govt Div., 1985–87; Personnel Management, 1987–90; Housing Corp. finance, 1990–91; Under-Sec., 1992. *Address:* Department of the Environment London Regional Office, Millbank Tower, SW1P 4QU. *T:* 0171–217 4529.

HEATH, Sir Mark, KCVO 1980; CMG 1980; Minister, then Ambassador, to the Holy See, 1980–85; *b* 22 May 1927; *m* 1954, Margaret Alice Bragg; two *s* one *d. Educ:* Marlborough; Queens' Coll., Cambridge. RNVR, 1945–48. HM Foreign (subseq. Diplomatic) Service, 1950–85; served in Indonesia, Denmark, Bulgaria, Canada, France; with Hong Kong Government, 1985–88. Chm., Friends of Anglican Centre, Rome, 1984–90. *Address:* St Lawrence, Lansdown Road, Bath, Avon BA1 5TD. *Club:* Athenæum.

HEATH, Air Marshal Sir Maurice (Lionel), KBE 1962 (OBE 1946); CB 1957; CVO 1978; DL; Gentleman Usher to the Queen, 1966–79, Extra Gentleman Usher to the Queen since 1979; *b* 12 Aug. 1909; *s* of Lionel Heath, Artist and Principal of the Mayo Sch. of Arts, Lahore, India; *m* 1st, 1938, Kathleen Mary (*d* 1988), *d* of Boaler Gibson, Bourne, Lincs; one *s* one *d*; 2nd, 1989, Lisa, *widow* of Col J. M. B. Cooke, MC. *Educ:* Sutton Valence Sch.; Cranwell. Commissioned RAF, 1929; service with Nos 16 and 28 Squadrons; Specialist Armament duties, 1933–42; Chief Instructor, No 1 Air Armament Sch., 1942; Station Commander, Metheringham, No 5 Group, Bomber Comd, 1944 (despatches). Dep. to Dir-Gen. of Armament, Air Min., 1946–48; CO Central Gunnery Sch., 1948–49; Sen. Air Liaison Officer, Wellington, NZ, 1950–52; CO Bomber Comd Bombing Sch., 1952–53; idc, 1954; Dir of Plans, Air Min., 1955; Deputy Air Secretary, Air Ministry, 1955–57; Commander, British Forces, Arabian Peninsula, 1957–59; Commandant, RAF Staff Coll., 1959–61; Chief of Staff, HQ Allied Air Forces Central Europe, 1962–65, retd. Dir, Boyd and Boyd, Estate Agents, 1971–76; Private Agent, Henderson Financial Management, 1980–89. Chief Hon. Steward, Westminster Abbey, 1965–74. Appeal Dir, Voluntary Res. Trust, King's Coll. Hosp. and Med. Sch., 1977–79, Appeal Consultant, 1979–84; Pres., Storrington Br., RAFA, 1966–84, Life Vice Pres., 1984–. DL West Sussex, 1977. *Recreation:* keeping in touch with family and friends.

HEATH, Michael John; freelance cartoonist, since 1956; Cartoons Editor, The Spectator, since 1989; Political Cartoonist, The Independent, since 1991; *b* 13 Oct. 1935; *s* of George Heath and Alice (Queenie) Stewert Morrison Bremner; *m* 1959, Hanne Sternkopf (marr. diss. 1992); two *d. Educ:* no education to speak of (Devon, Hampstead and Brighton); Brighton Art Coll. Trained as animator, Rank Screen Services, 1955; started placing cartoons in Melody Maker, 1955; contributed to: Lilliput; Tatler; John Bull; Man about Town; Men Only; Honey; Punch, 1958–89; Spectator, 1958–; Private Eye, 1964– (strips include The Gays, The Regulars, Great Bores of Today, Baby); Sunday Times, 1967–; London Standard, 1976–86; Mail on Sunday, 1985–; The Independent, 1986–; London Daily News, 1987. Pocket Cartoonist of the Year, Cartoonist Club of GB, 1977; Glen Grant Cartoonist of the Year, 1978; What the Papers Say Cartoonist of the Year, 1982. *Publications:* Private Eye Cartoon Library, 1973, 2nd edn 1975; The Punch Cartoons of Michael Heath, 1976; Book of Bores, No 1, 1976, No 2, Star Bores, 1979, No 3, Bores Three, 1983; Love All, 1982; Best of Heath (foreword by Malcolm Muggeridge), 1984; Welcome to America, 1985. *Recreations:* listening to Charlie Parker and Thelonious Monk, walking. *Address:* 1 Bassett Chambers, 27 Bedfordbury, Covent Garden, WC2N 4BJ. *T:* 0171–379 0087. *Club:* Colony Room.

HAY, Michael John; His Honour Judge Heath; a Circuit Judge, since 1995; *b* Grimsby, 12 June 1948; *s* of Norman and Dorothy Heath; *m* 1972, Heather, *d* of late Christopher Croft and of Mrs D. Croft, Hetton-le-Hole; two *s. Educ:* Barcroft County Sch., Wintringham; Grammar Sch., Grimsby; Leeds Univ. (LLB). FCIArb. Asst Solicitor, R. A. C. Symes and Co., Scunthorpe, 1975, Partner, 1977; Dep. Dist Judge, 1985–95; a Recorder, 1993–95; Solicitor Advocate (All Courts), 1994. *Recreations:* soccer, cricket, window shopping. *Address:* Lincoln Combined Court Centre, 360 High Street, Lincoln. *T:* Lincoln (01522) 521500.

HEATH, Maj.-Gen. Michael Stuart, CB 1994; CBE 1991; CEng, FIEE; Director General, Engineering Council, since 1995; *b* 7 Sept. 1940; *s* of late Bernard Stuart Heath and of Blanche Dorothy Ellen Heath (*née* Fairey); *m* 1965, Frances Wood; one *s* one *d. Educ:* St Albans Sch.; Welbeck Coll.; Royal Military Coll. of Science (BSc Eng Upper 2nd cl. Hons London). Commissioned REME, 1961; served Malaya, BAOR, Edinburgh, to 1971; RMCS and Staff Coll., 1972–73; Armour Sch., Bovington, 1974–75; Comd 7 Field Workshop, BAOR, 1976–77; Nat. Defence Coll., 1978; Berlin Field Force, 1978–80; Comd Maint., HQ 2 Armd Div., BAOR, 1981–82; MoD, 1982–85; RCDS, 1986; Dir, Support Planning (Army), MoD, 1987–89; Comd Maint., HQ BAOR, 1990–91; Dir Gen., Electrical and Mechanical Engrg. subseq. Equipment Support (Army), MoD, 1991–93; Team Leader, Army Costs Study Team, 1994. FIMgt. *Recreations:* walking, music, photography, restoring antique furniture. *Address:* c/o Barclays Bank, 167 High Street, Bromley, Kent BR1 1NL. *Clubs:* Army and Navy, Commonwealth Trust.

HEATH, Oscar Victor Sayer, FRS 1960; DSc (London); Professor of Horticulture, University of Reading, 1958–69, now Emeritus; *b* 26 July 1903; *s* of late Sir (Henry) Frank Heath, GBE, KCB, and Frances Elaine (*née* Sayer); *m* 1930, Sarah Margery, (*d* 1984), *d* of Stephen Bumstead, Guestling, Hastings; two *s* one *d. Educ:* Imperial Coll., London (Forbes Medallist), Fellow, 1973. Asst Demonstrator in Botany, Imperial Coll., 1925–26; Empire Cotton Growing Corp. Sen. Studentship, Imperial Coll. of Tropical Agriculture, Trinidad, 1926–27; Plant Physiologist, Empire Cotton Growing Corp., Cotton Experiment Station, Barberton, S Africa, 1927–36; Research Student, Imperial Coll., London, 1936–39; Leverhulme Research Fellow, 1937–39; Research Asst, 1939–40, and Mem. of Staff, Research Inst. of Plant Physiology of Imperial Coll., Rothamsted, 1940–46, London, 1946–58; Sen. Principal Scientific Officer, 1948–58; Special Lectr in Plant Physiology, Imperial Coll., 1946–58; Dir, ARC Unit of Flower Crop Physiology, 1962–70; Mem. ARC, 1965–70; Leverhulme Emeritus Res. Fellow, 1970–72. *Publications:* chapters on physiology of leaf stomata in Encyclopædia of Plant Physiology (ed Ruhland) 1959, in Plant Physiology: a Treatise (ed Steward), 1959, and (with T. A. Mansfield) in Physiology of Plant Growth (ed Wilkins), 1969; The Physiological Aspects of Photosynthesis, 1969 (trans. German, 1972, Russian, 1972); Investigation by Experiment, 1970 (trans. Spanish, 1977, Portuguese, 1981); Stomata, 1975, 2nd edn 1981; papers in scientific jls. *Address:* 10 St Peter's Grove, W6 9AZ. *T:* 0181–748 0471.

HEATH-BROWN, Dr David Rodney, (Roger), FRS 1993; Fellow and Tutor in Pure Mathematics, Magdalen College, Oxford, since 1979; Reader in Pure Mathematics, University of Oxford, since 1990; *b* 12 Oct. 1952; *s* of Basil Heath-Brown and Phyllis Joan (*née* Watson); *m* 1992, Ann Louise Sharpley; one *d. Educ:* Welwyn Garden City

Grammar Sch.; Trinity Coll., Cambridge (BA, MA, PhD). Jun. Res. Fellow, Trinity Coll., Cambridge, 1977–79. Jun. Berwick Prize, London Math. Soc., 1981. *Publications:* numerous mathematical papers in learned jls. *Recreations:* field botany, nature conservation, gardening. *Address:* Magdalen College, Oxford OX1 4AU. *T:* Oxford (01865) 276026.

HEATH-STUBBS, John (Francis Alexander), OBE 1989; poet; Lecturer in English Literature, College of St Mark and St John, Chelsea, 1963–73; *b* 9 July 1918; *s* of Francis Heath Stubbs and Edith Louise Sara (*née* Marr). *Educ:* Bembridge School; Worcester Coll. for the Blind, and privately; Queen's Coll., Oxford. English Master, Hall Sch., Hampstead, 1944–45; Editorial Asst, Hutchinson's, 1945–46; Gregory Fellow in Poetry, Leeds Univ., 1952–55; Vis. Prof. of English: University of Alexandria, 1955–58; University of Michigan, 1960–61. Pres., Poetry Soc., 1993–. FRSL 1953. Queen's Gold Medal for Poetry, 1973; Oscar Williams/Jean Durwood Award, 1977; Cholmondeley Award, 1989; Commonwealth Poetry Prize, 1989; Howard Sargeant Award, 1989. *Publications: verse:* Wounded Thammuz, 1942; Beauty and the Beast, 1943; The Divided Ways, 1946; The Swarming of the Bees, 1950; A Charm against the Toothache, 1954; The Triumph of the Muse, 1958; The Blue Fly in his Head, 1962; Selected Poems, 1965; Satires and Epigrams, 1968; Artorius, 1973; A Parliament of Birds, 1975; The Watchman's Flute, 1978; Mouse, the Bird and the Sausage, 1978; Birds Reconvened, 1980; Buzz Buzz, 1981; Naming the Beasts, 1982; The Immolation of Aleph, 1985; Cats' Parnassus, 1987; Time Pieces, 1988; Collected Poems, 1988; A Partridge in a Pear Tree, 1988; A Ninefold of Charms, 1989; Selected Poems, 1990; The Parson's Cat, 1992; Sweetapple Earth, 1993; Chimeras, 1994; *drama:* Helen in Egypt, 1958; *criticism:* The Darkling Plain, 1950; Charles Williams, 1955; The Pastoral, 1969; The Ode, 1969; The Verse Satire, 1969; *translations:* (with Peter Avery) Hafiz of Shiraz, 1952; (with Iris Origo) Leopardi, Selected Prose and Poetry, 1966; (with Carol A. Whiteside) The Poems of Anyte, 1974; (with Peter Avery) The Rubaiyat of Omar Khayyam, 1979; *edited:* Selected Poems of Jonathan Swift, 1948; Selected Poems of P. B. Shelley, 1948; Selected Poems of Tennyson, 1948; Selected Poems of Alexander Pope, 1964; (with David Wright) The Forsaken Garden, 1950; Images of Tomorrow, 1953; (with David Wright) Faber Book of Twentieth Century Verse, 1953; (with Martin Green) Homage to George Barker on his Sixtieth Birthday, 1973; Selected Poems of Thomas Gray, 1983; (with Phillips Salman) Poems of Science, 1984; David Gray, In the Shadows, 1991; *autobiography:* Hindsights, 1993. *Recreation:* taxonomy. *Address:* 22 Artesian Road, W2 5AR. *T:* 0171–229 6367.

HEATHCOAT AMORY, Lady; *see* Wethered, J.

HEATHCOAT-AMORY, David Philip, FCA; MP (C) Wells, since 1983; HM Paymaster General, since 1994; *b* 21 March 1949; *s* of Roderick and Sonia Heathcoat-Amory; *m* 1978, Linda Adams; two *s* one *d*. *Educ:* Eton Coll.; Oxford Univ. (MA PPE). Qual. as Chartered Accountant with Price Waterhouse & Co., 1974; FCA 1980. Worked in industry, becoming Asst Finance Dir of British Technology Gp, until 1983 when resigned to fight Gen. Election. PPS to the Financial Sec. to the Treasury, 1985–87, to the Home Secretary, 1987–88; an Asst Govt Whip, 1988–89; a Lord Comr of HM Treasury, 1989; Parly Under Sec. of State, DoE, 1989–90, Dept. of Energy, 1990–92; Dep. Govt Chief Whip and Treasurer, HM Household, 1992–93; Minister of State, FCO, 1993–94. *Recreations:* fishing, shooting, music, growing trees. *Address:* 12 Lower Addison Gardens, W14 8BQ. *T:* 0171–603 3083. *Clubs:* Avalon (Glastonbury); Shepton Mallet Conservative; Wells Conservative.

HEATHCOAT AMORY, Sir Ian, 6th Bt *cr* 1874; DL; *b* 3 Feb. 1942; *s* of Sir William Heathcoat Amory, 5th Bt, DSO, and of Margaret Isabel Dorothy Evelyn, *yr d* of Sir Arthur Havelock James Doyle, 4th Bt; *S* father, 1982; *m* 1972, Frances Louise, *d* of J. F. B. Pomeroy; four *s*. *Educ:* Eton. Chairman: Lowman Manufacturing Co. Ltd, 1976–; DevonAir Radio Ltd, 1983–90; Dir, Watts Blake Bearne & Co. PLC, 1984–88. Mem., Devon CC, 1973–85. JP Devon, 1980–93; DL Devon, 1981. *Heir:* *s* William Francis Heathcoat Amory, *b* 19 July 1975. *Address:* Calverleigh Court, Tiverton, Devon EX16 8BB.

HEATHCOTE, Dr Frederic Roger; Head of Services Management Division, Department of Trade and Industry, since 1992; *b* 19 March 1944; *s* of Frederic William Trevor Heathcote and late Kathleen Annie Heathcote; *m* 1st, 1970, Geraldine Nixon (marr. diss. 1986); 2nd, 1986, Mary Campbell Syme Dickson; one *s* one step *d*. *Educ:* Bromsgrove Sch.; Birmingham Univ. (BSc (Hons) Physics, PhD). Res. Associate, Birmingham Univ., 1969–70; joined CS as Asst Principal, Min. of Technology (later DTI), 1970; Private Secretary to: Secretary (Industrial Develt), 1973; Permanent Under Sec. of State, Dept of Energy, 1974; Department of Energy: Principal, 1974; Asst Sec., 1978; Dir of Resource Management (Grade 4), 1988; Under Sec., Coal Div., 1989–91; Prin. Estabt and Finance Officer, 1991–92. Non-Exec. Dir, Trafalgar House Property Ltd, 1988–94. *Recreations:* reading, gardening, painting. *Address:* c/o Department of Trade and Industry, Kingsgate House, 66–74 Victoria Street, SW1E 6SW. *T:* 0171–215 3609.

HEATHCOTE, Brig. Sir Gilbert (Simon), 9th Bt *cr* 1733; CBE 1964 (MBE 1941); *b* 21 Sept. 1913; *s* of Col R. E. M. Heathcote, DSO (*d* 1970), Manton Hall, Rutland and Millicent Heathcote (*d* 1977), *d* of William Walton, Horsley Priory, Nailsworth, Glos; *S* to baronetcy of 3rd Earl of Ancaster, KCVO, 1983; *m* lst, 1939, Patricia Margaret (*née* Leslie) (marr. diss. 1984); one *s* one *d*; 2nd, 1984, Ann, *widow* of Brig. J. F. C. Mellor, DSO, OBE. *Educ:* Eton; RMA Woolwich. Commnd RA, 1933, War Service in Europe, 1939–44; Comdr RA, 1960–62; Chief of Staff, Middle East Comd, 1962–64; retd. Vice-Pres., Royal Star and Garter Home, Richmond, 1990–. *Recreations:* writing, travel. *Heir:* *s* Mark Simon Robert Heathcote, OBE [*b* 1 March 1941; *m* 1975, Susan, *d* of late Lt-Col George Ashley; two *s*]. *Address:* The Coach House, Tillington, near Petworth, Sussex GU28 0RA. *Clubs:* Garrick, Army and Navy.

HEATHCOTE, Sir Michael Perryman, 11th Bt, *cr* 1733; *b* 7 Aug. 1927; *s* of Leonard Vyvyan Heathcote, 10th Bt, and Joyce Kathleen Heathcote (*d* 1967); *S* father, 1963; *m* 1956, Victoria Wilford, *e d* of Comdr J. E. R. Wilford, RN, Retd; two *s* one *d*. *Educ:* Winchester Coll.; Clare Coll., Cambridge. Started farming in England, 1951, in Scotland, 1961. Is in remainder to Earldom of Macclesfield. *Recreations:* fishing, shooting and farming. *Heir:* *s* Timothy Gilbert Heathcote, *b* 25 May 1957. *Address:* Warborne Farm, Boldre, Lymington, Hants SO41 5QD. *T:* Lymington (01590) 673478.

HEATHCOTE-DRUMMOND-WILLOUGHBY, family name of **Baroness Willoughby de Eresby.**

HEATHCOTE-SMITH, Clifford Bertram Bruce, CBE 1963; HM Diplomatic Service, 1936–72; acting Senior Clerk, Department of Clerk of House of Commons, 1973–77; *b* 2 Sept. 1912; *s* of late Sir Clifford E. Heathcote-Smith, KBE, CMG; *m* 1940, Thelma Joyce Engström; two *s*. *Educ:* Malvern; Pembroke Coll., Cambridge. Entered Consular Service, 1936; served in China, 1937–44; Foreign Office, 1944–47; Political Adviser, Hong-Kong, 1947–50, Montevideo, 1951–56; Commercial Counsellor: Ankara, 1956–60; Copenhagen, 1960–64; Washington, 1964–65; Dep. High Comr, Madras, 1965–68; a Diplomatic Service Inspector, 1969–72. *Address:* 4 Britts Farm Road, Buxted, E Sussex TN22 4LZ. *T:* Buxted (01825) 733635.

HEATHER, Stanley Frank, CBE 1980; Comptroller and City Solicitor, City of London Corporation, 1974–80; Attorney and General Counsel, City of London (Arizona) Corporation, 1974–81; *b* 8 Jan. 1917; *s* of Charles and Jessie Heather; *m* 1946, Janet Roxburgh Adams (*d* 1989), Perth; one *s* one *d*. *Educ:* Downhills Sch.; London Univ. Commnd Reconnaissance Corps, RAC, 1941; India/Burma Campaign, 1942–45. Admitted Solicitor, 1959. Asst Solicitor, City of London, 1963; Dep. Comptroller and City Solicitor, 1968. FRSA 1981. *Recreations:* golf, fishing. *Address:* 71 Rosehill, Billingshurst, W Sussex RH14 9QQ. *T:* Billingshurst (01403) 783981. *Clubs:* City Livery, Guildhall.

HEATLEY, Brian Antony; Head of Adults and Training Strategy, Department for Education and Employment (formerly of Employment), since 1993; *b* 20 April 1947; *s* of Thomas Russell Heatley and Margaret Ross (*née* Deacon); *m*; one *d*. *Educ:* Sheen Grammar Sch.; St John's Coll., Cambridge (BA); Balliol Coll., Oxford; Warwick Univ. (MPhil). Volunteer teacher, Ethiopia, 1969–71; Department of Trade and Industry, 1974–89: appts include Financial Services, Consumer Protection and Radio Communications; Head, Small Firms and Enterprise Br., 1989–90, Head, Resource Planning Br., 1990–93, Dept of Employment. *Recreations:* running, walking, history, photography, food. *Address:* Room E932, Moorfoot, Department for Education and Employment, Sheffield S1 4PQ; 47 Canterbury Avenue, Sheffield S10 3RU. *T:* Sheffield (0114) 263 0278.

HEATLY, Sir Peter, Kt 1990; CBE 1971; DL; Director, Peter Heatly & Co. Ltd, since 1958; Chairman, Commonwealth Games Federation, 1982–90; *b* 9 June 1924; *s* of Robert Heatly and Margaret Ann Heatly; *m* 1st, 1948, Jean Robertha Hermiston (*d* 1979); two *s* two *d*; 2nd, 1984, Mae Calder Cochrane. *Educ:* Leith Academy; Edinburgh Univ. (BSc). CEng, FICE. Chm., Scottish Sports Council, 1975–87. DL City of Edinburgh, 1984–. Dr *hc* Edinburgh, 1992; Hon. DLitt Queen Margaret Coll., 1994. *Recreations:* swimming, golf, gardening. *Address:* Lanrig, Balerno, Edinburgh EH14 7AJ. *T:* 0131–449 3998. *Club:* New (Edinburgh).

HEATON, David, OBE 1993; Consultant, Museums and Galleries Commission, 1984–93; *b* 22 Sept. 1923; *s* of late Dr T. B. Heaton, OBE, MD; *m* 1961, Joan, *d* of Group Captain E. J. Lainé, CBE, DFC; two *s* one *d*. *Educ:* Rugby Sch. Served RNVR, 1942–46. Ghana, 1948–58; Cabinet Office, 1961–69; Home Office, 1969–83; Under Sec. of State, 1976–83. *Address:* 53 Murray Road, SW19 4PF. *T:* 0181–947 0375.

HEATON, Rev. Eric William; Dean of Christ Church, Oxford, 1979–91; Pro-Vice-Chancellor, Oxford University, 1984–91; *b* 15 Oct. 1920; *s* of late Robert William Heaton and late Ella Mabel Heaton (*née* Brear); *m* 1951, Rachel Mary, *d* of late Rev. Charles Harold Dodd, CH, FBA; two *s* two *d*. *Educ:* Ermysted's, Skipton; (Exhibnr) Christ's Coll., Cambridge (MA). English Tripos, Part I; Theological Tripos, Part I (First Class). Deacon, 1944; Priest, 1945; Curate of St Oswald's, Durham, 1944–45; Staff Sec., Student Christian Movement in University of Durham, 1944–45; Chaplain, Gonville and Caius Coll., Cambridge, 1945–46; Dean and Fellow, 1946–53; Tutor, 1951–53; Bishop of Derby's Chaplain in University of Cambridge, 1946–53; Canon Residentiary, 1953–60, and Chancellor, 1956–60, Salisbury Cathedral; Tutor in Theology, Official Fellow and Chaplain, 1960–74, Senior Tutor, 1967–73, St John's College, Oxford; Dean of Durham, 1974–79. Chm. Council, Headington Sch., Oxford, 1968–74; Chm. Governors, High Sch., Durham, 1975–79. Moderator, Gen. Ordination Exam., 1971–81. Examining Chaplain to: Archbishop of York, 1951–56; Bishop of Portsmouth, 1947–74; Bishop of Salisbury, 1949–64; Bishop of Norwich, 1960–71; Bishop of Wakefield, 1961–74; Bishop of Rochester, 1962–74. Select Preacher: Cambridge University, 1948, 1958; Oxford Univ., 1958–59, 1967, 1971. Hon. Lectr, Univ. of Durham, 1975–79. Hon. Fellow, Champlain Coll., Univ. of Trent, Ont, Canada, 1973–; Hon. Fellow: St John's Coll., Oxford, 1979; Christ's Coll., Cambridge, 1983; Hon. Student, Christ Church, Oxford, 1991. DD Lambeth, 1991. Cavaliere Ufficiale, Order of Merit (Italy), 1991. *Publications:* His Servants the Prophets, 1949 (revised and enlarged Pelican edn, The Old Testament Prophets, 1958, 2nd rev. edn, 1977); The Book of Daniel, 1956; Everyday Life in Old Testament Times, 1956; Commentary on the Sunday Lessons, 1959; The Hebrew Kingdoms, 1968; Solomon's New Men, 1974; The School Tradition of the Old Testament (Bampton Lectures), 1994; articles in Jl of Theological Studies, Expository Times, etc. *Address:* Tree Cottage, Elsfield, Oxford OX3 9UH. *T:* Oxford (01865) 351604.

HEATON, Frances Anne; Director: Lazard Brothers & Co. Ltd, since 1987; Bank of England, since 1993; *b* 11 Aug. 1944; *d* of John Ferris Whidborne and Marjorie Annie (*née* Maltby); *m* 1969, Martin Heaton; two *s*. *Educ:* Queen Anne's, Caversham; Trinity Coll., Dublin (BA, LLB). Called to the Bar, Inner Temple, 1967. Dept. of Econ. Affairs, 1967–70; HM Treasury, 1970–80; seconded to S. G. Warburg & Co. Ltd, 1977–79; Lazard Brothers & Co. Ltd, 1980–; seconded as Dir Gen., Panel on Takeovers and Mergers, 1992–94. *Recreations:* riding, gardening, bridge. *Address:* Lazard Brothers & Co. Ltd, 21 Moorfields, EC2P 2HT.

HEATON, Sir Yvo (Robert) Henniker-, 4th Bt *cr* 1912; *b* 24 April 1954; *s* of Sir (John Victor) Peregrine Henniker-Heaton, 3rd Bt, and of Margaret Patricia, *d* of late Lieut Percy Wright, Canadian Mounted Rifles; *S* father, 1971; *m* 1978, Freda, *d* of B. Jones; one *s* one *d*. Mem., North West Leics DC, 1987–. Chm., Kegworth Cons. Assoc., 1988–94. *Publication:* Corporate Computer Insurance, 1990. *Heir:* *s* Alastair (John) Henniker-Heaton, *b* 4 May 1990. *Address:* 7 Brendon Way, Ashby de la Zouch, Leics LE65 1EY.

HEATON-WARD, Dr William Alan, FRCPsych; Lord Chancellor's Medical Visitor, 1978–89; *b* 19 Dec. 1919; *s* of Ralph Heaton-Ward, MA, and Mabel Orton; *m* 1945, Christine Edith Fraser; two *d*. *Educ:* Sefton Park Jun. Sch.; Queen Elizabeth's Hosp., Bristol; Univ. of Bristol Med. Sch. MB, ChB, 1944; DPM 1948; FRCPsych 1971. Jun. Clerk, Messrs W. D. & H. O. Wills, 1936–38; House Phys., Bristol Royal Inf., 1944–45; MO, Littlemore Mental Hosp., 1945–46; served RNVR, 1946–48: Surg. Lt-Comdr; Neuropsychiatrist, Nore Comd; Sen. Registrar, St James Hosp., Portsmouth, 1948–50; Dep. Med. Supt, Hortham Brentry Gp, 1950–54; Stoke Park Hosp. Group: Consultant Psych., 1954–78, Hon. Consultant Psych., 1978–; Med. Supt, 1954–61; Cons. Psych. i/c, 1963–74; Clinical Teacher in Mental Health, Univ. of Bristol, 1954–78; Cons. Psych., Glos Royal Hosp., 1962–67. Mem., SW Mental Health Review Tribunal, 1960–78, 1985–92. Hon. Cons. Adviser: NAMH, 1966–73; CARE, 1970–78; British Council Vis. Lectr, Portugal, 1971. Royal Coll. of Psychiatrists: Vice Pres., 1976–78; Blake Marsh Lectr, 1976; Burden Res. Gold Medal and Prize Winner, 1978. Pres., Brit. Soc. for Study of Mental Subnormality, 1978–79; Vice-Pres., Fortune Centre of Riding Therapy, 1980–; Mem. Council, Inst. of Mental Subnormality, 1972–76; Hon. Mem., Amer. Assoc. of Physician Analysts, 1976–. Mem., Adv. Council, Radio Bristol, 1985–88. *Publications:* Notes on Mental Deficiency (jtly), 1952, 3rd edn 1955; Mental Subnormality, 1960, 5th edn, (jtly) as Mental Handicap, 1984; Left Behind, 1977; papers on all aspects of care and treatment of mentally handicapped people and on gen. psychiatric topics; book revs. *Recreations:* following all forms of outdoor sport, gardening, seeking the sun, philately, asking Why? *Address:* Flat 2, 38 Apsley Road, Clifton, Bristol BS8 2SS. *T:* Bristol (0117) 973 8971. *Clubs:* Savages (Bristol); Bristol Football.

HEAVEN, Derick; High Commissioner for Jamaica in London, since 1994, and Ambassador (non-resident) to Scandinavia, Spain and Portugal; *b* 19 Dec. 1940; *m* 1966, Thyra Reid; two *s* one *d*. *Educ:* Cornwall Coll.; Jamaica Sch. of Agriculture. Mem., St Catherine Parish Council, 1973–76; MP for South St Catherine, 1976–80; Parly Sec., Min. of Foreign Affairs, then Minister of Industry and Commerce, 1980; involved in farming and business interests, 1980–89; Consul-General, New York, 1989–92; Ambassador to Japan and (non-resident) to People's Republic of China and Republic of Korea, 1992–94. *Recreations:* reading, travelling, sports. *Address:* c/o Jamaican High Commission, 1–2 Prince Consort Road, SW7 2BZ. *T:* 0171–823 9911.

HEAVENER, Rt. Rev. Robert William; Bishop of Clogher, 1973–80, retired; *b* 28 Feb. 1905; *s* of Joseph and Maria Heavener; *m* 1936, Ada Marjorie, *d* of Rev. Chancellor Thomas Dagg; one *s* one *d*. *Educ:* Trinity Coll., Dublin (MA). Ordained, 1929; Curate, Clones; Diocesan Curate, 1930; Curate-in-charge, Lack, 1933–38; Rector, Derryvullen N, 1938–46; Rector, Monaghan, 1946–73; Rural Dean, 1946. Examining Chaplain and Canon of Clogher, 1951–62; Canon of St Patrick's Cathedral, Dublin, 1962–68; Archdeacon of Clogher, 1968–73. OCF, 1938–43; Member of Staff of Command Welfare Officer, NI District, 1938–43. *Publications:* Co. Fermanagh, 1940 (a short topographical and historical account of NI); Diskos, 1970 (a collection of material for Adult Education); (as Robert Cielou) Spare My Tortured People, 1983 (an attempt to understand the Ulster situation today); Credo, 1993 (local history viewed in context of past and present). *Recreations:* tennis, rare book collecting. *Address:* 12 Church Avenue, Newtownabbey, Co. Antrim BT57 0PJ. *T:* Belfast (01232) 863242. *Club:* Friendly Brother House (Dublin).

HEBBLETHWAITE, Rev. Canon Brian Leslie; University Lecturer in Divinity, Cambridge, since 1977 and Life Fellow of Queens' College, since 1994; *b* 3 Jan. 1939; *s* of Alderman Cyril Hebblethwaite and Sarah Anne Hebblethwaite; *m* 1991, Emma Sîan, *d* of John Ivor Disley, *qv*; one *d*. *Educ:* Clifton Coll.; Magdalen Coll., Oxford (BA LitHum 1961; MA 1967); Magdalene Coll., Cambridge (BA Theol 1963; MA 1968; BD 1984); Westcott House, Cambridge; Univ. of Heidelberg. Curate, All Saints', Elton, Bury, 1965–68; Bye-Fellow and Chaplain, 1968, Fellow and Dean of Chapel, 1969–94, Queens' Coll., Cambridge; Univ. Asst Lectr in Divinity, Cambridge, 1973–77; Examng Chaplain to Bishop of Manchester, 1977–; Canon Theologian, Leicester Cathedral, 1982–. Pres., Soc. for Study of Theology, 1989–91. Editor for Ethics, Theologische Realenzyklopädie, 1980–. *Publications:* Evil, Suffering and Religion, 1976; The Problems of Theology, 1980; (ed jtly) Christianity and Other Religions, 1980; The Adequacy of Christian Ethics, 1981; (ed jtly) The Philosophical Frontiers of Christian Theology, 1982; The Christian Hope, 1984; Preaching Through the Christian Year 10, 1985; The Incarnation, 1987; The Ocean of Truth, 1988; (ed jtly) Divine Action, 1990. *Recreations:* fell-walking, opera, cathedral and church architecture, books. *Address:* Queens' College, Cambridge CB3 9ET. *T:* Cambridge (01223) 335511.

HEBDITCH, Maxwell Graham, CBE 1994; Director, Museum of London, since 1977 (Deputy Director, 1974–77); *b* 22 Aug. 1937; *s* of late Harold Hebditch, motor engr, Yeovil, and Lily (*née* Bartle); *m* 1963, Felicity Davies; two *s* one *d*. *Educ:* Yeovil Sch.; Magdalene Coll., Cambridge. MA, FSA, FMA. Field Archaeologist, Leicester Museums, 1961–64; Asst Curator in Archaeology, later Curator in Agricultural and Social History, City Museum, Bristol, 1965–71; Dir, Guildhall Mus., London, 1971–74. Mem., EC Cttee of Cultural Consultants, 1990–92. Chm., UK Nat. Cttee, ICOM, 1981–87; Mem. Bd, Museum Trng Inst., 1990–; Pres., Museums Assoc., 1990–92 (Vice-Pres., 1988–90). Hon. DLitt City, 1992. *Publications:* contribs to archaeological and museological jls and books. *Recreation:* archaeology. *Address:* Museum of London, London Wall, EC2Y 5HN. *T:* 0171–600 3699, *Fax:* 0171–606 7523.

HEBER-PERCY, Algernon Eustace Hugh; Vice Lord-Lieutenant for Shropshire, since 1990; *b* 2 Jan. 1944; *s* of Brig. A. G. W. Heber-Percy, DSO and Daphne Wilma Kenyon (*née* Parker Bowles); *m* 1966, Hon. Margaret Jane Lever, *y d* of 3rd Viscount Leverhulme, *qv*; one *s* three *d*. *Educ:* Harrow; Mons OTC. Lieut Grenadier Guards, 1962–66. Farmer and landowner. Chm., Mercia Regional Cttee, Nat. Trust, 1990–; Trustee, Nat. Gardens Scheme, 1990–; Mem., Historic Houses Gardens Cttee, 1980–94; Pres., Shropshire and Mid Wales Hospice, 1988–; Chairman: Walker Trust Cttee, 1990– (Mem., 1990–); Pines and Lyneal Trusts for Disabled, 1980–. DL Shropshire, 1986; High Sheriff of Shropshire, 1987. *Recreations:* gardening, country sports. *Address:* Hodnet Hall, Hodnet, Market Drayton, Shropshire TF9 3NN. *T:* Hodnet (01630) 685202. *Club:* Cavalry and Guards.

HECTOR, Gordon Matthews, CMG 1966; CBE 1961 (OBE 1955); Secretary to the Assembly Council, General Assembly of the Church of Scotland, 1980–85; *b* 9 June 1918; *m* 1954, Mary Forrest, MB, ChB, *o d* of late Robert Gray, Fraserburgh, Aberdeenshire; one *s* two *d*. *Educ:* Edinburgh Academy; Lincoln Coll., Oxford. Military Service with East Africa Forces, 1940–45. Apptd Dist Officer, Kenya, 1946; Asst Sec., 1950; Sec. to Road Authority, 1951; Sec. to Govt of Seychelles, 1952; Acting Governor, 1953; Dep. Resident Comr and Govt Sec., Basutoland, 1956; Chief Sec., Basutoland, 1964; Deputy British Government Representative, Lesotho (lately Basutoland), 1965. Sec., Basutoland Constitutional Commn, 1957–58. Clerk to the Univ. Court, Aberdeen, 1967–76; Dep. Sec. and Establishment Officer, Aberdeen Univ., 1976–80. Fellow of the Commonwealth Fund, 1939. Chm., Council of Victoria League in Scotland, 1983–88; Vice-Pres., St Andrew Soc., 1983–93. Chm., Great N of Scotland Rly Assoc., 1989–92. Mem., West End Community Council, 1983–89 (Chm., 1986–89). Member: Ct of Dirs, Edinburgh Acad., 1967–75; Bd of Governors, Oakbank D List Sch., 1969–90. Burgess of Guild, Aberdeen City. *Recreations:* railways ancient and modern, grandchildren. *Address:* 4 Montgomery Court, 110 Hepburn Gardens, St Andrews, Fife KY16 9LT. *Clubs:* Royal Over-Seas League; Vincent's (Oxford).

HEDDY, Brian Huleatt; HM Diplomatic Service, retired; Regional Co-ordinator and Resettlement Officer, British Refugee Council, 1979–82; *b* 8 June 1916; *o s* of late Dr William Reginald Huleatt Heddy, Barrister-at-Law, and Ruby Norton-Taylor; *m* 1st, 1940, Barbara Ellen Williams (*d* 1965); two *s* one *d*; 2nd, 1966, Ruth Mackarness (*née* Hogan) (*d* 1967); (one step *s* two step *d*); 3rd, 1969, Horatia Clare Kennedy. *Educ:* St Paul's Sch.; Pembroke Coll., Oxford. Commissioned in 75th (Highland) Field Regt, Royal Artillery, Nov. 1939; served in France 1940; WA, 1943; War Office and France, 1944–45; Mem. of Gray's Inn. Entered Foreign Service, 1945. Appointed to Brussels, 1946; Denver, 1948; Foreign Office, 1952; Tel Aviv, 1953; UK Delegation to ECSC, Luxembourg, 1955; Foreign Office, 1959; promoted Counsellor, 1963; Consul-Gen. at Lourenço Marques, 1963–65; Head of Nationality and Consular Dept, Commonwealth Office, 1966–67; Head of Migration and Visa Dept, FCO, 1968–71; Consul-Gen. in Durban, 1971–76. *Recreations:* travel, reading. *Address:* Wynyards, Winsham, near Chard, Somerset TA20 4JG. *T:* Winsham (01460) 30260. *Clubs:* East India, Devonshire, Sports and Public Schools, MCC.

HEDGECOE, Prof. John, Dr RCA; FCSD; Professor of Photography, Royal College of Art, London, 1975–94, now Emeritus; Pro Rector, 1981–93, Acting Rector, 1983–84; *b* 24 March 1937; *s* of William Hedgecoe and Kathleen Don; *m* 1960, Julia Mardon; two *s* one *d*. *Educ:* Gulval Village Sch., Cornwall; Guildford Sch. of Art. Staff Photographer, Queen Magazine, 1957–72; Freelance: Sunday Times and Observer, 1960–70; most internat. magazines, 1958–; Portrait, HM the Queen, for British and Australian postage stamps, 1966; photographed The Arts Multi-Projection, British Exhibn, Expo Japan Show, 1970. Royal College ofArt: started Photography Sch., 1965: Head of Dept and Reader in Photography, 1965–74; Fellow, 1973; awarded Chair of Photography, 1975; started Audio/Visual Dept, 1980; started Holography Unit, 1982; Managing Trustee, 1983; Sen. Fellow, 1992. Vis. Prof., Norwegian Nat. Television Sch., Oslo, 1985. Man. Dir, Lion & Unicorn Press Ltd, 1986; Director: John Hedgecoe Ltd, 1965–; Perennial Pictures Ltd, 1980, 1991. Mem. Photographic Bd, CNAA, 1976–78; Gov., W Surrey Coll. of Art (and Mem. Acad. Adv. Bd), 1975–; Acad. Gov., Richmond Coll., London; Trustee, The Minories Victor Batte-Lay Trust, 1985–88. Consultant, English Heritage, 1995. Has illustrated numerous books, 1958–; has contributed to numerous radio broadcasts. Television: Tonight, Aust. TV, 1967; Folio, Anglia, 1980; 8 progs on Photography, Channel Four, 1983, repeated 1984; Winners, Channel Four, 1984; Light and Form, US Cable TV, 1985. Exhibitions: London, Sydney, Toronto, Edinburgh, Venice, Prague; Collections: V&A Museum; Art Gall. of Ontario; Nat. Portrait Gall., London; Citibank, London; Henry Moore Foundn; Museum of Modern Art, NY; Leeds City Art Gall.; Ministry of Culture, Morocco. FRSA. Hon. FIIPC. Laureate and Medal for contribution to photography, Govt of Czechoslovakia, 1989. *Publications:* Henry Moore, 1968 (prize best art book, world-wide, 1969); (jtly) Kevin Crossley-Holland book of Norfolk Poems, 1970; Sculptures of Picasso, 1970; (jtly) Photography, Material and Methods, 1971–74 edns; Henry Moore, Energy in Space, 1973; The Book of Photography, 1976; Handbook of Photographic Techniques, 1977, 3rd edn 1992; The Art of Colour Photography, 1978 (Kodak Photobuchpreis Stuttgart 1979); Grand Prix Technique de la Photographie, Musée Français de la Photographie, Paris 1980); Possessions, 1978; The Pocket Book of Photography, 1979; Introductory Photography Course, 1979; Master Classes in Photography: Children and Child Portraiture, 1980; (illus.) Poems of Thomas Hardy, 1981; (illus.) Poems of Robert Burns, 1981; The Book of Advanced Photography, 1982; What a Picture!, 1983; The Photographer's Work Book, 1983; Aesthetics of Nude Photography, 1984; The Workbook of Photo Techniques, 1984; The Workbook of Darkroom Techniques, 1984; Pocket Book of Travel and Holiday Photography, 1986; Henry Moore: his ideas, inspirations and life as an artist, 1986; The Three Dimensional Pop-up Photography Book, 1986; (with A. L. Rowse) Shakespeare's Land, 1986; Photographer's Manual of Creative Ideas, 1986; (with A. L. Rowse) Rowse's Cornwall, 1987; Practical Portrait Photography, 1987; Practical Book of Landscape Photography, 1988; Hedgecoe on Video, 1988; Hedgecoe on Photography, 1988; Complete Photography Guide, 1990; Video Photographer's Handbook, 1992; Zillij, 1992; (jtly) The Art of Moroccan Ceramics, 1993; John Hedgecoe's Basic Photography, 1993; The New Book of Photography, 1994; The Spirit of the Garden, 1994; Black and White Photography, 1994; Camcorder Basics, 1995. *Recreations:* sculpture, building, gardening. *Address:* c/o Royal College of Art, Kensington Gore, SW7 2EU. *T:* 0171–584 5020. *Club:* Arts.

HEDGELAND, Air Vice-Marshal Philip Michael Sweatman, CB 1978; OBE 1957 (MBE 1948); CEng, FIEE; *b* 24 Nov. 1922; *s* of Philip and Margaret Hedgeland, Maidstone, Kent; *m* 1946, Jean Riddle Brinkworth, *d* of Leonard and Anne Brinkworth, Darlington, Co. Durham; two *s*. *Educ:* Maidstone Grammar Sch.; City and Guilds Coll., Imperial Coll. of Science and Technology, London. BSc(Eng), ACGI (Siemens Medallist). Served War: commnd into Technical Br., RAF, 1942; Radar Officer, Pathfinder Force and at TRE, Malvern. Radar Develt Officer, Central Bomber Estabt, 1945–48; Radio Introd. Unit Project Officer for V-Bomber Navigation and Bombing System, 1952–57; Wing Comdr Radio (Air) at HQ Bomber Comd, 1957–60; jssc 1960; Air Ministry Technical Planning, 1961–62; aws 1963; Dir of Signals (Far East), Singapore, 1963–65; commanded RAF Stanbridge (Central Communications Centre), 1966–67; SASO, HQ Signals Comd/90 Gp, 1968–69; IDC, 1970; MoD Procurement Exec., Project Dir for Airborne Radar, 1971–74, Vice-Pres., Ordnance Bd, 1975–77, Pres., 1977–78. FCGI 1977. Pres., Pathfinder Assoc., 1985–87. *Recreations:* audio engineering, horticulture, amateur radio. *Club:* Royal Air Force.

HEDGER, Eric Frank, CB 1979; OBE 1960; Director General of Defence Contracts, Under Secretary, Ministry of Defence, 1969–80; *b* 15 Sept. 1919; *s* of late Albert Frank Hedger and Ellen Agnes Hedger (*née* Laffey); *m* 1945, Joan Kathleen Bernas; two *s* one *d*. *Educ:* St Luke's, Southsea. War Service, 1939–46 (despatches 1945): Adjutant, 10 Air Formation Signals; Adjutant, then 2nd i/c, 7 Indian Air Formation Signals. Secretary, Admiralty Awards Council, 1946–49; Admin. Staff Coll., 1958; Dir of Navy Contracts, 1968. Mem. of Council and Bd of Management, Inst. of Purchasing and Supply, 1974–75. Advr, Defence Manufacturers Assoc., 1983–88. FInstPS. *Recreations:* music, reading, gardening. *Address:* Helere House, Ridgeway Mead, Sidmouth, Devon EX10 9DT. *T:* Sidmouth (01395) 577741.

HEDGER, John Clive; Deputy Secretary, Department for Education and Employment (formerly of Education and Science, then for Education), since 1992; *b* 17 Dec. 1942; *s* of late Leslie John Keith Hedger and of Iris Hedger (*née* Friedlos); *m* 1966, Jean Ann Felstead; two *s* one *d*. *Educ:* Quirister Sch., Winchester; Victoria Coll., Jersey; Univ. of Sussex (BA 1965; MA 1966). Dept of Educn and Science, 1966; Asst Private Sec., 1970; Sec., Cttee of Enquiry on Educn of Handicapped, 1974–76; Under Sec. and Head of Schs Br. 1, DES 1988–92. *Recreations:* coarse acting, walking, coarse sailing, growing things. *Address:* c/o Department for Education and Employment, Sanctuary Buildings, Great Smith Street, SW1P 3BT; Poultons, Cookham, Berks SL6 9HW. *T:* Bourne End (016285) 23911. *Club:* Odney (Cookham).

HEDGES, Anthony (John); Reader in Composition, University of Hull, 1978–95; *b* 5 March 1931; *s* of late S. G. Hedges; *m* 1957, Delia Joy Marsden; two *s* two *d*. *Educ:* Bicester Grammar Sch.; Keble Coll., Oxford. MA, BMus, LRAM. National Service as solo pianist and arranger Royal Signals Band, 1955–57. Teacher and Lecturer, Royal Scottish Academy of Music, 1957–63. During this period became a regular contributor to Scotsman, Glasgow Herald, Guardian, Musical Times, etc. Lecturer in Music, Univ. of Hull, 1963, Sen. Lectr, 1968. The Composers' Guild of Great Britain: Chm., Northern Br., 1966–67; Mem. Exec. Cttee of Guild, 1969–73, 1977–81, 1982–87; Chm. of Guild, 1972, Jt Chm., 1973. Member: Council, Central Music Library, Westminster, 1970; Council, Soc. for Promotion of New Music, 1974–81; Music Bd, CNAA, 1974–77; Music Panel, Yorks Arts Assoc., 1974–75, Lincs and Humberside Arts Assoc., 1975–78; Founder-conductor, The Humberside Sinfonia, 1978–81. Wrote regularly for Yorkshire Post, 1963–78, and contributed to many jls, incl. Composer, Current Musicology, etc, and also broadcast on musical subjects. *Publications include: (works): orchestral:* Comedy Overture, 1962 (rev. 1967); Overture, October '62, 1962 (rev. 1968); Sinfonia Semplice, 1963; Expressions for Orchestra, 1964; Prelude, Romance and Rondo, strings, 1965; Concertante Music, 1965; Four Miniature Dances, 1967; A Holiday Overture, 1968; Variations on a theme of Rameau, 1969; Kingston Sketches, 1969; An Ayrshire Serenade, 1969; Four Diversions, strings, 1971; Celebrations, 1973; Symphony, 1972–73; Festival Dances, 1976; Overture, Heigham Sound, 1978; Four Breton Sketches, 1980; Sinfonia Concertante, 1980; Scenes from the Humber, 1981; A Cleveland Overture, 1984;

Concertino for Horn and String Orchestra, 1987; Sinfonia Giovanile, 1992; Showpiece, 1995; *choral:* Gloria, unaccompanied, 1965; Epithalamium, chorus and orch. (Spencer), 1969; To Music, chorus and orch. (various texts), 1972; Psalm 104, 1973; A Manchester Mass, chorus, orch. and brass band, 1974; A Humberside Cantata, 1976; Songs of David, 1978; The Temple of Solomon, 1979; I Sing the Birth: canticles for Christmas, 1985; I'll make me a world, 1990; *chamber music:* Five Preludes, piano, 1959; Four Pieces, piano, 1966; Rondo Concertante, violin, clarinet, horn, violoncello, 1967; Sonata for violin and harpsichord, 1967; Three Songs of Love, soprano, piano (from Song of Songs), 1968; String Quartet, 1970; Rhapsody, violin, piano, 1971, revd 1988; piano sonata, 1974; Song Cycle, 1977; Piano Trio, 1977; Fantasy for Violin and Piano, 1981; Sonatinas for Flute, Viola, Cello, 1982; Wind Quintet, 1984; Flute Trios, 1985, 1989; Fantasy Sonata for bassoon and piano, 1986; Clarinet Quintet, 1987; Flute Sonata, 1988; Five Aphorisms, piano, 1990; In such a night, string quartet, 1990; Bassoon Quintet, 1991; Piano Quartet, 1992; Trombone Sonata, 1994; *opera:* Shadows in the Sun (lib. Jim Hawkins), 1976; *musical:* Minotaur (lib. Jim Hawkins), 1978; *miscellaneous:* many anthems, partsongs, albums of music for children; music for television, film and stage. *Recreations:* family life, reading, walking. *Address:* Malt Shovel Cottage, 76 Walkergate, Beverley, HU17 9ER. *T:* Beverley (01482) 860580.

HEDLEY, Prof. Anthony Johnson, MD; FRCPE, FRCPGlas, FRCP, FFPHM; Professor of Community Medicine, University of Hong Kong, since 1988; *b* 8 April 1941; *s* of Thomas Johnson Hedley and Winifred Duncan; *m* 1967, Elizabeth-Anne Walsh (marr. diss. 1992). *Educ:* Rydal Sch.; Aberdeen Univ. (MB, ChB 1965; MD 1972); Edinburgh Univ. (Dip. Soc. Med. 1973). MRCP 1973; FRCPE 1981; FRCPGlas, 1985; FRCP 1987; FFPHM (FFCM 1981; MFCM 1975). Lectr in Community Medicine, Univ. of Aberdeen, 1974–76; Sen. Lectr in Community Health, Univ. of Nottingham, 1976–83; Prof.-Designate in Community Medicine, 1983–84, Henry Mechan Prof. of Public Health, 1984–88, Univ. of Glasgow. Med. Adviser (Thailand), ODA, 1977–. Hon. MD Khon Kaen Univ., 1983. *Publications:* papers and chapters on endocrine disease, surveillance of chronic disease and on med. educn. *Recreations:* long-distance running, photography, rifle shooting, flying (private pilot's licence, 1992). *Address:* 39 Foxhill Road, Burton Joyce, Nottinghamshire NG14 5DB. *T:* Burton Joyce (0160231) 2558; Flat B6, Block 2, Tam Towers, 25 Sha Wan Drive, Victoria Road, Pok fu Lam, Hong Kong. *T:* 8194708, *Fax:* 8559014. *Clubs:* Rydal Veterans (Colwyn Bay); Freelancers (Nottingham); Hong Kong Aviation (Hong Kong).

HEDLEY, Mark; His Honour Judge Hedley; a Circuit Judge, since 1992; *b* 23 Aug. 1946; *s* of Peter and Eve Hedley; *m* 1973, Erica Britton; three *s* one *d*. *Educ:* Framlingham College; Univ. of Liverpool (LLB Hons). Called to the Bar, Gray's Inn, 1969; VSO, Sudan, 1969–70; practice at Liverpool Bar, 1971–92; Head of Chambers, 1983–92; a Recorder, 1988–92. *Recreations:* cricket, railways. *Address:* 55 Everton Road, Liverpool L6 2EH. *T:* 0151–260 6266.

HEDLEY, Prof. Ronald; Director, Trent Polytechnic, Nottingham, 1970–80, Emeritus Professor, 1980; *b* 12 Sept. 1917; *s* of Francis Hedley, Hebburn, Co. Durham; *m* 1942; one *s* one *d*. *Educ:* Jarrow Grammar Sch.; Durham Univ. (MA, DipEd); Ecole Normale d'Instituteurs, Evreux. Various appts in teaching and educational administration, 1947–64; Dep. Dir of Education, Nottingham, 1964–70. Chm., Regional Acad. Bd, Regional Adv. Council for Further Educn in E Midlands, 1972–76; Member: Central Council for Educn and Trng in Social Work, 1971–77; Nat. Adv. Council for Educn for Ind. and Commerce, 1973–77; Central Council for Educn and Trng of Health Visitors, 1972–77; Cttee for Arts and Social Studies, CNAA, 1974–76; Personal Social Services Council, 1974–78; Cttee on Recreation Management Training, 1977–80; Local Govt Trng Bd, 1978–81; Adv. Cttee for Supply and Educn of Teachers, 1980–81, Chm., Local Cttee for Teacher Educn, King Alfred's Coll., Winchester, 1986–89. FRSA 1970. Hon. Fellow: Trent Polytechnic, 1980; Nottingham Trent, 1992. Hon. Senator, Fachhochschule, Karlsruhe, Germany, 1980. Hon. LLD Nottingham, 1981; DUniv Nottingham Trent, 1993. *Address:* Evergreen, Haydn Close, Kings Worthy, Hants SO23 7RD. *T:* Winchester (01962) 884142.

HEDLEY, Ronald Henderson, CB 1986; DSc, PhD; FIBiol; Director, British Museum (Natural History), 1976–88; *b* 2 Nov. 1928; *s* of Henry Armstrong Hedley and Margaret Hopper; *m* 1957, Valmai Mary Griffith, New Zealand; one *s*. *Educ:* Durham Johnston Sch.; King's Coll., Univ. of Durham. Commissioned in Royal Regt of Artillery, 1953–55. Sen. Scientific Officer, British Museum (Natural History), 1955–61; New Zealand Nat. Research Fellow, 1960–61; Principal Scientific Officer, 1961–64; Dep. Keeper of Zoology, 1964–71; Dep. Dir, 1971–76. Vis. Lectr in Microbiology, Univ. of Surrey, 1968–75. Mem. Council, Fresh Water Biological Assoc., 1972–76; Trustee, Percy Sladen Meml Fund, 1972–77; Pres., British Section, Soc. of Protozoology, 1975–78; Member Council: Marine Biolog. Assoc., 1976–79, 1981–92; Zoological Soc., London, 1981–85 (Hon. Sec., 1977–80; Vice-Pres., 1980–85); Mem., Internat. Trust for Zoological Nomenclature, 1977–90. Member: Council, Royal Albert Hall, 1982–88; National Trust, 1985–88. *Publications:* (ed with C. G. Adams) Foraminifera, vols 1–3, 1974, 1976, 1978; (with C. G. Ogden) Atlas of Testate Amoebae, 1980; technical papers, mainly on biology, cytology and systematics of protozoa, 1956–. *Recreations:* horology, horticulture, humour. *Club:* Civil Service.

HEDLEY-MILLER, Dame Mary (Elizabeth), DCVO 1989; CB 1983; Ceremonial Officer, Cabinet Office, 1983–88; *b* 5 Sept. 1923; *d* of late J. W. Ashe; *m* 1950, Roger Latham Hedley-Miller; one *s* two *d*. *Educ:* Queen's Sch., Chester; St Hugh's Coll., Oxford (MA). Joined HM Treasury, 1945; served in UK Treasury Delegn, Washington DC, 1947–49; Under-Sec., HM Treasury, 1973–83. Alternate Dir, Monetary Cttee, EEC, and Alternate Exec. Dir, European Investment Bank, 1977–83. *Recreations:* family, including family music; reading. *Address:* 108 Higher Drive, Purley, Surrey CR8 2HL. *T:* 0181–660 1837. *Club:* United Oxford & Cambridge University.

HEENAN, Maurice, CMG 1966; QC (Hong Kong) 1962; The General Counsel, United Nations Relief and Works Agency for Palestine Refugees in the Near East, 1973–77; *b* NZ, 8 Oct. 1912; 2nd *s* of late David Heenan and of Anne Frame; *m* 1951, Claire, 2nd *d* of late Emil Ciho and Irene Rotbauer, Trenčín, Bratislava; two *d*. *Educ:* Canterbury Coll., University of New Zealand. Law Professional, LLB, Barrister and Solicitor of Supreme Court of New Zealand, Practised law in NZ, 1937–40. War of 1939–45; Major, 2nd NZEF; active service Western Desert, Libya, Cyrenaica and Italy, 1940–45 (despatches). Crown Counsel, Palestine, 1946–48. Solicitor-Gen., Hong Kong, 1961; HM's Attorney-Gen., Hong Kong, and *ex officio* MEC and MLC, Hong Kong, 1961–66; Dep.-Dir, Gen. Legal Div., Office of Legal Affairs, Offices of the Sec.-Gen., UN, NY, 1966–73. *Recreations:* Rugby football, tennis, squash, ski-ing, golf. *Address:* Plane Trees, West Road, New Canaan, CT 06840, USA. *Clubs:* Hong Kong; Country (New Canaan).

HEES, Hon. George Harris, PC (Canada) 1957; OC (Can.) 1989; Ambassador-at-Large, Canada, since 1988; *b* Toronto, 17 June 1910; *s* of Harris Lincoln Hees, Toronto, and Mabel Good, New York; *m* 1934, Mabel, *d* of late Hon. E. A. Dunlop; three *d*. *Educ:* Trinity Coll. Sch., Port Hope, Ont; RMC, Kingston, Ont; University of Toronto; Cambridge Univ. Formerly Dir, George H. Hees & Son & Co. Served War of 1939–45: Royal Canadian Artillery, 1941–44; 3rd Anti-Tank Regt, Royal Canadian Artillery; Bde Major, 5th Infantry Bde, Holland (wounded); retd as Major. Contested (Prog. C) Spadina Riding, 1945; MP (Prog. C): Toronto–Broadview, May 1950–1963; Prince Edward—Hastings Riding, subseq. Northumberland, Ont, Nov. 1965–88; Minister of Transport, Canada, 1957–60; Minister of Trade and Commerce, 1960–63; Minister of Veterans Affairs, 1984–88. Pres., Montreal and Canadian Stock Exchanges, 1964–65. Executive with George H. Hees Son & Co., Toronto; Dir, Expo 67. Hon. LLD Waterloo UC (now Sir Wilfrid Laurier Univ.), 1961; Hon. DMilSc Royal Mil. Coll., Kingston, Ont, 1988. *Recreations:* reading, ski-ing, swimming, golf, tennis, riding, bridge; formerly boxing. *Clubs:* Toronto Golf, Toronto Badminton and Racquet (Toronto); Royal Ottawa Golf.

HEGARTY, John Kevin; Creative Director, since 1982, and Chairman, since 1991, Bartle Bogle Hegarty Ltd; *b* 20 May 1944; *s* of Matthew and Anne Hegarty; *m* 1970, Kari Bergesen; one *s* one *d*. *Educ:* Challoner Grammar Sch.; Hornsey Sch. of Art; London Coll. of Printing. Junior Art Dir, Benton & Bowles, 1965–66; Art Director: John Collings and Partners, 1966–67; Cramer Saatchi, 1967–70; Saatchi & Saatchi: Founding Shareholder, 1970; Dep. Creative Dir, 1971–73; Founding Partner and Creative Dir, TBWA, London, 1973–82. FRSA 1992. *Recreations:* tennis, ski-ing. *Address:* (office) 24–27 Great Pulteney Street, W1R 3DB. *Club:* Groucho.

HEGARTY, Most Rev. Séamus; *see* Derry, Bishop of, (RC).

HEGARTY, Thomas Brendan; QC 1992; a Recorder, since 1988; *b* 6 June 1943; *s* of Thomas Hegarty and Louise (*née* Conlan); *m* 1972, Irene Letitia Hall; one *s* one *d*. *Educ:* St Joseph's Coll., Dumfries; St John's Coll., Cambridge (BA 1964; LLB 1965; MA 1970). Called to the Bar, Middle Temple, 1970. *Address:* 8 King Street, Manchester M2 6AQ. *Club:* Manchester Tennis and Racquet.

HEGGS, Geoffrey Ellis; Chairman of Industrial Tribunals, since 1977, Regional Chairman, London North, since 1990; a Recorder of the Crown Court, since 1983; *b* 23 Oct. 1928; *s* of George Heggs, MBE and Winifred Grace Heggs; *m* 1953, Renée Fanny Madeleine Calderan (*see* R. F. M. Heggs); two *s* one *d*. *Educ:* Elizabeth Coll., Guernsey; LLB London. Admitted Solicitor, 1952. Rotary Foundn Fellow, Yale Univ., 1953–54; LLM Yale; Asst Sec., Law Soc., 1956–58; practised as solicitor in London, 1958–77. Member: Law Society; City of London Solicitors' Company. *Recreations:* military history, music, painting. *Address:* 19/21 Woburn Place, WC1H 0LU. *T:* 0171–239 9265.

HEGGS, Renée Fanny Madeleine; a Social Security Commissioner, since 1981; a Child Support Commissioner, since 1993; Legal Member, Mental Health Review Tribunal, since 1985; *b* 29 Nov. 1929; *d* of E. and G. Calderan; *m* 1953, Geoffrey Ellis Heggs, *qv*; two *s* one *d*. *Educ:* Notting Hill and Ealing High Sch., GPDST; London Univ. (LLB 1952). Admitted Solicitor, 1955; practising Solicitor, 1955–81. Chm., Nat. Insce Local Tribunal, 1976–81; pt-time Chm. of Industrial Tribunals, 1978–81; Pres., Appeal Tribunal under London Building Acts, 1979–81. *Recreations:* music, travelling. *Address:* (office) Harp House, 83 Farringdon Street, EC4A 4DH. *T:* 0171-353 5145.

HEGINBOTHAM, Christopher John; Chief Executive, Riverside Mental Health NHS Trust, since 1993; *b* 25 March 1948; *s* of Joseph William and Marjorie Heginbotham; *m* 1988, Barbara Joyce, *d* of Charles and Lois-Ella Gill, Cincinnati, Ohio; two *d*. *Educ:* Univ. of Birmingham (BSc Hons); Univ. of Essex (MSc); MA Wales 1989. Area Manager, Circle Thirty Three Housing Trust, 1977–80; Assistant Borough Housing Officer, London Borough of Haringey, 1980–82; Nat. Dir, MIND (Nat. Assoc. for Mental Health), 1982–88; Fellow in Health Services Management, King's Fund Coll., London, 1989–93. Member: Hampstead DHA, 1981–87; Waltham Forest DHA, 1989–92 (Vice-Chm., 1991–92); Chm., Redbridge and Waltham Forest FHSA, 1992–93. Member: Nat. Adv. Council on Employment of Disabled People, 1983–90; Bd, World Fedn for Mental Health, 1985–89 (rep., UN Commn on Human Rights, 1985–91); Bd, Internat. Acad. of Law and Mental Health, 1987–89. Vis. Res. Fellow, Univ. of Glasgow Inst. of Law and Ethics in Medicine, 1987–91. *Publications:* Housing Projects for Mentally Handicapped People, 1981; Promoting Residential Services for Mentally Handicapped People, 1982; Webs and Mazes: approaches to community care, 1984; The Rights of Mentally Ill People, 1987; Return to Community, 1990; (with T. Campbell) Mental Illness: prejudice, discrimination and the law, 1990; (with C. Ham) Purchasing Dilemmas, 1992. *Recreations:* creative writing, walking. *Address:* (office) Commonwealth House, Chalkhill Road, W6 8DW. *T:* 0181–746 5554.

HEGINBOTHAM, Prof. Wilfred Brooks, OBE 1978; FEng 1985; Director General, Production Engineering Research Association of Great Britain (PERA), Melton Mowbray, 1979–84; *b* 9 April 1924; *s* of Fred and Alice Heginbotham; *m* 1957, Marjorie Pixton; three *d*. *Educ:* Manchester Univ. (UMIST). BScTech 1949; MScTech 1950; PhD (Manchester) 1956; DSc (Manchester) 1979. FIProdE; MIMechE; FRSA. Started in industry as wood pattern maker; part-time courses to HNC, 1938–46; Walter Preston Schol., Manchester Coll. of Tech., 1946; joined staff, 1951; Lectr in Production Engineering subjects, UMIST, 1951–58; industrial experience for 10 years; Nottingham University: Sen. Lectr, 1958; started first BSc course in Prod. Engrg in UK, 1961; Head of Dept of Prod. Engrg and Prod. Management, 1961–63; Cripps Prof., 1963–79; Dean, Faculty of Applied Science, 1967–71; Special Prof. of Prodn Engrg, 1983–86; Prof. Emeritus, 1990. Hon. Prof., Dept of Engrg, Univ. of Warwick, 1984–89; Vis. Prof., Univ. of RI, USA, 1987; Vis. Sen. Res. Fellow, Dept of Mech. Engrg, Univ. of Birmingham, 1989–. Developed group to study Automatic Assembly Systems and Industrial Robot devices, including computer vision and tactile sense, and co-operated with industry in development of advanced automation equipment. Chm. Org. Cttee for establishment of Brit. Robot Assoc., 1977, Chm. of Council, 1977–80, Pres., 1980–84. Editor-in-Chief: The Industrial Robot; Assembly Automation; Advanced Manufacturing Technology Journal. Hon. DTech Scis Eindhoven, 1981; Hon. DSc Aston, 1983. Engelberger Award, Robot Inst. of America, 1983. *Publications:* Programmable Assembly, 1984; (ed with D. T. Pham) Robot Grippers, 1986; contribs to Encyc. Brit. on Robot Devices and to prof. pubns on metal cutting, automated assembly, industrial robots, artificial intelligence and production processes. *Recreations:* gliding, model aircraft construction and operation (radio controlled). *Address:* 7 Paddocks View, Eaton Grange, Long Eaton, Notts NG10 3QF. *T:* Nottingham (0115) 946 3250.

HEGLAND, David Leroy, DFC 1944; Director: Kemtron Ltd; Galena; Massey-Ferguson Holdings (Australia) Ltd; Carlton and United Breweries Holdings Ltd; Plessey Pacific Pty Ltd; cattle grazier; *b* 12 June 1919; *s* of Lee and Jennie Hegland; *m* 1944, Dagmar Cooke; two *s* one *d*. *Educ:* Whitman Coll., Washington, USA (BA). Served War, 1942–45; USN aircraft pilot in Pacific Ocean areas; Lt Comdr USNR, 1945. Managing Director: GM International, Copenhagen, 1956–58; GM South African, Port Elizabeth, 1958–61; GM Holden's Pty Ltd, Melbourne, 1962–65; Chm. and Man. Dir, Vauxhall Motors Ltd, Luton, 1966–70; Dir, General Motors Ltd, London, 1966–70; Chm., GKN Australia Ltd, and Dir, Ajax GKN Holdings Pty Ltd, and Guest, Keen & Nettlefolds (Overseas) Ltd, 1972–80. Member: Albury-Wodonga Develt Corp., 1980–81; Industry Forum, Aust. Acad. of Science, 1972–; Aust. Inst. of Dirs; Delta Sigma Rho. FIMI. Richard Kirby medal for production engrg, 1964. *Recreations:* flying, tennis, riding. *Clubs:* Royal &

1957; Men of Tomorrow, 1958; In the Wake of a Stranger, 1958; No Trees in the Street, 1959; Some People, 1962; Play it Cool, 1962; Live it Up, 1963; Two Left Feet, 1963; The System, 1964; Be my Guest, 1965; Eye of the Devil, 1966; Blow Up, 1966; Camelot, 1967; Barbarella, 1967; Only When I Larf, 1968; The Charge of the Light Brigade, 1968; The Long Day's Dying, 1968; The Best House in London, 1968; Alfred the Great, 1969; Fragment of Fear, 1970; The Walking Stick, 1970; Unman, Wittering & Zigo, 1971; The Love Machine, 1971; Voices, 1973; Don't Worry Momma, 1973; Juggernaut, 1974; Quilp, 1974; Profundo Rosso, 1975; Islands in the Stream, 1975; The Squeeze, 1976; Jeeves (musical), Her Majesty's, 1975; Power Play, 1978; Thirst, 1979; Beyond Reasonable Doubt, 1980; Jekyll and Hyde, 1980; Harlequin, 1980. BBC TV, Scott Fitzgerald, 1975; ITV, The Rime of the Ancient Mariner, 1978; ITV, Charlie Muffin, 1979. Directed: Running Scared, 1972; The 14, 1973 (Silver Bear Award, Berlin Film Festival, 1973); Disappearance, 1977; Power Play, 1977; Just a Gigolo, 1978; David Bowie Stage, 1979; Murder By Decree, 1979; Survivor, 1979; Race to the Yankee Zephyr, 1980; also in Australia, NZ etc. Produced: Strange Behaviour, 1981; Turkey Shoot, 1981. Director: International Home Video FGH Pty Ltd (Melbourne); Film and General Holdings Inc. (California). *Recreation:* painting. *Clubs:* Chelsea Arts, Magic Circle.

HEMP, Prof. William Spooner, MA, FRAeS; Stewarts and Lloyds Professor of Structural Engineering, Oxford University, 1965–83; Emeritus Fellow of Keble College, Oxford, since 1984 (Professorial Fellow, 1965–83); *b* 21 March 1916; *s* of late Rev. William James Hemp and Daisy Lilian Hemp; *m* 1938, Dilys Ruth Davies; one *s*. *Educ:* Paston Grammar Sch., North Walsham; Jesus Coll., Cambridge (Scholar, MA). Aeronautical Engineer, Bristol Aeroplane Co., 1938–46. Coll. of Aeronautics: Senior Lecturer, 1946–50; Prof. of Aircraft Structures and Aeroelasticity, 1950–65; Head of Dept of Aircraft Design, 1951–65; Dep. Principal, 1957–65. Mem. of various cttees of Aeronautical Research Council since 1948. Visiting Prof., Stanford Univ., Calif, 1960–61. *Publications:* Optimum Structures, 1973; research papers in the Theory of Structures, Solid Mechanics and Applied Mathematics. *Recreations:* mountain walking, music. *Address:* Duffryn House, Church Lane, Horton-cum-Studley, Oxford OX33 1AW.

HEMPHILL, 5th Baron *cr* 1906, of Rathkenny and Cashel; **Peter Patrick Fitzroy Martyn Martyn-Hemphill;** *b* 5 Sept. 1928; *o s* of 4th Baron Hemphill and Emily, *d* of F. Irving Sears, Webster, Mass; *S* father 1957; *m* 1952, Olivia Anne, *er d* of Major Robert Francis Ruttledge, MC, Cloonee, Ballinrobe, County Mayo; one *s* two *d*; assumed surname of Martyn in addition to Hemphill, 1959. *Educ:* Downside; Brasenose Coll., Oxford (MA Jurisp.). Sen. Steward, Irish Turf Club, 1985–88; Steward, Irish Nat. Hunt Steeplechase Cttee, 1973–76 and 1978–81. *Heir: s* Hon. Charles Andrew Martyn Martyn-Hemphill [*b* 8 Oct. 1954; *m* 1985, Sarah J. F., *e d* of Richard Lumley; one *s* three *d*]. *Address:* Raford, Kiltulla, Co. Galway, Eire. *Clubs:* White's; Royal Irish Automobile (Dublin); Irish Cruising.

HEMSLEY, Thomas Jeffrey; free-lance opera and concert singer; Professor: Guildhall School of Music and Drama, since 1987; Trinity College of Music, 1988–93; *b* 12 April 1927; *s* of Sydney William Hemsley and Kathleen Annie Hemsley (*née* Deacon); *m* 1960, Hon. Gwenllian Ellen James, *d* of 4th Baron Northbourne; three *s*. *Educ:* Ashby de la Zouch Grammar Sch.; Brasenose Coll., Oxford (MA). Vicar Choral, St Paul's Cathedral, 1950–51; Prin. Baritone, Stadttheater, Aachen, 1953–56; Deutsche Oper am Rhein, 1957–63; Opernhaus, Zurich, 1963–67; Glyndebourne, Bayreuth, Edinburgh Festivals, etc. Vis. Prof., RCM, 1986; Guest Prof., Royal Danish Acad. of Music, 1990–91. Mem., Roy. Philharmonic Soc., 1968–. Hon. RAM 1974; Hon. FTCL 1988. FRSA 1991. *Address:* 10 Denewood Road, N6 4AJ. *T:* 0181–348 3397. *Club:* Garrick.

HENAO, Rev. Sir Ravu, Kt 1982; OBE 1975; Executive Secretary, Bible Society of Papua New Guinea, 1980–87; retired; *b* 27 March 1927; *s* of Boga Henao and Gaba Asi; *m* 1944, Lahui Peri; four *s* five *d*. *Educ:* Port Moresby (completed standard 5); Lawes Theol Coll., Fife Bay, Milne Bay Province. Primary sch. teacher, various schs in Central Dist, 1944–66 (pastor as well as teacher, 1946); Chm. (full-time), Papua Ekalesia (national church related to London Missionary Soc.), 1967; Bishop of United Church for Papua Mainland Region, 1968–80. Hon. DTech PNG Univ. of Technology, 1987. *Publications:* (with Raymond Perry) Let's Discuss These Things, 1966; (with Alan Dunstan) Paul's Letter to the Galatians, 1974. *Recreations:* fishing, hunting, gardening. *Address:* c/o PO Box 18, Port Moresby, Papua New Guinea. *T:* 217893.

HENBEST, Harold Bernard; *see* Herbert, H. B.

HENDER, John Derrik, CBE 1986; DL; public sector consultant; Chief Executive, West Midlands Metropolitan County Council, 1973–86; *b* 15 Nov. 1926; *s* of late Jessie Peter and late Jennie Hender; *m* 1949, Kathleen Nora Brown; one *d*. *Educ:* Great Yarmouth Grammar School. IPFA, FCA, FIMgt. Deputy Borough Treasurer: Newcastle-under-Lyme, 1957–61; Wolverhampton County Borough, 1961–64; City Treas. 1965–69, Chief Exec. and Town Clerk 1969–73, Coventry County Borough. DL West Midlands, 1975. *Publications:* numerous articles relating to various aspects of local govt and related matters. *Recreation:* gardening. *Address:* Endwood, South Avenue, Thorpe St Andrew, Norwich NR7 0EZ.

HENDERSON, family name of **Barons Faringdon** and **Henderson of Brompton.**

HENDERSON OF BROMPTON, Baron *cr* 1984 (Life Peer), of Brompton in the Royal Borough of Kensington and Chelsea and of Brough in the County of Cumbria; **Peter Gordon Henderson,** KCB 1975; Clerk of the Parliaments, 1974–83; *b* 16 Sept. 1922; *m* 1950, Susan Mary Dartford; two *s* two *d*. *Educ:* Stowe Sch.; Magdalen Coll., Oxford. Served War, Scots Guards, 1942–44. Clerk, House of Lords, 1954–60; seconded to HM Treasury as Sec. to Leader and Chief Whip, House of Lords, 1960–63; Reading Clerk and Clerk of Public Bills, 1964–74; Clerk Asst, 1974. Mem., Cttee on Preparation of Legislation, 1973–74. Gov., Lake District Art Gall. and Mus. Trust, 1984–. President: New Bridge, 1990–; Progress, 1991–; Vice-Pres., Nat. Assoc. of Motor Projects, 1991–.

See also Hon. L. D. J. Henderson.

HENDERSON, Barry; *see* Henderson, J. S. B.

HENDERSON, Bernard Vere, CBE 1987; Chairman: Anglian Water, 1981–94; British Waterways Board, since 1994; *b* 8 July 1928; *s* of late Percy Cecil and Ruth Elizabeth Henderson; *m* 1952, Valerie Jane Cairns; two *s* one *d*. *Educ:* Ampleforth Coll.; Harvard Business Sch. Served Army, RE, 1946–48. P. C. Henderson Group, 1949–80 (Man. Dir, 1958–80). Chm., Water Services Assoc., 1990–91. Chm., Australia and NZ Trade Adv. Cttee, 1994–95. *Recreations:* countryside, narrow boat cruising.

HENDERSON, Charles Edward, CB 1992; FIA; Deputy Secretary, Department of Trade and Industry, since 1992; *b* 19 Sept. 1939; *s* of late David Henderson and of Giorgiana Leggatt Henderson; *m* 1966, Rachel Hilary Hall, *d* of Dr Stephen Hall, FRCP and late Dr Mary Hall, Boarstall Tower, Bucks; one *d* one *s*. *Educ:* Charterhouse; Pembroke Coll., Cambridge (MA). FIA 1965. Actuarial Trainee, subseq. Asst Investment Sec., Equity & Law Life Assurance Soc., 1960–70; ECGD, 1971–73; DTI, 1973–74; Dept of Energy, 1974–88: Asst Sec., 1975; Under Sec., 1982; Atomic Energy Div., 1982; Oil Div., 1985; Prin. Estabt and Finance Officer, 1986–88; Head, Office of Arts and Libraries, 1989–92. Dir, Aluminium Corp. Ltd, 1981–84. *Recreations:* making and listening to music, mountaineering, golf. *Address:* 33 Fairfax Road, Bedford Park, W4 1EN. *T:* 0181–994 1345.

See also Julian Hall.

HENDERSON, Rt. Rev. Charles Joseph; Auxiliary Bishop in Southwark, (RC), since 1972; Titular Bishop of Tricala, since 1972; Area Bishop with responsibility for South East Metropolitan London, since 1980; *b* 14 April 1924; *s* of Charles Stuart Henderson and Hanora Henderson (*née* Walsh). *Educ:* Mount Sion Sch., Waterford; St John's Seminary, Waterford. Priest, 1948; Curate, St Stephen's, Welling, Kent, 1948–55; English Martyrs, Streatham, SW16, 1955–58; Chancellor, RC Diocese of Southwark, 1958–70; Vicar General, RC Diocese of Arundel and Brighton, 1965–66; Episcopal Vicar for Religious, Southwark, 1968–73; Vicar General, RC Archdiocese of Southwark, 1969; Parish Priest, St Mary's, Blackheath, 1969–82; Canon of Cathedral Chapter, 1972; Provost of Cathedral Chapter, 1973. Member: Ecumenical Commn for England and Wales, 1976–92; Nat. Catholic Commn for Racial Justice, 1978–81; English Anglican/RC Cttee, 1982–, Co. Chm. 1983–92; Methodist/RC Nat. Ecumenical Cttee, 1983 and Co. Chm. 1984–92; Chairman: RC Cttee for Dialogue with Other Faiths, 1984–; RC Nat. Cttee for Catholic–Jewish Relations, 1992; RC Consultant-Observer, BCC, 1982–86; Exec. Cttee, interfaith network for UK, 1987–; Member: Pontifical Council for Inter-religious Dialogue, 1990–; Exec. Cttee, CCJ, 1992–. Papal Chamberlain, 1960; Prelate of Papal Household, 1965. Freeman, City of Waterford, 1973. Kt Comdr with Star of Equestrian Order of Holy Sepulchre, Jerusalem, 1973 (Prior, Southwark Sect., 1994–). *Recreation:* special interest in sport. *Address:* Park House, 6A Cresswell Park, Blackheath, SE3 9RD. *T:* 0181–318 1094.

HENDERSON, David; *see* Henderson, P. D.

HENDERSON, Sir Denys (Hartley), Kt 1989; Chairman: Rank Organisation, since 1995; Imperial Chemical Industries PLC, 1987–95; ZENECA Group plc, 1993–95; *b* 11 Oct. 1932; *s* of John Hartley Henderson and Nellie Henderson (*née* Gordon); *m* 1957, Doreen Mathewson Glashan, *o d* of Robert and Mary Glashan; two *d*. *Educ:* Aberdeen Grammar School; Univ. of Aberdeen (MA, LLB). Solicitor; Mem., Law Soc. of Scotland. Joined ICI as lawyer in Secretary's Dept, London, 1957; commercial appts at Agricl Div. and Nobel Div.; Dir, Fertiliser Sales and Marketing, Agricl Div., 1972; Corporate Gen. Manager, Commercial, 1974; Chm., ICI Paints Div., 1977; ICI Main Bd Dir, 1980; Dep. Chm., 1986–87. Non-Exec. Director: Dalgety plc, 1981–87; Barclays Bank, 1983–; Barclays, 1985–; Barclays International, 1985–87; RTZ Corp., 1990–; MORI, 1995–. Chm., Stock Exchange Listed Companies Adv. Cttee, 1987–91; Mem., NY Stock Exchange Listed Co. Adv. Cttee, 1988–90. Trustee, Natural Hist. Mus., 1989–. Member: BBC's Consultative Group on Industrial and Business Affairs, 1984–86; CEFIC Presidential Adv. Gp, 1987; CBI President's Cttee, 1987–; Advertising Assoc. President's Cttee, 1988–; Opportunity Japan Campaign Cttee, 1988–; Japan Fest. 1991 Council, 1989–; Industry and Commerce Gp, SCF, 1988–; Adv. Council, Prince's Youth Business Trust, 1986–; Appeal Council, Winston Churchill Meml Trust, 1988–; Council, British Malaysian Soc., 1987–; President's Adv. Gp, SCOPE (formerly Spastics Soc.), 1993–; Adv. Cttee on Business Appointments, 1994–; Greenbury Cttee on Directors' Remuneration, 1994–. Mem., European Round Table, 1992–. Pres., Soc. of Business Economists, 1990–. Pres. and Chm. Bd, British Quality Foundn, 1993–. Patron, Assoc. Internationale des Etudiants en Sciences Economiques et Commerciales, 1989–. Chancellor, Bath Univ., 1993–; Mem. Court of Governors, Henley Management Coll., 1986– (Chm., 1989–); Chm., Univ. of Aberdeen Quincentenary Appeal Cttee, 1993–. Hon. Vice-Pres., Chartered Inst. of Marketing, 1989–. CIMgt (CBIM 1981); FInstM 1987; FRSA 1987. Hon. FCGI 1990. DUniv: Brunel, 1987; Strathclyde, 1993; Hon. LLD: Aberdeen, 1987; Nottingham, 1990; Manchester, 1991; Bath, 1993; Hon. DSc: Cranfield Inst. of Technol., 1989; Teesside, 1993. Centenary Medal, SCI, 1993. *Recreations:* family life, swimming, reading, travel, minimal gardening, unskilled but enjoyable golf. *Address:* Rank Organisation, 6 Connaught Place, W2 2EZ. *Clubs:* Athenæum, Royal Automobile.

HENDERSON, Derek, FDSRCS; Senior Consultant Oral and Maxillo-facial Surgeon, St Thomas' Hospital, 1975–93; Consultant, St George's Hospital, 1975–86; Hon. Consultant, Charing Cross Hospital, since 1977; Recognised Teacher, University of London, since 1977; Hon. Civilian Consultant in Oral Surgery: Royal Navy, since 1971; Army, since 1981; *b* 9 April 1935; *s* of Robert Henderson and Dorothy Edith Henderson; *m* 1961, Jennifer Jill Anderson; one *s* one *d*. *Educ:* Dulwich Coll.; London Univ. (BDS Hons 1956, MB, BS Hons 1963). FDSRCS (Eng) 1960 (LDS 1956); MRCS, LRCP 1963. Dental and med. trng, KCH, London, 1952–56 and 1959–63 (Prizeman); house surg. appts, KCH and Royal Dental Hosp., 1956–59; King's Coll. Hospital: Lectr in Dental Materials, 1958–65; ENT House Officer, and Casualty Off., 1964; Registrar in Oral Surg., Queen Mary's Hosp., Roehampton, and Westminster Hosp., 1965; Sen. Registrar in Oral Surg., United Cardiff Hosps, 1965–67; Consultant Oral Surgeon to Eastern Reg. Hosp. Bd, Scotland, and Dundee Dental Hosp., 1967–69 (Hon. Sen. Lectr, Univ. of Dundee); Consultant i/c Reg. Maxillo-facial Service to Glasgow and West of Scotland, based on Canniesburn Plastic and Oral Surg. Unit, Glasgow, 1969–75 (Hon. Clinical Teacher, Glasgow Univ.); Consultant, Royal Dental Hosp., 1975–85. Hon. Civilian Consultant, Queen Elizabeth Mil. Hosp., Woolwich (formerly Queen Alexandra Mil. Hosp., Millbank), 1976–81; Hon. Sen. Lectr in Oral Surg., Royal Dental Sch., London, 1977–85. Vis. Prof. and Lectr, Brazil, Argentina, Chile, USA, Spain, Venezuela, Australia, Holland, Saudi Arabia, Uruguay, Italy, SA. Mem. Senate, Royal Surgical Colls of GB and Ire., 1993–; Royal College of Surgeons: Hunterian Prof., 1975–76; Mem. Council, 1984–86 (Collyer Gold Medal, 1995); Kelsey Fry Adviser in Postgraduate Educnl Trng, 1975–80, Mem. Bd, 1978–86, Mem. Exec. Cttee, 1983–86, and Vice-Dean, 1984–85, Faculty of Dental Surgery (also Examr, FDSRCS). Member: Central Cttee for Hospital Dental Services, 1978–85 (Mem. Exec. Cttee, 1980–85); Central Cttee for Univ. Dental Teachers and Research Workers, 1978–81; Negotiating Subcttee, CCHMS, 1980–85; European Assoc. for Maxillo-Facial Surg.; BMA; BDA; Craniofacial Soc. (Mem. Council, 1973–77); Oral Surgery Club GB (Pres., 1992–93). Fellow: BAOMS (Pres., 1994–95; Mem. Council, 1974–76, 1977–80, 1984–86; Downs Prize, 1992). Internat. Assoc. of Oral Surgeons. Hon. Mem., Amer. Assoc. of Oral Surgeons in Europe; Hon. Associate Life Mem., Soc. of Maxillo-facial and Oral Surgeons of SA; Hon. Pres., Inst. of Maxillo-Facial Technol., 1977–78. *Publications:* An Atlas and Textbook of Orthognathic Surgery, 1985 (Astra Prize, Soc. of Authors, 1986); contribs on general oral surgery to British Jl of Oral Surgery and British Dental Jl, and especially on surgery of facial and jaw deformity to Brit. Jl of Oral Surg. and Brit. Jl of Plastic Surg. *Recreation:* fly fishing. *Address:* Mallington, Headley Road, Leatherhead, Surrey KT22 8PU. *T:* Leatherhead (01372) 378513; 107 Harley Street, W1N 1DG. *T:* 0171–935 6906. *Clubs:* Royal Navy Medical; Piscatorial Soc.

HENDERSON, Dr Derek Scott, FRSSAf; Principal and Vice-Chancellor, Rhodes University, Grahamstown, South Africa, since 1975; *b* 28 Oct. 1929; *s* of late Ian Scott and Kathleen Elizabeth Henderson (*née* White); *m* 1958, Thelma Muriel, *d* of W. E. B.

Mullins; two *d.* *Educ:* St John's Coll., Johannesburg; Rhodes University Coll. (BSc); Oxford Univ. (MA); Cambridge Univ. (MA); Harvard Univ. (PhD). FRSSAf 1994. Exec. Trainee, Anglo American Corp. of S Africa, 1953–56; Engr, Advanced Systems Develt, IBM Corp., Poughkeepsie, NY, 1960–62; Univ. of the Witwatersrand: Dir of Computer Centre, 1964–69; Prof. of Computer Science, 1967–75; Dean of Science Faculty, 1974–75. Chm., J. L. B. Smith Inst. of Ichthyology, 1976–; Mem. Council, CSIR, 1982–87; Mem., Scientific Adv. Council, 1988–; Mem. Bd, SABC, 1990–93; Vice-Chm., Leather Res. Inst., 1976–; Mem. Council, Grahamstown (formerly 1820) Foundn (Vice-Chm., 1976–89); Pres., SA Council of Automation and Computation, 1974. Chairman: Hillbrow Br., Progressive Party, 1964–65; Johannesburg Br., Kolbe Assoc. of Catholic Graduates, 1964; Mem. Council, St Andrew's Coll., 1986–; Trustee, SA Foundn, 1976–; Patron, All Saints Coll., Bisho, 1986–. Dir, Sabinet, 1983–88. Fellow, Computer Soc. of SA, 1974. *Recreation:* golf. *Address:* Rhodes University, PO Box 94, Grahamstown, 6140, S Africa. *T:* (461) 22023. *Club:* Port Elizabeth (Port Elizabeth, S Africa).

HENDERSON, Douglas John; MP (Lab) Newcastle upon Tyne North, since 1987; *b* 9 June 1949; *s* of John and Joy Henderson; *m* 1974, Janet Margaret Graham; one *s.* *Educ:* Waid Academy, Anstruther, Fife; Central Coll., Glasgow; Univ. of Strathclyde. Apprentice, Rolls Royce, 1966–68; Clerk, British Rail, 1969; Research Officer, GMWU, 1973–75; Regional Organiser, GMWU, then GMB, 1975–87. Mem. Exec., Scottish Council, Labour Party, 1979–87 (Chm., 1984–85). Opposition spokesman on trade and industry, 1988–92, on local govt, 1992–94, on public service, 1994–. Sec., GMB Parly Gp, 1987–. *Recreations:* athletics, mountaineering. *T:* 0191–267 2427. *Clubs:* Elswick Harriers, Lemington Labour, Newburn Memorial, Dinnington, Union Jack (Newcastle).

HENDERSON, Douglas Mackay, CBE 1985; FRSE 1966; FLS; HM Botanist in Scotland, since 1987; *b* 30 Aug. 1927; *s* of Captain Frank Henderson and Adine C. Mackay; *m* 1952, Julia Margaret Brown; one *s* two *d.* *Educ:* Blairgowrie High Sch.; Edinburgh Univ. (BSc). Scientific Officer, Dept of Agriculture and Fisheries for Scotland, 1948–51. Royal Botanic Garden, Edinburgh, 1951–87, Regius Keeper, 1970–87; Adminr, Inverewe, Nat. Trust for Scotland, 1987–92. Hon. Prof., Edinburgh Univ., 1983–. Sec., Internat. Assoc. of Botanical Gardens, 1969–81. Curator of Library and Museum, Royal Soc. of Edinburgh, 1978–87. VMH, 1985. *Publications:* British Rust Fungi (with M. Wilson), 1966; (with J. H. Dickson) A Naturalist in the Highlands: the life and travels of James Robertson in Scotland 1767–1771, 1993; many papers on taxonomy of cryptogams. *Recreations:* music, hill walking, cooking, painting, sailing. *Address:* Larachan, 54 Lonemore, Gairloch, W Ross IV22 2DB. *T:* Gairloch (01445) 712391; 38E Cramond Vale, Edinburgh EH4 6RB. *T:* 0131–312 8432.

HENDERSON, Ven. Edward Chance, BD, ALCD; Archdeacon of Pontefract, 1968–81, now Archdeacon Emeritus; *b* 15 Oct. 1916; *s* of William Edward and Mary Anne Henderson; *m* 1942, Vera Massie Pattison; two *s* three *d.* *Educ:* Heaton Grammar Sch.; London University. Asst Curate, St Stephen, Newcastle upon Tyne, 1939–42; Organising Sec., CPAS, 1942–45; Vicar of St Mary of Bethany, Leeds, 1945–51; Priest i/c: Armley Hall, Leeds, 1948–51; St John, New Wortley, Leeds, 1949–51; Vicar of: All Souls, Halifax, 1951–59; Dewsbury, 1959–68; Darrington with Wentbridge, 1968–75. Examining Chaplain to Bishop of Wakefield, 1972–81. *Address:* 12 Park Lane, Balne, Goole, North Humberside DN14 0EP. *T:* Goole (01405) 861934.

HENDERSON, Gavin Douglas; Principal, Trinity College of Music, since 1994; *b* 3 Feb. 1948; *s* of Magnus Reg Henderson and Sybil (*née* Horton); *m* 1st, 1973, Jane Williams (marr. diss. 1977); 2nd, 1983, Carole Becker (marr. diss. 1992); two *s;* 3rd, 1992, Mary Jane Walsh. *Educ:* Brighton Coll.; Brighton Coll. of Art; Kingston Art Coll.; University Coll. London; Slade Sch. of Fine Art. Leader and Dir, Henderson Brass Consort, 1968–75; Principal Trumpet, Worthing Municipal and Concert Orchs, 1969–70; Dep. Front of House and Publicity Manager, Victoria Theatre, Stoke-on-Trent, 1970–71; Founder and Dir, Crawley Fest., 1971–73; Artistic Director: York Fest. Mystery Plays, 1972–76; Portsmouth Fest., 1974–76; Chief Exec., New Philharmonia and Philharmonia Orchs, 1975–78; Dir, S Hill Park Arts Centre and Founder, Wilde Theatre, Bracknell, 1979–84; Artistic Director: Brighton Internat. Fest., 1983–94; Dartington Internat. Summer Sch., 1985–; Court in the Act, Royal Acad. of Arts, 1993; Bournemouth Fest., 1994–. Chairman: Clarion Concert Agency, 1972–75; Palindrome Prodns Ltd, 1994–. Writer and presenter, A View of . . ., BBC TV Series, 1983. Member: Music Panel and Opera Cttee, Arts Council of GB, 1973–75; Arts Council of England, 1994– (Chm., Music Panel, 1994–); Arts Cttee, RSA, 1991–94; Chm., British Arts Fests Assoc., 1994– (Dep. Chm., 1987–94); Member: Exec. Cttee, SE Arts Assoc., 1982–89; Exec. Bd, European Fests Assoc., 1988–94 (Vice Pres., 1994–); Southern Arts Bd, 1990–93. Pres., Nat. Piers Soc., 1986–. One-man exhibitions: Gall. 185, Brighton, 1968; Mulberry Gall., Lancaster, 1969. Governor: Brighton Univ. (formerly Poly.), 1987–; Chetham's Sch., Manchester, 1994–. Hon. Fellow: Univ. of Sussex, 1991; Univ. of Brighton, 1993. Hon. MA Sussex, 1992. Europe Award, E Sussex CC, 1992. *Publications:* Picasso and the Theatre, 1982; articles for Classical Music, Tempo, Musical Times, Stage, and Listener. *Recreations:* seaside pierage, cooking seafood, vintage motor-racing. *Address:* Trinity College of Music, Mandeville Place, W1M 6AQ. *T:* 0171–935 5773. *Clubs:* Garrick, Savile.

HENDERSON, Prof. George David Smith, FSA; Professor of Medieval Art, Cambridge, since 1986; Fellow of Downing College, Cambridge, 1974–94; *b* 7 May 1931; *yr s* of late Very Rev. Prof. George David Henderson, DLitt, DTh, DD and Jenny Holmes McCulloch Henderson (*née* Smith); *m* 1957, Isabel Bisset Murray; one *s* one *d.* *Educ:* Aberdeen Grammar Sch.; Univ. of Aberdeen (MA 1953); Courtauld Inst., Univ. of London (BA 1956); Trinity Coll., Cambridge (MA, PhD 1961). Research Fellow, Barber Inst. of Art, Univ. of Birmingham, 1959–60; Graham Robertson Research Fellow, Downing Coll., Cambridge, 1960–63; University of Manchester: Asst Lectr in History of Art, 1962–64; Lectr, 1964–66; University of Edinburgh: Lectr in Fine Arts, 1966–71; Reader in Fine Arts, 1971–73; University of Cambridge: Lectr in History of Art, 1974–79; Head of Dept, 1974–88; Reader in Medieval Art, 1979–86; a Syndic, Fitzwilliam Museum, 1974–. Mem., Ely Cathedral Fabric Adv. Cttee, 1990–. *Publications:* Gothic, 1967; Chartres, 1968; Early Medieval, 1972, repr. 1993; (ed with Giles Robertson) Studies in Memory of David Talbot Rice, 1975; Bede and the Visual Arts (Jarrow Lect.), 1980; Losses and Lacunae in Early Insular Art (Garmonsway Lect.), 1982; Studies in English Bible Illustration, 1985; From Durrow to Kells, 1987; (contrib.) The Eadwine Psalter, 1992; Emulation and Innovation in Carolingian Culture, 1993; articles in UK and Amer. jls and papers in procs of internat. confs. *Recreations:* listening to Wagner, porphyrology, looking for agates. *Address:* Department of History of Art, 1 Scroope Terrace, Cambridge CB2 1PX. *T:* Cambridge (01223) 332975.

HENDERSON, Rt. Rev. George Kennedy Buchanan, MBE 1974; Bishop of Argyll and the Isles, 1977–92; Primus of the Episcopal Church in Scotland, 1990–92; *b* 5 Dec. 1921; *s* of George Buchanan Henderson and Anna Kennedy Butters; *m* 1950, Isobel Fergusson Bowman. *Educ:* Oban High School; University of Durham (BA, LTh). Assistant Curate, Christ Church, Glasgow, 1943–48; Priest in Charge, St Bride's, Nether Lochaber, 1948–50; Chaplain to Bishop of Argyll and The Isles, 1948–50; Rector, St Andrew's, Fort William, 1950–77; Canon, St John's Cathedral, Oban, 1960; Synod Clerk, 1964–73; Dean of Argyll and The Isles, 1973–77. JP of Inverness-shire, 1963–; Hon. Sheriff, 1971–; Provost of Fort William, 1962–75; Hon. Burgess of Fort William, 1973. *Address:* Benvoulin, Achnalea, Onich, by Fort William PH33 6SA. *T:* Onich (018553) 240.

HENDERSON, Prof. George Patrick, FRSE 1980; Professor of Philosophy in the University of Dundee (formerly Queen's College, Dundee), 1959–80, Dean, Faculty of Arts and Social Sciences, 1973–76; *b* 22 April 1915; *e s* of Rev. George Aitchison Henderson, MA, and Violet Margaret Mackenzie; *m* 1939, Hester Lowry Douglas McWilliam, BSc (*d* 1978), *d* of Rev. John Morell McWilliam, BA. *Educ:* Elgin Academy; St Andrews Univ. (Harkness Scholar); Balliol Coll., Oxford. 1st Class Hons in Philosophy, University of St Andrews, 1936; Miller Prize and Ramsay Scholarship; MA 1936; Ferguson Scholarship in Philosophy, 1936; 2nd Class Lit Hum, University of Oxford, 1938; BA 1938. Asst in Logic and Metaphysics, University of St Andrews, 1938; Shaw Fellow in Mental Philosophy, University of Edinburgh, 1938. MA Oxon, 1943. Army Service, 1940–46; Royal Artillery (commissioned 1940, Adjutant 1942–43) and Gen. Staff (GSO 3 1945); served in UK, Italy and Greece. Lecturer in Logic and Metaphysics, University of St Andrews, 1945; Senior Lecturer, 1953. Corresp. Member: Acad. of Athens, 1973; Ionian Acad., 1975. Editor of the Philosophical Quarterly, 1962–72. *Publications:* The Revival of Greek Thought 1620–1830, 1970 (trans. Greek, 1994); The Ionian Academy (trans. Greek), 1980; E. P. Papanoutsos, 1983; The Ionian Academy, 1988 (2nd edn, trans. Greek, 1994); numerous articles and reviews in learned jls. *Recreations:* modern Greek studies, gardening. *Address:* The Pendicle, Waterside Road, Invergowrie, Dundee DD2 5DQ.

HENDERSON, Giles Ian, CBE 1992; Senior Partner, Slaughter and May, since 1993; *b* 20 April 1942; *s* of late Charles David Henderson and Joan K. Firmin; *m* 1971, Lynne Fyfield; two *s* one *d.* *Educ:* Michaelhouse, Natal; Univ. of Witwatersrand (BA); Magdalen Coll., Oxford (MA, BCL). Associate in Law, Univ. of California at Berkeley, 1966–67; joined Slaughter and May, 1968; admitted Solicitor, 1970; Partner, Slaughter and May, 1975. *Recreations:* sport, opera, ballet. *Address:* Slaughter and May, 35 Basinghall Street, EC2V 5DB. *T:* 0171–710 3011. *Clubs:* City Law; Wildernesse Golf.

HENDERSON, Ian Dalton, ERD 1960 (1st clasp 1966, 2nd clasp 1972); FRCS; Consultant Surgeon, Tunbridge Wells District, 1956–82, now Honorary Consultant Surgeon; *b* 4 Nov. 1918; *s* of Stewart Dalton Henderson and Grace Aird (*née* Masterson); *m* 1951, Rosa Hertz, MB, BS, MRCOG; two *d.* *Educ:* Fettes Coll., Edinburgh; Guy's Hosp., Univ. of London (MB, BS 1943). LMSSA 1943; FRCS 1949. Served War, RAMC, 1943–46: served India; Major, 1945–46. Lectr in Anatomy and Surg. Registrar, Guy's Hosp., 1947–50; Sen. Surg. Registrar, Royal Postgrad. Med. Sch. of London, 1952–56. Hon. Surgeon to the Queen, 1971–73. Member: Kent AHA, 1973–82; Société Internat. de Chirurgie, 1972–. FRSM 1947–. Served TA and AER, subseq. T&AVR, 1948–79; former Hon. Col and OC 308 Gen. Hosp., T&AVR. Silver Jubilee Medal, 1978. *Recreations:* archaeology, skiing, golf, photography. *Address:* 5 Thornbury Court, Chepstow Villas, W11 2RE. *T:* 0171–221 3822.

HENDERSON, James Ewart, CVO 1988; MA, DSc; President, Mastiff Electronic Systems Ltd, since 1995 (Managing Director, 1982–90; Chairman, 1985–95); *b* 29 May 1923; *s* of late Rev. James Ewart Henderson, MA, BD and Agnes Mary (*née* Crawford); *m* 1st, 1949, Alice Joan Hewlitt; one *d;* 2nd, 1966, Nancy Maude Dominy; two *s.* *Educ:* private sch.; Glasgow Univ.; Edinburgh Univ. Research on air rockets and guns, MAP, 1943–44; hon. commn in RAFVR, 1944–46; operational assessment of air attacks in Belgium, Holland and Germany, 2TAF, 1944–45; exper. research on fighter and bomber capability, and on the use of radar and radio aids: RAF APC Germany, 1945–46, Fighter Comd, 1946–49 and CFE, 1949–52; research on weapons effects and capability: Air Min., 1952–54, AWRE 1955, Air Min., 1955–58; Asst Scientific Adviser (Ops), Air Min., 1958–63; Dep. Chief Scientist (RAF), MoD, 1963–69; Chief Scientist (RAF) and Mem., Air Force Bd, 1969–73. Aviation Consultant, Hawker Siddeley Aviation Ltd, 1973–77; Financial Consultant, Charles Stapleton & Co. Ltd, 1973–78; freelance Operational Res. and Management Consultant, 1975–78; Scientific Advr, BAe, 1978–82; Director: Lewis Security Systems Ltd, 1976–77; Mastiff Security Systems Ltd, 1977–82; Pres. and Chief Exec., Mastiff Systems US Inc., 1982–88; Chm., TIB Netherlands, 1982–86. Life Vice-Pres., Air League, 1994 (Mem. Council, 1979–80; Chm., 1981–87; Pres., 1987–94); Chm., Air League Educational Trust, 1983–87. FInstD 1978. *Publications:* technical papers on operational capability of aircraft and weapons; UK manual on Blast Effects of Nuclear Weapons. *Recreations:* sailing, golf, opera, photography. *Clubs:* Naval and Military; Royal Scottish Automobile (Glasgow); Moor Park Golf; New Zealand Golf; Royal Western Yacht.

HENDERSON, (James Stewart) Barry; management consultant; politician; *b* 29 April 1936; *s* of James Henderson, CBE and Jane Stewart (*née* McLaren); *m* 1961, Janet Helen Sprot Todd; two *s.* *Educ:* Lathallan Sch.; Stowe Sch. Nat. Service, Scots Guards, 1954–56; electronics and computer industries, 1957–65; Scottish Conservative Central Office, 1966–70; computer industry, 1971–74; management consultant, 1975–86; paper industry, 1987–90; Dir, British Paper and Board Industry Fedn, 1990–92; Partner, Henderson Consulting, 1993–. Contested (C): E Edinburgh, 1966; E Dunbartonshire, 1970; Fife NE, 1987. MP (C): East Dunbartonshire, Feb.-Sept. 1974; E Fife, 1979–83; Fife NE, 1983–87. PPS to Economic Sec. to HM Treasury, 1984–87. Member: Select Cttee on Scottish Affairs, 1979–87; H of C Chairmen's Panel, 1981–83; Chm., Scottish Cons. Back Bench Cttee, 1983–84; Vice-Chm., PITCOM, 1986–87. Trustee, St Andrews Links Trust, 1979–87. Comr, Gen. Assembly of Church of Scotland, 1986. *Publications:* various pamphlets on Scottish, European and environmental issues. *Address:* 10 White Hart Court, Fairford, Glos GL7 4NH. *T:* and *Fax:* Cirencester (01285) 713385.

HENDERSON, Dame Joan; *see* Kelleher, Dame Joan.

HENDERSON, Sir (John) Nicholas, GCMG 1977 (KCMG 1972; CMG 1965); KCVO 1991; HM Diplomatic Service, retired; re-appointed, Ambassador to Washington, 1979–82; author and company director; *b* 1 April 1919; *s* of Prof. Sir Hubert Henderson; *m* 1951, Mary Barber (*née* Cawadias) (OBE 1988); one *d.* *Educ:* Stowe Sch.; Hertford Coll., Oxford (Hon. Fellow 1975). Mem. HM Diplomatic Service. Served Minister of State's Office, Cairo, 1942–43; Asst Private Sec. to the Foreign Sec., 1944–47; HM Embassy, Washington, 1947–49; Athens, 1949–50; Permanent Under Secretary's Dept, FO, 1950–53; HM Embassy, Vienna, 1953–56; Santiago, 1956–59; Northern Dept, FO, 1959–62; Permanent Under Secretary's Dept, 1962–63; Head of Northern Dept, Foreign Office, 1963; Private Sec. to the Sec. of State for Foreign Affairs, 1963–65; Minister in Madrid, 1965–69; Ambassador to Poland, 1969–72, to Federal Republic of Germany, 1972–75, to France, 1975–79. Lord Warden of the Stannaries, Keeper of the Privy Seal of the Duke of Cornwall, and Mem. of Prince's Council, 1985–90. Mem., BBC General Adv. Council, 1983–87; Chm., Channel Tunnel Gp, 1985–86; Director: Foreign & Colonial Investment Trust, 1982–88; M&G Reinsurance, 1982–90; Hambros, 1983–89; Tarmac, 1983–89; F&C Eurotrust, 1984–; Eurotunnel, 1986–88; Supervisory Bd, Fuel-Tech NV, 1987–; Sotheby's, 1989–. Trustee, Nat. Gallery, 1985–89. Pres., Hertford Soc., 1984–89. Romanes Lectr, 1986. Hon. DCL Oxford, 1987. *Publications:* Prince Eugen of

Savoy (biography), 1964; The Birth of Nato, 1982; The Private Office, 1984; Channels and Tunnels, 1987; Mandarin: the diaries of Nicholas Henderson, 1994; various stories and articles in Penguin New Writing, Horizon, Apollo, Country Life, The Economist and History Today. *Recreations:* tennis, gardening. *Address:* 6 Fairholt Street, SW7 1EG. *T:* 0171–589 4291; School House, Combe, near Newbury, Berks RG15 0EH. *T:* Inkpen (01488) 668330. *Clubs:* Brooks's, Garrick, Pratt's.

See also Earl of Drogheda.

HENDERSON, John Ronald, CVO 1985; OBE 1985 (MBE 1945); Lord-Lieutenant of Berkshire, 1989–95; Chairman, Henderson Administration (Group), 1983–90; *b* 6 May 1920; *s* of Major R. H. W. Henderson and Mrs Marjorie Henderson (*née* Garrard); *m* 1st, 1949, Sarah Katherine Beckwith-Smith (*d* 1972); two *s* one *d*; 2nd, 1976, Catherine Christian; one step *s* two step *d*. *Educ:* Eton; Cambridge Univ. Served War: ADC to Field Marshal Montgomery, 1942–46; retd Major, 12th Royal Lancers, 1946. Trustee, Winston Churchill Meml Trust, 1985–. Vice Lord-Lieutenant, Berks, 1979–89. KStJ 1989. *Recreations:* racing, shooting, golf, tennis. *Address:* West Woodhay House, Newbury, Berks RG15 0BS. *T:* Inkpen (01488) 668271. *Club:* White's.

HENDERSON, John Stuart Wilmot; Under Secretary, Ministry of Defence, and Director General of Ordnance Factories, Finance, Procurement and Administration, retired 1976; *b* 31 March 1919; *s* of Bruce Wilmot Henderson and Sarah (*née* Marchant); *m* 1st, 1941, Elsie Kathleen (*née* Rose) (*d* 1981); one *s* three *d*; 2nd, 1984, Yvonne Crawley (*née* Smith), *widow* of Victor James Crawley. *Educ:* Wade Deacon Grammar Sch., Widnes. Exec. Officer, Royal Ordnance Factories, 1938–39; served War of 1939–45: Royal Fusiliers, 1939–43; Intell. Corps, 1944–47; various appts in Ministries of Supply, Aviation, Technology and Defence, 1947–76. *Recreations:* gardening, enjoying music. *Address:* Tregaron, Llantrissent, near Usk, Gwent NP5 1LG. *T:* Usk (01291) 672297.

HENDERSON, Hon. Launcelot Dinadan James; QC 1995; *b* 20 Nov. 1951; *er s* of Baron Henderson of Brompton, *qv*; *m* 1989, Elaine Elizabeth Webb; two *s* one *d*. *Educ:* Westminster Sch.; Balliol Coll., Oxford (MA). Fellow of All Souls Coll., Oxford, 1974–81 and 1982–89; called to the Bar, Lincoln's Inn, 1977; practised as Barrister (Chancery), 1978–; Standing Junior Counsel: to Inland Revenue (Chancery), 1987–91; to Inland Revenue, 1991–95. *Address:* 5 Stone Buildings, Lincoln's Inn, WC2A 3XT. *T:* 0171–242 6201.

HENDERSON, Leslie Edwin, CBE 1982; Director of Contracts, Property Services Agency, 1978–82, retired; *b* 16 Dec. 1922; *s* of Thomas Edwin and Mabel Mary Henderson; *m* 1946, Marjorie (*née* Austin); two *s*. *Educ:* Ealing County Sch., London. Entered Civil Service (BoT) as Clerical Officer, 1939; Min. of Shipping, 1939; served in RAF, 1941–46; Min. of War Transport, 1946; subsequently in: Min. of Transport and Civil Aviation, MoT, DoE; Head of Contracts, Highways, Dept of Transport, 1968–78. *Recreations:* gardening, do-it-yourself. *Address:* 61 Greenacres Avenue, Ickenham, Mddx UB10 8HH. *T:* Ruislip (01895) 672536.

HENDERSON, Michael John Glidden, FCA; Director: Ronar Services Ltd, since 1991; Republic of Kajakhstan Trade and Economic Development Co. Ltd, since 1991; *b* 19 Aug. 1938; *s* of William Glidden Henderson and Aileen Judith Henderson (*née* Malloy); *m* 1965, Stephanie Maria Henderson; four *s*. *Educ:* St Benedict's Sch., Ealing. FCA 1971. Took articles with William Dyson Jones & Co., 1956; qual. as chartered accountant, 1961; Whinney Smith & Whinney & Co., 1963; Goodlass Wall & Lead Industries, later Cookson Group plc, 1965; Cookson Group: Dir, 1975; Man. Dir, 1979; Gp Man. Dir, 1984; Chief Exec., 1987–90; Chm., 1990; Director: Tioxide Gp, 1987–90; Guinness Mahon Holdings, 1988–; Chm., Three Counties Ltd, 1991–. Mem., Innovation Adv. Bd, DTI, 1988–93. Trustee, Natural History Mus. Develt Trust, 1990–. Governor: St George's Coll., Weybridge, 1990–; Cranmore Sch., W Horsley, 1992–. *Recreations:* tennis, cricket, golf, watching all sports. *Address:* Langdale, Woodland Drive, East Horsley, Surrey KT24 5AN. *T:* East Horsley (01483) 283844. *Clubs:* MCC; Wisley Golf.

HENDERSON, Sir Nicholas; *see* Henderson, Sir J. N.

HENDERSON, (Patrick) David, CMG 1992; economist, author and consultant; Visiting Fellow, Centre for European Policy Studies; *b* 10 April 1927; *s* of late David Thomson Henderson and late Eleanor Henderson; *m* 1960, Marcella Kodicek; one *s* one *d*. *Educ.* Ellesmere Coll., Shropshire; Corpus Christi Coll., Oxford. Fellow and Tutor in Economics, Lincoln Coll., Oxford, 1948–65 (Hon. Fellow, 1991); Univ. Lectr in Economics, Oxford, 1950–65; Commonwealth Fund Fellow (Harvard), 1952–53; Junior Proctor, Oxford Univ., 1955–56; Economic Adviser, HM Treasury, 1957–58; Chief Economist, Min. of Aviation, 1965–67; Adviser Harvard Development Advisory Service (Athens and Kuala Lumpur), 1967–68; Vis. Lectr, World Bank, 1968–69; Economist, World Bank, 1969–75, Dir of Economics Dept 1971–72; Prof. of Political Economy, UCL, 1975–83; Hd of Econs and Stats Dept, OECD, 1984–92. Mem., Commn on Environmental Pollution, 1977–80; Special Adviser, Sec. of State for Wales, 1978–79; Member: Nat. Ports Council, 1979–81; Bd, Commonwealth Develt Corp., 1980–83. Reith Lectr, BBC, 1985; Copland Meml Address, 1989. *Publications:* India: the energy sector, 1975; Innocence and Design: the influence of economic ideas on policy, 1986; (jointly) Nyasaland: The Economics of Federation, 1960; ed and contrib.: Economic Growth in Britain, 1965; contrib: The British Economy in the 1950's, 1962; Public Enterprise, 1968; Public Economics, 1969; Unfashionable Economics, 1970; The World Bank, Multilateral Aid and the 1970's, 1973; The Economic Development of Yugoslavia, 1975; Contemporary Problems of Economic Policy, 1983; Protectionism and Growth, 1985; Economic Policies for the 1990s, 1991; articles in economic and other jls. *Address:* c/o CEPS, 33 rue Ducale, 1000 Brussels, Belgium.

HENDERSON, Prof. Paul, DPhil; Director of Science, Natural History Museum, since 1995; *b* 7 Nov. 1940; *s* of Thomas William Henderson and Dorothy Violet (*née* Marriner); *m* 1966, Elizabeth Kathryn Ankerson; one *s* one *d*. *Educ:* King's Coll. Sch., Wimbledon; Univ. of London (BSc 1963); Univ. of Oxford (DPhil 1966). FGS 1990; CGeol 1990. Asst Lectr in Chemistry, Glasgow Univ., 1967–68; Lectr in Geochem., Chelsea Coll., Univ. of London, 1968–76; British Museum (Natural History), subseq. Natural History Museum: PSO, 1977, Grade 6, 1984, Dep. Keeper, 1987, Keeper, 1989–95, Dept of Mineralogy; Associate Dir, Earth Scis, 1992–95. Visiting Professor: Univ. of Bern, Switzerland, 1989; UCL, 1990–; Vis. Res. Fellow, Univ. of Alberta, Canada, 1976; Hon. Research Fellow: Chelsea Coll., Univ. of London, 1979–85; RHBNC, Univ. of London, 1985–86. Pres., Mineralogical Soc., 1989–91 (Mem. Council, 1974–76 and 1986–89); Member Council: Eur. Assoc. for Geochem., 1986–; Internat. Mineralog. Assoc., 1989–94. Fourmarier Medal, Belgian Geol Soc., 1989. *Publications:* Inorganic Geochemistry, 1982; (ed) Rare Earth Element Geochemistry, 1984; contribs to jls on geochem. and mineral chem. *Recreations:* music, Paris, wine. *Address:* Science Directorate, Natural History Museum, Cromwell Road, SW7 5BD. *T:* 0171–938 9010.

HENDERSON, Dr Richard, FRS 1983; Member of Scientific Staff, Medical Research Council Laboratory of Molecular Biology, Cambridge, since 1973; Fellow of Darwin College, Cambridge, since 1981; *b* 19 July 1945; *s* of John and Grace Henderson; *m* 1969, Penelope FitzGerald; one *s* one *d* (and one *d* decd). *Educ:* Hawick High Sch.; Boroughmuir Secondary Sch.; Edinburgh Univ. (BSc); Cambridge Univ. (PhD). Helen Hay Whitney Fellow, Yale, 1970–73. William Bate Hardy Prize, Cambridge Phil Soc., 1978; Ernst Ruska Prize for Electron Microscopy, Ernst Ruska Foundn, 1981; Lewis S. Rosenstiel Award, Brandeis Univ., 1991; Louis Jeantet Award, Jeantet Foundn, Geneva, 1993. *Publications:* research pubns and reviews in scientific jls. *Recreations:* canoeing, wine-tasting. *Address:* MRC Laboratory of Molecular Biology, Hills Road, Cambridge CB2 2QH. *T:* Cambridge (01223) 248011.

HENDERSON, Major Richard Yates, TD 1966; JP; Lord-Lieutenant of Ayrshire and Arran, since 1991; *b* 7 July 1931; *s* of late John Wishart Henderson and Dorothy (*née* Yates); *m* 1957, Frances Elizabeth Chrystal; two *s* one *d* (and one *s* decd). *Educ:* Rugby; Hertford Coll., Oxford (BA); Glasgow Univ. (LLB). Served Royal Scots Greys, 1950–52; Ayrshire Yeomanry TA, 1953–69. Partner, Mitchells Robertson, Solicitors, Glasgow, 1958–90; Trustee, TSB, Glasgow, 1966–74; Dir, West of Scotland TSB, 1974–83. Mem., Royal Company of Archers, Queen's Body Guard for Scotland. DL Ayrshire, 1970–90. *Recreations:* shooting, tennis, golf. *Address:* Blairston, by Ayr KA7 4EF. *T:* Alloway (01292) 441601. *Club:* Western (Glasgow).

HENDERSON, Robert Alistair; Chairman: Kleinwort, Benson, Lonsdale plc, 1978–88; Kleinwort Development Fund PLC (formerly Cross Investment Trust Ltd), 1969–91; Merchants Trust PLC, since 1985; Deputy Chairman, Cadbury Schweppes plc, 1983–92 (Director, 1977–92); *b* 4 Nov. 1917; *s* of Robert Evelyn Henderson and Beatrice Janet Elsie Henderson; *m* 1947, Bridget Elizabeth, *d* of late Col J. G. Lowther, CBE, DSO, MC, TD, and Hon. Lilah White, *er d* of 3rd Baron Annaly; one *s* one *d* (one *s* decd). *Educ:* Eton; Magdalene Coll., Cambridge. Hons degree in History. Served War: 60th Rifles, 1940–45, Captain. Jessel Toynbee & Co. Ltd, 1945–48; Borneo Co. Ltd, 1948–51 (Dir, 1956–66; then, on merger, Dir, Inchcape, 1966–87); Robert Benson, Lonsdale & Co. Ltd, 1951 (Dir, 1957); Dir, Kleinwort, Benson Ltd, 1961 (on merger of Robert Benson, Lonsdale & Co. Ltd with Kleinwort Sons & Co.; Vice-Chm., 1970–71, Dep. Chm., 1971–75, Chm., 1975–83). Dir, 1958–81, Pres., 1974–79, Equitable Life Assurance Soc.; Dir, 1981–89, Dep. Chm., 1985–89, British Airways; Chm., MT Oil & Gas, 1985–87. *Recreations:* gardening, shooting, fishing. *Address:* 7 Royal Avenue, Chelsea, SW3 4QE; North Ecchinswell Farm, Ecchinswell, near Newbury, Berks RG15 8UJ. *T:* Headley (0163523) 244. *Clubs:* White's, Brooks's.

HENDERSON, Robert Brumwell, CBE 1979; Managing Director, 1959–83, Chairman, 1983–91, Ulster TV; *b* 28 July 1929; *s* of late Comdr Oscar Henderson, CVO, CBE, DSO, RN, and of Mrs Henderson; *m* 1st, 1953, Joy Frances Duncan (marr. diss. 1969); two *d*; 2nd, 1970, Patricia Ann Davison. *Educ:* Brackenber House Sch., Belfast; Bradfield Coll., Berks; Trinity Coll., Dublin. BA (Hons) 1951, MA 1959. Journalism: London, Liverpool, Glasgow and Belfast, 1951–59. Director: ITN, 1964–68; Independent Television Publications, 1969–86. Dep. Chm., Powerscreen Internat., 1989–92; Director: Ulster Cablevision, 1985–93; Laganside Corp., 1988–92; Airtronics Internat., 1990–95, etc. Chm., Publicity Assoc. of NI, 1959–60; Vice-Pres., Co-operation North, 1984–; President: Radio Industries Club of NI, 1963–70, 1972–80; NI Chamber of Commerce and Industry, 1980–81; NI Chartered Inst. of Marketing, 1984–92; Assoc. of Ulster Drama Festivals, 1984–; Chm., NI Millenium Bid Cttee, 1994–; Member: Exec. Council, Cinema and Television Benevolent Fund, 1980–84; Council for Continuing Educn, 1975–85; NI Council for Educnl Develt, 1980–; Cttee to Review Higher Educn in NI, 1964; various cttees of Trinity Coll. Dublin, Univ. of Ulster; Senate, Queen's Univ. of Belfast, 1980–; Council, Inst. of Dirs, 1973–93 (Chm., NI Br., 1973–79); Design Council (NI), 1980–92; Governor, Ulster Polytechnic, 1979–84. FRTS 1977 (Mem. Council, 1981–84, Chm., 1982–84, Vice Pres., 1986–91). Hon. DLitt Ulster, 1982. *Publications:* Midnight Oil, 1961; A Television First, 1977; Amusing, 1984. *Recreations:* reading, theatre and cinema, golf. *Address:* 8 Crabtree Road, Ballynahinch, Co. Down, N Ireland BT24 8RH. *Clubs:* Royal County Down Golf; Malone Golf.

HENDERSON, Robert Ewart, QC (Scot.) 1982; *b* 29 March 1937; *s* of William Ewart Henderson and Agnes Ker Henderson; *m* 1st, 1958, Olga Sunter; two *s* two *d*; 2nd, 1982, Carol Black. *Educ:* Larchfield Sch., Helensburgh; Morrison's Acad., Crieff; Glasgow Univ. (BL 1962). Admitted to Faculty of Advocates, 1963. National Service, 2nd Lieut RA, 1956–58. Hon. Sheriff-Substitute, Stirling, Dunbarton and Clackmannan, 1968; Standing Jun. Counsel in Scotland, DTI, 1970–74, Dept of Trade, 1974–77; Temp. Sheriff, 1978. Pres., Glasgow Univ. Law Soc., 1961–62; Chairman: NHS Appeal Tribunal, 1972; Medical Appeal Tribunal (Scotland), 1985–; War Pensions Appeal Tribunal, 1986–. Contested (C) Inverness-shire, Feb. and Oct. 1974. *Recreations:* golf, sailing. *Address:* The Old Schoolhouse, Gullane, East Lothian EH31 2AF. *T:* Gullane (01620) 842012. *Clubs:* New (Edinburgh); Hon. Company of Edinburgh Golfers (Muirfield); Royal St George's Golf (Sandwich).

HENDERSON, Roger Anthony, QC 1980; a Recorder of the Crown Court, since 1983; a Deputy High Court Judge, since 1987; *b* 21 April 1943; *s* of late Dr Peter Wallace Henderson and of Dr Stella Dolores Henderson; *m* 1968, Catherine Margaret Williams; three *d* (and one *d* decd). *Educ:* Radley Coll.; St Catharine's Coll., Cambridge (Scholar; 1st Cl. Hons degree in Law, MA; Adderley Prize for Law, 1964). Inner Temple: Duke of Edinburgh Award, 1962; Major Scholarship, 1964; called to the Bar, 1964; Bencher, 1985. Counsel to King's Cross Inquiry, 1988. Mem., Bar Council, 1988–91; Chm., Public Affairs Cttee of Bar, 1989–90. Chm., Civil Service Arbitration Tribunal, 1994–; Member: Exec. Council, British Acad. of Forensic Sciences, 1977–90 (Pres., 1986–87); Council of Legal Educn, 1983–90. Gov., London Hosp. Med. Coll., 1989– (Chm., Council, 1993–); Chm., Special Cttee, St Peter's Hosps, 1989–92; Mem. Council, QMW, 1993–. FRSA 1994. *Recreations:* fly-fishing, gardening, shooting. *Address:* 2 Harcourt Buildings, Temple, EC4Y 9DB. *T:* 0171–583 9020; 9 Brunswick Gardens, W8 4AS; Holbury Mill, Lockerley, Romsey, Hants SO52 0JR. *T:* Lockerley (01794) 340583; Upper Round Road, St John's Parish, Nevis, West Indies.

HENDERSON, Roy (Galbraith), CBE 1970; FRAM; retired baritone and Teacher of Singing (private); Professor of Singing, RAM, London, 1940–74; *b* Edinburgh, 4 July 1899; *er s* of late Rev. Dr Alex. Roy Henderson, formerly Principal of Paton Coll., Nottingham; *m* 1926, Bertha Collin Smyth (*d* 1985); one *s* two *d*. *Educ:* Nottingham High Sch.; Royal Academy of Music, London (Worshipful Company of Musicians Medal). Debut as baritone singer, Queen's Hall, London, 1925; has sung at all leading Festivals in England, Internat. Festival for contemporary music, Amsterdam, 1933; recitals at first two Edinburgh Festivals, 1947 and 1948; principal parts in all Glyndebourne Opera festivals, 1934–40, associated chiefly with works of Delius, Elgar and Vaughan Williams, and sang many first performances of contemp. music. Retired from concert platform, 1952, to devote his whole time to teaching (among his pupils was late Kathleen Ferrier). Conductor, Huddersfield Glee and Madrigal Soc., 1932–39; Founder and Conductor, Nottingham Oriana Choir, 1937–52. Conductor of Bournemouth Municipal Choir, 1942–53. Adjudicator at International Concours, Geneva, 1952, and Triennially, 1956–65. Mem. of the Jury of the International Muziekstad s'Hertogenbosch, Holland, 1955–62, 1965, and Barcelona, 1965. Master classes in singing: Royal Conservatory of Music, Toronto, 1956;

Toonkunst Conservatorium, Rotterdam, 1957, 1958; s'Hertogenbosch, 1967. Awarded the Sir Charles Santley memorial by Worshipful Company of Musicians for distinguished services to the art of singing, 1958. *Publications:* contributed to: Kathleen Ferrier, ed Neville Cardus, 1954; Opera Annual, 1958; The Voice, ed Sir Keith Falkner, 1983. *Recreations:* watching cricket, television, radio, reading. *Address:* Ivor Newton House, 10 Edward Road, Bromley BR1 3NQ. *T:* 0181–460 9150.

HENDERSON, Sir William (MacGregor), Kt 1976; FRS 1976; FRSE 1977; President, Zoological Society of London, 1984–89; *b* 17 July 1913; *s* of late William Simpson Henderson and late Catherine Alice Marcus Berry; *m* 1941, Alys Beryl Goodridge; four *s*. *Educ:* George Watson's Coll., Edinburgh; Royal (Dick) Veterinary Coll., Edinburgh (MRCVS); Univ. of Edinburgh (BSc, DSc). Assistant, Dept of Medicine, Royal (Dick) Veterinary Coll., Edinburgh, 1936–38; Member Scientific Staff, Animal Virus Research Inst., Pirbright, 1939–56, Dep. Dir, 1955–56; Director, Pan American Foot-and-Mouth Disease Center, Rio de Janeiro, 1957–65; Head, Dept of Microbiology, ARC Inst. for Research on Animal Diseases, Compton, 1966–67, Director, 1967–72; Sec., ARC, 1972–78. Visiting Prof., Univ. of Reading, 1970–72. Chm., Genetic Manipulation Adv. Gp, 1979–81. Mem., Science Council, 1980–82, Bd Mem., 1982–84, Celltech Ltd; Bd Mem., Wellcome Biotechnology Ltd, 1983–89; Chm., Woodstock Breeding Services, 1988–89. Pres., Royal Assoc. of British Dairy Farmers, 1985–87. Corresp. Member: Argentine Assoc. of Microbiology, 1959; Argentine Soc. of Veterinary Medicine, 1965; Foreign Mem., Argentine National Acad. of Agronomy and Veterinary Science, 1980; Hon. Mem. Brasilian Soc. of Veterinary Medicine, 1965; FRCVS, by election, 1973; FIBiol; Hon. Fellow, RASE, 1979. Hon. DVMS Edinburgh, 1974; Hon. DVSc Liverpool, 1977; Hon. DSc Bristol,. 1985; DUniv Stirling, 1989. Orden de Mayo, Argentina, 1962. Dalrymple-Champneys Award, 1974; Massey-Ferguson National Award, 1980; Underwood-Prescott Award, 1981. *Publications:* Quantitative Study of Foot-and-Mouth Disease Virus, 1949; Man's Use of Animals, 1981; British Agricultural Research and the Agricultural Research Council, 1981; A Man of the Country, 1994; contribs to scientific jls principally on foot-and-mouth disease. *Recreation:* gardening. *Address:* Culvers, Croft Road, Goring-on-Thames, Reading RG8 9ES. *Club:* Athenæum.

HENDERSON, William Ross, CBE 1988; TD 1972, clasps 1978, 1984; Conservative Central Office Agent, Western Area, since 1989; *b* 15 Sept. 1936; *s* of Major William Ross Henderson and Jean Elizabeth Doxford Henderson; *m* 1969, Valerie Helen Thomas; one *s* one *d*. *Educ:* Argyle House School, Sunderland. Agent and Secretary, Newcastle upon Tyne West Cons. Assoc., 1961–68; Dep. Central Office Agent, Greater London Area, 1968–76; Cons. Party Training Officer, 1976–80; Central Office Agent, East of England Area, 1980–84; Dir, Scottish Cons. and Unionist Central Office, 1984–87. Cross of Merit, Gold Class, Poland, 1972. *Recreations:* gardening, reading. *Address:* Applegarth, Priesthill, Kentisbeare, Cullompton, Devon EX15 2BG. *Club:* St Stephen's Constitutional.

HENDERSON-STEWART, Sir David (James), 2nd Bt *cr* 1957; *b* 3 July 1941; *s* of Sir James Henderson-Stewart, 1st Bt, MP, and of Anna Margaret (*née* Greenwell); *S* father, 1961; *m* 1972, Anne, *d* of Count Serge de Pahlen; three *s* one *d*. *Educ:* Eton Coll.; Trinity Coll., Oxford. *Heir: s* David Henderson-Stewart, *b* 2 Feb. 1973. *Address:* 90 Oxford Gardens, W10 5UW. *T:* 0181–960 1278.

HENDRICK, Mark Phillip, CEng; Member (Lab and Co-op) Lancashire Central, European Parliament, since 1994; *b* 2 Nov. 1958; *s* of Brian Francis Hendrick and Jennifer (*née* Chapman). *Educ:* Liverpool Poly. (BSc Hons Electrical and Electronic Engrg); Univ. of Manchester (MSc Computer Sci.; Cert Ed). CEng 1987; MIEE 1987. Trainee Technician, Signal and Telecommunications, BR, 1975–78; Student Engr, 1979–81; RSRE Malvern, MoD, 1979; Special Systems Unit, STC plc, 1980; AEG Telefunken, Seligenstadt, Germany, 1981; Design Engr, Daresbury Lab., SERC, 1982–84 and 1985–88; Lectr, Stockport Coll., 1989–94. *Recreations:* football supporter (Manchester City), travel, chess, German and French. *Address:* 20 Milton Avenue, Weaste, Salford, Lancs M5 2HG. *T:* 0161–743 1648. *Clubs:* Lostock Hall Labour, Penwortham Sports and Social (Preston).

HENDRICKSE, Prof. Ralph George, MD; FRCP, FRCPE; Professor and Head of Department of Tropical Paediatrics, 1974–91, and Dean, 1988–91, Liverpool School of Tropical Medicine, now Professor Emeritus; *b* 5 Nov. 1926; *s* of William George Hendrickse and Johana Theresa Hendrickse (*née* Dennis); m 1948, Begum Johanara Abdurahman; one *s* four *d*. *Educ:* Livingstone High Sch.; Univ. of Cape Town (MD). FMCPaed (Hon. Foundn Fellow). Res. MO, McCord Zulu Hosp., Durban, 1949–54, incl. secondment to Willis F. Pierce Meml Hosp., S Rhodesia, as MO i/c, 1951; postgrad. studies, Glasgow and Edinburgh, 1955; Sen. Registrar, UCH, Ibadan, Nigeria, 1955–57; Sen. Lectr, Univ. of Ibadan, 1957–62, and Hon. Consultant Paediatrician, UCH, 1957–69; Prof. and Head of Paediatrics, Univ. of Ibadan, 1962–69. Dir, Inst. of Child Health, 1964–69; Sen. Lectr, Liverpool Univ. Sch. of Trop. Med., 1969–74. Mem., Standing Panel of Experts in Public Health Medicine, Univ. of London, 1990–. Hon. Vis. Prof., Santo Tomas Univ., Philippines. Hon. Member: BPA, 1995; Philippines Paed. Soc. Founder and Editor-in-Chief, Annals of Tropical Paediatrics, 1981–. Frederick Murgatroyd Prize, RCP, 1970. *Publications:* Paediatrics in the Tropics: current review, 1981; (ed and contrib.) Paediatrics in the Tropics, 1991; papers in learned jls. *Recreations:* photography, sketching, theatre, swimming, travel. *Address:* Beresford House, 25 Riverbank Road, Heswall, Wirral, Merseyside L60 4SQ. *T:* 0151–342 5510.

HENDRIE, Dr Gerald Mills; Professor of Music, The Open University, 1969–90; *b* 28 Oct. 1935; *s* of James Harold Hendrie and Florence Mary MacPherson; *m* 1st, 1962, Dinah Florence Barsham, BMus, PhD (*d* 1985); two *s*; 2nd, 1986, Dr Lynette Anne Maddern, MB, BS. *Educ:* Framlingham Coll., Suffolk; Royal Coll. of Music; Selwyn Coll., Cambridge (MA, MusB, PhD). FRCO, ARCM. Director of Music, Homerton Coll., Cambridge, 1962–63; Lectr in the History of Music, Univ. of Manchester, 1963–67; Prof. and Chm., Dept of Music, Univ. of Victoria, BC, Canada, 1967–69; Reader in Music, subseq. Prof., The Open Univ., 1969–90; Dir of Studies in Music, St John's Coll., Cambridge, 1981–84, Supervisor, 1977–84. Vis. Fellow in Music, Univ. of WA, 1985. *Publications:* Musica Britannica XX, Orlando Gibbons: Keyboard Music, 1962, 2nd rev. edn, 1967; G. F. Handel: Anthems für Cannons, 3 vols, 1985, 1987, 1991; Anthems für die Chapel Royal, 1992; articles for Die Musik in Geschichte und Gegenwart; musical compositions include: Five Bagatelles for piano, 1980; Four Excursions for piano, 1983; Three Pieces for flute and piano, 1985; Specula Petro for organ, 1988; Quintet for Brass, 1988; Choral: Hommage à César Franck for organ, 1990; Le Tombeau de Marcel Dupré (for organ): Toccata and Fugue, 1991; Prelude and Fugue, 1991; Prelude and Fugue on the name BACH, 1992; Two Sketches on the name BACH, 1993; In Praise of St Asaph, 1994; choral music. *Recreations:* windsurfing, walking, gardening, needlepoint. *Address:* The Garth, 17 The Avenue, Dallington, Northampton NN5 7AJ. *T:* Northampton (01604) 587267.

HENDRIE, Robert Andrew Michie; HM Diplomatic Service; Ambassador to Uruguay, since 1994; *b* 4 May 1938; *s* of John Hendrie, Edinburgh and Effie Campbell (*née* Mackay); *m* 1964, Consuelo Liaño Solórzano; two *d*. *Educ:* Bradford Grammar Sch.; Trinity Hall, Cambridge (BA, MA). Joined HM Diplomatic Service, 1961; MECAS, Beirut, 1961–62; Political Residency, Bahrain, 1962–65; Tehran, 1965–68; Tripoli, 1968–69; Latin America Dept, FCO, 1969–73; Lima, 1973–75; Buenos Aires, 1975–80; Asst Hd, Central Africa Dept, ME Dept and Inf. Dept, FCO, 1980–86; Consul-General: Lille, 1986–90; Dubai, UAE, 1990–94. MIL 1987. MIMgt 1979. *Recreations:* reading, walking, watching Rugby, languages. *Address:* c/o Foreign and Commonwealth Office, King Charles Street, SW1A 2AH.

HENDRON, Joseph Gerard; MP (SDLP) Belfast West, since 1992; *b* 12 Nov. 1932; *m* 1974, Sally (*née* Lennon); three *s* one *d*. *Educ:* St Malachy's Coll.; Queen's Univ., Belfast (MB 1957). FRCGP 1987. Formerly GP, W Belfast. Mem. (SDLP) Belfast CC, 1981–. Contested (SDLP) Belfast W, 1983, 1987. *Address:* House of Commons, SW1A 0AA.

HENDRY, Prof. Arnold William; Professor of Civil Engineering, University of Edinburgh, 1964–88, now Emeritus; *b* 10 Sept. 1921; *s* of late Dr George Hendry, MB, ChB, Buckie, Scotland; *m* 1st, 1946, Sheila Mary Cameron Roberts (*d* 1966), Glasgow; one *s* one *d* (and one *s* decd); 2nd, 1968, Elizabeth Lois Alice Inglis, Edinburgh. *Educ:* Buckie High Sch.; Aberdeen Univ. Civil engineer with Sir William Arrol & Co. Ltd, Bridge builders and Engineers, Glasgow, 1941–43; Asst in Engineering, University of Aberdeen, 1943–46; Lecturer in Civil Engineering, 1946–49; Reader in Civil Engineering, Univ. of London, King's Coll., 1949–51; Prof. of Civil Engrg and Dean of Fac. of Engrg, Univ. of Khartoum, 1951–57; Prof. of Building Science, University of Liverpool, 1957–63. *Publications:* An Introduction to Photo-Elastic Analysis, 1948; (with L. G. Jaeger) The Analysis of Grid Frameworks, 1958; The Elements of Experimental Stress Analysis, 1964, 2nd edn 1977; Structural Brickwork, 1981; An Introduction to the Design of Load Bearing Brickwork, 1981; Structural Masonry, 1990; (ed) Reinforced and Prestressed Masonry, 1991; about 150 papers and articles in professional and technical jls. *Address:* c/o Department of Civil Engineering, School of Engineering, The King's Buildings, Edinburgh EH9 3JL; 146/6 Whitehouse Loan, Edinburgh EH9 2AN.

HENDRY, Charles; MP (C) High Peak, since 1992; *b* 6 May 1959; *s* of late Charles William Righton Hendry and of Margaret Anne Hendry; *m* 1995, Mrs Sallie A. Moores. *Educ:* Rugby Sch.; Univ. of Edinburgh (BCom Hons 1981). Account Dir, Ogilvy and Mather PR, 1983–86; Burson-Marsteller: Associate Dir (PR), 1986–88; Sen. Counsellor, Public Affairs, 1990–92. Special Adviser to: Rt Hon. John Moore, 1988; Rt Hon. Anthony Newton, 1988–89. Vice-Chm., Battersea Cons. Assoc., 1981–83. Contested (C): Clackmannan, 1983; Mansfield, 1987. PPS to Sec. of State for Educn and Employment, 1995–. Mem. Select Cttee on Procedure, 1994, on NI Affairs, 1994–. Secretary: Conservative Back bench Social Services Cttee, 1992–94; Cons. Back bench Home Improvement Sub-Cttee, 1993–94; Cons. Back bench Urban Affairs Cttee, 1994; Jt Chm., All-Party Parly Gp on Homelessness, 1992–. Sec., E Midlands Area Cons. MPs, 1992–94. Pres., British Youth Council, 1992–; Trustee: Drive for Youth, 1989–; Friends of NACAB, 1992–. FRSA. *Recreations:* tennis, ski-ing, theatre. *Address:* House of Commons, SW1A 0AA. *T:* 0171–219 4581.

HENDRY, Prof. David Forbes, PhD; FBA 1987; Professor of Economics, University of Oxford, since 1982; Fellow, Nuffield College, Oxford, since 1982; *b* 6 March 1944; *s* of Robert Ernest Hendry and Catherine Helen (*née* Mackenzie); *m* 1966, Evelyn Rosemary (*née* Vass); one *d*. *Educ:* Aberdeen Univ. (MA 1st Cl. Hons); LSE (MSc Distinction, PhD). Fellow, Econometric Soc., 1975. Lectr, LSE, 1969, Reader, 1973, Prof. of Econometrics, 1977. Vis. Professor: Yale Univ., 1975; Univ. of Calif, Berkeley, 1976; Catholic Univ. of Louvain, 1980; Univ. of Calif, San Diego, 1981, 1989–90; Vis. Research Prof., Duke Univ., 1987–91. Pres., Royal Economic Soc., 1992–95. Hon. Foreign Member: Amer. Economic Assoc., 1991; Amer. Acad. of Arts and Scis. Hon. LLD Aberdeen, 1987. Guy Medal in Bronze, Royal Statistical Soc., 1986. Editor: Rev. of Econ. Studies, 1971–75; Econ. Jl, 1976–80; Oxford Bulletin of Economics and Statistics, 1983–. *Publications:* (ed with K. F. Wallis) Econometrics and Quantitative Economics, 1984; PC-GIVE, 1989; (with A. J. Neale and N. R. Ericsson) PC-NAIVE, 1991; Econometrics: alchemy or science?, 1993; (jtly) Cointegration, Error Correction and the Econometric Analysis of Non-stationary Data, 1993; Dynamic Econometrics, 1995; papers in econometrics, statistics and economics jls. *Recreations:* squash, cricket. *Address:* Nuffield College, Oxford OX1 1NF; 26 Northmoor Road, Oxford OX2 6UR. *T:* Oxford (01865) 515588.

HENDRY, Stephen Gordon, MBE 1993; professional snooker player, since 1986; *b* 13 Jan. 1969; *s* of Gordon John Hendry and Irene Agnes (*née* Anthony); *m* 1995, Amanda Elizabeth Theresa. *Educ:* Inverkeithing High Sch. Embassy World Champion, 1990, 1992, 1993, 1994, 1995; Benson & Hedges Masters Champion, 1989, 1990, 1991, 1992, 1993; UK Professional Champion, 1989, 1990, 1994; World Doubles Champion, 1987. *Publication:* Remember My Name, 1989. *Recreations:* golf, music, cars. *Address:* Stephen Hendry Snooker Ltd, Kerse Road, Stirling FK7 7SG. *T:* Stirling (01786) 462634, *Fax:* (01786) 450068. *Club:* Lord's Taverners (Scotland).

HENDY, John Giles; QC 1987; *b* 11 April 1948; *s* of late Jack and of Mary Hendy; *m*; one *d*. *Educ:* Ealing Technical College (LLB); Queen's Univ., Belfast (DipLL, LLM). Called to the Bar, Gray's Inn, 1972; Dir, Newham Rights Centre, 1973–76; Lectr, Middlesex Polytechnic, 1976–77; Barrister, 1977–. Chm., Inst. of Employment Rights, 1989–. *Address:* Old Square Chambers, 1 Verulam Buildings, Gray's Inn, WC1R 5LQ. *T:* 0171–831 0801, *Fax:* 0171–405 1387.

HENES, John Derek; Director, Civil Aviation, Department of Transport, since 1995; *b* 8 June 1937; *s* of Frederick William Kingaby Henes and Joan Elizabeth Henes (*née* Colbourne); *m* 1981, Virginia Elizabeth Evans; one *s* one *d*. *Educ:* Christ's Hospital; Gonville and Caius College, Cambridge (MA). Ministry of Aviation, 1963; Dept of Trade, 1971; Private Sec. to Christopher Chataway, 1973–74, to Lord Beswick, 1974–75; Asst Sec., 1975; Dept. of Transport, 1983–; Under Sec., 1989. *Recreations:* reading, music. *Address:* Department of Transport, 76 Marsham Street, SW1P 4DR.

HENHAM, John Alfred; His Honour Judge Henham; a Circuit Judge, since 1983; *b* 8 Sept. 1924; *s* of Alfred and Daisy Henham; *m* 1946, Suzanne Jeanne Octavie Ghislaine Pinchart (*d* 1972); two *s*. Stipendiary Magistrate for S Yorks, 1975–82; a Recorder of the Crown Court, 1979–82. *Address:* Crown Court, Castle Street, Sheffield S3 8LW.

HENIG, Prof. Stanley; Professor of European Politics, since 1982 and Head of Department of European Studies, since 1990, University of Central Lancashire (formerly Preston, then Lancashire, Polytechnic); *b* 7 July 1939; *s* of Sir Mark Henig and Grace (*née* Cohen); *m* 1966, Ruth Beatrice Munzer; two *s*. *Educ:* Wyggeston Grammar Sch.; Corpus Christi Coll., Oxford. BA 1st Cl. Hons, 1961; MA 1965 Oxon. Teaching Asst, Dept of Politics, Univ. of Minnesota, 1961; Research Student, Nuffield Coll., 1962; Lecturer in Politics, Lancaster Univ., 1964–66; MP (Lab) Lancaster, 1966–70; Lectr in Politics, Warwick Univ., 1970–71; Lectr, Civil Service Coll., 1972–75; Preston, subseq. Lancashire, Polytechnic: Head of Div. of Social Admin, later Sch. of Social Studies, 1976–82; Dean, Faculty of Social Studies, 1985–90. Mem., Lancaster CC, 1981– (Leader, 1991–). Governor, British Inst. of Recorded Sound, 1975–80. Secretary: Historic Masters Ltd, 1983–; Historic Singers Trust, 1985–. Chm., Court, RNCM, 1986–89. Asst Editor, Jl of Common Market Studies, 1964–72, Editor, 1973–76. *Publications:* (ed) European Political

Parties, 1969; External Relations of the European Community, 1971; (ed) Political Parties in the European Community, 1979; Power and Decision in Europe, 1980. *Recreation:* collector of old gramophone records. *Address:* 10 Yealand Drive, Lancaster LA1 4EW. *T:* Lancaster (01524) 69624.

HENLEY, 8th Baron (Ire.), *cr* 1799; **Oliver Michael Robert Eden;** Baron Northington (UK) 1885; Minister of State, Department for Education and Employment, since 1995; *b* 22 Nov. 1953; *er s* of 7th Baron Henley and of Nancy Mary, *d* of Stanley Walton, Gilsland, Cumbria; *S* father, 1977; *m* 1984, Caroline Patricia, *d* of A. G. Sharp, Mackney, Oxon; two *s* one *d*. *Educ:* Clifton; Durham Univ. (BA 1975). Called to the Bar, Middle Temple, 1977. A Lord in Waiting (Govt Whip), 1989; Parliamentary Under-Secretary of State: DSS, 1989–93; Dept of Employment, 1993–94; MoD, 1994–95. Mem., Cumbria CC, 1986–89. Chm., Penrith and the Border Conservative Assoc., 1987–89. Pres., Cumbria Assoc. of Local Councils, 1981–89. Pres., Cumbria Trust for Nature Conservation, 1988–89. *Heir: s* Hon. John Michael Oliver Eden, *b* 30 June 1988. *Address:* Scaleby Castle, Carlisle, Cumbria CA6 4LN. *Clubs:* Brooks's; Pratt's.

HENLEY, Sir Douglas (Owen), KCB 1973 (CB 1970); Comptroller and Auditor General, 1976–81; *b* 5 April 1919; *m* 1942, June Muriel Ibbetson; four *d*. *Educ:* Beckenham County Sch.; London Sch. of Economics (Hon. Fellow, 1974). BSc (Econ.), 1939; Gerstenberg Studentship and Leverhulme Res. Studentship (not taken up). Served Army, 1939–46; Queen's Own Royal West Kent Regt and HQ 12th Inf. Bde (despatches twice, 1945). Treasury, 1946; Treas. rep. (Financial Counsellor) in Tokyo and Singapore, 1956–59; Asst Under-Sec. of State, DEA, 1964–69, Dep. Under-Sec. of State, 1969; Second Permanent Sec., HM Treasury, 1972–76. Mem. Council, GPDST, 1982–. Hon. LLD Bath, 1981. *Address:* Walwood House, Park Road, Banstead, Surrey SM7 3ER. *T:* Burgh Heath (01737) 352626.

HENLEY, Rear-Adm. Sir Joseph (Charles Cameron), KCVO 1963; CB 1962; *b* 24 April 1909; *e s* of Vice-Adm. J. C. W. Henley, CB; *m* 1934, Daphne Ruth (marr. diss. 1965), *d* of late A. A. H. Wykeham, of Pitt Place, Brighstone, IW; one *s* three *d*; *m* 1966, Patricia Sharp, MBE 1952, *d* of late Roy Eastman, Alberta, Canada. *Educ:* Sherborne. Joined Royal Navy, 1927. Served War of 1939–45, in HMS Birmingham and King George V. Capt., 1951, in command HMS Defender, 1954–55; Naval Attaché; Washington (as Commodore), 1956–57; Dir, Royal Naval Staff Coll., 1958; Chief of Staff, Mediterranean Station, 1959–61, as Commodore; Rear-Adm. 1960; Flag Officer, Royal Yachts and Extra Naval Equerry to the Queen, 1962–65; retd 1965. *Address:* 11A/13 Thornton Street, Darling Point, Sydney, NSW 2027, Australia. *T:* (2) 3631068. *Clubs:* Royal Yacht Squadron; Royal Sydney Golf.

HENLEY, Rt Rev. Michael Harry George; *see* St Andrews, Dunkeld and Dunblane, Bishop of.

HENN, Charles Herbert; Assistant Under Secretary of State, Ministry of Defence, 1979–88; *b* 11 July 1931; *s* of Herbert George Henn and Ellen Anne Henn; *m* 1955, Ann Turner; one *s* one *d*. *Educ:* King's Coll. Sch., Wimbledon; Queen's Coll., Oxford (BA). National Service, REME, 1952–54 (2/Lieut). Scientific Officer, WO, 1954; Sen. Scientific Officer, 1957; Principal, 1964; Private Sec. to Minister of State for Defence, 1969; Asst Sec., 1972. *Recreations:* walking, running, listening to music.

HENNELL, Rev. Canon Michael Murray; Residentiary Canon, Manchester Cathedral, 1970–84, Canon Emeritus, since 1984; *b* 11 Sept. 1918; *s* of Charles Murray and Jessie Hennell; *m* 1950, Peggy Glendinning; four *s*. *Educ:* Bishops Stortford Coll. (Prep.); Royal Masonic Sch., St Edmund Hall and Wycliffe Hall, Oxford. MA Oxon and, by incorporation, MA Cantab. Asst Curate: St Stephen's With St Bartholomew's, Islington, N1, 1942–44; All Saints, Queensbury, Middx, 1944–48; Tutor, Ridley Hall, Cambridge, 1948–51. St Aidan's Coll., Birkenhead: Sen. Tutor, 1951; Vice-Principal, 1952–59; Principal, 1959–63; Principal, Ridley Hall, Cambridge, 1964–70. *Publications:* John Venn and the Clapham Sect, 1958; Sons of the Prophets, 1979; ed and contrib., Charles Simeon, 1759–1836, 1959; The Deans and Canons of Manchester Cathedral 1840–1948, 1989; contribs to: The Anglican Synthesis, 1964; Popular Belief and Practice, 1972; A Dictionary of Christian Spirituality, 1983; The Study of Spirituality, 1986; The Blackwell Dictionary of Evangelical Biography, 1994. *Address:* 53 Cleveley Road, Meols, Wirral, Merseyside L47 8XN.

HENNESSY, family name of **Baron Windlesham.**

HENNESSY, Christopher; journalist; Chairman, Associated Catholic Newspapers (1912) Ltd, 1970–79; Trustee, The Universe, 1979–87 (Editor, 1954–72); *b* 29 Dec. 1909; *e s* of Daniel and Anne Hennessy; *m* 1942, Kathleen Margaret Cadley, Liverpool. *Educ:* St Edward's Coll., Liverpool. Served War of 1939–45 as Commissioned Officer in British and Indian Armies; commanded a Territorial Army Unit in the North-West, 1950–55. KCSG 1975. *Recreation:* travel. *Address:* Flat 49, The Metropole, The Leas, Folkestone, Kent CT20 2LU.

HENNESSY, Sir James (Patrick Ivan), KBE 1982 (OBE 1968; MBE 1959); CMG 1975; HM Diplomatic Service, retired; *b* 26 Sept. 1923; *s* of late Richard George Hennessy, DSO, MC; *m* 1947, Patricia, *o d* of late Wing Comdr F. H. Unwin, OBE; five *d* (one *s* decd). *Educ:* Bedford Sch.; King's Coll., Newcastle; Sidney Sussex Coll., Cambridge; LSE. Served RA, 1942–44; seconded IA, 1944–46, Adjt and Battery Comdr, 6th Indian Field Regt. Apptd to HM Overseas Service, Basutoland, District Officer, 1948; Judicial Comr, 1953; Dist Comr, 1954–56; Jt Sec., Constitutional Commn, 1957–59; Supervisor of Elections, 1959; Sec. to Exec. Council, 1960; seconded to Office of High Comr, Cape Town/Pretoria, 1961–63; Perm. Sec. for local govt, 1964; MLC, 1965; Sec. for External Affairs, Defence and Internal Security, 1967; Prime Minister's Office, 1968. Retired, later apptd to HM Diplomatic Service; FO, 1968–70; Chargé d'Affaires, Montevideo, 1971–72; High Comr to Uganda and Ambassador (non-resident), Rwanda, 1973–76; Consul-Gen., Cape Town, 1977–80; Governor and C-in-C, Belize, 1980–81; HM Chief Inspector of Prisons for England and Wales, 1982–87. Mem., Parole Bd, 1988–91. Trustee, Butler Trust, 1989–. *Clubs:* Naval and Military, Commonwealth Trust.

HENNESSY, Brig. Mary Brigid Teresa, (Rita), CBE 1988 (MBE 1967); RRC 1982; Matron-in-Chief, Queen Alexandra's Royal Army Nursing Corps, 1985–89 and Director of Defence Nursing Service, 1986–89; *b* 27 Jan. 1933; *d* of late Bartholomew and Nora Agnes Hennessy. *Educ:* Convent of Mercy, Ennis, Co. Clare; Whittington Hosp., Highgate, London; Victoria Maternity Hosp., Barnet. SRN; SCM. Joined QARANC, 1959; service in Britain, Singapore, Malaya, Germany; various hosp. appts, 1959–74; seconded to office of Chargé d'affaires, Peking, 1965–67; Dep. Matron, Hongkong, 1976; Lt-Col 1979; Col 1982; Brig., Matron-in-Chief and Dir of Army Nursing Services, 1985. QHNS 1985–89. *Recreations:* music, theatre, gardening.

HENNESSY, Prof. Peter John, FRHistS; Professor of Contemporary History, Queen Mary and Westfield College, University of London, since 1992; Chairman, Kennedy Memorial Trust, since 1995; *b* 28 March 1947; *s* of William Gerald and Edith Hennessy; *m* 1969, Enid Mary Candler; two *d*. *Educ:* Marling Sch., Stroud; St John's Coll., Cambridge (BA 1969), PhD Cantab 1990; LSE; Harvard, 1971–72 (Kennedy Meml Scholar). FRHistS 1993. Reporter, THES, 1972–74, The Times, 1974–76; Lobby corresp., Financial Times, 1976; Whitehall corresp., The Times, 1976–82; journalist, The Economist, 1982; home leader writer and columnist, The Times, 1982–84; columnist: New Statesman, 1986–87; The Independent, 1987–91; Director, 1989–93. Co-Founder and Co-Dir, 1986–89, Mem. Bd, 1989–, Inst. of Contemporary British Hist. (Hon. Fellow, 1995). Vis. Prof. of Govt, Strathclyde Univ., 1989–; Gresham Prof. of Rhetoric, Gresham Coll., 1994–Sept. 1996; Vis. Lectr, Dept of Politics, Univ. of Strathclyde, 1983–84 (Hon. Res. Fellow, 1985–89); Visiting Fellow: Policy Studies Inst., 1986–91 (Sen. Fellow, 1984–85; Council Mem., 1991–); Univ. Depts of Politics, Reading 1988–94, Nottingham 1989–; RIPA, 1989–92; Hon. Res. Fellow, Dept of Politics and Sociology, Birkbeck Coll., London, 1990–91; Vis. Scholar, Centre for Australian Public Sector Management, Griffith Univ., Brisbane, 1991. Vice-Pres., Politics Assoc., 1985–. Trustee, Attlee Foundn, 1985–. Partner, Intellectual R and D, 1990–. Mem. Bd, Inst. of Histl Res., 1992–. FRSA 1992. Presenter: Under Fire, TV, 1985–87; Radio 4 Analysis programme, 1986–92; writer and presenter, What Has Become of Us, TV, 1994; numerous other radio and TV productions. Hon. DLitt Univ. of W England, 1995. *Publications:* (with Keith Jeffery) States of Emergency, 1983; (with Michael Cockerell and David Walker) Sources Close to the Prime Minister, 1984; What the Papers Never Said, 1985; Cabinet, 1986; (ed with Anthony Seldon) Ruling Performance, 1987; Whitehall, 1989; Never Again: Britain, 1945–51, 1992 (Duff Cooper Prize, 1993; NCR Book Award for Non-Fiction, 1993); The Hidden Wiring: unearthing the British Constitution, 1995. *Recreations:* reading, listening to music, running, searching for the British Constitution. *Address:* Department of History, Queen Mary and Westfield College, Mile End Road, E1 4NS. *T:* 0171–975 5555. *Clubs:* Savile; Attlee Memorial Runners.

HENNIG, Dr Georg, Hon. LVO 1969; Ambassador of the Republic of Austria to the Court of St James's, since 1993; *b* 3 Sept. 1937; *s* of late Max Hennig and of Eva (*née* Weinberger, now Mrs F. W. Mayer); *m* 1968, Ilona Esterhazy; one *s*. *Educ:* Schottengymnasium, Vienna; Univ. of Vienna (Dr jur 1960); Bologna Centre, Sch. of Advanced Internat. Studies, Johns Hopkins Univ. (Dip.). Protocol Div., Legal Dept, Federal Min. for Foreign Affairs, Vienna, 1961–63; Perm. Mission to UN, NY, 1963–66; Personal Asst to Foreign Minister, 1966–70; First Sec., Madrid, 1970–71; Sen. Dir, Office of Sec.-Gen. of UN, 1972–75; Minister, Hd of Office of Sec.-Gen. for Foreign Affairs, Vienna, 1976–79; Ambassador to: India, and accredited to Bangladesh, Sri Lanka and Nepal, 1979–83; Japan, and accredited to Republic of Korea, 1983–86; Special Advr to Federal Pres. of Austria, 1987–92; Ambassador at Federal Min. for Foreign Affairs, Vienna, 1992–93. Grand Decoration of Honour in Gold (Austria), 1992. *Recreations:* reading, shooting. *Address:* 18 Belgrave Square, SW1X 8PX. *T:* 0171–235 7268. *Clubs:* Travellers; St Johann's (Vienna).

HENNIKER, 8th Baron *cr* 1800; **John Patrick Edward Chandos Henniker-Major,** KCMG 1965 (CMG 1956); CVO 1960; MC 1945; Bt 1765; Baron Hartismere (UK) 1866; DL; Director, Wates Foundation, 1972–78; *b* 19 Feb. 1916; *s* of 7th Baron Henniker, and Molly (*d* 1953), *d* of Sir Robert Burnet, KCVO; *S* father, 1980; *m* 1946, Margaret Osla Benning (*d* 1974); two *s* one *d*; *m* 1976, Julia Marshall Poland (*née* Mason). *Educ:* Stowe; Trinity Coll., Cambridge. HM Foreign Service, 1938; served 1940–45, Army (Major, The Rifle Brigade). HM Embassy Belgrade, 1945–46; Asst Private Secretary to Secretary of State for Foreign Affairs, 1946–48; Foreign Office, 1948–50; HM Embassy, Buenos Aires, 1950–52; Foreign Office, 1952–60 (Counsellor and Head of Personnel Dept, 1953); HM Ambassador to Jordan, 1960–62; to Denmark, 1962–66; Civil Service Commission, 1966–67; Asst Under-Secretary of State, FO, 1967–68. Dir-Gen., British Council, 1968–72. Lay Mem., Mental Health Review Tribunal (Broadmoor), 1975–81; Member: Parole Bd, 1979–83; Council and Finance Bd, Univ. of E Anglia, Norwich, 1979–86; Council, Toynbee Hall, 1978–90, Dep. Chm., 1982–86. Chairman/President: Suffolk Community Alcohol Services, 1983–93; Suffolk Rural Housing Assoc., 1984–; President: Suffolk Community Council (Suffolk ACRE), 1988–93; Suffolk Agricl Assoc., 1989; Rainer Foundn, 1985–90 (Chm., Intermediate Treatment Fund, 1985–90); Vice-Pres., Suffolk Trust for Nature Conservation, 1985–. Trustee: City Parochial Foundn, 1973–90; London Festival Ballet, 1975–85. Governor: Cripplegate Foundn, 1979–90; Stowe Sch., 1982–90. Hon. (Lay) Canon of St Edmundsbury Cathedral, 1986–92. DL Suffolk, 1988. Hon. DCL UEA, 1989; Hon. LLD New England Coll., NH, 1993. *Recreations:* gardening, ornithology. *Heir: s* Hon. Mark Ian Philip Chandos Henniker-Major [*b* 29 Sept. 1947; *m* 1973, Lesley Antoinette Masterton-Smith, *d* of Wing Comdr G. W. Foskett; two *s* three *d*]. *Address:* Red House, Thornham Magna, Eye, Suffolk IP23 8HH. *Club:* Special Forces.

HENNIKER, Sir Adrian Chandos, 9th Bt *cr* 1813, of Newton Hall, Essex; *b* 18 Oct. 1946; *s* of Brig. Sir Mark Chandos Auberon Henniker, 8th Bt, CBE, DSO, MC and of Kathleen Denys, *d* of John Anderson; *S* father, 1991; *m* 1971, Ann, *d* of Stuart Britton; twin *d*. *Educ:* Marlborough. *Heir: cousin* Richard Frederick Henniker [*b* 10 June 1906; *m* 1938, Daphne Irene, *d* of Captain C. J. Maxwell]. *Address:* Llwyndu Court, Abergavenny, Gwent.

HENNIKER HEATON, Sir Yvo Robert; *see* Heaton.

HENNIKER-MAJOR, family name of **Baron Henniker.**

HENREY, Mrs Robert; authoress; *b* Paris, 13 Aug. 1906; maiden name Madeleine Gal; *m* 1928, Robert Selby Henrey (*d* 1982), *o s* of Rev. Thomas Selby Henrey, Vicar of Old Brentford, Mddx, and Euphemia, *d* of Sir Coutts and Lady Lindsay of Balcarres; one *s*. *Educ:* Protestant Girls' Sch., Clichy; Convent of The Holy Family, Tooting, SW. *Publications:* autobiographical sequence in the following chronological order: The Little Madeleine, 1951, New York, 1953; An Exile in Soho, 1952; Julia, 1971; A Girl at Twenty, 1974; Madeleine Grown Up, 1952, New York 1953; Green Leaves, 1976; Madeleine Young Wife, New York 1954, London 1960; London under Fire 1940–45, 1969; A Month in Paris, 1954; Milou's Daughter, 1955, New York 1956; Her April Days, 1963; Wednesday at Four, 1964; Winter Wild, 1966; She Who Pays, 1969; The Golden Visit, 1979 (read in the above order these volumes make one consecutive narrative); *other books:* A Farm in Normandy, 1941; A Village in Piccadilly, 1943; The Incredible City, 1944; The Foolish Decade, 1945; The King of Brentford, 1946; The Siege of London, 1946; The Return to the Farm, 1947; London (with illustrations by Phyllis Ginger RWS) 1948, New York, 1949; A Film Star in Belgrave Square, 1948; A Journey to Vienna, 1950; Matilda and the Chickens, 1950; Paloma, 1951, New York, 1955; A Farm in Normandy and the Return, 1952; Madeleine's Journal, 1953; This Feminine World, 1956; A Daughter for a Fortnight, 1957; The Virgin of Aldermanbury (illustrations by Phyllis Ginger), 1958; Mistress of Myself, 1959; The Dream Makers, 1961; Spring in a Soho Street, 1962. *Recreations:* most feminine occupations: sewing, knitting, ironing, gardening. *Address:* c/o J. M. Dent & Sons, Aldine House, 33 Welbeck Street, W1M 8LX; Ferme Robert Henrey, 14640 Villers-sur-Mer, Calvados, France. *T:* Calvados 31870388.

HENRI, Adrian Maurice; President, Liverpool Academy of Arts, 1972–81; *b* Birkenhead, 10 April 1932; *s* of Arthur Maurice Henri and Emma Johnson; *m* 1959, Joyce Wilson (*d*

1987). *Educ:* St Asaph Grammar Sch., N Wales; Dept of Fine Art, King's Coll., Newcastle upon Tyne, 1951–55. Hons BA Fine Art (Dunelm) 1955; DLitt Liverpool, 1990. Worked for ten seasons in Rhyl fairground, later as a scenic-artist and secondary school teacher; taught at Manchester then Liverpool Colls of Art, 1961–67. Led the poetry/rock group, Liverpool Scene, 1967–70; since then, freelance poet/painter/singer/songwriter/lecturer. Tour of USA, 1973; Bicentennial Poetry Tour of USA, 1976; exchange tour of Canada, 1980. Pres., Merseyside Arts Assoc., 1978–80; Writer-in-Residence: Tattenhall Centre, Cheshire, 1980–82; Liverpool Univ., 1989. *Exhibitions:* include: Biennale della Giovane Pintura, Milan, 1968; Pen as Pencil, Brussels, 1973; John Moores Liverpool Exhibns, 1962, 1965, 1967, 1974, 1978, 1980, 1989, 1993; Peter Moores Project, Real Life, Liverpool, 1977; Art and the Sea, 1980–81; Hedgerow mural, 1980, Summer Terrace mural, 1983. Royal Liverpool Hosp. John Moores Liverpool £2000 prize, 1972. *Major One-Man Shows:* ICA, London, 1968; ArtNet, London, 1975; Williamson Art Gall., Birkenhead, 1975; Retrospective 1960–76, Wolverhampton City Art Gall., 1976; Demarco Gall., Edinburgh, 1978; Touring Retrospective, The Art of Adrian Henri, South Hill Park and elsewhere, 1986–87; Hanover Gall., Liverpool, 1987; Library Centre, Skelmersdale, 1989; Poetry Soc., 1990; Acorn Gall., Liverpool, 1992; Storey Inst., Lancaster, 1994; Merkmal Gall., Liverpool, 1994. Various recordings. *Publications:* Tonight at Noon, 1968; City, 1969 (out of print); Autobiography, 1971; (with Nell Dunn) I Want (novel), 1972; World of Art Series: Environments and Happenings, 1974; The Best of Henri, 1975; City Hedges 1970–76, 1977; From The Loveless Motel, poems 1976–79, 1980; Penny Arcade, poems 1978–82, 1983; Collected Poems, 1986; Wish You Were Here (poems), 1990; Not Fade Away (poems), 1994; *for children:* Eric, the Punk Cat, 1982; The Phantom Lollipop-Lady (poems), 1986; Eric and Frankie in Las Vegas, 1987; Rhinestone Rhino (poems), 1989; The Postman's Palace, 1990; Dinner with the Spratts (poems), 1993; *for teenagers:* Box (poems), 1990; The Wakefield Mysteries (playscript), 1991; *anthologies:* The Oxford Book of Twentieth Century Verse, 1973; The Liverpool Scene (ed Edward Lucie-Smith), 1967; Penguin Modern Poets No 10: The Mersey Sound, 1967, rev. and enlarged edn, 1974, rev. edn, 1983; British Poetry since 1945 (ed Edward Lucie-Smith: Penguin), 1970; New Volume, 1983; *plays:* I Wonder, a Guillaume Apollinaire Show (with Mike Kustow), 1968; (with Nell Dunn) I Want, 1983; The Wakefield Mysteries, 1988; (jtly) Fears and Miseries of the Third Term, 1989; *TV plays:* Yesterday's Girl, 1973; The Husband, the Wife and the Stranger, 1986. *Recreations:* watching Liverpool FC; visiting Shropshire and Normandy; old movies; SF, Gothic and crime novels. *Address:* 21 Mount Street, Liverpool L1 9HD. *T:* 0151–709 6682; (literary agent) Rogers, Coleridge and White Ltd, 20 Powis Mews, W11 1JN. *Clubs:* Chelsea Arts; Private Chauffeurs' (Liverpool).

HENRIQUES, Richard Henry Quixano; QC 1986; barrister; a Recorder of the Crown Court, since 1983; *b* 27 Oct. 1943; *s* of Cecil Quixano Henriques and late Doreen Mary Henriques; *m* Joan Hilary, (Toni), (*née* Senior); one *s* and one step *s*. *Educ:* Bradfield Coll., Berks; Worcester Coll., Oxford (BA). Called to the Bar, Inner Temple, 1967; Bencher, 1994. Mem., Northern Circuit. Member: Gen. Council of the Bar, 1993–; Criminal Justice Liaison Cttee, 1993–; Northern Circuit Exec. Cttee, 1993–. Council Mem., Rossall Sch. *Recreations:* bridge, golf. *Address:* Ilex House, Woodhouse Road, Thornton-Cleveleys, Lancs FY5 5LQ. *T:* Cleveleys (01253) 826199. *Clubs:* The Manchester (Manchester); North Shore Golf (Blackpool).

HENRISON, Dame (Anne) Rosina (Elizabeth), DBE 1984; *b* 7 Dec. 1902; *d* of Amelina Marie (*née* Malepa) and Julius Marie; *m* 1st, 1931, Charles Duval; three *s* one *d*; 2nd, 1943, Edward Henrison. *Educ:* Loreto Convent, Port Louis. Hon. Citizen, Town of Bangui, Central Africa, 1975; Ordre de Mérite, Centre Africaine; Mother Gold Medal. *Recreations:* reading, travelling. *Address:* Melville, Grandgaube, Mauritius. *T:* 039518. *Club:* Port Louis Tennis (Mauritius).

HENRY, David; Senior Director, Postal Services, 1978–82, retired; *b* 19 April 1925; *s* of Thomas Glanffrwd Henry and Hylda Frances Henry. *Educ:* Midhurst Grammar Sch.; St John's Coll., Cambridge (MA Hons). Assistant Postal Controller, 1950; Head Postmaster, Norwich, 1961; Postal Controller, 1966; Controller Operations, 1968; Director, Midlands Postal Region, 1969; Chairman, Midlands Postal Board, 1974; Dir, London Postal Region, 1977. *Recreations:* Rugby football, cricket.

HENRY, Sir Denis (Aynsley), Kt 1975; OBE 1962; QC Grenada 1968; barrister-at-law; Senior Partner, Henry, Henry & Bristol, St George's, Grenada, WI; *b* 3 Feb. 1917; *s* of Ferdinand H. Henry and Agatha May Henry; *m* 1966, Kathleen Carol (*née* Sheppard); two *s* three *d*. *Educ:* Grenada Boys' Secondary Sch.; King's Coll., London (LLB Hons). Called to Bar, Inner Temple (Certif. of Honour), 1939. In practice at Bar, Grenada, 1939–. Served three terms as nominated MLC, Grenada, 1952–65; Sen. nominated Mem. Exec. Council, 1956–65; Senator in First Parlt of Associated State of Grenada, 1966–67. Mem. Council, Univ. of West Indies, 1956–68. Pres. and Dir, Windward Islands Banana Growers Assoc., 1957–75; Pres., Commonwealth Banana Exporters Assoc., 1973–75; Chairman: Grenada Banana Co-operative Soc., 1953–75; Grenada Cocoa Assoc., 1973–75. Vice-Pres., Commonwealth Caribbean Society for the Blind, 1972–75; Mem. Exec., West India Cttee, London, 1972–75. *Recreations:* golf, swimming, tennis. *Clubs:* Commonwealth Trust; Grenada Golf, Richmond Hill Tennis (Grenada).

HENRY, Rt. Hon. Sir Denis (Robert Maurice), Kt 1986; PC 1993; **Rt. Hon. Lord Justice Henry;** a Lord Justice of Appeal, since 1993; *b* 19 April 1931; *o s* of late Brig. Maurice Henry and Mary Catherine (*née* Irving); *m* 1963, Linda Gabriel Arthur; one *s* one *d* (and one *d* decd). *Educ:* Shrewsbury; Balliol Coll., Oxford (MA). 2nd Lieut, KORR, 1950–51. Called to the Bar, Inner Temple, 1955, Bencher, 1985; QC 1977; a Recorder, 1979–86; a Judge of the High Court, QBD, 1986–93. Chm., Judicial Studies Bd, 1994–. Part-time Tutor, New Coll., Oxford, 1985–. *Recreation:* golf. *Address:* Royal Courts of Justice, Strand, WC2A 2LL.

HENRY, Sir Geoffrey (Arama), KBE 1992; Prime Minister, Cook Islands, 1983, and since 1989; *b* Aitutaki, Cook Is, 16 Nov. 1940; *s* of Arama Henry and Mata Uritaua; *m* 1965, Louisa Olga Hoff; four *s* two *d*. *Educ:* St George's Prep. Sch., Wanganui, NZ; Wanganui Collegiate Sch.; Victoria Univ., Wellington, NZ (BA English and Educn). School Teacher, 1965–67; entered politics, 1965–68; public service, 1970–72; returned to politics, and Cabinet Minister, 1972–78; Leader of Opposition, 1978–83, 1983–84; Dep. Prime Minister in Coalition Govt, 1984; Leader of Opposition, 1985–89. Chm., Standing Cttee, Pacific Is Develt Prog. (EWC), 1989; Organiser, Jt Commercial Commn, USA and Pacific Is, 1990; Chm., Econ. Summit of Small Island States, 1992. Chancellor, Univ. of S Pacific, 1992. Chambellan de l'Ordre des Coteaux de Champagne, 1991. Silver Jubilee Medal, 1977; NZ Commemoration Medal, 1990. *Recreations:* golf, Rugby, Rugby league, other sports, reading, music. *Address:* PO Box 281, Rarotonga, Cook Islands. *Clubs:* Rarotonga Golf, Rarotonga Bowling, Rarotonga Fishing, Lions, Rarotonga (Cook Islands).

HENRY, Sir James Holmes, 2nd Bt, *cr* 1922; CMG 1960; MC 1944; TD 1950; QC (Tanganyika) 1953, (Cyprus) 1957; Chairman, Foreign Compensation Commission, 1977–83 (Commissioner, 1960–77); *b* 22 Sept. 1911; *er s* of Rt Hon. Sir Denis Stanislaus Henry, 1st Baronet, Cahore, Draperstown, Co. Londonderry, 1st Lord Chief Justice of Northern Ireland, and Violet (*d* 1966), 3rd *d* of late Rt Hon. Hugh Holmes, Court of Appeal, Ireland; *S* father, 1925; *m* 1st, 1941 (marriage terminated by divorce and rescript of Holy Office in Rome); 2nd, 1949, Christina Hilary, *widow* of Lieut-Commander Christopher H. Wells, RN, and *e d* of late Sir Hugh Holmes, KBE, CMG, MC, QC (formerly Mixed Courts, Egypt); three *d*. *Educ:* Mount St Mary's Coll., Chesterfield; Downside Sch.; University College, London. BA (Hons) Classics (1st Class), University Scholarships. Called to Bar, Inner Temple, 1934; practised, London, 1934–39. Served War of 1939–45, London Irish Rifles (wounded). Crown Counsel, Tanganyika, 1946; Legal Draftsman, 1949; jt comr, Revised Edn of Laws of Tanganyika (1947–49), 1950; Solicitor-General, 1952; Attorney-General, Cyprus, 1956–60. *Heir: nephew* Patrick Denis Henry, *b* 20 Dec. 1957. *Address:* Kandy Lodge, 18 Ormond Avenue, Hampton on Thames, Mddx TW12 2RU. *Club:* Travellers'.

HENRY, John Philip; Principal Finance Officer, Department of the Environment, since 1994; *b* 8 Oct. 1946; *s* of late L. Henry, MD, FRCS and P. M. Henry, MB, ChB; *m* 1992, Gillian Mary Richardson; one *d*. *Educ:* Cheltenham Coll.; Queen's Coll., Oxford (MA). Psychologist, Road Research Lab., 1968; Admin Trainee, DoE, 1972; Principal, 1976; Private Sec., Minister for Housing and Construction, 1981–83; Asst Sec., 1983–89; Regl Dir, Yorks and Humberside Regl Office, Depts of the Envmt and Transport, 1990–94. *Address:* 2 Marsham Street, SW1P 3EB.

HENRY, Lenworth George, (Lenny); stand-up comedian, since 1975; actor; *b* 29 Aug. 1958; *s* of Winston Henry and Winifred Henry; *m* 1984, Dawn R. French; one adopted *d*. *Educ:* Bluecoat Secondary Mod. Sch.; W. R. Tewson Sch.; Preston Coll. Won New Faces Talent Show, 1975; *TV appearances* include: Fosters, 1976–77; Tiswas, 1978–81; 3 of a Kind, 1981–84; Lenny Henry Show, 1984, 1985, 1987, 1988, 1995; Lenny Henry Tonight, 1986; Xmas Specials, 1987, 1988, 1994; Chef, 1992, 1994; *films:* Coast to Coast, 1984; Work Experience, 1989; Alive and Kicking, 1990; True Identity, 1990. *Publications:* Quest for the Big Woof; Charlie and the Big Chill. *Recreations:* funkateer, reading quality graphic novels, going to nursery, books, pretending to be a soul singer, being with friends and family, cooking. *Address:* c/o James Sharkey Associates, 3rd Floor Suite, 15 Golden Square, W1R 3AG. *Clubs:* Groucho, Soho House; Tuffy (Reading).

HENRY, Hon. Sir Trevor (Ernest), Kt 1970; Judge, Fiji Court of Appeal, 1974–85; *b* 9 May 1902; *s* of John Henry and Edith Anna (*née* Eaton); *m* 1930, Audrey Kate Sheriff; one *s* one *d*. *Educ:* Rotorua District High Sch.; Univ. of New Zealand (Auckland). LLB 1925, LLM Hons 1926, NZ. Solicitor of Supreme Court of NZ, 1923, Barrister, 1925. Judge of the Supreme Court of NZ, 1955–77. *Recreation:* fishing. *Address:* Arbour Vale, Old North Road, Waimauki RD2, Auckland, New Zealand. *Club:* Northern (Auckland).

HENRY, Wendy Ann; *d* of Bernard and Elsa Henry; *m* 1980, Tim Miles; one *d*. *Educ:* Queen Mary School, Lytham. Reporter, Daily Mail, Manchester, 1975, News of the World, 1976; Features Editor, Woman Magazine, 1979; Asst Editor, The Sun, 1981; Editor: Sunday Magazine, 1986; The News of the World, 1987–88; Dep. Editor, The Sun, 1988; Editor: The People, 1989; The Globe, Florida, 1990. Mem., Weight Watchers. *Recreation:* sleeping.

HENRY, William Robert, CBE 1979; Chairman: Coats Patons Ltd, 1975–81; Scottish Amicable Life Assurance Society, 1981–84; *b* 30 April 1915; *s* of William Henry and Sarah (*née* Lindsay); *m* 1947, Esther Macfayden; two *s* one *d*. *Educ:* Govan High Sch.; London Univ. Entered Company's service, 1934; Head of Financial Dept, 1953; Asst Accountant, 1957; Dir, J. & P. Coats Ltd (Parent Co.), 1966; Dep. Chm., Coats Patons Ltd, 1970. FIMgt (FBIM 1976). *Recreations:* golf, gardening. *Address:* Hawkstone Lodge, Ascog, Isle of Bute, Scotland PA20 9EU.

HENSCHEL, Ruth Mary; *see* Ashton, R. M.

HENSHALL, Rt. Rev. Michael; *see* Warrington, Bishop Suffragan of.

HENSHAW, Frank Charles, CBE 1993; FRICS; General Manager, Milton Keynes Development Corporation, 1980–92; *b* 28 Aug. 1930; *s* of Frank and Edith Annie Henshaw; *m* 1966, Patricia Jane McDonald; one *s* one *d*. *Educ:* Towcester Grammar Sch.; Coll. of Estate Management. FRICS 1959. Nat. service, RAF, 1948–50. Quantity Surveyor: Northants CC, 1947–53; Coventry City Council, 1953–63; Prin. Quantity Surveyor, Midlands Housing Consortium, 1963–65; Chief Quantity Surveyor: Runcorn Develt Corp., 1965–70; Sheffield City Council, 1970–71; Milton Keynes Development Corporation: Chief Quantity Surveyor, 1971–74; Exec. Dir, 1974–78; Dep. Gen. Manager, 1978–80. Chm., Milton Keynes Housing Assoc., 1985–88; Dep. Chm., Central Milton Keynes Shopping Man. Co., 1978–89. Pres., Milton Keynes and N Bucks TEC, 1992–95 (Dir, 1990–92). Hon. Fellow, De Montfort Univ., 1993. DUniv Open, 1994. OON 1989. *Recreations:* golf, travel. *Address:* Pondwykes, Willen Road, Milton Keynes Village, Milton Keynes MK10 9AF. *Club:* Woburn Golf and Country.

HENSLEY, John; *b* 28 Feb. 1910; *s* of late Edward Hutton and Marion Hensley; *m* 1st, 1940, Dorothy Betty (*d* 1969), *d* of Percy George and Dorothy Coppard; one *s*; 2nd, 1971, Elizabeth, *widow* of Charles Cross and *d* of Harold and Jessie Coppard. *Educ:* Malvern; Trinity Coll., Cambridge (Chancellor's Classical Medal, MA). Entered Min. of Agriculture and Fisheries, 1933; Priv. Sec. to Chancellor of Duchy of Lancaster and Minister of Food, 1939; Priv. Sec. to Minister of Agriculture and Fisheries, 1945; Asst Sec., 1946; Under Sec., 1957. Member: Agricultural Research Council, 1957–59; Council, Nat. Inst. of Agricultural Botany, 1970–73; Sec., Cttee of Inquiry into Veterinary Profession, 1971–75; retired 1975. *Recreations:* theatre, opera, genealogy, gardening. *Address:* 109 Markfield, Courtwood Lane, Croydon CR0 9HP. *T:* 0181–657 6319.

HENSON, Marguerite Ann, (Mrs Nicky Henson); *see* Porter, M. A.

HENSON, Nicholas Victor Leslie, (Nicky); actor; *b* 12 May 1945; *s* of Leslie Henson and Billie Collins; *m* 1st, 1968, Una Stubbs (marr. diss.); two *s*; 2nd, 1986, Marguerite Porter, *qv*; one *s*. *Educ:* St Bede's, Eastbourne; Charterhouse. Formerly popular song writer; Founder Mem., Young Vic; first stage appearance, 1962; *London stage:* All Square, Vandeville, 1963; Camelot, Drury Lane, 1964; Passion Flower Hotel, Prince of Wales, 1965; Canterbury Tales, Phoenix, 1968; Ride Across Lake Constance, Mayfair, 1973; Hamlet, Greenwich, 1973; Midsummer Night's Dream, Regent's Park, 1973; Cinderella, Casino, 1973; Mardi Gras, Prince of Wales, 1976; Rookery Nook, Her Majesty's, 1980; Noises Off, Savoy, 1982; The Relapse, Lyric, 1983; Sufficient Carbohydrate, Albery, 1984; Journey's End, Whitehall, 1986; The Three Sisters, Royal Court, 1990; Matador, Queen's, 1991; Reflected Glory, Vaudeville, 1992; An Ideal Husband, Globe, 1993; Rage, Bush, 1994; *Young Vic:* Scapino, Waiting for Godot, She Stoops to Conquer, Taming of the Shrew, Measure for Measure, Soldier's Tale, Oedipus, Romeo and Juliet, The Maids, Look Back in Anger, Rosencrantz and Guildenstern are Dead, Charley's Aunt; *National Theatre:* Cherry Orchard, Macbeth, The Woman, The Double Dealer, A Fair Quarrel, Browning Version, Provok'd Wife, Elephant Man, Mandragola; *Royal Shakespeare Co.:* Man and Superman, Merry Wives of Windsor, As You Like It; *television series:* Life of Balzac, 1976; Seagull Island, 1981; Happy Apple, 1983; Thin Air, 1988; The Green Man,

1990; The Healer, 1994; Preston Front, 1994; Shine on Harvey Moon, 1994; 25 films. *Recreation:* music. *Address:* c/o Richard Stone, 25 Whitehall, SW1A 2BS. *T:* 0171–839 6421.

HENTY, Jonathan Maurice; Commissioner of Social Security and Child Support, since 1993; *b* 22 Dec. 1933; *s* of Richard Iltid Henty and Lettice Ellen (*née* Moore Gwyn); *m* 1st, 1956, Margaret Louise Sadler (*d* 1972); one *s* one *d* (and one *s* decd); 2nd, 1977, Veronica Mary Francis Miller; two *d. Educ:* Eton; New Coll., Oxford (MA). Called to the Bar, Lincoln's Inn, 1957, Bencher, 1989. Chancellor, Dio. Hereford, 1977–. *Recreations:* fishing, art and architecture. *Address:* Fisher Hill House, Northchapel, Petworth, W Sussex GU28 9EJ. *Club:* Athenæum.

HENZE, Hans Werner; composer; Professor of Composition, Royal Academy of Music, 1987–91; *b* 1 July 1926; *s* of Franz Gebhard Henze and Margarete Geldmacher. *Educ:* Bünde i/W; Bielefeld i/W; Braunschweig. Studying music in Heidelberg, 1945; First Work performed (Chamber Concerto), at Darmstadt-Kranichstein, 1946; Musical Dir, Municipal Theatre, Constance, 1948; Artistic Dir of Ballet, Hessian States Theatre, Wiesbaden, 1950; Prof. of Composition, Acad. Mozarteum, Salzburg, 1962–67. Definite departure for Italy, living first in Forio d'Ischia, then Naples, then Castelgandolfo as a composer; Artistic Director: Internat. Art Workshop, Montepulciano, Tuscany, 1976–80, Munich, 1989–; Philharmonic Acad., Rome, 1981–82; Munich Biennale, Internat. Fest. of New Music Theatre, 1988, 1990, 1992, 1994; Prof. of Composition, Hochschule für Musik, Cologne, 1980–91; Composer-in-Residence, Berlin Philharmonic Orchestra, 1991–92. Frequent international conducting tours. Member: German Acad. of Arts, Berlin; Philharmonic Acad., Rome; Acad. Scientiarum et Artium Europaea, Salzburg, 1992. Hon. Member: Deutsche Oper, Berlin, 1982; AAIL, 1982; Internat. Soc. for New Music, 1991. Hon. DMus Edinburgh, 1970. Robert Schumann Prize, 1952; Prix d'Italia, 1953; Nordrhein-Westphalien Award, 1955; Berlin Prize of Artists, 1958; Great Prize for Artists, Hanover, 1962; Louis Spohr Prize, Brunswick, 1977; Bach Prize, Hamburg, 1983; Siemens Prize, 1990. *Compositions:* 8 symphonies; 13 full length operas, 3 one-act operas, 1 children's opera, 2 radio-operas; ballets; chamber music; choral works; concerti for piano, violin, viola, violoncello, double bass, oboe, clarinet, trumpet, guitar and harp; various symphonic works; song cycle; music theatre works incl. The Magic Theatre, Boulevard Solitude, The Prince of Homburg, Elegy for Young Lovers, The Bassarids, The Young Lord, Natascha Ungeheuer, Moralities, La Cubana, The Ocean Betrayed. *Publications:* a book of Essays; El Cimarrón: ein Werkstatt-bericht, 1971; Neue Aspeckte der musikalischen Ästhetic: vol. I, Zwischen den Kulturen, 1979; vol. II, Die Zeichen, 1981; vol. III, Lehrgänge, 1986; vol. IV, Chiffren, 1990. *Address:* Schott Musik International, 55116 Mainz, Weihergarten 5, Germany.

HEPBURN, Sir John Alastair Trant Kidd B.; *see* Buchan-Hepburn.

HEPBURN, John William; Under Secretary, Ministry of Agriculture, Fisheries and Food, since 1982; *b* 8 Sept. 1938; *s* of late Dugald S. Hepburn and Margarita R. Hepburn; *m* 1972, Isla Marchbank; one *s. Educ:* Hutchesons' Grammar Sch.; Glasgow Univ. (MA); Brasenose Coll., Oxford. Assistant Principal, 1961, Principal, 1966, MAFF; First Secretary, UK Delegn to European Communities, Brussels, 1969–71; Private Sec. to Minister of Agriculture, Fisheries and Food, 1971–73; Asst Sec., MAFF, 1973–81. *Recreation:* golf. *Address:* c/o Ministry of Agriculture, Fisheries and Food, SW1A 2HH.

HEPBURN, Katharine; actress; *b* 9 Nov. 1909; *d* of late Dr Thomas N. Hepburn and Katharine Houghton; *m* Ludlow Ogden Smith (marr. diss.). *Educ:* Hartford; Bryn Mawr College. First professional appearance on stage, Baltimore, 1928, in Czarina; first New York appearance, 1928, in Night Hostess (under name Katherine Burns). The Millionairess, New Theatre, London, 1952. Entered films, 1932; notable films: A Bill of Divorcement; Morning Glory; Little Women; The Little Minister; Mary of Scotland; Quality Street; Stage Door; The Philadelphia Story; Keeper of the Flame; Dragon Seed; Woman of the Year; Under-current; Without Love; Sea of Grass; Song of Love; State of the Union; Adam's Rib; The African Queen; Pat and Mike; Summer Madness; The Iron Petticoat; The Rainmaker; His Other Woman; Suddenly, Last Summer; Long Day's Journey into Night; Guess Who's Coming to Dinner; The Madwoman of Chaillot; The Lion in Winter; The Trojan Women; A Delicate Balance; Rooster Cogburn; On Golden Pond. *Stage:* Warrior's Husband; The Philadelphia Story; Without Love; As You Like It; Taming of the Shrew; Merchant of Venice; Measure for Measure, Australia, 1955; Coco, 1970; A Matter of Gravity, NY, 1976, tour, 1977; The West Side Waltz, NY, 1981. Academy Awards for performances in Morning Glory, Guess Who's Coming to Dinner, The Lion in Winter, On Golden Pond. *Publications:* The Making of The African Queen, 1987; Me: stories of my life, 1991.

HEPBURN, Surg. Rear-Adm. Nicol Sinclair, CB 1971; CBE 1968; *b* 2 Feb. 1913; *s* of late John Primrose and Susan Hepburn, Edinburgh; *m* 1939, Dorothy Blackwood (*d* 1989); two *s. Educ:* Broughton; Edinburgh Univ. MB, ChB 1935; DPH London, 1948; DIH London, 1952. Barrister-at-law, Gray's Inn, 1956. Joined RN, 1935; served during war in Atlantic and Pacific Stations; SMO, HM Dockyard: Plymouth, 1952; Portsmouth, 1955; Naval Medical Officer of Health: Portsmouth, 1959; Malta, 1962; Surg. Cdre and Dep. Med. Dir-Gen., 1966; Surg. Rear-Adm. 1969; MO i/c, RN Hosp., Haslar, 1969–72; retd. MO, DHSS, 1972–80. FFPHM (FFCM 1973). *Address:* Mallows, 10 Chilbolton Avenue, Winchester, Hants SO22 5HD.

HEPBURN, Prof. Ronald William; Professor of Moral Philosophy, University of Edinburgh, since 1975 (Professor of Philosophy, 1964–75); *b* 16 March 1927; *s* of late W. G. Hepburn, Aberdeen; *m* 1953, Agnes Forbes Anderson; two *s* one *d. Educ:* Aberdeen Grammar Sch.; University of Aberdeen. MA 1951, PhD 1955 (Aberdeen). National service in Army, 1944–48. Asst, 1952–55, Lecturer, 1955–60, Dept of Moral Philosophy, University of Aberdeen; Visiting Associate Prof., New York University, 1959–60; Prof. of Philosophy, University of Nottingham, 1960–64. Stanton Lecturer in the Philosophy of Religion, Cambridge, 1965–68. *Publications:* (jointly) Metaphysical beliefs, 1957; Christianity and Paradox, 1958; Wonder and Other Essays: eight studies in aesthetics and neighbouring fields, 1984; contrib. to learned journals; broadcasts. *Recreations:* music, hill-walking. *Address:* Department of Philosophy, University of Edinburgh, David Hume Tower, George Square, Edinburgh EH8 9JX.

HEPBURNE-SCOTT, family name of **Lord Polwarth.**

HEPHER, Michael Leslie; Group Managing Director, British Telecommunications, since 1991; *b* 17 Jan. 1944; *s* of Leslie and Edna Hepher; *m* 1971, Janice Morton; one *s* two *d. Educ:* Kingston Grammar School. FIA; Associate, Soc. of Actuaries; FLIA. Provident Life Assoc., UK, 1961–67; Commercial Life Assurance, Canada, 1967–70; Maritime Life Assurance Co., Canada, 1970–79; Chm. and Man. Dir, Abbey Life Group, UK, subseq. Lloyds Abbey Life, 1980–91. Non-exec. Dir, Grand Metropolitan, 1994. *Recreations:* reading, golf.

HEPPEL, Peter John Merrick; QC 1992; a Recorder, since 1988; *b* 31 March 1948; *s* of late John Edward Thomas and Ida Florence Heppel, Romford, Essex; *m* 1980, Janice Coulton; two *s* two *d. Educ:* Royal Liberty Sch., Romford; Univ. of Hull (LLB Hons); University Coll. London (LLM). Called to the Bar, Middle Temple, 1970 (Harmsworth Scholar); in practice, NE Circuit, 1972–. *Recreations:* music, reading, cricket. *Address:* Warriston, Parkfield Avenue, North Ferriby, Humberside HU14 3AL; Paradise Chambers, 12 Paradise Square, Sheffield S1 2DE. *T:* Sheffield (0114) 273 8951; 4 King's Bench Walk, Temple, EC4Y 7DL. *T:* 0171–353 0478; Wilberforce Chambers, 171 High Street, Hull HU1 1NE. *T:* Hull (01482) 23264. *Club:* Sloane.

HEPPELL, John; MP (Lab) Nottingham East, since 1992; *b* 3 Nov. 1948; *m* 1974, Eileen Golding; two *s* one *d. Educ:* Rutherford Grammar Sch.; SE Northumberland Technical Coll.; Ashington Technical Coll. Fitter: NCB, 1964–70; various cos, 1970–75; diesel fitter, 1975–78, workshop supervisor, 1978–89, British Rail. Mem. (Lab) Nottinghamshire CC, 1981–93. *Address:* House of Commons, SW1A 0AA.

HEPPELL, (Thomas) Strachan, CB 1986; Consultant, Department of Health; Chairman, Management Board, European Medicines Evaluation Agency; *b* 15 Aug. 1935; *s* of late Leslie Thomas Davidson Heppell and Doris Abbey Heppell (*née* Potts); *m* 1963, Felicity Ann Rice; two *s. Educ:* Acklam Hall Grammar Sch., Middlesbrough; The Queen's Coll., Oxford. National Assistance Board, Ministry of Social Security/DHSS: Asst Principal, 1958; Principal, 1963–73 (seconded to Cabinet Office, 1967–69); Asst Director of Social Welfare, Hong Kong, 1971–73; Asst Sec., DHSS, 1973–78 (Social Security Adviser, Hong Kong Govt, 1977); Under Sec., DHSS, 1979–83; Dep. Sec., DHSS, later DoH, 1983. *Publications:* contribs on health and social welfare. *Recreations:* gardening, travelling. *Address:* Department of Health, Richmond House, 79 Whitehall, SW1A 2NS.

HEPPER, Anthony Evelyn, CEng, FIMechE; CIMgt; Chairman, Hyde Sails Ltd, since 1984; *b* 16 Jan. 1923; *s* of Lieut-Col J. E. Hepper; *m* 1970, Jonquil Francisca Kinloch-Jones. *Educ:* Wellington Coll., Berks. Royal Engrs, 1942–47 (retd as Hon. Major); Courtaulds Ltd, 1947–53; Cape Asbestos Co. Ltd 1953–57; Thomas Tilling Ltd, 1957–68 (Dir from 1963 until secondment), seconded as Industrial Adviser, DEA, 1966–67, and Mem., SIB, 1967; Chairman: Upper Clyde Shipbuilders Ltd, 1968–71; Henry Sykes Ltd, 1972–81; Richardsons Westgarth plc, 1982–85; Lamont & Partners plc, 1986–90. Director: Cape plc, 1968–94; Cardinal Investment Trust plc, 1982–84; General Investors Trustees plc, 1982–84; F. & Pacific Investment Trust PLC, 1984–87. *Recreation:* golf. *Address:* 70 Eaton Place, SW1X 8AT. *T:* 0171–235 7518. *Club:* Boodle's.

HEPPLE, Prof. Bob Alexander, LLD; Master of Clare College, Cambridge, since 1993; Professor of Law, University of Cambridge, since 1995; *b* 11 Aug. 1934; *s* of late Alexander Hepple and Josephine Zwarenstein; *m* 1st, 1960, Shirley Goldsmith; one *s* one *d*; 2nd, 1993, Mary Coussey. *Educ:* Univ. of Witwatersrand (BA 1954, LLB *cum laude* 1957); Univ. of Cambridge (LLB 1966; MA 1969; LLD 1993). Attorney, S Africa, 1958; Lectr in Law, Univ. of Witwatersrand, 1959–62; Advocate, S Africa, 1962–63. Left S Africa after detention without trial for anti-apartheid activities, 1963. Called to Bar, Gray's Inn, 1966; Lectr in Law, Nottingham Univ., 1966–68; Fellow of Clare Coll., Cambridge and Univ. Lectr in Law, 1968–76; Prof. of Comparative Social and Labour Law, Univ. of Kent, 1976–77 (Hon. Prof., 1978–83); Prof. of English Law, 1982–93, Dean of Faculty of Laws and Head of Dept of Laws, 1989–93, Vis. Prof., 1993–, UCL; Chm., Cttee of Heads of Univ. Law Schs, 1992–93. Chairman: Industrial Tribunals (England and Wales), pt-time 1975–77 and 1982–93, full-time 1977–82; Cttee, Justice Report on Industrial Tribunals, 1987. Member: Judicial Studies Bd (Tribunals Cttee), 1988–93; Lord Chancellor's Adv. Cttee on Legal Educn and Conduct, 1994–. Mem., CRE, 1986–90. Expert consultant to EC Commn, 1974–, and to ILO, 1990–; Advr to Russian Fedn, 1992, to S African Govt, 1994–. *Publications:* various books and articles on labour law, race relations, law of tort, etc; Founding Editor, Industrial Law Jl, 1972–77; Gen. Ed (jtly) Encyclopedia of Labour Relations Law, 1972–90; Chief Editor, International Encyclopedia of Comparative Law, Vol. XV, Labour Law, 1979–. *Address:* The Master's Lodge, Clare College, Cambridge CB2 1TL. *Club:* Reform.

HEPPLESTON, Prof. Alfred Gordon; Professor of Pathology, University of Newcastle upon Tyne (formerly Durham), 1960–77, now Emeritus Professor; *b* 29 Aug. 1915; *s* of Alfred Heppleston, Headmaster, and Edith (*née* Clough); *m* 1942, Eleanor Rix Tebbutt; two *s. Educ:* Manchester Grammar Sch. Chief Asst, Professorial Medical Unit, University of Manchester; Asst Lecturer in Pathology, Welsh Nat. Sch. of Medicine, Univ. of Wales, 1944–47; Dorothy Temple Cross Research Fellow, Univ. of Pennsylvania, 1947–48; Sen. Lectr in Pathology, Univ. of Wales, 1948–60. *Publications:* on pathological topics, largely in reference to pulmonary disorders. *Recreations:* ornithology, cricket and music. *Address:* Bridgeford Gate, Bellingham, Hexham, Northumberland NE48 2HT. *T:* Bellingham (01434) 220431.

HEPPLEWHITE, Rosalind Mary Joy, (Ros); Chief Executive, Child Support Agency, 1992–94; *b* 20 Dec. 1952; *d* of Anne and Anthony Phillips; *m* 1971, Julian Hepplewhite; one *s* one *d. Educ:* University College London (BA Hons). Asst House Governor, 1980–83, and Hosp. Sec., 1983–84, Bethlem Royal and Maudsley Hosps; Unit Administrator (Mental Health), Hammersmith and Fulham HA, 1984–85; Unit Gen. Manager (Mental Health and Mental Handicap), 1985–88, Dir, Corporate Develt, 1988–89, Brighton HA; Nat. Dir, MIND (Nat. Assoc. of Mental Health), 1989–91. *Recreation:* home and family.

HEPTINSTALL, Leslie George; HM Diplomatic Service, retired; *b* 20 Aug. 1919; *s* late Victor George Heptinstall and Maud Maunder; *m* 1949, Marion Nicholls (*d* 1986); one *d. Educ:* Thames Valley County Sch.; London Univ. (BSc Econ.). Served War of 1939–45: Capt., Royal Artillery; Middle East, Mediterranean, North-West Europe. Asst Principal, Colonial Office, 1948; Principal, 1951; seconded to West African Inter-Territorial Secretariat, Accra, 1955; Acting Chief Sec., 1958; Acting Administrator, W African Research Office, 1959; Principal, CRO, 1961; First Sec. on Staff of Brit. High Comr, Wellington, NZ, 1962–64; Brit. Dep. High Comr, Lahore, 1964–65; Head of South Asia Dept, ODM, 1966–68; Dep. Senior Trade Comr, Montreal, 1968–70; Internat. Coffee Orgn, 1971–73. *Recreations:* sailing, golf and tennis. *Address:* 34 Church Street, Leatherhead, Surrey KT22 8DW.

HEPWORTH, Rear-Adm. David, CB 1976; retired from RN, 1976; *b* 6 June 1923; *s* of Alfred Ernest Hepworth and Minnie Louisa Catherine Bennet Tanner (*née* Bowden); *m* 1st, 1946, Brenda June Case (marr. diss. 1974); one *s* one *d*; 2nd, 1975, Eileen Mary Macgillivray (*née* Robson). *Educ:* Banbury Grammar School. Boy Telegraphist, RN, 1939; HMS Ganges, 1939–40; served in Atlantic, Mediterranean and E Indies Fleets; commnd 1944; submarines and midget submarines, 1945–50; Home, Australian and Far East Stns, 1951–58; Sen. Officer Submarines Londonderry, 1959–61; CO HMS Ashanti, 1961–64; jssc 1964; Dep. Dir Undersea Warfare, MoD, 1964–66; idc 1967; CO HMS Ajax and Captain (D) 2nd Far East Destroyer Sqdn, 1968–69; Dir RN Tactical Sch. and Maritime Tactical Sch., 1969–71; Dir Naval Warfare, MoD, 1971–73; Staff of Vice-Chief of Naval Staff, 1973–76. Lt-Comdr 1952; Comdr 1958; Captain 1964; Rear-Adm. 1974. Naval Advr to Internat. Military Services Ltd, 1977–83. *Recreations:* home and garden. *Address:* Darville House, Lower Heyford, Oxon OX6 3PD. *T:* Steeple Aston (01869) 347460.

HEPWORTH, Noel Peers, OBE 1980; Director, Chartered Institute of Public Finance and Accountancy, since 1980; *b* 22 Dec. 1934; *m* 1963, Jean Margaret Aldcroft; one *s* three *d.* *Educ:* Crewe County Grammar Sch.; London Univ. IPFA 1958; DPA 1963. Nat. Service, RAF, 1953–55. NW Gas Bd, 1951–58; Asst City Treasurer, Manchester, 1965–72; Dir of Finance, Croydon, 1972–80. Financial Advr to London Boroughs Assoc. and AMA, 1972–80; Mem., London Treasurers' Adv. Body, 1972–80; Member: Dept of Envt Property Adv. Group, 1980–88; Audit Commn, 1983–91. Pres., Internat. Consortium on Governmental Financial Management, 1987–92. Chm., FEE Public Sector Cttee, 1988–. FRSA 1985. Freeman, City of London, 1991. *Publications:* Finance of Local Government, 1970, 7th edn 1984, Japanese edn 1983; Housing Rents, Costs and Subsidies, 1978, 2nd edn 1981; contribs to technical and financial jls, local govt press and nat. and internat press. *Recreations:* gardening, walking. *Address:* Chartered Institute of Public Finance and Accountancy, 2–3 Robert Street, WC2N 6BH. *T:* 0171–895 8823.

HERALD, John Pearson; Sheriff of North Strathclyde, since 1992; *b* 12 July 1946; *s* of Andrew James Herald and Martha Wilson or Herald; *m* 1969, Catriona McDougall Anderson; one *d.* *Educ:* Hillhead High Sch., Glasgow; Univ. of Glasgow (LLB). Partner, Carlton Gilruth, Dundee, 1971–91; Dir, William Halley & Sons, Dundee, 1988–91. Depute Town Clerk, Newport-on-Tay, 1970–75; Temp. Sheriff, 1984–91; Chm., Industrial Tribunals, 1984–91. Sec., Angus Legal Aid Cttee, 1979–87; Mem., Legal Aid Central Cttee, 1981–87; Chm., Dundee CAB, 1972–79 and 1982–91. *Recreations:* reading, golf, soccer. *Address:* Sheriff's Chambers, Sheriff Court House, 1 Nelson Street, Bogston, Greenock PA15 1TR. *T:* Greenock (01475) 787073.

HERAT, (James Edward) Harold, MP (United National Party) Puttalam District, Sri Lanka, since 1989; Minister of Justice, 1993–94; State Minister of Finance, 1989–94; *b* 10 Nov. 1930; *s* of Dr Albert Edward Herat and Enid Evangeline Henrietta Dagmar Herat; *m* 1965, Gwendoline; one *s* two *d.* *Educ:* Maris Stella Coll., Negombo; St Joseph's Coll., Colombo. Attorney-at-Law. MP (UNP) Nattandiya, NW Province, 1977; Minister of Coconut Industries, 1978, and concurrently Dep. Minister, Janatha Estates Develt, 1980; Minister of Foreign Affairs, 1990–93. Mem., Court of Univ. of Sri Lanka, 1980, 1981, 1982. JP and Unofficial Magistrate, 1968. *Recreations:* tennis, riding, swimming. *Address:* Mudukatuwa Estate, Marawila, Sri Lanka. *Clubs:* Sri Lanka Tennis Association (Vice-Patron), Marawila Sports (Patron).

HERBECQ, Sir John (Edward), KCB 1977; a Church Commissioner, 1982–March 1996; *b* 29 May 1922; *s* of late Joseph Edward and Rosina Elizabeth Herbecq; *m* 1947, Pamela Filby; one *d.* *Educ:* High Sch. for Boys, Chichester. Clerical Officer, Colonial Office, 1939; Asst Principal, Treasury, 1950; Private Sec. to Chm., UK Atomic Energy Authority, 1960–62; Asst Sec., Treasury, 1964; Asst Sec., 1968, Under Sec., 1970, Dep. Sec., 1973, Second Permanent Sec., 1975–81, CSD. Dep. Chm., Review Body for Nursing Staff, Midwives, Health Visitors and Professions Allied to Medicine, 1986–91 (Mem., 1983–91); Chm., Malaŵi Civil Service Review Commn, 1984–85. Member: C of E Pensions Bd, 1985–89; Chichester Diocesan Bd of Finance, 1983– (Chm., 1989–). *Recreations:* Scottish country dancing (ISTD Supreme Award with Hons), walking, watching cricket. *Address:* Maryland, Ledgers Meadow, Cuckfield, Haywards Heath, West Sussex RH17 5EW. *T:* Haywards Heath (01444) 413387.

HERBERT, family name of **Earls of Carnarvon, Pembroke,** and **Powis,** and **Baron Hemingford.**

HERBERT, Lord; William Alexander Sidney Herbert; *b* 18 May 1978; *s* and *heir* of Earl of Pembroke and Montgomery, *qv.*

HERBERT, Alfred James; British Council Representative, Portugal, 1980–84, retired; *b* 16 Oct. 1924; *s* of Allen Corbyn Herbert and Betty Herbert; *m* 1st, 1958, Helga Elberling (*d* 1981); two *s*; 2nd, 1982, Dr Wanda Wolska. *Educ:* Royal Masonic Schs; University Coll. London (BA 1950, MA 1952). Guest Prof. of English Lit., Univs of Yokohama and Tokyo, 1958–60; Lectr, English Dept, Birmingham Univ., 1960–62; joined British Council, 1962: Sierra Leone, 1962–65; Brazil, 1965–68; Representative: Somalia, 1968–70; Pakistan, 1974–77; Poland, 1977–80. *Publications:* Modern English Novelists, (Japan), 1960; Structure of Technical English, 1965. *Recreations:* travelling, reading. *Address:* Quinta do Val do Riso, São Simão, Azeitão, 2900 Setubal, Portugal.

HERBERT, Brian Douglas; Director of Performance Review, East Anglian Regional Health Authority, 1989–91; *b* 29 May 1930; *s* of Stanley and Kathleen Herbert; *m* 1st, 1952, Linda (marr. diss.); two *s* one *d*; 2nd, 1973, Lila; one *d.* *Educ:* Ipswich School. IPFA. Local Govt Finance, 1946–63; Health Service: Asst Treasurer, NW Metropolitan RHB, 1963; Group Treasurer, SW Middlesex HMC, 1967; Area Treasurer, Ealing, Hammersmith and Hounslow AHA(T), 1973; Regional Treasurer, 1981, Dir of Finance and Administration, 1985, E Anglian RHA. *Address:* 3 Dane Drive, Cambridge CB3 9LP. *T:* Cambridge (01223) 355823.

HERBERT, Rt Rev. Christopher William; *see* St Albans, Bishop of.

HERBERT, (Dennis) Nicholas; (3rd Baron Hemingford, *cr* 1943, of Watford); Deputy Chief Executive, Westminster Press, 1992–95 (Editorial Director, 1974–92); *b* 25 July 1934; *s* of 2nd Baron Hemingford and Elizabeth McClare (*d* 1979), *d* of Col J. M. Clark, Haltwhistle, Northumberland; *S* father, 1982; remains known professionally as Nicholas Herbert; *m* 1958, Jennifer Mary Toresen Bailey, *d* of F. W. Bailey, Harrogate; one *s* three *d.* *Educ:* Oundle Sch.; Clare Coll., Cambridge (MA). Reuters Ltd, 1956–61; The Times: Asst Washington Corresp., 1961–65; Middle East Corresp., 1965–68; Dep. Features Editor, 1968–70; Editor, Cambridge Evening News, 1970–74. Vice-Pres., Guild of British Newspaper Editors, 1979, Pres., 1980–81. Mem. Bd, Assoc. of British Editors (Hon. Sec., 1985–95). Pres., Huntingdonshire Family History Soc., 1985–. Chm., East Anglia Regl Cttee, Nat. Trust, 1990–. Trustee, Bell Educnl Trust, 1985–90. *Heir:* *s* Hon. Christopher Dennis Charles Herbert, *b* 4 July 1973. *Address:* Old Rectory, Hemingford Abbots, Huntingdon PE18 9AH. *T:* St Ives (Hunts) (01480) 466234. *Clubs:* Commonwealth Trust, City Livery.

See also Hon. Lady Goodhart.

HERBERT, Frederick William; Emeritus Fellow in Industrial Relations, International Management Centre, Buckingham, 1985–92; Chairman, NALGO Insurance Association Ltd, 1981–93; *b* London, 18 Dec. 1922; *s* of late William Herbert and Alice Herbert; *m* 1948, Nina Oesterman; two *d.* *Educ:* Ealing Boys' Grammar Sch. Served RAFVR, 1942–46. Local Govt Finance, Mddx CC, 1939–65; Greater London Council: Local Govt Finance, 1965–72; Personnel Management, Estabt Officer, 1972–77; Asst Dir of Personnel, 1977–80; Head of Industrial Relations, 1980–82; Controller of Personnel, 1982–84. Parly Correspondent, Eurotunnel (UK), 1986–87. FRSA 1986. *Recreations:* cricket, music (classical and jazz), theatre, Antient Society of Cogers (debating). *Address:* 20 Priory Hill, Wembley, Mddx HA0 2QF. *T:* 0181–904 8634. *Clubs:* Royal Over-Seas League, MCC.

HERBERT, Prof. Harold Bernard; consultant, holistic learning; *b* 10 March 1924; *s* of late A. Bernard Henbest and Edith Winifred Henbest (*née* Herbert); *m* 1948, Rosalind Eve Skone James; two *s* one *d.* *Educ:* Barking Abbey Sch.; Imperial Coll. of Science, London. Beit Research Fellow, 1947–48; Lectr, University of Manchester, 1948–56; Research Fellow, Harvard Univ., 1953–54; Vis. Prof., UCLA, 1954; Reader, KCL, 1956–57; Prof of Organic Chemistry, QUB, 1958–73. Founder, The Learning Soc., 1988. *Publications:* Organic Chemistry (with M. F. Grundon), 1968; contribs to Jl of Chemical Soc. *Address:* 5 Witley Court, Coram Street, WC1N 1HD. *T:* 0171–278 0888.

HERBERT, Jeffrey William, FEng, FIMechE; Chief Executive, Charter plc, since 1990; *b* 21 July 1942; *s* of Alexander William John Herbert and Amy (*née* Whitwell); *m* 1965, Sheila Heane; one *s* two *d.* *Educ:* Loughborough Univ. (DLC, BEng Mech. and Prodn Engrg). MIEE 1968; FIMechE 1992; FEng 1993. Managing Director: Rover-Triumph Cars Ltd, 1976–81; GEC Diesels Ltd, 1981–85; Exec. Dir, Industry, Charter Consolidated PLC, 1985–89. Chairman: Cape, 1985–; Anderson Gp, 1987–; Non-Executive Director: Vickers, 1991–; M & G Investment Trust, 1992–. FRSA 1993. Freeman, City of London, 1993; Liveryman, Wheelwrights' Co., 1993. *Recreations:* shooting, jogging, tennis, veteran and classic cars. *Address:* Charter plc, 7 Hobart Place, SW1W 0HH. *T:* 0171–838 7000.

HERBERT, Jocelyn, Hon. ARCA 1964; RDI 1971; *b* 22 Feb. 1917; *d* of Sir Alan Patrick Herbert, CH, and Gwendolen (*née* Quilter); *m* 1937, Anthony Lousada (marr. diss. 1960); one *s* three *d.* *Educ:* St Paul's Girls' Sch.; Paris and Vienna; London Theatre Studio; Slade School of Art. Started painting at André L'Hote's Sch., Paris, 1932–33; studied drawing and painting with Leon Underwood, 1934; trained as theatre designer with Michel St Denis and George Devine, London Th. Studio, 1936–37; joined staff of English Stage Co., Royal Court Th., 1956; became freelance designer, 1958, centred largely on Royal Court. Hon. FRA, 1991. *Plays designed,* 1957–: *Royal Court Theatre:* Ionesco: The Chairs, The Lesson, Exit the King; W. B. Yeats: Purgatory; Ann Jellico: Sport of My Mad Mother; Samuel Beckett: Krapp's Last Tape, Happy Days, Not I, Footfalls, That Time; Arnold Wesker: Roots, The Kitchen, I'm Talking about Jerusalem, Chips with Everything; Arden: Serjeant Musgrave's Dance; Christopher Logue: Trials by Logue, Antigone, The Trial of Cob and Leach; Middleton: The Changeling; Shakespeare: Midsummer Night's Dream, Julius Caesar; John Osborne: Luther, A Patriot for Me, Inadmissible Evidence; Barry Reckford: Skyvers; W. Solvonka: The Lion and the Jewel; O'Neil and Seabrook: Life Price; Donald Howarth: Three Months Gone; David Storey: Home, The Changing Room, Cromwell, Life Class; Christopher Hampton: Savages, The Portage to San Cristobal of A. H.; Joe Orton: What the Butler Saw; David Hare: Teeth 'n' Smiles; Mustapha Matura: Rum and Coca Cola; *RSC:* Richard III; Ibsen's Ghosts; *Phoenix:* Brecht's Baal; Ronald Harwood's J. J. Fahr; *National Theatre:* Othello; Brecht's Mother Courage and Life of Galileo; A Woman Killed with Kindness; Adrian Mitchell's Tyger; David Storey's Early Days; Aeschylus' The Oresteia; Tony Harrison: The Trackers of Oxyrhynchus; Square Rounds; David Storey: Early Days; The March on Russia; Stages; *Queen's:* The Seagull; Brecht's Joan of the Stockyard; *Round House:* Hamlet; *Albery:* Pygmalion; *Aldwych:* Saratoga; (New York) Wesker's The Merchant; *Haymarket:* Heartbreak House; *Lyric, Hammersmith:* The Devil and the Good Lord; *Lyric, Shaftesbury Ave:* Gigi; *Haymarket, Leicester:* Timon of Athens; Julius Caesar; Sophocles' Creon. *Opera,* 1967, and 1975–: Sadler's Wells: Gluck's Orpheus and Euridice; Paris Opera: Verdi's The Force of Destiny, 1975; Metropolitan, NY: Alban Berg's Lulu, 1977; Mozart's The Abduction, 1979; Brecht and Weil's Rise and Fall of the City of Mahagonny, 1979; Coliseum: Birtwistle's The Mask of Orpheus, 1986. *Films:* Tony Richardson: (colour cons. and costumes) Tom Jones, 1961, (prodn designer) Hamlet, 1969, Ned Kelly, 1970, Hotel New Hampshire, 1983; Karel Reiss: (prodn designer) Isadora, 1968; Lindsay Anderson: (prodn designer) If . . . , 1969, O Lucky Man!, 1972; Whales of August, 1987. Retrospective exhibn of theatre work, Royal Nat. Theatre, 1993. *Relevant publication:* Jocelyn Herbert: a theatre workbook, ed Cathy Courtney, 1993. *Recreations:* the country, painting. *Address:* 45 Pottery Lane, W11 4LY. *T:* 0171–727 1104.

HERBERT, Mark Jeremy; QC 1995; *b* 12 Nov. 1948; *yr s* of late Kenneth Falkner Herbert and of Kathleen Ellis Herbert; *m* 1977, Shiranikha Pullenayegum. *Educ:* Lancing Coll,; King's Coll., London (BA). Called to the Bar, Lincoln's Inn, 1974; in practice at Chancery Bar, 1975–. *Publications:* (contrib.) Whiteman on Capital Gains Tax, 4th edn 1988; Drafting and Variation of Wills, 1989. *Recreation:* bell-ringing. *Address:* 5 Stone Buildings, Lincoln's Inn, WC2A 3XT. *T:* 0171–242 6201. *Club:* Royal Automobile.

HERBERT, Nicholas; *see* Herbert, D. N.

HERBERT, Adm. Sir Peter (Geoffrey Marshall), KCB 1983; OBE 1969; Non-Executive Director: Radamec Group plc, since 1985; Forces Safeguard Trust, since 1992; consultant; *b* 28 Feb. 1929; *s* of A. G. S. Herbert and P. K. M. Herbert; *m* 1953, Ann Maureen (*née* McKeown); one *s* one *d.* *Educ:* Dunchurch Hall; RN Coll., Dartmouth. Specialised in submarines, 1949; served in submarines, 1950–68: Comd HM Submarines Scythian, Porpoise and Excalibur, 1956–60; Submarine Staff, 1960–62; Comd nuclear submarine, HMS Valiant, 1963–68; Comd HMS Venus, 1964; Dep. Dir, Naval Equipment, 1969; Comd 10th (Polaris) Submarine Squadron, 1970–72; COS to Flag Officer Submarines, 1972–74; Comd HMS Blake, 1974–75; Dep. Chief, Polaris Exec., 1976–78; Flag Officer Carriers and Amphibious Ships, 1978–79; Dir Gen., Naval Manpower and Training, 1980–81; Flag Officer Submarines and Comdr Submarines Eastern Atlantic, 1981–83; VCDS (Personnel and Logistics), 1983–84. Chm., SSAFA, 1985–93. Pres., Glos Br., King George's Fund for Sailors, 1990–. Governor: Cheam School, 1987– (Chm., 1992–); Cheltenham Ladies' Coll., 1993–. Chm. Parent Body, Royal Soc. of St George, 1995–. CIMgt; MINucE. *Recreations:* woodwork, gardening, swimming. *Address:* Dolphin Square, SW1. *T:* 0171–798 8330. *Club:* Army and Navy.

HERBERT, Prof. Robert Louis, PhD; Professor, Department of Art, Mount Holyoke College, Mass., since 1990; *b* 21 April 1929; *s* of John Newman Herbert and Rosalia Harr Herbert; *m* 1953, Eugenia Randall Warren; one *s* two *d.* *Educ:* Wesleyan Univ., Middletown, Conn (BA 1951); Yale Univ. (MA 1954, PhD 1957). Fulbright Scholar, Paris, 1951–52; Faculty, Yale Univ., 1956–90: Associate Prof., 1963; Prof., 1966; Departmental Chm., 1965–68; Robert Lehman Prof. of Hist. of Art, 1974–90. Guggenheim Fellow, 1971–72; Slade Prof. of Fine Art, Oxford, 1978. Organizer of exhibitions: Barbizon Revisited, Boston Museum of Fine Arts and others, 1962–63; Neo-Impressionism, Solomon R. Guggenheim Mus., 1968; J. F. Millet, Musées Nationaux, Paris, and Arts Council, London, 1975–76; Léger's Le Grand Déjeuner, Minneapolis Inst. of Arts and Detroit Inst. of Arts, 1980; Seurat, Museés Nationaux, Paris and Metropolitan Mus., NY, 1991. Fellow, Amer. Acad. of Arts and Sciences, 1978; Mem., Amer. Philosophical Soc., 1993. Chevalier, 1976, Officier, 1990, Ordre des Arts et des Lettres. *Publications:* Barbizon Revisited, 1962–63; Seurat's Drawings, 1963; The Art Criticism of John Ruskin, 1964; Modern Artists on Art, 1964; Neo-Impressionism, 1968; David, Voltaire, 'Brutus' and the French Revolution, 1972; J. F. Millet, 1975; (ed jtly) Société Anonyme and Dreier Bequest at Yale University: a catalogue raisonné, 1984; Impressionism: art, leisure and Parisian society, 1988; Monet on the Normandy Coast, 1994; articles in learned jls. *Address:* Department of Art, Mount Holyoke College, South Hadley, MA 01075, USA.

HERBERT, Robin Arthur Elidyr, CBE 1994; DL; JP; Chairman: Leopold Joseph Holdings PLC, since 1978; Union PLC (formerly Union Discount Company of London), since 1990 (Director, since 1989); *b* 5 March 1934; *s* of late Sir John Arthur Herbert, GCIE and Lady Mary Herbert; *m* 1st, 1960, Margaret Griswold Lewis (marr. diss. 1988);

two *s* two *d*; 2nd, 1988, Philippa Harriet King. *Educ:* Eton; Christ Church, Oxford (MA); Harvard Business School (MBA). ARICS. 2nd Lieut Royal Horse Guards, 1953–54; Captain Royal Monmouthshire RE, 1962–68. Chairman: Lands Improvement Gp Ltd, 1991–; Foreign & Colonial Income Growth Investment Trust, 1994–; Director: Nat. Westminster Bank, 1972–92; Agricl Mortgage Corp., 1985–93; Marks & Spencer, 1986–91; Consolidated Gold Fields, 1986–89 (Dep. Chm., 1988–89); F&C Smaller Companies Investment Trust, 1985–; Federated Aggregates, 1991–; SWOAC Holdings, 1990–. Financial Advisor: Water Superannuation Fund, 1986–89; Nat. Rivers Authy. Mem. Council, BBA, 1992–. Dep. Chm., Countryside Commn, 1971–80; Member: Council, National Trust, 1969–87 (Mem., Exec. Cttee, 1969–84; Chm. Cttee for Wales, 1969–84); Nat. Water Council, 1980–83; Welsh Develt Agency, 1980–86; Darwin Initiative Adv. Cttee, 1993–; Royal Parks Agency Adv. Gp, 1993–. Royal Horticultural Society: Mem. Council, 1971–74 and 1979–94; Pres. and Chm. Council, 1984–94; Pres. Emeritus, 1994–. Trustee, Royal Botanic Gardens, Kew, 1987– (Chm., 1991–). DL 1968, JP 1964, High Sheriff 1972, Monmouthshire. *Recreations:* dendrology, walking. *Address:* Llanover, Abergavenny, Gwent NP7 9EF. *T:* Nantyderry (01873) 880232. *Clubs:* Brooks's, Pratt's.

HERBERT, Walter William, (Wally Herbert); *b* 24 Oct. 1934; *s* of Captain W. W. J. Herbert and Helen (*née* Manton); *m* 1969, Marie, *d* of Prof. C. A. McGaughey; one *d* (and one *d* decd). Trained as surveyor in RE; Egypt, 1953–54, demob. 1955; travelled in Middle East, 1955; Surveyor with Falkland Is Dependencies Survey; Hope Bay, Antarctica, 1955–58; travelled in S America, 1958–59; Mem. expedn to Lapland and Spitzbergen, 1960; travelled in Greenland, 1960; Surveyor, NZ Antarctic Expedn, 1960–62; leader Southern Party; mapped 26,000 sq. miles of Queen Maud Range and descended Amundsen's route to Pole on 50th anniv.; led expedn to NW Greenland, 1966–67; dog-sledged 1,400 miles Greenland to Canada in trng for trans-Arctic crossing; led British Trans-Arctic Expedn, 1968–69, which made 3,800–mile first surface crossing of Arctic Ocean from Alaska via North Pole to Spitzbergen; led Ultima Thule expedn (filming Eskimos, Thule District), 1971–73; led expedn to Lapland, 1975; led expedn to Greenland, 1978–82 (attempting first circumnavigation by dog sledge and skin boat); led filming expedn to NW Greenland, Ellesmere Island and North Pole, 1987. One-man exhibitions: QE-2, 1994; Explorers Club, NY, 1994; Jamestown Coll., NY, 1994; Australian Geographic Soc., 1994. Hon. Mem., British Schools Exploring Soc.; Jt Hon. Pres., World Expeditionary Assoc. FRGS. Hon. Fellow, New World Acad., 1993. Polar Medal 1962, and clasp 1969; Livingstone Gold Medal, RSGS, 1969; Founder's Gold Medal, RGS, 1970; City of Paris Medal, 1983; French Geog. Soc. Medal, 1983; Explorers' Medal, Explorers' Club, 1985; Finn Ronne Award, 1985. *Publications:* A World of Men, 1968; Across the Top of the World, 1969; (contrib.) World Atlas of Mountaineering, 1969; The Last Great Journey on Earth, 1971; Polar Deserts, 1971; Eskimos, 1976 (Jugendbuchpreis, 1977); North Pole, 1978; (contrib.) Expeditions the Expert's Way, 1977; (contrib.) Bell House Book, 1978; Hunters of the Polar North, 1982; The Noose of Laurels, 1989. *Recreation:* painting. *Address:* c/o Royal Geographical Society, SW7 2AR. *Clubs:* Lansdowne; Explorers (NY).

HERBERT, William Penry Millwarden; Member, Cardiff City Council, 1970–March 1996; Lord Mayor of Cardiff, 1988–89; *b* 31 March 1921; *s* of William John Herbert and Esabella Marinda Francis; *m* 1945, Ellen Vera McCarthy; two *d* (one *s* decd). *Educ:* Argoed Elementary Sch., Blackwood, Monmouthshire. Cert. of Professional Competence, Transport, 1977. Miner, 1934–37; Railwayman, 1937–45. Served RE, 1945–47. 1947–78: Guest Keen Iron and Steel Works; Guest Keen and Baldwins British Steel Corp.; Plant Supervisor, Traffic Foreman, Transport Manager. *Recreations:* dancing, gardening, reading, travel. *Address:* 27 Wellwood, Llanedeyrn, Cardiff, South Glamorgan CF3 7JP. *Club:* City Social (Cathays, Cardiff).

HERBERT-JONES, Hugh Jarrett, (Hugo), CMG 1973; OBE 1963; HM Diplomatic Service, retired, company director; *b* 11 March 1922; *s* of late Dora Herbert-Jones (*née* Rowlands), MBE and Captain Herbert-Jones; *m* 1954, Margaret, *d* of Rev. J. P. Veall; one *s* two *d*. *Educ:* Bryanston; Worcester Coll., Oxford. History Scholar. Commnd Welsh Guards, 1941; served NW Europe and Middle East; wounded 1944; demobilised 1946 (Major). Entered Foreign (later Diplomatic) Service, 1947; served: Hamburg, 1947; Berlin, 1949; Hong Kong, 1951; Phnom Penh, 1955; Saigon, 1956; Nairobi, 1959; Pretoria/Cape Town, 1963; FCO, 1966; Paris, 1973; FCO, 1975–79; Internat. Affairs Dir, CBI, 1979–87. Chm., Aldeburgh Soc., 1988–93. *Recreations:* sailing, golf, shooting, music, spectator sports. *Address:* Prior's Hill, Aldeburgh, Suffolk IP15 5ET. *T:* Aldeburgh (01728) 453335; 408 Nelson House, Dolphin Square, SW1V 3NZ. *T:* 0171–798 8625. *Clubs:* Garrick, MCC; London Welsh Rugby Football; Aldeburgh Golf; Aldeburgh Yacht.

HERBISON, Dame Jean (Marjory), DBE 1985; CMG 1976; Associate Director, Christchurch Polytechnic, New Zealand, 1975–84, retired; *b* 29 April 1923; *d* of William Herbison and Sarah Jane Herbison (*née* McKendry). *Educ:* Univ. of Canterbury (BA); Auckland Teachers' Coll. (Dip Teaching); Univ. of Northern Iowa (MA); Inst. of Education, Univ. of London. AIE 1974. Teaching, Avonside Girls' High School, Christchurch, 1952–59; Dean, 1960–68, Vice-Principal, 1968–74, Christchurch Teachers' Coll.; Assoc. Dir, Christchurch Polytechnic, 1975–84; Mem. Council, 1970–84, Chancellor, 1979–84, Univ. of Canterbury. Chairperson, NZ Council for Educnl Research, 1986–88 (Mem., 1977–88); Member: UGC, 1985–90; Ministerial Cttee of Inquiry into Curriculum, Assessment and Qualifications in the Senior Secondary Sch., 1985–87; Commonwealth Council for Educnl Admin, 1970– (Vice-Pres., 1982–86); NZ Vice-Chancellors' Cttee, Univ. Review Panel, 1987. Fellow: Commonwealth Council for Educnl Admin., 1986; NZ Educnl Admin. Soc., 1990; Hon. Fellow: NZ Educnl Inst.; NZ Inst. of Management. Hon. DLitt Canterbury, 1987. Queen's Silver Jubilee Medal, 1977. *Recreations:* gardening, walking, reading. *Address:* 2/172 Soleares Avenue, Christchurch 8, New Zealand. *T:* (3) 3849086.

HERBISON, Rt. Hon. Margaret McCrorie, PC 1964; Lord High Commissioner to the General Assembly of the Church of Scotland, 1970–71; *b* 11 March 1907. *Educ:* Dykehead Public Sch., Shotts; Bellshill Acad.; Glasgow Univ. Teacher of English and History in Glasgow Schs; MP (Lab) North Lanark, 1945–70; Jt Parly Under-Sec. of State, Scottish Office, 1950–51; Minister of Pensions and National Insurance, Oct. 1964–Aug. 1966, of Social Security, 1966–67. Chm., Select Cttee on Overseas Aid, 1969–. Member National Executive Cttee, Labour Party; Chm. Labour Party, 1957. Mem., Royal Commn on Standards of Conduct in Public Life, 1974–. Scotswoman of the Year, 1970. Hon. LLD Glasgow, 1970. *Recreations:* reading, gardening. *Address:* 8 Mornay Way, Shotts, Lanarkshire ML7 4EG. *T:* Shotts (01501) 821944.

HERCUS, Hon. Dame (Margaret) Ann, DCMG 1988; international consultant, since 1991; *b* 24 Feb. 1942; *d* of Horace Sayers and Mary (*née* Ryan); *m* John Hercus; two *s*. *Educ:* Victoria Univ. of Wellington; Univs. of Auckland (BA) and Canterbury (LLB). Lawyer and Staff Training Officer, Beath & Co., Christchurch, 1969–70; Mem., Price Tribunal and Trade Practices Commn, 1973–75; Dep. Chm., Commerce Commn, 1975–78; Chm., Consumer Rights Campaign, 1975; MP (Lab) Lyttleton, 1978–87; in opposition, 1978–84; Minister of Social Welfare, Police and Women's Affairs, 1984–87; Ambassador to UN, 1988–90. *Address:* 8 Park Terrace, Christchurch 1, New Zealand.

HERD, Frederick Charles; Assistant Under-Secretary of State (Civilian Management, General), Ministry of Defence, 1970–75; *b* 27 April 1915. *Educ:* Strode's Sch., Egham; Sidney Sussex Coll., Cambridge. Asst Principal, Admiralty, 1937; Principal, 1941; Asst. Sec., 1950; Asst Under-Sec. of State, 1964. *Recreations:* music, lawn tennis, bridge. *Address:* 11 Bloemfontein Avenue, W12 7BJ.

HERDMAN, (John) Mark (Ambrose), CBE 1990; LVO 1979; HM Diplomatic Service, retired; *b* 26 April 1932; *s* of late Comdr Claudius Alexander Herdman, DL, RN, and Joan Dalrymple Herdman (*née* Tennant); *m* 1963, Elizabeth Anne Dillon; one *s* two *d*. *Educ:* St Edward's Sch., Oxford; Trinity Coll., Dublin (BA, MA); Queen's Coll., Oxford (postgrad.). HMOCS, Kenya, 1954–64; joined HM Diplomatic Service, 1964; Second, later First Sec., CRO, 1964–65; ODM, 1965; MECAS, 1965–66; Amman, 1966–68; FCO, 1969–71; Lusaka, 1971–74; Hd of Chancery, Jedda, 1974–76; FCO, 1976–78; Lilongwe, 1978–81; FCO, 1981–83; Dep. Governor, Bermuda, 1983–86; Gov., British Virgin Is, 1986–91; Hd of British Delegn to EC Monitoring Mission in Yugoslavia, 1991–92. *Recreations:* fishing, golf, philately. *Address:* Tullywhisker House, Berry Lane, Fox Corner, Worplesdon, Surrey GU3 3PU. *T:* Worplesdon (01483) 232900. *Clubs:* Commonwealth Trust, Ebury Court.

HERDON, Christopher de Lancy, OBE 1971; HM Diplomatic Service, retired; contributor to The Tablet, since 1983, editorial assistant, since 1986; *b* 24 May 1928; *s* of Wilfrid Herdon and Clotilde (*née* Parsons); *m* 1953, Virginia Grace; two *s* two *d* (and one *s* decd). *Educ:* Ampleforth; Magdalen Coll., Oxford. Foreign Office, 1951; Vienna, 1953; 2nd Sec., Baghdad, 1957; Beirut, 1961; 1st Sec., Amman, 1962; FO, 1965; Aden, 1967; FCO, 1970; Counsellor: Rome, 1973; FCO, 1977; retired 1983. Clerk to Lurgashall Parish Council, 1988–94. RC Observer, BCC, 1984–90; Mem., Assembly of Council of Churches for Britain and Ireland, 1990–94. *Recreations:* painting, music, sailing, long-distance walking. *Address:* Moses Farm, Lurgashall, Petworth, W Sussex GU28 9EP. *T:* Northchapel (01428) 707323. *Club:* Reform.

HEREFORD, 18th Viscount *cr* 1550; **Robert Milo Leicester Devereux;** Bt 1611; Premier Viscount of England; *b* 4 Nov. 1932; *o s* of Hon. Robert Godfrey de Bohun Devereux (*d* 1934) and Audrey Maureen Leslie, DStJ 1963 (*d* 1978) (she *m* 2nd 1961, 7th Earl of Lisburne, who *d* 1965), *y d* of late James Meakin, Westwood Manor, Staffs and of late Countess Sondes; *S* grandfather, 1952; *m* 1969, Susan Mary (marr. diss. 1982), *o c* of Major Maurice Godley, Ide Hill, Sevenoaks, Kent, and of Mrs Glen Godley, Ascott, Shipston-on-Stour, Warwicks; two *s*. *Educ:* Eton. Served Royal Horse Guards (The Blues), 1960–63. Member: Royal Philharmonic Soc.; Royal Philharmonic Orchestra Assoc. OStJ. *Heir:* *s* Hon. Charles Robin de Bohun Devereux, *b* 11 Aug. 1975. *Address:* c/o House of Lords, SW1A 0PW.

HEREFORD, Bishop of, since 1990; **Rt. Rev. John Keith Oliver;** *b* 14 April 1935; *s* of Walter Keith and Ivy Oliver; *m* 1961, Meriel Moore; two *s* one *d*. *Educ:* Westminster School; Gonville and Caius Coll., Cambridge (MA, MLitt); Westcott House. Asst Curate, Hilborough Group of Parishes, Norfolk, 1964–68; Chaplain and Asst Master, Eton College, 1968–72; Team Rector: South Molton Group of Parishes, Devon, 1973–82; Parish of Central Exeter, 1982–85; Archdeacon of Sherborne, 1985–90. Chm., ABM, 1993–. *Publications:* The Church and Social Order, 1968; contribs to Theology, Crucible. *Recreations:* railways, music, architecture, motorcycling. *Address:* Bishop's House, The Palace, Hereford HR4 9DN. *Clubs:* United Oxford & Cambridge, Worcester CC.

HEREFORD, Dean of; *see* Willis, Very Rev. R. A.

HEREFORD, Archdeacon of; *see* Moss, Ven. L. G.

HERFORD, Geoffrey Vernon Brooke, CBE 1956 (OBE 1946); MSc; FIBiol; Director of Pest Infestation Research, Agricultural Research Council, 1940–68, retired; *b* 18 Nov. 1905; *s* of late Henry J. R. Herford, Hampstead; *m* 1933, Evelyn Cicely (*d* 1969), *d* of W. G. Lambert. *Educ:* Gresham's School, Holt; Magdalen College, Oxford (BA); Minnesota University (MSc). *Address:* Rose Cottage, Wells Road, Eastcombe, Stroud, Glos GL6 7ED.

HERFT, Rt. Rev. Roger Adrian; *see* Newcastle, NSW, Bishop of.

HERITAGE, John Langdon, CB 1991; Chairman, Chesham Building Society, since 1992; *b* 31 Dec. 1931; *s* of Frank and Elizabeth Heritage; *m* 1956, Elizabeth Faulkner, *d* of Charles and Ethel Robertson; two *s* one *d*. *Educ:* Berkhamsted Sch., Exeter Coll., Oxford (MA). Called to the Bar, Middle Temple, 1956. National Service, Royal Hampshire Regt and Royal W African Frontier Force. Legal Asst, Treasury Solicitor's Office, 1957, Sen. Legal Asst 1964; Asst Solicitor, Lord Chancellor's Dept, 1973; Sec., Royal Commn on Legal Services, 1976–79; Under Sec., 1983; Circuit Administrator, South Eastern Circuit, 1983–88; Hd of Judicial Appts, Lord Chancellor's Dept, 1989–92. *Publications:* articles in legal jls. *Recreation:* making things. *Address:* c/o Chesham Building Society, 12 Market Square, Chesham Bucks HP5 1ER. *T:* Chesham (01494) 725165. *Club:* United Oxford & Cambridge University.

HERITAGE, Robert, CBE 1980; RDI 1963; DesRCA, FCSD; Professor, School of Furniture Design, Royal College of Art, 1974–85; *b* 2 Nov. 1927; *m* Dorothy; two *s* one *d*. *Educ:* Royal College of Art, RCA, 1950; freelance designer, 1961. *Recreations:* tennis, fishing. *Address:* 12 Jay Mews, Kensington Gore, SW7 2EP.

HERITAGE, Rev. Canon Thomas Charles; Canon Residentiary of Portsmouth Cathedral, 1964–76, now Canon Emeritus; *b* 3 March 1908; *s* of Thomas and Sarah Ellen Heritage; *m* 1934, Frances Warrington (*d* 1979); twin *d*. *Educ:* The King's Sch., Chester; St Edmund Hall, Oxford. BA 1929; MA 1944; Diploma in Education (Oxford), 1930; ATCL 1931. Deacon, 1934; Priest, 1938. Curate of Christ Church, Chesterfield and Asst Master, Chesterfield Grammar Sch., 1934–38; Asst Master, Portsmouth Grammar Sch., 1938–64; Curate of St Mark, Portsmouth, 1938–40, St Christopher, Bournemouth, 1940–44; Chaplain of Portsmouth Cathedral, 1945–64. Hon. Canon, 1958–64. Examining Chaplain to the Bishop of Portsmouth, 1965–74. Warden, Portsmouth Diocesan Readers' Assoc., 1966–76. *Publications:* A New Testament Lectionary for Schools, 1943; The Early Christians in Britain (with B. E. Dodd), 1966. *Recreations:* music, the theatre, reading. *Address:* 117 The Close, Salisbury, Wilts SP1 2EY. *T:* Salisbury (01722) 329104.

HERLIE, Eileen; actress; *b* 8 March 1920; *d* of Patrick Herlihy (Irish) and Isobel Cowden (Scottish); *m* 1st, 1942, Philip Barrett; 2nd, 1951, Witold Kuncewicz. *Educ:* Shawlands Academy, Glasgow. Varied repertoire with own company, 1942–44; Old Vic, Liverpool, 1944–45; Lyric Theatre, Hammersmith, 1945–46; Andromache in Trojan Women, Alcestis in Thracian Horses, Queen in Eagle has Two Heads, 1946–47; Gertrude in Hamlet (film), 1948; Medea, 1949; Angel with the Trumpet (film), 1949; Paula in The Second Mrs Tanqueray, Haymarket, 1950–51; Helen D'Oyly Carte in Gilbert and Sullivan (film), 1952; Mother in Isn't Life Wonderful? (film), 1952; John Gielgud Season, 1953: Mrs Marwood in The Way of the World; Belvidera in Venice Preserv'd; Irene in Sense of Guilt, 1953; Mrs Molloy in The Matchmaker, 1954; She Didn't Say No! (film), 1958;

acted in George Dillon (New York), 1958; Take Me Along (New York), 1959; All America (New York), 1963; The Queen in Hamlet (New York), 1964; Halfway up the Tree, 1967; Emperor Henry IV, NY, 1973; Crown Matrimonial, 1973; The Seagull (film). *Recreations:* riding, reading, music.

HERMAN, David Joseph; Chairman and Managing Director, Adam Opel AG, since 1992; *b* 10 Jan. 1946; *m* Isabel Roehrenbach; two *d*. *Educ:* New York Univ. (BA Govt Affairs); LSE; Harvard Univ. Grad. Sch. (JD). Attorney, Legal Staff, General Motors, NY, 1973; Manager, Sales Develt, USSR, GM Internat. Ops, 1976; Special Asst to Man. Dir, GM España, 1979–82; Managing Director: GM Chile, Santiago, 1982; GM Colombia, 1984–86; GM Continental, Antwerp, 1986–88; Exec. Dir, Europ. Parts & Accessories, GM Europe, 1988–89; Pres. and Chief Exec. Officer, SAAB Automobile, 1989–92. *Recreations:* golf, opera, bridge. *Address:* Adam Opel AG, Bahnhofsplatz, 65423 Ruesselsheim, Germany. *T:* (6142) 664500.

HERMAN, Josef, OBE 1980; RA 1990; painter; *b* 3 Jan. 1911; *m* 1955, Eleanor Ettlinger; one *s* (one *d* decd). *Educ:* Warsaw. First exhibition, Warsaw, 1932; left for Belgium, 1938; arrived in Britain, June 1940; lived in: Glasgow, 1940–43; Ystradgynlais (mining village, Wales), 1944–53. Exhibitions include: Glasgow, 1942; Edinburgh, 1942; London, 1943; Roland, Browse and Delbanco Gallery, 1946–; British Council; Arts Council; (retrospective) Whitechapel Art Gallery, 1956; (retrospective) Camden Arts Centre, 1980; contrib. to British Mining exhbn, Science Museum, 1983. Work in permanent collections: Arts Council; British Council; British Museum; National Museum, Cardiff; Contemporary Art Society; National Museum Bezalel, Jerusalem; National Gallery, Johannesburg; Tate Gallery, London; Victoria and Albert Museum, London; National Gallery, Melbourne; National Gallery, Ottawa; National Gallery, Wellington, etc. Gold Medal, Royal National Eisteddfod, Llanelly, 1962; Contemporary Art Society prize, 1952 and 1953; prize, John Moore Exhibition, 1956; Trust House Award, 1962. *Publications:* Related Twilights (autobiog.), 1975; Reflections on Drawing, 1985; Notes from a Welsh Diary, 1988. *Address:* 120 Edith Road, W14 9AP.

HERMANN, Alexander Henry Baxter; HM Diplomatic Service, retired; *b* 28 Dec. 1917; *m* Rita Rosalind Fernandes. Joined Foreign Service, 1939; served 1942–55; Peking, Ahwaz, Chengtu, Chungking, Shanghai, Quito, Panama, Tamsui; Foreign Office, 1956; Commercial Counsellor and Consul-General, Rangoon, 1957–61; HM Consul-General at Marseilles, also to Monaco, 1961–65; Diplomatic Service Inspector, 1965–66; Counsellor, Hong Kong Affairs, Washington, 1967–70, 1974–77; Consul-General, Osaka, 1971–73. *Address:* Old Place, Aldwick, Sussex.

HERMER, Julius; solicitor; Partner with Grossman, Hermer & Seligman; Lord Mayor of Cardiff, 1987–88; *b* 18 Nov. 1933; *s* of Saul and Cissie Hermer; *m* 1960, Gloria Cohen; three *s* one *d*. *Educ:* St Illtyd's Coll., Cardiff; Peterhouse, Cambridge (BA, MA). Partner, 1959–, Grossman & Hermer, later Crowley, Grossman & Hermer, later Grossman, Hermer & McCarthy. Member: Cardiff City Council, 1964–88, 1991–Apr. 1996 (Chm., Planning Cttee, 1980–84, 1986–87; Dep. Lord Mayor of Cardiff, 1979–80); S Glam CC, 1974–Apr. 1996 (Vice-Chm. of Council and Dep. Leader of Cons. Party, 1977–78). Dep. Chm., Cardiff W Cons. Assoc., 1985. *Recreations:* sport, wine, food, travel. *Address:* 28 Palace Road, Llandaff, Cardiff CF5 2AF. *T:* Cardiff (01222) 566198.

HERMON, Sir John (Charles), Kt 1982; OBE 1975; QPM 1988; Chief Constable, Royal Ulster Constabulary, 1980–89; *b* 23 Nov. 1928; *s* of late William Rowan Hermon and Agnes Hermon; *m* 1954, Jean Webb (*d* 1986); one *s* one *d*; *m* 1988, Sylvia Paisley, LLB; two *s*. *Educ:* Larne Grammar Sch. Accountancy training and business, 1946–50; joined RUC, 1950. Pres., Internat. Professional Security Assoc., 1993–. CStJ 1984. *Recreations:* boating, reading, walking. *Clubs:* Royal Ulster Yacht (Bangor, Co. Down); Donaghadee Golf.

HERMON, Peter Michael Robert; Head of Information Systems, CL-Alexanders Laing and Cruickshank Holdings Ltd, 1989–90; *b* 13 Nov. 1928; British; *m* 1954, Norma Stuart Brealey; two *s* two *d*. *Educ:* Nottingham High Sch.; St John's and Merton Colls, Oxford. 1st cl. hons Maths Oxon. Leo Computers Ltd, 1955–59; Manager, Management and Computer Divs, Dunlop Co., 1959–65; Information Handling Dir, BOAC, 1965–68; Management Services Dir, BOAC, and Mem. Bd of Management, 1968–72; Mem. of Board, BOAC, 1972; British Airways: Gp Management Services Dir, 1972–78; Board Mem., 1978–83; Management Services Dir, 1978–82; Man. Dir, European Services Div., 1982–83. Man. Dir, Tandem Computers Ltd, 1983–84; Dir, Tandem UK, 1983–85; Head of Systems and Communications, Lloyd's of London, 1984–86; Informations Systems Dir, Harris Queensway, 1986–88. Mem. Bd of Dirs, Internat. Aeradio Ltd, 1966–83, Chm., 1982–83; Chm., Internat. Aeradio (Caribbean) Ltd, 1967–83; Mem. Bd, SITA, 1972–83, Chm., 1981–83. *Publication:* Hill Walking in Wales, 1991. *Recreations:* hill walking, music, cats. *Address:* White Flints, Quentin Way, Wentworth, Virginia Water, Surrey GU25 4PS.

HERMON-HODGE, family name of **Baron Wyfold.**

HERMON-TAYLOR, Prof. John, FRCS; Professor of Surgery, St George's Hospital Medical School, since 1976; *b* 16 Oct. 1936; *s* of Hermon Taylor, *qv*; *m* 1971, Eleanor Ann Pheteplace, of Davenport, Iowa; one *s* one *d*. *Educ:* Harrow Sch. (Shepherd-Churchill Open Major Entrance Schol.); St John's Coll., Cambridge (travelling schol., 1955; BA 1957, MB BChir 1960, MChir 1968); London Hosp. Med Coll. (Open Entrance Schol., 1957, prizes in Med., Path., and Obst.). FRCS 1963 (Hallett Prize, 1962). Training in surgery, 1962–68; MRC Travelling Fellow to Mayo Clinic, USA, 1968–69 (Vis. Prof., 1980, 1985); Senior Lectr, 1970, Reader in Surgery, 1971–76, London Hosp. Med. Coll. Pearce-Gould Vis. Prof., Middlesex Hosp., 1982; Vis. Prof., Pakistan Inst. of Med. Scis, Islamabad, 1989. Hon. Consultant in Gen. Surgery to RN, 1989–. Mem. Council, Assoc. of Surgeons of GB and Ireland, 1981–84; Dir, James IV Assoc. of Surgeons, 1983–86; Mem., Clinical Panel, Wellcome Trust, 1985–88. Mem., Council, Action Research, 1988–; Mem., Scientific Cttee, British Digestive Foundn, 1991–; British Liver Trust, 1995–. Dir, BioScience Internat. Inc. Mem., numerous professional bodies, UK and overseas. Innovator of the Year award, Times Newspaper/Barclays Bank, 1988. *Publications:* scientific papers on purification and biochem. of enteropeptidase, diseases of pancreas, peptide chem., enzymeactivation in gastric disorders, on causation and specific treatment of Crohn's disease, mycobacterial genetics, epidemiology of breast cancer, biolog. res. on common solid tumours. *Recreations:* sailing, shooting, growing soft fruit and vegetables. *Address:* 11 Parkside Avenue, Wimbledon, SW19 5ES. *T:* 0181–767 7631.

HERN, Jane Carolyn; Assistant Secretary-General, Law Society, since 1992; *b* 22 Sept. 1954; *d* of George Kenneth Hern and Elizabeth Ellen Hern (*née* Byford). *Educ:* Girton Coll., Cambridge (BA Hons Law 1976; MA). Articles with Lovell, White & King, 1977–79; admitted as solicitor, 1979; LCD, 1979–87, Law Commn, 1981–86; Law Soc., 1987–. *Recreations:* eating, drinking, reading crime thrillers, visiting places of historic interest. *Address:* Law Society's Hall, 113 Chancery Lane, WC2A 1PL. *T:* 0171–242 1222.

HERN, Major William Richard, (Dick), CVO 1980; racehorse trainer; *b* Holford, Somerset, 20 Jan. 1921. Served War of 1939–45, North Irish Horse. Asst Trainer to Major M. B. Pope, MC, 1952–57; licence to train under Jockey Club rules, 1957–; leading trainer, 1962, 1972, 1980, 1983. Races won include: Derby, 1979, 1980, 1989 (Troy, Henbit, Nashwan); 2,000 Guineas, 1971, 1989 (Brigadier Gerard, Nashwan); 1,000 Guineas, 1974 (Highclere); St Leger, 1962, 1965, 1974, 1977, 1981, 1983 (Hethersett, Provoke, Bustino, Dunfermline, Cut Above, Sun Princess); Epsom Oaks, 1977, 1980, 1983 (Dunfermline, Bireme, Sun Princess); King George VI and Queen Elizabeth Diamond Stakes, 1972, 1979, 1980, 1985, 1989 (Brigadier Gerard, Troy, Ela-Mana-Mou, Petoski, Nashwan); Champion Stakes, 1971, 1972 (Brigadier Gerard); Eclipse Stakes, 1972, 1980, 1989, 1990 (Brigadier Gerard, Ela-Mana-Mou, Nashwan, Elmaamul); Coronation Cup, 1974, 1975 (Buoy, Bustino). Leading Trainer, Flat Seasons, 1962, 1972, 1980, 1983. *Address:* Kingwood House Stables, Lambourn, Newbury, Berks RG16 7RS. *T:* (office) Lambourn (01488) 73300; (home) East Ilsley (0163528) 251.

HERNIMAN, Ven. Ronald George; Archdeacon of Barnstaple 1970–88; *b* 18 April 1923; *s* of George Egerton and Rose Herniman; *m* 1949, Grace Jordan-Jones; one *s* two *d*. *Educ:* Geneva; Bideford, Devon. Served RAF, 1941–46. Birkbeck Coll., London Univ., 1948–51 (BA); Oak Hill Theological Coll., 1951–53; Tutor, Oak Hill Coll., 1953–54; Asst Curate, Christ Church, Cockfosters, 1954–56; Dir of Philosophical Studies, Oak Hill, 1956–61; Rector of Exe Valley Group of Churches (Washfield, Stoodleigh, Withleigh, Calverleigh Oakford, Morebath, Rackenford, Loxbeare and Templeton), 1961–72; Rector of Shirwell with Loxhore, 1972–82. *Recreations:* sailing; making and mending things. *Address:* Castleland House, Oakfordbridge, Tiverton, Devon EX16 9JA.

HERON, Sir Conrad (Frederick), KCB 1974 (CB 1969); OBE 1953; Permanent Secretary, Department of Employment, 1973–76; *b* 21 Feb. 1916; *s* of Richard Foster Heron and Ida Fredrika Heron; *m* 1948, Envye Linnéa Gustafsson; two *d*. *Educ:* South Shields High Sch.; Trinity Hall, Cambridge. Entered Ministry of Labour, 1938; Principal Private Secretary to Minister of Labour, 1953–56; Under-Secretary, Industrial Relations Dept, 1963–64 and 1965–68, Overseas Dept, 1964–65; Dep. Under-Sec. of State, Dept of Employment, 1968–71; Dep. Chm., Commn on Industrial Relations, 1971–72; Second Permanent Sec., Dept of Employment, 1973. *Address:* Old Orchards, West Lydford, Somerton, Somerset TA11 7DG. *T:* Wheathill (01963) 240387.

HERON, Michael Gilbert; Chairman, Post Office, since 1993; *b* 22 Oct. 1934; *s* of Gilbert Thwaites Heron and Olive Lilian (*née* Steele); *m* 1958, Celia Veronica Mary Hunter; two *s* one *d* (and one *d* decd). *Educ:* St Joseph's Acad., Blackheath; New Coll., Oxford (MA Hist.). Lieut RA, 1953–55. Dir, BOCM Silcock, 1971–76; Chm., Batchelors Foods, 1976–82; Dep. Co-ordinator, Food & Drinks Co-ordination, Unilever, 1982–86; Dir, Unilever, 1986–92. Food and Drink Federation: Mem. Cttee, 1986–92; Mem. Council, 1986–92; Chm., Food Policy Res. Cttee, 1987–92. Mem., Armed Forces Pay Rev. Bd, 1981–82. Dep. Chm. and Mem. Bd, BITC, 1991–; Member: Policy Steering Bd, BESO, 1992–93; CBI Council, 1992–; Dep. Chm., NACETT, 1993–; Chm., NCVQ, 1994–. Chm. Council, St George's Hosp. Med. Sch., 1992–; Mem., Governing Body, Douai Abbey, 1991–. *Recreation:* avid Rugby football watcher. *Address:* (office) 148 Old Street, EC1V 9HQ; Smithincott, The Avenue, Bucklebury, Berks RG7 6NP; Garden Flat, 19 Kensington Court, W8 5DW. *T:* 0171–250 2518.

HERON, Patrick, CBE 1977; painter; *b* 30 Jan. 1920; *e s* of late T. M. and Eulalie Heron; *m* 1945, Delia Reiss (*d* 1979); two *d*. *Educ:* St Ives, Cornwall; Welwyn Garden City; St Georges, Harpenden; Slade School. Art criticism in: New English Weekly, 1945–47; New Statesman and Nation, 1947–50 (Art Critic); London correspondent, Arts (NY), 1955–58. John Power Lectr, Sydney Univ., 1973; Doty Prof., Univ. of Texas at Austin, 1978. Trustee, Tate Gall., 1980–87. *One-man exhibitions:* Redfern Gallery, London, 1947, 1948, 1950, 1951, 1954, 1956 and 1958; Waddington Galleries, London, 1959, 1960, 1963, 1964, 1965, 1967, 1968, 1970 (canvases), 1970 (prints), 1973, 1975, 1977, 1979, 1983, 1987; Bertha Schaefer Gallery, NY, 1960, 1962 and 1965; Galerie Charles Lienhard, Zürich, 1963; Traverse Theatre Gallery, Edinburgh, 1965; São Paulo Bienal VIII, 1965 (Silver Medal) (exhibn toured S Amer., 1966); Harrogate Festival, 1970; Rudy Komon Gall., Sydney, 1970; Waddington Fine Arts, Montreal, 1970; Whitechapel Gallery, 1972; Bonython Art Gall., Sydney, 1973; Rutland Gall., London, 1975; Galerie le Balcon des Arts, Paris, 1977; *retrospective exhibitions:* Wakefield City Art Gallery, Leeds, Hull, Nottingham, 1952; Richard Demarco Gallery, Edinburgh, 1967; Kunstnernes Hus, Oslo, 1967; Museum of Modern Art, Oxford, 1968; Univ. of Texas at Austin Art Mus., 1978 (69 works); Oriel Gallery, Cardiff, 1979; Barbican Art Gall., 1985. Twelve paintings shown at São Paulo Bienal II, Brazil, 1953–54. Carnegie International, Pittsburgh, 1961; British Art Today, San Francisco, Dallas, Santa Barbara, 1962–63; Painting and Sculpture of a Decade, 1954–64, Tate Gallery, 1964; British Painting and Sculpture, 1960–70, National Gallery of Art, Washington DC; British Painting 1952–1977, RA, 1977; Color en la Pintura Británica (tour of S Amer.), 1977–78. Exhibited in group and British Council exhibitions in many countries; *works owned by:* Tate Gallery; Arts Council; British Council; V&A Museum; British Museum; Gulbenkian Foundation; Leeds City Art Gallery; Stuyvesant Foundation; National Portrait Gallery; Broadcasting House; Wakefield City Art Gallery; Manchester City Art Gallery; Contemporary Art Society; Oldham Art Gallery; CEMA, N Ireland; Abbot Hall Art Gallery, Kendal; The Art Gallery, Aberdeen; National Gallery of Wales, Cardiff; Art Gall. of Ont., Toronto; Scottish Nat. Portrait Gall., Scottish Nat. Gall. of Modern Art; Univ. of Galway; Eliot Coll., Univ. of Kent; Montreal Museum of Fine Art; Vancouver Art Gallery; Toledo Museum of Art, Ohio; Smith College Museum of Art, Mass; Brooklyn Museum, NY; Albright-Knox Art Gallery, Buffalo, NY; Univ. of Michigan Museum of Art; Univ. of Texas at Austin Art Museum; Museum of Art, Carnegie Inst., Pittsburgh; Yale Center for British Art, New Haven, Conn; Stuyvesant Foundn, Holland; Boymans Museum, Rotterdam; Musée d'Art Contemporain, Montreal; Western Australian Art Gallery, Perth; Art Gall. of NSW, Sydney; Pembroke, Merton and Nuffield Colleges, Oxford; Bristol City Art Gall.; Exeter Art Gallery; Exeter Univ. (Cornwall House); Plymouth City Art Gallery; Power Collection, Sydney; London Art Gall., London, Ont.; Hatton Art Gall., Newcastle Univ.; Southampton Art Gall.; Norwich Art Gall; also represented in Fitzwilliam Museum, Cambridge, and in municipal collections at Glasgow, Reading and Sheffield. Hon. FRIBA 1991. Hon. DLitt: Exeter, 1982; Kent, 1986; Hon. Dr RCA, 1987. Awarded Grand Prize by international jury, John Moores' 2nd Liverpool Exhibition, 1959. *Publications:* Vlaminck: Paintings, 1900–1945, 1947; The Changing Forms of Art, 1955; Ivon Hitchens, 1955; Braque, 1958; The Shape of Colour, 1973; Paintings by Patrick Heron 1965–1977, 1978; The Colour of Colour, 1978; Patrick Heron, 1988; contrib. The Guardian, Studio International, etc. *Address:* Eagles Nest, Zennor, near St Ives, Cornwall TR26 3BP. *T:* Penzance (01736) 796921; 12 Edith Mansions, Edith Grove, SW10 0NN. *T:* 0171–352 1787.

HERON, Raymond, CBE 1984; retired; Deputy Director, Propellants, Explosives and Rocket Motor Establishment, Ministry of Defence (Procurement Executive), 1977–84; *b* 10 April 1924; *s* of Lewis and Doris Heron; *m* 1948, Elizabeth MacGathan; one *s* one *d*. *Educ:* Heath Grammar Sch., Halifax; Queen's Coll., Oxford (BA Physics). Shell Refining and Marketing Co., 1944–47; RN, Instructor Branch, 1947–52; Rocket Propulsion Estabt, Min. of Supply (later Min. of Technology), 1952–67; Cabinet Office, 1967; Asst Dir, Min. of Technology, 1967–73; Dep. Dir, Explosives Research and Development

Estabt, MoD, 1973; Special Asst to Sec. (Procurement Exec.), MoD, 1973–74; Head of Rocket Motor Exec. and Dep. Dir/2, Rocket Propulsion Estabt, MoD (PE), 1974–76. *Publications:* articles in scientific and technical jls. *Recreations:* music, hill walking, golf. *Address:* 9 Grange Gardens, Wendover, Aylesbury, Bucks HP22 6HB. *T:* Wendover (01296) 622921. *Club:* Ashridge Golf.

HERON, Robert, CVO 1988; MA; Director, Duke of Edinburgh's Award Scheme, 1978–87; *b* 12 Oct. 1927; *s* of James Riddick Heron and Sophie Leathem; *m* 1953, Patricia Mary Pennell; two *s* one *d.* *Educ:* King Edward's Sch., Birmingham; St Catharine's Coll., Cambridge. Housemaster: Strathallan, Perthshire, 1952–59; Christ Coll., Brecon, 1959–62; Headmaster, King James I Sch., IOW, 1962–66. Head of Educational Broadcasting, ATV Network Ltd, 1966–69, responsible for production of TV programme series in the scis, langs, soc. documentary, leisure interests, music, drama; Deleg., EBU study gps on educnl broadcasting, 1967–69; Programme Dir, The Electronic Video Recording Partnership (CBS Inc. USA/ICI/Ciba-Geigy UK), 1970–77; Managing Dir, EVR Ltd, 1974–77, and of EVR Enterprises Ltd, 1975–77. Freeman, City of London, 1981. Formerly 6/7th Bn, The Black Watch (RHR) TA. *Recreations:* travel, gardening, sport. *Address:* The Oast, Ingleden Park, Tenterden, Kent TN30 6SN. *Clubs:* Rugby; Hawks (Cambridge); Achilles.

HERON-MAXWELL, Sir Nigel (Mellor), 10th Bt *cr* 1683; *b* 30 Jan. 1944; *s* of Sir Patrick Ivor Heron-Maxwell, 9th Bt and of D. Geraldine E., *yr d* of late Claud Paget Mellor; *S* father, 1982; *m* 1972, Mary Elizabeth Angela, *o d* of late W. Ewing, Co. Donegal; one *s* one *d.* *Educ:* Milton Abbey. *Heir: s* David Mellor Heron-Maxwell, *b* 22 May 1975. *Address:* 50 Watlington Road, Old Harlow, Essex CM17 0DY.

HERRIDGE, Geoffrey Howard, CMG 1962; Chairman, Iraq Petroleum Co. Ltd and Associated Companies, 1965–70, retired (Managing Director, 1957–63; Deputy Chairman, 1963–65); *b* 22 Feb. 1904; 3rd *s* of late Edward Herridge, Eckington, Worcestershire; *m* 1935, Dorothy Elvira Tod; two *s* two *d.* *Educ:* Crypt Sch., Gloucester; St John's Coll., Cambridge. Joined Turkish Petroleum Co. Ltd (later Iraq Petroleum Co. Ltd), Iraq, 1926; served in Iraq, Jordan, Palestine, 1926–47; General Manager in the Middle East, Iraq Petroleum Co. and Associated Companies, 1947–51; Executive Director, 1953–57; Member of London Cttee, Ottoman Bank, 1964–79. Chairman, Petroleum Industry Training Board, 1967–70. *Address:* Flint, Sidlesham Common, Chichester, West Sussex PO20 7PY. *Club:* Oriental.

HERRIES OF TERREGLES, Lady (14th in line, of the Lordship *cr* 1490); **Anne Elizabeth Fitzalan-Howard;** *b* 12 June 1938; *e d* of 16th Duke of Norfolk, KG, GCVO, GBE, TD, PC, and of Lavinia Duchess of Norfolk, *qv*; *S* to lordship upon death of father, 1975; *m* 1985, Sir Colin Cowdrey, *qv*. Racehorse trainer. *Recreations:* riding, golf, breeding spaniels. *Heir: sister* Lady Mary Katharine Mumford, *qv*. *Address:* Angmering Park, Littlehampton, West Sussex BN16 4EX. *T:* Patching (0190674) 421.

HERRING, Cyril Alfred; Chairman and Managing Director, Southern Airways Ltd, since 1978; *b* Dulwich, 17 Jan. 1915; *s* of Alfred James Herring and Minnie Herring (*née* Padfield); *m* 1939, Helen (*née* Warnes); three *s.* *Educ:* Alleyn's Sch.; London School of Economics. BSc(Econ); FCMA; JDipMA; IPFA; FCIT. Chief Accountant, Straight Corporation Ltd, 1936–46; joined BEA, 1946; Chief Accountant, 1951–57; Personnel Director, 1957–65; Financial Director, 1965–71; Executive Board Member, 1971–74; Mem., British Airways Bd, 1972–78; Chief Executive, British Airways Regional Div., 1972–74; Finance Dir, 1975–78; Chm. and Man. Dir, British Air Services Ltd, 1969–76; Chairman: Northeast Airlines Ltd, 1969–76; Cambrian Airways Ltd, 1973–76; London Rail Adv. Cttee, 1976–80; CIPFA Public Corporations Finance Group, 1976–78. Member Council: Chartered Inst. of Transport, 1971–74; Inst. of Cost and Management Accountants, 1967–77 (Vice-Pres., 1971–73, Pres., 1973–74); CBI, 1975–78 (Mem. Financial Policy Cttee, 1975–78, Finance and General Purposes Cttee, 1977–78). Freeman, City of London; Liveryman, Guild of Air Pilots and Air Navigators. *Recreations:* flying, motoring, boating. *Address:* Cuddenbeake, St Germans, Cornwall PL12 5LY. *Clubs:* Reform, Royal Aero.

HERRINGTON, Air Vice-Marshal Walter John, CB 1982; RAF retd; aviation and security consultant; *b* 18 May 1928; *s* of Major H. Herrington, MBE, MM and Daisy Restal Gardiner; *m* 1958, Joyce Maureen Cherryman; two *s.* *Educ:* Woking Grammar Sch.; RAF Coll., Cranwell. FBIM. Commnd RAF, 1949, Pilot; 1950–69: Long Range Transp. Sqdns; ADC to C-in-C Bomber Comd; Reconnaissance Sqdns; RAF Staff Coll.; Exchange Officer, USAF Acad., Colo; Comd 100 Sqdn; Jt Services Staff Coll.; Air Sec.'s Dept; Stn Comdr RAF Honnington, 1969–71; Ops Dept, MoD, 1971–73; RCDS (student) 1974; Defence Attaché, Paris, 1975–77. Hon. ADC to the Queen, 1971–74; Senior RAF Mem., Directing Staff, RCDS, 1978–80; Dir of Service Intelligence, 1980–82. Aviation Advr, Internat. Mil. Services, 1982–89. Member: European Security Study, 1982–83; Central Council, TA&VRA, 1984–90; Council, Officers Pensions Soc., 1983–89. *Publications:* The Future for the Defence Industry, 1991; text books for courses on air power for USAF Academy. *Recreations:* reading, international affairs, sport. *Address:* c/o Lloyds Bank, Obelisk Way, Camberley, Surrey GU15 3SE. *Club:* Royal Air Force.

HERROD, Donald, QC 1972; **His Honour Judge Herrod;** a Circuit Judge, since 1978; *b* 7 Aug. 1930; *o s* of Wilfred and Phyllis Herrod, Doncaster; *m* 1959, Kathleen Elaine Merrington, MB, ChB; two *d.* *Educ:* grammar schs, Doncaster and Leeds. Called to Bar, 1956. A Recorder of the Crown Court, 1972–78. Member: Parole Bd, 1978–81; Judicial Studies Bd, 1982–86. *Recreation:* golf. *Address:* The Castle, York YO1 1RY.

HERRON, Very Rev. Andrew; Clerk to the Presbytery of Glasgow, 1959–81; Editor, Church of Scotland Year Book, 1961–92; *b* 29 Sept. 1909; *s* of John Todd Herron and Mary Skinner Hunter; *m* 1935, Joanna Fraser Neill; four *d.* *Educ:* Glasgow Univ. (MA, BD, LLB). ATCL 1930. Minister: at Linwood, 1936–40, at Houston and Killellan, 1940–59; Clerk to the Presbytery of Paisley, 1953–59; Moderator of General Assembly of Church of Scotland, 1971–72. Convener: Dept of Publicity and Publications, 1959–68; Gen. Admin Cttee; Business Cttee, Gen. Assembly, 1972–76, 1978; Gen. Trustee, Church of Scotland. Barclay Trust Lectr, 1989. Hon. DD: St Andrews, 1975; Glasgow, 1989. Hon. LLD Strathclyde, 1983. *Publications:* Record Apart, 1974; Guide to the General Assembly of the Church of Scotland, 1976; Guide to Congregational Affairs, 1978; Guide to Presbytery, 1983; Kirk by Divine Right (Baird lectures), 1985; A Guide to the Ministry, 1987; A Guide to Ministerial Income, 1987; Minority Report, 1990; Houston and Killellan: a handful of yesterdays, 1993; The Law and Practice of the Kirk: a guide and commentary, 1995. *Address:* 36 Darnley Road, Glasgow G41 4NE. *T:* 0141–423 6422. *Club:* Caledonian (Edinburgh).

HERRON, Henry, CBE 1975; Procurator-Fiscal, Glasgow, 1965–76, retired; Deputy Chairman of Traffic Commissioners and Licensing Authority for Scottish Traffic Area, 1978–81; *b* 6 May 1911; *s* of William and Jessie Herron; *m* 1942, Dr Christina Aitkenhead Crawford; one *s* two *d.* *Educ:* Hamilton Academy; Glasgow Univ. (MA, LLB). Solicitor. Depute Procurator-Fiscal, Glasgow, 1946; Procurator-Fiscal, Banff, 1946–51; Asst Procurator-Fiscal, Glasgow, 1951–55; Procurator-Fiscal, Paisley, 1955–65. *Recreations:* gardening, jurisprudence, criminology. *Address:* 51 Craw Road, Paisley PA2 6AE. *T:* 0141–889 3091.

HERSCHBACH, Prof. Dudley Robert; Baird Professor of Science, Harvard University, since 1976; *b* 18 June 1932; *s* of Robert D. Herschbach and Dorothy E. Herschbach; *m* 1964, Georgene L. Botyos; two *d.* *Educ:* Campbell High School; Stanford Univ. (BS Math 1954, MS Chem 1955); Harvard Univ. (AM Physics 1956, PhD Chem Phys 1958). Junior Fellow, Soc. of Fellows, Harvard, 1957–59; Asst Prof., 1959–61, Associate Prof., 1961–63, Univ. of California, Berkeley; Prof. of Chemistry, Harvard Univ., 1963–76. Hon. DSc: Univ. of Toronto, 1977; Dartmouth Coll., 1992; Charles Univ., Prague, 1993. (Jtly) Nobel Prize for Chemistry, 1986; US Nat. Medal of Sci., 1991; Heyrovský Medal, Czech Acad. of Scis, 1992; Walker Prize, 1994. *Publications:* over 300 research papers, chiefly on quantum mechanics, chemical kinetics, reaction dynamics, molecular spectroscopy, collision theory, in Jl of Chemical Physics. *Recreations:* hiking, canoeing, chess, poetry, viola. *Address:* 116 Conant Road, Lincoln, MA 01773, USA. *T:* (home) (617) 2591386; (office) (617) 4953218.

HERSCHELL, family name of **Baron Herschell.**

HERSCHELL, 3rd Baron, *cr* 1886; **Rognvald Richard Farrer Herschell;** late Captain Coldstream Guards; *b* 13 Sept. 1923; *o s* of 2nd Baron and Vera (*d* 1961), *d* of Sir Arthur Nicolson, 10th Bt, of that Ilk and Lasswade; *S* father, 1929; *m* 1948, Lady Heather, *d* of 8th Earl of Dartmouth, CVO, DSO; one *d.* *Educ:* Eton. Page of Honour to the King, 1935–40. *Heir:* none. *Address:* Westfield House, Ardington, Wantage, Oxon OX12 8PN. *T:* Abingdon (01235) 833224.

HERSEY, David Kenneth; lighting designer; founder Chairman, DHA Lighting, since 1972; *b* 30 Nov. 1939; *s* of Ella Morgan Decker and C. Kenneth Hersey; *m* Demetra Maraslis; one *s* two *d.* *Educ:* Oberlin Coll., Ohio. Left NY for London, 1968; lighting designer for theatre, opera and ballet cos, incl. Royal Opera House, ENO, Glyndebourne, Ballet Rambert, London Contemporary Dance, Scottish Ballet; lighting consultant to Nat. Theatre, 1974–84; many productions for RSC. Chm., Assoc. of Lighting Designers, 1984–86. *Designs include:* Evita, 1978 (Tony award, 1980); Nicholas Nickleby, 1980; Cats, 1981 (Tony and Drama Desk awards, 1983); Song and Dance, 1982; Guys and Dolls, 1982; Starlight Express, 1984; Les Misérables, 1985 (Tony award, 1987); Porgy and Bess, 1986; Chess, 1986; Miss Saigon, 1989 (Drama Desk award, 1991); Oliver, 1995. *Recreation:* sailing. *Address:* 2 Elm Tree Road, St John's Wood, NW8 9JX.

HERSHEY, Dr Alfred Day; Director, Genetics Research Unit, Carnegie Institution of Washington, 1962–74, retired; *b* 4 Dec. 1908; *s* of Robert D. Hershey and Alma (*née* Wilbur); *m* 1945, Harriet Davidson; one *s.* *Educ:* Michigan State Coll. (now Univ.). BS 1930; PhD 1934. Asst Bacteriologist, Washington Univ. Sch. of Medicine, St Louis Missouri, 1934–36; Instructor, 1936–38; Asst Prof., 1938–42; Assoc. Prof., 1942–50; Staff Mem., Dept of Genetics (now Genetics Research Unit), Carnegie Instn of Washington, 1950–. Albert Lasker Award, Amer. Public Health Assoc., 1958; Kimber Genetics Award, Nat. Acad. Sci., US, 1965. Hon. DSc, Chicago, 1967; Hon. Dr Med. Science, Michigan State, 1970. Nobel Prize for Physiology or Medicine (jtly), 1969. *Publications:* numerous articles in scientific jls or books. *Address:* RD Box 1640, Moores Hill Road, Syosset, NY 11791, USA. *T:* (516) 6926855.

HERTFORD, 8th Marquess of, *cr* 1793; **Hugh Edward Conway Seymour;** Baron Conway of Ragley, 1703; Baron Conway of Killultagh, 1712; Earl of Hertford, Viscount Beauchamp, 1750; Earl of Yarmouth, 1793; DL Warwick, 1959; formerly Lieutenant Grenadier Guards, *b* 29 March 1930, *s* of late Brig.-General Lord Henry Charles Seymour, DSO (2nd *s* of 6th Marquess) and Lady Helen Frances Grosvenor (*d* 1970), *d* of 1st Duke of Westminster; *S* uncle, 1940; *m* 1956, Comtesse Louise de Caraman Chimay, *o d* of late Lt-Col Prince Alphonse de Chimay, TD; one *s* three *d.* *Educ:* Eton. Chm., Hertford Public Relations Ltd, 1962–73. Chief interests are estate management (Diploma, Royal Agricultural Coll., Cirencester, 1956) and fox hunting. *Heir: s* Earl of Yarmouth, *qv*. *Address:* North Wing, Ragley Hall, Alcester, Warwickshire B49 5NJ. *T:* Alcester (01789) 762455/762090. *Clubs:* White's, Pratt's, Turf.

HERTFORD, Bishop Suffragan of, since 1990; **Rt. Rev. Robin Jonathan Norman Smith;** *b* 14 Aug. 1936; *s* of Richard Norman and Blanche Spurling Smith; *m* 1961, Hon. Lois Jean, *d* of Baron Pearson, CBE, PC; three *s* one *d.* *Educ:* Bedford Sch.; Worcester Coll., Oxford (MA); Ridley Hall, Cambridge. RAF Regiment Commission, 1955–57. Curate, St Margaret's, Barking, 1962–67; Chaplain, Lee Abbey, 1967–72; Vicar, Chesham St Mary, 1972–80; Rector, Great Chesham, 1980–90. Hon. Canon, Christ Church, Oxford, 1988–90. *Recreations:* gardening, walking. *Address:* Hertford House, Abbey Mill Lane, St Albans AL3 4HE.

HERTFORDSHIRE, Bishop in, (RC); *see* O'Brien, Rt Rev. J. J.

HERVEY, family name of **Marquess of Bristol.**

HERVEY, Rear Adm. John Bethell, CB 1982; OBE 1970; independent naval consultant; *b* 14 May 1928; *s* of late Captain Maurice William Bethell Hervey, RN, and Mrs Joan Hervey (*née* Hanbury); *m* 1950, (Audrey) Elizabeth Mote; two *s* one *d.* *Educ:* Marlborough Coll., Wilts. Joined RN, 1946; specialised in submarines, 1950, nuclear submarines, 1968; command appointments: HMS Miner VI, 1956; HMS Aeneas, 1956–57; HMS Ambush, 1959–62; HMS Oracle, 1962–64; Sixth Submarine Div., 1964–66; HMS Cavalier, 1966–67; HMS Warspite, 1968–69; Second Submarine Sqdn, 1973–75; HMS Kent, 1975–76; staff appointments: Course Officer, Royal Naval Petty Officers Leadership Sch., 1957–59; Submarine Staff Officer to Canadian Maritime Comdr, Halifax, NS, 1964–66; Ops Officer to Flag Officer Submarines, 1970–71; Def. Op. Requirements Staff, 1971–73; Dep. Chief of Allied Staff to C-in-C Channel and C-in-C Eastern Atlantic (as Cdre), 1976–80; Comdr British Navy Staff, and British Naval Attaché, Washington, and UK Nat. Liaison Rep. to SACLANT, 1980–82, retired. Comdr 1964, Captain 1970, Rear Adm. 1980. Marketing Vice-Pres., Western Hemisphere, MEL, 1982–86. FIMgt (FBIM 1983). *Publication:* Submarines, 1994. *Recreations:* walking, talking, reading. *Address:* c/o National Westminster Bank, 1 St James's Square, SW1Y 4JX. *Clubs:* Army and Navy, Royal Navy of 1765 and 1785, Anchorites (Pres., 1988).

HERVEY, Sir Roger Blaise Ramsay, KCVO 1991; CMG 1980; HM Diplomatic Service; Ambassador to Mexico, 1992–94; *b* 3 Oct. 1934. HM Forces, 1953–55. Joined Diplomatic Service, 1958; Bonn, 1958; FO, 1961; Prague, 1963; First Sec., FO, 1965; Office of Political Advr, Singapore, 1968; FCO, 1970; First Sec. and Head of Chancery, Bogotá, 1974; Counsellor, FCO, 1976; Counsellor, The Hague, 1979; Minister, Madrid, 1982; Asst Under Sec. of State (Protocol) and Vice Marshal of Diplomatic Corps, 1986. *Address:* c/o Foreign and Commonwealth Office, SW1A 2AH.

HERVEY-BATHURST, Sir Frederick Peter Methuen; *see* Bathurst.

HERWARTH von BITTENFELD, Hans Heinrich; Grand Cross (2nd Class), Order of Merit, Federal Republic of Germany, 1963; Hon. GCVO 1958; State Secretary, retired; *b* Berlin, 14 July 1904; *s* of Hans Richard Herwarth von Bittenfeld and Ilse Herwarth von

Bittenfeld (*née* von Tiedemann); *m* 1935, Elisabeth Freiin von Redwitz; one *d. Educ:* Universities of Berlin, Breslau and Munich (Law and Nat. Econ.). Entered Auswärtiges Amt, Berlin, 1927; Attaché, Paris, 1930; Second Secretary and Personal Secretary to Ambassador, Moscow, 1931–39. Military Service, 1939–45. Oberregierungsrat, Regierungsdirektor, Bavarian State Chancellery, 1945–49; Ministerialdirigent and Chief of Protocol, Federal Government, 1950, Minister Plenipotentiary, 1952; German Ambassador to Court of St James's, 1955–61; State Secretary and Chief of German Federal Presidential Office, 1961–65; German Ambassador to Republic of Italy, 1965–69; Pres., Commn for Reform of German Diplomatic Service, 1969–71. Chm., Supervisory Council, Unilever, Germany, 1969–77. Chm., Venice Cttee, German Unesco Commn; Pres., Internat. Adv. Cttee for Venice. Pres., Goethe Institut, Munich, 1971–77. Cavaliere di San Marco, 1989; Hon. Citizen, Augsburg Univ., 1989. *Publications:* Against Two Evils: memoirs of a diplomat-soldier during the Third Reich, 1981 (German edn, Zwischen Hitler und Stalin, 1982); Von Adenauer zu Brandt, 1990. *Recreation:* antiques. *Address:* Schloss, 96328 Küps, Germany. *T:* (9264) 7174.

HERZBERG, Charles Francis; consultant; Chairman, Unique Business Services Ltd (formerly Newcastle upon Tyne Polytechnic Products Ltd), since 1988; *b* 26 Jan. 1924; *s* of Dr Franz Moritz Herzberg and Mrs Marie Louise Palache; *m* 1956, Ann Linette Hoare; one *s* two *d. Educ:* Fettes Coll., Edinburgh; Sidney Sussex Coll., Cambridge (MA). CEng, FIMechE, MIGasE. Alfred Herbert Ltd, 1947–51; Chief Engr and Dir, Hornflowa Ltd, Maryport, 1951–55; Chief Engr, Commercial Plastics Gp of Cos, and Dir, Commercial Plastics Engrg Co. at Wallsend on Tyne, North Shields, and Cramlington, Northumberland, 1955–66; Corporate Planning Dir, Appliance Div., United Gas Industries, and Works Dir, Robinson Willey Ltd, Liverpool, 1966–70; Man. Dir and Chief Exec., Churchill Gear Machines Ltd, Blaydon on Tyne, 1970–72; Regional Industrial Director, Dept of Industry, N Region, 1972–75; Dir of Corporate Develt, Clarke Chapman Ltd, 1975–77; Gp Industrial Planning Adviser, 1977–84, Dir Industrial Planning, 1984–88, Northern Engineering Industries plc; Dir, Northern Investors Co. Ltd, 1984–89; Pres., Tyne & Wear Chamber of Commerce and Industry, 1989–90 (Vice-Pres., 1986–89). Gov., Univ. of Northumbria (formerly Newcastle upon Tyne Poly.), 1986– (Hon. Fellow, 1991). *Recreation:* shooting. *Address:* 3 Furzefield Road, Gosforth, Newcastle upon Tyne NE3 4EA. *T:* 0191–285 5202. *Club:* East India, Devonshire, Sports and Public Schools.

HERZBERG, Hon. Gerhard, CC (Canada), 1968; PC (Can.) 1992; FRS 1951; FRSC 1939; Director, Division of Pure Physics, 1949–69, Distinguished Research Scientist, 1969–95, now Emeritus, National Research Council of Canada; *b* Hamburg, Germany, 25 Dec. 1904; *s* of late Albin Herzberg and Ella Herzberg; *m* 1929, Luise Herzberg, *née* Oettinger (*d* 1971); one *s* one *d*; *m* 1972, Monika Herzberg, *née* Tenthoff. *Educ:* Inst. of Technology, Darmstadt, Germany; Univ. of Göttingen, Germany; Univ. of Bristol, England. Lecturer, Darmstadt Inst. of Technology, 1930; Research Professor, Univ. of Saskatchewan, 1935; Prof. of Spectroscopy, Yerkes Observatory, Univ. of Chicago, 1945; Principal Research Officer, National Research Council of Canada, 1948. University Medal, Univ. of Liège, Belgium, 1950; President, RSC, 1966 (Henry Marshall Tory Medal, 1953). Joy Kissen Mookerjee Gold Medal of Indian Association for Cultivation of Science, 1954 (awarded 1957). Gold Medal of Canadian Association Phys., 1957; Bakerian Lecture, Royal Society, 1960; Faraday Lecture and Medal, Chem. Soc., 1970; Nobel Prize for Chemistry, 1971; Royal Medal, Royal Soc., 1971. Hon. Fellow: Indian Academy of Science, 1954; Indian Physical Society, 1957; Chemical Society of London, 1968. Hon. Member: Hungarian Academy of Sciences, 1964; Optical Society of America, 1968; Royal Irish Acad., 1970; Japan Acad., 1976; Chem. Soc. of Japan, 1978; Hon. Foreign Member American Academy Arts and Sciences, 1965; Foreign Associate, National Academy of Sciences, US, 1968; Foreign Mem. (Physics), Royal Swedish Acad. of Sciences, 1981. President, Canadian Association of Physicists, 1956; Vice-Pres., International Union of Pure and Applied Physics, 1957–63. Holds numerous hon. degrees, including Hon. ScD Cantab, 1972. *Publications:* Atomic Spectra and Atomic Structure, 1st edition (USA) 1937, 2nd edition (USA) 1944; Molecular Spectra and Molecular Structure: I, Spectra of Diatomic Molecules, 1st edition (USA), 1939, 2nd edition (USA), 1950; II, Infra-red and Raman Spectra of Polyatomic Molecules (USA), 1945; III, Electronic Spectra and Electronic Structure of Polyatomic Molecules (USA), 1966; IV, (with K. P. Huber) Constants of Diatomic Molecules (USA), 1979; The Spectra and Structures of Simple Free Radicals: an introduction to Molecular Spectroscopy (USA), 1971; original research on atomic and molecular spectra published in various scientific journals. *Address:* National Research Council, Ottawa, Ontario K1A 0R6, Canada. *T:* (613) 9900917; 190 Lakeway Drive, Rockcliffe Park, Ottawa, Ontario K1L 5B3, Canada. *T:* (613) 7464126.

HERZOG, Chaim, Hon. KBE 1970; President of Israel, 1983–93; *b* Ireland, 17 Sept. 1918; *s* of Rabbi Isaac Halevy Herzog, first Chief Rabbi of Israel and formerly of Ireland, and Sarah Herzog (*née* Hillman); *m* 1947, Aura (*née* Ambache); three *s* one *d. Educ:* Univ. of London (LLB). Called to the Bar, Lincoln's Inn, 1942 (Hon. Bencher, 1987); Advocate, Israel Bar. Immigrated to Palestine, 1935; Army service: Jerusalem, 1936–38; British Army, war of 1939–45; RMC; served 2nd Army, NW Europe; Israel Defence Forces: Defence Attaché, USA, 1950–54; Dir of Mil. Intell., 1948–50 and 1959–62; Comdr, Jerusalem Brigade, 1954–57; Chief of Staff, Southern Comd, 1957–59; retired 1962 (Maj.-Gen.); 1st Mil. Governor, W Bank and Jerusalem, 1967. Ambassador and Perm. Rep. to UN, 1975–78; Mem. Tenth Knesset, 1981–83. Director, 1962–83: Israel Aircraft Industries; Industrial Development Bank of Israel; Israel Discount Bank; Man. Dir, G. U. S. Industries, 1962–72; Senior Partner, Herzog, Fox and Neeman, 1972–83. President: Variety Club of Israel, 1967–72; ORT Israel, 1968–83; World ORT Union, 1980–83. Hon. Fellow, UCL, 1986. Hon. degrees from home and overseas univs. *Publications:* Israel's Finest Hour, 1967; Days of Awe, 1973; (ed) Judaism, Law and Ethics, 1974; The War of Atonement, 1975; Who Stands Accused?, 1978; (with Mordechai Gichon) Battles of the Bible, 1978; The Arab–Israeli Wars, 1982; Heroes of Israel, 1990. *Recreations:* sailing, flying light aircraft, golf. *Address:* Beit Ammot Mishpat, 8 King Saul Boulevard, Tel Aviv 64733, Israel.

HERZOG, Roman; President of the Federal Republic of Germany, since 1994; *b* 5 April 1934. *Educ:* Munich, Berlin and Tübingen Univs. DJur. Mem. for Rhineland-Palatinate, Bundestag, 1973–78; Minister for Culture and Sport, 1978–80, for the Interior, 1980–83, Baden-Württemberg; Vice-Pres, 1983–87, Pres., 1987–94, Federal Constitutional Court. Mem. Federal Cttee, CDU, 1979–83. *Publications:* (jtly) Kommentar zur Grundgesetz, 1966, 3rd edn 1987; Allgemeine Staatslehre, 1971; Staaten der Frühzeit, 1988. *Address:* Office of the President, Kaiser-Friedrich-Strasse 16, 53113 Bonn, Germany.

HESELTINE, Rt Hon. Michael (Ray Dibdin); PC 1979; MP (C) Henley, since 1974 (Tavistock, 1966–74); First Secretary of State and Deputy Prime Minister, since 1995; *b* 21 March 1933; *s* of late Col R. D. Heseltine, Swansea, Glamorgan; *m* 1962, Anne Harding Williams; one *s* two *d. Educ:* Shrewsbury Sch.; Pembroke Coll., Oxford (BA PPE; Hon. Fellow 1986). Pres. Oxford Union, 1954. National Service (commissioned), Welsh Guards, 1959. Contested (C): Gower, 1959; Coventry North, 1964. Director of Bow Publications, 1961–65; Chm., Haymarket Press, 1966–70. Vice-Chm., Cons. Parly Transport Cttee, 1968; Opposition Spokesman on Transport, 1969; Parly Sec., Min. of Transport, June–Oct. 1970; Parly Under-Sec. of State, DoE, 1970–72; Minister for Aerospace and Shipping, DTI, 1972–74; Opposition Spokesman on: Industry, 1974–76; Environment, 1976–79; Sec. of State for the Environment, 1979–83 and 1990–92, for Defence, 1983–86; Pres., BoT, 1992–95. Pres., Assoc. of Conservative Clubs, 1978; Vice-Pres., 1978, Pres., 1982–84, Nat. Young Conservatives. Mem. Council, Zoological Soc. of London, 1987–90. Hon. Fellow, Leeds Polytechnic, 1988. Hon. FRIBA 1991. Hon. LLD Liverpool, 1990. *Publications:* Reviving the Inner Cities, 1983; Where There's a Will, 1987; The Challenge of Europe, 1989. *Address:* c/o House of Commons, SW1A 0AA. *Club:* Carlton.

HESELTINE, Rt. Hon. Sir William (Frederick Payne), GCB 1990 (KCB 1986; CB 1978); GCVO 1988 (KCVO 1982; CVO 1969; MVO 1961); AC 1988; QSO 1990; PC 1986; Chairman, NZI Insurance Australia Ltd, since 1992 (Deputy Chairman, 1991–92); Director: P&O Australia Ltd, since 1990; West Coast Telecasters Ltd, since 1991; *b* E Fremantle, W Australia, 17 July 1930; *s* of late H. W. Heseltine; *m* 1st, Ann Elizabeth (*d* 1957), *d* of late L. F. Turner, Melbourne; 2nd, Audrey Margaret, *d* of late S. Nolan, Sydney; one *s* one *d. Educ:* Christ Church Grammar Sch., Claremont, WA; University of Western Australia (1st class hons, History). Prime Minister's dept, Canberra, 1951–62; Private Secretary to Prime Minister, 1955–59; Asst Information Officer to The Queen, 1960–61; Acting Official Secretary to Governor-General of Australia, 1962; Asst Federal Director of Liberal Party of Australia, 1962–64; attached to Household of Princess Marina for visit to Australia, 1964; attached to Melbourne Age, 1964; Asst Press Secretary to the Queen, 1965–67, Press Secretary, 1968–72; Assistant Private Secretary to the Queen, 1972–77, Dep. Private Secretary, 1977–86, Private Sec., and Keeper of the Queen's Archives, 1986–90. *Address:* PO Box 35, York, WA 6302, Australia. *Club:* Weld (Perth).

HESKETH, 3rd Baron, *cr* 1935, of Hesketh; **Thomas Alexander Fermor-Hesketh;** Bt 1761; PC 1991; Captain of the Gentlemen at Arms (Government Chief Whip in the House of Lords), 1991–93; *b* 28 Oct. 1950; *s* of 2nd Baron and Christian Mary, OBE 1984, *o d* of Sir John McEwen, 1st Bt of Marchmont, DL, JP; *S* father 1955; *m* 1977, Hon. Claire, *e d* of 3rd Baron Manton, *qv*; one *s* two *d. Educ:* Ampleforth. A Lord in Waiting (Govt Whip), 1986–89; Parly Under-Sec. of State, DoE, 1989–90; Minister of State, DTI, 1990–91. Hon. FSE. *Heir: s* Hon. Frederick Hatton Fermor-Hesketh, *b* 13 Oct. 1988. *Address:* Easton Neston, Towcester, Northamptonshire NN12 7HS. *T:* Towcester (01327) 350445. *Clubs:* White's, Turf.

HESLAM, (Mary) Noelle, (Mrs David Heslam); *see* Walsh, M. N.

HESLOP, David Thomas, OBE 1987; CompIGasE; Regional Chairman, British Gas plc Southern, since 1989; *b* 16 Sept. 1932; *s* of late John Heslop and Frances Mary (*née* Brooks); *m* 1952, Barbara Mary Seddon; one *s* one *d. Educ:* Henley Management Coll. (GMC 1974); Harvard Business Sch. (AMP 1981). CompIGasE 1990. Commercial Sales Officer, Scottish Gas, 1960; Marketing Develt Man., West Midlands Gas, 1965; Sales Man., South Eastern Gas, 1972; Dir of Sales, North Western Gas, 1976; HQ Dir of Sales, British Gas, 1982. Pres., Internat. Gas Marketing Colloquium, 1986–89. FCIM 1977; CIMgt (CBIM 1990). *Recreations:* chess, choral singing, walking, Rugby. *Address:* British Gas plc Southern, 80 St Mary's Road, Southampton SO9 5AT.

HESLOP, Martin Sydney; QC 1995; Senior Treasury Counsel, since 1993; a Recorder of the Crown Court, since 1993; *b* 6 Aug. 1948; *s* of late Sydney Heslop and of Patricia (*née* Day). *Educ:* St George's Coll., Weybridge; Bristol Univ. LLB Hons 1971. Called to the Bar, Lincoln's Inn, 1972; Jun. Treasury Counsel, 1987; First Jun. Treasury Counsel, 1992–93. Asst Recorder, 1989–93. *Recreations:* sailing, travel, photography. *Address:* 1 Hare Court, Temple, EC4Y 7BE. *T:* 0171–353 5324. *Club:* Bar Yacht.

HESLOP, Philip Linnell; QC 1985; *b* 24 April 1948; *s* of late Richard Norman Heslop and of Ina Winifred Heslop, Merstham, Surrey. *Educ:* Haileybury; Christ's Coll., Cambridge (schol.; BA Hons (Law Tripos) 1970; LLM 1971). Called to the Bar, Lincoln's Inn, 1970, Bencher, 1993; Jt Jun. Counsel (Chancery), DTI, 1979–85. Dep. Chm., Membership Tribunal, IMRO, 1988–; DTI Inspector, Consolidated Goldfields PLC. Chm., CU Cons. Assoc., 1969; Pres., Cambridge Union Soc., 1971; Chm., Coningsby Club, 1976; contested (C) Lambeth Vauxhall, 1979. *Publication:* (ed jtly) Crew on Meetings, 1975. *Recreations:* travel, sailing, ski-ing, history. *Address:* 4 Stone Buildings, Lincoln's Inn, WC2A 3XT. *T:* 0171–242 5524.

HESLOP-HARRISON, Prof. John, MSc, PhD, DSc; FRS 1970; FRSE, MRIA, FRSA, FLS; Royal Society Research Professor, University College of Wales, Aberystwyth, 1977–85; *b* 10 Feb. 1920; *s* of late Prof. J. W. Heslop-Harrison, FRS; *m* 1950, Yolande Massey; one *s. Educ:* Grammar School, Chester-le-Street, King's Coll. (University of Durham), Newcastle upon Tyne. MSc (Dunelm), PhD (Belfast), DSc (Dunelm). Army service, 1941–45. Lecturer in Agricultural Botany, King's Coll., Univ. of Durham, 1945–46; Lecturer in Botany: Queen's Univ., Belfast, 1946–50; UCL, 1950–53; Reader in Taxonomy, UCL, 1953–54; Prof. of Botany, Queen's Univ., Belfast, 1954–60; Mason Prof. of Botany, Univ. of Birmingham, 1960–67; Prof. of Botany, Inst. of Plant Develt, Univ. of Wisconsin, 1967–71; Dir, Royal Botanic Gardens, Kew, 1971–76. Visiting Professor: (Brittingham) Univ. of Wisconsin, 1965; US Dept of Agriculture Institute of Forest Genetics, Rhinelander, Wis, 1968; Univ. of Massachusetts, Amherst, Mass, 1976–77, 1978–79; Lectures: Sigma Xi, Geneva, NY, 1969; William Wright Smith, Edinburgh, 1972; George Bidder, Soc. Exptl Biol., Leeds, 1973; Ghosh, Univ. of Calcutta, 1973; Kennedy Orton Meml, UCW, Bangor, 1974; Croonian, Royal Society, 1974; Amos Meml, E Malling, 1975; Holden, Univ. of Nottingham, 1976; Bewley, Glasshouse Crops Res. Inst., 1978; Hooker, Linnean Soc., 1979; Bateson, John Innes Inst., 1979; Waller Meml, Univ. of Ohio, 1980; Blackman, Univ. of Oxford, 1980. Mem., ARC, 1977–82; Vice-President: Botanical Soc. of British Isles, 1972; Linnean Soc., 1973; President: Inst. of Biology, 1974–75; Sect. K, British Assoc. for Advancement of Science, 1974. Editor, Annals of Botany, 1961–67. Corresp. Mem., Royal Netherlands Botanical Soc., 1968; For. Fellow, Indian Nat. Sci. Acad., 1974; For. Associate, National Acad. of Sciences, USA, 1983; Mem., German Acad. of Science, 1975; For. Mem., American Botanical Soc., 1976; For. Hon. Mem., Amer. Acad. Arts and Scis., 1982; For. Mem., Acad. Royale de Belgique (Sci. Div.), 1985. Hon. DSc: Belfast, 1971; Bath, 1982; Edinburgh, 1984; Hull, 1986. Trail-Crisp Award, Linnean Soc., 1967; Univ. of Liège Medal, 1967; Erdtman Internat. Medal for Palynology, 1971; Cooke Award, Amer. Acad. of Allergy, 1974; Darwin Medal, Royal Soc., 1983; Keith Medal, RSE, 1984; Navashin Medal, Komarov Inst., USSR Acad., 1991. *Publications:* papers and monographs on botanical and cell physiological subjects in various British and foreign journals. *Recreations:* hill walking, photography and painting. *Address:* The Pleasaunce, 137 Bargates, Leominster, Herefordshire HR6 8QS. *T:* Leominster (01568) 611566; Institute of Grassland and Environmental Research, Plas Gogerddan, near Aberystwyth SY23 3EB.

HESS, Ellen Elizabeth, NDH; Administrator, Studley College Trust, 1970–80; Principal, Studley College, Warwickshire, 1956–69; *b* 28 Dec. 1908; *d* of Charles Michael Joseph Hess and Fanny Thompson Hess (*née* Alder). *Educ:* Grammar School for Girls, Dalston; Royal Botanic Society, Regents Park. Lecturer in Horticulture, Swanley Horticultural College for Women, 1934–39; Agricultural Secretary, National Federation of Women's

Institutes, 1939–46; Ellen Eddy Shaw Fellowship, Brooklyn Botanic Gardens, New York, USA, 1946–47; School of Horticulture, Ambler, Pa., USA, 1947–48; HM Inspector of Schools (Agriculture and Further Education), 1948–56. Veitch Meml Medal, RHS, 1967. *Recreations:* travel, photography, walking. *Address:* Augusta Court, Winterbourne Road, Chichester, West Sussex PO19 4TT.

HESSAYON, Dr David Gerald; gardening author; Chairman: Expert Publications Ltd, since 1988; Hessayon Books, since 1993; *b* 13 Feb. 1928; *s* of Jack and Lena Hessayon; *m* 1951, Joan Parker Gray; two *d. Educ:* Salford Grammar Sch.; Leeds Univ. (BSc 1950); Manchester Univ. (PhD 1954). FRMS 1960; FRES 1960; FRSA 1970; FIBiol 1971; FIMgt (FBIM 1972); FIHort 1986. Res. Fellow, UC of Gold Coast, 1953. Pan Britannica Industries Ltd: Technical Man., 1955–60; Tech. Dir, 1960–64; Man. Dir, 1964–91; Chm., 1972–93; Chm., Turbair Ltd, 1972–93. Chm., British Agrochemicals Assoc., 1980–81. Vice-Patron, Royal Nat. Rose Soc., 1987–. Mem., Guild of Freemen, City of London, 1977–; Liveryman, Gardeners' Co., 1985. Hon. DSc: Manchester, 1990; Hertfordshire, 1994. Lifetime Achievement Trophy, Nat. British Book Awards, 1992; Veitch Gold Meml Medal, RHS, 1992. *Publications:* Be Your Own Gardening Expert, 1959, revd edn 1977; Be Your Own House Plant Expert, 1960; Potato Growers Handbook, 1961; Silage Makers Handbook, 1961; Be Your Own Lawn Expert, 1962, revd edn 1979; Be Your Own Rose Expert, 1964, revd edn 1977; (with J. P. Hessayon) The Garden Book of Europe, 1973; Vegetable Plotter, 1976; Be Your Own House Plant Spotter, 1977; Be Your Own Vegetable Doctor, 1978; Be Your Own Garden Doctor, 1978; The House Plant Expert, 1980; The Rose Expert, 1981; The Lawn Expert, 1982; The Cereal Disease Expert, 1982; The Tree and Shrub Expert, 1983; The Armchair Book of the Garden, 1983; The Flower Expert, 1984; The Vegetable Expert, 1985; The Indoor Plant Spotter, 1985; The Garden Expert, 1986; The Gold Plated House Plant Expert, 1987; The Home Expert, 1987; Vegetable Jotter, 1989; Rose Jotter, 1989; House Plant Jotter, 1989; The Fruit Expert, 1990; Be Your Own Greenhouse Expert, 1990; The Bio Friendly Gardening Guide, 1990; The Bedding Plant Expert, 1991; The New House Plant Expert, 1991; The Garden DIY Expert, 1992; The Rock and Water Garden Expert, 1993; The Flowering Shrub Expert, 1994; The Greenhouse Expert, 1994; The Flower Arranging Expert, 1994; The Container Expert, 1995; The Bulb Expert, 1995; The Labour-saving Gardening Expert, 1995. *Recreations:* American folk music, cartophily, thinking about the book I should be writing. *Address:* c/o Transworld Publishers Ltd, 61–63 Uxbridge Road, W5 5SA.

HESSE, Prof. Joachim Jens, PhD; Professor of European Politics and Comparative Government, University of Oxford, since 1991; Official Fellow, Nuffield College, Oxford, since 1991; Director, Centre for European Studies, Nuffield College, since 1991; *b* 20 Nov. 1942; *s* of Joachim Hesse and Frieda Hesse (*née* Madrowski); *m* 1981, Irmgart Wethmar-von Hagen; one *s* one *d. Educ:* Schadow Gymnasium, Berlin; Univ. of Goettingen; Univ. of Kiel; Univ. of Berlin (Dipl. Volkswirt. 1967); Univ. of Cologne (PhD Econs 1972). Res. Associate, German Inst. of Urbanism, Berlin, 1968–73; Professor of: Pol and Admin. Scis, Univ. of Constance, 1973–77; Pol Sci. and Comparative Govt, Duisburg, 1978–83; Exec. Dir, Rhine–Ruhr Inst. for Social Res. and Public Policy Studies, 1980–84; Prof. of Pol and Admin. Scis, German Post-Grad. Sch. of Admin. Scis, Speyer, 1984–90. Vis. Prof., Coll. of Europe, Bruges, 1987–90; Visiting Scholar: Harvard Univ., 1984–85; Oxford Univ., 1988–89. Consultant: OECD, UN, EEC, ILO, 1972–. Man. Editor, Staatswissenschaften und Staatspraxis, 1990–; Internat. Editor, Public Admin., 1992–; General Editor: Jahrbuch zur Staatswissenschaft und Staatspraxis, 1987–; European Yearbook on Comparative Govt and Public Admin., 1994–. *Publications:* include: (ed) Local Government and Urban Affairs in International Perspective, 1991; Das Regierungssystem der Bundesrepublik Deutschland, 7th edn, 1992; Administrative Transformation in Central and Eastern Europe, 1993. *Address:* Stockwell, The Ridgeway, Boars Hill, Oxford OX1 5EZ. *T:* Oxford (01865) 326544.

HESSE, Mary Brenda, MA, MSc, PhD; FBA 1971; Professor of Philosophy of Science, University of Cambridge, 1975–85; Fellow of Wolfson College (formerly University College), Cambridge, 1965–92, subseq. Hon. Fellow; *b* 15 Oct. 1924; *d* of Ethelbert Thomas Hesse and Brenda Nellie Hesse (*née* Pelling). *Educ:* Imperial Coll., London; University Coll., London. MSc, PhD (London); DIC; MA (Cantab). Lecturer: in Mathematics, Univ. of Leeds, 1951–55; in Hist. and Philosophy of Science, UCL, 1955–59; in Philosophy of Science, Univ. of Cambridge, 1960–68; Reader in Philosophy of Sci., Cambridge Univ., 1968–75; Vice-Pres., Wolfson Coll., 1976–80. Member: Council, British Acad., 1979–82; UGC, 1980–85. Visiting Professor: Yale Univ., 1961; Univ. of Minnesota, 1966; Univ. of Chicago, 1968. Stanton Lectr, Cambridge, 1977–80; Joint Gifford Lectr, Edinburgh, 1983. Mem., Academia Europaea, 1989. Hon. DSc: Hull, 1984; Guelph, Ontario, 1987. Editor, Brit. Jl for the Philosophy of Science, 1965–69. *Publications:* Science and the Human Imagination, 1954; Forces and Fields, 1961; Models and Analogies in Science, 1963; The Structure of Scientific Inference, 1974; Revolutions and Reconstructions in the Philosophy of Science, 1980; (jtly) The Construction of Reality, 1987; articles in jls of philosophy and of the history and the philosophy of science. *Recreations:* walking, local archaeology. *Address:* Wolfson College, Cambridge CB3 9BB. *Club:* Commonwealth Trust.

HESTER, Rev. Canon John Frear; Canon Residentiary and Precentor of Chichester Cathedral, since 1985; Chaplain to the Queen, since 1984; *b* 21 Jan. 1927; *s* of William and Frances Mary Hester; *m* 1959, Elizabeth Margaret, *d* of Sir Eric Riches, MC, MS, FRCS; three *s. Educ:* West Hartlepool Grammar School; St Edmund Hall, Oxford (MA); Cuddesdon Coll., Oxford. Captain RAEC, 1949–50. Personal Asst to Bishop of Gibraltar, 1950; Deacon, 1952; Priest, 1953; Assistant Curate: St George's, Southall, 1952–55; Holy Redeemer, Clerkenwell, 1955–58; Sec., Actors' Church Union, 1958–63; Chaplain, Soc. of the Sisters of Bethany, Lloyd Sq., 1959–62; Dep. Minor Canon of St Paul's Cathedral, 1962–75; Rector of Soho, 1963–75; Priest-in-charge of St Paul's, Covent Garden, 1969–75; Senior Chaplain, Actors' Church Union, 1970–75; Chaplain to Lord Mayor of Westminster, 1970–71; in residence at St George's Coll. and the Ecumenical Inst., Tantur, Jerusalem, 1973; Chm., Covent Garden Conservation Area Adv. Ctee, 1971–75; Vicar of Brighton, 1975–85; Canon and Prebendary of Chichester Cathedral, 1976–85; RD of Brighton, 1976–85. Chm., Chichester Diocesan Overseas Council, 1985–94. Editor, Christian Drama, 1957–59. Lectr and preacher, US, 1961–; Leader of Pilgrimages to the Holy Land, Turkey, etc, 1962–. Mem., Worshipful Co. of Parish Clerks, 1970–86; Chaplain, Brighton and Hove Albion FC, 1979–. Vice-Pres., 1979– and Hon. Chaplain, 1975–79 and 1988–, Royal Theatrical Fund (formerly Royal Gen. Theatrical Fund Assoc.); Chm. of Trustees, Chichester Centre of Arts, 1989–; Chm., Chichester Arts Liaison Gp, 1990–95; Pres., Forum Soc., 1985–; Vice-Pres., Guild of Sussex Craftsmen, 1991–; Gov., Lavant House Sch., 1993– (Chm. Govs, 1995–). Hon. Mem., British Actors' Equity Assoc. *Publication:* Soho Is My Parish, 1970. *Recreations:* sitting down; pulling legs; watching soccer and other drama; Middle Eastern studies. *Address:* The Residentiary, Canon Lane, Chichester PO19 1PX. *T:* Chichester (01243) 782961.

HESTER, Prof. Ronald Ernest, DSc,. PhD; CChem, FRSC; Professor of Chemistry, University of York, since 1983; *b* 8 March 1936; *s* of Ernest and Rhoda Hester; *m* 1958, Bridget Ann Maddin; two *s* two *d. Educ:* Royal Grammar Sch., High Wycombe; London Univ. (BSc; DSc 1979); Cornell Univ. (PhD 1962). CChem 1975; FRSC 1971. Res. Fellow, Cambridge Univ., 1962–63; Asst Prof., Cornell Univ., 1963–65; University of York: Lectr, 1965–71; Sen. Lectr, 1971–76; Reader, 1976–83. Science and Engineering Research Council: Chm., Chemistry Cttee, 1988–90; Mem., Science Bd, 1988–90; Mem., Council, 1990–94. Chm., Envmt Group, RSC, 1982–85. European Editor, BioSpectroscopy, 1994–. *Publications:* (jtly) Inorganic Chemistry, 1965; (ed with R. J. H. Clark) Advances in Infrared and Raman Spectroscopy, 12 vols, 1975–85; (ed with R. J. H. Clark) Advances in Spectroscopy, 12 vols, 1986–95; (ed with R. M. Harrison) Issues in Environmental Science and Technology, Vols 1 and 2, 1994, Vols 3 and 4, 1995; 250 research papers. *Recreations:* tennis, squash, golf, ski-ing, travel. *Address:* Department of Chemistry, University of York, York YO1 5DD. *T:* York (01904) 432557.

HESTON, Charlton; actor (films, stage and television), USA; *b* Evanston, Ill, 4 Oct. 1924; *s* of Russell Whitford Carter and Lilla Carter (*née* Charlton); *m* 1944, Lydia Marie Clarke (actress), Two Rivers, Wisconsin; one *s* one *d. Educ:* New Trier High Sch., Ill; Sch. of Speech, Northwestern Univ., 1941–43. Served War of 1939–45, with 11th Army Air Forces in the Aleutians. Co-Dir (with wife), also both acting, Thomas Wolfe Memorial Theatre, Asheville, NC (plays: the State of the Union, The Glass Menagerie, etc.). In Antony and Cleopatra, Martin Beck Theatre, New York, 1947; also acting on Broadway, 1949 and 1950, etc.; London stage début (also dir.), The Caine Mutiny Court Martial, Queen's, 1985; A Man for All Seasons, Savoy, 1987, tour 1988. *Films:* (1950–) include: Dark City, Ruby Gentry, The Greatest Show on Earth, Arrowhead, Bad For Each Other, The Savage, Pony Express, The President's Lady, Secret of the Incas, The Naked Jungle, The Far Horizons, The Private War of Major Benson, The Ten Commandments (Moses), The Big Country, Ben Hur (Acad. Award for best actor, 1959), The Wreck of the Mary Deare, El Cid, 55 Days at Peking, The Greatest Story Ever Told, Major Dundee, The Agony and the Ecstacy, Khartoum, Will Penny, Planet of the Apes, Soylent Green, The Three Musketeers, Earthquake, Airport 1975, The Four Musketeers, The Last Hard Men, Battle of Midway, Two-Minute Warning, Gray Lady Down, Crossed Swords, The Mountain Men, The Awakening, Mother Lode, Music Box. TV appearances, esp. in Shakespeare. Mem., Screen Actors' Guild (Pres., 1966–69); Mem., Nat. Council on the Arts, 1967–; Chm., Amer. Film Inst., 1961–; Chm., Center Theatre Group, LA, 1963; Chm. on the Arts for Presidential Task Force on the Arts and Humanities, 1981–. Is interested in Shakespearian roles. Hon. Dr: Jacksonville Univ., Fla; Abilene Christian Univ., Texas. Academy Award, 1978; Jean Hersholt Humanitarian Award, 1978. *Publications:* (ed Hollis Alpert) The Actor's Life: Journals 1956–1976, 1979; Beijing Diary, 1990. *Address:* c/o ICM, 388–396 Oxford Street, W1 9HE. *Club:* All England Lawn Tennis.

HETHERINGTON, Alastair; *see* Hetherington, H. A.

HETHERINGTON, (Arthur) Carleton, CBE 1971 (MBE 1945); Secretary of Association of County Councils, 1974–80; *b* 13 Feb. 1916; *s* of late Arthur Stanley and Mary Venters Hetherington, Silloth, Cumberland; *m* 1941, Xenia, *d* of late Nicholas Gubsky, Barnes; three *s. Educ:* St Bees Sch. Admitted Solicitor 1938. Asst Solicitor: Peterborough, 1938–39; Stafford, 1939. Served Royal Artillery, 1939–46 (Hon. Lt-Col); Temp. Lt-Col 1944–46. Dep. Clerk of the Peace and Dep. Clerk of County Council: of Cumberland, 1946–52; of Cheshire, 1952–59; Clerk of the Peace and Clerk of County Council of Cheshire, 1959–64. Sec., County Councils Assoc., 1964–74. Mem., Departmental Cttee on Jury Service, 1963–64; Sec., Local Authorities Management Services and Computer Cttee, 1965–80. *Recreations:* music, golf, family. *Address:* 33 Campden Hill Court, W8 7HS.

HETHERINGTON, Sir Arthur (Ford), Kt 1974; DSC 1944; FEng 1976; Chairman, British Gas Corporation, 1973–76 (Member 1961, Deputy Chairman 1967–72, Chairman 1972, Gas Council); *b* 12 July 1911; *s* of late Sir Roger Hetherington and Lady Hetherington; *m* 1937, Margaret Lacey; one *s* one *d. Educ:* Highgate Sch.; Trinity Coll., Cambridge (BA). Joined staff of Gas Light & Coke Company, 1935. Served War, RNVR, 1941–45. North Thames Gas Board, 1945–55; joined staff of Southern Gas Board, 1955; Deputy Chairman, 1956; Chairman 1961–64; Chairman, E Midlands Gas Board, 1964–66. Hon. FIGasE. Hon. DSc London, 1974. *Address:* 32 Connaught Square, W2 2HL. *T:* 0171–723 3128. *Club:* Athenæum.

HETHERINGTON, Carleton; *see* Hetherington, A. C.

HETHERINGTON, (Hector) Alastair; journalist; Research Professor in Media Studies, Stirling University, 1982–87, now Emeritus; former Editor of The Guardian; *b* Llanishen, Glamorganshire, 31 Oct. 1919; *yr s* of late Sir Hector Hetherington and Lady Hetherington; *m* 1st, 1957, Miranda (marr. diss. 1978), *d* of Professor R. A. C. Oliver, *qv*; two *s* two *d*; 2nd, 1979, Sheila Janet Cameron, *widow* of Hamish Cameron; one step *s* two step *d. Educ:* Gresham's Sch., Holt; Corpus Christi Coll., Oxford (Hon. Fellow, 1971). Royal Armoured Corps, 1940–46. Editorial staff, The Glasgow Herald, 1946–50; joined Manchester Guardian, 1950, Asst Editor and Foreign Editor, 1953–56, Editor, 1956–75; Director: Guardian and Manchester Evening News Ltd, 1956–75; Guardian Newspapers Ltd, 1967–75; Controller, BBC Scotland, 1975–78; Manager, BBC Highland, 1979–80. Member, Royal Commission on the Police, 1960–62. Vis. Fellow, Nuffield Coll., Oxford, 1973–79. Trustee, Scott Trust, 1970–89 (Chm., 1984–89). Dr *hc* Univ. of Lille 3, 1989. Journalist of the Year, Nat. Press awards, 1970; Special Award, Bank of Scotland Press awards, 1992. *Publications:* Guardian Years, 1981; News, Newspapers and Television, 1985; News in the Regions, 1989; Highlands and Islands: a generation of progress, 1990; Cameras in the Commons, 1990; BBC Scotland 1975–80, 1992; A Walker's Guide to Arran, 1994. *Recreations:* hill walking, golf. *Address:* Tigh na-Fraoich, High Corrie, Isle of Arran KA27 8JB. *T:* Brodick (01770) 810652. *Club:* Athenæum.

HETHERINGTON, Sir Thomas Chalmers, (Tony), KCB 1979; CBE 1970; TD; QC 1978; Director of Public Prosecutions, 1977–87; Head of the Crown Prosecution Service, 1986–87; *b* 18 Sept. 1926; *er s* of William and Alice Hetherington; *m* 1953, June Margaret Ann Catliff; four *d. Educ:* Rugby Sch.; Christ Church, Oxford. Served in Royal Artillery, Middle East, 1945–48; Territorial Army, 1948–67. Called to Bar, Inner Temple, 1952; Bencher, 1978. Legal Dept, Min. of Pensions and Nat. Insce, 1953; Law Officers' Dept, 1962, Legal Sec., 1966–75; Dep. Treasury Solicitor, 1975–77. Jt Head, War Crimes Inquiry, 1988–89. Pres., Old Rugbeians Soc., 1988–90. *Publication:* Prosecution and the Public Interest, 1989. *Address:* Rosemount, Mount Pleasant Road, Lingfield, Surrey RH7 6BH.

HETZEL, Phyllis Bertha Mabel, (Mrs R. D. Hetzel, jr); Registrar of the Roll, and Bye-Fellow, Newnham College, Cambridge, since 1993; President, Lucy Cavendish College, Cambridge, 1979–84; *b* 10 June 1918; *d* of Stanley Ernest and Bertha Myson; *m* 1st, 1941, John Henry Lewis James (*d* 1962); one *d*; 2nd, 1974, Baron Bowden (marr. diss. 1983, he *d* 1989); 3rd, 1985, Ralph Dorn Hetzel (*d* 1994). *Educ:* Wimbledon High Sch.; Newnham Coll., Cambridge (MA). Commonwealth (now Harkness) Fellow, 1957–58. BoT, 1941; Principal 1947; Asst Sec., 1960; DEA, 1964–69; Min. of Technology, 1969–70; Dept of Trade and Industry, 1970–75; Asst Under-Sec. of State 1972; Regional Dir, NW Region, DTI, subseq. DoI, 1972–75. Member: Monopolies and Mergers

Commn, 1975–78; Local Govt Boundary Commn for England, 1977–81; W Midlands Cttee, National Trust, 1976–81. Chm., Manchester, Marriage Guidance Council, 1976–79. Member: Court, Manchester Univ., 1976–83; Court and Council, UMIST, 1978–80; Council of Senate, Cambridge Univ., 1983–84; Bd, American Friends of Cambridge University Inc., 1985–. Vice-Pres., Oxford and Cambridge Club of Los Angeles, 1986–92. *Publications:* The Concept of Growth Centres, 1968; Gardens through the Ages, 1971; Regional Policy in Action, 1980; contrib. Public Administration, Cambridge Review, Encycl. Britannica. *Recreations:* landscape architecture, conservation, writing, piano, family. *Address:* 18 Trafalgar Road, Cambridge CB4 1EU. *T:* Cambridge (01223) 69878; Newnham College, Cambridge CB3 9DF.

HEUSTON, Prof. Robert Francis Vere, DCL Oxon 1970; MRIA 1978; Regius Professor of Laws, Trinity College, Dublin, 1970–83; *b* Dublin, 17 Nov. 1923; *e s* of late Vere Douglas Heuston and late Dorothy Helen Coulter; *m* 1962, Bridget Nancy (*née* Bolland), *widow* of Neville Ward-Perkins; four step *c. Educ:* St Columba's Coll.; Trinity Coll., Dublin; St John's Coll., Cambridge. Barrister, King's Inns, 1947 (Hon. Bencher, 1983), Gray's Inn, 1951 (Hon. Bencher, 1988); Hon. Member, Western Circuit, 1966. Fellow, Pembroke Coll., Oxford, 1947–65 (Hon. Fellow, 1982), Dean, 1951–57, Pro-Proctor, 1953; Professor of Law, Univ. of Southampton, 1965–70. Arthur Goodhart Prof. of Legal Sci., and Fellow, Jesus Coll., Cambridge, 1986–87. Member, Law Reform Cttee (England), 1968–70, (Ireland), 1975–81. Visiting Professor: Univ. of Melbourne, 1956; Univ. of British Columbia, 1960, 1985; ANU, 1977; Gresham Professor in Law, 1964–70. Corresponding FBA, 1988. Hon. QC 1995. Hon. LLD Buckingham. *Publications:* (ed) Salmond and Heuston on Torts, 11th edn 1953, to 20th edn 1992; Essays in Constitutional Law, 2nd edn 1964; Lives of the Lord Chancellors, vol. I, 1885–1940, 1964, vol. II, 1940–70, 1987; various in learned periodicals. *Address:* Kentstown House, Brownstown, Navan, Co. Meath, Ireland. *T:* Drogheda (41) 25195. *Clubs:* Beefsteak, United Oxford & Cambridge University; Royal Irish Yacht.

HEWARD, Air Chief Marshal Sir Anthony Wilkinson, KCB 1972 (CB 1968); OBE 1952; DFC and bar; AFC; Air Member for Supply and Organisation, Ministry of Defence, 1973–76; *b* 1 July 1918; *s* of late Col E. J. Heward; *m* 1944, Clare Myfanwy Wainwright, *d* of late Maj.-Gen. C. B. Wainwright, CB; one *s* one *d*. Gp Captain RAF, 1957; IDC 1962; Air Cdre 1963; Dir of Operations (Bomber and Reconnaissance) MoD (RAF), 1963; Air Vice-Marshal 1966; Dep. Comdr, RAF Germany, 1966–69; AOA, HQ RAF Air Support Command, 1969–70; Air Marshal 1970; Chief of Staff, RAF Strike Command, 1970–72; AOC, No 18 (Maritime) Group, 1972–73; Air Chief Marshal, 1974. County Councillor, Wilts, 1981–89. *Address:* Home Close, Donhead St Mary, near Shaftesbury, Dorset SP7 9DL. *Clubs:* Royal Air Force, Flyfishers'.

HEWARD, Edmund Rawlings, CB 1984; Chief Master of the Supreme Court (Chancery Division), 1980–85 (Master, 1959–79); *b* 19 Aug. 1912; *s* of late Rev. Thomas Brown Heward and Kathleen Amy Rachel Rawlings; *m* 1945, Constance Mary Sandiford, *d* of late George Bertram Crossley, OBE. *Educ:* Repton; Trinity Coll., Cambridge. Admitted a solicitor, 1937. Enlisted Royal Artillery as a Gunner, 1940; released as Major, DAAG, 1946. Partner in Rose, Johnson and Hicks, 9 Suffolk St, SW1, 1946. LLM 1960. *Publications:* Guide to Chancery Practice, 1962 (5th edn 1979); Matthew Hale, 1972; (ed) Part 2, Tristram and Coote's Probate Practice, 24th edn, 1973, 26th edn, 1983; (ed) Judgments and Orders in Halsbury's Laws of England, 4th edn; Lord Mansfield, 1979, paperback 1985; Chancery Practice, 1983, 2nd edn 1990; Chancery Orders, 1986; Lord Denning—A Biography, 1990; Masters in Ordinary, 1991; The Great and the Good—a life of Lord Radcliffe, 1995. *Address:* 36a Dartmouth Row, Greenwich, SE10 8AW. *T:* 0181–692 3525. *Clubs:* United Oxford & Cambridge University, Travellers'.

HEWES, Robin Anthony Charles; Director, Finance, Lloyd's of London, and Member of Lloyd's Market Board, since 1994; *b* 15 April 1945; *s* of late Leslie Augustus Hewes and Lily Violet Hewes (*née* Norfolk); *m* 1967, Christine Diane Stonebridge; one *s* two *d*. *Educ:* Colchester Royal Grammar School; Bristol Univ. (LLB Hons 1966). Inspector of Taxes, 1966; Department of Industry, 1974; Cabinet Office (Management and Personnel Office), 1985–87; Dir, Enterprise and Deregulation Unit, DTI, 1987–88; Head, later Dir, Regulatory Services, Lloyd's of London, 1988–94 (nominated Member, Council of Lloyd's and Lloyd's Regulatory Bd, 1993–94). Non-exec. Dir, Comforto-Vickers (formerly Vickers Business Equipment Div.), 1984–88. *Recreation:* swimming. *Address:* 38 Plovers Mead, Wyatts Green, Brentwood, Essex CM15 0PS. *T:* Brentwood (01277) 822891.

HEWETSON, Ven. Christopher; Archdeacon of Chester, since 1994; *b* 1 June 1937; *s* of Edward and Mary Hewetson; *m* 1963, Alison Mary Croft; four *d*. *Educ:* Shrewsbury Sch.; Trinity Coll., Oxford (MA); Chichester Theol Coll. Assistant Master: Dragon Sch., Oxford, 1960–64 and 1966–67; The Craig, Windermere, 1964–66. Ordained deacon, 1969, priest, 1970; Assistant Curate: SS Peter and Paul, Leckhampton, 1969–71; All Saints, Wokingham, 1971–73; Vicar, St Peter's, Didcot, 1973–82; Rector, All Saints, Ascot Heath, 1982–90; Chaplain, St George's Sch., Ascot, 1985–88; RD, Bracknell, 1986–90; Priest i/c, Holy Trinity, Headington Quarry, 1990–94; Hon. Canon, Christ Church, Oxford, 1992–94; RD, Cowley, 1994. *Recreations:* fell walking, restoring old pictures, opera. *Address:* 25 Bartholomew Way, Westminster Park, Chester CH4 7RJ. *T:* Chester (01244) 675417.

HEWETSON, Sir Christopher (Raynor), Kt 1984; TD 1967; DL; Partner, Lace Mawer (formerly Laces), Solicitors, Liverpool, 1961–95; President, Law Society, 1983–84; *b* 26 Dec. 1929; *s* of Harry Raynor Hewetson and Emma Hewetson; *m* 1962, Alison May Downie, *d* of late Prof. A. W. Downie, FRCP, FRS; two *s* one *d*. *Educ:* Sedbergh Sch.; Peterhouse, Cambridge (MA). National Service, 2nd Lieut 4th RHA, 1951–53; Territorial Service, 1953–68: Lt-Col commanding 359 Medium Regt, RA, TA, 1965–68. Qualified as solicitor, 1956. Mem. Council, Law Society, 1966–87; Vice-Pres., 1982–83; President, Liverpool Law Society, 1976. Gov., Coll. of Law, 1969–94 (Chm., 1977–82). Hon. Col, 33 Signal Regt (V), 1992–94. DL Merseyside, 1986. *Recreations:* golf, walking. *Address:* 24c Westcliffe Road, Birkdale, Southport, Merseyside PR8 2BU. *T:* Southport (01704) 567179. *Clubs:* Army and Navy; Athenæum (Liverpool); Royal Birkdale Golf (Southport).

HEWETT, Sir Peter (John Smithson), 6th Bt *cr* 1813, of Nether Seale, Leicestershire, MM 1956; *b* 27 June 1931; *s* of Sir John George Hewett, 5th Bt, MC and Yuilleen Maude (*d* 1980), *d* of late Samuel Frederick Smithson; *S* father, 1990; *m* 1958, Jennifer Ann Cooper, *o c* of late Emrys Thomas Jones, OBE; two *s* one *d*. *Educ:* Bradfield Coll.; Jesus Coll., Cambridge (BA). Called to Bar, Gray's Inn, 1954; now a practising Advocate in Kenya. *Heir: s* Richard Mark John Hewett, *b* 15 Nov. 1958. *Address:* PO Box 15669, Nairobi, Kenya.

HEWETT, Major Richard William; Vice President and Director, International Operations, Reader's Digest Association Inc., 1986–88; *b* 22 Oct. 1923; *s* of late Brig. W. G. Hewett, OBE, MC, and Louise S. Hewett (*née* Wolfe); *m* 1954, Rosemary Cridland; two *d*. *Educ:* Wellington Coll., Berks. Enlisted RA, 1941; commnd RA, 1943; regular commn 1944: served Normandy, India, UK, Malaya; regtl duty, flying duties Air OP, Instr, OCTU, Mons, 1954; sc 1955; Staff and regtl duties, Germany, 1956–59; Mil. Mission, USA, 1959–61. Joined Reader's Digest Assoc. Ltd, 1962; Dir 1976; Man. Dir, 1981–84; Chm. and Man. Dir, 1984–86. *Recreations:* tennis, fishing, travelling.

HEWISH, Prof. Antony, MA, PhD; FRS 1968; Professor of Radioastronomy, University of Cambridge, 1971–89, now Emeritus (Reader, 1969–71); Fellow of Churchill College since 1962; *b* 11 May 1924; *s* of late Ernest William Hewish and Frances Grace Lanyon Pinch; *m* 1950, Marjorie Elizabeth Catherine Richards; one *s* one *d*. *Educ:* King's Coll., Taunton; Gonville and Caius Coll., Cambridge (Hon. Fellow, 1976). BA (Cantab.) 1948, MA 1950, PhD 1952; Hamilton Prize, Isaac Newton Student, 1952. RAE Farnborough, 1943–46; Research Fellow, Gonville and Caius Coll., 1952–54; Asst Dir of Research, 1954–62; Fellow, Gonville and Caius Coll., 1955–62; Lectr in Physics, Univ. of Cambridge, 1962–69. Dir, Mullard Radio Astronomy Observatory, Cambridge, 1982–87. Visiting Prof. in Astronomy, Yale, 1963; Prof. of the Royal Instn, 1977; Vikram Sarabhai Prof., Physical Res. Lab., Ahmedabad, India, 1988. Lectures: Karl Schwarzschild, Bonn, 1971; Lindsay Meml, Maryland, 1972; Larmor, Cambridge, 1973; Harland, Exeter, 1974; Kelvin, IEE, 1975; Halley, Oxford, 1979; Selby, Cardiff, 1983; Krishnan Meml, New Delhi, 1989; Gold, Cornell, 1992; Saha Meml, Calcutta, 1993; Birla Meml, Hyderabad, 1993. Foreign Mem., Belgian Royal Acad., 1990; Foreign Hon. Mem., Amer. Acad. of Arts and Sciences; Foreign Fellow, Indian Nat. Sci. Acad., 1982; Hon. Fellow, Instn of Electronics and Telecommunication Engrs, India, 1985. Hon. DSc: Leicester, 1976; Exeter, 1977; Manchester, 1989; Santa Maria, Brazil, 1989. Eddington Medal, Royal Astronomical Soc., 1969; Charles Vernon Boys Prize, Inst. of Physics and Physical Soc., 1970; Dellinger Gold Medal, Internat. Union of Radio Science, 1972; Michelson Medal, Franklin Inst., 1973; Hopkins Prize, Cambridge Phil Soc., 1973; Holweck Medal and Prize, Soc. Française de Physique, 1974; Nobel Prize for Physics (jtly), 1974; Hughes Medal, Royal Soc., 1977. *Publications:* Papers in Proc. Royal Society, Phys. Soc., Mon. Not. Royal Astr. Soc., etc. *Recreations:* music, gardening, sailing. *Address:* Pryor's Cottage, Kingston, Cambridge CB3 7NQ. *T:* Cambridge (01223) 262657.

HEWITT, family name of **Viscount Lifford.**

HEWITT, Sir (Cyrus) Lenox (Simson), Kt 1971; OBE 1963; company chairman and director; *b* 7 May 1917; *s* of Cyrus Lenox Hewitt and Ella Louise Hewitt; *m* 1943, Alison Hope (*née* Tillyard); one *s* two *d* (and one *d* decd). *Educ:* Scotch Coll., Melbourne; Melbourne Univ. (BCom). FASA, FCIS, CPA. Broken Hill Proprietary Co. Ltd, 1933–46; Asst Sec., Commonwealth Prices Br., Canberra, 1939–46; Economist, Dept of Post War Reconstruction, 1946–49; Official Sec. and Actg Dep. High Comr, London, 1950–53; Commonwealth Treasury: Asst Sec., 1953–55; 1st Asst Sec., 1955–62; Dep. Sec., 1962–66; Chm., Australian Univs Commn, 1967; Secretary to: Prime Minister's Dept, 1968–71; Dept of the Environment, Aborigines and the Arts, 1971–72; Dept of Minerals and Energy, 1972–75. Lectr, Econs and Cost Accountancy, Canberra UC, 1940–49, 1954. Acting Chairman: Pipeline Authority, 1973–75; Petroleum and Minerals Authority, 1974–75; Chairman: Qantas Airways Ltd, 1975–80 (Dir, 1973–80); Qantas Wentworth Hldgs Ltd, 1975–80; QH Tours Ltd, 1975–80 (Dir, 1974–80); Petroleum and Minerals Co. of Aust. Pty Ltd, 1975; Austmark Internat. Ltd, 1983–88; Northern Mining Corp. NL, 1984–85; State Rail Authority of NSW, 1985–88; Director: East/Aust. Pipeline Corp. Ltd, 1974–75; Mary Kathleen Uranium Ltd, 1975–80; Aust. Industry Develt Corp., 1975; Santos Ltd, 1981–82; Pontello Constructions Ltd, 1980–82; Aberfoyle Ltd, 1981–89; Endeavour Resources Ltd, 1982–86; Ansett Transport Industries Ltd, 1982–88; Short Brothers (Australia) Ltd, 1981–91; Airship Industries PLC, 1984–88; Qintex Australia Ltd, 1985–90; British Midland Airways (Australia) Pty Ltd, 1985–; Universal Telecasters Securities Ltd, 1986–90; Mirage Management Ltd, 1986–91; Qintex Ltd, 1987–90; Qintex America Ltd, 1987–90; Fortis Pacific Aviation Ltd, 1987–; Fortis Aviation Group Ltd, 1988–; Hope Downs Ltd, 1993–; Hancock Minerals Ltd, 1993–. Dep. Chm., Aust. Atomic Energy Commn, 1972–77; Chairman: Exec. Cttee, IATA, 1976–77 (Mem., 1975–80); Orient Airlines Assoc., 1977; State Rail Authority of NSW, 1985–88; Mem., Judicial Commn of NSW, 1986–89. *Recreations:* tennis, farming. *Address:* 9 Torres Street, Red Hill, Canberra, ACT 2603, Australia. *T:* (6) 2952446; (office) 3, 70 Pitt Street, Sydney, NSW 2000, Australia. *T:* (2) 2313233. *Clubs:* Brooks's; Melbourne (Melbourne); Union (Sydney).

See also P. H. Hewitt.

HEWITT, Eric John, PhD, DSc; FRS 1982; Head of Biochemistry Group in Plant Sciences Division, Long Ashton Research Station, and Reader in Plant Physiology, University of Bristol, 1967–84, retired; *b* London, 27 Feb. 1919; *s* of Harry Edward Hewitt, OBE, MD, DPH, and Blanche (*née* Du Roveray); *m* 1943, Hannah Eluned (*née* Williams); one *s*. *Educ:* Whitgift Sch., S Croydon; King's Coll., Univ. of London, 1936–40 (BSc 1st Cl., AKC; DipEd); PhD, DSc Bristol; FIBiol. Asst Chemist/Chemist, MoS, 1940–42; Long Ashton Research Station: ARC Res. Grant Research Asst, 1942–45; Sen. Plant Physiologist, 1945–84; seconded to ARC Unit of Plant Nutrition (Micronutrients), 1952–59; SPSO (merit promotion), 1967. *Publications:* Sand and Water Culture Methods Used in the Study of Plant Nutrition, 1952, 2nd edn 1966; (with T. A. Smith) Plant Mineral Nutrition, 1975; (ed, with C. V. Cutting): (sympos.) Nitrogen Metabolism in Plants, 1968; (sympos.) Nitrogen Assimilation of Plants, 1979; approx. 150 research contribs to jls. *Recreations:* squash, gardening, fell walking, TV and records. *Address:* Langdales, 63 Ridgeway Road, Long Ashton, Bristol BS18 9EZ. *T:* Long Ashton (01275) 392274.

HEWITT, Francis Anthony; Deputy Chief Executive, Industrial Development Board for Northern Ireland, since 1988; *b* 1 July 1943; *s* of Joseph and Mary Hewitt; *m* 1968, Carol Burch; two *d*. *Educ:* Queen's Univ., Belfast (BScEcon). NI Min. of Agriculture, 1961–63; HM Customs and Excise, 1963–72; NI Min. of Commerce Rep. in W Germany, 1973–78; NI Dept of Commerce, 1978–82; HM Consulate-Gen., LA, 1982–84; Exec. Dir, Marketing, Industrial Develt Bd for NI, 1984–88. *Recreations:* music, walking.

HEWITT, Gavin Wallace, CMG 1995; HM Diplomatic Service; Ambassador to the Republic of Croatia, since 1994; *b* 19 Oct. 1944; *s* of George Burrill and Elisabeth Murray Hewitt; *m* 1973, Heather Mary Clayton; two *s* two *d*. *Educ:* George Watson's Boys' Coll., Edinburgh; Edinburgh Univ. (MA). Min. of Transport, 1967–70; on secondment from MoT as Third, later Second, Sec. to UK Delegn, EEC, Brussels, 1970–72; FCO, 1972–73; First Sec., British High Commn, Canberra, 1973–78; FCO, 1978–81; First Sec. and Head of Chancery, HM Embassy, Belgrade, 1981–84; Mem., Jt FCO/BBC Review Gp, BBC External Services, 1984; Counsellor on loan to Home Civil Service, 1984–87; Counsellor, Head of Chancery and Dep. Perm. Rep., UK Mission to UN, Geneva, 1987–91; Head, SE Asia Dept, FCO, 1992–94. Mem., Bd of Geneva English Sch., 1989–91 (Vice-Chm., 1990–91). *Recreations:* music, tinkering, walking. *Address:* c/o Foreign and Commonwealth Office, SW1A 2AH.

HEWITT, Prof. Geoffrey Frederick, FRS 1989; FEng 1984; Courtaulds Professor of Chemical Engineering, Imperial College of Science, Technology and Medicine, since 1993 (Professor of Chemical Engineering, 1985–93); *b* 3 Jan. 1934; *s* of Frederick and Elaine Hewitt; *m* 1956, Shirley Foulds; two *d*. *Educ:* Boteler Grammar School, Warrington; UMIST (BScTech, PhD). FIChemE, FRSC, FIMechE, CEng, CChem. Scientist, Group

Leader, Div. Head, Harwell Lab., specialising in heat transfer and fluid flow in multiphase systems, 1957–90. Pres., IChemE, 1989–90. Hon. DSc Louvain, 1988. *Publications:* (with N. S. Hall Taylor) Annular Two Phase Flow, 1970; (co-author) Two Phase Flow, 1973; Measurement of Two Phase Flow Parameters, 1978; (with J. G. Collier) Introduction to Nuclear Power, 1986; (jtly) Process Heat Transfer, 1994; contribs to books, numerous papers. *Recreations:* bridge, music. *Address:* Department of Chemical Engineering and Chemical Technology, Imperial College of Science, Technology and Medicine, Prince Consort Road, SW7 2BY. *T:* 0171–589 5111.

HEWITT, Rev. Canon George Henry Gordon; Residentiary Canon, Chelmsford Cathedral, 1964–78, Canon Emeritus since 1978; *b* 30 May 1912; *s* of Rev. G. H. Hewitt; *m* 1942, Joan Ellen Howden; two *s* one *d*. *Educ:* Trent Coll.; Brasenose, Oxford; Wycliffe Hall, Oxford. Asst Curate, St Clement, Leeds, 1936–39; Chaplain, Ridley Hall, Cambridge, 1939–41; Asst Curate, Leeds Parish Church, 1941–43; Religious Book Editor, Lutterworth Press, 1943–52; Diocesan Education Sec., Sheffield, 1952–58; Residentiary Canon, Sheffield Cathedral, 1953–58; Vicar of St Andrew, Oxford, 1958–64. Chaplain to the Queen, 1969–82. *Publications:* Let the People Read, 1949; The Problems of Success: a history of the Church Missionary Society, 1910–1942, vol. I, 1971, vol. II, 1977. *Address:* 8 Rainsford Avenue, Chelmsford, Essex CM1 2PJ.

HEWITT, His Honour Harold; a Circuit Judge, 1980–90; *b* 14 March 1917; *s* of George Trueman Hewitt and Bertha Lilian Hewitt; *m* 1946, Doris Mary Smith; two *s*. *Educ:* King James I Grammar Sch., Bishop Auckland. Admitted solicitor (Hons), 1938; HM Coroner, S Durham, 1948–80; a Recorder of the Crown Court, 1974–80. Chm. (part-time), Industrial Tribunal, 1975–80. Member Council, Law Society, 1976–80. Pres., NE Region, YMCA, 1981–. *Recreations:* music, gardening, French literature. *Address:* Longmeadows, Etherley, Bishop Auckland, Co. Durham DL14 0HD. *T:* Bishop Auckland (01388) 832386. *Club:* Carlton.

HEWITT, Harry Ronald, FEng; Chairman, Johnson Matthey PLC, 1983–84; retired; *b* 12 April 1920; *s* of Charles William Hewitt and Florence Hewitt; *m* 1954, Rosemary Olive, *d* of Walter George Hiscock and Olive Mary Hiscock; two *s* one *d*. *Educ:* City of Leeds High Sch,; Leeds Coll. of Technol. (BSc London 1941). FEng 1982; MIChemE 1949; MRSC 1944; CBIM 1983 (MBIM 1947). Jun. Chemist, Joseph Watson & Sons, soap manufrs, Leeds, 1936–41; Chemist, Royal Ordnance Factories (explosive manuf.), 1941–45; Control Officer, Chemical Br., Control Commn, Germany, 1945–47; Works Manager, Consolidated Zinc Corp., Avonmouth and Widnes, 1947–58; Johnson Matthey: Gen. Man., 1958–62; Exec. Dir, 1962–76; Gp Man. Dir, 1976–83. Freeman, City of London, 1979; Liveryman, Worshipful Co. of Clockmakers, 1979. FRSA. *Recreations:* golf, tennis, skiing, music. *Address:* 6 Loom Lane, Radlett, Herts WD7 8AD. *T:* Radlett (01923) 5243.

HEWITT, Sir Lenox; *see* Hewitt, Sir C. L. S.

HEWITT, Michael Earling; Director of Central Banking Studies, Bank of England, since 1990; *b* 28 March 1936; *s* of late Herbert Erland Hewitt and Dorothy Amelia Hewitt; *m* 1961, Elizabeth Mary Hughes Batchelor; one *s* one *d*. *Educ:* Christ's Hospital; Merton College, Oxford (Chancellor's Prize for Latin Prose, 1958; MA (Modern Hist.)); BSc Econ London. Entered Bank of England, 1961; Economic Adviser, Govt of Bermuda, 1970–74; Financial Forecaster, 1976–78; Adviser, Financial Instns, 1981–83; Head of Financial Supervision, Gen. Div., 1984–87; Head of Finance and Industry Area, 1987–88; Senior Advr, Finance and Industry, 1988–90. Chm., OECD Gp of Experts on Securities Markets, 1988–90. *Recreations:* chess, wine, travel. *Address:* Bank of England, Threadneedle Street, EC2R 8AH. *T:* 0171–601 4444.

HEWITT, Sir Nicholas Charles Joseph, 3rd Bt *cr* 1921; *b* 12 Nov. 1947; *s* of Sir Joseph Hewitt, 2nd Bt and of Marguerite, *yr d* of Charles Burgess; *S* father, 1973; *m* 1969, Pamela Margaret, *o d* of Geoffrey J. M. Hunt, TD; two *s* one *d*. *Heir:* *s* Charles Edward James Hewitt, *b* 15 Nov. 1970. *Address:* Colswayn House, Huttons Ambo, Yorks YO6 7HJ. *T:* Malton (01653) 696557.

HEWITT, Patricia Hope; Head of Research, Andersen Consulting, since 1994; *b* 2 Dec. 1948; *d* of Sir (Cyrus) Lenox (Simson) Hewitt, *qv*, and Alison Hope Hewitt; *m* 1981, William Birtles; one *s* one *d*. *Educ:* C of E Girls' Grammar Sch., Canberra; Australian Nat. Univ.; Newnham Coll., Cambridge (MA). MA Oxon; AMusA (piano). Public Relations Officer, Age Concern (Nat. Old People's Welfare Council), 1971–73; Women's Rights Officer, Nat. Council for Civil Liberties, 1973–74, Gen. Secretary 1974–83; Press and Broadcasting Sec., 1983–88, Policy Co-ordinator, 1988–89, to Leader of Opposition; Sen. Res. Fellow, 1989, Dep. Dir, 1989–94, Inst. for Public Policy Res. Vis. Fellow, Nuffield Coll., Oxford, 1992–. Trustee: Cobden Trust, 1974–83; Areopagitica Trust, 1981–84; Member: Sec. of State's Adv. Cttee on Employment of Women, 1977–84; Unofficial Cttee of Enquiry into Southall, 23 April 1979; National Labour Women's Cttee, 1979–83; Labour Party Enquiry into Security Services, 1980–81; Council, Campaign for Freedom of Information, 1983–89; Bd, Internat. League for Human Rights, 1984–; Exec. Cttee, Fabian Soc., 1988–93; Co-Chm., Human Rights Network, 1979–81; Dep. Chair, Commn on Social Justice, 1993–; Vice-Chm., Healthcare 2000, 1995–. Contested (Lab) Leicester East, 1983. Mem., Editorial Adv. Panel, New Socialist, 1980–90. Associate, Newnham Coll., Cambridge, 1984–. FRSA 1992. *Publications:* Your Rights (Age Concern), 1973, 14th edn 1986; Rights for Women (NCCL), 1975; Civil Liberties, the NCCL Guide (co-ed 3rd edn), 1977; The Privacy Report (NCCL), 1977; Your Rights at Work (NCCL), 1978, 2nd edn 1981; The Abuse of Power, 1981; (jtly) Your Second Baby, 1990; About Time: the revolution in work and family life, 1993. *Recreations:* reading, theatre, music, politics, gardening. *Address:* 21 Rochester Square, NW1 9SA. *T:* 0171–267 2567.

HEWITT, Penelope Ann; Stipendiary Magistrate, Leeds, since 1990; *b* 4 May 1932; *d* of late William Mottershead, JP, MB ChB and Eileen Mottershead; *m* 1954, Peter Nisbet Hewitt; one *s* two *d*. *Educ:* Howell's Sch., Denbigh; BA Open Univ., 1975. Called to the Bar, Gray's Inn, 1978; in practice, Liverpool, 1978–90; Mem., Northern Circuit. Lay Chm., Bolton Deanery Synod, 1984–90. Mem., British Acad. of Forensic Scis, 1979. JP Bolton, 1968–90. *Recreations:* music, reading, choral singing, opera, embroidery. *Address:* Leeds Magistrates' Court, PO Box 97, Westgate, Leeds LS1 3JP. *T:* Leeds (0113) 245 9653. *Club:* Leeds (Leeds).

HEWITT, Peter McGregor, OBE 1967; Regional Director, East Midlands, Departments of the Environment and Transport, 1984–89; *b* 6 Oct. 1929; *e s* of late Douglas McGregor Hewitt and Audrey Vera Hewitt; *m* 1962, Joyce Marie Gavin; three *d*. *Educ:* De Aston Sch., Market Rasen, Lincs; Keble Coll., Oxford (MA). National Service (Army), 1947–49. HM Overseas Civil Service, 1952–64: served in Malaya and N Borneo; HM Diplomatic Service, 1964–71: served in FO, Shanghai and Canberra; Home Civil Service: Principal, 1971–77; Asst Sec., 1977–83; Grade 4, 1984. *Recreations:* cricket, music, gardening. *Address:* 14 Dovedale Road, West Bridgford, Nottingham NG2 6JA. *Club:* Commonwealth Trust.

HEWITT, Stephen Geoffrey; Director of Personnel, Department of Social Security, since 1993; *b* 9 March 1950; *s* of late Geoffrey Gordon Hewitt and Doreen Brinsdon Hewitt; *m* 1992, Jill Elizabeth Harris. *Educ:* Weymouth Grammar Sch.; Dulwich Coll.; Sussex Univ. (BSc Chem. 1971; MSc Hist. of Science 1972). Admin trainee, N Ireland Office, 1975; Private Sec. to Ray Carter, MP, 1977–78; transf. to Dept of Social Security, 1990. *Address:* c/o Department of Social Security, Richmond House, Whitehall, SW1A 2NS. *T:* 0171–210 5831.

HEWLETT-DAVIES, Mrs Janet Mary; Deputy Shop Manager, Age Concern; journalist; public affairs consultant; *b* 13 May 1938; *d* of Frederick Charles and Margaret Ellen Hewlett; *m* 1964, Barry Davies. *Educ:* King Edward VI High School for Girls, Birmingham. Journalist, West Midlands 1956–59; BBC, 1959–65; Films Division, Central Office of Information, 1966–67; Press Officer: Prime Minister's Office, 1967–72; HM Customs and Excise, 1972–73; Principal Information Officer, Dept of Trade and Industry, 1973–74; Dep. Press Secretary to Prime Minister, 1974–76; Head of Information, Dept of Transport, 1976–79; Director of Information: DoE, 1979–82; DHSS, 1982–86; Dir of Public Affairs, Pergamon, BPCC and Mirror Gp of Cos, 1986–87. Vice-Chm., WHO Working Gp on Information and Health, 1983. Mem., Austerity Club, 1987–. FRSA 1985. *Recreations:* cooking, theatre, needlework, Radio 4. *Address:* 44 Sussex Square, Brighton BN2 1GE. *T:* Brighton (01273) 693792.

HEWSON, John Robert, PhD; MP (L) Wentworth, New South Wales, 1987–95; Leader of the Opposition, Australia, 1990–94; Shadow Minister for Industry, Commerce, Infrastructure and Customs, 1994–95; *b* 28 Oct. 1946; *m* 1988, Carolyn Somerville; two *s* one *d* by previous marriage. *Educ:* Univ. of Sydney (BEc); Univ. of Saskatchewan (MA 1969); Johns Hopkins Univ. (MA, PhD 1971). Lecturer: Towson State Coll., 1972–73; Monash Univ., 1975; Res. Economist, Reserve Bank of Australia, 1976; Economic Advr to Fed. Treas., 1976–77; University of New South Wales: Prof. of Econs, 1978–87; Head, Sch. of Econs, 1983–86; Dir, Japanese Econs Management Studies Centre, 1984–87. Shadow Minister for Finance, 1988–89; Shadow Treas., 1989–90. *Publications:* Liquidity Creation and Distribution in the Eurocurrency Market, 1975; (jtly) The Eurocurrency Markets and their Implications, 1975; Offshore Banking in Australia, 1981. *Address:* c/o Parliament House, Canberra, ACT 2600, Australia.

HEXHAM AND NEWCASTLE, Bishop of, (RC), since 1992; **Rt. Rev. (Michael) Ambrose Griffiths,** OSB; *b* 4 Dec. 1928; *s* of Henry and Hilda Griffiths. *Educ:* Ampleforth Coll.; Balliol Coll., Oxford (MA, BSc Chemistry). Entered monastery at Ampleforth, 1950; theological studies at S Anselmo, Rome, 1953–56; ordained priest, 1957; Prof. of Theology at Ampleforth, 1963; Sen. Science Master, Ampleforth Coll., 1967; Inspector of Accounts for English Benedictine Congregation, 1971 and 1985–92; Procurator (Bursar) at Ampleforth, 1972; Abbot of Ampleforth, 1976–84; Parish Priest, St Mary's, Leyland, Preston, 1984–92. Mem. Public School Bursars' Assoc. Cttee, 1975. *Recreation:* walking. *Address:* Bishop's House, East Denton Hall, 800 West Road, Newcastle upon Tyne NE5 2BJ.

HEXHAM AND NEWCASTLE, Auxiliary Bishop of, (RC); *see* Swindlehurst, Rt Rev. O. F.

HEY, Air Vice-Marshal Ernest, CB 1967; CBE 1963 (OBE 1954); CEng; Air Member for Technical Services, Department of Air, Canberra, 1960–72, retired; *b* Plymouth, Devon, 29 Nov. 1912; *s* of Ernest Hey, Terrigal, NSW; *m* 1936, Lorna, *d* of Sqdn Ldr A. Bennett, Melbourne; one *s* one *d*. *Educ:* Sydney Technical High Sch.; Sydney University. RAAF cadet, 1934; served War of 1939–45; Dir Technical Services, 1947–54, AOC Maintenance Comd, 1956–57; Imp. Defence Coll., 1957; Liaison Air Materiel Comd, USAF, 1958–59. *Recreations:* painting, lawn bowls.

HEY, James Stanley, MBE 1945; DSc; FRS 1978; retired; Research Scientist at Royal Radar Establishment, 1952–69, Chief Scientific Officer, 1966–69; *b* 3 May 1909; *s* of William Rennie Hey and Barbara Elizabeth Hey (*née* Matthews); *m* 1934, Edna Heywood. *Educ:* Rydal Sch.; Manchester Univ. BSc (Physics), 1930; MSc (X-ray Crystallography), 1931; DSc (Radio Astronomy and Radar Research), 1950. Army Operational Research Group, 1940–52 (Head of Estab., 1949–52). Hon. DSc: Birmingham, 1975; Kent, 1977. Eddington Medal, RAS, 1959. *Publications:* The Radio Universe, 1971, rev. 3rd edn 1983; The Evolution of Radio Astronomy, 1973; The Secret Man (autobiog.), 1992; research papers in scientific jls (RAS, Royal Society, Phys Soc., Philosophical Magazine, Nature, etc) including pioneering papers in radio astronomy. *Address:* 4 Shortlands Close, Willingdon, Eastbourne, East Sussex BN22 0JE.

HEY, Prof. John Denis; Professor of Economics and Statistics, University of York, since 1984; *b* 26 Sept. 1944; *s* of George Brian Hey and Elizabeth Hamilton Hey (*née* Burns); *m* 1968, Margaret Robertson Bissett; one *s* two *d*. *Educ:* Manchester Grammar Sch.; Cambridge Univ. (MA); Edinburgh Univ. (MSc). Econometrician, Hoare & Co., 1968–69; Lectr in Economics, Univ. of Durham, 1969–73, Univ. of St Andrews, 1974–75; Lectr in Social and Economic Statistics, Univ. of York, 1975–81, Sen. Lectr, 1981–84. Co-Dir, Centre for Experimental Economics, Univ. of York, 1986–. Economic Consultant, Wise Speke & Co., 1972–87. Editor: Bulletin of Economic Research, 1984–86; Economic Journal, 1986–. *Publications:* Statistics in Economics, 1974; Uncertainty in Microeconomics, 1979; Britain in Context, 1979; Economics in Disequilibrium, 1981; Data in Doubt, 1983; (ed jtly) Surveys in the Economics of Uncertainty, 1987; (ed) Current Issues in Microeconomics, 1989; (ed jtly) A Century of Economics, 1990; Experiments in Economics, 1991; (ed) The Future of Economics, 1992; (ed jtly) Recent Developments in Experimental Economics, 1993; articles in academic economics jls. *Recreations:* squash, walking, eating. *Address:* Department of Economics and Related Studies, University of York, Heslington, York YO1 5DD. *T:* York (01904) 433786.

HEYERDAHL, Thor; author and anthropologist, since 1938; *b* Larvik, Norway 6 Oct. 1914; *s* of Thor Heyerdahl and Alison Heyerdahl (*née* Lyng); *m* 1st, 1936, Liv Coucheron Torp (*d* 1969); two *s*; 2nd, 1949, Yvonne Dedekam-Simonsen; three *d*. *Educ:* University of Oslo, 1933–36. Researches in the Marquesas Islands (Pacific), 1937–38; Researches among Coast Indians of Brit. Columbia, 1939–40. Active service Free Norwegian Army-Air Force parachute unit, 1942–45. Organised and led Kon-Tiki expedition, 1947. Continued research in USA and Europe, with authorship, 1948–. Organised and led Norwegian Archæological Expedition to the Galapagos Islands, 1952; experiments revealing tacking principles of balsa raft in Ecuador, 1953; field research, Bolivia, Peru, Colombia, 1954. Organised and led Norwegian Archæological Expedition to Easter Island and the East Pacific, 1955–56. Continued research, 1957–59. Made crossing from Safi, Morocco, to W Indies in papyrus boat, Ra II, 1970; sailed from Qurna, Iraq, to Djibouti in reed boat, Tigris, 1977–78; organised and led two archaeol expedns to Maldive Islands, 1982–84; leader, organiser jt Norwegian/Chilean archaeol expedn, Easter Island, 1986–88; organiser Kon-Tiki Mus.—Museo Brüning archaeol project, Tucume, Peru, 1988–; organiser, archaeol project, Tenerife, Canary Is, 1990–. Participation in: Internat. Congress of Americanists, 1952–; Pacific Science Congresses, 1961–, all with lectures subseq. publ. in Proc. Congress. Vice-President: World Assoc. of World Federalists, 1966–; Foundn for Exploration and Research on Cultural Origins, 1990–; Trustee, Internat. Bd, World

Wildlife Fund, 1977–; Internat. Patron, United World Colls, 1980. Mem., Royal Norwegian Acad. of Science, 1958; Fellow: New York Acad. of Sciences, 1960; Amer. Anthropological Assoc., 1966. Hon. Prof., Inst. Politecnico Nacional, Mexico, 1972. Hon. Dir, Explorers' Club, NY, 1982. Hon. Mem. Geog. Soc.: Peru, 1953; Norway, 1953; Brazil, 1954; USSR, 1964. Hon. Doctor: Oslo, 1961; USSR Acad. of Scis, 1980; Lima, 1990; Havana, 1992. Retzius Medal, Swedish Soc. for Anthropology and Geography, 1950; Mungo Park Medal, Royal Scottish Geographical Society, 1951; Prix Bonaparte-Wyse from Société de Géographie, Paris, 1951; Elish Kent Kane Gold Medal, Geog. Soc. of Philadelphia, 1952; Vega Medal, Swedish Soc. of Anthropology and Geography, 1962; Lomonosov Medal, Moscow Univ., 1962; Royal Gold Medal, Royal Geog. Society, London, 1964; Officer of El Orden por Méritos Distinguidos, Peru, 1953; Gold Medal City of Lima; Gr.-Officer, Order Al Merito della Repubblica Italiana, Italy, 1965; Comdr, Knights of Malta, 1970; Comdr with Star, Order of St Olav, Norway, 1970; Order of Merit, Egypt, 1971; Grand Officer, Royal Alaouites Order, Morocco, 1971; Hon. Citizen, Larvik, Norway, 1971; Kiril i Metodi Order, Bulgaria, 1972; Internat. Pahlavi Environment Prize, UN, 1978; Order of Golden Ark, Netherlands, 1980; Bradford Washburn Award, Boston Mus. of Science, USA, 1982. *Films:* The Kon-Tiki Expedition (Oscar award for camera achievement, Nat. Acad. Motion Picture Arts and Scis, 1951); Galapagos Expedition; Aku-Aku, The Secret of Easter Island; The Ra Expeditions; The Tigris Expedition; The Maldive Mystery. *Publications:* Paa Jakt efter Paradiset, 1938; The Kon-Tiki Expedition, 1948; American Indians in the Pacific: the theory behind the Kon-Tiki expedition, 1952; (with A. Skjolsvold) Archæological Evidence of Pre-Spanish Visits to the Galapagos Islands, 1956; Aku-Aku: The Secrets of Easter Island, 1957; Co-editor (with E. N. Ferdon, Jr) Reports of the Norwegian Achæological Expedition to Easter Island and the East Pacific, Vol. I: The Archæology of Easter Island, 1961, vol. II: Miscellaneous Papers, 1965; Navel of the World (Chapter XIV) in Vanished Civilizations, 1963; Indianer und Alt-Asiaten im Pazifik: Das Abenteuer einer Theorie, 1965 (Vienna); Sea Routes to Polynesia, 1968; The Ra Expeditions, 1970; Chapters in Quest for America, 1971; Fatu-Hiva Back to Nature, 1974; Art of Easter Island, 1975; Zwischen den Kontinenten, 1975; Early Man and the Ocean, 1978; The Tigris Expedition, 1980; The Maldive Mystery, 1986; Easter Island: the mystery solved, 1989; (jtly) Pyramids of Tucume, 1995; contrib. National Geographical Magazine, Royal Geographical Journal, The Geographical Magazine, Archiv für Völkerkunde, Ymer, Swedish Geogr. Year-book, South-western Journal of Anthropology, Russian Academy of Sciences Yearbook, American Antiquity, Antiquity (Cambridge); works trans. into numerous languages; *relevant publication:* Senor Kon-Tiki, by Arnold Jacoby, 1965; The Kon-Tiki Man, by Christopher Ralling, 1990. *Recreations:* outdoor life, travelling. *Address:* Kon-Tiki Museum, Bygdøynesveien 36, 0286 Oslo, Norway.

HEYGATE, Sir Richard John Gage, 6th Bt *cr* 1831, of Southend, Essex; Principal, McKinsey and Company Inc., since 1987; *b* 30 Jan. 1940; *s* of Sir John Edward Nourse Heygate, 4th Bt and his 2nd wife, Gwyneth Eliot (*d* 1994), 2nd *d* of J. E. H. Lloyd; *S* brother, 1991; *m* 1st, 1968, Carol Rosemary (marr. diss. 1972), *d* of Comdr Richard Michell; 2nd, 1974, Jong Ja (marr. diss. 1988), *d* of In Suk, Seoul; one *d*; 3rd, 1988, Susan Fiona, *d* of late Robert Buckley; two *s*. *Educ:* Repton; Balliol Coll., Oxford. IBM (UK) Ltd, 1967–70; McKinsey & Company Inc., 1970–77; Director: Olaf Foods, 1977–85; Index Gp, 1985–87. Mem., Finance Cttee, Cancer Res., 1992–. *Heir: s* Frederick Carysfort Gage Heygate, *b* 28 June 1988. *Address:* 29 Rossetti Garden Mansions, Flood Street, SW3 5QX.

HEYHOE, David Charles Ross; Assistant Under Secretary of State, Ministry of Defence, since 1986; *b* 29 June 1938; *s* of late Cecil Ross Heyhoe and Clara Beatrice (*née* Woodard Knight); *m* 1972, Pauline Susan (*née* Morgan); one *s* one *d*. *Educ:* Beckenham and Penge Grammar Sch.; Worcester Coll., Oxford (Schol.; MA LitHum). Served HM Forces, RAEC, 1957–59. Asst Principal, War Office, 1963; Asst Private Sec. to Minister (Army), 1966; Principal, MoD, 1967; Asst Sec., 1975; Res. Associate, Inst. for Strategic Studies, 1975–76; Private Sec. to Leader of H of C, 1981–84. *Recreations:* books, sports, antiques. *Address:* c/o Ministry of Defence, SW1A 2HB. *Clubs:* Roehampton, Rosslyn Park FC.

HEYHOE FLINT, Rachael, MBE 1972; public relations and sports marketing consultant; journalist, broadcaster, public speaker, sportswoman; *b* 11 June 1939; *d* of Geoffrey Heyhoe and Roma (*née* Crocker); *m* 1971, Derrick Flint, BSc; one *s* and one step *s* two step *d*. *Educ:* Wolverhampton High Sch. for Girls; Dartford Coll. of Physical Educn (Dip. in Phys. Educn). Head of Phys. Education: Wolverhampton Municipal Grammar Sch., 1960–62; Northicote Sch., 1962–64; US Field Hockey Assoc. Coach, 1964 and 1965; Journalist, Wolverhampton Express & Star, 1965–72; Sports Editor, Wolverhampton Chronicle, 1969–71; first woman Sports Reporter, ITV, 1972; Daily Telegraph Sports Writer, 1967–; Vice-Chm., 1981–86, and Public Relations Officer, 1982–86, Women's Cricket Assoc.; Promotions Consultant, Hyatt La Manga Club, Southern Spain, 1983–; PR Executive: Wolverhampton Wanderers Football Club; Patshull Park Hotel, 1985; Dep. Chm., Charities Unit Trust Adv. Bd, 1993–; Mem. Cttee of Management, Family Assurance Soc., 1992–. Mem., Sportswriters Assoc., 1967. Mem. Council, Malvern Coll., 1989–. England Hockey rep., 1964 (goalkeeper); Mem., England Women's Cricket team, 1960–83, Captain, 1966–77. Hit first 6 in Women's Test Cricket 1963 (England *v* Australia, Oval); scored highest test score by England player in this country and 3rd highest in world, 1976 (179 runs for England *v* Australia, Oval). Best After Dinner Speakers Award, Guild of Professional Toastmasters, 1972. *Publications:* Just for Kicks, (Guide to hockey goalkeeping), 1966; Women's Hockey, 1975; (with Netta Rheinberg) Fair Play, The Story of Women's Cricket, 1976; (autobiog.) "Heyhoe!", 1978. *Recreations:* golf, cricket; former county squash player (Staffs). *Address:* Danescroft, Wergs Road, Tettenhall, Wolverhampton, West Midlands WV6 9BN. *T:* Wolverhampton (01902) 752103. *Clubs:* Lord's Taverners; Patshull Park Golf; South Staffs Golf; Hyatt La Manga (Spain).

HEYMAN, Allan, QC 1969; *b* 27 Feb. 1921; *e s* of late Erik Heyman and Rita Heyman (*née* Meyer); *m* 1958, Anne Marie (*née* Castenschiold); one *d*. *Educ:* Stenhus Kostskole, Denmark; Univ. of Copenhagen. Master of Law (Univ. of Copenhagen), 1947. Called to Bar, Middle Temple, 1951, Bencher, 1975, Treasurer, 1992. Pres., Internat. Lawn Tennis Fedn, 1971–74, Hon. Life Vice-Pres., 1979. Kt Comdr, Royal Order of Dannebrog (Denmark). *Recreations:* shooting, stalking, reading, music. *Address:* 1 New Square, Lincoln's Inn, WC2A 3SA; Marshland House, Sudbourne, Woodbridge, Suffolk IP12 2HA. *Clubs:* Naval and Military, Shikar; All England Lawn Tennis and Croquet.

HEYMAN, Sir Horace (William), Kt 1976; CEng, FIEE; Chairman, English Industrial Estates Corporation, 1970–77; Hotelplan International AG: Member, Supervisory Board, Zurich, 1955–84; Director: UK Group, 1965–86; Ingham Travel, 1965–77; *b* 13 March 1912; *m* 1st, 1939; one *s* one *d*; 2nd, 1966, Dorothy Forster Atkinson. *Educ:* Ackworth Sch.; Technische Hochschule, Darmstadt; Birmingham Univ. BSc hons, electrical engrg, 1936. Electricars Ltd, 1936–40; Metropolitan Vickers Ltd, Sheffield, 1940–45; Smith's Electric Vehicles Ltd and Subsids, 1945–64 (Man. Dir, 1949–64); Co-Founder, Sevcon Engineering Ltd, 1960; Vice-Pres., Battronic Corp., Philadelphia, 1960–64. Export Marketing Adviser for Northern Region, BoT, 1969–70; Consultant: DoI Invest in Britain Bureau, 1977–79; Elmwood Sensors Ltd, 1977–86; Thermal Quarz Schmelz GmbH, 1983–86; Chm., Newcastle Polytechnic Products Ltd, 1983–86. Newcastle Polytechnic: Governor, 1974–86; Vice-Chm., 1983–86; Hon. Fellow, 1985. Mem. Council, Soc. of Motor Manufrs and Traders, 1949–64 (Man. Cttee, 1952–64); Chm., Electric Vehicle Assoc. of Gt Britain, 1953–55. Witness at US Senate hearings on air and water pollution, 1967. Chairman: N Region Energy Conservation Group, 1973–77; NEDO Working Party on House Bldg Performance, 1976–79. Pres., Northumbria Tourist Bd, 1983–86. FIEE 1952; FRSA 1969. *Address:* 20 Whitburn Hall, Whitburn, Sunderland SR6 7JQ.

HEYMAN, Prof. Jacques, MA, PhD; FICE; FSA; FEng; Professor of Engineering, 1971–92, and Head of Department of Engineering, 1983–92, University of Cambridge, now Emeritus Professor; Fellow of Peterhouse, 1949–51, and 1955–92, now Emeritus Fellow; *b* 8 March 1925; *m* 1958, Eva Orlans (*d* 1982); three *d*. *Educ:* Whitgift Sch.; Peterhouse, Cambridge. Senior Bursar, Peterhouse, 1962–64; University Demonstrator, Engineering Dept, Cambridge Univ., 1951, University Lectr, 1954, Reader, 1968. Vis. Professor: Brown Univ., USA, 1957–58; Harvard Univ., 1966. Consultant Engineer: Ely Cathedral, 1972–; St Albans Cathedral, 1978–; Lichfield Cathedral, Worcester Cathedral, 1986–; Gloucester Cathedral, 1989–. Member: Architectural Adv. Panel, Westminster Abbey, 1973–; Cathedrals Fabric Commn (formerly Cathedrals Adv. Commn) for England, 1981–; Council, ICE, 1960–63 and 1975–78; Smeatonian Soc. of Civil Engrs, 1982–. Hon. DSc Sussex, 1975. James Watt Medal, 1973. *Publications:* The Steel Skeleton, vol. 2 (with Lord Baker, M. R. Horne), 1956; Plastic Design of Portal Frames, 1957; Beams and Framed Structures, 1964, 2nd edn 1974; Plastic Design of Frames, vol. 1, 1969 (paperback 1980), vol. 2, 1971; Coulomb's Memoir on Statics, 1972; Equilibrium of Shell Structures, 1977; Elements of Stress Analysis, 1982; The Masonry Arch, 1982; The Stone Skeleton, 1995; articles on plastic design, masonry construction and general structural theory. *Address:* 3 Banhams Close, Cambridge CB4 1HX. *T:* Cambridge (01223) 357360.

HEYMANN, Prof. Franz Ferdinand, PhD; CPhys, FInstP; Quain Professor of Physics, and Head of Department of Physics and Astronomy, University College, University of London, 1975–87, now Professor Emeritus; *b* 17 Aug. 1924; *s* of Paul Gerhard Heymann and Magdalena Petronella Heymann; *m* 1950, Marie Powell. *Educ:* Univ. of Cape Town (BScEng with Distinction, 1944); Univ. of London (PhD 1953). FInstP 1966. Engr, Cape Town, 1944–45; Jun. Lectr in Engrg, Univ. of Cape Town, 1945–47; Special Trainee, Metropolitan Vickers, Manchester, 1947–50; University Coll. London: Asst Lectr in Physics, 1950–52; Lectr, 1952–60; Reader, 1960–66; Prof. of Physics, 1966–75; Fellow, 1987. *Publications:* scientific papers on res. done mainly in fields of particle accelerators and elementary particle physics. *Recreations:* music, gemmology, gardening. *Address:* Sunnybank, Gayle, Hawes, N Yorks DL8 3RS.

HEYTESBURY, 6th Baron *cr* 1828; **Francis William Holmes à Court;** Bt 1795; *b* 8 Nov. 1931; *s* of 5th Baron Heytesbury and Beryl (*d* 1968), *y d* of late A. E. B. Crawford, LLD, DCL, Aston Clinton House, Bucks; *S* father, 1971; *m* 1962, Alison, *e d* of Michael Graham Balfour, CBE; one *s* one *d*. *Educ:* Bryanston; Pembroke College, Cambridge (BA 1954). *Heir: s* Hon. James William Holmes à Court, *b* 30 July 1967.

HEYWARD, Rt. Rev. Oliver Spencer; Bishop of Bendigo, 1975–91; Assistant to Primate of Anglican Church of Australia, since 1991; *b* Launceston, Tasmania, 16 March 1926; *s* of Harold and Vera Heyward; *m* 1952, Peggy Butcher; four *s*. *Educ:* Church Gram. Sch., Launceston; Univ. of Tasmania (BA Hons 1949); Oriel Coll., Univ. of Oxford (BA 1953, MA 1956); Cuddesdon Coll., Oxford. RAAF, 1944–46. Rhodes Scholar, 1949. Deacon 1953, priest 1954, dio. Chichester; Asst Curate, St Peter's, Brighton, 1953–56; Rector of Sorell, Tasmania, 1956–60; Rector of Richmond, Tasmania, 1960–62; Precentor, St David's Cathedral, Hobart, 1962–63; Warden, Christ Coll., Univ. of Tasmania, 1963–74. Chm., Brotherhood of St Laurence, 1993–. Pres., Bendigo Coll. of Advanced Educn, 1976–86; Comr, Victorian Post-Secondary Educn Commn, 1982–93. *Recreation:* gardening. *Address:* 7 Waltham Street, Richmond, Vic 3121, Australia.

HEYWOOD, Francis Melville, MA; Warden of Lord Mayor Treloar College, 1952–69, retired 1969; *b* 1 Oct. 1908; 4th *s* of late Rt Rev. B. O. F. Heywood, DD; *m* 1937, Dorothea Kathleen (*d* 1983), *e d* of late Sir Basil Mayhew, KBE; one *s* two *d* (and one *s* decd). *Educ:* Haileybury Coll. (Scholar); Gonville and Caius Coll. Cambridge (Scholar), 1st Class Hons, Classical Tripos, Part I, 1929; Part II, 1931; Rugby Football blue, 1928. Asst Master, Haileybury Coll., 1931–35; Fellow, Asst Tutor and Praelector, Trinity Hall, Cambridge, 1935–39; Master of Marlborough Coll., 1939–52. *Publication:* A Load of New Rubbish, 1985. *Recreations:* walking, writing. *Address:* 30 The Bayle, Folkestone, Kent CT20 1SQ.

HEYWOOD, Geoffrey, MBE (mil.) 1945; JP; Consulting Actuary; *b* 7 April 1916; *s* of Edgar Heywood and Annie (*née* Dawson), Blackpool; *m* 1941, Joan Corinna Lumley; one *s* one *d*. *Educ:* Arnold Sch., Blackpool; Open Univ. (BA). Served War, 1940–46: Royal Artillery, N Africa, Italy, Greece; commissioned, 1941, Major, 1944; despatches, 1945. Refuge Assce Co. Ltd, 1933–40; Duncan C. Fraser & Co. (Consulting Actuaries), 1946–86 (Sen. Partner, 1952–86). Pres., Manchester Actuarial Soc., 1951–53; Chm., Assoc. of Consulting Actuaries, 1959–62; Chm., Internat. Assoc. of Consulting Actuaries, 1968–72; Pres., Inst. of Actuaries, 1972–74 (Vice-Pres., 1964–67). Mem. Page Cttee to Review National Savings. Dep. Chm., Mersey Docks & Harbour Co., 1975–85; Mem., Nat. Bus Co., 1978–85. Chm., Merseyside Cable Vision, 1982–90; Director: Barclays Bank Trust Co., 1967–86; Liverpool Bd Barclays Bank, 1972–86; Barclays Unicorn Gp, 1977–85; Universities Superannuation Scheme, 1974–86. Corresp. Mem., Assoc. des Actuaires Suisses, 1973. FFA 1939; FIA 1946; FRAS 1982; FRSA 1986. Founder Master, Actuaries Co., 1979; Liveryman, Clockmakers' Co. JP Liverpool 1962. *Publications:* contribs to Jl Inst. Actuaries. *Recreation:* antiquarian horology. *Address:* Drayton, Croft Drive East, Caldy, Wirral, Merseyside L48 1LS. *T:* 0151–625 6707. *Clubs:* Army and Navy, Royal Automobile.

HEYWOOD, Sir Peter, 6th Bt *cr* 1838, of Claremont, Lancashire; account director, since 1986; *b* 10 Dec. 1947; *s* of Sir Oliver Kerr Heywood, 5th Bt and Denise Wymondham, 2nd *d* of late Jocelyn William Godefroi; *S* father, 1992; *m* 1970, Jacqueline Anne, *d* of Sir Robert Hunt, *qv*; two *d*. *Educ:* Bryanston Sch.; Keble Coll., Oxford (BA Hons). *Heir:* twin *b* Michael Heywood [*b* 10 Dec. 1947; *m* 1972, Caroline Awdry Greig; one *s* one *d*]. *Address:* 64 Newbridge Road, Bath, Avon BA1 3LA. *T:* Bath (01225) 421581.

HEYWOOD, Dr Ronald Barry; Director, British Antarctic Survey, since 1994; *b* 28 Sept. 1937; *s* of Ronald Heywood and Edith Henrietta Heywood (*née* Bradbury); *m* 1965, Josephine Despina Panagopoulos; two *d*. *Educ:* Ashby Grammar Sch., Leics; Birmingham Univ. (BSc 1959; MSc 1961); Queen Mary Coll., London Univ. (PhD 1970). MIBiol 1967. British Antarctic Survey: Biologist, 1961–68; Hd, Freshwater Res., 1968–83; Chief Scientist, Offshore Biol Prog., 1978–86; Hd, Marine Life Scis Div., 1986–87; Dep. Dir, 1988–94. UK Delegate, IOC Regl Cttee for Southern Ocean, 1987–; Mem., British Nat. Cttee Antarctic Res., 1994–. Hon. Associate, RHC, 1981. Polar Medal, 1967 and Clasp, 1986. *Publications:* University Research in Antarctica, 1993; papers on freshwater and marine physics and biol. *Recreations:* walking, music. *Address:* British Antarctic Survey, High Cross, Madingley Road, Cambridge CB3 0ET. *T:* Cambridge (01223) 251524;

Grove Close House, Church Street, Woodhurst, Cambs PE17 3BN. *T:* Ramsey (01487) 823669. *Club:* Antarctic.

HEYWOOD, Prof. Vernon Hilton; Executive Editor, Global Biodiversity Assessment, United Nations Environment Programme, since 1993; Emeritus Professor, University of Reading, since 1988; *b* 24 Dec. 1927; *s* of Vernon William and Marjorie Elizabeth Heywood; *m* 1st, 1952, María de la Concepción Salcedo Manrique; four *s*; 2nd, 1980, Christine Anne Brighton. *Educ:* George Heriot's Sch., Edinburgh; Edinburgh Univ. (BSc, DSc); Pembroke Coll., Cambridge (PhD). Lecturer 1955–60, Sen. Lectr 1960–63, Reader 1963–64, Professor 1964–68, Dept of Botany, Univ. of Liverpool; University of Reading: Prof. of Botany and Hd of Dept of Botany, 1968–88; Dean, Faculty of Science, 1978–81. Dir, 1987–92, Consultant Dir, 1993, Botanic Gardens Conservation Internat.; Chief Scientist (Plant Conservation), IUCN, 1988–92. Hon. Prof., Botanical Inst., Nanjing, 1989–. Storer Lecturer, Univ. of California, Davis, 1990. Chm., European Plants Specialist Gp, Species Survival Commn of IUCN, 1984–87; Pres., Internat. Council on Medicinal and Aromatic Plants, 1994–; Member of Board: Genetic Resources Communications Systems Inc., 1990–94; Yves Rocher Foundn, 1991–; Conservatoire Botanique National, Porquerolles, 1991–, Bailleul, 1993–. Trustee: Royal Botanic Gardens, Kew, 1983–87; IUCN, UK, 1993–. Corresponding Mem., Botanical Soc. of Amer., 1987–. Councillor of Honour, Consejo Superior de Investigaciones Científicas, Spain, 1970. Linnean Medal, Linnean Soc. of London, 1987; Hutchinson Medal, Chicago Hortl Soc., 1989. Order of the Silver Dog (Gran Canaria), 1989. *Publications:* Principles of Angiosperm Taxonomy (with P. H. Davis), 1963, 2nd edn 1965; (ed jtly) Flora Europaea: vol. 1 1964 (2nd edn 1993), vol. 2 1968, vol. 3 1972, vol. 4 1976, vol. 5 1980; Plant Taxonomy, 1967, 2nd edn 1976; Flowering Plants of the World, 1978, 2nd edn 1985; (jtly) Our Green and Living World, 1984; Las Plantas con Flores, 1985; (jtly) Botanic Gardens and the World Conservation Strategy, 1987; The Botanic Gardens Conservation Strategy, 1989; (jtly) International Directory of Botanic Gardens V, 1990; (jtly) Conservation of Medicinal Plants, 1991; (jtly) Conservation Techniques in Botanic Gardens, 1991; (jtly) Tropical Botanic Gardens: their role in conservation and development, 1991; (jtly) Proceedings of the International Symposium on Botanical Gardens, 1991; (jtly) Conservation des ressources végétales, 1991; (jtly) Centres of Plant Diversity: a guide and strategy for their conservation: vol. 1 1994, vol. 2 1995, vol. 3 1995; nearly 300 papers in sci. jls. *Recreations:* cooking, travel, music, writing. *Address:* White Mead, 22 Wiltshire Road, Wokingham RG11 1TP. *T:* Wokingham (01734) 780185.

HEYWOOD-LONSDALE, Lt-Col Robert Henry, MBE 1952; MC 1945; Vice Lord-Lieutenant for Oxfordshire, since 1989; *b* 18 Dec. 1919; *s* of Col John Pemberton Heywood-Lonsdale, DSO, OBE, TD and Hon. Helen Annesley; *m* 1952, Hon. Jean Helen Rollo, *d* of 12th Lord Rollo; one *s* three *d*. *Educ:* Eton. Grenadier Guards, 1938–56; Royal Wilts Yeo., 1961–67. Farmer. High Sheriff, Wilts, 1975; DL Wilts, 1972, Oxon, 1983. *Recreation:* country pursuits. *Address:* Mount Farm, Churchill, Oxon OX7 6NP. *T:* Kingham (01608) 658316. *Club:* Boodle's.

HEZLET, Vice-Admiral Sir Arthur Richard, KBE 1964; CB 1961; DSO 1944 (Bar 1945); DSC 1941; *b* 7 April 1914; *s* of late Maj.-Gen. R. K. Hezlet, CB, CBE, DSO; *m* 1948, Anne Joan Patricia, *e d* of late G. W. N. Clark, Carnabane, Upperlands, Co. Derry; two adopted *d*. *Educ:* RN College, Dartmouth. Comd HM Submarines: H44, Ursula, Trident, Thrasher and Trenchant, 1941–45; comd HMS Scorpion, 1949–50; Chief Staff Officer to Flag Officer (Submarines), 1953–54; Capt. (D), 6th Destroyer Squadron 1955–56; Dir, RN Staff Coll., Greenwich, 1956–57; comd HMS Newfoundland, 1958–59; Rear-Adm. 1959; Flag Officer (Submarines), 1959–61; Flag Officer, Scotland, 1961–62; Vice-Adm. 1962; Flag Officer, Scotland and Northern Ireland, 1963–64; retired 1964. Legion of Merit (Degree of Commander) (US), 1945. *Publications:* The Submarine and Sea Power, 1967; Aircraft and Sea Power, 1970; The 'B' Specials, 1972; Electron and Sea Power, 1975. *Address:* Bovagh House, Mullaghinch Road, Aghadowey, Co. Londonderry, N Ireland. *T:* Aghadowey (01265) 868206. *Clubs:* Army and Navy, Royal Ocean Racing.

HIBBARD, Prof. Bryan Montague, MD, PhD; FRCOG; Professor of Obstetrics and Gynaecology, University of Wales College of Medicine (formerly Welsh National School of Medicine), 1973–91, now Emeritus Professor; *b* 24 April 1926; *s* of Montague Reginald and Muriel Irene Hibbard; *m* 1955, Elizabeth Donald Grassie. *Educ:* Queen Elizabeth's Sch., Barnet; St Bartholomew's Hosp. Med. Coll., London (MD); PhD (Liverpool). MRCS. Formerly: Sen. Lectr, Liverpool Univ.; Consultant Obstetrician and Gynaecologist, Liverpool RHB, and Univ. Hosp. of Wales. Chairman, Joint Standing Committee: Obstetric Anaesthesia, RCOG/RCAnaes, 1988–91; RCOG/RCM, 1988–91; Member: Cttee on Safety of Medicines, 1979–83; Maternity Services Adv. Cttee, 1981–85; Council, RCOG, 1982–88, 1989–92; S Glam HA, 1983–88; Medicines Commn, 1986–89. President: Welsh Obst. and Gynaecol Soc., 1985–86; History of Medicine Soc. of Wales, 1995–Oct. 1996. Hon. Curator of Museum, RCOG, 1986– (Hon. Librarian, 1992–94). Mem. Editl Bd, Confidential Enquiries into Maternal Deaths, 1985– (Chm., Clinical Sub-Group, 1990–). *Publications:* Principles of Obstetrics, 1988; The Obstetric Forceps, 1988; numerous contribs to world medical literature. *Recreations:* collecting 18th century drinking glasses, fell walking, coarse gardening. *Address:* The Clock House, Cathedral Close, Llandaff, Cardiff CF5 2ED. *T:* Cardiff (01222) 566636.

HIBBERT; *see* Holland-Hibbert, family name of Viscount Knutsford.

HIBBERT, Rev. Barrie Edward; Minister, Bloomsbury Central Baptist Church, London, since 1987; *b* 9 June 1935; *s* of Joseph and Eva Hibbert, Gisborne, NZ; *m* 1957, Ellen Judith Eade; one *s* two *d*. *Educ:* Victoria Univ. of Wellington, NZ (BA); Melbourne Coll. of Divinity, Vic, Australia (LTh); NZ Baptist Theol Coll. Minister: Baptist churches in Gore, Tawa and Dunedin, NZ, 1962–79; Flinders St Baptist Church, Adelaide, SA, 1979–87. *Address:* 11 Mornington Crescent, NW1 7RH. *T:* 0171–388 9278.

HIBBERT, Christopher, MC 1945; author; *b* 5 March 1924; *s* of late Canon H. V. Hibbert; *m* 1948, Susan Piggford; two *s* one *d*. *Educ:* Radley; Oriel Coll., Oxford (MA). Served in Italy, 1944–45; Capt., London Irish Rifles. Partner in firm of land agents, auctioneers and surveyors, 1948–59. Fellow, Chartered Auctioneers' and Estate Agents' Inst., 1948–59. Pres., Johnson Soc., 1980. FRSL, FRGS. Heinemann Award for Literature, 1962; McColvin Medal, LA, 1989. *Publications:* The Road to Tyburn, 1957; King Mob, 1958; Wolfe at Quebec, 1959; The Destruction of Lord Raglan, 1961; Corunna, 1961; Benito Mussolini, 1962; The Battle of Arnhem, 1962; The Roots of Evil, 1963; The Court at Windsor, 1964; Agincourt, 1964; (ed) The Wheatley Diary, 1964; Garibaldi and His Enemies, 1965; The Making of Charles Dickens, 1967; (ed) Waterloo: Napoleon's Last Campaign, 1967; (ed) An American in Regency England: The Journal of Louis Simond, 1968; Charles I, 1968; The Grand Tour, 1969; London: Biography of a City, 1969; The Search for King Arthur, 1970; (ed) The Recollections of Rifleman Harris, 1970; Anzio: the bid for Rome, 1970; The Dragon Wakes: China and the West, 1793–1911, 1970; The Personal History of Samuel Johnson, 1971; (ed) Twilight of Princes, 1971; George IV, Prince of Wales, 1762–1811, 1972; George IV, Regent and King, 1812–1830, 1973; The Rise and Fall of the House of Medici, 1974; (ed) A Soldier of the Seventy-First, 1975; Edward VII: a portrait, 1976; The Great Mutiny: India 1857, 1978; Disraeli and His World, 1978; The Court of St James's, 1979; (ed) Boswell's Life of Johnson, 1979; The French Revolution, 1981; (ed) Greville's England, 1981; Africa Explored: Europeans in the Dark Continent, 1769–1889, 1982; (ed with Ben Weinreb) The London Encyclopaedia, 1983; Queen Victoria in Her Letters and Journals, 1984; Rome, Biography of a City, 1985; Cities and Civilizations, 1986; The English: A Social History 1066–1945, 1987; A Guide to Royal London, 1987; The Grand Tour, 1987; London's Churches, 1988; (ed) The Encyclopaedia of Oxford, 1988; Venice: biography of a city, 1988; Redcoats and Rebels: the war for America 1770–1781, 1990; The Virgin Queen: the personal history of Elizabeth I, 1990; (ed) Captain Gronow: his reminiscences of Regency and Victorian Life 1810–60, 1991; The Story of England, 1992; Cavaliers and Roundheads: the English at war 1642–1649, 1993; Florence: biography of a city, 1993; Nelson: a personal history, 1994. *Recreations:* gardening, travel, cooking, crosswords. *Address:* 6 Albion Place, West Street, Henley-on-Thames, Oxon RG9 2DT. *Clubs:* Garrick, Army and Navy.

HIBBERT, Sir Jack; KCB 1990; Director, Central Statistical Office, and Head of Government Statistical Service, 1985–92; *b* 14 Feb. 1932; *s* of late William Collier Hibbert and Ivy Annie (*née* Wigglesworth); *m* 1957, Joan Clarkson; two *s* one *d*. *Educ:* Leeds Grammar Sch.; London Sch. of Economics (BScEcon). Served Royal Air Force, 1950–52. Exchequer and Audit Dept, 1952–60; Central Statistical Office, 1960–65; LSE, 1965–66; CSO, 1966; Chief Statistician, 1970; Asst Dir, 1977; Under Sec., DTI, 1982–85. OECD and EUROSTAT Consultant, 1981 and 1993. *Publications:* Measuring the Effects of Inflation on Income, Saving and Wealth (OECD), 1983; articles in economic and statistical pubns. *Recreations:* golf, bridge. *Club:* Reform.

HIBBERT, Sir Reginald (Alfred), GCMG 1982 (KCMG 1979; CMG 1966); HM Diplomatic Service, retired; *b* 21 Feb. 1922; *s* of Alfred Hibbert, Sawbridgeworth, Herts; *m* 1949, Ann Alun Pugh, *d* of late Sir Alun Pugh; two *s* one *d*. *Educ:* Queen Elizabeth's Sch., Barnet; Worcester Coll., Oxford (Hon. Fellow, 1991). Served with SOE and 4th Hussars in Albania and Italy, 1943–45. Entered Foreign Service, 1946; served in Bucharest, Vienna, Guatemala, Ankara, Brussels; Chargé d'Affaires, Ulan Bator, 1964–66; Research Fellow, Leeds Univ., 1966–67; Political Adviser's Office, Singapore, 1967–69; Political Adviser to C-in-C Far East, 1970–71; Minister, Bonn, 1972–75; Asst Under-Sec. of State, FCO, 1975–76; Dep. Under-Sec. of State, FCO, 1976–79; Ambassador to France, 1979–82; Dir, Ditchley Foundn, 1982–87. Vis. Fellow, Nuffield Coll., Oxford, 1984–88; Hon. Res. Fellow, UC, Swansea, 1988–. Chm., Franco-British Soc., 1990–. *Publication:* The Albanian National Liberation Struggle: the bitter victory, 1991. *Address:* Frondeg, Pennal, Machynlleth, Powys SY20 9JX. *T:* Pennal (01654) 791220. *Club:* Reform.

HICHENS, Antony Peverell, RD 1969; Chairman, Caradon (formerly MB-Caradon) plc, since 1990; *b* 10 Sept. 1936; *s* of late Lt-Comdr R. P. Hichens, DSO (and Bar), DSC (and 2 Bars), RNVR, and Catherine Gilbert Enys; *m* 1963, Sczerina Neomi Hobday; one *d*. *Educ:* Stowe; Magdalen Coll., Oxford (MA Law); Univ. of Pennsylvania, Wharton Sch. (MBA). Midshipman, RNVR, 1954–56. Called to Bar, Inner Temple, 1960. Rio Tinto-Zinc Corp., 1960–72; Financial Dir, Redland, 1972–81; Man. Dir and Chief Financial Officer, Consolidated Gold Fields, 1981–89; Chm., Y. J. Lovell (Holdings), 1990–94. Mem. (non-exec.), British Coal Corp., 1992–. *Recreations:* travel, wine, shooting. *Address:* Slape Manor, Netherbury, near Bridport, Dorset DT6 5HL. *T:* Netherbury (01308) 88232. *Clubs:* Brooks's, City of London.

HICK, Prof. John Harwood; Danforth Professor, 1979–92, and Director of Blaisdell Programs in World Religions and Cultures, 1983–92, Claremont Graduate School, California, now Professor Emeritus; *b* 20 Jan. 1922; *s* of Mark Day Hick and Mary Aileen (Hirst); *m* 1953, (Joan) Hazel, *d* of F. G. Bowers, CB, CBE, and Frances Bowers; two *s* one *d* (and one *s* decd). *Educ:* Bootham Sch., York; Edinburgh Univ. (MA 1948 (1st cl. hons Philos); DLitt 1974); Oriel Coll., Oxford (Campbell Fraser schol.; DPhil 1950), Westminster Coll., Cambridge. Friends' Ambulance Unit, 1942–45. Ordained, Presb. C of E, 1953; Minister, Belford Presb. Church, Northumberland, 1953–56; Asst Prof. of Philosophy, Cornell Univ., 1956–59; Stuart Prof. of Christian Philosophy, Princeton Theolog. Seminary, 1959–64; S. A. Cook Bye-Fellow, Gonville and Caius Coll., Cambridge, 1963–64; PhD by incorporation; Lectr in Divinity, Cambridge Univ., 1964–67; H. G. Wood Prof. of Theology, Univ. of Birmingham, 1967–82. Guggenheim Fellow, 1963–64, and 1985–86; Leverhulme Res. Fellow, 1976; Scholar-in-residence, Rockefeller Foundn Research Center, Bellagio, Italy, 1986; Fellow, Inst. for Advanced Res. in the Humanities, Birmingham Univ., 1988–; Hon. Prof., Univ. of Wales, Lampeter, 1995–. Lectures: Mead-Swing, Oberlin Coll., USA, 1962–63; Mary Farnum Brown, Haverford Coll., USA 1964–65; James W. Richard, Univ. of Virginia, 1969; Distinguished Vis., Univ. of Oregon, 1969; Arthur Stanley Eddington Meml, 1972; Stanton, Cambridge Univ., 1974–77; Teape, Delhi and Madras, 1975; Ingersoll, Harvard, 1977; Hope, Stirling, 1977; Younghusband, London, 1977; Mackintosh, East Anglia, 1978; Riddell, Newcastle, 1978–79; Berkeley, TCD, 1979; Greenhoe, Louisville Pres. Sem., 1979; Potter, Washington State Univ., 1980; Montefiore, London, 1980; Brooks, Univ. of S California, 1982; Mars and Shaffer, Northwestern Univ., 1983; Niebuhr, Elmhurst Coll., 1986; Gifford, Edinburgh, 1986–87; Kegley, Calif State Univ.; Bakersfield, 1988; Suarez, Spring Hill Coll., 1988; Gates, Grinnell Coll., 1989; Birks, McGill Univ., 1989; Fritz Marti, Univ. of Southern Illinois, 1989; Brooke Anderson, Brown Univ., 1990; Eliot, Reed Coll., 1990; Resler, Ohio State Univ., 1991; Showers, Univ. of Indianapolis, 1993; McMartin, Ottawa Univ., 1993; Auburn, Union Theol Seminary, NY, 1994; Lily Montagu, London, 1994; Killeen, St Norbert Coll., Wis, 1995. Visiting Professor: Banares Hindu Univ., 1971; Visva Bharati Univ., 1971; Punjabi Univ., Patiala, 1971; Goa Univ., 1990; Visiting Fellow: British Acad. Overseas, 1974 and 1990; Univ. of Ceylon, 1974. Hulsean Preacher, Cambridge Univ., 1969; Select Preacher, Oxford Univ., 1970. Chairman: Religious and Cultural Panel, Birmingham Community Relations Cttee, 1969–74; Coordinating Working Party, Statutory Conf. for Revision of Agreed Syllabus of Religious Educn, Birmingham, 1971–74; Birmingham Inter-Faiths Council, 1975; President: Soc. for the Study of Theology, 1975–76; All Faiths for One Race, 1980–85 (Chm., 1972–73, 1978–80); Vice-President: World Congress of Faiths, 1993–; British Soc. for Philosophy of Religion, 1995–; Mem., Amer. Acad. of Religion, 1980–; Member Emeritus: Amer. Soc. for the Study of Religion, 1992 (Mem., 1983); Amer. Philosophical Assoc., 1992 (Mem., 1980). Mem. Council, Selly Oak Colls, 1967–80; Governor, Queen's Coll., Birmingham, 1972–80. Member Editorial Board: The Encyclopedia of Philosophy; Religious Studies. Hon. Teol. Dr Uppsala, 1977. Louisville Grawemeyer Award in Religion, Univ. of Louisville and Louisville Theol Seminary, 1991. *Publications:* Faith and Knowledge, 1957, 2nd edn 1966; Philosophy of Religion, 1963, 4th edn 1990 (Spanish, Portuguese, Chinese, Japanese, Korean, Finnish and Swedish edns); (ed) Faith and the Philosophers, 1963; (ed) The Existence of God, 1963; (ed) Classical and Contemporary Readings in the Philosophy of Religion, 1963, 3rd edn 1990; Evil and the God of Love, 1966, 2nd edn 1977; (ed) The Many-Faced Argument, 1967; Christianity at the Centre, 1968, 2nd edn as The Centre of Christianity, 1977 (trans. Dutch, Korean and Chinese); Arguments for the Existence of God, 1971; Biology and the Soul, 1972; God and the Universe of Faiths, 1973; (ed) Truth and Dialogue, 1974; Death and Eternal Life, 1976 (trans. Dutch); (ed) The Myth of God Incarnate, 1977 (trans. German and Arabic); God has Many Names, 1980 (trans. German, Japanese); (ed with Brian Hebblethwaite) Christianity and Other Religions, 1980; The Second Christianity, 1983 (trans. Japanese); (with Michael Goulder) Why Believe in God?, 1983; Problems of Religious Pluralism, 1985 (trans. Japanese); (ed with Hasan Askari) The Experience of Religious Diversity, 1985; An Interpretation of Religion, 1989; (ed with Edmund Meltzer) Three Faiths—One God, 1989; (ed with Lamont Hempel) Gandhi's Significance for Today, 1989; (ed with Paul Knitter) The Myth of Christian Uniqueness, 1992 (trans. Japanese, Italian); Disputed Questions in Theology and the Philosophy of Religion, 1993; The Metaphor of God Incarnate, 1993; The Rainbow of Faiths, 1995. *Address:* 144 Oak Tree Lane, Selly Oak, Birmingham B29 6HU.

HICKEY, Most Rev. Barry James; *see* Perth (Australia), Archbishop of, (RC).

HICKEY, Sir Justin, Kt 1979; Chairman and Managing Director, Hickey Group; *b* 5 April 1925; *s* of Hon. Simon Hickey, Speaker, New South Wales Parliament, and Hilda Ellen Hickey (*née* Dacey); *m* 1964, Barbara Standish Thayer; one *s* four *d*. *Educ:* De La Salle College, Sydney. Chairman: Australian Family Trust, 1965; Thayer Foundation (US), 1972; Director: Biocom Internat. Ltd (Bermuda), 1987–; Chemical Fuels Corp. (Atlanta, Ga), 1987–. Mem., Lloyd's of London, 1979. FRSA 1978. JP 1950. *Recreations:* yachting, art collection. *Address:* 78 Cabana Boulevard, Benowa Waters, Qld 4217, Australia.

HICKEY, Dr Stephen Harald Frederick; Chief Executive, Civil Service College, since 1994; *b* 10 July 1949; *s* of late Rev. Dr James Peter Hickinbotham and Ingeborg Hickinbotham; name changed by Deed Poll to Hickey, 1976; *m* 1976, Dr Janet Elizabeth Hunter; three *s*. *Educ:* St Lawrence Coll., Ramsgate; Corpus Christi Coll., Oxford (BA, MA); St Antony's Coll., Oxford (DPhil). Joined DHSS, 1974; Asst Sec., DHSS, later DSS, 1985–94; seconded to Rank Xerox (UK), 1989–90. *Publication:* Workers in Imperial Germany: the miners of the Ruhr, 1985. *Recreations:* music, swimming, walking, history. *Address:* Civil Service College, Larch Avenue, Ascot, Berks SL5 0QE. *T:* Ascot (01344) 634000.

HICKLIN, Denis Raymond, OBE 1969; Partner, Middle Greadow Dairy Farm, Lanlivery, Cornwall, since 1986; *b* 15 April 1918; *s* of Joseph Herbert and Florence May Hicklin; *m* 1949, Joyce Grisdale Smith; two *s*. *Educ:* Merchant Taylors' Sch. Served War, 1939–46, RA (Major; despatches). John Dickinson, 1936–48; St Anne's Board Mill Co. Ltd, 1948–78 (Chm. and Man. Dir, 1966–78). Pt-time Mem., Forestry Commn, 1978–81. *Recreations:* gardening, golf. *Address:* 1 Bumpers Batch, Midford Road, Bath BA2 5SQ. *T:* Bath (01225) 833123.

HICKLING, Rev. Canon Colin John Anderson; Vicar of All Saints, Arksey, Sheffield, since 1986; Hon. Lecturer in Biblical Studies, University of Sheffield, since 1986; Canon Theologian, Leicester Cathedral, since 1983; *b* 10 July 1931; *s* of late Charles Frederick Hickling, CMG, ScD, and late Marjorie Ellerington, *d* of late Henry Blamey. *Educ:* Taunton Sch.; Epsom Coll.; King's Coll., Cambridge; Chichester Theol Coll. BA 1953, MA 1957. Deacon 1957, Priest 1958. Asst Curate, St Luke's, Pallion, Sunderland, 1957–61; Asst Tutor, Chichester Theol Coll., 1961–65; Asst Priest Vicar, Chichester Cath., 1964–65; Asst Lectr in New Testament Studies, King's Coll., Univ. of London, 1965–68, Lectr, 1968–84; Dep. Minor Canon, St Paul's Cath., 1969–78; Dep. Priest in Ordinary to the Queen, 1971–74; Priest in Ordinary to the Queen, 1974–84; Subwarden of King's Coll. Hall, 1969–78; Warden of King's Coll. Hostel, 1978–81; Tutor in Biblical Studies, Queen's Coll., Birmingham, 1984–85; E. W. Benson Fellow, Lincoln Theol Coll., 1985–86. Mem., Liturgical Commn, 1981–86. Boyle Lectr, 1973–76; Select Preacher: Univ. of Cambridge, 1979; Univ. of Oxford, 1983. *Publications:* contributed to: Church without Walls, 1968; Catholic Anglicans Today, 1968; Bible Bibliography 1967–73, 1974; (also ed jtly) What About the New Testament?, 1975; St Paul: Teacher and Traveller, 1975; L'Evangile de Jean, 1977; Les Actes des Apôtres, 1979; The Ministry of the Word, 1979; This is the Word of the Lord, 1980; Studia Biblica 1978, Vol. III, 1980; Logia: the sayings of Jesus, 1982; Studia Evangelica, Vol. VII, 1982; A Dictionary of Biblical Interpretation, 1990; The Bible in Three Dimensions, 1990; Memorial Volume for J. Anastasiou, 1992; Resurrection, 1994; The Corinthian Correspondence, 1995; reviews and articles. *Recreation:* music. *Address:* All Saints Vicarage, Station Road, Arksey, by Doncaster, S Yorks DN5 0SP. *T:* Doncaster (01302) 874445.

HICKLING, Reginald Hugh, CMG 1968; PhD (London); QC (Gibraltar) 1970; *b* 2 Aug. 1920; *er s* of late Frederick Hugh Hickling and Elsie May Hickling, Malvern, Worcs; *m* 1945, Beryl Iris (*née* Dennett); two *s* one *d* (and one *s* decd). *Educ:* Buxton Coll.; Nottingham Univ. RNVR, 1941–46. Dep. Solicitor, Evening Standard, London, 1946–50; Asst Attorney-Gen., Sarawak, 1950–55; Legal Adviser, Johore, 1956; Legal Draftsman, Malaya, 1957; Parly Draftsman, Malaya, 1959; Comr of Law Revision, Malaya, 1961; Commonwealth Office, 1964; Legal Adviser to High Comr, Aden and Protectorate of S Arabia, 1964–67; Maritime Law Adviser: Thailand, 1968–69; Malaysia, 1969; Sri Lanka, 1970; Yemen Arab Republic, 1984, 1986; Attorney-General, Gibraltar, 1970–72. Lectr in SE Asian Law, SOAS, 1976–78, 1981–82; Visiting Professor, Faculty of Law: Univ. of Singapore, 1974–76 and 1978–80; Univ. of Malaya, 1983–84, 1986–88; Nat. Univ. of Malaysia, 1988–94. Consumer Law Advr, Fiji, 1990 and 1992. Hon. JMN (Malaya), 1960. *Publications:* The Furious Evangelist, 1950; The English Flotilla, 1954 (US as Falconer's Voyage, 1956); Sarawak and Its Government, 1955; Festival of Hungry Ghosts, 1957; An Introduction to the Federal Constitution, 1960; Lieutenant Okino, 1968; A Prince of Borneo, 1985; The Ghost of Orchard Road and other stories, 1985; Malaysian Law, 1987; Essays in Malaysian Law, 1991; Essays in Singapore Law, 1992; So Lucky and Other Stories, 1992; The Dog Satyricon, 1994; Finding Hobbes, 1994. *Recreation:* not watching TV. *Address:* 1 Highfield Road, Malvern, Worcs WR14 1HR. *T:* Malvern (01684) 573477.

HICKMAN, Sir Glenn; *see* Hickman, Sir R. G.

HICKMAN, John Kyrle, CMG 1977; HM Diplomatic Service, retired; Director, Anaconda (South America) Inc., since 1988; *b* 3 July 1927; *s* of late J. B. Hickman and Joan Hickman; *m* 1956, Jennifer Love; two *s* one *d*. *Educ:* Tonbridge; Trinity Hall, Cambridge. Served in RA, 45th Field Regt, Commonwealth Bde, 1948–50. Asst Principal, WO, 1950; Principal, 1955; transf. to CRO, 1958; UK High Commn, Wellington, 1959–62; HM Diplomatic Service, 1965; British Embassy, Madrid, 1966; Counsellor and HM Consul-General, Bilbao, 1967; Dep. High Comr, Singapore, 1969–71; Head of SW Pacific Dept, FCO, 1971–74; Counsellor, Dublin, 1974–77; Ambassador to Ecuador, 1977–81, to Chile, 1982–87. Alternate Chm., Belize Independence Conf., 1981. Chairman: Anglo-Ecuadorian Soc., 1988–91; Anglo-Chilean Soc., 1991–. Consultant to World Fedn of Engrg Orgns, 1988–89. Gran Oficial, Order of Merit (Chile), 1992. *Publications:* The Enchanted Islands: the Galápagos Discovered, 1985; occasional historical articles. *Recreations:* history, golf. *Address:* 48A Fitzgeorge Avenue, W14. *T:* 0171–602 5624. *Clubs:* Garrick; Los Leones Golf (Santiago).

HICKMAN, His Honour Michael Ranulf; a Circuit Judge, 1974–93; *b* 2 Oct. 1922; *s* of John Owen Hickman and Nancy Viola Hickman (*née* Barlow); *m* 1943, Diana Richardson; one *s* one *d*. *Educ:* Wellington; Trinity Hall, Cambridge. 2nd cl. Hons in Law. Served War, RAFVR, 1940–46. Cambridge Univ., 1946–48; called to Bar, Middle Temple, 1949. Actg Dep. Chm., Hertfordshire QS, 1965–72; a Recorder of Crown Court, 1972–74. *Recreations:* shooting, fishing, gun dog training. *Address:* The Acorn, Bovingdon, Herts HP3 0NA. *T:* Hemel Hempstead (01442) 832226.

HICKMAN, Sir (Richard) Glenn, 4th Bt *cr* 1903; *b* 12 April 1949; *s* of Sir Alfred Howard Whitby Hickman, 3rd Bt, and of Margaret D., *o d* of Leonard Kempson; *S* father, 1979; *m* 1981, Heather Mary Elizabeth, *er d* of late Dr James Moffett, Swindon, and late Dr Gwendoline Moffett; two *s* one *d*. *Educ:* Eton. *Heir:* *s* Charles Patrick Alfred Hickman, *b* 5 May 1983. *Address:* Grains Farm, Lower Blunsdon, near Swindon, Wilts SN2 4DF. *Club:* Turf.

HICKMET, Richard Saladin; barrister-at-law; *b* 1 Dec. 1947; *s* of Ferid and Elizabeth Hickmet; *m* 1973, Susan (*née* Ludwig); three *d*. *Educ:* Millfield Sch.; Sorbonne; Hull Univ. (BA). Called to the Bar, Inner Temple, 1974. Mem., Wandsworth Borough Council, 1978–83 (Chm., Leisure and Amenities Cttee, 1980–83; privatised street cleansing, refuse collection, parks maintenance). Contested (C): Glanford and Scunthorpe, 1987; Eastbourne, Oct. 1990. MP (C) Glanford and Scunthorpe, 1983–87. *Recreations:* squash, hunting. *Address:* 12 Middle Street, Taunton TA1 1SH. *T:* Taunton (01823) 331919.

HICKOX, Richard Sidney, FRCO(CHM); conductor; Music Director: City of London Sinfonia, since 1971; City of London Sinfonia (formerly Richard Hickox) Singers, since 1971; London Symphony Chorus, since 1976; Bradford Festival Choral Society, since 1978; Associate Conductor, London Symphony Orchestra, since 1985; *b* Stokenchurch, Bucks, 5 March 1948; *m* 1976, Frances Ina Sheldon-Williams (marr. diss.); one *s*; *m* 1995, Pamela Helen Stephen. *Educ:* in organ, piano and composition, Royal Acad. of Music (LRAM); Organ Scholar, Queens' Coll., Cambridge (MA). Début as professional conductor, St John's Smith Square, 1971; Organist and Master of the Music, St Margaret's, Westminster, 1972–82; Prom début, 1973. Artistic Director: Wooburn Fest., 1967–; St Endellion Fest., 1974–; Christ Church Spitalfields Fest., 1978–94; Truro Fest., 1981–; Chester Summer Fest., 1989–; City of London Fest., 1994–; Principal Guest Conductor: Dutch Radio Orch., 1980–84; Northern Sinfonia, 1990– (Artistic Dir, 1982–90); Associate Conductor, San Diego Symphony Orch., 1983–84; also regularly conducts Philharmonia, RPO, Bournemouth Symphony Orch. and Sinfonietta, Royal Liverpool Phil. Orch., BBC Symphony, Concert, Scottish and Welsh Orchs, BBC Singers, Hallé Orch.; San Francisco Symphony Orch.; Detroit Symphony Orch.; Houston Symphony Orch.; National Symphony Orch., Washington; Rotterdam Philharmonic; Oslo Philharmonic; Turku Philharmonia; Salzburg Mozarteum; Suisse Romande; Stockholm Philharmonic. Conducted: ENO, 1979; Opera North, 1982, 1986, 1995; Scottish Opera, 1985, 1987; Royal Opera, 1985; has appeared at many music festivals incl. Proms, Flanders, Bath and Cheltenham. Co-founder, Opera Stage, 1985. Many recordings of choral and orchestral music. *Address:* 35 Ellington Street, N7 8PN.

HICKS; *see* Joynson-Hicks.

HICKS, Dr Colin Peter, CChm, FRSC; Head of Environment and Energy Technologies Division, Department of Trade and Industry, since 1994; *b* 1 May 1946; *s* of George Stephen Frederick Hicks and Irene Maud (*née* Hargrave); *m* 1967, Elizabeth Joan Payne; two *d*. *Educ:* Rutlish Grammar Sch., Merton; Univ. of Bristol (BSc, PhD). Lectr in Chemistry, Univ. of W Indies, Jamaica, 1970–73; ICI Res. Fellow, Univ. of Exeter, 1973–75; DTI, 1975–; NPL, 1975–80; Laboratory of Govt Chemist, 1984–87; Sec., Ind. Develt Adv. Bd, 1988–90; Hd, Res. and Technol. Policy Div., 1990–94. *Address:* Environment and Energy Technologies Division, Department of Trade and Industry, 1–17 Victoria Street, SW1H 0ET.

HICKS, Gp Captain David; *see* Hicks, Gp Captain H. D.

HICKS, David (Nightingale); interior decorator, designer, author, garden and jewellery designer; Director, David Hicks Ltd, since 1960; *b* 25 March 1929; 3rd surv. *s* of late Herbert Hicks (stockbroker and twice past Master Salter's Company) and late Mrs Hicks; *m* 1960, Lady Pamela Carmen Louise Mountbatten, *yr d* of Admiral of the Fleet Earl Mountbatten of Burma, KG, GCB, OM, GCSI, GCIE, GCVO, DSO, PC, FRS; one *s* two *d*. *Educ:* Charterhouse; Central School of Arts and Crafts, London. Interiors for: Helena Rubinstein; QE2; HRH the Prince of Wales; Govt of NSW; British Steel Corp.; Aeroflot Offices; Marquess of Londonderry; Library in British Embassy, Washington, and Royal Yacht for HM King Fahd. Designer of gardens, jewellery, fabrics, carpets, furniture, etc. Master, Salters' Co., 1977–78. FRSA. CoID (now Design Council) design award, 1970. *Publications:* David Hicks on Decoration, 1966; David Hicks on Living—with taste, 1968; David Hicks on Bathrooms, 1970; David Hicks on Decoration—with fabrics, 1971; David Hicks on Decoration—5, 1972; David Hicks Book of Flower Arranging, 1976; David Hicks Living with Design, 1979; David Hicks Garden Design, 1982; David Hicks Style and Design, 1988. *Recreations:* gardening, preservation. *Address:* Albany, Piccadilly, W1V 9RP. *T:* (office) 0171–437 2499, (home) Wallingford (01491) 824555, *Fax:* 0171–734 4893.

HICKS, Group Captain (Harry) David, MBE 1967; Director General, English-Speaking Union, 1990–91 (Deputy Director General, 1985–90); *b* 13 July 1923; *s* of Walter Hicks and Clara Ann (*née* Jagger); *m* 1948, Jane Irene Mary Tibbs; one *s* one *d*. *Educ:* Grange Grammar Sch., Bradford; London Univ. (BA Hons 1947); Nottingham Univ. (PGCE 1948). Served War, 1942–45, as Pilot, 149 Sqdn, Bomber Comd. Schoolmaster, Surbiton Grammar Sch., 1948–49; Royal Air Force: Educn Br., 1950–54; Admin. Br., 1954–76, finally as Dep. Dir, Recruiting; Dir of Educn, E-SU, 1976–85; Gen. Dir, Internat. Shakespeare Globe Centre, 1991–92. Special Consultant to BBC English, 1991–; German Language Consultant to Callon Sch., 1992–. Pres., Windsor and S Bucks Br., ESU, 1991–; speaker, Bucks Fedn of WI Panels. *Recreations:* golf, tennis, playing piano. *Address:* Highgrove, 24 Clifton Road, Chesham Bois, Bucks HP6 5PU. *T:* Chesham (01494) 727239. *Clubs:* Royal Air Force, English-Speaking Union.

HICKS, John Charles; QC 1980; **His Honour Judge Hicks;** a Judge of the Official Referees' Courts, since 1993; a Circuit Judge, since 1988; *b* 4 March 1928; *s* of late Charles Hicks and late Marjorie Jane Hicks; *m* 1957, Elizabeth Mary, *o d* of late Rev. J. B. Jennings; one *d* (one *s* decd). *Educ:* King Edward VI Grammar Schs, Chelmsford and Totnes; London Univ. LLM 1954. Served RA (National Service), 1946–48. Admitted solicitor, 1952; called to the Bar, Middle Temple, 1966; a Recorder, 1978–88. Legal Dept, Thomas Tilling Ltd, 1953–54; Partner in Messrs Burchells, solicitors, 1955–65; Methodist Missionary Soc., Caribbean, 1965–66. Jl Sec., Methodist Conf., 1989–. *Publications:* (ed jtly) The Constitution and Discipline of the Methodist Church in the Caribbean and the Americas, 1967, with annual supplements to 1987; (ed) The Constitutional Practice and Discipline of the Methodist Church, 6th edn 1974, 7th edn 1988, with annual supplements, 1974–; articles in Mod. Law Rev., Cambridge Law Jl, Conveyancer, and Epworth Rev. *Recreations:* squash rackets, music, theatre, opera, the Methodist Constitution. *Address:* Flat 3, 17 Montagu Square, W1H 1RD. *T:* 0171–935 6008.

HICKS, Maureen Patricia; Project Director, Stratford-upon-Avon Visitor Management National Pilot Project, since 1992; *b* 23 Feb. 1948; *d* of Ron and Nora Cutler; *m* 1973, Keith Hicks; one *s* one *d*. *Educ:* Ashley Secondary School; Brockenhurst Grammar School; Furzedown College of Education. Teacher's Cert. Secondary Teacher, Drama and English, 1969–70; Marks & Spencer Management, 1970–74; Asst Area Educn Officer, 1974–76; Dir, Motor Museum, 1976–82. Mem., Stratford DC, 1979–84. MP (C) Wolverhampton North East, 1987–92; contested (C) Wolverhampton NE, 1992. PPS to Minister of State and Parly Under-Sec. of State, FCO, 1991–92; Sec., H of C Tourism Cttee, 1987–92. Non-executive Director: David Clarke Associates, 1992–; S Warwicks Mental Health Services NHS Trust, 1994–. Mem., Women In Management Assoc. Hon. Fellow, Wolverhampton Univ., 1992. *Recreations:* amateur dramatics, music, golf, travel.

HICKS, Maj.-Gen. Michael; *see* Hicks, Maj.-Gen. W. M. E.

HICKS, Robert; MP (C) Cornwall South-East, since 1983 (Bodmin, 1970–Feb. 1974 and Oct. 1974–1983); *b* 18 Jan. 1938; *s* of W. H. Hicks; *m* 1st, 1962, Maria Elizabeth Ann Gwyther (marr. diss. 1988); two *d*; 2nd, 1991, Mrs Glenys Foote. *Educ:* Queen Elizabeth Grammar Sch., Crediton; University Coll., London; Univ. of Exeter. Taught at St Austell Grammar Sch., 1961–64; Lecturer in Regional Geography, Weston-super-Mare Technical Coll., 1964–70. An Asst Govt Whip, 1973–74; Member: Select Cttee of House of Commons, European Legislation, 1973, 1976–; Speaker's Panel, 1992–; Vice-Chm., Cons. Parly European Affairs Cttee, 1979–81; Chairman: Cons. Parly Agric. Cttee, 1988–90 (Vice-Chm., 1972–73 (Chm., Horticultural Sub-Cttee), and 1974–82); Westcountry Gp of Cons. MPs, 1976–77; UK Gp, Parly Assoc. for Euro-Arab Co-operation, 1982–; Vice-Chm., Cons. Party ME Council, 1992– (Treasurer , 1980–92); Parly Adviser to British Hotels, Restaurants and Caterers Assoc., 1974–, to Milk Marketing Bd, 1985–. Pres., Plymouth Albion RFC, 1991–. *Recreations:* cricket, gardening, golf. *Address:* 7 Carew Wharf, Marine Drive, Torpoint, Cornwall PL11 2EH. *Club:* MCC.

HICKS, Robin Edgcumbe; Director, Royal Smithfield Show, since 1992; *b* 6 Dec. 1942; *s* of late Ronald Eric Edgcumbe Hicks and of Fredrica Hicks; *m* 1970, Sue (*née* Dalton); one *s* one *d*. *Educ:* Bancrofts' Sch.; Seale Hayne Coll. (NDA; Dip. Farm Management); Univ. of Reading (DipAgric Extension). ARAgS. Farm worker, 1961–63; Agricl Advr, MAFF, 1967–69; Producer/Presenter, BBC Farming Today, 1969–71; Churchill Fellow, 1973; various production posts, radio and television, 1973–77; Hd of Marketing and Develt, RASE, 1977–79; Hd of Network Radio, BBC South and West, 1979–88; Chief Exec., RASE, 1989–91. Mem., Bristol and Weston HA, 1986–88; Vice-Chm., Radio Acad., 1986–88; Trustee: St George's Music Trust, 1981–88; Rural Housing Trust, 1990–; Member: Exec. Cttee, SW Arts, 1981–85; SW Concerts Bd, 1981–88; Trustee, Head Injury Recovery Trust, 1986–. Freeman, City of London, 1977; Liveryman, Drapers' Co, 1981. *Recreations:* family, photography, gardening, theatre. *Address:* 271 Lauderdale Mansions,W9 1LZ. *Club:* Farmers'.

HICKS, Thomas; *see* Steele, Tommy.

HICKS, William David Antony; QC 1995; *b* 11 June 1951; *s* of Maj.-Gen. William Michael Ellis Hicks, *qv*; *m* 1982, Jennifer Caroline Ross; one *s* two *d*. *Educ:* Eton Coll.; Magdalene Coll., Cambridge (MA Econs). Called to the Bar, Inner Temple, 1975. *Recreations:* fishing, tennis, ski-ing. *Address:* 1 Serjeants' Inn, EC4Y 1NH. *T:* 0171–583 1355. *Club:* Vanderbilt Racquets.

HICKS, Maj.-Gen. (William) Michael (Ellis), CB 1982; OBE 1967; Secretary, Royal College of Defence Studies, 1983–93; *b* 2 June 1928; *s* of late Group Captain William Charles Hicks, AFC, and Nellie Kilbourne (*née* Kay), *m* 1950, Jean Hilary Duncan; three *s*. *Educ:* Eton Coll.; RMA Sandhurst. Commnd 2 Lieut Coldstream Guards, 1948; served, 1948–67: regtl service, UK, Tripoli and Canal Zone; Instr, Sch. of Inf. (Captain); Staff Coll. (Major); GSO2 (Ops) HQ 4 Div.; regtl service, BAOR, UK and Kenya; JSSC; GSO (DS) Staff Coll.; GSO1 MO1, MoD, 1967–70 (Lt-Col); CO 1st Bn Coldstream Guards, 1970–72; RCDS, 1973 (Col); comd 4th Guards Armoured Bde, 1974–76 (Brig.); BGS Trng HQ UKLF, 1977–79; BGS (Author) attached to DMO, MoD, 1979; GOC NW Dist, 1980–83, retd. *Recreation:* gardening. *Address:* c/o Lloyds Bank, Cox's & King's, PO Box 1190, 7 Pall Mall, SW1Y 5NA.

HICKS BEACH, family name of **Earl St Aldwyn.**

HIDDEN, Hon. Sir Anthony Brian, Kt 1989; **Hon. Mr Justice Hidden;** a Judge of the High Court of Justice, Queen's Bench Division, since 1989; *b* 7 March 1936; *s* of late James Evelyn Harold Hidden, GM and Gladys Bessie (*née* Brooks); *m* 1982, Mary Elise Torriano Pritchard, *d* of R. C. Pritchard of Barton Abbotts, Tetbury, Glos; three *s* one *d*. *Educ:* Reigate Grammar Sch.; Emmanuel Coll., Cambridge (BA Hons 1957, MA 1960). 2nd Lieut, 1st Royal Tank Regt, Far East Land Forces, Hong Kong, 1958–59. Called to the Bar, Inner Temple, 1961, Bencher, 1985; Mem., Hon. Soc. of Inner Temple, 1956–, and of Lincoln's Inn (*ad eundem*), 1973–. QC 1976; a Recorder, 1977–89; Leader, SE Circuit, 1986–89. *Recreations:* reading, playing bad golf. *Address:* Royal Courts of Justice, Strand, WC2A 2LL.

HIDE, Prof. Raymond, CBE 1990; FRS 1971; Research Professor, Departments of Physics and Earth Sciences, Oxford University, 1992–94, now Emeritus Professor of Physics; Fellow, Jesus College, Oxford, since 1983 (Senior Research Fellow, since 1994); *b* 17 May 1929; *s* of late Stephen Hide and of Rose Edna Hide (*née* Cartlidge; now Mrs Thomas Leonard); *m* 1958, (Phyllis) Ann Licence; one *s* two *d*. *Educ:* Percy Jackson Grammar Sch., near Doncaster; Manchester Univ.; Caius Coll., Cambridge. BSc 1st cl. hons Physics Manchester, 1950; PhD 1953, ScD 1969, Cantab. Res. Assoc. in Astrophysics, Univ. of Chicago, 1953–54; Sen. Res. Fellow, AERE Harwell, 1954–57; Lectr in Physics, Univ. of Durham (King's Coll., Newcastle), 1957–61; Prof. of Geophysics and Physics, MIT, 1961–67; Hd of Geophysical Fluid Dynamics Lab., Met. Office, 1967–90 (CSO 1975); Dir, Robert Hooke Inst. and Vis. Prof., Dept of Physics, Oxford Univ., 1990–92. Short-term vis. appts at Princeton Inst. for Advanced Study, 1954, MIT and UCLA, 1960, CIT, 1993 (Fairchild Schol.); Visiting Professor: UCL, 1967–84; Reading Univ., 1976–91; Leeds Univ., 1986–91; Gresham Prof. of Astronomy, Gresham Coll., City of London, 1985–90; Adrian Fellow, Univ. of Leicester, 1980–83. Distinguished Vis. Scientist, Jet Propulsion Lab., CIT, 1985–; Hon. Sen. Res. Fellow, Inst. of Oceanographic Scis Deacon Lab., 1990–; Hon. Scientist, Rutherford Appleton Lab., 1992–. Member Council: RAS, 1969–72 and 1983–86 (Pres., 1983–85); Royal Meteorological Soc., 1969–72 and 1974–77 (Pres., 1974–76; Hon. Mem., 1989); NERC, 1972–75; Eur. Geophysical Soc., 1981–85 (Pres., 1982–84, Hon. Mem., 1988); Royal Soc., 1988–90. Lectures: Symons Meml, RMetS, 1970; R. A. Fisher Meml, 1977; Halley, Oxford, 1980; Jeffreys, RAS, 1981; Union, Internat. Union of Geodesy and Geophysics, Hamburg, 1983; Scott, Cambridge, 1984; Thompson, Toronto, 1984; Lindsay, NASA, 1988. Fellow: Amer. Acad. of Arts and Sciences, 1964; Amer. Geophys. Union, 1967; Academia Europaea, 1988. Hon. DSc: Leicester, 1985; UMIST, 1994. Charles Chree Medal, Inst. Physics, 1975; Holweck Medal, Soc. Franç. de Physique, 1982; Gold Medal, RAS, 1989. *Publications:* papers in scientific jls. *Address:* Jesus College, Oxford OX1 3DW. *T:* (home) Oxford (01865) 56521.

HIDER, David James; Director, Internal Communications Project, British Gas, since 1994; *b* 5 Nov. 1934; *s* of Edward James Hider and Marguerite Noel Hider (*née* James); *m* 1963, Margaret Gilbert Macdonald Watson; two *s* one *d*. *Educ:* Roan Sch., Greenwich; King Edward VII Nautical Coll., Poplar. Master Mariner; DMS; CIGasE. Merchant Navy, 1952–67 (to Chief Officer); South Eastern Gas: Commercial Asst, 1967; Conversion Unit Manager, 1969; Area Service Manager, Sussex, 1973; Regl Service Manager, 1976; Dir of Marketing, 1981; British Gas: Dir of Service, 1983; Dir of Domestic Marketing, 1990; Regl Chm., British Gas S Western, 1990–94. *Publications:* contribs to Jl IGasE. *Recreations:* squash, swimming, walking, cooking. *Address:* British Gas plc, Riverside, Temple Street, Keynsham, Bristol BS18 1EQ. *T:* Bristol (0117) 986 1717.

HIDER, Prof. Robert Charles, PhD; CChem, FRSC; Professor of Medicinal Chemistry, since 1987 and Head, School of Life, Basic Medical and Health Sciences, since 1994, King's College, London; *b* 14 Aug. 1943; *s* of Charles Thomas Hider and Josephine Mary (*née* Breitbach); *m* 1967, Shirley Christine Nickels; one *s* one *d*. *Educ:* King's Coll., London (BSc Chem. and Physics 1964; PhD Chem. 1967). Wellcome Res. Fellow, St Thomas' Hosp., 1967–70; Lectr, then Reader, Dept of Chem., Essex Univ., 1970–87. Vis. Prof., Dept of Biochem., Univ. of Calif, Berkeley, 1977 and 1980. *Publications:* contrib. articles on pharmaceutically active peptides and metal chelating agents to pharmaceutical, biochem. and chem. jls. *Recreations:* arachnology, natural history, Australian philately. *Address:* 257 Point Clear Road, St Osyth, Essex C016 8JL. *T:* St Osyth (01255) 821335.

HIELSCHER, Sir Leo (Arthur), Kt 1987; Chairman, Queensland Treasury Corporation, since 1988; *b* 1 Oct. 1926; *s* of Leslie Charles Hielscher and Elizabeth Jane Petersen; *m* 1948, Mary Ellen Pelgrave; one *s* one *d* (and one *s* decd). *Educ:* Brisbane State High Sch.; Univ. of Queensland (BComm, AAUQ). AASA, FAIM. Queensland Public Service, 1942; RAAF, 1945–47; Asst Under Sec. (Budget), Qld Treasury, 1964, Dep. Under Treasurer, 1969–74; Under Treas. of Qld (CS Hd of Treasury Dept of Qld Govt), 1974–88. Eisenhower Exchange Fellow, 1973. Director: Freshmark; Qld Provincial Newspapers; Crusader; Chairman: Gladstone Special Steel Corp.; Autsafe Pty; Southern Cross Airlines Hldgs; Sugar North. Councillor, Griffith Univ. Council. Chairman: Brisbane Cricket Ground; Lyric Opera, Qld. *Recreations:* golf, fishing, boating, theatre. *Address:* 8 Silverash Court, Capalaba, Brisbane, Qld 4157, Australia. *T:* (home) (7) 32060104, *Fax:* (7) 32064241, (business) (7) 32245760, *Fax:* (7) 32100262. *Clubs:* Brisbane, Gailes Golf, Tattersalls (Brisbane).

HIGGINBOTHAM, Prof. James Taylor, PhD; FBA 1995; Professor of General Linguistics, University of Oxford, since 1993; Fellow, Somerville College, Oxford, since 1993; *b* 17 Aug. 1941; *s* of William Rufus Higginbotham and Eunice Taylor Higginbotham; *m* 1st, 1972, Jenni W. Caldwell (marr. diss. 1988); two *s*; 2nd, 1988, Nancy L. Roberts; two *s* two *d*. *Educ:* Columbia Univ., NY (BS 1967; PhD 1973). Columbia University, New York: Instructor in Philosophy, 1970–73; Asst Prof., 1973–80; Fellow in Humanities, 1975–77 and 1979–80; Massachusetts Institute of Technology: Vis. Associate Prof. of Philosophy, 1980–82; Associate Prof., 1982–87; Prof. of Philosophy and Linguistics, 1987–93. *Publications:* articles in Jl Philosophy, Linguistic Inquiry, Mind and Language, Linguistics and Philosophy; contribs to several collections in linguistics and in philosophy. *Recreations:* chess, music. *Address:* Centre for Linguistics and Philology, Walton Street, Oxford OX1 2HG. *T:* Oxford (01865) 280401; Somerville College, Oxford OX2 6HD. *T:* Oxford (01865) 270589; 31 Leckford Road, Oxford OX2 6HX. *T:* Oxford (01865) 510763.

HIGGINBOTTOM, Donald Noble; HM Diplomatic Service, retired; Counsellor, Foreign and Commonwealth Office, 1976–79; *b* 19 Dec. 1925; *s* of late Harold Higginbottom and Dorothy (*née* Needham); *m* 1950, Sarah Godwin. *Educ:* Calday Grange Grammar Sch., Cheshire; King's Coll., Cambridge (1st Cl. Hons Hist.); Yale Univ., USA (MA Hist.). Lectr in Humanities, Univ. of Chicago, 1951. Entered Foreign Office, 1953; Buenos Aires, 1955; Peking, 1958; Saigon, 1960; Phnom Penh, 1962, Singapore, 1964; Bangkok, 1971; Buenos Aires, 1974. *Recreations:* electronic clocks, power boating. *Address:* Apartado 54, 12580 Benicarló, Castellón, Spain. *Clubs:* Athenæum; Yacht Club Olivos (Buenos Aires).

HIGGINS; *see* Longuet-Higgins.

HIGGINS, Alec Wilfred, MBE 1944; MC 1940; TD 1945; Deputy Chairman of Lloyd's, 1975, 1976, 1980 and 1981; Chairman: Higgins, Brasier & Co. Ltd (formerly Higgins & Doble Ltd), 1962–88; M. J. Marchant Underwriting Ltd, 1982–88; *b* 1 Nov. 1914; *s* of late Frederick Gladstone Higgins and Beatrice Louisa Scriven; *m* 1939, Denise May Philcox; two *s* one *d*. *Educ:* Merton Court Sch., Sidcup; Sutton Valence Sch. Joined Woods & Maslen Ltd, 1937, Chm., 1963–80. Underwriting Mem. of Lloyd's, 1948 (Mem. Cttee, 1967–73, 1975–77, 1980–83); Mem. Cttee, Lloyd's Insce Brokers Assoc., 1960–63 and 1965–68 (Dep. Chm. 1965, Chm. 1966); Mem., Gen. Cttee, Lloyd's Register of Shipping, 1978–81; Chm., Insce Section, London Chamber of Commerce, 1963–64; Vice-Pres., Insce Inst. of London, 1967; Member: Council, Chartered Insce Inst., 1972–80; Insce Industry Trng Council, 1969; Export Guarantee Adv. Council, 1977–83 (Dep. Chm., 1982–83). Mem., Court of Assistants, Insurers' Co., 1980, Master 1984. Councillor, Chislehurst and Sidcup UDC, 1962–65 (Vice-Chm. of Council, 1964); Alderman, London Borough of Bexley, 1968–78; JP Bexley, 1967–84; DL Greater London, 1973, Representative DL, Havering, 1978–89. *Recreation:* swimming. *Address:* Farthings, Beaulieu Road, Cooden, E Sussex TN39 3AD. *T:* Cooden (01424) 842659. *Clubs:* City of London, Royal Automobile.

HIGGINS, Andrew James, PhD; MRCVS; Director, Animal Health Trust, Newmarket, since 1988; *b* 7 Dec. 1948; *s* of late Edward James Higgins and of Gabrielle Joy, *d* of late Sir John Kelland; *m* 1981, Nicola, *d* of late Peter Eliot and of Jenifer Eliot; one *s* three *d*. *Educ:* St Michael's Coll., Leeds; Royal Veterinary Coll., Univ. of London (BVetMed 1973; PhD 1985); Centre for Tropical Med., Univ. of Edinburgh (MSc 1977). CBiol 1993; FIBiol 1993. Commnd RAVC 1973. Vet. Officer to Sultan of Oman, 1975–76; Vet. Advr, ME and N Africa, Wellcome Foundn, 1977–82; Cons., FAO 1981–. Member: Council, Soc. for Protection of Animals in N Africa, 1985– (Vice-Chm., 1986–89); Conservation and Welfare Cttee, Zoological Soc. of London, 1987–; Vet. Res. Club, 1989–. Hon. Vet. Advr to Jockey Club, 1988– (Mem. Vet. Cttee, 1992–); Hon. Scientific Advr, FEI, 1990–. Editor, British Vet. Jl, 1991– (Dep. Ed., 1990–91). Gov., St Edmunds Hosp. and Nursing Home, Bury St Edmunds, 1993–. Univ. of London Laurel, 1971; Ciba-Geigy Prize for Res. in Animal Health, 1985; Equine Veterinary Jl Open Award and medal, 1986; Centenary Prize, Central Vet. Soc., 1986; George Flemming Prize, British Vet. Jl, 1987. *Publications:* (contrib.) An Anatomy of Veterinary Europe, 1972; (ed and contrib.) The Camel in Health and Disease, 1986; (ed) The Equine Mammal, 1995; papers in sci. and gen. pubns and communications to learned socs. *Recreations:* ski-ing, riding, opera, camels. *Address:* Animal Health Trust, PO Box 5, Newmarket, Suffolk CB8 7DW. *T:* Newmarket (01638) 661111. *Club:* Buck's.

HIGGINS, Prof. Christopher Francis, PhD; FRSE; Professor of Clinical Biochemistry, and Fellow, Hertford College, Oxford University, since 1993; *b* 24 June 1955; *s* of Prof. Philip John Higgins and Betty Ann Higgins (*née* Edmonds); *m* 1978, Elizabeth Mary Joy (marr. diss. 1994); two *d*; *m* 1994, Suzanne Wilson Higgins; two *d*. *Educ:* Univ. of Durham (BSc 1st Cl. Hons Botany 1976; PhD 1979). FRSE 1989. NATO-SERC postdoctoral Fellow, Univ. of California, Berkeley, 1979–81; University of Dundee: Lectr, 1981–87; Reader and Prof. of Molecular Genetics, 1987–89; Lister Inst. Res. Fellow, 1983–89; Principal Scientist, ICRF, and Dep. Dir, ICRF Labs, Inst. of Molecular Medicine, Oxford, 1989–93 (Hon. Dep. Dir, 1993–); Fellow, Keble Coll., Oxford, 1989–93. Howard Hughes Internat. Res. Scholar; Fellow, EMBO, 1988. Founding Editor and Editor-in-Chief, Molecular Microbiology, 1987–. Fleming Medal, Soc. for Gen. Microbiol., 1987; CIBA Medal and Prize, Biochemical Soc., 1995. *Publications:* numerous research papers in learned jls. *Recreation:* playing the violin. *Address:* Institute of Molecular Medicine, University of Oxford, John Radcliffe Hospital, Oxford OX3 9DU. *T:* Oxford (01865) 222423, *Fax:* (01865) 222431.

HIGGINS, Sir Christopher (Thomas), Kt 1977; Chairman, Peterborough Development Corporation, 1968–81; *b* 14 Jan. 1914; *s* of late Thomas Higgins and Florence Maud Higgins; *m* 1936, Constance Joan Beck; one *s* one *d*. *Educ:* West Kensington Central Sch.; London Univ. Executive with Granada Group Ltd, 1939–68. Served War of 1939–45: with RA, 1940–46. Member: Acton Borough Council, 1945–65; GLC, 1964–67; Hemel Hempstead Develt Corp., 1947–52; Bracknell Develt Corp., 1965–68. Chm., North Thames Gas Consumers' Council, 1969–79. *Recreations:* reading, gardening, walking; watching most sports. *Address:* 2 North Lodge, Bicester House, Kings End, Bicester, Oxon OX6 7HZ.

HIGGINS, Colin Kirk; Sheriff for North Strathclyde at Paisley, since 1990; *b* 9 Nov. 1945; *s* of late William Higgins and Janet Currie (*née* Lenney); *m* 1971, Anne McMahon; one *s* two *d*. *Educ:* St Patrick's High Sch., Coatbridge; Glasgow Univ. (LLB). Apprenticed to Town Clerk, Coatbridge, 1967–69, Legal Asst, 1969–70; Assistant, 1970–73, Partner, 1974–90, James Bell & Sons, later Bell, Russell & Co. Dean, Airdrie Soc. of Solicitors, 1989–90. *Recreations:* walking, travel, theatre, racquet sports. *Address:* Paisley Sheriff Court, St James' Street, Paisley, Strathclyde PA3 2HW. *T:* 0141–887 5291.

HIGGINS, Frank, FCIT 1979; *b* 30 Aug. 1927; *s* of Wilfred and Hilda Higgins; *m* 1948, Betty Pulford; one *s* one *d*; *m* 1985, Margaret Roberts. *Educ:* Hanley High Sch., Stoke-on-Trent; St Paul's Coll., Cheltenham. Teacher: Stoke-on-Trent, 1946; Notts, 1948–58; Organising Sec., Youth Gp, 1958–60; Teacher, Nottingham, Derby, 1960–73; Mem. Nat. Bus Co., 1974–79. Contested (Lab) Harborough 1966, Grantham 1970. Mem., Nottingham City Council, 1971–74, 1979–87 (Chm. Transportation Cttee, 1972–74, 1979–81); Lord Mayor of Nottingham, 1986–87; Mem., Notts CC, 1973–77 and 1981–89 (Chm. Environment Cttee, 1973–77; Chm. Resources Cttee, 1981–86; Chm., Police Cttee, 1987–89); Chm., E Midlands Airport Jt Cttee, 1986–87. Chm., Central Transport Consultative Cttee, 1977–80. Chairman: Bridge Housing Assoc., 1987–; Notts Building Preservation Trust, 1988–. *Recreations:* travelling, talking. *Address:* 8 River View, The Embankment, Nottingham NG2 2GF. *T:* Nottingham (0115) 986 3135.

HIGGINS, Jack; *see* Patterson, Harry.

HIGGINS, John Andrew; Assistant Auditor General, National Audit Office, since 1989; *b* 19 Feb. 1940; *s* of George Henry and Mildred Maud Higgins; *m* 1965, Susan Jennifer Mathis; one *s*. *Educ:* Hendon County Sch.; Hastings Grammar Sch. ARCO. Exchequer and Audit Department: Asst Auditor, 1958; Auditor, 1968; Sen. Auditor, 1971; Chief Auditor, 1977; Dep. Dir, 1981; Office of Auditor Gen. of Canada, 1983–84; Dir, Nat. Audit Office, 1984. Hon. Mem., CIPFA, 1984–. Mem., Crawley and Horsham Dist Organists' Assoc., 1989–. *Recreations:* classical organ playing, golf, bridge, gardening, supporting Crystal Palace. *Address:* Zaria, 65 Milton Mount Avenue, Pound Hill, Crawley, Sussex RH10 3DP. *T:* Crawley (01293) 883869. *Club:* Ifield Golf and Country.

HIGGINS, Prof. John Christopher, CEng, FIEE; CIMgt; Director of Management Centre, University of Bradford, and Professor of Management Sciences, 1972–89, Emeritus Professor, since 1992; *b* 9 July 1932; *s* of Sidney James Higgins and Margaret Eileen Higgins (*née* Dealtrey); *m* 1960, Margaret Edna Howells; three *s*. *Educ:* Gonville and Caius Coll., Cambridge (MA); Univ. of London (BSc, MSc); PhD Bradford. Short service commission, RAF, 1953–56; 1956–70: Electronics Industry; Dept of Chief Scientist (RAF) in MoD; management consultancy; Director of Economic Planning and Research for IPC Newspapers Ltd. Member: Final Selection Bd for Civil Service Commn, 1976–91; Defence Scientific Adv. Council's Assessments Bd, 1976–83 (Chm. of its Cttee on Operational Analysis, 1980–83); UGC Sub-Cttee on Management and Business Studies, 1979–85; Yorks, Humberside and Midlands Industrial Develt Bd, 1988–91; Chm., Social Sciences Res. Council's Accountancy Steering Cttee and Member of its Management and Industrial Relns Cttee, 1976–80. Vis. Fellow, Wolfson Coll., Cambridge, 1985; Vis. Prof., Open Business School, Open Univ., 1991–. *Publications:* Information Systems for Planning and Control: concepts and cases, 1976, new edn as Computer-Based Planning Systems, 1985; Strategic and Operational Planning Systems: Principles and Practice, 1980; numerous papers and articles on corporate planning, information systems and management educn. *Recreations:* violin/viola (ex National Youth Orchestra of Great Britain), cricket, fell-walking. *Address:* Woodfield, 36 Station Road, Baildon, West Yorkshire BD17 5NW. *T:* Bradford (01274) 592836.

HIGGINS, Prof. Julia Stretton, DPhil; FRS 1995; CChem, FRSC; CEng, FIM; Professor of Polymer Science, since 1989, and Dean, City and Guilds College, since 1993, Imperial College of Science, Technology and Medicine, University of London; *b* 1 July 1942; *d* of George Stretton Downes, *qv* and late Sheilah D. M. Downes (*née* Gavigan). *Educ:* Somerville Coll., Oxford (MA, DPhil 1968). CChem 1991; FRSC 1991; CEng 1994; FIM 1994; FCGI 1994. Physics teacher, Mexborough Grammar Sch., 1966–68; Dept of Chemistry, Univ. of Manchester, 1968–72; Res. Fellow, Centre de Recherche sur les Macromolecules, Strasbourg, 1972–73; physicist, Inst Laue-Langevin, Grenoble, 1973–76; Dept of Chem. Engrg, Imperial Coll., Univ. of London, 1976–. Vis. Academic, Institut für Makromoleculare Chemie, Freiburg, 1988. Science and Engineering Research Council: Member: Neutron Beam Res. Cttee, 1979–83 and 1988–91; Polymers and Composites Cttee, 1989–94 (Chm., 1991–94); Materials Commn, 1991–94; Facilities Commn, 1993–94; Member: EPSRC, 1994–; Council for Central Lab. of the Res. Councils, 1995–; Sci. and Engrg Cttee, British Council, 1993–. *Publications:* (with H. Benoît) Polymers and Neutron Scattering, 1994; contrib. articles on polymer science to learned jls. *Address:* Department of Chemical Engineering, Imperial College of Science, Technology and Medicine, Prince Consort Road, SW7 2BY. *T:* 0171–594 5565.

HIGGINS, Sir Malachy (Joseph), Kt 1993; **Hon. Mr (Justice), Higgins;** Judge of the High Court of Justice in Northern Ireland, since 1993; *b* 30 Oct. 1944; *er s* of late James and May Higgins; *m* 1980, Dorothy Ann, *d* of Dr Leslie Grech, Malta; three *d*. *Educ:* St MacNissi's Coll., Garron Tower; Queen's Univ., Belfast (LLB); Middle Temple (BL). Called to NI Bar, 1969 (Bencher, 1993), to Irish Bar, 1978; QC (NI), 1985; County Court Judge, 1988–93; Recorder of Londonderry, 1990–93; County Court Judge for Co. Armagh, 1993. *Recreations:* gardening, golf, sailing, walking. *Address:* Royal Courts of Justice, Belfast BT1 3JF; Ashdene, Comber, Co. Down. *Clubs:* Ulster Reform (Belfast); Royal Ulster Yacht.

HIGGINS, Very Rev. Michael John; Dean of Ely, since 1991; *b* 31 Dec. 1935; *s* of Claud John and Elsie Higgins; *m* 1976, Bevyl Margaret Stringer; one *d*. *Educ:* Whitchurch Grammar Sch., Cardiff; Univ. of Birmingham (LLB 1957); Gonville and Caius Coll., Cambridge (LLB 1959, PhD 1962); Harvard Univ.; Ridley Hall, Cambridge. Lectr in English Law, Univ. of Birmingham, 1961–63. Ordained, 1965; Curate, Ormskirk Parish Church, dio. of Liverpool, 1965–68; Selection Sec., ACCM, 1968–74; Vicar, Frome and Priest-in-charge of Woodlands, dio. of Bath and Wells, 1974–80; Rector of Preston, and Leader of Preston Town Centre Team Ministry, dio. of Blackburn, 1980–91. *Publication:* The Vicar's House, 1988. *Recreations:* music, walking, travel. *Address:* The Deanery, Ely, Cambridgeshire CB7 4DN. *T:* (01353) 662432.

HIGGINS, Prof. Peter Matthew, OBE 1987; Bernard Sunley Professor and Chairman of Department of General Practice, United Medical Schools of Guy's and St Thomas' Hospitals (formerly Guy's Hospital Medical School), University of London, 1974–88, now Emeritus Professor; *b* 18 June 1923; *s* of Peter Joseph Higgins and Margaret Higgins; *m* 1952, Jean Margaret Lindsay Currie; three *s* one *d*. *Educ:* St Ignatius' Coll., London; UCH, London. MB, BS; FRCP, FRCGP. House Phys., Medical Unit, UCH, 1947; RAMC, 1948–49; House Phys., UCH, St Pancras, 1950; Resident MO, UCH, 1951–52; Asst Med. Registrar, UCH, 1953; Gen. Practice, Rugeley, Staffs, 1954–66, and Castle Vale, Birmingham, 1966–68; Sen. Lectr, Guy's Hosp. Med. Sch., 1968–74. Vice-Chm., SE Thames RHA, 1976–92. Chm., Kent FHSA, 1990–92. Mem., National Council, 1985–, Nat. Exec. Cttee, 1991–, Family Service Units. Mem. Court, Kent Univ., 1984–. *Publications:* articles in Lancet, BMJ, Jl RCGP. *Recreations:* squash, swimming, sailing. *Address:* Wallings, Heathfield Lane, Chislehurst, Kent BR7 6AH. *T:* 0181–467 2756.

HIGGINS, Dame Rosalyn, DBE 1995; JSD; FBA 1995; QC 1986; a Judge of the International Court of Justice, since 1995; Professor of International Law at the London School of Economics, University of London, since 1981; *b* 2 June 1937; *d* of Lewis Cohen and Fay Inberg; *m* 1961, Rt Hon. Sir Terence Langley Higgins, *qv*; one *s* one *d*. *Educ:* Burlington Grammar Sch., London; Girton Coll., Cambridge (Scholar; BA 1958, 1st Cl. Law Qualifying 1, 1st Cl. Tripos Pt II; 1st Cl. LLB 1959); Yale Law Sch., (JSD 1962). UK Intern, Office of Legal Affairs, UN, 1958; Commonwealth Fund Fellow, 1959; Vis. Fellow, Brookings Instn, Washington, DC, 1960; Jun. Fellow in Internat. Studies, LSE, 1961–63; Staff Specialist in Internat. Law, RIIA, 1963–74; Vis. Fellow, LSE, 1974–78; Prof. of Internat. Law, Univ. of Kent at Canterbury, 1978–81. Gen. course, Hague Acad. of Internat. Law, 1991. Visiting Professor of International Law: Stanford Univ., 1975; Yale Univ., 1977. Bencher, Inner Temple, 1989. Mem., UN Cttee on Human Rights, 1985–. Hague Lectures on Internat. Law, 1982. Vice Pres., Amer. Soc. of Internat. Law, 1972–74 (Certif. of Merit, 1971). Associé de l'Institut de Droit International, 1987. Dr *hc* Univ. of Paris XI, 1980. Membre de l'Ordre des Palmes Académiques (France), 1988. *Publications:* The Development of International Law through the Political Organs of the United Nations, 1963; Conflict of Interests: international law in a divided world, 1965; The Administration of the United Kingdom Foreign Policy through the United Nations, 1966; (ed with James Fawcett) Law in Movement—essays in memory of John McMahon, 1974; UN Peacekeeping: documents and commentary: Vol. I, Middle East, 1969; Vol. II, Asia, 1971; Vol. III, Africa, 1980; Vol. IV, Europe, 1981; Problems and Process, 1994; articles for law jls and jls of internat. relations. *Recreations:* golf, cooking, eating. *Address:* c/o Essex Court Chambers, 24 Lincoln's Inn Fields, WC2A 3ED. *T:* 0171–813 8000.

HIGGINS, Rt. Hon. Sir Terence (Langley), KBE 1993; PC 1979; DL; MP (C) Worthing since 1964; *b* 18 Jan. 1928; *s* of late Reginald and Rose Higgins, Dulwich; *m* 1961, Dame Rosalyn Higgins, *qv*; one *s* one *d*. *Educ:* Alleyn's Sch., Dulwich; Gonville and Caius Coll., Cambridge. Brit. Olympic Team (athletics) 1948, 1952; BA (Hons) 1958. MA 1963; Pres. Cambridge Union Soc., 1958. NZ Shipping Co., 1948–55; Lectr in Economic Principles, Dept of Economics, Yale Univ., 1958–59; Economist with Unilever, 1959–64. Dir, 1980–92, Consultant, 1992–, Lex Service Group (Chm., Lex Pension Fund Trustees, 1994–); Dir, First Choice Holidays (formerly Owners Abroad), 1992–. Sec., Cons. Parly Finance Cttee, 1965–66; Opposition Spokesman on Treasury and Economic Affairs, 1966–70; Minister of State, Treasury, 1970–72; Financial Sec. to Treasury, 1972–74; Opposition Spokesman: on Treasury and Econ. Affairs, 1974; for Trade, 1974–76; Chairman: Cons. Parly Cttees, on Sport, 1979–81, Transport, 1979–91; Select Cttee on Procedure, 1980–83; Select Cttee on Treasury and CS, 1983–92 (Mem., 1980–92); House of Commons Liaison Cttee, 1984–; Member: Public Accounts Commn, 1984–; Exec. Cttee, 1922 Cttee, 1980–. Member: Council, RIIA, 1979–85; Council, IAM, 1979–. Governor: NIESR, 1989–; Dulwich Coll., 1980–. Special Fellow, PSI, 1986; (Mem. Council, 1989–); Trustee, Industry and Parlt Trust, 1985–91; Hon. Mem., Keynes College, Univ. of Kent, 1976–. DL W Sussex, 1989. *Address:* c/o House of Commons, SW1A 0AA. *Clubs:* Yale; Hawks (Cambridge); Royal Blackheath Golf, Worthing Golf.

HIGGINS, Wilfred Frank; *see* Higgins, Frank.

HIGGINS, Rear-Adm. William Alleyne, CB 1985; CBE 1980; *b* 18 May 1928; *s* of Comdr H. G. Higgins, DSO, RN, and Mrs L. A. Higgins; *m* 1963, Wiltraud Hiebaum; two *s* one *d*. *Educ:* Wellington College. Joined Royal Navy, 1945; Commander 1965; Captain 1973; Commodore, HMS Drake, 1980–82; Flag Officer Medway and Port Adm. Chatham, 1982–83; Dir. Gen. Naval Personal Services, 1983–86; Chief Naval Supply and Secretariat Officer, 1983–86. Sec., Defence, Press and Broadcasting Cttee, 1986–92. *Recreations:* skiing, mountaineering, Austin Sevening. *Club:* Royal Naval and Royal Marines Mountaineering.

HIGGINSON, Sir Gordon (Robert), Kt 1992; DL; PhD; FEng; Vice-Chancellor, University of Southampton, 1985–94; *b* 8 Nov. 1929; *s* of Frederick John and Letitia Higginson; *m* 1954, Marjorie Forbes Rannie; three *s* two *d*. *Educ:* Leeds Univ. BSc, PhD. FICE; FIMechE; FEng 1991. Scientific Officer, then Sen. Scientific Officer, Min. of Supply, 1953–56; Lectr, Leeds Univ., 1956–62; Associate Prof., RMCS, Shrivenham, 1962–65; Durham University: Prof. of Engrg, 1965–85; Dean of Faculty of Science, 1972–75. Dir (non-exec.), Rolls-Royce, 1988–. DL Hants, 1994. Hon. FRCP 1992. Hon. DSc Durham, 1991; Hon. DEng Portsmouth, 1993; Hon. LLD Leeds, 1994. IMechE James Clayton Fund Prize, 1963 and 1979; Gold Medal, Brit. Soc. of Rheology, 1969. *Publications:* Elastohydrodynamic Lubrication (with D. Dowson), 1966, 2nd edn 1977; Foundations of Engineering Mechanics, 1974; papers on mechanics in various jls. *Address:* 29 Oak Vale, West End, Southampton SO30 3SE.

HIGGS, Air Vice-Marshal Barry, CBE 1981; Director General, Fertiliser Manufacturers Association, since 1987; *b* 22 Aug. 1934; *s* of late Percy Harold Higgs and of Ethel Eliza Higgs; *m* 1957, Sylvia May Wilks; two *s*. *Educ:* Finchley County Secondary Grammar Sch. Served with Nos 207, 115, 138, 49 and 51 Sqdns, 1955–70; sc 1968; Forward Policy (RAF), 1971–73; ndc 1974; Comd No 39 (PR) Sqdn, 1975–77; Asst Dir Defence Policy, 1978–79; Comd RAF Finningley, 1979–81; RCDS 1982; Dep. Dir of Intelligence, 1983–85; ACDS (Overseas), 1985–87. *Recreations:* cruising, bridge, gardening, the outdoors, theatre. *Address:* 33 Parsonage Street, Cambridge CB5 8DN. *T:* Cambridge (01223) 69062. *Clubs:* Royal Air Force, Farmers'.

HIGGS, Brian James, QC 1974; a Recorder of the Crown Court, since 1974; Barrister-at-Law; *b* 24 Feb. 1930; *s* of James Percival Higgs and Kathleen Anne Higgs; *m* 1st, 1953, Jean Cameron DuMerton; two *s* three *d*; 2nd, 1980, Vivienne Mary Johnson; one *s*. *Educ:* Wrekin Coll.; London Univ. Served RA, 1948–50 (2nd Lieut). Called to Bar, Gray's Inn, 1955, Bencher, 1986; Mem., Hon. Soc. of Inner Temple (*ad eundem*), 1987. Contested (C) Romford, 1966. *Recreations:* gardening, golf, wine, chess, bridge. *Address:* 5 Paper Buildings, Temple, EC4Y 7HB. *T:* 0171–353 5638. *Club:* Thorndon Park Golf.

HIGGS, Sir (John) Michael (Clifford), Kt 1969; DL; solicitor, retired; *b* 30 May 1912; *s* of late Alderman A. W. Higgs, Cranford House, Stourton, Staffs; *m* 1st, 1936, Diana Louise Jerrams (*d* 1950); two *d*; 2nd, 1952, Rachel Mary Jones, OBE; one *s* one *d*. *Educ:* St Cuthberts, Malvern; Shrewsbury. LLB (Birmingham), 1932. Admitted solicitor, 1934. Served War of 1939–45 with 73 HAA Regt RA (TA), 1939–42; JAG Staff, 1942–46; demobilised, 1946, with rank of Lieut-Col. Mem. of Staffs County Council, 1946–49; MP (C) Bromsgrove Div. of Worcs, 1950–55; Member: Worcs CC, 1953–73 (Chm. 1959–73; Alderman, 1963); Hereford and Worcester CC, 1973–85 (Chm., 1973–77); West Midlands Economic Planning Council, 1965–79; Chm., W Midlands Planning Authorities' Conf., 1969–73. DL Worcs 1968, Hereford and Worcester, 1974. *Address:* Pixham Cottage, Callow End, Worcester WR2 4TH. *T:* Worcester (01905) 830645.

HIGGS, Sir Michael; *see* Higgs, Sir J. M. C.

HIGGS, Prof. Peter Ware, PhD; FRS 1983; FRSE; Professor of Theoretical Physics, University of Edinburgh, since 1980; *b* 29 May 1929; *s* of Thomas Ware Higgs and Gertrude Maud (*née* Coghill); *m* 1963, Jo Ann, *d* of Jo C. and Meryl Williamson, Urbana, Ill; two *s*. *Educ:* Cotham Grammar Sch., Bristol; King's Coll., Univ. of London (BSc, MSc; PhD 1954). FRSE 1974. Royal Commn for Exhibn of 1851 Sen. Student, KCL, 1953–54 and Univ. of Edinburgh, 1954–55; Sen. Res. Fellow, Univ. of Edinburgh, 1955–56; ICI Res. Fellow, UCL, 1956–57 and Imperial Coll., 1957–58; Lectr in Maths, UCL, 1958–60; Lectr in Mathematical Physics, 1960–70, and Reader in Math. Physics, 1970–80, Univ. of Edinburgh. Hughes Medal, Royal Soc., 1981; Rutherford Medal, Inst. of Physics, 1984; James Scott Prize, RSE, 1993. *Publications:* papers on molecular vibrations and spectra, classical and quantum field theories, and on spontaneous breaking of gauge symmetries in theories of elementary particles. *Recreations:* walking, swimming, listening to music. *Address:* 2 Darnaway Street, Edinburgh EH3 6BG. *T:* 0131–225 7060.

HIGHAM, Geoffrey Arthur; Chairman, Rugby Group PLC, since 1986 (Director, since 1979); Director and Trustee, Building Centre Group, since 1982 (Chairman, 1984–88); *b* 17 April 1927; *s* of Arthur and Elsie Higham; *m* 1951, Audrey Hill; one *s* and *d*. *Educ:* King William Coll., IOM; St Catharine's Coll., Cambridge (MA MechScis). CBIM 1975. Served RE, 1945–48. Metal Box Co., 1950–64; Montague Burton, 1964–65; Cape Industries, 1965–85: Man. Dir, 1971–80; Chm., 1980–85; Industrial Dir, Charter Consolidated, 1980–87; Director: Pirelli General, 1987–; Travers Morgan, 1988–91; Try Gp, 1989–. Chm., BIM Foundn, 1981–83; Vice Chm., Council, BIM, 1984–88; Mem. Council, 1978–88, Chm., 1980–82, UK S Africa Trade Assoc. Trustee, Mansfield Coll., Oxford, 1988–. FRSA 1989. *Recreations:* music, cricket, gardening. *Address:* 32 East St Helen Street, Abingdon, Oxfordshire OX14 5EB. *Clubs:* Army and Navy, Middlesex CC.

HIGHAM, John Arthur; QC 1992; barrister; *b* 11 Aug. 1952; *s* of late Frank Greenhouse Higham and of Muriel (*née* King); *m* 1st, 1982, Francesca Mary Antonietta Ronan (decd); one *s* two *d*; 2nd, 1988, Catherine Mary Ennis; two *s* one *d*. *Educ:* Shrewsbury Sch.; Churchill Coll., Cambridge (MA, LLM). Called to the Bar, Lincoln's Inn, 1976. *Publications:* (ed jtly) Loose on Liquidators, 2nd edn 1981; (ed jtly) The Law and Practice of Corporate Administrations, 1994. *Recreations:* opera, cricket, gardening, children. *Address:* 3–4 South Square, Gray's Inn, WC1R 5HP. *T:* 0171–696 9900.

HIGHAM, John Drew, CMG 1956; *b* 28 Nov. 1914; *s* of Richard and Margaret Higham, Pendleton, Lancs; *m* 1st, 1936, Mary Constance Bromage (*d* 1974); three *d*; 2nd, 1976, Katharine Byard Pailing, FRTPI. *Educ:* Manchester Grammar Sch.; Gonville and Caius Coll., Cambridge (Scholar). Asst Principal, Admiralty, 1936; Asst Private Sec. to First Lord, 1939; Private Sec. to Parliamentary Sec. and Parliamentary Clerk, 1940; Principal, Admiralty, 1941; transferred to Colonial Office, 1946; Asst Sec. Colonial Office, 1948; seconded to Singapore as Under Sec., 1953, and as Dir of Personnel, 1955–57 (acted on various occasions as Chief Sec.); Asst Sec., Min. of Housing and Local Govt, 1965; Head of Development Control Div., DoE, 1970–74. Vice-Chm., Bredon Parish Council, 1985–87. Chevalier 1st Cl. Order of St Olaf (Norway), 1948. *Address:* 17 Bannister Close, Oxford OX4 1SH. *T:* Oxford (01865) 251311. *Club:* National Liberal.

HIGHAM, Norman, OBE 1984; External Professor, Department of Information and Library Studies, Loughborough University, since 1993; Librarian, University of Bristol, 1966–89; *b* 14 June 1924; *s* of John Henry Higham, MM, and Edith Fanny (*née* Hubbard); *m* 1954, Jean Elizabeth, *d* of Frederick William and Isabel Traylen; one *s* one *d*. *Educ:* Firth Park Grammar Sch., Sheffield; Univ. of Sheffield (BA 1st Cl. Hons English, Philos., Spanish); MA Leeds 1961. ALA 1956. Served RNVR, 1942–46 (Lieut Coastal Forces). Assistant Librarian: Univ. of Sheffield, 1953–57; Univ. of Leeds, 1957–62; Librarian, Loughborough Coll. of Advanced Technology, 1962–63; Dep. Librarian, Univ. of Leeds, 1963–66. Mem. Council, Standing Conf. on Nat. and Univ. Libraries, 1972–75 and 1979–86 (Chm., 1976–79); Pres., LA, 1983 (Mem. Council, 1975–86, Chm., 1978–81 and 1985–87); Member: UGC Steering Gp on Liby Res., 1977–83; Brit. Liby Bd, 1986–89 (Adv. Council, 1976–79, and 1990–94); Liby and Inf. Services Council (England), 1977–83; Sci. Inf. Cttee, Royal Soc., 1982–91; Standing Cttee on Libraries, CVCP, 1982–89; Nat. Cttee on Regl Liby Co-operation, 1985–89; Council, Liby and Inf. Co-operation Council, 1989– (Chm., 1989–92). Mem. Council and Trustee, Oxfam, 1973–79 and 1980–86. Hon. DLitt Bristol, 1989. *Publications:* A Very Scientific Gentleman: the major works of Henry Clifton Sorby, 1963; Computer Needs for University Library Operations, 1973; The Library in the University: observations on a service, 1980; articles and reviews in librarianship and history of science. *Recreations:* literature and the arts, music, golf. *Address:* 30 York Gardens, Clifton, Bristol BS8 4LN. *T:* Bristol (0117) 973 6264. *Clubs:* Commonwealth Trust; Bristol and Clifton Golf.

HIGHAM, Rear-Adm. Philip Roger Canning, CB 1972; *b* 9 June 1920; *s* of Edward Higham, Stoke Bishop, Bristol; *m* 1942, Pamela Bracton Edwards, *er d* of Gerald Edwards, Southport, Lancs; two *s*. *Educ:* RNC Dartmouth. Cadet, 1937; Midshipman, 1938; Sub-Lt 1940; Lieut 1942; qual. Gunnery Officer, 1944; Second Gunnery Off., HMS Vanguard, Royal Tour of S Africa, 1947; psc 1948; Exper. Dept, HMS Excellent, 1951–52; Comdr, Devonport Gunnery Sch., 1953; Trials Comdr, RAE Aberporth, 1954–55; jssc 1956; Exper. Comdr, HMS Excellent, 1957–59; Admty (DTWP), 1960–61; Naval Attaché, Middle East, 1962–64; idc 1965; Dep. Chief Polaris Exec., 1966–68; Cdre i/c Hong Kong, 1968–70; Asst Chief of Naval Staff (Op. Requirements), 1970–72; retired list 1973; Dir, HMS Belfast Trust, 1973–78; Keeper, HMS Belfast, Imperial War Mus., 1978–83. Trustee, Portsmouth Naval Base Property Trust, 1985–92. *Address:* 1 John King Shipyard, King Street, Emsworth, Hants PO10 7AY. *T:* Emsworth (01243) 372195.

HIGHET, Helen Clark; *see* MacInnes, H. C.

HIGHGATE, Sir James (Brown), Kt 1994; CBE 1981; Consultant to Miller Beckett & Jackson, Solicitors, Glasgow, since 1985; *b* 18 June 1920; *s* of William Highgate and Margaret H. C. Highgate (*née* Brown). *Educ:* High Sch. of Glasgow; Glasgow Univ. (MA 1941; LLB 1949). Served War, 1941–45, RA; Royal Indian 8th Rajput Regt, 1945–47, demobilised as Maj. RA. Partner, Brownlie Watson & Beckett, Solicitors, Glasgow, 1951–75, Sen. Partner, 1975–85. General Comr of Income Tax, 1969– (Chm., Glasgow N Div., 1981–). Scottish Conservative and Unionist Association: Jt Hon. Sec., 1973–86; Pres., 1987–89; Hon. Pres., Motherwell N Cons. Assoc. Mem., Strathclyde Adv. Bd, Salvation Army, 1970–. Gov., High Sch. of Glasgow, 1981–90. Elder, Park Church of Scotland, Uddingston, 1947– (Chm., Bd of Mgt, 1960–). *Recreations:* golf, travel. *Address:* c/o Messrs Miller Beckett & Jackson, Solicitors, 190 St Vincent Street, Glasgow G2 5SP; Broomlands, 121 Kylepark Drive, Uddingston, Glasgow G71 7DD. *T:* Uddingston (01698) 813377. *Club:* Royal Over-Seas League.

HIGMAN, Prof. Graham, MA, DPhil; FRS 1958; Waynflete Professor of Pure Mathematics, Oxford University, and Fellow of Magdalen College, Oxford, 1960–84, now Professor Emeritus; *b* 1917; 2nd *s* of Rev. Joseph Higman; *m* 1941, Ivah May Treleaven (*d* 1981); five *s* one *d*. *Educ:* Sutton Secondary Sch., Plymouth; Balliol Coll., Oxford (Hon. Fellow 1984). Meteorological Office, 1940–46; Lecturer, University of Manchester, 1946–55; Reader in Mathematics at Oxford Univ., 1955–60; Senior Research Fellow, Balliol Coll., Oxford, 1958–60. George A. Miller Vis. Prof., Univ. of Illinois, 1984–86. Hon. DSc: Exeter, 1979; NUI, 1992. De Morgan Medal, London Mathematical Soc., 1974; Sylvester Medal, Royal Soc., 1979. *Publications:* papers in Proc. London Math. Soc., and other technical jls. *Address:* 64 Sandfield Road, Oxford OX3 7RL.

HIGNETT, John Mulock, FCA; Chairman, Schroder Income Growth Fund plc, since 1995; Deputy Chairman, TI Group plc, since 1993 (non-executive Director, since 1989); *b* 9 March 1934; *s* of late Reginald and Marjorie Hignett; *m* 1961, Marijke Inge de Boer; one *s* one *d*. *Educ:* Harrow Sch.; Magdalene Coll., Cambridge (MA). Kemp Chatteris & Co., 1958–61; Deloitte & Co., 1961–63; joined Lazard Brothers & Co. Ltd, 1963; Manager, Issues Dept, 1971; Dir, 1972; Head of Corporate Finance Div., 1980; Man. Dir, 1984–88; Finance Dir, 1988–92, Man. Dir, Corporate Funds, 1992–94, Glaxo Holdings plc. Non-executive Director: Emerging World Trust Fund Ltd, 1994–; Sedgwick Group plc, 1993–; London American Growth Trust plc, 1994–; Alfred McAlpine plc, 1994–. Director-General: Panel on Take-Overs and Mergers, 1981–83; Council for the Securities Industry, 1983. Chm., Internat. Shakespeare Globe Centre Ltd, 1992–; Dir, Inst. of Neurology and Brain Res. Trust. *Address:* Flat 3, 44 Lowndes Square, SW1X 9JT. *Clubs:* MCC; Hawks (Cambridge); Royal Southern Yacht.

HIGNETT, Peter George; Regional Veterinary Officer, People's Dispensary for Sick Animals, 1982–90, retired; *b* 3 June 1925; *s* of Harry Sutton Hignett and Annie Hignett; *m* 1948, Patricia Bishop (marr. diss. 1988); two *s* one *d*. *Educ:* Pontesbury C of E Sch.; King Edward VI Sch., Birmingham; Univ. of Liverpool (MRCVS). General practice, 1947–49; Wellcome Veterinary Res. Station, 1949–54; Reader in Veterinary Reproduction, Univ. of Glasgow, 1954–76; Gen. Man., Hampshire Cattle Breeders' Soc., 1976–82. Mem. Council, RCVS, 1972–, Pres., 1981–82; President: Soc. for Study of Animal Breeding, 1966–68; Southern Counties Veterinary Soc., 1983–84; Secretary: Associated AI Centres, 1977–82; Edgar Meml Trust, 1977–82; Member: Trehane Cttee, 1979–82; Scientific Adv. Cttee, Animal Health Trust, 1983–85; Banner Cttee on Ethics of Emerging Technologies in Animal Breeding, 1993–95; Gov., Berks Coll. of Agric., 1990–93. *Publications:* scientific papers on fertility in domestic animals. *Recreations:* gardening, sailing, music. *Address:* 70 Stonerock Cottages, Chilgrove, Chichester, W Sussex PO18 9NA. *T:* East Marden (01243) 535330. *Club:* Farmers'.

HIGSON, Gordon Robert; consultant on medical technology; Chairman, Medical Technology Consultants Europe, since 1989; *b* 10 June 1932; *s* of Robert and Agnes Higson; *m* 1955, Eileen Mary Warrington; two *s* one *d*. *Educ:* Thornleigh Coll., Bolton; Manchester Univ. (BSc 1954). FInstP 1968; FIEE 1978. Fairey Aviation Co., 1954–59; NCB Mining Res. Estabt, 1959–68; Department of Health and Social Security: Scientific and Tech. Services Br., 1969; Dir of Scientific and Tech. Services, 1980–84; Controller of Supply, 1984–85; Dir, Supplies Technology Div., 1986–88; Sec. Gen., Internat. Assoc. of Med. Prosthesis Manufacturers, 1988–90. Mayneord Lectr, BIR, 1986. *Publications:* The Medical Devices Directives—a Manufacturers' Handbook, 1994; papers in scientific and tech. jls. *Recreations:* walking, theatre. *Address:* Burnden, Bridge of Canny, Banchory, Aberdeenshire AB31 4AT. *T:* Banchory (01330) 824952.

HIGTON, Dennis John, CEng, FIMechE, FRAeS; aeronautical mechanical engineer, retired; *b* 15 July 1921; *s* of John William and Lillian Harriett Higton; *m* 1945, Joy Merrifield Pickett; one *s* one *d*. *Educ:* Guildford Technical Sch.; RAE Farnborough Technical Sch. Mid-Wessex Water Co., 1937–38. RAE Engineering Apprentice, 1938–42; RAE Aerodynamics Dept (Aero Flight), 1942–52; learned to fly at No 1 EFTS RAF Panshangar, 1946; A&AEE Boscombe Down, Head of Naval Test and Supt of Performance, 1953–66; British Defence Staff, Washington DC, USA, 1966–70; MoD(PE) Anglo-French Helicopter Production, 1970–72; Director Aircraft Production, 1972–75; Under-Sec. and Dir-Gen. of Mil. Aircraft Projects, MoD, 1976–79, of Aircraft 4, 1979–80, of Aircraft 3, 1980–81; Hd, Engrg Profession, Air Systems Controllerate, MoD, 1976–81; aeronautical consultant and company dir, 1981–93. Chm., Technology Div., CS Commn, 1984–89. Mem., Fleet Air Arm Officers Assoc., 1960–. Chm., S Wilts and Salisbury Br., NSPCC, 1982–. Mem., Exec. Cttee, Salisbury Gp of Artists, 1987–92. *Publications:* research and memoranda papers mainly on aerodynamic flight testing. *Recreations:* beekeeping, skiing, sailing, gardening, walking on Salisbury Plain, shooting, painting (Diploma in Fine Art, Southampton). *Address:* Jasmine Cottage, Rollestone Road, Shrewton, Salisbury, Wiltshire SP3 4HG. *T:* Shrewton (01980) 620276.

HILBORN, Rev. Dr David Henry; Minister, The City Temple United Reformed Church, since 1994; *b* 4 Jan. 1964; *s* of Edwin Henry and Constance May Hilborn; *m* 1988, Mia Alison Kyte; one *s*. *Educ:* Langley Park Sch. for Boys; Nottingham Univ. (BA English; PhD); Mansfield Coll., Oxford (MA Theol.). Ordinand, Mansfield Coll., Oxford, 1985–89; Minister, Keyworth URC, 1989–92; research and teaching, Nottingham Univ., 1992–94. *Publications:* articles in theological books and jls. *Recreations:* cricket, poetry. *Address:* The City Temple, Holborn Viaduct, EC1A 2DE. *T:* 0171–583 5532; 18 Wynyatt Street, EC1V 7HU. *T:* 0171–278 8684

HILD, Maj.-Gen. John Henry, MBE 1969; CEng, FIEE; FIMgt; Director: Siemens (UK) plc, since 1984; Siemens Plessey Electronic Systems Ltd, since 1989; consultant, since 1984; *b* 28 March 1931; *m* 1954, Janet Macdonald Brown; one *s* one *d*. *Educ:* Blackfriars, Laxton; Sandhurst. Joined Army, 1949; commissioned, 1952; Korea, 1952–53; sc 1961; MoD, DAQMG, 1962–64; Borneo, 1965; Hong Kong, 1966–67; 1 (BR) Corps, DAQMG, 1968–69; CO 18 Sig. Regt, 1969–71; DS, Staff Coll., 1972–73; Comd 1 Sig. Gp, 1974–76; Comdt, Sch. of Sigs, 1976–78; RCDS 1979; HQ BAOR, DQMG and CSO, 1980–84. Col Comdt, RCS, 1984–90. Dir, RCS Assoc. Trustee Ltd, 1989–. Mem.,

Caravan Club Council, 1985–. *Recreations:* entertaining friends, travel, sport. *Address:* c/o Lloyds Bank, 5 The Square, Petersfield, Hants GU32 3HL. *Club:* Army and Navy.

HILDRETH, (Henry) Jan (Hamilton Crossley); independent consultant; Chairman: Scallop Kings PLC, since 1987; Pathfinder NHS Trust, since 1994; High Performance Sports Ltd, since 1995; non-executive Director, Grampian Assured PLC, and other companies; *b* 1 Dec. 1932; *s* of Maj.-Gen. Sir (Harold) John (Crossley) Hildreth, KBE, and late Mrs Joan Elise Hallett (*née* Hamilton); *m* 1958, Wendy Moira Marjorie, *d* of late Arthur Harold Clough, CMG, OBE; two *s* one *d*. *Educ:* Wellington Coll.; The Queen's Coll., Oxford. National Service in RA, BAOR, 1952–53; 44 Parachute Bde (TA), 1953–58. Oxford, Hon. Mods (Nat. Sci.), BA (PPE) 1956, MA. Baltic Exchange, 1956; Royal Dutch Shell Group, 1957: served Philippines (marketing) and London (finance); Kleinwort, Benson Ltd, 1963; NEDO, 1965; Member of Economic Development Cttees for the Clothing, the Hosiery and Knitwear, and the Wool Textile industries; Mem., London Transport Bd, subseq. LTE, 1968–72: main responsibilities Finance, Marketing, Corp. Plan, Data Processing, and Estates; Asst Chief Exec., John Laing & Son Ltd, 1972–74; Dir-Gen., Inst. of Directors, 1975–78. Director: Minster Trust Ltd, 1979–94; Monument Oil and Gas plc, 1984–88; Chairman: Carroll Securities Ltd, 1986–91; Sea Catch PLC, 1987–94. Member: Cttee, GBA, 1978–86; Council, ISIS, 1979–82; Exec. Cttee, Industrial Soc., 1973–84; Council, British Exec. Service Overseas, 1975–91; Council, Spastic Soc., 1980–83, 1985–; Revue Body for Nursing and Midwifery Staff and Professions Allied to Medicine, 1989–95; Council, St George's Hosp. Med. Sch.; Dir, Contact A Family, 1980–89. Constituency Chm., 1986–89, Pres., 1989–92, Wimbledon Cons. Assoc. Governor: Wellington Coll., 1974–; Eagle House Sch., 1986–. FCIT. FRSA. *Recreations:* cross-country, mountain and road running, photography, water mills, and others. *Address:* 50 Ridgway Place, Wimbledon, SW19 4SW. *Clubs:* Athenæum; Vincent's (Oxford); Thames Hare and Hounds.

HILDREW, Bryan, CBE 1977; FEng 1976; Managing Director, Lloyds Register of Shipping, 1977–85; *b* 19 March 1920; *s* of Alexander William Hildrew and Sarah Jane (*née* Clark); *m* 1950, Megan Kathleen Lewis; two *s* one *d*. *Educ:* Bede Collegiate Sch., Sunderland; Technical Coll., Sunderland; City and Guilds, Imperial Coll., London (MSc, DIC). FIMechE, FIMarE. Engineer Officer, RN, 1941–46. Lloyds Register of Shipping: Research Surveyor, 1948–67 (Admiralty Nuclear Submarine Project, 1956–61); Chief Engineer Surveyor, 1967–70; Technical Dir, 1970–77. Chm., Abbeyfield, Orpington, 1985–. President: IMechE, 1980–81; IMarE, 1983–85; Chm., CEI, 1981–82. FCGI 1990. Hon. DEng Newcastle, 1987; DUniv Surrey, 1994. *Recreations:* orienteering, walking. *Address:* 8 Westholme, Orpington, Kent BR6 0AN. *T:* Orpington (01689) 825451.

HILDYARD, Sir David (Henry Thoroton), KCMG 1975 (CMG 1966); DFC 1943; HM Diplomatic Service, retired; *b* 4 May 1916; *s* of late His Honour G. M. T. Hildyard, QC, and Sybil, *d* of H. W. Hamilton Hoare; *m* 1947, Millicent (*née* Baron), *widow* of Wing Commander R. M. Longmore, OBE; one *s* one *d*. *Educ:* Eton; Christ Church, Oxford. Served with RAF, 1940–46. Entered HM Foreign (subseq. Diplomatic) Service, 1948; Montevideo, 1950; Madrid, 1953; FO, 1957; Counsellor, Mexico City, 1960–65; Head of Economic Relations Dept, FO, 1965–68; Minister and Alternate UK Rep. to UN, 1968–70; Ambassador to Chile, 1970–73; Ambassador and Permanent UK Rep. to UN and other International Organisations, Geneva, 1973–76; Head, UK Delegn to CSCE, 1974–75. *Address:* 97 Onslow Square, SW7 3LU. *Clubs:* Brooks's, Reform, Hurlingham.

See also C. L. Falconer, R. H. T. Hildyard.

HILDYARD, Robert Henry Thoroton; QC 1994; *b* 10 Oct. 1952; *s* of Sir David (Henry Thoroton) Hildyard, *qv*; *m* 1980, Isabella Jane Rennie; two *d* (and one *d* decd). *Educ:* Eton Coll.; Christ Church, Oxford (BA Hons Hist.). Called to the Bar, Inner Temple, 1977; Jun. Counsel to Crown (Chancery), 1992–94. *Recreations:* family, tennis, shooting. *Address:* 4 Stone Buildings, Lincoln's Inn, WC2A 3XT. *T:* 0171–242 5524. *Club:* Hurlingham.

HILL, family name of **Marquess of Downshire** and **Baron Sandys.**

HILL; *see* Clegg-Hill, family name of Viscount Hill.

HILL; *see* Erskine-Hill.

HILL, 8th Viscount *cr* 1842; **Antony Rowland Clegg-Hill;** Bt 1726–27; Baron Hill 1814; *b* 19 March 1931; *s* of 7th Viscount Hill and Elisabeth Flora (*d* 1967), *d* of Brig.-Gen. George Nowell Thomas Smyth-Osbourne, CB, CMG, DSO; *S* father, 1974; *m* 1st, 1963, Juanita Phyllis (marr. diss. 1976), *d* of John W. Pertwee, Salfords, Surrey; 2nd, 1989, Elizabeth Harriett, *d* of Ronald L. Offer, Salisbury, Wilts. *Educ:* Kelly Coll.; RMA, Sandhurst. Formerly Captain, RA. Freeman of Shrewsbury, 1957. *Heir: cousin* Peter David Raymond Charles Clegg-Hill [*b* 17 Oct. 1945; *m* 1973, Sharon Ruth Deane, Kaikohe, NZ; two *s* five *d*]. *Address:* House of Lords, SW1A OPW.

HILL, Prof. Alan Geoffrey, MA; FBA 1994; Professor of English Language and Literature in the University of London at Royal Holloway and Bedford New College (formerly Royal Holloway College), since 1981; *b* 12 Dec. 1931; *yr s* of Thomas Murton Hill and Alice Marion Hill (*née* Nunn); *m* 1960, Margaret Vincent Rutherford, MA; three *d*. *Educ:* Dulwich Coll.; St Andrews Univ. (MA 1st Cl. Hons English Lang. and Lit.); Merton Coll., Oxford (BLitt). Asst Lectr/Lectr in English, Exeter Univ., 1958–62; Lectr in English, St Andrews Univ., 1962–68; Sen. Lectr in English, Dundee Univ., 1968–80. Vis. Professor of English, Univ. of Saskatchewan, 1973–74; Ext. Examr in English, Univ. of Buckingham, 1986–90. Lectures: Crowsley, Charles Lamb Soc., 1981; Warton, British Acad., 1986; Newman Centenary, Univ. of Malta, 1990; Lambeth Palace Library, 1992. Founded Centre for Study of Victorian Art, RHC, 1981. Trustee, Dove Cottage Trust, 1969–; General Editor, The Letters of William and Dorothy Wordsworth, 1979–. Member: Editl Bd, Forum for Modern Language Studies, 1964–69; Publications Bd, Tennyson Res. Bulletin, 1993–. *Publications:* The Letters of William and Dorothy Wordsworth, vol. III, The Middle Years, Part 2, 1812–1820, 2nd edn (rev. and ed with Mary Moorman), 1970; vol. IV, The Later Years, Part 1, 1821–1828, 2nd edn (rev. and ed), 1978; vol. V, The Later Years, Part 2, 1829–1834, 2nd edn (rev. and ed), 1979; vol. VI, The Later Years, Part 3, 1835–1839, 2nd edn (rev. and ed), 1982; vol. VII, The Later Years, Part 4, 1840–1853, 2nd edn (rev. and ed), 1988; vol. VIII, A Supplement of New Letters, 1993; (ed) Selected Letters of Dorothy Wordsworth, 1981; (ed) Selected Letters of William Wordsworth, 1984; (ed) John Henry Newman, Loss and Gain, 1986; Wordsworth's Grand Design, 1987; (ed with Ian Ker) Newman After A Hundred Years, 1990; (ed) Ford Madox Ford, The Soul of London, 1995; contrib. DNB, articles and reviews in lit. and theological jls. *Recreations:* music, fine arts, ecclesiology. *Address:* 1a Northcroft Road, Englefield Green, Surrey TW20 0DP. *T:* Egham (01784) 431659. *Club:* Savile.

HILL, Alastair Malcolm; QC 1982; *b* 12 May 1936; *s* of Prof. Sir Ian George Wilson Hill, CBE, LLD, FRCP, FRSE and Lady (Audrey) Hill; *m* 1969, Elizabeth Maria Innes; one *s* one *d*. *Educ:* Trinity Coll., Glenalmond; Keble Coll., Oxford (Stevenson-Chatterton Schol.; BA Hons Jurisp. 1959). Nat. Service, RHA, 1954–56. Called to the Bar, Gray's Inn, 1961; South Eastern Circuit; a Recorder, 1982. *Recreations:* collecting prints and watercolours, opera, fly-fishing. *Address:* New Court, Temple, EC4Y 9BE. *T:* 0171–583 6166.

HILL, Allen; *see* Hill, H. A. O.

HILL, Antony James de Villiers; Headmaster, St Mark's School, Southborough, Mass, since 1994; *b* 1 Aug. 1940; *s* of James Kenneth Hill and Hon. Yvonne Aletta Hill, *d* of 2nd Baron de Villiers; *m* 1974, Gunilla Els-Charlotte Emilie (Elsa) Nilsson; one *d*. *Educ:* Sydney Grammar School; Sydney Univ. (BA Hons); Boston Univ. (MEd). Law Clerk, 1962–64; Antarctic Expedition, 1964–65; Master, Canberra Grammar Sch., 1965–66; Instructor, Himalayan Mountaineering Inst., Darjeeling, 1967–68; Master, Sydney C of E Grammar Sch., 1967–72, 1977; Mem. Faculty: Phillips Acad., Andover, Mass, 1972–74; Boston Univ., 1974–76; Senior Master, King's Sch., Parramatta, 1977–81; Headmaster: Christ Church Grammar Sch., WA, 1982–87; Melbourne C of E Grammar Sch., later Melbourne Grammar Sch., 1988–94. *Recreations:* running, climbing, sailing, theatre, music, reading. *Address:* St Mark's School, 25 Marlborough Road, PO Box 9105, Southborough, MA 01772, USA. *T:* (508) 4850050, *Fax:* (508) 4853884. *Clubs:* Weld (Perth, WA); Savage (Melbourne).

HILL, Sir Arthur (Alfred), Kt 1989, CBE 1980; Chairman, Walsall District Health Authority, 1982–92; *b* 14 May 1920; *s* of Arthur James Hill and Phoebe Mary Hill (*née* Prees); *m* 1947, Alma M. E. Bate, CBE; one *s* two *d*. *Educ:* Langley High Sch.; Halesowen Technical Coll. Served RAFVR, 1939–45. Joint Company Director: Arthur Brook Cars Ltd, 1948–68; Abro Finance Ltd, 1950–65; Cradley Heath Motor Co. Ltd, 1956–65. Chm., CPC, 1969–72, Treas., 1973–76, Chm., 1976–79, Pres., 1985–88, W Midlands Area Cons. Council; Mem., Cons. Nat. Union, 1966–80; Chairman: Kidderminster Cons. Assoc., 1964–67; Walsall S Cons. Assoc., 1981–84. Mem., Rowley Regis BC, 1948–57. Chm., Bd of Govs, Rowley Regis Grammar Sch., 1961–64. *Recreations:* travelling, golf. *Address:* Lichfield, 1 Mellish Road, Walsall, West Midlands WS4 2DQ. *T:* Walsall (01922) 34949.

HILL, (Arthur) Derek; artist, writer, and organiser of exhibitions; *b* Bassett, Hampshire, 6 Dec. 1916; *s* of A. J. L. Hill and Grace Lilian Mercer. *Educ:* Marlborough Coll. Has designed sets and dresses for Covent Garden and Sadler's Wells. *One-man exhibitions:* Nicholson Gall., London, 1943; Leicester Galls, London, 1947, 1950, 1953 and 1956. *Organised exhibitions:* 1934 onwards: Dégas Exhibn for Edinburgh Fest. and Tate Gall., London, 1952; Landseer exhibn (with John Woodward) at Royal Academy, 1961, etc. Represented in exhibns, Europe and USA, 1957–; exhibns in New York, 1966 and 1969; retrospective exhibitions: Whitechapel Gall., London, 1961; Arts Council of NI, Belfast, 1970; Municipal Gall., Dublin, 1971; portraits, Marlborough Fine Arts, London, 1978; King's Lynn Fest., 1986. *Pictures owned by:* Tate Gall.; Nat. Gall. of Canada; Arts Council; Fogg Museum, Harvard; Nat. Portrait Gall. of Denmark; Liechtenstein Gall., Vaduz; National Gall. of Ireland and Municipal Gall. of Dublin; Ulster Mus., Belfast; Walker Gall., Liverpool; City Art Galleries of: Southampton, Birmingham, Bradford, Coventry, Carlisle, Sheffield, etc. FRGS. Hon. DLit TCD, 1990. *Publications:* Islamic Architecture and Its Decoration (with Prof. Oleg Grabar), 1965; Islamic Architecture in North Africa (with L. Golvin), 1976; articles in Illustrated London News, Apollo, Burlington Magazine, etc.; *relevant publication:* Derek Hill: an appreciation, by the Earl of Gowrie, 1987. *Recreations:* gardening, travelling.

HILL, Brian, CBE 1990; DL; Chief Executive and Clerk, Lancashire County Council, 1977–90; *b* 16 Oct. 1930; *m* 1954, Barbara (*née* Hickson); one *d*. *Educ:* Wigan Grammar Sch.; Univ. of Manchester (LLB). Solicitor. Asst Solicitor, Manchester Corp., 1953–56; Lancashire County Council: Sen. Solicitor appts, finally Second Dep. Clerk of CC, 1956–74; Dep. Clerk, 1974–76. Clerk of Lancs Lieutenancy, 1977–90; County Electoral Returning Officer, 1977–90. Secretary: Lancs Adv. Cttee, 1977–90; Lord Chancellor's Adv. Cttee on Gen. Comrs of Income Tax, 1977–91; Lancs Probation and After Care Cttee, 1977–90; Co. Sec., Lancashire County Enterprises Ltd (formerly Lancashire Enterprises), 1982–90, Mem., MSC Area Manpower Bd, 1983–86. Member: Council on Tribunals, 1990–July 1996; Local Govt Commn for England, 1992–. Chairman: Local Govt Legal Soc., 1970–71; Soc. of County Secs, 1976–77; NW Br., SOLACE, 1985; Assoc. of County Chief Execs, 1989–90. Mem., Lancs Community Council, 1990–92. Vice-Pres., Lancs Youth Clubs Assoc., 1977–; Clerk to Court, 1977–89, Mem. of Council, 1990–, RNCM, Manchester (Hon. RNCM 1979); Member: Court, Univ. of Lancaster, 1977–; Council, Univ. of Central Lancashire (formerly Lancs Poly.), 1990–93. Chm., S Pennine Pack Horse Trails Trust, 1990–93. Dep. Chm., Hallé Concerts Soc., 1990–. Mem., Rossall Sch. Council, 1990–. DL Lancs, 1977. FRSA 1983; CIMgt (CBIM 1987). Hon. Fellow, Univ. of Central Lancashire (formerly Lancs Poly.), 1990. *Recreation:* music. *Address:* The Cottage, Bruna Hill, Garstang, near Preston, Lancs PR3 1QB. *Club:* Royal Over-Seas League.

HILL, Sir Brian (John), Kt 1989; FRICS; FCIOB; President, Higgs and Hill plc, since 1993; *b* 19 Dec. 1932; *s* of Doris Winifred Hill and Gerald Aubrey Hill, OBE; *m* 1959, Janet J. Newman; two *s* one *d*. *Educ:* Stowe School; Emmanuel College, Cambridge. BA (Land Economy); MA. Managing Director, Higgs and Hill Building Ltd, 1966–86; Higgs and Hill plc: Group Managing Dir, 1972–83; Chm. and Chief Exec., 1983–89; Exec. Chm., 1989–91; non-exec. Chm., 1991–92. Director: Etonbrook Properties, 1991–93; Southern Reg. Nat. Westminster Bank, 1990–92; Chm., Goldsborough Healthcare plc, 1994–. President: London Region, Nat. Fedn of Building Trades Employers, 1981–82; CIOB, 1987–88; Building Employers Confedn, 1992–95; Chairman: Vauxhall Coll. of Building and Further Educn, 1976–86; Nat. Contractors Group, 1983–84; Director: Building Centre, 1977–85; LDDC, 1994. Property Services Agency: Mem. Adv. Bd, 1981–86; Mem. Bd, 1986–88. Mem. Cttee, Lazard Property Unit Trust, 1982–. Dir (formerly Gov.), Great Ormond Street Hosp. for Sick Children, 1985– (Chm., 1992–); Gov., Aberdour Sch. Hon. FIStructE; Hon. FCGI. Hon. DSc.*Recreations:* travelling, tennis, gardening, amateur dramatics. *Address:* Barrow House, The Warren, Kingswood, Surrey KT20 6PQ. *T:* Mogador (01737) 832424. *Club:* Royal Automobile.

HILL, Charles; *see* Hill, R. C.

HILL, Christopher; *see* Hill, J. E. C.

HILL, Rev. Canon Christopher John; a Canon Residentiary, since 1989 and Precentor, since 1990, of St Paul's Cathedral; a Chaplain to the Queen, since 1987; *b* 10 Oct. 1945; *s* of Leonard and Frances V. Hill; *m* 1976, Hilary Ann Whitehouse; three *s* one *d*. *Educ:* Sebright Sch., Worcs; King's Coll., London (BD Hons; Relton Prize for Theology, 1967; MTh 1968; AKC 1967). Deacon 1969, priest 1970. Asst Curate, Dio. of Lichfield: St Michael's, Tividale, 1969–73; St Nicholas, Codsall, 1973–74; Asst Chaplain to Archbp of Canterbury for Foreign Relations, 1974–81; Archbp's Sec. for Ecumenical Affairs, 1982–89; Hon. Canon of Canterbury Cathedral, 1982–89. Anglican Secretary: Anglican-RC Internat. Commn (I), 1974–81, Internat. Commn (II), 1983–90 (Mem., 1990–91); Anglican-Lutheran Eur. Commn, 1981–82; Consultant: C of E—German Churches Commn, 1987–90; C of E—Nordic–Baltic Churches Commn, 1989–; Co-Chm., C of E—French Lutheran and Reformed Conversations, 1994–. Mem., Legal Adv. Commn,

Gen. Synod of C of E, 1991–. Guestmaster, Nikaean Club, 1982–89. Co-Chm., London Soc. of Jews and Christians, 1991–; Vice-Chm., Ecclesiastical Law Soc., 1993–. *Publications:* (ed jtly) Anglicans and Roman Catholics: the search for unity, 1995; miscellaneous ecumenical articles. *Recreations:* Radio 3, mountain walking, detective stories, Italian food, unaffordable wine. *Address:* 3 Amen Court, EC4M 7BU. *T:* 0171–236 4532. *Club:* Athenæum.

HILL, Rev. Canon Colin Arnold Clifford; Vicar of Croydon and Chaplain to Archbishop Whitgift Foundation, 1973–94; Chaplain to the Queen, since 1990; *b* 13 Feb. 1929; *s* of William and May Hill; *m* 1st, 1957, Shirley (*d* 1961); one *s*; 2nd, 1971, Irene Chamberlain; one step *s*. *Educ:* Reading Sch.; Bristol Univ.; Ripon Hall Theol Coll., Oxford. Ordained deacon, Sheffield Cathedral, 1957, priest, 1958; Rotherham Parish Church; Vicar of Brightside, 1960; Rector of Easthampstead, Bracknell, 1964; Chaplain, RAF Staff Coll., Bracknell, 1968. Hon. Canon, Canterbury, 1975, Canon Emeritus, 1984; Hon. Canon, Southwark, 1984; Proctor in Convocation and General Synod, Dio. Oxford, 1970–73, Dios of Canterbury and Southwark, 1980–84. Religious Advr, London Borough of Croydon, 1973–94; Chairman: Church Tenements Trust, 1973–94; Croydon Industrial Mission, 1975–94. Chm., Croydon Crime Prevention Initiative, 1989–94; Vice Chm., Croydon Police Consultative Cttee, 1985–94. *Recreations:* boating, walking, reading. *Address:* Silver Birches, 70 Preston Crowmarsh, Wallingford, Oxon OX10 6SL. *T:* Wallingford (01491) 836102. *Club:* Naval and Military.

HILL, Prof. David Keynes, ScD; FRS 1972; Professor of Biophysics, Royal Postgraduate Medical School, University of London, 1975–82; *b* 23 July 1915; *s* of late Prof. Archibald Vivian Hill, CH, OBE, ScD, FRS, and Margaret Neville, *d* of late Dr J. N. Keynes; *m* 1949, Stella Mary Humphrey; four *d*. *Educ:* Highgate Sch.; Trinity Coll., Cambridge. ScD Cantab 1965. Fellow, Trinity Coll., Cambridge, 1940–48; Physiologist on staff of Marine Biological Assoc., Plymouth, 1948–49; Sen. Lectr, 1949–62, Reader in Biophysics, 1962–75, Vice-Dean, 1969–74, Royal Postgrad. Med. Sch., London Univ. Physiological Society: Editor of Journal, 1969–76; Chm., Bd of Monographs, 1979–81. *Publications:* Scientific papers in Jl Physiology. *Recreations:* woodworking, photography. *Address:* Ivy Cottage, Winksley, Ripon, N Yorks HG4 3NR. *T:* Kirkby Malzeard (01765) 658562.

See also Polly Hill.

HILL, David Neil, MA, FRCO; Organist and Master of Music, Winchester Cathedral, since 1988; *b* 13 May 1957; *s* of James Brian Greatrex Hill and Jean Hill; *m* 1st, 1979, Hilary Llystyn Jones (marr. diss.); one *s* one *d*; 2nd, 1994, Alice Mary Wills. *Educ:* Chetham's School of Music, Manchester; St John's College, Cambridge (organ student; toured Aust. 1977, USA and Canada, 1978, Japan, 1979; MA). Sub-Organist, Durham Cathedral, 1980–82; Organist and Master of Music, Westminster Cathedral, 1982–88. Conductor: Alexandra Choir, 1979–87; Waynflete Singers, Winchester, 1988–; Associate Chorus Master, 1987–, Artistic Dir, 1992–, Philharmonia Chorus. Mem. Council, RCO, 1984–. Recordings with Westminster Cathedral Choir (Gramophone award, 1985); concerts abroad; toured Aust. as organist, 1984; USA tour with Cathedral Choir, 1985; toured Aust., Philippines and USA, 1988; toured Aust., NZ and Germany, 1989. *Recreations:* wine, beer, cricket, reading, snooker, walking. *Address:* 10 The Close, Winchester, Hants SO23 9LS. *T:* Winchester (01962) 854392, *Fax:* Winchester (01962) 856003.

HILL, David Rowland; Chief Spokesperson for Labour Party, since 1993; *b* 1 Feb. 1948; *s* of Rowland Foster Hill and Rita Maud Hill; *m* 1974, Janet Gibson (marr. diss. 1992); one *s* one *d*. *Educ:* King Edward VI Sch., Birmingham; Brasenose Coll., Oxford Univ. (BA PPE). Unigate Ltd, 1970–72; Asst to Rt Hon. Roy Hattersley, MP, 1972–76; Political Advr, Dept of Prices and Consumer Protection, 1976–79; Head of Staff, Rt Hon. Roy Hattersley, 1979–83; Dep. Leader of Labour Party's Office, 1983–91; Dir of Campaigns and Communications, Lab Party, 1991–93. *Recreations:* cinema, watching sport, foreign travel. *Address:* 1 Rectory Road, Walthamstow, E17 3BG. *T:* 0181–520 8753.

HILL, Derek; *see* Hill, A. D.

HILL, Prof. Dorothy, AC 1993; CBE 1971; FRS 1965; FAA 1956; Research Professor of Geology, University of Queensland, 1959–72, now Emeritus Professor; President, Professorial Board, 1971–72, Member of Senate, 1976–77; *b* 10 Sept. 1907; *d* of R. S. Hill, Brisbane; unmarried. *Educ:* Brisbane Girls' Grammar Sch.; Univs of Queensland and Cambridge. BSc (Qld) 1928, 1st Cl. Hons in Geol. and Univ. Gold Medal. Foundn Trav. Fellowship of Univ. of Queensland held at Newnham Coll., Cambridge, 1930–32; PhD Cantab 1932; Old Students' Res. Fellowship, Newnham Coll., Cambridge, 1932–35; Sen. Studentship (Exhibn of 1851) held at Cambridge, 1935–37; Coun. for Sci. and Indust. Res. Fellowship, held at Univ. of Queensland, 1937–42; DSc (Qld) 1942. WRANS, Second Off., 1942–45 (RAN Ops Staff). Univ. of Queensland: Lectr in Geol., 1946–56, Reader, 1956–59. Hon. Editor, Geol. Soc. of Aust., 1958–64; Mem. Council, Australian Acad. of Science, 1968–70, Pres. 1970; Pres., Geol Soc. of Aust., 1973–75. Lyell Medal, Geol. Soc. of London, 1964; Clarke Medal, Royal Society of NSW, 1966; Mueller Medal, ANZAAS, 1967; Foreign and Commonwealth Mem. Geol. Soc. London, 1967; Hon. Fellow, Geol Soc. of America, 1971. Hon. LLD Queensland, 1974. W. R. Browne Medal, Geol. Soc. of Australia, 1980; ANZAAS Medal, 1983. *Publications:* numerous, in geology and palæontology jls on fossil corals, archæocyatha, brachiopods, reef sediments and Australian geology and stratigraphy. *Recreations:* travel, reading. *Address:* 66 Sisley Street, St Lucia, Brisbane, Qld 4067, Australia.

HILL, Col (Edward) Roderick, DSO 1944; JP; Lord-Lieutenant of Gwent, 1974–79 (HM Lieutenant for Monmouthshire, 1965–74); Patron, Chepstow Race Course Co. Ltd (Director, 1958–83; Chairman, 1964–81); *b* 1904; *s* of late Capt. Roderick Tickell Hill; *m* 1934, Rachel (*d* 1983), *e d* of Ellis Hicks Beach, Witcombe Park, Glos; one *s* one *d*. *Educ:* Winchester; Magdalen Coll., Oxford. Gazetted to Coldstream Guards, 1926; served War of 1939–45, with regt (despatches, DSO); commanded 5th Bn and 1st Bn Coldstream Guards and Guards Training Bn; comd Regt, 1949–52. JP Co. Monmouth; High Sheriff of Monmouthshire, 1956; DL Monmouthshire, 1957; Vice-Lieut, 1963–65. Chm. of the Curre Hunt, 1959–65. Chm. of Governors, Monmouth Sch. and Monmouth Sch. for Girls, 1961–66; Chm. Chepstow RDC, 1962–63. Hon. Col, 104 Light AD Regt RA(V), 1967–69. Freeman and Liveryman, Haberdashers Co., 1969. Pres., Royal Welsh Agric. Soc., 1970–71. Pres., TA&VRA for Wales and Monmouthshire, 1971–74. Officer, Order of Orange-Nassau (with swords), 1946. KStJ 1972. *Publication:* (with the Earl of Rosse) The Story of the Guards Armoured Division, 1941–1945, 1956. *Address:* Manor Farm Cottage, Stanford in the Vale, Faringdon, Oxfordshire SN7 8NN. *Club:* Cavalry and Guards.

See also Baron Raglan.

HILL, (Eliot) Michael; QC 1979; QC (NSW) 1991; a Recorder of the Crown Court, since 1977; *b* 22 May 1935; *s* of Cecil Charles Hill and Rebecca Betty Hill; *m* 1965, Kathleen Irene (*née* Hordern); one *s* two *d*. *Educ:* Bancroft's Sch., Essex; Brasenose Coll., Oxford (MA). Called to the Bar, Gray's Inn, 1958, Bencher, 1986; Member: Senate of the Inns of Court and the Bar, 1976–79 and 1982–86; Bar Council, 1986–87 and 1989–90. South-Eastern Circuit. Prosecuting Counsel to Crown, Inner London Sessions, 1969–74; Jun. Pros. Counsel to Crown, Central Criminal Court, 1974–77; a Sen. Pros. Counsel to Crown, 1977–79. Chm., Criminal Bar Assoc., 1982–86 (Sec., 1973–75; Vice-Chm., 1979–82); Member: Council of Legal Educn, 1977–86; Criminal Law Revision Cttee, 1983–; Exec. Cttee, Soc. for Reform of Criminal Law, 1988– (Chm., Management Cttee, 1991–). Dir, Bar Mutual Indemnity Fund Ltd, 1987– (Chm., Investment Cttee, 1991–). *Recreations:* family, friends, riding, fishing and just living. *Address:* (chambers) 36 Essex Street, WC2R 3AS. *T:* 0171–413 0353, *Fax:* 0171–413 0374. *Club:* Garrick.

HILL, Dame Elizabeth (Mary), DBE 1976; Emeritus Professor of Slavonic Studies, Cambridge; *b* 24 Oct. 1900; *m* 1984, Stojan J. Veljković. *Educ:* University and King's Colls, London Univ. BA London 1924, PhD London 1928; MA Cantab 1937. War of 1939–45: Slavonic specialist, Min. of Information. University Lecturer in Slavonic, 1936–48; Prof. of Slavonic Studies, Univ. of Cambridge, 1948–68; Andrew Mellon Prof. of Slavic Languages and Literatures, Pittsburgh Univ., 1968–70. Fellow of University Coll., London; Fellow, Girton Coll., Cambridge; Hon. Fellow, SSEES, Univ. of London, 1990. Hon. LittD East Anglia, 1978. *Address:* 10 Croft Gardens, Cambridge CB3 9LD.

HILL, Air Cdre Dame Felicity (Barbara), DBE 1966 (OBE 1954); Director of the Women's Royal Air Force, 1966–69; *b* 12 Dec. 1915; *d* of late Edwin Frederick Hill and late Mrs Frances Ada Barbara Hill (*née* Cocke). *Educ:* St Margaret's Sch., Folkestone. Joined WAAF, 1939; commnd, 1940; served in: UK, 1939–46; Germany, 1946–47; Far East Air Force, 1949–51; other appts included Inspector of WRAF, 1956–59; OC, RAF Hawkinge, 1959–60; OC, RAF Spitalgate, 1960–62; Dep. Dir, 1962–65. Hon. ADC to the Queen, 1966–69. *Address:* Worcester Cottage, Mews Lane, Winchester, Hants SO22 4PS. *Club:* Royal Air Force.

HILL, Prof. Geoffrey (William), FRSL; University Professor, and Professor of Literature and Religion, Boston University, since 1988; *b* 18 June 1932; *s* of late William George Hill and late Hilda Beatrice Hill (*née* Hands); *m* 1st, 1956, Nancy Whittaker (marr. diss. 1983); three *s* one *d*; 2nd, 1987, Alice Goodman; one *d*. *Educ:* County High Sch., Bromsgrove; Keble Coll., Oxford (BA 1953, MA 1959; Hon. Fellow, 1981). Mem., academic staff, Univ. of Leeds, 1954–80 (Prof. of Eng. Lit., 1976–80); Univ. Lectr in English and Fellow of Emmanuel College, Cambridge, 1981–88. Churchill Fellow, Univ. of Bristol, 1980. Clark Lectr, Trinity Coll., Cambridge, 1986. FRSL 1972. English version of Ibsen's Brand produced at National Theatre, London, 1978. Hon. Fellow, Emmanuel Coll., Cambridge, 1990. Whitbread Award, 1971; RSL Award (W. H. Heinemann Bequest), 1971; Loines Award, Amer. Acad. and Inst. of Arts and Letters, 1983; Ingram Merrill Foundn Award in Literature, 1985. Hon. DLitt Leeds, 1988. *Publications: poetry:* For the Unfallen, 1959 (Gregory Award, 1961); King Log, 1968 (Hawthornden Prize, 1969; Geoffrey Faber Meml Prize, 1970); Mercian Hymns, 1971 (Alice Hunt Bartlett Award, 1971); Somewhere is Such a Kingdom: Poems 1952–1971, 1975; Tenebrae, 1978 (Duff Cooper Meml Prize, 1979); The Mystery of the Charity of Charles Péguy, 1983; Collected Poems, 1985; New and Collected Poems 1952–1992, 1994; *poetic drama:* Henrik Ibsen, Brand: a version for the English Stage, 1978; *criticism:* The Lords of Limit, 1984; The Enemy's Country, 1991. *Address:* The University Professors, Boston University, 745 Commonwealth Avenue, Boston, MA 02215, USA.

HILL, George Geoffrey David, CMG 1971; late Assistant Secretary, Department of the Environment (Head of International Transport Division, Ministry of Transport, 1964); *b* 15 Aug. 1911; *o s* of late William George Hill, JP; *m* 1935, Elisabeth Wilhelmina (*née* Leuwer) (*d* 1988); one *d*. *Educ:* Manchester Grammar Sch.; Gonville and Caius Coll., Cambridge (BA (Hons)). Entered Ministry of Transport as Asst Principal, 1934; Principal, 1941; Asst Sec., 1954; retired 1972. *Recreations:* bridge, languages. *Address:* 125 Ember Lane, Esher, Surrey KT10 8EH. *T:* 0181–398 1851.

HILL, George Raymond, FCA, FCIT; FHCIMA; Director, Ashford International Hotel PLC, since 1987; *b* 25 Sept. 1925; *s* of George Mark and Jill Hill; *m* 1948, Sophie (*née* Gilbert); two *d*. *Educ:* St Dunstan's Coll., London. Royal Marines, 1943–46 (Lieut). Distillers Co. Ltd (Industrial Group), 1952–66; BP Chemicals Ltd, 1967–69; British Transport Hotels Ltd: Chief Exec., 1970–76; Chm., 1974–76; Dir, Bass PLC, 1976–84 (Mem. Exec. Cttee); Chm., Bass UK Ltd, 1978–80; Chairman: Howard Machinery PLC (later H. M. Holdings PLC), 1984–85; Sims Catering Butchers plc, 1985–87; Director: Prince of Wales Hotels PLC, 1985–86; Chester Internat. Hotel, 1987–92; Regal Hotel Gp, 1989–92 (non-exec. Chm.). Member Boards: British Railways (Scottish), and British Rail Hovercraft Ltd, 1972–76; British Tourist Auth., 1981–89 (Chm., Marketing Cttee, 1985–89); Chairman: Liquor Licensing Working Party, 1985–; Channel Tunnel Nat. Tourism Working Pty, 1986–89. Member: Hotel and Catering Industry Trng Bd, 1973–80; Civil Service Final Selection Bd, 1973–80; Cttee of Inquiry on Motorway Service Areas, 1978; BHRCA (Bd Chm., 1979–80; Nat. Council Chm., 1985–86); Pres., Licensed Victuallers Schs, 1982–83. Mem., HAC. FRSA 1980. *Recreations:* music, theatre, works of art, country life. *Address:* 23 Sheffield Terrace, W8 7NQ. *T:* 0171–727 3986. *Club:* Royal Automobile.

HILL, Gladys, MA, MD; FRCS, FRCOG; retired as Obstetrician and Gynæcologist, Royal Free Hospital (1940–59); *b* 28 Sept. 1894; *d* of late Arthur Griffiths Hill and Caroline Sutton Hill. *Educ:* Cheltenham Ladies' Coll.; Somerville Coll., Oxford; Royal Free Hosp. Med. Sch. MA Oxon, MD, BS London, FRCS 1936; FRCOG 1943. *Publications:* contribs to medical journals. *Recreations:* architecture, amateur dramatics, reading. *Address:* The Manor Nursing Home, Haydon Close, Bishops Hull, Taunton TA1 5HF.

HILL, Graham Chadwick, FRSC; Headmaster, Dr Challoner's Grammar School, Amersham, since 1993; *b* 11 Jan. 1942; *s* of Harold Hill and Harriet Chadwick; *m* 1964, Elizabeth Wadsworth; three *d*. *Educ:* Bacup and Rawtenstall Grammar Sch.; Trinity Coll., Cambridge (BA, MA, PGCE Dist, AdvDipEd). Asst Science Master, Marlborough Coll., 1965–70; Sen. Chemistry Master, 1970–75, Sen. Science Master, 1975–78, Bristol Grammar Sch.; Dep. Headmaster, Dr Challoner's Grammar Sch., 1978–86, 1989–93; Sen. Fellow, Univ. of York, 1986–87. Chm., 1987–89, Trustee, 1991–93, ASE. FRSA 1993. Guinness Award for Sci. Teachers, 1968; Bronze Medallion, RSC, 1986. *Publications:* Chemistry in Context, 1978; Chemistry in Context Laboratory Manual and Study Guide, 1982; Chemistry Counts, 1986; Letts Revise Science, 1990; Science Scene (booklets, books and teachers' guides), 1990–92; Materials, 1992; contribs to learned jls. *Recreations:* walking, gardening, theatre. *Address:* Dr Challoner's Grammar School, Chesham Road, Amersham, Bucks HP6 5HA. *T:* Amersham (01494) 721685.

HILL, Graham Starforth; Resident Consultant, office in Rome 1992–94, and in Milan, 1990–94, Frere Cholmeley, later Frere Cholmeley Bischoff, solicitors; Consultant: to Monaco office, Frere Cholmeley, later Frere Cholmeley Bischoff, solicitors, 1984–94; to Rodyk and Davidson, solicitors, Singapore, since 1985; *b* 22 June 1927; *s* of late Harold Victor John Hill and Helen Dora (*née* Starforth); *m* 1952, Margaret Elise Ambler (marr. diss.); one *s* one *d*. *Educ:* Dragon Sch., Oxford; Winchester Coll.; St John's Coll., Oxford (MA Hons). Called to the Bar, Grays Inn, 1951; admitted solicitor, 1961; also admitted solicitor Malaysia, Singapore and Hong Kong; Notary Public and Comr for Oaths, Singapore. Flying Officer, RAF, 1948–50. Crown Counsel, Colonial Legal Service,

Singapore, 1953–56; Partner, subseq. Sen. Partner, Rodyk and Davidson, Advocates and Solicitors, Singapore, 1957–76. Chm., Guinness Mahon & Co. Ltd, 1979–83 (Dir, 1977–79); non-exec. Dir, Phelan, Lewis and Peat Ltd, 1984–86. Mem., Malayan Bd of Income Tax, 1957–60. Formerly (all Singapore): Hon. Legal Adviser to High Commn; Law Reform Comr; dir of numerous cos; Member: Univ. Faculty of Law; Constitutional Commn; Council, Law Soc. (Pres., 1970–74, Hon. Mem. 1978); Courts Martial Mil. Ct of Appeal; Council, Internat. Bar Assoc.; Discip. Cttee and Appeal Cttee, ICA, 1980–86. Trustee: Southwark Cathedral Develt Trust Fund, 1980–85; Royal Opera House Trust, 1982–85. FRSA. Cavaliere dell'Ordine della Stella della Solidarieta, and Commendatore dell'Ordine al Merito, Italy. *Publications:* co-editor, The Laws of Singapore, revised edition 1970; report of Constitutional Commission of Singapore. *Recreations:* music, Italy. *Address:* 36 Terrazze del Porto, CP 24, 07020 Porto Cervo, Sardegna, Italy. *T:* (0789) 92626; 10 St Thomas Street, Winchester, Hants SO23 9HE. *T:* Winchester (01962) 854146. *Clubs:* Garrick; Costa Smeralda Yacht (Italy).

See also I. S. Hill.

HILL, Rt. Rev. Henry Gordon; Co-Chairman, Anglican-Orthodox Joint Doctrinal Commission, 1980–90; *b* 14 Dec. 1921; *s* of Henry Knox Hill and Kathleen Elizabeth (*née* Cunningham); unmarried. *Educ:* Queen's Univ., Kingston, Ont. (BA 1945); Trinity Coll., Toronto (LTh 1948); St John's Coll., Cambridge (MA 1952). Deacon, Dio. Ont., 1948; Priest (Bp of Ely for Ontario), 1949; Curate, Belleville, Ont., 1950; Rector of Adolphustown, Ont., 1951; Chaplain, St John's Coll., Cambridge, Eng., 1952; Curate, Wisbech, Cambs, 1955; Rector, St Thomas, Reddendale, Ont., 1957; Asst Prof., Canterbury Coll., Assumption Univ., Windsor, 1962–68; (Vice-Principal, 1965–68); Associate Prof. of History, Univ. of Windsor, Ont., 1968–74; Bishop of Ontario, 1975–81; Asst Bishop of Montreal, 1981–83. Warden, Sisters of St John the Divine, 1976; Vice-Pres., Fellowship of St Alban and St Sergius, 1980. Episcopal Consultant for the Eastern and Oriental Orthodox Churches, Lambeth Conf., 1988; formerly on staff of Primate of Canada, episcopal liaison with non-Chalcedonian orthodox church; estabd Scholarship of St Basil the Great, 1992 (for interchange of scholars between Oriental Orthodox Churches of ME and Anglican Church of Canada). Hon. DD: Trinity Coll., Toronto, 1976; Montreal Dio. Theol Coll., 1976; Hon. LLD Univ. of Windsor, 1976; Hon. Dr, Theological Inst., Bucharest, 1977. KLJ 1980. Patriarchal Cross of Romanian Orthodox Church, 1969. *Publications:* Contemplation and Ecumenism (Monastic Studies No 15), 1984; Light Out of the East: chapters on the life and worship of the ancient orthodox churches, 1988; Engolpion, HH Ignatius Zakka Ivas, Syrian Orthodox Patriarch of Damascus, 1988; (contrib.) Dictionary of the Ecumenical Movement, 1991; articles in Cdn Jl of Theology, Sobornost, Jl Fellowship of St Alban and St Sergius. *Recreations:* walking, reading. *Address:* St John's Convent, 1 Botham Road, Willowdale, Ontario M2N 2J5, Canada.

HILL, Prof. (Hugh) Allen (Oliver), FRS 1990; CChem, FRSC; Professor of Bioinorganic Chemistry, Oxford, since 1992; Fellow and Praelector, The Queen's College, Oxford, since 1965; *b* 23 May 1937; *s* of Hugh Rankin Stewart Hill and Elizabeth Hill (*née* Burns); *m* 1967, Boglárka Anna Pinter; two *s* one *d*. *Educ:* Royal Belfast Academical Institution; QUB (BSc 1959; PhD 1962); Univ. of Oxford (MA 1964; DSc 1986). Research Fellowships, 1962–65; Oxford University: Deptl Demonstrator, 1965–67, Lectr, 1967–90, in Inorganic Chemistry; Reader in Bioinorganic Chemistry, 1990–92; Sen. Proctor, 1976–77. Vis. appts, Harvard, Univ. of Sydney, Univ. of California, 1970–82. Robinson Lectr, RSC, 1994. Interdisciplinary Award, RSC, 1987; Chemistry and Electrochemistry of Transition Metals Award, RSC, 1990; Mullard Award, Royal Soc., 1993; Breyer Medal, RACI, 1994. *Publications:* Physical Methods in Advanced Inorganic Chemistry (with P. Day), 1968; papers in professional jls. *Recreations:* gardening, music. *Address:* The Queen's College, Oxford OX1 4AW. *T:* Oxford (01865) 279177.

HILL, Ian Macdonald, MS, FRCS; Consulting Cardiothoracic Surgeon, St Bartholomew's Hospital, since 1984 (Consultant Cardio-thoracic Surgeon, 1950–84); Hon. Consultant Thoracic Surgeon, SE Thames Regional Health Authority, since 1984 (Consultant Thoracic Surgeon, 1950–84); *b* 8 June 1919; British; *m* 1944, Agnes Mary Paice; three *s* one *d*. *Educ:* Stationers' Company Sch.; St Bartholomew's Hosp. Medical Coll. Undergrad. schols and medals, 1937–41; MB, BS (Hons) London, 1942; MRCS, LRCP 1942; FRCS 1944; MS London 1945. Demonstrator of Anatomy, St Bartholomew's, 1943; Surgical Chief Asst, St Bart's Hosp., 1944; RAF Medical Branch, 1946; Wing Comdr i/c Surg. Div. No 1 RAF Gen. Hosp., 1947; Senior Registrar, Thoracic Surg. Unit, Guy's Hosp., 1948; Surgical Chief Asst, Brompton Hosp. and Inst. of Diseases of the Chest, 1950. Sub-Dean, St Bart's Hosp. Med. Coll., 1964–73. FRSocMed. Member: Soc. of Apothecaries; Soc. of Thoracic Surgeons; Thoracic and Cardiac Socs. Governor, St Bartholomew's Hosp. Med. Coll., 1985–. Freeman of City of London. *Publications:* articles in professional jls, mainly relating to lung and cardiac surgery, 1942–61. *Recreations:* old cars, furniture, keyboard instruments; gardening and house care. *Address:* Bracken Wood, Church Lane, Fernham, Faringdon, Oxon SN7 7PB. *T:* Faringdon (01367) 820475.

HILL, His Honour (Ian) Starforth, QC 1969; a Circuit Judge, 1974–94; Resident Judge, Winchester Combined Court Centre, 1992–94; *b* 30 Sept. 1921; *s* of late Harold Victor John Hill; *m* 1st, 1950, Bridget Mary Footner; one *s* two *d*; 2nd, 1982, Greta Grimshaw; 3rd, 1986, Wendy Elizabeth Stavert. *Educ:* Shrewsbury Sch.; Brasenose Coll., Oxford (MA). 11th Sikh Regt, Indian Army, 1940–45, India, Africa, Italy (despatches). Called to Bar, Gray's Inn, 1949; Dep. Chm., Isle of Wight QS, 1968–71; Western Circuit; a Recorder of the Crown Court, 1972–74. Mem., Parole Bd, 1983–84. *Address:* Tulls Hill, Preston Candover, Hants RG25 2EW. *T:* Preston Candover (01256) 389309.

See also G. S. Hill.

HILL, Ivan Conrad, CBE 1960; Chairman, Industrial Coal Consumers Council, 1965, retired; *b* 22 Jan. 1906; *s* of Wilfred Lawson Hill and Annie Jane (*née* England); *m* 1st, 1931, Alexandrina Ewart (marr. diss. 1962); four *d*; 2nd, 1963, Sheila Houghton. *Educ:* Oakham Sch.; St John's Coll., Cambridge. Exhibitioner and Open Scholar of St John's Coll. 1st cl. Hons Law Tripos Cantab 1928. Apptd Jt Man. Dir, Kelsall & Kemp Ltd, 1933. Chm. Wool Industries Research Assoc., 1950–53; Mem. Monopolies and Restrictive Practices Commn, and Monopolies Commn, 1951–63; Chairman: British Rayon Research Assoc., 1956–61; Samuel Courtauld & Co. Ltd, 1962–66; Illingworth Morris & Co. Ltd, 1976–80; Convoy Woollen Co. Ltd, 1984–90. Liveryman, Weavers' Company, 1938–. *Recreations:* travel, architecture, sport. *Address:* Crystal Spring, Duchy Road, Harrogate, N Yorks HG1 2HE.

HILL, Brig. James; *see* Hill, Brig. S. J. L.

HILL, James; *see* Hill, S. J. A.

HILL, Sir James Frederick, 4th Bt *cr* 1917; DL; Chairman, Sir James Hill (Wool) Ltd, since 1991; Director: Yorkshire Building Society, since 1972; Airedale NHS Trust, since 1992; *b* 5 Dec. 1943; *s* of Sir James Hill, 3rd Bt and of Marjory, *d* of late Frank Croft; *S* father, 1976; *m* 1966, Sandra Elizabeth, *o d* of J. C. Ingram; one *s* three *d*. Chm., British Wool Fedn, 1987–90. DL West Yorks, 1994. *Heir: s* James Laurence Ingram Hill, *b* 22 Sept. 1973. *Address:* Roseville, Moor Lane, Menston, Ilkley, West Yorks LS29 6AP. *T:* Menston (01943) 874624. *Clubs:* Royal Automobile; Bradford (Yorks); Ilkley Golf.

HILL, James William Thomas, (Jimmy), OBE 1995; Chairman: Jimmy Hill Ltd, since 1972; Fulham Football Club (1987) Ltd, since 1987; Soccer analyst to the BBC, since 1973; *m* 1st, 1950, Gloria Mary (marr. diss. 1961); two *s* one *d*; 2nd, 1962, Heather Christine (marr. diss. 1982); one *s* one *d*; 3rd, 1991, Bryony Ruth Jarvis. *Educ:* Henry Thornton School, Clapham. Player, Brentford FC, 1949–52, Fulham FC, 1952–61; Gen. Manager, Coventry City FC, 1961–67, Managing Director, 1975–83, Chm., 1980–83. London Weekend Television: Head of Sport, 1967–72; Controller of Press, Promotion and Publicity, 1971–72; Deputy Controller, Programmes, 1972–73. Mem., Sports Council, 1971–76. Hon. Chm., The Professional Footballers Assoc., 1957–61. *Publications:* Striking for Soccer, 1961; Improve your Soccer, 1964; Football Crazy, 1985. *Recreations:* golf, riding, tennis, soccer, bridge. *Address:* c/o BBC Television, Kensington House, Richmond Way, W14 0AX. *Clubs:* Wig and Pen, The Sportsman, All England Lawn Tennis and Croquet; The Berkshire, Addington Golf.

HILL, Jimmy; *see* Hill, James William Thomas.

HILL, John; *b* 28 April 1922; *s* of William Hallett Hill and Emily Hill (*née* Massey); *m* 1952, Hilda Mary Barratt; one *s*. *Educ:* Merchant Taylors' Sch., Crosby; Liverpool Univ. (BCom); Inst. of Public Finance and Accountancy, 1954. City Treasurer of Liverpool, 1974–82. Mem., Merseyside Residuary Body, 1985–88. Hon. Sen. Res. Fellow, Inst. of Local Govt Studies, Birmingham Univ., 1982–93. *Recreation:* music. *Address:* 325 Northway, Lydiate, Merseyside L31 0BW. *T:* 0151–526 3699.

HILL, Sir John Alfred Rowley, 11th Bt *cr* 1779, of Brook Hall, Londonderry; *b* 1940; *s* of Sir George Alfred Rowley Hill, 9th Bt and of his 2nd wife, Jessie Anne (*née* Roberts); *S* half-brother, 1992. *Heir: kinsman* Allan Claude Hill [*b* 1936; *m* 1970, Rachel St Just; one *s* one *d*].

HILL, John Cameron, TD 1959; FRICS; Part-time Member, Lands Tribunal, since 1987; *b* 8 April 1927; *s* of Raymond Cameron Hill and Margaret (*née* Chadwick); *m* 1954, Jane Edna Austin; one *s* one *d*. *Educ:* Trinity Coll., Oxford; College of Estate Management, London Univ. (BSc EstMan). Hillier Parker May & Rowden, 1953–88, Partner, 1962–88. Served TA (Major), 1949–73; Metropolitan Special Constabulary (Comdt), 1973–86. Liveryman, Co. of Chartered Surveyors, 1992. *Publication:* (jtly) Valuations: Principles into Practice, 1980, 4th edn 1993. *Recreations:* shooting, DIY. *Address:* Hastoe House, Hastoe, Tring, Herts HP23 6LU. *T:* Tring (0144282) 2084. *Clubs:* Army and Navy, Honourable Artillery Company.

HILL, John Edward Bernard; farming in Suffolk since 1946; *b* 13 Nov. 1912; *o s* of late Capt. Robert William Hill, Cambs Regt, and Marjorie Jane Lloyd-Jones, *d* of Edward Scott Miller; *m* 1944, Edith Luard, *widow* of Comdr R. A. E. Luard, RNVR, and 5th *d* of late John Maxwell, Cove, Dunbartonshire; one adopted *d*. *Educ:* Charterhouse; Merton Coll., Oxford (MA). Various journeys; Middle East, Far East, India, USA, 1935–37; Far East, 1956–57; USA, 1958. Called to Bar, Inner Temple (Certificate of Honour), 1938. RA (TA), 1939; Air Observation Post Pilot, 1942; War Office, 1942; 651 (Air OP) RAF, Tunisia, 1942; wounded, 1943; invalided out, 1945. MP (C) South Norfolk, Jan. 1955–Feb. 1974; Mem. Parliamentary delegns: W Germany and Berlin, 1959; Ghana, 1965; IPU Conf., Teheran, 1966; CPA Conf., Uganda, 1967; Bulgaria, 1970; Council of Europe and WEU, 1970–72; Mem., European Parlt, 1973–74; Chm., Cons. Educn Cttee, 1971–73; Member: Select Cttee on Agriculture, 1967–69; Select Cttee on Procedure, 1970–71; Asst Govt Whip, 1959–60; a Lord Comr of the Treasury, 1960–64. Mem. East Suffolk and Norfolk River Board, 1952–62. Mem. Exec. Cttee, CLA, 1957–59, 1977–82. Member: Governing Body, Charterhouse Sch., 1958–90; Langley Sch., Norfolk, 1962–77; Governing Body, Sutton's Hosp., Charterhouse, 1966–; GBA Cttee, 1966–79, 1980–83; Council, Univ. of East Anglia, 1975–82. *Recreations:* association football (Blue; Sec., OUAFC 1934); shooting, concerts, picture galleries. *Address:* Watermill Farm, Wenhaston, Halesworth, Suffolk IP19 9BY. *T:* Blythburgh (01502) 478207. *Club:* Garrick.

HILL, Prof. (John Edward) Christopher, DLitt; FBA 1966; Master of Balliol College, Oxford, 1965–78; *b* 6 Feb. 1912; *m* 1st, 1944, Inez Waugh; (one *d* decd); 2nd, 1956, Bridget Irene Sutton; one *s* one *d* (and one *d* decd). *Educ:* St Peter's Sch., York; Balliol Coll., Oxford. BA 1931, DLitt 1965. Fellow of All Souls Coll., Oxford, 1934; Asst Lectr, University Coll., Cardiff, 1936; Fellow and Tutor in Modern History, Balliol Coll., Oxford, 1938. Private in Field Security Police, commissioned Oxford and Bucks Light Inf., 1940, Major; seconded to Foreign Office, 1943. Returned to Balliol, 1945; University Lectr in 16th- and 17th-century history, 1959; Ford's Lectr, 1962. Vis. Prof., Open Univ., 1978–80. Hon. Fellow, Lancs Polytechnic, 1988. Hon. DLitt: Hull, 1966; E Anglia, 1968; Glasgow, 1976; Exeter, 1979; Wales, 1979; Hon. LittD Sheffield, 1967; Hon. LLD Bristol, 1976; DUniv York, 1978; Hon. Dr Sorbonne Nouvelle, 1979; DUniv Open, 1982. Foreign Hon. Member: Amer. Acad. of Sciences, 1973; Hungarian Acad. of Sciences, 1982; Acad. of Sciences, GDR, 1988. *Publications:* The English Revolution 1640, 1940; (under name K. E. Holme) Two Commonwealths, 1945; Lenin and the Russian Revolution, 1947; The Good Old Cause (ed jointly with E. Dell), 1949; Economic Problems of the Church, 1956; Puritanism and Revolution, 1958; Oliver Cromwell, 1958; The Century of Revolution, 1961; Society and Puritanism in Pre-Revolutionary England, 1964; Intellectual Origins of the English Revolution, 1965; Reformation to Industrial Revolution, 1967; God's Englishman, 1970; Antichrist in 17th Century England, 1971; The World Turned Upside Down, 1972; ed, G. Winstanley, The Law of Freedom and other writings, 1973; Change and Continuity in Seventeenth Century England, 1975; Milton and the English Revolution, 1978 (Heinemann award; Milton Soc. of America award); Some Intellectual Consequences of the English Revolution, 1980; (with B. Reay and W. M. Lamont) The World of the Muggletonians, 1983; The Experience of Defeat: Milton and some contemporaries, 1984; Collected Essays Vol. I: Writing and Revolution in 17th Century England, 1985, Vol. II: Religion and Politics in 17th Century England, 1986, Vol. III: People and Ideas in 17th Century England, 1986; A Turbulent, Seditious, and Factious People: John Bunyan and his Church, 1988 (W. H. Smith Literary Award, 1989); A Nation of Change and Novelty: radical politics, religion and literature in 17th century England, 1990; The English Bible and the 17th Century Revolution, 1993; articles in learned journals, etc. *Address:* Woodway House, Sibford Ferris, Banbury, Oxon OX15 5RA.

HILL, John Lawrence; Chairman, Britannia Building Society, 1990–94; Chief Executive, Loss Prevention Council, since 1986; *b* 21 July 1934; *s* of late Sidney Hill and Hilda Wardle Hill; *m* 1960, Elizabeth Godfrey; one *s* three *d*. *Educ:* Abbotsholme Sch.; Sidney Sussex Coll., Cambridge (MA). CEng, MIMechE; CIMgt; FIRM. National Service, Royal Corps of Signals, 1953–55. Royal Dutch Shell Group, 1959–67; PA Consulting Group, 1967–86; Director: Britannia Building Soc., 1984–94; Britannia Life, 1989–94. Director: Loss Prevention Certification Bd, 1986–; Nat. Approval Council for Security Systems, 1990–. Governor, Inst. of Risk Management, 1987–93. *Recreations:* golf, music, opera. *Address:* Warwick Lodge, Warwicks Bench, Guildford, Surrey GU1 3TG. *T:* Guildford (01483) 66413. *Clubs:* Royal & Ancient Golf, Worplesdon Golf.

HILL, Sir John McGregor, Kt 1969; BSc, PhD; FRS 1981; FEng 1982; FInstP; FInstE; Chairman: Rea Brothers Group, since 1987; British Nuclear Fuels PLC, 1971–83; Amersham International PLC, 1975–88; Aurora Holdings PLC, 1984–88; *b* 21 Feb. 1921; *s* of late John Campbell Hill and Margaret Elizabeth Park; *m* 1947, Nora Eileen Hellett; two *s* one *d*. *Educ:* King's Coll., London; St John's Coll., Cambridge. Flt Lieut, RAF, 1941. Cavendish Laboratory, Cambridge, 1946; Lecturer, London Univ., 1948. Joined UKAEA, 1950, Mem. for Production, 1964–67, Chm., 1967–81. Member: Advisory Council on Technology, 1968–70; Nuclear Power Adv. Bd, 1973–81; Energy Commn, 1977–79. Pres., British Nuclear Forum, 1984–92. Hon. FIChemE 1977; Hon. FIEE 1981; Foreign Associate, US Nat. Acad. of Engineering, 1976. Hon. DSc Bradford, 1981. Melchett Medal, Inst. of Energy, 1974; Sylvanus Thompson Medal, Inst. of Radiology, 1978. *Recreation:* golf. *Address:* Dominic House, Sudbrook Lane, Richmond, Surrey TW10 7AT. *T:* 0181–940 7221. *Club:* East India.

HILL, Sir John (Maxwell), Kt 1974; CBE 1969; DFC 1945; QPM; Chief Inspector of Constabulary, Home Office, 1972–75; *b* 25 March 1914; *s* of late L. S. M. Hill, Civil Servant, Plymouth; *m* 1939, Marjorie Louisa (*d* 1992), *d* of late John Oliver Reynolds, Aylesbury, Bucks; one *s* one *d*. *Educ:* Plymouth Coll. Metropolitan Police Coll., Hendon, 1938–39; joined Metropolitan Police, 1933. Served with RAF, 1942–45. Dep. Comdr, New Scotland Yard, 1959; Metropolitan Police: Comdr, No 3 District, 1963, Comdr, No 1 District, 1964; HM Inspector of Constabulary, 1965; Asst Comr (Administration and Operations), 1966–68; Asst Comr (Personnel and Training), 1968–71; Dep. Comr, 1971–72. *Recreations:* walking, golf. *Address:* 4 The Kingsway, Epsom, Surrey KT17 1LT. *Clubs:* Royal Automobile, Royal Air Force.

HILL, Rear-Adm. John Richard; Editor, The Naval Review, since 1983; *b* 25 March 1929; *s* of Stanley Hill and May Hill (*née* Henshaw); *m* 1956, Patricia Anne Sales; one *s* two *d*. *Educ:* Royal Naval College, Dartmouth. China Station as midshipman, 1946–47; Sub-Lieut's Courses, 1948–49; Lieut, HM Ships: Gambia, 1950; Chevron, 1950–52; Tintagel Castle, 1952–54; Dryad (Navigation Specialist), 1954; Cardigan Bay, 1954–56; Albion, 1956–58; Roebuck, 1958–59; Lt-Comdr, Pembroke Dock, 1959–60; HMS Duchess, 1960–62; Comdr, MoD, 1963–65 and 1967–69; IDC 1965–67; HMS Dryad, 1969–71; Captain, MoD, 1973–75; Defence and Naval Attaché, The Hague, 1975–77; Cdre, MoD, 1977–80; Rear-Adm. 1981; Flag Officer, Admiralty Interview Bd, 1981–83. Under-Treas., Middle Temple, 1984–94 (Hon. Bencher, 1994); Sec., Council of Inns of Court, 1987–93; Member: Bd of War Studies, London Univ., 1986–94; Council, Foundn for Internat. Security, 1987–; Council, Navy Records Soc., 1993–; Council, Soc. for Nautical Res., 1993– (Chm., 1994–). Defence Fellow, University of London King's College, 1972. *Publications:* The Royal Navy Today and Tomorrow, 1981; Anti-Submarine Warfare, 1984; British Sea Power in the 1980s, 1985; Maritime Strategy for Medium Powers, 1986; Air Defence at Sea, 1988; Arms Control at Sea, 1988; (Gen. Ed.) Oxford Illustrated History of the Royal Navy, 1995; articles in Survival, Navy International, Brassey's Annual, NATO's 15 Nations, Naval Review, Naval Forces. *Recreation:* amateur theatre. *Address:* Cornhill House, The Hangers, Bishop's Waltham, Southampton SO32 1EF. *Club:* Commonwealth Trust.

HILL, Jonathan Hopkin, CBE 1995; Senior Consultant, Lowe Bell Communications, since 1994; *b* 24 July 1960; *s* of Rowland Louis Hill and Paddy Marguerite (*née* Henwood); *m* 1988, Alexandra Jane Nettelfield; one *s* two *d*. *Educ:* Highgate Sch.; Trinity Coll., Cambridge. MA Cantab. RIT & Northern, 1983; Hamish Hamilton, 1984–85; Conservative Research Dept, 1985–86; Special Advr to Rt Hon. Kenneth Clarke at Dept of Employment, DTI and DoH, 1986–89; Lowe Bell Communications, 1989–91; No 10 Policy Unit, 1991–92, Political Sec. to Prime Minister, 1992–94. *Recreations:* reading, gardening, walking on Exmoor, fencing. *Address:* Lowe Bell Communications, 7 Hertford Street, W1Y 8LP.

HILL, Keith; *see* Hill, T. K.

HILL, Len; *see* Hill, R. K. L.

HILL, Leslie Francis; Chairman and Chief Executive, Central Independent Television plc and subsidiaries, since 1991 (Managing Director, 1987–91); Director, ITN, since 1987; *b* 2 Sept. 1936; *s* of late Elizabeth May and Francis Alfred Hill; *m* 1972, Christine Susan (*née* Bush); two *s*. *Educ:* Cotham Grammar School. FCA. Qualified as Chartered Accountant; with Ware, Ward (now Ernst & Young), 1952–62, Peat, Marwick, Mitchell, 1962–65; IPC Group, 1965–70, finally Finance Director, Music for Pleasure, continuing as such with EMI Group to 1971; EMI Group: Exec. Dir, 1972–73; Man. Dir, EMI NZ, 1973–74; Asst Dir, Group Music, 1975–76; Man. Dir, EMI Records (UK), 1976–78, EMI Music, Europe, 1979–80; Director, 1980–84, Jt Man. Dir, 1984–86, HAT Group plc. Dir, ITVA, 1987– (Chm., 1994–). *Recreations:* listening to music, reading, playing and watching cricket. *Address:* Central Independent Television plc, Central House, Broad Street, Birmingham B1 2JP. *T:* 0121–643 9898.

HILL, Martyn Geoffrey; tenor singer; *b* 14 Sept. 1944; *s* of Norman S. L. Hill and Gwendoline A. M. Hill (*née* Andrews); *m* 1974, Marleen M. J. B. (*née* De Maesschalck); three *s* one *d*. *Educ:* Sir Joseph Williamson's Mathematical School, Rochester, Kent; King's College, Cambridge; Royal College of Music (ARCM); vocal studies with Audrey Langford. Concert, oratorio, recital and operatic appearances throughout the world with major orchestras, conductors and choirs; numerous radio, TV and gramophone recordings.

HILL, Michael; *see* Hill, E. M.

HILL, Ven. Michael Arthur; Archdeacon of Berkshire, since 1992; *b* 17 April 1949; *s* of Arthur and Hilda Hill; *m* 1972, Anthea Jean Hill (*née* Longridge); one *s* four *d*. *Educ:* N Cheshire Coll. of FE (Dip. in Business Studies); Brasted Place Coll.; Ridley Hall, Cambridge (GOE); Fitzwilliam Coll., Cambridge (Postgrad. Cert. in Theology). Junior Exec. in printing industry, 1968–72. Mem., Scargill House Community, 1972–73; ordained deacon, 1977, priest, 1978; Curate: St Mary Magdalene, Addiscombe, Croydon, 1977–80; St Paul, Slough, 1980–83; Priest in charge, 1983–90, Rector, 1990–92, St Leonard, Chesham Bois. *Recreations:* playing guitar, listening to music, cricket, soccer, Rugby League and Union, reading. *Address:* Foxglove House, Love Lane, Donnington, Newbury RG13 2JG. *T:* Newbury (01635) 552820, *Fax:* (01635) 522165.

HILL, Michael William, President, Fédération Internationale d'Information et de Documentation, 1985–90; *b* 1928; *o s* of late Geoffrey William Hill, Ross on Wye and Torquay; *m* 1st, 1957, Elma Jack Forrest (*d* 1967); one *s* one *d*; 2nd, 1969, Barbara Joy Youngman. *Educ:* Nottingham High Sch.; Lincoln Coll., Oxford (MA, MSc). MRIC 1953; CChem; FIInfSc 1982. Research Chemist, Laporte Chemicals Ltd, 1953–56; Morgan Crucible Group: Laboratory Head, 1956; Asst Process Control Manager, 1958; Group Technical Editor, 1963. Asst Keeper, British Museum, 1964. Dep. Librarian, Patent Office Library, 1965; Keeper, Nat. Ref. Library of Science and Invention, 1968–73; British Library: Dir, Science Ref. Library, 1973–86; Associate Dir, Sci. Technology and Industry, 1986–88. Member: Exec. Cttee, Nat. Central Library, 1971–74; EEC/CIDST Working Parties on Patent documentation, 1973–80, and on Information for Industry, 1976–80; Board, UK Chemical Inf. Service, 1974–77; Adv. Cttee for Scottish Science Reference Library, 1983–; Chairman: Circle of State Librarians, 1977–79; Council, Aslib, 1979–81; Vice Pres., IATUL, 1976–81; Founder, Western European Round Table on Information and Documentation, subseq. European Council of Information Assocs, 1980. Series Editor (with I. McIlwaine), Guides to Information Sources. *Publications:* Patent Documentation (with Wittmann and Schiffels), 1979; Michael Hill on Science, Technology and Information (ed by P. Ward), 1988; National Information Policies and Strategies, 1994; papers on librarianship, documentation and information science in jls and conf. proceedings. *Address:* 137 Burdon Lane, Cheam, Surrey SM2 7DB. *T:* 0181–642 2418. *Club:* United Oxford & Cambridge University.

HILL, Dr Polly; Fellow, Clare Hall, Cambridge, since 1965; *b* 10 June 1914; *d* of Prof. A. V. Hill, CH, OBE, FRS, and Margaret, *d* of Dr J. N. Keynes and F. A. Keynes; *m* 1953, Kenneth Humphreys (marr. diss. 1961; he *d* 1985); one *d*. *Educ:* Newnham Coll., Cambridge. PhD Cantab 1967. Editorial Asst, REconS, 1936–38; research, Fabian Soc., 1938–39; temp. civil servant, 1940–51; editorial staff, West Africa (weekly), 1951–53; Res. Fellow, then Sen. Res. Fellow, Econs Dept, followed by Inst. of African Studies, Univ. of Ghana, 1954–65; financed by Center for Research on Econ. Devel, Univ. of Mich, Ann Arbor, mainly working in Cambridge and northern Nigeria, 1965–70, and by SSRC, mainly working in northern Nigeria, 1970–72; Smuts Reader in Commonwealth Studies, Cambridge Univ., 1973–79; fieldwork in villages in Karnataka, S India, 1977–78, and (as Leverhulme Emeritus Fellow) in Kerala, S India, 1981–82. *Publications:* The Unemployment Services, 1940; The Gold Coast Cocoa Farmer, 1956; The Migrant Cocoa-Farmers of Southern Ghana, 1963, 3rd edn 1977; Rural Capitalism in West Africa, 1970, 2nd edn 1976; Rural Hausa, 1972; Population, Prosperity and Poverty: rural Kano, 1900 and 1970, 1977 (Amaury Talbot prize for African anthropology, 1977); Dry Grain Farming Families, 1982; Development Economics on Trial, 1986, 5th edn 1992; (ed with R. Keynes) Lydia and Maynard: letters between Lydia Lopokova and J. M. Keynes, 1989; Who were the Fen People? (Proc. Cambridge Antiquarian Soc.), 1993; articles on rural W Africa and India in learned jls; monographs and chapters in books. *Address:* 4 Earl Street, Cambridge CB1 1JR. *T:* Cambridge (01223) 315151.
See also D. K. Hill.

HILL, (Robert) Charles; QC (NI) 1974; Member, since 1991, Chairman, since 1992, Standing Advisory Commission on Human Rights under Northern Ireland Constitution Act 1973; *b* 22 March 1936; *s* of Benjamin Morrison Hill and Mary A. Hill (*née* Roche); *m* 1961, Kathleen Allen; three *s* one *d*. *Educ:* St Malachy's Coll., Belfast; Queen's Univ. Belfast (LLB); Trinity Coll., Dublin (MA). Called to the Bar: Inn of Court, NI, 1959, Bencher, 1988; Gray's Inn, 1971; King's Inns, Dublin, 1986; Sen. Counsel, Ireland, 1987. Official Referee under Finance Acts, 1976; Dep. County Court Judge, 1979–80. Chairman: Statutory Body, Pharmaceutical Soc. of NI, 1977–92; Poison Bd of NI, 1982–92. *Recreations:* history of art, forestry, shooting. *Address:* The Bar Library, Royal Courts of Justice, Chichester Street, Belfast BT1 3JP. *T:* Belfast (01232) 241523. *Club:* Kildare Street and University (Dublin).

HILL, Sir Robert (Charles Finch), KBE 1991; FEng 1992; FIMechE, FIMarE; reliability consultant; President, Institute of Marine Engineers, 1995–March 1996; *b* 1 May 1937; *s* of Frances Margaret Hill (*née* Lumsden) and Ronald Finch Hill; *m* 1971, Deborah Mary (*née* Windle); one *s* one *d*. *Educ:* Nautical Coll., Pangbourne; RNEC Manadon. BSc(Eng), CEng. HMS Thermopylae, 1964–65; HMS Repulse, 1967–71; MoD (PE), 1971–74; RNEC Manadon, 1975–77; HMS Cleopatra, 1977–78; Nuclear Power Manager, Chatham, 1979–80; MoD (PE), 1980–84; RCDS 1985; HMS Raleigh in Comd, 1986–87; CSO (Engrg) to C-in-C Fleet, 1987–89; Chief Abovewater Systems Exec., 1989–91; Dep. Controller of the Navy (Vice-Adm.), 1989–93; Dir Gen. Submarines, 1991–93; retd. *Recreations:* rhythm guitar, theatre, sailing. *Club:* Royal Over-Seas League.

HILL, Robert Williamson, (Robin), CEng, FIGasE; Regional Chairman, British Gas, North Western, 1990–93; *b* 8 Dec. 1936; *s* of William Hill and Mary Duncanson (*née* Williamson); *m* 1961, Janette Margaret (*née* Bald); one *s* two *d*. *Educ:* Dumbarton Acad.; Strathclyde Univ. (BSc 1st Cl. Hons). CEng, FIGasE 1958. Scottish Gas Board: various appts, 1958–70; Area Service Manager, subseq. Regional Service Manager, 1970–73; British Gas Corporation: Service Ops Manager, 1973–75; Asst Service Dir, 1975–76; Service Dir, 1977–82; Regl Chm., Scotland, 1982–89. Pres., Assoc. for Sci. Educn, Scotland, 1985–86. Pres., IGasE, 1989–90 (Vice-Pres., 1987–89). Mem. Court, Heriot-Watt Univ., 1987–. Hon. Mem., CGLI, 1981. *Recreation:* golf. *Address:* 5 Grange View, Linlithgow, W Lothian EH49 7HY. *T:* Linlithgow (01506) 671173.

HILL, Roderick; *see* Hill, Colonel E. R.

HILL, Rodney, FRS 1961; PhD; ScD; Professor of Mechanics of Solids, University of Cambridge, 1972–79 (Reader, 1969–72); Fellow, Gonville and Caius College, since 1972; *b* 11 June 1921; *o s* of Harold Harrison Hill, Leeds; *m* 1946, Jeanne Kathlyn, *yr d* of C. P. Wickens, Gidea Park; one *d*. *Educ:* Leeds Grammar Sch.; Pembroke Coll., Cambridge. MA, PhD, ScD Cambridge. Armament Research Dept, 1943–46; Cavendish Laboratory, Cambridge, 1946–48; British Iron and Steel Research Assoc., 1948–50; University of Bristol: Research Fellow, 1950–53, Reader, 1953; Univ. of Nottingham: Prof. of Applied Mathematics, 1953–62; Professorial Research Fellow, 1962–63; Berkeley Bye-Fellow, Gonville and Caius Coll., Cambridge, 1963–69. Hon. DSc: Manchester, 1976; Bath, 1978. Von Karman Medal, ASCE, 1978; Gold Medal and Internat. Modesto Panetti Prize, Accademia delle Scienze di Torino, 1988; Royal Medal, Royal Soc., 1993. Editor, Jl of Mechanics and Physics of Solids, 1952–68. *Publications:* Mathematical Theory of Plasticity, 1950; Principles of Dynamics, 1964. *Address:* Department of Applied Mathematics and Theoretical Physics, Silver Street, Cambridge CB3 9EW.

HILL, Roy Kenneth Leonard, (Len), CBE 1983; JP; Chairman, South West Water Authority, 1977–87; *b* 28 May 1924; *m* 1944, Barbara May Kendall. Mem., ASLEF; Plymouth City Councillor, 1961–68, 1970–74 (formerly Dep. Lord Mayor); County Councillor, Devon, 1974 (formerly Leader of Labour Gp). Chm., Water Authorities Assoc., 1983–86. Mem., SW Econ. Planning Council. Chm. Council, Coll. of St Mark and St John, Plymouth; Governor, Plymouth Polytechnic; Mem. Bd of Visitors, Dartmoor Prison. JP Plymouth, 1968. *Address:* 5 Revell Park Road, Plympton, Plymouth PL7 4EH. *T:* Plymouth (01752) 339125.

HILL, (Stanley) James (Allen); MP (C) Southampton Test, 1970–Oct. 1974, and since 1979; company director; *b* 21 Dec. 1926; *s* of James and Florence Cynthia Hill; *m* 1958, Ruby Susan Evelyn Ralph, CBE; two *s* three *d*. *Educ:* Regents Park Sch., Southampton; Southampton Univ.; North Wales Naval Training Coll. Former Pilot. Mem., Southampton City Council, 1966–70, 1976–79, Chm. of Housing, 1967–70, 1976–79; Mem. Cttee, Southampton Conservative and Ratepayers Fedn. Mem., Speaker's Panel of Chairmen, 1990–. Secretary: Cons. Parly Cttee on Housing and Construction, 1971–73; Cons. Industry Cttee, 1979–81; Member, Select Committee: on European Legislation, 1979–84; on Transport, 1993–; on Procedure, 1993–; Chm., Cons. Cttee on Housing Improvement, 1985–; Chm./Sec., Constitutional Affairs Cons. Backbench Cttee, 1993–. Vice Chm., 1988–92, Chm., 1992–, All Party Anglo-Sri Lanka Gp; Vice Chm., All Party Anglo-Singapore Gp, 1992–; Mem., British Delegn to European Parlt, Strasbourg, and Chm.,

Regional Policy and Transport Cttee, 1973–75; Member: Hon. Cttee for Europe Day, Council of Europe, 1973–75; Scientific, Technol and Aerospace Cttee, Western European Defence, 1979–89; Political and Legal Affairs Cttee, Council of Europe, 1984–89, 1994–; Govt Whip to Council of Europe and WEU, 1980–89. Pres., Motor Schools Assoc., 1980–85; Mem. Council, IAM, 1982–89. *Recreations:* private aviation, farming. *Address:* Gunsfield Lodge, Melchet Park, Plaitford, near Romsey, Hants SO51 0ES. *Club:* St Stephen's Constitutional.

HILL, Brig. (Stanley) James (Ledger), DSO 1942, and Bars, 1944, 1945; MC 1940; Vice-Chairman, Powell Duffryn Ltd, 1970–76 (Director, 1961–76); Chairman, Pauls & Whites Ltd, 1973–76 (Director, since 1970); Director: Lloyds Bank, 1972–79; Lloyds Bank UK Management Committee Ltd, 1979–81; *b* 14 March 1911; *s* of late Maj.-Gen. Walter Pitts Hendy Hill, CB, CMG, DSO, West Amesbury House, Wilts; *m* 1st, 1937, Denys, *d* of late E. Hubert Gunter-Jones, MC, JP, Gloucester House, Ledbury; one *d*; 2nd, 1986, Joan Patricia Haywood. *Educ:* Marlborough; RMC Sandhurst (Sword of Honour). 2nd Bn, Royal Fusiliers, 1931–35; 2nd Bn, RF, BEF, 1939; DAAG, GHQ, BEF, 1940; comd 1st Bn, Parachute Regt, N Africa landing, 1942; comd 3rd Parachute Bde, 1943–45; took part in Normandy and Rhine crossing (wounded thrice); comdr 4th Parachute Bde (TA), 1947–48. Apptd to Bd of Associated Coal & Wharf Cos Ltd, 1948; Pres., Powell Duffryn Group of Cos in Canada, 1952–58. Legion of Honour (France), 1942; Silver Star (USA), 1945; King Haakon VII Liberty Cross (Norway), 1945. *Recreation:* birdwatching. *Address:* Hidden House, Guilden Road, Chichester PO19 4LA. *T:* Chichester (01243) 789083. *Clubs:* Army and Navy; Island Sailing (IoW).

HILL, Starforth; *see* Hill, Ian S.

HILL, Susan Elizabeth, (Mrs Stanley Wells); novelist and playwright; *b* 5 Feb. 1942; *d* of late R. H. and Doris Hill; *m* 1975, Prof. Stanley W. Wells, *qv*; two *d* (and one *d* decd). *Educ:* grammar schs in Scarborough and Coventry; King's Coll., Univ. of London. BA Hons English 1963; Fellow, 1978. FRSL 1972. Literary critic, various jls, 1963–; numerous plays for BBC, 1970–; Presenter, Bookshelf, Radio 4, 1986–87. *Publications:* The Enclosure, 1961; Do me a Favour, 1963; Gentleman and Ladies, 1969; A Change for the Better, 1969; I'm the King of the Castle, 1970; The Albatross, 1971; Strange Meeting, 1971; The Bird of Night, 1972; A Bit of Singing and Dancing, 1973; In the Springtime of the Year, 1974; The Cold Country and Other Plays for Radio, 1975; (ed) The Distracted Preacher and other stories by Thomas Hardy, 1979; The Magic Apple Tree, 1982; The Woman in Black: a ghost story, 1983 (adapted for stage, 1989); (ed) Ghost Stories, 1983; (ed) People, an anthology, 1983; Through the Kitchen Window, 1984; Through the Garden Gate, 1986; The Lighting of the Lamps, 1987; Lanterns Across the Snow, 1987; Shakespeare Country, 1987; The Spirit of the Cotswolds, 1988; Family (autobiog.), 1989; Air and Angels, 1991; The Mist in the Mirror: a ghost story, 1992; Mrs de Winter, 1993; (ed) Contemporary Women's Short Stories, 1995; (with Rory Stuart) Reflections from a Garden, 1995; *for children:* One Night at a Time, 1984; Mother's Magic, 1986; Can it be True?, 1988; Susie's Shoes, 1989; Stories from Codling Village, 1990; I've Forgotten Edward, 1990; I Won't Go There Again, 1990; (ed) The Walker Book of Ghost Stories, 1990; Pirate Poll, 1991; The Glass Angels, 1991; Beware, Beware!, 1993; King of King's, 1993; *play:* The Ramshackle Company, 1981. *Address:* Longmoor Farmhouse, Ebrington, Chipping Campden, Glos GL55 6NW. *T:* Evesham (01386) 593352.

HILL, (Trevor) Keith; MP (Lab) Streatham, since 1992; *b* 28 July 1943; *s* of George Ernest Hill and Ena Ida (*née* Dakin); *m* 1972, Lesley Ann Shephard. *Educ:* Corpus Christi Coll., Oxford (BA, MA); UCW, Aberystwyth (DipEd). Res. Asst in Politics, Univ. of Leicester, 1966–68; Belgian Govt Scholar, Brussels, 1968–69; Lectr in Politics, Univ. of Strathclyde, 1969–73; Res. Officer, Labour Party Internat. Dept, 1974–76; Political Liaison Officer, NUR, subseq. Nat. Union of Rail, Maritime and Tspt Workers, 1976–92. *Publications:* (contrib.) European Political Parties, 1969; (contrib.) Electoral Behaviour, 1974. *Recreations:* walks, books, films. *Address:* 110 Wavertree Road, Streatham Hill, SW2 3ST. *T:* 0181–674 0434.

HILL, Prof. William George, FRS 1985; FRSE 1979; Professor of Animal Genetics, since 1983, and Head, Division of Biological Sciences, since 1993, University of Edinburgh; *b* 7 Aug. 1940; *s* of late William Hill and Margaret Paterson Hill (*née* Hamilton); *m* 1971, Christine Rosemary Austin; one *s* two *d*. *Educ:* St Albans School; Wye Coll., Univ. of London (BSc 1961); Univ. of California, Davis (MS 1963); Iowa State Univ.; Univ. of Edinburgh (PhD 1965; DSc 1976). University of Edinburgh: Asst Lectr, 1965–67, Lectr, 1967–74, Reader, 1974–83, in Genetics; Hd, Dept of Genetics, 1989–90; Hd, Inst. of Cell, Animal and Population Biol., 1990–93. Visiting Professor/Research Associate: Univ. of Minnesota, 1966; Iowa State Univ., 1967–78; N Carolina State Univ., 1979, 1985, 1992–. Consultant Geneticist: Cotswold Pig Develt Co., 1965–; British Friesian Cattle Soc., 1978–88; Holstein Friesian Soc., 1988–. Chm., Org Cttee, 4th World Congress, 1990, Pres., 5th World Congress, Genetics Applied to Livestock Prodn. Member: Scientific Study Group, Meat and Livestock Commn, 1969–72; Cattle Res. Consultative Cttee, 1985–86; AFRC Animals Res. Grant Bd, 1986–92; Dir's Adv. Gp, AFRC Animal Breeding Res. Orgn, 1983–86; Inst. Animal Physiology and Genetics Res., 1986–93; Roslin Inst., 1994–; Council, Royal Soc., 1993–94. *Publications:* (ed) Benchmark Papers in Quantitative Genetics, 1984; (ed) Evolution and Animal Breeding, 1989; numerous papers on quantitative and population genetics, biometrics and animal breeding, in sci. jls. *Recreations:* farming, bridge. *Address:* 4 Gordon Terrace, Edinburgh EH16 5QH. *T:* 0131–667 3680. *Club:* Farmers'.

HILL-NORTON, family name of **Baron Hill-Norton.**

HILL-NORTON, Baron *cr* 1979 (Life Peer), of South Nutfield, Surrey; **Admiral of the Fleet Peter John Hill-Norton,** GCB 1970 (KCB 1967; CB 1964); Chairman, Military Committee of NATO, 1974–77; *b* 8 Feb. 1915; *s* of Capt. M. J. Norton and Mrs M. B. Norton; *m* 1936, Margaret Eileen Linstow; one *s* one *d*. *Educ:* RNC Dartmouth. Went to sea, 1932; commnd, 1936; specialised in Gunnery, 1939; War of 1939–45: Arctic Convoys; NW Approaches; Admiralty Naval Staff. Comdr 1948; Capt. 1952; Naval Attaché, Argentine, Uruguay, Paraguay, 1953–55; comd HMS Decoy, 1956–57; comd HMS Ark Royal, 1959–61; Asst Chief of Naval Staff, 1962–64; Flag Officer, Second-in-Command, Far East Fleet, 1964–66; Dep. Chief of the Defence Staff (Personnel and Logistics), 1966; Second Sea Lord and Chief of Naval Personnel, Jan.-Aug. 1967; Vice-Chief of Naval Staff, 1967–68; C-in-C Far East, 1969–70; Chief of the Naval Staff and First Sea Lord, 1970–71; Chief of the Defence Staff, 1971–73. President: Sea Cadets Assoc., 1977–84; Defence Manufacturers' Assoc., 1980–84; British Maritime League, 1982–85; Vice-Pres., RUSI, 1977–90. Liveryman, Shipwrights' Co., 1973, Mem. Court, 1979; Freeman, City of London, 1973. *Publications:* No Soft Options, 1978; Sea Power, 1982. *Recreations:* gardening, shooting. *Address:* Cass Cottage, Hyde, Fordingbridge, Hants SP6 2QH. *Clubs:* Army and Navy; Royal Navy of 1765.

See also Vice-Adm. Hon. Sir N. J. Hill-Norton.

HILL-NORTON, Vice-Adm. Hon. Sir Nicholas (John), KCB 1991; Deputy Chief of Defence Staff, Ministry of Defence, 1992–95; *b* 13 July 1939; *s* of Admiral of the Fleet Baron Hill-Norton, *qv*; *m* 1966, Ann Jennifer, *d* of Vice-Adm. D. H. Mason, *qv*; two *s* one *d*. *Educ:* Marlborough Coll.; RNC, Dartmouth; US Naval War Coll., Newport, RI. Royal Navy, 1957–95; Flag Officer, Gibraltar, 1987–90; Flag Officer Surface Flotilla and Comdr, Anti-Submarine Warfare Striking Force, 1990–92. *Recreations:* country sports, family pursuits. *Club:* Farmers'.

HILL-SMITH, His Honour Derek Edward, VRD 1958; a Circuit Judge, 1972–87; *b* 21 Oct. 1922; *s* of Charles Hill-Smith and Ivy (*née* Downs); *m* 1950, Marjorie Joanna, *d* of His Honour Montague Berryman, QC; one *s* one *d*. *Educ:* Sherborne; Trinity Coll., Oxford (MA). RNVR, 1942–46; Lt-Comdr RNR. Trinity Coll., Oxford, 1941–42 and 1946–47 (MA, Classics and Modern Greats); BEA, 1947–48; business, 1948–50; teaching, 1950–54; called to Bar, Inner Temple, 1954; Dep. Chm., Kent QS, 1970; Recorder, 1972. Chm., Mental Health Review Tribunals, 1987–. FCIArb 1994 (ACIArb 1993). *Publications:* contrib. Law Guardian. *Recreations:* the theatre, food and wine, collecting and restoring Old Masters and New Mistresses, the study of mediaeval church frescoes in Cyprus and Asia Minor. *Address:* c/o National Westminster Bank, North Street, Bishop's Stortford, Herts. *Clubs:* Garrick; Bar Yacht.

HILL-TREVOR, family name of **Baron Trevor.**

HILL-WOOD, Sir David (Basil), 3rd Bt *cr* 1921; Director, Guinness Mahon & Co. Ltd (Bankers), since 1977; *b* 12 Nov. 1926; *s* of Sir Basil Samuel Hill Hill-Wood, 2nd Bt, and Hon. Joan Louisa Brand, *e d* of 3rd Viscount Hampden; *S* father, 1954; *m* 1970, Jennifer, 2nd *d* of late Peter McKenzie Strang, Adelaide; two *s* one *d*. *Educ:* Eton. Served in Army (Grenadier Guards), 1945–48. Morgan Grenfell & Co. Ltd, 1948–55; Myers & Co., Stockbrokers, 1955–71, Sen. Partner, 1971–74; Dir, Capel-Cure Myers Ltd, 1974–77. Aust. Rep., FA Council, 1978–. High Sheriff Berks, 1982. *Recreations:* soccer, farming, forestry. *Heir:* *s* Samuel Thomas Hill-Wood, *b* 24 Aug. 1971. *Address:* Dacre Farm, Farley Hill, Reading, Berks RG7 1XJ. *T:* Eversley (01734) 733185. *Clubs:* White's; Melbourne (Australia).

HILLABY, John; writer, naturalist and traveller; *b* 24 July 1917; *er s* of late Albert Ewart Hillaby, Pontefract, and Mabel Colyer; *m* 1940, Eleanor Riley, Leeds (marr. diss.); two *d*; *m* 1966, Thelma Gordon (*d* 1972), child analyst, London and Montreal; *m* 1981, Kathleen Burton, Easingwold, Yorks. *Educ:* Leeds; Woodhouse Grove, Yorkshire. Served War, RA, 1939–44. Local journalism up to 1939; magazine contributor and broadcaster, 1944–; Zoological Corresp., Manchester Guardian, 1949; European science writer, New York Times, 1951–; biological consultant, New Scientist, 1953–. Formerly a dir, Universities Fedn for Animal Welfare; Founder Pres., Backpackers Club. Has travelled on foot through parts of boreal Canada, Appalachian Trail, USA, Congo, traversed Ituri Forest and Mountains of the Moon (Ruwenzori), Sudan, Tanzania; three months foot safari with camels to Lake Rudolf, Kenya, and walked from Lands End to John o'Groats, from The Hague to Nice via the Alps, from Provence to Tuscany, from Lake District to London, and from Athens to Mt Olympus via the Pindos mountains. Woodward Lectr, Yale, 1973. Radio and TV series include: Men of the North, Expedition South, Alpine Venture, Hillaby Walks, Globetrotter, etc. FZS (scientific). Hon. DL:tt City, 1993. *Publications:* Within The Streams, 1949; Nature and Man, 1960; Journey to the Jade Sea, 1964; Journey through Britain, 1968; Journey through Europe, 1972; Journey through Love, 1976; Journey Home, 1983; John Hillaby's Yorkshire: the moors and dales, 1986; John Hillaby's London, 1987; Journey to the Gods, 1991; Hillaby's World, 1992. *Recreations:* talking, reading, music, walking; observing peculiarities of man, beast, fowl and flora. *Club:* Savage.

HILLARD, His Honour Richard Arthur Loraine, MBE 1946; a Circuit Judge (formerly a County Court Judge), 1956–72; *b* 1906; *e s* of Frederick Arthur Hillard, Puriton Manor, Bridgwater, Som; *m* 1st, 1936, Nancy Alford (*d* 1964), *d* of Dr Alford Andrews, Cambridge; one *s* one *d*; 2nd, 1969, Monica Constance, *er d* of John Healey Carus, Darwen, and *widow* of Paul Hillard; one step *s* one step *d*. *Educ:* Worcester Royal Grammar Sch.; Christ Church, Oxford. Barrister, Gray's Inn, 1931; South-Eastern circuit. Served, 1940–45: Military Dept, Judge Advocate General's Office, 1941–45, Lt-Col 1945. Asst Reader and Lecturer, Council of Legal Education, 1945–55. Chm. Agricultural Land Tribunal, South Eastern Province, 1955. *Recreation:* gardening. *Address:* Oakchurch House, Staunton-on-Wye, Hereford HR4 7NE. *T:* Moccas (01981) 500345. *Club:* United Oxford & Cambridge University.

HILLARY, Sir Edmund (Percival), KG 1995; ONZ 1987; KBE 1953; author; lecturer; mountaineer; *b* 20 July 1919; *s* of Percival Augustus Hillary and Gertrude Hillary (*née* Clark); *m* 1st, 1953, Louise Mary Rose (*d* 1975), *d* of J. H. Rose; one *s* one *d* (and one *d* decd); 2nd, 1989, June Mulgrew, *widow* of Peter Mulgrew. *Educ:* Auckland Grammar Sch., Auckland, New Zealand. Apiarist, 1936–43. RNZAF, navigator on Catalina flying boats in Pacific Area, 1944–45. Apiarist (in partnership with brother W. F. Hillary), 1951–70. NZ High Comr to India, Nepal and Bangladesh, 1985–88. Himalayan Expeditions: NZ Gawhal Expedition, 1951; British Everest Reconnaissance, 1951; British Cho Oyu Expedition, 1952; Everest Expedition, 1953; with Sherpa Tenzing reached summit of Mount Everest, May 1953 (KBE). Leader of NZ Alpine Club Expedition to Barun Valley, East of Everest, 1954. Appointed, 1955, leader of New Zealand Transantarctic Expedition; completed overland journey to South Pole, Jan. 1958. Expeditions in Everest region, 1960–61, 1963, 1964, 1965, 1981; led expedition to Antarctic for geological and mountaineering purposes incl. first ascent of Mt Herschel, 1967; expedition to E Nepal (explored Himalayan rivers with two jet boats; first ascent of 180 miles of Sun Kosi river from Indian border to Katmandu), 1968; jet boat expedition up the Ganges, 1977. Built first hosp. for Sherpas in Everest area, with public subscription and NZ doctor, 1966; latterly Everest region has 25 schools, 2 hosps, 12 med. clinics, bridges, difficult access paths, fresh water pipelines; also re-afforestation prog. in Sagarmatha (Everest) Nat. Park. Internat. Dir, WWF; UNICEF Special Rep., Children of the Himalayas, 1991–. Consultant to Sears Roebuck & Co., Chicago, on camping and outdoor equipment. Hon. LLD: Univ. of Victoria, BC, Canada, 1969; Victoria Univ., Wellington, NZ, 1970. Hubbard Medal (US), 1954; Star of Nepal 1st Class; US Gold Cullum Geographical Medal, 1954; Founder's Gold Medal, Royal Geographical Society, 1958; Polar Medal, 1958. *Publications:* High Adventure, 1955; East of Everest, 1956 (with George Lowe); The Crossing of Antarctica, 1958 (with Sir Vivian Fuchs); No Latitude for Error, 1961; High in the Thin Cold Air, 1963 (with Desmond Doig); School House in the Clouds, 1965; Nothing Venture, Nothing Win (autobiog.), 1975; From the Ocean to the Sky: jet boating up the Ganges, 1979; (with Peter Hillary) Two Generations, 1983; Sagarmatha. *Recreations:* mountaineering, ski-ing, camping. *Address:* 278A Remuera Road, Auckland 5, New Zealand. *Clubs:* New Zealand Alpine (Hon. Mem.; Pres. 1965–67); Explorers (New York) (Hon. Pres); Hon. Mem. of many other NZ and US clubs.

HILLER, Dame Wendy, DBE 1975 (OBE 1971); actress; *b* 15 Aug. 1912; *d* of Frank Watkin and Marie Hiller, Bramhall, Cheshire; *m* 1937, Ronald Gow (*d* 1993); one *s* one *d*. *Educ:* Winceby House, Bexhill. Manchester Repertory Theatre; Sir Barry Jackson's tour of Evensong; Sally Hardcastle in Love on the Dole, London and New York; leading parts in Saint Joan and Pygmalion at Malvern Festival, 1936. *Plays include:* Twelfth Night (war factory tour); Cradle Song (Apollo); The First Gentleman (Savoy); Tess of the d'Urbervilles (Piccadilly); The Heiress (Biltmore, NY, and Haymarket, London); Ann Veronica

(Piccadilly); Waters of the Moon (Haymarket), 1951–53; The Night of the Ball (New), 1955; Old Vic Season, 1955–56; Moon for the Misbegotten (NY), 1957; Flowering Cherry (Haymarket), 1958; Toys in the Attic (Piccadilly), 1960; Aspern Papers (NY), 1962; The Wings of the Dove (Lyric), 1963; The Sacred Flame (Duke of York's), 1967; When We Dead Awaken (Edinburgh Festival), 1968; The Battle of Shrivings (Lyric), 1970; Crown Matrimonial (Haymarket), 1972; John Gabriel Borkman (National), 1975; Lies! (Albery), 1975; Waters of the Moon (Chichester), 1977, (Haymarket) 1978; The Old Jest, 1980; The Importance of Being Earnest (Watford), 1981, (Royalty), 1987; The Aspern Papers (Haymarket), 1984; Driving Miss Daisy (Apollo), 1988. *Films:* Pygmalion; Major Barbara; I Know Where I'm Going; Outcast of the Islands; Separate Tables (Academy Award); Sons and Lovers; Toys in the Attic; A Man for All Seasons; David Copperfield; Murder on the Orient Express; The Elephant Man; The Lonely Passion of Judith Hearne, etc. *TV:* When We Dead Awaken, 1968; Peer Gynt, 1972; Clochemerle, 1973; Last Wishes, 1978; Richard II, 1979; Miss Morison's Ghosts, 1981; The Kingfisher, Witness for the Prosecution, Attracta, 1982; The Comedy of Errors, 1983; Death of the Heart, 1985; Darley's Folly, All Passion Spent, The Importance of Being Earnest, 1986; Ending Up, 1989; The Best of Friends, 1991; The Countess Alice, 1992. Hon. LLD Manchester, 1984. *Address:* c/o ICM, 388/396 Oxford Street, W1N 9HE.

HILLERY, Dr Patrick John; Uachtarán na hÉireann (President of Ireland), 1976–90; *b* Miltown Malbay, Co. Clare, 2 May 1923; *s* of Dr Michael Joseph Hillery and Ellen (*née* McMahon); *m* 1955, Dr Mary Beatrice Finnegan; one *s* one *d*. *Educ:* Miltown Malbay National Sch.; Rockwell Coll.; University Coll., Dublin. BSc; MB BCh, BAO, DPH. Mem. Health Council, 1955–57; MO, Miltown Malbay, 1957–59; Coroner for West Clare, 1958–59; TD (Mem. Dáil Eireann), Clare, 1951–73; Minister: for Educn, 1959–65; for Industry and Commerce, 1965–66; for Labour, 1966–69; of Foreign Affairs, 1969–72 (negotiated Ireland's accession to European Communities); Comr for Social Affairs and a Vice-Pres., Commn of the European Communities, 1973–76. MRIA 1963; Life Fellow, Irish Management Inst., 1981. Hon. FRCSI 1977; Hon. FFDRCSI 1977; Hon. FRCPI 1978; Hon. FRCGP 1982; Hon. FFCM RCSI, 1986; Hon. Fellow: Pharmaceutical Soc. of Ireland, 1984; All-India Inst. of Medical Sciences, 1978. Hon. LLD: NUI, 1962; Univ. of Dublin, 1977; Univ. of Melbourne, 1985; Hon. DPh Pontifical Univ. of Maynooth, 1988. Robert Schuman Gold Medal (France), 1986. Grand Cross and Grand Cordon, Order of Merit (Italy), 1986; Grand Cross of the Netherlands Lion, 1986; Grand Cross of the Legion of Honour (France), 1988; Collar of the Pian Order (Vatican State), 1989. *Address:* Grasmere, Greenfield Road, Sutton, Dublin 13, Ireland.

HILLHOUSE, Sir (Robert) Russell, KCB 1991; Permanent Under-Secretary of State, Scottish Office, since 1988; *b* 23 April 1938; *s* of Robert Hillhouse and Jean Russell; *m* 1966, Alison Janet Fraser; two *d*. *Educ:* Hutchesons' Grammar Sch., Glasgow; Glasgow Univ. (MA). FRSE 1995: Scottish Education Dept, 1962; HM Treasury, 1971; Asst Secretary, Scottish Office, 1974; Scottish Home and Health Dept, 1977; Under Sec. (Principal Finance Officer), Scottish Office, 1980; Under Sec., 1985–87, Sec., 1987–88, Scottish Educn Dept. CIMgt (CBIM 1990). FRSA 1992. *Recreation:* making music. *Address:* c/o Scottish Office, St Andrew's House, Edinburgh EH1 3DG. *T:* 0131–556 8400. *Club:* New (Edinburgh).

HILLIER, Bevis; author, art historian, journalist; *b* 28 March 1940; *s* of late J. R. Hillier and of Mary Louise Hillier. *Educ:* Reigate Grammar Sch.; Magdalen Coll., Oxford (demy). Gladstone Memorial Prize, 1961. Editorial staff, The Times, 1963–68 (trainee, Home News Reporter, Sale Room Correspondent); Editor, British Museum Society Bulletin, 1968–70; Guest Curator, Minneapolis Inst. of Arts, USA, 1971; Editor, The Connoisseur, 1973–76; Antiques Correspondent, 1970–84, Dep. Literary Editor, 1980–82, The Times; Editor, The Times Saturday Review, 1982; Features Editor, 1982–83, Exec. Editor, 1983–84, Telegraph Sunday Magazine; Associate Editor, Los Angeles Times, 1984–88; Editor, Sotheby's Preview, 1990–93. Commendatore, Order of Merit (Italy), 1976. FRSA 1967. *Publications:* Master Potters of the Industrial Revolution: The Turners of Lane End, 1965; Pottery and Porcelain 1700–1914, 1968; Art Deco of the 1920s and 1930s, 1968; Posters, 1969; Cartoons and Caricatures, 1970; The World of Art Deco, 1971; 100 Years of Posters, 1972; introduction to A Boy at the Hogarth Press by Richard Kennedy, 1972; Austerity/Binge, 1975; (ed with Mary Banham) A Tonic to the Nation: The Festival of Britain 1951, 1976; The New Antiques, 1977; Greetings from Christmas Past, 1982; The Style of the Century 1900–1980, 1983; John Betjeman: a life in pictures, 1984; Young Betjeman, 1988; contributor to The Connoisseur, Apollo, Trans English Ceramic Circle, Proc. Wedgwood Soc., etc. *Recreations:* piano, collecting. *Address:* c/o The Maggie Noach Literary Agency, 21 Redan Street, W14 0AB. *Club:* Garrick.

HILLIER, Malcolm Dudley; designer and author; *b* 1 Aug. 1936. *Educ:* St Paul's School; Guildhall School of Music (LGSM). Advertising career, Colman Prentis and Varley; later Dir of Television, S. H. Benson, 1958–74; started garden design co. (with Colin Hilton), and opened flower shop, specialising in dried flowers, 1974; formed design partnership with Quentin Roake, 1992; writer since 1985. *Publications:* Complete Book of Dried Flowers, 1986; Malcolm Hillier's Guide to Arranging Dried Flowers, 1987; Flowers, 1988; Container Gardening, 1991; Roses, 1991; Pot Pourri, 1991; Malcolm Hillier's Christmas, 1992; Little Scented Library, 1992; Garlands, 1994; Container Gardening throughout the Year, 1995; Good Food Fast, 1995; Malcolm Hillier's Colour Garden, 1995. *Recreations:* poetry, pottery. *Address:* 101 Cheyne Walk, SW10 0DQ. *T:* 0171–352 9031. *Club:* PEN.

HILLIER, Prof. Paul Douglas; singer; Professor of Music, University of California, Davis, since 1990; *b* 9 Feb. 1949; *s* of Douglas and Felicity Hillier; *m* 1977, Lena-Liis Kiesel; two *d*. *Educ:* Guildhall School of Music and Drama, London (AGSM). Vicar-Choral, St Paul's Cathedral, 1974–76; Musical Dir, Hilliard Ensemble, 1974–90; Conductor: Western Wind Chamber Choir, 1985–89; Klemetti Inst. Chamber Choir, Finland, 1989–93; Dir, Theatre of Voices, 1989–. Gen. Editor, Fazer Editions of Early Music, Helsinki, 1992–. Edison Prize (Holland), 1989. *Publications:* 300 Years of English Partsongs, 1983; Romantic English Partsongs, 1986; The Catch Book, 1987; The Music of Arvo Pärt, 1996. *Recreations:* reading, spending time in the countryside. *Address:* Music Department, University of California, Davis, CA 95616, USA.

HILLIER, William Edward, CEng, FIEE; Corporate Industrial Marketing, Engineering and Physical Sciences Research Council, since 1994; *b* 11 April 1936; *s* of William Edward and Ivy Hillier; *m* 1958, Barbara Mary Thorpe; one *s* one *d*. *Educ:* Acton Grammar School; Open Univ. (BA). FIEE 1990. Missile Electronics Engineer, De Havilland Propellers, 1958–60; Semiconductor Test Equipment Design and Production Manager, 1960–64, Semiconductor Production Manager, 1965–70, Texas Instruments; Computer Aided Engineering Services Manager, up to Tech. Dir, CAD, Racal Redac, 1970–85 (Dep. Man. Dir, 1982–85); Dir, Application of Computers and Manufg Engrg Directorate, 1985–94, and Hd of IT, 1991–94, SERC. Chm., Computing and Control Div., IEE, 1993–. FIMgt. *Publications:* articles in professional papers. *Recreation:* railway preservation (company secretary to standard gauge railway operating company, Gloucestershire Warwickshire Steam Railway plc). *Address:* 19 Simon de Montfort Drive, Evesham, Worcs WR11 4NR. *T:* Evesham (01386) 443449.

HILLIER-FRY, (William) Norman, CMG 1982; HM Diplomatic Service, retired; High Commissioner in Uganda, 1980–83; *b* 12 Aug. 1923; *o s* of William Henry and Emily Hillier Fry; *m* 1948, Elizabeth Adèle Misbah; two *s* two *d*. *Educ:* Colfe's Grammar School, Lewisham; St Edmund Hall, Oxford (BA 1946). Served Army, 1942–45; commissioned, Loyal Regt, 1942. HM Foreign Service, 1946; served: Iran, 1947–52; Strasbourg (Delegation to Council of Europe), 1955–56; Turkey, 1956–59; Czechoslovakia, 1961–63; Counsellor, UK Disarmament Delegn, Geneva, 1968–71; Hd of ME Dept, ODA, 1971–74; Consul-Gen., Hamburg, 1974–79; Ambassador to Afghanistan, 1979–80. *Recreations:* music, theatre. *Address:* 127 Coombe Lane West, Kingston-upon-Thames, Surrey KT2 7HF.

HILLIS, Arthur Henry Macnamara, CMG 1961; Comptroller General, National Debt Office, 1961–68; *b* 29 Dec. 1905; *s* of late John David Hillis, FRCS, Dublin; *m* 1936, Mary Francis (*d* 1990); no *c*. *Educ:* Trinity Coll., Dublin. Called to Bar, Inner Temple, 1931. HM Treasury, 1941; Harkness Fund Fellow, USA, 1950–51; Minister (Treasury Adviser), UK Permanent Mission to United Nations, 1958–61; Under-Sec., Treasury, 1961. Mem., Internat. CS Commn (UN), 1974–81. *Address:* 2 Hare Court, Temple, EC4Y 7BH. *T:* 0171–353 3443. *Club:* Athenæum.

HILLMAN, Ellis Simon; consultant on city infrastructures; Principal Lecturer in Environmental Studies, University of East London (formerly North East London Polytechnic, then Polytechnic of East London), since 1972 (Head of International Office, 1981–84); *b* 17 Nov. 1928; *s* of David and Annie Hillman; *m* 1967, Louise; one *s*. *Educ:* University Coll. Sch.; Chelsea Coll. of Science and Technol. (BSc). Served RAF, 1947–49. Scientific Technical Officer: Soil Mechanics Ltd; NCB Field Investigation Group; Architectural Assoc.; Organiser of Conference NELP/British Telecom on Rewiring Britain—Technical Challenge of Cable TV; Chm., London Subterranean Survey Assoc., 1968–. Elected to LCC, 1958; GLC Cllr, 1964–81; Councillor (Lab), Colindale, 1986–; Mayor, London Borough of Barnet, 1994–95. Chairman: GLC Arts and Recreation Cttee, 1973–77; AMA Arts and Recreation Cttee, 1974–78; Further and Higher Educn Sub-Cttee, ILEA, 1977–81 (Bldgs Section, 1970–73); London Br. ACFHE, 1987–88 (Vice Chm., 1986–87); Vice-Chm., ILEA, 1980–81. Member: Lee Conservancy Catchment Bd, 1966–67; Lee Valley Reg. Park Authority, 1973–81; Sports Council, 1975–81; TWA, 1975–78; Water Space Amenity Commn, 1977–80; Inland Waterways Amenity Adv. Council, 1977–80; ARCUK Bd of Educn, 1973–82, 1986–94; Exec. Cttee, Field Studies Council, 1962–70; Exec. Cttee, Greater London Arts Assoc., 1973–77, 1982–86; Adv. Bd, NFT, 1973–78; Council, Science Fiction Foundn, 1986–; Sen. Vice-Pres., Hackney Soc., 1987– (Vice-Pres., 1984–87). Invited Member: Green Alliance, 1984–; Soc. of Educn Consultants, 1994–. Founder and Hon. Pres., Lewis Carroll Soc., 1969–. Consultant, London the Underground City Exhibn, 1992–93. Founding Gov., Museum of London, 1973– (Mem., Archaeol. Cttee, 1982–92); Chm. Governors, Hackney Coll., 1974–82, 1985–. Governor: Imperial Coll. of Science and Technol., later Imperial Coll. of Science, Technol. and Medicine, 1969–91, and Queen Mary Coll., 1973–82, Univ. of London; Coombe Lodge Staff Further Educn Coll., 1978–82; Hendon Coll., 1986–93; London Festival Ballet, 1973–77. Trustee, Contemporary Dance Trust, 1981–. Chm., Colson Trust and Mem. Editl Bd, Colson News: Two Way Numbers, 1984–. Guest Editor, The Built Environment (one edn), 1984. FRSA 1979. *Publications:* Essays in Local Government Enterprise, 1964–67; (ed) Towards a Wider Use, 1976; Novellae on the Scroll of Esther, 1982; (ed) Space for the Living or Space for the Dead, 1977; (jtly) London Under London, 1985; contrib. Underground Services; Architects Jl, Arch. Design, Municipal Rev., Municipal Jl and Structural Survey and the Environmentalist. *Recreations:* walking, gardening, allotment cultivation, classical music, reading, writing poetry. *Address:* 29 Haslemere Avenue, NW4 2PU. *T:* 0181–202 7792.

HILLMAN, Prof. John Richard, PhD; CBiol; FRSE; FLS; Director, Scottish Crop Research Institute, since 1986; *b* 21 July 1944; *s* of late Robert Hillman and of Emily Irene (*née* Barrett); *m* 1967, Sandra Kathleen Palmer; two *s*. *Educ:* Chislehurst and Sidcup Grammar Sch. for Boys; University Coll. of Wales, Aberystwyth (BSc; PhD 1968). FRSE, FIBiol, CBiol, 1985; FLS 1982; FIMgt (FBIM 1987). Univ. of Nottingham: Asst Lectr in Physiology and Environmental Studies, 1968; Lectr, 1969; Univ. of Glasgow: Lectr in Botany, 1971; Sen. Lectr, 1977; Reader, 1980; Prof. of Botany, 1982. Visiting Professor: Univ. of Dundee, 1986–; Univ. of Strathclyde, 1986–; Univ. of Edinburgh, 1988–; Univ. of Glasgow, 1991–. Chm., Agric., Nat. Resources and Envmt Sector Panel, UK Technology Foresight Prog.; Dep. Chm., Mylnefield Research Services Ltd. Hon. DSc Strathclyde, 1994. *Publications:* (ed) Isolation of Plant Growth Substances, 1978; (ed with A. Crozier) The Biosynthesis and Metabolism of Plant Hormones, 1984; (ed with C. T. Brett) Biochemistry of Plant Cell Walls, 1985; papers in Nature, Planta, Jl of Experimental Botany, Physiologia Plantarum, Annals of Botany. *Recreations:* landscaping, building renovations, horology, reading. *Address:* Scottish Crop Research Institute, Invergowrie, Dundee DD2 5DA. *T:* Dundee (01382) 562731. *Club:* Farmers'.

HILLS, Andrew Worth; Executive Director, Corporate Development, AEA Technology, since 1995; Member, United Kingdom Atomic Energy Authority, 1991–94; *b* 1 Sept. 1949; *s* of Roland Frederick Hills and Margaret Eunice (*née* Johnson); *m* 1st, 1974, Frances Mary Ralston (marr. diss. 1992); three *s*; 2nd, 1992, Mary Sandra Caraffi. *Educ:* Abingdon Sch.; Corpus Christi Coll., Cambridge (BA 1971; MA 1975). United Kingdom Atomic Energy Authority, 1971–: Gen. Sec., AEE Winfrith, 1981–84; Principal Finance and Programmes Officer, 1984–86; Authority Personnel Officer, 1986–89; Exec. Dir, Finance and Personnel, 1989–91; Man. Dir, Sites and Personnel, AEA Technol., 1991–92; Man. Dir, Corporate Services, 1992–94, Services Div., 1994–95. *Recreations:* church-crawling, music, reading. *Address:* AEA Technology, Corporate HQ, Harwell, Oxon OX11 0RA.

HILLS, Barrington William; racehorse trainer, since 1969; *b* 2 April 1937; *s* of William George Hills and Phyllis (*née* Biddle); *m* 1st, 1959, Maureen (marr. diss. 1977), *d* of late Patrick Newson; three *s*; 2nd, 1977, Penelope Elizabeth May, *d* of John Richard Woodhouse; two *s*. *Educ:* Robston Hall, Gloucester; St Mary's Convent, Newmarket; Mr Whittaker's, Worcester. National Service, King's Troop, RHA. Major race winners include: Prix de l'Arc de Triomphe, 1973 (Rheingold); 1,000 Guineas, 1978 (Enstone Spark); 2,000 Guineas, 1979 (Tap on Wood). Irish Derby, 1987 (Sir Harry Lewis); Irish 1,000 Guineas, 1993 (Nicer); St Leger, 1994 (Moonax); Irish Oaks, 1994 (Bolas); Prix Royal-Oak, 1994 (Moonax). *Recreations:* hunting, shooting, golf. *Address:* B. W. Hills Southbank Ltd, Southbank, Lambourn, Newbury, Berks RG16 7LL. *T:* Lambourn (01488) 71548. *Club:* Turf.

HILLS, Air Vice-Marshal David Graeme Muspratt, CB 1985; OBE 1965; Director, Medical Policy and Plans, Ministry of Defence, 1983–85; *b* 28 Feb. 1925; *s* of late Arthur Ernest Hills and Muriel Steinman Hills (*née* Fisher); *m* 1960, Hilary Enid Mary, *d* of Rev. Raymond Morgan Jones and Mary Jones (*née* Ritson); two *s* one *d*. *Educ:* Salisbury Cathedral School; Epsom College; Middlesex Hosp. Medical School. MB BS 1949; MFCM, DPH, AFOM. Commissioned RAF Med. Branch, 1950; served UK, Korea (Casualty Evacuation and MO to 77 Sqn, RAAF), A&AEE, RAF Stanmore Park, RAF Tengah and MoD, 1951–68; OC RAF Hosp., Muharraq Bahrain, 1968–70; SMO RAF Cranwell, 1970–72; Dep. Dir Medical Personnel, RAF, 1972–75; PMO RAF Germany,

1975–78; Dep. Dir Gen., RAF Medical Services, 1979–83. QHS, 1980–85. CStJ. *Recreations:* music, painting, gardening, golf. *Club:* Royal Air Force.

HILLS, David Henry, CBE 1993; Director-General of Intelligence, Ministry of Defence, 1988–93; *b* 9 July 1933; *s* of Henry Stanford Hills and Marjorie Vera Lily Hills; *m* 1957, Jean Helen Nichols; one *s* two *d. Educ:* Varndean Sch., Brighton; Univ. of Nottingham (BA Econs). Served Army Intell. Corps, 1954–56. Entered MoD, 1956; other appointments include: NBPI, 1967–70; National Indust. Relations Court, 1971–73; Dir of Marketing, Defence Sales Orgn, MoD, 1979–82; Dir of Economic and Logistic Intell., MoD, 1982–88. *Recreations:* gardening, music.

HILLS, Air Vice-Marshal (Eric) Donald, CB 1973; CBE 1968 (MBE 1941); SASO Maintenance Command, 1971–73, retired; *b* 26 Jan. 1917; *s* of late Henry James Hills; *m* 1st, 1945, Pamela Mary (*d* 1989), *d* of late Col A. P. Sandeman, Cape Town; one *s* one *d*; 2nd, 1991, Lady Cynthia Way. *Educ:* Maidstone Grammar Sch. Joined RAF 1939; Group Captain 1962; Dir of Equipment 3 (RAF), 1968–69; Air Cdre 1969; Dir of Equipment (Policy) (RAF), MoD, 1969–71; Air Vice-Marshal 1971. *Recreations:* gardening, sport as spectator. *Club:* Royal Air Force.

HILLS, Sir Graham (John), Kt 1988; PhD, DSc; FRSE, CChem, FRSC; Principal and Vice-Chancellor of the University of Strathclyde, 1980–91; Scottish Governor of the BBC, 1989–94; *b* 9 April 1926; *s* of Albert Victor Hills and Marjorie Hills (*née* Harper); *m* 1st, 1950, Brenda Stubbington (*d* 1974); one *s* three *d*; 2nd, 1980, Mary Jane McNaughton. *Educ:* Birkbeck Coll., London Univ. (BSc 1946, PhD 1950, DSc 1962; Hon. Fellow 1984). Lecturer in Physical Chemistry, Imperial College, 1949–62; Professor of Physical Chemistry, Univ. of Southampton, 1962–80; Visiting Professor: Univ. of Western Ontario, 1968; Case Western Reserve Univ., 1969; Univ. of Buenos Aires, 1977. President: Internat. Soc. of Electrochemistry, 1983–85; Soc. of Chemical Industry, 1991–; Design Industries Assoc., 1992–. Member: ACOST, 1987–; Council, RSC, 1983–86; Council, CNAA, 1988–; Design Council, 1989–90; Scottish Enterprise, 1991–. Non-Executive Director: Scottish Post Office Bd, 1986–; Scottish Develt Agency, 1988–90; Glasgow Action, 1986–90; Britoil, 1988–90. Chm. Council, Quarrier's Homes, 1992–. Hon. ScD Technical Univ. of Łodz, Poland, 1984; Hon. DSc: Southampton, 1984; Lisbon, 1994; Hon. LLD: Glasgow, 1985; Waterloo, Canada, 1991; Strathclyde, 1991; DUniv Paisley, 1993. Hon. Medal, Univ. of Pavia, 1988. Commander: Polish Order of Merit, 1984; Royal Norwegian Order of Merit, 1986. *Publications:* Reference Electrodes, 1961; Polarography, 1964; contrib. Faraday Transactions, on physical chemistry, espec. electrochemistry. *Recreations:* country life, European political history, rocking the boat. *Address:* Sunnyside of Threepwood, Laigh Threepwood, Beith, Ayrshire KA15 2JW. *T:* Beith (015055) 3479. *Clubs:* Athenæum, Caledonian.

HILLS, Prof. Richard Edwin; Professor of Radio Astronomy, since 1990, and Fellow of St Edmund's College, since 1993, University of Cambridge; *b* 30 Sept. 1945; *s* of Ronald Hills and Betty Dorothy Hills (*née* Davies); *m* 1973, Beverly Bevis; two *s. Educ:* Bedford Sch.; Queen's Coll., Cambridge (BA Physics); Univ. of California, Berkeley (PhD Astronomy). Research Scientist, Max Planck Inst. for Radio Astronomy, Bonn, 1972–74; Research Associate, 1974–84, Asst Dir of Research, 1984–90, Cavendish Lab., Cambridge; Project Scientist, James Clerk Maxwell Telescope, 1975–87. FRAS. Jackson-Gwilt Medal, RAS, 1989; MacRobert Award, Fellowship of Engineers, 1990. *Publications:* contribs to professional jls. *Recreations:* travel, DIY, music. *Address:* Cavendish Laboratory, Madingley Road, Cambridge CB3 0HE. *T:* Cambridge (01223) 337300.

HILLSBOROUGH, Earl of; Arthur Francis Nicholas Wills Hill; Finance Director, Scheduling Technology Group Ltd, since 1989 (Finance Controller, 1988–89); *b* 4 Feb. 1959; *s* and *heir* of Marquess of Downshire, *qv*; *m* 1990, Janey, *d* of Gerald Bunting; two *d. Educ:* Eton College; Royal Agricultural Coll., Cirencester; Central London Polytechnic. ACA 1985. Touche Ross & Co., 1981–87. *Recreations:* country pursuits, sport. *Heir: b* Lord Anthony Ian Hill [*b* 20 Oct. 1961; *m* 1992, Annabel Priscilla Angela, *d* of Hon. David Nall-Cain; one *s*].

HILSUM, Prof. Cyril, CBE 1990; PhD; FRS 1979; FEng 1978; FInstP, FIEE; Corporate Research Adviser, GEC plc, since 1993; *b* 17 May 1925; *s* of Benjamin and Ada Hilsum; *m* 1947, Betty Cooper (*d* 1987); two *d. Educ:* Raines Sch., London; University Coll., London (BSc, PhD). FIEE 1967; FIEEE 1984; FInstP 1960. Joined Royal Naval Scientific Service, 1945; Admiralty Res. Lab., 1947–50, and Services Electronics Res. Lab., 1950–64, working first on infra-red res., then on semiconductors; Royal Signals and Radar Estab., 1964–83, working first on compound semiconductors, later on flat panel electronic displays; CSO, 1974–83; Chief Scientist, Gen. Electric Co. Res. Labs, 1983–85; Dir of Res., GEC plc, 1985–93. Vis. Prof. in Physics, UCL, 1988–. Mem., SERC, 1984–88. Pres., Inst. of Physics, 1988–90. Foreign Associate, US National Acad. of Engrg, 1983. Hon. DEng Sheffield, 1992. Max Born Medal and Prize, Inst. of Physics, 1987; Faraday Medal, IEE, 1988. *Publications:* Semiconducting III-V Compounds, 1961; over 100 scientific and technical papers. *Recreations:* ballroom dancing, tennis. *Address:* 12 Eastglade, Moss Lane, Pinner, Mddx HA5 3AN. *T:* 0181–866 8323, *Fax:* 0181–933 6114.

HILTON OF EGGARDON, Baroness *cr* 1991 (Life Peer), of Eggardon in the County of Dorset; **Jennifer Hilton,** QPM 1989; *b* 12 Jan. 1936; *d* of John Robert Hilton, CMG. *Educ:* Bedales Sch.; Manchester Univ. (BA Hons Psychology 1970; MA (Research) 1971); London Univ. (Dip. Criminology 1972; Dip. History of Art 1982). Joined Metropolitan Police, 1956; Univ. Scholarship, 1967; Police Staff Coll. (Directing Staff), 1973–74; Met. Police Management Services Dept, 1975–76; Supt then Chief Supt, Heathrow Airport, Battersea, Chiswick, 1977–83; New Scotland Yard (Traffic, Courts, Obscene Publications, Planning, Neighbourhood Policing), 1983–87; Comdr, 1984; Head of Training, Metropolitan Police, 1988–90. House of Lords: opposition spokesperson on the envmt, 1991–; Member: European Community Sub-Cttee on Envmt, 1991–; Science and Technol. Cttee, 1993– (Mem., Forensic Science Cttee, 1993–). *Publications:* The Gentle Arm of the Law, 1967, 2nd edn 1973; (with Sonya Hunt) Individual Development and Social Experience, 1975, 2nd edn 1981; articles in Police Jl, Police Review, etc. *Recreations:* gardening, history, art, travel. *Address:* House of Lords, SW1A 0PW.

HILTON, (Alan) John Howard; QC 1990; a Recorder, since 1986; *b* 21 Aug. 1942; *s* of Alan Howard Hilton and Barbara Mary Campbell Hilton; *m* 1st, 1968, Jasmina Laila Hamzavi; 2nd, 1978, Nicola Mary Bayley, *qv*; one *s. Educ:* Haileybury and Imperial Service Coll.; Manchester Univ. (LLB Hons). Called to the Bar, Middle Temple, 1964. *Recreations:* opera, cooking, magic, 19th century paintings of ladies, enjoying adjournments. *Address:* Queen Elizabeth Building, Temple, EC4Y 9BS. *T:* 0171–583 5766.

HILTON, Anthony Victor; Managing Director, Evening Standard, since 1989; *b* 26 Aug. 1946; *s* of Raymond Walwork Hilton and Miriam Eileen Norah Hilton (*née* Kydd); *m* 1st, 1969, Patricia Moore; one *s*; 2nd, 1989, Cynthia June Miles; two *s* one *d. Educ:* Univ. of Aberdeen (MA Hons Econs 1968). Financial columnist: Guardian, 1968; Observer, 1969; Daily Mail, 1971; Sunday Express, 1972; Editor, Accountancy Age, 1974–79; NY corresp., Sunday Times, 1979–82; City Editor: The Times, 1982–83; Evening Standard, 1984–89; Dir, Associated Newspapers, 1989. Director: London Forum, 1993–94; London First, 1993–. Mem. Cttee, St John's Ambulance Charity Appeal, 1992–. *Publications:* How to communicate financial information to employees, 1979; City within a state: a portrait of the City of London, 1987. *Recreations:* canal cruising, cycling, bonfires. *Address:* Priory Farm, Hadleigh, Suffolk IP7 5AZ. *T:* Hadleigh (01473) 823185. *Club:* Lansdowne.

HILTON, Brian James George, CB 1992; Deputy Secretary, Department of Trade and Industry, since 1994; *b* 21 April 1940; *s* of Percival William Hilton and late Gladys Hilton (*née* Haylett); *m* 1965, Mary Margaret Kirkpatrick; one *s* two *d. Educ:* St Marylebone Grammar Sch., London. Export Credits Guarantee Dept, 1958–68; Board of Trade, 1968–71; Foreign and Commonwealth Office, 1971–74: First Secretary to UK Delegn to OECD, Paris; Asst Sec., Dept of Industry, 1976–84; RCDS 1981; Hd, Financial Services Div., DTI, 1984–87; Hd, Central Unit (Under Sec.), DTI, 1987–89; Dep. Sec., MAFF, 1989–91; Dir, Citizen's Charter Unit, Cabinet Office, 1991–94. Foundation Governor, Hampden Gurney Primary Sch., London W1, 1976–. *Recreations:* cricket, Rugby, music, opera, gardening. *Address:* Department of Trade and Industry, 151 Buckingham Palace Road, SW1W 9SS.

HILTON, John Howard; *see* Hilton, A. J. H.

HILTON, Rear-Adm. John Millard Thomas, FIMechE, FIEE; consulting engineer; Hon. Senior Visiting Fellow, School of Engineering, City University, since 1993; *b* 24 Dec. 1934; *s* of late Edward Thomas Hilton and of Margaret Norah Attrill (*née* Millard); *m* 1st, 1958, Patricia Anne Kirby (marr. diss. 1979); one *s* one *d*; 2nd, 1985, Cynthia Mary Caroline Seddon-Brown (*née* Hargreave); one step *d. Educ:* Wyggeston Grammar Sch. for Boys, Leicester; County High Sch., Clacton; RNC Dartmouth; RNEC Manadon; RNC Greenwich; City Univ. (MSc 1968); Imperial Coll. of Science and Technology (DIC 1973). Joined RN 1951; various sea and shore appts, 1951–80; Dep. Chief Naval Signal Officer, MoD, London, 1980–83; Project Dir, ARE Portsdown, 1984–87; Vice-Pres. (Navy), Ordnance Bd, 1987–88; Pres., Ordnance Bd, 1988–90. ADC to the Queen, 1985–88. Asst, Scientific Instrument Makers' Co., 1994–. *Publications:* professional papers. *Recreations:* gardening, personal computing, photography, Christian apologetics, family life. *Address:* Pennyfold, Church Road, Steep, near Petersfield, Hants GU32 2DF. *Club:* Royal Navy and Royal Albert Yacht (Portsmouth).

HILTON, Nicola Mary; *see* Bayley, N. M.

HILTON, Prof. Peter John, MA, DPhil Oxon, PhD Cantab; Distinguished Professor of Mathematics, State University of New York at Binghamton, 1982–93, Emeritus since 1993; *b* 7 April 1923; *s* of late Dr Mortimer Hilton and Mrs Elizabeth Hilton; *m* 1949, Margaret (*née* Mostyn); two *s. Educ:* St Paul's Sch.; Queen's Coll., Oxford. Asst Lectr, Manchester Univ., 1948–51, Lectr, 1951–52; Lectr, Cambridge Univ., 1952–55; Senior Lecturer, Manchester Univ., 1956–58; Mason Prof. of Pure Mathematics, University of Birmingham, 1958–62; Prof. of Mathematics, Cornell Univ., 1962–71, Washington Univ., 1971–73; Beaumont Univ. Prof., Case Western Reserve Univ., 1972–82. Distinguished Prof. of Maths, Univ. of Central Florida, 1994–. Visiting Professor: Cornell Univ., USA, 1958–59; Eidgenössische Techn. Hochschule, Zürich, 1966–67, 1981–82, 1988–89; Courant Inst., NY Univ., 1967–68; Univ. Aut. de Barcelona, 1989. Mathematician-in-residence, Battelle Research Center, Seattle, 1970–82. Chairman: US Commn on Mathematical Instruction, 1971–74; NRC Cttee on Applied Maths Trng, 1977–; First Vice-Pres., Math. Assoc. of Amer., 1978–80. Corresp. Mem., Brazilian Acad. of Scis, 1979; Hon. Mem. Belgian Mathematical Soc., 1955. Hon. DHum N Michigan, 1977; Hon. DSc: Meml Univ. of Newfoundland, 1983; Univ. Aut. de Barcelona, 1989. Silver Medal, Univ. of Helsinki, 1975; Centenary Medal, John Carroll Univ., 1985. *Publications:* Introduction to Homotopy Theory, 1953; Differential Calculus, 1958; Homology Theory (with S. Wylie), 1960; Partial Derivatives, 1960; Homotopy Theory and Duality, 1965; (with H. B. Griffiths) Classical Mathematics, 1970; General Cohomology Theory and K- Theory, 1971; (with U. Stammbach) Course in Homological Algebra, 1971; (with Y.-C. Wu) Course in Modern Algebra, 1974; (with G. Mislin and J. Roitberg) Localization of Nilpotent Groups and Spaces, 1975; (with J. Pedersen) Fear No More, 1983; Nilpotente Gruppen und Nilpotente Räume, 1984; (with J. Pedersen) Build Your Own Polyhedra, 1987; (ed) Miscellanea Mathematica, 1991; numerous research articles on algebraic topology, homological algebra and category theory in British and foreign mathematical journals. *Recreations:* travel, sport, reading, theatre, chess, bridge, broadcasting. *Address:* Department of Mathematical Sciences, State University of New York, Binghamton, NY 13902–6000, USA.

HILTON, Prof. Rodney Howard, FBA 1977; Professor of Medieval Social History, University of Birmingham, 1963–82, now Emeritus; *b* 1916; *s* of John James Hilton and Anne Hilton. *Educ:* Manchester Grammar Sch.; Balliol Coll. and Merton Coll., Oxford (BA, DPhil). Army, 1940–46; Lectr and Reader in Medieval History, 1946–63, Dir, Inst. for Advanced Res. in the Humanities, 1984–87, Univ. of Birmingham. *Publications:* The Economic Development of Some Leicestershire Estates in the 14th and 15th Centuries, 1947; (with H. Fagan) The English Rising of 1381, 1950; (ed) Ministers' Accounts of the Warwickshire Estates of the Duke of Clarence, 1952; (ed) The Stoneleigh Leger Book, 1960; A Medieval Society, 1966, rev. edn 1983; The Decline of Serfdom in Medieval England, 1969, rev. edn 1983; Bondmen Made Free, 1973; The English Peasantry in the Later Middle Ages, 1975; (ed) Peasants, Knights and Heretics, 1976; (ed) The Transition from Feudalism to Capitalism, 1976; (ed with T. H. Aston) The English Rising of 1381, 1984; Class Conflict and the Crisis of Feudalism, 1985; English and French Towns in Feudal Society 1992; articles and reviews in Past and Present, English Historical Review, Economic History Review, etc. *Address:* School of History, University of Birmingham, Birmingham B15 2TT. *T:* 0121–414 5736.

HILTON, Tessa, (Mrs G. Ball); Editor, Sunday Mirror, since 1994; *b* 18 Feb. 1951; *d* of Michael and Phyllis Hilton; *m* 1976, Graham Ball; two *s* one *d. Educ:* St Mary's Sch., Gerrards Cross. Trainee reporter, Mirror Gp Trng Scheme, Devon, 1970–74; Reporter, Sunday Mirror, 1974–78; freelance writer, 1978–85; Editor, Mother mag., 1985–87; Features Editor, then Asst Editor, Today, 1987–91; Femail Editor, Daily Mail, 1991–94; Asst Editor, Sun, 1994. *Publication:* Great Ormond Street Book of Child Health, 1990. *Recreation:* family life. *Address:* Sunday Mirror, 1 Canada Square, Canary Wharf, E14 5AP. *T:* 0171–293 3144.

HILTON, William (Samuel); Director General, Federation of Master Builders, 1987–91 (National Director, 1970–87); Managing Director: Trade Press (FMB) Ltd, 1972–91; National Register of Warranted Builders Ltd, 1980–91; *b* 21 March 1926; *m* 1948, Agnes Aitken Orr; three *s. Educ:* Kyleshill, Saltcoats; Ardrossan Academy. Railway Fireman until 1949; Labour Party Agent to late Lord Kirkwood, 1949–52; Research and Education Officer for Building Trade Operatives, 1952–66. MP (Lab and Co-op) Bethnal Green, 1966–Feb. 1974. Director: Trade Debt Recovery Services Ltd, 1986; Construction Industry Services Ltd, 1986. Member: Agrément Bd for Building Industry, 1965–66; EDC for Building Industry, 1964–66; Construction ITB, 1985–91; Employers' Sec., Building and Allied Trades Jt Industrial Council, 1979–91. Editor, Builders Standard, 1954–66. *Publications:* Building by Direct Labour, 1954; Foes to Tyranny, 1964; Industrial Relations in Construction, 1968; The Plug Dropper, 1986. *Address:* Pilgrim Cottage, 18 Court Hill, Coulsdon, Surrey CR5 3NQ.

HIME, Martin, CBE 1987; HM Diplomatic Service, retired; *b* 18 Feb. 1928; *s* of Percy Joseph Hime and Esther Greta (*née* Howe); *m* 1st, 1960, Henrietta Fehling (marr. diss.); one *s* three *d*; 2nd, 1971, Janina Christine Majcher; one *d*. *Educ:* King's Coll. Sch., Wimbledon; Trinity Hall, Cambridge (MA). Served RA, 1946–48. Called to the Bar, Inner Temple, 1951; Marks and Spencer Ltd, 1952–58; joined HM Diplomatic Service, 1960; served in Tokyo, Kobe, Frankfurt and Buenos Aires, 1960–69; 2nd Sec., FCO, 1970–72; Consul, Johannesburg, 1972–74; 1st Sec. (Econ.), Pretoria, 1974–76; Asst Head, S Pacific Dept, FCO, 1976–79; Dep. High Comr in Bangladesh, 1979–82; Consul-General: Cleveland, Ohio, 1982–85; Houston, Texas, 1985–88; Personnel Assessor, FCO, 1988–93. *Recreations:* golf, lawn tennis, books, table games. *Address:* Field House, 248 Dover House Road, Roehampton, SW15 5DA. *Clubs:* All England Lawn Tennis; Hawks (Cambridge); Royal Wimbledon Golf.

HIMSWORTH, Prof. Richard Lawrence, MD; FRCP; Professor of Health Research and Development, Cambridge University, 1993–95; Fellow, Girton College, Cambridge, since 1995; *b* 14 June 1937; *s* of Sir Harold Himsworth, KCB, FRS; *m* 1966, Sara Margaret Tattersall; two *s* one *d*. *Educ:* Westminster Sch.; Trinity Coll., Cambridge (MD 1971); University Coll. Hosp. Med. Sch. FRCP 1977; FRCPE 1988; FRCPGlas 1990. Lectr in Medicine, UCH Med. Sch., 1967–71; MRC Travelling Fellow, New York, 1969–70; MRC Scientific Staff, Clinical Res. Centre, 1971–85: Asst Dir, 1978–82; Head, Endocrinology Res. Gp, 1979–85; Consultant Physician, Northwick Park Hosp., 1972–85; Regius Prof. of Medicine, Univ. of Aberdeen, and Hon. Consultant Physician, Aberdeen Royal Infirmary, 1985–93. Hon. Prof., UEA, 1994. Associate Dir, R&D, Anglia and Oxford RHA, 1994–. Member: NW Thames RHA, 1982–85; Scottish Nat. Med. Adv. Cttee, 1990–92. Liveryman, 1976–, Mem. Ct of Assts, 1995–, Goldsmiths' Co. *Publications:* scientific and medical papers. *Recreation:* painting. *Address:* Park House, 39 High Street, Balsham, Cambridge CB1 6DJ. *T:* Cambridge (01223) 893975.

HINCHINGBROOKE, Viscount; Luke Timothy Charles Montagu; *b* 5 Dec. 1969; *er s* and *heir* of Earl of Sandwich, *qv*.

HINCHCLIFFE, Peter Robert Mossom, CMG 1988; CVO 1979; HM Diplomatic Service; Ambassador to Jordan, since 1993; *b* 9 April 1937; *s* of Herbert Peter and Jeannie Hinchcliffe; *m* 1965, Archbold Harriet Siddall; three *d*. *Educ:* Elm Park, Killylea, Co. Armagh, Prep. Sch.; Radley Coll.; Trinity Coll., Dublin (BA (Hons), MA). Military service, short service commission, W Yorks Regt, 1955–57; TCD, Dublin Univ., 1957–61; HMOCS: West Aden Protectorate, South Arabian Fedn, 1961–67; Admin. Asst, Birmingham Univ., 1968–69; FCO: 1st Sec., Near Eastern Dept, 1969–70; 1st Sec., UK Mission to UN, 1971–74; 1st Sec. and Head of Chancery, Kuwait, 1974–76; Asst Head of Science and Technology and Central and Southern African Depts, FCO, 1976–78; Dep. High Comr, Dar es Salaam, 1978–81; Consul-Gen., Dubai, 1981–85; Hd of Information Dept, FCO, 1985–87; Ambassador to Kuwait, 1987–90; High Comr to Zambia, 1990–93. *Recreations:* golf, tennis, writing poetry. *Address:* c/o Foreign and Commonwealth Office, SW1A 2AH. *Clubs:* East India, Devonshire, Sports and Public Schools; North Middlesex Golf; Royal Co. Down Golf (Newcastle, Co. Down).

HINCHINGBROOKE, Viscount; *see* Montagu, J. E. H.

HINCHLIFF, Rev. Prof. Peter Bingham, MA, DD Oxon, PhD Rhodes; Canon of Christ Church and Regius Professor of Ecclesiastical History, Oxford University, 1992–Oct. 1996; *b* 25 Feb. 1929; *e s* of Rev. Canon Samuel Bingham Hinchliff and Brenda Hinchliff; *m* 1955, Constance, *d* of E. L. Whitehead, Uitenhage, S Africa; three *s* one *d*. *Educ:* St Andrew's Coll., Grahamstown, S Africa; Rhodes Univ., Grahamstown; Trinity Coll., Oxford. Deacon, 1952; Priest, 1953, in Anglican Church in S Africa; Asst in Parish of Uitenhage, 1952–55. Subwarden, St Paul's Theological Coll., Grahamstown, 1955–59; Lectr in Comparative Religion, Rhodes Univ., 1957–59; Prof. of Ecclesiastical History, Rhodes Univ., 1960–69; Canon and Chancellor, Grahamstown Cathedral, 1964–69; Sec., Missionary and Ecumenical Council of the General Synod (formerly the Church Assembly), 1969–72; Fellow and Tutor, 1972–92, Chaplain, 1972–87, Balliol Coll., Oxford. Examg Chaplain to Bishop of Newcastle, 1973, to Bishop of Oxford, 1974–. Public Orator, Rhodes Univ., 1965; Hulsean Lectr, Cambridge Univ., 1975–76; Bampton Lectr, Oxford Univ., 1982. Provincial Hon. Canon, Cape Town Cathedral, 1959–; Hon. Canon, Grahamstown Cathedral, 1969–; Canon Theologian, Coventry Cathedral, 1972–92. Mem., Gen. Synod, 1988–90. Pres., Oxford Soc. of Historical Theol., 1978–79. *Publications:* The South African Liturgy, 1959; The Anglican Church in South Africa, 1963; John William Colenso, 1964; The One-Sided Reciprocity, 1966; A Calendar of Cape Missionary Correspondence, 1967; The Church in South Africa, 1968; The Journal of John Ayliff, 1970; Cyprian of Carthage, 1974; (with D. Young) The Human Potential, 1981; Holiness and Politics, 1982; Benjamin Jowett and the Christian Religion, 1987; God and History, 1992; contributor to: Jl of Ecclesiastical History; Studia Liturgica, etc. *Recreations:* crossword puzzles, odd jobbery. *Address:* Christ Church, Oxford OX1 1DP.

HINCHLIFF, Stephen, CBE 1976; Chairman and Managing Director, Dexion Group, 1976–91, retired; *b* 11 July 1926; *s* of Gordon Henry and Winifred Hinchliff; *m* 1987, Anne Fiona Maudsley; one *d* and one *s* one *d* from a previous marriage. *Educ:* Almondbury Grammar Sch., Huddersfield; Boulevard Nautical Coll., Hull; Huddersfield Coll. of Technology; Cranfield Inst. of Technology (MSc). FIMechE, FIEE. Production Engr, Dowty Auto Units Ltd, 1953–54; Dowty Seals Ltd: Chief Prodn Engr, 1953–54; Works Manager, 1954–56; Dir, 1956–76; Dep. Man. Dir, 1966–67; Man. Dir, 1967–76; Dep. Chm., Dowty Gp Ltd, 1973–76; Man. Dir, Dowty Gp Industrial Div., 1973–76. CIMgt; FRSA. *Recreations:* squash, badminton, tennis. *Address:* Cedar House, Little Gaddesden, Berkhamsted, Herts HP4 1PE. *T:* Little Gaddesden (01442) 843728.

HINCHLIFFE, David Martin; MP (Lab) Wakefield, since 1987; *b* 14 Oct. 1948; *s* of late Robert Victor Hinchliffe and Muriel Hinchliffe; *m* 1982, Julia (*née* North); one *s* one *d*. *Educ:* Lawefield Lane Primary Sch., Wakefield; Cathedral C of E Secondary Modern Sch., Wakefield; Leeds Polytechnic (Cert. in Social Work); Bradford Univ. (MA Social Work and Community Work); Huddersfield Polytechnic (Cert Ed). Social Work with Leeds Social Services, 1968–79; Social Work Tutor, Kirklees Metropolitan Borough Council, 1980–87. An opposition front bench spokesman on personal social services and community care, 1992–. *Recreation:* Rugby League—supporter of Wakefield Trinity RLFC. *Address:* 18 King Street, Wakefield, W Yorks WF1 2SQ. *T:* Wakefield (01924) 295722. *Club:* Wakefield Labour.

HIND, Rt. Rev. John William; *see* Gibraltar in Europe, Bishop of.

HIND, Kenneth Harvard, CBE 1995; barrister; *b* 15 Sept. 1949; *s* of George Edward and Brenda Hind; *m* 1977, Patricia Anne (*née* Millar); one *s* one *d*. *Educ:* Woodhouse Grove Sch., Bradford; Leeds Univ. (LLB 1971); Inns of Court Sch. of Law. Pres., Leeds Univ. Union, 1971–72. Called to the Bar, Gray's Inn, 1973; practised North Eastern circuit, 1973–83. MP (C) West Lancashire, 1983–92; contested (C) W Lancashire, 1992. PPS to Minister of State: for Defence Procurement, 1986–87; for Employment, 1987–89; for Northern Ireland, 1989–90; PPS to Sec. of State for Northern Ireland, 1990–92. Member: Liverpool Univ. Senate, 1983–; Soc. of Conservative Lawyers, 1983–; Justice, Internat. Commn of Jurists, 1983–; Hon. Mem., Anglo Hellenic Assoc., 1983–. Hon. Vice-President: Merseyside Chamber of Commerce, 1983–; Central and West Lancs Chamber of Industry and Commerce, 1983–. Chm., De Keyser Europe, 1989–. MInstD. *Recreations:* music, sailing Enterprise, cricket; Hon. Vice-Pres. Headingley RUFC. *Address:* Ben Lane Farmhouse, Intake Lane, Bickerstaffe, near Ormskirk, Lancs L39 0HW; 54 Red Post Hill, Dulwich, SE24 9JQ. *Clubs:* Farmers (Ormskirk); Ormskirk Conservative.

HINDE, Prof. Robert Aubrey, CBE 1988; FRS 1974; Master of St John's College, Cambridge, 1989–94 (Fellow, 1951–54, 1958–89 and since 1994); *b* 26 Oct. 1923; *s* of late Dr and Mrs E. B. Hinde, Norwich; *m* 1st, 1948, Hester Cecily (marr. diss. 1971), *d* of late C. R. V. Coutts; two *s* two *d*; 2nd, 1971, Joan Gladys, *d* of F. J. Stevenson; two *d*. *Educ:* Oundle Sch.; St John's Coll., Cambridge; Balliol Coll., Oxford (Hon. Fellow, 1986). Served Coastal Comd, RAF, Flt-Lt, 1941–45. Research Asst, Edward Grey Inst., Univ. of Oxford, 1948–50; Curator, Ornithological Field Station (now sub-Dept of Animal Behaviour), Madingley, Cambridge, 1950–65; St John's Coll., Cambridge: Steward, 1956–58; Tutor, 1958–63; Royal Soc. Res. Prof., Cambridge Univ., 1963–89. Hon. Dir, MRC Unit on Develt and Integration of Behaviour, 1970–89. Hitchcock Prof., Univ. of California, 1979; Green Vis. Scholar, Univ. of Texas, 1983. Mem. Council, Royal Soc., 1985–87. Croonian Lect., Royal Soc., 1990. Mem., Academia Europaea, 1990. Hon. Member: Assoc. for the Study of Animal Behaviour, 1987; Deutsche Ornithologische Ges., 1988; For. Hon. Mem., Amer. Acad. of Arts and Sciences, 1974; For. Associate, Nat. Acad. of Scis, USA, 1978; Hon. Fellow, Amer. Ornithologists' Union, 1977; Hon FBPsS 1981; Hon. FRCPsych 1988; Hon. FTCD, 1990. Hon. ScD: Univ. Libre, Brussels, 1974; Univ. of Paris (Nanterre), 1979; Stirling Univ., 1991; Göteborg Univ., 1991; Edinburgh Univ., 1992. Scientific Medal, Zoological Soc., 1961; Leonard Cammer Medal in Psychiatry, Columbia Coll., NY, 1980; Osman Hill Award, Primate Soc. of GB, 1980; Albert Einstein Award for Psychiatry, Albert Einstein Coll. of Medicine, NY, 1987; Huxley Medal, RAI, 1990; Distinguished Scientists Award, Soc. for Res. in Child Develt, 1991; Distinguished Career Award, Internat. Soc. for Study of Personal Relationships, 1992; Frink Medal, Zool Soc., 1992; G. Stanley Hall Medal, Amer. Psychol Assoc., 1993. *Publications:* Animal Behaviour: a synthesis of Ethology and Comparative Psychology, 1966; (ed) Bird Vocalizations: their relations to current problems in biology and psychology, 1969; (ed jtly) Short Term Changes in Neural Activity and Behaviour, 1970; (ed) Non-Verbal Communication, 1972; (ed jtly) Constraints on Learning, 1973; Biological Bases of Human Social Behaviour, 1974; (ed jtly) Growing Points in Ethology, 1976; Towards Understanding Relationships, 1979; Ethology: its nature and relations with other sciences, 1982; (jtly) Defended to Death, 1982; (ed and contrib.) Primate Social Relationships: an integrated approach, 1983; (ed jtly) Social Relationships and Cognitive Development, 1985; Individuals, Relationships and Culture, 1987; (ed jtly) Relationships within Families, 1988; (ed jtly) Aggression and War, 1989; (ed jtly) Education for Peace, 1989; (ed and contrib) The Institution of War, 1991; (ed jtly) Co-operation and Prosocial Behaviour, 1991; (ed jtly) War: a necessary evil? 1994; sundry papers in biological and psychological journals. *Address:* St John's College, Cambridge CB2 1TP. *T:* Cambridge (01223) 338635; Park Lane, Madingley, Cambridge CB3 8AL. *T:* Madingley (01954) 211816.

HINDE, Thomas; *see* Chitty, Sir Thomas Willes.

HINDLEY, Prof. Colin Boothman; Director of Centre for Study of Human Development since 1967, and Professor of Child Development, 1972–84, now Professor Emeritus, Institute of Education, London; *b* Bolton, 1923; *m* 1945; two *s*. *Educ:* Bolton Sch.; Manchester Univ.; University Coll., London. MB, ChB Manchester 1946; BSc London 1949 (1st cl. Psychol.). Asst Med. Officer, Hope Hosp., Salford; Res. Psychologist and subseq. Sen. Lectr, London Univ. Inst. of Educn, 1949–72; Head of Adolescent Development Dip. Course, 1968–72. Psychol. Adviser, Internat. Children's Centre Growth Studies, Paris, 1954–; Editor, Jl of Child Psychol. and Psychiat., 1959–69; Mem. Council, Brit. Psychol. Soc., 1970–73; Mem. Cttee, Internat. Soc. for Study Behavioural Develt, 1969–75; Mem. Assoc. Child Psychol. and Psychiat. (Chm. 1967–68). FBPsS. *Publications:* Conceptual and Methodological Issues in the Study of Child Development, 1980; chapters in Child Development: International Method of Study, ed Falkner, 1960; Learning Theory and Personality Development, in Psychosomatic Aspects of Paediatrics, ed Mackeith and Sandler, 1961; The Place of Longitudinal Methods in the Study of Development, in Determinants of Behavioural Development, ed Mönks, Hartup and de Wit, 1972; (jt ed. and contrib.) Development in Adolescence, 1983; contribs to jls. *Recreations:* jazz, literature, gardening, walking, travel, cinema, modern art, science, philosophy. *Address:* Department of Child Development and Primary Education, Institute of Education, Bedford Way, WC1H 0AL. *T:* 0171–636 1500.

HINDLEY, Estella Jacqueline, (Mrs J. G. Harvey); QC 1992; a Recorder of the Crown Court, since 1989; *b* 11 Oct. 1948; *d* of Arthur John Hindley and Olive Maud (*née* Stanley); *m* 1980, John Gilbert Harvey; one *s*. *Educ:* Univ. of Hull (LLB Hons). *Recreations:* book collecting, music, theatre. *Address:* 5 Fountain Court, Steelhouse Lane, Birmingham B4 6DR. *T:* 0121–606 0500.

HINDLEY, Michael John; Member (Lab) European Parliament, Lancashire South, since 1994 (Lancashire East, 1984–94); *b* 11 April 1947; *s* of John and Edna Hindley; *m* 1980, Ewa Agnieszka (*née* Leszczyc-Grabianka); one *d*. *Educ:* Clitheroe Royal Grammar School; London University (BA Hons); Lancaster University (MA); Free University of West Berlin. Labour Councillor, Hyndburn District Council, 1979–84 (Leader, 1981–84); contested (Lab) Blackpool North, 1983. *Recreations:* swimming, walking, reading, music, travel. *Address:* 27 Commercial Road, Great Harwood, Lancs BB6 7HX. *T:* Great Harwood (01254) 887017.

HINDLEY-SMITH, David Dury, CBE 1972; Registrar, General Dental Council (formerly Dental Board of the UK), 1947–81; *b* 20 Feb. 1916; *e s* of late James Dury Hindley-Smith; *m* 1947, Dorothy Westwood Legge (*d* 1987), *e d* of Arthur Collins and Mary Fielding; two *d*. *Educ:* Uppingham; King's Coll., Cambridge (MA); Paris and Vienna. Passed examination for Diplomatic Service, 1939. War Service: Artists' Rifles, 1939; commissioned Royal Fus., 1940; liaison officer to Gén. Leclerc, 1942, to Gén. de Gaulle's first administration, 1944; Acting Col. Mem., W Suffolk HA, 1982–86; Chm., Mental Health Cttee, W Suffolk HA, 1982–86. Mem. Council, Royal Dental Hosp., London Sch. of Dental Surgery, 1976–84 (Chm., 1981–84). Vice-Chm., Surrey Assoc. of Youth Clubs, 1950–70 (Vice-Pres., 1970–); Executive Chm., Nat. Assoc. of Youth Clubs, 1970–74 (Vice-Pres., 1974–); Chm., Sembal Trust, 1972–81; Vice-Pres., Suffolk Assoc. of Youth, 1984– (Chm., 1982–84). Hon. Mem., BDA, 1975; Hon. FDSRCSE 1977; Hon. FDSRCS, 1980. Cecil Peace Prize, 1938. *Recreations:* gardening, cooking. *Address:* The Ark House, Whepstead, Bury St Edmunds, Suffolk IP29 4UB. *T:* Horringer (01284) 735351. *Club:* Royal Society of Medicine.

HINDLIP, 6th Baron *cr* 1886; **Charles Henry Allsopp;** Bt 1880; Chairman, Christie, Manson & Woods, since 1986; Director, Christies International, since 1986; *b* 5 Aug.

1940; *e s* of 5th Baron Hindlip and of Cecily Valentine Jane, *o d* of Lt-Col Malcolm Borwick, DSO; *S* father, 1993; *m* 1968, Fiona Victoria Jean Atherley, *d* of late Hon. William Johnston McGowan, 2nd *s* of 1st Baron McGowan, KBE; one *s* three *d*. *Educ:* Eton. Coldstream Guards, 1959–62; joined Christie's, 1962; Gen. Manager, Christie's New York, 1965–70; Christie, Manson & Woods: Dir, 1970; Dep. Chm., 1985. Trustee, Chatham Historic Dockyard, 1989–. *Recreations:* painting, shooting, ski-ing. *Heir: s* Hon. Henry William Allsopp, *b* 8 June 1973. *Address:* Christie, Manson & Woods, 8 King Street, St James's, SW1Y 6QT. *T:* 0171–839 9060; 55 Campden Hill Road, W8 7DY. *T:* 0171–937 6038; The Cedar House, Inkpen, Berks RG15 0DT. *Clubs:* White's, Pratt's.

HINDMARSH, Frederick Bell; Under-Secretary, Department of Health and Social Security, 1973–79, retired; *b* 31 Jan. 1919; *yr s* of Frederick Hindmarsh and Margaret May Hindmarsh; *m* 1947, Mary Torrance Coubrough; one *d*. *Educ:* County Grammar Sch., Acton. Clerical Officer, Min. of Health, 1936; Exec. Officer, 1937. Served war, Army, 1939–46. Min. of Pensions and Nat. Insurance and Min. of Social Security: Higher Exec. Officer, 1946; Sen. Exec. Officer, 1947; Chief Exec. Officer, 1951; Sen. Chief Exec. Officer, 1959; Prin. Exec. Officer, 1964; Asst Sec., DHSS, 1969. *Recreation:* music.

HINDMARSH, Irene, JP, MA; Principal, St Aidan's College, University of Durham, 1970–88; Second Pro-Vice-Chancellor, University of Durham, 1982–85; *b* 22 Oct. 1923; *d* of Albert Hindmarsh and Elizabeth (*née* White). *Educ:* Heaton High Sch.; Lady Margaret Hall, Oxford (MA Hons French); King's Coll., Univ. of Durham (PGCE). Taught at St Paul's Girls' Sch., London, 1947–49, Rutherford High Sch., Newcastle upon Tyne, 1949–59; Interchange Teacher, Lycée de Jeunes Filles, Dax, Landes, France, 1954–55; Lectr in Educn and French, King's Coll., Durham, 1959–64; Headmistress, Birkenhead High Sch., GPDST, 1964–70. Vis. Prof., New York State Univ., Syracuse, Cornell, Harvard, 1962; Delegate of Internat. Fedn of Univ. Women to UNO, NY, to Commns on Human Rights and Status of Women, 1962; Vis. Professor: Fu-Dan Univ., Shanghai, 1979, and again, 1980; SW China Teachers' Univ., Beibei, Sichuan, and Fu-Dan Univ., Shanghai, 1986. Delegate/Translator to internat. confs of FIPESO, 1963–70; Chairman: Internat. Cttee of Headmistresses' Assoc., 1966–70; Internat. Panel of Joint Four, 1967–70. Editor, Internat. Bull. of AHM, 1966–70. JP Birkenhead 1966, Durham 1974. FRSA 1989. *Publications:* various articles on educnl topics in AGM papers of Assoc. of Head Mistresses; contribs to prelim. papers of FIPESO meetings; seminar papers to symposia on lit. topics, Sèvres, under auspices of Council of Europe; contrib. re St Aidan's to Durham History from the Air. *Recreations:* travel, music, theatre, films, art, architecture, quality of life. *Address:* 8 Dickens Wynd, Merryoaks, Elvet Moor, Durham DH1 3QR. *T:* Durham (0191) 3861881.

HINDSON, William Stanley, CMG 1962; BScEng, MIM, FIMechE; engineering and metallurgical consultant, 1974–94; *b* 11 Jan. 1920; *s* of late W. A. L. Hindson, Darlington; *m* 1944, Mary Sturdy (*d* 1961); one *s* one *d*; *m* 1965, Catherine Leikine, Paris, France; one *s*. *Educ:* Darlington Grammar Sch.; Coatham Sch., Redcar. With Dorman Long (Steel) Ltd, Middlesbrough, 1937–55; Metallurgical Equipment Export Co. Ltd and Indian Steelworks Construction Co. Ltd, 1956–62; Wellman Engineering Corp. Ltd, 1963–69; Cementation Co. Ltd, 1970–71; Humphreys & Glasgow, 1971–74. *Recreations:* chess, philately. *Address:* 36 Eresby House, Rutland Gate, SW7 1BG. *T:* 0171–589 3194.

HINE, Deirdre Joan, FRCP, FFPHM; Chief Medical Officer, Welsh Office, since 1990; *b* 16 Sept. 1937; *d* of late David Alban Curran and of Noreen Mary Curran (*née* Cliffe); *m* 1963, Raymond Hine; two *s*. *Educ:* Heathfield House, Cardiff; Charlton Park, Cheltenham; Welsh Nat. Sch. of Medicine (MB BCh). DPH 1964; FFPHM 1978; FRCP 1993. Asst MO, Glamorgan CC, 1963–74; Specialist in Community Medicine, S Glam HA, 1974–82; Sen. Lectr in Geriatric Medicine, Univ. of Wales Coll. of Medicine, 1982–84; Dep. Chief MO, Welsh Office, 1984–87; Dir, Welsh Breast Cancer Screening Service, 1987–90. *Publications:* papers on health promotion, health care of elderly, breast cancer screening, epidemiol. of old age in jls and text books. *Recreations:* sheep farming, reading, canal cruising. *Address:* c/o Welsh Office, Cathays Park, Cardiff CF1 3NG. *T:* Cardiff (01222) 228391.

HINE, Air Chief Marshal Sir Patrick (Bardon), GCB 1989 (KCB 1983); GBE 1991; Air Officer Commanding-in-Chief, RAF Strike Command and Commander-in-Chief, United Kingdom Air Forces, 1988–91; Military Adviser to British Aerospace plc, since 1992; *b* 14 July 1932; parents decd; *m* 1956, Jill Adèle (*née* Gardner); three *s*. *Educ:* Peter Symonds Sch., Winchester. Served with Nos 1, 93 and 111 Sqns, 1952–60; Mem., Black Arrows aerobatic team, 1957–59; commanded: No 92 Sqn, 1962–64; No 17 Sqn, 1970–71; RAF Wildenrath, 1974–75; Dir, Public Relations (RAF), 1975–77; RCDS 1978; SASO, HQ RAF, Germany, 1979; ACAS (Policy), 1979–83; C-in-C RAF Germany and Comdr, Second Allied Tactical Air Force, 1983–85; VCDS, 1985–87; Air Mem. for Supply and Orgn, 1987–88. Air ADC to the Queen, 1989–91. Queen's Commendation for Valuable Service in the Air, 1960. CBIM; FRAeS. Winner, Carris Trophy, Hants, IoW and Channel Islands Golf Championship, and Brabazon Trophy, 1949; English Schoolboy Golf Internat., 1948–49; Inter-Services Golf, 1952–57. *Recreations:* golf, ski-ing, caravanning, photography. *Clubs:* Royal Air Force; Colonels (Founder Mem.); Brokenhurst Manor Golf.

HINES, Barry Melvin, FRSL; writer; *b* 30 June 1939; *s* of Richard and Annie Hines; *m* (marr. diss.); one *s* one *d*. *Educ:* Ecclesfield Grammar Sch.; Loughborough Coll. of Educn (Teaching Cert.). FRSL 1977. Teacher of Physical Educn, London, 1960–62 and S Yorks, 1962–72; Yorkshire Arts Fellow in Creative Writing, Sheffield Univ., 1972–74; E Midlands Arts Fellow in Creative Writing, Matlock Coll. of Higher Educn, 1975–77; Sheffield City Polytechnic: Arts Council Fellow in Creative Writing, 1982–84; Hon. Fellow in Creative Writing, 1984; Hon. Fellow, 1985. *Television scripts:* Billy's Last Stand, 1971; Speech Day, 1973; Two Men from Derby, 1976; The Price of Coal (2 films), 1977; The Gamekeeper, 1979; A Question of Leadership, 1981; Threads, 1984; Shooting Stars, 1990; Born Kicking, 1992; *screenplays:* Kes, 1970; Looks and Smiles, 1981. *Publications:* (fiction): The Blinder, 1966; A Kestrel for a Knave, 1968; First Signs, 1972; The Gamekeeper, 1975; The Price of Coal, 1979; Looks and Smiles, 1981; Unfinished Business, 1983; The Heart of It, 1994. *Recreation:* supporting Sheffield United Football Club. *Address:* c/o Lemon and Durbridge Ltd, 24 Pottery Lane, Holland Park, W11 4LZ. *T:* 0171–229 9216. *Club:* Hoyland Common Workingmen's (near Barnsley).

HINES, Sir Colin (Joseph), Kt 1976; OBE 1973; President: NSW Returned Services League Clubs Association, 1971–90; NSW Branch, Returned Services League of Australia, 1971–90; Vice-President of the National Executive, Returned Services League of Australia, 1971–90 (Deputy National President, 1974–90); *b* 16 Feb. 1919; *s* of J. Hines and Mrs Hines, Lyndhurst, NSW; *m* 1942, Jean Elsie, *d* of A. Wilson, Mandurama, NSW; two *s*. *Educ:* All Saints' Coll., Bathurst, NSW. Farmer and grazier. Army, 1937–45. Hon. Officer, Returned Services League of Aust., 1946–, Trustee, 1990–. State Comr, Aust. Forces Overseas Fund, 1971–; Trustee, Anzac Meml Trust, 1971–. Pres., War Veterans Homes, Narrabeen, 1976– (Chm., 1971–76); Chm., Clubs Mutual Services Ltd, 1972–. *Recreations:* rifle shooting, golf. *Address:* The Meadows, Lyndhurst, NSW 2741, Australia. *T:* (63) 675151. *Club:* Imperial Services (Sydney, NSW).

HINKLEY, Prof. David Victor, PhD; Professor of Statistical Science, Oxford University, since 1989; Fellow, St Anne's College, Oxford, since 1989; *b* 10 Sept. 1944; *s* of Eric Samson Hinkley and Edna Gertrude (*née* Alger); *m*; one *s* one *d*. *Educ:* Birmingham Univ. (BSc 1965); Imperial Coll., London (PhD 1969). MA Oxon 1990. Asst Lectr in Maths, Imperial Coll., London, 1967–69; Asst Prof. in Stats, Stanford Univ., 1969–71; Lectr in Maths, Imperial Coll., 1971–73; Associate Prof. and Prof. in Stats, Univ. of Minnesota, 1973–80; Prof. in Maths, Univ. of Texas, 1980–91. Editor: Annals of Statistics, 1980–82; Biometrika, 1991–92. *Publications:* Theoretical Statistics, 1973; Problems and Solutions in Theoretical Statistics, 1977; Statistical Theory and Modelling, 1990; articles in statistical and scientific jls. *Recreations:* philately, football, botanical observation. *Address:* Department of Statistics, 1 South Parks Road, Oxford OX1 3TG. *T:* Oxford (01865) 272860.

HINSLEY, Prof. Sir (Francis) Harry, Kt 1985; OBE 1946; FBA 1981; Master of St John's College, Cambridge, 1979–89 (Fellow, 1944–79; President, 1975–79); *b* 26 Nov. 1918; *s* of Thomas Henry and Emma Hinsley; *m* 1946, Hilary Brett, *d* of H. F. B. and Helena Brett-Smith, Oxford; two *s* one *d*. *Educ:* Queen Mary's Grammar Sch., Walsall; St John's Coll., Cambridge. HM Foreign Office, war service, 1939–46. University of Cambridge: Research Fellow, St John's Coll., 1944–50, Tutor, 1956–63; University Lectr in History, 1949–65; Reader in the History of International Relations, 1965–69; Prof., History of Internat. Relations, 1969–83; Vice-Chancellor, 1981–83; Chm., Faculty Bd of History, 1970–72; Lees-Knowles Lectr on Military Science, Trinity Coll., 1970–71. Lectures: Cecil Green, Univ. of BC, 1976; Sir Douglas Robb, Univ. of Auckland, and Yencken Meml, ANU, 1980; Martin Wight Meml, Univ. of Sussex, 1981; Lindsay Meml, Univ. of Keele, 1985; Chancellor's, Univ. of Witwatersrand, 1985; Earl Grey Meml, Univ. of Newcastle-upon-Tyne, 1985; Chettiar Meml, Univ. of Madras, 1988; Harmon Meml, USAF Acad., Colorado, 1988; Liddell Hart, KCL, 1992; Montague Burton, Univ. of Nottingham, 1992. UK Rep., Provisional Academic Cttee for European Univ. Inst., 1973–75. Trustee, BM, 1984–89. Hon. Fellow: TCD, 1981; Darwin Coll., Cambridge, 1987. Hon. DLitt Witwatersrand, 1985. Hon. D Mil. Sci. Royal Roads Mil. Coll., Canada, 1987. Editor, The Historical Jl, 1960–71. *Publications:* Command of the Sea, 1950; Hitler's Strategy, 1951; (ed) New Cambridge Modern History, Vol. XI, 1962; Power and the Pursuit of Peace, 1963; Sovereignty, 1966, 2nd edn 1986; Nationalism and the International System, 1973; (ed) British Foreign Policy under Sir Edward Grey, 1977; (jtly) British Intelligence in the Second World War, vol. 1, 1979, vol. 2, 1981, vol. 3 (Pt 1), 1984, (Pt 2), 1988, vol. 4, 1990, abridged edn 1993; (ed) Codebreakers: the inside story of Bletchley Park, 1993. *Address:* St John's College, Cambridge CB2 1TP. *T:* Cambridge (01223) 355075.

HINTON, Prof. Denys James, FRIBA; Chairman, Redditch New Town Development Corporation, 1978–85; *b* 12 April 1921; *s* of James and Nell Hinton; *m* 1971, Lynette Payne (*née* Pattinson); one *d*. *Educ:* Reading Sch.; Architectural Assoc. (MSc; AADip.). FRIBA. Asst, Wells Coates, 1950–52; Birmingham Sch. of Architecture: Lectr, 1952–57; Sen. Lectr, 1957–64; Dir, 1964–72; Prof. of Architecture, Univ. of Aston, 1966–81, now Emeritus. Sen. Partner, Hinton Brown Langstone, Architects, Warwick, 1960–86. Chairman: Architects Registration Council of UK, 1983–86; Fabric Adv. Cttee, St Philip's Cathedral, Birmingham, 1992–; Pres., EC Architects' Directive Adv. Cttee, 1992–93; Vice-Pres. (formerly Vice-Chm.), Exec. Cttee, Internat. New Towns Assoc., 1980–85. *Publications:* Performance Characteristics of the Athenian Bouleterion, RIBA Athens Bursary, 1962; Great Interiors: High Victorian Period, 1967; contrib. RIBA and Architects Jl, papers on architectural education, Inst. Bulletin (worship and religious architecture), Univ. of Birmingham. *Recreations:* travel, moving house, water colours. *Address:* Hill Farm Barns, 33 Main Street, Greetham, near Oakham, Leics LE15 7NJ. *T:* Oakham (01572) 813267.

HINTON, Michael Herbert, JP; FCA; FICM; FRSA; FFA; ACIArb; *b* 10 Nov. 1934; *s* of late Walter Leonard Hinton and of Freda Millicent Lillian Hinton; *m* 1st, 1955, Sarah Sunderland (marr. diss. 1982); one *s* two *d*; 2nd, 1984, Jane Margaret Manley, *d* of Arthur Crichton Howell. *Educ:* Ardingly Coll. Liveryman: Farmers' Co., 1964 (Master, 1981–82); Wheelwrights' Co.; Arbitrators' Co.; Mem. Court of Common Council, 1970–71, Alderman, 1971–79, Ward of Billingsgate; Clerk to Wheelwrights' Co., 1965–71; Sheriff, City of London, 1977–78. JP City of London, 1971. *Recreations:* cricket, Association football, theatre, travel. *Address:* Quags, Lower Oddington, Glos GL56 0UP. *T:* Cotswold (01451) 831692. *Clubs:* Farmers, MCC, City Livery (Pres., 1976–77).

HINTON, Nicholas John, CBE 1985; President, International Crisis Group, since 1995; *b* 15 March 1942; *s* of late Rev. Canon Hinton and Mrs J. P. Hinton; *m* 1971, Deborah Mary Vivian; one *d*. *Educ:* Marlborough Coll., Wiltshire; Selwyn Coll., Cambridge (MA). Asst Dir, Northorpe Hall Trust, 1965–68; Nat. Assoc. for Care and Resettlement of Offenders, 1968–77, Dir, 1973–77; Dir, NCVO (formerly Nat. Council of Social Service), 1977–84; Dir-Gen., SCF, 1985–94. Member: Central Council for Educn and Trng in Social Work, 1974–79; Stonham Housing Assoc., 1976–79; Cttee of Inquiry into UK Prison Services, 1978–79; Exec Cttees, Councils of Social Service, NI, Scotland and Wales, 1977–84; Council, VSO, 1981–86; Exec. Cttee, Business in the Community, 1982–88; Parole System Review, 1987–88; Council, Industrial Soc., 1987–; Council, RSA, 1988–94; Trustee: Charities Aid Foundn, 1977–84. Dir, Edington Music Festival, 1965–70. Contested (SDP-Liberal Alliance) Somerton and Frome, 1983. FRSA 1981. *Recreation:* music. *Address:* 22 Westmoreland Place, SW1V 4AE. *T:* 0171–828 3965.

HIPKIN, John; Head of English, Meridian School, Royston, Herts, since 1977; *b* 9 April 1935; *s* of Jack Hipkin and Elsie Hipkin; *m* 1963, Bronwyn Vaughan Dewey (marr. diss. 1985); four *s* one *d*; one *d*. *Educ:* Surbiton Grammar Sch. for Boys; LSE (BScEcon). Asst Teacher, 1957–65; Research Officer: King's Coll., Cambridge, 1965–68; Univ. of East Anglia, 1968–71; Sec., Schools Council Working Party on Whole Curriculum, 1973–74; Dir, Adv. Centre for Educn, 1974–77. *Publications:* (jtly) New Wine in Old Bottles, 1967; The Massacre of Peterloo (a play), 1968, 2nd edn 1974; (ed jtly) Education for the Seventies, 1970. *Recreations:* theatre, photography, history, medieval music. *Address:* 15 Oxford Road, Cambridge CB4 3PH. *T:* Cambridge (01223) 321407.

HIPPISLEY-COX, Peter Denzil John; Partner: Dyson Bell Martin (formerly Dyson, Bell & Co.), London, 1953–92; Bircham & Co., 1989–92; *b* 22 May 1921; *s* of late Col Sir Geoffrey Hippisley Cox, CBE, and Lady Hippisley Cox; *m* 1st, 1948, Olga Kay (marr. diss. 1956); one *d*; 2nd, 1956, Frieda Marion Wood; two *d*. *Educ:* Stowe; Trinity Coll., Cambridge (MA). Served War, RAF (Signals), 1941–46 (Flt Lieut). Admitted a solicitor, 1949. Dir, Equity & Law Life Assurance Soc., 1965–87 (Dep. Chm. 1973; Chm., 1977–85). Member: Council, Law Soc., 1956–81; Court, Drapers' Co., 1972– (Master, 1983–84). Governor, Bancroft's Sch., 1975–93. *Recreation:* music. *Address:* 48D Whistlers Avenue, SW11 3TS. *T:* 0171–585 2142. *Club:* Carlton.

HIRD, Dame Thora, (Dame Thora Scott), DBE 1993 (OBE 1983); actress; *b* 28 May 1911; *d* of James Henry Hird and Mary Jane Mayor; *m* 1937, James Scott (*d* 1994); one *d*. *Educ:* The Misses Nelson's Prep. Sch., Morecambe, Lancs. Royalty Theatre Repertory Co., Morecambe; first appeared in West End of London, 1940–42: No Medals, Vaudeville; The Queen Came By, Duke of York's; Tobacco Road, Playhouse; The Trouble-Makers,

Ancient Golf (St Andrews); Melbourne, Victoria Racing (Melbourne); Albury (Albury, NSW).

HEILBRON, Hilary Nora Burstein; QC 1987; *b* 2 Jan. 1949; *d* of Dr Nathaniel Burstein and Dame Rose Heilbron, *qv*. *Educ:* Huyton College; Lady Margaret Hall, Oxford (MA). Called to the Bar, Gray's Inn, 1971. DTI Inspector into Blue Arrow plc, 1989–91. Chairman: London Common Law and Commercial Bar Assoc., 1992–93; Jt Gen. Council of Bar and Law Soc. indep. working party into civil justice, 1993. Dir, The City Disputes Panel Ltd, 1994–. *Recreations:* travel, gardening. *Address:* Brick Court Chambers, 15/19 Devereux Court, WC2R 3JJ. *T:* 0171–583 0777.

HEILBRON, Dame Rose, DBE 1974; a Judge of the High Court of Justice, Family Division, 1974–88; *b* 19 Aug. 1914; *d* of late Max and Nellie Heilbron; *m* 1945, Dr Nathaniel Burstein; one *d*. *Educ:* Belvedere Sch., GPDST; Liverpool University, LLB 1st Class Hons, 1935; Lord Justice Holker Scholar, Gray's Inn, 1936; LLM 1937. Called to Bar, Gray's Inn, 1939, Bencher, 1968, Treasurer, 1985; joined Northern Circuit, Leader, 1973–74, Presiding Judge, 1979–82; QC 1949; Recorder of Burnley, 1956–71, a Recorder, and Hon. Recorder of Burnley, 1972–74. Mem., Bar Council, 1973–74. Chm., Home Sec's Adv. Gp on Law of Rape, 1975–. Hon. Fellow: Lady Margaret Hall, Oxford, 1976; UMIST, 1986; Hon. LLD: Liverpool, 1975; Warwick, 1978; Manchester, 1980; CNAA, 1988. Formerly Hon. Col, WRAC(TA).
See also H. N. B. Heilbron.

HEIM, Most Rev. Bruno Bernard, PhD, JCD; Apostolic Pro-Nuncio to the Court of St James's, 1982–85 (Apostolic Delegate, 1973–82); *b* Olten, Switzerland, 5 March 1911; *s* of Bernard and Elisabeth Heim-Studer. *Educ:* Olten, Engelberg and Schwyz; St Thomas of Aquino Univ.; Gregorian Univ.; Univ. of Fribourg; Papal Acad. of Diplomacy. Priest 1938; Vicar in Basle and Arbon, 1938–42; Chief Chaplain for Italian and Polish Internees in Switzerland, 1943–45; Sec., Papal Nunciature in Paris; Auditor at Nunciature in Vienna; Counsellor and Chargé d'affaires at Nunciature in Germany; titular Archbp of Xanthos, 1961; Apostolic Delegate to Scandinavia, 1961–69; Apost. Pro-Nuncio (Ambassador): to Finland, 1966–69; to Egypt, 1969–73; President of Caritas Egypt, 1969–73. Lauréat, French Acad.; Corresp. Mem., Real Academia de la Historia, Madrid, 1950; Mem. Council, Internat. Heraldic Acad.; Patron, Cambridge Univ. Heraldic and Genealogical Soc. Grand Cross: Order of Malta, 1950; Teutonic Order, 1961; Order of Finnish Lion, 1969; Order of St Maurice and Lazarus, 1973; (1st Class) Order of the Republic, Egypt, 1975; Bailiff Grand Cross and Grand Prior, Constantinian Order of St George; Sub-Prelate, Order of St John; Comdr, Order of Isabel la Catolica; Gr. Officer Order of Holy Sepulchre; Orders of Merit: Germany, Italy, Austria; Officier Légion d'honneur, etc. *Publications:* Die Freundschaft nach Thomas von Aquin, 1934; Wappenbrauch und Wappenrecht in der Kirche, 1947; Coutumes et droit héraldiques de l'Eglise, 1949; L'oeuvre héraldique de Paul Boesch, 1973; Heraldry in the Catholic Church, 1978, rev. and enlarged edn 1981; Armorial Liber Amicorum, 1981; Or and Argent, 1994; contrib. Adler, Zeitschrift f. Heraldik und Genealogie, Heraldisk Tidskrift. *Recreations:* heraldry, heraldic painting, cooking, gardening. *Address:* Zehnderweg 31, 4600 Olten, Switzerland.

HEIM, Paul Emil, CMG 1988; a Chairman: Financial Services Tribunal, since 1988; Value Added Tax Tribunal, since 1989; President, FIMBRA Appeal Tribunals, since 1990; a Deputy Chairman, PIA Appeal Tribunal, since 1994; Visiting Professor, Leicester University, since 1988; *b* 23 May 1932; *s* of George Heim and Hedy Heim (*née* Herz); *m* 1962, Elizabeth, *er d* of late Lt-Col G. M. Allen, MBE; one *s* two *d*. *Educ:* Prince of Wales School, Nairobi; King's Coll., Univ. of Durham (LLB). Called to the Bar, Lincoln's Inn, 1955, Bencher, 1986. Dep. Registrar, Supreme Court of Kenya, then Sen. Dep. Registrar, Magistrate and Acting Registrar (HMOCS), 1954–65; admitted Advocate, Supreme Court, 1959; Administrator, European Court of Human Rights, Strasbourg, 1965, European Commn of Human Rights, Strasbourg, 1966; Principal Administrator, Political Directorate, Council of Europe, 1967, Dep. Head, Private Office, 1969; Head of Div., then Dir, European Parlt, 1973–81; Registrar, European Court of Justice, 1982–88; Pres., Heads of Admin of EC Instns, 1986–88; Special Advr, European Court of Justice, 1988–89. *Address:* Wearne Wych, Langport, Somerset TA10 9AA.

HEINE, Prof. Volker, FRS 1974; Professor of Theoretical Physics, University of Cambridge, since 1976; Fellow of Clare College, Cambridge, since 1960; *b* 19 Sept. 1930; *m* 1955, M. Daphne Hines; one *s* two *d*. *Educ:* Otago Univ. (MSc, DipHons); Cambridge Univ. (PhD). FInstP. Demonstrator, Cambridge Univ., 1958–63, Lectr 1963–70; Reader in Theoretical Physics, 1970–76. Vis. Prof., Univ. of Chicago, 1965–66; Vis. Scientist, Bell Labs, USA, 1970–71. For. Mem., Max-Planck Inst., Stuttgart, 1980–. Fellow, Amer. Phys. Soc., 1987. Royal Medal, Royal Soc., 1993; Paul Dirac Medal, Inst. of Physics, 1993. *Publications:* Group Theory in Quantum Mechanics, 1960; (jtly) Solid State Physics Vol. 24, 1970, Vol. 35, 1980; articles in Proc. Royal Soc., Jl Physics, Physical Review, etc. *Address:* Cavendish Laboratory, Madingley Road, Cambridge CB3 0HE.

HEISBOURG, François; Senior Vice-President, Matra Défense-Espace, Paris, since 1992; *b* 24 June 1949; *s* of Georges Heisbourg, *qv*; *m* 1989, Elyette, *d* of Georges Levy; one *s*. *Educ:* Landon School, Bethesda, Maryland; Collège Stanislas, Paris; Inst. d'Etudes Politiques, Paris; Ecole Nationale d'Administration, Paris. French Foreign Ministry: Asst to Head of Economics Dept, 1978; Mem., Policy Planning Staff, 1979; 1st Sec., French Mission to UN, NY, 1979–81; Diplomatic Adviser to Minister of Defence, 1981–84. Vice-Pres., Thomson SA, Paris, 1984–87; Dir, IISS, 1987–92. Numerous foreign orders. *Publications:* Emiliano Zapata et la Révolution mexicaine, 1978; (with P. Boniface) La Puce, les Hommes et la Bombe, 1986; (contrib.) The Conventional Defence of Europe, 1986; (contrib.) Conventional Arms Control and East-West Security, 1989; (ed) The Changing Strategic Landscape, 1989; (ed) The Strategic Implications of Change in the Soviet Union, 1990; (contrib.) The Shape of the New Europe, 1992; (contrib.) Western Europe and the Gulf War, 1992; contribs to internat. jls. *Recreations:* hiking, old atlas collecting. *Club:* Travellers' (Paris).

HEISBOURG, Georges; Ambassador of Luxembourg, retired; *b* 19 April 1918; *s* of Nicolas Heisbourg and Berthe (*née* Ernsterhoff); *m* 1945, Hélène Pinet; two *s* one *d*. *Educ:* Athénée, Luxembourg; Univs of Grenoble, Innsbruck and Paris. Head of Govt Press and Information Office, Luxembourg, 1944–45; Attaché 1945–48, Sec. 1948–51, of Legation, London; Head of Internat. Organisations Section, Dir of Political Affairs, Min. of For. Affairs, Luxembourg, 1951–58; Luxembourg Ambassador to USA, Canada and Mexico, 1958–64; Perm. Rep. to UN, 1958–61; Luxembourg Ambassador: to Netherlands, 1964–67; to France, 1967–70; Perm. Rep. to OECD, 1967–70; Sec. Gen., WEU, 1971–74; Ambassador to USSR, Finland, Poland and Outer Mongolia, 1974–77; Perm. Rep. to Council of Europe, 1978–79; Ambassador to Fed. Rep. of Germany and to Denmark, 1979–83. Médaille de l'Ordre de la Résistance, Grand Officer, Nat. Order of Crown of Oak, 1980 (Chevalier, 1958), Comdr, Order of Adolphe de Nassau, 1963, and Grand Officer, Order of Merit, 1976, Luxembourg; also holds decorations from Austria, Belgium, France, Germany, Italy, Mexico, and the Netherlands. *Publication:* Le Gouvernement Luxembourgeois en exil 1940, Vol. I, 1986, Vol. II, 1987, Vol. III, 1989, Vol. IV, 1991. *Recreation:* swimming. *Address:* 9A Boulevard Joseph II, 1840 Luxembourg.
See also F. Heisbourg.

HEISER, Sir Terence Michael, (Sir Terry Heiser), GCB 1992 (KCB 1987; CB 1984); Permanent Secretary, Department of the Environment, 1985–92; *b* 24 May 1932; *s* of David and Daisy Heiser; *m* 1957, Kathleen Mary Waddle; one *s* two *d*. *Educ:* Grafton Road Primary Sch., Dagenham; London Evacuee Sch., Sunninghill, Berks; Windsor County Boy's Sch., Berks; Birkbeck Coll., Univ. of London; BA (Hons English). Served in RAF, 1950–52; joined Civil Service 1949, served with Colonial Office, Min. of Works, Min. of Housing and Local Govt; Principal Private Sec. to Sec. of State for the Environment, 1975–76; Under Secretary: Housing Directorate, 1976–79; Local Govt Finance Directorate, 1979–81; Dep. Sec., DoE, 1981–85. Non-exec. Director: Abbey National plc, 1992–; Sainsbury plc, 1992–; Wessex Water plc, 1993–; Smith New Court plc, 1993–; McDonnell Information Systems Gp plc, 1993–; Costain Gp plc, 1994–. Mem. Bd, PIA, 1994–. Chm., Gen. Adv. Council, BBC, 1992–. Mem. Exec. Cttee, Nat. Trust, 1993–; Trustee, V&A Mus., 1993–. Governor, Birkbeck Coll., London, 1990–. Freeman, City of London, 1990. Hon. Fellow, Birkbeck Coll., London, 1988. Hon. DLitt Bradford, 1988. *Recreations:* reading, walking, talking. *Clubs:* Reform, Garrick.

HEISKELL, Andrew; Chairman Emeritus, New York Public Library (Chairman, 1981–90); Chairman of the Board, 1960–80, and Chief Executive Officer, 1969–80, Time Inc., retired; *b* Naples, 13 Sept. 1915; *s* of Morgan Heiskell and Ann Heiskell (*née* Hubbard); *m* 1937, Cornelia Scott (marr. diss.); one *s* one *d*; *m* 1950, Madeleine Carroll (marr. diss.); *m* 1965, Marian, *d* of Arthur Hays Sulzberger, and *widow* of Orvil E. Dryfoos. *Educ:* Switzerland; France; University of Paris. Science teacher, Ecole du Montcel, Paris, 1935. Life Magazine: Science and Medicine Editor, 1937–39; Asst Gen. Manager, 1939–42; Gen. Manager, 1942–46; Publisher, 1946–60; Vice-Pres., Time, Inc., 1949–60. Fellow, Harvard Coll., 1979–89. Chm., President's Cttee on Arts and Humanities, 1982–90; Vice-Chm., Vivian Beaumont Theater; Director: Enterprise Foundn; People for the American Way. Chm., Bryant Park Restoration Corp.; Vice Chm., Hon. Chm., and Hon. Trustee, Brookings Instn; Trustee, Inst. of Internat. Educn. Mem. Bd of Visitors, Graduate Sch. and University Center, City Univ. of New York; Chm., Exec. Cttee, Amer. Acad. in Rome; eponymous Andrew Heiskell Library for Blind and Physically Handicapped, opened 1991. Gold Medal Award of Merit, Wharton Sch. Alumni Soc., Univ. of Pennsylvania, 1968; John W. Gardner Leadership Award. Hon. LLD: Shaw Univ., 1968; Lake Erie Coll., 1969; Hofstra Univ., 1972; Hobart and William Smith Colls, 1973; Harvard, 1989; Hon. DLitt Lafayette Coll., 1969. *Address:* Time and Life Building, Rockefeller Center, New York, NY 10020; 870 United Nations Plaza, New York, NY 10017; Darien, CT, USA.

HELAISSI, Sheikh Abdulrahman Al-; Hon. GCVO; retired; Saudi Arabian Ambassador to the Court of St James's, 1966–76; *b* 24 July 1922. *Educ:* Universities of Cairo and London. Secretary to Embassy, London, 1947–54; Under-Sec., Min. of Agriculture, 1954–57; Head of Delegn to FAO, 1955–61; Ambassador to Sudan, 1957–60; Representative to UN, and to various confs concerned with health and agriculture; Delegate to Conf. of Non-aligned Nations, Belgrade, 1961; Ambassador: Italy and Austria, 1961–66; UK and Denmark (concurrently), 1966–76. Versed in Islamic Religious Law. *Publication:* The Rehabilitation of the Bedouins, 1959. *Address:* PO Box No 8062, Riyadh-11482, Saudi Arabia.

HELE, Desmond George K.; *see* King-Hele.

HELE, James Warwick, CBE 1986; High Master of St Paul's School 1973–86; *b* 24 July 1926; *s* of John Warwick Hele, Carlisle; *m* 1948, Audrey Whalley; four *d*. *Educ:* Sedbergh Sch.; Hertford Coll., Oxford; Trinity Hall, Cambridge (Schol., MA). 1st cl. hons History Tripos 1951. 5th Royal Inniskilling Dragoon Guards, 1946–48. Asst Master, Kings College Sch., Wimbledon, 1951–55; Rugby School: Asst Master, 1955–73; Housemaster, Kilbracken, 1965–73; 2nd Master, 1970–73. Chairman: Headmasters' Conference, 1982 (Chm., Acad. Cttee, 1979–81); Indep. Schs Adv. Cttee, 1983–88; Member: Secondary Exams Council, 1986–88; Exec. Cttee, GBA, 1988–. Chm., Westminster Centre for Educn, 1991–. Mem., Dorset FHSA, 1990–92. Trustee, Brathay Hall, 1977–91. Gov., Port Regis Sch., Shaftesbury, 1986–; Chm. of Govs, Sherborne Sch., 1990–; Chm., Clouds House, East Knoyle, 1992–. *Recreations:* Rugby football (Oxford Univ. XV 1944), hill walking. *Address:* Hillside, Hawkesdene Lane, Shaftesbury, Dorset SP7 8EX. *T:* Shaftesbury (01747) 854205. *Club:* East India, Devonshire, Sports and Public Schools.

HELEY, (Neil) Patrick; Stipendiary Magistrate for Norfolk, since 1994; *b* 25 April 1949; *s* of John William Heley and late Hilary Heley (*née* Stretton); *m* 1975, Jane Louise Holliday-Rhodes; one *s* one *d*. *Educ:* Leeds Univ. (LLB). Qualified as solicitor, 1973; Asst Solicitor, W Yorks County Prosecuting Solicitor's Office, 1974–82; Partner, Green Williamson & Way, Wakefield, 1984–93. Member: Bd of Visitors, Wakefield Prison, 1984–91; Duty Solicitor Cttee, Legal Aid Bd, 1992–94. *Recreations:* opera, music, literature, the countryside, small French restaurants. *Address:* The Magistrates' Court, Bishopgate, Norwich NR3 1UP. *T:* Norwich (01603) 632421. *Club:* Norfolk (Norwich).

HELLABY, Sir (Frederick Reed) Alan, Kt 1981; Managing Director, 1963–83, and Chairman, 1983–85, R. & W. Hellaby Ltd; Chairman, P & O New Zealand, since 1986; Director, Bank of New Zealand, since 1993; *b* 21 Dec. 1926; *s* of Frederick Allan Hellaby and Mavis Reed; *m* 1954, Mary Dawn Trotter; three *s* one *d*. *Educ:* King's Coll., Auckland; Auckland Univ. Joined R. & W. Hellaby Ltd, 1948, Dir, 1960–87, Dep. Chm., 1969–87. Chairman: NZ Steel Ltd, 1974–86 (Dir, 1964–86); NZ Insurance Co., 1979–81 (Dir, 1966); NZI Corp. (formed from merger of NZ Insurance and S British Insurance Gp), 1981–87 (Dir, 1981–89); NZ Steel Develt Co. Ltd, 1981–86; Director: Rheem NZ Ltd, 1979–88; IBM (NZ) Ltd, 1981–94; Alcan NZ Ltd, 1985–88; P&O Australia, 1986–94; NZ Guardians Trust, 1987–; Alcan Australia Ltd, 1988–93; NZI Bank Ltd, 1989–90; Nat. Australia Bank NZ Ltd, 1991–93; former Director: NZ Steel Mining; Pacific Steel Ltd. Mem., Commn of Inquiry into Meat Industry, 1973. Chm., NZ Export Year Cttee, 1978–79. President: Auckland Chamber of Commerce, 1985–87; NZ Chamber of Commerce, 1990–93 (Mem., 1987–93; Life Mem., 1993). Chm. Bd of Governors, King's Coll.; Chm. and Trustee, NZ Police Centennial Trust, 1986; Former Trustee: Massey Univ. Agricl Res. Foundn (also Patron); NZ Red Cross Foundn. Hon. DSc Massey, 1982. *Recreation:* weekend farming. *Address:* 519 Remuera Road, Auckland, New Zealand. *T:* (9) 5247423, *Fax:* (9) 5244245. *Clubs:* Northern, Royal NZ Yacht Squadron, Auckland Golf (all Auckland).

HELLAWELL, Keith, QPM 1990; Chief Constable, West Yorkshire Police, since 1993; *b* 18 May 1942; *s* of Douglas Hellawell and Ada Alice Hellawell (*née* Battye); *m* 1963, Brenda Hey; one *s* two *d*. *Educ:* Kirkburton Sec. Mod. Sch.; Dewsbury Tech. Coll.; Barnsley Coll. of Mining; London Univ. (LLB 1972); Cranfield Inst. of Tech. (MSc 1982); Police Staff Coll. Huddersfield Borough Police, 1962; seconded to Home Office, 1975–78, incl. service in NI; Asst Chief Constable, W Yorks Police, 1983; Dep. Chief Constable, Humberside Police, 1985; Chief Constable, Cleveland Police, 1990. Nat. Police Advr, Common Purpose, 1993–. Mem. Bd, Community Action Trust; Mem., Adv. Council on Misuse of Drugs. Mem., St John's Council, W Yorks, 1983–85 and 1993–; Trustee,

NSPCC, 1993–. SBStJ. *Recreations:* design, gardening, reading, sport. *Address:* West Yorkshire Police HQ, Laburnum Road, Wakefield WF1 3QP. *T:* Wakefield (01924) 292002.

HELLIER, Maj.-Gen. Eric Jim, CBE 1977 (OBE 1970, MBE 1967); Regional Manager, International Military Services, 1981–92; *b* 23 July 1927; *s* of Harry and Elizabeth Hellier; *m* 1952, Margaret Elizabeth Leadeham; one *s* one *d* (and one *s* decd). *Educ:* Hugh Saxons Sch.; Cardiff Univ. Served, 1945–66: Navigating Officer, RNVR; regtl duty, Royal Signals; Staff Coll. and Jt Services Staff Coll; GSO2 WO; DAA&QMG 39 Inf. Bde; CO, 24 Signals Regt, 1967–69; GSO1 Plans (Operational Requirements) MoD, 1970; Col A/Q HQ 4 Div, 1971–72; Comd Bde Royal Signals and Catterick Garrison, 1973–74; RCDS, 1975; Brig A/Q HQ 1(BR), Corps, 1976–79; Maj. Gen. Admin, UKLF, 1979–81. Col Comdt, 1981–87, Rep. Col Comdt, 1983, Royal Corps of Signals. Chairman: Gen. Purposes Cttee, Regular Forces Employment Assoc., 1983–91; Royal Signals Instn, 1984–89; Fund Raising Cttee, Nat. Mus. of Signal Communication, 1991–. *Recreations:* golf, squash, ski-ing, sailing. *Address:* Goddards, 27 Church Street, Wherwell, Hants SP11 7JJ. *T:* Chilbolton (01264) 860710. *Club:* Army and Navy.

HELLINGA, Dr Lotte, FBA 1990; a Deputy Keeper, Humanities and Social Sciences, British Library, since 1986; *b* 9 Sept. 1932; *d* of Arie Querido and Catharina Geertruida Querido (*née* Nagtegaal); *m* Wytze Hellinga (*d* 1985); one *s*. *Educ:* Univ. of Amsterdam. Lectr, then Sen. Lectr, Univ. of Amsterdam, 1967–76; Asst Keeper, British Liby, 1976–86. Sec., Consortium of European Res. Libraries, 1994–. Gutenberg Preis, Mainz, 1989. *Publications:* The Fifteenth Century Printing Types of the Low Countries, 1966; Caxton in Focus, 1982; numerous articles in learned jls. *Address:* 40A Canonbury Square, N1 2AW. *T:* 0171–359 2083.

HELLIWELL, Prof. John Richard, DPhil; FInstP; Professor of Structural Chemistry, Manchester University, since 1989; *b* 19 Sept. 1953; *s* of Henry Smith Helliwell and Amy (*née* Southam); *m* 1978, Madeleine Berry; two *s* one *d*. *Educ:* Ossett Sch.; Univ. of York (BSc 1st cl. Hons Physics 1974); Balliol Coll., Univ. of Oxford (DPhil Molecular Biophysics 1978). CPhys; FInstP 1986; CChem; MRSC 1991. MRC Res. Asst and Jun. Res. Fellow, Linacre Coll., Oxford, 1978; Lectr in Biophysics, Keele Univ., jtly with SERC Daresbury Lab., 1979–83; SSO, then PSO, SERC Daresbury Lab., 1983–85; Lectr in Physics, York Univ., 1985–88; jtly with SERC Daresbury Lab., 1985–93. Vis. Res. Scholar, Cornell Univ., 1994; Vis. Prof., Univ. of Chicago, 1994. Consultant to: industrial cos in UK, Denmark and Japan; EMBL, Grenoble, 1991–. Co-editor: Acta Crystallographica, 1990–; Jl Applied Crystallography, 1995–; Main Ed., Jl of Synchrotron Radiation, 1993–. Chm., Internat. Union of Crystallography's Commn on Synchrotron Radiation, 1989–93; Vice-Chm., then Chm., European Synchrotron Radiation Facility's Scientific Adv. Cttee, Grenoble, 1991–92; Chm., MacChess Adv. Cttee, Cornell Univ., 1992–. Chm., Manchester and Dist Br., Inst. Physics, 1991–; Vice-Pres., British Crystallographic Assoc., 1989–93. Plenary Lectures: Synchrotron Radiation 90 Conf., Moscow, 1990; Italian Chem. Soc., 1991; 4th internat. conf., Biophys and Synchrotron Radiation, Tsukuba, 1992; Conference Lecture: Yugoslav-Italian Crystallographic Assoc., 1989; Soc. of Crystallographers of Australia, 1994 (Fellow, 1987); Ilyas Haneef Meml Lecture, Univ. of Leeds, 1993. *Publications:* Macromolecular Crystallography with Synchrotron Radiation, 1992; (ed jtly) Time-Resolved Macromolecular Crystallography, 1992; (ed jtly) Synchrotron Radiation in the Biosciences, 1994; 125 res. papers in learned jls. *Recreations:* squash (Squash Champion, Univ. of Keele, 1982), cycling, swimming. *Address:* Department of Chemistry, University of Manchester, Manchester M13 9PL. *T:* 0161–275 4694, *Fax:* 0161–275 4734.

HELLYER, Hon. Paul Theodore, PC (Canada) 1957; FRSA 1973; Syndicated Columnist, Toronto Sun, 1974–84; *b* Waterford, Ont, Canada, 6 Aug. 1923; *s* of A. S. Hellyer and Lulla M. Anderson; *m* 1945, Ellen Jean, *d* of Henry Ralph, Toronto, Ont; two *s* one *d*. *Educ:* Waterford High Sch., Ont; Curtiss-Wright Techn. Inst. of Aeronautics, Glendale, Calif; University of Toronto (BA). Fleet Aircraft Mfg Co., Fort Erie, Ont. Wartime service, RCAF and Cdn Army. Propr Mari-Jane Fashions, Toronto, 1945–56; Treas., Curran Hall Ltd, Toronto, 1950 (Pres., 1951–62). Elected to House of Commons, 1949; re-elected, 1953; Parly Asst to Hon. Ralph Campney, Minister of Nat. Defence, 1956; Associate Minister of Nat. Defence, 1957; defeated in gen. elections of June 1957 and March 1958; re-elected to House of Commons in by-election Dec. 1958 and again re-elected June 1962, April 1963, Nov. 1965, June 1968, and Oct. 1972; defeated gen. election July 1974; Minister of National Defence, 1963–67; Minister of Transport, 1967–69, and Minister i/c Housing, 1968–69; resigned 1969 on question of principle relating to housing. Chm., Federal Task Force on Housing and Urban Develt, 1968. Served as a Parly Rep. to NATO under both L and C administrations. Joined Parly Press Gallery, Oct. 1974. Distinguished visitor, York Univ., 1969–70. Founder and Leader, Action Canada, 1971; joined Progressive Cons. Party, 1972; Candidate for leadership of Progressive Cons. Party, Feb. 1976; re-joined Liberal Party, Nov. 1982. Exec. Dir, The Canada Uni Assoc., 1991–. *Publications:* Agenda: a Plan for Action, 1971; Exit Inflation, 1981; Jobs for All—Capitalism on Trial, 1984; Canada at the Crossroads, 1990; Damn the Torpedoes, 1990; Funny Money: a common sense alternative to mainline economics, 1994. *Recreations:* philately, music. *Address:* Suite 506, 65 Harbour Square, Toronto, Ont M5J 2L4, Canada. *Club:* Ontario.

HELMORE, Roy Lionel, CBE 1980; Principal, Cambridgeshire College of Arts and Technology, 1977–86; Fellow of Hughes Hall, Cambridge, 1982–94, now Emeritus Fellow; *b* 8 June 1926; *s* of Lionel Helmore and Ellen Helmore (*née* Gibbins); *m* 1969, Margaret Lilian Martin. *Educ:* Montrose Academy; Edinburgh Univ. (BScEng); MA (Cantab). FIEE. Crompton Parkinson Ltd, 1947–49; Asst Lectr, Peterborough Techn. Coll., 1949–53; Lectr, subseq. Sen. Lectr, Shrewsbury Techn. Coll., 1953–57; Head of Electrical Engrg and Science, Exeter Techn. Coll., 1957–61; Principal, St Albans Coll. of Further Education, 1961–77. Association of Principals of Colleges: Hon. Sec., 1968–71; Pres., 1972–73; Hon. Treasurer, 1983–86; Chm., of Council, Assoc. of Colls of Further and Higher Educn, 1987–88. Member: BBC Further Educn Adv. Council, 1967–73; Air Transport and Travel ITB, 1967–73; Technician Educn Council, 1973–79 (Vice-Chm.); Manpower Services Commn, 1974–82; RAF Trng and Educn Adv. Cttee, 1976–79; Chm., Trng and Further Educn Cons. Gp, 1977–82. JP St Albans, 1964–78. *Publication:* CCAT—a brief history, 1989. *Recreations:* gardening, watercolours, bowls. *Address:* 5 Beck Road, Saffron Walden, Essex CB11 4EH. *T:* Saffron Walden (01799) 523981.

HELTAY, Laszlo Istvan; Director of Music, Royal Choral Society, 1985–95; Founder and Music Director, Academy of St Martin in the Fields Chorus, since 1975; *b* Budapest, 5 Jan. 1930; *s* of Laszlo Heltay and Gizella Somogy; *m* 1964, Hilary Nicholson. *Educ:* Franz Liszt Acad. of Music, Budapest (MA); Merton Coll., Oxford (MLitt). Associate Conductor, NZBC Symphony Orchestra and Dir, NZ Opera Co., 1964–67; Conductor, Phoenix Opera Co., 1970–73; Founder and Music Director: Brighton Fest. Chorus, 1968; British Choral Acad., 1994. Has conducted major orchestras including: Philharmonia, Royal Philharmonic, London Philharmonic, Dresden Philharmonic, Dallas Symphony, Budapest Philharmonic; also radio orchestras and choirs. Choral music for film, Amadeus, 1984. Has made recordings. Hon. DMus Sussex, 1995. Internat. Kodaly Medal, 1982. *Recreations:* chess, tennis. *Address:* 85 Cholmley Gardens, Fortune Green Road, NW6 1UN.

HELY, Air Commodore Arthur Hubert McMath, CB 1962; OBE 1945; Air Commodore Operations, HQ Maintenance Command, 1961–64, retired; *b* 16 Feb. 1909; *s* of Hamilton McMath Hely, OBE, RD and Lubie Thrine Hely (*née* Jörgensen); *m* 1935, Laura Mary Sullivan, 6th *d* of Serjeant A. M. Sullivan, QC; two *s* two *d*. *Educ:* Truro Sch.; Mt Albert GS, Auckland, NZ; Auckland University. Joined Royal Air Force, 1934; Staff Coll., 1942; HQ SACSEA, 1944, 1945; Joint Chiefs of Staff, Australia, 1946–48; Joint Services Staff Coll., 1948; Group Capt. 1950; HQ Fighter Command, 1953–56; HQ Far East Air Force, 1956, 1958; ADC to HM the Queen, 1957–59; Air Ministry (acting Air Commodore), 1958; Air Commodore, 1959. *Recreations:* golf, painting. *Address:* 5 Brewer's Yard, Storrington, West Sussex RH20 4DN. *Club:* West Sussex Golf.

HELY-HUTCHINSON, family name of **Earl of Donoughmore.**

HELY HUTCHINSON, Hon. Timothy Mark; Group Chief Executive, Hodder Headline PLC, since 1993; *b* 26 Oct. 1953; *s* of Earl of Donoughmore, *qv* and Sheila (*née* Parsons). *Educ:* Eton Coll. (Oppidan Schol.); Magdalen Coll., Oxford (William Doncaster Schol.; MA Mod. Langs and Phil.). Various appts, Macmillan Publishers, 1975–82; Managing Director: Macdonald & Co. (Publishers) Ltd, 1982–86; Headline Book Publishing PLC, 1986–93. Venturer of the Year Award, Brit. Venture Capital Assoc., 1990. *Recreations:* opera, horse-racing. *Address:* 25 Royal Crescent, Holland Park, W11 4SN. *Club:* Groucho.

HEMANS, Simon Nicholas Peter, CMG 1992; CVO 1983; HM Diplomatic Service; High Commissioner to Kenya, since 1995; *b* 19 Sept. 1940; *s* late of Brig. P. R. Hemans, CBE, and of Mrs M. E. Hemans (*née* Melsome); *m* 1970, Ursula Martha Naef; three *s* one *d*. *Educ:* Sherborne; London School of Economics (BScEcon). Joined Foreign Office, 1964; British Embassy, Moscow, 1966–68; FO, 1968–69; Dep. Commissioner, Anguilla, March–Oct. 1969; FO, 1969–71; UK Mission to UN, New York, 1971–75; British Embassy, Budapest, 1975–79; FO, 1979–81; Dep. High Comr, Nairobi, 1981–84; Head of Chancery, Moscow, 1985–87; Head of Soviet Dept, FCO, 1987–90; Asst Under-Sec. of State (Africa), FCO, 1990–92; Ambassador, Ukraine, 1992–95. *Recreation:* travel. *Address:* c/o Foreign and Commonwealth Office, SW1A 2AH.

HEMINGFORD, 3rd Baron; *see* Herbert, D. N.

HEMINGWAY, Peter, FCA; Director and Chief General Manager, Leeds Permanent Building Society, 1982–87; *b* 19 Jan. 1926; *s* of William Edward and Florence Hemingway; *m* 1952, June Maureen, *d* of Maurice and Lilian A. Senior. *Educ:* Leeds College of Commerce. With John Gordon, Walton & Co., Chartered Accountants, Leeds, 1941–62, Partner 1959–62; Director, Provincial Registrars Ltd, 1955–62; joined Leeds Permanent Bldg Soc. as Secretary, 1962. Local Dir (Leeds), Royal Insurance (UK) Ltd, 1983–93; Dir, Homeowners Friendly Soc., 1983–86. Hon. Sec. 1970–82, Vice-Chm. 1982–84, Chm. 1984–86, Yorkshire and North Western Assoc. of Building Societies; Vice Pres., Northern Assoc. of Building Socs, 1988–; Mem. Council: Building Societies Assoc., 1981–87; Chartered Building Societies Inst., 1982–87. *Recreations:* travel, motor racing, music, gardening. *Address:* Old Barn Cottage, Kearby, near Wetherby, Yorks LS22 4BU. *T:* Leeds (0113) 288 6380.

HEMLOW, Prof. Joyce; Professor Emerita, McGill University, Montreal, Canada; author; *b* 30 July 1906; *d* of William Hemlow and Rosalinda (*née* Redmond), Liscomb, NS. *Educ:* Queen's Univ., Kingston, Ont (MA; Hon. LLD 1967); Harvard Univ., Cambridge, Mass (AM, PhD). Preceding a univ. career, period of teaching in Nova Scotia, Canada; lecturer in English Language and Literature at McGill Univ.; Prof. of English Language and Literature, McGill Univ., 1955, Greenshields Professor 1965. FRSC 1960. Guggenheim Fellow, 1951–52, 1960–62 and 1966. Member, Phi Beta Kappa, The Johnsonians, and of other literary and professional organizations. Hon. LLD Dalhousie, 1972. James Tait Black Memorial Book Prize, 1958; Brit. Academy Award (Crawshay Prize), 1960. *Publications:* The History of Fanny Burney, 1958 (GB); (ed with others) The Journals and Letters of Fanny Burney (Madame d'Arblay), vols i–xii, 1972–84; (ed) Fanny Burney: selected letters and journals, 1986; articles in learned jls on Fanny Burney's novels and unpublished plays. *Address:* (home) Liscomb, NS B0J 2A0, Canada; 1521 Le Marchant Street, Apt 3-G, Halifax, NS B3H 3R2, Canada. *Club:* English-Speaking Union (Canadian Branch).

HEMMING, Air Commodore Idris George Selvin, CB 1968; CBE 1959 (OBE 1954); retired; *b* 11 Dec. 1911; *s* of late George Hemming, Liverpool; *m* 1939, Phyllis, *d* of Francis Payne, Drogheda, Eire; two *s*. *Educ:* Chalford, Glos.; Wallasey, Cheshire. Joined RAF, 1928; served War of 1939–45, UK, India and Burma; Gp Capt. 1957; Air Cdre 1962; Dir of Equipment (Pol.) (RAF), MoD, 1962–66; Dir of Equipment (1) (RAF), MoD, Harrogate, 1966–68. *Recreations:* cricket, golf. *Address:* Ash House, St Chloe Green, Amberley, near Stroud, Glos GL5 5AP. *T:* Amberley (01453) 873581. *Club:* Royal Air Force.

HEMMING, John Henry, CMG 1994; DLitt; Joint Chairman: Hemming Publishing Ltd (formerly Municipal Journal Ltd), since 1976 (Director, since 1962; Deputy Chairman, 1967–76); Hemming Group Ltd (formerly Municipal Publications Ltd), since 1976; Director and Secretary, Royal Geographical Society, since 1975; *b* 5 Jan. 1935; *s* of late Henry Harold Hemming, OBE, MC, and Alice Louisa Weaver, OBE; *m* 1979, Sukie, *d* of late M. J. Babington Smith, CBE; one *s* one *d*. *Educ:* Eton College; McGill University; Oxford University (DLitt 1981). Chairman: Brintex Ltd, 1979– (Man. Dir, 1963–70, Dep. Chm. 1976–78); Newman Books, 1979–. Member, Iriri River Expedition, Brazil, 1961; Leader, Maracá Rainforest Project, Brazil, 1987–88. Member Council: British Council; Goldsmiths' Educn Commn; Anglo-Brazilian Soc.; Pro Natura Internat. Corres. Mem., Academia Nacional de la Historia, Venezuela. Sponsor, Survival International; Trustee: L. S. B. Leakey Trust; Gilchrist Educnl Trust; Greencard Trust; Chm., Empire and Commonwealth Mus. Trust. Hon. DLitt Warwick, 1989; DUniv. Stirling, 1991. Mungo Park Medal, RSGS, 1988; Founder's Medal, RGS, 1990; Washburn Medal, Boston Mus. of Sci., 1990. Orden de Mérito (Peru). *Publications:* The Conquest of the Incas, 1970 (Robert Pitman Literary Prize, 1970, Christopher Award, NY, 1971); (jt) Tribes of the Amazon Basin in Brazil, 1972; Red Gold: The Conquest of the Brazilian Indians, 1978; The Search for El Dorado, 1978; Machu Picchu, 1981; Monuments of the Incas, 1982; The New Incas, 1983; (ed) Change in the Amazon Basin (2 vols), 1985; Amazon Frontier: the defeat of the Brazilian Indians, 1987; Maracá, 1988; Roraima: Brazil's northernmost frontier, 1990; Maracá Rainforest Island, 1993; (ed) The Rainforest Edge, 1994. *Recreations:* writing, travel. *Address:* 10 Edwardes Square, W8 6HE. *T:* 0171–602 6697. *Clubs:* Boodle's, Beefsteak, Geographical (Mem. Council).

See also L. A. Service.

HEMMINGS, David Leslie Edward; actor, director and producer; engaged in entertainment industry since 1949; *b* 18 Nov. 1941; *m* 1st, 1960, Genista Ouvry; one *d*; 2nd, 1969, Gayle Hunnicutt (marr. diss. 1975); one *s*; 3rd, 1976, Prudence J. de Casembroot; two *s*. *Educ:* Glyn Coll., Epsom, Surrey. The Turn of the Screw, English Opera Group, 1954; Five Clues to Fortune, 1957; Saint Joan, 1957; The Heart Within,

Strand; The Same Sky, Duke of York's; The Love Match, Palace. Film contract, Ealing Studios, 1940; many *films include:* Blacksheep of Whitehall; They Came in Khaki; A Kind of Loving; Once a Jolly Swagman; Maytime in Mayfair; Wide-eyed and Legless; *TV series and serials:* Meet the Wife; The First Lady; In Loving Memory; Hallelujah!; Last of the Summer Wine; Flesh and Blood; Praise Be!; Thora on the Straight and Narrow; Goggle Eyes; many plays, incl. Cream Cracker under the Settee (BAFTA Award for Best TV Actress, 1988). Pye Female Comedy Star Award, 1984. Hon. DLitt Lancaster, 1989. *Publications:* Scene and Hird (autobiog.), 1976; Praise Be Notebook, 1991; Praise Be Year Book, 1991; Praise Be Christmas Book, 1991; Praise Be Book of Prayers, 1992; Praise Be I Believe, 1993. *Recreations:* reading, gardening, travelling. *Address:* c/o Felix de Wolfe, Manfield House, 376–378 Strand, WC2R 0LR. *T:* 071–723 5561.

HIRSCH, Prof. Sir Peter (Bernhard), Kt 1975; MA, PhD; FRS 1963; Isaac Wolfson Professor of Metallurgy in the University of Oxford, 1966–92, Emeritus, 1992; Fellow, St Edmund Hall, Oxford, 1966–92, now Emeritus; *b* 16 Jan. 1925; *s* of Ismar Hirsch and Regina Meyerson; *m* 1959, Mabel Anne Kellar (*née* Stephens), *widow* of James Noel Kellar; one step *s* one step *d*. *Educ:* Sloane Sch., Chelsea; St Catharine's Coll., Cambridge (Hon. Fellow, 1982). BA 1946; MA 1950; PhD 1951. Reader in Physics in Univ. of Cambridge, 1964–66; Fellow, Christ's Coll., Cambridge, 1960–66, Hon. Fellow, 1978. Has been engaged on researches with electron microscope on imperfections in crystalline structure of metals and on relation between structural defects and mechanical properties. Chairman: Metallurgy and Materials Cttee (and Mem., Eng. Bd), SRC, 1970–73; UKAEA, 1982–84 (pt-time Mem., 1982–94); Technical Adv. Gp on Structl Integrity, 1993–; Member: Elec. Supply Res. Council, 1969–82; Tech. Adv. Cttee, Advent, 1982–89; Tech. Adv. Bd, Monsanto Electronic Materials, 1985–88. Chm., Isis Innovation Ltd, 1988–; Director: Cogent Ltd, 1985–89; Rolls Royce Associates, 1994–. FIC 1988. Hon. Fellow: RMS, 1977; Japan Soc. of Electron Microscopy, 1979. Hon. DSc: Newcastle, 1979; City, 1979; Northwestern, 1982; Hon. ScD East Anglia, 1983; Hon. DEng: Liverpool, 1991; Birmingham, 1993. Rosenhain Medal, Inst. of Metals, 1961; C. V. Boys Prize, Inst. of Physics and Physical Soc., 1962; Clamer Medal, Franklin Inst., 1970; Wihuri Internat. Prize, Helsinki, 1971; Royal Soc. Hughes Medal, 1973; Metals Soc. Platinum Medal, 1976; Royal Medal, Royal Soc., 1977; Arthur Von Hippel Award, Materials Res. Soc., 1983; (jtly) Wolf Prize in Physics, Wolf Foundn, 1983–84; Dist. Scientist Award, Electron Microscopy Soc. of America, 1986; Holweck Prize, Inst. of Physics and French Physical Soc., 1988; Gold Medal, Japan Inst. of Metals, 1989. *Publications:* Electron Microscopy of Thin Crystals (with others), 1965; (ed) The Physics of Metals, vol. 2, Defects, 1975; numerous contribs to learned jls. *Recreation:* walking. *Address:* 104A Lonsdale Road, Oxford OX2 7ET.

HIRSCH, Prof. Steven Richard, FRCP; FRCPsych; Professor of Psychiatry, Charing Cross and Westminster Medical School, since 1975; *b* 12 March 1937; *m* Theresa Hirsch; one *s* three *d*. *Educ:* Amherst Coll., Mass (BA Hons); Johns Hopkins Univ. (MD); London Univ. (MPhil). Res. worker, MRC Social Psychiatry, 1971–73; Hon. Sen. Registrar, Maudsley Hosp., 1971–73; Lectr in Psychiatry, Inst. of Psychiatry, Univ. of London, 1972–73; Sen. Lectr and Hon. Cons., Depts of Psychiatry, Westminster Hosp. and Queen Mary's Hosp., 1973–75. *Publications:* (ed with M. Shepherd) Themes and Variations in European Psychiatry: an anthology, 1974; (with J. Leff) Abnormalities in parents of schizophrenics: review of the literature and an investigation of communication defects and deviances, (monograph) 1975; (ed with R. Farmer) The Suicide Syndrome, 1980; (ed with P. B. Bradley) The Psychopharmacology and Treatment of Schizophrenia, 1986; Psychiatric Beds and Resources: factors influencing bed use and service planning (report of a working party, RCPsych), 1988; (ed with J. Harris) Consent and the Incompetent Patient: ethics, law and medicine, 1988; (ed with D. Weinberger) Schizophrenia, 1995. *Address:* Department of Psychiatry, Charing Cross and Westminster Medical School, St Dunstan's Road, W6 8RP. *T:* 0181–846 7390.

HIRST, Rt. Hon. Sir David (Cozens-Hardy), Kt 1982; PC 1992; **Rt. Hon. Lord Justice Hirst;** a Lord Justice of Appeal, since 1992; *b* 31 July 1925; *er s* of late Thomas William Hirst and Margaret Joy Hirst, Aylsham, Norfolk; *m* 1951, Pamela Elizabeth Molesworth Bevan, *d* of Col T. P. M. Bevan, MC; three *s* two *d*. *Educ:* Eton (Fellow, 1976); Trinity Coll., Cambridge. MA. Served 1943–47; RA and Intelligence Corps, Capt. 1946. Barrister, Inner Temple, 1951, Bencher, 1974, Reader, 1994, Treas., 1995; QC 1965; a Judge of the High Court, QBD, 1982–92. Vice-Chm. of the Bar, 1977–78, Chm., 1978–79. Member: Lord Chancellor's Law Reform Cttee; Council on Tribunals, 1966–80; Cttee to review Defamation Act, 1952, 1971–74; Hon. Life Mem., Amer. Bar Assoc. *Recreations:* shooting, theatre and opera, growing vegetables. *Address:* Royal Courts of Justice, Strand, WC2A 2LL. *Clubs:* Boodle's, MCC.

See also J. W. Hirst.

HIRST, David Michael Geoffrey, FBA 1983; Professor of the History of Art, University of London at the Courtauld Institute, since 1991 (Reader, 1980–91); *b* 5 Sept. 1933; *s* of Walter Hirst; *m* 1st, 1960, Sara Vitali (marr. diss. 1970); one *s*; 2nd, 1972, Jane Martineau (marr. diss. 1984); 3rd, 1984, Diane Zervas. *Educ:* Stowe Sch.; New Coll., Oxford; Courtauld Inst. of Art. Lectr, Courtauld Inst., 1962–80. Fellow at Villa I Tatti, 1969–70; Mem., Inst. for Advanced Study, Princeton, 1975. Mem., Pontifical Commn for Restoration of Sistine Ceiling, 1987–90. Arranged exhibn, Michelangelo Draftsman, Nat. Gall., Washington, 1988, Louvre, Paris, 1989; co-curated exhibn, The Young Michelangelo, Nat. Gall., 1994. *Publications:* Sebastiano del Piombo, 1981; Michelangelo and his Drawings, 1988; Michelangelo Draftsman, Milan, 1988 (French edn 1989); (jtly) The Young Michelangelo, 1995; many contribs to British and continental books and periodicals. *Address:* 3 Queensdale Place, W11 4SQ.

HIRST, Prof. John Malcolm, DSC 1945; PhD; FRS 1970; FIBiol; Consultant on aerobiology and international agriculture; Director, Long Ashton Research Station, and Professor of Agricultural and Horticultural Science, Bristol University, 1975–84, now Professor Emeritus; *b* 20 April 1921; *s* of Maurice Herbert Hirst and Olive Mary (*née* Pank); *m* 1957, Barbara Mary Stokes; two *d*. *Educ:* Solihull Sch.; Reading University (BSc Hons Agric. Bot., 1950); PhD London 1955. Royal Navy (Coastal Forces), 1941–46. Rothamsted Exper. Stn, Harpenden, 1950–75, Hd of Plant Pathology Dept, 1967–75. Vice-Chm. Tech. Adv. Cttee, Consultative Gp, Internat. Agricl Research, 1981–82; Chm., Scientific Adv. Bd, Twyford Plant Labs. Pres., British Aerobiology Fedn, 1990–93. Jakob Eriksson Gold Medal (Internat. Botanical Congress), 1959; Research Medal, RASE, 1970. *Publications:* papers in scientific jls mainly in Trans British Mycological Soc., Annals of Applied Biology, Jl of General Microbiology. *Address:* The Cottage, Butcombe, Bristol BS18 6XQ. *T:* Lulsgate (01275) 472880. *Club:* Farmers'.

HIRST, Jonathan William; QC 1990; *b* 2 July 1953; *s* of Rt Hon. Sir David (Cozens-Hardy) Hirst, *qv*; *m* 1974, Fiona Christine Mary Hirst (*née* Tyser); one *s* (and one *s* decd). *Educ:* Eton Coll.; Trinity Coll., Cambridge (MA). Called to the Bar, Inner Temple, 1975; Bencher, 1994. Mem., Gen. Council of the Bar, 1987– (Chm., Law Reform Cttee, 1992–94). Gov., Taverham Hall Sch., Norfolk, 1991–. *Recreations:* shooting, gardening, other country pursuits. *Address:* Brickcourt Chambers, 15/19 Devereux Court, Temple, WC2R 3JJ. *T:* 0171–583 0777. *Club:* Boodle's.

HIRST, Sir Michael (William), Kt 1992; LLB, CA; company director; business consultant; Founder, Michael Hirst Associates; Chairman, Scottish Conservative Party, since 1993; *b* 2 Jan. 1946; *s* of late John Melville Hirst and of Christina Binning Torrance or Hirst; *m* 1972, Naomi Ferguson Wilson; one *s* two *d*. *Educ:* Glasgow Acad., Glasgow; Univ. of Glasgow (LLB). CA 1970. Exchange Student, Univ. of Iceland, 1967; Partner, Peat, Marwick Mitchell & Co., 1978–83; Consultant, Peat Marwick UK, 1983–92. Pres., Glasgow Univ. Conservative Club, 1967; National Vice-Chm., Scottish Young Conservatives, 1971–73; Chm., Scottish Conservative Candidates Assoc., 1978–81; Vice-Chairman: Pty Organisation Cttee, 1985; Conservative Party in Scotland, 1987–89; Pres., Scottish Cons. & Unionist Assoc., 1989–92. Contested (C): Central Dunbartonshire, Feb. and Oct. 1974; E Dunbartonshire, 1979; Strathkelvin and Bearsden, 1987 and 1992. MP (C) Strathkelvin and Bearsden, 1983–87. PPS to Parly Under-Secs of State, DoE, 1985–87. Mem., Select Cttee on Scottish Affairs, 1983–87. Dir, Children's Hospice Assoc., Scotland, 1993–; Member: Bd of Trustees, British Diabetic Assoc. (Hon. Sec., 1993–); Exec. Cttee, Princess Louise Scottish Hosp., 1980–; Court, Glasgow Caledonian Univ., 1993– (Chm., Audit Cttee, 1993–). Chm., Park Sch. Educnl Trust, 1988–. FRSA 1993. *Recreations:* golf, walking, ski-ing. *Address:* Enderley, Baldernock Road, Milngavie, Glasgow G62 8DU. *T:* 0141–956 1213; 712 Howard House, Dolphin Square, SW1V 3LX. *T:* 0171–798 8021. *Clubs:* Carlton; The Western (Glasgow).

HIRST, Prof. Paul Heywood; Professor of Education, University of Cambridge, 1971–88, now Emeritus, and Fellow of Wolfson College (formerly University College), Cambridge, since 1971; *b* 10 Nov. 1927; *s* of late Herbert and Winifred Hirst, Birkby, Huddersfield. *Educ:* Huddersfield Coll.; Trinity Coll., Cambridge. BA 1948, MA 1952, Certif. Educn 1952, Cantab; DipEd 1955, London; MA Oxon (by incorporation), Christ Church, Oxford, 1955. Asst Master, William Hulme's Grammar Sch., Manchester, 1948–50; Maths Master, Eastbourne Coll., 1950–55; Lectr and Tutor, Univ. of Oxford Dept of Educn, 1955–59; Lectr in Philosophy of Educn, Univ. of London Inst. of Educn, 1959–65; Prof. of Educn, King's Coll., Univ. of London, 1965–71. Visiting Professor: Univ. of British Columbia, 1964, 1967; Univ. of Malawi, 1969; Univ. of Puerto Rico, 1984; Univ. of Sydney, 1989; Univ. of Alberta, 1989; Inst. of Educn, Univ. of London, 1991–93. De Carle Lectr, Univ. of Otago, 1976; Fink Lectr, Univ. of Melbourne, 1976. Vice-Pres., Philosophy of Educn Soc. of GB; Member: UGC Educn Sub-Cttee, 1971–80; Educn Cttee, 1972–82, Academic Policy Cttee, 1981–87, Chm., Research Cttee, 1988–92, CNAA; Swann Cttee of Inquiry into Educn of Children from Ethnic Minorities, 1981–85. Chm., Univs Council for Educn of Teachers, 1985–88. Hon. DEd CNAA, 1992. *Publications:* (with R. S. Peters) The Logic of Education, 1970; (ed with R. F. Dearden and R. S. Peters) Education and the Development of Reason, 1971; Knowledge and the Curriculum, 1974; Moral Education in a Secular Society, 1974; (ed) Educational Theory and its Foundation Disciplines, 1984; (with V. J. Furlong) Initial Teacher Training and the Role of the School, 1988; papers in: Philosophical Analysis and Education (ed R. D. Archambault), 1965; The Study of Education (ed J. W. Tibble), 1965; The Concept of Education (ed R. S. Peters), 1966; Religious Education in a Pluralistic Society (ed M. C. Felderhof), 1985; Education, Values and Mind (ed D. E. Cooper), 1986; Partnership in Initial Teacher Training (ed M. Booth *et al*), 1990; Beyond Liberal Education (ed R. Barrow and P. White), 1993. *Recreation:* music, especially opera. *Address:* Flat 3, 6 Royal Crescent, Brighton BN2 1AL. *T:* Brighton (01273) 684118. *Club:* Athenæum.

HIRST, Prof. Rodney Julian, MA; Professor of Logic and Rhetoric, University of Glasgow, 1961–81; *b* 28 July 1920; *s* of Rev. William Hirst and Elsie Hirst; *m* 1st, 1942, Jessica (*d* 1978), *y d* of Charles Alfred Podmore; two *d*; 2nd, 1985, Mary, *widow* of John Patrick. *Educ:* Leeds Grammar Sch.; Magdalen Coll., Oxford, Demy, 1938–47; 1st Cl. Hons Classical Mods, 1940. War Service, 1940–45, mainly as REME Officer (Radar) at home and in Italy. First Class Hons Lit. Hum., Dec. 1947. Lectr in Logic and Metaphysics, St Andrews Univ., 1948; Glasgow University: Lectr, 1949, and Sen. Lectr, 1959, in Logic; Dean of Arts, 1971–73; Senate Assessor on Univ. Court, 1973–78; Vice-Principal, 1976–79. *Publications:* Problems of Perception, 1959; (co-author) Human Senses and Perception, 1964; Perception and the External World, 1965; Philosophy: an outline for the intending student, 1968; contribs to Encyclopedia of Philosophy and philosophical journals. *Address:* 26 Riverside Court, Netherlee, Glasgow G44 3PH. *T:* 0141–637 9433.

HISCOCKS, Prof. Charles Richard, MA, DPhil; Professor of International Relations, University of Sussex, 1964–72, now Emeritus; *b* 1 June 1907; *y s* of F. W. Hiscocks; unmarried. *Educ:* Highgate Sch.; St Edmund Hall, Oxford; Berlin University. Asst Master, Trinity Coll. Sch., Port Hope, Ont, 1929–32; Bradfield Coll., 1936–39; Marlborough Coll., 1939–40. Served with Royal Marines, 1940–45, Lieut-Col; seconded to army for mil. govt duties in Germany, 1945; Brit. Council Rep. in Austria, 1946–49, S India, 1949–50; Prof. of Polit. Sci. and Internat. Relations, Univ. of Manitoba, 1950–64. UK Mem., UN Sub-Commn for Prevention of Discrimination and Protection of Minorities, 1953–62. Pres., Winnipeg Art Gall., 1959–60. Vis. Fellow, Princeton Univ., 1970–71; Fellow, Adlai Stevenson Inst. of Internat. Affairs, Chicago, 1971–72. Vice-Pres., UNA 1977–. *Publications:* The Rebirth of Austria, 1953; Democracy in Western Germany, 1957; Poland: Bridge for the Abyss?, 1963; Germany Revived, 1966; The Security Council: a study in adolescence, 1973. *Recreations:* music, art, gardening. *Address:* Dickers, Hunworth, Melton Constable, Norfolk NR24 2AA. *T:* Holt (01263) 712503. *Club:* Garrick.

HISCOX, Robert Ralph Scrymgeour; Chairman, Hiscox Group and subsidiary companies, since 1970; *b* 4 Jan. 1943; *s* of Ralph Hiscox, CBE and Louisa Jeanie Hiscox (*née* Boal); *m* 1st, 1966, Lucy Mills (marr. diss. 1978); two *s*; 2nd, 1985, Lady Julia Elizabeth Meade, 3rd *d* of Earl of Clanwilliam; three *s*. *Educ:* Rugby Sch.; Corpus Christi Coll., Cambridge (MA). ACII. Member of Lloyd's, 1967– (Dep. Chm., 1993–95; Dep. Chm., First Market Bd, 1993–95); Chm., Lloyd's Underwriting Agents' Assoc., 1991. Director: Hiscox Dedicated Insurance Fund; Hiscox Select Insurance Fund. Treasurer, Friends of the Tate Gallery, 1990–93. Gov., St Francis Sch., Pewsey. *Recreations:* family life, country life, 20th century paintings. *Address:* Hiscox Holdings, 52 Leadenhall Street, EC3A 2BJ. *T:* 0171–929 5531, *Fax:* 0171–626 2222; Rainscombe Park, Oare, Marlborough, Wilts SN8 4HZ. *T:* Marlborough (01672) 563491, *Fax:* (01672) 564120. *Club:* City of London.

HISLOP, George Steedman, CBE 1976; PhD; FEng, FIMechE; FRSE; Director, Aviall Airline Services (Caledonian) (formerly Caledonian Airmotive), 1978–94; *b* 11 Feb. 1914; *s* of George Alexander Hislop and Marthesa Maria Hay; *m* 1942, Joan Daphne, *d* of William Beer and Gwendoline Fincken; two *s* one *d*. *Educ:* Clydebank High Sch.; Royal Technical Coll., Glasgow (ARTC); Cambridge Univ. (PhD). BScEng London. CEng, FIMechE 1949; FRAeS 1955; Fellowship of Engrg, 1976; FRSE 1976; FRSA 1959. A&AEE, RAF Boscombe Down, 1939–45; RAE, Farnborough, 1945–46; BEA, 1947–53; Chief Engr/Dir, Fairey Aviation Ltd, 1953–60; Westland Aircraft Ltd, 1960–79: Technical Dir (Devel), 1962–66; Dep. Man. Dir, 1966–68; Man. Dir, 1968–72; Vice-Chm., 1972–76. Chm., CEI, 1979–80 (Vice-Chm., 1978–79); Mem., Airworthiness Requirements Bd, CAA, 1976–83 (Chm., 1982–83). Vis. Prof., Univ. of Strathclyde, 1978–84. Mem. Council, RAeS, 1960–83 (Pres., 1973–74; Hon. FRAeS, 1983); Gov., Inveresk Res. Foundn, 1980–90. LRPS 1992. Hon. DSc Strathclyde, 1976. *Publications:* contrib. R & M series and RAeS Jl. *Recreations:* hill walking, photography, bird watching.

Address: Hadley, St John's Hill, Old Coulsdon, Surrey CR5 1HD. *T:* 0181–660 1008. *Clubs:* Royal Air Force, MCC.

HISLOP, Ian David; Editor, Private Eye, since 1986; writer and broadcaster; *b* 13 July 1960; *s* of late David Atholl Hislop and of Helen Hislop; *m* 1988, Victoria Hamson; one *s* one *d.* *Educ:* Ardingly College; Magdalen College, Oxford (BA Hons Eng. Lang. and Lit.; Underhill Exhibn; Violet Vaughan Morgan Scholarship). Joined Private Eye, 1981, Dep. Editor, 1985–86. Columnist, The Listener, 1985–89. *Radio:* Newsquiz, 1985–; 4th Column, 1992–; (scriptwriter, with Nick Newman) Gush, 1994; *television:* scriptwriter: Spitting Image, 1984–89; (with Nicholas Newman) The Stone Age, 1989; Briefcase Encounter, 1990; The Case of the Missing, 1991; He Died a Death, 1991; Harry Enfield's Television Programme, 1990–92; Harry Enfield and Chums, 1994; Mangez Merveillac, 1994; Dead on Time, 1995; performer, Have I Got News For You, 1990–. *Publications:* (ed) Secret Diary of a Lord Gnome, 1985; (ed) Gnome of the Rose, 1987; (with Nicholas Newman) Battle for Britain, 1987; (ed) Satiric Verses, 1989; (ed) Fib and Lie Diet, 1991; Secret Diary of John Major, 1992; Second Secret Diary of John Major, 1993; (ed) Gnome in Provence, 1993; (ed) Absolutely Libellous, 1994; Third and Last Secret Diary of John Major, 1994; contribs to newspapers and magazines on books, current affairs, arts and entertainment. *Address:* c/o Private Eye, 6 Carlisle Street, W1V 5RG. *T:* 0171–437 4017.

HISS, Alger; Commercial printing, 1959–80 (manufacturing, 1957–59); Lecturer, 1970–80; retired; *b* 11 Nov. 1904; *s* of Charles Alger Hiss and Mary L. Hughes; *m* 1929, Priscilla Fansler Hobson; one *s.* *Educ:* Johns Hopkins Univ. (AB 1926, Hon. LLD 1947); Harvard Univ. (LLB 1929). Sec. and law clerk to Supreme Court Justice Holmes, 1929–30; law practice, 1930–33; asst to gen. counsel and asst gen. counsel, Agricultural Adjustment Admin., 1933–35; legal asst, special Senate cttee investigating munitions industry, 1934–35; special attorney, US Dept of Justice, 1935–36; asst to Asst Sec. of State, 1936; asst to Adviser on Political Relations, 1939; special asst to Dir, Office of Far Eastern Affairs, 1944; special asst to Dir, Office of Special Political Affairs, May 1944; Dep. Dir, Nov. 1944, Dir, 1945; accompanied Pres. Roosevelt and Sec. of State Stettinius to Malta and Yalta Conferences, Feb. 1945; exec. sec., Dumbarton Oaks Conversations, Aug.–Oct. 1944; sec.-gen., United Nations Conference on International Organization, San Francisco, 1945; Principal Adviser to US Delegation, Gen. Assembly of United Nations, London, 1946; elected Pres. and Trustee of Carnegie Endowment for Internat. Peace, Dec. 1946 (Pres. until 1949). Mem., Massachusetts Bar. Mem., Alpha Delta Phi, Phi Beta Kappa. *Publications:* The Myth of Yalta, 1955; In the Court of Public Opinion, 1957, new edn 1972; Holmes-Laski Letters (abridged edn), 1963; Recollections of a Life, 1988. *Address:* 303 East 83 Street, New York, NY 10028, USA.

HITCH, Brian, CMG 1985; CVO 1980; HM Diplomatic Service, retired; Director, Diploma in European Studies, and Fellow of Kellogg College (formerly Rewley House), University of Oxford, since 1991; *b* 2 June 1932; *m* 1954, Margaret Kathleen Wooller; two *d.* *Educ:* Wisbech Grammar Sch. (FRCO, LRAM); Magdalene Coll., Cambridge. Joined FO, 1955; 3rd/2nd Sec., Tokyo, 1955–61; FO, 1961–62; 2nd/1st Sec., Havana, 1962–64; 1st Sec., Athens, 1965–68; 1st Sec. and Head of Chancery, Tokyo, 1968–72; Asst Head, Southern European Dept, FCO, 1972–73; Dep. Head, later Head, Marine and Transport Dept, FCO, 1973–75; Counsellor, Bonn, 1975–77 and Algiers, 1977–80; Consul-Gen., Munich, 1980–84; Minister, Tokyo, 1984–87; High Comr to Malta, 1988–91. *Recreation:* music. *Address:* 19 Moreton Road, Oxford OX2 7AX. *T:* Oxford (01865) 56764.

HITCHCOCK, Dr Anthony John Michael; Principal Consultant, AHS Safety Ltd, since 1994; *b* 26 June 1929; *s* of Dr Ronald W. Hitchcock and Hilda (*née* Gould); *m* 1st, 1953, Audrey Ellen Ashworth (*d* 1990); one *s* two *d*; 2nd, 1992, Louise Nickel. *Educ:* Bedales; Manchester Grammar Sch.; Trinity Coll., Cambridge; Univ. of Chicago. PhD, BA; MInstP; MCIT. Asst, Univ. of Chicago, 1951–52; AEA, 1953–67; Department of Transport: Head of Traffic Dept, 1967–71, Head of Transport Ops Dept, 1971–75, TRRL; Head, Res. Policy (Transport) Div., DoE/DoT, 1975–78; Head of Safety and Transportation Dept, TRRL, 1978–89; Vis. Researcher, Program for Advanced Technol. on the Highway, Univ. of Calif at Berkeley, 1990–94. Vis. Prof., Transport Studies, Cranfield Inst. of Technology, 1978–81. *Publications:* Nuclear Reactor Control, 1960; research reports and articles in learned jls. *Recreation:* bridge. *Address:* Seal Point, Comeragh Close, Golf Club Road, Woking, Surrey GU22 0LZ.

HITCHEN, Brian, CBE 1990; Editor, Sunday Express and Sunday Express Magazine, since 1994; *b* 8 July 1936; *s* of Fred and Alice Hitchen, Lancs; *m* 1962, Ellen Josephine O'Hanlon, Kildare, Eire; one *s* one *d.* *Educ:* Hegginbottom Sch., Ashton-under-Lyne, Lancs, and elsewhere. Served Army, WO, Whitehall, 1954–56. Copy Boy, Daily Despatch, 1951; Gen. Reporter, Bury Times, 1952–54; Reporter, Manchester Evening News, 1957; Reporter, 1958–63, Foreign Correspondent, Paris Bureau, 1963–64, Daily Mirror; For. Corresp., Mirror US Bureaux, New York and Washington, 1964–72; Dep. News Editor, Daily Mirror, 1972; News Editor, Daily Express, 1973–76; Asst Editor, National Enquirer, USA, 1976, European Bureau Chief, 1977; Asst Editor, Now! magazine, 1978–80; London Editor, The Daily Star, 1981–86; Dep. Editor, Sunday Express, 1986–87; Ed., Daily Star, 1987–94. Director: Airspeed Internat. Corp., 1973–; Express Newspapers, 1988–; Independent Star, Eire, 1988–95. Member: Press Complaints Commn, 1991–95; Defence, Press and Broadcasting Adv. Cttee, 1993–. *Recreations:* watercolours, still thinking about writing the Great British Novel, golf. *Address:* Ludgate House, 245 Blackfriars Road, SE1 9UX. *Clubs:* St James's, Variety of Great Britain, London Press; Sussex Yacht.

HITCHEN, John David; a Recorder of the Crown Court, since 1978; *b* 18 July 1935; *s* of late Harold Samuel and Frances Mary Hitchen; *m* 1966, Pamela Ann Cellan-Jones. *Educ:* Woodhouse Grove Sch., nr Bradford; Pembroke Coll., Oxford (BA(Hons)). Called to Bar, Lincoln's Inn, 1961. *Recreations:* music, reading. *Address:* 39 Rutland Drive, Harrogate, Yorks HG1 2NX. *T:* Harrogate (01423) 66236.

HITCHENS, Rear Adm. Gilbert Archibald Ford, CB 1988; Director General Ship Refitting, Ministry of Defence, 1985–87, retired; *b* 11 April 1932; *m* 1960, Patricia Hamilton; one *s* one *d.* BA Hons. Joined Royal Navy, 1950; Commander, 1968; Guided Weapons Staff Officer, Min. of Technology, 1968–70; Exec. Officer, RNEC, 1970–72; Senior Officer while building and Weapon Engineer Officer, HMS Sheffield, 1973–75; MoD (Navy), 1975–77; Naval Attaché, Tokyo and Seoul, 1977–79; Asst Dir, Manpower Requirements, MoD (Navy), 1979–80; Dir, Officers' Appts (Eng.), 1980–82; Captain, HMS Defiance, 1982–84; CSO Engrg to C-in-C Fleet, 1984–85. Mem., Plymouth DHA, 1989–90. Admiralty Gov., Royal Naval Benevolent Trust, 1989–. Chm. Govs, Devonport High Sch. for Boys, 1993–. *Recreation:* any activity in the high hills.

HITCHIN, Prof. Aylwin Drakeford, CBE 1970; Boyd Professor of Dental Surgery, Director of Dental Studies, University of Dundee (formerly University of St Andrews), 1947–77, Professor Emeritus, 1978 and Dean of Dundee Dental Hospital, 1947–73; Dental Consultant, Dundee Royal Infirmary, 1947–77; Civil Consultant Dental Surgeon to Royal Navy, 1957–77; *b* 31 Dec. 1907; *s* of Alfred Leonard Hitchin, FRPS, and Ruth Drakeford; *m* 1942, Alice Stella Michie; one *s* one *d.* *Educ:* Rutherford College, Newcastle upon Tyne; Durham University Coll. of Medicine. LDS (Dunelm) 1931, BDS 1932, MDS 1935; DDSc 1957; FDSRCS Edinburgh 1951; FFDRCS Ire 1964; FDSRCPS Glasgow 1967. Asst Hon. Dental Surgeon and Demonstrator of Dental Surgery, Newcastle upon Tyne Dental Hosp., 1932–36; Private Dental Practice, Newcastle upon Tyne, 1932–46 (except for 6 yrs with AD Corps during War of 1939–45); Dental Surgical Specialist, Scottish Command, 1943–45, with rank of Major. Chairman: Dental Educn Advisory Council, 1951–52; Dental Hosp. Assoc., 1959–60; Chm., Dental Cttee, Scot. Post-Grad. Med. Council, 1969–79; Member: Dental Cttee of MRC, 1966–72; Advisory Cttee on Medical Research (Scotland), 1967–71; Dental Adv. Cttee, Scottish Health Services Council, 1952–57, 1968–74; Convener, Dental Council, RCSE, 1971–74; Jt Cttee on Higher Training in Dentistry, 1969–74; East Scotland Regional Hosp. Bd, 1948–52; Dental Sub Cttee, UGC, 1969–73; Nominated Mem., Gen. Dent. Council, 1956–74; External Examiner Dental Subjects, Universities, Durham, Edinburgh, Queen's, Belfast, Dublin, Manchester, Liverpool, Birmingham, Leeds, Newcastle, Bristol, Wales, RCS in Ireland; Examiner, LDS, FDSRCS Edinburgh, FFDRCS Ire, and FDSRCPS Glasgow. William Guy Meml Lectr, RCSE, 1972; Founders and Benefactors Lectr, Univ. of Newcastle upon Tyne Dental Sch., 1973. President: Oral Surgery Club, 1956–57; Christian Dental Fellowship, 1966–69; Brit. Soc. Dental Radiology, 1961–63; Royal Odonto-Chir. Soc. of Scotland, 1969–70; Pres., Inter-Varsity Fellowship, 1966–67; Foundation Fellow of the British Assoc. of Oral Surgeons; Hon. Mem., Swedish Dental Soc. Dr Odont (*hc*) Lund, 1977; Hon. FDSRCPS Glasgow, 1979. *Publications:* contribs to dental periodical literature. *Address:* Coniston, Prieston Road, Bridge of Weir, Renfrewshire PA11 3AJ. *T:* Bridge of Weir (01505) 614936.

HITCHIN, Prof. Nigel James, DPhil; FRS 1991; Rouse Ball Professor of Mathematics, University of Cambridge, since 1994; Fellow of Gonville and Caius College, Cambridge, since 1994; *b* 2 Aug. 1946; *s* of Eric Wilfred Hitchin and Bessie (*née* Blood); *m* 1973, Nedda Vejarano Bernal; one *s* one *d.* *Educ:* Ecclesbourne Sch., Duffield; Jesus Coll., Oxford (BA 1968); Wolfson Coll., Oxford (MA, DPhil 1972). Res. Asst, Inst. for Advanced Study, Princeton, 1971–73; Instructor, Courant Inst., New York Univ., 1973–74; SRC Res. Asst, 1974–77, SRC Advanced Res. Fellow, 1977–79, Oxford Univ.; Fellow and Tutor in Maths, St Catherine's Coll., Oxford, 1979–90; Prof. of Maths, Univ. of Warwick, 1990–94. Vis. Prof., SUNY, Stony Brook, 1983. London Mathematical Society: Pres., 1994–Nov. 1996; Jun. Whitehead Prize, 1981; Sen. Berwick Prize, 1990. *Publications:* Monopoles, Minimal Surfaces and Algebraic Curves, 1987; (with M. F. Atiyah) The Geometry and Dynamics of Magnetic Monopoles, 1988; articles in learned jls. *Address:* Department of Pure Mathematics and Mathematical Statistics, 16 Mill Lane, Cambridge CB2 1SB. *T:* Cambridge (01223) 337999.

HITCHING, Alan Norman; His Honour Judge Hitching; a Circuit Judge, since 1987; *b* 5 Jan. 1941; *s* of late Norman Henry Samuel Hitching and Grace Ellen Hitching; *m* 1967, Hilda Muriel (*née* King); one *d* two *s.* *Educ:* Forest Sch., Snaresbrook; Christ Church, Oxford (BA 1962; Radcliffe Exhibnr and Dixon Scholar, 1962; BCL 1963; MA). Harmsworth Entrance Scholar, Middle Temple, 1960; Astbury Scholar and Safford Prize, Middle Temple, 1964; called to the Bar, Middle Temple, 1964; Standing Counsel, Inland Revenue, SE Circuit, 1972–87; a Recorder, 1985–87. Cropwood Fellow, Inst. of Criminology, Cambridge, 1990. Vice-Pres., John Grooms Assoc. for the Disabled, 1991– (Chm., 1981–89; Vice-Chm., 1978–81 and 1989–91). Licensed Reader, Dio. of Chelmsford, 1987–. *Address:* 9 Monkhams Drive, Woodford Green, Essex IG8 0LG. *T:* 0181–504 4260.

HITCHINGS, Dr George Herbert; Scientist Emeritus and Consultant, Burroughs Wellcome Co., since 1975; Director, The Burroughs Wellcome Fund, 1971–94 (President, 1971–90); *b* 18 April 1905; *m* 1st, 1933, Beverly Reimer (*d* 1985); one *s* one *d*; 2nd, 1989, Joyce Shaver. *Educ:* Univ. of Washington (BS *cum laude* Chem 1927; MS 1928); PhD Biochem Harvard 1933. Teaching Fellow, Univ. of Washington, 1926–28; Harvard University: Teaching Fellow, 1928–34; Instructor and Tutor, 1932–36; Res. Fellow, 1934–36; Associate, 1936–39; Sen. Instructor, Western Reserve Univ., 1939–42; Burroughs Wellcome Co.: Biochemist, 1942–46; Chief Biochemist, 1946–55; Associate Res. Dir, 1955–63; Res. Dir (Chemotherapy Div.), 1963–67; Vice-Pres. in charge of Res., 1967–75; Dir, 1968–77. Prof. of Pharmacology, Brown Univ., 1968–80; Adjunct Prof. of Pharmacology and Adjunct Prof. of Experimental Medicine, Duke Univ., 1970–85; Staff, Dept of Medicine, Roger Williams Gen. Hosp., Brown Univ., 1970–80; Adjunct Prof. of Pharmacology, Univ. of N Carolina at Chapel Hill, 1972–85; Vis. Prof. of Clinical Pharmacology, Chuang-Ang Univ., Seoul, 1974–77; Vis. Lectr, Pakistan, Iran, Japan, India, Republic of S Africa. Mem., US and internat scientific bodies, incl. Royal Soc., RSocMed, RSC. Hon. degrees from univs in US, UK and Italy. Numerous medals and awards; (jtly) Nobel Prize in Physiology or Medicine, 1988; Albert Schweitzer Internat. Prize for Medicine, 1989. Member, Editorial Boards: Research Communications in Chemical Pathology and Pharmacology, 1969–; Molecular Pharmacology, 1967–; Biochemical Pharmacology, 1967–; Life Sciences, 1978. *Publications:* contribs to learned jls on chemotherapy, antimetabolites, organic chemistry of heterocycles, nucleic acids, antitumor, antimalarial and antibacterial drugs. *Address:* 1 Carolina Meadows, Apt 102, Chapel Hill, NC 27514, USA. *T:* (home) (919) 9335023.

HIVES, family name of **Baron Hives.**

HIVES, 2nd Baron, *cr* 1950, of Duffield; **John Warwick Hives,** CBE 1989; *b* 26 Nov. 1913; *s* of 1st Baron Hives and of Gertrude Ethel (*d* 1961), *d* of John Warwick; *S* father, 1965; *m* 1st, 1937, Olwen Protheroe Llewellin (*d* 1972); no *c*; 2nd, 1972, Gladys Mary Seals. *Educ:* Manor School, Mickleover, Derby. *Recreation:* shooting. *Heir: nephew* Matthew Peter Hives, *b* 25 May 1971. *Address:* Langdale House, Sutton-on-the-Hill, Derby DE6 5JA. *Club:* Farmers'.

HNATYSHYN, Rt. Hon. Ramon John, PC (Can.) 1979; CC 1990; CMM 1990; CD 1990; QC (Can.) 1988; Governor General and Commander-in-Chief of Canada, 1990–95; *b* 16 March 1934; *s* of John Hnatyshyn and Helen Constance Hnatyshyn (*née* Pitts); *m* 1960, Karen Gerda Nygaard Andreasen; two *s.* *Educ:* Victoria Public Sch.; Nutana Collegiate Inst., Univ. of Saskatchewan (BA 1954; LLB 1956). Royal Canadian Air Force: trng, 1951–56; 23 Wing Auxiliary, 1956–58. Called to the Bar of Saskatchewan, 1957; QC Sask, 1973; practised to 1990; Private Sec. and Exec. Asst to Senate Leader of Govt, 1958–60; Lectr in Law, Univ. of Saskatchewan, 1966–74; MP (PC Party) Saskatoon-Biggar, 1974, Saskatoon West, 1979, 1980, 1984 elections; Minister of State for Science and Technology, 1979; Minister of Energy, Mines and Resources, 1979–80; Govt House Leader, 1984–86; Minister responsible for Regulatory Affairs, 1986; Minister of Justice and Attorney General of Canada, 1986–88. Pres., Queen's Privy Council for Canada, 1985–86. *Address:* Suite 2600, 160 Elgin Street, Ottawa, Ont K1P 1C3, Canada.

HO, Eric Peter, CBE 1981; Chairman, Public Service Commission, Hong Kong, 1987–91, retired; *b* 30 Dec. 1927; *s* of Sai-Ki Ho and Doris (*née* Lo); *m* 1956, Grace Irene, *d* of Mr and Mrs A. V. Young; two *s* one *d.* *Educ:* Univ. of Hong Kong (BA 1950). Inspector of Taxes (under training), London, 1950–53; Hong Kong Civil Service, 1954–87: Sec. for Social Services, 1977–83; Sec. for Trade and Industry, 1983–87. RCDS, London, 1976.

Recreations: swimming, lawn tennis. *Address:* 26 Greenways Drive, Sunningdale, Berks SL5 9QS.

HOAD, Air Vice-Marshal Norman Edward, CVO 1972; CBE 1969; AFC 1951 and Bar, 1956; artist; *b* 28 July 1923; *s* of Hubert Ronald Hoad and Florence Marie (*née* Johnson); two *s*. *Educ:* Brighton. Joined RAF, 1941, pilot trng, S Rhodesia; Lancaster pilot until shot down and taken prisoner in Germany, 1944; various flying and instructional duties, 1945–51; Sqdn Ldr 1951; OC No 192 Sqdn, 1953–55; psc 1956; Wing Comdr, HQ 2 ATAF, 1957–59; pfc 1960; OC No 216 Sqdn, 1960–62; jssc 1963; Gp Capt., MoD, 1963–65; idc 1966; Stn Comdr: RAF Lyneham, 1967, RAF Abingdon, 1968; Defence and Air Attaché, British Embassy, Paris, 1969–72; Dir, Defence Policy (A), 1972–74; Chief of Staff, 46 Gp, RAF Strike Comd, April-Oct. 1974; AOC No 46 Group, and Comdr, UK Jt Airborne Task Force, 1974–75; Senior RAF Mem., RCDS, 1976–78. Director, Air League, 1978–82. Founder Mem., Guild of Aviation Artists; Chm., Soc. of Equestrian Artists. MBIM 1970. *Address:* Little Meadow, Stowupland, Stowmarket, Suffolk IP14 5DF. *T:* Stowmarket (01449) 612006. *Club:* Royal Air Force.

HOAR, Rev. Ronald William Cecil; Chairman, Manchester and Stockport Methodist District, 1979–95; President of the Methodist Conference, 1991–92; *b* 31 Oct. 1931; *s* of Cecil Herbert William and Lilian Augusta Hoar; *m* 1956, Peggy Jean (*née* Stubbington); three *s* two *d*. *Educ:* Shedfield Church of England Primary Sch., Hants; Prices Sch., Fareham, Hants; Richmond Coll., Univ. of London (BD). Methodist Minister: Wells, Somerset, 1955–58; Bermondsey, London, 1958–62; Westminster and Chelsea, 1962–67; Bristol Mission, 1967–76; Great Yarmouth and Gorleston, 1976–79. *Publications:* Methodism in Chelsea to 1963, 1963; A Good Ideal: a history of the Bristol Methodist Mission, 1973; Advertising the Gospel, 1991. *Recreations:* DIY, watching sport, oil painting, gardening. *Address:* 43 Green Lanes, Prestatyn, Clwyd LL19 7BH. *T:* Prestatyn (01745) 886923.

HOARE, Rev. Brian Richard; President of the Methodist Conference, 1995–June 1996; *b* 9 Dec. 1935; *s* of William Charles Hoare and Kathleen Nora Hoare (*née* Thwaites); *m* 1962, Joyce Eleanor Davidson; one *s* one *d*. *Educ:* Southwell Minster Grammar Sch., Notts; Westminster Coll., London (Teacher's Cert.); Richmond Coll., Univ. of London (BD 1971). Ops Clerk, RAF, 1954–56. Teacher, Col Frank Seely Secondary Sch., Calverton, Notts, 1959–62; Travelling Sec., subsequently Nat. Sec., Colls of Educn Christian Union, Inter-Varsity Fellowship, London, 1962–68. Methodist Minister, 1971–: Chaplain Hunmanby Hall Sch., Filey, 1971–74; Minister, Endike Hall and Thornton Hall, 1974–77; New Testament Tutor, Cliff Coll., Sheffield, 1977–86; Superintendent Minister, Longton Central Hall, Stoke-on-Trent, 1986–88; Divl Sec. 1988–89, Dep. Gen. Sec. 1989–95, Home Mission Div. Member: World Methodist Council, Nairobi, 1986, Singapore, 1991; World Methodist Exec. Cttee, Bulgaria, 1992, Estonia, 1994. Has served on numerous Methodist cttees. *Publications:* (ed) Methods of Mission, 1979; Evangelism in New Testament Practice and Methodist Tradition, 1984; Hymns and Songs for Worship, 1985; Celebrate and Sing, 1991; 20 Things to do in a Decade of Evangelism, 1991; By the Way: six studies in incidental evangelism, 1995; New Creation: a full length musical presentation, 1995; hymns and songs (words and music) and tunes published in a variety of books. *Recreations:* music, literature, travel, walking. *Address:* 1 St Peter's Close, Staines, Middx TW18 2ED. *T:* Staines (01784) 461340.

HOARE, Prof. Charles Antony Richard, (Tony), FRS 1982; James Martin Professor of Computing (formerly Professor of Computation), Oxford University, since 1977; Fellow of Wolfson College, since 1977; *b* 11 Jan. 1934; *s* of Henry S. M. Hoare and Marjorie F. Hoare; *m* 1962, Jill Pym; one *s* one *d* (and one *s* decd). *Educ:* King's Sch., Canterbury; Merton Coll., Oxford (MA, Cert. Stats). Computer Div., Elliott Brothers, London, Ltd, 1959–68: successively Programmer, Chief Engr, Tech. Man., Chief Scientist; National Computer Centre, 1968; Prof. of Computer Science, QUB, 1968–77; Dir, Oxford Univ. Computing Lab., 1982–87. Lee Kuan Yew Distinguished Visitor, Singapore, 1992. Dist. FBCS 1978; MAE 1989; For. Mem., Accademia Nazionale dei Lincei, 1988. Hon. DSc: Southern California, 1979; Warwick, 1985; Pennsylvania, 1986; Belfast, 1987; York, 1989; Essex 1991; Bath, 1993. A. M. Turing Award, Assoc. Comp. Mach., 1980; Harry Goode Meml Award, Amer. Fedn of Inf. Processing Socs, 1981; Faraday Medal, IEE, 1985. *Publications:* Structured Programming (with O.-J. Dahl and E. W. Dijkstra), 1972; Communicating Sequential Processes, 1985; Essays in Computing Science, 1988; articles in Computer Jl, Commun. ACM, and Acta Informatica. *Recreations:* walking, swimming, reading, listening to music. *Address:* 8–11 Keble Road, Oxford OX1 3QD. *T:* Oxford (01865) 273841.

HOARE, Henry Cadogan; Chairman and Chief Executive, C. Hoare & Co., Bankers, since 1988; *b* 23 Nov. 1931; *s* of late Henry Peregrine Rennie Hoare and of Lady Beatrix Fanshawe, *d* of 6th Earl Cadogan, CBE; *m* 1st, 1959, Pamela Bunbury (marr. diss. 1970); two *s* one *d*; 2nd, 1977, Caromy Maxwell Macdonald. *Educ:* Eton; Trinity Coll., Cambridge (MA). Career in banking. *Address:* c/o C. Hoare & Co., 37 Fleet Street, EC4P 4DQ.

HOARE, John Michael; independent consultant, health services management, since 1990; *b* 23 Oct. 1932; *s* of Leslie Frank Hoare and Gladys Hoare; *m* 1963, Brita Hjalte; one *s* one *d*. *Educ:* Raynes Park; Christ's Coll., Cambridge (BA). Asst Sec., United Bristol Hosps, 1961; House Governor, St Stephen's Hosp., 1963; Asst Clerk, St Thomas' Hosp., 1965; Administrator, Northwick Park Hosp., 1967; Wessex Regional Health Authority: Administrator, 1974–84; Gen. Man., 1984–89; Quality Advr, 1989–90. Mem., Defence Medical Services Inquiry, 1971–73. *Recreations:* reading, walking, music, squash. *Address:* 24 Clausentum Road, Winchester, Hants SO23 9QE. *T:* Winchester (01962) 54192.

HOARE, Hon. Marcus Bertram, CMG 1965; Justice of Supreme Court of Queensland, 1966–80; *b* 3 March 1910; *s* of John George and Emma Hoare; *m* 1936, Eileen Parker; four *s*. *Educ:* Brisbane Grammar Sch. Solicitor, 1933; Barrister-at-Law, 1944; QC (Australia) 1960. *Address:* 13 Mortlake Road, Graceville, Brisbane, Qld 4068, Australia. *T:* (7) 33794181.

HOARE, Sir Peter Richard David, 8th Bt *cr* 1786; *b* 22 March 1932; *s* of Sir Peter William Hoare, 7th Bt, and Laura Ray (*d* 1992), *o d* of Sir John Esplen, 1st Bt, KBE; *S* father, 1973; *m* 1st, 1961, Jane (marr. diss. 1967), *o d* of late Daniel Orme; 2nd, 1978, Katrin Alexa, Lady Hodson (marr. diss. 1982), *o d* of late Erwin Bernstiel; 3rd, 1983, Angela Francesca de la Sierra, *d* of late Fidel Fernando Ayarza. *Educ:* Eton. *Recreations:* travelling, shooting, skiing. *Heir:* *b* David John Hoare [*b* 8 Oct. 1935; *m* 1st, 1965, Mary Vanessa (marr. diss. 1978), *y d* of Peter Gordon Cardew; one *s*; 2nd, 1984, Virginia Victoria Graham Labes, *d* of late Michael Menzies]. *Address:* c/o Crèdit Andorrà, Avinguda Princep Benlloch 25, Andorra la Vella, Principality of Andorra. *Club:* Royal Automobile.

HOARE, Rt. Rev. Rupert William Noel; *see* Dudley, Suffragan Bishop of.

HOARE, Sir Timothy Edward Charles, 8th Bt *cr* 1784; Director: Career Plan Ltd, since 1970; New Metals and Chemicals Ltd, since 1968; *b* 11 Nov. 1934; *s* of Sir Edward O'Bryen Hoare, 7th Bt and of Nina Mary, *d* of late Charles Nugent Hope-Wallace, MBE; *S* father, 1969; *m* 1969, Felicity Anne, *o d* of late Peter Boddington; one *s* twin *d*. *Educ:* Radley College; Worcester College, Oxford (MA Modern Hist.); Birkbeck Coll., London (MA Manpower Studies). FLS 1980; FZS 1982. Dir, World Vision of Britain, 1983–95. Member: Gen. Synod of Church of England, 1970– (Chairman: Law of Marriage Gp; Clergy Conditions of Service Steering Gp); Chadwick Commn on Church and State, 1970; Crown Appointments Commn, 1987–92. Treas., dio. of London, 1994–. Deleg., WCC, Canberra, 1991. *Heir:* *s* Charles James Hoare, *b* 15 March 1971. *Address:* 10 Belitha Villas, N1 1PD. *Clubs:* National, MCC.

HOARE, Tony; *see* Hoare, C. A. R.

HOBAN, Brian Michael Stanislaus; Head Master of Harrow, 1971–81; *b* 7 Oct. 1921; 2nd *s* of late Capt. R. A. Hoban; *m* 1947, Jasmine, 2nd *d* of J. C. Holmes, MC, Charterhouse, Godalming; one *s* one *d* (and one *d* decd). *Educ:* Charterhouse (Scholar); University Coll., Oxford (Sch.). 2nd Cl. Hon. Mods, 1947; 2nd Cl. Lit. Hum., 1949; BA 1949, MA 1957. Served War of 1939–45: Capt., Westminster Dragoons; NW Europe, 1944–45 (despatches); demobilised, Nov. 1945. Capt. Northants Yeomanry, TA, 1950–56. Asst Master: Uppingham Sch., 1949–52; Shrewsbury Sch., 1952–59; Headmaster, St Edmund's Sch., Canterbury, 1960–64; Head Master, Bradfield Coll., 1964–71. Pt-time Chm., CSSBs, 1984–91. Hon. Associate Mem., HMC, 1981– (Hon. Treasurer, 1975–80). Sometime Mem., Central Adv. Bd, RAF Coll., Cranwell; Governor: Wellington Coll., 1981–92; St Edmund's Sch., Canterbury, 1975–; St Margaret's Sch., Bushey, 1975–. JP Berks, 1967–71. *Publication:* (with Donald Swann) Jesu Parvule, 1965. *Recreations:* music, cooking, watching amateur cricket, walking, gardening. *Address:* Upcot, Wantage Road, Streatley, Berks RG8 9LD. *T:* Goring-on-Thames (01491) 873419. *Clubs:* East India, Devonshire, Sports and Public Schools; Vincent's (Oxford).

HOBAN, Russell Conwell, FRSL 1988; writer; *b* 4 Feb. 1925; *s* of Abram Hoban and Jenny Dimmerman; *m* 1st, 1944, Lillian Aberman (marr. diss. 1975); one *s* three *d*; 2nd, 1975, Gundula Ahl; three *s*. *Educ:* Lansdale High Sch.; Philadelphia Museum Sch. of Industrial Art. Served US Army, 1943–45: 339th Inf., 85th Div., Italy (Bronze Star Medal, 1945). Various jobs, 1945–56; free-lance illustration, 1956–65; copywriter with Doyle, Dane, Bernbach, New York, 1965–67; resident in London, 1969–. Drama: (television) Come and Find Me, 1980; (stage) The Carrier Frequency, 1984; opera: The Second Mrs Kong (music by Sir Harrison Birtwistle), Glyndebourne, 1994. *Publications: children's books:* What Does It Do and How Does It Work?, 1959; The Atomic Submarine, 1960; Bedtime for Frances, 1960; Herman the Loser, 1961; The Song in My Drum, 1962; London Men and English Men, 1963; Some Snow Said Hello, 1963; A Baby Sister for Frances, 1964; Nothing To Do, 1964; Bread and Jam for Frances, 1964; The Sorely Trying Day, 1964; Tom and the Two Handles, 1965; The Story of Hester Mouse, 1965; What Happened When Jack and Daisy Tried To Fool the Tooth Fairies, 1965; Goodnight, 1966; Henry and the Monstrous Din, 1966; Charlie the Tramp, 1966; The Little Brute Family, 1966; Save My Place, 1967; The Mouse and His Child, 1967; The Pedalling Man and Other Poems, 1968, 2nd edn 1991; The Stone Doll of Sister Brute, 1968; A Birthday for Frances, 1968; Ugly Bird, 1969; Best Friends for Frances, 1969; Harvey's Hideout, 1969; The Mole Family's Christmas, 1969; A Bargain for Frances, 1970; Emmet Otter's Jug-Band Christmas, 1971; Egg Thoughts and Other Frances Songs, 1972; The Sea-Thing Child, 1972; Letitia Rabbit's String Song, 1973; How Tom Beat Captain Najork and His Hired Sportsmen, 1974 (Whitbread Literary Award); Ten What?, 1974; Dinner at Alberta's, 1975; Crocodile and Pierrot, 1975; A Near Thing for Captain Najork, 1975; The Twenty-Elephant Restaurant, 1977; Arthur's New Power, 1978; The Dancing Tigers, 1979; La Corona and Other Tin Tales, 1979; Ace Dragon Ltd, 1980; Flat Cat, 1980; The Serpent Tower, 1981; The Great Fruit Gum Robbery, 1981; They Came from Aargh!, 1981; The Flight of Bembel Rudzuk, 1982; The Battle of Zormla, 1982; Jim Frog, 1983; Big John Turkle, 1983; Charlie Meadows, 1984; Lavinia Bat, 1984; The Rain Door, 1986; The Marzipan Pig, 1986; Ponders, 1988; Monsters, 1989; Jim Hedgehog's Supernatural Christmas, 1989; Jim Hedgehog and the Lonesome Tower, 1990; M.O.L.E. (Much Overworked Little Earthmover), 1993; The Court of the Winged Serpent, 1994; *novels:* The Lion of Boaz-Jachin and Jachin-Boaz, 1973; Kleinzeit, 1974; Turtle Diary, 1975 (filmed, 1985); Riddley Walker, 1980 (John W. Campbell Meml Award, 1981, Best Internat. Fiction, Aust. Sci. Fiction Achievement Award, 1983; adapted for stage, 1986); Pilgermann, 1983; The Medusa Frequency, 1987; *verse:* contribs to Six of the Best (ed A. Harvey), 1989; *anthology:* The Moment Under the Moment, 1992; stories and essays in Fiction Magazine and Granta. *Recreation:* rewriting yesterday's pages. *Address:* David Higham Associates Ltd, 5–8 Lower John Street, Golden Square, W1R 4HA. *T:* 0171–437 7888, *Fax:* 0171–437 1072.

HOBART (Australia), Archbishop of, (RC), since 1988; **Most Rev. Eric D'Arcy;** *b* 25 April 1924; *s* of late Joseph D'Arcy, MM and Eileen (*née* McCoy). *Educ:* De La Salle Coll. and Corpus Christi Coll., Melbourne; Univs of Melbourne (BA Hons; MA), Oxford (DPhil), and Gregoriana (PhD). Asst priest, Melbourne, 1949–55; Chaplain, Nat. Civic Council, 1955–59; Lectr, 1962, Sen. Lectr, 1966, Reader in Philosophy, 1975–81, Univ. of Melbourne; Bishop of Sale, 1981–88. Danforth Prof of Philosophy, Univ. of Minnesota, 1968. Member: Vatican Pontifical Congregation for Bishops, 1993–; Pontifical Congregation for Catholic Educn, 1989–94; Pontifical Commn for Cultural Heritage of the Church, 1994–. *Publications:* Conscience, Right to Freedom, 1961 (trans. Spanish 1964, French 1965); Human Acts, 1963; (ed and trans.) St Thomas Aquinas, Pleasure, 1967, The Emotions, 1975. *Recreations:* walking, reading. *Address:* Mount St Canice, GPO Box 62A, Hobart, Tas 7001, Australia. *T:* (02) 251920. *Clubs:* United Oxford & Cambridge University; University House (Melbourne).

HOBART, Sir John Vere, 4th Bt *cr* 1914, of Langdown, Co. Southampton; *b* 9 April 1945; *s* of Lt-Comdr Sir Robert Hampden Hobart, 3rd Bt, RN and Sylvia (*d* 1965), *d* of Harry Argo; *heir-pres.* to Earl of Buckinghamshire, *qv*; *S* father, 1988; *m* 1980, Kate, *o d* of late George Henry Iddles; two *s*. *Heir:* *s* George Hampden Hobart, *b* 10 June 1982. *Address:* 63 Queens Road, Cowes, Isle of Wight PO31 8BW.

HOBART-HAMPDEN, family name of **Earl of Buckinghamshire.**

HOBBS, Prof. Frederick David Richard, FRCGP; Professor and Head of Department of General Practice, since 1992, Assistant Dean, School of Medicine, since 1993, University of Birmingham; *b* 2 Nov. 1953; *s* of Frederick Derek Hobbs and Nancy Elizabeth (*née* Wilde); *m* 1977, Jane Marilyn Porter; one *s* one *d*. *Educ:* King Edward VI Camp Hill Sch., Birmingham; Bristol Univ. (MB, ChB 1977). MRCGP 1981, FRCGP 1990. House officer posts, Bath Royal United Hosp., 1977–78; Sen. house officer posts, Selly Oak Hosp., Birmingham, 1978–80; GP trainee, Univ. Health Centre, Birmingham, 1980–81; Principal in general practice, Bellevue Med. Centre, Birmingham, 1981– (part-time, 1992–); part-time Sen. Lectr in General Practice, Univ. of Birmingham, 1985–92. *Publications:* (with M. Drury) Treatment and Prognosis in General Practice, 1990; (with B. Stillwell): Nursing in general practice, 1990; Practice Nurse Programme, 1990; (with M. Barrowcliffe) Managing practice information, 1992; (with L. Beeley) Treatment: a handbook of drug therapy, 1993; contrib. jls incl. BMJ, Brit. Jl Gen. Pract., Archives of Disease in Childhood, Gut, Jl RSM. *Recreations:* gardening, travel, interests in music (passive), wine and good food. *Address:* Department of General Practice, University of Birmingham, Edgbaston, Birmingham B15 2TT. *T:* 0121–414 6764.

HOBBS, Herbert Harry, CB 1956; CVO 1972; Director, Ancient Monuments and Historic Buildings, 1970–72, retired; *b* 7 Nov. 1912; *s* of late Bertie Hobbs and Agnes Dora (*née* Clarke); *m* 1937, Joan Hazel Timmins (*d* 1979); two *s* one *d*. *Educ:* Bedford Sch.; Corpus Christi Coll., Oxford. Entered War Office, 1935; Comptroller of Lands and Claims, 1956–60; Asst Under-Sec. of State (Works), War Office, 1960–63; Under-Sec., MPBW, later DoE, 1963–72. Medal of Freedom with bronze palm (USA), 1946. *Recreations:* music, gardening. *Address:* 9 Hemp Garden, Minehead, Som TA24 5JG. *T:* Minehead (01643) 705350.

HOBBS, John Charles; Chief Insurance Officer, Department of Health and Social Security, 1971–76; *b* 28 May 1917; British; *m* 1961, Doris Gronow. *Educ:* Portsmouth Southern Grammar Sch.; Portsmouth Coll. of Technology. 1st cl. hons BSc, 1936; 1st cl. hons BSc (Spec.) Maths, 1944. FIS 1950. Asst Principal, 1946; Principal, 1947; Asst Sec., 1957.

HOBBS, Rev. Canon Keith; Archdeacon of Chichester, 1981–91; Canon Residentiary of Chichester Cathedral, 1981–91, now Canon Emeritus; *b* 3 March 1925; *s* of late Percival Frank and Gwennyth Mary Hobbs; *m* 1950, Mary, *d* of late Louis Lingg and Mary Elizabeth Ruderman; one *s* (and one *s* one *d* decd). *Educ:* St Olave's Grammar School; Exeter Coll., Oxford (MA); Wells Theological Coll. Instr Branch, RN, 1946; retired (Lt Comdr), 1956. Curate, Clewer St Stephen, 1958–60; Soho, 1960–62; St Stephen, S Kensington, 1962–78; Lectr and Co-ordinator of Counselling, Borough Road Coll., 1964–77; Actg Gen. Secretary, Church Union, 1977–78; Chaplain to Bishop of Chichester, 1978–81. *Address:* 10 St Martin's Square, Chichester, W Sussex PO19 1NR. *T:* Chichester (01243) 784260.

HOBBS, Prof. Kenneth Edward Frederick, ChM, FRCS; Professor of Surgery, Royal Free Hospital School of Medicine, University of London, and Consultant Surgeon, Royal Free Hampstead NHS Trust (formerly Royal Free Hospital), since 1973; Chairman, Joint Board of Surgery, University College London Medical School and Royal Free Hospital School of Medicine, since 1993; Dean, University of London Faculty of Medicine, since 1994; *b* 28 Dec. 1936; *s* of late Thomas Edward Ernest Hobbs and Gladys May Hobbs (*née* Neave). *Educ:* West Suffolk County Grammar Sch., Bury St Edmunds; Guy's Hosp. Med. Sch., Univ. of London (MB BS 1960). ChM Bristol 1970; FRCS 1964. Lectr in Surgery, Univ. of Bristol, 1966–70; Surgical Res. Fellow, Harvard Univ., 1968–69; Sen. Lectr in Surgery, Univ. of Bristol, 1970–73; University of London: Vice-Dean, Faculty of Medicine, 1986–90; Mem. Senate, 1985–; Chm., Acad. Adv. Bd in Medicine, 1986–90; Dep. Chm., Acad. Council Standing Sub-Cttee in Medicine, 1986–90. Mem., Systems Bd, MRC, 1982–86; Chm., Grants Cttee A, MRC, 1984–86; Member: Med. Sub-Cttee, UGC, 1986–89; Med. Cttee, UFC, 1991–92; Mason Med. Res. Foundn, 1988– (Chm., 1993–). Vis. Prof., Univs in China, Ethiopia, S Africa, Europe, USA, West Indies. Secretary: Patey Soc., 1979–82; 1942 Club, 1985–88; Trustee and Bd Mem., Stanley Thomas Johnson Foundn, Berne, 1976–. *Publications:* chapters on aspects of liver surgery in textbooks; contribs to professional jls. *Recreations:* gourmet dining, the countryside. *Address:* The Rookery, New Buckenham, Norfolk NR16 2AE. *T:* East Harling (01953) 860558. *Club:* Athenæum.

HOBBS, Maj.-Gen. Michael Frederick, CBE 1982 (OBE 1979, MBE 1975); Director, Duke of Edinburgh's Award, since 1988; *b* 28 Feb. 1937; *s* of late Brig. Godfrey Pennington Hobbs and Elizabeth Constance Mary Hobbs; *m* 1967, Tessa Mary Churchill; one *s* two *d*. *Educ:* Eton College. Served Grenadier Guards, 1956–80; Directing Staff, Staff Coll., 1974–77; MoD, 1980–82; Commander 39 Inf. Bde, 1982–84; Dir of PR (Army), 1984–85; Commander, 4th Armoured Div., 1985–87; retired. *Recreations:* field sports, horticulture. *Address:* (office) Gulliver House, Madeira Walk, Windsor, Berks SL4 1EU. *T:* Windsor (01753) 810753. *Club:* MCC.

HOBDAY, Sir Gordon (Ivan), Kt 1979; Lord Lieutenant and Keeper of the Rolls for Nottinghamshire, 1983–91; Chancellor, Nottingham University, 1979–92 (President of the Council, 1973–82); *b* 1 Feb. 1916; *e s* of late Alexander Thomas Hobday and Frances Cassandra (*née* Meads); *m* 1940, Margaret Jean Joule; one *d*. *Educ:* Long Eaton Grammar Sch.; UC Nottingham. BSc, PhD London; FRSC. Joined Boots Co., 1939; Dir of Research, 1952–68; Man. Dir, 1970–72; Chm., 1973–81; Chm., Central Independent Television, 1981–85; Dir, Lloyds Bank, 1981–86. A Dep. Chm., Price Commn, 1977–78. Pres., Portland Trng Coll., 1990–93. DL Notts, 1981. KStJ 1983. Hon. LLD Nottingham, 1977. *Recreations:* handicrafts, gardening. *Address:* Newstead Abbey Park, Nottingham NG15 8GD.

HOBDEN, Reginald Herbert, DFC 1944; HM Diplomatic Service, retired; *b* 9 Nov. 1919; *s* of William Richard and Ada Emily Hobden; *m* 1945, Gwendoline Ilma Vowles; two *s* one *d*. *Educ:* Sir William Borlase's Sch., Marlow. Apptd Colonial Office, Dec. 1936. Served War of 1939–45 (despatches, DFC): RAFVR, Sept. 1940–Jan. 1946 (Sqdn Ldr). Returned to Colonial Office, 1946; seconded to Dept of Technical Co-operation, 1961; First Sec., UK Commn, Malta, 1962–64; HM Diplomatic Service, Nov. 1964: CRO until April 1968; Head of British Interests Section, Canadian High Commn, Dar es Salaam, April 1968; British Acting High Comr, Dar es Salaam, July–Oct. 1968, and Counsellor, Dar es Salaam, Oct. 1968–69; Counsellor (Economic and Commercial), Islamabad, 1970–75; Inst. of Develt Studies, Sussex Univ., 1975; High Comr, Lesotho, 1976–78. Clerk in Clerk's Dept, House of Commons, 1978–84. *Recreations:* chess, bridge. *Address:* 14 Belmont Close, Uxbridge, Mddx UB8 1RF. *T:* Uxbridge (01895) 234754.

HOBHOUSE, Sir Charles (John Spinney), 7th Bt *cr* 1812, of Broughton-Gifford, Bradford-on-Avon and of Monkton Farleigh, Wiltshire; *b* 27 Oct. 1962; *s* of Sir Charles Chisholm Hobhouse, 6th Bt, TD and of Elspeth Jean, *yr d* of late Thomas George Spinney; *S* father, 1991; *m* 1993, Katrina, *d* of Maj.-Gen. Sir Denzil Macarthur-Onslow, CBE, DSO and of Lady Macarthur-Onslow. *Heir: uncle* John Spencer Hobhouse [*b* 15 Nov. 1910; *m* 1940, Mary, *yr d* of late Llewelyn Robert, MD]. *Address:* Monkton Farleigh Manor, Bradford-on-Avon, Wilts BA15 2QE.

HOBHOUSE, Rt. Hon. Sir John Stewart, Kt 1982; PC 1993; **Rt. Hon. Lord Justice Hobhouse;** a Lord Justice of Appeal, since 1993. *Educ:* Christ Church, Oxford (BCL 1958; MA 1958). Called to the Bar, Inner Temple, 1955; QC 1973; a Judge of the High Court, Queen's Bench Div., 1982–93. *Address:* Royal Courts of Justice, Strand, WC2A 2LL.

HOBHOUSE, (Mary) Hermione, MBE 1981; FSA; writer and conservationist; General Editor, Survey of London, 1983–94; *d* of late Sir Arthur Lawrence Hobhouse and Konradin, *d* of Rt Hon. Frederick Huth Jackson; *m* 1958, Henry Trevenen Davidson Graham (marr. diss. 1988); one *s* one *d*. *Educ:* Ladies' Coll., Cheltenham; Lady Margaret Hall, Oxford (Hons Mod. Hist.). Researcher/Writer, Associated-Rediffusion TV and Granada TV, 1957–65; Tutor in Architectural History, Architectural Assoc. Sch., London, 1973–78; Sec., Victorian Soc., 1977–82. Member: Royal Commn for Exhibn of 1851, 1983–; Council, Nat. Trust, 1983–; Council, Soc. of Antiquaries, 1984–87; London DAC, 1988–. *Publications:* Thomas Cubitt: Master Builder, 1971 (Hitchcock Medal, 1972); Lost London, 1971; History of Regent Street, 1975; Oxford and Cambridge, 1980; Prince Albert: his life and work, 1983; (ed) Survey of London, vol. 42, Southern Kensington: Kensington Square to Earls Court, 1986, vol. 17, County Hall, 1991, vols 42 and 43, Poplar, Blackwall and the Isle of Dogs, 1994; London Survey'd: the work of the Survey of London 1894–1994, 1994; contrib. Architectural Jl, Architectural Review. *Recreations:* gardening, looking at buildings of all periods. *Address:* 61 St Dunstan's Road, W6 8RE. *T:* 0181–741 2575. *Club:* Reform.

HOBHOUSE, Penelope, (Mrs John Malins); gardener, garden writer and garden consultant, since 1976; *b* 20 Nov. 1929; *d* of late Captain J. J. L.-C. Chichester-Clark, DSO and Bar, MP and Marion Chichester-Clark (later Mrs C. E. Brackenbury); *m* 1st, 1952, Paul Hobhouse (marr. diss. 1982); two *s* one *d*; 2nd, 1983, Prof. John Malins (*d* 1992). *Educ:* Girton Coll., Cambridge (BA Hons Econs, 1951). National Trust tenant of Tintinhull House garden, 1980–93. *Publications:* The Country Gardener, 1976, revd edn 1989; The Smaller Garden, 1981; Gertrude Jekyll on Gardening, 1983; Colour in your Garden, 1985; The National Trust: A Book of Gardening, 1986; Private Gardens of England, 1986; Garden Style, 1988; Painted Gardens, 1988; Borders, 1989; The Gardens of Europe, 1990; Flower Gardens, 1991; Plants in Garden History, 1992; Penelope Hobhouse on Gardening, 1994. *Recreations:* reading Trollope and Henry James, Italy. *Address:* The Coach House, Bettiscombe, Bridport, Dorset DT6 5NT.

See also Sir R. Chichester-Clark, Baron Moyola.

HOBKIRK, Michael Dalgliesh; *b* 9 Dec. 1924; *s* of Roy and Phyllis Hobkirk; *m* 1952, Lucy Preble; two *d*. *Educ:* Marlborough Coll.; Wadham Coll., Oxford. BA (Social Studies), MA 1949. Served War of 1939–45: Army (RAC, RAEC, Captain), 1943–47. Civil Service: War Office, 1949–63; MoD, 1963–70; Directing Staff, Nat. Defence Coll., 1970–74; Brookings Instn, Washington, DC, USA, 1974–75; Lord Chancellor's Dept, 1975–80 (Principal Establishment and Finance Officer, 1977–80); Asst Under-Sec. of State, MoD, 1980–82. Sen. Fellow, Nat. Defense Univ., Washington, DC, USA, 1982–83. *Publication:* (contrib.) The Management of Defence (ed L. Martin), 1976; The Politics of Defence Budgeting, 1984; Land, Sea or Air?, 1992. *Address:* 48 Woodside Avenue, Beaconsfield, Bucks HP9 1JH. *Club:* United Oxford & Cambridge University.

HOBLER, Air Vice-Marshal John Forde, CB 1958; CBE 1943; *b* Rockhampton, Qld, Australia, 26 Sept. 1907; *s* of late L. E. Hobler, Rockhampton; *m* 1939, Dorothy Evelyn Diana Haines, Wilsford, Wilts; two *s* one *d*. *Educ:* Rockhampton, Qld. Served whole of War of 1939–45 in Bomber Command; commanded RAF Lossiemouth; Palestine, 1945; Staff Coll., 1946–48; Air Ministry, 1948–50; Comd Habbaniya, Iraq, 1950–52; HQ Flying Trg Comd, 1952–54; Air Ministry, 1954–56; AO i/c Administration, Middle East Air Force, 1956–58; Air Officer Commanding No 25 Gp, 1958–61; Air Officer i/c Administration, Far East Air Force, 1961–63, retd. Mem., RAF Escaping Soc.; Founder Mem., Central Queensland Aero Club, 1929–. FRGS. *Address:* Unit P8, The Domain Country Club, 74 Wardoo Street, Ashmore, Qld 4214, Australia. *Club:* United Services (Brisbane).

HOBLEY, Brian, FSA; historical and archaeological researcher and writer; Director, Hobley Archaeological Consultancy Services Ltd, 1989–92; *b* 25 June 1930; *s* of William Hobley and Harriet (*née* Hobson); *m* (marr. diss. 1992); one *s* one *d*; partner, Dr Elizabeth Greene. *Educ:* Univ. of Leicester (BA Hons 1965); Univ. of Oxford (MSt 1994). FSA 1969; AMA 1970. Field Officer, Coventry Corp., 1965; Keeper, Dept Field Archaeology, Coventry Museum, 1970; Chief Urban Archaeologist, City of London, 1973–89. Lectr, Birmingham Univ. Extra-mural Dept, 1965–74. Chm. Standing Cttee, Arch. Unit Managers, 1986–89; Jt Sec., British Archaeologists and Developers Liaison Gp, 1986–89. MBIM 1978; MIFA 1982. *Publications:* (ed jtly) Waterfront Archaeology in Britain and Northern Europe, 1981; Roman Urban Defences in the West, 1983; Roman Urban Topography in Britain and the Western Empire, 1985; Roman and Saxon London: a reappraisal, 1986; British Archaeologists and Developers Code of Practice, 1986; The Rebirth of Towns in the West AD 700–1050, 1988; reports in learned jls incl. Proc. 7th, 8th, 9th and 12th Internat. Congresses of Roman Frontier Studies, Tel Aviv, Univ. Israel and Bucharest Univ., Rumania on excavations and reconstructions at The Lunt Roman fort, Baginton near Coventry. *Recreations:* classical music, chess. *Address:* 4 Farm Court, Church Road, Weston-on-the-Green, Oxon OX6 8FH.

HOBMAN, David Burton, CBE 1983; Director, Age Concern England (National Old People's Welfare Council), 1970–87; *b* 8 June 1927; *s* of J. B. and D. L. Hobman; *m* 1954, Erica Irwin; one *s* one *d*. *Educ:* University College Sch.; Blundell's. Community work, Forest of Dean, 1954–56; British Council for Aid to Refugees, 1957; Nat. Council of Social Service, 1958–67; Visiting Lectr in Social Admin, Nat. Inst. for Social Work, 1967; Dir, Social Work Adv. Service, 1968–70. Vis. Prof., Sch. of Social Work, McGill Univ., Montreal, 1977; Vis. Fellow, Univ. of Sussex, 1994–July 1996. Member: BBC/ITA Appeals Adv. Council, 1965–69; Steering Cttee, Enquiry into Homelessness, Nat. Asstce Bd, 1967–68; Adv. Council, Nat. Corp. for Care of Old People, 1970–74; Metrication Bd, 1974–80; Lord Goodman's Cttee Reviewing Law of Charity, 1975–76; Chairman: Social Welfare Commn Conf. of Bishops, 1968–71; Family Housing Assoc., 1969–70; Oftel Adv. Cttee for Disabled and Elderly Persons, 1984–92; Home Concern Housing Assoc., 1985–87; Jt Chm., Age Concern Inst. of Gerontology, KCL, 1986–87; Consultant, UN Div. of Social Affairs, 1968–69; Observer, White House Congress on Ageing, 1971–; Pres., Internat. Fedn on Ageing, 1977–80, 1983–87 (Vice-Pres., 1974–77); Member: Personal Social Services Council, 1978–80; Exec. Cttee, Nat. Council of Voluntary Orgns, 1981–83; Anchor Housing, 1984–86; Exec. Sec., Charities Effectiveness Review Trust, 1987–92. Producer, Getting On (television programme), 1987–88. Special Advr, British delegn to World Assembly on Ageing, 1982. Mem. Adv. Bd, Saga Magazine, 1985–; Dir, Cinetel Ltd. Governor: Newman Comp. Sch., Hove, 1971–76 (Chm); Volunteer Centre, 1975–79; Conciliator, Sheltered Housing Adv. and Conciliation Service, 1990–94; Counsellor, Helen Hamlyn Foundn, 1991–; Company Ombudsman, Peverel Gp, 1995–. KSG. *Publications:* A Guide to Voluntary Service, 1964, 2nd edn 1967; Who Cares, 1971; The Social Challenge of Ageing, 1978; The Impact of Ageing, 1981; The Coming of Age, 1989; Planning Your Retirement, 1990; Intergenerational Solidarity—fact and fiction, 1993; (with Dorothy Jerrome) The More We Are Together: a study of partnerships in later life, 1995; numerous papers, broadcasts. *Recreations:* caravanning, travel, grandchildren. *Address:* Robinswood, George's Lane, Storrington, Pulborough, W Sussex RH20 3JH. *T:* Storrington (01903) 742987. *Club:* Reform.

HOBSBAWM, Prof. Eric John Ernest, FBA 1976; Emeritus Professor of Economic and Social History, University of London, since 1982; *b* 9 June 1917; *s* of Leopold Percy Hobsbawm and Nelly Grün; *m* 1962, Marlene Schwarz; one *s* one *d*. *Educ:* Vienna; Berlin; St Marylebone Grammar Sch.; Univ. of Cambridge (BA, PhD). Lectr, Birkbeck Coll., 1947; Fellow, King's Coll., Cambridge, 1949–55, Hon. Fellow, 1973; Reader, Birkbeck Coll., 1959, Prof., 1970–82. Hon. DPhil Univ. of Stockholm, 1970; Hon. Dr Hum. Let.: Univ. of Chicago, 1976; New Sch. of Social Res., 1982; Bard Coll., 1986; Hon. LittD: UEA, 1982; York Univ., Canada, 1986; Hon. DLit London, 1993; D*hc* Univ. of Pisa, 1987. Foreign Hon. Mem., American Academy of Arts and Sciences, 1971; Hon. Mem., Hungarian Acad. of Sciences, 1979. Palmes Académiques, France, 1993. *Publications:*

Labour's Turning Point, 1948; Primitive Rebels, 1959; (*pseud.* F. Newton) The Jazz Scene, 1959; The Age of Revolution, 1962; Labouring Men, 1964; (ed) Karl Marx, Precapitalist Formations, 1964; Industry and Empire, 1968; (with G. Rudé) Captain Swing, 1969; Bandits, 1969; Revolutionaries, 1973; The Age of Capital, 1975; (with T. Ranger) The Invention of Tradition, 1983; Worlds of Labour, 1984; The Age of Empire, 1987; Politics for a Rational Left, 1989; Nations and Nationalism since 1780, 1990; Echoes of the Marseillaise, 1990; Age of Extremes: the short Twentieth Century, 1994; contribs to jls. *Recreation:* travel. *Address:* Birkbeck College, Malet Street, WC1E 7HX. *T:* 0171–580 6622.

HOBSLEY, Prof. Michael, TD 1969; PhD; FRCS; David Patey Professor of Surgery, University of London, 1986–94 (Professor of Surgery, 1984–94); Head, Department of Surgery, University College and Middlesex School of Medicine, University College London, 1984–93; *b* 18 Jan. 1929; *s* of Henry Hobsley and Sarah Lily Blanchfield; *m* 1953, Jane Fairlie Cambell; one *s* three *d. Educ:* La Martinière Coll., Calcutta; Sidney Sussex Coll., Cambridge (MA, MB, MChir); Middlesex Hosp. Med. Sch. PhD London, 1961; DSc London, 1989. FRCS 1958. Training posts in RAMC and at Middlesex, Whittington and Chace Farm Hosps, 1951–68; Comyns Berkeley Fellow, Gonville and Caius Coll., Cambridge and Mddx Hosp. Med. Sch., 1965–66; posts at Mddx Hosp. and Med. Sch., 1968–88: Hon. Consultant Surgeon, 1969–94; Reader in Surgical Science, 1970–75; Prof. of Surg. Science, 1975–83; Dir, Dept of Surgical Studies, 1983–88. Howard C. Naffziger Surg. Res. Fellow, Univ. of Calif, 1966; Windermere Foundn Travelling Prof. of Surgery, 1984; Glaxo Visitor, Univ. of Witwatersrand, 1985; Vis. Professor: Univ. of Calif, 1980; Univ. of Khartoum, 1976; McMaster Univ., 1982; Monash Univ., 1984; Univ. of Louisville, 1995. Non-exec. Mem., Enfield HA, 1990–93. Pres., British Soc. of Gastroenterology, 1992–93; Chm., Assoc. of Profs of Surgery, 1990–94. Royal College of Surgeons: Hunterian Prof., 1962–63; Penrose May Tutor, 1973–78; Sir Gordon Taylor Lectr, 1980; Examr, 1968–94. Examiner: Univ. of London, 1978–94; Univ. of Nigeria, 1977–94; Univ. of the WI, 1978–94; Univ. of Bristol, 1986–88; Univ. of Cambridge, 1986–94; St Mary's Hosp. Med. Sch., 1989–91; St George's Hosp. Med. Sch., 1990–93; Univ. of Birmingham, 1992–94; Univ. of Newcastle, 1992–94. Mem., Professional and Linguistics Assessment Bd and Chm., Multiple Choice Questions Panel, 1993–. Hon. Fellow: Assoc. of Surgeons of India, 1983; Amer. Surgical Assoc., 1989. FRSM 1960. *Publications:* Pathways in Surgical Management, 1979, 2nd edn 1986; Disorders of the Digestive System, 1982; Colour Atlas of Parotidectomy, 1983; Physiology in Surgical Practice, 1992; articles in BMJ, Lancet, British Jl of Surgery, Gut, Klinische Wochenschrift. *Recreation:* cricket. *Address:* Fieldside, Barnet Lane, Totteridge, N20 8AS. *T:* 0181–445 6507. *Clubs:* Athenæum, MCC.

HOBSON, Anthony Robert Alwyn, DLitt; FBA 1992; bibliographical historian; *b* 5 Sept. 1921; *s* of Geoffrey Dudley Hobson, MVO and Gertrude Adelaide, *d* of Rev. Thomas Vaughan, Rector of Rhuddlan, Flintshire; *m* 1959, Elena Pauline Tanya (*d* 1988), *d* of Igor Vinogradoff; one *s* two *d. Educ:* Eton Coll. (Oppidan Scholar); New Coll., Oxford (MA); DLitt Oxon, 1992. Served Scots Guards, 1941–46, Captain; Italy, 1943–46 (mentioned in despatches). Joined Sotheby & Co., 1947: Dir, 1949–71, Associate, 1971–77. Sandars Reader in Bibliography, Univ. of Cambridge, 1974–75; Franklin Jasper Walls Lectr, Pierpont Morgan Library, NY, 1979; Vis. Fellow, All Souls Coll., Oxford, 1982–83; Rosenbach Fellow, Univ. of Pennsylvania, 1990; Lyell Reader in Bibliography, Univ. of Oxford, 1990–91. President: Bibliographical Soc., 1977–79; Association internationale de Bibliophilie, 1985–; Hon. Pres., Edinburgh Bibliographical Soc., 1971–; Trustee: Eton Coll. Collections Trust, 1977–; Lambeth Palace Library, 1984–90. Hon. Fellow, Pierpont Morgan Library, 1983; For. Associate, Ateneo Veneto, 1987. Cavaliere Ufficiale, Al Merito della Repubblica Italiana, 1979. *Publications:* French and Italian Collectors and their Bindings, 1953; Great Libraries, 1970; Apollo and Pegasus, 1975; Humanists and Bookbinders, 1989 (Premio Felice Feliciano, Verona, 1991; Triennial Prize, Internat. League of Antiquarian Booksellers, 1991); (with Paul Culot) Italian and French Sixteenth-century Bookbindings, 1990; contrib. The Library, TLS, etc. *Recreations:* travel, opera, visiting libraries founded before 1800. *Address:* The Glebe House, Whitsbury, Fordingbridge, Hants SP6 3QB. *T:* Rockbourne (017253) 221. *Clubs:* Brooks's, Beefsteak, Roxburghe; Grolier (New York).

HOBSON, David Constable, CBE 1991; Chartered Accountant; Partner, Coopers & Lybrand, 1953–84, Senior Partner, 1975–83; *b* 1 Nov. 1922; *s* of late Charles Kenneth and Eileen Isabel Hobson; *m* 1961, Elizabeth Anne Drury; one *s* one *d. Educ:* Marlborough Coll.; Christ's Coll., Cambridge (Scholar). MA. ACA 1950; FCA 1958. Served War, REME, 1942–47 (Captain). Joined Cooper Brothers & Co. (later Coopers & Lybrand), 1947; Mem., Exec. Cttee, Coopers & Lybrand (International), 1973–83. Chairman: Cambrian & General Securities, 1986–89; Fleming High Income Investment Trust, 1991–93 (Dir, 1989–93); Dir, The Laird Gp, 1985–. Inspector (for Dept of Trade), London & County Securities Group Ltd, 1974; Advr, Prime Minister's Policy Unit, 1983–86. Member: Accounting Standards Cttee, 1970–82; City Capital Markets Cttee, 1980–84; Nat. Biological Standards Bd, 1983–88; Building Socs Commn, 1986–92; Board Mem. (repr. UK and Ireland), Internat. Accounting Standards Cttee, 1980–85. Hon. Treasurer, Lister Inst., 1986–. Member of Council: Marlborough Coll., 1967–92 (Chm., 1987–92); Francis Holland Schools, 1975–. *Recreations:* travel, gardening, reading, occasional golf. *Address:* Magnolia, Chiswick Mall, W4 2PR. *T:* 0181–994 7511. *Club:* Reform.

HOBSON, John; Under Secretary, Department of the Environment, since 1986; *b* 30 March 1946; *s* of late John Leslie Hobson and of Beatrice Edith Hobson; *m* 1970, Jeanne Gerrish; one *s* one *d. Educ:* Northampton Grammar Sch.; Manchester Grammar Sch.; King's Coll., Cambridge (MA Mathematics). Joined Min. of Transport, 1967; Asst Private Sec. to Sec. of State for the Environment, 1970–72; Private Sec. to Head of CS, 1974–78; Assistant Secretary: Dept of Transport, 1979–80; DoE, 1980–86. *Address:* Department of the Environment, 2 Marsham Street, SW1P 3EB.

HOBSON, Peter; Headmaster, Charterhouse, 1993–95; *b* 2 Oct. 1944; *er s* of late William Hobson and of Sheila (*née* Surtees); *m* 1976, Amanda Rosemary, *d* of Michael Thomas Emilius Clayton, CB, OBE. *Educ:* Rossall Sch.; Queen's Coll., Oxford (Fletcher Exhibnr; BA LitHum 1967; MA 1972). Wellington College: Classics Dept, 1968–86; Housemaster, 1971–86; Industrial Liaison Officer, 1978–86; Headmaster, Giggleswick Sch., 1986–93. Chm., ISIS N, 1991–93. Schoolmaster Fellow, Queen's Coll., Oxford, 1982. FRSA 1991. *Recreations:* travel, holidays in Cornwall, reading biography, watching sport. *Address:* c/o Charterhouse, Godalming, Surrey GU7 2DJ. *Club:* East India, Devonshire, Sports and Public Schools.

HOBSON, Valerie Babette Louise, (Mrs Profumo); film and stage actress; *b* Larne, Ireland; *d* of Comdr R. G. Hobson, RN, and Violette Hamilton-Willoughby; *m* 1st, 1939, Sir Anthony James Allan Havelock-Allan, Bt (marr. diss. 1952), *qv*; one *s* (and one *s* decd); 2nd, 1954, John Dennis Profumo, *qv*; one *s. Educ:* St Augustine's Priory, London; Royal Academy of Dramatic Art. Was trained from early age to become ballet dancer; first stage appearance at Drury Lane in Ball at the Savoy, aged 15. The King and I, Drury Lane, 1953. First film, Badgers Green; went to Hollywood and appeared in Werewolf of London, Bride of Frankenstein, The Mystery of Edwin Drood, etc; at 18 returned to England. Films include: The Drum, This Man is News, This Man in Paris, The Spy in Black, Q Planes, Silent Battle, Contraband, Unpublished Story, Atlantic Ferry, The Adventures of Tartu, The Years Between, Great Expectations, Blanche Fury, The Small Voice, Kind Hearts and Coronets, Train of Events, Interrupted Journey, The Rocking Horse Winner, The Card, Who Goes There?, Meet Me Tonight, The Voice of Merrill, Background, Knave of Hearts. *Recreations:* listening to music, writing, reading, painting.
See also A. M. D. Havelock-Allan.

HOCHHAUSER, Victor, CBE 1994; impresario; *b* 27 March 1923; *m* 1949, Lilian Hochhauser (*née* Shields); three *s* one *d. Educ:* City of London Coll. Impresario for: David Oistrakh; Sviatoslav Richter; Mstislav Rostropovich; Gilels, Kogan; Margot Fonteyn; Natalia Makarova; Nureyev Festival; Bolshoi Ballet season at Covent Garden, 1963, 1969; Leningrad State Kirov Ballet, Covent Garden, 1961, 1966; Kirov Ballet, 1993, 1995; Birmingham Royal Ballet, 1994–95; concerts, Royal Albert Hall, Barbican and Royal Festival Hall; Peking Opera and other Chinese companies, 1972–; co-presenter, Aida, Earls Court, 1988, Birmingham Arena, 1991. *Recreations:* reading, swimming, sleeping. *Address:* 4 Oak Hill Way, NW3 7LR. *T:* 0171–794 0987.

HOCKADAY, Sir Arthur (Patrick), KCB 1978 (CB 1975); CMG 1969; Secretary and Director-General, Commonwealth War Graves Commission, 1982–89; *b* 17 March 1926; *s* of late William Ronald Hockaday and Marian Camilla Hockaday, *d* of Rev. A. C. Evans; *m* 1955, Peggy, *d* of late H. W. Prince. *Educ:* Merchant Taylors' Sch.; St John's Coll., Oxford. BA (1st cl. Lit. Hum.) 1949, MA 1952. Apptd to Home Civil Service, 1949; Admty, 1949–62; Private Sec. to successive Ministers of Defence and Defence Secretaries, 1962–65; NATO Internat. Staff, 1965–69 (Asst Sec. Gen. for Defence Planning and Policy, 1967–69); Asst Under-Sec. of State, MoD, 1969–72; Under-Sec., Cabinet Office, 1972–73; Dep. Under-Sec. of State, MoD, 1973–76; 2nd Permanent Under-Sec. of State, MoD, 1976–82. Chm., British Group, Council on Christian Approaches to Defence and Disarmament, 1989–. Chm., Gallipoli Meml Lecture Trust, 1990–93. *Publications:* (contrib.) Ethics and Nuclear Deterrence, 1982; The Strategic Defence Initiative, 1985; (contrib.) Ethics and European Security, 1986; (contrib.) Ethics and International Relations, 1986; (contrib.) Just Deterrence, 1990; occasional articles and reviews. *Recreation:* fell-walking. *Address:* 11 Hitherwood Court, Hitherwood Drive, SE19 1UX. *T:* 0181–670 7940. *Clubs:* Naval and Military, Civil Service.

HOCKÉ, Jean-Pierre; international consultant; United Nations High Commissioner for Refugees, 1986–89; *b* 31 March 1938; *s* of Charles and Marie Rose Hocké; *m* 1961, Michèle Marie Weber; two *s. Educ:* Univ. of Lausanne (grad. Econ. and Business Admin). With commercial firms in Switzerland and Nigeria, 1961–67; joined Internat. Cttee of Red Cross, 1968: Hd of Operations Dept, 1973; Mem., Directorate, 1981. Mem., Jean Monnet Foundn, Lausanne, 1984–; Vice-Chm., CASIN (internat. negotiations inst.), Geneva, 1986–; Chm., Bd, InterAssist, Bern, 1990–. Hon. Dr Lausanne, 1987. *Address:* Chemin des Baules, 1268 Begnins, Switzerland. *T:* (22) 3662130.

HOCKENHULL, Arthur James Weston, OBE 1966; HM Diplomatic Service, retired; *b* 8 Aug. 1915; *s* of late Frederick Weston Hockenhull and late Jessie Gibson Kaye Hockenhull (*née* Mitchell); *m* 1955, Rachel Ann Kimber; two *d. Educ:* Clifton Coll.; Exeter Coll., Oxford (MA). HM Overseas Civil Service; various appts in Far East, Cyprus and British Guiana, 1936–57. Interned by Japanese, in Singapore, 1942–45; First Sec., UK Commn, Singapore, 1958–63; Counsellor, British High Commn, Malaysia, 1964–68; HM Consul-Gen., Houston, 1969–74. *Recreations:* golf, gardening, swimming. *Club:* United Oxford & Cambridge University.

HOCKER, Dr Alexander; Grosses Verdienstkreuz mit Stern des Verdienstordens der Bundesrepublik Deutschland, 1973; Director-General, European Space Research Organisation (ESRO), 1971–74; *m* 1940, Liselotte Schulze; five *s* one *d. Educ:* Univs of Innsbruck, Hamburg and Leipzig. Asst, Law Faculty, Leipzig Univ.; County Court Judge; Officer, Advanced Scientific Study Div., Min. of Educn, Hannover, 1947–49; Dep. of Sec.-Gen. of German Res. Assoc. (Deutsche Forschungsgemeinschaft), 1949–56; Ministerialrat and Ministerialdirigent (responsible for res., trng and sci. exchanges), Fed. Min. for Atomic Energy, 1956–61; Mem. Directorate, Nuclear Res. Centre (Kernforschungsanlage) Jülich, 1961–69; Sci. Adviser to Foundn Volkswagenwerk, 1969–71. German Deleg. to CERN, Geneva, 1952–61 (Chm. of Finance Cttee, 1960–61); Chm. of Legal, Admin. and Financial Working Gp of COPERS, 1961–63; Chm. of Council, ESRO, 1965–67 (Vice-Chm. 1964); Member: German Commn for Space Res., 1964–71; Kuratorium Max-Planck-Institut für Physik und Astrophysik, 1968–71; Max-Plank-Institut für Plasmaphysik, 1971–80, Hon. Member 1980–. *Publication:* (jtly) Taschenbuch für Atomfragen, 1968. *Address:* Bad Godesberg, Augustastrasse 63, 53173 Bonn, Germany. *T:* (228) 363961.

HOCKING, Frederick Denison Maurice; formerly Cornwall County Pathologist; Consulting Biologist and Toxicologist, Devon River Board; late Consulting Pathologist, South-Western Regional Hospital Board; Acting Director Public Health Laboratory Service, Cornwall, and other hospitals in Cornwall; late Chemical Pathologist, Biochemist, and Assistant Pathologist, Westminster Hospital; Lecturer in General and Clinical Pathology, Westminster Hospital Medical School, University of London; *b* 28 Feb. 1899; *o s* of late Rev. Almund Trevosso Hocking and Gertrude Vernon Mary, *o d* of J. Parkinson; *m* 1st, 1927, Amy Gladys (*d* 1956), *y d* of A. T. Coucher; one *d*; 2nd, 1957, Kathleen, *e d* of Dr G. P. O'Donnell. *Educ:* High Sch., Leytonstone; City and Guilds of London Coll., Finsbury; Middlesex Hospital Medical Sch. RN Experimental and Anti-gas Station, 1917–18; Asst Laboratory Dir to the Clinical Research Assoc. MB, BS, BSc, MSc London, MRCS, LRCP, CChem, FRSC, FCS, FRMS; FRSA, MIBiol, FRSH. Associate of the City and Guilds of London Tech. Coll., Finsbury; Member: Pathological Soc. of Great Britain and Ireland; Association of Clinical Pathologists (Councillor, 1944–46); Society of Public Analysts; Medico-Legal Society; Brit. Assoc. in Forensic Medicine; former Mem. Court, Univ. of Exeter (representing Royal Institute of Chemistry); Pres. South-Western Branch, British Medical Association, 1946; Chm. South-Western Branch, RIC, 1955–57; Mem. Council, RIC, 1959–62, 1965–68. Mem. Brit. Acad. of Forensic Sciences; Mem. Soc. for Forensic Science. *Publications:* The Employment of Uranium in the Treatment of Malignant New Growths, British Empire Cancer Campaign International Conference, London, 1928; Disseminated Sclerosis (with Sir James Purves-Stewart), 1930; Seaside Accidents, 1958; Delayed Death due to Suicidal Hanging, 1961; Hanging and Manual Strangulation, 1966; Christmas Eve Crime in Falmouth (Murder in the West Country), 1975; The Porthole Murder: Gay Gibson (Facets of Crime), 1975; Bodies and Crimes: a pathologist speaks, 1993; numerous scientific papers in medical journals, etc. *Recreations:* hotels, good food, wine, conversation. *Address:* Strathaven, Carlyon Bay, Cornwall. *Clubs:* National Liberal (Associate Mem.), English-Speaking Union.

HOCKING, Philip Norman; *b* 27 Oct. 1925; *s* of late Fred Hocking, FIOB; *m* 1950, Joan Mable (marr. diss. 1970), *d* of Horace Ernest Jackson, CBE, Birmingham; three *d. Educ:* King Henry VIII Sch., Coventry; Birmingham Sch. of Architecture. Formerly Dir of building and develt cos. Mem. Coventry City Council, 1955–60. Prominent Mem.

Young Con. Movement. MP (C) Coventry South, 1959–64; PPS to Minister of State, FO, 1963–64. Contested Coventry S, 1964 and 1966. Chm., Conservative Back Benchers' Housing and Local Govt Cttee, 1962–64. Life Mem., Shropshire Sheep Breeders' Soc.; show judge of sheep. *Recreations:* gardening, field sports, hunting with foot hound packs (Chm., Leadon Vale Basset Hounds), observing nature. *Address:* 2A Homepiece Cottages, Snowshill, Broadway, Worcs WR12 7JX.

HOCKLEY, Sir Anthony Heritage F.; *see* Farrar-Hockley.

HOCKLEY, Rev. Canon Raymond Alan; Canon Residentiary, Precentor, Succentor Canonicorum and Chamberlain of York Minster, 1976–95, Canon Emeritus, since 1995; *b* 18 Sept. 1929; 2nd *s* of late Henry Hockley and Doris (*née* Stonehouse); unmarried. *Educ:* Firth Park School, Sheffield; Royal Academy of Music, London; Westcott House, Cambridge. MA, LRAM. Macfarren Schol., Royal Acad. of Music, 1951–54; Charles Lucas Medal, William Corder Prize, Cuthbert Nunn Prize, etc; Theodore Holland Award, 1955. Clements Memorial Prize for Chamber Music by a British subject, 1954. Curate of St Augustine's, Sheffield, 1958–61; Priest-in-charge of Holy Trinity, Wicker, with St Michael and All Angels, Neepsend, 1961–63; Chaplain of Westcott House, Cambridge, 1963–68; Fellow, Chaplain and Dir of Studies in Music, Emmanuel Coll., Cambridge, 1968–76. Works performed include: Songs for Tenor, Soprano; String Quartet; Divertimento for piano duet; Cantata for Easter and the Ascension; Symphony; My Enemies pictured within, a Bitter-Suite for Orchestra; various anthems and motets; incidental music for plays. Other works include: two more Symphonies, A Woman's Last Word for three sopranos; Oratorio on the Destruction and Salvation of the World; nine Suites for piano; Mass for four voices. *Publications:* Six Songs of Faith; New Songs for the Church; Divertimento; Intercessions at Holy Communion; contribs to theological and musical jls. *Recreations:* cooking, talking, unfinished work. *Address:* 2A Sycamore Terrace, York YO3 7DN.

HOCKMAN, Stephen Alexander; QC 1990; *b* 4 Jan. 1947; *s* of Nathaniel and Trude Hockman. *Educ:* Eltham Coll.; Jesus Coll., Cambridge (MA). Called to the Bar, Middle Temple, 1970. *Recreations:* philosophy, politics, the arts. *Address:* 6 Pump Court, Temple, EC4Y 7AR. *T:* 0171–797 8400. *Club:* Royal Automobile.

HOCKNEY, David, RA 1991 (ARA 1985); artist; *b* Bradford, 9 July 1937; *s* of Kenneth and Laura Hockney. *Educ:* Bradford Grammar Sch.; Bradford Sch. of Art; Royal Coll. of Art. Lecturer: Maidstone Coll. of Art, 1962; Univ. of Iowa, 1964; Univ. of Colorado, 1965; Univ. of California, Los Angeles, 1966, Berkeley, 1967. One-man shows: Kasmin Ltd, London, 1963, 1965, 1966, 1968, 1969, 1970, 1972; Alan Gallery, New York, 1964–67; Museum of Modern Art, NY, 1964–68; Stedlijk Museum, Amsterdam, 1966; Whitworth Gallery, Manchester, 1969; Louvre, Paris, 1974; Galerie Claude Bernard, Paris, 1975 and 1985; Nicholas Wilder, LA, 1976; Galerie Neundorf, Hamburg, 1977; Warehouse Gall., 1979; Knoedler Gall., 1979, 1981, 1982, 1983, 1984, 1986 and 1988; André Emmerich Gall., 1979, 1980, annually 1982–; Tate, 1986, 1988; Hayward Gall., 1983 and 1985; L. A. Louver, LA, 1986, 1989 and 1995, etc; touring show of drawings and prints: Munich, Madrid, Lisbon, Teheran, 1977; USA and Canada, 1978; Tate, 1980; Saltaire, Yorks, New York and LA, 1994. Retrospective Exhibitions: Whitechapel Art Gall., 1970; LA County Museum of Art, Metropolitan Mus. of Art, Tate Gall., 1988–89. Exhibitions of photographs: Hayward Gall., 1983; Nat. Mus. of Photography, Film and Television, 1991. 1st Prize, John Moores Exhibn, Liverpool, 1967. Designer: The Rake's Progress, Glyndebourne, 1975, La Scala, 1979; The Magic Flute, Glyndebourne, 1978; L'Enfant et les sortilèges and Nightingale, Double Bill, and Varii Capricci, Covent Garden, 1983; Tristan und Isolde, LA, 1987; Turandot, Chicago, San Francisco, Die Frau ohne Schatten, Covent Garden, 1992, LA, 1993; designing costumes and sets for Parade and Stravinsky triple bills, Metropolitan Opera House, NY, 1981. Films: A Bigger Splash, 1975; A Day on the Grand Canal with the Emperor of China or surface is illusion but so is depth, 1988. Shakespeare Prize, Hamburg Foundn, 1983; First Prize, Internat. Center of Photography, NY, 1985; Silver Progress Medal, RPS, 1988; Praemium Imperiale, Japan Art Assoc., 1989; Fifth Annual Gov. CA Visual Arts Award, 1994. *Publications:* (ed and illustrated) 14 Poems of C. P. Cavafy, 1967; (illustrated) Six Fairy Tales of the Brothers Grimm, 1969; 72 Drawings by David Hockney, 1971; David Hockney by David Hockney (autobiog.), 1976; The Blue Guitar, 1977; David Hockney: Travels with Pen, Pencil and Ink: selected prints and drawings 1962–77, 1978; Paper Pools, 1980; (with Stephen Spender) China Diary, 1982; Hockney Paints the Stage, 1983; David Hockney: Cameraworks, 1984 (Kodak Photography Book Award); David Hockney: A Retrospective, 1988; Hockney on Photography (conversations with Paul Joyce), 1988; Hockney's Alphabet, 1991 (ed Stephen Spender); That's the way I see it (autobiog.), 1993. *Address:* c/o 7508 Santa Monica Boulevard, Los Angeles, CA 90046, USA; Tradhart Ltd, 19B Buckingham Avenue, Slough, Berks SL1 4QB.

HODDER, Prof. Bramwell William, PhD; Professor of Geography, School of Oriental and African Studies, University of London, 1970–83, now Emeritus; *b* 25 Nov. 1923; *s* of George Albert Hodder and Emily Griggs, Eastbourne; *m* 1971, Elizabeth (*née* Scruton); three *s* two *d* by previous marriages. *Educ:* Oldershaw, Wallasey; Oriel Coll., Oxford (MA, BLitt); PhD London. Served War, 1942–47, commissioned in Infantry (Cameronians), Lieut. Lecturer, Univ. of Malaya, Singapore, 1952–56; Lectr/Sen. Lectr, Univ. of Ibadan, Nigeria, 1956–63; Lectr, Univ of Glasgow, 1963–64; Lectr/Reader, Queen Mary Coll., Univ. of London, 1964–70. Chm., Commonwealth Geog. Bureau, 1968–72; Hon. Dir, 1981–82, Mem. Exec. Council, 1981–84, Internat. African Inst. Joint Hon. Pres., World Expeditionary Assoc., 1972–. *Publications:* Man in Malaya, 1959; Economic Development in the Tropics, 1968, 3rd edn 1980; (jtly) Markets in West Africa, 1969; (jtly) Africa in Transition, 1967; (jtly) Economic Geography, 1974; Africa Today, 1979; articles in various learned jls. *Recreations:* music, hill walking. *Address:* Maris House, Trumpington, Cambridge CB2 2LB. *T:* Cambridge (01223) 841306.

See also I. R. Hodder.

HODDER, Dr Ian Richard; Reader in Prehistory, University of Cambridge, since 1990; Fellow of Darwin College, Cambridge, since 1990; *b* 23 Nov. 1948; *s* of Bramwell William Hodder and Noreen Victoria Hodder; *m* 1st, 1975, Françoise Marguerite Hivernel; two *s*; 2nd, 1987, Christine Ann Hastorf; two *s*. *Educ:* Inst. of Archaeology, London (BA 1971); Peterhouse, Cambridge (PhD 1975). Lectr, Dept of Archaeology, University of Leeds, 1974–77; University of Cambridge: Univ. Asst, then Univ. Lectr, Dept of Archaeology, 1977–90; Dir, Cambridge Archaeol. Unit, 1990–. Adjunct Asst Prof. of Anthropology, SUNY, 1984–89; Visiting Professor: Dept of Anthropology, Univ. of Minnesota (and Adjunct Prof.), 1986–93; Van Giffen Inst. for Pre- and Proto-history, Amsterdam, 1980; Univ. of Paris I, Sorbonne, 1985; Fellow, Centre for Advanced Study in Behavioural Scis, Calif., 1987. *Publications:* Spatial Analysis in Archaeology (with C. Orton), 1976; Symbols in Action, 1982; The Present Past, 1982; Reading the Past, 1986; The Domestication of Europe, 1990; Theory and Practice in Archaeology, 1992. *Recreations:* music (playing violin and piano), tennis, golf, sailing, travel. *Address:* Department of Archaeology, Downing Street, Cambridge CB2 3DZ. *T:* Cambridge (01223) 333520/333529.

HODDER-WILLIAMS, Paul, OBE 1945; TD; publisher; *b* 29 Jan. 1910; *s* of late Frank Garfield Hodder Williams, sometime Dean of Manchester, and late Sarah Myfanwy (*née* Nicholson); *m* 1936, Felicity (*d* 1986), 2nd *d* of late C. M. Blagden, DD, sometime Bishop of Peterborough; two *s* two *d*. *Educ:* Rugby; Gonville and Caius Coll., Cambridge (MA). Joined Hodder & Stoughton Ltd, 1931; Dir, 1936, Chm., 1961–75, Consultant, 1975–93. Served with HAC (Major, 1942), 99th (London Welsh) HAA Regt RA (Lt-Col Comdg, 1942–45). *Recreation:* gardening. *Address:* Court House, Exford, Minehead, Somerset TA24 7LY. *T:* Exford (01643) 831268.

HODDINOTT, Prof. Alun, CBE 1983; DMus; Hon. RAM; FRNCM; Professor of Music, University College, Cardiff, 1967–87, now Emeritus (Fellow, 1983); *b* 11 Aug. 1929; *s* of Thomas Ivor Hoddinott and Gertrude Jones; *m* 1953, Beti Rhiannon Huws; one *s*. *Educ:* University Coll. of S Wales and Mon. Lecturer: Cardiff Coll. of Music and Drama, 1951–59; University Coll. of S Wales and Mon, 1959–65; Reader, University of Wales, 1965–67. Member: BBC Music Central Adv. Cttee, 1971–78; Welsh Arts Council, 1968–74; Member Council: Welsh Nat. Opera, 1972–75; Composers' Guild of GB, 1972–; Nat. Youth Orchestra, 1972–. Chm., Welsh Music Archive, 1977–78, 1983–87. Artistic Dir, 1967–89, Pres., 1990–, Cardiff Music Festival. Governor: Welsh Nat. Theatre, 1968–74; St John's Coll., 1991–. FRNCM 1981; Fellow, Welsh Coll. of Music and Drama, 1991. Hon. DMus Sheffield, 1993. Walford Davies Prize, 1954; Arnold Bax Medal, 1957; John Edwards Meml Award, 1967; Hopkins Medal, St David's Soc., NY, 1980. *Publications: opera:* The Beach of Falesá, 1974; The Magician, 1975; What the Old Man does is always right, 1975; The Rajah's Diamond, 1979; The Trumpet Major, 1981; *choral:* Rebecca, 1961; oratorio, Job, 1962; Medieval Songs, 1962; Danegeld, 1964; Four Welsh Songs, 1964; Cantata: Dives and Lazarus, 1965; An Apple Tree and a Pig, 1968; Ballad, Black Bart, 1968; Out of the Deep, 1972; The Tree of Life, 1971; Four Welsh Songs, 1971; The Silver Swimmer, 1973; Sinfonia Fidei, 1977; Dulcia Iuventutis, 1978; Voyagers, 1978; Hymnus ante Somnum, 1979; Te Deum, 1982; Charge of the Light Brigade, 1983; In Parasceve Domini, 1983; King of Glory, 1984; Bells of Paradise, 1984; Jubilate, 1985; Lady and Unicorn, 1985; In Gravescentem Aetatem, 1985; Ballad of Green Broom, 1985; Christ is Risen, 1986; Sing a New Song, 1986; Flower Songs, 1986; In Praise of Music, 1986; The Legend of St Julian, 1987; Lines from Marlowe's Dr Faustus, 1988; Emynau Pantycelyn, 1990; Advent Carols, 1990; Vespers Canticle, 1992; Gloria, 1992; Three Motets, 1993; Missa Sancti David, 1994; Three Hymns for mixed choir and organ, 1994; Shakespeare Songs for unaccompanied voices, 1994; *vocal:* Roman Dream, 1968; Ancestor Worship, 1972; Ynys Mon, 1975; A Contemplation upon Flowers, 1976; Six Welsh Songs, 1982; The Silver Hound, 1986; Songs of Exile (tenor and orch.), 1989; The Silver Swimmer (soprano and ensemble), 1994; Five Poems of Becquer (baritone and piano), 1994; One Must Always Have Love: songs for high voice and piano, 1994; *orchestral:* Symphonies 1955, 1962, 1968, 1969, 1973, 1984; Nocturne, 1952; Welsh Dances I, 1958, II 1969; Folk Song Suite, 1962; Variations, 1963; Night Music, 1966; Sinfonietta I, 1968, II, 1969, III, 1970, IV, 1971; Fioriture, 1968; Investiture Dances, 1969; Divertimento, 1969; the sun, the great luminary of the universe, 1970; the hawk is set free, 1972; Welsh Airs and Dances for Symphonic Band, 1975; Landscapes, 1975; French Suite, 1977; Passaggio, 1977; Nightpiece, 1977; Lanterne des Morts, 1981; Five Studies, 1983; Four Scenes, 1983; Quodlibet, 1984; Hommage à Chopin, 1985; Welsh Dances–3rd Suite, 1985; Scena, 1986; Fanfare with Variants; Concerto for Orchestra; Star Children, 1989; Symphony for Organ and Orchestra, 1989; Symphony for brass and percussion, 1992; A Vision of Eternity (symphony), 1993; *concertos:* Clarinet I, 1951, II, 1987; Oboe, 1954; Harp, 1958; Viola, 1958; Piano I, 1950, II, 1960, III, 1966; Violin, 1961; Organ, 1967; Horn, 1969; Nocturnes and Cadenzas (cello), 1969; Ritornelli (trombone), 1974; The Heaventree of Stars, for violin and orchestra, 1980; Doubles (oboe); Scenes and Interludes (trumpet), 1985; Violin, Cello, Piano (Triple Concerto); Divisions (horn); Noctis Equi ('cello and orch.), 1989; MISTRAL: concerto for violin and orch., 1995; *chamber:* Septet, 1956; Sextet, 1960; Variations for Septet, 1962; Wind Quartet, 1963; String Quartet, 1965; Nocturnes and Cadenzas for Clarinet, Violin and Cello, 1968; Divertimento for 8 instruments, 1968; Piano Trio, 1970; Piano Quintet, 1972; Scena for String Quartet, 1979; Ritornelli for Brass Quintet, 1979; Ritornelli for four double basses, 1981; String Quartet no 2, 1984; Masks for oboe, bassoon, piano, 1985; Piano Trio no 2, 1985; Divertimenti for flute, bassoon, double-bass and percussion, 1985; Sonata for Four Clarinets; String Quartet no 3, 1988; chorales, variants and fanfares, 1992; Wind Quintet, 1993; six Bagatelles for string quartet, 1994; *instrumental:* sonatas for: piano, 1959, 1962, 1965, 1966, 1968, 1972, 1984, 1986, 1989 (two), 1993, 1994; harp, 1964; clarinet and piano, 1967; violin and piano, 1969, 1970, 1971, 1976, 1992; cello and piano, 1970, 1977; horn and piano, 1971; organ, 1979; two pianos, 1986; flute and piano, 1991; sonatinas for: clavichord, 1963; 2 pianos, 1978; guitar, 1978; Suite for Harp, 1967; Fantasy for Harp, 1970; Italian Suite for Recorder and Guitar, 1977; Nocturnes and Cadenzas for Solo Cello, 1983; Bagatelles for Oboe and Harp, 1983; Passacaglia and Fugue for Organ, 1986; Little Suite (trumpet and piano), 1988; Sonata Notturna for Harp, 1990. *Address:* Maesawelon, 86 Mill Road, Lisvane, Cardiff CF4 5UG.

HODDINOTT, Rear-Adm. Anthony Paul, CB 1994; OBE 1979; Executive Director, International Bar Association, since 1995; Naval Attaché and Commander British Naval Staff, Washington, 1990–94; retired; *b* 28 Jan. 1942; *s* of Comdr Peter Hoddinott, RN and Marjorie Hoddinott (*née* Kent); *m* 1965, Ellen Ruby Burton (Rue); one *s* two *d*. *Educ:* St Michael's, Otford; Bloxham; BRNC Dartmouth. Served HM Ships Chawton, Trump, Dreadnought, Repulse, Porpoise; in Comd, HMS Andrew, 1973–75; Staff of Comdr Third Fleet, USN, 1975–76; in Comd, HMS Revenge, 1976–79; Comdr, Submarine Tactics and Weapons Gp, 1979–81; in Comd, HMS Glasgow, 1981–83 (South Atlantic, 1982); Asst Dir, Naval Warfare, 1983–85; NATO Defence Coll., Rome, 1985; Dep. UK Mil. Rep. to NATO, Brussels, 1986–88; COS (Submarines), 1988–90. Dir, Warship Preservation Trust, 1995. *Recreations:* theatre, golf, swimming, family, beagles. *Address:* 45 Oaklands Road, Petersfield, Hants GU32 2EY. *Club:* Naval.

HODGART, Prof. Matthew John Caldwell; Professor of English, Concordia University, Montreal, 1970–76; *b* 1 Sept. 1916; *s* of late Matthew Hodgart (Major RE), MC, and Katherine Barbour Caldwell (*née* Gardner); *m* 1st, 1940, Betty Joyce Henstridge (*d* 1948); one *s* one *d*; 2nd, 1949, Margaret Patricia Elliott; one adopted *d*. *Educ:* Rugby Sch. (Scholar); Pembroke Coll., Cambridge (Scholar; BA 1938, MA 1945). Jebb Studentship, Cambridge, 1938–39. Served War, 1939–45: Argyll and Sutherland Highlanders and in Intelligence (mentioned in despatches). Cambridge University: Asst Lectr in English, 1945–49; Lectr in English, and Fellow of Pembroke Coll., 1949–64; Prof. of English, Sussex Univ., 1964–70. Vis. Professor: Cornell Univ., 1961–62 and 1969; Univ. of Calif, Los Angeles, 1977–78; Stanford Univ., 1979; La Trobe Univ., Australia, 1979–80; Hinckley Prof., Johns Hopkins Univ., 1982. Chevalier de la Légion d'honneur, and Croix de guerre, 1945. *Publications:* The Ballads, 1950; (with Prof. M. Worthington) Song in the Work of James Joyce, 1959; Samuel Johnson, 1962; (ed) Horace Walpole, Memoirs, 1963; (ed) Faber Book of Ballads, 1965; Satire, 1969 (trans. various languages); A New Voyage (fiction), 1969; James Joyce, Student Guide, 1978; contrib. Rev. of English Studies, and TLS. *Recreations:* travel, music, computers. *Address:* 13 Montpelier Villas, Brighton BN1 3DG. *T:* Brighton (01273) 326993.

HODGE, Alexander Mitchell, GC 1940; VRD; DL; Captain RNVR, retired; WS; Member of firm of Cowan & Stewart, WS, Edinburgh, 1946–84; Director, Standard Life Assurance Co., 1965–87 (Chairman, 1977–82); *b* 23 June 1916; *y s* of James Mackenzie Hodge, Blairgowrie, Perthshire; *m* 1944, Pauline Hester Winsome, *o d* of William John Hill, Bristol; one *s* two *d*. *Educ:* Fettes Coll.; Edinburgh Univ. (MA 1936, LLB 1938). Joined RNVR, 1938; served with Royal Navy, 1939–45 (despatches, GC). Comdr RNVR, 1949, Capt. RNVR, 1953; CO of the Forth Div. RNVR, 1953–57. Chm., Edinburgh Dist Sea Cadet Cttee, 1959–63; Chm., Lady Haig's Poppy Factory, 1961–67; Mem. Council, Earl Haig Fund (Scotland), 1963–67; Chm., Livingston New Town Licensing Planning Cttee, 1963–69; Dir, Edinburgh Western Gen. Hosp. Assoc. of Friends, 1962– (Chm., 1962–68); Trustee and Mem. Cttee of Management: Royal Victoria Hosp. Tuberculosis Trust, 1964–87 (Pres., 1970–87); Royal Edinburgh Inst. for Sailors, Soldiers and Airmen, 1964–71; Chm. General Comrs of Income Tax, Edinburgh South Div., 1967–85; Pres., Edinburgh Chamber of Commerce, 1968–70; Chm., The Cruden Foundn, 1983–92 (Dir, 1969–72, 1973–83). Governor, Fettes Coll., 1970–75; Mem. Court, Heriot-Watt Univ., 1982–88. DL Edinburgh, 1972. *Address:* Springbank, Barnton, Edinburgh EH4 6DJ. *T:* 0131–339 3054. *Clubs:* Royal Automobile; New (Edinburgh).

HODGE, Sir Andrew (Rowland), 3rd Bt *cr* 1921, of Chipstead, Kent; *b* 4 Dec. 1968; *o s* of Sir John Rowland Hodge, 2nd Bt, MBE and of his 4th wife, Vivien Jill, *d* of A. S. Knightley. *Educ:* Stella Maris Coll., Malta; Benjamin Britten High Sch., Suffolk. Estate agent, 1986–91 and 1993–94. *Recreations:* tennis, ski-ing. *Address:* 16 Sutherland Drive, Gunton Park, Lowestoft, Suffolk NR32 4LP. *T:* Lowestoft (01502) 568943.

HODGE, Henry Egar Garfield, OBE 1993; Senior Partner, Hodge Jones & Allen, Solicitors, since 1977; *b* 12 Jan. 1944; *s* of late Raymond Garfield Hodge and of Ruth (*née* Egar); *m* 1st, 1971, Miranda Tufnell (marr. diss. 1975); 2nd, 1978, Margaret Eve Hodge, *qv*; two *d*, and one step *s* one step *d*. *Educ:* Chigwell Sch., Essex; Balliol Coll., Oxford (BA Law 1965). Admitted solicitor, 1970; Legal Sec., Justice, 1971; Solicitor and Dep. Dir, CPAG, 1972–77; Asst Recorder, 1993–. Mem. (Lab), Islington Borough Council, 1974–78 (Vice-Chm., Housing Cttee, 1976–78). Member: Lord Chancellor's Legal Aid Adv. Cttee, 1977–83; Matrimonial Causes Rules Ctee, 1986–90. Law Society: Mem. Council, 1984– (Legal Aid Specialist); Chm., Courts and Legal Services Cttee, 1987–90; Chairman: Race Relns Cttee, 1992–94; Equal Opportunities Cttee, 1994–95. Member: Supplementary Benefits Commn, 1978–80; Social Security Adv. Cttee, 1980–92. Chairman: NCCL, 1974–75; Nat. CAB Trng Cttee, 1982–84; Camden CAB, 1983–88. Vice-Chm., Soc. of Labour Lawyers, 1992–; Dep. Vice-Pres., Law Soc. of England and Wales, 1994–95. Contested (Lab) Croydon S, Feb. 1974. Gov., Coll. of Law, 1991–. *Publications:* Legal Rights, 1974; numerous articles on legal aid and legal rights. *Recreations:* Arsenal supporter, motor-cycling, golf, gardening. *Address:* 10 Richmond Crescent, N1 0LZ. *T:* 0171–607 8806; (office) 0171–482 1974.

HODGE, James William; HM Diplomatic Service; Minister, British Embassy, Peking, since 1995; *b* 24 Dec. 1943; *s* of late William Hodge and Catherine Hodge (*née* Carden); *m* 1970, Frances Margaret, *d* of Michael Coyne and Teresa Coyne (*née* Walsh); three *d*. *Educ:* Holy Cross Academy, Edinburgh; Univ. of Edinburgh (MA(Hons) English Lang. and Lit.). Commonwealth Office, 1966; Third Secretary, Tokyo, 1967; Second Secretary (Information), Tokyo, 1970; FCO, 1972; First Sec. (Development, later Chancery), Lagos, 1975; FCO, 1978; First Sec. (Economic), 1981, Counsellor (Commercial), 1982, Tokyo; Counsellor: Copenhagen, 1986; FCO, 1990; RCDS, 1994. *Recreations:* books, music. *Address:* c/o Foreign and Commonwealth Office, SW1A 2AH. *Club:* MCC.

HODGE, John Dennis; President, J. D. Hodge & Co., International Management and Aerospace Consultants, since 1987; *b* 10 Feb. 1929; *s* of John Charles Henry Hodge and Emily M. Corbett Hodge; *m* 1952, Audrey Cox; two *s* two *d*. *Educ:* Northampton Engineering Coll., University of London (now The City Univ.). Vickers-Armstrong Ltd, Weybridge, England (Aerodynamics Dept), 1950–52; Head, Air Loads Section, Avro Aircraft Ltd, Toronto, Canada, 1952–59; Tech. Asst to Chief, Ops Div., Space Task Group, NASA, Langley Field, Va, USA, 1959; Chief, Flight Control Br., Space Task Group, NASA, 1961; Asst Chief of Flight Control, 1962, Chief, Flight Control Div., Flight Ops Directorate, NASA, MSC, 1963–68; Manager, Advanced Missions Program, NASA, Manned Spacecraft Centre, 1968–70; Dir, Transport Systems Concepts, Transport Systems Center, 1970; Vice-Pres., R&D, The Ontario Transportation Develt Corp., 1974–76; Department of Transportation, Washington, 1976–82; Chief, R&D Plans and Programs Analysis Div., 1976–77; Actg Dir, Office of Policy, Plans and Admin, 1977–79; Associate Administrator, for Policy, Plans and Program Management, Res. and Special programs Admin, 1979–82; Dir, Space Station Task Force, NASA, Washington, 1982–84; Dep. Associate Administrator for Space Station, NASA, Washington, 1984–85, Actg Associate Administrator, 1985–86. FAIAA 1991. Hon. ScD, The City Univ., London, Eng., 1966; NASA Medal for Exceptional Service, 1967 and 1969; Dept of Transportation Meritorious Achievement Award, 1974; Special Achievement Award, 1979; Presidential Rank Award of Meritorious Executive, NASA, 1985. *Publications:* contribs to NASA publications and various aerospace jls. *Recreation:* reading. *Address:* 1105 Challendon Road, Great Falls, VA 22066, USA.

HODGE, Sir Julian Stephen Alfred, Kt 1970; Merchant banker; Chairman: Avana Group Ltd, 1973–81; Carlyle Trust (Jersey) Ltd, since 1977; St Aubins Investment Co. Ltd, since 1986; Founder and Chairman, Bank of Wales, 1971–85; Chairman, Bank of Wales (Jersey) Ltd, 1974–87; Director, Bank of Wales (IoM) Ltd, 1974–85; *b* 15 Oct. 1904; *s* of late Alfred and Jane Hodge; *m* 1951, Moira (*née* Thomas); two *s* one *d*. *Educ:* Cardiff Technical Coll. Certified Accountant, 1930. Fellow, Inst. of Taxation, 1941–. Founded Hodge & Co., Accountants and Auditors; Man. Dir, 1963–75, Exec. Chm., 1975–78, Hodge Group Ltd; former Chairman: Julian S. Hodge & Co. Ltd; Gwent Enterprises Ltd; Hodge Finance Ltd; Hodge Life Assurance Co. Ltd; Carlyle Trust Ltd, 1962–85; Dir, Standard Chartered Bank, 1973–75. Founder and Chairman: The Jane Hodge Foundation, 1962; Sir Julian Hodge Charitable Trust, 1964; Chairman: Aberfan Disaster Fund Industrial Project Sub-Cttee; Member: Welsh Economic Council, 1965–68; Welsh Council, 1968–79; Council, Univ. of Wales Inst. of Science and Technology (Treasurer, 1968–76; Pres., 1981–85); Foundation Fund Cttee, Univ. of Surrey; Duke of Edinburgh Conf., 1974; Prince of Wales Cttee, 1979–85. Pres., S Glamorgan Dist, St John Ambulance Bde; Trustee, Welsh Sports Trust. Former Governor, All Hallows (Cranmore Hall) Sch. Trust Ltd. FTII 1941. FRSA. Hon. LLD Univ. of Wales, 1971. KStJ 1977 (CStJ 1972); KSG 1978. *Publication:* Paradox of Financial Preservation, 1959. *Recreations:* golf, walking, reading, gardening. *Address:* Clos des Seux, Mont du Coin, St Aubin, St Brelade, Jersey, JE3 8BE. *Clubs:* Victoria (St Helier, Jersey); La Moye Golf (Jersey).

HODGE, Margaret Eve, MBE 1978; MP (Lab) Barking, since June 1994; Visiting Fellow, Institute for Public Policy Research, since 1992; *b* 8 Sept. 1944; *d* of late Hans and Lisbeth Oppenheimer; *m* 1st, 1968, Andrew Watson (marr. diss. 1978); one *s* one *d*; 2nd, 1978, Henry Egar Garfield Hodge, *qv*; two *d*. *Educ:* Bromley High Sch.; Oxford High Sch.; LSE (BSc Econ 1966). Teaching and internat. market research, 1966–73. London Borough of Islington: Councillor, 1973–94; Chair of Housing, 1975–79; Dep. Leader, 1981; Leader, 1982–92. Chair: Assoc. of London Authorities, 1984–92; London Res. Centre, 1985–92; Vice-Chair, AMA, 1991–92. Member: HO Adv. Cttee on Race Relations, 1988–92; Local Govt Commn, 1993–94; Board, Central and Inner London North TEC, 1990–92; Labour Party Local Govt Cttee, 1983–92; former mem., govt and local govt bodies. Sen. Consultant, Price Waterhouse, 1992–94. Director: London First, 1992–; (non-exec.) UCH and Middlesex Hosp., 1992–94. Chair, Circle 33 Housing Trust, 1993–. Gov., LSE, 1990–; Mem. Council, Univ. of London. Hon. Fellow, Polytechnic of North London. Hon. DCL City, 1993. *Publications:* Quality, Equality and Democracy, 1991; Beyond the Town Hall, 1994; contribs to numerous jls and newspapers. *Recreations:* family, opera, piano, travel, cooking. *Address:* 10 Richmond Crescent, N1 0LZ. *T:* 0171–607 8806.

HODGE, Michael John Davy V.; *see* Vere-Hodge.

HODGE, Patricia; actress; *b* 29 Sept. 1946; *d* of Eric and Marion Hodge; *m* 1976, Peter Owen; two *s*. *Educ:* Wintringham Girls' Grammar Sch., Grimsby; St Helen's Sch., Northwood, Mddx; Maria Grey Coll., Twickenham; London Acad. of Music and Dramatic Art. Theatre début, No-one Was Saved, Traverse, Edinburgh, 1971; *West End* theatre includes: Popkiss, Globe, 1972; Two Gentlemen of Verona (musical), 1973; Pippin, Her Majesty's, 1973; Hair, Queen's, 1974; The Mitford Girls, Globe, 1981 (transf. from Chichester); Benefactors, Vaudeville, 1984; Noël and Gertie, Comedy, 1989–90; Shades, Albery, 1992; Separate Tables, Albery, 1993; The Prime of Miss Jean Brodie, Strand, 1994; *other appearances* include: The Beggar's Opera, Nottingham Playhouse, 1975; Pal Joey, and Look Back In Anger, Oxford Playhouse, 1976; Then and Now, Hampstead, 1979; As You Like It, Chichester Fest., 1983; Lady in the Dark, Edinburgh Fest., 1988; *television plays and films* include: The Girls of Slender Means, 1975; The Naked Civil Servant, 1975; Hay Fever, 1984; The Death of the Heart, 1985; Hotel du Lac, 1986; Heat of the Day, 1988; The Shell Seekers, 1989; The Secret Life of Ian Fleming, 1989; *television series and serials* include: Rumpole of the Bailey, 7 series, 1978–90; Edward and Mrs Simpson, 1978; Holding the Fort, 3 series, 1979–82; The Other 'Arf, 1979–80, 1981; Nanny, 1980; Jemima Shore Investigates, 1982; The Life and Loves of a She-Devil, 1986; Rich Tea and Sympathy, 1991; The Cloning of Joanna May, 1992; *films* include: Betrayal, 1983. *Address:* c/o Michael Foster, ICM Ltd, Oxford House, 76 Oxford Street, W1R 1RB. *T:* 0171–636 6565.

HODGES, C(yril) Walter; free-lance writer, book illustrator, theatrical historian and designer; *b* 18 March 1909; *s* of Cyril James and Margaret Mary Hodges; *m* 1936, Greta (*née* Becker); two *s*. *Educ:* Dulwich Coll.; Goldsmiths' Coll. Sch. of Art. Commenced as stage designer, 1929, then illustrator for advertising, magazines (esp. Radio Times) and children's books; began writing, 1937; served with Army, 1940–46 (despatches); has designed stage productions (Mermaid Theatre, 1951, 1964), permanent Elizabethan stage, St George's Theatre, 1976; exhibns (Lloyds, UK Provident Instn; retrospective of theatre designs, Folger Shakespeare Library, Washington, 1988); mural decorations painted for Chartered Insce Inst., UK Provident Instn; Art Dir, Encyclopædia Britannica Films, 1959–61; reconstruction drawings for model of excavated Elizabethan Rose Theatre, Museum of London, 1989–91; consultant designer, Globe Theatre, Alexander Mills, N Carolina, USA, 1993–. Judith E. Wilson Lectr in Poetry and Drama, Cambridge, 1974; Co-ordinator, Symposium for the Reconstruction of Globe Playhouse, 1979, Adjunct Prof. of Theatre, 1980–83, Wayne State University, USA; Vis. Scholar, Univ. of Maryland, 1983. Hon. DLitt Sussex, 1979. Kate Greenaway Medal for illustration, 1965; Hons List, Hans Christian Andersen Internat. Award, 1966. *Publications:* Columbus Sails, 1939; The Flying House, 1947; Shakespeare and the Players, 1948; The Globe Restored, 1953 (rev. edn 1968); The Namesake, 1964; Shakespeare's Theatre, 1964; The Norman Conquest, 1966; Magna Carta, 1966; The Marsh King, 1967; The Spanish Armada, 1967; The Overland Launch, 1969; The English Civil War, 1972; Shakespeare's Second Globe, 1973; Playhouse Tales, 1974; The Emperor's Elephant, 1975; Plain Lane Christmas, 1978; The Battlement Garden, 1979; (ed) The Third Globe, 1981; contributor, Shakespeare Survey; Theatre Notebook; (illus.) The New Cambridge Shakespeare, 1984–. *Recreations:* music (listening), letters (writing), museums (visiting). *Address:* 36 Southover High Street, Lewes, East Sussex BN7 1HX. *T:* Lewes (01273) 6530.

HODGES, Elaine Mary, OBE 1975; HM Diplomatic Service; Counsellor, Foreign and Commonwealth Office, 1981–83; retired; *b* 12 Nov. 1928; *d* of late Lancelot James Hodges and of Edith Mary (*née* Crossland). *Educ:* Nottingham High School for Girls; St Anne's Coll., Oxford (BA Hons, MA). Joined Foreign Office, 1952; served in: Germany, 1952–53; Switzerland, 1955–56; Warsaw, 1959; New Delhi, 1963–64; Paris, 1967–69; Brussels, 1974–79. *Recreations:* gardening, antiques, travel. *Address:* 46 Westbridge Road, SW11 3PW. *T:* 0171–228 3771.

HODGES, Gerald; Director of Finance, City of Bradford Metropolitan Council, 1974–85; *b* 14 June 1925; *s* of Alfred John Hodges and Gertrude Alice Hodges; *m* 1950, Betty Maire (*née* Brading); one *s* (and one *s* decd). *Educ:* King's Sch., Peterborough. IPFA. Accountancy Asst, Bexley Borough Council, 1941–48, and Eton RDC, 1948–49; Sen. Accountancy Asst, Newcastle upon Tyne, 1949–53; Chief Accountant, Hemel Hempstead, 1953–56; Dep. Treas., Crawley UDC, 1956–70; Treas., Ilkley UDC, 1970–74. Pres., Soc. of Metropolitan Treasurers, 1984–85. Hon. Treasurer: Yorkshire Arts, 1973–86; Univ. of Bradford, 1986–; Chm., Bradford Flower Fund Homes; Trustee, Bradford Disaster Appeal, 1985. *Publications:* occasional articles in professional jls. *Recreations:* travelling, ornithology, reading. *Address:* 23 Victoria Avenue, Ilkley, West Yorks LS29 9BW. *T:* Ilkley (01943) 607346.

HODGES, Lew; Finance Director, Arts Council of England (formerly of Great Britain), since 1989; *b* 29 Feb. 1956. *Educ:* University Coll. London (BA (Hons) Classics); MBA London Business Sch., 1990. Chartered Accountant 1981. Subsidy Officer, then Asst Dir of Finance, Arts Council, 1981–87; Head of Finance, CNAA, 1987–89. *Address:* Arts Council of England, 14 Great Peter Street, SW1P 3NQ.

HODGES, Air Chief Marshal Sir Lewis (Macdonald), KCB 1968 (CB 1963); CBE 1958; DSO 1944 and Bar 1945; DFC 1942 and Bar 1943; DL; *b* 1 March 1918; *s* of late Arthur Macdonald Hodges and Gladys Mildred Hodges; *m* 1950, Elisabeth Mary, *e d* of late G. H. Blackett, MC; two *s*. *Educ:* St Paul's Sch.; RAF Coll., Cranwell. Bomber Command, 1938–44; SE Asia (India, Burma, Ceylon), 1944–45; Palestine, 1945–47; Air Ministry and Min. of Defence, 1948–52; Bomber Command, 1952–59; Asst Comdt, RAF Coll., Cranwell, 1959–61; AO i/c Admin., Middle East Comd, Aden, 1961–63; Imperial Def. Coll., 1963; SHAPE, 1964–65; Ministry of Defence, Asst Chief of Air Staff (Ops), 1965–68; AOC-in-C, RAF Air Support Comd, 1968–70; Air Mem. for Personnel, MoD, 1970–73; Dep. C-in-C, Allied Forces Central Europe, 1973–76, retired. Air ADC to the Queen, 1973–76. Dir, Pilkington Bros Ltd (Optical Div.), 1979–83; Governor, BUPA Med. Foundn Ltd, 1987–; Chm. of Governors, Duke of Kent School, 1979–86; Chm., RAF Benevolent Fund Educn Cttee, 1979–86; Pres., RAF Escaping Soc., 1979–; Pres., Royal Air Forces Assoc., 1981–84. DL Kent, 1992. Grand Officier, Légion d'Honneur (France), 1988 (Commandeur, 1950); Croix de Guerre (France), 1944. *Recreations:*

gardening, shooting, bee-keeping. *Address:* c/o Lloyds Bank, High Street, Tonbridge, Kent. *Clubs:* Royal Air Force (Vice Patron, 1993–), Special Forces.

HODGES, Mark Willie; Head of the Office of Arts and Libraries, 1982–84; *b* 23 Oct. 1923; *s* of William H. and Eva Hodges; *m* 1948, Glenna Marion (*née* Peacock); one *s* one *d. Educ:* Cowbridge Grammar Sch.; Jesus Coll., Oxford (MA 1948). Served War, RN, 1942–45. Lectr, Univ. of Sheffield, 1950–54; DSIR, 1954–56; Asst Scientific Attaché, Washington, 1956–61; Office of Minister for Science, 1961–64; Sec., Royal Commn on Med. Educn, 1965–68; Asst Sec., DES, 1968–79 (Arts and Libraries Br., 1977–79); Office of Arts and Libraries, 1979–84, Under Sec., 1982, Dep. Sec., 1983. Member: South Bank Theatre Bd, 1982–93 (Chm., 1984–93); Council, Royal Albert Hall, 1983–93; Council and Management Cttee, Eastern Arts Assoc., 1986–89. *Recreations:* woodwork, computer programming, listening to music. *Address:* The Corner Cottage, Church Way, Little Stukeley, Cambs PE17 5BQ. *T:* Huntingdon (01480) 459266.

HODGES, Prof. Richard Andrew, OBE; PhD; FSA 1984; Professor of Archaeology and Prehistory, Sheffield University, since 1993; Director, British School at Rome (on secondment), 1988–95; *b* 29 Sept. 1952; *s* of Roy Clarence Hodges and Joan (*née* Hartnell); *m* 1976, Deborah Peters; one *s* one *d. Educ:* City of Bath Boys' Sch.; Univ. of Southampton (BA, PhD). Lectr in Prehistory and Archaeology, 1976–86, Sen. Lectr, 1986–93, Sheffield Univ. Leverhulme Res. Fellow, British Sch. at Rome, 1980; Visiting Professor: in Medieval Studies, SUNY-Birmingham, 1983; in Medieval Archaeology, Siena Univ., 1984–87; in Archaeology, Copenhagen Univ., 1987–88. Director: Roystone Grange landscape project, Derbyshire, 1978–88; San Vincenzo excavations, S Italy, 1980–95; co-director: Sheffield-Siena archaeological project, Montarrenti, Tuscany, 1982–87; Butsint excavations, Albania, 1994–. *Publications:* Walks in the Cotswolds, 1976; The Hamwih Pottery, 1981; (with G. Barker) Archaeology and Italian Society, 1981; Dark Age Economics, 1982, 2nd edn 1989; (with P. Davey) Ceramics and trade, 1983; (with D. Whitehouse) Mohammed, Charlemagne and the origins of Europe, 1983; (with John Mitchell) San Vincenzo al Volturno, 1985; Primitive and Peasant Markets, 1988; (with B. Hobley) Rebirth of the town in the West, 1988; The Anglo-Saxon Achievement, 1989; Wall to Wall History, 1991 (British Archaeological Book of the Year, 1992); (with K. Smith) Recent Developments in the Archaeology of the Peak District, 1991; (ed) San Vincenzo 1, 1993; (ed) San Vincenzo 2, 1995; (with J Mitchell) San Vincenzo Maggiore, 1995. *Recreations:* hill walking, music, watching cricket. *Address:* Department of Archaeology and Prehistory, University of Sheffield, Sheffield S10 2TN.

HODGETTS, Robert Bartley; Clerk to Worshipful Company of Glaziers, 1979–85; *b* 10 Nov. 1918; *s* of late Captain Bartley Hodgetts, MN and Florence Hodgetts (*née* Stagg); *m* 1st, 1945, A. K. Jeffreys; one *d;* 2nd, 1949, Frances Grace, *d* of late A. J. Pepper, Worcester; two *d. Educ:* Merchant Taylors' Sch., Crosby; St John's Coll., Cambridge (Scholar, MA). Served RNVR (A), 1940–45. Asst Principal, Min. of Nat. Insce, 1947; Principal 1951; Asst Sec. 1964; Under-Sec., DHSS, 1973–78. *Recreations:* watching cricket and Rugby football. *Address:* 9 Purley Bury Close, Purley, Surrey CR8 1HW. *T:* 0181–668 2827.

HODGINS, Ven. Michael Minden; Archdeacon of Hackney, 1951–71; Secretary of London Diocesan Fund, 1946–74; *b* 26 Aug. 1912; *yr s* of late Major R. Hodgins, Indian Army, and Margaret Hodgins (*née* Wilson); unmarried. *Educ:* Wellington; Cuddesdon Theological Coll. Deacon, 1939; Priest, 1940; Curate, S Barnabas, Northolt Park, 1939; Asst Secretary, London Diocesan Fund, 1943. MA Lambeth 1960. *Address:* 5 Up, The Quadrangle, Morden College, Blackheath, SE3 0PW. *T:* 0181–858 4762.

HODGKIN, Sir Alan (Lloyd), OM 1973; KBE 1972; FRS 1948; MA, ScD Cantab; Master of Trinity College, Cambridge, 1978–84 (Fellow, 1936–78 and since 1984); Chancellor, University of Leicester, 1971–84; *b* 5 Feb. 1914; *s* of G. L. Hodgkin and M. F. Wilson; *m* 1944, Marion de Kay, *d* of late F. P. Rous; one *s* three *d. Educ:* Gresham's Sch., Holt; Trinity Coll., Cambridge. Scientific Officer working on Radar for Air Ministry and Min. of Aircraft Production, 1939–45. Lecturer and then Asst Dir of Research at Cambridge, 1945–52; Foulerton Research Prof., Royal Soc., 1952–69; John Humphrey Plummer Prof. of Biophysics, Univ. of Cambridge, 1970–81. Baly Medal, RCP, 1955; Royal Medal of Royal Society, 1958; Nobel Prize for Medicine (jointly), 1963; Copley Medal of Royal Society, 1965. Pres., Royal Society, 1970–75; Pres., Marine Biological Assoc., 1966–76. Foreign Member: Royal Danish Acad. of Sciences, 1964; Amer. Acad. of Arts and Sciences, 1962; Amer. Philosophical Soc.; Royal Swedish Acad. of Sciences; Member: Physiological Soc.; Leopoldina Acad., 1964; Hon. Mem., Royal Irish Acad., 1974; Hon. For. Mem., USSR Acad. of Scis, 1976. Fellow, Imperial Coll. London, 1972; Hon. FRSE, 1974; Hon. Fellow: Indian National Science Acad., 1972; Girton Coll., Cambridge, 1979; Pharmaceutical Soc.; For. Assoc., Nat. Acad. of Scis, USA, 1974. Hon. MD: Berne 1956, Louvain 1958; Hon. DSc: Sheffield 1963, Newcastle upon Tyne 1965, E Anglia 1966, Manchester 1971, Leicester 1971, London 1971, Newfoundland 1973, Wales 1973, Rockefeller Univ., 1974, Bristol 1976; Oxford, 1977; Hon. LLD: Aberdeen 1973; Salamanca, 1984; Pisa, 1987; Cambridge, 1991. Lord Crook Medal, 1983; Helmerich Prize, Retina Res. Foundn, USA, 1988. *Publications:* The Conduction of the Nervous Impulse, 1963; Chance and Design, 1992; scientific papers dealing with the nature of nervous conduction, muscle and vision, Jl Physiology, etc. *Recreations:* travel, ornithology and fishing. *Address:* Physiological Laboratory, Downing Street, Cambridge CB2 3EG; 18 Panton Street, Cambridge CB2 1HP. *T:* Cambridge (01223) 352707.

See also J. A. Hodgkin.

HODGKIN, Sir Howard, Kt 1992; CBE 1977; painter; *b* 6 Aug. 1932; *m* 1955, Julia Lane; two *s. Educ:* Camberwell Sch. of Art; Bath Academy of Art. Taught at Charterhouse Sch., 1954–56; taught at Bath Academy of Art, 1956–66; occasional tutor, Slade Sch. of Art and Chelsea Sch. of Art. Vis. Fellow in Creative Art, Brasenose Coll. Oxford, 1976–77. A Trustee: Tate Gall., 1970–76; National Gall., 1978–85. Mem., Exec. Cttee, Nat. Art Collections Fund, 1988. One-man exhibitions include: Arthur Tooth & Sons, London, 1961, 1962, 1964, 1967; Kasmin Gallery, 1969, 1971, 1976; Arnolfini Gall., Bristol, 1970, 1975; Dartington Hall, 1970; Galerie Müller, Cologne, 1971; Kornblee Gall., NY, 1973; Museum of Modern Art, Oxford, 1976, 1977; Serpentine Gall., London and provincial tour, Waddington Gall., 1976; André Emmerich Gall., Zürich and NY, 1977; Third Sydney Biennale, Art Gall. of NSW, 1979; Waddington Galls, 1972, 1980, 1988; Knoedler Gall. NY, 1981, 1982, 1984, 1988, 1990; Bernard Jacobson NY, 1980, 1981, LA, 1981, London, 1982; Tate Gall., 1982, 1985; Bath Fest., 1984; Phillips Collection, Washington DC, 1984; XLI Venice Biennale, 1984; Yale Centre for British Art, New Haven, 1985; Kestner-Gesellschaft, Hanover, 1985; Whitechapel Art Gall., 1985; Michael Werner Gall., Cologne, 1990; Nantes, Barcelona, Edinburgh and Dublin tour, 1990–91; Anthony D'Offay Gall., 1993; Knoedler Gall., NY, 1993. Group Exhibitions include: The Human Clay, Hayward Gall., 1976; British Painting 1952–1977, RA, 1977; A New Spirit in Painting, RA, 1981; Hard Won Image, Tate Gall., 1984; An International Survey of Recent Paintings and Sculpture, Mus. of Mod. Art, 1984; NY, Carnegie International, Mus. of Art, Carnegie Inst., 1985–86; and in exhibns in: Australia, Austria, Belgium, Canada, Denmark, France, Germany, GB, Holland, India, Italy, Japan, Malta, Norway, Sweden, Switzerland, USA. Designs for: Pulcinella, Ballet Rambert, 1987; Piano, Royal Ballet, 1989; mural for British Council building, New Delhi, 1992. Works in public collections: Arts Council of GB; British Council, London; Contemp. Arts Soc.; Kettering Art Gall.; Peter Stuyvesant Foundn; São Paulo Museum; Oldham Art Gall.; Tate; V&A Museum; Swindon Central Lib.; Bristol City Art Gall.; Walker Art Center, Minneapolis; Nat. Gall. of S Aust., Adelaide; Fogg Art Museum, Cambridge, Mass; BM; Louisiana Museum, Denmark; Museum of Modern Art, Edinburgh; Southampton Art Gall.; Museum of Modern Art, NY; Mus. of Art, Carnegie Inst.; Whitworth Art Gall., Manchester; City of Manchester Art Galls; Govt Picture Coll., London; Saatchi Coll., London. Hon. Fellow, Brasenose Coll., Oxford, 1988. Hon. DLitt London, 1985. 2nd Prize, John Moore's Exhibn, 1976 and 1980; Turner Prize, 1985. *Address:* 32 Coptic Street, WC1A 1NP. *T:* 0171–580 7970.

HODGKIN, Jonathan Alan, PhD; FRS 1990; Staff Scientist, Medical Research Council Laboratory of Molecular Biology, since 1977; *b* 24 Aug. 1949; *s* of Sir Alan Hodgkin, *qv* and Marion Hodgkin, *d* of late F. P. Rous. *Educ:* Bryanston Sch., Dorset; Merton Coll., Oxford (BA); Darwin Coll., Cambridge (PhD). SRC Res. Fellowship, 1974–76. Vis. Prof., Univ. of Wisconsin, 1990. Mem., EMBO, 1989–. *Publications:* contribs to scientific jls. *Recreations:* archaeology, cooking, cinema. *Address:* 7 Little Saint Mary's Lane, Cambridge CB2 1RR. *T:* Cambridge (01223) 313360.

HODGKINS, David John, CB 1993; Director, Resources and Planning, Health and Safety Executive, 1992–94; *b* 13 March 1934; *s* of Rev. Harold Hodgkins and of late Elsie Hodgkins; *m* 1963, Sheila Lacey; two *s. Educ:* Buxton Coll.; Peterhouse, Cambridge. BA 1956, MA 1960. Entered Min. of Labour as Asst Principal, 1956; Principal: Min. of Lab., 1961–65; Treasury, 1965–68; Manpower and Productivity Services, Dept of Employment, 1968–70; Assistant Secretary: Prices and Incomes Div., Dept of Employment, 1970–72; Industrial Relns Div., 1973–76; Under Secretary, Overseas and Manpower Divisions, Dept of Employment, 1977–84; Safety Policy Div., HSE, 1984–92. *Address:* Four Winds, Batchelors Way, Amersham, Bucks HP7 9AJ. *T:* Amersham (01494) 725207. *Club:* Commonwealth Trust.

HODGKINSON, Rev. Canon Arthur Edward; Retired Priest-in-Charge of St Ebba's, Eyemouth, Diocese of Edinburgh, 1982–86; *b* 29 Oct. 1913; *s* of Arthur and Rose Hodgkinson. *Educ:* Glasgow High School; Edinburgh Theol College. LTh Durham 1942. Deacon 1939; Priest 1940. Curate, St George's, Maryhill, Glasgow, 1939–43; Choir Chaplain, 1943, and Precentor of St Ninian's Cath., Perth, 1944–47; Curate-in-Charge, St Finnian's, Lochgelly, 1947–52, and Rector, 1952–54; Rector, Holy Trinity, Motherwell, 1954–65; Provost of St Andrew's Cathedral, Aberdeen, 1965–78; Area Sec., Dioceses of Monmouth, Llandaff, Swansea and Brecon, and St Davids, USPG, 1978–82. Commissary to Bp of St John's, 1961–78; Mem., Anglican Consultative Council, 1971–77; Canon of St Mary's Cath., Glasgow, 1963–65. Hon. Canon of Christ Church Cathedral, Connecticut, 1965–78; Hon. Canon of Aberdeen, 1981. *Recreations:* motoring, travel. *Address:* 36 Forbes Road, Edinburgh EH10 4ED.

HODGKINSON, Sir Derek; *see* Hodgkinson, Sir W. D.

HODGKINSON, Terence William Ivan, CBE 1958; Trustee, The Burlington Magazine, since 1986 (Editor, 1978–81; Member, Editorial Board, 1978–86); *b* 7 Oct. 1913; *s* of late Ivan Tattersall Hodgkinson, Wells, Som, and of late Kathryn Van Vleck Townsend, New York (who *m* 2nd, 1929, Sir Gilbert Upcott, KCB); unmarried. *Educ:* Oundle Sch.; Magdalen Coll., Oxford. Served War of 1939–45 Major, Gen. Staff 1943. Joined staff of Victoria and Albert Museum (Dept of Architecture and Sculpture) 1946; Asst to the Dir, 1948–62; Secretary to the Advisory Council, 1951–67; Keeper, Dept of Architecture and Sculpture, 1967–74; Dir, Wallace Collection, 1974–78. Member: Exec. Cttee, Nat. Art Collections Fund, 1975–88; Museums and Galleries Commn, 1981–88 (Vice-Chm., 1987–88). *Publications:* (part author) Catalogue of Sculpture in the Frick Collection, New York, 1970; Catalogue of Sculpture at Waddesdon Manor, 1970; articles in Burlington Magazine, Bulletin and Yearbook of the Victoria and Albert Museum and for Walpole Society. *Recreation:* music. *Address:* 9 The Grove, N6 6JU.

HODGKINSON, Air Chief Marshal Sir (William) Derek, KCB 1971 (CB 1969); CBE 1960; DFC 1941; AFC 1942; *b* 27 Dec. 1917; *s* of late Ernest Nicholls Hodgkinson; *m* 1939, Nancy Heather Goodwin; one *s* one *d. Educ:* Repton. Joined RAF 1936; served war of 1939–45, POW Germany, 1942–45; OC 210 and 240 (GR) Sqns; DS Aust. Jt Anti-Sub. Sch. and JSSC, 1946–58; Gp Captain, 1958; OC RAF St Mawgan, 1958–61; Staff of CDS, and ADC to the Queen, 1961–63; Air Cdre, 1963; IDC, 1964; Comdt RAF Staff Coll., Andover, 1965; Air Vice-Marshal, 1966; ACAS, Operational Requirements, 1966–68; SASO, RAF Training Command, 1969; Air Marshal, 1970; AOC-in-C, Near East Air Force, Commander British Forces Near East, and Administrator, Sovereign Base Areas, Cyprus, 1970–73; Air Secretary, 1973–76; Air Chief Marshal, 1974; retired 1976. Report on RAF Officer Career Structure, 1969. Pres., Regular Forces Employment Assoc., 1982–86 (Vice-Chm., 1977–80; Chm., 1980–82). *Recreations:* fishing, cricket. *Clubs:* Royal Air Force, MCC.

HODGSON, (Adam) Robin; Chief Executive, Hampshire County Council, since 1985; *b* 20 March 1937; *s* of Thomas Edward Highton Hodgson, CB; *m* 1962, Elizabeth Maureen Linda Bovenizer; one *s* two *d. Educ:* William Ellis Sch., London; Worcester Coll., Oxford (MA). Admitted Solicitor, 1964. Asst Solicitor, LCC and GLC, 1964–66; Sen. Asst Solicitor, Oxfordshire CC, 1966–71; Asst Clerk, Northamptonshire CC, 1972–74; Dep. County Sec., E Sussex CC, 1974–77; Dep. Chief Exec. and Clerk, Essex CC, 1977–85. *Recreations:* music, drama, geology. *Address:* The Castle, Winchester SO23 8UJ. *T:* Winchester (01962) 847373.

HODGSON, Arthur Brian, CMG 1962; Consultant, League of Red Cross Societies, 1982–92; *b* 24 Aug. 1916; *s* of late Major Arthur H. F. Hodgson, Westfields, Iffley, Oxford, and Isabel, *d* of late W. H. Kidston, Rosebank, Helensburgh; *m* 1945, Anne Patricia Halse, *d* of late Lt-Col Edward Marlborough Ley, DSO, KRRC and Marjorie (*née* Broadbridge); two *s* two *d. Educ:* Edinburgh Academy; Eton Coll.; Oriel Coll., Oxford; Trinity Coll., Cambridge. Colonial Civil Service, Tanganyika Administration, 1939–62, retiring as Principal Sec. and Dir of Establishments. British Red Cross Society: Sec., 1964; Dep. Dir-Gen., 1966–70; Dir-Gen., 1970–75; Counsellor, 1975–91. Steward, Henley Royal Regatta, 1970. FRGS 1991. Henry Dunant Medal, Internat. Red Cross, 1993. *Recreations:* rowing, gardening, messing about in boats. *Address:* Chandlers, Furners Green, near Uckfield, Sussex TN22 3RH. *T:* Danehill (01825) 790310. *Clubs:* Naval; Leander.

HODGSON, Hon. Sir Derek; *see* Hodgson, Hon. Sir W. D. T.

HODGSON, George Charles Day, CMG 1961; MBE 1950; lately an Administrative Officer, Nyasaland; retired from HMOCS, Nov. 1964; Secretary, Old Diocesans' Union, Diocesan College, Rondebosch, Cape, South Africa, 1964–86; *b* 21 Sept. 1913; *s* of late P. J. Hodgson and of A. E. Joubert; *m* 1st, 1940, Edna Orde (*d* 1977), *d* of late G. H. Rushmere; one *s;* 2nd, 1978, Cecile Paston Dewar (*née* Foster). *Educ:* Diocesan Coll., Rondebosch, Capetown, S Africa; Rhodes Univ., Grahamstown, S Africa; Cambridge Univ. Joined Colonial Administrative Service as Cadet, 1939. Military Service, 1940–42; Lieut, 1st Bn King's African Rifles. Returned to duty as Distr. Officer, Nyasaland, 1943;

seconded for special famine relief duties in Nyasaland, 1949–50; Provincial Commissioner, 1952; Adviser on Race Affairs to Govt of Federation of Rhodesia and Nyasaland, 1958–59; Nyasaland Govt Liaison Officer to Monckton Commn, 1960; Permanent Sec., Ministry of Natural Resources and Surveys, Nyasaland, 1961–62; Permanent Sec., Ministry of Transport and Communications, Nyasaland, 1963–64. *Recreations:* Rugby football, cricket, golf. *Address:* 308 Grosvenor Square, College Road, Rondebosch, 7700, South Africa. *Clubs:* Royal Cape Golf, Western Province Cricket (Cape Town).

HODGSON, Gordon Hewett; Master of the Supreme Court, Queen's Bench Division, since 1983; *b* 21 Jan. 1929; *s* of late John Lawrence Hodgson and Alice Joan Hodgson (*née* Wickham); *m* 1958, Pauline Audrey Gray; two *s*. *Educ:* Oundle School; University College London. LLB (Hons). National Service, RAEC, 1947–49; called to the Bar, Middle Temple, 1953; private practice, South Eastern Circuit, 1954–83; Asst Boundary Commissioner, 1976; Asst Recorder, 1979. Mem. Cttee, Bentham Club, 1987– (Chm., 1990–95). *Publication:* (ed jtly) Supreme Court Practice, 1991 and 1995. *Recreations:* sailing, enjoying Tuscany. *Address:* Royal Courts of Justice, Strand WC2A 2LL. *T:* 0171–936 6031. *Clubs:* East India; Royal Corinthian Yacht, Bar Yacht.

HODGSON, Guy Andrew Keith; Stipendiary Magistrate for Bradford, since 1993; *b* 19 March 1946; *s* of Herbert and Kathleen Hodgson; *m* 1968, Kay Bampton; three *s*. *Educ:* Pocklington Sch.; Nottingham Poly. (LLB London Ext.). Articled to M. M. Rossfield, Solicitor, York; Legal Asst, Thames Valley Police, 1970–71; Asst Prosecutor, Suffolk Police, 1971–72; Asst Solicitor, Gotelee & Goldsmith, Ipswich, 1972–74; Partner, Close Thornton, Darlington, 1974–93. Formerly Member: Legal Aid Bd Appeals Cttee; Monitoring of Articles Cttee, Law Soc.; Child Care Panel; Solicitors' Family Law Assoc. *Recreations:* reading, painting, horse riding, hobby farming, vintage tractors, family interests. *Address:* Bradford Magistrates Court, The Tyrls, Bradford, W Yorks BD1 1JL. *T:* Bradford (01274) 390111.

HODGSON, Howard Osmond Paul; Chief Executive, Halkin Holdings, since 1993; *b* 22 Feb. 1950; *s* of late Osmond Paul Charles Hodgson and of Sheila Mary (*née* Ward; now Mrs Baker); *m* 1972, Marianne Denise Yvonne, *d* of Samuel Katibien, Aix-en-Provence, France; two *s* one *d* (and one *s* decd). *Educ:* Aiglon Coll., Villars, Switzerland. DipFD 1970; MBIFD; Affiliated MRSH, 1970. Asst Man., Hodgson & Sons Ltd, 1969–71; life assce exec., 1971–75; acquired: Hodgson & Sons Ltd, 1975 (floated USM, 1986); Ingalls from House of Fraser, 1987; launched Dignity in Destiny Ltd, 1989; merger with Pompes Funèbres Générales, France, Kenyon Securities and Hodgson Hldgs plc to form PFG Hodgson Kenyon Internat. plc, 1989; launched: Bereavement Support Service, 1990; PHKI Nat. Training Sch., 1990; retd, 1991, to pursue career in broadcasting and writing. Chief Exec., Hoskins Brewery, 1993; acquired Ronsen plc and LGW plc, 1994. Presenter, How Euro Are You, BBC2, 1991. Hon. Vice Pres., Royal Soc. of St George, 1989. USM Entrepreneur of the Year, 1987. *Publication:* How to Become Dead Rich, 1992. *Recreations:* cricket, yachting, ski-ing, history. *Clubs:* Carlton; RMYC.

HODGSON, James, CBE 1984; Vice-Chairman, British Telecom, 1983–85; Chairman, Printing Equipment Economic Development Committee, 1986–88; *b* 14 Oct. 1925; *s* of late Frederick and Lucy Hodgson; *m* Brenda Dawn (*née* Giles). *Educ:* Exeter Sch.; St John's Coll., Cambridge. Entered GPO, 1950; Private Sec. to Asst PMG, 1952–55 and to Dir Gen. GPO, 1955–56; seconded to Cabinet Office, 1961–63; Head of Telephone Operating Div. of GPO Headquarters, 1965–67; Dir, later Sen. Dir, PO Internat. Telecommunications, 1969–81; Man. Dir, British Telecom Internat., 1981–83. Dir (non-exec.), Cable and Wireless Ltd, 1970–78. FRSA 1984. *Recreations:* travel, archaeology. *Address:* 2 Park Place, Bath BA1 2TY.

HODGSON, John Bury; Special Commissioner of Income Tax, 1970–78; *b* 17 March 1912; *s* of Charles Hodgson and Dorothy Hope Hodgson; *m* 1948, Helen Sibyl Uvedale Beaumont. *Educ:* Derbyshire Grammar Sch.; Manchester Univ. Solicitor, 1942; Asst Solicitor of Inland Revenue, 1956–70. *Publications:* (contrib.) Halsbury's Laws of England; (Consulting Editor) Sergeant on Stamp Duties. *Recreations:* sailing, beekeeping. *Address:* Five Thorns Cottage, North Weirs, Brockenhurst, Hants SO42 7QA. *T:* Lymington (01590) 22653. *Clubs:* various yacht.

HODGSON, Ven. John Derek; Archdeacon of Durham, since 1993, and Canon Residentiary of Durham Cathedral, since 1983; *b* 15 Nov. 1931; *s* of Frederick and Hilda Hodgson; *m* 1956, Greta Wilson; two *s* one *d*. *Educ:* King James School, Bishop Auckland; St John's Coll., Durham (BA Hons History); Cranmer Hall, Durham (Dip. Theology). Short service commission, DLI, 1954–57. Deacon 1959, priest 1960; Curate: Stranton, Hartlepool, 1959–62; St Andrew's, Roker, 1962–64; Vicar: Stillington, 1964–66; Consett, 1966–75; Rector of Gateshead, 1975–83; RD of Gateshead, 1976–83; Hon. Canon of Durham, 1978–83; Archdeacon of Auckland, 1983–93. *Recreations:* walking, music, theatre, country houses. *Address:* 15 The College, Durham DH1 3EQ. *T:* Durham (0191) 3847534.

HODGSON, Sir Maurice (Arthur Eric), Kt 1979; Chairman, British Home Stores plc, 1982–87, and Chief Executive, 1982–85; *b* 21 Oct. 1919; *s* of late Walter Hodgson and of Amy Hodgson (*née* Walker); *m* 1945, Norma Fawcett; one *s* one *d*. *Educ:* Bradford Grammar Sch.; Merton Coll., Oxford (Hon. Fellow, 1979). MA, BSc; FEng, FIChemE; CChem, FRSC. Joined ICI Ltd Fertilizer & Synthetic Products Gp, 1942; seconded to ICI (New York) Ltd, 1955–58; Head of ICI Ltd Technical Dept, 1958; Develt Dir, ICI Ltd Heavy Organic Chemicals Div., 1960, Dep. Chm., 1964; Gen. Man., Company Planning, ICI Ltd, 1966; Commercial Dir and Planning Dir, ICI Ltd, 1970; Dep. Chm., ICI Ltd, 1972–78, Chm., 1978–82; Director: Carrington Viyella Ltd, 1970–74; Imperial Chemicals Insce Ltd, 1970–78 (Chm. 1972); Dunlop Holdings plc, 1982–84 (Chm. 1984); Storehouse, 1985–89; Member: Internat. Adv. Bd, AMAX Inc., 1982–85; European Adv. Council, Air Products and Chemicals Inc., 1982–84; Council, Lloyd's of London, 1987–94. Chm., Civil Justice Review Adv. Cttee, 1985–88; Member: Court, British Shippers' Council, 1978–82; Council, CBI, 1978–82; Internat. Council, Salk Inst., 1978–; Court, Univ. of Bradford, 1979–. Vis. Fellow, Sch. of Business and Organizational Studies, Univ. of Lancaster, 1970–. Governor, London Grad. Sch. of Business Studies, 1978–87. Hon. DUniv Heriot-Watt, 1979; Hon. DTech Bradford, 1979; Hon. DSc Loughborough, 1981; Hon. FUMIST, 1979. Messel Medal, Soc. of Chemical Industry, 1980; George E. Davis Medal, IChemE, 1982. *Recreations:* horse-racing, swimming, fishing. *Address:* Suite 75/76, Kent House, 87 Regent Street, W1R 7HF. *T:* 0171–734 7777.

HODGSON, Patricia Anne, (Mrs George Donaldson), CBE 1995; Director of Policy & Planning, BBC, since 1993; *b* 19 Jan. 1947; *d* of Harold Hodgson and Pat Smith; *m* 1979, George Donaldson; one *s*. *Educ:* Brentwood High Sch.; Newnham Coll., Cambridge (MA); LRAM (Drama) 1968. Conservative Res. Dept, Desk Officer for public sector industries, 1968–70; freelance journalism and broadcasting in UK and USA during seventies; Chm., Bow Gp, 1975–76; Editor, Crossbow, 1976–80. Joined BBC as educn producer for Open Univ. (part of founding team pioneering distance learning techniques), 1970; most of prodn career in educn, specialising in history and philosophy, with spells in current affairs on Today and Tonight. BBC Secretariat, 1982–83, Dep. Sec., 1983–85, The Sec., 1985–87; Hd of Policy & Planning, 1987–92. Dir, BARB, 1987–. Mem., (C) Haringey BC, 1974–77. Mem., Monopolies and Mergers Commn, 1993–. Vice Chm., RTS, 1992–94. Mem., London Arts Bd, 1991–; Trustee, Prince's Youth Business Trust, 1992–95. Associate Fellow, Newnham Coll., Cambridge, 1994–. *Television series* include: English Urban History, 1978; Conflict in Modern Europe, 1980; Rome in the Age of Augustus, 1981. *Publications:* contribs to The Spectator, Daily Telegraph and Guardian. *Recreation:* quietness. *Address:* Broadcasting House, Portland Place, W1A 1AA. *T:* 0171–580 4468. *Club:* Reform.

HODGSON, Prof. Phyllis; Professor of English Language and Mediæval Literature, Bedford College, University of London, 1955–72, retired; *b* 27 June 1909; *d* of late Herbert Henry Hodgson, MA, BSc, PhD, FRIC. *Educ:* Bolling Grammar Sch. for Girls, Bradford; Bedford Coll., University of London (BA); (Sen. Schol.) Lady Margaret Hall, Oxford (BLitt, DPhil). Tutor of St Mary's Coll., Durham Univ., 1936–38; Jex-Blake Fellow, Girton Coll., Cambridge (MA), 1938–40; Lecturer in English Language (Part-time), Queen Mary Coll., University of London, and Lecturer in English, Homerton Coll., Cambridge, 1940–42; Lecturer in English Language and Mediæval Literature, Bedford Coll., University of London, 1942–49; Reader in English Language in the University of London, 1949–55; External examiner for Reading Univ., 1955–57, 1961–63. Mem. Council of Early English Text Soc., 1959–79; Chm., Bd of Studies in English, 1964–66. Sir Israel Gollancz Prize, British Academy, 1971. *Publications:* The Cloud of Unknowing (EETS), 1944, 1958; Deonise Hid Divinite (EETS), 1955, 1958, 1973; The Franklin's Tale, 1960; The Orcherd of Syon and the English Mystical Tradition (Proc. Brit. Acad. 1964), 1965; The Orcherd of Syon (EETS), 1966; Three 14th Century English Mystics, 1967; The General Prologue to the Canterbury Tales, 1969; The Cloud of Unknowing and Related Treatises (Analecta Cartusiana), 1982; articles in Review of English Studies, Modern Language Review, Contemporary Review, etc. *Recreations:* music, walking, travel.

HODGSON, Robin; *see* Hodgson, A. R.

HODGSON, Robin Granville, CBE 1992; Chairman, Granville Holdings plc (Director, since 1972; Group Chief Executive, 1979–95); Director, Johnson Bros & Co. Ltd, Walsall, since 1970; *b* 25 April 1942; *s* of late Henry Edward and of Natalie Beatrice Hodgson; *m* 1982, Fiona Ferelith, *o d* of K. S. Allom, Dorking, Surrey; three *s* one *d* (and one twin *s* decd). *Educ:* Shrewsbury Sch.; Oxford Univ. (BA Hons 1964); Wharton Sch. of Finance, Univ. of Pennsylvania (MBA 1969). Investment Banker, New York and Montreal, 1964–67; Industry in Birmingham, England, 1969–72; Director: Community Hospitals plc, 1982–85 and 1995–; Domnick Hunter Gp, 1992–; Staffordshire Building Soc., 1995–. Mem., W Midlands Industrial Develt Bd, 1989–. Contested (C) Walsall North, Feb. and Oct. 1974; MP (C) Walsall North, Nov. 1976–1979. Chm., Birmingham Bow Gp, 1972–73; National Union of Conservative Associations: Member: Central Council, 1979–; Exec. Cttee, 1988–; Gen. Purposes Cttee, 1990–; Vice Pres., 1995–; Asst Treas., 1985–88, Treas., 1988–91, Chm., 1991–94, W Midlands Area. Member: Council for the Securities Industry, 1980–85; Securities and Investments Board, 1985–89; Dir, SFA, 1991–; Chm., Nat. Assoc. of Security Dealers and Investment Managers, 1979–85. Trustee, Friends of Shrewsbury Sch.; Associate, St. George's House, Windsor. Liveryman, Goldsmiths' Co., 1983. *Publication:* Britain's Home Defence Gamble, 1978. *Recreations:* squash, theatre. *Address:* 15 Scarsdale Villas, W8 6PT. *T:* 0171–937 2964; Nash Court, Ludlow, Salop SY8 3DG. *T:* Ludlow (01584) 811677.

HODGSON, Stanley Ernest, CBE 1974 (OBE 1966); retired; Education Adviser, British High Commission, New Delhi, 1971–77; *b* 11 July 1918; *s* of Harold Frederick Hodgson, MPS, and Winifred Caroline (*née* Gale); *m* 1945, Joan Beryl (*née* Ballard); two *d*. *Educ:* Brentwood Grammar Sch.; London Univ. Teacher's Certif., London, 1941; BA Hons Russian, London, 1949. RA, 1941–46. British Council: India, 1949–54; Uganda, 1956–60; Reg. Rep., South India, 1965–68; Controller Estabts, 1969–71. Dir, Fest. of India in Britain 1982. *Recreations:* reading, gardening, walking. *Address:* Clarendon, Netherfield Road, Battle, East Sussex TN33 0HJ. *T:* Battle (01424) 772631. *Club:* Commonwealth Trust.

HODGSON, Col Terence Harold Henry, DSO 1945; MC 1944; TD 1953; DL; FSVA; Vice Lord-Lieutenant of Cumbria, 1983–91; *b* 10 Dec. 1916; *s* of late Michael C. L. Hodgson, Grange-over-Sands; *m* 1st, 1942, Joan Winsome Servant (marr. diss. 1969; she *d* 1974); 2nd, 1972, Doreen Jacqueline Pollit Brŭnzel (*d* 1985); three *s* three *d*; 3rd, 1985, Elizabeth Robinson. *Educ:* Kendal Grammar Sch. FSVA 1953; FRSH 1954. Served War with Border Regt, Ceylon, India and Burma; Comdr, 4th Bn Border Regt, TA, 1953–56; Dep. Comdr, 126 Inf. Bde, TA, 1956–59; Col TA, 1959; Hon. Colonel: King's Own Royal Border Regt, 1976–82; Cumbria Cadet Force, 1977–86. Dir, Cartmel Steeplechasers Ltd, 1959–; Local Dir, Royal Insurance, 1960–. Chairman: Governors, Kirkbie Kendal Sch., 1970–86; Kendal Almshouse Charities, 1975–86; Cumbria Appeal Cttee, Army Benevolent Fund, 1987–93. Past Pres., Cumberland and Westmorland Rugby Union. DL Westmorland, 1958. *Recreations:* Rugby football, horse racing. *Address:* Abbotsrood, Grange-over-Sands, Cumbria LA11 7HH. *T:* Grange-over-Sands (015395) 32843. *Club:* Army and Navy.

HODGSON, Ven. Thomas Richard Burnham; Archdeacon of West Cumberland, 1979–91, now Archdeacon Emeritus; *b* 17 Aug. 1926; *s* of Richard Shillito Hodgson and Marion Thomasina Bertram Marshall; *m* 1952, Margaret Esther, *o d* of Evan and Caroline Margaret Makinson; one *s* one *d*. *Educ:* Heversham Grammar School; London Coll. of Divinity, Univ. of London. BD, ALCD. Deacon 1952, priest 1953, dio. Carlisle; Curate of Crosthwaite, Keswick, 1952–55; Curate of Stanwix, Carlisle, 1955–59; Vicar of St Nicholas', Whitehaven, 1959–65; Rector of Aikton, 1965–67; Vicar of Raughtonhead with Gaitsgill, 1967–73; Hon. Canon of Carlisle, 1973–91; Vicar of: Grange-over-Sands, 1973–79; Mosser, 1979–83. Mem., General Synod of C of E, 1983–90. Domestic Chaplain to Bishop of Carlisle, 1967–73, Hon. Chaplain 1973–79; Director of Ordination Candidates, 1970–74; RD of Windermere, 1976–79; Surrogate, 1962–91. FRMetS 1988–91. *Recreations:* listening to music, watching drama, geology, meteorological observing, watercolour painting. *Address:* 58 Greenacres, Wetheral, Carlisle CA4 8LD. *T:* Carlisle (01228) 561159.

HODGSON, Hon. Sir (Walter) Derek (Thornley), Kt 1977; a Judge of the High Court of Justice, Queen's Bench Division, 1977–92; *b* 24 May 1917; *s* of late Walter Hodgson, Whitefield, Manchester; *m* 1951, Raymonde Valda (*née* de Villiers) (*d* 1965); no *c*. *Educ:* Malvern Coll.; Trinity Hall, Cambridge. Scholar, Trinity Hall; Harmsworth Scholar, Middle Temple; 1st Cl. Law Tripos, Part II, 1938; 1st Cl. LLB, 1939. Served throughout War 1939–46, Royal Artillery; Burma 1942–45; released with rank of Captain, 1946. Called to Bar, Middle Temple, 1946 (Master of the Bench, 1967); QC 1961. Member: Senate of Inns of Court, 1966–69; Gen. Council of the Bar, 1965–69. Judge of the Salford Hundred Court of Record, 1965–71; a Law Comr, 1971–77; a Recorder of the Crown Court, 1972–77. Member: Lord Chancellor's Cttees on: Legal Educn, 1968–71; Contempt of Court, 1971–74; Butler Cttee on Mentally Abnormal Offenders, 1973–75; Parole Board, 1981–83 (Vice-Chm., 1982–83). Chm., Howard League Wkg Pty on Forfeiture (report published as The Profits of Crime and their Recovery, 1984). *Recreation:* travel.

Address: Carpmael Building, Middle Temple Lane, EC4Y 7AT. *T:* 0171–583 1613. *Clubs:* United Oxford & Cambridge University, MCC; Tennis and Racquets (Manchester); Hawks (Cambridge).

HODGSON, William Donald John; Broadcasting Consultant; *b* 25 March 1923; *s* of James Samuel Hodgson and Caroline Maud Albrecht; *m* 1946, Betty Joyce Brown; two *s* six *d.* *Educ:* Beckenham Grammar School. Served Beds and Herts Regt, 1940–42; pilot, RAF and Fleet Air Arm, 1942–46. Documentary and feature film editor (with Jean Renoir on The River, Calcutta), 1946–50; Organiser, Festival of Britain Youth Programme, 1950–51; Asst Sec., Central Bureau for Educational Visits and Exchanges, 1951–54; Asst Gen. Man., Press Assoc., 1954–60; Gen. Man., ITN, 1960–82; Dir of Develt, ITN, 1982–86 (Dir, 1972–86). Dir, UPITN Corp., 1967–73. Executive Producer: Battle for the Falklands, 1982; Theft of a Thoroughbred, 1983; Victory in Europe, 1985; writer and producer, Welcome to the Caley (Royal Caledonian Schs), 1987. *Recreations:* grandchildcare, private flying, cricket, swimming. *Address:* 38 Lakeside, Wickham Road, Beckenham, Kent BR3 2LX. *T:* 0181–650 8959.

HODIN, Prof. Josef Paul, LLD; author, art historian, art critic; *b* 17 Aug. 1905; *s* of Eduard D. Hodin and Rosa (*née* Klug); *m* 1945, Doris Pamela Simms; one *s* one *d.* *Educ:* Kleinseitner Realschule and Neustädter Realgymnasium, Prague; Charles Univ., Prague; London Univ.; Art Academies of Dresden and Berlin. Press Attaché to Norwegian Govt in London, 1944–45; Dir of Studies and Librarian, Inst. of Contemporary Arts, London, 1949–54; Hon. Mem. Editorial Council of The Journal of Aesthetics and Art Criticism, Cleveland, 1955–; Mem. Exec. Cttee British Soc. of Aesthetics; Pres., British Section, AICA; Editor: Prisme des Arts, Paris, 1956–57; Quadrum, Brussels, 1956–66. 1st internat. prize for art criticism, Biennale, Venice, 1954. Hon. PhD Uppsala, 1969; Hon. Prof. Vienna, 1975. DSM 1st cl. Czechoslovakia, 1947; St Olav Medal, Norway, 1958; Comdr, Order of Merit, Italy, 1966; Grand Cross, Order of Merit, Austria, 1968; Order of Merit, 1st cl., Germany, 1969; Silver Cross of Merit, Austria, 1972; Comdr, Order of Merit, Germany, 1986. *Publications:* Monographs on Sven Erixson (Stockholm), 1940; Ernst Josephson (Stockholm), 1942, Edvard Munch (Stockholm), 1948, (Frankfurt a/M), 1951; Isaac Grünewald (Stockholm), 1949; Art and Criticism (Stockholm), 1944; J. A. Comenius and Our Time (Stockholm), 1944; The Dilemma of Being Modern (London), 1956, (New York), 1959; Henry Moore (Amsterdam, Hamburg), 1956, (London, New York), 1958, (Buenos Aires), 1963; Ben Nicholson (London), 1957; Barbara Hepworth (Neuchatel, London, New York), 1961; Lynn Chadwick (Amsterdam, Hamburg, London, New York), 1961; Bekenntnis zu Kokoschka (Mainz), 1963; Edvard Munch (Mainz), 1963; Oskar Kokoschka: A Biography (London, New York), 1966; Walter Kern (Neuchatel, London), 1966; Ruszkowski (London), 1967; Bernard Leach (London), 1967; Oskar Kokoschka: Sein Leben Seine Zeit (Mainz), 1968; Kafka und Goethe (Hamburg), 1968; Giacomo Manzú (Rome), 1969; Die Brühlsche Terrasse, Ein Künstlerroman, 1970; Emilio Greco, Life and Work (London, New York), 1971; Edvard Munch (London, New York, Oslo), 1972; Modern Art and the Modern Mind (London, Cleveland), 1972; Alfred Manessier (London, NY, Paris), 1972; Bernard Stern (London), 1972; Ludwig Meidner (Darmstadt), 1973; Hilde Goldschmidt (Hamburg), 1974; Paul Berger-Bergner, Leben und Werk (Hamburg), 1974; Die Leute von Elverdingen (Hamburg), 1974; Kokoschka und Hellas (Vienna), 1977; John Milne (London), 1977; Else Meidner, 1979; Elisabeth Frink, 1983; Douglas Portway, 1983; Franz Luby (Vienna), 1983; Dieses Mütterchen hat Krallen, Die Geschichte einer Prager Jugend (Hamburg), 1985; Verlorene Existenzen, Erzählungen (Hamburg), 1986; Friedrich Karl Gotsch (Hamburg), 1987; Manzú Pittore (Bergamo, London, Hamburg), 1988; Jan Brazda (London, Stockholm), 1989; contribs on literary and art subjects to internat. periodicals. *Address:* 12 Eton Avenue, NW3 3EH. *T:* 0171–794 3609. *Clubs:* Athenæum, Arts.

HODKIN, Rev. Canon Hedley; Residentiary Canon, Manchester Cathedral, 1957–70, Canon Emeritus, since 1970; Sub-Dean, 1966–70; *b* 3 Jan. 1902; *s* of Walter and Elizabeth Hodkin; *m* 1932, Mary M., *d* of Dr J. A. Findlay; one *s* one *d.* *Educ:* University of Sheffield; Christ's Coll. and Westcott House, Cambridge. Curate of: Morpeth, 1935–38; St George's, Newcastle, 1938–40; Vicar of: St Luke's, Newcastle, 1940–47; Holy Trinity, Millhouses, Sheffield, 1947–57. Examining Chaplain: to Bishop of Newcastle, 1939–47; to Bishop of Sheffield, 1951–57; to Bishop of Manchester, 1957. Hon. Canon of Sheffield, 1955–57. Select Preacher, Cambridge, 1968. *Recreation:* music. *Address:* Dulverton Hall, St Martin's Square, Scarborough YO11 2DQ. *T:* Scarborough (01723) 360364.

HODKINSON, Prof. Henry Malcolm, DM; FRCP; Barlow Professor of Geriatric Medicine, University College London, 1985–91, now Emeritus; *b* 28 April 1931; *s* of Charles and Olive Hodkinson; *m* 1st, (marr. diss.); four *d*; *m* 2nd, 1986, Judith Marie Bryant, *qv.* *Educ:* Manchester Grammar Sch.; Brasenose Coll., Oxford (DM 1975); Middlesex Hospital. FRCP 1974. Consultant Physician in Geriatrics to: Enfield and Tottenham Gps of Hosps, 1962–70; Northwick Park Hosp., 1970–78 (also Mem., Scientific Staff of Clin. Res. Centre); Sen. Lectr in Geriatric Medicine, 1978–79, Prof. of Geriatric Medicine, 1979–84, RPMS. Gov., Research into Ageing, 1983–. *Publications:* An Outline of Geriatrics, 1975, 2nd edn 1981 (trans. Spanish, Dutch, German, Italian and Japanese); Common Symptoms of Disease in the Elderly, 1976, 2nd edn 1980 (trans. Turkish); Biochemical Diagnosis of the Elderly, 1977; (ed) Clinical Biochemistry of the Elderly, 1984; (with J. M. Hodkinson) Sherratt? A Natural Family of Staffordshire Figures, 1991; approx. 100 papers in learned jls, 1961–. *Recreations:* English glass and ceramics. *Address:* 8 Chiswick Square, Burlington Lane, Chiswick, W4 2QG. *T:* 0181–747 0239.

HODKINSON, Judith Marie, (Mrs H. M. Hodkinson); *see* Bryant, J. M.

HODSON, Clive, CBE 1992; FCCA; FCIT; Managing Director: London Buses Ltd, since 1989; London Transport Buses, since 1994; Chairman, Victoria Coach Station Ltd, since 1995; *b* 9 March 1942; *s* of late Stanley Louis Hodson and of Elsie May Hodson (*née* Stratford); *m* 1976, Fiona Mary Pybus; one *s* one *d.* *Educ:* Erith Grammar Sch. FCCA 1967; FCIT 1969; ATII 1968. LT, 1960–69; Asst Sec. and Accountant, London Country Bus Services Ltd, 1970–74; Mgt Accountant, LT, 1974–78; Finance Dir, London Buses, 1978–89. LT Project Dir, Bus Privatisation, 1993–95. Freeman, City of London, 1995; Co. of Carmen, 1995. *Recreations:* travel, walking, reading. *Address:* 172 Buckingham Palace Road, Westminster, SW1W 9TN. *T:* 0171–918 3872.

HODSON, Christopher Robert; His Honour Judge Hodson; a Circuit Judge, since 1993; *b* 3 Nov. 1946; *s* of James and Elizabeth Hodson; *m* 1970, Jean Patricia Anne Dayer; one *s* one *d.* *Educ:* King's Sch., Worcester. Called to the Bar, Lincoln's Inn, 1970; practised, Birmingham, 1971–93; a Recorder, 1988–93. *Recreations:* gardening, learning French. *Address:* 6 Fountain Court, Steelhouse Lane, Birmingham B4 6DR. *T:* 0121–233 3282.

HODSON, Daniel Houghton, FCT; Chief Executive, London International Financial Futures and Options Exchange, since 1993; *b* 11 March 1944; *s* of Henry Vincent Hodson, *qv* and Margaret Elizabeth (*née* Honey); *m* 1979, Diana Mary Ryde; two *d.* *Educ:* Eton; Merton Coll., Oxford (MA Hons PPE). FCT 1979. Chase Manhattan Bank, 1965–73; joined Edward Bates & Sons Ltd, 1973, Dir 1974–76; Unigate plc: Gp Treas., 1976–81; Gp Finance Dir, 1981–87; Pres., Unigate Inc., 1986–87; Chief Exec., 1987–88, Chm. 1988, Davidson Pearce Gp plc; Dep. Chief Exec., Nationwide Building Soc., 1989–92. Director: The Post Office, 1984–; Ransomes plc, 1993–. Association of Corporate Treasurers: Chm., 1985–86; Pres., 1992–93. Gov., Yehudi Menuhin Sch., 1984–. Founding Editor, Corporate Finance and Treasury Management, 1984–. *Recreations:* music, travel, ski-ing, gardening. *Address:* Treyford Manor, Midhurst, W Sussex GU29 0LD. *T:* Midhurst (01730) 825436. *Clubs:* Brooks's, City of London.

HODSON, Denys Fraser, CBE 1981; Director, Arts and Recreation, Thamesdown Borough Council, 1974–92; *b* 23 May 1928; *s* of Rev. Harold Victor Hodson, MC and Marguerite Edmée Ritchie; *m* 1954, Julie Compton Goodwin; one *s* one *d.* *Educ:* Marlborough Coll.; Trinity Coll., Oxford (MA). After a career in commerce and industry, apptd first Controller of Arts and Recreation, Swindon Bor. Council, 1970. Chairman: Southern Arts Assoc., 1974–80 and 1985–87; Council, Regional Arts Assocs, 1975–80; Chief Leisure Officers' Assoc., 1974 and 1982–84; Chm., Public Arts Commns Agency, 1993–; Vice-Chm., Arts Council of England (formerly of GB), 1989–94 (Mem., 1987–94); a Director: Oxford Playhouse Co., 1974–86; Oxford Stage Co., 1988–89; Chairman: Brewery Arts, 1994–; Voluntary Arts Network, 1994– (Vice-Chm., 1992–94); a Governor: BFI, 1976–87; Wyvern Arts Trust, 1984–95. *Publications:* (contrib.) Arts Centres, 1981; (contrib.) The Future of Leisure Services, 1988; conf. papers and articles. *Recreations:* bird-watching, fishing, the arts. *Address:* Manor Farm House, Fairford, Glos GL7 4AR. *T:* Cirencester (01285) 712462.

HODSON, Prof. Frank, BSc London 1949; PhD Reading 1951; Professor of Geology in the University of Southampton, 1958–81, now Emeritus; *b* 23 Nov. 1921; *s* of late Matthew and Gertrude Hodson; *m* 1945, Ada Heyworth; three *d.* *Educ:* Burnley Grammar Sch.; Reading Univ.; London Univ. (external student). Demonstrator, Reading Univ., 1947–49; Lecturer, Reading Univ., 1949–58. Dean, Faculty of Science, 1972–74, and 1976–77, Public Orator, 1970–73, Univ. of Southampton. Murchison Fund, Geol. Soc., 1962; Founder Mem. and first Hon. Sec., Palaeontol. Assoc., 1957. Pres. Sect. C (geology), British Assoc. for Adv. of Science, 1975. Hon. Mem. Geol. Soc. de Belg. *Publications:* geological papers in publications of learned societies. *Recreation:* book collecting. *Address:* Department of Geology, The University, Southampton SO9 5NH.

HODSON, Henry Vincent; Provost of Ditchley (Director, Ditchley Foundation), 1961–71; *b* 12 May 1906; *er s* of late Prof. T. C. Hodson; *m* 1933, Margaret Elizabeth Honey, Sydney; four *s.* *Educ:* Gresham's Sch.; Balliol Coll., Oxford. Fellow of All Souls Coll., Oxford, 1928–35; Staff of Economic Advisory Council, 1930–31; Asst Editor of the Round Table, 1931, Editor, 1934–39; Director, Empire Div., Ministry of Information, 1939–41; Reforms Commissioner, Govt of India, 1941–42; Principal Asst Sec., and later head of Non-Munitions Div., Min. of Production, 1942–45; Asst Editor, Sunday Times, 1946–50, Editor, 1950–61. Sole Partner, Hodson Consultants, 1971–. Editor, 1973–88, Consultant Editor, 1988–93, Annual Register (of world events); Consultant Editor, The International Foundation Directory, 1974–89. Past Master, Mercers' Co. *Publications:* Economics of a Changing World, 1933; (part) The Empire in the World, 1937; Slump and Recovery, 1929–37, 1938; The British Commonwealth and the Future, 1939; Twentieth Century Empire, 1948; Problems in Anglo-American Relations, 1963; The Great Divide: Britain-India-Pakistan, 1969 (reissued 1985); The Diseconomics of Growth, 1972; many articles in reviews, etc. *Address:* Flat 1, 105 Lexham Gardens, W8 6JN. *T:* 0171–373 2859.

See also D. H. Hodson.

HODSON, John; Chief Executive, Singer & Friedlander Holdings, since 1990; *b* 19 May 1946; *s* of Arthur and Olga Hodson; *m* 1971, Christina McLeod; one *s* two *d.* *Educ:* Worcester Coll., Oxford (PPE). Joined Singer & Friedlander, 1969: Asst Dir, 1974–83; Dir, 1983–; Head of Investment Dept, 1985–90; Chief Exec., Singer & Friedlander Gp PLC, 1993– (Dir, 1987–). *Recreations:* tennis, family. *Address:* 21 New Street, EC2M 4HR. *T:* 0171–623 3000.

HODSON, Sir Michael (Robin Adderley), 6th Bt *cr* 1789; Captain, Scots Guards, retired; *b* 5 March 1932; *s* of Major Sir Edmond Adair Hodson, 5th Bt, DSO, and Anne Elizabeth Adderley (*d* 1984), *yr d* of Lt-Col Hartopp Francis Charles Adderley Cradock, Hill House, Sherborne St John; *S* father, 1972; *m* 1st, 1963, Katrin Alexa (marr. diss. 1978), *d* of late Erwin Bernstiel, Dinas Powis, Glamorgan; three *d*; 2nd, 1978, Catherine, *d* of late John Henry Seymour, Wimpole St, W1. *Educ:* Eton. *Heir:* *b* Patrick Richard Hodson [*b* 27 Nov. 1934; *m* 1961, June, *o d* of H. M. Shepherd-Cross; three *s*]. *Address:* The White House, Awbridge, Romsey, Hants SO51 0HF.

HODSON, Thomas David Tattersall; His Honour Judge Hodson; a Circuit Judge, since 1987; *b* 24 Sept. 1942; *s* of late Thomas Norman Hodson and Elsie Nuttall Hodson; *m* 1969, Patricia Ann Vint; two *s* one *d.* *Educ:* Sedbergh Sch.; Manchester Univ. (LLB). Leader Writer, Yorkshire Post, 1964–65; called to the Bar, Inner Temple 1966; in practice on Northern Circuit, 1967–87; Junior, 1969; a Recorder, 1983–87. Pres., S Lancs Br., Magistrates' Assoc., 1994–. *Recreations:* music, genealogy, fell-walking. *Address:* c/o Manchester Crown Court, Crown Square, Manchester M3 3FL. *T:* 0161–954 1800. *Club:* Lancashire CC.

HOEKMAN, Johan Bernard; Knight, Order of Netherlands Lion; Officer, Order of Orange Nassau; Netherlands Ambassador to the Court of St James's, 1990–94, and concurrently to Iceland; *b* 11 Sept. 1931; *m* 1957, Jeanne van Gelder; three *s* one *d.* *Educ:* Univ. of Groningen (degree in Social Geography). Foreign Service, 1961; served Baghdad, Washington, Jeddah; Counsellor, Cairo, 1972–74; Deputy, later Head, Dept for Financial Economic Develt Co-operation, Min. of Foreign Affairs, 1974–80; Ambassador, Dakar, 1980–81, Paramaribo, 1981–84; Dir-Gen. for Internat. Co-operation, 1984–88; Ambassador, Paramaribo, 1988–90. Holds foreign decorations. *Address:* Staten Laan 102, 2582 GV The Hague, Netherlands.

HOERNER, John Lee; Chief Executive, Burton Group PLC, since 1992; *b* 23 Sept. 1939; *s* of Robert Lee Hoerner and Lulu Alice (*née* Stone); *m* 1st 1959, Susan Kay Morgan (marr. diss. 1971); one *s* one *d*; 2nd, 1973, Anna Lea Thomas. *Educ:* Univ. of Nebraska (BS, BA). Hahnes Department Stores: senior buying and merchandising positions: Hovland Swanson, Lincoln, Neb, 1959–68; Woolf Bros, Kansas City, Mo, 1968–72; Hahnes, NJ, 1972–73; Pres. and Chief Exec. Officer, First 21st Century Corp., Hahnes, 1974–81; Chairman and Chief Executive Officer: H. & S. Pogue Co., Cincinnati, Ohio, 1981–82; L. S. Ayres & Co., Indianapolis, Ind., 1982–87; Burton Group PLC: Chairman: Debenhams, 1987–92; Harvey Nichols, 1988–91; Chief Exec., Stores, 1989–92. Member: Governing Cttee, Dogs' Home, Battersea, 1991–; Air Sqdn. *Publications:* Ayres Adages, 1983; The Director's Handbook, 1991. *Recreations:* riding, flying. *Address:* 10 Great Castle Street, W1N 7AD. *T:* 0171–927 0501. *Clubs:* Groucho; Woodstock (Indianapolis).

HOEY, Catharine Letitia; MP (Lab) Vauxhall, since June 1989; *b* 21 June 1946; *d* of Thomas Henry and Letitia Jane Hoey. *Educ:* Lylehill Primary Sch.; Belfast Royal Acad.; Ulster Coll. of Physical Educn (Dip. in PE); City of London Coll. (BSc Econs). Lectr, Southwark Coll., 1972–76; Sen. Lectr, Kingsway Coll., 1976–85; Educnl Advr, London Football Clubs, 1985–89. *Recreations:* watching soccer, keeping fit. *Address:* House of Commons, SW1A 0AA. *T:* 0171–219 3000. *Club:* Barbican Health and Fitness Centre.

HOFF, Harry Summerfield; *see* Cooper, William.

HOFFBRAND, Prof. (Allan) Victor, DM; FRCP, FRCPath; Professor of Haematology and Honorary Consultant, Royal Free Hospital School of Medicine, since 1974; *b* 14 Oct. 1935; *s* of late Philip Hoffbrand and Minnie (*née* Freedman); *m* 1963, Irene Jill Mellows; two *s* one *d*. *Educ:* Bradford Grammar Sch.; Queen's Coll., Oxford (BA 1956; MA 1960; BM BCh 1959; DM 1972); Royal London Hospital; DSc London 1987. FRCP 1976; FRCPath 1980; Hon. FRCPE 1986. Jun. hosp. posts, Royal London Hosp., 1960–62; Res. and Registrar posts, RPMS, 1962–66; Lectr, St Bartholomew's Hosp., 1966–67; MRC Fellow, New England Med. Centre, Boston, 1967–68; Sen. Lectr, RPMS, 1968–74. Visiting Professor: Sanaa, Yemen, 1986; Armed Forces Inst. Path., Rawalpindi, 1988; Royal Melbourne Hosp., 1991. Lectures: Los Braun Meml, Johannesburg, 1978; Sir Stanley Davidson, Edinburgh, 1983; G. Izak Meml, Jerusalem, 1984; K. J. R. Wightman, Toronto, 1988. Chairman: Standing Intercollegiate Cttee on Med. Oncology, 1993–94; Jt Haematology Cttee, RCP, RCPath, 1994–; Member: Systems Bd, MRC, 1986–89; Council, RCPath, 1987–90; Council, Royal Free Sch. of Med., 1991–. Medical Adviser: UK Thalassaemia Soc.; Gaucher Foundn. Member: Amer. Soc. Haematology; Brit. Soc. Haematology; Internat. Soc. Haematology. Member, Editorial Board: Brit. Jl Haematology (Chm.); Clinical Haematology; Blood Reviews; Leukaemia Res.; Leukaemia and Lymphoma; Haematologica; Qly Jl Medicine; Jl Lab. and Clin. Medicine. *Publications:* (ed with S. M. Lewis) Postgraduate Haematology, 1972, 3rd edn 1989; (ed) Recent Advances in Haematology, 1977, 7th edn 1993; (with J. E. Pettit): Essential Haematology, 1980, 3rd edn 1993; Blood Diseases Illustrated, 1987; Sandoz Atlas of Clinical Haematology, 1988, 2nd edn 1944; papers on megaloblastic anaemia, iron chelation, leukaemia and related disorders. *Recreations:* music, antiques, chess, bridge. *Address:* Department of Haematology, Royal Free Hospital, NW3 2QG. *T:* 0171–794 0500.

HOFFENBERG, Sir Raymond, (Bill), KBE 1984; President, Wolfson College, Oxford, 1985–93, Hon. Fellow, 1993; Professor of Medical Ethics, University of Queensland, since 1993; *b* 6 March 1923; *er s* of Ben and Dora Hoffenberg; *m* 1949; two *s*. *Educ:* Grey High Sch., Port Elizabeth; Univ. of Cape Town. MB, ChB 1948, MD, PhD; MA Oxon. FRCP 1971; FRCPE, FRCPI; Hon. FRACP 1984; Hon. FACP 1985; Hon. FRCP(C) 1986; Hon. FFOM 1990; Hon. FFPM 1990; Hon. FRCPsych 1991; Hon. FRCSE 1993. Wartime Service with S African Armed Forces, N Africa and Italy. Sen. Lectr, Dept of Medicine, Univ. of Cape Town, 1955–67; Carnegie Corp. of NY Trav. Fellow, 1957–58; banned by S African Govt, 1967; emigrated to UK, 1968. Sen. Scientist, MRC (UK), 1968–72; William Withering Prof. of Medicine, Univ. of Birmingham, 1972–85. Member: West Midlands RHA, 1976–83; MRC, 1978–82. Member: Central and Exec. Cttee, Internat. Soc. for Endocrinology, 1976–88; Royal Soc. Med., Endocr. Sect. (Pres., 1978–80); Med. Res. Soc. (Chm., 1978–83); Assoc. of Physicians (Pres., 1985–86); Amer. Assoc. of Physicians; Academia Europaea, 1990; Chm. Council, British Heart Foundn, 1987–; President: Mental Health Foundn, 1989–; Med. Campaign against Nuclear War, 1989–. Member, Editorial Board of several journals. Hon. Mem., Acad. of Medicine of Malaysia, 1989. Royal College of Physicians: Oliver-Sharpey Lectr, 1973; Senior Censor, 1981–82; Pres., 1983–89; Harveian Orator, 1991. Freeman, City of London, 1983. Hon. DSc: Leicester, 1985; City, 1985; Cape Town, 1993; Hon. MD Bristol, 1989. *Publications:* Clinical Freedom, 1987 (Rock Carling Fellowship, Nuffield Provincial Hospitals Trust); papers on endocrinology and metabolism. *Recreations:* (largely nostalgic) reading, walking, gardening, golf, tennis. *Address:* c/o Wolfson College, Oxford OX2 6UD. *T:* Oxford (01865) 274102.

HOFFMAN, Dustin Lee; actor, *b* 8 Aug. 1937; *s* of Harry Hoffman and Lillian Hoffman; *m* 1st, 1969, Anne Byrne (marr. diss. 1980), two *d*, 2nd, 1980, Lisa Gottsegen; two *s* two *d*. *Educ:* Santa Monica City Coll.; Pasadena Playhouse. Stage début in Sarah Lawrence Coll. prodn, Yes is For a Very Young Man; Broadway début, A Cook for Mr General, 1961; appeared in: Harry, and Noon and Night, Amer. Place Theatre, NY, 1964–65; Journey of the Fifth Horse, and Star Wagon, 1965; Fragments, Berkshire Theatre Festival, Stockbridge, Mass, 1966; Eh?, 1966–67; Jimmy Shine, Broadway, 1968–69; Death of a Salesman, Broadway, 1984; London début, Merchant of Venice, Phoenix, 1989. Dir, All Over Town, Broadway, 1974. Films: The Graduate, 1967; Midnight Cowboy, 1969; John and Mary, 1969; Little Big Man, 1971; Who Is Harry Kellerman and Why Is He Saying Those Terrible Things About Me?, 1971; Straw Dogs, 1972; Alfredo, Alfredo, 1972; Papillon, 1973; Lenny, 1974; All The President's Men, 1975; Marathon Man, 1976; Straight Time, 1978; Agatha, 1979; Kramer vs Kramer, 1979 (Academy Award); Tootsie, 1983; Death of a Salesman, 1985 (Emmy Award); Ishtar, 1987; Rain Man, 1989 (Academy Award; Golden Globe Award); Family Business, 1990; Billy Bathgate, 1991; Hook, 1992; Accidental Hero, 1993; Outbreak, 1995. Record: Death of a Salesman. Obie Award as best off-Broadway actor, 1965–66, for Journey of the Fifth Horse; Drama Desk, Theatre World, and Vernon Rice Awards for Eh?, 1966; Oscar Award nominee for The Graduate, Midnight Cowboy, and Lenny. *Address:* Punch Productions, 540 Madison Avenue, New York, NY 10022, USA.

HOFFMAN, Michael Richard, FEng; Chief Executive, since 1989, and Deputy Chairman, since 1993, Thames Water plc (formerly Thames Water Authority); *b* 31 Oct. 1939; *s* of Sydney William Hoffman and Ethel Margaret Hoffman (*née* Hill); *m* 1st, 1963, Margaret Edith Tregaskes (marr. diss. 1978); one *d*; 2nd, 1982, Helen Judith Peters. *Educ:* Hitchin Grammar Sch.; Univ. of Bristol (BScEng Hons). Eur Ing; FIMechE, FIEE. Rolls Royce, 1961; AE Ltd, 1973; Perkins Engines Group: Managing Director, 1976; Chairman, 1977; Massey Ferguson Ltd: Vice President, 1980; President, Farm Machinery Div., 1981; Chief Exec. and Man. Dir, Babcock Internat., 1983–87; Deputy Chairman: Airship Industries, 1988–90 (Chief Exec., 1987–88); Cosworth Engrg Ltd, 1988–91; Director: Cray Electronics, 1990–; Power Gen, 1993–. Pres., IProdE, 1987–88 (Vice Pres., 1985–87); Vice-Pres., EEF, 1985–87. Chm., UK S African Trade Assoc., 1987; Member: Technology Requirements Bd, 1985–88; Monopolies and Mergers Commn, 1988–; BOTB, 1986–89; Engrg Council, 1991–. Chm. Council, Brunel Univ., 1991– (Mem., 1984–). Freeman, City of London, 1984; Liveryman, Engineers' Co., 1984–. *Recreations:* Real tennis, shooting, sailing. *Address:* 43 De Vere Gardens, W8 5AW. *T:* 0171–581 4612. *Clubs:* Reform, Royal Automobile, MCC.

HOFFMAN, Rev. Canon Stanley Harold, MA; Chaplain in Ordinary to the Queen, 1976–87; Hon. Canon of Rochester Cathedral, 1965–80, now Emeritus; *b* 17 Aug. 1917; *s* of Charles and Ellen Hoffman, Denham, Bucks; *m* 1943, Mary Mifanwy Patricia, *d* of late Canon Creed Meredith, Chaplain to the Queen, and of Mrs R. Creed Meredith, Windsor; one *s* one *d*. *Educ:* The Royal Grammar Sch., High Wycombe, Bucks; St Edmund Hall, Oxford (BA 1939, MA 1943); Lincoln Theol Coll., 1940–41. Deacon, 1941; Priest, 1942; Curate: Windsor Parish Ch., 1941–44; All Saints, Weston, Bath, 1944–47; Chertsey (in charge of All SS), 1947–50; Vicar of Shottermill, Haslemere, Sy, 1951–64; Diocesan Director of Education, Rochester, 1965–80; Warden of Readers, 1974–80. Proctor in Convocation, Church Assembly, 1969–70; Exam. Chaplain to Bp of Rochester, 1973–80. Member: Kent Educn Cttee, 1965–80; Bromley Educn Cttee, 1967–80; Kent Council of Religious Educn, 1965–80; Archbps' Commn on Christian Initiation, 1970. Vice-Chm., Christ Church Coll., Canterbury, 1973–80. Hon. MA Kent, 1982. *Publications:* Morning Shows the Day: the making of a priest (autobiog.), 1995; (pt-author): A Handbook of Thematic Material, 1968; Christians in Kent, 1972; Teaching the Parables, 1974; contrib. various pubns on Preaching and Religious Educn; numerous Dio. study papers. *Recreations:* music, walking. *Address:* Zansizzey, Trevone, Padstow, Cornwall PL28 8QJ. *T:* Padstow (01841) 520864.

HOFFMANN, family name of **Baron Hoffmann**.

HOFFMANN, Baron *cr* 1995 (Life Peer), of Chedworth in the County of Gloucestershire; **Leonard Hubert Hoffmann;** Kt 1985; PC 1992; a Lord of Appeal in Ordinary, since 1995; *b* 8 May 1934; *s* of B. W. and G. Hoffmann; *m* 1957, Gillian Lorna Sterner; two *d*. *Educ:* South African College Sch., Cape Town; Univ. of Cape Town (BA); The Queen's Coll., Oxford (Rhodes Scholar; MA, BCL, Vinerian Law Scholar; Hon. Fellow, 1992). Advocate of Supreme Court of S Africa, 1958–60. Called to the Bar, Gray's Inn, 1964, Bencher, 1984; QC 1977; a Judge, Courts of Appeal of Jersey and Guernsey, 1980–85; a Judge of the High Court of Justice, Chancery Div., 1985–92; a Lord Justice of Appeal, 1992–95. Stowell Civil Law Fellow, University Coll., Oxford, 1961–73. Member: Royal Commn on Gambling, 1976–78; Council of Legal Educn, 1983–92 (Chm., 1989–92). Pres., British-German Jurists Assoc., 1991–. Dir, ENO, 1985–90, 1991–94. Chm., Arts Council Adv. Cttee on London Orchs, 1993. Hon. DCL City, 1992. *Publication:* The South African Law of Evidence, 1963. *Address:* Surrey Lodge, 23 Keats Grove, NW3 2RS.

HOFFMANN, Prof. Roald; John A. Newman Professor of Physical Science, Cornell University, since 1974; *b* 18 July 1937; *s* of Hillel Safran and Clara (*née* Rosen, who *m* 2nd, Paul Hoffmann); *m* 1960, Eva Börjesson; one *s* one *d*. *Educ:* Columbia Univ. (BA); Harvard Univ. (MA, PhD). Junior Fellow, Society of Fellows, Harvard Univ., 1962–65; Associate Professor, to Professor, Cornell Univ., 1965–74. Member: Nat. Acad. of Sciences; Amer. Acad. of Arts and Sciences. Foreign Member: Royal Soc., 1984; Indian Nat. Acad. of Sciences; Royal Swedish Acad. of Sciences; USSR Acad. of Sciences; Finnish Acad. of Sciences. Hon. DTech Royal Inst. of Technology, Stockholm, 1977; Hon. DSc: Yale, 1980; Hartford, 1982; Columbia, 1982; City Univ. of NY, 1983; Puerto Rico, 1983; La Plata, 1984; Uruguay, 1984; State Univ. of NY at Binghamton, 1985; Colgate, 1985; Rennes, 1986; Ben Gurion, 1989; Lehigh Univ., 1989; Carleton Coll., 1989; Maryland, 1990; Athens 1991; Thessaloniki, 1991; Bar Ilan, 1991; St Petersburg, 1991; Barcelona, 1992; Ohio State, 1993. Nobel Prize for Chemistry, 1981. *Publications:* The Conservation of Orbital Symmetry, 1970; The Metamict State (poetry), 1987; Solids and Surfaces, 1988; Gaps and Verges (poetry), 1990; Chemistry Imagined, 1993; The Same and Not the Same, 1995; many scientific articles. *Address:* Department of Chemistry, Cornell University, Ithaca, NY 14853, USA.

HOFFMEISTER, Maj.-Gen. Bertram Meryl, OC 1982; CB 1945; CBE 1944; DSO 1943; ED; *b* 15 May 1907; *s* of Flora Elizabeth Rodway and Louis George Hoffmeister; *m* 1935, Donalda Strauss; one *s* one *d*. *Educ:* Public Schs, Vancouver. Previous to war of 1939–45 employed by H. R. MacMillan Export Co. Ltd, Vancouver, BC. 1st Lieut Seaforth Highlanders of Canada, 1927; Capt. 1934; Major 1939 and given command of a rifle Co. Served with Seaforth Highlanders in England as Co. Comdr, 1939–40; returned to Canada, 1942, to attend Canadian Junior War Staff Course; given Command of Seaforth Highlanders of Canada and commanded this Bn in assault on Sicily in July 1943 (DSO); Brig. Oct. 1943 and assumed command 2 Canadian Infantry Brigade (Bar to DSO battle of Ortona); Maj.-Gen. and commanded 5 Cdn Armoured Div. March 1944; operations on Hitler Line, May–June 1944 (2nd Bar to DSO, CBE), in NW Europe until conclusion of hostilities (CB). GOC Canadian Army Pacific Force, 1945. Gen. Manager, Canadian White Pine Co. Ltd, and MacMillan Industries Ltd (Plywood Div.), 1945–47; H. R. MacMillan Export Co. Ltd; Gen. Mgr Prod., 1947–49 and Vice-Pres. Prod., 1949; Pres., 1949–51; MacMillan & Bloedel Ltd; Pres. 1951–56; Chm. Bd, 1956–57. Agent-Gen. for British Columbia, 1958–61. Pres., Council of the Forest Industries of BC, Vancouver, 1961–71. Chm., Nature Trust of BC (formerly Nat. Second Century Fund of BC, 1971–92). *Recreations:* rugby, rowing, shooting, skiing. *Address:* 1501–2240 Bellevue Avenue, West Vancouver, BC V7V 1C7, Canada. *Clubs:* Vancouver, Capilano Golf and Country, Vancouver Rowing (Vancouver).

HOFMEYR, Murray Bernard; Member, Executive Committee, Anglo American Corporation of South Africa Limited, since 1972; Chairman, Johannesburg Consolidated Investment Co. Ltd, since 1987; *b* 9 Dec. 1925; *s* of William and Margareta Hofmeyr; *m* 1953, Johanna Hendrika Hofmeyr (*née* Verdurmen); two *s* two *d*. *Educ:* BA (Rhodes), MA (Oxon). Joined Anglo American Corp., 1962; in Zambia, 1965–72; in England, 1972–80; Man. Dir, 1972–76, Chm. and Man. Dir, 1976–80, Charter Consolidated Ltd. *Recreations:* golf, tennis; Captain Oxford Univ. Cricket, 1951; played Rugby for England, 1950. *Address:* 54 Melville Road, Illovo, Johannesburg, South Africa.

HOGAN, Michael Henry; Member, Gaming Board for Great Britain, 1986–94 (Secretary, 1980–86); *b* 31 May 1927; *s* of James Joseph Hogan and Edith Mary Hogan; *m* 1st, 1953, Nina Spillane (*d* 1974); one *s* three *d*; 2nd, 1980, Mollie Burtwell. *Educ:* Ushaw Coll.; LSE. Certif. Social Sci., Certif. Mental Health. Asst Warden, St Vincent's Probation Hostel, 1949–50; London Probation Service, 1953–61; Home Office Inspectorate, 1961–80, Chief Probation Inspector, 1972–80. *Recreation:* golf. *Address:* Yew Tree Cottage, The Street, Capel, Surrey RH5 5LD. *T:* Dorking (01306) 711523.

HOGARTH, (Arthur) Paul, OBE 1989; RA 1984 (ARA 1974); RDI 1979; FRSA 1984; painter, illustrator and draughtsman; *b* Kendal, Cumbria, 4 Oct. 1917; *s* of Arthur Hogarth and Janet Bownass; *m* 1963, one *s*. *Educ:* St Agnes Sch., Manchester; Coll. of Art, Manchester; St Martin's Sch. of Art, London. Travels in: Poland and Czechoslovakia, 1953; USSR and China, 1954; Rhodesia and S Africa, 1956; Ireland, with Brendan Behan, 1959; USA, 1961–79. Senior tutor of Drawing: Cambridge Sch. of Art, 1959–61; RCA, 1964–71; Associate Prof., Philadelphia Coll. of Art, 1968–69; Vis. Lectr, RCA, 1971–81. Hon. Pres., Assoc. of Illustrators, 1982. Exhibitions: one-man, Leicester Gall., London, 1955; Agnews, London, 1957; Amer. Embassy, London, 1964; retrospectives, Time-Life Bldg, London, 1968; World of Paul Hogarth, Arts Council, RCA Gall., 1970; Travels through the Seventies, Kyle Gall., London; The Other Hogarth, Northern Arts Council, 1985–86; Cold War Reports: drawings 1947–67, Norfolk Inst. of Art & Design, Eastern Arts Council, 1989–90; exhibits regularly at Francis Kyle Gall., London. Dr RCA, 1971. *Publications:* Defiant People, 1953; Looking at China, 1956; People Like Us, 1958; (illus.) Brendan Behan's Island, 1962; Creative Pencil Drawing, 1964 (6th edn 1979); (illus.) Brendan Behan's New York, 1964; (with Robert Graves) Majorca Observed, 1965; (with M. Muggeridge) London à la Mode, 1966; Artist as Reporter, 1967, revised and enlarged edn, 1986; (with A. Jacob) Russian Journey, 1969; Drawing People, 1971; Artists on Horseback, 1972; Drawing Architecture, 1973; Paul Hogarth's American Album, 1974; Creative Ink Drawing, 1974 (5th edn 1979); Walking Tours of Old Philadelphia, 1976; Walking Tours of Old Boston, 1978; (with Stephen Spender) America Observed, 1979; Arthur Boyd Houghton, 1982; (with Graham Greene) Graham Greene Country, 1986; (with Laurence Durrell) The Mediterranean Shore, 1988. *Recreation:* sailing. *Address:* c/o Tessa Sayle, 11 Jubilee Place, SW3 3TE. *T:* 0171–823 3883. *Club:* Arts.

HOGARTH, James, CB 1973; Under-Secretary, Scottish Home and Health Department, 1963–74, retired; *b* 14 Aug. 1914; *s* of George Hogarth; *m* 1940, Katherine Mary Cameron; two *s* one *d*. *Educ:* George Watson's, Edinburgh; Edinburgh Univ.; Sorbonne, Paris. Joined Dept of Health for Scotland as Asst Principal, 1938; Principal, 1944; Asst Sec., 1948; Under-Sec., 1963. *Publications:* Payment of the General Practitioner, 1963; translations from French, German, Russian, etc. *Recreation:* travel. *Address:* 6A Crawfurd Road, Edinburgh EH16 5PQ. *T:* 0131–667 3878.

HOGARTH, Paul; *see* Hogarth, A. P.

HOGBEN, Ven. Peter Graham; Archdeacon of Dorking, 1982–90, now Archdeacon Emeritus; *b* 5 July 1925; *s* of Harold Henry and Winifred Minnie Hogben; *m* 1948, Audree Sayers; two *s*. *Educ:* Harvey Grammar School, Folkestone; Bishops' College, Cheshunt. Served Royal Engineers, 1943–47 (three years in Far East). Office Manager for two firms of Agricultural Auctioneers in Kent and Herts, 1948–59; theological college, 1960–61; ordained, 1961; Asst Curate of Hale, 1961–64; Vicar of Westborough, Guildford, 1964–71; Chaplain to WRAC, 1964–71; Vicar of Ewell, 1971–82; Editor, Guildford Diocesan Leaflet, 1978–82; Hon. Canon of Guildford, 1979–90, Canon Emeritus, 1990. RD of Epsom, 1980–82. *Recreations:* walking, gardening, water colour painting. *Address:* 3 School Road, Rowledge, Farnham, Surrey GU10 4EJ. *T:* Frensham (01252) 793533.

HOGBIN, Walter, CBE 1990; FEng 1994; FICE; Chairman, Taylor Woodrow International Ltd, since 1985; *b* 21 Dec. 1937; *s* of Walter Clifford John Hogbin and Mary Hogbin; *m* 1968, Geraldine Anne-Marie Castley; two *s*. *Educ:* Kent Coll., Canterbury; Queen's Coll., Cambridge (MA). Joined Taylor Woodrow, 1961; Taylor Woodrow International Ltd: Divl Dir, 1975–77; Dir, 1977–79; Man. Dir, 1979–85; Dir, 1987–, Jt Man. Dir, 1988–92, Taylor Woodrow plc; Chm., Taylor Woodrow Construction Supervisory Bd, 1991–93. Vice-President: Europ. Construction Industry Fedn, 1992–94; Europ. Internat. Contractors Council, 1992– (Mem., 1988–91); Member: Adv. Council, ECGD, 1983–88; Overseas Projects Bd, 1986–91; Export Gp for Construction Ind., 1980– (Chm., 1988–90); Europ. Internat. Contractors Fedn, 1988– (Pres., 1994–). Col, Engr and Transport Staff Corps, RE, 1986–. FRSA. Telford Gold Medal, ICE, 1979. *Recreations:* golf, tennis, gardening. *Address:* Arendal, 65 Penn Road, Beaconsfield, Bucks HP9 2LW. *T:* Beaconsfield (01494) 671064. *Club:* Athenæum.

HOGG, family name of **Hailsham Viscountcy** and of **Baron Hailsham of Saint Marylebone** and **Baroness Hogg.**

HOGG, Baroness *cr* 1995 (Life Peer), of Kettlethorpe, in the county of Lincolnshire; **Sarah Elizabeth Mary Hogg;** Head of Prime Minister's Policy Unit, 1990–95; *b* 14 May 1946; *d* of Baron Boyd-Carpenter, *qv*; *m* 1968, Rt Hon. Douglas Martin Hogg, *qv*; one *s* one *d*. *Educ:* St Mary's Convent, Ascot; Lady Margaret Hall, Oxford University. 1st Cl. Hons PPE. Staff writer, Economist, 1967, Literary Editor, 1970, Economics Editor, 1977; Economics Editor, Sunday Times, 1981; Presenter, Channel 4 News, 1982–83; Econs Editor, and Dep. Exec. Editor, Finance and Industry, The Times, 1984–86; Asst Editor, and Business and City Editor, The Independent, 1986–89; Econs Editor, Daily Telegraph and Sunday Telegraph, 1989–90. Director: London Broadcasting Co., 1982–90; Royal Nat. Theatre, 1988–91; Governor: Centre for Economic Policy Research, 1985–92; IDS, 1987. Hon. MA Open Univ., 1987; Hon. DLitt Loughborough, 1992. Wincott Foundation Financial Journalist of the Year, 1985. *Address:* House of Lords, SW1A 0PW.
See also Hon. Sir T. P. J. Boyd-Carpenter.

HOGG, Sir Arthur (Ramsay), 7th Bt *cr* 1846; MBE (mil.) 1945; retired; *b* 24 Oct. 1896; *s* of Ernest Charles Hogg (*d* 1907) (*g s* of 1st Bt) and Lucy (*d* 1924), *d* of late William Felton Peel; *S* cousin, Sir Kenneth Weir Hogg, 6th Bt, OBE, 1985; *m* 1924, Mary Aileen Hester Lee (*d* 1980), *d* of late P. H. Lee Evans; three *s* one *d*. *Educ:* Sherborne; Christ Church, Oxford (BA 1921; MA 1929). Served European War, 1914–18 (twice wounded), Captain Royal West Kent Regt; War of 1939–45 (MBE), Major, General List. *Heir: s* Michael David Hogg [*b* 19 Aug. 1925; *m* 1956, Elizabeth Anne Thérèse, *d* of Lt-Col Sir Terence Falkiner, 8th Bt; three *s*]. *Address:* c/o 19 Woodlands Road, SW13 0JZ.

HOGG, Sir Christopher (Anthony), Kt 1985; Chairman: Courtaulds plc, since 1980; Reuters Holdings PLC, since 1985 (Director, since 1984); *b* 2 Aug. 1936; *s* of Anthony Wentworth Hogg and Monica Mary (*née* Gladwell); *m* 1961, Anne Patricia (*née* Cathie) (separated 1992); two *d*. *Educ:* Marlborough Coll.; Trinity Coll., Oxford (MA; Hon. Fellow 1982); Harvard Univ. (MBA). National Service, Parachute Regt, 1955–57. Harkness Fellow, 1960–62; IMEDE, Lausanne, 1962–63; Hill, Samuel Ltd, 1963–66; IRC, 1966–68; Courtaulds plc, 1968– (Chm., Courtaulds Textiles, 1990–95); Dir, SmithKline Beecham, 1993–; Dep. Chm., Allied Domecq, 1995–. Member: Indust. Develt Adv. Bd, 1976–81; Cttee of Award for Harkness Fellowships, 1980–86; Internat. Council, J. P. Morgan, 1988–; Court, Bank of England, 1992–. Trustee, Ford Foundn, 1987–. For. Hon. Mem., Amer. Acad. of Arts and Scis, 1991. Hon. FCSD 1987; Hon. Fellow, London Business Sch., 1992; Hon. FCGI 1992. Hon. DSc: Cranfield Inst. of Technol., 1986; Aston, 1988. BIM Gold Medal, 1986; Centenary Medal, Soc. of Chemical Industry, 1989; Hambro Businessman of the Year, 1993. *Publication:* Masers and Lasers, 1963. *Recreations:* theatre, reading, walking, ski-ing. *Address:* Reuters Holdings PLC, 85 Fleet Street, EC4P 4AJ.

HOGG, Rt. Hon. Douglas (Martin); PC 1992; QC 1990; MP (C) Grantham, since 1979; Minister of Agriculture, Fisheries and Food, since 1995; *b* 5 Feb. 1945; *er s* of Baron Hailsham of Saint Marylebone, *qv*; *m* 1968, Sarah Boyd-Carpenter (*see* Baroness Hogg); one *s* one *d*. *Educ:* Eton (Oppidan Schol.); Christ Church, Oxford (Schol.; Pres., Oxford Union). Called to the Bar, Lincoln's Inn, 1968 (Kennedy Law Schol.). Mem., Agric. Select Cttees, 1979–82; PPS to Chief Sec., HM Treasury, 1982–83; an Asst Govt Whip, 1983–84; Parly Under-Sec. of State, Home Office, 1986–89; Minister of State (Minister for Industry and Enterprise), DTI, 1989–90; Minister of State, FCO, 1990–95. *Address:* House of Commons, SW1A 0AA.

HOGG, Sir Edward William L.; *see* Lindsay-Hogg.

HOGG, Gilbert Charles; Director of Regulatory Operations, British Gas plc, since 1990; *b* 11 Feb. 1933; *s* of Charles and Ivy Ellen Hogg; *m* 1st, Jeanne Whiteside; one *s* one *d*; 2nd, 1979, Angela Christina Wallace. *Educ:* Victoria University Coll., Wellington, NZ (LLB 1956). Called to the New Zealand Bar and admitted Solicitor, 1957; admitted Solicitor, GB, 1971. Served RNZAC (TF), 1955–62 (Lieut). Partner, Phillips, Shayle-George and Co., Solicitors, Wellington, 1960–66; Sen. Crown Counsel, Hong Kong, 1966–70; Editor, Business Law Summary, 1970–72; Divl Legal Adviser, BSC, 1974–79; British Gas Corporation, subseq. British Gas: Dir of Legal Services, 1979–84; Sec., 1984–90. Mem. Council, Energy Section, Internat. Bar Assoc., 1990–. *Publication:* A Smell of Fraud (novel), 1974. *Address:* 23 Ellerby Street, SW6 6EU. *T:* 0171–736 8903. *Club:* Royal Automobile.

HOGG, Vice-Adm. Sir Ian (Leslie Trower), KCB 1968 (CB 1964); DSC 1941, Bar to DSC 1944; *b* 30 May 1911; 3rd *s* of Col John M. T. Hogg, IA, and Elma (*née* Brand); *m* 1945, Mary G. J., *e d* of Col and Mrs Marsden; two *s*. *Educ:* Cheltenham Coll. Entered Royal Navy, 1929; specialised in Navigation, 1937; HMS Cardiff, 1939; HMS Penelope, 1940; HMAS Napier, 1941–43; HMS Mauritius, 1944–45; Master of the Fleet, 1946–47; British Admiralty Delegation, Washington, DC, 1948–49; HMS Sluys, in comd, 1950–51; Staff of C-in-C Med., 1952–53; Captain RN, Dec. 1953; Brit. Joint Staff, Washington, DC, 1955–57; idc 1958; Staff of Chief of Defence Staff, 1959–60; Cdre, Cyprus, 1961–62; Dir, Chief of Defence Staff's Commonwealth Exercise, 1962–63; Rear-Adm. 1963; Flag Officer, Medway, and Admiral Superintendent, HM Dockyard, Chatham, 1963–66; Vice-Adm. 1966; Defence Services Sec., 1966–67; Vice-Chief of the Defence Staff, 1967–70, retired. Comptroller, Royal Soc. of St George, 1971–74; Dir, Richard Unwin Internat. Ltd, 1975–86. *Address:* 21 Chapel Side, Titchfield, Hants PO14 4AP. *T:* Titchfield (01329) 847515.

HOGG, Sir John (Nicholson), Kt 1963; TD 1946; Deputy Chairman: Williams & Glyn's Bank Ltd, 1970–83; Gallaher Ltd, 1964–78; Chairman, Banque Française de Crédit International Ltd, 1972–83; *b* 4 Oct. 1912; *o s* of late Sir Malcolm Hogg and of Lorna Beaman; *m* 1948, Barbara Mary Elisabeth, *yr d* of Capt. Arden Franklyn, Shedfield, Southampton and *widow* of Viscount Garmoyle (*d* of wounds, 1942); one *s* one *d*. *Educ:* Eton; Balliol Coll., Oxford. Joined Glyn, Mills and Co., 1934. Served War of 1939–45, with KRRC in Greece, Crete, Western Desert, Tunisia, NW Europe. Rejoined Glyn, Mills and Co. 1945, a Man. Dir., 1950–70, Dep. Chm. 1963–68, Chm. 1968–70; Director: Royal Bank of Scotland Gp Ltd, 1969–82; Prudential Corp. Ltd, 1964–85. Fellow of Eton Coll., 1951–70. Mem. of Commonwealth War Graves Commission, 1958–64; A Trustee Imperial War Graves Endowment Fund, 1965–87. Sheriff County of London, 1960; Chm., Export Credits Guarantee Department's Adv. Council, 1962–67. Chm., Abu Dhabi Investment Bd, 1967–75. Hon. Treasurer, Inst. of Child Health, 1974–87 (Hon. Fellow 1987). *Recreations:* cricket, tennis, fishing. *Address:* The Red House, Shedfield, Southampton SO32 2HN. *T:* Wickham (01329) 832121. *Club:* Brooks's.

HOGG, Hon. Dame Mary (Claire), (Hon. Dame Mary Koops), DBE 1995; **Hon. Mrs Justice Hogg;** a Judge of the High Court of Justice, Family Division, since 1995; *b* 15 Jan. 1947; *d* of Rt Hon. Baron Hailsham of St Marylebone, *qv*; *m* 1987, Eric Koops; one *s* one *d*. *Educ:* St Paul's Girls' Sch. Called to the Bar, Lincoln's Inn, 1968, NI, 1993; QC 1989; Asst Recorder, 1986–90; Recorder, 1990–95. Mem. Council, Children's Soc., 1990–; Trustee, Harrison Homes, 1986–. Gov., Univ. of Westminster, 1992– (Poly. of Central London, 1983–92). FRSA 1991. Freeman, City of London, 1981. *Address:* Royal Courts of Justice, Strand, WC2A 2LL.

HOGG, Norman; MP (Lab) Cumbernauld and Kilsyth, since 1983 (Dunbartonshire East, 1979–83); *b* 12 March 1938; *s* of late Norman Hogg, CBE, LLD, DL, JP, and of Mary Wilson; *m* 1964, Elizabeth McCall Christie. *Educ:* Causewayend Sch., Aberdeen; Ruthrieston Secondary Sch., Aberdeen. Local Government Officer, Aberdeen Town Council, 1953–67; District Officer, National and Local Govt Officers Assoc., 1967–79. Select Cttee on Scottish Affairs, 1979–82; Scottish Labour Whip, 1982–83; Chm., Scottish Parly Lab Gp, 1981–82; Dep. Chief Opposition Whip, 1983–87; Scottish Affairs spokesman, 1987–88; Member: Chairman's Panel, 1988–; Public Accounts Cttee, 1991–92. *Recreation:* music. *Address:* House of Commons, SW1A 0AA. *T:* 0171–219 5095.

HOGG, Rear-Adm. Peter Beauchamp, CB 1980; Head of British Defence Liaison Staff and Defence Adviser, Canberra, 1977–80, retired; *b* 9 Nov. 1924; *s* of Beauchamp and Sybil Hogg; *m* 1951, Gabriel Argentine Alington; two *s* two *d*. *Educ:* Connaught House, Weymouth; Bradfield Coll., Berks; Royal Naval Engineering Coll., Keyham. Lieut, HMS Sirius, 1947–49; Advanced Engrg Course, RNC Greenwich, 1949–51; HMS Swiftsure and HMS Pincher, 1951–53; Lt Comdr, Loan Service with Royal Canadian Navy, 1953–56; Staff of RN Engrg Coll., Manadon, 1956–58; Comdr (Trng Comdr), HMS Sultan, 1959–62; Marine Engr Officer, HMS Hampshire, 1962–64; JSSC, Latimer, 1964; Ship Dept, Bath, 1965–67; Captain, Ship Dept, Bath, 1968–69; CO, HMS Tyne, 1970–71; RCDS, 1972; CO, HMS Caledonia, 1973–74; Dir of Naval Recruiting, 1974–76. Sec., Sixth Centenary Appeal, and Bursar i/c building works, Winchester Coll., 1980–88. Chm., Hereford Cathedral Fabric Adv. Cttee, 1991–. *Address:* c/o National Westminster Bank, 14 Old Town Street, Plymouth PL1 1DG.

HOGG, Prof. Richard Milne, FBA 1994; Smith Professor of English Language and Medieval Literature, University of Manchester, since 1980; *b* 20 May 1944; *s* of Charles Milne Hogg and Norenne Hogg (*née* Young); *m* 1969, Margaret Kathleen White; two *s*. *Educ:* Royal High Sch., Edinburgh; Univ. of Edinburgh (MA, Dip. Gen. Linguistics, PhD). Lecturer in English Language: Univ. Van Amsterdam, 1969–73; Univ. of Lancaster, 1973–80. Gen. Editor, Cambridge History of the English Language, 1992–. *Publications:* English Quantifier Systems, 1977; Metrical Phonology, 1986; A Grammar of Old English, 1992; contribs to learned jls. *Recreation:* Altrincham Football Club. *Address:* Department of English Language and Literature, University of Manchester, Oxford Road, Manchester M13 9PL. *T:* 0161–275 3164.

HOGG, Rear-Adm. Robin Ivor Trower, CB 1988; FNI, FIMgt; Managing Director, Raidfleet Ltd, since 1988; Chief Executive Officer, Colebrand Ltd, since 1988; *b* 25 Sept. 1932; *s* of Dudley and Nancy Hogg; *m* 1st, 1958, Susan Bridget Beryl Grantham; two *s* two *d*; 2nd, 1970, Angela Sarah Patricia Kirwan. *Educ:* The New Beacon, Sevenoaks; Bedford School. Directorate of Naval Plans, 1974–76; RCDS 1977; Captain RN Presentation Team, 1978–79; Captain First Frigate Sqdn, 1980–82; Director Naval Operational Requirements, 1982–84; Flag Officer, First Flotilla, 1984–86; COS to C-in-C Fleet, 1986–87, retd. *Recreation:* private life. *Address:* c/o Barclays Bank, Blenheim Gate, 22/24 Upper Marlborough Road, St Albans AL1 3AL. *T:* St Albans (0727) 863315.

HOGGART, Richard, LittD; Warden, Goldsmiths' College, University of London, 1976–84; *b* 24 Sept. 1918; 2nd *s* of Tom Longfellow Hoggart and Adeline Emma Hoggart; *m* 1942, Mary Holt France; two *s* one *d*. *Educ:* elementary and secondary schs, Leeds; Leeds Univ. (MA, LittD 1978). Served 1940–46, RA; demobilised as Staff Capt. Staff Tutor and Sen. Staff Tutor, University Coll. of Hull and University of Hull, 1946–59; Sen. Lectr in English, University of Leicester, 1959–62; Prof. of English, Birmingham Univ., 1962–73, and Dir, Centre for Contemporary Cultural Studies, 1964–73; an Asst Dir-Gen., Unesco, 1970–75. Vis. Fellow, Inst. of Development Studies, Univ. of Sussex, 1975. Visiting Prof., University of Rochester (NY), USA, 1956–57; Reith Lectr, 1971. Member: Albemarle Cttee on Youth Services, 1958–60; (Pilkington) Cttee on Broadcasting, 1960–62; Arts Council, 1976–81 (Chm., Drama Panel, 1977–80; Vice-Chm., 1980–82); Statesman and Nation Publishing Co. Ltd, 1977–81 (Chm., 1978–81); Chairman: Adv. Council for Adult and Continuing Educn, 1977–83; European Museum of the Year Award, 1977–; Broadcasting Research Unit, 1981–91. Governor, Royal Shakespeare Theatre, 1962–88. Pres., British Assoc. of Former UN Civil Servants, 1979–86. Hon. Professor: UEA, 1984; Univ. of Surrey, 1985; Hon. Fellow: Sheffield Polytechnic, 1983; Goldsmiths' Coll., 1987; DUniv: Open, 1973; Surrey, 1981; Leeds Metropolitan, 1995; Hon DèsL: Univ. of Bordeaux, 1975; Paris, 1987; Hon. LLD: CNAA, 1982; York (Toronto), 1988; Hon. LittD: East Anglia, 1986; Leicester, 1988; Hull, 1988; Keele, 1995. *Publications:* Auden, 1951; The Uses of Literacy, 1957; W. H.

Auden, 1957; W. H. Auden—A Selection, 1961; chap. in Conviction, 1958; chapter in Pelican Guide to English Literature, 1961; Teaching Literature, 1963; chapter in Of Books and Humankind, 1964; The Critical Moment, 1964; How and Why Do We Learn, 1965; The World in 1984, 1965; Essays by Divers Hands XXXIII; Guide to the Social Sciences, 1966; Technology and Society, 1966; Essays on Reform, 1967; Your Sunday Paper (ed), 1967; Speaking to Each Other: vol. I, About Society; vol. II, About Literature, 1970; Only Connect (Reith Lectures), 1972; An Idea and Its Servants, 1978; (ed with Janet Morgan) The Future of Broadcasting, 1982; An English Temper, 1982; (ed) The Public Service Idea in British Broadcasting: main principles, 1986; Writers on Writing, 1986; (jtly) The British Council and The Arts, 1986; (with Douglas Johnson) An Idea of Europe, 1987; A Local Habitation (autobiog.), 1988; (ed) Liberty and Legislation, 1989; (ed) Quality in Television: programmes, programme makers, systems, 1989; A Sort of Clowning: life and times 1940–59 (autobiog.), 1990; An Imagined Life: life and times 1959–91 (autobiog.), 1992; Townscape with Figures, 1994; numerous introductions, articles, pamphlets and reviews. *Recreation:* pottering about the house and garden. *Address:* Mortonsfield, Beavers Hill, Farnham, Surrey GU9 7DF.

See also S. D. Hoggart.

HOGGART, Simon David; Parliamentary Reporter, The Guardian, since 1993; *b* 26 May 1946; *s* of Richard Hoggart, *qv*; *m* 1983, Alyson Clare Corner; one *s* one *d*. *Educ:* Hymer's College, Hull; Wyggeston Grammar Sch., Leicester; King's College, Cambridge. MA. Reporter, The Guardian, 1968–71, N Ireland corresp., 1971–73, political corresp., 1973–81; feature writer, The Observer, 1981–85; political columnist, Punch, 1979–85; US correspondent, 1985–89, columnist, 1989–92, Political Editor, 1992–93, The Observer. Presenter, Fourth Column, Radio 4, 1991–. *Publications:* The Pact (with Alistair Michie), 1978; Michael Foot: a portrait (with David Leigh), 1981; On the House, 1981; Back on the House, 1982; House of Ill Fame, 1985; (ed) House of Cards, 1988; America: a user's guide, 1990; House of Correction, 1994. *Recreations:* reading, writing, occasional broadcasting. *Address:* The Guardian, 119 Farringdon Road, EC1R 3ER. *T:* 0171–239 9588.

HOGGE, Maj.-Gen. (Arthur) Michael (Lancelot), CB 1979; DL; *b* 4 Aug. 1925; *s* of late Lt-Col A. H. F. Hogge, Punjab Regt, Indian Army, and Mrs K. M. Hogge; *m* 1952, Gunilla Jeane Earley; two *s*. *Educ:* Wellington Coll.; Brasenose Coll., Oxford (war-time course). Commissioned, Oct. 1945; 6th Airborne Armoured Recce Regt and 3rd Hussars, Palestine, 1945–48; regimental appts, 3rd Hussars, BAOR, 1948–58; Queen's Own Hussars, BAOR, and Staff appts, 1958–65; comd Queen's Own Hussars, UK and Aden, 1965–67; Col GS, Staff Coll., 1969–71; Royal Coll. of Defence Studies, 1972; Dir of Operational Requirements, MoD, 1973–74, rank of Brig.; Dir Gen. Fighting Vehicles and Engineer Equipment, 1974–77; Dep. Master-General of the Ordnance, 1977–80; Gen. Man., Regular Forces Employment Assoc., 1981–87. Chm., Surrey Branch, SSAFA, 1992–. DL Surrey, 1993. *Recreations:* sailing, horticulture.

HOGGER, Henry George; HM Diplomatic Service; High Commissioner to Namibia, since 1992; *b* 9 Nov. 1948; *s* of late Rear-Adm. Henry Charles Hogger, CB, DSC and Ethel Mary Hogger; *m* 1972, Fiona Jane McNabb; two *s* two *d*. *Educ:* Winchester Coll.; Trinity Hall, Cambridge (MA Hons). Joined FCO 1969; MECAS, Lebanon, 1971–72; served Aden, Caracas, Kuwait; FCO, 1978–82; Head of Chancery, Abu Dhabi, 1982–86; FCO, 1986–89; Counsellor and Dep. Head of Mission, Amman, 1989–92. Mem., Inst. of Advanced Motorists. *Recreations:* golf, sailing, music, travel. *Address:* c/o Foreign and Commonwealth Office, SW1A 2AH.

HOGGETT, Anthony John Christopher, PhD, QC 1986; a Recorder, since 1988; *b* 20 Aug. 1940; *s* of late Christopher Hoggett and Annie Marie Hoggett; *m* 1968, Brenda Marjorie Hale (Hon. Dame Brenda Hale, DBE) (marr. diss. 1992); one *d*. *Educ:* Leeds Grammar Sch.; Hymers Coll., Hull; Clare Coll., Cambridge (MA, LLB); PhD Manchester. Asst Juridique, Inst. of Comparative Law, Paris, 1962–63; Lectr in Law, Univ. of Manchester, 1963–69; called to Bar, Gray's Inn, 1969, Head of Chambers, 1985; Asst Recorder, 1982. Res. Fellow, Univ. of Michigan, 1965–66. Mem., Civil Service Final Selection Bd for Planning Inspectors, 1987–. Dir, Europ. Youth Parlt Internat., 1993–. Mem. Editl Bd, Envmtl Law Reports, 1992–. *Publications:* articles in Criminal Law Rev., Mod. Law Rev. and others. *Recreations:* swimming, music, walking. *Address:* Flat 29, Chepstow House, Chepstow Street, Manchester M1 5JF. *T:* 0161–236 7973; 57 Brooksby Street, N1 1EX.

HOGGETT, Brenda Marjorie; *see* Hale, Hon. Dame B. M.

HOGWOOD, Christopher Jarvis Haley, CBE 1989; harpsichordist, conductor, musicologist, writer, editor and broadcaster; Founder and Director, Academy of Ancient Music, since 1973; *b* 10 Sept. 1941; *s* of Haley Evelyn Hogwood and Marion Constance Higgott. *Educ:* Pembroke Coll., Cambridge (MA; Hon. Fellow, 1992); Charles Univ., Prague. Keyboard and orchestral recordings. Editor of books and music. Artistic Director: King's Lynn Festival, 1976–80; Handel and Haydn Soc., Boston, USA, 1986–; Summer Mozart Fest., Nat. Symphony Orch., USA, 1993–; Dir of Music, St Paul Chamber Orchestra, USA, 1987–92, Prin. Guest Conductor, 1992–. Internat. Prof. of Early Music Performance, RAM, 1992–; Vis. Prof., Dept of Music, KCL, 1992–; Hon. Prof. of Music, Keele Univ., 1986–90; Hon. Fellow, Jesus Coll., Cambridge, 1989. FRSA 1982. Hon. DMus Keele, 1991. Freeman, Co. of Musicians, 1989. Walter Willson Cobbett Medal, Co. of Musicians, 1986. *Publications:* Music at Court (Folio Society), 1977; The Trio Sonata, 1979; Haydn's Visits to England (Folio Society), 1980; (ed with R. Luckett) Music in Eighteenth-Century England, 1983; Handel, 1984; (ed) Holmes' Life of Mozart (Folio Society), 1991. *Address:* 10 Brookside, Cambridge CB2 1JE. *T:* Cambridge (01223) 63975.

HOHLER, Henry Arthur Frederick, CMG 1954; HM Diplomatic Service, retired; Ambassador to Switzerland 1967–70; *b* 4 Feb. 1911; *e s* of late Lt-Col Arthur Preston Hohler, DSO; *m* 1st, 1932, Mona Valentine (*d* 1944), *d* of late Lieut-Col Arthur Murray Pirie, DSO; two *s*; 2nd, 1945, Eveline Susan, *d* of late Lieut-Col Hon. Neville Albert Hood, CMG, DSO; two *d*. *Educ:* Eton; Sandhurst. 2nd Lieut Grenadier Guards, 1931. 3rd Sec. in Foreign Office, 1934; Budapest, 1936; 2nd Sec., 1939; Foreign Office, 1941; 1st Sec., 1945; Berne, 1945; Helsinki, 1948; Moscow, 1949; Counsellor, 1950; Head of Northern Dept, Foreign Office, 1951; Minister in Rome, 1956–60; Ambassador in Saigon, 1960–63; Minister in Paris, 1963–65; Asst Under-Sec., Foreign Office, 1966–67. Liveryman, Grocers' Company. *Address:* 7835 Berkshire Lane, Gloucester, VA 23061, USA. *Clubs:* Boodle's; Metropolitan (Washington).

HOLBOROW, Eric John, MD, FRCP, FRCPath; Emeritus Professor of Immunopathology and Honorary Consultant Immunologist, London Hospital Medical College, E1, retired 1983; *b* 30 March 1918; *s* of Albert Edward Ratcliffe Holborow and Marian Crutchley; *m* 1943, Cicely Mary Foister; two *s* one *d*. *Educ:* Epsom Coll.; Clare Coll., Cambridge; St Bart's Hosp. MA, MD (Cantab). Served War of 1939–45, Major, RAMC. Consultant Bacteriologist, Canadian Hosp., Taplow, 1953; Mem. Scientific Staff, MRC Rheumatism Unit, Taplow, 1957; Director, 1975; Head, MRC Group, Bone and Joint Res. Unit, London Hosp. Med. Coll., 1976–83. Visiting Prof., Royal Free Hosp. Med. Sch., 1975. Bradshaw Lectr, RCP, 1982. Chm., Smith Kline Foundn, 1987–89 (Trustee, 1977–89). Editor, Jl Immunol. Methods, 1971–85. *Publications:* Autoimmunity and Disease (with L. E. Glynn), 1965; An ABC of Modern Immunology, 1968, 2nd edn 1973; (with W. G. Reeves) Immunology in Medicine, 1977, 2nd edn 1983; (with A. Maroudas) Studies in Joint Disease, vol. 1, 1981, vol. 2, 1983; books and papers on immunology. *Recreations:* glebe terriers, ecclesiastical records.

See also J. Holborow.

HOLBOROW, Jonathan; Editor, Mail on Sunday, since 1992; *b* 12 Oct. 1943; *s* of Prof. Eric John Holborow, *qv* and Cicely Mary (*née* Foister); *m* 1st, 1965, Susan Ridings (*d* 1993); one *s* one *d*; 2nd, 1994, Vivien Ferguson. *Educ:* Charterhouse. Reporter, Maidenhead Advertiser, 1961–65; Lincs Echo, 1965–66; Lincoln Chronicle, 1966–67; Daily Mail, Manchester, 1967–69; Scottish News Editor, Daily Mail, Glasgow, 1969–70; Daily Mail, Manchester: Northern Picture Editor, 1970–72; Northern News Editor, 1972–74; Daily Mail, London: Dep. News Editor, 1974–75; News Editor, 1975–80; Editor, Cambrian News, Aberystwyth, 1980–82; Asst Editor, then Associate Editor, Mail on Sunday, 1982–86; Dep. Editor, Today, 1986–87; Daily Mail: Asst Editor, then Associate Editor, 1987–88; Dep. Editor, 1988–92. *Recreation:* golf. *Address:* The Mail on Sunday, Northcliffe House, 2 Derry Street, W8 5TT. *T:* 0171–938 6000.

HOLBOROW, Prof. Leslie Charles, MA; Vice-Chancellor, Victoria University of Wellington, since 1985; *b* 28 Jan. 1941; *s* of George and Ivah Vivienne Holborow; *m* 1965, Patricia Lynette Walsh; one *s* two *d*. *Educ:* Henderson High Sch.; Auckland Grammar Sch.; Univ. of Auckland (MA 1st Cl. Hons Philosophy); Oxford Univ. (BPhil). Jun. Lectr, Auckland Univ., 1963; Commonwealth schol. at Merton Coll., Oxford, 1963–65; Lectr, then Sen. Lectr, Univ. of Dundee (until 1967 Queen's Coll., Univ. of St Andrews), 1965–74, Mem. Court, 1972–74; University of Queensland, Brisbane: Prof. of Philosophy, 1974–85; Pres., Academic Bd, 1980–81; Pro-Vice-Chancellor (Humanities), 1983–85. Pres., Qld Br., Aust. Inst. of Internat. Affairs, 1984–85; Nat. Pres., NZ Inst. of Internat. Affairs, 1987–90; Member: NZ Cttee for Pacific Economic Co-operation, 1986–; Bd, Inst. of Policy Studies, 1986–; Bd, NZ Inst. of Econ. Res., 1986–91. NZ Cttee for Security Co-operation in Asia Pacific, 1994–. Chair: NZ Vice-Chancellors' Cttee, 1990; Cttee on Univ. Academic Progs, 1993–; Mem., Council, ACU, 1990–91. Member: Musica Viva Nat. Bd, 1984–85; Bd of Management, Music Fedn of NZ, 1987–90. Trustee, NZ String Quartet, 1990–. *Publications:* various articles in philosophical and legal jls. *Recreations:* tramping, listening to music. *Address:* 11 Kinross Street, Wellington, New Zealand. *Clubs:* Wellington, Victoria University Staff (Wellington).

HOLBOROW, Lady Mary (Christina); JP; Lord-Lieutenant of Cornwall, since 1994; *b* 19 Sept. 1936; *d* of 8th Earl of Courtown, OBE, TD, DL, and Christina Margaret Tremlett (*née* Cameron); *m* 1959, Geoffrey Jermyn Holborow, OBE; one *s* one *d*. *Educ:* Tudor Hall Sch., Banbury. Mem., Regional Board, TSB, 1981–87; Director: SW Water, 1989–95; Devon and Cornwall TEC, 1990–; Vice-Chm., Cornwall and Isles of Scilly HA, 1990–; Chm., Cornwall Rural Develt Cttee, 1987–. JP Cornwall 1970. DStJ 1987 (Comr, St John Ambulance, 1982–87). *Address:* Ladock House, Ladock, Truro, Cornwall TR2 4PL. *T:* St Austell (01726) 882274.

HOLBROOK, David Kenneth, MA; author; *b* 9 Jan. 1923; *o s* of late Kenneth Redvers and late Elsie Eleanor Holbrook; *m* 1949, Margot Davies-Jones; two *s* two *d*. *Educ:* City of Norwich Sch.; Downing Coll., Cambridge (Exhibr). Intell., mines and explosives officer, ER Yorks Yeo., Armd Corps, 1942–45. Asst Editor, Our Time, 1948; Asst Editor, Bureau of Current Affairs, 1949; Tutor organiser, WEA, 1952–53; Tutor, Bassingbourn Village Coll., Cambs, 1954–61; Fellow, King's Coll., Cambridge, 1961–65; Sen. Leverhulme Res. Fellow, 1965; College Lectr in English, Jesus Coll., Cambridge, 1968–70; Compton Poetry Lectr, Hull Univ., 1969 (resigned); Writer in Residence, Dartington Hall, 1970–73 (grant from Elmgrant Trust); Downing Coll., Cambridge: Asst Dir, English Studies, 1973–75; Fellow and Dir of English Studies, 1981–88, Emeritus Fellow, 1988–; Leverhulme Emeritus Res. Fellow, 1988–90. Hooker Distinguished Vis. Prof., McMaster Univ., Ontario, 1984. Arts Council Writers Grants, 1970, 1976, 1979. Mem. Editorial Bd, New Universities Qly, 1976–86. *Publications: poetry:* Imaginings, 1961; Against the Cruel Frost, 1963; Object Relations, 1967; Old World, New World, 1969; Moments in Italy, 1976; Chance of a Lifetime, 1978; Selected Poems, 1980; *fiction:* Lights in the Sky Country, 1963; Flesh Wounds, 1966; A Play of Passion, 1978; Nothing Larger than Life, 1987; Worlds Apart, 1988; A Little Athens, 1990; Jennifer, 1991; The Gold in Father's Heart, 1992; Even If They Fail, 1994; *on education:* English for Maturity, 1961; English for the Rejected, 1964; The Secret Places, 1964; The Exploring Word, 1967; Children's Writing, 1967; English in Australia Now, 1972; Education, Nihilism and Survival, 1977; English for Meaning, 1980; Education and Philosophical Anthropology, 1987; Further Studies in Philosophical Anthropology, 1988; *literary criticism:* Llareggub Revisited, 1962; The Quest for Love, 1965; The Masks of Hate, 1972; Dylan Thomas: the code of night, 1972; Sylvia Plath: poetry and existence, 1976; Lost Bearings in English Poetry, 1977; The Novel and Authenticity, 1987; Images of Woman in Literature, 1989; The Skeleton in the Wardrobe: the fantasies of C. S. Lewis, 1991; Edith Wharton and the Unsatisfactory Man, 1991; Where D. H. Lawrence was Wrong about Woman, 1991; Charles Dickens and The Image of Woman, 1993; *music criticism:* Gustav Mahler and the Courage to Be, 1975; *general:* Children's Games, 1957; Human Hope and the Death Instinct, 1971; Sex and Dehumanization, 1972; The Pseudo-revolution, 1972; (ed) The Case Against Pornography, 1972; Evolution and the Humanities, 1987; (ed) What is it to be Human?: report on a philosophy conference, 1990; Creativity and Popular Culture, 1994; *anthologies:* edited: Iron, Honey, Gold, 1961; People and Diamonds, 1962; Thieves and Angels, 1963; Visions of Life, 1964; (with Elizabeth Poston) The Cambridge Hymnal, 1967; Plucking the Rushes, 1968; (with Christine Mackenzie) The Honey of Man, 1975; *opera libretti:* (with Wilfrid Mellers) The Borderline, 1958; (with John Joubert) The Quarry, 1967. *Recreations:* painting, cooking, gardening. *Address:* Denmore Lodge, Brunswick Gardens, Cambridge CB5 8DQ. *T:* Cambridge (01223) 328341.

HOLCROFT, Sir Peter (George Culcheth), 3rd Bt *cr* 1921; JP; *b* 29 April 1931; *s* of Sir Reginald Culcheth Holcroft, 2nd Bt, TD, and Mary Frances (*d* 1963), *yr d* of late William Swire, CBE; *S* father, 1978; *m* 1956, Rosemary Rachel (marr. diss. 1987), *yr d* of late G. N. Deas; three *s* one *d*. *Educ:* Eton. High Sheriff of Shropshire, 1969; JP 1976. *Recreation:* the countryside. *Heir:* *s* Charles Antony Culcheth Holcroft [*b* 22 Oct. 1959; *m* 1986, Mrs Elizabeth Carter, *y d* of John Raper, Powys; one *s* one *d*]. *Address:* Berrington House, Berrington, Shrewsbury SY5 6HA.

HOLDEN, Anthony Ivan; writer; *b* 22 May 1947; *s* of late John Holden and Margaret Lois Holden (*née* Sharpe); *m* 1st, 1971, Amanda Juliet (marr. diss. 1988), *d* of Sir Brian Warren, *qv*, and Dame Josephine Barnes, *qv*; three *s*; 2nd, 1990, Cynthia Blake, *d* of Mrs George Blake, Brookline, Mass. *Educ:* Tre-Arddur House Sch., Anglesey; Oundle Sch.; Merton Coll., Oxford (MA Hons Eng. Lang. and Lit.; Editor, Isis). Trainee reporter, Thomson Regional Newspapers, Evening Echo, Hemel Hempstead, 1970–73; home and foreign corresp., Sunday Times, 1973–77; columnist (Atticus), Sunday Times, 1977–79; Washington corresp. and chief US corresp., Observer, 1979–81; columnist, Punch, 1979–81; Features Editor and Asst Editor, The Times, 1981–82; freelance journalist and author, 1982–85 and 1986–; Exec. Editor, Today, 1985–86. Broadcaster, radio and TV;

TV documentaries include: The Man Who Would Be King, 1982; Charles at Forty, 1988; Anthony Holden on Poker, 1992; Who Killed Tchaikovsky, 1993. Young Journalist of 1972; commended for work in NI, News Reporter of the Year, British Press Awards, 1976; Columnist of the Year, British Press Awards, 1977. Opera translations: Don Giovanni, 1985; La Bohème, 1986; The Barber of Seville, 1987. *Publications:* (trans. and ed) Aeschylus' Agamemnon, 1969; (contrib.) The Greek Anthology, 1973; (trans. and ed) Greek Pastoral Poetry, 1974; The St Albans Poisoner, 1974; Charles, Prince of Wales, 1979; Of Presidents, Prime Ministers and Princes, 1984; The Queen Mother, 1985, 2nd edn 1990; Don Giovanni, 1987; Olivier, 1988; Charles, 1988; Big Deal, 1990; (ed) The Last Paragraph, 1990; The Oscars, 1993; The Tarnished Crown, 1993; (contrib.) Power and the Throne, 1994; Tchaikovsky, 1995. *Recreations:* poker, Arsenal FC, Lancashire CC. *Address:* c/o Rogers Coleridge White, 20 Powis Mews, W11 1JN. *T:* 0171–221 3717. *Clubs:* Victoria Casino, Barracuda.

HOLDEN, Basil Munroe; Rector, Glasgow Academy, 1959–75, retired; *b* 10 Nov. 1913; *m* 1951, Jean Watters; two *s* two *d.* *Educ:* Queen Elizabeth's Grammar Sch., Blackburn; King's Coll., Cambridge (Foundation Scholar). BA 1935, Maths Tripos (Wrangler), MA 1939. Mathematical Master, Highgate Sch., 1937. Instructor Lieut RN, 1940. Head of Mathematical Dept, Oundle Sch., 1947; Housemaster, Oundle Sch., 1956. *Address:* Orchard House, Blennerhasset, Carlisle, Cumbria CA5 3QX. *T:* Kirkbride (01697) 320735.

HOLDEN, Sir David (Charles Beresford), KBE 1972; CB 1963; ERD 1954; *b* 26 July 1915; *s* of Oswald Addenbrooke Holden and Ella Mary Beresford; *m* 1948, Elizabeth Jean Odling; one *s* one *d.* *Educ:* Rossall Sch.; King's Coll., Cambridge. Northern Ireland Civil Service, 1937–76; Permanent Sec., Dept of Finance, NI, and Head of NI Civil Service, 1970–76; Dir, Ulster Office, 1976–77. Royal Artillery, 1939–46. *Address:* Falcons, Wilsford Cum Lake, Amesbury, Salisbury SP4 7BL. *T:* Amesbury (01980) 622493.

HOLDEN, Derek; His Honour Judge Holden; a Circuit Judge, since 1984; *b* 7 July 1935; *s* of Frederic Holden and Audrey Holden (*née* Hayes); *m* 1961, Dorien Elizabeth Holden (*née* Bell); two *s.* *Educ:* Cromwell House; Staines Grammar Sch. Served Army; Lieut East Surrey Regt, 1953–56. Qualified as Solicitor, 1966; Derek Holden & Co., Staines, Egham, Camberley, Feltham and Ashford, 1966–84; Consultant, Batt Holden & Co., 1966–84. A Recorder, 1980–84. President: Social Security Appeal Tribunals and Medical Appeal Tribunals, 1990–92; Vaccine Damage Tribunals, 1990–92; Disability Appeals Tribunal, 1992; Chm., Tribunals Cttee, Judicial Studies Bd, 1990–92. Mem., Royal Yachting Assoc., 1975– (Dept of Trade Yachtmaster, Instr and Ocean certs). Principal, Chandor Sch. of Sailing, Lymington, 1978–85. *Recreations:* sailing, ski-ing, photography, music. *Address:* c/o Kingston Courts Administrator's Office, 10 Sundial Court, Tolworth Rise, South Tolworth, Surbiton, Surrey KT5 9NN. *Clubs:* Law Society; Western (Glasgow); Leander, Remenham (Henley); Burway Rowing (Laleham); Eton Excelsior Rowing (Windsor); Staines Boat; Royal Solent Yacht (Yarmouth, IoW); Queen Mary Sailing (Ashford).

HOLDEN, Sir Edward, 6th Bt, *cr* 1893; Consultant Anæsthetist, Darlington & Northallerton Group Hospitals, 1957–74; *b* 8 Oct. 1916; *s* of Sir Isaac Holden Holden, 5th Bt, and Alice Edna Byrom (*d* 1971); *S* father, 1962; *m* 1942, Frances Joan, *e d* of John Spark, JP, Ludlow, Stockton-on-Tees; two adopted *s.* *Educ:* Leys Sch. and Christ's Coll., Cambridge (MA); St Thomas's Hosp. MRCS; LRCP 1942; DA Eng., 1946; FRCA (FFARCS, 1958). Formerly Vis. Anæsth., Cumb. Infirm., Carlisle; Cons. Anæsth. W Cumb. Hospital Group. Mem. Council, Harlow Car Gardens. *Recreations:* fishing and gardening. *Heir:* *b* Paul Holden [*b* 3 March 1923; *m* 1950, Vivien Mary Oldham; one *s* two *d*]. *Address:* Moorstones, Osmotherley, Northallerton, N Yorks DL6 3BG. *Club:* Farmers'.

HOLDEN, Sir John David, 4th Bt *cr* 1919; *b* 16 Dec. 1967; *s* of David George Holden (*d* 1971) (*e s* of 3rd Bt), and of Nancy, *d* of H. W. D. Marwood, Foulrice, Whenby, Brandsby, Yorks; *S* grandfather, 1976; *m* 1987, Suzanne Cummings; one *d.* *Heir:* *uncle* Brian Peter John Holden [*b* 12 April 1944; *m* 1984, Bernadette Anne Lopez, *d* of George Gerard O'Malley].

HOLDEN, Patrick Brian, MA, FCIS; Chairman: Ainsfield PLC, since 1991; Holden Homes (Southern) Ltd, since 1984; *b* 16 June 1937; *s* of Reginald John and Winifred Isabel Holden; *m* 1972, Jennifer Ruth (*née* Meddings), MB, BS. *Educ:* Allhallows Sch. (Major Schol.); St Catharine's Coll., Cambridge (BA Hons Law 1960, MA 1963). FCIS 1965. Served Royal Hampshire Regt, 1955–57 regular commn), seconded 1 Ghana Regt, RWAFF. Fine Fare Group: Sec., 1960–69; Legal and Property Dir, 1965–69; Pye of Cambridge Gp, 1969–74; Dir, Pye Telecom. Ltd, 1972–74; Dir and Sec., Oriel Foods Gp, 1975–81; Gp Sec., Fisons plc, 1981–83. Sec., New Town Assoc., 1974–75. FIMgt. *Recreations:* dogs, bridge, walking. *Address:* The Old School House, Lower Green, Tewin, Herts AL6 0LD. *T:* Tewin (01438) 717573. *Club:* Naval and Military.

HOLDEN-BROWN, Sir Derrick, Kt 1979; Chairman, Allied-Lyons PLC, 1982–91 (Chief Executive, 1982–88); Director, Allied Breweries, 1967–91 (Chairman, 1982–86); *b* 14 Feb. 1923; *s* of Harold Walter and Beatrice Florence (*née* Walker); *m* 1950, Patricia Mary Ross Mackenzie; one *s* one *d.* *Educ:* Westcliff. Mem., Inst of Chartered Accountants of Scotland. Served War, Royal Navy, 1941–46, Lt RNVR, Coastal Forces. Chartered Accountant, 1948; Hiram Walker & Sons, Distillers, 1949; Managing Director: Cairnes Ltd, Brewers, Eire, 1954; Grants of St James's Ltd, 1960; Dir, Ind Coope Ltd, 1962; Chm., Victoria Wine Co., 1964; Finance Dir, 1972, Vice-Chm., 1975–82, Allied Breweries; Director: Sun Alliance & London Insurance plc, 1977– (Vice Chm., 1983, Dep. Chm., 1985–92); Midland Bank, 1984–88. Chm., FDIC, 1984–85 (Dep. Chm. 1974–76). President: Food and Drink Fedn, 1985–86; Food Manufacturers' Fedn Inc., 1985. Chairman: Brewers' Soc., 1978–80 (Master, Brewers' Co., 1987–88); White Ensign Assoc., 1987–90; Portsmouth Naval Heritage Trust, 1989–. *Recreations:* sailing, offshore cruising. *Address:* Copse House, Milford-on-Sea, Lymington, Hants SO41 0PS. *T:* Lymington (01590) 642247. *Clubs:* Boodle's; Royal Yacht Squadron; Royal Lymington Yacht; Royal Canadian Yacht.

HOLDER, Sir (John) Henry, 4th Bt *cr* 1898, of Pitmaston, Moseley, Worcs; Production Director and Head Brewer, Elgood & Sons Ltd, North Brink Brewery, Wisbech, 1975–93, retired; *b* 12 March 1928; *s* of Sir John Eric Duncan Holder, 3rd Bt and Evelyn Josephine (*d* 1994), *er d* of late William Blain; *S* father, 1986; *m* 1960, Catharine Harrison (*d* 1994), *yr d* of late Leonard Baker; twin *s* one *d.* *Educ:* Eton Coll.; Birmingham Univ. (Dip. Malting and Brewing); Dip. in Safety Management, British Safety Council. Diploma Mem., Inst. of Brewing. National Service, RAC; commnd 5th Royal Tank Regt, 1947. Shift Brewer, Mitchells & Butlers Ltd, 1951–53; Brewer, Reffels Bexley Brewery Ltd, 1953–56; Asst Manager, Unique Slide Rule Co., 1956–62; Brewer, Rhymney Brewery Co. Ltd, 1962–75. *Recreations:* sailing, computing. *Heir:* *er* twin *s* Nigel John Charles Holder, *b* 6 May 1962. *Address:* 47 St Paul's Road North, Walton Highway, Wisbech, Cambs PE14 7DN. *T:* Wisbech (01945) 583493. *Club:* Brancaster Staithe Sailing (King's Lynn).

HOLDER, Air Marshal Sir Paul (Davie), KBE 1965; CB 1964; DSO 1942; DFC 1941; *b* 2 Sept. 1911; *s* of Hugh John and Frances Rhoda Holder; *m* 1940, Mary Elizabeth Kidd; two *s.* *Educ:* Bristol Univ.; University of Illinois, USA. MSc Bristol, 1933; Robert Blair Fellow, 1934; PhD Bristol, 1935. Commissioned RAF, 1936; Flt Comdr 84 Sqdn, Iraq 1938–39; Stn Admin. Officer, Habbiniya, Iraq, 1940–41; OC 218 Sqdn Bomber Comd, 1941–42 (1st thousand bomber raid, Cologne); SASO Force 686, Ankara, Turkey, 1943; Group Capt. Plans, MEAF; formed Marshal Tito's first Hurricane Fighter Sqdn, Benina, Libya, 1944; DS RAF Staff Coll., 1945; CO RAF Broadwell, Transport Comd, 1946; Vice-Pres., RAF Selection Bd, 1947–48; Student, Admin. Staff Coll., Henley-on-Thames, 1947; Chief Instr, RAF Officer Cadet Training Sch., 1948–49; CO, RAF, Shallufa, Egypt, 1950–51; CO, RAF, Kabrit, Egypt, 1952; Dep. Dir, Air Staff Policy, Air Min., 1953–55; Student, Imperial Defence Coll., 1956; AOC, Singapore, 1957; AOC, Hong Kong, 1958–59; ACAS (Trng), Air Min., 1960–62; AOC No 25 Gp, RAF Flying Trng Comd, 1963–64; AOC-in-C, RAF Coastal Comd, NATO Comdr Maritime Air, Channel Comd, and Comdr Maritime Air, Eastern Atlantic Area, 1965–68, retired 1968. FRAeS 1966. *Recreations:* gardening, bridge. *Address:* Innisfree, Bramshott Chase, Hindhead, Surrey GU26 6DG. *T:* Hindhead (01428) 604579. *Club:* Royal Air Force.

HOLDERNESS, Baron *cr* 1979 (Life Peer), of Bishop Wilton in the County of Humberside; **Richard Frederick Wood;** PC 1959; DL; *b* 5 Oct. 1920; 3rd *s* of 1st Earl of Halifax, KG, PC, OM, GCSI, GCMG, GCIE, TD; *m* 1947, Diana, *d* of late Col E. O. Kellett, DSO, MP, and Hon. Mrs W. J. McGowan; one *s* one *d.* *Educ:* Eton; New College, Oxford. Hon. Attaché, British Embassy, Rome, 1940; served War of 1939–45 as Lieutenant, KRRC, 1941–43; retired, wounded, 1943; toured US Army hospitals, 1943–45; New College, Oxford, 1945–47. MP (C) Bridlington, Yorkshire, 1950–79; Parliamentary Private Secretary: to Minister of Pensions, 1951–53; to Minister of State, Board of Trade, 1953–54; to Minister of Agriculture and Fisheries, 1954–55; Joint Parliamentary Secretary: Ministry of Pensions and National Insurance, 1955–58; Ministry of Labour, 1958–59; Minister of Power, October 1959–63, of Pensions and National Insurance, Oct. 1963–64; Minister of Overseas Develt, ODM, June–Oct. 1970, FCO, 1970–74. Dir, Hargreaves Group Ltd, 1974–86; Regional Dir, Yorkshire and Humberside regional board, Lloyds Bank, 1981–90. Chairman: Disablement Services Authy, 1987–91; Adv. Gp on Rehabilitation, DoH, 1991–. Pres., Queen Elizabeth's Foundn for the Disabled, 1983–. DL E Riding Yorks, 1967. Hon. LLD: Sheffield Univ., 1962; Leeds, 1978; Hull, 1982. Hon. Colonel: Queen's Royal Rifles, 1962; 4th (Volunteer) Bn Royal Green Jackets, 1967–89. *Address:* Flat Top House, Bishop Wilton, York YO4 1RY. *T:* Bishop Wilton (01759) 368266; 65 Les Collines de Guerrevieille, 83120 Ste Maxime, France.

See also Sir E. N. Brooksbank, Bt.

HOLDERNESS, Sir Richard William, 3rd Bt, *cr* 1920; Partner, Whiteheads, Estate Agents and Surveyors, 1967–86; retired; *b* 30 Nov. 1927; *s* of Sir Ernest William Elsmie Holderness, 2nd Bt, CBE, and Emily Carlton (*d* 1950), *y d* of late Frederick McQuade, Sydney, NSW; *S* father, 1968; *m* 1953, Pamela, *d* of late Eric Chapman, CBE; two *s* one *d.* *Educ:* Dauntsey's Sch.; Corpus Christi Coll., Oxford. ARICS 1976. *Recreations:* golf, gardening, travel. *Heir:* *s* Martin William Holderness, CA [*b* 24 May 1957; *m* 1984, Elizabeth, BSc, DipHV, *d* of Dr William and Dr Maureen Thornton, Belfast; one *s* one *d.* *Educ:* Bradfield Coll., Berks]. *Address:* Bramfold Court, Nutbourne Road, Pulborough, West Sussex RH20 2HA. *Clubs:* East India; West Sussex Golf.

HOLDGATE, Sir Martin (Wyatt), Kt 1994; CB 1979; PhD; FIBiol; President, Zoological Society of London, since 1994; *b* 14 Jan. 1931; *s* of late Francis Wyatt Holdgate, MA, JP, and Lois Marjorie (*née* Bebbington); *m* 1963, Elizabeth Mary (*née* Dickason), *widow* of Dr H. H. Weil; two *s.* *Educ:* Arnold Sch., Blackpool; Queens' Coll., Cambridge. BA Cantab 1952; MA 1956; PhD 1955; FIBiol 1967. Jt Leader and Senior Scientist, Gough Is Scientific Survey, 1955–56; Lecturer in Zoology: Manchester Univ., 1956–57; Durham Colleges, 1957–60; Leader, Royal Society Expedition to Southern Chile, 1958–59; Asst Director of Research, Scott Polar Research Institute, Cambridge, 1960–63; Senior Biologist, British Antarctic Survey, 1963–66; Dep. Dir (Research), The Nature Conservancy, 1966–70; Director: Central Unit on Environmental Pollution, DoE, 1970–74; Inst. of Terrestrial Ecology, NERC, 1974–76; Dep. Sec., 1976, Dir-Gen. of Res., 1976–79, Chief Scientist, 1979–85, Depts of the Environment and of Transport; Dep. Sec., Environment Protection and Chief Envmt Scientist, DoE, and Chief Scientific Advr, Dept of Transport, 1985–88; Dir Gen., IUCN, 1988–94. Hon. Professorial Fellow, UC Cardiff, 1976–83. Member: NERC, 1976–87; SERC (formerly SRC), 1976–86; ABRC, 1976–88; Bd, World Resources Inst., Washington, 1985–94; China Council for Internat. Co-operation on Envmt and Develt, Beijing, 1992–94; Chairman: Review of Scientific Civil Service, 1980; Renewable Energy Adv. Gp, 1992; Energy Adv. Panel, 1993–; Internat. Inst. for Envmt and Develt, 1994–; Mem., Royal Commn on Envmtl Pollution, 1994–. Chm., British Schools Exploring Society, 1967–78; Vice-Pres., Young Explorer's Trust, 1981–90 (Chm., 1972, 1979–81). President: Governing Council, UN Environment Prog., 1983–84; Global 500 Forum, 1992–; Chm., Commonwealth Expert Gp on Climate Change, 1988–89. Hon. DSc: Durham, 1991; Sussex, 1993. Bruce Medal, RSE, 1964; UNEP Silver Medal, 1983; UNEP Global 500, 1988; Patron's Medal, RGS, 1992; Livingstone Medal, RSGS, 1993. Comdr, Order of the Golden Ark (Netherlands), 1991. *Publications:* A History of Appleby, 1956, 2nd edn 1970; Mountains in the Sea, The Story of the Gough Island Expedition, 1958; (ed jtly) Antarctic Biology, 1964; (ed) Antarctic Ecology, 1970; (with N. M. Wace) Man and Nature in the Tristan da Cunha Islands, 1976; A Perspective of Environmental Pollution, 1979; (ed jtly) The World Environment 1972–82, 1982; (ed jtly) The World Environment 1972–92, 1992; numerous papers and articles on Antarctica, environment and conservation. *Address:* 35 Wingate Way, Trumpington, Cambridge CB2 2HD. *Club:* Athenæum.

HOLDING, John Francis; HM Diplomatic Service; Consul-General, Auckland, and Director of UK Trade Promotion in New Zealand, since 1990; *b* 12 August 1936; *s* of late Francis George Holding, CA, Inland Revenue, and Gwendoline Elizabeth Holding (*née* Jenkins); *m* 1st, 1970, Pamela Margaret Straker-Nesbit (marr. diss. 1984); two *d;* 2nd, 1993, Susan Ann Clark. *Educ:* Colwyn Bay Grammar Sch.; LSE (externally). Mil. service, 1955–57; Min. of Housing and Local Govt, 1957; CRO (later FCO), 1964; served Karachi, Islamabad and Kinshasa; First Sec., 1973; Canberra, 1973–78; Dep. High Comr, Banjul, The Gambia, 1978–80; Grenada and Barbados, 1984–87; Dep. High Comr, Dhaka, 1987–90. *Recreations:* tennis, sailing, walking, pianoforte. *Address:* c/o Foreign and Commonwealth Office, SW1A 2AH.

HOLDING, Malcolm Alexander; HM Diplomatic Service, retired; Consul-General, Naples, 1986–90; *b* 11 May 1932; *s* of Adam Anderson Holding and Mary Lillian (*née* Golding); *m* 1955, Pamela Eve Hampshire; two *d.* *Educ:* King Henry VIII Sch., Coventry. Foreign Office, 1949–51; HM Forces, 1951–53; FO, 1953–55; Middle East Centre for Arab Studies, 1956–57; Third Secretary (Commercial), Tunis, 1957–60; Second Sec. (Commercial), Khartoum, 1960–64; Second, later First Sec. (Commercial), Cairo, 1964–68; Consul, Bari, 1969; FCO, 1970–73; First Sec., British Dep. High Commission, Madras, 1973–75; FCO, 1976–78; Canadian National Defence Coll., Kingston, Ontario,

1978–79; Counsellor (Commercial), Rome, 1979–81; Consul-Gen., Edmonton, 1981–85. Commendatore, Order of Merit of the Republic of Italy, 1980. *Recreations:* sailing, skiing. *Address:* Theatre Cottage, Powderham, Exeter EX6 8JJ.

HOLDRIDGE, Ven. Bernard Lee; Archdeacon of Doncaster, since 1994; *b* 24 July 1935; *s* of Geoffrey and Lucy Medlow Holdridge. *Educ:* Grammar Sch., Thorne; Lichfield Theol Coll. Ordained deacon, 1967, priest, 1968; Curate, Swinton, S Yorks, 1967–71; Vicar, St Jude, Hexthorpe, Doncaster, 1971–81; Rector, St Mary, Rawmarsh with Parkgate, 1981–88; RD of Rotherham, 1986–88; Vicar, Priory Church of St Mary and St Cuthbert, Worksop, with St Giles, Carburton and St Mary the Virgin, Clumber Park, dio. of Southwell, 1988–94. Chm., DAC for Care of Churches and Churchyards, Southwell, 1990–94. *Recreations:* foreign travel, reading, theatre, a glass of wine with friends. *Address:* Fairview House, 14 Armthorpe Lane, Wheatley Hills, Doncaster DN2 5LZ. *T:* Doncaster (01302) 325787.

HOLDSWORTH, Lt-Comdr (Arthur) John (Arundell), CVO 1980; OBE 1962; an Extra Gentleman Usher to the Queen, since 1985 (Gentleman Usher, 1967–85); Vice Lord-Lieutenant for Devon, 1982–90; *b* 31 March 1915; *s* of Captain F. J. C. Holdsworth, JP, DL, Totnes, and M. W. Holdsworth (*née* Arundell); *m* 1940, Barbara Lucy Ussher, *d* of Col and Mrs W. M. Acton; one *s* one *d*. *Educ:* Stanmore Park Prep. Sch.; Royal Naval Coll., Dartmouth. Entered RN, 1928; served War at sea (despatches); Asst Naval Attaché Warsaw, 1947–49; BJSM Washington, 1950–51; Naval Staff, Germany, 1954–56; Flag Lieut to Bd of Admiralty, 1956–65; retired 1965. Steward, Newton Abbot Race Course, 1967–85; Dep. Pres., Devon Br., BRCS, 1971–85 (Patron, 1985–); Chm., Silver Jubilee Trust Council, Devon, 1978–85. DL 1973, High Sheriff, 1976–77, Devon. *Address:* Holbeam Mill, Ogwell, Newton Abbot, Devon TQ12 6LX. *T:* Newton Abbot (01626) 65547.

HOLDSWORTH, Sir (George) Trevor, Kt 1982; Chairman: Allied Colloids Group PLC, since 1983; Beauford PLC, since 1991; Lambert Howarth Group PLC, since 1993; Director: Prudential Corporation, since 1986 (Joint Deputy Chairman, 1988–92); Owens-Corning Fiberglas Corp., since 1994; *b* 29 May 1927; *s* of late William Albert Holdsworth and Winifred Holdsworth (*née* Bottomley); *m* 1st, 1951, Patricia June Ridler (*d* 1993); three *s*; 2nd, 1995, Jenny Watson. *Educ:* Hanson Grammar Sch., Bradford; Keighley Grammar Sch. FCA 1950. Rawlinson Greaves & Mitchell, Bradford, 1944–51; Bowater Paper Corp., 1952–63 (financial and admin. appts; Dir and Controller of UK paper-making subsids); joined Guest, Keen & Nettlefolds (later GKN plc), 1963; Dep. Chief Accountant, 1963–64; Gp Chief Accountant, 1965–67; General Man. Dir, GKN Screws & Fasteners Ltd, 1968–70; Dir, 1970–88; Gp Controller, 1970–72; Gp Exec. Vice Chm., Corporate Controls and Services, 1973–74; Dep. Chm., 1974–77; Man. Dir and Dep. Chm., 1977–80; Chm., 1980–88. Chairman: British Satellite Broadcasting, 1987–90; National Power, 1990–95; Director: Equity Capital for Industry, 1976–84; THORN EMI, 1977–87; Midland Bank plc, 1979–88. Member: AMF Inc. Europ. Adv. Council, 1982–85; European Adv. Bd, Owens Corning Fiberglas Inc., 1990–93; Adv. Bd, LEK, 1992–. Confederation of British Industry: Mem. Council, 1974–; Mem., Econ. and Financial Policy Cttee, 1978–80; Mem., Steering Gp on Unemployment, 1982; Mem., Special Programmes Unit, 1982; Chm., Tax Reform Working Party, 1984–86; Dep. Pres., 1987–88; Pres., 1988–90. Chairman: Review Body on Doctors' and Dentists' Remuneration, 1990–93; Adv. Council, Foundn for Manufacturing and Industry, 1993–; Dep. Chm., Financial Reporting Council, 1990–93; Mem., Business in the Community, 1984–92; British Institute of Management: Mem. Council, 1974–84; Vice-Chm., 1978; Mem., Bd of Fellows, 1979; Chm., 1980–82; a Vice Pres., 1982–; Gold Medal, 1987; Vice Pres., Engineering Employers' Fedn, 1980–88; Jt Dep. Chm., Adv. Bd, Inst. of Occupational Health, 1980; Duke of Edinburgh's Award: Mem., Internat. Panel, 1980 (Chm., 1987); Internat. Trustee, 1987–94; UK Trustee, 1988–; Member: Exec. Cttee, SMMT, 1980–83; Engineering Industries Council, 1980– (Chm., 1985); Court of British Shippers' Council, 1981–89; British-North American Cttee, 1981–85; Council, RIIA, 1983–; Internat. Council of INSEAD, 1985–92; Eur. Adv. Cttee, New York Stock Exchange, 1985–; Chm., Wigmore Hall Trust, 1992–; Member: Council, Royal Opera House Trust (Trustee, 1981–84); Council, Winston Churchill Meml Trust, 1985–; Hon. Pres., Council of Mechanical and Metal Trade Assocs, 1987. Dir, UK–Japan 2000 Gp, 1987. Trustee: Anglo-German Foundn for the Study of Industrial Society, 1980–92; Brighton Fest. Trust, 1980–90 (Chm. 1982–87); Philharmonia Trust, 1982–93; Thrombosis Res. Trust, 1989–. Governor, Ashridge Management Coll., 1978; Chancellor, Bradford Univ., 1992–. Vice-Pres., Ironbridge Gorge Museum Develt Trust, 1981–. Internat. Counsellor, Conference Bd, 1984. CIEx 1987. FRSA 1988. Freeman, City of London, 1977; Liveryman, Worshipful Co. of Chartered Accountants in England and Wales, 1978. Hon. DTech Loughborough, 1981; Hon. DSc: Aston, 1982; Sussex, 1988; Hon. DEng: Bradford, 1983; Birmingham, 1992; Hon. DBA Internat. Management Centre, Buckingham, 1986. Chartered Accountants Founding Socs' Centenary Award, 1983; Hon. CGIA 1989. *Recreations:* music, theatre. *Address:* Old School House, Offham, Lewes, Sussex. *Club:* Athenæum.

HOLDSWORTH, Lt-Comdr John; *see* Holdsworth, Lt-Comdr A. J. A.

HOLDSWORTH, Sir Trevor; *see* Holdsworth, Sir G. T.

HOLE, Very Rev. Derek Norman; Provost of Leicester Cathedral, since 1992; *b* 5 Dec. 1933; *s* of Frank Edwin Hole and Ella Evelyn Hole (*née* Thomas). *Educ:* Public Central Sch., Plymouth; Lincoln Theological College. Deacon, 1960; Priest, 1961; Asst Curate, St Mary Magdalen, Knighton, 1960–62; Domestic Chaplain to Archbishop of Cape Town, 1962–64; Asst Curate, St Nicholas, Kenilworth, 1964–67; Rector, St Mary the Virgin, Burton Latimer, 1967–73; Vicar, St James the Greater, Leicester, 1973–92; Chaplain to the Queen, 1985–92. Hon. Canon, Leicester Cathedral, 1983–92. Rural Dean, Christianity South, Leicester, 1983–92; Chm., House of Clergy, 1986–94; Vice-Pres., Diocesan Synod and Mem., Bishop's Council, 1986–94. Chaplain to: Lord Mayor of Leicester, 1976–77, 1994–95; High Sheriffs of Leics, 1980–85 and 1987; Leicester High Sch., 1984–92; Haymarket Theatre, Leicester, 1980–83, 1993–95; Leicester Br., RAFA, 1978–92; Master of Merchant Taylors' Co., 1995–96. Priest Associate, Actors' Church Union, 1995–; Vice-Pres., English Clergy Assoc., 1993–. Chm. Leicester Diocesan Redundant Churches Uses Cttee, 1985–. Mem., Leicester Charity Orgn Soc. 1983–; Trustee: Leicester Church Charities, 1983–; Leicester GS, 1992–; Pres., Leicester Rotary Club, 1987–88. Mem., Victorian Soc., 1986–; Hon. Life Mem., Leics Br., BRCS, 1995. Governor: Alderman Newton's Sch., Leicester, 1976–82; Alderman Newton Foundn, 1993–; Leicester High Sch., 1992–. *Recreations:* music, walking, reading biographies and Victorian history. *Address:* Provost's House, 1 St Martin's East, Leicester LE1 5FX. *T:* Leicester (0116) 262 5294, *Fax:* (0116) 262 5295. *Clubs:* Leicestershire (Leicester); Royal Western Yacht.

HOLFORD, Surgeon Rear-Adm. John Morley, CB 1965; OBE 1954; Senior Principal Medical Officer, Department of Health and Social Security, 1973–74, retired; *b* 10 Jan. 1909; *o s* of late Rev. W. J. Holford and Amy Finnemore Lello; *m* 1935, Monica Peregrine (*d* 1986), *d* of late Preb. P. S. G. Propert; two *s*. *Educ:* Kingswood, Bath; Trinity Hall, Cambridge. MA, MB, Cantab; FRCP; joined RN 1935. War service in HMS Nelson, 1940–42; RN Hosp. Plymouth, 1942–44; consultant in Medicine to RN, 1954–66; Surgeon Capt., 1957; Surgeon Rear-Adm. 1963; Medical Officer in Charge, RN Hosp. Haslar, 1963–66. Retired, 1966. MO, Min. of Health, 1966, SMO, 1967, SPMO, 1973. Gilbert Blanc Medal, 1956; F. E. Williams Prize in Geriatric Medicine, RCP, 1972. CStJ 1964. *Publications:* Articles in medical journals. *Recreations:* chess (jt champion of South Africa, 1946), bridge. *Address:* c/o Lloyds Bank, 84 Park Lane, W1. *Club:* Army and Navy.

HOLGATE, Hon. Harold Norman, AO 1994; *b* 5 Dec. 1933; *s* of late H. W. Holgate; *m* 1963, Rosalind, *d* of E. C. Wesley; two *s* two *d*. *Educ:* Maitland (NSW) High Sch.; Univ. of Tasmania (BA). Journalist: Sydney Morning Herald, 1952–55; Melbourne Herald, 1955–62; Political Journalist, Dep. Chief of Staff, Launceston Examiner, 1963–66; Public Relns Manager, Tasmanian Directorate of Industrial Development, 1966–70; Exec. Producer, ABC TV Public Affairs Programme, This Day Tonight, Hobart, 1970–73; Press Sec. to Dep. Prime Minister and Minister for Defence, Govt of Australia, Mr Lance Barnard, 1973–74; MHA (Lab) for Bass, Tasmania, 1974–92; Speaker of House of Assembly, 1975–76; Minister (Govt of Tasmania): for Housing and Construction and Minister assisting the Dep. Premier, 1976–77; for Education, Recreation and the Arts and for Racing and Gaming, 1977–79; for Education, Recreation and the Arts, and for Police and Emergency Services, 1979–80; for Education, for Police and Emergency Services, for Racing and Gaming, 1980–81; for Police and Emergency Services, for Local Govt, for the Environment, for Water Resources, for Racing and Gaming, 1981; Premier of Tasmania, Treasurer and Minister for Racing and Gaming, 1981–82; Dep. Leader of the Opposition, Tasmanian House of Assembly, 1982–86; Chm., Tasmanian Parly Labor Party, 1986–89; Minister for Tourism, Sport and Recreation, 1989–92, for Roads and Transport, 1990, for Parks, Wildlife and Heritage, 1991–92. *Recreations:* horse racing, music, reading, swimming. *Address:* 3 Jacques Road, Hillwood, Tasmania 7252, Australia. *T:* (03) 948208.

HOLGATE, Dr Sidney, CBE 1981; Master of Grey College, University of Durham, 1959–80; Member, Academic Advisory Committee, Open University, 1969–81 (Vice-Chairman, 1972–75; Chairman, 1975–77); *b* Hucknall, Notts, 9 Sept. 1918; *e s* of late Henry and Annie Elizabeth Holgate; *m* 1942, Isabel Armorey; no *c*. *Educ:* Henry Mellish Sch., Nottingham; Durham Univ. Open Scholar, Hatfield Coll., Durham, 1937; Univ. Mathematical Scholarship, 1940; BA (1st Cl. Hons Mathematics) 1940; MA 1943; PhD 1945. Asst Master, Nottingham High Sch., 1941–42; Lecturer in Mathematics, University of Durham, 1942–46; Sec. of the Durham Colls, 1946–59; Pro-Vice-Chancellor, Univ. of Durham, 1964–69. Member: Schools Council Gen. Studies Cttee, 1967–70; Chm., BBC Radio Durham Council, 1968–72; Vice-Chm., BBC Radio Newcastle Council, 1972–74. Hon. DUniv. Open, 1980. *Publications:* mathematical papers in Proc. Camb. Phil. Soc. and Proc. Royal Soc. *Recreations:* cricket and other sports, railways, bridge. *Address:* 6 Howlcroft Villas, Neville's Cross, Durham DH1 4DU.

HOLLAMBY, Edward Ernest, OBE 1970; FRIBA, FRTPI, FCSD; Chief Architect and Planner to London Docklands Development Corporation, 1981–85, retired; architectural consultant; *b* 8 Jan. 1921; *s* of late Edward Thomas Hollamby and Ethel May (*née* Kingdom); *m* 1941, Doris Isabel Parker; one *s* two *d*. *Educ:* School of Arts and Crafts, Hammersmith; University Coll. London. DipTP London. Served RM Engrs, 1941–46. Architect, Miners' Welfare Commn, 1947–49; Sen. Architect, LCC, 1949–62; Borough Architect, Lambeth, 1963–65, Bor. Architect and Town Planning Officer, 1965–69, Dir of Architecture, Planning and Develt, 1969–81. Works, 1957–, incl.: Christopher Wren and N Hammersmith Sec. Schs; Brandon Estate, Southwark; Housing at Elephant and Castle; study for Erith Township, Kent (prototype study for Thamesmead); pioneered rehabil. old houses, LCC Brixton Town Centre Develt Plan, housing schemes, Lambeth, 1965–, incl.: Lambeth Towers, Central Hill, Norwood, Stockwell, Brixton, Clapham, Tulse Hill and Vauxhall; also conservation and historic bldgs restoration, parks and open spaces, sheltered housing, old people's homes, health centres, doctors' gp practices, community centres, commercial and civic offices. Area rehabil. and renewal schemes, Clapham Manor and Kennington; Norwood Libr. and Nettlefold Hall; schs for mentally retarded, Clapham and Kennington; rehabil. centre for disabled, Clapham; recreation centre, Brixton; study, Civic Centre, Brixton; holiday hotel for severely disabled, Netley, near Southampton; Girls' Secure Unit, Croydon, 1978; scheme for village development, Shirley Oaks, Croydon, 1979; Isle of Dogs Urban Design Guide, 1982; develt strategies for Limehouse, Surrey and Greenland Docks, Bermondsey and Wapping, 1982–83; refurbishment of exterior and landscape, St George's in the East, 1983; Royal Docks Develt Strategy, 1984; overall layout, Western Dock, Wapping; Chm., Design Gp, Docklands Light Railway, 1982–84. Assessor, numerous architectural competitions and award schemes. Has lectured on architecture and environmental planning; numerous radio and TV appearances. RIBA: Mem. Council, 1961–70, Hon. Treas., 1967–70. Vice-Pres., London Forum of Amenity and Civic Socs, 1991–; Member: Historic Buildings Council, 1972–82; London Adv. Cttee, English Heritage, 1986–90; Founder Member: William Morris Soc.; Bexley Civic Soc. Hon. ALI; FRSA. Numerous design and Civic Trust awards. *Publications:* (with Raphaele Gorjux) La Red House, 1983; Docklands Heritage: conservation and regeneration in Docklands, 1987; Red House, Bexleyheath by Philip Webb: the home of William Morris, 1991; contrib. architectural and town planning jls. *Recreations:* travel, classical music, opera, gardening. *Address:* Red House, Red House Lane, Upton, Bexleyheath, Kent DA6 8JF. *T:* 0181–303 8808. *Club:* Arts.

HOLLAND, Hon. Sir Alan (Douglas), Kt 1995; Judge, High Court (formerly Supreme Court) of New Zealand, 1978–94, retired; *b* 20 June 1929; *s* of Clarence Cyril Holland and Marjorie Evelyn Holland; *m* 1961, Felicity Ann Ower; one *s*. *Educ:* Waitaki Boys' High Sch.; Canterbury Coll., Univ. of New Zealand (LLB). Part-time Lectr in Law and Commerce Faculties of Canterbury Univ., 1953–63; Partner, Wynn Williams & Co., Solicitors, Christchurch, 1956–78. Pres., Canterbury Dist Law Soc., 1973 (Mem. Council, 1963–73); Mem. Council and associated cttees, NZ Law Soc., 1970–74. *Recreations:* general. *Address:* 39 McDougall Avenue, Christchurch 8001, New Zealand. *T:* (3) 3557102. *Club:* Christchurch.

HOLLAND, Rt. Rev. Alfred Charles; Bishop of Newcastle, NSW, 1978–92; *b* 23 Feb. 1927; *s* of Alfred Charles Holland and Maud Allison; *m* 1954, Joyce Marion Embling; three *s* one *d*. *Educ:* Raine's Sch., London; Univ. of Durham (BA 1950, DipTh 1952). RNVR, 1945–47; Univ. of Durham, 1948–52; Assistant Priest, West Hackney, London, 1952–54; Rector of Scarborough, WA, 1955–70; Asst Bishop, Dio. Perth, WA, 1970–77. Life Member: Stirling Rugby Football Club, 1969; Durham Univ. Society, 1984. *Publications:* Luke Through Lent, 1980; (ed) The Diocese Together, 1987. *Recreations:* reading, painting. *Address:* 21 Sullivan Crescent, Wanniassa, ACT 2903, Australia. *Club:* Australian (Sydney).

HOLLAND, Anthony; *see* Holland, J. A.

HOLLAND, Arthur David, CB 1973; TD 1947; Chief Highway Engineer, Department of the Environment, 1970–74; *b* 1 Nov. 1913; *o s* of Col. Arthur Leslie Holland, MC, TD, and Dora Helena Hassé; *m* 1938, Jean Moyra Spowart; two *s*. *Educ:* Malvern Coll.; University of Bristol (BSc(Eng)Hons). Asst Engineer, Great Western Railway Co, 1935–36; N Devon CC, 1936–37; Min. of Transport: Manchester, 1937–38; London,

1938–39. Served War: with RE, 1939–46; in Air Defence Gt Britain, 1939–42; with Middle East Forces, 1942–46, finally as Lt-Col RE (now Hon. Lt-Col), Sen. Staff Officer to Chief Engineer, Italy. Min. of Transport, Nottingham, 1946–47; Bridge Section, London, 1947–61; Divl Road Engr, E Midland Div., Nottingham, 1961–63; Asst Chief Engr (Bridges), 1963–65; Dep. Chief Engr, HQ London, 1965–70. FICE, FIStructE, FInstHE; Mem., Smeatonian Soc. of Civil Engrs, 1972– (Pres., 1991). *Publications:* contribs to Proc. Instn of Civil Engineers and Instn of Highway Engineers. *Address:* Pine Tree Cottage, Pembroke Road, Woking, Surrey GU22 7DS. *T:* Woking (01483) 762403.

HOLLAND, Brian Arthur; Solicitor to the Post Office, 1981–93; postal law consultant; *b* 14 June 1935; *s* of late George Leigh Holland and Hilda Holland, MBE; *m* 1964, Sally Edwards; one *s* one *d. Educ:* Manchester Grammar Sch.; Manchester Univ. (LLB Hons). Admitted Solicitor, 1961. Joined Solicitor's Dept, GPO, 1961; Solicitor's Office, Post Office: Head of Civil Litigation Div., 1977–79; Dir, Litigation and Prosecution Dept, 1979–81. *Publication:* (contrib.) Halsbury's Laws of England, 4th edn, vol. 36. *Recreations:* photography, studying railways, sketching, gardening. *Address:* 23 Grasmere Road, Purley, Surrey CR8 1DY. *T:* 0181–660 0479.

HOLLAND, Hon. Sir Christopher (John), Kt 1992; **Hon. Mr Justice Holland;** a Judge of the High Court of Justice, Queen's Bench Division, since 1992; a Judge of the Employment Appeal Tribunal, since 1994; *b* 1 June 1937; *er s* of late Frank and Winifred Mary Holland; *m* 1967, Jill Iona Holland; one *s* one *d. Educ:* Leeds Grammar Sch.; Emmanuel Coll., Cambridge (MA, LLB). National Service (acting L/Cpl), 3rd Royal Tank Regt, 1956–58. Called to the Bar, Inner Temple, 1963, Bencher, 1985; commenced practice on North Eastern Circuit (Presiding Judge, 1993–); QC 1978; a Recorder, 1992. Mem., Criminal Injuries Compensation Bd, 1992. Vice Chm., Cttee of Inquiry into Outbreak of Legionnaires' Disease at Stafford, 1985. Chm., Lower Washburn Parish Council, 1975–91. *Address:* c/o Royal Courts of Justice, Strand, WC2A 2LL.

HOLLAND, Sir Clifton Vaughan, (Sir John), AC 1988; Kt 1973; BCE; CPEng, FTS, Hon. FIE(Aust), FAIM, FAIB; Chairman, John Holland Holdings Limited, 1963–86; *b* Melbourne, 21 June 1914; *s* of Thomas and Mabel Ruth Elizabeth Holland; *m* 1942, Emily Joan Atkinson; three *s* one *d. Educ:* Flinders State Sch.; Frankston High Sch.; Queen's Coll., Univ. of Melbourne (BCE); Monash Univ. (Hon. DEng 1978). Junior Engineer, BP, 1936–39. Served War of 1939–45, RAE and 'Z' Special Force, Middle East, SW Pacific (Lt-Col). Construction Engr, BP Aust. 1946–49; Founder, John Holland (Constructions) Pty Ltd, 1949, Man. Dir 1949–73, Chm., 1949–86; Chm., Process Plant Constructions Pty Ltd, 1949–82; Director: T & G Life Soc., 1972–82; Aust. and NZ Banking Gp, 1976–81. Foundn Pres., Australian Fedn of Civil Contractors (Life Mem., 1971); Chm., Nat. Construction Industry Conf. Organising Cttee, 1982; Mem., Construction Industry Res. Bd, 1982. Chm., Econ. Consultative Adv. Gp to the Treasurer, 1975–81; Mem., Rhodes Scholar Selection Cttee, 1970–73; Mem. Bd, Royal Melbourne Hosp., 1963–79; Nat. Chm., Outward Bound, 1973–74, Chm. Victorian Div., 1964–77; Councillor, Inst. of Public Affairs, 1980; Mem., Churchill Fellowship Selection Cttee, 1968–82; Director: Winston Churchill Meml Trust, 1976–82 (Chm., Vic. Br., 1977–82); Child Accident Prevention Foundn of Australia, 1979–81; Chairman: La Trobe Centenary Commemoration Council, 1975–76; Matthew Flinders Bi-Centenary Council, 1973–75; History Adv. Council of Victoria, 1975–85; Loch Ard Centenary Commemoration Cttee, 1976–78; Citizens' Council, 150th Anniversary Celebrations, Victoria, 1979–82; Victorian Cttee for Anzac Awards, 1982–; Nat. Chm., Queen's Silver Jubilee Trust for Young Australians, 1981–87 (Vic. Chm., 1977–80; Life Mem., 1992); Mem., Centenary Test Co-ordinating Cttee, 1976–77. Dep. Chm., Melbourne Univ. Engineering Sch. Centenary Foundn and Appeal Cttee, 1982–90. Director: Corps of Commissionaires (Victoria) Ltd, 1978–89; Australian Bicentenary Celebrations, 1980–82 (Vic. Chm., 1980–82). Pres., Stroke Res. Foundn, 1983–90; Patron, Bone Marrow Foundn, 1992–. Construction projects include: Jindabyne pumping station; Westgate Bridge; Tasman Bridge restoration, New Parliament House. Foundation Fellow, Australian Acad. of Technological Scis. Hon. DEng Monash, 1976. Peter Nicoll Russell Meml Medal, 1974; Kernot Meml Medal, Univ. of Melbourne, 1976; Consulting Engineers Advancement Soc. Medal, 1983. *Recreations:* golf, music, gardening, cricket. *Address:* Bunkers, 29 George Road, Flinders, Vic 3929, Australia. *Clubs:* Australian, Naval and Military (Melbourne); Royal Melbourne Golf, Frankston Golf, Flinders Golf.

HOLLAND, David Cuthbert Lyall, CB 1975; Librarian of the House of Commons, 1967–76; *b* 23 March 1915; *yr s* of Michael Holland, MC, and Marion Holland (*née* Broadwood); *m* 1949, Rosemary Griffiths, *y d* of David Ll. Griffiths, OBE; two *s* one *d. Educ:* Eton; Trinity Coll., Cambridge (MA). War service, Army, 1939–46; PoW. Appointed House of Commons Library, 1946. Chm., Study of Parlt Gp, 1973–74. *Publications include:* book reviews, etc. *Recreation:* book collecting. *Address:* The Barn, Milton Street, Polegate, East Sussex. *T:* Alfriston (01323) 870379. *Club:* Athenæum.

HOLLAND, David George, CMG 1975; Chairman, Securities Standards Advisory Board, 1993–94; *b* 31 May 1925; *s* of late Francis George Holland and Mabel Ellen Holland; *m* 1954, Marian Elizabeth Rowles; two *s* one *d. Educ:* Taunton Sch.; Wadham Coll., Oxford. Inst. of Economics and Statistics, Oxford, 1949–63; Internat. Bank for Reconstruction and Development, Washington, DC, 1963–65; Min. of Overseas Development, 1965–67; Chief Economic Adviser, FCO, 1967–75; Dep. Chief, Economic Intelligence and Overseas Depts, Bank of England, 1975–80; Chief Adviser, Bank of England, 1980–85; Exec. Dir, 1986–90, consultant, 1990–93, The Group of Thirty. *Address:* Coombe Cottage, Missenden Road, Butlers Cross, Aylesbury, Bucks HP17 0UP.

HOLLAND, Rt. Rev. Edward; *see* Colchester, Area Bishop of.

HOLLAND, Edward Richard Charles, OBE 1983 (MBE 1969); HM Diplomatic Service, retired; *b* 26 March 1925; *s* of Cecil Francis Richard Holland and Joyce Mary (*née* Pyne); *m* 1952, Dorothy Olive Branthwaite; two *s. Educ:* Launceston Coll. Served RAF, 1943–48. Joined FO, 1948; served in Batavia, Bangkok, Oslo, Prague and Helsinki, 1949–57; Consul, Saigon, 1957; FO, 1959; Cape Town, 1962; First Sec., Monrovia, 1964; Consul: Stuttgart, 1969; Düsseldorf, 1971; FCO, 1972; First Sec., Islamabad, 1977; Consul-Gen., Alexandria, 1981–82. *Recreations:* gardening, walking, reading, painting. *Address:* 25 Stafford Road, Seaford, E Sussex BN25 1UE. *T:* Seaford (01323) 897631. *Club:* Civil Service.

HOLLAND, Einion; *see* Holland, R. E.

HOLLAND, Frank Robert Dacre; Chairman, C. E. Heath & Co. PLC, 1973–84, Non-Executive Director, 1984–86; *b* 24 March 1924; *s* of Ernest Albert Holland and Kathleen Annie (*née* Page); *m* 1948, Margaret Lindsay Aird; one *d. Educ:* Whitgift Sch., Croydon. Joined C. E. Heath & Co. Ltd, 1941; entered Army, 1942; Sandhurst, 1943; commissioned 4th Queen's Own Hussars, 1944; served, Italy, 1944–45, Austria and Germany, 1945–47; returned to C. E. Heath & Co. Ltd, 1947; Joint Managing Director, North American Operation, 1965; Director, C. E. Heath & Co. Ltd, 1965, Dep. Chm., 1969. Liveryman, Insurers' Co., 1980– (Master, 1985–86). *Recreations:* travel, gardening. *Address:* Moatside, 68 Ashley Road, Walton-on-Thames, Surrey KT12 1HR. *T:* Walton-on-Thames (01932) 227591. *Clubs:* Oriental, Cavalry and Guards.

HOLLAND, Sir Geoffrey, KCB 1989 (CB 1984); Vice-Chancellor, Exeter University, since 1994; *b* 9 May 1938; *s* of late Frank Holland, CBE and of Elsie Freda Holland; *m* 1964, Carol Ann Challen. *Educ:* Merchant Taylors' Sch., Northwood; St John's Coll., Oxford (BA 1st cl. Hons; MA; Hon. Fellow, 1991). 2nd Lieut, RTR, 1956–58. Entered Min. of Labour, 1961, Asst Private Sec., 1964–65; Principal Private Sec. to Sec. of State for Employment, 1971–72; Manpower Services Commission: Asst Sec., Hd of Planning, 1973; Dir of Special Progs, 1977; Dep. Sec., 1981; Dir, 1981; Second Perm. Sec., 1986; Perm. Sec., Dept of Employment, subseq. Employment Dept Gp, 1988–93; Perm. Sec., DFE, 1993. Dir, Shell UK, 1994–. Consultant, Industrial Cttee, C of E Bd of Social Responsibility, 1985–. Liveryman, Merchant Taylors' Co., 1967– (Jun. Renter Warden, 1990–91). CIMgt (CBIM 1987). Fellow, Eton Coll., 1994–; Hon. Fellow: Polytechnic of Wales, 1986; Inst. of Training Develt, 1986. Hon. FCGI 1994. Hon. LLD Sheffield, 1994. *Publications:* Young People and Work, 1977; many articles on manpower, educn, training, management etc in professional jls. *Recreations:* journeying, opera, exercising the dog. *Address:* Northcote House, The Queen's Drive, Exeter EX4 4QJ. *Club:* East India, Devonshire, Sports and Public Schools.

HOLLAND, Sir Guy (Hope), 3rd Bt *cr* 1917; farmer; art dealer; *b* 19 July 1918; *s* of Sir Reginald Sothern Holland, 1st Bt and Stretta Aimée Holland (*née* Price) (*d* 1949); *S* brother, 1981; *m* 1945, Joan Marianne Street, *d* of late Captain Herbert Edmund Street, XXth Hussars, and of Lady Tottenham; two *d. Educ:* privately and Christ Church, Oxford. Served War of 1939–45 (wounded); Captain, Royal Scots Greys; ADC to Gen. Sir Andrew Thorne, 1944. *Heir:* none. *Address:* Sheepbridge Barn, Eastleach, Cirencester, Gloucestershire GL7 3PS. *T:* Southrop (01367) 850296. *Clubs:* Boodle's, Pratt's.

HOLLAND, Sir John; *see* Holland, Sir C. V.

HOLLAND, (John) Anthony; Partner, Foot & Bowden, solicitors, Plymouth, since 1964; *b* 9 Nov. 1938; *s* of John and Dorothy Rita Holland; *m* 1963, Kathleen Margaret Anderson; three *s. Educ:* Ratcliffe Coll., Leics; Nottingham Univ. (LLB). Admitted Solicitor of Supreme Court, 1962; notary public. Joined Foot & Bowden, 1964. Chairman: Young Solicitors Gp, Law Soc., 1972; Social Security Appeals Tribunal, 1974–; South Western Regl Adv. Council, BBC, 1984–87; a Chm., SFA, 1993–; Member: Council, Law Soc., 1976– (Vice-Pres., 1989–90; Pres., 1990–91); Marre Cttee on future of the Legal Profession, 1986–88; Council, Justice, 1991–; Hon. Solicitor and Mem. Council, Howard League for Penal Reform, 1992–; Hon. Mem., SPTL, 1992. President: Plymouth Law Soc., 1986–87; Cornwall Law Soc., 1988–89. Member: Plymouth Diocesan Finances Cttee, 1986–94; Univ. of Nottingham Vice Chancellor's Adv. Bd, 1990–. Chm., Plymouth Chamber of Commerce and Industry, 1994–. Governor: Plymouth Coll., 1976–93; Coll. of Law, 1991–. Hon. Mem., Canadian Bar Assoc., 1990. Jt Adv. Editor, Mines and Quarries Section, Butterworth's Encyclopædia of Forms and Precedents, 1989–. *Publications:* (jtly) Principles of Registered Land Conveyancing, 1966; (jtly) Landlord and Tenant, 1968; (Gen. Ed.) Cordery on Solicitors, 9th edn. *Recreations:* opera, literature, journalism, broadcasting. *Address:* 46 Thornhill Way, Mannamead, Plymouth PL3 5NP. *T:* Plymouth (01752) 220529; 66 Andrewes House, Barbican, EC2Y 8AY. *T:* 0171–638 5044. *Club:* Royal Western Yacht (Plymouth).

HOLLAND, John Lewis; Managing Director, Herts & Essex Newspapers, since 1990; *b* 23 May 1937; *s* of George James Holland and Esther Holland; *m* 1958, Maureen Ann Adams; one *s* one *d. Educ:* Nottingham Technical Grammar Sch. Trainee Reporter, Nottingham Evening News, subseq. Jun. Reporter, Mansfield Br. Office, 1953–55; Sports Reporter, Mansfield Reporter Co., 1955–56; Sports Reporter, subseq. Sports Editor, Aldershot News Group, 1956–59; News Editor, West Bridgford & Clifton Standard, Nottingham, 1959–61; Chief Sports Sub Editor, Bristol Evening Post, and Editor, Sports Green 'Un (sports edn), 1961–64; Editor, West Bridgford & Clifton Standard, Nottingham, and Partner, Botting & Turner Sports Agency, Nottingham, 1964–66; Birmingham Evening Mail: Dep. Sports Editor, 1966–71; Editor, Special Projects Unit (Colour Prodn Dept), 1971–75; Editor, 1975–79, and Gen. Man., 1979–81, Sandwell Evening Mail; Marketing/Promotions Gen. Man., Birmingham Post & Mail, 1981–82; Editor, The Birmingham Post, 1982–86. Director: Birmingham Post & Mail Circulation and Promotions, 1986–88; Birmingham Post & Mail Publications and Promotions, 1988–90; Birmingham Convention and Visitor Bureau, 1982–90. Pres., Chartered Inst. of Marketing, 1989–90; Vice-Pres., Chiltern Newspaper Proprietors Assoc., 1994–95 (Pres., 1995–). *Recreations:* journalism, most sports (more recently playing golf), keeping horses, gardening, keep fit. *Address:* Malting House, Malting Lane, Litlington, Royston, Herts SG8 0QT. *Clubs:* Press (Birmingham); Heydon Grange Golf (Royston).

HOLLAND, Sir Kenneth (Lawrence), Kt 1981; CBE 1971; QFSM 1974; Consultant, Fire Safety Engineering, since 1981; Director: Gent Ltd, 1981–93; Bas/Firelaw Ltd, since 1993; *b* 20 Sept. 1918; *s* of Percy Lawrence and Edith Holland; *m* 1941, Pauline Keith (*née* Mansfield); two *s* one *d. Educ:* Whitcliffe Mount Grammar Sch., Cleckheaton, Yorks. Entered Fire Service, Lancashire, 1937; Divisional Officer: Suffolk and Ipswich, 1948; Worcestershire, 1952; Dep. Chief Fire Officer, Lancashire, 1955; Chief Fire Officer: Bristol, 1960; West Riding of Yorkshire, 1967; HM Chief Inspector of Fire Services, 1972–80. Chm., Firelaw Ltd, 1988–93. President: Commonwealth Overseas Fire Services Assoc., 1983–90; Assoc. of Structural Fire Protection Contractors and Manufacturers, 1986–90; Nat. Assoc. for Safety in the Home, 1988–90; Trustee: Fire Services Res. Trng Trust, 1983–; Ivy Owen Award Trust, 1989–; Chairman: ISO Technical Cttee TC/21 Fire Equipment, 1983–94; Loss Prevention Certification Bd, 1984–92; Multi-technics Council, BSI, 1984–90; Visitor, Fire Res. Station, 1984–90; Vice President: Fire Brigade Soc., 1969; Fire Services Nat. Benevolent Fund, 1973–. FIFireE. Hon. Treasurer, Poole Arts Fedn, 1985–88. Mem., Past Rotarians Club, 1992–. OStJ 1964. Defence Medal; Fire Brigade Long Service and Good Conduct Medal. *Recreations:* sports, gardening, the Arts. *Club:* St John House.

HOLLAND, Kevin John William C.; *see* Crossley-Holland.

HOLLAND, Norman James Abbott, IEng, FIEIE; Group Standards Manager, Philips UK, 1983–90; President, British National Electrotechnical Committee, since 1993; *b* 16 Dec. 1927; *s* of James George Holland and May Stuart Holland; *m* 1951, Barbara Florence Byatt; one *s* one *d. Educ:* Sir Walter St John's Grammar Sch.; Regent Street Polytechnic. Chm., Incorp. Engrg and Engrg Technicians Adv. Cttee, Engrg Council, 1985–91; UK Delegate: IEC Council, 1987–92 (Delegn Leader, 1993–); CENELEC Gen. Assembly, 1987–92; Member: IEC Finance Cttee, 1985–91; Engrg Council, 1985–91; Bd, Electronic Engrg Assoc., 1985–92 (Chm., Standards Policy Gp); NACCB, 1987–92; Standards Bd, BSI, 1993–. *Recreation:* golf. *Address:* Pinehaven, 94 Hiltingbury Road, Chandler's Ford, Hants SO5 1NZ. *Clubs:* Bramshaw Golf, Ampfield Golf.

HOLLAND, Sir Philip (Welsby), Kt 1983; retired; *b* 14 March 1917; *s* of late John Holland, Middlewich, Cheshire; *m* 1943, Josephine Alma Hudson; one *s. Educ:* Sir John Deane's Grammar Sch., Northwich. Enlisted RAF 1936; commissioned 1943. Factory

Manager, Jantzen Knitting Mills, 1946–47; Management Research, 1948–49; Manufacturers' Agent in Engineering and Refractories Products, 1949–60. Contested (C) Yardley Div. of Birmingham, Gen. Election, 1955; MP (C): Acton, 1959–64; Carlton, 1966–83; Gedling, 1983–87. PPS: to Minister of Pensions and Nat. Insurance, 1961–62; to Chief Sec. to Treasury and Paymaster-Gen., 1962–64; to Minister of Aviation Supply, 1970; to Minister for Aerospace, 1971; to Minister for Trade, 1972. Pres., Cons. Trade Union Nat. Adv. Cttee, 1972–74. Personnel Manager, The Ultra Electronics Group of Companies, 1964–66; Personnel Consultant to Standard Telephones and Cables Ltd, 1969–81. Chm., Cttee of Selection, H of C, 1979–84; Standing Cttee Chm., 1983–87. Councillor, Royal Borough of Kensington, 1955–59. Rector's Warden, St Margaret's Church, Westminister, 1990–95. *Publications:* The Quango Explosion (jtly), 1978; Quango, Quango, Quango, 1979; Costing the Quango, 1979; The Quango Death List, 1980; The Governance of Quangos, 1981; Quelling the Quango, 1982; (jtly) A–Z Guide to Parliament, 1988; Lobby Fodder?, 1988; St Margaret's Westminster, 1993; The Hunting of the Quango, 1994. *Recreations:* travel, writing. *Address:* 53 Pymers Mead, West Dulwich, SE21 8NH.

HOLLAND, (Robert) Einion, FIA; Chairman: Pearl Assurance PLC, 1983–89; Pearl Group PLC, 1985–89 (Director, since 1985); *b* 23 April 1927; *s* of late Robert Ellis Holland and Bene Holland; *m* 1955, Eryl Haf Roberts (*d* 1988); one *s* two *d*. *Educ:* University Coll. of N Wales, Bangor (BSc). FIA 1957. Joined Pearl Assurance Co. Ltd, 1953: Dir, 1973; Chief Gen. Manager, 1977–83. Chm., Industrial Life Offices Assoc., 1976–78; Director: Aviation & General Insurance Co. Ltd, 1972–89 (Chm. 1976–78, 1984–85); British Rail Property Board, 1987–90; Community Reinsurance Corp. Ltd, 1973–89 (Chm., 1973–76); Crawley Warren Group, 1987–; Pearl American Corp., 1972–84. Member: Welsh Develt Agency, 1976–86; CS Pay Research Unit Bd, 1980–81; Council, Univ. of Wales, 1990–. *Recreations:* golf and Welsh literature. *Address:* 55 Corkscrew Hill, West Wickham, Kent BR4 9BA. *T:* 0181–777 1861.

HOLLAND, Stuart (Kingsley); political economist; Director, Associate Research in Economy and Society Ltd, since 1993; *b* 25 March 1940; *y s* of late Frederick Holland and May Holland, London; *m* 1976, Jenny Lennard; two *c*. *Educ:* state primary schs; Christ's Hosp.; Univ. of Missouri (Exchange Scholar); Balliol Coll., Oxford (Domus Scholar; 1st Cl. Hons Mod. History); St Antony's Coll., Oxford (Sen. Scholar; DPhil Econs). Econ. Asst, Cabinet Office, 1966–67; Personal Asst to Prime Minister, 1967–68; Res. Fellow, Centre for Contemp. European Studies, Univ. of Sussex, 1968–71, Assoc. Fellow and Lectr, 1971–79. Vis. Scholar, Brookings Instn, Washington, DC, 1970. Adviser to Commons Expenditure Cttee, 1971–72; Special Adviser to Minister of Overseas Develt, 1974–75. MP (Lab) Vauxhall, 1979–89; Opposition frontbench spokesman on overseas develt and co-operation, 1983–87, on treasury and economic affairs, 1987–89; Prof. of Econs, Eur. Univ. Inst., Florence, 1989–93. Res. Specialist, RIIA, 1972–74; Associate, Inst. of Develt Studies, 1974– (Gov., 1983–91). Consultant: Econ. and Social Affairs Cttee, Council of Europe, 1973; Open Univ., 1973. Rapporteur, Trades Union Adv. Cttee, OECD, 1977. Chm., Public Enterprise Gp, 1973–75. European Community Commission: Mem., Expert Cttee on Inflation, 1975–76; Consultant to Directorate Gen. XVI, 1989; Dir, Proj. on Econ. and Social Cohesion, 1991–93; Advr to Merger Task Force, DG IV, 1991–. Member: Council, Inst. for Workers' Control, 1974–; UN Univ. Working Party on Socio-Cultural Factors in Develt, Tokyo, 1977. Lubbock Lectr, Oxford Univ., 1975; Tom Mann Meml Lectr, Australia, 1977. Mem., Labour Party, 1962–; Mem. sub-cttees (inc. Finance and Econ. Policy, Indust. Policy, EEC, Economic Planning, Defence, Development Cooperation, Public Sector), Nat. Exec. Cttee, Labour Party, 1972–89; Executive Member: Labour Coordinating Cttee, 1978–81; European Nuclear Disarmament Campaign, 1980–83; Mem., Economic Cttee, Socialist International, 1984–. Hon. MRTPI 1980. Dr *hc* Roskilde Univ., Denmark, 1992. *Publications:* (jtly) Sovereignty and Multinational Corporations, 1971; (ed) The State as Entrepreneur, 1972; Strategy for Socialism, 1975; The Socialist Challenge, 1975; The Regional Problem, 1976; Capital versus the Regions, 1976; (ed) Beyond Capitalist Planning, 1978; Uncommon Market, 1980; (ed) Out of Crisis, 1983; (with Donald Anderson) Kissinger's Kingdom, 1984; (with James Firebrace) Never Kneel Down, 1984; The Market Economy, 1987; The Global Economy, 1987; The European Imperative: economic and social cohesion in the 1990s, 1993; Towards a New Bretton Woods: alternatives for the global economy, 1994; contrib. symposia; articles in specialist jls and national and internat. press. *Recreation:* singing in the bath. *Address:* Associate Research in Economy and Society Ltd, 91–93 Buckingham Palace Road, SW1W 0RP. *T:* 0171–733 5829, *Fax:* 0171–274 9659.

HOLLAND, Rt. Rev. Thomas, DSC 1944; DD (Gregorian); retired Bishop of Salford; *b* 11 June 1908; *s* of John Holland and Mary (*née* Fletcher). *Educ:* Upholland; Valladolid; Rome. PhD Valladolid, 1929; DD Gregorian, Rome 1936. Taught theology: Spain, 1936–41; Lisbon, 1941–43. Chaplain, RN, 1943–46; Port Chaplain, Bombay, 1946–48; CMS, 1948–56; Secretary to Apostolic Delegate, 1956–60; Coadjutor Bp of Portsmouth, 1960–64; Bishop of Salford, 1964–83; Apostolic Administrator, 1983–84. Privy Chamberlain to the Pope, 1958. Member of Vatican Secretariat for Promoting Christian Unity, 1961–73, for Unbelievers, 1965–73; Mem., Vatican Synod, 1974. Hon. DLitt Salford, 1980. *Publications:* Great Cross, 1958; For Better and For Worse (autobiog.), 1989. *Address:* Nazareth House, Scholes Lane, Prestwich, Manchester M25 8AP.

HOLLAND, Prof. Walter Werner, CBE 1992; MD; FRCP, FRCPE, FRCGP, FRCPath, FFPHM; Professor of Public Health Medicine, 1991–94, now Emeritus, and Hon. Director, 1968–94, Social Medicine and Health Service Research Unit, United Medical and Dental Schools of Guy's and St Thomas' Hospitals (formerly St Thomas's Hospital Medical School); *b* 5 March 1929; *s* of Henry Holland and Hertha Zentner; *m* 1964, Fiona Margaret Auchinleck Love; three *s*. *Educ:* St Thomas's Hosp. Med. Sch., London (BSc Hons 1951; MB, BS Hons 1954; MD 1964). FFCM 1972; FRCP 1973; FRCGP 1982; FRCPE 1990; FRCPath 1992. House Officer, St Thomas' Hosp., 1954–56; MRC Clin. Res. Fellow, London Sch. of Hygiene, 1959–61; Lectr, Johns Hopkins Univ., Md, USA, 1961–62; St Thomas's Hospital Medical School, later United Medical and Dental Schools of Guy's and St Thomas' Hospitals: Sen. Lectr, Dept of Medicine, 1962–64; Reader and Chm., Dept of Clin. Epidemiol. and Social Medicine, 1965–68; Prof. of Clin. Epidemiol., 1968–91. Fogarty Scholar-in-Residence, NIH, Bethesda, Md, 1984–85; Sawyer Scholar-in-Residence, Case Western Reserve Med. Sch., Cleveland, Ohio, 1985. President: Internat. Epidemiol Assoc., 1987–90; Faculty of Public Health (formerly Community) Medicine, RCP, 1989–92. Non-exec. Mem., Glos HA, 1992–. Life Mem., Soc. of Scholars, Johns Hopkins Univ., 1970; Hon. Mem., Amer. Epidemiol Soc., 1985. Hon. FFPHMI 1993. Dr *hc* Univ. of Bordeaux, 1981; Free Univ. of Berlin, 1990. *Publications:* Data Handling in Epidemiology, 1970; Air Pollution and Respiratory Disease, 1972; Epidemiology and Health, 1977; Health Care and Epidemiology, 1978; Measurement of Levels of Health, 1979; Evaluation of Health Care, 1983; Chronic Obstructive Bronchopathies, 1983; Oxford Textbook of Public Health, 1984, 2nd edn 1991; (with Susie Stewart) Screening in Health Care, 1990; pubns on health services res., epidemiol methods and on respiratory disease. *Recreations:* reading, walking. *Address:* 11 Ennerdale Road, Kew, Richmond, Surrey TW9 3PG. *Club:* Athenæum.

HOLLAND-HIBBERT, family name of **Viscount Knutsford.**

HOLLAND-MARTIN, Robert George, (Robin); Director, Henderson Administration Group plc, since 1983; *b* 6 July 1939; *y s* of late Cyril Holland-Martin and of Rosa, *d* of Sir Gerald Chadwyck-Healey, 2nd Bt, CBE; *m* 1976, Dominique, 2nd *d* of Maurice Fromaget; two *d*. *Educ:* Eton. Cazenove & Co., 1960–74 (partner, 1968–74); Finance Director, Paterson Products Ltd, 1976–86; Consultant, Newmarket Venture Capital plc (formerly Newmarket Co.), 1982–94. Hon. Dep. Treasurer, Cons. and Unionist Party, 1979–82. Member of Council: Metropolitan Hospital-Sunday Fund, 1963– (Chm. of Council, 1977–); Homoeopathic Trust, 1970–90 (Vice Chm., 1975–90). Victoria & Albert Museum: Mem. Adv. Council, 1972–83; Mem. Cttee, Associates of V&A, 1976–85 (Chm., 1981–85); Dep. Chm., Trustees, 1983–85. Mem., Visiting Cttee for Royal Coll. of Art, 1982–93 (Chm., 1984–93). Trustee, Blackie Foundn Trust, 1971– (Chm., 1987–). *Address:* 18 Tite Street, SW3 4HZ. *T:* 0171–352 7871. *Clubs:* White's, Royal Automobile.

HOLLAND-MARTIN, Rosamund Mary, (Lady Holland-Martin), DBE 1983 (OBE 1947); DL; Member, Central Executive Committee, National Society for the Prevention of Cruelty to Children, since 1947 (Chairman of the Society, 1969–87); *b* 26 June 1914; *d* of Charles Harry St John Hornby and Cicely Rachel Emily Barclay; *m* 1951, Adm. Sir Deric Holland-Martin, GCB, DSO, DSC (*d* 1977), Lord Lieutenant of Hereford and Worcester; one *s* one *d*. *Educ:* privately. WVS Administrator, South East, 1946–51; Vice-Chm., WRVS, 1978–81; Pres., Friends of Worcester Cathedral, 1978–; Pres., Worcester Sea Cadets, 1978–; Mem. Council, Malvern College, 1979–90. DL Hereford and Worcester, 1983. *Recreations:* needlework, photography, collecting things. *Address:* Bells Castle, Kemerton, Tewkesbury, Glos GL20 7JW. *T:* Overbury (01386) 725333.

HOLLANDS, Maj.-Gen. Graham Spencer; Chief Executive, West Kent College, since 1994; *b* 14 Feb. 1942; *s* of Ernest Darrell Hollands and Gwendoline Isobel Hollands (*née* Matheson); *m* 1969, Lesley Clair Billam; one *s* one *d*. *Educ:* King Edward VI Sch., Bath; RMA Sandhurst; RMCS; Staff Coll., Camberley. Commissioned RA, 1963; served BAOR and UK; MoD, 1980–81; CO 25 Field Regt RA, 1981–84; CO 3rd Regt RHA, 1984–85; COS Artillery Div., HQ 1 (BR) Corps, 1985–86; Comdr, British Adv. Trng Teams, Nigeria, 1986–87; CRA 2nd Inf. Div., 1987–89; DCOS, HQ BAOR, 1989–92; Comdr Artillery, 1st British Corps, 1992–94. Vice-Pres., British Winter Sports Cttee, 1955–. Mem. Bd, Children in Crisis, 1994–. *Recreations:* golf, ski-ing, country pursuits. *Address:* National Westminster Bank, Chatteris Branch, Chatteris, Cambs PE16 6BA.

HOLLENDEN, 3rd Baron *cr* 1912; **Gordon Hope Hope-Morley;** I. & R. Morley Ltd, 1933–67, retired as Chairman; *b* 8 Jan. 1914; *s* of Hon. Claude Hope-Morley (*d* 1968) (*yr s* of 1st Baron) and Lady Dorothy Edith Isabel (*d* 1972), *d* of 7th Earl of Buckinghamshire; *S* uncle, 1977; *m* 1945, Sonja Sundt, Norway; three *s*. *Educ:* Eton. War medals of 1939–45; King Haakon of Norway Liberation medal. *Heir:* *s* Hon. Ian Hampden Hope-Morley [*b* 23 Oct. 1946; *m* 1st, 1972, Beatrice Saulnier (marr. diss. 1985); one *s* one *d*; 2nd, 1988, Caroline Ash; two *s*]. *Address:* Hall Place, Leigh, Tonbridge, Kent TN11 8HH. *T:* Hildenborough (01732) 832255. *Clubs:* Brooks's, Beefsteak.

See also Sir Michael Hanley.

HOLLENWEGER, Prof. Walter Jacob; Professor of Mission, University of Birmingham, 1971–89; *b* 1 June 1927; *s* of Walter Otto and Anna Hollenweger-Spörri; *m* 1951, Erica Busslinger. *Educ:* Univs. of Zürich and Basel. Dr theol Zürich 1966 (and degrees leading up to it). Stock Exchange, Zürich, and several banking appts, until 1948. Pastor, 1949–57; ordained, Swiss Reformed Church, 1961. Study Dir, Ev. Acad., Zürich, 1964–65; Research Asst, Univ. of Zürich, 1961–64; Exec. Sec., World Council of Churches, Geneva, 1965–71; regular guest prof. in Switzerland, Germany and USA. *Publications:* Handbuch der Pfingstbewegung, 10 vols, 1965/66; (ed) The Church for Others, 1967 (also German, Spanish and Portuguese edns); (ed) Die Pfingstkirchen, 1971; Kirche, Benzin und Bohnensuppe, 1971; The Pentecostals, 1972, 1988 (also German and Spanish edns); Pentecost between Black and White, 1975 (also German and Dutch edns); Glaube, Geist und Geister, 1975; (ed) Studies in the Intercultural History of Christianity, 100 vols, 1975–; Evangelism Today, 1976 (also German edn); (with Th. Ahrens) Volkschristentum und Volksreligion in Pazifik, 1977; Interkulturelle Theologie, vol. I, 1979, vol. II, 1982, vol. III, 1988 (abridged French edn); Erfahrungen in Ephesus, 1979; Wie Grenzen zu Brücken werden, 1980; Besuch bei Lukas, 1981; Conflict in Corinth—Memoirs of an Old Man, 1982 (also German, Italian, Indonesian and French edns); Jüngermesse/Gomer: Das Gesicht des Unsichtbaren, 1983 (music edns 1994 and 1995); Zwingli zwischen Krieg und Frieden, 1983, 1988; Das Fest der Verlorenen, 1984; Der Handelsreisende Gottes, 1985 (music edn 1994); Das Wagnis des Glaubens, 1986 (music edn 1993); Weihnachtsoratorium, 1986; Mirjam, Mutter, and Michal: Die Frauen meines Mannes (zwei Monodramen), 1987 (music edn 1994); Bonhoeffer Requiem, 1990 (music edn 1992); Ostertanz der Frauen/Veni Creator Spiritus, 1990; Kommet her zu mir/Die zehn Aussätzigen, 1990; Fontana (musical), 1991; Jona (musical), 1992; Hiob im Kreuzfeuer der Religionen, 1993; Jürg Rathgeb (oratorio), 1993; Der Kommissar auf biblischer Spurensuche, 1993; Ruth, die Ausländerin, 1993; Kamele und Kapitalisten, 1994; The Pentecostals, vol. II: promise and problem, 1995; Johannestexte, 1995. *Address:* 3704 Krattigen, Switzerland. *T:* (33) 544302.

HOLLEY, Rear Adm. Ronald Victor, CB 1987; FRAeS; Independent Inspector, Lord Chancellor's Panel, since 1992; *b* 13 July 1931; *s* of late Mr and Mrs V. E. Holley; *m* 1954, Sister Dorothy Brierley, QARNNS; two *s* twin *d*. *Educ:* Rondebosch, S Africa; Portsmouth GS; RNEC Manadon; RAFC Henlow (post graduate). MIMechE, MIEE; FRAeS 1988. Served HM Ships Implacable, Finisterre, Euryalus, Victorious, Eagle (899 Sqdn); NATO Defence Coll., Rome, 1968; Naval Plans, 1969–71; Aircraft Dept, 1971–73; Air Engr Officer, HMS Seahawk, 1973–75; Naval Asst to Controller of the Navy, 1975–77; RCDS, 1978; Seaman Officer Develt Study, 1979; Dir, Helicopter Projects, Procurement Exec., 1979–82; RNEC in command, 1982–84; Sen. Naval Mem., Directing Staff, RCDS, 1984–85; Dir Gen. Aircraft (Navy), 1985–87. Tech. Dir, Shell Aircraft, 1987–92. Sec., European Helicopter Operators Cttee, 1988–91. President: RN Volunteer Bands, 1983–87; RN Amateur Fencing Assoc., 1986–87 (Chm., 1983–86). Mem., Parly Gp for Engrg Develt, 1993–. Henson and Stringfellow Lectr, RAeS, 1987. *Publications:* contribs to Naval Jls, and Seaford House Papers, 1978. *Recreations:* playing the bassoon; dinghy sailing, rowing.

HOLLEY, (William) Stephen, CBE 1979; General Manager, Washington Development Corporation, 1965–80; *b* 26 March 1920; *m* 1947, Dinah Mary Harper; three *s*. *Educ:* King William's Coll. Student Accountant, 1937–39. War service, RA (TA), 1939–45 (Major). Colonial Service, and Overseas Civil Service, 1945–64; Mem. Legislature and State Sec., Head of Civil Service, Sabah, Malaysia, 1964. Hon. ADK (Malaysia). DL Tyne and Wear, 1975–81. *Publications:* Washington—Quicker by Quango, 1983; Entente Cordiale, 1990; contribs to Sarawak Museum Jl and press articles on New Town Development. *Recreations:* golf, writing, gardening, theatre. *Address:* Forge Cottage, The Green, Abthorpe, Northants NN12 8QP. *Club:* Commonwealth Trust.

HOLLICK, family name of **Baron Hollick.**

HOLLICK, Baron *cr* 1991 (Life Peer), of Notting Hill in the Royal Borough of Kensington and Chelsea; **Clive Richard Hollick;** Chief Executive, MAI PLC (formerly Mills & Allen International PLC), since 1974; *b* 20 May 1945; *s* of Leslie George Hollick and Olive Mary (*née* Scruton); *m* 1977, Susan Mary (*née* Woodford); three *d*. *Educ:* Taunton's Sch., Southampton; Univ. of Nottingham (BA Hons). Joined Hambros Bank Ltd, 1968, Dir, 1973; Chairman: Shepperton Studios Ltd, 1976–84; Garban Ltd (USA), 1983–; Meridian Broadcasting Ltd, 1992–; Director: Logica plc, 1987–91; Avenir Havas Media SA, 1989–92; Satellite Information Systems Ltd, 1990–94; British Aerospace, 1992–; Anglia Television, 1994–. Member: Nat. Bus Co. Ltd, 1984–91; Adv. Cttee, Dept of Applied Econs, Univ. of Cambridge, 1989–; Financial Law Panel, 1993–. Chm., Galleon Trust, 1992–. Founding Trustee, Inst. for Public Policy Res., 1988–. Hon. LLD Nottingham, 1993. *Recreations:* reading, theatre, cinema, tennis, countryside. *Address:* House of Lords, SW1A 0PW.

HOLLIDAY, Sir Frederick (George Thomas), Kt 1990; CBE 1975; FRSE; Chairman, Northumbrian Water plc, since 1993 (Director, since 1991); *b* 22 Sept. 1935; *s* of Alfred C. and Margaret Holliday; *m* 1957, Philippa Mary Davidson; one *s* one *d*. *Educ:* Bromsgrove County High Sch.; Sheffield Univ. BSc 1st cl. hons Zool. 1956; FIBiol 1970, FRSE 1971. Fisheries Research Trng Grant (Develt Commn) at Marine Lab., Aberdeen, 1956–58; Sci. Officer, Marine Lab., Aberdeen, 1958–61; Lectr in Zoology, Univ. of Aberdeen, 1961–66; Prof. of Biology, 1967–75, Dep. Principal, 1972, Acting Principal, 1973–75, Univ. of Stirling; Prof. of Zoology, Univ. of Aberdeen, 1975–79; Vice-Chancellor and Warden, Univ. of Durham, 1980–90. Member: Scottish Cttee, Nature Conservancy, 1969; Council, Scottish Field Studies Assoc., 1970–78 (Pres., 1981–); Council, Scottish Marine Biol Assoc., 1967–85 (Pres., 1979–85); Scottish Wildlife Trust (Vice-Pres.); Council, Freshwater Biol Assoc., 1969–72, and 1993–; NERC Oceanography and Fisheries Research Grants Cttee, 1971; Council, NERC, 1973–79; Nature Conservancy Council, 1975–80 (Dep. Chm., 1976–77, Chm., 1977–80); Scottish Economic Council, 1975–80; Council, Marine Biol Assoc. UK, 1975–78 (Vice-Pres., 1994–); Oil Develt Council for Scotland, 1976–78; Standing Commn on Energy and the Environment, 1978–; Adv. Cttee, Leverhulme Trust Res. Awards, 1978–95 (Chm., 1989–95); PCFC, 1989–93; Awards Council, Royal Anniv. Trust, 1993–95; Council, Water Aid, 1994–; Envmtl Cttee, CBI, 1994–; Chm., Independent Review of Disposal of Radioactive Waste at Sea, 1984; Ind. Chm., Jt Nature Conservation Cttee, 1991. Dir, Shell UK, 1980–; Mem., Shell UK Audit Cttee, 1993–94; Chm., Investors' Cttee, Northern Venture Partnership Fund, 1990; Dep. Chm., Northern Regional Bd, Lloyd's Bank, 1989–91 (Mem., 1985–91; Chm., 1986–89); Member: Bd, Northern Investors Ltd, 1984–90; BRB, 1990–94 (Chm., BR (Eastern), 1986–90); Union Railways Bd, 1993–. Trustee, Nat. Heritage Meml Fund, 1980–91; Vice-Pres., Civic Trust for NE. Member: Bd of Governors, Rowett Res. Inst., 1976–84; Scottish Civic Trust, 1984–87. DUniv Stirling, 1984; Hon. DSc: Sheffield, 1987; Cranfield, 1991. DL Durham, 1985–90. *Publications:* (ed and contrib.) Wildlife of Scotland, 1979; numerous on fish biology and wildlife conservation in Adv. Mar. Biol., Fish Physiology, Oceanography and Marine Biology, etc. *Recreations:* walking, gardening. *Address:* Northumbrian Water, Regent Centre, Gosforth, Newcastle upon Tyne NE3 3PX. *T:* 0191–284 3151. *Club:* Commonwealth Trust.

HOLLIDAY, Leslie John, FCIOB, CIMgt; Chairman and Chief Executive, John Laing plc, 1982–85 (Director, 1978); Chairman, John Laing Construction Ltd, since 1980 (Director, 1966); *b* 9 Jan. 1921; *s* of John and Elsie Holliday; *m* 1943, Kathleen Joan Marjorie Stacey; two *s*. *Educ:* St John's, Whitby. FCIOB 1969; CIMgt (CBIM 1982). Denaby & Cadby Colliery, 1937–40; served Merchant Navy, 1940–45; joined John Laing & Son Ltd, 1947, Dir 1977; Chairman: Laing Homes Ltd, 1978–81; Super Homes Ltd, 1979–81; Laing Management Contracting Ltd, 1980–81; John Laing Internat. Ltd, 1981–82; Director: Declan Kelly Holdings, 1985–89; RM Douglas Holdings, 1986–89; Admiral Homes Ltd, 1989–; Redrow Gp, 1989–92. Mem., EDC for Bldg, 1979–82. Freeman, City of London, 1984; Liveryman, Plaisterers' Co., 1984–. *Recreations:* yachting, golf. *Address:* The White House, Frithsden Copse, Berkhamsted, Herts HP4 2RQ. *Clubs:* Porters Park Golf, Berkhamsted Golf.

HOLLIDAY, Dr Robin, FRS 1976; Chief Research Scientist, Commonwealth Scientific and Industrial Research Organisation (Australia), since 1988; *b* 6 Nov. 1932; *s* of Clifford and Eunice Holliday; *m* 1st, 1957, Diana Collet (*née* Parsons) (marr. diss. 1983); one *s* three *d*; 2nd, 1986, Lily Irene (*née* Huschtscha); one *d*. *Educ:* Hitchin Grammar Sch.; Univ. of Cambridge (BA, PhD); Fulbright Scholar, 1962. Member, Scientific Staff: Dept of Genetics, John Innes Inst., Bayfordbury, Herts, 1958–65; Division of Microbiology, Nat. Inst. for Med. Research, 1965–70; Head, Div. of Genetics, Nat. Inst. for Med. Research, 1970–88. Mem., EMBO, 1982. For. Fellow, INSA, 1995. Lord Cohen Medal, 1987. *Publications:* The Science of Human Progress, 1981; Genes, Proteins and Cellular Aging, 1986; Understanding Ageing, 1995; over 180 scientific papers on genetic recombination, repair, gene expression and cellular ageing. *Recreations:* travel, writing. *Address:* CSIRO Division of Biomolecular Engineering, PO Box 184, North Ryde, Sydney, NSW 2113, Australia. *T:* (2) 8864888, *Fax:* (2) 8864818; 12 Roma Court, West Pennant Hills, NSW 2125, Australia. *T:* (2) 873376.

HOLLIGER, Heinz; oboist, composer and conductor; *b* Langenthal, Switzerland, 1939; *m* Ursula Holliger, harpist. *Educ:* Berne Conservatoire; Paris; Basle; studied with Cassagnaud, Lefébure, Veress, Pierlot and Boulez. Played with Basle Orch., 1959–63; Prof. of oboe, Freiburg Music Acad., 1965–. Has appeared as soloist and conductor at all major European music festivals, and with Chamber Orch. of Europe, English Chamber Orch., etc; has directed all major Swiss orchs, Cleveland Orch., Philharmonia, etc. Has inspired compositions by Berio, Penderecki, Stockhausen, Henze, Martin and others. *Compositions include:* Der magische Tänzer, Trio, Dona nobis pacem, Pneuma, Psalm, Cardiophonie, Kreis, Siebengesang, H for wind quintet, string quartet Atembogen, Jahreszeiten, Come and Go. Has won many international prizes, including: Geneva Competition first prize, 1959; Munich Competition first prize, 1961; Sonning Prize; Frankfurt Music Prize; Ernst von Siemens Prize. *Address:* Konzertgesellschaft Zürich, Steinwiesstrasse 2, 8032 Zürich, Switzerland.

HOLLINGS, Sir (Alfred) Kenneth, Kt 1971; MC 1944; Judge of the High Court of Justice, Family Division (formerly Probate, Divorce and Admiralty Division), 1971–93; *b* 12 June 1918; *s* of Alfred Holdsworth Hollings and Rachel Elizabeth Hollings; *m* 1949, Harriet Evelyn Isabella, *d* of W. J. C. Fishbourne, OBE, Brussels; one *s* one *d*. *Educ:* Leys Sch., Cambridge; Clare Coll., Cambridge. Law Qualifying and Law Tripos, Cambridge, 1936–39; MA. Served RA (Shropshire Yeomanry), 1939–46. Called to Bar, Middle Temple, 1947 (Harmsworth Schol.); Master of the Bench, 1971. Practised Northern Circuit; QC 1966; Recorder of Bolton, 1968; Judge of County Courts, Circuit 5 (E Lancs), 1968–71; Presiding Judge, Northern Circuit, 1975–78. *Recreations:* walking, swimming, music. *Clubs:* Garrick, Hurlingham; Tennis and Racquets (Manchester).

HOLLINGS, Rev. Michael Richard, MBE 1993; MC 1943; Parish Priest, St Mary of the Angels, Bayswater, since 1978; Dean of North Kensington, since 1980; *b* 30 Dec. 1921; *s* of Lieut-Commander Richard Eustace Hollings, RN, and Agnes Mary (*née* Hamilton-Dalrymple). *Educ:* Beaumont Coll.; St Catherine's Society, Oxford (MA). St Catherine's, 1939; Sandhurst, 1941. Served War of 1939–45 (despatches): commnd Coldstream Guards, 1941; served N Africa, Italy, Palestine, 1942–45; Major. Trained at Beda Coll., Rome, 1946–50. Ordained Rome, 1950; Asst Priest, St Patrick's, Soho Square, W1, 1950–54; Chaplain, Westminster Cathedral, 1954–58; Asst Chaplain, London Univ., 1958–59; Chaplain to Roman Catholics at Oxford Univ., 1959–70; Parish Priest, St Anselm's, Southall, Middx, 1970–78. Religious Adviser: ATV, 1958–59; Rediffusion, 1959–68; Thames Television, 1968; Advr, Prison Christian Fellowship, 1983–. Member: Nat. Catholic Radio and TV Commn, 1968; Westminster Diocesan Schools Commn, 1970–; Southall Chamber of Commerce, 1971–78; Oxford and Cambridge Catholic Educn Bd, 1971–78; Executive, Council of Christians and Jews, 1971–79, 1984–; Lay Mem., Press Council, 1969–75; Nat. Conf. of Priests Standing Cttee, 1974–76; Rampton Cttee, 1979–81; Swann Cttee, 1981–84; Exec., Ealing Community Relations Council, 1973–76; Exec., Notting Hill Social Council, 1980–; Chairman: N Kensington Action Group, 1980–81; W London Family Service Unit, 1984–; Portobello Trust, 1988–. Mem. Bd, Christian Aid, 1984–87. Chaplain: to Sovereign Military Order of Malta, 1957; to Nat. Council of Lay Apostolate, 1970–74; to Catholic Inst. of Internat. Relations, 1971–80. Chm., Bd of Govs, Sion-Manning Sch., 1991–; Gov., St Charles Catholic Sixth Form Coll., 1990–93. *Publications:* Hey, You!, 1955; Purple Times, 1957; Chaplaincraft, 1963; The One Who Listens, 1971; The Pastoral Care of Homosexuals, 1971; It's Me, O Lord, 1972; Day by Day, 1972; The Shade of His Hand, 1973; Restoring the Streets, 1974; I Will Be There, 1975; You Must Be Joking, Lord, 1975; The Catholic Prayer Book, 1976; Alive to Death, 1976; Living Priesthood, 1977; His People's Way of Talking, 1978; As Was His Custom, 1979; St Thérèse of Lisieux, 1981; Hearts not Garments, 1982; Chaplet of Mary, 1982; Path to Contemplation, 1983; Go In Peace, 1984; Christ Died at Notting Hill, 1985; Athirst for God, 1985; Prayers before and after Bereavement, 1986; By Love Alone, 1986; Prayers for the Depressed, 1986; You Are Not Alone, 1988; Dying to Live, 1990; Thoughts of Peace, 1991; Love Heals, 1993; contrib. Tablet, Clergy Review, Life of the Spirit, The Universe. *Recreations:* reading, walking, people. *Address:* St Mary of the Angels, Moorhouse Road, Bayswater, W2 5DJ. *T:* 0171–229 0487.

HOLLINGSWORTH, Michael Charles; Chief Executive, Venture Television (formerly Venture Broadcasting) Ltd, since 1989; *b* 22 Feb. 1946; *s* of Albert George Hollingsworth and Gwendoline Marjorie Hollingsworth; *m* 1st, 1968, Patricia Margaret Jefferson Winn (marr. diss. 1987); one *d*; 2nd, 1989, Anne Margaret Diamond; four *s* (and one *s* decd). *Educ:* Carlisle Grammar Sch. Programme Editor, Anglia Television, 1964–67; Producer, BBC Local Radio, 1967–74; Northern Editor, Today, Radio Four, 1974–75; Editor, News and Current Affairs: Southern Television Ltd, 1975–79; ATV Network/Central, 1979–82; Sen. Producer, Current Affairs, BBC TV, 1982–84; Dir of Programmes, TV-am Ltd, 1984–86; Man. Dir, Music Box Ltd, 1986–89. Consultant on television matters to indep. television cos. *Recreations:* DIY (house renovation), gardening, polo. *Address:* The Old Manor, Armscote, Warwickshire CV37 8DH; 67 Parkway, NW1 7PP.

HOLLINGWORTH, Clare, OBE 1984; Far Eastern Correspondent in Hong Kong for Sunday Telegraph, since 1981; Research Associate (formerly Visiting Scholar), Centre of Asian Studies, University of Hong Kong, since 1981; *b* 10 Oct. 1911; *d* of John Albert Hollingworth and Daisy Gertrude Hollingworth; *m* 1st, 1936, Vyvyan Derring Vandeleur Robinson (marr. diss. 1951); 2nd, 1952, Geoffrey Spencer Hoare (*d* 1966). *Educ:* Girls' Collegiate Sch., Leicester; Grammar Sch., Ashby de la Zouch, Leics; Sch. of Slavonic Studies, Univ. of London. On staff, League of Nations Union, 1935–38; worked in Poland for Lord Mayor's Fund for Refugees from Czechoslovakia, 1939; Correspondent in Poland for Daily Telegraph: first to report outbreak of war from Katawice; remained in Balkans as Germans took over; moved to Turkey and then Cairo, 1941–50, covering Desert Campaigns, troubles in Persia and Iraq, Civil War in Greece and events in Palestine; covered trouble spots from Paris for Manchester Guardian, 1950–63, incl. Algerian War, Egypt, Aden and Vietnam (Journalist of the Year Award and Hannan Swaffer Award, 1963); Guardian Defence Correspondent, 1963–67; Daily Telegraph: foreign trouble shooter, 1967–73, covering war in Vietnam; Correspondent in China, 1973–76; Defence Correspondent, 1976–81. Hon. DLitt Leicester, 1993. James Cameron Award for Journalism, 1994. *Publications:* Poland's Three Weeks War, 1940; There's a German Just Behind Me, 1945; The Arabs and the West, 1951; Mao and the Men Against Him, 1984; Front Line, 1990. *Recreations:* visiting second-hand furniture and bookshops, collecting modern pictures and Chinese porcelain, music. *Address:* 19 Dorset Square, NW1 6QB. *T:* 0171–262 6923; 302 Ridley House, 2 Upper Albert Road, Hong Kong. *T:* 28681838. *Clubs:* Cercle de l'Union Interalliée (Paris); Foreign Correspondents (Hong Kong and Tokyo).

HOLLINGWORTH, John Harold; *b* 11 July 1930; *s* of Harold Hollingworth, Birmingham; *m* 1969, Susan Barbara (marr. diss. 1985), *d* of late J. H. Walters, Ramsey, IoM. *Educ:* Chigwell House Sch.; King Edward's Sch., Edgbaston. MP (C) All Saints Division of Birmingham, 1959–64; contested (C) Birmingham, All Saints, 1966 and 1970. Chairman: Birmingham Young Conservatives, 1958–62; Edgbaston Div. Conservative Assoc., 1967–72; Vice-Chm., Birmingham Conservative Assoc., 1958–61, 1972–78 (Vice-Pres. 1960–66). Dir and Gen. Manager, Cambridge Symphony Orch. Trust, 1979–82 (Gov., 1982–92); Dir, Thaxted Fest. Foundn, 1987–93. Chm., Elmdon Trust Ltd, 1984–91; dir of other cos; mem. of various charitable activities. Trustee, 1991–, Hon. Treas., 1993–, British Performing Arts Medicine Trust (Hon. Chief Exec., 1992–93). Mem., Cttee of ISSTIP. *Publications:* contributions to political journals. *Recreations:* exercising Rough Collie dogs, planning third British Empire. *Address:* 16A Hockerill Street, Bishops Stortford, Herts CM23 2DW. *T:* Bishops Stortford (01279) 501689. *Club:* Lansdowne.

HOLLINGWORTH, Most Rev. Peter John; *see* Brisbane, Archbishop of.

HOLLINS, Rear-Adm. Hubert Walter Elphinstone, CB 1974; marine consultant; *b* 8 June 1923; *s* of Lt-Col W. T. Hollins; *m* 1963, Jillian Mary McAlpin; one *s* one *d*. *Educ:* Stubbington House; Britannia RNC Dartmouth. Cadet RN, 1937; Comdr 1957; Captain 1963; Rear-Adm. 1972; comd HM Ships Petard, Dundas, Caesar and Antrim; Flag Officer, Gibraltar, 1972–74; Admiral Commanding Reserves, 1974–77; Gen. Man., ME Navigation Aids Service, Bahrain, 1977–84. Younger Brother of Trinity House; Mem., Trinity House Lighthouse Bd, 1985–91. Commodore, Bahrain Yacht Club, 1981–83. Master Mariner. Trustee, Royal Merchant Navy Sch., Bearwood, 1985–92; President: Newbury RN Assoc., 1985–90; Newbury Sea Cadet Corps, 1985–91 (Patron, 1991). FIMgt. *Recreation:* fishing. *Address:* Waunllan, Llandyfriog, Newcastle Emlyn, Dyfed SA38 9HB. *T:* Newcastle Emlyn (01239) 710456.

HOLLIS, family name of **Baroness Hollis of Heigham.**

HOLLIS OF HEIGHAM, Baroness *cr* 1990 (Life Peer), of Heigham in the City of Norwich; **Patricia Lesley Hollis;** DL; DPhil; Senior Fellow, Modern History, University of East Anglia; *b* 24 May 1941; *d* of (Harry) Lesley (George) Wells and Queenie Rosalyn Wells; *m* 1965, (James) Martin Hollis, *qv*; two *s*. *Educ:* Plympton Grammar Sch.; Cambridge Univ. (MA); Univ. of California; Columbia Univ., NY; Nuffield Coll.,

Oxford (DPhil). Harkness Fellow, 1962–64; Nuffield Scholar, 1964–67. University of East Anglia: Lectr, 1967, then Reader; Dean, School of English and American Studies, 1988–90. Councillor: Norwich City Council, 1968–91 (Leader, 1983–88); Norfolk CC, 1981–85. Member: Regional Econ. Planning Council, 1975–79; Govt Commn on Housing, 1975–77; RHA, 1979–83; BBC Regional Adv. Cttee, 1979–83. Vice-President: ADC, 1990–; AMA, 1990–; Envmtl Health Officers, 1992–; NFHA, 1993–. Dir, Radio Broadland, 1983–. Nat. Comr, English Heritage, 1988–91; Mem. Press Council, 1989–90. Contested (Lab) Gt Yarmouth, Feb. and Oct. 1974, 1979. An opposition whip, 1990–; opposition frontbench spokesperson on social security, local govt and housing. FRHistS. DL Norfolk, 1994. Hon. DLitt Anglia Poly. Univ. *Publications:* The Pauper Press, 1970; Class and Conflict, 1815–50, 1973; Pressure from Without, 1974; Women in Public 1850–1900, 1979; (with Dr B. H. Harrison) Robert Lowery, Radical and Chartist, 1979; Ladies Elect: Women in English Local Government 1865–1914, 1987. *Recreations:* boating, singing, domesticity. *Address:* House of Lords, SW1A 0PW. *T:* 0171–219 3000.

HOLLIS, Hon. Sir Anthony Barnard, Kt 1982; **Hon. Mr Justice Hollis;** a Judge of the High Court of Justice, Family Division, since 1982; *b* 11 May 1927; *er s* of late Henry Lewis Hollis and of Gladys Florence Hollis (*née* Barnard); *m* 1956, Pauline Mary (*née* Skuce); one step *d*. *Educ:* Tonbridge Sch.; St Peter's Hall, Oxford (Hon. Fellow, St Peter's Coll., 1993). Called to the Bar, Gray's Inn, 1951 (Bencher, 1979); QC 1969; a Recorder of the Crown Court, 1976–82. Chm., Family Law Bar Assoc., 1974–76. *Recreation:* golf. *Address:* Royal Courts of Justice, Strand, WC2A 2LL. *Clubs:* Garrick; Woking Golf; Royal St George's Golf (Sandwich).

HOLLIS, Rt. Rev. Crispian; *see* Portsmouth, Bishop of, (RC).

HOLLIS, Daniel Ayrton, QC 1968; a Recorder of the Crown Court, since 1972; *b* 30 April 1925; *m* 1st, 1950, Gillian Mary Turner (marr. diss., 1961); one *d* (one *s* decd); 2nd, 1963, Stella Hydleman; one *s*. *Educ:* Geelong Grammar Sch., Australia; Brasenose Coll., Oxford. Served N Atlantic and Mediterranean, 1943–46. Lieut-Commander, RNVR. Called to Bar, Middle Temple, 1949; Bencher, 1975; Treas., 1994. Mem., Criminal Injuries Compensation Bd, 1995–. Mem., Home Sec.'s Adv. Bd on Restricted Patients, 1986–92. *Recreation:* travel. *Address:* Queen Elizabeth Building, Temple, EC4Y 9BS.

HOLLIS, Geoffrey Alan; Under Secretary and Head of Livestock (formerly Meat) Group, Ministry of Agriculture, Fisheries and Food, since 1991; *b* 25 Nov. 1943; *s* of late William John Hollis and of Elsie Jean Hollis (*née* Baker); *m* 1967, Ann Josephine Prentice; two *s*. *Educ:* Hastings Grammar Sch.; Hertford Coll., Oxford (MA); Polytechnic of Central London (Dip. Management Studies). International Computers, 1966; International Publishing Corp., 1967; Gulf Oil, 1969; MAFF, 1974–; seconded to FCO, First Sec., 1977–80, UK Perm. Rep., EC, Brussels. Non-Exec. Dir, Lucas Ingredients (Dalgety plc), 1991–. *Recreations:* chess, golf, horology. *Address:* Ministry of Agriculture, Fisheries and Food, Whitehall Place, SW1A 2HH. *T:* 0171–270 8679.

HOLLIS, Ven. Gerald; Archdeacon of Birmingham, 1974–84; *b* 16 May 1919; *s* of Canon Walter Hollis and Enid (*née* Inchbold); *m* 1946, Doreen Emmet Stancliffe; one *s* three *d*. *Educ:* St Edward's Sch., Oxford; Christ Church, Oxford (MA); Wells Theological College. RNVR, 1940–45. Curate: All Saints, Stepney, E1, 1947–50; i/c St Luke's, Rossington, 1950–55; Rector, Armthorpe, 1955–60; Vicar of Rotherham and Rural Dean, 1960–74. Hon. Canon, Birmingham Cathedral, 1984–. Mem. Gen. Synod, C of E, 1975–84. *Publication:* Rugger: do it this way, 1946. *Recreation:* gardening. *Address:* 68 Britford Lane, Salisbury, Wilts SP2 8AH. *T:* Salisbury (01722) 338154. *Club:* Vincent's (Oxford).

HOLLIS, Prof. James Martin, FBA 1990; Professor of Philosophy, University of East Anglia, since 1982; *b* 14 March 1938; *s* of Hugh Marcus Noel Hollis and Ruth Margaret Hollis; *m* 1965, Patricia Lesley Wells (*see* Baroness Hollis of Heigham); two *s*. *Educ:* Winchester Coll.; New Coll., Oxford (BA 1961; MA 1964). Harkness Commonwealth Fund Fellow, Berkeley and Harvard, 1961; FCO, 1964; Extraordinary Lectr, New Coll., Oxford, 1964; Lectr, Balliol Coll., Oxford, 1965; University of East Anglia: Lectr, 1967; Sen. Lectr, 1972; Pro-Vice-Chancellor, 1992–95. Dist. Vis. and Lectr, Univs of British Columbia, 1980; Kingston, 1982, Bayreuth, 1988. Pres., Aristotelian Soc., 1986. Mem. Council, Univ. of Bayreuth, 1989–; Gov., Eaton (CNS) Sch., 1972–75. JP Norwich, 1972–82. Editor, Ratio, 1980–87. *Publications:* The Light of Reason, 1971; (with E. J. Nell) Rational Economic Man, 1975; Models of Man, 1977; (with F. Hahn) Philosophy and Economic Theory, 1979; (with S. Lukes) Rationality and Relativism, 1982; Invitation to Philosophy, 1985; The Cunning of Reason, 1988; (with S. Smith) Explaining and Understanding International Relations, 1990; Rationalität und soziales Verstehen, 1991; The Philosophy of Social Science, 1994. *Recreation:* puzzles. *Address:* School of Economic and Social Studies, University of East Anglia, Norwich NR4 7TJ. *T:* Norwich (01603) 456161.

HOLLIS, Posy; *see* Simmonds, P.

HOLLIS, Most Rev. Reginald; Rector, St Paul's Church, New Smyrna Beach, Florida, since 1994; *b* 18 July 1932; *s* of Jesse Farndon Hollis and Edith Ellen Lee; *m* 1957, Marcia Henderson Crombie; two *s* one *d*. *Educ:* Selwyn Coll., Cambridge; McGill Univ., Montreal. Chaplain and Lectr, Montreal Dio. Theol Coll., 1956–60; Chaplain to Anglican Students, McGill Univ.; Asst Rector, St Matthias' Church, Westmount, PQ, 1960–63; Rector, St Barnabas' Church, Pierrefonds, PQ, 1963–70; Rector, Christ Church, Beaconsfield, PQ, 1971–74; Dir of Parish and Dio. Services, Dio. Montreal, 1974–75; Bishop of Montreal, 1975; Metropolitan of the Ecclesiastical Province of Canada and Archbishop of Montreal, 1989–90; Asst Bishop, dio. of Central Florida and Episcopal Dir, Anglican Fellowship of Prayer, 1990–94. Hon. DD 1975. *Publication:* Abiding in Christ, 1987. *Address:* PO Box 1559, New Smyrna Beach, FL 32170, USA.

HOLLIS, Rt. Rev. (Roger Francis) Crispian; *see* Portsmouth, Bishop of, (RC).

HOLLMAN, Arthur, MD; FRCP; FLS; Consultant Cardiologist, University College Hospital, London, 1962–87, now Consulting Cardiologist, Consultant Cardiologist, Hospital for Sick Children, London, 1978–88, now Consulting Cardiologist; Hon. Senior Lecturer, University College London Medical School (formerly University College and Middlesex School of Medicine), since 1962; *b* 7 Dec. 1923; *s* of W. J. and I. R. Hollman; *m* 1949, Catharine Elizabeth Large; four *d*. *Educ:* Tiffin Boys' Sch., Kingston upon Thames; University Coll. London (Fellow, 1978); UCH Med. Sch. (MD). FRCP 1967. FLS 1983. Jun. hosp. appts, London, Banbury and Taplow, 1946–57; Bilton Pollard Fellow of UCH Med. Sch. at Children's Meml Hosp., Montreal, 1951–52; Clinical Asst, National Heart Hosp., 1954–56; Sen. Registrar and Asst Lectr, Royal Postgraduate Med. Sch., 1957–62; Hon. Consultant Cardiologist, Kingston Hosp., 1964–87. Advisor in Cardiology: to Mauritius Govt, 1966–86; to Republic of Seychelles, 1974–. Councillor, RCP, 1976–79. Member: Cttee of Management, Chelsea Physic Garden, 1971–; Council, British Heart Foundn, 1975–80; British Cardiac Soc. (Mem. Council, Asst Sec., and Sec., 1971–76); Assoc. of Physicians of GB and Ireland. Pres., Osler Club, 1983–84. *Publications:* articles on cardiology, the history of cardiology and the use of plants in medical practice. *Recreations:* gardening, especially medicinal plants; medical history. *Address:* Seabank, Chick Hill, Pett, Hastings, East Sussex TN35 4EQ. *T:* Hastings (01424) 813228. *Club:* Athenæum.

HOLLOM, Sir Jasper (Quintus), KBE 1975; Chairman: Eagle Star Holdings PLC, 1985–87; Eagle Star Insurance Co. Ltd, 1985–87; *b* 16 Dec. 1917; *s* of Arthur and Kate Louisa Hollom; *m* 1954, Patricia Elizabeth Mary Ellis. *Educ:* King's Sch., Bruton. Entered Bank of England, 1936; appointed Deputy Chief Cashier, 1956; Chief Cashier, 1962–66; Director, 1966–70, 1980–84; Deputy Governor, 1970–80. Director: BAT Industries plc, 1980–87; Portals Hldgs plc, 1980–88. Chairman: Panel on Take-overs and Mergers, 1980–87; Council for the Securities Industry, 1985–86; Commonwealth Develt Finance Co. Ltd, 1980–86; Pres., Council of Foreign Bondholders, 1983–89. *Address:* High Wood, Selborne, Alton, Hants GU34 3LA. *T:* Selborne (01420) 511317.

HOLLOWAY, Hon. Sir Barry (Blyth), KBE 1984 (CBE 1974); *b* 26 Sept. 1934; *s* of Archibald and Betty Holloway; *m* 1974, Ikini Aikel; three *s* four *d*. *Educ:* Launceston Church Grammar Sch., Tasmania; Sch. of Pacific Administration, Sydney, 1957; Univ. of Papua New Guinea. Dip., Pacific Admin. District Officer in Papua New Guinea, 1953–64. Elected to first PNG Parliament, 1964; Foundn Mem., Pangu Pati, 1966; MP Eastern Highlands Province, Member of various parliamentary cttees, incl. Public Accounts; Speaker of Parliament, 1972–77; Finance Minister, 1977–80; Minister for Educn, 1982–85. Chairman of Constituent Assembly responsible for the formation of Constitution of the Independent State of Papua New Guinea, 1974–75. Director of various companies. *Recreations:* reading, agriculture. *Address:* PO Box 6361, Boroko, Papua New Guinea. *T:* Port Moresby 272338. *Club:* Papua (Port Moresby).

HOLLOWAY, Derrick Robert Le Blond; Registrar of the Family Division, Principal Registry, 1966–83; retired; *b* 29 May 1917; *s* of Robert Fabyan Le Blond and Mary Beatrice Holloway; *m* 1942, Muriel Victoria Bower; one *s*. *Educ:* Brentwood; Univ. of London (LLB (Hons)). Principal Probate Registry, 1937. Served War of 1939–45: DCLI, RASC, Claims Commn. Sec., Cttee on Law of Intestate Succession, 1951; Sec., Cttee on Ancient Probate Records, 1953; Asst Sec., Royal Commn on Marriage and Divorce, 1952–56; Acting Registrar, Probate, Divorce and Admiralty Div., 1965. Gp Chm. (Amersham), Civil Service Retirement Fellowship, 1985; Chm., S Bucks Br., CS Retirement Fellowship, 1990. *Publications:* (ed jtly) Latey on Divorce (14th edn), 1952; Editor: Proving a Will (2nd edn), 1952; Obtaining Letters of Administration, 1954; Divorce Forms and Precedents, 1959; Probate Handbook (now Holloway's Probate Handbook), 1961, 7th edn 1984, (Consultant Editor) 8th edn 1987; Phillips' Probate Practice (6th edn), 1963; contrib. to Butterworths' Costs (4th edn), 1971; Acting in Person: how to obtain an undefended divorce, 1977. *Recreations:* marriage, gardening, foreign travel, music, photography. *Address:* 1 Chiltern Manor Park, Great Missenden, Bucks HP16 9BL.

HOLLOWAY, Frank, FCA; Managing Director, Supplies and Transport, 1980–83 and Board Member, 1978–83, British Steel Corporation; *b* 20 Oct. 1924; *s* of Frank and Elizabeth Holloway; *m* 1949, Elizabeth Beattie; three *d*. *Educ:* Burnage High Sch., Manchester. Served War, Royal Navy, 1943–46. Various senior finance appts in The United Steel Companies Ltd and later in British Steel Corp., 1949–72. Managing Director: Supplies and Production Control, 1973–76, Finance and Supplies, 1976–80, British Steel Corp. *Recreations:* cricket, collecting books.

HOLLOWAY, Frederick Reginald Bryn; His Honour Judge Holloway; a Circuit Judge, since 1992; *b* 9 Jan. 1947; *s* of William Herbert Holloway and Audrey (*née* Hull-Brown); *m* 1971, Barbara Bradley; two *s*. *Educ:* Mill Mead, Shrewsbury; Wrekin Coll., Wellington, Salop; Coll. of Law. Entered chambers in Liverpool, 1972; Asst Recorder, 1984–89; Recorder, 1989–92. *Recreations:* gardening, Shrewsbury Town FC, cricket, tennis. *Address:* Queen Elizabeth II Law Courts, Derby Square, Liverpool L2 1XA.

HOLLOWAY, Prof. John, MA, DPhil, DLitt, LittD; Professor of Modern English, Cambridge, 1972–82 (Reader, 1966–72); Fellow of Queens' College, 1955–82, Life Fellow, 1982; *b* 1 Aug. 1920; *s* of George Holloway and Evelyn Astbury; *m* 1946, Audrey Gooding; one *s* one *d*; *m* 1978, Joan Black. *Educ:* County Sch., Beckenham, Kent; New Coll., Oxford (Open History Scholar). 1st class Modern Greats, 1941; DPhil Oxon 1947; DLitt Aberdeen 1954; LittD Cambridge, 1969. Served War of 1939–45, commnd RA, 1942; subsequently seconded to Intelligence. Temporary Lecturer in Philosophy, New Coll., 1945; Fellow of All Souls Coll., 1946–60; John Locke Scholar, 1947; University Lecturer in English: Aberdeen, 1949–54; Cambridge, 1954–66; Sec., 1954–56, Librarian, 1964–66, Chm., 1970, 1971, English Faculty. FRSL 1956. Lecture Tours: Ceylon, India, Pakistan, 1958; Middle East, 1965; France, 1970; Tunisia, 1972; Hong Kong, NZ, Fiji, 1984; Kyoto, 1986; India, 1988; California, 1989; Visiting appointments: Byron Professor, University of Athens, 1961–63; Alexander White Professor, Chicago, 1965; Hinkley Prof., Johns Hopkins Univ., 1972; Virginia Lectr, Charlottesville, 1979; Berg Prof., New York Univ., 1987. *Publications:* Language and Intelligence, 1951; The Victorian Sage, 1953; (ed) Poems of the Mid-Century, 1957; The Charted Mirror (Essays), 1960; (ed) Selections from Shelley, 1960; Shakespeare's Tragedies, 1961; The Colours of Clarity (essays), 1964; The Lion Hunt, 1964; Widening Horizons in English Verse, 1966; A London Childhood, 1966; Blake, The Lyric Poetry, 1968; The Establishment of English, 1972; (ed with J. Black) Later English Broadside Ballads, vol. I, 1975, vol. II, 1979; The Proud Knowledge, 1977; Narrative and Structure, 1979; The Slumber of Apollo, 1983; (ed) The Oxford Book of Local Verses, 1987; contributions to journals; *verse:* The Minute, 1956; The Fugue, 1960; The Landfallers, 1962; Wood and Windfall, 1965; New Poems, 1970; Planet of Winds, 1977; Civitatula—Cambridge, the little city, 1994. *Recreation:* enjoyment. *Address:* Queens' College, Cambridge CB3 9ET.

HOLLOWAY, Reginald Eric, CMG 1984; HM Diplomatic Service, retired; business consultant, since 1992; President, Holloway Pacificwest Inc., since 1992; *b* 22 June 1932; *s* of late Ernest and Beatrice Holloway; *m* 1958, Anne Penelope, *d* of late Walter Robert and Doris Lilian Pawley; one *d*. *Educ:* St Luke's, Brighton. Apprentice reporter, 1947–53; served RAF, 1953–55; journalist in Britain and E Africa, 1955–61; Press Officer, Tanganyika Govt, 1961–63; Dir, British Inf. Service, Guyana, 1964–67; Inf. Dept, FCO, 1967–69 (Anguilla, 1969); 2nd, later 1st Sec., Chancery in Malta, 1970–72; E African Dept, FCO, 1972–74; Consul and Head of Chancery, Kathmandu, 1974–77 (Chargé d'Affaires *ai*, 1975 and 1976); Asst Head, S Asian Dept, FCO, 1977–79; Counsellor, 1979; Inspector, 1979–81; Consul-Gen., Toronto, 1981–85; Sen. British Trade Comr, Hong Kong, 1985–89, and Consul-Gen. (non-resident), Macao, 1986–89; Consul-Gen., Los Angeles, 1989–92. Chm., Canadian Urban Inst., 1993–. *Recreations:* woodworking, old wirelesses, old cameras. *Address:* 900 Yonge Street, Suite 601, Toronto, Ontario M4W 3P5, Canada.

HOLLOWAY, Most Rev. Richard Frederick; *see* Edinburgh, Bishop of.

HOLLOWAY, Dr Robin Greville; composer; Fellow of Gonville and Caius College, Cambridge, since 1969, and Lecturer in Music, University of Cambridge, since 1975; *b* 19 Oct. 1943; *s* of Robert Charles Holloway and Pamela Mary Jacob. *Educ:* St Paul's Cathedral Choir Sch.; King's Coll. Sch., Wimbledon; King's Coll., Cambridge (MA 1968;

PhD 1972; MusD 1976); New Coll., Oxford. *Compositions* include: Garden Music, 1962; First Concerto for Orchestra, 1966–69; Scenes from Schumann, 1969–70; Evening with Angels, 1972; Domination of Black, 1973–74; Sea Surface full of Clouds, 1974–75; Clarissa, 1976 (premièred ENO, 1990); Romanza, 1976; The Rivers of Hell, 1977; Second Concerto for Orchestra, 1978–79; Serenade in C, 1979; Aria, 1980; Brand, 1981; Women in War, 1982; Second Idyll, 1983; Seascape and Harvest, 1984; Viola Concerto, 1984; Serenade in E flat, 1984; Ballad for harp and orch., 1985; Inquietus, 1986; Double Concerto for clarinet and saxophone, 1988; The Spacious Firmament, 1989; Violin Concerto, 1990; Third Concerto for Orchestra, 1994. *Publications:* Wagner and Debussy, 1978; numerous articles and reviews. *Recreation:* playing on two pianos. *Address:* Gonville and Caius College, Cambridge CB2 1TA. *T:* Cambridge (01223) 335424.

HOLLOWAY, Maj.-Gen. Robin Hugh Ferguson, CB 1976; CBE 1974; *b* Hawera, 22 May 1922; *s* of late Hugh Ferguson Holloway and Phyllis Myrtle Holloway; *m* 1947, Margaret Jewell, *d* of late E. G. Monk, Temple Cloud, Somerset; one *s* two *d*. *Educ:* Hawera Technical High Sch.; RMC, Duntroon, Australia. Commnd NZ Staff Corps, 1942; served in 2nd NZEF, Solomon Is, Italy and Japan, 1943–47; qual. Air Observation Post Pilot, 1948–49; Staff Coll., Camberley, 1952; Jt Services Staff Coll., Latimer, 1958; Dir of Mil. Intelligence, 1959–61; Dep. Adjt Gen., 1962–63; Head, NZ Defence Liaison Staff, Singapore and Malaysia, 1964–65; ACDS, 1967–68; IDC, 1969; Comdr Northern Mil. Dist, and Comdr 1st Inf. Bde Gp, 1970; DCGS, 1971–73; CGS, 1973–76; R of O, March 1977; Dir of Civil Defence, NZ, 1977–83. Referee, Small Claims Tribunal: Lower Hutt, 1982–91; Wellington, 1985–91. Pres., Scout Assoc. of NZ, 1979–89; Dep. Chief Scout, 1979–89. *Recreations:* gardening, walking, bowls. *Address:* 435 Te Moana Road, Waikanae, New Zealand. *T:* (4) 2934089. *Club:* Wellington (NZ).

HOLM, Sir Carl Henry, (Sir Charles Holm), Kt 1987; OBE 1975; land developer, dairy farmer, cane farmer; *b* 1 Aug. 1915; *s* of Frederick Otto Holm and Johanna Jamieson (formerly Stickens); *m* 1st, 1938, Myrtle Phyllis Murtha (*d* 1987); one *s*; 2nd, 1988, Joyce Elaine Blackbeard (*née* Shell). *Educ:* Baralaba State Sch.; Ipswich Boys' Sch.; Pimpana State Sch.; Coomera State Sch. Sgt, Volunteer Defence Corp., 1942–45. Albert Shire Council: Councillor, 1967–82; Mem., Town Planning Cttee, 1975–82; Chm., Works Cttee, 1975–82; National Party of Australia: Senior Vice-Pres., Qld, 1972–90; Federal Sen. Vice-Pres., 1975–; Past Chm., Tranport Cttee; Past Chm., Conservation Cttee. Queensland Dairymen's Organisation: Mem., 1946–; Chm., SE District Council, 1961–; Mem., State Council, 1972–; Mem., State Milk Exec., 1967–; Chm., United Milk Producers Co-operative Assoc., 1972–; Pres., Metrop. Milk Producers Co-operative Assoc., 1976–79, Dir, 1979–. *Recreation:* riding horses. *Address:* Kingsholme, Upper Ormeau Road, Kingsholme, Qld 4208, Australia. *T:* (7) 55466237. *Club:* National (Southport, Qld) (Foundn Mem. and Chm., 1973–91).

HOLM, Ian, CBE 1989; actor, since 1954; *b* 12 Sept. 1931; *s* of Dr James Harvey Cuthbert and Jean Wilson Cuthbert; *m* 1st, 1955, Lynn Mary Shaw (marr. diss. 1965); two *d*; and one *s* one *d*; 2nd, 1982, Sophie Baker (marr. diss. 1986); one *s*; 3rd, 1991, Penelope Wilton; one step *d*. *Educ:* Chigwell Grammar Sch., Essex. Trained RADA, 1950–53 (interrupted by Nat. Service); joined Shakespeare Memorial Theatre, 1954, left after 1955; Worthing Rep., 1956; tour, Olivier's Titus Andronicus, 1957; re-joined Stratford, 1958: roles include: Puck; Ariel; Gremio; Lorenzo; Prince Hal; Henry V; Duke of Gloucester; Richard III; The Fool in Lear; Lennie in The Homecoming (also on Broadway, 1966) (Evening Standard Actor of the Year, 1965); left RSC, 1967; Moonlight, Almeida, 1993 (Evening Standard Actor of the Year, Critics Circle Award). Major film appearances include: Young Winston, The Fixer, Oh! What a Lovely War, The Bofors Gun, Alien, All Quiet on the Western Front, Chariots of Fire (Best Supporting Actor: Cannes, 1981; BAFTA, 1982); Return of the Soldier; Greystoke; Brazil; Laughterhouse; Dance With a Stranger; Wetherby; Dreamchild; Another Woman; Hamlet; Kafka; Naked Lunch; Blue Ice; Mary Shelley's Frankenstein; The Madness of King George; Lochness. TV series include: J. M. Barrie in trilogy The Lost Boys (RTS Best Actor Award, 1979); We, the Accused, 1980; The Bell, 1981; Game, Set and Match, 1988; other TV appearances include: Lech Walesa in Strike, 1981; Goebbels in Inside the Third Reich, 1982; Mr and Mrs Edgehill, 1985; The Browning Version, 1986; Uncle Vanya, 1990; The Last Romantics, 1991; The Borrowers, 1992; The Deep Blue Sea, 1994; Landscape, 1995. *Recreations:* tennis, walking, general outdoor activities. *Address:* c/o Julian Belfrage Associates, 68 St James's Street, SW1A 1PH.

HOLMAN, Hon. Sir (Edward) James, Kt 1995; **Hon. Mr Justice Holman;** a Judge of the High Court of Justice, Family Division, since 1995; *b* 21 Aug. 1947; *o s* of Dr Edward Theodore Holman and Mary Megan Holman, MBE (*née* Morris), formerly of Ringwood, Hants, and Manaccan, Cornwall; *m* 1979, Fiona Elisabeth, *er d* of Dr Ronald Cathcart Roxburgh, FRCP; two *s* one *d*. *Educ:* Dauntsey's; Exeter College, Oxford (BA Jurisp., MA). Called to the Bar, Middle Temple, 1971, Bencher, 1995; QC 1991; Western Circuit; in practice, 1971–95; Standing Counsel to HM Treasury (Queen's Proctor), 1980–91; a Recorder, 1993–95. A Legal Assessor, UK Central Council for Nursing, Midwifery and Health Visiting, 1983–95. Member: Family Proceedings Rules Cttee, 1991–95; Supreme Court Procedure Cttee, 1992–; ex-officio Mem., Bar Council, 1992–95. Chm., Family Law Bar Assoc., 1992–95 (Sec., 1988–92). Mem., Council, RYA, 1980–83, 1984–87, 1988–91. *Recreations:* sailing, ski-ing, music. *Address:* Royal Courts of Justice, Strand, WC2A 2LL. *Clubs:* Royal Ocean Racing (Mem. Cttee, 1984–87); Royal Yacht Squadron.

HOLMAN, Richard Christopher; His Honour Judge Holman; a Circuit Judge, since 1994; *b* 16 June 1946; *s* of Frank Harold Holman and Joan (*née* Attrill); *m* 1969, Susan Whittaker, MBE; two *s*. *Educ:* Watford Grammar Sch. for Boys; Eton Coll.; Gonville and Caius Coll., Cambridge (MA 1968). Admitted as solicitor, 1971; Partner, Foysters, later Davies Wallis Foyster, 1973–94, Man. Partner, 1988–89; Dep. Dist Registrar of High Court and Dep. Registrar of County Court, 1982–88; Asst Recorder, 1988–92; a Recorder, 1992–94. Mem., NW Legal Aid Area Cttee, 1980–94. Mem. Council, Manchester Law Soc., 1983–90. Gov., Pownall Hall Sch., Wilmslow, 1990– (Chm., 1993–). *Recreations:* golf, gardening, theatre, music. *Address:* Queen Elizabeth II Law Courts, Derby Square, Liverpool L2 1XA. *T:* 0151–473 7373. *Club:* Wilmslow Golf.

HOLMBERG, Eric Robert Reginald; Deputy Chief Scientist (Army), Ministry of Defence, 1972–77; *b* 24 Aug. 1917; *s* of Robert and May Holmberg; *m* 1940, Wanda Erna Reich; one *s* one *d*. *Educ:* Sandown (Isle of Wight) Grammar Sch.; St John's Coll., Cambridge (MA); Imperial Coll., London (PhD). Joined Mine Design Department, Admiralty, 1940; Admiralty Gunnery Establishment, 1945; Operational Research Department, Admiralty, 1950; appointed Chief Supt Army Operational Research Group, 1956; Dir, Army Operational Science and Res., subseq. Asst Chief Scientist (Army), MoD, 1961–72. *Publications:* The Trouble with Relativity, 1986; papers in Proc. Royal Astronomical Society. *Address:* 29 Westmoreland Road, Barnes, SW13 9RZ. *T:* 0181–748 2568.

HOLME, family name of Baron Holme of Cheltenham.

HOLME OF CHELTENHAM, Baron *cr* 1990 (Life Peer), of Cheltenham in the County of Gloucestershire; **Richard Gordon Holme**, CBE 1983; Chairman: Threadneedle Publishing Group, since 1988; Prima Europe, since 1992; *b* 27 May 1936; *s* of J. R. Holme and E. M. Holme (*née* Eggleton); *m* 1958, Kathleen Mary Powell; two *s* two *d*. *Educ:* Royal Masonic Sch.; St John's Coll., Oxford; Harvard Business Sch. (PMD). Commnd 10th Gurkha Rifles, Malaya, 1954–56. Vice-Chm., Liberal Party Exec., 1966–67; Pres., Liberal Party, 1980–81; contested: East Grinstead (L) 1964 and by-election, 1965; Braintree (L) Oct. 1974; Cheltenham (L) 1983, (L/Alliance) 1987. Lib Dem spokesman on NI, H of L, 1992–. Dir, Campaign for Electoral Reform, 1976–85; Sec., Parly Democracy Trust, 1977–; Chm., Constitutional Reform Centre, 1985–94; Hon. Treasurer, Green Alliance, 1978–90. Chairman: DPR Publishing (formerly Dod's Publishing and Research), 1988–; Black Box Publishing, 1988–95; Hollis Directories, 1989–; Data Management Services Gp Ltd, 1995–; Director: AVI Hldgs Ltd, 1987–; Political Quarterly, 1988–. Vis. Prof. in Business Administration, Middlesex Polytechnic, 1990–94. Associate Mem., Nuffield Coll., 1985–89; Exec. Mem., Campaign for Oxford, 1990–. Vice-Chm., Hansard Soc. for Parly Govt, 1991–. Chm., English Coll. Foundn, Prague, 1991–. *Publications:* No Dole for the Young, 1975; A Democracy Which Works, 1978; The People's Kingdom, 1987; (ed jtly) 1688–1988, Time for a New Constitution, 1988. *Address:* House of Lords, SW1A 0PW. *Club:* Brooks's, Reform.

HOLME, Maj.-Gen. Michael Walter, CBE 1966; MC 1945; *b* 9 May 1918; *s* of Thomas Walter Holme and Ruth Sangster Holme (*née* Rivington); *m* 1948, Sarah Christian Van Der Gucht; one *s* two *d*. *Educ:* Winchester College. Directing Staff, Staff Coll., Camberley, 1952–55; Comdr 1st Bn 3rd East Anglian Regt, 1960–62; Comdr Land Forces Persian Gulf, 1963–66; Chief of Staff, Western Comd, 1966–67; Divisional Brig., The Queen's Div., 1968–69; GOC Near East Land Forces, 1969–72, retired; Dep. Col, The Royal Anglian Regiment, 1970–77. *Recreations:* various. *Address:* c/o C. Hoare & Co., 37 Fleet Street, EC4. *Club:* Army and Navy.

HOLMER, Paul Cecil Henry, CMG 1973; HM Diplomatic Service, retired; Ambassador to Romania, 1979–83; *b* 19 Oct. 1923; *s* of late Bernard Cecil and Mimi Claudine Holmer; *m* 1946, Irene Nora, *e d* of late Orlando Lenox Beater, DFC; two *s* two *d*. *Educ:* King's Sch., Canterbury; Balliol Coll., Oxford. Served in RA, 1942–46. Entered Civil Service, 1947; Colonial Office, 1947–49; transferred to HM Foreign Service, 1949; FO, 1949–51; Singapore, 1951–55; FO, 1955–56; served on Civil Service Selection Bd, 1956; FO, 1956–58; Moscow, 1958–59; Berlin, 1960–64; FO, 1964–66; Counsellor, 1966; Dep. High Comr, Singapore, 1966–69; Head of Security Dept, FCO, 1969–72; Ambassador, Ivory Coast, Upper Volta and Niger, 1972–75; Minister and UK Dep. Perm. Rep. to NATO, 1976–79. Dir, African Develt Fund, 1973–75.

HOLMES, Anthony, CBE 1982; Head of Passport Department, Home Office (formerly Chief Passport Officer, Foreign and Commonwealth Office), 1980–88, retired; *b* 4 Sept. 1931; *s* of Herbert and Jessie Holmes; *m* 1954, Sheila Frances Povall. *Educ:* Calday Grange Grammar School. Joined HM Customs and Excise, 1949; served HM Forces, 1950–52; Passport Office, 1955; Dep. Chief Passport Officer, 1977. *Recreations:* golf, sailing. *Address:* Hilbre, Mill Road, West Chiltington, Pulborough, West Sussex RH20 2PZ. *Clubs:* Cowdray Park Golf (Midhurst); West Sussex Golf (Pulborough).

HOLMES, Barry Trevor; HM Diplomatic Service, retired; business development consultant; *b* 23 Sept. 1933; *s* of Edwin Holmes and Marion (*née* Jones); *m* 1st, 1956, Dorothy Pitchforth (marr. diss. 1989); three *d*; 2nd, 1992, Sherie Shortridge. *Educ:* Bishopshalt Grammar School. Entered HM Foreign Service, 1950; Personnel Services Dept, 1950–53; Foreign Office, 1955–58; Quito, 1958–62; FO, 1962–65; Vancouver, 1965–68; First Secretary, FCO, 1968–72; Nairobi, 1972–75; FCO, 1975–80; Commercial Counsellor, Helsinki, 1980–85; Consul-Gen., Atlanta, 1985–92. National Service: Captain, Royal Artillery, Egypt, 1953–55. *Recreations:* chess, light opera, walking. *Address:* 3751 Haddon Hall Road NW, Atlanta, GA 30327, USA.

HOLMES, Christopher John; Director, Shelter, since 1995; *b* 13 July 1942; *s* of Gordon Holmes and Doris Holmes (*née* Waite); *m* 1969, Ann Warden (marr. diss. 1989); one *s* one *d*; partner, Hattie Llewelyn-Davies; one *s*. *Educ:* Clare Coll., Cambridge (MA Hons Econs 1964); Univ. of Bradford (Dip. in Industrial Admin 1966). Asst Gen. Sec., Student Christian Movement, 1964–65; John Laing Construction, 1966–68; NE Islington Community Project, then N Islington Housing Rights Project, 1969–74; Dep. Dir, Shelter, 1974–76; Director: Soc. for Co-operative Dwellings, 1976–79; E London Housing Assoc., 1979–82; CHAR, 1982–87; Consultant, Priority Estates Project, 1988–89; Dir of Housing, London Borough of Camden, 1990–95. Mem., Nat. Consumer Council, 1975–80. *Recreations:* my family, reading, walking, theatre, cricket. *Address:* 2 Carpenters Yard, Park Street, Tring, Herts HP23 6AR.

HOLMES, David, CB 1985; Director, Government and Industry Affairs, British Airways plc, since 1991; *b* 6 March 1935; *s* of late George A. Holmes and Annie Holmes; *m* 1963, Ann Chillingworth; one *s* two *d*. *Educ:* Doncaster Grammar Sch.; Christ Church, Oxford (MA). Asst Principal, Min. of Transport and Civil Aviation, 1957; Private Sec. to Jt Parly Sec., 1961–63; HM Treasury, 1965–68; Principal Private Sec. to Minister of Transport, 1968–70; Asst Sec., 1970, Under Sec., 1976, Dep. Sec., 1982–91, Dept of Transport. *Recreation:* music. *Address:* British Airways plc, PO Box 10, Heathrow Airport (London), Hounslow TW6 2JA. *Clubs:* United Oxford & Cambridge University, Royal Automobile.

HOLMES, David Vivian; Member, Broadcasting Complaints Commission, 1987–92; *b* 12 Oct. 1926; *s* of Vivian and Kathleen St Clair Holmes; *m* 1st, 1957, Rhoda Ann, *d* of late Col N. J. Gai; two *d*; 2nd, 1979, Linda Ruth Alexander (*née* Kirk). *Educ:* Ipswich Sch.; Allhallows Sch. Served KRRC, 1944–47. Entered journalism, 1948; Evening Standard, 1951–56; Reporter, BBC News, 1956–61; BBC political reporter, 1961–72; Asst Head, BBC Radio Talks and Documentary Programmes; launched Kaleidoscope arts programme, 1973; Political Editor, BBC, 1975–80; Chief Asst to Dir-Gen., BBC, 1980–83; Sec. of the BBC, 1983–85. Chm., Parly Lobby Journalists, 1976–77. Member: Council, Hansard Soc., 1981–83; MoD Censorship Study Gp, 1983; Adv. Cttee, W Yorks Media in Politics Gp, Leeds Univ., 1985–90; Exec. Cttee, Suffolk Historic Churches Trust, 1989–90. *Recreations:* music, gardening. *Address:* 5 Salters Lane, Walpole, Halesworth, Suffolk IP19 9BA. *T:* Bramfield (01986) 784412. *Club:* Farmers'.

HOLMES, Sir Frank (Wakefield), Kt 1975; JP; company director; consultant; Emeritus Professor, since 1985, Visiting Fellow, since 1986, and Chairman, 1989–91, Institute of Policy Studies, Victoria University of Wellington; *b* 8 Sept. 1924; *s* of James Francis Wakefield and Marie Esme Babette Holmes; *m* 1947, Nola Ruth Ross; two *s*. *Educ:* Waitaki Boys' Jun. High Sch. (Dux 1936); King's High Sch. (Dux 1941); Otago Univ.; Auckland University Coll. (Sen. Schol. 1948); Victoria University Coll. MA (1st Cl. Hons) 1949. Flying Officer, Royal NZ Air Force, 1942–45 (despatches). Economic Div., Prime Minister's and External Affairs Depts 1949–52; Lectr to Prof., Victoria Univ. of Wellington, 1952–67; Macarthy Prof. of Economics, 1959–67; Dean, Faculty of Commerce, 1961–63; Economics Manager, Tasman Pulp & Paper Co Ltd, 1967–70; Victoria Univ. of Wellington: Prof. of Money and Finance, 1970–77; Vis. Prof. and Convener, Master of Public Policy Programme, 1982–85. Adviser, Royal Commn on

Monetary, Banking and Credit Systems, 1955; Consultant, Bank of New Zealand, 1956–58 and 1964–67; Chm., Monetary and Economic Council, 1961–64 and 1970–72; Jt Sec., Cttee on Universities, 1959; Mem., NZ Council Educnl Research, 1965–77 (Chm. 1970–74); Chairman: Adv. Council on Educnl Planning and Steering Cttee, Educnl Develt Conf., 1973–74; NZ Govt Task Force on Economic and Social Planning, 1976; NZ Planning Council, 1977–82; Asia 2000 Foundn, NZ, 1994–; Nat. Adv. Cttee on Post-Entry Clinical Trng, 1995–; Dep. Chm., Inst. of Policy Studies, 1984–89. President: NZ Assoc. of Economists, 1961–63; Economic Section, ANZAAS, 1967, Education Section, 1979; Central Council, Economic Soc. of Australia and NZ, 1967–68. Chairman: South Pacific Merchant Finance Ltd, 1985–89 (Dir, 1984–89); Hugo Consulting Group Ltd, 1989– (Exec. Dir., 1986–); State Insurance Ltd, 1990–94; Norwich Holdings Ltd, 1990–94; Norwich Union Life Insce (NZ) Ltd, 1993–94; Director: National Bank of NZ Ltd, 1982–95; Norwich Union Life Insce Soc. 1983–92 (Chm., 1990–92); Lloyds Bank NZA Ltd, Sydney, 1992–95. Mem., Internat. Organising Cttee, Pacific Trade and Develt Confs, 1982–. FNZIM 1986. Life Mem., VUW Students' Assoc., 1967. JP 1960. FRSA. *Publications:* Money, Finance and the Economy, 1972; Government in the New Zealand Economy, 1977, 2nd edn 1980; Closer Economic Relations with Australia, 1986; Partners in the Pacific, 1988; (ed) Stepping Stones to Freer Trade, 1989; (jtly) Meeting the East Asia Challenge, 1989; Meeting the European Challenge, 1991; NAFTA, CER and a Pacific Basin Initiative, 1992; A New Approach to Central Banking, 1994; CER: Trends and Linkages, 1994; pamphlets and articles on econs, finance, educn and internat. affairs. *Recreations:* touring, walking, swimming, music. *Address:* 61 Cheviot Road, Lowry Bay, Lower Hutt, New Zealand. *T:* Wellington (4) 5684719. *Club:* Wellington (Wellington).

HOLMES, Prof. George Arthur, PhD; FBA 1985; Chichele Professor of Medieval History, University of Oxford, and Fellow of All Souls College, 1989–94; *b* 22 April 1927; *s* of late John Holmes and Margaret Holmes, Aberystwyth; *m* 1953, Evelyn Anne, *d* of late Dr John Klein and Audrey Klein; one *s* two *d* (and one *s* decd). *Educ:* Ardwyn County Sch., Aberystwyth; UC, Aberystwyth; St John's Coll., Cambridge (MA, PhD). Fellow, St John's Coll., Cambridge, 1951–54; Tutor, St Catherine's Society, Oxford, 1954–62; Fellow and Tutor, St Catherine's Coll., Oxford, 1962–89 (Vice-Master, 1969–71; Emeritus Fellow, 1990). Mem., Inst. for Advanced Study, Princeton, 1967–68. Vis. Prof., Harvard Univ. Centre for Italian Renaissance Studies, Florence, 1995–. Chm., Victoria County Hist. Cttee, Inst. of Hist. Res., 1979–89. Jt Editor, English Historical Review, 1974–81; Delegate, Oxford Univ. Press, 1982–91. Serena Medal for Italian Studies, British Acad., 1993. *Publications:* The Estates of the Higher Nobility in Fourteenth-Century England, 1957; The Later Middle Ages, 1962; The Florentine Enlightenment 1400–1450, 1969; Europe: hierarchy and revolt 1320–1450, 1975; The Good Parliament, 1975; Dante, 1980; Florence, Rome and the Origins of the Renaissance, 1986; (ed) The Oxford Illustrated History of Medieval Europe, 1988; The First Age of the Western City 1300–1500, 1990; (ed) Art and Politics in Renaissance Italy, 1993; articles in learned jls. *Address:* Highmoor House, Bampton, Oxon OX18 2HY. *T:* Bampton Castle (01993) 850408.

HOLMES, George Dennis, CB 1979; FRSE; Director-General and Deputy Chairman, Forestry Commission, 1977–86, retired; *b* 9 Nov. 1926; *s* of James Henry Holmes and Florence Holmes (*née* Jones); *m* 1953, Sheila Rosemary Woodger; three *d*. *Educ:* John Bright's Sch., Llandudno; Univ. of Wales (BSc (Hons)); FRSE 1982; FICFor. Post-grad Research, Univ. of Wales, 1947; appointed Forestry Commission, 1948; Asst Silviculturist, Research Div., 1948; Asst Conservator, N Wales, 1962; Dir of Research, 1968; Comr for Harvesting and Marketing, 1973. Mem., Scottish Legal Aid Bd, 1989–94. Hon. Prof., Univ. of Aberdeen, 1984. Chm., Scottish Council for Spastics, 1986–. Hon. DSc Wales, 1985. *Publications:* contribs to Forestry Commission publns and to Brit. and Internat. forestry jls. *Recreations:* golf, fishing. *Address:* (office) 22 Corstorphine Road, Edinburgh EH12 6HP. *T:* 0131–337 9876.

HOLMES, John Eaton; HM Diplomatic Service; European Union Department (External), Foreign and Commonwealth Office, since 1995; *b* 29 April 1951; *s* of Lesley Howard Holmes and Joyce Mary (*née* Stone); *m* 1976, Margaret Penelope Morris; three *d*. *Educ:* Preston Grammar Sch.; Balliol Coll., Oxford (BA 1st Cl. Hons Lit. Hum., MA). Joined HM Diplomatic Service, 1973; FCO, 1973–76; 3rd Sec., then 2nd Sec., Moscow, 1976–78; Near East and N Africa Dept, FCO, 1978–82; Asst Private Sec. to Foreign Sec., 1982–84; 1st Sec. (Economic), Paris, 1984–87; Asst Hd of Soviet Dept, FCO, 1987–89; seconded to Thomas de la Rue & Co., 1989–91; Counsellor, Econ. and Commercial, New Delhi, 1991–95. *Recreations:* sport (tennis, squash, cricket, golf), music, reading. *Address:* c/o Foreign and Commonwealth Office, King Charles Street, SW1A 2AH.

HOLMES, Dr John Ernest Raymond; Director, Quality and Performance, United Kingdom Atomic Energy Authority, 1989–90; *b* Birmingham, 13 Aug. 1925; *s* of late Dr John K. Holmes and of Ellen R. Holmes; *m* 1949, Patricia Clitheroe; one *s* one *d*. *Educ:* King Edward's School, Birmingham; University of Birmingham (BSc, PhD). Asst Lectr in Physics, Manchester Univ., 1949–52; Research Scientist, AERE Harwell, 1952–59; Atomic Energy Establishment, Winfrith: Research Scientist, 1959–66; Chief Physicist, 1966–73; Dep. Dir, 1973–86; Dir, 1986–89. *Publications:* technical papers on nuclear power. *Address:* The Mount, Durlston Road, Swanage, Dorset BH19 2HX. *T:* Swanage (01929) 423330.

HOLMES, John Wentworth, MBE 1983; Chief Agent, Liberal Party, and Deputy Head, Party HQ, 1974–86; *b* 14 Jan. 1925; *s* of Arthur and Annie Holmes; *m* 1969, Sonia Pratt; four *d*. *Educ:* Caverswall Church School. Foxwell Colliery Co., 1941–47, NCB 1947–51; Labour Agent, Rugby and Meriden, 1951–62; Liberal Agent, Leicester, 1963–65; Regional Sec., Liberal Party, Home Counties Region, 1965–74. Member: National Exec., Liberal Party, 1986–88; Council, Liberal Party, 1986–88. Mem., North Staffs District and Midland Area Council, NUM, 1947–50; formerly Mem., Warwickshire CC; Dir, Rugby Co-operative Soc. Ltd and its subsidiary interests, 1952–70 (Pres. and Chm., Bd of Dirs, 1964–70). *Recreations:* gardening, cooking. *Address:* Crossways, Parsonage Lane, Icklesham, Winchelsea, Sussex TN36 4BL. *T:* Hastings (01424) 814415.

HOLMES, Prof. Kenneth Charles, PhD; FRS 1981; Director of the Department of Biophysics, Max-Planck-Institute for Medical Research, Heidelberg, since 1968; Professor of Biophysics, Heidelberg University, since 1972; *b* 19 Nov. 1934; *m* 1957, Mary Scruby; one *s* three *d*. *Educ:* St John's Coll., Cambridge (MA 1959); London Univ. (PhD 1959). Res. Associate, Childrens' Hosp., Boston, USA, 1960–61; Mem., Scientific Staff, MRC Lab. of Molecular Biology, Cambridge, 1962–68. Mem., European Molecular Biol. Organisation. Scientific mem., Max Planck Gesellschaft, 1972–; Corresp. Mem., Soc. Royale des Scis, Liège. *Publications:* (with D. Blow) The Use of X-ray Diffraction in the Study of Protein and Nucleic Acid Structure, 1965; papers on virus structure, molecular mechanism of muscular contraction and the structure of actin. *Recreations:* rowing, singing. *Address:* Biophysics Department, Max-Planck-Institute for Medical Research, Jahnstrasse 29, 69120 Heidelberg, Germany. *T:* (6221) 486270.

HOLMES, Sir Maurice (Andrew), Kt 1969; Barrister-at-Law; *b* 28 July 1911; *o s* of Rev. A. T. Holmes and Ellen Holmes; *m* 1935, Joyce Esther, *d* of late E. C. Hicks, JP, CC; no *c*. *Educ:* Felsted Sch., Essex. Served with RASC, 1941–45 (Major, despatches). Called to Bar, Gray's Inn, 1948; Practised at Bar, 1950–55. Director, 1955–60, Chairman, 1960–65, The Tilling Association Ltd; Chairman, London Transport Board, 1965–69. Circuit Administrator, South Eastern Circuit, 1970–74. *Recreations:* golf, music. *Address:* The Limes, Felsted, near Dunmow, Essex CM6 3HB. *T:* Great Dunmow (01371) 820352. *Club:* Forty.

HOLMES, Maurice Colston, OBE 1985; Director, Safety, British Railways Board, 1989–92; *b* 15 Feb. 1935; *s* of Charles Edward Holmes and Ellen Catherine Mary Holmes (*née* Colston); *m* 1985, Margaret Joan Wiscombe. *Educ:* Presentation Coll., Reading. British Rail: Divl Man., Liverpool Street, 1976–79; Chief Operating Man., 1979–80, Dep. Gen. Man., 1980–82, Southern Region; Dir of Operations, BRB, 1982–88. Dir and Trustee, Railway Pension Trustee Co. Ltd. Pres., British Transport Pension Fedn, 1993–. Lt-Col, RE, Engrg and Transport Staff Corps (TA), 1990–. *Recreations:* travel, transport, gardens. *Address:* 9 High Tree Drive, Earley, Reading, Berks RG6 1EU. *T:* Reading (01734) 668887.

HOLMES, Prof. Patrick, PhD; Professor of Hydraulics, Imperial College of Science, Technology and Medicine, since 1983; Dean, City and Guilds College, 1988–91; *b* 23 Feb. 1939; *s* of Norman Holmes and Irene (*née* Shelbourne); *m* 1963, Olive (*née* Towning); one *s* one *d*. *Educ:* University Coll. of Swansea, Univ. of Wales (BSc 1960, PhD 1963). CEng, MICE. Res. Engr, Harbour and Deep Ocean Engrg, US Navy Civil Engrg Lab., Port Hueneme, Calif, 1963–65; Lectr, Dept of Civil Engrg, Univ. of Liverpool, 1966–72, Sen. Lectr, 1972–74, Prof. of Maritime Civil Engrg, 1974–83. Chm., Environment Cttee, SERC, 1981–85. Pres., Conf. of European Schs of Advanced Engrg Educn and Res., 1993–95. Hon. Mem., C&G, 1992. *Publications:* (ed) Handbook of Hydraulic Engineering (English edn), by Lencastre, 1987; articles on ocean and coastal engineering, wave motion, wave loading, coastal erosion and accretion, and harbour and breakwater design, in Proc. ICE and Proc. Amer. Soc. of Civil Engrs. *Recreations:* hockey, yachting, walking, choral music. *Address:* Department of Civil Engineering, Imperial College of Science, Technology and Medicine, SW7 2AZ; West Winds, The Green, Steeple Morden, near Royston, Herts SG8 0ND. *T:* Steeple Morden (01763) 852582. *Club:* Athenæum.

HOLMES, Sir Peter (Fenwick), Kt 1988; MC 1952; Managing Director, 1982–93 and Chairman, Committee of Managing Directors, 1992–93, Royal Dutch/Shell Group; Director, Shell Transport and Trading Co., since 1982 (Chairman, 1985–93); *b* 27 Sept. 1932; *s* of Gerald Hugh Holmes and Caroline Elizabeth Holmes; *m* 1955, Judith Millicent (*née* Walker); three *d*. *Educ:* Trinity Coll., Cambridge (MA). Various posts in Royal Dutch/Shell Group, 1956–, including: Gen. Man., Shell Markets, ME, 1965–68; Chief Rep., Libya, 1970–72; Man. Dir, Shell-BP, Nigeria, 1977–81; Pres., Shell Internat. Trading, 1981–83. Trustee, WWF–UK, 1989–. FRGS. Hon. DSc Cranfield, 1993. *Publications:* Mountains and a Monastery, 1958; Nigeria, Giant of Africa, 1985; Turkey, A Timeless Bridge, 1988. *Recreations:* mountaineering, ski-ing, travel to remote areas, photography, 19th century travel books, golf. *Address:* c/o Shell Centre, SE1 7NA. *T:* 0171–934 5611. *Clubs:* Athenæum, Alpine, Himalayan, Climbers, Kandahar; Sunningdale Golf.

HOLMES, Peter Rodney; HM Diplomatic Service; Ambassador to Honduras, since 1995; *b* 29 July 1938; *m* 1957, Anne Cecilia Tarrant; one *s* three *d*. Vice-Consul, Strasbourg, 1959; served Belgrade, Paris, Cento, Ankara; First Sec., Stockholm, 1974; Consul, Douala, 1978; First Sec., Bahrain, 1983; Commercial Counsellor, Santiago, 1987. *Address:* c/o Foreign and Commonwealth Office, SW1A 2AH.

HOLMES, Peter Sloan; Under Secretary, Department of Education for Northern Ireland, since 1987; *b* 8 Dec. 1942; *s* of George H. G. and Anne S. Holmes; *m* 1966, Patricia McMahon; two *s*. *Educ:* Rossall Sch.; Magdalen Coll., Oxford (BA English Lang. and Lit.). Teacher, Eastbourne Coll., 1965–68; Head of English, Grosvenor High Sch., Belfast, 1968–71; Lectr, then Sen. Lectr, Stranmillis Coll. of Educn, Belfast, 1971–75; Department of Education for Northern Ireland: Inspector, 1975–83 (Sen. Inspector, 1980; Staff Inspector, 1982); Asst Sec., 1983–87. *Recreations:* singing, sailing, walking. *Address:* (office) Rathgael House, Bangor, Co. Down BT19 7PR. *T:* Bangor (01247) 279317. *Club:* United Oxford & Cambridge University.

HOLMES, Richard Gordon Heath, OBE 1992; FRSL; writer; *b* 5 Nov. 1945; *s* of Dennis Patrick Holmes and Pamela Mavis Holmes (*née* Gordon). *Educ:* Downside Sch.; Churchill Coll., Cambridge (BA). FRSL 1975. Reviewer and historical features writer for The Times, 1967–92. Mem. Cttee, Royal Literary Fund. Ernest Jones Meml Lecture, British Inst. of Psycho-Analysis, 1990; John Keats Meml Lect., RCS, 1995. *Publications:* Thomas Chatterton: the case re-opened, 1970; One for Sorrow (poems), 1970; Shelley: the pursuit, 1974 (Somerset Maugham Award, 1977); Gautier: my fantoms (trans.), 1976; Inside the Tower (radio drama documentary), 1977; (ed) Shelley on Love, 1980; Coleridge, 1982; (with Peter Jay) Nerval: the chimeras, 1985; Footsteps: adventures of a romantic biographer, 1985; (ed) Mary Wollstonecraft and William Godwin, 1987; (ed with Robert Hampson) Kipling: something of myself, 1987; De Feministe en de Filosoof, 1988; Coleridge: early visions (Whitbread Book of the Year Prize), 1989; To the Tempest Given (radio drama documentary), 1992; Dr Johnson & Mr Savage, 1993 (James Tait Black Meml Prize, 1994); (ed) Coleridge: selected poems, 1996. *Recreations:* sailing, hill-walking, rooftop gardening, stargazing. *Address:* c/o HarperCollins, 77 Fulham Palace Road, W6 8JB.

HOLMES, Robin Edmond Kendall; Head of Judicial Appointments, Lord Chancellor's Department, since 1992; *b* 14 July 1938; *s* of Roy Frederick George Holmes; *m* 1964, Karin Kutter; two *s*. *Educ:* Wolverhampton Grammar Sch.; Clare Coll., Cambridge (BA); Birmingham Univ. (LLM). Articles, Wolverhampton CBC, 1961–64; admitted solicitor, 1964; Min. of Housing and Local Govt, subseq. DoE, 1965–73 and 1976–82; Colonial Secretariat, Hong Kong, 1973–75; Lord Chancellor's Dept, 1982–; Grade 3, 1983–; Circuit Administrator, Midland and Oxford Circuit, 1986–92. *Recreation:* travelling. *Address:* Lord Chancellor's Department, Southside, 105 Victoria Street, SW1E 6QT. *T:* 0171–210 1602.

HOLMES, Roger de Lacy; Deputy Master and Comptroller, Royal Mint, since 1993; *b* 15 Jan. 1948; *s* of Stephen and Muriel Holmes; *m* 1970, Jennifer Anne Heal; one *s* one *d*. *Educ:* Huddersfield New Coll.; Balliol Coll., Oxford (BA). DTI, 1969–74; Dept of Prices and Consumer Protection, 1974–77; Dept of Industry, 1977–79; Asst to Chm., British Leyland, 1980–82; Company Sec., Mercury Communications, 1982–83; Jt Sec and Dir, Corporate Affairs, ICL, 1984; Exec. Dir, Dunlop Holdings, 1984–85; Euroroute, 1985–86; Chloride Group: Man. Dir, Power Electronics, 1986–88; Corporate Affairs Dir, 1989–92. Non-exec. Dir, Cygnet Health Care, 1993–. *Recreations:* golf, cricket, chess. *Address:* Royal Mint, 7 Grosvenor Gardens, SW1W 0BH. *T:* 0171–828 8724.

HOLMES, Timothy Charles; HM Diplomatic Service; Deputy Head of Mission and Commercial and Economic Counsellor, Seoul, since 1994; *b* 26 April 1951; *s* of late Ronald William Holmes and of Barbara Jean (*née* Mickleburgh); *m* 1973, Anna-Carin Magnusson; one *s* one *d*. *Educ:* Bec Sch.; Selwyn Coll., Cambridge (MA); Univ. of Aix-

Marseille. Joined FCO, 1974; Second, later First, Sec., Tokyo, 1976–80; seconded to Invest in Britain Bureau, Dept of Industry, 1981–83; FCO, 1983–86; First Sec., Islamabad, 1986–90; FCO, 1990–94. *Publication:* The Wild Flowers of Islamabad, 1990. *Recreations:* botany, ornithology, reading. *Address:* c/o Foreign and Commonwealth Office, King Charles Street, SW1A 2AH.

HOLMES, Prof. William; Professor of Agriculture, Wye College, University of London, 1955–87, Professor Emeritus, since 1985, Fellow, 1993; *b* Kilbarchan, Renfrewshire, 16 Aug. 1922; *s* of William John Holmes, Bank Manager; *m* 1949, Jean Ishbel Campbell, BSc; two *d*. *Educ:* John Neilson Sch., Paisley; Glasgow Univ.; West of Scotland Agricultural Coll. BSc (Agric), NDD, 1942; NDA (Hons), 1943; PhD Glasgow, 1947; DSc London, 1966. FIBiol 1974. Asst Executive Officer, S Ayrshire AEC, 1943–44; Hannah Dairy Research Inst.: Asst in Animal Husbandry, 1944–47; Head of Department of Dairy and Grassland Husbandry, 1947–55. Member, Cttee on Milk Composition in the UK, 1958–60; Governor, Grassland Research Inst., 1960–75; Pres., British Grassland Soc., 1968–69 (1st recipient, British Grassland Soc. Award, 1979); Pres., British Soc. of Animal Production, 1969–70; Member technical cttees of ARC, JCO MAFF, MMB and Meat and Livestock Commn, 1960–. Correspondent Étranger, Acad. d'Agric. de France, 1984. *Publications:* (ed) Grass, its production and utilization, 1980, 2nd edn 1989; (ed) Grassland Beef Production, 1984; papers in technical agricultural journals. *Recreations:* woodland ecology, gardening, beekeeping, travel. *Address:* Amage, Wye, Kent TN25 5DF. *T:* Wye (01233) 812372.

HOLMES, Prof. William Neil; Professor of Physiology, University of California, since 1964; *b* 2 June 1927; *s* of William Holmes and Minnie Holmes (*née* Lloyd); *m* 1955, Betty M. Brown, Boston, Mass; two *s* two *d*. *Educ:* Adams Grammar Sch., Newport, Salop; Liverpool Univ. (BSc, MSc, PhD, DSc); Harvard Univ., Cambridge, Mass. National Service, 2nd Bn RWF, 1946–48. Visiting Scholar in Biology, Harvard Univ., 1953–55; Post-grad. Research Schol., Liverpool Univ., 1955–56; ICI Fellow, Glasgow Univ., 1956–57; Asst Prof. of Zoology, 1957–63, Associate Prof. of Zoology, 1963–64, Univ. of British Columbia, Canada; John Simon Guggenheim Foundn Fellow, 1961–62; Visiting Professor of Zoology: Univ. of Hull, 1970; Univ. of Hong Kong, 1973, 1982–83 and 1987. Scientific Fellow, Zoological Soc. of London, 1967; External examiner: for undergraduate degrees, Univ. of Hong Kong, 1976–79, 1985–88; for higher degrees, Univs of Hong Kong and Hull, 1976–; Consultant to: Amer. Petroleum Inst., Washington, DC (environmental conservation), 1972–74; US Nat. Sci. Foundn (Regulatory Biology Prog.), 1980–83; US Bureau of Land Management (petroleum toxicity in seabirds), 1982–. Mem. Editorial Bd, American Journal of Physiology, 1967–70. Member: Endocrine Soc., US, 1957–; Soc. for Endocrinology, UK, 1955–; Amer. Physiological Soc., 1960–; Zoological Soc. of London, 1964–. *Publications:* numerous articles and reviews in Endocrinology, Jl of Endocrinology, Gen. and Comp. Endocrinology, Cell and Tissue Res., Archives of Environmental Contamination and Toxicology, Environmental Res., Jl of Experimental Biology. *Recreations:* travel, old maps and prints, carpentry and building. *Address:* 117 East Junipero Street, Santa Barbara, CA 93105, USA. *T:* (805) 6827256. *Club:* Tennis (Santa Barbara).

HOLMES à COURT, family name of **Baron Heytesbury.**

HOLMES SELLORS, Patrick John; *see* Sellors.

HOLMPATRICK, 4th Baron *cr* 1897; **Hans James David Hamilton;** *b* 15 March 1955; *s* of 3rd Baron Holmpatrick and of Anne Loys Roche, *o d* of Commander J. E. P. Brass, RN (retd); *S* father, 1991; *m* 1984, Mrs Gill du Feu, *e d* of K. J. Harding; one *s* and one step *s*. *Heir: b* Hon. Ion Henry James Hamilton, *b* 12 June 1956.

HOLROYD, Air Marshal Sir Frank (Martyn), KBE 1989; CB 1985; FEng 1992; Chairman: Composite Technology Ltd, since 1992; Elettronica (UK), since 1992; *b* 30 Aug. 1935; *s* of George L. Holroyd and Winifred H. Holroyd (*née* Ford); *m* 1958, Veronica Christine, *d* of Arthur Booth; two *s* one *d*. *Educ:* Southend-on-Sea Grammar Sch.; Cranfield Inst. of Technology (MSc). FIEE; FRAeS. Joined RAF, 1956; Fighter Comd units, 1957–60; Blind Landing Development RAE Bedford, 1960–63; Cranfield Inst. of Tech., 1963–65; HQ Fighter Comd, 1965–67; Far East, 1967–69; Wing Comdr, MoD, 1970–72; RAF Brize Norton, 1972–74; Gp Captain Commandant No 1 Radio School, 1974–76; SO Eng. HQ 38 Gp, 1976–77; Air Cdre Director Aircraft Engrg, MoD, 1977–80; RCDS 1981; Dir Weapons and Support Engrg, MoD, 1982, Air Vice-Marshal 1982; DG Strategic Electronics Systems, MoD (Procurement Exec.), 1982–86; AO Engrg, Strike Comd, 1986–88; Chief Engr, 1988–91, and Chief of Logistics Support, 1989–91, RAF. Chm., AVR Communications Ltd, 1992–95; Director: Admiral plc, 1992–; Ultra Electronics Hldgs, 1995–. Mem., Engrg Council, 1990–. Pres., RAeS, 1992–93. Member: Court, 1988–, and Council, 1990–, Inst. of Technology, now Univ., Cranfield; Adv. Council, RMCS, Shrivenham, 1988–91; BBC Engrg Adv. Bd, 1984–90. Trustee, Macrobert Award Trust, Royal Acad. of Engrg, 1993. CIMgt. *Recreations:* travel, gardening, maintaining 14th century house. *Club:* Royal Air Force.

HOLROYD, John Hepworth, CB 1993; Secretary for Appointments to the Prime Minister, and Ecclesiastical Secretary to the Lord Chancellor, since 1993; *b* 10 April 1935; *s* of Harry Holroyd and Annie Dodgshun Holroyd; *m* 1963, Judith Mary Hudson; one *s* one *d*. *Educ:* Kingswood Sch., Bath; Worcester Coll., Oxford (Open Schol.; BA(Hist.); MA 1987). Joined MAFF, 1959; Asst Private Sec. to Minister, 1961–63; Principal, Forestry Commn and MAFF, 1963–69; Asst. Sec., 1969–78; Under Secretary, 1978; Resident Chm., Civil Service Selection Bd, 1978–80; Dir of Establishments, MAFF, 1981–85; Cabinet Office: Under Sec., European Secretariat, 1985–89; First CS Comr and Dep. Sec., 1989–93. Sen. Fellow, European Inst. of Public Admin, 1993. Gov., Kingswood Sch., 1985–. Lay Reader, St Albans Abbey. Trustee, St Albans Cathedral Trust, 1980–. *Recreations:* music, carpentry, bee-keeping, travel. *Address:* c/o Cabinet Office, 70 Whitehall, SW1A 2AS.
See also W. A. H. Holroyd.

HOLROYD, Margaret, (Mrs Michael Holroyd); *see* Drabble, M.

HOLROYD, Michael (de Courcy Fraser), CBE 1989; author; *b* London, 27 Aug. 1935; *s* of Basil Holroyd and Ulla (*née* Hall); *m* 1982, Margaret Drabble, *qv*. *Educ:* Eton Coll.; Maidenhead Public Library. Vis. Fellow, Pennsylvania State Univ., 1979. Chm., Soc. of Authors, 1973–74; Chm., Nat. Book League, 1976–78; Pres., English PEN, 1985–88. Chm., Strachey Trust, 1990–95. Member: BBC Archives Adv. Cttee, 1976–79; Arts Council of England (formerly of GB), 1992–95 (Vice-Chm., 1982–83, Chm., 1992–95, Literature Panel). Nat. Gov., Shaw Fest. Theatre, Ontario, 1993–. FRSL 1968 (Mem. Council, 1977–87); FRHistS; FRSA. Hon. DLitt: Ulster, 1992; Sheffield, 1993; Warwick, 1993; East Anglia, 1994. *Publications:* Hugh Kingsmill: a critical biography, 1964; Lytton Strachey, 2 vols, 1967, 1968, rev. edn 1994; A Dog's Life: a novel, 1969; (ed) The Best of Hugh Kingsmill, 1970; (ed) Lytton Strachey By Himself, 1971; Unreceived Opinions, 1973; Augustus John (2 vols), 1974, 1975, rev. edn 1996; (with M. Easton) The Art of Augustus John, 1974; (ed) The Genius of Shaw, 1979; (ed with Paul Levy) The Shorter Strachey, 1980; (ed with Robert Skidelsky) William Gerhardie's God's Fifth Column, 1981; (ed) Essays by Divers Hands, vol. XLII, 1982; Bernard Shaw: Vol. I, The Search for Love 1856–1898, 1988; Vol. II, The Pursuit of Power 1898–1918, 1989; Vol. III, The Lure of Fantasy 1918–1950, 1991; Vol. IV, The Last Laugh 1950–1991, 1992; Vol. V, The Shaw Companion, 1992; various radio and television scripts. *Recreations:* listening to stories, watching people dance, avoiding tame animals, being polite, music, siestas. *Address:* c/o A. P. Watt Ltd, 20 John Street, WC1N 2DL.

HOLROYD, William Arthur Hepworth, FHSM; Chief Executive, North Durham Health Authority, 1992–93; *b* 15 Sept. 1938; *s* of late Rev. Harry Holroyd and Annie Dodgshun Holroyd; *m* 1967, Hilary Gower; three *s*. *Educ:* Kingswood Sch., Bath; Trinity Hall, Cambridge (MA History); Manchester Univ. (DSA). Hospital Secretary: Crewe Memorial Hosp., 1963–65; Wycombe General Hosp., 1965–67; secondment to Dept of Health, 1967–69; Dep. Gp Sec., Blackpool and Fylde HMC, 1969–72; Regional Manpower Officer, Leeds RHB, 1972–74; District Administrator, York Health Dist, 1974–82; Regional Administrator, Yorkshire RHA, 1982–85; Dist Gen. Man., Durham HA, 1985–92. Member: National Staff Cttee for Admin. and Clerical Staff in NHS, 1973–82; General Nursing Council for England and Wales, 1978–83; English Nat. Board for Nursing, Midwifery and Health Visiting, 1980–87; NHS Trng Authority, 1988–91. Director, Methodist Chapel Aid Assoc. Ltd, 1978–. *Publication:* (ed) Hospital Traffic and Supply Problems, 1968. *Recreations:* walking, music, visiting the Shetland Isles. *Address:* Forge House, Ferryman's Walk, Main Street, Nether Poppleton, York YO2 6HZ.
See also J. H. Holroyd.

HOLROYDE, Geoffrey Vernon; Director of Coventry Cathedral Chapter House Choir, since 1982; student at Birmingham Conservatoire, since 1992; *b* 18 Sept. 1928; *s* of late Harold Vincent Holroyde and Kathleen Olive (*née* Glover); *m* 1960, Elizabeth Mary, *d* of Rev. E. O. Connell; two *s* two *d*. *Educ:* Wrekin Coll.; Birmingham Univ.; BSc. ARCO. Royal Navy, 1949–54 and 1956–61; School-master, Welbeck Coll., 1954–56; English Electric, becoming Principal of Staff Coll., Dunchurch, 1961–70; British Leyland, Head Office Training Staff, 1970–71; Head, Sidney Stringer Sch. and Community Coll., Coventry, 1971–75; Dir, Coventry (formerly Coventry Lanchester) Polytechnic, 1975–87; Higher Educn Adviser to Training Commn, 1987–88; Dir, GEC Management Coll., Dunchurch, 1989–92. Chairman: Industrial Links Adv. Gp to Cttee of Dirs of Polytechnics, 1980–87; National Forum for the Performing Arts in Higher Educn, 1987–91; Develt Training Steering Gp, 1983–88; Mem., W Midlands RHA, 1986– (Chm., Non Clinical Res. Cttee; Vice-Chm., AIDS Task Force); Mem., RSA Educn Industry Forum, 1986–90. Dir of Music, St Mary's Church, Warwick, 1962–72. Mem., Exec. Cttee, British Fedn of Young Choirs, 1993–. Mem. Council, Upper Avon Navigation Trust, 1994–. Governor, 1978–91, Trustee, 1979–91, Chm., Governing Body, 1984–89, Brathay Hall Trust; Chm. Trustees, St Mary's Hall, Warwick, 1984–90; Governor: Mid Warwicks Coll. of Further Educn, 1976–87; Kings School, Worcester, 1983–88. Hon. Life Mem., RSCM, 1970. *Publications:* Managing People, 1968; Delegations, 1968; Communications, 1969; Organs of St Mary's Church, Warwick, 1969. *Recreations:* music (organ and choir), canals, sailing, outdoor pursuits. *Address:* 38 Coten End, Warwick CV34 4NP. *T:* Warwick (01926) 492329.

HOLT, Christopher Robert Vesey, CVO 1976; VRD 1952; Member of London Stock Exchange, 1938–82; *b* 17 Oct. 1915; *s* of late Vice-Adm. R. V. Holt, CB, DSO, MVO, and Evelyn Constance Holt; *m* 1945, Margaret Jane Venetia, *d* of late Sir Michael Albert James Malcolm, 10th Bt; one *s* one *d*. *Educ:* Eton. Partner, James Capel & Co., Stockbrokers, 1938, Sen. Partner, 1968–70, Chm. (on firm becoming a company), 1970–75, Dir, 1975–76. Served RNVR, War of 1939–45, mostly in destroyers; retd with rank of Lieut-Comdr, 1957. *Recreations:* painting, wildlife. *Address:* Westbury Manor, West Meon, Petersfield, Hants GU32 1ND. *Clubs:* Boodle's, Lansdowne.

HOLT, Constance, CBE 1975; Area Nursing Officer, Manchester Area Health Authority (Teaching), 1973–77; *b* 5 Jan. 1924; *d* of Ernest Biddulph and of Ada Biddulph (*née* Robley); *m* 1975, Robert Lord Holt, OBE, FRCS. *Educ:* Whalley Range High Sch. for Girls, Manchester; Manchester Royal Infirmary (SRN); Queen Charlotte's Hosp., London; St Mary's Hosp., Manchester (SCM); Royal Coll. of Nursing, London Univ. (Sister Tutor Dipl.); Univ. of Washington (Florence Nightingale Schol., Fulbright Award). Nursing Officer, Min. of Health, 1959–65; Chief Nursing Officer: United Oxford Hosps, 1965–69; United Manchester Hosps, 1969–73. Pres., Assoc. of Nurse Administrators (formerly Assoc. of Hosp. Matrons), 1972–. Reader licensed by Bishop of Sodor and Man. Hon. Lectr, Dept of Nursing, Univ. of Manchester, 1972. Hon. MA Manchester, 1980. *Publications:* articles in British and internat. nursing press. *Recreations:* reading, gardening, music. *Address:* Seabank, Marine Terrace, Port St Mary, Isle of Man.

HOLT, Prof. David, (Tim), PhD; FSS: Director, Central Statistical Office and Head, Government Statistical Service, since 1995; Leverhulme Professor of Social Statistics, Southampton University, since 1980 (on leave of absence); *b* 29 Oct. 1943; *s* of late Ernest Frederick Holt and of Catherine Rose (*née* Finn); *m* 1966, Jill Blake; one *s* one *d*. *Educ:* Coopers' Company's Sch.; Exeter Univ. (BSc Maths 1966; PhD Mathematical Stats 1969). FSS 1973. Res. Fellow, Univ. of Exeter, 1969–70; Survey Statistician, Statistics Canada, 1970–73 (Consultant, 1974–75); University of Southampton: Lectr in Social Stats, 1973–80; Dean, Social Sci. Faculty, 1981–83; Dep. Vice Chancellor, 1990–95. Consultant: NZ Dept of Stats, 1981; OPCS, 1983, 1987, 1991; ESRC, 1990; Australian Bureau of Stats, 1990; Scientific Advr to Chief Scientist, DHSS, 1983–88. Associate Editor: Jl Royal Statistical Soc. B, 1983–88; Survey Methodology, 1988–; Editor, Jl Royal Statistical Soc. A: Stats and Society, 1991–94. Vice-Pres., Internat. Assoc. of Survey Statisticians, 1989–91 (Scientific Sec., 1985–87); Mem., Internat. Statistical Inst., 1985; Fellow, Amer. Statistical Assoc., 1990. Trustee, Newitt Trust, 1990–. *Publications:* (jtly) Analysis of Complex Surveys, 1989; numerous papers in learned jls. *Recreation:* orienteering. *Address:* Central Statistical Office, Government Offices, Great George Street, SW1P 3AQ. *T:* 0171–270 6155.

HOLT, Jack; *see* Holt, John Lapworth.

HOLT, Sir James (Clarke), Kt 1990; FBA 1978; Professor of Medieval History, 1978–88, and Master of Fitzwilliam College, 1981–88 (Hon. Fellow, 1988), Cambridge University; *b* 26 April 1922; *s* of late Herbert and Eunice Holt; *m* 1950, Alice Catherine Elizabeth Suley; one *s*. *Educ:* Bradford Grammar Sch.; Queen's Coll., Oxford (Hastings Schol.). MA 1947; 1st cl. Modern Hist.; DPhil 1952. Served with RA, 1942–45 (Captain). Harmsworth Sen. Schol., Merton Coll., Oxford, 1947; Univ. of Nottingham: Asst Lectr, 1949; Lectr, 1951; Sen. Lectr, 1961; Prof. of Medieval History, 1962; Reading University: Prof. of History, 1966–78; Dean, Faculty of Letters and Soc. Scis, 1972–76; Professorial Fellow, Emanuel Coll., Cambridge, 1978–81 (Hon. Fellow, 1985). Vis. Prof., Univ. of Calif, Santa Barbara, 1977; Vis. Hinkley Prof., Johns Hopkins Univ., 1983; Vis. JSPS Fellow, Japan, 1986. Raleigh Lectr, British Acad., 1975. Mem., Adv. Council on Public Records, 1974–81. Pres., Royal Historical Soc., 1980–84; Vice-Pres., British Academy, 1987–89. Corres. Fellow, Medieval Acad. of America, 1983. Hon DLitt Reading, 1984. Comdr, Order of Civil Merit (Spain), 1988. *Publications:* The Northerners: a study in the reign of King John, 1961, 2nd edn 1992; Praestita Roll 14–18 John, 1964; Magna Carta, 1965,

2nd edn 1992; The Making of Magna Carta, 1966; Magna Carta and the Idea of Liberty, 1972; The University of Reading: the first fifty years, 1977; Robin Hood, 1982, 2nd edn 1989; (ed with J. Gillingham) War and Government in the Middle Ages, 1984; Magna Carta and Medieval Government, 1985; (with R. Mortimer) Acta of Henry II and Richard I, 1986; (ed) Domesday Studies, 1987; papers in English Historical Review, Past and Present, Economic History Review, Trans Royal Hist. Soc. *Recreations:* mountaineering, cricket, fly-fishing, music. *Address:* 5 Holben Close, Barton, Cambridge CB3 7AQ. *T:* Cambridge (01223) 332041. *Clubs:* National Liberal, MCC; Wayfarers' (Liverpool).

HOLT, (James) Richard (Trist); President, Pensions Appeal Tribunals (England & Wales), since 1993; *b* 17 Aug. 1924; *s* of George Richard Holt and Gladys Floyd Holt (*née* Bennetts); *m* 1st, 1952, Helen Worswick (marr. diss); one *s* one *d*; 2nd, 1977, Patricia Mary Hartley. *Educ:* Giggleswick Sch.; Queen's Coll., Oxford (MA 1950); London Univ. (ext. LLB 1952). Served Royal Signals, 1942–47, commnd 1945. Articled clerk, 1941; admitted solicitor, 1951; called to the Bar, Gray's Inn, 1973. Part-time Chairman: Med. Appeal Tribunals, 1979–; Vaccine Damage Tribunals, 1982–; Pensions Appeal Tribunals, 1985–; Disability Appeal Tribunals, 1992–; Immigration Appeals Adjudicator, 1982–90; Mem., Mental Health Act Commn, 1985–86. Contested (C), Rossendale, 1959. *Publication:* contrib. Law Soc. Gazette. *Recreations:* walking, reading history. *Address:* The Hey Farm, Newton-in-Bowland, near Clitheroe, Lancs BB7 3EE. *T:* Slaidburn (01200) 446213; 48/49 Chancery Lane, WC2A 1JR. *T:* 0171–936 7031. *Club:* Victory Services.

HOLT, John Lapworth, (Jack Holt), OBE 1979; Founder and Director of Jack Holt Ltd and Holt group of companies, designers and suppliers of small boats and their fittings (Managing Director, 1946–76); *b* 18 April 1912; *s* of Herbert Holt and Annie (*née* Dawson); *m* 1936, Iris Eileen Thornton; one *s* one *d*. *Educ:* St Peter's Sch., London; Shoreditch Techn. Inst. (Schol.). Joiner, boat builder and designer, 1929–46; formed Jack Holt Ltd, 1946; designed: first British post-war sailing dinghy class, Merlin; first British factory-made do-it-yourself boat building kit to construct Internat. Cadet, for Yachting World magazine; International Enterprise, National Solo and Hornet, Heron, Rambler, Diamond, Lazy E, GP14, Vagabond, International Mirror Dinghy, Mirror 16, and Pacer; Pandamaran, for World Wildlife Fund. Techn. Adviser to Royal Yachting Assoc. dinghy cttee, 1950–. Jt winner (with Beecher Moore) of 12ft Nat. Championship, 1946 and Merlin Championships, 1946, 1947 and 1949; Merlin Silver Tiller series winner, 1954–56; won Solo Dutch Nat. Championships, 1962. Yachtsman's Award for service to yachting, RYA, 1977. *Recreation:* small boat sailing. *Address:* 17 Elmstead Park Road, West Wittering, West Sussex PO20 8NQ. *T:* Birdham (01243) 3559. *Clubs:* Ranelagh Sailing, Wraysbury Lake Sailing, Chichester Yacht, Aldenham Sailing.

HOLT, John Michael, MD, FRCP; Consultant Physician, John Radcliffe Hospital, Oxford; Fellow of Linacre College, Oxford, since 1968; *b* 8 March 1935; *s* of late Frank Holt, BSc and of Constance Holt; *m* 1959, Sheila Margaret Morton; one *s* three *d*. *Educ:* St Peter's Sch., York; Univ. of St Andrews. MA Oxon; MD St Andrews; MSc Queen's Univ. Ont. Registrar and Lectr, Nuffield Dept of Medicine, Radcliffe Infirmary, Oxford, 1964–66, Cons. Physician 1968; Chm., Medical Staff, Oxford Hosps, 1982–84. University of Oxford: Med. Tutor, 1967–73; Dir of Clinical Studies, 1971–76; Mem., Gen. Bd of Faculties, 1987–91; Chm., Clinical Medicine Bd, 1992–94. Examiner in Medicine: Univ. of Oxford; Hong Kong; London; Glasgow; TCD; RCP. Member: Assoc. of Physicians; Soc. of Apothecaries; Cttee on Safety of Medicines, 1979–86; Oxford RHA, 1984–88. Editor, Qly Jl of Medicine, 1975–92. *Publications:* papers on disorders of blood and various med. topics in BMJ, Lancet, etc. *Recreation:* sailing. *Address:* Old Whitehill, Tackley, Oxon OX5 3AB. *T:* Tackley (0186983) 241. *Club:* Royal Cornwall Yacht (Falmouth).

HOLT, Prof. John Riley, FRS 1964; Professor of Experimental Physics, University of Liverpool, 1966–83, now Emeritus; *b* 15 Feb. 1918; *er s* of Frederick Holt and Annie (*née* Riley); *m* 1949, Joan Silvester Thomas; two *s*. *Educ:* Runcorn Secondary Sch.; University of Liverpool. PhD 1941. British Atomic Energy Project, Liverpool and Cambridge, 1940–45. University of Liverpool: Lecturer, 1945–53, Senior Lecturer, 1953–56, Reader, 1956–66. *Publications:* papers in scientific journals on nuclear physics and particle physics. *Recreation:* gardening. *Address:* Rydalmere, Stanley Avenue, Higher Bebington, Wirral L63 5QE. *T:* 0151–608 2041.

HOLT, Mary; Her Honour Judge Holt; a Circuit Judge, since 1977; *d* of Henry James Holt, solicitor, and of Sarah Holt (*née* Chapman); unmarried. *Educ:* Park Sch., Preston; Girton Coll., Cambridge (MA, LLB, 1st cl. Hons). Called to the Bar, Gray's Inn, 1949 (Atkin Scholar). Practised on Northern circuit. Former Vice-Chm., Preston North Conservative Assoc.; Member: Nat. Exec. Council, 1969–72; Woman's Nat. Advisory Cttee, 1969–70; representative, Central Council, 1969–71. MP (C) Preston N, 1970–Feb. 1974. Contested (C) Preston N, Feb. and Oct. 1974. Dep. Pres., Lancs Br., BRCS, 1976–. Freedom of Cities of Dallas and Denton, Texas, 1987. Badge of Honour, BRCS, 1989. *Publication:* 2nd edn, Benas and Essenhigh's Precedents of Pleadings, 1956. *Recreation:* walking. *Address:* The Sessions House, Preston, Lancs. *Clubs:* Commonwealth Trust, Royal Over Seas League.

HOLT, Sir Michael, Kt 1995; CBE 1981; FCA; Chairman, Eastern Area Conservative Provincial Council, since 1992; *b* 23 Dec. 1927; *s* of Frank Holt, MM, FCA and Helen Gertrude Holt (*née* Wheeler); *m* 1955, Janet Michelle Simon; two *s* one *d*. *Educ:* Epsom Coll.; Downing Coll., Cambridge (MA, LLM). Called to the Bar, Inner Temple, 1953; qualified as Chartered Accountant, 1958; Sen. Partner, Arthur Goddard & Co., Chartered Accountants, 1966–83. Dir, Lay and Wheeler Gp Ltd, 1983, and other cos. External Mem., Lloyds, 1983–. Member: NE Essex HA, 1982–89, 1990–93; Bd of Govs, St John's Hosp. for Diseases of the Skin, 1980–82. Conservative Party: Hon. Treas., 1965–76, Chm., 1983–85, Vice Pres., 1985–95, Colchester Assoc.; Vice Chm., then Chm., N Colchester Assoc., 1985–90; Hon. Treas., 1975–80, Vice Chm., then Dep. Chm., 1986–92, Eastern Area; Pres., N Essex and S Suffolk Eur. Constituency Council, 1994– (Pres., NE Essex, 1991–94); Vice Pres., N Essex Constituency, 1995–; Mem. Exec. Cttee, Nat. Union of Cons. and Unionist Assocs, 1975–83, 1986–. *Recreations:* politics, gardening, book collecting. *Address:* Alresford Grange, Colchester, Essex CO7 8BG. *T:* Colchester (01206) 824200. *Clubs:* St Stephen's Constitutional; Colchester Garrison Officers'.

HOLT, Prof. Peter Malcolm, FBA 1975; FSA; Professor of History of the Near and Middle East, University of London, 1975–82, now Professor Emeritus; *b* 28 Nov. 1918; *s* of Rev. Peter and Elizabeth Holt; *m* 1953, Nancy Bury (*née* Mawle); one *s* one *d*. *Educ:* Lord Williams's Grammar Sch., Thame; University Coll., Oxford (Schol.) (MA, DLitt). Sudan Civil Service: Min. of Education, 1941–53; Govt Archivist, 1954–55. School of Oriental and African Studies, London, 1955–82; Prof. of Arab History, 1964–75. FRHistS 1973; FSA 1980. Hon. Fellow, SOAS, 1985. Gold Medal of Science, Letters and Arts, Repub. of Sudan, 1980. *Publications:* The Mahdist State in the Sudan, 1958, 2nd edn 1970; A Modern History of the Sudan, 1961, 4th edn (with M. W. Daly) as A History of the Sudan from the Coming of Islam to the Present Day, 1988; (co-ed with Bernard Lewis) Historians of the Middle East, 1962; Egypt and the Fertile Crescent, 1966; (ed) Political and Social Change in Modern Egypt, 1968; (co-ed with Ann K. S. Lambton and Bernard Lewis) The Cambridge History of Islam, 1970; Studies in the History of the Near East, 1973; (ed) The Eastern Mediterranean Lands in the period of the Crusades, 1977; The Memoirs of a Syrian Prince, 1983; The Age of the Crusades, 1986; trans. P. Thorau, The Lion of Egypt, 1992; Early Mamluk Diplomacy, 1995; articles in: Encyclopaedia of Islam, Bulletin of SOAS, Sudan Notes and Records, Der Islam, English Historical Rev., etc. *Address:* Dryden Spinney, Kirtlington, Oxford OX5 3HG. *T:* Bletchington (01869) 350477. *Club:* United Oxford & Cambridge University.

HOLT, Richard; *see* Holt, J. R. T.

HOLT, Richard Anthony Appleby; Chairman, 1959–78, Managing Director, 1978–80, Hutchinson Ltd; Chairman: Hutchinson Publishing Group, 1965–80; Hutchinson Printing Trust, 1957–80; *b* 11 March 1920; *s* of Frederick Appleby Holt and Rae Vera Franz (*née* Hutchinson); *m* 1945, Daphne Vivien Pegram; three *s* two *d*. *Educ:* Harrow Sch.; King's Coll., Cambridge. Served War of 1939–45, commissioned 60th Rifles, 1941; demobilised, 1946 (Major). Admitted Solicitor, 1949. Dir, Constable & Co., 1968–90. Gov., Harrow Sch., 1952–82. *Recreation:* lawn tennis. *Address:* 55 Queen's Gate Mews, SW7 5QN. *T:* 0171–589 8469. *Clubs:* All England Lawn Tennis & Croquet (Vice-Pres., 1982–), MCC.

HOLT, Prof. Stephen Campbell, PhD; Rector and Chief Executive, Roehampton Institute, London, since 1988; *b* 27 Sept. 1935; *s* of late E. S. Holt and E. C. Holt; *m* 1st, 1959, Moira Jill Ditchburn (marr. diss.); two *s* one *d*; 2nd, 1989, Anne Ashcroft, two step *d*. *Educ:* Mill Hill Sch.; Emmanuel Coll., Cambridge (MA); PhD Manchester 1966. Nat. Service, RM, 1954–56, 2nd Lieut; worked in family hosiery business, The Holt Hosiery Co., 1959–61; research, Dept of Govt, Univ. of Manchester, 1961–63; Asst Lectr and Lectr, Dept of Political Theory and Instns, Univ. of Sheffield, 1963–69; Vis. Prof., Univ. of Colorado, 1969–70; University of Bradford: Prof. of Eur. Studies, 1970–80; Pro Vice-Chancellor, 1976–78; University of Kent at Canterbury: Prof. of Eur. Studies, 1980–88; Pro Vice-Chancellor, 1986–88. Vis. Prof., Coll. of Europe, Bruges, 1984–88. *Publications:* The Common Market, 1967; Six European States, 1970; (with J. E. Farquharson) Europe from Below, 1975; articles in acad. jls. *Recreations:* family, music, reading. *Address:* Heath Bank, 37 Seymour Road, SW19 5JL.

HOLT, Thelma, CBE 1994; Managing Director, Thelma Holt Ltd, since 1990; *b* 4 Jan. 1932; *d* of David Holt and Ellen Finagh Doyle; *m* 1st, 1956, Patrick Graucob (marr. diss. 1968); 2nd, 1969, David Pressman (marr. diss. 1970). *Educ:* St Ann's Sch., Lytham; RADA. Actress, 1953; Founder, Open Space Theatre (with Charles Marowitz), 1968; Dir, Round House Theatre, 1977; Exec. Producer, Theatre of Comedy, 1983; Head of Touring and Commercial Exploitation, Royal Nat. Theatre, 1985 (Laurence Olivier/Observer Award for Outstanding Achievement, 1987); Exec. Producer, Peter Hall Co., 1989; formed Thelma Holt Ltd, 1990. Member: Arts Council, 1993– (Chm., Drama Adv. Panel, 1994–); Council, RADA. Director: Theatre Investment Fund Ltd; Citizens Theatre, Glasgow. DUniv Middlesex, 1994; Hon. MA Open, 1988. *Recreation:* bargain hunting at antique fairs. *Address:* Waldorf Chambers, 11 Aldwych, WC2B 4DA. *T:* 0171–379 0438.

HOLT, Tim; *see* Holt, David.

HOLTAM, Rev. Nicholas Roderick; Vicar of St Martin-in-the-Fields, since 1995; *b* 8 Aug. 1954; *s* of Sydney Holtam and Kathleen (*née* Freeberne); *m* 1981, Helen Harris; three *s* one *d*. *Educ:* Latymer Grammar Sch., Edmonton; Collingwood Coll., Univ. of Durham (BA Geog.; MA Theol.); King's Coll. London (BD, AKC); Westcott House, Cambridge. Ordained deacon, 1979, priest, 1980; Asst Curate, St Dunstan and All Saints, Stepney, 1979–82; Tutor, Lincoln Theol Coll., 1983–87; Vicar, Christ Church and St John with St Luke, Isle of Dogs, 1988–95. *Recreations:* walking, cycling, reading, exploring London. *Address:* 6 St Martin's Place, WC2N 4JJ. *T:* 0171–930 0089.

HOLTBY, Very Rev. Robert Tinsley, FSA; Dean of Chichester, 1977–89, Dean Emeritus, 1989; *b* 25 Feb. 1921; *o s* of William and Elsie Holtby, Thornton-le-Dale, Yorkshire; *m* 1947, Mary, *er d* of late Rt Rev. Eric Graham; one *s* two *d*. *Educ:* York Minster Choir Sch.; Scarborough Coll. and High School. St Edmund Hall, Oxford, 1939; MA (2nd Class Mod. Hist.), 1946; BD 1957. Choral Scholar, King's Coll., Cambridge, 1944; MA (2nd Class Theol.), 1952. Cuddesdon Theological Coll. and Westcott House, Cambridge, 1943–46. FSA 1990. Deacon, 1946; Priest, 1947. Curate of Pocklington, Yorks, 1946–48. Chaplain to the Forces, 1948–52: 14/20th King's Hussars, Catterick; Singapore; Priest-in-charge, Johore Bahru. Hon. CF, 1952–; Acting Chaplain, King's Coll., Cambridge, 1952; Chaplain and Asst Master, Malvern Coll., 1952–54; Chaplain and Assistant Master, St Edward's Sch., Oxford, 1954–59; Canon Residentiary of Carlisle and Diocesan Dir of Educn, 1959–67, Canon Emeritus, 1967–; Gen. Sec., Nat. Soc. for Promoting Religious Education, 1967–77; Sec., Schs Cttee, 1967–74, Gen. Sec., 1974–77, Church of England Bd of Educn. Vis. Fellow, W Sussex Inst. of Higher Educn, 1990–93. Select Preacher: Cambridge, 1984; Oxford, 1989. Chm., Cumberland Council of Social Service, 1962–67. Chaplain to High Sheriff of Cumberland, 1964, 1966. *Publications:* Daniel Waterland, A Study in 18th Century Orthodoxy, 1966; Carlisle Cathedral Library and Records, 1966; Eric Graham, 1888–1964, 1967; Carlisle Cathedral, 1969; Chichester Cathedral, 1980; Robert Wright Stopford, 1988; Bishop William Otter, 1989; Eric Milner-White, 1991. *Recreations:* music, walking, history. *Address:* 4 Hutton Hall, Huttons Ambo, York YO6 7HW. *T:* Malton (01653) 696366. *Club:* United Oxford & Cambridge University.

HOLTHAM, Gerald Hubert; Director, Institute for Public Policy Research, since 1994; *b* Aberdare, 28 June 1944; *s* of Denis Arthur Holtham and Dilys Maud Holtham (*née* Bull); *m* 1st, 1969, Patricia Mary Blythin (marr. diss. 1976); one *d*; 2nd, 1979, Edith Hodgkinson; one *s* one *d*. *Educ:* King Edward's Sch., Birmingham; Jesus Coll., Oxford (BA 1st Cl. PPE); Nuffield Coll., Oxford (MPhil Econ). ODI, 1973–75; Economist, OECD, Paris, 1975–82; Head, Gen. Econ. Div., Dept of Econs, OECD, 1982–85; Vis. Fellow, Brookings Inst., Washington, 1985–87; Chief Internat. Economist, Shearson Lehman, 1988–91; Econs Fellow, Magdalen Coll., Oxford, 1991–92; Chief Economist, Lehman Brothers, Europe, 1992–94. Vis. Prof., Univ. of Strathclyde, 1990–; Affiliated Prof., London Business Sch., 1992–. *Publications:* (with Roger Busby) Main Line Kill (novel), 1967; (with Arthur Hazlewood) Aid and Inequality in Kenya, 1975; (jtly) Empirical Macroeconomics for Interdependent Economies, 1988; (with Ralph Bryant and Peter Hooper) External Deficits and the Dollar, 1988; articles on economics in learned jls. *Recreations:* gardening, windsurfing, listening to jazz. *Address:* 13 Lansdowne Gardens, SW8 2EQ. *T:* 0171–622 8673.

HOLTON, Michael; Assistant Secretary, Ministry of Defence, 1976–87, retired; *b* 30 Sept. 1927; 3rd *s* of late George Arnold Holton and Ethel (*née* Fountain); *m* 1st, 1951, Daphne Bache (marr. diss. 1987); one *s* two *d*; 2nd, 1987, Joan Catherine Thurman (*née* Hickman), Huddersfield. *Educ:* Finchley County Grammar Sch.; London Sch. of Economics. National Service, RAF, 1946–48; Min. of Food, 1948–54; Air Ministry, 1955–61; MoD, 1961–68; Sec., Countryside Commn for Scotland, 1968–70; Sec., Carnegie UK Trust, 1971–75. Sec., European Conservation Year Cttee for Scotland, 1970; Mem. Council, 1976–93, Hon. Sec., 1988–93, RSNC; Member: YHA, 1946–; Consultative Cttee, Family Fund, 1973–75; Bd, Cairngorm Chairlift Co., 1973–; Museums Assoc., 1976–; Inverliever Lodge

Trust, 1979–90. Hon. Secretary: RAF Mountaineering Assoc., 1952–54; British Mountaineering Council, 1954–59; RAF Mountain Rescue Assoc., 1993–. *Publication:* Training Handbook for RAF Mountain Rescue Teams, 1953. *Address:* 4 Ludlow Way, Hampstead Garden Suburb, N2 0LA. *T:* 0181–444 8582. *Clubs:* Athenæum, Alpine; Himalayan (Bombay).

HOLWELL, Peter, FCA; Principal, University of London, since 1985; *b* 28 March 1936; *s* of Frank Holwell and Helen (*née* Howe); *m* 1959, Jean Patricia Ashman; one *s* one *d*. *Educ:* Palmers Endowed Sch., Grays, Essex; Hendon Grammar Sch.; London Sch. of Econs and Pol Science (BSc Econ). FCA 1972; MBCS 1974; FZS 1988; FRSM 1991. Articled Clerk, 1958–61, Management Consultant, 1961–64, Arthur Andersen and Co.; University of London: Head of Computing, Sch. Exams Bd, 1964–67; Head of University Computing and O & M Unit, 1967–77; Sec. for Accounting and Admin. Computing, 1977–82; Clerk of the Court, 1982–85; Dir, School Exams Council, 1988–94; Mem., Univ. of London Exams and Assessments Council, 1991–. Chm., UCCA Computing Gp, 1977–82. Chm., City and E London FHSA, 1994–. Director: Zoo Operations Ltd, 1988–92; London E Anglian Gp Ltd, 1990–93; Non-exec. Mem., NE Thames RHA, 1990–94. Treas., Zool. Soc. of London, 1991–92. Trustee, Samuel Courtauld (formerly Home House) Trust, 1985–. *Recreations:* walking, music, horology. *Address:* University of London, Malet Street, WC1E 7HU. *T:* 0171–636 8000.

HOLZACH, Dr Robert; Hon. Chairman, Union Bank of Switzerland, since 1988; *b* 28 Sept. 1922. *Educ:* Univ. of Zürich (Dr of Law). Union Bank of Switzerland: trainee, Geneva, London, 1951–52; Vice-Pres., 1956; Senior Vice-Pres., Head of Commercial Div., Head Office, 1962; Mem., Exec. Board, 1966; Exec. Vice-Pres., 1968; President, 1976; Chm. of Board, 1980–88. *Publication:* Herausforderungen, 1988. *Address:* Union Bank of Switzerland, PO Box, 8021 Zurich, Switzerland. *T:* (1) 2341111.

HOMA, Peter Michael; Chief Executive, Leicester Royal Infirmary NHS Trust, since 1993; *b* 3 Jan. 1957; *s* of late Karol Anthony Homa and of Anne Kathleen Homa (*née* Dixon); *m* 1985, Carol Pamela Brunt; one *s* one *d*. *Educ:* Ernest Bevin Sch., London; Univ. of Sussex (BA Hons Econs 1979); Univ. of Hull (MBA 1993). MHSM 1985. Self-employed, 1979–81; nat. admin. trainee, SW Thames RHA, 1981–82; Operational Services Adminr, St George's Hosp., London, 1983–84; Dep. Unit Adminr, Bristol Children's and Maternity Hosps, 1984–86; Dep. Unit Gen. Manager, Acute Services, Bromsgrove and Redditch HA, 1986–89; Leicester Royal Infirmary: Associate Gen. Manager, 1989–90; Unit. Gen. Manager, 1990–93. Pres., Leicester Royal Infirmary Drama, Operatic and Literary Soc., 1991–. *Recreations:* running, cycling, climbing, reading, writing, picture framing. *Address:* Chief Executive's Office, Leicester Royal Infirmary NHS Trust, Leicester LE1 5WW. *T:* Leicester (0116) 258 6311, *Fax:* (0116) 258 5631.

HOMAN, Maj.-Gen. John Vincent, CB 1980; CEng, FIMechE; Facilities Manager, Matra Marconi Space (formerly Marconi Space Systems), Portsmouth, 1982–92; *b* 30 June 1927; *s* of Charles Frederic William Burton Homan and Dorothy Maud Homan; *m* 1953, Ann Bartlett; one *s* two *d*. *Educ:* Haileybury; RMA Sandhurst; RMCS Shrivenham. BSc (Eng). Commnd, REME, 1948; Lt-Col 1967; Comdr REME 2nd Div., 1968–70; Col 1970; MoD 1970–72; CO 27 Comd Workshop REME, 1972–74; Brig. 1974; Dep. Dir, Electrical and Mechanical Engineering, 1st British Corps, 1974–76; Dir of Equipment Management, MoD, 1976–77; Dir Gen., Electrical and Mechanical Engrg, MoD, 1978–79; Maj.-Gen. 1978; Sen. Army Mem., RCDS, 1980–82. Col Comdt, REME, 1982–88. *Recreations:* hill walking, woodwork. *Address:* Roedean, 25 The Avenue, Andover, Hants SP10 3EW. *T:* Andover (01264) 351196. *Club:* Army and Navy.

HOMAN, Rear-Adm. Thomas Buckhurst, CB 1978; *b* 9 April 1921; *s* of late Arthur Buckhurst Homan and Gertrude Homan, West Malling, Kent; *m* 1945, Christine Oliver; one *d*. *Educ:* Maidstone Grammar Sch. RN Cadet, 1939; served War of 1939–45 at sea; Comdr 1958; Captain 1965; Defence Intell. Staff, 1965; Sec. to Comdr Far East Fleet, 1967; idc 1970; Dir Naval Officer Appts (S), 1971; Captain HMS Pembroke, 1973; Rear-Adm. 1974; Dir Gen., Naval Personal Services, 1974–78. Sub-Treasurer, Inner Temple, 1978–85. *Recreations:* reading, theatre, staying at home, cooking. *Address:* 602 Hood House, Dolphin Square, SW1V 3NJ. *T:* 0171–798 8434. *Clubs:* Army and Navy, Garrick.

HOME; *see* Douglas-Home.

HOME, 14th Earl of [disclaimed his peerages for life, 23 Oct. 1963]; *see under* Home of the Hirsel, Baron and Douglas-Home, Hon. D. A. C.

HOME OF THE HIRSEL, Baron *cr* 1974 (Life Peer), of Coldstream; **Alexander Frederick Douglas-Home,** KT 1962; PC 1951; DL; Chancellor, Order of the Thistle, 1973–92; First Chancellor of Heriot-Watt University, 1966–77; *b* 2 July 1903; *e s* of 13th Earl of Home (*d* 1951), KT, and Lilian (*d* 1966), *d* of 4th Earl of Durham; *S* father, 1951, but disclaimed his peerages for life, 23 Oct. 1963; *m* 1936, Elizabeth Hester (*d* 1990), 2nd *d* of late Very Rev. C. A. Alington, DD; one *s* three *d*. *Educ:* Eton; Christ Church, Oxford. MP (U) South Lanark, 1931–45; MP (C) Lanark Div. of Lanarkshire, 1950–51; Parliamentary Private Sec. to the Prime Minister, 1937–40; Joint Parliamentary Under-Sec., Foreign Office, May-July 1945; Minister of State, Scottish Office, 1951–April 1955; Sec. of State for Commonwealth Relations, 1955–60; Dep. Leader of the House of Lords, 1956–57; Leader of the House of Lords, and Lord Pres. of the Council, 1959–60; Sec. of State for Foreign Affairs, 1960–63; MP (U) Kinross and W Perthshire, Nov. 1963–Sept. 1974; Prime Minister and First Lord of the Treasury, Oct. 1963–64; Leader of the Opposition, Oct. 1964–July 1965; Sec. of State for Foreign and Commonwealth Affairs, 1970–74. Hon. Pres., NATO Council, 1973. Captain, Royal Co. of Archers, Queen's Body Guard for Scotland, 1973. Mem., National Farmers' Union, 1964. DL Lanarkshire, 1960. Hon. DCL Oxon., 1960; Hon. Student of Christ Church, Oxford, 1962; Hon. LLD: Harvard, 1961; Edinburgh, 1962; Aberdeen, 1966; Liverpool, 1967; St Andrews, 1968; Hon. DSc Heriot-Watt, 1966. Hon. Master of the Bench, Inner Temple, 1963; Grand Master, Primrose League, 1966–84; Pres. of MCC, 1966–67. Freedom of Selkirk, 1963; Freedom of Edinburgh, 1969; Freedom of Coldstream, 1972. Hon. Freeman: Skinners' Co., 1968; Grocers' Co., 1977. *Publications:* The Way the Wind Blows (autobiog.), 1976; Border Reflections, 1979; Letters to a Grandson, 1983. *Address:* House of Lords, SW1A 0PW; The Hirsel, Coldstream, Berwickshire TD12 4LP. *T:* Coldstream (01890) 882345; Castlemains, Douglas, Lanarkshire. *T:* Douglas, (Lanarks) (01555) 851241.
See also Hon. D. A. C. Douglas-Home, Duke of Sutherland.

HOME, Anna Margaret, OBE 1993; Head of Children's Programmes, BBC Television, since 1986; *b* 13 Jan. 1938; *d* of James Douglas Home and Janet Mary (*née* Wheeler). *Educ:* Convent of Our Lady, St Leonard's-on-Sea, Sussex; St Anne's Coll., Oxford (MA (Hons) Mod. Hist.). BBC Radio Studio Man., 1960–64; Res. Asst, Dir, Producer, Children's TV, 1966–70; Exec. Producer, BBC Children's Drama Unit, 1970–81: responsible for series such as Lizzie Dripping, Bagthorpe Saga, Moon Stallion; started Grange Hill, 1977; Controller of Programmes SE, later Dep. Dir of Programmes, TVS (one of the original franchise gp), 1981–86. FRTS 1987. Pye Award for distinguished services to children's television, 1984; Eleanor Farjeon Award for services to children's literature, 1989; Judges Award, RTS, 1993. *Publication:* Into the Box of Delights: a history of children's television, 1993. *Recreations:* theatre, literature, travel, gardening. *Address:* c/o BBC Television, Television Centre, Wood Lane, W12 7RJ. *T:* 0181–576 1875.

HOME, Prof. George, BL; FCIBS; Professor of International Banking, Heriot-Watt University, Edinburgh, 1978–85, Professor Emeritus, since 1985; *b* 13 April 1920; *s* of George Home and Leah Home; *m* 1946, Muriel Margaret Birleson; two *s* one *d*. *Educ:* Fort Augustus Village Sch.; Trinity Academy, Edinburgh; George Heriot's Sch., Edinburgh; Edinburgh Univ. (BL 1952). FCIBS; FIMgt. Joined Royal Bank of Scotland, 1936; served RAF, 1940–46; Dep. Man. Dir, Royal Bank of Scotland Ltd, 1973–80; Dep. Gp Man. Dir, Royal Bank of Scotland Gp Ltd, 1976–80; Director: Williams & Glyn's Bank Ltd, 1975–80; The Wagon Finance Corp. plc, 1980–85. Vice-Pres., Inst. of Bankers in Scotland, 1977–80. Chm., George Heriot's Trust, 1989–. *Recreations:* fishing, gardening, reading, travel. *Address:* Bickley, 12 Barnton Park View, Edinburgh EH4 6HJ. *T:* 0131–312 7648.

HOME, John Gavin M.; *see* Milne Home.

HOME, Sir William (Dundas), 14th Bt *cr* 1671 (NS), of Blackadder, Co. Berwick; consultant tree surgeon and horticulturalist; *b* 19 Feb. 1968; *s* of late John Home, *er s* of 13th Bt, and of Nancy Helen, *d* of H. G. Elliott, Perth, WA and *widow* of Comdr Ian Macgregor, RAN; *S* grandfather, 1992. *Educ:* Cranbrook Sch., Sydney, NSW. Member: Internat. Soc. of Arboriculture, 1991; Aust. Inst. of Horticulture, 1992. *Recreations:* golf, scuba diving, fishing, tennis. *Heir: uncle* Patrick Home [*b* 4 July 1941; *m* 1984, Catherine Mary, *d* of J. M. Henderson; one *s* one *d*]. *Address:* 32 Parsley Road, Vaucluse, NSW 2030, Australia. *T:* (2) 3373195, 3376740. *Club:* Royal Sydney Golf (Sydney).

HOME ROBERTSON, John David; MP (Lab) East Lothian, since 1983 (Berwick and East Lothian, Oct. 1978–1983); *b* 5 Dec. 1948; *s* of late Lt-Col J. W. Home Robertson and Mrs H. M. Home Robertson; *m* 1977, Catherine Jean Brewster; two *s*. *Educ:* Ampleforth Coll.; West of Scotland Coll. of Agriculture. Farmer. Mem., Berwicks DC, 1975–78; Mem., Borders Health Bd, 1976–78. Chm., Eastern Borders CAB, 1977. Opposition Scottish Whip, 1983–84; opposition spokesman on agric., 1984–87, 1988–90, on Scotland, 1987–88. Member: Select Cttee on Scottish affairs, 1980–83; Select Cttee on Defence, 1990–. Chm., Scottish Gp of Lab MPs, 1983. Founder, Paxton Trust, 1989. *Address:* House of Commons, SW1A 0AA. *T:* 0171–219 4135. *Clubs:* East Lothian Labour, Prestonpans Labour.

HONDERICH, Prof. Edgar Dawn Ross, (Ted), PhD; Grote Professor of the Philosophy of Mind and Logic, University College London, since 1988; *b* 30 Jan. 1933; *s* of John William Honderich and Rae Laura Armstrong, Baden, Canada; *m* 1st, 1964, Pauline Ann Marina Goodwin (marr. diss. 1972), *d* of Paul Fawcett Goodwin and Lena Payne, Kildare; one *s* one *d*; 2nd, 1989, Jane Elizabeth O'Grady, *d* of Major Robert O'Grady and Hon. Joan Ramsbotham, Bath. *Educ:* Kitchener Sch., Kitchener, Canada; Lawrence Park Sch., Toronto; University Coll., Univ. of Toronto (BA 1959); University Coll. London (PhD 1968). Literary Editor, Toronto Star, 1957–59; Lectr in Phil., Univ. of Sussex, 1962–64; Lectr in Phil., 1964–73, Reader in Phil., 1973–83, Prof. of Phil., 1983–88, and Head of Dept of Philosophy, 1988–93, UCL; Chm., Bd of Phil Studies, Univ. of London, 1986–89. Vis. Prof., Yale Univ., and CUNY, 1970. Editor: Internat. Library of Philosophy and Scientific Method, 1966–; Penguin philosophy books, 1967–; The Arguments of the Philosophers, 1968–; The Problems of Philosophy: their past and present, 1984–; radio, television, journalism. *Publications:* Punishment: the supposed justifications, 1969, 4th edn 1989; (ed) Essays on Freedom of Action, 1973; (ed) Social Ends and Political Means, 1976; Violence for Equality: inquiries in political philosophy (incorporating Three Essays on Political Violence, 1976), 1980, 2nd edn 1989; (ed with Myles Burnyeat) Philosophy As It Is, 1979; (ed) Philosophy Through Its Past, 1984; (ed) Morality and Objectivity, 1985; A Theory of Determinism: the mind, neuroscience, and life-hopes, 1988, 2nd edn, as The Consequences of Determinism, 1990; Mind and Brain, 1990; Conservatism, 1990; How Free Are You? The Determinism Problem, 1993; (ed) The Oxford Companion to Philosophy, 1995; phil articles in Amer. Phil Qly, Analysis, Inquiry, Jl of Theoretical Biol., Mind, Phil., Pol Studies, Proc. Aristotelian Soc., etc. *Recreations:* cycling, wine. *Address:* Department of Philosophy, University College London, Gower Street, WC1E 6BT. *T:* 0171–380 7115/7116; 4 Keats Grove, NW3 2RT. *T:* 0171–435 2687. *Clubs:* Beefsteak, Garrick.

HONDROS, Ernest Demetrios, DSc; FRS 1984; Director: Petten Establishment, Commission of European Communities' Joint Research Centre, 1985–95; Institute of Advanced Materials, Petten (Netherlands) and Ispra (Italy), 1988–95; Visiting Professor, Department of Materials, Imperial College of Science, Technology and Medicine, since 1988; *b* 18 Feb. 1930; *s* of Demetrios Hondros and Athanasia Paleologos; *m* 1968, Sissel Kristine Garder-Olsen; two *s*. *Educ:* Univ. of Melbourne (DSc MSc); Univ. of Paris (Dr d'Univ.). CEng, FIM. Research Officer, CSIRO Tribophysics Laboratory, Melbourne, 1955–59; Research Fellow, Univ. of Paris, Lab. de Chimie Minérale, 1959–62; National Physical Laboratory: Sen. Research Officer, Metallurgy Div., 1962–65; Principal Res. Fellow, 1965–68; Sen. Principal Res. Officer (Special Merit), 1974; Supt, Materials Applications Div., 1979–85. Membre d'Honneur, Société Française de Métallurgie, 1986; Mem., Academia Europaea, 1988. Rosenhain Medallist, Metals Soc., 1976; Howe Medal, Amer. Soc. for Metals, 1978; A. A. Griffiths Medal and Prize, Inst. of Metals, 1987. *Publications:* numerous research papers and reviews in learned jls. *Recreations:* music, literature, walking. *Address:* 37 Ullswater Crescent, Kingston Vale, SW15 3RG. *T:* and *Fax:* 0181–549 9526.

HONE, David; landscape and portrait painter; President, Royal Hibernian Academy of Arts, 1978–83; *b* 14 Dec. 1928; *s* of Joseph Hone and Vera Hone (*née* Brewster); *m* 1962, Rosemary D'Arcy; two *s* one *d*. *Educ:* Baymount School; St Columba's College; University College, Dublin. Studied art at National College of Art, Dublin, and later in Italy. Hon. RA, HRSA (ex-officio). *Recreations:* fishing, photography. *Address:* 25 Lower Baggot Street, Dublin 2, Ireland. *T:* (1) 6763746.

HONE, Michael Stuart, OBE 1993 (MBE 1978); HM Diplomatic Service; Ambassador and Consul-General, Iceland, since 1993; *b* 19 May 1936; *s* of William John Hone and Marguerite (*née* Howe); *m* 1st, 1957; three *s*; 2nd, 1983, Dr Elizabeth Ann Balmer; one *s* one *d*. *Educ:* Westham Secondary Sch. Entered RN 1951; joined CRO, 1961; served Kingston, Nairobi, Lisbon, Bridgetown; FCO 1972; served Beirut, Baghdad, Canberra; Resident British Rep., St Vincent and Grenadines; Chief Secretary, St Helena, 1990. *Recreations:* family, walking, golf, water colour painting. *Address:* c/o Foreign and Commonwealth Office, SW1A 4AH.

HONE, Robert Monro, MA; Headmaster, Exeter School, 1966–79; *b* 2 March 1923; *s* of late Rt Rev. Campbell R. Hone; *m* 1958, Helen Isobel, *d* of late Col H. M. Cadell of Grange, OBE; three *d*. *Educ:* Winchester Coll. (Scholar); New Coll., Oxford (Scholar). Rifle Brigade, 1942–45. Asst Master, Clifton Coll., 1948–65 (Housemaster, 1958–65). *Address:* St Madron, Throwleigh, Okehampton, Devon EX20 2HX.

HONEY, Michael; Chief Executive, Gloucestershire County Council, since 1990; *b* 18 Nov. 1941; *s* of Denis Honey and Mary Honey (*née* Henderson); four *d*. *Educ:* Clifton

College; Regent Street Polytechnic (DipArch); Columbia Univ. MArch (Urban Design); MSc (City Planning). City Planner, Boston Redevelopment Authority, 1968–70; Corporate Planning Manager, Bor. of Greenwich, 1970–74; Head, Exec. Office, Bor. of Croydon, 1974–80; Chief Executive: Bor. of Richmond upon Thames, 1980–88; LDDC, 1988–90. *Recreations:* flying, sailing. *Address:* Shire Hall, Gloucester GL1 2TG.

HONEY, Air Vice-Marshal Robert John, CB 1991; CBE 1987; Director, RAF Sports Board, since 1994; *b* 3 Dec. 1936; *s* of F. G. Honey; *m* 1956, Diana Chalmers; one *s* one *d*. *Educ:* Ashford Grammar Sch. Joined RAF as pilot, 1954; served: Germany, 1956–59; Singapore, 1961–64; Canada, 1968–69; India, 1982; UK intervening years; Dep. Commander RAF Germany, 1987–89; Air Sec., 1989–94. Mountaineering expedns to Mulkila, India, 1979, Masherbrum, Pakistan, 1981. *Recreations:* climbing, mountaineering, ski-ing. *Club:* Royal Air Force.

HONEYCOMBE, Gordon; *see* Honeycombe, R. G.

HONEYCOMBE, Sir Robert (William Kerr), Kt 1990; FRS 1981; FEng 1980; Goldsmiths' Professor of Metallurgy, University of Cambridge, 1966–84, now Emeritus; *b* 2 May 1921; *s* of William and Rachel Honeycombe (*née* Kerr); *m* 1947, June Collins; two *d*. *Educ:* Geelong Coll.; Univ. of Melbourne. Research Student, Department of Metallurgy, University of Melbourne, 1941–42; Research Officer, Commonwealth Scientific and Industrial Research Organization, Australia, 1942–47; ICI Research Fellow, Cavendish Laboratory, Cambridge, 1948–49; Royal Society Armourers and Brasiers' Research Fellow, Cavendish Laboratory, Cambridge, 1949–51; Senior Lecturer in Physical Metallurgy, University of Sheffield, 1951–55; Professor, 1955–66. Fellow of Trinity Hall, Cambridge, 1966–73, Hon. Fellow, 1975; Pres. 1973–80, Fellow, 1980–88, Emeritus Fellow, 1988, Clare Hall, Cambridge. Pres., Instn of Metallurgists, 1977; Pres., Metals Soc., 1980–81; Vice-Pres., Royal Institution, 1977–78; Treas., 1986–92, a Vice Pres., 1986–92, Royal Soc. Visiting Professor: University of Melbourne, 1962; Stanford Univ., 1965; Monash Univ., 1974; Hatfield Meml Lectr, Sheffield Univ., 1979. Hon. Member: Iron and Steel Inst. of Japan, 1979; Soc. Française de Métallurgie, 1981; Japan Inst. of Metals, 1983 (Gold Medallist, 1983); Indian Inst. of Metals, 1984. Mem. Ct of Assts, Goldsmiths' Co., 1977– (Prime Warden, 1986–87). Hon. DAppSc Melbourne, 1974; Hon. DMet Sheffield, 1983; Dr *hc* Montanistischen Wissenschaften Leoben, 1990. Rosenhain Medal of Inst. of Metals, 1959; Sir George Beilby Gold Medal, 1963; Ste-Claire-Deville Medal, 1971; Inst. of Metals Lectr and Mehl Medallist, AIME, 1976; Sorby Award, Internat. Metallographic Soc., 1986. *Publications:* The Plastic Deformation of Metals, 1968, 2nd edn 1984; Steels—Microstructure and Properties, 1981, 2nd edn (with H. K. D. H. Bhadeshia) 1995; papers in Proc. Royal Soc., Metal Science, etc. *Recreations:* gardening, photography, walking. *Address:* Barrabool, 46 Main Street, Hardwick, Cambridge CB3 7QS. *T:* Madingley (01954) 210501.

HONEYCOMBE, (Ronald) Gordon; author, playwright, television presenter, actor and narrator; *b* Karachi, British India, 27 Sept. 1936; *s* of Gordon Samuel Honeycombe and Dorothy Louise Reid Fraser. *Educ:* Edinburgh Acad.; University Coll., Oxford (MA English). National Service, RA, mainly in Hong Kong, 1955–57. Announcer: Radio Hong Kong, 1956–57; BBC Scottish Home Service, 1958; actor: with Tomorrow's Audience, 1961–62; with RSC, Stratford-on-Avon and London, 1962–63; Newscaster with ITN, 1965–77; Newscaster, TV-am, 1984–89. Acted in TV plays, series and shows including: That Was the Week that Was, 1964; The Brack Report, 1982; CQ, 1984; Nice People, 1993; appearances as TV presenter include: (also writer), A Family Tree and Brass Rubbing (documentaries), 1973; The Late Late Show (series), and Something Special (series), 1978; Family History (series), 1979; appearances as TV narrator include: Arthur C. Clarke's Mysterious World (series), 1980; A Shred of Evidence, 1984; stage appearances include: Play-back 625, Royal Court, 1970; Paradise Lost, York and Old Vic, 1975; Suspects, Swansea, 1989; Aladdin, Wimbledon, 1989–90, Bournemouth, 1990–91; Run For Your Wife!, tour, 1990; film appearances include: The Medusa Touch, The Fourth Protocol. Author of stage productions: The Miracles, Oxford, 1960 and (perf. by RSC), Southwark Cath., 1963 and Consett, 1970; The Princess and the Goblins (musical), Great Ayton, 1976; Paradise Lost, York, Old Vic and Edinburgh Fest., 1975–77; Waltz of my Heart, Bournemouth, 1980; Lancelot and Guinevere, Old Vic, 1980; author of TV plays: The Golden Vision (with Neville Smith), 1968; Time and Again, 1974 (Silver Medal, Film and TV Fest., NY, 1975); The Thirteenth Day of Christmas, 1986; radio dramatisations (all Radio 4): Paradise Lost, 1975; Lancelot and Guinevere, 1976; A King shall have a Kingdom, 1977; devised Royal Gala performances: God save the Queen!, Chichester, 1977; A King shall have a Kingdom, York, 1977. Directed and prod, The Redemption, Fest. of Perth, 1990. Pres., Bournemouth Operatic Soc., 1979–81. *Publications: non-fiction:* Nagasaki 1945, 1981; Royal Wedding, 1981; The Murders of the Black Museum, 1982; The Year of the Princess, 1982; Selfridges, 1984; TV-am's Official Celebration of the Royal Wedding, 1986; More Murders of the Black Museum, 1993; *documentary novels:* Adam's Tale, 1974; Red Watch, 1976; Siren Song, 1992; *fiction:* The Redemption (play), 1964; Neither the Sea nor the Sand, 1969; Dragon under the Hill, 1972; The Edge of Heaven, 1981; contrib. national newspapers and magazines. *Recreations:* brass-rubbing, bridge, crosswords. *Address:* c/o Jules Bennett, 19 Lainson Street, W4 4NL. *T:* 0181–875 9515.

HONEYSETT, Martin; cartoonist and illustrator, since 1969; *b* 20 May 1943; *s* of Donovan Honeysett and Kathleen Ethel Ivy Probert; *m* 1970, Maureen Elizabeth Lonergan (marr. diss. 1988); one *s* one *d* (and one *s* decd). *Educ:* Selhurst Grammar Sch.; Croydon Art Coll. (for one year). After leaving Art Coll., 1961, spent several years in NZ and Canada doing variety of jobs; returned to England, 1968; started drawing cartoons part-time, 1969; became full-time freelance, working for Punch, Private Eye and other magazines and newspapers, 1972; illustrator of series of books by the author/poet, Ivor Cutler. *Publications:* Private Eye Cartoonists No 4, 1974; Honeysett at Home, 1976; The Motor Show Book of Humour, 1978; The Not Another Book of Old Photographs Book, 1981; Microphobia, 1982; The Joy of Headaches, 1983; Fit for Nothing, 1984; Animal Nonsense Rhymes, 1984; The Best of Honeysett, 1985. *Recreations:* walking, swimming. *Address:* 52 Eversfield Place, St Leonards-on-Sea, East Sussex TN37 6DB. *T:* Hastings (01424) 717266.

HONIG, His Honour Frederick; a Circuit Judge (formerly a County Court Judge), 1968–86; *b* 22 March 1912; 2nd *s* of late Leopold Honig; *m* 1940, Joan, *o d* of late Arthur Burkart. *Educ:* Berlin and Heidelberg Univs. LLD (Hons) Heidelberg, 1934. Barrister, Middle Temple, 1937. War service, 1940–47: Capt., JAG's Dept; Judge Advocate in civilian capacity, 1947–48; subseq. practised at Bar. *Publications:* (jtly) Cartel Law of the European Economic Community, 1963; contribs to Internat. Law Reports (ed. Lauterpacht) and legal jls, incl. Amer. Jl of Internat. Law, Internat. and Comparative Law Quarterly, Law Jl, Propriété Industrielle, etc. *Recreations:* foreign languages, country walking. *Address:* Lamb Building, Temple, EC4Y 7AS. *T:* 0171–353 1612.

HONIGMANN, Prof. Ernst Anselm Joachim, DLitt; FBA 1989; Joseph Cowen Professor of English Literature, University of Newcastle upon Tyne, 1970–89, now Professor Emeritus; *b* Breslau, Germany, 29 Nov. 1927; *s* of Dr H. D. S. Honigmann and U. M. Honigmann (*née* Heilborn); *m* 1958, Dr Elsie M. Packman (*d* 1994); two *s* one *d*. *Educ:* Glasgow Univ. (MA 1948; DLitt 1966); Merton Coll., Oxford (BLitt 1950). Asst Lectr, 1951, Lectr, Sen. Lectr and Reader, 1954–67, Glasgow Univ.; Fellow, Shakespeare Inst., Birmingham Univ., 1951–54; Reader, Univ. of Newcastle upon Tyne, 1968–70. Jt Gen. Ed., The Revels Plays, 1976–. *Publications:* The Stability of Shakespeare's Text, 1965; Shakespeare: Seven Tragedies, the dramatist's manipulation of response, 1976; Shakespeare's Impact on his Contemporaries, 1982; Shakespeare: the lost years, 1985; John Weever: a biography, 1987; Myriad-minded Shakespeare, 1989; The Texts of Othello, 1996; *editor:* King John, 1954; Milton's Sonnets, 1966; The Masque of Flowers, 1967; Richard III, 1968; Twelfth Night, 1971; Paradise Lost, Book 10 (with C. A. Patrides), 1972; Shakespeare and his Contemporaries: essays in comparison, 1986; (with Susan Brock) Playhouse Wills 1558–1642, 1993; Othello, 1996. *Recreations:* grandchildren, gardening, travel. *Address:* 18 Wilson Gardens, Newcastle upon Tyne NE3 4JA.

HONORÉ, Prof. Antony Maurice; QC 1987; DCL Oxon; FBA 1972; Regius Professor of Civil Law, University of Oxford, 1971–88; Fellow, 1971–89, Acting Warden, 1987–89, All Souls College, Oxford; *b* 30 March 1921; *o s* of Frédéric Maurice Honoré and Marjorie Erskine (*née* Gilbert); *m* 1st, Martine Marie-Odette Genouville; one *s* one *d*; 2nd, Deborah Mary Cowen (*née* Duncan). *Educ:* Diocesan Coll., Rondebosch; Univ. of Cape Town; New Coll., Oxford. Rhodes Scholar, 1940. Union Defence Forces, 1940–45; Lieut, Rand Light Infantry, 1942. BCL 1948. Vinerian Scholar, 1948. Advocate, South Africa, 1951; called to Bar, Lincoln's Inn, 1952, Hon. Bencher, 1971. Lectr, Nottingham Univ., 1948; Rhodes Reader in Roman-Dutch Law, 1957–70, Fellow of Queen's Coll., Oxford, 1949–64, of New Coll., 1964–70. Visiting Professor: McGill, 1961; Berkeley, 1968. Lectures: Hamlyn, Nottingham, 1982; J. H. Gray, Cambridge, 1985; Blackstone, Oxford, 1988; H. L. A. Hart, University Coll., Oxford, 1992. Member: Internat. Acad. of Comparative Law; Accademia Costantiniara. Corresp. Member: Bavarian Acad. of Scis; Serbian Phil. Soc. Hon. LLD: Edinburgh; South Africa; Stellenbosch; Cape Town. *Publications:* (with H. L. A. Hart) Causation in the Law, 1959, 2nd edn 1985; Gaius, 1962; The South African Law of Trusts, 1965, 4th edn 1992; Tribonian, 1978; Sex Law, 1978; (with J. Menner) Concordance to the Digest Jurists, 1980; Emperors and Lawyers, 1981, 2nd edn 1994; The Quest for Security, 1982; Ulpian, 1982; Making Law Bind, 1987. *Address:* 94C Banbury Road, Oxford OX2 6JT. *T:* Oxford (01865) 59684.

HONOUR, (Patrick) Hugh, FRSL; writer; *b* 26 Sept. 1927; *s* of late Herbert Percy Honour and Dorothy Margaret Withers. *Educ:* King's Sch., Canterbury; St Catharine's Coll., Cambridge (BA). Asst to Dir, Leeds City Art Gall. and Temple Newsam House, 1953–54. Guest Curator for exhibn, The European Vision of America, National Gall. of Art, Washington, Cleveland Museum of Art, and, as L'Amérique vue par l'Europe, Grand Palais, Paris, 1976. FRSL 1972. Corresp. FBA 1986 (Serena Medal, 1995). *Publications:* Chinoiserie, 1961 (2nd edn 1973); Companion Guide to Venice, 1965 (rev. edn 1990); (with Sir Nikolaus Pevsner and John Fleming) The Penguin Dictionary of Architecture, 1966 (4th rev. edn 1991); Neo-classicism, 1968 (4th edn 1977); The New Golden Land, 1976; (with John Fleming) The Penguin Dictionary of Decorative Arts, 1977 (rev. edn 1989); Romanticism, 1979; (with John Fleming) A World History of Art, 1982 (Mitchell Prize, 1982) (USA as The Visual Arts: a history, 4th edn 1994); The Image of the Black in Western Art IV, from the American Revolution to World War I, 1989 (Anisfield-Wolf Book Award in Race Relations, 1990); (with John Fleming) The Venetian Hours of Henry James, Whistler and Sargent, 1991; (ed) Edizione Nazionale delle Opere di Antonio Canova, vol. I, Scritti, 1994. *Recreation:* gardening.

HONYWOOD, Sir Filmer (Courtenay William), 11th Bt *cr* 1660; FRICS; Regional Surveyor and Valuer, South Eastern Region, Central Electricity Generating Board, 1978–88; *b* 20 May 1930; *s* of Col Sir William Wynne Honywood, 10th Bt, MC, and Maud Naylor (*d* 1953), *d* of William Hodgson Wilson, Hexgreave Park, Southwell, Notts; *S* father, 1982; *m* 1956, Elizabeth Margaret Mary Cynthia, *d* of Sir Alastair George Lionel Joseph Miller of Glenlee, 6th Bt; two *s* two *d*. *Educ:* Downside; RMA Sandhurst; Royal Agricultural College, Cirencester (MRAC Diploma). Served 3rd Carabiniers (Prince of Wales' Dragoon Guards). Asst Surveyor, Min. of Agriculture, Fisheries and Food, Maidstone, 1966–73; Surveyor, Cockermouth, Cumbria, 1973–74; Senior Lands Officer, South Eastern Region, CEGB, 1974–78; pt time Sen. Valuer, Inland Revenue Valuation Service, Folkestone, 1989–90. Consultant on agricultural compensation/restoration, UK Nirex Ltd, 1988–90. Examiner in Agric., Incorporated Soc. of Estates & Wayleaves Officers, 1989–. *Heir: s* Rupert Anthony Honywood, *b* 2 March 1957. *Address:* Greenway Forstal Farmhouse, Hollingbourne, Maidstone, Kent ME17 1QA. *T:* Maidstone (01622) 880418.

HOOD, family name of **Viscounts Bridport** and **Hood.**

HOOD, 7th Viscount *cr* 1796; **Alexander Lambert Hood;** Bt 1778; Baron (Ire.) 1782, (GB) 1795; Chairman, Petrofina (UK) Ltd, 1982–87 (Director, 1958–87); *b* 11 March 1914; *s* of Rear-Adm. Hon. Sir Horace Hood, KCB, DSO, MVO (*d* 1916) (3rd *s* of 4th Viscount) and Ellen Floyd (*d* 1950), *d* of A. E. Touzalin; *S* brother, 1981; *m* 1957, Diana Maud, CVO 1957, *d* of late Hon. G. W. Lyttelton; three *s*. *Educ:* RN Coll., Dartmouth; Trinity Coll., Cambridge; Harvard Business Sch. RNVR, 1939–45. Director: J. Henry Schroder Wagg & Co., 1957–75; George Wimpey, 1957–90; Tanks Consolidated Investments PLC, 1971–84 (Chm., 1976–83); Benguela Railway Co., 1979–84; Union Minière, 1973–84; Abbott Laboratories Inc., 1971–83; Abbott Laboratories Ltd, 1964–85. Part-time Mem., British Waterways Bd, 1963–73. *Heir: s* Hon. Henry Lyttelton Alexander Hood [*b* 16 March 1958; *m* 1991, Flora, *yr d* of Comdr M. B. Casement; one *s*]. *Address:* 67 Chelsea Square, SW3 6LE. *T:* 0171–352 4952; Loders Court, Bridport, Dorset DT6 3RZ. *T:* Bridport (01308) 22983. *Club:* Brooks's.

HOOD, Sir Harold (Joseph), 2nd Bt *cr* 1922, of Wimbledon, Co. Surrey; TD; Circulation Director: Universe, 1953–60; Catholic Herald, 1961–87; *b* 23 Jan. 1916; *e s* of Sir Joseph Hood, 1st Bt, and Marie Josephine (*d* 1956), *e d* of Archibald Robinson, JP, Dublin; *S* father, 1931; *m* 1946, Hon. Ferelith Rosemary Florence Kenworthy, *o d* of 10th Baron Strabolgi and Doris, *o c* of late Sir Frederick Whitley-Thomson, MP; two *s* two *d* (and one *s* decd). *Educ:* Downside Sch. Mem. Editorial Staff, The Universe, 1936–39; Asst Editor, The Catholic Directory, 1950, Managing Ed., 1959–60; Editor, The Catholic Who's Who, 1952 Edition. 2nd Lieutenant 58th Middx Battalion RE (AA) (TA) 1939; Lieut RA, 1941. GCSG (Holy See) 1986; (KSG 1964; KCSG 1978); Kt of Magistral Grace, SMO Malta, 1972. *Heir: s* John Joseph Harold Hood, *b* 27 Aug. 1952. *Address:* 31 Avenue Road, NW8 6BS. *T:* 0171–722 9088. *Clubs:* Royal Automobile, MCC.

HOOD, James; MP (Lab) Clydesdale, since 1987; *b* 16 May 1948; *m* 1967, Marion McCleary; one *s* one *d*. *Educ:* Lesmahagow Higher Grade, Coatbridge; Motherwell Tech. Coll.; Nottingham Univ. WEA. Miner, Nottingham; NUM official, 1973–85 (Mem., NEC, 1990–92). Mem., Newark and Sherwood Dist Council, 1979–87. Mem., Select Cttee on European Legislation, 1987– (Chm., 1992–); Chairman: All Party Gp on ME (Myalgic Encephalomyetis); Miners Parly Gp, 1990–92. *Recreations:* reading, gardening. *Address:* House of Commons, SW1A 0AA; Ras-al-Ghar, 57 Biggar Road, Symington, Lanarks. *Club:* Lesmahagow Miners Welfare Social (Hon. Mem.).

HOOD, Rear-Adm. John, CBE 1981; CEng, FIMechE; Director General Aircraft (Naval), 1978–81; *b* 23 March 1924; *s* of Charles Arthur Hood, architect, and Nellie Ormiston Brown Lamont; *m* 1948, Julia Mary Trevaskis (*d* 1993); three *s*. *Educ:* Plymouth Coll.; RN Engineering Coll., Keyham. Entered Royal Navy, 1945; RNEC, 1945–48; served in Illustrious, 1948; RN Air Stations, Abbotsinch, Anthorn, RAF West Raynham (NAFDU), 1948–51; HQ Min. of Supply, 1951–53; Air Engineer Officer, 1834 Sqdn, 1953–55, Aeroplane and Armament Experimental Estabt, 1955–57; Staff of Dir Aircraft Maintenance and Repair, 1957–59; AEO, HMS Albion, 1959–61; Sen. Air Engr, RNEC, Manadon, 1961–62; Development Project Officer, Sea Vixen 2, Min. of Aviation, 1962–65; AEO, RNAS, Lossiemouth, 1965–67; Staff of Dir of Officer Appointments (E), 1967–70; Defence and Naval Attaché, Argentina and Uruguay, 1970–73; Sen. Officers War Course, 1973; Asst Dir, Naval Manpower Requirements (Ships), 1974–75; Head of Aircraft Dept (Naval), 1975–78. Comdr 1962, Captain 1969, Rear-Adm. 1979. *Recreations:* sailing, gardening. *Club:* RN Sailing Association.

HOOD, (Martin) Sinclair (Frankland), FSA; FBA 1983; archaeologist; *b* 31 Jan. 1917; *s* of late Lt-Comdr Martin Hood, RN, and late Mrs Martin Hood, New York; *m* 1957, Rachel Simmons; one *s* two *d*. *Educ:* Harrow; Magdalen Coll., Oxford. FSA 1953. British Sch. at Athens: student, 1947–48 and 1951–53; Asst Dir, 1949–51; Dir, 1954–62. Student, British Inst. Archaeology, Ankara, 1948–49. Geddes-Harrower Vis. Prof. of Greek Art and Archaeology, Univ. of Aberdeen, 1968. Took part in excavations at: Dorchester, Oxon, 1937; Compton, Berks, 1946–47; Southwark, 1946; Smyrna, 1948–49; Atchana, 1949–50; Sakca-Gozu, 1950; Mycenae, 1950–52; Knossos, 1950–51, 1953–55, 1957–61, 1973 and 1987; Jericho, 1952; Chios, 1952–55. *Publications:* The Home of the Heroes: The Aegean before the Greeks, 1967; The Minoans, 1971; The Arts in Prehistoric Greece, 1978; various excavation reports and articles. *Address:* The Old Vicarage, Great Milton, Oxford OX44 7PB. *T:* Great Milton (01844) 279202. *Club:* Athenæum.

HOOD, Prof. Neil, FRSE; Professor of Business Policy, since 1979, and Director, Strathclyde International Business Unit, since 1992, University of Strathclyde; *b* 10 Aug. 1943; *s* of Andrew Hood and Elizabeth Taylor Carruthers; *m* 1966, Anna Watson Clark; one *s* one *d*. *Educ:* Wishaw High Sch.; Univ. of Glasgow. MA, MLitt; FRSE 1987. Res. Fellow, Scottish Coll. of Textiles, 1966–68; Lectr, later Sen. Lectr, Paisley Coll. of Technol., 1968–78; Economic Advr, Scottish Economic Planning Dept, 1979; University of Strathclyde: Associate Dean, 1982–85, Dean, 1985–87, Strathclyde Business Sch.; Co-Dir, Strathclyde Internat. Business Unit, 1983–87; Special Advr to Dep. Principal (Develt), then Principal (Develt), 1991–94. Dir, Locate In Scotland, 1987–89, and Dir, Employment and Special Initiatives, 1989–90, Scottish Develt Agency (on secondment). Vis. Prof. of Internat. Business, Univ. of Texas, Dallas, 1981; Vis. Prof., Stockholm Sch. of Economics, 1983–89. Trade Adviser, UNCTAD-GATT, 1980–85; Economic Consultant to Sec. of State for Scotland, 1980–87; Consultant to: Internat. Finance Corp., World Bank, 1982–84, 1991–; UN Centre on Transnational Corporations, 1982–84. Mem., Irvine Develt Corp., 1985–87. Non-executive Director: Euroscot Meat Exports Ltd, 1983–86; Scottish Develt Finance Ltd, 1984–90, 1993–; Lanarkshire Industrial Field Executive Ltd, 1984–86; Prestwick Holdings PLC, 1986–87; Lamberton (Hldgs) Ltd, 1989–92; GA (Hldgs) Ltd, 1990–92; Shanks & McEwan Gp PLC, 1990–94; First Charlotte Assets Trust plc, 1990–92; Charlotte Marketing Services Ltd, 1991–94; Kwik-Fit plc, 1991–; I & S UK Smaller Cos Trust plc, 1992–; Grampian Hldgs plc, 1993–; I & S Trustlink Ltd, 1994–; Chm., John Drinkel Gp Ltd, 1995–. Investment Advr, Castleforth Fund Managers Ltd, 1984–88; Corporate Advr, Scottish Power plc, 1990–; Chm., Scottish Adv. Council, FI Gp, 1992–. Member: various boards, CNAA, 1971–83; Industry and Employment Cttee, ESRC, 1985–87. Pres., European Internat. Business Assoc., 1986. Fellow, European Inst. of Advanced Studies in Management, Brussels, 1985–87. *Publications:* (with S. Young): Chrysler UK: Corporation in transition, 1977; Economics of Multinational Enterprise, 1979; European Development Strategies of US-owned Manufacturing Companies Located in Scotland, 1980; Multinationals in Retreat: the Scottish experience, 1982; Multinational Investment Strategies in the British Isles, 1983; (ed) Industrial Policy and the Scottish Economy, 1984; (with P. Draper, I. Smith and W. Stewart) Scottish Financial Sector, 1987; (ed with J. E. Vahlne) Strategies in Global Competition, 1987; (with S. Young and J. Hamill) Foreign Multinationals and the British Economy, Impact and Policy, 1988; articles on internat. business, marketing and business policy, in various jls. *Recreations:* reading, writing, swimming, golf, gardening. *Address:* Teviot, 12 Carlisle Road, Hamilton ML3 7DB. *T:* Hamilton (01698) 424870.

HOOD, Nicholas; *see* Hood, W. N.

HOOD, Roger Grahame, CBE 1995; FBA 1992; University Reader in Criminology, Director of the Centre for Criminological Research, and Fellow of All Souls College, Oxford, since 1973; *b* 12 June 1936; 2nd *s* of Ronald and Phyllis Hood; *m* 1963, Barbara Blaine Young (marr. diss. 1985); one *d*; *m* 1985, Nancy Stebbing (*née* Lynah). *Educ:* King Edward's Sch., Five Ways, Birmingham; LSE (BSc Sociology); Downing Coll., Cambridge (PhD). Research Officer, LSE, 1961–63; Lectr in Social Admin, Univ. of Durham, 1963–67; Asst Dir of Research, Inst. of Criminology, Univ. of Cambridge, 1967–73; Fellow of Clare Hall, Cambridge, 1969–73. Vis. Prof., Univ. of Virginia Sch. of Law, 1980–90. Expert Consultant, UN, on death penalty, 1988. Member: Parole Bd, 1972–73; SSRC Cttee on Social Sciences and the Law, 1975–79; Judicial Studies Bd, 1979–85; Parole System Review, 1987–88; Pres., British Soc. of Criminology, 1986–89. Sellin-Glueck Award, Amer. Soc. of Criminology, 1986. Mem. Editorial Bd, Crime and Justice. *Publications:* Sentencing in Magistrates' Courts, 1962; Borstal Re-assessed, 1965; (with Richard Sparks) Key Issues in Criminology, 1970; Sentencing the Motoring Offender, 1972; (ed) Crime, Criminology and Public Policy: Essays in Honour of Sir Leon Radzinowicz, 1974; (with Sir Leon Radzinowicz) Criminology and the Administration of Criminal Justice: a bibliography, 1976; (with Sir Leon Radzinowicz) A History of English Criminal Law, vol. 5, The Emergence of Penal Policy, 1986; The Death Penalty: a world-wide perspective, 1989; Race and Sentencing, 1992. *Address:* 63 Iffley Road, Oxford OX4 1EF. *T:* Oxford (01865) 246084.

HOOD, Samuel Harold; Director, Defence Operational Analysis Establishment, Ministry of Defence, 1985–86; *b* 21 Aug. 1926; *s* of Samuel N. and Annie Hood; *m* 1959, Frances Eileen Todd; two *s* four *d*. *Educ:* Larne Grammar Sch., Co. Antrim; Queen's Univ., Belfast (BA Hons Maths). Joined Civil Service, staff of Scientific Advr, Air Min., 1948; Staff of Operational Res. Br., Bomber Comd, 1950; Scientific Officer, BCDU, RAF Wittering, 1954; Operational Res. Br., Bomber Comd, 1959; Staff of Chief Scientist (RAF), 1964; joined DOAE, 1965; Supt, Air Div., DOAE, 1969; Dir, Defence Sci. Divs 1 and 7, MoD, 1974; Head, Systems Assessment Dept, RAE, 1981. *Recreations:* walking, gardening, bird watching. *Address:* 17 Newman Avenue, Brightwater, Nelson, New Zealand.

HOOD, Sinclair; *see* Hood, M. S. F.

HOOD, (William) Nicholas, CBE 1991; FIWEM; Chairman, Wessex Water Plc, since 1989; *b* 3 Dec. 1935; *s* of Sir Tom Hood, KBE, CB, TD and of Joan, *d* of Richmond P. Hellyar; *m* 1st, 1963, Angela Robinson (marr. diss. 1990); one *s* one *d*; 2nd, 1994, Ann E. H. Reynolds. *Educ:* Clifton Coll. FIWEM 1992. CIMgt (CBIM 1990). Served DCLI, 1955–57. NEM General Insce Assoc. Ltd and Credit Insce Assoc. Ltd, 1958–64; G. B. Britton UK Ltd, eventually Sales and Marketing Dir, 1964–70; UBM Gp Plc, eventually Dir of Central Reg., 1970–84; Man. Dir, UBM Overseas Ltd, 1972–82; Dir, HAT Gp Ltd, 1984–86; Chm ., Wessex Water Authy, 1987–89. Director: Bremhill Industries Plc, 1987–93; Provident Life Assoc. Ltd, 1988–; Western Adv. Bd, Nat. Westminster Bank, 1990–92; CU Environmental Trust Plc, 1992–; APV plc, 1994–. Dep. Chm., BITC, 1993–. Mem., DTI/DoE Adv. Cttee on Business and the Envmt, 1991–93. Chm., Water Aid Council, 1990–95; Vice-Chm., Water Services Assoc., 1994; Vice-Pres., IWSA, 1993–; Member: Water Trng Council, 1987–; Foundn for Water Res., 1989–. Mem., Prince of Wales Council, 1993–. *Recreations:* fishing, painting. *Address:* Wessex Water Plc, Wessex House, Passage Street, Bristol BS2 0JQ. *T:* Bristol (0117) 929 0611. *Club:* Army and Navy.

HOOK, David Morgan Alfred, FEng 1985; Consultant, G. Maunsell & Partners, since 1991 (Managing Director, 1984–88; Deputy Chairman, 1989–90); *b* 16 April 1931; *m* 1957, Winifred (*née* Brown); two *s* one *d*. *Educ:* Bancroft's School; Queens' College, Cambridge (MA). FICE, FIStructE. Holland & Hannen and Cubitts, 1954–58; Nuclear Civil Constructors, 1958–62; G. Maunsell & Partners (Consulting Engineers), 1962–, Partner, 1968–. Liveryman, Engineers' Co., 1985. *Publications:* papers in Jl of IStructE. *Recreations:* private flying, golf. *Club:* United Oxford & Cambridge University.

HOOK, Neil Kenneth, MVO 1983; HM Diplomatic Service; Ambassador to Turkmenistan, since 1995; *b* 24 April 1945; *s* of George Edward Hook and Winifred Lucy Hook (*née* Werrell); *m* 1973, Pauline Ann Hamilton; one *s* one *d*. *Educ:* Varndean Grammar Sch., Brighton; Sheffield Univ. (Dip. Management Studies). Joined Diplomatic Service, 1968; served FCO, Moscow, Tokyo; Dhaka, 1980–83; S Africa Dept, FCO, 1984; S Asia Dept, FCO, 1985–86; Tokyo, 1987–92; N America Dept, FCO, 1993–95. *Recreations:* ballads, bridge, Hash House Harriers, photography. *Address:* c/o Foreign and Commonwealth Office, SW1A 2AH.

HOOK, Rt. Rev. Ross Sydney, MC 1945; *b* 19 Feb. 1917; *o s* of late Sydney Frank and Laura Harriet Hook; *m* 1948, Ruth Leslie, *d* of late Rev. Herman Masterman Biddell and Violet Marjorie Biddell; one *s* one *d*. *Educ:* Christ's Hosp.; Peterhouse, Cambridge (MA); Ridley Hall, Cambridge. Asst Curate, Milton, Hants, 1941–43. Chaplain, RNVR (Royal Marine Commandos), 1943–46. Chaplain, Ridley Hall, Cambridge, 1946–48. Select Preacher, University of Cambridge, 1948; Rector, Chorlton-cum-Hardy, Manchester, 1948–52; Rector and Rural Dean, Chelsea, 1952–61; Chaplain: Chelsea Hosp. for Women, 1954–61; St Luke's Hosp., Chelsea, 1957–61; Residentiary Canon of Rochester and Precentor, 1961–65; Treasurer, 1965; Diocesan Dir of Post Ordination Training, 1961–65; Bishop Suffragan of Grantham, 1965–72; Bishop of Bradford, 1972–80; Chief of Staff to Archbishop of Canterbury, 1980–84. Examining Chaplain to Bishop of Rochester, 1961–65, to Bishop of Lincoln, 1966–72; Prebendary of Brampton (Lincoln Cathedral), 1966–72; Dean of Stamford, 1971–72. Chm., Inspections Cttee, Central Advisory Council for the Ministry, 1966–71 (Sec., 1960–66). Hon. DLitt Bradford, 1981. *Recreation:* cricket. *Address:* 23A White Cliff Mill Street, Blandford, Dorset DT11 7BQ.

HOOKER, Michael Ayerst, PhD; Cultural Director, Shi-tennoji International, since 1992; *b* 22 Jan. 1923; *s* of late Albert Ayerst Hooker, late of Broomsleigh Park, Seal Chart, Kent, and Marjorie Mitchell Hooker (*née* Gunson). *Educ:* Marlborough; St Edmund Hall, Oxford (MA 1944); Univ. of the Witwatersrand (PhD 1952). Home Guard, Oxford Univ. Sen. Trng Corps and Army Cadet Force (TARO), 1940–48. British Council, 1945–47; Schoolmaster, England and S Africa, 1947–51; London Diocesan Bd of Educn, 1952–66; Visual Aids and Public Relations, 1953–59. Chm., Fedn of Conservative Students, 1944; Parly Candidate (C) Coventry East, 1955; various offices, Conservative Commonwealth Council, 1955–60. Wells Organisation, fund raising in UK and NZ, 1957–58; Man. Dir, Hooker Craigmyle & Co. Ltd (first institutional fund raising consultants in UK), 1959–72; Man. Dir, Michael Hooker and Associates Ltd, 1972–79; Develt Dir, The Look Wide Trust, 1979–80; Chief Exec. Gov., Truman and Knightley Educn Trust, 1981–87 (Gov., 1977–87); Exec. Dir, 1988–91, Sen. Educnl Advr, 1991–93, Jerwood Award. From 1957, has helped to raise nearly £70 million for various good causes, incl. 13 historic cathedrals, univs, colleges, schools, medical causes, welfare charities, etc. Mem., Adv. Cttee on Charitable Fund Raising, Nat. Council of Social Service, 1971–73. Jt Founder and Chm., Friends of Friends, subseq. Routledge Soc., 1985–90; Trustee: Ross McWhirter Foundn, 1976–; Dicey Trust, 1978–93; Jerwood Oakham Foundn, 1981–92; Police Convalescence and Rehabilitation Trust, 1985–92; Hon. Councillor, NSPCC, 1981–; Governor: Oakham Sch., 1971–83; Shi-tennoji Sch., 1986–; All Hallows House, 1991–; Newton Prep. Sch., 1991–93. Patron, Elton John AIDS Foundn, 1993–. *Publications:* various pamphlets and broadcasts on charities, historic churches, educnl issues, law and taxation, Christian stewardship of money. *Address:* Flat 8, 85 Marine Parade, Brighton BN2 1AJ.

HOOKER, Prof. Morna Dorothy, DD; Lady Margaret's Professor of Divinity, University of Cambridge, since 1976; Fellow of Robinson College, Cambridge, since 1976; *b* 19 May 1931; *d* of Percy Francis Hooker, FIA, and Lily (*née* Riley); *m* 1978, Rev. Dr W. David Stacey, MA (*d* 1993). *Educ:* Univ. of Bristol (research schol.); Univ. of Manchester (research studentship). MA (Bristol 1956, Oxford 1970 and Cambridge 1976); PhD (Manchester 1966); DD (Cambridge 1993). Research Fellow, Univ. of Durham, 1959–61; Lectr in New Testament Studies, King's Coll., London, 1961–70; Lectr in Theology, Oxford, and Fellow, Linacre Coll., 1970–76 (Hon. Fellow, 1980); Lectr in Theology, Keble Coll., 1972–76. Visiting Fellow, Clare Hall, Cambridge, 1974; Visiting Professor: McGill Univ., 1968; Duke Univ., 1987 and 1989. FKC 1979. Lectures: T. W. Manson meml, 1977; A. S. Peake meml, 1978; Henton Davies, 1979; Ethel M. Wood, 1984; James A. Gray, Duke Univ., 1984; W. A. Sanderson, Melbourne, 1986; Didsbury, Manchester, 1988; Brennan, Louisville, 1989; St Paul's, 1989; Perkins, Texas, 1990; Shaffer, Yale, 1995. Pres., SNTS, 1988–89. Jt Editor, Jl of Theological Studies, 1985–. Hon. DLitt Bristol, 1994. *Publications:* Jesus and the Servant, 1959; The Son of Man in Mark, 1967; (ed jtly) What about the New Testament?, 1975; Pauline Pieces, 1979; Studying the New Testament, 1979; (ed jtly) Paul and Paulinism, 1982; The Message of Mark, 1983; Continuity and Discontinuity, 1986; From Adam to Christ, 1990; A Commentary on the Gospel according to St Mark, 1991; Not Ashamed of the Gospel, 1994; contribs to New Testament Studies, Jl of Theological Studies, Theology, Epworth Review, etc. *Recreations:* Molinology, walking, music. *Address:* Divinity School, St John's Street, Cambridge CB2 1TW.

HOOKER, Ronald George, CBE 1985; FEng; CIMgt; FRSA; Chairman: Management & Business Services Ltd, since 1972; Thomas Storey Ltd, since 1984; EAC Ltd, since 1993; Co-ordinated Land and Estates, since 1985; Warner Howard plc, since 1987; company directorships; *b* 6 Aug. 1921; *m* 1954, Eve Pigott; one *s* one *d*. *Educ:* Wimbledon Technical Coll.; London Univ. (external). Hon. FIEE (FIProdE 1980); FEng 1984. CIMgt (CBIM 1972). Apprentice, Philips Electrical Ltd, 1937–41, Develt Engr, 1945–48; FBI, 1948–50; Dir and Gen. Man., Brush Electrical Engineering Co. Ltd, 1950–60; Man. Dir, K & L Steelfounders & Engineers Ltd, 1960–65; Man. Dir, Associated Fire Alarms Ltd, 1965–68; Chm. and Man. Dir, Crane Fruehauf Trailers Ltd, 1968–71; Dir of Manufacture,

Rolls Royce (1971) Ltd, 1971–73. Chm. and Man. Dir, John M. Henderson (Holdings) Ltd, 1973–75. Dir, Computing Devices Hldgs Ltd, 1986–. Pres., Engrg Employers' Fedn, 1986–88 (Mem. Management Bd, 1977–); Mem., Engrg Council, 1982–86. Past Pres., IProdE, 1974–75 (Hon. Life MIProdE 1980). Freeman, City of London. *Publications:* papers on management and prodn engrg to BIM, ICMA, IProdE and IMechE. *Recreations:* gardening, reading, music. *Address:* Loxborough House, Bledlow Ridge, near High Wycombe, Bucks HP14 4AA. *T:* Bledlow Ridge (0124027) 486; 6 Tufton Court, Tufton Street, SW1P 3QH. *T:* 0171–222 6669. *Clubs:* Athenæum, Lansdowne.

HOOKS, Air Vice-Marshal Robert Keith, CBE 1979; CEng, FRAeS; RAF retired; *b* 7 Aug. 1929; *s* of late Robert George Hooks and Phyllis Hooks; *m* 1954, Kathleen (*née* Cooper); one *s* one *d. Educ:* Acklam Hall Sch.; Constantine Coll., Middlesbrough. Bsc(Eng) London. Commissioned RAF, 1951; served at RAF stations West Malling, Fassberg, Sylt, 1952–55; RAF Technical Coll., Henlow, 1956; Fairey Aviation Co., 1957–58; Air Ministry, 1958–60; Skybolt Trials Unit, Eglin, Florida, 1961–63; Bomber Command Armament Sch., Wittering, 1963–65; OC Engrg Wing, RAF Coll., Cranwell, 1967–69; HQ Far East Air Force, 1969–71; Supt of Armament A&AEE, 1971–74; Director Ground Training, 1974–76; Director Air Armament, 1976–80; Vice-Pres. (Air), Ordnance Board, 1980; Dir Gen. Aircraft 2, MoD (Procurement Exec.), 1981–84; Divl Dir (European Business), Westland Helicopters, 1984–85; Projects Dir, Helicopter Div., Westland plc, 1985–87. Dep. Man. Dir, E H Industries Ltd, 1987–94. *Address:* c/o Lloyds Bank, Cox's & King's Branch, 7 Pall Mall, SW1Y 5NA. *Club:* Royal Air Force.

HOOKWAY, Sir Harry (Thurston), Kt 1978; Pro-Chancellor, Loughborough University of Technology, 1987–93; *b* 23 July 1921; *s* of William and Bertha Hookway; *m* 1956, Barbara Olive (*d* 1991), *o d* of late Oliver and Olive Butler; one *s* one *d. Educ:* Trinity Sch. of John Whitgift; London Univ. (BSc, PhD). Various posts in industry, 1941–49; DSIR, 1949–65; Asst Dir, National Chemical Laboratory, 1959; Dir, UK Scientific Mission (North America), Scientific Attaché, Washington, DC, and Scientific Adviser to UK High Comr, Ottawa, 1960–64; Head of Information Div., DSIR, 1964–65; CSO, DES, 1966–69; Asst Under-Sec. of State, DES, 1969–73; Dep. Chm. and Chief Exec., The British Library Bd, 1973–84; Chairman: Publishers Databases Ltd, 1984–87; LA Publishing Ltd, 1986–89. Chairman: UNESCO Internat. Adv. Cttee for Documentation, Libraries and Archives, 1975–79; British Council Libraries Adv. Cttee, 1982–86; President: Inst. of Information Scientists, 1973–76; Library Assoc., 1985. Mem., Royal Commn on Historical Monuments (England), 1981–89. Governor, British Inst. for Recorded Sound, 1981–86. Dir, Arundel Castle Trustees Ltd, 1976–. Hon. FLA, 1982; Hon. FIInfSc. Hon. LLD Sheffield, 1976; Hon. DLitt Loughborough, 1980. Gold Medal, Internat. Assoc. of Library Assocs, 1985. *Publications:* various contribs to jls of learned societies. *Recreations:* music, travel. *Address:* 3 St James Green, Thirsk, N Yorks YO7 1AF. *Club:* Athenæum.

HOOLAHAN, Anthony Terence, QC 1973; a Recorder of the Crown Court, since 1976; a Social Security Commissioner, since 1986; a Child Support Commissioner, since 1993; *b* 26 July 1925; *s* of late Gerald and Val Hoolahan; *m* 1949, Dorothy Veronica Connochie; one *s* one *d. Educ:* Dorset House, Littlehampton, Sussex; Framlingham Coll., Suffolk; Lincoln Coll., Oxford (MA). Served War, RNVR, 1943–46. Oxford Univ., 1946–48. Called to Bar, Inner Temple, 1949, Bencher, 1980; called to the Bar of Northern Ireland, 1980, QC (Northern Ireland) 1980. Chairman: Richmond Soc., 1976–80; Trustees, Richmond Museum, 1988–. Gov., St Elizabeth's Sch., Richmond, 1990–. *Publications:* Guide to Defamation Practice (with Colin Duncan, QC), 2nd edn, 1958; contrib. to Halsbury's Laws of England, Atkin's Court Forms. *Recreation:* swimming. *Address:* Harp House, 83 Farringdon Street, EC4A 4DH. *T:* 0171–353 5145.

HOOLE, Alan Norman, OBE 1991, Governor and Commander-in-Chief, St Helena and its Dependencies, since 1991, *b* 25 April 1942; *s* of Walter Norman and Elsie Hoole; *m* 1st, 1962, Pauline Claire Bettison (marr. diss.); one *s* one *d*; 2nd, 1982, Delia Rose Clingham. *Educ:* Chesterfield Grammar Sch.; Lady Manners Grammar Sch., Bakewell; Sheffield Univ.; Coll. of Law, London. Admitted as Solicitor, 1964 (S. H. Clay Prize, Law Soc., 1963). Partner, Blakesley & Booth, Solicitors, Chesterfield, 1965–78, Attorney General: St Helena, 1978–83; Anguilla, 1983–85; Chief Sec., Turks and Caicos Is, 1986–88; Attorney Gen., Anguilla, 1989–90; Dep. Gov., Anguilla, 1990–91. *Recreations:* fishing, tennis. *Address:* Plantation House, Island of St Helena, South Atlantic. *T:* 290 4444, *Fax:* 290 2598. *Club:* Commonwealth Trust.

HOOLE, Sir Arthur (Hugh), Kt 1985; Consultant, Tuck & Mann, Epsom, since 1989 (Partner, 1951–88); *b* 14 Jan. 1924; *s* of Hugh Francis and Gladys Emily Hoole; *m* 1945, Eleanor Mary Hobbs; two *s* two *d. Educ:* Sutton County School; Emmanuel College, Cambridge. MA, LLM. Served RAFVR, 1943–46; admitted solicitor, 1951; Mem. Council, Law Society, 1969–87 (Vice-Pres., 1983–84; Pres., 1984–85); Governor, College of Law, 1976–93 (Chm., 1983–90); Member: Adv. Cttee on Legal Educn, 1977–90; Common Professional Examination Bd, 1977–81 (Chm., 1978–81); Criminal Injuries Compensation Bd, 1985–. Governor: St John's Sch., Leatherhead, 1987–94; Sutton GS for Boys (formerly Sutton Manor High Sch.), 1987–. *Recreations:* cricket, books, music. *Address:* Yew Tree House, St Nicholas Hill, Leatherhead, Surrey KT22 8NE. *T:* Leatherhead (01372) 373208. *Club:* Royal Automobile.

HOOLE, John George Aldick; Curator, Barbican Art Gallery, since 1982; *b* 3 Feb. 1951; *s* of John Aldick Hoole and Pamela Betty Coleman; *m* 1975, Lindsey G. Rushworth; one *s* one *d. Educ:* Univ. of East Anglia (BA Hons History of Art). Asst Keeper of Art, Southampton Art Gall., 1974–78; Asst Dir, Museum of Modern Art, Oxford, 1978–82. *Recreations:* parenthood, books. *Address:* Barbican Art Gallery, Barbican Centre, Silk Street, EC2Y 8DS. *T:* 0171–638 4141.

HOOLEY, Prof. Christopher, FRS 1983; Professor of Pure Mathematics, since 1967, Head of School of Mathematics, since 1988, and Deputy Principal, since 1991, University of Wales College of Cardiff (formerly University College, Cardiff); *b* 7 Aug, 1928; *s* of Leonard Joseph Hooley, MA, BSc, and Barbara Hooley; *m* 1954, Birgitta Kniep; two *s. Educ:* Wilmslow Preparatory Sch.; Abbotsholme Sch.; Corpus Christi Coll., Cambridge (MA, PhD, ScD). Captain, RAEC, 1948–49 (SO III, British Troops in Egypt). Fellow, Corpus Christi Coll., Cambridge, 1955–58; Lectr in Mathematics, Univ. of Bristol, 1958–65; Prof. of Pure Mathematics, Univ. of Durham, 1965–67; University College, Cardiff: Hd of Dept of Pure Maths, 1967–88; Dean of Faculty of Science, 1973–76; Dep. Principal, 1979–81. Visiting Member: Inst. for Advanced Study, Princeton, 1970–71, and Fall Terms, 1976, 1977, 1982, 1983; Institut des Hautes Etudes Scientifiques, Paris, 1984. Adams Prize, Cambridge, 1973; Sen. Berwick Prize, London Mathematical Soc., 1980. *Publications:* Applications of Sieve Methods to the Theory of Numbers, 1976; (ed with H. Halberstam) Recent Progress in Analytic Number Theory, 1981; memoirs in diverse mathematical jls. *Recreations:* classic cars; antiquities. *Address:* Rushmoor Grange, Backwell, Bristol BS19 3BN. *T:* Flax Bourton (01275) 462363.

HOOLEY, Frank Oswald; retired; *b* 30 Nov. 1923; *m* 1945, Doris Irene Snook; two *d. Educ:* King Edward's High Sch., Birmingham; Birmingham Univ. Admin. Asst, Birmingham Univ., 1948–52; Sheffield Univ.: Asst Registrar, 1952–65; Sen. Asst Registrar, 1965–66; Registrar, Fourah Bay Coll., Sierra Leone, 1960–62 (secondment from Sheffield); Sen. Admin. Asst, Manchester Poly., 1970–71; Chief Admin. Offr, Sheffield City Coll. of Educn, 1971–74. Res. Asst to John Tomlinson, MEP, 1984–88. MP (Lab) Sheffield, Heeley, 1966–70 and Feb. 1974–1983. Chm., Parly Liaison Gp for Alternative Energy Strategies, 1978; formerly Member, Select Committees on Public Accounts, Estimates, Sci. and Technol., Overseas Aid, Foreign Affairs, and Procedure. Contested (Lab) Stratford-on-Avon, 1983. Chm., Co-ordinating Cttee, Internat. Anti-Apartheid Year, 1978. *Address:* 6 Mayland Drive, Sutton Coldfield B74 2DG. *T:* 0121–353 0982.

HOOLEY, John Rouse, DL; Chief Executive, West Sussex County Council, 1975–90; Clerk to the Lieutenancy of West Sussex, 1976–90; *b* 25 June 1927; *s* of Harry and Elsie Hooley; *m* 1953, Gloria Patricia Swanston; three *s* one *d. Educ:* William Hulme's Sch., Manchester; Lincoln Coll., Oxford; Manchester Univ. LLB London. Admitted Solicitor (Hons), 1952. Served Lancashire Fusiliers, 1946–48. Asst Solicitor, Chester, Carlisle and Shropshire, 1952–65; Asst Clerk, Cornwall, 1965–67; Dep. Clerk and Dep. Clerk of the Peace, W Sussex, 1967–74; County Sec., W Sussex, 1974–75. Member: Chichester HA, 1990–95 (Chm., 1993–95); W Sussex HA, 1995–. Chm., Downland Housing Soc., 1994–. FRSA. DL W Sussex, 1991. *Recreations:* gardening, music. *Address:* Bosvigo, Lavant Road, Chichester PO19 1RQ.

HOON, Geoffrey William; MP (Lab) Ashfield, since 1992; *b* 6 Dec. 1953; *s* of Ernest and June Hoon; *m* 1981, Elaine Ann Dumelow; one *s* two *d. Educ:* Nottingham High Sch.; Jesus College, Cambridge (MA). Called to the Bar, Gray's Inn, 1978. Labourer at furniture factory, 1972–73; Lectr in Law, Leeds Univ., 1976–82. Vis. Prof. of Law, Univ. of Louisville, 1979–80. In practice at Nottingham, 1982–84. An Opposition Whip, 1994–. European Parliament: Mem. (Lab) Derbyshire, 1984–94; Mem., Legal Affairs Cttee, 1984–94; President: Standing Delegn to China, 1987–89; Standing Delegn to US, 1989–92. Chm., Friends of Music, 1992–; Vice-Chm. and Gov., Westminster Foundn, 1994–. *Recreations:* football, cricket, running, cinema, music. *Address:* 8 Station Street, Kirkby-in-Ashfield, Notts NG17 7AR.

HOOPER, family name of **Baroness Hooper.**

HOOPER, Baroness *cr* 1985 (Life Peer), of Liverpool and of St James's in the City of Westminster; **Gloria Dorothy Hooper;** *b* 25 May 1939; *d* of late Frances and Frederick Hooper. *Educ:* University of Southampton (BA Hons Law); Universidad Central, Quito, Ecuador (Lic. de Derecho Internacional). Admitted to Law Society, Solicitor, 1973; Partner, Taylor Garrett (formerly Taylor and Humbert), 1974–84. MEP (C) Liverpool, 1979–84; Vice-Chm., Environment and Consumer Affairs Cttees, European Parlt, 1979–84; EDG Whip, European Parlt, 1982–84; contested (C) Merseyside West, European Parly elecn, 1984. Baroness in Waiting, 1985–87; Parly Under Sec. of State, DES, 1987–88, Dept of Energy, 1988–89, DoH, 1989–92. Mem., Parly Delegns to Council of Europe and WEU, 1992–. FRGS 1982; Fellow, Industry and Parlt Trust, 1983; FRSA 1986. *Publications:* Cases on Company Law, 1967; Law of International Trade, 1968. *Recreations:* theatre and walking. *Address:* House of Lords, Westminster, SW1A 0PW. *T:* 0171–219 3000.

HOOPER, Hon. Sir Anthony, Kt 1995; **Hon. Mr Justice Hooper;** a Judge of the High Court of Justice, Queen's Bench Division, since 1995; *b* 16 Sept 1937; *s* of late Edwin Morris Hooper and of Greta Lillian Chissim; *m* 1st, Margrethe Frances (*née* Hansen) (marr. diss. 1986); one *s* one *d*; 2nd, Heather Christine (*née* Randall). *Educ:* Sherborne; Trinity Hall, Cambridge (Scholar; MA, LLB). 2nd Lieut, 7th RTR, 1956–57. Called to the Bar, Inner Temple, 1965, Bencher, 1993; admitted to Law Society of British Columbia, 1969; QC 1987; a Recorder, 1986–95. Asst Lectr and Lectr, Univ. of Newcastle upon Tyne, 1962–65; Asst and Associate Prof., Faculty of Law, Univ. of British Columbia, 1965–68; Prof. Associé, Univ. de Laval, 1969–70; Prof., Osgoode Hall Law Sch., York Univ., 1971–73. Visiting Professor: Univ. de Montréal, 1972, 1973; Osgoode Hall, 1984. *Publications:* (ed) Harris's Criminal Law, 21st edn 1968; articles in legal jls. *Address:* Royal Courts of Justice, Strand, WC2A 2LL.

See also R. Hooper.

HOOPER, Noel Barrie; Judge of the High Court, Hong Kong, 1981–93; *b* 9 Nov. 1931; twin *s* of late Alfred Edward Hooper and Constance Violet Hooper; *m* 1959, Pauline Mary (*née* Irwin); two *d. Educ:* Prince of Wales Sch., Kenya; St Peter's Hall, Oxford (BA 1954). Called to the Bar, Gray's Inn, 1956. Advocate of High Court, Uganda, 1956–61; Magistrate, Basutoland, 1961–64 and Hong Kong, 1964–68; Sen. Magistrate, Hong Kong, 1968–73; Principal Magistrate, 1973–76; Dist Judge, 1976–81; Comr of the Supreme Court of Brunei, 1983–86, 1986–89, 1990–93, 1994–. *Recreations:* tennis, cricket, golf, reading. *Clubs:* MCC, Royal Automobile.

HOOPER, Richard; Managing Partner, Hooper Communications, since 1988; *b* 19 Sept. 1939; *s* of late Edwin Morris Hooper and of Greta Lillian (*née* Goode): *m* 1964, Meredith Jean Rooney; two *s* one *d. Educ:* Sherborne Sch.; Worcester Coll., Oxford (BA German and Russian, 1963; MA). National Service, 2nd Lieut 7th RTR, BAOR, 1958–59. Gen. trainee, BBC, 1963; Radio Producer, BBC Further Educn, 1964–66; Harkness Fellow, USA, 1967–68; Sen. Radio and TV Producer, BBC Open Univ. Prodns, 1969–72; Dir, National Develt Prog. in Computer Assisted Learning, 1973–77; Man. Dir, Mills & Allen Communications, 1978–79; Dir, Prestel, Post Office Telecommunications, 1980–81; Chief Exec., Value Added Systems and Services, BT, 1982–86; Man. Dir, Super Channel, 1986–88. Mem., Radio Authority, 1990–94. Chm. (non-exec.), ABFL, 1994–; non-exec. Dir, MAI, 1993–. Special Staff Consultant to President Lyndon Johnson's Commn on Instructional Technology, 1968. Chairman: UK Chapter, Internat. Inst. of Communications, 1992–; The Pluralists, 1992–. Mem., Inst. of Dirs; FRSA. *Publications:* (ed) Colour in Britain, 1965; (ed) The Curriculum, Context, Design and Development, 1971; Unnatural Monopolies, 1991; contrib. to books and jls. *Recreations:* the family, theatre.

See also Sir A. Hooper.

HOOSON, family name of **Baron Hooson.**

HOOSON, Baron *cr* 1979 (Life Peer), of Montgomery in the County of Powys and of Colomendy in the County of Clwyd; **Hugh Emlyn Hooson;** QC 1960; a Recorder of the Crown Court, 1972–93 (Recorder of Swansea, 1971); *b* 26 March 1925; *s* of late Hugh and Elsie Hooson, Colomendy, Denbigh; *m* 1950, Shirley Margaret Wynne, *d* of late Sir George Hamer, CBE; two *d. Educ:* Denbigh Gram. Sch.; University Coll. of Wales; Gray's Inn (Bencher, 1968; Vice-Treasurer, 1985; Treasurer, 1986). Called to Bar, 1949; Wales and Chester Circuit (Leader, 1971–74); Dep. Chm., Flint QS, 1960–71; Dep. Chm., Merioneth QS, 1960–67, Chm., 1967–71; Recorder of Merthyr Tydfil, 1971. MP (L) Montgomery, 1962–79. Leader, 1966–79, Pres., 1983–86, Welsh Liberal Party. Vice-Chm. Political Cttee, North Atlantic Assembly, 1975–79. Dir (non-exec.), Laura Ashley (Holdings) Ltd, 1985–; Chm., Severn River Crossing, 1991–. Pres., Llangollen Internat. Eisteddfod, 1987–93. Gov., Inst. of Grassland and Envmtl Res., 1989–92. Hon. Professorial Fellow, University Coll. of Wales, 1971. Farms Pen-Rhiw farm, Llanidloes. *Address:* Summerfield, Llanidloes, Powys SY18 6AQ. *T:* Llanidloes (01686) 2298; *T:* (office) 0171–219 5226; (home) 0171–405 4160.

HOOTON, Patrick Jonathan; His Honour Judge Hooton; a Circuit Judge, since 1994; *b* 30 June 1941; *s* of late John Charles Hooton, CMG, MBE, QC (Bermuda) and of Patricia Jessica Hooton (*née* Manning); *m* 1st, 1970, Anne Josephine Wells; one *s*; 2nd, 1980, Jocely Margaret East; one *s* one *d*. *Educ:* Downside Sch., Somerset; Trinity Coll., Cambridge. Commonwealth Develt Corp., 1964–68; Van Moppes & Co., 1969–71; called to the Bar, Gray's Inn, 1973; practised on Western Circuit, 1973–94. Mem., Club Taurino. *Recreations:* field sports, sailing, ski-ing, Southampton FC and Hampshire CC. *Clubs:* Lawyers' Fishing; Hampshire CC.

HOOVER, Herbert William, Jr; President, 1954–66, and Chairman of the Board, 1959–66, The Hoover Company, North Canton, Ohio; *b* 23 April 1918; *s* of late Herbert William Hoover and Grace Hoover (*née* Steele); *m* 1941, Carl Maitland Good; one *s* one *d*. *Educ:* Choate Sch., Wallingford, Conn.; Rollins Coll. (AB). Served in US Army, 1943–45. Offices held with Hoover Co.: Exec. Sales, 1941; Dir Public Relations, 1945; Asst Vice-Pres., 1948; Vice-Pres. Field Sales, 1952; Exec. Vice-Pres., 1953. The Hoover Co. Ltd, Canada: Pres., 1954; Dir, 1952; Hoover Ltd, England: Dir 1954, Chm. 1956. Hoover Inc., Panama: Dir and Pres., 1955; Hoover (America Latina) SA, Panama: Dir and Pres., 1955; Hoover Mexicana, Mexico: Dir and Pres., 1955; Hoover Industrial y Comercial SA, Colombia: Dir and Pres., 1960; Hoover Worldwide Corp., NY City: Pres. and Chm., 1960; Dir, S. A. Hoover, France, 1965. Past Regional Vice-Chm., US Cttee for the UN. Dir, Miami Heart Inst.; Mem., Bd of Trustees, Univ. of Miami. Hon. LLD, Mount Union Coll., 1959. Chevalier Légion d'Honneur, France, 1965. *Address:* 20 Indian Creek Island, Surfside, FL 33154–2904, USA.

HOPCROFT, George William; HM Diplomatic Service, retired; consultant on international relations; *b* 30 Sept. 1927; *s* of late Frederick Hopcroft and Dorothy Gertrude (*née* Bourne); *m* 1951, Audrey Joan Rodd; three *s* one *d*. *Educ:* Chiswick Grammar Sch.; London Univ. (BCom); Brasenose Coll., Oxford; INSEAD, Fontainebleau. Auditor with Wm R. Warner, 1946; entered Export Credits Guarantee Dept, 1946; Asst Trade Comr, Madras, 1953–57; Sen. Underwriter, ECGD, 1957–65; joined FO, 1965; First Sec. (Commercial), Amman, 1965–69; First Sec. (Econ.), Bonn, 1969–71; First Sec. (Comm.), Kuala Lumpur, 1971–75; FCO, 1975–78; Counsellor (Comm. and Econ.), Bangkok, 1978–81; FCO 1981. Founder Mem., Export and Overseas Trade Adv. Panel (EOTAP), 1982–; operational expert in for. affairs, attached to Govt of Belize, 1982–83. *Recreations:* leisure and circumnavigation, athletics (Civil Service 880 yds champion, 1947), serendipity. *Address:* Ffrogs, Pond Road, Hook Heath, Woking, Surrey GU22 0JT. *T:* Woking (014862) 715121. *Club:* British (Bangkok).

HOPE, family name of **Barons Glendevon** and **Hope of Craighead, Marquess of Linlithgow** and **Baron Rankeillour.**

HOPE OF CRAIGHEAD, Baron *cr* 1995 (Life Peer), of Bamff in the District of Perth and Kinross; **James Arthur David Hope;** PC 1989; Lord Justice-General of Scotland and Lord President of the Court of Session, since 1989; *b* 27 June 1938; *s* of Arthur Henry Cecil Hope, OBE, WS, Edinburgh and Muriel Ann Neilson Hope (*née* Collie); *m* 1966, Katharine Mary Kerr, *d* of W. Mark Kerr, WS, Edinburgh; twin *s* one *d*. *Educ:* Edinburgh Acad.; Rugby Sch.; St John's Coll., Cambridge (Scholarship 1956, BA 1962, MA 1978; Hon. Fellow, 1995); Edinburgh Univ. (LLB 1965). National Service, Seaforth Highlanders, 1957–59 (Lieutenant 1959). Admitted Faculty of Advocates, 1965; Standing Junior Counsel in Scotland to Board of Inland Revenue, 1974–78; Advocate-Depute, 1978–82; QC (Scotland) 1978; Dean, Faculty of Advocates, 1986–89. Chm., Med. Appeal Tribunal, 1985–86; Legal Chm., Pensions Appeal Tribunal, 1985–86. Pres., Stair Soc., 1993–. Hon. Prof. of Law, Aberdeen, 1994. Hon. Member: Canadian Bar Assoc., 1987; SPTL, 1991; Hon. Bencher: Gray's Inn, 1989; Inn of Court of NI, 1995. Hon. LLD: Aberdeen, 1991; Strathclyde, 1993; Edinburgh, 1995. *Publications:* (ed jtly) Gloag & Henderson's Introduction to the Law of Scotland, 7th edn 1968, asst editor, 8th edn 1980 and 9th edn 1987; (ed jtly) Armour on Valuation for Rating, 4th edn 1971, 5th edn 1985; (with A. G. M. Duncan) The Rent (Scotland) Act 1984, 1986; (contrib.) Stair Memorial Encyclopaedia of Scots Law. *Recreations:* walking, ornithology, music. *Address:* 34 India Street, Edinburgh EH3 6HB. *T:* 0131–225 8245; Parliament House, Edinburgh EH1 1RQ. *T:* 0131–225 2595. *Club:* New (Edinburgh).

HOPE, Alan, JP; Leader, West Midlands County Council Opposition Group (C), since 1981; *b* 5 Jan. 1933; *s* of George Edward Thomas Hope and Vera Hope; *m* 1960, Marilyn Dawson; one *s* one *d*. *Educ:* George Dixon Grammar Sch., Birmingham. Councillor, Birmingham CC, 1964–73; West Midlands County Council: Councillor, 1973; Leader, 1980–81; Chairman: Trading Standards, 1977–79; Finance, 1979–80. JP Birmingham 1974. *Address:* Whitehaven, Rosemary Drive, Little Aston Park, Sutton Coldfield, West Midlands B74 3AG. *T:* 0121–353 3011. *Club:* Commonwealth Trust; Birmingham (Birmingham).

HOPE, Bob, (Leslie Townes Hope), CBE (Hon.) 1976; Congressional Gold Medal, US, 1963; film, stage, radio, TV actor; *b* England, 29 May 1903; family migrated to US, 1907; *m* 1934, Dolores Reade; two adopted *s* two adopted *d*. *Educ:* Fairmont Gram. Sch. and High Sch., Cleveland, O. Started career as dance instructor, clerk, amateur boxer; formed dancing act for Fatty Arbuckle review. After Mid-West tours formed own Company in Chicago; toured New York and joined RKO Vaudeville and Keith Circuit; first important stage parts include: Ballyhoo, 1932; Roberta, 1933; Ziegfield Follies, 1935; first radio part, 1934. Entered films, 1938. *Films include:* Big Broadcast of 1938; Some Like It Hot; The Cat and the Canary; Road to Singapore; The Ghost Breakers; Road to Zanzibar; Star Spangled Rhythm; Nothing but the Truth; Louisiana Purchase; My Favorite Blonde; Road to Morocco; Let's Face It; Road to Utopia; Monsieur Beaucaire; My Favorite Brunette; They Got Me Covered; The Princess and the Pirate; Road to Rio; Where There's Life; The Great Lover; My Favorite Spy; Road to Bali; Son of Paleface; Here Come the Girls; Casanova's Big Night; The Seven Little Foys; The Iron Petticoat; That Certain Feeling; Beau James; The Facts of Life; Bachelor in Paradise; The Road to Hong Kong; Call Me Bwana; A Global Affair; Boy, Did I Get a Wrong Number!; Eight on the Run; How to Commit Marriage; Cancel My Reservation. *TV series:* The Bob Hope Show, 1950–93; numerous guest appearances. Five Royal Command Performances. Awarded 44 honorary degrees; more than a thousand awards and citations for humanitarian and professional services. *Publications:* They've Got Me Covered, 1941; I Never Left Home, 1944; So This is Peace, 1946; This One's on Me, 1954; I Owe Russia $1200, 1963; Five Women I Love, 1966; The Last Christmas Show, 1974; Road to Hollywood, 1977; Confessions of a Hooker, 1985; Don't shoot, it's only me, 1990. *Address:* Hope Enterprises, Inc., 3808 Riverside Drive, Burbank, CA 91505, USA.

HOPE, Sir (Charles) Peter, KCMG 1972 (CMG 1956); TD 1945; Ambassador to Mexico, 1968–72; *b* 29 May 1912; *s* of G. L. N. Hope and H. M. V. Riddell, Weetwood, Mayfield, Sussex; *m* 1936, H. M. Turner, *d* of late G. L. Turner, company director; three *s*. *Educ:* Oratory Sch., Reading; London and Cambridge Univs. BSc (Hons), ACGI. Asst War Office, 1938; RA, TA, 1939; served until 1946 (TD). Transferred to Foreign Office and posted HM Embassy, Paris, as Temp. First Sec., 1946; transferred to United Nations Dept, Foreign Office, 1950; to HM Embassy, Bonn, as Counsellor, 1953; Foreign Office Spokesman (Head of News Dept Foreign Office), 1956–59; Minister, HM Embassy, Madrid, 1959–62; Consul-General, Houston, USA, 1963–64; Minister and Alternate UK Rep. to UN, 1965–68. Mem., Acad. of International Law. Pres., British Assoc. of Sovereign Military Order of Malta, 1983–89; KStJ 1984. Grand Cross: Order of the Aztec Eagle, 1972; Constantine Order of St George, 1981; Grand Cross, Order of Malta, 1984; Grand Officer, Order of Merito Militense, 1975. *Recreations:* shooting and fishing. *Address:* Guillard's Oak House, Midhurst, W Sussex GU29 9JZ. *Club:* White's.

HOPE, Christopher, FRSL; writer; *b* 26 Feb. 1944; *s* of Dennis Tully and Kathleen Mary Hope (*née* McKenna); *m* 1967, Eleanor Klein; two *s*. *Educ:* Christian Brothers College, Pretoria; Univ. of Natal (BA Hons 1970); Univ. of Witwatersrand (MA 1973). FRSL 1990. Pringle Prize, English Acad. of Southern Africa, 1972; Cholmondeley Award, Soc. of Authors, 1974; Arts Council Bursary, 1982. *Publications:* Cape Drives, 1974; A Separate Development, 1981 (David Higham Prize for Fiction); In the Country of the Black Pig, 1981; Private Parts and Other Tales, 1982 (rev. edn as Learning to Fly and Other Tales, 1990) (Internat. PEN Silver Pen Award); Kruger's Alp, 1984 (Whitbread Prize for Fiction); Englishmen, 1985; The Hottentot Room, 1986; Black Swan, 1987; White Boy Running, 1988 (CNA Award, S Africa); My Chocolate Redeemer, 1989; Moscow! Moscow!, 1990; Serenity House, 1992; The Love Songs of Nathan J. Swirsky, 1993; contribs to BBC, newspapers, jls. *Recreation:* getting lost. *Address:* c/o Rogers, Coleridge & White, 20 Powis Mews, W11 1JN.

HOPE, Colin Frederick Newton, MA; CEng, FIMechE; FIMI; Chairman and Chief Executive, T & N plc (formerly Turner & Newall), since 1989 (Group Managing Director, 1985–89); *b* 17 May 1932; *s* of Frederick and Mildred Hope; *m* 1959, Gillian Carden; two *s*. *Educ:* Stowe Sch.; St Catharine's College, Cambridge (MA). Glacier Metal Co., 1963–70; Managing Dir, 1970–73, Exec. Chm., 1973–75, Covrad; Director: Engineering Group, Dunlop, 1975–79; Tyres UK Dunlop, 1979–82; Tyres Europe Dunlop Holdings, 1982–84; Chief Exec., Dunlop Engineering International, 1984–85. Chairman: Bryant Gp, 1992–; Ibstock Johnsen, 1993–. Pres., SMMT, 1991–93. *Recreations:* theatre, music, travel. *Address:* Hornby Cottage, High Street, Welford-on-Avon, Warwickshire CV37 8EF. *T:* Stratford upon Avon (01789) 750301. *Club:* Royal Automobile.

HOPE, Most Rev. and Rt Hon. David Michael; *see* York, Archbishop of.

HOPE, Sir John (Carl Alexander), 18th Bt *cr* 1628 (NS), of Craighall; *b* 10 June 1939; *s* of Sir Archibald Philip Hope, 17th Bt, OBE, DFC, AE and of Ruth, *y d* of Carl Davis; *S* father, 1987; *m*1968, Merle Pringle, *d* of late Robert Douglas, Holbrook, Ipswich; one *s* one *d*. *Educ:* Eton. *Heir: s* Alexander Archibald Douglas Hope, *b* 16 March 1969. *Address:* 9 Westleigh Avenue, SW15 6RF.

HOPE, Laurence Frank, OBE 1968; HM Diplomatic Service, retired; HM Consul General, Seattle, 1975–76; *b* 18 May 1918; *y s* of late Samuel Vaughan Trevylian Hope and late Ellen Edith Hope (*née* Cooler); *m* 1940, Doris Phyllis Rosa Hulbert; one *s* one *d*. Served War, reaching rank of Major, in British Army (12th (2nd City of London Regt) Royal Fusiliers, TA and York and Lancaster Regt); Indian Army (7th Rajput Regt); Mil. Govt of Germany (Economic Div.), 1939–46. Bd of Trade, London, 1946–47; Asst Brit. Trade Comr, Pretoria, 1947–51; Cape Town, 1951–53; Bd of Trade, London, 1953–56; British Trade Comr, Sydney, 1956–60; Canberra, 1960–61; Lahore, 1961–63; Singapore, 1964; transferred to HM Diplomatic Service; Head of Commercial Section, High Commn, Singapore, 1965–68; Counsellor (Economic and Commercial), Lagos, 1969–72; HM Consul-Gen., Gothenburg, 1972–75. *Recreations:* oil painting, reading. *Address:* 22 Cranford Avenue, Exmouth, Devon EX8 2HU.

See also M. L. H. Hope.

HOPE, Marcus Laurence Hulbert; HM Diplomatic Service; Head of Western European Department, Foreign and Commonwealth Office, since 1992; *b* 2 Feb. 1942; *s* of Laurence Frank Hope, *qv*; *m* 1980, Uta Maria Luise Müller-Unverfehrt; one *s*. *Educ:* City of London Sch.; Sydney C of E Grammar Sch.; Univ. of Sydney (BA); Univ. of London (BA Hons). Joined HM Diplomatic Service, 1965; Third Sec., CRO, 1965; MECAS, 1966; Second Sec., Tripoli, 1968; FCO, 1970; First Sec., 1972; Head of Chancery, Dubai, 1974; First Sec. (Commercial), Bonn, 1976; FCO, 1980; NATO Defence Coll., Rome, 1984; Counsellor, Beirut, 1984–85; Counsellor and Head of Chancery, Berne, 1985–89; Dep. Head of Mission and Counsellor (Commercial and Aid), Jakarta, 1989–92. *Recreation:* classical guitar. *Address:* c/o Foreign and Commonwealth Office, King Charles Street, SW1A 2AH.

HOPE, Sir Peter; *see* Hope, Sir C. P.

HOPE-DUNBAR, Sir David, 8th Bt *cr* 1664; *b* 13 July 1941; *o s* of Sir Basil Douglas Hope-Dunbar, 7th Bt, and of his 2nd wife, Edith Maude Maclaren (*d* 1989), *d* of late Malcolm Cross; *S* father, 1961; *m* 1971, Kathleen, *yr d* of late J. T. Kenrick; one *s* two *d*. *Educ:* Eton; Royal Agricultural College, Cirencester. ARICS 1966. Founder, Dunbar & Co., now Allied Dunbar PLC. *Recreations:* fishing, shooting. *Heir: s* Charles Hope-Dunbar, *b* 11 March 1975. *Address:* Banks Farm, Kirkcudbright DG6 4XF. *T:* Kirkcudbright (01557) 30424.

HOPE JOHNSTONE, family name of **Earl of Annandale and Hartfell.**

HOPE-JONES, Ronald Christopher, CMG 1969; HM Diplomatic Service, retired; *b* 5 July 1920; *s* of William Hope-Jones and Winifred Coggin; *m* 1944, Pamela Hawker; two *s* one *d*. *Educ:* Eton (scholar); King's Coll., Cambridge (scholar). Served with HM Forces, 1940–45. 3rd Sec., Foreign Office, 1946, Paris, 1947; 2nd Sec., Beirut, 1949; 1st Sec., FO, 1952; Head of Chancery and Consul, Quito, 1955; Commercial Sec., Budapest, 1959; Head of Chancery, 1960; FO, 1961, Counsellor, 1963; UK Rep. to Internat. Atomic Energy Agency, Vienna, 1964–67; FCO 1967; Head of Disarmament Dept, 1967–70; Head of N African Dept, 1970–71; Counsellor, Brasilia, 1972–73; Ambassador in La Paz, 1973–77. *Address:* Wellfield House, Mill Lane, Headley, Bordon, Hants GU35 0PD. *T:* Bordon (01420) 472793.

HOPE-MORLEY, family name of **Baron Hollenden.**

HOPE-WALLACE, (Dorothy) Jaqueline, CBE 1958; *b* 1909; 2nd *d* of Charles Nugent Hope-Wallace and Mabel Chaplin. *Educ:* Lady Margaret Hall, Oxford. Entered Ministry of Labour, 1932; transferred to National Assistance Board, 1934; Under-Sec., 1958–65; Under-Sec., Min. of Housing and Local Govt, 1965–69, retired. Commonwealth Fellow, 1952–53. Comr, Public Works Loan Bd, 1974–78; Member Board: Corby Develt Corp., 1969–80; Governors, UCH, 1970–74; Inst. for Recorded Sound, 1971–74, 1979–83 (Chm. 1975–76); Nat. Corp. for Care of Old People (now Centre for Policy on Ageing), 1973–81 (Chm., 1978–80); Mem., Nat. Sound Archive Adv. Cttee, 1983–84; Chm., Friends of UCH, 1973–85. *Recreations:* arts, travel, gardening. *Address:* 17 Ashley Court, Morpeth Terrace, SW1P 1EN.

HOPETOUN, Earl of; Andrew Victor Arthur Charles Hope; *b* 22 May 1969; *s* and *heir* of Marquess of Linlithgow, *qv*; *m* 1993, Skye Laurette, *e d* of Major Bristow Bovill. *Educ:* Eton; Exeter Coll., Oxford. A Page of Honour to the Queen Mother, 1985–87.

HOPEWELL, John Prince; Consultant Surgeon, Royal Free Hospital, 1957–88 (Hon. Consulting Surgeon (Urology), since 1988); *b* 1 Dec. 1920; *s* of Samuel Prince and Wilhelmina Hopewell; *m* 1st, 1959, Dr Natalie Bogdan (*d* 1975); one *s* one *d*; 2nd, 1984, Dr Rosemary Radley-Smith. *Educ:* Bradfield Coll., Berks; King's Coll. Hosp., London. RAMC, 1945–48. Postgrad. education at King's Coll. Hosp. and Brighton, Sussex, and Hosp. for Sick Children, Gt Ormond Street. Formerly Cnslt Surgeon, Putney Hosp. and Frimley Hosp., Surrey. Mem., Hampstead DHA, 1982–85; Chm., Camden Div., BMA, 1985–93; Past Chairman: Med. Cttee, Royal Free Hosp.; N Camden Dist Med. Cttee; Chm., Hon. Med. Staff Cttee, Hosp. of St John and St Elizabeth, 1993–. Founder Mem., British Transplantation Soc., 1972; Member: Internat. Soc. of Urology; British Assoc. Urol. Surgeons; Past President: Chelsea Clinical Soc.; Section of Urology, RSM, 1982–83; Fellowship of Postgrad. Medicine. Founder Mem., Assoc. of Univ. Hospitals. Hon. Mem., NY Section, AUA. Hunterian Prof., RCS, 1958. Mem. Court of Examiners, RCSE, 1969–75. Member: Friends of St Helena; Soc. of Ornamental Woodturners. *Publications:* Three Clinical Cases of Renal Transplantation, British Medical Jl, 1964, and contribs to various medical journals. *Address:* 30 Hillfield Court, Belsize Avenue, NW3 4BJ. *T:* 0171–435 8809.

HOPKIN, Sir Bryan; *see* Hopkin, Sir W. A. B.

HOPKIN, Sir David (Armand), Kt 1987; Chief Metropolitan Stipendiary Magistrate, 1982–92; *b* 10 Jan. 1922; *s* of Daniel and Edmée Hopkin; *m* 1948, Doris Evelyn (*née* Whitaker); one *s* three *d*. *Educ:* St Paul's Sch., W Kensington; University Coll., Aberystwyth; Corpus Christi Coll., Cambridge (BA). Called to the Bar, Gray's Inn, 1949. Served in Army, 1942–47, Hon. Major, 1947. Member of Staff of Director of Public Prosecutions, 1950–70; Metropolitan Stipendiary Magistrate, 1970–92. Pres., British Boxing Board of Control, 1991– (Chm., 1983–). *Recreations:* fencing, tennis. *Address:* 8 Crane Grove, N7 8LE. *T:* 0171–607 0349.

HOPKIN, John Raymond; His Honour Judge Hopkin; a Circuit Judge, since 1979; *b* 23 June 1935; *s* of George Raymond Buxton Hopkin and Muriel Hopkin; *m* 1965, Susan Mary Limb; one *s* one *d*. *Educ:* King's Sch., Worcester. Called to Bar, Middle Temple, 1958; in practice at the Bar, 1959–. A Recorder of the Crown Court, 1978–79. A Chm. of Disciplinary Tribunals, Council of Inns of Court, 1987–. Chm. of Governors, Nottingham High Sch. for Girls, 1992–. *Recreations:* fell walking and climbing, gardening, golf, the theatre. *Address:* c/o The Crown Court, Canal Street, Nottingham NG1 7EJ. *Club:* Nottingham and Notts Services.

HOPKIN, Royston Oliver, CMG 1995; Chairman and Managing Director, Spice Island Inn, since 1987; Owner, Blue Horizons Cottage Hotel, since 1978; *b* 10 Jan. 1945; *s* of late Curtis Hopkin and of Audrey Hopkin; *m* 1st, 1975, Floreen (decd); two *c*; 2nd, 1983, Betty; one *c*. *Educ:* Grenada Boys' Secondary Sch. British Amer. Insce Co., 1963–65; joined family business, Ross Point Inn, 1965, Manager, 1969–78. Mem., Grenada Tourist Bd, 1965–83; Pres., Grenada Hotel Assoc., 1969–89; Caribbean Hotel Association: Dir, 1970–; Pres., 1994–96; Caribbean Tourism Organization: Dir, 1990–; Exec. Cttee, 1994–. Numerous awards incl. Caribbean Hotelier of the Year, 1991. *Recreations:* reading, tennis. *Address:* Mace Point Villa, True Blue, Box 41, St George's, Grenada, West Indies. *T:* (home) 4444584; (business) 4444316.

HOPKIN, Sir (William Aylsham) Bryan, Kt 1971; CBE 1961; Hon. Professorial Fellow, University College, Swansea, since 1988; *b* 7 Dec. 1914; *s* of late William Hopkin and Lilian Hopkin (*née* Cottelle); *m* 1938, Renée Ricour; two *s*. *Educ:* Barry (Glam.) County Sch.; St John's Coll., Cambridge (Hon. Fellow, 1982); Manchester Univ. Ministry of Health, 1938–41; Prime Minister's Statistical Branch, 1941–45; Royal Commn on Population, 1945–48; Econ. Sect., Cabinet Office, 1948–50; Central Statistical Office, 1950–52; Dir, Nat. Inst. of Econ. and Soc. Research, 1952–57; Sec., Council on Prices, Productivity, and Incomes, 1957–58; Dep. Dir, Econ. Sect., HM Treasury, 1958–65; Econ. Planning Unit, Mauritius, 1965, Min. of Overseas Devlt, 1966–67, Dir-Gen. of Economic Planning, ODM, 1967–69; Dir-Gen., DEA, 1969; Dep. Chief Econ. Adviser, HM Treasury, 1970–72; Prof. of Econs, UC Cardiff, 1972–82 (on leave of absence, Head of Govt Economic Service and Chief Economic Advr, HM Treasury, 1974–77). Mem., Commonwealth Develt Corp., 1972–74. Chm., Manpower Services Cttee for Wales, 1978–79. *Address:* 15 St John's Close, Cowbridge, South Glamorgan CF7 7HL. *T:* Cowbridge (01446) 772303.

HOPKINS, Alan Cripps Nind, MA Cantab, LLB Yale; Chairman, Wellman Engineering Corporation, 1972–83 (Director, 1968); *b* 27 Oct. 1926; *s* of late Rt Hon. Sir Richard V. N. Hopkins, GCB and Lady Hopkins; *m* 1st, 1954, Margaret Cameron (from whom divorced, 1962), *d* of E. C. Bolton, Waco, Texas, USA; one *s*; 2nd, 1962, Venetia, *d* of Sir Edward Wills, 4th Bt; twin *s*. *Educ:* Winchester Coll.; King's Coll., Cambridge; Yale University Law Sch., USA. BA Cantab 1947, MA 1950; LLB Yale 1952. Barrister, Inner Temple, 1948. MP (C and Nat L) Bristol North-East, 1959–66; PPS to Financial Sec. to Treasury, 1960–62. Dir, Dexion-Comino Internat. Ltd, 1973–85. *Recreation:* travelling. *Address:* Chalet Topaze, 1972 Anzere, Valais, Switzerland. *T:* (27) 381651. *Club:* Brooks's.

HOPKINS, Sir Anthony (Philip), Kt 1993; CBE 1987; actor since 1961; *b* Port Talbot, S Wales, 31 Dec. 1937; *s* of late Richard and of Muriel Hopkins; *m* 1st, 1968, Petronella (marr. diss. 1972); one *d*; 2nd, 1973, Jennifer, *d* of Ronald Lynton. *Educ:* Cowbridge, S Wales; RADA; Cardiff Coll. of Drama. London debut as Metellus Cimber in Julius Caesar, Royal Court, 1964; National Theatre: Juno and the Paycock, A Flea in Her Ear, 1966; The Dance of Death, The Three Sisters, As You Like It (all male cast), 1967; The Architect and the Emperor of Assyria, A Woman Killed with Kindness, Coriolanus, 1971; Macbeth, 1972; Pravda, 1985 (Laurence Olivier/Observer Award for outstanding achievements, 1985; (jtly) Best Actor, British Theatre Assoc. and Drama Magazine Awards, 1985; Royal Variety Club Stage Actor Award, 1985); King Lear, 1986; Antony and Cleopatra, 1987. Other stage appearances include: The Taming of the Shrew, Chichester, 1972; Equus, USA, 1974–75, 1977 (Best Actor Award, NY Drama Desk, Amer. Authors and Celebrities Forum Award, Outer Critics Circle Award, 1975; LA Drama Critics' Award, 1977); The Tempest, LA, 1979; Old Times, New York, 1984; The Lonely Road, Old Vic, 1985; M. Butterfly, Shaftesbury, 1989; Director: Dylan Thomas: return journey, Lyric, Hammersmith, 1992; August, Theatr Clwyd, 1994. *Films:* The Lion in Winter, 1967; The Looking Glass War, 1968; Hamlet, 1969; When Eight Bells Toll, 1971; Young Winston, 1972; A Doll's House, The Girl from Petrovka, 1973; All Creatures Great and Small, 1974; Dark Victory, 1975; Audrey Rose, A Bridge Too Far, 1976; International Velvet, 1977; Magic, 1978; The Elephant Man, A Change of Seasons, 1980; The Bounty (Variety Club Film Actor Award), 1984; The Good Father, 1986; 84 Charing Cross Road (Best Actor Award, Moscow Film Fest.), 1987; The Dawning, 1988; A Chorus of Disapproval, 1989; Desperate Hours, 1990; The Silence of the Lambs, (Acad., BAFTA and NY Film Critics Circle, Awards for Best Actor, 1992), One Man's War, 1991; Freejack, Howard's End, Charlie, 1992; Bram Stoker's Dracula, The Trial, The Innocent, The Remains of the Day, 1993 (BAFTA Best Actor Award); Shadowlands, 1994; The Road to Wellville, Legends of the Fall, August, 1995. *American television films:* QB VII, 1973; Bruno Hauptmann in The Lindbergh Kidnapping Case (Emmy Award), 1976; The Voyage of the Mayflower, 1979; The Bunker (Emmy Award, 1981), The Acts of Peter and Paul, 1980; The Hunchback of Notre Dame, 1981; The Arch of Triumph, 1984; Hollywood Wives, 1984; Guilty Conscience, 1984; The Tenth Man, 1988; To Be the Best, 1991; *BBC television:* Pierre Bezuhov in serial, War and Peace (SFTA Best TV Actor award), 1972; Kean, 1978; Othello, 1981; Little Eyolf, 1982; Guy Burgess in Blunt (film), 1987; Donald Campbell in Across the Lake, 1988; Heartland, 1989; Gwyn Thomas: a few selected exits, 1993; Indep. TV performances incl. A Married Man (series), 1983. Hon. Fellow, St David's Coll., Lampeter, 1992. Hon. DLitt Wales, 1988. *Recreations:* reading, walking, piano. *Address:* (office) c/o 25 St George' Court, Brompton Road, SW3 2AT. *Club:* Garrick.

HOPKINS, Dr Anthony Philip, MD; FRCP, FFPHM, FACP; Director, Research Unit, Royal College of Physicians, since 1988; Consultant Neurologist, St Bartholomew's Hospital, since 1972; *b* 15 Oct. 1937; *s* of Gerald Hopkins and Barbara Isobel Hopkins; *m* 1965, Elizabeth Ann Wood; three *s*. *Educ:* Sherborne Sch.; Guy's Hospital Med. Sch. MD London. FRCP 1976; FACP 1991; FFPHM 1991. Postgraduate work: Hammersmith and National Hosps, 1961–69; Salpetrière Hosp., Paris, 1962–63; Mayo Foundn, Rochester, Minn, 1970. St Bartholomew's Hospital: Cons. Neurologist, 1972–76; Physician-in-charge, Dept of Neurological Scis, 1976–88. Res. into experimental pathology, headache, epilepsy, and into the evaluation of the effectiveness and quality of med. care. *Publications:* Epilepsy, 1987, 2nd edn 1995; Measuring the quality of medical care, 1990; Clinical neurology: a modern approach, 1993; contribs to sci. and med. literature. *Recreations:* walking, dining. *Address:* Research Unit, Royal College of Physicians, 11 St Andrews Place, NW1 4LE; 149 Harley Street, W1N 2DE. *T:* 0171–935 4444. *Club:* Garrick.

See also Sir M. J. Hopkins.

HOPKINS, Anthony Strother, BSc(Econ); FCA; Managing Partner, Touche Ross & Co., Northern Ireland, Chartered Accountants, since 1992; *b* 17 July 1940; *s* of Strother Smith Hopkins, OBE, and Alice Roberta Hopkins; *m* 1965, Dorothy Moira (*née* McDonough); one *s* two *d*. *Educ:* Campbell Coll., Belfast; Queen's University of Belfast (BScEcon). Manager, Thomson McLintock & Co., Chartered Accountants, London, 1966–70; Principal, Dept of Commerce, N Ireland, 1970–74; Northern Ireland Development Agency, 1975–82, Chief Executive, 1979–82; Under Secretary, 1982–88, Second Perm. Sec., 1988–92, Dept of Economic Development for N Ireland; Dep. Chief Exec., 1982–88, Chief Exec., 1988–92, Industrial Develt Bd for NI. Chm., MMB for NI, 1995–. Member: NI Tourist Bd, 1992–; Council, NI Chamber of Commerce and Industry, 1992–. Vis. Prof., Univ. of Ulster, 1992–. Mem. Adv. Bd, Ulster Business Sch., 1992–. CIMgt (CBIM 1990; Chm. NI Regl Bd, 1992–). *Recreations:* golf, tennis, sailing. *Club:* Royal Belfast Golf (Co. Down).

HOPKINS, Antony, CBE 1976; composer and conductor; *b* 21 March 1921; *s* of late Hugh and of Marjorie Reynolds; adopted *c* of Major and Mrs T. H. C. Hopkins since 1925; *m* 1947, Alison Purves (*d* 1991). *Educ:* Berkhamsted Sch.; Royal Coll. of Music. Won Chappell Gold Medal and Cobbett Prize at RCM, 1942; shortly became known as composer of incidental music for radio; numerous scores composed for BBC (2 for programmes winning Italia prize for best European programme of the year, 1952 and 1957). Composed music for many productions at Stratford and in West End. Dir, Intimate Opera Co., 1952–, and has written a number of chamber operas for this group; *ballets:* Etude and Café des Sports, for Sadler's Wells; *films (music) include:* Pickwick Papers, Decameron Nights, Cast a Dark Shadow, Billy Budd; John and the Magic Music Man (narr. and orch.; Grand Prix, Besançon Film Festival, 1976). Regular broadcaster with a series of programmes entitled Talking about Music. Hon. FRCM 1964; Hon. RAM 1979; Hon. Fellow, Robinson Coll., Cambridge, 1980. DUniv. Stirling, 1980. *Publications:* Talking about Symphonies, 1961; Talking about Concertos, 1964; Music All Around Me, 1968; Lucy and Peterkin, 1968; Talking about Sonatas, 1971; Downbeat Guide, 1977; Understanding Music, 1979; The Nine Symphonies of Beethoven, 1980; Songs for Swinging Golfers, 1981; Sounds of Music, 1982; Beating Time (autobiog.), 1982; Pathway to Music, 1983; Musicamusings, 1983; The Concertgoer's Companion: Vol. I, 1984; Vol. II, 1985. *Recreations:* motoring, golf. *Address:* Woodyard Cottage, Ashridge, Berkhamsted, Herts HP4 1PS. *T:* Little Gaddesden (0144284) 2257.

HOPKINS, Prof. Antony Gerald, PhD; Smuts Professor of Commonwealth History, Cambridge, since 1994; *b* 21 Feb. 1938; *s* of George Henry Hopkins and Queenie Ethel Knight; *m* 1964, Wendy Beech; two *s*. *Educ:* St Paul's Sch.; Univ. of London (BA, PhD). Asst Lectr, Lectr, then Reader, 1964–77, Prof. of Economic History, 1977–88, Univ. of Birmingham; Prof. of Internat. History, Grad. Inst. of Internat. Studies, Univ. of Geneva, 1988–94. *Publications:* An Economic History of West Africa, 1973, revd 1988; (with P. J. Cain) British Imperialism: innovation and expansion 1688–1914, 1993; (with P. J. Cain) British Imperialism: crisis and deconstruction 1914–90, 1993; articles in learned jls. *Recreation:* worrying. *Address:* Pembroke College, Cambridge CB2 1RF.

HOPKINS, David Rex Eugène; Director of Quality Assurance/Administration, Ministry of Defence, 1983–90; *b* 29 June 1930; *s* of Frank Hopkins and Vera (*née* Wimhurst); *m* 1955, Brenda Joyce Phillips; two *s* one *d* (one *d* decd). *Educ:* Worthing High Sch.; Christ Church, Oxford (MA 1950; Dip. in Econs and Pol. Science, 1951). National Service Commn, RA, 1952; service in Korea. Asst Principal, WO, 1953; Principal, WO, 1957, MoD 1964; Asst Sec., 1967; Home Office, 1969–70; RCDS, 1971; Defence Equipment Secretariat, 1972; Dir, Headquarters Security, 1975; Financial Counsellor, UK Delegn to NATO, 1981–83. *Recreations:* church work, archaeological digging, fell-walking, military history. *Address:* 16 Hitherwood Drive, SE19 1XB. *T:* 0181–670 7504.

HOPKINS, Elizabeth Ann; Financial Management Adviser, Department of Transport, South Africa, since 1995; *b* 25 Sept. 1941; *d* of Philip G. H. Hopkins and Edith A. I. (Nessie) Hopkins (*née* Holmes). *Educ:* Parkstone Grammar Sch.; King Edward VI High Sch., Birmingham; Lady Margaret Hall, Oxford (BA Hons); Univ. of Ibadan (MSc); Univ. of Sussex (DPhil). Asst Lectr, Univ. of Sussex, 1965–68; Res. Officer, Inst. of Develt Studies, Sussex, 1968–72; Economist, Govt of Zambia, 1972–76; DoE, 1977–86; Dept of Transport (Channel Tunnel; Internat. Aviation), 1986–90; Regl Dir (SW), Depts of the Envmt and of Transport, 1990–93; Dir of Finance, Dept of Transport, 1993–95. *Recreation:* travel. *Address:* Department of Transport, Forum Building, Private Bag X193, Pretoria 0001, S Africa. *T:* (12) 2902801.

HOPKINS, John; writer; *b* 27 Jan. 1931. *Plays:* This Story of Yours, Royal Court, 1968, Long Wharf Theatre, 1981, Hampstead Theatre, 1987; Find Your Way Home, Open Space, 1970, NY, 1974; Economic Necessity, Haymarket Theatre, Leicester, 1973; Next of Kin, Nat. Theatre, 1974; Losing Time, Manhattan Theatre Club, 1979, Deutsches Schauspielhaus, 1984; Valedictorian, Williston-Northampton Sch., 1982; Absent Forever, Great Lakes Theatre Festival, 1987; *TV:* includes: Talking to a Stranger (quartet), 1968; That Quiet Earth; Walk into the Dark; Some Distant Shadow; The Greeks and their Gifts, 1966; A Story to Frighten the Children, 1976; Fathers and Families (sextet), 1977; Codename Kyril, 1987; scripts for Z-Cars (series); (with John Le Carré) Smiley's People (series), 1982; adaptations of classic novels; *film scripts:* The Offence, 1973; Murder by

Decree, 1979; The Holcroft Covenant, 1985. *Publications:* Talking to a Stranger, 1967; This Story of Yours, 1969; Find Your Way Home, 1971; Losing Time, 1982.

HOPKINS, John Humphrey David; Golf Correspondent, The Times, since 1993; *b* 26 March 1945; *s* of Leslie Charles Hopkins and Mary Eileen Hopkins (*née* Ellis); *m* 1970, Suzanne Ernestine Kommenda; one *s* one *d*. *Educ:* Llandaff Cathedral Sch., Cardiff (Choral Schol.); Wrekin Coll., Telford, Salop. Sunday Times: Rugby Corresp., 1976–80; Golf Corresp., 1980–91; golf and Rugby writer, Financial Times, 1991–93. *Publications:* Life with the Lions, 1977; The British Lions, 1980; Nick Faldo in Perspective, 1985; Golf: the four Majors, 1988; Golfers Companion, 1990; Golf in Wales: the Centenary 1895–1995, 1995. *Recreations:* squash, golf, Rugby, theatre, reading. *Address:* c/o The Times, 1 Pennington Street, E1 9XN. *T:* 0171–782 5944. *Clubs:* Royal Automobile, MCC; Jesters.

HOPKINS, Julian; *see* Hopkins, R. J.

HOPKINS, Keith; *see* Hopkins, M. K.

HOPKINS, Sir Michael (John), Kt 1995; CBE 1989; RA 1992; RIBA; RWA; Founding Partner, Michael Hopkins & Partners, 1976; *b* 7 May 1935; *s* of late Gerald and Barbara Hopkins; *m* 1962, Patricia Ann Wainwright (*see* P. A. Hopkins); one *s* two *d*. *Educ:* Sherborne Sch.; Architectural Assoc. (AA Dip. 1964). RIBA 1966; RWA 1989. Worked in offices of Sir Basil Spence, Leonard Manasseh and Tom Hancock; partnership with Norman Foster, 1969–75 and with Patricia Hopkins, 1976–; *projects include:* own house and studio, Hampstead, 1976; brewery bldg for Greene King, 1979; Patera Bldg System, 1984; Res. Centre for Schlumberger, Cambridge, 1984; infants sch., Hampshire, 1986; Bicentenary Stand, Lord's Cricket Ground, 1987; R & D Centre, Solid State Logic, 1988; London office and country workshop for David Mellor, 1989 and 1991; redevelt of Bracken House, St Paul's, for Ohbayashi Corp., 1992; offices at New Square, Bedfont Lakes, 1992; Glyndebourne Opera House, 1994; *current projects:* New Parliamentary Building, Westminster, 1989–; Inland Revenue offices, Nottingham, 1992–; lecture theatre, Emmanuel Coll., Cambridge, 1993–. Exhibited, Venice Biennale, 1991. Member: Royal Fine Art Commn, 1986–; London Adv. Cttee, English Heritage; Architectural Adv. Gp, Arts Council, 1992–. Vice Pres., Architectural Assoc., 1987–93; Trustee: Thomas Cubitt Trust, 1987–; British Mus., 1993–. Dr *hc* RCA 1994. Awards include: RIBA, 1977, 1980, 1988, 1993; Civic Trust, 1979, 1988, 1990, 1994; FT, 1980, 1982, 1993; Structural Steel, 1980, 1988, 1993; Royal Acad. Architectural, 1982; (with Patricia Hopkins) Royal Gold Medal, RIBA, 1994. *Recreations:* sailing, Catureglio. *Address:* 49A Downshire Hill, NW3 1NX. *T:* 0171–794 1494; (office) 27 Broadley Terrace, NW1 6LG. *T:* 0171–724 1751.
See also A. P. Hopkins.

HOPKINS, Prof. (Morris) Keith, FBA 1984; Professor of Ancient History, University of Cambridge, and Fellow of King's College, since 1985; *b* 20 June 1934; *s* of late Albert Thomas Hopkins and Hélène Dorothy Pratt; *m* 1963, Juliet, *d* of Sir Henry Phelps Brown, MBE, FBA; two *s* one *d*. *Educ:* Brentwood School; King's College, Cambridge. BA 1958; MA 1961. Asst Lectr in Sociology, Leicester Univ., 1961–63; Research Fellow, King's College, Cambridge, 1963–67; Lectr and Senior Lectr in Sociology, LSE, 1963–67, 1970–72; Prof. of Sociology: Univ. of Hong Kong, 1967–69; Brunel Univ., 1972–85 (Dean, Faculty of Social Sciences, 1981–85). Mem., Inst. for Advanced Study, Princeton, 1969–70, 1974–75, 1983. *Publications:* Hong Kong: The Industrial Colony (ed), 1971; Conquerors and Slaves, 1978; Death and Renewal, 1983. *Recreation:* drinking wine. *Address:* King's College, Cambridge CB2 1ST. *T:* Cambridge (01223) 350411.

HOPKINS, Patricia Ann, (Lady Hopkins); Partner, Michael Hopkins & Partners, since 1976; *b* 7 April 1942; *d* of Denys Wainwright, MB, Dsc, FRCS and Dr Shelagh Wainwright, MB, ChB; *m* 1962, Michael John Hopkins (*see* Sir Michael Hopkins); one *s* two *d*. *Educ:* Wycombe Abbey Sch.; Architectural Assoc. (AA Dip. 1968). Own practice, 1968–76; in partnership with Michael Hopkins, 1976–. Projects include: own house and studio, Hampstead, 1976; brewery bldg for Greene King, 1979; Patera Bldg System, 1984; Res. Centre for Schlumberger, Cambridge, 1984; infant's sch., Hants, 1986; Bi-centenary Stand, Lord's Cricket Ground, 1987; R & D Centre, Solid State Logic, 1988; London office and country workshop for David Mellor, 1980–91; New Parliamentary Bldg, Westminster, 1989–; redevelt of Bracken Hse, St Paul's, for Ohbayashi Corp., 1992; offices at New Square, Bedfont Lakes, 1992; Glyndebourne Opera Hse, 1994; projects in progress: Inland Revenue offices, Nottingham, 1992–; Lecture Theatre, Emmanuel Coll., Cambridge, 1993–. Exhibited, Venice Biennale, 1991. Member: Nat. Lottery Bd, Arts Council, 1994–; Foundn Campaign Bd, AA, 1994–. Building Awards include: RIBA, 1977, 1980, 1988, 1989, 1993; Civic Trust, 1979, 1988, 1990, 1994; Structural Steel, 1980, 1988, 1993; Royal Acad. Architectural, 1982; (with Michael Hopkins) Royal Gold Medal for Architecture, 1994. *Recreations:* family, friends, Catureglio. *Address:* (office) 27 Broadley Terrace, NW1 6LG. *T:* 0171–724 1751; 49a Downshire Hill, NW3 1NX. *T:* 0171–435 1109.

HOPKINS, (Richard) Julian; Director, ORBIS USA, ORBIS International, New York, since 1994; *b* 12 Oct. 1940; *s* of Richard Robert Hopkins and late Grace Hilda (*née* Hatfield); *m* 1971, Maureen Mary (*née* Hoye); two *s* one *d*. *Educ:* Bedford School. Asst Manager, London Palladium, 1963; Central Services Manager, BBC, 1965; joined RSPCA as Accounts Manager, 1972, appointed Admin. and Finance Officer, 1976; Exec. Dir, 1978–82; Gen. Manager, Charity Christmas Card Council, 1982–83; Finance Dir, War on Want, 1984–88; Dir, CARE Britain, 1988–94. Dir, and Mem. Exec. Cttee, World Soc. for Protection of Animals, 1980–82. Mem., Farm Animal Welfare Council, 1980–83. FIMgt. *Recreation:* all theatre, but especially opera, concert-going. *Address:* ORBIS, 330 West 42nd Street, New York, NY 10036, USA. *T:* (212) 2442525; 560 West 43rd Street, Apt #41B, New York, NY 10036–4320, USA. *T:* (212) 7149113; Rowan, 33 Needham Terrace, NW2 6QL.

HOPKINS, Russell, OBE 1989; FDSRCS; Consultant Oral and Maxillo-Facial Surgeon, Cardiff Royal Infirmary, 1968–95; Director of Medical Audit, South Glamorgan Health Authority, 1991–95; *b* 30 April 1932; *s* of Charles Albert Hopkins and Frances Doris Hopkins; *m* 1970, Jill Margaret Pexton; two *s* one *d*. *Educ:* Barnard Castle Sch.; King's Coll., Durham Univ. (BDS 1956); Royal Free Hosp., London Univ. LRCP, MRCS 1964; FDSRCS 1961. Gen. dental practice, 1956–58; SHO, Oral Surgery, Nottingham Gen. Hosp., 1958–59; Registrar, Oral Surgery, St Peter's Hosp., Chertsey, 1959–61; Sen. Registrar, Royal Victoria Infirmary, Newcastle upon Tyne, 1965–68; Consultant, 1970–95, Gen. Manager, 1985–91, Univ. Hosp. of Wales, Cardiff. Member: Central Cttee, Hosp. Med. Services, 1975–88; Jt Consultant Cttee, London, 1980–93 (Chm., Welsh Sub-Cttee, 1986–93); Chairman: Med. Bd, S Glamorgan, 1980–82; Welsh Council, BMA, 1991–94 (Chm., Welsh Consultant and Specialist Cttee, 1989–93); BMA Gen. Managers' Gp, 1988–90. Pres., BAOMS 1992–93; Mem., Eur. Assoc. of Max.-Fac. Surgery. Ext. Examr, Univ. of Hong Kong, 1990–93. *Publications:* Pre-Prosthetic Oral Surgery, 1986; chapters in numerous medical works. *Recreations:* golf, sea fishing, walking, photography, reading. *Address:* 179 Cyncoed Road, Cardiff CF2 6AH. *T:* (home) Cardiff (01222) 752319. *Clubs:* Cardiff Golf, Newport Golf; Newport Boat.

HOPKINS, Sidney Arthur; Managing Director, Guardian Royal Exchange plc, 1990–94; *b* 15 April 1932; *m* 1955, Joan Marion Smith; one *d*. *Educ:* Battersea Grammar Sch. ACII. Joined Royal Exchange Assce, 1948, Man., Organisation and Methods, 1966; Guardian Royal Exchange Assurance Ltd: Chief Claims Man. (UK), 1974; Man., Home Motor, 1976; Asst Gen. Man. (Life), 1979; Guardian Royal Exchange Assurance plc: Asst Gen. Man. (Field Operations), 1983; Gen. Man. (UK), 1985; Guardian Royal Exchange (UK) Ltd: Man. Dir, 1987; Guardian Royal Exchange plc: Dir, 1986; Dep. Chief Exec., 1989. Freeman, City of London; Liveryman, Company of Insurers. *Recreations:* sports, films. *Address:* Woodlands, 8 Littleworth Lane, Esher, Surrey KT10 9PF. *Club:* Royal Automobile.

HOPKINSON, family name of **Baron Colyton.**

HOPKINSON, Ven. Barnabas John; Archdeacon of Sarum, since 1986; Priest-in-charge, Stratford-sub-Castle, since 1987; *b* 11 May 1939; *s* of Prebendary Stephan Hopkinson and late Mrs Anne Hopkinson; *m* 1968, Esmé Faith (*née* Gibbons); three *d*. *Educ:* Emanuel School; Trinity Coll., Cambridge (MA); Lincoln Theological Coll. Curate: All Saints and Martyrs, Langley, Manchester, 1965–67; Great St Mary's, Cambridge, 1967–70; Chaplain, Charterhouse School, 1970–75; Team Vicar of Preshute, Wilts, 1975–81; RD of Marlborough, 1977–81; Rector of Wimborne Minster, Dorset, 1981–86; RD of Wimborne, 1985–86. Canon of Salisbury Cathedral, 1983–. *Recreations:* mountaineering, camping. *Address:* Russell House, Stratford-sub-Castle, Salisbury, Wilts SP1 3LG. *T:* Salisbury (01722) 328756.

HOPKINSON, Prof. David Albert, MD; Director, Medical Research Council Human Biochemical Genetics Unit, since 1976; Professor of Human Biochemical Genetics, University College London, since 1993; *b* 26 June 1935; *s* of George Albert and Lily Hopkinson; *m* 1st, 1959, Josephine Manze; two *s* one *d*; 2nd, 1980, Yvonne Edwards. *Educ:* Chesterfield Grammar Sch.; St Catharine's Coll., Cambridge; Royal London Hosp. Med. Coll. (MA, MD). Royal London Hospital: House Surgeon and House Physician, 1959–60; Jun. Lectr, Biochem., 1960; Resident Pathologist, 1961; Scientific Staff, MRC Human Biochemical Genetics Unit, 1962–. Hon. Life Mem., Internat. Forensic Haemogenetics Soc., 1992. *Publication:* Handbook of Enzyme Electrophoresis in Human Genetics, 1976. *Recreations:* allotment gardening, hill and mountain walking, furniture restoration, watching Rugby. *Address:* 10 Princes Court, 68 Pilgrims Lane, NW3 1SP. *T:* (office) 0171–387 7050.

HOPKINSON, David Hugh; Chief Night Editor of The Times, 1982; *b* 9 June 1930; *er s* of late C. G. Hopkinson. *Educ:* Sowerby Bridge Grammar Sch. Entered journalism on Huddersfield Examiner, 1950; Yorkshire Observer, 1954; Yorkshire Evening News, 1954; Evening Chronicle, Manchester, 1956; Chief Sub-Editor, Sunday Graphic, London, 1957; Asst Editor, Evening Chronicle, Newcastle upon Tyne, 1959; Chief Asst Editor, Sunday Graphic, 1960; Dep. Editor, Sheffield Telegraph, 1961, Editor, 1962–64; Editor, The Birmingham Post, 1964–73; Dir, Birmingham Post & Mail Ltd, 1967–80; Editor, Birmingham Evening Mail, 1974–79; Editor-in-Chief, Evening Mail series, 1975–79, Birmingham Post and Evening Mail, 1979–80; Asst to Editor of The Times, 1981. Member: Lord Justice Phillimore's Cttee inquiring into law of contempt; International Press Institute; Associate Mem., Justice (British br. of Internat. Commn of Jurists). National Press Award, Journalist of the Year, 1963. *Address:* c/o The Times, 1 Pennington Street, E1 9XN.

HOPKINSON, David Hugh Laing, CBE 1986; RD 1965; DL; Deputy Chairman and Chief Executive, M&G Group PLC, 1979–87; Chairman, Harrisons and Crosfield, 1988–91 (Deputy Chairman, 1987–88, Director, 1986–91); Deputy Chairman, ECC Group (formerly English China Clays), 1986–91 (Director, since 1975); *b* 14 Aug. 1926; *s* of late Cecil Hopkinson and Leila Hopkinson; *m* 1951, Prudence Margaret Holmes; two *s* two *d*. *Educ:* Wellington Coll.; Merton Coll., Oxford (BA 1949). RNVR and RNR, 1944–65. A Clerk of the House of Commons, 1948–59; Robert Fleming, 1959–62; M&G Investment Management, 1963–87 (Chm., 1975–87); Director: Lloyds Bank Southern Regional Board, 1977–88; BR (Southern) Bd, 1978–87 (Chm., 1983–87); Wolverhampton and Dudley Breweries, 1987–; Mem., Adv. Gp of Governor of Bank of England, 1984. Mem., Housing Corp., 1986–88. Director: English Chamber Orchestra and Music Soc., 1970–89; Charities Investment Managers, 1970–; Merchants Trust, 1976–; SE Arts Board, 1994–. Member: General Synod of C of E, 1970–90; Central Bd of Finance, 1970–90; a Church Comr, 1973–82, 1984–94; Mem., Chichester Dio. Bd of Finance, 1970– (Chm., 1977–88); Chm., Church Army Bd, 1987–89. Trustee: Nat. Assoc. of Almshouses; Chichester Cathedral Development Trust; Pallant House Museum, Chichester; Royal Pavilion, Brighton; RAM Foundn; Edward James Foundn; Weald and Downland Mus. Governor: Sherborne Sch., 1970– (Vice-Chm., Bd, 1987–); Wellington Coll., 1978–. DL 1986, High Sheriff, 1987–88, W Sussex. Hon. Fellow, St Anne's Coll., Oxford, 1984–. *Recreations:* travelling, walking, opera. *Address:* St John's Priory, Poling, Arundel, W Sussex BN18 9PS. *T:* Arundel (01903) 882393. *Club:* Brooks's.

HOPKINSON, George William; Assistant Under-Secretary of State (Policy), Ministry of Defence, since 1993; *b* 13 Sept. 1943; *s* of William Hartley Hopkinson and Mary (*née* Ashmore); *m* 1973, Mary Agnes Coverdale; one *s*. *Educ:* Tupton Hall Grammar Sch.; Pembroke Coll., Cambridge (MA 1965). Inland Revenue, 1965–73; CSD, 1973–81; HM Treasury, 1981–86; Ministry of Defence, 1986–: Hd, Defence Arms Control Unit, 1988–91; Vis. Fellow, Global Security Programme, Cambridge Univ., 1991–92 (on secondment); Hd, Defence Lands Service, 1992–93. *Publications:* contribs to books on security policy, arms control and Global Security Programme; occasional papers. *Recreations:* reading, walking. *Address:* c/o Ministry of Defence, Main Building, Whitehall, SW1A 2HB. *T:* 0171–218 2505. *Club:* United Oxford & Cambridge University.

HOPKINSON, Giles, CB 1990; Under-Secretary, Departments of the Environment and Transport, 1976–90, retired; *b* 20 Nov. 1931; *s* of late Arthur John Hopkinson, CIE, ICS, and of Eleanor (*née* Richardson); *m* 1956, Eleanor Jean Riddell; three *d*. *Educ:* Marlborough Coll.; Leeds Univ. (BSc). E. & J. Richardson Ltd, 1956–57; Forestal Land, Timber and Rly Co. Ltd, 1957–58; DSIR: Scientific Officer, 1958–61; Sen. Scientific Officer, 1961–64; Private Sec. to Perm. Sec., 1963–64; Principal, MoT, 1964–71; Asst Sec., DoE, 1971; Under-Secretary: DoE, 1976; Dept of Transport (Ports and Freight Directorate), 1979; Dir, London Region, PSA, DoE, 1983–90. *Recreations:* music, landscape gardening; restoration of antique furniture. *Address:* Digswell Water Mill, Digswell Lane, Welwyn Garden City, Herts AL7 1SW. *Club:* Commonwealth Trust.

HOPKINSON, Maj.-Gen. John Charles Oswald Rooke, CB 1984; Director, British Field Sports Society, 1984–93; *b* 31 July 1931; *s* of Lt-Col John Oliver Hopkinson and Aileen Disney Hopkinson (*née* Rooke); *m* 1956, Sarah Elizabeth, *d* of Maj.-Gen. M. H. P. Sayers, *qv*; three *s* one *d*. *Educ:* Stonyhurst Coll.; RMA, Sandhurst. sc 1963, jssc 1968, rcds 1979. Commanding Officer, 1st Bn Queen's Own Highlanders, 1972–74 (despatches); Dep. Comdr 2nd Armoured Division, and Comdr Osnabrück Garrison, 1977–78; Director Operational Requirements 3 (Army), 1980–82; Chief-of-Staff, HQ Allied Forces Northern Europe, 1982–84. Colonel, Queen's Own Highlanders, 1983–94. Chm., Wye Salmon

Fishing Owners, 1993–. *Recreations:* shooting, fishing, sailing. *Address:* Bigsweir, Gloucestershire. *Club:* Army and Navy.

HOPKINSON, John Edmund; Judge of the High Court, Hong Kong, 1985–89, retired; *b* 25 Oct. 1924; *s* of Captain E. H. Hopkinson, OBE, RN and Mrs E. H. Hopkinson; *m* 1961, Inge Gansel; one *s* one *d*. *Educ:* Marlborough Coll., Wilts; Pembroke Coll., Cambridge (MA). Called to the Bar, Lincoln's Inn, 1949. Served War, RN, 1943–46: Ordinary Seaman, Midshipman RNVR, 1943; Sub-Lt RNVR, 1944–46. Prudential Assurance Co., 1949–50; Legal Asst, Colonial Office, 1950–55; Hong Kong, 1962–89: Crown Counsel, 1962; Principal Crown Counsel, 1972; Dist Judge, 1974. *Recreations:* golf, tennis, ski-ing, music. *Address:* 41 Clavering Avenue, SW13 9DX. *Clubs:* Roehampton; Shek O Country (Hong Kong); Royal Hong Kong Golf; Royal Cinque Ports Golf.

HOPKIRK, Joyce, (Mrs W. J. Lear); Director, Editors' Unlimited, since 1990; *b* 2 March; *d* of Walter Nicholson and Veronica (*née* Keelan); *m* 1st, 1962, Peter Hopkirk; one *d*; 2nd, 1974, William James Lear; one *s*. *Educ:* Middle Street Secondary Sch., Newcastle upon Tyne. Reporter, Gateshead Post, 1955; Founder Editor, Majorcan News, 1959; Reporter, Daily Sketch, 1960; Royal Reporter, Daily Express, 1961; Ed., Fashion Magazine, 1967; Women's Ed., Sun, 1967; Launch Ed., Cosmopolitan, 1971–72 (launched 1972); Asst Ed., Daily Mirror, 1973–78; Women's Ed., Sunday Times, 1982; Editl Dir, Elle, 1984; Asst Ed., Sunday Mirror, 1985; Ed.-in-Chief, She Magazine, 1986–89; Founder Ed., Chic Magazine 1994. Editor of the Year, 1972; Women's Magazines Editor of the Year, 1988. FRSA. *Publications:* Successful Slimming, 1976; Successful Slimming Cookbook, 1978; (jtly) Splash!, 1995. *Recreations:* conversation, sleeping, gardening, hockey, ski-ing, boating. *Address:* Gadespring, 109 Piccotts End, Hemel Hempstead, Herts HP1 3AT. *T:* Hemel Hempstead (01442) 245608; Jury's Gap, Sussex; Puerto Andraitx, Mallorca. *Club:* Groucho.

HOPPER, Prof. Frederick Ernest, MDS, FDSRCS; FFDRCSI; Professor of Dental Surgery and Dean of the School of Dentistry, University of Leeds, 1959–85, now Professor Emeritus; Consultant Dental Surgeon, Leeds Area Health Authority, 1959–85; Chairman, Board of Faculty of Medicine, University of Leeds, 1975–78; *b* 22 Nov. 1919; *s* of Frederick Ernest Hopper, MPS and Margaret Ann Carlyle; *m* 1949, Gudrun Eik-Nes, LDSRCS, *d* of Prost Knut Eik-Nes and Nina Eik-Nes, Trondheim, Norway; three *s*. *Educ:* Dame Allan's Sch., Newcastle upon Tyne; King's Coll., University of Durham. BDS (with dist.) 1943; FDSRCS 1948; MDS 1958. House Surg., Newcastle upon Tyne Dental Hosp. and Royal Dental Hospital, 1943–44; served in EMS in Maxillo-Facial Centres at E Grinstead and Shotley Bridge, 1944–46; successively Lecturer, 1946, and Sen. Lecturer, 1956, in Periodontal Diseases, King's Coll., University of Durham; Lecturer in Dental Pharmacology and Therapeutics, 1947–59; Examiner in Dental subjects, Univs of Durham, Edinburgh, St Andrews, Bristol, Liverpool; Dental Surgeon in charge Parodontal Dept, Newcastle upon Tyne Dental Hosp., and Sen. Dental Surg., Plastic and Jaw Unit, Shotley Bridge, 1946–59; Cons. Dent. Surg., United Newcastle Hosps, 1955–59. Hon. Treas., Brit. Soc. of Periodontology, 1949–53, Pres. 1954. Member: General Dental Council, 1959–85 (Chm., Educn Cttee, 1980–85); Brit. Dental Assoc., 1943–; Internat. Dental Fedn, 1948–; Pres., British Soc. for Oral Medicine, 1986. GDC Visitor, 1986–87, to Medical Univ. of Southern Africa and to Univs of Pretoria, Stellenbosch, Western Cape, the Witwatersrand, Otago, Hong Kong and Singapore. *Publications:* contribs to med. and dental jls. *Recreations:* photography (still and ciné); golf. *Address:* 23 Ancaster Road, Leeds LS16 5HH. *Club:* Alwoodley Golf (Leeds).

HOPPER, William Joseph; Executive Chairman, W. J. Hopper & Co. Ltd, since 1991; *b* 9 Aug. 1929; *s* of I. Vance Hopper and Jennie Josephine Hopper; one *d* by a former marriage. *Educ:* Langside Elementary Sch., Glasgow; Queen's Park Secondary Sch., Glasgow; Glasgow Univ. (MA 1st Cl. Hons (Mod. Langs) 1953). Financial Analyst, W. R. Grace & Co., NY, 1956–59; London Office Manager, H. Hentz & Co., Members, NY Stock Exchange, 1960–66; Gen. Manager, S. G. Warburg & Co. Ltd, 1966–69; Director: Hill Samuel & Co. Ltd, 1969–74; Morgan Grenfell & Co. Ltd, 1974–79 (Adviser, 1979–86) (bond issue for EIB selected as Deal of the Year by Institutional Investor, 1976); Wharf Resources Ltd, Calgary, 1984–87; Manchester Ship Canal Co., 1985–87; Chm., Robust Mouldings, 1986–90; Exec. Chm., Shire Trust, 1986–91; Advr, Yamaichi Internat. (Europe), 1986–88. MEP (C), Greater Manchester West, 1979–84. Co-founder (1969) and first Chm. (now Mem., Exec. Cttee), Inst. for Fiscal Studies, London; Treasurer, Action Resource Centre, 1985–94; Trustee: Nat. Hosp. for Nervous Diseases Develt Fund, 1986–90; Hampstead, Wells and Campden Trust, 1989– Chm., Rosslyn Hill Unitarian Chapel, 1995–. Governor, Colville Primary Sch., Notting Hill Gate, 1978–80. *Publication:* A Turntable for Capital, 1969. *Recreations:* listening to music, garden design. *Address:* 43 Flask Walk, Hampstead, NW3 1HH. *T:* 0171–435 6414. *Club:* Garrick.

HOPWOOD, Prof. Anthony George; Professor of Management Studies and Deputy Director of the School of Management, and Fellow, Templeton College, Oxford University, since 1995; *b* 18 May 1944; *s* of late George and Violet Hopwood; *m* 1967, Caryl Davies; two *s*. *Educ:* Hanley High School; LSE (BSc Econ); Univ. of Chicago (MBA, PhD). Lectr in Management Accounting, Manchester Business Sch., 1970–73; Senior Staff, Admin. Staff Coll., Henley, 1973–76; Professorial Fellow, Oxford Centre for Management Studies, 1976–78; ICA Prof. of Accounting and Financial Reporting, London Business Sch., 1978–85; Arthur Young, subseq. Ernst and Young, Prof. of Internat. Accounting and Financial Management, LSE, 1985–95. Vis. Prof. of Management, European Inst. for Advanced Studies in Management, Brussels, 1972–; Associate Fellow, Industrial Relations Research Unit, Univ. of Warwick, 1978–80; Amer. Accounting Assoc. Dist. Internat. Vis. Lectr, 1981; Distinguished Vis. Prof. of Accounting, Pennsylvania State Univ., 1983–88. Mem., Management and Industrial Relations Cttee, SSRC, 1975–79; Chm., Management Awards Panel, SSRC, 1976–79; Pres., European Accounting Assoc., 1977–79 and 1987–88; Member: Council, Tavistock Inst. of Human Relations, 1981–91; Research Bd, ICA, 1982–; Dir, Greater London Enterprise Bd, 1985–87. Accounting Advr, EC, 1989–90; Accounting Cons., OECD, 1990–91. Hon. DEcon: Turku Sch. of Econs, Finland, 1989; Gothenburg, 1992. Editor-in-Chief, Accounting, Organizations and Society, 1976–. *Publications:* An Accounting System and Managerial Behaviour, 1973; Accounting and Human Behaviour, 1973; (with M. Bromwich) Essays in British Accounting Research, 1981; (with M. Bromwich and J. Shaw) Auditing Research, 1982; (with M. Bromwich) Accounting Standard Setting, 1983; (with H. Schreuder) European Contributions to Accounting Research, 1984; (with C. Tomkins) Issues in Public Sector Accounting, 1984; (with M. Bromwich) Research and Current Issues in Management Accounting, 1986; Accounting from the Outside: the collected papers of Anthony G. Hopwood, 1988; International Pressures for Accounting Change, 1989; (with M. Page and S. Turley) Understanding Accounting in a Changing Environment, 1990; (with M. Bromwich) Accounting and the Law, 1992; (with P. Miller) Accounting as Social and Institutional Practice, 1994; articles in learned and professional jls. *Address:* School of Management Studies, University of Oxford, Radcliffe Infirmary, Woodstock Road, Oxford OX2 6HE. *T:* Oxford (01865) 228470.

HOPWOOD, Sir David (Alan), Kt 1994; FRS 1979; John Innes Professor of Genetics, University of East Anglia, Norwich, and Head of the Genetics Department, John Innes Centre, Institute, since 1968; *b* 19 Aug. 1933; *s* of Herbert Hopwood and Dora Hopwood (*née* Grant); *m* 1962, Joyce Lilian Bloom; two *s* one *d*. *Educ:* Purbrook Park County High Sch., Hants; Lymm Grammar Sch., Cheshire; St John's Coll., Cambridge (MA, PhD). DSc (Glasgow). Whytehead Major Scholar, St John's Coll., Cambridge, 1951–54; John Stothert Bye-Fellow, Magdalene Coll., Cambridge, 1956–58 (Hon. Fellow, 1991); Res. Fellow, St John's Coll., 1958–61; Univ. Demonstrator, Univ. of Cambridge, 1957–61; Lectr in Genetics, Univ. of Glasgow, 1961–68. Pres., Genetical Soc. of GB, 1985–87. Foreign Fellow, Indian Nat. Science Acad., 1987. Hon. Professor: Chinese Acad. of Med. Scis, 1987; Insts of Microbiology and Plant Physiology, Chinese Acad. of Scis, 1987; Huazhong Agricl Univ., Wuhan, China, 1989. Hon. Fellow: UMIST, 1990; Magdalene Coll., Cambridge, 1992. Hon. Mem., Hungarian Acad. of Scis, 1990. Hon. DSc Eidgenössische Technische Hochschule, Zürich, 1989. *Publications:* numerous articles and chapters in scientific jls and books. *Address:* John Innes Institute, John Innes Centre, Colney Lane, Norwich NR4 7UH. *T:* Norwich (01603) 52571, *Fax:* Norwich (01603) 56844.

HORAM, John Rhodes; MP (C) Orpington, since 1992; Parliamentary Secretary, Office of the Deputy Prime Minister, since 1995; *b* 7 March 1939; *s* of Sydney Horam, Preston; *m* 1987, Judith Jackson. *Educ:* Silcoates Sch., Wakefield; Univ. of Cambridge. Marketing Executive, Rowntree & Co., 1960–62; leader and feature writer: Financial Times, 1962–65; The Economist, 1965–68; Man. Dir, Commodities Research Unit Ltd, 1968–70 and 1983–92; Dep. Chm., CRU Internat. Ltd, 1992–95. MP Gateshead West, 1970–83 (Lab, 1970–81, SDP, 1981–83). Parly Under-Sec. of State, Dept of Transport, 1976–79; Labour spokesman on econ. affairs, 1979–81; Parly spokesman on econ. affairs, SDP, 1981–83. Contested (SDP) Newcastle upon Tyne Central, 1983. Joined Conservative Party, Feb. 1987. *Address:* 6 Bovingdon Road, SW6 2AP.

HORAN, Rt. Rev. Forbes Trevor; *b* 22 May 1905; *s* of Rev. Frederick Seymour Horan and Mary Katherine Horan; *m* 1st, 1939, Veronica (*d* 1983), *d* of late Rt Rev. J. N. Bateman-Champain, sometime Bishop of Knaresborough; two *s* two *d*; 2nd, 1988, Elizabeth Lyona Lancaster, Cheltenham. *Educ:* Sherborne and Trinity Hall, Cambridge. RMC Sandhurst, 1924–25; Oxford and Bucks Lt Infantry, Lieutenant, 1925–29; Trinity Hall, Cambridge, 1929–32; Westcott House, Cambridge, 1932–33; Curate, St Luke's, Newcastle upon Tyne, 1933–35; Curate, St George's, Jesmond, Newcastle upon Tyne, 1935–37; Priest-in-charge, St Peter's, Balkwell, 1937–40; RNVR, 1940–45; Vicar of St Chad's, Shrewsbury, 1945–52; Vicar of Huddersfield Parish Church, 1952–60; Bishop Suffragan of Tewkesbury, 1960–73. *Recreations:* listening to the Third Programme on the radio, bicycling in order to maintain some semblance of independence, cooking and housekeeping. *Address:* 3 Silverthorn Close, Shurdington Road, Cheltenham, Glos GL53 0JL. *T:* Cheltenham (01242) 527313.

HORD, Brian Howard, CBE 1989; FRICS; Director General, Bureau of European Building Consultants and Experts, since 1991; *b* 20 June 1934; *s* of late Edwin Charles and of Winifred Hannah Hord; *m* 1960, Christine Marian Lucas; two *s*. *Educ:* Reedham Sch.; Purley Grammar Sch. County Planning Dept, Mddx CC, 1950–51; Surveyor, private practice, 1951–57; National Service, RAF, 1957–59; Estates Surveyor, United Drapery Stores, 1959–66; Richard Costain Ltd, 1966–70; Director, Capcount UK Ltd, principal subsid. of Capital & Counties Property Co. Ltd, 1970–75; Partner, Howard Hord & Palmer, Chartered Surveyors, 1975–84. Chm., Bexley HA, 1986–92; Mem., London Rent Assessment Panel, 1985–. Contested (C) Darlington, Feb. and Oct. 1974. MEP (C) London West, 1979–84; Whip of European Democratic Gp, 1982–83; Mem., Agric. and Budgets Cttees, Eur. Parlt. *Publication:* (jtly) Rates-Realism or Rebellion. *Recreations:* photography, top-fruit growing, bee-keeping. *Address:* Whitesides, Pilgrims Way East, Otford, Sevenoaks, Kent TN14 5QN. *Club:* Carlton.

HORDEN, Prof. John Robert Backhouse, FSA; FRSL; Emeritus Professor of Bibliographical Studies, University of Stirling, since 1988; Editor, Dictionary of Scottish Biography, since 1982; *o s* of late Henry Robert Horden and Ethel Edith Horden (*née* Backhouse), Warwicks; *m* 1948, Aileen Mary (*d* 1984), *o d* of late Lt Col and Mrs W. J. Douglas, Warwicks and S Wales; one *s*. *Educ:* Oxford, Cambridge, Heidelberg, Sorbonne, Lincoln's Inn. Revived and ed The Isis, 1945–46. Previously: Tutor and Lectr in English Literature, Christ Church, Oxford; Director, Inst. of Bibliography and Textual Criticism, Univ. of Leeds; Dir, Centre for Bibliographical Studies, Univ. of Stirling. Vis. professorial appts, Univs of Pennsylvania State, Saskatchewan, Erlangen-Nürnberg, Texas at Austin, Münster; Cecil Oldman Meml Lectr in Bibliography and Textual Criticism, 1971. Hon. Life Mem., Modern Humanities Res. Assoc., 1976. DHL (*hc*) Indiana State Univ., 1974. Marc Fitch Prize for Bibliography, 1979. Devised new academic discipline of Publishing Studies and designed first British degree course at Univ. of Leeds, 1972 (MA); initiated first British degree in Public Relations (MSc), Univ. of Stirling, 1987. *Publications:* Francis Quarles: a bibliography of his works to 1800, 1953; (ed) Francis Quarles' Hosanna and Threnodes, 1960, 3rd edn 1965; (ed) Annual Bibliography of English Language and Literature, 1967–75; (ed) English and Continental Emblem Books (22 vols), 1968–74; Art of the Drama, 1969; Everyday Life in Seventeenth-century England, 1974; (contrib.) New Cambridge Bibliography of English Literature, 1974; Techniques of Bibliography, 1977; (ed) Dictionary of Concealed Authorship, vol. 1, 1980 (1st vol. of rev. Halkett and Laing); (initiator and first editor) Index of English Literary Manuscripts (7 vols), 1980–90; John Freeth: political ballad writer and inn keeper, 1985, 2nd edn 1993; (ed) Bibliographia, 1992; (ed jtly) Francis Quarles' Emblemes and Hieroglyphikes, 1993; numerous contribs to learned jls. *Recreations:* golf (represented England, Warwicks, Oxford and Cambridge), music, painting. *Address:* Department of English Studies, University of Stirling, Stirling FK9 4LA. *T:* Stirling (01786) 467495. *Clubs:* Athenæum; Vincent's (Oxford); Hawks' (Cambridge).

HORDEN, Richard, RIBA; Chairman and Managing Director, Richard Horden Associates, since 1985; *b* 26 Dec. 1944; *s* of Peter Horden and Irene Horden (*née* Kelly); *m* 1972, Kathleen Gibson Valentine; one *s* one *d*. *Educ:* Perrott Hill Sch.; Bryanston Sch.; Architectural Assoc. (AA Dip.). RIBA 1974. Work with Sir Norman Foster, 1974–84: Design Assistant for the Sainsbury Centre for Visual Arts, UEA; Stansted Airport; estabd Richard Horden Associates, 1985. RIBA Commendation for Courtyard House, Poole, 1974; FT Award and RIBA Nat. Award for Architecture for Queen's Stand, Epsom, 1993. *Recreations:* yachting, ski-ing, running. *Address:* Richard Horden Associates, 4 Golden Square, W1R 3AE. *T:* 0171–439 0241. *Club:* Royal Motor Yacht (Poole).

HORDER, family name of **Baron Horder.**

HORDER, 2nd Baron *cr* 1933, of Ashford in the County of Southampton; **Thomas Mervyn Horder;** Bt, of Shaston, 1923; *b* 8 Dec. 1910; *s* of 1st Baron Horder, GCVO, MD, FRCP, and Geraldine Rose (*d* 1954), *o d* of Arthur Doggett, Newnham Manor, Herts; *S* father, 1955. *Educ:* Winchester; Trinity Coll., Cambridge. BA 1932; MA 1937. Served War of 1939–45: HQ, RAF Fighter Comd, 1940–42 (despatches); Air HQ, India, 1942–44; Headquarters, South-East Asia Command, 1944–45; United Kingdom Liaison

Mission, Tokyo, 1945–46; Chairman, Gerald Duckworth & Co. Ltd, 1948–70. *Publications:* The Little Genius, 1966; (ed) Ronald Firbank: memoirs and critiques, 1977; On Their Own: shipwrecks & survivals, 1988; *music:* (ed) The Orange Carol Book, 1962; Six Betjeman Songs, 1967; A Shropshire Lad (songs), 1980; (ed) The Easter Carol Book, 1982; Seven Shakespeare Songs, 1988; Black Diamonds (six Dorothy Parker songs), 1990; Five Burns Songs, 1995. *Recreations:* music, idling. *Address:* 4 Hamilton Close, NW8 8QY.

HORDER, Dr John Plaistowe, CBE 1981 (OBE 1971); FRCP, FRCPE, FRCGP, FRCPsych; general practitioner of medicine, 1951–81, retired; President, National Centre for the Advancement of Interprofessional Education (Chairman, 1987); *b* 9 Dec. 1919; *s* of Gerald Morley Horder and Emma Ruth Horder; *m* 1940, Elizabeth June Wilson; two *s* two *d. Educ:* Lancing Coll.; University Coll., Oxford (BA 1945); London Hosp. (BM BCh 1948). FRCP 1972 (MRCP 1951); FRCGP 1970 (MRCGP 1957); FRCPsych 1980 (MRCPsych 1975); FRCPE 1982. Consultant, 1959, Travelling Fellow, 1964, WHO; Lectr, London School of Economics and Pol. Sci., 1964–69; Sir Harry Jeffcott Vis. Prof., Univ. of Nottingham, 1975; Visiting Professor: Royal Free Hosp. Med. Sch., 1982–91; Zagreb Univ., 1990–. Consultant Adviser, DHSS, 1978–84. Pres., Medical Art Soc., 1990–. Pres., RCGP, 1979–82 (John Hunt Fellow, 1974–77; Wolfson Travelling Prof., 1978); Hon. Fellow, RSM, 1983 (Vice-Pres., 1987–89; Pres., Sect. of Gen. Practice, 1970). Hon. Fellow, Green Coll., Oxford, 1988. Hon. MD Free Univ. Amsterdam, 1985. Hon. Mem., Coll. of Family Physicians of Canada, 1982. *Publications:* ed and co-author, The Future General Practitioner—learning and teaching, 1972; articles on general practice—training for and psychiatry in. . . . , 1953–. *Recreations:* painting, music. *Address:* 98 Regent's Park Road, NW1 8UG. *T:* 0171–722 3804.

HORDERN, (Alfred) Christopher (Willoughby); QC 1979; **His Honour Judge Hordern;** a Circuit Judge, since 1983; *m*; one *s* two *d. Educ:* Oxford Univ. (MA). Called to the Bar, Middle Temple, 1961; a Recorder of the Crown Court, 1974–83. *Address:* c/o South Eastern Circuit Office, New Cavendish House, 18 Maltravers Street, WC2R 3EU.

HORDERN, Rt. Hon. Sir Peter (Maudslay), Kt 1985; PC 1993; DL; MP (C) Horsham, 1964–74 and since 1983 (Horsham and Crawley, 1974–83); *b* 18 April 1929; British; *s* of C. H. Hordern, MBE; *m* 1964, Susan Chataway; two *s* one *d. Educ:* Geelong Grammar Sch., Australia; Christ Church, Oxford, 1949–52 (MA). Mem. of Stock Exchange, London, 1957–74. Chairman: F. & C. Smaller Cos (formerly F. & C. Alliance Investment), 1986– (Dir, 1976–); Fina (formerly Petrofina (UK)), 1987– (Dir, 1973–); Dir, TR Technology, 1975–. Chm., Cons. Parly Finance Cttee, 1970–72; Member: Exec., 1922 Cttee, 1968– (Jt Sec., 1988–); Public Accts Cttee, 1970–; Public Accounts Commn, 1984– (Chm., 1988–). DL West Sussex, 1988. *Recreations:* golf, reading and travel.

HORE-RUTHVEN, family name of **Earl of Gowrie.**

HORLICK, Vice-Adm. Sir Edwin John, (Sir Ted Horlick), KBE 1981; FEng, FIMechE, MIMarE; part-time consultant; *b* 28 Sept. 1925; *m* Jean Margaret (*née* Covington) (*d* 1991); four *s. Educ:* Bedford Modern Sch. Joined RN, 1943; Sqdn Eng. Officer, 2nd Frigate Sqdn, 1960–63; Ship Dept, MoD, 1963–66; First Asst to Chief Engineer, HM Dockyard, Singapore, 1966–68; Asst Dir Submarines, 1969–72; SOWC 1973; Fleet Marine Engineering Officer, Staff of C-in-C Fleet, 1973–75; RCDS 1976; Dir Project Team Submarine/Polaris, 1977–79; Dir Gen. Ships, 1979–83; Chief Naval Engineer Officer, 1981–83. *Recreations:* golf, Rugby administration, DIY. *Address:* Garden Apt, 74 Great Pulteney Street, Bath BA2 4DL. *Club:* Army and Navy.

HORLICK, Sir James Cunliffe William, 6th Bt *cr* 1914, of Cowley Manor, Gloucester; *b* 19 Nov. 1956; *o s* of Sir John James Macdonald Horlick, 5th Bt and of June, *d* of Douglas Cory-Wright, CBE; *S* father, 1995; *m* 1985, Fiona Rosalie, *e d* of Andrew McLaren; three *s. Educ:* Eton. *Heir: s* Alexander Horlick, *b* 8 April 1987.

HORLICK, Sir Ted; *see* Horlick, Sir Edwin John.

HORLOCK, Henry Wimburn Sudell; Underwriting Member of Lloyd's, since 1957; Director, Stepping Stone School, 1962–87; *b* 19 July 1915; *s* of Rev. Henry Darrell Sudell Horlock, DD, and Mary Haliburton Laurie; *m* 1960, Jeannetta Robin, *d* of F. W. Tanner, JP. *Educ:* Pembroke Coll., Oxford (MA). Army, 1939–42. Civil Service, 1942–60. Court of Common Council, City of London, 1969– (Chm., West Ham Park Cttee, 1979–82; Chm., Police Cttee, 1987–90); Deputy, Ward of Farringdon Within, 1978–; Sheriff, City of London, 1972–73; Chm., City of London Sheriffs' Soc., 1985–; Liveryman: Saddlers Co., 1937–, Master, 1976–77; Plaisterers' Co. (Hon.), 1975–; Fletchers' Co., 1977–; Gardeners' Co., 1980–; Member: Parish Clerks' Co., 1966–, Master, 1981–82; Guild of Freemen, 1972–, Master, 1986–87; Farringdon Ward Club, 1970–, Pres., 1978–79; United Wards Club, 1972–, Pres., 1980–81; City Livery Club, 1969–, Pres., 1981–82; City of London Br., Royal Society of St George, 1972–, Chm., 1989–90. Commander: Order of Merit, Federal Republic of Germany, 1972; National Order of the Aztec Eagle of Mexico, 1973; Order of Wissam Alouite, Morocco, 1987. *Recreations:* gardening, travel. *Address:* 97 Defoe House, Barbican, EC2Y 8DN. *T:* 0171–588 1602. *Clubs:* Athenæum, Guildhall, City Livery.

HORLOCK, Prof. John Harold, FRS 1976; FEng 1977; Vice-Chancellor, 1981–90, and Fellow, since 1991, Open University; Hon. Professor of Engineering, Warwick University, since 1991; *b* 19 April 1928; *s* of Harold Edgar and Olive Margaret Horlock; *m* 1953, Sheila Joy Stutely; one *s* two *d. Educ:* Edmonton Latymer Sch.; (Scholar) St John's Coll., Cambridge (Hon. Fellow 1989). 1st Class Hons Mech. Sci. Tripos, Pt I, 1948, Rex Moir Prize; Pt II, 1949; MA 1952; PhD 1955; ScD 1975. Design and Development Engineer, Rolls Royce Ltd, Derby, 1949–51; Fellow, St John's Coll., Cambridge, 1954–57 and 1967–74; Univ. Demonstrator, 1952–56; University Lecturer, 1956–58, at Cambridge Univ. Engineering Lab.; Harrison Prof. of Mechanical Engineering, Liverpool Univ., 1958–66; Prof. of Engineering, and Dir of Whittle Lab., Cambridge Univ., 1967–74; Vice-Chancellor, Univ. of Salford, 1974–80. Visiting Asst Prof. in Mech. Engineering, Massachusetts Inst. of Technology, USA, 1956–57; Vis. Prof. of Aero-Space Engineering, Pennsylvania State Univ., USA, 1966. Chm., ARC, 1979–80 (Mem., 1960–63, 1969–72); Member: SRC, 1974–77; Cttee of Inquiry into Engineering Profession, 1977–80; Engineering Council, 1981–83; Chm., Adv. Cttee on Safety in Nuclear Installations, 1984–93. Director: BICERA Ltd, 1964–65; Cambridge Water Co., 1971–74; British Engine Insurance Ltd, 1979–84; Gaydon Technology Ltd, 1978–88; Open University Educational Enterprises Ltd, 1981–88; Co-ax Cable Communications Ltd, 1983–89 (Chm.); National Grid Co., 1989–94. A Vice-Pres., 1981–83, 1992–, Treas., 1992–, Royal Soc. Calvin Rice Lectr, ASME, 1994. FIMechE; Fellow ASME; Foreign Associate, US Nat. Acad. of Engrg. Hon. Fellow, UMIST, 1991 (a Pro-Chancellor, 1995–). Hon. DSc: Heriot-Watt, 1980; Salford, 1981; CNAA, 1991; de Montfort, 1995; Hon. ScD East Asia, 1987; Hon. DEng Liverpool, 1987; DUniv Open, 1991. Clayton Prize, 1962; Thomas Hawksley Gold Medal, IMechE, 1969. *Publications:* The Fluid Mechanics and Thermodynamics of Axial Flow Compressors, 1958; The Fluid Mechanics and Thermodynamics of Axial Flow Turbines, 1966; Actuator Disc Theory, 1978; (ed) Thermodynamics and Gas Dynamics of Internal Combustion Engines, vol. I, 1982, vol. II, 1986; Cogeneration—Combined Heat and Power, 1987; Combined Power Plants, 1992; contribs to mech. and aero. engineering jls and to Proc. Royal Society. *Recreations:* music, watching sport. *Address:* 2 The Avenue, Ampthill, Bedford MK45 2NR. *T:* Ampthill (01525) 841307. *Clubs:* Athenæum, MCC.

HORN, Prof. Gabriel, MA, MD, ScD; FRS 1986; Master of Sidney Sussex College, Cambridge, since 1992; Deputy Vice-Chancellor, University of Cambridge, since 1994; *b* 9 Dec. 1927; *s* of late Abraham and Anne Horn; *m* 1st, 1952, Ann Loveday Dean Soper (marr. diss. 1979); two *s* two *d*; 2nd, 1980, Priscilla Barrett. *Educ:* Handsworth Technical Sch. and Coll., Birmingham (Nat. Cert. in Mech. Engrg); Univ. of Birmingham (BSc Anatomy and Physiology; MD, ChB). MA, ScD Cantab. Served in RAF (Educn Br.), 1947–49. House appts, Birmingham Children's and Birmingham and Midland Eye Hosps, 1955–56; University of Cambridge: Univ. Demonstrator in Anat., 1956–62; Lectr in Anat., 1962–72; Reader in Neurobiology, 1972–74; Fellow of King's Coll., 1962–74, 1978–92; Prof. and Head of Dept of Anat., Univ. of Bristol, 1974–77; Prof. of Zoology, 1978–94, and Hd of Dept, 1979–94, Cambridge Univ. Sen. Res. Fellow in Neurophysiol., Montreal Neurol Inst., McGill Univ., 1957–58; Leverhulme Res. Fellow, Laboratoire de Neurophysiologie Cellulaire, France, 1970–71. Vis. Prof. of Physiol Optics, Univ. of Calif, Berkeley, 1963; Vis. Res. Prof., Ohio State Univ., 1965; Vis. Prof. of Zool., Makerere University Coll., Uganda, 1966; Dist. Vis. Prof., Univ. of Alberta, Edmonton, Canada, 1988; Vis. Miller Prof., Univ. of Calif, Berkeley, USA, 1989. Charnock Bradley Lectr, Edinburgh Univ., 1988; Crisp Lectr, Univ. of Leeds, 1990. Member: Biol Sciences Cttee, SRC, 1973–75; Jt MRC and SRC Adv. Panel on Neurobiol., 1971–72; Res. Cttee, Mental Health Foundn, 1973–78; Council, Anatomical Soc., 1976–78; Adv. Gp, ARC Inst. of Animal Physiology, Babraham, 1981–87; AFRC, 1991–94; Chairman: Wkg Party on Biol. of Spongiform Encephalopathies, 1991–95; Animal Scis and Psychol. Res. Grants Cttee, BBSRC, 1994–. Dir, Co. of Biologists, 1980–93. FIBiol 1978. Kenneth Craik Award in Physiol Psychol., 1962. *Publications:* (ed with R. A. Hinde) Short-Term Changes in Neural Activity and Behaviour, 1970; Memory, Imprinting and the Brain, 1985; (ed with J. R. Krebs) Behavioural and Neural Aspects of Learning and Memory, 1991; contrib. scientific jls, mainly on topics in neurosciences. *Recreations:* walking, cycling, music, riding. *Address:* Sidney Sussex College, Cambridge CB2 3HU.

HORN, Dr Heinz; Chairman, Executive Board, Ruhrkohle AG, since 1985. *Educ:* Univs. of Frankfurt and Munster. Financial Dir, Eschweiler Bergwerks-Verein, 1965–68; Member, Executive Board: Krupp Industrie und Stahlbau, 1968–72; Eisen & Metall AG, 1972–74; Mem., Exec. Bd, later Chm., Eschweiler Bergwerks-Verein, 1974–83; Dep. Chm., Exec. Bd, Ruhrkohle AG, 1983–85. *Address:* Ruhrkohle AG, Rellinghauser Strasse 1, 45128 Essen, Germany. *T:* (201) 1771.

HORNBY, Sir Derek (Peter), Kt 1990; Chairman, British Overseas Trade Board, since 1990 (Member, since 1987; Chairman, North American Group, 1987); Chairman, Partnership Sourcing Ltd, since 1993; *b* 10 Jan. 1930; *s* of F. N. Hornby and V. M. Pardy; *m* 1st, 1953, Margaret Withers (marr. diss.); one *s* one *d*; 2nd, 1971, Sonia Beesley; one *s* one *d. Educ:* Canford School. With Mobil Oil, Mars Industries and Texas Instruments; Xerox Corp., 1973 (Dir, Internat. Ops); Exec. Dir, Rank Xerox, 1980–84; Chm., Rank-Xerox (UK), 1984–90. Mem. Bd, British Rail, 1985–90; Civil Service Comr, 1986–90; Chm., NACCB. Chm., Video Arts, 1993–; Director: Cogent Elliott, 1988–; London and Edinburgh Insurance Gp, 1989–; Kode International, 1989–; Dixons plc, 1990–; Sedgwick Group, 1993–. Mem. Bd, Savills, 1988–95. CIMgt (Chm., 1990–93). FRSA. Hon. DSc Aston, 1993. *Recreations:* Real tennis, theatre, cricket. *Address:* Badgers Farm, Idlicote, Shipston-on-Stour, Warwicks CV36 5DT. *Clubs:* Garrick, MCC; Leamington Real Tennis, Moreton Morell Real Tennis.

HORNBY, Derrick Richard; *b* 11 Jan. 1926; *s* of late Richard W. Hornby and Dora M. Hornby; *m* 1948, June Steele; two *s* one *d. Educ:* University Coll., Southampton (DipEcon). Early career in accountancy; Marketing Dir, Tetley Tea Co. Ltd, 1964–69; Man. Dir, Eden Vale, 1969–74; Chm., Spillers Foods Ltd, 1974–77; Divisional Managing Director: Spillers Internat., 1977–80; Spillers Grocery Products Div., 1979–80; Chm., Carrington Viyella Ltd, 1979. Pres., Food Manufrs Fedn Incorp., 1977–79; Mem., Food and Drinks EDC. Member Council: CBI, to 1979; Food and Drinks Industry Council, to 1979. Chairman: Appeal Fund, Nat. Grocers Benefit Fund, 1973–74; London Animal Trust, 1978–80. FIMgt, FIGD, ACommA. *Recreations:* golf, fly-fishing. *Address:* 54 Cerne Abbas, The Avenue, Branksome Park, Poole, Dorset BH13 6HE.

HORNBY, Prof. James Angus; Professor of Law in the University of Bristol, 1961–85, now Emeritus; *b* 15 Aug. 1922; twin *s* of James Hornby and Evelyn Gladys (*née* Grant). *Educ:* Bolton County Grammar Sch.; Christ's Coll., Cambridge. BA 1944, LLB 1945, MA 1948 Cantab. Called to Bar, Lincoln's Inn, 1947. Lecturer, Manchester Univ., 1947–61. *Publications:* An Introduction to Company Law, 1957, 5th edn 1975; contribs to legal journals. *Recreations:* listening to music, reading, walking. *Address:* 6 Henbury Gardens, Henbury Road, Bristol BS10 7AJ. *Club:* United Oxford & Cambridge University.

HORNBY, Keith Anthony Delgado; His Honour Judge Hornby; a Circuit Judge, since 1995; *b* 18 Feb. 1947; *s* of late James Lawrence Hornby and of Naomi Ruth Hornby (*née* Delgado); *m* 1970, Judith Constance Fairbairn; two *s* one *d. Educ:* Oratory Sch.; Trinity Coll., Dublin (BA Hons Legal Sci.). Lectr in Commercial Law, PCL, 1969–70; called to the Bar, Gray's Inn, 1970; practised on SE Circuit, 1970–95; Asst Recorder, 1982–92; Recorder, 1992–95. *Recreations:* art, theatre, cricket, squash, golf. *Address:* Snaresbrook Crown Court, 75 Holly Bush Hill, E11 1QW. *T:* 0181–982 5500. *Club:* Hurlingham.

HORNBY, Richard Phipps, MA; Chairman, Halifax Building Society, 1983–90 (Director, 1976; Vice-Chairman, 1981–83); *b* 20 June 1922; *e s* of late Rt Rev. Hugh Leycester Hornby, MC; *m* 1951, Stella Hichens; two *s* one *d* (and one *s* decd). *Educ:* Winchester Coll.; Trinity Coll., Oxford (Scholar). Served in King's Royal Rifle Corps, 1941–45. 2nd Cl. Hons in Modern History, Oxford, 1948 (Soccer Blue). History Master, Eton Coll., 1948–50; with Unilever, 1951–52; with J. Walter Thompson Co., 1952–63, 1964–81 (Dir, 1974–81); Director: McCorquodale plc, 1982–86; Cadbury Schweppes plc, 1982–93. Contested (C) West Walthamstow: May 1955 (gen. election) and March 1956 (by-election); MP (C) Tonbridge, Kent, June 1956–Feb. 1974. PPS to Rt Hon. Duncan Sandys, MP, 1959–63; Parly Under-Sec. of State, CRO and CO, Oct. 1963–Oct. 1964. Member: BBC Gen. Adv. Council, 1969–74; Cttee of Inquiry into Intrusions into Privacy, 1970–72; British Council Exec. Cttee, 1971–74. *Recreations:* shooting, fishing, walking. *Address:* Ebble Thatch, Bowerchalke, near Salisbury, Wilts SP5 5BW.

HORNBY, Sir Simon (Michael); Kt 1988; Director, 1974–94, Chairman, 1982–94, W. H. Smith Group (formerly W. H. Smith & Son (Holdings) plc); Director: Pearson plc (formerly S. Pearson & Son Ltd), since 1978; Lloyds Bank, since 1988; Lloyds Abbey Life PLC, since 1991 (Chairman, since 1992); *b* 29 Dec. 1934; *s* of late Michael Hornby and Nicolette Joan, *d* of Hon. Cyril Ward, MVO; *m* 1968, Sheran Cazalet. *Educ:* Eton; New Coll., Oxford; Harvard Business Sch. 2nd Lieut, Grenadier Guards, 1953–55. Entered W. H. Smith & Son, 1958, Dir, 1965; Gp Chief Exec., W. H. Smith & Son (Holdings), 1978–82. Mem. Exec. Cttee, 1966–93, Property Cttee, 1979–86, Council 1976–, National Trust; Mem. Adv. Council, Victoria and Albert Museum, 1971–75; Council, RSA,

1985–90; Trustee, British Museum, 1975–85; Chairman: Design Council, 1986–92; Assoc. for Business Sponsorship of the Arts, 1988–; Nat. Literary Trust, 1993–; President: Book Trust, 1990– (Dep. Chm., 1976–78, Chm., 1978–80, NBL); Newsvendors' Benevolent Instn, 1989–94; RHS, 1994– (Mem. Council, 1992–); Chelsea Soc., 1994–. Mem. Court of Assistants, Goldsmiths' Co., 1990–. DUniv Stirling, 1992; Hon. DLitt Hull, 1994. *Recreations:* gardening, golf. *Address:* 8 Ennismore Gardens, SW7 1NL. *T:* 0171–584 1597; The Ham, Wantage, Oxon OX12 9JA.

HORNE, Sir (Alan) Gray (Antony), 3rd Bt *cr* 1929; *b* 11 July 1948; *s* of Antony Edgar Alan Horne (*d* 1954) (*o s* of 2nd Bt), and of Valentine Antonia, *d* of Valentine Dudensing; *S* grandfather, 1984; *m* 1980, Cecile Rose, *d* of Jacques Desplanche. *Heir:* none. *Address:* Château du Basty, Thenon, Dordogne, France.

HORNE, Alistair Allan, CBE 1992; LittD; author, journalist, lecturer; *b* 9 Nov. 1925; *s* of late Sir (James) Allan Horne and Lady (Auriol Camilla) Horne (*née* Hay); *m* 1st, 1953, Renira Margaret (marr. diss. 1982), *d* of Adm. Sir Geoffrey Hawkins, KBE, CB, MVO, DSC; three *d*; 2nd, 1987, Hon. Mrs Sheelin Eccles. *Educ:* Le Rosey, Switzerland; Millbrook, USA; Jesus Coll., Cambridge (MA); LittD Cantab 1993. Served War of 1939–45: RAF, 1943–44; Coldstream Gds, 1944–47; Captain, attached Intelligence Service (ME). Dir, Ropley Trust Ltd, 1948–77; Foreign Correspondent, Daily Telegraph, 1952–55. Founded Alistair Horne Res. Fellowship in Mod. History, St Antony's Coll., Oxford, 1969, Hon. Fellow, 1988. Fellow, Woodrow Wilson Center, Washington, DC, USA, 1980–81. Lectures: Lees Knowles, Cambridge, 1982; Goodman, Univ. of West Ontario, 1983. Member: Management Cttee, Royal Literary Fund, 1969–; Franco-British Council, 1979–; Cttee of Management, Soc. of Authors, 1979–82; Trustee, Imperial War Museum, 1975–82. FRSL. Chevalier, Légion d'Honneur (France), 1993. *Publications:* Back into Power, 1955; The Land is Bright, 1958; Canada and the Canadians, 1961; The Price of Glory: Verdun 1916, 1962 (Hawthornden Prize, 1963); The Fall of Paris: The Siege and The Commune 1870–71, 1965, rev. 2nd edn 1990; To Lose a Battle: France 1940, 1969, rev. 2nd edn 1990; Death of a Generation, 1970; The Terrible Year: The Paris Commune, 1971; Small Earthquake in Chile, 1972, rev. 2nd edn 1990; A Savage War of Peace: Algeria 1954–62, 1977 (Yorkshire Post Book of Year Prize, 1978; Wolfson Literary Award, 1978), rev. 2nd edn 1987; Napoleon, Master of Europe 1805–1807, 1979; The French Army and Politics 1870–1970, 1984 (Enid Macleod Prize, 1985); Macmillan: the official biography, Vol. I, 1894–1956, 1988, Vol. 2, 1957–1986, 1989; A Bundle from Britain, 1993; (with David Montgomery) The Lonely Leader: Monty 1944–45, 1994; *contribs to books:* Combat: World War I, ed Don Congdon, 1964; Impressions of America, ed R. A. Brown, 1966; Marshal V. I. Chuikov, The End of the Third Reich, 1967; Sports and Games in Canadian Life, ed N. and M. L. Howell, 1969; Decisive Battles of the Twentieth Century, ed N. Frankland and C. Dowling, 1976; The War Lords: Military Commanders of the Twentieth Century, ed Field Marshal Sir M. Carver, 1976; Regular Armies and Insurgency, ed R. Haycock, 1979; Macmillan: a life in pictures, 1983; contribs various periodicals. *Recreations:* ski-ing, painting, gardening, travel. *Address:* The Old Vicarage, Turville, near Henley-on-Thames, Oxon RG9 6QU. *Clubs:* Garrick, Beefsteak.

HORNE, David Oliver, FCA; Chairman and Chief Executive, Lloyds Merchant Bank, 1988–92; *b* 7 March 1932; *s* of Herbert Oliver Horne, MBE and Edith Marion Horne (*née* Sellers); *m* 1959, Joyce Heather (*née* Kynoch); two *s* two *d*. *Educ:* Fettes College, Edinburgh. Director: S. G. Warburg & Co., 1966–70; Williams & Glyn's Bank, 1970–78; Lloyds Bank International, 1978–85; Managing Dir, Lloyds Merchant Bank, 1985–87. *Recreation:* golf. *Address:* Four Winds, 5 The Gardens, Esher, Surrey KT10 8QF. *T:* Esher (01372) 463510.

HORNE, Frederic Thomas; Chief Taxing Master of the Supreme Court, 1983–88 (Master, 1967–83); *b* 21 March 1917; *y s* of Lionel Edward Horne, JP, Moreton-in-Marsh, Glos; *m* 1944, Madeline Hatton; two *s* two *d*. *Educ:* Chipping Campden Grammar Sch. Admitted a Solicitor (Hons), 1938. Served with RAFVR in General Duties Branch (Pilot), 1939–56. Partner in Iliffe Sweet & Co., 1956–67. Mem., Lord Chancellor's Adv. Cttee on Legal Aid, 1983–91; Chm., Working Party on the Simplification of Taxation, 1980–83 (Horne Report, 1983). Pres., Assoc. of Law Costs Draftsmen. *Publications:* Cordery's Law Relating to Solicitors, 7th edn (jtly) 1981, 8th edn 1987; (contrib.) Atkins Encyclopaedia of Court Forms, 2nd edn, 1983; (ed jtly) The Supreme Court Practice, 1985 and 1988 edns; (contrib.) Private International Litigation, 1987. *Recreations:* cricket, music, archaeology. *Address:* Dunstall, Quickley Lane, Chorleywood, Herts WD3 5AF. *Club:* MCC.

HORNE, Sir Gray; *see* Horne, Sir A. G. A.

HORNE, Marilyn (Bernice); mezzo-soprano; *b* 16 Jan. 1934; *m* 1960, Henry Lewis (marr. diss.); one *d*; *m* Nicola Zaccaria. *Educ:* Univ. of Southern California. US opera début, 1954; sings at Covent Garden, La Scala, Metropolitan Opera and other major venues; rôles include Adalgisa, Amneris, Carmen, Eboli, Isabella, Mignon, Orlando, Rosina, Tancredi, concerts and recitals. *Address:* c/o Colombia Artists Management, Wilford Division, 165 West 57th Street, New York, NY 10019, USA.

HORNE, Prof. Michael Rex, OBE 1981; MA, PhD, ScD Cantab; MSc (Manchester); FRS 1981; FEng, FICE; FIStructE; Professor of Civil Engineering, University of Manchester, 1960–83 (Beyer Professor, 1978–83); *b* 29 Dec. 1921; *s* of late Rev. Ernest Horne, Leicester; *m* 1947, Molly, *d* of late Mark Hewett, Royston, Herts; two *s* two *d*. *Educ:* Boston (Lincs) Grammar Sch.; Leeds Grammar Sch.; St John's Coll., Cambridge. MA Cantab 1945; PhD Cantab 1950, ScD Cantab 1956. John Winbolt Prize for Research, Cambridge Univ., 1944. Asst Engineer, River Great Ouse Catchment Bd, 1941–45; Scientific Officer, British Welding Research Assoc., 1945–51; Asst Dir of Research in Engineering, 1951–56, Lectr in Engineering, 1957–60, Fellow of St John's Coll., 1957–60, Univ. of Cambridge. Royal Soc. Vis. Prof., Univ. of Hong Kong, 1986. Instn of Civil Engineers, Telford Premiums, 1956, 1966, 1978. Chm., NW Branch, 1969–70, Pres., 1980–81, IStructE; Pres., Section G, BAAS, 1981–82; Mem., Merrison Cttee on Box Girders, 1970–73; Chm., Review for Govt of Public Utility Streetworks Act, 1984. Hon. DSc Salford, 1981. Diploma, 1971, Bronze Medal, 1973, Gold Medal, 1986, IStructE; Baker Medal, ICE, 1977. *Publications:* (with J. F. Baker and J. Heyman) The Steel Skeleton, 1956; (with W. F. Merchant) The Stability of Frames, 1965; The Plastic Theory of Structures, 1971; (with L. J. Morris) Plastic Design of Low Rise Frames, 1981; contribs on structures, strength of materials and particulate theory of soils to learned journals. *Recreations:* photography, theatre-going, foreign travel. *Address:* 19 Park Road, Hale, Altrincham, Cheshire WA15 9NW.

HORNE, Dr Nigel William, FEng 1982; FIEE; Special Adviser, KPMG Peat Marwick, since 1992; Chairman, Alcatel Network Systems UK, since 1992; Director: FI Group Plc, since 1992; Abingworth Management Ltd, since 1992; *b* 13 Sept. 1940; *s* of late Eric Charles Henry and Edith Margaret Horne; *m* 1965, Jennifer Ann Holton; one *s* two *d*. *Educ:* John Lyon Sch., Harrow; Univ. of Bristol (BScEng 1962); Univ. of Cambridge (PhD 1968). FIEE 1984. GEC Telecommunications, 1958–70; Management Systems Manager, 1970–72; Manufg Gen. Manager, 1972–75; Dir and Gen. Manager, Switching, 1976–82; Managing Dir, GEC Inf. Systems, 1982–83; Director: Technical and Corporate Develt, STC, 1983–90; Abingworth, 1985–90; LSI Logic, 1986–90; IT Partner, KPMG Peat Marwick, 1990–92. Vis. Prof., Univ. of Bristol, 1990. Member: Nat. Electronics Council, 1985–90; EC Esprit Adv. Bd, 1988–; Cabinet Office Adv. Council on Sci. and Technology, 1991–; Chairman: Computing and Control Div., IEE, 1988–89; DTI/SERC IT Adv. Bd, 1988–91. FRSA. Freeman, City of London; Mem., Co. of Inf. Technologists. Hon. DEng Bristol, 1992; Hon. DSc: Hull, 1992; City, 1995. Caballeros del Monasteria de Juste (Spain), 1992. *Publications:* papers in learned jls. *Recreations:* piano, walking, gardening. *Address:* KPMG Peat Marwick, PO Box 486, 1 Puddle Dock, EC4V 3PD. *T:* 0171–236 8000. *Club:* United Oxford & Cambridge University.

HORNE, Robert Drake; Accountant-General, Department for Education (formerly of Education and Science), since 1993; *b* 23 April 1945; *s* of late Harold Metcalfe Horne and Dorothy Katharine Horne; *m* 1972, Jennifer Mary (*née* Gill); three *d*. *Educ:* Mill Hill Sch.; Oriel Coll., Oxford (MA Classics). Asst Master, Eton Coll., Windsor, 1967–68; DES, 1968–; seconded to Cabinet Office, 1979–80. *Recreations:* running, entertaining Australians. *Address:* Department for Education, Sanctuary Buildings, Great Smith Street, SW1.

HORNER, Arthur William, CMG 1964; TD and clasp 1946; *b* 22 June 1909; *s* of Francis Moore and Edith Horner; *m* 1938, Patricia Denise (*née* Campbell); two *s* one *d*. *Educ:* Hardenwick; Felsted. Marine Insurance, 1926–39. Served War, 1939–46, Rifle Brigade; Lieut-Col; psc. Farming in Kenya, 1948–50. Colonial Administrative Service (later HM Overseas Civil Service), Kenya, 1950–64; Commissioner of Lands, 1955–61; Permanent Sec., 1961–64; Dir of Independence Celebrations, 1963; Principal, ODM, 1964–73; seconded Diplomatic Service, 1968–70, retired 1973. *Recreations:* music, gardening. *Address:* St Margaret's Cottage, Northiam, Rye, East Sussex TN31 6NJ.

HORNER, Douglas George, FCIB; Chairman, Mercantile Credit Company, 1980–84; Vice-Chairman, 1979–81, Director, 1975–84, Barclays Bank UK Limited; *b* Dec. 1917; *s* of Albert and Louise Horner; *m* 1941, Gwendoline Phyllis Wall; one *s*. *Educ:* Enfield Grammar Sch. Commissioned, Royal Norfolk Regt, 1940. Asst Manager/Manager at various bank branches, 1954–71; Local Dir, Lombard Street, 1971; Regional Gen. Manager, London, 1973; Gen. Man., 1975; Senior Gen. Man., 1977; Dir Barclays Bank plc, 1977–83. *Recreations:* golf, gardening. *Address:* Barclays Bank plc, 54 Lombard Street, EC3P 3AH.

HORNER, Frederick, DSc; CEng, FIEE; Director, Appleton Laboratory, Science Research Council, 1977–79; *b* 28 Aug. 1918; *s* of late Frederick and Mary Horner; *m* 1946, Elizabeth Bonsey; one *s* one *d*. *Educ:* Bolton Sch.; Univ. of Manchester (Ashbury Scholar, 1937; Fairbairn Engrg Prize, 1939; BSc 1st Cl. Hons 1939; MSc 1941; DSc 1968). CEng, FIEE 1959. On staff of DSIR, NPL, 1941–52; UK Scientific Mission, Washington DC, 1947; Radio Research Station, later Appleton Lab. of SRC, 1952–79, Dep. Dir, 1969–77; Admin. Staff Coll., Henley, 1959. Delegate: Internat. Union of Radio Science, 1950– (Chm., Commn VIII, 1966–69); Internat. Radio Consultative Cttee, 1953–90 (Internat. Chm., Study Group 2, 1980–90). Member: Inter-Union Commn on Frequency Allocations for Radio Astronomy and Space Science, 1965–92 (Sec., 1975–82); Electronics Divl Bd, IEE, 1970–76. Mem. Council: RHC, 1979–85 (Vice-Chm., 1982–85); RHBNC, 1985–89; Hon. Associate, Physics: RHC, 1975–85; RHBNC, 1985–. Diplôme d'Honneur, Internat. Radio Cons. Cttee, 1989. *Publications:* more than 50 scientific papers. *Recreations:* genealogy, gardening. *Address:* Gordano Lodge, Clevedon Road, Weston-in-Gordano, Bristol BS20 8PZ.

HORNER, John; *b* 5 Nov. 1911; *s* of Ernest Charles and Emily Horner; *m* 1936, Patricia, *d* of Geoffrey and Alice Palmer; two *d*. *Educ:* elementary sch. and Sir George Monoux Grammar Sch., Walthamstow. Apprenticed Merchant Navy, 1927; Second Mate's Certificate, 1932. Joined London Fire Brigade, 1933; Gen. Sec. Fire Brigades Union, 1939–64; MP (Lab) Oldbury and Halesowen, 1964–70. Mem. Select Cttee on Nationalised Industries. *Publication:* Studies in Industrial Democracy, 1974. *Recreations:* gardening, reading history. *Address:* c/o Barclays Bank, Ross-on-Wye, Herefordshire.

HORNSBY, Timothy Richard, MA; Chief Executive, National Lottery Charities Board, since 1995; *b* 22 Sept. 1940; *s* of late Harker William Hornsby and Agnes Nora French; *m* 1971, Dr Charmian Rosemary Newton; one *s* one *d*. *Educ:* Bradfield Coll.; Christ Church, Oxford Univ. (MA 1st C1. Hons Modern History). Harkness Fellow, USA, at Harvard, Columbia, Henry E. Huntington Research Inst., 1961–63; Asst Prof., Birmingham Southern Coll., Alabama, 1963–64; Research Lectr, Christ Church, Oxford, 1964–65; Asst Principal, Min. of Public Building and Works, 1965–67; Private Sec. to Controller General, 1968–69; HM Treasury, 1971–73; Prin., then Asst Sec., DoE, 1975; Dir, Ancient Monuments and Historic Buildings, 1983–88, and Dir of Rural Affairs, 1984–88, DoE; Dir Gen., Nature Conservancy Council, 1988–91; Dir, Construction Policy Directorate, DoE, 1991; Chief Exec., Royal Bor. of Kingston upon Thames, 1991–95. FRSA. *Recreations:* conservation, skiing, talking. *Address:* National Lottery Charities Board, 7th Floor, St Vincent House, 30 Orange Street, WC2H 7HH. *T:* 0171–839 8481. *Club:* Athenæum.

HOROWITZ, Gillian Mary, (Mrs M. Horowitz); *see* Darley, G. M.

HOROWITZ, Michael; QC 1990; a Recorder, since 1991; *b* 18 Oct. 1943; *s* of David Horowitz and late Irene Horowitz; *m* 1986, Gillian Mary Darley, *qv*; one *d* (one *s* decd). *Educ:* St Marylebone Grammar School; Pembroke College, Cambridge (BA 1966; LLB 1967). Pres., Cambridge Union Soc., 1967; English-Speaking Union Debating Tour of USA, 1967. Called to the Bar, Lincoln's Inn, 1968; Asst Recorder, 1987. Senate of Inns of Court and Bar, 1982–85. *Recreations:* music, history, listening. *Address:* 1 Mitre Court Buildings, Temple, EC4Y 7BS. *T:* 0171–797 7070.

HOROWITZ, Prof. Myer, OC 1990; EdD; President, 1979–89, Professor Emeritus of Education, since 1990, University of Alberta, Canada; *b* 27 Dec. 1932; *s* of Philip Horowitz and Fanny Cotler; *m* 1956, Barbara, *d* of Samuel Rosen and Grace Midvidy, Montreal; two *d*. *Educ:* High Sch., Montreal; Sch. for Teachers, Macdonald Coll.; Sir George Williams Univ. (BA); Univ. of Alberta (MEd); Stanford Univ. (EdD). Teacher, Schs in Montreal, Sch. Bd, Greater Montreal, 1952–60. McGill University: Lectr in Educn, 1960–63; Asst Prof., 1963–65; Associate Prof., 1965–67; Asst to Dir, 1964–65; Prof. of Educn, 1967–69 and Asst Dean, 1965–69; University of Alberta: Prof. and Chm., Dept Elem. Educn, 1969; Dean, Faculty of Educn, 1972–75; Vice-Pres. (Academic), 1975–79. Hon. Dr: McGill, 1979; Concordia, 1982; Athabasca, 1989; British Columbia, 1990; Alberta, 1990. *Address:* 845 Education Centre, University of Alberta, Edmonton, Alberta T6G 2G5, Canada; 14319, 60 Avenue, Edmonton, Alberta T6H 1J8.

HORRELL, John Ray, CBE 1979; TD; DL; farmer; *b* 8 March 1929; *er s* of late Harry Ray Horrell and of Phyllis Mary Horrell (*née* Whittome); *m* 1951, Mary Elizabeth Noëlle Dickinson; one *s* one *d*. Director: Horrell's Farmers Ltd; Horrell's Dairies Ltd. Mem., Board, Peterborough New Town Develt Corp., 1970–88; formerly Mem. Oakes and Taylor Cttees of Enquiry. Mem., Cambs (formerly Huntingdon and Peterborough) CC, 1963– (Chm., 1971–77; Chm., Educn Cttee; Leader, 1989–93); Chairman: Council of Local Educn Authorities, 1976–79; ACC, 1981–83 (Vice-Chm., 1979–81); E of England Agricl Soc., 1984–87. Mem. Council, CGLI, now C&G, 1975–. Major, TA; a Vice-

Chm., 1977–86, Chm., 1986–91, E Anglia TA&VRA. FRSA 1981. High Sheriff, Cambs, 1981–82; DL Cambs, 1973. *Address:* The Grove, Longthorpe, Peterborough PE3 6LZ. *T:* Peterborough (01733) 262618.

HORRELL, Roger William, CMG 1988; OBE 1974; HM Diplomatic Service, retired; *b* 9 July 1935; *s* of William John Horrell and Dorice Enid (*née* Young); *m* 1970, Patricia Mildred Eileen Smith (*née* Binns) (marr. diss. 1975); one *s* one *d*. *Educ:* Shebbear College; Exeter College, Oxford. MA. Served in Devonshire Regt, 1953–55; HM Colonial Service, Kenya, 1959–64; joined Foreign Office, 1964; Economic Officer, Dubai, 1965–67; FCO, 1967–70; First Sec., Kampala, 1970–73; FCO, 1973–76; First Sec., Lusaka, 1976–80; Counsellor, FCO, 1980–93. *Recreations:* cricket, reading, walking, bridge. *Club:* Reform.

HORRIDGE, Prof. (George) Adrian, FRS 1969; FAA 1971; Professor, Research School of Biological Sciences, Australian National University, 1969–92, Emeritus Professor and University Fellow, since 1993; *b* Sheffield, England, 12 Dec. 1927; *s* of George William Horridge and Olive Stray; *m* 1954, Audrey Anne Lightburne; one *s* three *d*. *Educ:* King Edward VII Sch., Sheffield. Fellow, St John's Coll., Cambridge, 1953–56; on staff, St Andrews Univ., 1956–69; Dir, Gatty Marine Laboratory, St Andrews, 1960–69. Vis. Fellow, Churchill Coll., Cambridge, 1993–94. *Publications:* Structure and Function of the Nervous Systems of Invertebrates (with T. H. Bullock), 1965; Interneurons, 1968; (ed) The Compound Eye and Vision of Insects, 1975; Monographs of the Maritime Museum at Greenwich nos 38, 39, 40, 54, 1979–82; The Prahu: traditional sailing boat of Indonesia, 1982 (Oxford in Asia); Sailing Craft of Indonesia, 1985 (Oxford in Asia); Outrigger Canoes of Bali & Madura, Indonesia, 1986; contribs numerous scientific papers on behaviour and nervous systems of lower animals, to jls, etc. *Recreations:* optics, mathematics, marine biology; sailing, language, arts, boat construction in Indonesia. *Address:* PO Box 475, Canberra City, ACT 2601, Australia. *T:* Canberra (6) 2494532, *Fax:* (6) 2493808.

HORROCKS, Raymond, CBE 1983; Chairman, Chloride Group, since 1988 (Director, since 1986; Chief Executive, 1989–91); Chairman, Owenbell Ltd, since 1987; *b* 9 Jan. 1930; *s* of Elsie and Cecil Horrocks; *m* 1953, Pamela Florence Russell; three *d*. *Educ:* Bolton Municipal Secondary School. Textile Industry, 1944–48 and 1950–51; HM Forces, Army, Intelligence Corps, 1948–50; Sales Rep., Proctor & Gamble, 1951–52; Merchandiser, Marks & Spencer, 1953–58; Sub Gp Buying Controller, Littlewoods Mail Order Stores, 1958–63; various plant, departmental and divisional management positions, Ford Motor Co., 1963–72; Regional Dir, Europe and Middle East, Materials Handling Gp, Eaton Corp., 1972–77; Chm. and Man. Dir, Austin Morris Ltd, 1978–80; Man. Dir, BL Cars, 1980–81; Chm. and Chief Exec., BL Cars Gp, 1981–82; Exec. Dir and Bd Mem., BL, 1981–86; Gp Chief Exec., Cars, 1982–86; Chairman: Unipart Group Ltd, 1981–86; Austin Rover Gp Hldgs, 1981–86; Jaguar Cars Holdings Ltd, 1982–84; Kay Consultancy Group, 1989–91; Dir, Nuffield Services, 1982–86; non-executive Director: Jaguar plc, 1984–85; The Caravan Club, 1983–87; Electrocomponents, 1986–; Lookers, 1986–; WOL Hldgs Ltd, 1988–89; Burtree Caravans, 1988–; Applied Hldgs (UK) Pty, 1988–96; Smith Millington Motor Co. Ltd (formerly SMAC Gp), 1988– (Chm., 1988–89); Applied Chemicals, 1988–96 (Dep. Chm., 1988–94); Jabiru UK, 1989–96. Member: Council, CBI, 1981–86; Europe Cttee, CBI, 1985–86. FIMI; CIMgt; FRSA. *Recreations:* fly fishing, gardening, walking. *Address:* Far End, Riverview Road, Pangbourne, Reading, Berks RG8 7AU.

HORSBRUGH, Ian Robert; Principal, Guildhall School of Music and Drama, since 1988; *b* 16 Sept. 1941; *s* of Walter and Sheila Horsbrugh; *m* 1965, Caroline Everett; two *s* two *d*. *Educ:* St Paul's Sch.; Guildhall Sch. of Music and Drama (AGSM); Royal Coll. of Music (ARCM). FGSM 1988; FRCM 1988; FRSAMD 1993; FRNCM 1993. Head of Music: St Mary's Sch., Hendon, 1969–72; Villiers High Sch., Southall, 1972–79; Dep. Warden, ILEA Music Centre, 1979–84; Vice-Dir, Royal Coll. of Music, 1985–88. Mem., Music Panel and Chm., New Music Sub-Cttee, Arts Council, 1981–87; Member: Music Adv. Cttee, British Council, 1987–; Steering Cttee, Nat. Studio for Electronic Music, 1986–89; Bd, City Arts Trust, 1989–; Management Bd, London Internat. String Quartet Competition, 1989–; Council, NYO, 1989–; Arts and Entertainment Training Council, 1990–; Dep. Chm., London Arts Bd, 1991–; Vice-Pres., Nat. Assoc. of Youth Orchestras, 1989–; Trustee, Parkhouse Award, 1990– (Chm., 1990–92). Treasurer, 1977–79, Chm., 1979–84, New Macnaghten Concerts. Hon. RAM 1933; FRSA. *Publication:* Leoš Janáček: the field that prospered, 1981. *Recreations:* watching Rugby football and cricket, reading, walking. *Address:* Guildhall School of Music and Drama, Barbican, Silk Street, EC2Y 8DT. *T:* 0171–628 2571. *Club:* MCC.

HORSBRUGH-PORTER, Sir John (Simon), 4th Bt *cr* 1902; *b* 18 Dec. 1938; *s* of Col Sir Andrew Marshall Horsbrugh-Porter, 3rd Bt, DSO and Bar, and Annette Mary (*d* 1992), *d* of Brig.-Gen. R. C. Browne-Clayton, DSO; *S* father, 1986; *m* 1964, Lavinia Rose, *d* of Ralph Turton; one *s* two *d*. *Educ:* Winchester College; Trinity Coll., Cambridge (BA Hons History). School Master. *Recreations:* gliding, literature, music. *Heir:* *s* Andrew Alexander Marshall Horsbrugh-Porter, *b* 19 Jan. 1971. *Address:* Bowers Croft, Coleshill, Amersham, Bucks HP7 0LS. *T:* Amersham (01494) 724596.

HORSBURGH, John Millar Stewart, QC (Scot.) 1980; Sheriff of Lothian and Borders at Edinburgh, since 1990; *b* 15 May 1938; *s* of late Alexander Horsburgh and Helen Margaret Watson Millar or Horsburgh; *m* 1966, Johann Catriona Gardner, MB, ChB, DObst RCOG; one *s* one *d*. *Educ:* Hutchesons' Boys' Grammar Sch., Glasgow; Univ. of Glasgow (MA Hons, LLB). Admitted to Scots Bar, 1965; Advocate-Depute, 1987–89. Part-time Mem., Lands Tribunal for Scotland, 1985–87. *Address:* 8 Laverockbank Road, Edinburgh EH5 3DG. *T:* 0131–552 5328.

HORSEFIELD, John Keith, CB 1957; Historian, International Monetary Fund, 1966–69; *b* 14 Oct. 1901; *s* of Rev. Canon F. J. Horsefield, Bristol; *m* 1934, Lucy G. G. Florance. *Educ:* Monkton Combe Sch.; University of Bristol; MA 1948, DSc 1971; London Sch. of Economics. Lecturer, LSE, 1939; Min. of Aircraft Production, 1940; International Monetary Fund, 1947; Under-Sec., Min. of Supply, 1951; Dep. Asst Sec.-Gen. for Economics and Finance, NATO, 1952; Supply and Development Officer, Iron and Steel Bd, 1954; Dir of Finance and Accounts, Gen. Post Office, 1955–60; Chief Editor, International Monetary Fund, 1960–66. Hon. Treas., Carisbrooke Castle Museum, 1971–92. *Publications:* The Real Cost of the War, 1940; British Monetary Experiments, 1650–1710, 1960; The International Monetary Fund, 1945–1965, 1970; articles in Economica, etc. *Address:* 60 Clatterford Road, Carisbrooke, Newport, Isle of Wight PO30 1PA. *T:* Isle of Wight (01983) 523675.

HORSEY, Gordon, JP; a District Judge, since 1991; *b* 20 July 1926; *s* of late E. W. Horsey, MBE, and of H. V. Horsey; *m* 1951, Jean Mary (*née* Favill); one *d*. *Educ:* Magnus Grammar Sch., Newark, Notts; St Catharine's Coll., Cambridge. BA, LLB. Served RN, 1944–45, RE, 1945–48 (Captain). Admitted solicitor, 1953; private practice in Nottingham, 1953–71; Registrar: Coventry County Court, 1971; Leicester County Court, 1973; a Recorder, 1978–84. JP Leics, 1975. *Recreation:* fly-fishing. *Address:* The Old Woodyard, 55 Swithland Lane, Rothley, Leics LE7 7SG. *T:* Leicester (0116) 230 2545.

HORSFALL, Sir John (Musgrave), 3rd Bt *cr* 1909; MC 1946; TD 1949 and clasp 1951; JP; *b* 26 Aug. 1915; *s* of Sir (John) Donald Horsfall, 2nd Bt, and Henrietta (*d* 1936), *d* of William Musgrave; *S* father, 1975; *m* 1940, Cassandra Nora Bernardine, *d* of late G. E. Wright; two *s* one *d*. *Educ:* Uppingham. Major, Duke of Wellington's Regt. Dir, Skipton Building Society, 1960–85, retd. Mem. Skipton RDC, 1952–74; Pres. Skipton Divl Conservative Assoc., 1966–79. Pres., Worsted Spinners Fedn, 1961–64. JP North Yorks, 1959. *Heir:* *s* Edward John Wright Horsfall [*b* 17 Dec. 1940; *m* 1965, Rosemary, *d* of Frank N. King; three *s*]. *Address:* Greenfield House, Embsay, Skipton, North Yorkshire BD23 6SD. *T:* Skipton (01756) 794560.

HORSFIELD, Maj.-Gen. David Ralph, OBE 1962; FIEE; *b* 17 Dec. 1916; *s* of late Major Ralph B. and Morah Horsfield (*née* Baynes); *m* 1948, Sheelah Patricia Royal Eagan; two *s* two *d*. *Educ:* Oundle Sch.; RMA Woolwich; Cambridge Univ. (MA). Commnd in Royal Signals, 1936; comd Burma Corps Signals, 1942; Instr, Staff Coll., 1944–45; comd 2 Indian Airborne Signals, 1946–47; Instr, RMA Sandhurst, 1950–53 (Company Comdr to HM King Hussein of Jordan); comd 2 Signal Regt, 1956–59; Principal Army Staff Officer, MoD, Malaya, 1959–61; Dir of Telecommunications (Army), 1966–68; ADC to the Queen, 1968–69; Deputy Communications and Electronics, Supreme HQ Allied Powers, Europe, 1968–69; Maj.-Gen. 1969; Chief Signal Officer, BAOR, 1969–72; Col Comdt, Royal Signals, 1972–78. Pres., Indian Signals Assoc. of GB, 1978–; Vice Pres., Nat. Ski Fedn, 1978–81. *Recreations:* ski-ing (British Ski Champion, 1949), the visual arts. *Address:* Southill House, Cranmore, Shepton Mallet, Somerset BA4 4QS. *T:* Cranmore (01749) 880395. *Club:* Ski Club of Great Britain.

HORSFIELD, Peter Muir Francis, QC 1978; *b* 15 Feb. 1932; *s* of Henry Taylor Horsfield, AFC, and Florence Lily (*née* Muir); *m* 1962, Anne Charlotte, *d* of late Sir Piers Debenham, 2nd Bt, and Lady (Angela) Debenham; three *s*. *Educ:* Beaumont; Trinity Coll., Oxford (BA 1st Cl. Hons Mods and Greats). Served RNR, 1955–57; Lieut RNR, 1960. Called to the Bar, Middle Temple, 1958, Bencher, 1984; in practice at Chancery Bar, 1958–. *Recreations:* painting, observational astronomy. *Address:* (chambers) 8 Stone Buildings, Lincoln's Inn, WC2A 3TA. *Club:* Garrick.

HORSFORD, Alan Arthur; Group Chief Executive, Royal Insurance plc, 1985–89; *b* 31 May 1927; *s* of Arthur Henry Horsford and Winifred Horsford; *m* 1957, Enid Maureen Baker; one *s* one *d*. *Educ:* Holt School; Liverpool University. BA; FCII. Secretary, Royal Insurance Co. Ltd, 1970–72; Dep. General Manager, 1972–74, General Manager, 1974–79, Royal Insurance Canada; General Manager and Director, 1979–83, Dep. Chief Gen. Manager, 1983–84, Royal Insurance plc. Dep. Chm., Assoc. of British Insurers, 1985–88. *Recreations:* theatre, music, cycling, golf. *Address:* 17 Darnhills, Watford Road, Radlett, Herts WD7 8LQ.

HORSFORD, Maj.-Gen. Derek Gordon Thomond, CBE 1962 (MBE 1953); DSO 1944 and Bar 1945; *b* 7 Feb. 1917; *s* of late Captain H. T. Horsford, The Gloucestershire Regt, and Mrs V. E. Horsford; *m* 1948, Sheila Louise Russell Crawford; one *s* (and one step *s* two step *d*). *Educ:* Clifton Coll.; RMC, Sandhurst. Commissioned into 8th Gurkha Rifles, 1937; despatches 1943 and 1945; comd 4/1 Gurkha Rifles, Burma, 1944–45; transf. to RA, 1948; Instructor Staff Coll., 1950–52; transf. to King's Regt, 1950; GSO1, 2nd Infantry Div., 1955–56; comd 1st Bn, The King's Regt, 1957–59; AAG, AG2, War Office, 1959–60; Comdr 24th Infantry Brigade Group, Dec. 1960–Dec. 1962; Imperial Defence Coll., 1963; Brig., Gen. Staff, HQ, BAOR, 1964–66. Maj.-Gen. 1966; GOC 50 (Northumbrian) Div./Dist, 1966–67; GOC Yorks Dist, 1967–68; GOC 17 Div./Malaya District, 1969–70; Maj.-Gen., Brigade of Gurkhas, 1969–71; Dep. Comdr Land Forces, Hong Kong, 1970–71, retired. Col, The King's Regt, 1965–70; Col, The Gurkha Transport Regt, 1973–78. *Recreations:* travel, outdoor life.

HORSHAM, Bishop Suffragan of, since 1993; **Rt Rev. Lindsay Goodall,** OGS; *b* 13 March 1956. *Educ:* Camberwell GS, Australia; Ripon Coll., Cuddesdon. Ordained deacon, 1980, priest, 1981; Curate, St Peter, Walworth, 1980-83; Vicar, St Faith, N Dulwich, 1983–88; Diocesan Missioner, Chichester, 1988–93. Mem., OGS, 1991–. *Address:* Bishop's House, 21 Guildford Road, Horsham RH12 1LU. *T:* Horsham (01403) 211139, *Fax:* (01403) 217349.

HORSHAM, Archdeacon of; *see* Filby, Ven. W. C. L.

HORSHAM, Jean, CBE 1979; Deputy Parliamentary Commissioner for Administration, 1981–82, retired; Chairman, Solicitors Complaints Bureau, 1986–89; *b* 25 June 1922; *d* of Albert John James Horsham and Janet Horsham (*née* Henderson). *Educ:* Keith Grammar Sch. Forestry Commn, 1939–64, seconded to Min. of Supply, 1940–45; Min. of Land and Natural Resources, 1964–66; Min. of Housing and Local Govt, 1966; Office of Parly Comr for Administration, 1967–82. Member: Subsidence Compensation Review Cttee, 1983–84; Law Soc. Professional Purposes Cttee, 1984–86; Council on Tribunals, 1986–92; Chorus Enquiry at Royal Opera House, 1988–89; Tribunals Cttee, Judicial Studies Bd, 1990–92. *Address:* 14 Cotelands, Chichester Road, Croydon, Surrey CRO 5UD. *T:* 0181–681 0806.

HORSLEY, Rev. Canon Alan Avery; Vicar, Mill End and Heronsgate with West Hyde, since 1991; *b* 13 May 1936; *s* of Reginald James and Edith Irene Horsley; *m* 1966, Mary Joy Marshall, MA; two *d*. *Educ:* St Chad's Coll., Durham (BA 1958); Birmingham Univ.; Pacific Western Univ., Calif (MA 1984; PhD 1985); Queen's Coll., Birmingham. Deacon 1960, priest 1961, Peterborough; Assistant Curate: Daventry, 1960–63; St Giles, Reading, 1963–64; St Paul's, Wokingham, 1964–66; Vicar of Yeadon, dio. Bradford, 1966–71; Rector of Heyford and Stowe Nine Churches, dio. Peterborough, 1971–78; RD of Daventry, 1976–78; Vicar of Oakham with Hambleton and Egleton (and Braunston and Brooke from 1980), 1978–86; Non-Residentiary Canon of Peterborough, 1979–86; Chaplain: Catmose Vale Hosp., 1978–86; Rutland Memorial Hosp., 1978–86; Vicar of Lanteglos-by-Fowey, dio. Truro, 1986–88; Canon Emeritus of Peterborough, 1986–; Provost of St Andrew's Cathedral, Inverness, 1988–91; Priest in Charge: St Mary in the Fields, Culloden, 1988–91; St Paul, Strath Nairn, 1988–91. *Publications:* (with Mary J. Horsley) A Lent Course, 1967, 2nd edn 1982; Lent with St Luke, 1978, 2nd edn 1984; Action at Lanteglos and Polruan, 1987; contribs to Rutland Record Soc. Jl. *Recreations:* music, piano and organ, cultivation of flowers, historical research. *Address:* St Peter's Vicarage, Berry Lane, Rickmansworth WD3 2HQ. *T:* Rickmansworth (01923) 772785.

HORSLEY, Air Marshal Sir (Beresford) Peter (Torrington), KCB 1974; CBE 1964; LVO 1956; AFC 1945; idc; psc; pfc; *b* 26 March 1921; *s* of late Capt. Arthur Beresford Horsley, CBE; *m* 1st, 1943, Phyllis Conrad Phinney (marr. diss. 1976); one *s* one *d*; 2nd, 1976, Ann MacKinnon, *d* of Gareth and Frances Crwys-Williams; two step *s* two step *d*. *Educ:* Wellington Coll. Joined Royal Air Force, 1940; served in 2nd TAF and Fighter Command. Adjt Oxford Univ. Air Sqdn, 1948; Commands: No 9 and No 29 Sqdns, RAF Wattisham, RAF Akrotiri. Equerry to Princess Elizabeth and to the Duke of Edinburgh, 1949–52; Equerry to the Queen, 1952–53; Equerry to the Duke of Edinburgh, 1953–56. Dep. Comdt, Jt Warfare Establishment, RAF Old Sarum, 1966–68; Asst CAS (Operations), 1968–70; AOC No 1 (Bomber) Gp, 1971–73; Dep. C-in-C, Strike Comd, 1973–75. Retired RAF, 1975. Chairman: National Printing Ink Co., 1987–; Osprey

Aviation Ltd, 1991–; Director: Horsley Hldgs, 1985–; RCR Internat., 1984–. Pres., Yorkshire Sports, 1986–. Croix de Guerre, 1944. Holds Orders of Christ (Portugal), North Star (Sweden), and Menelik (Ethiopia). *Publication:* (as Peter Beresford) Journal of a Stamp Collector, 1972. *Recreations:* ski-ing, philately. *Address:* c/o Barclays Bank, High Street, Newmarket CB8 8NH.

HORSLEY, Colin, OBE 1963; FRCM 1973; Hon. RAM 1977; pianist; Professor, Royal College of Music, London, 1953–90; *b* Wanganui, New Zealand, 23 April 1920. *Educ:* Royal College of Music. Debut at invitation of Sir John Barbirolli at Hallé Concerts, Manchester, 1943. Soloist with all leading orchestras of Great Britain, the Royal Philharmonic Soc. (1953, 1959), Promenade Concerts, etc. Toured Belgium, Holland, Spain, France, Scandinavia, Malta, Ceylon, Malaya, Australia and New Zealand. Festival appearances include Aix-en-Provence, International Contemporary Music Festival, Palermo, British Music Festivals in Belgium, Holland and Finland. Broadcasts frequently, and has made many records. *Recreation:* gardening. *Address:* Belmont, Dreemskerry, Maughold, Isle of Man. *T:* Ramsey (01624) 813095.

HORSLEY, (George) Nicholas (Seward); Chairman, 1970–86, Deputy Chairman, 1986–88, Northern Foods plc, retired; non-executive Chairman, Millway Foods Limited, 1988–89; *b* 21 April 1934; *s* of Alec Stewart Horsley and Ida Seward Horsley; *m* 1st, 1958, Valerie Anne Edwards (marr. diss. 1975); two *s* one *d*; 2nd, 1975, Sabita Sarkar (marr. diss. 1987); 3rd, 1988, Alwyne Marjorie Law. *Educ:* Keswick Grammar Sch.; Bootham Sch., York; Worcester Coll., Oxford (BA). Freelance journalist, 1957–58. Northern Dairies Ltd: Trainee Manager, 1958; Director, 1963; Vice-Chairman, 1968–70 (Northern Dairies Ltd changed its name to Northern Foods Ltd in 1972). Chm., News on Sunday Publishing, 1986–87. Pres., Dairy Trade Fedn, 1975–77 and 1980–85. Chm., BBC Consultative Group on Industrial and Business Affairs, 1980–83; Mem., BBC Gen. Adv. Council, 1980–83. *Recreations:* music, bridge, watching cricket, reading. *Address:* Barbados, West Indies.

HORSLEY, Sir Peter; *see* Horsley, Sir B. P. T.

HORSLEY, Stephen Daril; Consultant in Public Health, Morecambe Bay Health Authority, since 1994; *b* 23 June 1947; *s* of Donald Vincent Horsley and Marie Margaret Horsley; *m* 1974, Vivienne Marjorie Lee; one *s* two *d*. *Educ:* Guy's Hosp.; Manchester Business Sch. (MBSc 1985). FRCP 1988 (MRCP 1976); FFPHM. Gen. Hosp. Medicine, Truro, 1971–75; Community Medicine, Yorks RHA, 1975–79; District Community Physician, E Cumbria HA, 1979–82; District MO, S Cumbria HA, 1982–85; Specialist in Community Medicine, Oxford RHA, 1985–86; Regl MO, N Western RHA, 1986–94. *Publications:* contribs to BMJ, Community Medicine. *Recreations:* wind surfing, walking. *Address:* Ulverston, Cumbria. *Club:* Border & County (Carlisle).

HORSMAN, Malcolm; *b* 28 June 1933. Director, Slater Walker Securities Ltd, 1967–70; Chairman: Ralli International Ltd, 1969–73; Alice Hoffman Homes Ltd, 1992–; Director: The Bowater Corporation Ltd, 1972–77; Tozer Kemsley & Millbourn (Holdings) Ltd, 1975–82. Member: Study Group on Local Authority Management Structures, 1971–72; South East Economic Planning Council, 1972–74; Royal Commission on the Press, 1974–77; Institute of Contemporary Arts Ltd, 1975–78; Council, Oxford Centre for Management Studies, 1973–84; Chm., British Centre, Internat. Theatre Inst., 1982–84 (Mem. Exec. Council, 1980–87). Visiting Fellow, Cranfield Univ. (formerly Cranfield Institute of Technology)/The School of Management, 1977–. Vis. Lectr, Univ. of Transkei, 1977. Chm., Nat. Youth Theatre, 1982–90 (Dep. Chm. 1971–82); Dir, Hackney New Variety Ltd (Hackney Empire Trust), 1995–; Member: Court, RCA, 1977–80; Editorial Bd, DRAMA, 1978–81; Council, Birthright, 1974–85. *Clubs:* Reform, Royal Automobile; Harlequins Rugby Football, Knickerbocker (New York).

HORSMAN, Michael John; Director, Office of Manpower Economics, since 1992; *b* 3 March 1949; *s* of Graham Joseph Vivian Horsman and Ruth (*née* Guest); *m* 1977, Dr Anne Margaret Marley; three *s*. *Educ:* Dollar Acad.; Glasgow Univ. (MA Hist. and Politics, 1st cl. Hons, 1971); Balliol Coll., Oxford (Snell Exhibnr, Brackenbury Scholar). Entered Civil Service, 1974; Private Sec. to Chm., MSC, 1978–79; Dept of Employment, 1979–84, on secondment to Unilever, 1981–82; Dir, PER, 1984–85; Hd, Finance Policy, and Resource Controller, MSC, 1985–87; Hd, Ops Br., Employment Service, 1987–89; Regl Dir, London and SE, Employment Service, 1989–92. *Recreations:* historical research, literature, cycling. *Address:* Office of Manpower Economics, Oxford House, 76 Oxford Street, W1N 9FD. *T:* 0171–636 1742.

HORT, Sir Andrew (Edwin Fenton), 9th Bt *cr* 1767, of Castle Strange, Middlesex; *b* 15 Nov. 1954; *e s* of Sir James Fenton Hort, 8th Bt and of Joan, *d* of Edward Peat; *S* father, 1995; *m* 1986, Mary, *d* of Jack Whibley; one *s* one *d*. *Heir: s* James John Fenton Hort, *b* 26 Nov. 1989. *Address:* Westerlee, 77 Fortis Green, E Finchley, N2 9JD.

HORTON, Dr Eric William; retired; Director of Regulatory Affairs, Glaxo Group Research Ltd, 1980–83, Member Board, 1982–83; *b* 20 June 1929; *e s* of late Harold and Agnes Horton; *m* 1956, Thalia Helen, *er d* of late Sir George Lowe; two *s* one *d*. *Educ:* Sedbergh Sch.; Edinburgh Univ. BSc, MB, ChB, PhD, DSc, MD, FRCPE. Mem. Scientific Staff, MRC, Nat. Inst. for Med. Res., London, 1958–60; Dir of Therapeutic Res. and Head of Pharmacology, Miles Labs Ltd, Stoke Poges, 1960–63; Sen. Lectr in Physiology, St Bartholomew's Hosp., London, 1963–66; Wellcome Prof. of Pharmacology, Sch. of Pharmacy, Univ. of London, 1966–69; Prof. of Pharmacology, Univ. of Edinburgh, 1969–80. Hon. Sen. Res. Fellow, Med. Coll. of St Bartholomew's Hosp., London, 1980–; Hon. Lectr in Pharmacol., Royal Free Hosp. Med. Sch., London, 1960–63. Member, Governing Body, Inveresk Res. Foundn (formerly International), 1971–80; Non-executive Director: Inveresk Res. Internat. Ltd, 1977–80; GLP Systems Ltd, 1978–80. Member: Adv. Cttee on Pesticides, MAFF, 1970–73; Biological Research and Cell Boards, MRC, 1973–75; Pharmacy Panel, SRC, 1980–81; Editorial Bd, British Jl of Pharmacology, 1960–66; Editorial Bd, Pharmacological Reviews, 1968–74. Hon. Treasurer, Brit. Pharmacological Soc., 1976–80. Baly Medal, RCP, 1973. *Publications:* Prostaglandins, 1972; papers in learned jls on peptides and prostaglandins. *Recreations:* listening to music and books on cassette, computer programming.

HORTON, Matthew Bethell; QC 1989; *b* 23 Sept. 1946; *s* of Albert Leslie Horton, BSc, FRICS and Gladys Rose Ellen Harding; *m* 1972, Liliane Boleslawski (marr. diss. 1984); one *s* one *d*. *Educ:* Sevenoaks School; Trinity Hall, Cambridge (Open Exhibn, Hist.; Squire Law Scholar; 1st Cl. Hons Law 1967; MA 1967; LLM 1968); Astbury Scholar, Middle Temple, 1968. Called to the Bar, Middle Temple, 1969. Western Circuit; Mem., Parly Bar Mess. Member: Cttee, Jt Planning Law Conf.; European Environmental Law Cttee, Internat. Bar Assoc.; Admin. Law Cttee of Justice. *Recreations:* ski-ing, windsurfing, tennis. *Address:* 2 Mitre Court Buildings, Temple, EC4Y 7BX. *T:* 0171–583 1380. *Club:* Tramp.

HORTON, Robert Baynes, FCIT; Chairman, Railtrack, since 1993; Chancellor, University of Kent at Canterbury, since 1990; *b* 18 Aug. 1939; *s* of late William Harold Horton and of Dorothy Joan Horton (*née* Baynes); *m* 1962, Sally Doreen (*née* Wells); one *s* one *d*. *Educ:* King's School, Canterbury; University of St Andrews (BSc); Massachusetts Inst. of Technology (SM; Sloan Fellow, 1970–71). British Petroleum, 1957–92: General Manager, BP Tankers, 1975–76; Gen. Manager, Corporate Planning, 1976–79; Man. Dir and Chief Exec. Officer, BP Chemicals, 1980–83; a Man. Dir, 1983–86 and 1988–92; Chm. and Chief Exec. Officer, 1990–92; Chairman: Standard Oil, 1986–88; BP America, 1988–89; Dep. Chm., BP, 1989–90; Vice-Chm., BRB, 1992–93. Director: ICL plc, 1982–84; Pilkington Brothers plc, 1985–86; National City Corp., 1986–88; Emerson Electric Company, 1987–; Partner Re, 1993–. Pres., Chemicals Industry Assoc., 1982–84; Vice-Chm., BIM, 1985–91 (CIMgt (CBIM 1982)); Member: SERC, 1985–86; UFC, 1989–92; Bd and Management Cttee, Amer. Petroleum Inst., 1986–88; US Business Roundtable, 1986–88; Nat. Petroleum Council, USA, 1986–88; MIT Corp., 1987–. Pres., BESO, 1993–. Trustee: Cleveland Orchestra, 1986–93; Case Western Reserve Univ., 1987–93; Chairman: Tate Foundation, 1988–92; Business in the Arts, 1988–. Gov., King's Sch., Canterbury, 1984–. Hon. FCGI 1992. Hon. LLD Dundee, 1988; Hon. DCL Kent, 1990; Hon. DBA N London Poly., 1991; Hon. LLD Aberdeen, 1992; Hon. DSc Cranfield, 1992; Hon. DCL Kingston, 1994. Corporate Leadership Award, MIT, 1987; Civic Award, Cleveland, 1988. *Recreations:* music, country activities. *Address:* Railtrack, 40 Bernard Street, WC1N 1BY. *Clubs:* Athenæum, Leander.

HORWICH, Prof. Alan, PhD; FRCR, FRCP; Professor of Radiotherapy, since 1986, and Director of Clinical Research and Clinical Tutor, since 1994, Institute of Cancer Research and Royal Marsden Hospital; Dean, Institute of Cancer Research, since 1992; *b* 1 June 1948; *s* of William and Audrey Horwich; *m* 1981, Pauline Amanda Barnes; two *s* one *d*. *Educ:* William Hulme's Grammar Sch., Manchester; University College Hosp. Med. Sch. (MB BS 1971; PhD 1981). MRCP 1974, FRCP 1994; FRCR 1981. Postgrad. medicine, London, 1971–74; Fellowship in Oncology, Harvard, 1975; res. on ribonucleic acid tumour viruses, ICRF, 1976–79; radiation oncology, Royal Marsden Hosp. and Inst. Cancer Res., 1979–. Chm., MRC Testicular Tumour Working Party, 1988–94. Civilian Consultant to RN, 1989–. *Publications:* Testicular Cancer: investigation and management, 1991; Combined Radiotherapy and Chemotherapy in Clinical Oncology, 1992; Oncology: a multidisciplinary text book, 1995; numerous articles in med. jls on urological cancers and lymphomas. *Address:* Royal Marsden Hospital, Downs Road, Sutton, Surrey SM2 5PT. *T:* 0181–642 6011.

HORWOOD, Hon. Owen Pieter Faure, DMS; President, Council of Governors, Development Bank of Southern Africa, 1983–93; Chancellor, University of Durban-Westville, 1973–88; *b* 6 Dec. 1916; *e s* of late Stanley Ebden Horwood and of Anna Johanna Horwood (*née* Faure); *m* 1946, Helen Mary Watt; one *s* one *d*. *Educ:* Boys' High Sch., Paarl, CP; University of Cape Town (BCom). South African Air Force, 1940–42. Associate Prof. of Commerce, University of Cape Town, 1954–55; Prof. of Economics, University Coll. of Rhodesia and Nyasaland, 1956–57; Univ. of Natal: William Hudson Prof. of Economics, 1957–65; Dir of University's Natal Regional Survey; Principal and Vice-Chancellor, 1966–70. Mem., 1970–80, Leader, 1978–80, South African Senate; Minister of Indian Affairs and Tourism, 1972–74; Minister of Economic Affairs, 1974–75; Minister of Finance, 1975–84. Financial Adviser to Govt of Lesotho, 1966–72. Past Chairman: Nedbank Gp; Cape Wine and Distillers Ltd; Nedbank Ltd; Finansbank Ltd; UAL Merchant Bank Ltd; Past Director: South African Mutual Life Assurance Soc.; Rembrandt Group; South African Permanent Building Soc.; Director: Macsteel Group; Bank of Taiwan (SA) Ltd; TNT Express International. Patron, S Africa Sports Assoc. for Physically Disabled. Hon. DCom: Port Elizabeth, 1980; Stellenbosch, 1983; Hon. Scriptural degree, Israel Torah Res. Inst. and Adelphi Univ., 1980; Hon. DEcon Rand Afrikaans, 1981. Order of the Brilliant Star (Republic of China), 1982. *Publications:* (jtly) Economic Systems of the Commonwealth, 1962; contribs to SA Jl of Economics, SA Bankers' Jl, Economica (London), Optima, etc. *Recreations:* cricket, gardening, sailing. *Address:* PO Box 130694, Bryanston 2021, South Africa. *Clubs:* Durban (Durban); Pretoria Country; Western Province Cricket; Cape Town Cricket (Captain 1943–48).

HOSE, John Horsley, CBE 1987; Forest Craftsman, Forestry Commission, 1975–88 (Forest Worker, 1949, Skilled Forest Worker, 1950); President, National Union of Agricultural and Allied Workers, 1978–82; *b* 21 March 1928; *s* of Harry and Margaret Eleanor Hose; *m* 1st, 1967, Margaret Winifred Gaskin (marr. diss. 1987); 2nd, 1987, Linda Sharon Morris. *Educ:* Sneinton Boulevard Council Sch.; Nottingham Bluecoat Sch. Architects' Junior Asst, 1943–46. National Service, with Royal Engineers, 1946–48. Chm., Nat. Trade Gp, Agricultural and Allied Workers/TGWU, 1982–86 (Mem., 1982–89); Mem., Gen. Exec. Council, TGWU, 1986–88. *Recreations:* walking, reading, drinking real ale. *Address:* 140 Sneinton Dale, Nottingham NG2 4HJ. *T:* Nottingham (0115) 958 0494.

HOSIER, John, CBE 1984; Director and Member of Council, Hong Kong Academy for Performing Arts, 1989–93 (Fellow, 1993); *b* 18 Nov. 1928; *s* of Harry J. W. Hosier and Constance (*née* Richmond). *Educ:* Preston Manor Sch.; St John's Coll., Cambridge. MA 1954. Taught in Ankara, Turkey, 1951–53; Music Producer, BBC Radio for schools, 1953–59; seconded to ABC, Sydney, to advise on educational music programmes, 1959–60; Music Producer, subseq. Sen. and Exec. Producer, BBC TV, pioneering first regular music broadcasts to schools, 1960–73; ILEA Staff Inspector for music, and Dir of Centre for Young Musicians, 1973–76; Principal, Guildhall Sch. of Music and Drama, 1978–89. Vice-Chm., Kent Opera, 1985–87; Founder Mem. and Vice-Chm., UK Council for Music Educn and Training, 1975–81; Member: Gulbenkian Enquiry into training musicians, 1978; Music Panel, British Council, 1984–88; Music Panel, GLAA, 1984–86; Council of Management, Royal Philharmonic Soc., 1982–89; Cttee, Hong Kong Philharmonic Orch., 1990–93; Conservatoires Adv. Gp, HEFCE, 1993–; Board, Trinity Coll. of Music, 1993–; Council, Early Music Centre, 1994–; Governing Body, Chetham's Sch., 1983–88. Trustee, Kathleen Ferrier Meml Scholarship Fund, 1994–. FRSA 1976; FGSM 1978; Hon. RAM 1980; FRCM 1981; FRNCM 1985; Hon. FTCL 1986. Hon. DMus City, 1986. *Compositions:* music for: Cambridge revivals of Parnassus, 1949, and Humorous Lovers, 1951; Something's Burning, Mermaid, 1974; many radio and TV productions. *Publications:* The Orchestra, 1961, revd edn 1977; various books, songs and arrangements for children; contribs on music to educnl jls. *Address:* 5 Royal Crescent, Brighton BN2 1AL. *Clubs:* City Livery; Hong Kong.

HOSKER, Sir Gerald (Albery), KCB 1995 (CB 1987); HM Procurator General, Treasury Solicitor and Queen's Proctor, since 1992; *b* 28 July 1933; *s* of Leslie Reece Hosker and Constance Alice Rose Hosker (*née* Hubbard); *m* 1956, Rachel Victoria Beatrice Middleton; one *s* one *d*. *Educ:* Berkhamsted Sch., Berkhamsted, Herts. Admitted Solicitor, 1956; Corporate Secretary 1964; Associate of the Faculty of Secretaries and Administrators 1964. Articled to Derrick Bridges & Co., 1951–56; with Clifford-Turner & Co., 1957–59; entered Treasury Solicitor's Dept as Legal Asst, 1960; Sen. Legal Asst, 1966; Asst Solicitor, 1973; Under Sec. (Legal), 1982; Dep. Treasury Solicitor, 1984–87; Solicitor to the DTI, 1987–92. FRSA 1964. Hon. QC 1991. *Recreations:* the study of biblical prophecy, herbalism. *Address:* Queen Anne's Chambers, 28 Broadway, SW1H 9JS. *Club:* Royal Over-Seas League.

HOSKING, Barbara Nancy, OBE 1985; non-executive Director, Westcountry Television, since 1992; *b* 4 Nov. 1926; *d* of late William Henry Hosking and Ada Kathleen

Hosking (*née* Murrish). *Educ:* West Cornwall School for Girls, Penzance; Hillcroft College, Surbiton; and by friends. Secretary to Town Clerk, Council of Isles of Scilly, and local corresp. for BBC and Western Morning News, 1945–47; Editl Asst, The Circle, Odeon and Gaumont cinemas, 1947–50; Asst to Inf. Officer, Labour Party, 1952–55; Asst to Gen. Manager, Uruwira Minerals Ltd, Tanzania, 1955–57; Res. Officer, Broadcasting Section, Labour Party, 1958–65; Science Press Officer, DES, 1965; Press Officer, Min. of Technology, 1967; Press and Publicity Officer, Metrication Board, 1970; Senior Inf. Officer, 10 Downing Street, 1970; Principal Inf. Officer, DoE, 1972; Private Sec. to Parly Secs, Cabinet Office, 1973; Chief Inf. Officer, DoE, 1974–77; Controller of Inf. Services, IBA, 1977–86. Non-Exec. Dir, Camden and Islington Community Health Services NHS Trust, 1992–93. Pres., Media Soc., 1987–88; Hon. Vice Pres., London Cornish Assoc., 1992; Jt Vice-Chm., NCVO, 1987–92. Mem. Council, Family Policy Studies Centre, 1994–. Trustee: Charities Aid Foundn, 1987–92; 300 Gp, 1988–91; Nat. Literacy Trust, 1993–. Associate, Women's Advertising Club of London, 1994–. Patron, Clean-Break Theatre Co., 1992–. Radio broadcaster, incl. BBC Radio 4 Any Questions. FRTS 1988; FRSA (Mem. Council, 1992–). Special citation, American Women's Forum, NY, 1983. *Publications:* contribs to Punch, New Scientist, Spectator. *Recreations:* opera, lieder, watching politics, watching sport. *Address:* 9 Highgate Spinney, Crescent Road, N8 8AR. *T:* 0181–340 1853. *Club:* Reform.

HOSKING, Prof. Geoffrey Alan, FBA 1993; Professor of Russian History, University of London, since 1984; *b* 28 April 1942; *s* of Stuart William Steggall Hosking and Jean Ross Hosking; *m* 1970, Anne Lloyd Hirst; two *d*. *Educ:* Maidstone Grammar Sch.; King's Coll., Cambridge (MA, PhD); St Antony's Coll., Oxford. Asst Lectr in Government, 1966–68, Lectr in Government, 1968–71, Univ. of Essex; Vis. Lectr in Political Science, Univ. of Wisconsin, Madison, 1971–72; Lectr in History, Univ. of Essex, 1972–76; Sen. Research Fellow, Russian Inst., Columbia Univ., New York, 1976; Sen. Lectr and Reader in Russian History, Univ. of Essex, 1976–84; Vis. Professor, Slavisches Inst., Univ. of Cologne, 1980–81. BBC Reith Lectr, 1988 (The Rediscovery of Politics: authority, culture and community in the USSR). Member: Council, Writers and Scholars Educnl Trust, 1985–; Overseas Policy Cttee, British Acad., 1994–; Jury, Booker Prize for Russian Fiction, 1993. Member: East-West Adv. Cttee, BCC, 1987–89; Council of Management, Keston Coll., 1987–89; Internat. Academic Council, Mus. of the Revolution, Moscow, 1994–; Admin. Bd, Moscow Sch. of Pol Studies, 1992–. Trustee, J. S. Mill Inst., 1992–; Governor, Camden Sch. for Girls, 1989–94. Member: Editl Bd, Jl of Contemporary History, 1988; Editl Cttee, Nations and Nationalism, 1994–. *Publications:* The Russian Constitutional Experiment: Government and Duma 1907–14, 1973; Beyond Socialist Realism: Soviet fiction since Ivan Denisovich, 1980; A History of the Soviet Union, 1985, 3rd edn 1992 (Los Angeles Times Hist. Book Prize, 1986); The Awakening of the Soviet Union, 1990, 2nd edn 1991; (with J. Aves and P. J. S. Duncan) The Road to Post-Communism: independent political movements in the Soviet Union 1985–91, 1992. *Recreations:* music, chess, walking. *Address:* School of Slavonic Studies, University of London, Senate House, Malet Street, WC1E 7HU. *T:* 0171–637 4934.

HOSKING, John Everard, CBE 1990; JP; DL; Chairman, Agra Europe (London) Ltd, 1989–94 (Director and Chief Executive, 1974–89); Vice-President, Magistrates' Association, since 1990 (Chairman of Council, 1987–90); *b* 23 Oct. 1929; *s* of J. Everard Hosking, OBE and E. Margaret (*née* Shaxson); *m* 1953, Joan Cecily Whitaker, BSc; two *s*. *Educ:* Marlborough Coll.; London Univ. (BScA 1953). NDA 1954. Farmer and landowner in Kent, 1953–69; Man. Dir, Eastes and Loud Ltd, 1965–69; Director: Newgrain-Kent, 1969–74; Ashford Corn Exchange Co., 1965–69; Agroup Ltd, 1987–94; Bureau Européen de Recherches SA, 1987–90; European Intelligence Ltd, 1987–94. Tax Comr, 1980–. Chairman: Centre for European Agricultural Studies Assoc., 1977–83; Kent Br., Magistrates' Assoc., 1973–78; Kent Magistrates' Courts Cttee, 1984–88; Member: Kent Police Authority, 1970–74; Lord Chancellor's Adv. Cttee on the Appointment of Magistrates, 1977–89; Central Council, Magistrates' Courts Cttees, 1980–83; Bar Council Professional Conduct Cttee, 1983–86; Senate of Inns of Court and the Bar Disciplinary Tribunal, 1983–86; Council, Commonwealth Magistrates' and Judges' Assoc., 1989–92; Lord Chief Justice's Working Party on Mode of Trial, 1989; Lord Chancellor's Adv. Cttee on Legal Educn and Conduct, 1991–94. Member: CLA, 1958–; RASE, 1960–. Governor, Ashford Sch., 1976– (Chm., 1994–). JP Kent, 1962 (Chm., Ashford Bench, 1975–85); DL Kent, 1992. British Univs Ploughing Champion, 1952. *Publications:* (ed) Rural Response to the Resource Crisis in Europe, 1981; The Agricultural Industry of West Germany, 1990. *Recreations:* the arts, the countryside. *Address:* 28 Fitzroy Square, W1P 6DD. *Club:* Farmers'.

HOSKINS, Prof. Brian John, PhD; FRS 1988; FRMetS; Professor of Meteorology, since 1981, Head of Department of Meteorology, since 1990, University of Reading; *b* 17 May 1945; *s* of George Frederick Hoskins and Kathleen Matilda Louise Hoskins; *m* 1968, Jacqueline Holmes; two *d*. *Educ:* Univ. of Cambridge (MA; PhD 1970). FRMetS 1970; Fellow, Amer. Meteorol Soc, 1985. Post-doctoral Fellow, Nat. Center for Atmospheric Res., Boulder, Colo, 1970–71; Vis. Scientist, GFD Program, Univ. of Princeton, 1972–73; Univ. of Reading: Post-doctoral Fellow, 1971–72, Gp Leader, 1973–, Atmospheric Modelling Gp; Reader in Atmospheric Modelling, 1976–81. Special Advr to Sec. of State for Transport, 1990. Member: NERC, 1988–94; Meteorol Cttee, Meteorol Office, 1994– (Chm., Meteorol. Res. Sub-Cttee, 1994–); Jt Scientific Cttee, World Climate Res. Prog., 1995–. Pres., IAMAS, 1991–95. Mem., Academia Europaea, 1989; Corresp. Academician, Real Acad. de Ciencias y Artes de Barcelona, 1994. Starr Meml Lecture, MIT, 1989; Bernard Haurwitz Meml Lecture, Amer. Meteorol Soc., 1995. Royal Meteorological Society: Symons Meml Lecture, 1982; L. F. Richardson Prize, 1972; Buchan Prize, 1976; Charles Chree Silver Medal, Inst. of Physics, 1987; Carl-Gustaf Rossby Res. Medal, Amer. Meteorol Soc., 1988. *Publications:* (ed with R. P. Pearce) Large-scale Dynamical Processes in the Atmosphere, 1983; 60 papers in meteorol jls. *Recreations:* music, sport, gardening. *Address:* 32 Reading Road, Wokingham, Berks RG11 1EH. *T:* Wokingham (01734) 791015.

HOSKINS, Robert William, (Bob); actor; *b* 26 Oct. 1942; *s* of Robert Hoskins and Elsie Lilian Hoskins; *m* 1st, 1970, Jane Livesey; one *s* one *d*; 2nd, 1982, Linda Banwell; one *s* one *d*. *Educ:* Stroud Green School. *Stage:* Intimate Theatre, Palmers Green, 1966; Victoria, Stoke on Trent, 1967; Century Travelling Theatre, 1969; Royal Court, 1972; Doolittle in Pygmalion, Albery, 1974; RSC season, Aldwych, 1976; The World Turned Upside Down, NT, 1978; Has Washington Legs?, NT, 1978; True West, NT, 1981; Guys and Dolls, NT, 1981; *television:* On the Move, 1976; Pennies from Heaven, 1978; Flickers, 1980; The Dunera Boys, 1985; *films:* Zulu Dawn, 1980; The Long Good Friday, 1981; The Honorary Consul, 1982; Lassiter, 1984; Cotton Club, 1984; Sweet Liberty, 1986; Mona Lisa, 1986 (Best Actor award, Cannes Fest.; Golden Globe Award); A Prayer for the Dying, 1988; The Raggedy Rawney (writer, dir, actor), 1988; Who Framed Roger Rabbit, 1988; The Lonely Passion of Judith Hearne, 1989; Heart Condition, 1990; Mermaids, 1991; The Favour, the Watch and the Very Big Fish, 1992; Hook, 1992; The Inner Circle, 1992; Super Mario Brothers, 1993. *Recreations:* photography, gardening, playgoing. *Address:* c/o Anne Hutton, Hutton Management, 200 Fulham Road, SW10.

HOSKYNS, Sir Benedict (Leigh), 16th Bt, *cr* 1676; *b* 27 May 1928; *s* of Rev. Sir Edwyn Clement Hoskyns, 13th Bt, MC, DD and Mary Trym (*d* 1994), *d* of Edwin Budden, Macclesfield; *S* brother 1956; *m* 1953, Ann Wilkinson; two *s* two *d*. *Educ:* Haileybury; Corpus Christi Coll., Cambridge; London Hospital. BA Cantab 1949; MB, BChir Cantab 1952. House Officer at the London Hospital, 1953. RAMC, 1953–56. House Officer at Royal Surrey County Hospital and General Lying-In Hospital, York Road, SE1, 1957–58; DObstRCOG 1958; in general practice, 1958–93. *Heir: s* Edwyn Wren Hoskyns [*b* 4 Feb. 1956; *m* 1981, Jane, *d* of John Sellars; one *s* one *d*. *Educ:* Nottingham Univ. Medical School (BM, BS 1979; MRCP 1984). Cons. Paediatrician, Leicester Gen. Hosp, 1993–]. *Address:* Russell House, High Street, Manningtree, Essex CO11 1AJ. *T:* Colchester (01206) 396432.

HOSKYNS, Sir John (Austin Hungerford Leigh), Kt 1982; Director-General, Institute of Directors, 1984–89; Chairman: The Burton Group plc, since 1990; EMAP, since 1994 (Director, since 1993); *b* 23 Aug. 1927; *s* of Lt-Colonel Chandos Benedict Arden Hoskyns and Joyce Austin Hoskyns; *m* 1956, Miranda Jane Marie Mott; two *s* one *d*. *Educ:* Winchester College. Served in The Rifle Brigade, 1945–57 (Captain); IBM United Kingdom Ltd, 1957–64; founded John Hoskyns & Co. Ltd, later part of Hoskyns Group Ltd (Chm. and Man. Dir), 1964–75; Director: ICL plc, 1982–84; AGB Research plc, later Pergamon AGB plc, 1983–89; Clerical Medical & General Life Assurance Soc., 1983–; McKechnie plc, 1983–93; Ferranti Internat. plc, 1986–94. Hd of PM's Policy Unit, 1979–82. Hon. DSc Salford, 1985; DU Essex, 1987. *Recreations:* opera, shooting. *Address:* c/o Child & Co., 1 Fleet Street, EC4Y 1BD. *Club:* Travellers'.

HOTHAM, family name of **Baron Hotham.**

HOTHAM, 8th Baron, *cr* 1797; **Henry Durand Hotham;** Bt 1621; DL; *b* 3 May 1940; *s* of 7th Baron Hotham, CBE, and Lady Letitia Sibell Winifred Cecil (*d* 1992), *er d* of 5th Marquess of Exeter, KG; *S* father, 1967; *m* 1972, Alexandra Stirling Home, *d* of late Maj. Andrew S. H. Drummond Moray; two *s* one *d*. *Educ:* Eton; Cirencester Agricultural Coll. Late Lieut, Grenadier Guards; ADC to Governor of Tasmania, 1963–66. DL Humberside, 1981. *Heir: s* Hon. William Beaumont Hotham, *b* 13 Oct. 1972. *Address:* Dalton Hall, Dalton Holme, Beverley, Yorks; Scorborough Hall, Driffield, Yorks.

HOTHFIELD, 6th Baron *cr* 1881; **Anthony Charles Sackville Tufton;** Bt 1851; *b* 21 Oct. 1939; *s* of 5th Baron Hothfield, TD and Evelyn Margarette (*d* 1989), *e d* of late Eustace Charles Mordaunt; *S* father, 1991; *m* 1975, Lucinda Marjorie, *d* of Captain Timothy John Gurney; one *s* one *d*. *Educ:* Eton; Magdalene Coll., Cambridge (MA). MICE. *Recreations:* Real tennis, lawn tennis, bridge, shooting. *Heir: s* Hon. William Sackville Tufton, *b* 14 Nov. 1977. *Address:* House of Lords, SW1A 0PW. *Clubs:* Hawks (Cambridge); Jesters; Cockermouth Lawn Tennis, almost every Real tennis club.

HOTSPUR; *see* McGrath, J. A.

HOTTEN, Christopher Peter; QC 1994; a Recorder, since 1990; *b* 7 July 1949; *s* of Alan John Hotten and Ida Lydia Hotten; *m* 1973, Lone Elisabeth Nielsen; one *s* two *d*. *Educ:* Hornchurch Grammar Sch.; Leicester Univ. (LLB). Called to the Bar, Inner Temple, 1972. *Recreations:* golf, tennis, snooker. *Address:* 7 Fountain Court, Steelhouse Lane, Birmingham B4 6DR. *T:* 0121–236 8531. *Club:* Stetchford (Birmingham).

HOTTER, Hans; opera and concert singer, retired 1972, but still gives occasional concert performances; teaches masterclasses in USA, Japan, Great Britain, Austria, Germany and other countries; *b* Offenbach, Germany, 19 Jan. 1909; *m* 1936, Helga Fischer; one *s* one *d*. *Educ:* Munich. Concert career began in 1929 and opera career in 1930. Prof. at Vienna Musik-Hochschule, 1977–80. Mem. of Munich, Vienna and Hamburg State Operas; guest singer in opera and concerts in all major cities of Europe and USA; concert tours in Australia; for 10 years, connected with Columbia Gramophone Co., England; guest singer, Covent Garden Opera, London, 1947–72. Festivals: Salzburg, Edinburgh and Bayreuth. *Relevant publication:* Hans Hotter: man and artist, by Penelope Turing, 1984. *Address:* Emil Dittlerstrasse 26, 81479 München, Germany.

HOTUNG, Sir Joseph (Edward), Kt 1993; Chairman, Inter-Continental Capital Co. Ltd; *b* 25 May 1930; *s* of Edward Sai-kim Hotung and Maud Alice (*née* Newman); *m* 1st, 1957, Mary Catherine McGinley (marr. diss. 1969); two *s* two *d*; 2nd, 1970, Ann Virginia Carlo (marr. diss. 1981). *Educ:* St Francis Xavier Coll., Shanghai; St Louis Coll., Tientsin; Catholic Univ. of America (BA); Univ. of London (LLB). With Marine Midland Bank, 1957–60; Ho Hung Hing Estates Ltd, 1960–. Director: HSBC Hldgs plc; Hongkong & Shanghai Banking Corp. Ltd; Hongkong Electric Hldgs Ltd; China & Eastern Investment Co. Ltd. Member: Judicial Services Commn; Inland Revenue Bd of Review. University of Hong Kong: Mem. Council; Mem., Finance Cttee; Chm. and Trustee, Staff Terminal Benefits Scheme; Mem. Council, Business Sch. Chm., Arts Develt Council, Hong Kong, 1994–; Dir, E Asian Hist. of Sci. Foundn, 1991–; Member: Internat. Council, and Trustee, Asia Soc., NY; UK Adv. Council, Asia House, London, 1993–; Chm's Council and Vis. Cttee, MMA; Vis. Cttee, Freer Gall. of Art, Washington DC. Trustee, British Mus., 1994–. NACF Award, 1993. *Recreation:* Oriental art. *Address:* 3310 Edinburgh Tower, The Landmark, 15 Queen's Road, Central, Hong Kong. *T:* 5229929. *Clubs:* Hong Kong, Royal Hong Kong Jockey (Hong Kong); Century (New York).

HOUGH, George Hubert, CBE 1965; PhD; FRAeS; Chairman: Forthstar Ltd, since 1980; Abasec Ltd, since 1988; *b* 21 Oct. 1921; *m* Hazel Ayrton (*née* Russel); one *s* two *d*. *Educ:* Winsford Grammar Sch.; King's Coll., London. BSc (Hons Physics), PhD. Admiralty Signals Estabt, 1940–46. Standard Telecommunication Laboratories Ltd (ITT), 1946–51 (as external student at London Univ. prepared thesis on gaseous discharge tubes); de Havilland Propellers Ltd: early mem. Firestreak team in charge of develt of guidance systems and proximity fusing, 1951–59; Chief Engr (Guided Weapons), 1959; Chief Executive (Engrg), 1961; Dir, de Havilland Aircraft Co., 1962; Hawker Siddeley Dynamics Ltd: Technical Dir, 1963; Dep. Managing Dir, 1968; Man. Dir, 1977; Dep. Chief Exec., Dynamics Group British Aerospace, 1977. Chief Exec., 1977–80, Chm., 1978–80, British Smelter Constructions Ltd; Chairman: Magnetic Components Ltd, 1986–89; Fernau Hldgs Ltd, 1989–94; Fernau Avionics Ltd, 1989–94; Director: Sheepbridge Engrg Ltd, 1977–79; Scientific Finance Ltd, 1979–84; Programmed Neuro Cybernetics (UK) Ltd, 1979–85; Landis & Gyr Ltd, 1980–85; Leigh Instruments Ltd (Canada), 1987–88. *Publication:* (with Dr P. Morris) The Anatomy of Major Projects, 1987. *Recreation:* golf. *Address:* Trelyon, Rock, near Wadebridge, Cornwall PL27 6LB. *T:* Trebetherick (01208) 863454.

HOUGH, John Patrick; Secretary, Institute of Chartered Accountants in England and Wales, 1972–82; *b* 6 July 1928; *s* of William Patrick Hough, MBE, Lt-Comdr RN and Eva Harriet Hough; *m* 1956, Dorothy Nadine Akerman; four *s* one *d*. *Educ:* Purbrook High School. FCA, MIMC, FBCS. Articled M. R. Cobbett & Co., Portsmouth, 1950–53; Derbyshire & Co., 1953–54; Turquand Youngs & Co., 1954–57; Computer Specialist, IBM United Kingdom Ltd, 1957–61; Consultant 1961–62, Partner 1962–69, Robson Morrow & Co.; Dep. Sec., Inst. of Chartered Accountants in England and Wales, 1969–71. *Recreations:* music, food. *Address:* 5 South Row, Blackheath, SE3 0RY; Coastguard Cottage, Newtown, Newport, Isle of Wight PO30 4PA. *Club:* London Rowing.

HOUGH, Julia Marie, (Judy); *see* Taylor, Judy.

HOUGH, Richard Alexander; writer; *b* 15 May 1922; *s* of late George and Margaret May Hough; *m* 1st, 1943, Helen Charlotte (marr. diss.) *o d* of Dr Henry Woodyatt; four *d*; 2nd, 1980, Judy Taylor, *qv*. *Educ:* Frensham Heights. Served War, RAF Pilot, Fighter Command, home and overseas, 1941–46. Publisher, 1947–70: Bodley Head until 1955; Hamish Hamilton as Dir and Man. Dir, Hamish Hamilton Children's Books Ltd, 1955–70. Contrib. to: Guardian; Observer; Washington Post; NY Times; Encounter; History Today; New Yorker. Mem. Council, 1970–73, 1975–84, Vice-Pres., 1977–82, Navy Records Society. Chm., Auxiliary Hospitals Cttee, King Edward's Hospital Fund, 1975–80 (Mem. Council, 1975–86). *Publications:* The Fleet that had to Die, 1958; Admirals in Collision, 1959; The Potemkin Mutiny, 1960; The Hunting of Force Z, 1963; Dreadnought, 1964; The Big Battleship, 1966; First Sea Lord: an authorised life of Admiral Lord Fisher, 1969; The Pursuit of Admiral von Spee, 1969; The Blind Horn's Hate, 1971; Captain Bligh and Mr Christian, 1972 (Daily Express Best Book of the Sea Award) (filmed as The Bounty, 1984); Louis and Victoria: the first Mountbattens, 1974; One Boy's War: per astra ad ardua, 1975; (ed) Advice to a Grand-daughter (Queen Victoria's letters), 1975; The Great Admirals, 1977; The Murder of Captain James Cook, 1979; Man o' War, 1979; Nelson, 1980; Mountbatten: Hero of Our Time, 1980; Edwina: Countess Mountbatten of Burma, 1983; The Great War at Sea 1914–1918, 1983; Former Naval Person: Churchill and the Wars at Sea, 1985; The Longest Battle, 1986; The Ace of Clubs: a history of the Garrick, 1986; Born Royal, 1988; (with Denis Richards) The Battle of Britain: the jubilee history, 1989; Winston and Clementine: the triumph of the Churchills, 1990; Bless our Ship: Mountbatten and HMS Kelly, 1991; Other Days Around Me: a memoir, 1992; Edward & Alexandra: their private and public lives, 1992; Captain James Cook: a biography, 1994; *novels:* Angels One Five, 1978; The Fight of the Few, 1979; The Fight to the Finish, 1979; Buller's Guns, 1981; Razor Eyes, 1981; Buller's Dreadnought, 1982; Buller's Victory, 1984; The Raging Sky, 1989; numerous books on motoring history; also books for children under *pseudonym* Bruce Carter. *Address:* 31 Meadowbank, Primrose Hill, NW3 1AY. *T:* 0171–722 5663, *Fax:* 0171–722 7750. *Clubs:* Garrick, MCC.
See also D. Moggach.

HOUGH, Stephen; concert pianist; *b* 22 Nov. 1961; *s* of Colin Hough and Annetta (*née* Johnstone). *Educ:* Chetham's Sch. Music, Manchester; Royal Northern Coll. of Music (Fellow, 1993); Juilliard Sch. Numerous recitals and concerto appearances with LSO, LPO, RPO, Philharmonia, Chicago Symphony, Philadelphia Orchestra, Cleveland Orchestra, LA Philharmonic, San Francisco Symphony; festival performances incl.: Ravinia, Mostly Mozart, Hollywood Bowl, Blossom, Proms, Le Grange de Meslay, La Roque d'Antheron. Recordings: Hummel Piano Concertos; 2 Liszt Recitals; 2 Piano Albums; Schumann Recital; Brahms Piano Concertos Nos 1 and 2; Complete Britten Piano Music; (with Robert Mann) Complete Beethoven and Brahms Violin Sonatas; Scharwenka Piano Concerto No 4; Sauer Piano Concerto No 1; (with Steven Isserlis) Cello Sonatas of Grieg and Rubinstein; piano music of York Bowen. RNCM Dayas Gold Medal, 1981; Internat. Terence Judd Award, 1982; Naumburg Internat. Piano Competition, 1983. *Recreations:* reading, pipe-smoking. *Address:* Harrison Parrott Ltd, 12 Penzance Place, W11 4PA.

HOUGHAM, John William; Chairman, Advisory, Conciliation and Arbitration Service, since 1993; *b* 18 Jan. 1937; *s* of William George Hougham and Emily Jane (*née* Smith); *m* 1961, Peggy Edith Grove; one *s* one *d*. *Educ:* Sir Roger Manwood's Sch., Sandwich; Leeds Univ. (BA Hons). National Service: commnd 2nd Lieut RA, 1955–57. British Home Stores, 1960–63; Ford Motor Company Ltd, 1963–93: Director: Industrial Relns, Ford España SA, 1976–80; Industrial Relns, Mfg, Ford of Europe Inc., 1982–86; Personnel, and Exec. Bd Mem., 1986–93. Mem. Bd, Personnel Mgt Services Ltd, 1989–93. Member: Review Body on Doctors' and Dentists' Remuneration, 1992–93; Adv. Bd of CS Occupational Health Service, 1992–; Employment Appeal Tribunal, 1992–93. Member: Engrg ITB, 1987–90; IPM Nat. Cttee for Equal Opportunities, 1987–92; CBI Employment Policy Cttee, 1987–93; Council, CRAC, 1988–; Bd, Trng and Employment Agency for NI, 1990–93; Council, Engrg Trng Auth., 1990–93; Chm., Employment Occupational Standards Council, 1994–. Vis. Prof., Univ. (formerly Poly.) of E London, 1991–; Vis. Fellow, City Univ., 1991–. Vice-Pres., Involvement & Participation Assoc., 1994–. FIPD (CIPM 1986); CIMgt 1986. Freeman, City of London, 1995. Member, Editorial Advisory Board: Human Resource Mgt Jl, 1991–; Personnel Mgt Mag., 1993–. *Publication:* (contrib.) Legal Intervention in Industrial Relations (ed William McCarthy), 1992. *Recreations:* collecting books on Kent, walking, watching cricket and Rugby football, family history. *Address:* 27 Wilton Street, SW1X 7AZ. *T:* 0171–210 3670. *Club:* Harlequin Football.

HOUGHTON, family name of **Baron Houghton of Sowerby.**

HOUGHTON OF SOWERBY, Baron *cr* 1974 (Life Peer), of Sowerby, W Yorks; **Arthur Leslie Noel Douglas Houghton,** PC 1964; CH 1967; *b* 11 Aug. 1898; *s* of John and Martha Houghton, Long Eaton, Derbyshire; *m* 1939, Vera Travis (CBE 1986); no *c*. Inland Revenue, 1915–22; Civil Service Rifles, 1916–19; 1st 60th Rifles, 1919–20; Sec., Inland Revenue Staff Fedn, 1922–60. Broadcaster in "Can I Help You?" Programme, BBC, 1941–64. Alderman LCC, 1947–49; Mem. Gen. Council, TUC, 1952–60. Chm., Staff Side, Civil Service National Whitley Council, 1956–58. MP (Lab) Sowerby, WR Yorks, March 1949–Feb. 1974; Chm. Public Accounts Cttee, 1963–64; Chancellor of the Duchy of Lancaster, 1964–66; Minister Without Portfolio, 1966–67. Chm., Parly Lab. Party, 1967–70, Nov. 1970–1974. Chairman: British Parly Gp, Population and Develt, 1978–84; House of Lords Industry Study Gp, 1979–87. Member: Commn on the Constitution, 1969–73; Royal Commn on Standards of Conduct in Public Life, 1974–75. Chairman: Commonwealth Scholarships Commn, 1967–68; Young Volunteer Force Foundation, 1967–70 (Jt Vice-Chm. 1970–71); Teachers' Pay Inquiry, 1974; Cttee on aid to Political Parties, 1975–76; Cttee on Security of Cabinet Papers, 1976; Cttee for Reform of Animal Experimentation, 1977–; Vice-Pres., RSPCA, 1978–82. *Publication:* Paying for the Social Services, 2nd edn, 1968. *Address:* 110 Marsham Court, SW1P 4LA. *T:* 0171–834 0602; Becks Cottage, Whitehill Lane, Bletchingley, Surrey RH1 4QS. *T:* Godstone (01883) 743340. *Club:* Reform.

HOUGHTON, Brian Thomas, CB 1991; Director, International Division (formerly International Tax Policy Division), Inland Revenue, 1987–91; *b* 22 Aug. 1931; *s* of Bernard Charles Houghton and Sadie Houghton; *m* 1953, Joyce Beryl (*née* Williams); three *s* one *d*. *Educ:* City Boys' Sch., Leicester; Christ's Coll., Cambridge. BA (Mod. Langs), MA 1957. Inland Revenue, 1957; Private Sec. to Chief Sec., HM Treasury, 1966–68; Assistant Secretary: Inland Revenue, 1968–75; HM Treasury, 1975–77; Under Sec., 1977, Principal Finance Officer and Dir of Manpower, Inland Revenue, 1977–83; Policy Div. Dir, Inland Revenue, 1983–87. Consultant, OECD, 1991–93. Vis. Professorial Fellow, QMW, 1992–. *Address:* 19 Rookes Lane, Lymington, Hants SO41 8FP. *T:* Lymington (01590) 670375.

HOUGHTON, Herbert; Director: Stenhouse Holdings Ltd, 1979–83; Reed Stenhouse Cos Ltd, 1977–86; Chancellor Insurance Co. Ltd, 1984; *b* 4 Oct. 1920; *s* of Herbert Edward and Emily Houghton; *m* 1939, Dorothy Ballantyne; one *s* one *d*. *Educ:* William Hulmes' Grammar School. Director, Cockshoots Ltd, 1955; Man. Dir, Stenhouse Northern Ltd, 1968; Chairman: Sir Wm Garthwaite (Holdings) Ltd, 1973; Sten-Re Ltd, 1973; Director and Chief Executive, A. R. Stenhouse & Partners Ltd, 1977; Dir, British Vita Co. Ltd, 1969–84. *Recreations:* overseas travel, golf, reading, gardening. *Address:* 2 Orchard Court, Grindleford, Sheffield S30 1JH. *T:* Hope Valley (01433) 631142.

HOUGHTON, Dr John, JP; Director, Teesside Polytechnic, 1971–79, retired (Principal, Constantine College of Technology, 1961–70); *b* 12 June 1922; *s* of George Stanley Houghton and Hilda (*née* Simpson); *m* 1951, Kathleen Lamb; one *s* one *d*. *Educ:* King Henry VIII Sch., Coventry; Hanley High Sch.; Coventry Techn. Coll.; King's Coll., Cambridge; Queen Mary Coll., London Univ. BSc (hons) Engrg 1949; PhD 1952. CEng, MIMechE, FRAeS. Aircraft Apprentice, Sir W. G. Armstrong-Whitworth Aircraft Ltd, 1938–43; design and stress engr, 1943–46; student at univ. (Clayton Fellow), 1946–51; Lectr, Queen Mary Coll., London Univ., 1950–52; Sen. Lectr and Head of Aero-Engrg, Coventry Techn. Coll., 1952–57; Head of Dept of Mech. Engrg, Brunel Coll. Advanced Technology, 1957–61. Freeman, City of Coventry, 1943. JP Middlesbrough, 1962. *Publications:* (with D. R. L. Smith) Mechanics of Fluids by Worked Examples, 1959; various research reports, reviews and articles in professional and learned jls. *Recreations:* keen sportsman (triple Blue), do-it-yourself activities, gardening, pottery, oil painting. *Club:* Middlesbrough Rotary.

HOUGHTON, Sir John (Theodore), Kt 1991; CBE 1983; FRS 1972; Chief Executive (formerly Director General) of the Meteorological Office, 1983–91; Chairman, Royal Commission on Environmental Pollution, since 1992 (Member, since 1991); *b* 30 Dec. 1931; *s* of Sidney M. Houghton, schoolmaster, and Miriam Houghton; *m* 1st, 1962, Margaret Edith Houghton (*née* Broughton) (*d* 1986), MB, BS, DPH; one *s* one *d*; 2nd, 1988, Sheila Houghton (*née* Thompson). *Educ:* Rhyl Grammar Sch.; Jesus Coll., Oxford (Scholar). BA hons Physics 1951, MA, DPhil 1955. Research Fellow, RAE Farnborough, 1954–57; Lectr in Atmospheric Physics, Oxford Univ., 1958–62; Reader, 1962–76; Professor, 1976–83; Fellow, Jesus Coll., Oxford, 1960–83, Hon. Fellow 1983; on secondment as Dir (Appleton), 1979–83, and Dep. Dir, 1981–83, Rutherford Appleton Laboratory, SERC, Hon. Scientist, 1992–. Member: Astronomy, Space and Radio Bd, SERC (formerly SRC), 1970–73 and 1976–81; Exec. Cttee, WMO, 1983–91 (Vice-Pres., 1987–91); Astronomy and Planetary Sci. Bd, SERC, 1987–93; Meteorological Cttee, 1975–80; Jt Organising Cttee, Global Atmospheric Res. Programme, 1976–79; Exec. Management Bd, British Nat. Space Centre, 1986–91; Chairman: Jt Scientific Cttee, World Climate Research Programme, 1981–84; Earth Observation Adv. Cttee, ESA, 1982–93; Scientific Assessment, Intergovtl Panel for Climate Change, 1988–; Jt Scientific and Tech. Cttee, Global Climate Observing System, 1992–. Pres., RMetS, 1976–78. FInstP; Fellow, Optical Soc. of America; Hon. Fellow, Univ. of Wales, Lampeter, 1994. MAE 1988. Lectures: Cherwell-Simon Meml, 1983–84, Halley, 1992, Templeton, 1992, Oxford Univ.; Bakerian, Royal Soc., 1991. Hon. DSc: Wales, 1991; UEA, 1993; Leeds, 1995; DUniv Stirling, 1992. Buchan Prize, RMetS, 1966; Charles Chree medal and prize, Inst. of Physics, 1979; (with F. W. Taylor, C. D. Rodgers and G. D. Peskett) Rank Prize for opto-electronics, 1989; Symons Meml Medal, RMetS, 1991; Glazebrook Medal and Prize, Inst. of Phys, 1990; Gold Medal, RAS, 1995. *Publications:* (with S. D. Smith) Infra-Red Physics, 1966; The Physics of Atmospheres, 1977, 2nd edn 1986; (with F. W. Taylor and C. D. Rodgers) Remote Sounding of Atmospheres, 1984; Does God play dice?, 1988; Global Warming: the complete briefing, 1994; The Search for God: can science help?, 1995; papers in learned jls on atmospheric radiation, spectroscopy, remote sounding from satellites and climate change. *Recreations:* walking, sailing. *Address:* Royal Commission on Environmental Pollution, Church House, Great Smith Street, SW1P 3BZ.

HOUGHTON, Maj.-Gen. Robert Dyer, CB 1963; OBE 1947; MC 1942; DL; *b* 7 March 1912; *s* of late J. M. Houghton, Dawlish, Devon; *m* 1940, Dorothy Uladh, *y d* of late Maj.-Gen. R. W. S. Lyons, IMS; two *s* one *d*. *Educ:* Haileybury Coll. Royal Marines Officer, 1930–64; Col Comdt, Royal Marines, 1973–76. Gen. Sec., Royal UK Beneficent Assoc., 1968–78. DL East Sussex, 1977. *Recreations:* gardening, sailing, model engineering. *Address:* Vert House, Whitesmith, near Lewes, East Sussex BN8 6JQ. *Club:* Army and Navy.

HOULDEN, Rev. Prof. (James) Leslie; Professor of Theology, King's College, London, 1987–94, now Emeritus; *b* 1 March 1929; *s* of James and Lily Alice Houlden. *Educ:* Altrincham Grammar Sch.; Queen's Coll., Oxford. Asst Curate, St Mary's, Hunslet, Leeds, 1955–58; Chaplain, Chichester Theological Coll., 1958–60; Chaplain Fellow, Trinity Coll., Oxford, 1960–70; Principal, Cuddesdon Theol Coll., later Ripon Coll., Cuddesdon, 1970–77; King's College, London: Lectr, 1977; Sen. Lectr in New Testament Studies, 1985; Dean, Faculty of Theology and Religious Studies, 1986–88; Head, Dept of Biblical Studies, 1988–89; FKC 1994. Hon. Canon of Christ Church Oxford, 1976–77. Member: Liturgical Commn, 1969–76; Doctrine Commn of C of E, 1969–76; Gen. Synod of C of E, 1980–90. Editor, Theology, 1983–91. *Publications:* Paul's Letters from Prison, 1970; (ed) A Celebration of Faith, 1970; Ethics and the New Testament, 1973; The Johannine Epistles, 1974; The Pastoral Epistles, 1976; Patterns of Faith, 1977; Explorations in Theology 3, 1978; What Did the First Christians Believe?, 1982; Connections, 1986; Backward into Light, 1987; (ed) The World's Religions, 1988; History, Story and Belief, 1988; (ed) Dictionary of Biblical Interpretation, 1990; Truth Untold, 1991; (ed) Austin Farrer: the essential sermons, 1991; Bible and Belief, 1991; Jesus: a question of identity, 1992; (ed jtly) Austin Farrer, Words for Life, 1993; (ed) The Interpretation of the Bible in the Church, 1995; (ed) Companion Encyclopedia of Theology, 1995; *contributed to:* The Myth of God Incarnate, 1977; Incarnation and Myth, 1979; Alternative Approaches to New Testament Study, 1985; The Reality of God, 1986; A New Dictionary of Christian Ethics, 1986; The Trial of Faith, 1988; God's Truth, 1988; Embracing the Chaos, 1990; Tradition and Unity, 1991; Using the Bible Today, 1991; Fundamentalism and Tolerance, 1991; Anchor Bible Dictionary, 1992; The Resurrection of Jesus Christ, 1993; Crossing the Boundaries, 1994; reviews and articles in learned jls. *Address:* 33 Raleigh Court, Lymer Avenue, SE19 1LS. *T:* 0181–265 9869. *Club:* Athenæum.

HOULDER, Bruce Fiddes; QC 1994; a Recorder, since 1991; *b* 27 Sept. 1947; *s* of Charles Alexander Houlder and Jessie Houlder (*née* Fiddes); *m* 1974, Stella Catherine Mattinson; two *d*. *Educ:* Felsted Sch., Dunmow. Called to the Bar, Gray's Inn, 1969. Mem., Bar Council. *Recreations:* painting, sailing, theatre, music. *Address:* 6 King's Bench Walk, Temple, EC4Y 7DR. *T:* 0171–583 0410.

HOULDER, John Maurice, CBE 1977 (MBE (mil.) 1941); Chairman, Houlder Offshore Engineering Ltd, since 1984; *b* 20 Feb. 1916; *m* 1981, Rody, *d* of late Major Luke White. Private Pilot's Licence, 1938–; instrument rating, 1949–; Lessee, Elstree Aerodrome, 1951–. Chm., Houlder Diving Research Facility Ltd, 1978–. Vis. Prof., Dept of Ship and Marine Technol., Univ. of Strathclyde, 1982–. Chm., London Ocean Shipowners Joint Dock Labour Piecework Cttee, 1950–60; first Chm., River Plate Europe Freight Conf., 1961–70; Chm., Bulk Cargo Cttee, Continental River Plate Conf., 1954–70. Member: Exec. Board, 1970–93, and Technical Cttee, 1970–, Lloyds Register of Shipping; Light

Aircraft Requirements Cttee, CAA, 1955–84; Adv. Cttee on R&D to Sec. of State for Energy, 1987–90. Member, Council: RSPB, 1974–79; RINA, 1981–87; Pres., Soc for Underwater Technology, 1978–80 (President's Award, 1987). Hon. DSc Strathclyde, 1986. Stanley Gray Award, Inst. of Marine Engrs, 1982. *Recreations:* ski-ing, flying, bird-watching, computer programming. *Address:* 59 Warwick Square, SW1V 2AL. *T:* 0171–834 2856. *Clubs:* Air Squadron; Kandahar Ski, 1001.

HOULDSWORTH, Sir Richard (Thomas Reginald), 5th Bt *cr* 1887, of Reddish and Coodham; Farm Manager since 1988; *b* 2 Aug. 1947; *s* of Sir Reginald Douglas Henry Houldsworth, 4th Bt, OBE, TD and Margaret May (*d* 1995), *d* of late Cecil Emilius Laurie; *S* father, 1989; *m* 1st, 1970, Jane Elizabeth (marr. diss. 1982), *o d* of Alistair Orr; two *s*; 2nd, 1992, Ann Catherine Tremayne; one *s*. *Educ:* Bredon School, Tewkesbury, Glos; Blanerne School, Denholm, Roxburghshire. *Recreations:* shooting, fishing, tennis, squash, horse racing. *Heir:* *s* Simon Richard Henry Houldsworth, *b* 6 Oct. 1971. *Address:* Kirkbride, Glenburn, Crosshill, Ayrshire KA19 7QA. *T:* Crosshill (016554) 202.

HOULSBY, Prof. Guy Tinmouth, PhD; Professor of Civil Engineering, and Fellow of Brasenose College, Oxford, since 1991, *b* 28 March 1954; *s* of Thomas Tinmouth Houlsby and Vivienne May Houlsby (*née* Ford); *m* 1985, Jenny Lucy Damaris Nedderman; two *s*. *Educ:* Trinity College, Glenalmond; St John's College, Cambridge (MA, PhD). CEng, MICE. Engineer, Binnie and Partners, 1975–76, Babtie Shaw and Morton, 1976–77; Research Student, Cambridge, 1977–80; Oxford University: Jun. Res. Fellow, Balliol Coll., 1980–83; Lectr in Engineering, 1983–91; Fellow, Keble College, 1983–91. *Publications:* BASIC Soil Mechanics (with G. W. E. Milligan), 1984; contribs to learned jls on soil mechanics. *Recreations:* ornithology, woodwork, Northumbrian small pipes. *Address:* 25 Purcell Road, Marston, Oxford OX3 0HB. *T:* Oxford (01865) 722128.

HOUNSFIELD, Sir Godfrey (Newbold), Kt 1981; CBE 1976; FRS 1975; Consultant to Laboratories, THORN EMI Central Research Laboratories (formerly Central Research Laboratories of EMI), Hayes, Mddx, since 1986 (Head of Medical Systems section, 1972–76; Chief Staff Scientist, 1976–77, Senior Staff Scientist, 1977–85); Consultant (part-time), National Heart & Chest Hospitals, Chelsea, since 1986; *b* 28 Aug. 1919; *s* of Thomas Hounsfield, Newark, Notts. *Educ:* Magnus Grammar Sch., Newark; City and Guilds Coll., London (Radio Communications qualif.); Faraday House Electrical Engineering Coll. (Diploma); grad. for IEE. Volunteered for RAF, 1939; served 1939–46 (incl. period as Lectr at Cranwell Radar Sch.); awarded Certificate of Merit (for work done in RAF), 1945. Attended Faraday House, where he studied elec. and mech. engrg, 1947–51. Joined EMI Ltd, 1951, working initially on radar systems and, later, on computers; led design team for the first large, all transistor computer to be built in Great Britain, the EMIDEC 1100, 1958–59; invented the EMI-scanner computerised transverse axial tomography system for X-ray examination, 1969–72 (now used at Atkinson Morley's Hosp., Wimbledon, and leading hosps in the USA and European continent, which are buying the invention); the technique can be applied to cranial examinations and the whole of the body; the system has overcome obstacles to the diagnosis of disease in the brain which have continued since Roentgen's day (1895); it includes a patient-scanning unit; developer of a new X-ray technique (the EMI-scanner system) which won the 1972 MacRobert Award of £25,000 for the invention, and a Gold Medal for EMI Ltd; working on Nuclear Magnetic Resonance Imaging, 1976–; Magnetic Resonance Imaging Advr, Nat. Heart Hosp. and Brompton Hosp. Professorial Fellow in imaging sciences, Manchester Univ., 1978–. Hon. FRCP 1976; Hon. FRCR 1976; Hon. FEng 1994. Dr Medicine (*hc*) Universität Basel, 1975; Hon. DSc: City, 1976; London, 1976; Hon. DTech Loughborough, 1976. Wilhelm-Exner Medal, Austrian Industrial Assoc., 1974; Ziedses des Plantes Medal, Physikalisch Medizinische Gesellschaft, Würzburg, 1974; Prince Philip Medal Award, CGLI, 1975; ANS Radiation Industry Award, Georgia Inst. of Technology, 1975; Lasker Award, Lasker Foundn, 1975; Duddell Bronze Medal, Inst. Physics, 1976; Golden Plate Award, Amer. Acad. of Achievement, 1976; Reginald Mitchell Gold Medal, Stoke-on-Trent Assoc. of Engrs, 1976; Churchill Gold Medal, 1976; Gairdner Foundn Award, 1976; (jtly) Nobel Prize for Physiology or Medicine, 1979; Ambrogino d'Oro Award, City of Milan, 1980; Deutsche Roentgen Plakette, Deutsche Roentgen Museum, 1980. *Publications:* contribs: New Scientist; Brit. Jl of Radiology; Amer. Jl of Röntgenology. *Recreation:* mountain walking. *Address:* THORN EMI Central Research Laboratories, Dawley Road, Hayes, Mddx UB3 1HH. *T:* 0181–848 6404; 15 Crane Park Road, Twickenham TW2 6DF. *T:* 0181–894 1746.

HOURSTON, Gordon Minto, FRPharmS; Member since 1989, Chairman since 1993, Armed Forces Pay Review Body; *b* 24 July 1934; *s* of William A. M. Hourston and Vera W. (*née* Minto); *m* 1962, Sheila Morris; two *s*. *Educ:* Daniel Stewart's Coll., Edinburgh; Heriot-Watt Univ. FRPharmS 1982 (MRPharmS 1957). Joined Boots The Chemists, 1958: Dir, 1978; Dep. Man. Dir, 1984–88; Chm. and Man. Dir, 1988–95; Dir, Boots Co. plc, 1981–95. Chm., Company Chemists' Assoc., 1988–95. Mem., Sen. Salaries Rev. Body, 1993–. *Recreations:* golf, walking, modern history, reading. *Address:* c/o Office of Manpower Economics, Oxford House, 76 Oxford Street, W1N 9FD. *T:* 0171–467 7200.

HOUSDEN, Peter James; Chief Executive, Nottinghamshire County Council, since 1994; *b* 7 Dec. 1950; *s* of Gordon Arthur James Housden and Mary Archibald; *m* 1st, 1970, Kate Toon (marr. diss. 1974); one *s*; 2nd, 1974, Maureen McMorrow; one *s* one *d*. *Educ:* Univ. of Essex (BA Hons Sociology). Teacher, Madeley Court Sch., Telford, 1975–79; Professional Asst, Humberside LEA, 1979–82; Asst Dir of Educn, Notts LEA, 1982–86; Sen. Educn Officer, Lancs LEA, 1986–88; Dep. Chief Educn Officer, Notts LEA, 1988–91; Dir of Educn, Notts CC, 1991–94. Advr, Educn Cttee, ACC, 1993–94; Chm., Midlands Soc. of Educn Officers, 1993–94. *Recreations:* ironing, Nottingham Forest. *Address:* County Hall, West Bridgford, Nottingham NG2 7QP. *T:* Nottingham (0115) 977 3582.

HOUSE, Lt-Gen. Sir David (George), GCB 1977 (KCB 1975); KCVO 1985; CBE 1967; MC 1944; Gentleman Usher of the Black Rod, House of Lords, 1978–85; Serjeant-at-Arms, House of Lords, and Secretary to the Lord Great Chamberlain, 1978–85; *b* 8 Aug. 1922; *s* of A. G. House; *m* 1947, Sheila Betty Darwin; two *d*. *Educ:* Regents Park Sch., London. War service in Italy; and thereafter in variety of regimental (KRRC and 1st Bn The Royal Green Jackets) and staff appts. Comd 51 Gurkha Bde in Borneo, 1965–67; Chief BRIXMIS, 1967–69; Dep. Mil. Sec., 1969–71; Chief of Staff, HQ BAOR, 1971–73; Dir of Infantry, 1973–75; GOC Northern Ireland, 1975–77. Colonel Commandant: The Light Division, 1974–77; Small Arms School Corps, 1974–77. Dir, Yorks and Humberside, Lloyds Bank, 1985–91. *Address:* Dormer Lodge, Aldborough, near Boroughbridge, N Yorks YO5 9EP. *Club:* Army and Navy.

HOUSE, Ven. Francis Harry, OBE 1955; MA; Officer Royal (Hellenic) Order of Phoenix, 1947; Archdeacon of Macclesfield, 1967–78, now Archdeacon Emeritus; Rector of St James, Gawsworth, 1967–78; *b* 9 Aug. 1908; *s* of late Canon William Joseph House, DD; *m* 1938, Margaret Neave; two *d*. *Educ:* St George's Sch., Harpenden; Wadham Coll., Oxford; Cuddesdon Theological Coll. Sec. of Student Christian Movement of Gt Britain and Ireland, 1931–34; Deacon, 1936; Priest, 1937. Asst Missioner, Pembroke Coll. (Cambridge) Mission, Walworth, 1936–37; Travelling sec. of World's Student Christian Federation, Geneva, 1938–40; Curate of Leeds Parish Church, 1940–42; Overseas Asst, Religious Broadcasting Dept, BBC, London, 1942–44; representative of World Student Relief in Greece, 1944–46; Sec. Youth Dept World Council of Churches, Geneva, and World Conference of Christian Youth, Oslo, 1946–47; Head of Religious Broadcasting BBC, London, 1947–55; Associate Gen. Sec. of the World Council of Churches, Geneva, 1955–62; Vicar of St Giles, Pontefract, 1962–67. Select Preacher, Cambridge Univ., 1949. Member: Gen. Synod of Church of England, 1970–78; Gen. Synod's Commn on Broadcasting, 1971–73; Bd for Mission and Unity, 1971–80 (Vice-Chm., 1971–75). *Publications:* The Russian Phoenix, 1988; articles contributed to: The Student Movement, The Student World, East and West, the Ecumenical Review, Theology, Crucible, One in Christ, etc. *Address:* 11 Drummond Court, Far Headingley, Leeds LS16 5QE. *T:* Leeds (0113) 278 3646.

HOUSE, Dr John Peter Humphry; Reader, Courtauld Institute of Art, University of London, since 1987 (Lecturer, 1980–87); *b* 19 April 1945; *s* of Madeline Edith Church and Arthur Humphry House; *m* 1968, Jill Elaine Turner; two *s*. *Educ:* Westminster Sch.; New Coll., Oxford (BA); Courtauld Inst. of Art (MA, PhD). Lecturer: UEA, 1969–76; UCL, 1976–80. Slade Prof. of Fine Art, Univ. of Oxford, 1986–87; British Acad. Res. Reader, 1988–90. Organiser: Impressionism Exhibn, RA, 1974; Landscapes of France exhibn, Hayward Gall., 1995; Co-organiser: Post Impressionism exhibn, RA, 1979–80; Renoir exhibn, Arts Council, 1985. *Publications:* Monet, 1977, 2nd edn 1981; Monet: nature into art, 1986; (jtly) Impressionist and Post-Impressionist Masterpieces from the Courtauld Collection, 1987; (jtly) Impressionism for England: Samuel Courtauld as Patron and Collector, 1994; author/co-author, exhibition catalogues; articles in Burlington Magazine, Art History, Art in America. *Recreation:* second hand bookshops. *Address:* Courtauld Institute of Art, University of London, Somerset House, Strand, WC2R 0RN. *T:* 0171–872 0220.

See also E. H. O. Parry.

HOUSE, Roger Keith; a Metropolitan Stipendiary Magistrate, since 1995; *b* 24 Jan. 1944; *s* of Donald Stuart House and Kathleen Mary House; *m* 1971, Elizabeth Anne Hall; two *s*. *Educ:* Wychwood Prep. Sch.; Sherborne. Admitted Solicitor, 1972; Asst Solicitor with various firms, 1972–76; sole practitioner, 1976–95. *Recreations:* singing, reading, walking the countryside, shooting, surfing, travelling. *Address:* c/o Camberwell Magistrates' Court, Camberwell Green, SE5 7UP. *T:* 0171–703 0909.

HOUSEMAN, Alexander Randolph, CBE 1984; FEng, FIMechE, FIEE; Deputy Chairman, British Rail Engineering Ltd, since 1985 (Director, since 1979); *b* 9 May 1920; *e s* of Captain Alexander William Houseman and Elizabeth Maud (*née* Randolph); *m* 1942, Betty Edith Norrington; one *d*. *Educ:* Stockport Grammar School and College. FIMC, CIMgt. Apprenticed Crossley Motors, 1936–40; Production Engineer: Ford Motor Co. (Aero Engines) Ltd, 1940–43; Saunders-Roe Ltd, 1943–48, General Works Manager, 1948–54; Consultant, Director, Man. Dir and Dep. Chm., P-E International Ltd, 1954–81; Dir, P-E Consulting Gp Ltd, 1968–85; Chm., W. Canning Ltd, 1975–80; Dir, Record Ridgway Ltd, 1978–81. Chm., NEDO EDC for Gauge and Tool Industry, 1979–85; Institution of Production Engineers: Chm., Technical Policy Bd, 1978–82; Vice-Pres., 1982–83; Pres., 1983–84. Member: Industrial Adv. Panels of Fellowship of Engineering, 1980–82; Council, Inst. of Management Consultants, 1968–83; Inst. of Directors; Life Member: Soc. of Manufg Engrs, USA, 1985; Inst. of Industrial Engrs, USA, 1985. Distinguished Engrg Management Award, Nat. Soc. of Professional Engrs, USA, 1983; Distinguished Achievements Award, LA Council of Engrs and Scientists, 1984; Nuffield Award, 1984. *Publications:* articles to learned jls and technical and management press on manufacturing technology and management. *Recreations:* DIY, sailing, photography, walking. *Address:* 11 Kings Avenue, Ealing, W5 2SJ. *T:* 0181–997 3936. *Clubs:* Caledonian; Royal Anglesey Yacht (Beaumaris).

HOUSSEMAYNE du BOULAY, (Edward Philip) George, CBE 1985; FRCR, FRCP; Professor of Neuroradiology, University of London at Institute of Neurology, 1975–84, now Emeritus; Hon. Research Fellow, Zoological Society of London (Head, X-Ray Department, Nuffield Laboratories, Institute of Zoology, 1965–86); Director, Radiological Research Trust, since 1985; *b* 28 Jan. 1922; *yr s* of Philip Houssemayne du Boulay and Mercy Tyrrell (*née* Friend); *m* 1944, Vivien M. Glasson (marr. diss.); four *s* (and two *s* decd); *m* 1968, Pamela Mary Verity; two *d*. *Educ:* Christ's Hospital; King's Coll., London; Charing Cross Hosp. (Entrance Schol. 1940; MB, BS, DMRD). Served RAF (Medical), 1946–48; Army Emergency Reserve, 1952–57. House appts, Charing Cross Hosp. and Derby City Hosp., 1945–46; Registrar (Radiology), Middlesex Hosp., 1948–49; Sen. Registrar (Radiology): St Bartholomew's Hosp., 1949–54; St George's Hosp., 1951–52; Consultant Radiologist: Nat. Hosp. for Nervous Diseases, Maida Vale, 1954–68; Bartholomew's Hosp., 1954–71; Nat. Hosp. for Nervous Diseases, Queen Square, 1968–75 (Head, Lysholm Radiol Dept, 1975–84). Editor, Neuroradiology, 1974–91. Pres., Brit. Inst. of Radiology, 1976–77, Appeal Co-ordinator 1976–84; Hon. Member: Société Française de Neuroradiologie; Amer. Soc. of Neuroradiology; Swedish Soc. of Neuroradiology; German Soc. Neuroradiology. Trustee, Nat. Hosp. Devel Foundn. Glyn Evans Meml Lectr, RCR, 1970; Ernestine Henry Lectr, RCP, 1976. Hon. FACR. Hon. DSc Leicester Polytechnic, 1992. Barclay Medal, BIR, 1968. *Publications:* Principles of X-Ray Diagnosis of the Skull, 1965, 2nd edn 1979; (jtly) 4th edn of A Text Book of X-Ray Diagnosis by British Authors: Neuroradiology Vol. 1, 5th edn 1984; (jtly) The Cranial Arteries of Mammals, 1973; (jtly) An Atlas of Normal Vertebral Angiograms, 1976; works in specialist jls. *Recreation:* gardening. *Address:* Old Manor House, Brington, Huntingdon, Cambs PE18 0PX. *T:* Bythorn (01832) 710353.

HOUSSEMAYNE du BOULAY, Sir Roger (William), KCVO 1982 (CVO 1972); CMG 1975; HM Diplomatic Service, retired; Vice Marshal of the Diplomatic Corps, 1975–82; *b* 30 March 1922; *s* of Charles John Houssemayne du Boulay, Captain, RN, and Mary Alice Veronica, *née* Morgan; *m* 1957, Elizabeth, *d* of late Brig. Home, late RM, and Molly, Lady Pile; one *d*, and two step *s*. *Educ:* Winchester; Oxford. Served RAFVR, 1941–46 (Pilot). HM Colonial Service, Nigeria, 1949–58; HM Foreign, later Diplomatic, Service, 1959; FO, 1959; Washington, 1960–64; FCO 1964–67; Manila, 1967–71; Alternate Director, Asian Development Bank, Manila, 1967–69, and Director, 1969–71; Counsellor and Head of Chancery, Paris, 1971–73; Resident Comr, New Hebrides, 1973–75. Adviser: Solomon Is Govt, 1986; Swaziland Govt, 1992. *Address:* Anstey House, near Buntingford, Herts SG9 0BJ.

HOUSTON, Maj.-Gen. David, CBE 1975 (OBE 1972); JP; Lord-Lieutenant of Sutherland, since 1991; *b* 24 Feb. 1929; *s* of late David Houston and late Christina Charleson Houston (*née* Dunnett); *m* 1959, Jancis Veronica Burn; two *s*. *Educ:* Latymer Upper Sch. Commissioned, Royal Irish Fusiliers, 1949; served Korea, Kenya, BAOR, N Africa; Staff Coll., Camberley, 1961; commanded 1 Loyals and newly amalgamated 1st QLR, 1969–71; in comd 8th Inf. Bde, Londonderry, N Ireland, 1974–75; Mem. RCDS, 1976; Military Attaché and Commander, British Army Staff, Washington, 1977–79; HQ UKLF, 1979–80; Pres., Regular Commissions Bd, 1980–83; retd 1984. Hon. Col, Manchester and Salford Univs OTC (TA), 1985–90; Col, The Queen's Lancashire Regt,

1983–92. DL Sutherland, 1991; JP Sutherland, 1991. *Recreations:* fishing, golf. *Address:* c/o Bank of Scotland, Bonar Bridge, Sutherland IV24 3EB.

HOUSTON, James Caldwell, CBE 1982; MD, FRCP; Physician to Guy's Hospital, 1953–82, now Emeritus Physician; Dean, United Medical and Dental Schools, Guys and St Thomas's Hospitals, 1982–84 (Hon. Fellow, 1993; Dean, Medical and Dental Schools, Guy's Hospital, 1965–82); *b* 18 Feb. 1917; *yr s* of late David Houston and Minnie Walker Houston; *m* 1946, Thelma Cromarty Cruickshank, MB, ChB, 2nd *d* of late John Cruickshank, CBE; four *s*. *Educ:* Mill Hill Sch.; Guy's Hosp. Medical Sch. MRCS, LRCP 1939; MB, BS (London) 1940; MRCP 1944; MD 1946; FRCP 1956. Late Major RAMC; Medical Registrar, Guy's Hospital, 1946; Asst Ed., 1954, Jt Ed., 1958–67, Guy's Hosp. Reports; Member: Bd of Governors, Guy's Hosp., 1965–74; SE Metropolitan Regional Hosp. Bd, 1966–71; Lambeth, Lewisham and Southwark AHA (Teaching), 1974–78; Court of Governors, London Sch. of Hygiene and Tropical Med., 1969–84; Senate, Univ. of London, 1970–84; Bd of Faculty of Clinical Medicine, Cambridge Univ., 1975–81; Cttee of Vice-Chancellors and Principals, 1977–80; Special Trustee, Guy's Hosp., 1974–82; Trustee, Hayward Foundn, 1978–. Dir, Clerical, Medical & Gen. Life Assurance Soc., 1965–87; Vice-Pres., Medical Defence Union, 1970–92. *Publications:* Principles of Medicine and Medical Nursing (jtly), 1956, 5th edn 1978; A Short Text-book of Medicine (jtly), 1962, 8th edn 1984; articles in Quart. Jl Med., Brit. Med. Bull., Lancet, etc. *Recreations:* golf, gardening. *Address:* Keats House, Guy's Hospital, St Thomas Street, SE1 9RT. *T:* 0171–955 4290; Cockhill Farm, Detling, Maidstone, Kent ME14 3HG. *T:* Medway (01634) 231395.

HOUSTOUN-BOSWALL, Sir (Thomas) Alford, 8th Bt *cr* 1836; international economics and business consultant; *b* 23 May 1947; *s* of Sir Thomas Houstoun-Boswall, 7th Bt, and of Margaret Jean, *d* of George Bullen-Smith; *S* father, 1982; *m* 1971, Eliana Michele, *d* of Dr John Pearse, New York; one *s* one *d*. *Educ:* Lindisfarne College. Chairman, Metropolitan Car Parks and Excelsior Properties Ltd, UK; Partner, Rosedale-Engel, Houstoun-Boswall Partnership, Bermuda; Director, Stair & Co., New York (specialising in fine 18th century English furniture and works of art); Pres., Houstoun-Boswall Inc. (Fine Arts), New York. Lecturer, New York Univ. and Metropolitan Museum of Art, New York. *Heir: s* Alexander Alford Houstoun-Boswall, *b* 16 Sept. 1972. *Address:* 18 rue Basse, 06410 Biot, France; 15 East 77 Street, New York, NY 10021, USA.

HOVELL-THURLOW-CUMMING-BRUCE, family name of **Baron Thurlow,** and *see* Cumming-Bruce.

HOVEN, Helmert Frans van den; Knight, Order of Netherlands Lion, 1978; Commander, Order of Orange Nassau, 1984; Hon. KBE 1980; President, International Chamber of Commerce, Paris, 1985–86; Chairman, Unilever NV, 1975–84; Vice-Chairman, Unilever Ltd, 1975–84; *b* 25 April 1923; *m* 1st, 1950, Dorothy Ida Bevan (marr. diss. 1981); one *s*; 2nd, 1981, Cornelia Maria van As. *Educ:* Grammar and Trade schs in The Netherlands. Joined Unilever N. V., Rotterdam, 1938; transf. to Unilever Ltd, London, 1948, then to Turkey, 1951, becoming Chm. of Unilever's business there, 1958; Chm., Unilever's Dutch margarine business, Van den Bergh en Jurgens B. V., 1962; sen. marketing post, product gp, Margarine, Edible Fats and Oils, 1966; Mem. Bds of Unilever, and responsible for product gp, Sundry Foods and Drinks, 1970; Mem. Supervisory Bd of Shell; Chm. Supervisory Bds of ABN/Amro Bank and various other cos; Mem., Eur. Adv. Bd, A.T., T. and Rockwell; Mem. Council, North Western (Kellogg) Business Sch. *Recreations:* summer and winter sports in general. *Address:* Marevista 35, 2202 BX, Noordwijk, Netherlands.

HOVING, Thomas; President Hoving Associates, Inc., since 1977, Editor-in-Chief, Connoisseur, 1982–91; *b* 15 Jan. 1931; *s* of late Walter Hoving and Mary Osgood (*née* Field); *m* 1953, Nancy Melissa Bell; one *d*. *Educ:* Princeton Univ. BA Highest Hons, 1953; Nat. Council of the Humanities Fellowship, 1955; Kienbusch and Haring Fellowship, 1957; MFA 1958; PhD 1959. Dept of Medieval Art and The Cloisters, Metropolitan Museum of Art: Curatorial Asst, 1959; Asst Curator, 1960; Associate Curator, 1963; Curator, 1965, Commissioner of Parks, New York City, 1966; Administrator of Recreation and Cultural Affairs, New York City, 1967; Dir, Metropolitan Museum of Art, 1967–77. Distinguished Citizen's Award, Citizen's Budget Cttee, 1967. Hon. Mem. AIA, 1967. Hon. LLD, Pratt Inst., 1967; Dr *hc* Princeton; New York Univ. Middlebury and Woodrow Wilson Awards, Princeton. *Publications:* The Sources of the Ada Group Ivories (PhD thesis), 1959; Guide to The Cloisters, 1962; The Chase and The Capture, 1976; Two Worlds of Andrew Wyeth, 1977; Tutankhamun, the Untold Story, 1978; King of the Confessors, 1981; Masterpiece (novel), 1986; Discovery (novel), 1989; Making the Mummies Dance: inside the Metropolitan Museum of Art, 1993; articles in Apollo magazine and Metropolitan Museum of Art Bulletin. *Recreations:* sailing, ski-ing, bicycling, flying. *Address:* (office) Hoving Associates, 150 East 73rd Street, New York, NY 10021, USA.

HOWARD; *see* Fitzalan-Howard.

HOWARD, family name of **Earls of Carlisle, Effingham,** and **Suffolk,** and of **Barons Howard of Penrith** and **Strathcona.**

HOWARD DE WALDEN, 9th Baron *cr* 1597, **AND SEAFORD,** 5th Baron *cr* 1826; **John Osmael Scott-Ellis,** TD; *b* 27 Nov. 1912; *s* of 8th Baron and Margherita, CBE 1920 (*d* 1974), *d* of late Charles van Raalte of Brownsea Island, Dorset; *S* father, 1946; *m* 1st, 1934, Countess Irene Harrach (*d* 1975), *y d* of Count Hans Albrecht Harrach; four *d*; 2nd, 1978, Gillian Viscountess Mountgarret. *Educ:* Eton; Magdalene Coll., Cambridge (BA 1934, MA). Member of the Jockey Club (Senior Steward, 1957, 1964, 1976). *Heir:* (to Barony of Howard de Walden) four co-heiresses; (to Barony of Seaford) *cousin* Colin Humphrey Felton Ellis [*b* 19 April 1946; *m* 1971, Susan Magill; two *s* two *d*]. *Address:* Avington Manor, Hungerford, Berks RG17 0UL. *T:* Kintbury (01488) 58229; Flat K, 90 Eaton Square, SW1W 9AG. *T:* 0171–235 7127. *Clubs:* Turf, White's.

See also Capt. D. W. S. Buchan of Auchmacoy.

HOWARD OF PENRITH, 2nd Baron, *cr* 1930; **Francis Philip Howard,** DL; Captain late RA; *b* 5 Oct. 1905; *s* of 1st Baron and Lady Isabella Giustiniani-Bandini (*d* 1963) (*d* of Prince Giustiniani-Bandini, 8th Earl of Newburgh); *S* father, 1939; *m* 1944, Anne, *widow* of Anthony Bazley; four *s*. *Educ:* Downside; Trinity Coll., Cambridge (BA); Harvard Univ. Called to Bar, Middle Temple, 1931; served in War, 1939–42 (wounded). DL County of Glos, 1960. *Heir: s* Hon. Philip Esme Howard [*b* 1 May 1945; *m* 1969, Sarah, *d* of late Barclay Walker and of Mrs Walker, Perthshire; two *s* two *d*]. *Address:* Dean Farm, Coln St Aldwyns, Glos GL7 5AX.

See also Hon. Edmund B. C. Howard.

HOWARD, Alan (Mackenzie); actor; Associate Artist, Royal Shakespeare Company, since 1967; *b* 5 Aug. 1937; *s* of late Arthur John Howard and of Jean Compton Mackenzie; *m* 1st, Stephanie Hinchcliffe Davies (marr. diss. 1976); 2nd, Sally Beauman; one *s*. *Educ:* Ardingly Coll. Belgrade Theatre, Coventry, 1958–60, parts incl. Frankie Bryant in Roots (also at Royal Court and Duke of York's); Wesker Trilogy, Royal Court, 1960; A Loss of Roses, Pembroke, Croydon, 1961; The Changeling, Royal Court, 1961; The Chances, and The Broken Heart, inaugural season, Chichester Festival, 1962; Virtue in Danger, Mermaid and Strand, 1963; Bassanio in The Merchant of Venice, Lysander in A Midsummer Night's Dream, in tour of S America and Europe, 1964; Simon in A Heritage and its History, Phoenix, 1965; Angelo in Measure for Measure, Bolingbroke in Richard II, Nottingham, 1965–66; Cyril Jackson in The Black and White Minstrels, Traverse, Edinburgh, 1972, Hampstead, 1973; A Ride Across Lake Constance, Hampstead and Mayfair, 1973; The Silver King, Chichester, 1990; Scenes from a Marriage, Chichester, transf. Wyndhams, 1990; Kings, 1991; *Royal Shakespeare Company:* joined company, 1966, playing Orsino in Twelfth Night, Lussurioso in The Revenger's Tragedy; 1967: Jaques in As You Like It (also LA, 1968), Young Fashion in The Relapse; 1968: Edgar in King Lear, Achilles in Troilus and Cressida, Benedick in Much Ado about Nothing; 1969: Benedick (also in LA and San Francisco), Achilles, Lussurioso, and Bartholomew Cokes in Bartholomew Fair; 1970: Mephistophilis in Dr Faustus, Hamlet, Theseus/Oberon in A Midsummer Night's Dream, Ceres in The Tempest; 1971: Theseus/Oberon (NY debut); 1971–72: Theseus/Oberon, Nikolai in Enemies, Dorimant in The Man of Mode, The Envoy in The Balcony; 1972–73: Theseus/Oberon, in tour of E and W Europe, USA, Japan, Australia; 1974: Carlos II in The Bewitched; 1975: Henry V, Prince Hal in Henry IV parts I and II; 1976: Prince Hal (SWET Award for Best Actor in revival), Henry V in tour of Europe and USA, Jack Rover in Wild Oats (also Piccadilly); 1977: Henry V, Henry VI parts I, II and III, Coriolanus (Plays and Players London Critics Award, SWET Award for Best Actor in revival, Evening Standard Best Actor Award, 1978); 1978: Antony in Antony and Cleopatra; 1979: Coriolanus in tour of Europe, The Children of the Sun; 1980: title rôles in Richard II and Richard III (Variety Club Best Actor Award); 1981–82: Neschastlivsev in The Forest; Good (Standard Best Actor Award, 1981); 1985: Nikolai in Breaking the Silence; *Royal National Theatre:* Prof. Higgins in Pygmalion, 1992; title rôle in Macbeth, 1993; Calogero in La Grande Magia, 1995. Best Actor (jt), 1981, Drama (British Theatre Assoc.) awards for Richard II, Good and The Forest. *Films include:* The Heroes of Telemark; Work is a Four Letter Word; The Return of the Musketeers; The Cook, The Thief, his Wife and her Lover. *Television appearances include:* The Way of the World; Comet Among the Stars; Coriolanus; The Holy Experiment; Poppyland; Sherlock Holmes, Evensong, The Double Helix, 1986; A Perfect Spy, 1987; The Dog it Was That Died, 1988. *Radio includes:* Soames in Forsyte Chronicles, 1990–91. *Address:* c/o Julian Belfrage Associates, 68 St James's Street, SW1. *T:* 0171–491 4400.

HOWARD, Alexander Edward, CBE 1972; Lecturer in Education, London University Centre for Teachers, 1977–81; *b* 2 Aug. 1909; *o s* of Alexander Watson Howard and Gertrude Nellie Howard; *m* 1937, Phyllis Ada Adams; no *c*. *Educ:* Swindon Coll.; University Coll. and Westminster Coll., London Univ. BSc (London) 1930; Pt I, BSc (Econ.) 1934. Flt-Lieut, RAF, 1940–46. Asst Master, Sanford Boys' Sch., Swindon, 1931–34; Lectr in Maths, Wandsworth Techn. Coll., 1935–40; Maths Master, Wilson's Grammar Sch., 1946–48; Headmaster: Northfleet Sch. for Boys, Kent, 1948–51; Borough-Beaufoy Sch., London, 1951–54; Forest Hill Sch., London, 1955–63; Wandsworth Sch., 1963–74. Co-ordinating Officer Teaching Practice Organisation, London Univ. Inst. of Educn, 1975–77. Member: Naval Educn Adv. Cttee, 1966–80; Army Educational Adv. Bd, 1957–74. Academic Council, RMA, 1970–75. FRSA 1970. Hon. Mem., CGLI, 1979. *Publications:* The Secondary Technical School in England, 1955; Longman Mathematics Stages 1–5, 1962–67, new Metric edns, 1970–71; Teaching Mathematics, 1968; articles in Times Educational Supplement, The Teacher, Technology, Inside the Comprehensive Sch. *Recreations:* amateur theatre, old-time dancing, music, cricket, travel, rotary. *Address:* 19 Downsway, Sanderstead, Surrey CR2 0JB. *T:* 0181–657 3399.

HOWARD, Ann; freelance opera singer (mezzo-soprano), since 1971; *b* 22 July 1936, *d* of William Alfred and Gladys Winifred Swadling; *m* 1954, Keith Giles; one *d*. *Educ:* privately; with Topliss Green, Rodolfa Lhombino (London) and Dominic Modesti (Paris) via scholarship from Royal Opera House, Covent Garden. Principal Mezzo-Soprano, Sadler's Wells Opera, 1964–73. Main rôles: Carmen, Dalila (Samson et Dalila), Azucena (Il Trovatore), Amneris (Aida), Fricka (Das Rheingold and Die Walküre), La Grande Duchesse de Gerolstein, Brangäne (Tristan und Isolde), Kabanicha (Káta Kabanová), Eboli (Don Carlos), Katisha (Mikado), La Belle Hélène, Babulenka (The Gambler), Dulcinée (Don Quichotte), Hérodiade, Klytemnestra (Electra), Isabella (Italian Girl in Algiers), Old Lady (Candide), Prince Orlofsky (Die Fledermaus), Hostess and Marina (Boris Godunov), Step-Mother (Into the Woods), Auntie (Peter Grimes), Baba (Rake's Progress), Emma Jones (Street Scene), Begbick (Rise and Fall of the City of Mahagonny); world premières: Madam Leda (The Mines of Sulphur), Sadler's Wells, 1965; Mrs Danvers (Rebecca), Opera North, 1983; Caliban (The Tempest), Santa Fé Festival Opera, USA, 1985; Mrs Worthing (The Plumber's Gift), ENO, 1989; British premières: Cassandra (The Trojans, Pts 1 and 2), Scottish Opera, 1969; Mescalina (Le Grand Macabre), ENO, 1982; début Metropolian Opera, NY, 1994 (Auntie); also performances in France, Italy, Belgium, Germany, USA (incl. series of Gilbert and Sullivan operas at Performing Arts Center, NY State Univ., 1993–94), Canada, Mexico, Chile, Portugal; many recordings and videos. *Recreations:* gardening, cooking. *Address:* c/o Stafford Law Associates, 6 Barham Close, Weybridge, Surrey KT13 9PR. *T:* Weybridge (01932) 854489, *Fax:* (01932) 858521.

HOWARD, Anthony Michell; Obituaries Editor, The Times, since 1993; *b* 12 Feb. 1934; *s* of late Canon Guy Howard and Janet Rymer Howard; *m* 1965, Carol Anne Gaynor. *Educ:* Westminster Sch.; Christ Church, Oxford. Chm., Oxford Univ. Labour Club, 1954; Pres., Oxford Union, 1955. Called to Bar, Inner Temple, 1956. Nat. Service, 2nd Lieut, Royal Fusiliers, 1956–58; Political Corresp., Reynolds News, 1958–59; Editorial Staff, Manchester Guardian, 1959–61 (Harkness Fellowship in USA, 1960); Political Corresp., New Statesman, 1961–64; Whitehall Corresp., Sunday Times, 1965; Washington Corresp., Observer, 1966–69 and Political Columnist, 1971–72; Asst Editor, 1970–72, Editor, 1972–78, New Statesman; Editor, The Listener, 1979–81; Dep. Editor, The Observer, 1981–88; Presenter: Face the Press, Channel Four, 1982–85; The Editors, Sky News TV, 1989–90; Reporter, BBC TV News and Current Affairs (Panorama and Newsnight), 1989–92; Chief Political book reviewer, Sunday Times, 1990–. *Publications:* (contrib.) The Baldwin Age, 1960; (contrib.) Age of Austerity, 1963; (with Richard West) The Making of the Prime Minister, 1965; (ed) The Crossman Diaries: selections from the Diaries of a Cabinet Minister, 1979; Rab: the life of R. A. Butler, 1987; Crossman: the pursuit of power, 1990; (ed with David Heaton) The Times Lives Remembered, 1993. *Address:* 17 Addison Avenue, W11 4QS. *T:* 0171–603 3749; Dinham Lodge, Ludlow, Shropshire SY8 1EA. *T:* Ludlow (01584) 878457. *Club:* Garrick.

HOWARD, Dame Christian; *see* Howard, Dame R. C.

HOWARD, Rear-Adm. Christopher John, (Jack); Director of Operations, Devon and Cornwall Training and Enterprise Council, since 1992; Chief of Staff, C-in-C Naval Home Command, 1987–89, retired; *b* 13 Sept. 1932; *s* of late Claude Albert Howard and Hilda Mabel Howard (*née* Norton); *m* 1st, 1960, Jean Webster (marr. diss. 1987); two *d*; 2nd, 1987, Hilary Troy; one *s* one *d*. *Educ:* Newton Abbot Grammar School; King's College London; Imperial College, London. MSc, DIC. MIEE. Entered RN 1954; served in HM Ships Ocean, Pukaki, Roebuck, Urchin, Tenby; Officer i/c RN Polaris School, 1978–80; Dean, RN Engineering College, 1980–82; Dir, Naval Officer Appts (Instructor),

1982–84; Commodore, HMS Nelson, 1985–87. NDC Latimer, 1975; Chief Naval Instructor Officer, 1987. Consultant, PA Consulting Group, 1989–91. *Recreations:* shooting, Rugby. *Club:* Army and Navy.

HOWARD, David John; Director, Excise and Central Policy, HM Customs and Excise, since 1994; *b* 1 June 1941; *s* of late Albert Henry Howard and Olive Mary Howard (*née* Chase); *m* 1969, Anne Westmore; two *s* two *d*. *Educ:* Whitgift Sch., Croydon. Exchequer and Audit Dept, 1960–69; HM Customs and Excise, 1969–72: Asst Principal, 1969; Principal, 1969–72; Private Sec. to Chief Sec. to HM Treasury, 1972–74; Customs & Excise, 1974–91: Asst Sec., 1976–84; Director: VAT Control, 1985–87; Personnel, 1987–90; Organisation, 1990–91; Dep. Dir of Savings, Principal Estabt and Finance Officer, Dept for Nat. Savings, 1991–94. Chm. Govs, Coulsdon High Sch., 1993–. *Recreations:* vintage films, walking. *Address:* HM Customs & Excise, 22 Upper Ground, SE1 9PJ. *T:* 0171–865 5018, *Fax:* 0171–865 4841.

HOWARD, Rev. Canon Donald; Provost, St Andrew's Cathedral, Aberdeen, 1978–91, retired; *b* 21 Jan. 1927; *s* of William Howard and Alexandra Eadie (*née* Buchanan); unmarried. *Educ:* Hull Coll. of Technology; London Univ. (BD, AKC). AFRAeS, 1954–58. Design Engineer, Blackburn Aircraft, 1948–52; Hunting Percival Aircraft, 1952–54; English Electric Co., 1954–55. Assistant Minister, Emmanuel Church, Saltburn-by-the-Sea, Yorks, 1959–62; Rector and Mission Director, Dio. Kimberley and Kuruman, S Africa, 1962–65; Rector of St John the Evangelist, East London, S Africa, 1965–72; Rector of Holy Trinity Episcopal Church, Haddington, Scotland, 1972–78. Honorary Canon: Christ Church Cathedral, Hartford, Conn, USA, 1978–91; St Andrew's Cathedral, Aberdeen, 1991. *Address:* 42 Waterside, Bondgate, Ripon, North Yorkshire HG4 1RA. *T:* Ripon (01765) 692144.

HOWARD, Hon. Edmund Bernard Carlo, CMG 1969; LVO 1961; HM Diplomatic Service, retired; *b* 8 Sept. 1909; *s* of 1st Baron Howard of Penrith, PC, GCB, GCMG, CVO, and Lady Isabella Giustiniani-Bandini (*d* of Prince Giustiniani-Bandini, 8th Earl of Newburgh); *m* 1936, Cécile Geoffroy-Dechaume; three *s* one *d* (and one *d* decd). *Educ:* Downside Sch.; Newman Sch., Lakewood, NJ; New Coll., Oxford. Called to the Bar, 1932; Sec., Trustees and Managers, Stock Exchange, 1937. Served in HM Forces, KRRC, 1939–45. Joined HM Diplomatic Service, 1947; served in: Rome, 1947–51; Foreign Office, 1951–53; Madrid, 1953–57; Bogotá, 1957–59; Florence, 1960–61; Rome, 1961–65; Consul-Gen., Genoa, 1965–69. Comdr, Order of Merit, Italy, 1973. *Publications:* Genoa: history and art in an old seaport, 1971 (Duchi di Galliera prize, 1973); trans. The Aryan Myth, 1974. *Recreations:* travel, gardening. *Address:* Jerome Cottage, Marlow Common, Bucks SL7 2QR. *T:* Marlow (01628) 482129.

HOWARD, Sir Edward; *see* Howard, Sir H. E. de C.

HOWARD, Elizabeth Jane, FRSL; novelist; *b* 26 March 1923; *d* of David Liddon and Katharine M. Howard; *m* 1st, 1942, Peter M. Scott (marr. diss. 1951; later Sir Peter Scott, CH, CBE, FRS (*d* 1989)); one *d*; 2nd, 1959, James Douglas-Henry; 3rd, 1965, Kingsley Amis (*see* Sir Kingsley Amis) (marr. diss. 1983). *Educ:* home. FRSL 1994. Trained at London Mask Theatre Sch. Played at Stratford-on-Avon, and in repertory theatre in Devon; BBC, Television, modelling, 1939–46; Sec. to Inland Waterways Assoc., 1947; subsequently writing, editing, reviewing, journalism and writing plays for television, incl. serials of After Julius in three plays and Something in Disguise in six plays. John Llewellyn Rhys Memorial Prize for The Beautiful Visit, 1950. Hon. Artistic Dir, Cheltenham Literary Festival, 1962; Artistic co-Dir, Salisbury Festival of Arts, 1973. Film script, The Attachment, 1986. *Publications:* The Beautiful Visit, 1950; The Long View, 1956; The Sea Change, 1959; After Julius, 1965; Something in Disguise, 1969 (TV series, 1982); Odd Girl Out, 1972; Mr Wrong, 1975; (ed) A Companion for Lovers, 1978; Getting It Right, 1982 (Yorkshire Post Prize) (film script, 1985); (jtly) Howard and Maschler on Food: cooking for occasions, 1987; The Light Years, 1990; Green Shades (anthology), 1991; Marking Time, 1991; Confusion, 1993. *Recreations:* music, gardening, enjoying all the arts, travelling, natural history. *Address:* c/o Jonathan Clowes, Iron Bridge House, Bridge Approach, NW1 8BD.

HOWARD, Sir (Hamilton) Edward (de Coucey), 2nd Bt *cr* 1955; GBE 1972; Director of Stockbroking Firm of Charles Stanley and Company Ltd; Chairman, LRC International Ltd, 1971–82; *b* 29 Oct. 1915; *s* of Sir (Harold Walter) Seymour Howard, 1st Bt, and Edith M. (*d* 1962), *d* of Edward Turner; *S* father 1967; *m* 1943, Elizabeth Howarth Ludlow; two *s*. *Educ:* Le Rosey, Rolle, Switzerland; Radley Coll., Abingdon; Worcester Coll., Oxford. Mem. of the Stock Exchange, London, 1946. Sheriff of the City of London, 1966 (Common Councilman, 1951; Alderman, 1963); Lord Mayor of London, 1971–72; one of HM Lieutenants, City of London, 1976–90. Master of the Gardeners' Company, 1961. DSc City Univ., 1971. KStJ 1972. *Recreation:* gardening. *Heir: s* David Howarth Seymour Howard [*b* 29 Dec. 1945; *m* 1968, Valerie Picton, *o d* of Derek W. Crosse; two *s* two *d*]. *Address:* Courtlands, Bishops Walk, Shirley Hills, Surrey CR0 5BA. *T:* 0181–656 4444. *Clubs:* Guildhall, City Livery, United Wards.

HOWARD, Rear-Adm. Jack; *see* Howard, Rear-Adm. C. J.

HOWARD, James Boag, CB 1972; Assistant Under-Secretary of State, Home Office, 1963–75; *b* 10 Jan. 1915; *yr s* of William and Jean Howard, Greenock; *m* 1943, Dorothy Jean Crawshaw; two *d*. *Educ:* Greenock High Sch.; Glasgow Univ. (MA, BSc; 1st cl. Hons Mathematics and Natural Philosophy). Asst Principal, Home Office, 1937; Private Sec. to Permanent Sec., Ministry of Home Security, 1940–41; Principal, 1941; Asst Sec., 1948. *Address:* 12 Windhill, Bishop's Stortford, Herts CM23 2NG. *T:* Bishop's Stortford (01279) 651728.

HOWARD, Dr James Griffiths, FRS 1984; Programme Director, The Wellcome Trust, 1986–90, retired; *b* 25 Sept. 1927; *s* of late Joseph Griffiths Howard and Kathleen Mildred Howard; *m* 1951, Opal St Clair (*née* Echalaz); two *d* (one *s* decd). *Educ:* Middlesex Hosp. Med. Sch., Univ. of London (MB, BS 1950; PhD 1957; MD 1960). Public Health Lab. Service, 1951–53; Jun. Specialist in Pathology, RAMC, 1953–55; Res. Fellow, Wright-Fleming Inst., St Mary's Hosp., 1955–58; Edinburgh University: Immunologist (Lectr, Sen. Lectr and Reader), Dept of Surgical Science, 1958–66; Reader and Head of Immunobiology Section, Dept of Zoology, 1966–69; Wellcome Research Laboratories: Head, Experimental Immunobiology Dept, 1969–74; Head, Exp. Biology Div., 1974–83; Dir, Biomedical Res., 1984–85. *Publications:* some 130 scientific articles, reviews and chapters in books, pre-dominantly on immunology. *Recreations:* fine arts, music, cooking, hill walking. *Address:* Sarnesfield Grange, Sarnesfield, Herefordshire HR4 8RG. *T:* Weobley (01544) 318302.

HOWARD, (James) Kenneth, RA 1991 (ARA 1983); painter; *b* 26 Dec. 1932; *s* of Frank and Elizabeth Howard; *m* Ann Howard (*née* Popham), dress designer (marr. diss. 1974); *m* 1990, Christa Gaa (*née* Köhler), RWS (*d* 1992). *Educ:* Kilburn Grammar School; Hornsey School of Art; Royal College of Art. ARCA. NEAC 1962, ROI 1966, RWA 1981, RWS 1983. British Council scholarship to Florence, 1958–59; taught various London Art Schools, 1959–73; Official Artist for Imperial War Museum in N Ireland, 1973, 1978; painted for the British Army in N Ireland, Germany, Cyprus, Hong Kong, Brunei, Nepal, Belize, Norway, Lebanon, Canada, Oman, 1973–; one man exhibitions: Plymouth Art Centre, 1955; John Whibley Gallery, 1966, 1968; New Grafton Gallery, 1971–; Jersey, 1978, 1980, 1983; Hong Kong, 1979; Nicosia, 1982; Delhi, 1983; Lowndes Lodge Gall., 1987, 1989, 1990, 1991; Sinfield Gall., 1991, 1993, 1995. Works purchased by Plymouth Art Gall., Imperial War Mus., Guildhall Art Gall., Ulster Mus., Nat. Army Mus., Hove Mus., Sheffield Art Gall., Southend Mus.; commissions for UN, BAOR, Drapers' Co., Stock Exchange, States of Jersey, Banque Paribas, Royal Hosp. Chelsea. Hon. ROI 1988; Hon. RBA 1989; RSBA 1991. First Prize: Hunting Group Award, 1982; Sparkasse Karlsruhe, 1985. Gen. Editor, Art Class series, 1988. *Publications:* contribs to: The War Artists, 1983; 60th Vol. of The Old Water-Colour Societies' Club, 1985; Painting Interiors, 1989; Art of Landscape and Seascape, 1989; Visions of Venice, 1990; Venice: the artist's vision, 1990; 20th Century Painters and Sculptors, 1991; *relevant publication:* The Paintings of Ken Howard, by Michael Spender, 1992. *Recreations:* cinema, opera. *Address:* 8 South Bolton Gardens, SW5 0DH. *T:* 0171–373 2912 (studio); St Clements Hall, Mousehole, Cornwall TR19 6TR. *T:* Penzance (01736) 731596. *Clubs:* Arts, Chelsea Arts.

HOWARD, John James, CBE 1985; Chief General Manager, Royal Insurance plc, 1980–84; *b* 9 March 1923; *s* of late Sir Henry Howard, KCIE, CSI, and Lady Howard; *m* 1949, Julia Tupholme Mann; one *s* one *d* (and one *d* decd). *Educ:* Rugby Sch.; Trinity Hall, Cambridge (MA). Pilot, RAFVR, 1942–46 (Flt Lieut). Royal Insurance Company Ltd: Financial Secretary, 1964–69; General Manager, 1970–80, Director, 1970–84. Chm., British Insurance Assoc., 1983–84 (Dep. Chm., 1981–83). Chm., YWCA Central Club, 1986–90. *Recreations:* golf, competitive bridge, gardening, grandchildren. *Address:* Highfields, High Barn Road, Effingham, Surrey KT24 5PX.

HOWARD, Hon. John Winston; MP (Lib) for Bennelong, NSW, since 1974; Leader of the Opposition, Australia, 1985–89 and since 1995 (Deputy Leader, 1983–85); *b* 26 July 1939; *m* 1971, Alison Janette Parker; two *s* one *d*. *Educ:* Canterbury Boys' High Sch.; Sydney Univ. Solicitor of NSW Supreme Court. Minister for Business and Consumer Affairs, Australia, 1975; Minister assisting Prime Minister, May 1977; Minister for Special Trade Negotiations, July 1977; Federal Treasurer, 1977–83; Leader, Parly Liberal Party, Australia, 1985–89, 1995– (Dep. Leader, 1982–85). Chm., Manpower and Labour Market Reform Gp, 1990–. *Recreations:* reading, tennis, cricket. *Address:* Parliament House, Canberra, ACT 2600, Australia; 19 Milner Crescent, Wollstonecraft, NSW 2065, Australia. *T:* (2) 4394360. *Club:* Australian (Sydney).

HOWARD, Prof. Jonathan Charles, DPhil; FRS 1995; Professor of Genetics, Institute for Genetics, University of Cologne, since 1994; *b* 24 June 1943; *s* of John Eldred Howard and Marghanita (*née* Laski); *m* 1990, Maria Leptin; two *s*. *Educ:* Westminster Sch.; Magdalen Coll., Oxford (BA Zool. 1964; DPhil Medicine 1969). Mem., Scientific Staff, MRC, at Cellular Immunology Res. Unit, Sir William Dunn Sch. of Pathology, Univ. of Oxford, 1968–73; Weir Jun. Res. Fellow, University Coll., Oxford, 1970–73; Babraham Institute, Cambridge: Mem. Staff, Dept of Immunology, 1974–94; Head of Dept, 1985–94; Res. Fellow, Clare Hall, Cambridge, 1975–78; sabbaticals at: Depts of Pathology and Cell Biol., Stanford Univ., 1983, 1987; Div. of Biol., CIT, 1983; EMBL, 1992. Mem., EMBO, 1993. *Publications:* Darwin, 1982; papers in learned jls on immunology and evolution. *Recreation:* fishing. *Address:* Institut für Genetik, Universität zu Köln, Zülpicher Strasse 47, 50674 Köln, Germany. *T:* (221) 4704864; Heinestrasse 19, 50931 Köln, Germany. *T:* (221) 4200320.

HOWARD, Kenneth; *see* Howard, J. K.

HOWARD, Margaret; freelance broadcaster, since 1969; *b* 29 March 1938; *d* of John Bernard Howard and Ellen Corwena Roberts. *Educ:* St Mary's Convent, Rhyl, N Wales; St Teresa's Convent, Sunbury; Guildhall Sch. of Music and Drama; Indiana Univ., Bloomington, USA. LGSM; LRAM 1960. BBC World Service Announcer, 1967–69; Reporter: The World This Weekend, BBC Radio 4, 1970–74; Edition, BBC TV, 1971; Tomorrow's World, BBC TV, 1972; Presenter: Pick of the Week, BBC Radio 4, 1974–91; It's Your World, BBC World Service, 1981–; Masterclass, Classic FM, 1994–; Interviewer/Presenter, Strictly Instrumental, occasional series, 1980–85; Editor and Presenter: Classic Reports, Classic FM, 1992–94; Howard's Week, 1994–. Radio critic, The Tablet; columnist, The Universe. Female UK Radio Personality of the Year, Sony Awards, 1984; Sony Radio Awards Roll of Honour, 1988; Voice of the Listener Award for excellence, 1991. *Publications:* Margaret Howard's Pick of the Week, 1984; Court Jesting, 1986. *Recreations:* riding, tasting wine, walking the Jack Russell. *Address:* 215 Cavendish Road, SW12 0BP. *T:* 0181–673 7336.

HOWARD, Rt. Hon. Michael, PC 1990; QC 1982; MP (C) Folkestone and Hythe, since 1983; Secretary of State for the Home Department, since 1993; *b* 7 July 1941; *s* of late Bernard Howard and of Hilda Howard; *m* 1975, Sandra Clare, *d* of Wing-Comdr Saville Paul; one *s* one *d* (and one step *s*). *Educ:* Llanelli Grammar School; Peterhouse, Cambridge. MA, LLB; President of the Union, 1962. Major Scholar, Inner Temple, 1962; called to the Bar, Inner Temple, 1964, Bencher, 1992. Junior Counsel to the Crown (Common Law), 1980–82; a Recorder, 1986–. Contested (C) Liverpool, Edge Hill, 1966 and 1970; Chm., Bow Group, 1970–71. PPS to Solicitor-General, 1984–85; Parly Under-Sec. of State, DTI, 1985–87; Minister of State, DoE, 1987–90; Secretary of State for: Employment, 1990–92; the Environment, 1992–93. Jt Sec., Cons. Legal Cttee, 1983–84; Jt Vice-Chm., Cons. Employment Cttee, 1983–84; Vice-Chm., Soc. of Cons. Lawyers, 1985. *Recreations:* watching football (Swansea, Liverpool) and baseball (New York Mets). *Address:* House of Commons, SW1A 0AA. *T:* 0171–219 5493. *Clubs:* Carlton, Coningsby (Chm., 1972–73).

HOWARD, Sir Michael (Eliot), Kt 1986; CBE 1977; MC 1943; DLitt; FBA 1970; FRHistS; Emeritus Professor of Modern History, University of Oxford, since 1989; *b* 29 Nov. 1922; *y s* of late Geoffrey Eliot Howard, Ashmore, near Salisbury, and of Edith Julia Emma, *o d* of Otto Edinger. *Educ:* Wellington; Christ Church, Oxford (BA 1946, MA 1948; Hon. Student, 1990). Served War, Coldstream Guards, 1942–45. Asst Lecturer in History, University of London, King's Coll., 1947; Lecturer, 1950; Lecturer, then Reader, in War Studies, 1953–63; Prof. of War Studies, 1963–68; University of Oxford: Fellow of All Souls Coll., 1968–80; Chichele Prof. of History of War, 1977–80; Regius Prof. of Modern History and Fellow of Oriel Coll., 1980–89 (Hon. Fellow, 1990); Robert A. Lovett Prof. of Military and Naval Hist., Yale Univ., 1989–93. Vis. Prof. of European History, Stanford Univ., 1967. Ford's Lectr in English History, Oxford, 1971; Radcliffe Lectr, Univ. of Warwick, 1975; Trevelyan Lectr, Cambridge, 1977; FKC. Pres. and co-Founder, Internat. Institute for Strategic Studies; Vice-Pres., Council on Christian Approaches to Defence and Disarmament. For. Hon. Mem., Amer. Acad. of Arts and Scis, 1983. Hon. LittD Leeds, 1979; Hon. DLit London, 1988; Hon. DHumLit Lehigh Univ., Pa, USA, 1990. Chesney Meml Gold Medal, RUSI, 1973; NATO Atlantic Award, 1989. *Publications:* The Coldstream Guards, 1920–46 (with John Sparrow), 1951; Disengagement in Europe, 1958; Wellingtonian Studies, 1959; The Franco-Prussian War, 1961 (Duff Cooper Memorial Prize, 1962); The Theory and Practice of War, 1965; The Mediterranean Strategy in the Second World War, 1967; Studies in War and Peace, 1970; Grand Strategy, vol IV (in UK History of 2nd World War, Military series), 1971 (Wolfson Foundn History

Award, 1972); The Continental Commitment, 1972; War in European History, 1976; (with P. Paret) Clausewitz On War, 1977; War and the Liberal Conscience, 1978; (ed) Restraints on War, 1979; The Causes of Wars, 1983; Clausewitz, 1983; Strategic Deception in World War II, 1990; The Lessons of History, 1991. *Address:* The Old Farm, Eastbury, Newbury, Berks RG16 7JN. *Clubs:* Athenæum, Garrick; Yale (New York).

HOWARD, Michael Newman; QC 1986; a Recorder, since 1993; *b* 10 June 1947; *s* of Henry Ian Howard and Tilly Celia Howard. *Educ:* Clifton College; Magdalen College, Oxford (MA, BCL). Lecturer in Law, LSE, 1970–74; called to the Bar, Gray's Inn, 1971; in practice at Bar, 1971–. Vis. Prof. of Law, Univ. of Essex, 1987–92. Mem. of Panel, Lloyd's Salvage Arbitrators, 1987–. *Publications:* (ed jtly) Phipson on Evidence, 12th edn 1976 to 14th edn 1990; (contrib.) Frustration and Force Majeure (ed McKendrick), 1991, 2nd edn 1995; articles and reviews in legal periodicals. *Recreations:* books, music, sport. *Address:* 4 Essex Court, Temple, EC4Y 9AJ. *T:* 0171–797 7970. *Club:* Royal Automobile.

HOWARD, Michael Stockwin; organ recitalist and recording artist; Co-founder and Artistic Director, Rye Spring Music, 1976; *b* London, 14 Sept. 1922; *er s* of late Frank Henry Howard (viola, Internat. String Quartet, Foundn principal, Beecham's Philharmonic) and Florence Mabel Howard. *Educ:* Ellesmere; Royal Acad. of Music; privately. Organist, Tewkesbury Abbey, 1943–44; Dir of Music, Ludgrove Sch.; Founder, Renaissance Society, and conductor, Renaissance Singers, 1944–64; Organist and Master of the Choristers, Ely Cath., 1953–58; Dir of Music, St George's Sch., Harpenden, 1959–61; Dir, Cantores in Ecclesia, 1964–86; Asst, Music Presentation, BBC, 1968–78; Dir of Music, St Marylebone Parish Church, 1971–79, Dir Emeritus, 1979; Organist to the Franciscans of Rye, 1979–83; Organist and Rector Chori, St Michael's Abbey, Farnborough, 1984–86. Freelance harpsichordist, conductor, broadcaster and writer. Hon. ARAM 1976. Prix Musicale de Radio Brno, 1967; Gustave Charpentier Grand Prix du Disque, 1975. Recordings with essays include: Tallis/Byrd 1575 Cantiones Sacrae, 1969; Tallis at Waltham Abbey, 1974; Palestrina, The Garden of Love, 1974; recordings at Farnborough: Widor, Vierne, Tournemire, Saint-Saëns, Franck, Bach, all performed on England's only Cavaillé-Coll organ, 1988–92. *Principal compositions include:* Mass, Sonnet VIII, 1961; Scaena Dramatis for Antoinette Michael, 1978; Dances for a Mountain Goat, 1979; opera, The Lion's Mouth, 1980; Sequentia de Insomnia, 1981; Diptych (Arnold and St Ambrose), 1981; Discourse on Chorale by Judith Earley, 1982; Cantiones Iudithae, 1983; In Memoriam Duncan Thomson, 1983; Missa de Ecclesia Christi, 1984; *organ:* Cantique d'un Oiseau matinal, 1982; Carillon des Larmes, 1982; Te Deum Cardinalis, 1987. *Publications:* The Private Inferno (autobiog.), 1974; Tribute to Aristide Cavaillé-Coll, 1985; contrib. Musical Times, Monthly Musical Record, Dublin Review, Listener, EMG Monthly Letter, The Organists' Review. *Recreations:* steam railway traction, village fairgrounds. *Address:* 9 Wallis Field, Groombridge, Sussex TN3 9SE.

HOWARD, Air Vice-Marshal Peter, CB 1989; OBE 1957; FRCP, FRAeS; Commandant, RAF Institute of Aviation Medicine, 1975–88; The Senior Consultant, RAF, 1987–88; *b* 15 Dec. 1925; *s* of late Edward Charles Howard and Doris Mary Howard (*née* Cure); *m* 1950, Norma Lockhart Fletcher; one *s* one *d*. *Educ:* Farnborough Grammar Sch.; St Thomas's Hosp. Med. Sch. (MB BS 1949, PhD 1964); FRCP 1977; FFOM 1981; FRAeS 1973. House Physician, 1950, Registrar, 1951. St Thomas' Hosp.; RAF Medical Branch, 1951–88; RAF Consultant in Aviation Physiology, 1964; RAF Consultant Adviser in Occupational Medicine, 1983–85; Dean of Air Force Medicine, 1985–87. QHP 1982–88. Chm., Defence Med. Services Postgraduate Council, 1986–87; Registrar, Faculty of Occupational Medicine, RCP, 1986–91. *Publications:* papers and chapters in books on aviation physiology, medicine, occupational medicine. *Recreations:* fly fishing, computing. *Address:* 135 Aldershot Road, Church Crookham, Hants GU13 0JU. *T:* Fleet (01252) 617309. *Club:* Royal Air Force.

HOWARD, Peter Milner; Editor, Jane's Defence Weekly, since 1989; *b* 27 June 1937; *s* of Thomas Roland Howard and Margaret A. Howard (*née* Potter); *m* 1965, Janet Crownshaw; one *s* one *d*. *Educ:* St Thomas C of E Sch., Heaton Chapel; Dialstone Lane Mod. Sec., Stockport; Woodseats Co., Sheffield; Sheffield Coll. of Commerce and Tech. (NCTJ Prof. Cert. 1960). Copy boy, reporter, sports reporter and sub-editor, The Star, Sheffield, 1952–58; Nat. Service, Army, 1958–60; The Star, Sheffield: sports reporter and sub-editor, 1960–73; Sports Editor, 1973–75; Inf. Officer, MoD, 1975–83; Sen. Inf. Officer and Editor, Soldier Mag., 1983–85; Jane's Defence Weekly: Features Editor, 1985–87; Man. Editor, 1987–89. *Recreations:* military history, military music, golf, walking. *Address:* Jane's Information Group, 163 Brighton Road, Coulsdon, Surrey CR5 2NH. *T:* 0181–763 1030.

HOWARD, Philip Nicholas Charles, FRSL; leader writer and columnist, The Times, since 1992; *b* 2 Nov. 1933; *s* of Peter Dunsmore Howard and Doris Emily Metaxa; *m* 1959, Myrtle, *d* of Sir Reginald Houldsworth, 4th Bt, OBE, TD; two *s* one *d*. *Educ:* Eton Coll. (King's Scholar); Trinity Coll., Oxford (Major Scholar; first cl. Lit. Hum; MA). Glasgow Herald, 1959–64; The Times, 1964–: reporter, writer, columnist; Literary Ed., 1978–92. Member: Classical Assoc.; Horatian Soc.; Soc. of Bookmen; Literary Soc. Founder Patron, Friends of Classics, 1991. FRSL 1987. Liveryman, Wheelwrights' Co. London Editor, Verbatim, 1977–. *Publications:* The Black Watch, 1968; The Royal Palaces, 1970; London's River, 1975; New Words for Old, 1977; The British Monarchy, 1977; Weasel Words, 1978; Words Fail Me, 1980; A Word in Your Ear, 1983; The State of the Language, English Observed, 1984; (jtly) The Times Bicentenary Stamp Book, 1985; We Thundered Out, 200 Years of The Times 1785–1985, 1985; Winged Words, 1988; Word-Watching, 1988; (jtly) London, The Evolution of a Great City, 1989; A Word in Time, 1990; (ed) The Times Bedside Book, 1991; Reading a Poem, 1992; (ed) The Times Bedside Book, 1992; *Recreations:* walking, reading, talking, music, the classics, beagles not beagling, Jack Russells, stand at Twickenham. *Address:* Flat 1, 47 Ladbroke Grove, W11 3AR. *T:* 0171–727 1077. *Clubs:* Garrick; Ad Eundem (Oxford and Cambridge).

HOWARD, Robert, (Bob); Northern Regional Secretary, Trades Union Congress, since 1980; *b* 4 April 1939; *s* of Robert and Lily Howard; *m* 1984, Valerie Stewart; two *s* one *d*. *Educ:* Gregson Lane County Primary Sch.; Deepdale Secondary Modern Sch.; Queen Elizabeth's Grammar Sch., Blackburn, Lancs; Cliff Training Coll., Calver via Sheffield, Derbyshire. British Leyland, Lancs, 1961–68: Member, Clerical and Admin. Workers' Union Br. Exec.; Councillor, Walton le Dale UDC, 1962–65; GPO, Preston, Lancs, 1969–80: Telephone Area UPW Telecomms Representative Member: Jt Consultative Council, Jt Productivity Council, Council of PO Unions Area Cttee, Delegate to Preston Trades Council; Secretary, Lancashire Assoc. of Trades Councils, 1977–79; created 14 specialist cttees for LATC; appointment as N Reg. Sec., Trades Union Congress, 1980–, by Gen. Sec., TUC, first full-time secretary to a TUC region. Member: Industrial Tribunals, 1979–80; Northumbria Regional Cttee, Nat. Trust, 1989–; Council, Northern Exams Assoc., 1986–; Bd, Durham Univ. Business Sch., 1987–; Bd, Tyneside TEC, 1989–; Bd, Northern Develt Co., 1991–. Northern Region Coordinator, Jobs March, 1983; Exec. Organiser, Great North Family Gala Day, 1986–90. JP Duchy of Lancaster, 1969–74. *Publications:* North-East Lancashire Structure Plan—The Trades Councils' View (with Peter Stock), 1979; Organisation and Functions of TUC Northern Regional Council, 1980. *Recreations:* fell walking, opera, ballet, classical music, camping, cricket, football, spectating outdoor sports, reading, chess. *Address:* 8 Caxton Way, North Lodge, Chester le Street, County Durham DH3 4BW. *Club:* Durham CC.

HOWARD, Dame (Rosemary) Christian, DBE 1986; *b* 5 Sept. 1916; *d* of Hon. Geoffrey Howard, *s* of 9th Earl of Carlisle, and Hon. Christian, *d* of 3rd Baron Methuen. *Educ:* Westbourne House, Folkestone; Villa Malatesta, Florence; Ozannes, Paris; and privately. STh Lambeth 1943; MA Lambeth 1979. Divinity Teacher, Chichester High Sch. for Girls, 1943–45; Licensed Lay Worker, Dio. York, 1947–; Sec., Bd of Women's Work, 1947–72; Sec., Lay Ministry, 1972–79; retired 1980. Deleg. to WCC Assemblies, 1961 and 1968; Member: Faith and Order Commn, WCC, 1961–75; BCC, 1974–87; Church Assembly, 1960–70, General Synod, 1970–85; Churches' Council for Covenanting, 1978–82. Governor, Slingsby School. *Publications:* The Ordination of Women to Priesthood, 1972, Supplement 1978, Further Report 1984; Praise and Thanksgiving, 1972; contribs to Ecumenical Review, Year Book of Social Policy, Crucible, New Directions, Chrysalis. *Recreations:* woodwork, gardening, foreign travel. *Address:* Coneysthorpe, York YO6 7DD. *T:* Coneysthorpe (01653) 648264.

HOWARD, William Brian; Deputy Chairman, Northern Foods plc, since 1988 (Director, since 1987); Deputy Chairman, 1984–87, Joint Managing Director, 1976–86, Marks & Spencer plc; *b* 16 July 1926; *s* of William James and Annie Howard; *m* 1952, Audrey Elizabeth (*née* Jenney); one *s* one *d*. *Educ:* Revoe Junior Sch., Blackpool; Blackpool Grammar Sch.; Manchester Univ. (BA (Hons) Mod. Hist., Economics and Politics); Harvard Graduate Business Sch., 1973. Royal Signals, 1944–47. Marks & Spencer Ltd, 1951–87; Dir, 1973–87. A Church Comr, 1977–93. *Address:* c/o Beverley House, St Stephen's Square, Hull HU1 3XG. *Club:* MCC.

HOWARD-DOBSON, Gen. Sir Patrick John, GCB 1979 (KCB 1974; CB 1973); *b* 12 Aug. 1921; *s* of late Canon Howard Dobson, MA; *m* 1946, Barbara Mary Mills; two *s* one *d*. *Educ:* King's Coll. Choir Sch., Cambridge; Framlingham College. Joined 7th Queen's Own Hussars, Egypt, Dec. 1941; served in: Burma, 1942; Middle East, 1943; Italy, 1944–45; Germany, 1946; psc 1950; jssc 1958; comd The Queen's Own Hussars, 1963–65 and 20 Armoured Bde, 1965–67; idc 1968; Chief of Staff, Far East Comd, 1969–71; Comdt, Staff Coll., Camberley, 1972–74; Military Secretary, 1974–76; Quartermaster General, 1977–79; Vice-Chief of Defence Staff (Personnel and Logistics), 1979–81; ADC Gen. to the Queen, 1978–81. Col Comdt, ACC, 1976–82. Nat. Pres., Royal British Legion, 1981–87. Virtuti Militari (Poland), 1945; Silver Star (US), 1945. *Recreations:* sailing, golf. *Address:* 1 Drury Park, Snape, Saxmundham, Suffolk IP17 1TA. *Clubs:* Royal Cruising; Senior Golfers' Society.

HOWARD-DRAKE, Jack Thomas Arthur; Assistant Under-Secretary of State, Home Office, 1974–78; *b* 7 Jan. 1919; *o s* of Arthur Howard and Ruby (*née* Cherry); *m* 1947, Joan Mary, *o d* of Hubert and Winifred Crook; one *s* two *d*. *Educ:* Hele's Sch., Exeter. Asst Inspector, Ministry of Health Insurance Dept, 1937–39 and 1946–47. Served War, RA, 1939–46 (Major, despatches). Colonial Office: Asst Principal, 1947; Principal, 1949; Private Sec. to Sec. of State, 1956–62; Asst Sec., 1962; Asst Sec., Cabinet Office, 1963–65; Asst Sec., Home Office, 1965–72; Asst Under-Sec. of State, NI Office, 1972–74. Chairman: Oxfordshire Local History Assoc., 1984–91; Wychwoods Local History Soc., 1984–92. *Publications:* Oxford Church Courts: Depositions 1542–1550, 1991; Oxford Church Courts: Depositions 1570–1574, 1993; Oxford Church Courts: Depositions 1581–1586, 1994. *Recreations:* gardening, local history, golf. *Address:* 26 Sinnels Field, Shipton-under-Wychwood, Chipping Norton, Oxon OX7 6EJ. *T:* Shipton-under-Wychwood (01993) 830792.

HOWARD-JOHNSTON, Rear-Admiral Clarence Dinsmore, CB 1955; DSO 1942; DSC 1940; *b* 13 Oct. 1903; *m* 1955, Paulette, *d* of late Paul Helleu. *Educ:* Royal Naval Colls Osborne and Dartmouth. Midshipman, 1921; Commander, 1937; Dir of Studies, Greek Naval War Coll., Athens, 1938–40; Naval staff, anti-submarine Warfare Div., Admlty, 1940; detached to set up anti-sub. trng, Quiberon, 1940; i/c ops for destruction port facilities St Malo, evacuation British troops St Malo and Jersey (despatches); anti-sub. ops, Norwegian fjords, evacuation troops and wounded, Molde and Andalsnes (DSC); in comd anti-sub. escort group, N Atlantic, 1941–42; escorted 1,229 ships (DSO for sinking U651); staff, Battle of Atlantic Comd, Liverpool, 1942–43; Captain, 1943; Dir, Anti-U-boat Div., Admlty, 1943–45, anti-sub. specialist, PM's Cabinet U-boat meetings; in Comd, HMS Bermuda, British Pacific Fleet and occupation of Japan forces, 1946–47; Naval Attaché, Paris, 1947–50; Naval ADC to the Queen, 1952; Rear-Adm., 1953; Chief of Staff to Flag Officer, Central Europe, 1953–55, retired, 1955. Inventor of simple hydraulic mechanisms; commended by Lords Comrs of the Admiralty for invention and develt of anti-submarine training devices including Johnston Mobile A/S target, 1937. Participated in and prepared maritime historical programmes on French TV, 1967–81. Order of Phœnix (Greece), 1940; Legion of Merit (USA), 1945. *Recreations:* fishing, pisiculture, hill-walking, gardening. *Address:* 45 Rue Emile Ménier, 75116 Paris, France; Le Coteau, Chambre d'Amour, 64600 Anglet, France. *Clubs:* White's, Naval and Military, (Naval Member) Royal Yacht Squadron; Jockey (Paris).

HOWARD-LAWSON, Sir John (Philip), 6th Bt *cr* 1841, of Brough Hall, Yorkshire; *b* 6 June 1934; *s* of Sir William Howard Lawson, 5th Bt and Joan Eleanor (*d* 1989), *d* of late Maj. Arthur Cowie Stamer, CBE; assumed by Royal Licence surname and arms of Howard, 1962, of Howard-Lawson, 1992; *S* father, 1990; *m* 1960, Jean Veronica (*née* Marsh); two *s* one *d*. *Educ:* Ampleforth. *Heir: s* Philip William Howard [*b* 28 June 1961; *m* 1st, 1988, Cara Margaret Browne (marr. diss. 1992); 2nd, 1993, Isabel Anne de la Hey]. *Address:* Hunter Hall, Great Salkeld, Penrith, Cumbria CA11 9NA. *T:* Penrith (01768) 897135. *Club:* Farmers'.

HOWARTH, Alan Thomas, CBE 1982; MP (C) Stratford-on-Avon, since 1983; *b* 11 June 1944; *e s* of late T. E. B. Howarth, MC, TD and Margaret Howarth; *m* 1967, Gillian Martha, *d* of Mr and Mrs Arthur Chance, Dublin; two *s* two *d*. *Educ:* Rugby Sch. (scholar); King's Coll., Cambridge (major scholar in History; BA 1965). Sen. Res. Asst to Field-Marshal Montgomery on A History of Warfare, 1965–67; Asst Master, Westminster Sch., 1968–74; Private Sec. to Chm. of Conservative Party, 1975–79; Dir, Cons. Res. Dept, 1979–81; Vice-Chm., Conservative Party, 1980–81. PPS to Dr Rhodes Boyson, MP, 1985–87; an Asst Govt Whip, 1987–88; Lord Comr of HM Treasury, 1988–89; Parly Under-Sec. of State, DES, 1989–92. Sec., Cons. Arts and Heritage Cttee, 1984–85; Mem., Nat. Heritage Select Cttee, 1992–93; Chm., All Party Parly Gp on Charities and Vol. Sector, 1992–; Treasurer, All Party Arts and Heritage Gp, 1993–. Chm., Friends, Huntington's Disease Assoc., 1988–; Mem. Adv. Council, Nat. Listening Library, 1992–; Vice-Pres., British Dyslexia Assoc., 1992–. Mem. Court: Univ. of Warwick, 1987–; Univ. of Birmingham, 1992–. Mem. Bd., Inst. of Historical Res., 1992–. Governor, Royal Shakespeare Theatre, 1984–. *Publications:* (jtly) Monty at Close Quarters, 1985; jt author of various CPC pamphlets. *Recreations:* books, the arts, running. *Address:* House of Commons, SW1A 0AA.

HOWARTH, Elgar; freelance musician; *b* 4 Nov. 1935; *s* of Oliver and Emma Howarth; *m* 1958, Mary Bridget Neary; one *s* two *d*. *Educ:* Manchester Univ. (MusB); Royal Manchester Coll. of Music (ARMCM 1956; FRMCM 1970). Royal Opera House,

Covent Garden (Orchestra), 1958–63; Royal Philharmonic Orchestra, 1963–69; Mem., London Sinfonietta, 1968–71; Mem., Philip Jones Brass Ensemble, 1965–76; freelance conductor, 1970–; Principal Guest Conductor, Opera North, 1985–88; Musical Advisor, Grimethorpe Colliery Brass Band, 1972–. FRAM 1989; FRNCM 1994. DUniv Birmingham, 1993. *Publications:* various compositions mostly for brass instruments. *Address:* 27 Cromwell Avenue, N6 5HN.

HOWARTH, George Edward; MP (Lab) Knowsley North, since Nov. 1986; *b* 29 June 1949; *m* 1977, Julie Rodgers; two *s* one *d*. *Educ:* Liverpool Polytechnic. Formerly: engineer; teacher; Chief Exec., Wales TUC's Co-operative Centre, 1984–86. Former Mem., Huyton UDC; Mem., Knowsley Bor. Council, 1975–86 (Dep. Leader, 1982). *Address:* House of Commons, SW1A 0AA.

HOWARTH, (James) Gerald (Douglas); Joint Managing Director, Taskforce Communications, since 1993; *b* 12 Sept. 1947; *s* of late James Howarth and of Mary Howarth, Hurley, Berks; *m* 1973, Elizabeth Jane, *d* of Michael and Muriel Squibb, Crowborough, Sussex; two *s* one *d*. *Educ:* Haileybury and ISC Jun. Sch.; Bloxham Sch.; Southampton Univ. (BA Hons). Commnd RAFVR, 1968. Gen. Sec., Soc. for Individual Freedom, 1969–71; entered internat. banking, 1971; Bank of America Internat., 1971–77; European Arab Bank, 1977–81 (Manager, 1979–81); Syndication Manager, Standard Chartered Bank, 1981–83. Dir, Richard Unwin Internat., 1983–87. Dir, Freedom Under Law, 1973–77; estabd Dicey Trust, 1976. Mem., Hounslow BC, 1982–83. MP (C) Cannock and Burntwood, 1983–92. Parliamentary Private Secretary: to Parly Under-Sec. of State for Energy, 1987–90; to Minister for Housing and Planning, 1990–91; to Rt Hon. Margaret Thatcher, MP, 1991–92. Mem., Select Cttee on Sound Broadcasting, 1987–92. Jt Sec., Cons. Parly Aviation Cttee, 1983–87. Prospective Parly Candidate (C) Aldershot, 1993–. Britannia Airways Parly Pilot of the Year, 1988. Contributor to No Turning Back Gp pubns. *Recreations:* flying (private pilot's licence, 1965), squash, walking up hills, normal family pursuits.

HOWARTH, Judith; soprano. *Educ:* Royal Scottish Acad. of Music and Drama. Rôles include: *Royal Opera:* Adele; Aennchen; Gilda; Liu; Marguerite de Valois; Marzelline; Morgana; Musetta; Norina; Oscar; *Opera North:* Cressida; Norina; Susanna; *Scottish Opera:* Zerlina. Many concerts and festival appearances. *Address:* c/o Lies Askonas, 6 Henrietta Street, WC2E 8LA.

HOWARTH, Prof. Leslie, OBE 1955; BSc, MA, PhD; FRS 1950; FRAeS; CMath; Henry Overton Wills Professor of Mathematics, University of Bristol, 1964–76, now Emeritus; *b* 23 May 1911; *s* of late Fred and Elizabeth Ellen Howarth; *m* 1934, Eva Priestley; two *s*. *Educ:* Accrington Grammar Sch.; Manchester Univ.; Gonville and Caius Coll., Cambridge. Mathematical tripos, 1933; Smith's Prize, 1935; PhD, 1936. FRAeS 1951. Berry-Ramsey Research Fellow, King's Coll., Cambridge, 1936–45; Lecturer in Mathematics in the University of Cambridge, 1936–49; Fellow of St John's Coll., Cambridge, 1945–49; Prof. of Applied Mathematics, University of Bristol, 1949–64; Adams Prize, 1951. Worked at External Ballistics Dept, Ordnance Board, 1939–42, and at Armament Research Dept, 1942–45. Hon. FIMA 1979. *Publications:* (ed) Modern Developments in Fluid Dynamics: High Speed Flow; papers on aerodynamics. *Address:* 10 The Crescent, Henleaze, Bristol BS9 4RW. *T:* Bristol (0117) 962 9621.

HOWARTH, Nigel John Graham; His Honour Judge Howarth; a Circuit Judge, since 1992; *b* 12 Dec. 1936; *s* of Vernon and Irene Howarth; *m* 1962, Janice Mary Hooper; two *s* one *d*. *Educ:* Manchester Grammar Sch,; Manchester Univ. (LLB, LLM). Called to the Bar, Gray's Inn, 1960; private practice at Chancery Bar, Manchester, 1961–92; Actg Deemster, IOM, 1985, 1989; a Recorder, 1989–92. Chm., Northern Chancery Bar Assoc., 1990–92. *Recreations:* music, theatre, fell walking.

HOWARTH, Peter James, CBE 1995; Managing Director, Royal Mail, 1992–July 1996, and Board Member, 1991–July 1996, Post Office; *b* 27 July 1935; *s* of late Sidney and Margaret Howarth; *m* 1964, Susan Mary Briggs; one *s* one *d*. *Educ:* St Joseph's Coll., Blackpool. Entered Post Office, 1953; held junior and middle management positions; Head Postmaster, Manchester, 1979–85; Chm., NW Postal Bd, 1985–86; Gen. Manager, West and London Letters Territories, 1986–88; Dir Ops, Royal Mail, 1988–91; Asst Man. Dir, Royal Mail, 1991; Man. Dir, Parcelforce, 1991–92. Mem., Billericay Mayflower Rotary Club. *Recreations:* golf, fishing, reading. *Address:* Royal Mail House, 148 Old Street, EC1V 9HQ. *T:* 0171–250 2200. *Club:* Warren Danbury Golf.

HOWARTH, Robert Lever; Leader, Labour Group, Bolton Metropolitan Borough, since 1975; Leader, Bolton Metropolitan Borough Council, since 1980; *b* 31 July 1927; *s* of James Howarth and Bessie (*née* Pearson); *m* 1952, Josephine Mary Doyle; one *s* one *d*. *Educ:* Bolton County Grammar Sch.; Bolton Technical Coll. Draughtsman with Hawker Siddeley Dynamics. MP (Lab) Bolton East, 1964–70. Lectr in Liberal Studies, Leigh Technical Coll., 1970–76; Senior Lectr in General Studies, Wigan Coll. of Technology, 1977–87. Dep. Chm., 1986–87, Chm., 1987–88, Manchester Airport. *Recreations:* gardening, reading, walking, films. *Address:* 93 Markland Hill, Bolton, Lancs BL1 5EQ. *T:* Bolton (01204) 844121.

HOWAT, Prof. Henry Taylor, CBE 1971; MSc (Manch.); MD, FRCP, FRCPE; Professor of Gastroenterology, University of Manchester, 1972–76, now Emeritus; Physician, Manchester Royal Infirmary, 1948–76; *b* 16 May 1911; *s* of late Adam Howat, MA, and late Henrietta Howat, Pittenweem, Fife; *m* 1940, Rosaline, *o d* of late Miles Green, Auckland, NZ; two *s* one *d*. *Educ:* Cameron Public Sch. and Madras Coll., St Andrews; Univ. of St Andrews. MB, ChB (St And) 1933; MD with Hons and Univ. Gold Medal (St And), 1960; MRCP 1937, FRCP 1948; MRCPE 1961, FRCPE 1965. Resident MO, Manchester Royal Infirmary, 1938–40. Served War, MEF and BLA; RMO, Physician Specialist, Officer in charge of Med. Div., Mil. Hosps, 1940–46; temp. Lt-Col, RAMC. Univ. of Manchester: Asst Lectr in Applied Physiology, 1946–48; Lectr in Med., 1948–69 (Chm., Faculty of Med., 1968–72); Reader, 1969–72; Physician, Ancoats Hosp., Manchester, 1946–62. United Manchester Hospitals, 1948–76: Chm., Med. Exec. Cttee, 1968–73; Mem., Bd of Governors, 1966–74. President: European Pancreatic Club, 1965; British Soc. of Gastroenterology, 1968–69; Assoc. of Physicians of GB and Ireland, 1975–76; Manchester Med. Soc., 1975–76; Pancreatic Soc. of GB and Ireland, 1978–79. Hon. MD, Univ. of Louvain, Belgium, 1945. Manchester Man of the Year, 1973. Medallist, J. E. Purkyně Czechoslovak Med. Soc., 1968; Diploma and Medallion of Hungarian Gastroenterol Soc., 1988. *Publications:* (ed) The Exocrine Pancreas, 1979; articles on gastrointestinal physiology and disease. *Recreation:* golf. *Address:* 3 Brookdale Rise, Hilton Road, Bramhall, Cheshire SK7 3AG. *T:* 0161–439 2853; 40 High Street, Pittenweem, Fife KY10 2PL. *T:* Anstruther (01333) 311325. *Club:* Royal and Ancient Golf (St Andrews).

HOWD, Mrs Isobel; Regional Nursing Officer, Yorkshire Regional Health Authority, 1973–83; *b* 24 Oct. 1928 (*née* Young); *m* 1951, Ralph Howd. SRN, RMN, BTA Cert. Matron, Naburn Hosp., York, 1960–63; Asst Regional Nursing Officer, Leeds Regional Hosp. Bd, 1963–70; Chief Nursing Officer, South Teesside Hosp. Management Cttee, 1970–73. Mem., Mental Health Act Commn, 1983–87. *Address:* Yew Tree Cottage, Upper Dunsforth, York YO5 9RU. *T:* Boroughbridge (01423) 322534.

HOWDEN, Timothy Simon; Group Chief Executive for Europe, The Albert Fisher Group plc, since 1992; *b* 2 April 1937; *s* of Phillip Alexander and Rene Howden; *m* 1958, Penelope Mary Wilmott (marr. diss. 1984); two *s* one *d*. *Educ:* Tonbridge Sch. Served RA, 1955–57, 2nd Lieut. Floor Treatments Ltd, 1957–59; joined Reckitt & Colman, 1962; France, 1962–64; Germany, 1964–70; Dir, Reckitt & Colman Europe, 1970–73; Ranks Hovis McDougall, 1973–92: Dir, RHM Flour Mills, 1973–75; Man. Dir, RHM Foods, 1975–81; Chm. and Man. Dir, British Bakeries, 1981–85; Planning, then Dep. Man. Dir, 1985–89; Man. Dir, 1989–92. *Recreations:* ski-ing, scuba diving, tennis, sailing. *Address:* The Albert Fisher Group plc, C Sefton Park, Bells Hill, Stoke Poges, Bucks SL2 4HS. *T:* Slough (01753) 677877. *Club:* Annabel's.

HOWE, family name of **Baron Howe of Aberavon**.

HOWE, 7th Earl *cr* 1821; **Frederick Richard Penn Curzon;** Baron Howe, 1788; Baron Curzon, 1794; Viscount Curzon, 1802; Parliamentary Under-Secretary of State, Ministry of Defence, since 1995; farmer; *b* 29 Jan. 1951; *s* of Chambré George William Penn Curzon (*d* 1976) (*g s* of 3rd Earl) and of Enid Jane Victoria Curzon (*née* Fergusson); *S* cousin, 1984; *m* 1983, Elizabeth Helen Stuart; one *s* three *d*. *Educ:* Rugby School; Christ Church, Oxford (MA Hons Lit. Hum.; Chancellor's Prize for Latin Verse, 1973). AIB. Entered Barclays Bank Ltd, 1973; Manager, 1982; Sen. Manager, 1984–87. Director: Adam & Co., 1987–90; Provident Life Assoc. Ltd, 1988–91. A Lord in Waiting (Govt Whip), 1991–92; front bench spokesman, H of L, on employment and transport, 1991, on environment and defence, 1992; Parly Sec., MAFF, 1992–95. Governor: King William IV Naval Foundation, 1984–; Milton's Cottage, 1985–; Trident Trust, 1985–; President: S Bucks Assoc. for the Disabled, 1984–; Chilterns Br., RNLI, 1985–; Nat. Soc. for Epilepsy, 1986– (Vice-Pres., 1984–86); Penn Country Br., CPRE, 1986–92; Abbeyfield Beaconsfield Soc., 1991–. *Recreation:* spending time with family. *Heir:* *s* Viscount Curzon, *qv*. *Address:* c/o House of Lords, SW1A 0PW.

HOWE OF ABERAVON, Baron *cr* 1992 (Life Peer), of Tandridge, in the County of Surrey; **Richard Edward Geoffrey Howe**, PC 1972; Kt 1970; QC 1965; *b* 20 Dec. 1926; *er s* of late B. E. Howe and Mrs E. F. Howe, JP (*née* Thomson), Port Talbot, Glamorgan; *m* 1953, Elspeth Rosamund Morton Shand (*see* Lady Howe of Aberavon); one *s* two *d*. *Educ:* Winchester Coll. (Exhibitioner); Trinity Hall, Cambridge (Scholar, MA, LLB; Hon. Fellow, 1992); Pres., Trinity Hall Assoc., 1977–78. Lieut Royal Signals 1945–48. Chm. Cambridge Univ. Conservative Assoc., 1951; Chm. Bow Group, 1955; Managing Dir, Crossbow, 1957–60, Editor 1960–62. Called to the Bar, Middle Temple, 1952, Bencher, 1969, Reader, 1993; Mem. General Council of the Bar, 1957–61; Mem. Council of Justice, 1963–70. Dep. Chm., Glamorgan QS, 1966–70. Contested (C) Aberavon, 1955, 1959; MP (C): Bebington, 1964–66; Reigate, 1970–74; Surrey East, 1974–92. Sec. Conservative Parliamentary Health and Social Security Cttee, 1964–65; an Opposition Front Bench spokesman on labour and social services, 1965–66; Solicitor-General, 1970–72; Minister for Trade and Consumer Affairs, DTI, 1972–74; opposition front bench spokesman on social services, 1974–75, on Treasury and economic affairs, 1975–79; Chancellor of the Exchequer, 1979–83; Sec. of State for Foreign and Commonwealth Affairs, 1983–89; Lord Pres. of the Council, Leader of H of C, and Dep. Prime Minister, 1989–90. Chm., Interim Cttee, IMF, 1982–83. Chm., Framlington Russian Investment Fund, 1994–; Director: Sun Alliance & London Insce Co. Ltd, 1974–79; AGB Research Ltd, 1974–79; EMI Ltd, 1976–79; BICC plc, 1991–; Glaxo Hldgs, 1991–. Special Advr, Internat. Affairs, Jones, Day, Reavis and Pogue, 1991–; Member: J. P. Morgan Internat. Adv. Council, 1992–; Bertelsmann Foundn, 1992–. Member: (Latey) Interdeptl Cttee on Age of Majority, 1965–67; (Street) Cttee on Racial Discrimination, 1967; (Cripps) Cons. Cttee on Discrimination against Women, 1968–69; Chm. Ely Hospital, Cardiff, Inquiry, 1969. Visitor, SOAS, Univ. of London, 1991–; Vis. Fellow, John F. Kennedy Sch. of Govt, Harvard Univ., 1991–92; Herman Phleger Vis. Prof., Stanford Law Sch., Calif, 1993. Member, International Advisory Council: Inst. of Internat. Studies, Stanford Univ., Calif, 1990–; Centre for Eur. Policy Studies, 1992–; Chm., Adv. Bd, English Centre for Legal Studies, Warsaw Univ., 1992–; Vice-President: RUSI, 1991–; English Coll. Foundn in Prague, 1992–. President: Cons. Political Centre Nat. Adv. Cttee, 1977–79; Nat. Union of Cons. and Unionist Assocs, 1983–84; Jt Pres., Wealth of Nations Foundn, 1991–. Mem., Adv. Council, Presidium of Supreme Soviet of Ukraine, 1991–. Mem. Council of Management, Private Patients' Plan, 1969–70; Mem., Steering Cttee, Project Liberty, 1991–; Patron, Enterprise Europe, 1990–. Pres., Assoc. for Consumer Res., 1992– (an Hon. Vice-Pres., 1974–92). Hon. Freeman, Port Talbot, 1992. Hon. LLD Wales, 1988; Hon. DCL City, 1993. Joseph Bech Prize, FVS Stifting, Hamburg, 1993. Grand Cross, Order of Merit (Germany), 1992. *Publications:* Conflict of Loyalty (memoirs), 1994; various political pamphlets for Bow Group and Conservative Political Centre. *Address:* House of Lords, SW1A 0PW. *Clubs:* Athenæum, Garrick.

HOWE OF ABERAVON, Lady; Elspeth Rosamund Morton Howe, JP; Chairman: Broadcasting Standards Council, since 1993; BOC Foundation for the Environment and Community, since 1990; President, UNICEF UK, since 1993; *b* 8 Feb. 1932; *d* of late Philip Morton Shand and Sybil Mary (*née* Sissons); *m* 1953, Baron Howe of Aberavon, *qv*; one *s* two *d*. *Educ:* Bath High Sch.; Wycombe Abbey; London Sch. of Econs and Pol Science (BSc 1985). Vice-Chm., Conservative London Area Women's Adv. Cttee, 1966–67, also Pres. of the Cttee's Contact Gp, 1973–77; Mem., Conservative Women's Nat. Adv. Cttee, 1966–71. Member: Lord Chancellor's Adv. Cttee on appointment of Magistrates for Inner London Area, 1965–75; Lord Chancellor's Adv. Cttee on Legal Aid, 1971–75; Parole Board, 1972–75. Dep. Chm., Equal Opportunities Commn, 1975–79. Co-opted Mem., ILEA, 1967–70; Member: Briggs Cttee on Nursing Profession, 1970–72; Justice Cttee on English Judiciary, 1992. Chairman: Hansard Soc. Commn on Women at the Top, 1989–90; The Quality of Care, Local Govt Management Bd Inquiry and Report, 1991–92; Archbishop's Commn on Cathedrals, 1992–94. Director: Kingfisher (formerly Woolworth Holdings) PLC, 1986–; United Biscuits (Holdings) PLC, 1988–; Legal & General Group, 1989–; Chm., Opportunity 2000 Target Team, Business in the Community, 1990–. President: Peckham Settlement, 1976–; Women's Gas Fedn, 1979–93; Fedn of Personnel Services, subseq. of Recruitment and Employment Services, 1980–94; Member Council: NACRO, 1974–93; PSI, 1983–92; St George's House, Windsor, 1987–92; Vice-Pres., Pre-Sch. Playgroups Assoc., 1979–83. Trustee, Westminster Foundn for Democracy, 1992–. Has served as chm. or mem. of several sch. governing bodies in Tower Hamlets; Governor: Cumberlow Lodge Remand Home, 1967–70; Wycombe Abbey, 1968–90; Froebel Educn Inst., 1968–75; LSE, 1985–; Mem. Bd of Governors, James Allen's Girls' Sch., 1988–93. JP Inner London Juvenile Court Panel, 1964–92 (Chm. of Court, 1970–90). Hon. LLD London, 1990; DUniv Open, 1993; Hon. DLitt Bradford, 1993. *Publication:* Under Five (a report on pre-school education), 1966. *Address:* The BOC Foundation, 5–8 The Sanctuary, SW1P 3JS.

See also B. M. H. Shand.

HOWE, Allen; Circuit Administrator, Wales and Chester Circuit, 1974–82; Chairman, Medical Appeals Tribunal for Wales, 1982–92; *b* 6 June 1918; *s* of late Frank Howe and

inventing Australia, trailing his coat. *Address:* c/o Duet Productions, 2nd Floor, 20 Young Street, Neutral Bay, NSW 2089, Australia. *Clubs:* Athenæum, Garrick, Beefsteak.

HUMPHRIES, John Charles Freeman; Editor, Western Mail, 1988–92; *b* 2 Jan. 1937; *s* of Charles Montague Humphries and Lilian Clara Humphries; *m* 1959, Eliana Paola Julia Mifsud; two *s* one *d*. *Educ:* St Julian's High Sch., Newport, Gwent. Western Mail: News Editor, 1966–73; Dep. Editor, 1973–80; Thomson Regional Newspapers: European Bureau Chief, 1980–86; London/City Editor, 1986–87; Launch Editor, Wales on Sunday, 1989. Trustee and Founder, British Bone Marrow Donor Appeal, 1987–. *Recreations:* walking, opera, reading, Rugby, cricket. *Address:* Plas Cwm Coed, Usk Road, Tredunnock, Gwent NP1 5BE.

HUMPHRYS, John; Presenter: Today Programme, Radio 4, since 1987; On the Record, BBC TV, since 1993; John Humphrys Interview, Radio 4, since 1995; *b* 17 Aug. 1943; *s* of George and Winifred Humphrys; *m* 1965, Edna Wilding (marr. diss. 1991); one *s* one *d*. *Educ:* Cardiff High School. BBC TV: Washington Correspondent, 1971–77; Southern Africa Correspondent, 1977–80; Diplomatic Correspondent, 1980–81; Presenter, 9 o'Clock News, 1981–86. *Recreations:* music, attempting to play the 'cello, organic dairy farming (masochism). *Address:* c/o BBC Radio, Broadcasting House, W1A 1AA.

HUNN, Sir Jack (Kent), Kt 1976; CMG 1964; LLM; Retired as Secretary of Defence, New Zealand (1963–66); *b* 24 Aug. 1906; *m* 1st, 1932, Dorothy Murray; two *s*; 2nd, 1985, Mabel Duncan. *Educ:* Wairarapa Coll.; Auckland Univ. Public Trust Office, 1924–46; Actg Sec. of Justice, 1950; Public Service Comr, 1954–61; Actg Sec. of Internal Affairs and Dir of Civil Defence, 1959; Sec. for Maori Affairs and Maori Trustee, 1960–63. Reviewed Cook Islands Public Service, 1949 and 1954; Mem. NZ delegn to Duke of Edinburgh's Conf, 1956; Mem. UN Salary Review Cttee, 1956; reviewed organisation of South Pacific Commn, Noumea and Sydney, 1957, and of SEATO, Bangkok, 1959. Chairman: Wildlife Commission of Inquiry, 1968; Fire Safety Inquiry, 1969; Fire Service Council, 1973; Fire Service Commn, 1974; Electricity Distribution Enquiry, 1987. *Publications:* Hunn Report on Maori Affairs, 1960; Not Only Affairs Of State, 1982. *Address:* 17 Kereru Street, Waikanae 6154, New Zealand. *T:* (4) 2935033.

HUNNISETT, Dr Roy Frank, FSA, FRHistS; on staff of Public Record Office, 1953–88; *b* 26 Feb. 1928; *s* of Frank Hunnisett and Alice (*née* Budden); *m* 1st, 1954, Edith Margaret Evans (marr. diss. 1989); 2nd, 1989, Janet Heather Stevenson. *Educ:* Bexhill Grammar Sch.; New Coll., Oxford (1st Cl. Hons Mod. Hist., 1952; Amy Mary Preston Read Scholar, 1952–53; MA, DPhil 1956). FRHistS 1961; FSA 1975. Lectr, New Coll., Oxford, 1957–63. Royal Historical Society: Alexander Prize, 1957; Mem. Council, 1974–77; Vice-Pres., 1979–82; Selden Society: Mem. Council, 1975–84, 1987–; Vice-Pres., 1984–87; Treasurer, Pipe Roll Soc., 1973–87. *Publications:* Calendar of Inquisitions Miscellaneous: (ed jtly) vol. IV, 1957 and vol. V, 1962; (ed) vol. VI, 1963 and vol. VII, 1968; The Medieval Coroners' Rolls, 1960; The Medieval Coroner, 1961; (ed) Bedfordshire Coroners' Rolls, 1961; (ed) Calendar of Nottinghamshire Coroners' Inquests 1485–1558, 1969; (contrib.) The Study of Medieval Records: essays in honour of Kathleen Major, 1971; Indexing for Editors, 1972; Editing Records for Publication, 1977; (ed jtly and contrib.) Medieval Legal Records edited in memory of C.A.F. Meekings, 1978; (ed) Wiltshire Coroners' Bills 1752–1796, 1981; (ed) Sussex Coroners' Inquests 1485–1558, 1985; articles and revs in historical and legal jls. *Recreations:* Sussex, music, cricket. *Address:* 23 Byron Gardens, Sutton, Surrey SM1 3QG. *T:* 0181–661 2618.

HUNSDON OF HUNSDON, Baron; *see* Aldenham, Baron.

HUNSWORTH, John Alfred; Director, Banking Information Service, 1954–81; *b* 23 Dec. 1921; *s* of late Fred Sheard Hunsworth and Lillian Margaret (*née* Wetmon); *m* 1972, Phyllis Sparshatt (*d* 1994). *Educ:* Selhurst Grammar Sch.; LSE (BCom). Served War, 1941–46: commnd E Surrey Regt; served 2nd Punjab Regt, Indian Army, 1942–45. Dep. Editor, Bankers' Magazine, 1948–54. Freeman, City of London. *Publications:* contrib. prof. jls. *Recreations:* gardening, world travel, philately; formerly lawn tennis and Rugby football. *Address:* 29 West Hill, Sanderstead, Surrey CR2 0SB. *T:* 0181–657 2585. *Clubs:* Reform, Royal Over-Seas League; Surrey County Cricket.

HUNT, family name of **Barons Hunt** and **Hunt of Tanworth.**

HUNT, Baron, *cr* 1966, of Llanfair Waterdine (Life Peer); **(Henry Cecil) John Hunt,** KG 1979; Kt 1953; CBE 1945; DSO 1944; *b* 22 June 1910; *s* of late Capt. C. E. Hunt, MC, IA, and E. H. Hunt (*née* Crookshank); *m* 1936, Joy Mowbray-Green; four *d*. *Educ:* Marlborough Coll.; RMC, Sandhurst. Commissioned King's Royal Rifle Corps, 1930; seconded to Indian Police, 1934–35 and 1938–40 (Indian Police Medal, 1940). War of 1939–45: Comd 11th Bn KRRC, 1944; Comd 11th Indian Inf. Bde, 1944–46. Staff Coll., 1946; Joint Services Staff Coll., 1949; GSO 1, Jt Planning Staffs, MELF, 1946–48; Western Europe C's-in-C Cttee, 1950–51; Allied Land Forces, Central Europe, 1951–52; Col, Gen. Staff, HQ I (British) Corps, 1952; Asst Comdt, The Staff Coll., 1953–55; Comdr 168 Inf. Bde, TA, 1955–56; retired, 1956; Hon. Brigadier. Dir, Duke of Edinburgh's Award Scheme, 1956–66. Rector, Aberdeen Univ., 1963–66. Personal Adviser to Prime Minister during Nigerian Civil War, 1968–70. Chairman: Parole Bd for England and Wales, 1967–74; Adv. Cttee on Police in N Ireland, 1969; President: Nat. Assoc. of Youth Clubs, 1954–70; Council for Volunteers Overseas, 1968–74; Nat. Assoc. of Probation Officers, 1974–80; Rainer Foundn, 1971–85; Council for Nat. Parks, 1980–86; Nat. Assoc. for Outdoor Educn, 1991–93; Mem., Royal Commn on the Press, 1974–77; Pres., Britain and Nepal Soc., 1960–75. Joined Social Democratic Party, 1981, Social and Liberal Democrats, 1988. Leader, British Expedition to Mount Everest, 1952–53. President: The Alpine Club, 1956–58; Climbers' Club, 1963–66; British Mountaineering Council, 1965–68; The National Ski Fedn, 1968–72; RGS, 1977–80 (Hon. Mem., 1984). Hon. DCL Durham 1954; Hon. LLD: Aberdeen 1954; London 1954; City 1976; Leeds 1979; Hon. DSc Sheffield, 1989. Order 1st Class Gurkha Right Hand, 1953; Indian Everest Medal, 1953; Hubbard Medal (US), 1954; Founder's Medal, RGS, 1954; Lawrence Memorial Medal, RCAS, 1954; King Albert I Meml Medal for Mountaineering, 1994. *Publications:* The Ascent of Everest, 1953; Our Everest Adventure, 1954; (with C. Brasher) The Red Snows, 1959; Life is Meeting, 1978; (ed) My Favourite Mountaineering Stories, 1978; In Search of Adventure, 1989. *Recreation:* mountain activities. *Address:* Highway Cottage, Aston, Henley-on-Thames RG9 3DE. *Clubs:* Alpine, Ski Club of Great Britain.

HUNT OF TANWORTH, Baron *cr* 1980 (Life Peer), of Stratford-upon-Avon in the county of Warwickshire; **John Joseph Benedict Hunt,** GCB 1977 (KCB 1973; CB 1968); Secretary of the Cabinet, 1973–79; Chairman: Banque Nationale de Paris plc, since 1980; BNP UK Holdings Ltd, since 1991; *b* 23 Oct. 1919; *er s* of Major Arthur L. Hunt and Daphne Hunt; *m* 1st, 1941, Hon. Magdalen Mary Lister Robinson (*d* 1971), *yr d* of 1st Baron Robinson; two *s* one *d*; 2nd, 1973, Madeleine Frances, *d* of Sir William Hume, CMG, FRCP, and *widow* of Sir John Charles, KCB, FRCP; one step *s* one step *d*. *Educ:* Downside; Magdalene College, Cambridge (Hon. Fellow, 1977). Served Royal Naval Volunteer Reserve, 1940–46, Lieut; Convoy escort, Western Approaches and in Far East. Home Civil Service, Admin. Class, 1946; Dominions Office, 1946; Priv. Sec. to Parly Under-Sec., 1947; 2nd Sec., Office of UK High Comr in Ceylon, 1948–50; Principal, 1949; Directing Staff, IDC, 1951–52; 1st Sec., Office of UK High Comr in Canada, 1953–56; Private Secretary to: Sec. of Cabinet and Perm. Sec. to Treasury and Head of Civil Service, 1956–58; Asst Secretary: CRO 1958; Cabinet Office, 1960; HM Treasury, 1962–67, Under-Sec., 1965; Dep. Sec., 1968 and First Civil Service Comr, Civil Service Dept, 1968–71; Third Sec., Treasury, 1971–72; Second Permanent Sec., Cabinet Office, 1972–73. Dir, 1980–92, Dep. Chm., 1982–85, Chm., 1985–90, Prudential Corp., Dep. Chm., Prudential Assurance Co. Ltd, 1982–85; Dir, IBM (UK) Ltd, 1980–90; Adv. Dir, Unilever plc, 1980–90. Chm., Disasters Emergency Cttee, 1981–89. Chm., Inquiry into Cable Expansion and Broadcasting Policy, 1982. Chm., European Policy Forum, 1992–. Chm., Ditchley Foundn, 1983–91. Chm., The Tablet Publishing Co. Ltd, 1984–. Officier, Légion d'Honneur (France), 1987. *Recreation:* gardening. *Address:* 8 Wool Road, Wimbledon, SW20 0HW. *T:* 0181–947 7640.

HUNT, Alan Charles, CMG 1990; HM Diplomatic Service; Senior Directing Staff (Civilian), Royal College of Defence Studies, since 1995; *b* 5 March 1941; *s* of John Henry Hunt and Nelly Elizabeth Hunt (*née* Hunter); *m* 1978, Meredith Margaret Claydon; two *d*. *Educ:* Latymer Upper School, Hammersmith; Univ. of East Anglia. First Cl. Hons BA in European Studies. Clerical Officer, Min. of Power, 1958–59; FO, 1959–62; Vice-Consul, Tehran, 1962–64; Third Sec., Jedda, 1964–65; floating duties, Latin America, 1965–67; University, 1967–70; Second, later First Sec., FCO, 1970–73; First Sec., Panama, 1973–76; FCO 1976–77; First Sec. (Commercial), Madrid, 1977–81; FCO, 1981–83; Counsellor (Econ. and Commercial), Oslo, 1983–87; Head of British Interests Section, subseq. Chargé d'Affaires, Buenos Aires, 1987–90; Counsellor, FCO, 1990–91; Consul-Gen., Düsseldorf, and Dir-Gen. of Trade and Investment Promotion in Germany, 1991–95. *Recreations:* tennis, sailing, skiing, travel, reading, music. *Address:* c/o Foreign and Commonwealth Office, SW1A 2AH.

HUNT, Anthony James, CEng; FIStructE; Chairman: Anthony Hunt Associates, since 1988; YRM plc, 1993–94; *b* 1932; *s* of late James Edward Hunt and of Joan Margaret (*née* Cassidy); *m* 1st, 1957, Patricia Daniels (marr. diss. 1972; remarried 1975; marr. diss. 1982); one *s* one *d*; 3rd, 1985, Diana Joyce Collett. *Educ:* Salesian Coll., Farnborough; Westminster Tech. Coll. CEng 1961. FIStructE 1973. Articled via Founders' Co. to J. L. Wheeler Consulting Engr, 1948–51; F. J. Samuely and Partners, Consulting Engrs, 1951–59; Morton Lupton, Architects, 1960–62; founded Anthony Hunt Associates, Consulting Engrs, 1962; acquired by YRM plc, Bldg Design Consultants, 1988. FRSA 1989. Hon. FRIBA 1989. Gold Medallist, IStructE, 1995. *Recreations:* furniture restoration, music, sailing, ski-ing. *Address:* Anthony Hunt Associates, Gloucester House, 60 Dyer Street, Cirencester, Glos GL7 2PF. *Club:* Chelsea Arts.

HUNT, Arthur James, OBE 1971; FRTPI, FRICS; Chief Reporter for Public Inquiries, Scottish Office, 1974–79; *b* 18 Nov. 1915; *s* of Edward Henry and Norah Hunt; *m* 1946, Fanny Betty Bacon; one *s* three *d*. *Educ:* Tauntons Sch., Southampton. Ordnance Survey, 1938–44; Planning Officer with West Sussex, Kent and Bucks County Councils, 1944–48; Asst County Planning Officer, East Sussex CC, 1948–52; Town Planning Officer, City of Durban, SA, 1953–61; Sen. and Principal Planning Inspector, Min. of Housing and Local Govt, 1961–68; Mem., Roskill Commn on the Third London Airport, 1968–70; Superintending Inspector, Dept of the Environment, 1971–74. *Recreations:* sailing, gardening, caravan touring. *Address:* Pentlands, 4 West Avenue, Middleton-on-Sea, West Sussex PO22 6EF.

HUNT, Christopher John; Director and University Librarian, John Rylands University Library of Manchester, since 1991; *b* 28 Jan. 1937; *s* of Richard John Hunt and Dorothy (*née* Pendleton); *m* 1963, Kathleen Mary Wyatt. *Educ:* Rutlish Sch., Merton; Univ. of Exeter (BA); King's Coll., Univ. of Durham (MLitt). Asst Librarian, Univ. of Newcastle upon Tyne, 1960–67; Sub Librarian, Univ. of Manchester, 1967–74; University Librarian: James Cook Univ. of N Queensland, 1974–81; La Trobe Univ., 1981–85; Librarian, British Library of Political and Economic Science, LSE, 1985–91. Chairman: Internat. Cttee for Social Sci. Inf. and Documentation, 1989–; Library Panel, Wellcome Trust. Academic Gov., LSE, 1989–91; Feoffee of Chetham's Hosp. and Library, Manchester, 1993–. *Publications:* The Leadminers of the Northern Pennines, 1970; The Book Trade in Northumberland and Durham to 1860, 1975; papers in professional and learned jls. *Recreations:* book collecting, scuba diving, wine. *Address:* John Rylands University Library, Oxford Road, Manchester M13 9PP. *T:* 0161–275 3700; 18 Stanneylands Road, Wilmslow, Cheshire SK9 4ER.

HUNT, Rt. Hon. David James Fletcher, MBE 1973; PC 1990; MP (C) Wirral West, since 1983 (Wirral, March 1976–1983); Chancellor of the Duchy of Lancaster and Minister for Public Service and Science, 1994–95; *b* 21 May 1942; *s* of late Alan Nathaniel Hunt, OBE and Jessie Edna Ellis Northrop Hunt; *m* 1973, Patricia, (Paddy), Margery (*née* Orchard); two *s* two *d*. *Educ:* Liverpool Coll.; Montpellier Univ.; Bristol Univ. (LLB); Guildford Coll. of Law. Solicitor of Supreme Court of Judicature, admitted 1968; Partner: Stanleys & Simpson North, 1977–88; Beachcroft Stanleys, 1988–; Partner, then Consultant, Stanley Wasbrough & Co., 1965–85; Dir, BET Omnibus Services Ltd, 1980–81. Chm., Cons. Shipping and Shipbuilding Cttee, 1977–79; Vice-Chm., Parly Youth Lobby, 1978–80; Vice-Pres., Cons. Group for Europe, 1984–87 (Vice-Chm., 1978–81; Chm, 1981–82); a Vice-Chm., Cons. Party, 1983–85. PPS to Sec. of State for Trade, 1979–81, to Sec. of State for Defence, 1981; an Asst Govt Whip, 1981–83; a Lord Comr of HM Treasury, 1983–84; Parly Under-Sec. of State, Dept of Energy, 1984–87; Treasurer of HM Household and Dep. Chief Whip, 1987–89; Minister for Local Govt and Inner Cities, DoE, 1989–90; Secretary of State: for Wales, 1990–93; for Employment, 1993–94. Chm., Bristol Univ. Conservatives, 1964–65; winner of Observer Mace for British Universities Debating Competition, 1965–66; Nat. Vice-Chm., FUCUA, 1965–66; Chm., Bristol City CPC, 1965–68; Nat. Vice-Chm., YCNAC, 1967–69; Chm., Bristol Fedn of YCs, 1970–71; Chm., British Youth Council, 1971–74 (Pres., 1978–80); Vice-Pres., Nat. YCs, 1986–88 (Chm., 1972–73); Vice-Chm., Nat. Union of Cons. and Unionist Assocs, 1974–76. Pres., Tory Reform Gp, 1991–. Vice-Pres., Nat. Playbus Assoc., 1981–. Contested (C) Bristol South, 1970, Kingswood, 1974. Member: South Western Economic Planning Council, 1972–76; Adv. Cttee on Pop Festivals, 1972–75. *Publications:* Europe Right Ahead, 1978; A Time for Youth, 1978. *Recreations:* cricket, walking. *Address:* Hoylake Conservative Club, Meols Drive, Hoylake, Wirral. *T:* 0151–632 1052; House of Commons, SW1A 0AA. *T:* 0171–219 5132. *Club:* Hurlingham.

HUNT, David Roderic Notley; QC 1987; a Recorder, since 1991; *b* 22 June 1947; *s* of Dr Geoffrey Notley Hunt and Deborah Katharine Rosamund Hunt; *m* 1974, Alison Connell Jelf; two *s*. *Educ:* Charterhouse School; Trinity College, Cambridge (MA Hons). Called to the Bar, Gray's Inn, 1969. *Recreations:* sailing, ski-ing, golf. *Address:* 2 Hare Court, Temple, EC4Y 7BH. *T:* 0171–583 1770.

HUNT, Sir David (Wathen Stather), KCMG 1963 (CMG 1959); OBE 1943; HM Diplomatic Service, retired; Director: Observer Newspapers, 1982–94; Trigraph Ltd, since 1988; *b* 25 Sept. 1913; *s* of late Canon B. P. W. Stather Hunt, DD, and late Elizabeth Milner; *m* 1st, 1948, Pamela Muriel Medawar; two *s*; 2nd, 1968, Iro Myrianthousis. *Educ:* St Lawrence Coll.; Wadham Coll., Oxford. 1st Class Hon. Mods. 1934; 1st Class Lit.

Dora Howe, Monk Bretton, Yorks; *m* 1952, Katherine, *d* of late Griffith and Catherine Davies, Pontypridd; two *d*. *Educ:* Holgate Grammar Sch., Barnsley. Served with E Yorks Regt and RWAFF, 1939–46, France, Africa, India and Burma (Major). HM Colonial Admin. Service, Gold Coast, 1946–55 (Sen. Dist Comr). Called to Bar, Middle Temple, 1953; Judicial Adviser, Ashanti, 1954–55; practised Wales and Chester Circuit, 1955–59; Legal Dept, Welsh Bd of Health, 1959–65; Legal Dept, Welsh Office, 1965–74. *Recreations:* golf, gardening, walking. *Address:* 2 Orchard Drive, Whitchurch, Cardiff CF4 2AE. *T:* Cardiff (01222) 626626. *Clubs:* Cardiff and County; Radyr Golf.

HOWE, Hon. Brian Leslie; MP (Lab) Batman, Victoria, since 1977; Deputy Prime Minister, Australia, since 1991; *b* 28 Jan. 1936; *s* of John P. Howe and Lillian M. Howe; *m* 1962, Renate Morris; one *s* two *d*. *Educ:* Melbourne High Sch.; Melbourne Univ. (BA, DipCrim); McCormick Theol Seminary, Chicago (MA). Ordained Minister of Methodist Church, 1963; parishes at Eltham, Morwell and Fitzroy, 1960–69; Dir, Centre for Urban Research and Action, Fitzroy, and Lectr in Sociology, Swinburne Inst. of Technology, 1970–77. Minister: for Defence Support, 1983–84; for Social Security, 1984–89; for Community Services and Health, 1990–91; for Health, Housing and Community Services, 1991–93; for Housing, Local Govt and Community Services, 1993–94; for Housing and Regl Develt, 1994–; Minister assisting the Prime Minister for Social Justice, 1988–, for Commonwealth-State Relations, 1991–. *Recreations:* tennis, reading, films, Australian Rules football. *Address:* Parliament House, Canberra, ACT 2600, Australia. *T:* (6) 2777680.

HOWE, Prof. Christopher Barry, PhD; Professor of Economics with reference to Asia, University of London, since 1979; *b* 3 Nov. 1937; *s* of Charles Roderick Howe and Patricia (*née* Creeden); *m* 1967, Patricia Anne Giles; one *s* one *d*. *Educ:* William Ellis Sch., London; St Catharine's Coll., Cambridge (MA). PhD London. Economic Secretariat, FBI, 1961–63; Sch. of Oriental and African Studies, London Univ., 1963–: Head, Contemp. China Inst., 1972–78. Member: Hong Kong Univ. and Polytechnic Grants Cttee, 1974–; UGC, 1979–84; ESRC Res. Develt Gp, 1987–88; Hong Kong Res. Grants Council, 1991–. Chm., Japan and SE Asia Business Gp, 1983–87. *Publications:* Employment and Economic Growth in Urban China 1949–57, 1971; Industrial Relations and Rapid Industrialisation, 1972; Wage Patterns and Wage Policy in Modern China 1919–1972, 1973; China's Economy: a basic guide, 1978; (ed) Studying China, 1979; (ed) Shanghai: revolution and development, 1980; (ed) The Readjustment in the Chinese Economy, 1984; (ed) China and Japan: history, trends and prospects, 1990; The Origins of Japanese Trade Supremacy, 1994. *Recreations:* music, Burmese cats. *Address:* 12 Highgate Avenue, N6 5RX. *T:* 0181–340 8104.

HOWE, Prof. Daniel Walker; Rhodes Professor of American History, and Fellow of St Catherine's College, Oxford, since 1992; *b* 10 Jan. 1937; *s* of Maurice Langdon Howe and Lucie Walker Howe; *m* 1961, Sandra Shumway; two *s* one *d*. *Educ:* Harvard (BA); Magdalen Coll., Oxford (MA); Univ. of California at Berkeley (PhD). Lieut, US Army, 1959–60. Yale University: Instructor, 1966–68; Asst Prof., 1968–73; University of California at Los Angeles: Associate Prof., 1973–77; Prof., 1977–92; Chm., History Dept, 1983–87. Harmsworth Vis. Prof., Oxford, 1989–90. Fellow: Charles Warren Center, Harvard, 1970–71; Nat. Endowment for Humanities, 1975–76; Guggenheim Foundn, 1984–85; Res. Fellow, Huntington Library, 1991–92. *Publications:* The Unitarian Conscience, 1970, 2nd edn 1988; The Political Culture of the American Whigs, 1980; articles in learned jls. *Recreation:* music. *Address:* St Catherine's College, Oxford OX1 3UJ. *T:* Oxford (01865) 271700; 3814 Cody Road, Sherman Oaks, CA 91403, USA.

HOWE, Prof. Denis; Professor of Aircraft Design, 1973–92, College of Aeronautics, Cranfield Institute of Technology, now Professor Emeritus, Cranfield University; *b* 3 Sept. 1927; *s* of Alfred and Alice Howe; *m* 1st, 1954, Audrey Marion Wilkinson; two *s* three *d*; 2nd, 1981, Catherine Bolton. *Educ:* Watford Grammar Sch.; MIT (SM); College of Aeronautics (PhD). CEng, FIMechE, FRAeS. Project Engineer, Fairey Aviation Co., 1945–54, College of Aeronautics, Cranfield Institute of Technology: Lectr, Sen. Lectr and Reader, 1954–73, Head of College, 1986–90; Dean of Engineering, 1988–91. *Publications:* contribs to learned jls. *Recreations:* gardening, church administration. *Address:* College of Aeronautics, Cranfield, Bedford MK43 0AL; 57 Brecon Way, Bedford MK41 8DE. *T:* Bedford (01234) 56747.

HOWE, Derek Andrew, CBE 1991; public affairs and political consultant; company director; *b* 31 Aug. 1934; *o s* of late Harold and Elsie Howe; *m* 1st, 1958, Barbara (*née* Estill); two *d*; 2nd, 1975, Sheila (*née* Digger), MBE (*d* 1990); one *s*. *Educ:* City of Leeds Sch.; Cockburn High Sch., Leeds. Journalist, Yorkshire Evening News, 1951–61; Conservative Central Office, 1962–70; Parliamentary Liaison Officer, 1970–73; Special Adviser, 1973–75; Press Officer, Leader of HM Opposition, 1975–79; special adviser to: Paymaster Gen., 1979–81; Chancellor of Duchy of Lancaster, 1981; Political Secretary, 10 Downing Street, 1981–83 and Special Adviser to Leader of the House of Commons, 1982–83. Trustee, London Youth Trust, 1985– (Chm., 1988). Freeman of the City of London. *Recreations:* gardening, reading, philately. *Address:* The Vines, Kimpton, near Andover, Hampshire SP11 8NU. *Club:* St Stephen's Constitutional.

HOWE, Elspeth Rosamund Morton; *see* Lady Howe of Aberavon.

HOWE, Eric James, CBE 1990; Data Protection Registrar, 1984–94; *b* 4 Oct. 1931; *s* of Albert Henry Howe and Florence Beatrice (*née* Hale); *m* 1967, Patricia Enid (*née* Schollick); two *d*. *Educ:* Stretford Grammar Sch.; Univ. of Liverpool (BA Econs 1954). FIDPM 1990; FBCS 1972. NCB, 1954–59; British Cotton Industry Res. Assoc., 1959–61; English Electric Computer Co., 1961–66; National Computing Centre, 1966–84: Dep. Dir, 1975–84; Mem. Bd of Dirs, 1976–84. Chairman: National Computer Users Forum, 1977–84; Focus Cttee for Private Sector Users, DoI, 1982–84; Member: User Panel, NEDO, 1983–84; Council, British Computer Soc., 1971–74 and 1980–83; NW Regional Council, CBI, 1977–83. Rep. UK, Confedn of Eur. Computer Users Assocs, 1980–83. *Recreations:* gardening, piano, local community work.

HOWE, Prof. Geoffrey Leslie, TD 1962 (Bars 1969 and 1974); Professor of Oral Surgery and Oral Medicine, since 1987, and Dean, since 1988, Jordan University of Science and Technology; *b* 22 April 1924; *e s* of late Leo Leslie John Howe, Maidenhead, Berks; *m* 1948, Heather Patricia Joan Hambly; one *s*. *Educ:* Royal Dental and Middlesex Hospitals. LDS RCS 1946; LRCP, MRCS 1954; FDS RCS 1955; MDS Dunelm, 1961; FFD RCSI 1964; FICD 1981. Dental and Medical Sch. Prizeman; Begley Prize, RCS, 1951; Cartwright Prize, RCS, 1961. Dental Officer, Royal Army Dental Corps, 1946–49. House appointments, etc., Royal Dental and Middlesex Hospitals, 1949–55. Registrar in Oral Surgery, Eastman Dental Hosp. (Institute of Dental Surgery), 1955–56; Senior Registrar in Oral Surgery, Plastic and Oral Surgery Centre, Chepstow, Mon, 1956; Senior Registrar in Oral Surgery, Eastman Dental Hospital, 1956–59; Professor of Oral Surgery, University of Newcastle upon Tyne (formerly King's Coll., University of Durham), 1959–67; Prof. of Oral Surgery, Royal Dental Hosp., London Sch. of Dental Surgery, 1967–78 (Dean of School, 1974–78); Prof. of Oral Surgery and Oral Medicine, and Dean of Dental Studies, Univ. of Hong Kong, 1978–83; Dir, Prince Philip Dental Hosp., 1981–83. Cons. Oral Surgeon, United Newcastle upon Tyne Hosps, 1959–67; Chm., Central Cttee for Hosp. Dental Services, 1971–73; Vice-Pres., BDA, 1979– (Vice-Chm., 1971–73; Chm., 1973–78); Pres., Internat. Assoc. of Oral Surgeons, 1980–83. Hon. Col Comdt, RADC, 1975–89. Mem., Probus Club, Sanderstead and Purley Oaks. OStJ. *Publications:* The Extraction of Teeth, 1961, 2nd edn 1970; Minor Oral Surgery, 1966, 3rd edn 1985; (with F. I. H. Whitehead) Local Anaesthesia in Dentistry, 1972, 3rd edn 1990; contribs to: Medical Treatment Yearbook, 1959; Modern Trends in Dental Surgery, 1962, and to numerous medical and dental journals. *Recreations:* sailing; Territorial Army Volunteer Reserve (lately Col, OC 217 (L) Gen. Hosp. RAMC (V), graded Cons. Dental Surgeon RADC, TAVR). *Address:* 70 Croham Manor Road, South Croydon, Surrey CR2 7BF. *Clubs:* Gents, Oral Surgery; Hong Kong; Royal Hong Kong Yacht.

HOWE, Geoffrey Michael Thomas; Managing Partner, Clifford Chance, since 1989; *b* 3 Sept. 1949; *s* of Michael Edward Howe and Susan Dorothy Howe (*née* Allan). *Educ:* Manchester Grammar Sch.; St John's Coll., Cambridge (MA). Solicitor. Stephenson Harwood, 1971–75; joined Clifford Chance, 1975; Partner, Corporate Dept, 1980. *Recreations:* cricket, golf, squash, opera, wine, antiques. *Address:* 107 Seddon House, Barbican, EC2Y 8BX. *Club:* United Oxford & Cambridge University.

HOWE, George Edward; HM Diplomatic Service, retired; Counsellor, Foreign and Commonwealth Office, 1977–82; *b* 18 June 1925; *s* of late George Cuthbert Howe and Florence May (*née* Baston); *m* 1949, Florence Elizabeth Corrish; one *s*. *Educ:* Highbury Grammar Sch.; Westminster Coll. Served British Army, 1943; Indian Army, 2nd Bn The Burma Rifles, 1945–48 (Major). HMOCS, Malaya, 1949; joined Foreign Service, later Diplomatic Service, 1957; served Pnomn Penh, Hong Kong, Singapore, Paris, Milan and FCO. *Recreations:* fishing, shooting, military history. *Clubs:* Army and Navy, Travellers'.

HOWE, Prof. G(eorge) Melvyn, PhD, DSc; FRSE, FRGS, FRSGS, FRMetS; Professor of Geography, University of Strathclyde, 1967–85, now Emeritus; *b* Abercynon, 7 April 1920; *s* of Reuben and Edith Howe, Abercynon; *m* 1947, Patricia Graham Fennell, Pontypridd; three *d*. *Educ:* Caerphilly Boys' Grammar Sch.; UCW Aberystwyth (BSc 1940; BSc 1st cl. hons Geog. and Anthrop., 1947; MSc 1949; PhD 1957); DSc Strathclyde 1974. Served with RAF, 1940–46: Meteorological Br., 1940–42; commnd Intell. (Air Photographic Interpretation) Br., 1942–46, in Middle East Comd. Lectr, later Sen. Lectr, in Geography, UCW Aberystwyth, 1948; Reader in Geog., Univ. of Wales, 1964. Vis. Prof. (Health and Welfare, Canada), 1977. Mem. Council, Inst. of British Geographers (Pres., 1985); Mem. Medical Geography Cttee, RGS, 1960–; British Rep. on Medical Geog. Commn of IGU, 1970–; Mem., British Nat. Cttee for Geography, Royal Soc., 1978–83. Gill Memorial Award, RGS, 1964. *Publications:* Wales from the Air, 1957, 2nd edn 1966; (with P. Thomas) Welsh Landforms and Scenery, 1963; National Atlas of Disease Mortality in the United Kingdom, 1963, 2nd edn 1970; The Soviet Union, 1968, 2nd edn 1983; The USSR, 1971; Man, Environment and Disease in Britain, 1972, 2nd edn 1976; (ed and contrib.) Atlas of Glasgow and the West of Scotland, 1972; (contrib.) Wales (ed E. G. Bowen), 1958; (contrib.) Modern Methods in the History of Medicine (ed E. Clarke), 1970; (ed with J. A. Loraine, and contrib.) Environmental Medicine, 1973, 2nd edn 1980; (contrib.) Environment and Man (ed J. Lenihan and W. W. Fletcher), 1976; (ed and contrib.) A World Geography of Human Diseases, 1977; (ed and contrib.) Global Geocancerology, 1986; articles in geographical, meteorological, hydrological and medical jls. *Recreation:* travel. *Address:* Hendre, 50 Heol Croes Faen, Nottage, Porthcawl CF36 3SW. *T:* Porthcawl (01656) 772377. *Club:* Royal Air Force.

HOWE, Jack, RDI 1961; FRIBA 1953; Architect and Industrial Designer; *b* 24 Feb. 1911; *s* of Charles Henry and Florence Eleanor Howe; *m* 1960, Margaret Crosbie Corrie (*d* 1979); one *s* one *d* (by former marriage); *m* 1981, Jennifer Mary Dixon (*née* Hughes D'Aeth). *Educ:* Enfield Grammar Sch.; Polytechnic Sch. of Architecture. FSIAD 1955. Asst to E. Maxwell Fry, 1933–37; Chief Asst to Walter Gropius and Maxwell Fry, 1937–39; Drawing Office Manager to Holland, Hannan & Cubitts Ltd for Royal Ordnance Factories at Wrexham and Ranskill, 1939–43; Associate Partner, Arcon, 1944–48; private practice, 1949; Partnership with Andrew Bain, 1959–76. Architectural work includes: Highbury Quadrant Primary School, (LCC); Windmill House, Lambeth (LCC Housing Scheme); Television Research Lab. for AEI Ltd; Kodak Pavilion, Brussels Exhibn, 1958; Official Architects for British Trade Fair, Moscow, 1961; Industrial Designs include: Diesel Electric Locomotives and Express Pullman Trains; also Rly equipment. Industrial Design Consultant to various large firms and to BR Board. Mem. Design Index Cttee and Street Furniture Cttee, Design Council (formerly CoID), 1956–; Member: Cttee on Traffic Signs, Min. of Transport, 1962, 1963; Nat. Council for Diplomas in Art and Design. Pres., SIAD, 1963–64; Master of Faculty, RDI, 1975–77. Duke of Edinburgh's design prize, 1969. *Publications:* articles for various architectural and design jls. *Recreations:* music, theatre. *Address:* 4 Leopold Avenue, Wimbledon, SW19 7ET. *T:* 0181–946 7116.

HOWE, John Francis, OBE 1974; Deputy Under-Secretary of State (Civilian Management), Ministry of Defence, since 1992; *b* 29 Jan. 1944; *s* of late Frank and Marjorie Howe; *m* 1981, Angela Ephrosini (*née* Nicolaides); one *d* one step *d*. *Educ:* Shrewsbury Sch.; Balliol Coll., Oxford (Scholar; MA). Pirelli General Cable Works, 1964; joined MoD as Asst Principal, 1967; Principal, 1972; Civil Adviser to GOC NI, 1972–73; Private Sec. to Perm. Under-Sec. of State, 1975–78; Asst Sec., 1979; seconded to FCO as Defence Counsellor, UK Delegn to NATO, 1981–84; Head, Arms Control Unit, MoD, 1985–86; Private Sec. to Sec. of State for Defence, 1986–87; Asst Under-Sec. of State (Personnel and Logistics), 1988–91. *Recreations:* travel, garden labour.

HOWE, Air Vice-Marshal John Frederick George, CB 1985; CBE 1980; AFC 1961; Commandant-General, RAF Regiment and Director General of Security (RAF), 1983–85, retired; *b* 26 March 1930; *m* 1961, Annabelle Gowing; three *d*. *Educ:* St Andrew's Coll., Grahamstown, SA. SAAF, 1950–54 (served in Korea, 2nd Sqdn SAAF and 19 Inf. Regt, US Army, 1951); 222 Sqdn, Fighter Comd, 1956; 40 Commando RM, Suez Campaign, 1956; Fighter Command: Flt Comdr, 222 Sqdn, 1957; Flt Comdr, 43 Sqdn, 1957–59; Sqdn Comdr, 74 Sqdn, 1960–61; Air Staff, HQ Fighter Command, 1961–63; RAF Staff Coll., 1964; USAF Exchange Tour at Air Defence Comd HQ, Colorado Springs, 1965–67; 229 Operational Conversion Unit, RAF Chivenor, 1967–68; OC 228 OCU, Coningsby, 1968–69; Central Tactics and Trials Org., HQ Air Support Comd, 1969–70; MoD, 1970–72; Station Comdr, RAF Gutersloh, 1973–74; RCDS, 1975; Gp Capt. Ops, HQ No 11 Gp, 1975–77; Comdt, ROC, 1977–80; Comdr, Southern Maritime Air Region, 1980–83. Hon. Colonel: Field Sqns (Airfield Damage Repair) (Vol.) (South), 1988–93; 77 Engr Regt (Vol.), 1993. American DFC 1951; Air Medal 1951. *Recreations:* country pursuits, skiing, sailing. *Club:* Royal Air Force.

HOWE, Rt. Rev. John William Alexander; Assistant Bishop, diocese of Ripon, 1985–91; *b* 1920. *Educ:* Westcliff High Sch.; St Chad's Coll., Durham Univ. BA 1943; MA, BD 1948. Ordained, 1943; Curate, All Saints, Scarborough, 1943–46; Chaplain, Adisadel Coll., Gold Coast, 1946–50; Vice-Principal, Edinburgh Theological Coll., 1950–55; Hon. Chaplain, St Mary's Cathedral, Edinburgh, 1951–55; Bishop of St Andrews, Dunkeld and Dunblane, 1955–69. Hon. Canon, St Mary's Cath., Glasgow, 1969; Exec. Officer of the Anglican Communion, 1969–71; Secretary General, Anglican Consultative Council, 1971–82; Research Fellow of the Research Project, ACC, 1983–85, retd. Hon. DD:

General Theological Seminary, NY, 1974; Lambeth, 1978. *Publication:* Highways and Hedges: Anglicanism and the Universal Church, 1985. *Address:* Stuart Court, High Street, Kibworth Beauchamp, Leicester LE8 0LE. *T:* Leicester (0116) 279 6205.

HOWE, Josephine Mary O'C.; *see* O'Connor Howe.

HOWE, Martin, CB 1995; PhD; Director, Competition Policy Division, Office of Fair Trading, since 1984; *b* 9 Dec. 1936; *s* of late Leslie Wistow Howe and Dorothy Vernon Howe (*née* Taylor Farrell); *m* 1959, Anne Cicely Lawrenson; three *s*. *Educ:* Leeds Univ. (BCom (Accountancy), PhD). Asst Lectr, Lectr, Sen. Lectr, in Economics, Univ. of Sheffield, 1959–73; Senior Economic Adviser: Monopolies Commn, 1973–77; Office of Fair Trading, 1977–80; Asst Secretary, OFT and DTI, 1980–84. *Publications:* Equity Issues and the London Capital Market (with A. J. Merrett and G. D. Newbould), 1967; articles on variety of topics in learned and professional jls. *Recreations:* theatre (including amateur dramatics), cricket, gardening. *Address:* Office of Fair Trading, Field House, Breams Buildings, EC4A 1PR. *T:* 0171–242 2858.

HOWE, Ronald William; His Honour Judge Howe; a Circuit Judge, since 1991; *b* 19 June 1932; *s* of William Arthur and Lilian Mary Howe; *m* 1956, Jean Emily Goodman; three *s* one *d*. *Educ:* Morpeth Sch.; Coll. of Law, London. Admitted Solicitor, 1966; partner with Ronald Brooke & Co., Ilford, then Brooke, Garland & Howe, 1966–75; Registrar of County Court, subseq. Dist Judge, 1975–91. Mem., Judicial Studies Bd, 1990–91 (Mem., Civil and Family Cttee, 1988–91). *Recreations:* tennis, badminton, golf.

HOWE, Stephen Douglas; Editor, Farmers Weekly, since 1991; *b* 28 Feb. 1948; *m* 1971, Susan Jane Apps; one *s* one *d*. *Educ:* Brymore Sch., Somerset; Seale-Hayne Coll. (DipAgr); NDA, Dip Farm Management. Lectr in Crop Husbandry and Farm Manager, Lackham Coll. of Agric., Wilts, 1969–72; Power Farming magazine: Management Specialist, 1972–82; Managing Editor, 1982–85; Agricultural Machinery Jl, 1985–87; Editor, Crops, 1987–91. Fellow, Guild of Agricultural Journalists, 1991. *Recreations:* gardening, sailing, farming, flying. *Address:* Springfield Cottage, Byers Lane, South Godstone, Surrey RH9 8JH. *T:* South Godstone (01342) 893018. *Club:* Farmers'.

HOWELL, family name of **Baron Howell**.

HOWELL, Baron *cr* 1992 (Life Peer), of Aston Manor in the City of Birmingham; **Denis Herbert Howell;** PC 1976; *b* 4 Sept. 1923; *s* of Herbert and Bertha A. Howell; *m* 1955, Brenda Marjorie, *d* of Stephen and Ruth Willson, Birmingham; two *s* one *d* (and one *s* decd). *Educ:* Gower Street Sch.; Handsworth Grammar Sch., Birmingham. Mem., Birmingham City Council, 1946–56; Hon. Sec. Birmingham City Council Labour Group, 1950–55 (served Catering Establishment, General Purposes, Health and Watch Cttees); Chm. Catering Cttee, 1952–55; Health (Gen. Purposes) Sub-Cttee for setting up of first smokeless zones. MP (Lab): All Saints Div., Birmingham, 1955–Sept. 1959; Birmingham, Small Heath, March 1961–1992. Jt Parly Under-Sec. of State, Dept of Educn and Science (with responsibility for sport), 1964–69; Minister of State, Min. of Housing and Local Govt (with responsibility for sport), 1969–70; Opposition Spokesman for Local Govt and Sport, 1970–74; Minister of State, DoE (responsible for environment, water resources and sport), 1974–79; Opposition Spokesman on Environment (Environment and Services, Water Resources, Sport, Recreation and Countryside), 1979–83, on Home Affairs, 1983–84; Opposition front bench spokesman on the Environment (specializing in Sport), 1984–92. Opposition Defence spokesman, H of L, 1993–94. Mem., Labour Party NEC, 1982–83. Pres., Labour Movement for Europe, 1995 (Chm., 1979–95); Vice Pres., European Movt, 1979–. Member: Dudley Road Hosp. Group Management Cttee, 1948–64; the Albemarle Cttee on the Youth Service; Management Cttee, City of Birmingham Symphony Orchestra, 1950–55; Pres., Canoldir Choir, 1980–. Governor, Handsworth Grammar Sch., 1948–56. Chairman: Birmingham Assoc. of Youth Clubs, 1963–64; Birmingham Settlement, 1963–64; Sports Council, 1965–70; Youth Service Develt Council, 1964–69 (report: Youth and Community Work in the 70's); Central Council of Physical Recreation, 1973–74 (Vice Pres., 1985); Cttee of Enquiry into Sponsorship of Sport, 1981–83 (report: The Howell Report on Sports Sponsorship); St Peter's Urban Village Trust, 1985–; President: Birmingham Olympic Council, 1985–86; Middlesex Wanderers FC, 1993–; Midland Club Cricket Conf., 1993–94; Council of Cricket Socs, 1993–; Vice-President: Warwicks CCC, 1986–; Birchfield Harriers, 1987–; Aston Villa FC, 1994–. Pres., Assoc. of Professional, Exec. Clerical and Computer Staffs (APEX) (formerly CAWU), 1971–83. FIPR 1987 (MIPR 1961). Football League Referee, 1956–70. Hon. Freeman, City of Birmingham, 1991. Silver Medal, Olympic Order, 1981. Midlander of the Year Award, 1987. *Publications:* Soccer Refereeing, 1968; Made in Birmingham (autobiog.), 1990. *Recreations:* sport, theatre, music. *Address:* 33 Moor Green Lane, Moseley, Birmingham B13 8NE. *Clubs:* Reform; Warwickshire County Cricket (Birmingham); Birmingham Press.

HOWELL, Rt. Hon. David Arthur Russell; PC 1979; MP (C) Guildford since 1966; journalist and economic consultant; *b* 18 Jan. 1936; *s* of late Colonel A. H. E. Howell, DSO, TD, DL and Beryl Howell, 5 Headfort Place, SW1; *m* 1967, Davina Wallace; one *s* two *d*. *Educ:* Eton; King's Coll., Cambridge. BA 1st class hons Cantab, 1959. Lieut Coldstream Guards, 1954–56. Joined Economic Section of Treasury, 1959; resigned, 1960. Leader-Writer and Special Correspondent, The Daily Telegraph, 1960; Chm. of Bow Gp, 1961–62; Editor of Crossbow, 1962–64; contested (C) Dudley, 1964. A Lord Comr of Treasury, 1970–71; Parly Sec., CSD, 1970–72; Parly Under-Sec.: Dept of Employment, 1971–72; NI Office, March–Nov. 1972; Minister of State: NI Office, 1972–74; Dept of Energy, 1974; Secretary of State: for Energy, 1979–81; for Transport, 1981–83. Chairman: Select Cttee on Foreign Affairs, 1987–; Cons. One Nation Gp, 1987–; UK-Japan 2000 Group, 1990–. Sen. Vis. Fellow, PSI, 1983–85; Vis. Fellow, Nuffield Coll., Oxford, 1993–. Dir of Conservative Political Centre, 1964–66. Director: Trafalgar House, 1990–; Jardine Insurance Brokers, 1991–; Monks Investment Trust, 1993–. Mem., Internat. Adv. Council, Swiss Bank Corp., 1988–. *Publications:* (co-author) Principles in Practice, 1960; The Conservative Opportunity, 1965; Freedom and Capital, 1981; Blind Victory: a study in income, wealth and power, 1986; various pamphlets and articles. *Recreations:* writing, DIY, golf. *Address:* House of Commons, SW1A 0AA. *Club:* Buck's.

HOWELL, Air Vice-Marshal Evelyn Michael Thomas, CBE 1961; CEng, FRAeS; *b* 11 Sept. 1913; *s* of Sir Evelyn Berkeley Howell, KCIE, CSI; *m* 1st, 1937, Helen Joan, *o d* of late Brig. W. M. Hayes, CBE, FRICS (marr. diss. 1972); one *s* three *d*; 2nd, 1972, Rosemary, *e d* of I. A. Cram, CEng, MICE; one *s* one *d*. *Educ:* Downside Sch.; RAF Coll., Cranwell. Commissioned, 1934; Dir of Air Armament Research and Devt, Min. of Aviation, 1960–62; Comdt, RAF Techn. Coll., 1963–65; SASO, HQ Technical Training Command RAF, 1966–67; retired, 1967. Gen. Manager, Van Dusen Aircraft Supplies, Oxford, Minneapolis, St Louis, Helsingborg, 1967–79. Mem. Livery of Clothworkers' Co., 1938. *Recreations:* swimming, conservation, boating. *Address:* 47 Captain French Lane, Kendal, Cumbria LA9 4HP. *Club:* Royal Air Force.

HOWELL, Gareth, CBE 1993; PhD; CChem; Director, British Council, Malaysia, 1990–95; *b* 22 April 1935; *s* of Amwel John and Sarah Blodwen Howell; *m* 1957, Margaret Patricia Ashelford; one *s* two *d*. *Educ:* Ferndale Grammar Sch., Rhondda; University College London; Inst. of Education, Univ. of London. BSc, PhD; PGCE London. MRSC. Asst Master, Canford Sch., Wimborne, Dorset, 1957–61; Lectr, Norwich City Coll., 1961–65; British Council: Science Educn Officer, London, 1965–66; Science Educn Officer, Nigeria, 1966–70; Head, Science Educn Section, 1970–74; Director, Science and Technology Dept, 1974; Representative, Malawi, 1974–76; on secondment to Min. of Overseas Development as Educn Adviser, 1976–79; Counsellor and Dep. Educn Adviser, British Council Div., British High Commn, India, 1979–83; Controller: Sci., Technol. and Educn Div., 1983–87; Americas, Pacific and E Asia Div., 1987–90. *Recreations:* photography, philately, gardening, tennis, running, travel. *Address:* 9 Alderway, West Cross, Swansea SA3 5PD.

HOWELL, Gwynne Richard; Principal Bass, Royal Opera House, since 1971; *b* Gorseinon, S Wales, 13 June 1938; *s* of Gilbert and Ellaline Howell; *m* 1968, Mary Edwina Morris; two *s*. *Educ:* Pontardawe Grammar Sch.; Univ. of Wales, Swansea (BSc; Hon. Fellow 1986); Manchester Univ. (DipTP); MRTPI 1966. Studied singing with Redvers Llewellyn while at UCW; pt-time student, Manchester RCM, with Gwilym Jones, during DipTP trng at Manchester Univ.; studied with Otakar Kraus, 1968–72. Planning Asst, Kent CC, 1961–63; Sen. Planning Officer, Manchester Corp., 1965–68, meanwhile continuing to study music pt-time and giving public operatic performances which incl. the rôle of Pogner, in Die Meistersinger; as a result of this rôle, apptd Principal Bass at Sadler's Wells, 1968; also reached final of BBC Opera Singers competition for N of Eng., 1967. In first season at Sadler's Wells, sang 8 rôles, incl. Monterone and the Commendatore; appearances with Hallé Orch., 1968 and 1969; Arkel in Pelleas and Melisande, Glyndebourne and Covent Garden, 1969; Goffredo, in Il Pirato, 1969. *Royal Opera House, Covent Garden:* début as First Nazarene, Salome, 1969–70 season; the King, in Aida; Timur, in Turandot; Mephisto, in Damnation of Faust; Prince Gremin, in Eugene Onegin; High Priest, in Nabucco; Reinmar, in Tannhauser, 1973–74 (later rôle, Landgraf); Colline, in La Boheme; Pimen, in Boris Godunov; Ribbing, Un ballo in maschera; Padre Guardiano, in La forza del destino; Hobson, in Peter Grimes, 1975; Sparafucile, in Rigoletto, 1975–76 season; Ramfis in Aida, 1977; Tristan und Isolde, 1978, 1982; Luisa Miller, 1978; Samson et Delilah, 1981; Fiesco in Simon Boccanegra, 1981; Pogner in Die Meistersinger, 1982; Arkell in Pelléas et Mélisande, 1982; Dossifei in Khovanshchina, 1982; Semele, 1982; Die Zauberflöte, 1983; Raimondo, in Lucia di Lammermoor, 1985; Rocco in Fidelio, 1986; Marcel in Les Huguenots, 1991; Daland in Der Fliegende Holländer, 1992; Katya Kabanova, 1994; Stiffelio, 1995; *English National Opera:* Don Carlos, Die Meistersinger, 1974–75; The Magic Flute, Don Carlos, 1975–76; Duke Bluebeard's Castle, 1978, 1991; The Barber of Seville, 1980; Tristan and Isolde, 1981; Hans Sachs in Die Meistersinger, 1984; Parsifal, 1986; Don Carlos, 1992; Banquo in Macbeth, 1993; *Metropolitan Opera House, New York:* début as Lódovico in Otello, and Pogner in Die Meistersinger, 1985; *sacred music:* Verdi and Mozart Requiems, Missa Solemnis, St Matthew and St John Passions; sings in Europe and USA; records for BBC and for major recording companies. *Recreations:* tennis, squash, golf, Rugby enthusiast, gardening. *Address:* 197 Fox Lane, N13 4BB. *T:* 0181–886 1981.

HOWELL, Prof. John Bernard Lloyd, CBE 1991; Chairman: Southampton and SW Hampshire District Health Authority, since 1983; Southampton and SW Hampshire Health Commission, since 1992; Foundation Professor of Medicine, University of Southampton, 1969–91, now Emeritus (Dean of the Faculty of Medicine, 1978–83); Hon. Consultant Physician, Southampton General Hospital, 1969–92, now Emeritus; *b* 1 Aug. 1926; *s* of late David John Howells and Hilda Mary Hill, Ynystawe, Swansea; *m* 1952, Heather Joan Rolfe; two *s* one *d*. *Educ:* Swansea Grammar Sch.; Middx Hosp. Med. Sch. (Meyerstein Scholar 1946). BSc, MB, BS, PhD; FRCP. House Officer posts, Middx and Brompton Hosps; MO RAMC, 1952–54; Lectr in Physiol Medicine, 1954–56, in Pharmacol Medicine, 1958–60, Middlesex Hosp. Med. Sch.; Manchester Royal Infirmary: Sen. Lectr in Medicine and Hon. Consultant Physician, 1960–66; Consultant Physician, 1966–69. Eli Lilly Travelling Fellow, Johns Hopkins Hospital, 1957–58; Goulstonian Lectr, RCP, 1966. Member: Physiol Soc., 1956–; Med. Res. Soc., 1956–; Assoc. of Physicians of GB and Ire., 1964–; GMC, 1978–83. President: British Thoracic Soc., 1988–89; BMA, 1989–90 (Chm., Bd of Sci. and Educn, 1991–). Hon. Life Mem., Canadian Thoracic Soc., 1978; Hon. FACP 1982. *Publications:* (ed jtly) Breathlessness, 1966; chapters in: Cecil and Loeb's Textbook of Medicine, 13th edn 1970, 14th edn 1974; Recent Advances in Chest Medicine, 1976; Thoracic Medicine, 1981; Oxford Textbook of Medicine, 1982; scientific papers on respiratory physiology and medicine. *Recreations:* DIY, wine. *Address:* The Coach House, Bassett Wood Drive, Southampton SO2 3PT. *T* and *Fax:* Southampton (01703) 768878.

HOWELL, John Frederick; Director, Overseas Development Institute, since 1987; Visiting Professor in Agricultural Development, Wye College, University of London, since 1988; *b* 16 July 1941; *s* of Frederick John Howell and late Glenys Howell (*née* Griffiths); *m* 1993, Paula Wade; two *s*, and one step *s*. *Educ:* Univ. of Wales (BA Hons 1963); Univ. of Manchester (MA Econ. Dist. 1965); Univ. of Reading, (external; PhD). Lectr, Univ. of Khartoum, 1966–73; correspondent, Africa Confidential, 1971–75; Sen. Lectr and Head of Pol. and Admin. Studies, Univ. of Zambia, 1973–77; Res. Fellow, 1977–84, Dep. Dir, 1984–87, ODI. Vis Lectr, Mananga Agric. Management Centre, Swaziland, 1978–80; Consultant on aid and agricl develt: World Bank; FAO; Commonwealth Secretariat; ODA in India, Nepal, Nigeria, Brazil, Tanzania, Sudan; Adviser: All-Party Parly Gp on Overseas Develt, 1985–86; Princess Royal's Africa Review Gp, 1987–89. Mem. Council, VSO, 1991–. Pres., UK Chapter, Soc. of Internat. Develt, 1991–93. Co-editor, Develt Policy Review, 1985–87. *Publications:* Local Government and Politics in the Sudan, 1974; (ed) Borrowers and Lenders: rural financial markets and institutions in developing countries, 1980; Administering Agricultural Development for Small Farmers, 1981; (ed) Recurrent Costs and Agricultural Development, 1985; (ed) Agricultural Extension in Practice, 1988; (with Alex Duncan) Structural Adjustment and the African Farmer, 1992. *Recreations:* cricket, gardening, modern jazz, Arsenal FC. *Address:* Overseas Development Institute, Regent's College, Inner Circle, Regent's Park, NW1 4NS. *T:* 0171–487 7413.

HOWELL, Maj.-Gen. Lloyd, CBE 1972; Consultant, Technical Education Development, University College, Cardiff, 1980–86 (Fellow, 1981); *b* 28 Dec. 1923; *s* of Thomas Idris Howell and Anne Howell; *m* 1st, 1945, Hazel Barker (*d* 1974); five *s* three *d*; 2nd, 1975, Elizabeth June Buchanan Husband (*née* Atkinson); two step *s*. *Educ:* Barry Grammar Sch.; University Coll. of S Wales and Monmouthshire (BSc); Royal Military Coll. of Science. CEng, MRAeS. Commissioned RA, 1944; Field Regt, RA, E Africa, 1945–46; Staff, Divl HQ, Palestine, 1946–47; RAEC 1949; Instr, RMA Sandhurst, 1949–53; TSO II Trials Estabt, 1954–57; SO II (Educn), Divl HQ, BAOR, 1957–59; DS, Royal Mil. Coll. of Science, 1960–64; SEO, Army Apprentices Coll., 1964–67; Headmaster/Comdg, Duke of York's Royal Mil. Sch., 1967–72; Col (Ed), MoD (Army), 1972–74; Chief Educn Officer, HQ UKLF, 1974–76; Dir, Army Educn, 1976–80. Col Comdt, RAEC, 1982–86. Dir (non-exec.), Building Trades Exhibitions Ltd, 1980–93. Mem. Council, CGLI, 1977–90; Mem., Ct of Governors, University of Wales Coll., Cardiff, 1980–. Hon. MA Open Univ., 1980. *Recreations:* gardening, golf, reading. *Address:* c/o Midland Bank, The Forum, Old Town, Swindon, Wilts SN3 1QT.

HOWELL, Michael Edward, CMG 1989; OBE 1980; HM Diplomatic Service; High Commissioner, Mauritius, 1989–93; *b* 2 May 1933; *s* of Edward and Fanny Howell; *m* 1958; Joan Little; one *s* one *d. Educ:* Newport High Sch. Served RAF, 1951–53. Colonial Office, 1953; CRO, 1958; Karachi, 1959; 2nd Secretary: Bombay, 1962; UK Delegn to Disarmament Cttee, Geneva, 1966; 1st Sec. (Parly Clerk), FCO, 1969; Consul (Comm.), New York, 1973; ndc 1975; FCO, 1976; Hd of Chancery, later Chargé d'Affaires, Kabul, 1978; Consul-General: Berlin, 1981; Frankfurt, 1983; High Comr to Papua New Guinea, 1986. *Recreation:* tennis. *Address:* c/o Foreign and Commonwealth Office, SW1A 2AH.

HOWELL, Patrick Leonard; QC 1990; *b* 4 Dec. 1942; *s* of Leonard Howell, MC, and Mary Isobel (*née* Adam); *m* 1966, Sandra Marie McColl; two *s* one *d. Educ:* Radley; Christ Church, Oxford (MA); London Sch. of Econs and Pol Science (LLM). Called to the Bar: Inner Temple, 1966; Lincoln's Inn, 1968. Teaching Fellow, Osgoode Hall Law Sch., Toronto, 1965–66. Social Security Comr and Child Support Comr, 1994–. *Recreation:* building things. *Address:* Office of the Social Security Commissioners, 83 Farringdon Street, EC4A 4DH. *T:* 0171–353 5145.

HOWELL, Paul Frederic; farmer; *b* 17 Jan. 1951; *s* of Sir Ralph Howell, *qv*; *m* 1987, Johanna Youlten Turnbull; two *s. Educ:* Gresham's Sch., Holt, Norfolk; St Edmund Hall, Oxford (BA Agric. and Econ.). Conservative Research Dept, 1973–75. MEP (C) Norfolk, 1979–94; contested (C) Eur. Parly elecns, 1994. Mem., Agricl, Foreign Affairs and Fisheries Cttees, European Parlt, 1979–94; spokesman for EDG: on youth culture, educn, information and sport, 1984–86; on agriculture, 1989–92; on fisheries, 1989–94; Mem. and EDG spokesman, Regl Cttee, 1992–94; Member, European Parliament's delegation: to Central America, 1987–94; to Soviet Union, 1989–91; to CIS, 1991–94; to Russia, Ukraine, Georgia, Armenia and Azerbaijan, 1993–94; Vice-Chm., Europ. Parlt/Comecon Delegn, 1984; Pres., Council of Centre for Eur. Educn, 1985–87. Mem. Council, and Trustee, RSPB, 1992–95; Trustee, Nuffield Russia Trust, 1991–. *Recreations:* all sports. *Address:* The White House Farm, Bradenham Road, Scarning, East Dereham, Norfolk NR19 2LA.

HOWELL, Peter Adrian; Senior Lecturer, Department of Classics, Royal Holloway and Bedford New College, University of London, since 1994 (Lecturer, 1985–94); *b* 29 July 1941; *s* of Lt-Col Harry Alfred Adrian Howell, MBE and Madge Maud Mary, *d* of Major-Gen. R. L. B. Thompson, CB, CMG, DSO. *Educ:* Downside School; Balliol College, Oxford (BA 1963; MA; MPhil 1966). Asst Lectr and Lectr, Dept of Latin, Bedford Coll., Univ. of London, 1964–85. Dep. Chm., Jt Cttee, Nat. Amenity Socs, 1991–93; Member: Cttee, Victorian Soc., 1968– (Chm., 1987–93); Westminster Cathedral Art Cttee, 1974–91, 1993–; Dept of Art and Architecture, Liturgy Commn, RC Bishops' Conf., 1977–84; Churches Cttee, English Heritage, 1984–88. *Publications:* Victorian Churches, 1968; (with Elisabeth Beazley) Companion Guide to North Wales, 1975; (with Elisabeth Beazley) Companion Guide to South Wales, 1977; A Commentary on Book I of the Epigrams of Martial, 1980; (ed with Ian Sutton) The Faber Guide to Victorian Churches, 1989; articles in Architectural History, Country Life. *Recreations:* art, architecture, music. *Address:* 127 Banbury Road, Oxford OX2 6JX. *T:* Oxford (01865) 515050.

HOWELL, Sir Ralph (Frederic), Kt 1993; MP (C) North Norfolk since 1970; *b* 25 May 1923; *m* 1950, Margaret (*née* Bone); two *s* one *d. Educ:* Diss Grammar Sch., Norfolk. Navigator/Bomb-aimer, RAF, 1941–46; farmer, 1946–. Mem., European Parlt, 1974–79. Member: Treasury and Civil Service Select Cttee, 1981–87; Select Cttee on Employment, 1994–. Vice-Chm., Cons. Parly Finance Cttee, 1979–84; Chairman: Cons. Parly Employment Cttee, 1984–87; Cons. Parly Agriculture Cttee, 1988; Mem. Exec., 1922 Cttee, 1984–90; Mem., Council of Europe and WEU, 1987–. *Publications:* Why Work, 1976, 2nd edn 1981; Why Not Work, 1991. *Address:* Wendling Grange, Dereham, Norfolk NR19 2NH. *Clubs:* Carlton, Farmers'.
See also P. F. Howell.

HOWELLS, family name of **Baron Geraint**.

HOWELLS, Anne, (Mrs Stafford Dean), FRMCM (ARMCM); opera, concert and recital singer; *b* 12 Jan. 1941; *d* of Trevor William Howells and Mona Hewart; *m* 1st, 1966, Ryland Davies, *qv* (marr. diss. 1981); 2nd, 1981, Stafford Dean; one *s* one *d. Educ:* Sale County Grammar Sch.; Royal Manchester Coll. of Music. Three seasons (Chorus), with Glyndebourne, 1964–66; at short notice, given star rôle there, in Cavalli's L'Ormindo, 1967; rôles, there, also include: Dorabella in Così fan Tutte; Cathleen in (world première of) Nicholas Maw's Rising of the Moon, 1970; also the Composer in Ariadne; Diana in Calisto; Unitel Film of Salzburg prodn of Mozart's Clemenza di Tito. Royal Opera House, Covent Garden: under contract for three years, 1969–71. Rôles include: Lena in (world première of) Richard Rodney Bennett's Victory; Rosina in Barber of Seville; Cherubino in Marriage of Figaro; Der Rosenkavalier (video recording), 1985. Currently, 1973–, Guest artist with Royal Opera House. Recitals in Brussels and Vienna; operatic guest performances in Chicago, Metropolitan (NY), San Francisco, Geneva, Brussels, Salzburg, Amsterdam, Hamburg (W German début), W Berlin, Paris; sings with Scottish Opera, English Nat. Opera, major orchestras in UK. *Recreations:* cinema, tennis, reading. *Address:* c/o Harrison Parrott, 12 Penzance Place, W11 4PA.

HOWELLS, Sir Eric (Waldo Benjamin), Kt 1993; CBE 1986; farmer and landowner, since 1966; *b* 9 Aug. 1933; *s* of Vincent Vaughan Howells and Amy (*née* Jones); *m* 1960, Margaret Maisie Edwards; one *s* twin *d.* Sec. and Gen. Manager of a limited co., 1959–66; former Chm., Pembrokeshire NFU; Councillor for 28 years, Llanddewi Velfrey Council (Chm. 4 times); Pres., Wales Cons. Area Exec. Cttee, 1994– (Mem., 1979–; Chm., 1988–93); Chm., Wales Cons. European Co-ordinating Cttee, 1992–; Mem. of numerous other local and nat. Cons. bodies; broadcaster in English and Welsh. *Recreations:* music, bee keeping, DIY, reading. *Address:* Upper Fron, Llanddewi Velfrey, Narberth, Dyfed SA67 7EJ. *T:* Whitland (01994) 240205.

HOWELLS, Dr Gwyn, CB 1979; MD; FRCP, FRACP; Director-General and Permanent Head, Federal Department of Health, Canberra, Australia, 1973–83; Chairman, Cochlear Pty Ltd, Sydney, since 1984; Director, Nucleus Ltd, Sydney, since 1984; *b* 13 May 1918; *s* of Albert Henry and Ruth Winifred Howells; *m* 1942, Simone Maufe; two *s* two *d. Educ:* University College Sch., London; St Bartholomew's Hosp., Univ. of London (MB BS 1942, MD 1950). MRCS 1941; FRCP 1974 (MRCP 1950, LRCP 1941); FRACP 1971 (MRACP 1967). Cons. Phys., Thoracic Annexe, Toowoomba, Qld, Aust.; Chest Phys., Toowoomba Gen. Hosp., Qld, 1957–66; Federal Dept of Health, Canberra: First Asst Director-General, 1966–73; Dep. Dir-Gen., Feb.-Sept. 1973. Chairman, Nat. Health and Med. Res. Council, 1973–83; Director of Quarantine for Australia, 1973–83. *Publications:* several articles in Lancet, BMJ, Aust. Med. Jl and other specialist jls. *Recreations:* squash, tennis, reading. *Address:* 23 Beauchamp Street, Deakin, ACT 2600, Australia. *T:*(6) 2812575. *Clubs:* Commonwealth, National Tennis and Squash Centre (Canberra).

HOWELLS, Kim Scott, PhD; MP (Lab) Pontypridd, since Feb. 1989; *b* 27 Nov. 1946; *s* of Glanville James and Joan Glenys Howells; *m* 1983, Eirlys Howells (*née* Davies); two *s* one *d. Educ:* Mountain Ash Grammar Sch.; Hornsey College of Art; Cambridge College of Advanced Technology (BA (Jt Hons)); Warwick Univ. (PhD). Steel-worker, 1969–70; Coal-miner, 1970–71; Lectr, 1975–79; Research Officer: Swansea Univ., 1979–82; NUM, S Wales Area, 1982–89. Opposition Front bench spokesman on aid and develt, 1993–, on foeign affairs, 1994, on home affairs, 1994–. *Recreations:* climbing, jazz, cinema, literature. *Address:* 30 Berw Road, Pontypridd, Mid-Glamorgan CF37 2AA. *Clubs:* Llantwit Fadre Cricket, Pontypridd Rugby Football (Pontypridd); Hopkinstown Cricket (Pontypridd).

HOWES, Prof. Christopher Kingston, CB 1993; Second Commissioner and Chief Executive of the Crown Estate, since 1989; *b* 30 Jan. 1942; *yr s* of Leonard Howes, OBE and Marion Howes (*née* Bussey); *m* 1967, Clare Cunliffe; two *s* one *d* (and one *d* decd). *Educ:* Gresham's Sch.; LSE; Coll. of Estate Management (BSc 1965); Univ. of Reading (MPhil 1976). ARICS 1967, FRICS 1977. Valuation and Planning Depts, GLC, 1965–67; Partner and Sen. Partner, Chartered Surveyors, Norwich, 1967–79; Department of the Environment: Dep. Dir, Land Economy, 1979–81; Chief Estates Officer, 1981–85; Dir, Land and Property Div., 1985–89. Sen. Vis. Fellow, Sch. of Envtl Scis, UEA, 1975; Vis. Lectr, Univs of Reading, 1976, Aberdeen 1980–; Vis. Prof., Bartlett Sch. of Architecture and Planning. UCL, 1984–. Mem., Sec. of State for the Envmt's Thames Adv. Cttee, 1995–. Member: CNAA Surveying Bd, 1978–82; Planning and Develt Divl Council, RICS, 1983–92; Policy Review Cttee, RICS, 1984–90; Norfolk Archaeological Trust, 1979–; HRH Prince of Wales's Council, 1990–; Council, British Property Fedn, 1992–. Hon. Mem., Cambridge Univ. Land Soc., 1989–. Founder Mem., Norwich Third World Centre, 1970; dir of various housing assocs, 1970–80; Dir, Theatre Royal Trust, 1969–79; Steward and Hon Surveyor to Dean and Chapter, Norwich Cathedral, 1973–79; Member: Court of Advisers, St Paul's Cathedral, 1980–; Court, UEA, 1992–; Council, Duchy of Lancaster, 1993–. Mem., Court of Advisers, HRH The Prince of Wales's Inst. of Architecture, 1992–. Norwich CC, 1969–73; JP Norfolk 1973–80. Hon. FRIBA 1995. Mem. of various editorial bds. *Publications:* (jtly) Acquiring Office Space, 1975; Value Maps: aspects of land and property values, 1979; Economic Regeneration (monograph), 1988; Urban Revitalization (monograph), 1988; papers on land and property policy in learned jls. *Recreations:* music, art, architecture, sailing. *Address:* Highfield House, Woldingham, Surrey CR3 7BE; Flint Cottage, Aldeburgh, Suffolk. *Clubs:* Athenæum; Norfolk (Norwich); Aldeburgh Yacht; Aldeburgh Golf.

HOWES, Sally Ann; actress (stage, film and television); *b* 20 July; *d* of late Bobby Howes; *m* 1958, Richard Adler (marr. diss.); *m* 1969, Andrew Maree (marr. diss.). *Educ:* Glendower, London; Queenswood, Herts; privately. *Films include:* Thursday's Child; Halfway House; Dead of Night; Nicholas Nickleby; Anna Karenina; My Sister and I; Fools Rush In; History of Mr Polly; Stop Press Girl; Honeymoon Deferred; The Admirable Crichton; Chitty, Chitty Bang Bang. First appeared West End stage in (revue) Fancy Free, at Prince of Wales's, and at Royal Variety Performance, 1950. *Stage Shows include:* Caprice (musical debut); Paint Your Wagon; Babes in the Wood; Romance by Candlelight; Summer Song; Hatful of Rain; My Fair Lady; Kwamina, NY; What Makes Sammy Run?, NY; Brigadoon (revival), NY City Center, 1962; Sound of Music, Los Angeles and San Francisco, 1972; Lover, St Martin's; The King and I, Adelphi, 1973, Los Angeles and San Francisco, 1974; Hans Andersen, Palladium, 1977; Hamlet (tour), 1983. Has appeared on television: in England from 1949 (Short and Sweet Series, Sally Ann Howes Show, etc); in USA from 1958 (Dean Martin Show, Ed Sullivan Show, Mission Impossible, Marcus Welby MD); Play of the Week; Panel Shows: Hollywood Squares; Password; Bell Telephone Hour; US Steel Hour, etc. *Recreations:* reading, riding, theatre.

HOWICK OF GLENDALE, 2nd Baron *cr* 1960; **Charles Evelyn Baring;** a Director, Northern Rock Building Society, since 1987; a Managing Director, Baring Brothers & Co. Ltd, 1969–82; *b* 30 Dec. 1937; *s* of 1st Baron Howick of Glendale, KG, GCMG, KCVO, and of Lady Mary Cecil Grey, *er d* of 5th Earl Grey; *S* father, 1973; *m* 1964, Clare Nicolette, *y d* of Col Cyril Darby; one *s* three *d. Educ:* Eton; New Coll., Oxford. Director: The London Life Association Ltd, 1972–82; Swan Hunter Group Ltd, 1972–79. Member: Exec. Cttee, Nat. Art Collections Fund, 1973–86; Council, Friends of Tate Gall., 1973–78. Council, Baring Foundn, 1982–. Dir. Chelsea Physic Garden, 1994–. *Heir: s* Hon. David Evelyn Charles Baring, *b* 26 March 1975. *Address:* Howick, Alnwick, Northumberland NE66 3LB. *T:* Longhoughton (01665) 577624; 42 Bedford Gardens, W8. *T:* 0171–221 0880.
See also Sir E. H. T. Wakefield.

HOWIE, family name of **Baron Howie of Troon.**

HOWIE OF TROON, Baron *cr* 1978 (Life Peer), of Troon in the District of Kyle and Carrick; **William Howie;** civil engineer, publisher, journalist; Director (Internal Relations), Thomas Telford Ltd, since 1987 (General Manager, 1976–87); *b* Troon, Ayrshire, 2 March 1924; *er s* of late Peter and Annie Howie, Troon; *m* 1951, Mairi Margaret, *o d* of late Martha and John Sanderson, Troon; two *d* two *s. Educ:* Marr Coll., Troon; Royal Technical Coll., Glasgow (BSc, Diploma). MP (Lab) Luton, Nov. 1963–70; Asst Whip, 1964–66; Lord Comr of the Treasury, 1966–67; Comptroller, HM Household, 1967–68. A Vice-Chm., Parly Labour Party, 1968–70. MICE 1951, FICE 1984; Member: Council, Instn of Civil Engineers, 1964–67; Cttee of Inquiry into the Engineering Profession, 1977–80; President: Assoc. of Supervisory and Exec. Engrs, 1980–85; Assoc. for Educnl and Trng Technol., 1982–93; Indep. Publishers Guild, 1987–93; Vice-Pres., PPA, 1990–. Member: Governing Body, Imperial Coll. of Science and Technology, 1965–67; Pro-Chancellor, City Univ., 1984–91 (Mem. Council 1968–91). MSocIS (France), 1978. Hon. FIStructE 1995. Hon. DSc City Univ., 1992; Hon. LLD Strathclyde, 1994. *Publications:* (jtly) Public Sector Purchasing, 1968; Trade Unions and the Professional Engineer, 1977; Trade Unions in Construction, 1981; (ed jtly) Thames Tunnel to Channel Tunnel, 1987. *Recreation:* opera. *Address:* 34 Temple Fortune Lane, NW11 7UL. *T:* 0181–455 0492. *Clubs:* Luton Labour, Lighthouse, Architecture.

HOWIE, Prof. Archibald, PhD; FRS 1978; Professor of Physics, since 1986, and Head of Department, since 1989, Cavendish Laboratory, University of Cambridge; Fellow of Churchill College, Cambridge, since 1960; *b* 8 March 1934; *s* of Robert Howie and Margaret Marshall McDonald; *m* 1964, Melva Jean Scott; one *d* (one *s* decd). *Educ:* Kirkcaldy High Sch.; Univ. of Edinburgh (BSc); California Inst. of Technology (MS); Univ. of Cambridge (PhD). English Speaking Union, King George VI Memorial Fellow (at Calif. Inst. of Technology), 1956–57; Cambridge University: Research Scholar, Trinity Coll., 1957–60; Research Fellow, Churchill Coll., 1960–61; Cavendish Laboratory: ICI Research Fellow, 1960–61; Demonstrator in Physics, 1961–65; Lecturer, 1965–79; Reader, 1979–86. Visiting Scientist, Nat. Research Council, Canada, 1966–67; Vis. Prof. of Physics, Univ. of Aarhus, Denmark, 1974. Hon. FRMS 1978 (Pres., 1984–86); Hon. FRSE 1995. Hon. Dr (Physics), Bologna, 1989. (Jtly with M. J. Whelan): C. V. Boys Prize, Inst. of Physics, 1965; Hughes Medal, Royal Soc., 1988; Distinguished Scientist Award, Electron Microscopy Soc. of America, 1991; Guthrie Medal, Inst. of Physics, 1992. *Publications:* (co-author) Electron Microscopy of Thin Crystals, 1965, 2nd edn 1977; papers on electron microscopy and diffraction in scientific jls. *Recreations:* gardening, wine-making. *Address:* 194 Huntingdon Road, Cambridge CB3 0LB. *T:* Cambridge (01223) 570977.

HOWIE, Prof. John Garvie Robertson, MD, PhD; FRCGP; FRCPE; Professor of General Practice, University of Edinburgh, since 1980; *b* 23 Jan. 1937; *s* of Sir James Howie and of Isabella Winifred Mitchell, BSc; *m* 1962, Elizabeth Margaret Donald; two *s* one *d*. *Educ:* High School of Glasgow; Univ. of Glasgow (MD); PhD Aberdeen. House officer, 1961–62; Laboratory medicine, 1962–66; General practitioner, Glasgow, 1966–70; Lectr/Sen. Lectr in General Practice, Univ. of Aberdeen, 1970–80. *Publications:* Research in General Practice, 1979, 2nd edn 1989; articles on appendicitis, prescribing and general medical practice and education, in various jls. *Recreations:* golf, gardening, music. *Address:* 4 Ravelrig Park, Balerno, Midlothian EH14 7DL. *T:* 0131–449 6305.

HOWIE, Prof. John Mackintosh, CBE 1993; Regius Professor of Mathematics, University of St Andrews, since 1970; Dean, Faculty of Science, 1976–79; *b* 23 May 1936; *s* of Rev. David Y. Howie and Janet McD. Howie (*née* Mackintosh); *m* 1960, Dorothy Joyce Mitchell Miller; two *d*. *Educ:* Robert Gordon's Coll., Aberdeen; Univ. of Aberdeen; Balliol Coll., Oxford. MA, DPhil, DSc; FRSE 1971. Asst in Mathematics: Aberdeen Univ., 1958–59; Glasgow Univ., 1961–63; Lectr in Mathematics, Glasgow Univ., 1963–67; Visiting Asst Prof., Tulane Univ., 1964–65; Sen. Lectr in Mathematics, Stirling Univ., 1967–70; Visiting Professor: Monash Univ., 1979; N Illinois Univ., 1988. Mem., Cttee to Review Examination Arrangements (Dunning Cttee), 1975–77; Chairman: Scottish Central Cttee on Mathematics, 1975–82; Cttee to Review Curriculum and Exams in Fifth and Sixth Years (Howie Cttee), Scottish Office Educn Dept, 1990–92. Vice-Pres., London Mathematical Soc., 1984–86. Chm., Bd of Governors, Dundee Coll. of Educn, 1983–87. Keith Prize for 1979–81, RSE, 1982. *Publications:* An Introduction to Semigroup Theory, 1976; Automata and Languages, 1991; Fundamentals of Semigroup Theory, 1995; articles in British and foreign mathematical jls. *Recreations:* music, gardening. *Address:* Mathematical Institute, North Haugh, St Andrews, Fife KY16 9SS. *T:* St Andrews (01334) 76161.

HOWIE, Prof. Robert Andrew, PhD, ScD; FGS; FKC; Lyell Professor of Geology, Royal Holloway and Bedford New College, University of London, 1985–87, now Emeritus Professor of Mineralogy; *b* 4 June 1923; *s* of Robert Howie; *m* 1952, Honor Eugenie, *d* of Robert Taylor; two *s*. *Educ:* Bedford Sch.; Trinity Coll., Cambridge (MA, PhD, ScD). FGS 1950. Served War, RAF, 1941–46. Research, Dept of Mineralogy and Petrology, Univ. of Cambridge, 1950–53; Lectr in Geology, Manchester Univ., 1953–62; King's College, London: Reader in Geol., 1962–72; Prof. of Mineralogy, 1972–85; Fellow 1980; Dean, Faculty of Science, Univ. of London, 1979–83; Chairman: Academic Council, Univ. of London, 1983–86; Computer Policy Cttee, Univ. of London, 1987–93; Vice-Chm., Bd of Management, Univ. of London Computer Centre, 1989–93. Mem., Commonwealth Scholarships Commn, 1988–. Geological Society: Mem. Council, 1968–71, 1972–76; Vice-Pres., 1973–75. Mineralogical Society: Mem. Council, 1958–61, 1963–; Gen. Sec., 1965; Vice-Pres., 1975–77; Pres., 1978–80; Managing Trustee, 1978–87. Fellow, Mineral Soc. of America, 1962. Member: Council, Internat. Mineral Assoc., 1974–82; Senate, Univ. of London, 1974–78, 1980–90; Court, Univ. of London, 1984–89. Hon. Mem., Mineralogical Soc. of India, 1973, of USSR, 1982, of France, 1986, of Bulgaria, 1991. Murchison Medal, Geol Soc., 1976. Editor, Mineralogical Abstracts, 1966–. *Publications:* Rock-forming Minerals (with Prof. W. A. Deer and Prof. J. Zussman), 5 vols, 1962–63 (2nd edn, 1978–); An Introduction to the Rock-forming Minerals, 1966, 2nd edn 1992; scientific papers dealing with charnockites and with silicate mineralogy. *Recreations:* mineral collecting, writing abstracts. *Address:* Ashcroft, Glebe Close, Church Street, Bonsall, Matlock, Derbyshire DE4 2AE. *Club:* Geological.

HOWITT, Anthony Wentworth; Senior Consultancy Partner, Peat, Marwick, Mitchell & Co., Management Consultants, 1957–84; *b* 7 Feb. 1920; *o s* of late Sir Harold Gibson Howitt, GBE, DSO, MC, and late Dorothy Radford; *m* 1951, June Mary Brent. *Educ:* Uppingham; Trinity Coll., Cambridge (MA). FCA, FCMA, JDipMA, CBIM, FIMC, FBCS. Commissioned RA; served in UK, ME and Italy, 1940–46 (Major). With Peat, Marwick, Mitchell & Co., Chartered Accountants, 1946–57. British Consultants Bureau: Vice-Chm., 1981–83; Mem. Council, 1968–75 and 1979–84; led mission to Far East, 1969. Member Council: Inst. of Management Consultants, 1964–77 (Pres., 1967–68); Inst. of Cost and Management Accountants, 1966–76 (Pres., 1972–73; Gold Medal, 1991); Management Consultants Assoc., 1966–84 (Chm., 1976); Mem., Devlin Commn of Inquiry into Industrial Representation, 1971–72. Member: Bd of Fellows of BIM, 1973–76; Adv. Panel to Overseas Projects Gp, 1973–76; Price Commn, 1973–77; Domestic Promotions Cttee, British Invisible Exports Council, 1984. Mem., Court of Assistants, Merchant Taylors' Co., 1971– (Master 1980–81). *Publications:* papers and addresses on professional and management subjects. *Recreations:* fox-hunting, tennis, golf. *Address:* 17 Basing Hill, Golders Green, NW11 8TE. *Clubs:* Army and Navy; MCC; Harlequins.

HOWITT, Fowler; *see* Howitt, W. F.

HOWITT, Richard; Member (Lab) Essex South, European Parliament, since 1994; *b* 5 April 1961. *Educ:* Lady Margaret Hall, Oxford. Former community worker. Mem. (Lab), Harlow DC, 1984–94 (Leader, 1991–94). Contested (Lab) Billericay, 1987. *Address:* European Parliament, 97 Rue Belliard, 1040 Brussels, Belgium.

HOWITT, W(illiam) Fowler, DA (Dundee), FRIBA; architect and hospital planning consultant, retired; *b* Perth, Scotland, May 1924; *s* of late Frederick Howitt, Head Postmaster, Forfar; *m* 1951, Ann Elizabeth, *o d* of late A. J. Hedges, Radipole, Dorset; three *s* one *d*. *Educ:* Perth Academy. Royal Marines, 1943–46. Sch. of Architecture, Dundee, 1948; RIBA Victory Scholar, 1949. Asst Louis de Soissons, London (housing and flats), 1949–52; Prin. Asst to Vincent Kelly, Dublin (hosps & offices), 1952–55; Architect to St Thomas' Hosp. (Hosp. rebuilding schemes, flats, offices), 1955–64; Partner, Cusdin Burden and Howitt, Architects, 1965–90. Projects include: design and supervision of Coll. of Medicine and King Khalid Hosp., King Saud Univ., Riyadh, Saudi Arabia; design of teaching hospitals: Abuja city and Niger State, Nigeria; children's hospitals, Anambra and Imo States, Nigeria; Addenbrooke's Hosp., Cambridge; Royal Victoria Hosp., Belfast; planning consultancy, 1980–: gen. hosps, Sharjah and Fujairah, UAE; King Fahad Medical City, Riyadh, Saudi Arabia; Polyclinico Teaching Hosp., Milan; private hosp., Milan; gen. hosps Como and Varese. *Recreations:* reading, golf. *Address:* 32 Gloucester Road, Teddington, Mddx TW11 0NU. *T:* 0181–977 5772.

HOWKINS, John, MD, FRCS; Gynæcological Surgeon to St Bartholomew's Hospital, 1946–69 (Hon. Consultant Gynæcologist since 1969), to Hampstead General Hospital 1946–67 (Hon. Consultant Gynæcologist, since 1968), and to Royal Masonic Hospital, 1948–73; *b* 17 Dec. 1907; *m* 1940, Lena Brown; one *s* two *d*. *Educ:* Shrewsbury Sch.; London Univ. Arts Scholar, Middlesex Hospital, 1926; MRCS, LRCP, 1932; MB, BS, London, 1933; FRCS, 1936; MS London, 1936; MD (Gold Medal) London, 1937; MRCOG 1937, FRCOG 1947. House Surgeon and Casualty Surgeon, Middlesex Hosp., 1932–34; RMO Chelsea Hosp. for Women, 1936; Gynæcological Registrar, Middlesex Hosp., 1937–38; Resident Obstetric Surg., St Bartholomew's Hosp., 1938 and 1945; Temp. Wing-Comdr, RAFVR Med. Br., 1939–45. Hunterian Prof., RCS 1947. William Meredith Fletcher Shaw Lectr, RCOG, 1975. Sometime Examiner in Midwifery to Univs of Cambridge and London, RCOG, Conjoint Bd of England. Chm., Council Ski Club of Great Britain, 1964–67 (Hon. Life Member, 1968, Trustee, 1969–); Mem., Gynaecological Travellers' Club. *Publications:* Shaw's Textbook of Gynæcology, 7th edn 1956 to 9th edn 1971; Shaw's Textbook of Operative Gynaecology, 2nd edn 1960 to 5th edn 1983 (jtly, 4th edn–); (jtly) Bonney's Textbook of Gynæcological Surgery, 7th edn 1964, 8th edn 1974. *Recreations:* ski-ing, salmon fishing and sheep farming. *Address:* Caen Hen, Abercegir, Machynlleth, Powys, Wales SY20 8NR. *Clubs:* Ski Club of Great Britain; Wilks XV (Hon. Mem.).

HOWKINS, John Anthony; consultant and writer; *b* 3 Aug. 1945; *s* of Col Ashby Howkins and Lesley (*née* Stops); *m* 1st, 1971, Jill Liddington; 2nd, 1977, Annabel Whittet. *Educ:* Rugby Sch.; Keele Univ.; Architectural Association's Sch. of Architecture (Dip.). Marketing Manager, Lever Bros, 1968–70; founder, TV4 Conf., 1971: TV/Radio Editor, Books Editor, Time Out, 1971–74; Sec., Standing Conf. on Broadcasting, 1975–76; Editor, InterMedia, Journal of IIC, 1975–84. Gov., London Internat. Film Sch., 1976– (Chm., 1979–84); Member: Interim Action Cttee on the Film Industry, DTI, 1980–84; British Screen Adv. Council, DTI, 1985– (Dep. Chm., 1991–); Vice-Chm. (New Media), Assoc. of Independent Producers, 1984–85. Exec. Editor, National Electronics Review, 1981–; TV Columnist, Illustrated London News, 1981–83; Exec. Dir, Internat. Inst. of Communications, 1984–89. Dir. Television Investments, 1993–; Specialist Advr, Select Cttee on European Communities, House of Lords, 1985–87; Adviser: Broadcasting Reform Commn, Poland, 1989–90; Polish-Radio-and-Television, 1991–94; Minister of Film, Poland, 1991–92. Associate, Coopers Lybrand Deloitte, 1990–91. *Publications:* Understanding Television, 1977; The China Media Industry, 1980; Mass Communications in China, 1982; New Technologies, New Policies, 1982; Satellites International, 1987; (with Michael Foster) Television in '1992': a guide to Europe's new TV, film and video business, 1989. *Address:* E6 Albany, Piccadilly, W1V 9RH. *T:* 0171–434 1400.

HOWLAND, Lord; Andrew Ian Henry Russell; Partner, Bloomsbury Stud, since 1985; Director, Tattersalls Ltd, since 1992; *b* 30 March 1962; *s* and *heir* of Marquess of Tavistock, *qv*. *Educ:* Heatherdown; Harrow; Harvard. *Recreations:* shooting, racing. *Address:* 6 Fairlawns, Dullingham Road, Newmarket, Suffolk CB8 9JS; (office) Tattersalls Ltd, Terrace House, High Street, Newmarket, Suffolk CB8 9BT. *Clubs:* White's, Turf; AD (Cambridge, Mass).

HOWLAND JACKSON, Anthony Geoffrey Clive; Chairman, Bain Hogg plc, since 1994; *b* 25 May 1941; *s* of Arthur Geoffrey Howland Jackson and Pamela (*née* Wauton); *m* 1963, Susan Ellen Hickson; one *s* two *d*. *Educ:* Sherborne Sch. Chief Executive: H. Clarkson Insurance Hldgs, 1979–81; Clarkson Puckle, 1981–83; Dir, Gill & Duffus plc, 1983–87; Man. Dir, Bain Clarkson Ltd, 1987; Dep. Chm. and Chief Exec., 1987–93, Chm., 1993–94, Hogg Group plc. Lloyd's: Mem., 1976–; Mem., Regulatory Bd, 1993–. Mem., Worshipful Co. of Insurers, 1981–. *Recreations:* shooting, cricket, racing, golf. *Address:* Bain Hogg Ltd, Lloyd's Chambers, 1 Portsoken Street, E1 8DF. *T:* 0171–480 4000. *Club:* Turf.

HOWLETT, Anthony Douglas, RD 1971; Remembrancer of the City of London, 1981–86; *b* 30 Dec. 1924; *s* of late Ernest Robert Howlett and Catherine (*née* Broughton), Grantham, Lincs; *m* 1952, Alfreda Dorothy Pearce, *yr d* of Arthur W. Pearce, Hove, Sussex. *Educ:* King's Sch., Rochester; Wellingborough; King's Sch., Grantham; Trinity Coll., Cambridge. BA Hons 1948, LLB 1949, MA 1950. Served War, 1939–46, RNVR; RNVSR, 1951–60; RNR, 1960–75 (Lt Comdr 1968). Hon. Mem., HMS President. Called to the Bar, Gray's Inn, 1950; joined Legal Br., BoT, 1951; Sen. Legal Assistant, 1960; Asst Solicitor, 1972, i/c Export Credit Guarantees Br., 1972–75, i/c Merchant Shipping Br., 1975–81. UK delegate: London Diplomatic Conf. on Limitation of Liability for Maritime Claims, 1976; Geneva Diplomatic Conf. on Multi-Modal Transport, 1980, and other internat. maritime confs. Vice-Chm., Enfield HA, 1987–93; Chm., Enfield Dist Res. Ethics Cttee, 1990–93. Founder Mem., Sherlock Holmes Soc. of London, 1951 (Chm., 1960–63, 1986–89; Pres., 1992–); Mem., City Pickwick Club, 1988–. Freedom of City of London, 1981; Liveryman, Scriveners' Co., 1981–. OStJ 1986. Order of King Abdul Aziz (II) (Saudi Arabia), 1981; Order of Oman (III), 1982; Comdr, Order of Orange-Nassau (Netherlands), 1982; Officier, Légion d'Honneur (France), 1984; Comdr, Order of the Lion of Malaŵi, 1985; Order of Qatar (III), 1985. *Publications:* articles on Conan Doyle and Holmesiana. *Recreations:* book browsing, Sherlock Holmes, opera, photography, sailing and maritime history, foreign travel. *Address:* Rivendell, 37 Links Side, Enfield, Middlesex EN2 7QZ. *T:* 0181-363 5802. *Club:* Naval.

HOWLETT, Gen. Sir Geoffrey (Hugh Whitby), KBE 1984 (OBE 1972); MC 1952; Chairman: Leonard Cheshire Foundation, 1990–95; Services Sound & Vision Corporation, since 1991 (Vice-Chairman, 1989–91); President, Regular Forces Employment Association, since 1993 (Vice-Chairman, 1989–90; Chairman, 1990–93); *b* 5 Feb. 1930; *s* of Brig. B. Howlett, DSO, and Mrs Joan Howlett (later Latham); *m* 1955, Elizabeth Anne Aspinal; one *s* two *d*. *Educ:* Wellington Coll.; RMA, Sandhurst. Commnd Queen's Own Royal W Kent Regt, 1950; served, 1951–69: Malaya, Berlin, Cyprus and Suez; 3 and 2 Para, 16 Parachute Bde and 15 Para (TA); RAF Staff Coll. and Jt Services Staff Coll.; Mil. Asst to CINCNORTH, Oslo, 1969–71; CO 2 Para, 1971–73; RCDS, 1973–75; Comd 16 Parachute Bde, 1975–77; Dir, Army Recruiting, 1977–79; GOC 1st Armoured Div., 1979–82; Comdt, RMA, Sandhurst, 1982–83; GOC SE District, 1983–85; C-in-C Allied Forces Northern Europe, 1986–89, retd. Colonel Commandant: ACC, 1981–89; Parachute Regt, 1983–90. Comr, Royal Hosp., Chelsea, 1989–95. President: CCF, 1989–; Army Benevolent Fund for Dorset, 1992–; Army Cricket Assoc., 1984–85; Combined Services Cricket Assoc., 1985; Stragglers of Asia Cricket Club, 1989–94. Chm. of Govs, Milton Abbey Sch., 1994–. Liveryman, Cooks' Co., 1991–. Cross of Merit, 1st cl. (Lower Saxony), 1982. *Recreations:* cricket, shooting. *Address:* c/o Lloyds Bank, Tonbridge, TN9 1DB. *Clubs:* Naval and Military, MCC.

HOWLETT, Jack, CBE 1969; MA Oxon, PhD Manchester; MIEE, FSS, FBCS, FIMA; Consultant to International Computers Ltd, since 1975 and Editor, ICL Technical Journal, since 1978; Managing Editor, Journal of Information Technology for Development, since 1985; *b* 30 Aug. 1912; *s* of William Howlett and Lydia Ellen Howlett; *m* 1939, Joan Marjorie Simmons; four *s* one *d*. *Educ:* Stand Grammar Sch., Manchester; Manchester Univ. Mathematician, LMS Railway, 1935–40 and 1946–48; mathematical work in various wartime research estabts, 1940–46; Head of Computer Group, Atomic Energy Research Estabt, Harwell, 1948–61; Dir, Atlas Computer Lab., Chilton Didcot, Berks, 1961–75 (under SRC, 1965–75). Chm., Nat. Cttee on Computer Networks, 1976–78. Fellow by special election, St Cross Coll., Oxford, 1966. Hon. Sec., British Cttee of Honour for Celebration of 1300th Anniversary of Foundn of Bulgarian State, 1980–82; 1300th Anniversary Medal of Bulgarian State, 1982. *Publications:* reviews and gen. papers on numerical mathematics and computation; trans of French books on computational subjects. *Recreations:* hill walking, music. *Address:* 20B Bradmore Road, Oxford OX2 6QP. *T:* Oxford (01865) 52893. *Clubs:* New Arts, Savile.

HOWLETT, Air Vice-Marshal Neville Stanley, CB 1982; RAF retired, 1982; Member: Lord Chancellor's Panel of Independent Inquiry Inspectors, 1982–95; Pensions Appeal

Tribunal, since 1988; *b* 17 April 1927; *s* of Stanley Herbert Howlett and Ethel Shirley Howlett (*née* Pritchard); *m* 1952, Sylvia, *d* of J. F. Foster; one *s* one *d*. *Educ:* Liverpool Inst. High Sch.; Peterhouse, Cambridge. RAF pilot training, 1945–47; 32 and 64 (Fighter) Squadrons, 1948–56; RAF Staff Coll. Course, 1957; Squadron Comdr, 229 (Fighter) OCU, 1958–59; OC Flying Wing, RAF Coltishall, 1961–63; Directing Staff, RAF Staff Coll., 1967–69; Station Comdr, RAF Leuchars, 1970–72; RCDS, 1972; Dir of Operations (Air Defence and Overseas), 1973–74; Air Attaché, Washington DC, 1975–77; Dir, Management Support of Intelligence, MoD, 1978–80; Dir Gen. of Personal Services (RAF), MoD, 1980–82. Vice-Pres., RAFA, 1984– (Chm., Exec. Cttee, 1990–). *Recreations:* golf, fishing. *Address:* Milverton, Bolney Trevor Drive, Lower Shiplake, Oxon RG9 3PG. *Clubs:* Royal Air Force; Phyllis Court (Henley); Huntercombe Golf.

HOWLETT, Ronald William, OBE 1986; Managing Director, Cwmbran Development Corporation, 1978–88, retired; *b* 18 Aug. 1928; *s* of Percy Edward Howlett and Lucy Caroline Howlett; *m* 1954, Margaret Megan Searl (marr. diss. 1990); two *s*. *Educ:* University Coll. London. BSc Eng.(Hons); CEng; FICE. Crawley Develt Corp., 1953–56; Exec. Engr, Roads and Water Supply, Northern Nigeria, 1956–61; Bor. of Colchester, 1961–64; Cwmbran Develt Corp., 1964–65; Bor. of Slough, 1965–69; Dep. Chief Engr and Chief Admin. Officer, Cwmbran Develt Corp., 1969–78. *Recreations:* fishing, music. *Address:* Llangronwin, Llanbadoc, Usk, Gwent NP5 1TL. *T:* Usk (01291) 673493.

HOWSE, Lt-Comdr Humphrey Derek, MBE 1954; DSC 1945; FSA, FRIN, FRAS; RN retired; Caird Research Fellow, National Maritime Museum, 1982–86; *b* Weymouth, 10 Oct. 1919; *s* of late Captain Humphrey F. Howse, RN and late Rose Chicheliana (*née* Thornton); *m* 1946, Elizabeth de Warrenne Waller; three *s* one *d*. *Educ:* RN Coll., Dartmouth. FRIN 1976; FRAS 1967; FSA 1986. Midshipman, RN, 1937–39; Sub-Lt, 1939, Lieut 1941; war service in HMS Boadicea, Sardonyx, Garth, Inconstant, Rinaldo, 1939–45; specialized in navigation, 1944, in aircraft direction, 1947 (despatches 3 times 1943–45); Lt-Comdr 1949; HMS Newcastle, Korean War, 1952–54, Inshore Flotilla, 1954–56; retd 1958. Atomic Energy Div., Gen. Electric Co., 1958–61; Associated Industrial Consultants, 1961–62; Continental Oil Co., 1962–63; Asst Keeper, Dept of Navigation and Astronomy, National Maritime Museum, 1963; Head of Astronomy, 1969; Dep. Keeper and Head of Navigation and Astronomy, 1976; Keeper, 1979–82. Clark Library Vis. Prof., UCLA, 1983–84. Member Council: IUHPS (Pres., Scientific Instrument Commn, 1977–82); British Astronomical Assoc., 1980–88 (Pres., 1980–82); Antiquarian Horological Soc., 1976–82; Royal Astronomical Soc., 1982–83; Royal Inst. of Navigation, 1982–83; Soc. for Nautical Research, 1982–86 (Vice-Pres., 1992); Hakluyt Soc., 1984–88; Scientific Instrument Soc., 1987–90. Liveryman, Clockmakers' Co., 1981. *Publications:* Clocks and Watches of Captain James Cook, 1969; The Tompion Clocks at Greenwich, 1970; (with M. Sanderson) The Sea Chart, 1973; Greenwich Observatory: the buildings and instruments, 1975; Francis Place and the Early History of Greenwich Observatory, 1975; Greenwich Time and the Discovery of the Longitude, 1980; Nevil Maskelyne: the seaman's astronomer, 1989; (ed) Background to Discovery, 1990; (with N. J. W. Thrower) A Buccaneer's Atlas, 1992; Radar at Sea, 1993; papers to Mariners' Mirror, L'Astronomie, Antiquarian Horology, Jl of Navigation and Jl of British Astronomical Assoc. *Recreations:* reading, writing, sticking in photos, pottering in the vegetable beds. *Address:* 12 Barnfield Road, Riverhead, Sevenoaks, Kent TN13 2AY. *T:* Sevenoaks (01732) 454366.

HOY, Rev. David, SJ; Superior, St John's, Beaumont, since 1984; *b* 1 March 1913; *s* of Augustine Hilary Hoy and Caroline Lovelace. *Educ:* Mount St Mary's Coll. Entered Society of Jesus, 1931. Senior English Master, Wimbledon Coll., 1947, Asst Head Master, 1957–59. Rector of St Robert Bellarmine, Heythrop, Chipping Norton, 1959–64; Rector of Stonyhurst College, 1964–71 and 1980–84; Superior of Farm St Church, 1972–75. *Recreation:* walking. *Address:* St John's, Beaumont, Old Windsor, Berks SL4 2JN.

HOYES, Thomas, PhD; FRICS; Member, Lands Tribunal, since 1989; *b* 19 Nov. 1935; *s* of late Fred Hoyes and Margaret Elizabeth (*née* Hoyes); *m* 1960, Amy Joan (*née* Wood); two *d*. *Educ:* Queen Elizabeth's Grammar Sch., Alford, Lincs; Downing Coll., Cambridge (BA 1956; MA 1960; PhD 1963). FRICS 1969 (ARICS 1964). Partner, Hallam Brackett, Chartered Surveyors, Nottingham, 1963–83; Prof. of Land Management, Univ. of Reading, 1983–88 (Head of Dept, 1986–88). Royal Institution of Chartered Surveyors: Mem., Gen. Council, 1982–85; Pres., Planning and Develt Div., 1983–84. President: Cambridge Univ. Land Soc., 1973; Land Inst., 1991; Mem., Rating Surveyors Assoc., 1968–. Governor, Nottingham High Sch. for Girls (GPDST), 1976–82. *Publications:* The Practice of Valuation, 1979; articles and papers in Estates Gazette, Chartered Surveyor Weekly, and Jl of Planning and Environment Law. *Recreations:* gardening, adapting houses. *Address:* (office) 48–49 Chancery Lane, WC2A 1JR. *T:* 0171–936 7200. *Club:* Farmers'.

HOYLAND, John, RA 1991 (ARA 1983); *b* 12 Oct. 1934; *s* of John Kenneth and Kathleen Hoyland; *m* 1957, Airi Karkkainen (marr. diss. 1968); one *s*. *Educ:* Sheffield Coll. of Art (NDD 1956); Royal Academy Schs (RA Cert. 1960). Taught at: Hornsey Coll. of Art, 1960–62; Chelsea Sch. of Art, 1962–69, Principal Lectr, 1965–69; St Martin's Sch. of Art, 1974–77; Slade Sch. of Art, 1974–77, 1980, 1983, resigned 1989; Charles A. Dana Prof. of Fine Arts, Colgate Univ., NY, 1972. Artist in residence: Studio Sch., NY, 1978; Melbourne Univ., 1979. Selector: Hayward Annual, 1979; RA Silver Jubilee exhibn, 1979; organized and curated Hans Hofman exhibn, Lateworks, Tate Gall., 1988. *One-man exhibitions* include: Marlborough New London Gall., 1964; Whitechapel Gall., 1967; Waddington Galls, 1967, annually 1969–71 and 1973–76, 1978, 1978, 1981, 1983, 1985; retrospective: Serpentine Gall., 1979; and in Canada, USA, Brazil, Italy, Portugal, W Germany and Australia. *Group exhibitions* include: Tate Gall., 1964; Hayward Gall., 1974; Walker Art Gall., Liverpool (in every John Moores exhibn, 1963–); British Art in the 20th Century, Royal Acad., 1987; Waddington Gall., 1987; also in Belgium, France, Japan and Norway. Work in public collections incl. RA, Tate Gall., V&A Mus. and other galls and instns in UK, Europe, USA and Australia. *TV appearances:* 6 Days in September, BBC TV, 1979; Signals, Channel 4, 1989. Designs for Zansa, Ballet Rambert, 1986. Gulbenkian Foundn purchase award, 1963; Peter Stuyvesant travel bursary, 1964, 1964; John Moores Liverpool exhibn prize, 1965, 1st prize, 1983; Open Paintings exhibn prize, Belfast, 1966; (jtly) 1st prize, Edinburgh Open 100 exhibn, 1969; 1st prize, Chichester Nat. Art exhibn, 1975; Arts Council purchase award, 1979; Athena Art Award, 1987. Order of the Southern Cross (Brazil), 1986. *Relevant publication:* John Hoyland, by Mel Gooding, 1990. *Address:* 41 Charterhouse Square, EC1M 6EA.

HOYLE, Prof. Eric; Professor of Education, School of Education, University of Bristol, since 1971; *b* 22 May 1931; *s* of Percy and Bertha Hoyle; *m* 1954, Dorothy Mary Morley; one *s* two *d*. *Educ:* Preston Grammar Sch.; Univ. of London (BSc Sociology, MA). Taught, Harehills Secondary Sch., Leeds, 1953–58 (Head of English Dept, 1956–58); Head, English Dept, Batley High Sch., 1958–60; Lectr and Sen. Lectr in Educn, James Graham Coll., Leeds, 1961–64; Lectr and Sen. Lectr in Educn, Univ. of Manchester, 1965–71; Bristol University: Hd, Sch. of Educn, 1971–91; Dean, Faculty of Educn, 1974–82, 1983–86. Member: Avon Educn Cttee, 1977–80; Educnl Res. Bd, SSRC, 1973–78 (Vice-Chm., 1976–78); Bd of Management, NFER, 1976–; Council, Exec. Council for Educn of Teachers, 1971 (Mem. Exec., 1978–81, 1987–90); Adviser to Public Schools Commn, 1968–70. Editor, World Yearbook of Educn, 1980–86; founding Co-Editor, Research in Educn, 1969. *Publications:* The Role of the Teacher, 1969; (with J. Wilks) Gifted Children and their Education, 1974; The Politics of School Management, 1986; (with Peter John) Professional Knowledge and Professional Practice, 1995; contribs to professional jls. *Recreations:* music, reading, collecting first editions, wine-drinking, watching sport. *Address:* 1 The Crescent, Henleaze, Bristol BS9 4RN. *T:* Bristol (0117) 962 0614; School of Education, University of Bristol, 35 Berkeley Square, Bristol BS8 1JA. *T:* Bristol (0117) 930 3030.

HOYLE, (Eric) Douglas (Harvey); MP (Lab) Warrington North, since 1983 (Warrington, July 1981–1983); consultant; *b* 17 Feb. 1930; *s* of late William Hoyle and Leah Ellen Hoyle; *m* 1953, Pauline Spencer (*d* 1991); one *s*. *Educ:* Adlington C of E Sch.; Horwich and Bolton Techn. Colls. Engrg apprentice, British Rail, Horwich, 1946–51; Sales Engr, AEI, Manchester, 1951–53; Sales Engr and Marketing Executive, Charles Weston Ltd, Salford, 1951–74. Mem., Manchester Regional Hosp. Bd, 1968–74; Mem., NW Regional Health Authority, 1974–75. Contested (Lab): Clitheroe, 1964; Nelson and Colne, 1970 and Feb. 1974; MP (Lab) Nelson and Colne, Oct. 1974–1979. Chm., PLP, 1992– (Mem., Trade and Industry Cttee, 1987–92); Mem., Select Cttee on Trade and Industry, 1984–92. Mem. Nat. Exec., Labour Party, 1978–82, 1983–85. Pres., ASTMS, 1977–81, 1985–88 (Vice-Pres., 1981–85), MSF, 1988–91 (Jt Pres., 1988–90); Chm., ASTMS Parly Cttee, 1975–76. Pres., Adlington Cricket Club, 1974–. JP 1958. *Recreations:* sport, cricket, theatre-going, reading. *Address:* 30 Ashfield Road, Anderton, Chorley, Lancs PR6 9PN.

HOYLE, Prof. Sir Fred, Kt 1972; FRS 1957; MA Cantab; Hon. Research Professor: Manchester University, since 1972; University College, Cardiff, since 1975; Visiting Associate in Physics, California Institute of Technology, since 1963; *b* 24 June 1915; *s* of Ben Hoyle, Bingley, Yorks; *m* 1939, Barbara Clark; one *s* one *d*. *Educ:* Bingley Grammar Sch.; Emmanuel Coll., Cambridge (Hon. Fellow, 1983). Mayhew Prizeman, Mathematical Tripos, 1936; Smith's Prizeman, Goldsmith Exhibnr, Senior Exhibnr of Royal Commn for Exhibn of 1851, 1938. War Service for British Admiralty, 1939–45. Fellow, St John's Coll., Cambridge, 1939–72; University Lecturer in Mathematics, Cambridge, 1945–58; Plumian Prof. of Astronomy and Exptl Philosophy, Cambridge Univ., 1958–72; Dir, Inst. of Theoretical Astronomy, Cambridge, 1967–73; Prof. of Astronomy, Royal Instn of GB, 1969–72; Staff Mem., Mount Wilson and Palomar Observatories, 1957–62. California Institute of Technology: Vis. Prof. of Astrophysics, 1953, 1954; Vis. Prof. of Astronomy, 1956; Sherman Fairchild Scholar, 1974–75; Addison White Greenaway Vis. Prof. of Astronomy; Andrew D. White Prof.-at-Large, Cornell Univ., 1972–78. Mem. SRC, 1967–72. Vice-Pres., Royal Society, 1970–71; Pres., Royal Astronomical Soc., 1971–73. Hon. MRIA (Section of Science), 1977; Mem., Amer. Philos. Soc., 1980; Hon. Member: Amer. Acad. of Arts and Sciences, 1964; Mark Twain Soc., 1978; Foreign Associate, US Nat. Acad. of Sciences, 1969. Hon. Fellow, St John's Coll., Cambridge, 1973. Hon. ScD E Anglia, 1967; Hon DSc: Leeds 1969; Bradford 1975; Newcastle 1976. Royal Astronomical Soc. Gold Medal, 1968; UN Kalinga Prize, 1968; Bruce Gold Medal, 1970, Klumphe-Roberts Award, 1977, Astronomical Soc. of Pacific; Royal Medal, Royal Soc., 1974; Dag Hammarskjöld Gold Medal, Académie Diplomatique de la Paix, 1986; Karl Schwarzehild Medal, German Astronomical Soc., 1992; Balzan Prize, 1994. *Publications: general:* Some Recent Researches in Solar Physics, 1949; The Nature of the Universe, 1951; A Decade of Decision, 1953; Frontiers of Astronomy, 1955; Man and Materialism, 1956; Astronomy, 1962; Star Formation, 1963; Of Men and Galaxies, 1964; Encounter with the Future, 1965; Galaxies, Nuclei and Quasars, 1965; Man in the Universe, 1966; From Stonehenge to Modern Cosmology, 1972; Nicolaus Copernicus, 1973; The Relation of Physics and Cosmology, 1973; (with J. V. Narlikar) Action-at-a-Distance in Physics and Cosmology, 1974; Astronomy and Cosmology, 1975; Highlights in Astronomy, 1975 (in England, Astronomy Today, 1975); Ten Faces of the Universe, 1977; On Stonehenge, 1977; Energy or Extinction, 1977; (with N. C. Wickramasinghe) Lifecloud, 1978; The Cosmogony of the Solar System, 1978; (with N. C. Wickramasinghe) Diseases From Space, 1979; (with G. Hoyle) Commonsense and Nuclear Energy, 1979; (with J. V. Narlikar) The Physics-Astronomy Frontier, 1980; (with N. C. Wickramasinghe) Space Travellers: the Bringers of Life, 1981; Ice, 1981; (with N. C. Wickramasinghe) Evolution from Space, 1981; The Intelligent Universe, 1983; (with N. C. Wickramasinghe) Archaeopteryx, the Primordial Bird: a case of fossil forgery, 1986; (with N. C. Wickramasinghe) Cosmic Life Force, 1988; (with N. C. Wickramasinghe) The Theory of Cosmic Grains, 1991; (with N. C. Wickramasinghe) Our Place in the Cosmos, 1993; *novels:* The Black Cloud, 1957; Ossian's Ride, 1959; (with J. Elliot) A for Andromeda, 1962; (with G. Hoyle) Fifth Planet, 1963; (with J. Elliot) Andromeda Breakthrough, 1964; October the First is Too Late, 1966; Element 79, 1967; (with G. Hoyle) Rockets in Ursa Major, 1969; (with G. Hoyle) Seven Steps to the Sun, 1970; (with G. Hoyle) The Molecule Men, 1971; (with G. Hoyle) The Inferno, 1973; (with G. Hoyle) Into Deepest Space, 1974; (with G. Hoyle) The Incandescent Ones, 1977; (with G. Hoyle) The Westminster Disaster, 1978; *children's stories with G. Hoyle:* The Energy Pirate, 1982; The Giants of Universal Park, 1982; The Frozen Planet of Azuron, 1982; The Planet of Death, 1982; Comet Halley, 1985; (with N. C. Wickramasinghe) Cosmic Life Force, 1988; *autobiography:* The Small World of Fred Hoyle, 1986; Home is Where the Wind Blows, 1994; *play:* Rockets in Ursa Major, 1962; *libretto:* The Alchemy of Love; space serials for television; scientific papers. *Address:* c/o The Royal Society, 6 Carlton House Terrace, SW1Y 5AG.

HOYLE, Susan; Deputy Secretary-General, Arts Council of England, since 1994; *b* 7 April 1953; *d* of Roland and Joan Hoyle. *Educ:* Univ. of Bristol (BA Drama and French). Education Officer, London Festival Ballet, 1980–83; Administrator, Extemporary Dance Th., 1983–86; Dance and Mime Officer, 1986–89, Dir of Dance, 1989–94, Arts Council of GB. *Address:* (office) 14 Great Peter Street, SW1P 3NQ.

HOYOS, Hon. Sir (Fabriciano) Alexander, Kt 1979; former Lecturer, Cave Hill, University of the West Indies; retired History Teacher, Lodge School, St John; *b* Brazil, 5 July 1912; *s* of Emigdio and Adelina Hoyos, Peru; *m* 1st, 1940, Kathleen Carmen (*d* 1970); three *s* one *d*; 2nd, 1973, Gladys Louise. *Educ:* Wesley Hall Boys' School; Harrison Coll.; Codrington Coll., Durham Univ. (Sen. Island Schol.). BA 1936; MA 1943; Hon. MEd 1963; DLitt UWI, 1982. Taught at: Combermere Sch., Barbados; St Benedict's Coll., Trinidad; Lodge Sch., 1943–72; Moderator, Caribbean History Survey Course, Cave Hill, UWI, 1963–70. Leader-writer of Daily Advocate, 1937–43; Correspondent, London Times, 1938–65. Chm., Nat. Adv. Commn on Educn, 1983–86; Member: Barbados Christian Council, 1976–80; Privy Council for Barbados, 1977–86; Constitution Review Commn, 1977–78. Queen's Jubilee Medal, 1977. *Publications:* Some Eminent Contemporaries, 1944; Two Hundred Years, 1945; Story of Progressive Movement, 1948; Our Common Heritage, 1953; Memories of Princess Margaret and Our Past, 1955; Road to Responsible Government, 1960; Barbados, Our Island Home, 1960; Rise of West Indian Democracy, 1963; Background to Independence, 1967; Builders of Barbados, 1972; Grantley Adams and the Social Revolution, 1974; Barbados: From the Amerindians to Independence, 1978; Visitor's Guide to Barbados, 1982; The Quiet Revolutionary (autobiog.), 1984; Tom Adams (biog.), 1988. *Recreations:* gardening, walking, talking, swimming. *Address:* Beachy Crest, Belair Cross Road, St Philip, Barbados, WI. *T:* 4236323. *Club:* Barbados Yacht.

HOYT, Hon. William Lloyd; Chief Justice of New Brunswick, since 1993; *b* 13 Sept. 1930; *m* 1954, Joan Millier; three *d. Educ:* Woodstock High Sch.; Acadia Univ. (BA, MA); Emmanuel Coll., Cambridge (BA Hons, MA). Called to New Brunswick Bar, 1957; QC (NB) 1972; Associate, Limerick & Limerick, 1957–59; Partner, Limerick, Limerick & Hoyt and successor firm, Hoyt, Mockler, Allen & Dixon, 1959–81; Judge, 1981–84, Court of Appeal, 1984–, New Brunswick. Member: Fredericton Barristers' Soc., 1957–81 (Pres., 1970–71); New Brunswick Barristers' Soc., 1957–81 (Council, 1970–72, 1975–79); Cttee on Canadian Constitution, Canadian Bar Assoc., 1977–78; Director: Canadian Inst. for Admin of Justice, 1979–83; Canadian Judges' Conf., 1985–89; Chm., New Brunswick Judicial Council, 1993– (Vice-Chm., 1988–93). *Publications:* Married Women's Property, 1961; Professional Negligence, 1973. *Address:* Justice Building, 423 Queen Street, PO Box 6000, Fredericton, New Brunswick E3B 5H1, Canada. *T:* (506) 4532776.

HOYTE, Hugh Desmond, SC; President, Co-operative Republic of Guyana, 1985–92; Leader, People's National Congress, 1985–92; *b* 9 March 1929; *s* of George Alphonso Hoyte and Gladys Marietta Hoyte; *m* Joyce Hoyte. *Educ:* St Barnabas Anglican Sch.; Progressive High Sch.; Univ. of London (BA extl 1950, LLB 1959). Called to the Bar, Middle Temple, 1959. QC 1970, now SC. Civil servant and teacher; practised at Guyana Bar, 1960–; Chm., Legal Practitioners' Cttee, 1964; Mem., Nat. Elections Commn, 1966. Elected to Parliament, 1968; Minister: Home Affairs, 1969–70; Finance, 1970–72; Works and Communications, 1972–74; Economic Develt, 1974–80; Vice-Pres., Economic Planning and Finance, 1980–83, Production, 1983–84; First Vice-Pres. and Prime Minister, 1984. *Recreations:* reading, music, swimming, walking. *Address:* 14 North Road, Bourda, Georgetown, Guyana.

HU DINGYI; Secretary-General, All-China Federation of Industry & Commerce, since 1988; *b* Dec. 1922; *m* Xie Heng; one *s* one *d. Educ:* Central Univ., Sichuan Province, China (graduate). 3rd Secretary, Embassy of People's Republic of China in India, 1950–54; 2nd Sec., Office of the Chargé d'Affaires of People's Republic of China in UK, 1954–58; Section Chief, Dept of Western European Affairs, Min. of Foreign Affairs, 1958–60; 1st Sec., Ghana, 1960–66; Division Chief, Dept of African Affairs, 1966–71; 1st Sec., then Counsellor, UK, 1972–79; Consul General, San Francisco, 1979–83; Minister, US, 1983–85; Ambassador to UK, 1985–87. *Recreation:* reading. *Address:* c/o All-China Federation of Industry & Commerce, 93 Bei He Yan Dajie, 100006, Beijing, China.

HUANG, Rayson Lisung, Hon. CBE 1976; DSc, DPhil; FRCPE; Vice-Chancellor, University of Hong Kong, 1972–86; *b* 1 Sept. 1920; *s* of Rufus Huang; *m* 1949, Grace Wei Li; two *s. Educ:* Munsang Coll., Hong Kong; Univ. of Hong Kong (BSc); Univ. of Oxford (DPhil, DSc); Univ. of Chicago. DSc (Malaya) 1956. FRCPE 1984. Demonstrator in Chemistry, Nat. Kwangsi Univ., Kweilin, China, 1943; Post-doctoral Fellow and Research Associate, Univ. of Chicago, 1947–50; Univ. of Malaya, Singapore: Lecturer in Chemistry, 1951–54; Reader, 1955–59; Univ. of Malaya, Kuala Lumpur: Prof. of Chemistry, 1959–69, and Dean of Science, 1962–65; Vice-Chancellor, Nanyang Univ., Singapore, 1969–72. Chm. Council, ACU, 1980–81; Pres., Assoc. of SE Asian Instns of Higher Learning, 1970–72, 1981–83. Mem. Drafting Cttee (Beijing) and Vice Chm. Consulting Cttee (Hong Kong), for the Basic Law for Special Administrative Region of Hong Kong, 1985–90. Mem. Adv. Bd, IBM China/Hong Kong Corp., 1989–93. Vice Chm. Council, Shantou Univ., China, 1987–94; Life Member: Court, Univ. of Hong Kong; Bd of Trustees, Croucher Foundn, Hong Kong. MLC Hong Kong, 1977–83. JP. Hon. DSc Hong Kong, 1968; Hon. LLD East Asia, Macao, 1987. *Publications:* Organic Chemistry of Free Radicals, 1974 (London); about 50 research papers on chemistry of free radicals, molecular rearrangements, etc, mainly in Jl of Chem. Soc. (London). *Recreation:* music. *Address:* Raycrest II, 10 The Stables, Selly Park, Birmingham B29 7JW. *Club:* Hong Kong.

HUBBARD, family name of **Baron Addington.**

HUBBARD, David; *see* Hubbard, R. D. C.

HUBBARD, Michael Joseph; QC 1985; a Recorder of the Crown Court, since 1984; *b* 16 June 1942; *s* of Joseph Thomas Hubbard and late Gwendoline Hubbard; *m* 1967, Ruth Ann; five *s. Educ:* Lancing College. Articled with Morris Bew & Baily, 1961; admitted Solicitor, 1966, Partner in Hubbard & Co., Chichester, 1966–71; called to the Bar, Gray's Inn, 1972, practising Western Circuit; Prosecuting Counsel to Inland Revenue, 1983–85. *Recreations:* messing about in boats and living on Herm Island. *Address:* (chambers) 1 Paper Buildings, Temple, EC4Y 7EP; Bartons, Stoughton, Chichester, West Sussex PO18 9JQ. *Club:* Chichester Sailing.

HUBBARD, (Richard) David (Cairns), OBE 1995; Chairman, Powell Duffryn, since 1986; *b* 14 May 1936; *s* of John Cairns Hubbard and Gertrude Emilie Hubbard; *m* 1964, Hannah Neale (*née* Dennison); three *d. Educ:* Tonbridge. FCA. Commissioned, Royal Artillery, 1955–57; Peat Marwick Mitchell & Co., 1957–65; Cape Asbestos Co., 1965–74; Bache & Co., 1974–76; Powell Duffryn, 1976–; Chairman: Andrew Sykes Group, 1991–94; London and Manchester Group, 1993– (Dir, 1989–); non-exec. Director: Blue Circle Industries, 1986–; TR City of London Trust, 1989–; Slough Estates, 1994–; Mem., Southern Adv. Bd, Nat. Westminster Bank, 1988–91. Mem., Bd of Crown Agents for Overseas Govts and Admins, 1986–88. Mem. Council, Inst. of Dirs, 1991–. Dep. Chm., CRC, 1992– (Council Mem., 1982–). Liveryman, Skinners' Co.; Freeman, City of London. *Recreation:* golf. *Address:* Meadowcroft, Windlesham, Surrey GU20 6BJ. *T:* Bagshot (01276) 472198. *Clubs:* Berkshire Golf, Lucifer Golfing Society.

HUBBARD-MILES, Peter Charles, CBE 1981; self-employed small businessman, since 1948; *b* 9 May 1927; *s* of Charles Hubbard and Agnes (*née* Lewis); *m* 1948, Pamela Wilkins; two *s* three *d. Educ:* Lewis' Sch., Pengam. Served RAF, 1945–48. County Councillor, Mid Glamorgan CC (formerly Glamorgan CC), 1967– (Leader, Conservative Group, 1974–83); Leader, Cons. Gp, Ogwr Borough Council, 1974–83, first Cons. Mayor 1979–80. Chm., Wales Cons. Local Govt Adv. Council, 1979–83. Contested (C) Bridgend, 1987. MP (C) Bridgend, 1983–87. PPS to Sec. of State for Wales, 1985–87. Chm. Governors, Bridgend Tech. Coll., 1977–81. *Recreations:* theatre, showbusiness. *Address:* 18 Lougher Gardens, Porthcawl CF36 3BJ.

HUBEL, Prof. David Hunter, MD; John Franklin Enders University Professor, Harvard Medical School, since 1982; *b* Canada, 27 Feb. 1926; US citizen; *s* of Jesse H. Hubel and Elsie M. Hunter; *m* 1953, S. Ruth Izzard; three *s. Educ:* McGill Univ. (BSc Hons Maths and Physics, 1947); McGill Univ. Med. Sch. (MD 1951). Rotating Intern, Montreal Gen. Hosp., 1951–52; Asst Resident in Neurology, Montreal Neurol Inst., 1952–53, and Fellow in Electroencephalography, 1953–54; Asst Resident in Neurol., Johns Hopkins Hosp., 1954–55; Res. Fellow, Walter Reed Army Inst. of Res., 1955–58; Res. Fellow, Wilmer Inst., Johns Hopkins Univ. Med. Sch., 1958–59; Harvard Medical School: Associate in Neurophysiology and Neuropharmacology, 1959–60; Asst Prof. of Neurophys. and Neuropharm., 1960–62; Associate Prof. of Neurophys. and Neuropharm., 1962–65; Prof. of Neurophys., 1965–67; George Packer Berry Prof. of Physiol. and Chm., Dept of Physiol., 1967–68; George Packer Berry Prof. of Neurobiol., 1968–82. George Eastman Vis. Prof., Univ. of Oxford, and Fellow, Balliol Coll., 1990–91. Sen. Fellow, Harvard Soc. of Fellows, 1971–; Mem., Bd of Syndics, Harvard Univ. Press, 1979–83. Associate, Neurosciences Res. Program, 1974. Fellow, Amer. Acad. of Arts and Sciences, 1965; Member: Amer. Physiol Soc., 1959–; National Acad. of Sciences, USA, 1971; Deutsche Akademie der Naturforscher Leopoldina, DDR, 1971; Soc. for Neuroscience, 1970; Assoc. for Res. in Vision and Ophthalmology, 1970; Amer. Philosophical Soc., 1982; Foreign Mem., Royal Soc., 1982; Hon. Member: Physiology. Soc., 1983; Amer. Neurol Assoc. Lectures: George H. Bishop, Washington Univ., St Louis, 1964; Bowditch, Amer. Physiol Soc., 1966; Jessup, Columbia Univ., 1970; Ferrier, Royal Soc., 1972; James Arthur, Amer. Mus. of Nat. Hist., 1972; Harvey, Rockefeller Univ., 1976; Grass Foundn, Soc. for Neuroscience, 1976; Weizmann Meml, Weizmann Inst. of Science, Israel, 1979; Vanuxem, Princeton Univ., 1981; Hughlings Jackson, Montreal Neurol Inst., 1982; first David Marr, Cambridge Univ., 1982; first James S. McDonnell, Washington Univ. Sch. of Medicine, 1982; James A. F. Stevenson Meml, Univ. of W Ont, 1982; Keys Meml, Trinity Coll., Toronto, 1983; Nelson, Univ. of Calif. Davis, 1983; Deane, Wellesley Coll., 1983; first James M. Sprague, Univ. of Pa, 1984; Vancouver Inst., Univ. of BC, 1985. Hon. DSc: McGill, 1978; Manitoba, 1983; Oxford, 1994; Hon. DHL Johns Hopkins, 1990. Awards: Res. to Prevent Blindness Trustees, 1971; Lewis S. Rosenstiel for Basic Med. Res., Brandeis Univ., 1972; Friedenwald, Assoc. for Res. in Vision and Ophthalmol., 1975; New England Ophthalmol Soc. Annual, 1983; Paul Kayser Internat. Award of Merit for Retina Res., 1989. Prizes: Karl Spencer Lashley, Amer. Phil Soc., 1977; Louisa Gross Horwitz, Columbia Univ., 1978; Dickson in Medicine, Univ. of Pittsburgh, 1979; Ledlie, Harvard Univ., 1980; Nobel Prize in Medicine or Physiol., 1981. *Publications:* Eye, Brain and Vision, 1987; articles in scientific jls. *Recreations:* music, photography, astronomy, amateur radio, Japanese. *Address:* Harvard Medical School, 220 Longwood Avenue, Boston, MA 02115, USA. *T:* (617) 4321655.

HUBER, Prof. Robert; Director, Max-Planck-Institut für Biochemie, and Scientific Member, Max-Planck Society, since 1972; *b* 20 Feb. 1937; *s* of Sebastian and Helene Huber; *m* 1960, Christa Essig; two *s* two *d. Educ:* Grammar Sch. and Humanistisches Gymnasium, München; Technische Univ., München (Dr rer. nat. 1963). Lecturer, 1968, Associate Prof., 1976–, Technische Univ., München. Scientific Mem., Max-Planck Soc. Member: EMBO (also Mem. Council); Deutsche Chem. Ges.; Ges. für Biologische Chem.; Bavarian Acad. of Scis, 1988; Deutsche Akademie der Naturforscher Leopoldina; Accademia Nazionale dei Lincei, Rome; Orden pour le mérite für Wissenschaft und Künste; Corresp. Mem., Croation Acad. of Scis and Arts; Associate Fellow, Third World Acad. of Scis, 1995. Hon. Member: Amer. Soc. of Biolog. Chemists; Swedish Soc. for Biophysics; Japanese Biochem. Soc. Dr *hc*: Catholic Univ. of Louvain, 1987; Univ. of Ljubljana, Jugoslavia, 1989; Univ. Tor Vergata, Rome, 1991. E. K. Frey Medal, Ges. für Chirurgie, 1972; Otto-Warburg Medal, Ges. für Biolog. Chem., 1977; Emil von Behring Medal, Univ. of Marburg, 1982; Keilin Medal, Biochem. Soc., 1987; Richard Kuhn Medal, Ges. Deutscher Chem., 1987; (jtly) Nobel Prize for Chemistry, 1988; E. K. Frey-E. Werle Gedächtnismedaille, 1989; Kone Award, Assoc. of Clin. Biochemists, 1990; Sir Hans Krebs Medal, FEBS, 1992; Bayerischer Maximiliansorden für Wissenschaft und Kunst, 1993; Distinguished Service Award, Miami Winter Symposia, 1995. Editor, Jl of Molecular Biology, 1976–. *Publications:* numerous papers in learned jls on crystallography, immunology and structure of proteins. *Recreations:* cycling, hiking, ski-ing. *Address:* Max-Planck Institut für Biochemie, Am Klopferspitz 18a, 82152 Martinsried, Germany. *T:* (089) 85782677/8.

HUCKER, Michael; His Honour Judge Hucker; a Circuit Judge, since 1994; *b* 25 Oct. 1937; *o s* of Ernest George Hucker, CBE and Mary Louise Hucker (*née* Jowett); *m* 1961, Hazel Zoë Drake, JP; one *s* one *d* (and one *s* decd). *Educ:* St Dunstan's Coll.; LSE. Regular Commission, RE, 1957–76; served BAOR, Cameroons, Malaysia, NI, MoD; attached Army Legal Services, 1974–76; retired 1976. Called to the Bar, Lincoln's Inn, 1974, Gibraltar, 1988; Head, Common Law Chambers,, 1978–91; Counsel for Army and Air Force Boards in CMAC and House of Lords, 1979; Judge Advocate, 1983; Asst Recorder, 1988; Recorder, 1992. Freeman, City of London, 1978. *Address:* Hardwicke Building, Lincoln's Inn, WC2A 3SB.

HUCKER, Rev. Michael Frederick, MBE 1970; Principal Chaplain, Church of Scotland and Free Churches, Royal Air Force, 1987–90; Secretary, Forces Board, Methodist Church, since 1990; *b* 1 May 1933; *s* of William John and Lucy Sophia Hucker; *m* 1961, Katherine Rosemary Parsons; one *s* one *d. Educ:* City of Bath Boys' Sch.; Bristol Univ. (MA); London Univ. (BD). Ordained Methodist minister, 1960; commnd as RAF chaplain, 1962. QHC 1987–90. *Recreations:* gardening, music. *Address:* 1 Central Buildings, Westminster, SW1H 9NH.

HUCKFIELD, Leslie (John); European Officer, Merseyside Colleges, since 1994; *b* 7 April 1942; *s* of Ernest Leslie and Suvla Huckfield. *Educ:* Prince Henry's Grammar Sch., Evesham; Keble Coll., Oxford; Univ. of Birmingham. Lectr in Economics, City of Birmingham Coll. of Commerce, 1963–67. Advertising Manager, Tribune, 1983; Co-ordinator, CAPITAL (transport campaign against London Transport Bill), 1983–84. Prin. Officer, External Resources, St Helen's Coll., Merseyside, 1989–93. Contested (Lab) Warwick and Leamington, 1966; MP (Lab) Nuneaton, March 1967–83. PPS to Minister of Public Building and Works, 1969–70; Parly Under-Secretary of State, Dept of Industry, 1976–79. MEP (Lab) Merseyside E, 1984–89. Member: Nat. Exec. Cttee, Labour Party, 1978–82; W Midlands Reg. Exec. Cttee, Labour Party, 1978–82; Political Sec., Nat. Union Lab. and Socialist Clubs, 1979–81. Chairman: Lab. Party Transport Gp, 1974–76; Independent Adv. Commn on Transport, 1975–76; Pres., Worcs Fedn of Young Socialists, 1962–64; Member: Birmingham Regional Hosp. Bd, 1970–72; Political Cttee, Co-op. Retail Soc. (London Regional), 1981–93. *Publications:* various newspaper and periodical articles. *Recreation:* running marathons. *Address:* PO Box 200, Northwich, Cheshire, CW9 6RL.

HUCKSTEP, Prof. Ronald Lawrie, CMG 1971; MD, FRCS, FRCSE, FRACS, FTS; Professor of Traumatic and Orthopaedic Surgery, University of New South Wales, 1972–92, now Emeritus Professor and Emeritus Orthopaedic Consultant, Prince of Wales/Prince Henry Hospital Group; Chairman of Departments of Orthopaedic Surgery and Director of Accident Services, Prince of Wales and Prince Henry Hospitals, Sydney, Australia, 1972–92; Consultant Orthopaedic Surgeon, Royal South Sydney and Sutherland Hospitals, 1972–92; *b* 22 July 1926; *er s* of late Herbert George Huckstep and Agnes Huckstep (*née* Lawrie-Smith); *m* 1960, Margaret Ann, *e d* of Ronald Græme Macbeth, DM, FRCS; two *s* one *d. Educ:* Cathedral Sch., Shanghai, China; Queens' Coll., Cambridge; Mddx Hosp. Med. Sch., London. MA, MB, BChir (Cantab) 1952; MD (Cantab) 1957; FRCS (Edinburgh) 1957; FRCS 1958; FAOrthA 1972; FRACS 1973. Registrar and Chief Asst, Orthopaedic Dept, St Bartholomew's Hosp., and various surgical appts Middx and Royal Nat. Orthopaedic Hosps, London, 1952–60; Hunterian Prof., RCS of Eng., 1959–60. Makerere Univ. Coll., Kampala, Uganda: Lectr, 1960–62, Sen. Lectr, 1962–65 and Reader, 1965–67, in Orthopaedic Surgery, with responsibility for starting orthopaedic dept in Uganda; Prof. of Orthopaedic Surgery, Makerere Univ., Kampala, 1967–72. Became Hon. Cons. Orthopaedic Surgeon, Mulago and Mengo

Hosps, and Round Table Polio Clinic, Kampala; Adviser on Orthopaedic Surgery, Ministry of Health, Uganda, 1960–72. Corresp. Editor: Brit. and Amer. jls of Bone and Joint Surgery, 1965–72; Jl Western Pacific Orthopædic Assoc.; British Jl of Accident Surgery. Fellow, British Orthopaedic Assoc., 1967; Hon. Fellow, Western Pacific Orthopaedic Assoc., 1968. Commonwealth Foundn Travelling Lectr, 1970, 1978–79 and 1982. FRSM; FTS 1982. Patron Med. Soc., Univ. of NSW; Founder, World Orthopaedic Concern, 1973 (Hon. Mem. 1978); Vice-Pres., Australian Orthopaedic Assoc., 1982–83 (Betts Medal, 1983); Pres., Coast Med. Assoc., Sydney, 1985–86; Chairman, Fellow or Mem. various med. socs and of assocs, councils and cttees concerned with orthopaedic and traumatic surgery, accident services and rehabilitation of physically disabled. Inventions incl. Huckstep femoral fracture nail, hip, knee, shoulder and circlip. Irving Geist Award, 11th World Congress, Internat. Soc. for Rehabilitation of the Disabled, 1969; James Cook Medal, Royal Soc. of NSW, 1984; Sutherland Medal, Australian Acad. of Technological Scis, 1986; Paul Harris Fellow and Medal, Rotary Internat., 1987; Humanitarian Award, Orthopaedics Overseas, 1991. Hon. MD NSW, 1988. Hon. Mem., Mark Twain Soc., 1978. Rotary Vocational Service Award, 1994. *Publications:* Typhoid Fever and Other Salmonella Infections, 1962; A Simple Guide to Trauma, 1970, 5th edn 1995 (trans. Italian 1978, Japanese 1982); Poliomyelitis A Guide for Developing Countries, Including Appliances and Rehabilitation, 1975 (ELBS and repr. edns 1979, 1983, French edn 1983); A Simple Guide to Orthopaedics, 1993; Colour Test in Orthopaedics and Trauma, 1994; various booklets, chapters in books, papers and films on injuries, orthopaedic diseases, typhoid fever, appliances and implants. *Recreations:* photography, designing orthopaedic appliances and implants for cripples in developing and developed countries, swimming, travel. *Address:* 108 Sugarloaf Crescent, Castlecrag, Sydney, NSW 2068, Australia. *T:* (2) 99581786, *Fax:* (2) 99672971. *Club:* Australian (Sydney).

HUDD, Roy; actor; *b* 16 May 1936; *s* of Harold Hudd and Evelyn Barham; *m* 1st, 1963, Ann Lambert (marr. diss. 1983); one *s*; 2nd, 1988, Deborah Flitcroft. *Educ:* Croydon Secondary Technical School. Entered show business, 1957, as half of double act Hudd & Kay; Butlin Redcoats; started as a solo comedian, 1959; first pantomime, Empire Theatre, Leeds, 1959; 4 years' concert party Out of the Blue, 1960–63; first radio broadcast Workers Playtime, 1960; *stage includes:* The Merchant of Venice, 1960; The Give Away, 1969; At the Palace, 1970; Young Vic Co. seasons, 1973, 1976, 1977; Oliver!, 1977; Underneath the Arches, 1982 (SWET Actor of the Year); Run For Your Wife, 1986, 1989; The Birth of Merlin, Theatre Clwyd, 1989; The Fantasticks, 1990; Midsummer Night's Dream, 1991; *films include:* Blood Beast Terror, 1967; Up Pompeii; The Seven Magnificent Deadly Sins; Up the Chastity Belt; The Garnet Saga; An Acre of Seats in a Garden of Dreams, 1973; What'll You Have, 1974; Up Marketing, 1975; *television series include:* Not So much a Programme, More a Way of Life, 1964; Illustrated Weekly Hudd, 1966–68; Roy Hudd Show, 1971; Comedy Tonight, 1970–71; Up Sunday, 1973; Pebble Mill, 1974–75; Hold the Front Page, 1974–75; The 60 70 80 show, 1974–77; Movie Memories, 1981–85; Halls of Fame, 1985; The Puppet Man, 1985; Cinderella, 1986; Hometown, 1987, 1988–89; What's My Line?, 1990; Lipstick On Your Collar, 1993; Common as Muck, 1994; What's My Line, 1994–95; Karaoke, 1995; *radio series:* The News Huddlines, 1975–; *author of stage shows:* Victorian Christmas, 1978; Just a Verse and Chorus, 1979; Roy Hudd's Very Own Music Hall, 1980; Beautiful Dreamer, 1980; Underneath the Arches, 1982; While London Sleeps, 1983; They Called Me Al, 1987; numerous pantomimes, 1980–. Chm., Entertainment Artistes Benevolent Fund, 1980–90. Pres., British Music Hall Soc., 1992–. King Rat, Grand Order of Water Rats, 1989. Variety Club BBC Radio Personality, 1976, 1993; Gold Badge of Merit, BASCA, 1981; Sony Gold Award, 1990; British Comedy Lifetime Achievement, LWT, 1990. *Publications:* Music Hall, 1976; Roy Hudd's Book of Music Hall, Variety and Show Biz Anecdotes, 1993. *Recreations:* collecting old songs and sleeping. *Address:* 652 Finchley Road, NW11 7NT. *T:* 0181–458 7288. *Club:* Green Room.

HUDDIE, Sir David (Patrick), Kt 1968; FEng 1981; retired; *b* 12 March 1916; *s* of James and Catherine Huddie; *m* 1941, Wilhelmina Betty Booth; three *s*. *Educ:* Mountjoy Sch., Dublin; Trinity Coll., Dublin. FIQA 1980; FIMechE 1974. Aero Engine Division, Rolls-Royce Ltd: Asst Chief Designer, 1947; Chief Development Engineer, 1953; Commercial Dir, 1959; General Manager, 1962; Dir, Rolls-Royce Ltd, 1961; Man. Dir, Aero Engine Div., 1965; Chm. Rolls-Royce Aero Engines Inc., 1969–70; Senior Res. Fellow, Imperial Coll., London, 1971–80, Hon. Fellow, 1981. Hon. DSc Dublin, 1968. *Recreations:* gardening, music, archaeology. *Address:*The Croft, Butts Road, Bakewell, Derbyshire DE45 1EB. *T:* Bakewell (01629) 813330.

HUDDLESTON, Most Rev. (Ernest Urban) Trevor, CR; DD; Chairman, International Defence and Aid Fund for Southern Africa, since 1983; *b* 15 June 1913; *s* of late Capt. Sir Ernest Huddleston, CIE, CBE; unmarried. *Educ:* Lancing; Christ Church, Oxford (Hon. Student, 1993); Wells Theological College. 2nd class Hon. Mod. Hist., Oxford, 1934 (BA), MA 1937. Deacon, 1936; Priest, 1937. Joined Community of the Resurrection; Professed, 1941. Apptd Priest-in-charge Sophiatown and Orlando Anglican Missions, diocese Johannesburg, Nov. 1943; Provincial in S Africa, CR, 1949–55; Guardian of Novices, CR, Mirfield, 1956–58; Prior of the London House, Community of the Resurrection, 1958–60; Bishop of Masasi, 1960–68; Bishop Suffragan of Stepney, 1968–78; Bishop of Mauritius, 1978–83; Archbishop of the Indian Ocean, 1978–83. Provost, Selly Oak Colls, 1983–. President: Anti-Apartheid Movement, 1981–94 (Vice-Pres., 1969–81); Nat. Peace Council, 1983–; IVS, 1984–; Chm., Internat. Defence and Aid Fund, 1983–. Trustee, Runnymede Trust, 1972–90. Fellow, Queen Mary and Westfield Coll., London Univ., 1990. Hon. DD: Aberdeen, 1956; City, 1987; Exeter, 1992; Oxford, 1993; Birmingham, 1993; Whittier Coll., Calif, 1994; Dundee, 1994; Hon. DLitt: Lancaster, 1972; Warwick, 1988; CNAA, 1989; City of London Polytechnic, 1989; Hon. DHL Denison Univ., USA, 1989; Hon. LLD Leeds, 1991. Indira Gandhi Meml Prize, 1995. *Publications:* Naught for Your Comfort, 1956; The True and Living God, 1964; God's World, 1966; I Believe: reflections on the Apostles Creed, 1986; Return to South Africa, 1991. *Recreation:* listening to music. *Address:* House of the Resurrection, Mirfield, W Yorks WF14 0BN.

HUDSON, Prof. Anne Mary, DPhil; FRHistS; FBA 1988; Professor of Medieval English, Oxford, since 1989; Fellow of Lady Margaret Hall, Oxford, since 1963; *b* 28 Aug. 1938; *d* of late R. L. and K. M. Hudson. *Educ:* Dartford Grammar Sch. for Girls; St Hugh's Coll., Oxford (BA English cl. I; MA; DPhil 1964). FRHistS 1976. Lectr in Medieval English, 1961–63, Tutor, 1963–91, LMH, Oxford; Oxford University: CUF Lectr, 1963–81; Special Lectr, 1981–83; British Acad. Reader in the Humanities, 1983–86; Lectr in Medieval English, 1986–89. Exec. Sec., 1969–82, Mem. Council, 1982–, EETS. Sir Israel Gollancz Prize, British Acad., 1985, 1991. *Publications:* (ed) Selections from English Wycliffite Writings, 1978; (ed) English Wycliffite Sermons, i, 1983, iii, 1990; Lollards and their Books, 1985; (ed jtly) From Ockham to Wyclif, 1987; The Premature Reformation, 1988; (ed) Two Wycliffite Texts, 1993. *Address:* Lady Margaret Hall, Oxford OX2 6QA.

HUDSON, Prof. Anthony Hugh, PhD; Professor of Common Law, Liverpool University, 1977–92, now Emeritus (Dean of Faculty of Law, 1971–78 and 1984–91); *b* 21 Jan. 1928; *s* of late Dr Thomas A. G. Hudson and Bridget Hudson; *m* 1962, Joan O'Malley; one *s* three *d*. *Educ:* St Joseph's Coll., Blackpool; Pembroke Coll., Cambridge (LLB 1950, MA 1953); PhD Manchester 1966. Called to Bar, Lincoln's Inn, 1954. Lecturer in Law: Hull Univ., 1951–57; Birmingham Univ., 1957–62; Manchester Univ., 1962–64; Liverpool University: Sen. Lectr, 1964–71; Professor of Law, 1971–77. *Publications:* (jtly) Hood Phillips: A First Book of English Law, 7th edn 1977, 8th edn 1988; (jtly) Commercial Banking Law, 1978; (jtly) Stevens and Borrie Mercantile Law, 17th edn 1978; contribs to various legal periodicals. *Recreations:* gardening, walking, history. *Address:* 18 Dowhills Road, Blundellsands, Crosby, Liverpool L23 8SW. *T:* 0151–924 5830.

HUDSON, (Eleanor) Erlund, RE 1946 (ARE 1938); RWS 1949 (ARWS 1939); ARCA (London) 1937; artist; *b* 18 Feb. 1912; *d* of Helen Ingeborg Olsen, Brookline, Boston, USA, and Harold Hudson. *Educ:* Torquay; Dorking; Royal College of Art (Diploma 1937, Travelling Scholarship 1938). Mem. Chicago Print Soc. and Soc. of Artist Print-Makers. Studied and travelled in Italy summer 1939. Interrupted by war. Exhibited in London, Provinces, Scandinavia, Canada, USA, etc.; works purchased by War Artists Advisory Council, 1942–43. Formerly Artistic Dir and designer, Brooking Ballet Sch., W1. *Recreations:* music, country life. *Address:* 6 Hammersmith Terrace, W6. *T:* 0181–748 3778; Meadow House, Old Bosham, W Sussex. *T:* Bosham (01243) 573558.

HUDSON, Erlund; *see* Hudson, E. E.

HUDSON, Frank Michael Stanislaus; a Recorder of the Crown Court, 1981–87; *b* 28 Sept. 1916; *s* of Frederick Francis Hudson and Elizabeth Frances (*née* O'Herlihy); *m* 1947, Jean Colburn (*née* Gordon); one *d*. *Educ:* Wimbledon Coll.; London Univ. (BA). Called to the Bar, Middle Temple, 1961; practised Northern Circuit, 1969–86. Served War: 77th Field Regt RA, 1939–42; Glider Pilot Regt, 1942–45. Post-war employment in local govt and in trade assocs; Dep. Circuit Judge, 1977–80.

HUDSON, Prof. George, FRCP, FRCPath; Professor of Experimental Haematology, University of Sheffield, 1975–89, now Emeritus; *b* 10 Aug. 1924; *s* of George Hudson, blacksmith, and Edith Hannah (*née* Bennett); *m* 1955, Mary Patricia Hibbert (decd); one *d*. *Educ:* Edenfield C of E Sch.; Bury Grammar Sch.; Manchester Univ. (MSc, MB, ChB); MD, DSc Bristol. House Officer, Manchester Royal Inf., 1949–50; Demonstr in Anatomy, Univ. of Bristol, 1950–51; RAMC, 1951–53; University of Bristol: Lectr, later Reader, in Anatomy, 1953–68; Preclinical Dean, 1963–68; Vis. Prof., Univ. of Minnesota (Fulbright Award), 1959–60; Sheffield University: Admin. Dean, 1968–83; Hon. Clinical Lectr in Haematology, 1968–75; Head, Dept of Haematology, 1981–89; Postgrad. Dean, 1984–91. Hon. Cons. Haematologist, United Sheffield Hosps, 1969–89. Chm., Conf. of Deans of Provincial Med. Schs, 1980–82; Member: Sheffield RHB, 1970–74; Sheffield HA, 1974–84; DHSS Working Party on NHS Adv. and Representative Machinery, 1980–81; Council for Postgraduate Med. Educn for England and Wales, 1980–83. Hon. LLD Sheffield, 1993. *Publications:* papers in medical and scientific jls on haematological subjects. *Recreations:* lay reader since 1953, history of medicine, cavies, garden. *Address:* 275 Ringinglow Road, Sheffield S11 7PZ. *T:* Sheffield (0114) 236 8004.

HUDSON, Sir Havelock (Henry Trevor), Kt 1977; Lloyd's Underwriter 1952–88; Chairman of Lloyd's, 1975, 1976 and 1977 (Deputy Chairman, 1968, 1971, 1973); *b* 4 Jan. 1919; *er s* of late Savile E. Hudson and Dorothy Hudson (*née* Cheetham); *m* 1st, 1944, Elizabeth (marr. diss., 1956), *d* of Brig. W. Home; two *s*; 2nd, 1957, Cathleen Blanche Lily (*d* 1994), *d* of 6th Earl of St Germans; one *s* one *d*. *Educ:* Rugby. Merchant Service, 1937–38. Served War of 1939–45: Royal Hampshire Regt (Major), 1939–42; 9 Parachute Bn, 1942–44. Member: Cttee Lloyd's Underwriters Assoc., 1963; Cttee of Lloyd's, 1965–68, 1970–73, 1975–78; Exec. Bd, Lloyd's Register of Shipping, 1967–78. Dir, Ellerman Lines Ltd, 1979–84. Vice Pres., Chartered Insurance Inst., 1973–76, Dep. Pres., 1976–77; Chairman: Arvon Foundn, 1973–85; Oxford Artificial Kidney and Transplant Unit, 1976–90; Pres., City of London Outward Bound Assoc., 1979–88; Member, Board of Governors: Pangbourne Coll., 1976–88; Bradfield Coll., 1978–88. Lloyd's Gold Medal, 1977. *Recreation:* shooting. *Address:* The Old Rectory, Stanford Dingley, Reading, Berkshire RG7 6LX. *T:* Bradfield (01734) 744346. *Club:* Boodle's.

HUDSON, Ian Francis, CB 1976; Deputy Secretary, Department of Employment, 1976–80; *b* 29 May 1925; *s* of Francis Reginald Hudson and Dorothy Mary Hudson (*née* Crabbe); *m* 1952, Gisela Elisabeth Grettka; one *s* one *d*. *Educ:* City of London Sch.; New Coll., Oxford. Royal Navy, 1943–47. Customs and Excise, 1947–53; Min. of Labour, 1953–56, 1959–61, 1963–64; Treasury, 1957–58; Dept of Labour, Australia, 1961–63; Asst Sec., 1963; DEA, 1964–68; Under-Sec., 1967; Dept of Employment, 1968–73; Dep. Sec. 1973; Sec., Pay Board, 1973–74; Sec., Royal Commn on Distribution of Income and Wealth, 1974–76.

See also J. A. Hudson.

HUDSON, James Ralph, CBE 1976; FRCS; Surgeon, Moorfields Eye Hospital, 1956–81, now Honorary Consulting Surgeon; Ophthalmic Surgeon, Guy's Hospital, 1963–76; Hon. Ophthalmic Surgeon: Hospital of St John and St Elizabeth, since 1953; King Edward VII Hospital for Officers, 1970–86; Teacher of Ophthalmology, Guy's Hospital, 1964–76, Institute of Ophthalmology, University of London, 1961–81; Consultant Adviser in Ophthalmology, Department of Health and Social Security, 1969–82; *b* 15 Feb. 1916; *o s* of late William Shand Hudson and Ethel Summerskill; *m* 1946, Margaret May Oulpé; two *s* two *d*. *Educ:* The King's Sch., Canterbury; Middlesex Hosp. (Edmund Davis Exhibnr), Univ. of London, MRCS, LRCP 1939; MB, BS London 1940; DOMS (England) 1948; FRCS 1949; FRCOphth (FCOphth 1988; Hon. FCOphth 1990). Res. Med. Appts, Tindal House Emergency Hosp. (Mddx Hosp. Sector), 1939–42. RAFVR Med. Service, 1942–46; Sqdn Ldr, 1944–46. Moorfields Eye Hosp., Clin. Asst, 1947, Ho. Surg., 1947–49; Sen. Resident Officer, 1949, Chief Clin. Asst, 1950–56; Middlesex Hosp., Clin. Asst Ophth. Outpatients, 1950–51; Ophth. Surg., W Middlesex Hosp., 1950–56, Mount Vernon Hosp., 1953–59. Civil Consultant in Ophthalmology to RAF, 1970–82. Examr in Ophthalmology (Dipl. Ophth. of Examg Bd of Eng., RCP and RCS, 1960–65; Mem. Court of Examrs, RCS, 1966–72). FRSocMed 1947 (Vice-Pres. Sect. of Ophthalmology, 1965); Member: Ophthal. Soc. UK, 1948–88 (Hon. Sec. 1956–58, Vice-Pres., 1969–71, Pres., 1982–84); Faculty of Ophthalmologists, 1950–88 (Mem. Council, 1960–82; Hon. Sec. 1960–70; Vice-Pres., 1970–74; Pres., 1974–77; Rep. on Council of RCS, 1968–73; Hon. Mem., 1982–); Soc. Française d'Ophtal., 1950– (membre délégué étranger, 1970–92); Cttee d'Honneur Les Entretiens Annuels d'Ophtalmologie, 1970–; Internat. Council of Ophthalmology, 1978–86; UK Rep., Union Européenne des Médecins Spécialistes (Ophthalmology Section), 1973–91 (Pres., 1982–86); Hon. Fellow, Royal Aust. Coll. Ophthalmologists; Pilgrims of Gt Britain; Hon. Steward, Westminster Abbey, 1972–88. Liveryman, Soc. of Apothecaries, and Freeman of City of London. *Publications:* (with T. Keith Lyle) chapters in Matthews's Recent Advances in the Surgery of Trauma; contrib. to chapters in Rob and Rodney Smith's Operative Surgery, 1969; articles in: Brit. Jl of Ophthalmology; Trans Ophth. Soc. UK; Proc. Royal Soc. Med. *Recreations:* motoring, travel. *Address:* Flat 2, 17 Montagu Square, W1H 1RD. *T:* 0171–487 2680. *Club:* Garrick.

HUDSON, John Arthur, CB 1970; Deputy Under-Secretary of State, Department of Education and Science, 1969–80; *b* 24 Aug. 1920; *s* of Francis Reginald Hudson and Dorothy Mary (*née* Crabbe); *m* 1960, Dwynwen Davies; one *s* one *d*. *Educ:* City of

London Sch.; Jesus Coll., Oxford. Served Royal Corps of Signals, 1941–45 (despatches). Entered Ministry of Education, 1946. Mem., South Bank Theatre Bd, 1967–89. *Address:* The Rosary, Green Lane, Leominster, Herefordshire HR6 8QN. *T:* Leominster (01568) 614413.

See also I. F. Hudson.

HUDSON, Prof. John Pilkington, CBE 1975 (MBE (mil.) 1943); GM 1944 and Bar 1945; BSc, MSc, PhD; NDH; FIBiol; now Emeritus Professor; former Director, Long Ashton Research Station, and Professor of Horticultural Science, University of Bristol, 1967–75; *b* 24 July 1910; *o s* of W. A. Hudson and Bertha (*née* Pilkington); *m* 1936, Mary Gretta, *d* of late W. N. and Mary Heath, Westfields, Market Bosworth, Leics; two *s*. *Educ:* New Mills Grammar Sch.; Midland Agricultural Coll.; University Coll., Nottingham. Hort. Adviser, E Sussex CC, 1935–39. Served War of 1939–45, Royal Engineers Bomb Disposal (Major). Horticulturist, Dept of Agric., Wellington, NZ, 1945–48; Lecturer in Horticulture, University of Nottingham Sch. of Agric., 1948–50; Head of Dept of Horticulture, University of Nottingham, 1950–67 (as Prof. of Horticulture, 1958–67, Dean, Faculty of Agriculture and Horticulture, 1965–67); seconded part-time to Univ. of Khartoum, Sudan, to found Dept of Horticulture, 1961–63. Associate of Honour, Royal New Zealand Institute of Horticulture, 1948. Chm., Jt Advisory Cttee on Agricultural Education (HMSO report published, 1973); Mem., RHS Exam. Bd; PP and Hon. Mem., Hort. Educn Assoc. Hon. Fellow: RASE, 1977; Inst. of Hort., 1985. VMH, 1976. Editor, Experimental Agriculture, 1965–82; Past Mem. Editorial Bds, Jl Hort. Sci, SPAN. *Publications:* (ed) Control of the Plant Environment, 1957; numerous technical instructions on dealing with unexploded bomb fuses, where unambiguity was a matter of life and death; many contribs on effects of environment on plant growth and productivity to scientific jls. *Recreations:* choral singing, gardening. *Address:* The Spinney, Wrington, Bristol BS18 7LB.

See also R. A. Hudson.

HUDSON, Keith William, FRICS; Technical Secretary, Cost Commission, Comité Européen des Economistes de la Construction, since 1989; *b* 2 June 1928; *s* of William Walter Hudson and Jessie Sarah Hudson; *m* 1952, Ailsa White; two *s* two *d*. *Educ:* Sir Charles Elliott Sch.; Coll. of Estate Management. FRICS 1945. Served Army, 1948–50 (Lieut). Private practice, 1945–48 and 1950–57; Min. of Works, Basic Grade, 1957–64; Min. of Health (later DHSS), 1964–: Main Grade, 1964–66; Sen. Grade, 1966–74; Superintending, 1974–76; Dir B, 1976–79; Under Sec., 1979; Dir of Construction and Cost Intelligence, and Chief Surveyor, DHSS, 1979–86, retd. *Publications:* articles in Chartered Surveyor and in Building. *Recreations:* Rugby coaching, athletics coaching. *Address:* Silver Birch, Mill Lane, Felbridge, East Grinstead, West Sussex RH19 2PE. *T:* East Grinstead (01342) 325817.

HUDSON, Prof. Liam, MA, PhD; psychologist and writer; partner, Balas Co-partnership, since 1987; *b* 20 July 1933; *er s* of Cyril and Kathleen Hudson; *m* 1st, 1955, Elizabeth Ward; 2nd 1965, Bernadine Jacot de Boinod; three *s* one *d*. *Educ:* Whitgift Sch.; Exeter Coll., Oxford. Post-graduate and post-doctoral research, Psychological Laboratory, Cambridge, 1957–65, and Research Centre, King's Coll., Cambridge, 1965–68; Fellow, King's Coll., Cambridge, 1966–68; Bell Prof. of Educnl Scis, Univ. of Edinburgh, 1968–77 and Dir, Res. Unit on Intellectual Develt, 1964–77; Prof. of Psychology, Brunel Univ., 1977–87. Mem., Inst. for Advanced Study, Princeton, 1974–75; Vis. Prof., Tavistock and Portman Clinics, London, 1987–. Maurice Hille Award, SIAD, 1983. *Publications:* Contrary Imaginations, 1966; Frames of Mind, 1968; (ed) The Ecology of Human Intelligence, 1970; The Cult of the Fact, 1972; Human Beings, 1975; The Nympholepts, 1978; Bodies of Knowledge, 1982; Night Life, 1985; The Way Men Think, 1991; Intimate Relations, 1995. *Recreations:* painting and photography, making things, otherwise largely domestic. *Address:* 34 North Park, Gerrards Cross, Bucks SL9 8JN.

HUDSON, Norman Barrie; Under Secretary, International Division, Overseas Development Administration, since 1993; *b* 21 June 1937; *s* of William and Mary Hudson; *m* 1963, Hazel (*née* Cotterill); two *s* one *d*. *Educ:* King Henry VIII Sch., Coventry; Univ. of Sheffield (BA Hons 1958); University Coll., London (MScEcon 1960). Economist, Tube Investments Ltd, 1960; Economist, Economist Intell. Unit, 1962; National Accounts Statistician (UK Technical Assistance to Govt of Jordan), 1963; Statistician, ODM, 1966; Econ. Adviser, ME Develt Div., Beirut, 1967; Overseas Development Administration: Econ. Adviser, 1972, Sen. Econ. Adviser, 1973; Head, SE Asia Develt Div., Bangkok, 1974; Asst Sec., 1977; Under Sec. (Principal Establishments Officer), 1981; Under Sec. for Africa, 1986. *Recreations:* theatre, reading, music, watching football and cricket. *Address:* The Galleons, Sallows Shaw, Sole Street, Cobham, Kent DA13 9BP. *T:* Meopham (01474) 814419.

HUDSON, Pamela May; *see* Hudson-Bendersky, P. M.

HUDSON, Lt-Gen. Sir Peter, KCB 1977; CBE 1970 (MBE 1965); DL; Lieutenant of the Tower of London, 1986–89; *b* 14 Sept. 1923; *s* of Captain William Hudson, late The Rifle Bde, and Ivy (*née* Brown); *m* 1949, Susan Anne Knollys; one adopted *s* one *d* and one adopted *d*. *Educ:* Wellingborough; Jesus Coll., Cambridge. Commnd into The Rifle Bde, 1944; psc 1954; comd company in Mau Mau and Malayan campaigns, 1955–57; jssc 1963; comd 3rd Bn The Royal Green Jackets, 1966–67; Regimental Col The Royal Green Jackets, 1968; Comdr 39 Infantry Bde, 1968–70; IDC 1971; GOC Eastern Dist, 1973–74; Chief of Staff, Allied Forces Northern Europe, 1975–77; Dep. C-in-C, UKLF, 1977–80; Inspector-Gen., T&AVR, 1978–80. Col Comdt, The Light Div., 1977–80; Hon. Colonel: Southampton Univ. OTC, 1980–85; 5 (Volunteer) Bn, The Royal Green Jackets, TA, 1985–93. Mem., Gen. Adv. Council, BBC, 1981–85. Mem., Rifle Bde Club and Assoc. (Chm., 1979–85); Trustee, Rifle Bde Museum (Chm., Trustees, 1979–85); Chairman: Green Jacket Club, 1979–85; Council, TA&VRA, 1981–90; Pres., Reserve Forces Assoc., 1985–91. Vice Chm., St John Fellowship, 1994–. Governor: Royal Sch. Bath, 1976– (Chm., 1981–88); Bradfield Coll., 1983–94. Mem., Frilsham Parish Council, 1988–. Freeman of City of London, 1965. DL Berks, 1984. FIMgt. KStJ (Sec.-Gen., Order of St John, 1981–88, Mem. Council, Royal Berks, 1988–). *Recreations:* travel, fishing, most games. *Address:* Little Orchard, Frilsham, Newbury, Berks RG16 9XB. *Clubs:* Naval and Military, St John House, MCC; I Zingari; Green Jackets; Free Foresters.

HUDSON, Peter Geoffrey; Member, Panel of Chairmen, Civil Service Selection Board, 1987–94; *b* 26 July 1926; *s* of late Thomas Albert Hudson and late Gertrude Hudson; *m* 1954, Valerie Mary, *yr d* of late Lewis Alfred Hart and late Eva Mary Hart; two *s*. *Educ:* King Edward VII Sch., Sheffield; Queen's Coll., Oxford (Hastings Scholar, MA). Gold Medallist, Royal Schs of Music, 1940. Sub-Lt RNVR, 1944–46. Min. of Transport, 1949; Private Sec. to Minister of Transport and Civil Aviation, 1951–53; Principal, Min. of Transport and Civil Aviation, 1953–57; Admin. Staff Coll., Henley, 1957; British Civil Air Attaché, SE Asia and Far East, 1958–61; Asst Sec., Overseas Policy Div. and Estabt Div., Min. of Aviation and BoT, 1963–68; Counsellor (Civil Aviation), British Embassy, Washington, 1968–71; Under-Sec., DTI, 1971–84; Dir of Resources, British Tourist Authority and English Tourist Bd, 1984–86. Indep. Advr to Lady Marre Cttee on Future of Legal Profession, 1987–88. Vice Chm., Bromley CAB, 1989–95. Governor, Coll. of Air Trng, Hamble, 1974–75. *Recreation:* music. *Address:* Candle Hill, Raggleswood, Chislehurst, Kent BR7 5NH. *T:* 0181–467 1761.

HUDSON, Peter John, CB 1978; Deputy Under-Secretary of State (Finance and Budget), Ministry of Defence, 1976–79; *b* 29 Sept. 1919; *o s* of late A. J. Hudson; *m* 1954, Joan Howard FitzGerald; one *s* one *d*. *Educ:* Tollington Sch.; Birkbeck Coll., London. Exchequer and Audit Dept, 1938; RNVR, 1940–46 (Lieut); Asst Principal, Air Min., 1947; Private Sec. to Perm. Under Sec. of State for Air, 1948–51; Asst Sec., 1958; Head of Air Staff Secretariat, 1958–61; Imperial Defence Coll., 1962; Head of Programme and Budget Div., MoD, 1966–69; Under-Sec., Cabinet Office, 1969–72; Asst Under-Sec. of State, MoD, 1972–75; Dep. Under-Sec. of State (Air), MoD, 1975–76. *Address:* Folly Hill, Haslemere, Surrey GU27 2EY. *T:* Haslemere (0142864) 2078. *Club:* Royal Air Force.

HUDSON, Prof. Richard Anthony, FBA 1992; Professor of Linguistics, University College London, since 1989; *b* 18 Sept. 1939; *s* of Prof. John Pilkington Hudson, *qv*; *m* 1970, Gaynor Evans; two *d*. *Educ:* Loughborough Grammar Sch.; Corpus Christi Coll., Cambridge (BA); Sch. of Oriental and African Studies, London (PhD). University College London: Research Asst, Linguistics, 1964–70; Lectr 1970, Reader 1980, Dept of Phonetics and Linguistics. *Publications:* English Complex Sentences: an introduction to systemic grammar, 1971; Arguments for a Non-Transformational Grammar, 1976; Sociolinguistics, 1980; Word Grammar, 1984; An Invitation to Linguistics, 1984; English Word Grammar, 1990; Teaching Grammar: a guide for the national curriculum, 1992; Word Meaning, 1995; articles in jls. *Recreations:* running, walking, cycling, music. *Address:* Department of Phonetics and Linguistics, University College London, Gower Street, WC1E 6BT. *T:* 0171–380 7172.

HUDSON, Prof. Robert Francis, PhD; FRS 1982; Professor of Organic Chemistry, University of Kent at Canterbury, 1967–85 (part-time, 1981–85), now Emeritus; *b* 15 Dec. 1922; *s* of late John Frederick Hudson and Ethel Hudson; *m* 1945, Monica Ashton Stray; one *s* twin *d*. *Educ:* Brigg Grammar Sch.; Imperial Coll. of Science and Technol., London (BSc, ARCS, PhD, DIC). Asst Lectr, Imperial Coll., London, 1945–47; Consultant, Wolsey Ltd, Leicester, 1945–50; Lectr, Queen Mary Coll., London, 1947–59; Res. Fellow, Purdue Univ., 1954; Gp Dir, Cyanamid European Res. Inst., Geneva, 1960–66. Vis. Professor: Rochester, USA, 1970; Bergen, 1971; CNRS, Thiais, Paris, 1973; Calgary, 1975; Mainz, 1979; Queen's, Kingston, Ont, 1983. Lectures: Frontiers, Case-Western Reserve Univ., USA, 1970; Nuffield, Canada, 1975; Quest, Queen's, Ont, 1983. Vice-Pres., Inst. of Science Technol., 1970–76; Member: Council, Chemical Soc., 1967–70 (Foundn Chm., Organic Reaction Mechanism Gp, 1973); Dalton Council, 1973–76; Perkin Council, 1980–83. *Publications:* (with P. Alexander) Wool—its physics and chemistry, 1954, 2nd edn 1960; Structure and Mechanism in Organophosphorus Chemistry, 1965; papers mainly in Jl of Chem. Soc., Helvetica Chemica Acta and Angewandte Chemie. *Address:* The Chemical Laboratory, University of Kent at Canterbury, Canterbury, Kent CT2 7NH. *T:* Canterbury (01227) 764000; 37 Puckle Lane, Canterbury CT1 3LA. *T:* Canterbury (01227) 761340. *Club:* Athenæum.

HUDSON, Thomas Charles, CBE 1975; Chairman, ICL Ltd, 1972–80; Chartered Accountant (Canadian); *b* Sidcup, Kent, 23 Jan. 1915; British parents; *m* 1st, 1944, Lois Alma Hudson (marr. diss. 1973); two *s* one *d*; 2nd, 1986, Susan Gillian van Kan. *Educ:* Middleton High Sch., Nova Scotia. With Nightingale, Hayman & Co, Chartered Accountants, 1935–40. Served War, Royal Canadian Navy, Lieut, 1940–45. IBM Canada, as Sales Rep., 1946–51 (transf. to IBM, UK, as Sales Manager, 1951, and Managing Dir, 1954–65). Plessey Company: Financial Dir, 1967; Dir, 1969–76; Dir, ICL, 1968. Councillor for Enfield, GLC, 1970–73. *Recreations:* tennis, ski-ing, gardening. *Address:* Hele Farm, North Bovey, Devon TQ13 8RW. *T:* Moretonhampstead (01647) 440249. *Club:* Carlton.

HUDSON-BENDERSKY, Pamela May, CBE 1988; JP; Regional Nursing Director, North West Thames Regional Health Authority, 1985–88, retired; *b* 1 June 1931; *d* of late Leonard Joshua Hudson and of Mabel Ellen Hudson (now Baker). *Educ:* South West Essex High School. SRN. Nursing Officer, Charing Cross Hosp., 1966–67; Matron, Fulham Hosp., 1967–70; Principal Regl Nursing Officer, SE Thames RHB, 1970–73; Area Nursing Officer, Lambeth, Southwark and Lewisham AHA(T), 1973–82; Regional Nursing Officer, NW Thames RHA, 1982–85. Member, Alcohol Education and Research Council, 1982–87. JP Inner London SE Div., 1983–88; Cheltenham Petty Sessional Div., 1989–. *Publications:* contribs to nursing profession jls. *Recreations:* embroidery, theatre. *Address:* Uluru, 13 Northcot Lane, Draycott, near Moreton-in-Marsh, Glos GL56 9LR. *T:* Blockley (0138670) 0142.

HUDSON DAVIES, (Gwilym) Ednyfed; *see* Davies, G. E. H.

HUDSON-WILLIAMS, Prof. Harri Llwyd, MA; Professor of Greek in the University of Newcastle upon Tyne (formerly King's College, Newcastle upon Tyne, University of Durham), 1952–76 and Head of Department of Classics, 1969–76; now Emeritus Professor; *b* 16 Feb. 1911; *yr s* of late Prof. T. Hudson-Williams; *m* 1946, Joan, *er d* of late Lieut-Col H. F. T. Fisher; two *d*. *Educ:* University College of North Wales; King's Coll., Cambridge (Browne Medallist; Charles Oldham Scholar); Munich University. Asst Lectr in Greek, Liverpool Univ., 1937–40; Intelligence Corps, 1940–41; Foreign Office, 1941–45; Lectr in Greek, Liverpool Univ., 1945–50; Reader in Greek, King's Coll., Newcastle upon Tyne, 1950–52; Dean of the Faculty of Arts, 1963–66. *Publications:* contribs to various classical jls, etc. *Recreation:* gardening. *Address:* The Pound, Mill Street, Islip, Oxon OX5 2SZ. *T:* Oxford (01865) 375893.

HUEBNER, Michael Denis, CB 1994; Deputy Secretary, since 1989, Chief Executive (formerly Head) of the Court Service and Deputy Clerk of the Crown in Chancery, since 1993, Lord Chancellor's Department; *b* 3 Sept. 1941; *s* of late Dr Denis William Huebner and Rene Huebner (*née* Jackson); *m* 1965, Wendy Ann, *d* of Brig. Peter Crosthwaite; one *s* one *d*. *Educ:* Rugby Sch.; St John's Coll., Oxford (BA Modern History). Called to the Bar, Gray's Inn, 1965, Bencher, 1994. Lord Chancellor's Department, 1966–68, 1970–: Law Officers' Dept, 1968–70; Asst Solicitor, 1978; Under Sec., Circuit Administrator, NE Circuit, 1985–88; Prin. Estabt and Finance Officer, 1988–89; Sec. of Commns, 1989–91. *Publications:* brief guide to Ormesby Hall (Nat. Trust); contrib. (jtly) Courts, Halsbury's Laws of England, 4th edn 1975; legal articles in New Law Jl. *Recreations:* looking at pictures, architecture. *Address:* Lord Chancellor's Department, Southside, 105 Victoria Street, SW1E 6QT.

HUFFINLEY, Beryl; President, National Assembly of Women; Vice President, British Peace Assembly; *b* 22 Aug. 1926; *d* of Wilfred and Ivey Sharpe; *m* 1948, Ronald Brown Huffinley. Secretary: Leeds Trades Council, 1966; Yorkshire and Humberside TUC Regional Council, 1974. Chairman: Leeds and York Dist Cttee, T&GWU, 1974; Regional Cttee, T&GWU No 9 Region, 1972. Member: Regional Econ. Planning Council (Yorkshire and Humberside), 1975–79; Leeds AHA, 1977; Press Council, 1978–84. Exec. Cttee, Labour Action for Peace. Trustee Yeadon Trade Council Club.

Address: Cornerways, South View, Menston, Ilkley, Yorks. *T:* Menston (01943) 75115. *Club:* Trades Council (Leeds).

HUFTON, Prof. Olwen, (Mrs B. T. Murphy), PhD; Professor of History, European University Institute, Florence, since 1991; *d* of Joseph Hufton and Caroline Hufton; *m* 1965, Brian Taunton Murphy; two *d. Educ:* Hulme Grammar Sch., Oldham; Univ. of London (BA 1959; PhD 1962). Lectr, Univ. of Leicester, 1963–66; Reading University: Lectr, then Reader, 1966–75; Prof. of Modern Hist., 1975–88; Vis. Fellow, All Souls Coll., Oxford, 1986–87; Prof. of Modern Hist. and Women's Studies, Harvard Univ., 1987–91. Corresp. FBA 1993. *Publications:* Bayeux in the Late Eighteenth Century, 1967; The Poor of Eighteenth Century France, 1974; Europe, Privilege and Protest, 1730–1789, 1980; Women and the Limits of Citizenship in the French Revolution, 1992; articles in Past and Present, Eur. Studies Rev., and French Hist. Studies. *Address:* 40 Shinfield Road, Reading, Berks RG2 7BW. *T:* Reading (01734) 871514.

HUGGINS, family name of **Viscount Malvern.**

HUGGINS, Sir Alan (Armstrong), Kt 1980; Justice of Appeal: Gibraltar and British Antarctica, since 1988; Falkland Islands, since 1988 (President, since 1991); Bermuda, since 1989; British Indian Ocean Territory (President), since 1991; *b* 15 May 1921; *yr s* of late William Armstrong Huggins and Dare (*née* Copping); *m* 1st, 1950, Catherine Davidson (marr. diss.), *d* of late David Dick; two *s* one *d*; 2nd, 1985, Elizabeth Low, *d* of late Christopher William Lumley Dodd, MRCS, LRCP. *Educ:* Radley Coll.; Sidney Sussex Coll., Cambridge (MA). TARO (Special List), 1940–48 (Actg Major); Admiralty, 1941–46. Called to Bar, Lincoln's Inn, 1947. Legal Associate Mem., TPI, 1949–70. Resident Magistrate, Uganda, 1951–53; Stipendiary Magistrate, Hong Kong, 1953–58; District Judge, Hong Kong, 1958–65. Chm., Justice (Hong Kong Br.), 1965–68; Judicial Comr, State of Brunei, 1966–; Judge of Supreme Court, Hong Kong, 1965–76; Justice of Appeal, Hong Kong, 1976–80; Vice-Pres., Court of Appeal, Hong Kong, 1980–87. Hon. Lectr, Hong Kong Univ., 1979–87. Chm., Adv. Cttee on Legal Educn, 1972–87. Diocesan Reader, Dio. of Hong Kong and Macao, 1954–87; Reader, Dio. of Exeter, 1988–. Past Pres., YMCAs of Hong Kong. Hon. Life Governor, Brit. and For. Bible Soc; Hon. Life Mem., Amer. Bible Soc. Liveryman, Leathersellers' Company, 1942–91. *Recreations:* forestry, boating, archery, amateur theatre, tapestry. *Address:* Widdicombe Lodge, Widdicombe, Kingsbridge, Devon TQ7 2EF. *T:* Kingsbridge (01548) 580727. *Club:* Royal Over-Seas League.

HUGGINS, Prof. Charles B.; Professor Emeritus, Ben May Institute and Department of Surgery, University of Chicago, since 1969; William B. Ogden Distinguished Service Professor since 1962; *b* Halifax, Canada, 22 Sept. 1901; *s* of Charles Edward Huggins and Bessie Huggins (*née* Spencer); citizen of USA by naturalization, 1933; *m* 1927, Margaret Wellman; one *s* one *d. Educ:* Acadia (BA 1920; DSc 1946); Harvard (MD 1924). University of Michigan: Interne in Surgery, 1924–26; Instructor in Surgery, 1926–27; Univ. of Chicago, 1927–: Instructor in Surgery, 1927–29; Asst Prof., 1929–33; Assoc. Prof., 1933–36; Prof. of Surgery, 1936–69; Dir, Ben May Laboratory for Cancer Research, 1951–69. Chancellor, Acadia Univ., 1972–79. Alpha Omega Alpha, 1942; Mem. Nat. Acad. of Sciences, 1949; Mem. Amer. Philosophical Soc., 1962. Sigillum Magnum, Bologna Univ., 1964; Hon. Prof., Madrid Univ., 1956; Hon. FRSocMed (London), 1956; Hon. FRCSE 1958; Hon. FRCS 1959; Hon. FACS 1963; Hon. FRSE 1983. Hon. MSc, Yale, 1947; Hon. DSc: Washington Univ., St Louis, 1950; Leeds Univ., 1953; Turin Univ., 1957; Trinity Coll., Hartford, Conn., 1965; Wales, 1967; Univ. of California, Berkeley, 1968; Univ. of Michigan, 1968; Medical Coll. of Ohio, 1973; Gustavus Adolphus Coll., 1975; Wilmington Coll. of Ohio, 1980; Univ. of Louisville, 1980; Hon. LLD: Aberdeen Univ., 1966; York Univ., Toronto, 1968; Hon. DPS, George Washington Univ., 1967. Has given many memorial lectures and has won numerous gold medals, prizes and awards for his work on urology and cancer research, including Nobel Prize for Medicine (jtly), 1966. Holds foreign orders. *Publications:* Experimental Leukemia and Mammary Cancer: Induction, Prevention, Cure, 1979; over 275 articles. *Address:* Ben May Institute, University of Chicago, 5841 South Maryland Avenue, Chicago, IL 60637, USA.

HUGH-JONES, Sir Wynn Normington, (Sir Hugh Jones), Kt 1984; LVO 1961; Joint Hon. Treasurer, Liberal Party, 1984–87; *b* 1 Nov. 1923; *s* of Huw Hugh-Jones and May Normington; *m* 1st, 1958, Ann (*née* Purkiss) (marr. diss. 1987); one *s* two *d*; 2nd, 1987, Oswynne (*née* Buchanan). *Educ:* Ludlow; Selwyn Coll., Cambridge (Scholar; MA) Served in RAF, 1943–46. Entered Foreign Service (now Diplomatic Service), 1947; Foreign Office, 1947–49; Jedda, 1949–52; Paris, 1952–56; FO, 1956–59; Chargé d'Affaires, Conakry, 1959–60; Head of Chancery, Rome, 1960–64; FO, 1964–66, Counsellor, 1964; Consul, Elizabethville (later Lubumbashi), 1966–68; Counsellor and Head of Chancery, Ottawa, 1968–70; FCO, 1971, attached Lord President's Office; Cabinet Office, 1972–73; Director-Gen., E-SU, 1973–77; Sec.-Gen., Liberal Party, 1977–83. A Vice-Chm., European-Atlantic Gp, 1985–92; Vice-Chm., Lib. Internat. British Gp, 1986–89. Chm., Avebury in Danger, 1988–89. Gov., Queen Elizabeth Foundn for Disabled People, 1985–; Trustee, Wilts Community Foundn, 1991–93. FIMgt. *Recreations:* golf, gardening. *Address:* Fosse House, Avebury, Wilts SN8 1RF. *Clubs:* English-Speaking Union; N Wilts Golf.

HUGH SMITH, Sir Andrew (Colin), Kt 1992; Chairman, London Stock Exchange (formerly International Stock Exchange), 1988–94 (Member, 1970, Member of Council, 1981–91); Chairman: Holland & Holland PLC, since 1987; Penna plc, since 1995; *b* 6 Sept. 1931; *s* of late Lt-Comdr Colin Hugh Smith and Hon. Mrs C. Hugh Smith; *m* 1964, Venetia, *d* of Lt-Col Peter Flower; two *s. Educ:* Ampleforth; Trinity Coll., Cambridge (BA). Called to Bar, Inner Temple, 1956; Hon. Bencher, 1995. Courtaulds Ltd, 1960–68; with Capel-Cure Carden (later Capel-Cure Myers), 1968–85; ANZ Merchant Bank, 1985–88. Director: Matheson Lloyds Investment Trust, 1994–; J. Bibby & Sons, 1995–. *Recreations:* gardening, shooting, fishing, reading. *Clubs:* Brooks's, Pratt's.

See also H. O. Hugh Smith.

HUGH SMITH, Col Henry Owen, LVO 1976; Defence Adviser to British High Commissioner, Nairobi, 1987–90; *b* 19 June 1937; *s* of Lt-Comdr Colin Hugh Smith and late Hon. Mrs C. Hugh Smith. *Educ:* Ampleforth; Magdalene Coll., Cambridge. BA Hons 1961. Commnd Royal Horse Guards, 1957; Blues and Royals, 1969; psc 1969; served Cyprus and Northern Ireland (wounded); Equerry in Waiting to The Duke of Edinburgh, 1974–76; CO The Blues and Royals, 1978–80; GSO1, MoD, 1980–87. *Recreation:* sailing. *Clubs:* Boodle's, Pratt's; Royal Yacht Squadron.

See also Sir A. C. Hugh Smith.

HUGHES, family name of **Barons Hughes** and **Cledwyn of Penrhos.**

HUGHES, Baron, *cr* 1961, of Hawkhill (Life Peer); **William Hughes,** PC 1970; CBE 1956 (OBE 1942); DL; President: Scottish Federation of Housing Associations, since 1975; Scottish Association for Mental Health, since 1975; company director; *b* 22 Jan. 1911; *e s* of late Joseph and Margaret Hughes; *m* 1951, Christian Clacher (*d* 1994), *o c* of late James and Sophia Gordon; two *d. Educ:* Balfour Street Public Sch., Dundee; Dundee Technical Coll. ARP Controller Dundee, 1939–43; Armed Forces, 1943–46; Commissioned RAOC, 1944; demobilised as Capt., 1946. Hon. City Treasurer, Dundee, 1946–47; Chairman, Eastern Regional Hospital Board, Scotland, 1948–60; Lord Provost of Dundee and HM Lieut of County of City of Dundee, 1954–60; Member: Dundee Town Council, 1933–36 and 1937–61; Court of St Andrews Univ., 1954–63; Council of Queen's Coll., Dundee, 1954–63; Cttee on Civil Juries, 1958–59; Cttee to Enquire into Registration of Title to Land in Scotland, 1960–62; North of Scotland Hydro-Electric Bd, 1957–64; Scottish Transport Council, 1960–64; Chairman: Glenrothes Develt Corp., 1960–64; East Kilbride Develt Corp., 1975–82; Royal Commn on Legal Services in Scotland, 1976–80. Contested (Lab) E Perthshire, 1945 and 1950. Jt Parly Under-Sec. of State for Scotland, 1964–69; Minister of State for Scotland, 1969–70, 1974–75. Mem., Council of Europe and WEU, 1976–87. Hon. LLD St Andrews, 1960. JP County and City of Dundee, 1943–76; DL Dundee 1960. Chevalier, Légion d'Honneur, 1958. *Recreation:* gardening. *Address:* The Stables, Ross, Comrie, Perthshire PH6 2JU. *T:* Comrie (01764) 70557.

HUGHES, Aneurin Rhys; Ambassador and Head of Delegation of Commission of European Communities in Oslo, Norway, since 1987; *b* 11 Feb. 1937; *s* of William and Hilda Hughes; *m* 1964, Jill (*née* Salisbury); two *s. Educ:* University College of Wales, Aberystwyth (BA). President, National Union of Students, 1962–64. Research in S America, 1964–66; HM Diplomatic Service, 1967–73: served, Singapore and Rome; Commission of the European Communities, 1973–: Head of Division for Internal Coordination in Secretariat-General, 1973–77; Adviser to Dir. Gen. for Information, 1977–80; Chef de Cabinet to Mr Ivor Richard, Comr responsible for Employment, Social Affairs and Educn, 1981–85; Adviser to Dir Gen. for Information, and Chm., Selection Bd for Candidates from Spain and Portugal, 1985–87. Organiser, Conf. on Culture, Economy and New Technologies, Florence, 1986–87. *Recreations:* squash, golf, music, hashing. *Address:* European Commission Delegation, Haakon VII's Gate 6, PO Box 1643 Vika, 0119 Oslo 1, Norway.

HUGHES, Anthony Philip Gilson; QC 1990; a Recorder, since 1988; *b* 11 Aug. 1948; *s* of Patrick and late Patricia Hughes; *m* 1972, Susan Elizabeth March; one *s* one *d. Educ:* Tettenhall Coll., Staffs; Van Mildert Coll., Durham (BA 1969). Sometime Lectr, Durham Univ. and QMC. Called to the Bar, Inner Temple, 1970. *Recreations:* garden labouring and mechanics, campanology. *Address:* 1 Fountain Court, Steelhouse Lane, Birmingham B4 6DR. *T:* 0121–236 5721.

HUGHES, Dr Antony Elwyn; Director, Engineering and Science, and Deputy Chief Executive, Engineering and Physical Sciences Research Council, since 1994; *b* 9 Sept. 1941; *s* of Ifor Elwyn Hughes and Anna Betty Hughes (*née* Ambler); *m* 1963, Margaret Mary Lewis; two *s* two *d. Educ:* Newport High Sch., Gwent; Jesus Coll., Oxford (MA; DPhil). CPhys; FInstP. Harkness Fellow, Cornell Univ., 1967–69. United Kingdom Atomic Energy Authority, Atomic Energy Research Establishment (Harwell): Scientific Officer, 1963–67; Sen. Scientific Officer, 1969–72; Principal Scientific Officer, 1972–75; Leader: Defects in Solids Gp, 1973; Solid State Sciences Gp, 1978; Individual Merit Appointment, 1975–81; Sen. Personal Appointment, 1981–83; Head, Materials Physics Div., 1983–86; Dir, Underlying Res. and Non-Nuclear Energy Res., 1986–87; Authority Chief Scientist and Dir, Nuclear Res., 1987–88. Science and Engineering Research Council: Dir, Labs, 1988–91; Dir. Progs and Dep. Chm., 1991–93; acting Chief Exec., 1993–94. *Publications:* Real Solids and Radiation, 1975; (ed) Defects and their Structure in Non-Metallic Solids, 1976; review articles in Contemporary Physics, Advances in Physics, Jl of Materials Science, Jl of Nuclear Materials, Reports on Progress in Physics. *Recreations:* hill walking, watching Rugby and cricket, playing the trumpet, gardening. *Address:* Engineering and Physical Sciences Research Council, Polaris House, North Star Avenue, Swindon SN2 1ET. *T:* Swindon (01793) 444178.

HUGHES, Catherine Eva, CMG 1984; HM Diplomatic Service, retired; Principal, Somerville College, Oxford, 1989–Sept. 1996; *b* 24 Sept. 1933; *d* of Edmund Ernest Pestell and Isabella Cummine Sangster; *m* 1991, Dr (John) Trevor Hughes. *Educ:* Leeds Girls' High Sch.; St Hilda's Coll., Oxford (MA). FO, 1956; Third Sec., The Hague, 1958; Second Sec., Bangkok, 1961; FO, 1964; First Sec., UK Delegn to OECD, Paris, 1969; FCO, 1971; St Antony's Coll., Oxford, 1974; Counsellor, East Berlin, 1975–78; Cabinet Office, 1978–80; Diplomatic Service Inspector, 1980–82; Minister (Economic), Bonn, 1983–87; Asst Under-Sec. (Public Depts), FCO, 1987–89. *Address:* Somerville College, Oxford OX2 6HD; (from June 1996) 2 Bishop Kirk Place, Oxford OX2 7HJ. *Club:* Reform.

See also J. E. Pestell.

HUGHES, Sir David (Collingwood), 14th Bt *cr* 1773; heraldic sculptor; Managing Director, Louis Lejeune Ltd, since 1978; *b* 29 Dec. 1936; *s* of Sir Richard Edgar Hughes, 13th Bt and Angela Lilian Adelaide Pell (*d* 1967); *S* father, 1970; *m* 1964, Rosemary Ann Pain, MA, LLM, *d* of late Rev. John Pain; three *s* (and one *s* decd). *Educ:* Oundle and Magdalene College, Cambridge (MA). National Service, RN, 1955–57. United Steel Cos Ltd, 1960–65; Unicam Instruments Ltd (subsequently Pye Unicam Ltd), export executive, 1965–70, E Europe manager, 1970–73. Builder, 1974–76. *Recreations:* shooting, fishing. *Heir: s* Dr Thomas Collingwood Hughes, *b* 16 Feb. 1966. *Address:* The Berristead, Wilburton, Ely, Cambs CB6 3RP. *T:* Ely (01353) 740770. *Clubs:* Flyfishers'; Cambridge County (Cambridge).

HUGHES, (David Evan) Peter, MA; Assistant Master, Westminster School, 1994; *b* 27 April 1932; *s* of late Evan Gwilliam Forrest-Hughes, OBE; *m* 1956, Iris (*née* Jenkins); one *s* two *d. Educ:* St Paul's Sch.; St John's Coll., Oxford (Gibbs Schol. in Chemistry; MA). National Service, 5 RHA, 1954. Assistant Master, Shrewsbury School, 1956; Head of Chemistry, 1958, Science, 1965; Nuffield Foundation, 1967–68; Second Master, Shrewsbury Sch., 1972; Headmaster, St Peter's Sch., York, 1980–84; Head of Science, Westminster Sch., 1984–89; Dir, Understanding Science Project, and Leverhulme Res. Fellow, Imperial Coll. and Westminster Sch., 1989–94. Chief Examr, Univ. of Cambridge Local Exam. Syndicate, 1968–. Chm., Friends' Cttee, Imperial Coll., 1992–94. *Publications:* Advanced Theoretical Chemistry (with M. J. Maloney), 1964; Chemical Energetics, 1967; (ed) Awareness of Science, 1993, 1994. *Recreations:* music, bridge, hill-walking. *Address:* Flat 1, 63 Millbank, SW1P 4RW.

HUGHES, David Glyn; National Agent, 1979–88, Senior National Officer, 1986–88, the Labour Party; *b* 1 March 1928; *s* of Richard and Miriam Hughes; *m* 1958, Mary Atkinson; one *d. Educ:* Darwin St Secondary Modern Sch. Apprentice, later fitter and turner, 1944–52; Labour Party Agent: Northwich, Bolton, Tonbridge, Portsmouth, 1952–69; Asst Regional Organiser, 1969–75, Regional Organiser, 1975–79, Northern Region. *Recreations:* gardening, walking. *Address:* 42 Langroyd Road, SW17 7PL. *T:* 0181–672 2959. *Clubs:* Stella Maris Social (Life-Mem.), Usworth and District Workmen's (Washington, Tyne and Wear).

HUGHES, David John, FRSL; writer; *b* 27 July 1930; *o s* of late Gwilym Fielden Hughes and of Edna Frances Hughes; *m* 1st, 1957, Mai Zetterling; 2nd, 1980, Elizabeth Westoll; one *s* one *d. Educ:* Eggar's Grammar Sch., Alton; King's College Sch., Wimbledon; Christ Church, Oxford (MA; Editor, Isis). FRSL 1986. Editorial Asst, London Magazine,

1953–55; Reader with Rupert Hart-Davis, 1956–60; Editor, Town magazine, 1960–61; script-writer and stills photographer of BBC documentaries and Scandinavian feature-films directed by Mai Zetterling, 1960–72; Editor, New Fiction Society, 1975–78, 1981–82. Asst Visiting Professor: Writers' Workshop, Univ. of Iowa, 1978–79, 1987; Univ. of Alabama, 1979; Vis. Assoc. Prof., Univ. of Houston, 1986. Film Critic, Sunday Times, 1982–83; Fiction Critic, Mail on Sunday, 1982–. Mem. Council, RSL, 1989–. Editor, Letters, jl of RSL, 1992–. *Publications: fiction:* A Feeling in the Air, 1957; Sealed with a Loving Kiss, 1958; The Horsehair Sofa, 1961; The Major, 1964; The Man Who Invented Tomorrow, 1968; Memories of Dying, 1976; A Genoese Fancy, 1979; The Imperial German Dinner Service, 1983; The Pork Butcher, 1984 (Welsh Arts Council Fiction Prize, 1984; W. H. Smith Literary Award, 1985; filmed as Souvenir, 1989); But for Bunter, 1985; The Little Book, 1996; (ed) Winter's Tales: New Series I, 1985; (ed with Giles Gordon): Best Short Stories, annually 1986–; The Best of Best Short Stories 1986–1995, 1995; *non-fiction:* J. B. Priestley, an informal study, 1958; The Road to Stockholm (travel), 1964; The Seven Ages of England (cultural history), 1967; The Rosewater Revolution, 1971; Evergreens, 1976. *Address:* 163 Kennington Road, SE11 6SF. *Clubs:* Savile, Academy; Surrey CC.

HUGHES, David Morgan; His Honour Judge Morgan Hughes; a Circuit Judge, since Nov. 1972; *b* 20 Jan. 1926; *s* of late Rev. John Edward Hughes and Mrs Margaret Ellen Hughes; *m* 1956, Elizabeth Jane Roberts; one *s* two *d*. *Educ:* Beaumaris Grammar Sch.; LSE (LLB). Army, 1944–48: Captain, Royal Welch Fusiliers; attached 2nd Bn The Welch Regt; Burma, 1945–47. London Univ., 1948–51; Rockefeller Foundn Fellowship in Internat. Air Law, McGill Univ., 1951–52; called to Bar, Middle Temple, 1953; practised Wales and Chester Circuit; Dep. Chm., Caernarvonshire QS, 1970–71; a Recorder, Jan.–Nov. 1972; Dep. Chm., Agricultural Lands Tribunal, 1972; Mem., Mental Health Review Tribunal, 1989–. Pres., Council, HM Circuit Judges for England and Wales, 1995–. *Recreations:* tennis, cricket, gardening. *Address:* Bryn, Kelsall, Cheshire CW6 0PA. *T:* Kelsall (01829) 751349.

HUGHES, David Richard; Group Political Editor, Thomson Regional Newspapers, since 1994; Political Editor, Daily Mail, since 1994; *b* 3 April 1951; *s* of John Arfon Hughes and Lilian Elvira Hughes (*née* Jones); *m* 1973, Christine O'Brien; two *s*. *Educ:* Cowbridge Grammar Sch.; Univ. of Leicester (BA Hons Hist.). Reporter, Merthyr Express, 1973–76; Leader Writer, 1976–79, Political Corresp., 1979–84, Western Mail; Political Reporter, Daily Mail, 1984–86; Political Corresp., 1986–89, Chief Political Corresp., 1989–92, Sunday Times; Editor, Western Mail, 1992–94. *Recreations:* hill walking, music, family, surfing. *Address:* 7 Southfield Gardens, Strawberry Hill, Twickenham TW1 4SZ. *T:* 0181–892 5726.

HUGHES, Dr David Treharne Dillon, FRCP; Consultant Physician, Royal London (formerly London) Hospital, since 1970; Director, Respiratory Medicine, Royal Hospitals Trust, since 1995; Head, Department of Clinical Investigation, Wellcome Research Laboratories, since 1978; *b* 31 Oct. 1931; *s* of Maj.-Gen. W. D. Hughes, *qv*; *m* 1959, Gloria Anna Bailey; one *s* two *d*. *Educ:* Cheltenham Coll.; Trinity Coll., Oxford (BSc, MA); London Hosp. Medical Coll. (BM BCh); RPMS. MRCP 1959, FRCP 1972. Jun. hosp. posts, London Hosp., 1957–59; Capt. RAMC, 1959–61 (jun. med. specialist, BMH Hong Kong); Res. Fellow, Univ. of Calif., 1963–64; jun. hosp. appts, London Hosp., 1964–70. Mem., GMC, 1993–. Past President: Internat. Soc. Internal Medicine; Hunterian Soc. Chm., Bd of Govs, Moving Theatre Trust, 1994–. Master, Soc. of Apothecaries, 1992–93. *Publications:* Tropical Health Science, 1967; Human Biology and Hygiene, 1969; Lung Function for the Clinician, 1981; numerous scientific papers on respiratory function and chest disease. *Recreations:* cricket, rowing, horse racing. *Address:* The Royal London Hospital, Whitechapel, E1 1BB. *T:* 0171–377 7000; 94 Overbury Avenue, Beckenham, Kent BR3 2PY. *T:* 0181–650 3983. *Clubs:* Savage; Leander (Henley-on-Thames).

HUGHES, Hon. Sir Davis, Kt 1975; Agent-General for New South Wales, in London, 1973–78; *b* 24 Nov. 1910; *m* 1940, Joan Philip Johnson; one *s* two *d*. *Educ:* Launceston High Sch., Tasmania; Phillip Smith Teachers' Coll., Hobart, Tas. Teacher, Tasmania, incl. Friends' Sch., Hobart, 1930–35; Master, Caulfield Grammar Sch., Melbourne, 1935–40. Served War, Sqdn Ldr, RAAF, Australia and overseas, 1940–45. Dep. Headmaster, Armidale Sch., Armidale, NSW, 1946–49; Mayor of Armidale, 1953–56. MLA, NSW, 1950–53 and 1956–65; Minister for Public Works, NSW, 1965–73. Rep., Derek Crouch Aust. Ltd, 1979–. Freeman: City of Armidale, NSW, 1965; City of London, 1975. *Recreations:* tennis, golf, fishing, racing. *Address:* 19/15 Koolang Road, Green Point, NSW 2250, Australia. *Club:* Australasian Pioneers (Sydney).

HUGHES, Dr (Edgar) John; HM Diplomatic Service; Counsellor, Consul-General and Deputy Head of Mission, Norway, since 1993; *b* 27 July 1947; *s* of William Thomas Hughes and Martha Hughes (*née* Riggs); *m* 1982, Lynne Evans; two *s*. *Educ:* Lewis Sch., Pengam, Wales; LSE (BSc Econ 1969); Lehigh Univ., USA (MA 1970); Pembroke Coll., Cambridge (Univ. of Cambridge Sara Norton Res. Prize in Amer. Hist., 1972; PhD 1973). FCO, 1973; on secondment to Cabinet Office, 1979; First Sec., UK Delegn to CSCE, Madrid, 1981; FCO, 1982; First Sec. and Head of Chancery, Santiago, 1983; First Sec. (Inf.), Washington, 1985; FCO, 1989–93, Counsellor and Hd of Aviation and Maritime Dept, 1990–93. *Publications:* The Historian as Diplomat (with P. A. Reynolds), 1976; articles in internat. affairs jls. *Recreations:* running, ski-ing, tennis, watching Rugby, reading. *Address:* c/o Foreign and Commonwealth Office, SW1A 2AH. *Club:* Rhymney Rugby Football.

HUGHES, Edmwnd Goronwy M.; *see* Moelwyn-Hughes.

HUGHES, Prof. Sir Edward (Stuart Reginald), Kt 1977; CBE 1971; Chairman and Professor, Department of Surgery, Monash University, Alfred Hospital, 1973–84, now Emeritus Professor of Surgery; *b* 4 July 1919; *s* of Reginald Hawkins Hughes and Annie Grace Langford; *m* 1944, Alison Clare Lelean; two *s* two *d*. *Educ:* Melbourne C of E Grammar Sch.; Univ. of Melbourne. MB, BS 1943; MD 1945; MS 1946; FRCS 1946 (Hon. FRCS 1985); FRACS 1950. Resident Medical Officer, Royal Melbourne Hosp., 1943–45, Asst Surgeon 1950–53, Surgeon 1954–74; Surgeon, Alfred Hosp., 1973–84. Consultant Surgeon to Australian Army, 1976–82. Royal Australasian College of Surgeons: Mem. Council, 1967–78; Chm. Exec. Cttee, 1971–78; Sen. Vice-Pres., 1974–84; Pres., 1975–78. First Dir, Menzies Foundn for Health, Fitness and Physical Achievement, 1979–. Cabrini Surgical Lectures, 1989. Fellow, Queens Coll. 1955. Hon. FACS, Hon. FRCS(C), Hon. FRCSE, Hon. FRCSI; Hon. FPCS 1977. Hon. LLD Monash, 1985. Sir Hugh Devine Medal, RACS, 1977. *Publications:* Surgery of the Anal Canal and Rectum, 1957; All about an Ileostomy, 1966, 3rd edn 1971; All about a Colostomy, 1970, 2nd edn 1977; Ano-Rectal Surgery, 1972; Colo-Rectal Surgery, 1983; Rectal Cancer, 1989. *Recreations:* tennis, racing. *Address:* 24 Somers Avenue, Malvern, Victoria 3144, Australia. *T:* (3) 8227688. *Clubs:* Melbourne, Melbourne Cricket, Victoria Racing, Victoria Amateur Turf (Melbourne).

HUGHES, George; Chairman and Chief Executive, Hughes Technology Ltd, since 1984; *b* 4 May 1937; *s* of Peter and Ann Hughes; *m* 1963, Janet; two *s*. *Educ:* Liverpool Collegiate (Sen. City Scholar; Open State Schol. with 3 distinctions); Gonville and Caius Coll., Cambridge (Open Scholar; MA Hons 1st Cl. German Mod. Lang. Tripos); Harvard Business Sch. (MBA 1968). Ski instructor, 1959; lead in J. Arthur Rank film, Holiday with Pay, 1959–60; Banking, Paris, 1960; IBM, London, 1960–69 (Strategy Develt Man., 1968–69; IBM European Salesman of the Year, Rome, 1965); Merchant Banking, London, 1969–70; Vice-Chm., Chief Exec. and Gp Man. Dir, Duple Gp Ltd, 1970–71; Chairman and Chief Executive: Hughes International, 1970–83; Willowbrook International, 1970–83; Willowbrook World Wide, 1971–83; Hampton Court Farms (formerly Castle Hughes Gp), 1975–87; Hughes Truck and Bus, 1976–84. Mem., Mensa, 1961. Chm., Derbys CCC, 1976–77; Mem., TCCB, 1976–77. *Publications:* The Effective Use of Computers, 1968; Military and Business Strategy, 1968; many papers on technical and management topics. *Recreations:* perception of visual patterns in thinking, creativity and innovation, historic buildings, Renoir, soccer, tennis, cricket. *Address:* Xanadu, Matthews Green, Wokingham RG11 1JU; Château de Beauchamps, Sarthe, France. *Clubs:* MCC, Carlton, Annabel's.

HUGHES, Prof. George Morgan; Professor of Zoology, Bristol University, 1965–85, now Emeritus; *b* 17 March 1925; *s* of James Williams Hughes and Edith May Hughes; *m* 1954, Jean Rosemary, *d* of Rowland Wynne Frazier and Jessie Frazier; two *s* one *d*. *Educ:* Liverpool Collegiate Sch.; King's Coll., Cambridge (Scholar). Martin Thackeray Studentship, 1946–48, MA, PhD, ScD (Cantab); Frank Smart Prize, 1946. Cambridge Univ. Demonstrator, 1950–55, Lectr, 1955–65; successively Bye-Fellow, Research Fellow and Fellow of Magdalene Coll., Cambridge, 1949–65; University of Bristol: Head of Dept of Zoology, 1965–70; Head of Res. Unit for Comparative Animal Respiration, 1970–90. Research Fellow, California Inst. of Technology, 1958–59; Visiting Lectr in Physiology, State Univ. of New York, at Buffalo, 1964; Visiting Professor: Duke Univ., 1969; Japan Society for the Promotion of Science, Kochi, Kyoto, Kyushu and Hokkaido Univs, 1974; Univ. of Regensburg, 1977; Univs of Bhagalpur and Bretagne Occidentale, 1979; Kuwait, 1983; Nairobi, 1985. Invited Prof., Nat. Inst. of Physiolog. Sciences, Okazaki, 1980; Hon. Prof., Univ. of Wales Coll. of Cardiff, 1991–. Mem., Internat. Cœlacanth Expdn, 1972. *Publications:* Comparative Physiology of Vertebrate Respiration, 1963; (jtly) Physiology of Mammals and other Vertebrates, 1965; (jtly) Air-breathing Fishes of India, 1992; (ed) several symposium vols; papers in Jl of Experimental Biology and other scientific jls, mainly on respiration of fishes. *Recreations:* travel, golf, photography; hockey for Cambridge Univ., 1945, and Wales, 1952–53. *Address:* 11 Lodge Drive, Long Ashton, Bristol BS18 9JF. *T:* Bristol (01275) 393402.

HUGHES, Glyn Tegai, MA, PhD; Warden of Gregynog, University of Wales, 1964–89; *b* 18 Jan. 1923; *s* of Rev. John Hughes and Keturah Hughes; *m* 1957, Margaret Vera Herbert, Brisbane, Qld; two *s*. *Educ:* Newtown and Towyn County Sch.; Liverpool Institute; Manchester Grammar Sch.; Corpus Christi Coll., Cambridge (Schol., MA, PhD). Served War, Royal Welch Fusiliers, 1942–46 (Major). Lector in English, Univ. of Basel, 1951–53; Lectr in Comparative Literary Studies, Univ. of Manchester, 1953–64, and Tutor to Faculty of Arts, 1961–64. Contested (L) Denbigh Div., elections 1950, 1955 and 1959. Mem., Welsh Arts Council, 1967–76; Nat. Governor for Wales, BBC, and Chm., Broadcasting Council for Wales, 1971–79; Member: Bd, Channel Four Television Co., 1980–87; Welsh Fourth TV Channel Auth., 1981–87. Chm., Welsh Broadcasting Trust, 1988–; Vice-Pres., N Wales Arts Assoc., 1977–94; Chm., Undeb Cymru Fydd, 1968–70. *Publications:* Eichendorffs Taugenichts, 1961; Romantic German Literature, 1979; (ed) Life of Thomas Olivers, 1979; Williams Pantycelyn, 1983; articles in learned journals and Welsh language periodicals. *Recreation:* book-collecting. *Address:* Rhyd-y-gro, Tregynon, Newtown, Powys SY16 3PR. *T:* Tregynon (01686) 650609.

HUGHES, (Harold) Paul; Chairman, Pan European Property Unit Trust, since 1987; Director: Lazard Select Investment Trust Ltd, since 1988; Keystone Investment Co. PLC, since 1988; *b* 16 Oct. 1926; *o s* of Edmund and Mabel Hughes; *m* 1955, Beryl Winifred Runacres; one *s* one *d*. *Educ:* Stand Grammar Sch., Whitefield, near Manchester. Certified Accountant. Westminster Bank Ltd, 1942–45; Royal Marines and Royal Navy, 1945–49; Arthur Guinness Son & Co. Ltd, 1950–58; British Broadcasting Corporation: Sen. Accountant, 1958–61; Asst Chief Accountant, Finance, 1961–69; Chief Accountant, Television, 1969–71; Dir of Finance, 1971–84; Pension Fund Consultant, 1984–89; Chm., BBC Enterprises Ltd, 1979–82; Chm., Visnews Ltd, 1984–85; Chief Exec., BBC Pension Trust Ltd, 1987–89; Dir, Kleinwort Benson Farmland Trust (Managers) Ltd, 1976–89. *Recreations:* opera, gardening. *Address:* 26 Downside Road, Guildford, Surrey GU4 8PH. *T:* Guildford (01483) 69166.

HUGHES, (Harold) Victor, CBE 1989; FRAgS; Principal, Royal Agricultural College, Cirencester, 1978–90, Principal Emeritus 1990; *b* 2 Feb. 1926; *s* of Thomas Brindley Hughes and Hilda Hughes (*née* Williams). *Educ:* Tenby County Grammar Sch.; UCW, Aberystwyth (BSc). FRAgS 1980. Lectr, Glamorgan Training Centre, Pencoed, 1947–49; Crop Husbandry Adv. Officer, W Midland Province, Nat. Agricultural Adv. Service, 1950; Lectr in Agric., RAC, 1950–54; Vice Principal, Brooksby Agricultural Coll., Leics, 1954–60; Royal Agricultural College: Farms Dir and Principal Lectr in Farm Management, 1960–76; Vice Principal and Farms Dir, 1976–78. Hon. ARICS 1984. FIAgrM 1992. *Publications:* articles in learned jls and agric. press. *Recreation:* shooting. *Address:* No 17 Quakers Row, Coates, Cirencester, Glos GL7 6JX.

HUGHES, Henry Andrew Carne M.; *see* Meyric Hughes.

HUGHES, Herbert Delauney, MA; Principal of Ruskin College, Oxford, 1950–79; *b* 7 Sept. 1914; *s* of late Arthur Percy Hughes, BSc, and late Maggie Ellen Hughes; *m* 1937, Beryl Parker. *Educ:* Cheadle Hulme Sch.; Balliol Coll., Oxford (State and County Major Scholar). BA (Hons) in Modern History, 1936. Served War of 1939–45, with 6 Field Regt Royal Artillery. Asst Sec., New Fabian Research Bureau, 1937–39; Organising Sec., Fabian Soc., 1939–46; Mem. Exec. Fabian Soc., 1946– (Vice-Chm. 1950–52, 1958–59, Chm. 1959–60, Vice-Pres., 1971–88, Pres., 1988–93); MP (Lab) Wolverhampton (West), 1945–50; Parliamentary Private Sec. to Minister of Education, 1945–47; to Financial Sec. to War Office, 1948–50; Mem. Lambeth Borough Council, 1937–42. Governor of Educational Foundation for Visual Aids, 1948–56. Member: Civil Service Arbitration Tribunal, 1955–81; Commonwealth Scholarship Commn, 1968–74; Cttee on Adult Educn, 1969–73. Workers' Educational Association: Vice-Pres., 1958–67; Dep. Pres., 1968–71; Pres., 1971–81; Hon. Treasurer, 1981–91; Hon. Mem., 1992–. Chm. Management Cttee, Adult Literacy Resource Agency, 1975–78; Mem., Adv. Council on Adult and Continuing Educn, 1978–83; Vice-Pres., Nat. Inst. of Adult and Continuing Educn, 1986–90. Chm., Webb Meml Trust, 1987–92. Hon. Fellow Sheffield Polytechnic, 1979. *Publications:* (part author) Democratic Sweden, 1937, Anderson's Prisoners, 1940, Six Studies in Czechoslovakia, 1947. Advance in Education, 1947; Towards a Classless Society, 1947; A Socialist Education Policy, 1955; The Settlement of Disputes in The Public Service, 1968; (jt author) Planning for Education in 1980, 1970; (part author) Education Beyond School, 1980. *Recreations:* drinking, reading, foreign travel. *Address:* Crossways, Mill Street, Islip, Oxford OX5 2SZ. *T:* Kidlington (01865) 376935.

HUGHES, Howard; World Managing Partner, Price Waterhouse, since 1992; *b* 4 March 1938; *s* of Charles William Hughes and Ethel May Hughes (*née* Howard); *m* 1st, 1964, Joy

Margaret Pilmore-Bedford (*d* 1984); two *s* one *d*; 2nd, 1988, Christine Margaret Miles; one *s*. *Educ:* Rydal School. FCA. Articled Bryce Hanmer & Co., Liverpool, 1955; joined Price Waterhouse, London, 1960: Partner, 1970; Dir, London Office, 1982; Managing Partner, UK, 1985–91; Member: World Bd, 1988–; Mgt Cttee, 1990–. Auditor, Duchy of Cornwall, 1983–. Member: Agricl Wages Bd, 1990–; Council, Royal London Soc. for the Blind, 1985–. *Recreations:* golf, music. *Address:* Witham, Woodland Rise, Seal, near Sevenoaks, Kent TN15 0HZ. *T:* Sevenoaks (01732) 61161. *Clubs:* Carlton; MCC; Wildernesse Golf (Sevenoaks).

HUGHES, Prof. Ieuan Arwel, FRCP, FRCP(C); Professor and Head of Department of Paediatrics, University of Cambridge, since 1989; Fellow of Clare Hall, Cambridge, since 1994; *b* 9 Nov. 1944; *s* of Arwel Hughes and Enid Phillips (*née* Thomas); *m* 1969, Margaret Maureen Davies; two *s* one *d*. *Educ:* Univ. of Wales Coll. of Medicine, Cardiff (MB, BCh, MD); MA Cantab, 1991. FRCP(C) 1974; FRCP 1984 (MRCP); MRSocMed. Medical Registrar, UCH, 1970–72; Senior Paediatric Resident, Dalhousie Univ., Canada, 1972–74; Endocrine Research Fellow, Manitoba Univ., Canada, 1974–76; MRC Fellow, Tenovus Inst., Cardiff, 1976–78; Consultant Paediatrician, Bristol, 1978–79; Senior Lectr in Child Health, 1979–85, Reader in Child Health, 1985–89, Univ. of Wales Coll. of Medicine, Cardiff. Pres., European Soc. for Paediatric Endocrinology, 1993 (Sec., 1987–92). *Publications:* Handbook of Endocrine Tests in Children, 1986; articles on paediatric endocrine disorders, steroid biochemistry and mechanism of steroid hormone action. *Recreations:* music, travel, walking, squash. *Address:* c/o Department of Paediatrics, Level 8, Addenbrooke's Hospital, Hills Road, Cambridge CB2 2QQ; 4 Latham Road, Cambridge CB2 2EQ.

HUGHES, Sir Jack (William), Kt 1980; chartered surveyor; Director, South Bank Estates and subsidiary companies, since 1960; Consultant, Jones, Lang, Wootton, since 1976 (a Senior Partner, 1949–76); *b* 26 Sept. 1916; 2nd *s* of George William Hughes and Isabel Hughes, Maidstone, Kent; *m* 1939, Marie-Theresa (Slade School scholar) (*d* 1987), *d* of Graham Parmley and Jessie Thompson. *Educ:* Maidstone Grammar Sch.; Univ. of London. BSc (Est. Man.). BA 1994. FRICS; FRIPHH. Served with Special Duties Br., RAF, 1940–46; demobilised Squadron Leader. Chairman: Bracknell Develt Corp., 1971–82; Property Adv. Gp, DoE, 1978–82; Director: URPT, 1961–86; MEPC, 1971–86; Housing Corporation (1974) Ltd, 1974–78; BR Property Bd, 1976–86; BR Investment Co., 1981–84; Property and Reversionary Investments, 1982–87; TR Property Investment Trust and subsid. cos, 1982–91; Brighton Marina Co. (Rep., Brighton Corp.), 1974–86; Undercliff Hldgs Ltd, 1986–93; Mem. Cttee, Mercantile Credit Gp Property Div.; Mem. Cttee of Management, Charities Property Unit Trust, 1967–74; Chm., South Hill Park Arts Centre Trust, 1972–79; Member: Adv. Gp to DoE on Commercial Property Develt, 1974–78; DoE Working Party on Housing Tenure, 1976–77; Founder Mem., Continuing Professional Develt Foundn (Mem. Adv. Bd, 1980–). Trustee, New Towns Pension Fund, 1975–82. Freeman, City of London, 1959–; Liveryman, Painter Stainers Guild, 1960–. FRSA. *Publications:* (jtly) Town and Country Planning Act 1949 (RICS); (Chm. of RICS Cttee) The Land Problem: a fresh approach; (co-ed) Glossary of Property Terms, 1990; techn. articles on property investment, develt and finance. *Recreations:* golf, travel, reading. *Address:* Challoners, The Green, Rottingdean, Brighton, Sussex BN2 7DD. *Clubs:* Carlton, Royal Air Force, Buck's.

HUGHES, James Ernest, PhD; FEng 1981; Director, 1973–85 and Managing Director and Chief Executive, 1983–84, Johnson Matthey PLC; *b* 3 Nov. 1927; *s* of Herbert Thomas Hughes and Bessie Beatrice Hughes; *m* 1950, Hazel Aveline (*née* Louguet-Layton), three *d*. *Educ:* Spring Grove Sch., Imperial Coll., London Univ. (BSc, ARSM (Bessemer Medalist), DIC), PhD London 1952. FIM, MIMM. Associated Electrical Industries, 1952–63; Johnson Matthey PLC, 1963–85. Vis. Professor, Univ. of Sussex, 1974–80. President: Inst. of Metals, 1972–73; Metals Soc., 1981–82; Instn of Metallurgists, 1982–83. FRSA 1978. *Publications:* scientific papers in learned jls. *Recreations:* antiques, music, gardening. *Address:* Lower Farm, Rimpton, near Yeovil, Somerset BA22 8AB.

HUGHES, John; *see* Hughes, E. J. and Hughes, R. J.

HUGHES, John; *b* 29 May 1925; *m*; two *s*. *Educ:* Durham. Served with Fleet Air Arm, 1943–45. Apprentice joiner; then miner and mechanic; worked for GEC, and Unipart (TGWU convener). Mem., Coventry City Council, 1974–82; Chm., Coventry NE Lab Party, 1978–81. MP (Lab) Coventry North East, 1987–92; contested (Ind. Lab) Coventry North East, 1992. *Address:* 15 Stafford Close, Bulkington, Bedworth, Nuneaton, Warwicks CV12 9QX.

HUGHES, Very Rev. John Chester; Vicar of Bringhurst with Great Easton and Drayton, 1978–87; *b* 20 Feb. 1924; *m* 1950, Sybil Lewis McClelland; three *s* two *d* (and one *s* decd). *Educ:* Dulwich Coll.; St John's Coll., Durham. Curate of Westcliffe-on-Sea, Essex, 1950–53; Succentor of Chelmsford Cathedral, 1953–55; Vicar of St Barnabas, Leicester, 1955–61; Vicar of Croxton Kerrial with Branston-by-Belvoir, 1961–63; Provost of Leicester, 1963–78. ChStJ 1974. *Address:* 29 High Street, Hallaton, Market Harborough, Leics LE16 8UD. *T:* Hallaton (01858) 555622.

HUGHES, John Dennis; Consultant, Trade Union Research Unit; Principal, Ruskin College, Oxford, 1979–89 (Tutor in Economics and Industrial Relations, 1957–70, and Vice Principal, 1970–79); *b* 28 Jan. 1927; *m* 1949, Violet (*née* Henderson); four *d*. *Educ:* Westminster City Sch.; Lincoln Coll., Oxford (MA). Lieut, RAEC, 1949–50. Extramural Tutor, Univs of Hull and Sheffield, 1950–57. Founded, Trade Union Res. Unit, 1970; Dep. Chm., Price Commn, 1977–79. Member: Industrial Develt Adv. Bd, 1975–79; Nat. Consumer Council, 1982–94. Governor, London Business Sch., 1979–92. Mem. Council, St George's House, 1978–83; Trustee Dir, NUMAST (formerly Merchant Navy and Airline Officers Assoc.), 1981–. *Publications:* Trade Union Structure and Government, 1968; (with R. Moore) A Special Case? Social Justice and the Miners, 1972; (with H. Pollins) Trade Unions in Great Britain, 1973; Industrial Restructuring: some manpower aspects, 1976; Britain in Crisis, 1981; The Social Charter and the European Single Market, 1991; contrib. Eur. Labour Forum jl. *Recreation:* cycling. *Address:* Rookery Cottage, Stoke Place, Old Headington, Oxford OX3 9BX. *T:* Oxford (01865) 63076.

HUGHES, Prof. John Pinnington-, PhD; FRS 1993; Director, Parke-Davis Neuroscience Research Centre (formerly Parke-Davis Research Unit), Cambridge University Forvie Site, Cambridge, since 1983; Senior Research Fellow, Wolfson College, University of Cambridge, since 1983; Vice President, Drug Discovery, Warner-Lambert, Europe, since 1988; *b* 6 Jan. 1942; *s* of Joseph and Edith Hughes; *m* 1967, Madelaine Carol Jennings (marr. diss. 1981); one *d*; and three *s* one *d* by Julie Pinnington-Hughes. *Educ:* Mitcham County Grammar Sch. for Boys; Chelsea Coll., London (BSc); Inst. of Basic Med. Sciences, London (PhD). MA Cantab, 1988. Res. Fellow, Yale Univ. Med. Sch., 1967–69; University of Aberdeen: Lectr in Pharmacology, 1969–77; Dep.-Dir, Drug Res. Unit, 1973–77; Imperial College, London University: Reader in Pharmacol Biochemistry, 1977–79; Prof. of Pharmacol Biochemistry, 1979–82; Vis. Prof., 1983–. Hon. Prof. of Neuropharmacology, Univ. of Cambridge, 1989–. Member: Substance Abuse Cttee, Mental Health Foundn, 1986–; Scientific Cttee, Assoc. of British Pharmaceutical Industry, 1990–; Chm., Res. Cttee, Persistent Virus Disease Res. Foundn, 1992–. Mem. Council, Internat. Sch. Neuroscience, 1988–. Editor: Brit. Jl Pharmacol., 1977–83; Brain Res., 1976–; Jt Chief Exec. Editor, Neuropeptides, 1980–. J. Y. Dent Meml Lectr, Soc. for Study of Drug Addiction, 1976; Oliver-Sharpey Lectr, RCP, 1980; Gaddum Lectr and Medal, British Pharmacol Soc., 1982. Mem., Royal Acad. of Medicine, Belgium, 1983. Dr *hc* Univ. of Liège, 1978. Sandoz Prize, British Pharmacol Soc., 1975; Pacesetter Award, US Nat. Inst. on Drug Abuse, 1977; Lasker Prize, Albert and Mary Lasker Foundn, NY, 1978; Scientific Medal, Soc. for Endocrinology, 1980; W. Feldberg Foundn Award, 1981; Lucien Dautrebande Prize, Fondation de Pathophysiologie, Belgium, 1983; Lilly Award, European Coll. of Neuropsychopharmacology, 1992. *Publications:* Centrally Acting Peptides, 1978; Opioids Past, Present and Future, 1984; (ed jtly) The Neuropeptide Cholecystokinin (CCK), 1989; articles in Nature, Science, Brit. Jl Pharmacol., and Brain Res. *Recreations:* dogs, gardening. *Address:* Parke-Davis Neuroscience Research Centre, Cambridge University Forvie Site, Robinson Way, Cambridge CB2 2QB. *T:* Cambridge (01223) 210929.

HUGHES, John Richard Poulton; DL; County Clerk and Chief Executive, Staffordshire County Council, and Clerk to the Lieutenancy, 1978–83; *b* 21 Oct. 1920; *s* of Rev. John Evan Hughes and Mary Grace Hughes; *m* 1943, Mary Margaret, *e d* of Thomas Francis Thomas; one *s*. *Educ:* Bromsgrove Sch.; LLB Hons London; DPA; LMRTPI. Solicitor. Served War, RN and RNVR, 1940–46; discharged with rank of Lieut, RNVR. Articled in private practice, 1937–40; Asst Solicitor: West Bromwich County Borough Council, 1947–48; Surrey CC, 1948–50; Staffs County Council: Sen. Asst Solicitor, subseq. Chief Asst Solicitor, and Dep. Clerk, 1950–74; Dir of Admin, 1974–78; Sec., Staffs Probation and After Care Cttee, 1978–83. Sec., Staffs Historic Bldgs Trust, 1983–89; Trustee and Advr, Soc. for the Prevention of Solvent Abuse, 1984– (Vice-Pres., 1989). DL Staffs, 1979. *Recreations:* forestry, antiques restoration, sailing, fishing. *Address:* Plas Isa Cottage, Llanbedr DC, near Ruthin, Clwyd LL15 1UP.

See also Sir T. P. Hughes.

HUGHES, Rt. Rev. John Taylor, CBE 1975; an Assistant Bishop, Diocese of Southwark, since 1986; *b* 12 April 1908; *s* of Robert Edward and Annie Hughes. *Educ:* Castle Hill Sch., Ealing; Uxbridge County Sch.; Bede Coll., University of Durham (BA 1931, MA 1935). Ordained 1931; Asst Chaplain and Tutor, Bede Coll., Durham, 1931–34; Lecturer, Bede Coll., 1934–35; Curate, St John's, Shildon, Co. Durham, 1934–37; Vicar, St James, West Hartlepool, 1937–48; Canon Residentiary and Missioner of Southwark Cathedral and Warden of Diocesan Retreat House, Southwark, 1948–56; Bishop Suffragan of Croydon, 1956–77; Archdeacon of Croydon, 1967–77; Bishop to the Forces, 1966–75; an Asst Bishop, Diocese of Canterbury, 1977–86. *Recreations:* music, reading. *Address:* The Hospital of the Holy Trinity, North End, Croydon CR0 1UB. *T:* 0181–686 8313.

HUGHES, Judith Caroline Anne, (Mrs M. G. Warwick); QC 1994; a Recorder, since 1995; *b* 13 Oct. 1950; 3rd *d* of Frank and Eva Hughes; *m* 1977, Mark G. Warwick; two *d*. *Educ:* Univ. of Leeds (LLB 1973). Called to the Bar, Inner Temple, 1974 (Bencher, 1994); Asst Recorder, 1991–95. *Recreations:* theatre, reading, handicrafts, travel, gardening. *Address:* 1 Mitre Court Buildings, Temple, EC4Y 7BS. *T:* 0171–797 7070.

HUGHES, Kevin Michael; MP (Lab) Doncaster North, since 1992; *b* 15 Dec. 1952; *s* of Leonard and Annie Hughes; *m* 1972, Lynda Saunders; one *s* one *d*. *Educ:* local state schs; Sheffield Univ. (3 yrs day release). Coal miner, 1970–90. Branch delegate, 1981–90, Mem., Yorks Area Exec. Cttee, 1983–86, NUM. Councillor, Doncaster MBC, 1986–92 (Chm., Social Services, 1987–92). *Recreations:* golf, walking, listening to opera. *Address:* House of Commons, SW1A 0AA. *Clubs:* Doncaster Trade Union and Labour; Skellow Grange Workingmen's.

HUGHES, Prof. Leslie Ernest, FRCS, FRACS; Professor of Surgery, University of Wales College of Medicine (formerly Welsh National School of Medicine), 1971–92; *b* 12 Aug. 1932; *s* of Charles Joseph and Vera Hughes; *m* 1955, Marian Castle; two *s* two *d*. *Educ:* Parramatta High Sch., Sydney Univ. MB, BS (Sydney); DS (Queensland), 1975; FRCS, 1959; FRACS, 1959. Reader in Surgery, Univ. of Queensland, 1965–71. Hunterian Prof., RCS, 1986. Eleanor Roosevelt Internat. Cancer Fellow, 1970. President: Welsh Surgical Soc., 1991–93; Surgical Res. Soc., 1992–94. Audio-visual Aid Merit Award, Assoc. of Surgeons of GB and Ireland, 1983, 1986. Educn Editor and Chm., Editl Bd, European Jl of Surgical Oncology, 1992–. *Publications:* (jtly) Benign Disorders of the Breast, 1988; numerous papers in medical jls, chiefly on immune aspects of cancer, and diseases of the colon. *Recreations:* music, travel. *Address:* Brook House, 14 Millwood, Lisvane, Cardiff CF4 5TL.

HUGHES, Lewis Harry; Assistant Auditor General, National Audit Office, since 1990; *b* 6 March 1945; *s* of Reginald Harry Hughes, retired MoD official, and Gladys Lilian Hughes; *m* 1975, Irene June Nash, violinist and teacher; one *s*. *Educ:* Devonport High Sch. for Boys; City of London Coll. CIPFA. Exchequer and Audit Dept, 1963–83 (Associate Dir, 1982–83); National Audit Office, 1983–; Dir of Health Audit and of Defence Audit to 1990. *Recreations:* golf, music, family life. *Address:* 1 Wood End Road, Harpenden, Herts AL5 3EB. *T:* Harpenden (01582) 764992. *Club:* Tavistock Golf.

HUGHES, Louis Ralph; President, General Motors International Operations, since 1994; Executive Vice President, General Motors Corporation, since 1992; *b* Cleveland, Ohio, 10 Feb. 1949. *Educ:* General Motors Inst., Flint (BMechEng); Harvard Univ. (MBA). General Motors Corp.: financial staff, 1973; Asst Treasurer, 1982; Vice-Pres., of Finance, Gen. Motors of Canada, 1985; Vice-Pres. of Finance, General Motors Europe, Zürich, 1987; Chm. and Man. Dir, Adam Opel AG, Rüsselsheim, 1989; Pres., General Motors Europe, 1992. *Recreations:* ski-ing, climbing, cuisine, antiques. *Address:* General Motors (Europe) AG, Stelzenstrasse 4, 8152 Glattbrugg (Zurich), Switzerland. *T:* (1) 8282600.

HUGHES, Nigel Howard; Director of Technology, Smiths Industries Aerospace and Defence Systems Ltd, since 1992; *b* 11 Aug. 1937; *s* of late William Howard Hughes and of Florence Hughes (*née* Crawshaw); *m* 1962, Margaret Ann Fairmaner; three *d*. *Educ:* St Paul's Sch.; Queen's Coll., Oxford (MA). CEng, FIMechE; FRAeS 1993. Pilot Officer, RAF, 1956–58. RAE, Bedford, 1961–73; Head of Radio and Navigation Div., 1973–77, Head of Flight Systems Dept, 1977–80, RAE, Farnborough; MoD Central Staffs, 1980–82; Asst Chief Scientific Advr (Projects), MoD, 1982–84; Dep. Chief Scientific Advr, MoD, 1985–86; Dir, RSRE, 1986–89; Chief Exec., Defence Res. Agency, 1989–91. *Recreations:* Rolls-Royce enthusiast; model engineering, amateur radio, music. *Address:* Smiths Industries Aerospace, Bishops Cleeve, Cheltenham, Gloucestershire GL52 4SF.

HUGHES, Owain Arwel; orchestral conductor, since 1970; Principal Conductor, Aalborg Symphony Orchestra, Denmark, since 1995; *b* 21 March 1942; *s* of Arwel Hughes and Enid Hughes (*née* Thomas); *m* 1966, Jean Lewis; one *s* one *d*. *Educ:* Howardian High Sch., Cardiff; University Coll., Cardiff (BA Hons); Royal Coll. of Music. Has conducted all major UK orchs and their choirs and also orchs throughout Europe; Associate Conductor: BBC Welsh Symphony Orch, 1980–86; Philharmonia Orch., London, 1985–90; Musical Dir, Huddersfield Choral Soc., 1980–86; Founder and Artistic Dir, Annual Welsh Proms, 1986–. Television: Blodeugerdd (series), BBC Wales, 1974–76; Development of English Choral Tradition, 1975; Music in Camera, 1976–86; Much Loved Music Show, 1977–83;

Requiem series, 1987; Easter series, 1988. Has made numerous recordings and videos. Vice-Pres., NCH Action for Chidren, 1988–. Founding Fellow, George Thomas Soc., 1989. FWCMD 1995. Hon. Fellow: Univ. of Glamorgan (formerly Poly. of Wales), 1986; UC, Cardiff, 1991. Hon. DMus: CNAA, 1986; Wales, 1991. Gold Medal, Welsh Tourist Bd, 1988. *Recreations:* Rugby, cricket, golf. *Address:* c/o Clarion/Seven Muses, 47 Whitehall Park, N19 3TW. *T:* 0171–272 4413. *Club:* Lord's Taverners.

HUGHES, Paul; *see* Hughes, H. P.

HUGHES, Peter; *see* Hughes, D. E. P.

HUGHES, Peter Thomas; QC 1993; a Recorder, since 1992; *b* 16 June 1949; *s* of late Peter Hughes, JP, and of Jane Blakemore Hughes (*née* Woodward); *m* 1974, Christine Stuart Taylor; one *s* one *d. Educ:* Bolton Sch.; Bristol Univ. (LLB Hons). Called to the Bar, Gray's Inn, 1971; Mem., Wales and Chester Circuit, 1971–, Junior, 1991; Asst Recorder, 1988–92. Chairman: Medical Appeal Tribunals, 1988–93; Registered Homes Tribunals, 1993–. Mem., Gen. Council of the Bar, 1993–. *Recreations:* fell-walking, books, taming an unruly garden. *Address:* 3 Paper Buildings, Temple, EC4Y 7EU. *T:* 0171–583 8055; 40 King Street, Chester CH1 2AH. *T:* Chester (01244) 323886. *Clubs:* Army and Navy; Lancashire County Cricket.

HUGHES, Philip Arthur Booley, CBE 1982; artist; Director: Logica plc, since 1990 (Chairman, 1972–90); Thames and Hudson Ltd, since 1991; *s* of Leslie Booley Hughes and Elizabeth Alice Hughes (*née* Whyte); *m* 1964, Psiche Maria Anna Claudia Bertini; two *d* and two step-*d. Educ:* Bedford Sch.; Clare Coll., Cambridge (BA). Engineer, Shell Internat. Petroleum Co., 1957–61; Computer Consultant, SCICON Ltd (formerly CEIR), 1961–69; Co-Founder, Logica, 1969; Man. Dir, Logica Ltd, 1969–72. Vis. Prof., UCL, 1981–90. Member: SERC, 1981–85; Nat. Electronics Council, 1981–88. Governor, Technical Change Centre, 1980–88. Mem. Council, RCA, 1988–92. Trustee: Design Museum, 1990–; Inst. for Public Policy Res., 1988–. Exhibn of paintings with Beryl Bainbridge, Monks Gall., Sussex, 1972; exhibited: Contemp. British Painting, Madrid, 1983; Contemp. Painters, Ridgeway Exhibn Museum and Art Gall., Swindon, 1986; one-man exhibitions: Parkway Focus Gall., London, 1976; Angela Flowers Gall., London, 1977; Gal. Cance Manguin, Vaucluse, France, 1979, 1985; Francis Kyle Gall., London, 1979, 1982, 1984, 1987, 1989, 1992, 1994; Gal. La Tourdes Cardinaux, Vaucluse, France, 1993; retrospective, Inverness Mus. and Art Gall., 1990. Companion of Operational Research, 1985. Hon. Fellow, QMC, 1987. DUniv Stirling, 1985; Hon. DSc Kent, 1988. *Publications:* articles in nat. press and learned jls on management scis and computing.

HUGHES, Major Richard Charles, MBE 1951; TD 1945; Director, Federation of Commodity Associations, 1973–78; *b* 24 Dec. 1915; *s* of late Frank Pemberton Hughes and Minnie Hughes, Northwich. *Educ:* Wrekin Coll., Wellington, Telford. TA commn, 4/5th (E of C) Cheshire Regt, 1935; regular commn, 22nd (Cheshire) Regt, 1939. Served War of 1939–45: 2 i/c 5th, 2nd and 1st Bns 22nd (Cheshire) Regt. Palestine, 1945–47; S/Captain MS and DAAG Western Comd, 1948–51; Korea, 1954; GSO2 Sch. of Infantry, 1955–56; Sec. of Sch. of Inf. Beagles, 1955–56; retd pay, 1958. Apptd Sec. to Sugar Assoc. of London, British Sugar Refiners Assoc. and Refined Sugar Assoc., 1958; formed British Sugar Bureau and apptd Sec., 1964–66. Hon. Treas., W Kensington Environment Cttee, 1974–75; Mem. Barons Keep Management Cttee, 1975. Member: City Liaison Cttee, Bank of England and City EEC Cttee, 1975; City Adv. Panel to City Univ., and Adviser to City of London Polytechnic, 1975; City Communications Consultative Gp, 1976. *Recreations:* travel, sailing, antiques. *Address:* Stone Cottage, 3 Bell Meadow Court, Tarporley, Cheshire, CW6 0DT.

HUGHES, Robert; MP (Lab) Aberdeen North since 1970; *b* Pittenweem, Fife, 3 Jan. 1932; *m* 1957, Ina Margaret Miller; two *s* three *d. Educ:* Robert Gordon's Coll., Aberdeen; Benoni High Sch., Transvaal; Pietermaritzburg Techn. Coll., Natal. Emigrated S Africa, 1947, returned UK, 1954. Engrg apprentice, S African Rubber Co., Natal; Chief Draughtsman, C. F. Wilson & Co. (1932) Ltd, Aberdeen, until 1970. Mem., Aberdeen Town Council, 1962–70; Convener: Health and Welfare Cttee, 1963–68; Social Work Cttee, 1969–70. Mem., AEU, 1952–. Contested (Lab) North Angus and Mearns, 1959. Member: Standing Cttee on Immigration Bill, 1971; Select Cttee, Scottish Affairs, 1971 and 1992–; introd. Divorce (Scotland) Bill 1971 (failed owing to lack of time); Parly Under-Sec. of State, Scottish Office, 1974–75; sponsored (as Private Member's Bill) Rating (Disabled Persons) Act 1978; Principal Opposition Spokesman: on agriculture, 1983–84; on transport, 1985–88 (Jun. Opp. Spokesman, 1981–83); Mem., PLP Shadow Cabinet, 1985–88. Chm., Aberdeen City Labour Party, 1961–69. Vice-Chm., Tribune Gp, 1984–. Founder Mem. and Aberdeen Chm., Campaign for Nuclear Disarmament; Vice-Chm., 1975–76, Chm., 1976–, Anti-Apartheid Movement; Member: Gen. Med. Council, 1976–79; Movement for Colonial Freedom, 1955– (Chm. Southern Africa Cttee); Scottish Poverty Action Group; Aberdeen Trades Council and Exec. Cttee, 1957–69; Labour Party League of Youth, 1954–57. *Recreation:* golf. *Address:* House of Commons, SW1A 0AA.

HUGHES, Robert Gurth; MP (C) Harrow West, since 1987; *b* 14 July 1951; *s* of Gurth Martin Hughes and Rosemary Dorothy Hughes (*née* Brown), JP; *m* 1986, Sandra Kathleen (*née* Vaughan); one *d. Educ:* Spring Grove Grammar Sch.; Harrow Coll. of Technology and Art. Trainee, then Film Producer, BAC Film Unit, 1968–73; Asst News Film Editor, subseq. News Film Editor and News Picture Editor, BBC Television News, 1973–87. Greater London Council: Mem., 1980–86; Opposition Dep. Chief Whip, 1982–86; Opposition spokesman on arts and recreation, 1984–86. An Asst Govt Whip, 1992–94; PPS to Chancellor of Duchy of Lancaster, 1994–95. National Chm., Young Conservatives, 1979–80. A Governor, BFI, 1990–92. *Recreations:* watching cricket, listening to music. *Address:* House of Commons, SW1A 0AA. *Clubs:* St Stephen's Constitutional; Harrow Borough Football.

HUGHES, (Robert) John; journalist; Syndicated Columnist, The Christian Science Monitor, since 1985; Director, International Media Studies Program, Brigham Young University, Utah, since 1991; *b* Neath, S Wales, 28 April 1930; *s* of Evan John Hughes and Dellis May Hughes (*née* Williams); *m* 1st, 1955, Vera Elizabeth Pockman (marr diss. 1987); one *s* one *d*; 2nd, 1988, Peggy Janeane Chu; one *s. Educ:* Stationers' Company's Sch., London. Reporter, sub-editor, corresp. for miscellaneous London and S African newspapers and news agencies (Natal Mercury, Durban; Daily Mirror, Daily Express, Reuter, London News Agency), 1946–54; joined The Christian Science Monitor, Boston, USA, 1954: Africa Corresp., 1955–61; Asst Foreign Editor, 1962–64; Far East Corresp., 1964–70; Man. Editor, 1970; Editor, 1970–76; Editor and Manager, 1976–79; Pres. and Publisher, Hughes Newspapers Inc., USA, 1979–81, 1984–85; Associate Dir, US Information Agency, 1981–82; Dir, Voice of America, 1982; Asst Sec. of State for Public Affairs, USA, 1982–84; Pres., Concord Communications Inc., 1989–91. Nieman Fellow, Harvard Univ., 1961–62. Pres., Amer. Soc. of Newspaper Editors, 1978–79. Pulitzer Prize for Internat. Reporting, 1967; Overseas Press Club of America award for best daily newspaper or wire service reporting from abroad, 1970; Sigma Delta Chi's Yankee Quill Award, 1977. Hon. LLD Colby Coll., 1978. *Publications:* The New Face of Africa, 1961; Indonesian Upheaval (UK as The End of Sukarno), 1967; articles in magazines and encyclopaedias. *Recreations:* reading, walking, raising Labrador retrievers. *Address:* Department of Communications, Brigham Young University, Provo, UT 84602, USA. *Clubs:* Foreign Correspondents', Hong Kong Country (Hong Kong); Overseas Press (New York).

HUGHES, Robert Studley Forrest; Senior Writer (Art Critic), Time Magazine, New York, since 1970; *b* Sydney, Aust., 28 July 1938; *s* of Geoffrey E. F. Hughes and Margaret Sealey Vidal; *m* (marr. diss. 1981); one *s*; *m* 1981, Victoria Whistler. *Educ:* St Ignatius' Coll., Riverview, Sydney; Sydney Univ. (architecture course, unfinished). Contributed articles on art to The Nation and The Observer, Sydney, 1958–62; to Europe, 1964, living in Italy until 1966, when moved to London; freelancing for Sunday Times, BBC and other publications/instns, 1966–70. TV credits include: Landscape with Figures, ten-part series on Australian art for ABC, Australia; Caravaggio, Rubens and Bernini, for BBC, 1976–77; The Shock of the New, eight-part series for BBC, 1980. Mem., Amer. Acad. of Arts and Scis, 1993. Hon. Dr Fine Arts, Sch. of Visual Arts, NY, 1982. Frank Jewett Mather Award, Coll. Art Assoc. of America, 1982, 1985; Golden Plate Award, Amer. Acad. of Achievement, 1988. *Publications:* The Art of Australia, 1966; Heaven and Hell in Western Art, 1969; The Shock of the New (BBC publication), 1980, rev. edn 1991; The Fatal Shore, 1987; Frank Auerbach, 1990; Nothing If Not Critical, 1991; Barcelona, 1992; Culture of Complaint: the fraying of America, 1993. *Recreations:* gardening, shooting, river and sea fishing, cooking. *Address:* Time Magazine, Room 23–26, 1271 Avenue of the Americas, New York, NY 10020, USA.

HUGHES, Robert Valentine, FCIS; Chief Executive, Kirklees Metropolitan Council, since 1988; *b* 13 Feb. 1943; *s* of Robert Canning Hughes and Betty Bertha Hughes; *m* 1968, Eryl Lumley. *Educ:* Univ. of Birmingham (DMS 1976; MSocSc 1979). FCIS 1982. Review Leader (Performance Rev.), W Midlands Co. Transport and Engrg Dept, 1977–81; Birmingham District Council: Principal Asst to Chief Exec., 1981–83; Develt and Promotion Officer, 1983–84; Town Clerk and Chief Exec., Great Grimsby BC, 1984–88. FRSA 1990. *Recreations:* composing music (jazz), cooking, ski-ing. *Address:* PO Box B24, Civic Centre III, Market Street, Huddersfield HD1 1WG. *T:* Huddersfield (01484) 442002/3.

HUGHES, Air Marshal Sir Rochford; *see* Hughes, Air Marshal Sir S. W. R.

HUGHES, Ronald Frederick, CEng, FICE; quality management consultant, since 1992; Systems Consultant, London Underground Ltd, 1992; *b* 21 Oct. 1927; *s* of Harry Frederick and Kate Hughes; *m* 1957, Cecilia Patricia, *d* of Maurice Nunis, MCS, State Treasurer, Malaya, and Scholastica Nunis; two *s* one *d. Educ:* Birmingham Central Technical College; Bradford College of Technology. Articled pupil, Cyril Boucher and Partners, 1943; Royal Engineers Engineering Cadet, 1946; commissioned RE, 1950; service in Malaya, 1950–53. Res. Asst, BISRA, 1954; Civil Engineer, H. W. Evans & Co. Ltd, Malaya, 1955, Man. Dir, 1958; War Office, 1959; Head of War Office Works Group, Singapore, 1963; Works Adviser to C-in-C, FARELF, 1964; District Civil Engineer, Malaya, 1966; Property Services Agency: Regional Site Control Officer, Midland Region, 1969; Principal Engineer, Post Office Services, 1970; Area Works Officer, Birmingham, 1977; Asst Dir, 1979, Dir, 1983–87, Civil Engineering Services; Dir and Quality Systems Manager, Mott MacDonald Consultants, 1987–92. Dir, Construction Industry Computing Assoc., 1982–86; Member: Standing Cttee for Structural Safety, 1985–88; Maritime Bd, ICE, 1985–90; Nat. Jt Consultative Cttee for Building, 1986–88; Member Council: Construction Industry Res. and Inf. Assoc., 1984–88; BSI, 1985; Perm. Internat. Assoc. of Navigation Congresses, 1983–; Parly Maritime Gp, 1988–; Vice Pres., Concrete Soc., 1989–. *Recreations:* squash, photography, music. *Address:* 9A The Street, West Horsley, Surrey KT24 6AY. *T:* East Horsley (014865) 2182. *Clubs:* Naval; Effingham (Surrey).

HUGHES, Royston John, (Roy); DL; MP (Lab) Newport East, since 1983 (Newport, Gwent, 1966–83); *b* 9 June 1925; *s* of John Hughes, Coal Miner; *m* 1957, Florence Marion Appleyard; three *d. Educ:* Ruskin Coll., Oxford. Mem. Coventry City Council, 1962–66; various offices in Transport and General Workers' Union, 1959–66. PPS to Minister of Transport, 1974–75; Mem., Speaker's panel, 1982–84, 1991–; opposition frontbench spokesman on Welsh affairs, 1984–88. Chairman: PLP Sports Gp, 1974–83; PLP Steel Group, 1978–87; Parly Gp, TGWU, 1979–82. Chm., Welsh Grand Cttee, 1982–84, 1991–. Exec. Mem., IPU, 1987– (Treas., 1990–92). Deleg., Council of Europe and WEU, 1991–. Jt Chm., Rugby Union Gp, 1993–; Vice President: Crawshays RFC; Glamorgan CCC. DL Gwent, 1992. *Recreations:* gardening, watching rugby and soccer. *Address:* Chapel Field, Chapel Lane, Abergavenny, Gwent NP7 7BT. *T:* Abergavenny (01873) 856502. *Clubs:* United Services Mess (Cardiff); Pontllanfraith Workingmen's Social.

HUGHES, Prof. Sean Patrick Francis, MS; FRCS, FRCSEd, FRCSI, FRCSEd (Orth); Professor of Orthopaedic Surgery, Royal Postgraduate Medical School, University of London, since 1991; Hon. Consultant Orthopaedic Surgeon, Hammersmith and Ealing Hospitals, since 1991; Hon. Consultant, National Hospital for Nervous Diseases, Queen Square; *b* 2 Dec. 1941; *s* of Patrick Joseph Hughes and Kathleen Ethel Hughes (*née* Bigg); *m* 1972, Felicity Mary (*née* Anderson); one *s* two *d. Educ:* Downside Sch.; St Mary's Hospital, Univ. of London (MB BS, MS). Senior Registrar in Orthopaedics, Middlesex and Royal National Orthopaedic Hosp., 1974–76; Research Fellow in Orthopaedics, Mayo Clinic, USA, 1975; Sen. Lectr, and Director Orthopaedic Unit, Royal Postgraduate Medical Sch., Hammersmith Hosp., 1977–79; George Harrison Law Prof. of Orthopaedic Surgery, Univ. of Edinburgh, 1979–91. Hon. Civilian Consultant, RN. Vice President: RCSE, 1994– (Mem. Council, 1984–); Assoc. Res. Circulation Bone, 1994–; Mem. Council: British Orthopaedic Assoc., 1989–92. Fellow: Brit. Orthopaedic Assoc.; Royal Soc. Med.; Member: Orthopaedic Research Soc.; British Orth. Res. Soc.; Soc. Internat. de Chirurgie Orth. et de Traumatologie; World Orth. Concern; Internat. Soc. for Study of the Lumbar Spine. *Publications:* Astons Short Text Book of Orthopaedics, 2nd edn 1976 to 5th edn (jtly) 1995; Basis and Practice of Orthopaedics, 1981; Basis and Practice of Traumatology, 1983; Musculoskeletal Infections, 1986; (ed jtly) Orthopaedics: the principles and practice of musculoskeletal surgery, 1987; (ed jtly) Orthopaedic Radiology, 1987; papers on blood flow and mineral exchange, fracture healing, bone scanning, antibiotics and injection in bone, external fixation of fractures, surgery of the lumbar and cervical spine. *Recreations:* walking, ski-ing, music. *Address:* 24 Fairfax Road, W4 1EW. *T:* 0181–995 2039. *Clubs:* Athenæum, Naval.

HUGHES, Shirley, (Mrs J. S. P. Vulliamy); free-lance author/illustrator; *b* 16 July 1927; *d* of Thomas James Hughes and Kathleen Dowling; *m* 1952, John Sebastian Papendiek Vulliamy; two *s* one *d. Educ:* West Kirby High Sch. for Girls; Liverpool Art Sch.; Ruskin Sch. of Art, Oxford. Illustrator/author; overseas edns or distribn in France, Spain, W Germany, Denmark, Holland, Sweden, Aust., NZ, Japan, USA, China and Canada. Lectures to Teacher Trng Colls, Colls of Further Educn, confs on children's lit. and to children in schs and libraries; overseas lectures incl. tours to Aust. and USA. Member: Cttee of Management, Soc. of Authors, 1983–86; Public Lending Right Registrar's Adv. Cttee, 1984–88; Library and Information Services Council, 1989–92. Children's Rights Other Award, 1976; Kate Greenaway Award, 1978; Silver Pencil Award, Holland, 1980;

Eleanor Farjeon Award for services to children's lit., 1984. *Publications:* illustrated about 200 books for children of all ages; written and illustrated: Lucy and Tom's Day, 1960, 2nd edn 1979; The Trouble with Jack, 1970, 2nd edn 1981; Sally's Secret, 1973, 3rd edn 1976; Lucy and Tom go to School, 1973, 4th edn 1983; Helpers, 1975, 2nd edn 1978; Lucy and Tom at the Seaside, 1976, 3rd edn 1982; Dogger, 1977, 4th edn 1980; It's Too Frightening for Me, 1977, 4th edn 1982; Moving Molly, 1978, 3rd edn 1981; Up and Up, 1979, 3rd edn 1983; Here Comes Charlie Moon, 1980, 3rd edn 1984; Lucy and Tom's Christmas, 1981; Alfie Gets in First, 1981, 2nd edn 1982; Charlie Moon and the Big Bonanza Bust-up, 1982, 2nd edn 1983; Alfie's Feet, 1982, 2nd edn 1984; Alfie Gives a Hand, 1983; An Evening at Alfie's, 1984; Lucy and Tom's abc, 1984; A Nursery Collection, 6 vols, 1985–86; Chips and Jessie, 1985; Another Helping of Chips, 1986; Lucy and Tom's 123, 1987; Out and About, 1988; The Big Alfie and Annie Rose Story Book, 1988; Angel Mae, 1989; The Big Concrete Lorry, 1989; The Snowlady, 1990; Wheels, 1991; The Big Alfie Out-of-Doors Story Book, 1992; Bouncing, 1993; Giving, 1993; Stories by Firelight, 1993; Chatting, 1994; Hiding, 1994. *Recreations:* looking at paintings, dressmaking, writing books for children.

HUGHES, Air Marshal Sir (Sidney Weetman) Rochford, KCB 1967 (CB 1964); CBE 1955 (OBE 1942); AFC 1947; *b* 25 Oct. 1914; *s* of late Capt. H. R. Hughes, Master Mariner, and late Mrs Hughes (*née* Brigham), Auckland, NZ; *m* 1942, Elizabeth, *d* of A. Duncum, Colombo, Ceylon; one *d*. *Educ:* Waitaki Boys' High School; Oamaru, NZ. Editorial Staff, NZ Herald, 1933–37; RNZ Air Force, 1937–38; RAF, Far East and Middle East, 1939–44 (despatches; Greek DFC); Chief Ops, USAF All Weather Centre, 1948–49; Air Min. and CO Farnborough, 1950–54; Imperial Defence Coll., 1955; CO RAF Jever, Germany, 1956–59; Air Mem. and Chm., Defence Res. Policy Staff, MoD, 1959–61; Air Officer Commanding No 19 Group, 1962–64; Dep. Controller Aircraft (RAF), Ministry of Aviation, 1964–66; Air Comdr, Far East Air Force, 1966–69, retd 1969. Air Adviser, Civil and Military, to Govt of Singapore, 1969–72; Commissioner, Northland Harbour Bd, NZ, 1974. Chm., Mazda Motors NZ, 1972–87; Director: NZ Steel, 1973–84; General Accident, 1975–84; Reserve Bank NZ, 1974–77; Whangarei Engrg Co., 1975–83; Lees Industries, 1976–84; First City Finance Corp., 1981–87. Patron: Taupo Brevet Club; Taupo Coastguard. Livery, Guild of Air Pilots and Air Navigators. *Recreations:* yachting, motoring, fishing. *Address:* 24 Scenic Heights, Acacia Bay, Taupo, New Zealand. *Club:* Royal NZ Yacht Squadron.

HUGHES, Simon Henry Ward; MP Southwark and Bermondsey, since Feb. 1983 (L 1983–88, Lib Dem since 1988); barrister; *b* 17 May 1951; *s* of James Henry Annesley Hughes and Sylvia (Paddy) Hughes (*née* Ward). *Educ:* Llandaff Cathedral Sch., Cardiff; Christ Coll., Brecon; Selwyn Coll., Cambridge (BA 1973, MA 1978); Inns of Court Sch. of Law; Coll. of Europe, Bruges (Cert. in Higher European Studies, 1975). Trainee, EEC, Brussels, 1976; Trainee and Mem. Secretariat, Directorate and Commn on Human Rights, Council of Europe, Strasbourg, 1976–77. Called to the Bar, Inner Temple, 1974; in practice, 1978–. Vice-Pres., Southwark Chamber of Commerce, 1987– (Pres., 1984–87). Spokesman: (L), on the environment, 1983–Jan. 1987 and June 1987–March 1988; (Alliance), on health, 1987; (Lib Dem), on education and science, 1988–92, on envmt, 1988–, on natural resources, 1992–. Jun. Counsel, Lib. Party application to European Commn on Human Rights, 1978–79; Chm., Lib. Party Adv. Panel on Home Affairs, 1981–83; Vice-Chm., Bermondsey Lib. Assoc., 1981–83. Jt Pres., British Youth Council, 1983–84. President: Young Liberals, 1986–88 (Vice-Pres., 1983–86, Mem. 1973–78); Democrats Against Apartheid, 1988–; Vice-President: Union of Liberal Students, 1983–88 (Mem., 1970–73); Southwark Chamber of Commerce, 1987– (Pres., 1984–87); Student Democrats, 1988–; Vice-Chm., Parly Youth Affairs Lobby, 1984–. Member: the Christian Church; Gen. Synod of Church of England, 1984–85; Southwark Area Youth Cttee, Council of Management, Cambridge Univ. Mission, Bermondsey; Anti-Apartheid Movement. Member to Watch Award, 1985. *Publications:* pamphlets on human rights in Western Europe, the prosecutorial process in England and Wales, Liberal values for defence and disarmament. *Recreations:* music, discotheques and good parties, history, sport, theatre, the countryside and open air, travel, spending time with family and friends. *Address:* House of Commons, SW1A 0AA. *T:* 0171–219 6256; 6 Lynton Road, Bermondsey, SE1 5QR.

HUGHES, Stephen Skipsey; Member (Lab) Durham, European Parliament, since 1984; Deputy Leader, Labour Party, European Parliament, 1991–93; *b* 19 Aug. 1952; *m* Cynthia; one *s* twin *d*. *Educ:* St Bede's School, Lanchester; Newcastle Polytechnic (DMA). Mem., EP Social Affairs and Employment Cttee; Substitute Member: Environment Cttee; Rules Cttee; Security and Defence Cttee. Member: EP Japan delegn, 1989–; EP Intergroup on Nuclear Disarmament, 1988– (Chm., 1988–90); Chm., EP Social Affairs and Employment Cttee, 1994–. Vice-President: Fedn of Industrial Develt Authorities, 1990–; Assoc. of District Councils, 1990–. *Address:* (office) 1/76 County Hall, Durham DH1 5UR; (home) 79 Greenbank Road, Darlington, Co. Durham DL3 6EN.

HUGHES, Ted, OBE 1977; author; Poet Laureate, since 1984; *b* 17 Aug. 1930; *s* of William Henry Hughes and Edith Farrar Hughes; *m* 1956, Sylvia Plath (*d* 1963); one *s* one *d*; *m* 1970, Carol Orchard. *Educ:* Pembroke Coll., Cambridge Univ. (Hon. Fellow, 1986). Author of Orghast (performed at 5th Festival of Arts of Shiraz, Persepolis, 1971). Awards: first prize, Guinness Poetry Awards, 1958; John Simon Guggenheim Fellow, 1959–60; Somerset Maugham Award, 1960; Premio Internazionale Taormina, 1973; The Queen's Medal for Poetry, 1974. *Publications: verse:* The Hawk in the Rain, (First Publication Award, NY), 1957; Lupercal, 1960 (Hawthornden Prize, 1961); Recklings, 1966; The Burning of the Brothel, 1966; Scapegoats and Rabies, 1967; Animal Poems, 1967; Wodwo, 1967 (City of Florence Internat. Poetry Prize, 1969); Poetry in the Making, 1967 (US as Poetry Is, 1970); Five Autumn Songs for Children's Voices, 1968; Crow, 1970; A Few Crows, 1970; Crow Wakes, 1970; Shakespeare's Poem, 1971; (with R. Fainlight and Alan Sillitoe) Poems, 1971; Eat Crow, 1971; Prometheus on His Crag, 1973; Spring Summer Autumn Winter, 1974; Cave Birds, with illustrations by Leonard Baskin, 1975, 1978; Season Songs, 1976; Earth-Moon, 1976; Gaudete, 1977; Orts, 1978; Moortown Elegies, 1978; Adam and the Sacred Nine, 1979; Remains of Elmet, 1979; Moortown, 1979 (Heinemann Bequest, RSL, 1980); (contrib.) Michael Morpurgo, All Around the Year, 1979; Selected Poems 1957–1981, 1982; River, 1983; Flowers and Insects, 1987; Wolfwatching, 1989; Moortown Diary, 1989; Rain-charm for the Duchy, 1992; New Selected Poems 1957–1994, 1995; *libretti:* The Demon of Adachigahara, 1969; The Story of Vasco, 1974; *stage:* adaptation of Seneca's Oedipus, 1969 (perf. NT, 1968); The Coming of the Kings (4 plays for children), 1970 (US as The Tiger's Bones, 1974); *for children: verse:* Meet My Folks!, 1961; The Earth-Owl and Other Moon People, 1963 (reissued as Moon Whales, 1988); Moon-Bells and other poems (Signal Award), 1978; Under the North Star (Signal Award), 1981; *verse story:* Nessie, The Mannerless Monster, 1964 (US as Nessie the Monster, 1974); *stories:* How the Whale Became, 1963; The Iron Man (US as The Iron Giant, 1968); What is the Truth, 1984 (Guardian Children's Fiction Award, 1985); Ffangs the Vampire Bat and the Kiss of Truth, 1986; Tales of the Early World, 1988; The Iron Woman, 1993; The Dreamfighter, 1995; *prose:* Shakespeare and the Goddess of Complete Being, 1992; Winter Pollen, 1994; *edited:* (jtly) Five American Poets, 1963; (with introd.) Selected Poems of Keith Douglas, 1964; A Choice of Emily Dickinson's Verse, 1968; A Choice of Shakespeare's Verse, 1971 (US as With Fairest Flowers while Summer Lasts); (introd and trans. jtly) János Pilinsky, Selected Poems, 1976; (with introd.) Sylvia Plath, Johnny Panic and the Bible of Dreams, 1977; (introd. and trans. jtly) Yehuda Amichai, Amen, 1978; Henry Williamson—A Tribute, 1979; Sylvia Plath, Collected Poems, 1981; (with Seamus Heaney) The Rattle Bag, 1982. *Address:* c/o Faber and Faber Ltd, 3 Queen Square, WC1N 3AU.

HUGHES, Thomas Lowe; Trustee, since 1971, and President Emeritus, since 1991, Carnegie Endowment for International Peace, Washington (President, 1971–91); *b* 11 Dec. 1925; *s* of Evan Raymond Hughes and Alice (*née* Lowe); *m* 1955, Jean Hurlburt Reiman (*d* 1993); two *s*. *Educ:* Carleton Coll., Minn (BA); Balliol Coll., Oxford (Rhodes Schol., BPhil); Yale Law Sch. (LLB, JD). USAF, 1952–54 (Major). Member of Bar: Supreme Court of Minnesota; US District Court of DC; Supreme Court of US. Professional Staff Mem., US Senate Sub-cttee on Labour-Management Relations, 1951; part-time Prof. of Polit. Sci. and Internat. Relations, Univ. of Southern California, Los Angeles, 1953–54, and George Washington Univ., DC, 1957–58; Exec. Sec. to Governor of Connecticut, 1954–55; Legislative Counsel to Senator Hubert H. Humphrey, 1955–58; Admin. Asst to US Rep. Chester Bowles, 1959–60; Staff Dir of Platform Cttee, Democratic Nat. Convention, 1960; Special Asst to Under-Sec. of State, Dept of State, 1961; Dep. Dir of Intelligence and Research, Dept of State, 1961–63; Dir of Intell. and Res. (Asst Sec. of State), 1963–69; Minister and Dep. Chief of Mission, Amer. Embassy, London, 1969–70; Mem., Planning and Coordination Staff, Dept of State, 1970–71. Chm., Nuclear Proliferation and Safeguards Adv. Panel, Office of Technology Assessment, US Congress; Chm., Bd of Editors, Foreign Policy Magazine; Sec., Bd of Dirs, German Marshall Fund of US; Dir, Arms Control Assoc. Chairman: Oxford-Cambridge Assoc. of Washington; US-UK Bicentennial Fellowships Cttee on the Arts. Member Bds of Visitors: Harvard Univ. (Center for Internat. Studies); Princeton Univ. (Woodrow Wilson Sch. of Public and Internat. Affairs); Georgetown Univ. (Sch. of Foreign Service); Bryn Mawr Coll. (Internat. Adv. Bd.); Univ. of Denver (Soc. Sci. Foundn); Atlantic Council of US (Exec. Cttee). Member Bds of Advisers: Center for Internat. Journalism, Univ. of S Calif; Coll. of Public and Internat. Affairs, Amer. Univ., Washington, DC; Washington Strategy Seminar; Cosmos Club Jl (Chm.). Member Bds of Trustees: Civilian Military Inst.; Amer. Acad. of Political and Social Sci.; Amer. Cttee, IISS; Hubert H. Humphrey Inst. of Public Affairs; Amer. Inst. of Contemp. German Studies, Washington, DC; Arthur F. Burns Fellowship Program. Mem. Adv. Bd, Fundacion Luis Munoz Marin, Puerto Rico. Member: Internat. Inst. of Strategic Studies; Amer. Assoc. of Rhodes Scholars; Amer. Political Sci. Assoc.; Amer. Bar Assoc.; Amer. Assoc. of Internat. Law; Amer. For. Service Assoc.; Amer. Acad. of Diplomacy; Internat. Studies Assoc.; Washington Inst. of Foreign Affairs; Trilateral Commn; Assoc. for Restoration of Old San Juan, Puerto Rico; Soc. Mayflower Descendants. Arthur S. Flemming Award, 1965. Hon. LLD Washington Coll., 1973; Denison Univ., 1979; Florida Internat. Univ., 1986; Hon. HLD: Carleton Coll., 1974; Washington and Jefferson Coll., 1979. KStJ 1984. *Publications:* occasional contribs to professional jls, etc. *Recreations:* swimming, tennis, music, 18th century engravings. *Address:* 5636 Western Avenue, Chevy Chase, MD 20815, USA. *T:* (301)6561420; 2400 N Street NW, Washington, DC 20037, USA. *T:* (office) (202) 8627911. *Clubs:* Yale, Century Association, Council on Foreign Relations (New York); Cosmos (Washington).

HUGHES, Thomas Merfyn; QC 1994; a Recorder, since 1991; *b* 8 April 1949; *s* of John Medwyn Hughes and Blodwen Jane Hughes (*née* Roberts); *m* 1977, Patricia Joan, *d* of John Talbot, surgeon, Brentwood; two *s* one *d*. *Educ:* Rydal Sch., Colwyn Bay; Liverpool Univ. (LLB Hons 1970); Council of Legal Educn. Called to the Bar, Inner Temple, 1968; in practice at the Bar, Chester, 1971–94, Temple, 1994–; Asst Recorder, 1987–91. Contested (Lab) Caernarfon, 1979. *Recreations:* sailing, Rugby. *Address:* Plas Llanfaes, Beaumaris, Anglesey LL58 8RH. *Clubs:* Royal Anglesey Yacht; Bangor Rugby Union Football.

HUGHES, Sir Trevor Denby L.; *see* Lloyd-Hughes.

HUGHES, Sir Trevor (Poulton), KCB 1982 (CB 1974); CEng, FICE; Chairman: Building and Civil Engineering Holidays Scheme Management Ltd, since 1987; Building and Civil Engineering Benefits Scheme Trustee Ltd, since 1987; *b* 28 Sept. 1925; *y s* of late Rev. John Evan and Mary Grace Hughes; *m* 1st, 1950, Mary Ruth Walwyn (marr. diss.); two *s*; 2nd, 1978, Barbara June Davison. *Educ:* Ruthin Sch. RE, 1945–48, Captain 13 Fd Svy Co. Municipal engineering, 1948–61; Min. of Transport, 1961–62; Min. of Housing and Local Govt: Engineering Inspectorate, 1962–70; Dep. Chief Engineer, 1970–71; Dir, 1971–72 and Dir-Gen., 1972–74, Water Engineering, DoE; Dep. Sec., DoE, 1974–77; Dep. Sec., Dept of Transport, 1977–80; Perm. Sec., Welsh Office, 1980–85. Mem., British Waterways Bd, 1985–88. Vice-Chm., Public Works Congress Council, 1975–89, Chm., 1989–91. Chief British Deleg., Perm. Internat. Assoc. of Navigation Congresses, 1985–91; Mem., Water Panel, Monopolies and Mergers Commn, 1991–. A Vice-Pres., ICE, 1984–86. Hon. Fellow, Univ. of Glamorgan (formerly Poly. of Wales), 1986. Hon. FCIWEM. *Recreations:* music, gardening, reading. *Address:* Clearwell, 13 Brambleton Avenue, Farnham, Surrey GU9 8RA. *T:* Farnham (01252) 714246.

See also J. R. P. Hughes.

HUGHES, Victor; *see* Hughes, H. V.

HUGHES, William, CB 1953; Chairman, Tooting Youth Project, 1981–87; *b* 21 Aug. 1910; *o s* of late William Hughes, Bishop's Stortford, Herts, and of Daisy Constance, *y d* of Charles Henry Davis; *m* 1941, Ilse Erna, *o d* of late E. F. Plohs; one *s* one *d*. *Educ:* Bishop's Stortford Coll.; Magdalen Coll., Oxford (demy). Board of Trade, 1933; Asst Sec., 1942; Under-Sec., 1948–63 (Sec., Monopolies and Restrictive Practices Commission, 1952–55); Second Sec., 1963–71. Consultant to British Overseas Trade Bd, 1972–73; Under-Sec., Prices Commn, 1973–75; Dep. Sec., DTI, 1970–71. *Recreation:* music. *Address:* 250 Trinity Road, SW18 3RQ. *T:* 0181–870 3652; Page's, Widdington, Essex CB11 3SN. *Clubs:* Reform; Leander.

HUGHES, Maj.-Gen. (Retd) William Dillon, CB 1960; CBE 1953; MD; FRCPI; DTM&H; Commandant, Royal Army Medical College, 1957–60; *b* 23 Dec. 1900; *s* of R. Hughes, JP; *m* 1929, Kathleen Linda Thomas (*d* 1976); one *s*. *Educ:* Campbell Coll., Belfast; Queen's Univ., Belfast. MB, BCh, BAO, 1923; Lieut, RAMC, 1928; Officer i/c Medical Div. 64 and 42 Gen. Hosps, MEF, 1940–42; Officer i/c Medical Div. 105 Gen. Hosp., BAOR, 1944–46; Sen. MO, Belsen, 1945; consulting Physician, Far East Land Forces, 1950–53; ADMS, Aldershot Dist, 1954. Prof. in Tropical Medicine and Consulting Physician, RAM Coll., 1955–56; Vice-Pres., Royal Society of Tropical Medicine and Hygiene, 1959–60; Col Comdt RAMC, 1961–65. QHP 1957; Mitchiner Medal, RCS, 1960. *Address:* Vine House, Summer Court, Tilford Road, Farnham GU9 8DS.

See also D. T. D. Hughes.

HUGHES, William Young, CBE 1987; Chief Executive, since 1976, and Chairman, since 1985, Grampian Holdings plc; Chairman, Aberforth Smaller Companies Trust plc, since 1990; Director, Central Scotland Healthcare NHS Trust (formerly Royal Scottish National Hospital and Community NHS Trust), since 1992; *b* 12 April 1940; *s* of Hugh

Prentice Hughes and Mary Henderson Hughes; *m* 1964, Anne Macdonald Richardson; two *s* one *d*. *Educ:* Firth Park Grammar Sch., Sheffield; Univ. of Glasgow (BSc Hons Pharmacy, 1963). MPS 1964. Research, MRC project, Dept of Pharmacy, Univ. of Strathclyde, 1963–64; Lectr, Dept of Pharmacy, Heriot-Watt Univ., 1964–66; Partner, R. Gordon Drummond (group of retail chemists), 1966–70; Man. Dir, MSJ Securities Ltd (subsid. of Guinness Gp), 1970–76; Grampian Holdings, Glasgow, 1977– (holding co. in transport, tourism, retail, sporting goods and veterinary medicines). Chm., CBI Scotland, 1987–89; Mem. Governing Council, Scottish Business in the Community, 1986–. Hon. Chm., European Summer Special Olympic Games (1990), Strathclyde, 1988–91. Pres., Work Wise. Treas., Scottish Conservative Party, 1993– (Dep. Chm., 1989–92). *Recreation:* golf. *Address:* The Elms, 12 Camelon Road, Falkirk FK1 5RX. *T:* 0141–357 2000. *Club:* Glenbervie Golf.

HUGHES JONES, Dr Nevin Campbell, FRS 1985; on scientific staff, Medical Research Council, 1954–88; Fellow of Hughes Hall, Cambridge, since 1987; *b* 10 Feb. 1923; *s* of William and Millicent Hughes Jones; *m* 1952, Elizabeth Helen Dufty; two *s* one *d*. *Educ:* Berkhampsted Sch., Herts; Oriel Coll., Univ. of Oxford; St Mary's Hosp. Med. School. MA, DM, PhD; FRCP. Medical posts held at St Mary's Hosp., Paddington, Radcliffe Infirmary, Oxford, and Postgrad. Med. Sch., Hammersmith, 1947–52; Member: MRC's Blood Transfusion Unit, Hammersmith, 1952–79 (Unit transferred to St Mary's Hosp. Med. Sch., Paddington, as MRC's Experimental Haematology Unit, 1960); MRC's Mechanisms in Immunopathology (formerly in Tumour Immunity) Unit, Cambridge, 1979–88, now Hon. Mem. *Publication:* Lecture Notes on Haematology, 1970, 5th edn 1991. *Recreations:* making chairs, walking the Horseshoe Path on Snowdon. *Address:* 65 Orchard Road, Melbourn, Royston, Herts SG8 6BB. *T:* Royston (01763) 260471.

HUGHES-MORGAN, Maj.-Gen. Sir David (John), 3rd Bt *cr* 1925; CB 1983; CBE 1973 (MBE 1959); **His Honour Judge Hughes-Morgan;** a Circuit Judge, since 1986; *b* 11 Oct. 1925; *s* of Sir John Hughes-Morgan, 2nd Bt and Lucie Margaret (*d* 1987), *d* of late Thomas Parry Jones-Parry; *S* father, 1969; *m* 1959, Isabel Jean (*d* 1994), *d* of J. M. Lindsay; three *s*. *Educ:* RNC, Dartmouth. Royal Navy, 1943–46. Admitted solicitor, 1950. Commissioned, Army Legal Services, 1955; Brig., Legal Staff, HQ UKLF, 1976–78; Dir, Army Legal Services, BAOR, 1978–80, MoD, 1980–84; a Recorder, 1983–86. *Heir:* *s* Ian Parry David Hughes-Morgan [*b* 22 Feb. 1960; *m* 1992, Julia, *er d* of R. J. S. Ward]. *Address:* c/o National Westminster Bank, 1 High Street, Bromley BR1 1LL.

HUGHES-YOUNG, family name of **Baron St Helens.**

HUGHESDON, Charles Frederick, AFC 1944; FRAeS; *b* 10 Dec. 1909; *m* 1st, 1937, Florence Elizabeth (actress, as Florence Desmond) (*d* 1993), *widow* of Captain Tom Campbell Black; one *s*; 2nd, 1993, Carol Elizabeth, *widow* of Baron Havers, QC. *Educ:* Raine's Foundation School. Entered insurance industry, 1927; learned to fly, 1932; Flying Instructor's Licence, 1934; commnd RAFO, 1934; Commercial Pilot's Licence, 1936. Joined Stewart, Smith & Co. Ltd, 1936; RAF Instructor at outbreak of war; seconded to General Aircraft as Chief Test Pilot, 1939–43; rejoined RAF, 1943–45 (AFC). Rejoined Stewart, Smith & Co. Ltd, 1946; retired as Chm. of Stewart Wrightson 1976. Dir, Aeronautical Trusts Ltd; Chm., The Charles Street Co. Hon. Treas., RAeS, 1969–85. Upper Freeman, City of London; Member: GAPAN; Gunmakers' Guild. Order of the Cedar, Lebanon, 1972. *Recreations:* shooting, horseracing, riding (dressage), yachting, water ski-ing. *Address:* Leckhampstead House, Leckhampstead, near Newbury, Berks RG16 8QH; Flat 12, 5 Grosvenor Square, W1X 9LA. *T:* 0171–493 1494. *Clubs:* Garrick, Royal Air Force, Royal Thames Yacht, Lloyd's Yacht.

HUGHFF, Victor William, FIA, CIMgt; Chief General Manager, Norwich Union Life Insurance Society, 1984–89; *b* 30 May 1931; *s* of William Scott Hughff and Alice Doris (*née* Kerry); *m* 1955, Grace Margaret (*née* Lambert) one *s* one *d*. *Educ:* City of Norwich School. Joined Norwich Union Life Insce Soc., 1949; Assistant Actuary, 1966; General Manager and Actuary, 1975; Main Board Director, 1981–89. Director: Stalwart Assurance Group, 1989–93; Congregational & General Insurance, 1989–; Norwich Centre Projects Ltd, 1994–. Served in RAF, 1951–53; commnd in Secretarial Br., National Service List. Elder of United Reformed Church. *Recreations:* tennis, badminton. *Address:* 18 Hilly Plantation, Thorpe St Andrew, Norwich NR7 0JN. *T:* Norwich (01603) 434517. *Club:* Royal Over-Seas League.

HUGILL, John; QC 1976; a Recorder of the Crown Court, since 1972; *b* 11 Aug. 1930; *s* of late John A. and Alice Hugill; *m* 1956, Patricia Elizabeth Hugill (*née* Welton); two *d*. *Educ:* Sydney C of E Grammar Sch., NSW; Fettes Coll.; Trinity Hall, Cambridge (MA). 2nd Lieut RA, 1948–49. Called to the Bar, Middle Temple, 1954 (Bencher, 1984); Northern Circuit, 1954; Assistant Recorder, Bolton, 1971; a Dep. High Court Judge, 1993–. Chairman: Darryn Clarke Inquiry, 1979; Stanley Royd Inquiry, 1985. Member: Senate of the Inns of Court and the Bar, 1984–86; Gen. Council of the Bar, 1987–89. *Recreation:* yachting. *Address:* Peel Court Chambers, 45 Hardman Street, Manchester M3 3HA.

HUGILL, Michael James; Assistant Master, Westminster School, 1972–86; *b* 13 July 1918; 2nd *s* of late Rear-Adm. R. C. Hugill, CB, MVO, OBE, and Winifred (*née* Backwell). *Educ:* Oundle; King's Coll., Cambridge, Exhibitioner, King's Coll., 1936–39; MA 1943. War Service in the RN; Mediterranean, Home and Pacific Fleets, 1939–46; rank on demobilisation, Lieut-Comdr. Mathematics Master, Stratford Grammar Sch., 1947–51; Senior Mathematics Master, Bedford Modern Sch., 1951–57; Headmaster, Preston Grammar Sch., 1957–61; Headmaster, Whitgift School, Croydon, 1961–70; Lectr, Inst. of Education, Keele Univ., 1971–72. *Publication:* Advanced Statistics, 1985. *Address:* 4 Glenmore, Kersfield Road, SW15 3HL. *Club:* Army and Navy.

HUGO, Lt-Col Sir John (Mandeville), KCVO 1969 (CVO 1959); OBE 1947; Gentleman Usher to the Queen, 1952–69, an Extra Gentleman Usher since 1969; *b* 1 July 1899; *s* of R. M. Hugo; *m* 1952, Joan Winifred, *d* of late D. W. Hill; two *d*. *Educ:* Marlborough Coll.; RMA, Woolwich, Commissioned RA, 1917; transf. to Indian Cavalry, 1925; Military Sec. to Governor of Bengal, 1938–40; rejoined 7th Light Cavalry, 1940; Military Sec. to Governor of Bengal 1946–47; Asst Ceremonial Sec., Commonwealth Relations Office, 1948–52; Ceremonial and Protocol Secretary, 1952–69. *Address:* Hilltop House, Vines Cross, Heathfield, East Sussex TN21 9EN. *T:* Horam Road (014353) 2562. *Club:* Army and Navy.

HUISMANS, Sipko; Chief Executive, Courtaulds PLC, since 1991 (Director, since 1984; Managing Director, 1990–91); *b* 28 Dec. 1940; *s* of Jouko and Roelofina Huismans; *m* 1969, Janet; two *s* one *d*. *Educ:* primary sch., Holland; secondary sch., Standerton, S Africa; Stellenbosch Univ., S Africa (BA Com). Shift chemist, Usutu Pulp Co. Ltd, 1961–68; Gen. Man., Springwood Cellulose Co., 1968–74; Man. Dir, Courtaulds Central Trading, 1974–80; Dir, 1980–, Man. Dir, 1982–84, Courtaulds Fibres; Chairman: Internat. Paints Ltd, 1987–90; Courtaulds Chemical and Industrial Exec., 1988–. *Recreations:* motor racing, sailing, competition. *Clubs:* Chichester Sailing, Royal Southampton Yacht.

HULDT, Bo Kristofer Andreas; Director, Swedish Institute of International Affairs, since 1988 (on leave of absence, 1992–95); *b* 24 April 1941; *s* of Bo and Martha Huldt; *m* Ingrid Mariana Neering; two *d*. *Educ:* Lund Univ., Sweden (PhD Hist.); Augustana Coll., USA (BA); graduate work, Princeton. Asst and Associate Prof. of History, Lund and Växjö Univs, 1974–79; Res. Associate, Swedish Secretariat for Future Studies, 1975–78; Swedish Institute of International Affairs: Res. Associate, 1979; Asst Dir, 1983; Dep. Dir and Dir of Studies, 1985; Dir, IISS, 1992–93; Dir, Dept of Security Policy, Strategy and Mil. Hist., Royal Swedish Mil. Staff and War Coll., Stockholm, 1994–95. Special Consultant to Swedish Dept of Defence, 1981–82. Member: Swedish Royal Acad. of War Science, 1984; Swedish Naval Acad., 1991. Editor, Yearbooks of Swedish Inst. of Internat. Affairs, 1983–92. *Publications:* Sweden, the United Nations and Decolonization, 1974; (jtly) Sweden in World Society, 1978; World History 1945–65, Norwegian edn, 1982, Swedish and Finnish edns, 1983, Icelandic edn, 1985; contribs to learned jls on history, internat. politics and security. *Recreations:* shooting, literature. *Address:* Box 1253, 11182 Stockholm, Sweden.

HULL, Bishop Suffragan of, since 1994; **Rt. Rev. James Stuart Jones;** *b* 18 Aug. 1948; *s* of Major James Stuart Anthony Jones and Helen Jones; *m* 1980, Sarah Caroline Rosalind Marrow; three *d*. *Educ:* Duke of York's Royal Mil. Sch., Dover; Exeter Univ. (BA Hons Theol.); Wycliffe Hall, Oxford. Teacher, Sevenoaks Sch., 1970–74; Producer, Scripture Union, 1975–81; ordained deacon, 1982, priest, 1983; Curate, Christ Church, Clifton, 1982–90; Vicar, Emmanuel Church, S Croydon, 1990–94. *Publications:* Finding God, 1987; Why do people suffer?, 1993; The Power and the Glory, 1994; A Faith that touches the World, 1994. *Recreations:* reading, the family. *Address:* Hullen House, Woodfield Lane, Hessle, N Humberside HU13 0ES. *T:* Hull (01482) 649019.

HULL, Prof. Sir David, Kt 1993; FRCP; Foundation Professor of Child Health, University of Nottingham, since 1972; *b* 4 Aug. 1932; *s* of late William and Nellie Hull; *m* 1960, Caroline Elena Lloyd; two *s* one *d*. *Educ:* Univ. of Liverpool (BSc Hons, MB ChB). DCH, DObstRCOG. Lectr in Paediatrics, Oxford, 1963–66; Consultant Paediatrician, Hosp. for Sick Children, London, 1966–72; Sen. Lectr, Inst. of Child Health, Univ. of London, 1966–72. President: Neonatal Soc., 1987–91; British Paediatric Assoc., 1991–94. *Publications:* (with D. I. Johnston) Essential Paediatrics, 1981, 3rd edn 1993; (with A. D. Milner) Hospital Paediatrics, 1984, 2nd edn 1992; (with E. F. St J. Adamson) Nursing Sick Children, 1984; (with L. Polnay) Community Paediatrics, 1984, 2nd edn 1993. *Recreations:* gardening, walking, drawing. *Address:* Department of Child Health, University Hospital, Queen's Medical Centre, Nottingham NG7 2UH. *T:* Nottingham (0115) 970 9255.

See also Derek Hull.

HULL, Air Vice-Marshal David Hugill, QHS 1991; FRCP; Dean of Air Force Medicine and Clinical Director, RAF, 1994–Aug. 1996; *b* 21 Aug. 1931; *s* of T. E. O. and M. E. Hull (*née* Dinsley); *m* 1957, Ann Thornton-Symington; two *d*. *Educ:* Rugby; Trinity Hall, Cambridge; St Thomas' Hosp. MA, MB BChir. Royal Waterloo and Kingston upon Thames Hosps, 1956–57; RAF 1957; Consultant in Medicine, PMRAF Hosp., Akrotiri, 1966–67; RAF Hosp., Cosford, 1967–74; Exchange Consultant, Aeromedical Consultation Service, USAF Sch. of Aerospace Medicine, 1974–77; PARAF Hosp., Wroughton, 1977–82; Consultant Advr in Medicine, RAF, 1983–93; Reader, Clinical Aviation Medicine, RAF IAM, 1981–93. Lady Cade Medal, RCS, 1973. Hon. Texas Citizen, 1977. *Publications:* chapters in books on aviation and aerospace medicine; papers in professional jls. *Recreations:* sailing, gardening, cross-country ski-ing. *Address:* 20 Chedworth Gate, Broome Manor, Swindon, Wilts SN3 1NE. *Club:* Royal Air Force.

HULL, Prof. Derek, FRS 1989; FEng 1986; FIM, FPRI; Senior Fellow, University of Liverpool, since 1991; Goldsmiths' Professor of Metallurgy, University of Cambridge, 1984–91, now Professor Emeritus; Fellow, Magdalene College, Cambridge, 1984–91; *b* 8 Aug. 1931; *s* of late William and Nellie Hull (*née* Hayes); *m* 1953, Pauline Scott; one *s* four *d*. *Educ:* Baines Grammar School, Poulton-le-Fylde; Univ. of Wales. PhD, DSc. AERE, Harwell and Clarendon Lab., Oxford, 1956–60; University of Liverpool: Senior Lectr, 1960–64; Henry Bell Wortley Prof. of Materials Engineering, 1964–84; Dean of Engineering,1971–74; Pro-Vice Chancellor, 1983–84. Dist. Vis. Prof. and Senior Vis. NSF Fellow, Univ. of Delaware, 1968–69; Monash Vis. Prof., Univ. of Monash, 1981; Hon. Fellow, University Coll. Cardiff, 1985. Andrew Laing Lecture, NECInst, 1989. Hon. DTech Tampere Univ. of Technology, Finland, 1987. Rosenhain Medal, 1973, A. A. Griffith Silver Medal, 1985, Inst. of Metals; Medal of Excellence in Composite Materials, Univ. of Delaware, 1990. *Publications:* Introduction to Dislocations, 1966, 3rd edn 1984; An Introduction to Composite Materials, 1981; numerous contribs to Proc. Roy. Soc., Acta Met., Phil. Mag., Jl Mat. Sci., MetalScience, Composites. *Recreations:* golf, music, fell-walking. *Address:* Department of Materials Science and Engineering, University of Liverpool, PO Box 147, Liverpool L69 3BX. *Club:* Heswall Golf.

See also Sir David Hull.

HULL, John Folliott Charles, CBE 1993; Deputy Chairman, Schroders plc, 1977–85; *b* 21 Oct. 1925; *er s* of Sir Hubert Hull, CBE, and of Judith, *e d* of P. F. S. Stokes; *m* 1951, Rosemarie Waring; one *s* three *d*. *Educ:* Downside; Aberdeen Univ.; Jesus Coll., Cambridge (Titular Schol.; 1st cl. hons Law; MA). Captain, RA, 1944–48; served with Royal Indian Artillery, 1945–48. Called to Bar, Inner Temple, 1952, *ad eund* Lincoln's Inn, 1954. J. Henry Schroder Wagg & Co. Ltd, 1957–72, 1974–85: a Man. Dir, 1961–72; Dep. Chm., 1974–77; Chm., 1977–83; Dir, 1984–85; Dir, Schroders plc, 1969–72, 1974–85; Dep. Chm., Land Securities plc, 1976–; Director: Lucas Industries plc, 1975–90; Legal and General Assurance Soc., 1976–79; Legal & General Group plc, 1979–90; Goodwood Racecourse Ltd, 1987–93. Dir-Gen., City Panel on Take-overs and Mergers, 1972–74 (Dep. Chm., 1987–); Chm., City Company Law Cttee, 1976–79. Lay Mem., Stock Exchange, 1983–84. Mem., Council, Manchester Business Sch., 1973–86. *Recreation:* reading 19th century novelists. *Address:* 33 Edwardes Square, W8 6HH. *T:* 0171–603 0715. *Club:* MCC.

See also Duke of Somerset.

HULL, John Grove, QC 1983; **His Honour Judge Hull;** a Circuit Judge, since 1991; *b* 21 Aug. 1931; *s* of Tom Edward Orridge Hull and Marjorie Ethel Hull; *m* 1961, Gillian Ann, *d* of Leslie Fawcett Stemp; two *d*. *Educ:* Rugby School; King's College, Cambridge. BA (1st cl. in Mech. Scis Tripos) 1953, MA 1957; LLB 1954. National Service, commissioned RE, 1954–56; called to the Bar, Middle Temple, 1958 (Cert. of Honour, Bar Final), Bencher, 1989; in practice, common law Bar, 1958–91; a Recorder, 1984–91. *Recreations:* gardening, English literature.

HULLAH, Rev. Peter Fearnley; Headmaster, Chetham's School of Music, since 1992; *b* 7 May 1949; *s* of Ralph and Mary Hullah; *m* 1971, Hilary Sargent Long; one *s* one *d*. *Educ:* Bradford Grammar Sch.; King's Coll., London (BD, AKC); Makerere Univ., Kampala; Cuddesdon Coll., Oxford. Curate, St Michael and All Angels, Summertown, Oxford, 1974–77; Asst Chaplain, St Edward's Sch., Oxford, 1974–77; Chaplain, 1977–82, Housemaster, 1982–87, Internat. Centre, Sevenoaks Sch.; Sen. Chaplain, King's Sch., Canterbury, 1987–92. Mem., Bloxham Project Steering Cttee, 1979–. Chm., Chaplains' Conf., 1987–92. Hon. Minor Canon, Canterbury Cathedral, 1987–92. FRSA 1993.

Recreations: pilgrimage, music, hill walking. *Address:* Chetham's School of Music, Long Millgate, Manchester M3 1SB. *T:* 0161–834 9644. *Club:* Athenæum.

HULME, Bishop Suffragan of, since 1984; **Rt. Rev. Colin John Fraser Scott;** *b* 14 May 1933; *s* of late Kenneth Miller Scott and Marion Edith Scott; *m* 1958, Margaret Jean MacKay; one *s* two *d*. *Educ:* Berkhamsted School; Queens' College, Cambridge; Ridley Hall, Cambridge. MA Cantab. Curate: St Barnabas, Clapham Common, 1958–61; St James, Hatcham, 1961–64; Vicar, St Mark, Kennington, 1964–71; Vice-Chm., Southwark Diocesan Pastoral Cttee, 1971–77; Team Rector, Sanderstead Team Ministry, 1977–84. Chm., Council for the Care of Churches, 1994–. *Address:* 1 Raynham Avenue, Didsbury, Manchester M20 6BW. *T:* 0161–445 5922.

HULME, Geoffrey Gordon, CB 1984; Consultant, Public Finance Foundation, since 1991; *b* 8 March 1931; *s* of Alfred and Jessie Hulme; *m* 1956, Shirley Leigh Cumberlidge; one *s* one *d*. *Educ:* King's Sch., Macclesfield; Corpus Christi Coll., Oxford (MA, 1st Cl Hons Mod. Langs). Nat. Service, Intelligence Corps, 1949–50; Oxford, 1950–53; Ministry of Health, subseq. Department of Health and Social Security, latterly Department of Health: Asst Principal, 1953–59; Principal, 1959–64; Principal Regional Officer, W Midlands, 1964–67; Asst Sec., 1967–74; Under-Sec., 1974–81; Principal Finance Officer, 1981–86; Dep. Sec., 1981–91; seconded to Public Finance Foundn as Dir, Public Expenditure Policy Unit, 1986–91. *Recreations:* the usual things and collecting edible fungi. *Address:* Stone Farm, Little Cornard, Sudbury, Suffolk CO10 0NW; 163A Kennington Park Road, SE11 4JJ. *T:* 0171–735 4461. *Club:* Royal Automobile.

HULME, Rev. Paul; Superintendent Minister, Wesley's Chapel, London, since 1988; *b* 14 May 1942; *s* of Harry Hulme and Elizabeth Hulme; *m* 1976, Hilary Frances Martin; three *s*. *Educ:* Hatfield House, Yorks; Didsbury Theological Coll., Bristol (BA). Minister: Bungay, Suffolk, 1968–70; Brighton, 1970–75; Newquay, Cornwall, 1975–79; Taunton, 1979–86; Enfield, 1986–88. Chaplain, Sussex Univ., 1970–75. Freeman, City of London, 1990. *Recreations:* walking, music. *Address:* Wesley's Chapel, 49 City Road, EC1Y 1AU. *T:* 0171–253 2262. *Clubs:* National Liberal.

HULSE, Sir (Hamilton) Westrow, 9th Bt, *cr* 1739; Barrister-at-Law, Inner Temple; *b* 20 June 1909; *o s* of Sir Hamilton Hulse, 8th Bt, and Estelle (*d* 1933) *d* of late William Lorillard Campbell, of New York, USA; *S* father, 1931; *m* 1st, 1932, Philippa Mabel (marr. diss. 1937), *y d* of late A. J. Taylor, Strensham Court, Worcs; two *s*; 2nd, 1938, Amber (*d* 1940), *o d* of late Captain Herbert Stanley Orr Wilson, RHA, Rockfield Park, Mon; 3rd, 1945 (marr. diss.); 4th, 1954, Elizabeth, *d* of late Col George Redesdale Brooker Spain, CMG, TD, FSA. *Educ:* Eton; Christ Church, Oxford. Wing Comdr RAFVR, served 1940–45 (despatches). *Heir: s* Edward Jeremy Westrow Hulse [*b* 22 Nov. 1932; *m* 1957, Verity Ann, *d* of William Pilkington, Ivy Well, St John, Jersey; one *s* one *d*]. *Address:* Breamore, Hants SP6 2BU. *TA:* Breamore. *T:* Downton (01725) 512773. *Clubs:* Carlton; Leander.

HULSE, Dr Russell Alan; Principal Research Physicist and Head, Advanced Modeling Sciences Laboratory, Plasma Physics Laboratory, Princeton University; *b* 28 Nov. 1950; *s* of Alan Earle Hulse and Betty Joan Hulse (*née* Wedemeyer). *Educ:* The Cooper Union, NY (BS Physics 1970); Univ. of Massachusetts, Amherst (MS Physics 1972; PhD Physics 1975; DSc 1994). National Radio Astronomy Observatory, 1975–77; Plasma Physics Lab., Princeton Univ., 1977–, Dist. Res. Fellow, 1994. Fellow, Amer. Physical Soc., 1993. (Jtly) Nobel Prize in Physics, 1993. *Publications:* papers in professional jls and conf. procs in fields of pulsar astronomy, controlled fusion plasma physics and computer modeling. *Recreations:* cross-country ski-ing, canoeing, nature photography, bird watching, other outdoor activities, target shooting, music. *Address:* Princeton University, Plasma Physics Laboratory, Princeton, NJ 08543, USA. *T:* (609) 2432621.

HULSE, Sir Westrow; *see* Hulse, Sir H. W.

HUM, Christopher Owen; HM Diplomatic Service; Assistant Under-Secretary of State (Northern Asia and Pacific), Foreign and Commonwealth Office, since 1994; *b* 27 Jan. 1946; *s* of late Norman Charles Hum and of Muriel Kathleen (*née* Hines); *m* 1970, Julia Mary, second *d* of Hon. Sir Hugh Park, *qv*; one *s* one *d*. *Educ:* Berkhamsted Sch.; Pembroke Coll., Cambridge (Foundn Scholar; 1st Cl. Hons; MA); Univ. of Hong Kong. Joined FCO, 1967; served in: Hong Kong, 1968–70; Peking, 1971–73; Office of the UK Perm. Rep. to the EEC, Brussels, 1973–75; FCO, 1975–79; Peking, 1979–81; Paris, 1981–83; Asst Head, Hong Kong Dept, FCO, 1983–85; Counsellor, 1985; Dep. Head, Falkland Is Dept, FCO, 1985–86; Head, Hong Kong Dept, FCO, 1986–89; Counsellor (Political) and Hd of Chancery, UK Mission to UN, New York, 1989–92; Asst Under-Sec. of State (Northern Asia), FCO, 1992–94. *Recreations:* music (piano, viola), walking. *Address:* c/o Foreign and Commonwealth Office, King Charles Street, SW1A 2AH.

HUMBLE, James Kenneth; Chief Executive, Local Authorities Coordinating Body on Food and Trading Standards (formerly Trading Standards), since 1982; *b* 8 May 1936; *s* of Joseph Humble and Alice (*née* Rhodes); *m* 1962, Freda (*née* Holden); three *d*. Fellow, Inst. of Trading Standards. Served RN, 1954–56. Weights and Measures, Oldham, 1956–62; Fed. Min. of Commerce and Industry, Nigeria, 1962–66; Chief Trading Standards Officer, Croydon, 1966–74; Asst Dir of Consumer Affairs, Office of Fair Trading, 1974–79; Dir of Metrication Bd, 1979–80; Dir, Nat. Metrological Co-ordinating Unit, 1980–87. Sec., Trade Descriptions Cttee, Inst. of Trading Standards, 1968–73; Examr, Dip. in Trading Standards, 1978–; Vice Chm., Council of Europe Cttee of Experts on Consumer Protection, 1976–79. Member: Council for Vehicle Servicing and Repair, 1972–75; Methven Cttee, 1974–76; OECD Cttee, Air Package Tours, 1978–79; BSI Divl Council, 1976–79; Eden Cttee on Metrology, 1984; Chairman: World Conf. on Safety, Sweden, 1989; Yugoslavian Conf. on 1992, 1989; Mem. Cttee, 1985–, Mem. Exec., 1987–, European Consumer Product Safety Assoc.; Member Executive: W European Legal Metrology Co-operation, 1989–; European Forum Food Law Enforcement Practitioners, 1990–. Organiser, First European Metrology Symposium, 1988. Conf. papers to USA Western States Conf. on Weights and Measures, 1989. Sport, Devonport Services, 1954–56; Captain, Oldham Rugby Union, 1957–59; Professional Rugby, Leigh RFC, 1959–65. *Publications:* (contrib.) Marketing and the Consumer Movement, 1978; European Inspection, Protection and Control, 1990; contrib. to various jls. *Recreations:* bridge, golf, opera. *Address:* PO Box 6, Token House, 1A Robert Street, Croydon CR9 1LG. *T:* 0181–688 1996.

HUME, Sir Alan (Blyth), Kt 1973; CB 1963; *b* 5 Jan. 1913; *s* of late W. Alan Hume; *m* 1943, Marion Morton Garrett; one *s* one *d*. *Educ:* George Heriot's Sch.; Edinburgh Univ. Entered Scottish Office, 1936. Under-Sec., Scottish Home Department, 1957–59; Asst Under-Sec. of State, Scottish Office, 1959–62; Under-Sec., Min. of Public Bldg and Works, 1963–64; Secretary, Scottish Develt Dept, 1965–73. Chairman: Ancient Monuments Bd, Scotland, 1973–81; Edinburgh New Town Conservation Cttee, 1975–90. *Recreations:* golf, fishing. *Address:* 12 Oswald Road, Edinburgh EH9 2HJ. *T:* 0131–667 2440. *Clubs:* English-Speaking Union; New (Edinburgh).

HUME, His Eminence Cardinal (George) Basil; *see* Westminster, Archbishop of, (RC).

HUME, James Bell; Under-Secretary, Scottish Office, 1973–83; *b* 16 June 1923; *s* of late Francis John Hume and Jean McLellan Hume; *m* 1950, Elizabeth Margaret Nicolson. *Educ:* George Heriot's Sch., Edinburgh; Edinburgh Univ. (MA Hons History, 1st Cl.). RAF, 1942–45. Entered Scottish Office, 1947; Jt Sec., Royal Commn on Doctors' and Dentists' Remuneration, 1958–59; Nuffield Trav. Fellowship, 1963–64; Head of Edinburgh Centre, Civil Service Coll., 1969–73. *Publication:* Mandarin Grade 3, 1993. *Recreations:* dance music, walking, enjoying silence. *Address:* 2/9 Succoth Court, Succoth Park, Edinburgh EH12 6BZ. *T:* 0131–346 4451. *Club:* New (Edinburgh).

HUME, John; MP (SDLP) Foyle, since 1983; Member (SDLP) Northern Ireland, European Parliament, since 1979; Leader, Social Democratic and Labour Party, since 1979; *b* 18 Jan. 1937; *s* of Samuel Hume; *m* 1960, Patricia Hone; two *s* three *d*. *Educ:* St Columb's Coll., Derry; St Patrick's Coll., Maynooth, NUI (MA). Res. Fellow in European Studies, TCD; Associate Fellow, Centre for Internat. Affairs, Harvard, 1976. Pres., Credit Union League of Ireland, 1964–68; MP for Foyle, NI Parlt, 1969–73; Member (SDLP), Londonderry: NI Assembly, 1973–75; NI Constitutional Convention, 1975–76; NI Assembly, 1982–86; Minister of Commerce, NI, 1974. Mem. (SDLP) New Ireland Forum, 1983–84. Contested (SDLP) Londonderry, UK elections, Oct. 1974. Member: Cttee on Regl Policy and Regl Planning, European Parlt, 1979–; ACP-EEC Jt Cttee, 1979–; Bureau of European Socialist Gp, 1979–. Mem., Irish T&GWU (now Services, Industrial, Professional & Technical Union). Hon. DLitt: Massachusetts, 1985; Catholic Univ. of America, 1986; St Joseph's Univ., Philadelphia, 1986; Tusculum Coll., Tennessee, 1988. St Thomas More Award, Univ. of San Francisco, 1991. *Address:* 6 West End Park, Derry, N Ireland BT48 9JF. *T:* Londonderry (01504) 265340.

HUME, Dr Robert, FRCPE, FRCPGlas, FRCPI, FRCPath, FRCSE; Consultant Physician, Southern General Hospital, Glasgow, 1965–93; *b* 6 Jan. 1928; *m* 1958, Kathleen Ann Ogilvie; two *s* one *d*. *Educ:* Univ. of Glasgow (MB, ChB, MD, DSc). FRCPGlas 1968; FRCPEd 1969; FRCPath 1992; FRCSEd 1992; FRCPI 1993. Nat. Service in India and Germany, 1946–48, commnd into Gordon Highlanders. Glasgow University: Hutcheson Res. Scholar, 1955–56; Hall Fellow, 1956–58; Hon. Clinical Sub-Dean, 1985–93. Pres., RCPSGlas, 1990–92. Mem., Acad. of Medicine, Malaysia, 1991. Hon. FACP; Hon. FRACP; Hon. FCSSA; Hon. FRCP&S (Canada). *Publications:* on haematological and vascular diseases. *Recreations:* hill-walking, swimming, reading, art appreciation, gardening, talking. *Address:* 6 Rubislaw Drive, Bearsden, Glasgow G61 1PR. *T:* 0141–942 5331. *Clubs:* Commonwealth Trust; Royal Automobile (Glasgow).

HUMFREY, Charles Thomas William; HM Diplomatic Service; Minister, Tokyo, since 1995; *b* 1 Dec. 1947; *s* of Brian and Marjorie Humfrey; *m* 1971, Enid Thomas; two *s* one *d*. *Educ:* The Lodge Sch., Barbados (Barbados Scholar, 1966); St Edmund Hall, Oxford (BA; Webb Medley Jun. Prize, 1968). FCO 1969; Tokyo, 1971–76; SE Asian Dept, FCO, 1976–79; Private Sec. to Minister of State, 1979–81; UK Mission, NY, 1981–85; Southern African Dept, FCO, 1985–87; Counsellor, Ankara, 1988–90; Counsellor (Econ.), Tokyo, 1990–94; Head of African Dept (Southern), FCO, 1994–95. *Address:* c/o Foreign and Commonwealth Office, SW1A 2AH.

HUMM, Roger Frederick; Vice-Chairman and Chief Executive, Alexanders Holdings, since 1992; Director, Imperial Hospitals Ltd, since 1991; *b* 7 March 1937; *s* of Leonard Edward Humm, MBE, and Gladys Humm; *m* 1966, Marion Frances (*née* Czechman) (marr. diss.). *Educ:* Hampton Sch., Hampton, Mddx; Univ. of Sheffield (BA Hons Econ). Graduate trainee, Ford Motor Co. Ltd (UK), 1960, Sales Manager, 1973; Marketing Dir, 1977, Internat. Gp Dir, N Europe, 1978, Ford of Europe Inc.; Exec. Dir of Sales, 1980, Man. Dir, 1986–90, Ford Motor Co. Ltd; Director: Ford Motor Credit Co. Ltd, 1980–90; Henry Ford & Son Ltd (Cork), 1982–90. FRSA 1987; CIMgt; FInstD; FIMI. Liveryman, Worshipful Co. of Carmen, 1986; Freeman, City of London, 1986. *Recreations:* golf, scuba diving, writing. *Address:* The Clock House, Kelvedon, Essex CO5 9DG. *Clubs:* Royal Automobile, Lord's Taverners, Variety Club of Great Britain; Harlequins.

HUMMEL, Frederick Cornelius, MA, DPhil, BSc; Head of Forestry Division, Commission of the European Communities, 1973–80, retired; *b* 28 April 1915; *s* of Cornelius Hummel, OBE, and Caroline Hummel (*née* Riefler); *m* 1st, 1941, Agnes Kathleen Rushforth (marr. diss., 1961); one *s* (and one *s* decd); 2nd, 1961, Floriana Rosemary Hollyer; three *d*. *Educ:* St Stephan, Augsburg, Germany; Wadham Coll., Oxford. District Forest Officer, Uganda Forest Service, 1938–46; Forestry Commn, 1946–73; Mensuration Officer, 1946; Chief, Management Sect., 1956; released for service with FAO as Co-Dir, Mexican Nat. Forest Inventory, 1961–66; Controller, Management Services, Forestry Commn, 1966–68, Comr for Harvesting and Marketing, 1968–73. Hon. Member: Société Royale Forestière de Belgique; Asociación para el Progreso Forestal, Spain; Corresponding Member: Mexican Acad. of Forest Scis; Italian Acad. of Forest Scis; Soc. of Forestry, Finland. Dr *hc* Munich, 1978. Bernard Eduard Fernow Plaquette, (jtly) Amer. Forestry Assoc. and Deutscher Forstverein, 1986; Alexander von Humboldt Gold Medal, 1995. *Publications:* Forest Policy, 1984; Biomass Forestry in Europe, 1988; Forestry Policies in Europe: an analysis, 1989. *Recreations:* walking, travel. *Address:* Ridgemount, 8 The Ridgeway, Guildford, Surrey GU1 2DG. *T:* Guildford (01483) 572383. *Club:* United Oxford & Cambridge University.

HUMPHREY, Arthur Hugh Peters, CMG 1959; OBE 1952; Hon. PMN (Malaya), 1958; Controller of Special Projects, Overseas Development Administration, Foreign and Commonwealth Office, 1961–71; Malayan Civil Service, 1934–60, retired; *b* 18 June 1911; *s* of late Arthur George Humphrey, Bank Manager; *m* 1948, Mary Valentine, *d* of late Lieut-Col J. E. Macpherson; three *d*. *Educ:* Eastbourne Coll.; Merton Coll., Oxford (Open Exhbr 1930, 1st class Maths, 1933; MA 1948). Appointed Malayan Civil Service, 1934; Private Sec. to Governor of Straits Settlements and High Comr for Malay States, 1936–38; Resident, Labuan, 1940–42; interned by Japanese in Borneo, 1942–45; idc 1948; Sec. for Defence and Internal Security, Fedn of Malaya, 1953–57; Mem. of Federal Legislative and Executive Councils, 1953–56; Sec. to the Treasury, Federation of Malaya, 1957–59; Director of Technical Assistance, Commonwealth Relations Office, 1960–61; Controller of Special Projects, ODM, 1961. Official Leader, United Kingdom delegations at Colombo Plan conferences: Tokyo, 1960, and Kuala Lumpur, 1961. Coronation Medal, 1953. *Recreations:* music, tennis. *Address:* 14 Ambrose Place, Worthing, Sussex BN11 1PZ. *T:* Worthing (01903) 233339. *Club:* East India, Devonshire, Sports and Public Schools.

HUMPHREYS, Arthur Leslie Charles, CBE 1970; Director: Computer Associated Systems Ltd, since 1982; Charles Babbage Institute, since 1978; *b* 8 Jan. 1917; *s* of late Percy Stewart Humphreys and late Louise (*née* Weston); *m* 1st, 1943, Marjorie Irene Murphy-Jones (decd); two *s* one *d*; 2nd, 1975, Audrey Norah Urquhart (*née* Dunningham) (decd); 3rd, Marion Terry Ruston. *Educ:* Catford Grammar Sch.; Administrative Staff Coll., Henley. International Computers & Tabulators Ltd: Dir 1963–83; Dep. Man. Dir 1964; Man. Dir 1967; ICL Ltd: Dir, 1968–82; Man. Dir, 1968–72; Dep. Chm., 1972–77; Dir, Data Recording Instrument Co. Ltd, 1957–84. *Recreations:* table tennis, bridge, music. *Address:* 24 Middle Street, Thriplow, Royston, Herts SG8 7RD. *T:* Fowlmere (0176382) 594.

HUMPHREYS, Prof. Colin John, FIM; FInstP; Goldsmiths' Professor of Materials Science, University of Cambridge, since 1992 (Professor of Materials Science, 1990–92); Head of Department of Materials Science and Metallurgy, since 1991; Fellow of Selwyn College, Cambridge, since 1990; *b* 24 May 1941; *s* of Arthur William Humphreys and Olive Annie (*née* Harton); *m* 1966, Sarah Jane Matthews; two *d*. *Educ:* Luton Grammar Sch.; Imperial Coll., London (BSc); Churchill Coll., Cambridge (PhD); Jesus Coll., Oxford (MA). Sen. Res. Officer 1971–80, Lectr 1980–85, in Metallurgy and Science of Materials, Univ. of Oxford; Sen. Res. Fellow, Jesus Coll., Oxford, 1974–85; Henry Bell Wortley Prof. of Materials Engrg and Hd of Dept of Materials Sci. and Engrg, Liverpool Univ., 1985–89. Visiting Professor: Univ. of Illinois, 1982–86; Arizona State Univ., 1979. Chm., Commn on Electron Diffraction, and Mem. Commn on Internat. Tables, Internat. Union of Crystallography, 1984–87. Member: SERC, 1988–92 (Chm., Materials Sci. and Engrg Commn, 1988–92; Mem., Science Bd, 1990–92); Adv. Cttee, Davy-Faraday Labs, Royal Instn, 1989–92; Scientific Adv. Cttee on Advanced Materials for EC Internat. Scientific Co-opn Prog., 1990–. Member Council: RMS, 1988–89; Inst. of Metals, 1989–91; Inst. of Materials, 1992– (Vice-Pres., 1993–). Mem., Academia Europaea, 1991. Member Court: Univ. of Bradford, 1990–92; Univ. of Cranfield, 1992–. Freeman, City of London. RSA Medal, 1963; Reginald Mitchell Meml Lecture and Medal, 1989; Rosenhain Medal and Prize, Inst. of Metals, 1989; D. K. C. MacDonald Meml Lectr, Toronto, 1993; Templeton Award, 1994. *Publications:* (ed) High Voltage Electron Microscopy, 1974; (ed) Electron Diffraction 1927–77, 1978; Creation and Evolution, 1985 (trans. Chinese 1988); patents and numerous sci. and tech. pubns mainly on electron microscopy, semiconductors, superconductors and nanometre scale electron beam lithography. *Recreations:* chronology of ancient historical events, contemplating gardening. *Address:* Department of Materials Science and Metallurgy, Pembroke Street, Cambridge CB2 3QZ. *T:* Cambridge (01223) 334457.

HUMPHREYS, Emyr Owen; author; *b* 15 April 1919; *s* of William and Sarah Rosina Humphreys, Prestatyn, Flints; *m* 1946, Elinor Myfanwy, *d* of Rev. Griffith Jones, Bontnewydd, Caerns; three *s* one *d*. *Educ:* University Coll., Aberystwyth; University Coll., Bangor (Hon. Fellow, Univ. of Wales, 1987). Gregynog Arts Fellow, 1974–75; Hon. Prof., English Dept, Univ. Coll. of N Wales, Bangor, 1988. Hon. DLitt Wales, 1990. *Publications:* The Little Kingdom, 1946; The Voice of a Stranger, 1949; A Change of Heart, 1951; Hear and Forgive, 1952 (Somerset Maugham Award, 1953); A Man's Estate, 1955; The Italian Wife, 1957; Y Tri Llais, 1958; A Toy Epic, 1958 (Hawthornden Prize, 1959); The Gift, 1963; Outside the House of Baal, 1965; Natives, 1968; Ancestor Worship, 1970; National Winner, 1971 (Welsh Arts Council Prize, 1972); Flesh and Blood, 1974; Landscapes, 1976; The Best of Friends, 1978; Penguin Modern Poets No 27, 1978 (Soc. of Authors Travelling Award, 1979); The Kingdom of Brân, 1979; The Anchor Tree, 1980; Pwyll a Riannon, 1980; Miscellany Two, 1981; The Taliesin Tradition, 1983 (Welsh Arts Council Non-Fiction Prize, 1984); Jones: a novel, 1984; Salt of the Earth, 1985; An Absolute Hero, 1986; Darn o Dir, 1986; Open Secrets, 1988; The Triple Net, 1988; The Crucible of Myth, 1990; Bonds of Attachment, 1991 (Book of the Year, Welsh Arts Council, 1992); Outside Time, 1991; Brodyr a Chwiorydd, 1994; Unconditional Surrender, 1996. *Recreations:* rural pursuits. *Address:* Llinon, Penyberth, Llanfairpwll, Ynys Môn, Gwynedd LL61 5YT.

HUMPHREYS, Janet, (Mrs V. W. Humphreys); *see* Anderson, Janet.

HUMPHREYS, Dr Keith Wood, CBE 1992; Deputy Chairman, AMEC plc, since 1995; Director, Hickson International plc, since 1995; *b* 5 Jan. 1934; *s* of William and Alice Humphreys; *m* 1964, Tessa Karen Shepherd; three *d*. *Educ:* Manchester Grammar School; Trinity Hall, Cambridge (MA, PhD). MRSC; CIMgt. Managing Dir, Plastics Div., Ciba-Geigy (UK), 1972–78; Jt Managing Dir, Ciba-Geigy (UK), 1979–82; Managing Dir, 1982–84, Chm. and Man. Dir, 1984–95, May & Baker, later Rhône-Poulenc Ltd. Mem., BBSRC, 1994–. *Recreations:* music, tennis, mountain walking.

HUMPHREYS, Sir Myles; see Humphreys, Sir R. E. M.

HUMPHREYS, Sir Olliver (William), Kt 1968; CBE 1957; BSc, FInstP, CEng, FIEE, FRAeS; *b* 4 Sept. 1902; *s* of late Rev. J. Willis Humphreys, Bath; *m* 1st, 1933, Muriel Mary Hawkins (*d* 1985); 2nd, 1993, Dr P. E. R. Read, AM. *Educ:* Caterham Sch.; University Coll., London. Joined staff GEC Research Labs, 1925, Dir, 1949–61; Director 1953, Vice-Chm., 1963–67, GEC Ltd; Chm. all GEC Electronics and Telecommunications subsidiaries, 1961–66 and GEC (Research) Ltd, 1961–67. Mem. Bd, Inst. Physics, 1951–60 (Pres., 1956–58); Mem. Coun., IEE, 1952–55 (Vice-Pres., 1959–63; Pres., 1964–65); Faraday Lectr, 1953–54. Mem., BoT Cttee on Organisation and Constitution of BSI, 1949–50; Chm., BSI Telecommunications Industry Standards Cttee, 1951–63 (Mem. Gen. Coun., 1953–56; Mem. Exec. Cttee, 1953–60); Chm., Internat. Special Cttee on Radio Interference (CISPR), 1953–61; Chm., Electrical Res. Assoc., 1958–61; Chm., DSIR Radio Res. Bd, 1954–62; Pres., Electronic Engrg Assoc., 1962–64; Founder Chm., Conf. of Electronics Industry, 1963–67; Mem., Nat. ERC, 1963–67. Fellow UCL, 1963. Sen. Freeman, Worshipful Co. of Makers of Playing Cards. *Publications:* various technical and scientific papers in proceedings of learned societies. *Recreations:* travel, walking, reading.

HUMPHREYS, Sir (Raymond Evelyn) Myles, Kt 1977; JP; DL; Chairman: Northern Ireland Railways Co. Ltd, 1967–90; Northern Ireland Transport Holding Company, 1988–93 (Dir, 1968–74); *b* 24 March 1925; *s* of Raymond and May Humphreys; *m* 1st, 1963, Joan Tate (*d* 1979); two *s*; 2nd, 1987, Sheila Clements-McFarland. *Educ:* Skegoniel Primary Sch.; Londonderry High Sch.; Belfast Royal Acad. Research Engineer: NI Road Transport Bd, 1946–48; Ulster Transport Authy, 1948–55; Transport Manager, Nestle's Food Products (NI) Ltd, 1955–59; Director: Walter Alexander (Belfast) Ltd, 1959–92; Quick Service Stations Ltd, 1971–85; Bowring Martin Ltd, 1978–88; Abbey National plc (formerly Abbey National Bldg Soc.), 1981–91 (Chm., NI Adv. Bd, 1981–92); NI Railways Leasing, 1986–90; Belfast Harbour Pension Fund Ltd, 1987–; NI Railways Travel Ltd, 1988–90. Chm., Belfast Marathon Ltd, 1981–85. Member of Board: Ulster Transport Authority, 1966–69. Chm., NI Police Authority, 1976–86. Mem., Belfast City Council, 1964–81; Chairman: Belfast Corp. Housing Cttee, 1966–69; City Council Planning Cttee, 1973–75; City Council Town Planning and Environmental Hlth Cttee, 1973–75; Finance and Gen. Purposes Cttee, 1978–80; High Sheriff of Belfast, 1969; Dep. Lord Mayor, 1970; Lord Mayor, 1975–77. Member: Nat. Planning and Town Planning Council, 1970–81 (Chm., 1976–77); NI Tourist Bd, 1973–80; NI Housing Exec., 1975–78; Chm., Ulster Tourist Develt Assoc., 1968–78; Belfast Harbour Comr, 1979–88. Mem., May Cttee of Inquiry into UK Prison Services, 1978–79. Past Chairman: Bd of Visitors, HM Prison, Belfast; Bd of Management, Dunlambert Secondary Sch. Past-Pres., Belfast Junior Chamber of Commerce; Mem. Exec., NI Chamber of Commerce and Industry (Pres., 1982); NI Rep., Motability Internat.; Senator, Junior Chamber Internat.; Pres., Belfast Br., BIM, 1983–. Member: TA&VRA for NI, 1980; Council, Queen's Silver Jubilee Appeal. Pres., NI Polio Fellowship, 1977–. Pres., City of Belfast Youth Orch., 1980; Dir, Ulster Orch. Soc., 1980–82; Trustee, Ulster Folk & Transport Mus., 1976–81; Vice Pres., Railway Preservation Soc. of Ire., 1994–; Patron, Model Engineers Soc., 1974–. Mem. Senate, QUB, 1975–77; Mem. Court, Ulster Univ., 1984–. District Transport Officer, St John Ambulance Brigade, 1946–66. Freeman of City of London, 1976. JP 1969; DL Belfast 1983. FCIT (Mem. Council); CIMgt. OStJ. *Address:* Mylestone, 23 Massey Avenue, Belfast BT4 2JT. *T:* Belfast (01232) 761166. *Club:* Ulster Reform (Belfast).

HUMPHREYS, Prof. Robert Arthur, OBE 1946; MA, PhD Cantab; Director, Institute of Latin-American Studies, University of London, 1965–74; Professor of Latin-American History in University of London, 1948–74, now Emeritus; *b* 6 June 1907; *s* of late Robert Humphreys and Helen Marion Bavin, Lincoln; *m* 1946, Elisabeth (*d* 1990), *er d* of late Sir Bernard Pares, KBE, DCL. *Educ:* Lincoln Sch.; Peterhouse, Cambridge (Scholar). Commonwealth Fund Fellow, Univ. of Michigan, 1930–32. Asst Lectr in American History, UCL, 1932, Lectr 1935; Reader in American History in Univ. of London, 1942–48; Prof. of Latin-American History, UCL, 1948–70. Research Dept, FO, 1939–45. Mem., UGC Cttee on Latin American Studies, 1962–64; Chairman: Cttee on Library Resources, Univ. of London, 1969–71; Management Cttee, Inst of Archæology, 1975–80; Mem. Adv. Cttee, British Library Reference Div., 1975–79. Governor, SOAS, 1965–80, Hon. Fellow 1981. Pres., RHistS, 1964–68 (Hon. Vice-Pres., 1968). Lectures: Enid Muir Meml, Univ. of Newcastle upon Tyne, 1962; Creighton, Univ. of London, 1964; Raleigh, Brit. Acad., 1965. Corresp. Member: Hispanic Soc. of America; Argentine Acad. of History; Instituto Histórico e Geográfico Brasileiro; Academia Chilena de la Historia; Sociedad Chilena de Historia y Geografia; Instituto Ecuatoriano de Ciencias Naturales; Sociedad Peruana de Historia; Instituto Histórico y Geográfico del Uruguay; Academia Nacional de la Historia, Venezuela. Hon. DLitt: Newcastle, 1966; Nottingham, 1972; Hon. LittD Liverpool, 1972; DUniv Essex, 1973. Comdr, Order of Rio Branco, Brazil, 1972. Machado de Assis Medal, Academia Brasileira de Letras, 1974. *Publications:* British Consular Reports on the Trade and Politics of Latin America, 1940; The Evolution of Modern Latin America, 1946; Liberation in South America, 1806–1827, 1952; Latin American History: A Guide to the Literature in English, 1958; The Diplomatic History of British Honduras, 1638–1901, 1961; (with G. S. Graham), The Navy and South America, 1807–1823 (Navy Records Soc.), 1962; (with J. Lynch) The Origins of the Latin American Revolutions, 1808–1826, 1965; Tradition and Revolt in Latin America and other Essays, 1969; The Detached Recollections of General D. F. O'Leary, 1969; The Royal Historical Society, 1868–1968, 1969; Robert Southey and his History of Brazil, 1978; Latin American Studies in Great Britain (autobiog.), 1978; Latin America and the Second World War, vol. I, 1939–1942, 1981, vol. II, 1942–1945, 1982; Elisabeth Humphreys, 1904–1990: a memoir, 1992; co-edited: (with A. D. Momigliano) Byzantine Studies and Other Essays by N. H. Baynes, 1955; (with Elisabeth Humphreys) The Historian's Business and Other Essays by Richard Pares, 1961; contrib. to The New Cambridge Modern History, vols VIII, IX and X. *Address:* 5 St James's Close, Prince Albert Road, NW8 7LG. *T:* 0171–722 3628.

HUMPHRIES, Barry; *see* Humphries, J. B.

HUMPHRIES, David Ernest; defence science consultant; Director, Materials Research Laboratory, Defence Science and Technology Organisation, Melbourne, Australia, 1992–94; *b* 3 Feb. 1937; *er s* of late Ernest Augustus Humphries and Kathleen Humphries; *m* 1959, Wendy Rosemary Cook; one *s* one *d*. *Educ:* Brighton Coll.; Corpus Christi Coll., Oxford (Scholar; MA). RAE Farnborough: Materials Dept, 1961; Avionics Dept, 1966; Head of Inertial Navigation Div., 1974; Head of Bombing and Navigation Div., 1975; Head of Systems Assessment Dept, 1978; Dir Gen. Future Projects, MoD PE, 1981–83; Chief Scientist (RAF) and Dir Gen. of Res. (C), MoD, 1983–84; Dir Gen. Res. Technol., MoD (PE), 1984–86; Asst Chief Scientific Advr (Projects and Research), MoD, 1986–90; Dir, Australian Aeronautical Res. Lab., 1990–92. *Recreations:* music, pipe organ building and playing. *Address:* Little Follies, East Liphook Road, Headley, Bordon, Hants GU35 8LL.

HUMPHRIES, Gerard William; His Honour Judge Humphries; a Circuit Judge since 1980; *b* 13 Dec. 1928; *s* of late John Alfred Humphries and Marie Frances Humphries (*née* Whitwell), Barrow-in-Furness; *m* 1957, Margaret Valerie, *o d* of late W. W. Gelderd and Margaret Gelderd (*née* Bell), Ulverston; four *s* one *d*. *Educ:* St Bede's Coll., Manchester; Manchester Univ. (LLB Hons). Served RAF, 1951–53, Flying Officer. Called to Bar, Middle Temple, 1952; admitted to Northern Circuit, 1954; Asst Recorder of Salford, 1969–71; a Recorder of the Crown Court, 1974–80. Chairman: Medical Appeals Tribunal, 1976–80; Vaccine Damage Tribunals, 1979–80. Charter Mem., Serra Club, N Cheshire, 1963– (Pres. 1968, 1973). Trustee, SBC Educnl Trust, 1979– (Chm., 1979–90). Foundn Governor, St Bede's Coll., Manchester, 1978–. KHS 1986. *Recreations:* tennis, golf, music, caravanning, gardening. *Clubs:* Lansdowne; Northern Lawn Tennis, Northenden Golf (Manchester).

HUMPHRIES, John Anthony Charles, OBE 1980; Senior Partner, Travers Smith Braithwaite, since 1980; *b* 15 June 1925; *s* of Charles Humphries; *m* 1951, Olga June, *d* of Dr Geoffrey Duckworth, MRCP; four *d*. *Educ:* Fettes; Peterhouse, Cambridge (1st Law). Served War, RNVR, 1943–46. Solicitor (Hons), 1951. Chairman: Water Space Amenity Commn, 1973–83; Southern Council for Sport and Recreation, 1987–92; Vice-Pres., Inland Waterways Assoc., 1973– (Chm., 1970–73); Mem. Inland Waterways Amenity Adv. Council, 1971–89; Adviser to HM Govt on amenity use of water space, 1972; Member: Nat. Water Council, 1973–83; Thames Water Authy, 1983–87. Mem., Sports Council, 1987–88. Chm., Evans of Leeds plc, 1982–; Mem., London Bd, Halifax Building Soc., 1985–92; Dep. Chm., Environment Council, 1985–94. Vice Chm., Council, Surrey Univ., 1995–. Governor, Sports Aid Foundn, 1990–. *Recreations:* inland waters, gardening. *Address:* 21 Parkside, Wimbledon, SW19 5NA. *T:* 0181–946 3764. *Clubs:* Naval, City.

HUMPHRIES, (John) Barry, AO 1982; music-hall artiste and author; *b* 17 Feb. 1934; *s* of J. A. E. Humphries and L. A. Brown; *m* 1st, 1959, Rosalind Tong; two *d*; 2nd, 1979, Diane Millstead; two *s*; 1990, Lizzie, *d* of Sir Stephen (Harold) Spender, CBE, CLit. *Educ:* Melbourne Grammar Sch.; Univ. of Melbourne. Repertory seasons, Union Theatre, Melbourne, 1953–54; Phillip Street Revue Theatre, Sydney, 1956; Demon Barber, Lyric, Hammersmith, 1959; Oliver, New Theatre, 1960. One-man shows (author and performer): A Nice Night's Entertainment, 1962; Excuse I, 1965; Just a Show, 1968; A Load of Olde Stuffe, 1971; At Least You Can Say That You've Seen It, 1974; Housewife Superstar, 1976; Isn't It Pathetic at His Age, 1979; A Night with Dame Edna, 1979; An Evening's Intercourse with Barry Humphries, 1981–82; Tears Before Bedtime, 1986; Back with a Vengeance, 1987; Look At Me When I'm Talking To You!, 1994. TV series, The Dame Edna Experience, 1987. Numerous plays, films and broadcasts. President: Arthur Machen Soc. (UK); Frans de Boever Soc. (Belgium). DUniv Griffith Univ., Qld, 1994. *Publications:* Bizarre, 1964; Innocent Austral Verse, 1968; (with Nicholas Garland) The Wonderful World of Barry McKenzie, 1970; (with Nicholas Garland) Bazza Holds His Own, 1972; Dame Edna's Coffee Table Book, 1976; Les Patterson's Australia, 1979; Treasury of Australian Kitsch, 1980; A Nice Night's Entertainment, 1981; Dame Edna's Bedside Companion, 1982; The Traveller's Tool, 1985; (with Nicholas Garland) The Complete Barry McKenzie, 1988; My Gorgeous Life: the autobiography of Dame Edna Everage, 1989; The Life and Death of Sandy Stone, 1991; More Please (autobiog.), 1992; Women in the Background, 1995. *Recreations:* reading secondhand booksellers' catalogues in bed,

Hum. 1936; Thomas Whitcombe Greene Prize, 1936; Diploma in Classical Archæology, 1937; Fellow of Magdalen Coll., 1937. Served 1st Bn Welch Regt and General Staff in Middle East, Balkans, North Africa, Sicily, Italy, 1940–46 (despatches 3 times, OBE, US Bronze Star); GSO1 18th Army Group, 1943; 15th Army Group, 1943–45; Col General Staff, Allied Force HQ, 1945–46; attached staff Governor-General Canada, 1946–47; released and granted hon. rank of Colonel, 1947. Principal, Dominions Office, 1947; 1st Secretary, Pretoria, 1948–49; Private Secretary to Prime Minister (Mr Attlee), 1950–51, (Mr Churchill) 1951–52; Asst Secretary, 1952; Deputy High Commissioner for UK, Lahore, 1954–56; Head of Central African Dept, Commonwealth Relations Office, 1956–59; Asst Under Secretary of State, Commonwealth Relations Office, 1959–60; accompanied the Prime Minister as an Adviser, on African tour, Jan.-Feb. 1960; Dep. High Comr for the UK in Lagos, Fedn of Nigeria, Oct. 1960–62; High Comr in Uganda, 1962–65; in Cyprus, 1965–67; in Nigeria, 1967–69; Ambassador to Brazil, 1969–73. Dep. Chm., Exim Credit Management and Consultants, 1974–77, Consultant, 1978–82. Chm., Bd of Governors, Commonwealth Inst., 1974–84. Mem. Appts Commn, Press Council, 1977–82. Montague Burton Vis. Prof. of Internat. Relations, Univ. of Edinburgh, 1980. President: Classical Assoc., 1981–82; Soc. for Promotion of Hellenic Studies, 1986–90. FSA 1984. Corresp. Mem., Brazilian Acad. of Arts, 1972. BBC TV Mastermind, 1977 and Mastermind of Masterminds, 1982. Hon. DHum Ball State Univ., 1991. US Bronze Star 1945; Grand Cross, Order of the Southern Cross, Brazil, 1985. *Publications:* A Don at War, 1966, 2nd edn 1990; On the Spot, 1975; Footprints in Cyprus, 1982, rev. edn 1990; (ed and trans.) Gothic Art and the Renaissance in Cyprus, by Camille Enlart, 1987; (ed with Iro Hunt) Caterina Cornaro: Queen of Cyprus, 1989; articles in Annual of British School of Archæology at Athens, Journal of Hellenic Studies, and Slavonic Rev.; Editor, The Times Yearbook of World Affairs, 1978–81. *Recreations:* reading, writing, roses. *Address:* Old Place, Lindfield, West Sussex RH16 2HU. *T:* Lindfield (01444) 482298. *Clubs:* Athenæum, Beefsteak; Pen Clube do Brasil.

HUNT, Derek Simpson; Chairman, MFI Furniture Group Ltd, since 1987 (Chief Executive, 1987–94); Chairman and Managing Director, MFI Furniture Centres Ltd, since 1987; *b* 9 June 1939; *s* of late John William Hunt and of Elizabeth (*née* Simpson); *m* 1967, Sandra Phyllis Jones; two *s*. *Educ:* Queen Elizabeth Grammar Sch., Darlington, Co. Durham. Joined MFI as Retail Area Controller, 1972; Branch Ops Controller, 1973; Dir, MFI Furniture Centres, 1974; MFI Furniture Group: Dir, 1976; Man. Dir, 1981; Chm., 1984; during merger with Asda, also Chief Exec. and Dep. Chm., Asda-MFI, 1985–87; returned to MFI and effected management buy-out, 1987. Gov., Ashridge Management Coll., 1986–. Founding Fellow, Nat. Children's Home George Thomas Soc., 1989. Hon. Fellow, Manchester Polytechnic, 1988. *Recreations:* sailing, Rugby Union, fishing. *Address:* Southon House, 333 The Hyde, Edgware Road, Colindale, NW9 6TD. *T:* 0181–200 8000.

HUNT, Donald Frederick, OBE 1993; FRCO; Master of the Choristers and Organist, Worcester Cathedral, since 1975; *b* 26 July 1930; *m* 1954, Josephine Benbow; two *s* two *d*. *Educ:* King's School, Gloucester. ARCM; ARCO 1951; FRCO(CHM) 1954. Asst Organist, Gloucester Cathedral, 1947–54; Director of Music: St John's Church, Torquay, 1954–57; Leeds Parish Church, 1957–75; Leeds City Organist, 1973–75. Chorus Dir, Leeds Festival, 1962–75; Conductor: Halifax Choral Soc., 1957–88; Leeds Philharmonic Soc., 1962–75; Worcester Festival Choral Soc., 1975–; Worcester Three Choirs Festival, 1975–; Artistic Dir, Bromsgrove Festival, 1981–91. Hon DMus Leeds 1975. *Publications:* Magnificat and Nunc Dimittis, 1972; Missa Brevis, 1973; Versicles and Responses, 1973; God be gracious, 1984; Missa Nova, 1985; Mass for Three Voices, 1986; S. S. Wesley: cathedral musician, 1990; anthems and carols. *Recreations:* cricket, poetry, travel. *Address:* 13 College Green, Worcester WR1 2LH. *T:* Worcester (01905) 23555.

HUNT, (Henry) Holman, CBE 1988; Deputy Chairman, 1985–91, Member, 1980–91, Monopolies and Mergers Commission; *b* 13 May 1924; *s* of Henry Hunt and Jessie Brenda Beale; *m* 1954, Sonja Blom; one *s* two *d*. *Educ:* Queens Park Sch., Glasgow; Glasgow Univ. (MA). FCMA, FIMC, FBCS, FInstAM. Caledonian Insce Co., 1940–43; RAF, 1943–46; Glasgow Univ., 1946–50; Cadbury Bros, 1950–51; PA Management Consultants: Consultant, 1952–57; Manager, Office Organisation, 1958–63; Dir, Computer Div., 1964–69; Bd Dir, 1970–83; Man. Dir, PA Computers and Telecommunications, 1976–83. Pres., Inst. of Management Consultants, 1974–75. FRSA 1988. *Recreations:* music, reading, walking, travel, photography. *Address:* 28 The Ridings, Epsom, Surrey KT18 5JJ. *T:* Epsom (01372) 720974. *Club:* Caledonian.

HUNT, James; *see* Hunt, P. J.

HUNT, Sir John (Leonard), Kt 1989; MP (C) Ravensbourne, since 1974 (Bromley, 1964–74); *b* 27 Oct. 1929; *s* of late William John Hunt and Dora Maud Hunt, Keston, Kent; unmarried. *Educ:* Dulwich Coll. Councillor, Bromley Borough Council, 1953–65; Alderman, Bromley Borough Council, 1961–65; Mayor of Bromley, 1963–64. Contested (C) S Lewisham, Gen. Election, 1959. Member: Select Cttee on Home Affairs (and Mem., Sub-Cttee on Race Relations and Immigration), 1979–87; Speaker's Panel of Chairmen, 1980–. Jt-Chm., British-Caribbean Assoc., 1968–77 and 1984–; Chm., Indo-British Parly Gp, 1979–91; UK Rep. at Council of Europe and WEU, 1973–77 and 1988–. Mem., BBC Gen. Adv. Council, 1975–87. Pres., Inst. of Administrative Accountants, subseq. of Financial Accountants, 1970–88. Mem. of London Stock Exchange, 1958–70. Freeman, City of London, 1986; Freeman, Haberdashers' Co., 1986. *Recreations:* foreign travel, gardening, good food. *Address:* House of Commons, SW1A 0AA. *T:* 0171–219 4530.

HUNT, John Maitland, MA, BLitt; Headmaster of Roedean, 1971–84; *b* 4 March 1932; *s* of Richard Herbert Alexander Hunt and Eileen Mary Isabelle Hunt (*née* Witt); *m* 1969, Sarah, *d* of Lt-Gen. Sir Derek Lang, *qv*; two *s*. *Educ:* Radley College; Wadham College, Oxford. BA 1956; BLitt 1959; MA 1960. Assistant Master, Stowe School, 1958–70 (Sixth Form tutor in Geography). Chm., Bd of Managers, Common Entrance Exam. for Girls' Schs, 1974–81. *Publications:* various articles on fine arts and architecture. *Recreations:* estate management, fine arts, writing, travel. *Address:* Logie, Dunfermline, Fife KY12 8QN. *Clubs:* Commonwealth Trust, Ski of GB.

HUNT, Judith Anne; Chief Executive, Local Government Management Board, since 1993; *b* 13 Sept. 1945; *d* of Philip E. Riley and late Amy Riley; *m* 1st, 1967, Alan J. Hunt (marr. diss. 1979); two *d*; 2nd, 1988, Daniel W. Silverstone. *Educ:* Cheadle Hulme Sch.; Leeds Univ. (BA Hons). Lectr, Stockport Coll. and Salford Coll. of Technology, and teacher, Salford, 1967–74; Nat. Organiser, 1974–80 and Asst Gen. Sec., 1980–82. AUEW (TASS); Equal Opportunities Advr and Dep. Head, Personnel Services, GLC, 1982–84; Dir of Personnel (Staffing), GLC, 1984–86; Acting Dir of Personnel, ILEA, 1986–87; Chief Exec., London Borough of Ealing, 1987–93. Parent Governor, ILEA; Member: Governing Body, Ruskin Coll.; Exec. Council, Solace; Women's Nat. Commn, 1976–82; W London TEC; W London Leadership, 1989–93; London First. Trustee, Common Purpose. FRSA. *Publications:* Organising Women Workers, 1985; (ed) Jackie West: work, women and the labour market; contribs to jls. *Recreations:* books, gardening, opera, theatre. *Address:* Local Government Management Board, 41 Belgrave Square, SW1X 8NZ. *Club:* Reform.

HUNT, Prof. Julian Charles Roland, PhD; FRS 1989; Chief Executive of the Meteorological Office, since 1992; Hon. Professor in Fluid Mechanics, University of Cambridge, since 1992; Fellow of Trinity College, Cambridge, since 1966; *b* 5 Sept. 1941; *s* of Roland Charles Colin Hunt, *qv*; *m* 1965, Marylla Ellen Shephard; one *s* two *d*. *Educ:* Westminster Sch.; Trinity Coll., Cambridge (BA 1963; PhD 1967); Univ. of Warwick. Post-doctoral res., Cornell Univ., USA, 1967; Res. Officer, Central Electricity Res. Labs, 1968–70; University of Cambridge: Lectr in Applied Maths and in Engrg, 1970–78; Reader in Fluid Mechanics, 1978–90; Prof. in Fluid Mechanics, 1990–92. Visiting Professor: Colorado State Univ., 1975; NC State Univ., and Envmtl Protection Agency, 1977; Univ. of Colorado, 1980; Nat. Center for Atmospheric Res., Boulder, Colo, 1983. Founder Dir, Cambridge Envmtl Res. Consultants Ltd, 1986–91. Pres., IMA, 1993– (Hon. Sec., 1984–89; Vice-Pres., 1989–93); Mem. Man. Bd, European Res. Community for Flow Turbulence and Combustion, 1988–; Mem., NERC, 1994– (Chm., Atom. Sci. and Tech. Bd). Councillor, Cambridge CC, 1971–74 (Leader, Labour Gp, 1972). *Publications:* (contrib.) New Applications of Mathematics, ed C. Bondi, 1991; scientific pubns in Jl of Fluid Mechanics, Atmospheric Envmt, Qly Jl of Royal Meteorol Soc., Proc. Royal Soc. *Address:* Meteorological Office, Bracknell, Berks, RG12 2SZ.

HUNT, Brig. Kenneth, OBE 1955; MC 1943; Vice-President, International Institute for Strategic Studies, since 1988 (Deputy Director, 1967–77); *b* 26 May 1914; *s* of late John Hunt and Elizabeth Hunt; *m* 1939, Mary Mabel Crickett (*d* 1995); two *s* (and one *d* decd). *Educ:* Chatham House Sch., Ramsgate; sc Camberley; idc. Commissioned into Royal Artillery, 1940; served, Africa, Italy, Austria, with HAC, 1 RHA and 2 RHA, 1942–46 (despatches thrice); Bt Lt-Col 1955; CO 40 Fd Regt RA, 1958–60; CRA 51 Highland Div., 1961–63; IDC 1963; Dep. Standing Gp Rep. to N Atlantic Council, 1964–66; resigned commission, 1967. Dir, British Atlantic Cttee, 1978–81. Specialist Adviser to House of Commons Defence Cttee, 1971–84. Visiting Professor: Fletcher Sch. of Law, Cambridge, Mass, 1975; Univ. of S California, 1978–79; Univ. of Surrey, 1978–87. Mem. Council, RUSI, 1977; Fellow, Inst. of Security, Tokyo, 1979–. Freeman, City of London, 1977; Mem., HAC. Hon. Dr (PolSci), Korea Univ., 1977. Order of Rising Sun (Japan), 1984. *Publications:* NATO without France, 1967; The Requirements of Military Technology, 1967; Defence with Fewer Men, 1973; (ed) The Military Balance, 1967–77; (jtly) The Third World War, 1978; (jtly) Asian Security, annually, 1979–89; Europe in the Western Alliance, 1988; contribs to learned jls, and chapters in books, in UK, USA, E Asia. *Recreations:* fly-fishing, listening to music. *Address:* 22 The Green, Ewell, Surrey KT17 3JN. *T:* 0181–393 7906. *Clubs:* Army and Navy; International House of Japan (Tokyo).

HUNT, Kevan; Corporation Member and Employee Relations Director, British Coal Corporation, since 1991; Chairman: British Coal Enterprise, since 1993; International Mining Consultants Group Holdings, since 1993; Centris Coal Benefits Ltd, since 1994; *b* Seaham Harbour, Co. Durham, 13 Oct. 1937; *s* of late Martin Hunt and of Mary Patilla (formerly Hunt, *née* Lavery); *m* 1958, Valerie Anne Scattergood; two *s*. *Educ:* William Rhodes Sch., Chesterfield; Chesterfield Coll. of Technology; Extramural Studies Dept, Sheffield Univ.; Derby and Dist Coll. of Art. National Coal Board, later British Coal: Mining Technician (Electrical), 1955–68; Personnel Manager, 1969–74; Industrial Relations Br. Head, 1974–76; Area IR Officer (S Notts), 1976–82; HQ IR Dir (Nat.), 1982–84; IR Dep. Dir-Gen. (Nat.), 1984–85; Head of IR, 1985–88; Exec. Dir, 1988–91. Chm., Nationalised Industry's Personnel Panel. Dist Councillor, 1964–76; Chm., Alfreton UDC, 1970–71; Leader, Amber Valley Dist Council, 1973–76. CIMgt (Pres., Notts Branch); FIPM; MIMEMME. *Publications:* papers in personnel, training and industrial relations field. *Recreations:* travel, walking, reading. *Address:* Craigside, 168 Greenhill Lane, Riddings, Alfreton, Derbys DE55 4EX.

HUNT, Maj.-Gen. Malcolm Peter John, OBE 1984; Royal Marines retired, 1992; General Secretary, Association of British Dispensing Opticians, since 1995; *b* 19 Nov. 1938; *s* of Peter Gordon Hunt and Rachel Margaret Hunt (*née* Owston); *m* 1962, Margaret Peat; two *s*. *Educ:* St John's Sch., Leatherhead; Staff Coll., Camberley. Joined Royal Marines, 1957; service in Malta, Aden and NI; OC RM Detachment, HMS Nubian, 1966–68; Instructor, Army Staff Coll., 1979–81; CO, 40 Commando RM, 1981–83 (Falklands, NI); Internat. Mil. Staff, HQ NATO, 1984–87; Dir, NATO Defence Commitments Staff, MoD, 1987–90; Comdr, British Forces Falkland Islands, 1990–91. Exec. Dir, Nat. Back Pain Assoc., 1993–94. Mem., Metropolitan Police Cttee, 1995–. Gov., St John's Sch., Leatherhead, 1993–. FRSA 1993. *Recreations:* sport, politics, reading, theatre. *Address:* c/o National Westminster Bank, 52 Royal Parade, Plymouth, Devon PL1 1ED.

HUNT, Martin Robert, RDI 1981; Partner, Queensberry Hunt, design consultancy, since 1966; *b* 4 Sept. 1942; *s* of Frederick and Frances Hunt; *m* 1st, 1963, Pauline Hunt; one *s* one *d*; 2nd, 1980, Glenys Barton; one *s*. *Educ:* Monmouth. DesRCA, FCSD. Graduated RCA 1966 (Hon. Fellow 1987); formed Queensberry Hunt Partnership, 1966; part time Tutor, RCA, 1968; Head of Glass Sch., RCA, 1974–86. *Recreation:* sailing. *Address:* 24 Brook Mews North, W2 3BW. *T:* 0171–724 3701.

HUNT, Maurice William; Deputy Director-General since 1989, and Secretary, since 1986, Confederation of British Industry; *b* 30 Aug. 1936; *s* of Maurice Hunt and Helen Hunt (*née* Andrews); *m* 1960, Jean Mary Ellis; one *s* one *d*. *Educ:* Selhurst Grammar School, Croydon; LSE (BSc Econ). ACIB. Nat. Service, RAF, 1955–57. ANZ Bank, 1953–66; Joint Iron Council, 1966–67; Board of Trade, 1967; Asst Sec., DTI, 1974; RCDS 1982; Dir, Membership, CBI, 1984; Exec. Dir (Ops), CBI, 1987. *Recreations:* walking, gardening, sailing. *Address:* 24 Fairford Close, Haywards Heath, W Sussex RH16 3EF. *T:* Haywards Heath (01444) 452916; (office) Centre Point, 103 New Oxford Street, WC1A 1DU. *Club:* Royal Automobile.

HUNT, Adm. Sir Nicholas (John Streynsham), GCB 1987 (KCB 1985); LVO 1961; Commander-in-Chief, Fleet, and Allied Commander-in-Chief, Channel and Eastern Atlantic, 1985–87, retired; Director-General, Chamber of Shipping, since 1991; Rear-Admiral of the United Kingdom, since 1994; *b* 7 Nov. 1930; *s* of Brig. and Mrs J. M. Hunt; *m* 1966, Meriel Eve Givan; two *s* one *d*. *Educ:* BRNC, Dartmouth. CO HMS Burnaston, HMS Palliser, HMS Troubridge, HMS Intrepid, and BRNC, Dartmouth; Asst Private Sec. to late Princess Marina, Duchess of Kent; Executive Officer, HMS Ark Royal, 1969–71; RCDS 1974; Dir of Naval Plans, 1976–78; Flag Officer, Second Flotilla, 1980–81; Dir-Gen., Naval Manpower and Training, 1981–83; Flag Officer, Scotland and NI, and Port Admiral Rosyth, 1983–85. Dep. Man. Dir (Orgn and Develt), Eurotunnel, 1987–89. Chm., SW Surrey DHA, 1990–95. Comr, CWGC, 1988–92; Vice-Pres., E-SU of Malta, 1988. CIMgt (CBIM, 1988). Freeman, City of London, 1988. *Recreation:* family. *Clubs:* Boodle's, Royal Navy of 1765 and 1785; Woodroffe's.

HUNT, Prof. Norman Charles, CBE 1975; Professor of Business Studies, 1967–84, Vice-Principal, 1980–84, University of Edinburgh, now Emeritus Professor; *b* 6 April 1918; *s* of Charles Hunt and Charlotte (*née* Jackson), Swindon, Wilts; *m* 1942, Lorna Mary, 2nd *d* of Mary and William Arthur Mann, Swindon, Wilts; two *s*. *Educ:* Commonweal Sch.; Swindon Coll.; University of London (Sir Edward Stern Schol., BCom 1st cl. hons); PhD

(Edinburgh). On Staff (Research Dept and Personal Staff of Chief Mechanical Engineer); former GWR Co., 1934–45. Lectr in Organisation of Industry and Commerce, University of Edinburgh, 1946–53; Dir of Studies in Commerce, 1948–53; Prof. of Organisation of Industry and Commerce, 1953–66; Dean of Faculty of Social Sciences, 1962–64. Member: Departmental Cttee on Fire Service, 1967–70; Rubber Industry NEDC, 1968–71; UGC, 1969–78 (Vice-Chm., 1974–76); ODM Working Party on Management Educn and Training in Developing Countries, 1968–69; Bd of Governors (and Chm., Management Develt Cttee), Council for Technical Educn and Training in Overseas Countries, 1971–75; Police Adv. Bd for Scotland, 1971–75; Council for Tertiary Educn in Scotland, 1979–84; CNAA, 1979–84. Consultant: UNIDO, 1973–; Hong Kong Baptist Coll., 1984–87; Hong Kong Management Assoc., 1986–. Chairman: R. and R. Clark Ltd, 1967–70; William Thyne Ltd, 1967–70; Director: William Thyne (Holdings) Ltd, 1963–70; William Thyne (Plastics) Ltd, 1967–70; INMAP Ltd, 1984–86; UnivEd Technologies Ltd, 1984– (Chm. 1984–86). Hon. DLitt Loughborough, 1975. *Publications:* Methods of Wage Payment in British Industry, 1951; (with W. D. Reekie) Management in the Social and Safety Services, 1974; articles in economic and management jls on industrial organisation, industrial relations, and management problems. *Recreations:* photography, motoring, foreign travel. *Address:* 65 Ravelston Dykes Road, Edinburgh EH4 3NU.

HUNT, (Patrick) James; QC 1987; a Recorder of the Crown Court, since 1982; *b* 26 Jan. 1943; *s* of Thomas Ronald Clifford Hunt and Doreen Gwyneth Katarina Hunt; *m* 1969, Susan Jennifer Goodhead; one *s* three *d*. *Educ:* Ashby de la Zouch Boys' Grammar Sch.; Keble Coll., Oxford (MA Mod. History). Called to the Bar, Gray's Inn, 1968; in practice on Midland and Oxford Circuit, from London chambers; Dep. Leader, Midland and Oxford Circuit, 1992–. Mem., Gen. Council of the Bar, 1989–91. Legal Assessor to Disciplinary Cttee, RCVS, 1990–. *Recreations:* singing, gardening, stonework. *Address:* Easton Hall, Easton on the Hill, Stamford, Lincs PE9 3LL. *T:* Stamford (01780) 52266; (chambers) 1 King's Bench Walk, Temple, EC4Y 7DB.

HUNT, Sir Peter John, Kt 1995; FRICS; Chairman and Managing Director, Land Securities PLC, since 1987 (Managing Director, since 1978); *b* 1 July 1933; *s* of Prof. Herbert James Hunt and Sheila Jessamine Hunt; *m*; one *s*. *Educ:* Bedford Sch.; College of Estate Management (BScEstMan). Borrett and Borrett, 1956–60; Chamberlain Gp, 1960–64; Land Securities Gp, 1964–. Member: Covent Garden Market Authority, 1975–; Council, British Property Fedn, 1978– (Pres., 1990–91). *Recreations:* boating, tennis. *Address:* 37 Devonshire Mews West, W1N 1FQ.

HUNT, Philip Alexander, OBE 1993; Director, National Association of Health Authorities and Trusts, since 1990; *b* 19 May 1949; *s* of Rev. Philip Lacey Winter Hunt and Muriel Hunt; *m* 1st, 1974 (marr. diss.); one *d*: 2nd, 1988, Selina Ruth Helen Stewart; two *s* one *d*. *Educ:* City of Oxford High Sch.; Oxford Sch.; Leeds Univ. (BA). MHSM. Oxford RHB, 1972–74; Nuffield Orthopaedic Centre, 1974–75; Mem., Oxfordshire AHA, 1975–77; Sec. Edgware/Hendon Community Health Council, 1975–78; Asst Sec., 1978–79, Asst Dir, 1979–84, Dir, 1984–90, NAHA. Member: Oxford City Council, 1973–79; Birmingham City Council, 1980–82; Council, Internat Hosp. Fedn, 1986–91; King's Fund Inst. Adv. Cttee, 1991–93; Council, Assoc. for Public Health, 1992– (Co-Chm., 1994–). *Publications:* The Health Authority Member (discussion paper) (with W. E. Hall), 1978; articles in Health Service publications. *Recreations:* music, cycling, swimming.

HUNT, Philip Bodley; Director, Welsh Office Industry Department, 1975–76; *b* 28 July 1916; *s* of Bernard and Janet Hunt; *m* 1940, Eleanor Margaret Parnell (*d* 1989); three *s* one *d*. *Educ:* Sedbergh Sch.; Christ Church, Oxford (Boulter Exhibnr; 1st cl. PPE; MA). Joined Board of Trade, 1946; Trade Commissioner, Montreal, 1952; Principal Trade Commissioner, Vancouver, 1955; Commercial Counsellor, Canberra, 1957; returned Board of Trade, 1962; Dept of Economic Affairs, 1964–65; Director, London & SE Region, BoT, 1968; Dir, DTI Office for Wales, 1972–75. Chm., S Wales Marriage Guidance Council, 1971 83; Mem. Nat. Exec., Nat. Marriage Guidance Council, 1977–83; Dept Mem. of Panel, County Structure Plans of S and W Glamorgan, 1978, of Gwent and Mid Glamorgan, 1979; Vice-Pres., Develt Corporation for Wales, 1980–83. Chm., John Macmurray Fellowship, 1993–. Silver Jubilee Medal, 1977. *Publication:* John Macmurray and the BBC: 1930–1941, 1995. *Recreations:* gardening, life and works of John Macmurray. *Address:* 93 Station Road, Llanishen, Cardiff CF4 5UU. *T:* Cardiff (01222) 750480.

HUNT, Sir Rex (Masterman), Kt 1982; CMG 1980; HM Diplomatic Service, retired; Civil Commissioner, Falkland Islands, 1982–Sept. 1985, and High Commissioner, British Antarctic Territory, 1980–85 (Governor and Commander-in-Chief, Falkland Islands, 1980–82; Governor, Oct. 1985); *b* 29 June 1926; *s* of H. W. Hunt and Ivy Masterman; *m* 1951, Mavis Amanda Buckland; one *s* one *d*. *Educ:* Coatham Sch.; St Peter's Coll., Oxford (BA). Served with RAF, 1944–48; Flt Lt RAFO. Entered HM Overseas Civil Service, 1951; District Comr, Uganda, 1962; CRO, 1963–64; 1st Sec., Kuching, 1964–65; Jesselton, 1965–67; Brunei, 1967; 1st Sec. (Econ.), Ankara, 1968–70; 1st Sec. and Head of Chancery, Jakarta, 1970–72; Asst ME Dept, FCO, 1972–74; Counsellor, Saigon, 1974–75, Kuala Lumpur, 1976–77; Dep. High Comr, Kuala Lumpur, 1977–79. Hon. Air Cdre, City of Lincoln Sqn, RAuxAF, 1987–. Hon. Freeman, City of London, 1981. *Publication:* My Falkland Days, 1992. *Recreations:* golf, gardening. *Address:* Old Woodside, Broomfield Park, Sunningdale, Berks SL5 0JS. *Club:* Wentworth.

HUNT, Richard Bruce; Chairman, R. B. Hunt and Partners Ltd, 1966–95; Deputy Chairman, Howe Robinson and Co. Ltd, since 1990; *b* 15 Dec. 1927; *s* of Percy Thompson Hunt and Thelma Constance Hunt; *m* 1972, Ulrike Dorothea Schmidt; two *d*. *Educ:* Christ's Hospital. FICS. Served Royal Signals, 1946–48; joined Merchant Bankers Ralli Brothers, 1949–66; formed own company, R. B. Hunt and Partners, 1966. Chm., Baltic Exchange Ltd, 1985–87 (Dir, 1977–80, re-elected, 1981–87). Liveryman, Shipwrights' Co. *Recreations:* golf, ski-ing. *Address:* Howe Robinson and Co. Ltd, 77 Mansell Street, E1 8AF. *T:* 0171–488 3444. *Clubs:* Hurlingham, Royal Wimbledon Golf; Royal Lymington Yacht.

HUNT, Richard Henry; Chief Registrar of the High Court of Justice in Bankruptcy, 1980–84, retired; *b* 19 Jan. 1912; *s* of late Francis John and Lucy Edwyna Louise Hunt; *m* 1947, Peggy Ashworth Richardson; two *s*. *Educ:* Marlborough Coll.; Queen's Coll., Oxford. Called to Bar, 1936. Served with RA, 1939–45: Western Desert, Greece and Crete campaigns (PoW, Crete, 1941). Elected Bencher, Middle Temple, 1964. Registrar of the High Court of Justice in Bankruptcy, 1966–80. *Recreations:* foreign travel, languages.

HUNT, (Richard) Tim(othy), PhD; FRS 1991; Principal (formerly Senior) Scientist, Imperial Cancer Research Fund, since 1990; Fellow of Clare College, Cambridge, since 1968; *b* 19 Feb. 1943; *s* of Richard William Hunt and Katherine Eva Rowland; *m* 1971, Missy Cusick (marr. diss. 1974). *Educ:* Dragon Sch.; Magdalen Coll. Sch., Oxford; Clare Coll., Cambridge (BA Nat. Sci. 1964; PhD 1968). Univ. Lectr in Biochem., Cambridge, 1981–90 (Junior Proctor, 1982–83). Mem., EMBO. *Publications:* Molecular Biology of the Cell Problems (with John Wilson), 1989; The Cell Cycle: an introduction (with Andrew Murray), 1993; articles in cell and molecular biology jls. *Recreation:* marine stations. *Address:* Imperial Cancer Research Fund, Clare Hall Laboratories, South Mimms, Herts EN6 3LD. *T:* 0171–269 3981, *Fax:* 0171–269 3804.

HUNT, Robert Alan, OBE 1984; QPM 1992; Assistant Commissioner, Territorial Operations Department, Metropolitan Police, 1990–95; *b* 6 July 1935; *s* of Peter and Minnie Hunt; *m* 1956, Jean White; one *s* three *d*. *Educ:* Dulwich Coll.; London Univ. (LLB external 1970). Served in RA. Joined Metropolitan Police, 1955: Chief Superintendent, 1973; Comdr, 1976; Dep. Asst Comr, 1981. *Recreations:* music—traditional and light classical, reading, the family. *Address:* c/o New Scotland Yard, Broadway, SW1H 0BG. *T:* 0171–230 1212.

HUNT, Sir Robert (Frederick), Kt 1979; CBE 1974; DL; Chairman, Dowty Group PLC, 1975–86; Deputy Chairman, Rover Group (formerly BL plc), 1982–90 (Director, 1980–90); Director, Charter Consolidated, 1983–90; *b* 11 May 1918; *s* of late Arthur Hunt, Cheltenham and Kathleen Alice Cotton; *m* 1st, 1947, Joy Patricia Molly (*d* 1984), *d* of late Charles Leslie Harding, Cheltenham; four *d*; 2nd, 1987, Joyce Elizabeth Baigent, *d* of Otto Leiske. *Educ:* Pates Grammar Sch., Cheltenham; N Glos Techn. Coll. Apprenticed Dowty Equipment Ltd, 1935; Chief Instructor to Co.'s Sch. of Hydraulics, 1940; RAF Trng Comd, 1940; Export Man., Dowty Equipment Ltd, 1946; Vice-Pres. and Gen. Man., 1949, Pres., 1954, Dowty Equipment of Canada Ltd; Dir, Dowty Gp Ltd, 1956, Dep. Chm., 1959–75, Chief Exec., 1975–83. Dir, Eagle Star Hldgs plc, 1980–87. Chm., Bd of Trustees, Improvement District of Ajax, Ont., 1954; Dir, Ajax and Pickering Gen. Hosp., 1954; Chm., Cheltenham Hosp. Gp Man. Cttee, 1959; Chm., Glos AHA, 1974–81; Pres., 1967–68, Treas., 1973, Vice-Pres., 1976, Pres., 1977–78, SBAC. FEng 1982; FCASI 1976; FRAeS 1968, Hon. FRAeS 1981. Hon. DSc Bath, 1979. DL Glos, 1977; Hon. Freeman of Cheltenham, 1980. *Recreations:* family interests, golf, gardening. *Address:* Maple House, Withington, Glos GL54 4DA. *T:* Cheltenham (01242) 890344. *Club:* New (Cheltenham).

HUNT, Roger; His Honour Judge Hunt; a Circuit Judge, since 1986; *b* 15 Jan. 1935; *s* of late Richard Henry Hunt and Monica Hunt; *m* 1963, Barbara Ann Eccles; two *d*. *Educ:* Giggleswick Sch.; Pembroke Coll., Oxford (MA). Commnd Royal Signals, 1955; served Germany, HQ 4th Guards Bde, 1956; TA 49th Inf. Div., Signal Regt, 1956–63. Called to the Bar, Lincoln's Inn, 1960; joined NE Circuit, 1961; a Recorder, 1978–86. *Recreations:* golf, gardening. *Club:* Moortown Golf.

HUNT, Roland Charles Colin, CMG 1965; HM Diplomatic Service, retired; Director, British National Committee, International Chamber of Commerce, 1973–76; *b* 19 March 1916; *s* of Colin and Dorothea Hunt, Oxford; *m* 1939, Pauline (*d* 1989), 2nd *d* of late Dr J. C. Maxwell Garnett, CBE; three *s* two *d*. *Educ:* Rugby Sch. (scholar); The Queen's Coll., Oxford (scholar). Entered Indian Civil Service, 1938. Served in various districts in Madras as Sub-Collector, 1941–45; Joint Sec. and Sec., Board of Revenue (Civil Supplies), Madras, 1946–47; joined Commonwealth Relations Office, 1948; served on staff of United Kingdom High Commissioner in Pakistan (Karachi), 1948–50; Mem. UK Delegation to African Defence Facilities Conference, Nairobi, 1951; served in Office of UK High Comr in S Africa, 1952–55; Asst Sec., 1955; attached to Office of High Comr for Fedn of Malaya, Kuala Lumpur, 1956; Dep. High Commisioner for the UK in the Federation of Malaya, Kuala Lumpur, 1957–59; Imperial Defence Coll., 1960; Asst Sec., Commonwealth Relations Office, 1961; British Dep. High Comr in Pakistan, 1962–65; British High Commissioner in Uganda, 1965–67; Asst Under-Sec. of State, CO and FCO, 1967–70; High Comr, Trinidad and Tobago, 1970–73. *Publication:* (ed jtly) The District Officer in India, 1930–1947, 1980. *Recreations:* ball-games, piano-playing. *Address:* Spindlewood, Whitchurch Hill, Reading, Berks RG8 7PG.

See also Baron Hacking, J. C. R. Hunt.

HUNT, Terence; National Director, NHS Supplies, since 1991; *b* 8 Aug. 1943; *s* of Thomas John Hunt and Marie Louise Hunt (*née* Potter); *m* 1967, Wendy Graeme George; one *s* one *d*. *Educ:* Huish's Grammar Sch., Taunton. Associate Mem. Inst. of Health Service Management. Tone Vale Group HMC, 1963–65; NE Somerset HMC, 1965–67; Winchester Gp HMC, 1967–69; Lincoln No 1 HMC, 1969–70; Hosp. Sec., Wycombe General Hosp., 1970–73; Dep. Gp Sec., Hillingdon Hosp., 1973–74; Area General Administrator, Kensington and Chelsea and Westminster AHA(T), 1974–77; District Administrator: NW Dist of KCW AHA(T), 1977–82; Paddington and N Kensington, 1982–84; Regl Gen. Manager, NE Thames RHA, 1984–91. Member: Steering Gp on Undergrad. Med. and Dental Educn and Res., 1987–91; NHS Central R&D Cttee, 1991–; Hosp. Cttee, EEC, 1991–93; Med. Cttee, UFC, 1989–91. Member: Twyford & Dist Round Table, 1975–84 (Chm., 1980–81; Pres., 1988–89); Cttee, Reading Town Regatta, 1984– (Treas., 1984–86; Chm., 1989–93). Member: Council of Govs, London Hosp. Med. Coll., 1985–91; Council, UCL, 1985–91. *Recreations:* sculling, cycling, all things practical with metal and wood. *Address:* 36 Old Bath Road, Charvil, Reading, Berks RG10 9QR. *T:* Reading (01734) 341062.

HUNT, Tim; *see* Hunt, R. T.

HUNT-DAVIS, Brig. Miles Garth, CBE 1990 (MBE 1977); Private Secretary to HRH The Duke of Edinburgh, since 1993 (Assistant Private Secretary, 1991–92); *b* Johannesburg, SA, 7 Nov. 1938; *s* of late Lt-Col Eric Hunt-Davis, OBE, ED and Mary Eleanor Turnbull (*née* Boyce); *m* 1965, Anita (Gay) Ridsdale, *d* of Francis James Ridsdale; two *s* one *d*. *Educ:* St Andrew's Coll., Grahamstown, SA. Commnd 6th QEO Gurkha Rifles, 1962; active service in Borneo and Malaya, 1964–66; student, Canadian Land Forces Comd and Staff Coll., 1969–70; Bde Maj., 48 Gurkha Inf. Bde, 1974–76; Comdt, 7th Duke of Edinburgh's Own Gurkha Rifles, 1976–79; School of Infantry: Chief Instructor, Tactics Wing, 1979–80; GSO 1 Tactics, 1980–82; Instr, Staff Coll., Camberley, 1982–83; Commander: British Gurkhas, Nepal, 1985–87; Bde of Gurkhas, 1987–90; retd, 1991. Col, 7th Duke of Edinburgh's Own Gurkha Rifles, 1991–94. Chm., Gurkha Bde Assoc., 1991–. *Recreations:* golf, walking, elephant polo. *Address:* 5B The Old Barracks, Kensington Palace, W8 4PU. *T:* (home) 0171–937 6258; (office) 071–930 4832. *Clubs:* Army and Navy, Commonwealth Trust; W Wiltshire Golf (Warminster); Royal Hong Kong Golf.

HUNTE, Joseph Alexander; Senior Community Relations Officer, Tower Hamlets, 1968–82, retired; *b* 18 Dec. 1917; *s* of Clement and Eunice Hunte; *m* 1967, Margaret Ann (formerly Jones); three *d* (and one *d* decd). *Educ:* Swansea University Coll., 1962–65 (BA Politics, Economics, Philosophy); PRO, 1964–65. West Indian Standing Conference: PRO, Sec., Chairman 1958–80; Executive Member: Jt Council for Welfare of Immigrants, 1968–74; CARD, 1969–70 (Grievance Officer); Anne Frank Foundn, 1965–70; Chm., Presentation Housing Assoc., 1981–; Governor, St Martin-in-the-Fields Girls' Sch., SW2, 1982–. Silver Jubilee Medal (for services in community relations), 1977. *Publication:* Nigger Hunting in England, 1965. *Recreations:* reading, watching television. *Address:* 43 Cambria Road, SE5 9AS. *T:* 0171–733 5436.

HUNTER, Hon. Lord; John Oswald Mair Hunter, VRD; a Senator of the College of Justice in Scotland, 1961–86; *b* 21 Feb. 1913; *s* of John Mair Hunter, QC(Scot) and Jessie Donald Frew; *m* 1939, Doris Mary Simpson (*d* 1988); one *s* one *d*. *Educ:* Edinburgh Acad.; Rugby; New Coll., Oxford (BA 1934, MA 1961); Edinburgh Univ. (LLB 1936, LLD

1975). Entered RNVR, 1933; served War 1939–45 (despatches); Lt-Comdr RNVR; retired list 1949. Called to Bar, Inner Temple, 1937; admitted to Faculty of Advocates, 1937; QC(Scot) 1951. Advocate Depute (Home), 1954–57; Sheriff of Ayr and Bute, 1957–61. Chairman: Deptl Cttee on Scottish Salmon and Trout Fisheries, 1962–65; Lands Valuation Appeal Court, 1966–71; Scottish Law Commn, 1971–81; Scottish Council on Crime, 1972–75; Dep. Chm., Boundary Commn for Scotland, 1971–76. Pres., Scottish Univs Law Inst., 1972–77; Member: Scottish Records Adv. Council, 1966–81; Statute Law Cttee, 1971–81; Chm., later Hon. Pres., Cttee, RNLI (Dunbar), 1969–80 and 1981–; Hon. Pres., Scottish Assoc. for Study of Delinquency, 1971–88.

HUNTER, (Adam) Kenneth (Fisher), CBE 1990; formerly Sheriff of North Strathclyde at Paisley, now retired; *b* 1920; *o s* of late Thomas C. Hunter, MBE, AMIEE, and Elizabeth Hunter; *m* 1949, Joan Stella Hiscock, MB, ChB; one *s* two *d*. *Educ:* Dunfermline High Sch.; St Andrews Univ. (MA Hons); Edinburgh Univ. (LLB). Called to Bar, 1946; Chm. of the Supreme Court Legal Aid Cttee of the Law Society of Scotland, 1949–53; Standing Junior Counsel to HM Commissioners of Customs and Excise, 1950–53; Sheriff-Substitute, later Sheriff, of Renfrew and Argyll (subseq. N Strathclyde) at Paisley, 1953–90. *Recreations:* photography, music, philately. *Address:* Ravenswood, Bridge of Weir, Renfrewshire PA11 3AN. *T:* Bridge of Weir (01505) 612017.

HUNTER, Dr Alan, CBE 1975; Director, Royal Greenwich Observatory, 1973–75; *b* 9 Sept. 1912; *s* of late George Hunter and Mary Edwards; *m* 1937, W. Joan Portnell (*d* 1985); four *s*. *Educ:* Imperial Coll. of Science and Technology. PhD, DIC; FRAS. Research Asst, Applied Mech. Dept, RNC, 1940–46; Royal Observatory, Greenwich: Asst, 1937–61; Chief Asst, 1961–67; Dep. Dir, 1967–73. Editor, The Observatory, 1943–49. Treas., Royal Astronomical Soc., 1967–76 (Sec. 1949–56, Vice-Pres. 1957, 1965, 1976); Pres., British Astronomical Assoc., 1957–59; Chm., Large Telescope Users' Panel, 1974–75 (sec. 1969–73). Liveryman, Worshipful Co. of Clockmakers, 1975. *Recreation:* gardening. *Address:* Thatched Cottage, Frettenham Road, Frettenham, Norwich NR12 7LZ. *T:* Norwich (01603) 890179.

HUNTER, Sir Alexander (Albert), KBE 1976; Representative, Pecten Belize Company, since 1983; Speaker of the House of Representatives of Belize, 1974–79; *b* Belize, British Honduras, 21 May 1920; *s* of Alexander J. Hunter, KSG, and Laura Hunter (*née* Reyes); *m* 1947, Araceli Marin Sanchez, Alajuela, Costa Rica; one *s* two *d*. *Educ:* St John's Coll. (Jesuit), Belize City; Regis Coll. (Jesuit), Denver, Colo; Queen's Univ., Kingston, Ont. In Accounting Dept, United Fruit Co., Costa Rica, 1940–41 and 1945–47. Served War, NCO, Radar Br., RCAF, 1941–45: active service in UK, Azores, Gibraltar, with 220 Sqdn Coastal Comd, RAF. Joined staff of James Brodie & Co. Ltd, as Accountant, 1947; Company Sec., 1948; Dir 1952–61; Consultant: James Brodie & Co. Ltd, 1975–83; Anschutz Overseas Corp., Denver, Colo, 1975–82; Chm., Belize Airways Ltd, 1978–80. MLA (PUP), Fort George Div., 1961; Minister of Natural Resources, Commerce and Industry, March 1961; MHR (PUP), Fort George, under new Constitution, 1965; Minister of Natural Resources and Trade, 1965–69; Minister of Trade and Industry, 1969–74; Mem., Constitutional Ministerial External Affairs Cttee, 1965–74. Represented Belize: Bd of Governors, Caribbean Develt Bank, 1969–74; Council of Ministers, CARIFTA, 1971–73; Council of Ministers, Caribbean Economic Community, 1973–74. Hon. Consul of El Salvador, 1951–78. Acted as Dep. Governor, Aug.–Sept. 1975, and as Dep. Premier on several occasions, 1969–74. Official observer to Salvadoran Elections, 1982 and 1984. People's United Party: Treasurer and Mem. Central Party Council, 1961–74; Mem. Exec. Cttee, 1961–74; Chm. Fort George Div., 1961–74. Former Vice-Pres., Belize Chamber of Commerce; Member: Property Valuation Appeal Bd, 1960; Citrus Industry Investigation Cttee, 1960. Member: West India Cttee; Nat. Geographic Soc.; Belize Ex-Servicemen's League. 1939–45 Star; Atlantic Star; Defence of Britain medal; Canadian Service medal and bar; British War medal. *Recreations:* target shooting, hunting, light and heavy tackle salt-water fishing. *Address:* 6 St Matthew Street, Caribbean Shores, PO Box 505, Belize City, Belize. *T:* (2) 44482.

HUNTER, Air Vice-Marshal Alexander Freeland Cairns, CBE 1982 (OBE 1981); AFC 1978; DL; Director: Newcastle Building Society, since 1993; Clyde Helicopters Ltd, since 1993; *b* 8 March 1939; *s* of late H. A. C. and L. E. M. Hunter; *m* 1964, Wilma Elizabeth Bruce Wilson. *Educ:* Aberdeen Grammar Sch.; Aberdeen Univ. (MA 1960, LLB 1962). Commissioned RAFVR 1959; RAF 1962; flying training 1962; Pilot, 81 (PR) Sqn, FEAF, 1964–67; Central Flying Sch., 1967–68; Instructor, Northumbrian Univ. Air Sqn, 1968–69; Asst Air Attaché, Moscow, 1971–73; RAF Staff Coll., 1974; Flight Comdr, 230 Sqn, 1975–77; OC 18 Sqn, RAF Germany, 1978–80; Air Warfare Course, 1981; MoD (Air), 1981; OC RAF Odiham, 1981–83; Gp Captain Plans, HQ Strike Comd, 1983–85; RCDS 1986; Dir of Public Relations (RAF), 1987–88; Comdt, RAF Staff Coll., 1989–90; Comdr British Forces Cyprus and Adminr of Sovereign Base Areas, 1990–93. Bd Mem., North Housing Assoc. Ltd, 1993–95 (Vice Chm. (NE), 1994); Chm., Home Housing Assoc., 1995–. DL Northumberland, 1994. OStJ 1994. *Recreations:* shooting, fishing, hill-walking, military history. *Address:* c/o Clydesdale Bank, Queen's Cross, Aberdeen. *Clubs:* Royal Air Force; Northern Counties (Newcastle upon Tyne); Tanglin (Singapore).

HUNTER, Sir Alistair John, KCMG 1994 (CMG 1985); HM Diplomatic Service; British Consul-General, New York, and Director-General of Trade and Investment, USA, since 1991; *b* 9 Aug. 1936; *s* of Kenneth Clarke Hunter and Joan Tunks; *m* 1st, 1963; one *s* two *d*; 2nd, 1978, Helge Milton (*née* Kahle). *Educ:* Felsted; Magdalen Coll., Oxford. Royal Air Force, 1955–57; CRO, 1961–65; Private Sec. to Permanent Under-Sec., 1961–63; 2nd Sec., Kuala Lumpur, 1963–65; 1st Sec. (Commercial), Peking, 1965–68; seconded to Cabinet Office, 1969–70; FCO, 1970–73; 1st Sec., Rome, 1973–75; FCO, 1975–80; Hd of Chancery, Bonn, 1980–85; seconded to DTI as Under Sec., Overseas Trade, 1985–88; Consul-Gen., Düsseldorf, and Dir-Gen. of British Trade and Investment Promotion in FRG, 1988–91. *Address:* c/o Foreign and Commonwealth Office, SW1A 2AH.

HUNTER, Andrew Robert Frederick; MP (C) Basingstoke, since 1983; company director and consultant; *b* 8 Jan. 1943; *s* of late Sqdn Leader Roger Edward Hunter, DFC and Winifred Mary Hunter (*née* Nelson); *m* 1972, Janet, *d* of late Samuel Bourne of Gloucester; one *s* one *d*. *Educ:* St George's Sch., Harpenden; Durham Univ.; Jesus Coll., Cambridge; Westcott House, Cambridge. In industry, 1969; Asst Master, St Martin's Sch., Northwood, 1970–71; Asst Master, Harrow Sch., 1971–83. Contested (C) Southampton, Itchen, 1979. PPS to Minister of State, DoE, 1985–86. Member: Agriculture Select Cttee, 1985, 1993–94; Environment Select Cttee, 1986–92; NI Select Cttee, 1994–. Chm., Cons. NI Cttee, 1992–; Dep. Chm., Monday Club, 1990–. Sponsored Private Members' Bills: Control of Smoke Pollution Act, 1989; Timeshare Act, 1992; Noise and Statutory Nuisance Act, 1993. Member: NFU; British Field Sports Soc. (Chm., Falconry Cttee, 1988–92). Vice-Pres., Nat. Prayer Book Soc., 1987–. Mem., Court, Univ. of Southampton, 1983–. Commnd Major, TAVR, 1973 (resigned commn, 1984). Hon. Mem., Soc. of the Sealed Knot, 1990–. Order of Polonia Restituta, 1980. *Recreations:* horse riding, watching cricket and Rugby football, collecting toy soldiers. *Address:* House of Commons, SW1A 0AA. *T:* 0171–219 5216. *Clubs:* Pratt's, St Stephen's Constitutional.

HUNTER, Rt. Rev. Anthony George Weaver; *b* 3 June 1916; *s* of Herbert George Hunter and Ethel Frances Weaver; *m* 1st, 1948, Joan Isobel Marshall (*d* 1981); 2nd, 1982, Emlyn Marianne Garton (*née* Dent). *Educ:* Wanstead; Leeds Univ. (BA); Coll. of the Resurrection, Mirfield. Deacon, 1941; Priest, 1942; Curate of St George's, Jesmond, 1941–43; Orlando Mission Dist, 1943–47; Johannesburg Coloured Mission, 1947–48; Curate of St George's, Jesmond, 1948–49; Vicar of Ashington, 1949–60; Proctor in Convocation, 1959–60; Vicar of Huddersfield, 1960–68; Rural Dean of Huddersfield, 1960–68; Hon. Canon of Wakefield, 1962–68; Proctor in Convocation, 1962–68; Bishop of Swaziland, 1968–75; Rector of Hexham, Dio. Newcastle, 1975–79; Asst Bishop, Dio. Newcastle, 1976–80; Supernumerary Bishop, 1980–81; Acting Archdeacon of Lindisfarne, 1981; retd Oct. 1981. OStJ. *Recreations:* walking, gardening, travel. *Address:* Hillside, Sheriff Hutton, N Yorks YO6 1PS. *T:* Sheriff Hutton (01347) 878226.

HUNTER, Anthony Rex; *see* Hunter, Tony.

HUNTER, Rt Rev. Barry Russell, AM 1992; Locum Tenens in the parish of Cudal, New South Wales, 1992–95; *b* Brisbane, Queensland, 15 Aug. 1927; *s* of late John Hunter; *m* 1961, Dorothy Nancy, *d* of B. P. Sanders, Brisbane; three *d*. *Educ:* Toowoomba Grammar Sch.; St Francis' Theological Coll., Brisbane; Univ. of Queensland (BA,ThL). Assistant Curate, St Matthew's, Sherwood, 1953–56; Member, Bush Brotherhood of St Paul, Cunnamulla, Queensland, 1956–61; Rector, St Cecilia's, Chinchilla, 1961–66; Rector, St Gabriel's, Biloela, 1966–71; Archdeacon of the East, Diocese of Rockhampton, 1969–71; Bishop of Riverina, 1971–92. DLitt (*hc*) Charles Sturt Univ., 1994. *Recreation:* music. *Address:* 27 Telopea Drive, Taree, NSW 2430, Australia.

HUNTER, Evan; writer; *b* New York, 15 Oct. 1926; *s* of Charles F. Lombino and Marie Lombino; *m* 1st, 1949, Anita Melnick (marr. diss.); three *s*; 2nd, 1973, Mary Vann Finley; one step *d*. *Educ:* Cooper Union; Hunter Coll. (BA 1950). Served USNR. Literary Father of the Year, 1961; Phi Beta Kappa. Grand Master Award, Mystery Writers of America, 1986. *Publications include: as Evan Hunter:* The Blackboard Jungle, 1954; Second Ending, 1956; Strangers When We Meet, 1958; A Matter of Conviction, 1959; The Remarkable Harry, 1960; The Wonderful Button, 1961; Mothers and Daughters, 1961; Happy New Year, Herbie, 1963; Buddwing, 1964; The Paper Dragon, 1966; A Horse's Head, 1967; Last Summer, 1968; Sons, 1969; Nobody Knew They Were There, 1971; Every Little Crook and Nanny, 1972; The Easter Man, 1972; Seven, 1972; Come Winter, 1973; Streets of Gold, 1974; The Chisholms, 1976; Me and Mr Stenner, 1977; Walk Proud, 1978; Love, Dad, 1981; Far From the Sea, 1983; Lizzie, 1984; Criminal Conversation, 1994; *as Ed McBain:* Cop Hater, 1956; The Mugger, 1956; The Pusher, 1956; The Con Man, 1957; Killer's Choice, 1958; Killer's Payoff, 1958; Lady Killer, 1958; Killer's Wedge, 1959; 'Til Death, 1959; King's Ransom, 1959; Give the Boys a Great Big Hand, 1960; The Heckler, 1960; See Them Die, 1960; Lady, Lady, I Did It, 1961; The Empty Hours, 1962; Like Love, 1962; Ten Plus One, 1963; Ax, 1964; The Sentries, 1965; He Who Hesitates, 1965; Doll, 1965; Eighty Million Eyes, 1966; Fuzz, 1968; Shotgun, 1969; Jigsaw, 1970; Hail, Hail, the Gang's All Here!, 1971; Sadie When She Died, 1972; Let's Hear It for the Deaf Man, 1972; Death of a Nurse, 1972; Hail to the Chief, 1973; Bread, 1974; Where There's Smoke, 1975; Blood Relatives, 1975; So Long as You Both Shall Live, 1976; Guns, 1976; Long Time No See, 1977; Goldilocks, 1978; Calypso, 1979; Ghosts, 1980; Even the Wicked, 1980; Rumpelstiltskin, 1981; Heat, 1981; Beauty and the Beast, 1982; Ice, 1983; Jack and the Beanstalk, 1984; Lightning, 1984; Snow White and Rose Red, 1985; Eight Black Horses, 1985; Cinderella, 1986; Another Part of the City, 1986; Poison, 1987; Tricks, 1987; Puss in Boots, 1987; McBain's Ladies, 1988; The House that Jack Built, 1988; Lullaby, 1989; McBain's Ladies, Too, 1989; Downtown, 1989; Vespers, 1990; Mary, Mary, 1992; Mischief, 1993; There was a Little Girl, 1994; Romance, 1995; *screenplays:* Strangers When We Meet, 1959; The Birds, 1962; Fuzz, 1972; Walk Proud, 1979; Dream West (TV mini-series), 1986; *plays:* The Easter Man, 1964; The Conjuror, 1969. *Recreation:* travelling. *Address:* William Morris Agency (UK) Ltd, 31/32 Soho Square, W1V 6HH.

HUNTER, Rear-Adm. Ian Alexander, CB 1993; Chief of Naval Staff, New Zealand, 1991–94; *b* 23 Oct. 1939; *s* of A. A. Hunter and late O. R. Hunter; *m* 1965, Hilary R. Sturrock; two *s*. *Educ:* Christchurch Boys' High Sch.; BRNC Dartmouth. Joined RNZN 1957; served HMNZS Otago, HMS Tabard, USS Arneb, HMNZS Rotoiti (Antarctic), N Ireland Anti-Submarine Sch., HM Ships Torquay and Eastbourne, HMNZ Ships Taranaki, Blackpool, Canterbury, Waikato (Command), Southland (Command); posts with Chief of Naval Staff; RCDS 1985; ACDS (Develt Plans), 1987–88; Commodore Auckland, 1988–91 (concerned with Govt financial reforms for RNZN, restructuring Dockyard, orgn of Whitbread Round the World Yacht Race). Trustee, Wellington Civic Trust; Chm. of Friends, Wellington Maritime Mus. *Address:* 108B Messines Road, Karori, Wellington, New Zealand.

HUNTER, Sir Ian (Bruce Hope), Kt 1983; MBE 1945; Impresario; President and Director, Harold Holt Ltd, since 1988 (Chairman and Chief Executive, 1953–88); Chairman, Tempo Video Ltd, since 1984; *b* 2 April 1919; *s* of late W. O. Hunter; *m* 1st, 1949, Susan (*d* 1977), *d* of late Brig. A. G. Russell; four *d*; 2nd, 1984, Lady Showering, *widow* of Sir Keith Showering. *Educ:* Fettes Coll., Edinburgh; abroad as pupil of Dr Fritz Busch and at Glyndebourne. Served War of 1939–45, Lieut-Col. Asst to Artistic Dir, Edinburgh Festival, 1946–48; Artistic Administrator, Edinburgh Festival, 1949–50; Artistic Dir, Edinburgh Festival, 1951–55. Director, Bath Festivals, 1948, 1955, 1958–68; Adviser, Adelaide Festivals, 1960–64; Dir-Gen., Commonwealth Arts Festival, 1965; Artistic Director: Festivals of the City of London, 1962–80; Brighton Festivals, 1967–83; (with Yehudi Menuhin) Windsor Festivals, 1969–72; Hong Kong Arts Festivals, 1973–75; Malvern Festival, 1977–82; American Festival, 1985; Festival of German Arts, London, 1987. Dir, British Nat. Day Entertainment, Expo' 67. Dir, Live Music Now, 1983–. Member: Opera/Ballet Enquiry for Arts Council, 1967–69; Arts Administration Course Enquiry for Arts Council, 1970–71; Arts Council Trng Cttee, 1974–76; Centenary Appeal Cttee, RCM, 1982–; Adv. Cttee, Britain Salutes New York, 1983; Chairman: Entertainments Cttee, Queen's Silver Jubilee Appeal; Musicians' Benevolent Fund, 1987–95. Royal Concert Cttee, 1988–93. Pres., British Arts Festivals Assoc., 1978–81; Dep. Chm., Stravinsky Festival Trust; Trustee, Chichester Festival Theatre Trust, until 1988; Founder and Trustee, Young Concert Artists Trust, 1984–; Chm. of Governors, London Festival Ballet (later English National Ballet), 1984–89; Vice-Chm., Japan Fest. UK 1991, 1989–92; Mem. Cttee, Spanish Arts Festival, London, 1994; Vice-Pres., Yehudi Menuhin Sch. R. B. Bennett Commonwealth Prize for 1966. FRCM 1991 (Hon. RCM 1984); Hon. Mem., GSMD, 1975. FRSA (Mem. Council, 1968–73, 1976–; Chm. Council, 1981–83; a Vice-Pres., 1981–). Mem. Ct of Assistants, Musicians' Co., 1981–84. *Recreations:* gardening, painting. *Address:* Harold Holt Ltd, 31 Sinclair Road, W14 0NS. *T:* 0171–603 4600. *Club:* Garrick.

HUNTER, Ian Gerald Adamson, QC 1980; SC (NSW) 1994; a Recorder, since 1986; *b* 3 Oct. 1944; *s* of Gerald Oliver Hunter and late Jessie Hunter; *m* 1975, Maggie (*née* Reed); two *s*. *Educ:* Reading Sch.; Pembroke Coll., Cambridge (Open Scholar, Squire Univ. Law Scholar, Trevelyan Scholar, BA (double first in Law), MA, LLB); Harvard Law Sch. (Kennedy Memorial Scholar, LLM). Called to the Bar, Inner Temple, 1967 (Duke of

Edinburgh Entrance Scholar, Major Scholar), Bencher, 1986. Mem. Bar, NSW, 1993. Chm., Consolidated Regulations and Transfer Cttee, Senate of Inns of Court, 1986–87 (Mem., 1982–85); Member: International Relations Cttee, Bar Council, 1982–90; Exec. Cttee, Bar Council, 1985–86. Mem. and Rapporteur, Internat. Law Assoc. Anti-Trust Cttee, 1968–72; Pres., Union Internat. des Avocats, 1989 (UK Vice-Pres., 1982–86; first Vice Pres., 1986–; Dir of Studies, 1990–91). Hon. Mem., Canadian Bar Assoc., 1990. *Publications:* articles on public international law. *Recreations:* bebop, other good music, French cooking. *Address:* Essex Court Chambers, 24 Lincoln's Inn Fields, WC2A 3ED. *T:* 0171–813 8000.

HUNTER, Brig. Ian Murray, CVO 1954; AM 1994; MBE 1943; psc 1943; fsc (US) 1955; FAIM 1964; FAICD 1990; FIM 1993; FAPRI 1994; Chairman, since 1970, and Managing Director, since 1981, Allied Rubber Products (Qld) Pty Ltd; *b* Sydney, Aust., 10 July 1917; *s* of late Dr James Hunter, Stranraer, Scotland; *m* 1947, Rosemary Jane Batchelor; two *s* two *d*. *Educ:* Cranbrook Sch., Sydney; RMC, Duntroon. Lieut Aust. Staff Corps, and AIF 1939; 2/1 MG Bn, 1939–40; T/Capt. 1940; Staff Capt., 25 Inf. Bde, 1940–41; Middle East Staff Coll., Haifa, 1941; DA QMG (1), HQ 6 Div., 1941–42; T/Major 1942; AQMG, NT Force (MBE), 1942–43; Staff Sch. (Aust.), 1943; Gen. Staff 3 Corps and Advanced HQ Allied Land Forces, 1943–44; Lieut-Col 1945; Instructor, Staff Sch., 1945; AQMG, and Col BCOF, 1946–47; AQMG, AHQ and JCOSA, 1947; AA & QMG, HQ, 3 Div., 1948–50; Royal Visit, 1949; Exec. Commonwealth Jubilee Celebrations, 1950–51; CO 2 Recruit Trg Bn, 1952; CO 4 RAR, 1953; Executive and Commonwealth Marshal, Royal Visit, 1952, and 1954; Command and Gen. Staff Coll., Fort Leavenworth, USA, 1954–55; Military Mission, Washington, 1955–56; Officer i/c Admin., N Comd, 1956–59; Comd 11 Inf. Bde, 1959–60; Command 2nd RQR 1960–62; Chief of Staff 1st Div., 1963; Commandant, Australian Staff Coll., 1963–65; Comdr, Papua New Guinea Comd, 1966–69; DQMG, Army HQ, 1969. Indep. Mem., Presbyterian Church Property Commn, 1974–84. Chm., Australian Red Cross Soc. (Qld), 1990–94. *Recreations:* golf, squash, swimming, riding. *Address:* Box 3053, Stafford Delivery Centre, Qld 4053, Australia; Garthland, 5 Sword Street, Ascot, Brisbane, Queensland 4007, Australia; Finchley, Hargreaves Street, Blackheath, NSW 2785, Australia. *Clubs:* Australian (Sydney); Queensland (Brisbane); Royal Sydney Golf.

HUNTER, Surg. Rear-Adm. (D) John, CB 1973; OBE 1963; Director of Naval Dental Services, Ministry of Defence, 1971–74; *b* 21 Aug. 1915; *s* of Hugh Hunter and Evelyn Marian Hunter (*née* Jessop), Hale, Cheshire; *m* 1947, Anne Madelaine Hardwicke, Friarmayne, Dorset; three *s* two *d*. *Educ:* Bowdon Coll., Cheshire; Manchester Univ. LDS 1939. Surg. Lieut (D) RNVR 1940; HMS Kenya and 10th Cruiser Sqdn, 1941–42; HMS Newcastle and HMS Howe, British Pacific Fleet, 1944–47; transf. to RN; HMS Forth on Staff of Rear-Adm. Destroyers, Mediterranean (Surg. Lt-Comdr), 1948–50; Dartmouth, Royal Marines; Surg. Comdr, Staff of Flag Officer Flotillas Mediterranean, 1956; service ashore in Admty, 1960–63; Surg. Captain (D), Staff of C-in-C Mediterranean, 1965–66; Staff of C-in-C Plymouth Comd, 1967–68; Fleet Dental Surgeon on Staff of C-in-C Western Fleet, 1969–70. QHDS 1971–74. Mem., South Hams DC, 1979–83. Chm., River Yealm Harbour Authority, 1982–85. *Recreations:* ocean racing, cruising, shooting. *Address:* Horsewells, Newton Ferrers, Plymouth PL8 1AT. *T:* Plymouth (01752) 872254. *Clubs:* Royal Ocean Racing; Royal Western Yacht.

HUNTER, His Honour John; a Circuit Judge, 1980–93; *b* 12 April 1921; *s* of Charles and Mary Hunter; *m* 1956, Margaret Cynthia Webb; one *s* two *d*. *Educ:* Fitzwilliam House, Cambridge (MA). Called to the Bar, Lincoln's Inn, 1952. Served War, Army, 1939–46. Industry, 1952–62; practised at the Bar, 1962–80. *Recreations:* sailing, gardening. *Address:* 6 Pump Court, Temple, EC4Y 7AP. *Clubs:* London Rowing, Royal Over-Seas League.

HUNTER, John Garvin; Chief Executive, Management Executive, Health and Personal Social Services, Northern Ireland, since 1990; *b* 9 Aug. 1947; *s* of Garvin and Martha Hunter; *m* 1976, Rosemary Alison Haire; one *s* two *d*. *Educ:* Merchant Taylors' Sch., Liverpool; Queen's Univ., Belfast (BA); Cornell Univ., NY (MBA). Asst Principal, NICS, 1970; Department of Health and Social Services: Dep. Principal, 1973; Harkness Fellow, 1977–79; Principal Officer, 1979; Asst Sec., 1982; Dir Gen., Internat. Fund for Ireland, 1986; Under Sec., 1988. *Publications:* contribs to conf. papers on the conflict in NI and on health service planning. *Recreations:* Corrymeela Community, church, swimming. *Address:* Department of Health and Social Services, Dundonald House, Upper Newtownards Road, Belfast BT4 3SF.

HUNTER, John Murray, CB 1980; MC 1943; Scottish Tourist Guide; *b* 10 Nov. 1920; *s* of Rev. Dr John Hunter and Frances Hunter (*née* Martin); *m* 1948, Margaret, *d* of late Stanley Cursiter, CBE, RSW, RSA, and Phyllis Eda (*née* Hourston); two *s* three *d*. *Educ:* Fettes Coll.; Clare Coll., Cambridge. Served Army, 1941–45: Captain, The Rifle Bde. Served in Diplomatic Service at Canberra, Bogotá, Baghdad, Prague, Buenos Aires and in FCO (Head of Consular Dept, 1966, and of Latin America Dept, 1971–73); idc 1961, sowc 1965, jssc (Senior Directing Staff), 1967–69. Sec., 1973–75, Comr for Admin and Finance, 1976–81, Forestry Commn. Vice- Chm., 1981–83, Chm., 1983–86, Edinburgh West End Community Council. *Recreations:* music, reading; formerly Rugby football (Cambridge 1946, Scotland 1947), curling. *Address:* 21 Glencairn Crescent, Edinburgh EH12 5BT.

HUNTER, John Oswald Mair; *see* Hunter, Hon. Lord.

HUNTER, Keith Robert, OBE 1981; British Council Director, Italy, since 1990; *b* 29 May 1936; *s* of Robert Ernest Williamson and Winifred Mary Hunter; *m* 1st, 1959, Ann Patricia Fuller (marr. diss. 1989); one *s* two *d*; 2nd, 1991, Victoria Solomonidis. *Educ:* Hymers Coll., Hull; Magdalen Coll., Oxford (MA). Joined British Council, 1962; Lectr, Royal Sch. of Admin, Phnom Penh, 1960–64; Schs Recruitment Dept, 1964–66; SOAS, 1966–67; Asst Rep., Hong Kong, 1967–69; Dir, Penang, 1970–72; Dep. Rep., Kuala Lumpur, 1972–74; London Univ. Inst. of Educn, 1974–75; Rep., Algeria, 1975–78; First Sec. (Cultural), subseq. Cultural Counsellor (British Council Rep.), China, 1979–82; Sec. of Bd, and Hd of Dir-Gen.'s Dept, 1982–85; Controller, Arts Div., 1985–90. *Recreation:* music. *Address:* British Council, Via Quattro Fontane 20, 00184 Rome, Italy.

HUNTER, Kenneth; *see* Hunter, A. K. F.

HUNTER, Sir Laurence (Colvin), Kt 1995; CBE 1987; FRSE 1986; Professor of Applied Economics, since 1970, and Director of External Relations, 1987–90, University of Glasgow; *b* 8 Aug. 1934; *s* of Laurence O. and Jessie P. Hunter; *m* 1958, Evelyn Margaret (*née* Green); three *s* one *d*. *Educ:* Hillhead High Sch., Glasgow; Univ. of Glasgow (MA); University Coll., Oxford (DPhil). Asst, Manchester Univ., 1958–59; National Service, 1959–61; Post-Doctoral Fellow, Univ. of Chicago, 1961–62; University of Glasgow: Lectr, 1962; Sen. Lectr, 1967; Titular Prof., 1969; Vice-Principal, 1982–86. Member: Ct of Inquiry into miners' strike, 1972; Council, Advisory, Conciliation and Arbitration Service, 1974–86; Royal Commn on Legal Services in Scotland, 1976–80; Council, ESRC, 1989–92; Chairman: Post Office Arbitration Tribunal, 1974–92; Police Negotiating Bd, 1987– (Dep. Chm., 1980–86). Pres., Scottish Econ. Soc., 1993–. *Publications:* (with G. L. Reid) Urban Worker Mobility, 1968; (with D. J. Robertson) Economics of Wages and Labour, 1969, 2nd edn (with C. Mulvey), 1981; (with G. L. Reid and D. Boddy) Labour Problems of Technological Change, 1970; (with A. W. J. Thomson) The Nationalised Transport Industries, 1973; (with R. B. McKersie) Pay, Productivity and Collective Bargaining, 1973; (with L. Baddon *et al.*) People's Capitalism, 1989; other pubns in economics and industrial relations. *Recreations:* golf, painting. *Address:* 23 Boclair Road, Bearsden, Glasgow G61 2AF. *T:* 0141–942 0793.

HUNTER, Muir Vane Skerrett; QC 1965; Lt-Col (Hon.); MA Oxon; MRI; Barrister-at-Law; *b* 19 Aug. 1913; *s* of late H. S. Hunter, Home Civil Service, and Bluebell M. Hunter, novelist; *m* 1st, 1939, Dorothea Eason, JP (*d* 1986), *e d* of late P. E. Verstone; one *d*; 2nd, 1986, Gillian Victoria Joyce Petrie, *d* of late Dr Alexander Petrie, CBE, MD, FRCS, FRCP. *Educ:* Westminster Sch.; Christ Church, Oxford (Scholar). Called, Gray's Inn, 1938 (*ad eundem* Inner Temple, 1965); Holker Senior Scholar; Bencher, Gray's Inn, 1976. Served 1940–46: Royal Armoured Corps; GS Intelligence, GHQ (India); GSO 1 attd War and Legislative Depts, Govt of India; returned to the Bar, 1946; standing counsel (bankruptcy) to Bd of Trade, 1949–65; Dep. Chm., Advisory Cttee on Service Candidates, HO; Member: EEC Bankruptcy Adv. Cttee, Dept of Trade, 1973–76; Insolvency Law Review Cttee, Dept of Trade, 1977–82; Advr, Law Reform Commn, Kenya Govt, 1991–; Consultant on law reform, Govt of The Gambia/USAID, 1992. Founder-Chairman, N Kensington Neighbourhood Law Centre, 1969–71; Mem., Exec. Cttee, British-Polish Legal Assoc., 1991–; Hon. Mem. of Council, Justice. Amnesty/ICJ International Observer: Burundi, 1962; Rhodesia, 1969; Turkey, 1972. Governor, Royal Shakespeare Theatre, 1978–; Mem. Council, Royal Shakespeare Theatre Trust, 1978–. Chairman: Gdansk Hospice Fund, 1989–92; Polish Hospices Fund, 1992–. Hon. Legal Advr, Nairobi Hospice, Kenya, 1989–92. Hon. Life Mem., Commercial Law League of America, 1985. Mem. Editl Board, Insolvency Law & Practice, 1985–. *Publications:* Senior Editor, Williams on Bankruptcy, 1958–78, Williams and Muir Hunter on Bankruptcy, 1979–84, Muir Hunter on Personal Insolvency, 1987–; Emergent Africa and the Rule of Law, 1963; Jt Editor: Halsbury's Laws, 4th edn, Vol 3; Atkins' Forms, Vol 7; Editor, Kerr, The Law and Practice as to Receivers and Administrators, 17th edn, 1988; Part Editor, Butterworth's County Court Precedents and Pleadings, 1984–; (contrib.) Years in the Fence (poetry), 1994. *Recreations:* writing poetry, theatre, travel, music. *Address:* (chambers) 3–4 South Square, Gray's Inn, WC1R 5HP. *T:* 0171–696 9900, *Fax:* 0171–696 9911; Hunterston, Donhead St Andrew, Shaftesbury, Dorset SP7 9EB. *T:* Donhead (01747) 828779, *Fax:* (01747) 828045. *Clubs:* Hurlingham; Oxford Union.

HUNTER, Dame Pamela, DBE 1981; Vice-President, National Union of Conservative and Unionist Associations, since 1985 (Vice-Chairman, 1981–84; Chairman, 1984–85); *b* 3 Oct. 1919; *d* of late Col T. G. Greenwell, TD, JP, DL, and M. W. Greenwell; *m* 1942, Gordon Lovegrove Hunter; one *s* one *d*. *Educ:* Westonbirt Sch., Tetbury; Eastbourne Sch. of Domestic Economy. Served WRNS, 1942–45. Mem., Conservative Nat. Union Exec. Cttee, 1972–88; Chairman: Northern Area Cons. Women's Adv. Cttee, 1972–75; Cons. Women's Nat. Adv. Cttee, 1978–81; Mem., Cons. Party Policy Cttee, 1978–85. President: Berwick-upon-Tweed Cons. Assoc., 1986–89; N Area Cons. Council, 1986–89. Mem., Northumbrian Water Authority, 1973–76. Member: Berwick-upon-Tweed Borough Council, 1973–83; Chatton Parish Council 1987–95 (Chm., 1993–95); Lay Chm., Parish of Chatton with Chillingham PCC, 1989–92, and 1993–, also Church warden. *Recreations:* charity work for NSPCC and RNLI, antiques. *Address:* The Coach House, Chatton, Alnwick, Northumberland NE66 5PY. *T:* Chatton (01668) 215259. *Club:* Lansdowne.

HUNTER, Philip Brown, TD; Chairman, John Holt & Co. (Liverpool) Ltd, 1967–71; *b* 30 May 1909; *s* of Charles Edward Hunter and Marion (*née* Harper); *m* 1937, Joyce Mary (*née* Holt); two *s* two *d*. *Educ:* Birkenhead Sch.; London University. Practised as Solicitor, 1933–80. Chm., Guardian Royal Exchange Assurance (Sierra Leone) Ltd, 1972–79; Director: Cammell Laird & Co. Ltd, 1949–70 (Chm. 1966–70); John Holt & Co. (Liverpool) Ltd, 1951–71 (Exec. Dir, 1960); Guardian Royal Exchange, 1969–79; Guardian Assurance Co. Ltd, 1967–69; Royal Exchange (Nigeria) Ltd, 1972–79; Lion of Africa Insurance Co. Ltd, 1972–79; Enterprise Insurance Co. Ltd, Ghana, 1972–79. *Address:* Bryn Hyfryd, Lixwm, Holywell, Clwyd CH8 8LT. *T:* Halkyn (01352) 780054.

HUNTER, Dr Philip John: Chief Education Officer, Staffordshire, since 1985; *b* 23 Nov. 1939; *m* Ruth Bailey; two *s* one *d*. *Educ:* Univ. of Durham (BSc 1962); Univ. of Newcastle upon Tyne (PhD 1965). Lectr, Univ. of Khartoum, 1965–67; Senior Scientific Officer: ARC, Cambridge, 1967–69; DES, 1969–71; Course Dir, CS Staff Coll., 1971–73; posts at DES, including science, schools, finance and Private Office, 1973–79; Dep. Chief Educn Officer, ILEA, 1979–85. Dir, Staffs TEC, 1990–; Member of Council: Keele Univ., 1987–; BTEC, 1990–; Member: Nat. Council for Educnl Technol., 1986–91; Nat. Curriculum Wkg Gp on Design and Technol., 1988–89; Design Council Educn Cttee, 1990–. *Publications:* (jtly) Terrestrial Slugs, 1970; (jtly) Pulmonates, 1978; papers on ecology of invertebrates; contrib. educnl jls on educn policy matters. *Recreation:* gardening. *Address:* Upmeads, Newport Road, Stafford ST16 1DD.

HUNTER, Rita, CBE 1980; prima donna; leading soprano, Australian Opera, since 1981; *b* 15 Aug. 1933; *d* of Charles Newton Hunter and Lucy Hunter; *m* 1960, John Darnley-Thomas (*d* 1994); one *d*. *Educ:* Wallasey. Joined Carl Rosa, 1950. Début: Berlin, 1970; Covent Garden, 1972; Metropolitan, NY, 1972; Munich, 1973; Australia, 1978 (returned 1980 and 1981); Seattle Wagner Fest., 1980. Joined Sadler's Wells as leading soprano, 1958, and sang Brünnhilde in first complete Ring cycle, 1973; first perf. of Norma, San Francisco then NY Metropolitan, 1975; first perf. of Tosca, Canberra, Aust., 1988. Has sung leading roles in Aida, Trovatore, Masked Ball, Cavalleria Rusticana, Lohengrin, Flying Dutchman, Idomeneo, Don Carlos, Turandot, Nabucco, Macbeth, Tristan and Isolde, Electra. Founded, 1986, and ran with husband, Maduo Sch. of Singing, Aust., now renamed John Darnley Thomas Singing Acad. and run with daughter; also gives world-wide master classes. Many recordings, including complete Ring, complete Euryanthe, and several recital discs. Hon. DLitt Warwick, 1978; Hon. DMus Liverpool, 1983. RAM 1978. *Publication:* Wait till the Sun Shines Nellie (autobiog.), 1986. *Recreations:* sewing, swimming, oil painting, reading, gardening (Mem. Royal Nat. Rose Soc.), caravanning (Mem. Caravan Club), swimming. *Address:* 305 Bobbin Head Road, North Turramurra, NSW 2074, Australia. *T:* (2) 445062; (Aust. Rep.) Avere, 26 Oxley Drive, Bowral, NSW 2576, Australia. *T:* (48) 621688. *Club:* White Elephant.

HUNTER, Dr Tony, (Anthony Rex Hunter), FRS 1987; Professor, Molecular Biology and Virology Laboratory, Salk Institute, San Diego, California, since 1982; concurrently Adjunct Professor of Biology, University of California, San Diego; *b* 23 Aug. 1943; *s* of Ranulph Rex Hunter and Nellie Ruby Elsie Hunter (*née* Hitchcock); *m* 1969, Philippa Charlotte Marrack (marr. diss. 1974); *m* 1992, Jennifer Ann Maureen Price; one *s*. *Educ:* Felsted Sch., Essex; Gonville and Caius Coll., Cambridge (BA, MA, PhD). Research Fellow: Christ's Coll., Cambridge, 1968–71 and 1973–74; Salk Inst., San Diego: Res. Associate, 1971–73; Asst Prof., 1975–78; Associate Prof., 1978–82. American Cancer Soc. Res. Prof., 1992–. Assoc. Mem., EMBO, 1992. FRSA 1989; Fellow, Amer. Acad. of Arts and Scis, 1992. Katharine Berkan Judd Award, Meml Sloan-Kettering Cancer Center, 1992; Gairdner Foundn Internat. Award, 1994; Hopkins Meml Medal, Biochemical Soc., 1994; Mott Prize, Gen. Motors Cancer Res. Foundn, 1994. *Publications:* numerous, in leading scientific jls. *Recreations:* white water rafting, exploring the Baja peninsula. *Address:* Molecular Biology and Virology Laboratory, The Salk Institute, PO Box 85800, San Diego, CA 92186, USA. *T:* (619) 4534100, *Fax:* (619) 4574765.

HUNTER, William Hill, CBE 1971; JP; DL; CA; Consultant, McLay, McAlister & McGibbon, Chartered Accountants, since 1991 (Partner, 1946–91); *b* 5 Nov. 1916; *s* of Robert Dalglish Hunter and Mrs Margaret Walker Hill or Hunter; *m* 1947, Kathleen, *d* of William Alfred Cole; two *s*. *Educ:* Cumnock Academy. Chartered Accountant, 1940. Served War: enlisted as private, RASC, 1940; commissioned RA, 1941; Staff Capt., Middle East, 1944–46. Director: Abbey National Building Soc. Scottish Adv. Bd, 1966–86; City of Glasgow Friendly Soc., 1966–88 (Pres., 1980–88); J. & G. Grant Glenfarclas Distillery, 1966–92. President: W Renfrewshire Conservative and Unionist Assoc., 1972–; Scottish Young Unionist Assoc., 1958–60; Scottish Unionist Assoc., 1964–65. Contested (U) South Ayrshire, 1959 and 1964. Chairman: Salvation Army Adv. Bd in Strathclyde, 1982–93 (Vice-Chm., 1972–82); Salvation Army Housing Assoc. (Scotland) Ltd, 1986–91. Hon. Treasurer, Quarrier's Homes, 1979–94 (Acting Chm., 1989–92). Deacon Convener, Trades House of Glasgow, 1986–87. Hon. Vice-Pres., Royal Scottish Agricl Benevolent Inst., 1993–; Hon. Pres., Friends of Glasgow Britannic Gardens, 1994–. JP 1970, DL 1987, Renfrewshire. *Recreations:* gardening, golf, swimming. *Address:* Armitage, Kilmacolm, Renfrewshire PA13 4PH. *T:* Kilmacolm (0150587) 2444. *Clubs:* Western, Royal Scottish Automobile (Glasgow).

HUNTER, William John, MB, BS; Director, Health and Safety Commission of the European Communities, since 1988; *b* 5 April 1937; *m*; two *s* one *d*. *Educ:* Westminster Medical Sch. (MB, BS); LRCP, MRCS; FFOM. Commission of the European Communities: Principal Administrator, 1974–82; Hd of Div., Industrial Medicine and Hygiene, 1982–88. OStJ 1994. *Publications:* many on health and safety at work. *Recreations:* squash, jogging, music. *Address:* Commission of the European Communities, Bâtiment Jean Monnet, 2920 Luxembourg.

HUNTER-BLAIR, Sir Edward (Thomas), 8th Bt *cr* 1786, of Dunskey; landowner and forester since 1964; *b* 15 Dec. 1920; *s* of Sir James Hunter Blair, 7th Bt and Jean Galloway (*d* 1953), *d* of T. W. McIntyre, Sorn Castle, Ayrshire; *S* father, 1985; *m* 1956, Norma (*d* 1972), *d* of late W. S. Harris; one adopted *s* one adopted *d*. *Educ:* Balliol Coll., Oxford (BA); Univ. of Paris (Diploma, French Lang. and Lit.). Temp. Civil Servant, 1941–43; journalist (Asst Foreign Editor), 1944–49; in business in Yorkshire, manager and director of own company, 1950–63. Mem. Council, Wyndham's Trust, 1992–. Mem., Kirkcudbright CC, 1970–71; former Pres., Dumfries and Galloway Mountaineering Club. 1939–45 Star, Gen. Service Medal, 1946. *Publications:* Scotland Sings, and A Story of Me, 1981; A Future Time (With an Earlier Life), 1984; A Mission in Life, 1987; Nearing the Year 2000, 1990; Our Troubled Future, 1993; articles on learned and other subjects. *Recreations:* gardening, hill-walking. *Heir:* *b* James Hunter Blair, *b* 18 March 1926. *Address:* Parton House, Castle Douglas, Scotland DG7 3NB. *T:* Parton (016447) 234. *Clubs:* Royal Over-Seas League; Western Meeting (Ayr).

HUNTER JOHNSTON, David Alan; *b* 16 Jan. 1915; *s* of James Ernest Johnston and Florence Edith Johnston (*née* Hunter); *m* 1949, Philippa Frances Ray; three *s* one *d*. *Educ:* Christ's Hospital; King's Coll., London. FKC 1970. Royal Ordnance Factories, Woolwich, 1936–39; S Metropolitan Gas Co., 1939–44; Min. of Economic Warfare (Economic and Industrial Planning Staff), 1944–45; Control Office for Germany and Austria, 1945–47; Sec. to Scientific Cttee for Germany, 1946; FO (German Section), Asst Head, German Gen. Economic Dept, 1947–49; HM Treasury, Supply, Estabt and Home Finance Divs, 1949–53. Central Bd of Finance of Church of England: Sec. (and Fin. Sec. to Church Assembly), 1953–59, and Investment Manager, 1959–65; concurrently, Dir, Local Authorities Mutual Investment Trust, 1961–65, and Investment Man. to Charities Official Investment Fund, 1963–65; a Man. Dir, J. Henry Schroder Wagg & Co. Ltd, 1965–74; Chairman: Schroder Executor & Trustee Co. Ltd, 1966–74; Reserve Pension Bd, 1974–75; Assoc. of Investment Trust Cos, 1975–77; Director: Trans-Oceanic Trust, subseq. Schroder Global Trust plc, 1965–88; Clerical, Medical & General Life Assurance Soc., 1970–74; Lindustries Ltd, 1970–79 and of other investment trust cos for many years. Mem., Monopolies Commn, 1969–73. A Reader, 1959–85, licensed in dio. St Albans, dio. Bath and Wells. *Publication:* Stewardship and the Gospel, 1995. *Address:* Eastfield, North Perrott, Crewkerne, Somerset TA18 7SW. *T:* Crewkerne (01460) 75156. *Clubs:* Farmers', City of London.

HUNTER SMART, Norman; *see* Hunter Smart, W. N.

HUNTER SMART, (William) Norman, CA; Chairman: Charterhouse Development Capital Fund Ltd, since 1987; C. J. Sims Ltd, since 1990; *b* 25 May 1921; *s* of William Hunter Smart, CA, and Margaret Thorburn Inglis; *m* 1st, 1948, Bridget Beryl Andreae (*d* 1974); four *s*; 2nd, 1977, Sheila Smith Stewart (*née* Speirs). *Educ:* George Watson's Coll., Edinburgh. Served War, 1939–45; 1st Lothians & Border Horse; Warwickshire Yeomanry; mentioned in despatches. Hays Allan, Chartered Accountants, 1950–86 (Senior Partner, 1983–86). Chm., Assoc. of Scottish Chartered Accountants in London, 1972–73; Institute of Chartered Accountants of Scotland: Council Mem., 1970–75; Vice-Pres., 1976–78; Pres., 1978–79. Member: Gaming Bd for GB, 1985–90; Scottish Legal Aid Bd, 1986–89. *Address:* Flat 1, Imperial Court, 12 Ravine Road, Canford Cliffs, Poole, Dorset BH13 7HX. *Club:* Caledonian.

HUNTER-TOD, Air Marshal Sir John (Hunter), KBE 1971 (OBE 1957); CB 1969; Head of Engineer Branch and Director-General of Engineering (RAF), 1970–73, retired; *b* 21 April 1917; *s* of late Hunter Finlay Tod, FRCS; *m* 1959, Anne, *d* of late Thomas Chaffer Howard; one *s*. *Educ:* Marlborough; Trinity Coll., Cambridge (MA). DCAe 1948. Commissioned, 1940; Fighter Command and Middle East, 1939–45. Group Capt. 1958; Air Cdre 1963. Dir, Guided Weapons (Air), Min. of Aviation, 1962–65; AOEng, RAF Germany, 1965–67; AOC No 24 Group, RAF, 1967–70; Air Vice-Marshal, 1968; Air Marshal, 1971. CEng. Hon. DSc Cranfield Inst. of Technol., 1974. *Address:* 21 Ridge Hill, Dartmouth, S Devon TQ6 9PE. *T:* Dartmouth (01803) 833130. *Club:* Royal Air Force.

HUNTING, (Lindsay) Clive; Non-executive Director, Hunting plc, since 1991 (Chairman, 1974–91); Director, Battle of Britain Memorial Ltd, since 1993; *b* 22 Dec. 1925; *s* of late Gerald Lindsay Hunting and Ruth (*née* Pyman); *m* 1952, Shelagh (*née* Hill Lowe); one *s* one *d*. *Educ:* Loretto; Trinity Hall, Cambridge (MA). Royal Navy, 1944–47; Cambridge, 1947–50; joined Hunting Group, 1950, Dir 1952, Vice-Chm. 1962, Chm., 1975. Chm., Field Aviation Ltd, 1970–94. President: British Independent Air Transport Assoc., 1960–62; Fedn Internationale de Transporte Aerien Privée, 1961–63; Air Educn and Recreation Organisation, 1970–90; SBAC, 1985–86 (Treas., 1988–); Chm., Air League, 1968–71; Mem. Ct, Cranfield Inst. of Technol., 1980– (Mem. Council, 1989–). Master, Coachmakers' and Coach Harness Makers' Co., 1983–84. CIMgt (CBIM 1980); CRAeS 1983. Nile Gold Medal for Aerospace Educn, 1982. *Recreations:* yachting, fishing. *Address:* April Cottage, Alderbourne Lane, Fulmer, Bucks SL3 6JB. *T:* Fulmer (01753) 662300; Hunting PLC, 3 Cockspur Street, SW1Y 5BQ. *T:* 0171–321 0123, *Fax:* 0171–839 2072. *Clubs:* Royal Yacht Squadron, Royal London Yacht (Cdre, 1989) (Cowes).

HUNTING, Richard Hugh; Chairman, Hunting plc, since 1991 (Deputy Chairman, 1989–91); *b* 30 July 1946; *s* of late Charles Patrick Maule Hunting, CBE, TD and of Diana, *d* of Brig. A. B. P. Pereira, DSO; *m* 1970, Penelope, *d* of Col L. L. Fleming, MBE, MC and Mrs S. E. Fleming; one *s* two *d*. *Educ:* Rugby Sch.; Sheffield Univ. (BEng); Manchester Business Sch. (MBA). Joined Hunting Gp, 1972; worked at Hunting Surveys and Consultants, Field Aviation, E. A. Gibson Shipbrokers, Hunting Oilfield Services, Hunting Engineering; Director: Hunting Associated Industries, 1986–89 (Chm., 1989); Hunting Petroleum Services, 1989; Hunting plc, 1989–. Mem. Council, CBI, 1992–. Mem. Court, Ironmongers' Co., 1986– (Sen. Warden, 1995). *Recreations:* ski-ing, board sailing, computing. *Address:* (office) 3 Cockspur Street, SW1Y 5BQ. *T:* 0171–321 0123. *Club:* Travellers'.

HUNTINGDON, 16th Earl of, *cr* 1529; **William Edward Robin Hood Hastings Bass;** racehorse trainer, since 1976; *b* 30 Jan. 1948; *s* of Capt. Peter Robin Hood Hastings Bass (who assumed additional surname of Bass by deed poll, 1954) (*d* 1964); *g s* of 13th Earl and of Priscilla Victoria, *d* of Capt. Sir Malcolm Bullock, 1st Bt, MBE; *S* kinsman, 1990; *m* 1989, Sue Warner. *Educ:* Winchester; Trinity Coll., Cambridge. Trainer, West Ilsley Stables, Berks, 1989–. *Heir:* *b* Hon. Simon Aubrey Robin Hood Hastings Bass, *b* 2 May 1950. *Address:* Hodcott House, West Ilsley, near Newbury, Berks RG16 0AE.

HUNTINGDON, Bishop Suffragan of, since 1980; **Rt. Rev. William Gordon Roe;** *b* 5 Jan. 1932; *s* of William Henry and Dorothy Myrtle Roe; *m* 1953, Mary Andreen; two *s* two *d*. *Educ:* Bournemouth School; Jesus Coll., Oxford (MA, DipTh (with distinction), DPhil); St Stephen's House, Oxford. Curate of Bournemouth, 1958–61; Priest-in-charge of St Michael's, Abingdon, 1961–69; Vice-Principal of St Chad's Coll., Durham, 1969–74; Vicar of St Oswald's, Durham, 1974–80; RD of Durham, 1974–80; Chaplain of Collingwood Coll., Durham, 1974–80; Hon. Canon of Durham Cathedral, 1979–80. Co-Chm., Meissen Commn, 1991–. *Publications:* Lamennais and England, 1966; (with A. Hutchings) J. B. Dykes, Priest and Musician, 1976. *Recreations:* French literature, painting, camping. *Address:* 14 Lynn Road, Ely, Cambs CB6 1DA. *T:* Ely (01353) 662137, *Fax:* (01353) 669357.

HUNTINGDON, Archdeacon of; *see* Sledge, Ven. R. K.

HUNTINGFIELD, 7th Baron *cr* 1796 (Ire.); **Joshua Charles Vanneck;** Bt 1751; accountant, NFU Mutual, Cambridge, since 1993; *b* 10 Aug. 1954; *o s* of 6th Baron Huntingfield and of Janetta Lois, *er d* of Captain R. H. Errington, RN; *S* father, 1994; *m* 1982, Arabella Mary, *d* of A. H. J. Fraser, MC; four *s* one *d* (incl. twin *s*). *Educ:* West Downs, Winchester; Eton; Magdalene Coll., Cambridge (MA). ACA. With Gerald Eve & Co., London, 1976, Chestertons, London, 1977–82; Highland Wineries, Inverness, 1982–87; accountant, Deloitte Haskin & Sells, later Coopers & Lybrand, Cambridge, 1987–91. *Recreations:* family, history. *Heir:* *s* Hon. Gerard Charles Alastair Vanneck, *b* 12 March 1985. *Address:* 69 Barrons Way, Comberton, Cambridge CB3 7EQ. *Clubs:* Pratt's.

HUNTINGTON-WHITELEY, Sir Hugo (Baldwin), 3rd Bt *cr* 1918; DL; *b* 31 March 1924; *e surv. s* of Captain Sir Maurice Huntington-Whiteley, 2nd Bt, RN, and Lady (Pamela) Margaret Huntington-Whiteley (*d* 1976), 3rd *d* of 1st Earl Baldwin of Bewdley, KG, PC; *S* father, 1975; *m* 1959, Jean Marie Ramsay, JP 1973, DStJ; two *d*. *Educ:* Eton. Royal Navy, 1942–47. Chartered Accountant; Partner, Price Waterhouse, 1963–83. Mem. Ct of Assts, Goldsmiths' Co., 1982– (Prime Warden, 1989–90). Worcs: High Sheriff 1971; DL 1972. *Recreations:* music, travel. *Heir:* *b* (John) Miles Huntington-Whiteley, VRD, Lieut-Comdr RNR [*b* 18 July 1929; *m* 1960, Countess Victoria Adelheid Clementine Louise, *d* of late Count Friedrich Wolfgang zu Castell-Rudenhausen; one *s* two *d*]. *Address:* Ripple Hall, Tewkesbury, Glos GL20 6EY. *T:* Tewkesbury (01684) 592431; 12 Stafford Terrace, W8 7BH. *T:* 0171–937 2918. *Club:* Brooks's.

HUNTLEY, Andrew John Mack, FRICS; Chairman, Richard Ellis, Chartered Surveyors, since 1993; *b* 24 Jan. 1939; *s* of William Mack Huntley and Murial Huntley (*née* Akehurst); *m* 1963, Juliet Vivien Collum; three *d*. *Educ:* Monkton Coombe Sch., Bath. FRICS 1963. Davis & Son, Bristol, 1956–58; D. Ward & Son, Plymouth, 1958–61; Davige & Partners, London, 1961–65; with Richard Ellis, 1965–. *Recreations:* shooting, tennis. *Address:* Ashurst, Fernhurst, Haslemere, Surrey GU27 3JB. *Club:* Boodle's.

HUNTLY, 13th Marquess of, *cr* 1599 (Scot.); **Granville Charles Gomer Gordon;** Earl of Huntly, 1450; Earl of Aboyne, Baron Gordon of Strathavon and Glenlivet, 1660; Baron Meldrum (UK), 1815; Premier Marquess of Scotland; Chief of House of Gordon; *b* 4 Feb. 1944; *s* of 12th Marquess of Huntly and of Hon. Mary Pamela Berry, *d* of 1st Viscount Kemsley; *S* father, 1987; *m* 1st, 1972, Jane Elizabeth Angela (marr. diss. 1990), *d* of late Col Alistair Gibb and Lady McCorquodale of Newton; one *s* two *d*; 2nd, 1991, Mrs Catheryn Millbourn; one *d*. *Educ:* Gordonstoun. *Heir:* *s* Earl of Aboyne, *qv*. *Address:* Aboyne Castle, Aberdeenshire AB34 5JP. *T:* Aboyne (01339) 886118.

See also Baron Cranworth.

HUNTSMAN, Peter William, FRICS; FAAV; Principal, College of Estate Management, 1981–92, Hon. Fellow, 1993; *b* 11 Aug. 1935; *s* of late William and Lydia Irene Huntsman (*née* Clegg); *m* 1st, 1961, Janet Mary Bell (marr. diss.); one *s* one *d*; 2nd, 1984, Cicely Eleanor (*née* Tamblin). *Educ:* Hymers Coll., Hull; Coll. of Estate Management, Univ. of London (BSc Estate Man.). Agricultural Land Service: Dorset and Northumberland, 1961–69; Kellogg Foundn Fellowship, USA, 1969–70; Principal Surveyor, London, ADAS, 1971–76; Divl Surveyor, Surrey, Middx and Sussex, 1976–81. Liveryman, Chartered Surveyors' Co., 1985; Freeman, City of London, 1985. Hon. FSVA 1993. *Publications:* (contrib.) Walmsley's Rural Estate Management, 6th edn 1978; contribs to professional jls. *Recreations:* sport, Dorset countryside, reading. *Address:* Radnor Cottage, Cauldon Road, Swanage, Dorset BH19 1PQ. *T:* Swanage (01929) 425857. *Club:* Farmers.

HUPPERT, Prof. Herbert Eric, ScD; FRS 1987; Professor of Theoretical Geophysics and Foundation Director, Institute of Theoretical Geophysics, Cambridge University, since 1989; Fellow of King's College, Cambridge, since 1970; *b* 26 Nov. 1943; *er c* of Leo Huppert and Alice Huppert (*née* Neuman); *m* 1966, Felicia Adina Huppert (*née* Ferster), PhD; two *s*. *Educ:* Sydney Boys' High Sch.; Sydney Univ. (BSc 1963); ANU (MSc 1964); Univ. of California at San Diego (MS 1966, PhD 1968); Univ. of Cambridge (MA 1971, ScD 1985). ICI Research Fellow, 1968–70; University of Cambridge: Asst Dir of Research, 1970–81; Lectr in Applied Maths, 1981–88; BP Venture Unit Sen. Res. Fellow, 1983–89; Reader in Geophysical Dynamics, 1988–89. Visiting research scientist: ANU; Univ. of California, San Diego; Canterbury Univ.; Caltech; MIT; Univ. of NSW; Woods Hole Oceanographic Inst.; Vis. Prof., Univ. of NSW, 1991–. Mem., NERC, 1993–. Co-Chm., Scientists for the Release of Soviet Refusniks, 1988– (Vice-Chm., 1985–88). Associate Editor, Jl Fluid Mechanics, 1971–90; Editor, Jl of Soviet Jewry, 1985–; Mem. Editl Bd, Philosophical Trans of Royal Soc. (series A), 1994–. *Publications:* approximately 140 papers on applied mathematics, crystal growth, fluid mechanics, geology, geophysics, oceanography and meteorology. *Recreations:* my children, squash, tennis, mountaineering, cycling. *Address:* Institute of Theoretical Geophysics, 20 Silver Street, Cambridge CB3

9EW; 46 De Freville Avenue, Cambridge CB4 1HT. *T:* Cambridge (01223) 356071; (office) Cambridge (01223) 337853, Cambridge (01223) 333463, *Fax:* Cambridge (01223) 337918.

HURD, Rt. Hon. Douglas (Richard), CBE 1974; PC 1982; MP (C) Witney, since 1983 (Mid-Oxon, Feb. 1974–1983); Secretary of State for Foreign and Commonwealth Affairs, 1989–95; *b* 8 March 1930; *e s* of Baron Hurd (*d* 1966) and Stephanie Corner (*d* 1985); *m* 1st, 1960, Tatiana Elizabeth Michelle (marr. diss. 1982), *d* of A. C. Benedict Eyre, Westburton House, Bury, Sussex; three *s*; 2nd, 1982, Judy, *d* of Sidney and Pamela Smart; one *s* one *d*. *Educ:* Eton (King's Scholar and Newcastle Scholar); Trinity Coll., Cambridge (Major Scholar). Pres., Cambridge Union, 1952. HM Diplomatic Service, 1952–66; served in: Peking, 1954–56; UK Mission to UN, 1956–60; Private Sec. to Perm. Under-Sec. of State, FO, 1960–63; Rome, 1963–66. Joined Conservative Research Dept, 1966; Head of Foreign Affairs Section, 1968; Private Sec. to Leader of the Opposition, 1968–70; Political Sec. to Prime Minister, 1970–74; Opposition Spokesman on European Affairs, 1976–79; Minister of State, FCO, 1979–83; Minister of State, Home Office, 1983–84; Sec. of State for NI, 1984–85, for Home Dept, 1985–89. Vis. Fellow, Nuffield Coll., Oxford, 1978–86. *Publications:* The Arrow War, 1967; Truth Game, 1972; Vote to Kill, 1975; An End to Promises, 1979; with Andrew Osmond: Send Him Victorious, 1968; The Smile on the Face of the Tiger, 1969, repr. 1982; Scotch on the Rocks, 1971; War Without Frontiers, 1982; (with Stephen Lamport) Palace of Enchantments, 1985. *Recreation:* writing thrillers. *Address:* House of Commons, SW1A 0AA. *Club:* Beefsteak.

HURFORD, Peter (John), OBE 1984; organist; *b* 22 Nov. 1930; *e c* of H. J. Hurford, Minehead; *m* 1955, Patricia Mary Matthews, *e d* of late Prof. Sir Bryan Matthews, CBE, FRS; two *s* one *d*. *Educ:* Blundells Sch.; Royal Coll. of Music; Jesus Coll., Cambridge. MA, MusB Cantab, FRCO. Director of Music, Bablake Sch., Coventry and Conductor, Leamington Spa Bach Choir, 1956–57; Master of the Music, Cathedral and Abbey Church of St Alban, 1958–78, Conductor, St Albans Bach Choir, 1958–78; Founder, Internat. Organ Festival Soc., 1963. Artist-in-Residence: Univ. of Cincinnati, 1967–68; Sydney Opera Ho., 1980, 1981, 1982; Acting Organist, St John's Coll., Cambridge, 1979–80; recital and lecture tours throughout Europe, USA, Canada, Japan, Philippines, Taiwan, Australia and NZ from 1960. Vis. Prof. of Organ, Univ. of Western Ontario, 1976–77; Prof., RAM, 1982–88, Consultant Prof., 1988–. Betts Fellow, Oxford Univ., 1992–93. Mem. Council, 1963–, Pres., 1980–82, RCO; Pres., IAO, 1995–; Mem., Hon. Council of Management, Royal Philharmonic Soc., 1983–87. Has made numerous LP records, incl. complete organ works of J. S. Bach (Gramophone Award, 1979; Silver Disc, 1983), F. Couperin, G. F. Handel, P. Hindemith. Hon. Dr, Baldwin-Wallace Coll., Ohio, 1981; Hon. DMus Bristol, 1992. Hon. FRSCM 1977; Hon. Mem., RAM, 1981; Hon. FRCM 1987. *Publications:* Making Music on the Organ, 1988; Suite: Laudate Dominum; sundry other works for organ; Masses for Series III and Rite II of Amer. Episcopal Church; sundry church anthems. *Recreations:* walking, wine, silence. *Address:* Broom House, St Bernard's Road, St Albans, Herts AL3 5RA.

HURLEY, Dame Rosalinde, (Dame Rosalinde Gortvai), DBE 1988; LLB, MD; FRCPath; Professor of Microbiology, University of London, at Institute of Obstetrics and Gynaecology, (Royal Postgraduate Medical School), since 1975; Consultant Microbiologist, Queen Charlotte's Maternity Hospital, since 1963; *b* 30 Dec. 1929; *o d* of late William Hurley and Rose Clancey; *m* 1964, Peter Gortvai, FRCS. *Educ:* Academy of the Assumption, Wellesley Hills, Mass, USA; Queen's Coll., Harley St, London; Univ. of London; Inns of Court. Called to the Bar, Inner Temple, 1958. House Surg., Wembley Hosp., 1955; Ho. Phys., W London Hosp., 1956; Sen. Ho. Officer, 1956–57, Registrar, 1957–58, Lectr and Asst Clin. Pathologist, 1958–62, Charing Cross Hosp. and Med. Sch. Chm., Medicines Commn, 1982–93, Mem., PHLS Bd, 1982–90 (Chm., Ethics Cttee, 1983–); Chm., Nuffield Council on Bioethics Working Gp on Human Tissues (report published, 1995). EP Rep., Management Bd, European Evaluation Agency. Examiner, RCPath, and univs at home and abroad; Mem. Council, 1977–, Asst Registrar, 1978–, and Vice-Pres., 1984–87, RCPath; Royal Society of Medicine: Pres., Section of Pathology, and Vice-Pres., 1979–; Mem. Council, 1980–; Hon. Sec., 1984–90; Chm., 1980–82, formerly Vice-Chm., Cttee on Dental and Surgical Materials; Pres., Assoc. of Clinical Pathologists, 1984– (Pres.-elect, 1983–84); Chm., Assoc. of Profs of Medical Microbiol., 1987–94. Mem. Governing Body, Postgrad. Med. Fed., 1985–90. FRCOG 1993. Hon. FFPM 1990. DUniv Surrey, 1984. C. ver Heyden de Lancey Prize, RSM, 1991. *Publications:* (jtly) Candida albicans, 1964; (jtly) Symposium on Candida Infections, 1966; (jtly) Neonatal and Perinatal Infections, 1979; chapters in med. books; papers in med. and sci. jls. *Recreations:* gardening, reading. *Address:* 2 Temple Gardens, Temple, EC4Y 9AY. *T:* 0171–353 0577.

HURN, (Francis) Roger; Chairman, since 1991, Chief Executive, since 1981, and Managing Director, since 1978, Smiths Industries Plc; *b* 9 June 1938; *s* of Francis James Hurn and Joyce Elsa Hurn (*née* Bennett); *m* 1980, Rosalind Jackson; one *d*. *Educ:* Marlborough Coll. Engrg apprentice, Rolls Royce Motors, 1956; joined Smiths Industries, 1958. National Service, 1959–61. Export Dir, Motor Accessory Div., Smiths Industries, 1969; Man. Dir, Internat. Operations, 1974; Exec. Dir, 1976. Non-executive Director: Ocean Transport & Trading, 1982–88; Pilkington, 1984–94; S. G. Warburg Gp, 1987–; ICI, 1993–. Gov., Henley Coll., 1986–. Liveryman, Coachmakers & Coach Harness Makers' Co., 1979–. *Recreations:* shooting, travel. *Address:* c/o Smiths Industries Plc, 765 Finchley Road, NW11 8DS. *T:* 0181–458 3232.

HURON, Archbishop of, since 1993; **Most Rev. Percival Richard O'Driscoll;** Metropolitan of Ontario, since 1993; Bishop of Huron, since 1990; *b* 4 Oct. 1938; *s* of T. J. O'Driscoll and Annie O'Driscoll (*née* Copley); *m* 1965, Suzanne Gertrude Savignac; one *s* one *d*. *Educ:* Bishop's Univ., Lennoxville, Quebec (BA, STB); Huron Coll., London, Ont. (DD). Ordained deacon 1964, priest 1966; Assistant Curate: St Matthias, Ottawa, 1965–67; St John Evan, Kitchener, 1967–70; Religious Educn Dir, St Paul's Cathedral and Bishop Cronyn Memorial, London, 1970; Rector: St Michael & All Angels, London, 1970–75; St Batholomew's, Sarnia, 1975–80; Rector, St Paul's Cathedral, and Dean of Huron, 1980–87; Suffragan Bishop of Huron, 1987; Coadjutor Bishop, 1989. *Recreations:* camping, hiking, photography. *Address:* 4–220 Dundas Street, London, Ont N6A 1H3, Canada. *T:* (519) 4330299, *Fax:* (519) 6734151. *Club:* London (Ontario).

HURRELL, Sir Anthony (Gerald), KCVO 1986; CMG 1984; HM Diplomatic Service, retired; *b* 18 Feb. 1927; *s* of late William Hurrell and Florence Hurrell; *m* 1951, Jean Wyatt; two *d*. *Educ:* Norwich Sch.; St Catharine's Coll., Cambridge. RAEC, 1948–50; Min. of Labour, 1950–53; Min. of Educn, 1953–64; joined Min. of Overseas Develt, 1964; Fellow, Center for International Affairs, Harvard, 1969–70; Head of SE Asia Develt Div., Bangkok, 1972–74; Under Secretary: Internat. Div. ODM, 1974–75; Central Policy Rev. Staff, Cabinet Office, 1976; Duchy of Lancaster, 1977; Asia and Oceans Div., ODA, 1978–83; Ambassador to Nepal, 1983–86. Pres., St Catharine's Soc., 1993–94 (Vice-Pres., 1992–93). *Recreations:* bird-ringing, bird-watching, digging ponds, music. *Address:* Lapwings, Dunwich, Saxmundham, Suffolk IP17 3DR.

HURRELL, Air Vice-Marshal Frederick Charles, CB 1986; OBE 1968; Director General, Royal Air Force Medical Services and Deputy Surgeon General (Operations), 1986–87; retired 1988; Director of Appeals, Royal Air Force Benevolent Fund, since 1988; *b* 24 April 1928; *s* of Alexander John Hurrell and Maria Del Carmen Hurrell (*née* De Biedma); *m* 1950, Jay Jarvis; five *d*. *Educ:* Royal Masonic School, Bushey; St Mary's Hosp., Paddington (MB BS 1952). MRCS, LRCP 1952; Dip Av Med (RCP) 1970; MFOM 1981, FFOM 1987. Joined RAF 1953; served UK, Australia and Singapore; Dep. Dir, Aviation Medicine, RAF, 1974–77; British Defence Staff, Washington DC, 1977–80; CO Princess Alexandra Hosp., RAF Wroughton, 1980–82; Dir, Health and Research, RAF, 1982–84; PMO Strike Command, 1984–86. QHP 1984–88. FRAeS 1987. CStJ 1986. Chadwick Gold Medal, 1970. *Recreations:* walking, climbing, painting, photography. *Address:* Hale House, 4 Upper Hale Road, Farnham, Surrey GU9 0NJ. *T:* Farnham (01252) 714190. *Club:* Royal Air Force.

HURST, George; conductor; *b* 20 May 1926; Rumanian father and Russian mother. *Educ:* various preparatory and public schs. in the UK and Canada; Royal Conservatory, Toronto, Canada. First prize for Composition, Canadian Assoc. of Publishers, Authors and Composers, 1945. Asst Conductor, Opera Dept, Royal Conservatory of Music, of Toronto, 1946; Lectr in Harmony, Counterpoint, Composition etc, Peabody Conservatory of Music, Baltimore, Md, 1947; Conductor of York, Pa, Symph. Orch., 1950–55, and concurrently of Peabody Conservatory Orch., 1952–55; Asst Conductor, LPO, 1955–57, with which toured USSR 1956; Associate conductor, BBC Northern Symphony Orchestra, 1957; Principal Conductor, BBC Northern Symphony Orchestra (previously BBC Northern Orchestra), 1958–68; Artistic Adviser, 1968–73, Staff Conductor, 1968–88, Vice-Pres., 1979, Western Orchestral Soc. (Bournemouth SO and Bournemouth Sinfonietta); Prin. Conductor, Nat. SO of Ireland, 1990–91. Consultant: Nat. Centre of Orchestral Studies, 1980–87; RAM conducting studies consultant, 1983–; Principal Guest Conductor, BBC Scottish Symphony Orchestra, 1986–89. Since 1956 frequent guest conductor in Europe, Israel, Canada. *Publications:* piano and vocal music (Canada). *Recreations:* yachting, horse-riding.

HURST, Henry Ronald Grimshaw; Overseas Labour Adviser, Foreign and Commonwealth Office, 1976–81, retired; *b* 24 April 1919; *s* of Frederick George Hurst and Elizabeth Ellen (*née* Grimshaw); *m* 1st, 1942, Norah Joyce (*d* 1984), *d* of John Stanley Rothwell; one *s* one *d*; 2nd, 1986, Joy Oldroyde (*d* 1991). *Educ:* Darwen and Blackpool Grammar Schs; St Catharine's Coll., Cambridge (MA). Served War, Army, 1940–46. Colonial Service, 1946–70: Permanent Sec., Min. of Labour, Tanzania, 1962–64; Labour Adviser, Tanzania, 1965–68, and Malaŵi, 1969–70; Dep. Overseas Labour Adviser, FCO, 1970–76. *Recreations:* cricket, gardening, golf. *Address:* Flat 1, Meriden, Weston Road, Bath, Avon BA1 2XZ. *T:* Bath (01225) 334429. *Clubs:* Civil Service; Bath and County (Bath); Lansdown Golf.

HURST, John Gilbert, FBA 1987; FSA 1958; Assistant Chief Inspector of Ancient Monuments, English Heritage (formerly Department of the Environment), 1980–87; *b* 15 Aug. 1927; *s* of late Charles Chamberlain and Rona Hurst; *m* 1955, Dorothy Gillian Duckett (*d* 1971); two *d*. *Educ:* Harrow; Trinity Coll., Cambridge (BA Hons Archaeol. 1951; MA 1954). Joined Ancient Monuments Inspectorate, Min. of Works, 1952; Asst Inspector, 1954, Inspector, 1964, (Medieval rescue excavations); Principal Inspector (rescue excavations), 1973–80; directed excavations: Northolt Manor, 1950–70; Norwich, 1951–55; Dir, Wharram Res. Project, 1953–90; Sec., (Deserted) Medieval Village Res. Gp, 1952–86; British Association for Advancement of Science (Sect. H Anthrop.): Sec., 1954–57; Recorder, 1958–62; Pres., 1974; Society for Medieval Archaeology: Treasurer, 1957–76; Pres., 1980–83; Hon. Vice-Pres., 1983–; Vice-Pres., Soc. of Antiquaries of London, 1969–73; President: Soc. for Post-Medieval Archaeology, 1970–72 (Hon. Life Mem., 1993); Medieval Pottery Res. Gp, 1977–80; Southwark and Lambeth Arch. Soc., 1982–84; Hon. Vice-Pres., Medieval Settlement Res. Gp, 1986–. Hon. MRIA 1991. DUniv York 1995. Hon. Mem., Asoc. Española de Arqueología Medieval, Madrid, 1993. Gen. Editor, Wharram Research Project Monographs, 1979–. Legal and General Silver Trowel Award, Archaeologist of the Year, 1990. *Publications include:* Deserted Villages of Oxfordshire, 1965 and Deserted Villages of Northamptonshire, 1966 (both with K. J. A. Allison and M. W. Beresford); (with M. W. Beresford) Deserted Medieval Villages: studies, 1971, 2nd edn 1989; (ed) B. Rackham, Medieval English Pottery, 2nd edn, 1972; (ed with H. Hodges and V. Evison) Medieval Pottery from Excavations, 1974; (with D. S. Neal and H. J. E. Van Beuningen) Pottery Produced and Traded in North West Europe 1350–1650, 1986; (with M. W. Beresford) Wharram Percy: deserted medieval village, 1990; numerous contribs to learned jls. *Recreations:* listening to music, gardening. *Address:* The Old Dairy, 14 Main Street, Great Casterton, Stamford, Lincs PE9 4AP. *T:* Stamford (01780) 57072.

HURST, Peter Thomas; Chief Master of the Supreme Court Taxing Office, since 1992 (Master, 1981–92); *b* Troutbeck, Westmorland, 27 Oct. 1942; *s* of Thomas Lyon Hurst and Nora Mary Hurst; *m* 1968, Diane Irvine; one *s* two *d*. *Educ:* Stonyhurst College. LLB London. Admitted as Solicitor of the Supreme Court, 1967; Partner: Hurst and Walker, Solicitors, Liverpool, 1967–77; Gair Roberts Hurst and Walker, Solicitors, Liverpool, 1977–81. *Publications:* (contrib.) Cordery on Solicitors, 8th edn 1988; (ed jtly) Legal Aid, Halsbury's Laws of England, 4th edn 1994; (ed jtly) Supreme Court Practice, 1995; Butterworth's Costs Service, vol. 2, Solicitors' Remuneration and Costs in Criminal Cases, 1995; Sweet & Maxwell's Civil Costs, 1995. *Recreations:* gardening, music. *Address:* Royal Courts of Justice, Strand, WC2A 2LL. *T:* 0171–936 6000.

HURST, Dr Robert, CBE 1973; GM 1944; FRSC; retired; *b* Nelson, NZ, 3 Jan. 1915; *s* of late Percy Cecil Hurst and late Margery Hurst; *m* 1946, Rachael Jeanette (*née* Marsh); three *s*. *Educ:* Nelson Coll.; Canterbury Coll., NZ (MSc); Cambridge Univ. (PhD). FRIC 1977. Experimental Officer, Min. of Supply, engaged in research in bomb disposal and mine detection, 1940–45. Group Leader Transuranic Elements Group, AERE, Harwell, 1948–55; Project Leader, Homogeneous Aqueous Reactor Project, AERE, Harwell, 1956–57; Chief Chemist, Research and Development Branch, Industrial Group UKAEA, 1957–58; Director, Dounreay Experimental Reactor Establishment, UKAEA, 1958–63; Dir of Res., British Ship Res. Assoc., 1963–76. *Publication:* Editor, Progress in Nuclear Engineering, Series IV (Technology and Engineering), 1957. *Recreation:* gardening. *Address:* 15 Elms Avenue, Parkstone, Poole, Dorset BH14 8EE.

HURT, John; actor; stage, films and television; Director, United British Artists, since 1982; *b* 22 Jan. 1940; *s* of Rev. Arnould Herbert Hurt and Phyllis Massey; *m* 1984, Donna Peacock (marr. diss. 1990); *m* 1990, Jo Dalton; two *s*. *Educ:* The Lincoln Sch., Lincoln; RADA. Started as a painter. *Stage:* début, Arts Theatre, London, 1962; Chips With Everything, Vaudeville, 1962; The Dwarfs, Arts, 1963; Hamp (title role), Edin. Fest., 1964; Inadmissible Evidence, Wyndhams, 1965; Little Malcolm and his Struggle Against the Eunuchs, Garrick, 1966; Belcher's Luck, Aldwych (RSC), 1966; Man and Superman, Gaiety, Dublin, 1969; The Caretaker, Mermaid, 1972; The Only Street, Dublin Fest. and Islington, 1973; Travesties, Aldwych (RSC), 1974; The Arrest, Bristol Old Vic, 1974; The Shadow of a Gunman, Nottingham Playhouse, 1978; The Seagull, Lyric, Hammersmith, 1985; A Month in the Country, Albery, 1994. *Films:* With The Wild and the Willing, 1962; A Man for All Seasons, 1966; Sinful Davey, 1967; Before Winter Comes, 1969; In Search of Gregory, 1970; Mr Forbush and the Penguins, 1971; (Evans in) 10 Rillington Place, 1971; The Ghoul, 1974; Little Malcolm, 1974; East of Elephant Rock, 1977; The Disappearance, The Shout, Spectre, Alien, and Midnight Express (BAFTA award, 1978), all 1978; Heaven's Gate, 1979; The Elephant Man, 1980 (BAFTA award, 1981); History of the World Part 1, 1981; Partners, 1982; Champions, Nineteen Eighty-Four, The Osterman Weekend and The Hit, all 1984; Jake Speed, 1986; Rocinate, 1986; Aria, 1987; White Mischief, 1988; Scandal, 1989; Frankenstein Unbound, 1990; The Field, 1990; King Ralph, 1991; Lapse of Memory, 1991; Dark at Noon, 1992; Second Best, 1994; Even Cowgirls Get the Blues, 1995; Rob Roy, 1995. *Television:* The Waste Places, 1968; The Naked Civil Servant, 1975 (Emmy Award, 1976); Caligula, in I Claudius (series), 1976; Treats, 1977; Crime and Punishment (series), 1979; Deadline, 1988; Poison Candy, 1988; Who Bombed Birmingham, 1990; Red Fox, 1991; Six Characters in Search of an Author, 1992. *Address:* c/o Julian Belfrage, 68 St James's Street, SW1A 1PH. *T:* 0171–491 4400.

HURWITZ, His Honour Vivian Ronald; a Circuit Judge, 1974–91; *b* 7 Sept. 1926; *s* of Alter Max and Dora Rebecca Hurwitz; *m* 1963, Dr Ruth Cohen, Middlesbrough; one *s* two *d*. *Educ:* Roundhay Sch., Leeds; Hertford Coll., Oxford (MA). Served RNVR: Univ. Naval Short Course, Oct. 1944–March 1945, followed by service until March 1947. Called to Bar, Lincoln's Inn, 1952, practised NE Circuit. A Recorder of Crown Court, 1972–74. *Recreations:* junior cricket, bowls, bridge, music (listening), art (looking at), sport—various (watching).

HUSBAND, Prof. Thomas Mutrie, PhD; FEng 1988; FIEE, FIMechE; Vice-Chancellor, University of Salford, since 1990; *b* 7 July 1936; *s* of Thomas Mutrie Husband and Janet Clark; *m* 1962, Pat Caldwell; two *s*. *Educ:* Shawlands Acad., Glasgow; Univ. of Strathclyde. BSc(Eng), MA, PhD. Weir Ltd, Glasgow: Apprentice Fitter, 1953–58; Engr/Jun. Manager, 1958–62; sandwich degree student (mech. engrg), 1958–61; various engrg and management positions with ASEA Ltd in Denmark, UK and S Africa, 1962–65; postgrad. student, Strathclyde Univ., 1965–66; Teaching Fellow, Univ. of Chicago, 1966–67; Lectr, Univ. of Strathclyde, 1967–70; Sen. Lectr, Univ. of Glasgow, 1970–73; Prof. of Manufacturing Organisation, Loughborough Univ., 1973–81; Prof. of Engrg Manufacture, 1981–90, Dir of Centre for Robotics, 1982–90, Hd of Dept of Mech. Engrg, 1983–90, Imperial Coll., London Univ. Member: Standing Cttee for Educn, Training and Competence to Practise, Royal Acad. of Engrg (formerly Fellowship of Engrg), 1989–93; Engrg Technol. Adv. Cttee, DTI, 1990–93; Council, Engrg Council, 1992–; Manufacturing Div. Bd, IEE, 1992–. Non-executive Director: Royal Exchange Theatre, Manchester, 1993–; Univs and Colls Employers Assoc., 1994–. *Publications:* Work Analysis and Pay Structure, 1976; Maintenance and Terotechnology, 1977; Education and Training in Robotics, 1986; articles in Terotechnica, Industrial Relations Jl, Microelectronics and Reliability, etc. *Recreations:* watching Arsenal FC, music, theatre. *Address:* University of Salford, Salford M5 4WT; 34 Hawthorn Lane, Wilmslow SK9 5DG.

HUSH, Prof. Noel Sydney, AO 1993; DSc; FRS 1988; FAA; Foundation Professor and Head of Department of Theoretical Chemistry, University of Sydney, 1971–92, now Professor Emeritus; *b* 15 Dec. 1924; *s* of Sidney Edgar Hush and Adrienne (*née* Cooper); *m* 1949, Thea L. Warman (decd), London; one *s* one *d*. *Educ:* Univ. of Sydney (BSc 1946; MSc 1948); Univ. of Manchester (DSc 1959). FAA 1977. Res. Fellow in Chemistry, Univ. of Sydney, 1946–49; Lectr in Phys. Chem., Univ. of Manchester, 1950–54; Lectr, subseq. Reader in Chem., Univ. of Bristol, 1955–71. Visiting Professor: ANU, 1960; Florida State Univ., 1965; Case Western Reserve Univ., 1968; Cambridge Univ., 1981; Stanford Univ., 1987; Vis. Fellow, Cavendish Lab., 1971; Vis. Sen. Scientist, Brookhaven Nat. Lab., USA, 1959–. Mem., Aust. Res. Grants Cttee, 1984–90 (Chm., Chem. Cttee, 1987–90). Centenary Medal, RSC, 1990; Flinders Medal, Australian Acad. of Science, 1994. Adv. Editor, Chemical Physics, 1973–. *Publications:* (ed) Reactions of Molecules at Electrodes, 1971; papers in Jl of Chemical Physics, Chemical Physics, Jl of Amer. Chemical Soc. *Recreations:* literature, music, travel. *Address:* 170 Windsor Street, Paddington, Sydney, NSW 2021, Australia. *T:* (2) 3281685; Department of Theoretical Chemistry, University of Sydney, Sydney, NSW 2006. *T:* (2) 6923330. *Club:* Athenæum.

HUSKISSON, Robert Andrews, CBE 1979; Chairman, Lloyd's Register of Shipping, 1973–83 (Deputy Chairman, 1972–73); *b* 2 April 1923; *y s* of Edward Huskisson and Mary Huskisson (*née* Downing); *m* 1969, Alice Marian Swaffin. *Educ:* Merchant Taylors' Sch.; St Edmund Hall, Oxford. Served Royal Corps of Signals, 1941–47 (Major). Joined Shaw Savill & Albion Co. Ltd 1947; Dir 1966–72; Dep. Chief Exec., 1971–72; Director: Overseas Containers Ltd, 1967–72; Container Fleets Ltd, 1967–72; Cairn Line of Steamships Ltd, 1969–72. Director: SMIT Internat. Gp (UK) Ltd, 1982–87; Harland and Wolff plc, 1983–87; Lloyd's of London Press, 1983–89. President: British Shipping Fedn, 1971–72 (Chm. 1968–71); International Shipping Fedn, 1969–73; Chairman: Hotels and Catering EDC, 1975–79; Marine Technology Management Cttee, SRC, 1977–81. Dir, Chatham Historical Dockyard Trust, 1984–91; Chm., Essex Nuffield Hosp. Local Adv. Cttee, 1987–91. *Recreations:* golf, music. *Address:* Lanterns, Luppitt Close, Hutton Mount, Brentwood, Essex CM13 2JU. *Clubs:* Vincent's (Oxford); Thorndon Park Golf.

HUSSAIN, Karamat, SQA 1983; retired; Councillor (Lab) Mapesbury Ward, London Borough of Brent, 1971–86; Chairman, National Standing Conference of Afro-Caribbean and Asian Councillors, 1980–86 (Founder Member); *b* Rawalpindi, 1926; *m* Shamim. *Educ:* Aligarh Muslim Univ., India (BA Hons Humanities, MPhil). Political Educn Officer, Brent E, 1967–70. Brent Council: Chm., Planning Cttee, 1978–86; Vice Chm., Develt Cttee, 1978–86; Mem., Housing and Finance Cttees, 1978–86; Mayor of Brent, 1981–82 (Dep. Mayor, 1980–81); formerly Mem. and Vice-Chm., Brent Community Relations Council. Former Member: Regl Adv. Council on Higher Technical Educn, London and Home Counties; ASTMS. Gov., Willesden Coll. of Technology, 1971–86. *Recreation:* research in political philosophy. *Address:* Bungalow 14, Tregwilym Road, Rogerstone, Newport, Gwent NP1 9DW. *T:* Newport (01633) 892187.

HUSSAIN, Mukhtar; QC 1992; a Recorder of the Crown Court, since 1989; *b* 22 March 1950; *s* of late Karam Dad and Rehmi Bi; *m* 1972, Shamim Akhtar Ali; three *d*. *Educ:* William Temple Secondary School. Came to UK, 1964. Called to the Bar, Middle Temple, 1971; Asst Recorder, 1986–89; Head of Chambers, 1992–. Presenter, Granada TV, 1982–87. *Recreations:* cricket, squash, bridge, reading. *Address:* Lincoln House, 1 Brazennose Street, Manchester M2 5EL.

HUSSEIN bin Talal; King of Jordan; *b* 14 Nov. 1935; *s* of late King Talal (*d* 1972) and Queen Zein (*d* 1994); *S* father, 1952; *m* 1st, 1955, Princess Dina (marr. diss.); one *d*; 2nd, 1961, Antoinette Gardiner (marr. diss. 1972); two *s* twin *d*; 3rd, 1972, Alia Baha Eddin Toukan (d 1977); one *s* one *d*; 4th, 1978, Lisa Hallaby, (Queen Noor); two *s* two *d*. *Educ:* Victoria Coll., Alexandria; Harrow; RMA, Sandhurst. Holds many foreign decorations. *Publications:* Uneasy Lies the Head, 1962; My War with Israel, 1969; Mon Metier de Roi, 1975. *Recreations:* water sports, karate, flying, driving, fencing, photography, ham radio. *Address:* Royal Hashemite Court, Amman, Jordan.

HUSSEY, Prof. Joan Mervyn, MA, BLitt, PhD; FSA; FRHistS; Professor of History in the University of London, at Royal Holloway College, 1950–74, now Emeritus. *Educ:* privately; Trowbridge High Sch.; Lycée Victor Duruy, Versailles; St Hugh's Coll., Oxford. Research Student, Westfield Coll., London, 1932–34; Internat. Travelling Fellow (FUW), 1934–35; Pfeiffer Research Fellow, Girton, 1934–37; Gamble Prize, 1935. Asst Lectr in Hist., Univ. of Manchester, 1937–43; Lectr in Hist., 1943–47, Reader in Hist., 1947–50, at Bedford Coll., Univ. of London. Visiting Prof. at Amer. Univ. of Beirut, 1966. Leverhulme Foundn Emeritus Res. Fellow, 1974. Pres., Brit. Nat. Cttee for Byzantine Studies, 1961–71; Hon. Vice-Pres., Internat. Cttee for Byzantine Studies, 1976. Governor, Girton Coll., Cambridge, 1935–37; Mem. Council, St Hugh's Coll., Oxford, 1940–46; Mem. Council, Royal Holloway Coll., 1966–86. Hon. Fellow, St Hugh's Coll., Oxford, 1968; Hon. Res. Associate, RHBNC, 1986. Hon. Fellow, Instituto Siciliano di Studi Bizantini, 1975. *Publications:* Church and Learning in the Byzantine Empire 867–1185, 1937 (repr. 1961); The Byzantine World, 1957, 3rd edn 1966; Cambridge Medieval History IV, Pts I and II: ed and contributor, 1966–67; The Finlay Papers, 1973; The Orthodox Church in the Byzantine Empire, 1986, rev. edn 1990; (ed) Journals and Correspondence of George Finlay, 1995; reviews and articles in Byzantinische Zeitschrift, Byzantinoslavica, Trans Roy. Hist. Soc., Jl of Theological Studies, Jahrbuch der Österreichischen Byzantinistik, Enc. Britannica, Chambers's Enc., New Catholic Enc., etc. *Address:* 16 Clarence Drive, Englefield Green, Egham, Surrey TW20 0NL.

HUSSEY, Marmaduke James; Chairman, Board of Governors: BBC, since 1986; Royal Marsden Hospital, since 1985; Director, Colonial Mutual Group, since 1982; *b* 1923; *s* of late E. R. J. Hussey, CMG and Mrs Christine Hussey; *m* 1959, Lady Susan Katharine Waldegrave (*see* Lady Susan Hussey); one *s* one *d*. *Educ:* Rugby Sch.; Trinity Coll., Oxford (Scholar, MA; Hon. Fellow 1989). Served War of 1939–45, Grenadier Guards, Italy. Joined Associated Newspapers, 1949, Dir 1964; Man. Dir, Harmsworth Publications, 1967–70; joined Thomson Organisation Exec. Bd, 1971; Chief Exec. and Man. Dir, 1971–80, Dir, 1982–86, Times Newspapers Ltd; Jt Chm., Great Western Radio, 1985–86; Dir, William Collins plc, 1985–89. Mem. Bd, British Council, 1983–. Member: Govt Working Party on Artificial Limb and Appliance Centres in England, 1984–86; Management Cttee and Educn Cttee, King Edward's Hosp. Fund for London, 1987–. Pres., Royal Bath and West of England Soc., 1990–91. Trustee: Rhodes Trust, 1972–91; Royal Acad. Trust, 1988–. *Address:* Waldegrave House, Chewton Mendip, near Bath, Somerset BA3 4PD; Flat 15, 45/47 Courtfield Road, SW7 4DB. *T:* 0171–370 1414. *Club:* Brooks's.

See also Sir Francis Brooke, Bt.

HUSSEY, Lady Susan Katharine, DCVO 1984 (CVO 1971); Lady-in-Waiting to the Queen, since 1960; *b* 1 May 1939; 5th *d* of 12th Earl Waldegrave, KG, GCVO; *m* 1959, Marmaduke James Hussey, *qv*; one *s* one *d*. *Address:* Flat 15, 45/47 Courtfield Road, SW7 4DB. *T:* 0171–370 1414.

See also Sir Francis Brooke, Bt.

HUTCHINGS, Andrew William Seymour, CBE 1973; General Secretary, Assistant Masters Association, 1939–78, Joint General Secretary, Assistant Masters and Mistresses Association, Sept–Dec. 1978; Vice-President, National Foundation for Educational Research in England and Wales, since 1983 (Chairman, 1973–83); *b* 3 Dec. 1907; *o s* of William Percy and Mellony Elizabeth Louisa Hutchings; unmarried. *Educ:* Cotham Sch., Bristol; St Catharine's Coll., Cambridge (MA). Asst Master: Downside Sch., 1929–30; Methodist Coll., Belfast, 1930–34; Holt Sch., Liverpool, 1934–36; Asst Sec., Asst Masters Assoc., 1936–39; Hon. Sec., Jt Cttee of Four Secondary Assocs, 1939–78; Sec.-Gen. 1954–65, Pres. 1965–71 and 1972–73, Internat. Fedn of Secondary Teachers; Member: Exec. Cttee, World Confedn of Organisations of Teaching Profession, 1954–80; Secondary Schs Examination Council, and subseq. of Schools Council, 1939–78; Norwood Cttee on Curriculum and Examinations in Secondary Schs, 1941–43; Chm., Teachers' Panel, Burnham Primary and Secondary Cttee, 1965–78; Vice-Pres., Associated Examining Bd, 1994– (Chm., 1992–94; Vice-Chm., 1982–92; Chm., Exec. Cttee, 1979–92). FEIS 1963; FCP 1975. *Publications:* educnl and professional articles and memoranda for Asst Masters Assoc. *Address:* Lower Eastacott House, Umberleigh, North Devon EX37 9AJ. *T:* Chittlehamholt (01769) 540486. *Club:* Kennel.

HUTCHINGS, Gregory Frederick; Chairman, Tomkins PLC (Director, since 1983; Chief Executive, 1984). *Educ:* Uppingham Sch.; University of Aston. BSc, MBA. *Address:* Tomkins PLC, East Putney House, 84 Upper Richmond Road, SW15 2ST. *T:* 0181–871 4544.

HUTCHINS, Captain Ronald Edward, CBE 1961; DSC 1943; RN; *b* 7 Jan. 1912; *s* of Edward Albert Hutchins and Florence Ada (*née* Sharman); *m* 1937, Irene (*née* Wood); two *s*. *Educ:* St John's (elem. sch.), Hammersmith; TS Mercury, Hamble, Hants (C. B. Fry); RN Coll., Greenwich. Royal Navy, 1928–61, service in submarines, then Exec. Br. specialising in gunnery; Computer Industry, 1961–79: Manager and Company Dir, ICL and some of its UK subsids, and associated engrg cos. *Recreations:* walking, gardening. *Address:* 11 Virginia Beeches, Callow Hill, Virginia Water, Surrey GU25 4LT.

HUTCHINSON; *see* Hely-Hutchinson.

HUTCHINSON, family name of **Baron Hutchinson of Lullington.**

HUTCHINSON OF LULLINGTON, Baron *cr* 1978 (Life Peer), of Lullington in the County of E Sussex; **Jeremy Nicolas Hutchinson,** QC 1961; *b* 28 March 1915; *o s* of late St John Hutchinson, KC; *m* 1st, 1940, Dame Peggy Ashcroft (marr. diss. 1966; she *d* 1991); one *s* one *d*; 2nd, 1966, June Osborn. *Educ:* Stowe Sch.; Magdalen Coll., Oxford. Called to Bar, Middle Temple, 1939, Bencher 1963. RNVR, 1939–46. Practised on Western Circuit, N London Sessions and Central Criminal Court. Recorder of Bath, 1962–72; a Recorder of the Crown Court, 1972–76. Member: Cttee on Immigration Appeals, 1966–68; Cttee on Identification Procedures, 1974–76. Prof. of Law, RA, 1987–. Mem., Arts Council of GB, 1974–79 (Vice-Chm., 1977–79); Trustee: Tate Gallery, 1977–84 (Chm., 1980–84); Chantrey Bequest, 1977–. *Address:* House of Lords, Westminster, SW1A 0PW. *Club:* MCC.

HUTCHINSON, Arthur Edward; QC 1979; **His Honour Judge Arthur Hutchinson;** a Circuit Judge, since 1984; *b* 31 Aug. 1934; *s* of late George Edward Hutchinson and Kathleen Hutchinson; *m* 1967, Wendy Pauline Cordingley, one *s* two *d*. *Educ:* Silcoates Sch.; Emmanuel Coll., Cambridge (MA). Commissioned, West Yorkshire Regt, 1953; served in Kenya with 5th Fusiliers, 1953–54. Called to Bar, Middle Temple, 1958; joined NE Circuit, 1959; a Recorder, 1974–84. *Recreations:* cricket, gardening, music. *Address:* c/o The Court House, Oxford Row, Leeds LS1 3BE. *T:* Leeds (0113) 245 1616.

HUTCHINSON, (George) Malcolm, CB 1989; CEng, FIEE; Managing Director, Docklands Light Railway, since 1992; *b* 24 Aug. 1935; *s* of Cecil George Hutchinson and Annie Hutchinson; *m* 1958, Irene Mary Mook; four *d*. *Educ:* Pocklington Sch.; Queens' Coll., Cambridge (MA). Develt Engr, Metropolitan Vickers, 1957; short service commn, 1958, regular commn, 1961, REME; RMCS, 1967; sc Camberley, 1968; CO 12 Armd Workshop, REME, 1968–70; Staff appts, 1970–74; British Liaison Officer, USA Army Materiel Comd, 1974–76; Comdr REME 1 British Corps troops, 1977–79; REME staff, 1979–82; Project Man., Software Systems, 1982–85; Dep. to DGEME, 1985–86; Dir Procurement Strategy MoD(PE), 1986–88; Vice Master-Gen. of the Ordnance, 1988–90.

Mem., Defence Prospect Team, 1990. Procurement and logistic consultant, 1991–92. Mem., Engrg Council, 1993–. Pres., IEEIE, 1990–94. Col Comdt, REME, 1991–. *Recreations:* Rugby, cricket, sailing. *Address:* Rectory Cottage, Little Ann, Andover, Hants SP11 7NR.

HUTCHINSON, Prof. George William, MA, PhD, Cantab; Professor of Physics, Southampton University, 1960–85, now Emeritus; *b* Feb. 1921; *s* of George Hutchinson, farmer, and Louisa Ethel (*née* Saul), Farnsfield, Notts; *m* 1943, Christine Anne (marr. diss. 1970), *d* of Matthew Rymer and Mary (*née* Proctor), York; two *s*. *Educ:* Abergele Grammar Sch.; Cambridge. MA 1946, PhD 1952, Cantab. State Schol. and Schol. of St John's Coll., Cambridge, 1939–42. Research worker and factory manager in cotton textile industry, 1942–47; Cavendish Lab., Cambridge, 1947–52; Clerk-Maxwell Schol. of Cambridge Univ., 1949–52; Nuffield Fellow, 1952–53, and Lecturer, 1953–55, in Natural Philosophy, University of Glasgow; Research Assoc. of Stanford Univ., Calif, 1954. Lecturer, 1955, Sen. Lectr, 1957, in Physics, University of Birmingham. Member: Nat. Exec. Cttee, AUT, 1978–84; Nat. Council, CND, 1981–84; Internat. Sec., Scientists Against Nuclear Arms, 1985–90; Exec. Cttee, British Peace Assembly, 1988–92 (Acting Chm., 1990–92; Chm., 1992); Exec. Cttee, World Disarmament Campaign UK, 1988. Exec. Cttee, Labour Action for Peace, 1990– (Membership Sec., 1992–). Duddell Medal, Physical Soc., 1959. FRAS; FRSA. *Publications:* papers on nuclear and elementary particle physics, nuclear instrumentation and cosmic rays, and disarmament and peace. *Recreations:* music, travel. *Address:* Physical Laboratory, University of Southampton, Southampton SO9 5NH. *T:* Southampton (0703) 595000.

HUTCHINSON, (John) Maxwell, PPRIBA; Founder Member, The Hutchinson Studio, Architects Ltd, since 1993; *b* 3 Dec. 1948; *s* of late Frank Maxwell Hutchinson and Elizabeth Ross Muir (*née* Wright); marr. diss. *Educ:* Wellingborough Prep. Sch.; Oundle; Scott Sutherland Sch. of Arch., Aberdeen; Architectural Assoc. Sch. of Arch. (AA Dip. 1972); RIBA 1972. Founder, Hutchinson and Partners, Chartered Architects, 1972, Chm., 1987–93. Chairman: Permarock Products Ltd, Loughborough, 1985. Royal Institute of British Architects: Mem. Council, 1978–93, Sen. Vice Pres., 1988–89, Pres., 1989–91; Chm., East Midlands Arts Bd Ltd, 1991–95. Vis. Prof., Arch. and Planning Dept, QUB, 1989–93; Special Prof. of Architecture, Nottingham Univ., 1993–. Chm., British Architectural Library Trust, 1991–. Associate Mem., PRS, 1988. Trustee, St George's, Bloomsbury, 1988–. FRSA. Liveryman, Co. of Chartered Architects. Regular radio and TV broadcaster and writer. *Compositions:* The Kibbo Kift, Edinburgh Fest., 1976; The Ascent of Wilberforce III, Lyric Hammersmith, 1982; Requiem in a Village Church (choral), 1986; St John's Cantata, 1987. *Publication:* The Prince of Wales: right or wrong?, 1989. *Recreations:* composing, recording, playing the guitar loudly, cooking. *Address:* (office) 15 Stukeley Street, WC2B 5LT. *T:* 0171–404 6727; Noel Gay Artists, 76 Oxford Street, WC2H 8NA. *Club:* Athenæum.

HUTCHINSON, Malcolm; *see* Hutchinson, G. M.

HUTCHINSON, Maxwell; *see* Hutchinson, J. M.

HUTCHINSON, Patricia Margaret, CMG 1981; CBE 1982; HM Diplomatic Service, retired; *b* 18 June 1926; *d* of late Francis Hutchinson and Margaret Peat. *Educ:* abroad; St Paul's Girls' Sch.; Somerville Coll., Oxford (PPE, MA, Hon Fellow, 1980). ECE, Geneva, 1947; Bd of Trade, 1947–48; HM Diplomatic Service, 1948: 3rd Sec., Bucharest, 1950–52; Foreign Office, 1952–55; 2nd (later 1st) Sec., Berne, 1955–58; 1st Sec. (Commercial), Washington, 1958–61; FO, 1961–64; 1st Sec., Lima, 1964–67 (acted as Chargé d'Affaires); Dep. UK Permanent Rep. to Council of Europe, 1967–69; Counsellor: Stockholm, 1969–72; UK Delegn to OECD, 1973–75; Consul-Gen., Geneva, 1975–80; Ambassador to Uruguay, 1980–83; Consul-Gen., Barcelona, 1983–86. Pres., Somerville ASM, 1988–91. *Recreations:* music, reading. *Address:* 118A Ashley Gardens, SW1P 1HL. *Club:* United Oxford & Cambridge University.

HUTCHINSON, Prof. Philip, CPhys, CEng; Head of School of Mechanical Engineering, Cranfield University (formerly Institute of Technology), since 1987; *b* 26 July 1938; *s* of George and Edna Hutchinson; *m* 1960, Joyce Harrison; one *s* one *d*. *Educ:* King James 1st Grammar Sch., Bishop Auckland, Co. Durham; King's Coll., Univ. of Durham (BSc); Univ. of Newcastle upon Tyne (PhD). MInstP. SO and SSO, Theoretical Phys. Div., AERE, Harwell, 1962–69; Vis. Fellow, Chem. Engrg Dept, Univ. of Houston, Texas, 1969–70; AERE, Harwell: SSO and PSO, Theoretical Phys Div., 1970–75; Hd of Thermodynamics and Fluid Mechanics Gp, Engrg Scis Div., 1975–80; Hd of Engrg Phys Br., Engrg Scis Div., 1980–85; Hd of Engrg Scis Div., 1985–87; Hd, Harwell Combustion Centre, 1980–87. Visiting Professor: Imperial Coll., London, 1980–85; Univ. of Leeds, 1985–. Chairman: Internat. Energy Agency Exec. Cttee on Fundamental Res. in Combustion, 1977–81; Combustion Phys Gp of InstP, 1985–89; MRI 1989; Mem., Combustion Inst., 1977–; Past Mem., Watt Cttee on Energy, representing InstP and Combustion Inst. respectively; Founding Bd Mem., Europ. Research Community on Flow Turbulence and Combustion, 1988 (Chm., 1994–). 27th Leonardo da Vinci Lectr for IMechE, 1983. *Publications:* papers in learned jls on statistical mechanics, fluid mechanics, combustion and laser light scattering. *Recreations:* squash, music, reading, Go, gadgets. *Address:* School of Mechanical Engineering, Cranfield University, Cranfield, Beds MK43 0AL; 127 Blackmoor Gate, Furzton, Milton Keynes MK4 1DJ. *T:* Milton Keynes (01908) 504060.

HUTCHINSON, Richard Hampson; His Honour Judge Hutchinson; a Circuit Judge, since 1974; *b* 31 Aug. 1927; *s* of late John Riley Hutchinson and May Hutchinson; *m* 1954, Nancy Mary (*née* Jones); two *s* three *d*. *Educ:* St Bede's Grammar Sch., Bradford; UC Hull. LLB London. National Service, RAF, 1949–51. Called to Bar, Gray's Inn, 1949; practised on NE Circuit, 1951–74. Recorder: Rotherham, 1971–72; Crown Court, 1972–74; Hon. Recorder of Lincoln, 1991; Resident Judge, Lincoln Crown Court. Mem., County Court Rules Cttee, 1990–94; Technical Rep., Central Council of Probation Cttees, 1989–. *Recreations:* reading, conversation. *Address:* c/o Lincoln Combined Court Centre, 360 High Street, Lincoln LN5 7RL.

HUTCHINSON, Hon. Sir Ross, Kt 1977; DFC 1944; Speaker, Legislative Assembly, Western Australia, 1974–77, retired; MLA (L) Cottesloe, 1950–77; *b* 10 Sept. 1914; *s* of Albert H. Hutchinson and Agnes L. M. Hutchinson; *m* 1939, Amy Goodall Strang; one *s* one *d*. *Educ:* Wesley Coll. RAAF, 1942–45. School teacher, 1935–49. Chief Sec., Minister for Health and Fisheries, 1959–65; Minister for Works and Water Supplies, 1965–71. Australian Rules Football, former Captain Coach; East Fremantle, West Perth and South Fremantle; Captain Coach, WA, 1939. *Recreations:* tennis, reading. *Address:* 42 Griver Street, Cottesloe, WA 6011, Australia. *T:* 312680. *Club:* Royal King's Park Tennis (Perth, WA).

HUTCHISON, Rt. Rev. Andrew; *see* Montreal, Bishop of.

HUTCHISON, Hon. Sir Douglas; *see* Hutchison, Hon. Sir J. D.

HUTCHISON, Geordie Oliphant; Managing Director, Calders & Grandidge, timber importers and manufacturers, since 1974; *b* 11 June 1934; *s* of late Col Ronald Gordon Oliphant Hutchison and of Ruth Gordon Hutchison-Bradburne; *m* 1964, Virginia Barbezat; two *s* one *d*. *Educ:* Eton Coll. Served RN, 1952–54: commnd as aircraft pilot, 1953. Calders Ltd, 1954–59; Calders & Grandidge Ltd, 1959–: Dir, 1969. Comr, Forestry Commn, 1981–89. *Recreations:* golf, shooting. *Address:* Swallowfield House, Welby, Grantham, Lincs NG32 3LR. *T:* Loveden (01400) 230510. *Club:* Royal and Ancient Golf (St Andrews).

HUTCHISON, Lt-Comdr Sir (George) Ian Clark, Kt 1954; Royal Navy, retired; Member of the Queen's Body Guard for Scotland, Royal Company of Archers; *b* 4 Jan. 1903; *e s* of late Sir George Clark Hutchison, KC, MP, Eriska, Argyllshire; *m* 1926, Sheena (*d* 1966), *o d* of late A. B. Campbell, WS; one *d*. *Educ:* Edinburgh Academy; RN Colleges, Osborne and Dartmouth. Joined Navy as Cadet, 1916; Lieut, 1926; Lieut-Comdr 1934; specialised in torpedoes, 1929; emergency list, 1931; Mem., Edinburgh Town Council, 1935–41; Chm., Public Assistance Cttee, 1937–39; contested Maryhill Div. of Glasgow, 1935; rejoined Navy Sept. 1939; served in Naval Ordnance Inspection Dept, 1939–43; MP (U) for West Div. of Edinburgh, 1941–59. Mem. National Executive Council of British Legion (Scotland), 1943–51; Governor of Donaldson's Sch. for the Deaf, Edinburgh, 1937–75; Mem. Cttee on Electoral Registration, 1945–46; Mem. Scottish Leases Cttee, 1951–52. DL County of City of Edinburgh, 1958–84. *Recreations:* golf, fishing, walking, philately. *Address:* 16 Wester Coates Gardens, Edinburgh EH12 5LT. *T:* 0131–337 4888. *Club:* New (Edinburgh).
See also *J. V. Paterson.*

HUTCHISON, Helena Ann, (Mrs Iain Hutchison); *see* Kennedy, H. A.

HUTCHISON, Lt-Comdr Sir Ian Clark; *see* Hutchison, Sir G. I. C.

HUTCHISON, (Joseph) Douglas, CBE 1972; MC 1944; TD 1952; Director, Ranks Hovis McDougall Ltd, 1956–83; *b* 3 April 1918; *s* of late John K. Hutchison, Kinloch, Collessie, Fife and late Ethel Rank, OBE; unmarried. *Educ:* Loretto; Clare Coll., Cambridge. BA Agric. 1939. Served Fife and Forfar Yeomanry, 1939–46 (Major); comd Regt, 1951–53. Director: R. Hutchison & Co. Ltd, 1951–73; Ranks Ltd (later RHM), 1956. Mem., ARC, 1973–78. Pres., Nat. Assoc. British and Irish Millers, 1963–64 and 1974–75; Pres., Research Assoc. Flour Millers and Bakers, 1967–72; Chm., Game Conservancy, 1970–75. *Recreations:* gardening, music. *Address:* Bolfracks, Aberfeldy, Perthshire PH15 2EX. *Club:* New (Edinburgh).

HUTCHISON, Rt Hon. Sir Michael, Kt 1983; PC 1995; **Rt Hon. Lord Justice Hutchison;** a Lord Justice of Appeal, since 1995; *b* 13 Oct. 1933; *s* of Ernest and Frances Hutchison; *m* 1957, Mary Spettigue; two *s* three *d*. *Educ:* Lancing; Clare College, Cambridge (MA). Called to Bar, Gray's Inn, 1958, Bencher, 1983; a Recorder, 1975–83; QC 1976; a Judge of the High Court, QBD, 1983–95; Judge, Employment Appeal Tribunal, 1984–87; Presiding Judge, Western Circuit, 1989–92. Member: Judicial Studies Bd, 1985–87; Parole Bd, 1987–89. *Address:* Royal Courts of Justice, Strand, WC2A 2LL.

HUTCHISON, Sir Peter, 2nd Bt, *cr* 1939; *b* 27 Sept. 1907; *er s* of Sir Robert Hutchison, 1st Bt, MD, CM, and Lady Hutchison; *S* father 1960; *m* 1949, Mary-Grace (*née* Seymour); two *s* two *d*. *Educ:* Marlborough; Lincoln Coll., Oxford (MA). Admitted as a Solicitor, 1933. Dep.-Clerk of the Peace and of the CC, E Suffolk, 1947–71, Clerk of the Peace, 1971. Mem., Suffolk Coastal DC, 1973–83. Chm. of Governors, Orwell Park Prep. Sch., 1975–85. *Recreations:* gardening, reading. *Heir:* *s* Robert Hutchison [*b* 25 May 1954; *m* 1987, Anne Margaret, *er d* of Sir Michael Thomas, Bt, *qv*; two *s*]. *Address:* Melton Mead, near Woodbridge, Suffolk IP12 1PF. *T:* Woodbridge (013943) 2746.

HUTCHISON, Sir Peter Craft, 2nd Bt *cr* 1956; CBE 1992; Chairman, Hutchison & Craft Ltd, Insurance Brokers, Glasgow, since 1979; Vice-Chairman, British Waterways Board, since 1989 (Member, since 1987); Chairman, Forestry Commission, since 1994; *b* 5 June 1935; *s* of Sir James Riley Holt Hutchison, 1st Bt, DSO, TD, and Winefryde Eleanor Mary (*d* 1988), *d* of late Rev. R. H. Craft; *S* father, 1979; *m* 1966, Virginia, *er d* of late John Millar Colville, Gribloch, Kippen, Stirlingshire; one *s*. *Educ:* Eton; Magdalene Coll., Cambridge. Mem., Scottish Tourist Bd, 1981–87; Chm., Loch Lomond and Trossachs Wkg Party, 1991–92. Chm. of Trustees, Royal Botanic Gdn, Edinburgh, 1985–94; Mem. Bd, Scottish Natural Heritage, 1994–. Deacon, Incorporation of Hammermen, 1984–85. *Heir:* *s* James Colville Hutchison, *b* 7 Oct. 1967. *Address:* Milton House, Milton, by Dumbarton G82 2TU.

HUTCHISON, Robert Edward; Keeper, Scottish National Portrait Gallery, 1953–82, retired; *b* 4 Aug. 1922; *y s* of late Sir William Hutchison; *m* 1946, Heather, *d* of late Major A. G. Bird; one *s* one *d*. *Educ:* Gresham's Sch., Holt. Served War, 1940–46, Infantry and RA; Asst Keeper, Scottish National Portrait Gallery, 1949. Hon. MA Edinburgh, 1972. *Publication:* (with Stuart Maxwell) Scottish Costume 1550–1850, 1958. *Address:* Ivory Court, Langriggs, Haddington, East Lothian EH41 4BY. *T:* Haddington (01620) 823213.

HUTCHISON, Sidney Charles, CVO 1977 (LVO 1967); Hon. Archivist, Royal Academy of Arts, since 1982; *b* 26 March 1912; *s* of late Henry Hutchison; *m* 1937, Nancy Arnold Brindley (*d* 1985); no *c*. *Educ:* Holloway Sch., London; London Univ. (Dip. in Hist. of Art, with Dist.). Joined staff of Royal Academy, 1929. Served War of 1939–45: Royal Navy, rising to Lieut-Comdr (S), RNVR. Librarian of Royal Academy, 1949–68, also Sec. of Loan Exhibitions, 1955–68; Sec., Royal Academy, 1968–82, Hon. Mem. (Antiquary), 1992–. Secretary: E. A. Abbey Meml Trust Fund for Mural Painting, 1960–87; Incorporated E. A. Abbey Scholarships Fund, 1965–92; E. Vincent Harris Fund for Mural Decoration, 1970–87; British Institution Fund, 1968–82; Chantrey Trustees, 1968–82; Richard Ford Award Fund, 1977–82. Lectr in the History of Art, for Extra-Mural Dept of Univ. of London, 1957–67. Gen. Comr of Taxes, 1972–87. Governor, Holloway Sch., 1969–81. Trustee, Chantrey Bequest, 1982–; Pres., Southgate Soc. of Arts, 1983–. Organist and Choirmaster of St Matthew's, Westminster, 1933–37. Associate Mem., ICOM, 1964. FRSA 1950; FSA 1955; FMA 1962; Fellow, Assoc. of Art Historians, 1974. Officer, Polonia Restituta, 1971; Chevalier, Belgian Order of the Crown, 1972; Grand Decoration of Honour (silver), Austria, 1972; Cavaliere Ufficiale, Al Merito della Repubblica Italiana, 1980. *Publications:* The Homes of the Royal Academy, 1956; The History of the Royal Academy, 1768–1968, 1968, enl. and updated, 1768–1986, 1986; articles for Walpole Society, Museums Jl, Encyclopædia Britannica, DNB, Apollo, etc. *Recreations:* music, travel. *Address:* 60 Belmont Close, Mount Pleasant, Cockfosters, Herts EN4 9LT. *T:* 0181–449 9821. *Clubs:* Athenæum, Arts.

HUTCHISON, Prof. Terence Wilmot, FBA 1992; Professor of Economics, University of Birmingham, 1956–78, now Emeritus Professor; Dean of the Faculty of Commerce and Social Science, 1959–61; *b* 13 Aug. 1912; *m* 1st, 1935, Loretta Hack (*d* 1981); one *s* two *d*; 2nd, 1983, Christine Donaldson. *Educ:* Tonbridge Sch.; Peterhouse, Cambridge. Lector, Univ. of Bonn, 1935–38; Prof., Teachers' Training Coll., Bagdad, 1938–41. Served Indian Army, in intelligence, in Middle East and India, 1941–46; attached to Govt of India, 1945–46. Lecturer, University Coll., Hull, 1946–47; Lecturer, 1947–51 and Reader, 1951–56, London Sch. of Economics. Visiting Professor: Columbia Univ., 1954–55; Univ. of Saarbrücken, 1962, 1980; Yale Univ., 1963–64; Dalhousie Univ., 1970; Keio Univ., Tokyo, 1973; Univ. of WA, 1975; Univ. of California, Davis, 1978; Visiting

Fellow: Univ. of Virginia, 1960; Aust. Nat. Univ., Canberra, 1967. Mem. Council, Royal Economic Soc., 1967–72. *Publications:* The Significance and Basic Postulates of Economic Theory, 1938 (2nd edn 1960); A Review of Economic Doctrines 1870–1929, 1953; Positive Economics and Policy Objectives, 1964; Economics and Economic Policy 1946–66, 1968; Knowledge and Ignorance in Economics, 1977; Keynes *v* the Keynesians, 1977; Revolutions and Progress in Economic Knowledge, 1978; The Politics and Philosophy of Economics, 1981; Before Adam Smith, 1988; Changing Aims in Economics, 1992; The Uses and Abuses of Academic Economics, 1994; articles, reviews in jls. *Address:* 75 Oakfield Road, Selly Park, Birmingham B29 7HL. *T:* 0121–472 2020.

See also Ven. W. C. L. Filby.

HUTCHISON, Thomas Oliver, FRSE; Deputy Governor, Bank of Scotland, since 1991 (Director, since 1985); Director, Bank of Wales, since 1993; *b* 3 Jan. 1931; *s* of late James Hutchison and Thomasina Oliver; *m* 1955, Frances Mary Ada Butterworth; three *s*. *Educ:* Hawick High Sch.; Univ. of St Andrews (BSc Hons First Cl. Natural Philosophy). Joined ICI General Chemicals Division, 1954; key prodn, technical and commercial appts on general chemicals side of the Company's business until apptd Head of ICI's Policy Groups Dept, London, 1974; Dep. Chm., ICI Plastics Div., 1977–79; Chairman: ICI Petrochemicals and Plastics Div., 1981–85; Phillips-Imperial Petroleum, 1982–85; Dir, ICI plc, 1985–91. Director: Océ Finance Ltd, 1977–79; ICI Australia, 1985–91; ICI Impkemix Investments Pty, 1985–91; Enterprise Oil, 1987–90; Hammerson Group, 1991–; AMP Asset Management, 1991–; Dep. Chm., Cadbury Schweppes, 1992–; (Dir, 1985–). Mem. Council, British Plastics Fedn, 1977–80; Pres., Assoc. of Plastics Manufacturers in Europe, 1980–82; Mem., Cttee of Dirs and Associate, Corporate Assembly Membership, CEFIC, 1986–91. FRSE 1991. *Recreations:* tennis, golf, opera, music. *Address:* Bank of Scotland, 38 Threadneedle Street, EC2P 2EH. *T:* 0171–601 6666. *Clubs:* Athenæum, Royal Automobile.

HUTCHISON, Prof. William McPhee; Personal Professor in Parasitology, University of Strathclyde, 1971–89, now Emeritus; *b* 2 July 1924; *s* of William Hutchison and Ann McPhee; *m* 1963, Ella Duncan McLaughland; two *s*. *Educ:* Eastwood High Sch.; Glasgow Univ. BSc, PhD, DSc; FLS, FIBiol, CBiol; FRSE. Glasgow Univ. Fencing Blue, 1949; Ford Epée Cup; Glasgow Univ. Fencing Champion, 1950 (McLure Foil Trophy, 1950). Strathclyde Univ.: Asst Lectr, 1952; Lectr, 1953; Sen. Lectr, 1969. Engaged in res. on Toxoplasma and toxoplasmosis; discoverer of life cycle of Toxoplasma, 1968–70. Robert Koch Medal, 1970. *Publications:* contrib. Trans Royal Soc. Trop. Med. and Hygiene, Ann. Tropical Med. Parasitology, BMJ. *Recreations:* general microscopy, academic heraldry, collection of zoological specimens. *Address:* 597 Kilmarnock Road, Newlands, Glasgow G43 2TH. *T:* 0141–637 4882.

HUTSON, John Whiteford, OBE 1966; HM Diplomatic Service, retired; Consul-General, Casablanca, 1984–87; *b* 21 Oct. 1927; *s* of John Hutson and Jean Greenlees Laird; *m* 1954, Doris Kemp; one *s* two *d*. *Educ:* Hamilton Academy; Glasgow Univ. (MA (Hons)). MIL 1987. HM Forces, 1949–51; Foreign Office, 1951; Third Secretary, Prague, 1953; FO, 1955; Second Sec., Berlin, 1956; Saigon, 1959; First Sec., 1961; Consul (Commercial) San Francisco, 1963–67; First Sec. and Head of Chancery, Sofia, 1967–69; FCO, 1969; Counsellor, 1970; Baghdad, 1971–72; Inspector, FCO, 1972–74; Head, Communications Operations Dept, FCO, 1974–76; Counsellor (Commercial), Moscow, 1976–79; Consul-Gen., Frankfurt, 1979–83.

HUTT, Rev. Canon David Handley; Canon and Steward, Westminster Abbey, since 1995; *b* 24 Aug. 1938; *s* of late Frank and of Evelyn Hutt. *Educ:* Brentwood; RMA Sandhurst; King's College London (Hanson Prize for Christian Ethics; Barry Prize for Theology; AKC). Regular Army, 1957–64. KCL, 1964–68. Deacon 1969, priest 1970; Curate: Bedford Park, W4, 1969–70; St Matthew, Westminster, 1970–73; Priest Vicar and Succentor, Southwark Cathedral, 1973–78; Sen. Chaplain, King's Coll., Taunton, 1978–82; Vicar: St Alban and St Patrick, Birmingham, 1982–86; All Saints, Margaret St, 1986–95. *Publications:* miscellaneous theol articles and reviews. *Recreations:* gardening, cooking, music, theatre. *Address:* 5 Little Cloister, SW1P 3PL. *T:* 0171–222 6939. *Club:* Athenæum.

HUTTER, Prof. Otto Fred, PhD; Regius Professor of Physiology, University of Glasgow, 1971–90, now Emeritus; *b* 29 Feb. 1924; *s* of Isak and Elisabeth Hutter; *m* 1948, Yvonne T. Brown; two *s* two *d*. *Educ:* Chajes Real Gymnasium, Vienna; Bishops Stortford Coll., Herts; University Coll., London (BSc, PhD). Univ. of London Postgrad. Student in Physiology, 1948; Sharpey Scholar, UCL, 1949–52; Rockefeller Travelling Fellow and Fellow in Residence, Johns Hopkins Hosp., Baltimore, 1953–55; Lectr, Dept of Physiology, UCL, 1953–61; Hon. Lectr, 1961–70. Visiting Prof., Tel-Aviv Univ., 1968, 1970; Scientific Staff, Nat. Inst. for Medical Research, Mill Hill, London, 1961–70. Hon. Mem., Physiological Soc., 1992. Hon. DSc Glasgow Caledonian, 1994. *Publications:* papers on neuromuscular and synaptic transmission, cardiac and skeletal muscle, in physiological jls. *Address:* Institute of Physiology, University of Glasgow, Glasgow G12 8QQ. *T:* 0141–339 8855.

HUTTON, Alasdair Henry, OBE 1990 (MBE 1986); TD 1977; Chairman, Calchon Electronics; Senior Consultant, Coutts Career Consultants, Scotland, since 1994; *b* 19 May 1940; *s* of Alexander Hutton and Margaret Elizabeth (*née* Henderson); *m* 1975, Deirdre Mary Cassels; two *s*. *Educ:* Dollar Academy; Brisbane State High Sch., Australia. Radio Station 4BH, Brisbane, 1956; John Clemenger Advertising, Melbourne, 1957–59; Journalist: The Age, Melb., 1959–61; Press and Journal, Aberdeen, Scotland, 1962–64; Broadcaster, BBC: Scotland, N Ireland, London, Shetland, 1964–79. MEP (C) S Scotland, 1979–89; European Democratic Gp spokesman on regional policy, 1983–87, on budgetary control, 1987–89; contested (C) S Scotland, European Parly Election, 1989 and 1994. Board Member: Scottish Agricl Coll., 1990–; UK 2000 Scotland, 1991–. Chm., Crime Concern, Scotland, 1990–95. Member: Internat. Relns Cttee, Law Soc. of Scotland, 1991–; Church and Nation Cttee, Church of Scotland, 1992–. Presenter, The Business Programme, BBC Radio Scotland, 1989–90; Narrator, Edinburgh Mil. Tattoo, 1992–. Mem., Queen's Body Guard for Scotland, Royal Co. of Archers. Member: Border Union Agricl Soc.; Royal Highland and Agricl Soc. of Scotland. Life mem., John Buchan Soc.; Mem., Edinburgh Sir Walter Scott Club. Trustee, Community Service Volunteers, 1985–. Elder, Kelso N, Church of Scotland. *Recreation:* TA: Watchkeepers and Liaison Officers Pool. *Address:* Rosebank, Shedden Park Road, Kelso, Roxburghshire TD5 7PX. *T:* Kelso (01573) 224369.

HUTTON, Anthony Charles, CB 1995; Deputy Secretary, Principal Establishment and Finance Officer, Department of Trade and Industry, since 1991; *b* 4 April 1941; *s* of Charles James Hutton and Athene Mary (*née* Hastie); *m* 1963, Sara Flemming; two *s* one *d*. *Educ:* Brentwood School; Trinity College Oxford (MA). HM Inspector of Taxes, 1962; Joined Board of Trade, 1964; Private Sec. to 2nd Perm. Sec., 1967–68; Principal Private Sec. to Sec. of State for Trade, 1974–77; Asst Sec., DoT, 1977, DTI, 1983; Under Sec., 84–91. *Recreations:* music, reading, 20th century history. *Address:* Department of Trade and Industry, Ashdown House, 123 Victoria Street, SW1E 6RB. *T:* 0171–215 5000. *Club:* Athenæum.

HUTTON, Brian Gerald; *b* Barrow-in-Furness, 1 Nov. 1933; *s* of James and Nora Hutton; *m* 1958, Serena Quartermaine May; one *s* one *d*. *Educ:* Barrow Grammar Sch.; Nottingham Univ. (BA Hons Hist. 1955); University Coll. London (Dip. Archive Admin. and Churchill Jenkinson prizeman, 1959); Oxford Brookes Univ. (LLB 1995). National Service as Russian Linguist, RN, 1955–57. Asst Archivist, Herts County Record Office, 1959–60; Asst Keeper and Dep. Dir, Public Record Office, N Ireland, also Administrator, Ulster Hist. Foundn and Lectr in Archive Admin., Queen's Univ., Belfast, 1960–74; National Library of Scotland: Asst Keeper, 1974–88; Sec., 1976–88; Dep. Librarian, 1983–88. Chm., Friends of Oxfordshire Museums, 1991–. Commissioned, Kentucky Colonel, 1982. *Publications:* contribs to library and archive jls. *Recreations:* walking in Chilterns, visiting art galleries, listening to music. *Address:* Elma Cottage, The Green, Kingston Blount, Oxon OX9 4SE. *T:* Kingston Blount (01844) 354173; La Casa Bianca, Groppoli, Tuscany, Italy. *Club:* New (Edinburgh).

HUTTON, Gabriel Bruce; His Honour Judge Hutton; a Circuit Judge, since 1978; *b* 27 Aug. 1932; *y s* of late Robert Crompton Hutton, and Elfreda Bruce; *m* 1st, 1963, Frances Henrietta Cooke (*d* 1963); 2nd, 1965, Deborah Leigh Windus; one *s* two *d*. *Educ:* Marlborough; Trinity Coll., Cambridge (BA). Called to Bar, Inner Temple, 1956; Dep. Chm., Glos QS, 1971. A Recorder of the Crown Court, 1972–77. Liaison Judge for Glos, 1987–, and Resident Judge for Gloucester Crown Court, 1990–. Chm., Glos and Wilts Area Criminal Justice Liaison Cttee, 1992–. Chm., Glos Br., CPRE, 1993–. *Recreations:* hunting (Chm., Berkeley Hunt), shooting, fishing. *Address:* Chestal, Dursley, Glos. *T:* Dursley (01453) 543285.

HUTTON, (Hubert) Robin, OBE 1993; Director-General, British Merchant Banking and Securities Houses Association, 1988–92; *b* 22 April 1933; *e s* of late Kenneth Douglas and of Dorothy Hutton; *m* 1st, 1956, Valerie Riseborough (marr. diss. 1967); one *s* one *d*; 2nd, 1969, Deborah Berkeley; two step *d*. *Educ:* Merchant Taylors' Sch.; Peterhouse, Cambridge (Scholar). MA Cantab 1960. Royal Tank Regt, 1952–53 (commnd). Economic Adviser to Finance Corp. for Industry Ltd, 1956–62; economic journalist and consultant; Dir, Hambros Bank Ltd, 1966–70; Special Adviser: to HM Govt, 1970–72; to Min. of Posts and Telecommunications, 1972–73. Chm., Cttee of Inquiry into Public Trustee Office, 1971; Dir of Banking, Insurance and Financial Instns in EEC, Brussels, 1973–78; Exec. Dir, S. G. Warburg & Co. Ltd, 1978–82; Chm., Soc. des Banques S. G. Warburg et Leu SA, Luxembourg, 1979–82; Director-General: Accepting Houses Cttee, 1982–87; Issuing Houses Assoc., 1983–88. Director: Ariel Exchange Ltd, 1982–86; Associated Book Publishers PLC, 1982–87; Northern Rock Building Soc, 1986–; Rock Asset Management Ltd, Rock Asset Management (Unit Trust) Ltd, 1988–93; Singer & Friedlander Hldgs Ltd, 1993–; Chairman: LondonClear Ltd, 1987–89; Homes Intown plc, 1989–94. Dir, IMRO, 1986–; Member: Exec. Cttee, BBA, 1982–92 (Chm., Securities Cttee, 1987–91); Council of Foreign Bondholders, 1983–89; Adv. Cttee, European Business Inst., 1983–94; Chm., Nat. Adv. Cttee on Telecommunications for England, 1985–93. FRSA 1990. *Recreations:* cricket, ski-ing, gardening, travel. *Address:* Church Farm, Athelington, Suffolk IP21 5EJ. *T:* Worlingworth (01728) 628361. *Club:* MCC.

HUTTON, Rt. Hon. Sir (James) Brian (Edward), PC 1988; Kt 1988; Lord Chief Justice of Northern Ireland, since 1988; *b* 29 June 1931; *s* of late James and Mabel Hutton, Belfast; *m* 1975, Mary Gillian Murland; two *d*. *Educ:* Shrewsbury Sch.; Balliol Coll., Oxford (1st Cl. final sch. of Jurisprudence; Hon. Fellow, 1988); Queen's Univ. of Belfast. Called to Northern Ireland Bar, 1954; QC (NI) 1970; Bencher, Inn of Court of Northern Ireland, 1974; called to English Bar, 1972. Junior Counsel to Attorney-General for NI, 1969; Legal Adviser to Min. of Home Affairs, NI, 1973; Sen. Crown Counsel in NI, 1973–79; Judge of the High Court of Justice (NI), 1979–88. Hon. Bencher: Inner Temple, 1988; King's Inns, Dublin, 1988. Mem., Jt Law Enforcement Commn, 1974; Dep. Chm., Boundary Commn for NI, 1985–88. Pres., NI Assoc. for Mental Health, 1983–. Hon. LLD QUB, 1992. *Publications:* articles in Modern Law Review. *Address:* Royal Courts of Justice (Ulster), Belfast BT1 3JF.

HUTTON, Janet; nursing/management adviser, self-employed consultant; *b* 15 Feb. 1938; *d* of Ronald James and Marion Hutton. *Educ:* Gen. Infirmary at Leeds Sch. of Nursing. SRN 1959. Ward Sister, Leeds Gen. Infirmary, 1962–64, 1966–68; Nursing Sister, Australia, 1964–66; Commng Nurse, Lister Hosp., Stevenage, 1968–71; Planning and Develts Nurse, N London, 1971–73; Divl Nursing Officer, Colchester, 1973–79; Dist Nursing officer, E Dorset, 1979–83; Regl Nursing Officer, 1983–88, Quality Assurance Manager, 1986–88, Yorks RHA. *Recreations:* music, needlework, tennis (spectator and participant). *Club:* Soroptimist International of Great Britain and Ireland (Harrogate). *Address:* (office) 62 Westminster Drive, Burn Bridge, Harrogate, HG3 1NW.

HUTTON, John Matthew Patrick; MP (Lab) Barrow and Furness, since 1992; *b* 6 May 1955; *m*; three *s* one *d* (and one *s* decd). *Educ:* Magdalen Coll., Oxford (BA, BCL). Research Associate, Templeton Coll., Oxford, 1980–81; Sen. Lectr, Newcastle Poly., 1981–92. Contested (Lab): Penrith and Borders, 1987; Cumbria and Lancs N (European Parlt), 1989. *Publications:* articles on labour law in Industrial Law Jl. *Recreations:* football, cricket, cinema, soul music. *Address:* House of Commons, SW1A 0AA; 17 Mikasa Street, Walney, Barrow-in-Furness, Cumbria LA14 3ED. *T:* Barrow-in-Furness (01229) 473006; 25 Holland Grove, SW9 9ER. *T:* 0171–820 8538. *Clubs:* Cemetery Cottages Working Men's, Barrow Labour (Barrow-in-Furness).

HUTTON, Prof. John Philip, MA; Professor of Economics and Econometrics, University of York, since 1982; *b* 26 May 1940; *s* of Philip Ernest Michelson Hutton and Hester Mary Black Hutton; *m* 1964, Sandra Smith Reid; one *s* one *d*. *Educ:* Daniel Stewart's Coll., Edinburgh; Edinburgh Univ. (MA 1st Cl.). York University: Junior Research Fellow, 1962; Lecturer, 1963; Sen. Lectr, 1973; Reader, 1976. Economic Adviser, HM Treasury, 1970, 1971; Advr to Malaysian Treasury, 1977, Mem., Technical Assistance Mission, Kenya, 1990, IMF; Consultant to: NEDO, 1963; Home Office, 1966; Royal Commission on Local Govt in England and Wales, 1967; NIESR, 1980. Chairman, HM Treasury Academic Panel, 1980, 1981; Mem. Council, Royal Economic Soc., 1981–86. Jt Managing Editor, Economic Journal, 1980–86; Jt Editor, Bulletin of Economic Research, 1986–91; Associate Editor, Applied Economics, 1986–. *Publications:* contribs to learned jls, incl. Economic Jl, Rev. of Economic Studies, Oxford Economic Papers. *Recreation:* family. *Address:* 1 The Old Orchard, Fulford, York Y01 4LT. *T:* York (01904) 638363.

HUTTON, Kenneth; Chairman, Peterborough Development Agency, 1987–92; *b* 11 May 1931; *s* of Wilks and Gertrude Hutton; *m* 1981, Georgia (*née* Hutchinson); one *s*, and two step *s* one step *d*. *Educ:* Bradford Belle Vue Grammar School; Liverpool University (Thomas Bartlett Scholar; BEng). FICE; FIHT. Graduate Asst, Halifax CBC, 1952–54; Royal Engineers, 1954–56; Sen Engineer, Halifax CBC, 1956–59; Sen. Asst Engineer, Huddersfield CBC, 1959–63; Asst Chief Engineer, Skelmersdale Develt Corp., 1963–66; Dep. Chief Engineer, Telford Develt Corp., 1966–68; Chief Engineer, 1968–84, Gen. Manager, 1984–88, Peterborough Develt Corp. Gov., Peterborough Enterprise Programme, 1988–92. *Recreations:* swimming, bridge, golf, woodworking. *Address:* 4

Sunningdale, Orton Waterville, Peterborough PE2 5UB. *T:* Peterborough (01733) 233719.

HUTTON, Robin; *see* Hutton, H. R.

HUTTON-WILLIAMS, Derek Alfred, MBE 1947; BSc, ACGI; CEng, FIMechE, MIEE; Director-General, Royal Ordnance Factories, 1969–75, retired; *b* 26 April 1914; *s* of William Hutton-Williams and Violet Woodfall Hutton-Williams; *m* 1936, Albrée Freeman; two *d*; *m* 1948, Yvonne Irene Anthony; one *s* one *d*. *Educ:* Oundle Sch.; London Univ. (Kitchener Scholar); grad. NATO Defence Coll., Paris. Pupil, Winget Ltd, Rochester, 1935; Techn. Asst, Royal Arsenal, Woolwich, 1938; Asst to Director, Small Arms and Fuzes, Ordance Factories, in charge of UK production of Sten carbine, 1939; Manager, Royal Ordnance Factory, Theale, Berks, 1942; Dep.-Dir, Housing Supplies, Ministry of Supply, 1945; Partner, Hutton-Williams and Partners (Industrial Consultant), 1946; Supt, Royal Ordnance Factory, Maltby, Yorks, 1949; NATO Defence Coll., 1957; Asst Dir, Guided Weapons Production, Min. of Aviation, 1958; Dir, Inspectorate of Armaments, 1959; Dir, Royal Small Arms Factory, Enfield, 1964. *Recreations:* gardening, building, clock repair, music; recognising and accepting the inevitable; admiring craftsmanship. *Address:* The School House, Palgrave, near Diss, Norfolk IP22 1AG.

HUWS JONES, Robin; *see* Jones.

HUXLEY, Sir Andrew Fielding, OM 1983; Kt 1974; FRS 1955; MA, Hon. ScD Cantab; Master, 1984–90, Fellow, 1941–60 and since 1990, Trinity College, Cambridge (Hon. Fellow, 1967–90); *b* 22 Nov. 1917; *s* of late Leonard Huxley and Rosalind Bruce; *m* 1947, Jocelyn Richenda Gammell Pease; one *s* five *d*. *Educ:* University College Sch.; Westminster Sch. (Hon. Fellow, 1991); Trinity Coll., Cambridge (MA). Operational research for Anti-Aircraft Command, 1940–42, for Admiralty, 1942–45. Demonstrator, 1946–50, Asst Dir of Research, 1951–59, and Reader in Experimental Biophysics, 1959–60, in Dept of Physiology, Cambridge Univ.; Dir of Studies, Trinity Coll., Cambridge, 1952–60; Jodrell Prof., 1960–69 (now Emeritus), Royal Soc. Research Prof., 1969–83, UCL (Hon. Fellow, 1980). Lectures: Herter, Johns Hopkins Univ., 1959; Jesup, Columbia Univ., 1964; Alexander Forbes, Grass Foundation, 1966; Croonian, Royal Society, 1967; Review Lectr on Muscular Contraction, Physiological Soc., 1973; Hans Hecht, Univ. of Chicago, 1975; Sherrington, Liverpool, 1977; Florey, ANU, 1982; John C. Krantz Jr, Maryland Univ. Sch. of Medicine, 1982; Darwin, Darwin Coll., Cambridge, 1982; Romanes, Oxford, 1983; Fenn, IUPS XXIX Internat. Congress, Sydney, 1983; Blackett, Delhi, 1984; Green Coll., Oxford, 1986; Tarner, Trinity Coll., Cambridge, 1988; Maulana Abul Kalam Azad Meml, Delhi, 1991; C. G. Bernhard, Stockholm, 1993. Fullerian Prof. of Physiology and Comparative Anatomy, Royal Institution, 1967–73; Cecil H. and Ida Green Vis. Prof., Univ. of British Columbia, 1980. President: BAAS, 1976–77; Royal Soc., 1980–85 (Mem. Council, 1960–62, 1977–79, 1980–85); Internat. Union of Physiological Scis, 1986–93; Vice-Pres., Muscular Dystrophy Gp of GB, 1980–. Member: ARC, 1977–81; Nature Conservancy Council, 1985–87. Trustee: BM (Nat. Hist.), 1981–91; Science Museum, 1984–88. Hon. Member: Physiolog. Soc., 1979; Amer. Soc. of Zoologists, 1985; Japan Acad., 1988; Hon. MRIA, 1986; Foreign Associate: Nat. Acad. of Scis, USA, 1979; Amer. Philosophical Soc., 1975; Foreign Hon. Member: Amer. Acad. of Arts and Sciences, 1961; Royal Acad. of Medicine, Belgium, 1978; Foreign Fellow, Indian Nat. Science Acad., 1985; Hon. MRI, 1981; Associate Mem., Royal Acad. of Scis, Letters and Fine Arts, Belgium, 1978; Mem., Leopoldina Academy, 1964; Foreign Member: Danish Acad. of Sciences, 1964; Dutch Soc. of Sciences, 1984. Hon. Fellow: Imperial Coll., London, 1980; Darwin Coll., Cambridge, 1981; QMW, London, 1987. Hon. FIBiol 1981; Hon. FRSC (Canada) 1982; Hon. FRSE 1983; Hon. FEng 1986. Hon. MD: University of the Saar, 1964; Ulm, 1993; Hon. DSc: Sheffield, 1964; Leicester, 1967; London, 1973; St Andrews, 1974; Aston, 1977; Western Australia, 1982; Oxford, 1983; Pennsylvania, 1984; Harvard, 1984; Keele, 1985; East Anglia, 1985; Humboldt, E Berlin, 1985; Maryland, 1987; Brunel, 1988; Hyderabad, 1991; Glasgow, 1993; Hon. LLD: Birmingham, 1979; Dundee, 1984; DUniv York, 1981; Hon. DHL New York, 1982; Hon. Dr Marseille Fac. of Medicine, 1979. Nobel Prize for Physiology or Medicine (jtly), 1963; Copley Medal, Royal Soc., 1973. *Publications:* Reflections on Muscle (Sherrington Lectures XIV), 1980; (contrib.) The Pursuit of Nature, 1977; papers in the Journal of Physiology, etc. *Recreations:* walking, shooting, designing scientific instruments. *Address:* Manor Field, 1 Vicarage Drive, Grantchester, Cambridge CB3 9NG. *T* and *Fax:* Cambridge (01223) 840207; Trinity College, Cambridge. *T:* Cambridge (01223) 338586.

HUXLEY, Air Vice-Marshal Brian, CB 1986; CBE 1981; Deputy Controller, National Air Traffic Services, 1985–86; retired 1987; *b* 14 Sept. 1931; *s* of Ernest and Winifred Huxley; *m* 1955, Frances (*née* Franklin); two *s*. *Educ:* St Paul's Sch.; RAF College, Cranwell. Commissioned 1952; No 28 Sqdn, Hong Kong, 1953–55; qual. Flying Instructor, 1956; Cranwell, Central Flying Sch. and No 213 Sqdn, 1956–65; MoD, 1966–68; Chief Flying Instr, Cranwell, 1969–71; Commanding RAF Valley, 1971–73; RAF Staff Coll., 1973–74; RCDS 1975; Defence Intelligence Staff, 1976–77; AOC Mil. Air Traffic Ops, 1978–80; Dir of Control (Airspace Policy), and Chm., Nat. Air Traffic Management Adv. Cttee, 1981–84. Mem., CAA Ops Adv. Cttee, 1987–. Chm., Review of Helicopter Offshore Safety and Survival, 1993–94. *Publications:* contribs to Children's Encyclopaedia Britannica, 1970–72, and to Railway Modeller, 1974–. *Recreations:* Flying Officer RAFVR(T), model-making. *Club:* Royal Air Force.

HUXLEY, Elspeth Josceline, (Mrs Gervas Huxley), CBE 1962; JP; *b* 23 July 1907; *d* of Major Josceline Grant, Njoro, Kenya; *m* 1931, Gervas Huxley (*d* 1971); one *s*. *Educ:* European Sch., Nairobi, Kenya; Reading Univ. (Diploma in Agriculture); Cornell Univ., USA. Asst Press Officer to Empire Marketing Board, London, 1929–32; subsequently travelled in America, Africa and elsewhere; Mem. BBC Gen. Advisory Council, 1952–59; UK Independent Mem., Monckton Advisory Commission on Central Africa, 1959. *Publications:* White Man's Country; Lord Delamere and the Making of Kenya, 2 vols, 1935; Murder at Government House (detective story), 1937, repr. 1987; Murder on Safari (detective story), 1938, repr. 1982; The African Poison Murders, 1939, repr. 1988; Red Strangers (novel), 1939; Atlantic Ordeal, 1943; (with Margery Perham) Race and Politics in Kenya, 1944; The Walled City (novel), 1948; The Sorcerer's Apprentice (travel), 1948; I Don't Mind If I Do (light novel), 1951; Four Guineas (travel), A Thing to Love, 1954; The Red Rock Wilderness, 1957; The Flame Trees of Thika, 1959 (filmed, 1981); A New Earth, 1960; The Mottled Lizard, 1962; The Merry Hippo, 1963; Forks and Hope, 1964; A Man from Nowhere, 1964; Back Street New Worlds, 1965; Brave New Victuals, 1965; Their Shining Eldorado: A Journey through Australia, 1967; Love Among the Daughters, 1968; The Challenge of Africa, 1971; Livingstone and his African Journeys, 1974; Florence Nightingale, 1975; Gallipot Eyes, 1976; Scott of the Antarctic, 1977; Nellie: letters from Africa, 1980; Whipsnade: captive breeding for survival, 1981; The Prince Buys the Manor, 1982; (with Hugo van Lawick) Last Days in Eden, 1984; Out in the Midday Sun: My Kenya, 1985; Nine Faces of Kenya (anthology), 1990; Peter Scott: painter and naturalist, 1993. *Recreations:* resting, gossip. *Address:* Green End, Oaksey, near Malmesbury, Wilts SN16 9TL. *TA:* Oaksey, Malmesbury. *T:* Crudwell (01666) 577252.

HUXLEY, Prof. George Leonard, FSA; MRIA; Hon. Professor, Trinity College Dublin, since 1989 (Research Associate, 1983–89); Professor Emeritus, Queen's University, Belfast, since 1988; *b* Leicester, 23 Sept. 1932; *s* of late Sir Leonard Huxley, KBE and Ella M. C., *d* of F. G. and E. Copeland; *m* 1957, Davina Best; three *d*. *Educ:* Blundell's Sch.; Magdalen Coll., Oxford. 2nd Mods, 1st Greats, Derby Scholar 1955. Commnd in RE, 1951. Fellow of All Souls Coll., Oxford, 1955–61; Asst Dir, British School at Athens, 1956–58; Prof. of Greek, QUB, 1962–83; Dir, Gennadius Library, Amer. Sch. of Classical Studies, Athens, 1986–89. Harvard University: Vis. Lectr, 1958 and 1961; Loeb Lectr, 1986; Leverhulme Fellow, European Sci. Foundn, 1980–81; Vis. Lectr, St Patrick's Coll., Maynooth, 1984–85 and 1993; Vis. Prof., UCSD, 1990. Mem. of Exec., NI Civil Rights Assoc., 1971–72. Member: Managing Cttee, British Sch. at Athens, 1967–79; Irish Nat. Cttee Greek and Latin Studies, 1972–86, 1991–; (Chm., 1976–79); Managing Cttee, Amer. Sch. of Classical Studies, Athens, 1991–; Irish Mem., Standing Cttee on Humanities, European Science Foundn, Strasbourg, 1978–86. Royal Irish Academy: Sec., Polite Literature and Antiquities Cttee, 1979–86; Sen. Vice-Pres., 1984–85; Hon. Librarian, 1990–94; Spl Envoy, 1994–; Member: Bureau, Fédn Internat. d'Etudes Classiques, 1981–89 (Senior Vice-Pres. 1984–89); Academia Europaea, 1990. Hon. LittD TCD, 1984. Cromer Greek Prize, British Acad., 1963. *Publications:* Achaeans and Hittites, 1960; Early Sparta, 1962; The Early Ionians, 1966; Greek Epic Poetry from Eumelos to Panyassis, 1969; (ed with J. N. Coldstream) Kythera, 1972; Pindar's Vision of the Past, 1975; On Aristotle and Greek Society, 1979; Homer and the Travellers, 1988; articles on Hellenic and Byzantine subjects. *Recreation:* siderodromophilia. *Address:* School of Classics, Trinity College, Dublin 2; Forge Cottage, Church Enstone, Oxfordshire OX7 4NN. *Club:* Athenæum.

HUXLEY, Mrs Gervas; *see* Huxley, Elspeth J.

HUXLEY, Hugh Esmor, MBE 1948; MA, PhD, ScD; FRS 1960; Professor of Biology, since 1987, Director, 1988–94, Rosenstiel Basic Medical Sciences Research Center, Brandeis University, Boston, Mass; *b* 25 Feb. 1924; *s* of late Thomas Hugh Huxley and Olwen Roberts, Birkenhead, Cheshire; *m* 1966, Frances Fripp, *d* of G. Maxon, Milwaukee; one *d*, and two step-*s* one step-*d*. *Educ:* Park High Sch., Birkenhead; Christ's Coll., Cambridge (Exhibitioner and Scholar; Hon. Fellow 1981). Natural Science Tripos, Cambridge, 1941–43 and 1947–48 (Pt II Physics); BA 1948, MA 1950, PhD 1952, ScD 1964. Served War of 1939–45, Radar Officer, RAF Bomber Command and Telecommunications Research Establishment, Malvern, 1943–47; Mem. Empire Air Armaments Sch. Mission to Australia and NZ, 1946. Research Student, MRC Unit for Molecular Biology, Cavendish Lab., Cambridge, 1948–52; Commonwealth Fund Fellow, Biology Dept, MIT, 1952–54; Research Fellow, Christ's Coll., Cambridge, 1953–56; Mem. of External Staff of MRC, and Hon. Res. Associate, Biophysics Dept, UCL, 1956–61; Fellow, King's Coll., Cambridge, 1961–67; Scientific Staff, MRC Lab. of Molecular Biol., Cambridge, 1961–87, Dep. Dir, 1977–87; Fellow, Churchill Coll., Cambridge, 1967–87. Ziskind Vis. Prof., Brandeis Univ., 1971; Lectures: Harvey Soc., New York, 1964–65; Hooke, Univ. of Texas, 1968; Dunham, Harvard Med. Sch., 1969; Croonian, Royal Soc., 1970; Mayer, MIT, 1971; Penn, Pennsylvania Univ., 1971; Carter-Wallace, Princeton Univ., 1973; Adam Muller, State Univ. of NY, 1973; Pauling, Stanford, 1980; Jesse Beams, Virginia, 1980; Ida Beam, Iowa, 1981. Member: Council, Royal Soc., 1973–75, 1984–85; President's Adv. Bd, Rosentiel Basic Med. Scis Center, Brandeis Univ., 1971–77; Scientific Adv. Council, European Molecular Biol. Lab., 1976–81. Mem., German Acad. of Sci., Leopoldina, 1964; Hon. Member: Amer. Soc. of Biol Chem., 1976; Amer. Assoc. of Anatomy, 1981; Amer. Physiol. Soc., 1981; Amer. Soc. of Zoologists, 1986; Foreign Hon. Member: Amer. Acad. of Arts and Scis, 1965; Danish Acad. of Scis, 1971; Foreign Associate, US Nat. Acad. of Scis, 1978. Hon. ScD: Harvard, 1969; Leicester, 1989; Hon. DSc: Chicago, 1974; Pennsylvania, 1976. Feldberg Foundation Award for Experimental Medical Research, 1963; William Bate Hardy Prize (Camb. Phil. Soc.) 1965; Louisa Gross Horwitz Prize, 1971; Internat. Feltrinelli Prize, 1974; Gairdner Foundn Award, 1975; Baly Medal, RCP, 1975; Royal Medal, Royal Soc., 1977; E. B. Wilson Award, Amer. Soc. Cell Biology, 1983; Albert Einstein Award, World Cultural Council, 1987; Franklin Medal, Franklin Inst., Philadelphia, 1990; Distinguished Scientist Award, Electron Microscope Soc. of America, 1991. *Publications:* contrib. to learned jls. *Recreations:* ski-ing, sailing. *Address:* Rosenstiel Basic Medical Sciences Research Center, Brandeis University, Waltham, MA 02254, USA. *T:* (617) 7362490.

HUXLEY, Rev. Keith; Rector of Gateshead, Diocese of Durham, since 1983; Chaplain to the Queen, since 1981; *b* 17 Sept. 1933; *s* of George and Eluned Huxley. *Educ:* Birkenhead Sch.; Christ's Coll., Cambridge (MA); Cuddesdon Theol Coll. Curate: St Mary's, Bowdon, 1959–61; Christ Church, Crewe, 1961–62; Chester Diocesan Youth Chaplain, 1962–68; Leader, Runcorn Ecumenical Team Ministry, 1968–75; Vicar, St Andrew's, Runcorn, 1968–73; Rector, East Runcorn Team Ministry, 1973–77; Home Secretary, Bd for Mission and Unity, C of E, 1977–83; RD of Gateshead, 1988–93. Secretary: NE Ecumenical Gp, 1983–94; Durham Ecumenical Relations Gp, 1985–. *Recreation:* ornithology. *Address:* Gateshead Rectory, 91 Old Durham Road, Gateshead, Tyne and Wear NE8 4BS. *T:* 0191–477 3990.

HUXLEY, Paul, RA 1991 (ARA 1987); artist; Professor of Painting, Royal College of Art, since 1986; *b* 12 May 1938; *m* 1st, 1957, Margaret Doria Perryman (marr. diss. 1972); two *s*; 2nd, 1990, Susan Jennifer Metcalfe. *Educ:* Harrow Coll. of Art; Royal Acad. Schs (Cert.). Vis. Prof., Cooper Union, New York, 1974; Vis. Tutor, RCA, 1976. Member: Serpentine Gallery Cttee, 1971–74; Art Panel and Exhibns Sub-Cttee, Arts Council of GB, 1972–76; Exhibn Cttee, Royal Acad., 1989–; Trustee, Tate Gall., 1975–82. Commnd by London Transport to design 22 ceramic murals for King's Cross Underground Stn, 1984; commnd by Rambert Dance Co. to design sets and costumes for Cat's Eye, 1992. *One-man exhibitions:* Rowan Gall., London, 1963, 1965, 1968, 1969, 1971, 1974, 1978, 1980; Juda Rowan Gall., London, 1982; Kornblee Gall., New York, 1967, 1970; Galeria da Emenda, Lisbon, 1974; Forum Kunst, Rottweil, W Germany, 1975; Mayor Rowan Gall., 1989; Galerie zur alten Deutchen Schule, Switzerland, 1992; Gillian Jason Gall., 1993; Gardner Art Centre, Sussex Univ., 1994; *group exhibitions:* Whitechapel Art Gall., London, and Albright-Knox Gall., Buffalo, NY, 1964; Paris Biennale, and Marlborough-Gerson Gall., New York, 1965; Galerie Milano, Milan, 1966; Carnegie Inst., Pittsburgh, 1967; UCLA, Calif (also USA tour), and touring show of Mus. of Modern Art, New York, 1968; Mus. am Ostwall, Dortmund (also Eur. tour), and Tate Gall., 1969; Walker Art Gall., Liverpool, 1973; Hayward Gall., 1974; São Paulo Bienal, and Forum Gall., Leverkusen, 1975; Palazzo Reale, Milan, 1976; Royal Acad., 1977; Nat. Theatre, 1979; Arts Council tour, Sheffield, Newcastle upon Tyne and Bristol, 1980; Museo Municipal, Madrid, and Eastern Arts 4th Nat. Exhibn and British tour, 1983; Juda Rowan Gall., 1985; Kunstlerhaus, Vienna, 1986; Mappin Art Gall., Sheffield, 1988; British Council tour, Eastern Europe, 1990–93; Ready Steady Go, Arts Council tour, 1992–93; *works in public collections:* Tate Gall., V&A Mus. (prints), Arts Council of GB, British Council, Contemp. Arts Soc., Camden Council, DoE, Nuffield Foundn, and Chase Manhattan Bank, London; Swedish Lloyd, London and Stockholm; Whitworth Art Gall., Manchester; Graves Art Gall., Sheffield; Walker Art Gall., Liverpool; City Art Gall., Leeds; Creasey Collection of Modern Art, Salisbury; Leics Educn Authority; Art Gall. of NSW, and Power Inst. of Fine Arts, Sydney; Art Gall. of SA, Adelaide; Stuyvesant Foundn, Holland; Mus. of Modern Art (prints), and Bristol Myers Corp., New York; Albright-Knox Gall., Buffalo, NY; Neuberger Mus., Purchase, NY; Museo Tamayo, Mexico City; Technisches Mus.,

Vienna. *Publication:* (ed) Exhibition Road: painters at the Royal College of Art, 1988. *Address:* 2 Dalling Road, W6 0JB.

HUXLEY, Dr Peter Arthur, PhD; CBiol; FIBiol; agroforestry research/teaching consultant; *b* 26 Sept. 1926; *s* of Ernest Henry Huxley and Florence Agnes (*née* King); *m* 1st, 1954, Betty Grace Anne Foot (marr. diss. 1980); three *s* one *d*; 2nd, 1980, Jennifer Margaret Bell (*née* Pollard); one *s* one *d*. *Educ:* Alleyn's Sch.; Edinburgh Univ.; Reading Univ. (BSc, PhD). FIBiol 1970. RNVR, 1944–46. Asst Lectr to Sen. Lectr, Makerere University Coll., Uganda, 1954–64; Dir of Res., Coffee Res. Foundn, Kenya, 1965–69; Prof. of Horticulture, Univ. of Reading, 1969–74; Prof. of Crop Science, Univ. of Dar es Salaam/FAO, 1974–76; Agric. Res. Adviser/FAO, Agric. Res. Centre, Tripoli, 1977–78; International Council for Research in Agroforestry, Nairobi, 1979–92: Dir, Res. Devlt Div., 1987–90; Principal Res. Advr, 1991–92; private consultant in agroforestry res., educn and trng. Member: Internat. Soc. Horticl Sci.; Internat. Soc. Tropical Forestry; Internat. Assoc. for Ecology; Tropical Agricl Assoc., UK; Associate Mem., Oxford Forestry Inst. FRSA. *Publications:* (ed jtly) Soils Research in Agroforestry, 1980; (ed) Plant Research and Agroforestry, 1983; (ed jtly) Manual of Research Methodology for the Exploration and Assessment of Multipurpose Trees, 1983; (ed jtly) Multipurpose trees: selection and testing for agroforestry, 1989; approx. 130 pubns in agric., horticult., agroforestry, meteorol and agricl botany jls. *Recreations:* music and music-making (double bass), canal narrowboating. *Address:* Flat 4, 9 Linton Road, Oxford OX2 6UH.

HUXSTEP, Emily Mary, CBE 1964; BA London: Headmistress of Chislehurst and Sidcup Girls' Grammar School, Kent, 1944–66; *b* 15 Sept. 1906; *d* of George T. and Nellie M. Huxstep (*née* Wood). *Educ:* Chatham Girls' Grammar Sch.; Queen Mary Coll. Headmistress, Hanson Girls' Grammar Sch., Bradford, Yorks, 1938–44. Hon. DCL Kent, 1974. *Address:* The Loose Valley Nursing Home, Linton Road, Loose, Maidstone, Kent ME15 0AG.

HUXTABLE, Gen. Sir Charles Richard, KCB 1984 (CB 1982); CBE 1976 (OBE 1972; MBE 1961); DL; Commander-in-Chief, United Kingdom Land Forces, 1988–90; Aide-de-Camp General to the Queen, 1988–90; *b* 22 July 1931; *m* 1959, Mary, *d* of late Brig. J. H. C. Lawlor; three *d*. *Educ:* Wellington Coll.; RMA Sandhurst; Staff College, Camberley; psc, jssc. Commissioned, Duke of Wellington's Regt, 1952; Captain, 1958, Major, 1965; GS02 (Ops), BAOR, 1964–65; GS01 Staff College, 1968–70; CO 1 DWR, 1970–72; Col, 1973; MoD, 1974; Brig., Comd Dhofar Bde, 1976–78; Maj.-Gen., 1980; Dir, Army Staff Duties, 1982–83; Comdr, Training and Arms Dirs (formerly Training Estabts), 1983–86; QMG, 1986–88. Colonel: DWR, 1982–90; Col, Royal Irish Regt, 1992–; Colonel Commandant: The King's Div., 1983–88; UDR, 1991–92. Pres., Ex-Services Mental Welfare Soc., 1990–. DL N Yorks, 1994. *Address:* c/o Lloyds Bank, 23 High Street, Teddington, Middlesex TW11 8EX.

HUYDECOPER, Jonkheer (Jan Louis) Reinier, Hon. GCVO 1982 (Hon. KCVO 1972); Commander, Order of Orange Nassau, 1986 (Officer, 1966); Chevalier, Order of Netherlands Lion, 1980; Ambassador of the Netherlands to the Court of St James's, and concurrently to Iceland, 1982–86; *b* 23 Feb. 1922; *s* of Jonkheer Louis Huydecoper and Jonkvrouwe Laurence B. W. Ram; *m* 1944, Baroness Constance C. van Wassenaer; one *s* two *d*. *Educ:* Univ. of Utrecht (LLM). Banking, 1942–44; Legal Dept, Min. of Finance, The Hague, 1945–46; entered Min. of For. Affairs, 1946; UN, NY, 1946; Ottawa, 1947–48; Mil. Mission, Berlin, 1949–50; Bonn, 1950–52; London, 1952–56; Djakarta, 1956–59; Washington, 1959–62; Rome, 1962–66; Min. of For. Affairs, 1966–70; London, 1970–73; Ambassador, Hd of Delegn to Conf. on Security and Co-operation in Europe, Helsinki and Geneva, 1973–74; Ambassador: Moscow, 1974–77; Lisbon, 1978–80; Inspector of For. Service, Min. of For. Affairs, 1981–82. Holds various foreign orders. *Address:* Wassenaarseweg 132, 2596 EA, The Hague, Netherlands.

HUYGHE, René; Grand Officier de la Légion d'Honneur; Member of the Académie Française since 1960; Hon. Professor of Psychology of Plastic Arts, Collège de France (Professor, 1950–76); Hon. Head Keeper, Musée du Louvre; Director, Museum Jacquemart-André, Paris, since 1974; *b* Arras, Pas-de-Calais, France, 3 May 1906; *s* of Louis Huyghe and Marie (*née* Delvoye); *m* 1950, Lydie Bouthet; one *s* one *d*. *Educ:* Sorbonne; École du Louvre, Paris. Attached to Musée du Louvre, 1927; Asst Keeper, 1930; Head Keeper, Département des Peintures, Dessins, Chalcographie, 1937. Mem., Conseil Artistique de la Réunion des Musées Nationaux, 1952 (Vice-Pres. 1964, Pres. 1975–89); Pres. Assoc. internationale du Film d'Art, 1958. Holds foreign decorations. Praemium Erasmianum, The Hague, 1966. *Publications:* Histoire de l'Art contemporain: La Peinture, 1935; Cézanne 1936 and 1961; Les Contemporains, 1939 (2nd edn 1949); Vermeer, 1948; Watteau, 1950; various works on Gauguin, 1951, 1952, 1959; Dialogue avec le visible, 1955 (trans. Eng.); L'Art et l'homme, Vol. I, 1957, Vol. II, 1958, Vol. III, 1961 (trans. Eng.); Van Gogh, 1959; Merveilles de la France, 1960; L'Art et l'Ame, 1960 (trans. Eng.); La peinture française aux XVIIe et XVIIIe Siècles, 1962; Delacroix ou le combat solitaire, 1963, 2nd edn 1990 (trans. Eng.); Puissances de l'Image, 1965; Sens et Destin de l'Art, 1967; L'Art et le monde moderne, Vol. I, 1970, Vol. II, 1971; Formes et Forces, 1971; La Relève du réel, 1974; La Relève de l'imaginaire, 1976; Ce que je crois, 1976; De l'Art à la Philosophie, 1980; (with D. Ikeda) La Nuit appelle l'Aurore, 1980; Les Signes du Temps et l'Art moderne, 1985; (with M. Brion) Se perdre dans Venise, 1987; Psychologie de l'Art, 1991. *Address:* 3 rue Corneille, Paris 75006, France. *Club:* Union interalliée (Paris).

HYAM, Michael Joshua; His Honour Judge Hyam; a Circuit Judge, since 1984; Resident Judge, Norwich, since 1991; Designated Family Judge, Norwich, since 1991; *b* 18 April 1938; *s* of Isaac J. Hyam and Rachel Hyam; *m* 1968, Diana Mortimer; three *s*. *Educ:* Westminster Sch.; St Catharine's Coll., Cambridge (MA). Called to Bar, Gray's Inn, 1962; a Recorder, 1983–84; practised on SE Circuit, 1962–84. Member: Council of Legal Education, 1980–86; Ethical Cttee, Cromwell Hosp., 1983–92; Chm., Area Criminal Justice Liaison Cttee, 1992–. Gov., Dulwich Coll. Prep. Sch., 1986–92. *Publication:* Learning the Skills of Advocacy, 1990, 3rd edn 1995. *Recreations:* book collecting, cricket, gardening, yeast cookery. *Address:* 5 Essex Court, Temple, EC4Y 9AH. *T:* 0171–353 2825. *Clubs:* Garrick, MCC; Norfolk (Norwich).

HYAMS, Daisy Deborah, (Mrs C. Guderley), OBE 1974; *b* 25 Nov. 1912; *d* of Hyman Hyams and Annie Burnett; *m* 1936, Sidney Hart; no *c*; *m* 1975, C. Guderley. *Educ:* Coborn Grammar Sch. for Girls, Bow. FGI. Joined Tesco, 1931; Man. Dir, Tesco (Wholesale) Ltd, 1965–82; Dir, Tesco Stores PLC, 1969–82. *Recreations:* travel, reading. *Address:* 10 Noblefield Heights, Great North Road, Highgate, N2 0NX. *T:* 0181–348 1591.

HYATALI, Sir Isaac (Emanuel), Kt 1973; TC 1974; barrister and attorney-at-law; Chief Justice and President, Court of Appeal, Trinidad and Tobago, 1972–83; Legal Consultant to law firm of Hyatali and Co.; Chairman, Elections and Boundaries Commission, since 1983; *b* 21 Nov. 1917; *s* of late Joseph Hyatali and Esther Hyatali; *m* 1943, Audrey Monica Joseph; two *s* one *d*. *Educ:* Naparima Coll., San Fernando; Gray's Inn and Council of Legal Education, London. Called to Bar, Gray's Inn, 1947. Private practice at the Bar, 1947–59; Judge, Supreme Court, 1959–62; Justice of Appeal, 1962–72; Pres., Industrial Court, 1965–72; Justice of Appeal, Seychelles Republic, 1983–86. Chairman: Arima Rent Assessment Bd, 1953–59; Agricultural Rent Bd (Eastern Counties), 1953–59; Agricultural Wages Council, 1958–59; Oil and Water Bd, 1959–62; Constitution Commn, 1987–90. Arbitrator and Umpire, ICAO, 1981–86. Hon. Chm., Amer. Life and Gen. Insce Co. (Trinidad) Ltd, 1983–91; Chm., Ansa McAl Foundn, 1992– (amalgamation of Ansa Foundn (Chm., 1987) and McEneaney-Alston Foundn (Chm., 1989)). Trinidad and Tobago Editor of West Indian Law Reports, 1961–65. Member: World Assoc. of Judges; Council of Management, British Inst. of Internat. and Comparative Law; Hon. Mem., World Peace through Law Center. Chm., St Ann's Hosp. Commn of Enquiry, 1992–93. *Recreations:* reading, social work. *Address:* (chambers) 63 Edward Street, Port of Spain, Trinidad and Tobago. *T:* (62) 34007; Election and Boundaries Commission, Salvatori Building, Port of Spain. *T:* (62) 38320; (home) 8 Pomme Rose Avenue, Cascade, St Anns, Republic of Trinidad and Tobago. *Clubs:* Commonwealth Trust; (Hon. Mem.) Union Park Turf (Trinidad); (Hon. Mem.) Union (Port of Spain); Rotary (Princes Town).

HYDE, Lord; George Edward Laurence Villiers; *b* 12 Feb. 1976; *s* and *heir* of 7th Earl of Clarendon, *qv*.

HYDE, Helen Yvonne, MA; Headmistress, Watford Grammar School, since 1987; *b* 11 May 1947; *d* of Henry and Tilly Seligman; *m* 1968, Dr John Hyde; two *d*. *Educ:* Parktown Girls' High Sch., Johannesburg; Witwatersrand Univ. (BA 1967; BA Hons 1969); King's Coll., London (MA 1974). Teacher of French, 1970, Head of Modern Languages, 1978, Acland Burghley; Dep. Headmistress, Highgate Wood, 1983. Mem., Steering Cttee for Central Bureau, 1994–. *Recreations:* tapestry, running, theology. *Address:* Watford Grammar School, Lady's Close, Watford, Herts WD1 8AE.

HYDE, Margaret Sheila; Director, Esmée Fairbairn Charitable Trust, since 1994; *b* 11 Sept. 1945; *er d* of late Gerry Tomlins and Sheila (*née* Thorpe); *m* 1966, Derek Hyde (marr. diss. 1976). *Educ:* Watford Grammar Sch. for Girls; London Sch. of Econs and Political Science (DSA 1969; BSc Hons Social Admin 1971; Mostyn Lloyd Meml Prize, 1969; Janet Beveridge Award, 1971). Blackfriars Settlement, 1965–67; Home Office, 1972–77: served in Probation, Prison and Gen. Depts, 1972–76; Private Sec. to Perm. Under Sec. of State, 1976–77; Head of Information, NCVO, 1977–85; Chief Exec., Action Resource Centre, 1985–91 (Trustee, 1992–94); Dep. Sec. Gen., Arts Council of GB, 1991–92; Prog. Consultant, Internat. Save the Children Alliance and Save the Children UK, 1992–94. Exec. Cttee, 300 Gp, 1984–87. Exec. Cttee, Assoc. of Charitable Foundns, 1995–; Trustee: Peter Bedford Trust, 1983–92 (Chm., 1985–87); Charities Effectiveness Review Trust, 1986–91. Mem. Ct of Govs, LSE, 1987–. FRSA 1991 (Mem. Council, 1994–). *Recreations:* walking, sailing. *Address:* 178 Dalling Road, W6 0EU. *Club:* Reform.

HYDE, W(illiam) Leonard, FCIB; Director, Leeds Permanent Building Society, 1972–90 (Chief General Manager, 1973–78; Vice-President, 1978–81; President, 1981–83). Joined Leeds Permanent Building Soc., 1936. Member Council: Building Socs Assoc., 1973–78; Nat. House Builders, 1973–78; Chm., Yorkshire County Assoc. of Building Socs, 1978–80. *Recreations:* golf, walking. *Address:* 5 Burn Bridge Road, Harrogate, Yorks HG3 1NS. *T:* Harrogate (01423) 871748. *Club:* Pannal Golf.

HYDE-CHAMBERS, Fredrick Rignold; Director, Industry and Parliament Trust, since 1987; *b* 12 May 1949; *s* of late Derek Christie Hyde-Chambers and Margaret M. Rignold; *m* 1976, Audrey Christine Martin (*née* Smith); two *s*. *Educ:* Buckingham Coll., Harrow; Arts Educnl Sch. Child actor, TV and stage, 1958–64; The Tibet Relief Fund, UK, 1965–68; Gen. Sec., Buddhist Soc., 1968–72; Private Sec. to MPs, 1974–80; Industry and Parliament Trust, 1980–. Member: Bd, Inst. of Citizenship; Adv. Bd, Motorola Youth Parlt Comp.; Adv. Bd, State Legis. Leaders' Foundn, USA; Steering Cttee, Arts Inform; Council, Buddhist Soc.; Tibet Soc. Script writer and consultant, BBC TV and Channel 4 documentaries. First Novel Award, Authors' Club, 1988; Airey Neave Trust Human Rights Scholarship, 1989. *Publications:* The Mouse King, 1976; (with Audrey Hyde-Chambers) Tibetan Folktales, 1979; Tibet and China, 1988; Lama, 1988. *Recreations:* Tortoises, my two children. *Address:* Industry and Parliament Trust, 1 Buckingham Place, SW1E 6HR. *T:* 0171–976 5311; 12 Gloucester Court, Swan Street, SE1 1DQ. *T:* 0171–407 5244. *Club:* Authors' (Mem. Cttee).

HYDE-PARKER, Sir Richard William; *see* Parker.

HYLTON, 5th Baron, *cr* 1866; **Raymond Hervey Jolliffe,** MA; ARICS; *b* 13 June 1932; *er s* of 4th Baron Hylton and of the Dowager Lady Hylton, *d* of late Raymond Asquith and *sister* of 2nd Earl of Oxford and Asquith, *qv*; *S* father, 1967; *m* 1966, Joanna Ida Elizabeth, *d* of late Andrew de Bertodano; four *s* one *d*. *Educ:* Eton (King's Scholar); Trinity Coll., Oxford (MA). Lieut R of O, Coldstream Guards. Asst Private Sec. to Governor-General of Canada, 1960–62; Trustee, Shelter Housing Aid Centre 1970–76; Chairman: Catholic Housing Aid Soc., 1972–73; Nat. Fedn of Housing Assocs, 1973–76; Housing Assoc. Charitable Trust; Help the Aged Housing Trust, 1976–82; Hugh of Witham Foundn, 1978–; Vice-Pres., Age Concern (Nat. Old People's Welfare Council), 1971–77; President: SW Reg. Nat. Soc. for Mentally Handicapped Children, 1976–79; NI Assoc. for Care and Resettlement of Offenders, 1989. Member, All Party Parliamentary Group: on Penal Affairs; on Human Rights. Chm., St Francis and St Sergius Trust Fund, 1993–. Founder and Mem., Mendip and Wansdyke Local Enterprise Gp, 1979–85. Hon. Treas., Study on Human Rights and Responsibilities in Britain and N Ireland, 1985–88. Mem., Nat. Steering Gp, Charter '87; Signatory of Charter '88. Trustee: Christian Internat. Peace Service, 1977–82; Acorn Christian Healing Trust, 1983; Action around Bethlehem among Children with Disabilities, 1993; Governor, Christian Coll. for Adult Educn, 1972–. Mem., Frome RDC, 1968–72. DL Somerset, 1975–90. *Heir:* *s* Hon. William Henry Martin Jolliffe, *b* April 1967. *Address:* Ammerdown, Radstock, Bath, Somerset BA3 5SH.

HYLTON-FOSTER, family name of **Baroness Hylton-Foster.**

HYLTON-FOSTER, Baroness, *cr* 1965, of the City of Westminster (Life Peer); **Audrey Pellew Hylton-Foster,** DBE 1990; British Red Cross Society: Director, Chelsea Division, 1950–60; President and Chairman, London Branch, 1960–83, Patron, since 1984; Hon. Consultant, National Headquarters, 1984–86; Convenor, Cross Bench Peers, 1974–95; *b* 19 May 1908; *d* of 1st Viscount Ruffside, PC, DL (*d* 1958), and Viscountess Ruffside (*d* 1969); *m* 1931, Rt Hon. Sir Harry Hylton-Foster, QC (*d* 1965); no *c*. *Educ:* St George's, Ascot; Ivy House, Wimbledon. Pres., Research into Blindness Fund, 1965–76. *Recreations:* gardening, fishing. *Address:* The Coach House, Tanhurst, Leith Hill, Holmbury St Mary, Dorking, Surrey RH5 6LU. *T:* Dorking (01306) 711975; 54 Cranmer Court, Whiteheads Grove, SW3 3HW. *T:* 0171–584 2889.

HYMAN, Howard Jonathan; Deputy Chairman, Charterhouse Bank Limited, since 1994; Managing Director, Charterhouse plc, since 1994; *b* 23 Oct. 1949; *s* of Joe Hyman, *qv* and Corrine Irene (*née* Abrahams); *m* 1972, Anne Moira Sowden; two *s* one *d*. *Educ:* Bedales Sch., Hants; Manchester Univ. (MA Hons Econs 1972). ACA 1975, FCA 1982. Price Waterhouse: articled clerk, 1972–75; Partner, 1984; seconded to HM Treasury as specialist privatisation adviser, 1984–87; Founder and Partner i/c of Privatisation Services Dept, 1987–90; Head of Corporate Finance, Europe, 1990; Member: E European Jt Venture

Bd, 1990–94; European Mgt Bd, 1991–94; China Bd, 1993–94; World Gen. Council, 1994; World Head, Corporate Finance, 1994. FRSA 1993. *Publications:* Privatisation The Facts, 1988; The Implications of Privatisation for Nationalised Industries, 1988; chapters in: Privatisation and Competition, 1988; Privatisation in the UK, 1988; articles in Electrical Rev., Equities Internat., Public Finance and Accountancy, Business and Govt, Administrator. *Recreations:* walking, golf, watching cricket, reading, gardening, classical music. *Address:* Charterhouse Bank Ltd, 1 Paternoster Row, EC4M 7DH. *T:* 0171–246 2425. *Clubs:* Reform, MCC; Cirencester Golf, Ilkley Golf.

HYMAN, Joe; *b* 14 Oct. 1921; *yr s* of late Solomon Hyman and Hannah Hyman; *m* 1st, 1948, Corinne I. Abrahams (marriage dissolved); one *s* one *d*; 2nd, 1963, Simone Duke; one *s* one *d*. *Educ:* North Manchester Grammar Sch. In textiles, 1939–80; Founder, Viyella International, and Chm., 1961–69; Chm., John Crowther Gp, 1971–80. Trustee, Pestalozzi Children's Village Trust, 1967–; Governor, LSE. FRSA 1968; FIMgt. Comp. TI. *Recreations:* music, golf, gardening. *Address:* 24 Kingston House North, Prince's Gate, SW7 1LN. *Club:* MCC.

See also H. J. Hyman.

HYMAN, Robin Philip; publisher; Chairman, Calmann & King Ltd, since 1991; Consultant, Hambro Group Investments Ltd, since 1991; *b* 9 Sept. 1931; *s* of late Leonard Hyman and Helen Hyman (*née* Mautner); *m* 1966, Inge Neufeld; two *s* one *d*. *Educ:* Henley Grammar Sch.; Christ's Coll., Finchley; Univ. of Birmingham (BA (Hons) 1955). National Service, RAF, 1949–51. Editor, Mermaid, 1953–54; Bookselling and Publishing: joined Evans Brothers Ltd, Publishers, 1955: Dir, 1964; Dep. Man. Dir, 1967; Man. Dir, 1972–77; Chm., Bell & Hyman Ltd, 1977–86, which merged with Allen & Unwin Ltd, 1986, to form Unwin Hyman Ltd, Man. Dir, 1986–88, Chm. and Chief Exec., 1989–90. Mem. Editorial Bd, World Year Book of Education, 1969–73. Publishers' Association: Mem. Council, 1975–92; Treasurer, 1982–84; Vice-Pres., 1988–89, 1991–92; Pres., 1989–91; Member: Exec. Cttee, Educnl Publishers' Council, 1971–76 (Treas., 1972–75); Publishers' Adv. Cttee, British Council, 1989–92; BBC Gen. Adv. Council, 1992–. Mem., First British Publishers' Delegn to China, 1978. FRSA. *Publications:* A Dictionary of Famous Quotations, 1962; (with John Trevaskis) Boys' and Girls' First Dictionary, 1967; Bell & Hyman First Colour Dictionary, 1985; Universal Primary Dictionary (for Africa), 1976; (with Inge Hyman) 11 children's books, incl. Barnabas Ball at the Circus, 1967; Runaway James and the Night Owl, 1968; The Hippo who Wanted to Fly, 1973; The Magical Fish, 1974; Peter's Magic Hide-and-Seek, 1982. *Recreations:* theatre, reading, cricket. *Address:* 101 Hampstead Way, NW11 7LR. *T:* 0181–455 7055. *Clubs:* Garrick, MCC, Samuel Pepys.

HYND, Ronald; choreographer; Ballet Director, National Theater, Munich, 1970–73 and 1984–86; *b* 22 April 1931; *s* of William John and Alice Louisa Hens; *m* 1957, Annette Page, *qv*; one *d*. *Educ:* erratically throughout England due to multiple wartime evacuation. Joined Rambert School, 1946; Ballet Rambert, 1949; Royal Ballet (then Sadlers Well's Ballet), 1952, rising from Corps de Ballet to Principal Dancer, 1959; danced Siegfried (Swan Lake), Florimund (Sleeping Beauty), Albrecht (Giselle), Poet (Sylphides), Tsarevitch (Firebird), Prince of Pagodas, Moondog (Lady and Fool), Tybalt (Romeo), etc; produced first choreography for Royal Ballet Choreographic Group followed by works for London Festival Ballet, Royal Ballet, Dutch National Ballet, Munich Ballet, Houston Ballet, Australian Ballet, Tokyo Ballet, Nat. Ballet of Canada, Grands Ballets Canadiens, Santiago Ballet, Cincinnati Ballet, Pact Ballet, Malmö Ballet, Ljubljania Ballet, Northern Ballet, Bonn Ballet and Vienna State Ballet. *Ballets include:* Le Baiser de la Fée, 1968, new production 1974; Pasiphaë, 1969; Dvorak Variations, 1970; Wendekreise, 1972; In a Summer Garden, 1972; Das Telefon, 1972; Mozartiana, 1973; Charlotte Brontë, 1974; Mozart Adagio, 1974; Galileo (film), 1974; Orient/Occident, 1975; La Valse, 1975; Valses Nobles et Sentimentales, 1975; The Merry Widow, 1975; L'Eventail, 1976; The Nutcracker (new version for Festival Ballet), 1976; ice ballets for John Curry, 1977; Rosalinda, 1978, La Chatte, 1978, Papillon, 1979; The Seasons, 1980; Alceste, 1981; Scherzo Capriccioso, 1982, Le Diable a Quatre, 1984; Fanfare für Tänzer, 1985; Coppelia (new prodn for Festival Ballet), 1985; Ludwig-Fragmente Eines Rätsels, 1986; The Hunchback of Notre Dame, 1988; Ballade, 1988; Liaisons Amoureuses, 1989; Sleeping Beauty (new prodn for English Nat. Ballet), 1993; *musical:* Sound of Music, 1981; *tv productions:* The Nutcracker, The Sanguine Fan (Fest. Ballet); The Merry Widow (Nat. Ballet of Canada). *Recreations:* the gramophone, garden. *Address:* Fern Cottage, Upper Somerton, Bury St Edmunds, Suffolk IP29 4ND.

HYND, Mrs Ronald; *see* Page, Annette.

HYNES, Ann Patricia, (Mrs T. P. Hynes); *see* Dowling, A. P.

HYNES, Prof. Richard Olding, FRS 1989; Professor of Biology, since 1983, and Director of Center for Cancer Research, since 1991, Massachusetts Institute of Technology; Investigator, Howard Hughes Medical Institute, since 1988; *b* 29 Nov. 1944; *s* of Hugh Bernard Noel and Mary Elizabeth Hynes; *m* 1966, Fleur Marshall; two *s*. *Educ:* Trinity Coll., Cambridge (BA 1966; MA 1970); MIT (PhD Biology 1971). Res. Fellow, Imperial Cancer Res. Fund, 1971–74; Massachusetts Institute of Technology: Asst Prof., 1975–78, Associate Prof., 1978–83, Dept of Biology and Center for Cancer Res.; Associate Hd, 1985–89, Head, 1989–91, of Biology Dept. Hon. Res. Fellow, Dept of Zoology, UCL, 1982–83. Guggenheim Fellow, 1982. FAAAS, 1987; Fellow, Amer. Acad. of Arts and Scis, 1994. *Publications:* (ed) Surfaces of Normal and Malignant Cells, 1979; (ed) Tumor Cell Surfaces and Malignancy, 1980; Fibronectins, 1990; over 100 articles in professional jls. *Recreations:* reading, music, gardening, ski-ing. *Address:* E17-227, Massachusetts Institute of Technology, Cambridge, MA 02139, USA. *T:* (617) 2536422, *Fax:* (617) 2538357.

HYNES, Prof. Samuel, DFC 1945; PhD; Woodrow Wilson Emeritus Professor of Literature, Princeton University, since 1990; *b* 29 Aug. 1924; *s* of Samuel Hynes and Margaret Turner Hynes; *m* 1944, Elizabeth Igleheart; two *d*. *Educ:* Univ. of Minnesota (AB 1947); Columbia Univ. (PhD 1956). Pilot, US Marine Corps: 2nd Lieut, 1943–46; Capt., then Major., 1952–53. Instructor to Prof. of English, Swarthmore Coll., 1949–52 and 1954–68; Professor: Northwestern Univ., 1968–76; Princeton Univ., 1976–90. Woodrow Wilson Prof. of Literature, 1977–90. FRSL 1978; Fellow. Amer. Acad. of Arts and Scis, 1993. Air Medal, 1945. *Publications:* (ed) Further Speculations by T. E. Hulme, 1955; The Pattern of Hardy's Poetry, 1961; The Edwardian Turn of Mind, 1962; William Golding, 1964; (ed) The Author's Craft and Other Critical Writings of Arnold Bennett, 1968; (ed) Romance and Realism, 1970; Edwardian Occasions, 1972; The Auden Generation, 1976; (ed) Complete Poetical Works of Thomas Hardy, Vol. I 1982, Vol. II 1984, Vol. III 1985, Vols. IV and V 1995; (ed) Thomas Hardy, 1984; Flights of Passage: reflections of a World War II aviator, 1988; A War Imagined, 1990; (ed) Joseph Conrad: complete short fiction, 4 vols, 1992–93. *Address:* 130 Moore Street, Princeton, NJ 08540, USA. *T:* (609) 9211930.

HYSLOP; *see* Maxwell-Hyslop.

HYSLOP, James Telfer, OBE 1968; HM Diplomatic Service, retired; Consul General, Detroit, 1971–76; *b* 21 Sept. 1916; *s* of Mr and Mrs John J. Hyslop; *m* 1942, Jane Elizabeth Owers; one *s* one *d*. *Educ:* Queen Elizabeth's Grammar Sch., Hexham. Royal Navy, 1939–46. Entered Diplomatic Service, 1948; served at: Baltimore, 1948; Valparaiso, 1951; Amman, 1954; Tegucigalpa, 1958; San Francisco, 1961; Johannesburg, 1964; Bogota, 1968. *Recreations:* reading, music. *Address:* 12 Quay Walls, Berwick-on-Tweed TD15 1HB. *T:* Berwick-on-Tweed (01289) 305197.

HYTNER, Benet Alan, QC 1970; a Recorder of the Crown Court, since 1972; Judge of Appeal, Isle of Man, since 1980; *b* 29 Dec. 1927; *s* of late Maurice and Sarah Hytner, Manchester; *m* 1954, Joyce Myers (marr. diss. 1980); three *s* one *d*. *Educ:* Manchester Grammar Sch.; Trinity Hall, Cambridge (Exhibr). MA. National Service, RASC, 1949–51 (commnd). Called to Bar, Middle Temple, 1952, Bencher, 1977, Reader, 1995; Leader, Northern Circuit, 1984–88. Member: Gen. Council of Bar, 1969–73, 1986–88; Senate of Inns of Court and Bar, 1977–81, 1984–86. *Recreations:* fell walking, music, theatre, reading. *Address:* Byrom Chambers, 61 Fleet Street, EC4Y 1JU.

See also N. R. Hytner.

HYTNER, Nicholas Robert; Associate Director, Royal National Theatre, since 1989; *b* 7 May 1956; *s* of Benet Hytner, *qv*. *Educ:* Manchester Grammar School, Trinity Hall, Cambridge (MA). Associate Dir, Royal Exchange Theatre, Manchester, 1985–89, Director of many theatre and opera productions including: *theatre:* As You Like It, 1985, Edward II, 1986, The Country Wife, 1986, Don Carlos, 1987, Royal Exchange; Measure for Measure, 1987, The Tempest, 1988, RSC; Ghetto, National Theatre, 1989; Miss Saigon, Drury Lane, 1989, Broadway, 1991; Volpone, Almeida, 1990; King Lear, RSC, 1990; The Wind in the Willows, NT, 1990; The Madness of George III, NT, 1991; The Recruiting Officer, NT, 1992; Carousel, NT, 1992, Shaftesbury, 1993; The Importance of Being Earnest, Aldwych, 1993; *opera:* English National Opera: Rienzi, 1983; Xerxes, 1985 (Laurence Olivier and Evening Standard Awards); The Magic Flute, 1988; The Force of Destiny, 1992; King Priam, Kent Opera, 1983; Giulio Cesare, Paris Opera, Houston Grand Opera, 1987; Le Nozze di Figaro, Geneva Opera, 1989; La Clemenza di Tito, Glyndebourne, 1991; Don Giovanni, Bavarian State Opera, 1994; The Cunning Little Vixen, Paris, 1995; *film:* The Madness of King George, 1994. Best Director, Evening Standard Awards, 1989; Best Director, Critics Circle Awards, 1989. *Address:* The Royal National Theatre of Great Britain, South Bank, SE1 9PX.

I

IBBOTSON, Lancelot William Cripps, CBE 1971 (MBE 1948); General Manager of Southern Region, British Railways, and Chairman, Southern Railway Board, 1968–72; *b* 10 Feb. 1909; *s* of William Ibbotson, FRCS and Mrs Dora Ibbotson (*née* Chapman), London; *m* 1st, 1931, Joan Marguerite Jeffcock (*d* 1989); one *s* one *d*; 2nd, 1990, Rhoda Margot Beck. *Educ:* Radley Coll. Traffic Apprentice, LNER, 1927; Chief Clerk to Dist. Supt, Newcastle, 1939; Asst Dist Supt, York, 1942; Dist Supt, Darlington, 1945; Asst to Operating Supt, Western Region, 1950; Asst Gen. Man., Western Region, 1959; Chief Operating Officer, British Railways, 1963; Gen. Man., Western Region, BR, and Chm., Western Railway Board, 1966–68. Gen. Man., A. Pearce, Partners & Assoc., 1975–79; Dir, Flameless Furnaces Ltd, 1976–84. *Recreations:* foreign travel, photography. *Address:* 60 Carlton Hill, St John's Wood, NW8 0ET. *T:* 0171–624 7853.

IBBOTSON, Peter Stamford; Director of Corporate Affairs, Carlton Television Ltd, 1991–94; *b* 13 Dec. 1943; *s* of Arthur Ibbotson and Ivy Elizabeth (*née* Acton); *m* 1975, Susan Mary Crewdson; two *s* one *d*. *Educ:* Manchester Grammar Sch.; St Catherine's Coll., Oxford (BA Modern History). BBC: Editor, Newsweek, 1978–82; Editor, Panorama, 1983–85; Asst Head, Television Current Affairs, 1985–86; Chief Asst to Dir of Programmes, Television, 1986–87; Dep. Dir of Progs, TV, 1987–88; Corporate Consultant, Channel 4, 1988–91. Director: Film and Television Completions PLC, 1990–; UK Radio Develts Ltd, 1990–. Dir, BARB, 1987–88. *Publication:* (jtly) The Third Age of Broadcasting, 1978. *Recreations:* silviculture, reading, photography. *Address:* Newnham Farm, Wallingford, Oxon OX10 8BW. *T:* Wallingford (01491) 833111. *Club:* Royal Automobile.

IBBOTT, Alec, CBE 1988; HM Diplomatic Service, retired; *b* 14 Oct. 1930; *s* of Francis Joseph Ibbott and Madge Winifred Ibbott (*née* Graham); *m* 1964, Margaret Elizabeth Brown; one *s* one *d*. Joined Foreign (subseq. Diplomatic) Service, 1949; served in HM Forces, 1949–51; FCO, 1951–54; ME Centre for Arab Studies, 1955–56; Second Secretary and Vice Consul, Rabat, 1956–60; Second Secretary, FO, 1960–61; Second Sec. (Information), Tripoli, 1961; Second Sec., Benghazi, 1961–65; First Sec. (Information), Khartoum, 1965–67; First Sec., FO (later FCO), 1967–71; Asst Political Agent, Dubai, 1971; First Secretary, Head of Chancery and Consul: Dubai, 1971–72; Abu Dhabi, 1972–73; First Secretary and Head of Chancery: Nicosia, 1973–74; FCO, 1975–77; Carácas, 1977–79; Counsellor, Khartoum, 1979–82; seconded to IMS Ltd, 1982–85; Ambassador to Liberia, 1985–87. High Comr to the Republic of Gambia, 1988–90. Chief Exec., Southern Africa Assoc., 1992–. *Address:* 15a Sanderstead Hill, South Croydon, Surrey CR2 0HD.

IBBS, Sir (John) Robin, KBE 1988; Kt 1982; Chairman, Lloyds Bank, since 1993 (Director, since 1985; Deputy Chairman, 1988–93); *b* 21 April 1926; *o s* of late Prof. T. L. Ibbs, MC, DSc, FInstP and of Marjorie Ibbs (*née* Bell); *m* 1952, Iris Barbara, *d* of late S. Hall; one *d*. *Educ:* Univ. of Toronto; Trinity Coll., Cambridge (MA Mech. Scis). Instr Lieut, RN, 1947–49. Called to the Bar, Lincoln's Inn. C. A. Parsons & Co. Ltd, 1949–51; joined ICI, 1952; Dir, 1976–80 and 1982–88; on secondment as Head, Central Policy Review Staff, Cabinet Office, 1980–82; Advr to Prime Minister on Efficiency and Effectiveness in Govt, 1983–88. Chm., Lloyds Merchant Bank Hldgs, 1989–92; Dep. Chm., Lloyds Bank Canada, 1989–90. Member: Governing Body and Council, British Nat. Cttee of ICC, 1976–80; Industrial Develt Adv. Bd, DoI, 1978–80; Council, CBI, 1982–87 (Mem. Companies Cttee, 1978–80); Council, CIA, 1976–79, 1982–87 (Vice Pres., 1983–87; Hon. Mem., 1987); Chemicals EDC, NEDO, 1982–88; Council, RIIA, Chatham House, 1983–89; Top Salaries Review Body, 1983–89; Leader, Review of H of C Services, 1990. Pres., Bankers Club, 1994–95. Vice Pres., CIB, 1993– (FCIB 1993). Trustee and Dep. Chm., Isaac Newton Trust, 1988–. Mem. Court, Cranfield Inst. of Technology, 1983–88; Chm. of Council, UCL, 1989–. CIMgt (CBIM 1985). Hon Fellow UCL, 1993. Hon. DSc Bradford, 1986; Hon LLD Bath, 1993. BIM Special Award, 1989. *Address:* Lloyds Bank, 71 Lombard Street, EC3P 3BS. *Club:* United Oxford & Cambridge University (Trustee, 1989–).

IBRAHIM, Sir Kashim, GCON 1963; KCMG 1962; CBE 1960 (MBE 1952); Governor of Northern Nigeria, 1962–66; Chancellor, Lagos University, 1976–84; *b* 10 June 1910; *s* of Mallam Ibrahim Lakkani; *m* 1st, 1943, Halima; 2nd, 1944, Khadija; 3rd, 1957, Zainaba; four *s* three *d* (and two *d* decd). *Educ:* Bornu Provincial Sch.; Katsina Teachers' Trng Coll. Teacher, 1929–32; Visiting Teacher, 1933–49; Educ. Officer, 1949–52. Federal Minister of Social Services, 1952–55; Northern Regional Minister of Social Develt and Surveys, 1955–56; Waziri of Bornu, 1956–62. Advr to Military Governor, N Nigeria, 1966. Chm. Nigerian Coll. of Arts, Science and Technology, 1958–62; Chancellor, Ibadan Univ., 1967–75; Chm. Provisional Council of Ahmadu Bello Univ. Hon. LLD: Ahmadu Bello, 1963; Univ. of Ibadan; Univ. of Nigeria (Nsukka); University of Lagos. *Publications:* Kanuri Reader Elementary, I-IV; Kanuri Arithmetic Books, I-IV, for Elementary Schs and Teachers' Guide for above. *Recreations:* walking, riding, polo playing. *Address:* PO Box 285, Maiduguri, Bornu State, Nigeria.

IDALIE, Mme Heinric; *see* Oldenbourg-Idalie, Zoë.

IDDESLEIGH, 4th Earl of, *cr* 1885; **Stafford Henry Northcote,** DL; Bt 1641; Viscount St Cyres, 1885; Director: Devon & Exeter Steeplechases Ltd, since 1975 (Vice Chairman, since 1990); Gemini Radio Ltd, since 1993; *b* 14 July 1932; *er s* of 3rd Earl of Iddesleigh and Elizabeth (*d* 1991), *er d* of late F. S. A. Lowndes and late Marie Belloc; *S* father, 1970; *m* 1955, Maria Luisa Alvarez-Builla y Urquijo (Condesa del Real Agrado in Spain), OBE, DL, *d* of late Don Gonzalo Alvarez-Builla y Alvera and of Viscountess Exmouth, *widow* of 9th Viscount Exmouth; one *s* one *d*. *Educ:* Downside. 2nd Lieut, Irish Guards, 1951–52. Director: Television South West, 1982–92; UDT, 1983–87; TSB Gp, 1986–87; TSB Commercial Hldgs, 1987; Mem., SW Region, TSB GP Bd (Chm., 1983–87). DL Devon, 1979. Kt SMO Malta. *Heir:* *s* Viscount St Cyres, *qv*. *Address:* Shillands House, Upton Pyne Hill, Exeter, Devon EX5 5EB. *T:* Exeter (01392) 58916. *Club:* Army and Navy.

IDIENS, Dale; Depute Director (Collections), since 1992 and Keeper, Department of History and Applied Art, since 1983, National Museums of Scotland (formerly Department of Art and Archaeology, Royal Scottish Museum); *b* 13 May 1942; *d* of Richard Idiens and Ruth Christine Idiens (*née* Hattersley). *Educ:* High Wycombe High Sch.; Univ. of Leicester. BA (Hons); DipEd. Royal Scottish Museum, Department of Art and Archaeology: Asst Keeper in charge of Ethnography, 1964; Dep. Keeper, 1979. *Publications:* Traditional African Sculpture, 1969; Ancient American Art, 1971; (ed with K. G. Ponting) African Textiles, 1980; The Hausa of Northern Nigeria, 1981; Pacific Art, 1982; (contrib.) Indians and Europe, an Interdisciplinary Collection of Essays, 1987; Cook Islands Art, 1990; (contrib.) No Ordinary Journey: John Rae, Arctic explorer 1813–1893, 1993; articles and papers in Jl of the Polynesian Soc., African Arts, Textile History; reviews and lectures. *Recreations:* travel, film, wine. *Address:* Sylvan House, 13 Sylvan Place, Edinburgh EH9 1LH. *T:* 0131–667 2399. *Clubs:* Naval and Military; University Staff (Edinburgh).

IDLE, Prof. Jeffrey Robert, PhD; CChem, FRSC; Professor in Medicine, University of Trondheim, since 1996; *b* 17 Sept. 1950; *s* of Robert William Idle and Margaret Joyce Idle (*née* Golightly); *m* Samar El-Sallab (marr. diss.); one *d*. *Educ:* Univ. of London (BSc 1972, BSc Hons 1973; PhD 1976). CChem 1987; FRSC 1987. St Mary's Hospital Medical School, London: Lectr in Biochem., 1976; Lectr in Biochemical Pharmacol., 1976–83; Wellcome Trust Sen. Lectr, 1983–88; Reader in Pharmacogenetics, Univ. of London, 1985–88; University of Newcastle upon Tyne: Prof. of Pharmacogenetics, 1988–95; Hd, Sch. of Clinical Med. Scis, 1992–95; Hd, Dept of Pharmacol. Scis, 1992–95. Founding Editor and Editor-in-Chief, Pharmacogenitics, 1991–. Chief Executive: Genotype Ltd, 1993–; VitOmega Internat., 1995–. *Publications:* articles in internat. scientific and med. jls. *Recreations:* language and culture of the Middle East, music. *Address:* Medisinisk Teknisk Senter, Universitetet I Trondheim, 7005 Trondheim, Norway.

IEVERS, Frank George Eyre, CMG 1964; Postmaster-General, East Africa, 1962–65, retired; *b* 8 May 1910; *s* of Eyre Francis and Catherine Ievers; *m* 1936, Phyllis Robinson; two *s*. *Educ:* Dover Coll. Asst Traffic Supt, Post Office, 1933; Traffic Supt, East Africa, 1946; Telecommunications Controller, 1951; Regional Dir, 1959. *Recreations:* golf, photography. *Address:* 20 Heron Close, Worcester WR2 4BW. *T:* Worcester (01905) 427121. *Clubs:* Nairobi (Kenya); Sudan (Khartoum).

IGGO, Prof. Ainsley, PhD, DSc; FRCPE; FRS 1978; FRSE; Professor of Veterinary Physiology, University of Edinburgh, 1962–90; *b* 2 Aug. 1924; *s* of late Lancelot George Iggo and late Catherine Josefine Fraser; *m* 1952, Betty Joan McCurdy, PhD, *d* of late Donald A. McCurdy, OBE; three *s*. *Educ:* Gladstone Sch., NZ; Southland Technical High Sch., NZ; Lincoln Coll., NZ (Sen. Scholar; MAgrSc 1947); Univ. of Otago (BSc 1949). PhD Aberdeen, 1954; DSc Edinburgh, 1962. FRSE 1962; FRCPE 1985. Asst Lectr in Physiology, Otago Univ. Med. Sch., 1948–50; NZ McMillan Brown Trav. Fellow, Rowett Inst., 1950–51; Lectr in Physiol., Univ. of Edinburgh Med. Sch., 1952–60; Nuffield Royal Soc. Commonwealth Fellow, ANU, 1959; Royal Soc. Locke Res. Fellow, 1960–62; Dean, Faculty of Veterinary Med., Univ. of Edinburgh, 1974–77 and 1985–90. Vis. Professor: Univ. of Ibadan, Nigeria, 1968; (also Leverhulme Res. Fellow) Univ. of Kyoto, 1970; Univ. of Heidelberg, 1972. Chm., IUPS Somatosensory Commn, 1974–. Mem. Council: RCVS, 1975–78 and 1985–; Royal Soc., 1982–83; Pres., Internat. Assoc. for Study of Pain, 1980–83. Governor, E of Scotland Coll. of Agriculture, 1968–77. Hon. DSc Pennsylvania. *Publications:* (ed) Sensory Physiology: Vol. II, Somatosensory System, 1973; articles on neurophysiol topics in Jl Physiol., etc. *Recreations:* bee-keeping, gardening. *Address:* 5 Relugas Road, Edinburgh EH9 2NE. *T:* 0131–667 4879.

IGNATIEFF, Michael, PhD; writer; *b* 12 May 1947; *s* of George Ignatieff and Alison (*née* Grant); *m* 1977, Susan Barrowclough; one *s* one *d*. *Educ:* Upper Canada Coll., Toronto; Univ. of Toronto (BA 1969); Cambridge Univ. (MA 1978); Harvard Univ. (PhD 1975). Associate Prof. of History, Univ. of BC, 1976–78; Sen. Res. Fellow, King's Coll., Cambridge, 1978–84; Vis. Fellow, Ecole des Hautes Etudes, Paris, 1985; Alistair Horne Fellow, St Antony's Coll., Oxford, 1993–95. Presenter: Voices, Channel 4, 1986; Thinking Aloud, BBC TV Series, 1987–88; The Late Show, BBC TV, 1989–; Blood and Belonging, BBC, 1993; Editorial Columnist, The Observer, 1990–93. *Publications:* A Just Measure of Pain, 1978; The Needs of Strangers, 1984; The Russian Album, 1987 (Canadian Governor General's Award, 1988; Heinemann Prize, RSL, 1988); Asya, 1991; Scar Tissue, 1993; Blood and Belonging, 1993. *Recreations:* tennis, talking, wine, gardening. *Address:* c/o Sheil Land Associates, 43 Doughty Street, WC1N 2LF. *Club:* Groucho.

IKERRIN, Viscount; Arion Thomas Piers Hamilton Butler; *b* 1 Sept. 1975; *s* and *heir* of 10th Earl of Carrick, *qv*.

ILCHESTER, 9th Earl of, *cr* 1756; **Maurice Vivian de Touffreville Fox-Strangways;** Baron Ilchester of Ilchester, Somerset, and Baron Strangways of Woodsford Strangways, Dorset, 1741; Baron Ilchester and Stavordale of Redlynch, Somerset, 1747; Group Captain, Royal Air Force (rtd); Managing Director, County Border Newspapers Ltd, since 1984; *b* 1 April 1920; *s* of 8th Earl of Ilchester and Laure Georgine Emilie (*d* 1970), *d* of late Evanghelos Georgios Mazaraki, sometime Treasurer of Suez Canal Company; *S* father, 1970; *m* 1941, Diana Mary Elizabeth, *e d* of late George Frederick Simpson, Cassington, Oxfordshire. *Educ:* Kingsbridge Sch. CEng; MRAeS; FINucE (Pres., 1982–84); FIMgt. Served RAF, 1936–76 (Gp Captain). Vice Chm., Biggin Hill Airport Consultative Cttee, 1976–95. Dir, 1982–90, Vice Chm., 1985–86, Nottingham Building Soc. Mem., H of L Select Cttee on Science and Technology, 1984–89. President: Soc. of Engineers, 1974 (Hon. FSE 1989); SE Area, RAF Assoc., 1978–; Darent River Preservation Soc., 1993–; Grant Maintained Schools Foundn, 1991–; Cannock Sch., 1992– (Chm.

Govs, 1978–92); Kent and Downs Reg. Newspaper Soc., 1994–. Liveryman, GAPAN. Hon. FCP 1994. *Recreations:* outdoor activities, enjoyment of the arts. *Heir: b* Hon. Raymond George Fox-Strangways [*b* 11 Nov. 1921; *m* 1941, Margaret Vera, *d* of late James Force, North Surrey, BC; two *s*]. *Address:* Farley Mill, Westerham, Kent TN16 1UB. *T:* Westerham (01959) 562314. *Club:* Royal Air Force.

ILERSIC, Prof. Alfred Roman; Emeritus Professor of Social Studies, Bedford College, University of London, since 1984 (Professor, 1965–84); *b* 14 Jan. 1920; *s* of late Roman Ilersic and Mary (*née* Moss); *m* 1st, 1944, Patricia Florence Bertram Liddle (marr. diss. 1976); one *s* one *d*; 2nd, 1976, June Elaine Browning. *Educ:* Polytechnic Sec. Sch., London; London Sch. of Economics, Lectr in Econs, University Coll. of S West, Exeter, 1947–53; Lectr in Social Statistics, Beford Coll., 1953; Reader in Economic and Social Statistics, Bedford Coll., London, 1963. Vis. Prof., Univ. of Bath, 1983–87. Mem., Cost of Living Adv. Cttee, 1970–88. Chm., Inst. of Statisticians, 1968–70. Mem., Wilts CC, 1989–93. Hon. Mem., Rating and Valuation Assoc., 1968. *Publications:* Statistics, 1953; Government Finance and Fiscal Policy in Post-War Britain, 1956; (with P. F. B. Liddle) Parliament of Commerce 1860–1960, 1960; Taxation of Capital Gains, 1962; Rate Equalisation in London, 1968; Local Government Finance in Northern Ireland, 1969. *Recreations:* listening to music, walking. *Club:* National Liberal.

ILIFFE, family name of **Baron Iliffe.**

ILIFFE, 2nd Baron, *cr* 1933, of Yattendon; **Edward Langton Iliffe;** Vice-Chairman of the Birmingham Post and Mail Ltd, 1957–74; Chairman: Coventry Evening Telegraph, 1957–75; Cambridge News, 1959–75; *b* 25 Jan. 1908; *er s* of 1st Baron Iliffe, GBE, and Charlotte Gilding (*d* 1972); *S* father 1960; *m* 1938, Renée, *er d* of René Merandon du Plessis, Mauritius. *Educ:* Sherborne; France; Clare Coll., Cambridge. Served, 1940–46, with RAFVR (despatches). Trustee, Shakespeare's Birthplace; Mem. Council, Univ. of Warwick, 1965–71; Past Pres., Internat. Lawn Tennis Club of Gt Britain. High Sheriff of Berks, 1957. Hon. Freeman, City of Coventry. *Heir: n* Robert Peter Richard Iliffe, *qv*. *Address:* Basildon Park, Lower Basildon, near Reading, Berks RG8 9NR. *T:* Pangbourne (01734) 844409. *Clubs:* Brooks's, Carlton; Royal Yacht Squadron.

ILIFFE, Barrie John; Controller, Arts Division, The British Council, 1983–85; *b* 9 Jan. 1925; *s* of Edward Roy Iliffe; *m* 1959, Caroline Fairfax-Jones; three *d*. *Educ:* Westcliff High Sch.; University College London. Concerts Manager, Liverpool Philharmonic Orchestra, 1951–55; Orchestral Manager, Philharmonia Orch., 1955–56; Manager, Cape Town Orch., 1956–58; Concerts Manager, Philharmonia Orch., 1958–60; Manager, London Mozart Players, 1961–63; General Manager, New Philharmonia Orch., 1964–65; British Council: Head of Music, 1966–77; Director, Music Dept, 1977–83; Dep. Controller, Arts Div., 1981–83. Sec., William and Mary Tercentenary Trust, 1985–86; Asst to Chm., John Lewis Partnership, 1988–90. Royal Philharmonic Society: Mem., Hon. Council of Management, 1987–94; Hon. Co-Treasurer, 1989–93; Hon. Sec., 1993–94. Trustee, Eric Thompson Charitable Trust for Organists and Organ Music, 1993–. *Recreation:* inland waterways. *Address:* 29 Murray Mews, NW1 9RH. *T:* 0171–485 5154.

ILIFFE, Prof. John, FBA 1989; Professor of African History, University of Cambridge, since 1990; Fellow of St John's College, Cambridge, since 1971; *b* 1 May 1939; 2nd *s* of late Arthur Ross Iliffe and Violet Evelyn Iliffe. *Educ:* Framlingham Coll.; Peterhouse, Cambridge (BA 1961; MA; PhD 1965; LittD 1990). Lectr, then Reader, in History, Univ. of Dar-es-Salaam, 1965–71; University of Cambridge: Asst Dir of Res. in Hist., 1971–80; Reader in African Hist., 1980–90. *Publications:* Tanganyika under German Rule, 1969; A Modern History of Tanganyika, 1979; The Emergence of African Capitalism, 1983; The African Poor: a history, 1987; Famine in Zimbabwe, 1989; Africans: the history of a continent, 1995. *Recreation:* cricket. *Address:* St John's College, Cambridge CB2 1TP. *T:* Cambridge (01223) 338714. *Club:* MCC.

ILIFFE, Robert Peter Richard, Chairman, Yattendon Investment Trust PLC, since 1984; *b* Oxford, 22 Nov. 1944; *s* of late Hon. W. H. R. Iliffe and Mrs Iliffe; *m* 1966, Rosemary Anne Skipwith; three *s* one *d* (of whom one *s* one *d* are twins). *Educ:* Eton; Christ Church, Oxford. Chairman: Marina Developments Ltd; Cambridge Newspapers Ltd; Herts & Essex Newspapers Ltd; Burton Daily Mail Ltd; Staffordshire Newsletter. Chm., Yattendon Estates Ltd, since 1987; Director: Scottish Provincial Press Ltd, 1990–; British Air Transport (Holdings), 1989–. Member of Council, RASE, 1972– (Chm., 1994–). High Sheriff of Warwicks, 1983–84. *Recreations:* yachting, shooting, fishing, old cars. *Address:* Yattendon Park, Yattendon, Thatcham, Berks RG18 0UT.

ILLINGWORTH, David Gordon, CVO 1987 (LVO 1980); MD, FRCPE; retired; Surgeon Apothecary to HM Household at Holyrood Palace, Edinburgh, 1970–86; *b* 22 Dec. 1921; *yr s* of Sir Gordon Illingworth; *m* 1946, Lesley Beagrie, Peterhead; two *s* one *d*. *Educ:* George Watson's Coll.; Edinburgh University. MB, ChB Edinburgh, 1943; MRCPE 1949; MD (with commendation) 1963; FRCPE 1965; FRCGP 1970. Nuffield Foundn Travelling Fellow, 1966. RN Medical Service, 1944–46 (2nd Escort Gp); medical appts, Edinburgh Northern Hosps Group, 1946–82. Dep. CMO, Scottish Life Assurance Co., 1973–92. Hon. Sen. Lectr in Rehabilitation Studies, Dept of Orthopaedic Surgery, Edinburgh Univ., 1977–82; Lectr in Gen. Practice Teaching Unit, Edinburgh Univ., 1965–82. Member: Cancer Planning Group, Scottish Health Service Planning Council, 1976–81; Tenovus, Edinburgh, 1978–92; ASH, Royal Colleges Jt Cttee, 1978–82; Specialty Sub-Cttee on Gen. Practice, 1980–82; Nat. Med. Cons. Cttee, 1980–82. AFOM, RCP, 1980. Mem., Harveian Soc. Life Governor, Imperial Cancer Res. Fund, 1978. *Publications:* Practice (jtly), 1978; contribs to BMJ, Jl of Clinical Pathology, Gut, Lancet, Medicine. *Recreations:* golf, gardening. *Address:* 19 Napier Road, Edinburgh EH10 5AZ. *T:* 0131–229 8102. *Clubs:* University (Edinburgh); Bruntsfield Links Golfing Soc.

ILLINGWORTH, Raymond, CBE 1973; cricketer; Manager, Yorkshire County Cricket Club, 1979–84; Chairman, England (Cricket) Committee, Test and County Cricket Board, since 1994; *b* 8 June 1932; *s* of late Frederick Spencer Illingworth and Ida Illingworth; *m* 1958, Shirley Milnes; two *d*. *Educ:* Wesley Street Sch., Farsley, Pudsey. Yorkshire County cricketer; capped, 1955. Captain: MCC, 1969; Leics CCC, 1969–78; Yorks CCC, 1982–83. Toured: West Indies, 1959–60; Australia twice (once as Captain), 1962–63 and 1970–71. Played in 66 Test Matches (36 as Captain). Hon. MA Hull, 1983. *Publications:* Spinners Wicket, 1969; The Young Cricketer, 1972; Spin Bowling, 1979; Captaincy, 1980; Yorkshire and Back, 1980; (with Kenneth Gregory) The Ashes, 1982; The Tempestuous Years 1977–83, 1987. *Recreations:* golf, bridge. *Address:* The Mistle, 4 Calverley Lane, Farsley, Pudsey, West Yorkshire LS28 5LB. *T:* Pudsey (0113) 257 8137.

ILLMAN, John; HM Diplomatic Service; Ambassador to Peru, since 1995; *b* 26 Oct. 1940; *s* of Reginald Thomas Illman and Hilda Kathleen Illman (*née* Targett); *m* 1962, Elizabeth Hunter Frame; one *s* two *d*. *Educ:* Reading Sch.; St Andrews Univ. Joined Foreign Office, 1961: Leopoldville, later Kinshasa, 1963–66; Dublin, 1967–71; Paris, 1971–73; First Sec., FCO, 1973–75; Buenos Aires, 1975–79; Lagos, 1979–82; Commonwealth Co-ordination Dept, FCO, 1982–86; Dep. Head of Mission and Consul-Gen., Algiers, 1986–90; Consul-Gen., Marseilles and for Principality of Monaco, 1990–94. *Recreations:* squash, tennis, Rugby, cricket, amateur dramatics. *Address:* c/o Foreign and Commonwealth Office, King Charles Street, SW1A 2AH. *Club:* Commonwealth Trust.

ILLSLEY, Eric Evlyn; MP (Lab) Barnsley Central, since 1987; *b* 9 April 1955; *s* of John and Maude Illsley; *m* 1978, Dawn Webb; two *d*. *Educ:* Barnsley Holgate Grammar Sch.; Leeds Univ. (LLB Hons 1977). NUM, Yorkshire Area: Compensation Officer, 1978–81; Asst Head of General Dept, 1981–84; Head of Gen. Dept and Chief Admin. Officer, 1984–87. An Opposition Whip, 1991–94; Opposition spokesperson on health, 1994–. Member, Select Committee: on televising proceedings of H of C, 1988–91; on Energy, 1987–91; on Procedure, 1991–; Jt Chm., All Party Parly Glass Gp, 1989–; Treas., All Party Parly Gp on Occupnl Pensions, 1993–. Sec., Barnsley Constit. Lab. Pty, 1980–83 (Treas., 1979–80); Sec. and Election Agent, Yorks S Eur. Constit. Lab. Pty, 1983–87; Treas., Yorks Gp of Lab. MPs, 1988–. *Recreation:* gymnasium. *Address:* House of Commons, Westminster, SW1A 0AA. *T:* (office) Barnsley (01226) 730692.

ILLSLEY, Prof. Raymond, CBE 1979; PhD; Professorial Fellow in Social Policy, University of Bath, since 1984; *b* 6 July 1919; *s* of James and Harriet Illsley; *m* 1948, Jean Mary Harrison; two *s* one *d*. *Educ:* St Edmund Hall, Oxford (BA 1948). PhD Aberdeen 1956. Served War, 1939–45: active service in GB and ME, 1939–42; PoW, Italy and Germany, 1942–45. Econ. Asst, Commonwealth Econ. Cttee, London, 1948; Social Res. Officer, New Town Develt Corp., Crawley, Sussex, 1948–50; Sociologist, MRC, working with Dept of Midwifery, Univ. of Aberdeen, as Mem., Social Med. Res. Unit and later Mem., Obstetric Med. Res. Unit, 1951–64; Prof. of Sociology, Univ. of Aberdeen, 1964–75, Prof. of Medical Sociology, 1975–84. Dir, MRC Medical Sociology Unit, 1965–83. Vis. Prof., Cornell Univ., NY, 1963–64; Vis. Scientist, Harvard Univ., 1968; Sen. Foreign Scientist, National Sci. Foundn, Boston Univ., 1971–72; Vis. Prof., Dept of Sociology, Boston Univ., 1971–72, Adjunct Prof., 1972–76. Chairman: Scottish TUC Inquiry on Upper Clyde Shipbuilders Ltd, 1971; Social Sciences Adv. Panel, Action for the Crippled Child, 1971–76; Health Services Res. Cttee, Chief Scientist's Org., SHHD, 1976–84. Member: Sec. of State's Scottish Council on Crime, 1972–76; Exec. Cttee, Nat. Fund for Res. into Crippling Diseases, 1972–76; Chief Scientist's Cttee, SHHD, 1973–85; EEC Cttee on Med. Res., 1974–77; SSRC, 1976–78 (Chairman: Sociol. and Soc. Admin Cttee, 1976–79; Social Affairs Cttee, 1982–85); Chief Scientist's Adv. Cttee, DHSS, 1980–81; European Adv. Cttee for Med. Res., WHO, 1981–85. Rock Carling Fellow, Nuffield Prov. Hosps Trust, 1980. Hon. DSc Univ. of Hull, 1984; DUniv Stirling, 1987; Hon. dr med. Copenhagen, 1992. *Publications:* Mental Subnormality in the Community: a clinical and epidemiological study (with H. Birch, S. Richardson, D. Baird et al), 1970; Professional or Public Health, 1980; (with R. G. Mitchell) Low Birth Weight, 1984; articles in learned jls on reproduction, migration, social mobility, mental subnormality. *Recreation:* rough husbandry. *Address:* University of Bath, Claverton Down, Bath BA2 7AY; *T:* (office) Bath (01225) 826752; Tisbut House, Box Hill, Wilts SN14 9HG. *T:* Bath (01225) 742313.

ILLSTON, Prof. John Michael, CEng, FICE; Director of the Hatfield Polytechnic, 1982–87, Professor and Professor Emeritus, 1987, Fellow, 1991; *b* 17 June 1928; *s* of Alfred Charles Illston and Ethel Marian Illston; *m* 1951, Olga Elizabeth Poulter; one *s* two *d*. *Educ:* Wallington County Grammar Sch.; King's Coll., Univ. of London (BScEng, PhD, DScEng; FKC 1985). CEng, FICE 1975. Water engr, then schoolmaster, 1949–59; Lectr, Sen. Lectr and Reader in Civil Engrg, King's Coll., London, 1959–77; Dir of Studies in Civil Engrg, Dean of Engrg, and Dep. Dir, Hatfield Polytechnic, 1977–82. Member: Commonwealth Scholarships Commn, 1983–92; Engrg Bd, SERC, 1983–86; Engrg Council, 1981–90; Council, BTEC, 1986–89; Chm., CNAA Cttee for Engrg, 1987–91; Visitor, Building Res. Stn, 1989–. Chm. Governing Body, Bishop Wordsworth Sch., 1994–. *Publications:* (with J. M. Dinwoodie and A. A. Smith) Concrete, Timber and Metals, 1979; (ed) Construction Materials, 2nd edn 1994; contrib. Cement and Concrete Res. and Magazine of Concrete Res. *Address:* 10 Merrifield Road, Ford, Salisbury, Wilts SP4 6DF.

IMBERT, Sir Peter (Michael), Kt 1988; QPM 1980; DL; Commissioner, Metropolitan Police, 1987–93 (Deputy Commissioner, 1985–87); *b* 27 April 1933; *s* of late William Henry Imbert and of Frances May (*née* Hodge); *m* 1956, Iris Rosina (*née* Dove); one *s* two *d*. *Educ:* Harvey Grammar Sch., Folkestone, Kent; Holborn College of Law, Languages and Commerce. Joined Metropolitan Police, 1953; Asst Chief Constable, Surrey Constabulary, 1976, Dep. Chief Constable, 1977; Chief Constable, Thames Valley Police, 1979–85. Metropolitan Police Anti-Terrorist Squad, 1973–75; Police negotiator at Balcome Street siege, Dec. 1975; visited Holland following Moluccan sieges, and Vienna following siege of OPEC building by terrorists, Dec. 1975. Lectures in UK to police and military on terrorism and siege situations; also in Europe (incl. Berlin, 1978); lecture tours to Australia, 1977, 1980 and 1986, to advise on terrorism and sieges, and to Canada, 1981 re practical effects on police forces of recommendations of Royal Commn on Criminal Procedure. Sec., Nat. Crime Cttee-ACPO Council, 1980–83 (Chm., 1983–85). Member: Gen. Advisory Council, BBC, 1980–87; Criminal Justice Consultative Cttee, 1992–93; Academic Consultative Cttee, King George VI and Queen Elizabeth Foundn of St Catharine's, Cumberland Lodge, Windsor, 1983–; Public Policy Cttee, RAC, 1993–. Trustee, Queen Elizabeth Foundn of St Catharine's, 1988–. CIMgt (CBIM 1982). DL Greater London, 1994. Hon. DLitt Reading, 1987; Hon. DBA IMCB, 1989. *Publications:* occasional articles and book reviews. *Recreations:* bad bridge, coarse golf, talking about my grandchildren. *Address:* c/o New Scotland Yard, Broadway, SW1H 0BG. *T:* 0171–230 1212.

IMBERT-TERRY, Sir Michael Edward Stanley, 5th Bt *cr* 1917, of Strete Ralegh, Whimple, Co. Devon; *b* 18 April 1950; *s* of Major Sir Edward Henry Bouhier Imbert-Terry, 3rd Bt, MC, and of Jean (who *m* 1983, Baron Sackville, *qv*), *d* of late Arthur Stanley Garton; *S* brother, 1985; *m* 1975, Frances Dorothy, *d* of late Peter Scott, Ealing; one *s* two *d*. *Educ:* Cranleigh. *Heir: s* Brychan Edward Imbert-Terry, *b* 1975.

IMBODEN, Dr Christoph Niklaus; Director-General, BirdLife International; *b* 28 April 1946; *s* of Max Imboden and Elisabeth Imboden-Stahel; *m* 1970, Eve Elisabeth Staub; one *s* one *d*. *Educ:* Univ. of Basel (PhD). New Zealand Wildlife Service: Sen. Scientist, 1977; Asst Dir (Research), 1978; Dir-Gen., ICBP, now BirdLife Internat., 1980–. Premio Gaia, Sicily, 1993; RSPB Conservation Medal, 1993. *Publications:* papers on ornithology, ecology, conservation. *Recreations:* classical music, bbirdwatching, hill-walking, travelling.

IMRAN KHAN, (Imran Ahmad Khan Niazi); Hilal-e-Imtiaz, Pakistan, 1993; *b* Lahore, 25 Oct. 1952; *m* 1995, Jemima, (Haiqa), *d* of Sir James Goldsmith, *qv*. *Educ:* Aitchison Coll.; Keble Coll., Oxford (BA Hons; cricket blue, 1973, 1974, 1975; Captain, Oxford XI, 1974). Début for Lahore A, 1969; played first Test for Pakistan, 1970, Captain, 1982–84, 1985–87, 1988–89, 1992; with Worcs CCC, 1971–76 (capped, 1976); with Sussex CCC, 1977–88 (capped, 1978; Hon. Life Mem., 1988). Editor-in-Chief, Cricket Life Internat., 1989–90. Mem., Internat. Cricket Council, 1993–. Hon. Fellow of Keble Coll., Oxford, 1988. Special Sports Rep., UNICEF; Founder, Imran Khan Cancer Hosp. Appeal, 1991–. Pride of Performance Award, Pakistan. *Publications:* Imran, 1983; All-Round View (autobiog.), 1988; Indus Journey, 1990; Warrior Race, 1993. *Recreations:*

shooting, films, music. *Address:* c/o Shankat Khanum Memorial Trust, 29 Shah Jamal, Lahore 54600, Pakistan. *Clubs:* Tramp; Gymkhana (Lahore).

IMRAY, Sir Colin (Henry), KBE 1992; CMG 1983; HM Diplomatic Service, retired; Secretary General, Order of St John, since 1993; *b* 21 Sept. 1933; *s* of late Henry Gibbon Imray and Frances Olive Imray; *m* 1957, Shirley Margaret Matthews; one *s* three *d. Educ:* Highgate Sch.; Hotchkiss Sch., Conn; Balliol Coll., Oxford (2nd cl. Hons PPE). Served in Seaforth Highlanders and RWAFF, Sierra Leone, 1952–54. CRO, 1957; Canberra, 1958–61; CRO, 1961–63; Nairobi, 1963–66; FCO, 1966–70; British Trade Comr, Montreal, 1970–73; Counsellor, Head of Chancery and Consul-Gen., Islamabad, 1973–77; RCDS, 1977; Commercial Counsellor, Tel Aviv, 1977–80; Rayner Project Officer, 1980; Dep. High Comr, Bombay, 1980–84; Asst Under-Sec. of State (Dep. Chief Clerk and Chief Inspector), FCO, 1984–85; High Commissioner: Tanzania, 1986–89; Bangladesh, 1989–93. KStJ 1993. *Address:* c/o Order of St John, St John's Gate, Clerkenwell, EC1M 4DA. *Clubs:* Commonwealth Trust, Travellers'.

INCH, Thomas David, CChem, FRSC; Secretary-General, Royal Society of Chemistry, since 1993; *b* 25 Sept. 1938; *s* of Thomas Alexander Inch and Sarah Lang Graves Inch; *m* 1964, Jacqueline Vivienne Pudner; one *d. Educ:* St Austell Grammar Sch.; Univ. of Birmingham (BSc 1st Cl. Hons Chem. 1960; PhD 1963; DSc 1971). Salters Fellow, Univ. of Birmingham, 1963–64; Vis. Fellow, NIH, USA, 1964–65; Chemical Defence Estabt, MoD, 1965–87 (RCDS 1985); Gen. Manager, Research Business Development, BP Research, 1987–90; Vice-Pres., R&D, BP America, 1990–93. Director: BP Ventures, 1987–89; Edison Polymer Innovation Corp., 1990–92; Ohio Science and Technology Commn, 1992. *Publications:* papers and reviews on chemistry and related topics. *Recreation:* golf. *Address:* Royal Society of Chemistry, Burlington House, Piccadilly, W1V 0BN. *T:* 0171–437 8656. *Clubs:* Athenæum; High Post Golf.

INCHBALD, Michael John Chantrey, FCSD; designer; *b* 8 March 1920; *s* of late Geoffrey H. E. Inchbald and Rosemary, *d* of Arthur Ilbert and *niece* of Sir Courtenay Ilbert, GCB, KCSI, CIE; *m* 1955, Jacqueline Bromley (marr. diss. 1964; *see* J. A. Duncan); one *s* one *d*; *m* 1964, Eunice Haymes (marr. diss. 1970). *Educ:* Sherborne; Architect. Assoc. Sch. of Architecture. FSIAD 1970. Work exhibited: Triennale, Milan; V & A Mus.; Design Centres London, New York, Helsinki. Design projects for: Bank of America; Crown Estate Comrs; Cunard; Dunhill worldwide; Ferragamo; Imperial Group; Justerini & Brooks; Law Soc.; John Lewis; Manufacturers Hanover Bank; Manufacturers Hanover Trust Bank; John Player; Plessey Co.; Pratt Burnard Engineering; Savoy Group—Berkeley, Claridges and Savoy hotels, and the restaurant complex Stones Chop House; Scottish Highland Industries; Trust House Forte—Post House, London Airport and several restaurants; Wolsey; ships, QE2, Carmania, Franconia and Windsor Castle; royal and private yachts and houses. Consultant to furniture and carpet manufacturers. Consulted *re* changes at Buckingham Palace; other projects, for the Duc de la Rochefoucauld, 13th Duke of St Albans, 6th Marquess of Bristol, 17th Earl of Perth, 9th Earl of Dartmouth, 2nd Earl St Aldwyn, etc. Inchbald schs founded under his auspices, 1960. Winner of four out of four nat. design competitions entered, including: Shapes of Things to Come, 1946; Nat. Chair Design Competition, 1955. Freeman, Clockmakers' Co., 1985. *Publications:* contrib. Arch. Rev., Arch. Digest, Connaissance des Arts, Connoisseur, Country Life, Harpers/Queen, House & Garden, Internat. Lighting Rev., Tatler, and Vogue. *Recreations:* arts, travel, antiques. *Address:* Stanley House, 10 Milner Street, SW3 2PU. *T:* 0171–584 8832.

INCHCAPE, 4th Earl of *cr* 1929; **Kenneth Peter Lyle Mackay,** AIB; Viscount Glenapp 1929; Viscount Inchcape 1924; Baron Inchcape 1911; Chairman, Duncan Macneill Holdings Ltd, since 1995; Director: Inchcape Family Investments Ltd, since 1985; Assam Investments Ltd, since 1985; Assam Company Ltd, since 1995; *b* 23 Jan. 1943; *er s* of 3rd Earl of Inchcape, and of his 1st wife, Mrs Aline Thorn Hannay, *d* of Sir Richard Pease, 2nd Bt; *S* father, 1994; *m* 1966, Georgina, *d* of S. C. Nisbet and late Mrs G. R. Sutton; one *s* two *d. Educ:* Eton. Late Lieut 9/12th Royal Lancers. Master, Grocers' Co., 1993–94. *Recreations:* shooting, fishing, golf, farming. *Heir: s* Viscount Glenapp, *qv. Address:* Manor Farm, Clyffe Pypard, near Swindon, Wilts SN4 7PY; 63E Pont Street, SW1X 0BD. *Clubs:* White's, Oriental, Pratt's; Royal Sydney (Sydney, NSW).

INCHIQUIN, 18th Baron of, *cr* 1543; **Conor Myles John O'Brien;** (The O'Brien); Bt 1686; Prince of Thomond; Chief of the Name; *b* 17 July 1943; *s* of Hon. Fionn Myles Maryons O'Brien (*d* 1977) (*y s* of 15th Baron) and of Josephine Reine, *d* of late Joseph Eugene Bembaron; *S* uncle, 1982; *m* 1988, Helen, *d* of Gerald Fitzgerald O'Farrell; two *d. Educ:* Eton. Served as Captain, 14th/20th King's Hussars. *Heir: cousin* Murrough Richard O'Brien [*b* 25 May 1910; *m* 1st, 1942, Irene Clarice (marr. diss. 1951), *o d* of H. W. Richards; 2nd, 1952, Joan, *d* of Charles Pierre Jenkinson and *widow* of Captain Woolf Barnato; one *s* one *d*]. *Address:* Thomond House, Dromoland, Newmarket on Fergus, Co. Clare, Ireland.

INCHYRA, 2nd Baron, *cr* 1962, of St Madoes, Co. Perth; **Robert Charles Reneke Hoyer Millar;** Chairman, NABC—Clubs for Young People, since 1994; *b* 4 April 1935; *er s* of 1st Baron Inchyra, GCMG, CVO and of Elizabeth de Marees van Swinderen; *S* father, 1989; *m* 1961, Fiona Mary, *d* of Major E. C. R. Sheffield; one *s* two *d. Educ:* Eton; New Coll. , Oxford. J. Henry Schroder Wagg & Co., 1958–64; Barclays Bank, 1964–88: Local Dir, Newcastle upon Tyne, 1967–75; Reg. Gen. Man., 1976–81; Dep. Chm., Barclays Bank Trust Co., 1982–85; Gen. Man. and Dir, UK Financial Services, 1985–88; Sec. (later Dir) Gen., BBA, 1988–94. Chm., Johnson Fry European Utilities Trust plc, 1994–; Dir, Witan Investment Co., 1979–. *Heir: s* Hon. Christian James Charles Hoyer Millar [*b* 12 Aug. 1962; *m* 1992, Caroline, *d* of Robin Swan; one *d*]. *Address:* Rookley Manor, Kings Somborne, Stockbridge, Hants SO20 6QX. *T:* Romsey (01794) 388319. *Clubs:* White's, Pratt's.

IND, Jack Kenneth; Headmaster of Dover College, 1981–91; *b* 20 Jan. 1935; *s* of late Rev. William Price Ind and Mrs Doris Maud Ind (*née* Cavell); *m* 1964, Elizabeth Olive Toombs; two *s* two *d. Educ:* Marlborough Coll.; St John's Coll., Oxford (BA Hons Mods, 2nd Cl. Class. Lit. and Lit. Hum.). Assistant Master: Wellingborough Sch., 1960–63; Tonbridge Sch., 1963–81 (Housemaster, 1970–81) and 1991–92; Eastbourne Coll., 1992–93; Teacher, Gymnásium, Nové Zámky, Slovakia, 1994. *Recreations:* tennis, Rugby football, music, reading. *Address:* Salvete, 39 Sandridge Road, Melksham, Wilts SN12 7BQ. *T:* Melksham (01225) 790417.

IND, Rt. Rev. William; *see* Grantham, Bishop Suffragan of.

INGAMELLS, John Anderson Stuart; Editor, Dictionary of British Visitors to Italy in the Eighteenth Century, Paul Mellon Centre for Studies in British Art, since 1992; *b* 12 Nov. 1934; *s* of late George Harry Ingamells and Gladys Lucy (*née* Rollett); *m* 1964, Hazel Wilson; two *d. Educ:* Hastings Grammar School; Eastbourne Grammar School; Fitzwilliam House, Cambridge. National Service, Army (Cyprus), 1956–58; Art Asst, York Art Gallery, 1959–63; Asst Keeper, Dept of Art, National Museum of Wales, 1963–67; Curator, York Art Gallery, 1967–77; Asst to the Director, 1977–78, Director, 1978–92, Wallace Collection. Mem. Exec. Cttee, NACF, 1992–. *Publications:* The Davies Collection of French Art, 1967; The English Episcopal Portrait, 1981; numerous catalogues, including Philip Mercier (with Robert Raines), 1969; Portraits at Bishopthorpe Palace, 1972; museum catalogues at York, Cardiff and the Wallace Collection; articles in Apollo, Connoisseur, Burlington Magazine, Walpole Soc., etc. *Address:* 39 Benson Road, SE23 3RL.

INGE, George Patrick Francis, FRICS; Chief Executive, 1987–91 and Chairman, 1987–95, Savills Plc; *b* 31 Aug. 1941; *s* of late John William Wolstenholme Inge and Alison Lilias Inge; *m* 1977, Joyce (*née* Leinster); one *s* one *d. Educ:* Old Malthouse Prep. Sch., Dorset; Sherborne Sch. Joined Alfred Savill & Sons, 1960; Partner, 1968; Man. Partner, Savills, 1985. Non-exec. Chm., Severn Trent Property Ltd, 1995–. Chm. of Governors, Old Malthouse Sch., Dorset, 1986–; Dep. Chm. Govs, Cothill House Sch., 1994–; Gov., Nottingham Trent Univ., 1994–. *Recreations:* shooting, fishing, golf. *Address:* The Old Vicarage, Little Milton, Oxford OX44 7QB. *T:* Great Milton (01844) 279538. *Clubs:* Buck's, Flyfishers', Farmers'.

INGE, Field-Marshal Sir Peter (Anthony), GCB 1992 (KCB 1988); DL; Chief of the Defence Staff, since 1994; *b* 5 Aug. 1935; *s* of Raymond Albert Inge and late Grace Maud Caroline Inge (*née* Du Rose); *m* 1960, Letitia Marion Beryl, *yr d* of late Trevor and Sylvia Thornton-Berry; two *d. Educ:* Summer Fields; Wrekin College; RMA Sandhurst. Commissioned Green Howards, 1956; served Hong Kong, Malaya, Germany, Libya and UK; ADC to GOC 4 Div., 1960–61; Adjutant, 1 Green Howards, 1963–64; student, Staff Coll., 1966; MoD, 1967–69; Coy Comdr, 1 Green Howards, 1969–70; student, JSSC, 1971; BM 11 Armd Bde, 1972; Instructor, Staff Coll., 1973–74; CO 1 Green Howards, 1974–76; Comdt, Junior Div., Staff Coll., 1977–79; Comdr Task Force C/4 Armd Bde, 1980–81; Chief of Staff, HQ 1 (BR) Corps, 1982–83; GOC NE District and Comdr 2nd Inf. Div., 1984–86; Dir Gen. Logistic Policy (Army), MoD, 1986–87; Comdr 1st (Br.) Corps, 1987–89; Comdr Northern Army Gp, and C-in-C, BAOR, 1989–92; CGS 1992–94. ADC Gen. to the Queen, 1991–94. Colonel, The Green Howards, 1982–94. Col Comdt: RMP, 1987–92; APTC, 1988–. DL N Yorks, 1994. *Recreations:* cricket, walking, music and reading, especially military history. *Address:* c/o Barclays Bank, Market Place, Leyburn, North Yorks DL8 5BQ. *Clubs:* Boodle's, Beefsteak, Army and Navy, MCC.

INGE-INNES-LILLINGSTON, George David, CVO 1993; CBE 1986; MA, DL; a Crown Estates Commissioner, 1974–93; *b* 13 Nov. 1923; *s* of late Comdr H. W. Innes-Lillingston, RN, and Mrs Innes-Lillingston, formerly of Lochalsh House, Balmacara, Kyle, Ross-shire; *m* 1st, 1946, Alison Mary (*d* 1947), *er d* of late Canon F. W. Green, MA, BD, Norwich; one *d*; 2nd, 1955, Elizabeth Violet Grizel Thomson-Inge, *yr d* of late Lt-Gen. Sir William Thomson, KCMG, CB, MC; two *s* one *d. Educ:* Stowe, Buckingham; Merton Coll., Oxford (MA Hons Agric.). Served War as Lieut RNVR, 1942–45, Lt-Comdr RNR, 1966. Member: Agricultural Land Tribunal, 1962–72; Minister's Agricultural Panel for W Midlands, 1972–76; Council for Charitable Support, 1985–90; Chairman: N Birmingham and District Hosps, 1968–74; Agric. and Hort. Cttee, BSI, 1980–86; President: Staffs Agricultural Soc., 1970–71; CLA, 1979–81 (Dep. Pres., 1977–79; Chm., 1968–71, Pres., 1983–94, Staffs Br.). Dir, Lands Improvement Gp Ltd, and associated cos, 1983–91; Chm., Croxden Horticultural Products Ltd, 1986–91. Chm., Midland Reg., STA, 1983–94. Trustee, Lichfield Cathedral, 1980–. FRAgS 1986. JP 1967–74, DL 1969, Staffs; High Sheriff, Staffs, 1966. Bledisloe Gold Medal for Landowners, RASE, 1991. *Recreation:* growing trees. *Address:* The Old Kennels, Thorpe Constantine, Tamworth, Staffs B79 0LH. *T:* Tamworth (01827) 830224. *Clubs:* Boodle's, Farmers', Royal Thames Yacht; Royal Highland Yacht (Oban).

INGESTRE, Viscount; James Richard Charles John Chetwynd-Talbot; *b* 11 Jan. 1978; *s* and *heir* of 22nd Earl of Shrewsbury and Waterford, *qv.*

INGHAM, Sir Bernard, Kt 1990; Chairman, Bernard Ingham Communications, since 1990; *b* 21 June 1932; *s* of Garnet and Alice Ingham; *m* 1956, Nancy Hilda Hoyle; one *s. Educ:* Hebden Bridge Grammar Sch., Yorks. Reporter: Hebden Bridge Times, 1948–52; Yorkshire Post and Yorkshire Evening Post, Halifax, 1952–59; Yorkshire Post, Leeds, 1959–61; Northern Industrial Correspondent, Yorkshire Post, 1961; Reporter, The Guardian, 1962–65; Labour Staff, The Guardian, London, 1965–67; Press and Public Relns Adviser, NBPI, 1967–68; Chief Inf. Officer, DEP, 1968–73; Dir of Information: Dept of Employment, 1973; Dept of Energy, 1974–77; Under Sec., Energy Conservation Div., Dept of Energy, 1978–79; Chief Press Sec. to Prime Minister, 1979–90; Head, Govt Inf. Service, 1989–90. Columnist, Daily Express, 1991–. Non-executive Director: McDonald's Restaurants Ltd, 1991–; Hill and Knowlton (UK) Ltd, public relations counsel, 1991–. Mem., Press Complaints Commn, 1995–. Vis. Fellow, Univ. of Newcastle, 1990–. Pres., British Franchise Assoc., 1993–. Mem. Council Univ. of Huddersfield, 1994–. *Publication:* Kill The Messenger, 1991. *Recreations:* walking, gardening, reading. *Address:* 9 Monahan Avenue, Purley, Surrey CR8 3BB. *T:* 0181–660 8970, *Fax:* 0181–668 4357. *Club:* Reform.

INGHAM, Prof. Kenneth, OBE 1961; MC 1946; Professor of History, 1967–84, Part-time Professor of History, 1984–86, now Emeritus Professor, and Head of History Department, 1970–84, University of Bristol; *b* 9 Aug. 1921; *s* of Gladson and Frances Lily Ingham; *m* 1949, Elizabeth Mary Southall; one *s* one *d. Educ:* Bingley Grammar Sch.; Keble Coll., Oxford (Exhibitioner). Served with West Yorks Regt, 1941–46 (despatches, 1945). Frere Exhibitioner in Indian Studies, University of Oxford, 1947; DPhil 1950. Lecturer in Modern History, Makerere Coll., Uganda, 1950–56, Prof., 1956–62; Dir of Studies, RMA, Sandhurst, 1962–67. MLC, Uganda, 1954–61. *Publications:* Reformers in India, 1956; The Making of Modern Uganda, 1958; A History of East Africa, 1962; The Kingdom of Toro in Uganda, 1975; Jan Christian Smuts: the conscience of a South African, 1986; Politics in Modern Africa, 1990; Obote: a political biography, 1994; contrib. to Encyclopædia Britannica, Britannica Book of the Year. *Address:* The Woodlands, 94 West Town Lane, Bristol BS4 5DZ.

INGHAM, Rt Rev. Michael; *see* New Westminster, Bishop of.

INGHAM, Stuart Edward; Chief Executive, United Leeds Teaching Hospitals NHS Trust, since 1991; *b* 9 Oct. 1942; *s* of Edward Ingham and Dorothy Mary (*née* Pollard); *m* 1969, Jane Stella Wilkinson; one *s* one *d. Educ:* Canon Slade Grammar Sch., Bolton. AHSM 1970. Bolton and District HMC: Trainee in Hosp. Admin, 1965–66; HCO, 1966–67; Dep. Gen. Supt, Ancoats Hosp., 1967–69; Sen. Admin Asst, Royal Bucks and Associated HMC, 1969–70; Hospital Secretary: Harefield Hosp., 1970–73; St James's Univ. Hosp., Leeds, 1973–74; Leeds Area Health Authority (Eastern): General Administrator, 1974–77; Dist Administrator, 1977–82; York Health Authority: Dist Administrator, 1982–84; Dist Gen. Manager, 1985–88; Dist Gen. Manager, Leeds Western HA, 1988–90. *Recreations:* horse riding, sailing. *Address:* Trust Headquarters, United Leeds Teaching Hospitals NHS Trust, Leeds General Infirmary, Great George Street, Leeds LS1 3EX; The Turnings, Woodacre Crescent, Bardsey, Leeds LS17 9DQ. *T:* Wetherby (01937) 572673.

INGILBY, Sir Thomas (Colvin William), 6th Bt *cr* 1866; MRAC; ARICS; FAAV; managing own estate; *b* 17 July 1955; *s* of Sir Joslan William Vivian Ingilby, 5th Bt, DL, JP, and of Diana, *d* of late Sir George Colvin, CB, CMG, DSO; *S* father, 1974; *m* 1984, Emma Clare Roebuck, *d* of Major R. R. Thompson, Whinfield, Strensall, York; four *s* one *d*. *Educ:* Aysgarth Sch., Bedale; Eton Coll. Student Teacher, Springvale School, Marandellas, Rhodesia, Sept. 1973–April 1974. Joined Army, May 1974, but discharged on death of father; student at Royal Agricultural Coll., Cirencester, until 1978. Assistant: Stephenson & Son, York, 1978–80; Strutt & Parker, Harrogate, 1981–83. Chm., Action Harrogate Ltd, 1992–; Dir, Heritage Placements (Structures) Ltd, 1991–. Dir, N Yorks TEC, 1989–94; Founder and Nat. Co-ordinator, Stately Homes Hotline, 1988–; Pres., Council for Prevention of Art Theft, 1991–. Lecture tours, USA, speaking on castles and historic houses, 1978, 1979. Gov., Ashville Coll., Harrogate, 1987–95. FRSA 1992. Internat. Hon. Citizen, New Orleans, 1979. *Recreations:* cricket, tennis, squash. *Heir: s* James William Francis Ingilby, *b* 15 June 1985. *Address:* Ripley Castle, Ripley, near Harrogate, North Yorkshire HG3 3AY. *T:* Harrogate (01423) 770152.

INGLEBY, 2nd Viscount, *cr* 1955, of Snilesworth; **Martin Raymond Peake;** Landowner; Director, Hargreaves Group Ltd, 1960–80; *b* 31 May 1926; *s* of 1st Viscount Ingleby, and Joan, Viscountess Ingleby (*d* 1979); *S* father, 1966; *m* 1952, Susan, *d* of late Henderson Russell Landale; four *d* (one *s* decd). *Educ:* Eton; Trinity Coll., Oxford (MA). Called to the Bar, Inner Temple, 1956. Sec., Hargreaves Group Ltd, 1958–61. Administrative Staff Coll., 1961. CC Yorks (North Riding), 1964–67. Mem., N Yorks Moors Nat. Park Planning Cttee, 1968–78. *Heir:* none. *Address:* Snilesworth, Northallerton, North Yorks DL6 3QD.

INGLEDOW, Anthony Brian, OBE 1969; HM Diplomatic Service, retired; Counsellor, Foreign and Commonwealth Office, 1983–93; *b* 25 July 1928; *s* of Cedric Francis Ingledow and Doris Evelyn Ingledow (*née* Worrall); *m* 1956, Margaret Monica, *d* of Sir Reginald Watson-Jones, FRCS; one *s* one *d*. *Educ:* St Bees School; London Univ. Served HM Forces, 1947–49. Joined Colonial Administrative Service, Nigeria, 1950; District Officer: Auchi, 1954; Oyo, 1956; Secretariat, Ibadan, 1958, retired 1960; joined HM Diplomatic Service, 1961; 2nd Secretary, Khartoum, 1962; FO, 1964; 1st Secretary, Aden, 1966; Lagos, 1967; FCO, 1970; Dakar, 1972; FCO, 1975. *Recreations:* reading, travel. *Address:* c/o Lloyds Bank, 8–10 Waterloo Place, SW1Y 4BE. *Club:* Athenæum.

INGLEFIELD-WATSON, Lt-Col Sir John (Forbes), 5th Bt *cr* 1895, of Earnock, Co. Lanarks; *b* 16 May 1926; *s* of Sir Derrick William Inglefield Watson, Bt, TD (who changed family surname to Inglefield-Watson by Deed Poll, 1945) and of Margrett Georgina (*née* Robertson-Aikman, now Savill); *S* father, 1987. *Educ:* Eton College. MIMgt. Enlisted RE, 1944; short course, Trinity Coll., Cambridge, 1944–45; commnd RE, 1946; served in Iraq, Egypt, Kenya, Libya, Cyprus, Germany, N Ireland; psc 1958; Major 1959; Lt-Col 1969; retired 1981. Association Football Referee: Class I, 1954; Chm. Army FA Referees Cttee, 1974–78; FA Staff Referee Instructor, 1978–. Mem. Council, Kent County FA, 1975–81; Hon. Vice-Pres., Army FA, 1982–92. *Recreations:* Association football refereeing; philately. *Heir: cousin* Simon Conran Hamilton Watson [*b* 11 Aug. 1939; *m* 1971, Madeleine Stiles, *e d* of late Wagner Mahlon Dickerson]. *Address:* The Ross, Hamilton, Lanarkshire ML3 7UF. *T:* Hamilton (01698) 283734.

INGLESE, Anthony Michael Christopher; Legal Director, Office of Fair Trading, since 1991; *b* 19 Dec. 1951; *s* of Angelo Inglese and Dora Inglese (*née* Di Paola); *m* 1974, Jane Elizabeth Kerry Bailes; one *s* one *d*. *Educ:* Salvatorian Coll., Harrow Weald; Fitzwilliam Coll., Cambridge (MA, LLB). Called to the Bar, Gray's Inn, 1976; Legal Advr's Br., Home Office, 1975–86; Legal Secretariat to Law Officers, 1986–88; Legal Advr's Br., Home Office, 1988–91. *Recreations:* organising theatricals, watching football. *Address:* Office of Fair Trading, 15–25 Bream's Buildings, EC4A 1PR. *T:* 0171–242 2858. *Club:* Institute of Contemporary Arts.

INGLEWOOD, 2nd Baron *cr* 1964; **(William) Richard Fletcher-Vane;** DL; Parliamentary Under-Secretary of State, Department of National Heritage, since 1995; *b* 31 July 1951; *e s* of 1st Baron Inglewood, TD and Mary (*d* 1982), *e d* of Major Sir Richard George Proby, 1st Bt, MC; *S* father, 1989; *m* 1986, Cressida, *y d* of late Desmond Pemberton-Pigott, CMG; one *s* two *d*. *Educ:* Eton; Trinity Coll., Cambridge (MA); Cumbria Coll. of Agriculture and Forestry. ARICS. Called to the Bar, Lincoln's Inn, 1975. Member: Lake Dist Special Planning Bd, 1984–90 (Chm., Develt Control Cttee, 1984–89); NW Water Authority, 1987–89. Contested (C) Houghton and Washington, 1983; Durham, European Parlt, 1984; MEP (C) Cumbria and Lancashire N, 1989–94; contested (C) Cumbria and Lancashire N, Eur. Parly elecns, 1994. Cons. spokesman on legal affairs, Eur. Parlt, 1989–94; Dep. Whip, EDG, 1992–94, Chief Whip, 1994. A Lord in Waiting (Govt Whip), 1994–95; Captain of the Yeomen of the Guard (Dep. Govt Chief Whip), 1995. DL Cumbria, 1993. *Heir: s* Hon. Henry William Frederick Fletcher-Vane, *b* 24 Dec. 1990. *Address:* Hutton-in-the-Forest, Penrith, Cumbria CA11 9TH. *T:* Skelton (017684) 84500, *Fax:* (017684) 84571. *Clubs:* Pratt's, Travellers'.

INGLIS, Sir Brian Scott, AC 1988; Kt 1977; FTS; Chairman: Optus Communications, since 1992; Scalzo Automotive Research Ltd, since 1986; *b* Adelaide, 3 Jan. 1924; *s* of late E. S. Inglis, Albany, WA; *m* 1953, Leila, *d* of E. V. Butler; three *d*. *Educ:* Geelong Church of England Grammar School; Trinity Coll., Univ. of Melbourne (BSc; Mem. Council, 1985). Served War of 1939–45; Flying Officer, RAAF, 453 Sqdn, 1942–45. Director and Gen. Manufacturing Manager, 1963–70, first Australian Man. Dir, Ford Motor Co. of Australia Ltd, 1970–81, Vice-Pres., 1981–83, Chm. 1981–85; Chm., Ford Asia-Pacific Inc., 1983–84. Chairman: Newcrest Mining (formerly Newmont Holdings), 1985–94; Aerospace Technologies of Aust. Pty Ltd, 1987–94; Amcor, 1989–94 (Dep. Chm., 1988–89; Dir, 1984–94); non-exec. Dir, Australian Paper, 1994–. Chm., Defence Industry Cttee, 1984–87 (Mem., 1982–87). Chm., Centre for Molecular Biology and Medicine, Monash Univ. James N. Kirby Medal, IProdE, 1979; Kernot Medal, Faculty of Engrg, Univ. of Melbourne, 1979. *Address:* 10 Bowley Avenue, Balwyn, Victoria 3103, Australia. *Clubs:* Australian (Melbourne); Barwon Heads Golf.

INGLIS, George Bruton; Senior Partner, Slaughter and May, 1986–92; *b* 19 April 1933; *s* of late Cecil George Inglis and Ethel Mabel Inglis; *m* 1968, Patricia Mary Forbes; three *s*. *Educ:* Winchester College; Pembroke College, Oxford (MA). Solicitor. Partner, Slaughter and May, 1966–92. *Recreation:* gardening.

INGLIS, Heather Hughson; *see* Swindells, H. H.

INGLIS, Ian Grahame, CB 1983; Chairman, State Grants Commission, Tasmania, since 1990; *b* 2 April 1929; *s* of late William and Ellen Jean Inglis; *m* 1952, Elaine Arlene Connors; three *s* one *d*. *Educ:* Hutchins Sch., Hobart; Univ. of Tasmania (BComm). Agricl Economist, Tasmanian Dept. of Agric., 1951–58; Economist, State Treasury, 1958–69; Chairman: Rivers and Water Supply Commn, and Metropolitan Water Bd, 1969–77; NW Regl Water Authority, 1977; State Under Treasurer, Tas, 1977–89. Dir, TGIO Ltd (formerly Tasmanian Govt Insce Bd), 1989–. Chm., Retirement Benefits Fund Investment Trust, 1989–95. Member: Ambulance Commn of Tasmania, 1959–65; Tasmanian Grain Elevators Bd, 1962–65; Clarence Municipal Commn, 1965–69; Motor Accidents Insurance Bd, 1991–95. Dir, Comalco Aluminium (Bell Bay) Ltd, 1980–. *Recreation:* yachting. *Address:* 5 Sayer Crescent, Sandy Bay, Hobart, Tas 7005, Australia. *T:* (02) 231928. *Clubs:* Tasmanian, Royal Yacht of Tasmania (Hobart).

INGLIS, James Craufuird Roger, WS; Partner, Shepherd & Wedderburn, WS, 1976–89; Chairman, British Assets Trust plc, since 1978; *b* 21 June 1925; *s* of Lt-Col John Inglis and Helen Jean Inglis; *m* 1952, Phoebe Aeonie Murray-Buchanan; two *s* four *d*. *Educ:* Winchester Coll.; Cambridge Univ. (BA); Edinburgh Univ. (LLB). Director: Scottish Provident Institution, 1962–; Selective Assets Trust plc, 1988–; Royal Bank of Scotland, 1967–89; Royal Bank of Scotland Gp plc, 1985–90. Chairman: European Assets Trust NV, 1972–; Investors Capital Trust, 1985–94; Ivory & Sime Optimum Income Trust, 1989–. *Recreation:* golf. *Address:* Inglisfield, Gifford, East Lothian, Scotland EH41 4JH. *T:* Gifford (01620) 810339. *Clubs:* Army and Navy; New (Edinburgh), Royal and Ancient Golf (St Andrews), Hon. Company of Edinburgh Golfers.

INGLIS, Prof. Kenneth Stanley, DPhil; Professor of History, Australian National University, 1977–94, retired; *b* 7 Oct. 1929; *s* of S. W. Inglis; *m* 1st, 1952, Judy Betheras (*d* 1962); one *s* two *d*; 2nd, 1965, Amirah Gust. *Educ:* Univ. of Melbourne (MA); Univ. of Oxford (DPhil). Sen. Lectr in History, Univ. of Adelaide, 1956–60; Reader in History, 1960–62; Associate Prof. of History, Australian National Univ., 1962–65; Prof., 1965–66; Prof. of History, Univ. of Papua New Guinea, 1966–72, Vice-Chancellor, 1972–75; Professorial Fellow in Hist., ANU, 1975–77. Vis. Prof. of Australian Studies, Harvard, 1982; Vis. Prof., Univ. of Hawaii, 1985; Vis. Fellow, St John's Coll., Cambridge, 1990–91. Jt Gen. Editor, Australians: a historical library, 1987–88. *Publications:* Hospital and Community, 1958; The Stuart Case, 1961; Churches and the Working Classes in Victorian England, 1963; The Australian Colonists, 1974; This is the ABC: the Australian Broadcasting Commission, 1932–1983, 1983; The Rehearsal: Australians at War in the Sudan 1885, 1985; (ed and introduced) Nation: the life of an independent journal 1958–1972, 1989. *Address:* 28 Nardoo Crescent, O'Connor, Canberra, ACT 2601, Australia.

INGLIS, Sheriff Robert Alexander; Sheriff of North Strathclyde (formerly Renfrew and Argyll) at Paisley, 1972–84; *b* 29 June 1918; *m* 1950, Shelagh Constance St Clair Boyd (marriage dissolved, 1956); one *s* one *d*. *Educ:* Malsis Hall, Daniel Stewart's Coll.; Rugby Sch.; Christ Church, Oxford (MA); Glasgow Univ. (LLB). Army, 1940–46; Glasgow Univ., 1946–48; called to Bar, 1948. Interim Sheriff-Sub., Dundee, 1955; perm. appt, 1956; Sheriff of Inverness, Moray, Nairn and Ross and Cromarty, 1968–72. *Recreations:* golf, fishing, bridge. *Address:* 1 Cayzer Court, Ralston, Paisley, Renfrewshire PA1 3DH. *T:* 0141–883 6498.

INGLIS of Glencorse, Sir Roderick (John), 10th Bt *cr* 1703 (then Mackenzie of Gairloch); MB, ChB; *b* 25 Jan. 1936; *s* of Sir Maxwell Ian Hector Inglis of Glencorse, 9th Bt and Dorothy Evelyn (*d* 1970), MD, JP, *d* of Dr John Stewart, Tasmania; *S* father, 1974; *m* 1960, Rachel (marr. diss. 1975), *d* of Lt-Col N. M. Morris, Dowdstown, Ardee, Co. Louth; twin *s* one *d* (and *e s* decd); *m* 1975 (marr. diss. 1977); one *d*; *m* 1986, Marilyn, *d* of A. L. Irwin, Glasgow; one *s*. *Educ:* Winchester; Edinburgh Univ. (MB, ChB 1960). *Heir: s* Ian Richard Inglis, *b* 9 Aug. 1965. *Address:* 18 Cordwalles Road, Pietermaritzburg, S Africa.

INGLIS-JONES, Nigel John, QC 1982; Barrister-at-Law; *b* 7 May 1935; 2nd *s* of Major John Alfred Inglis-Jones and Hermione Inglis-Jones; *m* 1st, 1965, Lenette Bromley-Davenport (*d* 1986); two *s* two *d*; 2nd, 1987, Ursula Culverwell; one *s*. *Educ:* Eton; Trinity Coll., Oxford (BA). Nat. Service with Grenadier Guards (ensign). Called to the Bar, Inner Temple, 1959, Bencher, 1981. A Recorder, 1976–93. Dep. Social Security Comr, 1993–; Gen. Comr of Income Tax, 1992–. *Publication:* The Law of Occupational Pension Schemes, 1989. *Recreations:* gardening, fishing, collecting English drinking glass, conversation. *Address:* 21 Elms Crescent, SW4 8QE. *T:* 0171–622 3013. *Club:* MCC.

INGMAN, David Charles, CBE 1993; Chairman, British Waterways Board, 1987–93; *b* 22 March 1928; *s* of Charles and Muriel Ingman; *m* 1951, Joan Elizabeth Walker; two *d*. *Educ:* Grangefield Grammar Sch., Stockton-on-Tees; Durham Univ. (BSc, MSc). Imperial Chemical Industries, 1949–85: Dir, then Dep. Chm., Plastics Div., 1975–81; Gp Dir, Plastics and Petrochemicals Div., 1981–85; Chm. and Chief Exec., Bestobell, 1985–86. Dir, Engineering Services Ltd, 1975–78; Alternative Dir, AECI Ltd, SA, 1978–82; Non-exec. Dir, Negretti-Zambra, 1979–81. Mem., Nationalised Industries Chairmen's Gp, 1987–93. *Recreations:* golf, walking, travel.

INGOLD, Cecil Terence, CMG 1970; DSc 1940; FLS; Professor of Botany in University of London, Birkbeck College, 1944–72; Vice-Master, Birkbeck College, 1965–70, Fellow, 1973; *b* 3 July 1905; *s* of late E. G. Ingold; *m* 1933, Leonora Mary Kemp; one *s* three *d*. *Educ:* Bangor (Co. Down) Grammar Sch.; Queen's Univ., Belfast. Graduated BSc, QUB, 1925; Asst in Botany, QUB, 1929; Lectr in Botany, University of Reading, 1930–37; Lecturer-in-charge of Dept of Botany, University Coll., Leicester, 1937–44; Dean of Faculty of Science, London Univ., 1956–60. Dep. Vice-Chancellor, London Univ., 1966–68, Chm. Academic Council, 1969–72. Chm., University Entrance and School Examinations Council, 1958–64; Vice-Chm., Inter-Univ. Council for Higher Educn Overseas, 1969–74. Chm., Council Freshwater Biolog. Assoc., 1965–74; Pres., Internat. Mycological Congress, 1971. Hooker Lectr, Linnean Soc., 1974. Linnean Medal (Botany), 1983. Hon. DLitt Ibadan, 1969; Hon. DSc Exeter, 1972; Hon. DCL Kent, 1978. *Publications:* Spore Discharge in Land Plants, 1939; Dispersal in Fungi, 1953; The Biology of Fungi, 1961; Spore Liberation, 1965; Fungal Spores: their liberation and dispersal, 1971. *Address:* 12 Chiltern Close, Benson, Oxon OX10 6LG.

INGOLD, Dr Keith Usherwood, OC 1994; FRS 1979; FRSC 1969; Distinguished Research Scientist, Steacie Institute for Molecular Sciences, since 1991; *b* Leeds, 31 May 1929; *s* of Christopher Kelk Ingold and Edith Hilda (*née* Usherwood); *m* 1956, Carmen Cairine Hodgkin; one *s* one *d* (and one *s* decd). *Educ:* University Coll. London (BSc Hons Chem., 1949; Fellow, 1987); Univ. of Oxford (DPhil 1951). Emigrated to Canada, 1951; Post-doctorate Fellow (under Dr F. P. Lossing), Div. of Pure Chem., Nat. Res. Council of Canada, 1951–53; Def. Res. Bd Post-doctorate Fellow (under Prof. W. A. Bryce), Chem. Dept, Univ. of BC, 1953–55; National Research Council of Canada: joined Div. of Appl. Chem., 1955; Head, Hydrocarbon Chem. Section of Div. of Chem., 1965; Associate Dir, Div. of Chemistry, 1977–90. Adjunct Professor: Brunel Univ., 1983–94; Univ. of Guelph, 1985–87; Carleton Univ., 1991–; Van Arkel Vis. Prof., Leiden Univ., Holland, 1992; Vis. Lectr, Japan Soc. for Promotion of Science, 1982. Hon. Treas., RSC, 1979–81; Canadian Society for Chemistry: Vice-Pres., 1985–87, Pres., 1987–88. Lectures: Frontiers in Chem., Case Western Res. Univ., and Frank Burnett Dains Meml, Univ. of Kansas, 1969; J. A. McRae Meml, Queen's Univ., Ont, 1980; Canadian Industries Ltd, Acadia Univ., NS, Imperial Oil, Univ. of Western Ont, and Douglas Hill Meml, Duke Univ., NC, 1987; Rayson Huang, Univ. of Hong Kong, 1988; 3M University, Univ. of Western Ont, Peter de la Mare Meml, Univ. of Auckland, and Gilman, Iowa State Univ., 1993; Marjerie Young Bell, Mount Allison Univ., NB, and Bergman, Yale Univ., 1994; Weissberger-Williams, Kodak, Rochester, NY, and Stanley J. Cristol, Univ. of Colorado, 1995. Hon. DSc: Univ. of Guelph, 1985; St Andrews, 1989; Carleton, 1992; McMaster,

1995; Hon. LLD Mount Allison, New Brunswick, 1987. Amer. Chemical Soc. Award in Petroleum Chem., 1968; Award in Kinetics and Mechanism, Chem. Soc., 1978; Medal of Chem. Inst. of Canada, 1981, Syntex Award for Physical Organic Chemistry, CIC, 1983; Centennial Medal, RSC, 1982; Henry Marshall Tory Medal, RSC, 1985; Pauling Award, ACS, 1988; Humboldt Res. Award, Alexander von Humboldt Foundn, W Germany, 1989; Alfred Bader Award in Organic Chem., Canadian Soc. for Chem., 1989; Sir Christopher Ingold Lectureship Award, RSC, 1989; VERIS Award, Vitamin E Res. Inf. Services, 1989; Lansdowne Visitor Award, Univ. of Victoria, Canada, 1990; Mangini Prize in Chem., Univ. of Bologna, 1990; Davy Medal, Royal Soc., 1990; Izaak Walton Killam Meml Prize, Canada Council, 1992; Arthur C. Cope Scholar Award, 1992, James Flack Norris Award in Physical Organic Chemistry, 1993, Amer. Chem. Soc. Silver Jubilee Medal, 1977. *Publications:* over 400 scientific papers in field of physical organic chemistry, partic. free-radical chemistry. *Recreation:* ski-ing. *Address:* 72 Ryeburn Drive, Gloucester, Ont K1G 3N3, Canada. *T:* (613) 8221123; (office) (613) 9900938.

INGRAHAM, Rt Hon. Hubert Alexander; PC 1993; Prime Minister, Commonwealth of the Bahamas, since 1992; Member, National Assembly, since 1977 (PLP, 1977–86, Ind, since 1987); *b* 4 Aug. 1947; *m* Delores Velma Miller; six *c*. *Educ:* Cooper's Town Public Sch.; Southern Senior Sch.; Govt High Sch. Evening Inst., Nassau. Called to Bahamas Bar, 1972; Sen. Partner, Christie, Ingraham & Co. Formerly: Mem., Air Transport Licensing Authy; Chm., Real Property Tax Tribunal. Chm., Bahamas Mortgage Corp., 1982. Mem., Progressive Liberal Party, 1975–86; Minister of Housing, Nat. Insurance and Social Services, 1982–84; Leader, Free National Movement, 1990; Leader of Opposition, 1990–92. *Address:* Office of the Prime Minister, PO Box CB–10980, Nassau, Bahamas.

INGRAM, Adam Paterson, JP; MP (Lab) East Kilbride, since 1987; *b* 1 Feb 1947; *s* of Bert Ingram and Lousia Paterson; *m* 1970, Maureen Georgina McMahon. *Educ:* Cranhill Secondary School. Commercial apprentice, 1965, computer programmer, 1966–69, J. & P. Coats, Glasgow; programmer/analyst, Associated British Foods, 1969–70; programmer/systems analyst, SSEB, 1970–77; Trade Union Official, NALGO, 1977–87. Sec., Jt Trades Union Side, Gas Staffs and Senior Officers, Scottish Gas, 1978–82; Chair, East Kilbride Constituency Labour Party, 1981–85; Councillor, E Kilbride DC, 1980–87, Leader, 1984–87; Mem., Policy Cttee, COSLA, 1984–87. An Opposition Whip, Feb.–Nov. 1988 (responsible for Scottish business and Treasury matters); PPS to Leader of the Opposition, 1988–92. Frontbench spokesman on social security, 1993–; Mem., Select Cttee on Trade and Industry, 1992–93; Vice-Chm., British–Japanese All-Party Parly Gp, 1992–; Sec., British–Singapore All-Party Parly Gp, 1992–. JP 1980. *Recreations:* fishing, cooking, reading. *Address:* 17 Weaver Place, East Kilbride G75 8SH. *T:* East Kilbride (013552) 35343.

INGRAM, Prof. David John Edward, CBE 1991; DL; MA, DPhil; DSc Oxon 1960; CPhys, FInstP; Vice-Chancellor, University of Kent at Canterbury, 1980–94, Emeritus Professor of Physics, since 1994; *b* 6 April 1927; *s* of late J. E. Ingram and late Marie Florence (*née* Weller); *m* 1952, Ruth Geraldine Grace, *d* of late Donald McNair; two *s* one *d*. *Educ:* King's Coll. Sch., Wimbledon; New Coll., Oxford. Postgraduate research at Oxford Univ., 1948–52; Research Fellow and Lectr, University of Southampton, 1952–57; Reader in Electronics, University of Southampton, 1957–59; Prof. and Head of Dept of Physics, Univ. of Keele, 1959–73; Dep. Vice-Chancellor, University of Keele, 1964–65, 1968–71; Principal, Chelsea Coll., London Univ., 1973–80 (Fellow, 1984). Mem., UGC, Physical Sciences Cttee, 1971–74. British Council: Mem. Bd, 1992–; Chm., Cttee on Higher Educn, 1991–. Chairman: London Univ. Cttee for Non-Teaching Staff, 1979–80; London Univ. Central Coordinating Cttee for Computers, 1978–80; Standing Conf. on Univ. Admissions, 1982–89; Kent County Consultative Cttee Industry Year, 1986; Hon. Treas., CVCP, 1987–94 (Chm., Sub-Cttee on Staff and Student Affairs, 1986–89; Chm., Universities Staff Develt Trng Unit, 1989–). Member: Carnegie UK Trust, 1980–; Camberwell DHA, 1982–85; Thanet Health Care Trust, 1992–94; Somerset and Taunton NHS Trust, 1995–; Esso Trust for Tertiary Educn, 1978–88; Univs Authorities Panel for Staff Salaries, 1987–89; Member Council: SPCK, 1980–93; CNAA, 1983–89; CET, 1983–85; UCCA, 1984–94 (Chm., 1991–94). Member, Governing Body: Wye Coll., London Univ., 1975–; King's Sch., Canterbury, 1983–; St Lawrence Coll., 1980–89 (a Vice-Pres., 1989–); Cobham Hall, 1989–92; King's Coll. Hosp. Medical Sch., 1982–; Roehampton Inst., 1978–88; London Sch. of Contemporary Dance, 1983–85; South Bank Univ. (formerly Poly.), 1989–; West Heath Sch., 1990–94. DL Kent, 1992. FKC 1986; Hon. Fellow, Roehampton Inst., 1988. Hon. DSc: Clermont-Ferrand, 1965; Keele, 1983; Hon. DCL Kent, 1994. *Publications:* Spectroscopy at Radio and Microwave Frequencies, 1955, 2nd edn, 1967; Free Radicals as Studied by Electron Spin Resonance, 1958; Biological and Biochemical Applications of Electron Spin Resonance, 1969; Radiation and Quantum Physics, 1973; Radio and Microwave Spectroscopy, 1976; various papers in Proc. Royal Soc., Proc. Phys. Soc., etc. *Recreations:* sailing, debating, DIY. *Address:* Cordwainers Cottage, Maundown, Wiveliscombe, Somerset TA4 2BU. *Club:* Athenæum (Mem., Gen. Cttee, 1985–89).

See also A. A. J. McNair.

INGRAM, Prof. David Stanley; Regius Keeper, Royal Botanic Garden, Edinburgh, since 1990; *b* 10 Oct. 1941; *s* of Stanley Arthur Ingram and Vera May Ingram (*née* Mansfield); *m* 1965, Alison Winifred Graham; two *s*. *Educ:* Yardley Grammar School, Birmingham; Univ. of Hull (BSc, PhD); MA, ScD Cantab. CBiol, FIBiol 1986; FLS 1991; FRSE 1993. Research Fellow, Univ. of Glasgow Dept of Botany, 1966–68; ARC Unit of Develt Botany, Cambridge, 1969–74; University of Cambridge: Research Fellow, Botany Sch., 1968–69; Univ. Lectr, 1974–88; Reader in Plant Pathology, 1988–90; Mem. Gen. Board, 1984–88; Fellow, Downing Coll., Cambridge, 1974–90 (Dean, 1976–82; Tutor for Graduate Students, 1982–88; Dir of Studies in Biology, 1976–89). Vis. Prof., Botany Dept, Univ. of Glasgow, 1991–; Hon. Prof., Univ. of Edinburgh, 1992– (Mem. Adv. Cttee, Div. of Biol Scis, 1991–); Prof. of Horticulture, RHS, 1995–. Chairman: Scientific Council, Sainsbury Lab. for Plant Pathology, 1990–92; Science and Plants for Schools Trust, 1991–; Member: Adv. Cttee, St Andrews Botanic Garden, 1990–; Exec. Cttee, Scotland's Nat. Gardens Scheme, 1990–; Adv. Cttee on SSSI in Scotland, 1992–; Scientific Cttee, RHS, 1992–; Council, Linnean Soc., 1992– (Vice Pres., 1993–94); Council, Internat. Assoc. of Botanic Gardens. Trustee: Grimesthorpe and Drummond Castle Trust, 1990–; John Fife Meml Trust, 1990–; Younger Botanic Garden Trust, 1990–; Royal Botanic Garden (Sibbald) Trust, 1990–; Botanic Gardens Conservation International, 1991–. Hon. Pres., 7th Internat. Congress of Plant Pathology, 1994–; Hon. Vice-Pres., Royal Caledonian Horticultural Soc., 1990. Member: Editl Cttee, Flora of China, 1992–; Editorial Board: Biol Revs, 1984–; Annals of Botany, 1992–; Advances in Plant Path, 1992–. *Publications:* (with D. N. Butcher) Plant Tissue Culture, 1974; (with J. P. Helgeson) Tissue Culture Methods for Plant Pathologists, 1980; (with A. Friday) Cambridge Encyclopedia of Life Sciences, 1985; (with P. H. Williams) Advances in Plant Pathology, vol. 1, 1982—vol. 9, 1993; (with A. Hudson) Shape and Form in Plants and Fungi, 1994; many papers dealing with research in plant pathology, plant tissue culture and botany, in learned jls. *Recreations:* listening to classical music and jazz, theatre, ceramics, gardening, travel, reading, strolling around capital cities. *Address:* Royal Botanic Garden, Edinburgh EH3 5LR. *T:* 0131–552 7171. *Clubs:* Caledonian; New (Edinburgh).

INGRAM, Edward John W.; *see* Winnington-Ingram.

INGRAM, Sir James (Herbert Charles), 4th Bt *cr* 1893; *b* 6 May 1966; *s* of (Herbert) Robin Ingram (*d* 1979) and of Shiela, *d* of late Charles Peczenik; *S* grandfather, 1980. *Educ:* Eton. *Recreations:* golf and shooting. *Heir:* *half b* Nicholas David Ingram, *b* 12 June, 1975. *Address:* 8 Lochaline Street, W6 9SH.

INGRAM, Sir John (Henderson), Kt 1994; CBE 1984; FIMechE, FIPENZ; company director; *b* 3 Sept. 1924; *s* of John Garden Ingram and Irene Caro Ingram (*née* Simpson); *m* 1952, Rosemary Clara Cuningham; three *d*. *Educ:* Nelson Coll., NZ; Canterbury Univ., Christchurch, NZ (BE). FIPENZ (FNZIE 1969); FAusIMM 1975; FIMechE 1991. Served RNZAF, NZ and Pacific, 1943–45. Man. Dir, NZ Steel Ltd, 1969–86; Dir, Nat Bank of NZ, 1983–95; Chm., Auckland Uniservices Ltd, 1988–. Chm., Youth Skills NZ; Mem., Auckland HA, 1990–91. President: Inst. of Professional Engrs, NZ, 1976–77; Auckland Manufacturers' Assoc., 1989–91. Member: Univ. of Auckland Council, 1979–; Waitangi Tribunal, 1993–. Commemoration Medal, NZ, 1990. *Publications:* contrib. papers in Inst. of Professional Engrs, NZ Jl, Conf. papers IISI, Inst. of Engrs, Australia, Aust. Inst. of Metals. *Recreations:* garden, ski-ing. *Address:* 732 Remuera Road, Remuera, Auckland 5, New Zealand. *T:* (9) 5200167. *Club:* Northern (Auckland).

INGRAM, Dame Kathleen Annie; *see* Raven, Dame Kathleen.

INGRAM, Paul; Head of Agricultural Services, Barclays Bank plc, 1988–94; *b* 20 Sept. 1934; *s* of John Granville Ingram and Sybil Ingram (*née* Johnson); *m* 1957, Jennifer (*née* Morgan) (*d* 1988); one *s* one *d*. *Educ:* Manchester Central High School; University of Nottingham (BSc 1956). Dept of Conservation and Extension, Fedn of Rhodesia and Nyasaland, 1956–63; Nat. Agricl Adv. Service, later ADAS, MAFF, 1965–; County Livestock Officer, Lancs, 1969–70; Policy Planning Unit, MAFF, 1970–72; Farm Management Adviser, Devon, 1972–76; Regional Farm Management Adviser, Wales, 1976–77; Dep. Sen. Livestock Advr, 1977–79, Sen. Agricl Officer, 1979–85, Chief Agricl Officer, 1985–87, Dir of Farm and Countryside Service, 1987–88, ADAS. *Address:* 14 Cumberland Street, Woodbridge, Suffolk IP12 4AB.

INGRAM, Stanley Edward; solicitor; *b* 5 Dec. 1922; *o s* of late Ernest Alfred Stanley Ingram and Ethel Ann Ingram; *m* 1948, Vera (*née* Brown); one *s* one *d*. *Educ:* Charlton Central School. Articled clerk with Wright & Bull, Solicitors; admitted Solicitor, 1950. Served RAF, 1942–46. Legal Asst, Min. of Nat. Insurance, 1953; Sen. Legal Asst, Min. of Pensions and Nat. Insurance, 1958; Asst Solicitor, 1971, Under Sec. (Legal), 1978–83, DHSS. Member Council: Civil Service Legal Soc. and of Legal Section of First Division Assoc., 1971–82; Mem., Salaried Solicitors' Cttee of Law Society, 1978–81. Secretary: Romsey Gp, CS Retirement Fellowship, 1989–; Test Valley Croquet Club, 1995– (Treas., 1994–95). *Recreations:* gardening, playing croquet. *Address:* 2 Little Woodley Farm, Winchester Hill, Romsey, Hants SO51 7NU. *Club:* Law Society.

INGRAM, Prof. Vernon Martin, FRS 1970; John and Dorothy Wilson Professor of Biology, Massachusetts Institute of Technology, since 1988; *b* Breslau, 19 May 1924; *s* of Kurt and Johanna Immerwahr; *m* 1st, 1950, Margaret Young; one *s* one *d*; 2nd, 1984, Elizabeth Hendee. *Educ:* Birkbeck Coll., Univ. of London. PhD Organic Chemistry, 1949; DSc Biochemistry, 1961. Analytical and Res. Chemist, Thos Morson & Son, Mddx, 1941–45; Lecture Demonstrator in Chem., Birkbeck Coll., 1945–47; Asst Lectr in Chem., Birkbeck Coll., 1947–50; Rockefeller Foundn Fellow, Rockefeller Inst., NY, 1950–51; Coxe Fellow, Yale, 1951–52; Mem. Sci. Staff, MRC Unit for Molecular Biology, Cavendish Lab., Cambridge, 1952–58; Assoc. Prof. 1958–61, Prof. of Biochemistry, 1961–, MIT; Lectr (part-time) in Medicine, Columbia, 1961–73; Guggenheim Fellow, UCL, 1967–68. Jesup Lectr, Columbia, 1962; Harvey Soc. Lectr, 1965. Member: Amer. Acad. of Arts and Sciences, 1964; Amer. Chem. Soc.; Chemical Soc.; Biochemical Soc.; Genetical Society. Fellow, Amer. Assoc. for Advancement of Science, 1987. William Allen Award, Amer. Soc. for Human Genetics, 1967. *Publications:* Haemoglobin and Its Abnormalities, 1961; The Hemoglobins in Genetics and Evolution, 1963; The Biosynthesis of Macromolecules, 1965, new edn, 1971; articles on human genetics, nucleic acids, differentiation and molecular biology of aging and developmental neurobiology, in Nature, Jl Mol. Biol., Jl Cell Biol., Develt Biol., Jl Biol Chem., etc. *Recreations:* music; photographer of abstract images. *Address:* Massachusetts Institute of Technology, Massachusetts Avenue, Cambridge, Mass 02139, USA. *T:* 617–253–3706.

INGRAMS, family name of **Baroness Darcy de Knayth.**

INGRAMS, Leonard Victor, OBE 1980; Director, Robert Fleming Holdings Ltd, since 1985; *b* 1 Sept. 1941; *s* of Leonard St Clair Ingrams and Victoria Susan Beatrice (*née* Reid); *m* 1964, Rosalind Ann Moore; one *s* three *d*. *Educ:* Stonyhurst Coll.; Corpus Christi Coll., Oxford (1st Cl. Classics (Mods) 1961; 1st Cl. Lit.Hum. 1963; MA; Derby Schol. 1963; Sen. Schol. 1964; BLitt). Asst Lectr, QMC, 1965–67; joined Baring Bros, 1967, Man. Dir, 1975–81. Sen. Advr, Saudi Arabian Monetary Agency, 1974–79, Chief Advr to Gov., 1981–84. Chairman: Deutschland Investment Corp., 1990–; Czechoslovakia Investment Corp., 1992–. Chm., Garsington Opera Ltd, 1990–. *Publications:* (ed) International Bond Portfolio Management, 1988; contribs to various vols of Oxyrhynchus Papyri. *Recreations:* gardening, music. *Address:* Garsington Manor, Garsington, Oxford OX44 9DH. *T:* Oxford (01865) 361234. *Club:* Beefsteak.

See also R. R. Ingrams.

INGRAMS, Richard Reid; journalist; Editor, Private Eye, 1963–86, Chairman, since 1974; Editor, The Oldie, since 1992; *b* 19 Aug. 1937; *s* of Leonard St Clair Ingrams and Victoria (*née* Reid); *m* 1962, Mary Morgan (marr. diss. 1993); one *s* one *d* (and one *s* decd). *Educ:* Shrewsbury; University Coll., Oxford. Joined Private Eye, 1962; columnist, Observer, 1988–90, 1992–. *Publications:* (with Christopher Booker and William Rushton) Private Eye on London, 1962; Private Eye's Romantic England, 1963; (with John Wells) Mrs Wilson's Diary, 1965; Mrs Wilson's 2nd Diary, 1966; The Tale of Driver Grope, 1968; (with Barry Fantoni) The Bible for Motorists, 1970; (ed) The Life and Times of Private Eye, 1971; (as Philip Reid, with Andrew Osmond) Harris in Wonderland, 1973; (ed) Cobbett's Country Book, 1974; (ed) Beachcomber: the works of J. B. Morton, 1974; The Best of Private Eye, 1974; God's Apology, 1977; Goldenballs, 1979; (with Fay Godwin) Romney Marsh and the Royal Military Canal, 1980; (with John Wells) Dear Bill: the collected letters of Denis Thatcher, 1980; (with John Wells) The Other Half: further letters of Denis Thatcher, 1981; (with John Wells) One for the Road, 1982; (with John Piper) Piper's Places, 1983; (ed) The Penguin Book of Private Eye Cartoons, 1983; (with John Wells) My Round!, 1983; (ed) Dr Johnson by Mrs Thrale, 1984; (with John Wells) Down the Hatch, 1985; (with John Wells) Just the One, 1986; John Stewart Collis: a memoir, 1986; (with John Wells) The Best of Dear Bill, 1986; (with John Wells) Mud in Your Eye, 1987; The Ridgeway, 1988; You Might As Well Be Dead, 1988; England (anthology), 1989; (with John Wells) Number 10, 1989; On and On . . ., 1990; (ed) The Oldie Annual, 1993; (ed) The Oldie Annual 2, 1994; Malcolm Muggeridge: the authorized biography, 1995. *Recreation:* piano. *Address:* c/o The Oldie, 45 Poland Street, W1V 3DF.

INGRESS BELL, Philip; *see* Bell.

INGROW, Baron *cr* 1982 (Life Peer), of Keighley in the County of West Yorkshire; **John Aked Taylor;** Kt 1972; OBE 1960; TD 1951; DL; JP; Chairman and Managing Director, Timothy Taylor & Co. Ltd; Lord-Lieutenant and Custos Rotulorum of West Yorkshire, 1985–92 (Vice Lord-Lieutenant, 1976–85); *b* 15 Aug. 1917; *s* of Percy Taylor, Knowle Spring House, Keighley, and Gladys Broster (who *m* 2nd, 1953, Sir (John) Donald Horsfall, 2nd Bt); *m* 1949, Barbara Mary, *d* of Percy Wright Stirk, Keighley; two *d*. *Educ:* Shrewsbury Sch. Served War of 1939–45: Duke of Wellington's Regt and Royal Signals, Major; Norway, Middle East, Sicily, NW Europe and Far East. Mem., Keighley Town Council, 1946–67 (Mayor, 1956–57; Chm., Educn Cttee, 1949–61; Chm., Finance Cttee, 1961–67); Mem. Council, Magistrates' Assoc., 1957–86 (Vice-Chm., Exec. Cttee, 1975–76; Chm., Licensing Cttee, 1969–76; Hon. Treasurer, 1976–86; Vice-Pres., 1986–; Past Pres. and Chm., WR Br.; Life Vice-Pres., W Yorks Br.); Chm., Keighley Conservative Assoc., 1952–56 and 1957–67 (Pres., 1971–76, Jt Hon. Treas., 1947–52, and Chm., Young Conservatives, 1946–47); Chm., Yorkshire West Conservative European Constituency Council, 1978–84 (Pres., 1984–85); Chm., Yorkshire Area, Nat. Union of Conservative and Unionist Assocs, 1966–71 (Vice-Chm., 1965–66); Chm., Exec. Cttee of Nat. Union of Conservative and Unionist Assocs, 1971–76 (Mem. 1964–83); Pres., Nat. Union of Conservative and Unionist Assocs 1982–83 (Hon. Vice-Pres., 1976–). Gen. Comr of Income Tax, 1965–92. Vice-Pres., Yorks and Humberside TAVRA, 1985–88, and 1991–92 (Pres., 1988–91). Mem. Court, Univ. of Leeds, 1986–. Pres., Council of Order of St John, S and W Yorks, 1985–92; KStJ 1986. JP Borough of Keighley 1949; DL West (formerly WR) Yorks, 1971. DUniv Bradford, 1990. *Address:* Fieldhead, Keighley, West Yorkshire BD20 6LP. *T:* Keighley (01535) 603895. *Club:* Carlton.

INKIN, Sir Geoffrey (David), Kt 1993; OBE 1974 (MBE 1971); Chairman: Cardiff Bay Development Corporation, since 1987; Land Authority for Wales, since 1986; *b* 2 Oct. 1934; *e s* of late Noel D. Inkin and of Evelyn Margaret Inkin; *m* 1961, Susan Elizabeth, *d* of Col L. S. Sheldon and late Margaret Sheldon, and step *d* of Mrs Rosemary Sheldon; three *s*. *Educ:* Dean Close Sch.; RMA, Sandhurst; Staff Coll., Camberley; Royal Agricl Coll., Cirencester. Commnd The Royal Welch Fusiliers, 1955; served Malaya, 1955–57 and Cyprus, 1958–59 (despatches); commanded 1st Bn The Royal Welch Fusiliers, 1972–74. Member: Gwent CC, 1977–83; Gwent Police Authority, 1979–83; Mem. Bd, 1980–83, Chm., 1983–87, Cwmbran Develt Corp.; Mem. Bd, Welsh Devlt Agency, 1984–87. Gov., Haberdashers' Monmouth Schs, 1977–90; Mem. Bd, WNO, 1987–91, 1993–; Member Council: UWIST, 1987–88; Univ. of Wales Coll. of Cardiff, 1988–. Parly Cand. (C) Ebbw Vale, 1977–79. FRSA; Hon. Mem., RICS, 1994. Gwent: DL, 1983–91; High Sheriff, 1987–88. *Address:* The Old Rectory, St George's-super-Ely, South Glam CF5 6EP. *T:* Peterston-super-Ely (01446) 760348. *Clubs:* Brooks's; Cardiff and County (Cardiff).

INMAN, Derek Arthur; His Honour Judge Inman; a Circuit Judge, since 1993; *b* 1 Aug. 1937; *s* of Arthur and Marjorie Inman; *m* 1st, 1963, Sarah Juliet Cahn (marr. diss. 1982); one *s* two *d*; 2nd, 1983, Elizabeth (*née* Dickinson), *widow* of Lt-Col C. Thomson. *Educ:* Roundhay Sch., Leeds; RNC, Dartmouth. RN; served in HM Ships Sheffield, Belfast and Bulwark; Staff of C-in-C Home Fleet; Sec. to Comdr Naval Forces Gulf and HMS Hermione; retired as Lieut Comdr, 1974. Called to the Bar, Middle Temple, 1968; in Chambers at 2 Harcourt Bldgs, 1974–93. *Recreations:* watching cricket and Rugby, compulsory gardening. *Address:* c/o Lloyd's Bank, High Street, Godalming, Surrey GU7 1AT.

INMAN, Edward Oliver; Director (formerly Keeper) of Duxford Airfield, Imperial War Museum, since 1978; *b* 12 Aug. 1948; *s* of John Inman and Peggy Inman (*née* Beard); *m* 1st, 1971 (marr. diss. 1982); one *s* one *d*; 2nd, 1984, Sherida Lesley (*née* Sturton); one *d*, and two step *d*. *Educ:* King's College Sch., Wimbledon; Gonville and Caius Coll., Cambridge (MA); School of Slavonic and East European Studies, London (MA). Joined Imperial War Museum as Res. Asst, 1972; Asst Keeper 1974; Keeper of Exhibits (Duxford) 1976. Gov., 2nd Air Div. Meml Liby, Norwich, 1990–. *Recreations:* tennis, travel, the family. *Address:* c/o Imperial War Museum, Duxford, Cambridge CB2 4QR. *T:* Cambridge (01223) 835000.

INMAN, Herbert, CBE 1977; Regional Administrator, Yorkshire Regional Health Authority, 1973–77; Hon. Adviser to the Sue Ryder Foundation, since 1977, and Member of Council, 1986–89; Member, Executive Committee, Sue Ryder Homes, 1983–88 (Chairman, 1983–87); *b* 8 Jan. 1917; *s* of Matthew Herbert Inman and Rose Mary Earle; *m* 1939, Beatrice, *d* of Thomas Edward Lee and Florence Lee; twin *s*. *Educ:* Wheelwright Grammar Sch., Dewsbury; Univ. of Leeds. FHSM (Nat. Pres. 1968–69); DPA. Various hosp. appts, Dewsbury, Wakefield and Aylesbury, 1933–48; Dep. Gp Sec., Leeds (A) Gp HMC and Dep. Chief Admin. Officer, 1948–62; Gp Sec. and Chief Admin. Officer, Leeds (A) Gp HMC, 1962–70; Gp Sec. and Chief Admin. Officer, Leeds (St James's) Univ. HMC, 1970–73. *Publications:* occasional articles in Hospital and Health Services jls. *Recreations:* Rugby and cricket (spectator), travel, gardening, swimming. *Address:* 7 Potterton Close, Barwick in Elmet, Leeds LS15 4DY. *T:* Leeds (0113) 281 2538.

INMAN, Roger, OBE (mil.) 1945 (MBE (mil.) 1944); TD 1945; Vice Lord-Lieutenant of South Yorkshire, 1981–90; Joint Managing Director, Harrison Fisher Group, since 1951; *b* 18 April 1915; *y s* of S. M. Inman, Sheffield; *m* 1939, Christine Lucas, *e d* of Lt-Col J. Rodgers, Sheffield; two *s*. *Educ:* King Edward VII Sch., Sheffield. Commissioned into 71st (WR) Field Bde, RA TA, 1935; served War, with RA and General Staff, Western Desert, Middle East, Italy, 1939–46; released, 1946, with rank of Lt-Col; reformed and commanded 271 (WR) Fd Regt, RA TA, 1947–51; Brevet Col 1953; Hon. Col, Sheffield Artillery Volunteers, 1964–70; Member, W Riding T&AFA, 1947–; Vice-Chm., Yorkshire and Humberside TA&VRA, 1973–80. JP 1954 (Chm. Sheffield City Bench, 1974–80), DL 1967, West Riding. General Commissioner of Income Tax, 1969–90; Chm. of Comrs, Don Div. of Sheffield, 1975–90. Chm., Guardians of Standard of Wrought Plate within the Town of Sheffield, 1988–. *Recreation:* golf. *Address:* Flat 1, Mayfield View, 15 Whitworth Road, Sheffield S10 3HD. *Clubs:* Sheffield, Hallamshire Golf (Sheffield).

INNES, Alistair Campbell M.; *see* Mitchell-Innes.

INNES of Coxton, Sir David (Charles Kenneth Gordon), 12th Bt *cr* 1686 (NS); consultant in electronics for petro-chemical and power generation fields; *b* 17 April 1940; *s* of Sir Charles Innes of Coxton, 11th Bt and Margaret Colquhoun Lockhart (*d* 1992), *d* of F. C. L. Robertson; *S* father, 1990; *m* 1969, Majorie Alison, *d* of E. W. Parker; one *s* one *d*. *Educ:* Haileybury Coll.; City & Guilds Coll. of Imperial Coll., London Univ. BSc(Eng); ACGI. Technical Dir, Peak Technologies, 1974–78; Man. Dir, Peak Combustion Controls, 1978–81. *Recreations:* electronics, aeronautics, astronomy. *Heir: s* Alastair Charles Deverell Innes, *b* 17 Sept. 1970. *Address:* 28 Wadham Close, Shepperton, Middlesex TW17 9HT. *T:* Walton-on-Thames (01932) 228273.

INNES, Hammond; *see* Hammond Innes, Ralph.

INNES of Edingight, Sir Malcolm (Rognvald), KCVO 1990 (CVO 1981); Lord Lyon King of Arms, since 1981; Secretary to the Order of the Thistle, since 1981; *b* 25 May 1938; 3rd *s* of late Sir Thomas Innes of Learney, GCVO, LLD, and Lady Lucy Buchan, 3rd *d* of 18th Earl of Caithness; *m* 1963, Joan, *o d* of Thomas D. Hay, CA, Edinburgh; three *s*. *Educ:* Edinburgh Acad.; Univ. of Edinburgh (MA, LLB). WS 1964. Falkland Pursuivant Extraordinary, 1957; Carrick Pursuivant, 1958; Lyon Clerk and Keeper of the Records, 1966; Marchmont Herald, 1971. Mem., Queen's Body Guard for Scotland (Royal Company of Archers), 1971. Pres., Heraldry Soc. of Scotland. Trustee, Sir William Fraser's Foundn. FSA (Scot.); KStJ. Grand Officer of Merit, SMO Malta. *Recreation:* visiting places of historic interest. *Address:* 35 Inverleith Row, Edinburgh EH3 5QH. *T:* 0131-552 4924. *Club:* New (Edinburgh).

INNES, Maughan William; Controller Finance, National Research Development Corporation, 1965–77; *b* 18 Nov. 1922; *s* of Leslie W. Innes and Bridget Maud (*née* Humble-Crofts); *m* 1950, Helen Mary, *d* of Roper Spyers; one *s* (and one *s* decd). *Educ:* Marlborough College. BA Open Univ., 1988. FCA 1960. RAF, 1941–46. Chartered Accountant, 1949; in Canada, 1953–60; retired 1977. *Recreations:* music, theatre. *Address:* Brook Cottage, Four Elms, Edenbridge, Kent TN8 6PA. *T:* Four Elms (01732) 700232. *Club:* MCC.

INNES, Sir Peter (Alexander Berowald), 17th Bt *cr* 1628, of Balvenie; FICE; Partner, Scott Wilson Kirkpatrick and Partners, Consulting Engineers, since 1987; *b* 6 Jan. 1937; *s* of Lt-Col Sir (Ronald Gordon) Berowald Innes, 16th Bt, OBE and Elizabeth Haughton (*d* 1958), *e d* of late Alfred Fayle; *S* father, 1988; *m* 1959, Julia Mary, *d* of A. S. Levesley; two *s* one *d*. *Educ:* Prince of Wales School, Nairobi, Kenya; Bristol Univ. (BSc). Scott Wilson Kirkpatrick and Partners, 1964–; Associate, 1982–87. Responsible for several airport projects in UK, Africa and Middle East, including major military airbases. Major, Engr and Transport Staff Corps, RE(TA). *Heir: s* Alexander Guy Berowald Innes, *b* 4 May 1960. *Address:* The Wheel House, Nations Hill, Kings Worthy, Winchester SO23 7QY. *T:* Winchester (01962) 881024. *Club:* Naval and Military.

INNES, Sheila Miriam; consultant (education and media), since 1991; *b* 25 Jan. 1931; *d* of Dr James Innes, MB, ChB, MA and Nora Innes. *Educ:* Talbot Heath School, Bournemouth; Lady Margaret Hall, Oxford (Exhibnr; BA Hons Mod. Langs; MA). BBC Radio Producer, World Service, 1955–61; BBC TV producer: family programmes, 1961–65; further education, 1965–73; exec. producer, further education, 1973–77; Head, BBC Continuing Educn, TV, 1977–84; Controller, BBC Educnl Broadcasting, 1984–87; Dir, BBC Enterprises Ltd, 1986–87; Chief Exec., 1987–89, Dep. Chm., 1989–92, Open Coll. Non-exec. Dir, Brighton Health Care NHS Trust, 1993–. Chairman: Cross-Sector Cttee for Development and Review, BTEC, 1986–87; Cross-Sector Cttee for Product Develt, BTEC, 1989–92; British Gas Training Awards, 1988–92. Member: Gen. Board, Alcoholics Anonymous, 1980–; Board of Governors, Centre for Information on Language Teaching and Research, 1981–84; Council, Open Univ., 1984–87; Council for Educational Technology, 1984–87; EBU Educational Working Party, 1984–87; Educn Cttee, 1990–, Women's Adv. Gp, 1992–, RSA; Standing Conf. on Schools' Science and Technol., 1990–93 (Mem. Council, 1993–); Age Concern Training Validation (later Quality) Cttee, 1992–94; IMgt Management Develt Proj., 1992–95. Vice-Pres., Educn Sect., BAAS, 1990–. Mem., Clothing and Allied Products ITB Management 2000 Cttee of Enquiry, 1989. Patron, One World Broadcasting Trust, 1988–. Gov., Talbot Heath Sch., Bournemouth, 1989–95. Mem., RTS, 1984; FRSA 1986; FITD 1987; CIMgt 1987. Hon. DLitt South Bank, 1992. *Publications:* BBC publications; articles for language jls and EBU Review. *Recreations:* music (classical and jazz), country pursuits, swimming, sketching, photography, travel, languages. *Address:* Wychwood, Barcombe, East Sussex BN8 5TP. *T:* Barcombe (01273) 400268. *Clubs:* Reform; Oxford Society.

INNES, Lt-Col William Alexander Disney; DL; Vice Lord-Lieutenant of Banffshire, 1971–86; *b* 19 April 1910; 2nd *s* of late Captain James William Guy Innes, CBE, DL, JP, RN, of Maryculter, Kincardineshire; *m* 1939, Mary Alison, *d* of late Francis Burnett-Stuart, Howe Green, Hertford; two *s*. *Educ:* Marlborough Coll., RMC, Sandhurst. Gordon Highlanders: 2nd Lieut, 1930; Captain 1938; Temp. Major 1941; Major, 1946; Temp. Lt-Col, 1951; retd, 1952. Served War of 1939–45: Far East (PoW Malaya and Siam, 1942–45). Chm., Banffshire T&AFA, 1959. DL 1959–87, JP 1964–86, Banffshire. *Recreations:* shooting, gardening. *Address:* Heath Cottage, Aberlour, Banffshire AB38 9QD. *T:* Aberlour (01340) 871266.

INNES, William James Alexander; Assistant Under Secretary of State, 1985–94, Head of Fire and Emergency Planning Department, 1992–94, Home Office, retired; *b* 11 Oct. 1934; *s* of late William Johnstone Innes and of Helen Margaret Meldrum Porter; *m* 1st, 1959, Carol Isabel Bruce (marr. diss. 1983); one *s* one *d*; 2nd, 1992, Mrs Ann Harrold. *Educ:* Robert Gordon's Coll., Aberdeen; Aberdeen Univ. (MA). Served Royal Air Force, 1956, Officer Commanding 45 Sqdn, 1967–70. Principal, Home Office, 1972; Private Sec. to Home Sec., 1974–76; Asst Sec., 1977; Asst Under Sec. of State, seconded to NI Office, 1985–88; Dir of Operational Policy, Prison Dept, Home Office, 1988–90; Dir of Custody, Prison Service HQ, Home Office, 1990–92. *Recreations:* opera, theatre, golf. *Address:* Nightingales, Nightingale Lane, Maidenhead, Berks SL6 7QL. *Clubs:* Royal Air Force; Burnham Beeches Golf.

INNES-KER, family name of **Duke of Roxburghe.**

INNISS, Sir Clifford (de Lisle), Kt 1961; retired; Judge of the Court of Appeal of Belize, 1974–81; Chairman, Integrity Commission, National Assembly of Belize, 1981–87; Member, Belize Advisory Council, Feb.–Oct. 1985; *b* Barbados, 26 Oct. 1910; *e s* of late Archibald de Lisle Inniss and Lelia Emmaline, *e d* of Elverton Richard Springer. *Educ:* Harrison Coll., Barbados; Queen's Coll., Oxford. BA (hons jurisprudence), BCL. Called to bar, Middle Temple, 1935. QC (Tanganyika) 1950, (Trinidad and Tobago) 1953; practised at bar, Barbados; subseq. Legal Draughtsman and Clerk to Attorney-Gen., Barbados, 1938; Asst to Attorney General and Legal Draughtsman, 1941; Judge of Bridgetown Petty Debt Court, 1946; Legal Draughtsman, Tanganyika, 1947; Solicitor Gen., Tanganyika, 1949; Attorney-Gen., Trinidad and Tobago, 1953; Chief Justice, British Honduras, later Belize, 1957–72; Judge of the Courts of Appeal of Bermuda, the Bahamas, and the Turks and Caicos Is, 1974–75. *Recreations:* music, gardening, tennis. *Address:* 11/13 Oriole Avenue, Belmopan, Belize. *Clubs:* Barbados Yacht; Kenya Kongonis (hon. mem.).

INSALL, Donald William, CBE 1995 (OBE 1981); FSA, RWA, FRIBA, FRTPI; architect and planning consultant; Principal, Donald W. Insall & Associates, since 1958; *b* 7 Feb. 1926; *o s* of late William R. Insall and Phyllis Insall, Henleaze, Bristol; *m* 1964, Amy Elizabeth, MA, *er d* of Malcolm H. Moss, Nanpantan, Leics; two *s* one *d*. *Educ:* private prep; Bristol Grammar Sch.; Bristol Univ.; RA; Sch. of Planning, London (Dip. (Hons)); SPAB Lethaby Schol. 1951. FRIBA 1968, FRTPI 1973. Coldstream Guards, 1944–47. Architectural and Town-Planning Consultancy has included town-centre studies, civic and univ., church, domestic and other buildings, notably in conservation of historic towns and buildings (incl. restoration of ceiling, House of Lords, and Windsor Castle); Medal (Min. of Housing and Local Govt), Good Design in Housing, 1962. Visiting

Lecturer: RCA, 1964–69; Internat. Centre for Conservation, Rome, 1969–; Coll. d'Europe, Bruges, 1976–81; Catholic Univ. of Leuven, 1982–; Adjunct Prof., Univ. of Syracuse, 1971–81. Mem., Council of Europe Working Party, 1969–70; Nat. Pilot Study, Chester: A Study in Conservation, 1968; Consultant, Chester Conservation Programme, 1970–87 (EAHY Exemplar; European Prize for Preservation of Historic Monuments, 1981; Europa Nostra Medals of Honour, 1983 and 1989). Member: Historic Buildings Council for England, 1971–84; Grants Panel, EAHY, 1974; UK Council, ICOMOS, 1988; Council, RSA, 1976–80 (FRSA, 1948); Council, SPAB, 1979–; Ancient Monuments Bd for England, 1980–84; Comr, Historic Blgs and Monuments Commn, 1984–89; Member: Standing Adv. Cttee, Getty Grant Program, 1988–92; EC Expert Cttee on Architectural Heritage, 1990, 1993– (Pres., 1992); Dept of Nat. Heritage Inquiry into Fire Protection at Royal Palaces, 1993; Vice-Chm., Conf. on Trng in Architectural Conservation, 1990– (Hon. Sec., 1959–89); Vice-Pres., Bldg Crafts and Conservation Trust, 1994–. RIBA: Banister Fletcher Medallist, 1949; Neale Bursar, 1955; Examnr, 1957; Competition Assessor, 1971. Conferences: White House (Natural Beauty), 1965; UNESCO, 1969; Historic Architectural Interiors, USA, 1988, 1993; Singapore, 1994. Lecture Tours: USA, 1964, 1972 (US Internat. Reg. Conf. on Conservation); Mexico, 1972; Yugoslavia, 1973; Canada, 1974; Argentina, 1976; India, 1979; Portugal, 1982. European Architectural Heritage Year Medal (for Restoration of Chevening), 1973; Queen's Silver Jubilee Medal, 1977. *Publications:* (jtly) Railway Station Architecture, 1966; (jtly) Conservation Areas 1967; The Care of Old Buildings Today, 1973; Historic Buildings: action to maintain the expertise for their care and repair, 1974; Conservation in Action, 1982; Conservation in Chester, 1988; contrib. to Encyclopædia Britannica, professional, environmental and internat. jls. *Recreations:* visiting, photographing and enjoying places; appreciating craftsmanship; Post-Vintage Thoroughbred Cars (Mem., Rolls Royce Enthusiasts' Club). *Address:* 73 Kew Green, Richmond, Surrey TW9 3AH; (office) 19 West Eaton Place, Eaton Square, SW1X 8LT. *T:* 0171–245 9888. *Club:* Athenæum.

INSKIP, family name of **Viscount Caldecote.**

INSOLE, Douglas John, CBE 1979; Marketing Director, Trollope & Colls Ltd, 1975–91; *b* 18 April 1926; *s* of John Herbert Insole and Margaret Rose Insole; *m* 1948, Barbara Hazel Ridgway (*d* 1982); two *d* (and one *d* decd). *Educ:* Sir George Monoux Grammar Sch.; St Catharine's Coll., Cambridge. MA Cantab. Cricket: Cambridge Univ., 1947–49 (Captain, 1949); Essex CCC, 1947–63 (Captain, 1950–60); played 9 times for England; Vice-Captain, MCC tour of S Africa, 1956–57. Chairman: Test Selectors, 1965–68; Test and County Cricket Bd, 1975–78 (Chm., Cricket Cttee, 1968–87; Chm., Internat. Cttee, 1988–); Mem., MCC Cttee, 1955–94; Manager, England cricket team, Australian tours, 1978–79 and 1982–83. Soccer: Cambridge Univ., 1946–48; Pegasus, and Corinthian Casuals; Amateur Cup Final medal, 1956. Member: Sports Council, 1971–74; FA Council, 1979–. JP Chingford, 1962–74. *Publication:* Cricket from the Middle, 1960. *Recreations:* cricket, soccer. *Address:* 8 Hadleigh Court, Crescent Road, Chingford, E4 6AX. *T:* 0181–529 6546. *Club:* MCC (Trustee, 1988–94).

INVERFORTH, 4th Baron *cr* 1919, of Southgate; **Andrew Peter Weir;** *b* 16 Nov. 1966; *s* of 3rd Baron Inverforth and of Jill Elizabeth, *o d* of late John W. Thornycroft, CBE; *S* father, 1982. *Educ:* Marlborough College; Trinity Coll., Cambridge; London Hosp. Med. Coll. *Heir: uncle* Hon. John Vincent Weir, *b* 8 Feb. 1935. *Address:* 27 Morgan Street, Bow, E3 5AA. *T:* 0181–983 0724.

INVERNESS (St Andrew's Cathedral), Provost of; *see* Grant, Very Rev. M. E.

INVERURIE, Lord; James William Falconer Keith; Master of Kintore; *b* 15 April 1976; *s* and *heir* of Earl of Kintore, *qv.*

INWOOD, Ven. Richard Neil; Archdeacon of Halifax, since 1995; *b* 4 March 1946; *s* of Cyril and Sylvia Inwood; *m* 1969, Elizabeth Joan Abram; three *d. Educ:* University Coll., Oxford (MA, BSc Chem.); Univ. of Nottingham (BA Theol.). Teacher, Uganda, 1969; Works R & D chemist, Dyestuffs Div., ICI, 1970–71; ministerial trng, St John's Coll., Nottingham, 1971–74; ordained deacon, 1974, priest, 1975; Curate: Christ Church, Fulwood, Sheffield, 1974–78; All Souls, Langham Place, W1, 1978–81; Vicar, St Luke's, Bath, 1981–89; Hon. Chaplain, Dorothy House Foundn, Bath, 1984–89; Rector, Yeovil with Kingston Pitney, 1989–95; Prebendary of Wells, 1990–95. *Publications:* Biblical Perspectives on Counselling, 1980; (jtly) The Church, 1987. *Recreations:* fell walking, gardening, music, family. *Address:* 2 Vicarage Gardens, Rastrick, Brighouse, West Yorks HD6 3HD. *T:* Brighouse (01484) 714553.

IONESCU, Prof. George Ghita; Professor of Government, University of Manchester, 1970–80, now Emeritus; Editor, Government and Opposition, since 1965; *b* 21 March 1913; *s* of Alexandre Ionescu and Hélène Sipsom; *m* 1950, Valence Ramsay de Bois Maclaren. *Educ:* Univ. of Bucharest (Lic. in Law and Polit. Sci.). Gen. Sec., Romanian Commn of Armistice with Allied Forces, 1944–45; Counsellor, Romanian Embassy, Ankara, 1945–47; Gen. Sec., Romanian Nat. Cttee, NY, 1955–58; Dir, Radio Free Europe, 1958–63; Nuffield Fellow, LSE, 1963–68. Chm., 1975–94, Hon. Life Chm., 1994, Res. Cttee, Internat. Pol Sci. Assoc.; Life Vice-Pres., British Pol Sci. Assoc., 1994. Hon. MA(Econ) Manchester; Dr *hc* Univ. of Bucharest, 1992. *Publications:* Communism in Romania, 1965; The Politics of the Eastern European Communist States, 1966; (jtly) Opposition, 1967; (jtly) Populism, 1970; (ed) Between Sovereignty and Integration, 1973; Centripetal Politics, 1975; The Political Thought of Saint-Simon, 1976; (ed) The European Alternatives, 1979; Politics and the Pursuit of Happiness, 1984; Leadership in an Independent World, 1991. *Recreations:* music, bridge, racing. *Address:* 36 Sandileigh Avenue, Manchester M20 9LW. *T:* 0161–445 7726. *Club:* Athenæum.

IPSWICH, Viscount; Henry Oliver Charles FitzRoy; *b* 6 April 1978; *s* and *heir* of Earl of Euston, *qv.*

IPSWICH, Bishop of; *see* St Edmundsbury and Ipswich.

IPSWICH, Archdeacon of; *see* Gibson, Ven. T. A.

IRBY, family name of **Baron Boston.**

IREDALE, Peter, PhD; FInstP, FIEE; Chairman, Oxfordshire District Health Authority, since 1992; Supernumerary Fellow, Wolfson College, Oxford, since 1991; *b* Brownhills, Staffs, 15 March 1932; *s* of late Henry Iredale and Annie (*née* Kirby); *m* 1957, Judith Margaret (*née* Marshall); one *s* three *d. Educ:* King Edward VIth Grammar Sch., Lichfield; Univ. of Bristol (BSc, PhD). AERE Harwell (subseq. Harwell Laboratory), 1955–92: research: on Nuclear Instrumentation, 1955–69; on Non Destructive Testing, 1969–70; Computer Storage, 1970–73; Commercial Officer, 1973–75; Gp Leader, Nuclear Instrumentation, 1975–77; Dep. Hd, Marketing and Sales Dept, 1977–79; Hd of Marine Technology Support Unit, 1979–81; Chm., UK Wave-Energy Steering Cttee, 1979–84; Dir, Engrg, 1981–84; Dir, Engrg and Non Nuclear Energy, 1984–86; Dep. Dir, 1986–87, Dir, 1987–90, Harwell Lab.; Dir, Culham/Harwell Sites, UKAEA, 1990–92. Hon. DSc Oxford Brookes, 1993. *Publications:* papers on high energy physics, nuclear instrumentation. *Recreations:* family, music, working with wood, gardening. *Address:* Oxfordshire Health Authority, Manor House, Headley Way, Headington, Oxford OX3 9DZ. *T:* Oxford (01865) 222148.

IREDALE, Prof. Roger Oliver, PhD; Professor of International Education, since 1993, and Dean, Faculty of Education, since 1994, University of Manchester; *b* 13 Aug. 1934; *s* of Fred Iredale and Elsie Florence (*née* Hills); *m* 1968, Mavis Potter; one *s* one *d. Educ:* Harrow County Grammar Sch.; Univ. of Reading (BA 1956, MA 1959, PhD 1971; Hurry Medal for Poetry; Early English Text Soc's Prize; Seymour-Sharman Prize for Literature; Graham Robertson Travel Award); Peterhouse Coll., Univ. of Cambridge (Cert. Ed. 1957). Teacher, Hele's Sch., Exeter, 1959–61; Lectr and Senior Lectr, Bishop Otter Coll., Chichester, 1962–70; British Council Officer and Maître de Conférences, Univ. of Algiers, 1970–72; Lectr, Chichester Coll. of Further Educn, 1972–73; British Council Officer, Madras, 1973–75; Dir of Studies, Educl Admin., Univ. of Leeds, 1975–79; Educn Adviser, 1979–83, Chief Educn Advr, 1983–93, ODA. Member: Commonwealth Scholarship Commn, 1984–93; Unesco-Unicef Jt Cttee, 1991–; Comr, Sino-British Friendship Scholarship Scheme Commn, 1986–. Governor: Sch. of Oriental and African Studies, 1983–; Queen Elizabeth House, Oxford, 1986–87; Commonwealth of Learning, 1988–93. Poetry Society's Greenwood Prize, 1974. *Publications:* Turning Bronzes (poems), 1974; Out Towards the Dark (poems), 1978; articles in Comparative Education and other jls; poems for BBC Radio 3 and in anthologies and jls. *Recreations:* poetry writing, restoring the discarded. *Address:* School of Education, University of Manchester, Oxford Road, Manchester M13 9PL. *T:* 0161–275 3459.

IRELAND, Frank Edward, BSc, CChem; FRSC; FEng; FIChemE; SFInstE; consultant in air pollution control, retired; HM Chief Alkali and Clean Air Inspector, 1964–78; *b* 7 Oct. 1913; *s* of William Edward Ireland and Bertha Naylor; *m* 1941, Edna Clare Meredith; one *s* three *d. Educ:* Liverpool Univ. (BSc). CChem, FRSC (FRIC 1945); FIChemE 1950; SFInstF 1956; Founder FEng 1976. Plant Superintendent, Orrs Zinc White Works, Widnes, Imperial Smelting Corp. Ltd, 1935–51; Prodn Man., Durham Chemicals Ltd, Birtley, Co. Durham, 1951–53; Alkali Inspector based on Sheffield, 1953–58; Dep. Chief Alkali Inspector, 1958–64. Pres., Inst. of Fuel, 1974–75; Vice Pres., Instn of Chem. Engrs, 1969–72. Freeman 1983, Liveryman, 1986–, Engineers' Co. George E. Davis Gold Medal, Instn of Chem. Engrs, 1969. *Publications:* Annual Alkali Reports, 1964–77; contrib. Jl of IChemE; papers to nat. and internat. organisations. *Recreations:* golf, gardening. *Address:* 59 Lanchester Road, Highgate, N6 4SX. *T:* 0181–883 6060.

IRELAND, Norman Charles; Chairman, BTR, since 1993 (Director, since 1969); *b* 28 May 1927; *s* of Charles and Winifred Ireland; *m* 1953, Gillian Margaret (*née* Harrison); one *s* one *d. Educ:* England, USA, India. CA (Scot.); Chartered Management Accountant. With Richard Brown & Co., Edinburgh, 1944–50; Brown Fleming & Murray, London, 1950–54; Avon Rubber Co., Melksham, 1955–64; Chief Accountant, United Glass, 1964–66; Finance Dir, BTR, 1967–87; Chm., Bowater plc, 1987–93. Chairman: The Housing Finance Corp., 1988–93; Intermediate Capital Gp, 1989–93; Dir, Meggitt, 1987–93. *Recreations:* gardening, ballet, opera, music.

IRELAND, Patrick Gault de C.; *see* de Courcy-Ireland.

IRELAND, Ronald David; QC (Scotland) 1964; Sheriff Principal of Grampian, Highland and Islands, 1988–93; *b* 13 March 1925; *o s* of William Alexander Ireland and Agnes Victoria Brown. *Educ:* George Watson's Coll., Edinburgh; Balliol Coll., Oxford (Scholar); Edinburgh Univ. Served Royal Signals, 1943–46. BA Oxford, 1950, MA 1958; LLB Edinburgh, 1952. Passed Advocate, 1952; Clerk of the Faculty of Advocates, 1957–58; Aberdeen University: Prof. of Scots Law, 1958–71; Dean of Faculty of Law, 1964–67; Hon. Prof., Faculty of Law, 1988–; Sheriff of Lothian and Borders (formerly Lothians and Peebles) at Edinburgh, 1972–88. Governor, Aberdeen Coll. of Education, 1959–64 (Vice-Chm., 1962–64). Comr, under NI (Emergency Provisions) Act, 1974–75. Member: Bd of Management, Aberdeen Gen. Hosps, 1961–71 (Chm., 1964–71); Departmental Cttee on Children and Young Persons, 1961–64; Cttee on the Working of the Abortion Act, 1971–74; Hon. Sheriff for Aberdeenshire, 1963–88. Member: North Eastern Regional Hosp. Bd, 1964–71 (Vice-Chm. 1966–71); After Care Council, 1962–65; Nat. Staff Advisory Cttee for the Scottish Hosp. Service, 1964–65; Chm., Scottish Hosps Administrative Staffs Cttee, 1965–72. Dir, Scottish Courts Admin, 1975–78. Hon. LLD Aberdeen, 1994. *Address:* 6A Greenhill Gardens, Edinburgh EH10 4BW. *Clubs:* New (Edinburgh); Royal Northern and University (Aberdeen); Highland (Inverness).

IREMONGER, Thomas Lascelles Isa Shandon Valiant; *b* 14 March 1916; *o s* of Lt-Col H. E. W. Iremonger, DSO, Royal Marine Artillery, and Julia St Mary Shandon, *d* of Col John Quarry, Royal Berks Regiment; *m* Lucille Iremonger (*d* 1989), MA (Oxon), FRSL, author and broadcaster; one *d. Educ:* Oriel Coll., Oxford (MA; Rear-Cdre. Oxford Univ. Yacht Club, 1937–38). HM Overseas Service (Western Pacific, Gilbert & Ellice Islands Colony and Colony of Fiji), 1938–46. RNVR (Lt), 1942–46. MP (C) Ilford North, Feb. 1954–Feb. 1974, Redbridge, Ilford North, Feb.–Sept. 1974; PPS to Sir Fitzroy Maclean, Bt, CBE, MP, when Under-Sec. of State for War, 1954–57. Contested (C Ind. Democrat) Redbridge, Ilford N, March 1978 and (C, independently), 1979. Mem., Royal Commn on the Penal System, 1964–66. Underwriting Mem. of Lloyd's. *Publications:* Disturbers of the Peace, 1962; Money, Politics and You, 1963. *Address:* Milbourne Manor, near Malmesbury, Wilts SN16 9JA; La Voûte, Montignac-le-Coq, 16390 St Séverin, France.

IRENS, Alfred Norman, CBE 1969; Chairman: South Western Electricity Board, 1956–73; British Approvals Board for Telecommunications, 1982–84; *b* 28 Feb. 1911; *s* of Max Henry and Guinevere Emily Irens; *m* 1934, Joan Elizabeth, *d* of John Knight, FRIBA, Worsley, Manchester; two *s. Educ:* Blundell's Sch., Tiverton; Faraday House, London. College apprentice, Metropolitan Vickers, Ltd, Manchester. Subsequently with General Electric Co., Ltd, until joining Bristol Aeroplane Co., Ltd, 1939, becoming Chief Electrical Engineer, 1943; Consulting Engineer to Govt and other organisations, 1945–56. Part-time mem., SW Electricity Bd, 1948–56. Past Chm. IEE Utilization Section and IEE Western Sub-Centre; Chairman: British Electrical Development Assoc., 1962–63; SW Economic Planning Council, 1968–71; BEAB for Household Equipment, 1974–84. Chm., Bristol Waterworks Co., 1975–81 (Dir, 1967–81); Dir, Avon Rubber Co. Ltd, 1973–81. JP Long Ashton, Som, 1960–66. Hon. MSc Bristol, 1957. *Recreations:* general outdoor activities. *Address:* Crete Hill House, Cote House Lane, Bristol BS9 3UW. *T:* Bristol (0117) 962 2419.

IRETON, Barrie Rowland; Under Secretary, since 1988, and Head of Africa Division, since 1993, Overseas Development Administration, Foreign and Commonwealth Office; *b* 15 Jan. 1944; *s* of Philip Thomas Ireton, CBE, and Marjorie Rosalind Ireton; *m* 1965, June Collins; one *s* one *d* (and one *s* decd). *Educ:* Alleyn's Grammar Sch., Stevenage; Trinity Coll., Cambridge (MA); London School of Economics (MSc 1970). Economic Statistician, Govt of Zambia, 1965–68; Economist, Industrial Develt Corp., Zambia, 1968–69; Development Sec., The Gambia, 1970–73; Overseas Development Administration, 1973–; Economic Advr, 1973–76; Sen. Economic Advr, 1976–84; Asst Sec., 1984–88; Principal Finance Officer, 1988–93. *Recreations:* tennis, gardening, walking.

Address: Overseas Development Administration, 94 Victoria Street, SW1E 5JL. *T:* 0171–917 0439.

IRONS, Jeremy; actor; *b* 19 Sept. 1948; *s* of late Paul Dugan Irons and of Barbara Anne Brereton (*née* Sharpe); *m* 1st (marr. diss.); 2nd, 1978, Sinead Cusack; two *s. Educ:* Sherborne; Bristol Old Vic Theatre Sch. *Theatre* appearances include: Bristol Old Vic Theatre Co., 1968–71; Godspell, Round House, transf. Wyndham's, 1971; The Taming of the Shrew, New Shakespeare Co., Round House, 1975; Wild Oats, RSC, 1976–77; The Rear Column, Globe, 1978; The Real Thing, Broadway, 1984 (Tony Award for Best Actor); The Rover, Mermaid, 1986; A Winter's Tale, RSC, 1986; Richard II, RSC, 1986; *television* appearances include: The Pallisers; Love for Lydia; Brideshead Revisited, 1981; The Captain's Doll, 1983; *films* include: The French Lieutenant's Woman, 1981; Moonlighting, 1982; Betrayal, 1982; Swann in Love, 1983; The Wild Duck, 1983; The Mission, 1986; A Chorus of Disapproval, 1988; Dead Ringers, 1988; Danny Champion of the World, 1988; Reversal of Fortune, 1990; Australia, 1991; Kafka, 1992; Waterland, 1992; Damage, 1993; M. Butterfly, 1994; The House of the Spirits, 1994. Member: Gaia Foundn; European Film Acad.; Patron: Prison Phoenix Trust; Archway Foundn. *Address:* c/o Hutton Management, 200 Fulham Road, SW10 9PN.

IRONS, Norman MacFarlane, CBE 1995; JP; CEng; Lord Provost and Lord Lieutenant of Edinburgh, 1992–March 1996; Partner, IFP Consulting Engineers, since 1983; *b* 4 Jan. 1941; *s* of Dugald Paterson Irons and Anne Galbraith Irons (*née* Rankin); *m* 1966, Anne Wyness Buckley; one *s* one *d. Educ:* George Heriot's Sch.; Borough Road Coll.; Napier Tech. Coll. CEng; MCIBSE 1968; MIMechE 1973. Building Services Engr, 1962–. Mem. (SNP) City of Edinburgh Council, 1976–96. JP 1983, DL 1988, Edinburgh. Pres., Lismore RFC, 1989–94. Hon. FRCSE 1994. Hon. DLitt Napier, 1993. *Recreations:* enjoying life with wife, Rugby. *Address:* (until April 1996) City Chambers, Edinburgh EH1 1PL. *T:* 0131–529 4000; 141 Saughtonhall Drive, Edinburgh EH12 5TS. *T:* 0131–337 6154.

IRONSIDE, family name of **Baron Ironside.**

IRONSIDE, 2nd Baron, *cr* 1941, of Archangel and of Ironside; **Edmund Oslac Ironside;** Defence Consultant, Rolls-Royce Industrial Power Group, since 1991; *b* 21 Sept. 1924; *o s* of 1st Baron Ironside, Field Marshal, GCB, CMG, DSO, and Mariot Ysabel Cheyne (*d* 1984); *S* father, 1959; *m* 1950, Audrey Marigold, *y d* of late Lt-Col Hon. Thomas Morgan-Grenville, DSO, OBE, MC; one *s* one *d. Educ:* Tonbridge Sch. Joined Royal Navy, 1943; retd as Lt, 1952. English Electric Gp, 1952–63; Cryosystems Ltd, 1963–68; International Research and Development Co., 1968–84; Market Co-ordinator (Defence), NEI plc, 1984–89. Vice-Pres., Parly and Scientific Cttee, 1984–87 (Dep. Chm., 1974–77); Chm., All Party Defence Study Gp, 1995– (Hon. Sec., 1992–95). Mem., Organising Cttee, British Library, 1971–72. President: Electric Vehicle Assoc., 1976–83; European Electric Road Vehicle Assoc., 1980–82; Vice-Pres., Inst. of Patentees and Inventors, 1977–91; Chm., Adv. Cttee, Science Reference Lib., 1976–84. Governor, Tonbridge Sch. and others; Member: Court, 1971–, Council, 1987–89, City Univ.; Court and Council Essex Univ., 1982–87. Master, Skinners' Co., 1981–82. Hon. FCGI (CGIA 1986). *Publication:* (ed) High Road to Command: the diaries of Major-General Sir Edmund Ironside, 1920–22, 1972. *Heir: s* Hon. Charles Edmund Grenville Ironside [*b* 1 July 1956; *m* 1985, Hon. Elizabeth Law, *e d* of Lord Coleraine, *qv*; one *s* one *d*]. *Address:* Priory House, Old House Lane, Boxted, Colchester, Essex CO4 5RB. *Club:* Royal Ocean Racing.

IRVINE, family name of **Baron Irvine of Lairg.**

IRVINE OF LAIRG, Baron *cr* 1987 (Life Peer), of Lairg in the District of Sutherland; **Alexander Andrew Mackay Irvine,** QC 1978; *b* 23 June 1940; *s* of Alexander Irvine and Margaret Christina Irvine; *m* 1974, Alison Mary, *y d* of Dr James Shaw McNair, MD, and Agnes McNair, MA; two *s. Educ:* Inverness Acad.; Hutchesons' Boys' Grammar Sch., Glasgow; Glasgow Univ. (MA, LLB); Christ's Coll., Cambridge (Scholar; BA 1st Cl. Hons with distinction; LLB 1st Cl. Hons; George Long Prize in Jurisprudence). Called to the Bar, Inner Temple, 1967, Bencher, 1985; a Recorder, 1985–88. Univ. Lectr, LSE, 1965–69. Contested (Lab) Hendon North, Gen. Election, 1970. Shadow Lord Chancellor, H of L, 1992–. *Recreations:* cinema, theatre, collecting paintings, travel. *Address:* 11 King's Bench Walk, Temple, EC4Y 7EQ. *T:* 0171–583 0610. *Club:* Garrick.

IRVINE, Alan Montgomery, RDI 1964; DesRCA, ARIBA; architect in private practice; *b* 14 Sept. 1926; *s* of Douglas Irvine and Ellen Marler; *m* 1st, 1955; one *s*; 2nd, 1966, Katherine Mary Buzas; two *s. Educ:* Regent Street Polytechnic, Secondary Sch. and Sch. of Architecture; Royal College of Art. RAF (Aircrew), 1944–47. Worked in Milan with BBPR Gp, 1954–55. In private practice since 1956, specialising in design of interiors, museums and exhibitions; partnership Buzas and Irvine, 1965–85. Work has included interior design for Schroder Wagg & Co., Lazards, Bovis, S Australian Govt, Nat. Enterprise Bd; Mem. of design team for QE2, 1966. Various exhibns for V&A Museum, Tate Gallery, Royal Academy, Imperial War Museum, RIBA, British Council, British Museum, Wellcome Inst., Olivetti, Fiat etc including: Treasures of Cambridge, 1959; Book of Kells, 1961; Architecture of Power, 1963; Mellon Collection, 1969; Age of Charles I, 1972; Pompeii AD79, 1976; Gold of El Dorado, 1978; Horses of San Marco (London, NY, Milan, Berlin), 1979–82; Great Japan Exhibition, 1981; Art and Industry, 1982; Cimabue Crucifix (London, Madrid, Munich), 1982–83; Treasures of Ancient Nigeria, 1983; The Genius of Venice, 1983; Leonardo da Vinci: studies for the Last Supper (Milan, Sydney, Toronto, Barcelona, Tokyo), 1984; Art of the Architect, 1984; Re dei Confessori (Milan, Venice), 1985; C. S. Jagger: War and Peace Sculpture, 1985; Queen Elizabeth II: portraits of 60 years, 1986; Eye for Industry, 1986; Glass of the Caesars (London, Cologne, Rome), 1988; Michaelangelo Drawings, Louvre, 1989; Conservation Today, 1989; Paul de Lamerie, 1990; Lion of Venice (London, Amsterdam), 1991; David Smith Medals, 1991; Leonardo and Venezia, Venice, 1992. Museum work includes: Old Master Drawings Gallery, Windsor Castle, 1965; New Galleries for Royal Scottish Museum, 1968; Crown Jewels display, Tower of London, 1968; Heinz Gallery for Architectural Drawings, RIBA, London, 1972; Museum and Art Gallery for Harrow School, 1975; Heralds' Museum, London, 1980; Housesteads Roman Fort Mus., 1982; Al Shaheed Museum, Baghdad, 1983; Cabinet War Rooms, London, 1984; West Wing Galls, Nat. Maritime Mus., Greenwich, 1986; Beatrix Potter Museum, Cumbria, 1988; George III Gall., Science Mus., 1993; Treasuries at: Winchester Cathedral, 1968; Christ Church, Oxford, 1975; Winchester Coll., 1982; Lichfield Cath., 1993. Retrospective personal exhibn: RIBA Heinz Gall., 1989. Consultant designer to Olivetti, Italy; Consultant architect to British Museum, 1981–84. Mem., Crafts Council, 1984–86. Liveryman, Worshipful Co. of Goldsmiths. Hon. Fellow, RCA. *Recreations:* travel, photography. *Address:* 2 Aubrey Place, St John's Wood, NW8 9BH. *T:* 0171–328 2229. *Club:* London Collie.

IRVINE, Sir Donald (Hamilton), Kt 1994; CBE 1987 (OBE 1979); MD; FRCGP; Principal in General Practice, Ashington, since 1960; Regional Adviser in General Practice, University of Newcastle, since 1973; President, General Medical Council, since 1995; *b* 2 June 1935; *s* of late Dr Andrew Bell Hamilton Irvine and of Dorothy Mary Irvine; *m* 1960; two *s* one *d*; *m* 1986, Sally Fountain. *Educ:* King Edward Sixth Grammar Sch., Morpeth; Medical Sch., King's Coll., Univ. of Durham (MB BS); DObstRCOG 1960; MD Newcastle 1964; FRCGP 1972 (MRCGP 1965). Ho. Phys. to Dr C. N. Armstrong and Dr Henry Miller, 1958–59. Chm. Council, RCGP, 1982–85 (Vice-Chm., 1981–82); Hon. Sec. of the College, 1972–78; Jt Hon. Sec., Jt Cttee on Postgraduate Trng for General Practice, 1976–82; Fellow, BMA, 1976; Mem., Gen. Medical Council, 1979– (Chm., Cttee on Standards and Medical Ethics, 1985–); Governor, MSD Foundn, 1982–89 (Chm., Bd of Governors, 1983–89). Vice-Pres., Medical Defence Union, 1974–78. Vis. Professor in Family Practice, Univ. of Iowa, USA, 1973; (first) Vis. Prof. to Royal Australian Coll. of General Practitioners, 1977; Vis. Cons. on Postgrad. Educn for Family Medicine to Virginia Commonwealth Univ., 1971, Univ. of Wisconsin-Madison, 1973, Medical Univ. of S Carolina, 1974. Mem., Audit Commn, 1990–. *Publications:* The Future General Practitioner: learning and teaching, (jtly), 1972 (RCGP); Managing for Quality in General Practice, 1990; (ed jtly) Making Sense of Audit, 1991; chapters to several books on gen. practice; papers on clinical and educnl studies in medicine, in BMJ, Lancet, Jl of RCGP. *Recreations:* bird watching, motor cars, politics, watching television. *Address:* Mole End, Fairmoor, Morpeth NE61 3JL; Flat 11, Cedarland Court, Roland Gardens, SW7 3RW.

IRVINE, Surg. Captain Gerard Sutherland, CBE 1970; RN retired; Medical Officer, Department of Health and Social Security, 1971–78; *b* 19 June 1913; *s* of Major Gerard Byrom Corrie Irvine and Maud Andrée (*née* Wylde); *m* 1939, Phyllis Lucy Lawrie (*d* 1988); one *s. Educ:* Imperial Service Coll., Windsor; Epsom Coll.; University Coll. and Hosp., London. MRCS, LRCP, MB, BS 1937; DLO 1940; FRCS 1967. Jenks Meml Schol. 1932; Liston Gold Medal for Surgery 1936. Surg. Sub-Lt RNVR 1935, Surg. Lt RNVR 1937; Surg Lt RN 1939; Surg. Lt-Comdr 1944; Surg. Comdr 1953; Surg. Capt. 1963. Served War of 1939–45 (1939–45 Star, Atlantic Star with Bar for France and Germany, Burma Star, Defence Medal, Victory Medal); subseq. service: Ceylon, 1946; Haslar, 1947–49 and 1957–60; Malta, 1953–56; HMS: Maidstone (Submarine Depot Ship), 1949–51; Osprey (T&A/S Trng Sch.), 1951–53; Collingwood, 1956–57; Lion, 1960–62; Vernon (Torpedo Sch.), 1962–63; Sen. Cons. in ENT, 1953–70; Adviser in ENT to Med. Dir-Gen. (Navy), 1966–70; Sen. MO i/c Surgical Div., RN Hosp. Haslar, 1966–70; QHS 1969–70; retd 1970. Member: BMA 1938; Sections of Otology and Laryngology, RSM, 1948–77 (FRSM 1948–77); British Assoc. of Otolaryngologists, 1945–71 (Council, 1958–70); S Western Laryngological Assoc., 1951–71; Hearing Sub-Cttee of RN Personnel Res. Cttee, 1947–70; Otological Sub-Cttee of RAF Flying Personnel Res. Cttee, 1963–70. OStJ 1969. *Publications:* numerous articles in various medical jls. *Recreations:* gardening, philately, do-it-yourself. *Address:* 9 Alvara Road, Alverstoke, Gosport PO12 2HY. *T:* Gosport (01705) 580342.

IRVINE, James Eccles Malise; His Honour Judge Irvine; a Circuit Judge, since 1972 (Leicester County and Crown Courts, 1972–82; Oxford and Northampton Combined Courts Centres, since 1982); *b* 10 July 1925; *y s* of late Brig.-Gen. A. E. Irvine, CB, CMG, DSO, Wotton-under-Edge; *m* 1954, Anne, *e d* of late Col G. Egerton-Warburton, DSO, TD, JP, DL, Grafton Hall, Malpas; one *s* one *d. Educ:* Stowe Sch. (Scholar); Merton Coll., Oxford (Postmaster). MA Oxon. Served Grenadier Guards, 1943–46 (France and Germany Star); Hon. Captain Grenadier Guards, 1946. Called to Bar, Inner Temple, 1949 (Poland Prizeman in Criminal Law, 1949); practised Oxford Circuit, 1949–71; Prosecuting Counsel for Inland Revenue on Oxford Circuit, 1965–71; Dep. Chm., Glos QS, 1967–71. Lay Judge of Court of Arches of Canterbury and Chancery Court of York, 1981–. *Publication:* Parties and Pleasures: the Diaries of Helen Graham 1823–26, 1957. *Address:* 2 Harcourt Buildings, Temple, EC4Y 9DB; c/o Oxford Combined Courts Centre, St Aldate's, Oxford OX1 1TL.

IRVINE, Maj.-Gen. John, OBE 1955; Director of Medical Services, British Army of the Rhine, 1973–75; *b* 31 May 1914; *s* of late John Irvine and late Jessie Irvine (*née* McKinnon); *m* 1941, Mary McNicol, *d* of late Andrew Brown Cossar, Glasgow; one *d. Educ:* Glasgow High Sch.; Glasgow Univ. MB, ChB 1940. MFCM 1973. Commnd into RAMC, 1940; served War of 1939–45 (despatches and Act of Gallantry, 1944): Egypt, Greece, Crete, Western Desert, 1941–43; Sicily, Italy and Yugoslavia, 1943–45; served with British Troops, Austria, 1947–49; Korea, 1953–54 (OBE); Malaya, 1954–56 (despatches); Germany, 1958–61; Ghana, 1961; Germany, 1962–64; DDMS, HQ BAOR, 1968–69; DDMS, 1st British Corps, 1969–71; Dep. Dir-Gen., AMS, 1971–73. QHS 1972–75. OStJ 1971. *Recreations:* tennis, ski-ing. *Address:* Greenlawns, 11 Manor Road, Aldershot, Hants GU11 3DG.

IRVINE, John Ferguson, CB 1983; public administration consultant; Chief Executive, Industrial Therapy Organisation (Ulster), 1984–94; *b* 13 Nov. 1920; *s* of Joseph Ferguson Irvine and Helen Gardner; *m* 1st, 1945, Doris Partridge (*d* 1973); one *s* one *d*; 2nd, 1980, Christine Margot Tudor; two *s* and two step *s. Educ:* Ardrossan Acad.; Glasgow Univ. (MA). RAF, 1941–46; Scottish Home Dept, 1946–48; NI Civil Service, 1948–66; Chief Exec., Ulster Transport Authority, 1966–68; Chief Exec., NI Transport Holding Co., 1968; NI Civil Service, 1969–83; Dep. Sec., DoE, NI, 1971–76; Permanent Secretary: attached NI Office, 1977–80; Dept of Manpower Services, 1980–81; DoE for NI, 1981–83. Chm. Management Cttee, 1974–75, and Vice-Chm. General Council, 1975, Action Cancer; Chm., Down Care and Aftercare Cttee, 1992–; Member: NI Marriage Guidance Council (Chm., 1976–78); Council, PHAB (NI), 1984–86; Council, PHAB (UK), 1984–86; Trustee, Heart Fund, Royal Victoria Hosp., Belfast, 1986–88. *Recreations:* swimming, yoga, Majorca, football. *Address:* 7 Bullseye Park, Downpatrick, Co. Down BT30 6RX.

IRVINE, Prof. John Maxwell, PhD; CPhys, FInstP; FRAS; FRSE; Principal and Vice-Chancellor, University of Aberdeen, since 1991; *b* 28 Feb. 1939; *s* of John MacDonald Irvine and Joan Paterson (*née* Adamson); *m* 1962, Grace Ritchie; one *s. Educ:* George Heriot's Sch., Edinburgh; Edinburgh Univ. (BSc Math. Phys. 1961); Univ. of Michigan (MSc 1962); Univ. of Manchester (PhD 1964). FInstP 1971; CPhys 1985; FRAS 1986; FRSE 1993. English-Speaking Union Fellow, Univ. of Michigan, 1961–62; Asst Lectr, Univ. of Manchester, 1964–66; Res. Associate, Cornell Univ., 1966–68; University of Manchester: Lectr, 1968–73; Sen. Lectr, 1973–76; Reader, 1976–83; Prof. of Theoretical Physics, 1983–91; Dean of Science, 1989–91. Director: Grampian Enterprise Ltd, 1992–; Rowett Res. Inst., 1992–. Member: Nuclear Physics Bd, SERC, 1983–88 (Chm., Nuclear Structure Cttee, 1984–88); Bd, Scottish Council for Develt and Industry, 1992–; Scottish Econ. Council, 1993–; Scottish Cttee, British Council, 1994–. Member Council: Inst. of Physics, 1981–87, 1988–94 (Vice-Pres., 1982–87); ACU, 1994–. FRSA 1993. *Publications:* The Basis of Modern Physics, 1967 (trans. Dutch and French, 1969); Nuclear Structure Theory, 1972; Heavy Nuclei, Superheavy Nuclei and Neutron Stars, 1975; Neutron Stars, 1978; research articles on nuclear physics, astrophysics and condensed matter physics. *Recreations:* hill walking, tennis, bridge. *Address:* Chanonry Lodge, The Chanonry, Old Aberdeen AB2 1RP; University Office, Regent Walk, Aberdeen AB9 1FX. *T:* Aberdeen (01224) 272134, *Fax:* Aberdeen (01224) 488605. *Clubs:* Athenæum, Caledonian; Royal Northern and University (Aberdeen).

IRVINE, Very Rev. (John) Murray; Provost and Rector of Southwell Minster, 1978–91, Emeritus, since 1991; Priest-in-Charge of Edingley and Halam, 1978–91; Priest-in-Charge of Rolleston with Fiskerton and Morton and Upton, 1990–91; *b* 19 Aug. 1924; *s* of Andrew Leicester Irvine and Eleanor Mildred (*née* Lloyd); *m* 1961, Pamela Shirley Brain (*d* 1992); one *s* three *d*. *Educ:* Charterhouse; Magdalene Coll., Cambridge; Ely Theological Coll. BA 1946, MA 1949. Deacon, 1948; Priest, 1949; Curate of All Saints, Poplar, 1948–53; Chaplain of Sidney Sussex Coll., Cambridge, 1953–60; Selection Sec. of CACTM, 1960–65; Canon Residentiary, Prebendary of Hunderton, Chancellor and Librarian of Hereford Cathedral, and Dir of Ordination Training, Diocese of Hereford, 1965–78; Warden of Readers, 1976–78. *Address:* 9 Salston Barton, Strawberry Lane, Ottery St Mary, Devon EX11 1RG. *T:* Ottery St Mary (01404) 815901.

IRVINE, Michael Fraser; barrister; *b* 21 Oct. 1939; *s* of Rt Hon. Sir Arthur Irvine, PC, QC, MP, and Lady Irvine. *Educ:* Rugby; Oriel College, Oxford (BA). Called to the Bar, Inner Temple, 1964. Contested (C): Bishop Auckland, 1979; Ipswich, 1992; MP (C) Ipswich, 1987–92. PPS to Attorney-Gen., 1990–92. *Recreation:* hill walking in Scotland. *Address:* 1 Crown Office Row, Temple, EC4Y 7HH. *T:* 0171-583 9292.

IRVINE, Very Rev. Murray; *see* Irvine, Very Rev. J. M.

IRVINE, Norman Forrest; QC 1973; a Recorder of the Crown Court, 1974–86; *b* 29 Sept. 1922; *s* of William Allan Irvine and Dorcas Forrest; *m* 1964, Mary Lilian Patricia Edmunds (*née* Constable); one *s*. *Educ:* High Sch. of Glasgow; Glasgow Univ. BL 1941. Solicitor (Scotland), 1943. Served War, 1942–45: Lieut Royal Signals, Staff Captain. HM Claims Commn, 1945–46; London Claims Supt, Provincial Insurance Co. Ltd, 1950–52. Called to Bar, Gray's Inn, 1955. *Recreations:* reading, piano, writing. *Address:* 11 Upland Park Road, Oxford OX2 7RU.

IRVINE, Dr Robin Francis, FRS 1993; Research Scientist, Biotechnology and Biological Sciences (formerly Agricultural and Food) Research Council Babraham Institute, since 1978; *b* 10 Feb. 1950; *s* of Charles Donald Irvine and June (*née* Ievers); *m* 1973, Sandra Jane Elder; two *s*. *Educ:* Stroud Sch., Romsey; Sherborne Sch., Dorset; St Catherine's Coll., Oxford (MA Biochem. 1972); Corpus Christi Coll., Cambridge (PhD Botany 1976). SRC Res. Student, ARC Unit of Developmental Botany, Cambridge, 1972–75; Beit Meml Fellow, ARC Inst. of Animal Physiol., Babraham, 1975–78; Mem. of Scientific Staff, 1978–, UG5, 1993–, AFRC Inst. of Animal Physiol. and Genetics Res., subseq. AFRC Babraham Inst., Cambridge. Mem., Wellcome Trust Cell and Molecular Panel, 1989–92. Morton Lectr, Biochem. Soc., 1994. Mem. Editl Bd, Biochemical Jl, 1988–. *Publications:* (ed) Methods in Inositide Research, 1990; contribs to Nature, Biochem. Jl and other scientific jls. *Recreations:* playing the lute and guitar, music (especially pre-1650), ornithology, reading. *Address:* Babraham Institute, Babraham, Cambridge CB2 4AT. *T:* Cambridge (01223) 832312.

IRVINE, Sir Robin (Orlando Hamilton), Kt 1989; FRCP, FRACP; Vice-Chancellor, University of Otago, Dunedin, New Zealand, 1973–93, Emeritus Professor 1994; *b* 15 Sept. 1929; *s* of late Claude Turner Irvine; *m* 1957, Elizabeth Mary, *d* of late Herbert Gray Corbett; one *s* two *d*. *Educ:* Wanganui Collegiate Sch.; Univ. of Otago. Otago University Med. Sch., 1948–53; MB, ChB, 1953; MD (NZ), 1958; FRCP, FRACP. House Phys., Auckland Hosp., 1954; Dept of Medicine, Univ. of Otago: Research Asst (Emily Johnston Res. Schol.), 1955; Asst Lectr and Registrar, 1956–57. Leverhulme Research Scholar, Middlesex Hosp., London, 1958; Registrar, Postgraduate Medical Sch., London, 1959–60; Isaacs Medical Research Fellow, Auckland Hosp., 1960–61; Med. Tutor and Med. Specialist, Auckland Hosp., 1962–63; Lectr, Sen. Lectr in Med., Univ. of Otago, 1963–67; Associate Prof., 1968; Clinical Dean and Personal Professor, Univ. of Otago Medical Sch., 1969–72. Girdlers' Co. Senior Vis. Res. Fellowship, Green Coll., Oxford, 1986–87. Consultant, Asian Development Bank, 1974–; Dir, Dunedin City Hldgs, 1993–; Chm. Bd of Dirs, Mercy Hospital Dunedin Ltd, 1994–. Member: Selwyn Coll. Bd, 1966–; Pharmacology and Therapeutic Cttee, Min. of Health, 1967–73; Otago Hosp. Bd, 1969–88; Med. Educn Cttee of Med. Council of NZ, 1969–73; Cent. Educn Cttee, NZ Med. Assoc., 1970–73; Social Council of Nat. Develt Council of NZ, 1971–74; Cttee on Nursing Educn, Min. of Educn, 1972; Social Develt Council, 1974–79; Commn for the Future, 1976–80; NZ Planning Council, 1977–82; Otago Polytech. Council, 1973–87; Dunedin Teachers Coll. Council, 1973–90; NZ Adv. Cttee, Nuffield Foundn, 1973–81; NZ Rhodes Scholarships Selection Cttee, 1976–81; Lottery Health Res. Distn Cttee, 1985–91; Hon. Adv. Bd, Royal NZ Plunket Soc., 1980–93; Council, Dunedin Coll. of Educn, 1991–92; Chairman: Otago Med. Res. Foundn, 1975–81; Ministerial working party on novel genetic techniques, 1977; NZ Vice-Chancellors' Cttee, 1979–80, 1992; Council, ACU, 1991–92 (Mem., 1979–80, 1991–93); Ross Dependency Res. Cttee, 1993–; Bd, Internat. Centre of Antarctic Information and Research, 1994–; Convenor, Med. Educn Mission to Univ. of S Pacific, 1971; Director: Otago Develt Corp., 1982–85; Inst. of Envmtl Science and Res. (formerly Envmtl Health and Forensic Sci.), 1991–. Trustee: McMillan Trust, 1973–93 (Chm., 1977–86, 1990–93); Mem., Investment Adv. Cttee, 1994–); Rowheath Trust, 1973–93; NZ Red Cross Foundn, 1988–; NZ Educn and Scholarship Trust, 1991–; Nat. Liby of NZ, 1992–; Antarctic Heritage Trust, 1993–. Hon. ADC 1969, and Hon. Physician 1970, to the Governor-General, Sir Arthur Porritt. Hon. Mem., Australian Soc. of Nephrology. Dr *hc* Edinburgh, 1976; Hon LLD Otago, 1993. FRSA 1980; FNZIM 1984. Silver Jubilee Medal, 1977. *Publications:* various papers on high blood pressure, renal med. and medical educn. *Recreations:* computing, walking, reading, music, travel. *Address:* 950 George Street, Dunedin, New Zealand. *T:* (03) 4021023. *Club:* Fernhill (Dunedin).

IRVING, Clifford; *see* Irving, E. C.

IRVING, Edward, ScD; FRS 1979; FRSC 1973; Research Scientist, Pacific Geoscience Centre, Sidney, BC, 1981–92, Emeritus since 1992; *b* 27 May 1927; *s* of George Edward and Nellie Irving; *m* 1957, Sheila Ann Irwin; two *s* two *d*. *Educ:* Colne Grammar Sch.; Cambridge Univ., 1948–54 (BA, MA, MSc, ScD). Served Army, 1945–48. Research Fellow, Fellow and Sen. Fellow, ANU, 1954–64; Dominion Observatory, Canada, 1964–66; Prof. of Geophysics, Univ. of Leeds, 1966–67; Res. Scientist, Dominion Observatory, later Earth Physics Br., Dept of Energy, Mines and Resources, Ottawa, 1967–81; Adjunct Professor: Carleton Univ., Ottawa, 1975–81; Univ. of Victoria, 1985–. FRAS 1958; Fellow: Amer. Geophysical Union, 1976 (Walter H. Bucher Medal, 1979); Geological Soc. of America, 1979. Hon. FGS 1989. Hon. DSc: Carleton, 1979; Memorial Univ. of Newfoundland, 1986. Gondwanaland Medal, Mining, Geological and Metallurgical Soc. of India, 1962; Logan Medal, Geol Assoc. of Canada, 1975; J. T. Wilson Medal, Canadian Geophys. Union, 1984. *Publications:* Paleomagnetism, 1964; numerous contribs to learned jls. *Recreations:* gardening, carpentry, choral singing. *Address:* Pacific Geoscience Centre, 9860 West Saanich Road, Box 6000, Sidney, BC V8L 4B2 Canada. *T:* (604) 3636508; 9363 Carnoustie Crescent, Sidney, BC V8L 5G7. *T:* (604) 6569645.

IRVING, (Edward) Clifford, CBE 1981; Member, Legislative Council, Isle of Man, 1987–95; *b* 24 May 1914; *s* of late William Radcliffe Irving and Mabel Henrietta (*née* Cottier); *m* 1941, Nora, *d* of Harold Page, Luton; one *s* one *d*. *Educ:* Isle of Man; Canada. Member: House of Keys, 1955–61, 1966–81, 1984–87 (Acting Speaker, 1971–81); Executive Council, IOM Govt, 1968–81 (Chm., 1977–81). Member, IOM Government Boards: Airports, 1955–58; Assessment, 1955–56; Social Security, 1956; Local Govt, 1956–62; Tourist, 1956–62; Finance, 1966–71; Member: Industrial Adv. Council, 1961–62, 1971–81, 1987–94; CS Commn, 1976–81. Chairman: IOM Tourist Bd, 1971–81; IOM Sports Council, 1971–81; IOM Harbours Bd, 1985–87. Chairman: Bank of Wales (IOM), 1985–87; Etam (IOM), 1985–; Refuge (IOM) Ltd, 1988–92; Director: Bank of Scotland (IOM) Ltd, 1987–95 (Chm., 1987–89); Bank of Scotland Nominees (IOM) Ltd, 1987–95 (Chm., 1987–89). President: Wanderers Male Voice Choir; Manx Nat. Powerboat Club; Manx Parascending Club; IOM Angling Assoc.; Douglas Br., RNLI; Past Patron: Manx Variety Club; IOM TT Races. *Recreations:* powerboating, angling. *Address:* Highfield, Belmont Road, Douglas, Isle of Man IM1 4NR. *T:* Douglas (01624) 673652. *Clubs:* Douglas and District Angling; Douglas Bay Yacht.

IRVING, Prof. John; Freeland Professor of Natural Philosophy (Theoretical Physics), University of Strathclyde, Glasgow, 1961–84; retired; *b* 22 Dec. 1920; *s* of John Irving and Margaret Kent Aird; *m* 1948, Monica Cecilia Clarke; two *s*. *Educ:* St John's Grammar Sch.; Hamilton Academy; Glasgow Univ. MA (1st Class Hons in Maths and Nat. Phil.), Glasgow Univ., 1940; PhD (Mathematical Physics), Birmingham Univ., 1951. FInstP 1980. Lectr, Stow Coll., Glasgow, 1944–45; Lectr in Maths, Univ. of St Andrews 1945–46; Lectr in Mathematical Physics, University of Birmingham, 1946–49; Nuffield Research Fellow (Nat. Phil.), University of Glasgow, 1949–51; Sen. Lectr in Applied Maths, University of Southampton, 1951–59; Prof. of Theoretical Physics and Head of Dept of Applied Mathematics and Theor. Physics University of Cape Town, 1959–61. Dean of Sch. of Mathematics and Physics, Strathclyde Univ., 1964–69. *Publications:* Mathematics in Physics and Engineering, 1959 (New York); contrib. to: Proc. Physical Soc.; Philosophical Magazine, Physical Review. *Recreations:* gardening, computing. *Address:* 12 Lomond Road, Wemyss Bay, Renfrewshire PA18 6BD.

IRVING, Sir Miles (Horsfall), Kt 1995; MD; FRCS, FRCSE; Professor of Surgery, University of Manchester, since 1974; National Director, NHS Health Technology Programme, since 1994; *b* 29 June 1935; *s* of Frederick William Irving and Mabel Irving; *m* 1965, Patricia Margaret Blaiklock; two *s* two *d*. *Educ:* King George V Sch., Southport; Liverpool Univ. (MB, ChB 1959; MD 1962; ChM 1968); Sydney Univ., Australia; MSc Manchester Univ., 1977. FRCS 1964; FRCSE 1964. Robert Gee Fellow, Liverpool Univ., 1962; Phyllis Anderson Fellow, Sydney Univ., 1967; St Bartholomew's Hospital, London: Chief Asst in Surgery, 1969–71; Reader in Surgery, Asst Dir of Professorial Surgical Unit, and Hon. Consultant Surgeon, 1972–74. Hon. Consultant Surgeon: Hope Hosp., Salford, 1974–; Manchester Royal Infirmary, 1993–; to the Army, 1989–. Hunterian Prof., 1967, Hunterian Orator, 1993, RCS; Sir Gordon Bell Meml Orator, NZ, 1982. Regl Dir of R & D, N Western RHA, 1992–94; Chm., Standing Gp on Health Technol., DoH, 1993–; Member: Expert Adv. Gp on AIDS, DoH, 1991–; MRC Health Services and Public Health Res. Bd, 1993–. Member: Council, RCS, 1984–95; GMC, 1989–92; President: Ileostomy Assoc. of GB and Ireland, 1982–92; Assoc. of Surgeons of GB and Ireland, 1995–May 1996; Internat. Surgical Gp, 1995–Sept. 1996. Hon. Fellow, Amer. Assoc. for Surgery of Trauma, 1985; Hon. FFAEM 1994. Moynihan Medal, Assoc. of Surgeons of GB and Ire., 1968; Pybus Medal, N of England Surgical Soc., 1986; John Loewenthal Medal, Sydney Univ., 1993; Canet Medal, Inst. of Mech. Incorp. Engrs, 1995. *Publications:* Gastroenterological Surgery, 1983; Intestinal Fistulas, 1985; ABC of Colorectal Diseases, 1993. *Recreations:* thinking about and occasionally actually climbing mountains, reading The Spectator, opera. *Address:* 18 Albert Road, Heaton, Bolton, Lancs BL1 5HE. *T:* Bolton (01204) 841182.

IRWIN, Lord; James Charles Wood; *b* 24 Aug. 1977; *s* and *heir* of 3rd Earl of Halifax, *qv*. *Address:* Garrowby, York YO4 1QD.

IRWIN, Maj.-Gen. Brian St George, CB 1975; Director General, Ordnance Survey, 1969–77, retired; *b* 16 Sept. 1917; *s* of late Lt-Col Alfred Percy Bulteel Irwin, DSO, and late Eileen Irwin (*née* Holberton); *m* 1939, Audrey Lilla (*d* 1994), *d* of late Lt-Col H. B. Steen, IMS; two *s*. *Educ:* Rugby Sch.; RMA Woolwich; Trinity Hall, Cambridge (MA). Commnd in RE, 1937; war service in Western Desert, 1941–43 (despatches); Sicily and Italy, 1943–44 (despatches); Greece, 1944–45; subseq. in Cyprus, 1956–59 (despatches) and 1961–63; Dir of Military Survey, MoD, 1965–69. Col Comdt, RE, 1977–82. FRICS (Council 1969–70, 1972–76); FRGS (Council 1966–70; Vice-Pres., 1974–77). *Recreations:* sailing, golf, gardening, genealogy. *Address:* 16 Northerwood House, Swan Green, Lyndhurst, Hants SO43 7DT. *T:* Lyndhurst (01703) 283499. *Club:* Army and Navy.

IRWIN, Helen Elizabeth; Second Clerk of Select Committees, House of Commons, since 1994; *b* 21 April 1948; *d* of Walter William Taylor and late Kathleen Taylor (*née* Moffoot); *m* 1972, Robert Graham Irwin; one *d*. *Educ:* Whalley Range Grammar Sch., Manchester; King's Coll., London (BA Hons Hist. 1969); SSEES, Univ. of London (MA Soviet Studies 1970). Asst Clerk, H of C, 1970–72; Admin Asst, Univ. of St Andrews, 1972–75; a Clerk, House of Commons, 1977–: Cttee of Public Accounts, 1977–81; served in Table Office, 1981–85; Social Services Cttee, 1985–89; Health Cttee, 1989–91; Foreign Affairs Cttee, 1991–94; Principal Clerk, 1994–. Mem. Council, Hansard Soc., 1990–. *Publications:* occasional contribs to books on parliamentary practice and procedure. *Recreations:* family, friends, travel. *Address:* Committee Office, House of Commons, SW1A 0AA. *T:* 0171–219 6257.

IRWIN, Ian Sutherland, CBE 1982; Executive Chairman (formerly Chairman and Chief Executive), Scottish Transport Group, since 1987; *b* Glasgow, 20 Feb. 1933; *s* of Andrew Campbell Irwin and Elizabeth Ritchie Arnott; *m* 1959, Margaret Miller Maureen Irvine; two *s*. *Educ:* Whitehill Sen. Secondary Sch., Glasgow; Glasgow Univ. BL; CA, IPFA, FCIT, CBIM, FInstD. Commercial Man., Scottish Omnibuses Ltd, 1960–64; Gp Accountant, Scottish Bus Gp, 1964–69; Gp Sec., 1969–75, Dep. Chm. and Man. Dir, 1975–87, Scottish Transport Gp; Chairman: Scottish Bus Gp Ltd, 1975–; Caledonian MacBrayne Ltd, 1975–90; STG Properties Ltd (formerly Scottish Transport Investments Ltd), 1975–; Dir, Scottish Mortgage & Trust plc, 1986–. Pres., Bus and Coach Council, 1979–80; Hon. Vice-Pres., Internat. Union of Public Transport; Member Council: CIT, 1978–87 (Vice Pres., 1984–87); CBI, 1987–93. Hon. Col, 154 Regt RCT (V), 1986–93. *Publications:* various papers. *Recreations:* golf, foreign travel, reading. *Address:* 10 Moray Place, Edinburgh EH3 6DT. *T:* 0131–225 6454. *Clubs:* Caledonian, MCC; Dalmahoy Golf and Country.

IRWIN, John Conran; Keeper, Indian Section, Victoria and Albert Museum, 1959–78, with extended responsibility for new Oriental Department, 1970–78; *b* 5 Aug. 1917; *s* of late John Williamson Irwin; *m* 1947, Helen Hermione Scott (*née* Fletcher) (separated 1982), *d* of late Herbert Bristowe Fletcher; three *s*. *Educ:* Canford Sch., Wimborne, Dorset. Temp. commission, Gordon Highlanders, 1939. Private Sec. to Gov. of Bengal, 1942–45; Asst Keeper, Victoria and Albert Museum, 1946; Exec. Sec., Royal Academy Winter Exhibition of Indian Art, 1947–48; UNESCO Expert on museum planning: on mission to Indonesia, 1956; to Malaya, 1962. British Acad. Travelling Fellowship, 1974–75; Leverhulme Res. Fellow, 1978–80; Sen. Fellow, Center for Advanced Study in the Visual Arts, Nat. Gall. of Art, Washington, DC, 1983–84; Vis. Prof., Univ. of Michigan, 1986. Working with research grants from Leverhulme Trust and British Acad., 1978–84. Lectures: Birdwood Meml, 1972; Tagore Meml, 1973; Lowell Inst., Boston,

Mass, 1974; guest lectr, Collège de France, 1976. Pres., Res. into Lost Knowledge Orgn, 1960; Hon. Pres., Indian Circle, SOAS, 1990. FRSA 1972; FRAS 1946; FRAI 1977; FSA 1978. *Publications:* Jamini Roy, 1944; Indian art (section on sculpture), 1947; The Art of India and Pakistan (sections on bronzes and textiles), 1951, Shawls, 1955; Origins of Chintz, 1970; (with M. Hall) Indian Painted and Printed Fabrics, 1972; Indian Embroideries, 1974; articles in Encyclopædia Britannica, Chambers's Encyclopædia, Enciclopedia Italiana (2nd Supplement), Jl of Royal Asiatic Soc., Burlington Magazine, Artibus Asiae etc. *Recreations:* music, walking.

IRWIN, Dr Michael Henry Knox; international health consultant; *b* 5 June 1931; *s* of late William Knox Irwin, FRCS and of Edith Isabel Mary Irwin; *m* 1958, Elizabeth Miriam (marr. diss. 1982), *d* of late John and Nancie Naumann; three *d*; *m* 1994, Lady (Patricia) Walters, *d* of late Frederick and Gwendoline Tulloch. *Educ:* St Bartholomew's Hosp. Med. Coll., London (MB, BS 1955); Columbia Univ., New York (MPH 1960). House Phys. and House Surg., Prince of Wales' Hosp., London, 1955–56; MO, UN, 1957–61; Dep. Resident Rep., UN Technical Assistance Bd, Pakistan, 1961–63; MO, 1963–66, SMO, 1966–69, and Med. Dir, 1969–73, United Nations; Dir, Div. of Personnel, UNDP, 1973–76; UNICEF Rep., Bangladesh, 1977–80; Sen. Advr (Childhood Disabilities), UNICEF, 1980–82; Sen. Consultant, UN Internat. Year of Disabled Persons, 1981; Med. Dir, UN, UNICEF and UNDP, 1982–89; Director: Health Services Dept, IBRD, 1989–90; Westside Action, 1991–93. Pres., Assistance for Blind Children Internat., 1978–84. Consultant, Amer. Assoc. of Blood Banks, 1984–90; Advr, ActionAid, 1990–91. Member, Executive Committee: UNA, 1994–; Voluntary Euthanasia Soc., 1995–. Mem. Editl Adv. Panel, Medicine and War, 1985–95. FRSM. Officer Cross, Internat. Fedn of Blood Donor Organizations, 1984. *Publications:* Check-ups: safeguarding your health, 1961; Overweight: a problem for millions, 1964; Travelling without Tears, 1964; Viruses, Colds and Flu, 1966; Blood: new uses for saving lives, 1967; The Truth About Cancer, 1969; What Do We Know about Allergies?, 1972; A Child's Horizon, 1982; Aspirin: current knowledge about an old medication, 1983; Can We Survive Nuclear War?, 1984; Nuclear Energy: good or bad?, 1985; Peace Museums, 1991; *novel:* Talpa, 1990. *Recreations:* politics, windmills, writing. *Address:* 26 First Street, SW3 2LD.

IRWIN, Rear-Adm. Richard Oran, CB 1995; CEng, FIEE; Chief, Strategic Systems Executive, Ministry of Defence, 1992–95; *b* 3 Sept. 1942; *s* of Lt Col Richard Arthur Irwin, TD and Catherine Millicent (*née* Palmer); *m* 1965, Coreen Jill Blackham, *d* of Rear-Adm. J. L. Blackham, *qv*; one *s* one *d*. *Educ:* Sherborne; Dartmouth; RN Engrg Coll., Manadon (BSc Engrg). FIEE 1986. Served in 7th, 3rd and 10th Submarine Sqdns, 1968–78; on Naval Staff, 1978–81; on staff of Flag Officer, Submarines, 1981–83; on staff, Strategic Systems Exec., 1983–86; RCDS, 1987; Dir, Nuclear Systems, 1988–91; Captain, HMS Raleigh, 1991–92. Mem., RNSA. *Recreations:* sailing, squash, tennis, ski-ing, bridge. *Address:* Linden Lodge, Salthill Road, Chichester PO19 3PY. *Clubs:* Lansdowne; Thorney Island Sailing (Thorney Island).

ISAAC, Alfred James; Director of Home Regional Services, Property Services Agency, Department of the Environment, 1971–75; *b* 1 Aug. 1919; *s* of Alfred Jabez Isaac and Alice Marie Isaac (both British); *m* 1943, Beryl Marjorie Rist; one *s* two *d*. *Educ:* Maidenhead Grammar Sch. Post Office Engineering Dept, 1936–49. Served War, RAFVR, Flt Lt (pilot), Coastal Command, 1941–46. Min. of Works, Asst Principal, 1949; Regional Dir, Southern Region, 1960–67; Dir of Professional Staff Management, 1967. Business Coordinator, Danbury Drilling Ltd, 1977–78; Chm. (part-time), Recruitment Bds, CS Commn, 1978–87. Vice-Chm., Bigbury Parish Council, 1987–91 (part-time Clerk, 1981–83). *Recreations:* 9 grandchildren, amateur radio. *Address:* Wave Crest, Marine Drive, Bigbury on Sea, Kingsbridge, Devon TQ7 4AS. *T:* Bigbury on Sea (01548) 810387. *Club:* Civil Service.

ISAAC, Anthony John Gower, CB 1985; fiscal consultant; a Deputy Chairman, Board of Inland Revenue, 1982–91 (a Commissioner of Inland Revenue, 1973–77 and 1979–91); *b* 21 Dec. 1931; *s* of Ronald and Kathleen Mary Gower Isaac; *m* 1963, Olga Elizabeth Sibley; one *s* two *d* (and two *d* decd). *Educ:* Malvern Coll.; King's Coll., Cambridge (BA). HM Treasury, 1953–70: Private Sec. to Chief Sec. to Treasury, 1964–66; Inland Revenue, 1971; on secondment to HM Treasury, 1976–78. *Publication:* A Local Income Tax, 1992. *Recreations:* gardening, fishing.

ISAAC, James Keith, CBE 1985; FCIT; President, International Union of Public Transport, since 1993 (Vice-President, 1989–93); *b* 28 Jan. 1932; *s* of late Arthur Burton Isaac and of Doreen (*née* Davies); *m* 1957, Elizabeth Mary Roskell; two *d*. *Educ:* Leeds Grammar Sch. Mem., Inst. of Traffic Admin; FCIT 1978. Asst to Traffic Manager, Aldershot and Dist Traction Co. Ltd, 1958–59; Asst Traffic Man., Jamaica Omnibus Services Ltd, Kingston, Jamaica, 1959–64; Dep. Traffic Man., Midland Red (Birmingham and Midland Motor Omnibus Co. Ltd), Birmingham, 1965–67; Traffic Manager: North Western Road Car Co. Ltd, Stockport, Cheshire, 1967–69; Midland Red, Birmingham, 1969–73; Dir of Ops, 1973–77, Dir Gen., 1977–86, W Midlands Passenger Transp. Exec., Birmingham; Man. Dir, 1986–90, Chief Exec., 1986–92, Chm., 1986–94, West Midlands Travel Ltd. Chm., Bus and Coach Services Ltd, 1986–90. Hon. Chm., Internat. Commn on Transport Economics, 1988– (Chm., 1981–88); President: Omnibus Soc., 1982; Bus and Coach Council, 1985–86; Mem. Council, CIT, 1982–85. *Recreations:* golf, walking, travel. *Address:* 24B Middlefield Lane, Hagley, Stourbridge, West Midlands DY9 0PX. *T:* Hagley (01562) 884757. *Clubs:* Army and Navy; Rotary of Hagley (Hereford/Worcester); Churchill and Blakedown Golf (near Kidderminster).

ISAAC, Maurice Laurence Reginald, MA; Headmaster, Latymer Upper School, Hammersmith, W6, 1971–88; *b* 26 April 1928; *s* of late Frank and Lilian Isaac; *m* 1954, Anne Fielden; three *d*. *Educ:* Selhurst Grammar Sch., Croydon; Magdalene Coll., Cambridge. BA Hist. Tripos, 1950; MA 1955, Cambridge; Certif. in Educn, 1952. Asst Master: Liverpool Collegiate Sch., 1952–56; Bristol Grammar Sch., 1956–62; Head of History, Colchester Royal Grammar Sch., 1962–65; Headmaster, Yeovil Sch., 1966–71. Mem. Council, Francis Holland Schools Trust, 1982–. *Publications:* A History of Europe, 1870–1950, 1960; contributor to The Teaching of History, 1965. *Address:* Glebe House, Crowcombe, near Taunton, Somerset TA4 4AA. *T:* Crowcombe (01984) 618230. *Club:* East India.

ISAAC, Prof. Peter Charles Gerald; Professor of Civil and Public Health Engineering, 1964–81, now Emeritus, and Head of Department of Civil Engineering, 1970–81, University of Newcastle upon Tyne; Partner, Watson Hawksley (consulting engineers), 1973–83; *b* 21 Jan. 1921; *s* of late Herbert George Isaac and Julienne Geneviève (*née* Hattenberger); *m* 1950, Marjorie Eleanor White; one *s* one *d*. *Educ:* Felsted Sch.; London and Harvard Universities. BSc(Eng), SM. Asst Engineer, GWR, 1940–45; Lecturer in Civil Engineering, 1946; Senior Lecturer in Public Health Engineering, 1953, Reader, 1960, Univ. of Durham; Dean of Faculty of Applied Science, Univ. of Newcastle upon Tyne, 1969–73; Sandars Reader in Bibliography, Univ. of Cambridge, 1983–84. Member: Industrial Health Adv. Cttee, Min. of Lab. and Nat. Service, 1959–66; Working Party on Sewage Disposal, 1969–70; WHO Expert Adv. Panel on Environmental Health, 1976–87; specialist advr, House of Lords Select Cttee on Sci. and Technol. II (Hazardous Waste), 1980–81 and House of Lords Select Cttee on Sci. and Technol. I (Water), 1982; DoE Long-Term Water-Research Requirements Cttee. Bibliograhical Society: Mem. Council, 1970–74, 1979–83; Vice-Pres., 1984–94; Pres., 1994–; Hon. Editor of Monographs, 1982–89. Chairman: History of the Book Trade in the North, 1965–; British Book Trade Index; Printing Historical Soc., 1989–91. Member of Council: ICE, 1968–71, 1972–75, 1977–80; IPHE, 1973–87 (Pres., 1977–78); Pres., British Occupational Hygiene Soc., 1962–63 (Hon. Mem., 1993); Mem. Bd, CEI, 1978–79. Trustee, Asian Inst. Technology, Bangkok, 1968–82 (Vice-Chm., 1979–82). Hon. Mem., Lit. and Philos. Soc., Newcastle upon Tyne. Director: Thorne's Students' Bookshop Ltd, 1969–74; Environmental Resources Ltd, 1972–74. Freeman, Worshipful Co. of Stationers and Newspaper Makers, 1984, Liveryman, 1986. FSA 1987; FICE 1956 (AMICE 1946); Hon. FIPHE 1986. Clemens Herschel Prize in Applied Hydraulics, 1952; Telford Premium, 1957; Thomas Bedford Award, 1978; Gold Medal, IPHE, 1987. *Publications:* Electric Resistance Strain Gauges (with W. B. Dobie), 1948; Public Health Engineering, 1953; Trade Wastes, 1957; Waste Treatment, 1960; River Management, 1967; William Davison of Alnwick: pharmacist and printer, 1968; Farm Wastes, 1970; Civil Engineering-The University Contribution, 1970; Management in Civil Engineering, 1971; Davison's Halfpenny Chapbooks, 1971; (ed) The Burman Alnwick Collection, 1973; William Davison's New Specimen, 1990; Six Centuries of the Provincial Book Trade in Britain, 1990; William Bulmer: the fine printer in context, 1993; contribs to various learned and technical jls. *Recreations:* bibliography, printing, Roman engineering. *Address:* 10 Woodcroft Road, Wylam, Northumberland NE41 8DJ. *T:* Wylam (01661) 853174. *Clubs:* Commonwealth Trust; Royal Scottish Automobile (Glasgow).

ISAAC, Rear-Adm. Robert Arthur, CB 1989; Director General Marine Engineering, Ministry of Defence (Procurement Executive), 1986–89; consultant (business with Japan), 1989–95; *b* 21 Feb. 1933; *s* of Frank and Florence Isaac; *m* 1960, Joy Little; one *s* one *d*. *Educ:* Oakham Sch.; Royal Naval Engrg Coll. (Dartmouth Special Entry). CEng, FIMechE, FIMarE. Entered RN, 1951; HMS Albion, 1957–59; HM Submarines Scotsman, Aurochs, nuclear trng, and HM Submarine Warspite, 1959–69; Dir Gen. Ships, MoD, 1970–74; HMS Blake, 1974–76; 2nd Sea Lord's Dept, MoD, 1976–78; Captain 1977; Naval Attaché, Tokyo and Seoul, 1979–81; Project Dir, Surface Ships, MoD (PE), 1981–84; HMS Thunderer, RNEC in comd, 1984–86; Rear-Adm. 1986. *Recreations:* sport, gardening. *Clubs:* Naval, Army and Navy.

ISAACS, family name of **Marquess of Reading.**

ISAACS, Dame Albertha Madeline, DBE 1974; former Senator, now worker for the community, in the Bahamas; *b* Nassau, Bahamas, 18 April 1900; *d* of late Robert Hanna and Lilla (*née* Minns); *m*; three *s* one *d*. *Educ:* Cosmopolitan High Sch. and Victoria High Sch., Nassau. Member: Progressive Liberal Party, Senator, 1968–72; also of PLP's Nat. Gen. Council, and of Council of Women. Mem. of a Good Samaritan Group.

ISAACS, Dr Anthony John; Regional Consultant (Service Policy and Clinical Audit), North East Thames Regional Health Authority, since 1993; Consultant Endocrinologist, Charing Cross and Chelsea & Westminster Hospitals, since 1993; Hon. Consultant Physician (Endocrinology), University College and Middlesex Hospitals, since 1986; *b* 22 Oct. 1942; *s* of Benjamin H. Isaacs, BSc and Lily Isaacs (*née* Rogol); *m* 1st, 1971, Jill Kathleen Elek; three *s*; 2nd, 1986, Dr Edie Friedman; one *d*. *Educ:* Wanstead County High Sch.; Hertford Coll., Oxford (Open Exhibnr; Domus Scholar; BA Animal Physiology, 1st Cl. Hons 1965; MA 1968); Westminster Med. Sch. (Barron Schol.). BM, BCh 1968; MRCP 1971; MSc (Public Health Medicine) 1992. House posts, Westminster, Whittington and Hammersmith Hosps, 1968–70, Med. Registrar, Westminster Hosp., 1971–73; Research Fellow (Endocrinology), Royal Free Hosp., 1973–75; Sen. Med. Registrar, Westminster Hosp., 1975–84; SMO, Medicines Div., 1984–85, PMO, and Med. Assessor, Cttee on Safety of Medicines, 1985–86, SPMO/Under Sec., and Hd, Med. Manpower and Educn Div., 1986–91, DHSS, subseq. DoH. Vice-Chm., Jt Planning Adv. Cttee, 1986–91; Member: Steering Gp for Implementation of Achieving a Balance (and Co-Chm., Technical sub-gp), 1986–91; 2nd Adv. Cttee on Med. Manpower Planning, 1986–89; Steering Gp on Undergrad. Med. and Dental Educn and Res., 1987–91 (Chm., Implementation Task Gp, 1989–90 and Working Gp, 1990–91); Ministerial Gp on Junior Doctors' Hours, 1990–91. Hon. Vis. Fellow, LSHTM, 1992–93. Chm., New End Sch. PTA, 1983–85; Parent Governor, 1987–92, First Gov., 1992–, Hendon Sch. FRSocMed (Mem., Endocrinology Section). *Publications:* Anorexia Nervosa (with P. Dally and J. Gomez), 1979; papers in med. jls on rheumatol and endocrinol topics. *Recreations:* music, cinema, table tennis, chess, travel. *Address:* North East Thames Regional Health Authority, 40 Eastbourne Terrace, W2 3QR.

ISAACS, Jeremy Israel; General Director, Royal Opera House, Covent Garden, since 1988 (Member, Board of Directors, since 1985); *b* 28 Sept. 1932; *s* of Isidore Isaacs and Sara Jacobs; *m* 1st, 1958, Tamara (*née* Weinreich) (*d* 1986), Cape Town; one *s* one *d*; 2nd, 1988, Gillian Mary Widdicombe. *Educ:* Glasgow Acad.; Merton Coll., Oxford (MA). Pres. of the Union, Hilary, 1955. Television Producer, Granada TV (What the Papers Say, All Our Yesterdays), 1958; Associated-Rediffusion (This Week), 1963; BBC TV (Panorama), 1965; Controller of Features, Associated Rediffusion, 1967; with Thames Television, 1968–78: Controller of Features, 1968–74; Producer, The World at War, 1974; Director of Programmes, 1974–78; Chief Exec., Channel Four TV Co., 1981–87; TV programmes: A Sense of Freedom, STV; Ireland, a Television History, BBC. Dir, Open College, 1987–. Governor, BFI, 1979– (Chm., BFI Production Bd, 1979–81). James MacTaggart Meml Lectr, Edinburgh TV Fest., 1979. FRSA 1983; Fellow: BAFTA, 1985; BFI, 1986; FRSAMD 1989; FGSM 1989. Hon. DLitt: Strathclyde, 1984; CNAA, 1987; Bristol, 1988. Desmond Davis Award for outstanding creative contrib. to television, 1972; George Polk Meml Award, 1973; Cyril Bennett Award for outstanding contrib. to television programming, RTS, 1982; Lord Willis Award for Distinguished Service to Television, 1985; Directorate Award, Internat. Council of Nat. Acad. of TV Arts and Scis, NY, 1987; Lifetime Achievement Award, Banff, 1988. Commandeur de l'Ordre des Arts et des Lettres (France), 1988. *Publication:* Storm over Four: a personal account, 1989. *Recreations:* reading, walking. *Address:* Royal Opera House, 45 Floral Street, WC2E 9DD.

ISAACS, Sir Kendal (George Lamon), KCMG 1993; CBE 1970; QC 1968; Member (FNM), Bahamas House of Assembly, 1972–76 and 1982–92; *b* 23 July 1925; *s* of Edward Adolphus and Julia Isaacs; *m* Patricia Eleanor Fountain. *Educ:* Queens' Coll., Cambridge (MA, LLB). Called to the Bar, Middle Temple; Stipendiary and Circuit Magistrate, Bahamas, 1952; Solicitor General, 1955; Attorney General, 1963; Acting Chief Justice, 1959; Acting Judge, Supreme Court, 1964–65, 1977–78; private practice, 1965; Mem., Senate, 1965; Vice-Pres., Senate, 1968–71. *Recreations:* tennis, golf, travel. *Address:* Sandyport, PO Box N1372, Nassau, Bahamas. *Clubs:* Gym Tennis; Cable Beach Golf.

ISAACS, Stuart Lindsay; QC 1991; *b* 8 April 1952; *s* of Stanley Leslie Isaacs and Marquette Isaacs. *Educ:* Haberdashers' Aske's Sch., Elstree; Downing Coll., Cambridge (Law, Double 1st cl. Hons); Univ. Libre de Bruxelles (License spécial en droit européen, grande distinction). Called to the Bar, Lincoln's Inn, 1975; admitted NY Bar, 1985. An Asst Recorder, 1992–. Consultant Editor, Butterworth's EC Case Citator, 1991–. *Publications:*

EC Banking Law, 1985, 2nd edn 1994; Banking and the Competition Law of the EEC, 1978; (contrib.) Commentary on the EEC Treaty, 1995. *Recreations:* travel, languages. *Address:* 4–5 Gray's Inn Square, Gray's Inn, WC1R 5AY. *T:* 0171–404 5252, *Fax:* 0171–242 7803. *Club:* St James's.

ISAACSON, Prof. Peter Gersohn, DM, DSc; FRCPath; Professor of Morbid Anatomy, University College London, since 1982; *b* 24 Nov. 1936; *s* of Robert and Freda Isaacson; *m* 1959, Maria de Lourdes Abranches Pinto; one *s* three *d. Educ:* Prince Edward Sch., Salisbury, Rhodesia; Univ. of Cape Town (MB ChB); DM Southampton, 1980; DSc London, 1992. FRCPath 1972. Sen. Lectr, then Reader, Southampton Univ. Med. Sch., 1974–82. *Publications:* Biopsy Pathology of the Lymphoreticular System, 1983; Oxford Textbook of Pathology, 1993; Extranodal Lymphoma, 1994; numerous contribs to med. jls. *Address:* Department of Histopathology, Rockefeller Building, University Street, WC1E 6JJ. *T:* 0171–209 6045.

ISAAMAN, Gerald Michael, OBE 1994; journalist and consultant; Editorial Consultant, Home Counties Newspapers plc, since 1994; Editor, 1968–94, and General Manager, 1990–94, Hampstead and Highgate Express; *b* 22 Dec. 1933; *s* of Asher Isaaman and Lily Finklestein; *m* 1962, Delphine Walker, *e d* of Cecile and Arnold Walker; one *s. Educ:* Dame Alice Owen's Grammar School. Reporter, North London Observer Series, 1950, Hampstead and Highgate Express, 1955. Dir, Pipistrel Retail Solutions, 1994–; non-exec. Dir, Whittington Hosp. NHS Trust, 1994–. Founder Trustee, Arkwright Arts Trust, 1971; Chairman: Camden Arts Trust Management Board, 1970–82; Exhibns Cttee, Camden Arts Centre, 1971–82; Russell Housing Soc., 1976–82; Trustees, King's Cross Disaster Fund, 1987–89; Member: Camden Festival Trust, 1982–; Council, Assoc. of British Editors, 1985–93; Press Complaints Commn, 1993–95. FRSA 1992. Special presentation, for distinguished services to journalism, British Press Awards, 1994. *Recreations:* cooking breakfast, listening to jazz, work. *Address:* 10 Salmon Mews, West End Lane, NW6 1RH. *T:* 0171–794 3950. *Club:* Garrick.

ISEPP, Martin Johannes Sebastian; Head of Music Studies, National Opera Studio, since 1979; Chief Guest Coach, Glyndebourne Festival Opera, since 1994; *b* Vienna, 30 Sept. 1930; *s* of Sebastian and Helene Isepp; *m* 1966, Rose Henrietta Harris; two *s. Educ:* St Paul's Sch.; Lincoln Coll., Oxford; Royal Coll. of Music, London (ARCM 1952). Studied piano with Prof. Leonie Gombrich, 1939–52. English Opera Gp, 1954–57; Glyndebourne Fest. Opera, 1957– (Head of Music Staff, 1973–93); Head of Opera Trng Dept, Juilliard Sch. of Music, New York, 1973–78; Hd, Acad of Singing, Banff Sch. of Fine Arts, Alberta, Canada, 1982–93. As accompanist, began career accompanying mother, Helene Isepp (the singer and voice teacher); has accompanied many of the world's leading singers and instrumentalists, notably Elisabeth Schwarzkopf, Elisabeth Söderström, Janet Baker and John Shirley-Quirk; harpsichordist with Handel Opera Soc. of New York in most of their Handel Festivals, 1966–; master classes in opera and song at Amer. univs, incl. Southern Calif, Ann Arbor, Maryland, Minnesota and Colorado, 1975–; lieder courses, Britten-Pears Sch. for Advanced Musical Studies, Aldeburgh, 1988–; coached Peking Opera and Peking Conservatory in Mozart operas, 1983; annual opera prodn, Centre de la Voix, Fondation Royaumont, France, 1992–; annual opera course (Music Dir), Walton Foundn, Ischia, Italy, 1992–. As conductor: Le Nozze di Figaro, Glyndebourne Touring Op., 1984; Don Giovanni, Glyndebourne Touring Op., 1986; Abduction from the Seraglio, Washington Op., 1986–87. Carroll Donner Stuchell Medal for Accompanists, Harriet Cohen Internat. Musical Foundn, 1965. *Recreations:* photography, walking. *Address:* 37A Steele's Road, NW3 4RG. *T:* 0171–722 3085.

ISHAM, Sir Ian (Vere Gyles), 13th Bt *cr* 1627; *b* 17 July 1923; *s* of Lt-Col Vere Arthur Richard Isham, MC (*d* 1968) and Edith Irene (*d* 1973), *d* of Harry Brown; *S* cousin, Sir Gyles Isham, 12th Bt, 1976. Served War of 1939–45, Captain RAC. *Heir: b* Norman Murray Crawford Isham, OBE [*b* 28 Jan. 1930; *m* 1956, Joan, *d* of late Leonard James Genet; two *s* one *d*]. *Address:* 40 Turnpike Link, Croydon, Surrey CR0 5NX.

ISHIGURO, Kazuo, OBE 1995; FRSL; author; *b* 8 Nov. 1954; *s* of Shizuo and Shizuko Ishiguro; *m* 1986, Lorna Anne MacDougall; one *d. Educ.* Univ. of Kent (BA English/Philosophy); Univ. of East Anglia (MA Creative Writing). Began publishing short stories, articles, in magazines, 1980; writer of TV plays, 1984–. Mem. Jury, Cannes Film Festival, 1994. FRSL 1989. FRSA. Hon. DLitt Kent, 1990. *Publications:* A Pale View of Hills, 1982 (Winifred Holtby Prize, RSL); An Artist of the Floating World, 1986 (Whitbread Book of the Year, Whitbread Fiction Prize); The Remains of the Day, 1989 (Booker Prize; filmed 1993); The Unconsoled, 1995. *Recreations:* music; playing piano and guitar. *Address:* c/o Faber & Faber, 3 Queen Square, WC1N 3AU.

ISHIHARA, Takashi; First Class, Order of the Rising Sun (Japan), 1991; Hon. KBE 1990; Counsellor, Nissan Motor Co., Ltd, since 1992 (Chairman, 1985–92); *b* 3 March 1912; *s* of Ichiji and Shigeyo Ishihara; *m* 1943, Shizuko Nakajo; one *s. Educ:* Law Dept, Tohoku Univ. (grad 1937). Joined Nissan Motor Co., Ltd, 1937; promoted to Gen. Man. of Planning and Accounting Depts respectively; Dir of Finance and Accounting, 1954; Man. Dir, 1963; Exec. Man. Dir, 1969; Exec. Vice Pres., 1973; Pres., 1977; Pres., Nissan Motor Corp. in USA, 1960–65; Chm., Nissan Motor Manufacturing Corp., USA, 1980–82. Exec. Dir, Keidanren (Fedn of Econ. Orgns), 1977–85; Chm., Keizai Doyukai (Japan Assoc. of Corporate Execs), 1985–91; Dir, Nikkeiren (Japan Fedn of Employers Assocs), 1978–85; President: Japan Automobile Manufacturers Assoc., Inc., 1980–86; Japan Motor Industrial Fedn, Inc., 1980–86. Hon. DCL Durham, 1987. Blue Ribbon Medal (Japan), 1974; First Order of Sacred Treasure (Japan), 1983; Grand Cross (Spain), 1985. *Recreations:* reading, golf, ocean cruising. *Address:* Nissan Motor Co., 17–1 Ginza 6–chome, Chuo-ku, Tokyo 104, Japan; 20–3, 2–chome, Shiroganedai, Minato-ku, Tokyo 108, Japan.

ISLE OF WIGHT, Archdeacon of; *see* Turner, Ven. A. H. M.

ISLES, Maj.-Gen. Donald Edward, CB 1978; OBE 1968; DL; *b* 19 July 1924; *s* of Harold and Kathleen Isles; *m* 1948, Sheila Mary Stephens (formerly Thorpe); three *s* one *d. Educ:* Roundhay; Leeds Univ.; RMCS; JSSC. Italian campaign, Palestine, Egypt, Sudan, Syria, with 1st Bn, Duke of Wellington's Regt, 1944–47; Asst Mil. Attaché, Paris, 1963–65; CO, 1DWR, BAOR and UN Forces in Cyprus, 1965–67; AMS, MoD, 1968; Col GS, MoD, 1968–71; Dir of Munitions, Brit. Defence Staff Washington, 1972–75; Dir-Gen. Weapons (Army), 1975–78, retired. Dep. Man. Dir, British Manufacture & Res. Co., 1979–89. Col, The Duke of Wellington's Regt, 1975–82; Col Comdt, The King's Div., 1975–79; Vice-Chm., Yorks and Humberside TA&VRA, 1984–87. Hon. Colonel: 3rd Bn, The Yorkshire Volunteers, 1977–83; Leeds Univ. OTC, 1985–90. Mem., Court, Leeds Univ., 1987–. Pres., Lincs and S Humberside RBL, 1990–. DL Lincs, 1990. *Recreations:* shooting, tennis, squash. *Clubs:* Army and Navy; Lincolnshire.

ISMAY, Walter Nicholas; Managing Director, Worcester Parsons Ltd, 1975–82, retired; *b* 20 June 1921; *s* of late John Ismay, Maryport, Cumberland. *Educ:* Taunton's Sch., Southampton; King's Coll., University of London (BSc). Royal Aircraft Establishment, 1939–40; Ministry of Supply, 1940–43; Served Army (Capt., General List), 1943–46; Imperial Chemical Industries, Metals Division, 1948–58 (Technical Dir, 1957–58); Dir, Yorkshire Imperial Metals, 1958–67; Dep. Chm. Yorkshire Imperial Plastics, 1966–67; Dep. Chm. and Man. Dir, Milton Keynes Develt Corp., 1967–71; McKechnie Britain Ltd, 1972–75. FIMechE. *Recreation:* sailing. *Address:* Pitlundie, Monument Lane, Walhampton, Lymington, Hampshire SO41 5SE. *T:* Lymington (01590) 673032. *Club:* Royal Lymington Yacht.

ISOLANI, Casimiro Peter Hugh Tomasi, CBE 1975 (OBE 1960; MBE (mil.) 1945); LVO 1961; HM Diplomatic Service, retired; *b* 2 Sept. 1917; *s* of late Umberto Tomasi Isolani, Bologna, and late Georgiana Eleanor Lyle-Smyth, Great Barrow, Ches; *m* 1943, Karin Gunni Signe Zetterström, *d* of Henry Zetterström, Gothenburg; one *s. Educ:* Aldenham Sch.; Clare Coll., Cambridge; Major open schol., 1936, 1st cl. Mod. and Med. Lang. Tripos 1; Senior Foundn schol., 1937; BA 1939. Commnd RA 1940, Intell. Corps 1941; attached 1st Canadian Div., 1943 (Sicily, Italy landings); Psychol Warfare Br., 1944; GS1 (Civil Liaison, Liaison Italian Resistance), 1945; Hon. Partisan, Veneto Corpo Volontari della Libertà; FO 1946; Vice-Consul, Bologna, 1946; Attaché, later 1st Sec. (Information), British Embassy, Rome, 1947–61; resigned Foreign Service; Dep. Dir, Inst. for Strategic Studies, 1961–63; rejoined Foreign Service; Regional Information Officer, Paris, 1963–72; Counsellor (Information), British Embassy (and UK delegn NATO and UK Representation, EEC), Brussels, 1972–77. United Nations University: Rep. (Europe), 1978–85; Sen. Consultant, 1985–87. *Address:* 44 Pont Street, SW1X 0AD. *T:* 0171–584 1543. *Clubs:* Anglo-Belgian, Special Forces.

ISRAEL, Prof. Jonathan Irvine, DPhil; FBA 1992; Professor of Dutch History and Institutions, University College London, since 1985; *b* 22 Jan. 1946; *s* of David and Miriam Israel; *m* 1985, Jenny Tatjana Winckel; one *s* one *d. Educ:* Kilburn Grammar Sch.; Queens' Coll., Cambridge; St Antony's Coll., Oxford (DPhil 1972). Lectr, Hull Univ., 1972–74; Lectr, 1974–81, Reader, 1981–84, UCL. *Publications:* Race, Class and Politics in Colonial Mexico, 1975; The Dutch Republic and the Hispanic World, 1982; European Jewry in the Age of Mercantilism 1550–1750, 1985; Dutch Primacy in World Trade 1585–1740, 1989; Empires and Entrepots: the Dutch, the Spanish monarchy and the Jews 1585–1713, 1990; (ed) The Anglo-Dutch Movement: essays on the Glorious Revolution and its world impact, 1991; The Dutch Republic, 1995. *Address:* Department of History, University College London, Gower Street, WC1E 6BT. *T:* 0171–387 7050.

ISRAEL, Rev. Dr Martin Spencer, FRCPath; Priest-in-Charge, Holy Trinity with All Saints Church, South Kensington, since 1983; *b* 30 April 1927; *s* of Elie Benjamin Israel, ophthalmic surgeon, and Minnie Israel. *Educ:* Parktown Boys' High Sch., Johannesburg; Univ. of the Witwatersrand (MB ChB). MRCP 1952, FRCPath 1972. Ho. Phys., Hammersmith Hosp., 1952; Registrar in Pathology, Royal Hosp., Wolverhampton, 1953–55; service in RAMC, 1955–57; Lectr and Sen. Lectr in Pathology, 1958–82, Hon. Sen. Lectr 1982–, RCS. Ordained priest in C of E, 1975. President: Guild of Health, 1983–90; Churches' Fellowship for Psychical and Spiritual Studies, 1983–. *Publications: medical:* General Pathology (with J. B. Walter), 1963, 6th edn 1987; *spiritual matters:* Summons to Life, 1974; Precarious Living, 1976; Smouldering Fire, 1978; The Pain that Heals, 1981; Living Alone, 1982; The Spirit of Counsel, 1983; Healing as Sacrament, 1984; The Discipline of Love, 1985; Coming in Glory, 1986; Gethsemane, 1987; The Pearl of Great Price, 1988; The Dark Face of Reality, 1989; The Quest for Wholeness, 1989; Creation, 1989; Night Thoughts, 1990; A Light on the Path, 1990; Life Eternal, 1993; Dark Victory, 1994; Angels—Ministers of Grace, 1995. *Recreations:* music, conversation. *Address:* Flat 2, 26 Tregunter Road, SW10 9LH. *T:* 0171–370 5160.

ISRAEL, Prof. Werner, OC 1994; FRS 1986; Professor of Physics, since 1972, University Professor, since 1985, University of Alberta; *b* 4 Oct. 1931; *s* of Arthur Israel and Marie Kappauf; *m* 1958, Inge Margulies; one *s* one *d. Educ:* Cape Town High Sch.; Univ. of Cape Town (BSc 1951, MSc 1954); Dublin Inst. for Advanced Studies; Trinity Coll., Dublin (PhD 1960). Lectr in Applied Maths, Univ. of Cape Town, 1954–56; Asst Prof., 1958, Associate Prof., 1964, Prof. of Maths, 1968–71, Univ. of Alberta. Sherman Fairchild Dist. Schol., CIT, 1974–75; Vis. Prof., Dublin Inst. for Advanced Studies, 1966–68; Sen. Visitor, Dept of Applied Maths and Theoretical Physics, Univ. of Cambridge, 1975–76; Maître de Recherche Associé, Inst. Henri Poincaré, Paris, 1976–77; Vis. Prof., Berne, 1980, Kyoto, 1986; Vis. Fellow, Gonville and Caius Coll., Cambridge, 1985. Fellow, Canadian Inst. for Advanced Research, 1986–. Hon. DSc Queen's, Kingston, Ont., 1987; Dr *hc* Tours, 1994. *Publications:* (ed) Relativity, Astrophysics and Cosmology, 1973; (ed with S. W. Hawking) General Relativity: an Einstein centenary survey, 1979; (ed with S. W. Hawking) 300 Years of Gravitation, 1987; numerous papers on black hole physics, general relativity, relativistic statistical mechanics. *Recreation:* music. *Address:* Avadh Bhatia Physics Laboratory, University of Alberta, Edmonton, Alberta T6G 2J1, Canada. *T:* (403) 4923552.

ISRAELACHVILI, Prof. Jacob Nissim, FRS 1988; FAA; Professor of Chemical Engineering and Materials Science, Department of Chemical and Nuclear Engineering and Materials Department, University of California, Santa Barbara, since 1986; *b* 19 Aug. 1944; *s* of Haim and Hela Israelachvili; *m* 1971, Karina (*née* Haglund); two *d. Educ:* Univ. of Cambridge (MA; PhD 1972). FAA 1982. Post-doctoral res. into surface forces, Cavendish Lab., Cambridge, 1971–72; EMBO Res. Fellow, Biophysics Inst., Univ. of Stockholm, 1972–74; Res. Fellow, subseq. Professorial Fellow, Res. Sch. of Physical Scis, Inst. of Advanced Studies, ANU, Canberra, 1974–86. Council Mem., 1983–87, Vice-Pres., 1986–87, Internat. Assoc. of Colloid and Interface Scientists. Pawsey Medal, 1977, Matthew Flinders Lectr medallist, 1986, Aust. Acad. of Sci.; (jtly) David Syme Res. Prize, 1983. *Publications:* Intermolecular and Surface Forces: with applications to colloidal and biological systems, 1985, 2nd edn 1991; about 150 pubns in learned jls, incl. Nature, Science, Procs Royal Soc. *Recreations:* history, backgammon. *Address:* 2233 Foothill Lane, Santa Barbara, CA 93105, USA. *T:* (residence) (805) 9639545, (office) (805) 8938407.

ISSERLIS, Steven John; 'cellist; *b* 19 Dec. 1958; *s* of George and Cynthia Isserlis; lives with Pauline Mara; one *s. Educ:* City of London School; International 'Cello Centre; Oberlin College. London recital début, Wigmore Hall, 1977; London concerto début, with English Chamber Orchestra, 1980; concerts in Europe, N America, Australia, 1978–; tours in USSR, 1984–; débuts, 1990–, in New York, Chicago, LA, Paris, Berlin, etc; numerous recordings (Gramophone Award (Contemporary Music), for John Tavener's The Protecting Veil, 1992). Piatigorsky Artist Award, USA, 1993; Instrumentalist Award, Royal Philharmonic Soc., 1993. *Recreations:* talking on the telephone, eating too much, regretting it, watching videos, reading, panicking about upcoming concerts, sleeping, jet-lag, telling people how tired I am, wondering if I should have any more worthwhile hobbies. *Address:* c/o Harrison & Parrott, 12 Penzance Place, W11 4PA. *T:* 0171–229 9166.

ISTEAD, Maj.-Gen. Peter Walter Ernest, CB 1989; OBE 1978; GM 1966; Chief Executive, Institute of Brewing, since 1990; *b* 7 Aug. 1935; *s* of Walter and Marie Istead; *m* 1961, Jennifer Mary Swinson; one *s* one *d. Educ:* Whitgift Trinity Sch., Croydon. Enlisted as boy soldier into Scots Guards, 1952; commnd Queen's Royal Regt, 1954; seconded to KAR, 1954–56; transf. RAOC, 1957; HQ 16 Parachute Bde, 1958–62; sc 1968; Directing Staff, Staff Coll., Camberley, 1971–73; DCS, 4 Armd Div., 1978–81; RCDS, 1982; Dir, Admin. Planning (Army), 1983–86; Comdr Supply, BAOR, 1986–87;

Dir Gen., Logistic Policy (Army), 1987–90. Hon. Col Comdt, RAOC, 1989–92. Freeman, City of London, 1986; Liveryman, Co. of Gold and Silver Wyre Drawers, 1990. *Recreations:* angling, squash. *Address:* Wandsworth, London. *Club:* Naval and Military.

IVAMY, Prof. Edward Richard Hardy; Professor of Law, University of London, 1960–86, now Emeritus; *b* 1 Dec. 1920; *o s* of late Edward Wadham Ivamy and late Florence Ivamy; *m* 1965, Christine Ann Frances, *o d* of William and late Frances Culver; one *s*. *Educ:* Malvern Coll.; University Coll., London. Served War of 1939–45, RA: 67 Field Regt, N Africa, Italy and Middle East; 2nd Lieut 1942; Temp. Capt. 1945; Staff Capt., GHQ, Cairo, 1946. LLB (1st cl. hons) 1947; PhD 1953; LLD 1967. Barrister, Middle Temple, 1949. University Coll., London: Asst Lectr in Laws, 1947–50; Lectr, 1950–56; Reader in Law, 1956–60; Dean of Faculty of Laws, 1964 and 1965; Fellow, 1969. Hon. Sec., Soc. of Public Teachers of Law, 1960–63; Hon. Sec., Bentham Club, 1953–58; Governor, Malvern Coll., 1982–. *Publications:* Show Business and the Law, 1955; (ed) Payne and Ivamy's Carriage of Goods by Sea, 7th edn 1963–13th edn, 1989; Hire-Purchase Legislation in England and Wales, 1965; Casebook on Carriage of Goods by Sea, 1965, 6th edn 1985; Casebook on Sale of Goods, 1966, 5th edn 1987; (ed) Chalmers's Marine Insurance Act 1906, 6th edn 1966–10th edn 1993; General Principles of Insurance Law, 1966, 6th edn 1993; (ed) Topham and Ivamy's Company Law, 13th edn 1967–16th edn 1978; Casebook on Commercial Law, 1967, 3rd edn 1979; Fire and Motor Insurance, 1968, 5th edn 1995; Casebook on Insurance Law, 1969, 4th edn 1984; Marine Insurance, 1969, 4th edn 1985; Casebook on Shipping Law, 1970, 4th edn 1987; Casebook on Partnership, 1970, 2nd edn 1982; Casebook on Agency, 1971, 3rd edn 1987; Personal Accident, Life and Other Insurances, 1973, 2nd edn 1980; (ed) Underhill's Partnership, 10th edn 1975 to 12th edn 1985; (ed) Halsbury's Laws of England, 4th edn 1978, vol. 25 (Insurance), 1977 and 1994, vol. 43 (Shipping and Navigation), 1983; Dictionary of Insurance Law, 1981; Dictionary of Company Law, 1983, 2nd edn 1985; Insurance Law Handbook, 1983; Dictionary of Shipping Law, 1984; Encyclopaedia of Shipping Law Sources (UK), 1985; Encyclopedia of Oil and Natural Gas Law, 1986; Encyclopedia of Carriage Law Sources, 1987; Merchant Shipping (Liner Conferences) Act 1982, 1987; Merchant Shipping Act 1970, 1987; Merchant Shipping Act 1979, 1987; (ed) Mozley and Whiteley's Law Dictionary, 10th edn 1988 and 11th edn 1993; contrib. to Encyclopædia Britannica, Chambers's Encyclopædia, Current Legal Problems, Jl of Business Law; Annual Survey of Commonwealth Law, 1967–77. *Recreations:* railways, cricket, tennis. *Address:* 7 Egliston Mews, SW15 1AP. *T:* 0181–785 6718.

IVANYI, Prof. Juraj, MD; PhD; Director, Tuberculosis and Related Infections Unit, MRC Clinical Sciences Centre, since 1984; Professor of Mycobacteriological Immunology, Royal Postgraduate Medical School, University of London, since 1990; *b* 20 June 1934; *s* of Dr Arnold Ivanyi and Maria (*née* Keszner); *m* 1960, Ludmila Svobodova. *Educ:* Charles Univ., Prague (MD); Acad. of Scis, Prague (PhD 1963). Czechoslovak Acad. of Scis, Prague, 1961–68; Wellcome Res. Labs, Beckenham, 1969–84; MRC, Hammersmith Hosp., 1984–. Hon. Mem., Slovak Soc. for Immunology, 1995. *Publications:* numerous in field of immunology. *Recreations:* theatre, ski-ing. *Address:* 3 Grotes Place, Blackheath, SE3 0QH. *T:* 0181–318 1088.

IVEAGH, 4th Earl of, *cr* 1919; **Arthur Edward Rory Guinness;** Bt 1885; Baron Iveagh 1891; Viscount Iveagh 1905; Viscount Elveden 1919; *b* 10 Aug. 1969; *s* of 3rd Earl of Iveagh and of Miranda Daphne Jane, *d* of Maj. Michael Smiley; *S* father, 1992. *Heir: b* Hon. Rory Michael Benjamin Guinness, *b* 12 Dec. 1974.

IVENS, Michael William, CBE 1983, Consultant, Aims of Industry, since 1994 (Director, 1971–91); Director, Foundation for Business Responsibilities, 1967–92; *b* 15 March 1924; *s* of Harry Guest Ivens and Nina Ailion; *m* 1st, 1950, Rosalie Turnbull (marr. diss. 1971); two *s* one *d* (and one *s* decd); 2nd, 1971, Katherine Laurence; two *s*. Jt Editor, Twentieth Century, 1967; Hon. Vice-Pres., Junior Hosp. Doctors Assoc., 1969; Director: Standard Telephone, 1970; Working Together Campaign, 1972–73. Jt Founder and Vice-Pres., Freedom Assoc.; Jt Founder and Trustee, Foundn for the Study of Terrorism, 1986; Member: Adv. Bd, US Industrial Council Educn Foundn, 1980–; Council and Hon. Treas., Poetry Soc., 1989–91; Adv. Cttee, Airey Neave Foundn, 1990–. *Publications:* Practice of Industrial Communication, 1963; Case Studies in Management, 1964; Case Studies in Human Relations, 1966; Case for Capitalism, 1967; Industry and Values, 1970; Which Way?, 1970; Prophets of Freedom and Enterprise, 1975; (ed jtly) Bachman's Book of Freedom Quotes, 1978; *poetry:* Another Sky, 1963; Last Waltz, 1964; Private and Public, 1968; Born Early, 1975; No Woman is an Island, 1983; New Divine Comedy, 1990; columns and articles under pseudonym Yorick. *Recreation:* campaigning. *Address:* 49 Ordnance Hill, NW8 6PS.

IVERSEN, Leslie Lars, PhD; FRS 1980; Senior Visiting Scientist, Department of Pharmacology, University of Oxford, since 1995; *b* 31 Oct. 1937; *s* of Svend Iversen and Anna Caia Iversen; *m* 1961, Susan Diana (*née* Kibble) (*see* S. D. Iversen); one *s* one *d* (and one *d* decd). *Educ:* Trinity Coll., Cambridge (BA Biochem, PhD Pharmacol). Harkness Fellow, United States: with Dr J. Axelrod, Nat. Inst. of Mental Health, and Dr E. Kravitz, Dept of Neurobiology, Harvard Med. Sch., 1964–66; Fellow, Trinity Coll., Cambridge, 1964–84; Locke Research Fellow of Royal Society, Dept of Pharmacology, Univ. of Cambridge, 1967–71; Dir, MRC Neurochemical Pharmacology Unit, Cambridge, 1971–82; Dir, Merck, Sharp & Dohme Neurosci. Res. Centre, Harlow, 1982–95. Foreign Associate, Nat. Acad. of Scis (USA), 1986. *Publications:* The Uptake and Storage of Noradrenaline in Sympathetic Nerves, 1967; (with S. D. Iversen) Behavioural Pharmacology, 1975, 2nd edn 1981. *Recreations:* reading, gardening. *Address:* Department of Pharmacology, University of Oxford, Mansfield Road, Oxford OX1 3QT.

IVERSEN, Prof. Susan Diana, PhD, ScD; Professor and Head of Department of Experimental Psychology, Oxford University, since 1993; Fellow of Magdalen College, Oxford, since 1993; *b* 28 Feb. 1940; *d* of Jack Bertram Kibble and Edith Margaret Kibble; *m* 1961, Leslie Lars Iversen, *qv*; one *s* one *d* (and one *d* decd). *Educ:* Girton Coll., Cambridge (BA Zoology, PhD Exp. Psych, ScD). NATO Science Fellow, Nat. Inst. Mental Health and Dept of Pharmacology, Harvard Med. Sch., 1964–66; Fellow: Girton Coll., Cambridge, 1964–75; Jesus Coll., Cambridge, 1981–93; Dept of Exp. Psychology, Cambridge, 1966–83; Merck Sharp & Dohme, Neuroscience Research Centre, Harlow, 1983–93. Member: Council, SERC, 1991–94; BBSRC, 1994–. *Publications:* (with L. L. Iversen) Behavioural Pharmacology, 1975, 2nd edn 1981; (ed with L. L. Iversen and S. H. Snyder) Handbook of Psychopharmacology, 20 vols. *Recreations:* history, wildlife, modern art, theatre. *Address:* Department of Experimental Psychology, South Parks Road, Oxford OX1 3UD.

IVES, Charles John Grayston, (Bill); Informator Choristarum, Organist, and Tutor in Music, Magdalen College, Oxford, since 1991; Fellow of Magdalen College, since 1991; *b* 15 Feb. 1948; *s* of Harold James Ives and Catherine Lilla Ives; *m* 1st, 1972, Bethan Eleri Jones (marr. diss. 1986); one *s* one *d*; 2nd, 1988, Janette Ann (*née* Buqué). *Educ:* King's Sch., Ely; Selwyn Coll., Cambridge. Asst Dir of Music, Reed's Sch., Cobham, 1971–76; Lectr in Music, Coll. of Further Educn, Chichester, 1976–78; tenor, The King's Singers, 1978–85; freelance composer, 1985–92. Examr, Associated Bd of Royal Schs of Music, 1988–. *Publications:* (as Grayston Ives) musical compositions of sacred choral music, including Canterbury Te Deum (commnd for Enthronement of Archbishop George Carey, Canterbury Cathedral, 1991). *Recreations:* books, wine, travel. *Address:* Magdalen College, Oxford OX1 4AU. *T:* Oxford (01865) 276007.

IVES, Prof. Kenneth James, FEng 1986; FICE; Chadwick Professor of Civil Engineering, University College London, 1984–92, retired; *b* 29 Nov. 1926; *s* of Walter Ives and Grace Ives (*née* Curson); *m* 1952, Brenda Grace Tilley; one *s* one *d*. *Educ:* William Ellis Grammar School, London; University College London. BSc Eng, PhD, DSc Eng. Junior Engineer, Metropolitan Water Board, London, 1948–55; Lectr, Reader, Prof., University Coll. London, 1955–92. Research Fellow, Harvard Univ., 1958–59; Visiting Professor: Univ. of North Carolina, 1964; Delft Technical Univ., 1977; Consultant Expert Adviser, WHO, 1966–92. Mem., Badenoch Cttee on Cryptosporidium in Water Supplies, 1989–90. Gans Medal, Soc. for Water Treatment, 1966; Gold Medal, Filtration Soc. Internat, 1983; Jenkins Medal, IAWPRC, 1990; Freese Award, ASCE, 1994. *Publications:* Scientific Basis of Filtration, 1975; Scientific Basis of Flocculation, 1978; Scientific Basis of Flotation, 1984; contribs to sci. and eng. jls on water purification. *Recreations:* squash, ballroom dancing. *Address:* Department of Civil and Environmental Engineering, University College London, Gower Street, WC1E 6BT. *T:* 0171–387 7050.

IVISON, David Malcolm; Chief Executive, Institute of Road Transport Engineers, 1985–89; *b* 22 March 1936; *s* of John and Ruth Ellen Ivison; *m* 1961, Lieselotte Verse; one *s* one *d*. *Educ:* King Edward VI School, Lichfield; RMA Sandhurst; Staff College, Camberley. Army, Gurkha Transport Regt, 1955–83 (Lt-Col). Tate & Lyle, 1984–85. Dir, British Metallurgical Plant Constructors' Assoc., 1994. *Recreations:* learning languages, tennis, reading. *Address:* 1 Dundaff Close, Camberley, Surrey GU15 1AF. *T:* Camberley (01276) 27778.

IVORY, Brian Gammell, CA; Group Chief Executive, The Highland Distilleries Co. plc, since 1994 (Managing Director, 1988–94); *b* 10 April 1949; *s* of late Eric James Ivory and Alice Margaret Joan, *d* of Sir Sydney James Gammell; *m* 1981, Oona Mairi Macphie, *d* of late Archibald Ian Bell-MacDonald; one *s* one *d*. *Educ:* Eton College; Magdalene College, Cambridge (MA). Director: The Highland Distilleries Co., 1978–; Matthew Gloag & Son, 1987–; Rémy Cointreau SA, 1991–. Scottish Arts Council: Mem., 1983–92 (Vice-Chm., 1988–92); Chm., Combined Arts Cttee, 1984–88; Mem., Arts Council of GB, 1988–92. FRSA 1993. *Recreations:* the arts, farming, hill walking. *Address:* Brewlands, Glenisla, by Blairgowrie, Perthshire PH11 8PL. *Clubs:* New (Edinburgh); Royal Scottish Automobile (Glasgow).

IVORY, James Francis; film director; Partner in Merchant Ivory Productions, since 1961; *b* 7 June 1928; *s* of Edward Patrick Ivory and Hallie Millicent De Loney. *Educ:* Univ. of Oregon (BA Fine Arts); Univ. of Southern California (MFA Cinema). Guggenheim Fellow, 1974. Collaborator with Ruth Prawer Jhabvala and Ismail Merchant on the following films: The Householder, 1963; Shakespeare Wallah, 1965; The Guru, 1969; Bombay Talkie, 1970; Autobiography of a Princess, 1975; Roseland, 1977; Hullabaloo over Georgie and Bonnie's Pictures, 1978; The Europeans, 1979; Jane Austen in Manhattan, 1980; Quartet, 1981; Heat and Dust, 1983; The Bostonians, 1984; A Room With a View, 1986; Mr and Mrs Bridge, 1990; Howards End, 1992; The Remains of the Day, 1993; Jefferson in Paris, 1995; collaborator with Ismail Merchant (producer) on: (with Nirad Chaudhuri) Adventures of a Brown Man in Search of Civilization, 1971; (with George W. S. Trow and Michael O'Donoghue) Savages, 1972; (with Walter Marks) The Wild Party, 1975; (with Kit Hesketh-Harvey) Maurice, 1987; (with Tama Janowitz) Slaves of New York, 1989; other films: (with Terence McNally) The Five Forty Eight, 1979; documentaries: Venice, Theme and Variations, 1957; The Sword and the Flute, 1959; The Delhi Way, 1964. *Publication:* Autobiography of a Princess (Also Being the Adventures of an American Film Director in the Land of the Maharajas), 1975. *Recreation:* looking at pictures. *Address:* PO Box 93, Claverack, NY 12513, USA. *T:* (office) (212) 5828049.

J

JABALÉ, Rt. Rev. (John) Mark, OSB; Abbot of Belmont, since 1993; *b* 16 Oct. 1933; *s* of John and Arlette Jabalé. *Educ:* Belmont Abbey Sch.; Fribourg Univ. (LèsL); St Mary's Coll., London (DipEd). Belmont Abbey Sch: Games Master and House Master, 1963–69; Headmaster, 1969–83; built Monastery of the Incarnation, in Tambogrande, Perú; Prior of Belmont Abbey, 1986–93. Steward and Mem., Cttee of Management, Henley Royal Regatta. *Recreations:* computers, rowing. *Address:* Belmont Abbey, Hereford HR2 9RZ. *T:* Hereford (01432) 277386. *Club:* Leander (Henley-on-Thames).

JACK, Hon. Sir Alieu (Sulayman), Grand Commander, 1972, and Chancellor, 1972–83, National Order of The Gambia; Kt 1970; Speaker, House of Representatives of the Republic of The Gambia, 1962–72, and 1977–83, retired; *b* 14 July 1922; *m* 1946, Yai Marie Cham; four *s* four *d* (and one *d* decd). *Educ:* St Augustine's School. Entered Gambia Civil Service, 1939; resigned and took up local appt with NAAFI, 1940–44; Civil Service, 1945–48; entered commerce, 1948; Man. Dir, Gambia National Trading Co. Ltd, 1948–72. Mem., Bathurst City Council, 1949–62. Minister for Works and Communications, The Gambia, 1972–77. Represented The Gambia Parlt at various internat. gatherings. Comdr, National Order of Senegal, 1967; Comdr, Order of Merit of Mauritania, 1967; Commander, Order of Fed. Republic of Nigeria, 1970; Kt Grand Band, Liberia, 1977. *Recreation:* golf. *Address:* PO Box 376, Banjul, The Gambia. *T:* (home) 92204, (office) 28431. *Club:* Bathurst (Banjul).

JACK, Sir David, Kt 1993; CBE 1982; PhD; FRS 1992; FRSE; pharmacologist; *b* 22 Feb. 1924; *s* of Andrew Jack and Mary McDougal Jack (*née* Maiden); *m* 1952, Lydia Downie Brown; two *d*. *Educ:* Markinch and Buckhaven Schools, Fife; Univ. of Glasgow (BSc); Univ. of London (PhD); Royal Technical Coll., Glasgow. FRSC, FIBiol, FRPharmS; FRSE 1978. Lectr in Pharmacology, Glasgow Univ. and RTC Glasgow, 1948–51; Scientist, Glaxo Labs, 1951–53; Head of Product Develt, Smith Kline and French, 1953–61; Res. Dir, Allen & Hanburys, 1961–73; Man. Dir, Allen & Hanburys Res., 1973–78; R&D Dir, Glaxo Holdings, 1978–87; associated with new medicines for asthma (Queen's Awards for salbutamol, 1973, inhaled beclomethasone dipropionate, 1975), hypertension, peptic ulcer (Queen's Award for ranitidine, 1985), nausea and migraine. Hon. Mem., British Pharm. Soc., 1990. Hon. DL Dundee, 1991. Hon. DSc: Strathclyde, 1982; Bath, 1987; CNAA, 1987. Harrison Medal, Royal Pharm. Soc., 1969; Medicinal Chem. Medal, RSC, 1980; Award for Drug Discovery, Soc. for Drug Research, 1985; Lilly Prize Medal, British Pharm. Soc., 1989; Mullard Medal, Royal Soc., 1991. *Publications:* papers in Br. Jl Pharmacology. *Recreations:* gardening, golf. *Address:* 6 The Slype, Gustard Wood, Wheathampstead, Herts AL4 8RY. *T:* Wheathampstead (01582) 832241.

JACK, Sir David (Emmanuel), GCMG 1991; MBE 1975; Governor General, St Vincent and The Grenadines, since 1989; *b* 16 July 1918; *s* of John Fitzroy Jack and Margaret Lewis Jack; *m* 1946, Esther Veronica McKay; two *s* two *d* (and one *s* decd). *Educ:* Stubbs Govt School; La Salle Extension Univ., Chicago (Dip. Higher Accountancy). Teacher's Cert., St Vincent Educn Dept. School Teacher, 1934–43; Engine Operator, Shell Oil Refinery, 1943–45; Commercial Accounting, 1945–69; Gen. Manager, A'Root Ind., 1969–79; in business and politics, 1979–84; elected to Parliament, 1984; Minister, 1984–89. Methodist local preacher, 1940–. *Recreations:* carpentry, music. *Address:* Government House, Montrose, St Vincent and The Grenadines. *T:* 61401.

JACK, David M.; *see* Morton Jack.

JACK, Ian Grant; Editor, Granta, since 1995; *b* 7 Feb. 1945; *s* of Henry Jack and Isabella Jack (*née* Gillespie); *m* 1979, Aparna Bagchi (marr. diss. 1992); partner, Rosalind Sharpe; one *s* one *d*. *Educ:* Dunfermline High School, Fife. Trainee journalist, Glasgow Herald, 1965; reporter, Cambuslang Advertiser and East Kilbride News, 1966; journalist, Scottish Daily Express, 1966–70; Sunday Times, 1970–86; Observer and Vanity Fair (NY), 1986–88; Dep. Editor, 1989–91, Exec. Editor, 1991–92, Editor, 1992–95, Independent on Sunday. Journalist of the Year, Granada TV What The Papers Say award, 1985; Colour Magazine Writer of the Year, 1985, Reporter of the Year, 1988, British Press Awards; Nat. Newspaper Editor of the Year, Newspaper Focus Awards, 1992. *Publication:* Before the Oil Ran Out, 1987. *Recreations:* travelling, steamships, imperial history, India. *Address:* c/o Rogers, Coleridge and White, 20 Powis Mews, W11 1JN; Granta Publications Ltd, 2–3 Hanover Yard, Noel Road, N1 8BE. *Club:* India International Centre (New Delhi).

JACK, Prof. Ian Robert James, FBA 1986; Professor of English Literature, University of Cambridge, 1976–89, Emeritus 1989; Fellow of Pembroke College, Cambridge, 1961–89, Emeritus 1989; *b* 5 Dec. 1923; *s* of John McGregor Bruce Jack, WS, and Helena Colburn Buchanan; *m* 1st, 1948, Jane Henderson MacDonald (marr. diss.); two *s* one *d*; 2nd, 1972, Margaret Elizabeth Crone; one *s*. *Educ:* George Watson's Coll. (John Welsh Classical Schol., 1942); Univ. of Edinburgh (James Boswell Fellow, 1946; MA 1947); Merton Coll., Oxford (DPhil 1950); LittD Cantab 1973. Brasenose College, Oxford: Lectr in Eng. Lit., 1950–55; Sen. Res. Fellow, 1955–61; Cambridge University: Lectr in English, 1961–73; Reader in English Poetry, 1973–76; Librarian, Pembroke Coll., 1965–75. Vis. Professor: Alexandria, 1960; Chicago (Carpenter Prof.), 1968–69; California at Berkeley, 1968–69; British Columbia, 1975; Virginia, 1980–81; Tsuda Coll., Tokyo, 1981; New York Univ. (Berg Prof.), 1989; de Carle Lectr, Univ. of Otago, 1964; Warton Lectr in English Poetry, British Acad., 1967; Guest Speaker, Nichol Smith Seminar, ANU, 1976; Guest Speaker, 50th anniversary meeting of English Literary Soc. of Japan, 1978; Leverhulme Emeritus Fellow, 1990, 1991; numerous lecture-tours for British Council and other bodies. President: Charles Lamb Soc., 1970–80; Browning Soc., 1980–83; Johnson Soc., Lichfield, 1986–87; Vice-Pres., Brontë Soc., 1973–. General Editor: Brontë novels (Clarendon edn), 7 vols, 1969–92; The Poetical Works of Browning, 1983–. *Publications:* Augustan Satire, 1952; English Literature 1815–1832 (Vol. X, Oxf. Hist. of Eng. Lit.), 1963; Keats and the Mirror of Art, 1967; Browning's Major Poetry, 1973; The Poet and his Audience, 1984; *edited:* Sterne: A Sentimental Journey, etc, 1968; Browning: Poetical Works 1833–1864, 1970; (with Hilda Marsden) Emily Brontë: Wuthering Heights, 1976; (ed) The Poetical Works of Browning, Vol. I 1983, Vol. II 1984, Vol. III 1988, Vol. IV 1991, Vol. V 1995; contrib. TLS, RES, etc. *Recreations:* collecting books, travelling hopefully, thinking about words. *Address:* Highfield House, High Street, Fen Ditton, Cambridgeshire CB5 8ST. *T:* Teversham (01223) 292697; Pembroke College, Cambridge CB2 1RF. *Club:* MCC.

JACK, (John) Michael, MP (C) Fylde, since 1987; Financial Secretary to HM Treasury, since 1995; *b* 17 Sept. 1946; *m* 1976, Alison Jane Musgrave; two *s*. *Educ:* Bradford Grammar Sch.; Bradford Tech. Coll.; Leicester Univ. BA(Econs); MPhil. Shipping, subseq. Advertising, Depts, Procter & Gamble, 1970–75; PA to Sir Derek Rayner, Marks & Spencer, 1975–80; Sales Dir, L. O. Jeffs Ltd, 1980–87. Mem., Mersey RHA, 1984–87. Contested (C) Newcastle upon Tyne Central, Feb. 1974. PPS to Minister of State, DOE, 1988–89, to Minister of Agric., Fisheries and Food, 1989–90; Parly Under Sec. of State, DSS, 1990–92; Minister of State: Home Office, 1992–93; MAFF, 1993–95. Sec., Cons. Back-bench Transport Cttee, 1987–88; Chm., Cons. Back-bench sub-cttee on Horticulture and Markets, 1987–88; Sec., Cons. NW Members Gp, 1988–90. Nat. Chm., Young Conservatives, 1976–77. Vice-Pres., Think Green, 1989–90. Pres., Clifton Hosp. League of Friends, 1991–. *Recreations:* dinghy sailing, motor sport, boule. *Address:* House of Commons, SW1A 0AA.

JACK, Prof. Kenneth Henderson, PhD, ScD; FRS 1980; CChem, FRSC; Professor of Applied Crystal Chemistry, University of Newcastle upon Tyne, 1964–84, and Director of Wolfson Research Group for High-Strength Materials, 1970–84; Leverhulme Emeritus Fellow, 1985–87; *b* 12 Oct. 1918; *e s* of late John Henderson Jack, DSC, and Emily (*née* Cozens), North Shields, Northumberland; *m* 1942, Alfreda Hughes (*d* 1974); two *s*. *Educ:* Tynemouth Municipal High Sch.; King's Coll., Univ. of Durham, Newcastle upon Tyne (BSc 1939, DThPT 1940, MSc 1944); Fitzwilliam Coll., Univ. of Cambridge (PhD 1950, ScD 1978). Experimental Officer, Min. of Supply, 1940–41; Lectr in Chemistry, King's Coll., Univ. of Durham, 1941–45, 1949–52, 1953–57; Sen. Scientific Officer, Brit. Iron and Steel Res. Assoc., 1945–49; research at Crystallographic Lab., Cavendish Laboratory, Cambridge, 1947–49; Research Engr, Westinghouse Elec. Corp., Pittsburgh, Pa, 1952–53; Research Dir, Thermal Syndicate Ltd, Wallsend, 1957–64. Consultant, Cookson Group, 1986–94; Lectures: J.W. Mellor Meml, Brit. Ceramic Soc., 1973; Harold Moore Meml, Metals Soc., 1984; W. Hume-Rothery Meml, Oxford Metallurgical Soc., 1986; Sosman Meml, Amer. Ceramic Soc., 1989. Fellow, Amer. Ceramic Soc., 1984; Membre d'Honneur, Société Française de Métallurgie, 1984; Mem., Internat. Acad. of Ceramics, 1990; Hon. Member: Materials Res. Soc. of India, 1991; Ceramic Soc. of Japan, 1991. Saville-Shaw Medal, Soc. of Chem. Industry, 1944; Sir George Beilby Meml Award, Inst. of Metals, RIC and Soc. of Chem. Industry, 1951; Kroll Medal and Prize, Metals Soc., 1979; (with Dr R.J. Lumby) Prince of Wales Award for Industrial Innovation and Production, 1984; Armourers & Brasiers' Co. Award, Royal Soc., 1988; World Materials Congress Award, ASM Internat., 1988; A. A. Griffith Silver Medal and Prize, Inst. of Metals, 1989; Centennial Award, Ceramic Soc. of Japan, 1991. *Publications:* papers in scientific jls and conf. proc. *Address:* 147 Broadway, Cullercoats, Tyne and Wear NE30 3TA. *T:* 0191–257 3664; Cookson House, Willington Quay, Wallsend, Tyne and Wear NE28 6UQ. *T:* 0191–262 2211.

JACK, Dr Malcolm Roy; Clerk of Standing Committees, House of Commons, since 1991; *b* 17 Dec. 1946; *s* of late Iain Ross Jack and Alicia Maria Eça da Silva, Hong Kong. *Educ:* school in Hong Kong; Univ. of Liverpool (Hong Kong Govt Scholar; BA Hons 1st Class); LSE, Univ. of London (PhD). A Clerk, House of Commons, 1967–; Private Sec. to Chm. of Ways and Means, 1977–80; Clerk to Agriculture Select Cttee, 1980–88; Clerk of Supply, 1989–91. Mem., Highgate Literary and Scientific Instn. *Publications:* The Social and Political Thought of Bernard Mandeville, 1987; Corruption and Progress: the eighteenth-century debate, 1989; (ed with Anita Desai) The Turkish Embassy Letters of Lady Mary Wortley Montagu, 1993; (ed) Vathek and Other Stories: a William Beckford Reader, 1993; (ed) The Episodes of Vathek of William Beckford, 1994; William Beckford: an English Fidalgo, 1995; articles and essays in books, learned and literary jls. *Recreations:* French and Scottish Enlightenment, Luso-Brasilian life, letters and drama, stories of old and new China hands, the civic virtue of bees, fine arts. *Address:* Public Bill Office, House of Commons, SW1A 0AA. *T:* 0171–219 3257. *Club:* English-Speaking Union.

JACK, Michael; *see* Jack, J. M.

JACK, Raymond Evan; QC 1982; **His Honour Judge Raymond Jack;** a Circuit Judge, since 1991; Judge of the Bristol Mercantile Court, since 1994; *b* 13 Nov. 1942; *s* of Evan and Charlotte Jack; *m* 1976, Elizabeth Alison, *d* of Rev. Canon James Seymour Denis Mansel, *qv*; one *s* two *d*. *Educ:* Rugby; Trinity Coll., Cambridge (MA). Called to Bar, Inner Temple, 1966; a Recorder, 1989. *Publication:* Documentary Credits, 1991, 2nd edn 1993. *Recreations:* words and wood. *Address:* c/o The Law Courts, Small Street, Bristol BS1 1DA.

JACK, Prof. Robert Barr, CBE 1988; Chairman, Scottish Mutual Assurance PLC, since 1992 (Director, since 1987); Deputy Chairman, Scottish Metropolitan Property plc, since 1991 (Director, since 1980); *b* 18 March 1928; *s* of Robert Hendry Jack and Christina Alexandra Jack; *m* 1958, Anna Thorburn Thomson; two *s*. *Educ:* Kilsyth Acad.; High Sch., Glasgow; Glasgow Univ. MA 1948, LLB 1951. Admitted a solicitor in Scotland, 1951; Partner, McGrigor Donald, Solicitors, Glasgow, Edinburgh and London, 1957–93 (Jt Sen. Partner, 1986–90; Sen. Partner, 1990–93). Prof. of Mercantile Law, Glasgow Univ., 1978–93. Member: Company Law Cttee of Law Society of Scotland, 1971– (Convener, 1978–85); Scottish Law Commn, 1974–77. Scottish observer on Dept of Trade's

Insolvency Law Review Cttee, 1977–82; Mem., DoT Adv. Panel on Company Law, 1980–83; Chm., Review Cttee on Banking Services Law, 1987–89. Lay Member: Council for the Securities Industry, 1983–85; Stock Exchange Council, 1984–86; Independent Mem. Bd, Securities Assoc., later SFA, 1987–94; Mem. Bd, SIB, 1994–; UK Mem., Panel of Arbitrators, ICSID, 1989–; Member: Takeover Panel, 1992–; Financial Law Panel, 1993–; MSI 1993. Chairman: Brownlee plc, Timber Merchants, Glasgow, 1984–86 (Dir, 1974–86); Joseph Dunn (Bottlers) Ltd, Soft Drink Manufacturers, Glasgow, 1983–; Director: Clyde Football Club Ltd, 1980–; Bank of Scotland, 1985–; Gartmore Scotland Investment Trust, 1991–; Glasgow Develt Agency, 1992–. Pres., Scottish Nat. Council of YMCAs, 1983– (Chm., 1966–73). Mem., SHEFC, 1992–. Chm., The Turnberry Trust; Governor, Hutchesons' Educational Trust, Glasgow, 1978–87 (Chm. 1980–87); Mem. Bd of Govs, Beatson Inst. for Cancer Res., Glasgow, 1989–. *Publications:* lectures on various aspects of company, insolvency and banking law and financial services regulation law. *Recreations:* golf, hopeful support of one of Scotland's less fashionable football teams; a dedicated lover of Isle of Arran. *Address:* 50 Lanton Road, Newlands, Glasgow G43 2SR. *T:* 0141–637 7302. *Clubs:* Caledonian; Western (Glasgow); Pollok Golf; Shiskine Golf and Tennis (Isle of Arran) (Captain 1973–75).

JACK, Stuart Duncan Macdonald, CVO 1994; HM Diplomatic Service; *b* 8 June 1949; *s* of William Harris Jack and Edith Florence Jack (*née* Coker); *m* 1977, Mariko Nobechi; one *s* two *d*. *Educ:* Westcliff High Sch. for Boys; Merton Coll., Oxford (BA 1971). VSO, Laos, 1971; joined HM Diplomatic Service, 1972: Eastern European and Soviet Dept, FO, 1972–73; Tokyo, 1974–79; Far Eastern Dept, FCO, 1979–81; Moscow, 1981–84; on secondment with Bank of England, 1984–85; Tokyo, 1985–89; Overseas Inspector, 1989–92; Consul Gen., St Petersburg, 1992–95. *Recreations:* reading, photography, music. *Address:* c/o Foreign and Commonwealth Office, King Charles Street, SW1A 2AH.

JACK, Dr William Hugh, CB 1988; Comptroller and Auditor General, Northern Ireland Audit Office, 1989–94; *b* 18 Feb. 1929; *s* of John Charles Jack and Martha Ann Jack; *m* 1953, Beatrice Jane Thompson; three *s* one *d*. *Educ:* Ballymena Acad.; Univ. of Edinburgh (BSc(For); PhD); Queen's Univ., Belfast (BSc (Econ)). MICFor 1959. Min. of Agriculture for NI, 1948–49; Colonial Forest Service, Gold Coast/Ghana, 1949–59 (Conservator of Forests, 1957); Dept of Agriculture for NI, 1959–89 (Permanent Sec., 1983). CIMgt. *Publications:* various articles in forestry research and economic jls. *Recreations:* walking, reading. *Address:* c/o Audit Office, 106 University Street, Belfast BT7 1HE.

JACKAMAN, Michael Clifford John; Chairman, Allied Domecq (formerly Allied-Lyons) plc, since 1991 (Vice-Chairman, 1988–91); *b* 7 Nov. 1935; *s* of Air Cdre Clifford Thomas Jackaman, OBE and Lily Margaret Jackaman; *m* 1960, Valerie Jane Pankhurst; one *s* one *d*. *Educ:* Felsted Sch., Essex; Jesus Coll., Cambridge (MA Hons). Dep. Man. Dir, Harveys of Bristol, 1976–78; Marketing Dir, Allied Breweries, 1978–83; Dir, Allied Domecq (formerly Allied Lyons) plc, 1978–; Chairman: Hiram Walker Allied Vintners, 1983–91; John Harvey & Sons Ltd, 1983–93; Mem., Council of Admin, Château Latour, 1983–93; Director: Fintex of London Ltd, 1986–92; Rank Orgn, 1992–; Kleinwort Benson Gp, 1994–. Governor, Bristol Polytechnic, 1988–91. Mem., Keepers of the Quaich (Scotland); Commanderie des Bontemps du Médoc et des Graves (France). *Recreations:* walking, tennis, potting. *Address:* c/o Allied Domecq plc, 24 Portland Place, W1N 4BB. *T:* 0171–323 9000.

JACKLIN, Anthony, CBE 1990 (OBE 1970); professional golfer, 1962–85 and since 1988; Director of Golf, San Roque Club, since 1988; *b* 7 July 1944; *s* of Arthur David Jacklin; *m* 1st, 1966, Vivien (*d* 1988); two *s* one *d*; 2nd, 1988, Astrid May Waagen; one *s*, one step *s* one step *d*. Successes include: British Assistant Pro Championship, 1965; Pringle Tournament, 1967; Dunlop Masters, 1967; Greater Jacksonville Open, USA, 1968; British Open Championship, 1969; US Open Championship, 1970; Benson & Hedges, 1971; British Professional Golfers Assoc., 1972, 1982; Gtr Jacksonville Open, 1972; Bogota Open, 1973 and 1974; Italian Open, 1973; Dunlop Masters, 1973; Scandinavian Open, 1975; Kerrygold International, 1976; English National PGA Championship, 1977; German Open, 1979; Jersey Open, 1981; PGA Champion, 1982; Ryder Cup player, 1967–80, Team Captain, Europe, 1983–89. Professional Golfers' Association: Life Vice-Pres., 1970; Hon. Life Mem., European Tournament Players Div. *Publications:* Golf with Tony Jacklin, 1969; The Price of Success, 1979; (with Peter Dobereiner) Jacklin's Golfing Secrets, 1983; Tony Jacklin: the first forty years, 1985. *Recreation:* shooting. *Clubs:* Potters Bar Golf; Hon. Mem. of others.

JACKLIN, William, (Bill), RA 1991 (ARA 1989); *b* 1 Jan. 1943; *s* of Harold and Alice Jacklin; *m* 1st, 1979, Lesley Sariwa (marr. diss. 1993); 2nd, 1993, Janet Ann Russo. *Educ:* Walthamstow Sch. of Art, Royal College of Art (NDD, MARCA). Part-time Lectr at various art colleges, 1967–75; Arts Council Bursary, 1975; lives and works in New York, 1985–; Artist in Residence, British Council, Hong Kong, 1993–94. One man exhibns, London galleries, 1970–, USA, 1985–, Hong Kong, 1995; retrospective exhibn, Mus. of Modern Art, Oxford, 1992; frequent shows in internat. exhibns; works in major collections including Arts Council, British Mus., Metropolitan Mus. NY, Mus. of Modern Art NY, Tate Gall., V&A. *Publications:* catalogues to one man exhibns, London and New York. *Recreations:* planting trees, running. *Address:* c/o Marlborough Fine Art, 6 Albemarle Street, W1X 4BY. *T:* 0171–629 5161. *Club:* Chelsea Arts.

JACKLING, Roger Tustin, CB 1995; CBE 1982; Deputy Under-Secretary of State (Resources and Programmes), Ministry of Defence, since 1991; *b* 23 Nov. 1943; *s* of Sir Roger Jackling, GCMG and late Joan (*née* Tustin) (Lady Jackling); *m* 1976, Jane Allen Pritchard; two *s*. *Educ:* Wellington Coll.; New York Univ. (BA); Jesus Coll., Oxford. Asst Principal, MoD, 1969, Principal, 1972; London Executive Prog., London Business Sch., 1974; Sec. of State's Office, MoD, 1976–79; Asst Sec. and Hd of DS11, 1979–82; Prime Minister's Office, 1983; Head of DS7/Resources and Programmes (Army), MoD, 1983–85; Fellow, Center for Internat. Affairs, Harvard Univ., 1985–86; Principal, CS Coll. and Under Sec., Cabinet Office (OMCS), 1986–89; Asst Under-Sec. of State (Progs), MoD, 1989–91. Mem. Council, RIPA, 1987–. *Recreations:* books, theatre, playing golf and watching cricket. *Address:* c/o Ministry of Defence, Whitehall, SW1. *Clubs:* Garrick; Highgate Golf.

JACKSON, Alan Robert, AO 1991; Chairman, Australian Trade Commission, since 1996; *b* 30 March 1936; *m* 1962, Esme Adelia Giles; four *d*. FCA, FASA, FAIM. Accountant to Man. Dir, Mather & Platt, 1952–77; Man. Dir, BTR Nylex, 1977–90; Man. Dir and Chief Exec. Officer, BTR plc, 1991–95. *Recreations:* tennis, golf. *Address:* Austrade, AIDC Tower, 201 Kent Street, Sydney, NSW 2000, Australia.

JACKSON, Albert Leslie Samuel, JP; Chairman, Birmingham Technology Ltd (Aston Science Park), since 1984; *b* 20 Jan. 1918; *s* of Bert Jackson and Olive Powell; *m* Gladys Burley; one *s* one *d*. *Educ:* Handsworth New Road Council Sch. War service, Radio Mechanic, RAF. Mem., Birmingham CC, 1952–86; Lord Mayor, 1975–76, Dep. Lord Mayor, 1978–79, Birmingham. Dir and Cttee Chm., NEC, 1984–87. JP 1968. *Recreations:* chess, sailing. *Address:* Dickies Meadow, Dock Lane, Bredon, near Tewkesbury GL20 7LG. *T:* Tewkesbury (01684) 72541.

JACKSON, Brig. Alexander Cosby Fishburn, CVO 1957; CBE 1954 (OBE 1943); *b* 4 Dec. 1903; *s* of late Col S. C. F. Jackson, CMG, DSO, and Lucy B. Jackson (*née* Drake); *m* 1934, Margaret Hastings Hervey (*d* 1984), Montclair, NJ, USA; one *s* (and one *s* decd). *Educ:* Yardley Court, Tonbridge; Haileybury Coll.; RMC Sandhurst. 2nd Lt, R Hants Regt, 1923; Brig. 1944; employed RWAFF, 1927–33; served in Middle East, 1940–45 (despatches twice, OBE); Dep. Dir of Quartering, War Office, 1945–48; Comdr Northern Area, Kenya, 1948–51; Comdr Caribbean Area, 1951–54; HBM Military Attaché, Paris, 1954–58. ADC to the Queen, 1955–58. Order of Kutuzov 2nd Class, USSR, 1944; Comdr Legion of Honour, France, 1957. *Publications:* Rose Croix: a history of the Ancient and Accepted Rite for England and Wales, 1981; English Masonic Exposures 1760–1769, 1986; A Glossary of the Craft and Holy Royal Arch Rituals of Freemasonry, 1992. *Address:* Glenwhern, Golf Lane, Grouville, Jersey JE3 9BD.

JACKSON, Anthony Geoffrey Clive H.; *see* Howland Jackson.

JACKSON, Mrs (Audrey) Muriel W.; *see* Ward-Jackson.

JACKSON, Barry Trevor, MS, FRCS; Serjeant Surgeon to The Queen, since 1991; Consultant Surgeon: St Thomas' Hospital, since 1973; Queen Victoria Hospital, East Grinstead, since 1977; King Edward VII Hospital for Officers, since 1983; *b* 7 July 1936; *er s* of Arthur Stanley Jackson and Violet May (*née* Fry); *m* 1962, Sheila May Wood; two *s* one *d*. *Educ:* Sir George Monoux Grammar Sch.; King's College London; Westminster Med. Sch. (Entrance Scholar). MB, BS 1963; MRCS, LRCP 1963; MS 1972; FRCS 1967. Down Bros Ltd, 1952–54; RAF 1954–56; junior surgical appts, Gordon Hosp., St James' Hosp., Balham, St Peter's Hosp., Chertsey, St Helier Hosp., Carshalton, St Thomas' Hosp. Surgeon to the Royal Household, 1983–91; Hon. Consultant in Surgery to the Army, 1990–. Royal College of Surgeons: Arris & Gale Lectr, 1973; Vicary Lectr, 1994; Examr Primary FRCS, 1977–83; Mem. Court of Examrs, 1983–89; Mem. Council, 1991–; Asst Editor 1984–91, Editor, 1992–, Annals RCS; Pres., Assoc. of Surgeons of GB and Ireland, 1994–95 (Mem. Council, 1982–85; Hon. Sec., 1986–91; Vice Pres., 1993–94); Mem. Council, RSocMed, 1987–92 (Pres., Sect. of Coloproctology, 1991–92). External examr in surgery: Khartoum, 1981; Ibadan, 1982; Colombo, 1984, 1988; Abu Dhabi, 1989. Mem., W Lambeth HA, 1982–83; Special Trustee, St Thomas' Hosp., 1982–84, 1994–; Chm., SE Thames Regional Med. Adv. Cttee, 1983–87. Mem. Council of Govs, UMDS of Guy's and St Thomas' Hosps, 1989–94. *Publications:* contribs to surgical jls and textbooks (surgery of gastro-intestinal tract). *Recreations:* book collecting, reading, medical history, music, especially opera. *Address:* The Consulting Rooms, York House, 199 Westminster Bridge Road, SE1 7UT. *T:* 0171–928 5485. *Club:* Athenæum.

JACKSON, Betty, MBE 1987; RDI 1988; Designer Director, Betty Jackson Ltd, since 1981; *b* 24 June 1949; *d* of Arthur and Phyllis Gertrude Jackson; *m* 1985, David Cohen; one *s* one *d*. *Educ:* Bacup and Rawtenstall Grammar Sch.; Birmingham Coll. of Art (DipAD fashion and textiles). Freelance fashion illustrator, 1971–73; design asst, 1973–75; chief designer, Quorum, 1975–81. Part-time Tutor, RCA, 1982–. Fellow, Birmingham Polytechnic, 1989. Hon. Fellow, RCA, 1989. Awards include: British Designer of the Year, Harvey Nichols and British Fashion Council, 1985; Viyella, 1987; Fil d'Or, Internat. Linen, 1989. *Address:* Betty Jackson Ltd, 33 Tottenham Street, W1P 9PE. *T:* 0171–631 1010; Betty Jackson Retail, 311 Brompton Road, SW3 2DY. *T:* 0171-589 7884. *Club:* Groucho.

JACKSON, Very Rev. Brandon Donald; Dean of Lincoln, since 1989; *b* 11 Aug. 1934; *s* of Herbert and Millicent Jackson; *m* 1958, Mary Lindsay, 2nd *d* of John and Helen Philip; two *s* one *d*. *Educ:* Stockport School; Liverpool Univ., St Catherine's Coll. and Wycliffe Hall, Oxford (LLB, DipTh). Curate: Christ Church, New Malden, Surrey, 1958–61; St George, Leeds, 1961–65; Vicar, St Peter, Shipley, Yorks, 1965–77; Provost of Bradford Cathedral, 1977–89. Religious Adviser to Yorkshire Television, 1969–79; Church Commissioner, 1971–73; Mem., Marriage Commn, 1975–78; Examining Chaplain to Bishop of Bradford, 1974–80; Member Council: Wycliffe Hall, Oxford, 1971–85; St John's Coll., Nottingham, 1987–89. Governor: Harrogate College, 1974–86; Bradford Grammar Sch., 1977–89; Bishop Grosseteste Coll., Lincoln, 1989–; Lincoln Christ's Hosp. Sch., 1989–. Hon. DLitt Bradford, 1990. *Recreations:* sport (cricket, squash), fell-walking, fishing. *Address:* The Deanery, Lincoln LN2 1QG. *T:* Lincoln (01522) 523608.

JACKSON, Air Chief Marshal Sir Brendan (James), GCB 1992 (KCB 1987); Air Member for Supply and Organisation, Ministry of Defence, 1988–93, retired; *b* 23 Aug. 1935; *m* 1959, Shirley Ann Norris; one *s* one *d*. *Educ:* Chichester High Sch. for Boys; London Univ. (BA Modern Japanese); qualified Interpreter. Joined RAF, 1956; flew Meteors, Canberras, Victors, B-52s; Sqdn Leader, 1965; RAF Staff Coll., 1966; PSO to C of S, HQ 2nd ATAF, 1969; Wing Comdr, 1972; US Armed Forces Staff Coll., 1972; PSO to CAS, 1974; Group Captain, 1977; Dir of Air Staff Plans, Dept of ACAS (Policy), MoD, 1980; Air Cdre, 1981; Air Vice-Marshal, 1984; ACOS (Policy), SHAPE, 1984; Air Marshal, 1986; COS and Dep. C-in-C, RAF Strike Comd, 1986–88; Air Chief Marshal, 1990. *Recreations:* reading, writing on defence, gardening, golf, ski-ing. *Club:* Royal Air Force.

JACKSON, Caroline Frances; Member (C) European Parliament, Wiltshire North and Bath, since 1994 (Wiltshire, 1984–94); *b* 5 Nov. 1946; *d* of G. H. Harvey; *m* 1975, Robert Victor Jackson, *qv;* one *s* decd. *Educ:* School of St Clare, Penzance; St Hugh's and Nuffield Colleges, Oxford. MA, DPhil. Elizabeth Wordsworth Research Fellow, St Hugh's College, Oxford, 1972. Oxford City Councillor, 1970–73; contested (C) Birmingham, Erdington, 1974. Secretariat of Cons. Group, European Parlt, 1974–79; Head, London Office, European Democratic Group, 1979–84. Dir, Peugeot Talbot (UK) Ltd, 1987–. Mem., Nat. Consumer Council, 1982–84. *Publications:* A Students Guide to Europe, 1988; Europe's Environment, 1989. *Recreations:* walking, painting, tennis, golf. *Address:* 74 Carlisle Mansions, Carlisle Place, SW1P 1HZ. *T:* 0171–828 6113, *Fax:* 0171–233 5244.

JACKSON, Christopher Murray; Chairman, CJA Consultants Ltd, since 1995; *b* 24 May 1935; *s* of Rev. Howard Murray Jackson and Doris Bessie Jackson (*née* Grainger); *m* 1971, Carlie Elizabeth Keeling; one *s* one *d*. *Educ:* Kingswood Sch., Bath; Magdalen Coll., Oxford (Open Exhibnr, BA Hons (Physics) 1959, MA 1964); Goethe Univ., Frankfurt; London Sch. of Economics. National Service, commnd RAF, Pilot, 1954–56. Unilever, 1959–69, Sen. Man., 1967; Gen. Marketing Man., Save and Prosper Gp, 1969–71; D. MacPherson Gp, 1971–74; Dir, Corporate Development Spillers Ltd, 1974–80. Contested (C): East Ham South, 1970; Northampton North, Feb. 1974. Member, Gen. Council, Cons. Gp for Europe, 1974–76. MEP (C) Kent E, 1979–94; contested (C) Kent E, Eur. Parly elecns, 1994; Hon. MEP, 1994–; European Parliament: EDG spokesman, on develt and co-op., 1981–87, on foreign affairs, 1991–92, on econ., monetary and indust. affairs, 1992–94; Cons. spokesman on agric., 1987–89, on foreign affairs, 1991–94; Mem., Bureau of EDG, 1984–91; Dep. Ldr, Cons. Members, 1989–91; Rapporteur-General, ACP-EEC Jt Assembly, 1985–86. Vice President: Assoc. of Dist Councils, 1980–95; Assoc. of Local Councils, 1984–; Assoc. of Port Health Authorities, 1989–. Treas. and Council Mem., St Martin-in-the-Fields, 1975–77. Pres., Kent Hotels and Restaurants Assoc., 1988–. *Publications:* Towards 2000—people centred development, 1986 (major report); (ed) Your European Watchdogs, 1990; The Maastricht Summit, 1992; Whose Job is it Anyway?—

decentralisation (or subsidiarity) and the EC, 1992; Working for the European Community, 1990, 2nd edn 1992; EDG Briefs on cars, Third World, and world hunger; pamphlets on Britain and Europe. *Recreations:* music, gardening, ski-ing, sailing. *Address:* (office) 8 Wellmeade Drive, Sevenoaks, Kent TN13 1QA. *T:* Sevenoaks (01732) 741117.

JACKSON, Daphne Diana; Assistant Personnel Officer, City Engineer's Department, City of Birmingham, 1986–93; *b* 8 Oct. 1933; *d* of Major Thomas Casey, MC, South Lancs Regt, and Agnes Nora Casey (*née* Gradden); *m* 1953, John Hudleston Jackson. *Educ:* Folkestone County Grammar School for Girls; South West London College. ACIS. Westminster Bank, 1951–53; Kent Educn Cttee, 1953–57; Pfizer Ltd, Sandwich, 1957–67; Southern Transformer Products, 1967–68; Borough of Hounslow, 1968–86, Personnel and Central Services Officer, Borough Engr and Surveyor's Dept, 1978–86. Mem., NACRO Employment Adv. Cttee, 1984–86; Chm., Gen. Adv. Council to IBA, 1985–89 (Mem., 1980). Mem., Soroptimists International (Vice Pres., Stratford-upon-Avon, 1994–95). Mem., Cleeve Prior PCC, 1991–; Gov., Cleeve Prior C of E Controlled First Sch., 1989–. Freeman, City of London, 1980; Liveryman, Chartered Secretaries and Administrators Co., 1980. *Recreations:* bereavement counselling, learning about antiques, reading. *Address:* 3 Manor Court, Cleeve Prior, Evesham, Worcs WR11 5LQ. *T:* Bidford-on-Avon (01789) 772817.

JACKSON, Prof. David Cooper; Vice-President, Immigration Appeal Tribunal, since 1984; Professor of Law (part time), since 1984, and Director, Institute of Maritime Law, 1987–90, University of Southampton; *b* 3 Dec. 1931; *s* of late Rev. James Jackson and of Mary Emma Jackson; *m* Roma Lilian (*née* Pendergast). *Educ:* Ashville Coll., Harrogate; Brasenose Coll., Oxford. MA, BCL; Senior Hulme Scholar, 1954. Called to the Bar, Inner Temple, 1957, and Victoria, Australia, 1967. Bigelow Fellow, Univ. of Chicago, 1955; Fellow, Assoc. of Bar of City of New York, 1956; National Service, 1957–59; Senior Lectr, Univ. of Singapore, 1963–64; Sir John Latham Prof. of Law, Monash Univ., 1965–70 (Carnegie Travelling Fellow, 1969); Prof. of Law, Southampton Univ., 1970–83 (Dean of Law, 1972–75, 1978–81; Dep. Vice-Chancellor, 1982–83); Consultant, UNCTAD, 1980, 1983. Visiting Professor: Queen Mary Coll., London, 1969; Arizona State Univ., 1976; Melbourne Univ., 1976. JP Hants 1980–84. Editor, World Shipping Laws, 1979– (and contrib.). *Publications:* Principles of Property Law, 1967; The Conflicts Process, 1975; Enforcement of Maritime Claims, 1985; Civil Jurisdiction and Judgments: maritime claims, 1987; articles in legal jls, Australia, UK, USA. *Recreations:* walking, travel, theatre. *Address:* Fleet House, 9A Captains Row, Lymington, Hants SO41 9RP.

JACKSON, Sir Edward; *see* Jackson, Sir J. E.

JACKSON, Francis Alan, OBE 1978; Organist and Master of the Music, York Minster, 1946–82, Organist Emeritus, since 1988; *b* 2 Oct. 1917; *s* of W. A. Jackson; *m* 1950, Priscilla, *d* of Tyndale Procter; two *s* one *d*. *Educ:* York Minster Choir Sch.; Sir Edward Bairstow. Chorister, York Minster, 1929–33; ARCO, 1936; BMus Dunelm 1937; FRCO (Limpus Prize), 1937; DMus Dunelm 1957. Organist Malton Parish Church, 1933–40. Served War of 1939–45, with 9th Lancers in Egypt, N Africa and Italy, 1940–46. Asst Organist, York Minster, 1946; Conductor York Musical Soc., 1947–82; Conductor York Symphony Orchestra, 1947–80. Pres. Incorp. Assoc. of Organists, 1960–62; Pres., RCO, 1972–74. Hon. FRSCM 1963; Hon. Fellow, Westminster Choir Coll., Princeton, NJ, 1970; Hon. FRNCM, 1982. DUniv York, 1983. Order of St William of York, 1983. *Publications:* organ music, including 4 sonatas, symphony, organ concerto, church music, songs, monodramas. *Recreation:* gardening. *Address:* Nether Garth, East Acklam, Malton, N Yorks YO17 9RG. *T:* Burythorpe (01653) 658395.

JACKSON, Gerald Breck; *b* 28 June 1916; *o s* of Gerald Breck Jackson and Mary Jackson, Paterson, NJ; *m* 1940, Brenda Mary, *o d* of William and Mary Titshall; one *s*. *Educ:* various schs in USA; Canford Sch., Dorset; Faraday House Engrg Coll. Graduate Trainee, Central Electricity Bd, 1938. HM Forces, RE, 1939–43. Various appts in HV transmission with CEB and BEA, 1943–55; Overhead Line Design Engr, BEA, 1955–61; Asst Regional Dir, CEGB, 1961–64; Chief Ops Engr, CEGB, 1964–66; Regional Dir, NW Region, CEGB, 1966–68; Dir Engineering, English Electric Co. Ltd, 1968–69; Sen. Exec., Thomas Tilling Ltd, and Dir subsid. cos, 1969–71; Man. Dir, John Mowlem & Co. Ltd, 1971–72; Man. Dir, NCB (Ancillaries) Ltd, 1972–78. DFH, CEng, FIEE. *Publications:* Network for the Nation, 1960; Power Controlled, 1966. *Recreations:* photography, pen-and-ink drawing. *Address:* Larchwood, 1A Lansdowne Square, Tunbridge Wells, Kent TN1 2NF.

JACKSON, Glenda, CBE 1978; MP (Lab) Hampstead and Highgate, since 1992; Director, United British Artists, since 1983; *b* Birkenhead, 9 May 1936; *d* of Harry and Joan Jackson; *m* 1958, Roy Hodges (marr. diss. 1976); one *s*. *Educ:* West Kirby Co. Grammar Sch. for Girls; RADA. Actress with various repertory cos, 1957–63, stage manager, Crewe Rep.; joined Royal Shakespeare Co., 1963. Pres., Play Matters (formerly Toy Libraries Assoc.), 1976–. *Plays:* All Kinds of Men, Arts, 1957; The Idiot, Lyric, 1962; Alfie, Mermaid and Duchess, 1963; Royal Shakespeare Co.: Theatre of Cruelty Season, LAMDA, 1964; The Jew of Malta, 1964; Marat/Sade, 1965, NY and Paris, 1965; Love's Labour's Lost, Squire Puntila and his Servant Matti, The Investigation, Hamlet, 1965; US, Aldwych, 1966; Three Sisters, Royal Ct, 1967; Fanghorn, Fortune, 1967; Collaborators, Duchess, 1973; The Maids, Greenwich, 1974; Hedda Gabler, Australia, USA, London, 1975; The White Devil, Old Vic, 1976; Stevie, Vaudeville, 1977; Antony and Cleopatra, Stratford, 1978; Rose, Duke of York's, 1980; Summit Conference, Lyric, 1982; Great and Small, Vaudeville, 1983; Strange Interlude, Duke of York's, 1984; Phedra, Old Vic, 1984, Aldwych, 1985; Across from the Garden of Allah, Comedy, 1986; The House of Bernarda Alba, Globe, 1986; Macbeth, NY, 1988; Scenes from an Execution, Almeida, 1990; Mother Courage, Mermaid, 1990; *films:* This Sporting Life, 1963; Marat/Sade, 1967; Negatives, 1968; Women in Love (Oscar Award, 1971), 1970; The Music Lovers, 1971; Sunday, Bloody Sunday, 1971; The Boyfriend, 1972; Mary, Queen of Scots, 1972; Triple Echo, 1972; Il Sorviso de Grande Tentatore (The Tempter), 1973; Bequest to the Nation, 1973; A Touch of Class (Oscar Award, 1974), 1973; The Maids, 1974; The Romantic Englishwoman, 1974; Hedda Gabler, 1975; The Incredible Sarah, 1976; House Calls, 1978; Stevie, 1978; The Class of Miss MacMichael, 1978; Lost and Found, 1979; Hopscotch, 1980; Return of the Soldier, 1982; Health, 1982; Giro City, 1982; Sacharov, 1983; Turtle Diary, 1985; Business as Usual, 1987; Beyond Therapy, 1987; Salome's Last Dance, 1988; The Rainbow, 1989; The Secret Life of Sir Arnold Bax, 1992; *TV:* Elizabeth in Elizabeth R, 1971; The Patricia Neal Story (Amer.). Best film actress awards: Variety Club of GB, 1971, 1975, 1978; NY Film Critics, 1971; Nat. Soc. of Film Critics, US, 1971. *Recreations:* cooking, gardening, reading Jane Austen. *Address:* c/o House of Commons, SW1A 0AA.

JACKSON, Gordon Noel, CMG 1962; MBE; HM Ambassador to Ecuador, 1967–70, retired; *b* 25 Dec. 1913; *m* 1959, Mary April Nettlefold, *er d* of late Frederick John Nettlefold and of Mrs Albert Coates; one *s* two *d*. Indian Political Service until 1947; then HM Foreign Service; Political Officer, Sharjah, 1947; transf. to Kuwait, Persian Gulf, 1949; transf. to Foreign Office, 1950; Consul, St Louis, USA, 1953; Foreign Service Officer, Grade 6, 1955; Consul-General: Basra, 1955–57; Lourenço Marques, 1957–60; Benghazi, 1960–63; HM Ambassador to Kuwait, 1963–67. *Publications:* Effective Horsemanship (for Dressage, Hunting, Three-day Events, Polo), 1967; (with W. Steinkraus) The Encyclopædia of the Horse, 1973. *Address:* Lowbarrow House, Leafield, Witney, Oxfordshire OX8 5NH. *T:* Asthall Leigh (01993) 878443. *Club:* Travellers'.

JACKSON, Helen Margaret, (Mrs Keith Jackson); MP (Lab) Sheffield, Hillsborough, since 1992; *b* 19 May 1939; *d* of Stanley Price and Katherine (*née* Thornton); *m* 1960, Keith Jackson; two *s* one *d*. *Educ:* St Hilda's Coll., Oxford (BA Hons Mod. Hist., MA); C. F. Mott Coll. of Educn, Prescot (Cert Ed 1972). Asst Librarian, 1961; mother, housewife and voluntary worker, 1961–72; teacher, 1972–80; City Cllr, Sheffield, 1980–91 (Chm., Public Works and Econ. Develt Cttees). Founder Mem. and Chair, Centre for Local Economic Strategies, 1986–91. Co-Chair, PLP Women's Gp, 1992–; Mem., Envmt Select Cttee, 1992–. *Recreations:* walking, music. *Address:* 6 Stephen Lane, Grenoside, Sheffield S30 3QZ. *T:* Sheffield (0114) 246 3162.
See also Christopher Price.

JACKSON, Ian (Macgilchrist), BA Cantab, MB, BChir, FRCS, FRCOG; Obstetric and Gynæcological Surgeon, Middlesex Hospital, 1948–79, retired; Gynæcological Surgeon: Chelsea Hospital for Women, 1948–79; King Edward VII Hospital for Officers, 1961–84; Royal Masonic Hospital, 1963–79; Consulting Gynæcologist, King Edward VII Hospital, Midhurst, 1959; Consultant Obstetrician and Gynæcologist, RAF, 1964–83; *b* Shanghai, 11 Nov. 1914; *s* of Dr Ernest David Jackson; *m* 1943 (marr. diss., 1967); two *s* one *d*; *m* 1970, Deirdre Ruth Heitz. *Educ:* Marlborough Coll.; Trinity Hall, Cambridge (scholar; double 1st cl. hons, Nat. Sci. tripos pts I, II). London Hospital: open scholarship, 1936; house appointments, 1939; First Asst, Surgical and Obstetric and Gynæcol Depts, 1940–43. Served as Surgical Specialist, RAMC, 1943–47 (Major); Parachute Surgical Team, 224 Para. Field Amb.; Mobile Surgical Unit, 3 Commando Brigade. Royal College of Obstetricians and Gynæcologists: Council, 1951–61, 1962–70; Hon. Sec., 1954–61; Chm., Examination Cttee, 1962–65, Hon. Treas., 1966–70; Hon. Librarian, RSM, 1969–75. Examiner for Univs of Cambridge, Oxford, and London, Conjoint Bd and RCOG. Mem., Court of Assts, Worshipful Soc. of Apothecaries, 1966, Senior Warden 1977, Master 1978, Hon. Treas., 1985–89; President: Chelsea Clinical Soc., 1979; Sydenham Medical Club, 1987–90. Order of the Star of Africa (Liberia), 1969; Grand Officer of Order of Istiqlal, Jordan, 1970. *Publications:* British Obstetric and Gynæcological Practice (jtly), 1963; Obstetrics by Ten Teachers (jtly), 1966, 2nd edn 1972; Gynæcology by Ten Teachers (jtly), 1971; numerous contribs to medical literature. *Recreations:* fishing, golf, photography. *Address:* 23 Springfield Road, NW8 0QJ. *T:* 0171–624 3580.

JACKSON, Jane Therese, (Tessa Jackson); Director, Arnolfini, Bristol, since 1991; *b* 5 Nov. 1955; *d* of John Nevil Jackson and Viva Christian Therese Jackson (*née* Blomfield). *Educ:* Univ. of East Anglia (BA Hons Fine Art); Univ. of Manchester (Dip. Museum Studies). Art Editor, OUP, 1979–80; Exhibns Organiser, SPAB, 1981–82; Curator, Eyemouth Museum, 1982; Curator, Collins Gallery, Univ. of Strathclyde, 1982–88; Visual Arts Officer, Glasgow 1990—European City of Culture, 1988–91. *Publications:* (with John R. Hume) George Washington Wilson and Victorian Glasgow, 1983; (jtly) Signs of the Times: art and industry in Scotland 1750–1985, 1985; (ed jtly) A Platform for Partnership (Glasgow City Council), 1991. *Recreations:* travel, walking, architecture. *Address:* Arnolfini, 16 Narrow Quay, Bristol BS1 4QA. *T:* Bristol (0117) 929 9191.

JACKSON, Sir (John) Edward, KCMG 1984 (CMG 1977); HM Diplomatic Service, retired; Chairman, Spadel Ltd (formerly Brecon Beacons Natural Waters Ltd), since 1985; *b* 24 June 1925; *s* of late Edward and Margaret Jackson; *m* 1952, Eve Stainton Harris, *d* of late George James Harris, MC and Mrs Friede Rowntree Harris, York; two *s* one *d*. *Educ:* Ardingly; Corpus Christi Coll., Cambridge. RNVR (Sub-Lt), 1943–46; joined Foreign (now Diplomatic) Service, 1947; FO, 1947–49; 3rd Sec., Paris, 1949–52; 2nd Sec., FO, 1952–56; 1st Sec., Bonn, 1956–59; Guatemala City, 1959–62; FO, 1963–68; Counsellor, 1968; NATO Defence Coll., Rome, 1969; Counsellor (Political Adviser), British Mil. Govt, Berlin, 1969–73; Head of Defence Dept, FCO, 1973–75; Ambassador to Cuba, 1975–79; Head of UK Delegn to Negotiations on Mutual Reduction of Forces and Armaments and Associated Measures in Central Europe, with personal rank of Ambassador, 1980–82; Ambassador to Belgium, 1982–85. Director: Herbert Mueller Ltd and associated cos, 1987–90. Dir, Armistice Festival, 1986–89. Chm., Anglo-Belgian Soc., 1987–; Dep. Chm., Belgo-Luxembourg Chamber of Commerce, 1987–. Trustee, Imperial War Museum, 1986–. Vice-Pres., Internat. Menuhin Assoc., 1991–. *Recreations:* the arts, tennis. *Address:* 17 Paultons Square, SW3 5AP. *Clubs:* Royal Anglo-Belgian (Dir, 1993–), Hurlingham.

JACKSON, John Henry; Company Secretary, British Gas, since 1990; *b* 7 Aug. 1948; *s* of John and May Jackson; *m* 1975, Patricia Mary Robinson; one *s* one *d*. *Educ:* Trinity School, Croydon; St Catherine's College, Oxford (MA). FCIS. Joined SE Gas Board, 1970; Asst Sec., 1977, Sen. Asst Sec., 1983, British Gas Corp., later British Gas plc. *Address:* Rivermill House, 152 Grosvenor Road, SW1V 3JL. *T:* 0171–611 2334.

JACKSON, (John) Patrick; Director, British Council, Portugal, since 1993; *b* 18 Sept. 1940; *s* of Godfrey Jackson and Mary Jackson (*née* Worthington); *m* 1st, 1963, Marieliese de Vos van Steenwyk (marr. diss.); three *d* (and one *d* decd); 2nd, 1978, Hélène Mellotte; two *d*. *Educ:* Worksop Coll.; Midhurst Grammar Sch.; New Coll., Oxford (MA); Moscow Univ. (postgrad. studies); London Univ. Inst. of Educn (postgrad. Cert Ed). British Council, 1963–: English Language Teaching Inst., London, 1964–66; Asst Dir, Bahrain, 1966–69; Asst Cultural Attaché, Moscow, 1969–71; Dep. Dir, Higher Educn Dept, 1971–73; Regl Dir, Calcutta, 1973–75; Dir, N Europe Dept, 1975–79; Rep., Senegal, 1979–83; Regl Dir, São Paulo, 1983–88; Dep. Controller, Home Div., 1988–91; Dir, Exchanges and Training Div., 1991–93. *Recreations:* birdwatching, windsurfing, bridge. *Address:* c/o British Council, 10 Spring Gardens, SW1A 2BN.

JACKSON, Judith Mary; QC 1994; *b* 18 Sept. 1950; *d* of Thomas Worthington Jackson and Betty Jackson (*née* Kinsey); one *d*. *Educ:* Queen Mary College, London. LLB, LLM. Called to the Bar, Inner Temple, 1975. Chm., Young Barristers' Cttee, 1984–85. *Recreations:* music, cycling, gardening, dog-walking. *Address:* 9 Old Square, Lincoln's Inn, WC2A 3SR. *T:* 0171–405 4682.

JACKSON, (Kevin) Paul; Managing Director: Carlton Television, since 1993; Carlton UK Productions, since 1994; *b* 2 Oct. 1947; *s* of late T. Leslie Jackson and of Jo (*née* Spoonley); *m* 1981, Judith Elizabeth Cain; two *d*. *Educ:* Gunnersbury Grammar Sch.; Univ. of Exeter (BA 1970); Stanford Univ. (Sen. Exec. Program 1993). Stage manager: Marlowe Theatre, Canterbury, 1970; Thorndike Theatre, Leatherhead, 1971. BBC Television: Production Assistant, 1971–79; Producer, 1979–82: programmes include: The Two Ronnies, Three of a Kind (BAFTA Award 1982), Carrot's Lib, The Young Ones (BAFTA Award 1984), Happy Families; freelance producer and director, 1982–84: programmes include: Cannon & Ball, Girls On Top; Producer and Chm., Paul Jackson Prodns Ltd, 1984–86: programmes include: Red Dwarf, Don't Miss Wax, Saturday Live; Man. Dir, Noel Gay TV, 1987–91: progs include The Appointments of Dennis Jennings (Oscar for Best Live Action Short, 1989); Dir of Progs, Carlton TV, 1991. Chairman: RTS, 1994–; Comic Relief, 1987–; Charity Projects, 1992–. FInstD 1992; FRTS 1993.

Recreations: my family, theatre, Rugby, travel, food and wine. *Address:* (office) 101 St Martin's Lane, WC2N 4AZ. *T:* 0171–240 4000. *Club:* Groucho.

JACKSON, Very Rev. Lawrence, AKC; Provost of Blackburn, 1973–92, Provost Emeritus 1992; *b* Hessle, Yorks, 22 March 1926; *s* of Walter and Edith Jackson; *m* 1955, Faith Anne, *d* of Philip and Marjorie Seymour; four *d*. *Educ:* Alderman Newton's Sch.; Leicester Coll. of Technology; King's Coll., Univ. of London (AKC 1950); St Boniface Coll., Warminster. Asst Curate, St Margaret, Leicester, and Asst Chaplain, Leicester Royal Infirmary, 1951–54; Vicar of: Wymeswold, Leicester, 1954–59; St James the Greater, Leicester, 1959–65; Coventry (Holy Trinity), 1965–73. Canon of Coventry Cath., 1967–73; Rural Dean of Coventry N, 1969–73. Senior Chaplain: Leicester and Rutland ACF, 1955–65; Warwickshire ACF, 1965–73; Chaplain, Coventry Guild of Freemen, 1968–73; Dio. Chaplain, CEMS, 1969–71. Mem., Gen. Synod of C of E, 1975–92; a Church Comr, 1981–92. Dir, The Samaritans of Leicester, 1960–65; Pres., Coventry Round Table, 1968; Governor, Queen Elizabeth Grammar Sch., Blackburn, 1973–92. *Publication:* Services for Special Occasions, 1982. *Recreations:* music, archæology, architecture, countryside, after dinner speaking. *Address:* Northcot, Brook Lane, Newbold-on-Stour, Stratford-upon-Avon, Warwicks CV37 8UA. *T:* Stratford-upon-Avon (01789) 450721. *Clubs:* Carlton, Forty, Lighthouse; Lord's Taverners'.

JACKSON, Michael; Controller, BBC 2, since 1993; *b* 11 Feb. 1958; *s* of Ernest Jackson and Margaret (*née* Kearsley). *Educ:* King's Sch., Macclesfield; Poly. of Central London (BA (Hons) Media Studies). Organiser, Channel Four Gp, 1979; Producer, The Sixties, 1982; Independent Producer, Beat Productions Ltd, 1983–87, produced Whose Town is it Anyway?, Open the Box, The Media Show; joined BBC Television; Editor: The Late Show (BFI Television Award), 1988–90; Late Show Productions, 1990–91, progs incl. The Nelson Mandela Tribute, Tales from Prague (Grierson Documentary Award), Moving Pictures, The American Late Show (PBS), Naked Hollywood (BAFTA Award, Best Factual Series); Head of Music and Arts, BBC Television, 1991–93; progs produced, 1991–, incl. Sounds of the Sixties, The Lime Grove Story, TV Hell. Hon. DLitt Westminster, 1995. *Recreations:* reading, walking. *Address:* c/o BBC TV, Room 6066, Television Centre, Wood Lane, W12 7RJ.

JACKSON, Maj.-Gen. Michael David, CBE 1992 (MBE 1979); General Officer Commanding 3 (UK) Division, since 1994; *b* 21 March 1944; *s* of George Jackson and Ivy (*née* Bower); *m* 1985, Sarah Coombe; two *s* one *d*. *Educ:* Stamford Sch.; RMA Sandhurst; Birmingham Univ. (BSocSc 1967). Commnd Intelligence Corps, 1963; transf. to Parachute Regt, 1970; Staff Coll., 1976; Bde Major, Berlin, 1977–78; ndc 1981; DS, Staff Coll., 1981–83; Comd 1st Bn Parachute Regt, 1984–86; Sen. DS, Jt Service Defence Coll., 1986–88; Services Fellow, Wolfson Coll., Cambridge, 1989; Comdr, 39 Inf. Bde, 1990–92; Dir Gen. Personal Services (Army), MoD, 1992–94. Hon. Col 10th (V) Bn, Parachute Regt TA, 1994–. Freeman, City of London, 1988. *Recreations:* travel, music, ski-ing, tennis. *Address:* RHQ The Parachute Regiment, Browning Barracks, Aldershot, Hants GU11 2BU.

JACKSON, (Michael) Rodney; a Recorder, since 1985; Consultant, Andrew M. Jackson & Co., Solicitors, since 1994 (Partner, 1964–94; Senior Partner, 1992–94); *b* 16 April 1935; *s* of John William Jackson and Nora Jackson (*née* Phipps); *m* 1968, Anne Margaret, *d* of Prof. E. W. Hawkins, *qv;* two *s*. *Educ:* Queen Elizabeth Grammar Sch., Wakefield; Queens' Coll., Cambridge (MA, LLM). Admitted Solicitor of the Supreme Court, 1962; Notary Public, 1967. *Recreations:* fell walking, railway photography. *Address:* Andrew M. Jackson & Co., PO Box 47, Essex House, Manor Street, Hull HU1 1XU. *T:* Hull (01482) 25242.

JACKSON, Sir Michael (Roland), 5th Bt *cr* 1902; MA; CEng, MIEE; FIQA; *b* 20 April 1919; *s* of Sir W. D. Russell Jackson, 4th Bt, and Kathleen (*d* 1975), *d* of Summers Hunter, CBE, Tynemouth; *S* father 1956; *m* 1st, 1942, Hilda Margaret (marr. diss. 1969), *d* of late Cecil George Herbert Richardson, CBE, Newark; one *s* one *d*; 2nd, 1969, Hazel Mary, *d* of late Ernest Harold Edwards. *Educ:* Stowe; Clare Coll., Cambridge. Served War of 1939–45; Flight-Lt, Royal Air Force Volunteer Reserve. *Heir: s* Thomas St Felix Jackson [*b* 27 Sept. 1946; *m* 1980, Victoria, *d* of George Scatliff, Wineham, Sussex; two *d*]. *Address:* Jolliffe's House, Stour Row, Shaftesbury, Dorset SP7 0QW.

JACKSON, Michael Walter; Under Secretary and Head of Marine Directorate, Department of Transport, 1993–94, retired; *b* 5 April 1934; *s* of late William Henry Jackson and Nellie Jackson; *m* 1963, Mary Bruce Hope Sinclair; one *s* one *d*. *Educ:* Queen Elizabeth Grammar Sch., Wakefield; Queen's Coll., Oxford (MA Lit. Hum.). UKAEA, 1959–68; joined MoT, 1968; Assistant Secretary: MoT, 1973–76; PSA, 1976–80; Dept of Transport, 1980–93. *Recreations:* hill-walking, opera. *Address:* 41 Elmwood, Welwyn Garden City, Herts, AL8 6LD. *T:* Welwyn Garden (01707) 323830.

JACKSON, Mrs Muriel W.; *see* Ward-Jackson.

JACKSON, Sir Nicholas (Fane St George), 3rd Bt *cr* 1913; organist, harpsichordist and composer; Director, Concertante of London, since 1987; *b* 4 Sept. 1934; *s* of Sir Hugh Jackson, 2nd Bt, and of Violet Marguerite Loftus, *y d* of Loftus St George; *S* father, 1979; *m* 1972, Nadia Françoise Genevieve (*née* Michard); one *s*. *Educ:* Radley Coll.; Wadham Coll., Oxford; RAM. LRAM; ARCM. Organist: St Anne's, Soho, 1963–68; St James's, Piccadilly, 1971–74; St Lawrence, Jewry, 1974–77; Organist and Master of the Choristers, St David's Cathedral, 1977–84. Musical Dir, St David's Cathedral Bach Fest., 1979; Dir, Bach Festival, Santes Creus, Spain, 1987–. Organ recitals and broadcasts: Berlin, 1967; Paris, 1972, 1975; USA (tour), 1975, 1978, 1980 and 1989; Minorca, 1977; Spain, 1979; Madrid Bach Festival, 1980; RFH, 1984; concert tours of Spain and Germany, annually 1980–. Début as harpsichordist, Wigmore Hall, 1963; directed Soho Concertante, Queen Elizabeth Hall, 1964–72. Mem. Music Cttee, Welsh Arts Council, 1981–. Examiner, Trinity Coll. of Music, 1985–. Recordings: Mass for a Saint's Day, 1971; organ and harpsichord music, incl. works by Arnell, Bach, Couperin, Langlais, Mozart, Vierne and Walther; Spanish organ music. Liveryman: Drapers' Co., 1965 (Master, 1994–95); Musicians' Co., 1985. Hon. Fellow, Hertford Coll., Oxford, 1995. *Publications: compositions:* Mass for a Saint's Day, 1966; 20th Century Merbecke, 1967; 4 Images (for organ), 1971; Solemn Mass, 1977; Divertissement (organ), 1983; Organ Mass, 1984; 2 Organ Sonatas, 1985; Suite, for brass quintet and organ, 1986; The Reluctant Highwayman (opera), 1992 (world première, 1995). *Recreations:* sketching, writing. *Heir: s* Thomas Graham St George Jackson, *b* 5 Oct. 1980.

JACKSON, Oliver James V.; *see* Vaughan-Jackson.

JACKSON, Patrick; *see* Jackson, J. P.

JACKSON, Patrick; *see* Jackson, W. P.

JACKSON, Paul; *see* Jackson, K. P.

JACKSON, Peter John Edward; His Honour Judge Jackson; a Circuit Judge, since 1992; *b* 14 May 1944; *s* of late David Charles Jackson and of Sarah Ann (*née* Manester); *m* 1967, Ursula, *y d* of late Paul and Henny Schubert, Hamburg, W Germany; two *d*. *Educ:* Brockley County Grammar Sch.; Sprachen und Dolmetscher Inst., Hamburg; London Univ. (LLB Hons 1967); Tübingen Univ., W Germany (Dr jur. 1987). Called to the Bar, Middle Temple, 1968 (Blackstone Scholar; Churchill Prize); called to the Bar of NI, 1982. Dep. Circuit Judge, 1979–81; Asst Recorder, 1982–83; a Recorder, 1983–92; Attorney Gen.'s List of Prosecuting Counsel, 1985–92; Partner, Campbell and Jackson Internat. Arbitral and Legal Consultants, Brussels, Stuttgart, Paris, 1985–90; Overseas Mem., Law Offices of Dr Brauner and Colleagues, Stuttgart, 1982–92. Mem., Arbitration Panel, ICC, 1990–92; Co-opted Mem., Internat. Practice Cttee, Bar Council, 1991–92. Approved Supervisor, Judicial and Legal Trainees in England, German Ministries of Justice and German Attorneys' Assoc., 1987–. Speaker/Chm., legal seminars in England and overseas, 1987–. Chm., St Leonard's Soc., Ilford, 1993–. Gov., Newbold Coll., Bracknell, 1991–. ACIArb 1983. *Recreations:* horse riding, German Law, the German language, travel. *Address:* 3 Pump Court, Temple, EC4Y 7AJ. *T:* 071–353 0711; D7000 Stuttgart 50, Seelbergstrasse 8, W Germany. *T:* (0711) 561456, *Fax:* (0711) 552407.

JACKSON, Peter (Michael); Senior Lecturer, in Industrial Studies, Institute of Extra-mural Studies, National University of Lesotho, 1980; *b* 14 Oct. 1928; *s* of Leonard Patterson Jackson; *m* 1961, Christine Thomas. *Educ:* Durham Univ.; University Coll., Leicester. Lecturer, Dept of Sociology, University of Hull, 1964–66; Fellow, Univ. of Hull, 1970–72; Tutor, Open Univ., 1972–74; Senior Planning Officer, S Yorks CC, 1974–77. MP (Lab) High Peak, 1966–70; contested (Lab) Birmingham North, European Parly elecns, 1979. Member: Peak Park Jt Planning Bd, 1973–77, 1979–82; Derby CC, 1973–77. *Recreations:* numismatics, book collecting, ski-ing. *Address:* 82 Vandon Court, Petty France, SW1H 9HG. *Club:* Maseru (Lesotho).

JACKSON, Raymond Allen, (JAK); Cartoonist, Evening Standard, since 1952; *b* 11 March 1927; *s* of Maurice Jackson and Mary Ann Murphy; *m* 1957, Claudie Sidone Grenier; one *s* two *d*. *Educ:* Lyulph Stanley Central; Willesden School of Art (NDD). Army, 1945–48. General artist, Link House Publishing, 1950–51; Keymers Advertising Agency, 1951–52; Evening Standard, 1952–. *Publications:* JAK Annual, 1969–. *Recreations:* golf, walking. *Clubs:* St James', Special Forces.

JACKSON, Richard Michael, CVO 1983; HM Diplomatic Service; Ambassador to Costa Rica, since 1995; *b* 12 July 1940; *s* of Richard William Jackson and Charlotte (*née* Wrightson); *m* 1961, Mary Elizabeth Kitchin; one *s* one *d*. *Educ:* Queen Elizabeth Grammar Sch., Darlington; Paisley Grammar Sch.; Glasgow Univ. (MA Hons 1961). Joined Home Civil Service, 1961; Scottish Office, 1961–70; seconded to MAFF, 1971–72; seconded to FCO and served in The Hague, 1973–74; trans. to HM Diplomatic Service, 1974; European Integration Dept (External), FCO, 1975–76; Panama City, 1976–79; Arms Control and Disarmament Dept, FCO, 1979–81; Buenos Aires, 1981–82; Falkland Islands Dept, FCO, 1982; Stockholm, 1982–87; Dep. Head of Mission, Seoul, 1987–91; Ambassador to Bolivia, 1991–95. *Recreations:* birdwatching, real ale. *Address:* c/o Foreign and Commonwealth Office, King Charles Street, SW1A 2AH.

JACKSON, Sir Robert, 7th Bt *cr* 1815; *b* 16 March 1910; *s* of Major Francis Gorham Jackson (*d* 1942) (2nd *s* of 4th Bt) and Ana Maria Biscar Brennan; *S* kinsman, Sir John Montrésor Jackson, 6th Bt, 1980; *m* 1943, Maria E. Casamayou; two *d*. *Educ:* St George's College. Career on estancia. *Heir: kinsman* Keith Arnold Jackson [*b* 1921; *m* Pauline Mona, *d* of B. P. Climo, Wellington, NZ; four *s* one *d*]. *Address:* Boulevard Artigas 266, Flat 601, Montevideo, Uruguay. *T:* (2) 715032. *Club:* English (Montevideo).

JACKSON, Robert Victor; MP (C) Wantage, since 1983; *b* 24 Sept. 1946; *m* 1975, Caroline Frances Harvey (*see* C. F. Jackson), one *s* decd. *Educ:* Falcon Coll., S Rhodesia; St Edmund Hall, Oxford (H. W. C. Davis Prize, 1966, 1st Cl. Hons Mod. Hist. 1968); President Oxford Union, 1967. Prize Fellowship, All Souls Coll., 1968 (Fellow, 1968–86). Councillor, Oxford CC, 1969–71; Political Adviser to Sec. of State for Employment, 1973–74; Member, Cabinet of Sir Christopher Soames, EEC Commn, Brussels, 1974–76, Chef de Cabinet, President of EEC Economic and Social Cttee, Brussels, 1976–78; Mem. (C) Upper Thames, European Parlt, 1979–84; Special Adviser to Governor of Rhodesia (Lord Soames), 1979–80; European Parlt's Rapporteur-Gen. on 1983 European Community Budget. Parly Under Sec. of State, DES, 1987–90, Dept of Employment, 1990–92, Office of Public Service and Sci., 1992–93. Contested (C) Manchester Central Div., Oct. 1974. Editor: The Round Table: Commonwealth Jl of Internat. Relations, 1970–74; International Affairs (Chatham House), 1979–80. *Publications:* South Asian Crisis: India, Pakistan, Bangladesh 1972, 1975; The Powers of the European Parliament, 1977; The European Parliament: Penguin Guide to Direct Elections, 1979; Reforming the European Budget, 1981; Tradition and Reality: Conservative philosophy and European integration 1982; From Boom to Bust?—British farming and CAP reform, 1983; Political Ideas in Western Europe Today, 1984. *Recreations:* reading, music, walking. *Address:* House of Commons, SW1A 0AA.

JACKSON, Rodney; *see* Jackson, M. R.

JACKSON, Roy Arthur; Assistant General Secretary, Trades Union Congress, 1984–92; *b* 18 June 1928; *s* of Charles Frederick Jackson and Harriet Betsy (*née* Ridewood); *m* 1956, Lilian May Ley; three *d*. *Educ:* North Paddington Central Sch.; Ruskin Coll., Oxford (DipEcon Pol Sci (Distinction)); Worcester Coll., Oxford (BA Hons, PPE). Post Office Savings Bank, 1942; RN, Ord. Signalman, 1946–48. Trades Union Congress: joined Educn Dept, 1956; Dir of Studies, 1964; Head of Educn, 1974–84. Member: Albemarle Cttee of Youth Service, 1958–60; Open Univ. Cttee on Continuing Educn, 1975–76; Adv. Cttee for Continuing and Adult Educn, 1977–83; Schools Council Convocation, 1978–82; Further Educn Unit, DES, 1980–; Employment Appeal Tribunal, 1992–; served on a number of MSC bodies, 1978–85; TUC Comr, MSC, 1987–88. Lay Mem., Council of Legal Educn, 1994–. Non-exec. Dir, Remploy Ltd, 1992–. *Recreations:* walking, reading, gardening. *Address:* 27 The Ryde, Hatfield, Herts AL9 5DQ. *T:* Hatfield (017072) 63790.

JACKSON, Rupert Matthew; QC 1987; a Recorder, since 1990; *b* 7 March 1948; *s* of late George Henry Jackson and Nancy Barbara Jackson (*née* May); *m* 1975, Claire Corinne Potter; three *d*. *Educ:* Christ's Hospital; Jesus College, Cambridge (MA, LLB). Pres., Cambridge Union, 1971. Called to the Bar, Middle Temple, 1972, Bencher, 1995. FRSA 1988. *Publication:* Professional Negligence, 1982, 3rd edn 1992. *Address:* 2 Crown Office Row, Temple, EC4Y 7HJ. *T:* 0171–797–8000. *Club:* Reform.

JACKSON, Tessa; *see* Jackson, J. T.

JACKSON, Sir Thomas; *see* Jackson, Sir W. T.

JACKSON, Thomas; General Secretary, Union of Communication Workers (formerly Post Office Workers), 1967–82; bookseller; *b* 9 April 1925; *s* of George Frederick Jackson and Ethel Hargreaves; *m* 1st, 1947, Norma Burrow (marr. diss. 1982); one *d*; 2nd, 1982, Kathleen Maria Tognarelli; one *d*. *Educ:* Jack Lane Elementary Sch. Boy Messenger, GPO, 1939; Royal Navy, 1943; Postman, 1946; Executive Mem., Union of Post Office Workers, 1955; Asst Sec., Union of Post Office Workers, 1964. HM Government Dir, British Petroleum, 1975–83. Member: Gen. Council of TUC, 1967–82 (Chm., 1978–79; Chm.,

Internat. Cttee, 1978–82); Press Council, 1973–76; Annan Cttee on the Future of Broadcasting, 1974–77; CRE, 1977–78; Broadcasting Complaints Commn, 1982–87; Yorks Water Authority, 1983–89. Non-exec. Dir, Yorks Water plc, 1989–. Member: Court and Council, Sussex Univ., 1974–78; Council, Bradford Univ., 1987–90. Vice-Pres., WEA, 1977–; Chm., Ilkley Literature Fest., 1984–87. A Governor: BBC, 1968–73; NIESR, 1974–85. *Recreations:* cooking, photography. *Address:* 22 Parish Ghyll Road, Ilkley, West Yorks LS29 9NE.

JACKSON, (Walter) Patrick, CB 1987; Under-Secretary, Department of Transport, 1981–89, retired; *b* 10 Feb. 1929; *m* 1952, Kathleen Roper; one *s* one *d*. *Educ:* University Coll., Oxford. John Lewis Partnership, 1952–66; Principal, Min. of Transport and DoE, 1966–72; Asst Sec., DoE, 1972–78; Under Sec. and Regional Dir (E Midlands), DoE and Dept of Transport, 1978–81. *Publication:* The Last of the Whigs, 1994. *Recreations:* concert- and theatre-going, historical research.

JACKSON, Gen. Sir William (Godfrey Fothergill), GBE 1975 (OBE 1958); KCB 1971; MC 1940, and Bar, 1943; Military Historian, Cabinet Office, 1977–78 and 1982–87; Governor and Commander-in-Chief, Gibraltar, 1978–82; *b* 28 Aug. 1917; *s* of late Col A. Jackson, RAMC, Yanwath, Cumberland, and E. M. Jackson (*née* Fothergill), Brownber, Westmorland; *m* 1946, Joan Mary Buesden; one *s* one *d*. *Educ:* Shrewsbury; RMA, Woolwich; King's Coll., Cambridge, King's medal, RMA Woolwich, 1937. Commnd into Royal Engineers, 1937; served War of 1939–45: Norwegian Campaign, 1940; Tunisia, 1942–43; Sicily and Italy, 1943–44; Far East, 1945; GSO1, HQ Allied Land Forces SE Asia, 1945–48; Instructor, Staff Coll., Camberley, 1948–50; Instructor, RMA, Sandhurst, 1951–53; AA & QMG (War Plans), War Office, during Suez ops, 1956; Comdr, Gurkha Engrs, 1958–60; Col GS, Minley Div. of Staff Coll., Camberley, 1961–62; Dep. Dir of Staff Duties, War Office, 1962–64; Imp. Def. Coll., 1965; Dir, Chief of Defence Staff's Unison Planning Staff, 1966–68; Asst Chief of General Staff (Operational Requirements), MoD, 1968–70; GOC-in-C, Northern Command, 1970–72; QMG, 1973–76. Colonel Commandant: RE, 1971–81; Gurkha Engrs, 1971–76; RAOC, 1973–78; Hon. Col, Engineer and Rly Staff Corps, RE, TAVR, 1977–83; ADC (Gen.) to the Queen, 1974–76. Kermit Roosevelt Lectr, USA, 1975. Chm., Friends of Gibraltar's Heritage, 1990–94. Reviewer of mil. books, The Times, 1987–93. *Publications:* Attack in the West, 1953; Seven Roads to Moscow, 1957; The Battle for Italy, 1967; Battle for Rome, 1969; Alexander of Tunis as Military Commander, 1971; The North African Campaigns, 1975; Overlord: Normandy 1944, 1978; (ed jtly) The Mediterranean and the Middle East (British Official History, vol. VI), Pt 1, 1984, Pt 2, 1987, Pt 3, 1988; Withdrawal From Empire, 1986; The Alternative Third World War 1985–2035, 1987; The Rock of the Gibraltarians, 1988; British Defence Dilemmas, 1990; The Chiefs, 1992; The Governor's Cat, 1992; The Pomp of Yesterday, 1995; Salvador, 1995; As Nineveh and Tyre, 1996; contribs to Royal United Service Instn Jl (gold medals for prize essays, 1950 and 1966). *Recreations:* fishing, writing, gardening. *Club:* Army and Navy.

JACKSON, William Gordon; QC (Scot) 1990; *b* 5 Aug. 1948; *s* of Alexander Jackson and Margaret Shillinglaw or Jackson; *m* 1972, Anne Stevely; one *s* two *d*. *Educ:* Ardrossan Academy; St Andrews Univ. (LLB). Advocate, 1979; called to the Bar, Lincoln's Inn, 1989; Advocate Depute, Scotland, 1987–90. *Address:* 5 Hermitage Gardens, Edinburgh EH10 6DL. *T:* 0131–447 7094.

JACKSON, William Theodore, CBE 1967 (MBE 1946); ARIBA; MRTPI; Director of Post Office Services, Ministry of Public Building and Works, 1969–71, retired; *b* 18 July 1906; *y s* of Rev. Oliver Miles Jackson and Emily Jackson; *m* 1932, Marjorie Campbell; one *s* two *d*. *Educ:* Cheltenham Gram. Sch. Chief Architect, Iraq Govt, 1936–38; Dir, Special Repair Service, Min. of Works, 1939–45; Min. of Public Building and Works, 1946–69; Dir, Mobile Labour Force; Dir of Maintenance; seconded to World Bank as Advr to Iran Technical Bureau of Development Plan organisation, 1956–57; Regional Dir; Dir, Regional Services; Dir, Headquarters Services, 1957–69. *Recreations:* gardening, painting. *Address:* 26 Roding Close, Elmbridge Road, Cranleigh, Surrey GU6 8TE. *T:* Cranleigh (01483) 276273.

JACKSON, Sir (William) Thomas, 8th Bt *cr* 1869; farmer, declined 1990; *b* 12 Oct. 1927; *s* of Sir William Jackson, 7th Bt, and Lady Ankaret Jackson (*d* 1945), 2nd *d* of 10th Earl of Carlisle; *S* father, 1985; *m* 1951, Gilian Malise, *d* of John William Stobart, MBE; three *s*. *Educ:* Mill Hill School; Royal Agricultural Coll., Cirencester. Qualified Associate Chartered Land Agents Soc., later ARICS; resigned, 1969. Nat. Service, 1947–49, 2/Lt Border Regt; Gen. Reserve as Lieut. Land Agent in various firms and on private estates till 1969, when he left the profession and started farming. Chairman: Cumberland Branch, CLA, 1984–86; Whitehaven Branch, NFU, 1983–85. *Recreation:* painting. *Heir: e s* (William) Roland Cedric Jackson, PhD [*b* 9 Jan. 1954; *m* 1977, Nicola Mary, *yr d* of Prof. Peter Reginald Davis, PhD, FRCS; three *s*]. *Address:* Fell End, Mungrisdale, Penrith, Cumbria CA11 0XR.

JACKSON, William Unsworth, CBE 1985; DL; Chief Executive, Kent County Council, 1974–86; *b* 9 Feb. 1926; *s* of William Jackson and Margaret Esplen Jackson (*née* Sunderland); *m* 1952, Valerie Annette (*née* Llewellyn); one *s* one *d*. *Educ:* Alsop High Sch., Liverpool. Solicitor. Entered local govt service, Town Clerk's Office, Liverpool, 1942; Dep. County Clerk, Kent, 1970. Pres., Soc. of Local Authority Chief Execs, 1985–86 (Hon. Sec., 1980–84). Adjudicator on political restrictions in local govt in England and Wales, 1989–. Trustee, Charities Aid Foundn, 1986–. Gov., Henley Management Coll., 1983–86. DL Kent, 1992. *Address:* 34 Yardley Park Road, Tonbridge, Kent TN9 1NF. *T:* Tonbridge (01732) 351078. *Club:* Royal Over-Seas League.

JACKSON, Yvonne Brenda, OBE 1985; DL; Chairman, West Yorkshire Metropolitan County Council, 1980–81; *b* 23 July 1920; *d* of Charles and Margaret Wilson; *m* 1946, Edward Grosvenor Jackson; twin *s* one *d*. *Educ:* Edgbaston C of E Coll., Birmingham; Manchester Teachers' Trng Coll. (Dip. Domestic Science and qualified teacher). School Meals Organizer, West Bromwich, Staffs, 1942–45. Mem., W Riding CC, 1967–73 (local govt reorganisation); Mem. W Yorks CC, 1973–86; Chm., Fire and Public Protection Cttee, 1977–80; Deputy Leader and Shadow Chairman: Fire Cttee, 1981–86; Trading Standards Cttee, 1981–86; Police Cttee, 1982–86. Chm., Yorks Electricity Consultative Council, 1982–90; Mem., Yorks RHA, 1982–87. Mem. Exec. Cttee, Nat. Union of Cons. Assocs, 1981–88 (Dep. Chm., Yorks Area Finance and Gen. Purposes Cttee, 1982–88; Divl Pres., Elmet, 1985–93). Mem. Council and Court, Leeds Univ. DL W Yorks, 1983, High Sheriff, 1986–87. *Recreations:* badminton, fishing; formerly County hockey and tennis player; former motor rally driver (competed in nat. and internat. events inc. Monte Carlo, Alpine and Tulip rallies). *Address:* East Garth, School Lane, Collingham, W Yorks LS22 5BQ. *T:* Collingham Bridge (01937) 573452.

JACKSON-LIPKIN, Miles Henry; QC (Hong Kong) 1974; JP; a Judge of the High Court of Hong Kong, 1981–87; *b* Liverpool; *s* of late I. J. Jackson-Lipkin, MD and F.A. Patley; *m* Lucille Yun-Shim Fung, DLJ, barrister; one *s*. *Educ:* Harrow; Trinity Coll., Oxford. FCIArb 1986; Chartered Arbitrator, Canada, 1995. Called to the Bar, Middle Temple, 1951; admitted Hong Kong Bar, 1963, NSW Bar, 1980. Comr, Supreme Court of Negara Brunei Darussalam, 1984–87. Panel Member: Inland Revenue Bd of Review, Hong Kong, 1975; London Court of Internat. Arbitration, 1994–. Chm. Exec. Cttee, and Man. Dir, Hong Kong Children and Youth Services, 1978–. Member: Medico-Legal Soc., 1952; Justice, 1956; Council of Honour, Monarchist League; Founder Member: Hong Kong Br., Justice, 1963; Hong Kong Medico-Legal Soc., 1974 (Mem. Cttee, 1976–). Vice-Chm., Hong Kong Island Br., Internat. Wine and Food Soc. Hon. Mem., Chinese Soc. for Wind Engrg. Liveryman: Meadmakers' Co. (Edinburgh), 1984; Arbitrators' Co., 1986; Freeman, City of London, 1986. JP Hong Kong, 1977. KCLJ 1983 (Grand Priory of Lochore) (KLJ 1977; CLJ 1973). Hon. Mem., Officers' Mess, HQBF, Hong Kong. *Publications:* The Beaufort Legitimation, 1957; Scales of Justice, 1958; Israel Naval Forces, 1959. *Recreations:* gardening, heraldry, classical music, philately, walking. *Address:* A2–19 Evergreen Villa, 43 Stubbs Road, Hong Kong; 62 Eaton Terrace, SW1W 8TZ; 309 The Capilano, 2024 Fullerton Avenue, West Vancouver, BC V7P 3G4, Canada. *Clubs:* Naval and Military, MCC; Hong Kong, Hong Kong Cricket, Royal Hong Kong Golf, Royal Hong Kong Jockey, American, Arts, Classic Car, Shanghai Fraternity Assoc. (Hon.) (Hong Kong).

JACKSON-STOPS, Timothy William Ashworth, FRICS; Chairman, Jackson-Stops & Staff, since 1978; *b* 1942; *s* of late Anthony and Jean Jackson-Stops; *m* 1987, Jenny MacArthur; two *s*. *Educ:* Eton; Agricultural Coll., Cirencester. Jackson-Stops & Staff, 1967–: Dir, 1974. *Recreations:* ski-ing, sailing, shooting. *Address:* Wood Burcote Court, Towcester, Northants NN12 7JP. *T:* Towcester (01327) 50443. *Club:* Buck's.

JACOB, David Oliver Ll.; *see* Lloyd Jacob, D. O.

JACOB, Prof. François; Croix de la Libération; Grand-Croix de la Légion d'Honneur; Head of Cellular Genetics Unit, Pasteur Institute, 1960–91; Professor of Cellular Genetics, at the College of France, 1964–91; *b* Nancy (Meurthe & Moselle), 17 June 1920; *m* 1947, Lysiane Bloch (*d* 1984); three *s* one *d*. *Educ:* Lycée Carnot, France. DenM 1947; DèsS 1954. Pasteur Institute: Asst, 1950–56; Head of Laboratory, 1956–60; Prof., 1960–; Pres., 1982–88. Mem., Acad. of Scis, Paris, 1977. Charles Léopold Mayer Prize, Acad. des Sciences, Paris, 1962; Nobel Prize for Medicine, 1965. Foreign Member: Royal Danish Acad. of Letters and Sciences, 1962; Amer. Acad. of Arts and Sciences, 1964; Nat. Acad. of Scis, USA, 1969; Royal Soc., 1973; Acad. Royale de Médecine, Belgique, 1973; Acad. of Sci., Hungary, 1986; Royal Acad. of Sci., Madrid, 1987. Holds hon. doctorates from several univs, incl. Chicago, 1965. *Publications:* La Logique du Vivant, 1970 (The Logic of Life, 1974); Le Jeu des Possibles, 1981 (The Possible and the Actual, 1982); La Statue Intérieure, 1987 (The Statue Within, 1988); various scientific. *Recreation:* painting. *Address:* 25 rue du Dr Roux, 75724 Paris, Cedex 15, France.

JACOB, Frederick Henry; CBiol; retired; Director, Ministry of Agriculture, Fisheries and Food's Pest Infestation Control Laboratory, 1968–77; *b* 12 March 1915; *s* of Henry Theodore and Elizabeth Jacob; *m* 1941, Winifred Edith Sloman (decd); one *s* one *d*. *Educ:* Friars Sch., Bangor; UC North Wales. BSc, MSc; CBiol, FIBiol. Asst Entomologist: King's Coll., Newcastle upon Tyne, 1942–44; Sch. of Agriculture, Cambridge, 1944–45; Adviser in Agric. Zoology, UC North Wales, 1945–46; Adv. Entomologist, Min. of Agriculture and Fisheries, Nat. Agric. Adv. Service, N Wales, 1946–50; Head of Entomology Dept, MAFF, Plant Pathology Lab., 1950–68. Pres., Assoc. of Applied Biologists, 1976–77. *Publications:* papers mainly on systematics of Aphididae in learned jls. *Recreations:* hill walking, fishing, gardening. *Address:* Hillside, Almondbury Common, Huddersfield HD4 6SN. *T:* Huddersfield (01484) 422021. *Clubs:* Farmers', Climbers; Wayfarers (Liverpool).

JACOB, Sir Isaac Hai, (Sir Jack Jacob), Kt 1979; QC 1976; Senior Master of the Supreme Court, Queen's Bench Division, and Queen's Remembrancer, 1975–80; Director, Institute of Advanced Legal Studies, University of London, 1986–88; Fellow of University College London, 1966; *b* 5 June 1908; 3rd *s* of late Jacob Isaiah and Aziza Jacob; *m* 1940, Rose Mary Jenkins (*née* Samwell) (*d* 1995); two *s*. *Educ:* Shanghai Public Sch. for Boys; London Sch. of Economics; University Coll., London. LLB (1st class Hons), London; Joseph Hume Scholar in Jurisprudence, University Coll., London, 1928 and 1930; Arden Scholar, Gray's Inn, 1930; Cecil Peace Prizeman, 1930. Pres., Univ. of London Law Students' Soc., 1930; Chm., Univ. of London Jewish Students Union, 1931. Called to the Bar, Gray's Inn, Nov. 1930; Hon. Bencher, 1978; Mem., Senate of Inns of Court and the Bar, 1975–78. Served in ranks from 1940 until commissioned in RAOC 1942; Staff Capt., War Office (Ord. I), 1943–45. Master, Supreme Court, Queen's Bench Div., 1957–80. Prescribed Officer for Election Petitions, 1975–80. Hon. Lectr in Law, UCL, 1959–74; teaching LLM subject, Principles of Civil Litigation, 1959–87; Hon. Lectr in Legal Ethics, Birmingam Univ., 1969–72; Hon. Visiting Lecturer: Imperial Coll. of Science and Technology, 1963–64; Birmingham Univ., 1964–65; Bedford Coll., 1969–71; European Univ. Institute, Florence, 1978; Visiting Professor: Sydney Univ., 1971; Osgoode Hall Law Sch., York Univ., Toronto, 1971; of English Law, UCL, 1974–87; Polytechnic of Central London, 1981–83. Member: Lord Chancellor's (Pearson) Cttee on Funds in Court, 1958–59; Working Party on the Revision of the Rules of the Supreme Court, 1960–65; (Payne) Cttee on Enforcement of Judgment Debts, 1965–69; (Winn) Cttee on Personal Injuries Litigation, 1966–68; (Kerr) Working Party on Foreign Judgments, 1976–80. Chm., Working Party on Form of the Writ of Summons and Appearance, 1977. Mem., Fourth Anglo-Amer. Legal Exchange on Trial of Civil Actions, 1973. Vice-President: Industrial Law Soc., 1968–; Selden Soc., 1978–84 (Mem. Council, 1976–78, 1985–); Inst. of Legal Executives, 1978–; Mansfield Law Club, City of London Polytechnic, 1965–; Governor, Polytechnic of Central London, 1968–88; Member, Cttee of Management: Inst. of Judicial Admin, 1968–; Brit. Inst. of Internat. and Comparative Law, 1965–; Law Adv. Cttee of Associated Examining Bd, 1964–84; Friends of Hebrew Univ., Jerusalem, 1965–85; Mem. Council, Justice; Mem. Gen. Cttee, Bar Assoc. of Commerce, Finance and Industry, 1981–85; Life Mem., Assoc. of Law Teachers, 1985 (Vice Pres., 1965–78; Pres., 1978–85). Chm., Bentham Club, UCL, 1964–84, Pres. 1985, Vice Pres. 1986–. Hon. Member: SPTL, 1981–; Council of Justice, 1988–; Internat. Assoc. of Procedural Law, 1985–. Hon. Freeman, City of London, 1976. Mem., Broderers' Co., 1977. FCIArb 1984. Hon. Fellow, Univ. of Westminster (formerly Polytechnic of Central London), 1988. Hon. LLD: Birmingham, 1978; London, 1981; Staffordshire, 1994; Dr Jur *hc* Würzburg, Bavaria, 1982. Chief Adv. Editor, Atkin's Court Forms, 1984– (Adv. Editor, 1962–83); Editor, Annual Practice, 1961–66; General Editor: Supreme Court Practice, 1967–; Civil Justice Quarterly, 1982–; Adv. Editor, Internat. Encyclopedia of Comparative Law (Civil Procedure vol.), 1968–; Consultant Editor, Malaysian Court Practice, 1995. *Publications:* Law relating to Rent Restrictions, 1933, 1938; Law relating to Hire Purchase, 1938; (ed jtly) Bullen and Leake, Precedents of Pleadings, 11th edn 1959; (ed) Bullen, Leake and Jacob, Precedents of Pleadings, 12th edn 1975, 13th edn (with Iain Goldrein) 1990; chapter on Civil Procedure, including Courts and Evidence, in Annual Survey of Commonwealth Law, 1965–77; Chitty and Jacob's Queen's Bench Forms, 19th edn 1965, to 21st edn 1986; The Reform of Civil Procedural Law and Other Essays in Civil Procedure, 1982; The Fabric of English Civil Justice (Hamlyn Lectures), 1986; (gen. ed.) Private International Litigation, 1988; (ed jtly) Trends in Enforcement of Non-Money Judgments and Orders, 1988; (with Ian Goldrein) Pleadings: principles and practice, 1990; Halsbury's Laws of England, 4th edition: Discovery, Vol. 13, 1975; (jtly)

Execution, Vol. 17, 1976; Practice and Procedure, Vol. 37, 1982; Atkin's Court Forms: Compromise and Settlement, Vol. 12, 1990; Default, Vol. 14, 1991; Discontinuance, and Discovery, Vol. 15, 1990; Interim Orders, and Interlocutory Proceedings (QBD), Vol. 22, 1991; Issues, and Judgments (QBD), Vol. 23, 1991; References and Inquiries, Vol. 33, 1989; Service of Process, Vol. 35, 1991; Stay of Proceedings, and Third Party Procedure, Vol. 37, 1990; Transfer and Consolidation, Vol. 39, 1991; Writs of Summons, Vol. 41, 1991; *festschrift:* International Perspectives on Civil Justice, ed Prof. I. R. Scott, 1990. *Recreation:* painting. *Address:* 16 The Park, Golders Green, NW11 7SU. *T:* 0181–458 3832. *Clubs:* City Livery, Reform, Royal Automobile.

See also Sir R. R. H. Jacob.

JACOB, Hon. Sir Robert Raphael Hayim, (Sir Robin), Kt 1993; **Hon. Mr Justice Jacob;** a Judge of the High Court of Justice, Chancery Division, since 1993; *b* 26 April 1941; *s* of Sir Jack I. H. Jacob, *qv*; *m* 1967, Wendy Jones; three *s*. *Educ:* King Alfred Sch., Hampstead; Mountgrace Secondary Comprehensive Sch., Potters Bar; St Paul's Sch.; Trinity Coll., Cambridge (BA, MA); LSE (LLB). Called to the Bar, Gray's Inn, 1965 (Atkin Scholar; Bencher, 1989); teacher of law, 1965–66; pupillage with Nigel (now Lord) Bridge, 1966–67, with A. M. Walton, 1967; entered chambers of Thomas Blanco White, 1967; Junior Counsel to Treasury in Patent Matters, 1976–81; QC 1981. Dep. Chm., Copyright Tribunal, 1989–93; apptd to hear appeals to Sec. of State under the Trade Marks Acts, 1988–93. Gov., LSE, 1994–. Jt Editor, Encyclopedia of UK and European Patent Law, 1977–. *Publications:* Kerly's Law of Trade Marks (ed jtly), 1972, 1983 and 1986 edns; Patents, Trade Marks, Copyright and Designs (ed jtly), 1970, 1978, 1986; Editor, Court Forms Sections on Copyright (1978), Designs and Trade Marks (1975–86); section on Trade Marks (ed jtly), 4th edn, Halsbury's Laws of England, 1985; Guidebook of Intellectual Property, 1993. *Recreations:* photography, country garden. *Address:* Royal Courts of Justice, Strand, WC2A 2LL.

JACOB, Rev. Canon William Mungo, PhD; Warden of Lincoln Theological College, 1986–June 1996; Canon of Lincoln, since 1986; Assistant Curate of St Michael-on-the-Mount, Lincoln, since 1987; *b* 15 Nov. 1944; *s* of John William Carey Jacob and Mary Marsters Dewar. *Educ:* King Edward VII School, King's Lynn; Hull Univ. (LLB); Linacre Coll., Oxford (MA); Exeter Univ. (PhD). Deacon 1970, priest 1971; Curate of Wymondham, Norfolk, 1970–73; Asst Chaplain, Exeter Univ., 1973–75; Lecturer, Salisbury and Wells Theological Coll., 1975–80, Vice-Principal, 1977–80; Sec. to Cttee for Theological Education, ACCM, 1980–86. *Address:* The Warden's House, Drury Lane, Lincoln LN1 3BP. *T:* Lincoln (01522) 538885.

JACOBI, Sir Derek (George), Kt 1994; CBE 1985; actor; Artistic Director, Chichester Festival Theatre, since 1995; *b* 22 Oct. 1938; *s* of Alfred George Jacobi and Daisy Gertrude Masters. *Educ:* Leyton County High Sch.; St John's Coll., Cambridge (MA Hons; Hon. Fellow, 1987). Artistic Associate, Old Vic Co. (formerly Prospect Theatre Co.), 1976–81; associate actor, RSC. Vice-Pres., Nat. Youth Theatre, 1982–. *Stage:* Birmingham Repertory Theatre, 1960–63 (first appearance in One Way Pendulum, 1961); National Theatre, 1963–71; Prospect Theatre Co., 1972, 1974, 1976, 1977, 1978; Hamlet (for reformation of Old Vic Co., and at Elsinore), 1979; Benedick in Much Ado About Nothing (Tony Award, 1985), title rôle in Peer Gynt, Prospero in The Tempest, 1982, title rôle in Cyrano de Bergerac, 1983 (SWET Award; Plays and Players Award), RSC; Breaking the Code, Haymarket, 1986, Washington and NY 1987; Dir, Hamlet, Phoenix, 1988; title rôle in Kean, Old Vic, 1990; title rôle in Becket, Haymarket, 1991; Byron, in Mad, Bad and Dangerous to Know, Ambassadors, 1992; Macbeth, RSC, 1993; title rôle in Hadrian VII, Playing the Wife, Chichester, 1995; *appearances include: TV:* She Stoops to Conquer, Man of Straw, The Pallisers, I Claudius, Philby, Burgess and Maclean, Richard II, Hamlet, Inside the Third Reich, Mr Pye, Cadfael; *films.* 1971–: Odessa File; Day of the Jackal; The Medusa Touch; Othello; Three Sisters; Interlude; The Human Factor; Charlotte; The Man Who Went Up in Smoke; Enigma; Little Dorrit (Best Actor Award, Evening Standard); Henry V; The Fool; Dead Again. *Awards:* BAFTA Best Actor, 1976–77; Variety Club TV Personality, 1976; Standard Best Actor, 1983. *Address:* c/o ICM Ltd, Oxford House, 76 Oxford Street, W1N 0AX; Chichester Festival Theatre, Oaklands Park, Chichester, W Sussex PO19 4AP.

JACOBI, Sir James (Edward), Kt 1989; OBE 1978; Medical Practitioner (private practice), since 1960; *b* 26 Aug. 1925; *s* of Edward William Jacobi and Doris Stella Jacobi; *m* 1946, Joy; one *s* two *d*; *m* 1974, Nora Maria; two *s*. *Educ:* Maryborough State High School; Univ. of Queensland (MB, BS, PhC). Clerk, Public Service, 1941; RAAF, 1943–46; served navigator-wireless operator, Beaufighter Sqdn, SW Pacific. Apprentice pharmaceutical chemist, 1946–50; pharm. chem., 1950–54, and Univ. student, 1954–60; Resident MO, Brisbane, 1961; MO, Dept of Health, Papua New Guinea, 1962–63; GP Port Moresby, 1963–. *Recreations:* National President, PNG Rugby Football League. *Address:* Jacobi Medical Centre, Box 1551, Boroko, Papua New Guinea. *T:* 255355. *Clubs:* United Services (Brisbane); City Tattersalls, NSW Leagues (Sydney); Brisbane Polo; Papua (Port Moresby).

JACOBS, Sir Anthony; *see* Jacobs, Sir D. A.

JACOBS, Prof. Arthur David; musicologist and critic; Member of Editorial Board, Opera, since 1961; *b* 14 June 1922; *s* of late Alexander S. and Estelle Jacobs; *m* 1953, Betty Upton Hughes; two *s*. *Educ:* Manchester Grammar Sch.; Merton Coll., Oxford (MA). Music Critic: Daily Express, 1947–52; Jewish Chronicle, 1963–75; critic, Hi-Fi News and Record Review (formerly Audio and Record Review), 1964–89; record reviewer, Sunday Times, 1968–89. Professor, RAM, 1964–79; Hd of Music Dept, Huddersfield Polytechnic, 1979–84, created Prof. 1984. Founder and Editor, British Music Yearbook (formerly Music Yearbook), 1971–79, Adv. Editor, 1979–83. Leverhulme Res. Fellow in Music, 1977–78; Leverhulme Emeritus Res. Fellow, 1991–93. Vis. Fellow, Wolfson Coll., Oxford, 1979, 1984–85, 1991–92; Centennial Lectr, Univ. of Illinois, 1967; Vis. Professor: Univ. of Victoria, BC, 1968; Univ. of California at Santa Barbara, 1969; Temple Univ., Philadelphia, 1970, 1971; UCLA, 1973; Univ. of Western Ontario, 1974; McMaster Univ., 1975, 1983; Univ. of Queensland, 1985. Hon. RAM 1969. *Publications:* Music Lover's Anthology, 1948; Gilbert and Sullivan, 1951; A New Dictionary of Music, 1958 (also Spanish, Portuguese, Danish and Swedish edns), new edn, as The New Penguin Dictionary of Music, 1978, 5th edn 1991; Choral Music, 1963 (also Spanish and Japanese edns); Libretto of opera One Man Show by Nicholas Maw, 1964; (with Stanley Sadie) Pan Book of Opera, 1966, expanded edn 1984 (US edns, Great Operas in Synopsis, The Limelight Book of Opera); A Short History of Western Music, 1972 (also Italian edn); (ed) Music Education Handbook, 1976; Arthur Sullivan: a Victorian musician, 1984; The Pan Book of Orchestral Music, 1987; Penguin Dictionary of Musical Performers, 1990; Henry J. Wood: Maker of the Proms, 1994; many opera translations incl. Berg's Lulu (first US perf. of complete work, Santa Fe, New Mexico, 1979); contributions to: A History of Song, 1960; Grove's Dictionary of Music and Musicians, 1980; Shakespeare and the Victorian Stage, 1986; The New Grove Dictionary of Opera, 1992; TLS, Musical Times, foreign jls, etc. *Recreations:* puns, swimming, walking, theatre. *Address:* 7 Southdale Road, Oxford OX2 7SE. *T:* Oxford (01865) 515240. *Club:* Commonwealth Trust.

JACOBS, Sir (David) Anthony, Kt 1988; FCA; *b* Nov. 1931; *s* of Ridley and Ella Jacobs; *m* 1954, Evelyn Felicity Patchett; one *s* one *d*. *Educ:* Clifton Coll.; London Univ. (BCom). Chairman: Nig Securities Gp, 1957–72; British Sch. of Motoring, 1973–90. Contested (L) Watford, Feb. and Oct. 1974. Jt Treas., Liberal Party, 1984–87; Vice-Pres., Soc. & Lib. Dem., 1988; Chm., Federal Exec., Soc. & Lib. Dem., 1988. *Recreations:* golf, reading, theatre, opera, travel. *Address:* 9 Nottingham Terrace, NW1 4QB. *T:* 0171–486 6323. *Clubs:* Coombe Hill Golf (Surrey); Palm Beach Country (USA).

JACOBS, David Lewis; DL; radio and television broadcaster; *b* 19 May 1926; *s* of David Jacobs and Jeanette Victoria Jacobs; *m* 1st, 1949, Patricia Bradlaw (marr. diss. 1972); three *d* (one *s* decd); 2nd, 1975, Caroline Munro (*d* 1975); 3rd, 1979, Mrs Lindsay Stuart-Hutcheson. *Educ:* Belmont Coll.; Strand Sch. RN, 1944–47. First broadcast, Navy Mixture, 1944; Announcer, Forces Broadcasting Service, 1944–45; Chief Announcer, Radio SEAC, Ceylon, 1945–47; Asst Stn Dir, Radio SEAC, 1947; News Reader, BBC Gen. Overseas Service, 1947, subseq. freelance. Major radio credits include: Book of Verse, Housewives' Choice, Journey into Space, Dateline London, Grande Gingold, Curioser and Curioser, Puffney Post Office, Follow that Man, Man about Town, Jazz Club, Midday Spin, Music Through Midnight, Scarlet Pimpernel, Radio 2 DJ Show, Pick of the Pops, Saturday Show Band Show, Melodies for You (12 years), Saturday Star Sounds, Any Questions (Chm. for 17 years), Any Answers; Internat. Fest. of Light Music. TV credits incl.: Focus on Hocus, Vera Lynn Show, Make up your Mind, Tell the Truth, Juke Box Jury, Top of the Pops, Hot Line, Miss World, Top Town, David Jacobs' Words and Music, Sunday Night with David Jacobs, Little Women, There Goes that Song Again, Make a Note, Where are they Now, What's My Line, Who What or Where, Frank Sinatra Show, Mario Lanza Show, Walt Disney Christmas Show, Wednesday Show, Wednesday Magazine, Eurovision Song Contest, TV Ice Time, Twist, A Song for Europe, Ivor Novello Awards, Aladdin, Airs and Graces, Tell Me Another, Those Wonderful TV Times, Blankety Blank, Come Dancing, Questions (TVS), Primetime, Countdown, Holiday Destinations (Sky). Numerous film performances incl. Golden Disc, You Must Be Joking, It's Trad Dad, Stardust; former commentator, British Movietone News. 6 Royal Command Performances; 6 yrs Britain's Top Disc Jockey on both BBC and Radio Luxembourg; Variety Club of Gt Brit., BBC TV Personality of Year, 1960, and BBC Radio Personality of the Year, 1975; Sony Gold Award for Outstanding Contribution to Radio over the Years, 1984; RSPCA Richard Martin Award, 1978. Director: Duke of York's Theatre, 1979–85; Man in the Moon (UK) Ltd, 1986–; Video Travel Guides, 1990–91; Kingston Theatre Trust, 1991– (Chm., 1990–); College of Driver Educn, 1991–. Vice-Pres., Stars Organisation for Spastics (Past Chm.); Mem. Council, RSPCA, 1969–77, Vice-Chm. 1975–76; Vice-Pres., The St John Ambulance London (Prince of Wales's), 1985–. Past Pres., Nat. Children's Orch.; Vice-Pres., Wimbledon Girls Choir. Chm., Think British Council, 1985–89 (Dep. Chm., 1983–85); Vice-Pres., Invest in Britain Campaign, 1992– (Chm., 1989–92). President: Kingston upon Thames Royal British Legion, 1984–; SW London Area, SSAFA 1995; Jt Pres., SW London Community Foundn, 1994–; Vice-President: Royal Star and Garter Home, Richmond, 1988–; Friends of Chelsea and Westminster Hosp., 1993–; Patron: Age Resource, 1990–; Kingston Wel-Care Assoc., 1995; Pres., Kingston Alcohol Adv. Service, 1993–; Vice Pres., Kingston Arts Council; Trustee, Dine-a-Mite, 1994–. Life Gov., ICRF, 1995. DL Greater London, 1983, Kingston upon Thames, 1984 (representative). Hon Dr Kingston, 1994. *Publications:* (autobiog.) Jacobs' Ladder, 1963; Caroline, 1978; (with Michael Bowen) Any Questions?, 1981. *Recreations:* talking and listening, hotels. *Address:* 203 Pavilion Road, SW1X 0BJ. *Clubs:* Garrick, St James'; Helford River Sailing.

JACOBS, Francis Geoffrey; an Advocate General, Court of Justice of the European Communities, since 1988; *b* 8 June 1939; *s* of late Cecil Sigismund Jacobs and of Louise Jacobs (*née* Fischhof); *m* 1st, 1964, Ruth (*née* Freeman); one *s;* 2nd, 1975, Susan Felicity Gordon (*née* Cox); one *s* three *d*. *Educ:* City of London Sch.; Christ Church, Oxford; Nuffield Coll., Oxford. MA, DPhil. Called to the Bar, Middle Temple, 1964, Bencher, 1990; in part-time practice, 1974–88; QC 1984; Lectr in Jurisprudence, Univ. of Glasgow, 1963–65; Lectr in Law, LSE, 1965–69; Secretariat, European Commn of Human Rights, and Legal Directorate, Council of Europe, Strasbourg, 1969–72; Legal Sec., Court of Justice of European Communities, Luxembourg, 1972–74; Prof. of European Law, Univ. of London, 1974–88; King's College, London: Dir, Centre of European Law, 1981–88; Vis. Prof., 1989–; Fellow, 1990. Hon. Sec. UK Assoc. for European Law, 1974–81 (a Vice-Pres., 1988–); UK Deleg., Conf. of Supreme Administrative Courts, EEC, 1984–88; Mem., Admin. Tribunal, Internat. Inst. for Unification of Private Law, Rome. Cooley Lectr, 1983, Bishop Lectr, 1989, Univ. of Mich. Governor, British Inst. of Human Rights, 1985–. Commandeur de l'Ordre de Mérite, Luxembourg, 1983. Editor, Yearbook of European Law, 1981–88; Mem. Editorial Board: Yearbook of European Law; Cahiers de Droit Européen; Common Market Law Review; European Law Review; Jl of Envmtl Law; King's Coll. Law Jl; Rivista di Diritto Europeo (formerly Human Rights Rev. and Jl of Common Market Studies). Gen. Ed., Oxford European Community Law series, 1986–. *Publications:* Criminal Responsibility, 1971; The European Convention on Human Rights, 1975; (jtly) References to the European Court, 1975; (ed) European Law and the Individual, 1976; (jtly) The Court of Justice of the European Communities, 1977; (jtly) The European Union Treaty, 1986; (joint editor): The European Community and GATT, 1986; The Effect of Treaties in Domestic Law, 1987; Liber Amicorum Pierre Pescatore, 1987. *Recreations:* family life, books, music, nature, travel. *Address:* Court of Justice of the European Communities, Kirchberg, Luxembourg; Wayside, 15 St Alban's Gardens, Teddington, Mddx TW11 8AE. *T:* 0181–943 0503.

JACOBS, Rabbi Irving, PhD; Principal, Jews' College, London, 1990–93; *b* 2 Aug. 1938; *s* of Solomon Jacobs and Bertha (*née* Bluestone); *m* 1963, Ann Klein; one *s* three *d*. *Educ:* Jews' Coll., London; Univ. of London (BA, PhD); Rabbinical Dip. Jews' College, London: Res. Fellow, 1966–69; Lectr, 1969–75; Sen. Lectr, 1975–84; Dean, 1984–90. *Publications:* articles on Midrash Apocryphal lit. and Jewish liturgy in scholarly jls. *Address:* c/o Jews' College, 44a Albert Road, NW4 2SJ.

JACOBS, Prof. John Arthur; Hon. Professor, Institute of Earth Studies, University of Wales (formerly University College of Wales), Aberystwyth, since 1989; Professor of Geophysics, 1974–83, and Fellow, Darwin College, since 1976 (Vice Master, 1978–82), University of Cambridge; *b* 13 April 1916; *m* 1st, 1941, Daisy Sarah Ann Montgomerie (*d* 1974); two *d*; 2nd, 1974, Margaret Jones (marr. diss. 1981); 3rd, 1982, Ann Grace Wintle. *Educ:* Univ. of London. BA 1937, MA 1939, PhD 1949, DSc 1961. Instr Lieut RN, 1941–46; Lectr, Royal Holloway Coll., Univ. of London, 1946–51; Assoc. Prof., Univ. of Toronto, 1951–57; Prof., Univ. of British Columbia, 1957–67; Dir, Inst. of Earth Sciences, Univ. of British Columbia, 1961–67; Killam Meml Prof. of Science, Univ. of Alberta, 1967–74; Dir, Inst. of Earth and Planetary Physics, Univ. of Alberta, 1970–74. Res. Fellow, RHBNC, 1987–89. Sec., Royal Astronomical Soc., 1977–82; Harold Jeffreys Lectr, RAS, 1983. FRSC 1958; DSc *hc* Univ. of BC, 1987. Centennial Medal of Canada, 1967; Medal of Canadian Assoc. of Physicists, 1975; J. Tuzo Wilson Medal, Canadian Geophys. Union, 1982; John Adam Fleming Medal, Amer. Geophys. Union, 1994; Price Medal, RAS, 1994. *Publications:* (with R. D. Russell and J. T. Wilson) Physics and Geology, 1959, 2nd edn 1974; The Earth's Core and Geomagnetism, 1963; Geomagnetic

Micropulsations, 1970; A Textbook on Geonomy, 1974; The Earth's Core, 1975, 2nd edn 1987; Reversals of the Earth's Magnetic Field, 1984, 2nd edn 1994; Deep Interior of the Earth, 1992. *Recreations:* walking, music. *Address:* Institute of Earth Studies, University of Wales, Aberystwyth, Dyfed SY23 3DB. *T:* Aberystwyth (01970) 622646.

JACOBS, John Robert Maurice; golf entrepreneur; *b* 14 March 1925; *s* of Robert and Gertrude Vivian Jacobs; *m* 1949, Rita Wragg; one *s* one *d.* *Educ:* Maltby Grammar School. Asst Professional Golfer, Hallamshire Golf Club, 1947–49; Golf Professional: Gezira Sporting Club, Cairo, 1949–52; Sandy Lodge Golf Club, 1952–64; Man. Dir, Athlon Golf, 1967–75; Professional Golfers' Association: Tournament Dir-Gen., 1971–76, Advr to Tournament Div., 1977; European Ryder Cup Captain, 1979–81 (player, 1955); Golf Instructor: Golf Digest Magazine Schs, 1971–76; Golf Magazine Schs, US, 1977. Adviser to: Walker Cup Team; Spanish and French nat. teams; Past Adviser to: Curtis Cup Team; English Golf Union team; Scottish Union team; German, Swedish and Italian teams. Golf Commentator, ITV, 1967–87. Currently associated with John Jacobs' Practical Golf Schools, based in USA. Golf adviser to Golf World Magazine, 1962–86. *Publications:* Golf, 1961; Play Better Golf, 1969; Practical Golf, 1973; John Jacobs Analyses the Superstars, 1974; Golf Doctor, 1979; The Golf Swing Simplified, 1993; Golf in a Nutshell, 1995. *Recreations:* shooting, fishing. *Address:* Stable Cottage, Chapel Lane, Lyndhurst, Hants SO43 7FG. *T:* Southampton (01703) 282743. *Clubs:* Sandy Lodge Golf, New Forest Golf, Brokenhurst Manor Golf, Bramshaw Golf, Burley Golf; Lake Nona Golf and Country (Florida).

JACOBS, Hon. Sir Kenneth (Sydney), KBE 1976; Justice of High Court of Australia, 1974–79; *b* 5 Oct. 1917; *s* of Albert Sydney Jacobs and Sarah Grace Jacobs (*née* Aggs); *m* 1952, Eleanor Mary Neal; one *d.* *Educ:* Knox Grammar Sch., NSW; Univ. of Sydney (BA, LLB). Admitted to NSW Bar, 1947; QC 1958; Supreme Court of NSW: Judge, 1960; Judge of Appeal, 1966; Pres., Court of Appeal, 1972. *Publication:* Law of Trusts, 1958. *Recreations:* printing and bookbinding; gardening. *Address:* Crooks Lane Corner, Axford, Marlborough, Wilts SN8 2HA.

JACOBS, Rabbi Dr Louis, CBE 1990; Rabbi, New London Synagogue, since 1964; Visiting Professor, University of Lancaster, since 1987; *b* 17 July 1920; *s* of Harry and Lena Jacobs; *m* 1944, Sophie Lisagorska; two *s* one *d.* *Educ:* Manchester Central High Sch.; Manchester Talmudical Coll.; BA Hons, PhD, London. Rabbinical Ordination; Rabbi, Central Synagogue, Manchester, 1948–54; New West End Synagogue, 1954–60; Tutor, Jews' Coll., London, 1959–62; Dir, Society Study of Jewish Theology, 1962–64. Vis. Prof., Harvard Divinity Sch., 1985–86. Hon. Fellow: UCL, 1988; Leo Baeck Coll., 1988. Hon. DHL: Spertus Coll., Chicago, 1987; Hebrew Union Coll., Cincinnati, 1989; Jewish Theol. Seminary, NY, 1989; Hon. DLitt Lancaster, 1991. Hon. Citizen: Texas, 1961; New Orleans, 1963. *Publications:* Jewish Prayer, 1955; We Have Reason to Believe, 1957; Guide to Rosh Hashanah, 1959; Guide to Yom Kippur, 1959; Jewish Values, 1960; (trans.) The Palm Tree of Deborah, 1960; Studies in Talmudic Logic, 1961; (trans.) Tract on Ecstasy, 1963; Principles of Jewish Faith, 1964; Seeker of Unity, 1966; Faith, 1968; Jewish Law, 1968; Jewish Ethics, Philosophy and Mysticism, 1969; Jewish Thought Today, 1970; What Does Judaism Say About . . .?, 1973; A Jewish Theology, 1973; Theology in the Responsa, 1975; Hasidic Thought, 1976; Hasidic Prayer, 1977; Jewish Mystical Testimonies, 1977; TEKYU: the unsolved problem in the Babylonian Talmud, 1981; The Talmudic Argument, 1985; A Tree of Life, 1985; Holy Living, 1990; Helping with Inquiries (autobiog.), 1989; God, Torah, Israel, 1990; Structure and Form of the Babylonian Talmud, 1991; Religion and the Individual, 1991; The Jewish Religion: a companion, 1995; contribs to learned jls, collections and festschriften. *Recreations:* reading thrillers, watching television, hill walking. *Address:* 27 Clifton Hill, St John's Wood, NW8 0QE. *T:* 0171–624 1299.

JACOBS, Prof. Patricia Ann, FRS 1993; Director, Wessex Regional Genetics Laboratory, since 1988; *b* 8 Oct. 1934; *d* of Cyril Jacobs and Sadie Jacobs (*née* Jones); *m* 1972, Newton Ennis Morton; three step *s* two step *d.* *Educ:* St Andrews Univ. (BSc 1st Cl. Hons 1956; D'Arcy Thomson Medal 1956; DSc 1966; Sykes Medal 1966). FRSE 1977; FRCPath 1987. Res. Asst, Mount Holyoke Coll., USA, 1956–57; Scientist, MRC, 1957–72; Prof., Dept of Anatomy and Reproductive Biology, Univ. of Hawaii Sch. of Medicine, 1972–85; Prof. and Chief of Div. of Human Genetics, Dept of Pediatrics, Cornell Univ. Med. Coll., 1985–87. Hon. Prof. of Human Genetics, Univ. of Southampton Med. Sch., 1993. Allan Award, Amer. Soc. of Human Genetics, 1981; Regents Medal, Univ. of Hawaii, 1983. *Publications:* numerous articles in learned jls. *Recreations:* walking, botany, gardening. *Address:* Wessex Regional Genetics Laboratory, Salisbury District Hospital, Salisbury SP2 8BJ. *T:* Salisbury (01722) 336262.

See also Peter A. Jacobs.

JACOBS, Peter Alan; Chief Executive, British United Provident Association, since 1991; *b* 22 Feb. 1943; *s* of Cyril and Sadie Jacobs; *m* 1966, Eileen Dorothy Naftalin; twin *s* one *d.* *Educ:* Glasgow Univ. (BSc Hons MechEng); Aston Univ. (Dip. Management Studies). Tube Investments: grad. trainee, 1965–67; Production Controller, Toy Div., 1968–70; Pedigree Petfoods: Production Shift Manager, 1970–72; Purchasing Dept, 1972–81; Production Manager, 1981–83; Sales Dir, Mars Confectionery, 1983–86; Berisford International: Man. Dir, British Sugar, 1986–89; Chief Exec., Berisford and Chm., British Sugar, 1989–91. *Recreations:* tennis, theatre, music. *Address:* 2 Norfolk Road, NW8 6AX. *Club:* Royal Automobile.

See also Patricia A. Jacobs.

JACOBS, Sir Piers, KBE 1989 (OBE 1981); JP; Vice Chairman and Director, China Light and Power Company, Ltd, since 1992; Chairman, Sir Elly Kadoorie & Sons Ltd, since 1995; *b* 27 May 1933; *s* of Dorothy and Selwyn Jacobs; *m* 1964, Josephine Lee; one *d.* *Educ:* St Paul's Sch. Solicitor (Hons), England and Wales, 1955; Solicitor, Hong Kong, 1976. Hong Kong: Registrar General, 1976; Sec. for Economic Services, 1982; Financial Sec., 1986–91; Mem., Exec. and Legislative Councils, 1986–91. JP Hong Kong, 1992. *Recreations:* walking, swimming, reading. *Address:* St George's Building, 24th Floor, 2 Ice House Street, Hong Kong. *Clubs:* Oriental; Hong Kong, Royal Hong Kong Jockey (Hong Kong).

JACOBS, Sir Wilfred (Ebenezer), GCMG 1981; GCVO 1985 (KCVO 1977); Kt 1967; OBE 1959; QC 1959; Governor-General of Antigua and Barbuda, 1981–93; *b* 19 Oct. 1919; 2nd *s* of late William Henry Jacobs and Henrietta Jacobs (*née* Du Bois); *m* 1947, Carmen Sylva, 2nd *d* of late Walter A. Knight and Flora Knight (*née* Fleming); one *s* two *d.* *Educ:* Grenada Boys' Secondary Sch.; Gray's Inn, London. Called to Bar, Gray's Inn, 1946; Registrar and Additional Magistrate, St Vincent, 1946; Magistrate, Dominica, 1947, and St Kitts, 1949; Crown Attorney, St Kitts, 1952; Attorney-Gen., Leeward Is, 1957–59, and Antigua, 1960. Acted Administrator, Dominica, St Kitts, Antigua, various periods, 1947–60. MEC and MLC, St Vincent, Dominica, St Kitts, Antigua, 1947–60; Legal Draftsman and Acting Solicitor-Gen., Trinidad and Tobago, 1960. Barbados: Solicitor-Gen., and Actg Attorney-Gen., 1961–63; PC and MLC, 1962–63; Dir of Public Prosecutions, 1964; Judge of Supreme Court of Judicature, 1967; Governor of Antigua, 1967–81. KStJ. *Recreations:* swimming, gardening, golf. *Address:* c/o Governor-General's Office, St John's, Antigua, West Indies. *Club:* Royal Commonwealth Society.

JACOBSEN, Frithjof Halfdan; Norwegian Ambassador, retired; *b* 14 Jan. 1914; *m* 1941, Elsa Tidemand Anderson; one *s* two *d.* *Educ:* Univ. of Oslo (Law). Entered Norwegian Foreign Service, 1938; Legation, Paris, 1938–40; Norwegian Foreign Ministry, London, 1940–45; held posts in Moscow, London, Oslo, 1945–55; Director-Gen., Political Affairs, Oslo, 1955–59; Norwegian Ambassador to: Canada, 1959–61; Moscow, 1961–66; Under-Sec. of State, Oslo, 1966–70; Ambassador to Moscow, 1970–75; Ambassador to the Court of St James's and to Ireland, 1975–82. *Address:* Schwachsgate 4, Oslo 3, Norway.

JACOBSON, Prof. Dan, FRSL; novelist, critic; Professor Emeritus, University College London, since 1994; *b* 7 March 1929; *s* of Michael Hyman Jacobson and Liebe Jacobson (*née* Melamed); *m* 1954, Margaret Dunipace Pye, two *s* one *d.* *Educ:* Kimberley Boys' High Sch., SA; Univ. of Witwatersrand, Johannesburg (BA 1949). Fellow in Creative Writing, Stanford Univ., Calif, 1956–57; University College London: Reader in English, 1979–86; Prof. of English, 1986–94. Vis. Prof., Syracuse Univ., NY, 1965–66; Visiting Fellow: State Univ. of NY, 1972; Humanities Research Centre, ANU, 1981. FRSL 1974. Llewellyn Rhys Award, Book Trust, 1958; W. Somerset Maugham Award, Soc. of Authors, 1962; H. H. Wingate Award, Jewish Chronicle, 1979; J. R. Ackerley Prize, PEN, 1986; Mary Elinore Smith Poetry Prize, Amer. Scholar, 1992. *Publications: fiction:* The Trap, 1955; A Dance in the Sun, 1956; The Price of Diamonds, 1957; The Evidence of Love, 1960; The Beginners, 1966; The Rape of Tamar, 1970; Inklings: selected stories, 1973; The Wonder-Worker, 1973; The Confessions of Josef Baisz, 1977; Her Story, 1987; Hidden in the Heart, 1991; The God-Fearer, 1992; *criticism:* The Story of the Stories, 1982; Adult Pleasures, 1988; *travel:* The Electronic Elephant, 1994. *Recreations:* tennis, walking, reading, talking. *Address:* c/o A. M. Heath & Co., 79 St Martin's Lane, WC2N 4AA. *T:* 0171–229 0113. *Clubs:* Athenæum; Templars Tennis.

JACOMB, Sir Martin (Wakefield), Kt 1985; Chairman: British Council, since 1992; Prudential Corporation, since 1995 (Director, since 1994); Delta plc, since 1994; *b* 11 Nov. 1929; *s* of Hilary W. Jacomb and Félise Jacomb; *m* 1960, Evelyn Heathcoat Amory; two *s* one *d.* *Educ:* Eton Coll.; Worcester Coll., Oxford (MA Law 1953; Hon. Fellow, 1994). 2nd Lieut, RA, 1948–49. Called to the Bar, Inner Temple, 1955; practised at the Bar, 1955–68. Kleinwort Benson Ltd, 1968–85; Dep. Chm., Barclays Bank PLC, 1985–93; Chairman: Barclays de Zoete Wedd, 1986–91; Postel Investment Management, 1991–94; Director: The Telegraph plc (formerly Daily Telegraph), 1986–95; RTZ Corp., 1988–; Marks and Spencer, 1991–. A Dir, Bank of England, 1986–95. External Mem., Finance Cttee, OUP, 1971–95. Trustee, Nat. Heritage Meml Fund, 1982–. Hon. Bencher, Inner Temple, 1987. Hon. Dr Humberside, 1993. *Recreations:* theatre, family bridge, tennis. *Address:* Prudential Corporation plc, 142 Holborn Bars, EC1N 2NH.

JACQUES, family name of **Baron Jacques.**

JACQUES, Baron *cr* 1968 (Life Peer), of Portsea Island; **John Henry Jacques;** Chairman of the Co-operative Union Ltd, 1964–70; *b* 11 Jan. 1905; *s* of Thomas Dobson Jacques and Annie Bircham; *m* 1st, 1929, Constance White (*d* 1987); two *s* one *d*; 2nd, 1989, Violet Jacques. *Educ:* Victoria Univ., Manchester; (BA(Com)); Co-operative Coll. Sec-Man., Moorsley Co-operative Society Ltd, 1925–29; Tutor, Co-operative Coll., 1929–42; Accountant, Plymouth Co-operative Soc. Ltd, 1942–45; Chief Executive, Portsea Island Co-operative Soc. Ltd, Portsmouth, 1945–65; Pres., Co-operative Congress, 1961. Pres., Retail Trades Education Council, 1971–75. A Lord in Waiting (Govt Whip), 1974–77 and 1979; a Dep. Chm. of Cttees, 1977–85. JP Portsmouth, 1951–75. *Publications:* Book-Keeping I, II and III, 1940; Management Accounting, 1966; Manual on Co-operative Management, 1969. *Recreations:* walking, snooker, gardening, West-Highland terriers. *Address:* 23 Hartford House, Blount Road, Pembroke Park, Portsmouth PO1 2TN. *T:* Portsmouth (01705) 738111. *Club:* Co-operative (Portsmouth).

JACQUES, Peter Roy Albert, CBE 1990; Secretary, TUC Social Insurance and Industrial Welfare Department, since 1971; *b* 12 Aug. 1939; *s* of George Henry Jacques and Ivy Mary Jacques (*née* Farr); *m* 1965, Jacqueline Anne Sears; one *s* one *d.* *Educ:* Archbishop Temple's Secondary Sch.; Newcastle upon Tyne Polytechnic (BSc Sociology); Univ. of Leicester. Building labourer, 1955–58; market porter, 1958–62; Asst, TUC Social Insce and Industrial Welfare Dept, 1968–71. Member: Industrial Injuries Adv. Council, 1972; Nat. Insce Adv. Cttee, 1972–78; Health and Safety Commn, 1974–95; Royal Commn on the Nat. Health Service, 1976–79; EEC Cttee on Health-Safety, 1976; NHS London Adv. Cttee, 1979; Social Security Adv. Cttee, 1980–95; Health Educn Council, 1984–87; Civil Justice Review Adv. Cttee, 1985–; Royal Commn on Envmtl Pollution, 1989–95. Jt Sec., BMA/TUC Cttee, 1972; Secretary: TUC Social Health and Envmt Protection Cttee (formerly Social Insurance and Industrial Welfare Cttee), 1972–93; TUC Health Services Cttee, 1979–; TUC Special Advr, 1992–95. Mem., Redbridge and Waltham Forest HA, 1993–. Mem. Exec. Cttee, Royal Assoc. for Disability and Rehabilitation, 1975–. *Publications:* responsible for TUC pubns Health-Safety Handbook; Occupational Pension Schemes. *Recreations:* reading, yoga, walking, camping, vegetable growing. *Address:* 7 Starling Close, Buckhurst Hill, Essex IG9 5TN. *T:* 0181–505 5327.

JAEGER, Prof. Leslie Gordon, FRSE 1966; Research Professor of Civil Engineering and Applied Mathematics, Technical University of Nova Scotia, 1988–92, Emeritus 1992; *b* 28 Jan. 1926; *s* of Henry Jaeger; *m* 1st, 1948, Annie Sylvia Dyson; two *d*; 2nd, 1981, Kathleen Grant. *Educ:* King George V Sch., Southport; Gonville and Caius Coll., Cambridge. PhD, DSc (Eng) London. Royal Corps of Naval Constructors, 1945–48; Industry, 1948–52; University College, Khartoum, 1952–56; Univ. Lectr, Cambridge, 1956–62; Fellow and Dir of Studies, Magdalene Coll., Cambridge, 1959–62; Prof. of Applied Mechanics, McGill Univ., Montreal, 1962–65; Regius Prof. of Engineering, Edinburgh Univ., 1965–66; Prof. of Civil Engineering, McGill Univ., 1966–70; Dean, Faculty of Engineering, Univ. of New Brunswick, 1970–75; Academic Vice-Pres., Acadia Univ., NS, 1975–80; Vice-Pres. (Res.), Technical Univ. of NS, 1980–88. Pres., Canadian Soc. for Civil Engrg, 1992–93. DEng *hc* Carleton Univ., Ottawa, 1991; Meml Univ., Newfoundland, 1994; Technical Univ. of NS, 1995. Telford Premium, ICE, 1959; A. B. Sanderson Award, Canadian Soc. for Civil Engrg, 1983; Gzowski Medal, Engrg Inst. of Canada, 1985. *Publications:* The Analysis of Grid Frameworks and Related Structures (with A. W. Hendry), 1958; Elementary Theory of Elastic Plates, 1964; Cartesian Tensors in Engineering Science, 1965; (with B. Bakht) Bridge Analysis Simplified, 1985; (with B. Bakht) Bridge Analysis by Microcomputer, 1989; various papers on grillage analysis in British, European and American Journals. *Recreations:* golf, curling, contract bridge. *Address:* PO Box 1000, Halifax, NS B3J 2X4, Canada. *T:* (902) 4207757. *Club:* Saraguay (Halifax, Canada).

JAFFÉ, (Andrew) Michael, CBE 1989; LittD; Director, Fitzwilliam Museum, Cambridge, 1973–90, now Emeritus; Professor of the History of Western Art, 1973–90, now Emeritus; Fellow of King's College, Cambridge, since 1952; *b* 3 June 1923; *s* of Arthur Daniel Jaffé, OBE, and Marie Marguerite Strauss; *m* 1964, Patricia Anne Milne-Henderson; two *s* two *d.* *Educ:* Eton Coll.; King's Coll., Cambridge (MA, LittD 1980); Courtauld Inst. of Art. Lt-Comdr, RNVR, retd. Commonwealth Fund Fellow, Harvard and New York Univ.,

1951–53; Asst Lectr in Fine Arts, Cambridge, 1956; Prof. of Renaissance Art, Washington Univ., St Louis, 1960–61; Vis. Prof., Harvard Univ., Summer 1961; Lectr in Fine Arts, Cambridge, 1961; Reader in History of Western Art, Cambridge, 1968; Head of Dept of History of Art, Cambridge, 1970–73; a Syndic, Fitzwilliam Museum, 1971–73. Mem., Adv. Council, V&A Museum, 1971–76. Organiser: (for Nat. Gall. of Canada) of Jordaens Exhibn, Ottawa, 1968–69; (for BM) of Old Master Drawings from Chatsworth, 1993. Vis. Prof., Harvard Univ., Fall 1968–69. Hon. Mem., Amer. Acad. of Arts and Scis, 1990. FRSA 1969. Officier, Ordre de Léopold (Belgium), 1980; Officier, Ordre des Arts et des Lettres (France), 1989. *Publications:* Van Dyck's Antwerp Sketchbook, 1966; Rubens, 1967; Jordaens, 1968; Rubens and Italy, 1977; Rubens: catalogo completo, 1989; (ed) The Devonshire Collection of Italian Drawings, 4 vols, 1994; articles and reviews (art historical) in European and N American jls, etc. *Recreation:* viticulture. *Address:* King's College, Cambridge CB2 1ST. *Clubs:* Brooks's, Turf, Beefsteak.

JAFFRAY, Alistair Robert Morton, CB 1978; Deputy Under-Secretary of State, Ministry of Defence, 1975–84; *b* 28 Oct. 1925; *s* of late Alexander George and Janet Jaffray; *m* 1st, 1953, Margaret Betty Newman (decd); two *s* one *d*; 2nd, 1980, Edna Mary, *e d* of late S. J. Tasker, Brasted Chart. *Educ:* Clifton Coll.; Corpus Christi Coll., Cambridge. BA First Cl. Hons., Mod. Langs. Served War, RNVR, 1943–46. Apptd Home Civil Service (Admty), 1948; Private Sec. to First Lord of Admty, 1960–62; Private Sec. to successive Secretaries of State for Defence, 1969–70; Asst Under-Sec. of State, MoD, 1971, Dep. Sec. 1975; Sec. to Admty Bd, 1981–84. Governor, Clifton Coll., 1980–; Chm. Management Cttee, Royal Hospital Sch., Holbrook, 1985–91. *Address:* Okeford, 10 Lynch Road, Farnham, Surrey GU9 8BZ.

JAFFRAY, Sir William Otho, 5th Bt, *cr* 1892; *b* 1 Nov. 1951; *s* of Sir William Edmund Jaffray, 4th Bt, TD, JP, DL; *S* father, 1953; *m* 1981, Cynthia Ross Corrington, Montreal, Canada; three *s* one *d*. *Educ:* Eton. *Heir: s* Nicholas Gordon Alexander Jaffray, *b* 18 Oct. 1982. *Address:* The Manor House, Priors Dean, Petersfield, Hants GU32 1BP. *T:* Hawkley (01730) 827483.

JAFFRÉ, Philippe Serge Yves; Ordres du Mérite et du Mérite Agricole; Chairman and Chief Executive Officer, Elf Aquitaine, since 1993; *b* 2 March 1945; *s* of Yves-Frédéric Jaffré and Janine Jaffré (*née* Alliot); *m* 1974, Elisabeth Coulon; one *s* two *d*. *Educ:* Faculté of Law, Paris; Inst. d'études politiques, Paris (diploma); Ecole Nat. d'Administration (Bachelor of Law). Inspecteur des Finances, 1974; Dept of the Treasury, 1977–88; Gen. Sec., Comité Interministeriel pour l'Aménagement des Structures Industrielles, 1978; Tech. Advr to Minister of Economy, 1979; Dep. Dir, Dept of Govt Holdings, 1984; Head of Dept for Monetary and Financial affairs, 1986–88; Dir, Banque Stern, 1988; Chief Exec. Officer, Crédit Agricole, 1988–93. *Publication:* La Monnaie et la politique Monétaire, 1990. *Recreation:* golf. *Address:* 2 place de la Coupole, 92078 Paris la Défense, France. *T:* 47442200.

JAGAN, Cheddi, DDS; Guyanese Politician; President, Co-operative Republic of Guyana, since 1992; *b* March 1918; *m* 1943; one *s* one *d*. *Educ:* Howard Univ.; YMCA Coll., Chicago (BSc); Northwestern Univ. (DDS). Member of Legislative Council, British Guiana, 1947–53; Leader of the House and Minister of Agriculture, Lands and Mines, May-Oct. 1953; Chief Minister and Minister of Trade and Industry, 1957–61; (first) Premier, British Guiana, and Minister of Development and Planning, 1961–64; Leader of Opposition in Nat. Assembly, 1964–92. Hon. Pres., Guyana Agricl and General Workers' Union; Pres., Guyana Peace Council. Order of Friendship, USSR, 1978. *Publications:* Forbidden Freedom, 1954; Anatomy of Poverty, 1964; The West on Trial, 1966; Caribbean Revolution, 1979; The Caribbean—Whose Backyard?, 1984. *Recreations:* swimming, tennis. *Address:* Office of the President, Vlissengen Road, Georgetown, Guyana.

JAGO, David Edgar John; Communar of Chichester Cathedral, 1987–92; *b* 2 Dec. 1937; *s* of late Edgar George Jago and of Violet Jago; *m* 1963, Judith Lissenden, DPhil (*d* 1995); one *s* one *d*. *Educ:* King Edward's Sch., Bath; Pembroke Coll., Oxford (MA). National Service, RA, 1956–58. Asst Principal, Admiralty, 1961; Private Sec. to Permanent Under Sec. of State (RN), 1964–65; Principal 1965; Directing Staff, IDC, 1968–70; Private Sec. to Parly Under Sec. of State for Defence (RN), 1971–73; Ministry of Defence: Asst Sec., 1973; Asst Under Sec. of State: Aircraft, 1979–82; Naval Staff, 1982–84; Under Sec., Cabinet Office, 1984–86. *Recreations:* theatre, opera, military history, supporting Arsenal FC. *Club:* United Oxford & Cambridge University.

JAHN, Dr Wolfgang; Managing Director, Commerzbank AG, Düsseldorf, 1969–84; *b* 27 Sept. 1918; *s* of Dr Georg Jahn and Ella (*née* Schick); *m* 1949, Gabriele (*née* Beck); two *s* one *d*. *Educ:* Zürich Univ.; Berlin Univ.; Heidelberg Univ. (DrEcon). Industrial Credit Bank, Düsseldorf, 1949–54; IBRD, Washington, 1954–57; Commerzbank AG, Düsseldorf, 1957–84; Chm., Internat. Commercial Bank, 1984–88. *Address:* c/o Commerzbank AG, PO Box 1137, 4000 Düsseldorf, Germany.

JAHODA, Prof. Gustav, FBA 1988; FRSE; Professor of Psychology, University of Strathclyde, 1964–85, now Emeritus Professor; *b* 11 Oct. 1920; *s* of late Olga and Leopold Jahoda; *m* 1950, Jean Catherine (*née* Buchanan) (*d* 1991); three *s* one *d*. *Educ:* Vienna, Paris, Univ. of London. MScEcon, PhD. FRSE 1993. Tutor, Oxford Extra-Mural Delegacy, 1946–68; Lectr, Univ. of Manchester, 1948–51; Univ. of Ghana, 1952–56; Sen. Lectr, Univ. of Glasgow, 1956–63. Visiting Professor, Universities of: Ghana, 1968; Tilburg, 1984; Kansai, Osaka, 1985; Ecole des Hautes Etudes, Paris, 1986; Saarbrücken, 1987; New York, 1987; Geneva, 1990. Fellow, Netherlands Inst. of Advanced Studies, 1980–81; Hon. Fellow, Internat. Assoc. for Cross-Cultural Psychology (Pres., 1972–74); Membre d'Honneur, Assoc. pour la Recherche Inter-culturelle, 1986. *Publications:* White Man, 1961, 2nd edn 1983; The Psychology of Supersitition, 1969, 8th edn 1979; Psychology and Anthropology, 1982 (French edn 1989; Japanese edn 1992); (with I. M. Lewis) Acquiring Culture, 1988; Crossroads between Culture and Mind, 1992; contribs to learned jls. *Recreations:* fishing, gardening. *Address:* c/o Department of Psychology, University of Strathclyde, Glasgow G1 1RD. *Club:* University of Strathclyde Staff.

JAHODA, Prof. Marie, (Mrs A. H. Albu), CBE 1974; DPhil; Professor Emeritus, University of Sussex; *b* 26 Jan. 1907; *d* of Carl Jahoda and Betty Jahoda; *m* 1st, 1927, Paul F. Lazarsfeld; one *d*; 2nd, 1958, Austen Albu (*d* 1994). *Educ:* Univ. of Vienna (DPhil). Prof. of Social Psychology, NY Univ., 1949–58; Res. Fellow and Prof. of Psychol., Brunel Univ., 1958–65; Prof. of Social Psychol., Sussex Univ., 1965–73. Sen. Res. Consultant to Sci. Policy Res. Unit, Sussex Univ., 1971–83. Hon. DLit: Sussex, 1973; Leicester, 1973; Bremen, 1984; Stirling, 1988. Grosse Silberne Ehrenzeichen für Verdienste (Austria), 1993. *Publications:* Die Arbeitslosen von Marienthal, 1933 (Eng. trans. 1971); Research Methods in Human Relations, 1953; Current Concepts of Positive Mental Health, 1958; Freud and the Dilemmas of Psychology, 1977; (ed) World Futures: the great debate, 1977; Employment and Unemployment, 1982. *Recreations:* cooking, chess. *Address:* 17 The Crescent, Keymer, West Sussex BN6 8RB. *T:* Hassocks (01273) 842267.

JAINE, Tom William Mahony; Proprietor, Prospect Books, since 1993; freelance writer; *b* 4 June 1943; *s* of William Edwin Jaine and Aileen (*née* Mahony); *m* 1st, 1965, Susanna F. Fisher; 2nd, 1973, Patience Mary Welsh (decd); two *d*; 3rd, 1983, Sally Caroline Agnew; two *d*. *Educ:* Kingswood Sch., Bath; Balliol Coll., Oxford (BA Hons). Asst Registrar, Royal Commn on Historical Manuscripts, 1967–73; Partner, Carved Angel Restaurant, Dartmouth, 1974–84; publisher, The Three Course Newsletter (and predecessors), 1980–89; Editor, Good Food Guide, 1989–93. *Publications:* Cooking in the Country, 1986; Cosmic Cuisine, 1988; contribs Sunday Telegraph, etc. *Recreations:* baking, buildings. *Address:* Allaleigh House, Blackawton, Totnes, Devon TQ9 7DL.

JAK; *see* Jackson, R. A.

JAKEMAN, Prof. Eric, FRS 1990; Deputy Chief Scientific Officer, Defence Research Agency (formerly Royal Signals and Radar Establishment), since 1985; *b* 3 June 1939; *s* of Frederick Leonard Jakeman and Hilda Mary Hays; *m* 1968, Glenys Joan Cooper; two *d*. *Educ:* Brunts Grammar Sch., Mansfield; Univ. of Birmingham (BSc, PhD). FInstP 1979. Asst Res. Physicist, UCLA, 1963–64. DRA (formerly RRE, subseq. RSRE), 1964–. Vice-Pres. for Publications, Inst. of Physics, 1989–93; Mem. Exec. Cttee, European Physical Soc., 1990–94. Fellow, Optical Soc. of America, 1988. Maxwell Medal and Prize, Inst. of Physics, 1977; (jtly) MacRobert Award, 1977; (jtly) Instrument Makers' Co. Award. *Publications:* numerous contribs to learned jls. *Recreations:* gardening, music, beekeeping. *Address:* The Knell, Upper Colwall, Malvern, Worcs WR13 6PR.

JAKOBOVITS, family name of **Baron Jakobovits.**

JAKOBOVITS, Baron *cr* 1988 (Life Peer), of Regent's Park in Greater London; **Immanuel Jakobovits;** Kt 1981; Chief Rabbi of the United Hebrew Congregations of the British Commonwealth of Nations, 1967–91; *b* 8 Feb. 1921; *s* of Rabbi Dr Julius Jakobovits and Paula (*née* Wreschner); *m* 1949, Amelie Munk; two *s* four *d*. *Educ:* London Univ. (BA; PhD 1955; Fellow, UCL, 1984–; Hon. Fellow, QMC, 1987); Jews' Coll. and Yeshivah Etz Chaim, London. Diploma, 1944; Associate of Jews' Coll. Minister: Brondesbury Synagogue, 1941–44; SE London Synagogue, 1944–47; Great Synagogue, London, 1947–49; Chief Rabbi of Ireland, 1949–58; Rabbi of Fifth Avenue Synagogue, New York, 1958–67. Hon. DD Yeshiva Univ., NY, 1975; Hon. DLitt City, 1986; DD Lambeth, 1987; Hon. DD Wales, 1993. Templeton Prize for Progress in Religion, 1991. *Publications:* Jewish Medical Ethics, 1959 (NY; 4th edn 1975); Jewish Law Faces Modern Problems, 1965 (NY); Journal of a Rabbi, 1966 (NY), 1967 (GB); The Timely and the Timeless, 1977; If Only My People . . . Zionism in My Life, 1984; (ed) Centenary Edition of the Authorised Daily Prayer-Book, 1990; contrib. learned and popular jls in America, England and Israel. *Address:* Jews' College, 44a Albert Road, NW4 2SJ.

JALLAND, His Honour William Herbert Wainwright; a Circuit Judge, Manchester, 1975–88 (sitting in Crown Court, Manchester, and County Courts, Manchester and Salford); *b* 1922; *o s* of Arthur Edgar Jalland, QC, JP and Elizabeth Hewitt Jalland; *m* 1945, Helen Monica, BEM 1984, *o d* of John and Edith Wyatt; one *s* one *d*. *Educ:* Manchester Grammar Sch.; Manchester Univ. LLB 1949. Served War of 1939–45, HM Forces at home and abroad, 1941–46: Captain, King's Own Royal Regt, attached 8th Bn Durham LI. Called to Bar, Gray's Inn, 1950; practised Northern Circuit; part-time Dep. Coroner, City of Salford, 1955–65; part-time Dep. Recorder, Burnley, 1962–70; part-time Dep. Chm., Lancs County Sessions, 1970–71; Recorder, 1972; a Circuit Judge, Liverpool and Merseyside, 1972–75. JP Lancs, 1970–88; Liaison Judge at Magistrates' Courts, Rochdale, Middleton and Heywood, 1974–86. Vice-Pres., Old Mancunians' Assoc., 1979–; Pres., Styal Sports and Social Club, 1979–88. *Recreations:* hillwalking, gardening, photography. *Address:* c/o Circuit Administrator, Northern Circuit, 15 Quay Street, Manchester M60 9FD.

JAMES, family name of **Baron Northbourne.**

JAMES OF HOLLAND PARK, Baroness *cr* 1991 (Life Peer), of Southwold in the County of Suffolk; **Phyllis Dorothy White, (P. D. James),** OBE 1983; JP; FRSL; author; *b* 3 Aug. 1920; *d* of Sidney Victor James and Dorothy Amelia James (*née* Hone); *m* 1941, Connor Bantry White (*d* 1964); two *d*. *Educ:* Cambridge Girls' High Sch. Administrator, National Health Service, 1949–68; Civil Service: apptd Principal, Home Office, 1968; Police Dept, 1968–72; Criminal Policy Dept, 1972–79. Associate Fellow, Downing Coll., Cambridge, 1986. A Gov., BBC, 1988–93; Member: BBC Gen. Adv. Council, 1987–88; Arts Council, 1988–92 (Chm., Literature Adv. Panel, 1988–92); Bd, British Council, 1988–93 (Mem., Literature Cttee, 1988–93). Chm., Booker Prize Panel of Judges, 1987. Chm., Soc. of Authors, 1984–86; Member: Detection Club; CWA. JP: Willesden, 1979–82; Inner London, 1984. FRSL 1987; FRSA. Hon. DLitt: Buckingham, 1992; London, 1993; Hertfordshire, 1994; Glasgow, 1995. Cartier Diamond Dagger, CWA, 1987. *Publications:* Cover Her Face, 1962 (televised 1985); A Mind to Murder, 1963 (televised 1995); Unnatural Causes, 1967 (televised 1993); Shroud for a Nightingale, 1971 (Silver Dagger, CWA; Edgar Allen Poe Scroll; televised 1984); (with T. A. Critchley) The Maul and the Pear Tree, 1971; An Unsuitable Job for a Woman, 1972 (filmed 1982); The Black Tower, 1975 (Silver Dagger, CWA; televised 1986); Death of an Expert Witness, 1977 (televised 1983); Innocent Blood, 1980; The Skull beneath the Skin, 1982; A Taste for Death, 1986 (televised 1988); Devices and Desires, 1989 (televised 1991); The Children of Men, 1992 (Deo Gloria Award); Original Sin, 1994. *Recreations:* exploring churches, walking by the sea. *Address:* c/o Greene & Heaton Ltd, 37 Goldhawk Road, W12 8QQ.

JAMES, Anne Eleanor S.; *see* Scott-James.

JAMES, Anthony Trafford, CBE 1979; PhD; FRS 1983; Member of Executive Committee of Unilever Research Colworth Laboratory, also Head of Division of Biosciences, 1972–85; *b* Cardiff, Wales, 6 March 1922; *s* of J. M. and I. James; *m* 1st, 1945, O. I. A. Clayton (*d* 1980); two *s* one *d*; 2nd, 1983, L. J. Beare; one *s*. *Educ:* University College Sch.; Northern Polytechnic; University Coll. London (BSc, PhD), Fellow 1975; Harvard Business Sch. (AMP). MRC Junior Fellowship at Bedford Coll., Univ. of London (with Prof. E. E. Turner, subject: Antimalarials), 1945–47; Jun. Mem. staff, Lister Inst. for Preventive Med., London (with Dr R. L. M. Synge, Nobel Laureate, subject: Structure of Gramicidin S), 1947–50; Mem. scientific staff, Nat. Inst. for Med. Res., London (special appt awarded, 1961), 1950–62 (with Dr A. J. P. Martin, FRS, Nobel Laureate, 1950–56); Unilever Research Lab., Sharnbrook: Div. Manager and Head of Biosynthesis Unit, 1962–67; Head of Div. of Plant Products and Biochemistry, 1967–69; Gp Manager, Biosciences Gp, 1969–72. Industrial Prof. of Chemistry, Loughborough Univ. of Technology, 1966–71. Non-exec. Dir, Wellcome Foundn, 1985–92. Member: SRC, 1973–77; Food Sci. and Technol. Bd, MAFF, 1975–80; Manpower Cttee, SERC, 1981–84; ABRC, 1983–; Council, Royal Soc., 1988–90; Chairman: Food Composition, Quality and Safety Cttee, MAFF, 1975–80; Biotechnol. Management Cttee, SERC, 1981–85. Hon. Dr Dijon, 1981; Hon. DSc Cranfield Inst. of Technology, 1985. Has had various awards incl. some from abroad. *Publications:* New Biochemical Separations (ed A. T. James and L. J. Morris), 1964; Lipid Biochemistry—an introduction (M. I. Gurr and A. T. James), 1972. *Recreations:* glass engraving, antique collecting, gardening. *Address:* 9 High Street, Harrold, Beds MK43 7DQ.

JAMES, (Arthur) Walter; Principal, St Catharine's, Windsor, 1974–82; *b* 30 June 1912; *s* of late W. J. James, OBE; *m* 1st, 1939, Elisabeth (marr. diss. 1956), *e d* of Richard Rylands

Howroyd; one *d*; 2nd, 1957, Ann Jocelyn, *y d* of late C. A. Leavy Burton; one *d* and one adopted *s* two adopted *d*. *Educ:* Uckfield Grammar Sch.; Keble Coll., Oxford (Scholar); 1st Cl. Mod. Hist.; Liddon Student; Arnold Essay Prizeman. Senior Demy of Magdalen Coll., 1935; Scholar in Mediæval Studies, British School at Rome, 1935; Editorial staff, Manchester Guardian, 1937–46. NFS 1939–45. Contested (L) Bury, Lancs, 1945. Dep. Editor, The Times Educational Supplement, 1947–51, Editor, 1952–69; Special Advisor on Educn, Times Newspapers, 1969–71; also Editor, Technology, 1957–60. Reader in Journalism, Univ. of Canterbury, NZ, 1971–74. Member: BBC Gen. Advisory Council, 1956–64; Council of Industrial Design, 1961–66; Council, Royal Society of Arts, 1964; Cttee, British-American Associates, 1964; Governor, Central School of Art and Design, 1966. Woodard Lecturer, 1965. *Publications:* (Ed.) Temples and Faiths 1958; The Christian in Politics, 1962; The Teacher and his World, 1962; A Middle-class Parent's Guide to Education, 1964; (contrib.) Looking Forward to the Seventies, 1967. *Recreation:* gardening. *Address:* 1 Cumberland Mews, The Great Park, Windsor, Berks SL4 2JD. *T:* Egham (01784) 431377. *Club:* National Liberal.

JAMES, Aubrey Graham Wallen; Deputy Chief Land Registrar, 1975–81; *b* 5 Jan. 1918; *s* of Reginald Aubrey James and Amelia Martha James; *m* 1952, Audrey Elizabeth, *er d* of Dr and Mrs A. W. F. Edmonds; two *s*. *Educ:* Nantgyle Grammar Sch.; London Univ. (LLB 1939). Solicitor, 1940. Served Second World War, 1940–46, Major, Cheshire Regt. Legal Asst, HM Land Registry, 1948; Asst Land Registrar, 1954; Land Registrar, 1963; Dist Land Registrar, Nottingham, 1963. Chm., E Midlands Region, CS Sports Council, 1970–75. *Recreations:* gardening, motoring, golf; has played Rugby, cricket and tennis with enthusiasm and in latter years, has turned to admin of these and other sports. *Address:* 11 Playle Chase, Great Totham, Maldon CM9 8UT.

JAMES, Basil; Special Commissioner, 1963–82, Presiding Special Commissioner, 1982–83; *b* 25 May 1918; *s* of late John Elwyn James, MA (Oxon.), Cardiff, and Mary Janet (*née* Lewis), Gwaelodygarth, Glam; *m* 1943, Moira Houlding Rayner, MA (Cantab.), *d* of late Capt. Benjamin Harold Rayner, North Staffs Regt, and Elizabeth (*née* Houlding), Preston, Lancs; one *s* twin *d*. *Educ:* Llandovery Coll.; Canton High Sch., Cardiff; Christ's Coll., Cambridge (Exhibnr). Tancred Law Student, Lincoln's Inn, 1936; Squire Law Scholar, Cambridge, 1936. BA 1939; MA 1942. Called to Bar, Lincoln's Inn, 1940. Continuous sea service as RNVR officer in small ships on anti-submarine and convoy duties in Atlantic, Arctic and Mediterranean, 1940–45. King George V Coronation Scholar, Lincoln's Inn, 1946. Practised at Chancery Bar, 1946–63. Admitted to Federal Supreme Court of Nigeria, 1962. *Publications:* contrib. to Atkin's Court Forms and Halsbury's Laws of England. *Recreations:* music, gardening.

See also J. E. R. James.

JAMES, Cecil; *see* James, T. C. G.

JAMES, Charles Edwin Frederic; His Honour Judge Charles James; a Circuit Judge, since 1993; *b* 17 April 1943; *s* of Frederic Crockett Gwilym James and Marjorie Peggy James (*née* Peace); *m* 1968, Diana Mary Francis (*née* Thornton); two *s*. *Educ:* Trent College, Long Eaton, Derbyshire; Selwyn College, Cambridge. MA 1968. Called to the Bar, Inner Temple, 1965; practised on Northern Circuit, 1965–93. A Recorder, 1982–93. *Recreation:* family pursuits. *Address:* Manchester Crown Court, Crown Square, Manchester M3 3FL. *Clubs:* Cambridge University Cricket; Royal Liverpool Golf, Royal Mersey Yacht.

JAMES, Christopher John; Chairman, Birmingham Midshires Building Society, since 1990; *b* 20 March 1932; *s* of John Thomas Walters James, MC and Cicely Hilda James; *m* 1958, Elizabeth Marion Cicely Thomson; one *s* one *d*. *Educ:* Clifton Coll., Bristol; Magdalene Coll., Cambridge (MA). Served RA, 2nd Lieut, 1951–52; TA, 1952–60. Admitted Solicitor, 1958; Partner, Johnson & Co., Birmingham, 1960–87 (Sen. Partner, 1985–87); Dep. Sen. Partner, Martineau Johnson, 1987–89, Sen. Partner, 1989–94. Director: Birmingham Midshires Building Soc. (formerly Birmingham Building Soc.), 1980– (Dep. Chm., 1988–90); R. Griggs Group Ltd, 1993– (Dep. Chm., 1994–). Gen. Comr for Income Tax, 1974–82. Pres., Birmingham Law Soc., 1983–84. Mem. Council, Edgbaston High Sch. for Girls, 1980–90 (Chm., 1987–90); Gov., Clifton Coll., 1980–. *Recreations:* photography, railways, golf. *Clubs:* Birmingham; Little Aston Golf.

JAMES, Christopher Philip; His Honour Judge James; a Circuit Judge, since 1980; *b* 27 May 1934; *yr s* of late Herbert Edgar James, CBE, and late Elizabeth Margaret James. *Educ:* Felsted School; Magdalene Coll., Cambridge (MA). Commnd RASC, 1953. Called to the Bar, Gray's Inn, 1959; a Recorder of the Crown Court, 1979. *Address:* Flat 8, 93 Elm Park Gardens, SW10 9QW. *Club:* United Oxford & Cambridge University.

JAMES, Clive Vivian Leopold; writer and broadcaster; feature writer for The Observer, since 1972 (also television critic, 1972–82); *b* 7 Oct. 1939; *s* of Albert Arthur James and Minora May (*née* Darke). *Educ:* Sydney Technical High Sch.; Sydney Univ.; Pembroke Coll., Cambridge. President of Footlights when at Cambridge. Record albums as lyricist for Pete Atkin: Beware of the Beautiful Stranger; Driving through Mythical America; A King at Nightfall; The Road of Silk; Secret Drinker; Live Libel; The Master of the Revels; Touch has a Memory, 1991. Song-book with Pete Atkin: A First Folio. *Television series:* Cinema, Up Sunday, So It Goes, A Question of Sex, Saturday Night People, Clive James on Television, The Late Clive James, The Late Show with Clive James, Saturday Night Clive, The Talk Show with Clive James, Clive James—Fame in the Twentieth Century; Review of the Year; Sunday Night Clive; *television documentaries:* Shakespeare in Perspective: Hamlet, 1980; The Clive James Paris Fashion Show, Clive James and the Calendar Girls, 1981; The Return of the Flash of lightning, 1982; Clive James Live in Las Vegas,1982; Clive James meets Roman Polanski, 1984; The Clive James Great American Beauty Pageant, 1984; Clive James in Dallas, 1985; Clive James Meets Katherine Hepburn, 1986; Clive James on Safari, 1986; Clive James and the Heroes of San Francisco, 1987; Clive James in Japan, 1987; Clive James meets Jane Fonda, Clive James on the 80s, 1989; Postcard series, 1989–: Rio, Chicago, Paris, Miami, Rome, Shanghai, Sydney, London, Cairo, New York, Bombay, Berlin. *Publications: non-fiction:* The Metropolitan Critic, 1974, 2nd edn 1994; The Fate of Felicity Fark in the Land of the Media, 1975; Peregrine Prykke's Pilgrimage through the London Literary World, 1976; Britannia Bright's Bewilderment in the Wilderness of Westminster, 1976; Visions Before Midnight, 1977; At the Pillars of Hercules, 1979; First Reactions, 1980; The Crystal Bucket, 1981; Charles Charming's Challenges on the Pathway to the Throne, 1981; From the Land of Shadows, 1982; Glued to the Box, 1982; Flying Visits, 1984; Snakecharmers in Texas, 1988; On Television, 1991; The Dreaming Swimmer, 1992; Fame, 1993; *fiction:* Brilliant Creatures, 1983; The Remake, 1987; Brrm! Brrm!, 1991; The Silver Castle, 1995; *verse:* Fan-Mail, 1977; Poem of the Year, 1983; Other Passports: poems 1958–85, 1986; *autobiography:* Unreliable Memoirs, 1980; Falling Towards England: Unreliable Memoirs II, 1985; May Week Was in June: Unreliable Memoirs III, 1990.

JAMES, Rt Rev. Colin Clement Walter; Bishop of Winchester, 1985–95; *b* 20 Sept. 1926; *yr s* of late Canon Charles Clement Hancock James and Gwenyth Mary James; *m* 1962, Margaret Joan, (Sally), Henshaw; one *s* two *d*. *Educ:* Aldenham School; King's College, Cambridge (MA, Hons History); Cuddesdon Theological College. Assistant Curate, Stepney Parish Church, 1952–55; Chaplain, Stowe School, 1955–59; BBC Religious Broadcasting Dept, 1959–67; Religious Broadcasting Organizer, BBC South and West, 1960–67; Vicar of St Peter with St Swithin, Bournemouth, 1967–73; Bishop Suffragan of Basingstoke, 1973–77; Canon Residentiary of Winchester Cathedral, 1973–77; Bishop of Wakefield, 1977–85. Member of General Synod, 1970–; Chairman: Church Information Cttee, 1976–79; C of E's Liturgical Commn, 1986–93. Chm., BBC and IBA Central Religious Adv. Cttee, 1979–84. President: Woodard Corp., 1978–93; RADIUS, 1980–93. Chm., USPG, 1985–88. *Recreations:* theatre, travelling. *Address:* 5 Hermitage Road, Lansdown, Bath BA1 5SN.

JAMES, Sir Cynlais Morgan, (Sir Kenneth), KCMG 1985 (CMG 1976); HM Diplomatic Service, retired; Director General, Canning House, 1987–92; *b* 29 April 1926; *s* of Thomas James and Lydia Ann James (*née* Morgan); *m* 1953, Mary Teresa, *d* of R. D. Girouard and Lady Blanche Girouard; two *d*. *Educ:* Trinity Coll., Cambridge (MA). Service in RAF, 1944–47. Cambridge 1948–51. Entered Senior Branch of Foreign Service, 1951; Foreign Office, 1951–53; Third Sec., Tokyo, 1953–56; Second Sec., Rio de Janeiro, 1956–59; First Sec. and Cultural Attaché, Moscow, 1959–62; FO, 1962–65; Paris, 1965–69; promoted Counsellor, 1968; Counsellor and Consul-General, Saigon, 1969–71; Head of W European Dept, FCO, 1971–75; NATO Defence Coll., Rome, 1975–76; Minister, Paris, 1976–81; Ambassador to Poland, 1981–83; Asst Under Sec. of State, FCO, 1983; Ambassador to Mexico, 1983–86. Director: Thomas Cook, 1986–91; Latin American Investment Trust, 1990–; Foreign and Colonial Emerging Markets, 1993–; Gemini Management Consultants, 1992–; Consultant, Darwin Instruments, 1986–. Chairman: British-Mexican Soc., 1987–90; British Inst. in Paris, 1988–; Bd, Inst. of Latin American Studies, 1992–; Mem., Franco-British Council, 1986–. Hon. Dr Mexican Acad. of Internat. Law, 1984. Order of the Aztec, 1st cl. (Mexico), 1985; Order of Andres Bello, 1st cl. (Venezuela), 1990; Order of Merit (Chile), 1991; Chevalier, Legion of Honour (France). *Recreation:* tennis. *Address:* 63 Eccleston Square, SW1V 1PH. *Clubs:* Brooks's, Beefsteak, Pratt's, MCC; Travellers' (Paris).

JAMES, Prof. David Edward; Professor (formerly Director) of Adult Education, University of Surrey, since 1969; *b* 31 July 1937; *s* of Charles Edward James and Dorothy Hilda (*née* Reeves); *m* 1963, Penelope Jane Murray; two *s* one *d*. *Educ:* Universities of Reading, Oxford, Durham, London (Bsc Hons Gen., BSc Hons Special, MEd, DipEd, DipFE); FRSH; FITD 1992. Lectr in Biology, City of Bath Tech. Coll. 1961–63; Lectr in Sci. and Educn, St Mary's Coll. of Educn, Newcastle upon Tyne, 1963–64; University of Surrey: Lectr in Educnl Psych., 1964–69; Hd, Dept of Educnl Studies, 1982–93. FRSA. *Publications:* A Student's Guide to Efficient Study, 1966, Amer. edn 1967; Introduction to Psychology, 1968, Italian edn 1972. *Recreation:* farming. *Address:* Department of Educational Studies, University of Surrey, Guildford, Surrey GU2 5XH.

JAMES, Dr (David) Geraint, FRCP; Consultant Physician since 1959, and Dean since 1968, Royal Northern Hospital, London; Consultant Ophthalmic Physician, St Thomas Hospital, London, since 1973; Teacher, University of London, since 1979; *b* 2 Jan. 1922; *s* of David James and Sarah (*née* Davies); *m* 1951, Sheila Sherlock, *qv*; two *d*. *Educ:* Jesus Coll., Cambridge (MA 1945); Mddx Hosp. Med. Sch., London (MD 1953); Columbia Univ., NYC. FRCP 1964. Adjunct Prof. of Medicine, Univ. of Miami, Fla, 1973–, and Prof. of Epidemiology, 1981–; Adjunct Prof., Royal Free Hosp. Med. Sch., 1987–; Consulting Phys. to RN, 1972–; Hon. Consultant Phys., US Veterans' Admin, 1978–; Hon. Consulting Phys., Sydney Hosp., Australia, 1969–. President: Internat. Cttee on Sarcoidosis, 1987– (World Exec. Sec., 1980–86); Italian Congress on Sarcoidosis, 1983; World Assoc. of Sarcoidosis, 1987–; Vice-Pres., Fellowship of Postgrad. Medicine; Past President: Med. Soc. of London; Harveian Soc.; Osler Club (Hon. Fellow); Vice-Pres., London Glamorgan Soc., 1989–; Mem. Council, Cymmrodorion Soc. Lectures: Tudor Edwards, RCP and RCS, 1983; George Wise Meml, New York City, 1983. Foreign Corresponding Mem., French Nat. Acad. of Medicine, 1987; Hon. Corresp. Mem., Thoracic Socs of Italy, France, Dominican Republic and Portugal; Hon. FACP 1990; Hon. FRCOphth, 1994. Editor, Internat. Rev. of Sarcoidosis, 1984–. Freeman, City of London, 1961. Hon. LLD Wales, 1982. Chesterfield Medal, Inst. of Dermatology, London, 1957; Gold Medal, Barraquer Inst. of Ophthalmology, 1958; Carlo Forlanini Gold Medal, Italian Thoracic Soc., 1983. Gold Medal, Milan, 1987. Kt of Order of Christopher Columbus (Dominican Republic), 1987. *Publications:* Diagnosis and Treatment of Infections, 1957; Sarcoidosis, 1970; Circulation of the Blood, 1978; Atlas of Respiratory Diseases, 1981, 2nd edn 1992; Sarcoidosis and other Granulomatous Disorders, 1985; Textbook on Sarcoidosis and other Granulomatous Disorders, 1994. *Recreations:* history of medicine, international Welshness, Rugby football. *Address:* 149 Harley Street, W1N 1HG. *T:* 0171-935 4444. *Club:* Athenæum.

JAMES, Dr David Gwynfor; Head of Meteorological Research Flight, Royal Aircraft Establishment, Farnborough, 1971–82; *b* 16 April 1925; *s* of William James and Margaret May Jones; *m* 1953, Margaret Vida Gower; two *d*. *Educ:* Univ. of Wales, Cardiff (BSc, PhD). Joined Meteorological Office, 1950; Met. Res. Flight, Farnborough, 1951; Forecasting Res., Dunstable, 1953; Christmas Island, Pacific, 1958; Satellite Lab., US Weather Bureau, 1961; Cloud Physics Res., Bracknell, 1966; Met. Res. Flight, RAE, 1971. Fellow, UC Cardiff, 1987. *Publications:* papers in Qly Jl Royal Met. Soc., Jl Atmospheric Sciences, Met. Res. Papers, and Nature. *Recreations:* golf, choral singing. *Address:* Tŷ'r Onnen, 56 Port Lion, Llangwm, Haverfordwest, Dyfed SA62 4JT.

JAMES, Dr David William Francis, OBE 1989; Chief Executive, British Ceramic Research Ltd (formerly British Ceramic Research Association), 1982–91 (Director of Research, 1978–82); *b* 29 March 1929; *s* of Thomas M. and Margaret A. James, Merthyr Tydfil; *m* 1953, Elaine Maureen, *d* of Thomas and Gladys Hewett, Swansea; two *d*. *Educ:* Cyfarthfa Castle Sch., Merthyr Tydfil; Univ. of Wales (BSc); Univ. of London (PhD). FICeram 1985; FIM 1991; LRPS 1993. Research Asst, Inst. of Cancer Research, Royal Marsden Hosp., 1950–54; Flying Officer, RAF, 1954–56; Research Officer, Imperial Chemical Industries (now Mond Div.), 1956–60; Lectr and Sen. Lectr, UC North Wales, Bangor, 1960–71; Dep. Principal, Glamorgan Polytechnic, 1971–72; Principal and Director, Polytechnic of Wales, 1972–78. Council for National Academic Awards: Mem., 1976–82; Mem., Cttee for Research, 1976–83; Mem., Cttee on Entry Qualifications, 1976–79; Mem., Cttee for Academic Policy, 1979–80; Mem., Gen. Cttee, 1979–83; Chm., Sub-Cttee on College Research Degrees, 1981–85 (Mem., Working Party on Res. Policy, 1982–84); Mem., Cttee for Instns, 1982–86; Mem., Research Adv. Cttee, 1985–87; Mem., Credit Accumulation and Transfer System Adv. Bd, 1986–87. Member: WJEC Techn. Educn Cttee, 1972–78, Techn. Examns Cttee and Management Adv. Cttee, 1972–75; SRC Polytechnics Cttee, 1975–78; Mid-Glamorgan Further Educn Cttee, 1974–78; F and GP Cttee, CDRA, 1983–86 (Vice-Chm., 1985–86); Exec. Cttee, AIRTO, 1986–91 (Pres., 1987–88); Council, CBI, 1986–88. Pres., Inst. of Ceramics, 1989–90 (Mem. Council, 1988–93; Mem., Editl Bd, 1985–93); Vice Pres., Inst. of Materials, 1992–93. Member: Court, Univ. of Wales; Court, UWIST, 1972–78; Court, Univ. of Surrey, 1978–91; Governor, Westminster Coll., 1983–88. *Publications:* research papers in various jls; several patents. *Recreations:* photography, reading, church work. *Address:* Fairways, Birchall, Leek, Staffs ST13 5RD. *T:* Leek (01538) 373311.

JAMES, Derek Claude, OBE 1989; Director of Social Services, Leeds, 1978–89; *b* 9 March 1929; *s* of Cecil Claude James and Violet (*née* Rudge); *m* 1954, Evelyn (*née*

Thomas); one *s* one *d*. *Educ:* King Edward's Grammar Sch., Camp Hill, Birmingham; Open Univ. (BA). Dip. in Municipal Admin. Local Government: Birmingham, 1946–60; Coventry, 1960–63; Bradford, 1963–69; Leeds, 1969–89. Mem., Yorks and Humberside RHA, 1976–82; Chm., Leeds Area Review Cttee (Child Abuse), 1978–89; Mem., Nat. Adv. Council on Employment of Disabled People, 1984–89; Pres., Nat. Assoc. of Nursery and Family Care, 1988–92; Chairman: Nightstop Homeless Persons Project, 1989–92; Council, Disabled Living Centre, Leeds, 1994–; Vice-Chm., Nat. Family Service Units, 1992– (Mem. Nat. Cttee, 1992–); Expert Panel Mem., Registered Homes Tribunal, 1990–; Adviser: AMA Social Services Cttee, 1983–89; Physical Disablement Res. Liaison Gp, 1986–89. Sanctuary Housing Association: Chm., North and West Yorks Area Cttee, 1992–; Mem., North Divl Cttee, 1992–; Mem., Central Council, 1993–. *Recreations:* watching sport, garden pottering, acceding to my grandchildren's wishes. *Address:* Hill House, Woodhall Hills, Calverley, Pudsey, West Yorks LS28 5QY. *T:* Pudsey (0113) 2578044.

JAMES, Air Vice-Marshal Edgar, CBE 1966; DFC 1945; AFC 1948 (Bar 1959); FRAeS; aviation consultant, retired; *b* 19 Oct. 1915; *s* of Richard George James and Gertrude (*née* Barnes); *m* 1941, Josephine M. Steel; two *s*. *Educ:* Neath Grammar School. Joined RAF, 1939; commnd; flying instr duties, Canada, until 1944; opl service with Nos 305 and 107 Sqdns, 1944–45. Queen's Commendation for Valuable Service in the Air (1943, 1944, 1956). Empire Flying Sch. and Fighter Comd Ops Staff, until Staff Coll., 1950. Ops Requirements, Air Min., 1951–53; 2nd TAF Germany, 1953–56; comd No 68 Night Fighter Squadron, 1954–56; CFE, 1956–58; HQ Fighter Comd Staff, 1958–59; Asst Comdt, CFS, 1959–61; CO, RAF Leeming, 1961–62; Dir Ops Requirements 1, Min. of Def. (Air Force Dept), 1962–66; Comdr British Forces, Zambia, Feb.–Sept. 1966. Dep. Controller of Equipment, Min. of Technology, 1966–69. Wing Comdr 1953; Gp Capt. 1959; Air Cdre 1963; Air Vice-Marshal 1967. FRAeS 1971. *Recreation:* sailing. *Address:* Lowmead, Traine Paddock, Modbury, Devon PL21 ORN. *T:* Modbury (01548) 830492. *Clubs:* Royal Air Force; Royal Western Yacht (Plymouth).

JAMES, Edison Chenfil; Prime Minister, Dominica, since 1995; *b* 18 Oct. 1943; *s* of David and Patricia James; *m* 1970, Wilma; one *s* two *d*. *Educ:* North East London Poly. (BSc Hons); Univ. of Reading (MSc); Imperial Coll., London (Dip. Pest Management). Teacher, St Mary's Acad., 1973; Agronomist, Min. of Agriculture, Dominica, 1974–76; Farm Improvement Officer, Caribbean Develt Bank and Agric. and Indust. Develt Bank, 1976–80; Project Co-ordinator, Coconut Rehabilitation; Gen. Manager, Dominica Banana Marketing Corp., 1980–87; Man. Dir, Agric. Managing Corp., 1987–95. *Recreations:* cricket, football, table tennis, politics, international affairs. *Address:* Prime Minister's Office, Roseau, Dominica, West Indies. *T:* 4482401. *Club:* Rotary Club of Dominica.

JAMES, Edward Foster, CMG 1968; OBE 1946; HM Diplomatic Service, retired; *b* 18 Jan. 1917; *s* of late Arthur Foster James; *m* 1985, Janet Mary Walls; one *s* two *d* by a previous marriage. Served HM Forces, 1939–46, India, Burma, Malaya, Indonesia; Lieut-Colonel (GSO1) (OBE, despatches twice). Joined HM Diplomatic Service, 1947; Rangoon, 1948; Hong Kong, 1951; Foreign Office, 1953; Rome, 1955; Foreign Office, 1958; Berlin, 1960; FO (later FCO), 1961–74. Exec. Dir, Inst. of Directors, 1975–76; Dep. Dir-Gen., CBI, 1976–83. Chm., Coastal Pollution Control plc, 1984–85; Dir, Tace plc, 1984–91. *Address:* 95 Gloucester Terrace, W2 3HB. *T:* 0171–262 0139. *Club:* Special Forces.

JAMES, Edwin Kenneth George; Chairman, Photon plc, 1986–89, retired; Chief Scientific Officer, Civil Service Department, 1970–76; *b* 27 Dec. 1916; *s* of late Edwin and Jessie Marion James; *m* 1941, Dorothy Margaret Pratt; one *d*. *Educ:* Latymer Upper Sch., Northern Polytechnic. BSc London; FRSC; FOR. Joined War Office, 1938; Chem. Defence Exper. Stn, 1942; Aust. Field Exper. Stn, 1944–46; Operational Research Gp, US Army, Md, 1950–54; Dir, Biol and Chem. Defence, WO, 1961; Army (later Defence) Op. Res. Estab., Byfleet, 1965; HM Treasury (later Civil Service Dept), 1968. Chm., PAG Ltd, 1984–87 (Dir, 1977–84). Silver Medal, Op. Res. Soc., 1979. *Recreations:* writing, walking. *Address:* 5 Watersmeet Road, East Harnham, Salisbury, Wilts SP2 8JH. *T:* Salisbury (01722) 334099. *Club:* Athenæum.

JAMES, Eleanor Mary; Lecturer in Mathematics, University College of Wales, Aberystwyth, 1957–92; *b* 31 Aug. 1935; *d* of Morris and Violet Mary Jones; *m* 1958, David Bryan James. *Educ:* Ardwyn Grammar Sch., Aberystwyth; University College of Wales, Aberystwyth (BSc 1955; PhD 1972). Member: Welsh Consumer Council, 1981–90; CECG, 1982–84; Consumer Develt Sub-Cttee, Nat. Consumer Council, 1983–85; Layfield Cttee of Enquiry, Local Govt Finance, 1974–76; Audit Commn for Local Authorities and NHS, 1988–91; Dyfed-Powys Police Authy, 1994–. Member: N Wales Area Cttee, NACAB (formerly CAD), 1987–90, 1991– (Chm., Aberystwyth, 1988–93); POUNC, 1991– (Chm., Council for Wales, 1991–); Radioactive Waste Management Adv. Cttee, 1991–94; Chairman: Ceredigion Br., Campaign for Protection of Rural Wales, 1992– (Sec., 1989–92); Wales Rural Forum, 1994–. National Federation of Women's Institutes: Mem., Envmt and Public Affairs Sub-Cttee, 1981–84; Vice Chm., Fedn of Wales Sub-Cttee, 1991–94; Chm., Dyfed Ceredigion Fedn of WIs, 1993– (Treas., 1989–92). University College of Wales: Mem. Council, 1982–86; Mem., Court of Governors, 1982–; Treas., Old Students' Assoc., 1975–. *Publication:* (with T. V. Davies) Nonlinear Differential Equations, 1966. *Recreations:* walking, swimming, the WI. *Address:* Dolhuan, Llandre, Bowstreet, Dyfed SY24 5AB. *T:* Aberystwyth (01970) 828362.

JAMES, Rev. Canon Eric Arthur; an Extra Chaplain to HM the Queen, since 1995 (Chaplain, 1984–95); Hon. Director, Christian Action, since 1990 (Director, 1979–90); *b* 14 April 1925; *s* of John Morgan James and Alice Amelia James. *Educ:* Dagenham County High School; King's Coll. London (MA, BD; FKC 1986). Asst Curate, St Stephen with St John, Westminster, 1951–55; Chaplain Trinity Coll., Cambridge, 1955–59; Select Preacher to Univ. of Cambridge, 1959–60; Vicar of St George, Camberwell and Warden of Trinity College Mission, 1959–64; Director of Parish and People, 1964–69; Proctor in Convocation, 1964–72; Canon Precentor of Southwark Cathedral, 1964–73; Canon Residentiary and Missioner, Diocese of St Albans, 1973–83; Hon. Canon, 1983–90; Canon Emeritus, 1990. Preacher to Gray's Inn, 1978–; Select Preacher to Univ. of Oxford, 1991–92. Commissary to Bishop of Kimberley, 1965–67, to Archbishop of Melanesia, 1969–93. Examining Chaplain to Bishop of St Albans, 1973–83, to Bishop of Truro, 1983–93. FRSA 1992. DD Lambeth, 1993. *Publications:* The Double Cure, 1957, 2nd edn 1980; Odd Man Out, 1962; (ed) Spirituality for Today, 1968; (ed) Stewards of the Mysteries of God, 1979; A Life of Bishop John A. T. Robinson: Scholar, Pastor, Prophet, 1987; (ed) God's Truth, 1988; Judge Not: a selection of sermons preached in Gray's Inn Chapel, 1989; Collected Thoughts: fifty scripts for BBC's Thought for The Day, 1990; (ed) A Last Eccentric: a symposium concerning the Rev. Canon F. A. Simpson: historian, preacher and eccentric, 1991; Word Over All: forty sermons 1985–1991, 1992; The Voice Said, Cry: forty sermons 1990–1993, 1994. *Address:* 11 Denny Crescent, SE11 4UY. *T:* 0171–582 3068. *Clubs:* Reform, Commonwealth Trust.

JAMES, Evan Maitland; *b* 14 Jan. 1911; *er s* of late A. G. James, CBE, and late Helen James (*née* Maitland); *m* 1st, 1939, Joan Goodnow (*d* 1989), *d* of late Hon. J. V. A. MacMurray, State Dept, Washington, DC; one *s* two *d*; 2nd, 1992, Miriam Beatriz Porter, *d* of late George and of Elizabeth Wansbrough. *Educ:* Durnford; Eton (Oppidan Scholar); Trinity Coll., Oxford (MA). Served War of 1939–45: War Reserve Police (Metropolitan), 1939; BBC Overseas (Propaganda Research) Dept, 1940–41; Ordinary Seaman/Lieut, RNVR, 1941–46. Clerk of the Merchant Taylors' Company, 1947–62; Steward of Christ Church, Oxford, 1962–78. *Address:* Upwood Park, Besselsleigh, Abingdon, Oxon OX13 5QE. *T:* Oxford (01865) 390535. *Club:* Travellers'.

JAMES, Geraint; *see* James, D. G.

JAMES, Geraldine; actress; *b* 6 July 1950; *d* of Gerald Trevor Thomas and Annabella Doogan Thomas; *m* 1986, Joseph Sebastian Blatchley; one *d*. *Educ:* Downe House, Newbury; Drama Centre London Ltd. *Stage:* repertory, Chester, 1972–74, Exeter, 1974–75, Coventry, 1975; Passion of Dracula, Queen's, 1978; The White Devil, Oxford, 1981; Turning Over, Bush, 1984; When I was a Girl I used to Scream and Shout, Whitehall, 1987; Cymbeline, National, 1988; Merchant of Venice, Phoenix, 1989, NY (Drama Desk Best Actress Award), 1990; Death and the Maiden, Duke of York's, 1992; Lysistrata, Old Vic and Wyndham's, 1993; Hedda Gabler, Royal Exchange, Manchester, 1993; *TV series:* The History Man, 1980; Jewel in the Crown, 1984; Blott on the Landscape, 1985; Echoes, 1988; Stanley and the Women, 1991; Kavanagh QC, 1994; Band of Gold, 1994; *TV films:* Dummy (Best Actress, BPG), 1977; Ex, Losing Track, 1991; A Doll's House, 1992; The Healer, 1994; Doggin' Around, 1994; *films:* Sweet William, 1978; Night Cruiser, 1978; Gandhi, 1981; The Storm, 1985; Wolves of Willoughby Chase, 1988; The Tall Guy, 1989; She's Been Away, 1989 (Best actress, Venice Film Festival, 1989); If Looks Could Kill, 1990; The Bridge, 1990; Prince of Shadows, 1991; No Worries Australia, 1993; Words on the Window Pane, 1994. *Recreation:* music. *Address:* c/o Julian Belfrage Associates, 68 St James's Street, SW1A 1PH; c/o Robert Duva Associates, 200 W 57th Street, Suite 1407, New York, NY 10019, USA.

JAMES, Rt. Rev. Graham Richard; *see* St Germans, Bishop Suffragan of.

JAMES, Henry Leonard, CB 1980; Associate Director, Godwins Ltd, since 1987; Consultant, Tolley Publishing, since 1987; Director, Pielle & Co. Ltd (PR Consultants), since 1989; *b* 12 Dec. 1919; *o s* of late Leonard Mark James and late Alice Esther James; *m* 1949, Sylvia Mary Bickell (*d* 1989). *Educ:* King Edward VI Sch., Birmingham. Entered Civil Service in Min. of Health, 1938; Founder Editor, The Window, Min. of Nat. Insce, 1948–51; Dramatic Critic and London Corresp. of Birmingham News, 1947–51; Press Officer, Min. of Pensions and Nat. Insce, 1951–55; Head of Films, Radio and Television, Admty, 1955–61; Head of Publicity, Min. of Educn, 1961–63; Chief Press Officer, Min. of Educn, 1963–64; Dep. Public Relations Adviser to Prime Minister, 1964; Dep. Press Sec. to Prime Minister, 1964–68; Chief Information Officer, Min. of Housing and Local Govt, 1969–70; Press Sec. to Prime Minister, 1970–71; Dir of Information, DoE, 1971–74; Dir-Gen., COI, 1974–78; Chief Press Sec. to the Prime Minister, 1979; Public Relations Advr to Main Bd, Vickers Ltd, 1978–80; Dir-Gen., Nat. Assoc. of Pension Funds, 1981–86; Dir-Gen., European Fedn for Retirement Provision, 1982–86. Vice-Pres., Retirement Trust, 1992–. Member: Pub. Cttee, Internat. Year of the Child, 1979; Council, RSPCA, 1980–84; BOTB, 1980–83. Alumni Guest Lectr, Gustavus Adolphus Coll., Minnesota, 1977. FCAM 1980 (Dep. Chm., 1979–84; Vice-Pres., 1984–). FRSA. FIPR (Pres., 1979; President's Medal, 1976). *Recreation:* visual arts. *Address:* 17 Beaumont Avenue, Richmond, Surrey TW9 2HE. *T:* 0181–940 9229.

JAMES, Howell Malcolm Plowden; Political Secretary to the Prime Minister, since 1994; *b* 13 March 1954; *s* of late T. J. and Virginia James. *Educ:* Mill Hill Sch., London. Head of Promotions, Capital Radio, 1978–82; Organiser, Help a London Child Charity, 1979–82; Head of Press and Publicity, TV-am, 1982–85; Special Adviser: Cabinet Office, 1985; Dept of Employment, 1985–87; DTI, 1987; Dir of Corporate Affairs, BBC, 1987–92; Dir of Corporate and Govt Affairs, Cable and Wireless, 1992–94. Dir, Broadcast Audience Res. Bd, 1987–92. Dir, English Nat. Ballet Sch., 1990–; Gov., George Eliot Sch., 1989–92. Trustee, Queen Elizabeth's Foundn for Disabled People Develt Trust, 1992–. *Recreations:* theatre, movies, food. *Address:* 10 Downing Street, SW1A 2AA. *Club:* Reform.

JAMES, Prof. Ioan Mackenzie, FRS 1968; MA, DPhil; Savilian Professor of Geometry, Oxford University, 1970–95, Professor Emeritus, since 1995; Fellow of New College, Oxford, 1970–95, Emeritus Fellow, since 1995; Editor, Topology, since 1962; *b* 23 May 1928; *o s* of Reginald Douglas and Jessie Agnes James; *m* 1961, Rosemary Gordon Stewart, Fellow of Templeton College, Oxford Centre for Management Studies; no *c*. *Educ:* St Paul's Sch. (Foundn Schol.); Queen's Coll., Oxford (Open Schol.). Commonwealth Fund Fellow, Princeton, Berkeley and Inst. for Advanced Study, 1954–55; Tapp Res. Fellow, Gonville and Caius Coll., Cambridge, 1956; Reader in Pure Mathematics, Oxford, 1957–69, and Senior Research Fellow, St John's Coll., 1959–69, Hon. Fellow, 1988. Hon. Prof., Univ. of Wales, 1989. London Mathematical Society: Treasurer, 1969–79; Pres., 1985–87; Whitehead Prize and Lectr, 1978. Mem. Council, Royal Soc., 1982–83. Gov., St Paul's Schs, 1970–. Hon. DSc Aberdeen, 1993. *Publications:* The Mathematical Works of J. H. C. Whitehead, 1963; The Topology of Stiefel Manifolds, 1976; Topological Topics, 1983; General Topology and Homotopy Theory, 1984; Aspects of Topology, 1984; Topological and Uniform Spaces, 1987; Fibrewise Topology, 1988; Introduction to Uniform Spaces, 1990; papers in mathematical jls. *Address:* Mathematical Institute, 24–29 St Giles, Oxford OX1 3LB. *T:* Oxford (01865) 273541.

JAMES, Jeffrey Russell, CMG 1994; HM Diplomatic Service; Charge d'Affaires, Tehran, since 1993; *b* 13 Aug. 1944; *s* of Lewis Charles James and Ruth James; *m* 1965, Mary Longden; two *d*. *Educ:* Whitgift Sch.; Keele Univ. (BA Hons Internat. Relations). FCO 1967; served Tehran and Kabul; Dep. Political Advr, BMG Berlin, 1978; FCO 1982; Counsellor on loan to Cabinet Office, 1984; Counsellor and Head of Chancery, Pretoria/Cape Town, 1986; Counsellor (Economic and Commercial), New Delhi, 1988; Head, Edinburgh European Council Unit, FCO, 1992. *Recreations:* bird watching, golf, tennis, hill walking. *Address:* c/o Foreign and Commonwealth Office, SW1A 2AH. *Clubs:* Commonwealth Trust; Tandridge Golf.

JAMES, John, CBE 1981; Founder and Chairman: John James Group of Companies Ltd, Bristol, 1961–79; Broadmead Group of Companies, 1946–60; Dawn Estates Ltd, since 1945; *b* 25 July 1906; *m* 1st (marr. diss.); one *s* two *d* (and one *d* decd); 2nd, Margaret Theodosia Parkes (*d* 1991). *Educ:* Merchant Venturers, Bristol. Chm. Bd of Trustees: Dawn James Charitable Foundn, 1965–; John James Bristol Foundn (formerly Bristol) Charitable Foundn) 1983–. Hon. LLD Bristol, 1983. *Recreations:* chess, swimming. *Address:* 7 Clyde Road, Redland, Bristol BS6 6RG. *T:* Bristol (0117) 923 9444.

JAMES, John A.; *see* Angell-James.

JAMES, John Christopher Urmston; Secretary, Lawn Tennis Association, since 1981 (Assistant Secretary, 1973–81); *b* 22 June 1937; *s* of John Urmston James and Ellen Irene James; *m* 1st, 1959, Gillian Mary Davies (marr. diss. 1982); two *s*; 2nd, 1982, Patricia Mary, *d* of late Arthur Leslie Walter White. *Educ:* St Michael's, Llanelli; Hereford Cathedral Sch. Harrods, 1954; Jaeger, 1961; Pringle, 1972. *Recreations:* tennis, Rugby football, walking, architecture, the countryside. *Address:* c/o Lawn Tennis Association, The Queen's Club, West Kensington, W14 9EG. *T:* 0171–385 2366. *Clubs:* Queen's, Questors, London Welsh, International of GB; West Hants (Bournemouth).

JAMES, John Douglas; Chief Executive, Woodland Trust, since 1992; *b* 28 July 1949; *s* of late William Antony James, ERD, MA and of Agnes Winifred James (*née* Mitchell); *m* 1971, Margaret Patricia Manton. *Educ:* Spalding Grammar School. Dip. in Co. Direction, Inst. of Dirs, 1994. Articled pupil, William H. Brown & Son, 1967–68; Marketing Dept, Geest Industries, 1969–71; Marketing Dept, John Player & Sons, 1971–77; Nat. Develt Officer, 1977, (first) Director, 1980, Exec. Dir, 1985, Woodland Trust. Nottingham Roosevelt Scholar, 1975; Churchill Fellow, 1980. Founder Mem., S Lincs Nature Reserves Ltd, 1968; Mem., Inst. of Charity Fundraising Managers. MInstD. Films: Locked up, 1964; The Story of Springfields, 1966; (producer) Woodland Rescue, BBC2 TV, 1980. Winner: Inst. of Amateur Cinematographers' Internat. Competition, 1964; Daily Mirror Childrens' Literary Competition, 1965. *Publications:* articles in countryside and gardening jls. *Recreation:* woodland walks. *Address:* The Woodland Trust, Autumn Park, Grantham, Lincs NG31 6LL. *T:* Grantham (01476) 74297.

JAMES, John Henry; Chief Executive, Kensington & Chelsea and Westminster Commissioning Agency, since 1992; *b* 19 July 1944; step *s* of George Arthur James and *s* of Doris May James; *m* 3rd, 1987, Anita Mary Stockton, *d* of Brian Scarth, QPM and Irene Scarth. *Educ:* Ludlow Grammar Sch.; Keble Coll., Oxford (BA Mod. Hist. 1965; postgrad. dip. in Econ. and Pol. Sci. 1966). AHSM 1991 (LHSM 1989). Entered Home Civil Service 1966; Asst Principal, Min. of Pensions and Nat. Insurance; Private Sec. to First Perm. Sec., 1969–71, Principal, 1971–74, DHSS; seconded to HM Treasury, 1974–76; Principal, 1976–78, Asst Sec., 1978–86, Under Sec., 1986–91, DHSS, later Dept of Health; Dir of Health Authority Finance, NHS Management Bd, 1986–89; General Manager: Harrow DHA, 1990–92; Parkside DHA, 1991–93. Co-ordinator, London Cardiac Specialty Rev., 1993. Non-Exec. Dir, Laing Homes Ltd, 1987–89. Member: Adv. Council, King's Fund Inst., 1990–93; Res. Task Force, 1994; Central R&D Council, 1994–. FRSA 1994. *Publications:* Transforming the NHS, 1994; contributed: Oxford Textbook of Public Health, 1985, 2nd edn 1991; Health Care UK, 1993; Rationing of Health and Social Care, 1993; Information Management in Health Services, 1994; articles in jls. *Recreations:* playing chess and cricket, travel, food and wine, collecting edible fungi. *Address:* KCW Commissioning Agency, 50 Eastbourne Terrace, W2 6LG.

JAMES, Prof. John Ivor Pulsford, MB, MS London; FRCS; FRCSE; George Harrison Law Professor of Orthopædic Surgery, Edinburgh University, 1958–79, now Emeritus Professor; Consultant in Orthopædic Surgery to the Navy, 1956–84; Head of Orthopaedic Services, Kuwait, 1980–83; *b* 19 Oct. 1913; *s* of late Stanley B. James and Jessica Heley; *m* 1968, Margaret Eiriol Samuel, MB, ChB; one *s* one *d*. *Educ:* Eggars Grammar Sch., Alton, Hants; University Coll. and Hosp., London, Hampshire County Schol., 1932–38; Ferrière Schol., University Coll., 1935; Goldsmid Schol., University Coll. Hosp., 1935; Magrath Schol., University Coll. Hosp., 1937; Rockefeller Fellowship, 1947–48; Consultant Orthopædic Surgeon, Royal National Orthopædic Hospital, 1946–58; Asst Dir of Studies, Institute of Orthopædics, University of London, 1948–58. Fellow Univ. Coll., London. Hunterian Prof., RCS, 1957; Past Pres., British Orthopædic Assoc. (Fellow); Past Pres., British Soc. for Surgery of the Hand; Mem. Société Internationale de Chirurgie Orthopédique et de Traumatologie; Corresp. Member: Amer. Orthopædic Assoc.; Austr. Orthopædic Assoc.; Scandinavian Orthopædic Assoc.; Hon. Member: Amer. Acad. of Orthopædic Surgeons; Dutch Orthopædic Assoc.; Assoc. for Orthopædic Surgery and Traumatology of Yugoslavia; Canadian Orthopædic Assoc.; New Zealand Orthopædic Assoc.; Hellenic Assoc. of Orthopædics and Traumatology; Société Française d'Orthopédie et de Traumatologie. Hon. FRACS. Late Temp. Lieut-Col RAMC. Golden Star, Order of Service to the Yugoslav People, 1970. *Publications:* Scoliosis, 1967, 2nd edn 1976; Poliomyelitis, 1987; A Surgeon in Yugoslavia in World War II, BMJ, 1992; articles relating to curvature of the spine and surgery of the hand in medical journals, etc. *Recreations:* beekeeping, gardening. *Address:* Abbey Farm, The Vatch, Slad Valley, Glos GL6 7LE. *T:* Stroud (01453) 764986.

JAMES, John Jocelyn S.; *see* Streatfeild-James.

JAMES, John Nigel Courtenay, CBE 1990; FRICS; Secretary and Keeper of the Records, Duchy of Cornwall, since 1993; Trustee of the Grosvenor Estate, since 1971; a Crown Estate Commissioner, since 1984; *b* 31 March 1935; *s* of Frank Courtenay James and Beryl May Wilford Burden; *m* 1961, Elizabeth Jane St Clair-Ford; one *s* one *d*. *Educ:* Sherborne Sch., Dorset. Chief Agent and Estate Surveyor, Grosvenor Estate, 1968–71. Director: Sun Alliance & London Insurance Gp, 1972–93 (a Vice-Chm., 1988–93); Woolwich Equitable Building Soc., 1982–89; Williams & Glyn's Bank plc, 1983–85; Royal Bank of Scotland, 1985–93. Member: Commn for the New Towns, 1978–86; Cttee of Management, RNLI, 1980–; Prince of Wales' Council, 1984–. Pres., RICS, 1980–81. *Recreation:* sailing. *Club:* Brooks's.

JAMES, Jonathan Elwyn Rayner; QC 1988; *b* 26 July 1950; *s* of Basil James, *qv*; *m* 1981, Anne Henshaw (*née* McRae); one *s*. *Educ:* King's College Sch., Wimbledon; Christ's Coll., Cambridge (MA, LLM); Brussels Univ. (Lic. Spécial en Droit Européen 1973). Called to Bar, Lincoln's Inn (Hardwicke Schol.), 1971, Bencher, 1994. Asst Recorder, 1994. Mem. Editl Bd, Entertainment Law Rev. *Publications:* (co-ed) EEC Anti-Trust Law, 1975; (co-ed) Copinger and Skone James on Copyright, 13th edn 1991; (jt consulting editor) Encyclopaedia of Forms and Precedents, Vol. 15 (Entertainment), 1989. *Recreations:* DIY, opera, 007, squash, travel (in a good year). *Address:* 5 New Square, Lincoln's Inn, WC2A 3RJ. *T:* 0171–404 0404.

JAMES, Sir Kenneth; *see* James, Sir C. M.

JAMES, Linda Elizabeth B.; *see* Blake-James.

JAMES, Lionel Frederic Edward, CBE 1977 (MBE (mil.) 1944); Comptroller, Forces Help Society and Lord Roberts Workshops, 1970–82; *b* 22 Feb. 1912; *s* of late Frederic James, Westmount, Exeter; *m* 1st, 1933, Harriet French-Harley (decd); one *s* one *d*; 2nd, 1992, Aurea Maidment. *Educ:* Royal Grammar Sch., Worcester. Investment Co., 1933–39. Served War with Royal Engineers, 1939–46: BEF; Planning Staff, Sicilian Invasion; N Africa, Sicily, Greece and Italy (Major). Dep. Dir, Overseas Service, Forces Help Soc., 1946, Dir, 1948; Asst Sec. of Society, 1953, Company Sec., 1963. *Recreation:* vetting and restoration of art and antiques.

JAMES, Michael; *see* James, R. M. and Jayston, M.

JAMES, Michael Francis; Stipendiary Magistrate, West Midlands, since 1991; *b* 30 Oct. 1933; *s* of Francis and Eveline James; *m* 1958, Lois Joy Elcock. *Educ:* King Charles I Grammar Sch., Kidderminster. Admitted solicitor, 1956. National Service: commnd RAF, 1957; qualified as air navigator, 1958. Partner, Ivens Morton & Greville-Smith (later Morton Fisher), 1959–86; Sen. Partner, 1986–91. *Recreations:* books, wine, walking, music. *Address:* Victoria Law Courts, Corporation Street, Birmingham B4 6QJ. *T:* 0121–212 6600.

JAMES, Michael Leonard, (Michael Hartland); writer; Chairman, Wade Hartland Films Ltd, since 1991; *b* 7 Feb. 1941; *s* of late Leonard and of Marjorie James, Portreath, Cornwall; *m* 1975, Jill Elizabeth (marr. diss. 1992), *d* of late George Tarján, OBE and Etelka Tarján, formerly of Budapest; two *d*. *Educ:* Latymer Upper Sch.; Christ's Coll., Cambridge. Entered British govt service, 1963; Private Sec. to Rt Hon. Jennie Lee, MP, Minister for the Arts, 1966–68; Principal, DES, 1968–71; Planning Unit of Rt Hon. Margaret Thatcher, MP, Sec. of State for Educn and Science, 1971–73; Asst Sec., 1973; DCSO 1974; Advr to OECD, Paris, and UK Governor, IIMT, Milan, 1973–75; specialist duties, 1975–78; Director, IAEA, Vienna, 1978–83; Advr on Internat. Relations, EEC, Brussels, 1983–85. Chm., The Hartland Press Ltd, 1985–95. Member: Exeter Social Security Appeal Tribunal, 1986–; Devon and Cornwall Rent Assessment Panel, 1990–; Child Support Appeal Tribunal, 1993–. Governor: East Devon Coll. of Further Educn, Tiverton, 1985–92; Colyton Grammar Sch., 1985–90; Sidmouth Community Coll., 1988–; Chm., Bd of Management, Axe Vale Further Educn Unit, Seaton, 1987–92. Feature writer and book reviewer for The Times (resident thriller critic, 1989–90), Daily Telegraph (resident thriller critic, 1993–), Sunday Times and Guardian, 1986–. Television and radio include: Sonja's Report (ITV), 1990; Masterspy, interviews with Oleg Gordievsky (BBC Radio 4), 1991. FRSA 1982. Hon. Fellow, Univ. of Exeter, 1985. *Publications: as M. L. James:* (jtly) Internationalization to Prevent the Spread of Nuclear Weapons, 1980; articles on internat. relations and nuclear energy; *as Michael Hartland:* Down Among the Dead Men, 1983; Seven Steps to Treason, 1985 (SW Arts Lit. Award; dramatized for BBC Radio 4, 1990); The Third Betrayal, 1986; Frontier of Fear, 1989; The Year of the Scorpion, 1991; The Price of Silence, 1995. *Address:* Cotte Barton, Branscombe, Devon EX12 3BH; Wade Hartland Films Ltd, Quay West Studios, Old Newnham, Plymouth PL7 5BH. *Clubs:* Athenæum, United Oxford & Cambridge University, International PEN; Devon & Exeter Institution, Honiton Working Men's (Devon).

JAMES, Prof. Michael Norman George, DPhil, FRS 1989; FRS(Can) 1985; Professor of Biochemistry, University of Alberta, since 1978, University Professor of Biochemistry, since 1993; *b* 16 May 1940; *s* of Claud Stewart Murray James and Mimosa Ruth Harriet James; *m* 1961, Patricia McCarthy; one *s* one *d*; *m* 1977, Anita Sielecki. *Educ:* Univ. of Manitoba (BSc, MSc); Linacre Coll., Oxford (DPhil). Asst Prof., Associate Prof., Univ. of Alberta, 1968–78. Mem., MRC of Canada Group in Protein Structure and Function, 1974. *Publications:* contribs to learned jls. *Address:* Department of Biochemistry, University of Alberta, Edmonton, Alberta T6G 2H7, Canada. *T:* (403) 4924550.

JAMES, Dame Naomi (Christine), (Dame Naomi Haythorne), DBE 1979; author and yachtswoman; *b* 2 March 1949; *d* of Charles Robert Power and Joan Power; *m* 1st, 1976, Robert Alan James (*d* 1983); one *d*; 2nd, 1990, Eric G. Haythorne, *o s* of G. V. Haythorne, Ottawa, Canada. *Educ:* Rotorua Girls' High Sch., NZ. Hair stylist, 1966–71; language teacher, 1972–74; yacht charter crew, 1975–77. Sailed single handed round the world via the three great Capes, incl. first woman solo round Cape Horn, on 53 ft yacht, Express Crusader, Sept. 1977–June 1978; sailed in 1980 Observer Transatlantic Race, winning Ladies Prize and achieving women's record for single-handed Atlantic crossing, on 53 ft yacht Kriter Lady; won 1982 Round Britain Race with Rob James, on multihull Colt Cars GB. Formerly: Trustee, Nat. Maritime Museum; Council Mem., Winston Churchill Meml Trust. Royal Yacht Sqdn Chichester Trophy, 1978; NZ Yachtsman of the Year, 1978. *Publications:* Woman Alone, 1978; At One with the Sea, 1979; At Sea on Land, 1981; Courage at Sea, 1987. *Recreations:* tennis, golf, skiing, antiques. *Address:* Shore Cottage, Currabinny, Carrigaline, Co. Cork, Ireland. *Clubs:* Royal Dart Yacht (Dartmouth); Royal Lymington Yacht (Lymington); Royal Western Yacht (Plymouth); Minchinhampton Golf (Amberley Section).

JAMES, P. D.; *see* Baroness James of Holland Park.

JAMES, Patrick Leonard, FRCS, FDS RCS; Hon. Consulting Oral and Maxillo-facial Surgeon: Royal London (formerly London) Hospital, Whitechapel (Senior Consultant Surgeon, 1963–91); North East Thames Regional Hospital Board Hospitals (Consultant Surgeon, 1963–91); Recognized Teacher in Oral Surgery, London University, since 1965; *b* 7 Jan. 1926; *s* of late John Vincent James and Priscilla Elsie (*née* Hill), Cuffley, Herts; *m* 1951, Jean Margaret, *er d* of Leslie and Ruth Hatcher, Woking, Surrey; one *s* two *d*. *Educ:* King's Coll., London; London Hosp. FDSRCS 1958; FRCS 1985 (MRCS 1956); LRCP 1956. Served RAF, Flt Lieut, ME Comd, 1949–51. Resident Ho. Surg., Ho. Phys., Cas. Officer, King George Hosp., 1956–57; Sen. Registrar, Queen Victoria Hosp., E Grinstead, 1959–63; Hon. Consulting Oral and Maxillo-facial Surgeon: to London Hosp., Honey Lane Hosp., Waltham Abbey, Herts and Essex Hosp., Bishop's Stortford (Consultant Surgeon, 1963); to King George Hosp. (Consultant Surgeon, 1967); St Margaret's Hosp., Epping (Consultant Surgeon, 1966); Black Notley Hosp. (Consultant Surgeon, 1969); St Luke's Hosp. for the Clergy; Hon. Civil Consultant (Oral and Maxillo-facial Surgery), RAF, 1989 (Civil Consultant in Oral Surgery, 1979–89). Exchange Fellow, Henry Ford Hosp., Detroit, Mich., 1962; Hunterian Prof., RCS, 1970–71. Member: Academic Bd, London Hosp. Med. Coll., 1968–71; Adv. Cttee in Plastic Surgery, NE Met. Reg. Hosp. Bd, 1969–77; NE Thames Reg. Manpower Cttee, 1975–. Fellow: BAOS, 1963– (Mem. Council, 1971–74); Internat. Assoc. of Oral Surgs (BAOS Rep. on Council, 1974–78); Chm., Sci. Session, 6th Internat. Congress of Oral Surgs, Sydney, 1977; Associate Mem., Brit. Assoc. of Plastic Surgs, 1958–77. FRSM; Member: Council, Chelsea Clin. Soc; Bd of Governors, Eastman Hosp., 1983–84. Liveryman, Soc. of Apothecaries, 1969; Freeman, City of London, 1978. *Publications:* (chapter in Oral Surgery) Malignancies in Odontogenic Cysts, 1967; (chapter in Oral Surgery) Correction of Apertognathia with Osteotomies and Bone Graft, 1970; (chapter in Oral Surgery, vol. 7) Surgical Treatment of Mandibular Joint Disorders, 1978; numerous articles on surgical treatment of mandibular joint disorders, surgery of salivary glands and maxillo facial surgery in med. and surg. jls. *Recreations:* shooting, fishing, sailing (Cdre, United Hosps Sailing Club, 1968–75), skiing. *Address:* Meesden Hall, Meesden, Buntingford, Herts SG9 0AZ; 149 Harley Street, W1N 2DE. *T:* 0171–935 4444. *Club:* Boodle's.

JAMES, Peter John; Principal, London Academy of Music and Dramatic Art, since 1994; *b* 27 July 1940; *s* of Arthur Leonard James and Gladys (*née* King); *m* 1964, Anthea Olive (marr. diss. 1972); one *d*; one *s* by Bernadette McKenna; partner, 1984, Yvonne Joyce. *Educ:* Birmingham Univ. (BA Hons English, Philosophy); Bristol Univ. (Postgrad. Cert. Drama). Founder Dir, Liverpool Everyman Theatre, 1964–71; Associate Dir, NT at Young Vic, 1971–73; Director: Crucible Theatre, Sheffield, 1974–81; Lyric Theatre, Hammersmith, 1981–94 (numerous first productions; Lyric Theatre Awards, 1986, 1992). Dir of plays, UK and overseas, incl. Russia. Former cttee memberships incl. Arts Council, European Theatre Convention, Internat. Theatre Inst. (Award for Excellence, 1990). *Recreations:* cooking, watching boxing and football matches. *Address:* LAMDA, Tower House, 226 Cromwell Road, SW5 0SRT. *T:* 0171–373 3465.

JAMES, Philip; *see* James, W. P. T.

JAMES, Prof. Philip Seaforth; Professor of English Law and Head of the Department of Law, University College at Buckingham, 1975–81, Professor Emeritus, University of

Buckingham, since 1989; *b* 28 May 1914; *s* of Dr Philip William James, MC, and Muriel Lindley James; *m* 1954. Wybetty, *d* of Claas P. Gerth, Enschede, Holland; two *s*. *Educ:* Charterhouse; Trinity Coll., Oxford (MA); Research Fellow, Yale Univ., USA, 1937–38. Called to the Bar, Inner Temple, 1939. Served War of 1939–45, in Royal Artillery, India, Burma (despatches). Fellow of Exeter Coll., Oxford, 1946–49; Prof. and Hd of Dept of Law, Leeds Univ., 1952–75. Visiting Professor: Univs of Yale and of Louisville, Kentucky, USA, 1960–61; Univ. of South Carolina, 1972–73; NY Law Sch., 1981–83. Chairman: Yorks Rent Assessment Panel, 1966–75; Thames Valley Rent Assessment Panel, 1976–; Assessor to County Court under Race Relations Acts. Pres., Soc. of Public Teachers of Law, 1971–72. Governor, Swinton Conservative College, 1961–73. Hon. LLD Buckingham, 1986. Hon. Mem., Mark Twain Soc., 1979. *Publications:* An Introduction to English Law, 1950 (trans. Japanese, 1985); General Principles of the Law of Torts, 1959; Shorter Introduction to English Law, 1969; Six Lectures on the Law of Torts, 1980 (trans. Spanish); various articles, notes and reviews on legal and biographical subjects. *Recreations:* golf and gardening. *Address:* Chestnut View, Mill Road, Whitfield, near Brackley, Northants NN13 5TQ. *Club:* National Liberal.

JAMES, Richard Austin, CB 1980; MC 1945; Receiver for Metropolitan Police District, 1977–80; *b* 26 May 1920; *s* of late Thomas Morris James, Headmaster of Sutton Valence Sch., and Hilda Joan James; *m* 1948, Joan Boorer; two *s* one *d*. *Educ:* Clifton Coll.; Emmanuel Coll., Cambridge. British American Tobacco Co., 1938; Royal Engrs, 1939–41; Queen's Own Royal W Kent Regt, 1941–46; Home Office, 1948; Private Sec. to Chancellor of Duchy of Lancaster, 1960; Asst Sec., 1961; Dep. Receiver for Metropolitan Police District, 1970–73; Asst Under-Sec. of State, Police Dept, Home Office, 1974–76; Dep. Under-Sec. of State, 1980. Vice-Pres., Distressed Gentlefolk's Aid Assoc., 1992– (Gen. Sec., 1981–82; Mem., Council of Mgt, 1982–88); Mem., Cttee of Management, Sussex Housing Assoc. for the Aged, 1985–88. Pres., Brunswick Boys Club Trust, Fulham, 1990–95. Freeman, City of London, 1980. *Recreation:* cricket. *Address:* 5 Gadge Close, Thame, Oxfordshire OX9 2BD. *T:* Thame (01844) 261776. *Clubs:* Athenæum, MCC.

JAMES, (Robert) Michael; Public Relations Executive, Timber Trade Federation, since 1990; Director, Forests Forever Campaign, since 1990; *b* 2 Oct. 1934; *s* of late Rev. B. V. James and Mrs D. M. James; *m* 1959, Sarah Helen (*née* Bell); two *s* one *d*. *Educ:* St John's, Leatherhead; Trinity Coll., Cambridge (BA Hons History). Schoolmaster: Harrow Sch., 1958–60; Cranleigh Sch., 1960–62; joined CRO, 1962; 3rd Sec., Wellington, NZ, 1963–65; 1st Sec., Colombo, Sri Lanka, 1966–69; FCO, 1969–71; Dep. High Comr and Head of Chancery, Georgetown, Guyana, 1971–73; Econ. Sec., Ankara, Turkey, 1974–76; FCO, 1976–80; Commercial Counsellor and Deputy High Commissioner: Accra, 1980–83; Singapore, 1984–87; Dep. High Comr, Bridgetown, Barbados, 1987–90. *Recreations:* sport (cricket Blue, 1956–58), drawing, travel. *Address:* Timber Trade Federation, 26/27 Oxendon Street, SW1Y 4EL. *T:* 0171–839 1891; 17 North Grove, Highgate, N6 4SH. *T:* 0181–348 8689. *Clubs:* MCC; Hunstanton Golf, Highgate Golf.

JAMES, Sir Robert Vidal R.; *see* Rhodes James.

JAMES, Roy Lewis; HM Chief Inspector of Schools in Wales, since 1992 (Chief Inspector of Schools (Wales), Welsh Office, 1990–92); *b* 9 Feb. 1937; *s* of David John and Eleanor James; *m* 1962, Mary Williams; one *d*. *Educ:* Llandysul Grammar School; University College of Wales, Aberystwyth (BSc Hons, DipEd). Asst Master, Strode's Grammar Sch., Egham, 1959–60; Head of Maths Dept, Lampeter Comp. Sch., 1960–62; Head of Maths Dept, Cyfarthfa Castle Sch., Merthyr Tydfil, 1962–70; HM Inspector of Schools, 1970–84, seconded as Sec., Schs Council Cttee for Wales, 1975–77; Staff Inspector, 1984–90. *Recreations:* travel, walking, reading, snooker. *Address:* Office of HM Chief Inspector of Schools in Wales, Government Buildings, Phase I, Tŷ-Glas Road, Llanishen, Cardiff CF4 5WE.

JAMES, Prof. Dame Sheila (Patricia Violet); *see* Sherlock, Prof. Dame S. P. V.

JAMES, Sir Stanislaus (Anthony), GCSL 1992; GCMG 1992 (CMG 1990); OBE 1985; Governor General of Saint Lucia, West Indies, since 1988; *b* 13 Nov. 1919; *s* of Raymond and Theresa James; *m* 1952, Lucille MacDonald; two *s* two *d*. *Educ:* St Mary's Coll., St Lucia; Govt Training Coll., Trinidad; Univ. of Wales, Swansea; Carleton Univ., Ottawa. Educn Dept, St Lucia, 1944–46; Head, Public Relations and Social Welfare Dept, Probation Officer, 1948–50; Chief Clerk, Govt Office, 1954–56; PR and Social Welfare Officer, 1956–65; Perm. Sec., Min. of Trade, Industry, Agric. and Tourism, Min. of Housing, Community, Social Affairs and Labour, Min. of Educn and Health, 1965–74; National Co-ordinator: for Non-Govt Orgns, 1974–88; for Emergency Services, 1979–88. *Recreation:* horticulture. *Address:* Government House, The Morne, St Lucia, West Indies; Sunny Acres, Choc, Castries, St Lucia, West Indies. *T:* 4522481/2, 451–9562.

JAMES, Stanley Francis; Head of Statistics Division 1, Department of Trade and Industry, 1981–84; *b* 12 Feb. 1927; *s* of H. F. James; unmarried. *Educ:* Sutton County Sch.; Trinity Coll., Cambridge. Maths Tripos Pt II; Dip. Math. Statistics. Research Lectr, Econs Dept, Nottingham Univ., 1951; Statistician, Bd of Inland Revenue, 1956; Chief Statistician: Bd of Inland Revenue, 1966; Central Statistical Office, 1968; Asst Dir, Central Statistical Office, 1970–72; Dir, Stats Div., Bd of Inland Revenue, 1972–77; Head, Econs and Stats Div. 6, Depts of Industry and Trade, 1977–81. Hon. Treasurer, Royal Statistical Soc., 1978–83. *Recreations:* travel, theatre, gardening. *Address:* 23 Hayward Road, Oxford OX2 8LN. *Club:* Royal Automobile.

JAMES, Stephen Lawrence; Consultant, Simmons & Simmons, Solicitors, since 1992 (Partner, 1961; Senior Partner, 1980–92); *b* 19 Oct. 1930; *s* of Walter Amyas James and Cecile Juliet (*née* Hillman); *m* 1955, Patricia Eleanor Favell James (marr. diss. 1986); two *s* two *d*. *Educ:* Clifton Coll.; St Catharine's Coll., Cambridge (BA History and Law). Mem., Gray's Inn, 1953, Bar finals, 1956; admitted Solicitor: England and Wales, 1959; Hong Kong, 1980. Director: Horace Clarkson PLC (formerly H. Clarkson (Holdings) PLC), 1975–; Shipping Industrial Holdings Ltd, 1972–82; Tradinvest Bank & Trust Co. of Nassau Ltd, 1975–85; Nodiv Ltd, 1975–78; Silver Line Ltd, 1978–82; Thompson Moore Associates Ltd, 1984–88; Greycoat PLC, 1994–; Kiln Capital PLC, 1994–. Mem., Law Soc., 1961–. Freeman City of London; Mem., Glaziers' Co., 1964–. *Recreations:* yachting, gardening. *Address:* (office) Simmons & Simmons, 21 Wilson Street, EC2M 2TQ; Widden, Shirley Holms, Lymington, Hampshire SO41 8NL. *Clubs:* Royal Thames Yacht; Royal Yacht Squadron (Cowes); Royal Lymington Yacht.

JAMES, Steven Wynne Lloyd; Circuit Administrator, North-Eastern Circuit, Lord Chancellor's Department, 1988–94; *b* 9 June 1934; *s* of late Trevor Lloyd James and Olwen James; *m* 1962, Carolyn Ann Rowlands (*d* 1995), *d* of late James Morgan Rowlands and of Mercia Rowlands; three *s*. *Educ:* Queen Elizabeth Grammar Sch., Carmarthen; LSE. LLB 1956. Admitted solicitor, 1959. Asst Solicitor in private practice, 1959–61; Legal Asst, HM Land Registry, 1961; Asst Solicitor, Glamorgan CC, 1962–70; Asst Clerk of the Peace, 1970–71; Lord Chancellor's Dept, 1971–94: Wales and Chester Circuit: Courts Administrator, (Chester/Mold), 1971–76; Asst Sec., 1976; Dep. Circuit Administrator, 1976–82; Under Sec., 1982; Circuit Adminstrator, 1982–88. *Address:* Westlake, 2 Heol-y-Bryn, The Knap, Barry, South Glam CF62 8SY. *T:* Barry (01446) 741515. *Club:* Civil Service.

JAMES, (Thomas) Cecil (Garside), CMG 1966; Assistant Under-Secretary of State, Ministry of Defence, 1968–77; *b* 8 Jan. 1918; *s* of Joshua James, MBE, Ashton-under-Lyne; *m* 1941, Elsie Williams, Ashton-under-Lyne; one *s* two *d*. *Educ:* Manchester Grammar Sch.; St John's Coll., Cambridge. Prin. Priv. Sec. to Sec. of State for Air, 1951–55; Asst Sec., Air Min., 1955; Civil Sec., FEAF, 1963–66; Chief of Public Relations, MoD, 1966–68. *Recreation:* golf. *Address:* 9 Knoll House, Uxbridge Road, Pinner, Middx HA5 3LR. *T:* 0181–868 3602.

JAMES, Thomas Garnet Henry, CBE 1984; FBA 1976; Keeper of Egyptian Antiquities, British Museum, 1974–88; *b* 8 May 1923; *s* of late Thomas Garnet James and Edith (*née* Griffiths); *m* 1956, Diana Margaret, *y d* of H. L. Vavasseur-Durell; one *s*. *Educ:* Neath Grammar Sch.; Exeter Coll., Oxford. 2nd Cl. Lit. Hum. 1947; 1st Cl. Oriental Studies 1950, MA 1948. Served War of 1939–45, RA; NW Europe; 2nd Lieut 1943; Captain 1945. Asst Keeper, Dept of Egyptian and Assyrian Antiquities, 1951; Dep. Keeper (Egyptian Antiquities), 1974. Laycock Student of Egyptology, Worcester Coll., Oxford, 1954–60; Wilbour Fellow, Brooklyn Museum, 1964; Visiting Professor: Collège de France, 1983; Memphis State Univ., 1990. Editor, Jl of Egyptian Archæology, 1960–70; Editor, Egyptological pubns of Egypt Exploration Soc., 1960–89. Vice-Pres., Egypt Exploration Soc., 1990– (Chm., 1983–89); Mem., German Archæological Inst., 1974. *Publications:* The Mastaba of Khentika called Ikhekhi, 1953; Hieroglyphic Texts in the British Museum I, 1961; The Hekanakhte Papers and other Early Middle Kingdom Documents, 1962; (with R. A. Caminos) Gebel es-Silsilah I, 1963; Egyptian Sculptures, 1966; Myths and Legends of Ancient Egypt, 1969; Hieroglyphic Texts in the British Museum, 9, 1970; Archæology of Ancient Egypt, 1972; Corpus of Hieroglyphic Inscriptions in the Brooklyn Museum, I, 1974; (ed) An Introduction to Ancient Egypt, 1979; (ed) Excavating in Egypt, 1982; (with W. V. Davies) Egyptian Sculpture, 1983; Pharaoh's People, 1984; Egyptian Painting, 1985; Ancient Egypt: the land and its legacy, 1988; Howard Carter, the Path to Tutankhamun, 1992; Egypt: the living past, 1992; A Short History of Ancient Egypt, 1995;(contrib.) W. B. Emery: Great Tombs of the First Dynasty II, 1954; (contrib.) T. J. Dunbabin: Perachora II, 1962; (contrib.) Cambridge Ancient History, 3rd edn, Vol. II, i, 1973, Vol III, ii, 1991; (contrib.) Encyclop. Britannica, 15th edn, 1974; (ed English trans.) H. Kees: Ancient Egypt, 1961; articles in Jl Egyptian Arch., etc; reviews in learned jls. *Recreations:* music, cooking. *Address:* 14 Turner Close, NW11 6TU. *T:* 0181–455 9221. *Club:* United Oxford & Cambridge University.

JAMES, Thomas Geraint Illtyd, FRCS; Hon. Surgeon, Central Middlesex Hospital; Late Teacher of Surgery, Middlesex Hospital, and Hon. Surgical Tutor, Royal College of Surgeons of England; *b* 12 July 1900; *s* of late Evan Thomas and Elizabeth James, Barry; *m* 1932, Dorothy Marguerite, *o d* of late David John, Cardiff; two *s*. *Educ:* Barry, Glam; University Coll., Cardiff; Welsh National Sch. of Medicine; St Mary's Hosp., London; Guy's Hosp., London. BSc Wales, 1921, Alfred Sheen Prize in Anat. and Physiol.; MRCS, LRCP, 1924; MB, ChB, 1925, Maclean Medal and Prize in Obst. and Gynæcol.; FRCSE, 1927; FRCS, 1928; MCh Wales, 1932; FRSocMed; Fellow Association of Surgeons of Great Britain and Ireland; Erasmus Wilson Lectr, RCS, 1972. Mem., Internat. Soc. for Surgery; Corr. Mem. Spanish-Portuguese Soc. of Neurosurgery. Mem. Soc. of Apothecaries; Freeman of City of London. Formerly: Assoc. Examr University of London; Mem. and Chm., Court of Examiners RCS of England; Examr in Surgery, University of Liverpool; Ho. phys., Ho. surg. and Resident Surgical Officer, Cardiff Royal Infirmary; Clinical Asst St Mark's, St Peter's and Guy's Hosps, London; Asst to Neurosurg. Dept, London Hosp.; Mem., Management Cttee, Leavesden Gp of Hosps. *Publications:* in various jls on surg. and neurosurg. subjects. *Recreations:* literature, travelling. *Address:* 1 Freeland Road, W5 3HR. *T:* 0181–992 2430.

JAMES, Prof. Vivian Hector Thomas; Professor and Head of Department of Chemical Pathology, St Mary's Hospital Medical School, London University, 1973–90, now Professor Emeritus; Hon. Chemical Pathologist, Paddington and North Kensington Health Authority, since 1973; *b* 29 Dec. 1924; *s* of William and Alice James; *m* 1958, Betty Irene Pike. *Educ:* Latymer Sch.; London Univ. BSc, PhD, DSc; FRCPath 1977. Flying duties, RAF, 1942–46. Scientific Staff, Nat. Inst. for Med. Res., 1952–56; St Mary's Hospital Medical School, London: Lectr, Dept of Chemical Pathol., 1956; Reader, 1962; Prof. of Chem. Endocrinol., 1967; Chm., Div. of Pathology, St Mary's Hosp., 1981–85. Emeritus Fellow, Leverhulme Trust, 1991. Mem., Herts AHA, 1974–77. Secretary: Clin. Endocrinol. Cttee, MRC, 1967–72; Cttee for Human Pituitary Collection, MRC, 1972–76 (Chm., 1976–82); Endocrine Sect., RSocMed, 1972–76 (Pres., 1976–78); Gen. Sec., Soc. for Endocrinology, 1979–85 (Treas., 1986–91); Sec.-Gen., European Fedn of Endocrine Socs, 1986–. Clinical Endocrinology Medal Lectr, Clin. Endocrinol. Trust, 1990; Jubilee Medal, Soc. for Endocrinology, 1992. Hon. MRCP 1989. Freeman, Haverfordwest, 1946. Fiorino d'oro, City of Florence, 1977. Editor, Clinical Endocrinology, 1972–74. Editor-in-Chief, Endocrine-Related Cancer, 1993–. *Publications:* (ed jtly) Current Topics in Experimental Endocrinology, 1971, 5th edn 1983; (ed) The Adrenal Gland, 1979, 2nd edn 1992; (ed jtly) Hormones in Blood, 1961, 3rd edn 1983; contribs to various endocrine and other jls. *Address:* Department of Metabolic Medicine, St Mary's Hospital Medical School, W2 1PG. *T:* 0171–723 1252. *Club:* Royal Society of Medicine.

JAMES, Walter; *see* James, Arthur Walter.

JAMES, Prof. Walter, CBE 1977; Dean and Director of Studies, Faculty of Educational Studies, 1969–77, Professor of Educational Studies, 1969–84, Open University; *b* 8 Dec. 1924; *s* of late George Herbert James and Mary Kathleen (*née* Crutch); *m* 1948, Joyce Dorothy Woollaston; two *s*. *Educ:* Royal Grammar Sch., Worcester; St Luke's Coll., Exeter; Univ. of Nottingham. BA 1955. School teacher, 1948–52; Univ. of Nottingham: Resident Tutor, Dept of Extra-Mural Studies, 1958–65; Lectr in Adult Educn, Dept of Adult Educn, 1965–69. Consultant on Adult Educn and Community Develt to Govt of Seychelles and ODA of FCO, 1973; Adviser: to Office of Educn, WCC, 1974–76; on Social Planning, to State of Bahrain, 1975; Council of Europe: UK Rep., Working Party on Develt of Adult Education, 1973–81; UK Rep. and Project Adviser, Adult Educn for Community Develt, 1982–87, Adult Educn for Social Change, 1988–93; Chairman: Nat. Council for Voluntary Youth Services, 1970–76; Review of Training of part-time Youth and Community Workers, 1975–77; Religious Adv. Bd, Scout Assoc., 1977–82; Inservice Training and Educn Panel for Youth and Community Service, 1978–82; Council for Educn and Trng in Youth and Community Work, 1982–85; Nat. Adv. Council for the Youth Service, 1985–88; Council for Local Non-Stipendiary Ministerial Training, dio. of Southwark, 1992–; Member: DES Cttee on Youth and Community Work in 70s, 1967–69; ILO Working Party on Use of Radio and TV for Workers' Educn, 1968; Gen. Synod, C of E, 1970–75; Exec. Cttee, Nat. Council of Social Service, 1970–75; Univs' Council for Educn of Teachers, 1970–84; Univs Council for Adult Educn, 1971–76; BBC Further Educn Adv. Council, 1971–75; Exec. Cttee and Council, Nat. Inst. of Adult Educn, 1971–77; Library Adv. Council for England, 1974–76; Adv. Council, HM Queen's Silver Jubilee Appeal, 1976–78; Bd of Educn, Gen. Synod of C of E, 1991–;

Community Develt Sub-Cttee, Scout Assoc., 1991–; Trustee: Young Volunteer Force Foundn, 1972–77; Trident Educnl Trust, 1972–86; Community Projects Foundn, 1977–90; Community Develt Foundn, 1990–; President: Inst. of Playleadership, 1972–74; Fair Play for Children, 1979–82; London and SE Regl Youth Work Unit, 1992–94. Councillor (Lib Dem), Eastbourne BC, 1994–. *Publications:* (with F. J. Bayliss) The Standard of Living, 1964; (ed) Virginia Woolf, Selections from her essays, 1966; (contrib.) Encyclopaedia of Education, 1968; (contrib.) Teaching Techniques in Adult Education, 1971; (contrib.) Mass Media and Adult Education, 1971; (with H. Janne and P. Dominice) The Development of Adult Education, 1980; (with others) The 14 Pilot Experiments, Vols 1–3, 1984; Some Conclusions from the Co-operation of 14 Development Projects, 1985; Handbook on Co-operative Monitoring, 1986; The Uses of Media for Community Development, 1988. *Recreation:* living. *Address:* 25 Kepplestone, Staveley Road, Eastbourne BN20 7JZ. *T:* Eastbourne (01323) 417029.

JAMES, Prof. (William) Philip (Trehearne), CBE 1993; MD, DSc; FRCP, FRCPEd; FRSE; FIBiol; Director, Rowett Research Institute, Aberdeen, since 1982; Research Professor, Aberdeen University, since 1983; *b* 27 June 1938; *s* of Jenkin William James and Lilian Mary James; *m* 1961, Jean Hamilton (*née* Moorhouse); one *s* one *d*. *Educ:* Ackworth Sch., Pontefract, Yorks; University Coll. London (BSc Hons 1959; DSc 1983); University Coll. Hosp. (MB, BS 1962; MD 1968). FRCP 1978; FRCPEd 1983; FRSE 1986; FIBiol 1988. Sen. House Physician, Whittington Hosp., London, 1963–65; Clin. Res. Scientist, MRC Tropical Metabolism Res. Unit, Kingston, Jamaica, 1965–68; Harvard Res. Fellow, Mass Gen. Hosp., 1968–69; Wellcome Trust Res. Fellow, MRC Gastroenterology Unit, London, 1969–70; Sen. Lectr, Dept of Human Nutrition, London Sch. of Hygiene and Trop. Medicine, and Hon. Consultant Physician, UCH, 1970–74; Asst Dir, MRC Dunn Nutrition Unit, and Hon. Consultant Physician, Addenbrooke's Hosp., Cambridge, 1974–82. Hon. Consultant on nutrition to Army, 1989–; Advr, Eur. Dirs of Agricl Res. on Diet and Health, 1995–. Chairman: FAO Consultation on internat. food needs, 1987; Nat. Food Alliance, 1988–90 (Pres., 1990–); Coronary Prevention Gp, 1988–; WHO Consultation on world food and health policies, 1989; DoH Panel on Novel Foods, 1992–; DoH Task Force on Obesity, 1994; RCPE Wkg Pty on Mgt of Obesity in NHS, 1994–; Internat. Task Force on Obesity Mgt, 1995–; Eur. Panel, Eur. Heart Foundn's Analysis of Cardiovascular Risk, 1994; Planning Gp, Eur. Young Nutrition Leadership Courses, 1994–; Assoc. of Profs of Human Nutrition, 1994–; Member: MAFF Adv. Cttee on Novel Foods and Processes, 1986–; EC Scientific Cttee for Food, 1992–; DoH (formerly MAFF) Nutrition Task Force, 1992–; DoH Cttee on Med. Aspects of Food Policy, 1990–; Internat. Panel on Diet and Cancer, World Cancer Res. Fund, 1994–. Hon. MFPHM. FRSA 1988. Hon. MA Cantab, 1977. *Publications:* The Analysis of Dietary Fibre in Food, 1981; The Body Weight Regulatory System: normal and disturbed mechanisms, 1981; Assessing Human Energy Requirements, 1990; (ed) Human Nutrition and Diatetics, 1992; documents on European national nutrition policy and energy needs for Scottish Office, DoH, FAO, NACNE and WHO; scientific pubns on energy metabolism, salt handling, and heart disease in Lancet, Nature, Clin. Science. *Recreations:* talking, writing reports; eating, preferably in France. *Address:* Wardenhill, Bucksburn, Aberdeen AB2 9SA. *T:* Aberdeen (01224) 712623. *Club:* Athenæum.

JAMES, William Seymour; Registrar in Bankruptcy, Royal Courts of Justice, since 1991; *b* 11 Dec. 1945; *s* of late Arthur Dyfrig James and of Ann Pamela Mary James (*née* Pincham); *m* 1st, 1973, Pamela Margaret Lord (marr. diss. 1986); one *d*; 2nd, 1989, Susan Amy Barr (*née* Jones); two step *s*. *Educ:* St Edward's Sch., Oxford; College of Law, Guildford. Articled to L. W. S. Parry-Williams, Solicitor, Middlewich, 1966–71; Solicitor in private practice, 1971–91; Under-Sheriff, City of Gloucester, 1988–89. *Recreations:* tennis, ski-ing, sailing. *Address:* 1st Floor, Thomas More Building, Royal Courts of Justice, Strand, WC2A 2LL. *T:* 0171–936 7319.

JAMES-MOORE, Jonathan Guy; Head of Light Entertainment, BBC Radio, since 1991; *b* 22 March 1946; *s* of Wilfrid Seward and Alana James-Moore; *m* 1975, Jenny Baynes; one *d*. *Educ:* Bromsgrove Sch.; Emmanuel Coll., Cambridge (MA). Founder Dir, Oxford & Cambridge Shakespeare Co., 1968–71; Gen. Manager, Sir Nicholas Sekers Theatre at Rosehill, 1971–72; Administrator: Mermaid Theatre, 1972–74; St George's Theatre, 1975–76; BBC Radio Light Entertainment, 1978–. *Recreations:* collecting wine labels, planning holidays. *Address:* Room 101, 16 Langham Street, W1A 1AA; 25 Harcourt Road, Alexandra Palace, N22 4XW. *T:* 0181–888 0196.

JAMESON, Antony; *see* Jameson, G. A.

JAMESON, Derek; news, TV and radio commentator; Co-Presenter, Jamesons, Radio 2, since 1992; *b* 29 Nov. 1929; *e s* of Mrs Elsie Jameson; *m* 1st, 1948, Jacqueline Sinclair (marr. diss. 1966); one *s* one *d*; 2nd, 1971, Pauline Tomlin (marr. diss. 1978); two *s*; 3rd, 1988, Ellen Petrie. *Educ:* elementary schools, Hackney. Office boy rising to Chief Sub-editor, Reuters, 1944–60; Editor, London American, 1960–61; features staff, Daily Express, 1961–63; Picture Editor, Sunday Mirror, 1963–65; Asst Editor, Sunday Mirror, 1965–72; Northern Editor, Sunday and Daily Mirror, 1972–76; Managing Editor, Daily Mirror, 1976–77; Editor, Daily Express, 1977–79; Editor-in-Chief, The Daily Star, 1978–80; Editor, News of the World, 1981–84. Presenter: Radio 2 Jameson Show, 1986–91; Jameson Tonight, Sky TV, 1989–90. *Publications:* Touched by Angels (autobiog.), 1988; Last of the Hot Metal Men (autobiog.), 1990. *Recreations:* opera, music, reading. *Address:* BBC Radio 2, Broadcasting House, W1A 1AA.

JAMESON, Prof. (Guy) Antony, PhD; FRS 1995; James S. McDonnell Distinguished University Professor of Aerospace Engineering, Princeton University, since 1982; *b* 20 Nov. 1934; *s* of Brig. Guy Oscar Jameson and Olive Maud Helen Jameson (*née* Turney); *m* 1st, 1964, Catharina Selander; one *s* one *d*; 2nd, 1985, Charlotte Ansted. *Educ:* Trinity Hall, Cambridge (MA; PhD 1963). Nat. Service, 2nd Lieut, RE, 1953–55. Research Fellow, Trinity Hall, Cambridge, 1960–63; Economist, TUC, 1964–65; Chief Mathematician, Hawker Siddeley Dynamics, Coventry, 1965–66; Aerodynamics Engineer, Grumman Aerospace, Bethpage, NY, 1966–72; Courant Institute of Mathematical Sciences, New York University: Research Scientist, 1972–74; Prof. of Computer Sci., 1974–80; Prof. of Aerospace Engrg, Princeton Univ., 1980–82. *Publications:* numerous articles in jls and conference proceedings. *Recreations:* squash, tennis, ski-ing. *Address:* Mechanical and Aerospace Engineering Department, D404 Engineering Quadrangle, Princeton University, Princeton, NJ 08544, USA. *T:* (609) 2585138.

JAMESON, John, QFSM 1995; FIMgt; Firemaster, Strathclyde Fire Brigade, since 1991; *b* 12 April 1946; *s* of John Jameson and Catherine Clark Jameson; *m* 1970, Helen Mulvey; one *s* one *d*. *Educ:* St Aloysius and St Patrick's High Sch., Coatbridge. FBIM 1991. Lanarkshire Fire Brigade, 1965–70; Glasgow Fire Service, 1970–75; Strathclyde Fire Brigade, 1975–: Asst Firemaster, 1987–88; Dep. Firemaster, 1988–91. Fire Brigade Long Service and Good Conduct Medal, 1985; Strathclyde Regl Medal for Bravery, 1987. Churchill Fellowship, 1983. *Recreations:* historic buildings, golf. *Address:* Brigade Headquarters, Strathclyde Fire Brigade, Bothwell Road, Hamilton ML3 0EA; Iona, 56 Dunellan Road, Douglas Mains Estate, Milngavie, Glasgow.

JAMESON, Air Cdre Patrick Geraint, CB 1959; DSO 1943; DFC 1940 (and Bar 1942), psa; Royal Air Force, retired, 1960; *b* Wellington, NZ, 10 Nov. 1912; *s* of Robert Delvin Jameson, Balbriggan, Ireland, and Katherine Lenora Jameson (*née* Dick), Dunedin, NZ; *m* 1941, Hilda Nellie Haiselden Webster, *d* of B. F. Webster, Lower Hutt, NZ; one *s* one *d*. *Educ:* Hutt Valley High Sch., New Zealand. Commissioned in RAF, 1936. War of 1939–45 (despatches 5 times, DFC and Bar, DSO): 46 Squadron, 1936–40 (one of 37 survivors of sinking of HM Aircraft Carrier Glorious by enemy action in Arctic Ocean); commanded 266 Sqaudron, 1940–41; Wing Commander Flying, Wittering, 1941–42; Wing Commander (Flying), Norwegian Wing, North Weald, 1942–43; Group Capt. Plans, HQ No 11 Group, 1943–44; 122 Wing in France, Belgium, Holland, Germany and Denmark, 1944–46; Staff Coll., Haifa, 1946; Air Ministry, 1946–48; CFE, West Raynham, 1949–52; Wunsdorf (2nd TAF), 1952–54; SASO, HQ No II Group, 1954–56; SASO HQ RAF Germany (2nd TAF) 1956–59; Task Force Comdr, Operation Grapple, Christmas Is., 1959–60. Norwegian War Cross, 1943; Netherlands Order of Orange Nassau, 1945; American Silver Star, 1945. *Recreations:* fishing, shooting, sailing, golf. *Address:* 70 Wai-Iti Crescent, Lower Hutt, New Zealand. *Clubs:* Royal Air Force; Hutt Golf; Hutt.

JAMIESON, Brian George, PhD; Deputy Chief Executive, Biotechnology and Biological Sciences Research Council, since 1994; *b* 7 Feb. 1943; *s* of George and Amy Jamieson; *m* 1966, Helen Carol Scott. *Educ:* Boroughmuir Sch.; Edinburgh Univ. (BSc, PhD). Research Assistant: Brigham Young Univ., Utah, 1967–68; Edinburgh Univ., 1968–70; Natural Environment Res. Council, 1970–73 and 1975–77; Principal, ARC, 1973–75; Cabinet Office, 1977–78; Agricultural and Food Research Council: Asst Sec., 1978–87; Dir, Central Office, 1987–91; Acting Sec., Oct.–Dec. 1990; Dir of Admin, 1991–94. *Publications:* papers on the origins of igneous rocks. *Recreations:* running, keeping fit, ski-ing, travelling. *Address:* 8 Orwell Close, Caversham, Reading, Berks RG4 7PU. *T:* Reading (01734) 477780.

JAMIESON, Major David Auldjo, VC 1944; CVO 1990; Member of HM Body Guard, Hon. Corps of Gentlemen at Arms, 1968–90, Lieutenant, 1986–90; *b* 1 Oct. 1920; *s* of late Sir Archibald Auldjo Jamieson, KBE, MC; *m* 1st, 1948, Nancy Elwes (*d* 1963), *y d* of Robert H. A. Elwes, Congham, King's Lynn; one *s* two *d*; 2nd, 1969, Joanna, *e d* of Edward Woodall. *Educ:* Eton Coll. Commissioned Royal Norfolk Regt May 1939; served War of 1939–45, incl. Normandy, 1944 (VC); retired, 1948. Director: Australian Agricultural Co., 1949–78 (Governor, 1952–76); UK Branch, Australian Mutual Provident Society, 1963–89 (Dep. Chm., 1973–89); National Westminster Bank PLC, 1983–87; Steetley plc, 1976–86 (Dep. Chm., 1983–86). Clerk of the Cheque and Adjutant, Hon. Corps of Gentlemen at Arms, 1981–86. High Sheriff of Norfolk, 1980. *Address:* St Andrew's House, Burnham Market, King's Lynn, Norfolk PE31 8HH. *T:* Fakenham (01328) 730606.

JAMIESON, David Charles; MP (Lab) Plymouth, Devonport, since 1992; *b* 18 May 1947; *s* of Frank and Eileen Jamieson; *m* 1971, Patricia Hofton; two *s* one *d*. *Educ:* Tudor Grange Sch., Solihull; St Peter's, Birmingham; Open Univ. (BA). Teacher, Riland Bedford Sch., 1970–76; Head, Maths Dept, Crown Hills Sch., Leicester, 1976–81; Vice-Principal, John Kitto Community Coll., Plymouth, 1981–92. Mem., Select Cttee on Educn, 1992–. *Recreations:* music, tennis, gardening. *Address:* House of Commons, SW1A 0AA. *T:* 0171–219 6252.

JAMIESON, Air Marshal Sir (David) Ewan, KBE 1986 (OBE 1967); CB 1981; Chief of Defence Staff, New Zealand, 1983–86, retired; *b* Christchurch, 19 April 1930; *s* of R. D. Jamieson; *m* 1957, Margaret Elaine, *d* of L. J. Bridge; three *s* one *d*. *Educ:* Christchurch and New Plymouth Boys' High Sch. Joined RNZAF, 1949; OC Flying, Ohakea, 1964; CO Malaysia, 1965–66; Jt Services Staff Coll., 1969; CO Auckland, 1971–72; AOC Ops Group, 1974–76; RCDS 1977; Chief of Air Staff, RNZAF, 1979–83. *Address:* 14 Hinerau Grove, Taupo, New Zealand.

JAMIESON, Air Marshal Sir Ewan; *see* Jamieson, Air Marshal Sir D. E.

JAMIESON, Rt. Rev. Hamish Thomas Umphelby; *see* Bunbury, Bishop of.

JAMIESON, Lt-Col Harvey Morro H.; *see* Harvey-Jamieson.

JAMIESON, Rear-Adm. Ian Wyndham, CB 1970; DSC 1945; Emeritus Fellow, Jesus College, Oxford, 1986 (Home Bursar and Fellow, 1972–86); *b* 13 March 1920; *s* of late S. W. Jamieson, CBE; *m* 1949, Patricia Wheeler, Knowle, Warwickshire; two *s* one *d*. *Educ:* RNC, Dartmouth. Served War of 1939–45: Anti Submarine Warfare Specialist, 1943. Comdr, 1953; Staff of RN Tactical Sch., 1953–56; HMS Maidstone, 1956–58; Dir, Jt Tactical Sch., Malta, 1958; Capt. 1959; Asst Dir, Naval Intelligence, 1959–61; Comd HMS Nubian and 6th Frigate Sqdn, 1961–64; Dir, Seaman Officers Appts, 1964–66; Comd Britannia RN Coll., Dartmouth, 1966–68; Rear-Adm. 1968; Flag Officer, Gibraltar, and Admiral Superintendent, HM Dockyard, Gibraltar; also NATO Comdr, Gibraltar (Mediterranean Area), 1968–69; C of S to C-in-C Western Fleet, 1969–71; retired. Mem., Southern Arts Council, 1985–91. Hon. MA Oxon, 1973. *Recreations:* hockey (Scotland and Combined Services), cricket, golf, tennis. *Address:* Buckels, East Hagbourne, near Didcot, Oxfordshire OX11 9LJ. *Clubs:* Army and Navy, MCC.

JAMIESON, John Kenneth; Chairman of Board and Chief Executive Officer, Exxon Corporation (formerly Standard Oil Co. (NJ)), 1969–75; *b* Canada, 28 Aug. 1910; *s* of John Locke and Kate Herron Jamieson; US citizen; *m* 1937, Ethel May Burns; one *s* one *d*. *Educ:* Univ. of Alberta; Massachusetts Inst. of Technology (BS). Northwest Stellarene Co. of Alberta, 1932; British American Oil Co., 1934; Manager, Moose Jaw Refinery; served War of 1939–45 in Oil Controller's Dept of Canadian Govt; subseq. Manager, Manufrg Dept, British American Oil Co.; joined Imperial Oil Co., 1948: Head of Engrg and Develt Div., Sarnia Refinery, 1949; Asst Gen. Man. of Manufrg Dept, 1950; on loan to Canadian Dept of Defence Production, 1951; Dir, Imperial Oil, 1952, Vice-Pres. 1953; Pres. and Dir International Petroleum Co., 1959; Vice-Pres., Dir and Mem. Exec. Cttee Exxon Co., USA (formerly Humble Oil & Refining Co.), 1961, Exec. Vice-Pres. 1962, Pres. 1963–64; Exec. Vice-Pres. and Dir 1964, Pres. 1965–69, Jersey Standard. *Address:* Kellogg Tower, 601 Jefferson, Suite 975, Houston, TX 77002, USA. *Clubs:* Augusta National Golf (Augusta); Ramada, Houston Country (Houston); Ristigouche Salmon (Matapedia, Quebec).

JAMIESON, Kenneth Douglas, CMG 1968; HM Diplomatic Service, retired; *b* 9 Jan. 1921; *s* of late Rt Hon. Lord Jamieson, PC, KC, Senator of College of Justice in Scotland and Violet Rhodes; *m* 1946, Pamela Hall; two *s* one *d*. *Educ:* Rugby; Balliol Coll., Oxford. War Service: 5th Regt RHA, 1941–45; HQ, RA 7th Armoured Div., 1945–46. Joined Foreign Service, 1946; served in: Washington, 1948; FO, 1952; Lima, 1954; Brussels, 1959; FO, 1961; Caracas, 1963; Dir of Commercial Training, DSAO, 1968; Head of Export Promotion Dept, FCO, 1968–70; Minister and UK Dep. Permanent Representative, UN, NY, 1970–74; Ambassador to Peru, 1974–77; Sen. Directing Staff, RCDS, 1977–80. *Address:* Mill Hill House, Bucks Green, Rudgwick, W Sussex RH12 3HZ.

JAMIESON, Rt. Rev. Penelope Ann Bansall; *see* Dunedin, Bishop of.

JAMISON, James Hardie, OBE 1974; chartered accountant; Partner, Coopers & Lybrand, Chartered Accountants, 1939–78, retired; *b* 29 Nov. 1913; *s* of late W. I. Jamison; *m* 1940, Mary Louise, *d* of late W. R. Richardson; two *s* one *d*. *Educ:* Sydney Church of England Grammar Sch. Chm., Commn of Inquiry into Efficiency and Admin of Hosps, 1979–80. Mem., Nat. Council, Aust. Inst. of Chartered Accountants, 1969–77, Vice Pres., 1973–75, Pres., 1975–76. *Recreation:* sailing. *Address:* 16 Tivoli Street, Mosman, NSW 2088, Australia. *Clubs:* Australasian Pioneers' (Pres. 1970–72), Australian, Royal Sydney Yacht Squadron (Sydney).

JAMISON, James Kenneth, OBE 1978; Director, Arts Council of Northern Ireland, 1969–91; *b* 9 May 1931; *s* of William Jamison and Alicia Rea Jamison; *m* 1964, Joan Young Boyd; one *s* one *d*. *Educ:* Belfast College of Art (DA). Secondary school teacher, 1953–61; Art Critic, Belfast Telegraph, 1956–61; Art Organiser, Arts Council of Northern Ireland, 1962–64, Dep. Director, 1964–69. Hon. DLitt Ulster, 1989. *Publications:* miscellaneous on the arts in the North of Ireland. *Recreations:* the arts, travel. *Address:* 64 Rugby Road, Belfast BT7 1PT. *T:* Belfast (01232) 323063.

JANES, (John) Douglas (Webster), CB 1975; Secretary, The Bach Choir, 1981–89; Deputy Secretary, Northern Ireland Office, 1974–79; *b* 17 Aug. 1918; *s* of late John Arnold Janes and Maud Mackinnon (*née* Webster); *m* 1st, 1943, Margaret Isabel Smith (*d* 1978); one *s* two *d*; 2nd, 1986, Mrs Joan Walker (*née* Bentley). *Educ:* Southgate County Sch., Mddx; Imperial Coll. of Science and Technology. 1st cl. BSc (Eng) London, ACGI, DIC. Entered Post Office Engineering Dept, Research Branch, 1939. Served Royal Signals, RAOC, REME, 1939–45: War Office, 1941–45; Major. Min. of Town and Country Planning, 1947; Min. of Housing and Local Govt, 1951; seconded to Min. of Power, 1956–58; HM Treasury, 1960–63; Min. of Land and Natural Resources, 1964–66; Prin. Finance Officer and Accountant Gen., Min. of Housing and Local Govt, 1968–70; Prin. Finance Officer (Local Govt and Develt), DoE, 1970–73, Dep. Sec., 1973; Chief Executive, Maplin Develt Authority, 1973–74. Chm., Home Grown Timber Adv. Cttee, 1981–93 (Mem., 1979–93); various management and organisation reviews, 1979–81. *Recreations:* singing, do-it-yourself.

JANES, Maj.-Gen. Mervyn, CB 1973; MBE 1944; *b* 1 Oct. 1920; *o s* of W. G. Janes; *m* 1946, Elizabeth Kathleen McIntyre; two *d*. *Educ:* Sir Walter St John's Sch., London. Commnd 1942; served with Essex Yeo. (104 Regt RHA), 1942–46, Middle East and Italy; psc 1951; served with 3 RHA, 1952–53; 2 Div., BMRA, 1954–55; Chief Instructor, New Coll., RMAS, 1956–57; Batt. Comd, 3 RHA, 1958–60; Asst Army Instructor (GSO1), Imperial Defence Coll., 1961–62; comd 1st Regt RHA, 1963–65; Comdr, RA, in BAOR, 1965–67; DMS2 (MoD(A)), 1967–70; GOC 5th Division, 1970–71; Dir, Royal Artillery, 1971–73. Col Comdt, RA, 1973–81. *Recreations:* music, ornithology. *Address:* Lucy's Cottage, North Street, Theale, Reading, Berks RG7 5EX. *Club:* Army and Navy.

JANMAN, Timothy Simon; Public Sector Business (formerly National Account) Manager, Manpower PLC, since 1993; *b* 9 Sept. 1956; *s* of Jack and Irene Janman; *m* 1990, Shirley Buckingham. *Educ:* Sir William Borlase Grammar Sch., Marlow, Bucks; Nottingham Univ. (BSc Hons Chemistry). Ford Motor Co., 1979–83; IBM UK Ltd, 1983–87. Nat. Sen. Vice-Chm., FCS, 1980–81; Chm., Selsdon Gp, 1983–87. Mem., Southampton City Council, May–July 1987. MP (C) Thurrock, 1987–92; contested (C) Thurrock, 1992. Mem., Select Cttee on Employment, 1989–92. Vice-Chm., Cons. Backbench Employment Cttee, 1988–92 (Sec., 1987–88); Sec., Cons. Backbench Home Affairs Cttee, 1989–92. *Publications:* contribs to booklets and pamphlets. *Recreations:* restaurants, theatre. *Address:* 40 Weltje Road, Hammersmith, W6 9LT.

JANNER, Hon. Greville Ewan, MA Cantab; QC 1971; MP (Lab) Leicester West, since 1974 (Leicester North West, 1970–74); barrister, author, lecturer, journalist and broadcaster; *b* 11 July 1928; *s* of Baron Janner and Lady Janner; *m* 1955, Myra Louise Sheink, Melbourne; one *s* two *d*. *Educ:* Bishop's Coll. Sch., Canada; St Paul's Sch. (Foundn Schol.); Trinity Hall, Cambridge (Exhbnr); Harvard Post Graduate Law School (Fulbright and Smith-Mundt Schol.); Harmsworth Scholar, Middle Temple, 1955. Nat. Service: Sgt RA, BAOR, War Crimes Investigator. Pres., Cambridge Union, 1952; Chm., Cambridge Univ. Labour Club, 1952; Internat. Sec., Nat. Assoc. of Labour Students, 1952; Pres., Trinity Hall Athletic Club, 1952. Contested (Lab) Wimbledon, 1955. Mem., Select Cttee on Employment, 1982– (Chm., 1992–); Chairman: All-Party Industrial Safety Gp, 1975–; All-Party Magic Group, 1991–; Founder, 1973, and former Chm., All-Party Cttee for Homeless and Rootless People; Founder, 1990, and Vice-Chm., 1990–92, All Party Race and Community Gp; Vice-Chairman: All-Party Parly Cttee for Jews in the Former Soviet Union (formerly Cttee for Release of Soviet Jewry), 1971–; (Jt), British-Israel Parly Gp, 1983–; British-India Parly Gp, 1991– (Jt Vice-Chm., 1987–91); British-Spanish Parly Gp, 1987– (Sec., 1986); All-Party British-Romanian Gp, 1990–92; All-Party Parly Cttee for E Europ. Jewry, 1990–; Sec., All-Party War Crimes Gp, 1987–; Founder, 1990, and Pres. of World Exec., Inter-Party Council Against Anti-Semitism. Vis. Law Fellow, Lancaster Univ., 1985–88. President: National Council for Soviet Jewry, 1979–85; Bd of Deputies of British Jews, 1979–85; Commonwealth Jewish Council, 1983–; Vice-President: Assoc. for Jewish Youth, 1970–; Assoc. of Jewish Ex-Servicemen; IVS, 1983–; World Jewish Congress: European Vice-Pres., 1984–86; Mem. World Exec., 1986–; Hon. Vice-Pres., 1990–. Partner, JSB Associates, 1984–; Chm., JSB Gp Ltd, 1988–; non-exec. Dir, Ladbroke Plc, 1986–. Member: Nat. Union of Journalists; Soc. of Labour Lawyers; Magic Circle; Pres., REACH, 1982–; Pres., Jewish Museum, 1985–; Mem. Bd of Dirs, Jt Israel Appeal, 1985–; Vice-Pres., Guideposts Trust, 1983–; Founder and Chm., Maimonides Foundn, 1992–; Founder Mem., Internat. Cttee for Human Rights in USSR; Chm., Holocaust Educnl Trust, 1987–. Formerly Dir, Jewish Chronicle Newspaper Ltd; Trustee, Jewish Chronicle Trust. Hon. Mem., Leics NUM, 1986–. FIPD (FIPM 1976). Hon. PhD Haifa Univ., 1984. Sternberg Award, CCJ, 1985. *Publications:* 64 books, mainly on employment and industrial relations law, presentational skills, and on public speaking, including: Employment Letters; Complete Speechmaker; Complete Letterwriter; Janner on Presentation; Communication; Chairing; Meetings. *Recreations:* swimming, magic, languages. *Address:* House of Commons, SW1A 0AA. *T:* 0171–219 3000.

JANSEN, Elly, (Mrs Elly Whitehouse-Jansen), OBE 1980; Founder and International Director, The Richmond Fellowship for community mental health, since 1959; *b* 5 Oct. 1929; *d* of Jacobus Gerrit Jansen and Petronella Suzanna Vellekoop; *m* 1969, Alan Brian Stewart Whitehouse (known as George); three *d*. *Educ:* Paedologisch Inst. of Free Univ., Amsterdam; Boerhave Kliniek (SRN); London Univ. Founded: Richmond Fellowship of America, 1968, of Australia, 1973, of New Zealand, 1978, of Austria, 1979, of Canada, 1981, of Hong Kong, 1981, of India, of Israel, 1984, and of the Caribbean, 1987; Richmond Fellowship Internat., 1981; Richmond Fellowship branches in France, Malta, Peru, Uruguay, Mexico, Ghana, Nigeria, Philippines and Bangladesh, 1981–93; Fellowship Charitable Foundn (later Community Housing and Therapy), 1983. Organised internat. confs on therapeutic communities, 1973, 1975, 1976, 1979, 1984, and 1988; acts as consultant to many govts on issues of community care. Fellowship, German Marshall Meml Fund, 1977–78. *Publications:* (ed) The Therapeutic Community Outside the Hospital, 1980; (contrib.) Mental Health and the Community, 1983; (contrib.) Towards a Whole Society: collected papers on aspects of mental health, 1985; contribs to Amer. Jl of Psychiatry, L'Inf. Psychiatrique, and other jls. *Recreations:* literature, music, interior design. *Address:* Clyde House, 109 Strawberry Vale, Twickenham, TW1 4SJ. *T:* 0181–744 9585, *Fax:* 0181–891 0500.

JANSEN, Peter Johan; Group Chief Executive, since 1989, and Deputy Chairman, since 1994, Caradon (formerly MB-Caradon); *b* 13 Feb. 1940; *s* of Eric Jansen and Elizabeth (*née* Keesman); *m* 1963, Françoise Marie-Paule; three *s*. *Educ:* Parktown Boys' High School, Johannesburg. Internat. marketing exec., Pfizer Corp., 1959–65; marketing Dir, Bristol Myers, 1966–69; Partner, Urwick Orr & Partners, 1969–72; Senior Partner, Lee, Jansen & Partners, 1972–77; Redland plc: Divl Man. Dir, 1977–80; plc Director, 1981–85; led management buy-out and subseq. flotation, Caradon plc; Dep. Chm. and Chief Exec., 1985–89. Dir, Burmah Castrol plc, 1993–; Chm. Supervisory Bd, Nutreco Holding BV, 1995–. Pres., Nat. Council of Bldg Material Producers, 1994–; Mem. Council, CBI, 1992–. Gov., St George's Coll., Weybridge, 1990–; Mem. Bd of Advrs, St Edmund Hall, Oxford, 1995–. CIMgt; FCIM; FRSA. *Recreations:* golf, opera, theatre. *Address:* Caradon House, Queens Road, Weybridge, Surrey KT13 9UX. *T:* Weybridge (01932) 850850.

JANSEN, Sir Ross (Malcolm), KBE 1989 (CBE 1986); Chairman, Midland Regional Health Authority, since 1992; Mayor of Hamilton City, New Zealand, 1977–89; *b* 6 Sept. 1932; *m* 1957, Rhyl Robinson; three *s* three *d*. *Educ:* Horowhenua Coll., Levin (Dux *proxime accessit* 1950); Victoria Univ., Wellington (LLB 1957); Univ. of Waikato (DPhil 1994). NZ Univ. Law Moot Prize, 1956. Practised law in partnership. Hamilton, 1958–77. Hamilton City Council: Mem., 1965–74, 1977–89; Chairman: Planning Cttee, 1965–68; Works Cttee, 1968–74; Dep. Mayor, 1971–74. Chairman: Waikato United Council, 1986–89; Hamilton Industrial Develt Prog., 1966–68; NZ Bldg Industry Commn, 1986–89; Lottery Community Facilities Cttee, 1989–; Waikato Regl Council, 1989–91. President: Municipal Assoc. of NZ, 1984–89; NZ Local Govt Assoc., 1988–89. Mem. Council, Univ. of Waikato, 1977–. Winston Churchill Trust Fellowship in Town Planning, 1968. FRSA; ACIArb. Hon. Dr Waikato Univ., 1984. Hon. Chieftain of Western Samoa (for services to the Samoan Community). Commemoration Medal, NZ, 1990. *Recreations:* reading (poetry and history), tennis, gardening. *Address:* Apartment 5, Waterford Estate, Grantham Street, Hamilton, New Zealand. *T:* (7) 8397418.

JANSONS, Mariss; conductor; Music Director, Oslo Philharmonic, since 1979; *b* Riga, Latvia, 14 Jan. 1943; *s* of Arvid Jansons. *Educ:* Leningrad Conservatory; studied in Vienna with Prof. Hans Swarowsky and in Salzburg with Herbert von Karajan. Leningrad Philharmonic (later renamed St Petersburg Philharmonic): Associate Conductor, 1973–85; Associate Principal Conductor, 1985–; Principal Guest Conductor, LPO, 1992–. Has conducted leading orchestras of Europe and America incl. Boston, Chicago and Pittsburgh Symphony Orchestras, Berlin and Vienna Philharmonic, Royal Concertgebouw, etc. Has toured extensively in Europe, America and Japan. Numerous recordings. Eddison Award for recording of Shostakovich's 7th Symphony, Holland, 1989; Dutch Luister Award for recording of Berlioz Symphonie fantastique with Royal Concertgebouw Orch., 1982; Norwegian Culture Prize of Anders Jahre, 1991. Comdr with Star, Royal Norwegian Order of Merit, 1995. *Address:* c/o IMG Artists Europe, Media House, 3 Burlington Lane, WA 2TH.

JANVRIN, Robin Berry, CVO 1994 (LVO 1983); Deputy Private Secretary to the Queen, since 1996; *b* 20 Sept. 1946; *s* of Vice Adm. Sir Richard Janvrin, KCB, DSC; *m* 1977, Isabelle de Boissonneaux de Chevigny, two *s* two *d*. *Educ:* Marlborough Coll.; Brasenose Coll., Oxford (MA). Royal Navy, 1964–75; joined Diplomatic Service, 1975; First Secretary: UK Delegn to NATO, 1976–78; New Delhi, 1981–84; Counsellor, 1985; Press Sec. to the Queen, 1987–90; Asst Private Sec. to the Queen, 1990–95. *Recreations:* family, painting. *Address:* c/o Buckingham Palace, SW1A 1AA.

JANZON, Mrs Bengt; *see* Dobbs, Mattiwilda.

JAPAN, Emperor of; *see* Akihito.

JAQUES, Prof. Elliott; Visiting Research Professor in Management Sciences, George Washington University, since 1989; *b* 18 Jan. 1917; one *d*. *Educ:* Univ. of Toronto (BA, MA); Johns Hopkins Med. Sch. (MD); Harvard Univ. (PhD). Qual. Psycho-analyst (Brit. Psycho-An. Soc.) 1951. Rantoul Fellow in Psychology, Harvard, 1940–41; Major, Royal Can. Army Med. Corps, 1941–45; Founder Mem., Tavistock Inst. of Human Relations, 1946–51; private practice as psycho-analyst and industrial consultant, 1952–65; Brunel University: Head of Sch. of Social Sciences, 1965–70; Prof. of Sociology, 1970–82; Dir, Inst. of Orgn and Social Studies, 1970–85, now Prof. Emeritus of Social Sciences. Adviser to BoT on organisation for overseas marketing, 1965–69; Mem. Management Study Steering Cttee on NHS Reorganisation, 1972. *Publications:* The Changing Culture of a Factory, 1951; Measurement of Responsibility, 1956; Equitable Payment, 1961; (with Wilfred Brown) Product Analysis Pricing, 1964; Time-Span Handbook, 1964; (with Wilfred Brown) Glacier Project Papers, 1965; Progression Handbook, 1968; Work, Creativity and Social Justice, 1970; A General Theory of Bureaucracy, 1976; Health Services, 1978; Levels of Abstraction and Logic in Human Action, 1978; The Form of Time, 1982; Free Enterprise, Fair Employment, 1982; Requisite Organisation, 1989; Executive Leadership, 1991; Human Capability, 1994; articles in Human Relations, New Society, Internat. Jl of Psycho-Analysis, etc. *Recreations:* art, music, ski-ing. *Address:* 6 Raven Lane, Gloucester, MA 01930, USA.

JARDINE of Applegirth, Sir Alexander Maule, (Sir Alec), 12th Bt *cr* 1672 (NS); 23rd Chief of the Clan Jardine; *b* 24 Aug. 1947; *s* of Col Sir William Edward Jardine of Applegirth, 11th Bt, OBE, TD, JP, DL, and of Ann Graham, *yr d* of late Lt-Col Claud Archibald Scott Maitland, DSO; *S* father, 1986; *m* 1982, Mary Beatrice, *d* of late Hon. John Michael Inigo Cross and of Mrs James Parker-Jervis; three *s* two *d*. *Educ:* Gordonstoun. Member of Queen's Body Guard for Scotland, Royal Co. of Archers. *Heir: s* William Murray Jardine, yr of Applegirth, *b* 4 July 1984. *Address:* Ash House, Thwaites, Millom, Cumbria LA18 5HY.

JARDINE, Sir Andrew (Colin Douglas), 5th Bt *cr* 1916; *b* 30 Nov. 1955; *s* of Brigadier Sir Ian Liddell Jardine, 4th Bt, OBE, MC, and of Priscilla Daphne, *d* of Douglas Middleton Parnham Scott-Phillips; *S* father, 1982. *Educ:* Charterhouse. Commissioned Royal Green Jackets, 1975–78; with Henderson Administration Gp, 1981–92; Dir, Gartmore Investment Trust Management Ltd, 1992–93. MSI 1993. Mem., Queen's Body Guard for Scotland, Royal Company of Archers, 1990–. *Heir: b* Michael Ian Christopher Jardine [*b* 4 Oct. 1958; *m* 1982, Maria Milky Pineda; two *s*]. *Address:* 99 Addison Road, W14 8DD. *T:* 0171–603 6434. *Club:* Boodle's.

See also Sir J. R. G. Baird, Bt.

JARDINE, Sir (Andrew) Rupert (John) Buchanan-, 4th Bt *cr* 1885; MC 1944; DL; landowner and farmer; *b* 2 Feb. 1923; *s* of Sir John William Buchanan-Jardine, 3rd Bt and Jean Barbara (*d* 1989), *d* of late Lord Ernest Hamilton; *S* father, 1969; *m* 1950, Jane Fiona (marr. diss. 1975), 2nd *d* of Sir Charles Edmonstone, 6th Bt; one *s* one *d*. *Educ:* Harrow;

Royal Agricultural College. Joined Royal Horse Guards, 1941; served in France, Holland and Germany; Major 1948; retired, 1949. Joint-Master, Dumfriesshire Foxhounds, 1950. JP Dumfriesshire, 1957; DL Dumfriesshire, 1978. Bronze Lion of the Netherlands, 1945. *Recreations:* country pursuits. *Heir:* *s* John Christopher Rupert Buchanan-Jardine [*b* 20 March 1952; *m* 1975, Pandora Lavinia, *d* of Peter Murray Lee; one *s* five *d*]. *Address:* Dixons, Lockerbie, Dumfriesshire DG11 2PR. *T:* Lockerbie (015762) 2508. *Club:* MCC.

JARDINE, James Christopher Macnaughton; Sheriff of Glasgow and Strathkelvin, 1979–95; *b* 18 Jan. 1930; *s* of James Jardine; *m* 1955, Vena Gordon Kight; one *d*. *Educ:* Glasgow Academy; Gresham House, Ayrshire; Glasgow Univ. (BL). National Service (Lieut RASC), 1950–52. Admitted as Solicitor, in Scotland, 1953. Practice as principal (from 1955) of Nelson & Mackay, and as partner of McClure, Naismith, Brodie & Co., Solicitors, Glasgow, 1956–69; Sheriff of Stirling, Dunbarton and Clackmannan, later N Strathclyde, at Dumbarton, 1969–79. A Vice-Pres., Sheriffs' Assoc., 1976–79. Sec., Glasgow Univ. Graduates Assoc., 1956–66; Mem., Business Cttee of Glasgow Univ. Gen. Council, 1964–67. Member: Consultative Cttee on Social Work in the Criminal Justice System (formerly Probation) for Strathclyde Region, 1980–94; Professional Advisory Cttee, Scottish Council on Alcoholism, 1982–85. *Recreations:* boating, enjoyment of music and theatre. *Address:* 26 Chesterfield Avenue, Kelvindale, Glasgow G12 0BL.

JARDINE, Prof. Nicholas, PhD; Professor of History and Philosophy of the Sciences, University of Cambridge, since 1992; Fellow, Darwin College, Cambridge, since 1975; *b* 4 Sept. 1943; *s* of Michael James Jardine and Jean Caroline (*née* Crook); *m* 1992, Marina Frasca-Spada; two *s* two *d* from previous marriages. *Educ:* Monkton Combe; King's Coll., Cambridge (BA 1965; PhD 1969). Jun. Res. Fellow, 1967–71, Sen. Res. Fellow, 1971–75, King's Coll., Cambridge; Royal Soc. Res. Fellow, 1968–73; University of Cambridge: Lectr, 1975–86; Reader, 1986–92. Mem., Internat. Acad. of Hist. of Sci., 1991–. Editor, Studies in Hist. and Philosophy of Sci., 1982–. *Publications:* (with R. Sibson) Mathematical Taxonomy, 1971; The Birth of History and Philosophy of Science, 1984, rev. edn 1988; The Fortunes of Inquiry, 1986; The Scenes of Inquiry, 1991. *Recreation:* plant hunting. *Address:* 63 The Broadway, Grantchester, Cambridge CB3 9NQ. *T:* Cambridge (01223) 845634.

JARDINE, Ronald Charles C.; *see* Cunningham-Jardine.

JARDINE, Sir Rupert Buchanan-; *see* Jardine, Sir A. R. J. B.

JARDINE PATERSON, Sir John (Valentine), Kt 1967; *b* 14 Feb. 1920; *y s* of late Robert Jardine Paterson, Balgray, Lockerbie, Dumfriesshire; *m* 1953, Priscilla Mignon, *d* of late Sir Kenneth Nicolson, MC; one *s* three *d*. *Educ:* Eton Coll.; Jesus Coll., Cambridge. Emergency commn, The Black Watch, RHR, 1939. Director: Jardine Henderson Ltd, Calcutta, 1952–67 (Chm. 1963–67); McLeod Russel PLC, 1967–84 (Chm., 1979–83). Chm., Indian Jute Mills Assoc., 1963; Pres., Bengal Chamber of Commerce and Industry and Associated Chambers of Commerce of India, 1966. *Recreations:* golf, shooting. *Address:* Norton Bavant Manor, Warminster, Wilts BA12 7BB. *T:* Warminster (01985) 840378. *Clubs:* Oriental; Bengal, Royal Calcutta Turf (Calcutta).

JARMAN, Nicholas Francis Barnaby; QC 1985; barrister; a Recorder of the Crown Court, since 1982; *b* 19 June 1938; *s* of late A. S. Jarman and of Helene Jarman; *m* 1st, 1973, Jennifer Michelle Lawrence-Smith (marr. diss. 1978); one *d*; 2nd, 1989, Julia Elizabeth MacDougall (*née* Owen-John). *Educ:* Harrow; Christ Church, Oxford (MA Jurisprudence). Commnd RA, 1956–58 (JUO Mons, 1957). Called to the Bar, Inner Temple, 1965 (Duke of Edinburgh Scholar). Bar Chm., Bucks, Berks and Oxon Jt Liaison Cttee, 1986–. *Recreations:* France, fly-fishing. *Address:* 13 Blithfield Street, W8 6RH. *T:* 0171–937 0982; Sous Château, Castelnau-Valence, 30190 St Chaptes, France. *T:* 66833293; 4 King's Bench Walk, Temple, EC4Y 7DL. *T:* 0171–353 3581.

JARMAN, Richard Neville; General Director, Scottish Opera, since 1991; *b* 24 April 1949; *s* of Dr Gwyn Jarman and Pauline (*née* Lane). *Educ:* King's Sch., Canterbury; Trinity Coll., Oxford (MA English). Sadler's Wells Opera and ENO, 1971–76; Touring Officer, Dance, Arts Council, 1976–77; Edinburgh International Festival: Artistic Asst, 1978–82; Fest. Adminr, 1982–84; Gen. Adminr, London Fest. and English Nat. Ballet, 1984–90. *Publications:* History of Sadler's Wells Opera, 1974; History of London Coliseum Theatre, 1979. *Recreations:* listening to music, going to the theatre, planting a new garden in France, food and drink, travel, reading. *Address:* 191 Wilton Street, North Kelvinside, Glasgow G20 6DF. *T:* 0141–946 4120.

JARMAN, Roger Whitney; Under Secretary, Local Government Finance, Housing and Social Services Group, Welsh Office, 1994–95; *b* 16 Feb. 1935; *s* of Reginald Cecil Jarman and Marjorie Dix Jarman; *m* 1959, Patricia Dorothy Odwell; one *s*. *Educ:* Cathays High Sch., Cardiff; Univ. of Birmingham (BSocSc Hons; Cert. in Educn). Recruitment and Selection Officer, Vauxhall Motors Ltd, 1960–64; Asst Sec., Univ. of Bristol Appts Bd, 1964–68; Asst Dir of Recruitment, CSD, 1968–72; Welsh Office: Principal, European Div., 1972–74; Asst Sec., Devolution Div., 1974–78; Asst Sec., Perm. Sec.'s Div., 1978–80; Under Secretary: Land Use Planning Gp, 1980–83; Transport, Highways and Planning Gp, 1983–88; Transport, Planning, Water and Environment Gp, 1988; Housing, Health and Social Services Policy Gp, 1988–94. *Recreations:* walking, reading, cooking. *Club:* Civil Service.

JARRATT, Sir Alexander Anthony, (Sir Alex), Kt 1979; CB 1968; DL; Director, Smiths Industries PLC, since 1984 (Chairman, 1985–91); Chancellor, University of Birmingham, since 1983; Chairman, Centre for Dispute Resolution, since 1990; *b* 19 Jan. 1924; *o s* of Alexander and Mary Jarratt; *m* 1946, Mary Philomena Keogh; one *s* two *d*. *Educ:* Royal Liberty Gram. Sch., Essex; University of Birmingham. War Service, Fleet Air Arm, 1942–46. University of Birmingham, BCom, 1946–49. Asst Principal, Min. of Power, 1949, Principal, 1953, and seconded to Treas., 1954–55; Min. of Power: Prin. Priv. Sec. to Minister, 1955–59; Asst Sec., Oil Div., 1959–63; Under-Sec., Gas Div., 1963–64; seconded to Cabinet Office, 1964–65; Secretary to the National Board for Prices and Incomes, 1965–68; Dep. Sec., 1967; Dep. Under Sec. of State, Dept of Employment and Productivity, 1968–70; Dep. Sec., Min. of Agriculture, 1970. Man. Dir, IPC, 1970–73; Chm. and Chief Executive, IPC and IPC Newspapers, 1974; Chm., Reed Internat., 1974–85 (Dir, 1970–85); a Dep. Chm., Midland Bank, 1980–91; Jt Dep. Chm., Prudential Corp. plc, 1987–91, 1992–94 (Dir, 1985–94); Director: ICI, 1975–91; Thyssen-Bornemisza Group, 1972–89; Mem., Ford European Adv. Council, 1983–88. Confederation of British Industry: Mem., Council, 1972–92; Mem., President's Cttee, 1983–86; Chairman: Economic Policy Cttee, 1972–74; Employment Policy Cttee, 1983–86; Mem., NEDC, 1976–80. Pres., Advertising Assoc., 1979–83. Chairman: Industrial Soc., 1975–79; Henley: The Management Coll., 1977–89; Gov., Ashridge Management Coll., 1975–91. Pres., Periodical Publishers Assoc., 1983–85; Vice-Pres., Inst. of Marketing; Chm., Adv. Bd, Inst. of Occup. Health. FRSA. DL Essex, 1995. Hon. CGIA 1990. Hon. DSc Cranfield, 1973; DUniv Brunel, 1979; Hon. LLD Birmingham, 1982. *Recreations:* walking, the countryside, reading, music. *Address:* c/o Smiths Industries PLC, 765 Finchley Road, Childs Hill, NW11 8DS. *T:* 0181–458 3232. *Club:* Savile.

JARRATT, Prof. Peter, CEng; FBCS; FSS; FIMA; Professor of Computing, since 1975, and Development Adviser to Vice-Chancellor, since 1991, University of Birmingham; *b* 2 Jan. 1935; *s* of Edward Jarratt and Edna Mary Jarratt; *m* 1972, Jeanette Debeir; one *s* two *d*. *Educ:* Univ. of Manchester (BSc, PhD). Programmer, Nuclear Power Plant Co. Ltd, 1957; Chief Programmer, Nuclear Power Gp, 1960; Lectr in Mathematics, Bradford Inst. of Technology, 1962; Asst Dir, Computing Lab., Univ. of Bradford, 1966; Dir, Computing Lab., Univ. of Salford, 1972; University of Birmingham: Dir, Computer Centre, 1975–91; Dep. Dean, Faculty of Science and Engrg, 1984; first Dean of Faculty of Science, 1985–88. Dir, Birmingham Res. and Develt Ltd, 1986–88; Chm., Birmingham Inst. for Conductive Educn, 1987–90. Mem., Birmingham Lunar Soc., 1991–. Gov., Royal Nat. Coll. for the Blind, 1986–; Patron, Henshaw's Soc. for the Blind, 1993–. *Publications:* numerous res. papers on mathematics and computer sci. *Recreations:* classical music, mountain walking, gardening, chess. *Address:* 42 Reddings Road, Moseley, Birmingham B13 8LN. *T:* 0121–449 7160. *Club:* Athenæum.

JARRETT, Rt. Rev. Martyn William; *see* Burnley, Suffragan Bishop of.

JARRETT, Prof. William Fleming Hoggan, FRS 1980; FRSE 1965; Professor of Veterinary Pathology, 1968–91, Senior Research Fellow, since 1991, University of Glasgow; *b* 2 Jan. 1928; *s* of James and Jessie Jarrett; *m* 1952, Anna Fraser Sharp; two *d*. *Educ:* Lenzie Academy; Glasgow Veterinary Coll.; Univ. of Glasgow; PhD, FRCVS, FRCPath. Gold Medal, 1949; John Henry Steele Meml Medal, 1961; Steele Bodger Meml Schol. 1955. ARC Research Student, 1949–52; Lectr, Dept of Veterinary Pathology, Univ. of Glasgow Vet. Sch., 1952–53; Head of Hospital Path. Dept of Vet. Hosp., Univ. of Glasgow, 1953–61; Reader in Pathology, Univ. of Glasgow, 1962–65; seconded to Univ. of E Africa, 1963–64; Titular Prof. of Experimental Vet. Medicine, Univ. of Glasgow, 1965. Lectures: Leeuwenhoek, Royal Soc., 1986; McFadyean Meml, RVC, 1986. Fogarty Scholar, NIH, 1985. Hon. FRCPSGlas 1988. Dr *hc* Liège Univ., 1986; DUniv Stirling, 1988; Hon. DSc: East Anglia, 1989; Edinburgh, 1989; Hon. DVSc RVC, London, 1991. Centennial Award, Univ. of Pennsylvania, 1984; Makdougall Brisbane Prize, RSE, 1984; J.T. Edwards Meml Medal, RCVS, 1984; Feldberg Prize, 1987; Tenovus-Scotland Margaret McLellan Award, 1989; Saltire Award, 1989; WSAVA Waltham Internat. Award, 1991. *Publications:* various, on tumour viruses, Leukaemia and immunology. *Recreations:* sailing, skiing, mountaineering, music. *Address:* Auchineden House, Blanefield G63 9AX. *T:* and *Fax:* Blanefield (01360) 770112. *Clubs:* Clyde Cruising; Glencoe Ski.

JARRING, Gunnar, PhD; Grand Cross, Order of the North Star, Sweden; Swedish Ambassador and Special Representative of the Secretary-General of the United Nations on the Middle East question, 1967–91; *b* S Sweden, 12 Oct. 1907; *s* of Gottfrid Jönsson and Betty Svensson; *m* 1932, Agnes, *d* of Prof. Carl Charlier, Lund; one *d*. *Educ:* Lund; Univ. of Lund (PhD). Family surname changed to Jarring, 1931. Associate Prof. of Turkish Langs, Lund Univ., 1933–40; Attaché, Ankara, 1940–41; Chief, Section B, Teheran, 1941; Chargé d'Affaires *ad interim:* Teheran and Baghdad, 1945; Addis Ababa, 1946–48; Minister: to India, 1948–51, concurrently to Ceylon, 1950–51; to Persia, Iraq and Pakistan, 1951–52; Dir, Polit. Div., Min. of Foreign Affairs, 1953–56; Permanent Rep. to UN, 1956–58; Rep. on Security Council, 1957–58; Ambassador to USA, 1958–64, to USSR, 1964–73, and to Mongolia, 1965–73. *Publications:* Studien zu einer osttürkischen Lautlehre, 1933; The Contest of the Fruits - An Eastern Turki Allegory, 1936; The Uzbek Dialect of Quilich, Russian Turkestan, 1937; Uzbek Texts from Afghan Turkestan, 1938; The Distribution of Turk Tribes in Afghanistan, 1939; Materials to the Knowledge of Eastern Turki (vols 1–4), 1947–51; An Eastern Turki-English Dialect Dictionary, 1964; Literary Texts from Kashghar, 1980; Return to Kashghar, 1986; Prints from Kashghar, 1991. *Address:* Pontus Ols väg 7, 26040 Viken, Sweden.

JARROLD, Kenneth Wesley; Director of Human Resources, NHS Executive, since 1994; *b* 19 May 1948; *s* of William Stanley Jarrold and Martha Hamilton Jarrold (*née* Cowan); *m* 1973, Patricia Hadaway; two *s*. *Educ:* St Lawrence Coll., Ramsgate; Sidney Sussex Coll., Cambridge (Whittaker Schol.; BA Hons Hist. 1st cl.; Pres., Cambridge Union Soc.) Dip. IHSM (Hons Standard). E Anglian RHB, 1969–70; Briggs Cttee on Nursing, 1970–71; Dep. Supt, Royal Hosp., Sheffield, 1971–74; Hosp. Sec., Derbyshire Royal Infirmary, 1974–75; Sector Administrator, Nottingham Gen. and Univ. Hosps, 1975–79; Asst Dist Administrator (Planning), S Tees HA, 1979–82; Dist Administrator, 1982–84, Dist Gen. Manager, 1984–89, Gloucester HA; Regl Gen. Manager, Wessex RHA, 1990–94. Mem., NHS Training Authy and Chm., Training Cttee, 1984–87; Chm., Management Educn System by Open Learning Project Group, 1986–89. Pres., IHSM, 1985–86 (Mem., Nat. Council, 1977–89. *Publications:* articles in professional jls. *Recreations:* being with family, fitness training. *Address:* 3 Randall Road, Chandler's Ford, Eastleigh, Hants SO5 1AJ.

JARROLD, Nicholas Robert; HM Diplomatic Service; Counsellor (Economic and Commercial), Brussels (and concurrently Luxembourg), since 1992; *b* 2 March 1946; *s* of late A. R. Jarrold and D. V. Roberts; *m* 1972, Anne Catherine Whitworth; two *s*. *Educ:* Shrewsbury Sch.; Western Reserve Acad., Ohio (ESU Scholar); St Edmund Hall, Oxford (Exhibnr, MA). Entered Diplomatic Service, 1968: FCO, 1968–69; The Hague, 1969–72; Dakar, 1972–75; FCO, 1975–79; Nairobi, 1979–83; FCO, 1983–89; Counsellor and Dep. Head of Mission, Havana, 1989–91; Vis. Fellow, St Antony's Coll., Oxford, 1991–92. *Recreations:* reading history, cricket, the theatre. *Address:* c/o Foreign and Commonwealth Office, King Charles Street, SW1A 2AH.

JARROW, Bishop Suffragan of, since 1990; **Rt. Rev. Alan Smithson;** *b* 1 Dec. 1936; *s* of Herbert and Mary Smithson; *m* 1964, Margaret Jean McKenzie; two *s* two *d*. *Educ:* Queen's Coll., Oxford (BA 1962; MA 1968); Queen's Coll., Birmingham (DipTh 1964). Deacon 1964, priest 1965; Curate: Christ Church, Skipton, 1964–68; St Mary the Virgin with St Cross and St Peter, Oxford, 1968–72; Chaplain: Queen's Coll., Oxford, 1969–72; Reading Univ., 1972–77; Vicar of Bracknell, 1977–84; Residentiary Canon, Carlisle Cathedral and Dir of Training and Diocesan Training Inst., 1984–90. *Recreations:* water colour painting, travel, camping, fell walking, 'cello playing. *Address:* The Old Vicarage, Hallgarth, Pittington, Durham DH6 1AB. *T:* Durham (0191) 3720225.

JÄRVI, Neeme; Music Director, Detroit Symphony Orchestra, since 1990; Chief Conductor, Gothenburg Symphony Orchestra, Sweden, since 1982; *b* Tallinn, Estonia, 7 June 1937; *s* of August and Elss Järvi; *m* 1961, Liilia Järvi; two *s* one *d*. *Educ:* Estonia-Tallinn Conservatory of Music; Leningrad State Conservatory. Chief Conductor: Estonian Radio Symphony Orch., 1963–77 (Conductor, 1960–63); Estonia opera house, Tallinn, 1963–77; toured USA with Leningrad Phil. Orch., 1973 and 1977; Chief Conductor, Estonian State Symph. Orch., 1977–80; since emigration to USA in 1980 has appeared as Guest Conductor with New York Phil. Orch., Philadelphia Orch., Boston Symph., Chicago Symph., Los Angeles Phil., Met. Opera (New York) and in San Francisco, Cincinnati, Indianapolis, Minneapolis and Detroit; has also given concerts in Vienna, London, Canada, Sweden, Finland, Norway, Denmark, Holland, Switzerland and W Germany; Principal Guest Conductor, City of Birmingham Symph. Orch., 1981–84; Musical Dir and Principal Conductor, Scottish Nat. Orch., 1984–88, Conductor Laureate,

1989. 1st Prize, Internat. Conductors Competition, Accademia Santa Cecilia, Rome, 1971. Over 250 recordings including: works by Bartok, Dvorak, Medtner, Barber, Prokofiev (symphonic cycle), Shostakovich; complete works of Sibelius and all symphonies of Nielsen and Mahler (Toblach Prize for best recording, 1993, for No 3); Saul and David, opera by Nielsen; Don Giovanni; Schmidt symphonies. *Recreation:* traveller. *Address:* c/o Columbia Artists Management Inc., 165 West 57th Street, New York, NY 10019, USA.

JARVIS, Frederick Frank, (Fred Jarvis); General Secretary, National Union of Teachers, 1975–89; Member of General Council, 1974–89, President, 1987, Trades Union Congress (Chairman, 1986–87); *b* 8 Sept. 1924; *s* of Alfred and Emily Ann Jarvis; *m* 1954, Elizabeth Anne Colegrove, Stanton Harcourt, Oxfordshire; one *s* one *d*. *Educ:* Plaistow Secondary Sch., West Ham; Oldershaw Grammar Sch., Wallasey; Liverpool Univ.; St Catherine's Society, Oxford. Dip. in Social Science with dist. (Liverpool Univ.); BA (Hons) in Politics, Philosophy and Economics (Oxon), MA (Oxon). Contested (Lab) Wallasey, Gen. Elec., 1951; Chm., Nat. Assoc. of Labour Student Organisations, 1951; Pres., Nat. Union of Students, 1952–54 (Dep. Pres., 1951–52); Asst Sec., Nat. Union of Teachers, 1955–59; Head of Publicity and Public Relations, 1959–70; Dep. Gen. Sec., NUT, 1970–74 (apptd Gen. Sec. Designate, March 1974). Pres., Eur. Trade Union Cttee for Educn, 1983–84, 1985–86 (Vice-Pres., 1981–83); Chairman, TUC Cttees: Local Govt, 1983–88; Educn Training, 1985–88; Chm., TUC Nuclear Energy Review Body, 1986–88. Member: Central Arbitration Cttee, 1985–94; Franco-British Council, 1986–. Mem. Council, Nat. Youth Theatre. FRSA. Hon. FEIS 1980; Hon. FCP 1982. *Publications:* The Educational Implications of UK Membership of the EEC, 1972; Education and Mr Major, 1993; Ed, various jls incl.: 'Youth Review', NUT Guide to Careers; NUT Univ. and Coll. Entrance Guide. *Recreations:* swimming, golf, tennis, gardening, cinema, theatre, photography. *Address:* 92 Hadley Road, New Barnet, Herts EN5 5QR. *Club:* Ronnie Scott's.

JARVIS, John Manners; QC 1989; a Recorder, since 1992; *b* 20 Nov. 1947; *s* of Donald Edward Manners Jarvis and late Theodora Brixie Jarvis; *m* 1972, Janet Rona Kitson; two *s*. *Educ:* King's Coll. Sch., Wimbledon; Emmanuel Coll., Cambridge (MA (Law)). Called to Bar, Lincoln's Inn, 1970. Practising barrister specialising in Commercial Law, particularly banking. An Asst Recorder, 1987–92. Treas., Commercial Bar Assoc., 1993–. Gov., King's Coll. Sch., Wimbledon, 1987–. Overseas Editor, Jl of Banking and Finance—Law and Practice, 1990–. *Publications:* (jtly) Lender Liability, 1993; (contrib.) Banks, Liability and Risk, 2nd edn 1995. *Recreations:* tennis, sailing, ski-ing, cycling, music. *Address:* 7 Lancaster Gardens, Wimbledon, SW19 5DG. *T:* 0181–946 6603; 3 Gray's Inn Place, Gray's Inn, WC1R 5EA. *T:* 0171–831 8441. *Club:* Hurlingham.

JARVIS, Martin; actor; *b* 4 Aug. 1941; *s* of Denys Jarvis and Margot Jarvis; *m*; two *s*; *m* 1974, Rosalind Ayres. *Educ:* Whitgift School; RADA (Hons Dip., 1962, Silver Medal, 1962, Vanbrugh Award, 1962; RADA Associate, 1980). Nat. Youth Theatre, 1960–62; played Henry V, Sadler's Wells, 1962; Manchester Library Theatre, 1962–63; *stage:* Cockade, Arts, 1963; Poor Bitos, Duke of York's, 1963; Man and Superman, Vaudeville, 1966; The Bandwagon, Mermaid, 1970; The Rivals, USA, 1973; Hamlet (title rôle), Fest. of British Th., 1973; The Circle, Haymarket, 1976; She Stoops to Conquer, Canada, and Hong Kong Arts Festival, 1977; Caught in the Act, Garrick, 1981; Importance of Being Earnest, NT, 1982; Victoria Station, NT, 1983; The Trojan War Will Not Take Place, NT, 1983; Woman in Mind, Vaudeville, 1986; The Perfect Party, Greenwich, 1987; Henceforward, Vaudeville, 1989; Exchange, Vaudeville, 1990, Los Angeles, 1992; You Say Potato, Los Angeles, 1990; Twelfth Night, Playhouse, 1991; Leo in Love, Southampton, 1992; Just Between Ourselves, Greenwich, 1992; Make and Break, 1993, Man of the Moment, 1994, Los Angeles; On Approval, Playhouse, 1994; Table Manners LA, 1995; recitals of Paradise Lost, Old Vic, Chichester and QEH, 1975–77; *films:* The Last Escape, Ike, The Bunker, Taste the Blood of Dracula, Buster; The Fool of the World and the Flying Ship, 1991 (Emmy Award); Emily's Ghost, 1992; Calliope; Absence of War, 1995; *television series:* The Forsyte Saga, 1967; Nicholas Nickleby, 1968; Little Women, 1969; The Moonstone, 1971; The Pallisers, 1974; David Copperfield, 1975; Killers, 1976; Rings on Their Fingers, 1978–80; Breakaway, 1980; The Black Tower, 1985; Chelworth, 1988; Countdown, 1990; Murder Most Horrid, 1991; The Good Guys, 1992; Woof!, 1992; Library of Romance, 1992; Girl from Ipanema (British Comedy Award); Scarlet and Black, 1993; Brillat Saverin, 1994; Lovejoy, 1994; Murder She Wrote, 1995; and numerous plays; *radio:* numerous performances, incl. one-man series, Jarvis's Frayn, as Charles Dickens in series, The Best of Times; in Redevelopment, Globe Theatre series; Gush, 1994; script writing and adaptations; commentaries for TV and film documentaries and for arts programmes; has adapted and read over 50 of Richmal Crompton's Just William stories for radio, TV and cassette; recorded one-man performance of David Copperfield for cassette, 1991; co-produced cassette 2nd World War Poetry, 1993; produced and directed cassettes, Tales from Shakespeare. Mem., Stars Organisation for Spastics, 1983–; Dir, Children's Film Unit. Pres., Croydon Histrionic Soc., 1984–; Vice-Pres., Salamander Oasis Trust, 1990–. Sony Silver Award, 1991; NY Internat. Award, for contribn to broadcasting, 1994. *Publications:* Bright Boy, 1977; William Stories: a personal selection, 1992; short stories for radio; contribs to many anthologies; articles in The Listener, Punch, Tatler, Daily Telegraph and London Evening Standard. *Recreations:* Indian food, Beethoven, Mozart, people-watching. *Address:* c/o ICM, 76 Oxford Street, W1N 0AX. *Clubs:* BBC; St James's (LA).

JARVIS, Patrick William, CB 1985; CEng, FIEE, FIMarE; FRINA; RCNC; Deputy Controller (Warships), Ministry of Defence (Procurement Executive), and Head of Royal Corps of Naval Constructors, 1983–86; *b* 27 Aug. 1926; *s* of Frederick Arthur and Marjorie Winifred Jarvis; *m* 1951, Amy (*née* Ryley); two *s*. *Educ:* Royal Naval Coll., Greenwich; Royal Naval Engrg Coll., Keyham, Devonport. BScEng. Trade apprentice, HM Dockyard, Chatham, 1942–46; Design Engineer, Admiralty, Bath, 1946–62; Warship Electrical Supt, Belfast, 1962–63; Suptg Engr, MoD(N), Bath, 1963–72; Ship Department, MoD (PE), Bath: Asst Dir and Dep. Dir, 1972–78; Under Sec., 1978; Dir of Naval Ship Production, 1979–81; Dir of Ship Design and Engrg, and Dep. Head of Royal Corps of Naval Constructors, 1981–83; Dep. Sec., 1983. *Recreations:* indoor sports, chess. *Address:* Ranworth, Bathampton Lane, Bath BA2 6ST.

JASON, David, OBE 1993; actor; *b* 2 Feb. 1940; *s* of Arthur and Olwyn White. Stage career began with a season in repertory; *theatre includes:* Under Milk Wood, Mayfair, 1971; The Rivals, Sadler's Wells, 1972; No Sex Please . . . We're British!, Strand, 1972; Darling Mr London, tour, 1975; Charley's Aunt, tour, 1975; The Norman Conquests, Oxford Playhouse, 1976; The Relapse, Cambridge Theatre Co., 1978; Cinderella, 1979; The Unvarnished Truth, Mid/Far East tour, 1983; Look No Hans!, tour and West End, 1985; *films:* Under Milk Wood, 1970; Royal Flash, 1974; The Odd Job, 1978; Only Fools and Horses; Wind in the Willows, 1983; *television includes:* Do Not Adjust Your Set, 1967; The Top Secret Life of Edgar Briggs, 1973–74; Mr Stabbs, 1974; Ronnie Barker Shows, 1975; Open All Hours, 1975; Porridge, 1975; Lucky Feller, 1975; A Sharp Intake of Breath, 1978; Del Trotter in Only Fools and Horses, 1981–91; Porterhouse Blue, 1986; Jackanory, 1988; A Bit of A Do, 1988–89; Single Voices: The Chemist, 1989; Amongst Barbarians, 1989; Pa Larkin in The Darling Buds of May, 1990–92; A Touch of Frost, 1992; *voice work:* Dangermouse, Count Duckula, The Wind in the Willows. Awards include Best Actor Award, BAFTA, 1988. *Recreations:* diving, flying, motorcycles. *Address:* c/o Richard Stone Partnership, 25 Whitehall, SW1A 2BS.

JASPAN, Andrew; Editor, The Observer, since 1995; *b* 20 April 1952; *s* of Mervyn and Helen Jaspan; *m* 1991, Karen Jane Grant; one *s*. *Educ:* Beverley GS; Manchester Univ. (BA Hons Politics). Co-Founder, New Manchester Review, 1976–79; Daily Telegraph features, 1979; Fellowship, Journalists in Europe, Paris, 1980–81; freelance journalist, Daily Mirror and Daily Telegraph, 1982; News Sub-Ed., The Times, 1983–85; Asst News Ed., Sunday Times, 1985–88; Editor: Sunday Times Scotland, 1988–89; Scotland on Sunday, 1989–94; The Scotsman, 1994–95. *Publications:* Exams and Assessment, 1975; Preparing for Higher Education, 1975. *Recreations:* tennis, squash, cycling, travel. *Address:* (office) 119 Farringdon Road, EC1R 3ER. *T:* 0171–278 2332. *Club:* Glasgow Art.

JASPER, Robin Leslie Darlow, CMG 1963; HM Diplomatic Service, retired; *b* 22 Feb. 1914; *s* of T. D. Jasper, Beckenham; *m* 1st, 1940, Jean Cochrane (marr. diss.); one *d*; 2nd, 1966, Diana Speed (*née* West), two step *d*. *Educ:* Dulwich; Clare Coll., Cambridge. Apprentice, LNER Hotels Dept, 1936–39; Bursar, Dominion Students Hall Trust (London House), 1939–40; RAFVR (Wing Comdr), 1940–45; Principal, India Office (later Commonwealth Relations Office), 1945; concerned with resettlement of the Sec. of State's Services in India, 1947–48; British Dep. High Commissioner, Lahore, Pakistan, 1949–52; Adviser to London Conferences on Central African Federation, and visited Central Africa in this connection, 1952–53; Counsellor, HM Embassy, Lisbon, 1953–55; visited Portuguese Africa, 1954; Commonwealth Relations Office, 1955–60 (Head of Information Policy Dept, 1958–60); attached to the United Kingdom delegation to the United Nations, 1955 and 1956; British Dep. High Commissioner, Ibadan, Nigeria, 1960–64; Counsellor, Commonwealth Office, 1965–67; Consul-Gen., Naples, 1967–71, retired 1972. Lived in Almuñécar, Granada, Spain, 1971–79. *Recreations:* tennis, Rugby fives, wind music, 17th Century Church Sculpture, claret. *Address:* 1 Stafford Court, 50 Eversfield Place, St Leonard's-on-Sea, East Sussex TN37 6DB. *T:* Hastings (01424) 443196. *Clubs:* MCC, Jesters.

JAUNCEY, family name of **Baron Jauncey of Tullichettle.**

JAUNCEY OF TULLICHETTLE, Baron *cr* 1988 (Life Peer), of Comrie in the District of Perth and Kinross; **Charles Eliot Jauncey;** PC 1988; a Lord of Appeal in Ordinary, since 1988; *b* 8 May 1925; *s* of late Captain John Henry Jauncey, DSO, RN, Tullichettle, Comrie, and Muriel Charlie, *d* of late Adm. Sir Charles Dundas of Dundas, KCMG; *m* 1st, 1948, Jean (marr. diss. 1969), *d* of Adm. Sir Angus Cunninghame Graham of Gartmore, KBE, CB; two *s* one *d*; 2nd, 1973, Elizabeth (marr. diss. 1977), *widow* of Major John Ballingal, MC; 3rd, 1977, Camilla, *d* of late Lt-Col Charles Cathcart of Pitcairlie, DSO; one *d*. *Educ:* Radley; Christ Church, Oxford (Hon. Student, 1990); Glasgow Univ. BA 1947, Oxford; LLB 1949, Glasgow. Served in War, 1943–46, Sub-Lt RNVR. Advocate, Scottish Bar, 1949; Standing Junior Counsel to Admiralty, 1954; QC (Scotland) 1963; Kintyre Pursuivant of Arms, 1955–71; Sheriff Principal of Fife and Kinross, 1971–74; Judge of the Courts of Appeal of Jersey and Guernsey, 1972–79; a Senator of College of Justice, Scotland, 1979–88. Hon. Sheriff-Substitute of Perthshire, 1962. Mem. of Royal Co. of Archers (Queen's Body Guard for Scotland), 1951. Mem., Historic Buildings Council for Scotland, 1971–92. *Recreations:* shooting, fishing, bicycling, genealogy. *Address:* Tullichettle, Comrie, Perthshire PH6 2HU. *T:* Comrie (01764) 670349; House of Lords, SW1A 0PW. *Club:* Royal (Perth).

JAWARA, Alhaji Sir Dawda Kairaba, Kt 1966; Hon. GCMG 1974; Grand Master, Order of the Republic of The Gambia, 1972; President of the Republic of The Gambia, 1970–94; Vice-President of the Senegambian Confederation, 1982; *b* Barajally, MacCarthy Island Div., 16 May 1924. *Educ:* Muslim Primary Sch. and Methodist Boys' Grammar Sch., Bathurst; Achimota Coll. (Vet. School); Glasgow Univ. FRCVS 1988 (MRCVS 1953); Dipl. in Trop. Vet. Med., Edinburgh, 1957. Veterinary Officer for The Gambia Govt, 1954–57, Principal Vet. Officer, 1957–60. Leader of People's Progressive Party (formerly Protectorate People's Party), The Gambia, 1960; MP 1960; Minister of Education, 1960–61; Premier, 1962–63; Prime Minister, 1963–70. Chairman: Permanent Inter State Cttee for Drought in the Sahel, 1977–79; Organisation pour la Mise en Valeur du Fleuve Gambie Conf., Heads of State and Govt, 1987–88; Authy of Heads of State and Govt, Economic Community of W African States, 1988–89. Patron, Commonwealth Vet. Assoc., 1967–. FRCVS 1988. Hon. LLD Ife, 1978; Hon. DSc Colorado State Univ., USA, 1986. Peutinger Gold Medal, Peutinger-Collegium, Munich, 1979; Agricola Medal, FAO, Rome, 1980. Grand Cross: Order of Cedar of Lebanon, 1966; Nat. Order of Republic of Senegal, 1967; Order of Propitious Clouds of China (Taiwan), 1968; Nat. Order of Republic of Guinea, 1973; Grand Cordon of Most Venerable Order of Knighthood, Pioneers of Republic of Liberia, 1968; Grand Comdr, Nat. Order of Federal Republic of Nigeria, 1970; Comdr of Golden Ark (Netherlands), 1979; Grand Gwanghwa Medal of Order of Diplomatic Service (Republic of Korea), 1984; Nishan-i-Pakistan (Pakistan), 1984; Grand Officer of Nat. Merit, Islamic Republic of Mauritania, 1992; Grant Comdr, Nat. Order of Republic of Portugal, 1993. *Recreations:* golf, gardening, sailing.

JAY, family name of **Baron Jay** and **Baroness Jay of Paddington**.

JAY, Baron *cr* 1987 (Life Peer), of Battersea in Greater London; **Douglas Patrick Thomas Jay,** PC 1951; *b* 23 March 1907; *s* of Edward Aubrey Hastings Jay and Isobel Violet Jay; *m* 1st, 1933, Margaret Christian (marr. diss. 1972), *e d* of late J. C. Maxwell Garnett, CBE, ScD; two *s* two *d*; 2nd, 1972, Mary Lavinia Thomas, *d* of Hugh Lewis Thomas. *Educ:* Winchester Coll.; New Coll., Oxford (Scholar). First Class, Litteræ Humaniores. Fellow of All Souls' Coll., Oxford, 1930–37, and 1968–; on the staff of The Times, 1929–33, and The Economist, 1933–37; City Editor of the Daily Herald, 1937–40; Asst Sec., Ministry of Supply, 1940–43; Principal Asst Sec., BoT, 1943–45; Personal Asst to Prime Minister, 1945–46. MP (Lab) Battersea N, July 1946–1974, Wandsworth, Battersea N, 1974–83; Economic Sec. to Treasury, 1947–50; Financial Sec. to Treasury, 1950–51; President, BoT, 1964–67. Chairman: Common Market Safeguards Campaign, 1970–77; London Motorway Action Group, 1968–80. Director: Courtaulds Ltd, 1967–70; Trades Union Unit Trust, 1967–79; Flag Investment Co., 1968–71. *Publications:* The Socialist Case, 1937; Who is to Pay for the War and the Peace, 1941; Socialism in the New Society, 1962; After the Common Market, 1968; Change and Fortune, 1980; Sterling: a plea for moderation, 1985. *Address:* Causeway Cottage, Minster Lovell, Oxon OX8 5RN. *T:* Witney (01993) 775235.

See also Hon. Peter Jay.

JAY OF PADDINGTON, Baroness *cr* 1992 (Life Peer), of Paddington in the City of Westminster; **Margaret Ann Jay;** *b* 18 Nov. 1939; *er d* of Baron Callaghan of Cardiff, *qv*; *m* 1961, Hon. Peter Jay, *qv* (marr. diss. 1986); one *s* two *d*; *m* 1994, Prof. M. W. Adler, *qv*. Dir, Nat. Aids Trust, 1988–92. Vice Chm., Parkside Health Authority, 1986–. *Address:* 44 Blomfield Road, W9 2PF.

JAY, Sir Antony (Rupert), Kt 1988; CVO 1993; freelance writer and producer, since 1964; Chairman, Video Arts Ltd, 1972–89; *b* 20 April 1930; *s* of Ernest Jay and Catherine

Hay; *m* 1957, Rosemary Jill Watkins; two *s* two *d*. *Educ:* St Paul's Sch.; Magdalene Coll., Cambridge (BA (1st cl. Hons) Classics and Comparative Philology, 1952; MA 1955). 2nd Lieut Royal Signals, 1952–54. BBC, 1955–64: Editor, Tonight, 1962–63; Head of Talks Features, TV, 1963–64; (with Jonathan Lynn) writer of BBC TV series, Yes, Minister and Yes, Prime Minister, 1980–88. Mem., Cttee on Future of Broadcasting, 1974–77. FRSA 1992; CIMgt 1992. Hon. MA Sheffield, 1987; Hon. DBA IMCB, 1988. *Publications:* Management and Machiavelli, 1967, 2nd edn 1987; (with David Frost) To England with Love, 1967; Effective Presentation, 1970; Corporation Man, 1972; The Householder's Guide to Community Defence against Bureaucratic Aggression, 1972; (with Jonathan Lynn): Yes, Minister, Vol. 1 1981, Vol. 2 1982, Vol. 3 1983; The Complete Yes, Minister, 1984; Yes, Prime Minister, Vol. 1 1986, Vol. 2 1987; The Complete Yes, Prime Minister, 1989; Elizabeth R, 1992. *Address:* c/o Video Arts Ltd, 68 Oxford Street, W1N 9LA. *T:* 0171–637 7288.

JAY, Prof. Barrie Samuel, MD, FRCS; FRCOphth; Professor of Clinical Ophthalmology, University of London, 1985–92, now Emeritus; Consulting Surgeon, Moorfields Eye Hospital, since 1992 (Consultant Surgeon, 1969–92); Hon. Secretary, Conference of Medical Royal Colleges, since 1994; *b* 7 May 1929; *er s* of late Dr M. B. Jay and Julia Sterling; *m* 1954, Marcelle Ruby Byre; two *s*. *Educ:* Perse Sch., Cambridge; Gonville and Caius Coll., Cambridge (MA, MD); University Coll. Hosp., London. FRCS 1962; FCOphth 1988 (Hon. FRCOphth 1994). House Surgeon and Sen. Resident Officer, Moorfields Eye Hosp., 1959–62; Sen. Registrar, Ophthalmic Dept, London Hosp., 1962–65; Institute of Ophthalmology, University of London: Shepherd Res. Scholar, 1963–64; Mem., Cttee of Management, 1972–77, 1979–91; Clinical Sub-Dean, 1973–77; Dean, 1980–85; Ophthalmic Surgeon, The London Hosp., 1965–79. Consultant Advr in Ophthalmol., DHSS, 1982–88. Examiner: Dip. in Ophthal., 1970–75; British Orthoptic Council, 1970–78; Ophthalmic Nursing Bd, 1971–87; Mem. Ct of Examrs, RCS, 1975–80. Brit. Rep., Monospecialist Section of Ophthal., Eur. Union of Med. Specialists, 1973–85. Mem. Council: Section of Ophthal., RSM, 1965–77 (Editorial Rep., 1966–77); Faculty of Ophthalmologists, 1970–88 (Asst Hon. Sec., 1976–78; Hon. Sec., 1978–86; Pres., 1986–88); RCS (co-opted Mem. for Ophthalmology), 1983–88; Coll. of Ophthalmologists, 1988–92 (Vice-Pres., 1988–92); Nat. Ophthalmic Treatment Bd Assoc., 1971–75; Internat. Pediatric Ophthal. Soc., 1975–92; Ophthal. Soc. UK, 1985–88; Member: Ophthal. Nursing Bd, 1974–88; Orthoptists Bd, Council for Professions Supplementary to Medicine, 1977–92 (Vice Chm., 1982–88); Specialist Adv. Cttee in Ophthalmology, 1979–88 (Chm., 1982–88); Standing Med. Adv. Cttee, DHSS, 1980–84; Transplant Adv. Panel, DHSS, 1983–88. Trustee: Fight for Sight, 1973–94; Wolfson Foundn, 1986–92; Wolfson Family Charitable Trust, 1992–. Fellow, Eugenics Soc.; FRPSL (Hon. Sec., 1992–); Hon. Member: British Paediatric Assoc., 1995; Canadian Ophthalmol Soc. Mem., Ct of Assts, Soc. of Apothecaries (Master, 1995–96); Liveryman, Co. of Barbers. Mem., Bd of Governors, Moorfields Eye Hosp., 1971–90. Mem. Editorial Board: Ophthalmic Literature, 1962–91 (Asst Editor, 1977–78; Editor, 1978–85); British Jl of Ophthalmology, 1965–90; Jl of Medical Genetics, 1971–76; Metabolic Ophthalmology, 1975–78; Survey of Ophthalmology, 1976–; Ophthalmic Paediatrics and Genetics, 1981–94; Editor, Postal History, 1994–. *Publications:* contrib. on ophthalmology and genetics to med. jls. *Recreations:* postal history, gardening. *Address:* 10 Beltane Drive, SW19 5JR. *T:* 0181–947 1771.

JAY, John Philip Bromberg; Managing Editor, Business News, and City Editor, Sunday Times, since 1995; *b* 1 April 1957; *s* of Alec Jay and June (*née* Bromberg); *m* 1st, 1987, Susy Streeter (marr. diss. 1992); 2nd, 1992, Judi Bevan (*née* Leader). *Educ:* University Coll. Sch.; Magdalen Coll., Oxford (BA Hons Mod. Hist.). Journalist, Western Mail, 1979–81; financial journalist: Thomson Regl Newspapers, 1981–84; Sunday Telegraph, 1984–86; City Editor, Sunday Times, 1986–89; City and Business Editor, Sunday Telegraph, 1989–95. *Publication:* (with Judi Bevan) The New Tycoons, 1989. *Recreations:* ski-ing, cinema, theatre, walking. *Address:* 202 Rotherhithe Street, SE16 1RA. *T:* 0171–252 1194.

JAY, Michael Hastings, CMG 1992; HM Diplomatic Service; Deputy Under-Secretary of State (Director for European Community and Economic Affairs), Foreign and Commonwealth Office, since 1994; *b* 19 June 1946; *s* of late Alan David Hastings Jay, DSO, DSC, RN and of Vera Frances Effa Vickery; *m* 1975, Sylvia Mylroie. *Educ:* Winchester Coll.; Magdalen Coll., Oxford (MA); School of Oriental and African Studies, London Univ. (MSc 1969). ODM, 1969–73; UK Delegn, IMF-IBRD, Washington, 1973–75; ODM, 1976–78; First Sec., New Delhi, 1978–81; FCO, 1981–85; Counsellor: Cabinet Office, 1985–87; (Financial and Commercial), Paris, 1987–90; Asst Under-Sec. of State for EC Affairs, FCO, 1990–93. *Address:* c/o Foreign and Commonwealth Office, SW1A 2AH. *T:* 0171–270 3000.

JAY, Hon. Peter; writer and broadcaster; Economics and Business Editor, BBC, since 1990; *b* 7 Feb. 1937; *s* of Baron Jay, *qv*; *m* 1st, 1961, Margaret Ann (*see* Baroness Jay of Paddington) (marr. diss. 1986), *d* of Baron Callaghan of Cardiff, *qv*; one *s* two *d*; one *s*; 2nd, 1986, Emma, *d* of P. K. Thornton, *qv*; three *s*. *Educ:* Winchester Coll.; Christ Church, Oxford. MA 1st cl. hons PPE, 1960. President of the Union, 1960. Nuffield Coll., 1960. Midshipman and Sub-Lt RNVR, 1956–57. Asst Principal 1961–64, Private Sec. to Jt Perm. Sec. 1964, Principal 1964–67, HM Treasury; Economics Editor, The Times, 1967–77, and Associate Editor, Times Business News, 1969–77; Presenter, Weekend World (ITV Sunday morning series), 1972–77; The Jay Interview (ITV series), 1975–76; Ambassador to US, 1977–79; Dir Economist Intelligence Unit, 1979–83. Consultant, Economist Gp, 1979–81; Chm. and Chief Exec., TV-am Ltd, 1980–83 and TV-am News, 1982–83, Pres., TV-am, 1983–; Presenter, A Week in Politics, Channel 4, 1983–86; COS to Robert Maxwell (Chm., Mirror Gp Newspapers Ltd), 1986–89; Supervising Editor, Banking World, 1986–89 (Editor, 1984–86). Chairman: NACRO Working Party on Children and Young Persons in Custody, 1976–77; NCVO, 1981–86 (Vice-Pres., 1986–92); Trustee, Charities Aid Foundn, 1981–86; Chm., Charities Effectiveness Review Trust, 1986–87. Vis. Scholar, Brookings Instn, Washington, 1979–80; Wincott Meml Lectr, 1975; Copland Meml Lectr, Australia, 1980; Shell Lectr, Glasgow, 1985. Governor, Ditchley Foundn, 1982–; Mem. Council, St George's House, Windsor, 1982–. Dir, New Nat. Theater, Washington, DC, 1979–81. Political Broadcaster of Year, 1973; Harold Wincott Financial and Economic Journalist of Year, 1973; RTS Male Personality of Year (Pye Award), 1974; SFTA Shell Internat. TV Award, 1974; RTS Home News Award, 1992. FRGS 1977. Hon. DH Ohio State Univ., 1978; Hon. DLitt Wake Forest Univ., 1979; Berkeley Citation, Univ. of Calif, 1979. *Publications:* The Budget, 1972; (contrib.) America and the World 1979, 1980; The Crisis for Western Political Economy and other Essays, 1984; (with Michael Stewart) Apocalypse 2000, 1987; contrib. Foreign Affairs jl. *Recreation:* sailing. *Address:* Hensington Farmhouse, Woodstock, Oxon OX20 1LH. *T:* Woodstock (01993) 811222, *Fax:* (01993) 812861. *Clubs:* Garrick; Royal Naval Sailing Association, Royal Cork Yacht.

JAYAWARDANA, Brig. Christopher Allan Hector Perera, CMG 1956; CVO 1954; OBE 1944 (MBE 1941); ED 1936; JP; FLS; KStJ; *b* 29 March 1898; 4th *s* of Gate Muhandiram Herat Perera Jayawardana; *m* 1924, Sylvia Dorothy Samarasinhe, *e d* of late Mudaliyar Soloman Dias Samarasinhe; (one *s* one *d* decd). *Educ:* Trinity Coll., Kandy, Ceylon; Keble Coll., Oxford (MA). Sen. Asst Conservator of Forests, Ceylon (retd); Dep. Warden of Wild Life, Ceylon (retd), 1924–29; served War of 1939–45; OC 1st Bn the Ceylon LI, 1938–43; Chief Comr, Ceylon Boy Scouts' Association, 1949–54; Extra Aide de Camp to HE the Governor Gen. of Ceylon, 1949; Equerry to HM the Queen, during Royal Visit to Ceylon, 1954; Hon. ADC to the Queen, 1954. Awarded Silver Wolf, 1949. FLS, 1924. Carnegie Schol., 1931; Smith-Mundt Schol., 1951; KStJ, 1959 (CStJ, 1954). Diploma of Forestry. *Recreations:* rifle shooting, big game hunting, deep sea fishing, golf, tennis, riding, painting, camping, photography. *Clubs:* Corona; Sea Anglers' (Sri Lanka).

JAYES, Percy Harris, MB, BS, FRCS; Plastic Surgeon: St Bartholomew's Hospital, London, 1952–73; Queen Victoria Hospital, East Grinstead, 1948–73; Consultant in Plastic Surgery to the Royal Air Force, since 1960; Consultant Plastic Surgeon, King Edward VII Hospital for Officers, 1966–85; *b* 26 June 1915; *s* of Thomas Harris Jayes; *m* 1945, Kathleen Mary Harrington (*d* 1963); two *s* one *d*; *m* 1964, Aileen Mary McLaughlin; one *s* one *d*. *Educ:* Merchant Taylors' Sch.; St Bartholomew's Hosp. Resid. Plastic Surg., EMS Plastic Unit, East Grinstead, 1940–48; Surgeon in Charge, UNRRA Plastic Unit, Belgrade, 1946; Mem. Council, Brit. Assoc. Plastic Surgeons, 1954–64 (Pres., Assoc., 1960). *Publications:* contrib. British Journal of Plastic Surgery, Annals of Royal College of Surgeons and other journals. *Recreation:* tennis. *Address:* Pierpoint House, 110 High Street, Lindfield, West Sussex RH16 2HS. *T:* Lindfield (01444) 483906.

JAYEWARDENE, Junius Richard; President of Sri Lanka, 1978–88; *b* Colombo, 17 Sept. 1906; *s* of Mr Justice E. W. Jayewardene, KC and A. H. Jayewardene; *m* 1935, Elina B. Rupesinghe; one *s*. *Educ:* Royal Coll., Colombo; Ceylon University Coll.; Ceylon Law Coll. Sworn Advocate of Supreme Court of Ceylon, 1932. Ceylon National Congress, later United National Party, 1938–89: Hon. Sec., 1940–47; Hon. Treasurer, 1946–48, 1957–58; Vice-Pres., 1954–56, 1958–72; Sec., 1972–73; Pres., 1973–88. Member: Colombo Municipal Council, 1940–43; State Council, 1943–47; House of Representatives, 1947–56, 1960–77 (Leader, 1953–56); Minister of: Agriculture and Food, 1953–56; Finance, 1947–52, 1952–53, 1960; Chief Opposition Whip, 1960–65; Minister of State and Parly Sec. to Prime Minister, Minister of Defence and External Affairs, and Chief Govt Whip, 1965–70; Leader of the Opposition, House of Representatives, 1970–72, Nat. State Assembly, 1972–77; Prime Minister, and Minister of Planning and Economic Affairs, 1977; Minister of: Defence, and Plan Implementation, 1977–88; Power and Energy, 1981–88; Higher Education, Janatha Estates Develt and State Plantations. Was a co-author of Colombo Plan, 1950; has been leader of delegations to many UN and Commonwealth conferences; Governor, World Bank and IMF, 1947–52. *Publications:* Some Sermons of Buddha, 1940; Buddhist Essays; In Council, 1946; Buddhism and Marxism, 1950, 3rd edn 1957; Golden Threads, 1986; Selected Speeches. *Address:* 66 Ward Place, Colombo 7, Sri Lanka.

JAYSON, Prof. Malcolm Irving Vivian, MD; FRCP; Professor of Rheumatology and Director, University Centre for the Study of Chronic Rheumatism, University of Manchester, since 1977; *b* 9 Dec. 1937; *s* of Joseph and Sybil Jayson; *m* 1962, Judith Tauber; two *s*. *Educ:* Middlesex Hosp. Med. Sch., Univ. of London (MB, BS 1961); MD Bristol, 1969; MSc Manchester, 1977. FRCP 1976. House Physician, 1961, House Surgeon, 1962, Middlesex Hosp.; House Physician: Central Middlesex Hosp., 1962; Brompton Hosp., 1963; Sen. House Officer, Middlesex Hosp, 1963; Registrar: Westminster Hosp., 1964; Royal Free Hosp., 1965; Lectr, Univ. of Bristol, Royal Nat.. Hosp. for Rheumatic Diseases, Bath, and Bristol Royal Infirmary, 1967; Sen. Lectr, Univ. of Bristol, and Consultant, Royal Nat. Hosp. for Rheumatic Diseases, Bath, and Bristol Royal Infirmary, 1979. Visiting Professor: Univ. of Iowa, 1984; Univ. of Queensland, 1985; Univ. of Cairo, 1992. Gen. Sec., Internat. Back Pain Soc., 1986–; President: Soc. of Chiropodists, 1984; Arachnoiditis Self-Help Gp, 1989–; Pres., Internat. Soc. for Study of the Lumbar Spine, 1995–June 1996. *Publications:* (with A. StJ. Dixon) Rheumatism and Arthritis, 1974, 8th edn 1991; The Lumbar Spine and Back Pain, 1976, 4th edn 1992; Back Pain: the facts, 1981, 3rd edn 1992; (with C. Black) Systemic Sclerosis: Scleroderma, 1988; contribs to Lancet, BMJ and other med. jls. *Recreations:* antiques (especially sundials), trout fishing. *Address:* The Gate House, 8 Lancaster Road, Didsbury, Manchester M20 8TY. *T:* 0161–445 1729. *Club:* Royal Society of Medicine.

JAYSTON, Michael, (Michael James); actor; *b* 29 Oct. 1935; *s* of Aubrey Vincent James and Edna Myfanwy Llewelyn; *m* 1st, 1965, Lynn Farleigh (marr. diss. 1970); 2nd, 1970, Heather Mary Sneddon (marr. diss. 1977); 3rd, 1978, Elizabeth Ann Smithson; three *s* one *d*. *Educ:* Becket Grammar School, Nottingham; Guildhall Sch. of Music and Drama (FGSM). *Stage:* Salisbury Playhouse, 1962–63 (parts incl. Henry II, in Becket); Bristol Old Vic, 1963–65; RSC, 1965–69 (incl. Ghosts, All's Well That Ends Well, Hamlet, The Homecoming (NY), The Relapse); Equus, NT, 1973, Albery, 1977; Private Lives, Duchess, 1980; The Sound of Music, Apollo, 1981; The Way of the World, Chichester, 1984, Haymarket, 1985; Woman in Mind, Vaudeville, 1987; Dancing at Lughnasa, Garrick, 1992; The Wind in the Willows, NT, 1994; *films include:* Midsummer Night's Dream, 1968; Cromwell, 1969; Nicholas and Alexandra, 1970; *television includes:* Beethoven, 1969; Mad Jack, 1970; Wilfred Owen, 1971; The Power Game, 1978; Tinker, Tailor, Soldier, Spy, 1979; Dr Who, 1986; A Bit of a Do, 1988, 1989; Haggard, 1990; Darling Buds of May, 1992. Life Mem., Battersea Dogs Home. *Recreations:* cricket, darts, chess. *Address:* c/o Michael Whitehall, 125 Gloucester Road, SW7 4TE. *Clubs:* MCC, Lord's Taverners', Cricketers'; Gedling Colliery CC (Vice-Pres.); Rottingdean CC (Pres.).

JEAFFRESON, David Gregory, CBE 1981; Deputy Chairman, Big Island Holdings (formerly Big Island Contracting) (HK) Ltd, since 1992; *b* 21 Nov. 1931; *s* of Bryan Leslie Jeaffreson, MD, FRCS, MRCOG and Margaret Jeaffreson; *m* 1959, Elisabeth Marie Jausions; two *s* two *d* (and one *d* decd). *Educ:* Bootham Sch., York; Clare Coll., Cambridge (MA). 2nd Lieut, RA, 1950. Dist Officer, Tanganyika, 1955–58; Asst Man., Henricot Steel Foundry, 1959–60; Admin. Officer, Hong Kong Govt, 1961; Dep. Financial Sec., 1972–76; Sec. for Economic Services, 1976–82; Sec. for Security, 1982–88; Comr, Independent Commn Against Corruption, 1988–92. *Recreations:* history, music, sailing, walking. *Address:* A2 Cherry Court, 12 Consort Rise, Hong Kong. *T:* 28188025. *Club:* Royal Hong Kong Yacht.

JEANES, Leslie Edwin Elloway, CBE 1982; Chief of Public Relations, Ministry of Defence, 1978–81, retired; *b* 17 Dec. 1920; *er s* of late Edwin Eli Jubilee Jeanes and of Mary Eunice Jeanes; *m* 1942, Valerie Ruth, *d* of Ernest and Ethel Vidler; one *d*. *Educ:* Westcliff High Sch. Entered Civil Service, 1939; Inf. Officer, DSIR, 1948–65; Chief Press Officer, Min. of Technol., 1965–68; Dep. Head of Inf., MoT, 1968–70; Head of News, DoE, 1970–73; Chief Inf. Officer, MAFF, 1973–78. *Recreations:* bowls, gardening, motoring, DIY. *Address:* 14 Whistley Close, Bracknell, Berks RG12 3LQ. *T:* Bracknell (01344) 429429.

See also R. E. Jeanes.

JEANES, Ronald Eric; Deputy Director, Building Research Establishment, 1981–86; *b* 23 Sept. 1926; *s* of Edwin and Eunice Jeanes; *m* 1951, Helen Field (*née* Entwistle); one *s* one *d*. *Educ:* University Coll., Exeter (BSc 1951). Served HM Forces, 1945–48. Royal Naval

Scientific Service, 1951–62; BRE, 1962–86. *Publications:* DoE and BRE reports. *Recreation:* amateur theatre. *Address:* 1 Wrensfield, Hemel Hempstead, Herts HP1 1RN. *T:* Hemel Hempstead (01442) 258713.

See also L. E. E. Jeanes.

JEANNIOT, Pierre Jean, OC 1988; Director General, International Air Transport Association, since 1993; *b* Montpellier, France, 9 April 1933; *s* of Gaston and Renée Jeanniot; *m* 1979, Marcia David; two *s* one *d*. *Educ:* Sir George Williams Univ. (BSc); McGill Univ. (Management Prog.). Sperry Gyroscope, 1952–55; Air Canada, 1955–68; Vice-Pres., Computers and Communications, Québec Univ., 1969; Air Canada: Vice-Pres., Computer and Systems Services, 1970–76; subseq. Exec., sales, marketing, planning subsid. cos; Exec. Vice-Pres. and Chief Operating Officer, 1980; Pres. and CEO, 1984–90; Pres. and CEO, JINMAG Inc., 1990–92; Director, Bank of Nova Scotia and M3i. Pres., Canadian OR Soc., 1966; Chm., Air Transport Assoc. of Canada, 1984; Mem., Exec. Cttee and Chm., Strategic Planning Sub-Cttee, IATA, 1988–90. Chm., Council for Canadian Unity, 1991–94. University of Québec: Chm. Bd, 1972–78; Pres., Foundn, 1978–92; Hon. Dr, 1988. Chm. and participant, numerous charitable bodies. Chevalier, Légion d'Honneur (France), 1991. *Address:* IATA, PO Box 672, 1215 Geneva 15 Airport, Switzerland. *T:* Geneva 7992903.

JEAPES, Maj.-Gen. Anthony Showan, CB 1987; OBE 1977; MC 1960; retired; Member, Lord Chancellor's Panel of Independent Inspectors, since 1991; *b* 6 March 1935; *s* of Stanley Arthur Jeapes; *m* 1959, Jennifer Clare White; one *s* one *d*. *Educ:* Raynes Park Grammar Sch.; RMA Sandhurst. Commissioned Dorset, later Devonshire and Dorset, Regt, 1955; joined 22 SAS Regt, 1958; attached US Special Forces, 1961; Staff College, 1966; Brigade Major, 39 Inf. Bde, NI, 1967; Sqn Comdr, 22 SAS Regt, 1968; Nat. Defence Coll., 1971; Directing Staff, Staff Coll., Camberley, 1972; CO 22 SAS Regt, 1974; Mem., British Mil. Adv. Team, Bangladesh, 1977; Dep. Comdr, Sch. of Infantry, 1979; Comdr, 5 Airborne Brigade, 1982; Comdr, Land Forces NI, 1985–87; GOC, SW Dist, 1987–90. Vice-Chm., Romanian Orphanage Trust, 1991–. *Publication:* SAS Operation, Oman, 1980. *Recreations:* offshore sailing, deer management, country pursuits. *Address:* c/o National Westminster Bank, Warminster, Wilts. *Club:* Army and Navy.

JEAVONS, (Robert) Clyde (Scott); Curator, National Film and Television Archive, British Film Institute, since 1990; *b* 30 June 1939; *s* of Frank Rechab Scott-Jeavons and Olive Edith (*née* Robins); *m* 1st, 1963, Hilary Coopey (marr. diss.); one *d*; 2nd, 1977, Orly Yadin. *Educ:* Royal Russell Sch.; University Coll. London (BA Hons Scandinavian Studies). Asst Stage Manager, Det Norske Riksteatret, Norway, 1962–63; financial journalist, Investors' Rev., 1963–64; Chief Sub, Features Ed. and book reviewer and film critic, She mag., 1964–69; Dep. Curator and Hd, Film and TV Acquisitions, Nat. Film Archive, BFI, 1969–85; freelance author and film programmer, 1986–90. Hon. Treas., Internat. Fedn of Film Archives. Mem., BAFTA; FRSA 1992. Hon. FBKS 1994. *Publications:* (with Michael Parkinson) A Pictorial History of Westerns, 1974; A Pictorial History of War Films, 1975; (with Jeremy Pascall) A Pictorial History of Sex in the Movies, 1976; British Film-Makers of the Eighties, 1990; contrib. Sight & Sound, Monthly Film Bull., Guardian, etc. *Recreations:* cricket, travel, dining, music, film, watching television, popular literature, New York Times crossword. *Address:* National Film and Television Archive, British Film Institute, 21 Stephen Street, W1P 1PL. *T:* 0171–957 8948. *Clubs:* Nomads, Barnes Cricket (Hon. Mem.).

JEBB, family name of **Baron Gladwyn.**

JEBB, Dom (Anthony) Philip, MA; Prior, Downside Abbey, since 1991; *b* 14 Aug. 1932; 2nd *s* of late Reginald Jebb and Eleanor, *d* of Hilaire Belloc. *Educ:* Downside; Christ's Coll., Cambridge, 1957–60 (MA Classics). Professed at Downside, 1951; priest, 1956; Curate, Midsomer Norton, 1960–62; teaching at Downside, 1960–; House master, 1962–75; Dep. Head Master, 1975–80; Headmaster, 1980–91. Archivist and Annalist, English Benedictine Congregation, 1972–; Mem., EBC Theological Commn, 1969–82 (Chm., 1979–82); Delegate to General Chapter, EBC, 1981–; Mem., Central Cttee, 1987–88, Chm., SW Div., 1988, HMC; Member: Council, Somerset Records Soc., 1975–; Cttee, Area 7, SHA, 1984–91; Court, Bath Univ., 1983–85. Trustee, Somerset Archaeol and Natural Hist. Soc., 1989– (Pres., 1993–94). Vice-Pres., SW Amateur Fencing Assoc., 1970–. Chaplain of Magistral Obedience, British Assoc., Sovereign Mil. Order of Malta, 1978–. Gov., St Antony's-Leweston Sch., 1980–. *Publications:* Missale de Lesnes, 1964; Religious Education, 1968; Widowed, 1973, 2nd edn 1976; contrib. Consider Your Call, 1978, 2nd edn 1979; A Touch of God, 1982; (ed) By Death Parted, 1986; contribs to Downside Review, The Way, The Sword. *Recreations:* fencing, archaeology, astronomy, canoeing. *Address:* Downside Abbey, Stratton-on-the-Fosse, Bath BA3 4RJ. *T:* Stratton-on-the-Fosse (01761) 232295.

JEDDERE-FISHER, Arthur; Solicitor, Customs and Excise, 1982–85; *b* 15 July 1924; *s* of late Major Harry and Sarah Jeddere-Fisher; *m* 1947, Marcia Vincent, *d* of Kenneth Clarence Smith; three *s* one *d*. *Educ:* Harrow Sch.; Christ Church, Oxford (MA). Served War of 1939–45, Air Engineer, Royal Navy, 1942–46 (despatches). Called to Bar, Inner Temple, 1949; Magistrate, Senior Magistrate and Chairman Land Tribunal, Fiji, 1953–69; joined Solicitor's Office, HM Customs and Excise, 1970, Principal Asst Solicitor, 1977–82. *Recreations:* the collection and use of historic machinery, cricket, bird photography. *Address:* Apsley Cottage, Kingston Blount, Chinnor OX9 4SJ. *T:* Kingston Blount (01844) 351300. *Clubs:* MCC, Vintage Sports Car.

JEELOF, Gerrit, CBE (Hon.) 1981; Member, Board of Directors, Philips Electronics NV, since 1990; *b* 13 May 1927; *m* 1951, Jantje Aleida Plinsinga (*d* 1992); two *d*. *Educ:* Dutch Trng Inst. for Foreign Trade, Nijenrode. Philips Industries: Eindhoven, Holland, 1950–53; Spain and S America, 1953–65; Eindhoven, Holland, 1965–70; Varese, Italy, 1970–76; Chm. and Man. Dir, Philips Industries UK, 1976–80; Exec. Vice-Pres., 1981–86, Vice-Chm., 1986–90, Philips Industries Eindhoven. Chm., European Chamber of Commerce in USA, 1990–; Director: VNU Publishing, Haarlem, 1985–; ROBECO Investment Fund, Rotterdam, 1988–; Centraal Beheer Insce, Naarden, 1990–; Cabot Corp., Boston, 1990–. Chm., Bd of Trustees, Univ. for Business Administration Nijenrode, Brenkelen, 1983–. Commendatore del Ordine al Merito della Repubblica Italiana, 1974; Officer, Order of Oranje-Nassau (Netherlands), 1985. *Recreations:* sailing, golf. *Address:* Apt 3F, Long Island Apartements, Le Zoute, Zwinlaan 11, 8300 Knokke-Heist, Belgium. *T:* 50610085. *Clubs:* Royal Ocean Racing; Royal Yacht Squadron; Koninklijke Nederlandsche Zeil-en Roeivereeniging (Holland).

JEEPS, Richard Eric Gautrey, CBE 1977; Chairman, Sports Council, 1978–85; *b* 25 Nov. 1931; *s* of Francis Herbert and Mildred Mary Jeeps; *m* 1954, Jean Margaret Levitt (marr. diss.); three *d*. *Educ:* Bedford Modern Sch. Rugby career: Cambridge City, 1948–49; Northampton, 1949–62 and 1964; Eastern Counties, 1950–62; England, 1956–62 (24 caps); Barbarians, 1958–62; British Lions: SA, 1955; NZ, 1959; SA 1962; 13 Tests. Rugby Football Union: Mem. Cttee, 1962–78; Pres., 1976–77. Formerly: Mem., English Tourist Bd; Trustee, Sports Aid Trust. *Recreations:* Rugby Union football, sport. *Address:* Stocks Restaurant, 78 High Street, Bottisham, Cambridge CB5 9BA. *Club:* Lord's Taverners.

JEEVES, Prof. Malcolm Alexander, CBE 1992; FBPsS; FRSE; Professor of Psychology, University of St Andrews, 1969–93, Hon. Research Professor, since 1993; *b* 16 Nov. 1926; *s* of Alderman Alexander Frederic Thomas Jeeves and Helena May Jeeves (*née* Hammond); *m* 1955, Ruth Elisabeth Hartridge; two *d*. *Educ:* Stamford Sch.; St John's Coll., Cambridge (MA, PhD). Commissioned Royal Lincs Regt, served 1st Bn Sherwood Foresters, BAOR, 1945–48. Cambridge University: Exhibnr, St John's Coll., 1948, Res. Exhibnr, 1952; Burney Student, 1952; Gregg Bury Prizeman, 1954; Kenneth Craik Res. Award, St John's Coll., 1955. Rotary Foundn Fellow, Harvard, 1953; Lectr, Leeds Univ., 1956; Prof. of Psychology, Adelaide Univ., 1959–69, and Dean, Faculty of Arts, 1962–64; Vice-Principal, St Andrews Univ., 1981–85; Dir, MRC Cognitive Neuroscience Res. Gp, St Andrews, 1984–89. Lectures: Abbie Meml, Adelaide Univ., 1981; Cairns Meml, Aust., 1986; New Coll., Univ. of NSW, 1987. Member: SSRC Psych. Cttee, 1972–76; Biol. Cttee, 1980–84, Science Bd, 1985–89, Council, 1985–89, SERC; MRC Neuroscience and Mental Health Bd, 1985–89; Council, 1984–88, Exec., 1985–87, Vice-Pres., 1990–93, RSE; ABRC Manpower Sub-Cttee, 1991–93; Pres., Section J, BAAS, 1988. Hon. Sheriff, Fife, 1986–. Hon. DSc Edinburgh, 1993. Editor-in-Chief, Neuropsychologia, 1990–93. *Publications:* (with Z. P. Dienes) Thinking in Structures, 1965 (trans. French, German, Spanish, Italian, Japanese); (with Z. P. Dienes) The Effects of Structural Relations upon Transfer, 1968; The Scientific Enterprise and Christian Faith, 1969; Experimental Psychology: an introduction for Biologists, 1974; Psychology and Christianity: the view both ways, 1976 (trans. Chinese); (with G. B. Greer) Analysis of Structural Learning, 1983; (with R. J. Berry and D. Atkinson) Free to be Different, 1984; Behavioural Sciences: a Christian perspective, 1984; (with D. G. Myers) Psychology—through the eyes of faith, 1987; Mind Fields, 1994; papers in sci. jls, mainly on neuropsychology and cognition. *Recreations:* music, fly fishing, walking. *Address:* Psychology Laboratory, The University, St Andrews KY16 9JU. *T:* St Andrews (01334) 62057.

See also E. R. Dobbs.

JEEWOOLALL, Sir Ramesh, Kt 1979; *b* 20 Dec. 1940; *s* of Shivprasad Jeewoolall; *m* 1971, Usweenee (*née* Reetoo); two *s*. *Educ:* in Mauritius; Inns of Court Sch. of Law. Called to the Bar, Middle Temple, 1968; practising at the Bar, 1969–71; Magistrate, 1971–72; practising at the Bar and Chm., Mauritius Tea Develt Authority, 1972–76. Mem., Mauritius Parlt, 1976–82; Dep. Speaker, 1977–79; Speaker, 1979–82. *Recreations:* reading, conversation, chess. *Address:* Q1, Farquhar Avenue, Quatre Bornes, Mauritius. *T:* 45918.

JEFFARES, Prof. Alexander Norman, (Derry Jeffares), Hon. AM 1988; MA, PhD, DPhil; Docteur de l'Université (*hc*) Lille, 1977; Hon. DLitt Ulster, 1990; FRSA 1963; FRSL 1965; FRSE 1981; Professor of English Studies, Stirling University, 1974–86, Hon. Professor, since 1986; Managing Director, Academic Advisory Services Ltd, since 1975; Director, Colin Smythe Ltd, since 1978; *b* 11 Aug. 1920; *s* of late C. Norman Jeffares, Dublin; *m* 1947, Jeanne Agnès, *d* of late E. Calembert, Brussels; one *d*. *Educ:* The High Sch., Dublin; Trinity Coll., Dublin (Hon. Fellow, 1978); Oriel Coll., Oxford. Lectr in Classics, Univ. of Dublin, 1943–44; Lector in English, Univ. of Groningen, 1946–48; Lectr in English, Univ. of Edinburgh, 1949–51; Jury Prof. of English Language and Literature, Univ. of Adelaide, 1951–56; Prof. of English Lit., Leeds Univ., 1957–74. Sec., Australian Humanities Res. Council, 1954–57; Corresp. Mem. for Great Britain and Ireland, 1958–70; Hon. Fellow, Aust. Acad. of the Humanities, 1970–. Mem. Council, RSE, 1985– (a Vice-Pres., 1988–89); Scottish Arts Council: Mem., 1979–84; Vice-Chm., 1980–84; Chm., Literature Cttee, 1979–83; Chm., Touring Cttee, 1983–84; Chm., Housing the Arts, 1980–84; Mem., Arts Council of GB, 1980–84. Chm., Book Trust Scotland (formerly NBL (Scotland)), 1984–89; Mem. Exec. Cttee, NBL, 1984–86; Mem. Bd, Book Trust, 1987–88. Pres., Internat. PEN Scottish Centre, 1986–89; Mem., Exec. Cttee, Scots Australian Council, 1992–. Vice-Pres., Film and Television Council of S Aust., 1951–56; Chairman: Assoc. for Commonwealth Literature and Language Studies, 1966–68, Hon. Fellow, 1971; Internat. Assoc. for Study of Anglo-Irish Literature, 1968–70, Co-Chm., 1971–73, Hon. Life Pres., 1973–; Dir, Yeats Internat. Summer Sch., Sligo, 1969–71. Editor, A Review of English Literature, 1960–67; General Editor: Writers and Critics, 1960–73; New Oxford English Series, 1963–; Macmillan History of Literature, 1983–; (with Michael Alexander) Macmillan Anthologies of English Literature, 1989; York Classics, 1988–; York Insights, 1989–; Joint Editor, Biography and Criticism, 1963–73; Literary Editor, Fountainwell Drama Texts, 1968–75; Co-Editor, York Notes, 1980–; Editor: Ariel, A Review of Internat. English Literature, 1970–72; York Handbooks, 1984–. *Publications:* Trinity College, Dublin: drawings and descriptions, 1944; W. B. Yeats: man and poet, 1949, rev. edn 1962; Seven Centuries of Poetry, 1955, rev. edn 1960; (with M. Bryn Davies) The Scientific Background, 1958; The Poetry of W. B. Yeats, 1961; (ed with G. F. Cross) In Excited Reverie: centenary tribute to W. B. Yeats, 1965; Fair Liberty was All His Cry: a tercentenary tribute to Jonathan Swift 1667–1743, 1967; A Commentary on the Collected Poems of W. B. Yeats, 1968; (ed) Restoration Comedy, 4 vols, 1974; (with A. S. Knowland) A Commentary on the Collected Plays of W. B. Yeats, 1975; (ed) Yeats: the critical heritage, 1977; A History of Anglo-Irish Literature, 1982; A New Commentary on the Poems of W. B. Yeats, 1984; Brought up in Dublin (poems), 1987; Brought up to Leave (poems), 1987; (ed with Antony Kamm) An Irish Childhood, 1987; (ed with Antony Kamm) A Jewish Childhood, 1988; W. B. Yeats: a new biography, 1988; (ed) Yeats's Poems, 1989; (ed) W. B. Yeats: the love poems, 1990; (ed) W. B. Yeats: A Vision and related writings, 1990; (ed) W. B. Yeats: poems of place, 1991; (ed with Anna White) Always Your Friend: the Gonne-Yeats letters 1893–1938, 1992; (ed) Jonathan Swift: the selected poems, 1992; (with Brendan Kennelly) (ed) Joycechoyce, 1992; (ed jtly) Ireland's Women: writings past and present, 1994; (ed with Anna White) Maud Gonne, a servant of the Queen, 1994; Images of Imagination: Irish essays, 1995; (ed with Martin Gray) The Collins Dictionary of Quotations, 1995; also: edns of works by Congreve, Farquhar, Goldsmith, Sheridan, Cowper, Maria Edgeworth, Disraeli, Whitman and Yeats; edns of criticisms of Swift, Scott and Yeats; various monographs on Swift, Goldsmith, George Moore, Yeats, Oliver St John Gogarty; contribs to learned jls. *Recreations:* drawing, motoring. *Address:* Craighead Cottage, Fife Ness, Crail, Fife KY10 3XN. *Clubs:* Athenæum, Commonwealth Trust.

JEFFCOTT, Prof. Leo Broof, PhD, DVSc; FRCVS; Professor of Veterinary Clinical Studies, and Dean of Veterinary School, University of Cambridge, since 1991; Professorial Fellow, Pembroke College, Cambridge, since 1993; *b* 19 June 1942; *s* of late Edward Ian Broof Jeffcott and of Pamela Mary (*née* Hull); *m* 1969, Tisza Jacqueline (*née* Hubbard); two *d*. *Educ:* Univ. of London (BVetMed 1967, PhD 1972); Univ. of Melbourne (DVSc 1989); MA Cantab 1994. FRCVS 1978. Animal Health Trust, Newmarket: Asst Pathologist, 1967–71; Clinician, 1972–77; Head, Clinical Dept, 1977–81; Professor: of Clinical Radiology, Swedish Univ. of Agricl Scis, Uppsala, 1981–82; of Veterinary Clinical Sciences, Univ. of Melbourne, 1982–91. Lectures: Sir Frederick Hobday Meml, BEVA, 1977; Peter Hernqvist, Swedish Univ. of Agricl Scis, Skara, 1991; Share-Jones, RCVS, 1993. FEI Official Veterinarian: Seoul Olympics, 1988; World Equestrian Games, Stockholm, 1990, The Hague, 1994; Barcelona Olympics, 1992; Atlanta Olympics, July 1996. Norman Hall Medal for Research, RCVS, 1978; Internat. Prize of Tierklinik Hochmoor, Germany, 1981; Equine Veterinary Jl Open Award, BEVA, 1982; John Hickman Orthopaedic Prize, BEVA, 1991; Internat. Hall of Fame Award for Equine Res.,

Univ. of Kentucky, 1991; UK Equestrian Award for Scientific Achievement, 1994. *Publications:* (with R. K. Archer) Comparative Clinical Haematology, 1977; (ed jtly) Equine Exercise Physiology 3, 1991; (with E. Dalin) Osteochondrosis in the 90s, 1993; (with A. F. Clarke) On to Atlanta '96, 1994. *Recreations:* swimming, photography, equestrian sports. *Address:* Department of Clinical Veterinary Medicine, University of Cambridge, Madingley Road, Cambridge CB3 0ES. *T:* Cambridge (01223) 337733.

JEFFERIES, David George, CBE 1990; FEng 1989; Chairman: National Grid Co. plc, since 1990; Northern Ireland Electricity plc, since 1994; *b* 26 Dec. 1933; *s* of Rose and George Jefferies; *m* 1959, Jeanette Ann Hanson. *Educ:* SE Coll. of Technology. FEng, FIEE, CIMgt, FInstE. Southern Electricity Board: Area Manager, Portsmouth, 1967–72; Staff Coll., Henley, 1970; Chief Engr, 1972–74; Dir, NW Region, CEGB, 1974–77; Dir Personnel, CEGB, 1977–81; Chm., London Electricity Bd, 1981–86; Dep. Chm., Electricity Council, 1986–89. Chm., Electricity Pension Scheme, 1986–. Pres., Energy Industries Club, 1991–93. Mem., Bd of Governors, London Business Sch., 1980–84. Liveryman, Wax Chandlers' Co., 1984–. Hon. DTech Brunel, 1992; Hon. LLD Manchester, 1993. *Recreations:* golf, gardening, music. *Address:* 185 Park Street, SE1 9DY. *T:* 0171–620 8323. *Clubs:* Athenæum, Royal Automobile.

JEFFERIES, Roger David; Housing Association Tenants' Ombudsman, since 1993; *b* 13 Oct. 1939; *s* of George Edward Jefferies and Freda Rose Jefferies (*née* Marshall); *m* 1st, 1962, Jennifer Anne Southgate (marr. diss.); one *s* two *d*; 2nd, 1974, Margaret Sealy (marr. diss.); 3rd, 1984, Pamela Mary Elsey (*née* Holden); one *s*. *Educ:* Whitgift School; Balliol College, Oxford. BA, BCL; solicitor. Mem., Law Society,1965–. Asst Solicitor, Coventry Corporation, 1965–68; Asst Town Clerk, Southend-on-Sea County Borough Council, 1968–70; Director of Operations, London Borough of Hammersmith, 1970–75; Chief Exec., London Borough of Hounslow, 1975–90; Under Secretary, DoE, 1983–85 (on secondment); Chief Exec., London Bor. of Croydon, 1990–93. Member: Regl Planning Bd, Arts Council of GB, 1986–88; Adv. Bd, Lewisham Theatre, 1994–; Council, RIPA, 1982–88; Bd, Public Finance Foundn, 1987–93; Pres., SOLACE, 1990–91. Clerk: Mortlake Crematorium Bd, 1973–90; W London Waste Authy, 1986–90. Director: Extemporary Dance Co., 1989–91; Croydon Business Venture, 1991–93; Solotec, 1992–93. Hon. Sec., Commn for Local Democracy, 1993–. Trustee, S African Advanced Educn Project, 1989–. *Publication:* Tackling the Town Hall, 1982. *Recreations:* the novel, theatre, travel. *Address:* 19 Cumberland Road, Barnes, SW13 9LY.

JEFFERIES, Sheelagh, CBE 1987; Deputy Director General, 1983–87, Acting Director General, Jan.–June 1987, Central Office of Information; *b* 25 Aug. 1926; *d* of late Norman and Vera Jefferies. *Educ:* Harrogate Grammar Sch.; Girton Coll., Cambridge (MA); Smith Coll., Northampton, Mass, USA (MA). FIPR; FCAM. Archivist, RIIA, 1947–50, 1951–52; COI, 1953–60; Office of Chancellor of Duchy of Lancaster, 1960–61; Press Officer, Prime Minister's Office, 1961–67; Principal Inf. Officer, Privy Council Office, 1967–69; Chief Press Officer, Min. of Housing and Local Govt, 1969–71; Head of Parly Liaison Unit and later Head of News, DoE, 1971–74; Chief Inf. Officer, Dept of Prices and Consumer Protection, 1974–77; Central Office of Information: Dir, Overseas Press and Radio, 1977–78; Controller (Home), 1978–83. Press Consultant, WRVS, 1988–92. *Recreations:* reading, conversation. *Address:* 17 Beaumont Avenue, Richmond, Surrey TW9 2HE. *T:* 0181–940 9229.

JEFFERIES, Stephen; Senior Principal Dancer, Royal Ballet, since 1979, Character Principal, since 1994 (Principal Dancer, 1973–76 and 1977–79); *b* 24 June 1951; *s* of George and Barbara Jefferies; *m* 1972, Rashna Homji; one *s* one *d*. *Educ:* Turves Green Sch., Birmingham; Royal Ballet Sch. ARAD (Advanced Hons). Joined Sadler's Wells Royal Ballet, 1969; created 10 leading roles whilst with Sadler's Wells; joined National Ballet of Canada as Principal Dancer, 1976; created role of Morris, in Washington Square, 1977; returned to Royal Ballet at Covent Garden, 1977; *major roles include:* Prince in Sleeping Beauty, Swan Lake and Giselle, Prince Rudolf in Mayerling, Petruchio in Taming of the Shrew, Romeo and Mercutio in Romeo and Juliet, Lescaut in Manon; lead, in Song and Dance, 1982; *roles created:* Yukinojo (mime role), in world première of Minoru Miki's opera An Actor's Revenge, 1979; male lead in Bolero, Japan, 1980 (choreographed by Yashiro Okamoto); Antonio in The Duenna, S Africa (chor. by Ashley Killar), 1980; lead, in Dances of Albion (chor. by Glen Tetley), 1980; Esenin in Kenneth Macmillan's ballet, Isadora, Covent Garden, 1981; lead, in L'Invitation au Voyage, Covent Garden, 1982; Consort Lessons, and Sons of Horos, 1986, Still Life at the Penguin Café, and The Trial of Prometheus, 1988 (chor. by David Bintley); title role in Cyrano (chor. by David Bintley), 1991. Choreographed ballets: Bits and Pieces, in Canada, 1977; Mes Souvenirs, in London, 1978; Magic Toyshop, 1987. Rehearsal Dir, Rambert Dance Co., Jan.–July 1995 (on leave of absence). Dances in Europe, USA, S America and Far East. *Film:* Anna, 1988. *Recreations:* golf, football, sleeping, gardening, swimming and various other sports. *Address:* c/o Royal Ballet, Royal Opera House, Covent Garden, WC2E 9DD.

JEFFERS, John Norman Richard, CStat; CBiol, FIBiol; FICFor; consultant; Visiting Professor: Mechanical, Materials and Manufacturing, University of Newcastle, since 1994; Mathematical Institute, University of Kent, since 1993; School of Mathematics, Statistics and Computing, University of Greenwich, since 1994; *b* 10 Sept. 1926; *s* of late Lt-Col John Harold Jeffers, OBE, and Emily Matilda Alice (*née* Robinson); *m* 1951, Edna May (*née* Parratt); one *d*. *Educ:* Portsmouth Grammar Sch.; Forestry Commission Forester Trng Sch., 1944–46. Forester in Forestry Commn Research Br., 1946–55; joined Min. of Agriculture, 1955, as Asst Statistician, after succeeding in limited competition to Statistician Class; rejoined Forestry Commn as Head of Statistics Section of Forestry Commn Research Br., 1956; Dir, Nature Conservancy's Merlewood Research Station, 1968; Dep. Dir, Inst. of Terrestrial Ecology, NERC, 1973, Dir, 1976–86. Hon. Prof., Commn of Integrated Survey of Natural Resources, Academia Sinica, 1987–. Editor, Internat. Jl of Sustainable Develt and World Ecology, 1994–. Hon. DSc Lancaster, 1988. *Publications:* Experimental Design and Analysis in Forest Research, 1959; Mathematical Models in Ecology, 1972; Introduction to Systems Analysis: with ecological applications, 1978; Modelling, 1982; Practitioner's Manual on the Modelling of Dynamic Change in Ecosystems, 1988; Microcomputers in Environmental Biology, 1990; numerous papers in stat., forestry and ecolog. jls. *Recreations:* military history and wargaming, amateur dramatics. *Address:* Glenside, Oxenholme, Kendal, Cumbria LA9 7RF. *T:* Kendal (01539) 734375. *Club:* Athenæum.

JEFFERSON, Bryan; *see* Jefferson, J. B.

JEFFERSON, Sir George Rowland, Kt 1981; CBE 1969; BSc Hons (London); FEng, Hon. FIMechE, FIEE, FRAeS; FRSA; CBIM; FCGI; Chairman, Videotron Corp., since 1990; *b* 26 March 1921; *s* of Harold Jefferson and Eva Elizabeth Ellen; *m* 1943, Irene Watson-Browne; three *s*. *Educ:* Grammar Sch., Dartford, Kent. Engrg Apprentice, Royal Ordnance Factory, Woolwich, 1937–42; commnd RAOC, 1942; transf. REME, 1942; served 1942–45, Anti-Aircraft Comd on heavy anti-aircraft power control systems and later Armament Design Dept, Fort Halstead, on anti-aircraft gun mounting development; subseq. Mem. Min. of Supply staff, Fort Halstead, until 1952; joined Guided Weapons Div., English Electric Co. Ltd, 1952; Chief Research Engr, 1953; Dep. Chief Engr, 1958; Dir, English Electric Aviation Ltd, 1961 (on formation of co.); British Aircraft Corporation: Dir and Chief Exec., BAC (Guided Weapons) Ltd, 1963 (on formation of Corp.), Dep. Man. Dir, 1964, Mem. Board, 1965–77, Man. Dir, 1966–68, Chm. and Man. Dir, 1968–77; a Dir, British Aerospace, and Chm. and Chief Exec., Dynamics Gp, British Aerospace, 1977–80 (Mem., Organizing Cttee, 1976–77); Chm., Stevenage/Bristol and Hatfield/Lostock Divs, Dynamics Gp, 1978–80; Chm., BAC (Anti-Tank), 1968–78; Dep. Chm., Post Office, 1980; Chm., 1981–87, Chief Exec., 1981–86, British Telecommunications plc. Chairman: Matthew Hall, 1987–88; City Centre Communications, 1988–90. Director: British Aerospace (Australia) Ltd, 1968–80; British Scandinavian Aviation AB, 1968–80; Hawker Siddeley Dynamics, 1977–80; Engineering Sciences Data Unit Ltd, 1975–80; Babcock International, 1980–87; Lloyds Bank, 1986–89; AMEC, 1988–91. Member: NEB, 1979–80; NEDC, 1981–84; NICG, 1980–84; Member Council: SBAC, 1965–80; Electronic Engineering Assoc., 1968–72; RAeS, 1977–79 (Vice-Pres., 1979). Freeman of the City of London. Hon. DSc Bristol, 1984; DUniv Essex, 1985. *Address:* 206 Kingsway, Landsdale, Perth, WA 6065, Australia.

JEFFERSON, Joan Ena; *see* Appleyard, J. E.

JEFFERSON, (John) Bryan, CB 1989; CBE 1983; PPRIBA; Architectural Advisor to Department of National Heritage, since 1993; Visiting Professor, School of Architecture, Sheffield University, since 1992; *b* 26 April 1928; *s* of John Jefferson and Marjorie Jefferson (*née* Oxley); *m* 1954, Alison Gray (marr. diss. 1965); three *s*. *Educ:* Lady Manners Sch., Bakewell; Sheffield Univ. DipArch 1954. ARIBA 1954. Morrison and Partners, Derby, 1955–57; established practice in Sheffield and London with Gerald F. Sheard, 1957; Sen. Partner, Jefferson Sheard and Partners, 1957–84; Dir-Gen. of Design, PSA, DoE, 1984–89; Chm., PSA Projects, DoE, 1989–92. President: Sheffield Soc. of Architects, 1973–74; Concrete Soc., 1977–78; RIBA, 1979–81; Chm., RIBA Yorks Region, 1974–75. Hon. FRAIC 1980; Hon. ARICS 1987. Hon. DEng Bradford, 1986; Hon. LittD Sheffield, 1992. *Publications:* broadcasts; articles in lay and professional jls. *Recreations:* music, sailing offshore. *Address:* 6 St Andrews Mansions, Dorset Street, W1H 3FD. *Club:* Royal Western Yacht.

JEFFERSON, Sir Mervyn Stewart D.; *see* Dunnington-Jefferson.

JEFFERSON SMITH, Peter, CB 1992; Deputy Chairman, HM Customs and Excise, 1988–94; *b* 14 July 1939; *m* 1964, Anna Willett; two *d*. *Educ:* Trinity College, Cambridge. HM Customs and Excise, 1960; Commissioner, 1980. *Address:* 22 Iveley Road, SW4 0EW. *T:* 0171–622 8285.

JEFFERY, David John; Chief Executive (formerly Chief Executive, River), and Board Member, Port of London Authority, since 1986; *b* 18 Feb. 1936; *s* of late Stanley John Friend Jeffery and Sylvia May (*née* Mashford); *m* 1959, Margaret (*née* Yates); one *s* two *d*. Educ: Sutton High Sch., Plymouth; Croydon Coll. of Technology. Nat. Service, RAOC, 1954–56; Admiralty Dir of Stores Dept, 1956–66; RN Staff Coll., 1967; MoD, 1968–70; on secondment, 1970–76: Treasury Centre for Admin. Studies, 1970–72; Management Science Training Adviser, Malaysian Govt, Kuala Lumpur, 1972–74; Civil Service Dept, 1974–76; MoD, 1976–83; RCDS, 1983; Dir, Armaments and Management Services, RN Supply and Transport Service 1984–86. Chm., Estuary Services Ltd, 1988–. Director: British Ports Fedn, 1988–91; UK Major Ports Ltd, 1993–; British Ports Industry Trng Ltd, 1993–; Trustee Dir, Pilots' Nat. Pension Fund, 1987–; Chm., Internat. Assoc. of Ports and Harbours Trade Facilitation Cttee, 1992–; Vice-Chm., European Sea Ports Orgn, 1993–; Mem., European Maritime Industries High Level Panel, 1994–. Mem., Co. of Watermen and Lightermen of River Thames, 1987. Freeman, City of London, 1987. *Recreations:* theatre, music, travel, children's work with the local church. *Address:* Port of London Authority, Devon House, 58–60 St Katharine's Way, E1 9LB.

JEFFERY, Maj.-Gen. Philip Michael, AO 1989; MC 1971; Govenor of Western Australia, since 1993; *b* 12 Dec. 1937; *s* of Philip Frederick Jeffery and Edna Mary Jeffery (*née* Johnson); *m* 1966, Marlena Joy Kerr; three *s* one *d*. *Educ:* Kent Street High Sch.; Royal Mil. Coll., Duntroon. Served Infantry, 1958–: jun. regtl appts, 17 Nat. Service Trng Co. and SAS Regt, 1959–62; Operational Service, Malaya, Borneo and Vietnam, 1962–72; psc 1972; Commanding Officer: 2nd Bn Pacific Islands Regt, PNG, 1974–75; SAS Regt, Perth, 1976–77; jssc 1978; Dir, Special Forces, 1979–81; Comd, 1 Bde, Sydney, 1983–84; rcds 1985; comd, 1 Div., Brisbane, 1986–88; DCGS, Canberra, 1990–91. Mem., United Services Inst., Canberra, 1978–. *Recreations:* golf, fishing, music. *Address:* Government House, Perth, WA 6000, Australia. *T:* (9) 3253222. *Clubs:* Naval & Military (Brisbane); Weld (Perth); Royal Queensland Golf.

JEFFERY, Very Rev. Robert Martin Colquhoun; Dean of Worcester, since 1987; *b* 30 April 1935; *s* of Norman Clare Jeffery and Gwenyth Isabel Jeffery; *m* 1968, Ruth Margaret Tinling; three *s* one *d*. *Educ:* St Paul's School; King's Coll., London (BD, AKC). Assistant Curate: St Aidan, Grangetown, 1959–61; St Mary, Barnes, 1961–63; Asst Sec., Missionary and Ecumenical Council of Church Assembly, 1964–68; Sec., Dept of Mission and Unity, BCC, 1968–71; Vicar, St Andrew, Headington, Oxford, 1971–78; RD of Cowley, 1973–78; Lichfield Diocesan Missioner, 1978–79; Archdeacon of Salop, 1980–87. Mem., Gen. Synod of C of E, 1982–87 and 1988–, Mem., Standing Cttee, 1990–. FRSA 1992. *Publications:* (with D. M. Paton) Christian Unity and the Anglican Communion, 1965, 3rd edn 1968; (with T. S. Garret) Unity in Nigeria, 1964; (ed) Lambeth Conference 1968 Preparatory Information; Areas of Ecumenical Experiment, 1968; Ecumenical Experiments: A Handbook, 1971; Case Studies in Unity, 1972; (ed) By What Authority?, 1987; Anima Christi, 1994. *Recreations:* local history, cooking. *Address:* 10 College Green, Worcester WR1 2LH. *T:* Worcester (01905) 27821.

JEFFORD, Barbara Mary, OBE 1965; actress; *b* Plymstock, Devon, 26 July 1930; *d* of late Percival Francis Jefford and Elizabeth Mary Ellen (*née* Laity); *m* 1953, Terence Longdon (marr. diss. 1961); *m* 1967, John Arnold Turner. *Educ:* Weirfield Sch., Taunton, Som. Studied for stage, Bristol and Royal Academy of Dramatic Art (Bancroft Gold Medal). *Royal Shakespeare Co.:* Stratford-on-Avon, 1950–54: Isabella in Measure for Measure; Anne Bullen in Henry VIII; Hero in Much Ado About Nothing; Lady Percy in Henry IV parts I and II; Desdemona in Othello; Rosalind in As You Like It; Helena in A Midsummer Night's Dream; Katharina in The Taming of the Shrew; Volumnia in Coriolanus, 1989 and 1990; Tatyana in Barbarians, 1990; Countess in All's Well That Ends Well, Mistress Quickly in The Merry Wives of Windsor, 1992; Katia in Misha's Party, 1993; Countess Terzky in Wallenstein, 1993–94; *Old Vic Company:* (1956–62) Imogen in Cymbeline; Beatrice in Much Ado About Nothing; Portia in The Merchant of Venice; Julia in Two Gentlemen of Verona; Tamora in Titus Andronicus; Lady Anne in Richard III; Queen Margaret in Henry VI parts I, II and III; Isabella in Measure for Measure; Regan in King Lear; Viola in Twelfth Night; Ophelia in Hamlet; Rosalind in As You Like It; St Joan; Lady Macbeth; Gwendoline in The Importance of Being Earnest; Beatrice Cenci; Lavinia in Mourning Becomes Electra; *for Prospect, at Old Vic:* (1977–79) Gertrude in Hamlet; Cleopatra in All for Love; Cleopatra in Antony and Cleopatra; Nurse in Romeo and Juliet; Anna in The Government Inspector; RSC Nat. Tour, 1980, Mistress Quickly in Henry IV pts 1 and 2; *National Theatre:* Gertrude in Hamlet, Zabina in Tamburlaine the Great, 1976; Mother in Six Characters in Search of an Author, Arina

Bazarov in Fathers and Sons, Salathiel in Ting Tang Mine (Clarence Derwent Award, 1988), 1987. *Other London stage appearances include:* Andromache in Tiger at the Gates, Apollo, 1955, NY, 1956; Lina in Misalliance, Royal Court and Criterion, 1963; step-daughter in Six Characters in Search of an Author, Mayfair, 1963; Nan in Ride a Cock Horse, Piccadilly, 1965; Patsy Newquist in Little Murders, Aldwych, 1967; Mother Vauzou in Mistress of Novices, Piccadilly, 1973; Filumena, Lyric, 1979; Duchess of York in Richard II, and Queen Margaret in Richard III, Phoenix, 1988–89; *other stage appearances include:* Hedda Gabler, Phèdre, Medea; has toured extensively in UK, Europe, USA, Near East, Far East, Africa, Australia, Russia, Poland and Yugoslavia. *Films:* Ulysses, 1967; A Midsummer Night's Dream, 1967; The Shoes of the Fisherman, 1968; To Love a Vampire, 1970; Hitler: the last ten days, 1973; And the Ship Sails On, 1983; Why the Whales Came, 1988; Reunion, 1988; Where Angels Fear to Tread, 1991. Has appeared in numerous television and radio plays. Pragnell Shakespeare Award, 1994. Silver Jubilee Medal, 1977. *Recreations:* music, swimming, gardening. *Address:* c/o Fraser and Dunlop Ltd, The Chambers, Chelsea Harbour, Lots Road, SW10 0XF.

JEFFREY, Dr Robin Campbell, FEng 1992; FIChemE; FIMechE; Chief Executive, Scottish Nuclear Ltd, since 1992; *b* 19 Feb. 1939; *s* of Robert Stewart Martin Jeffrey and Catherine Campbell McSporran; *m* 1962, Barbara Helen Robinson; two *s* one *d*. *Educ:* Kelvinside Acad.; Royal Technical Coll. (Glasgow Univ.) (BSc); Pembroke Coll., Cambridge (PhD). With Babcock & Wilcox, 1956–79, Engrg Res. Manager, 1964–79; South of Scotland Electricity Board, later Scottish Power: Technical Services Manager, 1979–80; Torness Project Manager, 1980–88; Chief Engr, 1988–89; Man. Dir, Engrg Resources Business, 1989–92. Vis. Prof., Univ. of Strathclyde. *Publications:* (jtly) Open Cycle MHD Power Generation, 1969; pubns on energy related issues. *Recreations:* squash, tennis, ski-ing, playing musical instruments. *Address:* Scottish Nuclear Ltd, 3 Redwood Crescent, Peel Park, E Kilbride, Glasgow G74 5PR. *Clubs:* Cambridge University Royal Tennis; Glasgow Academical Squash.

JEFFREY, William Alexander; Under Secretary, Economic and Domestic Affairs Secretariat, Cabinet Office, since 1994; *b* 28 Feb. 1948; *s* of Alexander and Joyce Jeffrey; *m* 1979, Joan MacNaughton. *Educ:* Alan Glen's, Glasgow; Univ. of Glasgow (BSc Hons). Home Office, 1971–94: Private Sec. to Permanent Under Sec. of State, 1975–76; Principal, 1976–84; Assistant Secretary: Criminal Policy Dept, 1984–88; HM Prison Service, 1988–91; Asst Under Sec. of State, Immigration and Nationality Dept, 1991–94. *Recreations:* reading, hill-walking, watching football. *Address:* c/o Cabinet Office, 70 Whitehall, SW1A 2AS.

JEFFREYS, family name of **Baron Jeffreys.**

JEFFREYS, 3rd Baron *cr* 1952, of Burkham; **Christopher Henry Mark Jeffreys;** Stockbroker, Raphael Zorn Hemsley, since 1992; *b* 22 May 1957; *s* of 2nd Baron Jeffreys and of Sarah Annabelle Mary, *d* of late Major Henry Garnett; *S* father, 1986; *m* 1985, Anne Elisabeth Johnson; one *s* one *d*. *Educ:* Eton. Futures Broker, GNI Ltd, 1985–90. *Recreations:* country sports. *Heir: s* Hon. Arthur Mark Henry Jeffreys, *b* 18 Feb. 1989. *Address:* Bottom Farm, Eaton, Grantham, Lincs NG32 1ET. *Club:* White's.

JEFFREYS, Sir Alec John, Kt 1994; FRS 1986; Wolfson Research Professor of the Royal Society, University of Leicester, since 1991 (Professor of Genetics, since 1987); *b* 9 Jan. 1950; *s* of Sidney Victor Jeffreys and Joan (*née* Knight); *m* 1971, Susan Miles; two *d*. *Educ:* Luton Grammar School; Luton VIth Form College; Merton College, Oxford (Postmaster; Christopher Welch Schol.; BA, MA, DPhil 1975; Hon. Fellow, 1990). EMBO Research Fellow, Univ. of Amsterdam, 1975–77; Leicester University: Lectr, Dept of Genetics, 1977–84; Reader, 1984–87; Lister Inst. Res. Fellow, 1982–91. Member: EMBO, 1983; Human Genome Orgn, 1989. Editor, Jl of Molecular Evolution, 1985. Fellow, Forensic Sci. Soc. of India, 1989. Colworth Medal for Biochemistry, Biochem. Soc., 1985; Davy Medal, Royal Soc., 1987; Linnean Soc. Bicentenary Medal, 1987; Analytika Prize, German Soc. for Clin. Chem., 1988; Press, Radio and TV Award, Midlander of the Year, 1989; Linnean Medal, 1994. UK Patents on genetic fingerprints. *Publications:* research articles on molecular genetics and evolution in Nature, Cell, etc. *Recreations:* walking, swimming, postal history, reading unimproving novels.

JEFFREYS, David Alfred, QC 1981; a Recorder of the Crown Court, since 1979; *b* 1 July 1934; *s* of Coleman and Ruby Jeffreys; *m* 1964, Mary Ann Elizabeth Long; one *s* one *d*. *Educ:* Harrow; Trinity Coll., Cambridge (BA Hons). Served, Royal Signals, 1952–54; City, 1958. Called to the Bar, Gray's Inn, 1958, Bencher, 1989; Junior Prosecuting Counsel to the Crown, Central Criminal Court, 1975; Sen. Prosecuting Counsel to the Crown, CCC, 1979–81. Member: Bar Council, 1977–80; Crown Court Rule Cttee; Magistrates' Courts Rule Cttee; Council of Legal Educn. *Address:* (chambers) Queen Elizabeth Building, Temple, EC4Y 9BS.

JEFFREYS, Mrs Judith Diana; Assistant Director (Keeper), the Tate Gallery, 1975–83; *b* 22 Sept. 1927; *d* of Prof. Philip Cloake, FRCP and Letitia Blanche (*née* MacDonald); *m* 1968, William John Jeffreys. *Educ:* Bedales; Courtauld Inst. of Art, Univ. of London (BA Hons History of Art). Tate Gallery: Asst Keeper, 1951–64; Publications Manager, 1960–65; Dep. Keeper, 1964–75. *Recreations:* reading, music, landscape gardening, water-colour painting. *Address:* Oak Ridge House, Sutton Mandeville, Salisbury, Wilts SP3 5LT.

JEFFRIES, Hon. Sir John (Francis), Kt 1993; New Zealand Police Complaints Authority, since 1992; *b* 28 March 1929; *s* of Frank Leon Jeffries and Mary Jeffries; *m* 1951, Joan Patricia Christensen; one *s* one *d*. *Educ:* St Patrick's Coll., Wellington; Victoria Univ. of Wellington (BA, LLB). Clerical, 1946–50; school teaching, 1950–55; Law, 1956–76; Judge of the High Court of New Zealand, 1976–92. Chm., Air New Zealand, 1975. Wellington City Council, 1962–74; Dep. Mayor, Wellington, 1971–74. Chm., Nat. Housing Commn, 1973–75. Vice-Pres., NZ Law Soc., 1973–76; Member: Trust for Intellectually Handicapped, 1980–88; NZ Inst. of Mental Retardation, 1984–88. Hon. Life Mem., Amer. Bar Assoc., 1974. *Recreations:* reading, music, sports generally, playing golf. *Address:* 44 Clutha Avenue, Khandallah, Wellington, New Zealand. *T:* (4) 4795732. *Clubs:* Wellington; Wellington Golf.

JEFFRIES, Lionel Charles; actor since 1949, screen writer since 1959, and film director since 1970; *b* 10 June 1926; *s* of Bernard Jeffries and Elsie Jackson; *m* 1951, Eileen Mary Walsh; one *s* two *d*. *Educ:* Queen Elizabeth's Grammar Sch., Wimborne, Dorset; Royal Academy of Dramatic Art (Dip., Kendal Award, 1947). War of 1939–45: commissioned, Oxf. and Bucks LI, 1945; served in Burma (Burma Star, 1945); Captain, Royal West African Frontier Force. Stage: (West End) *plays:* Carrington VC; The Enchanted; Blood Wedding; Brouhaha; Hello Dolly, Prince of Wales, 1984; See How They Run, Two Into One, Rookery Nook, Shaftesbury, 1985–86; Pygmalion, Broadway, 1987; The Wild Duck, Phoenix, 1990; *films:* Colditz Story; Bhowani Junction; Lust for Life; The Baby and The Battleship; Doctor at Large; Law and Disorder; The Nun's Story; Idle on Parade; Two Way Stretch; The Trials of Oscar Wilde; Fanny; The Notorious Landlady (Hollywood); The Wrong Arm of the Law; The First Men in the Moon; The Truth about Spring; Arrivederci Baby; The Spy with a Cold Nose; Camelot (Hollywood); Chitty, Chitty, Bang Bang; Eyewitness; Baxter (also dir. 1971; Golden Bear Award for Best Film, Europe); The Prisoner of Zenda; Ménage à Trois; Chorus of Disapproval; Danny Champion of the World; Ending Up; First and Last. Wrote and directed: The Railway Children, 1970 (St Christopher Gold Medal, Hollywood, for Best Film); The Amazing Mr Blunden, 1972 (Gold Medal for Best Screen Play, Internat. Sci. Fiction and Fantasy Film Fest., Paris, 1974); Wombling Free, 1977; co-wrote and directed: The Water Babies, 1979; *television:* Cream in my Coffee, 1980; Shillingbury Tales, 1981; Father Charlie; Tom, Dick, and Harriet, 1983; Rich Tea and Sympathy, 1991; Look at it This Way, 1993. *Recreations:* swimming, painting. *Address:* c/o Denis Selinger, ICM, Oxford House, 76 Oxford Street, W1R 1RB.

JEFFS, Group Captain (George) James (Horatio), CVO 1960 (LVO 1943); OBE 1950; *b* 27 Jan. 1900; *s* of late James Thomas Jeffs, Chilvers Coton, Warwicks; *m* 1921, Phyllis Rosina (*née* Bell); two *s* one *d*. *Educ:* Kedleston Sch., Derby. Served European War: RNAS, 1916–18; RAF, 1918–19. Air Ministry, 1919–23; Croydon Airport, 1923–34; Heston Airport, 1934–37; Air Ministry, 1937–39. Served War of 1939–45, RAF: Aircrew Mem. of flights of HM King George VI and Sir Winston Churchill; Fighter, Ferry, and Transport Commands, Group Captain. UK Delegate to Civil Aviation Conf., Chicago, 1944; Ministry of Transport and Civil Aviation, 1945. Nat. Air Traffic Control Officers' Licence No 1; Airport Commandant, Prestwick, 1950–57; Airport Commandant, London-Heathrow Airport, 1957–60. Pioneered the opening and early functioning of all the major civil airports in the UK; for many years responsible for safe functioning of air traffic control in UK. Legion of Merit, USA, 1944. Liveryman, GAPAN. *Address:* Pixham Firs Cottage, Pixham Lane, Dorking, Surrey RH4 1PH. *T:* Dorking (01306) 884084. *Club:* Naval and Military.

JEFFS, Julian, QC 1975; a Recorder of the Crown Court since 1975; arbitrator, author and editor; *b* 5 April 1931; *s* of Alfred Wright Jeffs, Wolverhampton, and Janet Honor Irene (*née* Davies); *m* 1966, Deborah, *d* of Peter James Stuart Bevan; three *s*. *Educ:* Mostyn House Sch.; Wrekin Coll.; Downing Coll., Cambridge (MA; Associate Fellow, 1986). Royal Navy (nat. service), 1949–50. Sherry Shipper's Asst, Spain, 1956. Barrister, Gray's Inn, 1958 (Bencher 1981), Inner Temple, 1971; Midland and Oxford Circuit; Hong Kong Bar; retired from practice, 1991. Chm., Patent Bar Assoc., 1980–89; Member: Senate of Inns of Court and Bar, 1984–85; Bar Council, 1988–89. Gen. Comr of Income Tax, 1983–91. Editor, Wine and Food, 1965–67; Mem., Cttee of Management, International Wine & Food Soc., 1965–67, 1971–82; Chm., 1970–72, Vice-Pres., 1975–91, Pres., 1992–, Circle of Wine Writers. Dep. Gauger, City of London, 1979. Lauréat de l'Office International de la Vigne et du Vin, 1962; Glenfiddich wine writer awards, 1974 and 1978. General Editor, Faber's Wine Series. *Publications:* Sherry, 1961, 4th edn 1992; (an editor) Clerk and Lindsell on Torts, 13th edn 1969 to 16th edn 1989; The Wines of Europe, 1971; Little Dictionary of Drink, 1973; (jtly) Encyclopedia of United Kingdom and European Patent Law, 1977. *Recreations:* wine, walking, old cars, musical boxes, follies, Iberian things. *Address:* Church Farm House, East Ilsley, Newbury, Berks. *T:* East Ilsley (01635) 281216, *Fax:* (01635) 281756. *Clubs:* Beefsteak, Garrick, Reform, Saintsbury.

JEFFS, Kenneth Peter, CMG 1983; FRAeS; Director, Studley Associates, since 1994; *b* 30 Jan. 1931; *s* of Albert Jeffs and Theresa Eleanor Jeffs; *m* Iris Woolsey; one *s* two *d*. *Educ:* Richmond and East Sheen County Sch. jssc. National Service, RAF, 1949–51. Entered CS as Clerical Officer, Bd of Control, 1947; Air Min., 1952; Principal, 1964; JSSC, 1966–67; Private Secretary: to Under-Sec. of State (RN), MoD, 1969–71; to Minister of Defence, 1971–72; Asst Sec., Dir Defence Sales, MoD, 1972–75; Counsellor, Defence Supply, Washington, DC, 1976–79; Dir Gen. (Marketing), MoD, 1979–83; Exec. Vice-Pres., (Mil. Affairs), 1984–87, Dir, 1985–87, British Aerospace Inc.; Pres., MLRS Internat. Corp., 1987–92. FRAeS 1985. *Recreations:* rowing, tennis, golf, flying, horse racing. *Address:* Old Studley, Howell Hill Grove, Ewell, near Epsom, Surrey KT17 3ET. *Clubs:* Royal Automobile; Bude and North Cornwall Golf.

JEGER, Baroness *cr* 1979 (Life Peer), of St Pancras in Greater London, **Lena May Jeger;** *b* 19 Nov. 1915; *e d* of Charles and Alice Chivers, Yorkley, Glos; *m* 1948, Dr Santo Wayburn Jeger (*d* 1953); no *c*. *Educ:* Southgate County Sch., Middx; Birkbeck Coll., London University (BA). Civil Service: Customs and Excise, Ministry of Information, Foreign Office, 1936–49; British Embassy Moscow, 1947; Manchester Guardian London Staff, 1951–54, 1961–; Mem. St Pancras Borough Council, 1945–59; Mem. LCC for Holborn and St Pancras South, 1952–55. Mem., Nat. Exec. Cttee, Labour Party, 1968–80 (Vice-Chm., 1978–79; Chm., 1980). MP (Lab) Holborn and St Pancras South, Nov. 1953–1959 and 1964–74, Camden, Holborn and St Pancras South, 1974–79. Mem., Chairmen's Panel, House of Commons, 1971–79. Chm., Govt Working Party on Sewage Disposal, 1969–70. Member, Consultative Assembly: Council of Europe, 1969–71; WEU, 1969–71; UK delegate, Status of Women Commn, UN, 1967. *Address:* 9 Cumberland Terrace, Regent's Park, NW1 4HS.

JEHANGIR, Sir Hirji, 3rd Bt, *cr* 1908; *b* 1 Nov. 1915; 2nd *s* of Sir Cowasjee Jehangir, 2nd Bt, GBE, KCIE, and Hilla, MBE, *d* of late Hormarji Wadia, Lowji Castle, Bombay; *S* father, 1962; *m* 1952, Jinoo, *d* of K. H. Cama; two *s*. *Educ:* St Xavier Sch., Bombay; Magdalene Coll., Cambridge. Chairman: Jehangir Art Gallery, Bombay; Parsi Public School Soc.; Cowasji Jehangir Charitable Trust. *Heir: s* Jehangir [*b* 23 Nov. 1953; *m* 1988, Jasmine, *d* of Bejan Billimoria; one *s* one *d*]. *Address:* Readymoney House, 49 Nepean Sea Road, Bombay 400036, India; 24 Kensington Court Gardens, Kensington Court Place, W8 5QF. *T:* 0171–937 9587. *Clubs:* Royal Over-Seas League, English-Speaking Union; Willingdon (Bombay).

JEJEEBHOY, Sir Jamsetjee, 7th Bt *cr* 1857; *b* 19 April 1913; *s* of Rustamjee J. C. Jamsetjee (*d* 1947), and Soonabai Rustomjee Byramjee Jeejeebhoy (*d* 1968); *S* cousin, Sir Jamsetjee Jejeebhoy, 6th Bt, 1968, and assumed name of Jamsetjee Jejeebhoy in lieu of Maneckjee Rustamjee Jamsetjee; *m* 1943, Shirin J. H. Cama; one *s* one *d*. *Educ:* St Xavier's Coll., Bombay (BA). Chairman: Sir Jamsetjee Jejeebhoy Charity Funds; Sir J. J. Parsee Benevolent Instn; Wadiaji's Atash-behram; M. F. Cama Athornan Instn; Iran League; Rustomjee Jamsetjee Jejeebhoy Gujarat Schools' Fund; Bombay Panjrapole; Zoroastrian Bldg Fund; Parsee Dhanda Rojgar Fund; K. R. Cama Oriental Instn; Trustee: Byramjee Jeejeebhoy Parsee Charitable Instn; A. H. Wadia Charity Trust; Parsi Surat Charity Fund; Framjee Cowasjee Inst.; Destitute Eranee's Charity Fund and Dharamshala; Cowasji Behramji Divecha Charity Trust; Exec. Cttee, B. D. Petit Parsee Gen. Hosp.; Director: Enjay Estates Pvte Ltd, 1972–; Beaulieu Investments Pvte Ltd, 1975–; Palmera Investment Pvte Ltd, 1984–; Dawn Threads Pvte Ltd, 1984–. Created Special Executive Magistrate, 1977. Hon. Freeman and Liveryman, Clockmakers' Co., 1994. *Heir: s* Rustom Jejeebhoy [*b* 16 Nov. 1957; *m* 1984, Delara, *d* of Jal N. Bhaisa; one *s*]. *Address:* (residence) Beaulieu, 95 Worli Sea Face, Bombay 25, India. *T:* 4930955; (office) Maneckjee Wadia Building, Mahatma Gandhi Road, Fort, Bombay 1. *T:* 273843. *Clubs:* Willingdon Sports, Royal Western India Turf, Ripon, Western India Automobile Association (Bombay).

JELLICOE, family name of **Earl Jellicoe.**

JELLICOE, 2nd Earl, *cr* 1925; **George Patrick John Rushworth Jellicoe,** KBE 1986; DSO 1942; MC 1944; PC 1963; FRS 1990; Viscount Brocas of Southampton, *cr* 1925; Viscount Jellicoe of Scapa, *cr* 1918; President: Royal Geographical Society, since 1993;

British Heart Foundation, since 1990; Chancellor, Southampton University, since 1984; Director, European Capital Ltd, since 1991 (Chairman, 1991–95); *b* 4 April 1918; *o s* of Admiral of the Fleet 1st Earl Jellicoe and late Florence Gwendoline, *d* of Sir Charles Cayzer, 1st Bt; godson of King George V; *S* father, 1935; *m* 1st, 1944, Patricia Christine (marr. diss., 1966), *o d* of Jeremiah O'Kane, Vancouver, Canada; two *s* two *d*; 2nd, 1966, Philippa, *o d* of late Philip Dunne; one *s* two *d*. *Educ:* Winchester; Trinity Coll., Cambridge (Exhibnr). Hon. Page to King George VI; served War of 1939–45, Coldstream Guards, 1 SAS Regt, SBS Regt (despatches (three times), DSO, MC, Légion d'Honneur, Croix de Guerre, Greek War Cross). Entered HM Foreign Service, 1947; served as 1st Sec. in Washington, Brussels, Baghdad (Deputy Sec. General Baghdad Pact). Lord-in-Waiting, Jan.-June 1961; Jt Parly. Sec., Min. of Housing and Local Govt, 1961–62; Minister of State, Home Office, 1962–63; First Lord of the Admiralty, 1963–64; Minister of Defence for the Royal Navy, April-Oct. 1964; Deputy Leader of the Opposition, House of Lords, 1967–70; Lord Privy Seal and Minister in Charge, Civil Service Dept, 1970–73; Leader of the House of Lords, 1970–73. Chairman: Brit. Adv. Cttee on Oil Pollution of the Sea, 1968–70; 3rd Int. Conf. on Oil Pollution of the Sea, 1968. Chm., MRC, 1982–90. Chairman: Tate & Lyle, 1978–83 (Dir, 1974–93); Davy Corp., 1985–90; Booker Tate, 1988–91; Director: Sotheby's, 1973–85; Smiths Industries, 1973–86; Morgan Crucible, 1973–87; S. G. Warburg, 1973–88. Chm., BOTB, 1983–86; President: London Chamber of Commerce and Industry, 1979–82; E European Trade Council, 1990– (Chm., 1986–90); Chm., 1978–86, Patron, 1986–, Anglo-Hellenic League. A Governor, Centre for Environmental Studies, 1967–70; President: National Federation of Housing Societies, 1965–70; Parly and Scientific Cttee, 1980–83; Review of Prevention of Terrorism Act, 1983. Chm. of Council, KCL, 1977–86. FKC 1979. Hon. LLD: Southampton, 1985; Long Island Univ., 1987. Grand Comdr, Order of Honour (Greece), 1992. *Recreations:* ski-ing, tennis, riding. *Heir: s* Viscount Brocas, *qv*. *Address:* Tidcombe Manor, Tidcombe, near Marlborough, Wilts SN8 3SL. *T:* Oxenwood (01264) 731225; 97 Onslow Square, SW7 3LT. *T:* 0171–584 1551. *Club:* Brooks's.

See also Adm. Sir Charles Madden, Bt.

JELLICOE, Ann; *see* Jellicoe, P. A.

JELLICOE, Sir Geoffrey (Alan), Kt 1979; CBE 1961; RA 1991; FRIBA (Dist TP); PPILA; FRTPI; formerly Senior Partner of Jellicoe & Coleridge, Architects; *b* London, 8 Oct. 1900; *s* of George Edward Jellicoe; *m* 1936, Ursula (*d* 1986), *d* of late Sir Bernard Pares, KBE, DCL. *Educ:* Cheltenham Coll.; Architectural Association. Bernard Webb Student at British School at Rome; RIBA Neale Bursar. Principal, Arch. Assoc. Schs, 1939–41. Pres., Inst. of Landscape Architects, 1939–49; Hon. Pres. Internat. Fed. of Landscape Architects; Mem. Royal Fine Art Commission, 1954–68; former Trustee of the Tate Gallery; Hon. Corr. Mem. American, Italian and Venezuelan Societies of Landscape Architects. Gardens for: Sandringham; Royal Lodge, Windsor; Ditchley Park; RHS central area, Wisley; Chequers; Horsted Place, Sussex; Hartwell House, Aylesbury; Shute House, Wilts; Tidcombe Manor, Wilts; St Paul's Walden, Herts; Delta Works, W Bromwich; Hilton Hotel, Stratford-upon-Avon; Dewlish House, Dorchester; The Grange, Winchester; Sutton Place, Surrey; Barnwell Manor, Northants; Giza, Egypt; Denbies, Surrey; Historica Park, Atlanta, Ga; historical gardens for Moody Foundn, Galveston, Texas, USA, 1984; Town Plans for: Guildford, Wellington (Salop), Hemel Hempstead New Town. Arch. Cons. to N Rhodesian Govt, 1947–52. Housing for Basildon, Scunthorpe, LCC; Plymouth Civic Centre; Chertsey Civic Centre; Cheltenham Sports Centre; GLC Comprehensive Sch., Dalston; Durley Park, Keynsham; Grantham Crematorium and Swimming Pool; comprehensive plans for central area, Gloucester, and for Tollcross, Edinburgh; civic landscapes for Modena, Brescia, Asolo and Turin, Italy; Kennedy Memorial, Runnymede; Plans for Sark, Isles of Scilly, and Bridgefoot, Stratford-upon-Avon. Medal of Amer. Soc. of Landscape Architects, 1981; Medal of Landscape Inst., 1985; VMH 1994. *Publications:* Italian Gardens of the Renaissance (joint), 1925, rev. edn 1986; (with J. C. Shepherd) Gardens and Design, 1927; Baroque Gardens of Austria, 1931; Studies in Landscape Design, Vol. I 1959, Vol. II 1966, Vol. III 1970; Motopia, 1961; (with Susan Jellicoe) Water, 1971; The Landscape of Man, 1975, rev. edn 1987; The Guelph Lectures on Landscape Design, 1983; (ed with Susan Jellicoe, Patrick Goode and Michael Lancaster) The Oxford Companion to Gardens, 1986; The Moody Historical Gardens, 1989; The Landscape of Civilisation, 1989; Writings, vol. 1, 1993. *Address:* 14 Highpoint, North Hill, Highgate, N6 4BA. *T:* 0181–348 0123.

JELLICOE, (Patricia) Ann, (Mrs Roger Mayne), OBE 1984; playwright and director; *b* 15 July 1927; *d* of John Andrea Jellicoe and Frances Jackson Henderson; *m* 1st, 1950, C. E. Knight-Clarke (marr. diss., 1961); 2nd, 1962, Roger Mayne; one *s* one *d*. *Educ:* Polam Hall, Darlington; Queen Margaret's, York; Central Sch. of Speech and Drama (Elsie Fogerty Prize, 1947). Actress, stage manager and dir, London and provinces, 1947–51; privately commnd to study relationship between theatre architecture and theatre practice, 1949; founded and ran Cockpit Theatre Club to experiment with open stage, 1952–54; taught acting and directed plays, Central Sch., 1954–56; Literary Manager, Royal Court Theatre, 1973–75; Founder, 1979, Director, 1979–85 and Pres., 1986, Colway Theatre Trust to produce community plays. *Plays:* The Sport of My Mad Mother (also dir. with George Devine), Royal Court, 1958; The Knack, Arts (Cambridge), 1961 (also dir. with Keith Johnstone), Royal Court, 1962, New York, 1964, Paris, 1967 (filmed, 1965; Palme d'Or, Cannes, 1965); Shelley or The Idealist (also dir.), Royal Court, 1965; The Rising Generation, Royal Court, 1967; The Giveaway, Garrick, 1969; Flora and the Bandits (also dir.), Dartington Coll. of Arts, 1976; The Bargain (also dir.), SW Music Theatre, 1979; *community plays:* (also directed): The Reckoning, Lyme Regis, 1978; The Tide, Seaton, 1980; (with Fay Weldon and John Fowles) The Western Women, Lyme Regis, 1984; Mark og Mønt (Money and Land), Holbæk, Denmark, 1988; Under the God, Dorchester, 1989; Changing Places, Woking, 1992; *plays for children:* (also directed): You'll Never Guess!, Arts, 1973; Clever Elsie, Smiling John, Silent Peter, Royal Court, 1974; A Good Thing or a Bad Thing, Royal Court, 1974; *translations:* Rosmersholm, Royal Court, 1960; The Lady from the Sea, Queen's, 1961; (with Ariadne Nicolaeff) The Seagull, Queen's, 1963; Der Freischütz, Sadlers Wells, 1964; *directed:* For Children, 1959; Skyvers, 1963; A Worthy Guest, 1974; (community plays): The Poor Man's Friend, Bridport, 1981; The Garden, Sherborne, 1982; Entertaining Strangers, Dorchester, 1985. *Publications:* Some Unconscious Influences in the Theatre, 1967; (with Roger Mayne) Shell Guide to Devon, 1975; Community Plays: how to put them on, 1987; *plays:* The Sport of My Mad Mother, 1958 (USA 1964); The Knack, 1962 (USA 1964; trans. various langs); Shelley or The Idealist, 1966; The Rising Generation, 1969; The Giveaway, 1970; 3 Jelliplays, 1975. *Address:* Colway Manor, Lyme Regis, Dorset DT7 3HD.

JENCKS, Charles Alexander, PhD; Lecturer in Architecture, Architectural Association, since 1970; Professor, University of California at Los Angeles School of Architecture, since 1985 (Lecturer in Architecture, 1974–85); *b* 21 June 1939; *s* of Gardner Platt Jencks and Ruth Pearl Jencks; *m* 1st, 1960, Pamela Balding (marr. diss. 1973); two *s*; 2nd, 1978, Margaret Keswick (*d* 1995); one *s* one *d*. *Educ:* Harvard University (BA Eng. Lit. 1961; BA, MA Arch. 1965); London University (PhD Arch. Hist., 1970). Architectural Association, 1968; writer on Post-Modern architecture, 1975–, Late-Modern architecture, 1978–; designer of furniture, and Alessi Tea and Coffee Set, 1983; numerous Univ. lectures, incl. Peking, Warsaw, Tokyo, USA, Paris; house designs incl. The Garagia Rotunda, 1976–77, The Elemental House, 1983, The Thematic House, 1984. Fulbright Schol., Univ. of London, 1965–67; Melbourne Oration, Australia, 1974; Bossom Lectr, RSA, 1980; Mem., Cttee for selection of architects, Venice Biennale, 1980; Curator, Post-Modern London, exhibn, 1991. Editor at Academy Editions, 1979–. Member: Architectural Assoc.; RSA. Gold Medal for Architecture, Nara, Japan, 1992. *TV films:* (wrote) Le Corbusier, BBC, 1974; (wrote and presented) Kings of Infinite Space (Frank Lloyd Wright and Michael Graves), 1983. *Publications:* Meaning in Architecture, 1969; Architecture 2000, 1971; Adhocism, 1972; Modern Movements in Architecture, 1973, 2nd edn 1985; Le Corbusier and the Tragic View of Architecture, 1974, 2nd edn 1987; The Language of Post-Modern Architecture, 1977, 6th edn 1991; Late-Modern Architecture, 1980; Post-Modern Classicism, 1980; Free-Style Classicism, 1982; Architecture Today (Current Architecture), 1982, 2nd edn 1988; Abstract Representation, 1983; Kings of Infinite Space, 1983; Towards a Symbolic Architecture, 1985; What is Post-Modernism? 1986, 3rd edn 1989; Post-Modernism—the new classicism in art and architecture, 1987; The Architecture of Democracy, 1987; The Prince, The Architects and New Wave Monarchy, 1988; The New Moderns, 1990; (ed) The Post Modern Reader, 1992; Heteropolis, Los Angeles, the Riots and the Strange Beauty of Heteroarchitecture, 1993; The Architecture of the Jumping Universe, 1995; Frank O. Gehry: cultural conservation and individual imagination, 1995; articles in Encounter, Connoisseur, l'Oeil, TLS. *Recreations:* travel, collecting Chinese (bullet-hole) rocks. *Address:* 19 Lansdowne Walk, W11 3AH; 519 Latimer Road, Santa Monica, CA 90402, USA.

JENKIN, family name of **Baron Jenkin of Roding.**

JENKIN OF RODING, Baron *cr* 1987 (Life Peer), of Wanstead and Woodford in Greater London; **Charles Patrick Fleeming Jenkin,** PC 1973; MA; Chairman, Friends' Provident Life Office, since 1988 (Deputy Chairman, Friends' Provident Life Office (Director, 1986–88) and UK Provident Institution (Director, 1987–88), 1987–88, when merged); *b* 7 Sept. 1926; *s* of late Mr and Mrs C. O. F. Jenkin; *m* 1952, Alison Monica Graham; two *s* two *d*. *Educ:* Dragon Sch., Oxford; Clifton Coll.; Jesus Coll., Cambridge. MA (Cantab.) 1951. Served with QO Cameron Highlanders, 1945–48; 1st Class Hons in Law, Cambridge, 1951; Harmsworth Scholar, Middle Temple, 1951; called to the Bar, 1952. Distillers Co. Ltd, 1957–70. Member: Hornsey Borough Council, 1960–63; London Coun. of Social Service, 1963–67. MP (C) Wanstead and Woodford, 1964–87. An Opposition front bench spokesman on Treasury, Trade and Economics, 1965–70; Jt Vice-Chm., Cons. Parly Trade and Power Cttee, 1966–67; Chm., All Party Parly Group on Chemical Industry, 1968–70; Financial Sec. to the Treasury, 1970–72; Chief Sec. to Treasury, 1972–74; Minister for Energy, 1974; Opposition front bench spokesman: on Energy, 1974–76; on Soc. Services, 1976–79; Secretary of State: for Social Services, 1979–81; for Industry, 1981–83; for the Environment, 1983–85. President: National CPC Cttee, 1983–86; Greater London Area, Nat. Union of Cons. Assocs, 1989– (Vice-Pres., 1987–89). Chm., Forest Healthcare NHS Trust, 1991–. Director: Tilbury Contracting Gp Ltd, 1974–79; Royal Worcester Ltd, 1975–79; Continental and Industrial Trust Ltd, 1975–79; Chairman: Crystalate Hldgs PLC, 1988–90 (Dir, 1987–90); Lamco Paper Sales Ltd, 1987–93; Consultant, Thames Estuary Airport Co. Ltd, 1994–; Mem. Internat. Adv. Bd, Marsh and McLennan, 1993–. UK Co-Chm., UK-Japan 2000 Gp, 1986–90 (Bd Mem., 1990–); Vice-Pres., 1991 Japan Festival Cttee, 1987–91. Adviser: Andersen Consulting, Management Consultants, 1985–; Sumitomo Trust and Banking Co. Ltd, 1989–; Mem., UK Adv. Bd, Nat. Economic Res. Associates Inc., 1985–. Mem. Council: UK CEED, 1987–; Guide Dogs for the Blind Assoc., 1987–; Chm., Visual Handicap Gp, 1990–; Pres., Friends of Wanstead Hosp., 1987–91; ICRF, 1991– (Dep. Chm., 1994–); Chm., Taverner Concerts Trust, 1987–; Chm., Target Finland Ltd, 1989–. Pres., British Urban Regeneration Assoc., 1990–; Sen. Vice Pres., World Congress on Urban Growth and Develt, 1992–95. Chm. Trustees, Westfield Coll. Trust, 1988– (Gov., Westfield Coll., 1964–70; Fellow, QMW, 1991); Gov., Clifton Coll., 1969– (Mem. Council, 1972–79; Pres. of School, 1994–; Pres., Old Cliftonian Soc., 1987–89); Mem. Internat. Adv. Bd, Nijenrode Univ., Netherlands, 1994–. Trustee, Monteverdi Choir, 1992–. Patron: St Clare West Essex Hospice Trust, 1991–; Stort Trust, 1991–. Freeman: City of London, 1985; London Bor. of Redbridge, 1988. FRSA 1985. *Recreations:* music, gardening, sailing, bricklaying. *Address:* (office) 15 Old Bailey, EC4M 7AP. *T:* 0171–329 4454, *Fax:* 0171–248 6332. *Club:* West Essex Conservative (Wanstead).

See also Hon. B. C. Jenkin, Rear-Adm. D. C. Jenkin.

JENKIN, Hon Bernard Christison; MP (C) Colchester North, since 1992; *b* 9 April 1959; *s* of Lord Jenkin of Roding, *qv*; *m* 1988, Anne Caroline, *d* of late Hon. Charles Strutt; two *s*. *Educ:* Highgate Sch.; William Ellis Sch.; Corpus Christi Coll., Cambridge (BA Hons Eng. Lit., MA). Ford Motor Co., 1983–86; 3i, 1986–88; Hill Samuel Bank, 1988–89; Legal & General Ventures, 1989–92. Contested (C) Glasgow Central, 1987. Mem., Select Cttee on Social Security, 1992–; Sec., Cons. Backbench Small Business Cttee, 1992–; Jt Sec., Cons. Backbench Foreign Affairs Cttee, 1994–. Pres., Cambridge Union Soc., 1982. *Recreations:* family, music (esp. opera), fishing, shooting, sailing, ski-ing, DIY, arguing the Conservative cause. *Address:* House of Commons, SW1A 0AA. *T:* 0171–219 3000. *Club:* Colchester Conservative.

See also Baron Rayleigh.

JENKIN, Conrad; *see* Jenkin, D. C.

JENKIN, Rear Adm. (David) Conrad, CB 1983; Commandant, Joint Service Defence College (formerly National Defence College), 1981–84, retired; *b* 25 Oct. 1928; *s* of Mr and Mrs C. O. F. Jenkin; *m* 1958, Jennifer Margaret Nowell; three *s* one *d*. *Educ:* Dragon Sch., Oxford; RNC, Dartmouth. Entered RN at age of 13½, 1942; qual. in Gunnery, 1953; commanded: HMS Palliser, 1961–63; HMS Cambrian, 1964–66; HMS Galatea, 1974–75; HMS Hermes (aircraft carrier), 1978–79; Flag Officer, First Flotilla, 1980–81. *Recreations:* sailing, skiing, do-it-yourself. *Address:* Knapsyard House, West Meon, Hants GU32 1LF. *T:* West Meon (01730) 829227.

See also Baron Jenkin of Roding.

JENKIN, Ian (Evers) Tregarthen, OBE 1984; Co-founder, 1986, and Vice-President, since 1991, Open College of the Arts (Director, 1986–89, retired; President, 1989–91); *b* 18 June 1920; *s* of Henry Archibald Tregarthen Jenkin, OBE and Dagmar Leggott. *Educ:* Stowe; Camberwell Sch. of Art and Crafts; Trinity Coll., Cambridge (MA Econ.); Slade Sch., University Coll. London. Royal Artillery, 1940–46. Sec. and Tutor, Slade School, 1949–75; Principal, Camberwell Sch. of Art and Crafts, 1975–85; Curator, RA Schools, 1985–86. Member: Art Panel, Arts Council (Vice-Chm.), 1979–82; Crafts Council, 1981–84 (Chm., Educn Cttee); Art and Design Working Gp, Nat. Adv. Body for Public Sector Higher Educn, 1982–85; Advisor, Member, Trustee, examiner, numerous educnl, art and conservation bodies. Pres., Dulwich Br., NADFAS, 1984–; Vice-Pres., Nine Elms Gp of Artists, 1990–; Dir, Guild of St George, 1986– (Companion, 1984). FRSA. Hon. Dr Arts CNAA 1987. *Publications:* Disaster Planning and Preparedness: a survey of practices and procedures (British Liby R&D report), 1986; An Outline Disaster Control Plan

(British Liby Inf. Guide), 1987; contribs to DNB. *Recreations:* gardening, painting. *Address:* Grove Farm, Fifield, Maidenhead, Berks SL6 2PF. *Clubs:* Athenæum, Arts, Buck's.

JENKIN, Simon William Geoffrey; Chief Education Officer, Devon County Council, since 1989; *b* 25 July 1943; *s* of Dudley Cyril Robert Jenkin and Muriel Grace (*née* Mather); *m* 1973, Elizabeth Tapsell; two *d*. *Educ:* Univ. of London (BSc Econs); Jesus Coll., Oxford (DipEd). Lectr, 1967–72, Sen. Lectr, 1972–75, Bournemouth Coll. of Technology; Educn Officer, Essex CC, 1975–80; Area Educn Officer, NE Essex, 1980–83; Principal Educn Officer, Derbys CC, 1983–87; Dep. Chief Educn Officer, Devon CC, 1988–89. Mem., SW Regl Cttee, FEFCE, 1993–. Gov., United World Coll. of the Atlantic, 1991–. FRSA 1992. *Recreation:* my wife. *Address:* 34 Wonford Road, St Leonard's, Exeter, Devon EX2 4LD. *T:* Exeter (01392) 499798.

JENKINS, family name of **Barons Jenkins of Hillhead** and **Jenkins of Putney.**

JENKINS OF HILLHEAD, Baron *cr* 1987 (Life Peer), of Pontypool in the County of Gwent; **Roy Harris Jenkins,** OM 1993; PC 1964; Chancellor, University of Oxford, since 1987; President, Royal Society of Literature, since 1988; Co-President, Royal Institute of International Affairs, since 1993; Leader, Social and Liberal Democratic Peers, since 1988; First Leader, Social Democratic Party, 1982–83 (Member of Joint Leadership, 1981–82); *b* 11 Nov. 1920; *o s* of late Arthur Jenkins, MP, and of Hattie Jenkins; *m* 1945, Jennifer Morris (*see* Dame Jennifer Jenkins); two *s* one *d*. *Educ:* Abersychan Grammar Sch.; University Coll., Cardiff (Hon. Fellow 1982); Balliol Coll., Oxford (Hon. Fellow 1969). Sec. and Librarian, Oxford Union Society; Chairman, Oxford Univ. Democratic Socialist Club; First Class in Hon. Sch. of Philosophy, Politics and Economics, 1941; DCL Oxford, 1987. Served War of 1939–45, in RA, 1942–46; Captain, 1944–46. Contested (Lab) Solihull Div. of Warwicks, at Gen. Election, 1945. Mem. of Staff of Industrial and Commercial Finance Corp. Ltd, 1946–48. Mem. Exec. Cttee of Fabian Soc., 1949–61; Chm., Fabian Soc., 1957–58; Mem. Cttee of Management, Soc. of Authors, 1956–60; Governor, British Film Institute, 1955–58; Adviser to John Lewis Partnership, 1954–62, Dir of Financial Operations, 1962–64. Dir, Morgan Grenfell Hldgs Ltd, 1981–82. MP (Lab): Central Southwark, 1948–50; Stechford, Birmingham, 1950–76; PPS to Sec. of State for Commonwealth Relations, 1949–50; Minister of Aviation, 1964–65; Home Sec., 1965–67, 1974–76; Chancellor of the Exchequer, 1967–70; Dep. Leader, Labour Party, 1970–72. Pres., European Commn, 1977–81. Contested: Warrington by-election as first Social Democratic candidate, July 1981; Glasgow Hillhead (SDP/Alliance), 1982. MP (SDP) Glasgow Hillhead, March 1982–1987. UK Deleg. to Council of Europe, 1955–57. Vice-Pres., Inst. of Fiscal Studies, 1970–. Formerly: Dep. Chm. Federal Union; Pres., Britain in Europe, Referendum Campaign, 1975; Chm., Labour European Cttee. A President of United Kingdom Council of the European Movement. Pres., UWIST, 1975–81. Trustee, Pilgrim Trust, 1973–. Lectures: G. M. Young, Oxford, 1963; Henry L. Stimson, Yale, 1971; Jean Monnet, Florence, 1977; Dimbleby, 1979; Churchill, Luxembourg, 1980; Rede, Cambridge, 1988; George Ball, Princeton, 1989; Goodman, 1989; Leverhulme, 1990; Stephenson, Glasgow, 1992; Paul-Henri Spaak, Havard, 1994. Liveryman, Goldsmiths' Co.; Freeman, City of London, 1965. Freeman, City of Brussels, 1980. Hon. Foreign Mem., Amer. Acad. Arts and Scis, 1973. Hon. FBA 1993; Hon. Fellow: Berkeley Coll., Yale, 1972; St Antony's Coll., Oxford, 1987. Hon. LLD: Leeds, 1971; Harvard, 1972; Pennsylvania, 1973; Dundee, 1973; Loughborough, 1975; Bath, 1978; Michigan, 1978; Wales, 1979; Bristol, 1980; Hon. DLitt: Glasgow, 1972; City, 1976; Warwick, 1978; Reading, 1979; Hon. DCL: Oxford, 1973; Kent, 1992; Hon. DSc Aston, 1977; DUniv: Keele, 1977; Essex, 1978; Open, 1979; Hon. DPhil Katholieke Univ., Leuven, 1979; Hon. doctorates: Urbino, 1979; TCD, 1979; Georgetown, 1988; W Virginia, 1992; Glamorgan, 1994; Bologna, 1994. Charlemagne Prize, 1972; Robert Schuman Prize, 1972; Prix Bentinck, 1978. Order of European Merit (Luxemburg), 1976; Grand Cross: Legion of Honour of Senegal, 1979; Legion of Honour of Mali, 1979; Order of Charles III (Spain), 1980; Order of Merit (Italy), 1990; Order of Infante D. Henrique (Portugal), 1993. *Publications:* (ed) Purpose and Policy (a vol. of the Prime Minister's Speeches), 1947; Mr Attlee: An Interim Biography, 1948; (contrib.) New Fabian Essays, 1952; Pursuit of Progress, 1953; Mr Balfour's Poodle, 1954; Sir Charles Dilke: A Victorian Tragedy, 1958; The Labour Case (Penguin Special), 1959; Asquith, 1964; (contrib.) Hugh Gaitskell: a memoir, 1964; Essays and Speeches, 1967; Afternoon on the Potomac?, 1972; What Matters Now, 1972; Nine Men of Power, 1975; Partnership of Principle, 1985; Truman, 1986; Baldwin, 1987; Gallery of Twentieth Century Portraits, 1988; European Diary 1977–81, 1989; A Life at the Centre (autobiog.), 1991; Portraits and Miniatures, 1993; Gladstone, 1995. *Address:* 2 Kensington Park Gardens, W11 2HB; St Amand's House, East Hendred, Oxon OX12 8LA. *Clubs:* Athenæum, Brooks's, Pratt's, Reform, Beefsteak.

JENKINS OF HILLHEAD, Lady; *see* Jenkins, Dame M. J.

JENKINS OF PUTNEY, Baron *cr* 1981 (Life Peer), of Wandsworth in Greater London; **Hugh Gater Jenkins;** *b* 27 July 1908; *s* of Joseph Walter Jenkins and Florence Emily (*née* Gater), Enfield, Middlesex; *m* 1st, 1936, Marie (*née* Crosbie) (*d* 1989), *d* of Sqdn Ldr Ernest Crosbie and Ethel (*née* Hawkins); 2nd, 1991, Helena Maria (*d* 1994), *d* of Nicolas and Katerina Pavlidis, Athens. *Educ:* Enfield Grammar Sch. Personal exploration of employment and unemployment, and political and economic research, 1925–30; Prudential Assce Co., 1930–40. ROC, 1938; RAF: Fighter Comd, 1941; became GCI Controller (Flt Lt); seconded to Govt of Burma, 1945, as Dir Engl. Programmes, Rangoon Radio. Nat. Union of Bank Employees: Greater London Organiser, 1947; Res. and Publicity Officer; Ed., The Bank Officer, 1948; British Actors' Equity Assoc.: Asst Sec., 1950; Asst Gen. Sec., 1957–64. LCC: Mem. for Stoke Newington and Hackney N, 1958–65 (Public Control and Town Planning Cttees). Fabian Soc. lectr and Dir of Summer Schools in early post-war years; Chairman: H Bomb Campaign Cttee, 1954; Campaign for Nuclear Disarmament, 1979–81 (Vice-Pres., 1981–); CND, Aldermaston Marcher, 1957–63; Chm. Victory for Socialism, 1956–60; Mem. Exec. Cttee Greater London Labour Party. Contested (Lab): Enfield W, 1950; Mitcham, 1955; MP (Lab) Wandsworth, Putney, 1964–79; Minister for the Arts, 1974–76. Former Mem., Public Accounts Cttee. Member: Arts Council, 1968–71; Drama Panel, 1972–74; Nat. Theatre Bd, 1976–80; Dep. Chm., Theatres Trust, 1977–79, Dir, 1979–86, Consultant, 1986–. Theatres' Advisory Council: Jt Sec., 1963; Chm., 1964–74, 1976–86; Vice-Pres., 1986–. Occasional broadcasts and lectures on communications, theatrical and disarmament subjects. *Radio plays:* series, Scenes from an Autobiography: Solo Boy, 1983; When You and I Were Seventeen, 1985; A Day in September, 1986; In Time of War, 1986; Lost Tune from Rangoon, 1987; View to a Death, 1989. *Publications:* Essays in Local Government Enterprise (with others), 1964; The Culture Gap, 1979; Rank and File, 1980; various pamphlets; contrib. to Tribune, New Statesman, Guardian, etc. *Recreations:* reading, writing, talking, viewing, listening, avoiding retirement. *Address:* House of Lords, SW1A 0PW. *T:* 0171–219 6706, (office) 0171–836 8591.

JENKINS, Alan Roberts; editorial consultant; *b* 8 June 1926; *s* of Leslie Roberts Jenkins and Marjorie Kate Cawston; *m* 1st, 1949, Kathleen Mary Baker (*d* 1969); four *s*; 2nd, 1971, Helen Mary Speed; one *s*. *Educ:* Aylesbury Grammar Sch. Commnd Royal Berks Regt, 1945; Captain, W African Liaison Service, GHQ India; Staff Captain Public Relations, Royal W African Frontier Force, Lagos; DADPR W Africa Comd (Major). Reporter, Reading Mercury and Berkshire Chronicle, 1948; Sub-editor, Daily Herald; Daily Mail: Sub-editor; Night Editor, 1962–69; Northern Editor, 1969–71; Asst Editor, Evening Standard, 1971; Dep. Editor, Sunday People, 1971–72; Asst Editor, Sunday Mirror, 1972–77; Editor, Glasgow Herald, 1978–80; Editorial exec., The Times, 1981–89; Gp Consultant, The New Straits Times, Malaysia, 1989–92. *Recreations:* golf, travel. *Address:* Old Rose Cottage, Kirkton of Balmerino, Fife DD6 8SA.

JENKINS, Prof. Aubrey Dennis; Professor of Polymer Science, University of Sussex, 1971–92, now Emeritus; *b* 6 Sept. 1927; *s* of Arthur William Jenkins and Mabel Emily (*née* Street); *m* 1st, 1950, Audrey Doreen Middleton (marr. diss. 1987); two *s* one *d*; 2nd, 1987, Jitka Horská, *er d* of late Josef Horský and of Anna Horská, Hradec Králové, Czechoslovakia. *Educ:* Dartford Grammar Sch.; Sir John Cass Technical Inst.; King's Coll., Univ. of London. BSc 1948, PhD 1951; DSc 1961. FRIC 1957. Research Chemist, Courtaulds Ltd, Fundamental Research Laboratory, Maidenhead, 1950–60; Head of Chemistry Research, Gillette Industries Ltd, Reading, 1960–64 (Harris Research Labs, Washington, DC, 1963–64); University of Sussex, 1964–92: Sen. Lectr in Chemistry, 1964–68; Reader, 1968–71; Dean, Sch. of Molecular Scis, 1973–78. Visiting Professor: Inst. of Macromolecular Chemistry, Prague, 1978 and 1986; Univ. of Massachusetts, Amherst, 1979. Member: Internat. Union of Pure and Applied Chemistry, Commn on Macromolecular Nomenclature, 1974–85 (Chm., 1977–85; Sec., Macromolecular Div., 1985–93); British Assoc. for Central and Eastern Europe; British, Czech and Slovak Assoc. Mem., Brighton HA, 1983–90. Examining chaplain to Bishop of Chichester, 1980–90. Hon. Fellow, Soc. of Organic Chemistry of Argentina. Heyrovský Gold Medal for Chemistry, Czechoslovak Acad. of Scis, 1990. *Publications:* Kinetics of Vinyl Polymerization by Radical Mechanisms (with C. H. Bamford, W. G. Barb and P. F. Onyon), 1958; Polymer Science, 1972; (with A. Ledwith) Reactivity, Mechanism and Structure in Polymer Chemistry, 1974; (with J. F. Kennedy) Macromolecular Chemistry, Vol. I 1980, Vol. II 1982, Vol. III 1984; Progress in Polymer Science (12 vols), 1967–85; papers in learned jls. *Recreations:* music, travel, photography. *Address:* Shoe Box Cottage, 115 Keymer Road, Keymer, Hassocks, West Sussex BN6 8QL. *T:* Hassocks (01273) 845410.

JENKINS, Sir Brian (Garton), GBE 1991; FCA; Partner, Coopers & Lybrand, Chartered Accountants, since 1969; Lord Mayor of London, 1991–92; *b* 3 Dec. 1935; *s* of late Owen Garton Jenkins and Doris Enid (*née* Webber); *m* 1967, (Elizabeth) Ann Prentice; one *s* one *d*. *Educ:* Tonbridge; Trinity Coll., Oxford (State Scholar; MA; Hon. Fellow, 1992). ACA Hons 1963; FCA 1974; MBCS. Served RA, Gibraltar, 1955–57 (2nd Lieut). Joined Cooper Brothers & Co. (now Coopers & Lybrand), 1960. Mem. Council, ICAEW, 1976– (Pres., 1985–86). Director: Royal Ordnance Factories, 1976–83; Woolwich BS, 1994–. Dep. Pres., London Chamber of Commerce, 1994; Member: Commn for the New Towns, 1990–; Financial Law Panel, 1993–; London First, 1993–. Chm., BPMF, 1993–. Alderman, City of London (Ward of Cordwainer), 1980– (Sheriff, 1987–88); Liveryman: Co. of Chartered Accountants in England and Wales, 1980– (Master, 1990–91); Merchant Taylors' Co., 1984– (Mem. Court, 1989–); Co. of Information Technologists, 1985– (Master, 1994–95); Mem., Court of Assts, Corp. of Sons of the Clergy, 1983–. Governor: Royal Shakespeare Theatre, 1981–; London Goodenough Trust (formerly London House) for Overseas Graduates, 1990–; Mem. Council, RSCM, 1987–. Dir, Blackheath Preservation Trust, 1985–; Mem. Council of Management, Architectural Heritage Fund, 1987–. Trustee, Community Service Volunteers, 1987–. Mem., Bd of Green Cloth Verge of the Palaces, 1984–. Hon. Bencher, Inner Temple, 1992; Hon. Mem., Baltic Exchange, 1993. Hon. DSc City Univ., 1991; Hon. DLitt London Guildhall Univ., 1991; Companion, De Montfort Univ., 1993. CIMgt; FRSA; Hon. FCIS 1992. Centenary Award, Chartered Accountants Founding Socs, 1993. Grand Conseiller Tutilaire des Neuf Nations de Bruxelles, 1992. *Publications:* An Audit Approach to Computers, 1978, 4th edn 1992; contrib. accountancy and business magazines. *Recreations:* garden construction, old books, large jigsaw puzzles, ephemera. *Address:* 1 Embankment Place, WC2N 6NN. *T:* 0171–583 5000. *Clubs:* Brooks's, City of London, City Livery.

JENKINS, Lt-Col Charles Peter de Brisay, MBE 1960; MC 1945; Clerk, Worshipful Company of Goldsmiths, 1975–88, retired; *b* 19 Aug. 1923; *s* of late Brig. A. de B. Jenkins and of Mrs Elizabeth Susan Jenkins; *m* 1949, Joan Mary, *e d* of late Col and Mrs C. N. Littleboy, Thirsk; one *s*. *Educ:* Cheltenham Coll.; Selwyn Coll., Cambridge. Commnd RE, 1944; served in Italy, 1944–45; subseq. Hong Kong, Kenya and Germany; jssc 1960; Instructor, Staff Coll., Camberley, 1961–63; Comdr, RE 1st Div., 1965–67; retd 1967. Asst Clerk, Goldsmiths' Co., 1968. Mem., Hallmarking Council, 1977–88; Vice-Chm., Goldsmiths' Coll. (Univ. of London) Council, 1983–91. Trustee Nat. Centre for Orchestral Studies, 1980–89. *Recreations:* swimming, gardening, Wagner. *Address:* Oak Hill, South Brent, Devon TQ10 9JL.

JENKINS, Christopher; *see* Jenkins, J. C.

JENKINS, Christopher Dennis Alexander M.; *see* Martin-Jenkins.

JENKINS, Clive; *see* Jenkins, D. C.

JENKINS, David, CBE 1977; MA; Librarian, National Library of Wales, 1969–79; *b* 29 May 1912; *s* of late Evan Jenkins and Mary (*née* James), Blaenclydach, Rhondda; *m* 1948, Menna Rhys, *o d* of late Rev. Owen Evans Williams, Penrhyn-coch, Aberystwyth; one *s* one *d*. *Educ:* Ardwyn Grammar Sch., Aberystwyth; UCW, Aberystwyth. BA Hons Welsh Lit. 1936, MA 1948; W. P. Thomas (Rhondda) Schol. 1936; Sir John Williams Research Student, 1937–38. Served War of 1939–45, Army; Major, 1943; NW Europe. National Library of Wales: Asst, Dept MSS, 1939–48; Asst Keeper, Dept of Printed Books, 1949, Keeper, 1957, Sen. Keeper, 1962. Professorial Fellow, UCW Aberystwyth, 1971–79. Gen. Comr of Income Tax, 1968–87; Chairman: Mid-Wales HMC, 1969–70; Welsh Books Council, 1974–80 (Vice-Chm. 1971–74); Library Adv. Council (Wales), 1979–82; Member: Court of Governors, Univ. of Wales; Ct and Council, UC Aberystwyth and Lampeter; Adv. Council, British Library, 1975–82; BBC Archives Adv. Cttee, 1976–79; Hon. Soc. of Cymmrodorion; Pantyfedwen Trust, 1969–; Coll. of Librarianship Wales; Governor: Ardwyn Grammar Sch., 1963–72; Penweddig Compreh. Sch., 1973–77. Editor: NLW Jl, 1968–79; Jl Welsh Bibliog. Soc., 1964–79; Ceredigion, Trans Cards Antiq. Soc., 1973–84. JP Aberystwyth 1959–82: Chm. Llanbadarn Bench 1965–69; Vice-Chm., Aberystwyth Bench, 1980; Member: Dyfed Magistrates' Courts Cttee, 1975–79; Dyfed-Powys Police Authority, 1977–81. Hon. DLitt Wales, 1979. Sir Ellis Griffith Meml Prize, Univ. of Wales, 1975. *Publications:* Cofiant Thomas Gwynn Jones, 1973, 2nd edn 1994 (Welsh Arts Council Prize, 1974); (ed) Erthyglau ac Ysgrifau Kate Roberts, 1978; Bardd a Bro: T. Gwynn Jones, Cyngor y Celfyddydau, 1984; Bro Dafydd ap Gwilym, 1992; O Blas Gogerddan i Horeb, 1993; articles in NLW Jl, Bull. Bd of Celtic Studies and many other jls; contrib. Dictionary of Welsh Biography, Cydymaith i lenyddiaeth Cymru, DNB. *Recreation:* walking. *Address:* Maesaleg, Penrhyn-coch, Aberystwyth, Dyfed SY23 3EH. *T:* Aberystwyth (01970) 828 766.

JENKINS, (David) Clive; Director, Green Independants Goshawk Trust, since 1990; Joint General Secretary, Manufacturing, Science and Finance, 1988–89, now General Secretary

Emeritus (Joint General Secretary, 1968–70, General Secretary, 1970–88, Association of Scientific, Technical and Managerial Staffs); Member of the General Council of the TUC, 1974–89 (Chairman, 1987–88); *b* 2 May 1926; *s* of David Samuel Jenkins and Miriam Harris Jenkins (*née* Hughes); *m* 1963, Moira McGregor Hilley (marr. diss. 1989); one *s* one *d*. *Educ:* Port Talbot Central Boys' Sch.; Port Talbot County Sch.; Swansea Techn. Coll. (evenings). Started work in metallurgical test house, 1940; furnace shift supervisor, 1942; i/c of laboratory, 1943; tinplate night shift foreman, 1945; Branch Sec. and Area Treas., AScW, 1946; Asst Midlands Divisional Officer, ASSET, 1947; Transport Industrial Officer, 1949; Nat. Officer, 1954; Gen. Sec., ASSET, 1961–68. Woodrow Wilson Fellow, 1968; Australian Commonwealth Fellow, 1989. Metrop. Borough Councillor, 1954–60 (Chm. Staff Cttee, St Pancras Borough Coun.); Chm., Nat. Jt Coun. for Civil Air Transport, 1967–68; Member: NRDC, 1974–80; Bullock Cttee on Industrial Democracy, 1975; Wilson Cttee to Review the Functioning of Financial Institutions, 1977–80; BNOC, 1979–82; BOTB, 1980–83; NEDC, 1983–89; Commn of Inquiry into Labour Party, 1979 (Chm., Finance Panel, 1979); TUC-Labour Party Liaison Cttee, 1980–89; Council, ACAS, 1986–89; Chairman: TUC Educnl Trust, 1979; Roosevelt Meml Trust, 1979–89; Friends of the Earth Trust, 1984–86; Trustee, Nat. Heritage Meml Fund, 1980–88; Governor, Sadler's Wells Foundn, 1985–88. Editor, Trade Union Affairs, 1961–63. Sometime columnist, Tribune, Daily Mirror, Daily Record. *Publications:* Power at the Top, 1959; Power Behind the Screen, 1961; (with J. E. Mortimer) British Trade Unions Today, 1965; (with J. E. Mortimer) The Kind of Laws the Unions Ought to Want, 1968; with B. D. Sherman: Computers and the Unions, 1977; Collective Bargaining: what you always wanted to know about trade unions and never dared ask, 1977; The Collapse of Work, 1979; The Rebellious Salariat: white collar unionism, 1979; The Leisure Shock, 1981; All Against the Collar (autobiog.), 1990. *Recreations:* working with the Green movements and keeping an eye on multinational exploiters and Fairy Penguins. *Address:* Villa de l'Est, Redbill Point, Bicheno on the Pacific, Tas 7215, Australia; 472 Chelsea Cloisters, Sloane Avenue, SW3 3DW.

See also T. H. Jenkins.

JENKINS, Rt. Rev. David Edward; Bishop of Durham, 1984–94; an Assistant Bishop, diocese of Ripon, since 1994; *b* 26 Jan. 1925; *er s* of Lionel C. Jenkins and Dora (*née* Page); *m* 1949, Stella Mary Peet; two *s* two *d*. *Educ:* St Dunstan's Coll., Catford; Queen's Coll., Oxford (MA; Hon. Fellow, 1991). EC, RA, 1943–45 (Captain). Priest, 1954. Succentor, Birmingham Cath. and Lectr, Queen's Coll., 1953–54; Fellow, Chaplain and Praelector in Theology, Queen's Coll., Oxford, 1954–69; Dir, Humanum Studies, World Council of Churches, Geneva, 1969–73 (Consultant, 1973–75); Dir, William Temple Foundn, Manchester, 1973–78 (Jt Dir, 1979–); Prof. of Theology, Univ. of Leeds, 1979–84, Emeritus Prof., 1985; Hon. Prof. of Divinity, Univ. of Durham, 1994–. Exam. Chaplain to Bps of Lichfield, 1956–69, Newcastle, 1957–69, Bristol, 1958–84, Wakefield, 1978–84, and Bradford, 1979–84; Canon Theologian, Leicester, 1966–82, Canon Emeritus, 1982–. Lectures: Bampton, 1966; Hale, Seabury-Western, USA, 1970; Moorehouse, Melbourne, 1972; Cadbury, Birmingham Univ., 1974; Lindsay Meml, Keele Univ., 1976; Heslington, York Univ., 1980; Drummond, Stirling Univ., 1981; Hibbert, Hibbert Trust, 1985; Hensley Henson, Oxford, 1987; Gore, Westminster Abbey, 1990. Chm., SCM Press, 1987–92; Trustee, Trinity Press Internat., 1989–91. Hon. Fellow: St Chad's Coll., Durham, 1986; Univ. of Sunderland (formerly Sunderland Poly.), 1986. Hon. DD: Durham, 1987; Trinity Coll., Toronto, 1989; Aberdeen, 1990; Hon. DLitt Teesside, 1994; Hon. DCL Northumbria, 1994. Jt Editor, Theology, 1976–82. *Publications:* Guide to the Debate about God, 1966; The Glory of Man, 1967; Living with Questions, 1969; What is Man?, 1970; The Contradiction of Christianity, 1976; God, Miracle and the Church of England, 1987; God, Politics and the Future, 1988; God, Jesus and Life in the Spirit, 1988; Still Living with Questions, 1990; (with Rebecca Jenkins) Free to Believe, 1991; contrib. Man, Fallen and Free, 1969, etc. *Recreations:* music, reading, walking, birdwatching. *Address:* Ashbourne, Cotherstone, Barnard Castle, Co. Durham DL12 9PR.

JENKINS, David Edward Stewart; Research Consultant to HM Chief Inspector of Prisons, since 1987; *b* 9 May 1949; *s* of late William Stephen Jenkins and of Jean Nicol Downie; *m* 1972, Maggie Lack, *d* of Dr C. H. and Mrs J. D. Lack; two *s* one *d*. *Educ:* Univ. of London Goldsmiths' College (BA(Soc) 1977); LSE. Warden, Ellison Hse Adult Probation Hostel, SE17, 1973–74; Lecturer: (part-time) in Sociology, Brunel Univ., 1980–81; (part-time) in Social Administration, LSE and Goldsmiths' Coll., 1980–81; in Criminology, Univ. of Edinburgh, 1981; Dir, Howard League, 1982–86; Res. Fellow, PSI, 1986–87. Morris Ginsburg Fellow in Sociology, LSE, 1986–87. *Recreations:* music, swimming, cycling. *Address:* HM Inspectorate of Prisons, 50 Queen Anne's Gate, SW1H 9AT. *T:* 0171–273 2641.

JENKINS, David John; General Secretary, Wales Trades Union Congress, since 1983; *b* 21 Sept. 1948; *s* of William and Dorothy Jenkins; *m* 1976, Felicity Anne (*née* Wood); two *s* one *d*. *Educ:* Canton High Sch., Cardiff; Liverpool Univ. (BA Hons); Garnett Coll., London (CertEd). Industrial Sales Organiser, ITT (Distributors), 1970–74; steel worker, GKN, 1974; Lectr, Peterborough Tech. Coll., 1975–78; Research and Admin. Officer, Wales TUC, 1978–83. Pt-time Mem., Monopolies and Mergers Commission, 1993–; Mem., Employment Appeal Tribunal, 1994–. *Recreation:* finding time to spend with family. *Address:* 1 Cathedral Road, Cardiff CF1 9SD. *T:* Cardiff (01222) 372345.

JENKINS, Maj.-Gen. David John Malcolm, CBE 1994; Commandant, Royal Military College of Science, since 1994; *b* 2 Jan. 1945. *Educ:* Sherborne Sch.; Reading Univ. (BA Hons); Magdalene Coll., Cambridge (MPhil). Commissioned The Queen's Own Hussars, 1964; regimental service, 1964–75; RMCS and Staff Coll., 1976–77; Allied Staff, Berlin, 1983–85; CO, The Queen's Own Hussars, 1985–87; COS, 3 Armd Div., 1988–90; Comdr Armd 1 (Br) Corps, 1990–91; Dir, Military Ops, 1991–93. *Recreations:* ski-ing, country sports, music, military history. *Address:* Royal Military College of Science, Shrivenham, Swindon, Wilts SN6 9AH. *T:* Swindon (01793) 785439. *Club:* Cavalry and Guards.

JENKINS, Ven. David Thomas Ivor; Archdeacon of Westmorland and Furness, since 1995; *b* 3 June 1929; *s* of Edward Evan and Edith Olwen Jenkins; *m* 1st, 1953, Rosemary German; one *d*; 2nd, 1992, Kathleen Theresa Sidey. *Educ:* King's Coll. London (BD, AKC); Birmingham Univ. (MA (Theol.)). Ordained deacon, 1953, priest, 1954; Asst Curate, St Mark's Bilton, Rugby, 1953–56; Vicar, St Margaret's, Wolston, Coventry, 1956–61; Asst Dir, Religious Educn, dio. of Carlisle, 1961–63; Vicar: St Barnabas, Carlisle, 1963–72; St Cuthbert's, Carlisle, 1972–91; Canon Residentiary, Carlisle Cathedral, 1991–95. Sec., Carlisle Diocesan Synod and Bishop's Council, 1972–95; Diocesan Synod Sec., 1984–95; Sec., Synod of Convocation of York, 1985–. *Recreations:* golf, reading, good food and wine with friends, foreign travel. *Address:* Woodcroft, Levens, Kendal, Cumbria LA8 8NQ. *T:* Sedgwick (01539) 561281, *Fax:* (01539) 561217; Irvings House, Sleagill, Penrith, Cumbria CA10 3HD. *T:* Penrith (01931) 714400.

JENKINS, Prof. Edgar William, CChem, FRSC; Professor of Science Education Policy, University of Leeds, since 1992; *b* 7 Jan. 1939; *s* of Lewis Morgan Jenkins and Eira Gwyn Thomas; *m* 1961, Isobel Harrison; two *d*. *Educ:* Univ. of Leeds (BSc, MEd). Teacher: Keighley Grammar Sch., 1961–62; Leeds Grammar Sch., 1962–67; University of Leeds: Lectr and Sen. Lectr, 1967–76; Reader in Science Education, 1980–92; Head, Sch. of Education, 1980–84, 1991–95. JP W Yorks, 1977. Editor: Studies in Science Education; Internat. Jl of Technology and Design Education. *Publications:* A Safety Handbook for Science Teachers, 1973, 4th edn 1991; From Armstrong to Nuffield, 1979; Inarticulate Science?, 1983; Technological Revolution?, 1985; A Magnificent Pile, 1985; Policy, Practice and Professional Judgement, 1993; books for schools. *Recreations:* choral music, walking, lay administration of justice. *Address:* School of Education, The University, Leeds LS2 9JT. *T:* Leeds (0113) 233 4561.

JENKINS, Elizabeth, OBE 1981. *Educ:* St Christopher School, Letchworth; Newnham College, Cambridge. *Publications:* The Winters, 1931; Lady Caroline Lamb, a Biography, 1932; Harriet (awarded the Femina Vie Heureuse Prize), 1934; The Phoenix' Nest, 1936; Jane Austen, a Biography, 1938; Robert and Helen, 1944; Young Enthusiasts, 1946; Henry Fielding (The English Novelists Series), 1947; Six Criminal Women, 1949; The Tortoise and the Hare, 1954; Ten Fascinating Women, 1955; Elizabeth the Great (biography), 1958; Elizabeth and Leicester, 1961; Brightness, 1963; Honey, 1968; Dr Gully, 1972; The Mystery of King Arthur, 1975; The Princes in the Tower, 1978; The Shadow and the Light, 1983; A Silent Joy, 1992. *Address:* 8 Downshire Hill, Hampstead, NW3 1NR. *T:* 0171–435 4642.

JENKINS, Emyr; *see* Jenkins, J. E.

JENKINS, Very Rev. Frank Graham; Dean of Monmouth and Vicar of St Woolos, 1976–90; *b* 24 Feb. 1923; *s* of Edward and Miriam M. Jenkins; *m* 1950, Ena Doraine Parry; two *s* one *d*. *Educ:* Cyfarthfa Sec. Sch., Merthyr Tydfil; Port Talbot Sec. Sch.; St David's Coll., Lampeter (BA Hist); Jesus Coll., Oxford (BA Theol., MA); St Michael's Coll., Llandaff. HM Forces, 1942–46. Deacon 1950, priest 1951, Llandaff; Asst Curate, Llangeinor, 1950–53; Minor Canon, Llandaff Cathedral, 1953–60; CF (TA), 1956–61; Vicar of Abertillery, 1960–64; Vicar of Risca, 1964–75; Canon of Monmouth, 1967–76; Vicar of Caerleon, 1975–76. *Address:* Rivendell, 209 Christchurch Road, Newport, Gwent NP9 7QL. *T:* Newport (01633) 255278.

JENKINS, Prof. George Charles, MB, BS, PhD; FRCPE, FRCPath; Consultant Haematologist, The Royal London (formerly London) Hospital, since 1965; Hon. Consultant, St Peter's Hospitals, 1972–86; Professor of Haematology in the University of London, 1974–92, now Emeritus; Consultant to the Royal Navy; *b* 2 Aug. 1927; *s* of late John R. Jenkins and Mabel Rebecca (*née* Smith); *m* 1956, Elizabeth, *d* of late Cecil J. Welch, London; one *s* two *d*. *Educ:* Wyggeston, Leicester; St Bartholomew's Hosp. Med. Coll. MB, BS, PhD; MRCS 1951; LRCP 1951; FRCPath 1975 (MRCPath 1964); FRCPE; FRSocMed. House Phys. and Ho. Surg., St Bart's Hosp., 1951–52. Sqdn Ldr, RAF Med. Br., 1952–54. Registrar in Pathology, St Bart's Hosp., 1954–57; MRC Research Fellow, Royal Postgraduate Med. Sch., 1957–60; Sen. Registrar, Haematology, London Hosp., 1960–63; Cons. Haematologist, N Middlesex Hosp., 1963–65. Examiner: Univ. of London, 1971–; Univ. of Cambridge, 1984–; Sen. Examiner, RCPath, 1971–, Mem. Council, 1979–84, Vice-Pres., 1981–84. Member, subcttee on biologicals, 1976–86, cttee on dental and surgical materials, 1988–92, Cttee on Safety of Medicines. Pres., British Acad. of Forensic Scis, 1990–91 (Mem., 1977–; Chm. Exec. Council, 1985–89); Member: British Soc. for Haematology, 1962– (formerly Hon. Sec.; Pres., 1988–89); Internat. Soc. of Haematology, 1975–; Assoc. of Clinical Pathologists, 1958–92. FRSA 1991. Gov. and Mem. Council, Home Farm Trust, 1993–. *Publications:* (jtly) Advanced Haematology, 1974; (jtly) Infection and Haematology, 1994; papers and contribs to med. and sci. books and jls. *Recreations:* theatre, music, talking to people. *Club:* Royal Navy Medical.

JENKINS, Gilbert Kenneth; Keeper, Department of Coins and Medals, British Museum, 1965–78; *b* 2 July 1918; *s* of late Kenneth Gordon Jenkins and of Julia Louisa Jenkins (*née* Colbourne); *m* 1939, Cynthia Mary, *d* of late Dr Hugh Scott, FRS; one *s* two *d*. *Educ:* All Saints Sch., Bloxham; Corpus Christi Coll., Oxford. Open Classical Scholar (Corpus Christi Coll.), 1936; First Class Honour Mods, 1938. War Service in Royal Artillery, 1940–46 (SE Asia, 1944–46). BA, 1946. Asst Keeper, British Museum, 1947; Dep. Keeper, 1956. An Editor of Numismatic Chronicle, 1964. Mem., German Archaeological Inst., 1967; Corresp. Mem., Amer. Numismatic Soc., 1958; Hon. Mem., Swiss Numismatic Soc., 1979; Hon. FRNS, 1980. Akbar Medal, Numismatic Soc. of India, 1966; Royal Numismatic Soc. Medal, 1975; Archer Huntington Medal, Amer. Numismatic Soc., 1976. *Publications:* Carthaginian Gold and Electrum Coins (with R. B. Lewis), 1963; Coins of Greek Sicily, 1966; Sylloge Nummorum Graecorum (Danish Nat. Museum), part 42, N Africa (ed), 1969, part 43, Spain-Gaul (ed), 1979; The Coinage of Gela, 1970; Ancient Greek Coins, 1972; (with U. Westermark) The Coinage of Kamarina, 1980; (jtly) A catalogue of the Calouste Gulbenkian Collection of Greek Coins, part II, 1989; articles in numismatic periodicals. *Recreations:* music, cycling. *Address:* 3 Beechwood Avenue, Kew Gardens, Surrey TW9 4DD.

JENKINS, Prof. Harold, MA, DLitt; FBA 1989; Professor Emeritus, University of Edinburgh; *b* 19 July 1909; *s* of Henry and Mildred Jenkins, Shenley, Bucks; *m* 1939, Gladys Puddifoot (*d* 1984); no *c*. *Educ:* Wolverton Grammar Sch.; University Coll., London (Fellow, 1991). George Smith Studentship, 1930. Quain Student, University Coll., London, 1930–35; William Noble Fellow, University of Liverpool, 1935–36; Lecturer in English, University of the Witwatersrand, South Africa, 1936–45; Lecturer in English, 1945–46, Reader in English, 1946–54, UCL; Prof. of English, University of London (Westfield Coll.), 1954–67; Regius Prof. of Rhetoric and English Lit., Edinburgh Univ., 1967–71. Visiting Prof., Duke Univ., USA, 1957–58, Univ. of Oslo, 1974. Pres., Malone Soc., 1989– (Mem. Council, 1955–89). Hon. LittD Iona Coll., New Rochelle, NY, 1983. Shakespeare Prize, FVS Foundn, Hamburg, 1986. Jt Gen. Editor, Arden Shakespeare, 1958–82. *Publications:* The Life and Work of Henry Chettle, 1934; Edward Benlowes, 1952; The Structural Problem in Shakespeare's Henry IV, 1956; The Catastrophe in Shakespearean Tragedy, 1968; John Dover Wilson (British Acad. memoir), 1973; (ed) Hamlet (Arden edn), 1982; articles in Modern Language Review, Review of English Studies, The Library, Shakespeare Survey, Studies in Bibliography, etc. *Address:* 22 North Crescent, Finchley, N3 3LL. *Club:* Athenæum.

JENKINS, Hon. Dr Henry Alfred, AM 1991; retired; *b* 24 Sept. 1925; *s* of Henry Alfred Jenkins and Eileen Clare Jenkins (*née* McCormack); *m* 1951, Hazel Eileen Winter; three *s* one *d*. *Educ:* Ormond, Eltham and Heidelberg State Schools; Ivanhoe Grammar Sch.; Univ. of Melbourne (MSc, MB BS); Deakin Univ. (BA). Tutor, Univ. of Melbourne, 1946–52; RMO Alfred Hosp., 1953; Medical Practitioner, 1953–61; MLA (Lab) Reservoir Parliament of Victoria, 1961–69; MP (Lab) Scullin, Federal Parliament of Australia, 1969–85; Chm. of Committees and Dep. Speaker, House of Representatives, 1975–76, Speaker, 1983–85; Aust. Ambassador to Spain, 1986–88. *Recreations:* reading, hobby farming, community service. *Address:* 61 Mill Park Drive, Mill Park, Vic 3082, Australia. *Clubs:* Royal Automobile of Victoria, Melbourne Cricket.

JENKINS, Hugh Royston, FRICS, FPMI; Chief Executive, Prudential Portfolio Managers, and Director, Prudential Corporation, since 1989; *b* 9 Nov. 1933; *m* 1988, Mrs Beryl Kirk. *Educ:* Llanelli Grammar Sch.; National Service, Royal Artillery, 1954–56. Valuer, London County Council, 1956–62; Assistant Controller, 1962–68, Managing

Director, 1968–72, Coal Industry (Nominees) Ltd; Dir Gen. of Investments, NCB, 1972–85. Vice Chm., National Assoc. of Pension Funds, 1979–80; Chief Exec. Officer, Heron Financial Corp., 1985–86; Gp Investment Dir, Allied Dunbar Assce, 1986–89; Dep. Chm. and Chief Exec., Allied Dunbar Unit Trusts, 1986–89; Chm., Dunbar Bank, 1988–89; Chm. and Chief Exec., Allied Dunbar Asset Management, 1987–89; Director: Unilever Pensions Ltd, 1985–89; IBM Pensions Trust PLC, 1985–89; Heron International, 1985–89. Chm., Property Adv. Gp, DoE, 1990–; Member: The City Capital Markets Cttee, 1982; Private Finance Panel, 1994–; Lay Mem. of the Stock Exchange, 1984–85. *Recreation:* golf. *Address:* (office) 142 Holborn Bars, EC1N 2NH. *Club:* Garrick.

JENKINS, Dr Ivor, CBE 1970; FEng 1979; freelance Consultant, since 1979; Group Director of Research, Delta Metal Co. Ltd, 1973–78; Managing Director, 1973–77, Deputy Chairman, 1977–78, Delta Materials Research Ltd; *b* 25 July 1913; *m* 1941, Caroline Wijnanda James; two *s*. *Educ:* Gowerton Grammar Sch.; Univ. of Wales, Swansea. BSc, MSc, DSc; Hon. Fellow, UC Swansea, 1986. Bursar, GEC Research Labs, Wembley, 1934; Mem. Scientific Staff, GEC, 1935; Dep. Chief Metallurgist, Whitehead Iron & Steel Co., Newport, Mon, 1944; Head of Metallurgy Dept, 1946, Chief Metallurgist, 1952, GEC, Wembley; Dir of Research, Manganese Bronze Holdings Ltd, and Dir, Manganese Bronze Ltd, 1961–69; Dir of Research, Delta Metal Co., and Dir, Delta Metal (BW) Ltd, 1969–73. Vis. Prof., Univ. of Surrey, 1978–. FIM 1948 (Pres. 1965–66); Fellow, Amer. Soc. of Metals, 1974; Pres., Inst. of Metals, 1968–69; Mem., Iron and Steel Inst., 1937– (Williams Prize, 1946). Platinum medallist, Metals Soc., 1978. *Publications:* Controlled Atmospheres for the Heat Treatment of Metals, 1946; (ed jtly) Selected Case Studies in Powder Metallurgy, 1991; (ed jtly) Powder Metallurgy: an overview, 1991; contribs to learned jls at home and abroad on metallurgical and related subjects. *Recreations:* music, gardening, swimming. *Address:* 31 Trotyn Croft, Aldwick Felds, Aldwick, Bognor Regis, Sussex PO21 3TX. *T:* Bognor Regis (01243) 828749. *Club:* Anglo-Belgian.

JENKINS, (James) Christopher, CB 1987; First Parliamentary Counsel, since 1994; *b* 20 May 1939; *s* of Percival Si Phillips Jenkins and Dela (*née* Griffiths); *m* 1962, Margaret Elaine Edwards, *yr d* of Rt Hon. L. John Edwards and Dorothy (*née* Watson); two *s* one *d*. *Educ:* Lewes County Grammar Sch.; Magdalen Coll., Oxford. Solicitor, 1965. Joined Office of Parly Counsel, 1967; at Law Commn, 1970–72 and 1983–86; Parly Counsel, 1978–91; Second Parly Counsel, 1991–94. Hon. QC 1994. *Address:* Parliamentary Counsel Office, 36 Whitehall, SW1A 2AY.

JENKINS, Dame Jennifer; *see* Jenkins, Dame M. J.

JENKINS, (John) Emyr; Chief Executive, Arts Council of Wales, since 1994; *b* 3 May 1938; *s* of Llewellyn Jenkins and Mary Olwen Jenkins; *m* 1964, Myra Bonner Samuel; two *d*. *Educ:* Machynlleth County Sch.; UCW, Aberystwyth (BSc Physics). BBC Studio Manager, 1961–63; BBC Announcer and Newsreader, 1963–71; Anchorman, Heddiw (Daily TV Mag.), 1968–69; BBC Wales Programme Organiser, 1971–77; First Dir, Royal Nat. Eisteddfod of Wales, 1978–93; Dir, Welsh Arts Council, 1993–94. Mem., IBA Welsh Adv. Cttee, 1986–90. Foundn Chm., Mudiad Ysgolion Meithrin (Assoc. of Welsh Playgroups), 1971–73; Member: Welsh Lang. Educn Develt Cttee, 1987–88; Council, UCW Aberystwyth, 1982–86; Steering Cttee/Council, Voluntary Arts Network, 1988–94. FRSA 1992. Hon. MA Wales, 1993. Hon. Mem., Gorsedd of Bards, 1982. Elder, Crwys Presbytarian Church of Wales, 1983. *Recreations:* music, theatre, walking, sport. *Address:* c/o Arts Council of Wales, 9 Museum Place, Cardiff CF1 3NX. *T:* Cardiff (01222) 394711.

JENKINS, John George, CBE 1971; farmer; *b* 26 Aug. 1919; *s* of George John Jenkins, OBE, FRCS and Alice Maud Jenkins, MBE; *m* 1948, Chloe Evelyn (*née* Kenward); one *s* three *d*. *Educ:* Winchester; Edinburgh University. Farmed in Scotland, 1939–62; farmed in England (Cambs and Lincs), 1957–. Pres., NFU of Scotland, 1960–61; Chm., Agricultural Marketing Development Exec. Cttee, 1967–73. Chm., United Oilseeds Ltd, 1984–87; Director: Childerley Estates Ltd, 1957–; Agricultural Mortgage Corporation Ltd, 1968–90. Compère, Anglia Television programme Farming Diary, 1963–80. *Publications:* contrib. Proc. Royal Soc., RSA Jl, etc. *Recreations:* tennis, bridge, music. *Address:* Childerley Hall, Dry Drayton, Cambridge CB3 8BB. *T:* Madingley (01954) 210271. *Club:* Farmers'.

JENKINS, John Owen, MBE 1978; FCSP; Chartered Physiotherapist; Senior Lecturer, St Mary's Hospital School of Physiotherapy, W2, 1975–88 (Lecturer, 1959); *b* 4 Nov. 1922; *s* of late J. O. Jenkins, JP, and M. E. Jenkins, Great House, Dilwyn, Hereford; *m* 1953, Catherine MacFarlane Baird, MCSP; three *d*. *Educ:* Worcester College for the Blind; NIB School of Physiotherapy, London. TMMG, TET, FCSP 1990. Chartered Society of Physiotherapy: Mem. Council, 1952–81; Chm., Finance and Gen. Purposes Cttee, 1955–79; Member: Education Cttee, 1953–71; Executive Cttee, 1955–79; Trustee, Members' Benevolent Fund, 1955–. CSP Examiner, 1954–88; Pres., Orgn of Chartered Physiotherapists in Private Practice, 1980–86. Physiotherapy Representative: Min. of Health Working Party on Statutory Registration, 1954; Council for Professions Supplementary to Medicine, 1961–76; Chm., Physiotherapists' Board, 1962–76. Director, LAMPS, 1969–, Chm., 1980–87, Pres., 1988–; Trustee, Moira Pakenham-Walsh Foundn, 1978–. Churchwarden, St James the Great, N20, 1974–81. *Publications:* contribs to Physiotherapy and Rehabilitation. *Recreations:* chess, rowing. *Address:* The New House, 34A Ravensdale Avenue, N12 9HT. *T:* 0181–445 6072.

JENKINS, John Robin; writer; *b* Cambuslang, Lanarks, 11 Sept. 1912; *s* of late James Jenkins and of Annie Robin; *m* 1937, Mary McIntyre Wyllie; one *s* two *d*. *Educ:* Hamilton Academy; Glasgow Univ. (MA Hons). *Publications:* (as Robin Jenkins) Happy for the Child, 1953; The Thistle and the Grail, 1954; The Cone-Gatherers, 1955; Guests of War, 1956; The Missionaries, 1957; The Changeling, 1958; Some Kind of Grace, 1960; Dust on the Paw, 1961; The Tiger of Gold, 1962; A Love of Innocence, 1963; The Sardana Dancers, 1964; A Very Scotch Affair, 1968; The Holy Tree, 1969; The Expatriates, 1971; A Toast to the Lord, 1972; A Far Cry from Bowmore, 1973; A Figure of Fun, 1974; A Would-be Saint, 1978; Fergus Lamont, 1979; The Awakening of George Darroch, 1985; Just Duffy, 1988; Poverty Castle, 1991; Willie Hogg, 1993. *Recreations:* travel, golf. *Address:* Fairhaven, Toward, by Dunoon, Argyll PA23 7UE. *T:* Toward (01369) 870288.

JENKINS, Katharine Mary; independent consultant; *b* 14 Feb. 1945; *d* of Daniel Jenkins and Nell Jenkins; *m* 1967, Euan Sutherland, *qv*; one *s* one *d*. *Educ:* South Hampstead High Sch.; St Anne's Coll., Oxford (BA Hons); London School of Economics (MScEcon). Called to Bar, Inner Temple, 1971. Asst Principal, 1968, Principal, 1973, Dept of Employment; Central Policy Review Staff, 1976; Asst Sec., Dept of Employment, 1979; Dep. Head of Efficiency Unit, 1984; Hd, Prime Minister's Efficiency Unit, and Under Sec., Cabinet Office, 1986–89; Dir, Personnel, Royal Mail, 1989–91. Member: NHS Policy Bd, 1992–; Audit Commn, 1993–. Dir, London and Manchester Gp, 1989–. Special Trustee, St Thomas' Hosp., 1992–. Mem., Ct of Governors, LSE, 1990–; Governor, Alleyn's Sch., Dulwich, 1990–. *Publications:* reports: Making Things Happen: the implementation of government scrutinies, 1985; Improving Management in Government: the next steps, 1988. *Address:* 108 Andrewes House, Barbican, EC2Y 8AY. *See also* S. D. Jenkins.

JENKINS, Dame (Mary) Jennifer, (Lady Jenkins of Hillhead), DBE 1985; Member of Council, National Trust, 1985–91 (Chairman, 1986–90); *b* 18 Jan. 1921; *d* of late Sir Parker Morris; *m* 1945, Baron Jenkins of Hillhead, *qv*; two *s* one *d*. *Educ:* St Mary's Sch., Calne; Girton Coll., Cambridge. Chm., Cambridge Univ. Labour Club. With Hoover Ltd, 1942–43; Min. of Labour, 1943–46; Political and Economic Planning (PEP), 1946–48; part-time extra-mural lectr, 1949–61; part-time teacher, Kingsway Day Coll., 1961–67. Chairman: Consumers' Assoc., 1965–76; Historic Buildings Council for England, 1975–84; Member: Exec. Bd, British Standards Instn, 1970–73; Design Council, 1971–74; Cttee of Management, Courtauld Inst., 1981–84; Ancient Monuments Bd, 1982–84; Historic Buildings and Monuments Commn, 1984–85 (Chm., Historic Buildings Adv. Cttee, 1984–85); Pres., Ancient Monuments Soc., 1985– (Sec., 1972–75). Chairman: N Kensington Amenity Trust, 1974–77; Royal Parks Review Gp, 1991–; Architectural Heritage Fund, 1994–. Trustee, Wallace Collection, 1977–83. Director: J. Sainsbury Ltd, 1981–86; Abbey National plc (formerly Abbey National Building Soc.), 1984–91. Liveryman, Goldsmiths' Co., 1980. Freeman, City of London, 1982. JP London Juvenile Courts, 1964–74. Hon. FRIBA, Hon. FRICS, Hon. MRTPI; Hon. FLI 1995. Hon. LLD: London, 1988; Bristol, 1990; DUniv: York, 1990; Strathclyde, 1993; Hon. DCL Newcastle, 1992; Hon. DArch Oxford Brookes, 1993. *Publication:* (with Patrick James) From Acorn to Oak Tree, 1994. *Address:* 2 Kensington Park Gardens, W11 3HB; St Amand's House, East Hendred, Oxon OX12 8LA.

JENKINS, Michael Nicholas Howard, OBE 1991; Chairman: London Commodity Exchange, since 1992; Futures and Options Association, since 1993; *b* 13 Oct. 1932; *s* of C. N. and M. E. S. Jenkins; *m* 1957, Jacqueline Frances Jones; three *s*. *Educ:* Tonbridge School; Merton College, Oxford (MA Jurisp.). Shell-Mex & BP, 1956–61; IBM UK, 1961–67; Partner, Robson, Morrow, Management Consultants, 1967–71; Technical Dir, Stock Exchange, 1971–77; Man. Dir, European Options Exchange, Amsterdam, 1977–79; Chief Executive, LIFFE, 1981–92. Director: London Clearing House, 1991–; Tradepoint Financial Networks plc, 1995–. Gov., Sevenoaks Sch., 1993–. *Recreations:* games, classical music and jazz, furniture making. *Address:* London Commodity Exchange, 1 Commodity Quay, St Katharine Docks, E1 9AX. *T:* 0171–481 2080. *Club:* Wildernesse (Sevenoaks).

JENKINS, Sir Michael (Romilly Heald), KCMG 1990 (CMG 1984); HM Diplomatic Service, retired; Executive Director: Kleinwort Benson Group PLC, since 1993; Kleinwort Benson Ltd, since 1993; Chairman: Kleinwort Benson Europe Ltd, since 1995; KB Holdings Inc., since 1995; *b* 9 Jan. 1936; *s* of Prof. Romilly Jenkins and Celine Juliette Haeglar; *m* 1968, Maxine Louise Hodson; one *s* one *d*. *Educ:* privately; King's Coll., Cambridge (Exhibr, BA). Entered Foreign (subseq. Diplomatic) Service, 1959; served in Paris, Moscow and Bonn; Deputy Chef de Cabinet, 1973–75, Chef de Cabinet, 1975–76, to Rt Hon. George Thomson, EEC; Principal Advr to Mr Roy Jenkins, Pres. EEC, Jan–Aug. 1977; Head of European Integration Dept (External), FCO, 1977–79; Hd of Central Adv. Gp, EEC, 1979–81; Dep. Sec. Gen., Commn of the Eur. Communities, 1981–83; Asst Under Sec. of State (Europe), FCO, 1983–85; Minister, Washington, 1985–87; Ambassador to the Netherlands, 1988–93. Dir, Aegon NV, 1995–. Member: Trilateral Commn, 1994–; President's Adv. Council, Atlantic Council, 1994–. Dir (Chm.), Action Centre for Europe, 1995–. *Publications:* Arakcheev, Grand Vizier of the Russian Empire, 1969; A House in Flanders, 1992; contrib. History Today. *Address:* c/o Kleinwort Benson PLC, 20 Fenchurch Street, EC3P 3DB. *Clubs:* Athenæum, MCC.

JENKINS, Neil Martin James; opera singer; tenor; *b* 9 April 1945; *s* of Harry James Jenkins and Mary Morrison Jenkins (*née* Terry); *m* 1st, 1969, Sandra Wilkes; one *s*; 2nd, 1982, Penny (*née* Underwood); one *s* and two step *s* one step *d*. *Educ:* Westminster Abbey Choir School; Dean Close School (music Scholar); King's College Cambridge (Choral Scholar; MA). Recital début, Kirkman Concert Series, Purcell Room, 1967; operatic debut, Menotti's The Consul, Israel Festival, 1968; major rôles with English Music Theatre, Glyndebourne Fest. Opera, Kent Opera, New Sussex Opera, Scottish Opera, WNO; ENO; numerous recordings, film sound tracks and videos. Prof. of Singing, RCM, 1975–76; teacher, summer schools, incl. Canford and Wellington, 1989–. Pres., Grange Choral Soc., Hants; Vice-President: Hunts Philharmonic; Brighton Competitive Music Festival. Geoffrey Tankard Lieder Prize, 1967; NFMS Award, 1972. *Publications: choral music* (edited and arranged): The Carol Singer's Handbook, 1993; O Praise God, 1994; O Holy Night, 1994; The Light of the World, 1995; The Easter Singer's Handbook, 1995. *Recreations:* visiting ancient monuments, 18th Century music research. *Address:* c/o Music International, 13 Ardilaun Road, N5 2QR. *T:* 0171–359 5813.

JENKINS, Sir Owain (Trevor), Kt 1958; *b* 1907; 5th *s* of late Sir John Lewis Jenkins, KCSI, ICS; *m* 1940, Sybil Léonie, *y d* of late Maj.-Gen. Lionel Herbert, CB, CVO. *Educ:* Charterhouse; Balliol Coll., Oxford. Employed by Balmer Lawrie & Co. Ltd, Calcutta, 1929; Indian Army, 1940–44; Man. Dir, Balmer Lawrie, 1948–58. Pres. of the Bengal Chamber of Commerce and Industry and Pres. of the Associated Chambers of Commerce of India, 1956–57. Formerly Director: Singapore Traction Co.; Calcutta Electric Supply Corp.; Macleod Russel PLC; retd 1982. Mem., Econ. Survey Mission to Basutoland, Bechuanaland Protectorate and Swaziland, 1959. *Publication:* Merchant Prince (memoirs), 1987. *Address:* Boles House, East Street, Petworth, West Sussex GU28 0AB. *Club:* Oriental.

JENKINS, Peter Redmond; HM Diplomatic Service; Minister-Counsellor and Consul General, Brasilia, 1992–95; *b* 2 March 1950; *s* of Denys Arthur Reali Jenkins and Monique Marie-Louise Jenkins; *m* 1990, Angelina Chee-Hung Yang; one *s* one *d*. *Educ:* Downside Sch.; Corpus Christi Coll., Cambridge (BA Hons, MA); Harvard Univ. (Harkness Fellow). Joined HM Diplomatic Service, 1973: FCO, 1973–75; UK Mission to Internat. Orgns, Vienna, 1975–78; FCO, 1978–82; Private Sec. to HM Ambassador, Washington, 1982–84; FCO, 1984–87; Paris, 1987–91. *Address:* c/o Foreign and Commonwealth Office, King Charles Street, SW1A 2AH. *Club:* Brooks's.

JENKINS, Peter White; management consultant; *b* 12 Oct. 1937; *s* of John White Jenkins, OBE, and Dorothy Jenkins; *m* 1961, Joyce Christine Muter; one *s* one *d*. *Educ:* Queen Mary's Grammar Sch., Walsall; King Edward VI Grammar Sch., Nuneaton. CIPFA. Local govt service in Finance Depts at Coventry, Preston, Chester, Wolverhampton; Dep. Treasurer, Birkenhead, 1969–73; County Treasurer, Merseyside CC, 1973–84; Dir. of Finance, Welsh Water Authority, 1984–87. *Recreations:* walking, gardening, reading. *Address:* 9 Camden Crescent, Brecon, Powys LD3 7BY.

JENKINS, Richard Peter Vellacott; His Honour Judge Richard Jenkins; a Circuit Judge, since 1989; Nominated Care Judge, 1994; *b* 10 May 1943; *s* of late Gwynne Jenkins and of Irene Lilian Jenkins; *m* 1975, Agnes Anna Margaret Mullan; one *s* one *d*. *Educ:* Edge Grove School, Aldenham; Radley College; Trinity Hall, Cambridge (MA). Called to the Bar, Inner Temple, 1966; Midland Circuit, 1968–72; Midland and Oxford Circuit, 1972–89 (Remembrancer and Asst Treasurer, 1984–89); a Recorder, 1988–89. *Address:* Hall Barn, Far End, Boothby Graffoe, Lincoln LN5 0LG. *Clubs:* MCC, London Welsh Rugby Football.

JENKINS, Robin; *see* Jenkins, J. R.

JENKINS, Simon David; columnist, The Times, since 1992 (Editor, 1990–92); *b* 10 June 1943; *s* of Dr Daniel Jenkins and Nell Jenkins; *m* 1978, Gayle Hunnicutt; one *s* and one step *s*. *Educ:* Mill Hill Sch.; St John's Coll., Oxford (BA Hons). Country Life magazine, 1965; Research Asst, Univ. of London Inst. of Educn, 1966; News Editor, Times Educational Supplement, 1966–68; Evening Standard, 1968–74; Insight Editor, Sunday Times, 1974–75; Dep. Editor, Evening Standard, 1976, Editor, 1976–78; Political Editor, The Economist, 1979–86; The Sunday Times: columnist, 1986–90; editor, Books Section, 1988–89. Member: British Railways Bd, 1979–90 (Chm., BR Environment Panel, 1984–90); LRT Bd, 1984–86; South Bank Bd, 1985–90; Calcutt Cttee on Privacy, 1989–90; Grade Cttee on Fear of Crime, 1989. Chm., Commn for Local Democracy, 1994–95. Director: Municipal Journal Ltd, 1980–90; Faber & Faber, 1980–90. Mem. Council, Bow Group, and Editor of Crossbow, 1968–70; Member: Cttee Save Britain's Heritage, 1976–85; Historic Buildings and Monuments Commn, 1985–90 (Dep. Chm., 1988–90); Millennium Commn, 1994–; Mem. Council: Inst. of Contemporary Arts, 1976–85; Old Vic Co., 1979–81; Dep. Chm., Thirties Soc., 1979–85; Founder and Dir, Railway Heritage Trust, 1985–90; Trustee, World Monuments Fund, 1995–. Governor: Mus. of London, 1985–87; Wycombe Abbey Sch., 1985–90; Bryanston Sch., 1986–. What The Papers Say Journalist of the Year, 1988. *Publications:* A City at Risk, 1971; Landlords to London, 1974; (ed) Insight on Portugal, 1975; Newspapers: the power and the money, 1979; The Companion Guide to Outer London, 1981; (with Max Hastings) The Battle for the Falklands, 1983; Images of Hampstead, 1983; (with Anne Sloman) With Respect Ambassador, 1985; The Market for Glory, 1986; The Times Guide to English Style and Usage, 1992; The Selling of Mary Davies, 1993; Against the Grain, 1994. *Recreation:* walking. *Address:* c/o The Times, Pennington Street, E1 9XN. *Club:* Garrick.
See also K. M. Jenkins.

JENKINS, Stanley Kenneth; HM Diplomatic Service, retired; *b* 25 Nov. 1920; *s* of Benjamin and Ethel Jane Jenkins; *m* 1957, Barbara Mary Marshall Webb; four *d*. *Educ:* Brecon; Cardiff Tech. Coll. President, Nat. Union of Students, 1949–51. LIOB 1950. Served War, Royal Artillery and Royal Engineers, 1942–46, retiring as Major. Joined Foreign (later Diplomatic) Service, 1951; Singapore, 1953; Kuala Lumpur, 1955; FO, 1957; Singapore, 1959; Rangoon, 1959; FO, 1964; Nicosia, 1967; FO, 1970–78, Counsellor. Chm., Ferring Sports and Leisure Assoc., 1988–. *Recreations:* gardening, tennis. *Address:* Willow Cottage, 1 Beehive Lane, Ferring, Worthing, W Sussex BN12 5NL. *T:* Worthing (01903) 247356. *Club:* Commonwealth Trust.

JENKINS, Very Rev. Thomas Edward; *b* 14 Aug. 1902; *s* of late David Jenkins, Canon of St David's Cathedral and Vicar of Abergwili, and of Florence Helena Jenkins; *m* 1928, Annie Laura, *d* of late David Henry, Penygroes, Carms; one *s*. *Educ:* Llandyssul Grammar Sch.; St David's Coll., Lampeter; Wycliffe Hall, Oxford. St David's Coll., Lampeter, BA 1922, BD 1932, Powys Exhibitioner, 1924; Welsh Church Scholar, 1921. Ordained, 1925; Curate of Llanelly, 1925–34; Rector of Begelly, 1934–38; Vicar: Christ Church, Llanelly, 1938–46; Lampeter, 1946–55 (Rural Dean, 1949–54); Canon, St David's Cathedral, 1951–57; Vicar of Cardigan, 1955–57; Dean of St David's, 1957–72. *Address:* 18 North Road, Cardigan, Dyfed SA43 1AA.

JENKINS, Thomas Harris, (Tom), CBE 1981; General Secretary, Transport Salaried Staffs' Association, 1977–82; *b* 29 Aug. 1920; *s* of David Samuel Jenkins and Miriam Hughes (*née* Harris); *m* 1946, Joyce Smith; two *d*. *Educ:* Port Talbot Central Boys' Sch.; Port Talbot County Sch.; Shrewsbury Technical Coll. (evenings); Pitmans Coll., London (evenings). MCIT 1980. Served War, RAMC, 1941–46 (Certif. for Good Service, Army, Western Comd, 1946). Railway clerk, 1937–41; railway/docks clerk, 1946–49. Full-time service with Railway Clerks' Assoc., subseq. re-named Transport Salaried Staffs' Assoc., 1949–82: Southern Reg. Divl Sec., 1959; Western Reg. Divl Sec., 1963; LMR Divl Sec., 1966; Sen. Asst Sec., 1968; Asst Gen. Sec., 1970, also Dep. to Gen. Sec., 1973. Member: Cttee of Transport Workers in European Community, 1976–82; Transport Industry, Nationalised Industries, and Hotel and Catering Industry Cttees of TUC, 1977–82; Management and Indus. Relns Cttee, SSRC, 1979–81; Air Transport and Travel Industry Trng Bd, 1976–82; Hotel and Catering Industry Trng Bd, 1978–82; Employment Appeal Tribunal, 1982–91; British Railways Midland and NW Reg. Bd, 1982–86; Police Complaints Bd, 1983–85; Central Arbitration Cttee, 1983–90; ACAS Arbitration Bd, 1983–90. Mem. Labour Party, 1946–; Mem., Lab. Party Transport Sub-Cttee, 1970–82. *Recreations:* watching cricket, athletics and Rugby football. *Address:* 23 The Chase, Edgware, Mddx HA8 5DW. *T:* 0181–952 5314. *Clubs:* MCC, Middlesex County Cricket.
See also D. C. Jenkins.

JENKINS, Vivian Evan, MBE 1945; Director of Social Services, Cardiff City Council, 1971–74, retired; *b* 12 Sept. 1918; *s* of late Arthur Evan Jenkins and late Mrs Blodwen Jenkins; *m* 1946, Megan Myfanwy Evans; one *s* one *d*. *Educ:* UC Cardiff (BA). Dipl. Social Science. Army, 1940; commnd Royal Signals, 1943; served with 6th Airborne Div. as parachutist, Europe, Far East and Middle East, 1943–46 (Lieut). Child Care Officer, Glamorgan CC, 1949; Asst Children's Officer, 1951; Mem. Home Office Children's Dept Inspectorate, 1952. *Recreations:* Rugby football (former Captain of Univ. XV and Pontypridd RFC; awarded two Wales Rugby caps as schoolboy, 1933 and 1937); cricket, golf. *Address:* 24 Windsor Road, Radyr, Cardiff CF4 8BQ. *T:* Radyr (01222) 842485. *Club:* Radyr Golf.

JENKINSON, Dr David Stewart, FRS 1991; Lawes Trust Fellow, Rothamsted Experimental Station, since 1988; Visiting Professor, University of Reading, since 1992; *b* 25 Feb. 1928; *s* of Hugh McLoughlin Jenkinson and Isabel Frances (*née* Glass); *m* 1958, Moira O'Brien; three *s* one *d*. *Educ:* Armagh Royal Sch.; Trinity Coll., Dublin (BA 1950; BSc 1950; PhD 1954). MRSC 1955. Asst Lectr, Univ. of Reading, 1955–57; on scientific staff, Rothamsted Exptl Station, 1957–88. Hannaford Res. Fellow, Univ. of Adelaide, 1976–77; Vis. Scientist, CSIRO, 1977. Lectures: Hannaford, Univ. of Adelaide, 1977; Distinguished Scholars, QUB, 1989; Univ. of Kent, 1992; Massey Ferguson Nat. Agricl Award, 1993. *Publications:* Nitrogen Efficiency in Agricultural Soils, 1988; numerous papers in jls of soil science, soil biochemistry and agronomy. *Recreations:* Irish history and literature, low input gardening. *Address:* 15 Topstreet Way, Harpenden, Herts AL5 5TU. *T:* Harpenden (01582) 715744.

JENKINSON, Jeffrey Charles, MVO 1977; Chief Executive, Harwich Haven Authority, since 1992; *b* 22 Aug. 1939; *s* of late John Jenkinson and Olive May Jenkinson; *m* 1962, Janet Ann (*née* Jarrett); one *s* two *d*. *Educ:* Royal Liberty Sch., Romford; City of London Coll. MCIT, MBIM. National Service, RN, 1957–59. Port of London Authority: Port operations and gen. management, 1959–71; British Transport Staff Coll., 1972; PLA Sec., 1972–81; Dir of Admin, 1982–86; Bd Mem., 1982–92; Chief Exec., Property, 1987–92; Dir, Placon Ltd and other PLA gp subsid. cos, 1978–92. Dir, E London Small Business Centre Ltd, 1977–92; Mem. Bd, Globe Centre Ltd, 1992–. Chm., NRA Essex Catchment Panel, 1994–. Member: Bd, and Council, London Chamber of Commerce and Industry, 1989–92; Council, British Ports Assoc., 1993–; Chm., Thames Riparian Housing Assoc., 1986–92; Member: Newham CHC, 1974–80; Committee of Management: Seamen's Gp of Hosps, 1972–74; Seamen's Hosp. Soc., 1974–. Freeman, City of London, 1975; Mem. Ct, Co. of Watermen and Lightermen of River Thames, 1990–. *Recreations:* sailing, walking, music. *Address:* Harwich Haven Authority, Harbour House, The Quay, Harwich, Essex CO12 3HH. *T:* Harwich (01255) 243030.

JENKINSON, Sir John (Banks), 14th Bt *cr* 1661; *b* 16 Feb. 1945; *o s* of Sir Anthony Banks Jenkinson, 13th Bt and of Frances, *d* of Harry Stremmel; *S* father, 1989; *m* 1979, Josephine Mary Marshall-Andrew; one *s* one *d*. *Educ:* Eton; Univ. of Miami. *Heir: s* George Samuel Anthony Banks Jenkinson, *b* 8 Nov. 1980.

JENKS, Sir (Maurice Arthur) Brian, 3rd Bt *cr* 1932, of Cheape in the City of London; chartered accountant in sole practice; *b* 28 Oct. 1933; *er s* of Sir Richard Atherley Jenks, 2nd Bt and of Marjorie Suzanne Arlette Jenks, *d* of Sir Arthur du Cros, 1st Bt; *S* father, 1993; *m* 1962, Susan Lois Allen; one *d* and one adopted *s*. *Educ:* Charterhouse. FCA. Qualified chartered accountant, 1956; Partner, Touche Ross & Co., 1979–93. Mem. Ct of Assts, Haberdashers' Co., 1961– (Master 1988–89 and 1992–93). Chm. of Governors, Haberdashers' Sch., 1994–. *Publication:* Small Businesses: how to survive and succeed, 1989. *Recreations:* wine, racing, gardening. *Heir: b* Richard John Peter Jenks [*b* 18 July 1936; *m* 1963, Juniper Li-Yung, *e d* of Tan Sri Y. C. Foo; one *s* two *d*]. *Address:* Warren House, Savernake, Marlborough, Wilts SN8 3BQ. *T:* Marlborough (01672) 870442.

JENKYNS, Henry Leigh; Under-Secretary, Department of the Environment, 1969–75; *b* 20 Jan. 1917; *y s* of H. H. Jenkyns, Indian Civil Service; *m* 1947, Rosalind Mary Home; two *s* one *d*. *Educ:* Eton and Balliol Coll., Oxford. War Service in Royal Signals; Lt-Col, East Africa Command, 1944. Treasury, 1945–66; Private Sec. to Chancellor, 1951–53. Treasury Representative in Australia and New Zealand, 1953–56; UK Delegation to OECD, Paris, 1961–63; Asst Under-Sec. of State, DEA, 1966–69; Chm., SE Economic Planning Bd, 1968–71. Mem., Southwark Diocesan Adv. Cttee for Care of Churches, 1977–78. Mem., Exmoor Study Team, 1977. *Recreations:* music, garden, sailing, mending things. *Address:* Westcroft, Priors Hill Road, Aldeburgh, Suffolk IP15 5EP. *T:* Aldeburgh (01728) 452357.

JENNER, Ann Maureen; Director, National Theater Ballet School, Melbourne, since 1988 (Associate Director, 1987); Guest Ballet Teacher, since 1980: Victorian College of the Arts, Melbourne; Australian Ballet; Queensland Ballet; and many other schools in Sydney and Melbourne; *b* 8 March 1944; *d* of Kenneth George Jenner and Margaret Rosetta (*née* Wilson); *m* 1980, Dale Robert Baker; one *s*. *Educ:* Royal Ballet Junior and Senior Schools. Royal Ballet Co., 1961–78: Soloist 1964; Principal Dancer 1970. Australian Ballet, 1978–80. Roles include: Lise, Fille Mal Gardée, 1966; Swanhilda, Coppelia, 1968; Cinderella, 1969; Princess Aurora, Sleeping Beauty, 1972; Giselle, 1973; Gypsy, Deux Pigeons, 1974; White Girl, Deux Pigeons, 1976; Juliet, Romeo and Juliet, 1977; Countess Larisch, Mayerling, 1978; Flavia, Spartacus, 1979; Kitri, Don Quixote, 1979; Anna, Anna Karenina, 1980; Poll, Pineapple Poll, 1980; one-act roles include: Symphonic Variations, 1967; Firebird, 1972; Triad, 1973; Les Sylphides; Serenade; Les Patineurs; Elite Syncopations, Concert, Flower Festival Pas de Deux, etc. Guest Teacher, San Francisco Ballet Co. and San Francisco Ballet Sch., 1985. *Address:* National Theater Ballet School, corner of Carlisle and Barkly Street, St Kilda, Melbourne, Vic 3182, Australia.

JENNER, Prof. Peter George, PhD, DSc; FRPharmS; Professor of Pharmacology and Head of Department, King's College London, since 1989; *b* 6 July 1946; *s* of late George Edwin Jenner and Edith (*née* Hallett); *m* 1973, Katherine Mary Philomena Snell; one *s*. *Educ:* Chelsea Coll., London Univ. (BPharm Hons 1967; PhD 1970; DSc 1987). FRPharmS 1994. Post-grad. Fellow, Dept of Pharmacy, Chelsea Coll., London, 1970–72; Lectr in Biochem., 1972–78, Sen. Lectr, 1978–85, Dept of Neurol., Inst. of Psychiatry, Univ. of London, 1972–78; Reader in Neurochem. Pharmacol., Inst. of Psychiatry and KCH Med. Sch., 1985–89; Hon. Sen. Lectr, Inst. of Neurol., 1988–. Dir, Exptl Res. Labs, Parkinson's Disease Soc., 1988–; Co-Dir, Neurodegenerative Diseases Res. Centre, 1993–. Parkinson's Disease Society: Mem. Council, 1993–; Mem., Med. Adv. Panel, 1993–. Mem., Molecular and Cellular Pharmacol. Gp Cttee, Biochem. Soc., 1993. Mem., Bd of Mgt, Inst. of Epileptology, KCL, 1994–. *Publications:* (with B. Testa) Drug Metabolism: chemical and biochemical aspects, 1976; (ed with B. Testa) Concepts in Drug Metabolism, Part A 1980, Part B 1981; (ed jtly) Approaches to the Use of Bromocriptine in Parkinson's Disease, 1985; (ed jtly) Neurological Disorders, 1987; (ed) Neurotoxins and their Pharmacological Implications, 1987; (ed jtly) Disorders of Movement, 1989; contrib. Lancet, Jl Neurochem., Annals Neurol., Biochem. Pharmacol., Brain Res., Psychopharmacol., Neuroscience. *Recreations:* gardening, driving. *Address:* Neurodegenerative Diseases Research Centre, Pharmacology Group, King's College London, Manresa Road, SW3 6LX. *T:* 0171–333 4716.

JENNETT, Frederick Stuart, CBE 1985; consultant architect and town planner in own firm, since 1990; *b* 22 April 1924; *s* of Horace Frederick Jennett and Jenny Sophia Jennett; *m* 1948, Nada Eusebia Phillips; two *d*. *Educ:* Whitchurch Grammar School; Welsh School of Architecture, UWIST (Dip. in Architecture (dist.)). FRIBA, MRTPI, FRSA. T. Alwyn Lloyd & Gordon, Architects, Cardiff, 1949; Cwmbran Develt Corp., 1951; Louis de Soissons Peacock Hodges & Robinson, Welwyn Garden City, 1955; S. Colwyn Foukes & Partners, Colwyn Bay, 1956; Associate, 1962, Partner, 1964, Sir Percy Thomas & Son, Bristol; Chm. and Sen. Partner, Percy Thomas Partnership, 1971–89; Consultant to Studio BAAD, architects, Hebden Bridge, 1990–93. Experience ranges over new town neighbourhood planning, public housing and private houses; ecclesiastical, university and hospital projects in the UK and overseas, and refurbishment of historic/listed buildings. *Publications:* papers on hospital planning. *Recreations:* running, water colour painting, hill walking. *Address:* Portland Lodge, Lower Almondsbury, Bristol BS12 4EJ. *T:* Almondsbury (01454) 615175. *Clubs:* Reform, Royal Over-Seas League.

JENNETT, Prof. (William) Bryan, CBE 1992; FRCS; Professor of Neurosurgery, University of Glasgow, 1968–91, now Emeritus (Dean of the Faculty of Medicine, 1981–86); *b* 1 March 1926; *s* of Robert William Jennett and Jessie Pate Loudon; *m* 1950, Sheila Mary Pope; three *s* one *d*. *Educ:* Univ. of Liverpool (MB ChB 1949, MD 1960). House Physician to Lord Cohen of Birkenhead, 1949; Ho. Surg. to Sir Hugh Cairns, 1950; Surgical Specialist, RAMC, 1951–53; Registrar in Neurosurgery, Oxford and Cardiff, 1954–56; Lectr in Neurosurgery, Univ. of Manchester, 1957–62; Rockefeller Travelling Fellow, Univ. of California, LA, 1958–59; Cons. Neurosurgeon, Glasgow, 1963–68. Member: MRC, 1979–83; GMC, 1984–91; Chief Scientists' Cttee, 1983–; Inst. of Med. Ethics, 1986–. Mem. Ct, Univ. of Glasgow, 1988–91. Rock Carling Fellow, London, 1983. *Publications:* Epilepsy after Blunt Head Injury, 1962, 2nd edn 1975; Introduction to Neurosurgery, 1964, 4th edn 1983; (with G. Teasdale) Management of Head Injuries, 1981; High Technology Medicine: benefits and burdens, 1984, 2nd edn 1986; many papers in Lancet, BMJ and elsewhere. *Recreations:* cruising under sail, writing. *Address:* 83 Hughenden Lane, Glasgow G12 9XN. *T:* 0141–334 5148. *Club:* Royal Society of Medicine.

JENNINGS, Audrey Mary; Metropolitan Stipendiary Magistrate, since 1972; *b* 22 June 1928; *d* of Hugh and late Olive Jennings, Ashbrook Range, Sunderland; *m* 1961, Roger

Harry Kilbourne Frisby, *qv* (marr. diss. 1980); two *s* one *d*. *Educ:* Durham High Sch.; Durham Univ. (BA); Oxford Univ. (DPA). Children's Officer, City and County of Cambridge, 1952–56. Called to Bar, Middle Temple, 1956 (Harmsworth Schol.); practised at Criminal Bar, London, 1956–61 and 1967–72. Mem., Criminal Law Revision Cttee, 1977–. Occasional opera critic, Musical Opinion. *Recreations:* theatre, music, gardening, writing short stories.

JENNINGS, Ven. David Willfred Michael; Archdeacon of Southend, since 1992; *b* 13 July 1944; *s* of late Rev. Willfred Jennings and Nona Jennings (*née* de Winton); *m* 1969, Sarah Catherine Fynn, *d* of Dr Robert Fynn of Harare, Zimbabwe; three *s*. *Educ:* Radley Coll.; King's Coll., London (AKC 1966). Ordained deacon, 1967, priest, 1968; Assistant Curate: St Mary, Walton on the Hill, Liverpool, 1967–69; Christchurch Priory, Christchurch, Hants, 1969–73; Vicar: Hythe, Southampton, 1973–80; St Edward's, Romford, 1980–92. Rural Dean of Havering, 1985–92. Non-residentiary Canon, Chelmsford Cathedral, 1987–92. *Recreation:* exploring the buildings of the British Isles. *Address:* 136 Broomfield Road, Chelmsford CM1 1RN. *T:* Chelmsford (01245) 258257.

JENNINGS, Elizabeth (Joan), CBE 1992; author; *b* 18 July 1926; *d* of Dr H. C. Jennings, Oxon. *Educ:* Oxford High Sch.; St Anne's Coll., Oxford. Asst at Oxford City Library, 1950–58; Reader for Chatto & Windus Ltd, 1958–60. *Publications: poetry:* Poems (Arts Council Prize), 1953; A Way of Looking, 1955 (Somerset Maugham Award, 1956); A Sense of the World, 1958; (ed) The Batsford Book of Children's Verse, 1958; Song for a Birth or a Death, 1961; a translation of Michelangelo's sonnets, 1961; Recoveries, 1964; The Mind Has Mountains, 1966 (Richard Hillary Prize, 1966); The Secret Brother (for children), 1966; Collected Poems, 1967; The Animals' Arrival, 1969 (Arts Council Bursary, 1969); (ed) A Choice of Christina Rossetti's Verse, 1970; Lucidities, 1970; Relationships, 1972; Growing Points, 1975; Consequently I Rejoice, 1977; After the Ark (for children), 1978; Selected Poems, 1980; Moments of Grace, 1980; (ed) The Batsford Book of Religious Verse, 1981; Celebrations and Elegies, 1982; In Praise of Our Lady (anthology), 1982; Extending the Territory, 1985; (contrib.) A Quintet (for children), 1985; Collected Poems, 1953–86, 1986 (W. H. Smith Award, 1987); Tributes, 1989; Times and Seasons, 1992; Familiar Spirits, 1994; *prose:* Let's Have Some Poetry, 1960; Every Changing Shape, 1961; Robert Frost, 1964; Christianity and Poetry, 1965; Seven Men of Vision, 1976; also poems and articles in: New Statesman, New Yorker, Botteghe Oscure, Observer, Spectator, Listener, Vogue, The Independent, etc. *Recreations:* travel, looking at pictures, the theatre, the cinema, music, collecting, conversation. *Address:* c/o David Higham Associates Ltd, 5–8 Lower John Street, W1R 4HA. *Club:* Society of Authors.

JENNINGS, James, JP; Convener, Strathclyde Regional Council, 1986–90; *b* 18 Feb. 1925; *s* of late Mark Jennings and Janet McGrath; *m* 1st, 1943, Margaret Cook Barclay (decd); three *s* two *d*; 2nd, 1974, Margaret Mary Hughes, JP; two *d*. *Educ:* St Palladius School, Dalry; St Michael's College, Irvine. In steel industry, 1946–79. Member: Ayr County Council, 1958; Strathclyde Regional Council, 1974–March 1996 (Vice-Convener, 1982–86); Chairman: Ayr CC Police and Law Cttee, 1964–70; Ayrshire Jt Police Cttee, 1970–75; N Ayrshire Crime Prevention Panel, 1970–82; Police and Fire Cttee, Strathclyde Regl Council, 1978–82, 1990–96. Convention of Scottish Local Authorities: Rep. for Strathclyde, 1974–96; Chm., Protective Services Cttee, 1977–82; Mem., Exec. Policy Cttee, 1982–96. Chm., Official Side, Police Negotiating Bd, 1986–88, 1992–94 (Vice-Chm., 1984–86). Chm., Garnock Valley Develt Exec., 1988–. Contested (Lab) Perth and East Perthshire, 1966. Hon. Sheriff, Kilmarnock, 1991–. Vice-Pres., St Andrew's Ambulance Assoc., Patron, Assoc. of Youth Clubs in Strathclyde, Hon. President. Scottish Retirement Council, Princess Louise Scottish Hosp. (Erskine Hosp.), Hon. Vice-President. SNO Chorus; Royal British Legion Scotland (Dalry and District Branch). JP Cunninghame, 1969 (Chm., Cunninghame Justices Cttee, 1974–). *Recreation:* local community involvement. *Address:* 4 Place View, Kilbirnie, Ayrshire KA25 6BG. *T:* Kilbirnie (01505) 3339. *Clubs:* Royal Scottish Automobile (Glasgow); Garnock Labour (Chairman).

JENNINGS, John Southwood, CBE 1985; PhD; FRSE; Chairman, Shell Transport and Trading Company plc, since 1993; Vice Chairman, Committee of Managing Directors, Royal Dutch/Shell Group of Companies, since 1993; *b* 30 March 1937; *s* of George Southwood Jennings and Irene Beatrice Jennings; *m* 1961, Gloria Ann Griffiths; one *s* one *d*. *Educ:* Oldbury Grammar Sch.; Univ. of Birmingham (BSc Hons Geology, 1958); Univ. of Edinburgh (PhD Geology, 1961); London Business Sch. (Sloan Fellow, 1970–71). Various posts, Royal Dutch/Shell Group, 1962–, including: Gen. Man. and Chief Rep., Shell cos in Turkey, 1976–78; Man. Dir, Shell UK Exploration and Prodn, 1979–84; Exploration and Prodn Co-ordinator, Shell Internationale Petroleum Mij., The Hague, 1985–90; Man. Dir, Royal Dutch/Shell Gp of Cos, 1987–. Vice Chm., Governing Body, London Business Sch., 1993– (Mem., 1992–); Vice Pres., Liverpool Sch. of Tropical Medicine, 1991–; Mem. Council, RIIA, 1994–. FRSE 1992. Hon. FGS 1992. Hon. DSc Edinburgh, 1991. Commandeur de l'Ordre National du Mérite (Gabon), 1989. *Recreations:* fly fishing, shooting, travel. *Address:* c/o Shell Centre, SE1 7NA. *T:* 0171–934 5554. *Clubs:* Brooks's, Flyfishers'.

JENNINGS, Very Rev. Kenneth Neal; Dean of Gloucester, since 1983; *b* 8 Nov. 1930; *s* of Reginald Tinsley and Edith Dora Jennings; *m* 1972, Wendy Margaret Stallworthy; one *s* one *d*. *Educ:* Hertford Grammar School; Corpus Christi College, Cambridge (MA); Cuddesdon College, Oxford. Asst Curate, Holy Trinity, Ramsgate, 1956–59; Lecturer 1959–61, Vice-Principal 1961–66, Bishop's College, Calcutta; Vice-Principal, Cuddesdon Theological Coll., 1967–73; Vicar of Hitchin, 1973–76; Team Rector of Hitchin, 1977–82. *Recreations:* music, fell-walking. *Address:* The Deanery, Miller's Green, Gloucester GL1 2BP. *T:* Gloucester (01452) 524167.

JENNINGS, Percival Henry, CBE 1953; *b* 8 Dec. 1903; *s* of late Rev. Canon H. R. Jennings; *m* 1934, Margaret Katharine Musgrave, *d* of late Brig.-Gen. H. S. Rogers, CMG, DSO; three *d*. *Educ:* Christ's Hospital. Asst Auditor, N Rhodesia, 1927; Asst Auditor, Mauritius, 1931; Auditor, British Honduras, 1934; Dep. Dir of Audit, Gold Coast, 1938; Dep. Dir of Audit, Nigeria, 1945; Dir of Audit, Hong Kong, 1948; Dep. Dir-Gen. of the Overseas Audit Service, 1955; Dir-Gen. of the Overseas Audit Service, 1960–63, retd. *Recreation:* golf. *Address:* Littlewood, Lelant, St Ives, Cornwall TR26 3JU. *T:* Hayle (01736) 753407. *Clubs:* Commonwealth Trust, Royal Over-Seas League.

JENNINGS, Peter; educational and interfaith consultant; *b* 9 Oct. 1937; *s* of Robert William Jennings and Margaret Irene Jennings; *m* 1963, Cynthia Margaret Leicester; two *s*. *Educ:* Manchester Grammar Sch.; Keble Coll., Oxford (MA); Hartley Victoria Methodist Theological Coll.; Manchester Univ. (MA). Ordained 1965. Minister: Swansea Methodist Circuit, 1963–67; London Mission (East) Circuit, 1967–78, and Tutor Warden, Social Studies Centre, 1967–74; Gen. Sec., Council of Christians and Jews, 1974–81; Associate Minister, Wesley's Chapel, 1978–81; Asst Minister, Walthamstow and Chingford Methodist Circuit, 1981–82; Superintendent Minister: Whitechapel Mission, 1982–91; Barking and Ilford Methodist Circuit, 1991–93. *Publications:* papers and articles on aspects of Christian-Jewish relations. *Recreations:* photography, being educated by Tim and Nick. *Address:* 49 The Coverdales, Barking, Essex IG11 7JY. *T* and *Fax:* 0181–507 3988.

JENNINGS, Peter Nevile Wake; Serjeant at Arms, House of Commons, since 1995; *b* 19 Aug. 1934; *s* of late Comdr A. E. de B. Jennings, RN and Mrs V. Jennings, MBE; *m* 1958, Shirley Anne, *d* of late Captain B. J. Fisher, DSO, RN and Mrs C. C. Fisher; one *s* two *d*. *Educ:* Marlborough College; psc (m)†, osc (US). Commissioned 2/Lt, RM, 1952; retired as Major, 1976. Appointed to staff of House of Commons, 1976; Dep. Serjeant at Arms, 1982–95. *Address:* House of Commons, SW1A 0AA.

JENNINGS, Sir Robert (Yewdall), Kt 1982; QC 1969; MA, LLB Cantab; a Judge, 1982–95, and President, 1991–94, the International Court of Justice; *b* 19 Oct. 1913; *o s* of Arthur Jennings; *m* 1955, Christine, *yr d* of Bernard Bennett; one *s* two *d*. *Educ:* Belle Vue Grammar Sch., Bradford; Downing Coll., Cambridge (scholar; 1st cl. pts I & II Law Tripos; LLB; Hon. Fellow, 1982). Served War, Intelligence Corps, 1940–46; Hon. Major, Officers' AER. Called to the Bar, Lincoln's Inn, 1943 (Hon. Bencher, 1970). Whewell Scholar in Internat. Law, Cambridge, 1936; Joseph Hodges Choate Fellow, Harvard Univ., 1936–37; Asst Lectr in Law, LSE, 1938–39; Jesus College, Cambridge: Fellow, 1939, Hon. Fellow, 1982; Sen. Tutor, 1949–55; Sometime Pres. Whewell Prof. of Internat. Law, Cambridge Univ., 1955–81; Reader in Internat. Law, Council of Legal Educn, 1959–70. Member: Permanent Court of Arbitration, 1982–; Inst. of Internat. Law, 1967– (Vice-Pres., 1979; Pres., 1981–83; Hon. Mem., 1985–); Hon. Mem., Indian Soc. of Internat. Law; Hon. Life Mem., Amer. Soc. of Internat. Law (Manley O. Hudson Medal, 1993). Hon. LLD: Hull, 1987; Cantab, 1993; Leicester, 1995; Hon. Dr jur: Saarland, W Germany, 1988; La Sapienza, Rome, 1990. Joint Editor: International and Comparative Law Quarterly, 1956–61; British Year Book of International Law, 1960–82. *Publications:* The Acquisition of Territory, 1963; General Course on International Law, 1967; articles in legal periodicals. *Address:* Jesus College, Cambridge CB5 8BL. *T:* Cambridge (01223) 62611. *Clubs:* United Oxford & Cambridge University; Haagsche (The Hague).

JEPHCOTT, Sir (John) Anthony, 2nd Bt *cr* 1962; *b* 21 May 1924; *s* of Sir Harry Jephcott, 1st Bt, and Doris (*d* 1985), *d* of Henry Gregory; *S* father, 1978; *m* 1st, 1949, Sylvia Mary, *d* of Thorsten Frederick Relling, Wellington, NZ; two *d*; 2nd, 1978, Josephine Agnes Sheridan. *Educ:* Aldenham; St John's Coll., Oxford; London School of Economics (BCom). Served with REME and RAEC, 1944–47. Director, Longworth Scientific Instrument Co. Ltd, 1946; Managing Director and Chairman, 1952–73; Managing Director and Chairman, Pen Medic Ltd (NZ), 1973–78. Hon. FFARACS 1990. *Publications:* A History of Longworth Scientific Instrument Co. Ltd, 1988; correspondence in Anaesthesia (UK), and Anaesthesia and Intensive Care (Australia). *Recreations:* gardening, photography. *Heir:* *b* Neil Welbourn Jephcott [*b* 3 June 1929; *m* 1st, 1951, Mary Denise (*d* 1977), *d* of Arthur Muddiman; two *s* one *d*; 2nd, 1978, Mary Florence Daly]. *Address:* 26 Sage Road, Kohimarama, Auckland 5, New Zealand.

JEREMIAH, Melvyn Gwynne, CB 1994; Special Adviser to Government of Republic of Namibia; *b* 10 March 1939; *s* of Bryn Jeremiah and Evelyn (*née* Rogers); *m* 1960, Lilian Clare (*née* Bailey) (marr. diss. 1966). *Educ:* Abertillery County Sch. Apptd to Home Office, 1958; HM Customs and Excise, 1963–75; Cabinet Office, 1975–76; Treasury, 1976–79; Principal Finance Officer (Under Sec.), Welsh Office, 1979–87; Under Sec., DHSS, later DoH, 1987–95; Chief Exec., Disablement Services Authy, 1987–91, on secondment from DoH. Sec., Assoc. of First Div. Civil Servants, 1967–70. *Recreation:* genealogy. *Club:* Reform.

JEROME, Hon. James Alexander; PC (Can.) 1981; **Hon. Mr Justice Jerome;** Associate Chief Justice, Federal Court of Canada, since 1980; lawyer, since 1958; *b* Kingston, Ont., 4 March 1933; *s* of Joseph Leonard Jerome and Phyllis Devlin; *m* 1958, Barry Karen Hodgins; three *s* two *d*. *Educ:* Our Lady of Perpetual Help Sch., Toronto; St Michael's Coll. High Sch., Toronto; Univ. of Toronto; Osgoode Hall. Alderman, Sudbury, Ont., 1966–67. MP, Sudbury, 1968–80; Parly Sec. to President of Privy Council, 1970–74; Speaker of the House of Commons, 1974–80. QC (Can.) 1976. Pres., Commonwealth Parly Assoc., 1976. *Recreations:* golf, piano. *Address:* 1051 Cahill Drive W, Ottawa, Ontario K1V 9J1, Canada. *T:* (613) 7372118.

JERSEY, 9th Earl of, *cr* 1697; **George Francis Child Villiers;** Viscount Grandison (of Limerick), 1620; Viscount Villiers (of Dartford), and Baron Villiers (of Hoo), 1691; *b* 15 Feb. 1910; *e s* of 8th Earl and Lady Cynthia Almina Constance Mary Needham (who *m* 2nd, 1925, W. R. Slessor (*d* 1945); she died 1947), *o d* of 3rd Earl of Kilmorey; *S* father, 1923; *m* 1st, 1932, Patricia Kenneth (who obtained a divorce, 1937; she *m* 2nd, 1937, Robin Filmer Wilson, who *d* 1944; 3rd, 1953, Col Peter Laycock, who *d* 1977; 4th, 1987, Roderick More O'Ferrall, who *d* 1990), *o d* of Kenneth Richards, Cootamundra, NSW, and of late Eileen Mary (who *m* later Sir Stephenson Kent, KCB); one *d*; 2nd, 1937, Virginia (who obtained a divorce, 1946), *d* of James Cherrill, USA; 3rd, 1947, Bianca Maria Adriana Luciana, *er d* of late Enrico Mottironi, Turin, Italy; one *s* one *d* (and one *s* decd). *Heir:* *s* Viscount Villiers, *qv*. *Address:* Radier Manor, Le Chemin du Radier, Grouville, Jersey, Channel Islands JE3 9DR. *T:* Jersey (01534) 853102.

JERUSALEM AND THE MIDDLE EAST, President Bishop of; *see* Kafity, Rt Rev. Samir.

JERVIS, family name of **Viscount St Vincent.**

JERVIS, Charles Elliott, OBE 1966; Editor-in-Chief, Press Association, 1954–65; *b* Liverpool, 7 Nov. 1907; *y s* of late J. H. Jervis, Liverpool; *m* 1931, Ethel Braithwaite (*d* 1979), Kendal, Westmorland; one *d*. Editorial Asst, Liverpool Express, 1921–23; Reporter, Westmorland Gazette, 1923–28; Dramatic Critic and Asst Editor, Croydon Times, 1928–37; Sub-Editor, Press Assoc., 1937–47; Asst Editor, 1947–54. Pres., Guild of British Newspaper Editors, 1964–65; Mem. of the Press Council, 1960–65. *Address:* The Old Vicarage, Allithwaite, Grange-over-Sands, Cumbria LA11 7QN.

JERVIS, Roger P.; *see* Parker-Jervis.

JERVIS, Simon Swynfen, FSA; Historic Buildings Secretary, National Trust, since 1995; *b* 9 Jan. 1943; *s* of late John Swynfen Jervis and Diana (*née* Marriott); *m* 1969, Fionnuala MacMahon; one *s* one *d*. *Educ:* Downside Sch.; Corpus Christi Coll., Cambridge (schol.) Student Asst, Asst Keeper of Art, Leicester Mus. and Art Gall., 1964–66; Department of Furniture, Victoria and Albert Museum: Asst Keeper, 1966–75; Dep. Keeper, 1975–89; Actg Keeper, 1989; Curator, 1989–90; Dir, Fitzwilliam Mus., Cambridge, 1990–95. Guest Schol., J. Paul Getty Mus., 1988–89; Chm., Nat. Trust Arts Panel, 1987–95. Dir, Burlington Magazine, 1993–. Editor, Furniture History, 1987–92. Trustee, Royal Collection Trust, 1993–. FSA 1983 (Pres., 1995–). FRSA 1990. *Publications:* Victorian Furniture, 1968; Printed Furniture Designs Before 1650, 1974; High Victorian Design, 1983; Penguin Dictionary of Design and Designers, 1984; many articles in learned jls. *Address:* c/o National Trust, 36 Queen Anne's Gate, SW1H 9AS. *T:* 0171–222 9251.

JESSEL, Sir Charles (John), 3rd Bt *cr* 1883; farmer; nutrition consultant, since 1987; *b* 29 Dec. 1924; *s* of Sir George Jessel, 2nd Bt, MC, and Muriel (*d* 1948), *d* of Col J. W. Chaplin, VC; *S* father, 1977; *m* 1st, 1956, Shirley Cornelia (*d* 1977), *o d* of John Waters, Northampton; two *s* one *d*; 2nd, 1979, Gwendolyn Mary (marr. diss. 1983), *d* of late

Laurance Devereux, OBE, and *widow* of Charles Langer, MA. *Educ:* Eton; Balliol College, Oxford; Northants Inst. of Agric., Moulton, 1952 (Dip with distinction). Served War of 1939–45, Lieut 15/19th Hussars (despatches). Chm., Ashford Br., NFU, 1963–64; Mem., Exec. Cttee, Kent Br., NFU, 1960–73; Mem., Canterbury Farmers' Club (Chm. 1972); Pres., Kent Br., Men of the Trees, 1979–85. Life Vice Pres., British Soc. of Dowsers, 1994 (Pres., 1987–93). Gov., Inst of Optimum Nutrition, 1994–. Life Mem., Internat. Dendrology Soc.; Mem., Inst. of Allergy Therapists, 1990–. Hon. Fellow, Psionic Med. Soc., 1977. Dip., Inst. of Optimum Nutrition, 1987. JP Kent 1960–78. *Publication:* (ed) An Anthology of Inner Silence, 1990. *Recreations:* gardening, planting trees. *Heir: s* George Elphinstone Jessel [*b* 15 Dec. 1957; *m* 1988, Rose (marr. diss. 1993), *yr d* of James Coutts-Smith]. *Address:* South Hill Farm, Hastingleigh, near Ashford, Kent TN25 5HL. *T:* Elmsted (01233) 750325. *Club:* Cavalry and Guards.

JESSEL, Oliver Richard; Chairman of numerous companies in the Jessel Group, since 1954; *b* 24 Aug. 1929; *s* of late Comdr R. F. Jessel, DSO, OBE, DSC, RN; *m* 1950, Gloria Rosalie Teresa (*née* Holden); one *s* five *d. Educ:* Rugby. Founded group of companies, 1954; opened office in City of London, 1960; Chm., London, Australian and General Exploration Co. Ltd., 1960–75; formed: New Issue Unit Trust and other trusts, 1962–68; Castle Communications, 1983; Standard Financial Holdings, 1987; responsible for numerous mergers, incl. Johnson & Firth Brown Ltd, and Maple Macowards Ltd; Chm., Charles Clifford Industries Ltd, 1978–81; reorganised Belvoir Petroleum Corp., 1987–89; Chm., Thomas Seager PLC, 1993–. *Address:* Sponden House, Sandhurst, Cranbrook, Kent TN18 5NR. *T:* Cranbrook (01580) 850366. *Club:* Garrick.

JESSEL, Dame Penelope, DBE 1987; International Officer, Liberal Party, 1985–88; *b* 2 Jan. 1920; *d* of Sir Basil Blackwell and late Marion Christine, *d* of John Soans; *m* 1940, Robert George Jessel (*d* 1954); two *s. Educ:* Dragon Sch., Oxford; St Leonard's, St Andrews, Fife; Somerville Coll., Oxford (MA). On staff of Oxford House, London, 1940–41; ATS, 1941–43; Lecturer: William Temple Coll., 1956–62; Plater Coll., Oxford, 1968–84. Pres., Women's Liberal Fedn, 1970–72. *Publication:* Owen of Uppingham, 1965. *Recreations:* looking at old churches, music, gardening, looking at gardens. *Address:* The Cottage, The Green, Cassington, Oxford OX8 1DW. *T:* Oxford (01865) 881322. *Club:* National Liberal.

JESSEL, Toby Francis Henry; MP (C) Twickenham since 1970; *b* 11 July 1934; *y s* of late Comdr R. F. Jessel, DSO, OBE, DSC, RN; *m* 1st, 1967 (marr. diss. 1973); one *d* decd; 2nd, 1980, Eira Gwen, *y d* of late Horace and Marigwen Heath. *Educ:* Royal Naval Coll., Dartmouth; Balliol Coll., Oxford (MA). Sub-Lt, RNVR, 1954. Conservative Candidate: Peckham, 1964; Hull (North), 1966. Parly delegate: to India and Pakistan, 1971; to India, 1982, 1992, 1994; to Belgium, 1994; Member: Council of Europe, 1976–93; WEU, 1976–93. Chm., South Area Bd GLC Planning and Transportation Cttee, 1968–70. (Co-opted) LCC Housing Cttee, 1961–65; Councillor, London Borough of Southwark, 1964–66; Mem. for Richmond-upon-Thames, GLC, 1967–73; Hon. Sec. Assoc. of Adopted Conservative Candidates, 1961–66; Chairman: Cons. Parly Arts and Heritage Cttee, 1983 (Vice-Chm., 1979); Anglo-Belgian Parly Gp, 1983; Indo-British Parly Gp, 1991– (Hon. Sec., 1972–87; Vice-Chm., 1987); Treas., Anglo-Chilean Parly Gp, 1991–93; Mem., Nat. Heritage Select Cttee, 1992–. Hon. Sec., Katyn Meml Fund, 1972–75. Mem. Metropolitan Water Bd, 1967–70; Mem., London Airport Consultative Cttee, 1967–70. Mem. Council, Fluoridation Soc., 1976–83. Dir, Warship Preservation Trust, 1994. Member: Exec. Cttee and Organizing Cttee, European Music Year, 1985; Council, Assoc. of British Orchestras, 1991–. Liveryman, Worshipful Co. of Musicians. Chevalier, Ordre de la Couronne (Belgium), 1980; Order of Polonia Restituta (Polish Govt in Exile); Order of Merit (Liechtenstein), 1979. *Recreations:* music (has performed Mozart, Beethoven and Schumann piano concertos; raised £30,000 for NSPCC, Nov. perf., 1993), gardening, croquet (Longworth Cup, Hurlingham, 1961), ski-ing. *Address:* Old Court House, Hampton Court, East Molesey, Surrey KT8 9BW. *Clubs:* Garrick, Hurlingham.

See also O. R. Jessel, J. H. Walford.

JESSOP, Alexander Smethurst; Sheriff of Grampian, Highland and Islands at Aberdeen, since 1990; *b* 17 May 1943; *s* of Thomas Alexander Jessop and Ethel Marion Jessop; *m* 1967, Joyce Isobel Duncan; two *s* one *d. Educ:* Montrose Acad.; Fettes Coll.; Aberdeen Univ. (MA, LLB). Solicitor in private practice, Montrose, 1966–76; Depute Procurator Fiscal, Perth, 1976–78; Asst Solicitor, Crown Office, 1978–80; Sen. Asst Procurator Fiscal, Glasgow, 1980–84; Regional Procurator Fiscal: Aberdeen, 1984–87; Glasgow, 1987–90. *Recreation:* sport. *Address:* (home) 79 Devonshire Road, Aberdeen AB1 6XP; Sheriff Court, Castle Street, Aberdeen AB9 1AP.

JEVONS, Prof. Frederic Raphael, AO 1986; Hon. Professorial Fellow, Department of Management, Monash University, Australia, since 1994; *b* 19 Sept. 1929; *s* of Fritz and Hedwig Bettelheim; *m* 1956, Grete Bradel; two *s. Educ:* Langley Sch., Norwich; King's Coll., Cambridge (Major Schol.). 1st Cl. Hons Nat. Scis Pt II (Biochem.) Cantab 1950; PhD Cantab 1953; DSc Manchester 1966. Postdoctoral Fellow, Univ. of Washington, Seattle, 1953–54; Fellow, King's Coll., Cambridge, 1953–59; Univ. Demonstrator in Biochem., Cambridge, 1956–59; Lectr in Biol Chem., Manchester Univ., 1959–66; Prof. of Liberal Studies in Science, Manchester Univ., 1966–75; Vice-Chancellor, Deakin Univ., Australia, 1976–85, subseq. Emeritus Prof.; consultant on distance educn in southern Africa, 1986–87; Prof. of Science and Technology Policy, Murdoch Univ., Australia, 1988–92. Simon Sen. Res. Fellow, Univ. of Manchester, 1992. Chairman: Gen. Studies Cttee, Schools Council, 1974–75; Grad. Careers Council of Aust., 1976–80; Policy Cttee, Victorian Technical and Further Educn Off-Campus Network, 1985–88; Member: Jt Matriculation Bd, Manchester, 1969–75; Jt Cttee, SRC and SSRC, 1974–75; Educn Res. and Develt Cttee, Aust., 1980–81; Council, Sci. Mus. of Vic., 1980–83; Council, Mus. of Vic., 1983–87; Aust. Vice-Chancellors' Exec. Cttee, 1981–82; Standing Cttee on External Studies, Commonwealth Tertiary Educn Commn, Canberra, 1985–87; Aust. Sci. and Technol. Council, 1986–89. Interviewer for Civil Service Commn on Final Selection Bds, 1970–75; Adviser to Leverhulme project on educnl objectives in applied science, Strathclyde Univ., 1972–75; British Council tours in India, E Africa, Nigeria, 1972–75. Mem., Editorial Advisory Boards: R and D Management, 1972–76; Studies in Science Educn, 1974–84; Scientometrics, 1978–; Australasian Studies in History and Philosophy of Science, 1980–86. Life Gov., Geelong Hosp., 1986. DUniv Open, 1985; Hon. DLitt Deakin, 1986; Hon. DSc Manchester, 1986. Inaugural winner, UNESCO prize for science and technology policy, 1992. *Publications:* The Biochemical Approach to Life, 1964, 2nd edn 1968 (trans. Italian, Spanish, Japanese, German); The Teaching of Science: education, science and society, 1969; (ed jtly) University Perspectives, 1970; (jtly) Wealth from Knowledge: studies of innovation in industry, 1972; (ed jtly) What Kinds of Graduates do we Need?, 1972; Science Observed: science as a social and intellectual activity, 1973; Knowledge and Power, 1976; numerous papers on biochem., history of science, science educn and science policy. *Recreations:* music, theatre, reading. *Address:* Department of Management, Monash University, Vic 3168, Australia.

JEWELL, David John, MA, MSc; Master of Haileybury and Imperial Service College, 1987–Aug. 1996; *b* 24 March 1934; *s* of late Wing Comdr John Jewell, OBE, FRAeS, and Rachel Jewell, Porthleven, Cornwall; *m* 1958, Katharine Frida Heller; one *s* three *d. Educ:* Blundell's Sch., Tiverton; St John's Coll., Oxford. Honours Sch. of Natural Science (Chemistry), BA 1957, MA 1961; BSc Physical Sciences, 1959, MSc 1981. National Service with RAF, 1952–54. Head of Science Dept, Eastbourne Coll., 1958–62; Winchester Coll., 1962–67; Dep. Head, Lawrence Weston Comprehensive Sch., Bristol, 1967–70; Head Master, Bristol Cathedral Sch., 1970–78; Headmaster, Repton Sch., 1979–87. Vis. Prof., Rollins Coll., Florida, 1987. Chairman: HMC, 1990 (Chairman: Direct Grant Sub-Cttee, 1977–78; Professional Develt Cttee, 1987–89); Choir Schools' Assoc., 1976–77. Gov., Truro Sch., 1990– (Vice-Chm., 1994–); Vice Chm., Blundell's Sch., 1994–. FRSA 1981. *Publications:* papers and articles in various scientific and educnl jls. *Recreations:* music, cricket, cooking, Cornwall. *Address:* (until Aug. 1996) The Master's Lodge, Haileybury, Hertford SG13 7NU. *T:* Hoddesdon (01992) 462352; Petros, Compton Martin, Bristol BS18 6JA. *T:* Mendip (01761) 221264. *Clubs:* East India, Devonshire, Sports and Public Schools, MCC; Bristol Savages.

JEWELL, Prof. Peter Arundel, PhD; CBiol, FIBiol; Mary Marshall and Arthur Walton Professor of Physiology of Reproduction, University of Cambridge, 1977–92, now Professor Emeritus; Fellow of St John's College, Cambridge, since 1977; *b* 16 June 1925; *s* of Percy Arundel Jewell and Ivy Dorothea Enness; *m* 1958, Juliet Clutton-Brock; three *d. Educ:* Wandsworth Sch.; Reading Univ. (BSc Agric.); Cambridge Univ. (BA, MA, PhD). Lectr, Royal Veterinary Coll., 1950–60; Research Fellow, Zoological Soc. of London, 1960–66; Prof. of Biological Sciences, Univ. of Nigeria, 1966–67; Sen. Lectr and Dir of Conservation Course, University Coll. London, 1967–72; Prof. of Zoology, Royal Holloway Coll., 1972–77. Pres., Mammal Soc., 1991–93; Vice-Pres., Rare Breeds Survival Trust, 1991–. *Publications:* The Experimental Earthwork on Overton Down, Wiltshire, 1960; Island Survivors: the Ecology of the Soay Sheep of St Kilda, 1974; Management of Locally Abundant Wild Mammals, 1981; scientific papers in Jl Animal Ecology, Jl Physiology, Jl Zoology, Ark, etc. *Recreations:* emulating Cornish ancestors, watching wild animals, saving rare breeds, life drawing, pottery, archaeology. *Address:* St John's College, Cambridge CB2 1TP.

JEWERS, William George, CBE 1982 (OBE 1976); Managing Director, Finance, and Member, British Gas plc (formerly British Gas Corporation), 1976–87; *b* 18 Oct. 1921; *s* of late William Jewers and Hilda Jewers (*née* Ellison); *m* 1955, Helena Florence Rimmer; one *s* one *d. Educ:* Liverpool Inst. High Sch. for Boys. Liverpool Gas Co., 1938–41. Served War: RAFVR Observer (Flying Officer), 1941–46: Indian Ocean, 265 Sqdn (Catalinas), 1943–44; Burma 194 Sqdn (Dakotas), 1945. Liverpool Gas Co./NW Gas Bd, Sen. Accountancy Asst, 1946–52; W Midlands Gas Bd: Cost Acct, Birmingham and Dist Div., 1953–62; Cost Acct, Area HQ, 1962–65; Asst Chief Acct, 1965–66; Chief Acct, 1967; Dir of Finance, 1968; Gas Council, Dir of Finance, 1969–73; British Gas Corp., Dir of Finance, 1973–76. FCMA, FCCA, JDipMA, CompIGasE. *Publications:* papers and articles to gas industry jls. *Recreations:* music, reading. *Address:* 17 South Park View, Gerrards Cross, Bucks SL9 8HN. *T:* Gerrards Cross (01753) 886169.

JEWKES, Sir Gordon (Wesley), KCMG 1990 (CMG 1980); HM Diplomatic Service, retired; Director: Slough Estates plc, since 1992; Walpole Committee, since 1992; *b* 18 Nov. 1931; *er s* of late Jesse Jewkes; *m* 1954, Joyce Lyons; two *s. Educ:* Barrow Grammar Sch.; Magnus Grammar Sch., Newark-on-Trent, and elsewhere. Colonial Office, 1948; commnd HM Forces, Army, 1950–52; Gen. Register Office, 1950–63; CS Pay Res. Unit, 1963–65; Gen. Register Office, 1965–68; transf. to HM Diplomatic Service, 1968; CO, later FCO, 1968–69; Consul (Commercial), Chicago, 1969–72; Dep. High Comr, Port of Spain, 1972–75; Head of Finance Dept, FCO, and Finance Officer of Diplomatic Service, 1975–79; Consul-General: Cleveland, 1979–82; Chicago, 1982–85; Gov., Falkland Is and High Comr, British Antarctic Territory, 1985–88; Dir-Gen. of Trade and Investment, USA, and Consul-Gen., NY, 1989–91. Dir, Hogg Group, 1992–94. *Recreations:* music, travel, walking. *Address:* 19 Furzefield Road, Beaconsfield, Bucks HP9 1PG. *T:* (01494) 681830. *Club:* Travellers'.

JEWSON, Richard Wilson; Chairman: Savills plc, since 1994; Ideal Harware plc, since 1994; Deputy Chairman, Anglian Water plc, since 1991; *b* 5 Aug. 1944; *s* of Charles Boardman and Joyce Marjorie Jewson; *m* 1965, Sarah Rosemary Spencer; one *s* three *d. Educ:* Rugby; Pembroke Coll., Cambridge (MA). Joined Jewson & Sons, 1965, Man. Dir, 1974–86; Meyer International: Dir, 1983–93; Group Man. Dir, 1986–91; Dep. Chm., 1990–91; Chm., 1991–93. Non-Executive Director: Eastern Counties Newspapers Group Ltd (formerly Eastern Daily Press), 1982–; Pro Share (UK), 1991–95; Delian Lloyds Investment Trust, 1993–; Queens Moat Houses, 1994–; Miller Insurance Group Ltd, 1995–. Mem., CBI London Region Cttee, 1986–93. CIMgt. *Recreations:* Real tennis, golf, gardening. *Address:* Dades Farm, Barnham Broom, Norfolk, NR9 4BT. *T:* Barnham Broom (01603) 759237, *Fax:* (01603) 759685. *Clubs:* Boodle's, Queen's; Royal West Norfolk Golf.

JHABVALA, Mrs Ruth Prawer; author; *b* in Germany, of Polish parents, 7 May 1927; *d* of Marcus Prawer and Eleonora Prawer (*née* Cohn); came to England as refugee, 1939; *m* 1951, C. S. H. Jhabvala; three *d. Educ:* Hendon County Sch.; Queen Mary Coll., London Univ. Started writing after graduation and marriage, alternating between novels and short stories; occasional original film-scripts (with James Ivory and Ismail Merchant), including: Shakespeare-wallah, 1965; The Guru, 1969; Bombay Talkie, 1971; Autobiography of a Princess, 1975; Roseland, 1977; Hullabaloo over Georgie and Bonnie's Pictures, 1978; The Europeans (based on Henry James' novel), 1979; Jane Austen in Manhattan, 1980; Quartet (based on Jean Rhys' novel), 1981; Heat and Dust (based on own novel), 1983; The Bostonians (based on Henry James' novel), 1984; A Room with a View (based on E. M. Forster's novel), 1986 (Academy Award, 1987); Mr and Mrs Bridge (based on Evan Connell's novels), 1991; Howards End (based on E. M. Forster's novel), 1992 (Academy Award, 1993); Remains of the Day (based on Kazuo Ishiguro's novel), 1993; Jefferson in Paris, 1995; film script (with John Schlesinger), Madame Sousatzka, 1988. *Publications: novels:* To Whom She Will, 1955; The Nature of Passion, 1956; Esmond in India, 1958; The Householder, 1960; Get Ready for Battle, 1962; A Backward Place, 1965; A New Dominion, 1973; Heat and Dust, 1975 (Booker Prize, 1975); In Search of Love and Beauty, 1983; Three Continents, 1987; Poet and Dancer, 1993; Shards of Memory, 1995; *short story collections:* Like Birds, like Fishes, 1964; A Stronger Climate, 1968; An Experience of India, 1971; How I became a Holy Mother and other Stories, 1976; Out of India: selected stories, 1986. *Recreation:* writing film-scripts. *Address:* 400 East 52nd Street, New York, NY 10022, USA.

See also Prof. S. S. Prawer.

JI Chaozhu; Under-Secretary General of the United Nations, since 1991; *b* Shanxi Province, 30 July 1929; *s* of Dr Chi Kung-Chuan, Commissioner of Education, and Chang Tao-Jan; *m* 1957, Wang Xiangtong; two *s. Educ:* Primary and secondary schools in Manhattan; Harvard Univ. (reading Chemistry); Tsinghua Univ. (graduated 1952). English stenographer at Panmunjom, Korea, for Chinese People's Volunteers, 1952–73; English interpreter for Chinese leaders, incl. Chairman Mao, Premier Chou En-Lai, 1954–73; Dep. Dir, Translation Dept, Foreign Ministry, 1970–73; Counsellor, Liaison Office, Washington DC, 1973–75; Dep. Dir, Dept of Internat. Organisations and Confs, Foreign

Min., 1975–79; Dep. Dir, Dept of American and Oceanic Affairs, Foreign Min., 1979–82; Minister-Counsellor, US Embassy, 1982–85; Ambassador to Fiji, Kiribati and Vanuatu, 1985–87; Ambassador to UK, 1987–91. *Recreations:* swimming, music. *Address:* United Nations, One UN Plaza, New York, NY 10017, USA.

JILANI, Asaf; journalist and broadcaster; Senior Producer, South Asia Region (formerly Eastern) Service, BBC World Service, 1988–94; *b* 24 Sept. 1934; *s* of Abdul Wahid Sindhi and Noor Fatima Jilani; *m* 1961, Mohsina Jilani; two *s* one *d*. *Educ:* Jamia Millia, Delhi; Sindh Madrasa, Karachi; Karachi Univ. (BA, Economics and Persian). Sub-Editor, Daily Imroze, Karachi (Progressive Papers Ltd), 1952; Political Corresp., Daily Imroze, 1954; Special Corresp., Daily Jang, Karachi (posted in India), 1959–65; held prisoner in Delhi during India/Pakistan War, 1965; London Editor: Daily Jang (Karachi, Rawalpindi, Quetta); Daily News, Karachi, and Akhbar-Jehan, Karachi, 1965–73; Editor, Daily Jang, London (first Urdu Daily in UK), 1973–82. Iqbal Medal (Pakistan), for journalistic contribution to exposition of Islamic poetic philosopher Dr Mohammed Iqbal, during his centenary celebrations, 1979. *Publication:* Wast Asia, Nai Azadi Nay Challenge (Central Asian Journey, in Urdu; based on 21 prog. series for BBC World Service), 1994. *Recreations:* cricket, swimming, painting. *Address:* 23 Horsham Avenue, N12 9BG. *T:* 0181–368 5697.

JILLINGS, Godfrey Frank; Director, Financial Services Initiative, Welsh Development Agency, since 1994; *b* 24 May 1940; *s* of late Gerald Frank Jillings and of Dorothy Marjorie Jillings; *m* 1967, Moira Elizabeth McCoy (*d* 1986); one *s*. *Educ:* Tiffin's Sch., Kingston; Inst. of Personnel Management. DMS; ACIB. S. G. Warburg & Co. Ltd, 1956–58; National Westminster Bank Ltd, 1958–90: Head of Industrial Section, 1983; Sen. Project Manager, 1985–86; Director: County Unit Trust Managers Ltd, 1986–87; Natwest Stockbrokers Ltd, 1986–89; Chief Exec., Natwest Personal Financial Management Ltd, 1987–89; Senior Exec., Group Chief Exec's Office, 1989–90; Chief Exec., FIMBRA, 1990–94. A Dep. Chief Exec., PIA, 1992–94. Chm., John Gater Holdings Ltd; Dir, DBS Management plc, 1994–. *Recreations:* travel, chess. *Address:* 6 Worcester Gardens, Worcester Park, Surrey KT4 7HN. *T:* 0181–337 8481. *Club:* Athenæum.

JIMÉNEZ DE ARÉCHAGA, Eduardo, DrJur; President, Court of Arbitration for the Delimitation of Maritime areas between Canada and France, since 1989; Professor of International Law, Montevideo Law School, since 1946; *b* Montevideo, 8 June 1918; *s* of E. Jiménez de Aréchaga and Ester Sienra; *m* 1943, Marta Ferreira; three *s* two *d*. *Educ:* Sch. of Law, Univ. of Montevideo. Under-Sec., Foreign Relations, 1950–52; Sec., Council of Govt of Uruguay, 1952–55; Mem., Internat. Law Commn of UN, 1961–69 (Pres., 1963); Cttee *Rapporteur*, Vienna Conf. on Law Treaties, 1968–69; Minister of the Interior, Uruguay, 1968; Pres. of the International Ct of Justice, The Hague, 1976–79 (Judge of the Ct, 1970–79). Mem., World Bank Admin. Tribunal, 1990– (Pres., 1981–90). *Publications:* Reconocimiento de Gobiernos, 1946; Voting and Handling of Disputes in the Security Council, 1951; Derecho Constitucional de las Naciónes Unidas, 1958; Curso de Derecho Internacional Público, 2 vols, 1959–61; International Law in the Past Third of a Century, vol. I, 1978; Derecho Internacional Contemporáneo, 1980. *Address:* Casilla de Correo 539, Montevideo, Uruguay.

JINKINSON, Alan Raymond; General Secretary, UNISON, since 1993; *b* 27 Feb. 1935; *s* of Raymond and Maggie Jinkinson; *m* 1968, Madeleine Gillian Douglas (*d* 1995). *Educ:* King Edward VII Sch., Sheffield; Keble Coll., Oxford (BA Hons). National and Local Government Officers' Association: Education Dept, 1960; District Officer, 1967; District Orgn Officer, 1973; National Officer (Local Govt), 1976; Asst Gen. Sec., 1981; Dep. Gen. Sec., 1983; Gen. Sec., 1990. *Recreations:* cinema, jogging, walking. *Address:* UNISON, 1 Mabledon Place, WC1H 9AJ. *T:* 0171–388 2366.

JIRIČNA, Eva Magdalena, CBE 1994; RDI 1991; architect; Principal of own practice, since 1984; *b* 3 March 1939; *d* of Josef Jiričny and Eva Jirična; *m* 1963, Martin Holub (marr. diss. 1973). *Educ:* Coll. of Architecture and Town Planners, Univ. of Prague (Engr Architect 1962); Acad. of Fine Arts, Prague (Acad. Architect 1967). Professional practice and management examination, RIBA, 1973. Main projects include: Harrods Way-In; Vidal Sassoon Salons, Germany; Joseph Shops, Brompton Cross and Sloane Street; offices for Fafalios Ltd, London; Retail System for Vitra International; Joan & David Inc. Shops, NY; 5th floor conversion of Bergdorf Goodman, NY. Hon. FRCA 1989. *Address:* 7 Dering Street, W1R 9AB. *T:* 0171–629 7077.

JOACHIM, Rev. Dr Margaret Jane; Senior Relationship Manager (Insurance), EDS (Electronic Data Systems) Ltd, since 1994; *b* 25 June 1949; *d* of late Reginald Carpenter and Joyce Margaret Carpenter; *m* 1970, Paul Joseph Joachim; one *d*. *Educ:* Brighton and Hove High School; St Hugh's College, Oxford (MA Geology); Univ. of Birmingham (PhD Geology), Southern Dioceses Ministerial Trng Scheme. FRES 1983; FGS 1991. Grammar school teacher, 1971–76; post-doctoral research Fellow, Univ. of Birmingham, 1976–79; computer consultant, 1979–84; Futures Database Manager, Rudolf Wolff & Co., 1984–87; Manager, UK Insurance Services, 1988–91, Leadership and Professional Develt Instr, 1991–93, EDS (Electronic Data Systems) Ltd. Training Officer, Liberal Parly Assoc., 1979–84; Mem., Exec. Cttee, Women's Liberal Fedn, 1984–85; Vice-Chair, Fawcett Soc., 1993–95 (Chair, 1984–87; Mem. Exec. Cttee, 1990–); Trustee, Fawcett Trust, 1995–; Chair, internat. working gp to set up EEC Women's Lobby, 1988–90; Chair, 1989–90, Vice-Chair, 1990–92, WLD (formerly SLD Women's Orgn). Co-ordinator, Women into Public Life Campaign, 1987–88; Vice-Chair, 1989, Mem. Exec. Cttee, 1989–91, 300 Gp. Contested: (L) West Gloucestershire, 1979; (L/Alliance) Finchley, 1983; (L/Alliance) Epsom and Ewell, 1987. Ordained deacon, 1994, priest, 1995; non-stipendiary Asst Curate, St Barnabas, Ealing. Mem., Exec. Cttee, Nat. Traction Engine Club, 1976–79; Founder, Steam Apprentice Club, 1978; Founder, Oxford Univ. Gilbert and Sullivan Soc., 1968. *Publications:* papers in: Studies in the Late-Glacial of North-West Europe, 1980; Holocene Palaeoecology and Palaeohydrology, 1986. *Recreations:* walking, sailing, reading, going to traction engine rallies, making jam. *Address:* 8 Newburgh Road, W3 6DQ. *T:* 0181–723 4514. *Club:* Reform.

JOB, Rev. (Evan) Roger (Gould); Canon Residentiary, Precentor and Sacrist, 1979–94, Vice Dean, 1991–94, Winchester Cathedral; *b* 15 May 1936; 2nd *s* of late Thomas Brian and Elsie Maud Job, Ipswich; *m* 1964, Rose Constance Mary, *o d* of late Stanley E. and Audrey H. Gordon, Hooton, Wirral; two *s*. *Educ:* Cathedral Choir School and King's Sch., Canterbury; Magdalen Coll., Oxford; Cuddesdon Theol Coll. BA 1960, MA 1964; ARCM 1955. Deacon 1962, priest 1963. Asst Curate, Liverpool Parish Church, 1962–65; Vicar of St John, New Springs, Wigan, 1965–70; Precentor of Manchester Cath., 1970–74; Precentor and Sacrist of Westminster Abbey, 1974–79; Chaplain of The Dorchester, 1976–79. Select Preacher, Univ. of Oxford, 1974, 1991. *Recreations:* gardening, piano. *Address:* Kitwood Farm, Ropley, Alresford, Hants SO24 0DB.

JOB, Peter James Denton; Chief Executive, Reuters Holdings, since 1991; *b* 13 July 1941; *s* of Frederick Job and Marion Job (*née* Pickard); *m* 1966, Christine Cobley; one *s* one *d*. *Educ:* Clifton College; Exeter College, Oxford (BA). Trainee Reuter journalist, 1963; posts in Buenos Aires, Hong Kong, Kuala Lumpur, London, New Delhi, Paris; Alternate Dir to Man. Dir, Reuters Holdings, 1988; Man. Dir, Reuters Asia, based in Hong Kong, 1988–91; Dir, Reuters Holdings, 1989–; Chm., Visnews Ltd, 1991–92. Non-exec. Dir, Grand Metropolitan PLC. *Recreations:* water sports, golf, tennis, music, theatre, shooting. *Address:* Reuters Holdings, 85 Fleet Street, EC4P 4AJ. *T:* 0171–250 1122. *Club:* Hong Kong (Hong Kong).

JOBERT, Michel; Officier de la Légion d'Honneur; Croix de Guerre (1939–45); politician, writer and lawyer; Founder and Leader, Mouvement des Démocrates, since 1974; *b* Meknès, Morocco, 11 Sept. 1921; *s* of Jules Jobert and Yvonne Babule; *m* Muriel Frances Green; one *s*. *Educ:* Lycées of Rabat and Meknès; Dip. de l'Ecole libre des sciences politiques; Ecole nationale d'Administration. Cour des comptes: Auditor, 1949; Conseiller Référendaire, 1953. Member of Ministerial Cabinets: Finance, Labour and Social Security, President of the Council, 1952–56; Director of the Cabinet of the High Commr of the Republic in French West Africa, 1956–58; Dir of Cabinet of Minister of State, 1959–61; Jt Dir, 1963–66, then Director, 1966–68, of the Prime Minister's Cabinet (Georges Pompidou); Pres., Council of Admin of Nat. Office of Forests, 1966–73; Administrator of Havas, 1968–73; Secretary-Gen., Presidency of the Republic, 1969–73; Minister for Foreign Affairs, 1973–74; Minister of State and Minister for Overseas Trade, 1981–83. Conseiller-maître, Cour des comptes, 1971– (Hon. Conseiller-maître, 1986). Arbitrator, Nat. Cttee, Internat. Chamber of Commerce, 1991. Former Board Member: SOFIRRAD, Radio Monte-Carlo; French Radio and TV Organisation. Editor, La Lettre de Michel Jobert, 1974–84; Editorialiste, Paris ce Soir, Jan.–Feb. 1985. Prix de la Langue de France, 1989. *Publications:* Mémoires d'avenir, 1974; L'autre regard, 1976; Lettre ouverte aux femmes politiques, 1976; Parler aux Français, 1977; La vie d'Hella Schuster (novel), 1977; Maroc: extrême Maghreb du soleil couchant, 1978; La rivière aux grenades, 1982; Chroniques du Midi Libre, 1982; Vive l'Europe Libre, 1984; Par Trente-six chemins, 1984; Maghreb, à l'ombre de ses mains, 1985; Les Américains, 1987; Journal immédiat . . . et pour une petite éternité, 1987; Vandales!, 1990; Journal du Golfe, 1991; Ni dieu ni diable, 1993; Chroniques de l'Espérance, 1988–1992: horizons mediterranées, 1993. *Address:* (home) 21 quai Alphonse-Le Gallo, 92100 Boulogne-sur-Seine, France; (office) 108 quai Louis Blériot, 75016 Paris, France.

JOBLING, Captain James Hobson, RN; Metropolitan Stipendiary Magistrate, 1973–87; *b* 29 Sept. 1921; *s* of late Captain and Mrs J. S. Jobling, North Shields, Northumberland; *m* 1946, Cynthia, *o d* of late F. E. V. Lean, Beacon Park, Plymouth; one *s* one *d*. *Educ:* Tynemouth High Sch.; London Univ. (LLB Hons, 1971). Entered Royal Navy, 1940; HMS Furious, 1941; HMS Victorious, 1941–45; awarded Gedge Medal and Prize, 1946; called to Bar, Inner Temple, 1955; Comdr, 1960; JSSC course, 1961–62; Dir, Nat. Liaison, SACLANT HQ, USA, 1962–65; Chief Naval Judge Advocate, in rank of Captain, 1969–72; retd, 1973. Planning Inspector, DoE, 1973; a Dep. Circuit Judge, 1976–82. *Recreations:* gardening, walking. *Address:* Pinewell Lodge, Wood Road, Hindhead, Surrey GU26 6PT. *T:* Hindhead (01428) 604426.

JOBSON, Roy; Chief Education Officer, Manchester Local Education Authority, since 1988; *b* 2 June 1947; *s* of James Jobson and Miriam H. Jobson; *m* 1971, Maureen Scott; one *s* two *d*. *Educ:* Bedlington Grammar Sch.; Univ. of Durham; Newcastle and Sunderland Polytechnics. King's Sch., Tynemouth, 1970–73; Norham High Sch., 1973–74; E Midland Regional Examining Bd, 1974–80; Gateshead Metropolitan Borough Council, 1980–84; Manchester City Council, 1984–. Adviser, AMA, 1993–. Member: Jt Council for GCSE, 1989–93; NEAB, 1992–93; Soc. of Educn Officers, 1988–. FRSA 1994. *Recreations:* children, family, church, music, Louis the Bassett Hound. *Address:* 34 Old Broadway, Didsbury, Manchester M20 9DF. *T:* 0161–234 7001.

JOCELYN, family name of **Earl of Roden.**

JOCELYN, Viscount; Shane Robert Henning Jocelyn; *b* 9 Dec. 1989; *s* and *heir* of Earl of Roden, *qv*.

JOCELYN, Dr Henry David, FBA 1982; Hulme Professor of Latin, University of Manchester, since 1973; *b* 22 Aug. 1933; *s* of late John Daniel Jocelyn and Phyllis Irene Burton; *m* 1958, Margaret Jill, *d* of Bert James Morton and Dulcie Marie Adams; two *s*. *Educ:* Canterbury Boys' High Sch.; Univ. of Sydney (BA); St John's Coll., Univ. of Cambridge (MA, PhD). Teaching Fellow in Latin, Univ. of Sydney, 1955; Cooper Travelling Scholar in Classics, 1955–57; Scholar in Classics, British Sch. at Rome, 1957–59; Univ. of Sydney: Lectr in Latin, 1960–64; Sen. Lectr in Latin, 1964–66; Reader in Latin, 1966–70; Prof. of Latin, 1970–73. Visiting Lectr in Classics, Yale Univ., 1967; Vis. Fellow, ANU, 1979; British Acad. Leverhulme Vis. Prof., *Thesaurus Linguae Latinae*, Munich, 1983; Vis. Lectr in Classics, Univ. of Cape Town, 1985; Visiting Professor: Univ. of Fribourg, 1990; Univ. of Catania, 1994. Corresp. Fellow, Accademia Properziana del Subasio, 1985. FAHA 1970. Member: Editorial Bd, Cambridge Classical Texts and Commentaries, 1982–; Adv. Bd, *Res Publica Litterarum*, 1992–; Scientific Cttee, *Sileno*, 1994–. Hon. DLitt Sydney, 1995. *Publications:* The Tragedies of Ennius, 1967 (corr. reprint 1969); (with B. P. Setchell) Regnier de Graaf on the Human Reproductive Organs, 1972; Philology and Education, 1988; (ed jtly) Studies in Latin Literature and its Tradition, 1989; (ed jtly) F. R. D. Goodyear: papers on Latin Literature, 1992; (ed) Tria Lustra: papers in honour of J. Pinsent, 1993; papers on Greek and Latin subjects in various periodicals. *Address:* 4 Clayton Avenue, Manchester M20 6BN. *T:* 0161–434 1526.

JOEL, Hon. Sir Asher (Alexander), KBE 1974 (OBE 1956); AO 1986; Kt 1971; Member of Legislative Council of New South Wales, 1957–78; Company Director and Public Relations Consultant; *b* 4 May 1912; *s* of Harry and Phoebe Joel, London and Sydney; *m* 1st, 1937 (marr. diss. 1948); two *s*; 2nd, 1949, Sybil, *d* of Frederick Mitchell Jacobs; one *s* one *d*. *Educ:* Enmore Public Sch.; Cleveland Street High Sch., Sydney. Served War of 1939–45: AIF, 1942, transf. RAN; Lieut RANVR, 1943; RAN PRO staff Gen. MacArthur, 1944–45, New Guinea, Halmaheras, Philippines. Chairman: Asher Joel Media Gp; Carpentaria Newspapers Pty Ltd; Nat. Pres., Anzac Mem. Forest in Israel; Dir, Royal North Shore Hosp. of Sydney, 1959–81. Mem., Sydney Cttee (Hon. Dir, 1956–64); Hon. Dir and Organiser, Pageant of Nationhood (State welcome to the Queen), 1963; Exec. Mem., Citizens Welcoming Cttee visit Pres. Johnson, 1966; Chm., Citizens Cttee Captain Cook Bi-Centenary Celebrations, 1970; Dep. Chm., Citizens Welcoming Cttee visit Pope Paul VI to Australia, 1970; Chm., Sydney Opera Hse Official Opening Citizens Cttee, 1972; Dep. Chm., Aust. Govt Adv. Commn on US Bi-Centenary Celebrations, 1976; Mem., Nat. Australia Day Cttee. Mem., Sydney Opera Hse Trust, 1969–79; Chm., Sydney Entertainment Centre, 1979–84. Chm. Emeritus, Organising Cttee 1988 Public Relations World Congress, 1985–88; Member: Adv. Council 31st IAA World Advertising Congress, 1984–88; Australia–US Coral Sea Commemorative Council, 1992. Life Mem., RSL, 1992. Gov., Sir David Martin Foundn, 1990–94 (Life Fellow, 1994). Fellow: Advertising Inst. of Austr. (Federal Patron); Public Relations Inst. of Austr.; FAIM; Foundn FAICD; FInstD; FRSA; Hon. Mem., Royal Australian Historical Soc., 1970. Hon. Fellow, Internat. Coll. of Dentists, 1975. Hon. DLitt Macquarie, 1988. Tel Aviv Univ. Presidential Citation, 1992; Archbishop of Sydney Citation, 1992. KSS 1994. US Bronze Star, 1943; Ancient Order of Sikatuna (Philippines), 1975; Kt Comdr, Order of Rizal (Philippines), 1978. *Publications:* Without Chains Free (novel), 1977; Australian Protocol and Procedures, 1982, 2nd edn 1988. *Recreations:* fishing, gardening, reading, writing. *Address:* 120 Clarence Street, Sydney, NSW 2000, Australia. *Clubs:* American, Journalists, Australasian Pioneers, Royal Agricultural Society (Sydney); Royal Sydney Yacht Squadron.

JOHANNESBURG, Bishop of, since 1986; **Rt. Rev. George Duncan Buchanan;** *b* 23 April 1935; *s* of Wyndam Kelsey Fraser Buchanan and Phyllis Rhoda Dale Buchanan (*née* Nichols); *m* 1959, Diana Margaret Dacombe; two *d*. *Educ:* St John's Coll., Johannesburg; Rhodes Univ., Grahamstown (BA 1957); Gen. Theological Seminary (MDiv 1959). Curate, St Paul's Church, Durban, 1960; Rector, Parish of Kingsway, Natal, 1961–65; Diocesan Theol Tutor, Dio. Natal, 1963–65; Sub Warden, St Paul's Theol Coll., Grahamstown, 1966–76, Warden, 1976–86; Dean, St Mary's Cathedral, Johannesburg, May–Sept. 1986; Archdeacon of Albany, Diocese of Grahamstown, 1975–86. Chairman: Church Unity Commn, 1989–; Theol Educn by Extension Coll., 1993–; SA Anglican Theol Commn, 1995–. Hon. DD General Theological Seminary, 1987. *Publication:* The Counselling of Jesus, 1985. *Recreations:* carpentry, hockey umpiring, reading. *Address:* PO Box 1131, Johannesburg 2000, South Africa; 4 Crescent Drive, Johannesburg 2193, South Africa. *T:* (office) (29) 8724, (home) (486) 1014.

JOHANSEN-BERG, Rev. John; Founder Member, since 1984, and Leader, since 1986, Community for Reconciliation; Moderator, Free Church Federal Council, 1987–88; Minister, Rubery United Reformed Church, since 1992; *b* 4 Nov. 1935; *s* of John Alfred and Caroline Johansen-Berg, Middlesbrough; *m* 1971, Joan, *d* of James and Sally Ann Parnham, Leeds; two *s* one *d*. *Educ:* Acklam Hall Grammar Sch., Middlesbrough; Leeds Univ. (BA Hons Eng. Lit., BD); Fitzwilliam Coll., Cambridge Univ. (BA Theol Tripos, MA); Westminster Theol Coll. (Dip. Theol.). Tutor, Westminster Coll., Cambridge, 1961; ordained, 1962; pastoral charges: St Ninian's Presbyterian Church, Luton, 1962–70 (Sec., Luton Council of Churches); Founder Minister, St Katherine of Genoa Church, Dunstable (dedicated 1968); The Rock Church Centre, Liverpool (Presbyterian, then United Reformed), 1970–77, work begun in old public house, converted into Queens Road Youth Club, new Church Centre dedicated 1972, a building designed for youth, community and church use; Minister, St Andrew's URC, Ealing, 1977–86. Convener, Church and Community Cttee of Presbyterian C of E, 1970–72; Chm. Church and Society Dept, URC, 1972–79; Moderator of the Gen. Assembly of the URC, 1980–81. British Council of Churches: Mem., Assembly, 1987–90; formerly Member: Div. of Internat. Affairs; Div. of Community Affairs; Chm. Gp on Violence, Non-violence and Social Change (for Britain Today and Tomorrow Programme, 1977); Convenor, Commission on Non-Violent Action (report published 1973); Mem., Forum of Churches Together in England, 1990–. Chm., Christian Fellowship Trust, 1981–87; Trustee, Nat. Assoc. of Christian Communities and Networks, 1989–; Mem., Exec., CCJ, 1989–; Mem. Council, Centre for Study of Judaism and Jewish Christian Relns, 1989–. Founder Mem. and Sponsor, Christian Concern for Southern Africa, 1972–94; Founder Sponsor, Clergy Against Nuclear Arms, 1982– (Chm., 1986–90); Founder: Romania Concern, 1990; Ecumenical Order of Ministry, 1990; Jt Leader, Ecumenical Festivals of Faith in: Putney and Roehampton, 1978; Stroud, 1980; Banstead, 1983; North Mymms, 1985; Guildford, 1986; Jesmond, 1987; Worth Abbey, 1988; Palmers Green, 1990; Poole, and Ballyholme, 1991; Finchley, 1992; South Wallasey, 1994. Jt Editor, Jl of Presbyterian Historical Soc. of England, 1964–70. *Publications:* Arian or Arminian? Presbyterian Continuity in the Eighteenth Century, 1969; Prayers of the Way, 1987 (rev. edn 1992); Prayers of Pilgrimage, 1988; Prayers of Prophecy, 1990; Prayers for Pilgrims, 1993. *Recreations:* mountain walking, badminton, drama. *Address:* Barnes Close, Chadwich Manor Estate, Bromsgrove, Worcs B61 0RA. *T:* Romsley (01562) 710231.

JOHANSON, Rev. Dr Brian; Minister of Christ Church, United Reformed Church, Tonbridge, 1987–94; *b* 8 March 1929; *s* of Bernard Johanson and Petra Johanson; *m* 1955, Marion Shirley Giles; one *s* two *d*. *Educ:* Univ. of South Africa (BA, DD); Univ. of London (BD). Parish Minister, S Africa, 1956–63; Sen. Lectr in Theology, 1964–69, Prof. of Theol., 1970–76, Univ. of SA; Minister of the City Temple, London, 1976–85; Dir of Ministerial Training, Presbyterian Church of Southern Africa, Johannesburg, 1985–86. Vis. Res. Fellow: Princeton Theol Seminary, 1970; Univ. of Aberdeen, 1976. *Publications:* univ. pubns in S Africa; booklets; essays in collections; articles in theol jls. *Address:* Treetops, 79 St Helens Wood Road, Hastings, E Sussex TN34 2QR.

JOHN, David Dilwyn, CBE 1961; TD; DSc; Director, National Museum of Wales, Cardiff, 1948–68; *b* 20 Nov. 1901; *e s* of Thomas John, St Bride's Major, Glam; *m* 1929, Marjorie, *d* of J. W. Page, HMI, Wellington, Salop; one *s* one *d*. *Educ:* Bridgend County Sch.; University Coll. of Wales, Aberystwyth. Zoologist on scientific staff, Discovery Investigations, engaged in oceanographical research in Antarctic waters, 1925–35; awarded Polar Medal. Appointed Asst Keeper in charge of Echinoderms at British Museum (Natural History), 1935; Deputy Keeper, 1948. Pres., Museums Assoc., 1964–65. Joined Territorial Army, 1936; promoted Major, RA, 1942. Pres., Cardiff Naturalists' Soc., 1952–53; Hon. Sec., Challenger Soc., 1946–48. Hon. LLD Univ. of Wales, 1969; Hon. Fellow, UC Cardiff, 1982. *Publications:* papers, chiefly on Echinoderms, in scientific journals. *Address:* 1 Gilfach Hill, Lampeter Velfrey, near Narberth, Dyfed SA67 8UL. *T:* Llanteg (0183483) 789.

JOHN, Elton Hercules, (Reginald Kenneth Dwight); musician, composer; *b* 25 March 1947; *s* of Stanley Dwight and Sheila (now Farebrother); *m* 1984, Renate Blauel. *Educ:* Pinner County Grammar Sch.; Royal Acad. of Music, London. Played piano in Northwood Hills Hotel, 1964; joined local group, Bluesology, 1965; signed to Dick James Music as writer and singer, 1967; visited America for concert and was overnight success, 1970; formed Elton John Band, 1970; regularly tours America, Europe, Australia and Japan; first internat. pop singer to perform in Russia, 1979. Vice-Pres. and Mem. Council, National Youth Theatre of GB, 1975–; Life Pres., Watford Football Club, 1990 (Dir, 1974; Chm., 1976–90); toured China with Watford Football Club, 1983. *Hit Records include: albums:* Empty Sky, 1969; Elton John, Tumbleweed Connection, 1970; Friends, 11.17.70, Madman Across the Water, 1971; Honky Chateau, 1972; Don't Shoot Me, Goodbye Yellow Brick Road, 1973; Caribou, Greatest Hits, 1974; Captain Fantastic, Rock of the Westies, 1975; Here and There, Blue Moves, 1976; Greatest Hits vol. II, 1977; A Single Man, 1978; Victim of Love, 1979; 21 at 33, Lady Samantha, 1980; The Fox, 1981; Jump Up, 1982; Too Low for Zero, 1983; Breaking Hearts, 1984; Ice on Fire, 1985; Leather Jackets, 1986; Live in Australia, 1987; Reg Strikes Back, 1988; Sleeping with the Past, 1989; Made in England, 1995; *singles:* Your Song, 1971; Rocket Man, Crocodile Rock, 1972; Daniel, Goodbye Yellow Brick Road, 1973; Candle in the Wind, Don't Let the Sun Go Down On Me, The Bitch is Back, Lucy in the Sky with Diamonds, 1974; Philadelphia Freedom, Someone Saved My Life Tonight, 1975; Don't Go Breaking My Heart, Sorry Seems to be the Hardest Word, 1976; Ego, Part Time Love, Song for Guy, 1978; Little Jeannie, 1980; Nobody Wins, 1981; Blue Eyes, Empty Garden, Princess, 1982; I Guess that's Why They Call It the Blues, 1983; Sad Songs (Say So Much), Passengers, Who Wears These Shoes, 1984; Breaking Hearts, Act of War, Nikita, Wrap Her Up, 1985; Cry to Heaven, Heartache all over the World, Slow Rivers, 1986; Your Song (live), Candle in the Wind (live), 1987; I Don't Wanna Go On With You Like That, 1988; Healing Hands, 1989; Sacrifice, 1989. *Films:* Goodbye to Norma Jean, 1973; To Russia with Elton, 1980; played Pinball Wizard, in Tommy, 1973. Recipient of gold discs for all albums; Ivor Novello Award, Best Pop Song, 1976–77, Best Instrumental, 1978–79. *Recreations:* include playing tennis. *Address:* c/o John Reid Enterprises, 32 Galena Road, W6 0LT. *T:* 0181–741 9933.

JOHN, Geoffrey Richards, CBE 1991; Chairman, Food From Britain, since 1993; *b* 25 March 1934; *s* of Reginald and Mabel John; *m* 1961, Christine Merritt; two *d*. *Educ:* Bromsgrove School, Worcs; University College Cardiff (BA 1st cl. Hons Econs). Flying Officer, RAF, 1955–57; Cadbury Schweppes, 1957–74; Man. Dir, Spillers Foods, 1974–80; Chief Exec., Foods Div., Dalgety-Spillers, 1980–82; Chm. and Chief Exec., Allied Bakeries, 1982–87; Chm., Dairy Crest, 1988–94; Director: Associated British Foods, 1982–87; Frizzell Gp, 1991–92; Morland & Co., 1993–. Mem., ARC, 1980–82; Chm., Meat and Livestock Commn, 1987–93. Dir, Hereford Hosps NHS Trust, 1994–. Governor, Bromsgrove School, 1965– (Chm., 1982–91; Pres., 1994–). *Recreations:* Rugby Football, music. *Address:* Food From Britain, 301/344 Market Towers, New Covent Garden, SW8 5NQ. *T:* 0171–720 2144. *Clubs:* Royal Air Force, Harlequin FC.

JOHN, Maldwyn Noel, FEng 1979, FIEE, FIEEE; Consultant, Kennedy & Donkin, since 1994 (Chairman, 1987–94); *b* 25 Dec. 1929; *s* of Thomas Daniel John and Beatrice May John; *m* 1953, Margaret Cannell; two *s*. *Educ:* University College Cardiff. BSc 1st Cl. Hons, Elec. Eng. Metropolitan Vickers Elec. Co. Ltd, Manchester, 1950–59; Atomic Energy Authy, Winfrith, 1959–63; AEI/GEC, Manchester, as Chief Engineer, Systems Dept, Chief Engineer, Transformer Div., and Manager, AC Transmission Div., 1963–69; Chief Elec. Engineer, 1969–72, Partner, 1972–86, Kennedy & Donkin. President: IEE, 1983–84; Convention of Nat. Socs of Engineering of Western Europe, 1983–84; Dir Bd, Nat. Inspection Council for Electrical Installation Contractors, 1988–91; Mem., Overseas Projects Bd, 1987–91. MConsE 1973. Freeman, City of London, 1987; Liveryman, Engineers' Co., 1987–. *Publications:* (jtly) Practical Diakoptics for Electrical Networks, 1969; (jtly) Power Circuit Breaker Theory and Design, 1st edn 1975, 2nd edn 1982; papers in IEE Procs. *Recreation:* golf. *Address:* 65 Orchard Drive, Horsell, Woking, Surrey GU21 4BS. *T:* Woking (01483) 773995.

JOHN, Sir Rupert (Godfrey), Kt 1971; Governor of St Vincent, 1970–76; Director, St Vincent Building and Loan Association, since 1977; Consultant to UNITAR, since 1978; *b* 19 May 1916; 2nd *s* of late Donelley John; *m* 1937, Hepsy (*d* 1988); three *s* one *d* (and one *s* decd). *Educ:* St Vincent Grammar Sch.; Univ. of London (BA, DipEd); Gray's Inn; New York University. First Asst Master, St Kitts/Nevis Grammar Sch., 1944; Asst Master, St Vincent Grammar Sch., 1944–52; private practice at Bar of St Vincent, 1952–58; Magistrate, Grenada, 1958–60; Actg Attorney-General, Grenada, 1960–62; Human Rights Officer, UN, 1962–69; Mem. Internat. Team of Observers, Nigeria, 1969–70; Senior Human Rights Officer, 1970. Has attended numerous internat. seminars and confs as officer of UN. President: Assoc. of Sen. Citizens of St Vincent and the Grenadines, 1981–; Caribbean Inst. for Promotion of Human Rights, 1987–88 (Human Rights Award, 1988). Mem., Barclays Bank Internat. Ltd Policy Adv. Cttee (St Vincent), 1977–86. Mem. Editorial Adv. Bd, Jl of Third World Legal Studies, 1981–. KStJ 1971. *Publications:* St Vincent and its Constitution, 1971; Pioneers in Nation-Building in a Caribbean Mini-State, 1979; Racism and its Elimination, 1980; papers in various jls. *Recreations:* cricket, walking, swimming. *Address:* PO Box 677, Cane Garden, St Vincent, West Indies. *T:* 61500. *Club:* Commonwealth Trust.

JOHN CHARLES, Rt. Rev. Brother; *see* Vockler, Rt. Rev. J. C.

JOHN PAUL II, His Holiness Pope, (Karol Jozef Wojtyla); *b* Wadowice, Poland, 18 May 1920; *s* of Karol Wojtyla. *Educ:* Jagiellonian Univ., Cracow; Pontificio Ateneo 'Angelicum' (Dr in Theology). Ordained Priest, 1946; Prof. of Moral Theology, Univs of Lublin and Cracow, 1954–58; titular Bishop of Ombi, and Auxiliary Bishop of Cracow, 1958; Vicar Capitular, 1962; Archbishop and Metropolitan of Cracow, 1964–78. Cardinal, 1967; elected Pope, 16 Oct. 1978. Formerly Member, Congregations Pro Institutione Catholica, Pro Sacramentis et Cultu Divino, and Pro Clero. *Publications:* The Goldsmith Shop (play), 1960; Love and Responsibility, 1962; Person and Act, 1969; The Foundations of Renewal, 1972; Sign of Contradiction, 1976; The Future of the Church, 1979; Easter Vigil and other poems, 1979; Collected Poems (trans. Jerzy Peterkiewicz), 1982; Crossing the Threshold of Hope (essays), 1994. *Address:* Apostolic Palace, 00120 Vatican City.

JOHNS, Alan Wesley, CMG 1990; OBE 1973; Executive Director, Royal Commonwealth Society for the Blind, 1984–94 (Deputy Director, 1978–83); *b* 27 March 1931; *s* of Harold Wesley and Catherine Louisa Johns; *m* 1954, Joan Margaret (*née* Wheeler); one *s* one *d*. *Educ:* Farnborough Grammar Sch., Hants. BScEcon, London; CertEd, Southampton Univ. Teaching in secondary schools, Wilts LEA, 1953–61; Educn Officer, Govt of St Helena, 1961–68; Director of Education: Govt of Seychelles, 1968–74; Govt of Gibraltar, 1974–78. Official Mem., Exec. and Adv. Councils, Govt of St Helena, 1963–68. Sec. Gen., Internat. Agency for the Prevention of Blindness, 1994– (Pres., 1990–94); Trustee, Motor Neurone Disease Assoc., 1994–. FRSA 1992. SQA (Pakistan), 1992. *Recreations:* travel in developing countries, house maintenance, sailing. *Address:* Sitwell, Courtmead Road, Cuckfield, West Sussex RH17 5LR. *T:* Haywards Heath (01444) 413355. *Club:* Rotary (Haywards Heath).

JOHNS, Prof. David John, FEng 1990; Vice-Chancellor and Principal, University of Bradford, since 1989; *b* 29 April 1931. *Educ:* Univ. of Bristol (BSc Eng, MSc Eng, Aeronautical Engineering); Loughborough Univ. of Technology (PhD, DSc). FRAeS, FAeSI, FHKIE. Bristol Aeroplane Co., 1950–57 (section leader); Project Officer, Sir W. G. Armstrong Whitworth Co., 1957–58; Lectr, Cranfield Inst. of Technology, 1958–63; Loughborough University of Technology: Reader, 1964–68; Prof. in Transport Technology, 1968–83; Senior Pro-Vice-Chancellor, 1982–83; (Foundation) Dir, City Polytechnic of Hong Kong, 1983–89. 2nd Brunel Lectr, British Assoc. Adv. Sci., 1970. Unofficial JP Hong Kong, 1988–89. *Publications:* Thermal Stress Analyses, 1965; contribs to learned jls. *Recreations:* bridge, walking, music. *Address:* The University, Bradford, West Yorks BD7 1DP. *T:* Bradford (01274) 383011. *Clubs:* Athenæum; Hong Kong; Royal Hong Kong Jockey.

JOHNS, Glynis; actress; *b* Pretoria, South Africa; *d* of late Mervyn Johns and Alice Maude (*née* Steel-Payne); *m* 1st, Anthony Forwood (marr. diss.); one *s*; 2nd, David Foster, DSO, DSC and Bar (marr. diss.); 3rd, Cecil Peter Lamont Henderson; 4th, Elliott Arnold. *Educ:* Clifton and Hampstead High Schs. First stage appearance in Buckie's Bears as a child ballerina, Garrick Theatre, London, 1935. Parts include: Sonia in Judgement Day, Embassy and Strand, 1937; Miranda in Quiet Wedding, Wyndham's, 1938 and in Quiet Weekend, Wyndham's, 1941; Peter in Peter Pan, Cambridge Theatre, 1943; Fools Rush In, Fortune; The Way Things Go, Phœnix, 1950; Gertie (title role), NY, 1952; Major Barbara (title role), NY, 1957; The Patient in Too True to Be Good, NY, 1962; The King's Mare, Garrick, 1966; Come as You Are, New, 1970; A Little Night Music, New York, 1973 (Tony award for best musical actress); Ring Round the Moon, Los Angeles, 1975; 13 Rue de l'Amour, Phœnix, 1976; Cause Célèbre, Her Majesty's, 1977 (Best Actress Award, Variety Club); Hayfever, UK; The Boy Friend, Toronto; The Circle, NY, 1989–90. Entered films as a child. *Films include:* South Riding, 49th Parallel, Frieda, An Ideal

Husband, Miranda (the Mermaid), State Secret, No Highway, The Magic Box, Appointment with Venus, Encore, The Card, Sword and the Rose, Personal Affair, Rob Roy, The Weak and the Wicked, The Beachcomber, The Seekers, Poppa's Delicate Condition, Cabinet of Dr Caligari, Mad About Men, Josephine and Men, The Court Jester, Loser Takes All, The Chapman Report, Dear Bridget, Mary Poppins, Zelly and Me, Nuki, While You Were Sleeping. Also broadcasts; television programmes include: Star Quality; The Parkinson Show (singing Send in the Clowns); Mrs Amworth (USA); All You Need is Love; Across a Crowded Room; Little Gloria, Happy at Last; Sprague; Love Boat; Murder She Wrote; The Cavanaughs; starring role, Coming of Age (series). *Address:* c/o A. Morgan Maree, Jr, and Associates, Inc., 4727 Wilshire Boulevard, Suite 600, Los Angeles, CA 90010, USA.

JOHNS, Jasper; painter; *b* 15 May 1930; *s* of Jasper Johns and Jean Riley. *Educ:* Univ. of South Carolina. Works in collections of Tate Gall., NY Mus. of Modern Art, Buffalo, Cologne, Washington, Amsterdam, Stockholm, Dallas, Chicago, Baltimore, Basle, Cleveland, Minneapolis; one-man exhibitions principally in Leo Castelli Gallery, NY; others in UK, USA, Canada, France, Germany, Italy, Japan, Switzerland. Hon. RA; Mem., Amer. Acad. of Arts and Letters (Gold Medal, 1986); Pittsburgh Internat. Prize, 1958; Wolf Foundn Prize, 1986; Venice Biennale, 1988; Nat. Medal of Arts, 1990; Praemium Imperiale Award, Japan, 1993. Officier, Ordre des Arts et des Lettres (France), 1990. *Address:* c/o Leo Castelli Gallery, 420 W Broadway, New York, NY 10012, USA.

JOHNS, Michael Alan; Director, Business Operations Division, Board of Inland Revenue, since 1993; *b* 20 July 1946; *s* of John and Kathleen Johns. *Educ:* Judd School, Tonbridge; Queens' College, Cambridge (MA Hist.). Inland Revenue, 1967–79; Central Policy Review Staff, 1979–80; Inland Revenue, 1980–84; seconded to Orion Royal Bank, 1985; Inland Revenue, 1986–; Under Sec., 1987; Dir, Oil and Financial Div., 1988–91; Dir, Central Div., 1991–93. Treasurer, Working Men's College, 1986–90. *Recreations:* ski-ing, teaching adults, moral philosophy. *Address:* Board of Inland Revenue, Somerset House, Strand, WC2R 1LB.

JOHNS, Rev. Patricia Holly, MA; Non-stipendiary Curate, Marlborough Team Ministry, since 1994; Headmistress, St Mary's School, Wantage, Oxon, 1980–94; *b* 13 Nov. 1933; *d* of William and Violet Harris; *m* 1958, Michael Charles Bedford Johns (*d* 1965), MA; one *s* one *d*. *Educ:* Blackheath High Sch.; Girton Coll., Cambridge (BA 1956, MA 1959, CertEd with distinction 1957). Asst Maths Mistress; Cheltenham Ladies' Coll., 1957–58; Macclesfield Girls' High Sch., 1958–60; Asst Maths Mistress, then Head of Maths and Dir of Studies, St Albans High Sch., 1966–75; Sen. Mistress, and Housemistress of Hopeman House, Gordonstoun, 1975–80. Ordained deacon, 1990, priest, 1994. *Recreations:* choral singing, walking, camping, dogs (corgis). *Address:* 15 Blowhorn Street, Marlborough, Wilts SN8 1BV. *T:* Marlborough (01672) 515837.

JOHNS, Paul; management consultant, since 1994; Chief Executive, Fairtrade Foundation, 1992–94; *b* 13 March 1934; *s* of Alfred Thomas Johns and Margherita Johns; *m* 1st, 1956, Ruth Thomas (marr. diss. 1973); two *s* one *d*; 2nd, 1984, Margaret Perry. *Educ:* Kingswood School, Bath; Oriel College, Oxford (MA Hons Modern Hist.). MIPM. Personnel Management, Dunlop Rubber Co., 1958–63 and Northern Foods Ltd, 1963–68; Senior Partner, Urwick Orr & Partners, 1968–83; Dir, Profile Consulting, 1983–89; Man. Dir, Traidcraft, 1988–91. Chairperson, 1985–87, Vice-Chairperson, 1987–88, CND. Lay preacher, Methodist Church. *Publications:* contribs to jls on management and on nuclear issue. *Recreations:* photography, listening to music, watching football (keen supporter of Nottingham Forest). *Address:* Flat 11, The Covers, Fox Road, West Bridgford, Nottingham NG2 6AJ. *T:* Nottingham (0115) 981 6944.

JOHNS, Air Chief Marshal Sir Richard (Edward), KCB 1994 (CB 1991); CBE 1985 (OBE 1978); LVO 1972; Commander-in-Chief, Allied Forces North Western Europe, since 1994; *b* 28 July 1939; *s* of late Lt-Col Herbert Edward Johns, RM and of Marjory Harley Johns (*née* Everett); *m* 1965, Elizabeth Naomi Anne Manning; one *s* two *d*. *Educ:* Portsmouth Grammar Sch.; RAF College, Cranwell. Commissioned 1959; Night Fighter and Fighter/Reconnaissance Sqns, UK, Cyprus, Aden, 1960–67; Flying Instructional duties, 1968–71; Flying Instructor to Prince of Wales, 1970–71; OC 3 (Fighter) Sqn (Harrier), 1975–77; Dir, Air Staff Briefing, 1979–81; Station Comdr and Harrier Force Comdr, RAF Gütersloh, 1982–84; ADC to the Queen, 1983–84; RCDS 1985; SASO, HQ RAF Germany, 1985–88; SASO, HQ Strike Comd, 1989–91; AOC No 1 Gp, 1991–93; COS and Dep. C-in-C, Strike Comd and UK Air Forces, 1993–94; AOC-in-C Strike Comd, 1994. Hon. Col, 73 Engr Regt (V), 1994–. *Recreations:* military history, Rugby, cricket. *Address:* c/o Lloyds Bank, Cox's & King's Branch, PO Box 1190, 7 Pall Mall, SW1Y 5NA. *Club:* Royal Air Force.

JOHNSON, Alan Arthur; Joint General Secretary, Communication Workers Union, since 1995 (General Secretary, Union of Communication Workers, 1993–95); *b* 17 May 1950; *s* of Lillian May and Stephen Arthur Johnson; *m* 1st, 1968, Judith Elizabeth Cox (marr. diss.); one *s* two *d*; 2nd, 1991, Laura Jane Patient. *Educ:* Sloane Grammar School, Chelsea. Postman, 1968; UCW Branch Official, 1976; UCW Exec. Council, 1981; UCW National Officer, 1987–93. Mem. Gen. Council, TUC; Exec. Mem., Postal, Telegraph and Telephone Internat.; Dir, Unity Trust Bank plc. Duke of Edinburgh Commonwealth Study Conf., 1992. Gov., Ruskin Coll. *Recreations:* music, tennis, reading, football, radio. *Address:* CWU House, Crescent Lane, Clapham, SW4 9RN. *T:* 0171–622 9977.

JOHNSON, Alan Campbell; *see* Campbell-Johnson.

JOHNSON, Air Vice-Marshal Alan Taylor, FRAeS; Director of Occupational Health, Metropolitan Police, 1991–95; *b* 3 March 1931; *s* of Percy and Janet Johnson; *m* 1954, Margaret Ellen Mee; two *s* three *d* (and one *s* decd). *Educ:* Mexborough Grammar Sch.; Univ. of Sheffield (MB, ChB); DipAvMed; FFOM, MFCM. Commnd RAF, 1957; MO, RAF Gaydon, 1957–59; Princess Mary's RAF Hosp., Akrotiri, Cyprus, 1959–61; No 1 Parachute Trng Sch., RAF Abingdon, 1961–65; RAF Changi, Singapore, 1965–67; RAF Inst. of Aviation Medicine, 1967–71; RAF Bruggen, Germany, 1971–74; Med. SO (Air) HQ RAF Support Comd, 1974–77; RAF Brize Norton, 1977–78; Chief of Aerospace Medicine HQ SAC Offutt AFB, USA, 1978–81; Dep. Dir of Health and Res. (Aviation Medicine), 1981–84; OC Princess Alexandra Hosp., RAF Wroughton, 1984–86; Asst Surg.-Gen. (Environmental Medicine and Res.), MoD, 1986; PMO, HQ RAF, Germany, 1986–88; PMO, HQ Strike Comd, RAF High Wycombe, 1988–91; retired. QHS 1986–91. OStJ 1976. *Recreations:* sport parachuting, music, cricket. *Address:* c/o Lloyds Bank, 99 High Street, Huntingdon, Cambs PE18 6DU. *Club:* Royal Air Force.

JOHNSON, Anne Montgomrey; Market Research, Harris Research Centre, 1983–92; *b* 12 June 1922; *y c* of late Frederick Harold Johnson and late Gertrude Le Quesne (*née* Martin). *Educ:* St John's, Bexhill-on-Sea; Queen Elizabeth Hosp. (SRN); Brompton Hosp. (BTA Hons); Simpson Memorial Maternity Pavilion, Edinburgh (SCM). Asst Matron, Harefield Hosp., 1956–59; Dep. Matron, St Mary's Hosp., Paddington, 1959–62; Matron, Guy's Hosp., 1962–68; Mem. Directing and Tutorial Staff, King Edward's Hosp. Fund for London, 1968–71; Regional Dir, Help the Aged, 1971–73; Matron, The Royal Star and Garter Home for Disabled Sailors, Soldiers and Airmen, 1975–82. Member: King's Fund Working Party, 'The Shape of Hospital Management 1980', 1966–67 (report publd 1967); Jt Cttee of Gen. Synod Working Party 'The Hospital Chaplain' (report publd 1974); Hosp. Chaplaincies Council, 1963–81; Nursing Cttee, Assoc. of Indep. Hosps, 1978–83. Gov., Orleans Park Sch., Twickenham, 1988–. *Recreations:* straight theatre, travel. *Address:* Flat 5, 6 Cardigan Road, Richmond-on-Thames, Surrey TW10 6BJ.

JOHNSON, WO1 Barry, GC 1990; RAOC; Warrant Officer 1 (Staff Sergeant Major), 1986, retired 1992; *b* 25 Jan. 1952; *s* of Charles William Johnson and Joyce Johnson; *m* 1971, Linda Maria Lane; one *s* one *d*. Mem., Inst. of Explosives Engineers. Army Apprentices College, Chepstow, 1967; Royal Army Ordnance Corps, 1970; served in UK, BAOR, NI, Canada and Belize. *Club:* Victoria Cross and George Cross Association.

JOHNSON, Prof. Barry Edward, PhD; FRS 1978; Professor of Pure Mathematics, University of Newcastle upon Tyne, since 1969; *b* 1 Aug. 1937; *s* of Edward Johnson and Evelyn May (*née* Bailey); *m* (marr. diss. 1979); two *s* one *d*. *Educ:* Epsom County Grammar Sch.; Hobart State High Sch.; Univ. of Tasmania (BSc 1956); Cambridge Univ. (PhD 1961). Instr, Univ. of Calif, Berkeley, 1961–62; Vis. Lectr, Yale Univ., 1962–63; Lectr, Exeter Univ., 1963–65; University of Newcastle upon Tyne: Lectr, 1965–68; Reader, 1968–69; Head of Dept of Pure Maths, 1976–83; Head of Sch. of Maths, 1983–86; Dean, Faculty of Sci., 1986–89. Vis. Prof., Yale Univ., 1970–71. Auditor, HEQC, 1993–. Mem., London Math. Soc. (Mem. Council, 1975–78; Pres., 1980–82). *Publications:* Cohomology of Banach Algebras, 1972; papers in Jl of London Math. Soc. and Amer. Jl of Maths. *Recreations:* reading, travel. *Address:* 63 Montagu Court, Gosforth, Newcastle upon Tyne NE3 4JL. *T:* 0191–213 1013.

JOHNSON, Brian; *see* Johnson, R. B.

JOHNSON, Prof. Brian Frederick Gilbert, PhD; FRS 1991; Crum Brown Professor of Inorganic Chemistry, University of Edinburgh, since 1991; *b* 11 Sept. 1938; *s* of Frank and Mona Johnson; *m* 1962, Christine Draper; two *d*. *Educ:* Northampton Grammar Sch.; Univ. of Nottingham (BSc, PhD). Lecturer: Univ. of Manchester, 1965–67; UCL, 1967–70; Cambridge University: Lectr, 1970–78; Reader, 1978–90; Fitzwilliam College: Fellow, 1970–90; Pres., 1988–89; Vice Master, 1989–90. Mem., EPSRC, 1994–. *Publication:* Transition Metal Clusters, 1982. *Recreations:* walking, cycling. *Address:* Department of Chemistry, University of Edinburgh, West Mains Road, Edinburgh EH9 3JJ. *T:* 0131–650 4706.

JOHNSON, Bruce Joseph F.; *see* Forsyth-Johnson.

JOHNSON, Carol Alfred, CBE 1951; *b* 1903; *m*. Admitted a Solicitor, 1933 (Hons); practised City of London; Hon. Solicitor to Housing Assocs in Southwark and Fulham; Asst Town Clerk, Borough of Southall, 1940–43; Secretary of the Parliamentary Labour Party, 1943–59. Alderman, Lambeth Borough Council, 1937–49 (sometime Leader). MP (Lab) Lewisham S, Sept. 1959–Feb. 1974; served on Chairman's Panel, presiding over cttees and occasionally the House; sometime Chm., History of Parliament Trust and Anglo-Italian Parly Cttee; Mem., Parly delegations to Nigeria, Persia (now Iran), the Cameroons and India. Served on Council of Europe; many years Jt Hon. Sec., British Council of European Movement, now Vice-Pres., Lab. Cttee for Europe. Sometime Hon. Sec., Friends of Africa and later Treasurer, Fabian Colonial Bureau; original Mem., Local Govt Adv. Panel, Colonial Office; Member: Fabian delegn to Czechoslovakia, 1946; British Council Lecture Tour to Finland, 1946. Exec. Mem., Commons (now Open Spaces) Soc. (formerly Chm.); Mem., Standing Cttee on Nat. Parks (now Council for Nat. Parks), Trustee, William Morris Soc.; Mem. Exec. Cttee, British-Italian Soc.; Life Governor, British Inst., Florence (Gov., 1965–86). Comdr, Italian Order of Merit. *Address:* 2 Henley House, 8 Devonshire Place, Eastbourne, E Sussex BN21 4AF. *T:* Eastbourne (01323) 417982.

JOHNSON, Charles Ernest, JP; Councillor, Salford, since 1986; Member, Police Authority, Greater Manchester Police, since 1986; *b* 2 Jan. 1918; adopted *s* of Henry and Mary Johnson; *m* 1942, Betty, *d* of William Nelson Hesford, farmer; one *s*. *Educ:* elementary school. Commenced work as apprentice coppersmith, 1932; called up to Royal Navy, 1940, demobilised, 1946. Councillor and Alderman, Eccles Town Council, 1952–73; Mayor, 1964–65; Chm. of various cttees, incl. Housing, for 14 years, and of Local Employment Cttee, for ten years; Councillor, Greater Manchester County Council, 1974–86 (Chairman, 1982–83). Mem., Assoc. of Municipal Councils, 1958–. JP Eccles, 1965. 1939–45 Medal, Atlantic Medal, Africa Star, Victory Medal; Imperial Service Medal, 1978. *Recreations:* gardening, watching football, swimming. *Address:* 17 Dartford Avenue, Winton, Eccles, Manchester M30 8NF. *T:* 0161–789 4229.

JOHNSON, Christopher Edmund; Director General, Defence Accounts, Ministry of Defence, 1984–89; *b* 17 Jan. 1934; *s* of Christopher and Phyllis Johnson; *m* 1956, Janet Yvonne Wakefield; eight *s* three *d*. *Educ:* Salesian Coll., Chertsey; Collyer's Sch., Horsham. Sub Lt, RNVR, 1952–54. Exec. Officer, 1954–58, Higher Exec. Officer, 1959–65, War Office; Principal, MoD, 1965–71; UK Jt Comd Sec., ANZUK Force, Singapore, 1971–74; Ministry of Defence: Asst Sec., 1974–84; Asst Under Sec. of State, 1984. *Recreations:* gardening, reading. *Address:* Rohannon Farm, Weston, Bath, Avon BA1 4EY. *T:* Bath (01225) 314247.

JOHNSON, Daniel, PhD; Member (L) for Vaudreuil, Quebec National Assembly, since 1981; Leader of Official Opposition, since 1994; *b* Montreal, 24 Dec. 1944; *s* of Daniel Johnson (Premier of Quebec, 1966–68) and Reine (*née* Gagne); *m* 1993, Suzanne Marcil; one *s* one *d* from former marriage. *Educ:* Stanislas Coll., Montreal; Saint-Laurent Coll. (BA Univ. of Montreal); Univ. of Montreal (LLL); University Coll. London (LLM, PhD); Harvard Business Sch. (MBA). A lawyer. Minister of Industry and Commerce, 1985–88; Dep. House Leader, 1985–94; Pres., Treasury Bd and Minister responsible for Admin, 1988–89; Minister reponsible for Admin and CS and Chm., Treasury Bd, 1989–94; Prime Minister and Pres. Exec. Council, Jan.–Sept. 1994. Leader, Quebec Liberal Party, 1993–. Vice-Pres., Budget and Admin Commn, 1984–85. Corp. Sec., 1973–81, Vice-Pres., 1978–81, Power Corp. of Canada. *Address:* 3335 Félix-Leclerc, Vaudreuil, Quebec J7V 8W5, Canada. *T:* (514) 4246666, *Fax:* (514) 4249274.

JOHNSON, Daniel Benedict; Literary Editor, The Times, since 1991; *b* 26 Aug. 1957; *s* of Paul Johnson, *qv* and Marigold Johnson (*née* Hunt); *m* 1988, Sarah Thompson, *d* of J. W. M. Thompson, *qv*; two *s* one *d*. *Educ:* Langley Grammar Sch.; Magdalen Coll., Oxford (BA 1st Cl. Hons Hist.). Res. Student, Peterhouse, Cambridge, 1978–81; Shakespeare Scholar, Berlin, 1979–80; taught German hist., QMC, 1982–84; Dir of Pubns, Centre for Policy Studies, 1983–84; Daily Telegraph: Leader Writer, 1986–87; Bonn Corresp., 1987–89; Eastern Europe Corresp., 1989; Leader Writer, The Times, 1990–91. *Publications:* co-edited: German Neo-Liberals and the Social Market Economy, 1989; Thomas Mann: Death in Venice and other stories, 1991. *Recreation:* chess. *Address:* The Times, 1 Pennington Street, E1 9XN; 46 Aldbourne Road, W12 0LN. *T:* 0181–743 4995.

JOHNSON, David Bryan; Chief Executive, St James's University Hospital NHS Trust, since 1992; *b* 27 Feb. 1957; *s* of Audrey and Bernard Johnson; *m* 1980, Gillian Pobgee; one *s*. *Educ:* Sheffield Univ. (BA Hons Politics 1978). Nat. Management Trainee, NHS,

1980–83; Asst, then Dep. Administrator, Manchester Royal Infirmary, 1983–85; Unit Gen. Manager, Pontefract HA Acute and Maternity Services, 1985–90; Dir of Ops, 1990–92, Acting Chief Exec., Feb.–May 1992, St James's Univ. Hosp. *Recreations:* golf, swimming, football, walking, travel. *Address:* Woodthorpe, 40 Thorp Arch Park, Thorp Arch, Wetherby, W Yorks LS23 7AN.

JOHNSON, David Burnham, QC 1978; a Recorder, since 1984; *b* 6 Aug. 1930; *s* of late Thomas Burnham Johnson and of Elsie May Johnson; *m* 1968, Julia Clare Addison Hopkinson, *o d* of late Col H. S. P. Hopkinson, OBE; one *s* three *d.* *Educ:* Truro Sch.; Univ. of Wales. Solicitor and Notary Public, Oct. 1952. Commissioned, National Service, with Royal Artillery, 1952–54. Private practice as solicitor, Cardiff and Plymouth, 1954–67; called to Bar, Inner Temple, 1967, Bencher, 1985. *Recreations:* sailing, walking, shooting, reading, music. *Address:* 25 Murray Road, Wimbledon, SW19 4PD. *T:* 0181–947 9188; (chambers) 20 Essex Street, WC2R 3AL. *T:* 0171–583 9294. *Club:* Royal Western Yacht (Plymouth).

JOHNSON, Prof. David Hugh Nevil; Professor of International Law, Sydney University, 1976–85, now Emeritus; *b* 4 Jan. 1920; 2nd *s* of James Johnson and Gladys Mary (*née* Knight); *m* 1952, Evelyn Joan Fletcher. *Educ:* Winchester Coll.; Trinity Coll., Cambridge; Columbia Univ., New York. MA, LLM Cantab. Served Royal Corps of Signals, 1940–46. Called to Bar, Lincoln's Inn, 1950. Asst Legal Adviser, Foreign Office, 1950–53; Reader in Internat. Law, 1953–59, in Internat. and Air Law, 1959–60, Prof., 1960–Dec. 1975, Dean of Faculty of Laws, 1968–72, Univ. of London. Sen. Legal Officer, Office of Legal Affairs, UN, 1956–57. Registrar, the Court of Arbitration, Argentine-Chile Frontier Case, 1965–68. *Publications:* Rights in Air Space, 1965; articles in legal jls. *Address:* 1 Flannel Flower Fairway, Shoal Bay, NSW 2315, Australia.

JOHNSON, David John, CMG 1995; CVO 1994; HM Diplomatic Service; High Commissioner to Guyana and Ambassador to Suriname, since 1993; *b* 2 March 1938; *s* of Herbert John Victor Johnson and Mildred Frances (*née* Boyd); *m* 1976, Kathleen Johanna Hicks; three *d.* *Educ:* Harvey Grammar Sch., Folkestone. Served RAF, 1957–59. Entered FO, 1959; Third Sec., Moscow, 1962; Third, later Second Sec., Dakar, 1965; Second Secretary: Ulan Bator, 1969; UK Mission to UN, Geneva, 1969; First Secretary: UK Mission to negotiations on mutual reduction of forces and armaments and associated measures, Vienna, 1973; Moscow, 1975; FCO, 1978; Counsellor, NATO Defence Coll., Rome, 1982; seconded to NATO Internat. Secretariat, Brussels, 1982; Counsellor and Head of Chancery, Islamabad, 1985–90; Head, CSCE Unit, FCO, 1990–92. *Recreations:* marquetry, music, reading. *Address:* c/o Foreign and Commonwealth Office, SW1A 2AH.

JOHNSON, Rt. Hon. Sir David Powell C.; *see* Croom-Johnson.

JOHNSON, David Robert W.; *see* Wilson-Johnson.

JOHNSON, (Denis) Gordon, CBE 1969; Chairman, Geo. Bassett Holdings Ltd, 1955–78 (Managing Director, 1955–71); Chairman: W. R. Wilkinson & Co. Ltd, Pontefract, 1961–78; Drakes Sweets Marketing Ltd, 1961–78; B. V. de Faam, Holland, 1964–78; Barratt & Co. Ltd, London, 1968–78; *b* 8 Oct. 1911; *s* of late Percy Johnson; *m* 1986, Joan Wilde (*née* Barringham). *Educ:* Harrow; Hertford Coll., Oxford (MA). President: Cocoa, Chocolate and Confectionery Alliance, 1964–66 (Hon. Treas., 1972–77); Confectioners' Benevolent Fund, 1967–68; Member: Yorks Electricity Bd, 1965–75; Food Manufacturing Economic Develt Cttee, 1967–70; Council of CBI, 1968–78; Council, Sheffield Univ., 1972–81; Chm., S Yorks Industrialists' Council, 1976–78. Chm., Hallam Conservative Assoc., 1966–69, and 1973–76; Hon. Treas., City of Sheffield Conservative Fedn, 1969–73; Chm., City of Sheffield Cons. Assocs, 1976–78. Pres., Sheffield and Hallamshire Lawn Tennis Club. Vis. Fellow, Yorks and Humberside Regional Management Centre. CIMgt; MInstD. *Publications:* address to British Assoc. (Economics Section), 1964; contributor to: Business Growth (ed Edwards and Townsend), 1966; Pricing Strategy (ed Taylor and Wills), 1969. *Recreations:* walking, travel, philosophy. *Address:* Ivy Cottage, Trolver Croft, Feock, Truro, Cornwall TR3 6RT. *T:* Truro (01872) 865669.

JOHNSON, Donald Edwin, RIBA, FRTPI; Under Secretary, 1978–80, and Deputy Chief Planner, 1975–80, Department of the Environment; *b* 4 July 1920; *s* of Henry William Johnson and Ann Catherine (*née* Lake); *m* 1947, Thérèse Andrée Simone Marquant; two *s* one *d.* *Educ:* Haberdashers' Aske's, Hatcham; School of Architecture, Regent Polytechnic; APRR School of Planning. Served War, Royal Artillery and Royal Engineers, 1940–45. Planning Officer, Min. of Town and Country Planning, 1947; Sen. Planning Officer, 1950, Principal Planner, 1965, Asst Chief Planner, 1972. *Publications: fiction:* Project 38, 1963; Crooked Cross, 1964; Flashing Mountain, 1965; Devil of Bruges, 1966. *Address:* Flat D, 1 Morpeth Terrace, SW1P 1EW. *T:* 0171–834 7300.

JOHNSON, Prof. Douglas William John; Professor of French History, University College London, 1968–90, now Emeritus; Visiting Professor, French Department, King's College, London, since 1993; *b* Edinburgh, 1 Feb. 1925; *o s* of John Thornburn Johnson and Christine Mair; *m* 1950, Madeleine Rébillard; one *d.* *Educ:* Royal Grammar Sch., Lancaster; Worcester Coll., Oxford (BA, BLitt); Ecole Normale Supérieure, Paris. Birmingham Univ.: Lectr in Modern History, 1949; Prof. of Modern History and Chm. of Sch. of History, 1963–68; Head of Dept of History, 1979–83, Dean, Faculty of Arts, 1979–82, UCL. Vis. Prof., Univs of Aix-en-Provence, Nancy, Paris, British Columbia, Toronto, Caen, Lyons, Montreal, Texas; Lectures: Zaharoff, Oxford Univ., 1989; Simon Cohen Meml, Kent Univ., 1990; Creighton, London Univ., 1991. Chm. Bd of Examrs in History, Univ. of London, 1973–75; Member: CNAA, 1974–79; Franco-British Council, 1976–; Scientific Council, Fondation Charles de Gaulle, 1993–. FRHistS. Ordre Nat. du Mérite (France), 1980; Commandeur des Palmes Académiques (France), 1987; Chevalier de la Légion d'Honneur (France), 1990. *Publications:* Guizot: Aspects of French History 1787–1874, 1963; France and the Dreyfus Affair, 1966; France, 1969; Concise History of France, 1970; The French Revolution, 1970; (ed jtly) Britain and France: Ten Centuries, 1980; (with Richard Hoggart) An Idea of Europe, 1987; (with Madeleine Johnson) The Age of Illusion, 1987; (with Geoffrey Best) The Permanent Revolution, 1988; Michelet and the French Revolution, 1990; (General Editor) The Making of the Modern World; (General Editor) The Fontana History of Modern France. *Recreations:* music, French politics. *Address:* 29 Rudall Crescent, NW3 1RR; 12 rue Delambre, Paris 75014, France. *Club:* Travellers'.

JOHNSON, Prof. Francis Rea; Professor of Anatomy, London Hospital Medical College, 1968–86, now Emeritus; Pre-clinical Sub-Dean, 1979–86; *b* 8 July 1921; *s* of Marcus Jervis Johnson and Elizabeth Johnson; *m* 1951, Ena Patricia Laverty; one *s* one *d.* *Educ:* Omagh Academy, N Ire.; Queen's Univ., Belfast. MB, BCh, BAO 1945, MD 1949. House appts, Belfast City Hosp., 1946; Demonstrator in Anatomy and Physiology, QUB, 1947–50; Lectr in Anatomy, Sheffield Univ., 1950–57; Reader in Anatomy, London Hosp. Med. Coll., 1957–64; Prof. of Histology, London Hosp. Med. Coll., 1964–68. *Publications:* papers on histochemistry and ultrastructure of tissues and organs in various jls. *Recreations:* motoring, camping, gardening. *Address:* 11 Beacon Rise, Sevenoaks, Kent TN13 2NJ. *T:* Sevenoaks (01732) 453343.

JOHNSON, Frank Robert; Deputy Editor, The Sunday Telegraph, since 1994 (Associate Editor, 1988–93; Deputy Editor (Comment), 1993–94); *b* 20 Jan. 1943; *s* of late Ernest Johnson, pastry cook and confectioner, and Doreen (*née* Skinner). *Educ:* Chartesey Secondary Sch., Shoreditch; Shoreditch Secondary Sch. Messenger Boy, Sunday Express, 1959–60; Reporter on local and regional newspapers, 1960–69; Political Staff, Sun, 1969–72; Parly Sketch Writer and Leader Writer, Daily Telegraph, 1972–79; Columnist, Now! Magazine, 1979–81; The Times: Parly Sketch Writer, 1981–83; Paris Diarist, 1984; Bonn Corresp., 1985–86; Parly Sketch Writer, 1986–87; Associate Editor, 1987–88. Parly Sketch Writer of the Year Award, Granada, What The Papers Say, 1977; Columnist of the Year, British Press Awards, 1981. *Publications:* Out of Order, 1982; Frank Johnson's Election Year, 1983. *Recreations:* opera, ballet. *Address:* The Sunday Telegraph, 1 Canada Square, Canary Wharf, E14 5DT. *T:* 0171–538 5000. *Clubs:* Garrick, Beefsteak.

JOHNSON, Air Vice-Marshal Frank Sidney Roland, CB 1973; OBE 1963; CIMgt; *b* 4 Aug. 1917; *s* of Major Harry Johnson, IA, and Georgina Marklew; *m* 1943, Evelyn Hunt; two *s.* *Educ:* Trinity County Secondary Sch., Wood Green. Enlisted, 1935; served in UK and India; commnd, 1943; Germany (Berlin Airlift), 1948; Western Union Defence Organisation, 1955–57; Directing Staff, RAF Staff Coll., 1958–60; comd 113 MU, RAF Nicosia, 1960–63; Chief Instructor Equipment and Secretarial Wing, RAF Coll. Cranwell, 1963–64; Dep. Dir MoD, 1965–66; idc 1967; Chief Supply Officer, Fighter and Strike Comds, 1968–70; Dir-Gen. of Supply, RAF, 1971–73; Supply Manager, BAC, Saudi Arabia, 1974–76; Base Manager, BAC RSAF, Khamis Mushayt, Saudi Arabia, 1976–77, Dhahran, 1978–82. *Recreations:* golf, squash, hockey, cricket. *Club:* Royal Air Force.

JOHNSON, Frederick Alistair, PhD; FInstP; Director, Special Projects, GEC-Marconi Research Centre, since 1995; *b* Christchurch, NZ, 9 April 1928; *s* of Archibald Frederick Johnson and Minnie, *d* of William Frederick Pellew; *m* 1952, Isobel Beth, *d* of Horace George Wilson; two *d.* *Educ:* Christchurch Boys' High Sch.; Univ. of Canterbury, New Zealand (MSc, PhD). Rutherford Meml Fellow, 1952; Lectr, Univ. of Otago, 1952; post graduate research, Bristol Univ., 1953–55. Royal Radar Establishment, 1956–75: Individual Merit Promotion, 1964; Head of Physics Dept, 1968–73; Dep. Director, 1973–75; Dep. Dir, Royal Armament Research & Development Estabt, 1975–77; Dir of Scientific and Technical Intell., MoD, 1977–79; Chief Scientist (Royal Navy) and Dir Gen. Research A, MoD, 1980–84; Dir, Marconi Maritime Applied Res. Lab., and Chief Scientist, Marconi Underwater Systems Ltd, 1985–87; Technical Dir, GEC Research, later GEC-Marconi Res. Centre, 1987–95. Visiting Professor, Massachusetts Inst. of Technology, 1967–68; Hon. Prof. of Physics, Birmingham Univ., 1969–75. *Publications:* numerous papers on spectroscopy, optics, lattice dynamics and ocean thermal energy conversion in Proc. Physical Soc. and Proc. Royal Soc. *Recreation:* sailing. *Address:* Otia Tuta, Grassy Lane, Sevenoaks, Kent TN13 1PL. *Club:* Athenæum.

JOHNSON, Gen. Sir Garry (Dene), KCB 1990; OBE 1977 (MBE 1971); MC 1965; Chairman, International Defence Advisory Board to the Baltic States, since 1995; *b* 20 Sept. 1937; *m* 1962, Caroline Sarah Frearson; two *s.* *Educ:* Christ's Hospital. psc, ndc, rcds. Commissioned 10th Princess Mary's Own Gurkha Rifles, 1956; Malaya and Borneo campaigns, 1956–67; Royal Green Jackets, 1970; command, 1st Bn RGJ, 1976–79; Comdr, 11 Armoured Brigade, 1981–82; Dep. Chief of Staff, HQ BAOR, 1983; ACDS (NATO/UK), 1985–87; Comdr, British Forces Hong Kong, and Maj.-Gen., Bde of Gurkhas, 1987–89; MEC, Hong Kong Govt, 1987–89; Comdr Trng and Arms Dirs, 1989–91; Inspector Gen. Doctrine and Trng, 1991–92; C-in-C, AFNORTH, 1992–94. Colonel, 10th PMO Gurkha Rifles, 1985–94; Col Comdt, Light Div., 1990–94. Chm., Ogilby Trust, 1991–. *Publication:* Brightly Shone the Dawn, 1979. *Address:* c/o Holt's Branch, Royal Bank of Scotland, Lawrie House, Victoria Road, Farnborough GU14 7NR. *Club:* Army and Navy.

JOHNSON, Gordon; *see* Johnson, D. G.

JOHNSON, Dr Gordon; President, Wolfson College, University of Cambridge, since 1994; *b* 13 Sept. 1943; *s* of Robert Johnson and Bessie (*née* Hewson); *m* 1973, Faith Sargent Lewis, New Haven, Conn; three *s.* *Educ:* Richmond Sch., Yorks; Trinity Coll., Cambridge (BA 1964; MA, PhD 1968). Fellow, Trinity Coll., Cambridge, 1966–74; Selwyn College, Cambridge: Fellow, 1974–94; Tutor, 1975–92; Hon. Fellow, 1994; University of Cambridge: Lectr in History of S Asia, 1974–; Dir, Centre of S Asian Studies, 1983–; Chairman, Faculty of: Oriental Studies, 1984–87; Architecture and History of Art, 1985–; Educn, 1994–; Member: Library Syndicate, 1978–; Press Syndicate, 1981– (Chm., 1993–); Syndicate on Govt of Univ., 1988–89; Statutes and Ordinances Revision Syndicate, 1990–; Gen. Bd of Faculties, 1979–82 and 1985–90; Council, Senate, 1985–92. Trustee: Cambridge Commonwealth Trust, 1983–; Cambridge Overseas Trust, 1989–. Editor, Modern Asian Studies, 1971–; Gen. Editor, The New Cambridge History of India, 1979–. *Publications:* Provincial Politics and Indian Nationalism, 1973; University Politics: F. M. Cornford's Cambridge and his advice to the young academic politician, 1994; Cultural Atlas of India, 1995. *Recreations:* reading, taking exercise. *Address:* Wolfson College, Cambridge CB3 9BB. *T:* Cambridge (01223) 35900.

JOHNSON, Gordon Arthur; Chief Executive and Clerk of the County Council, Lancashire, since 1991; *b* 30 Aug. 1938; *y s* of Annie Elizabeth Johnson and William Johnson; *m* 1963, Jennifer Roxane Bradley; two *d.* *Educ:* Bournemouth Sch.; University College London (BA Hons Hist.). Solicitor. Kent CC, 1962–64; Staffs CC, 1964–73; Dep. Dir of Admin, W Yorks MCC, 1973–76; Dep. Clerk, Lancs CC, 1976–90; Clerk, Lancs Lieutenancy, 1991–; Lancs County Electoral Returning Officer, 1991–. Secretary: Lancs Adv. Cttee, 1991–; Lord Chancellor's Adv. Cttee on Gen. Cmrs of Income Tax, 1991–; Lancs Probation Cttee; Lancs Cttee, Prince's Trust and Royal Jubilee Trust; Co. Sec., Lancs County Enterprises Ltd, 1991–; Mem., MSC Area Manpower Bd, 1986–88; Chm., Soc. of County Secretaries, 1987–88 (Hon. Treasurer, 1977–86); Dir, LAWTEC, 1991–. Mem. Court, Univ. of Lancaster, 1991–. *Recreations:* motor cycling, travel, reading. *Address:* Lancashire County Council, PO Box 78, County Hall, Preston, Lancs PR1 8XJ; Arandel, Manor Way, Wrea Green, Preston, Lancs PR4 2WH.

JOHNSON, Graham Rhodes, OBE 1994; concert accompanist; Professor of Accompaniment, Guildhall School of Music, since 1986; *b* 10 July 1950; *s* of late John Edward Donald Johnson and of Violet May Johnson (*née* Johnson). *Educ:* Hamilton High Sch., Bulawayo, Rhodesia; Royal Acad. of Music, London. FRAM 1984; FGSM 1988. Concert début, Wigmore Hall, 1972; has since accompanied Elisabeth Schwarzkopf, Jessye Norman, Victoria de los Angeles (USA Tour 1977), Dame Janet Baker, Sir Peter Pears, Felicity Lott, Felicity Palmer, Margaret Price (USA Tour 1985), Peter Schreier, John Shirley Quirk, Valerie Masterson, Mady Mesplé, Thomas Hampson, Robert Holl, Tom Krause, Sergei Leiferkus, Brigitte Fassbaender. Work with contemporaries led to formation of The Songmakers' Almanac (Artistic Director); has devised and accompanied over 150 London recitals for this group since Oct. 1976. Tours of US with Sarah Walker, Richard Jackson, and of Australia and NZ with The Songmakers' Almanac, 1981. Writer and presenter of major BBC Radio 3 series on Poulenc songs, and BBC TV programmes on Schubert songs (1978) and the songs of Liszt (1986). Lectr at song courses in Savonlinna (Finland), US and at Pears-Britten Sch., Snape; Artistic advr and accompanist, Alte Oper

Festival, Frankfurt, 1981–82; Song Adviser, Wigmore Hall, 1992–; Festival appearances in Aldeburgh, Edinburgh, Munich, Hohenems, Salzburg, Bath, Hong Kong, Bermuda. Many recordings incl. those with Songmakers' Almanac, Martyn Hill, Elly Ameling, Arleen Auger, Janet Baker, Philip Langridge, Marjana Lipovsek, Ann Murray, Sarah Walker, Anthony Rolfe Johnson, and of Schubert Lieder, with various artists, 1988–. Gramophone Award, 1989. *Publications:* (contrib.) The Britten Companion, ed Christopher Palmer, 1984; (contrib.) Gerald Moore, The Unashamed Accompanist, rev. edn 1984; (contrib.) The Spanish Song Companion, 1992; reviews in TLS, articles for music jls. *Recreation:* eating in good restaurants with friends and fine wine. *Address:* 83 Fordwych Road, NW2 3TL. *T:* 0181–452 5193.

JOHNSON, Howard Sydney; solicitor; Senior Partner, Howard Johnson & McQue, 1933–83; *b* 25 Dec. 1911; *s* of Sydney Thomas Johnson; *m* 1939, Betty Frankiss, actress. *Educ:* Brighton; Highgate. Served War of 1939–45, Africa; invalided out as Major. Joined TA before the war. Mem. of Brighton Town Council, 1945–50. MP (C) Kemptown Div. of Brighton, 1950–Sept. 1959. Director: Alliance BS, 1960–83; Alliance & Leicester (Isle of Man) Ltd, 1992–. *Publication:* (contrib.) Against Hunting, ed Patrick Moore, 1965. *Address:* Ballakinnag Cottage, Smeale, Andreas, Isle of Man IM7 3ED. *T:* Kirk Andreas (01624) 880712.

JOHNSON, Hugh Eric Allan; author, broadcaster and editor; *b* 10 March 1939; *s* of late Guy Francis Johnson, CBE and Grace Kittel; *m* 1965, Judith Eve Grinling; one *s* two *d*. *Educ:* Rugby Sch.; King's Coll., Cambridge (MA). Staff writer, Condé Nast publications, 1960–63; Editor, Wine & Food, and Sec., Wine and Food Soc., 1963–65; Wine Corresp., 1962–67, and Travel Editor, 1967, Sunday Times; Editor, Queen, 1968–70. Pres., The Sunday Times Wine Club, 1973–. Chairman: Saling Hall Press, 1975–; Conservation Cttee, Internat. Dendrology Soc., 1979–86; Winestar Productions Ltd, 1984–; The Hugh Johnson Collection Ltd, 1985–; Director: Société Civile de Château Latour, 1986–; Coldstream Winemakers Ltd, 1991–94. Editorial Director: Jl of RHS, 1975–89, Editl Cons., 1989–; The Plantsman, 1979–94. Wine Editor, Cuisine, New York, 1983–84; Wine Consultant: to Jardine Matheson Ltd, Hong Kong and Tokyo, 1985–; to British Airways, 1987–. Gardening Correspondent, New York Times, 1986–87. Video, How to Handle a Wine, 1984 (Glenfiddich Trophy, 1984; reissued as Understanding Wine, 1989); TV series: Wine—a user's guide (KQED, San Francisco), 1986; Vintage—a history of wine (Channel 4 and WGBH, Boston), 1989; TV documentary, Return Voyage (Star TV, Hong Kong), 1992. Hon. Chm., Wine Japan (Tokyo exhibn), 1989–94. Docteur ès Vins, Acad. du Vin de Bordeaux, 1987. *Publications:* Wine, 1966, rev. edn 1974; The World Atlas of Wine, 1971, 4th edn 1994; The International Book of Trees, 1973, rev. edn 1994; (with Bob Thompson) The California Wine Book, 1976; Hugh Johnson's Pocket Wine Book, annually 1977–; The Principles of Gardening, 1979, rev. edn 1984; Understanding Wine, 1980; (with Paul Miles) The Pocket Encyclopedia of Garden Plants, 1981, rev. edn 1995; Hugh Johnson's Wine Companion, 1983, 3rd edn 1991; How to Enjoy Your Wine, 1985; The Hugh Johnson Cellar Book, 1986; The Atlas of German Wines, 1986, rev. edn (with Stuart Pigott) 1995; Hugh Johnson's Wine Cellar, (US) 1986; (with Jan Read) The Wine and Food of Spain, 1987; (with Hubrecht Duijker) The Wine Atlas of France, 1987; The Story of Wine, 1989 (ten awards, incl. Glenfiddich Wine Award, 1990, Grand Prix de la Communication de la Vigne et du Vin, 1992); Hugh Johnson's Pop-up Wine Book, 1989; (with James Halliday) The Art and Science of Wine, 1992; Hugh Johnson on Gardening: the best of Tradescant's Diary, 1993; articles on gastronomy, travel and gardening. *Recreations:* travelling, staying at home. *Address:* Saling Hall, Great Saling, Essex CM7 5DT; 73 St James's Street, SW1A 1PH; Domaine des Boutons, 03190 Hérisson, Allier, France. *Clubs:* Garrick, Saintsbury.

JOHNSON, Air Vice-Marshal James Edgar, (Johnnie Johnson), CB 1965; CBE 1960; DSO 1943 and Bars, 1943, 1944; DFC 1941 and Bar, 1942; DL; Consultant, 'Johnnie' Johnson Housing; Director of Companies in Canada, South Africa and UK; *m* Pauline Ingate; two *s*. *Educ:* Loughborough Sch.; Nottingham Univ. Civil Engr and Mem. of RAFVR until 1939; served with 616 Sqdn AAF, 1940–42; 610 Sqdn AAF, 1943; Wing Comdr Flying: Kenley, 1943; 127 Wing, 1944; Officer Comdg: 125 Wing (2nd TAF), 1944–45; 124 Wing (2nd TAF), 1945–46; RCAF Staff Coll., 1947–48; USAF (Exchange Officer), 1948–50; served Korea (with USAF), 1950–51; OC, RAF Wildenrath (2nd TAF), 1952–54; Air Ministry, 1954–57; Officer Commanding, RAF Cottesmore, Bomber Command, 1957–60; idc 1960; Senior Air Staff Officer, No 3 Group, Bomber Command, Mildenhall, Suffolk, 1960–63; AOC, Air Forces Middle East, Aden, 1963–65; retired. DL Leicester, 1967. Order of Leopold, 1945, Croix de Guerre, 1945 (Belgium); Legion of Merit, 1950, DFC 1943, Air Medal, 1950 (USA); Légion d'Honneur (France), 1988. *Publications:* Wing Leader, 1956; Full Circle, 1964; The Story of Air Fighting, 1985; (jtly) Glorious Summer, 1990; (jtly) Courage in the Skies, 1992; (jtly) Winged Victory, 1995. *Recreations:* shooting, golf. *Address:* The Stables, Hargate, Buxton, Derbyshire SK17 8TA. *Club:* Royal Air Force.

JOHNSON, Rt. Rev. James Nathaniel; Vicar of Hockley, Essex, since 1992; Hon. Assistant Bishop, Chelmsford Diocese, since 1994; *b* 28 April 1932; *s* of William and Lydia Florence Johnson; *m* 1953, Evelyn Joyce Clifford; one *s* one *d*. *Educ:* Primary and Secondary Selective School, St Helena; Church Army College; Wells Theolog. Coll. Deacon 1864, priest 1965; Curate of St Peter's, Lawrence Weston, dio. Bristol, 1964–66; Priest-in-charge of St Paul's Cathedral, St Helena, 1966–69, Vicar 1969–71; Domestic Chaplain to Bishop of St Helena, 1967–71; USPG Area Sec. for Diocese of Exeter and Truro, 1972–74; Rector of Combe Martin dio. Exeter, 1974–80; Hon. Canon of St Helena, 1975–85; Vicar of St Augustine, Thorpe Bay, dio. Chelmsford, 1980–85; Bishop of St Helena, 1985–91; Rector of Byfield with Boddington and Aston-le-Walls, and Hon. Asst Bishop, Peterborough dio., 1991–92. Non-residentiary Canon, Chelmsford Cathedral, 1994–. *Recreations:* music, gardening, walking. *Address:* The Vicarage, 5A High Road, Hockley, Essex SS5 4SY.

JOHNSON, His Honour John Robin; a Circuit Judge, 1973–93; *b* 27 Nov. 1927; *s* of Sir Philip Bulmer Johnson, Hexham, Northumberland; *m* 1958, Meriel Jean, *d* of H. B. Speke, Aydon, Corbridge; one *s* one *d*. *Educ:* Winchester; Trinity Coll., Cambridge. Called to Bar, Middle Temple, 1950. Dep. Chm., Northumberland QS, 1966–71; a Recorder of the Crown Court, 1972–73. *Address:* Kirk Fenwick, Cambo, Morpeth NE61 4BN.

JOHNSON, Sir John (Rodney), KCMG 1988 (CMG 1981); HM Diplomatic Service, retired; Director, Foreign Service Programme, and specially elected Fellow, Keble College, University of Oxford, 1990–95; Chairman, Countryside Commission, 1991–95; *b* 6 Sept. 1930; *s* of Edwin Done Johnson, OBE and Florence Mary (*née* Clough); *m* 1956, Jean Mary Lewis; three *s* one *d*. *Educ:* Manchester Grammar Sch.; Oxford Univ. (MA). HM Colonial Service, Kenya, 1955–64; Dist Comr, Thika, 1962–64; Administrator, Cttee of Vice-Chancellors and Principals of UK Univs, 1965; First Sec., FCO, 1966–69; Head of Chancery, British Embassy, Algiers, 1969–72; Dep. High Comr, British High Commn, Barbados, 1972–74; Counsellor, British High Commn, Lagos, 1975–78; Head of W African Dept, FCO, and Ambassador (non-resident) to Chad, 1978–80; High Comr in Zambia, 1980–84; Asst Under Sec. of State (Africa), FCO, 1984–86; High Comr in Kenya, 1986–90. Mem., Jt Nature Conservation Cttee, 1991–. Chm., Kenya Soc., 1992–. FRGS 1990. *Recreations:* walking, reaching remote places. *Address:* The Gables, High Street, Amersham, Bucks HP7 0DP. *Clubs:* Travellers', Alpine; Climbers; Mombasa.

JOHNSON, Air Vice-Marshal Johnnie; *see* Johnson, James Edgar.

JOHNSON, Kenneth James, OBE 1966; Chairman, Crown Agents Pensions Trust, since 1984; *b* 8 Feb. 1926; *s* of Albert Percy Johnson and Winifred Florence (*née* Coole); *m* 1951, Margaret Teresa Bontoft Jenkins; three *s* two *d*. *Educ:* Rishworth School, near Halifax; Wadham Coll., Oxford; LSE; SOAS. Indian Army (14 Punjab Regt), 1945–47. Colonial Admin. Service, Nigeria, 1949–61, senior appts in Min. of Finance and Min. of Commerce and Industry; Head of Economic Dept, later Dir of Industrial Affairs, CBI, 1961–70; Courtaulds Ltd, 1970–73: Chm. and Man. Dir, various subsidiary cos; Dep. Chm., Pay Board, 1973–74. Dunlop Group: 1974–85: Personnel Dir, 1974–79; Overseas Dir, Dunlop Holdings plc, 1979–84; Chm., Dunlop International AG, 1984–85. Member: Bd of Crown Agents for Oversea Govts and Administrations, 1980–88; Crown Agents Hldg and Realisation Bd, 1980–88. FRSA 1972; FIPM 1976. *Recreations:* book-collecting, travel. *Address:* Snappers Field, Shipley, Horsham, West Sussex RH13 7BQ. *Club:* Oriental.

JOHNSON, Prof. Kenneth Langstreth, PhD; FRS 1982; FEng 1987; Professor of Engineering, Cambridge University, 1977–92, now Emeritus; Fellow of Jesus College, Cambridge, since 1957; *b* 19 March 1925; *s* of Frank Herbert Johnson and Ellen Howorth Langstreth; *m* 1954, Dorothy Rosemary Watkins; one *s* two *d*. *Educ:* Barrow Grammar Sch.; Manchester Univ. (MScTech, MA, PhD). FIMechE. Engr, Messrs Rotol Ltd, Gloucester, 1944–49; Asst Lectr, Coll. of Technology, Manchester, 1949–54; Lectr, then Reader in Engrg, Cambridge Univ., 1954–77. Hon. FUMIST, 1993. Tribology Trust Gold Medal, IMechE, 1985; Mayo Hersey Award, ASME, 1991. *Publications:* Contact Mechanics, 1985; contrib. scientific and engrg jls, and Proc. IMechE. *Recreations:* mountain walking, swimming. *Address:* 1 New Square, Cambridge CB1 1EY. *T:* Cambridge (01223) 355287.

JOHNSON, Prof. Louise Napier, FRS 1990; David Phillips Professor of Molecular Biophysics, and Professorial Fellow, Corpus Christi College, Oxford, since 1990; *b* 26 Sept. 1940; *m*; one *s*. one *d*. *Educ:* Wimbledon High Sch. for Girls; University College London (BSc 1962; Fellow, 1993); Royal Institution, London (PhD 1965). Research Asst., Yale Univ., 1966; University of Oxford: Demonstrator, Zoology Dept, 1967–73; Lectr in Molecular Biophysics, 1973–90; Reader, 1990; Additional Fellow, Somerville College, 1973–90, Hon. Fellow, 1991. Hon. DSc St Andrews, 1992. Kaj Linderström-Lang Prize, 1989. *Publications:* Protein Crystallography (jtly with T. L. Blundell), 1976; papers on lysozyme, glycogen phosphorylase, protein crystallography, enzyme mechanism and allosteric mechanisms. *Recreation:* family. *Address:* Laboratory of Molecular Biophysics, Rex Richards Building, University of Oxford, South Parks Road, Oxford OX1 3QU.

JOHNSON, Prof. Martin Hume, PhD; Professor of Reproductive Sciences, since 1992, and Head of Department of Anatomy, since 1995, University of Cambridge; Fellow, Christ's College, Cambridge, since 1969; *b* 19 Dec. 1944; *s* of Reginald Hugh Ben and Joyce Florence Johnson. *Educ:* Cheltenham Grammar Sch.; Christ's Coll., Cambridge (MA, PhD). Jun. Res. Fellow, Christ's Coll., Cambridge, 1969; MRC Jun. Res. Fellow, 1970; Harkness Fellow, 1971; University of Cambridge: Lectr in Anatomy, 1974–84; Reader in Exptl Embryology, 1984–92. Hon. Sen. Lectr in Obstetrics and Gynaecology, UMDS, 1991; Distinguished Vis. Fellow, La Trobe Univ., 1993. Chm., Brit. Soc. for Developmental Biol., 1984–89; Mem., HFEA, 1994–. Albert Brachet Prize, Belgian Royal Acad. Scis, Letters and Fine Arts, 1989. *Publications:* (with B. J. Everitt) Essential Reproduction, 1980, 4th edn 1995; contrib. to numerous scientific pubns. *Recreations:* opera, dance, walking. *Address:* Department of Anatomy, Downing Street, Cambridge CB2 3DY. *T:* Cambridge (01223) 333789.

JOHNSON, Merwyn; *see* Johnson, W. M.

JOHNSON, Michael York-; *see* York, M.

JOHNSON, Dame Monica; *see* Golding, Dame (Cecilie) Monica.

JOHNSON, Col Neil Anthony, OBE 1989; TD 1985, bar 1992; General Secretary, Royal Automobile Club, since 1994; *b* 13 April 1949; *s* of Anthony and Dilys Johnson, Glamorgan; *m* 1971, Gail Ferguson; three *d*. *Educ:* Canton High Sch., Cardiff; RMA Sandhurst. Graduate Trainee, Lex Gp, 1971–73; British Leyland Internat., 1973–75; Leyland Cars: Gen. Manager, Tech. Services and Marketing, 1975–77; Staff Dir, Marketing and Planning, 1977–79; Service Dir, 1979–80; Dir, Continental Europe Ops, BL, 1980–82; Dir, Sales and Marketing, Jaguar Cars, 1982–86; MoD, 1986–89; Main Bd Dir, Rover Gp, British Aerospace, resp. for European Ops, 1989–92; Dir-Gen., EEF, 1992–93. Director: Charter plc, 1994–; RAC Ltd, 1994–; Motor Sports Assoc.; Auto Cycle Union. Chm., Speedway Control Bd, 1994–. Territorial Army: Pembroke Yeomanry, 1971; 4th Bn RGJ, 1973; CO, 1986–89; ADC to the Queen, 1990; Hon. Col, 157 Transport Regt, RLC, 1993–. Trustee, Jaguar Daimler Heritage Trust, 1994–. FIMI, FIMgt, FRSA. Rep. DL, City of Westminster, 1993. Ordre de l'Encouragement Publique (France), 1987. *Recreations:* family, farming, shooting, riding, reading, music. *Address:* Royal Automobile Club, 89–91 Pall Mall, SW1Y 5HS. *T:* 0171–930 2345. *Clubs:* Royal Automobile, Army and Navy, Royal Green Jackets, Fadeaways, Cardiff & County (Cardiff).

JOHNSON, Nevil; Nuffield Reader in the Comparative Study of Institutions, University of Oxford, and Professorial Fellow, Nuffield College, 1969–Oct. 1996; *b* 6 Feb. 1929; *s* of G. E. Johnson and Doris Johnson, MBE, Darlington; *m* 1957, Ulla van Aubel; two *s*. *Educ:* Queen Elizabeth Grammar Sch., Darlington; University Coll., Oxford (BA PPE 1952, MA 1962). Army service, 1947–49. Admin. Cl. of Home Civil Service: Min. of Supply, 1952–57; Min. of Housing and Local Govt, 1957–62; Lectr in Politics, Univ. of Nottingham, 1962–66; Sen. Lectr in Politics, Univ. of Warwick, 1966–69. Chm. Board, Faculty of Social Studies, Oxford, 1976–78. Visiting Professor: Ruhr Univ. of Bochum, 1968–69; Univ. of Munich, 1980. Mem., ESRC (formerly SSRC), 1981–87 (Chm., Govt and Law Cttee, 1982–86). Civil Service Comr (pt-time), 1982–85. Mem. Exec. Council, RIPA, 1965–87; Chm., Study of Parlt Gp, 1984–87. FRSA 1993. Hon. Editor, Public Administration, 1967–81. *Publications:* Parliament and Administration: The Estimates Committee 1945–65, 1967; Government in the Federal Republic of Germany, 1973; In Search of the Constitution, 1977 (trans. German, 1977); (with A. Cochrane) Economic Policy-Making by Local Authorities in Britain and Western Germany, 1981; State and Government in the Federal Republic of Germany, 1983; The Limits of Political Science, 1989 (trans. Spanish, 1991); articles in Public Admin, Political Studies, Parly Affairs, Ztschr. für Politik, Die Verwaltung, and Der Staat. *Recreations:* walking, swimming, gardening. *Address:* 2 Race Farm Cottages, Kingston Bagpuize, Oxon OX13 5AU. *T:* Longworth (01865) 820777.

JOHNSON, Prof. Newell Walter, MDSc, PhD; FDSRCS, FRACDS, FRCPath; Nuffield Research Professor of Dental Science, Royal College of Surgeons of England, since 1984; Professor of Oral Pathology, University of London at King's College School of Medicine and Dentistry, since 1994; Director of Research and University Postgraduate Education, Dental Institute, King's College London, since 1994; *b* 5 Aug. 1938; *s* of Otto Johnson and Lorna (*née* Guy); *m* 1965, Pauline Margaret Trafford (marr. diss. 1984); two *d*. *Educ:* University High Sch., Melbourne; Univ. of Melbourne (BDSc Hons 1960; MDSc 1963); Univ. of Bristol (PhD 1967). FDSRCS 1964; FRACDS 1966; FRCPath 1982. Res. Fellow in Pathology, Univ. of Melbourne, 1961–63; Lectr in Dental Surgery, UCL, 1963–64; Scientific Officer, MRC Dental Res. Unit, Bristol, 1964–67; London Hospital Medical College: Reader in Experimental Oral Path., 1968–76; Prof. of Oral Path., 1976–83; Hon. Dir, MRC Dental Res. Unit, 1983–93; Governor, 1983 (Chm., Academic Div. of Dentistry, 1983); Chm., London Hosp. Div. of Dentistry, 1981–83. Hon. Consultant Dental Surgeon: Royal London (formerly London) Hosp., 1968–; King's Healthcare NHS Trust, 1993–. Consultant, Fédération Dentaire Internationale, 1984–. Consultant in Oral Health, WHO, 1984–; Dir, WHO Collaborating Centre for Oral Cancer and Precancer, 1995–. Pres., British Soc. of Periodontology, 1992–93. Chm., UK Cttee, Royal Australasian Coll. of Dental Surgeons, 1981–83; FRSM; Mem. Council, Section of Odontology, RSM, 1972– (Pres., 1988–89). Member, Editorial Board: Jl of Oral Pathology, 1982–93; Jl of Periodontal Research, 1986– (Associate Ed., 1993–); Jl of Clin. Periodontology, 1990–; Editor in Chief, Oral Diseases, 1994–. *Publications:* (jtly) The Oral Mucosa in Health and Disease, 1975; (jtly) The Human Oral Mucosa: structure, metabolism and function, 1976; (jtly) Dental Caries: aetiology, pathology and prevention, 1979; (ed jtly) Oral Diseases in the Tropics, 1992; (ed) Detection of High Risk Groups for Oral Diseases, 3 vols, 1991; articles in scientific jls. *Recreations:* music, theatre, visual arts, yoga, the environment, the Third World. *Club:* Blizard.

JOHNSON, Patrick, OBE 1945; MA; *b* 24 May 1904; 2nd *s* of A. F. W. Johnson, JP, and F. E. L. Cocking; unmarried. *Educ:* RN Colls, Osborne and Dartmouth; Tonbridge Sch.; Magdalen Coll., Oxford. Fellow and Lecturer in Natural Science, Magdalen Coll., 1928–47, Dean, 1934–38, Vice-Pres., 1946–47. Flying Officer, RAFO, 1929–34; commissioned in RA (TA), 1938; served War of 1939–45, in Middle East and NW Europe, Lt-Col, Asst Dir of Scientific Research, 21st Army Group and comdg No. 2 operational research section. Dir of Studies, RAF Coll., Cranwell, 1947–52; Dean of Inst. of Armament Studies, India, 1952–55; Scientific Adviser to the Army Council, 1955–58; Asst Scientific Adviser, SHAPE, 1958–62; Head of Experimental Develt Unit, Educnl Foundn for Visual Aids, 1962–70. *Recreations:* rowing (rowed against Cambridge, 1927), sailing, shooting. *Address:* 5 Linley Court, Rouse Gardens, SE21 8AQ. *Club:* Leander (Henley-on-Thames).

JOHNSON, Sir Patrick Eliot, 8th Bt *cr* 1818, of Bath; *b* 1955; *s* of Sir Robin Eliot Johnson, 7th Bt and of Barbara Alfreda, *d* of late Alfred T. Brown; *S* father, 1989. *Heir: cousin* Allen Antony Wynn Johnson [*b* 14 April 1916; *m* 1939, Helen Janet Margaret, *o d* of W. A. Annett; two *s*].

JOHNSON, Paul (Bede); author; *b* 2 Nov. 1928; *s* of William Aloysius and Anne Johnson; *m* 1957, Marigold Hunt; three *s* one *d*. *Educ:* Stonyhurst; Magdalen Coll., Oxford. Asst Exec. Editor, Réalités, 1952–55; Editorial Staff, New Statesman, 1955, Dir, Statesman and Nation Publishing Co., 1965, Editor of the New Statesman, 1965–70. Member: Royal Commn on the Press, 1974–77; Cable Authority, 1984–90. *Publications:* The Suez War, 1957; Journey into Chaos, 1958; Left of Centre, 1960; Merrie England, 1964; Statesmen and Nations, 1971; The Offshore Islanders, 1972; (with G. Gale) The Highland Jaunt, 1973; Elizabeth I, 1974; A Place in History, 1974; Pope John XXIII, 1975 (Yorkshire Post Book of the Year Award, 1975); A History of Christianity, 1976; Enemies of Society, 1977; The National Trust Book of British Castles, 1978; The Recovery of Freedom, 1980; British Cathedrals, 1980; Ireland: Land of Troubles, 1980; Pope John Paul II and the Catholic Restoration, 1982; A History of the Modern World from 1917 to the 1980s, 1983; The Pick of Paul Johnson, 1985; Oxford Book of Political Anecdotes, 1986; A History of the Jews, 1987; Intellectuals, 1988; The Birth of the Modern: world society 1815–30, 1991; Wake Up Britain! A Latterday Pamphlet, 1994. *Recreations:* hill-walking, painting. *Address:* 29 Newton Road, W2 5JR. *T:* 0171–229 3859; The Coach House, Over Stowey, near Bridgwater, Somerset TA5 1HA. *T:* Bridgwater (01278) 732393.
See also D. B. Johnson.

JOHNSON, Sir Peter (Colpoys Paley), 7th Bt *cr* 1755, of New York in North America; author; publishing consultant; *b* 26 March 1930; *s* of Sir John Paley Johnson, 6th Bt, MBE, and of Carol, *d* of late Edmund Haas; *S* father, 1975; *m* 1st, 1956, Clare (marr. diss. 1973), *d* of late Dr Nigel Bruce; one *s* two *d*; 2nd, 1973, Caroline Elisabeth, *d* of late Sir John Hodsoll, CB; one *s*. *Educ:* Wellington Coll.; Royal Military Coll. of Science. Served RA, 1949; retired 1961, Captain. Dir, Sea Sure Ltd, 1965–73; Dir and Editor, Nautical Publishing Co. Ltd, 1970–81; Publishing Dir, Nautical Books, London, 1981–86. British Delegate, Internat. Offshore (Yachting) Council, 1970–79 (Chm. Internat. Technical Cttee, 1973–76); Ocean Racing Correspondent, Yachting World, London, 1971–81. Hon. Col, King's Royal Regt of NY (Canada), 1988–; *Publications:* Ocean Racing and Offshore Yachts, 1970, 2nd edn 1972; Boating Britain, 1973; Guinness Book of Yachting Facts and Feats, 1975; Guinness Guide to Sailing, 1981; This is Fast Cruising, 1985; The Encyclopedia of Yachting, 1989; Whitbread Round the World 1973–93, 1993; Yacht Clubs of the World, 1995. *Recreation:* sailing. *Heir: s* Colpoys Guy Johnson [*b* 13 Nov. 1965; *m* 1990, Marie-Louise, *d* of John Holroyd; one *s*]. *Address:* Dene End, Buckland Dene, Lymington, Hampshire SO41 9DT. *T:* Lymington (01590) 675921, *Fax:* (01590) 672885. *Clubs:* Royal Ocean Racing; Royal Yacht Squadron.

JOHNSON, Philip Cortelyou; architect, with own firm, 1953–67, with Johnson/Burgee Architects, since 1967; *b* Cleveland, Ohio, 8 July 1906; *s* of Homer H. Johnson and Louise Pope Johnson. *Educ:* Harvard (AB 1927, *cum laude*). Dir, Dept of Architecture, The Museum of Modern Art, New York, 1932–54, Trustee, 1958–; Graduate Sch. of Design, Harvard, 1940–43 (BArch). Has taught and lectured at: Yale Univ.; Cornell Univ.; Pratt Inst. (Dr Fine Arts, 1962). Mem. AIA (New York Chapter); Architectural League, NY. Hon. Dr Fine Arts Yale, 1978. Gold Medal, AIA, 1978; Pritzker Architecture Prize, 1979. *Publications:* Machine Art, 1934; Mies van der Rohe, 1st edn 1947, 2nd edn 1953; (with Henry-Russell Hitchcock) The International Style, Architecture since 1922, 1932, new edn 1966; (with others) Modern Architects, 1932; Architecture 1949–65, 1966; Philip Johnson Writings, 1979; contributor to Architectural Review. *Address:* (business) Philip Johnson, 885 Third Avenue #300, New York, NY 10022–4834, USA; (home) Ponus Ridge Road, New Canaan, CT 06840, USA. *T:* (203) 9660565. *Clubs:* Athenæum, Century.

JOHNSON, (Reginald) Stuart, CBE 1985; Director of Education, Leeds City Council, 1973–93; *b* 12 April 1933; *s* of late Reginald Johnson and Sarah Anne Johnson; *m* 1960, Dr Jennifer Johnson (*née* Craig); one *s* one *d*. *Educ:* Durham Univ. (BSc Hons); London Univ. (PGCE, DipEd). Deputy Education Officer, Leeds CC, 1968–73. Member: UGC, 1979–89 (Chm., Educn Sub-Cttee, 1985–89); Advisory Cttee on Supply and Educn of Teachers, 1980– (Chm., Teacher Trng Sub-Cttee, 1981–); PPITB, 1977–80 (Chm., Trng Cttee, 1978–80). Member: BBC Schools and Further Educn Broadcasting Council, 1976–82; Social Security Tribunal. Adviser to Burnham Cttee, 1984. Administrator, Leeds International Pianoforte Competition, 1978–81. Mem. Council, Leeds Univ., 1986–. *Publications:* frequent articles in educnl press. *Recreations:* golf, cricket, fishing. *Address:* Mickleber House, Gargrave Road, Gargrave, Skipton, N Yorks BD23 3AQ. *T:* Skipton (01756) 748423. *Clubs:* Lansdowne; Leeds (Leeds).

JOHNSON, Richard Keith; actor and producer; *b* 30 July 1927; *s* of Keith Holcombe and Frances Louisa Olive Johnson; *m* 1st, 1957, Sheila Sweet (marr. diss); one *s* one *d*; 2nd, 1965, Kim Novak (marr. diss.); 3rd, 1982, Marie-Louise Norlund (marr. diss.); one *s* one *d*. *Educ:* Parkfield School; Felsted School; RADA. RN, 1945–48. 1st stage appearance, Opera House, Manchester, 1944; repertory, Haymarket, 1944–45; *stage:* contract, Royal Shakespeare Theatre, 1957–62; Antony in Antony and Cleopatra, RSC, 1972–73, and 1992–93; NT, 1976–78; The War That Still Goes On, Young Vic, 1991; King, in All's Well that Ends Well, RSC, 1992–93; An Inspector Calls, Aldwych, 1994; The Rivals, Albery, 1994–95; *films:* MGM contract, 1959–65; acted in: The Haunting; Moll Flanders; Operation Crossbow; Khartoum; The Pumpkin Eater; Danger Route; Deadlier than the Male; Oedipus the King; Hennessy (also wrote original story); Aces High; The Four Feathers; produced: Turtle Diary; Castaway (Exec. Producer); The Lonely Passion of Judith Hearne; *television:* Rembrandt (title rôle); Hamlet (king); Antony and Cleopatra (Antony); The Member for Chelsea (title rôle); The Camomile Lawn (Oliver); Anglo-Saxon Attitudes (Gerald). Jt Founder, United British Artists, 1982. Mem. Council, BAFTA, 1977–79. *Recreations:* reading, gardening, travelling. *Address:* c/o Conway, Van Gelder, Robinson Ltd, 18–21 Jermyn Street, SW1Y 6HP.

JOHNSON, (Robert) Brian, CBE 1990; QPM 1981; DL; Chief Constable, Lancashire Constabulary, 1983–95; *b* 28 July 1932; *s* of Robert and Hilda Johnson; *m* 1954, Jean Thew; two *d*. *Educ:* Stephenson Memorial Boys' Sch.; College of Commerce, Newcastle. Newcastle City Police: Police Cadet, 1948; Police Constable, 1952; Detective Constable, 1955; Detective Sergeant, 1962; Detective Inspector, 1966; Detective Chief Inspector, 1969; Detective Supt, Northumbria Police, 1971; Chief Supt, Northumbria Police, Home Office, 1976; Asst Chief Constable, Northumbria, 1977; Dep. Chief Constable, Lancashire, 1981. President: NW Area, National Assoc. of Retired Police Officers (also Pres., Blackpool Br.), 1983–95; ACPO, 1991–92; Lancs Assoc. of Boys Clubs, 1983–95; Lancs Outward Bound Assoc., 1983–95; Vice-Pres., Lancs Council for Voluntary Youth Services, 1985–; Patron: NW Counties Schools ABA, 1983–95; Blackburn Area, Road Safety Assoc., 1983–. DL Lancs, 1989. *Recreations:* reading, gardening.

JOHNSON, Hon. Sir Robert (Lionel), Kt 1989; **Hon. Mr Justice Johnson;** a Justice of the High Court, Family Division, since 1989; *b* 9 Feb. 1933; *er s* of late Edward Harold Johnson, MSc, FRIC, and of Ellen Lydiate Johnson, Cranleigh; *m* 1957, Linda Mary, *er d* of late Charles William Bennie and Ena Ethel Bennie, Egglescliffe; one *s* two *d*. *Educ:* Watford Grammar Sch. (1940–51); London Sch. of Econs and Polit. Science. 5th Royal Inniskilling Dragoon Guards, 1955–57, Captain; ADC to GOC-in-C Northern Comd, 1956–57; Inns of Court Regt, 1957–64. Called to the Bar, Gray's Inn, 1957, Bencher, 1986; QC 1978; a Recorder, 1977–89. Jun. Counsel to Treasury in Probate Matters, 1975–78; Legal Assessor, GNC, 1977–82. Chairman: Bar Fees and Legal Aid Cttee, 1984–86 (Vice-Chm., 1982–84); Family Law Bar Assoc., 1984–86; Family Law Cttee, Justice, 1990–93; Mem., Bar Council, 1981–88; Vice Chm., 1987, Chm., 1988, Gen. Council of Bar. Member: Supreme Court Procedure Cttee, 1982–87; Law Soc. Legal Aid Cttee, 1981–87; No 1 Legal Aid Area Cttee, 1980–87; Co-Chm., Civil and Family Cttee, Judicial Studies Bd, 1989–94. Pres., English Chapter, Internat. Acad. of Matrimonial Lawyers, 1986–89. Sec., Internat. Cystic Fibrosis Assoc., 1984–90; Trustee: Cystic Fibrosis Res. Trust, 1964–; Robert Luff Charitable Foundn, 1977–. *Publications:* (with James Comyn) Wills & Intestacies, 1970; Contract, 1975; (with Malcolm Stitcher) Atkin's Trade, Labour and Employment, 1975. *Recreations:* charitable work, gardening. *Address:* Royal Courts of Justice, Strand, WC2A 2LL.

JOHNSON, Prof. Roger Paul, FEng 1986; Professor of Civil Engineering, University of Warwick, since 1971; *b* 12 May 1931; *s* of Norman Eric Johnson and Eleanor Florence (*née* Paul); *m* 1958, Diana June (*née* Perkins); three *s*. *Educ:* Cranleigh Sch., Surrey; Jesus Coll., Cambridge (BA 1953; MA 1957). FIStructE 1972; FICE 1979. Holloway Bros (London), Civil Engineering Contractor, 1953–55; Ove Arup and Partners, Consulting Engineers, 1956–59; Lectr in Engineering, Cambridge Univ., 1959–71. Vis. Prof., Univ. of Sydney, 1982–83. *Publications:* Structural Concrete, 1967; Composite Structures of Steel and Concrete, vol. 1, 1975, 2nd edn 1994, vol. 2 (with R. J. Buckby), 1979, 2nd edn 1986; (with D. Anderson) Designers' Handbook to Eurocode 4, 1993; contribs to learned jls. *Recreations:* music, gardening, mountain walking. *Address:* Engineering Department, University of Warwick, Coventry CV4 7AL. *T:* Coventry (01203) 523129.

JOHNSON, Sir Ronald (Ernest Charles), Kt 1970; CB 1962; JP; *b* 3 May 1913; *o c* of Ernest and Amelia Johnson; *m* 1938, Elizabeth Gladys Nuttall; two *s* (and one *s* decd). *Educ:* Portsmouth Grammar Sch.; St John's Coll., Cambridge. Entered Scottish Office, 1935; Sec., Scottish Home and Health Dept, 1963–72. Chm., Civil Service Savings Cttee for Scotland, 1963–78. Sec. of Commissions for Scotland, 1972–78. Chm., Scottish Hosp. Centre, 1964–72. Member: Scottish Records Adv. Council, 1975–81; Cttee on Admin of Sheriffdoms, 1981–82; Chm., Fire Service Res. and Training Trust, 1976–89. Served RNVR on intelligence staff of C-in-C, Eastern Fleet, 1944–45. President: Edinburgh Bach Soc., 1973–86; Edinburgh Soc. of Organists, 1980–82. JP Edinburgh, 1972. *Publications:* articles in religious and musical jls. *Address:* 14 Eglinton Crescent, Edinburgh EH12 5DD. *T:* 0131–337 7733.

JOHNSON, Stanley, CBE 1970; FCA; FCIT; Managing Director, British Transport Docks Board, 1967–75; *b* 10 Nov. 1912; *s* of late Robert and Janet Mary Johnson; *m* 1940, Sheila McLean Bald (*d* 1994); two *s* two *d*. *Educ:* King George V Sch., Southport. Served as Lieut (S) RINVR, 1942–45. Joined Singapore Harbour Board, 1939; Asst Gen. Man. 1952; Chm. and Gen. Man. 1958–59; Chief Docks Man., Hull Docks, 1962; Asst Gen. Man. 1963, Mem. and Dep. Man. Dir 1966, British Transport Docks Board. Chm. Major Ports Cttee, Dock and Harbour Authorities Assoc., 1971–72. Mem., Exec. Council, British Ports Assoc., 1973–75; Vice-Pres., Internat. Assoc. of Ports and Harbours, 1975–77. Vice-Pres., CIT, 1973–75. *Recreations:* walking, reading, travel. *Address:* The Cottage, Waldley, near Doveridge, Derbys DE6 5LR. *T:* Rocester (01889) 590442. *Club:* Naval and Military.

JOHNSON, Stanley Patrick; Director, Environmental Resources Ltd, since 1992; *b* 18 Aug. 1940; *s* of Wilfred Johnson and Irène (*née* Williams); *m* 1st, 1963, Charlotte Offlow Fawcett (marr. diss.); three *s* one *d*; 2nd, 1981, Mrs Jennifer Kidd; one *s* one *d*. *Educ:* Sherborne Sch.; Exeter Coll., Oxford (Trevelyan Schol., Sen. Classics Schol.); Harkness Fellow, USA, 1963–64. MA Oxon 1963; Dip. Agric. Econs Oxon 1965. World Bank, Washington, 1966–68; Project Dir, UNA-USA Nat. Policy Panel on World Population, 1968–69; Mem. Conservative Research Dept, 1969–70; Staff of Internat. Planned Parenthood Fedn, London, 1971–73; Consultant to UN Fund for Population Activities, 1971–73; Mem. Countryside Commn, 1971–73; Head of Prevention of Pollution and Nuisances Div., EEC, 1973–77; Adviser to Head of Environment and Consumer Protection Service, EEC, 1977–79; Member (C) Wight and Hants E, Eur. Parlt, 1979–84; Advr to Dir Gen. for Envmt, Civil Protection and Nuclear Safety, EEC, 1984–90; Dir for

Energy Policy, EEC, 1990; Special Advr, Coopers & Lybrand, Deloitte, 1991. Newdigate Prize for Poetry, 1962; Richard Martin Award, RSPCA, 1982; Greenpeace Award, 1984. *Publications:* Life Without Birth, 1970; The Green Revolution, 1972; The Politics of the Environment, 1973; (ed) The Population Problem, 1973; The Pollution Control Policy of the EEC, 1979, 3rd edn 1989; Antarctica—the last great wilderness, 1985; The Earth Summit: the United Nations Conference on Environment and Development, 1993; World Population—turning the tide, 1994; *novels:* Gold Drain, 1967; Panther Jones for President, 1968; God Bless America, 1974; The Doomsday Deposit, 1980; The Marburg Virus, 1982; Tunnel, 1984; The Commissioner, 1987; Dragon River, 1989. *Recreations:* writing, travel. *Address:* Nethercote, Winsford, Minehead, Somerset TA24 7HZ. *Club:* Savile.

JOHNSON, Stuart; *see* Johnson, R. S.

JOHNSON, Sir Vassel (Godfrey), Kt 1994; CBE 1979 (OBE 1970); JP; Managing Director, Montpelier Properties (Cayman) Ltd, since 1983; Director, British American Bank, since 1983; *b* 18 Jan. 1922; *s* of late Charles McKintha Johnson and of Theresa Virginia Johnson (*née* McDoom); *m* 1952, Rita Joanna Hinds; two *s* four *d* (and one *s* decd). *Educ:* Govt Secondary Sch., Grand Cayman; Bennett Coll., England; Wolsey Hall; Sussex Univ. Entered Cayman Is CS, 1942; transferred to Cayman Co. of Jamaica Home Guard, 1942–45; Clerical Officer, Dept of Treasury, Customs and PO, 1945–55; Asst to Dep. Treas., 1955–59; Clerk of Courts, 1959–60; Public Recorder, 1962–76; Treas. and Collector of Taxes, 1965–82; Hd of Exchange Control, 1966–80; Inspector of Banks and Trust Cos, 1966–73; Chm., Cayman Is Currency Bd, 1971–82; Mem., Exec. Council, resp. for Finance and Develt, 1972–82; Actg Gov., Cayman Is, 1977; Chm., Govt Vehicles Funding Scheme, 1977–82; retd from CS, 1983. MLA, George Town, 1984–88; Mem., Exec. Council, resp. for Develt and Nat. Resources, 1984–88. Cayman Airways Ltd: Founding Dir, 1968; Chm., 1971–77 and 1984–85; Chm., Cayman Is Corp. (Airport), 1969–77; Trustee, Swiss Bank & Trust Corp., 1983–. JP Cayman Is, 1979. Chm., Bd of Govs, Cayman Prep. Sch., 1982–84 and 1993–. Silver Jubilee Medal, 1977. *Publication:* Cayman Islands Economic and Financial Review 1904–1981, 1982. *Recreations:* bridge, church work (Senior Elder, United Church). *Address:* PO Box 78G, Grand Cayman, Cayman Islands. *T:* 9499217; PO Box 2136G, Grand Cayman, Cayman Islands. *T:* 9495511/5521, *Fax:* 9492726.

JOHNSON, Walter Hamlet; *b* Hertford, 21 Nov. 1917; *s* of John Johnson; *m* 1945. *Educ:* Devon House Sch., Margate. Councillor, Brentford and Chiswick for 6 years. Nat. Treasurer, 1965–77, Pres., 1977–81, Transport Salaried Staffs' Assoc. Joined Labour Party, 1945. Contested (Lab) Bristol West, 1955 and South Bedfordshire, 1959, in General Elections; also Acton (Lab), 1968, in by-election. MP (Lab) Derby South, 1970–83; an Assistant Govt Whip, 1974–75. Is particularly interested in welfare services, transport, labour relations and aviation matters; Chm., PLP Aviation Cttee, 1979–83. Principal Executive Assistant, London Transport, 1980–83 (formerly a Sen. Exec., Staff Trng). Governor, Ruskin Coll., Oxford, 1966–85. *Recreation:* sport. *Address:* 9 Milton Court, Haywards Heath RH16 1EY. *T:* Haywards Heath (01444) 412629.

JOHNSON, Prof. William, DSc Manchester, MA Cantab; FRS 1982; FEng 1983; FIMechE; United Technologies Distinguished Professor of Engineering, Purdue University, Indiana, 1988 and 1989; Emeritus Professor, Cambridge University; *b* 20 April 1922; *er s* of James Johnson and Elizabeth Johnson (*née* Riley); *m* 1946, Heather Marie (*née* Thornber); three *s* two *d*. *Educ:* Central Grammar Sch., Manchester; Manchester Coll. of Science and Technology (BScTech). BSc Maths, London; CEng. Served War, Lt REME, UK and Italy, 1943–47. Asst Principal, Administrative Grade, Home Civil Service, 1948–50; Lecturer, Northampton Polytechnic, London, 1950–51; Lectr in Engineering, Sheffield Univ., 1952–56; Senior Lectr in Mechanical Engineering, Manchester Univ., 1956–60; Prof. of Mechanical Engrg, 1960–75, Chm. of Dept of Mechanical Engrg, 1960–69, 1971–73, Dir of Medical Engrg, 1973–75, UMIST; Prof. of Mechanics, Engrg Dept, Cambridge Univ., 1975–82; Professorial Fellow, Fitzwilliam Coll., 1975–82. Visiting Professor: McMaster Univ., Canada, 1969; Springer Prof., Univ. of Calif, Berkeley, 1980; Singapore, 1982; Taiwan, 1985; Allied Irish Banks Prof., Univ. of Belfast, 1983; Industrial Engrg Dept, Purdue Univ., Indiana, 1984 and 1985. Hon. Sec., Yorks Br. of IMechE, 1953–56, and Chm., NW Br., 1974–75; Vis. for DoI to Prodn Engrg Res. Assoc. and Machine Tool Res. Assoc., 1973–75; President: Manchester and Salford Med. Engrg Club, 1971–72; Manchester Assoc. of Engrs, 1972–73; Manchester Technol. Assoc., 1983–84. Founder, and Editor-in-Chief: Internat. Jl Mech. Sciences, 1960–87; Internat. Jl Impact Engineering, 1983–87; Chm., Internat. Jl Mech. Engrg Educn, 1960–84. Fellow UCL, 1982. For. Fellow, Nat. Acad. of Athens, 1982. For. Mem., Russian Acad. of Scis, 1993. Hon. DTech Bradford, 1976; Hon. DEng: Sheffield, 1986; UMIST, 1995. Premium Award, Jl RAeS, 1956; T. Constantine Medal, Manchester Assoc. of Engrs, 1962; Bernard Hall Prize (jt), IMechE, 1965–66 and 1966–67; James Clayton Fund Prize (jt), IMechE, 1972 and 1978; Safety in Mech. Engrg Prize, (jt) 1980, 1991; Silver Medal, Inst. of Sheet Metal Engrg, 1987; James Clayton Prize, IMechE, 1987; Gold Medal, Jl of Advanced Materials Processing Technology, 1995. *Publications:* Plasticity for Mechanical Engineers (with P. B. Mellor), 1962; Mechanics of Metal Extrusion (with H. Kudo), 1962; Plane Strain Slip Line Fields (with R. Sowerby and J. B. Haddow), 1970; Impact Strength of Materials, 1972; Engineering Plasticity (with P. B. Mellor), 1973; Lectures in Engineering Plasticity (with A. G. Mamalis), 1978; Crashworthiness of Vehicles (with A. G. Mamalis), 1978; Plane-Strain Slip-Line Fields for Metal-Deformation Processes (with R. Sowerby and R. Venter), 1982; papers in mechanics of metal forming, impact engineering, mechanics of sports and games, solids, medical and bioengineering, and history of engineering mechanics. *Recreation:* landscape gardening. *Address:* Ridge Hall, Chapel-en-le-Frith, Derbyshire SK12 6UD.

JOHNSON, (Willis) Merwyn; Agent General for Saskatchewan in the United Kingdom, 1977–83; *b* 9 May 1923; *s* of Robert Arthur Johnson and Gudborg Kolbinson; *m* 1946, Laura Elaine Aseltine; two *s* two *d*. *Educ:* McKenzie High Sch., Kindersley; Univ. of Saskatchewan. BSA, BA. MP for Kindersley, Parliament of Canada, 1953–57 and 1957–58. *Recreations:* fishing, golf. *Address:* 4044 Hollydene Place, Victoria, BC V8N 3Z7, Canada.

JOHNSON-FERGUSON, Sir Ian (Edward), 4th Bt *cr* 1906, of Springkell, Dumfries, of Kenyon, Newchurch-in-Culceth, Lancaster, and of Wiston, Lanark; *b* 1 Feb. 1932; *s* of Sir Neil Edward Johnson-Ferguson, 3rd Bt, TD and Sheila Marion (*d* 1985), *er d* of Col H. S. Jervis, MC; *S* father 1992; *m* 1964, Rosemary Teresa, *yr d* of C. J. Whitehead; three *s*. *Educ:* Ampleforth Coll.; Trinity Coll., Cambridge (BA 1953); Imperial Coll., London (DIC Geophysics 1954). Royal Dutch Shell, 1954–62; IBM UK Ltd, 1963–90. *Heir: s* Captain Mark Edward Johnson-Ferguson, RE [*b* 14 Aug. 1965; *m* 1995, Julia Catherine, *d* of T. D. Getley]. *Address:* Copthall Place, Upper Clatford, Andover, Hants SP11 7LR.

JOHNSON-GILBERT, Ronald Stuart, OBE 1976; Secretary, Royal College of Surgeons of England, 1962–88; *b* 14 July 1925; *s* of late Sir Ian A. Johnson-Gilbert, CBE and late Rosalind Bell-Hughes; *m* 1951, Ann Weir Drummond; three *d*. *Educ:* Edinburgh Acad.; Rugby; Brasenose Coll., Oxford (Classical Exhbnr and Open Schol., 1943; MA). Intelligence Corps, 1943–46. Trainee, John Lewis Partnership, 1950–51; Admin. Staff, RCS, 1951–88; Secretary: Faculties of Dental Surgery and of Anaesthetists, 1958; Jt Conf. of Surgical Colls, 1963–88; Internat. Fedn of Surgical Colls, 1967–74; Hon. Sec., Med. Commn on Accident Prevention, 1984–88. Mem. Ct of Patrons, RCS, 1990–; Hunterian Trustee, RCS, 1989–. Hon. FFARCS 1983; Hon. FRCS 1987; Hon. FDSRCS 1987; Hon. FRCSI 1989. John Tomes Medal, BDA, 1980; McNeill Love Medal, RCS, 1981; Royal Australasian Coll. of Surgeons Medal, 1982. *Recreations:* music, painting, literature, golf. *Address:* Home Farm, Castle Rising, near King's Lynn, Norfolk PE31 6AE.
See also T. I. Johnson-Gilbert.

JOHNSON-GILBERT, Thomas Ian; Joint Senior Partner, Clifford Chance, Solicitors, 1987–89; *b* 2 June 1923; *s* of Sir Ian Johnson-Gilbert, CBE, LLD and late Rosalind Bell-Hughes (Lady Johnson-Gilbert); *m* 1950, Gillian June Pool; one *s* one *d*. *Educ:* Edinburgh Academy; Rugby School; Trinity College, Oxford (1942 and 1946–47); Open Classical Scholarship; MA. RAFVR, 1943–46. Admitted solicitor, 1950; Coward Chance, 1950–87 (Partner, 1954, Senior Partner, 1980–87). Mem. Council, Law Society, 1970–88. *Recreations:* reading, arts, travel, spectator sport. *Clubs:* Athenæum, Garrick, MCC.
See also R. S. Johnson-Gilbert.

JOHNSON-LAIRD, Prof. Philip Nicholas, FRS 1991; FBA 1986; Stuart Professor of Psychology, Princeton University, since 1994 (Professor pf Psychology, since 1989); *b* 12 Oct. 1936; *s* of Eric Johnson-Laird and Dorothy (*née* Blackett); *m* 1959, Maureen Mary Sullivan; one *s* one *d*. *Educ:* Culford Sch.; University Coll. London (Rosa Morison Medal, 1964; James Sully Schol., 1964–66; BA (Hons) 1964; PhD 1967). MBPsS 1962. 10 years of misc. jobs, as surveyor, musician, hosp. porter (alternative to Nat. Service), librarian, before going to university. Asst Lectr, then Lectr, in Psychol., UCL, 1966–73; Reader, 1973, Prof., 1978, in Exptl Psychol., Univ. of Sussex; Asst Dir, MRC Applied Psychology Unit, Cambridge, 1983–89; Fellow, Darwin Coll., Cambridge, 1984–89. Vis. Mem., Princeton Inst. for Advanced Study, 1971–72; Vis. Fellow, Stanford Univ., 1980; Visiting Professor: Stanford Univ., 1985; Princeton Univ., 1986. Member: Psychol. Cttee, SSRC, 1975–79; Linguistics Panel, SSRC, 1980–82; Adv. Council, Internat. Assoc. for Study of Attention and Performance, 1984. Member: Linguistics Assoc., 1967; Exptl Psychol. Soc., 1968; Cognitive Sci. Soc., 1980; Assoc. for Computational Linguistics, 1981. Hon. DPhil Göteborg, 1983. Spearman Medal, 1974, President's Award, 1985, BPsS. *Publications:* (ed jtly) Thinking and Reasoning, 1968; (with P. C. Wason) Psychology and Reasoning, 1972; (with G. A. Miller) Language and Perception, 1976; (ed jtly) Thinking, 1977; Mental Models, 1983; The Computer and the Mind, 1988; (with Ruth Byrne) Deduction, 1991; Human and Machine Thinking, 1993; contribs to psychol, linguistic and cognitive sci. jls, reviews in lit. jls. *Recreations:* talking, arguing, laughing, playing modern jazz. *Address:* Department of Psychology, Princeton University, Princeton, NJ 08540, USA. *T:* (609) 2584432.

JOHNSON SMITH, Sir Geoffrey, Kt 1982; DL; MP (C) Wealden, since 1983 (East Grinstead, Feb. 1965–1983); *b* 16 April 1924; *s* of late J. Johnson Smith; *m* Jeanne Pomeroy, MD; two *s* one *d*. *Educ:* Charterhouse; Lincoln Coll., Oxford. Served War of 1939–45: Royal Artillery, 1942–47; Temp. Capt. RA, 1946. BA Hons, Politics, Philosophy and Economics, Oxford, 1949. Mem., Oxford Union Soc. Debating Team, USA, 1949. Information Officer, British Information Services, San Francisco, 1950–52; Mem. Production Staff, Current Affairs Unit, BBC TV, 1953–54; London County Councillor, 1955–58; Interviewer, Reporter, BBC TV, 1955–59. MP (C) Holborn and St Pancras South, 1959–64; PPS, Board of Trade and Min. of Pensions, 1960–63; Opposition Whip, 1965; Parly Under-Sec. of State for Defence for the Army, MoD, 1971–72; Parly Sec., CSD, 1972–74. Chm., Cons. Back-bench Defence Cttee, 1988–93 (Vice-Chm., 1980–88); Chm., Select Cttee on Members' Interests, 1980–; Vice-Chm., 1922 Cttee, 1988– (Mem. Exec., 1979–). A Vice-Chm., Conservative Party, 1965–71. Member: IBA Gen. Adv. Council, 1975–80; N Atlantic Assembly, 1980– (Chm., Military Cttee, 1985–89; Leader, UK Delegn to Assembly, 1987–). Governor, BFI, 1980–88. Freeman, City of London, 1980. DL East Sussex, 1986. *Address:* House of Commons, SW1A 0AA. *Club:* Travellers'.

JOHNSTON; *see* Lawson Johnston.

JOHNSTON, family name of **Baron Johnston of Rockport.**

JOHNSTON, Hon. Lord; Alan Charles Macpherson Johnston; a Senator of the College of Justice in Scotland, since 1994; *b* 13 Jan. 1942; *s* of Hon. Lord Dunpark, TD; *m* 1966, Anthea Jean Blackburn; three *s*. *Educ:* Edinburgh Academy; Loretto School; Jesus Coll., Cambridge (BA Hons); Edinburgh Univ. (LLB). Called to the Bar, 1967; QC (Scot.) 1980. Standing Junior, Scottish Home and Health Dept, 1974–79; Advocate Depute, 1979–82; Treasurer, 1977–89, Dean, 1989–94, Faculty of Advocates. Chairman: Industrial Tribunal, 1982–88; Med. Appeal Tribunal, 1985–89. *Publication:* (asst editor) Gloag and Henderson, Introduction to Scots Law, 7th edn 1968. *Recreations:* shooting, fishing, golf, walking. *Address:* 3 Circus Gardens, Edinburgh EH3 6TN. *Clubs:* University Pitt (Cambridge); New (Edinburgh).

JOHNSTON OF ROCKPORT, Baron *cr* 1987 (Life Peer), of Caversham in the Royal County of Berkshire; **Charles Collier Johnston;** Kt 1973; TD; *b* 4 March 1915; *e s* of late Captain Charles Moore Johnston and Muriel Florence Mellon; *m* two *s*; *m* 1981, Mrs Yvonne Shearman. *Educ:* Tonbridge Sch., Kent. Commissioned TA, 1938; served War of 1939–45 (TD); Major RA, retd 1946. Managing Dir, 1948–76, Chm., 1951–77, of Standex International Ltd (formerly Roehlen-Martin Ltd), Engravers and Engineers, Ashton Road, Bredbury, Cheshire; Chairman: Thames & Kennet Marina Ltd, 1982–94; James Burn International, 1986–; Standex Holdings Ltd, 1986– (Dir 1983). Jt Hon. Treas., Conservative Party, 1984–87. Chm., Macclesfield Constituency Conservative Assoc., 1961–65; Hon. Treas., NW Conservatives and Mem. Conservative Bd of Finance, 1965–71; Chm., NW Area Conservatives, 1971–76; Pres., Nat. Union of Conservative and Unionist Assocs, 1986–87 (Mem. Exec. Cttee, 1965–, Chm. 1976–81). Nat. Chm., Cons. Friends of Israel, 1983–86. Mem., Boyd Commn, as official observers of elecns held in Zimbabwe/Rhodesia, April 1980. *Recreations:* spectator sports, travelling, gardening. *Address:* House of Lords, SW1A 0PW.

JOHNSTON, Alexander Graham; Sheriff of Strathkelvin at Glasgow, since 1985; *b* 16 July 1944; *s* of Hon. Lord Kincraig, *qv*; *m* 1st, 1972, Susan (marr. diss. 1982); two *s*; 2nd, 1982, Angela; two step *d*. *Educ:* Edinburgh Acad.; Strathallan Sch.; Univ. of Edinburgh (LLB); University Coll., Oxford (BA). Admitted as Solicitor and Writer to the Signet, 1971; Partner, Hagart and Burn-Murdoch, Solicitors, Edinburgh, 1972–82. Sheriff of Grampian, Highland and Isles, 1982–85. Editor, Scottish Civil Law Reports, 1987–92. Hon. Fellow, Inst. of Professional Investigators, 1980. *Recreations:* photography, piping, bridge, puzzles. *Address:* 3 North Dean Park Avenue, Bothwell, Lanarkshire G71 8HH. *T:* Bothwell (01698) 852177. *Clubs:* Oxford and Cambridge Golfing Society; Vincent's (Oxford).

JOHNSTON, Most Rev. Allen Howard, CMG 1978; LTh; *b* Auckland, NZ, 1912; *s* of Joseph Howard Johnston; *m* 1937, Joyce Rhoda, *d* of John A. Grantley, Auckland; four *d*. *Educ:* Seddon Memorial Technical College; St John's College, Auckland; Auckland Univ. College. Deacon, 1935; Priest, 1936. Assistant Curate of St Mark's, Remuera, 1935–37;

Vicar of Dargaville, 1937–42; Vicar of Northern Wairoa, 1942–44; Vicar of Otahuhu, 1944–49; Vicar of Whangarei, 1949–53; Archdeacon of Waimate, 1949–53; Bishop of Dunedin, 1953–69; Bishop of Waikato, 1969–80; Primate and Archbishop of New Zealand, 1972–80. Fellow, St John's Coll., Auckland, 1970. Hon. LLD Otago, 1969. ChStJ 1974. *Address:* 3 Wymer Terrace, Hamilton, New Zealand.

JOHNSTON, Catherine Elizabeth; Parliamentary Counsel, since 1994; *b* 4 Jan. 1953; *d* of Sir Alexander Johnston, GCB, KBE and Betty Joan (Lady Johnston, CBE), *d* of Edward and Catherine Anne Harris; *m* 1989, Brendan Patrick Keith; one *s* one *d*. *Educ:* St Paul's Girls' Sch.; St Hugh's Coll., Oxford (Scholar 1970; BA 1974). Admitted as solicitor, 1978; joined Parliamentary Counsel Office, 1980; with Law Commn, 1983–85 and 1990–92; on secondment to Office of Parly Counsel, Canberra, 1987–88. *Address:* Office of the Parliamentary Counsel, 36 Whitehall, SW1A 2AY.

JOHNSTON, Rear-Adm. Clarence Dinsmore H.; *see* Howard-Johnston.

JOHNSTON, Prof. David, MD, ChM; FRCS, FRCSE, FRCSGlas; Professor of Surgery and Head of Department, University of Leeds at Leeds General Infirmary, since 1977; *b* Glasgow, 4 Sept. 1936; *s* of Robert E. and Jean Johnston; *m* (marr. diss); three *s* one *d*; *m* 1987, Dr Maureen Teresa Reynolds; two *s*. *Educ:* Hamilton Acad.; Glasgow Univ. (MB, ChB Hons; MD Hons, ChM). FRCSE 1963; FRCSGlas 1964; FRCS 1979. House Surgeon, Western Infirmary, Glasgow, 1961–62; Res. Asst and Registrar, Univ. Dept of Surg., Leeds Gen. Infirm., 1962–64; Lectr in Surg., Univ. of Sheffield, 1965–68; Sen. Lectr and Consultant, Univ. Dept of Surg., Leeds Gen. Infirm., 1968–75; Prof. of Surg. and Head of Dept, Univ. of Bristol (Bristol Royal Infirm.), 1975–77. *Publications:* papers on physiology and surgery of the stomach, colon and rectum, and on obesity. *Recreations:* reading, running, tennis, fishing. *Address:* 23 Shire Oak Road, Headingley, Leeds LS6 2DD. *T:* Leeds (0113) 275 4689.

JOHNSTON, David Alan H.; *see* Hunter Johnston.

JOHNSTON, Prof. David Eric Lothian; advocate; Regius Professor of Civil Law, University of Cambridge and Fellow of Christ's College, Cambridge, since 1993; *b* 10 March 1961; *e s* of Thomas Lothian Johnston, *qv*, and Joan (*née* Fahmy). *Educ:* Daniel Stewart's and Melville Coll., Edinburgh; St John's Coll., Cambridge (BA 1982; MA 1986; PhD 1986). Research Fellow, Christ's Coll., Cambridge, 1985–89. Visiting Fellow: Univ. of Freiburg, 1985–86; Univ. of Michigan Law Sch., 1987. Advocate, 1992. *Publications:* On a Singular Book of Cervidius Scaevola, 1987; The Roman Law of Trusts, 1988; articles in learned jls mainly on Roman law and legal history. *Recreations:* music, travel, tasting wine. *Address:* Christ's College, Cambridge CB2 3BU. *T:* Cambridge (01223) 334900; Advocates Library, Parliament House, Edinburgh EH1 1RF. *T:* 0131–226 5071.

JOHNSTON, David Lawrence, CEng, FIEE; FIMgt; RCNC; Director General, National Inspection Council for Electrical Installation Contracting, since 1989; Chairman, Quality Assurance Ltd, since 1993 (Director, since 1989); Director, National Approval Council, Security Systems Ltd, since 1990; *b* 12 April 1936; *s* of late Herbert David Johnston and of Hilda Eleanor Johnston (*née* Wood); *m* 1959, Beatrice Ann Witten; three *d*. *Educ:* Lancastrian Sch., Chichester; King's Coll., Durham (BSc). FIEE 1980. Short Service Commn (Lieut), RN, 1959–62. Joined Ministry of Defence, 1962; Overseeing, Wallsend, 1962–63; Design, Bath, 1963–66; Production and Project Management, Devonport Dockyard, 1966–73; Dockyard Policy, Bath, 1973–76; Design, Bath, 1976–79; Production and Planning, Portsmouth Dockyard, 1979–81; Planning and Production, Devonport Dockyard, 1981–84; Asst Under-Sec. of State, and Man. Dir, HM Dockyard, Devonport, 1984–87; Chm. and Man. Dir, Devonport Dockyard Ltd, Management Buy-out Co., 1985–87; Dep. Chm., Devonport Management Ltd, 1987–88; management consultant, 1988–89. Dir, NQA, USA Inc., 1993–. Dir, Nat. Supervisory Council, Intruder Alarms Ltd, 1989–90. Chm., BASEEFA Adv. Council, HSE, 1990–; Mem., Electrical Equipment Certification Management Bd, HSE, 1990–. FIMgt (FBIM 1980). *Recreations:* gardening, walking, modernizing houses. *Address:* The Old Orchard, Harrowbeer Lane, Yelverton, Devon PL20 6DZ. *T:* Yelverton (01822) 854310; National Inspection Council for Electrical Installation Contracting, Vintage House, 37 Albert Embankment, SE1 7UJ. *T:* 0171–582 7746.

JOHNSTON, Prof. David Lloyd; Professor of Law, McGill University, since 1979 (Principal and Vice-Chancellor, 1979–94); *b* 28 June 1941; *s* of Lloyd Johnston and Dorothy Stonehouse Johnston; *m* 1963, Sharon Downey; five *d*. *Educ:* Harvard Univ., Cambridge, Mass; Cambridge Univ.; Queen's Univ. at Kingston, Ont. Asst Prof., Faculty of Law, Queen's Univ., Kingston, 1966–68; Faculty of Law, Univ. of Toronto: Asst Prof., 1968–69; Associate Prof., 1969–72; Prof., 1972–74; Dean and Prof., Faculty of Law, Univ. of Western Ont, 1974–79. Chm., Nat. Round Table on Envmt and the Economy, 1988–. LLD *hc* Law Soc. of Upper Canada, 1980. *Publications:* Computers and the Law (ed), 1968; Canadian Securities Regulation, 1977; (jtly) Business Associations, 1979, 2nd edn 1989; (with R. Forbes) Canadian Companies and the Stock Exchange, 1980; (jtly) Canadian Securities Regulation, Supplement, 1982; articles and reports. *Recreations:* jogging, skiing, tennis. *Address:* McGill Centre for Medicine, Ethics and Law, 3690 Peel Street, Montreal, Que H3A 1W9, Canada. *T:* (514) 3984180, *Fax:* (514) 3984768; 18 Sunnyside Avenue, Montreal, Que H3Y 1C2. *T:* (514) 4852166. *Clubs:* University, Faculty (Montreal).

JOHNSTON, Sir (David) Russell, Kt 1985; MP Inverness, Nairn and Lochaber, since 1983 (Inverness, 1964–83) (L 1964–88, Lib Dem since 1988); *b* 28 July 1932; *s* of late David Knox Johnston and Georgina Margaret Gerrie Russell; *m* 1967, Joan Graham Menzies; three *s*. *Educ:* Carbost Public Sch.; Portree High Sch.; Edinburgh Univ. (MA). Commissioned into Intelligence Corps (Nat. Service), 1958; subseq., Moray House Coll. of Educn until 1961; taught in Liberton Secondary Sch., 1961–63. Research Asst, Scottish Liberal Party, 1963–64. Chm., Scottish Liberal Party, 1970–74 (Vice-Chm., 1965–70), Leader, 1974–88; Dep. Leader, Social and Liberal Democrats, 1988–92; Pres., Scottish Liberal Democrats, 1988–94. Mem., UK Delegn to European Parlt, 1973–75 and 1976–79, Vice Pres., Political Cttee, 1976–79; Mem., UK Delegn to Council of Europe and WEU, 1988; Pres., Council of Europe Sub-Cttee on Youth and Sport, 1992–; Ldr, Liberal, Democrat and Reform Gp, Council of Europe, 1994. Mem., Select Cttee of Privileges, 1988–92; Lib Dem spokesman: on foreign affairs, 1988–89; on European Community affairs, 1988–; on East-West relations, 1992–94; on Central and Eastern Europe, 1994–. Contested (L) Highlands and Islands, European Parly elecn, 1979, 1984. Chm., All Party Scottish Gaelic Parly Gp; Vice Chm., Europe Gp; Vice-President: Liberal Gp; European Lib Dem and Reform Parties, 1990–92; Liberal Internat., 1994–; Secretary: UK-Falkland Is Parly Gp; British–Hong Kong Parly Gp; Treasurer, All Party Photography Gp. Mem., Royal Commission on Local Govt in Scotland, 1966–69. *Publications:* (pamphlet) Highland Development, 1964; (pamphlet) To Be a Liberal, 1972; Scottish Liberal Party Conf. Speeches, 1979 and 1987. *Recreations:* reading, photography, shinty (Vice Chief, Camanachd Assoc., 1987–90). *Address:* House of Commons, SW1A 0AA. *Club:* Scottish Liberal (Edinburgh).

JOHNSTON, Hon. Donald (James); PC 1980; QC; Secretary-General, Organisation for Economic Co-operation and Development, from June 1996; *b* 26 June 1936; *s* of Wilbur Austin Johnston and Florence Jean Moffat Tucker; *m* 1965, Heather Bell Maclaren; four *d*. *Educ:* McGill Univ. (BA, LLB; Gold Medallist 1958); Univ. of Grenoble (schol.). Joined Strikeman & Elliott, 1961; founder of law firm, Johnston, Heenan and Blaikie; Counsel, Heenan Blaikie; Lectr, Fiscal Law, McGill Univ., 1964–77; MP (L) St Henri-Westmount, 1978–88; Pres., Treasury Bd of Canada, 1980–82; Minister of State for Econ. and Regl Develt and for Sci. and Techn., 1982; Minister of Justice and Attorney-Gen., 1984. Pres., Liberal Party, 1990. Mem., Bd of Dirs, BCE Inc. *Publications:* How to Survive Canada's Tax Chaos, 1974; Up the Hill, 1986; (ed) With a Bank, Not a Whimper: Pierre Trudeau speaks out, 1988. *Recreations:* writing, tennis, piano. *Address:* Heenan Blaikie, 1250 René Lévesque Boulevard West, Suite 2500, Montreal, PQ H3B 4Y1, Canada. *Clubs:* Mount-Royal, Montreal Indoor Tennis.

JOHNSTON, Very Rev. Frederick Mervyn Kieran; Dean of Cork, 1967–71, retired; *b* 22 Oct. 1911; *s* of Robert Mills Johnston and Florence Harriet O'Hanlon; *m* 1938, Catherine Alice Ruth FitzSimons; two *s*. *Educ:* Grammar Sch., Galway; Bishop Foy Sch., Waterford; Trinity Coll., Dublin. BA 1933. Deacon, 1934; Priest, 1936; Curate, Castlecomer, 1934–36; Curate, St Luke, Cork, 1936–38; Incumbent of Kilmeen, 1938–40; Drimoleague, 1940–45; Blackrock, Cork, 1945–58; Bandon, 1958–67; Rector of St Fin Barre's Cathedral and Dean of Cork, 1967; Examng Chaplain to Bishop of Cork, 1960–78. *Address:* 24 Lapps Court, Hartlands Avenue, Cork, Republic of Ireland.

JOHNSTON, Frederick Patrick Mair, CBE 1993; Chairman, Johnston Press plc (formerly F. Johnston & Co. Ltd), since 1973; *b* Edinburgh, 15 Sept. 1935; *e s* of late Frederick M. Johnston and of Mrs M. K. Johnston, Falkirk; *m* 1961, Elizabeth Ann Jones; two *s*. *Educ:* Morrison's Acad., Crieff; Lancing Coll., Sussex; New Coll., Oxford (MA, Mod. Hist.). Commissioned in Royal Scots Fusiliers, 1955; served in E Africa with 4th (Uganda) Bn, KAR, 1955–56. Joined Editorial Dept of Liverpool Daily Post & Echo, 1959; joined The Times Publishing Co. Ltd, as Asst Sec., 1960; F. Johnston & Co. Ltd, subseq. Johnston Press plc: Company Sec., 1969–73; Managing Dir, 1973–80; Chief Exec., 1980–91; Exec. Chm., 1991–. Chm., Dunn & Wilson Ltd, 1976–; Dir, Scottish Mortgage and Trust plc, 1991–. Dir, FIEJ, 1990–. President: Young Newspapermen's Assoc., 1968–69; Forth Valley Chamber of Commerce, 1972–73; Scottish Newspaper Proprietors' Assoc., 1976–78; Newspaper Soc., 1989–90; Chm., Central Scotland Manpower Cttee, 1976–83; Mem., Press Council, 1974–88; Treasurer: Soc. of Master Printers of Scotland, 1981–86; CPU, 1987–91. FRSA 1992. *Recreations:* reading, travelling. *Address:* Johnston Press plc, 53 Manor Place, Edinburgh EH3 7EG. *Clubs:* Caledonian; New (Edinburgh).

JOHNSTON, Gordon MacKenzie; HM Diplomatic Service; Ambassador to Slovenia, since 1992; *b* 24 June 1941; *s* of William Johnston and Betty Isabel Lamond (*née* MacKenzie); *m* 1963, Barbara Glenis Christie; one *s* one *d*. *Educ:* Robert Gordon's Coll., Aberdeen; Dingwall Acad. Joined HM Foreign, later Diplomatic, Service, 1959; FO, 1959–63; Berne, 1963–65; Pro-Consul, Tamsui, 1966–67; FCO, 1967–71; Entry Clearance Officer, Islamabad, 1971; FCO, 1972–74; Commercial Attaché, Paris, 1974–77; Second Sec., Georgetown, 1978–81; Press Officer, FCO, 1981–84; First Secretary: Commercial, Belgrade, 1984–88; Economic, Dublin, 1989–90; FCO, 1990–92. *Recreations:* golf, tennis, reading. *Address:* c/o Foreign and Commonwealth Office, King Charles Street, SW1A 2AH.

JOHNSTON, Henry Butler M.; *see* McKenzie Johnston.

JOHNSTON, Hugh Philip, CB 1977; FEng 1989; Deputy Secretary, Property Services Agency, Department of the Environment, 1974–87; *b* 17 May 1927; *s* of late Philip Rose-Johnston and Dora Ellen Johnston; *m* 1949, Barbara Frances Theodoridi; one *s* three *d*. *Educ:* Wimbledon Coll.; Faraday House. DFH (Hons). Air Ministry Works Dept: Asst Engr, 1951; Engr, 1956; Ministry of Public Buildings and Works: Prin. Engr, 1964; Asst Dir, 1969; Dir (Under-Sec.), Dept of Environment and Property Services Agency, Engrg Services Directorate, 1970. Pres., CIBSE, 1987–88. *Recreations:* motoring, music. *Address:* 9 Devas Road, Wimbledon, SW20 8PD. *T:* 0181–946 2021.

JOHNSTON, Ian; *see* Johnston, W. I. R.

JOHNSTON, Ian Alistair, CB 1995; PhD; Deputy Principal, Sheffield Hallam University, since 1995; *b* 2 May 1944; *s* of late Donald Dalrymple Johnston and Muriel Joyce Johnston (*née* Hill); *m* 1973, Mary Bridget Lube; one *s* one *d*. *Educ:* Royal Grammar Sch., High Wycombe; Birmingham Univ. (BSc, PhD). Joined Dept of Employment as Assistant Principal, 1969; Private Sec. to Permanent Secretary, Sir Denis Barnes, 1972–73; Principal, 1973; First Sec. (Labour Attaché), British Embassy, Brussels, 1976–77; Asst Sec. (Director, ACAS), 1978; Under-Sec. (Dir of Planning and Resources, MSC), 1984; Chief Exec., Vocational Educn Trng Gp, MSC, 1985; Dep. Dir Gen., MSC, subseq. Training Commn, then Training Agency, then Training Enterprise and Education Directorate of Department of Employment, 1987–92; Dir of Resources and Strategy (Dep. Sec.), Dept of Employment, 1992; Dir Gen., TEED, Dept of Employment, 1992–95. Hon. Treas. and Council Mem., Industrial Soc., 1992–. Gov. and Dep. Chm., Sheffield Hallam Univ. (formerly Sheffield Poly.), 1988–95. *Publications:* contribs to learned jls on atomic structure of metals, 1966–69, and subseq. on public admin. *Recreations:* birding, gardening, tennis. *Address:* Sheffield Hallam University, Pond Street, Sheffield S1 1WB.

JOHNSTON, Ian Henderson, CB 1981; Deputy Controller Aircraft, Procurement Executive, Ministry of Defence, 1982–84; *b* 29 April 1925; *s* of late Peter Johnston and Barbara Johnston (*née* Gifford); *m* 1949, Irene Blackburn; two *d*. *Educ:* George Heriot's Sch., Edinburgh; Edinburgh Univ. (BSc Eng); Imperial Coll., London (DIC Aeronautics). D. Napier & Sons, 1945–46; National Gas Turbine Estabt, 1947–64; Ramjet Project Officer, Min. of Aviation, 1964–66; Exchange Officer to Wright Patterson Air Force Base, Ohio, 1966–68; Asst Dir (Engine Develt), Min. of Technology, 1968–70; Dep. Dir, National Gas Turbine Estabt, 1970–73; Ministry of Defence: Dir-Gen., Multi-Role Combat Aircraft, (PE), 1973–76; Dir, Mil. Vehicles and Engrg Estabt, 1976–78; Dep. Controller, Estabts and Res. B, and Chief Scientist (Army), 1978–80; Dep. Controller, Estabt Resources and Personnel, MoD, 1980–82. *Publications:* papers on turbine research in Aeronautical Research Council Reports and Memoranda Series. *Recreations:* golf, bridge. *Address:* 49 Salisbury Road, Farnborough, Hants GU14 7AJ. *T:* Farnborough (01252) 541971.

JOHNSTON, James Campbell, CBE 1972; Chairman: Capel Court Corporation Ltd, 1969–84; Australian Foundation Investment Co., 1967–84; Director, National Mutual T&G Life Association of Australasia Ltd (formerly of T&G Mutual Life Society), 1976–84; *b* 7 July 1912; *s* of late Edwin and Estelle Johnston; *m* 1938, Agnes Emily, *yr d* of late Richard Thomas; two *s* one *d*. *Educ:* Prince Alfred Coll., Adelaide; Scotch Coll., Melbourne; University of Melbourne. Admitted to Inst. Chartered Accountants, Australia, 1933; joined J. B. Were & Son, Stock and Share Brokers, 1935, Sen. Partner, 1967–78; Stock Exchange of Melbourne: Mem., 1947; Chm., 1972–77; Hon. Fellow, Australian Stock Exchange, 1991. Comr, State Electricity Commn of Victoria, 1978–83. Chartered

Accountant of the Year, 1984. *Address:* 2/714 Orrong Road, Toorak, Vic 3142, Australia. *Clubs:* Melbourne, Victoria Racing, Royal Melbourne Golf (Melbourne).

JOHNSTON, James Frederick Junor, CB 1993; CBE 1984; Chairman, Westminster Gardens Ltd, since 1991; *b* 5 Aug. 1939; *s* of late William Johnston and Margaret Macrae Ward Johnston (*née* Junor). *Educ:* George Watson's College; Welbeck College; RMA Sandhurst. BSc, CEng, Eur Ing, FIMechE, psc, rcds. Commissioned REME, 1959; Comd 7 Field Workshop, 1974–76; Directing Staff, Staff Coll., 1976–79; Comd Maint., 3 Armd Div., 1979–81; Dep. Chief of Staff, 4 Armd Div., 1981–84; Asst Chief of Staff, HQ BAOR, 1986–89; Dir Manning (Army), 1989; Dir Gen., Army Manning and Recruiting, MoD, 1990–93, retd. Col Comdt, REME, 1994–. Chm., Crown Housing Trust, 1993–94; Mem. Cttee, Broomleigh Housing Assoc., 1995–. Trustee of several Service charities. FInstD; FIMgt. *Recreations:* travel, photography, postal history, genealogy. *Address:* c/o Royal Bank of Scotland, Lawrie House, Victoria Road, Farnborough, Hants GU14 7NR. *Clubs:* Army and Navy, Cavalry and Guards; Fadeaways.

JOHNSTON, Jennifer, (Mrs David Gilliland), FRSL; author; *b* 12 Jan. 1930; *d* of late (William) Denis Johnston, OBE; *m* 1st, 1951, Ian Smyth; two *s* two *d*; 2nd, 1976, David Gilliland, *qv*. *Educ:* Park House Sch., Dublin; Trinity Coll., Dublin. FRSL 1979. Mem., Aosdána. Plays: Indian Summer, performed Belfast, 1983; The Porch, prod Dublin, 1986. Hon. DLitt: Ulster, 1984: TCD, 1992; QUB, 1993. *Publications:* The Captains and the Kings, 1972; The Gates, 1973; How Many Miles to Babylon?, 1974; Shadows on Our Skin, 1978 (dramatised for TV, 1979); The Old Jest, 1979 (filmed as The Dawning, 1988); (play) The Nightingale and not the Lark, 1980; The Christmas Tree, 1981; The Railway Station Man, 1984; Fool's Sanctuary, 1987; The Invisible Worm, 1991. *Recreations:* theatre, cinema, gardening, travelling. *Address:* Brook Hall, Culmore Road, Derry, N Ireland BT48 8JE. *T:* Londonderry (01504) 351297.

JOHNSTON, Sir John (Baines), GCMG 1978 (KCMG 1966; CMG 1962); KCVO 1972; HM Diplomatic Service, retired; *b* 13 May 1918; *e s* of late Rev. A. S. Johnston, Banbury, Oxon; *m* 1969, Elizabeth Mary, *d* of late J. F. Crace; one *s*. *Educ:* Banbury Grammar Sch.; Queen's Coll., Oxford (Eglesfield Scholar). Served War, 1940–46: Adjt 1st Bn Gordon Highlanders, 1944; DAQMG HQ 30 Corps District, 1945. Asst Principal, Colonial Office, 1947; Principal, 1948; Asst Sec., West African Council, Accra, 1950–51; UK Liaison Officer with Commission for Technical Co-operation in Africa South of the Sahara, 1952; Principal Private Sec. to Sec. of State for the Colonies, 1953; Asst Sec., 1956; Head of Far Eastern Dept, Colonial Office, 1956; transferred to Commonwealth Relations Office, 1957; Dep. High Commissioner in S Africa, 1959–61; British High Commissioner: in Sierra Leone, 1961–63; in the Federation of Rhodesia and Nyasaland, 1963, Rhodesia, 1964–65; Asst, later Dep. Under-Secretary of State, FCO, 1968–71; British High Commissioner: in Malaysia, 1971–74; in Canada, 1974–78. A Governor, BBC, 1978–85. Chm., ARELS Exams Trust, 1982–94. Mem., Disasters Emergency Cttee, 1985–92. *Address:* 5 Victoria Road, Oxford OX2 7QF. *T:* Oxford (01865) 56927.

JOHNSTON, John Douglas Hartley; Under Secretary (Legal), Solicitor's Office, Inland Revenue, since 1986; *b* 19 March 1935; *s* of John Johnston and Rhoda Margaret Hartley. *Educ:* Manchester Grammar Sch.; Jesus Coll., Cambridge (MA, LLB, PhD); Harvard Law Sch. (LLM). Called to the Bar, Lincoln's Inn, 1963. Practised at Bar, 1963–67; joined Solicitor's Office, Inland Revenue, 1968; Asst Solicitor, 1976–86. *Recreations:* reading, music, gardening. *Address:* Solicitor's Office, Inland Revenue, Somerset House, WC2R 1LB. *T:* 0171–438 6228.

JOHNSTON, Lt-Col Sir John (Frederick Dame), GCVO 1987 (KCVO 1981; CVO 1977; MVO 1971), MC 1945; Comptroller, Lord Chamberlain's Office, 1981–87 (Assistant Comptroller, 1964–81); *b* 24 Aug. 1922; *m* 1949, Hon. Elizabeth Hardinge (*d* 1995), JP Windsor 1971, *d* of late 2nd Baron Hardinge of Penshurst, PC, GCB, GCVO, MC, and late Lady Hardinge of Penshurst; one *s* one *d*. *Educ:* Ampleforth. Served in Grenadier Guards, 1941–64. Extra Equerry to the Queen, 1965–. Director: Theatre Royal Windsor; Claridge's Hotel; President: King George's Pension Fund for Actors and Actresses; Hearing Dogs for the Deaf; Chm., Combined Theatrical Charities Appeals Council. *Publication:* The Lord Chamberlain's Blue Pencil, 1990. *Address:* Studio Cottage, The Great Park, Windsor, Berks SL4 2HP. *T:* Egham (01784) 431627; Stone Hill, Newport, Dyfed. *Clubs:* Boodle's; Swinley Forest Golf.

JOHNSTON, Kenneth Robert Hope; QC 1953; *b* 18 June 1905; *e s* of Dr J. A. H. Johnston, Headmaster of Highgate Sch., 1908–36, and Kate Winsome Gammon; *m* 1937, Dr Priscilla Bright Clark (*d* 1993), *d* of Roger and Sarah Clark, Street, Somerset; one *s* three *d*. *Educ:* Rugby Sch.; Sidney Sussex Coll., Cambridge Univ.; Harvard Univ., USA. Called to the Bar, Gray's Inn, 1933; Bencher, 1958. RAFVR, 1939–45. *Address:* 28 Leigh Road, Street, Somerset BA16 0HB. *T:* Street (01458) 443559. *Club:* MCC.

JOHNSTON, Margaret; *see* Parker, Margaret Annette McCrie J.

JOHNSTON, Lt-Gen. Sir Maurice (Robert), KCB 1982; OBE 1971; DL; Deputy Chief of Defence Staff, 1982–83, retired 1984; *b* 27 Oct. 1929; *s* of late Brig. Allen Leigh Johnston, OBE, and Gertrude Geraldine Johnston (*née* Templer); *m* 1960, Belinda Mary Sladen; one *s* one *d*. *Educ:* Wellington College; RMA Sandhurst. rcds, psc. Commissioned RA, 1949; transf. The Queen's Bays, 1954; served in Germany, Egypt, Jordan, Libya, N Ireland, Borneo. Instr, Army Staff Coll., 1965–67; MA to CGS, 1968–71; CO 1st The Queen's Dragoon Guards, 1971–73; Comdr 20th Armoured Brigade, 1973–75; BGS, HQ UKLF, 1977–78; Senior Directing Staff, RCDS, 1979; Asst Chief of Gen. Staff, 1980; Dep. Chief of Defence Staff (Op. Reqs), 1981–82. Col, 1st The Queen's Dragoon Guards, 1986–91. Chairman: Secondary Resources plc, 1988–91; Detention Corp., 1988–94; Managing Director: Freshglen Ltd, Wraxall Gp, 1984–85; Unit Security Ltd, 1985–88; Director: Multilift Ltd, 1984–; Shorrock Guards Ltd, 1988–91. Governor: Dauntsey's Sch., Wilts, 1987–, St Mary's Sch., Calne, 1988–94. DL Wilts, 1990, High Sheriff, 1993–94. *Recreations:* fishing, shooting, gardening, music. *Address:* Ivy House, Worton, Devizes, Wilts SN10 5RU. *Club:* Army and Navy.

JOHNSTON, Very Rev. Michael Alexander Ninian C.; *see* Campbell-Johnston.

JOHNSTON, Peter William; Chief Executive and Secretary, Institute of Chartered Accountants of Scotland, since 1989; *b* 8 Feb. 1943; *s* of late William Johnston and of Louisa Alice Johnston (*née* Pritchard); *m* 1967, Patricia Sandra Macdonald; one *s* one *d*. *Educ:* Univ. of Glasgow (MA, LLB). Partner, MacArthur & Co., Solicitors, Inverness, 1971–76; Procurator Fiscal Depute, Dumfries, 1976–78; Procurator Fiscal, Banff, 1978–86; Senior Procurator Fiscal Depute, Crown Office, Edinburgh, 1986–87; Asst Solicitor, Crown Office, 1987–89. FRSA. *Recreations:* music, foreign languages, sailing. *Address:* 34 York Road, Edinburgh EH5 3EQ. *T:* 0131–225 5673. *Club:* New (Edinburgh).

JOHNSTON, Rita Margaret; Premier, Province of British Columbia, 1991; *b* 22 April 1935; *d* of John and Annie Leichert; *m* 1951, George Johnston; one *s* two *d*. Businesswoman and Mem., Chamber of Commerce. Alderman, Surrey, BC, 1970–83; MLA for Surrey, 1983–91; Parly Sec. to Minister of Energy, Mines and Petroleum Resources, then to Minister of Municipal Affairs, 1983–86; Minister: Municipal Affairs and Transit, 1986–89, also Recreation and Culture, 1988–89; Transportation and Highways, 1989–90; Dep. Premier, 1990–91. *Address:* #1601, 3190 Gladwin Road, Matsqui, BC V2S 6W8, Canada.

JOHNSTON, Robert Alan, AC 1986; Governor, Reserve Bank of Australia, 1982–89; *b* 19 July 1924; *m* 1948, Verna, *d* of H. I. Mullin; two *s* two *d*. *Educ:* Essendon High School; University of Melbourne. BCom. Commonwealth Bank of Australia, 1940–60; RAAF, 1943–46; Reserve Bank of Australia, 1960–89: Dep. Manager and Manager, Investment Dept, 1964–70; Chief Manager, Internat. Dept, 1970–76; Adviser, 1973–82; Chief Representative, London, 1976–77; Exec. Dir, World Bank Group, Washington, 1977–79; Secretary, Reserve Bank of Aust., 1980–82. Director: Australian Mutual Prov. Soc., 1989–; John Fairfax Gp Pty, 1989–90; Westpac Banking Corp., 1992–. Pres., Cttee for Econ. Develt of Australia, 1990–.

JOHNSTON, Robert Gordon Scott, CB 1993; Executive Director, United Kingdom Major Ports Group, since 1993; *b* 27 Aug. 1933; *s* of late Robert William Fairfield Johnston, CMG, CBE, MC, TD; *m* 1960, Jill Maureen Campbell; one *s* one *d*. *Educ:* Clifton; Clare Coll., Cambridge (1st Cl. Hons Classical Tripos, MA). 2/Lieut Scots Guards (National Service), 1955–57. Entered Air Min. as Asst Principal, 1957; Private Sec. to Parly Under Sec. of State for Air, 1959–62; transf. to MPBW, Def. Works Secretariat, 1963; Sec., Bldg Regulation Adv. Cttee, 1964; Principal Private Sec. to successive Ministers of Public Bldg and Works, 1965–68; seconded to Shell Internat. Chemical Co., Finance Div., 1968–70; Asst Dir of Home Estate Management, Property Services Agency, 1970–73; seconded to Cabinet Office, 1973–75; Asst Sec., Railways Directorate, Dept of Transport, 1975–79; Under Sec., DoE, 1979–93; seconded to Price Commn, 1979; Dir of Civil Accommodation, 1979–88, Dir, Defence Services, 1988–90, PSA; Man. Dir, PSA Internat., 1990–93. *Address:* 5 Methley Street, SE11 4AL.

JOHNSTON, Robert Smith; *see* Kincraig, Hon. Lord.

JOHNSTON, Prof. Ronald John, PhD; Professor of Geography, Bristol University, since 1995; *b* 30 March 1941; *s* of Henry Louis Johnston and Phyllis Joyce (*née* Liddiard); *m* 1963, Rita Brennan; one *s* one *d*. *Educ:* Commonweal County Secondary Grammar Sch., Swindon; Univ. of Manchester (BA 1962; MA 1964); Monash Univ. (PhD 1967). Department of Geography, Monash University: Teaching Fellow, 1964; Sen. Teaching Fellow, 1965; Lectr, 1966; University of Canterbury, New Zealand: Lectr, 1967–68; Sen. Lectr, 1969–72; Reader, 1973–74; University of Sheffield: Prof. of Geography, 1974–92; Pro-Vice-Chancellor for Acad. Affairs, 1989–92; Vice-Chancellor, Essex Univ., 1992–95. Murchison Award, 1985, Victoria Medal, 1990, RGS; Honors Award for Distinction in Res., Assoc. Amer. Geographers, 1991. *Publications:* (with P. J. Rimmer) Retailing in Melbourne, 1970; Urban Residential Patterns: an introductory review, 1971; Spatial Structures: an introduction to the study of spatial systems in human geography, 1973; The New Zealanders: how they live and work, 1976; The World Trade System: some enquiries into its spatial structure, 1976; (with B. E. Coates and P. L. Knox) Geography and Inequality, 1977; Multivariate Statistical Analysis in Geography: a primer on the general linear model, 1978; Political, Electoral and Spatial Systems, 1979; (with P. J. Taylor) Geography of Elections, 1979; Geography and Geographers: Anglo-American human geography since 1945, 1979, 4th edn 1991; City and Society: an outline for urban geography, 1980; The Geography of Federal Spending in the United States of America, 1980; The American Urban System: a geographical perspective, 1982; Geography and the State, 1982; Philosophy and Human Geography: an introduction to contemporary approaches, 1983, 2nd edn 1986; Residential Segregation, the State and Constitutional Conflict in American Urban Areas, 1984; The Geography of English Politics: the 1983 General Election, 1985; On Human Geography, 1986; Bell Ringing: the English art of change-ringing, 1986; Money and Votes: constituency campaign spending and election results, 1987; (jtly) The United States: a contemporary human geography, 1988; (with C. J. Pattie and J. G. Allsopp) A Nation Dividing?: the electoral map of Great Britain 1979–1987, 1988; Environmental Problems: nature, economy and state, 1989; (jtly) An Atlas of Bells, 1990; A Question of Place: exploring the practice of human geography, 1991; (ed) The Dictionary of Human Geography, 1989, 3rd edn 1993; contrib. chapters in ed vols and numerous papers in learned jls. *Recreation:* bell-ringing. *Address:* Department of Geography, University of Bristol, Bristol BS8 1SS. *Fax:* Bristol (0117) 928 7878.

JOHNSTON, Sir Russell; *see* Johnston, Sir D. R.

JOHNSTON, Sir Thomas Alexander, 14th Bt *cr* 1626, of Caskieben; *b* 1 Feb. 1956; *s* of Sir Thomas Alexander Johnston, 13th Bt, and of Helen Torry, *d* of Benjamin Franklin Du Bois; *S* father, 1984. *Heir: cousin* William Norville Johnston [*b* 11 July 1922; *m* 1952, Kathrine Pauline, *d* of Herbert Sigfred Solberg; three *s* one *d*].

JOHNSTON, Thomas Lothian, DL; Principal and Vice-Chancellor of Heriot-Watt University, 1981–88; President, Royal Society of Edinburgh, since 1993; *b* 9 March 1927; *s* of late T. B. Johnston and Janet Johnston; *m* 1956, Joan, *d* of late E. C. Fahmy, surgeon; two *s* three *d*. *Educ:* Hawick High Sch.; Univs of Edinburgh and Stockholm. MA 1951, PhD 1955, Edinburgh. FRSE 1979; FRSA 1981; CBIM 1983; FIPM 1986; FEIS 1989. Served RNVR, 1944–47 (Sub-Lt). Asst Lectr in Polit. Economy, Univ. of Edinburgh, 1953–55, Lectr 1955–65; Res. Fellow, Queen's Univ., Canada, 1965; Prof. and Hd of Dept of Econs, Heriot-Watt Univ., 1966–76. Visiting Professor: Univ. of Illinois, 1962–63; Internat. Inst. for Labour Studies, Geneva, 1973; Western Australia Inst. of Technol., 1979. Sec., Scottish Econ. Soc., 1958–65 (Pres., 1978–81); Member: Scottish Milk Marketing Bd, 1967–72; Nat. Industrial Relations Court, 1971–74; Scottish Cttee on Licensing Laws, 1971–73; Scottish Telecommunications Bd, 1977–84; Scottish Economic Council, 1977–91; Council for Tertiary Educn in Scotland, 1979–83; Chm., Manpower Services Cttee for Scotland, 1977–80; Economic Consultant to Sec. of State for Scotland, 1977–81. Trustee, Nat. Galls of Scotland, 1989–. Director: First Charlotte Assets Trust, 1981–92; Universities Superannuation Scheme, 1985–88; Scottish Life Assurance, 1989–; Hodgson Martin Ltd, 1989–. A Dir, Edinburgh Sci. Festival, 1989–91. Chairman: Scottish Cttee, Industry Year 1986; Scottish Cttee, Industry Matters, 1987–89; Scottish Cttee, RSA, 1991–95; Univ. Authorities Pay Panel, 1985–88. Chairman: Enquiry into staff representation, London Clearing Banks, 1978–79; Water Workers' Enquiry, 1983; Mem., Review Cttee for NZ Univs, 1987; Arbitrator; Overseas Corresp., Nat. Acad. of Arbitrators, USA. For. Mem., Swedish Royal Acad. of Engrg Scis, 1985. DL Edinburgh, 1987. Dr *hc* Edinburgh, 1986; Hon. DEd CNAA, 1989; Hon. LLD Glasgow, 1989; DUniv Heriot-Watt, 1989. Comdr, Royal Swedish Order of the Polar Star, 1985. *Publications:* Collective Bargaining in Sweden, 1962; (ed and trans.) Economic Expansion and Structural Change, 1963; (jtly) The Structure and Growth of the Scottish Economy, 1971; Introduction to Industrial Relations, 1981; articles in learned jls. *Recreations:* gardening, walking. *Address:* 14 Mansionhouse Road, Edinburgh EH9 1TZ. *T:* 0131–667 1439.

See also D. E. L. Johnston.

JOHNSTON, Very Rev. William Bryce; Minister of Colinton Parish Church, Edinburgh, 1964–91; an Extra Chaplain to the Queen in Scotland, since 1991 (Chaplain-in-Ordinary, 1981–91); *b* 16 Sept. 1921; *s* of William Bryce Johnston and Isabel Winifred Highley; *m* 1947, Ruth Margaret, *d* of Rev. James Arthur Cowley; one *s* two *d*. *Educ:* George

Watson's Coll., Edinburgh; Edinburgh Univ. (MA Hons Classics 1942); New Coll., Edinburgh (BD (Dist.) 1945). Ordained as Chaplain to HM Forces, 1945; served in Germany and as Staff Chaplain, PoW Directorate, War Office, 1945–48; Minister: St Andrew's, Bo'ness, 1949; St George's, Greenock, 1955. Moderator of General Assembly of Church of Scotland, 1980–81. Convener: Board of St Colm's Coll., 1966–70; General Assembly: Cttee on Adult Educn, 1970; Church and Nation Cttee, 1972; Inter-Church Relations Cttee, 1978; Cttee on Role of Men and Women, 1976; Chm., Judicial Commn, 1988–93. Mem., British Council of Churches, 1970–90 (Chm., Exec. Cttee, 1981–84); Delegate to 5th Assembly of World Council of Churches, 1975; Cunningham Lectr, New Coll., 1968–71; Vis. Lectr in Social Ethics, Heriot-Watt Univ., 1966–88. Mem., Broadcasting Council for Scotland, 1983–87. President, Edinburgh Rotary Club, 1975–76. Trustee, Scottish Nat. War Memorial, 1981–94. Hon. DD Aberdeen, 1980; Hon. DLitt Heriot-Watt, 1989. *Publications:* (jtly) Devolution and the British Churches, 1978; (ed) Davies, Ethics and Defence, 1986; *translations:* K. Barth, Church Dogmatics, vol. 2, 1955; Calvin, Commentaries on Hebrews, 1 Peter, 1960; various Bible study pamphlets and theological articles for SCM, Scottish Jl of Theology. *Recreations:* organ music, bowls. *Address:* 15 Elliot Road, Edinburgh EH14 1DU. *T:* 0131–441 3387. *Clubs:* New, University Staff (Edinburgh).

JOHNSTON, Ven. William Francis, CB 1983; Vicar, Winslow with Great Horwood and Addington, diocese of Oxford, since 1991; *b* 29 June 1930; *m* 1963, Jennifer Morton; two *s* one *d*. *Educ:* Wesley Coll., Dublin; Trinity Coll., Dublin (BA 1955; MA 1969). Ordained 1955; Curate of Orangefield, Co. Down, 1955–59; commissioned into Royal Army Chaplains Dept, 1959; served, UK, Germany, Aden, Cyprus; ACG South East District, 1977–80; Chaplain-Gen. to the Forces, 1980–86; QHC 1980–86; Priest-in-charge, Winslow with Addington, 1987–91. *Recreations:* golf, fishing, gardening. *Address:* The Vicarage, Winslow, Bucks MK18 3BJ. *T:* Winslow (01296) 712564.

JOHNSTON, (William) Ian (Ridley), QPM 1995; Assistant Commissioner, Metropolitan Police, since 1994; *b* 6 Sept. 1945; *s* of William and Alice Johnston; *m* 1968, Carol Ann Smith; two *s*. *Educ:* Enfield Grammar Sch.; LSE (BSc 1st Cl. Hons). Joined Metropolitan Police 1965; ranks of PC to Chief Supt, 1965–88; Staff Officer to Sir Peter Imbert, 1988–89; Senior Command Course, 1989; Asst Chief Constable, Kent, 1989–92; Dep. Asst Comr, Met. Police, 1992–94. *Recreations:* jogging, tennis, football, squash. *Address:* New Scotland Yard, Broadway, SW1H 0BG. *Club:* Orpington Rovers Football.

JOHNSTON, William James; Secretary, Association of Local Authorities of Northern Ireland, 1979–82; Chairman, National House Building Council, Northern Ireland, 1989–95; *b* 3 April 1919; *s* of late Thomas Hamilton Johnston and of Mary Kathleen Johnston; *m* 1943, Joan Elizabeth Nancye (*née* Young); two *d*. *Educ:* Portora Royal Sch., Enniskillen. FCA(Ire.). Professional accountancy, 1937–44; Antrim CC, 1944–68, Dep. Sec., 1951–68; Dep. Town Clerk, Belfast, 1968–73, Town Clerk, 1973–79. Dir, NI Adv. Bd, Abbey Nat. Bldg Soc., 1982–89. Member: NI Adv. Council, BBC, 1965–69; Council, ICAI, 1967–71; NI Tourist Bd, 1980–85; Local Govt Staff Commn, 1974–85; Public Service Trng Council (formerly Public Service Trng Cttee), 1974–83 (Chm., 1974–83); Arts Council of NI, 1974–81. NI Rep., Duke of Edinburgh's Commonwealth Study Conf., Canada, 1962. *Recreations:* golf, live theatre. *Address:* 19A Windsor Avenue, Belfast BT9 6EE; 4 Riverside Close, Cushendall, Ballymena BT44 0NR. *T:* Cushendall (012667) 72013. *Club:* Ulster Reform (Belfast).

JOHNSTON, Sir William Robert Patrick K.; *see* Knox-Johnston.

JOHNSTONE; *see* Hope Johnstone, family name of Earl of Annandale and Hartfell.

JOHNSTONE, VANDEN-BEMPDE-, family name of **Baron Derwent.**

JOHNSTONE, Lord; David Patrick Wentworth Hope Johnstone; Master of Annandale and Hartfell; *b* 13 Oct. 1971; *s* and *heir* of Earl of Annandale and Hartfell, *qv*. *Educ:* Stowe; St Andrews Univ.

JOHNSTONE, Air Vice-Marshal Alexander Vallance Riddell, CB 1966; DFC 1940; AE; Chairman, Climax Cleaning Co., 1983–91 (Director, 1981–91); *b* 2 June 1916; *s* of late Alex. Lang Johnstone and Daisy Riddell; *m* 1940, Margaret Croll; one *s* two *d*. *Educ:* Kelvinside Academy, Glasgow. 602 (City of Glasgow) Sqdn, AAF, 1934–41; CO RAF Haifa, 1942; Spitfire Wing, Malta, 1942–43 (despatches, 1942); RAF Staff Coll., 1943; OC Fairwood Common, 1943–44; HQ AEAF, 1944; Air Attaché Dublin, 1946–48; OC RAF Ballykelly, 1951–52; OC Air/Sea Warfare Devel. Unit, 1952–54; SASO HQ No 12 Gp, 1954–55; Founder and First CAS Royal Malayan Air Force, 1957; OC Middleton St George, 1958–60; idc, 1961; Dir of Personnel, Air Min., 1962–64; Comdr, Air Forces, Borneo, 1964–65; AO Scotland and N Ireland, AOC No 18 Group, and Maritime Air Comdr N Atlantic (NATO), 1965–68. Vice-Chm. Council, TA&VRA, 1969–79. DL Glasgow, 1971–94. Johan Mengku Negara (Malaya), 1958. *Publications:* Television Series, One Man's War, 1964; Where No Angels Dwell, 1969; Enemy in the Sky, 1976; Adventure in the Sky, 1978; Spitfire into War, 1986; Diary of an Aviator, 1993. *Recreations:* golf, sailing. *Address:* 36 Castle Brooks, Framlingham, Suffolk IP13 9SE. *Club:* Royal Air Force.

JOHNSTONE, Sir (George) Richard (Douglas), 11th Bt *cr* 1700, of Westerhall, Dumfriesshire; Managing Director, DBI Associates Ltd, since 1990; *b* 21 Aug. 1948; *er s* of Sir Frederic Allan George Johnstone, 10th Bt and of Doris Johnstone (*née* Shortridge); *S* father, 1994; *m* 1976, Gwyneth Susan Bailey; one *s* one *d*. *Educ:* Leeds Grammar Sch.; Magdalen Coll., Oxford (MA; Dip. Physical Anthropology). MIMC. Production Control Manager, Wolsey Ltd, 1973; Section Head, ITT Consumer Products (UK) Ltd, 1979; Dir, Central Govt Gp, P-E International plc, 1988. MInstD; FRSA. *Recreations:* reading, travel, computing. *Heir: s* Frederic Robert Arthur Johnstone, *b* 18 Nov. 1981.

JOHNSTONE, Iain Gilmour; author and broadcaster; film critic, since 1983, and tennis writer, since 1994, Sunday Times; *b* 8 April 1943; *s* of Jack and Gilly Johnstone; *m* 1980, Mo Watson; one *s* two *d*. *Educ:* Campbell College, Belfast; Bristol Univ. (LLB Hons). Newscaster, ITN, 1966–68; Producer, BBC TV, 1968–74; Prof. of Broadcasting, Boston Univ., 1975; Man. Dir, Kensington Television, 1977; BBC presenter, Film 1983, 1984. *Publications:* The Arnhem Report, 1977; The Man With No Name, 1980; Cannes: The Novel, 1990; Wimbledon 2000, 1992. *Recreations:* lawn tennis, amateur actuary. *Address:* c/o Fish Productions, 84 Ladbroke Road, W11 3NU. *Clubs:* Queen's, Campden Hill, Groucho.

JOHNSTONE, Isobel Theodora, PhD; Curator, Arts Council Collection, since 1979; *b* 1944. *Educ:* James Gillespie's High School; Edinburgh Univ.; Edinburgh Coll. of Art (MA Hons Fine Art); Glasgow Univ. (PhD). Lectr in History of Art, Glasgow School of Art, 1969–73; Scottish Arts Council, 1975–79. Painter of landscapes and portraits. *Publications:* (as Isobel Spencer): Walter Crane, 1975; articles on late 19th century and 20th century British art. *Address:* South Bank Centre, Royal Festival Hall, SE1 8XX.

JOHNSTONE, Sir (John) Raymond, Kt 1993; CBE 1988; Chairman, Forestry Commission, 1989–94; Chairman, Lomond Underwriting plc, since 1994; *b* 27 Oct. 1929; *s* of Henry James Johnstone of Alva, Captain RN and Margaret Alison McIntyre; *m* 1979, Susan Sara Gore; five step *s* two step *d*. *Educ:* Eton Coll.; Trinity Coll., Cambridge (BA Maths). CA. Apprenticed Chiene & Tait, Chartered Accts, Edinburgh, 1951–54; Robert Fleming & Co. Ltd, London, 1955–59; Partner in charge of investment management, Brown Fleming & Murray CA (becoming Whinney Murray CA, 1965), Glasgow, 1959–68; Murray Johnstone Ltd, Glasgow, formed to take over investment management dept of Whinney Murray: Man. Dir, 1968–89; Chm., 1984–94; Pres., 1994–. Chm., Summit Gp, 1989–; Director: Shipping Industrial Holdings, 1964–75; Scottish Amicable Life Assce Soc., 1971– (Chm., 1983–85); Dominion Insurance Co. Ltd, 1973–95 (Chm., 1978–95); Scottish Financial Enterprise, 1986–91 (Chm., 1989–91); Glasgow Cultural Enterprise Ltd, 1988–; R J Kiln & Co., 1995–. Hon. Pres., Scottish Opera, 1986– (Dir, 1978–86; Chm., 1983–85). Member: Scottish Adv. Cttee, Nature Conservancy Council, 1987–89; Scottish Econ. Council, 1987–. *Recreations:* fishing, music, farming. *Address:* Wards, Gartocharn, Dunbartonshire G83 8SB. *T:* Gartocharn (01389) 830321.

JOHNSTONE, Michael Anthony; Metropolitan Stipendiary Magistrate, since 1980; *b* 12 June 1936; *s* of late Thomas Johnstone and Violet Johnstone. *Educ:* St Edmund's College, Ware. Called to the Bar, Inner Temple, 1968; formerly Solicitor of the Supreme Court, admitted 1960; former Dep. Circuit Judge. Member: Soc. for Nautical Res.; Navy Records Soc.; Army Records Soc.; Internat. Soc. for Mil. Law and the Law of War. Mem., Campaign for Real Ale. *Recreations:* real ale (weight permitting), the study and collection of books on military and naval history. *Address:* Old Street Magistrates' Court, 335 Old Street, EC1V 9LJ.

JOHNSTONE, Sir Raymond; *see* Johnstone, Sir J. R.

JOHNSTONE, Sir Richard; *see* Johnstone, Sir G. R. D.

JOHNSTONE, William, CBE 1981; *b* 26 Dec. 1915; *s* of late David Grierson Johnstone and Janet Lang Johnstone (*née* Malcolm); *m* 1942, Mary Rosamund Rowden; one *s* two *d*. *Educ:* Dalry High Sch.; Glasgow Univ. (BSc (Agric)). NDA, NDD. Technical Officer, Overseas Dept of Deutches Kalisyndikat, Berlin, 1938–39; joined ICI Ltd, 1940; seconded to County War Agricl Exec. Cttees in SE England on food prodn campaigns, 1940–45; Reg. Sales Management, ICI, 1950–61; Commercial Dir, Plant Protection Ltd, 1961–63, Man. Dir, 1963–73; Dir, ICI Billingham/Agricl Div., 1961–73; Dep. Chm., ICI Plant Protection Div., 1974–77. Chm. Subsid. Cos: Solplant (Italy), 1967–73; Sopra (France), 1971–75; Zeltia Agraria (Spain), 1976–77; Vis. Dir, ICI (United States) Inc., 1974–77; retd from ICI, 1977. Chairman: Meat and Livestock Commn, 1977–80; British Agricl Export Council, 1977–84; Member: European Trade Cttee, BOTB, 1982–85; Sino-British Trade Council, 1983–85. *Recreations:* sheep husbandry, gardening. *Address:* Oxenbourne Farm, East Meon, Petersfield, Hants GU32 1QL. *T:* East Meon (01730) 823216. *Club:* Farmers'.

JOHNSTONE, Rev. Prof. William; Professor of Hebrew and Semitic Languages, University of Aberdeen, since 1980; *b* 6 May 1936; *s* of Rev. T. K. Johnstone and Evelyn Hope Johnstone (*née* Murray); *m* 1964, Elizabeth Mary Ward; one *s* one *d*. *Educ:* Hamilton Academy; Glasgow Univ. (MA 1st Cl. Hons Semitic Langs, BD Distinction in New Testament and Old Testament); Univ. of Marburg. University of Aberdeen: Lectr 1962, Sen. Lectr 1972, in Hebrew and Semitic Languages; Dean, Faculty of Divinity, 1984–87. Member, Mission archéologique française: Ras Shamra, 1963, 1964, 1966; Enkomi, 1963, 1965, 1971; Member, Marsala Punic Ship Excavation, 1973–79. Pres., SOTS, 1990. *Publications:* Exodus, 1990; (ed, trans. and contrib.) William Robertson Smith: essays in reassessment, 1995; trans. Fohrer: Hebrew and Aramaic Dictionary of the Old Testament, 1973; contributions to: Ugaritica VI, 1969, VII, 1978, Alasia I, 1972; Festschriften for: W. McKane, 1986; R. Davidson, 1992; G. W. Anderson, 1993; articles in Aberdeen Univ. Review, Atti del I Congresso Internazionale di Studi Fenici e Punici, Dictionary of Biblical Interpretation, Expository Times, Kadmos, Notizie degli Scavi, Palestine Exploration Qly, Trans. Glasgow Univ. Oriental Soc., Scottish Jl of Theology, Studia Theologica, Theology, Vetus Testamentum, Zeitschrift für die alttestamentliche Wissenschaft. *Recreation:* alternative work. *Address:* 37 Rubislaw Den South, Aberdeen AB2 6BD. *T:* Aberdeen (01224) 316022; Makkevet Bor, New Galloway, Castle Douglas DG7 3RN.

JOHNSTONE, William Neill, RDI 1989; Founder Chairman, Neill Johnstone Ltd, since 1986; Chairman, Fabric Design Consultants International; *b* 16 May 1938; *s* of Harry McCall Johnstone and Ethel Mary Neill; *m* 1st, (marr. diss.); two *d*; 2nd, 1991, Mara Lukic; one *s* one *d*. *Educ:* Forfar Acad.; Edinburgh Acad.; Univ. of Edinburgh; Scottish Coll. of Textiles; RCA. Designer, then Design Dir, R. G. Neill & Son, 1961–70; Man. Dir and Deisgn Dir, Neill of Langholm, 1970–85; Design Dir, Illingworth Morris Gp and Co-ordinator of design training programme, 1982–85; IWS Design Consultant, 1978–90. Chm., CBWT Steering Cttee, 1982–85; Industrialist on Selection Panel, Designer Graduate Attachment Scheme, 1982–85. *Recreations:* climbing, hill walking, collecting Inuit carvings. *Address:* Neill Johnstone Ltd, William Street, Langholm DG13 0BN. *T:* Langholm (01387) 381122.

JOICEY, family name of **Baron Joicey.**

JOICEY, 5th Baron *cr* 1906, of Chester-le-Street, Co. Durham; **James Michael Joicey;** Bt 1893; *b* 28 June 1953; *s* of 4th Baron and of Elisabeth Marion Joicey (*née* Leslie Melville); *S* father, 1993; *m* 1984, Agnes Harriet Frances Mary, *yr d* of Rev. and Mrs W. M. D. Thompson; two *s* two *d*. *Educ:* Eton Coll.; Christ Church, Oxford. *Heir: s* Hon. William James Joicey, *b* 21 May 1990.

JOLLIFFE, family name of **Baron Hylton.**

JOLLIFFE, Sir Anthony (Stuart), GBE 1982; FCA; *b* Weymouth, Dorset, 12 Aug. 1938; *s* of Robert and Vi Dorothea Jolliffe. *Educ:* Porchester Sch., Bournemouth. Qualified chartered accountant, 1964; articled to Morison Rutherford & Co.; commenced practice on own account in name of Kingston Jolliffe & Co., 1965, later, Jolliffe Cork & Co., Sen. Partner, 1976. Director: Corel Corp.; Paccar UK Ltd; Corel Corp. Ltd; Abela Gp (UK) Ltd; Abela & Gate Gourmet Ltd; Farne Salmon & Trout Ltd; Princess d'Isenbourg et Cie; Chm., Causeway Capital Develt Fund. Chm., Stoke Mandeville NHS Trust, 1994–. Alderman, Ward of Candlewick, 1975–84; Sheriff, City of London, 1980–81; Lord Mayor of London, 1982–83. Pres., London Chamber of Commerce, 1985–88. Chm., Police Dependants' Trust; Trustee, Police Foundn. Pres., Soc. of Dorset Men. Member: Guild of Freemen; Ct, Worshipful Co. of Painter Stainers; Worshipful Co. of Wheelwrights. FRSA; KStJ 1983. *Clubs:* Garrick, City Livery (Pres., 1979–80), Saints and Sinners.

JOLLIFFE, Christopher, CBE 1971; Chairman, Abbeyfield Richmond Society, 1980–87; Director, Science Division, Science Research Council, 1969–72 (Director for University Science and Technology, 1965–69); *b* 14 March 1912; *s* of William Edwin Jolliffe and Annie Etheldreda Thompson; *m* 1936, Miriam Mabel Ash. *Educ:* Gresham's Sch., Holt; University Coll., London. Asst Master, Stowe Sch., 1935–37; Dept of Scientific and Industrial Research, 1937–65. Vice-Chm., Council for Science and Society, 1978–82;

Dir, Leverhulme Trust Fund, 1976–77. *Address:* 8 Broomfield Road, Kew, Richmond, Surrey TW9 3HR. *T:* 0181–940 4265.

JOLLIFFE, William Orlando, IPFA, FCA; County Treasurer of Lancashire, 1973–85; *b* 16 Oct. 1925; *s* of late William Dibble Jolliffe and Laura Beatrice Jolliffe; *m* 1st (marr. diss.); one *s* one *d*; 2nd, 1975, Audrey (*née* Dale); one step *d*. *Educ:* Bude County Grammar Sch. Institute of Public Finance Accountant. Chartered Accountant (first place in final exam. of (former) Soc. of Incorporated Accountants, 1956). Joined Barclays Bank Ltd, 1941. Served War of 1939–45 (HM Forces, 1944–48). Subseq. held various appts in Treasurers' depts of Devon CC, Winchester City Council, Doncaster CB Council, Bury CB Council (Dep. Borough Treas.), and Blackpool CB Council (Dep. 1959, Borough Treas., 1962). Mem. Council, Chartered Inst. of Public Finance and Accountancy, 1969–85 (Pres., 1979–80); Financial Adviser, ACC, 1976–85; Mem. Council (Pres. 1974–75), Assoc. of Public Service Finance Officers, 1963–76; Chm., Officers' Side, JNC for Chief Officers of Local Authorities in England and Wales, 1971–76; Mem. Exec. Cttee (Pres. 1970–71), NW Soc. of Chartered Accountants, 1966–76; Chm., NW and N Wales Region of CIPFA, 1974–76; Mem., Soc. of County Treasurers (Mem. Exec. Cttee, 1977–85); Hon. Treas., Lancashire Playing Fields Assoc., 1974–85. Financial Adviser to Assoc. of Municipal Corporations, 1969–74; Mem. (Govt) Working Party on Collab. between Local Authorities and the National Health Service, 1971–74. *Publications:* articles for Public Finance and Accountancy and other local govt jls. *Address:* Yew Tree Cottage, Askham, Penrith, Cumbria CA10 2PF. *T:* Hackthorpe (01931) 712292. *Club:* Penrith Golf.

JOLLY, (Arthur) Richard, PhD; development economist; Acting Executive Director, UNICEF, New York, since 1995 (Deputy Executive Director, 1982–94); *b* 30 June 1934; *s* of late Arthur Jolly and Flora Doris Jolly (*née* Leaver); *m* 1963, Alison Bishop, PhD; two *s* two *d*. *Educ:* Brighton Coll.; Magdalene Coll., Cambridge (BA 1956, MA 1959); Yale Univ. (MA 1960, PhD 1966). Community Develt Officer, Baringo Dist, Kenya, 1957–59; Associate Chubb Fellow, Yale Univ., 1961–62; Res. Fellow, E Africa Inst. of Social Res., Makerere Coll., Uganda, 1963–64; Res. Officer, Dept of Applied Econs, Cambridge Univ., 1964–68 (seconded as Advr on Manpower to Govt of Zambia, 1964–66); Fellow, 1968–, Dir, 1972–81, Inst. of Develt Studies; Professorial Fellow, Univ. of Sussex, 1971–. Advr on Manpower Aid, ODM, 1968; Sen. Economist, Min. of Develt and Finance, Zambia, 1970; Advr to Parly Select Cttee on Overseas Aid and Develt, 1974–75; ILO Advr on Planning, Madagascar, 1975; Member: Triennial Rev. Gp, Commonwealth Fund for Tech. Co-operation, 1975–76; UK Council on Internat. Develt, 1974–78; UN Cttee for Develt Planning, 1978–81; Special Consultant on N-S Issues to Sec.-Gen., OECD, 1978; sometime member and chief of ILO and UN missions, and consultant to various governments and international organisations. Sec., British Alpine Hannibal Expedn, 1959. Member: Founding Cttee, European Assoc. of Develt Insts, 1972–75; Governing Council, 1976–85, and N-S Round Table, SID, 1976– (Vice-Pres., 1982–85; Chm., N-S Round Table, 1988–). Mem., Editorial Bd, World Development, 1973–. Master, Curriers' Co., 1977–78. Hon. LittD E Anglia, 1988; Hon. DLitt Sussex, 1992. *Publications:* (jtly) Cuba: the economic and social revolution, 1964; Planning Education for African Development, 1969; (ed) Education in Africa: research and action, 1969; (ed jtly) Third World Employment, 1973; (jtly) Redistribution with Growth, 1974 (trans. French 1977); (ed) Disarmament and World Development, 1978, 3rd edn 1986; (ed jtly) Recent Issues in World Development, 1981; (ed jtly) Rich Country Interests in Third World Development, 1982; (ed jtly) The Impact of World Recession on Children, 1984; (ed jtly) Adjustment with a Human Face, 1987 (trans. French 1987, Spanish 1987); (ed jtly) The UN & the Bretton Woods Institutions, 1995; contributions to: Development in a Divided World, 1971; Employment, Income Distribution and Development Strategy, 1976; The Poverty of Progress, 1982, articles in professional and develt jls. *Recreations:* billiards, croquet, nearly missing trains and planes. *Address:* Institute of Development Studies, University of Sussex, Brighton, Sussex BN1 9RE. *T:* Brighton (01273) 606261; UNICEF, UNICEF House, 3 United Nations Plaza, New York, NY 10017, USA. *T:* (212) 3267017.

JOLLY, James Falcon; Editor, Gramophone, since 1989; *b* 12 Feb. 1961; *s* of Gordon and Enid Jolly. *Educ:* Pinewood Sch., Bourton; Bradfield Coll.; Univ. of Bristol (BA Hons); Univ. of Reading (MA). Asst Editor, Gramophone, 1985–88; Producer, BBC Radio 3, 1988–89. *Publications:* contrib. British Music Yearbook, 1986–88, Good CD Guide, Gramophone, Independent, Le Monde de la Musique, New Grove Dictionary of Opera. *Recreations:* food, wine, travel, cinema, gardening. *Address:* 19A Nelson Road, Harrow-on-the-Hill, Middx HA1 3ET. *T:* 0181–864 7587.

JOLLY, Richard; *see* Jolly, A. R.

JOLLY, Air Cdre Robert Malcolm, CBE 1969; retired; *b* 4 Aug. 1920; *s* of Robert Imrie Jolly and Ethel Thompson Jolly; *m* 1946, Josette Jacqueline (*née* Baindeky); no *c*. *Educ:* Skerry's Coll., Newcastle upon Tyne. Commnd in RAF, 1943; served in: Malta, 1941–45; Bilbeis, Egypt, 1945; Shaibah, Iraq, 1945–46; Malta, 1946–49; Air Cdre 1971; Dir of Personal Services, MoD, 1970–72; Dir of Automatic Data Processing (RAF), 1973–75, retd. Man. Dir, Leonard Griffiths & Associates, 1975–77; Vice-Pres., MWS Consultants Inc., 1978–80; Gen. Man., Diebold Europe SA and Dir, Diebold Research Program Europe, 1983–84. Hon. Archivist, St Paul's Anglican Pro-Cathedral, Malta GC, 1992–. FBCS 1972; CIMgt (CBIM 1973). *Address:* Villa Grey Golf, Triq Galata, High Ridge, St Andrews STJ 03, Malta GC. *T:* 370282. *Club:* Royal Air Force.

JOLOWICZ, Prof. John Anthony; QC 1990; Professor of Comparative Law, University of Cambridge, 1976–93; Fellow, Trinity College, Cambridge, since 1952; *b* 11 April 1926; *e s* of late Prof. Herbert Felix Jolowicz and Ruby Victoria Wagner; *m* 1957, Poppy Stanley; one *s* two *d*. *Educ:* Oundle Sch.; Trinity Coll., Cambridge (Scholar; MA; 1st Cl. Hons Law Tripos 1950). Served HM Forces (commnd RASC), 1944–48. Called to the Bar, Inner Temple and Gray's Inn, 1952; Bencher, Gray's Inn, 1978. Univ. of Cambridge: Asst Lectr in Law, 1955, Lectr, 1959; Reader in Common and Comparative Law, 1972. Professeur associé, Université de Paris 2, 1976; Lionel Cohen Lectr, Hebrew Univ. of Jerusalem, 1983. Pres., SPTL, 1986–87. Corresp. Mem., Institut de France, Acad. des Sciences morales et politiques, 1989; Mem., Academia Europea, 1988. Hon. Dr Universidad Nacional Autónoma de México, 1985. Editor, Jl of Soc. of Public Teachers of Law, 1962–80. *Publications:* (ed) H. F. Jolowicz's Lectures on Jurisprudence, 1963; Winfield and Jolowicz on Tort, 1971, 14th edn (ed W. V. H. Rogers) 1994; (with M. Cappelletti) Public Interest Parties and the Active Role of the Judge, 1975; (jtly) Droit Anglais, 1986, 2nd edn 1992; contrib. to Internat. Encyc. of Comparative Law and to legal jls. *Address:* Trinity College, Cambridge CB2 1TQ. *T:* Cambridge (01223) 338400; West Green House, Barrington, Cambridge CB2 5SA. *T:* Cambridge (01223) 870495. *Clubs:* Royal Automobile; Leander (Henley-on-Thames).

JONAS, Christopher William, CBE 1994; FRICS; Senior Partner, Drivers Jonas, since 1987; President, Royal Institution of Chartered Surveyors, 1992–93; *b* 19 Aug. 1941; *s* of late Philip Griffith Jonas, MC and of Kathleen Marjory Jonas (*née* Ellis); *m* 1968, (Jennifer Susan) Penny Barker, *d* of B. Leslie and Jose Barker; three *s* one *d*. *Educ:* Charterhouse; Coll. of Estate Management; London Business Sch. (Sloan Fellow). TA Inns of Court Regt, 1959–66. Jones Lang Wootton, 1959–67; Drivers Jonas: Partner, 1967–82; Managing Partner, 1982–87. Property Adviser, Staffs County Council, 1982–. Chm., Economics Research Associates, USA, 1987–93; Board Member: PLA, 1985–; Securities and Futures Authy, 1988–91; Business in the Community, 1991–; British Rail Property Bd, 1991–94; (part-time) BR, 1993–94; Railtrack, 1994–. Mem., FEFC, 1992–. Member: Urban Land Inst., USA; Amer. Soc. of Real Estate Counselors. Trustee, Property Centre, City Univ. Liveryman: Clothworkers' Co. (Warden, 1994–); Chartered Surveyors' Co. (Asst, 1990). FInstD; FRSA. *Recreations:* Wagner, other music, ski-ing, golf, tennis. *Address:* Drivers Jonas, 16 Suffolk Street, SW1Y 4HQ. *T:* 0171–930 9731. *Clubs:* Naval and Military; Toronto (Toronto).

See also R. W. Jonas.

JONAS, Peter, CBE 1993; General Director (Staatsintendant), Bavarian State Opera, since 1993; *b* 14 Oct. 1946; *s* of Walter Adolf Jonas and Hilda May Jonas; *m* 1989, Lucy, *d* of Christopher and Cecilia Hull. *Educ:* Worth School; Univ. of Sussex (BA Hons); Northern Coll. of Music (LRAM); Royal Coll. of Music (CAMS; Fellow, 1989); Eastman Sch. of Music, Univ. of Rochester, USA. Asst to Music Dir, 1974–76, Artistic Administrator, 1976–85, Chicago Symphony Orch.; Dir of Artistic Admin, Orchestral Assoc. of Chicago (Chicago Symph. Orch., Chicago Civic Orch., Chicago Symph. Chorus, Allied Arts Assoc., Orchestra Hall), 1977–85; Man. Dir, subseq. Gen. Dir, ENO, 1985–93. Mem. Adv. Bd, Bayerische Vereinsbank, 1994–. Member: Bd of Management, Nat. Opera Studio, 1985–93; Council, RCM, 1988–95; Council, London Lighthouse, 1990–94. FRSA 1989. Hon. DrMus Sussex, 1994. *Publication:* (with Mark Elder and David Pountney) Power House, 1992. *Recreations:* cinema, 20th century architecture. *Address:* Bayerische Staatsoper, Nationaltheater, Max-Joseph-Platz 2, 80539 München, Germany; Prinzregentenstrasse 72, 81675 München, Germany. *Club:* Athenæum.

JONAS, Richard Wheen; FRICS; Senior Partner, Cluttons, since 1992; *b* 10 April 1943; *s* of late Philip Griffith Jonas, MC and of Kathleen Marjory (*née* Ellis); *m* 1973, Bettina Banton; two *d*. *Educ:* Charterhouse; Royal Agricl Coll. Strutt & Parker, 1965–70; Carter Jonas, 1970–73; Cluttons, 1973–: Partner, 1978–. Liveryman, Clothworkers' Co., 1965–. Gold Medal, RASE, 1967. *Recreations:* shooting, golf, ornithology. *Address:* Cluttons, 45 Berkeley Square, W1X 5DB. *T:* 0171–408 1010. *Club:* City of London.

See also C. W. Jonas.

JONES; *see* Armstrong-Jones, family name of Earl of Snowdon.

JONES; *see* Avery Jones.

JONES; *see* Gwynne Jones, family name of Baron Chalfont.

JONES; *see* Lloyd Jones and Lloyd-Jones.

JONES; *see* Mars-Jones.

JONES; *see* Morris-Jones.

JONES; *see* Owen-Jones.

JONES, Adrianne Shirley, (Ann), MBE 1969; Women's Team Captain, Lawn Tennis Association, since 1990; BBC tennis commentator, since 1970; *b* 17 Oct. 1938; *d* of Adrian Arthur Haydon and Doris (*née* Jordan); *m* 1962, Philip Frank Jones (*d* 1993); two *s* one *d*. *Educ:* King's Norton Grammar Sch., Birmingham. Finalist, World Table Tennis Championships: Ladies Doubles, 1954; Singles, Ladies Doubles, Mixed Doubles, 1957, Tennis Championships: Winner, French Open, 1961, 1966; Winner, Italian Open, 1966, Finalist, US, 1961, 1967; Wimbledon: Finalist, Ladies Singles, 1967; Winner, 1969; semi-finalist nine times. Chm., Women's Internat. Professional Tennis Council, 1977–84; Dir, European Ops, Women's Tennis Assoc., 1976–84. *Publications:* Tackle Table Tennis My Way, 1957; Tennis: a game to love, 1970. *Recreations:* all sports, reading, music. *Address:* (home) 85 Westfield Road, Edgbaston, Birmingham B15 3JF. *T:* 0121–454 4964; (office) Lawn Tennis Association, Queen's Club, West Kensington, W14 9EG. *T:* 0171–381 7073. *Clubs:* All England Lawn Tennis, Queen's; Edgbaston Priory.

JONES, Alan Payan P.; *see* Pryce-Jones.

JONES, Alan Wingate, FEng 1989; FIEE; Chief Executive, BICC plc, since 1995; *b* 15 Oct. 1939; *s* of Gilbert Victor Jones and Isobel Nairn Jones; *m* 1974, Judi Ann Curtis; one *s* one *d*. *Educ:* Sutton Valence Sch.; King's Coll., Cambridge (MA MechScis). GEC, 1961–73; Plessey Co. Plc, 1973–89: Man. Dir, Plessey Marine, 1975–79; Divl Man. Dir, Plessey Displays and Sensors, 1979–85; Internat. Dir, 1985–87; Man. Dir, Plessey Electronic Systems, 1987–89; Dir, Plessey Plc, 1985–89; Chief Exec., Westland Gp, 1989–95; Dir, GKN, 1994–95. FRAeS 1993. *Recreations:* opera, ski-ing, sailing. *Address:* The Grange, North Cadbury, near Yeovil, Somerset BA22 7BY. *Club:* Royal Automobile.

JONES, Prof. Albert Stanley, PhD; DSc; Professor of Chemistry, University of Birmingham, 1969–87, now Emeritus; *b* 30 April 1925; *s* of Albert Ernest Jones and Florence Jones (*née* Rathbone); *m* 1950, Joan Christine Gregg; one *s* one *d*. *Educ:* Waverley Grammar Sch.; Univ. of Birmingham (BSc (1st Cl. Hons) 1944, PhD 1947, DSc 1957). Beit Memorial Fellow for Medical Research, 1949–52; University of Birmingham: Lectr in Chemistry, 1952–61; Sen. Lectr, 1961–63; Reader in Organic Chemistry, 1963–69. Chemical Society London: Birmingham Representative, 1959–62; Mem. Council, 1966–69; Chm., Nucleotide Group, 1967–72. *Publications:* 183 papers, incl. three review articles, in scientific jls, on various aspects of organic chemistry and biological chemistry, particularly concerning nucleic acid derivatives. *Recreations:* church activities, walking, music, reading. *Address:* Waverley, 76 Manor House Lane, Yardley, Birmingham B26 1PR. *T:* 0121–743 2030.

JONES, Allen, RA 1986 (ARA 1981); artist; *b* 1 Sept. 1937; *s* of William Jones and Madeline Jones (*née* Aveson); *m* 1964, Janet Bowen (marr. diss. 1978); two *d*; *m* 1994, Deirdre Morrow. *Educ:* Ealing Grammar Sch. for Boys; Hornsey Sch. of Art (NDD; ATD); Royal Coll. of Art. Teacher of Lithography, Croydon Coll. of Art, 1961–63; Teacher of Painting, Chelsea Sch. of Art, 1966–68; Tamarind Fellow in Lithography, Los Angeles, 1968; Guest Professor: Hochschule fur Bildend Kunst, Hamburg, 1968–70; Univs of S Florida, 1970, Calif at Irvine, 1973, Los Angeles, 1977; Hochschule fur Kunst Berlin, 1983; has travelled extensively. Sec., Young Contemporaries exhibn, London, 1961. One-man exhibns include: Arthur Tooth and Sons, London, 1963, 1964, 1967, 1970; Richard Feigen Gall., NY, Chicago and LA, 1964, 1965, 1970; Marlborough Fine Art, London, 1972; Arts Council sponsored exhibn tour, UK, 1974; Waddington Galls, London, 1976, 1980, 1982, 1983, 1985, 1993; James Corocan Gall., LA, 1977, 1987; UCLA Art Galls, LA, 1977; Graphic Retrospective 1958–78, ICA, 1978, tour incl. Waddington Galls, Toronto; Gall. Cavallino, Venice, 1981; Thorden and Wetterling, Gothenburg, 1983; Gall. Kammer, Hamburg, 1983, 1984; Gall. Wentzel, Cologne (sculpture), 1984; Gall. Patrice Trigano, Paris, 1985, 1986, 1989; Gall. Kaj Forsblom, Helsinki, 1985; Gall. Hete Hunermann, Dusseldorf, 1987, 1994; Charles Cowles Gall., NY, 1988; Heland Wetterling Gall., Stockholm, 1989; Gall. Wentzel, Cologne, 1992; Gall. Punto, Valencia, 1992; Gall. Levy, Hamburg and Madrid, 1993; Print Retrospective,

Barbican Centre and tour, 1995; first Retrospective of Painting, 1959–79, Walker Art Gall., Liverpool, and tour of England and Germany, 1979; first internat. exhibn, Paris Biennale, 1961 (Prix des Jeunes Artists); first professional exhibn (with Howard Hodgkin), Two Painters, ICA, 1962; first UK mus. exhibn, Decade of Painting and Sculpture, Tate Gall., 1964; museum and group exhibns in UK and abroad include: New Generation, Whitechapel, 1964; London, The New Scene, Minneapolis, 1965; British Drawing/New Generation, NY, 1967; Documenta IV, Kassel, 1968; Pop Art Redefined, Hayward Gall., 1969; British Painting and Sculpture, Washington, 1970; Metamorphosis of Object, Brussels, and tour, 1971; Seibu, Tokyo, 1974; Hyperealist/Realistes, Paris, 1974; Arte Inglese Oggi, Milan, 1976; El color en la pintura Britanica, British Council S American tour, 1977; British Painting 1952–77, Royal Academy, 1977; Arts Council sponsored exhibn tour, UK, 1978, Wales, 1992; British Watercolours, British Council tour, China, 1982; The Folding Image, Washington and Yale, 1984; Pop Art 1955–1970, NY, then Aust. tour, 1985; 40 Years of Modern Art, Tate Gall., 1986; British Art in the Twentieth Century, Royal Academy, then Stuttgart, 1987; Pop Art, Tokyo, 1987; Picturing People, British Council tour, Hong Kong, Singapore, Kuala Lumpur, 1990; New Acquisitions, Kunstmus., Dusseldorf, 1990; Seoul Internat. Art Fest., 1991; British Art since 1930, Waddington Gall., 1991; BM, 1991; Pop Art, Royal Academy, 1991, then Cologne, Madrid and Montreal, 1992; From Bacon to Now, Florence; Nat. Portrait Gall., 1994; exhibited annually at Royal Acad., 1981–; murals and sculptures for public places include: Fogal, Basel and Zurich; Liverpool Garden Fest., 1984; Perseverance Works, Hackney, 1986; Citicorp/Canadian Nat. Bank, London Bridge City, 1987; Milton Keynes, 1990; BAA, Heathrow, 1990; Chelsea/Westminster Hosp., 1993; LDDC, 1994; television and stage sets include: O Calcutta!, for Kenneth Tynan, London and Europe, 1970; Manner Wir Kommen, WDR, Cologne, 1970; Understanding Opera, LWT, 1988; Cinema/Eric Satie, for Ballet Rambert, 1989. Television films have been made on his work. Trustee, British Mus., 1990–. *Publications:* Allen Jones Figures, 1969; Allen Jones Projects, 1971; Waitress, 1972; Sheer Magic, 1979, UK 1980; Allen Jones, 1993; articles in various jls. *Recreations:* very private, also gardening. *Address:* 41 Charterhouse Square, EC1M 6EA. *Fax:* 0171–600 1204.

JONES, Alun; *see* Jones, R. A.

JONES, Dr Alun Denry Wynn, CPhys, FInstP; Chief Executive, Institute of Physics, since 1990; *b* 13 Nov. 1939; *s* of Thomas D. and Ray Jones; *m* 1964, Ann Edwards; two *d. Educ:* Amman Valley Grammar Sch.; Christ Church, Oxford (MA, DPhil). CPhys, FInstP 1973. Sen. Student, Commission for Exhibn of 1851, 1964–66; Sen. Research Fellow, UKAEA, 1966–67; Lockheed Missiles and Space Co., California, 1967–70; Tutor, Open Univ., 1971–82; joined Macmillan and Co., Publishers, 1971; Dep. Editor, Nature, 1972–73; British Steel Corp., 1974–77; British Steel Overseas Services, 1977–81; Asst Dir, Technical Change Centre, 1982–85; Dep. Dir, 1986–87, Dir, 1987–90, Wolfson Foundn. Sec. of working party on social concern and biological advances, 1972–74, Mem., Section X Cttee, 1981–92, BAAS. British Library: Adv. Council, 1983–85; Document Supply Centre Adv. Cttee, 1986–89; Mem. Council, Nat. Library of Wales, 1987–94 (Gov., 1986–94). Dir, Council for Sci. and Technol. Insts, 1990–; Mem. Council, Standing Conf., Schs of Sci. and Technol., 1992–. Governor: UCW, Aberystwyth, 1990–92; City Univ., 1991–. *Publication:* (with W. F. Bodmer) Our Future Inheritance: choice or chance, 1974. *Recreations:* gardening, theatre, cricket. *Address:* Institute of Physics, 76 Portland Place, W1N 4AA. *T:* 0171–235 6111; 4 Wheatsheaf Close, Woking, Surrey GU21 4BP. *Club:* Athenæum.

JONES, Most Rev. Alwyn Rice; *see* Wales, Archbishop of.

JONES, Angela; *see* Jones, S. A. M.

JONES, Ann; *see* Jones, Adrianne S.

JONES, Prof. Anne; Professor, since 1991, and Head of Department of Continuing Education, since 1993, Brunel University (Director of Continuing Education, 1991–93); *b* 8 April 1935; *d* of Sydney Joseph and Hilda Pickard; *m* 1958, C. Gareth Jones (marr. diss. 1989); one *s* two *d. Educ:* Harrow Weald County Sch.; Westfield Coll., London (BA; Fellow, QMW, 1992); DipSoc, PGCE London. Assistant Mistress: Malvern Girls' Coll., 1957–58; Godolphin and Latymer Sch., 1958–62; Dulwich Coll., 1964; Sch. Counsellor, Mayfield Comprehensive Sch., 1965–71; Dep. Hd, Thomas Calton Sch., 1971–74; Head: Vauxhall Manor Sch., 1974–81; Cranford Community Sch., 1981–87; Under Sec. (Dir of Educn), Dept of Employment, 1987–91; management consultant, 1991–93. Vis. Prof. of Educn, Sheffield Univ., 1989–. Director: CRAC, 1983–94; Grubb Inst. of Behavioural Studies, 1987–. Member Council: QMW, 1991–; W London Inst. of Higher Educn, 1991–95; NICEC, 1991–95. FRSA 1984 (Mem. Council, 1986–94); FIMgt 1992. Hon. FCP 1990. *Publications:* School Counselling in Practice, 1970; Counselling Adolescents in School, 1977, 2nd edn as Counselling Adolescents, School and After, 1984; Leadership for Tomorrow's Schools, 1987; (with Jan Marsh and A. G. Watts): Male and Female, 1974, 2nd edn 1982; Living Choices, 1976; Time to Spare, 1980; contribs to various books. *Recreations:* walking, boating, gardening, theatre, opera. *Address:* Brunel University, Uxbridge, Middx UB8 3PH. *T:* Uxbridge (01895) 274000; 23 Queen Street, Henley-on-Thames, Oxfordshire RG9 1AR. *T:* Henley-on-Thames (01491) 578672.

JONES, Prof. Anthony Edward, FRCA; Rector, Royal College of Art, since 1992; *b* 3 Aug. 1944; *s* of late Edward and Violet Jones; *m* 1st, 1972, Gwen Brandt (marr. diss. 1978); one *s*; 2nd, 1989, Patricia Jon Carroll. *Educ:* Goldsmiths' Coll., Univ. of London; Newport Coll. of Art, Newport (DipAD, BA); Tulane Univ., New Orleans (MFA). Artist-in-Residence, Loyola Univ., 1967–68; Teaching Fellow, Gloucester Coll. of Art, Cheltenham, 1968–69; Sen. Lectr and Dep. Head of Sculpture, Glasgow Sch. of Art, 1969–72; Chm., Dept of Art and Art Hist., Texas Christian Univ., 1972–80; Dir, Glasgow Sch. of Art, 1980–86; Pres. and Co-Chief Exec., Art Inst. of Chicago, 1986–92. Fulbright Scholar, USA, 1966–68. FRCA 1993; FRSA 1994; Hon. AIA 1991. Newbery Medal, Glasgow Univ., 1986. *Publications:* Chapel Architecture in the Merthyr Valley, 1964; Welsh Chapels (Capeli Cymru), 1984; Charles Rennie Mackintosh, 1990. *Recreation:* travel, reluctantly! *Address:* c/o Royal College of Art, Kensington Gore, SW7 2EU. *T:* 0171–584 5020. *Clubs:* Chelsea Arts; University (Chicago).

JONES, Maj.-Gen. Anthony George Clifford, CB 1978; MC 1945; President, Regular Commissions Board, 1975–78; *b* 20 May 1923; *s* of late Col R. C. Jones, OBE, and M. D. Jones; *m* Kathleen Mary, *d* of Comdr J. N. Benbow, OBE, RN; two *d. Educ:* St Paul's School; Trinity Hall, Cambridge. Commissioned RE, 1942; service includes: Troop Comdr, Guards Armd Div., Nijmegen, 1945 (MC 1945; despatches, 1947); Indian Sappers and Miners; Staff Coll., 1954; Bde Major, 63 Gurkha Inf. Bde, 1955 (despatches, 1957); jssc; OC 25 Corps Engineer Regt, 1965–67; Comdr, RE Trng Bde, 1968–72; Head of Ops Staff, Northern Army Group, 1972–74; Dep. Comdr SE District, 1974–75. Hon. Col, RE Volunteers (Sponsored Units), 1978–86. *Club:* Army and Navy.

JONES, Anthony Graham Hume; His Honour Judge Graham Hume Jones; a Circuit Judge, since 1993; *b* 16 Aug. 1942; *s* of Rt Hon. Sir Edward Jones, PC and Margaret Anne Crosland (*née* Smellie); *m* 1966, Evelyn Ann Brice Smyth; two *s* one *d. Educ:* Trinity Coll., Glenalmond; Trinity Coll., Dublin (BA 1966). Mardon, Son & Hall Ltd, 1966–71; called to the Bar, Gray's Inn, 1971; called to the Bar, NI, 1981; a Recorder, 1990–93. Vice-Pres., Avon Br., SSAFA, 1993–. *Recreations:* sailing, golf. *Address:* Yeowood, Wrington, Avon BS18 7NS; Craig-y-Mor, Trearddur Bay, Holyhead, Anglesey LL65 2UP. *Clubs:* Royal Ocean Racing; Trearddur Bay Sailing (Cdre, 1994–); Royal County Down Golf.

JONES, Anthony W.; *see* Whitworth-Jones.

JONES, Rt Rev. Arthur Lucas Vivian; *see* Gippsland, Bishop of.

JONES, Prof. Arthur Stanley, CBiol; Principal, Royal Agricultural College, Cirencester, since 1990; *b* 17 May 1932; *s* of John Jones and Anne Jones (*née* Hamilton); *m* 1962, Mary Margaret Smith; three *s* one *d. Educ:* Gosforth Grammar Sch.; Durham Univ. (BSc); Aberdeen Univ. (PhD). FIBiol; FIMgt. Rowett Research Institute: Res. Scientist, 1959; Hd, Applied Nutrition Dept, 1966; Chm., Applied Scis Div., 1975; Dep. Dir, 1983; Governor, 1987–; Strathcona-Fordyce Prof. of Agriculture, Univ. of Aberdeen, 1986–90; Head, Sch. of Agriculture, Aberdeen, and Principal, N of Scotland Coll. of Agriculture, 1986–90. Mem., House of Lords Rural Econ. Gp, 1992–94. Chairman: Scottish Beef Develts Ltd, 1988–91; RAC Enterprises Ltd, 1992–. Member: Council, RASE, 1991–; Bd, Arable Res. Centres, 1992–. Trustee: Trehane Trust, 1993–; Geoffrey Cragghill Meml Scholarship Trust, 1993–. FRSA; FIAgrM. *Publications:* Nutrition of Animals of Agricultural Importance (vol. 17, Internat. Encyc. of Food and Nutrition) (ed D. P. Cuthbertson), 1967; 115 articles in learned jls. *Recreations:* yachting, flying, gardening. *Address:* Royal Agricultural College, Cirencester, Glos GL7 6JS. *Club:* Farmers'.

JONES, Rt. Hon. Aubrey, PC 1955; Director: Thomas Tilling Ltd, 1970–82; Cornhill Insurance Company Ltd, 1971–82 (Chairman, 1971–74); *b* 20 Nov. 1911; *s* of Evan and Margaret Aubrey Jones, Merthyr Tydfil; *m* 1948, Joan, *d* of G. Godfrey-Isaacs, Ridgehanger, Hillcrest Road, Hanger Hill, W5; two *s. Educ:* Cyfarthfa Castle Secondary Sch., Merthyr Tydfil; London School of Economics. BSc (Econ.) 1st Cl. Hons, Gladstone Memorial Prizewinner, Gerstenberg Post-grad. Schol., LSE. On foreign and editorial staffs of The Times, 1937–39 and 1947–48. Joined British Iron and Steel Federation, 1949; General Dir, June-Dec. 1955. Served War of 1939–45, Army Intelligence Staff, War Office and Mediterranean Theatre, 1940–46. Contested (C) SE Essex in General Election, 1945 and Heywood and Radcliffe (by-election), 1946; MP (U) Birmingham, Hall Green, 1950–65; Parliamentary Private Sec. to Minister of State for Economic Affairs, 1952, and to Min. of Materials, 1953; Minister of Fuel and Power, Dec. 1955–Jan. 1957; Minister of Supply, 1957–Oct. 1959. Mem., Plowden Cttee of Inquiry into Aircraft Industry, 1965–66. Chairman: Staveley Industries Ltd, 1964–65 (Dir 1962–65); Laporte Industries (Holdings) Ltd, 1970–72; Director: Guest, Keen & Nettlefolds Steel Company Limited, 1960–65; Courtaulds Ltd, 1960–63; Black & Decker, 1977–81. Chm., Nat. Bd for Prices and Incomes, 1965–70; Vice-Pres., Consumers' Assoc., 1967–72; leading consultant to: Nigerian Public Service Commn, 1973–74; Iranian Govt, 1974–78; Plessey Ltd, 1978–80; Mem. Panel of Conciliators, Internat. Centre for Settlement of Investment Disputes, 1974–81. Pres., Oxford Energy Policy Club, 1976–88. Regent Lectr, Univ. of California at Berkeley, 1968. Vis. Fellow: New Coll., Oxford, 1978; Sci. Policy Res. Unit, Univ. of Sussex, 1986–92, Hon. Fellow, 1993; Sen. Res. Associate, St Antony's Coll., Oxford, 1979–82; Guest Scholar, Brookings Instn, Washington, DC, 1982. Fellow Commoner, Churchill Coll., Cambridge, 1972 and 1982–86. Hon. Fellow, LSE, 1959, Mem., Court of Governors, 1964–87. Hon. DSc Bath, 1968. Winston Churchill Meml Trust Award, 1985. *Publications:* The Pendulum of Politics, 1946; Industrial Order, 1950; The New Inflation: the politics of prices and incomes, 1973; (ed) Economics and Equality, 1976; (contrib.) My LSE, 1977; (contrib.) The End of the Keynesian Era, 1977; Oil: the missed opportunity, 1981; Britain's Economy: the roots of stagnation, 1985. *Address:* Arnen, 120 Limmer Lane, Felpham, Bognor Regis, West Sussex PO22 7LP. *T:* Middleton-on-Sea (0124358) 2722.

JONES, Barry; *see* Jones, Stephen B.

JONES, Beti, CBE 1980; *b* 23 Jan. 1919; *d* of Isaac Jones and Elizabeth (*née* Rowlands). *Educ:* Rhondda County Sch. for Girls; Univ. of Wales. BA (Hons) History, Teaching Diploma. Grammar Sch. teaching, 1941–43; S Wales Organiser, Nat. Assoc. of Girls' Clubs, 1943–47; Youth Officer, Educn Branch, Control Commission, Germany, 1947–49; Children's Officer, Glamorgan CC, 1949–68; Chief Adviser on Social Work, Scottish Office, 1968–80. Fellow, University Coll., Cardiff, 1982 (Hon. Fellow, Dept of Social Administration, 1970). *Address:* 5 Belgrave Crescent, Edinburgh EH4 3AQ. *T:* 0131–332 2696; Lochside Cottage, Craigie, Blairgowrie, Tayside PH10 6RQ. *T:* Essendy (01250) 884373. *Clubs:* Royal Over-Seas League (London and Edinburgh).

JONES, Brian Leslie; Judge of the High Court of Justice, Hong Kong, 1981–94; *b* 19 Oct. 1930; *s* of late William Leslie Jones and Gladys Gertrude Jones; *m* 1966, Yukiko Hirokane; one *s* two *d. Educ:* Bromsgrove Sch.; Birmingham Univ. Admitted Solicitor, 1956; called as Barrister and Solicitor, Supreme Court, Victoria, Australia, 1968. Solicitor, private practice, England, 1956–64; Asst Registrar, Supreme Court, Hong Kong, 1964–68; Legal Officer, Attorney General's Dept, Canberra, 1968–69; Asst Registrar, Hong Kong, 1969–74; District Judge, Hong Kong, 1974–81. Comr, Supreme Ct of Brunei, 1982, 1985, 1990. Chm., Standing Cttee on Company Law Reform, Hong Kong, 1991–94. *Recreations:* squash, chess, walking, reading. *Address:* 3 Mitchell Gardens, Slinfold, W Sussex RH13 7TY. *Clubs:* Hong Kong; Anyos (Andorra).

JONES, Brinley; *see* Jones, Robert B.

JONES, Charles Beynon Lloyd, CMG 1978; Chairman of Directors, David Jones Ltd, 1963–80; Consul General of Finland in Sydney, 1971–88; *b* 4 Dec. 1932; *s* of late Sir Charles Lloyd Jones and Lady (Hannah Beynon) Lloyd Jones, OBE. *Educ:* Cranbrook Sch., Sydney; Univ. of Sydney (not completed). Joined David Jones Ltd, 1951; Alternate Director, 1956; Director, 1957; Joint Managing Director, 1961. President: Retail Traders Assoc., NSW, 1976–78; Bd of Trustees, Art Gall. of NSW, 1980–83 (Trustee, 1972; Vice-Pres., 1976–80). Governor, London House for Overseas Graduates, 1983–92. Officer, Order of Merit, Republic of Italy (Cavaliere Ufficiale); Comdr, Order of the Lion, Finland. *Address:* Summerlees Farm, Yarramalong, NSW 2259, Australia. *Club:* Royal Sydney Golf.

JONES, Gen. Sir (Charles) Edward (Webb), KCB 1989; CBE 1985; Gentleman Usher of the Black Rod and Serjeant-at-Arms, House of Lords, and Secretary to the Lord Great Chamberlain, since 1995; *b* 25 Sept. 1936; *s* of Gen. Sir Charles Phibbs Jones, GCB, CBE, MC and of Ouida Margaret Wallace; *m* 1965, Suzanne Vere Pige-Leschallas; two *s* one *d. Educ:* Portora Royal School, Enniskillen. Commissioned Oxford and Bucks LI, 1956; 1st Bn Royal Green Jackets, 1958; served BAOR, 1968–70; served NI, 1971–72 (despatches 1972); Directing Staff, Staff Coll., 1972; CO 1st Bn RGJ, 1974–76; Comdr 6th Armd Brigade, 1981–83; Comdr, British Mil. Adv. and Training Team, Zimbabwe, 1983–85; Dir Gen., TA and Organisation, 1985–87; Comdr, 3rd Armoured Div., 1987–88; QMG, MoD, 1988–91; UK Mil. Rep. to NATO, 1992–95. Colonel Commandant: RAEC,

1986–92; RGJ, 1988–95; Dep. Col Comdt, AGC, 1992–93. *Recreations:* golf, tennis, fishing. *Address:* House of Lords, SW1A 0PW. *Club:* Army and Navy.

JONES, Charles Ian McMillan; Grants Administrator, CfBT Education Services, UK, since 1995; *b* 11 Oct. 1934; *s* of Wilfred Charles Jones and Bessie Jones (*née* McMillan); *m* 1962, Jennifer Marie Potter; two *s*. *Educ:* Bishop's Stortford Coll.; St John's Coll., Cambridge. Certif. Educn 1959, MA 1962; FBIM, FRSA. 2nd Lieut RA, 1953–55. Head of Geog. Dept, Bishop's Stortford Coll., 1960–70, Asst to Headmaster, 1967–70; Vice-Principal, King William's Coll., IoM, 1971–75; Head Master, Bedford School, 1975–86; Dir of Studies, BRNC, Dartmouth, 1986–88; Centre for British Teachers, subseq. CfBT: Project Dir, Brunei Darussalam, 1988–91, Malaysia, 1990–91; Regl Dir, Educn Services, SE Asia, 1991–94. Man., England Schoolboy Hockey XI, 1967–74; Man., England Hockey XI, 1968–69; Pres., English Schoolboys Hockey Assoc., 1980–88; Mem. IoM Sports Council, 1972–75. *Publications:* articles in Guardian. *Recreations:* hockey (Captain Cambridge Univ. Hockey XI, 1959; England Hockey XI, 1959–64, 17 caps; Gt Britain Hockey XI, 1959–64, 28 caps), cricket (Captain IoM Cricket XI, 1973–75), golf. *Address:* Churchgate Middle Barn, Briston Road, Wood Dalling, Norwich NR11 6SN. *Clubs:* MCC; Hawks (Cambridge); Royal Norwich Golf; Pantai Mentiri Golf (Brunei).

JONES, Rt Rev. Christopher; *see* Elphin, Bishop of (RC).

JONES, Sir Christopher L.; *see* Lawrence-Jones.

JONES, Clement; *see* Jones, John C.

JONES, Clive Lawson; Secretary General, European Energy Charter Conference, European Commission, since 1991; *b* 16 March 1937; *s* of Celyn John Lawson Jones and Gladys Irene Jones; *m* 1961, Susan Brenda (*née* McLeod); one *s* one *d*. *Educ:* Cranleigh School; University of Wales. BSc (Chemistry). With British Petroleum, 1957–61; Texaco Trinidad, 1961–68; Principal, Min. of Power, 1968–69; Min. of Technology, 1969–70; DTI, 1970–73; Asst Sec., Oil Emergency Group, 1973–74; Department Energy: Asst Sec., 1974–77; Under Sec., Gas Div., 1981–82; Counsellor (Energy), Washington, 1977–81; Dir for Energy Policy, EC, 1982–86; Dep. Dir Gen. for Energy, EC, 1987–94. Chm., European Consultative Cttees on Electricity and Gas Markets, 1990–91. *Recreations:* art, antiques. *Address:* Energy Charter Secretariat, c/o DG XVII CEC, 200 rue de la Loi, 1049 Brussels, Belgium.

JONES, Clive William; Managing Director, Carlton UK Broadcasting Ltd, since 1995; *b* 10 Jan. 1949; *s* of Kenneth David Llewellyn Jones and Joan Muriel Jones (*née* Withers); *m* 1st, 1971; Frances Mawer (marr. diss. 1988); two *s* one *d*; 2nd, 1988, Fern Britton; two *s*. *Educ:* Newbridge Grammar Sch.; LSE (BSc Econ.). Journalist, until 1978; with Yorks TV, 1978–82; Man. Editor, Editor, then Editor-in-Chief, TV-am Ltd, 1982–84; TVS: Controller, News, Current Affairs and Sport, 1984–87; Dep. Dir of Programmes, 1987–91; Dep. Man. Dir, 1991–92; Founding Man. Dir, London News Network, 1992–94; Man. Dir, Central Independent Television PLC, April–Dec. 1994. *Recreations:* Rugby, golf, films. *Address:* Central House, Broad Street, Birmingham B1 2JP. *T:* 0121–643 9898, 0171–240 4000. *Clubs:* Birmingham Press; Winchester Rugby Football.

JONES, Courtney John Lyndhurst, OBE 1989 (MBE 1980); President, National Ice Skating Association, since 1987; *b* 30 April 1933; *s* of Reginald Jones and Inez Jones (*née* Wilsher). *Educ:* Ringwood Grammar Sch.; Bournemouth Coll. of Art (NDD). NSA Gold Medals for Ice Dance and for Pair Skating; British Ice Dance Champion, with June Markham, 1956–57, with Doreen Denny, 1958–60; European Ice Dance Champion, with June Markham, 1957–58, with Doreen Denny, 1959–61; World Ice Dance Champion, with June Markham, 1957–58, with Doreen Denny, 1959–60. Free-lance fashion designer, 1977–. Mem., US Figure Skating Hall of Fame, 1987; George Hasler Medal, Internat. Skating Union, 1991. *Recreations:* reading, music, the arts. *Address:* 1 Wesley Square, Lancaster Road, W11 1TP. *T:* 0171–221 1705.

JONES, Daniel Gruffydd; Registrar and Secretary, University of Wales, Aberystwyth, since 1990; *b* 7 Dec. 1933; *o s* of late Ifor Ceredig Jones and Gwendolen Eluned Jones; *m* 1969, Maureen Anne Woodhall; three *d*. *Educ:* Ardwyn Grammar Sch., Aberystwyth; University Coll. of N Wales, Bangor (BA). Min. of Housing and Local Govt, 1960; Private Sec. to Parly Sec., 1962–63; Principal, 1963; Private Sec. to Sec. of Cabinet, 1967–69; Asst Sec., 1969; Sec., Water Resources Bd, 1969–73; DoE, 1973; Sec., Prime Minister's Cttee on Local Govt Rules of Conduct, 1973–74; Under Sec., 1975; Prin. Finance Officer, Welsh Office, 1975–79; Director: Local Govt Directorate, DoE, 1980–82; Central Directorate of Envmtl Protection, DoE, 1982–86; Regl Dir, SE Reg., DoE and Dept of Transport, 1986–90. Mem., Royal Commn on Ancient and Historical Monuments in Wales, 1991–. Chm., Hafod Adv. Cttee, Forest Enterprise, 1992–. FRSA 1985. *Address:* c/o University of Wales, King Street, Aberystwyth, Dyfed SY23 2AX. *T:* Aberystwyth (01970) 622004.

JONES, Prof. David, OBE 1986; Professor and Dean, School of Nursing and Midwifery, University of Sheffield, since 1995; *b* 27 July 1940; *s* of John Evan Jones and Edith Catherine (*née* Edwards); *m* 1962, Janet Mary Ambler; two *s* two *d*. *Educ:* Boys' Grammar Sch., Bala, N Wales; Univ. of Wales (BEd). SRN; RMN; RNT. Divl Nursing Officer, Gwynedd, 1974–78; Chief Admin. Nursing Officer, Gwynedd HA, 1979–87; first Chm., Welsh Nat. Bd for Nursing, Midwifery and Health Visiting, 1979–86; Chief Exec., English Nat. Bd for Nursing, Midwifery and Health Visiting, 1987–89; Principal, Sheffield and N Trent Coll. of Nursing and Midwifery, 1990–94. *Recreations:* public affairs, countryside, family. *Address:* Postgraduate Research Centre, 8 Brunswick Street, Sheffield S10 2FN.

JONES, Sir David A.; *see* Akers-Jones.

JONES, David Charles, FCCA, FCIS; Chief Executive, Next Plc, since 1988 (Deputy Chief Executive, 1986–88); *b* 2 Feb. 1943; *s* of Frederick Charles Thomas Jones and Annie Marcella Jones; *m* 1968, Jeanette Ann Crofts; two *s* one *d*. *Educ:* King's Sch., Worcester. FCIS 1974; FCCA 1975. Joined Kays Mail Order Co. (part of Great Universal Stores), 1960, Finance Dir, 1971–77; Man. Dir, BMOC, 1977–80; Chief Exec., Grattan Plc, 1980–86. *Recreations:* golf, snooker. *Address:* Hepworth House, Claypit Lane, Leeds LS2 8DE. *T:* Leeds (0113) 244 0265.

JONES, David Evan Alun, CBE 1985; DL; Commissioner for Local Administration in Wales, 1980–85; *b* 9 Aug. 1925; *s* of David Jacob Jones, OBE, Master Mariner, and Margaret Jane Jones; *m* 1952, Joan Margaret Erica (*née* Davies); two *s*. *Educ:* Aberaeron County Sch.; University Coll. of Wales, Aberystwyth (LLB; Sir Samuel Evans Prize, 1949). Solicitor. Served War, RAF, 1943–47 (Flt Lieut). Articled service, Exeter, 1949–52; asst solicitor posts with Ilford Bor., Southampton County Bor., Berks County and Surrey County Councils, 1952–61; Dep. Clerk, Denbighshire CC, subseq. Clerk of CC and Clerk of the Peace, 1961–74; Chief Exec., Gwynedd CC, 1974–80. Chm., All Wales Adv. Panel on Develt of Services for Mentally Handicapped People, 1985–90; Member: Broadcasting Council for Wales, 1980–85; Local Govt Boundary Commn for Wales, 1985–89; Prince of Wales's Cttee, 1985–92 (Chm., Gwynedd County Gp, 1990–92); Gwynedd HA, 1986–88. Pres., Gwynedd Voluntary Services, 1994–. Treasurer, UCNW, 1988–. DL Gwynedd, 1988. *Recreations:* gardening, travel, a little golf. *Address:* Min-y-Don, West End, Beaumaris, Gwynedd LL58 8BG. *T:* Beaumaris (01248) 810225. *Clubs:* National Liberal; Baron Hill Golf (Beaumaris).

JONES, David George; Director General Naval Bases, Ministry of Defence, since 1995; *b* 31 May 1941; *s* of Frederick George Jones and Dorothy Jones (*née* Steele); *m* 1962, Leonie Usherwood Smith; three *s*. *Educ:* High Storrs Grammar Sch., Sheffield. Joined War Office as Exec. Officer, 1960; Asst Private Sec. to Army Minister, 1970–71; Principal, MoD Central Financial Planning Div., 1973–77; Private Sec. to Minister of State for Defence, 1977–80; Regl Marketing Dir, Defence Sales Organisation, 1980–84; Asst Sec., Air Systems Controllerate, 1984–85; Dep. Dir Gen., Al Yamamah Project Office, 1985–88; Dir Gen. Aircraft 2, Air Systems Controllerate, MoD (PE), 1988–89; Civil Sec., British Forces Germany, 1989–92; Dir Gen. Supplies and Transport (Naval), MoD, 1993–95. FILog. *Recreations:* gardening, travel. *Address:* c/o Ministry of Defence, Whitehall, SW1A 2HB. *T:* 0171–218 9000. *Club:* Civil Service.

JONES, David Hugh; Associate Director, Royal Shakespeare Company, since 1966; *b* 19 Feb. 1934; *s* of John David Jones and Gwendolen Agnes Langworthy (*née* Ricketts); *m* 1964, Sheila Allen; two *s*. *Educ:* Taunton Sch.; Christ's Coll., Cambridge (MA 1st Cl. Hons English). 2nd Lieut RA, 1954–56. Production team of Monitor, BBC TV's 1st arts magazine, 1958–62, Editor, 1962–64; joined RSC, 1964; Aldwych Co. Dir, 1968–72; Artistic Dir, RSC (Aldwych), 1975–77; Producer, Play of the Month, BBC TV, 1977–78; Artistic Dir, Brooklyn Acad. of Music Theatre Co., 1979–81; Adjunct Prof. of Drama, Yale Univ., 1981. Productions for RSC incl. plays by Arden, Brecht, Gorky, Granville Barker, Günter Grass, Graham Greene, Mercer, O'Casey, Shakespeare, and Chekhov; dir. prodns for Chichester and Stratford, Ontario, Festival Theatres; other productions include: Old Times, Theatre Royal, Haymarket, and Los Angeles (LA Dramalogue Award for direction), 1985; No Man's Land, NY, 1994; The Hothouse, Chichester Fest., 1995. Dir, films for BBC TV, including: biography of poet, John Clare, 1969; adaptations of Hardy and Chekhov short stories, 1972 and 1973; Pinter's screenplay, Langrishe, Go Down, 1978; Merry Wives of Windsor, Pericles, 1982–83; The Devil's Disciple, 1987; Look Back in Anger, 1989 (ACE Award); directed for American TV: The Christmas Wife, 1988; Sensibility and Sense, 1990; The End of a Sentence, 1991; Fire in the Dark, 1991; And Then There Was One, 1994; Is There Life Out There?, 1994; Sophie and the Moonhanger, 1995. Feature films directed: Pinter's Betrayal, 1982; 84 Charing Cross Road (royal film performance), 1987 (Christopher and Scriptor Awards, 1988); Jacknife, 1989; Kafka's The Trial, 1993. Obie Awards, NY, for direction of RSC Summerfolk, 1975, for innovative programming at BAM Theatre Co., 1980. *Recreations:* restaurants, reading modern poetry, exploring mountains and islands. *Address:* 250 West 27th Street (# 6B), New York, NY 10001–5908, USA.

JONES, Rt. Rev. David Huw; Assistant Bishop, Diocese of St Asaph, since 1993; *b* 1 July 1934; *s* of Joseph Elfed and Ethel Jones; *m* 1959, Gwyneth Jones; two *d*. *Educ:* Pontardawe Grammar Sch.; University Coll. of North Wales, Bangor (BA); University Coll., Oxford (MA). Curate: Aberdare, 1959–61; Neath, 1961–65; Vicar: Crynant, 1965–69; Michaelstone-super-Avon, 1969–73; Sub-Warden, St Michael's Coll., Llandaff, 1973–78; Lectr in Sch. of Theology, Univ. of Wales, Cardiff, 1973–78 (Asst Dean, 1977–78); Vicar of Prestatyn, 1978–82; Dean of Brecon, Vicar of Brecon, Battle and Llanddew, 1982–93. *Publications:* (ed jtly and contrib.) This Land and People, 1979; Guide to Brecon Cathedral, 1988. *Recreations:* walking, bird watching, church crawling, supporting Neath RFC. *Address:* 24 Drws-y-Coed, Coed-y-glyn, Wrexham LL13 9QB. *T:* Wrexham (01978) 357522.

JONES, Rev. David Ian Stewart; Director of the Lambeth Charities, since 1985; *b* 3 April 1934; *s* of Rev. John Milton Granville Jones and Evelyn Moyes Stewart Jones (formerly Chedburn); *m* 1967, Susan Rosemary Hardy Smith; twin *s* and *d*. *Educ:* St John's Sch., Leatherhead; Selwyn Coll., Cambridge (MA). Commnd Royal Signals, 1952–54. Curate at Oldham Parish Church, 1959–62; Vicar of All Saints, Elton, Bury, 1963–66; Asst Conduct and Chaplain of Eton Coll., 1966–70; Conduct and Sen. Chaplain of Eton Coll., 1970–74; Headmaster of Bryanston School, 1974–82; Rector-designate of Bristol City, 1982–85. Spiritual Develt Advr, NABC, 1990–. *Recreations:* reading, music. *Address:* 127 Kennington Road, SE11 6SF. *T:* 0171–735 1925. *Club:* East India, Devonshire, Sports and Public Schools.

JONES, David le Brun, CB 1975; energy consultant; *b* 18 Nov. 1923; *s* of Thomas John Jones and Blanche le Brun. *Educ:* City of London Sch.; Trinity Coll., Oxford. Asst Principal, Min. of Power, 1947; Principal, MOP, 1952; Asst Sec., Office of the Minister for Science, 1962; Asst Sec., MOP, 1963; Under-Sec., MOP, later Min. of Technology and DTI, 1968–73; Dep. Sec., DTI, later DoI, 1973–76; Cabinet Office, 1976–77; Dept of Energy, 1978–82; Dir, Long Term Office, Internat. Energy Agency, 1982–88. Trustee, Nat. Energy Foundn, 1989–. *Recreations:* walking, reading, chess. *Address:* 47 Grove End Road, NW8 9NB. *Club:* United Oxford & Cambridge University.

JONES, David Lewis; Librarian, House of Lords, since 1991; *b* 4 Jan. 1945; *s* of late Gwilym Morgan Jones and of Joyce Jones (*née* Davies). *Educ:* Aberaeron County Sch.; Jesus Coll., Oxford (MA); Coll. of Librarianship, Wales. Asst Librarian, Inst. of Histl Res., 1970–72; University of Wales, Aberystwyth: Asst Librarian, 1972–75; Law Librarian, 1975–77; Dep. Librarian, H of L, 1977–91. Hon. Sec., Honourable Soc. of Cymmrodorion, 1994–. Freeman: City of London, 1993; Stationers' and Newspapermakers' Co., 1993. *Publications:* Books in English on the Soviet Union 1917–73, 1975; Paraguay: a bibliography, 1979; Debates and proceedings of the British Parliaments: a guide to printed sources, 1986; (ed jtly) Peers, politics and power: the House of Lords 1603–1911, 1986; A parliamentary history of the Glorious Revolution, 1988. *Address:* 10 Heathfield Court, Heathfield Terrace, W4 4LP. *T:* 0181–995 6029.

JONES, David M.; *see* Mansel-Jones.

JONES, David Martin, FIBiol; Director, North Carolina Zoological Park, since 1994; *b* 14 Aug. 1944; *s* of John Trevor Jones and Mair Carno Jones; *m* 1969, Janet Marian Woosley; three *s*. *Educ:* St Paul's Cathedral Choir Sch.; St John's Sch., Leatherhead; Royal Veterinary Coll., London (BSc, BVetMed). MRCVS. Veterinary Officer, Whipsnade, 1969; Sen. Veterinary Officer, 1975, Asst Dir of Zoos, 1981, Dir of Zoos, 1984, Gen. Dir, 1991, Dir, Conservation and Consultancy Div., 1992, Zoological Soc. of London. Trustee, WWF UK, 1986–92, 1993– (Chm., Conservation Review Gp, subseq. Conservation Cttee, 1990–). Chm., Brooke Hosp. for Animals, 1990– (Vice-Chm., 1973–90). *Publications:* over 100 papers on wildlife medicine, management and conservation, in veterinary, medical and zoological jls. *Recreations:* field conservation, travel, antiquarian books, driving, gardening. *Address:* North Carolina Zoological Park, 4401 Zoo Parkway, Asheboro, NC 27203, USA.

JONES, Prof. David Morgan, MA; Professor of Classics in the University of London (Westfield College), 1953–80; *b* 9 April 1915; *m* 1965, Irene M. Glanville. *Educ:* Whitgift Sch.; Exeter Coll., Oxford (Scholar). 1st Class, Classical Hon. Mods, 1936; 1st Class, Lit Hum, 1938; Derby Scholar, 1938; Junior Research Fellow, Exeter Coll., Oxford,

1938–40; Oxford Diploma in Comparative Philology, 1940; Lecturer in Classics, University Coll. of North Wales, 1940–48; Reader in Classics in the University of London (Birkbeck Coll.), 1949–53. *Publications:* papers and reviews in classical and linguistic journals. *Address:* Kemyell Vean, 3 Laregan Hill, Penzance TR18 4NY. *T:* Penzance (01736) 63389.

JONES, Dr (David) Timothy; Deputy Chairman, Lloyd's Register, since 1993; *b* 21 Aug. 1944; *s* of David Percy Jones and Elvair (*née* Evans); *m* 1968, Jean Margaret Whitehead; four *d. Educ:* Leeds Univ. (PhD Physical Chem.); INSEAD, Fontainebleau (MBA with Dist.). MRSC 1967. Gen. Manager, Deutsche BP, 1985–88; Dir, BP France, 1988–89; Chief Exec., BP Oil Supply and Trading, 1990; Dir, BP Oil Europe, 1990–93. *Recreations:* watching Rugby, walking, playing squash, golf. *Address:* (office) 71 Fenchurch Street, EC3M 4BS. *T:* 0171–423 2201.

JONES, Della; mezzo-soprano; *d* of Eileen Gething Jones and late Cyril Vincent Jones; *m* 1988, Paul Vigars; one *s. Educ:* Neath Girls' Grammar School; Royal College of Music. GRSM; LRAM (singing), ARCM (piano); Kathleen Ferrier Scholarship. Mem., ENO, 1977–82, leading roles; 1982–: guest artist, ENO; sings with major British opera companies; overseas concert and operatic appearances in all major European countries, also Russia, Japan and USA; radio and TV; prolific recordings with all major recording cos. *Recreations:* writing cadenzas, art galleries, animal welfare, soap operas. *Address:* c/o Music International, 13 Ardilaun Road, Highbury, N5 2QR. *T:* 0171–359 5183.

JONES, Sir Derek A.; *see* Alun-Jones.

JONES, Derek John Claremont, CMG 1979; Senior Fellow, Trade Policy Research Centre, 1986–90; retired; *b* 2 July 1927; *er s* of Albert Claremont Jones and Ethel Lilian Jones (*née* Hazell); *m* 1st, 1951, Jean Cynthia Withams; one *s* two *d*; 2nd, 1970, Kay Cecile Thewlis; one *s. Educ:* Colston Sch., Bristol; Bristol Univ.; London Sch. of Economics and Political Science. Economic Asst, Economic Section, Cabinet Office, 1950–53; Second Sec., UK Delegn to OEEC/NATO, Paris, 1953–55; Asst Principal, Colonial Office, 1955–57; Principal, Colonial Office, 1957–66; First Secretary, Commonwealth Office, 1966–67; Counsellor (Hong Kong Affairs), UK Mission, Geneva, 1967–71; Government of Hong Kong: Dep. Economic Sec., 1971–73; Sec. for Economic Services, 1973–76; Sec. for the Environment, 1976–81; Sec. for Transport, 1981–82; Minister for Hong Kong Relns with EC and Member States, 1982–86. *Recreations:* reading, travel, conversation. *Address:* Cliff House, Trevaunance Cove, St Agnes, Cornwall TR5 0RZ. *T:* St Agnes (0187255) 2334. *Clubs:* Hong Kong, Royal Hong Kong Jockey.

JONES, Derek R.; *see* Rudd-Jones.

JONES, Derek William; Director, Industry and Training Department, Welsh Office, since 1994; *b* 8 Dec. 1952; *s* of William Jones and Patricia Mary Jones (*née* Gill); *m* 1976, Fiona Christine Anne Laidlaw; two *s. Educ:* UC Cardiff, Univ. of Wales (BA Hons). Worked on regional policy, company law and privatisation, DTI, 1977–82; HM Treasury: Public Expenditure Control, 1982–84; Head, Financial Instns and Markets Br., 1984–87; Head, Japan Desk and Overseas Trade Policy Div., DTI, 1987–89; Welsh Office: Asst Sec., 1989; Head, Industrial Policy Div., 1989–92; Head, Finance Progs Div., 1992–94; Under Sec., 1994. *Recreations:* family life, reading, blues guitar. *Address:* c/o Welsh Office, Cathays Park, Cardiff CF1 3NQ. *T:* Cardiff (01222) 823325.

JONES, Rt. Rev. Derwyn Dixon, DD; Bishop of Huron, 1984–90; *b* 5 Aug. 1925; *s* of Rev. Walter Jones, DD, and Mary Rosalie Jones (*née* Dixon); *m* 1960, Arline Carole Dilamarter; one *s* one *d. Educ:* Univ. of Western Ontario (BA); Huron College (LTh, DD). Deacon 1946, priest 1947; Curate: Holy Trinity, Winnipeg, 1946–48; All Saints', Windsor, 1948–49; Rector, St Andrew's, Kitchener, 1949–52; Asst Rector, St Paul's Cathedral, London, Ont, 1952–55; Rector: Canon Davis Memorial Church, Sarnia, 1955–58; St Barnabas, Windsor, 1958–66; St Peter's, Brockville, 1966–69; St James, Westminster, London, Ont, 1969–82; Archdeacon of Middlesex, 1978–82; Suffragan Bishop of Huron, 1982; Coadjutor Bishop, 1983. *Recreation:* music. *Address:* 301–7 Picton Street, London, Ontario N6B 3N7, Canada. *T:* (519) 6422161. *Club:* London (London, Ont).

JONES, Rev. Prof. Douglas Rawlinson; Lightfoot Professor of Divinity, University of Durham, 1964–85, now Emeritus; Residentiary Canon of Durham Cathedral, 1964–85, now Emeritus; *b* 11 Nov. 1919; *s* of Percival and Charlotte Elizabeth Jones; *m* 1946, Hazel Mary Passmore; three *s* two *d. Educ:* Queen Elizabeth's Hosp., Bristol; St Edmund Hall, Oxford; Wycliffe Hall, Oxford. Squire Scholar, 1938; BA 1941; MA 1945; deacon, 1942; priest, 1943. Curate of St Michael and All Angels, Windmill Hill, Bristol, 1942–45; Lectr, Wycliffe Hall, Oxford, 1945–50; Chaplain, Wadham Coll., Oxford, 1945–50; Lectr in Divinity, 1948–50; University of Durham: Lectr, 1951; Sen. Lectr, 1963. Mem., Gen. Synod of C of E, 1970–80 and 1982–85. Chairman of the Liturgical Commn, 1981–86. DD Lambeth, 1985. *Publications:* Haggai, Zechariah and Malachi, 1962; Isaiah, 56–66 and Joel, 1964; Instrument of Peace, 1965; Jeremiah, 1992; contrib. to: Peake's Commentary on the Bible, 1962; Hastings' Dictionary of the Bible, 1963; The Cambridge History of the Bible, 1963; Thomas Cranmer, 1990; Sacrifice and Redemption, 1991; articles in Jl of Theolog. Studies, Zeitschrift für die Alttestamentliche Wissenschaft, Vetus Testamentum, Theology, Scottish Jl of Theology. *Recreation:* carpentry. *Address:* Whitefriars, Kings Road, Longniddry, E Lothian EH32 0NN. *T:* Longniddry (01875) 52149.

JONES, Prof. Douglas Samuel, MBE 1945; FRS 1968; Ivory Professor of Mathematics, University of Dundee, 1965–92, now Emeritus Professor; *b* 10 Jan. 1922; *s* of late J. D. Jones and B. Jones (*née* Streather); *m* 1950, Ivy Styles; one *s* one *d. Educ:* Wolverhampton Grammar Sch.; Corpus Christi Coll., Oxford (MA 1947; Hon. Fellow, 1980); DSc Manchester 1957. FIMA 1964, CMath 1992; FRSE 1967; CEng, FIEE 1989. Flt-Lt, RAFVR, 1941–45. Commonwealth Fund Fellow, MIT, 1947–48; Asst Lectr in Maths, University of Manchester, 1948–51; Lectr 1951–54, Research Prof. 1955, New York Univ.; Sen. Lectr in Maths, Univ. of Manchester, 1955–57; Prof. of Maths, Univ. of Keele, 1957–64. Vis. Prof., Courant Inst., 1962–63. Member: UGC, 1976–86 (Mem., 1971–86, Chm., 1976–86, Mathematical Scis Sub-Cttee); Computer Bd, 1977–82; Open Univ. Vis. Cttee, 1982–87. Member Council: Royal Soc., 1973–74; IMA, 1982–85, 1986– (Pres., 1988–89). Hon. DSc Strathclyde, 1975. Keith Prize, RSE, 1974; van der Pol Gold Medal, Internat. Union of Radio Sci., 1981; Naylor Prize, London Mathematical Soc., 1987. Trustee, Quarterly Jl of Mechanics and Applied Maths, 1980–92; Associate Editor: Jl IMA, 1964–; RSE, 1969–82; SIAM Jl on Applied Maths, 1975–92; Applicable Analysis, 1976–92; Mathematical Methods, 1977–; Royal Soc., 1978–83; Methods and Applications of Analysis, 1992–; Jl of Engrg Maths, 1992–. *Publications:* Electrical and Mechanical Oscillations, 1961; Theory of Electromagnetism, 1964; Generalised Functions, 1966; Introductory Analysis, vol. 1, 1969, vol 2, 1970; Methods in Electromagnetic Wave Propagation, 1979, 2nd edn 1994; Elementary Information Theory, 1979; The Theory of Generalised Functions, 1982; Differential Equations and Mathematical Biology, 1983; Acoustic and Electromagnetic Waves, 1986; Assembly Programming and the 8086 Microprocessor, 1988; 80x86 Assembly Programming, 1991; articles in mathematical and physical jls. *Recreations:* golf, walking, photography. *Address:* Department of Mathematics and Computer Science, The University, Dundee DD1 4HN. *T:* Dundee (01382) 23181; 1 The Nurseries, St Madoes, Glencarse, Perth PH2 7NX. *Club:* United Oxford & Cambridge University.

JONES, His Honour Judge Edward; *see* Jones, J. E.

JONES, Sir Edward; *see* Jones, Sir C. E. W.

JONES, Edward David Brynmor, RIBA; architect in private practice, since 1973; Principal, Jeremy Dixon. Edward Jones, since 1989; *b* 20 Oct. 1939; *s* of David Jones and Margot Derricourt; *m* 1st; one *s* two *d*; 2nd, Margot Griffin; one *s* two *d. Educ:* Haileybury and ISC; AA Sch. of Architecture (AADip Hons 1963); RIBA 1968; RAIC and Ont. Assoc. of Architects, Canada. Tutor, AA, PCL and UC Dublin, 1968–72; Sen. Tutor, Sch. of Environmental Design, RCA, 1973–83; Vis. Prof., 1973–82, Adjunct Prof., 1983–89, Univ. of Toronto; Visiting Professor: Cornell, Harvard, Princeton, Pennsylvania, Rice, Syracuse and Yale Univs, 1973–93; Portsmouth Univ., 1994–; External Examiner: AA 1985; RIBA, 1990–93; AA Council, 1993–; Portsmouth Univ.; Kingston Univ.; Heriot-Watt Univ. Hon. Librarian, AA, 1994–. Competitions, first prize: Northampton County Offices, 1973; Mississauga City Hall, Canada, 1982; Bus Stn, Venice, 1990; other projects include: Royal Opera House, Covent Garden, 1983–; buildings for: Henry Moore Foundn at Leeds, 1989–93 and Perry Green, 1989–; Darwin Coll., Cambridge, 1989, 1994; Robert Gordon Univ., Aberdeen, 1991; superstores for J. Sainsbury at Plymouth and Bath; Portsmouth Univ.; housing in New Delhi, 1994; Nat. Portrait Gall., 1994; rep. Britain at Biennale: Venice, 1980; Paris, 1981; Santiago, 1982. FRSA. Governor-General's Award for Architecture (Canada), 1988. *Publications:* A Guide to the Architecture of London (with C. Woodward), 1983, 2nd edn 1992; contribs to arch. jls. *Address:* 41 Gloucester Crescent, NW1 7DL. *T:* 0171–267 7015. *Club:* Royal Automobile.

JONES, Air Marshal Sir Edward G.; *see* Gordon Jones.

JONES, Sir Edward Martin F.; *see* Furnival Jones.

JONES, Edward W.; *see* Wilson Jones.

JONES, Eleri Wynne; Member, Independent Television Commission, with special responsibility for Wales, since 1990; trainer and practitioner in psychotherapy and counselling; *b* 9 Aug. 1933; *d* of Ellis Edgar and Elen Mary Griffith; *m* 1960, Bedwyr Lewis Jones (*d* 1992); two *s* one *d. Educ:* Howell's Sch., Denbigh (Foundn Schol.); University Coll. of Wales, Aberystwyth; University Coll., Cardiff. BA (Wales); DipIPM. Journalist, Canada, 1956–57; Careers Officer, Gwynedd, 1957–64; Tutor, Marr. Guidance Council, 1978–87; Lectr, Gwynedd Technical Coll., 1980–84; Member: Welsh Fourth Channel Authy, 1984–91; Bd of Channel Four, 1987–90. Dir, Cais Ltd, 1993–. Mem., Staff Commn for Local Govt Reorgn (Wales), 1994–. Mem., Council, Univ. of Wales, Aberystwyth, 1995–. *Recreations:* walking, travel, television, films. *Address:* Bodafon, Siliwen, Bangor, Gwynedd LL57 2BH. *T:* Bangor (N Wales) (01248) 370621.

JONES, Emlyn Bartley, MBE 1975; Director General, The Sports Council, 1978–83; sport and leisure consultant, since 1983; *b* 9 Dec. 1920; *s* of Ernest Jones and Sarah Bartley; *m* 1944, Constance Inez Jones; one *d. Educ:* Alun Grammar School, Mold, Clwyd; Bangor Normal Coll.; Loughborough Coll. of Physical Education. Diploma Loughborough Coll. (Hons). Flight Lieut, RAF, 1941–46; Teacher, Flint Secondary Modern Sch., 1946; Technical Representative, N Wales, 1947–51; Technical Adviser, Central Council of Physical Recreation, 1951–62; Dir, Crystal Palace Nat. Sports Centre, 1962–78. Television commentator, 1955–. Pres., British Inst. of Sports Admin (formerly British Assoc. of Nat. Sports Administrators), 1984–; Vice-Pres., NABC, 1989–. FIMgt (FBIM 1984). *Publications:* Learning Lawn Tennis, 1958; Sport in Space: the implications of cable and satellite television, 1984. *Recreations:* golf, ski-ing, travel, conversation, reading. *Address:* Chwarae Teg, 1B Allison Grove, Dulwich Common, SE21 7ER. *T:* 0181–693 7528. *Club:* Royal Air Force.

JONES, Sir Emrys; *see* Jones, Sir W. E.

JONES, Prof. Emrys, MSc, PhD (Wales); FRGS; Professor of Geography, University of London, at London School of Economics, 1961–84, now Emeritus; *b* Aberdare, 17 Aug. 1920; *s* of Samuel Garfield and Anne Jones; *m* 1948, Iona Vivien, *d* of R. H. Hughes; one *d* (and one *d* decd). *Educ:* Grammar Sch. for Boys, Aberdare; University Coll. of Wales, Aberystwyth. BSc (1st Class Hons in Geography and Anthropology), 1941; MSc, 1945; PhD, 1947; Fellow of the University of Wales, 1946–47; Asst Lectr at University Coll., London, 1947–50; Fellow, Rockefeller Foundation, 1948–49; Lectr at Queen's Univ., Belfast, 1950–58, Sen. Lectr, 1958; Reader, LSE, 1959–61. O'Donnel Lectr, Univ. of Wales, 1977. Chairman: Regional Studies Assoc., 1967–69; Council, Hon. Soc. of Cymmrodorion, 1984–89 (Mem., 1977–; Pres., 1989–); Mem. Council, RGS, 1973–77 (Vice-Pres., 1978–81). Mem. Council, University Coll. of Wales, Aberystwyth, 1978–85. Consultant on urbanisation and planning. Hon. Fellow, UCW, 1991. Hon. DSc Belfast, 1978; DUniv Open, 1990. Victoria Medal, RGS, 1977. *Publications:* Hon. Editor, Belfast in its Regional Setting, 1952; (jointly) Welsh Rural Communities, 1960; A Social Geography of Belfast, 1961; Human Geography, 1964; Towns and Cities, 1966; Atlas of London, 1968; (ed jtly) Man and his Habitat, 1971; (contrib.) The Future of Planning, 1973; (with E. van Zandt) The City, 1974; Readings in Social Geography, 1975; (with J. Eyles) Introduction to Social Geography, 1977; (Chief Editor) The World and its Peoples, 1979; Metropolis: the world's great cities, 1990; articles in geographical, sociological and planning jls. *Recreations:* books, music. *Address:* 2 Pine Close, North Road, Berkhamsted, Herts HP4 3BZ. *T:* Berkhamsted (01442) 875422. *Club:* Athenæum.

JONES, Prof. Emrys Lloyd, FBA 1982; Goldsmiths' Professor of English Literature, Oxford University, and Fellow, New College, Oxford, since 1984; *b* 30 March 1931; *s* of Peter Jones and Elizabeth Jane (*née* Evans); *m* 1965, Barbara Maud Everett; one *d. Educ:* Neath Grammar Sch.; Magdalen Coll., Oxford (BA, MA). Tutor in English, Magdalen Coll., 1955–77; Reader in Eng. Lit., Oxford Univ., 1977–84; Fellow, Magdalen Coll., Oxford, 1955–84. Dr *hc* Lund. *Publications:* (ed) Poems of Henry Howard, Earl of Surrey, 1964; Pope and Dulness, 1972; Scenic Form in Shakespeare, 1971; The Origins of Shakespeare, 1977; (ed) Antony and Cleopatra, 1977; (ed) The New Oxford Book of Sixteenth Century Verse, 1991; contribs to jls and books. *Recreations:* looking at buildings; opera. *Address:* New College, Oxford OX1 3BN. *T:* Oxford (01865) 279555.

JONES, Eric S.; *see* Somerset Jones.

JONES, Ernest Edward; Member, Doncaster Metropolitan Borough Council, since 1980; *b* 15 Oct. 1931; *s* of William Edward Jones and Eileen Gasser; *m* 1955, Mary Armstrong; one *s* one *d. Educ:* Bentley Catholic Primary Sch., Doncaster; Sheffield De La Salle Coll.; Hopwood Hall Coll. of Educn, Middleton, Lancs; Manch. Univ. Sch. of Educn; Management Studies Unit, Sheffield Polytech. Min. of Educn Teaching Certif. (CertEd); Univ. Dipl. in Science Studies (DipSc); Dipl. in Educn Management (DEM). School Master, 1953–92. Doncaster County Borough: Councillor, 1962–74 (Chm. Health Cttee, 1971–74; Chm. Social Services Cttee, 1972–73; served on 15 other cttees at various times). South Yorkshire CC: Mem. 1973–77; Dep. Chm., 1973–75; Chm., 1975–76;

Chm., Rec., Culture and Health Cttee, 1973–75; Doncaster Metropolitan Borough Council: Chairman: Libraries, Museums and Arts Cttee, 1982–91; Further Educn Cttee, 1983–85; Trent Regional Assoc. of Community Health Councils, 1988–90; Doncaster CHC, 1981–90; Mem., Educn Services Cttee (Vice-Chm., 1982–). Chairman: Co. and Council of Management, Northern Coll., 1986–88, 1991– (Vice-Chm., 1982–86, 1990–91); Doncaster College (formerly Inst. of Further and Higher Educn), 1985–93; Mem., Doncaster Coll. Corp., 1993–. Member: Nat. Health Exec. Council, 1964–74; Doncaster and Dist Water Bd, 1972–74; AMC (Social Services), 1972–74; Peak Park Planning Bd, 1973–77; Yorks and Humberside Museum and Art Gall. Service, 1973–77, 1984–; Yorks and Humberside Jt Libraries Cttee, 1973–75, 1983–; Yorks and Humberside Assoc. of Further and High Educn, 1982–; Yorks and Humberside Assoc. of Educn Authorities, 1982– (Chm., 1988–89); Council, Museums Assoc., 1986; S Yorks Jt Archaeol Cttee, 1987–91 (Chm., 1987–88); S Yorks Jt Archives Cttee, 1987–91 (Chm., 1987–88); NEAB, 1992–; Exec. Mem., Nat. Field Studies Council, 1988–. Exec. Mem., Yorks Arts Assoc., 1983–85; Former Member: Yorks Regional Land Drainage Cttee; Univ. of Hull Educn Delegacy; AMA; Yorks and Humberside Museums and Art Galleries Fedn; Yorks and Humberside Regional Sports Council; Yorks, Humberside and Cleveland Tourist Bd; Exec. Mem., Youth Assoc. of South Yorks. Member: Hull Univ. Ct, 1983–85; Sheffield Univ. Ct and Council, 1983–; Bradford Univ. Ct and Council, 1986–93; Governor: Sheffield Poly., 1982–90; Sheffield Hallam Univ., 1995–. FRSH; FRSA 1980. *Recreations:* music and fine arts, general interest in sport, fell-walking, keen caravanner. *Address:* 11 Norborough Road, Doncaster, South Yorks DN2 4AR. *T:* Doncaster (01302) 66122.

JONES, Eurfron Gwynne; Director of Education, BBC, 1992–94; *b* 24 Sept. 1934; *d* of William Gwynne Jones and Annie (*née* Harries); *m* 1968, Michael Coyle; one *s*. *Educ:* Aberdare Girls' Grammar Sch.; University Coll., Cardiff, Univ. of Wales (BSc (Zoology); PhD). Teaching Asst, Mount Holyoke Coll., Mass, 1955–56; joined BBC as gen. trainee, 1959; Producer, BBC Sch. Radio, Sch. Television and Continuing Educn, TV, 1959–75; freelance broadcaster, writer and cons., Media Cons. Internat. Children's Centre, Educn Commn of the States, 1975–83; Asst Hd, Sch. Radio, 1983–84; Hd of Sch. Television, 1984–87; Controller, Educnl Broadcasting, BBC, 1987–92. Member: Wyatt Commn on Violence, 1986; OU Council, 1987–94; Open Coll. Council, 1987–89; Council, Royal Instn, 1989–92, and 1994–; COPUS, 1992–. Vis. Prof., Inst. of Educn, Univ. of London, 1994. FRTS 1994 (Mem., 1984–94). Hon. LLD Exeter, 1990. *Publications:* Children Growing Up, 1973; The First Five Years, 1975; How Did I Grow?, 1977; Television Magic, 1978; Lifetime I, Lifetime II, 1982; numerous articles on children and educn. *Recreations:* photography, swimming, active family life.

JONES, Ewan Perrins W.; *see* Wallis-Jones.

JONES, Sir Ewart (Ray Herbert), Kt 1963; DSc Victoria, PhD Wales, MA Oxon; FRS 1950, FRSC; Waynflete Professor of Chemistry, University of Oxford, 1955–78, now Emeritus; Fellow of Magdalen College, 1955–78, Hon. Fellow, 1978; *b* Wrexham, Denbighshire, 16 March 1911; *m* 1937, Frances Mary Copp; one *s* two *d*. *Educ:* Grove Park Sch., Wrexham; University Coll. of North Wales, Bangor; Univ. of Manchester. Fellow of Univ. of Wales, 1935–37; Lecturer, Imperial Coll. of Science and Technology, 1938; Reader in Organic Chemistry, Univ. of London, and Asst Prof., 1945; Sir Samuel Hall Prof. of Chemistry, The University, Manchester, 1947–55. Arthur D. Little Visiting Prof. of Chemistry, MIT, 1952; Karl Folkers Lectr at Univs of Illinois and Wisconsin, 1957; Andrews Lectr, Univ. of NSW, 1960. Mem. Council for Scientific and Industrial Research, and Chm., Research Grants Cttee, 1961–65; Mem. SRC and Chm., Univ. Science and Technology Bd, 1965–69; Mem., Science Bd, 1969–72. Chemical Society: Tilden Lectr, 1949, Pedler Lectr, 1959; Robert Robinson Lectr, 1978; Dalton Lectr, 1985, Award for Service to the Society, 1973; Award in Natural Product Chem., 1974; Meldola Medal, Royal Institute of Chemistry, 1940; Davy Medal, Royal Society, 1966. Fritzsche Award, American Chemical Soc., 1962. President: Chemical Soc., 1964–66; RIC, 1970–72 (Chm., Chem. Soc./RIC Unification Cttee, 1975–80); Royal Soc. of Chemistry, 1980–82. Fellow, Imperial Coll., 1967; Foreign Mem. Amer. Acad. of Arts and Sciences, 1967. Chm., Anchor and Guardian Housing Assocs, 1979–84. Hon. DSc: Birmingham, 1965; Nottingham, 1966; New South Wales, 1967; Sussex, 1969; Salford, 1971; Wales, 1971; East Anglia, 1978; Ulster, 1978; Hon. LLD Manchester, 1972. *Publications:* scientific papers in Jl of the Chem. Soc. *Address:* 6 Sandy Lane, Yarnton, Kidlington, Oxon OX5 1PB. *T:* Oxford (01865) 372581.

JONES, Fielding; *see* Jones, N. F.

JONES, Francis John; Chairman, Telford Development Corporation, 1987–91; Chairman, Shropshire Health Authority, 1979–90; *b* 28 June 1928; *s* of John Francis and Mary Emma Jones; *m* 1st, 1953, Angela Mary Kelly (marr. diss.); one *s* one *d*; 2nd, 1970, Jean Elsie Sansome; two step *s* two step *d*. *Educ:* Manchester Grammar Sch.; Manchester Univ. Various marketing and sales positions; West African Colonies, 1950–52; Proctor & Gamble, 1952–54; Beecham Group, 1954–57; Crosse & Blackwell/Nestlé, 1957–64; W. Symington, 1964–69; Chm., Telford Foods, 1970–84, retired. *Recreations:* reading, music, opera. *Address:* 2 Swan Hill Gardens, Shrewsbury SY1 1NT. *T:* Shrewsbury (01743) 362159.

JONES, Prof. F(rank) Llewellyn-, CBE 1965; MA, DPhil, DSc Oxon; Hon. LLD; Principal, University College of Swansea, 1965–74 (Vice-Principal, 1954–56 and 1960–62; Acting Principal, 1959–60); Professor Emeritus, since 1974; *b* 30 Sept. 1907; *er s* of Alfred Morgan Jones, JP, Penrhiwceiber, Glamorgan; *m* 1st, 1938, Eileen (*d* 1982), *d* of E. T. Davies, Swansea; one *s* (one *d* decd); 2nd, 1983, Mrs Gwendolen Thomas, Rhossili. *Educ:* West Monmouth Sch.; Merton Coll., Oxford. Science Exhibnr 1925; 1st Cl. Nat. Sci. physics, BA 1929; Research Scholar, Merton Coll., 1929, DPhil, MA, 1931; Senior Demy, Magdalen Coll., 1931. DSc 1955. Demonstrator in Wykeham Dept of Physics, Oxford, 1929–32; Lecturer in Physics, University Coll. of Swansea, 1932–40; Senior Scientific Officer, Royal Aircraft Establishment, 1940–45; Prof. of Physics, Univ. of Wales, and Head of Dept of Physics, University Coll. of Swansea, 1945–65. Vice-Chancellor, Univ. of Wales, 1969–71. Member: Radio Research Board, DSIR, 1951–54; Standing Conference on Telecommunications Research, DSIR, 1952–55; Board of Institute of Physics, 1947–50; Council of Physical Society, 1951–58 (Vice-Pres., 1954–59). Visiting Prof. to Univs in Australia, 1956; Supernumerary Fellow, Jesus Coll., Oxford, 1965–66, 1969–70; Hon. Professorial Res. Fellow, Univ. of Wales, 1974–; Leverhulme Emeritus Fellow, 1977–79; Fellow, UC of Swansea, 1990. Regional Scientific Adviser for Home Defence, Wales, 1952–59, Sen. and Chief Reg. Sci. Adv., 1959–77; Pres., Royal Institution of South Wales, 1957–60; Mem. of Council for Wales and Mon, 1959–63, 1963–66; Dir (Part-time), S Wales Gp, BSC, 1968–70; Chm., Central Adv. Council for Education (Wales), 1961–64. Sen. Consultant in Plasma Physics, Radio and Space Research Station of SRC, 1964–65. Vice-Pres., Hon. Soc. of Cymmrodorian, 1982. Hon. LLD Wales, 1975. C. V. Boys' Prizeman, The Physical Soc., 1960; Inaugural Ragnar Holm Scientific Achievement Award, 6th Internat. Conf. on Electric Contact Phenomena, Chicago, 1972. *Publications:* Fundamental Processes of Electrical Contact Phenomena, 1953; The Physics of Electrical Contacts, 1957; Ionization and Breakdown in Gases, 1957, 2nd edn 1966; The Glow Discharge, 1966; Ionization, Avalanches and Breakdown, 1966; papers in scientific jls on ionization and discharge physics. *Recreation:* industrial archaeology. *Address:* Brynheulog, 24 Sketty Park Road, Swansea SA2 9AS. *T:* Swansea (01792) 202344. *Club:* Athenæum.

JONES, Fred, CB 1978; CBE 1966; Deputy Secretary, HM Treasury, 1975–80, retired; *b* 5 May 1920; *s* of late Fred Jones and of Harriet (*née* Nuttall); *m* 1954, Joy (*née* Field); two *s*. *Educ:* Preston Grammar Sch.; St Catherine's Coll., Oxford. Economist, Trades Union Congress, 1951–59; Tutor in Economics and Industrial Relations, Ruskin Coll., Oxford, 1960–62; Economist, National Economic Development Office, 1962–64; Dept of Economic Affairs: Senior Economic Adviser, 1964–66; Asst Sec., 1966–68; Asst Under-Sec. of State, 1968–69; HM Treasury, Asst Under-Sec. of State, 1969–75. *Recreations:* walking, gardening, reading. *Address:* The Glen, Haighton Green Lane, Haighton, Preston, Lancs PR2 5SQ.

JONES, Gareth; *see* Jones, J. G.

JONES, Prof. Gareth (Hywel), QC 1986; FBA 1982; Fellow of Trinity College, Cambridge, since 1961; Downing Professor of the Laws of England, Cambridge University, since 1975; *b* 10 Nov. 1930; *o c* of late B. T. Jones, FRICS, and late Mabel Jones, Tylorstown, Glam; *m* 1959, Vivienne Joy, *o d* of late C. E. Puckridge, FIA, Debden Green, Loughton; two *s* one *d*. *Educ:* Porth County Sch.; University Coll. London (PhD; Fellow 1987); St Catharine's Coll., Cambridge (Scholar); Harvard Univ. (LLM). LLB London 1951; MA, LLB 1953, LLD 1972, Cantab. Choate Fellow, Harvard, 1953; Yorke Prize, 1960. Called to Bar, Lincoln's Inn, 1955 (Scholar); Hon. Bencher 1975. Lecturer: Oriel and Exeter Colls, Oxford, 1956–58; KCL, 1958–61; Trinity College, Cambridge: Lectr, 1961–75; Tutor, 1967; Sen. Tutor, 1972; Vice-Master, 1986–92; Univ. Lectr, Cambridge, 1961–75; Chm., Faculty of Law, 1978–81. Visiting Professor: Harvard, 1966 and 1975; Chicago, 1976–94; California at Berkeley, 1967 and 1971; Indiana, 1971, 1975; Michigan, 1983; Georgia, 1983; Texas, 1993. Lectures: Harris, Indiana, 1981; Wright, Toronto, 1984; Lionel Cohen, Hebrew Univ., 1985; Butterworth, QMC, 1987; Nambyar, India, 1991; Richard O'Sullivan, Thomas More Soc., 1991. Mem., American Law Inst.; For. Mem., Royal Netherlands Acad. of Arts and Scis, 1991. *Publications:* (with Lord Goff of Chieveley) The Law of Restitution, 1966, 4th edn 1993; The History of the Law of Charity 1532–1827, 1969; The Sovereignty of the Law, 1973; (with Sir William Goodhart) Specific Performance, 1986; various articles. *Address:* Trinity College, Cambridge CB2 1TQ. *T:* Cambridge (01223) 338473; 9B Cranmer Road, Cambridge CB3 9BL. *T:* Cambridge (01223) 63932; Clay Street, Thornham Magna, Eye, Suffolk IP23 8HE. *Club:* Beefsteak.

JONES, Geoffrey; *see* Jones, John G.

JONES, Prof. Geoffrey M.; *see* Melvill Jones.

JONES, Geoffrey Rippon R.; *see* Rees-Jones.

JONES, George Briscoe, CBE 1988; Director: Job Ownership Ltd, 1983–95; Partnership in Business Ltd, 1988–95; *b* 1 June 1929; *s* of late Arthur Briscoe Jones and Mary Alexandra Jones (*née* Taylor); *m* 1955, Audrey Patricia Kendrick; two *d*. *Educ:* Wallasey and Caldy Grammar Schools. Army, 1947–49; Unilever, 1949–84 (on secondment to CDA, 1982–84); Dir, BOCM Silcocks, 1974–82; Chm., Unitrition, 1977–82; Director: Co-op. Devlt Agency, 1982–90; Chrisamer Ltd, 1989–93. Mem., Plunkett Foundn, 1985–. Governor: QMW, 1993–; Fort Hill Sch., 1993–. *Recreations:* painting, sculpture, chess, bridge. *Address:* 3 Beverley Close, Basingstoke, Hants RG22 4BT. *T:* Basingstoke (01256) 28239. *Club:* Farmers'.

JONES, George Quentin; Political Editor, Daily Telegraph, since 1988; *b* 28 Feb. 1945; *s* of John Clement Jones, *qv*; *m* 1st, 1972, Diana Chittenden (marr. diss. 1989); one *s* one *d*; 2nd, 1990, Teresa Grace Rolleston. *Educ:* Highfields Sch., Wolverhampton. Trainee journalist, Eastern Daily Press, 1963–67; journalist, S Wales Argus and Western Mail, 1967–69; Reuters, London, 1969; Parly Staff, The Times, 1969–73; Parly and Political Corresp., Scotsman, 1973–82; Political Correspondent: Sunday Telegraph, 1982–85; Sunday Times, 1985–86; Daily Telegraph, 1986–88. Regular broadcaster, BBC News and current affairs programmes, London Radio, RTE. Chm., Parly Lobby Journalists, 1987–88. *Recreations:* walking, travelling, time with family. *Address:* 92 Kyrle Road, SW11 6BA. *T:* 0171–223 6646. *Club:* Athenæum.

JONES, Prof. George William; Professor of Government, University of London, since 1976; *b* 4 Feb. 1938; *er s* of George William and Grace Annie Jones; *m* 1963, Diana Mary Bedwell; one *s* one *d*. *Educ:* Wolverhampton Grammar Sch.; Jesus Coll., Oxford; Nuffield Coll., Oxford. Oxf. BA 1960, MA 1965, DPhil 1965. Univ. of Leeds: Asst Lectr in Govt, 1963; Lectr in Govt, 1965; London Sch. of Economics and Political Science: Lectr in Political Science, 1966; Sen. Lectr in Polit. Sci., 1971; Reader in Polit. Sci., 1974. Sec., 1965–68, Mem. Exec. Cttee, 1969–75, Polit. Studies Assoc. of the UK; Mem., Exec. Council, Hansard Soc., 1968–70; Member, Editorial Committee: Local Government Studies, 1970–; The London Journal, 1973–80; Governance, 1987–92; Korean Jl of Public Policy, 1988–; Studies in Law and Politics, 1989–; Nonprofit Management and Leadership, 1989–; Hong Kong Jl of Public Admin, 1992–. Member: Layfield Cttee of Inquiry into Local Govt Finance, 1974–76; Exams Cttee, and Admin. Staff Qualifications Council, Local Govt Trng Bd, 1977–80; Political Science and Internat. Relns Cttee, SSRC, 1977–81; Jt Working Party on Internal Management of Local Authorities, 1992–93; Chm., Central-Local Govt Relations Panel, SSRC, 1978–81; Special Adviser, Select Cttee on Welsh Affairs, 1985–87. Member: Governing Council, Wolverhampton Polytechnic, 1978–83 (Hon. Fellow, 1986); Council, RIPA, 1984–90; Nat. Consumer Council, 1991– (Chm., Public Services Cttee, 1992–); Vice-Pres., Assoc. of Councillors, 1980–. Chm., LSE Graduate Sch., 1990–93. FRHistS 1980. Hon. Fellow, Inst. of Local Govt Studies, Birmingham Univ., 1979. *Publications:* Borough Politics, 1969; (with B. Donoughue) Herbert Morrison: portrait of a politician, 1973; (ed with A. Norton) Political Leadership in Local Authorities, 1978; (ed) New Approaches to the Study of Central-Local Government Relationships, 1980; (with J. Stewart) The Case for Local Government, 1983, 2nd edn 1985; (ed jtly) Between Centre and Locality, 1985; (ed) West European Prime Ministers, 1991; (with Tony Travers *et al*) The Government of London, 1991; Local Government and the Social Market, 1991; (with Tony Travers *et al*) The Impact of Population Size on Local Authority Costs and Effectiveness, 1993; Local Government: the management agenda, 1993; (with Tony Travers) Attitudes to Local Government in Westminster and Whitehall, 1994; contribs to Political Studies, Public Admin., Political Qly, Parliamentary Affairs, Government and Opposition, Jl of Admin Overseas; Local Govt Chronicle. *Recreations:* cinema, politics. *Address:* Department of Government, London School of Economics, Houghton Street, WC2A 2AE. *T:* 0171–955 7179.

JONES, Geraint Iwan, FRAM; *b* 16 May 1917; *s* of Rev. Evan Jones, Porth, Glam; *m* 1st, 1940, M. A. Kemp; one *d*; 2nd, 1949, Winifred Roberts. *Educ:* Caterham Sch.; Royal Academy of Music (Sterndale Bennett Scholar). National Gallery Concerts, 1940–44; played complete organ works of Bach in 16 recitals in London, 1946. Musical dir of Mermaid Theatre performances of Purcell's Dido and Aeneas with Kirsten Flagstad, 1951–53. Formed Geraint Jones Singers and Orchestra, 1951, with whom many broadcasts, and series of 12 Bach concerts, Royal Festival Hall, 1955; series of all Mozart's piano concertos, Queen Elizabeth Hall, 1969–70. Frequent European engagements, 1947– and regular US and Canadian tours, 1948–. Musical Director: Lake District Festival, 1960–78; Kirckman Concert Soc., 1963–; Artistic Director: Salisbury Festival, 1973–77; Manchester Internat. Festival, 1977–87. Prof., RAM, 1961–88. As consultant, has designed many organs, incl. RNCM, St Andrew's Univ., RAM, Acad. for Performing Arts, Hong Kong, and Tsim Sha Tsni culture centre, Hong Kong. Recordings as organist and conductor; Promenade Concerts; also concerts and recordings as harpsichordist, including sonatas with violinist wife, Winifred Roberts. Grand Prix du Disque, 1959 and 1966. *Publications:* translations: Clicquot's Théorie Pratique de la facture de l'orgue, 1985; Davy's Les Grandes Orgues de L'Abbatiale St Etienne de Caen, 1985. *Recreations:* motoring, photography, antiques, reading. *Address:* The Long House, Arkley Lane, Barnet Road, Arkley, Herts EN5 3JR.

JONES, Geraint Stanley, CBE 1993; Chief Executive, S4C, 1989–94; *b* 26 April 1936; *s* of Olwen and David Stanley Jones; *m* 1961, Rhiannon Williams; two *d*. *Educ:* Pontypridd Grammar Sch.; University Coll. of N Wales (BA Hons; DipEd; Hon. Fellow 1988). BBC-Wales: Studio Manager, 1960–62; Production Asst, Current Affairs (TV), 1962–65; TV Producer: Current Affairs, 1965–69; Features and Documentaries, 1969–73; Asst Head of Programmes, Wales, 1973–74; Head of Programmes, Wales, 1974–81; Controller, BBC Wales, 1981–85; Dir of Public Affairs, BBC, 1986–87; Man. Dir, Regl Broadcasting, BBC, 1987–89. Director: WNO, 1985–94; Welsh Film Council, 1992–; Screen Wales, 1992–. Mem., Arts Council of Wales, 1994–. Chm., EBU Television Commn, 1990–. Chm., Ryan Davies Trust, 1977–; Mem., UK Freedom from Hunger Campaign Cttee, 1978–. Chm., Bd of Govs, Welsh Coll. of Music and Drama, 1990–; Mem., Court and Council, Univ. of Wales, Aberystwyth, 1990–. Chm., Welsh Nat. Lang. Centre, 1994–. FRSA 1989; FRTS 1992. *Recreations:* music, painting, horse riding. *Address:* 12 Lady Mary Road, Roath Park, Cardiff CF2 5NS. *Club:* Cardiff and County (Cardiff).

JONES, Dr Gerald, FRCP; Senior Principal Medical Officer, Department of Health (formerly of Health and Social Security), since 1984; *b* 25 Jan. 1939; *s* of John Jones and Gladys Jones (*née* Roberts); *m* 1st, 1964, Anne Heatley (*née* Morris) (marr. diss. 1987); one *s* two *d*; 2nd, 1990, Jutta Friese. *Educ:* Swansea Grammar School; Merton College, Oxford; London Hosp. Med. Coll. (BA, BM, BCh, PhD, MSc). Appointments in hosp. medicine, 1965–69; research with MRC, 1969–73; pharmaceutical industry, 1974–75; medical staff, DHSS, later DoH, 1975–. *Publications:* papers on cardiopulmonary physiology, respiratory medicine, cellular immunology and drug regulation. *Recreations:* music, gardening, art history, economics, catching dragonflies, wine making. *Address:* Skipton House, 80 London Road, SE1 6LW.

JONES, Gerallt; *see* Jones, R. G.

JONES, Rev. Canon Glyndwr; Secretary General, The Missions to Seamen, since 1990; a Chaplain to the Queen, since 1990; *b* 25 Nov. 1935; *s* of late Bertie Samuel Jones and of Elizabeth Ellen Jones; *m* 1st, 1961, Cynthia Elaine Jenkins (*d* 1964); 2nd, 1966, (Marion) Anita Morris; one *s* one *d*. *Educ:* Dynefor Sch., Swansea; St Michael's Theol Coll., Llandaff, Univ. of Wales (DipTh). Nat. Service, 1954–56: RAPC, attached 19 Field Regt RA; served Korea, Hong Kong; demobbed Sgt AER. Deacon 1962, priest 1963; Curate: Clydach, 1962–64; Llangyfelach with Morriston, 1964–67; Sketty, 1967–70; Rector, Bryngwyn with Newchurch and Llanbedr, Painscastle with Llandewi Fach, 1970–72; The Missions to Seamen: Port Chaplain, Swansea and Port Talbot, 1972–76; Sen. Chaplain, Port of London, 1976–81; Auxiliary Ministries Sec., Central Office, 1981–85; Asst Gen. Sec., 1985–90. Member Council: Merchant Navy Welfare Bd, 1990–; Marine Soc., 1990–; Partnership for World Mission, 1990–; Internat. Christian Maritime Assoc., 1990–. Hon. Chaplain, Royal Alfred Seafarers Soc., 1987–93; Hon. Canon, St Michael's Cathedral, Kobe, Japan, 1988–. Hon. Mem., Co. of Master Mariners, 1990. Freeman, City of London, 1990. Chaplain: Co. of Information Technologists, 1989–; Co. of Innholders, 1990–; Co. of Farriers, 1990–; Co. of Carmen, 1990–. *Recreations:* sport, music, reading, theatre, travel. *Address:* The Missions to Seamen, St Michael Paternoster Royal, College Hill, EC4R 2RL. *T:* 0171–248 5202. *Club:* Little Ship.

JONES, Glynn, CBE 1992; Circuit Administrator, Western Circuit, Lord Chancellor's Department, 1987–93; *b* 5 March 1933; *s* of late Bertie Jones and Alice Maud Jones (*née* Griffiths); *m* 1957, Crystal Laura, *d* of late Edward William Kendall and Ivy Irene Kendall; one *s* one *d*. *Educ:* state schs in Monmouthshire. Local Govt service, 1950–71; Lord Chancellor's Department: Crown Court, Newport, 1971, Winchester, 1973; Courts Administrator: Nottingham Group of Courts, 1976; South Wales Group of Courts, 1980. *Recreations:* Rugby Union football, golf. *Address:* 17 Rockfield Glade, Penhow, Newport, Gwent NP6 3JF. *T:* Penhow (01633) 400835. *Clubs:* Civil Service; St Pierre Golf and Country, Newport Golf.

JONES, Gordon Frederick; architect; *b* 25 Aug. 1929; *s* of Harold Frederick and Rose Isabel Jones; *m* 1954, Patricia Mary (*née* Rowley); one *s* one *d*. *Educ:* Saltley Grammar Sch.; The School of Architecture, Birmingham (DipArch), and subseq. by BBC; Sch. of Planning, UCL (CLD). RIBA 1950. FRSA. Architect: in local government, 1952; War Office, 1959; Asst City Architect, Sheffield, 1966; private practice, London, 1968; Property Services Agency, DoE: Architect, 1970; Head of Student Training Office, 1976; Head of Architectural Services, 1979–85; Res. Dir, 1985–90, Editor, 1990–93, Product Design Review. Dir, Building Centre, 1984–87. Chm. of Standards, BDB/–, BSI, 1984–87. *Recreations:* watching cats, listening to music, re-building houses. *Address:* c/o Saunders & Williams, Belmont House, Station Road, Belmont, Sutton, Surrey SM2 6BS.

JONES, Sir Gordon (Pearce), Kt 1990; Chairman: Yorkshire Water, since 1983; Water Authorities Association, 1986–89; *b* 17 Feb. 1927; *s* of Alun Pearce Jones and Miriam Jones; *m* 1951, Gloria Stuart Melville; two *s* one *d*. *Educ:* Univ. of Wales (BSc (Hons) Chemistry). Royal Navy, 1947. British Iron & Steel Research Assoc., 1951; Esso Petroleum Co., 1961; English Steel Corp., 1964; Managing Director: Rotherham Tinsley Steels, 1970; Firth Vickers, 1974; Chm., Hickson Internat., 1991–94; Dir, T. W. Ward plc, 1979–83. Mem., President's Adv. Cttee, CBI, 1987–89. Mem., Adv. Cttee on Business and the Envmt, 1993–. Mem. Court of Governors, Univ. of Leeds, 1992–. CIMgt 1990; FRSA 1994. Hon. FIWEM 1990. Hon. Fellow, UC, Swansea, 1991. Hon. DSc Bradford, 1992. *Recreations:* gardening, music, opera, travel, railway history. *Address:* Bryngower, Sitwell Grove, Rotherham, S Yorks S60 3AY. *T:* Rotherham (01709) 364588. *Club:* Naval and Military.

JONES, Graham Edward, MA; Headmaster, Repton School, since 1987; *b* 22 Sept. 1944; *s* of late Edward Thomas Jones and of Dora Rachel Jones; *m* 1976, Vanessa Mary Heloise (*née* Smith). *Educ:* Birkenhead Sch.; Fitzwilliam Coll., Cambridge (schol.; 1st cl. Hons Econs Tripos 1966). Asst Master, Hd of Economics and Politics, Housemaster, Charterhouse, 1967–87; secondment to British Petroleum, 1981. Awarder in Economics, Oxford and Cambridge Schs Examination Bd, 1979–91; Reviser in Economics, JMB, 1981–91. FRSA 1988. *Publications:* various articles on economics and teaching economics. *Recreations:* painting, walking, music, cooking, the classics. *Address:* The Hall, Repton, Derby DE65 6FH. *T:* Burton upon Trent (01283) 702375/702187.

JONES, Graham Julian; His Honour Judge Graham Jones; a Circuit Judge, since 1985; an Official Referee, since 1993; Resident and Designated Judge, Cardiff County Court, since 1994; *b* 17 July 1936; *s* of late David John Jones, CBE, and of Edna Lillie Jones; *m* 1961, Dorothy, *o d* of late James Smith and of Doris Irene Tickle, Abergavenny; two *s* one *d*. *Educ:* Porth County Grammar Sch. (state scholarship); St John's Coll., Cambridge. MA, LLM (Cantab). Admitted Solicitor, 1961; Partner, Morgan Bruce and Nicholas, 1961 (represented Parents and Residents Assoc., Aberfan Disaster, 1966). Dep. Circuit Judge, 1975–78; a Recorder, 1978–85. Pres., Pontypridd Rhondda and Dist Law Soc., 1973–75; Member Council: Cardiff Law Soc., 1975–78, 1984–85; Associated Law Socs of Wales, 1974–85 (Pres., 1982–84); Mem., Lord Chancellor's Legal Aid Adv. Cttee, 1980–85. *Recreations:* golf, boats. *Address:* c/o Cardiff County Court, 2 Park Street, Cardiff. *Clubs:* Cardiff and County (Cardiff), Radyr Golf, Royal Porthcawl Golf.

JONES, (Graham) Wyn, QPM 1987; Assistant Commissioner of Police of the Metropolis, 1989–93; *b* Ystradgynlais, Brecon, 12 Oct. 1943; *s* of Thomas James and Mary Elizabeth (*née* Almrott); *m* 1970, Joan Goodbrook. *Educ:* Thornbury Grammar Sch.; Univ. of Exeter (LLB). Joined Glos Police, 1963; Chief Inspector, Glos, 1971; Supt, 1976; Chief Supt, Oxford, 1979; Asst Chief Constable (Ops), Thames Valley Police, 1982; Dep. Asst Comr (CID), New Scotland Yard, 1984; Dep. Asst Comr, 2 Area (East), Metropolitan Police, 1985. Comd Police Ops, Greenham Common, 1983–84, Wapping, 1985–86. Vis. Lectr on policing and public disorder to Police Foundn, USA, and to Germany. *Publications:* articles and contribs to jls on public disorder, forensic investigation, police and media. *Recreations:* ballet, opera, tennis, golf, horse riding.

JONES, Griffith R.; *see* Rhys Jones.

JONES, Griffith Winston Guthrie, QC 1963; a Recorder, 1972–74 (Recorder of Bolton, 1968–71); *b* 24 Sept. 1914; second *s* of Rowland Guthrie Jones, Dolgellau, Merioneth; *m* 1st, 1959, Anna Maria McCarthy (*d* 1969); 2nd, 1978, Janet, *widow* of Commodore Henry Owen L'Estrange, DSC. *Educ:* Bootham Sch., York; University of Wales; St John's Coll., Cambridge. Called to the Bar, Gray's Inn, 1939. Dep. Chm., Cumberland QS, 1963–71. War service in Royal Artillery, 1940–46. *Publication:* The Wynnes of Sligo and Leitrim, 1995. *Recreation:* gardening. *Address:* Culleenamore, Sligo, Ireland.

JONES, Gwilym Haydn; MP (C) Cardiff North, since 1983; Parliamentary Under-Secretary of State, Welsh Office, since 1992; *s* of Evan Haydn Jones and Mary Elizabeth Gwenhwyfar Jones (*née* Moseley); *m* 1974, Linda Margaret (*née* John); one *s* one *d*. Dir, Bowring Wales Ltd, 1980–93. Councillor, Cardiff CC, 1969–72 and 1973–83. PPS to Minister of State, Dept of Transport, 1991–92; Secretary: Welsh Cons. Members Gp, 1984–93; All Party Gp for Fund for Replacement of Animals in Medical Experiments, 1987–92. Founder Chm., Friendship Force in Wales, 1978–81; Vice Pres., Kidney Res. Unit for Wales Foundn, 1986–93. Rowed for Wales in Speaker's Regatta, 1986. Liveryman, Welsh Livery Guild, 1993–. *Recreations:* golf, model railways, watching Wales win at Rugby. *Address:* House of Commons, SW1A 0AA. *T:* 0171–219 3000. *Clubs:* Carlton; County Conservative, Cardiff and County, Rhiwbina Rugby, United Services Mess (Cardiff); Tongwynlais Football; Whitchurch Bowls, Whitchurch Golf.

JONES, Gwyn; *see* Jones, Miah G.

JONES, Prof. Gwyn, CBE 1965; Professor of English Language and Literature, University College, Cardiff, 1965–75, Fellow, 1980; *b* 24 May 1907; *s* of George Henry Jones and Lily Florence (*née* Nethercott); *m* 1st, 1928, Alice (*née* Rees) (*d* 1979); 2nd, 1979, Mair (*née* Sivell), *widow* of Thomas Jones. *Educ:* Tredegar Grammar School; University of Wales. Schoolmaster, 1929–35; Lecturer, University Coll. of S Wales and Monmouthshire, 1935–40; Prof. of Eng. Language and Lit., University Coll. of Wales, Aberystwyth, 1940–64, Fellow 1987. Ida Beam Vis. Prof., Iowa Univ., 1982. Dir of Penmark Press, 1939–. Mem. of various learned societies; Pres. of Viking Soc. for Northern Research, 1950–52 (Hon. Life Mem., 1979); Mem. of Arts Council and Chm. of Welsh Arts Council, 1957–67. Gwyn Jones Annual Lecture established 1978. Hon. DLitt: Wales, 1977; Nottingham, 1978; Southampton, 1983. Fellow, Institut Internat. des Arts et des Lettres, 1960. Christian Gauss Award, 1973; Cymmrodorion Medal, 1991. Hon. Freeman of Islwyn, 1988. Commander's Cross, Order of the Falcon (Iceland), 1987 (Knight, 1963). *Publications: novels:* Richard Savage, 1935; Times Like These, 1936, repr. 1979; Garland of Bays, 1938; The Green Island, 1946; The Flowers Beneath the Scythe, 1952; The Walk Home, 1962; *short stories:* The Buttercup Field, 1945; The Still Waters, 1948; Shepherd's Hey, 1953; Selected Short Stories, 1974; *non-fiction:* A Prospect of Wales, 1948; Welsh Legends and Folk-Tales, 1955; Scandinavian Legends and Folk-Tales, 1956; The Norse Atlantic Saga, 1964, new edn 1986; A History of the Vikings, 1968, rev. and enlarged edn 1984; Kings, Beasts and Heroes, 1972; Being and Belonging (BBC Wales Annual Radio Lecture), 1977; Background to Dylan Thomas and Other Explorations, 1992; *translations:* The Vatnsdalers' Saga, 1942; (with Thomas Jones) The Mabinogion, 1948; Egil's Saga, 1960; Eirik the Red, 1961; *edited:* Welsh Review, 1939–48; Welsh Short Stories, 1956; (with I. Ff. Elis) Twenty-Five Welsh Short Stories, 1971; The Oxford Book of Welsh Verse in English, 1977; Fountains of Praise, 1983; contrib. to numerous learned and literary journals. *Address:* Castle Cottage, Sea View Place, Aberystwyth, Dyfed SY23 1DZ.

JONES, Gwyn Idris M.; *see* Meirion-Jones.

JONES, Gwyn Owain, CBE 1978; MA, DSc Oxon; PhD Sheffield; Director, National Museum of Wales, 1968–77; *b* 29 March 1917; *s* of Dr Abel John Jones, OBE, HMI, and Rhoda May Jones, Cardiff and Porthcawl; *m* 1st, 1944, Sheila Heywood (marr. diss.); two *d*; 2nd, 1973, Elizabeth Blandino. *Educ:* Monmouth Sch.; Port Talbot Secondary Sch.; Jesus Coll., Oxford (Meyricke Schol.). Glass Delegacy Research Fellow of University of Sheffield, later mem. of academic staff, 1939–41; Mem. UK Government's Atomic Energy project, 1942–46; Nuffield Foundation Research Fellow at Clarendon Laboratory, Oxford, 1946–49; Reader in Experimental Physics in University of London, at Queen Mary Coll., 1949–53; Prof. of Physics in Univ. of London, and Head of Dept of Physics at Queen Mary Coll., 1953–68; Fellow of Queen Mary and Westfield (formerly Queen Mary) Coll. Visiting Prof. Univ. of Sussex, 1964. Member: Court and Council, UWIST, 1968–74; Court, University Coll., Swansea, 1981–84; Hon. Professorial Fellow, University Coll., Cardiff, 1969–79. Yr Academi Gymreig (English Language Section) 1971 (Chm., 1978–81); Gorsedd y Beirdd (Aelod er Anrhydedd) 1974; Governor, Commonwealth Institute, 1974–77. FMA 1976. *Publications:* Glass, 1956; (in collab.) Atoms and the Universe, 1956; papers on solid-state, glass, low-temperature physics; *novels:* The Catalyst, 1960; Personal File, 1962; Now, 1965; *story sequence:* The Conjuring Show, 1981. *Address:* 12 Squitchey Lane, Summertown, Oxford OX2 7LB. *T:* Oxford (01865) 510363.

JONES, Dame Gwyneth, DBE 1986 (CBE 1976); a Principal Dramatic Soprano: Royal Opera House, Covent Garden, since 1963; Vienna State Opera, since 1966; Bavarian State Opera, since 1967; *b* 7 Nov. 1936; *d* of late Edward George Jones and late Violet (*née* Webster); *m* Till Haberfeld; one *d*. *Educ:* Twmpath Sec. Mod. Sch., Pontypool, Mon; Royal College of Music, London; Accademia Chigiana, Siena; Zürich Internat. Opera Studio; Maria Carpi Prof., Geneva. Oratorio and recitals as well as opera. Guest Artiste: La Scala, Milan; Berlin State Opera; Munich State Opera; Bayreuth Festival; Salzburg

Festival; Verona; Tokyo; Zürich; Metropolitan Opera, New York; Paris; Geneva; Dallas; San Francisco; Los Angeles; Teatro Colon, Buenos Aires; Edinburgh Festival; Welsh National Opera; Rome; Hamburg; Cologne; Maggio Musicale, Florence; Chicago. Numerous recordings, radio and TV appearances. FRCM. Kammersängerin, Austria and Bavaria. Hon. DMus Wales. Shakespeare Prize, FVS Hamburg, 1987. Bundesverdienstkreuz (FRG), 1988; Comdr, Ordre des Arts et des Lettres (France), 1992. *Address:* PO Box, 8037 Zürich, Switzerland.

JONES, Gwynoro Glyndwr; Partner, Education Policy Publicity Consulting (education, policy and marketing consultancy), since 1993; Lay Inspector of Schools, since 1993; broadcaster and television interviewer on S4C; *b* 21 Nov. 1942; *s* of J. E. and late A. L. Jones, Minyrafon, Foelgastell, Cefneithin, Carms; *m* 1967, A. Laura Miles (marr. diss. 1991); two *s* one *d. Educ:* Gwendraeth Grammar Sch.; Cardiff Univ. BSc Econ (Hons) Politics and Economics. Market Research Officer with Ina Needle Bearings Ltd, Llanelli, 1966–67; Economist Section, Wales Gas Bd, 1967–69; Public Relations Officer, Labour Party in Wales, March 1969–June 1970; West Glamorgan County Council: Dir of Res., 1974–77; Assistant Education Officer: Develt Forward Planning, 1977–88; Capital and Property, 1988–93. Vice-Pres., Dist Council Assoc., 1974; Member: INLOGOV Working Gp on Res. and Intelligence Units in Local Govt, 1975–77; S Wales Standing Conf. Working Gp, 1975–77; Council of European Municipalities, 1975–77, 1980–; Local Govt Exec. Cttee of European movement, 1975–77, 1980–. MP (Lab) Carmarthen, 1970–Sept. 1974; Member: House of Commons Expenditure Cttee, 1972–74; Standing Orders Cttee, 1972–74; Council of Europe and WEU, 1974; PPS to Home Sec., 1974. Pres., Nat. Eisteddfod of Wales, 1974. Political Educn Officer, Swansea Labour Assoc., 1976–77. Mem., Soc. of Educn Officers, 1978–. Co-ordinator, Wales in Europe campaign, 1975; Sponsor, Wales Lab and TU Cttee for Europe, 1975; joined SDP, May 1981; contested: (SDP) Gower, Sept. 1982; (SDP/Alliance) Carmarthen, 1987; (Lib Dem) Hereford, 1992. Chairman: SDP Council for Wales, 1982–85, 1987–88; Alliance Cttee for Wales, 1983–88; Interim Chm., Welsh Soc & Lib Dem Exec., 1988; Member: Council for Social Democracy, 1982–88; SDP Nat. Cttee, 1982–85; SDP Orgn Cttee, 1987–88; Lib Dem Federal Exec., 1988–90; European Movement; Charter 88; IULA; Vice Chm., Lib Dem Policy Cttee, 1988–89. *Publications:* booklets: The Record Put Straight, 1973; SDP and the Alliance in Wales 1981–1986, 1986; SLD Golden Opportunities, 1988; A Movement in Crisis, 1989. *Recreations:* sport (played Rugby for both 1st and 2nd class teams). *Address:* Flat 2, 8 Richmond Villas, Swansea SA1 6DQ. *T:* Swansea (01792) 458828.

JONES, Sir Harry (Ernest), Kt 1971; CBE 1955; Agent in Great Britain for Northern Ireland, 1970–76; *b* 1 Aug. 1911; *m* 1935, Phyllis Eva Dixon (*d* 1987); one *s* one *d. Educ:* Stamford Sch.; St John's Coll., Cambridge. Entered Northern Ireland Civil Service, 1934; Min. of Commerce: Principal Officer 1940; Asst Sec. 1942; Perm. Sec. 1955; Industrial Development Adviser to Ministry of Commerce, 1969. *Recreation:* fishing. *Address:* 51 Station Road, Nassington, Peterborough PE8 6QB. *T:* Stamford (01780) 782675.

JONES, Rt. Rev. Haydn Harold; *b* 22 Aug. 1920; *s* of Charles Samuel and Blodwen Jones (*née* Williams), Penarth, Glam. *Educ:* Brotherhood of Saint Paul, Barton. RAF, 1941–44. Deacon 1947, priest 1948, Diocese of Bradford. Curate of St Barnabas, Heaton, Bradford, 1947–49; Tor Mohun, Torquay, 1949–51; Chaplain RN, 1951–53; Licence to Officiate, Diocese of London, 1954–62, Diocese of Coventry, 1962–63; Curate of St Peter's, Coventry, 1963–64; Rector of Clutton, Diocese of Bath and Wells, 1964–76, with Cameley, 1975–76; Surrogate, 1972–76. Dean of St Mary's Cathedral, Caracas, 1976–85; Bishop of Venezuela, 1976–86. *Recreations:* formerly tennis (rep. RN 1952), bridge, films, theatre. *Address:* Apartado 17.467 Parque Central, 1015–A Caracas, Venezuela. *T:* Caracas (2) 5731437. *Club:* Commonwealth of Venezuela.

JONES, Henry Arthur, CBE 1974; MA; Professor Emeritus, University of Leicester, since 1981 (Vaughan Professor of Education, 1967–81; Head of the Department of Adult Education, 1967–78; Pro-Vice-Chancellor, 1978–81); *b* 7 March 1917; *er s* of Henry Lloyd Jones; *m* 1st, 1942, Molly (*d* 1971), 4th *d* of Richard Shenton; two *s*; 2nd, 1972, Nancy Winifred (*née* Cox), *widow* of Lt R. B. B. Jack, RN. *Educ:* Chorlton Grammar Sch.; Manchester Univ. George Gissing Prizeman, Manchester Univ., 1936; Graduate Research Fellow, Manchester Univ., 1937, MA 1938. Served War of 1939–45 with Lancs Fusiliers and DLI, 1940–42. Sen. English Master, Chorlton Grammar Sch., 1942–47; Resident Staff Tutor, Manchester Univ., 1947–49; Asst Dir of Extra-Mural Studies, Liverpool Univ., 1949–52, Dep. Dir 1953–57; Principal, The City Literary Institute, 1957–67. Chairman: Assoc. for Adult Education, 1964–67; Adult Educn Cttee, IBA, 1973–77; Vice-Pres., Nat. Inst. of Adult Education (Exec. Chm., 1976–84); Hon. Life Mem., Educnl Centres Assoc.; Vice-Pres., Pre-retirement Assoc.; Member: Library Adv. Council, DES, 1965–68; Sec. of State's Cttee on Adult Educn, DES, 1968–72; Adv. Council for Adult and Continuing Educn, DES, 1977–83. Chm., Leics Consultative Cttee for Voluntary Orgns, 1974–77. Editor: Vaughan Papers in Educn, 1967–82; Studies in Adult Education, 1974–82. *Publications:* Adult Literacy: a study of the impact, 1978; The Concept of Success in Adult Literacy, 1978; Adult Literacy: the UK experience, 1978; Education and Disadvantage, 1978; Stage by Stage, 1993. *Address:* Stokes House, Great Bowden, Market Harborough, Leics LE16 7HF. *T:* Market Harborough (01858) 462846.

JONES, (Henry) John (Franklin); writer; *b* 6 May 1924; *s* of late Lt-Col James Walker Jones, DSO, IMS, and Doris Marjorie (*née* Franklin); *m* 1949, Jean Verity Robinson; one *s* one *d. Educ:* Blundell's Sch.; Colombo Public Library; Merton Coll., Oxford. Served War, Royal Navy: Ordinary Seaman, 1943; Intell. Staff, Eastern Fleet, 1944. Merton Coll., Oxford: Harmsworth Sen. Scholar, 1948; Fellow and Tutor in Jurisprudence, 1949; Univ. Sen. Lectr, 1956; Fellow and Tutor in Eng. Lit., 1962; Prof. of Poetry, Univ. of Oxford, 1979–84. Dill Meml Lectr, QUB, 1983. Football Correspondent, The Observer, 1956–59. TV appearances include The Modern World, 1988. *Publications:* The Egotistical Sublime, 1954, 5th edn 1978; (contrib.) The British Imagination, 1961; On Aristotle and Greek Tragedy, 1962, 5th edn 1980; (contrib.) Dickens and the Twentieth Century, 1962; (ed) H. W. Garrod, The Study of Good Letters, 1963; John Keats's Dream of Truth, 1969, 2nd edn 1980; (contrib.) The Morality of Art, 1969; The Same God, 1971; Dostoevsky, 1983, 2nd edn 1985; Shakespeare at Work, 1995. *Address:* Garden Flat, 41 Buckland Crescent, NW3 5DJ. *T:* 0171–586 1808; Yellands, Brisworthy, Shaugh Prior, Plympton, Devon PL7 5EL. *T:* Shaugh Prior (01752) 839310.

JONES, Sir Hugh; *see* Hugh-Jones, Sir W. N.

JONES, Hugh Duncan Hitchings; His Honour Judge Hugh Jones; a Circuit Judge, since 1991; *b* 25 May 1937; *s* of Norman Everard Jones and Ann Jones (*née* Hitchings); *m* 1966, Helen Margaret Payne; three *d. Educ:* Mountain Ash Grammar School (State Scholarship); University College London (LLB). Admitted Solicitor, 1961; Registrar, Cardiff County Court and Dist Registrar of the High Court, Cardiff Dist Registry, 1978; a Recorder, 1988–91. Mem., County Court Rules Cttee, 1994–. *Recreations:* cricket, gardening, golf, holidays in France. *Address:* The Cottage, Cwmpennar, Mountain Ash, Mid Glamorgan CF45 4DW.

JONES, Hugh (Hugo) Jarrett H.; *see* Herbert-Jones.

JONES, Ven. Hughie; *see* Jones, Ven. T. H.

JONES, Hywel Francis; Commissioner for Local Administration in Wales, 1985–91; *b* 28 Dec. 1928; *s* of late Brynmor and Beatrice Jones, Morriston, Swansea; *m* 1959, Marian Rosser Craven; one *d. Educ:* Bishop Gore Grammar School, Swansea; St John's College, Cambridge (BA 1949, MA 1953). IPFA 1953. Borough Treasurer's Dept, Swansea, 1949–56; Nat. Service, RAPC, 1953–55; Dep. County Treasurer, Breconshire, 1956–59; Asst County Treasurer, Carmarthenshire, 1959–66; Borough Treasurer, Port Talbot, 1966–75; Sec., Commn for Local Administration in Wales, 1975–85. Mem., Public Works Loan Board, 1971–75; Financial Adviser, AMC, 1972–74. Mem., Lord Chancellor's Adv. Cttee for West Glamorgan, 1990–. Treasurer, Royal National Eisteddfod of Wales, 1975–; Mem., Gorsedd of Bards, 1977 (Treasurer, 1992–). *Recreations:* music, reading, gardening. *Address:* Godre'r Rhiw, 1 Lon Heulog, Baglan, Port Talbot, West Glam SA12 8SY. *T:* Briton Ferry (01639) 813822.

JONES, Hywel Glyn; Chairman, Fixpoint Ltd, economic and marketing consultants, since 1988; Partner, Hywel Jones and Associates, economic consultants, since 1985; *b* 1 July 1948; *s* of late Thomas Glyndwr Jones and Anne Dorothy Jones (*née* Williams); *m* 1970, Julia Claire (*née* Davies). *Educ:* Trinity College, Cambridge (Open Scholar, Sen. Scholar, Res. Scholar; MA Hons Econ 1st cl; Wrenbury Scholarship in Political Economy). Lectr in Economics, Univ. of Warwick, 1971–73; Univ. Lectr in Economics of the Firm, Fellow of Linacre Coll., and Lectr, Worcester Coll., Oxford, 1973–77; Henley Centre for Forecasting: Dir of Internat. Forecasting, 1977–81; Dir and Chief Exec., 1981–85. *Publications:* Second Abstract of British Historical Statistics (jtly), 1971; An Introduction to Modern Theories of Economic Growth, 1975, trans Spanish and Japanese; Full Circle into the Future?: Britain into the 21st Century, 1984. *Recreations:* conversation, travel, military history, boating. *Address:* 59 Yarnells Hill, North Hinksey, Oxford OX2 9BE. *T:* Oxford (01865) 240916.

JONES, Rt. Rev. Hywel James; *b* 4 March 1918; *s* of Ifor James and Ann Jones; *m* 1946, Dorothy Margaret Wilcox; one *s* one *d. Educ:* Emmanuel Coll., Univ. of Saskatchewan (LTh). Deacon, then priest, 1942; Curate, Tofield, 1942; travelling priest, 1942–44; Incumbent of Parksville–Qualicum Beach, 1944–47; Colwood–Langford, 1947–56; Rector, St Mary the Virgin, Oak Bay, 1956–80. Hon. Canon of BC, 1959–68; Archdeacon of Quatsino, 1968–71, of Victoria, 1971–77; Archdeacon Emeritus, 1977–80; Bishop of British Columbia, 1980–84. DD (*hc*) Emmanuel Coll., Univ. of Saskatchewan, 1980. *Recreations:* reading, music, gardening. *Address:* 2028 Frederick Norris Road, Victoria, BC V8P 2B2, Canada. *T:* (604) 5927658. *Club:* Union (Victoria, BC).

JONES, Prof. Ian C.; *see* Chester Jones.

JONES, Ian Michael; Head, Textiles and Retail Division, Department of Trade and Industry, since 1994; *b* 5 Sept. 1949; *s* of Derek and Jean Jones; *m* 1976, Vivien Hepworth; two *s. Educ:* St Bartholomew's Grammar Sch., Newbury; Fitzwilliam Coll., Cambridge (BA Econs and Politics 1972). Home Office, 1972–83; DTI, 1983–85, Grade 5, 1985; Dept of Employment, 1985–89; Sec., BOTB, 1989–90; Department of Trade and Industry, 1989–: Regl Dir, SE Reg., 1990–94; Leader, London City Action Team, 1992–94; Grade 3, 1994. *Recreation:* cricket. *Address:* Department of Trade and Industry, 151 Buckingham Palace Road, SW1W 9SS. *T:* 0171–215 2969.

JONES, Ieuan Wyn; MP (Plaid Cymru) Ynys Môn, since 1987; *b* 22 May 1949; *s* of John Jones and Mair Elizabeth Jones; *m* 1974, Eirian Llwyd; two *s* one *d. Educ:* Pontardawe Grammar School; Ysgol-y-Berwyn, Y Bala, Gwynedd; Liverpool Polytechnic. LLB Hons. Qualified Solicitor, 1973; Partner in practice, 1974–87. Plaid Cymru National Vice-Chm., 1975–79, National Chm., 1980–82, 1990–92. Mem. Select Committee: on Welsh Affairs, 1990–92; on Agriculture, 1992–. Contested (Plaid Cymru) Ynys Môn (Anglesey), 1983. *Recreations:* sport, local history. *Address:* 45 Bridge Street, Llangefni, Ynys Môn, Gwynedd LL77 7RZ. *T:* Llangefni (01248) 722261.

JONES, Ilston Percival Ll.; *see* Llewellyn Jones.

JONES, Ivor R.; *see* Roberts-Jones.

JONES, Jack L.; *see* Jones, James Larkin.

JONES, Jacqui, (Mrs Peter Jones); *see* Lait, J.

JONES, Prof. James Eirug Thomas, FRCPath; Courtauld Professor of Animal Health, Royal Veterinary College, University of London, 1984–93, now Emeritus Professor; *b* 14 June 1927; *s* of David John and Mary Elizabeth Jones; *m* 1953, Marion Roberts; one *s* one *d. Educ:* Ystalyfera County Sch.; Royal Vet. Coll. MRCVS 1950, FRCVS 1994; PhD 1973. Gen. vet. practice, 1950–53; vet. officer, Birmingham Corp., 1953–54; Lectr in Path., RVC, 1954–58; Res. Officer, Animal Health Trust, 1958–63; Fulbright Scholar, Univ. of Pennsylvania, 1963–64; vis. worker, 1964, Sen. Lectr, 1967, Reader in Animal Health, 1975–84, RVC. J. T. Edwards Meml Medal, RCVS, 1985; Bledisloe Vet. Award, RASE, 1994. *Publications:* numerous papers in sci. jls on infectious diseases of farm animals. *Recreations:* travel, reading. *Address:* 283 Bury Street West, N9 9JN. *T:* 0181–360 2146.

JONES, James Larkin, (Jack), CH 1978; MBE 1950; FCIT 1970; General Secretary, Transport and General Workers' Union, 1969–78; Member, TUC General Council, 1968–78; Chairman, TUC International, Transport and Nationalised Industries Committees, 1972–78; Deputy Chairman, National Ports Council, 1967–79; *b* 29 March 1913; *m* 1938, Evelyn Mary Taylor; two *s. Educ:* elementary sch., Liverpool. Worked in engineering and docks industries, 1927–39. Liverpool City Councillor, 1936–39; served in Spanish Civil War; wounded Ebro battle, Aug. 1938; Coventry District Sec., Transport and General Workers' Union, also District Sec., Confedn of Shipbuilding and Engineering Unions, 1939–55; Midlands Regional Sec., Transport and General Workers' Union, 1955–63, Executive Officer, 1963–69. Mem., Midland Regional Bd for Industry, 1942–46, 1954–63; Chm., Midlands TUC Advisory Cttee, 1948–63. Coventry City Magistrate, 1950–63; Executive Chm., Birmingham Productivity Cttee, 1957–63; Member: Labour Party Nat. Exec. Cttee, 1964–67; Nat. Cttee for Commonwealth Immigrants, 1965–69; NEDC, 1969–78; Council, Advisory, Conciliation and Arbitration Service, 1974–78; Overseas Trade Board, 1974–79; Cttee of Inquiry into Industrial Democracy, 1976–77 (Chm., Labour Party Wkg Party on Industrial Democracy, 1967); Bd, Crown Agents, 1978–80; Royal Commn on Criminal Procedure, 1978–80; Jt Chm. (with Lord Aldington), Special Cttee on the Ports, 1972. Pres., EFTA Trade Union Council, 1972–73; Founder Mem., European TUC, 1973. Vice-President: ITF, 1974–79; Anti-Apartheid Movement, 1976–; Age Concern, England, 1978–; European Fed of Retired and Elderly Persons, 1991–; Pres., Retired Members Assocs, 1979–; Chm., Nat Pensioners' Convention, 1992–. Chm., Trustees, Nat. Museum of Labour History, 1988–. Vis. Fellow, Nuffield Coll., Oxford, 1970–78; Associate Fellow, LSE, 1978–82. Dimbleby Lecture, BBC, 1977. Hon. Fellow: Liverpool John Moores Univ. (formerly Liverpool Poly.); Central Lancs Univ. Hon. DLitt Warwick, 1978. Freeman, City of London, 1979. Award of Merit, City of Coventry, 1978. *Publications:* (contrib.) The Incompatibles, 1967; (contrib.) Industry's Democratic Revolution, 1974; (with Max Morris) A-Z of Trade

Unionism and Industrial Relations, 1982; Union Man (autobiog.), 1986. *Recreation:* walking. *Address:* 74 Ruskin Park House, Champion Hill, SE5 8TH. *T:* 0171–274 7067.

JONES, (James) Roger; Head of Antiques Department, Colefax and Fowler, since 1994; *b* 30 May 1952; *s* of Albert James Jones and late Hilda Vera Jones (*née* Evans). *Educ:* Shrewsbury; St Catharine's Coll., Cambridge (Sen. Schol.; MA). Called to the Bar, Middle Temple, 1974 (Lloyd Jacob Meml Exhibnr; Astbury Schol.); practised Oxford and Midland Circuit, 1975–83. Joined Office of Parly Counsel, 1983; with Law Commn, 1988–91; Dep. Parly Counsel, 1991–94. *Recreation:* walking the dog. *Address:* Colefax and Fowler, 39 Brook Street, W1Y 2JE.

JONES, Rt. Rev. James Stuart; *see* Hull, Bishop Suffragan of.

JONES, Hon. Jeffrey Richard, CBE 1978; MA; Chief Justice, 1980–85, and President of the Court of Appeal, 1982–85, Kiribati; Member, Appeal Court, Solomon Islands, 1982 and Vanuatu, 1983; *b* 18 Nov. 1921; *s* of Rev. Thomas Jones and Winifred (*née* Williams); *m* 1955, Anna Rosaleen Carberry; one *s* one *d*. *Educ:* Grove Park Sch., Wrexham; Denstone Coll., Staffs; Keble Coll., Oxford, 1940, 1946–49 (MA (Hons) PPE); Council of Legal Educn, 1950–52. Served RAFVR, Flt Lieut (Pilot), 1940–46. Schoolmaster, Mountgrace Comprehensive, Potters Bar, 1953–55. Called to the Bar, Middle Temple, 1954; private practice, Zaria, Nigeria, 1955–57; Magistrate, 1957, High Court Judge, 1965, Sen. Puisne Judge, 1970, Northern Nigeria; Chief Justice, Kano State, N Nigeria, 1975, Chief Judge (change of title, decree 41 of 1976), 1976–80; Puisne Judge, High Court, Solomon Is, 1982–85. President, Rotary Club, Kano, 1977. Editor, Northern Nigeria Law Reports, 1966–74. *Publications:* Some Cases on Criminal Procedure and Evidence in Northern Nigeria 1968, 1968; Some Cases on Criminal Procedure and Evidence in Northern Nigeria 1969, 1969, 2nd edn combining 1968–69, 1970; Criminal Procedure in the Northern States of Nigeria (annotated), 1975, repr. 1978, 2nd edn 1979. *Recreations:* painting, gardening, bridge, golf. *Address:* Bradley Cottage, Bradley Lane, Holt, near Trowbridge, Wilts BA14 6QE. *T:* North Trowbridge (01225) 782004.

JONES, Jennifer, (Mrs Norton Simon); film actress (US); *b* Tulsa, Okla; *d* of Philip R. Isley and Flora Mae (*née* Suber); *m* 1st, 1939, Robert Walker (marr. diss. 1945); two *s*; 2nd, 1949, David O. Selznick (*d* 1965); one *d* decd; 3rd, 1971, Norton Simon. *Educ:* schools in Okla and Tex; Northwestern Univ., Evanston, Illinois; American Academy of Dramatic Arts, New York City. Films, since 1943, include: The Song of Bernadette; Since You Went Away; Cluny Brown; Love Letters; Duel in the Sun; We Were Strangers; Madame Bovary; Portrait of Jenny; Carrie; Wild Heart; Ruby Gentry; Indiscretion of an American Wife; Beat the Devil; Love is a Many-Splendoured Thing; The Barretts of Wimpole Street; A Farewell to Arms; Tender is the Night; The Idol; The Towering Inferno. Awards include: American Academy of Motion Pictures, Arts and Sciences Award, 1943; 4 other Academy nominations, etc. Medal for Korean War Work.

JONES, John; *see* Jones, H. J. F.

JONES, (John) Clement, CBE 1972; FRSA 1970; writer, broadcaster, technical adviser to developing countries; *b* 22 June 1915; *o s* of Clement Daniel Jones; *m* 1939, Marjorie (*d* 1991), *d* of George Gibson, Llandrindod Wells; three *s*. *Educ:* Ardwyn, Aberystwyth; BA (Hons) Open Univ., 1983. Various journalistic positions; News Editor, Express and Star, Wolverhampton, 1955; Editor, 1960–71; Editorial Director, 1971–74; Exec. Dir, Beacon Broadcasting, Wolverhampton, 1974–83. Pres., Guild of British Newspaper Editors, 1966–67, Hon. Life Vice-Pres., 1972. Member: Press Council, 1965–74; Adv. Bd, Thomson Foundn, 1965–87; BBC W Midlands Adv. Council, 1971–75; (part-time) Monopolies and Mergers Commn (Newspaper Panel), 1973–86; W Midlands Arts Assoc., 1973–78; Exec. Cttee, Soc. Internat. Develt, 1974–78; Vice Chm., Lichfield Dio. Media Council, 1976–82; Mem. Council, and Chm. Press Freedom Cttee, Commonwealth Press Union, 1975–80; Chm., Media Panel, Commn for Racial Equality, 1981–84; Vice-Chm., British Human Rights Trust, 1975–78; Governor, British Inst. Human Rights, 1971–82. Mem. Senate, Open Univ., 1983–86. Founder Mem., Circle of Wine Writers, 1966. Pres., Staffordshire Soc., 1971–74. Founder and Pres., Frinton and Walton Heritage Trust, 1984–. *Publications:* UNESCO World Survey of Media Councils and Codes of Ethics, 1976; Racism and Fascism, 1981; Race and the Media: thirty years on, 1982; A History of the First Fifty Years of the Guild of Editors, 1995; pamphlets on local history, NE Anglia. *Recreations:* travel, gardening. *Address:* The Annex, Summerhaugh Cottage, St Mary Bourne, Hampshire SP11 6BG. *T:* St Mary Bourne (01264) 738190. *Club:* Athenæum.
See also G. Q. Jones.

JONES, His Honour (John) Edward; a Circuit Judge (formerly County Court Judge), 1969–84; *b* 23 Dec. 1914; *s* of Thomas Robert Jones, Liverpool; *m* 1945, Katherine Elizabeth Edwards, SRN, *d* of Ezekiel Richard Edwards, Liverpool; one *s* one *d*. *Educ:* Sefton Park Council Sch.; Liverpool Institute High School. ACIS 1939–70; BCom London 1942; LLB London 1945. Called to Bar, Gray's Inn, 1945; Member of Northern Circuit, 1946; Dep. Chm., Lancs QS, 1966–69. Dep. Chm., Workmen's Compensation (Supplementation) and Pneumoconiosis and Byssinosis Benefit Boards, 1968–69; Director: Chatham Building Soc., 1955–59; Welsh Calvinistic Methodist Assurance Trust, 1953–59. Vice-Pres., Merseyside Br., Magistrates' Assoc., 1974–84. Pres., Liverpool Welsh Choral Union, 1987– (Vice Pres., 1973–87); Mem., Cymmrodorion Soc., 1961–; Life Member: Welsh National Eisteddfod Court; Gorsedd of Bards (Ioan Maesgrug), 1987. Governor: Aigburth Vale Comprehensive Sch., 1976–85; Calderstones Community Comprehensive Sch., 1985–88. Pres., Merseyside Branch, British Red Cross Soc., 1980–88 (Mem. Nat. Council, 1983–86). Chm., World Friendship, 1990–. Exec. Cttee, Liverpool Free Church Federal Council, 1988– (Pres., 1992–94); Welsh Presbyterian Church: Deacon, 1947; Liverpool Presbytery Moderator, 1971. JP Lancs, 1966. *Address:* 45 Sinclair Drive, Liverpool L18 0HW. *Club:* Athenæum (Liverpool).

JONES, John Elfed, CBE 1987; DL; CEng, FIEE; FRSA; Chairman, Welsh Water plc (formerly Welsh Water Authority), 1982–93; *b* 19 March 1933; *s* of Urien Maelgwyn Jones and Mary Jones; *m* 1957, Mary Sheila (*née* Rosser); two *d*. *Educ:* Blaenau Ffestiniog Grammar Sch.; Denbighshire Technical Coll., Wrexham; Heriot Watts Coll., Edinburgh. Student apprentice, 1949–53, graduate trainee, 1953–55, CEGB; National Service, RAF, 1955–57 (FO); Rock Climbing Instr, Outward Bound Sch., Aberdyfi, 1957; Technical Engr with CEGB, 1957–59; Dep. Project Manager, Rheidol Hydro-Electric Project, 1959–61; Sen. Elec. Engr, Trawsfynydd Nuclear Power Station, 1961–63; Deputy Manager: Mid Wales Gp of Power Stations, 1963–67; Connah's Quay Power Station, 1967–69; Anglesey Aluminium Metal Ltd: Engrg Manager, 1969–73; Production Manager, 1973–76; Admin Director, 1976–77; Dep. Man. Dir, 1977–79; Industrial Dir, Welsh Office (Under Sec. rank), 1979–82. Chm., British Water International Ltd, 1983–88. Dep. Chm., HTV Gp, 1991–; Director: HTV Cymru/Wales Ltd, 1990– (Chm., 1992–); W Midlands and Wales Regl Adv. Bd, National Westminster Bank, 1990–91; BMSS plc, 1993–; Cwmni Rheilffordd Beddgelert Cyf., 1994–; Cwmni Rheilffordd Caernarfon Cyf., 1994–. Treasurer, Urdd Gobaith Cymru, 1964–67; Chm., Welsh Language Bd, 1988–93; Mem., Royal National Eisteddfod of Wales, 1981–90; Member: BBC Broadcasting Council for Wales, 1979–83; Council, Food from Britain, 1985–87; Prince of Wales Cttee, 1986–90. Pres., Univ. of Wales, Lampeter, 1992–; Member: Court and Council: UCNW, Bangor, 1978–; Nat. Lib. of Wales, 1983–88; Coleg Harlech, 1983–88; Court, Univ. Coll., Aberystwyth, 1984–. Mem., Civic Trust for Wales, 1982–88. FRSA 1984; CIMgt (CBIM 1990). DL Mid Glam, 1989. Fellow, Univ. of Wales, Aberystwyth, 1990. Hon. Col, Commonwealth of Kentucky, 1976. *Recreations:* fishing for salmon and trout, reading, attending Eisteddfodau. *Address:* Ty Mawr, Coity, Bridgend, Mid Glamorgan CF35 6BN.

JONES, Air Vice-Marshal John Ernest A.; *see* Allen-Jones.

JONES, John Ernest P.; *see* Powell-Jones.

JONES, Prof. (John) Gareth, MD; FRCP; FRCA; Professor of Anaesthesia, Cambridge University, since 1991; *b* 20 Aug. 1936; *s* of Dr John and Catherine Jones; *m* 1964, Susan Price; three *d*. *Educ:* Canton High Sch.; Welsh Nat. Sch. of Medicine, Univ. of Wales (MB BCh 1960); MD Birmingham, 1967. MRCP 1963, FRCP 1983; FRCA (FFARCS 1970). Res. Fellow, Dept of Medicine, 1964–68, Lectr, Anaesthesia, 1968–70, Univ. of Birmingham; North Sen. Fellow, Cardiovascular Res. Inst., Univ. of California, San Francisco, 1970–74; Scientific Staff, MRC, Northwick Park, 1974–86; Prof. of Anaesthesia, Univ. of Leeds, 1986–91. Vis. Scientist, Chest Service, Univ. of California, San Francisco, 1977–78; Consultant, Baragwanath Hosp., Soweto, 1986. Hon. FANZCA 1992. *Publications:* Effects of Anaesthesia and Surgery on Pulmonary Mechanisms, 1984; (with I. Hindmarch and E. Moss) Aspects of Recovery From Anaesthesia, 1987; Depth of Anaesthesia, 1989; Depth of Anesthesia, 1993; (with C. Hanning) The Upper Airway, 1995. *Recreations:* model engineering, low flying. *Address:* Cambridge University Department of Anaesthesia, Addenbrooke's Hospital, Hills Road, Cambridge CB2 2QQ. *T:* Cambridge (01223) 217889.

JONES, (John) Geoffrey; His Honour Judge Geoffrey Jones; a Circuit Judge since 1975; *b* 14 Sept. 1928; *s* of Wyndham and Lilias Jones; *m* 1954, Sheila (*née* Gregory); three *s*. *Educ:* Brighton and Hove Grammar Sch.; St Michael's Sch., Llanelli; St David's Coll., Lampeter; University Coll., London. LLB London 1955; LLM London 1985. Army service, 1946–48, commnd into RASC, 1947. Electrical wholesale business, 1948–52. Called to Bar, Gray's Inn, 1956; practised Leicester, 1958–70 and London, 1970–75. Sen. Academic Fellow, Leicester Polytechnic, 1989. *Recreation:* golf. *Address:* c/o The County Court, Lower Hill Street, Leicester LE1 3SJ.

JONES, Maj.-Gen. John H.; *see* Hamilton-Jones.

JONES, Sir John Henry H.; *see* Harvey-Jones.

JONES, John Hubert E.; *see* Emlyn Jones.

JONES, Sir (John) Kenneth (Trevor), Kt 1965; CBE 1956; QC 1976; Legal Adviser to the Home Office, 1956–77; *b* 11 July 1910; *s* of John Jones and Agnes Morgan; *m* 1940, Menna, *d* of Cyril O. Jones; two *s*. *Educ:* King Henry VIII Grammar Sch., Abergavenny; University Coll. of Wales, Aberystwyth; St John's Coll., Cambridge. Called to the Bar, Lincoln's Inn, 1937. Served Royal Artillery, 1939–45. Entered the Home Office as a Legal Asst, 1945. Mem. of the Standing Cttee on Criminal Law Revision, 1959–80. *Address:* 7 Chilton Court, Walton-on-Thames, Surrey KT12 1NG. *T:* Walton-on-Thames (01932) 226890. *Club:* Athenæum.

JONES, John Knighton C.; *see* Chadwick-Jones.

JONES, Sir John (Lewis), KCB 1983; CMG 1972; *b* 17 Feb. 1923; *m* 1948, Daphne Nora (*née* Redman). *Educ:* Christ's College, Cambridge (MA). Royal Artillery, 1942–46; Sudan Government, 1947–55; Ministry of Defence, 1955–85. *Recreation:* golf. *Club:* United Oxford & Cambridge University.

JONES, Air Vice-Marshal John Maurice, CB 1986; *b* 27 Jan. 1931; *s* of E. Morris Jones and Gladys Jones (*née* Foulkes); *m* 1962, Joan (*née* McCallum); one *s* one *d*. *Educ:* Liverpool Institute High Sch.; Univ. of Liverpool (BDS). LDSRCS, FDSRCS 1987. Hospital appt, Liverpool Dental Hosp., 1954; RAF Dental Branch: appts UK and abroad, incl. Christmas Island, Malta, Cyprus and Fontainebleau, 1955–73; Dep. Dir of RAF Dental Services, 1973; OC RAF Inst. of Dental Health and Training, 1976; Principal Dental Officer: HQ RAF Germany, 1979; HQ RAF Support Command, 1982; Dir, RAF Dental Services, 1982–88, and Dir, Defence Dental Services, MoD, 1985–88; QHDS, 1983–87. Sec., Ski Club of GB, 1988–91. Pres., RAF Squash Rackets Assoc., 1986–88. OBStJ 1978. *Recreations:* golf, fishing, ski-ing. *Address:* Wyckenhurst, St Michael's Close, Halton Village, Wendover, Bucks HP22 5NW. *T:* Wendover (01296) 624184. *Club:* Royal Air Force, Kandahar.

JONES, Sir John Prichard; *see* Prichard-Jones.

JONES, Prof. (John) Stephen, PhD; Professor of Genetics, since 1992, and Head of Department of Genetics and Biometry, since 1989, University College London; *b* 24 March 1944; *s* of Thomas Gwilym Jones and Lydia Anne Jones; partner, Norma Percy. *Educ:* Wirral Grammar Sch.; Univ. of Edinburgh (BSc, PhD). Postdoctoral Fellow, Univ. of Chicago, 1969–71; Lectr in Genetics, Royal Free Hosp. Med. Sch., 1971–78; Lectr then Reader in Genetics, UCL, 1978–92. Reith Lectr, 1991. *Publications:* (ed) Cambridge Encyclopedia of Human Evolution, 1992; The Language of the Genes, 1993 (Science Book Prize, 1994); scientific papers in learned jls. *Recreation:* not administrating. *Address:* Department of Genetics, University College London, Gower Street, WC1E 6BT. *T:* 0171–387 7050.

JONES, Jonathan Owen; MP (Lab) Cardiff Central, since 1992; *b* 19 April 1954; *s* of Gwynfor Owen Jones and Dorothy Mary (*née* Davies); *m* 1989, Allison Clement; two *s*. *Educ:* Univ. of East Anglia (BSc Hons Ecology); Cardiff Univ. (PGCE). Science and biology teacher, 1977–92. An Opposition Whip, 1993–. *Recreations:* cooking, walking, watching Rugby, my family. *Address:* (office) 199 Newport Road, Cardiff CF2 1AJ. *T:* Cardiff (01222) 452322; House of Commons, SW1A 0AA. *T:* 0171–219 4531. *Club:* Roath Labour.

JONES, Julia P.; *see* Peyton-Jones.

JONES, Karen Ida Boalth S.; *see* Spärck Jones.

JONES, Prof. Kathleen; Professor of Social Policy, University of York, 1981–89 (Professor of Social Administration, 1965–81), now Emeritus Professor; *b* 7 April 1922; *d* of William Robert Savage and Kate Lilian Barnard; *m* 1944, Rev. David Gwyn Jones (*d* 1976); one *s*. *Educ:* North London Collegiate Sch.; Westfield Coll., Univ. of London (BA, PhD). Research Asst in Social Administration, Univ. of Manchester, 1951–53, Asst Lectr 1953–55; Sen. History Teacher, Victoria Instn, Kuala Lumpur, 1956–58, also Asst Lectr in History, Univ. of Malaya (part-time); Lectr in Social Administration, Univ. of Manchester, 1958–62, Sen. Lectr 1962–65. Chm., Social Scis Cttee, UK Commn for UNESCO, 1966–69. Mem., Gen. Synod of C of E, 1975–80; Member: Archbishop's Commn on Church and State, 1966–71; Lord Gardiner's Ctte on NI, 1974–75; Archbishop's Commn on Marriage, 1976–78; Mental Health Act Commn, 1983–86 (NE Chm., 1983–85). Pres., Assoc. of Psychiatric Social Workers, 1968–70; Chm., Social

Admin Assoc., 1980–83. Hon. FRCPsych, 1976. *Publications:* Lunacy, Law and Conscience, 1955; Mental Health and Social Policy, 1960; Mental Hospitals at Work, 1962; The Compassionate Society, 1965; The Teaching of Social Studies in British Universities, 1965; A History of the Mental Health Services, 1972; Opening the Door: a study of new policies for the mentally handicapped, 1975; Issues in Social Policy, 1978; (ed) Living the Faith: a call to the Church, 1980; Ideas on Institutions, 1984; Eileen Younghusband: a biography, 1985; Experience in Mental Health, 1988; The Making of Social Policy, 1991; Asylums and After, 1993; Poems of St John of the Cross, 1993; (series editor) International Library of Social Policy, 1968–85; (ed) Year Book of Social Policy in Britain, 1971–76. *Address:* 44 West Moor Lane, Heslington, York YO1 5ER. *T:* York (01904) 411579.

JONES, Very Rev. Keith Brynmore; Dean of Exeter, since 1996; *b* 27 June 1944; *s* of John Brynmor Jones and Mary Emily Jones; *m* 1973, Viola Mary Jenkyns; three *d*. *Educ:* Selwyn Coll., Cambridge (BA 1965; MA 1969); Cuddesdon Coll., Oxford. Ordained deacon, 1969, priest, 1970; Asst Curate, Limpfield with Titsey, Surrey, 1969–72; Dean's Vicar, Cathedral and Abbey Church of St Alban, 1972–76; Priest-in-charge, 1976–79, Team Vicar, 1979–82, St Michael's, Boreham Wood; Vicar of St Mary-le-Tower, Ipswich, 1982–95. Rural Dean of Ipswich, 1992–95; Hon. Canon, St Edmundsbury Cathedral, 1993–. *Recreations:* music, gardening, theatre, walking. *Address:* The Deanery, Exeter, Devon EX1 1HT. *T:* Exeter (01392) 52891, 72697.

JONES, Keith H.; *see* Hamylton Jones.

JONES, Sir Keith (Stephen), Kt 1980; FRCSE; FRACS; *b* 7 July 1911; *s* of Stephen William and Muriel Elsy Jones; *m* 1936, Kathleen Mary Abbott; three *s*. *Educ:* Newington Coll.; Univ. of Sydney (MB, BS). General practitioner, Army MO, Surgeon; President, Aust. Medical Assoc., 1973–76; Chief MO, NSW State Emergency Service, 1966–74; Mem., NSW Medical Bd, 1971–81. Mem., Newington Coll. Council, 1951–72; Mem., Nat. Specialist Recognition Appeals Cttee, 1970–83 (Chm., 1980–83; Chm., Nat. Spec. Qualifications Cttee, 1980–83). Chairman: Australasian Medical Publishing Co., 1976–82; Manly Art Gall., 1982–85; President: Medical Benefits Fund of Aust., 1983–85; Blue Cross Assoc. of Aust., 1983–85. Acting Editor, Medical Jl of Aust., 1981. Fellow, Australian Coll. of Emergency Medicine, 1984; Hon. FRACGP 1975. Gold Medal, AMA, 1976. *Recreation:* swimming. *Address:* 123 Bayview Garden Village, Cabbage Tree Road, Bayview, NSW 2104, Australia. *T:* (2) 99972876.

JONES, Sir Kenneth; *see* Jones, Sir J. K. T.

JONES, Sir Kenneth (George Illtyd), Kt 1974; a Judge of the High Court, Queen's Bench Division, 1974–89; *b* 26 May 1921; *s* of late Richard Arthur Jones and Olive Jane Jones, Radyr, Cardiff; *m* 1st, 1947, Dulcie (*d* 1977); one *s* two *d*; 2nd, 1978, June Patricia (prev. marr. diss.), *o d* of late Leslie Arthur and Winifred Doxey, Harrogate. *Educ:* Brigg Gram. Sch.; University Coll., Oxford (1939–41, 1945–46), MA; Treas., Oxford Union Society, 1941; served in Shropshire Yeo. (76th Medium Regt RA), 1942–45; Staff Captain, HQ 13th Corps, 1945 (despatches). Called to Bar, Gray's Inn, 1946; joined Oxford Circuit, 1947; QC 1962; Mem. Gen. Council of the Bar, 1961–65, 1968–69; Bencher, 1969, Treas., 1987, Gray's Inn. Recorder of: Shrewsbury, 1964–66; Wolverhampton, 1966–71; the Crown Court, 1972; Dep. Chm., Herefordshire QS, 1961–71; a Circuit Judge, 1972–73. Dep. Chm., Boundary Commn for Wales, 1984–88. *Recreations:* theatre, opera, travel, fishing.

JONES, Air Marshal Sir Laurence (Alfred), KCB 1987 (CB 1984); AFC 1971; Lieutenant-Governor of the Isle of Man, 1990–95; *b* 18 Jan. 1933; *s* of Benjamin Howel and Irene Dorothy Jones; *m* 1956, Brenda Ann; two *d*. *Educ:* Trinity Sch., Croydon; RAF College, Cranwell. Entry to RAF Coll., 1951, graduated 1953; served as Jun. Officer Pilot with 208 Sqdn in Middle East, 1954–57, Fighter Weapons Sch., 74 Sqdn, until 1961; commanded: No 8 Sqdn, Aden, 1961–63; No 19 Sqdn, RAF Germany, 1967–70; Station Comdr, RAF Wittering, 1975–76; RCDS 1977; Director of Operations (Air Support), MoD, 1978–81; SASO, Strike Command, 1982–84; ACAS(Ops), MoD, 1984; ACDS(Progs), 1985–86; ACAS, 1986–87; Air Member for Personnel, 1987–89, retd. *Recreation:* golf. *Club:* Royal Air Force.

JONES, Lewis C.; *see* Carter-Jones.

JONES, Lilian Pauline N.; *see* Neville-Jones.

JONES, Dr Lynne Mary; MP (Lab) Birmingham, Selly Oak, since 1992; *b* 26 April 1951; two *s*. *Educ:* Birmingham Univ. (BSc, PhD Biochem.); Birmingham Polytechnic (Dip. Housing Studies). Joined Labour Party, 1974; ASTMS, then MSF, 1972. Birmingham City Councillor, 1980–94 (Chair, Housing Cttee, 1984–87). Former Exec. Mem., Labour Housing Gp. Mem., Select Cttee on Science and Technology, 1992–. *Address:* House of Commons, SW1A 0AA. *T:* 0171–219 6971.

JONES, Mark Ellis Powell; Director, National Museums of Scotland, since 1992; *b* 5 Feb. 1951; *s* of John Ernest Powell-Jones, *qv* and Ann Paludan; *m* 1983, Ann Camilla, *d* of Stephen Edelston Toulmin, *qv*; two *s* two *d*. *Educ:* Eton College; Worcester College, Oxford (MA); Courtauld Inst. of Art. Asst Keeper, 1974–90, Keeper, 1990–92, Dept of Coins and Medals, BM. Sec., British Art Medal Soc., 1982; Pres., Fédn Internat. de la Médaille, 1994–; Corresp. Mem., Amer. Numismatic Soc. Editor, The Medal, 1983–. *Publications:* The Art of the Medal, 1977; Impressionist Painting, 1979; Catalogue of French Medals in the British Museum, I, 1982, II, 1988; Contemporary British Medals, 1986; (ed) Fake?: the art of deception, 1990; (ed) Why Fakes Matter, 1992; (ed) Designs on Posterity, 1994. *Address:* 39 Regent Street, Portobello, Edinburgh EH15 2AY. *T:* 0131–225 7534.

JONES, Prof. Martin Kenneth, DPhil; FSA; George Pitt-Rivers Professor of Archaeological Science, University of Cambridge, since 1990; *b* 29 June 1951; *s* of John Francis Jones and Margaret Olive (*née* Baldwin); *m* 1985, Lucy Walker; one *s* one *d*. *Educ:* Eltham Coll., Univ. of Cambridge (MA); Univ. of Oxford (DPhil 1985). FSA 1991. Oxford Archaeological Unit, 1973–79; Res. Asst, Oxford Univ., 1979–81; Lectr, 1981–89, Sen. Lectr, 1989–90, Durham Univ. *Publications:* The Environment of Man: the Iron Age to the Anglo-Saxon period, 1981; Integrating the Subsistence Economy, 1983; England before Domesday, 1986; Archaeology and the Flora of the British Isles, 1988. *Recreations:* walking, botanising. *Address:* Department of Archaeology, Downing Street, Cambridge CB2 3DZ. *T:* Cambridge (01223) 333520.

JONES, Martyn David; MP (Lab) Clwyd South West, since 1987; *b* 1 March 1947; *m* 1974, Rhona Bellis (marr. diss. 1991); one *s* one *d*. *Educ:* Liverpool and Trent Polytechnics. MIBiol. Microbiologist, Wrexham Lager Beer Co., 1968–87. Mem., Clwyd CC, 1981–89. An Opposition Whip, 1988–92; Opposition spokesman on food, agric. and rural affairs, 1994–; Mem., Chairman's Panel, 1992–94. Mem., Select Cttee on Agriculture, 1987–94; Chm., Parly Labour Party Agriculture Cttee, 1987–94. *Address:* House of Commons, SW1A 0AA; 20 High Street, Johnstown, Wrexham, Clwyd LL14 2SN.

JONES, Maude Elizabeth, CBE 1973; Deputy Director-General, British Red Cross Society, 1970–77; *b* 14 Jan. 1921; 2nd *d* of late E. W. Jones, Dolben, Ruthin, North Wales. *Educ:* Brynhyfryd Sch. for Girls, Ruthin. Joined Foreign Relations Dept, Jt War Organisation BRCS and OStJ, 1940; Dep. Dir, Jun. Red Cross, BRCS, 1949; Dir, Jun. Red Cross, 1960; Dep. Dir-Gen. for Branch Affairs, BRCS, 1966. Member: Jt Cttee (and Finance and Gen. Purposes Sub-Cttee) OStJ and BRCS, 1966–77; Council of Nat. Council of Social Service; Council of FANY, 1966–77. Governor, St David's Sch., Ashford, Mddx. SSStJ 1959. *Recreations:* music, gardening, reading. *Address:* Dolben, Ruthin, Clwyd, North Wales LL15 1RB. *T:* Ruthin (01824) 702443. *Club:* New Cavendish.

JONES, Mervyn; author; *b* 27 Feb. 1922; *s* of Ernest Jones and Katharine (*née* Jokl); *m* 1948, Jeanne Urquhart; one *s* two *d*. *Educ:* Abbotsholme School; New York University. Assistant Editor: Tribune, 1955–59; New Statesman, 1966–68; Drama Critic, Tribune, 1959–67. *Publications:* No Time to be Young, 1952; The New Town, 1953; The Last Barricade, 1953; Helen Blake, 1955; On the Last Day, 1958; Potbank, 1961; Big Two, 1962; A Set of Wives, 1965; Two Ears of Corn, 1965; John and Mary, 1966; A Survivor, 1968; Joseph, 1970; Mr Armitage Isn't Back Yet, 1971; Life on the Dole, 1972; Holding On, 1973; The Revolving Door, 1973; Strangers, 1974; Lord Richard's Passion, 1974; The Pursuit of Happiness, 1975; Scenes from Bourgeois Life, 1976; Nobody's Fault, 1977; Today The Struggle, 1978; The Beautiful Words, 1979; A Short Time to Live, 1980; Two Women and their Man, 1982; Joanna's Luck, 1985; Coming Home, 1986; Chances, 1987; That Year in Paris, 1988; A Radical Life, 1991; Michael Foot, 1994. *Address:* 1 Evelyn Mansions, Carlisle Place, SW1P 1NH. *T:* 0171–821 9563.

JONES, Miah Gwynfor, (Gwyn Jones), PhD; FBCS; BBC National Governor for Wales, since 1992; *b* 2 Dec. 1948; *s* of Robert Jones and Jane Irene Jones (*née* Evans); *m* 1976, Maria Linda Johnson; two *d*. *Educ:* Ysgol Eifionydd, Porthmadog; Univ. of Manchester (BSc 1st Cl. Hons); Univ. of Essex (PhD). FBCS 1987. British Steel Corp., 1974–77; ICL, 1977–81; Chm., Business Micro Systems, 1981–85; Chm. and Chief Exec., Corporate Technology Gp plc, 1985–87; Chm., L. G. Software, 1985–87; Director: ACT Computers PLC, 1989–; Welsh Water Enterprises Ltd, 1990–93; Tesco plc, 1992–; S4C Authority, 1992; Drayton English and Internat. Trust plc, 1993–. Chm., Welsh Develt Agency, 1988–93. Member: Council, Univ. of Wales, 1989–; Court, UC of Swansea, 1989–; Prince of Wales Cttee, 1989–92; Prince's Youth Business Trust, 1989–92. *Recreations:* golf, tennis, ski-ing. *Address:* Broadcasting House, Llandaff, Cardiff CF5 2YQ.

JONES, Michael Abbott; Head of Corporate Affairs, Sun Alliance, since 1993; *b* 3 May 1944; *s* of Ronald and Irene Jones; *m* 1973, Wendy (*née* Saward); twin *d*. *Educ:* Felsted; Magdalen Coll., Oxford (BA, DipEd). Joined Life Offices' Assoc., 1968, Jt Sec. 1982; transf. to Assoc. of British Insurers on its formation, as Manager, Legislation, 1985, Chief Exec., 1987–93. *Recreations:* reading, photography, sailing, theatre. *Address:* 10 Parkhill Road, E4 7ED.

JONES, Dr Michael Barry; HM Chief Inspector of Mines, Health and Safety Executive, 1986–92; *b* 28 April 1932; *s* of Mynorydd Jones and Dorothy Anne Jones; *m* 1957, Josephine Maura (*née* Dryden); two *d*. *Educ:* Alsop High Sch., Liverpool; Leeds Univ. (BSc; PhD 1956). CEng, FIMinE 1959. Trainee, NCB, 1956; Underofficial, Whitwick Colliery, 1959; Undermanager, Rawdon, Ellistown and Donisthorpe Collieries, 1961; HM Inspector of Mines and Quarries, Lancs, 1965; HM Dist Inspector of Mines and Quarries, Yorks, 1974; HM Sen. Dist Inspector, Scotland, 1980; HM Dep. Chief Inspector, 1982. *Publications:* author and co-author of papers in The Mining Engineer. *Recreation:* growing and showing sweet peas. *Address:* The Old Farm, Christleton, Chester CH3 7AS. *T:* Chester (01244) 336204.

JONES, Michael Frederick; Political Editor, since 1984, Associate Editor, since 1990, The Sunday Times; *b* 3 July 1937; *s* of late Glyn Frederick Jones and of Elizabeth (*née* Coopey); *m* 1959, Sheila Joan Dawes; three *s*. *Educ:* Crypt Grammar Sch., Gloucester. Reporter: Maidenhead Advertiser, 1956–59; Northern Echo, Darlington, 1959–61; Manchester Evening News, 1961–64; Labour reporter, Financial Times, 1964–65; Industrial reporter, Daily Telegraph, 1965–67; News Editor, later Asst Editor, Times Business News, 1967–70; Managing Editor, The Asian, Hong Kong, 1971; Sunday Times: Associate News Editor, 1972–75; political correspondent, 1975–84. Chm., Parly Press Gallery, 1989–91. *Recreations:* exploring Britain, reading history. *Address:* The Sunday Times, 1 Pennington Street, E1 9XW. *T:* 0171–782 5000. *Club:* Buck's.

JONES, Rt. Rev. Michael Hugh Harold B.; *see* Bedford-Jones.

JONES, Hon. Mrs Miller; *see* Askwith, Hon. B. E.

JONES, Dr Nevin Campbell H.; *see* Hughes Jones.

JONES, Nigel David; MP (Lib Dem) Cheltenham, since 1992; *b* 30 March 1948; *m* 1981, Katy Grinnell; one *s* twin *d*. *Educ:* Prince Henry's Grammar Sch., Evesham. With Westminster Bank, 1965–67; computer programmer, ICL Computers, 1967–70; systems analyst, Vehicle and Gen. Insce, 1970–71; systems programmer, Atkins Computing, 1971; systems designer and consultant, ICL Computers, 1971–. Contested (L) Cheltenham, 1979. Lib Dem spokesman on sci., res. and new technologies, 1993–. *Address:* House of Commons, SW1A 0AA.

JONES, Nigel John I.; *see* Inglis-Jones.

JONES, Noel Andrew Stephen; HM Diplomatic Service; Ambassador to Kazakhstan, since 1993; *b* 22 Dec. 1940; *s* of Ernest Walter Jones and Merlyn Edith (*née* Jones); *m* 1963, Jean Rosemary Cheval; one *s* one *d*. *Educ:* St Joseph's Coll., London. With Jenkins Wood, Chartered Accountants, 1958–61; joined HM Diplomatic Service, 1962; served Zagreb, Hamburg, Bangkok, Taiwan, 1963–72; FCO, 1972–74; Sarajevo (lang. studies), 1975; Third Sec. (Commercial), Belgrade, 1975–79; Second Sec. (Econ. then Pol), Bonn, 1979–83; Russian lang. studies, Sussex Univ., 1984–85; Hd of Chancery and Dep. Hd of Mission, Ulan Baatar, 1985–87; Hd of Post, Seattle, 1987–90; Press Attaché and Hd of Press and Public Affairs, Moscow, 1991–93. *Recreations:* field sports, gardening, travelling, sailing. *Address:* c/o Foreign and Commonwealth Office, King Charles Street, SW1A 2AH.

JONES, Rt. Rev. Noël Debroy; *see* Sodor and Man, Bishop of.

JONES, Norman Arthur W.; *see* Ward-Jones.

JONES, Dr (Norman) Fielding, FRCP; Consultant Physician, St Thomas' Hospital, London, 1967–93, now Emeritus; *b* 3 May 1931; *s* of William John and Winifred Jones; *m* 1958, Ann Pye Chavasse; three *s*. *Educ:* Christ Coll., Brecon; King's Coll., Cambridge (MA 1957; MD 1966); St Thomas' Hosp., London. FRCP 1970. Rockefeller Fellow, Univ. of N Carolina, 1963–64. Physician, King Edward VII's Hosp. for Officers, 1977–; Consulting Physician, Metropolitan Police, 1980–92; Hon. Consulting Physician: to the Army, 1980–93; to Royal Hosp., Chelsea, 1987–93; CMO, Equitable Life Assurance Soc., 1985–. Vice Chm., West Lambeth HA, 1989–90. Royal College of Physicians: Sen. Censor and Vice Pres., 1989–90; Treasurer, 1991–; Chm., Cttee on Renal Disease, 1980–92; Chm., Cttee on Legal Aspects of Medicine, 1990–93. Special Trustee, St

Thomas' Hosp., 1990–94. Member: Med. Res. Soc., 1962–; Assoc. of Physicians of GB and Ire., 1968–. FRSA 1991. *Publications:* (ed) Recent Advances in Renal Disease, 1975; (ed with Sir Douglas Black) Renal Disease, 1979; (ed with D. K. Peters) Recent Advances in Renal Medicine, 1982. *Recreations:* iconology, music. *Address:* 1 Annesley Road, SE3 0JX. *T:* 0181–856 0583.

JONES, Norman Henry; QC 1985; **His Honour Judge Norman Jones;** a Circuit Judge, since 1992; *b* 12 Dec. 1941; *s* of Henry Robert Jones and Charlotte Isobel Scott Jones; *m* 1970, Trudy Helen Chamberlain; two *s* one *d. Educ:* Bideford Grammar School; North Devon Tech. Coll.; Univ. of Leeds (LLB, LLM). Called to the Bar, Middle Temple, 1968. A Recorder, 1987–92. Contested Leeds NW (SDP), 1983; Mem., Nat. Cttee, SDP, 1982–84. *Recreation:* boating. *Address:* The Crown Court, Oxford Road, Leeds.

JONES, Norman Stewart C.; *see* Carey Jones.

JONES, Sir (Owen) Trevor, Kt 1981; formerly Councillor, Liverpool Metropolitan District Council; *b* 1927; *s* of Owen and Ada Jones, Dyserth. Mem., Liverpool City Council, 1968, Liverpool Metropolitan District Council, 1973–91 (Leader, 1981–83). Pres., Liberal Party, 1972–73; contested (L): Liverpool, Toxteth, Feb. 1974 and Gillingham, Oct. 1974. *Address:* 221 Queen's Drive, Liverpool L15 6YE.

JONES, Penry; Chief Assistant (Television) (formerly Deputy Head of Programme Services), IBA (formerly ITA), 1971–82, retired; *b* 18 Aug. 1922; *s* of Joseph William and Edith Jones; *m* Beryl Joan Priestley; two *d. Educ:* Rock Ferry High Sch.; Liverpool Univ. Gen. Sec., YMCA, Altrincham, 1940; Sec., SCM, Southern Univs, 1945; Industrial Sec., Iona Community, 1948; Religious Programmes Producer, ABC Television, 1958; Religious Programmes Officer of ITA, 1964; Head of Religious Broadcasting, BBC, 1967. *Recreations:* hill-walking, swimming, watching Rugby football. *Address:* Erraid House, Isle of Iona, Argyll PA76 6SJ. *T:* Iona (01681) 700448.

JONES, Brig. Percival de Courcy, OBE 1953; Chief Secretary, The Royal Life Saving Society, 1965–75; *b* 9 Oct. 1913; *s* of P. de C. Jones, Barnsley; *m* 1st, 1947, Anne Hollins (marr. diss., 1951); one *s*; 2nd, 1962, Elaine Garnett. *Educ:* Oundle; RMC, Sandhurst. Commissioned KSLI 1933; Staff Coll., 1942; comd 1st Northamptons, Burma, 1945; Staff Coll. Instructor, 1949–50; AA & QMG, 11th Armoured Div., 1951–53; comd 1st KSLI, 1953–55; AQMG, War Office, 1955–58; NATO Defence Coll., 1958–59; Bde Comdr, 1959–62; retd 1962. Mem., Aylesbury Vale DC, 1976–79. Commonwealth Chief Sec., RLSS, 1965–75. Silver Medallion, Fedn Internat. de Sauvetage, 1976. *Recreation:* gardening. *Address:* 6 Port Hill Gardens, Shrewsbury, Shropshire SY3 8SH.

JONES, Peter Benjamin Gurner, CB 1991; Under Secretary; Director of Personnel, Board of Inland Revenue, 1984–92; *b* 25 Dec. 1932; *s* of Gurner Prince Jones and Irene Louise Jones (*née* Myall); *m* 1962, Diana Margaret Henly; one *s* one *d. Educ:* Bancroft's Sch.; St Catherine's Society, Oxford (BA (Hons) English Language and Literature). Inspector of Taxes, 1957; Inspector (Higher Grade), 1963; Sen. Inspector, 1969; Principal Inspector, 1975; Sen. Principal Inspector, 1980; Dir of Data Processing, Bd of Inland Revenue, 1981–84. Hon. Nat. Chm., CS Retirement Fellowship, 1994–. *Clubs:* Hampshire Rugby Union, Swanage and Wareham RFC.

JONES, Peter Derek; Deputy Chairman, Civil Service Appeal Board, since 1992; Secretary: Council of Civil Service Unions, 1980–92; Civil Service National Whitley Council (Trade Union Side), 1963–92; *b* 21 May 1932; *s* of Richard Morgan Jones and Phyllis Irene (*née* Lloyd); *m* 1962, Noreen Elizabeth (*née* Kemp). *Educ:* Wembley County Grammar School. National Service and TA, Green Jackets/Parachute Regt, 1950–56; Civil Service, Nat. Assistance Bd, 1952–59; Asst Sec., Civil Service Nat. Whitley Council, 1959–63. Chm., Civil Service Housing Assoc. Ltd, 1988– (Dir, 1963–81; Vice Chm., 1981–88); Dir, Civil Service Building Soc., 1963–87. Vice-Pres., RIPA, 1991–92 (Chm., 1987–90; Vice-Chm., 1986–87; Mem. Exec. Council, 1981–85); Member: Adv. Council, Civil Service Coll., 1982–92; Tourism and Leisure Industries EDC, 1987–92; Adv. Council, CS Occupational Health Service, 1988–92; Industrial Tribunals, 1992–. Trustee: Inst. of Contemporary Brit. History, 1985–; CS Benevolent Fund, 1992–. Editor: Whitley Bulletin, 1963–83; CCSU Bulletin, 1984–92. *Publications:* articles in RIPA and personnel management jls. *Recreations:* relaxing, reading, golf. *Address:* 10 Meyrick Park Crescent, Bournemouth BH3 7AQ. *T:* Bournemouth (01202) 554630, *Fax:* (01202) 311330. *Clubs:* Wig and Pen, Belfry; Mansion House (Poole); Middlesex CC.

JONES, Peter Eldon, FRIBA, FRTPI, FCSD, FRSA; Director, Association of Small Historic Towns and Villages of the UK, since 1993; *b* 11 Oct. 1927; *s* of Wilfrid Eldon Jones and Jessie Meikle (*née* Buchanan); *m* 1st, 1954, Gisela Marie von Arnswaldt; two *s* one *d*; 2nd, 1985, Claudia Milner-Brown (*née* Laurence). *Educ:* Surbiton County Grammar Sch.; Kingston Polytechnic; University College London. DipTP. Private practice, 1950–54; joined LCC Architects Dept, 1954; Dep. Schools Architect, LCC, 1960–65; Town Development Architect/Planner, 1965–71; Technical Policy Architect, GLC, 1971–74; Education Architect, ILEA, 1974–82; Acting Director of Architecture, 1980–82, Dir of Architecture and Superintending Architect of Metrop. Bldgs, 1982–86, GLC. Consultant, DES, subseq. DFE, 1988–92. Director: Interior Transformation Ltd, 1985–87; Watkins Gray Peter Jones, 1986–91. Part-time Lectr in Architectl Design, Kingston Poly., 1986–90. Mem., EC Adv. Cttee on Educn and Training in Architecture, 1987–92. Pres., Soc. of Chief Architects of Local Authorities, 1984–85; Mem. Council, Chm. Membership Cttee, and Vice-Pres., RIBA, 1985–87. *Publications:* articles and papers on town development, educn building, housing design and planning. *Recreations:* building, photography, travel, golf. *Address:* Dene Cottage, The Green, Pirbright, Surrey GU24 0JE. *Club:* Woking Golf.

JONES, Peter Ferry, MA, MChir, FRCS, FRCSE; Surgeon to the Queen in Scotland, 1977–85; Honorary Consulting Surgeon, Woodend Hospital and Royal Aberdeen Children's Hospital, Aberdeen (Consultant Surgeon, 1958–85); Clinical Professor of Surgery, University of Aberdeen, 1983–85, now Emeritus; *b* 29 Feb. 1920; *s* of Ernest and Winifred Jones; *m* 1950, Margaret Thomson; two *s* two *d. Educ:* Emmanuel Coll., Cambridge (MA); St Bartholomew's Hosp. Med. Sch., London (MB, MChir). FRCS 1948; FRCSE 1964. Served War, RAMC, 1944–46, Captain. House Surgeon, St Bartholomew's Hosp., 1943; Surg. Registrar, N Middlesex Hosp., 1948–51; Surg. Tutor, St Bartholomew's Hosp., 1951–53; Sen. Surg. Registrar, Central Middlesex Hosp. and the Middlesex Hosp., London, 1953–57; Reader in Surg. Paediatrics, Univ. of Aberdeen, 1965–83. *Publications:* Abdominal Access and Exposure (with H. A. F. Dudley), 1965; Emergency Abdominal Surgery in Infancy, Childhood and Adult Life, 1974, 2nd edn 1987; (jtly) Integrated Clinical Science: Gastroenterology, 1984; A Colour Atlas of Colo-Rectal Surgery, 1985; papers on paediatric and gen. surgery in Brit. Jl of Surg., BMJ, Lancet, etc. *Recreation:* hill walking. *Address:* 7 Park Road, Cults, Aberdeen AB1 9HR. *T:* Aberdeen (01224) 867702.

JONES, Peter George Edward Fitzgerald, CB 1985; Director, Atomic Weapons Research Establishment, 1982–87, retired; Consultant to the Ministry of Defence, since 1987; *b* 7 June 1925; *s* of John Christopher Jones and Isobel (*née* Howell); *m* 1st; two *s*; 2nd, Jacqueline Angela (*née* Gilbert); two *s* one *d. Educ:* various schs; Dulwich Coll.; London Univ. (BSc (Special) Physics 1st Cl. Hons 1951). FInstP. Served RAF, flying duties, 1943–47. GEC Res. Labs, 1951–54; AWRE and Pacific Test Site, 1955–63; Asst Dir of Res., London Communications Security, 1963; Atomic Weapons Research Establishment: Supt, Electronics Res., 1964; Head, Electronics Div., 1966; Head, Special Projs, 1971; Chief, Warhead Develt, 1974; Principal Dep. Dir, 1980. *Recreations:* flying, motoring. *Address:* Rhyd Felin, Upper Llanover, Abergavenny, Gwent NP7 9DD. *T:* Nantyderry (01873) 880779.

JONES, Peter Llewellyn G.; *see* Gwynn-Jones.

JONES, Peter Trevor S.; *see* Simpson-Jones.

JONES, Sir Philip; *see* Jones, Sir T. P.

JONES, Philip Graham, CEng, FIChemE, FIExpE; Deputy Director of Technology and Health Sciences Division (formerly Technology Division), Health and Safety Executive, 1986–95; *b* 3 June 1937; *s* of Sidney and Olive Jones; *m* 1961, Janet Ann Collins; one *s* three *d. Educ:* Univ. of Aston in Birmingham (BSc). Eur Ing 1989. Professional position in UK explosives industry, 1961–68 and 1972–76; service with Australian Public Service, 1969–71, with UK Civil Service, 1976–95; HM Chief Inspector of Explosives, HSE, 1981–86. Mem., Accreditation Bd, 1987–90, Professional Develt Cttee, 1988–91, IChemE. *Publications:* articles in The Chemical Engineer and Explosives Engineer. *Recreations:* bridge, reading, curling. *Address:* 4 Grenville Drive, Much Wenlock, Shropshire TF13 6HB. *T:* Much Wenlock (01952) 727592.

JONES, Philip James, DPhil; FBA 1984; FRHistS; Fellow and Tutor, Modern History, 1963–89, Librarian, 1965–89, Brasenose College, Oxford, now Emeritus Fellow; *b* 19 Nov. 1921; *s* of John David Jones and Caroline Susan Jones (*née* Davies); *m* 1954, Carla Susini; one *s* one *d. Educ:* St Dunstan's College; Wadham College, Oxford (1st class Hons Mod. Hist. 1945, MA, DPhil). Senior Demy, Magdalen College, Oxford, 1945–49; Amy Mary Preston Road Scholar, 1946; Bryce Research Student, 1947; Asst in History, Glasgow Univ., 1949–50; Leeds University: Lectr in Med. Hist., 1950–61; Reader in Med. Hist., 1961–63; Eileen Power Meml Student, 1956–57. Corresp. Mem., Deputazione Toscana di Storia Patria, 1975–. Serena Medal for Italian Studies, British Acad., 1988. *Publications:* The Malatesta of Rimini, 1974; Economia e Societa nell'Italia medievale, 1980; contribs to: Cambridge Economic History, Vol. 1, 2nd edn, 1966; Storia d'Italia, vol. 2, 1974; Storia d'Italia, Annali, Vol. 1, 1978; The Italian City-State: from commune to signoria, 1995; articles and reviews in hist. jls. *Address:* 167 Woodstock Road, Oxford OX2 7NA. *T:* Oxford (01865) 57953; Piazza Pitti 3, Florence, Italy. *T:* (55) 282924.

JONES, Philip (Mark), CBE 1986 (OBE 1977); Principal, Trinity College of Music, London, 1988–94; *b* 12 March 1928; *m* 1956, Ursula Strebi. *Educ:* Royal College of Music (FRCM 1983 (ARCM 1947)). Principal Trumpet with all major orchestras in London, 1949–72; Founder and Dir, 1951–86, Philip Jones Brass Ensemble; Head of Dept of Wind and Percussion, Royal Northern Coll. of Music, Manchester, 1975–77; Head of Wind and Percussion Dept, GSMD, 1983–88. Member: Arts Council of GB, 1984–88; Royal Soc. of Musicians of GB. Over 50 gramophone records. Vice-Chm., Musicians Benevolent Fund, 1993–. Gov., Chetham's Sch., Manchester, 1988–94. FRNCM 1977; FGSM 1984. Hon. FTCL 1988; Hon. FRAM 1991. FRSA. Freeman, City of London, 1988. Grand Prix du Disque, 1977; Composers Guild Award, 1979; Cobbett Medal, Musicians' Co., 1986; Cesare Bendinelli Award, Verona, 1993. *Publications:* Joint Editor, Just Brass series (for Chester Music London), 1975–89. *Recreations:* history, ski-ing, mountain walking. *Address:* 14 Hamilton Terrace, NW8 9UG. *T:* 0171–286 9155.

JONES, Piers Nicholas L.; *see* Legh-Jones.

JONES, Mrs Rachel (Marianne); *b* 4 Aug. 1908; *d* of John Powell Jones Powell, solicitor, Brecon, and Kathleen Mamie Powell; *m* 1935, Very Rev. William Edward Jones (*d* 1974); one *s* three *d. Educ:* Princess Helena Coll.; Bedford Coll., University of London. Subwarden, Time and Talents Settlement, Bermondsey, 1931–32; Member: Bd of Governors, Fairbridge Farm Sch., Western Australia, 1945–49; Council for Wales and Mon, 1959–66; Nat. Governor for Wales of BBC and Chm. of Broadcasting Council for Wales, 1960–65. Member: Governing Body of the Church in Wales, 1953–78; Court and Council of Nat. Museum of Wales, 1962–78; St Fagan's Welsh Folk Museum Cttee, 1978–83; Pres., St David's Diocesan Mothers' Union, 1965–70. *Recreations:* music, gardening. *Address:* 3 Albeny Gate, Belmont Hill, St Albans, Herts AL1 1BH.

JONES, Raymond Edgar; HM Diplomatic Service, retired; *b* 6 June 1919; *s* of Edgar George Jones, Portsmouth; *m* 1942, Joan Mildred Clark; one *s* two *d. Educ:* Portsmouth Northern Grammar Sch. Entered Admiralty service as Clerical Officer, 1936; joined RAF, 1941; commissioned, 1943; returned to Admty as Exec. Officer, 1946; transf. to Foreign Service, 1948; Singapore, 1949; Second Sec., Rome, 1950; Bahrain, 1952; Rio de Janeiro, 1955; Consul, Philadelphia, 1958; FO, 1961; First Sec., Copenhagen, 1963; Consul, Milan, 1965; Toronto (Dir of British Week), 1966; Dep. High Comr, Adelaide, 1967–71; FCO, 1971–76; Consul-Gen., Genoa, 1976–79. *Recreations:* music, gardening. *Address:* Oaklands, 3 Old Hall Drive, Dersingham, Norfolk PE31 6JT.

JONES, Raymond Francis, OBE 1986; HM Diplomatic Service; High Commissioner, Honiara, Solomon Islands, since 1991; *b* 15 Nov. 1935; *s* of late Hugh and Jessie Jones; *m* 1957, Maurag Annat (*d* 1994); two *d. Educ:* Liverpool Collegiate Sch. Nat. Service, RAF, 1954–56. Joined Foreign Office, 1953; served Amman, Tokyo, Cairo, Accra, 1956–70; Second Sec., FCO, 1970–73; Consul, Seattle, 1973–78; First Sec., 1978; on loan to DoI, 1978–82; New Delhi, 1982–86; Dep. Consul-Gen., Chicago, 1986–91. *Recreations:* music, sport, reading. *Address:* c/o Foreign and Commonwealth Office, SW1A 2AH.

JONES, Reginald Victor, CH 1994; CB 1946; CBE 1942; FRS 1965; Professor of Natural Philosophy, University of Aberdeen, 1946–81, now Emeritus; *b* 29 Sept. 1911; *s* of Harold Victor and Alice Margaret Jones; *m* 1940, Vera (*d* 1992), *d* of late Charles and Amelia Cain; one *s* two *d. Educ:* Alleyn's; Wadham Coll., Oxford (Exhibitioner; MA, DPhil, 1934; Hon. Fellow, 1968); Balliol Coll., Oxford (Skynner Senior Student in Astronomy, 1934–36; Hon. Fellow 1981). Air Ministry: Scientific Officer, 1936 (seconded to Admiralty, 1938–39); Air Staff, 1939; Asst Dir of Intelligence, 1941, Dir, 1946; Dir of Scientific Intelligence, MoD, 1952–53; Mem., Carriers Panel, 1962–63; Chm., Air Defence Working Party, 1963–64; Scientific Adv. Council, War Office, 1963–66. Chairman: Infra-Red Cttee, Mins of Supply and Aviation, 1950–64; British Transport Commn Res. Adv. Council, 1954–55; Safety in Mines Res. Advisory Bd, 1956–60 (Mem., 1950–56); Electronics Res. Council, Mins of Aviation and Technol., 1964–70. Royal Society: Chm., Paul Fund Cttee, 1962–84; a Vice-Pres., 1971–72; Chairman: Inst. of Physics Cttee on Univ. Physics, 1961–63; British Nat. Cttee for History of Science, Medicine and Technol., 1970–78 (Chm., Org. Cttee, Internat. Congress, 1977); President: Crabtree Foundation, 1958; Sect. A, British Assoc., 1971. Also a mem., various cttees on electronics, scientific res., measurement, defence and educn. Rapporteur, European Convention on Human Rights, 1970. Companion, Operational Res. Soc., 1983. Governor, Dulwich Coll., 1965–79; Life Governor, Haileybury Coll., 1978. Jt Editor, Notes and Records of the Royal Society, 1969–89. Vis. Prof., Univ. of Colorado, 1982;

Visitor, RMCS, 1983. Hon. Member: Manchester Lit. and Phil. Soc., 1981; American Soc. for Precision Engrg, 1990. Hon. Fellow: College of Preceptors, 1978; IERE, 1982; Inst. of Measurement and Control, 1984; British Horological Inst., 1985. Hon. Freeman, Clockmakers' Co., 1984. Hon. DSc: Strathclyde, 1969; Kent, 1980; Westminster Coll., Missouri, 1992; Aberdeen, 1996; DUniv: York, 1976; Open, 1978; Surrey, 1979; Hon. LLD Bristol, 1979. Bailie of Benachie, 1980. US Medal of Freedom with Silver Palm, 1946; US Medal for Merit, 1947; BOIMA Prize, Inst. of Physics, 1934; Duddell Medal, Physical Soc., 1960; Parsons Medal, 1967; Hartley Medal, Inst. of Measurement and Control, 1972; Mexican Min. of Telecommunications Medal, 1973; Rutherford Medal, USSR, 1977; R. G. Mitchell Medal, 1979; Old Crows Medal, 1980; R. V. Jones Intelligence Award, CIA, 1993. Hon. Mem., US Air Force, 1982; Hon. Mayor, San Antonio, Texas, 1983. *Publications:* Most Secret War (The Wizard War, USA, La Guerre Ultra Secrète, France), 1978; Future Conflict and New Technology, 1981; Some Thoughts on 'Star Wars', 1985; Instruments and Experiences, 1988; Reflections on Intelligence, 1989; lectures and papers on scientific subjects, defence, educn, engrg, history of science and policy. *Address:* 8 Queens Terrace, Aberdeen AB1 1XL. *T:* Aberdeen (01224) 648184. *Clubs:* Athenæum, Special Forces; Royal Northern (Aberdeen).

JONES, Rhona Mary; Chief Nursing Officer, St Bartholomew's Hospital, 1969–74, retired; *b* 7 July 1921; *d* of late Thomas Henry Jones and late Margaret Evelyn King; single. *Educ:* Liverpool; Alder Hey Children's Hosp.; St Mary's Hosp., Paddington. RSCN 1943; SRN 1945; SCM 1948. Post-Registration Training, and Staff Nurse, Queen Charlotte's Hosp., 1946–48; Ward Sister, 1948–50, Departmental Sister, 1950–52, St Mary's Hosp., Paddington; General Duty Nurse, Canada, 1952–53; Asst Matron, Gen. Infirmary, Leeds, 1953–57; Dep. Matron, Royal Free Hosp., London, 1957–59; Matron, Bristol Royal Hosp., 1959–67; Matron and Superintendent of Nursing, St Bartholomew's Hosp., 1968–69. Chm., Bristol Branch, Royal Coll. of Nursing, 1962–65; Member: Standing Nursing Adv. Cttee, Central Health Services Council, 1963–74; Exec. Cttee, Assoc. Nurse Administrators (formerly Assoc. Hosp. Matrons for England and Wales), 1963–74; Area Nurse Trng Cttee, SW Region, 1965–67; NE Metropolitan Area Nurse Training Cttee, 1969–74; E London Group Hosp. Management Cttee, 1969–74. Vice-Pres., Bristol Royal Hosp. Nurses League. *Recreations:* reading, travel, listening to music. *Address:* 26 Seaton Drive, Bedford MK40 3BG. *T:* Bedford (01234) 365868.

JONES, Air Vice-Marshal Rhys Tudor Brackley, CB 1990; FRCS; Senior Consultant, Royal Air Force Medical Branch, 1988–90; *b* 16 Nov. 1925; *s* of Sir Edgar Rees Jones, KBE and Lilian May Jones; *m* 1953, Irene Lilian, *d* of late Peter Valentine Spain Gammon; two *s*. *Educ:* King's Coll. Sch., Wimbledon; St Mary's Hosp., London (qualified 1950). House Surgeon to Mr Dickson-Wright and J. C. Goligher; joined RAF, 1952; Specialist in Surgery; Consultant, 1964; Hosp. service, Aden, Singapore, Germany, as gen. surgeon, special interest oncology; Hon. Consultant, Westminster Hosp., 1982; Cade Prof., RCS, 1981; Consultant Adviser in Surgery, 1982; Dean of Air Force Medicine, 1987. QHS, 1987–90. CStJ 1986. Lady Cade Medal, RCS, 1988. *Publications:* contribs to learned jls. *Address:* Glebelands, Wiveton Road, Blakeney, Norfolk NR25 7NJ. *T:* Cley (01263) 741093. *Club:* Royal Air Force.

JONES, Rev. Richard Granville; Chairman of East Anglia District, Methodist Church, 1983–93; President of the Methodist Conference, 1988–89; *b* 26 July 1926; *s* of Henry William and Ida Grace Jones; *m* 1955, Kathleen Stone; three *d*. *Educ:* Truro School, Cornwall; St John's Coll., Cambridge (MA); Manchester Univ. (BD). Instructor Officer, RN, 1947–49. Methodist Minister in Plymouth East, 1949–50; Area Sec., SCM, 1953–55; Minister: Sheffield North Circuit, 1955–59; Sheffield Carver Street, 1959–64; Birkenhead, 1964–69; Tutor, Hartley Victoria Coll., Manchester, 1969–70; Principal 1978–82; Minister, Fakenham and Wells Circuit, 1982–83. Editor, Epworth Review, 1991–. Hon. DD Hull, 1988. *Publications:* (ed) Worship for Today, 1968; (with A. Wesson) Towards a Radical Church, 1972; How goes Christian Marriage?, 1978; Groundwork of Worship and Preaching, 1980; Groundwork of Christian Ethics, 1984. *Recreations:* walking, reading, writing. *Address:* 35 Davies Road, West Bridgford, Nottingham NG2 5JE. *T:* West Bridgford (0115) 981 8597.

JONES, Richard M.; *see* Mansell-Jones.

JONES, Richard Phare D.; *see* Duncan-Jones.

JONES, Richard S.; *see* Stanton-Jones.

JONES, (Robert) Alun; QC 1989; a Recorder, since 1992; *b* 19 March 1949; *s* of late Owen Glyn Jones and of Violet Marion Jones (*née* Luxton); *m* 1974, Elizabeth Clayton; one *s* three *d*. *Educ:* Oldershaw Grammar Sch., Wallasey, Cheshire; Bristol Univ. (BSc 1970). Called to the Bar, Gray's Inn, 1972. Asst Recorder, 1988. Member: Senate of Inns of Court and the Bar, 1979–82; Gen. Council of the Bar, 1986–89; Sec., Criminal Bar Assoc., 1982–86. *Publication:* Jones on Extradition, 1995. *Recreations:* bridge, cricket, growing vegetables. *Address:* 3 Raymond Buildings, Gray's Inn, WC1R 5BH. *T:* 0171–831 3833.

JONES, Robert Brannock; MP (C) Hertfordshire West, since 1983; Minister of State (Minister for Construction and Planning), Department of the Environment, since 1995; *b* 26 Sept. 1950; *s* of Ray Elwin Jones and Iris Pamela Jones; *m* 1989, Jennifer Anne, *d* of late Lewis Emmanuel Sandercock and of Iris Delphia Sandercock, Braunton, Devon. *Educ:* Merchant Taylors' Sch.; Univ. of St Andrews (MA Hons Modern History). Marketing Develt Exec., Tay Textiles Ltd, Dundee, 1974–76; Head of Res., NHBC, 1976–78; Housing Policy Adviser, Conservative Central Office, 1978–79; Parly Adviser, Fedn of Civil Engrg Contractors, 1979–83. Member: St Andrews Burgh Council, 1972–75; Fife CC, 1973–75; Chiltern DC, 1979–83; Vice-Pres., Assoc. of Dist Councils, 1983–94. Parly Under-Sec. of State, DoE, 1994–95. Chairman: Environment Select Cttee, 1992–94 (Mem., 1983–94); Cons. Party Orgn Cttee, 1986–94. Pres., Dacorum Sports Council, 1984–. Vice-Pres., Wildlife Hosp. Trust, 1985–. Freeman, City of London; Liveryman, Merchant Taylors' Co. *Publications:* New Approaches to Housing, 1976; Watchdog: guide to the role of the district auditor, 1978; Ratepayers' Defence Manual, 1980; Economy and Local Government, 1981; Roads and the Private Sector, 1982; Town and Country Chaos: critique of the planning system, 1982. *Recreations:* squash, tennis, shove-halfpenny, music. *Address:* Davidson House, 168 Queensway, Hemel Hempstead, Herts HP2 5HX. *Clubs:* Rugby; Conservative (Tring).

JONES, Dr (Robert) Brinley, FSA; Chairman, Cathedrals and Churches Commission of the Church in Wales, since 1994; *b* 27 Feb. 1929; *yr s* of John Elias Jones and Mary Ann Jones (*née* Williams); *m* 1971, Stephanie Avril Hall; one *s*. *Educ:* Tonypandy Grammar Sch.; University Coll. Cardiff (BA Wales 1st cl. Hons 1950; DipEd 1951; Fellow 1984); Jesus Coll., Oxford (DPhil 1960); Internat. Inst. for Advanced Studies, Clayton, Mo (MA 1984). FSA 1971; FCP 1982. Commissioned RAF, 1955; Educn Officer, RAF Kidlington and Bicester, 1955–58. Asst Master, Penarth Grammar Sch., 1958–60; Lectr, UC Swansea, 1960–66; Asst Registrar, Univ. of Wales, 1966–69; Dir, Univ. of Wales Press, 1969–76; Warden, Llandovery Coll., 1976–88. Member: Literature Cttee, Welsh Arts Council, 1968–74, 1981–1987; Bd, British Council, 1987– (Chm., Welsh Cttee, 1987–); Broadcasting Standards Council, 1988–91. Chairman: European Assoc. of Teachers, 1965; Dinefwr Tourism Gp, 1988–. Member: Court and Council, Nat. Liby of Wales, 1974–82; Council, St David's UC, Lampeter, 1977– (Hon. Fellow 1987); Court, UC Swansea, 1983–; Council, Trinity Coll., Carmarthen, 1984–; Governing Body, Church in Wales, 1981– (Chm., Provincial Validating Bd for Ministerial Educn, 1990–); Managing Trustee, St Michael's Theol Coll., 1982–94. Hon. Mem., Druidic Order, Gorsedd of Bards, 1979–; Mem., Welsh Acad., 1981–; Vice-Pres., Llangollen Internat. Musical Eisteddfod, 1989–. Fellow, Royal Commonwealth Soc., 1988–91. Editor, The European Teacher, 1964–69. Hon. DD Faraston Theol Seminary, Longview, WA, 1993. *Publications:* The Old British Tongue, 1970; (ed and contrib.) Anatomy of Wales, 1972; (ed with M. Stephens) Writers of Wales, 1970– (80 titles published by 1994); (ed with R. Bromwich) Astudiaethau ar yr Hengerdd: studies in old Welsh poetry, 1978; Introducing Wales, 1978, 3rd edn 1988; Prifysgol Rhydychen a'i Chysylltiadau Cymreig, 1983; Certain Scholars of Wales, 1986; (ed with D. Ellis Evans) Cofio'r Dafydd, 1987; (contrib.) C. N. D. Cole, The New Wales, 1990; (introd.) Songs of Praises: the English hymns and elegies of William Williams Pantycelyn 1717–1791, 1991; Prize Days: a headmaster remembers his school 1976–1987, 1993; William Salesbury, 1994; A Lanterne to their Feete: remembering Rhys Prichard 1579–1644, 1994; articles and reviews in learned jls. *Recreations:* music, farming, walking. *Address:* Drovers Farm, Porthyrhyd, Llanwrda, Dyfed SA19 8DF. *T:* Pumpsaint (01558) 650649.

JONES, Sir Robert (Edward), Kt 1989; author; sporting and political commentator; Founder Chairman, Robt Jones Investments Ltd, 1982–92; *b* 24 Nov. 1939; *s* of Edward Llewyllan and Joyce Lillian Jones; *m*; two *s* two *d*. *Educ:* Victoria Univ. of Wellington. Leader, New Zealand Party, Gen. Elect., 1984. Chm., NZ Winter Olympics Cttee, 1988. New Zealand Commemoration Medal, 1990. *Publications:* New Zealand Boxing Yearbooks, 1972 and 1973; Jones on Property, 1977, 6th edn 1979; NZ The Way I Want It, 1978; Travelling, 1980; Letters, 1981; The Permit (a philosophic novel), 1984; Wimp Walloping, 1989; Prancing Pavonine Charlatons, 1990; 80's Letters, 1990; Punchlines, 1991; A Year of It, 1992; Treading Water, 1993. *Recreations:* reading, writing, gardening, trout-fishing, tennis, travel. *Address:* Melling, Lower Hutt, New Zealand; Turangi, Lake Taupo, New Zealand; Darling Point, Sydney, Australia.

JONES, (Robert) Gerallt; writer; Warden of Gregynog Hall, University of Wales, since 1989; *b* 11 Sept. 1934; *s* of Rev. R. E. Jones and Elizabeth Jones, Nefyn, Wales; *m* 1962, Susan Lloyd Griffith; two *s* one *d*. *Educ:* Denstone; University of Wales (University Student Pres., 1956–57). Sen. English Master, Sir Thomas Jones Sch., Amlwch, 1957–60; Lectr in Educn, University Coll., Aberystwyth, 1961–65; Prin., Mandeville Teachers' Coll., Jamaica, 1965–67; Warden and Headmaster, Llandovery Coll., 1967–76; Fellow in Creative Writing, Univ. of Wales, 1976–77; Sen. Tutor, Extra-Mural Dept, UCW, Aberystwyth, 1979–89. Director: Sgrîn 82, 1981–83; S4C, 1991–. Chm., Wales Film Council, 1992; Mem., Welsh Books Council, 1989–. Member: Gov. Body, Church in Wales, 1959–; Welsh Acad. (Yr Academi Gymreig), 1959– (Vice-Chm., 1981; Chm., 1982–87); Broadcasting Council for Wales; Welsh Arts Council (Chm., Film Cttee, 1989–); Univ. Council, Aberystwyth. FRSA. Editor: Impact (the Church in Wales quarterly); Taliesin, 1987–. Nat. Eisteddfod Prose Medal, 1977, 1979; Hugh McDiarmid Trophy, 1987; Welsh Arts Council Poetry Prize, 1990. *Publications: poetry:* Ymysg Y Drain, 1959; Cwlwm, 1962; Jamaican Landscape, 1969; Cysgodion, 1973; (ed) Poetry of Wales 1930–1970, 1975; Dyfal Gerddwyr y Maes, 1981; Cerddi 1955–89, 1989 (Poetry Prize, Welsh Arts Council, 1989): *novels:* Y Foel Fawr, 1960; Naddig Gwyn, 1963; Triptych, 1978; Cafflogion, 1979; *short stories:* Gwared Y Gwirion, 1966; *criticism:* Yn Ffrwd i'r Eos, 1962; (ed) Fy Nghymru, 1962; The Welsh Literary Revival, 1966; T. S. Eliot, 1981; Dathlu, 1985; Seicoleg Cardota, 1989; The Writer's Craft, 1992; *autobiography:* Jamaica, Y Flwyddyn Gyntaf, 1974; Bardsey, 1976; Jamaican Interlude, 1977; Murmur Llawer Man, 1980; *travel:* Teithiau Gerallt, 1978; Pererindota, 1978; *drama:* Tair Drama, 1988. *Recreations:* cricket, journalism. *Address:* Lerry Dale, Dolybont, Borth, Aberystwyth, Wales SY24 5LX.

JONES, Robert Gwilym L.; *see* Lewis-Jones.

JONES, Robert Hefin, CVO 1969; PhD; Under Secretary, Welsh Office, 1980–92; *b* 30 June 1932; *s* of late Owen Henry and Elizabeth Jones, Blaenau Ffestiniog. *Educ:* Ysgol Sir Ffestiniog; University Coll. of Wales, Aberystwyth (BSc); University of London (PhD). Asst Master, Whitgift Sch., 1957–63; HM Inspector of Schools (Wales), 1963; seconded to Welsh Office as Sec., Prince of Wales Investiture Cttee, and Personal Asst to the Earl Marshal, 1967; Welsh Office: Principal, 1969; Asst Sec. 1972; Hd, Educn Dept, 1980–92. Member: HEFCW, 1992–; Council on Tribunals, 1993–. Dir, WNO, 1992–94; Mem., Welsh Cttee, Live Music Now, 1992–. *Recreations:* music, reading, cooking. *Address:* 34 The Grange, Llandaff, Cardiff CF5 2LH. *T:* Cardiff (01222) 564573.

JONES, Prof. Robert Maynard, FBA 1993; Professor of Welsh Language and Literature, University of Wales, 1980–89, now Professor Emeritus; *b* 20 May 1929; *s* of Sydney Valentine Jones and Mary Edith Jones; *m* 1952, Anne Elizabeth James; one *s* one *d*. *Educ:* Univ. of Wales (BA 1949; MA 1951; PhD 1965; DLitt 1979); Univ. of Ireland; Laval Univ., Québec. Teaching in Llanidloes and Llangefni, 1952–54; Lectr, Trinity Coll., Carmarthen, 1954–56; University of Wales, Aberystwyth: Lectr in Educn, 1956–65; Lectr, Sen. Lectr, Reader, Prof. and Head of Dept of Welsh Language and Literature, 1965–89. Chm., Yr Academi Gymreig (Welsh Acad. of Letters), 1975–79; Vice-President, UCCF, 1990–. *Publications include:* Crwydro Môn, 1957; Nid yw Dŵr yn Plygu, 1958; I'r Arch, 1959; Y Tair Rhamant, 1960; Bad yn Wraig, 1960; Émile, 1963; Cyflwyno'r Gymraeg, 1964; Cymraeg i Oedolion, I & II, 1965–66; Y Dyn na Ddaeth Adref, 1966; Ci wrth y Drws, 1968; Highlights in Welsh Literature, 1969; Daw'r Pasg i Bawb, 1969; System in Child Language, 1970; Pedwar Emynydd, 1970; Sioc o'r Gofod, 1971; Allor Wydn, 1971; Traed Prydferth, 1973; Tafod y Llenor, 1974; (with M. E. Roberts) Cyfeiriadur i'r Athro Iaith I–III, 1974–79; Llenyddiaeth Gymraeg 1937–1972, 1975; Llên Cymru a Chrefydd, 1977; Pwy laddodd Miss Wales, 1977; Seiliau Beirniadaeth, 4 vols, 1984–88; Hunllef Arthur, 1986; (with Gwyn Davies) The Christian Heritage of Welsh Education, 1986; (with Gwyn Thomas) The Dragon's Pen, 1986; Llenyddiaeth Gymraeg 1902–1936, 1987; Selected Poems (trans. Joseph P. Clancy), 1987; Blodeugerdd Barddas o'r 19 Ganrif, 1988; (with Rhiannon Ifans) Gloywi Iaith I–III, 1988; Casgliad o Gerddi, 1989; Crio Chwerthin, 1990; Dawn Gweddwon, 1991; Language Regained, 1993; Cyfriniaeth Gymraeg, 1994; Canu Arnaf, 1994; Crist a Chenedlaetholdeb, 1994. *Recreation:* walking. *Address:* Tandderwen, Ffordd Llanbadarn, Aberystwyth SY23 1HB. *T:* Aberystwyth (01970) 623603.

JONES, Robin Francis McN.; *see* McNab Jones.

JONES, R(obin) Huws, CBE 1969; Associate Director, Joseph Rowntree Memorial Trust, 1972–76 (Consultant, 1976–78); *b* 1 May 1909; *m* 1944, Enid Mary Horton; one *s* two *d*. *Educ:* Liverpool Univ. Frances Wood Prizeman, Royal Statistical Society. Lectr, Social Science Dept, Liverpool Univ., 1937–39; Staff Tutor (City of Lincoln) Oxford Univ. Extra-mural Delegacy, 1939–47; Dir of Social Science Courses, University Coll., Swansea, 1948–61; Principal, Nat. Inst. for Social Work Training, 1961–72. Visiting Prof.,

University of Minnesota, 1964; Heath Clark Lectr, University of London, 1969. Member: Cttee on Local Authority and Allied Personal Social Services, 1965–68; NE Metropolitan Reg. Hosp. Bd, 1967–72; Chief Scientist's Cttee, DHSS, 1971–77; Scientific Advr to DHSS and to Welsh Office, 1977–82. Mem., Ciba Foundn Cttee on Compensation in Biomedical Research, 1979–80. Founder mem., Swansea Valley Project Cttee, 1961–. Pres., Internat. Assoc. of Schools of Social Work, 1976–80. Hon. Fellow, UC Swansea, 1986. Hon. LLD Wales, 1982. *Publications:* The Doctor and the Social Services, 1971; contributions to journals. *Recreation:* University of the Third Age. *Address:* 3 Clifton Lodge, York YO3 6NP. *T:* York (01904) 655023.

JONES, Roger; *see* Jones, James R.

JONES, Roger Charles M.; *see* Moylan-Jones.

JONES, Ronald Christopher H.; *see* Hope-Jones.

JONES, Brigadier Ronald M.; *see* Montague-Jones.

JONES, Group Captain Royden Anthony; RAF retired; Regional Chairman of Industrial Tribunals, London (Central) Region, 1975–86; *b* 11 June 1925; *s* of Daniel Richard Glyndwr Jones and Hilda Margaret Jones (*née* Carruthers); *m* 1st, 1948, Krystyna Emilia Kumor (decd); one *s*; 2nd, 1955, Peggy Elizabeth Martin; one *s*. *Educ:* Torquay Grammar Sch. Trooper, Household Cavalry, 1943; RMC, Sandhurst, 1944; Captain, Arab Legion armoured car squadron, 1945–48. Qualified as solicitor, 1949; joined RAF Legal Services as prosecuting officer, 1950; RAF Staff Coll., 1961; served as Dep. Dir of Legal Services (RAF), in Cyprus and Germany, retiring as Gp Captain, 1975. *Publication:* Manual of Law for Kenya Armed Forces, 1971. *Recreations:* country pursuits, reading, house maintenance, photography. *Address:* Hill Top House, Staunton Harold, Ashby-de-la-Zouch, Leics LE65 1RW. *T:* Melbourne (01332) 862583. *Club:* Royal Air Force.

JONES, Samuel, DL; Town Clerk, Corporation of London, since 1991; *b* 27 Dec. 1939; *s* of Samuel Jones and late Sarah Johnston Jones (*née* McCulloch); *m* 1964, Jean Ann Broadhurst; two *d*. *Educ:* Morpeth Grammar Sch.; Manchester Univ. (LLB); Kent Univ. (MA). Admitted Solicitor, 1964. Asst Solicitor, Macclesfield Bor. Council, 1964–67; Asst Town Clerk, Bedford Bor. Council, 1967–71; Head of Legal Div., Coventry CBC, 1971–73; Head of Admin and Legal Dept, Sheffield Dist Council, 1973–76; Chief Exec. and County Clerk, Leics CC, and Clerk of Lieutenancy, 1976–91. DL Leics, 1992. *Recreations:* dog and coastal walking. *Address:* Chapel Knoll, 26 Hobbs Hill, Croyde EX33 1LZ. *T:* Croyde (01271) 890210; 20 Harestone Valley Road, Caterham, Surrey CR3 6HB. *T:* Oxted (01883) 344864.

JONES, Schuyler, DPhil; Director (formerly Curator and Head of Department of Ethnology and Prehistory), Pitt Rivers Museum, since 1985, and Fellow of Linacre College, since 1970, Oxford University; *b* 7 Feb. 1930; *s* of Schuyler Jones Jr and Ignace Mead Jones; *m* 1955, Lis Margit Søndergaard Rasmussen; one *s* one *d*. *Educ:* Edinburgh Univ. (MA Hons Anthropology); Oxford Univ. (DPhil Anthropology). Anthropological expeditions to: Atlas Mountains, Southern Algeria, French West Africa, Nigeria, 1951; French Equatorial Africa, Belgian Congo, 1952; East and Southern Africa, 1953; Morocco High Atlas, Algeria, Sahara, Niger River, 1954; Turkey, Iran, Afghanistan, Pakistan, India, Nepal, 1958–59; ten expeditions to Nuristan in the Hindu Kush, 1960–70; to Chinese Turkestan, 1985; Tibet and Gobi Desert, 1986; Southern China, Xinjiang, and Pakistan, 1988; Western Greenland, 1991; Greenland and E Africa, 1993. Asst Curator, Pitt Rivers Mus., 1970–71; Asst Curator and Univ. Lectr in Ethnology, 1971–85. Mem. Council, Royal Anthropological Inst., 1986–89. Trustee, Horniman Mus., 1989–94. *Publications:* Sous le Soleil Africain, 1955 (Under the African Sun, 1956); Annotated Bibliography of Nuristan (Kafiristan) and The Kalash Kafirs of Chitral, pt 1 1966, pt 2 1969; The Political Organization of the Kam Kafirs, 1967; Men of Influence in Nuristan, 1974; (jtly) Nuristan, 1979; Afghanistan, 1992; numerous articles. *Recreation:* travel in remote places. *Address:* Old Close Cottage, Chapel Lane, Enstone OX7 4LY. *T:* Enstone (01608) 677453.

JONES, Air Cdre Shirley Ann, CBE 1990; Director, Women's Royal Air Force, 1986–89; *d* of late Wilfred Esmond Jones, FRICS, and Louise May Betty Jones (*née* Dutton). *Educ:* Micklefield Sch., Seaford, Sussex; Open Univ. (BA 1992). Joined Royal Air Force, 1962; commnd 1962; served UK and Libya, 1962–71; Netherlands and UK, 1971–74; sc 1975; served UK, 1975–82; Dep. Dir, 1982–86. ADC 1986–89. *Recreations:* golf, music, gardening, cookery. *Club:* Royal Air Force.

JONES, Sir Simon (Warley Frederick) Benton, 4th Bt *cr* 1919; JP; *b* 11 Sept. 1941; *o s* of Sir Peter Fawcett Benton Jones, 3rd Bt, OBE, and Nancy (*d* 1974), *d* of late Warley Pickering; *S* father, 1972; *m* 1966, Margaret Fiona (OBE 1995), *d* of David Rutherford Dickson; three *s* two *d*. *Educ:* Eton; Trinity College, Cambridge (MA). JP Lincolnshire, 1971; High Sheriff, Lincs, 1977. *Heir: s* James Peter Martin Benton Jones, *b* 1 Jan. 1973. *Address:* Irnham Hall, Grantham, Lincs NG33 4JD. *T:* Corby Glen (01476) 550212.

JONES, Stephen; *see* Jones, John S.

JONES, Stephen Barry; MP (Lab) Alyn and Deeside, since 1983 (Flint East, 1970–83); *b* 1938; *s* of late Stephen and Grace Jones, Mancot, Flintshire; *m* Janet Jones (*née* Davies); one *s*. PPS to Rt Hon. Denis Healey, 1972–74; Parly Under-Sec. of State for Wales, 1974–79; Opposition spokesman on employment, 1980–83; Chief Opposition spokesman on Wales, 1983–87, 1988–92. Mem., Labour Shadow Cabinet, 1983–87 and 1988–92. Mem., Speaker's Panel of Chairmen, 1993–. Member: Govs, Nat Mus., Wales; Court, Univ. of Wales; Nat. Liby of Wales. *Address:* House of Commons, SW1A 0AA. *T:* 0171–219 3556, *Fax:* 0171–219 4027. *Clubs:* Connah's Quay Labour Party, Shotton Royal British Legion.

JONES, Stephen Morris; Chief Executive, Wigan Metropolitan Borough Council, since 1990; *b* 12 March 1948; *s* of Owain Morris Jones and late Sylvia Blanche Jones (*née* Moss); *m* 1970, Rosemary Diana Pilgrim; one *s* two *d*. *Educ:* Univ. of Manchester (BA Hons Town Planning, 1970). MRTPI 1972. Asst Chief Exec., Bolton MBC, 1978–85; Chief Exec., Blackburn BC, 1985–90. Mem., Soc. of Local Govt Chief Execs, 1985–. *Recreations:* family, walking, sport, reading. *Address:* Wigan Metropolitan Borough Council, New Town Hall, PO Box 36, Library Street, Wigan WN1 1NN. *T:* Wigan (01942) 827000.

JONES, Stephen Roger Curtis; education consultant, since 1994; Head of International Relations, Youth and General Branch, Department for Education, 1992–94; *b* 31 March 1944; *s* of Roger Henry Curtis Jones and Kate Alice Jones (*née* Pearson); *m* 1973, Janet Corkett; two *d*. *Educ:* Brentwood Sch., Essex; Univ. of Southampton (BA Hons French 1967; MA French 1968). MoD, 1968–71; UK Delegn to NATO, 1971–73; DES, 1973–81 (Private Sec. to Sec. of State, Rt Hon. Shirley Williams, 1976–78); Asst Dir, City of London Poly., 1982–85; Department of Education and Science: Staff Inspector, HM Inspectorate, 1986–88; Head, Internat. Relations Div., 1988–92. *Recreations:* walking, choral singing, preparing for life in France. *Address:* Marne, Southdown Road, Woldingham, Surrey CR3 7DP. *T:* Woldingham (01883) 653145.

JONES, Stewart Elgan; QC 1994; a Recorder, since 1990; *b* 20 Jan. 1945; *s* of late Gwilym John Jones and of Elizabeth (*née* Davies); *m* 1979, Jennifer Anne (*née* Syddall); two *d*, and one step *s* one step *d*. *Educ:* Cheltenham Coll.; Queen's Coll., Oxford (MA Mod. Langs). Called to the Bar, Gray's Inn, 1972; Mem., Western Circuit. *Recreations:* home, hearth, the great outdoors. *Address:* 3 Paper Buildings, Temple, EC4Y 7EU. *T:* 0171–583 8055.

JONES, S(tuart) Lloyd; *b* 26 Aug. 1917; *s* of Hugh and Edna Lloyd Jones, Liverpool; *m* 1942, Pamela Mary Hamilton-Williams, Heswall; one *s* three *d*. *Educ:* Rydal Sch.; Univ. of Liverpool. Solicitor, 1940; Dep. Town Clerk, Nottingham, 1950–53; Town Clerk of Plymouth, 1953–70; Chief Exec. Officer and Town Clerk of Cardiff, 1970–74; Chm., Welsh Health Technical Services Orgn, 1973–76. Chief Counting Officer, Welsh Referendum, 1979. US State Dept Foreign Leader Scholarship, 1962. One of Advisers to Minister of Housing and Local Govt on Amalgamation of London Boroughs, 1962; Indep. Inspector, extension of Stevenage New Town, 1964; Member: Adv. Cttee on Urban Transport Manpower, 1967–69; Cttee on Public Participation in Planning, 1969; PM's Cttee on Local Govt Rules of Conduct, 1973–74. Pres., Soc. of Town Clerks, 1972. Chm. of Governors, Plymouth Polytechnic, 1982–87. Hon. Fellow, Plymouth Polytechnic, 1987. Distinguished Services Award, Internat. City Management Assoc., 1976. *Recreations:* gardening, bookbinding. *Address:* High Dolphin, Dittisham, near Dartmouth, Devon TQ6 0HR. *T:* Dittisham (01803) 722224. *Club:* Royal Western Yacht Club of England (Plymouth).

JONES, Dr (Sybil) Angela (Margaret), (Mrs Michael Pearson), FFPHM; Consultant in Public Health Medicine, North (formerly North West) Thames Regional Health Authority, since 1985; *b* 23 Aug. 1940; *d* of Cyril and Ida Jones; *m* 1964, Dr Michael Pearson; three *s* one *d*. *Educ:* Cranford House Sch.; King's College London (AKC); King's Coll. Hosp. (MB BS). Dist MO, Victoria Health Authy, 1982–85. Member: Tech. Sub-Gp of Achieving a Balance, 1988–92; Standing Cttee on Postgrad. Med. Educn, 1989 (Chm., working gp on Health of the Nation); Jt Planning Adv. Cttee, 1988–92; Chm., Regl Med. Manpower and Personnel Gp, 1988–92. *Publications:* articles on med. manpower and public health issues in learned jls. *Recreations:* opera, dining with friends. *Address:* Flat 8, 7 Weymouth Mews, W1N 3FS. *T:* 0171–436 0999. *Club:* Royal Society of Medicine.

JONES, Terence Leavesley; Under-Secretary, Department of the Environment, 1974–84; *b* 24 May 1926; *s* of late Reginald Arthur Jones and Grace Jones; *m* 1966, Barbara Hall; one *s*. *Educ:* Nottingham High Sch.; Jesus Coll., Cambridge (MA). RNVR, 1944–46 (Sub-Lt). Asst Inspector of Ancient Monuments, Min. of Works, 1949; Principal, 1957; Sec., Historic Buildings Council for England, 1961–67; Asst Sec., 1967; on loan to Housing Corp., 1979–81. *Recreations:* music, archæology. *Address:* Meadow View, Woodlands Road, Mildenhall, Marlborough, Wilts SN8 2LP. *T:* Marlborough (01672) 512481.

JONES, Prof. Terence Valentine; Donald Schultz Professor of Turbomachinery, since 1988, and Director, Technology Centre in Aerodynamics and Heat Transfer, since 1993, Oxford University; Professorial Fellow, St Catherine's College, Oxford, since 1988; *b* 14 Feb. 1939; *s* of Albert Duncalf Jones and Frances Jones; *m* 1962, Lesley Lillian (*née* Hughes); one *s* one *d*. *Educ:* William Hulme's Grammar School, Manchester; Lincoln College, Oxford (MA, DPhil 1966). Lecturer: Keble College, Oxford, 1971–77; Lincoln College, Oxford, 1976–80; Jesus College, Oxford, 1977–86; Rolls Royce Tutorial Fellow, St Anne's College, Oxford, 1979–88. Senior Academic Visitor, NASA Lewis Research Center, Ohio, 1986. *Publications:* articles on turbomachinery, heat transfer and fluid dynamics in NATO, ASME and ARC jls and conf. procs. *Recreations:* running, hiking, paragliding. *Address:* Department of Engineering Science, Parks Road, Oxford OX1 3PJ. *T:* Oxford (01865) 246561.

JONES, Terry, (Terence Graham Parry Jones); writer, film director and occasional performer; *b* 1 Feb. 1942; *s* of Alick George Parry Jones and Dilys Louisa Newnes; *m* Alison Telfer; one *s* one *d*. *Educ:* Esher C of E Primary Sch.; Royal Grammar Sch., Guildford; St Edmund Hall, Oxford. *Television:* wrote for various TV shows, 1966–68; wrote and performed in series: Do Not Adjust Your Set, 1968–69; The Complete and Utter History of Britain, 1969; Monty Python's Flying Circus, 1969–75; wrote (with Michael Palin): Secrets (play), BBC TV, 1974; Ripping Yarns, 1976–79; presented: Paperbacks, BBC TV; Victorian Values, BBC Radio; wrote and directed The Rupert Bear Story (documentary), 1981; wrote, directed and presented, So This Is Progress, BBC TV, 1991; co-wrote and presented, Crusades, BBC TV, 1995. *Films:* And Now For Something Completely Different, 1971; directed (with Terry Gilliam), co-wrote and performed, Monty Python and the Holy Grail, 1975; directed, co-wrote and performed: Monty Python's Life of Brian, 1978; Monty Python's Meaning of Life, 1983 (Grand Prix Spécial du Jury, Cannes); directed Personal Services, 1986; wrote, directed and performed, Erik the Viking, 1989. *Publications:* Chaucer's Knight, 1980, 3rd edn 1984; Fairy Tales, 1981, 4th edn 1987; The Saga of Erik the Viking, 1983, 3rd edn 1986; Nicobobinus, 1985, 2nd edn 1987; Goblins of the Labyrinth, 1986; The Curse of the Vampire's Socks, 1988; Attacks of Opinion, 1988; Fantastic Stories, 1992; (with Brian Froud) Lady Cottington's Pressed Fairy Book, 1994; (with Alan Ereira) Crusades, 1994; (with Michael Palin): Dr Fegg's Encyclopeadia (sic) of all World Knowledge, etc.; Ripping Yarns, etc.; contrib. to the various Monty Python books. *Recreation:* sleeping. *Address:* 68A Delancey Street, NW1 7RY.

JONES, Thomas E.; *see* Elder-Jones.

JONES, Thomas Glanville; a Recorder of the Crown Court, since 1972; *b* 10 May 1931; *s* of late Evan James and Margaret Olive Jones; Welsh; *m* 1964, Valma Shirley Jones; three *s*. *Educ:* St Clement Dane's Grammar Sch.; University Coll., London (LLB). Called to Bar, 1956. Sec., Swansea Law Library Assoc., 1963; Chm., Jt Professional Cttees of Swansea Local Bar and Swansea Law Soc. and W. Wales Law Soc.; Founder Mem. and Exec. Cttee Mem., Wales Medico-Legal Soc., 1990; Founder Mem. and Trustee, Swansea Legal Charitable Foundn, 1994. Exec. Mem., Swansea Festival of Music and the Arts, 1967; Chm., Guild for Promotion of Welsh Music, 1970; Mem., Grand Theatre Trust. *Recreations:* Welsh culture, Rugby, reading, music, poetry, gardening. *Address:* Angel Chambers, 94 Walter Road, Swansea SA1 5QA. *T:* Swansea (01792) 464623; Gelligron, 12 Eastcliff, Southgate, Swansea SA3 2AS. *T:* Bishopston (01441) 283118. *Club:* Ffynone (Swansea).

JONES, Ven. (Thomas) Hughie; Archdeacon of Loughborough, 1986–92, now Emeritus; *b* 15 Aug. 1927; *s* of Edward Teifi Jones and Ellen Jones; *m* 1949, Beryl Joan Henderson; two *d*. *Educ:* William Hulme's Grammar School, Manchester; Univ. of Wales (BA, LLM); Univ. of London (BD); Univ. of Leicester (MA). Warden and Lectr, Bible Trng Inst., Glasgow, 1949–54; Minister, John Street Baptist Church, Glasgow, 1951–54; RE specialist, Leicester and Leics schs, 1955–63; Sen. Lectr in RE, Leicester Coll. of Educn, 1964–70; deacon 1966, priest 1967; Vice-Principal, Bosworth Coll., 1970–75; Principal, Hind Leys College, Leics, 1975–81; Rector, The Langtons and Stonton Wyville, 1981–86. Hon. Canon of Leicester Cathedral, 1983–86. Hon. Exec. Officer, Ecclesiastical Law Soc.,

1993– (Vice-Chm., 1990); Member: Selden Soc., 1991; Canon Law Soc. of GB and Ireland, 1993. *Publications:* (contrib. OT articles) New Bible Dictionary, 1962, 2nd edn 1980; Old Testament, religious education and canon law articles in relevant jls. *Recreations:* entomology, genealogy, Welsh interests, canon law. *Address:* Four Trees, Main Street, Thorpe Satchville, Melton Mowbray, Leics LE14 2DQ. *Clubs:* Carlton, Millbank; Leicestershire (Leicester); Leicestershire County Cricket.

JONES, Sir (Thomas) Philip, Kt 1986; CB 1978; Chairman: Total Oil Marine plc, since 1990; Total Oil Holdings, since 1991; *b* 13 July 1931; *s* of William Ernest Jones and Mary Elizabeth Jones; *m* 1955, Mary Phillips; two *s*. *Educ:* Cowbridge Grammar Sch.; Jesus Coll., Oxford (MA; Hon. Fellow, 1990). 2nd Lieut, Royal Artillery, 1953–55; Asst Principal, Min. of Supply, 1955; Principal Min. of Aviation, 1959; on loan to HM Treasury, 1964–66; Principal Private Sec. to Minister of Aviation, 1966–67; Asst Sec., Min. of Technology, subseq. Min. of Aviation Supply, 1967–71; Under Secretary, DTI, 1971; Under Sec., 1974, Dep. Sec., 1976–83, Dept of Energy; Chm., Electricity Council, 1983–90. Dir, Ivo Energy Ltd, 1990–. Member: BNOC, 1980–82; BOTB, 1985–88; HEFCW, 1992–. Chm., Nationalized Industries' Chairmen's Gp, 1986–87. Gov., Henley Management Coll., 1986–. Curator, Oxford Univ. Chest, 1992–. Freeman, City of London, 1986. CIMgt (CBIM 1983); CompIEE 1987; FInstPet 1990. FRSA 1987. Hon. DEng Heriot-Watt, 1993. *Recreations:* walking, reading, watching Rugby football. *Address:* 62 Tachbrook Street, SW1V 2NA. *Clubs:* Travellers', Royal Over-Seas League.

JONES, Timothy; *see* Jones, D. T.

JONES, Timothy Fraser; Vice Lord-Lieutenant of East Sussex, since 1992; *b* 15 July 1931; *o s* of Lionel Herbert Jones, DFC and Mary Jones; *m* 1955, Mary Cobbold Nicolle; one *s* two *d*. *Educ:* Shrewsbury Sch.; St John's Coll., Cambridge (MA). Nat. Service, commnd 1st Bn Rifle Bde, 1950–51; London Rifle Bde Rangers, 1951–54. Buckmaster & Moore, 1954–57; Akroyd & Smithers, 1957, Jt Chm., 1981–86; Dir, S. G. Warburg Group, 1985–88. Trustee, Chichester Cathedral, 1988–92; Mem., Regl Cttee, NT for Kent and E Sussex, 1991–. High Sheriff, 1987–88, DL 1989, E Sussex. *Recreations:* travel, gardening, wine. *Address:* The Old Rectory, Berwick, Polegate, East Sussex BN26 6SR. *T:* Eastbourne (01323) 870523; 11 Ropers Orchard, Danvers Street, SW3 5AX. *T:* 0171–352 6539. *Clubs:* White's, Brooks's, Beefsteak.

JONES, Tom; *see* Woodward, T. J.

JONES, Sir Trevor; *see* Jones, Sir O. T.

JONES, Trevor; General Manager, Lothian Health Board, since 1995; *b* 23 Dec. 1950; *s* of John Jones and Florence Mary Jones (*née* Rogerson); *m* 1974, Hazel Oliver. Local Govt Finance, 1969–78; Sen. Asst Regl Treas., Northern RHA, 1978; Dep. Treas., S Manchester HA, 1983; Waltham Forest Health Authority: Dir of Finance, 1986; Dist Gen. Manager, 1989–92; Chief Exec., Forest Healthcare NHS Trust, 1992–95. IPFA, FCCA, ACIS; MIMgt. *Recreations:* golf, squash, photography. *Address:* The Moorings, Dunmow Road, Great Bardfield, Essex CM7 4SF. *T:* Dunmow (01371) 810677. *Clubs:* Durham CC; Sunderland AF.

JONES, Trevor David K.; *see* Kent-Jones.

JONES, Prof. Tudor Bowden, DSc; FInstP; CEng, FIEE; Professor of Ionospheric Physics, since 1980, Head of Department of Physics and Astronomy, since 1993, University of Leicester; *b* 8 Nov. 1934; *s* of Idris Jones and Tydvil Ann Jones (*née* Bowden); *m* 1960, Patricia Brown; two *s*. *Educ:* County Grammar Sch., Ystradgynlais; University Coll. of Wales, Swansea (BSc Hons, PhD, DSc). FInstP 1975; CEng 1967, FIEE 1987. Res. Asst, UCW, Aberystwyth, 1959; University of Leicester: Lectr in Physics, 1960–69; Sen. Lectr, 1969–75; Reader, 1975–80. Guest Res. Scientist at various Govt estabts in UK and overseas, 1970–; Sen. Resident Associate, Nat. Oceanic and Atmospheric Admin Lab., Boulder, Colo, 1971–72. Appleton Prize, Internat. Union of Radio Sci. and Royal Soc., 1993; Charles Chree Prize and Medal, Inst. of Physics, 1995. *Publications:* (ed) Oblique Incidence Radio Wave Propagation, 1966; numerous papers in scientific jls on ionospheric physics and radio wave propagation. *Recreation:* classical music. *Address:* Department of Physics and Astronomy, University of Leicester, University Road, Leicester LE1 7RH. *T:* Leicester (0116) 252 3561.

JONES, Prof. Vaughan Frederick Randal, FRS 1990; Professor of Mathematics, University of California, Berkeley, since 1985; *b* Gisborne, NZ, 31 Dec. 1952; *s* of J. H. Jones and J. A. Goodfellow (*née* Collins); *m* 1979, Martha Weare Jones (*née* Myers); one *s* two *d*. *Educ:* St Peter's Sch., Cambridge, NZ; Auckland Grammar Sch.; Univ. of Auckland (schol.; Gillies schol.; Phillips Industries Bursary; BSc, MSc 1st Cl. Hons); Ecole de Physique, Geneva (Swiss Govt schol.; F. W. W. Rhodes Meml schol.); Ecole de Mathématiques, Geneva (DèsSc Mathematics); Vacheron Constantin Prize, Univ. de Genève. Asst, Univ. de Genève, 1975–80; E. R. Hedrick Asst Prof., UCLA, 1980–81; University of Pennsylvania: Vis. Lectr, 1981–82; Asst Prof., 1981–84; Associate Prof., 1984–85. Alfred P. Sloan Res. Fellowship, 1983; Guggenheim Fellowship, 1986. Hon. Vice Pres., Internat. Guild of Knot-tyers, 1991. Fields Medal, 1990. *Publication:* Coxeter graphs and Towers of algebras, 1989. *Recreations:* music, tennis, squash, ski-ing. *Address:* Mathematics Department, University College Berkeley, Berkeley, CA 94720, USA. *T:* (415) 6424196.

JONES, Vera June, (Mrs Ernest Brynmor Jones); *see* Di Palma, V. J.

JONES, Most Rev. Walter Heath; Archbishop and Metropolitan of Rupert's Land, 1988–93; *b* 25 Dec. 1928; *s* of Harry Heath Jones and Anne Grace Evelyn Jones (*née* Stoddart); *m* 1951, L. Marilyn Jones (*née* Lunney); one *s* three *d*. *Educ:* Univ. of Manitoba (BA); St John's College (LTh); Nashotah House (STM). Received into Episcopal Church of USA, 1958; Rector, St Mary's Church, Mitchell, S Dak, 1958–62; Vice-Pres. of Chapter, 1962–67; Dean of Calvary Cathedral, Sioux Falls, S Dak, 1968–70; Bishop of South Dakota, Sioux Falls, 1970–83; Bishop of Rupert's Land, 1983. Hon. DD: St John's Coll., 1970; Nashotah House; Trinity Coll., 1990. Hon. Citizen of St Boniface, 1966; Bush Fellow, 1978. *Address:* 133 Yale Avenue, Winnipeg, Manitoba R3M 0L1, Canada.

JONES, Wilfred, CMG 1982; HM Diplomatic Service, retired; *b* 29 Nov. 1926; *m* 1952, Millicent Beresford; two *s*. Joined Foreign Office, 1949; served in Tamsui, Jedda, Brussels, Athens and FCO, 1950–66; First Sec. (Admin), Canberra, 1966–68; FCO, 1968–71; Copenhagen, 1971–74, Blantyre, 1974–75; Lilongwe, 1975–77; FCO, 1977–81; High Comr to Botswana, 1981–86. *Recreations:* sailing, golf, tennis. *Address:* Conifers, 16 The Hummicks, Dock Lane, Beaulieu, Hants SO4 7YJ. *Club:* RAF Yacht.

JONES, Rt. Hon. William Armand Thomas Tristan G.; *see* Garel-Jones.

JONES, Sir (William) Emrys, Kt 1971; BSc; Principal, Royal Agricultural College, Cirencester, 1973–78; *b* 6 July 1915; *s* of late William Jones and Mary Ann (*née* Morgan); *m* 1938, Megan Ann Morgan (marr. diss., 1966); three *s*; *m* 1967, Gwyneth George. *Educ:* Llandovery Gram. Sch.; University Coll. of Wales, Aberystwyth. Agricultural Instr, Gloucester CC, 1940–46; Provincial Grassland Adv. Officer, NAAS, Bristol, 1946–50; County Agricultural Officer, Gloucester, 1950–54; Dep. Dir, 1954–57, Dir 1957–59, NAAS, Wales; Sen. Advisory Officer, NAAS, 1959–61; Dir, 1961–66; Dir-Gen., Agricultural Develt and Adv. Service (formerly Chief Agricl Advr), MAFF, 1967–73. Mem., Adv. Council for Agriculture and Horticulture in England and Wales, 1973–79. Independent Chm., Nat. Cattle Breeders' Assoc., 1976–79. Dir, North and East Midlands Reg. Bd, Lloyds Bank, 1978–86. Hon. LLD Wales, 1973; Hon. DSc Bath, 1975. *Recreations:* golf, shooting. *Address:* 18 St Mary's Park, Louth, Lincs LN11 0EF. *T:* Louth (01507) 602043. *Club:* Farmers'.

JONES, William George Tilston; independent telecommunications consultant, since 1990; *b* 7 Jan. 1942; *s* of late Thomas Tilston Jones and Amy Ethel Jones; *m* 1965, Fiona Mary; one *d*. *Educ:* Portsmouth Grammar School; Portsmouth Polytechnic (BSc; Hon. Fellow 1989). CEng, FIEE. Post Office Engineering Dept, 1960; Head, Electronic Switching Gp, 1969; Head, System X Develt Div., 1978; Dir, System Evolution and Standards, 1983; Chief Exec., Technology, BT, 1984; seconded as Exec. in Residence, Internat. Management Inst., Geneva, 1987; Sen. Strategy Adviser, BT, 1988. Member: IEE Electronics Divl Bd, 1984–89; Parly IT Cttee, 1985–87; Chairman: IT Adv. Bd, Polytechnic of Central London, 1984–87; Adv. Gp, Centre of Communication and Information Studies, 1988–89; SE Centre, IEE, 1989–90; Dir, Technology Studies, British Telecom, 1988–90. Governor, Polytechnic of Central London, 1985–89. *Publications:* contribs on telecommunications to learned jls. *Recreations:* theatre, tennis, camping, making furniture. *Address:* Primavera, 1a The Drive, Radlett, Herts WD7 7DA. *T:* Radlett (01923) 854448.

JONES, William Pearce A.; *see* Andreae-Jones.

JONES, Wyn; *see* Jones, Graham W.

JONES, Sir Wynn Normington H.; *see* Hugh-Jones.

JONES PARRY, Dr Emyr, CMG 1992; HM Diplomatic Service; Minister, British Embassy, Madrid, since 1993; *b* 21 Sept. 1947; *s* of Hugh Jones Parry and Eirwen Jones Parry (*née* Davies); *m* 1971, Lynn Noble; two *s*. *Educ:* Gwedraeth Grammar Sch.; University Coll. Cardiff (BSc, Dip Crystallography); St Catharine's Coll., Cambridge (PhD). FO, 1973–74; First Sec., Ottawa, 1974–79; FO, 1979–82; First Sec., UK Rep. to EC, Brussels, 1982–86; Dep. Head, Office of Pres. of European Parlt, 1987–89; Head, EC Dept (External), FCO, 1989–93. *Publications:* various scientific articles. *Recreations:* gardening, theatre, reading, sport. *Address:* c/o Foreign and Commonwealth Office, King Charles Street, SW1A 2AH. *Club:* Glamorgan County Cricket.

JONES-WILLIAMS, Dafydd Wyn, OBE 1970; MC 1942; TD 1954; DL; Commissioner for Local Administration for Wales (Local Ombudsman), 1974–79; *b* 13 July 1916; *s* of late J. Jones-Williams, Dolgellau; *m* 1945, Rosemary Sally, *e d* of late A. E. Councell, Blaenau Hall, Rhydymain; two *d*. *Educ:* Dolgellau Grammar Sch.; UCW Aberystwyth (LLB). Served 1939–45 with HAC and X Royal Hussars (Western Desert). Formerly comdg 446 (Royal Welch) AB, LAA Regt, RA (TA). Solicitor, 1939. Clerk of County Council, Clerk of Peace, and Clerk to Lieutenancy, Merioneth, 1954–70; Circuit Administrator, Wales and Chester Circuit, 1970–74. Member: Hughes-Parry Cttee on Legal Status of Welsh Language, 1963–65; Lord Chancellor's Adv. Cttee on Trng of Magistrates, 1974–81; Council on Tribunals, 1980–86; BBC Gen. Adv. Council, 1979–85. Formerly: Mem., Nature Conservancy (Chm., Cttee for Wales); Mem., Nat. Broadcasting Council for Wales; Chm., Merioneth and Montgomeryshire T&AFA. DL Merioneth, 1958. *Recreations:* golf, snooker, reading. *Address:* Bryncoedifor, Rhydymain, near Dolgellau, Gwynedd LL40 2AN. *T:* Rhydymain (0134141) 635. *Clubs:* Royal St Davids Golf, Dolgellau Golf.

JONKMAN, (Pieter Jan) Hans, Hon. GCVO 1982; Commander, Order of Orange Nassau; Cross of Honour, Order of House of Orange Nassau; Secretary-General of the Permanent Court of Arbitration, The Hague, since 1990; *b* 2 June 1925; *s* of Jan A. Jonkman and Johanna L. M. de Bruïne; *m* 1959, Maria Elisabeth te Winkel; one *s* two *d*. *Educ:* Univ. of Leyden (law degree). Entered Min. of Foreign Affairs, 1955; served Paris, Pretoria, Leopoldville, Buenos Aires; Min. of Foreign Affairs, 1962–66; Brussels, Beirut, Jakarta; Min. of Foreign Affairs, 1975–80; Grand-Officer for Special Services of HM Queen of the Netherlands, 1980–82; Grand-Master, House of The Queen, 1982–87; Ambassador of the Netherlands to UK and concurrently to Iceland, 1987–90. Holds various foreign decorations. *Address:* Peace Palace, Carnegie-plein 2, 2517 KJ The Hague, Netherlands. *T:* (70) 3024242. *Club:* Societeit de Witte (The Hague).

JONZEN, Mrs Karin, FRBS; sculptor; *b* London (Swedish parents), 22 Dec. 1914; *d* of U. Löwenadler and G. Munck av Fulkila; *m* 1944, Basil Jonzen (*d* 1967); one *s*; *m* 1972, Åke Sucksdorff (*d* 1992). Studied Slade Sch., 1933; Slade Dipl. and Scholarship, 1937; studied Royal Academy, Stockholm, 1939. Lectr, Camden Arts Centre, 1968–72; extra mural lectures in art appreciation, London Univ., 1965–71. Mem. Accad. delle Arte e Lavore, Parma, Italy, 1980 (Gold Medal, 1980); Diploma of Merit, Università delle Arti, Parma, 1982; Gold Medal, Internat. Parliament for Safety and Peace, USA, 1983; Silver Medal, RBS, 1983. *Works in municipal museums and art galleries:* Tate Gall., Bradford, Brighton, Glasgow, Southend, Liverpool, Melbourne, Andrew White Museum, Cornell Univ., USA. *Works commissioned by:* Arts Council (reclining figure in terracotta), 1950; Festival of Britain for sports pavilion (standing figure), 1950; Modern Schs in Leics and Hertford, 1953 and Cardiff, 1954 (animals and figures in terracotta and stone); Selwyn Coll. Chapel, Cambridge (over-life size ascension group, bronze), 1956; St Michael's Church, Golders Green (carving on exterior), 1959; Arts Council (life size bronze mother and child for a housing estate in Lewisham), 1959; Guildford Cathedral (carving on exterior), 1961; WHO HQ, New Delhi (life size bronze torso), 1963 (gift of British Govt); St Mary le Bow, Cheapside (Madonna and child), 1969; City of London Corp. for London Wall site (life size bronze figure), 1971; Guildhall Forecourt (over-life size bronze group), 1972; Sadler's Wells Theatre (bronze of Dame Ninette de Valois, a gift from the sculptor), 1974; Swedish Church, Marylebone (three-quarter life size Pietà, bronze resin), 1975; Action Research (annual trophy), 1979; Cadogan Estate (figure of young girl for Sloane Gardens), 1981; St Mary and St Margaret Church, South Harting, Hants (Madonna and child), 1985; St Saviour's Church, Warwick Ave (Madonna and child), 1986; Nat. Portrait Gall. (over life size bronze of Lord Constantine), 1989; St Anne and St Mary Church, Lewes (St Anne and St Mary gp), 1990. *Works exhibited by invitation:* Battersea Park open air exhibns, 1948–51; Tate Gall., 1952 (Four Seasons), 1954 (Religious Art), and 1957–59; City of London Festival, 1968; (one man exhibn) Fieldbourne Gall., London, 1974, 1990 (Mainly Portraits); Poole Wills Gall., NY, 1983; Messum Gall., 1995. *Portrait busts include:* Sir Alan Herbert, Lord Constantine (purchased by Nat. Portrait Gall.), Dame Ninette de Valois, Sir Hugh Casson, Donald Trelford, Sir Monty Finniston, Samuel Pepys (over-life size bronze, Seething Lane, EC3), Max von Sydow, Yuki, Paul Scofield. *Relevant publications:* Karin Jonzen: sculptor, introd. Carel Weight, foreword by Norman St John-Stevas, 1976; Karin Jonzen: Sculpture, introd. Carel Weight, foreword by Edward Lucie-Smith, 1994. *Recreations:* music, travel. *Address:* The Studio, 6A Gunter Grove, SW10 0UJ.

JOPE, Prof. Edward Martyn, FBA 1965; FSA 1946; MRIA 1973; Professor of Archæology, The Queen's University of Belfast, 1963–81, now Emeritus; Visiting Professor in Archaeological Sciences, University of Bradford, 1974–81, Honorary Visiting Professor, since 1982; *b* 28 Dec. 1915; *s* of Edward Mallet Jope and Frances Margaret (*née* Chapman); *m* 1941, Margaret Halliday; no *c*. *Educ:* Whitgift Sch., Croydon; Kingswood Sch., Bath; Oriel Coll., Oxford (Open Schol., Chemistry, 1935). Staff of Royal Commission on Ancient Monuments (Wales), 1938; Biochemist, Nuffield and MRC Grants, 1940; Queen's Univ., Belfast: Lectr in Archæology, 1949; Reader, 1954. Member: Ancient Monuments Adv. Coun. (NI), 1950; Royal Commission on Ancient Monuments (Wales), 1963–86; Sci,-based Archaeology Cttee, SRC, 1976–82; Ancient Monuments Bd (England), 1980–84; Pres. Section H, British Assoc., 1965. Rhys Res. Fellow and Vis. Sen. Res. Fellow, Jesus Coll., Oxford, 1977–78. Lectures: Munro, Edinburgh, 1953; O'Donnell, Oxford, 1968; Rhŷs, British Acad., 1987; Davies, Belfast, 1992. Hon. DSc Bradford, 1980. *Publications:* Early Celtic Art in the British Isles, 1977; (ed) Studies in Building History, 1961; (ed and contrib.) Archaeological Survey of Co. Down, 1966; papers in Biochem. Jl, Proc. RSocMed, Phil. Trans Royal Soc., Spectrochemica Acta, Trans Faraday Soc., Proc. Prehistoric Soc., Antiquaries' Jl, Medieval Archæology, Oxoniensia, Ulster Jl of Archæology, Proc. Soc. of Antiquaries of Scotland, etc. *Recreations:* music, travel. *Address:* 1 Chalfont Road, Oxford OX2 6TL. *T:* Oxford (01865) 59024.

JOPLING, Rt. Hon. (Thomas) Michael; PC 1979; DL; MP (C) Westmorland and Lonsdale, since 1983 (Westmorland, 1964–83); farmer; *b* 10 Dec. 1930; *s* of Mark Bellerby Jopling, Masham, Yorks; *m* 1958, Gail, *d* of Ernest Dickinson, Harrogate; two *s*. *Educ:* Cheltenham Coll.; King's Coll., Newcastle upon Tyne (BSc Agric.). Mem., Thirsk Rural District Council, 1958–64; contested Wakefield (C), 1959; Mem. National Council, National Farmers' Union, 1962–64. Jt Sec., Cons. Parly Agric. Cttee, 1966–70; PPS to Minister of Agriculture, 1970–71; an Asst Govt Whip, 1971–73; a Lord Comr, HM Treasury, 1973–74; an Opposition Whip, March–June 1974; an Opposition spokesman on agriculture, 1974–75, 1976–79; Shadow Minister of Agriculture, 1975–76; Parly Sec. to HM Treasury, and Chief Whip, 1979–83; Minister of Agriculture, Fisheries and Food, 1983–87. Mem., Select Cttee on Foreign Affairs, 1987–; Chm., Select Cttee on Sittings of the House, 1991–92. Hon. Sec., British Amer. Parly Gp, 1987– (Vice Chm., 1983–86). Mem., UK Exec., Commonwealth Parly Assoc., 1974–79, 1987– (Vice Chm., 1977–79). Pres. Councils, EEC Agric. and Fishery Ministers, July–Dec. 1986. Pres., Auto Cycle Union, 1990–. DL Cumbria, 1991. Hon. DCL Newcastle, 1992. *Address:* Ainderby Hall, Thirsk, North Yorks. *T:* Thirsk (01845) 567224; Clyder Howe Cottage, Windermere, Cumbria. *T:* Windermere (019662) 2590. *Clubs:* Beefsteak, Buck's.

JORDAN, Dr Carole, FRS 1990; FInstP; Wolfson Tutorial Fellow in Natural Science, Somerville College, Oxford, since 1976, and Reader, Department of Physics (Theoretical Physics), Oxford, since 1994; *b* 19 July 1941; *d* of Reginald Sidney Jordan and Ethel May Jordan (*née* Waller). *Educ:* Harrow County Grammar School for Girls; University College London (BSc 1962; PhD 1965; Fellow 1991). FInstP 1973. Post-Doctoral Research Associate, Jt Inst. for Lab. Astrophysics, Boulder, Colorado, 1966; Asst Lectr, Dept of Astronomy, UCL, attached to Culham Lab., UKAEA, 1966–69; Astrophysics Research Unit, SRC, 1969–76; Univ. Lectr in Physics, Oxford, 1976–94. Member: SERC, 1985–90 (Chm., Solar System Cttee, 1983–86; Mem., Astronomy, Space and Radio Bd, 1979–86; Mem., Astronomy and Planetary Sci. Bd, 1986–90); PPARC, 1994–. Pres., Royal Astronomical Soc., 1994– (Sec., 1981–90; Vice-Pres., 1990–91). DUniv Surrey, 1991. *Publications:* scientific papers on astrophysical plasma spectroscopy and structure and energy balance in cool star coronae, in learned jls. *Address:* Department of Physics (Theoretical Physics), 1 Keble Road, Oxford OX1 3NP. *T:* Oxford (01865) 273980.

JORDAN, David Harold, CMG 1975; MBE 1962; *b* Sunderland, 27 Oct. 1924; *er s* of late H. G. Jordan, OBE, and Gwendolyn (*née* Rees); *m* 1st, 1951, Lorna Mary Holland (marr. diss.), *er d* of late W. R. Harvey; three *s* one *d*; 2nd, 1971, Penelope Amanda, *d* of late Lt-Col B. L. J. Davy, OBE, TD; one *d*. *Educ:* Roundhay Sch., Leeds; Berkhamsted; Magdalen Coll., Oxford (1st Cl. Chinese), MA 1956. 9th Gurkha Rifles, Indian Army, 1943–47. HMOCS (Hong Kong), 1951–79: Chinese Language Sch., Univ. of Hong Kong, 1951–52; Asst Sec. for Chinese Affairs, 1952–55; Colonial Secretariat, 1956–68: Asst Sec., 1956–60; jssc 1960; Defence Sec., 1961–66; Dep. Dir, Commerce and Industry, 1968–70; Dep. Economic Sec., 1970–71; Dep. Financial Sec., 1971–72; Dir of Commerce and Industry, later Trade, Industry and Customs, and MLC, Hong Kong, 1972–79. *Address:* The Lower Farm, Drayton Parslow, Milton Keynes, Bucks MK17 0JS. *T:* Mursley (01296) 720688. *Clubs:* Hong Kong; Royal Hong Kong Jockey.

JORDAN, Douglas Arthur, CMG 1977; Senior Partner, Douglas Jordan Consultants, since 1991; *b* 28 Sept. 1918; *s* of late Arthur Jordan and Elizabeth Jordan; *m* 1st, 1940, Violet Nancy (*née* Houston); one *d*; 2nd, 1970, Constance Dorothy (*née* Wallis). *Educ:* East Ham Grammar Sch., London. HM Customs and Excise: Officer, 1938; Surveyor, 1953; Inspector, 1960; Asst Collector, Manchester and London, 1962–68; Sen. Inspector, 1968–69; Chief Investigation Officer, 1969–77; Dep. Comr, 1977–79, Comr of Customs and Controls, 1979, Trade, Industry and Customs Dept, Hong Kong (Comr of Customs and Excise, Customs and Excise Dept, 1982–84); Special Anti-Piracy Advr, SE Asia, 1984, Customs and Anti-Piracy Consultant, 1985–90, Internat. Fedn of Phonogram and Videogram Producers. Freeman, City of London, 1964. *Recreations:* golf, music. *Address:* 10 Crouchmans Close, Sydenham Hill, SE26 6ST. *T:* 0181–670 9638. *Clubs:* Wig and Pen, Commonwealth Trust; Dulwich and Sydenham Golf.

JORDAN, Francis Leo, (Frank), CBE 1989; QPM 1982; Chief Constable of Kent, 1982–89, retired; *b* 15 June 1930; *s* of Leo Thomas and Mary Jordan; *m* 1951, Ruth Ashmore; one *s* two *d*. *Educ:* St Joseph's Coll., Trent Vale, Stoke-on-Trent. CBIM. Staffordshire Police to rank of Chief Supt, 1950; seconded to Cyprus Police during EOKA emergency, 1956–58; Sen. Course in Criminology, Cambridge Univ., 1972; Sen. Comd Course, Police Staff Coll., 1973; Staff Officer to Home Office Police Inspectorate, 1975; Asst Chief Constable, West Midlands Police, 1976; Dep. Chief Constable of Kent, 1979. Mem., Parole Bd, 1990–93. Mem., Kent County Cttee, SSAFA, 1985–89. FRSA 1990. OStJ 1988. *Recreations:* walking, old buildings, churches, etc, travel. *Club:* Royal Over-Seas League.

JORDAN, Gerard Michael, CEng; Site Director, AEA Technology Dounreay (formerly Director, Dounreay Nuclear Power Establishment, United Kingdom Atomic Energy Authority), 1987–92; *b* 25 Sept. 1929; *s* of Arthur Thomas and Ruby Eveline Jordan; *m* 1955, Vera Peers; one *s* one *d*. *Educ:* Grange Sch., Birkenhead; Univ. of Liverpool. BEng; CEng, MIMechE, 1974. Marine Engrg Officer, 1950–55; Gp Engr, Messrs Thomas Hedley Ltd, 1956–59; United Kingdom Atomic Energy Authority: Principal Professional and Technical Officer, 1959–73; Band Grade Officer, 1973–80; Asst Dir (Safety and Reliability Div.), 1980; Asst Dir (Engrg and Safety Dounreay), 1980–84; Dep. Dir (Engrg Northern Div.), 1984–85; Dir of Engrg (Northern Div.), 1985–87. *Publications:* Handbook on Criticality Data, 1974, 2nd edn 1979; various papers in Trans IMechE, Trans IChemE, Trans INucE. *Recreations:* hobby electronics, DIY, fishing.

JORDAN, Graham Harold Ben; Deputy Chief Scientist (Scrutiny and Analysis), Ministry of Defence, since 1995; *b* 1 April 1945; *s* of Harold Jordan and Violet Emily Jordan (*née* Wakefield); *m* 1977, Jean Anne Swale. *Educ:* Chislehurst and Sidcup Grammar Sch.; Downing Coll., Cambridge (Schol.; BA 1966 Nat. Scis and Chem. Eng; MA 1970); Brunel Univ. (MTech 1974 Op. Res.). DOAE, 1967–77; Dept of Chief Scientist, RAF, 1977–78; Supt, Land Air Studies Div., DOAE, 1978–82; Royal Aircraft Establishment: Supt, Air to Air Weapons Div., 1982–85; Head, Defensive Weapons Dept, 1985–87; Head, Civil Service Personnel Policy Div., HM Treasury, 1987–90; Scientific Advr (Command Inf. Systems), MoD, 1990–91; Asst Chief Scientific Advr (Capabilities), MoD, 1991–95. *Publication:* (with Lee and Cawsey) Learning from Experience (report), 1988. *Recreations:* riding horses, small scale farming, home maintenance, music. *Address:* Ministry of Defence, Main Building, Whitehall, SW1A 2HB.

JORDAN, Michael Anthony; Chairman and Senior Partner, Cork Gully, Chartered Accountants, 1983–93; Partner, Coopers & Lybrand, Chartered Accountants, 1980–93; *b* 20 Aug. 1931; *s* of Charles Thomas Jordan and Florence Emily (*née* Golder); *m* 1st, 1956, Brenda Gee (marr. diss. 1989); one *s* one *d*; 2nd, 1990, Dorothea Rosine Estelle Coureau. *Educ:* Haileybury. FCA 1956. Joined R. H. March Son & Co., 1958, Partner, 1959–68; Partner: Saker & Langdon Davis, 1963–93; W. H. Cork Gully & Co., 1968–80. Jt Inspector for High Court of IoM into the affairs of the Savings & Investment Bank Ltd, 1983. Gov., Royal Shakespeare Theatre, 1979–. *Publication:* (jtly) Insolvency, 1986. *Recreations:* opera, DIY, gardening. *Address:* Ballinger Farm, Ballinger, near Great Missenden, Bucks. *T:* Great Missenden (012406) 3298.

JORDAN, William Brian, CBE 1992; General Secretary, International Confederation of Free Trade Unions, since 1995; a Governor, BBC, since 1988; *b* 28 Jan. 1936; *s* of Walter and Alice Jordan; *m* 1958, Jean Ann Livesey; three *d*. *Educ:* Secondary Modern Sch., Birmingham. Convener of Shop Stewards, Guest Keen & Nettlefolds, 1966; full-time AUEW Divl Organiser, 1976; Pres., AEU, then AEEU, 1986–95. Mem., TUC General Council, 1986–95 (Chm., Cttee on European Strategy, 1988–95). Member: NEDC, 1986–92; Engrg Industry Training Bd, 1986–91; Council, Industrial Soc., 1987–; RIIA, 1987–; ACAS, 1987–95; Nat. Trng Task Force, 1989–92; Engrg Trng Authy, 1991–; NACETT, 1993–95; English Partnerships, 1993–. President: European Metal-Workers Fedn, 1986–95; Exec., Internat. Metalworkers Fedn, 1986–95. Governor: London School of Economics, 1987–; Manchester Business School, 1987–92; Ashridge Management Coll., 1992–; Mem. Ct of Govs, Henley Coll., 1991–. Hon. CGIA 1989. Hon. Dr: Univ. of Central England, 1993; Cranfield, 1995. *Recreations:* reading; keen supporter, Birmingham City FC. *Address:* ICFTU, Boulevard Emil Jacqmain 155 B1, 1210 Brussels, Belgium.

JORDAN-MOSS, Norman, CB 1972; CMG 1965; Director, Crown Financial Management, 1984–90; *b* 5 Feb. 1920; *o s* of Arthur Moss and Ellen Jordan Round; *m* 1st, 1965, Kathleen Lusmore (*d* 1974); one *s* one *d*; 2nd, 1976, Philippa Rands (*d* 1993); one *d*. *Educ:* Manchester Gram. Sch.; St John's Coll., Cambridge (MA). Ministry of Economic Warfare, 1940–44; HM Treasury, 1944–71; Asst Representative of HM Treas. in Middle East, 1945–48; Principal, 1948; First Sec. (Econ.), Belgrade, 1952–55; Financial Counsellor, Washington, 1956–60; Counsellor, UK Permanent Delegation to OECD, Paris, 1963–66; Asst Sec., 1956–68, Under-Sec., 1968–71, HM Treasury; Dep. Under-Sec. of State, DHSS, 1971–76; Dep. Sec., HM Treasury, 1976–80. Consultant, Hambros Bank, 1981–84; Dir, 1928 Investment Trust, 1981–84. *Publication:* Don't Kill the Cuckoos, 1991. *Recreations:* music, theatre. *Address:* Milton Way, Westcott, Dorking, Surrey RH4 3PZ. *Club:* Travellers'.

JORRE DE ST JORRE, Danielle Marie-Madeleine; Secretary of State, since 1986 and Minister of the Environment, Economic Planning and External Relations, since 1992, Republic of Seychelles; *b* 30 Sept. 1941; *d* of Henri Jorre De St Jorre and Alice Corgat; *m* 1965 (marr. diss. 1983); one *s* one *d*. *Educ:* Univ. of Edinburgh (MA 1965); Inst. of Education, Univ. of London (PGCE 1966); Univ. of York (BPhil 1972). French Teacher, Streatham Hill and Clapham High Sch. (GPDST), 1967–69; French and English Teacher, and Hd of French Dept, Seychelles Coll., 1969–71; Principal, Teacher Training College, Seychelles, 1974–76; Principal Educn Officer, Min. of Educn, Seychelles, 1976–77; Principal Secretary: Min. of Foreign Affairs, Tourism and Aviation, 1977–79; Min. of Education and Information, 1980–82; Dept of External Relations and Co-operation, Min. of Planning and External Relations: Principal Sec., External Relns, 1982–83; Principal Sec., Planning and External Relns, 1983–86; High Comr for Seychelles in UK, concurrently Ambassador to France, Canada, Cuba, Federal Republic of Germany, Greece and USSR, 1983–85; Minister for Planning and External Relns, 1989–. Mem. or Head of delegn at numerous overseas meetings and conferences. Mem. Exec. Cttee, Seychelles People's Progressive Front, 1991–. Gov. for Seychelles, Bd of Governors, World Bank and African Develt Bank, 1984–; Chairperson: Seychelles Nat. Printing Co., 1977–82; Nat. Bookshop, 1977–82; Nat. Consultancy Services, 1983–88; Seychelles Hotels Ltd, 1986–91; Nat. Monument Bd, 1987–88; Develt Bank of Seychelles, 1988–91; Dir, Internat. Centre for Ocean Develt, 1987–. Vice-President: Comité International des Etudes Créoles, 1984–; E African Reg., Adv. Cttee on Protection of the Sea, 1994–; Pres., Bannzil Kreyol, 1986–. *Publications:* Apprenons la nouvelle orthographe, 1978; Dictionnaire Créole Seychellois-français, 1982; (jtly) Lexique des Spécificités de la Langue Française aux Seychelles, 1989. *Address:* Ministry of Foreign Affairs, Planning and Environment, PO Box 656, Victoria, Mahé, Republic of Seychelles.

JOSCELYNE, Richard Patrick; British Council Director, Japan, 1991–94; *b* 19 June 1934; *s* of Dr Patrick C. Joscelyne and Rosalind Whitcombe; *m* 1st, 1961, Vera Lucia Mello (marr. diss. 1988); one *s* one *d*; 2nd, 1988, Irangani Dias. *Educ:* Bryanston; Queens' Coll., Cambridge. Teaching posts in France, Brazil and Britain, 1958–62. British Council: Montevideo, 1962; Moscow, 1967; Madrid, 1969; Director, North and Latin America Dept, 1973; Representative, Sri Lanka, 1977; Controller, Overseas Div. B (America, Pacific and Asia Div.), 1980; Controller, Finance Div., 1982; Representative, Spain, 1987. *Address:* The Lake House, 8 Lagoon Court, Samford, Qld 4520, Australia. *T:* (7) 32891710.

JOSEPH, (Hon. Sir) James Samuel, (3rd Bt *cr* 1943, of Portsoken, City of London); *b* 27 Jan. 1955; *o s* of Baron Joseph, CH (Life Peer) and of Hellen Louise (*née* Guggenheimer); *S* to baronetcy of father, 1994, but does not use the title.

JOSEPH, Leslie, QC 1978; *b* 13 Aug. 1925; *s* of Benjamin Francis Joseph and Sarah Edelman; *m* 1964, Ursula Mary Hamilton (*d* 1988); one *s* two *d*. *Educ:* Haberdashers' Aske's, Hampstead; University Coll. London (LLB Hons). Served Army, 1943–47: Infantry, 1943–45 (Sgt); AEC, 1945–47. Called to the Bar, Middle Temple, 1953, Bencher, 1986. *Recreations:* wine and water. *Address:* 34 Upper Park Road, NW3 2UT. *T:* 0171–722 3390.

JOSEPH, Thomas John Cedric; His Honour Judge Joseph; a Circuit Judge, since 1994; *b* 25 Aug. 1938; *s* of Thomas Rees Joseph and Katherine Ann Joseph; *m* 1960 Mary Weston; three *d*. *Educ:* Cardigan GS; LSE (LLB). Called to the Bar, Gray's Inn, 1960; Crown Counsel, Nyasaland, 1962–64; practised at the Bar, 1964–94; Asst Recorder, 1987–92; Recorder, 1992–94. *Recreations:* music, golf, travel. *Address:* Snaresbrook Crown Court, 75 Hollybush Hill, Snaresbrook, E11 1QW. *T:* 0181–982 5500. *Club:* Royal Wimbledon Golf.

JOSEPHS, Wilfred; composer; *b* 24 July 1927; *s* of Philip Josephs and Rachel (*née* Block); *m* 1956, Valerie Wisbey; two *d*. *Educ:* Rutherford Coll. Boys' Sch.; Univ. of Durham at Newcastle (now Newcastle Univ.) (BDS Dunelm). Qual. dentistry, 1951. Army service, 1951–53. Guildhall Sch. of Music (schol. in composition, prizes), 1954; Leverhulme Schol. to study musical comp. in Paris with Maître Max Deutsch, 1958–59; Harriet Cohen Commonwealth Medal (for 1st quartet) and prizes; First Prize, La Scala, Milan, for Requiem, 1963. Abandoned dentistry completely and has since been a full-time composer, writing many concert works (incl. choral and orchestral works and 11 symphonies), many film and television scores and themes, incl. music for: The Great War, I, Claudius, Disraeli, Cider with Rosie, All Creatures Great and Small, Sister Dora, Swallows and Amazons, The Brontë Series, The Somerset Maugham Series, Horizon, Chéri, A Place in Europe, The Inventing of America, The Norman Conquests, The Ghosts of Motley Hall, The House of Bernardo Alba, The Hunchback of Notre Dame, The Voyage of Charles Darwin, Enemy at the Door, People Like Us, Black Sun, The Uncanny, The Atom Spies, Churchill and the Generals, Pride and Prejudice, Strangled, A Walk in the Dark, Gift of Tongues, Miss Morison's Ghosts, The Human Race, Weekend Theatre, The Moles, The Home Front, The Making of Britain, Courts Martial series, A Married Man, The Gay Lord Quex, Pope John Paul II, Martin's Day, Mata Hari, Drummonds, Return of the Antelope, Art of the Western World, Horizon (Wasting the Alps; The Company of Ants and Bees; Red Star in Orbit), also a television opera, The Appointment; one-act opera, Pathelin; children's operas, Through the Looking-glass and What Alice Found There; Alice in Wonderland; children's musical, King of the Coast (Guardian/Arts Council Prize, 1969); Equus, the ballet (best ballet award, USA, 1980); Rebecca, 3-act opera, 1981–83; Cyrano de Bergerac, 3-act ballet, 1990–91. Vis. Prof. of Comp. and Composer-in-Residence at Univ. of Wisconsin-Milwaukee, 1970, at Roosevelt Univ., Chicago, 1972; Dist. Vis. Prof., Ohio State Univ., 1992; Music Consultant, London Internat. Film Sch., 1988–. Member: Council, RPS; BAFTA; RSM; ISM; Composer's Guild of GB; Assoc. of Professional Composers; Producers' Assoc. Hon. DMus Newcastle, 1978. *Publications:* Requiem, Symphonies 1–11, various sonatas, quartets, concertos etc. *Recreations:* writing music, swimming, reading, opera, theatre, films. *Address:* Mornington Music, 6 Grand Union Walk, Kentish Town Road, Camden Town, NW1 9LP. *T and Fax:* 0171–485 1634.

JOSEPHSON, Prof. Brian David, FRS 1970; Professor of Physics, Cambridge University, since 1974; Fellow of Trinity College, Cambridge, since 1962; *b* 4 Jan. 1940; *s* of Abraham Josephson and Mimi Josephson; *m* 1976, Carol Anne Olivier; one *d*. *Educ:* Cardiff High School; Cambridge Univ. BA 1960, MA, PhD 1964, Cantab. FInstP. Asst Dir of Res. in Physics, 1967–72, Reader in Physics, 1972–74, Univ. of Cambridge. Res. Asst Prof., Illinois Univ., 1965–66; Vis., Fellow, Cornell Univ., 1971; Vis. Faculty Mem., Maharishi European Res. Univ., 1975; Visiting Professor: Wayne State Univ., 1983; Indian Inst. of Sci., Bangalore, 1984. Hon. MIEEE, 1982; For. Hon. Mem., Amer. Acad. of Arts and Scis, 1974. Hon. DSc: Wales, 1974; Exeter, 1984. Awards: New Scientist, 1969; Research Corp., 1969; Fritz London, 1970; Nobel Prize for Physics, 1973. Medals: Guthrie, 1972; van der Pol, 1972; Elliott Cresson, 1972; Hughes, 1972; Holweck, 1973; Faraday, 1982; Sir George Thomson, 1984. *Publications:* Consciousness and the Physical World, 1980 (ed jtly); research papers on physics and theory of intelligence, the convergence of science and religion. *Recreations:* mountain walking, ice skating. *Address:* Cavendish Laboratory, Madingley Road, Cambridge CB3 0HE. *T:* Cambridge (01223) 337260, *Fax:* (01223) 337356.

JOSIPOVICI, Prof. Gabriel David; Professor of English, School of European Studies, University of Sussex, since 1984; *b* 8 Oct. 1940; *s* of Jean Josipovici and Sacha (*née* Rabinovitch). *Educ:* Victoria Coll., Cairo; Cheltenham Coll.; St Edmund Hall, Oxford (BA 1st Cl. Hons 1961). School of European Studies, University of Sussex: Asst Lectr in English, 1963–65; Lectr, 1965–74; Reader (part-time), 1974–84. Weidenfeld Vis. Prof. in Eur. Comparative Lit., Univ. of Oxford, Oct. 1996–. *Plays:* Dreams of Mrs Fraser, 1972; Evidence of Intimacy, 1973; Playback, 1973; A Life, 1974; Vergil Dying, 1976; A Moment, 1977; AG, 1977; Kin, 1982; Mr Vee, 1987; A Little Personal Pocket Requiem, 1989. *Publications: fiction:* The Inventory, 1968; Words, 1971; Mobius the Stripper, 1974; The Present, 1975; Migrations, 1977; The Air We Breathe, 1981; Conversations in Another Room, 1984; Contre-Jour, 1987; The Big Glass, 1989; In the Fertile Land, 1991; Steps, 1992; In a Hotel Garden, 1993; Moo Pak, 1994; *non-fiction:* The World and the Book, 1971, 3rd edn 1994; The Lessons of Modernism, 1977, 2nd edn 1986; Writing and the Body, 1982; The Mirror of Criticism, 1983; The Book of God, 1987, 2nd edn 1989; Text and Voice, 1992. *Recreations:* walking, swimming. *Address:* 60 Prince Edward's Road, Lewes, Sussex BN7 1BH.

JOSLIN, Peter David, QPM 1983; Chief Constable of Warwickshire, since 1983; *b* 26 Oct. 1933; *s* of Frederick William Joslin and Emma Joslin; *m* 1960, Kathleen Josephine Monaghan; two *s* one *d*. *Educ:* King Edward VI Royal Grammer School, Chelmsford; Essex University. BA hons. Joined Essex Police, 1954–74 (Police Constable to Superintendent); Chief Superintendent, Divl Comdr, Leicestershire Constabulary, 1974–76; Asst Chief Constable (Operations), Leics Constab., 1976–77; Dep. Chief Constable, Warwicks Constabulary, 1977–83. Chm., Traffic Cttee, ACPO, 1989–92. Pres., Warwickshire Assoc. for the Blind, 1993–; Vice-Pres., Warwickshire Outward Bound Assoc., 1993–; Member: Cttee, Warwickshire Assoc. of Boys Clubs, 1983–; Council for Warwickshire, St John Ambulance, 1983–. CIMgt. *Recreations:* sport (now mainly as a spectator), house renovation, good wines, after dinner speaking. *Address:* Chief Constable's Office, PO Box 4, Leek Wootton, Warwick CV35 7QB. *T:* Warwick (01926) 415000.

JOSS, William Hay; a Recorder of the Crown Court, since 1982; *b* 20 May 1927; *s* of William Taylor Barron Joss and Elizabeth Lindsay Lillie Joss; *m* 1961, Rosemary Sarah Joss; two *s*. *Educ:* Worksop Coll., Notts; Exeter Coll., Oxon (BA Jurisprudence). Served Army, commissioned into 14th/20th King's Hussars, 1945–48. Industry, production management, 1950–62; called to the Bar, Gray's Inn, 1957; practising barrister, 1962–. *Recreations:* golf, music, literature. *Address:* 49 Village Road, Clifton Village, Nottingham NG11 8NP. *T:* Nottingham (0115) 921 1894. *Club:* Nottingham and Notts United Services.

JOST, H. Peter, CBE 1969; DSc; CEng; FIMechE; FIM; Hon. FIEE; CIMgt; Chairman, K. S. Paul Products Ltd, since 1973 (Managing Director, 1955–89); Director of overseas companies; Hon. Industrial Professor, Liverpool John Moores University (formerly Liverpool Polytechnic), since 1983; Hon. Professor of Mechanical Engineering, University of Wales, since 1986; *b* 25 Jan. 1921; *o s* of late Leo and Margot Jost; *m* 1948, Margaret Josephine, *o d* of late Michael and Sara Kadesh, Norfolk Is, S Pacific; two *d*. *Educ:* City of Liverpool Techn. Coll.; Manchester Coll. of Technology. Apprentice, Associated Metal Works, Glasgow and D. Napier & Son Ltd, Liverpool; Methods Engr, K & L Steelfounders and Engrs Ltd, 1943; Chief Planning Engr, Datim Machine Tool Co. Ltd, 1946; Gen. Man. 1949, Dir 1952, Trier Bros Ltd; Lubrication Consultant: Richard Thomas & Baldwins Ltd, 1960–65; August Thyssen Hütte AG 1963–66; Chairman: Bright Brazing Ltd, 1969–76; Peppermill Brass Foundry Ltd, 1970–76; Centralube Ltd, 1974–77 (Man. Dir, 1955–77); Associated Technology Gp Ltd, 1976–; Engineering & General Equipment Ltd, 1977–; Director: Williams Hudson Ltd, 1967–75; Stothert & Pitt, 1971–85. Chairman: Lubrication Educn and Res. Working Gp, DES, 1964–65; Cttee on Tribology, DTI, 1966–74; Industrial Technologies Management Bd, DTI, 1972–74; Dep. Chm., Cttee for Industrial Technologies, DTI, 1972–74; Member: Adv. Council on Technology, 1968–70; Cttee on Terotechnology, 1971–72. Hon. Associate, Manchester Coll. of Science and Technology, 1962; Univ. of Salford: Privy Council's Nominee to Ct, 1970–83; Mem. Council, 1974–84. Mem. Council: IProdE, 1973–91 (Vice-Pres., 1975–77, Pres., 1977–78; Chm., Technical Policy Bd and Mem., Exec. Policy Cttee, 1974; Hon. Fellow, 1980); IMechE, 1974–92 (Member: Technical Bd, 1975; Finance Bd, 1979– (Chm., 1988–91); Disciplinary Bd, 1979–; Vice-Pres., 1987–92); Council of Engineering Institutions: Mem. Bd, 1977–83; Mem. Exec., 1979–83 (Mem. External Affairs Cttee, 1974–80; Chm. Home Affairs Cttee, 1980–83); Mem., Parly and Scientific Cttee, 1973– (Hon. Sec., 1990–93; Vice-Pres., 1993–95; Vice Chm., 1995–; Mem., Gen. Purposes Cttee, 1991–; Mem. Council (formerly Steering Cttee), 1983–). President: Internat. Tribology Council, 1973–; Manchester Technology Assoc., 1984–85; Chm., Manchester Technology Assoc. in London, 1976–90. CIMgt (CBIM 1984); Fellow, 1970, Life Fellow, 1986, ASME; FSME, USA, 1988 (Hon. Mem., 1977); Hon. MIPlantE, 1969; Hon. Member: Société Française de Tribologie, 1972; Gesellschaft für Tribologie, 1972; Chinese Mech. Engrg Soc., 1986; Russian (formerly USSR) Acad. of Engrg, 1991; Nat. Tribology Council of Bulgaria, 1991; Japanese Soc. of Tribologists, 1992; Slovak Tribology Soc., 1993; Ukrainian Acad. of Transport, 1994; Polish Tribolog. Soc., 1995. Rutherford Lectr, Manchester Technology Assoc., 1979; James Clayton Lectr, IMechE, 1981. Freeman, City of London, 1984; Liveryman, Engineers' Co., 1984. Hon. DSc: Salford, 1970; Slovak Technical Univ., 1987; Bath, 1990; Technical Univ. of Budapest, 1993; Hon. DTech CNAA, 1987; Hon. DEng Leeds, 1989; San Fernando Valley Engineers Council (USA) Internat. Achievement Award, 1978; State of California State Legislature Commendation, 1978; Georg Vagelpohl Insignia, Germany, 1979. Sir John Larking Medal 1944, Derby Medal 1955, Liverpool Engrg Soc.; Hutchinson Meml Medal 1952, Silver Medal for Best Paper 1952–53, 1st Nuffield Award 1981, IProdE; Merit Medal, Hungarian Scientific Soc. of Mech. Engrs, 1983; Gold Medal, Slovak Tech. Univ., 1984; Colclough Medal and Prize, Inst. of Materials, 1992; Louwe Alberts Award, S African Inst. of Tribology, 1992. Gold Insignia, Order of Merit of Poland, 1986; Officer Cross, Order of Merit (Germany), 1992; Officier, Palmes Académiques (France), 1995. *Publications:* Lubrication (Tribology) Report of DES Cttee, 1966 (Jost Report); The Introduction of a New Technology, Report of DTI Cttee, 1973; Technology *vs* Unemployment, 1986; various papers in Proc. IMechE, Proc.IProdE, technical jls, etc. *Recreations:* music, opera, gardening. *Address:* Hill House, Wills Grove, Mill Hill, NW7 1QL. *T:* 0181–959 3355. *Club:* Athenæum.

JOTIKASTHIRA, Tongchan; Kt Grand Cordon, Order of White Elephant, 1994; Kt Grand Cordon, Order of Crown of Thailand, 1989; Ambassador of Thailand to the Court of St James's, 1991–94; *b* 29 March 1933; *s* of Gen. Luang Sura Narong (Tongchai Jotikasthira) and Than Puying Charuay Sura Narong; *m* 1956, Supang (*née* Sukhum); one *d* (one *s* decd). *Educ:* Boston Univ., USA (BS Business Admin). Entered Foreign Service, 1958; Second Secretary, Royal Thai Embassy: Jakarta, 1962–64; Bern, 1964–68; Asst Sec. to Minister of Foreign Affairs, 1968–72; Chargé d'Affaires and established Royal Thai Embassy, Ankara, 1972–74; First Sec. and Dep. Chief of Mission, Copenhagen, 1974–77; Chief of Press Div., Dept of Information, 1977–79; Dir, Econ. and Commercial Information, Econ. Dept, 1979–80; Dep. Dir-Gen., Protocol Dept, 1980–81; Ambassador: Brazil and Peru, 1981–83; Burma, 1983–90; Denmark and Iceland, 1990–91. Commander, Order of Dannebrog, Denmark, 1977; Grand Cross, Order of the Southern Cross, Brazil, 1983. *Recreation:* golf. *Address:* 16 Sukhumvit 34, Bangkok 10110, Thailand.

JOUGHIN, Sir Michael, Kt 1991; CBE 1971; JP; Chairman, Scottish Hydro-Electric plc (formerly North of Scotland Hydro-Electric Board), 1983–93; farmer, 1952–90; *b* 26 April 1926; *s* of John Clague Joughin and May Joughin; *m* 1st, 1948, Lesley Roy Petrie; one *s* one *d*; 2nd, 1981, Anne Hutchison. *Educ:* Kelly Coll., Tavistock. Lieut, Royal Marines, 1944–52, RM pilot with Fleet Air Arm, 1946–49. Pres., NFU of Scotland, 1964–66. Chm. of Governors: N of Scotland Coll. of Agriculture, 1969–72; Blairmore Prep. Sch., 1966–72; Chairman: N of Scotland Grassland Soc., 1970–71; Elgin Market Green Auction Co., 1969–70; Scottish Agricl Develt Council, 1971–80; N of Scotland Milk Marketing Bd, 1974–83. Governor: Rowett Research Inst., 1968–74; Scottish Plant Breeding Inst., 1969–74; Animal Diseases Research Assoc., Moredun Inst., 1969–74; Member: Intervention Bd for Agric. Produce, 1972–76; Econ. Develt Council for Agriculture, 1967–70; Agric. Marketing Develt Exec. Cttee, 1965–68; Scottish Constitutional Cttee, 1969–70; British Farm Produce Council, 1965–66. Mem. Aberdeen Bd, 1988–91, East of Scotland Bd, 1991–95, Bank of Scotland. Contested (C) Highland and Islands, European Parly Elections, 1979. FRAgS 1975. CIMgt (CBIM 1988; FBIM 1979). JP Moray, 1965; DL Moray, 1974–80. *Recreation:* sailing. *Address:* Elderslie, Findhorn, Moray IV30 3TN. *T:* Findhorn (01309) 690277. *Clubs:* New (Edinburgh); Royal Naval Sailing Assoc., Royal Marines Sailing, Royal Findhorn Yacht, Goldfish.

JOULWAN, Gen. George Alfred; Supreme Allied Commander, Europe, since 1993; Commander-in-Chief, United States European Command, since 1993; *b* 16 Nov. 1939; *m* Karen E. Jones; three *d*. *Educ:* US Mil. Acad., West Point (BS 1961); Loyola Univ. (Master of Pol Sci. 1968); US Army War Coll., Washington. Joined US Army, 1961; served Europe, US and Vietnam, 1962–73; Special Assistant to: the Pres., 1973–74; Supreme Allied Comdr, SHAPE, 1974–75; Bn Comdr, Europe, 1975–77; US Army War College: student, 1977–78; Dir, Pol and Econ. Studies, 1978–79; Bde Comdr, Europe, 1979–81; COS, 3 Inf. Div., Europe, 1981–82; Washington, DC, 1982–86; US Army Europe and Seventh Army: DCS for Ops, 1986–88; Commanding General: 3rd Armoured Div., 1988–89; V Corps, 1989–90; C-in-C, US Southern Comd, Quarry Heights, Panama, 1990–93. Defense Distinguished Service Medal (USA); Distinguished Service Medal (USA); Silver Star (with Oak Leaf Cluster) (USA); Hessian Order of Merit (FRG); Legion of Honour (France). *Address:* Supreme Headquarters Allied Powers Europe, B7010 SHAPE, Belgium. *T:* (65) 444113/444088.

JOWELL, Prof. Jeffrey Lionel; Professor of Public Law, since 1975, and Vice Provost, since 1992, University College London; *b* 4 Nov. 1938; *s* of Jack and Emily Jowell, Cape Town; *m* 1963, Frances Barbara, *d* of Helen Suzman, *qv*; one *s* one *d*. *Educ:* Cape Town Univ. (BA, LLB 1961); Hertford Coll., Oxford (BA 1963, MA 1969), Pres., Oxford Union Soc., 1963; Harvard Univ. Law Sch. (LLM 1966, SJD 1971). Called to Bar, Middle Temple, 1965. Research Asst, Harvard Law Sch., 1966–68; Fellow, Jt Center for Urban Studies of Harvard Univ. and MIT, 1967–68; Associate Prof. of Law and Admin. Studies, Osgoode Hall Law Sch., York Univ., Toronto, 1968–72; Leverhulme Fellow in Urban Legal Studies, 1972–74, and Lectr in Law, 1974–75, LSE; University College London: Dean, Faculty of Laws, 1979–89; Head of Dept, 1982–89. Chairman, Social Sciences and The Law Cttee, 1981–84, and Vice-Chm., Govt and Law Cttee, 1982–84, Social Science Res. Council; Asst Boundary Comr, 1976–85; Chm., Cttee of Heads of University Law Schools, 1984–86; Member: Cttee of Management, Inst. of Advanced Legal Studies, 1978–89; Standing Cttee, Oxford Centre for Socio-Legal Studies, 1980–84; Gp for Study of Comparative European Admin., 1978–86; Nuffield Cttee on Town and Country

Planning, 1983–86. UK deleg., Cttee of Experts, CSCE, Oslo, 1991. Non-exec. Director: UCL Press, 1993–; Camden and Islington Community Health Services NHS Trust, 1994–. Trustee: John Foster Meml Trust, 1986–; Internat. Centre for Public Law, 1992–. Lionel Cohen Lecture, Jerusalem, 1988; Vis. Prof., Univ. of Paris II, 1991. Hon. QC 1993. Hon. DJur: Athens, 1987; Ritsumeikan, 1988. Member Editorial Bds: Public Law, 1977–93; Policy and Politics, 1976–83; Urban Law and Policy, 1978–83; Jl of Environmental Law, 1988–92; Jt Editor, Current Legal Problems, 1984–89. *Publications:* Law and Bureaucracy, 1975; (ed jtly) Welfare Law and Policy, 1979; (ed jtly) Lord Denning: the Judge and the Law, 1984; (ed jtly) The Changing Constitution, 1985, 3rd edn 1994; (ed jtly) New Directions in Judicial Review, 1988; (jtly) Judicial Review of Administrative Action, 1995; articles and reviews on public law and planning law. *Recreations:* tennis, London, Exmoor. *Address:* University College London, Gower Street, WC1E 6BT. *T:* 0171–391 1405.

JOWELL, Tessa Jane Helen Douglas, (Tessa Mills); MP (Lab) Dulwich, since 1992; *b* 17 Sept. 1947; *d* of Kenneth and Rosemary Palmer; *m* 1st, 1970, Roger Jowell (marr. diss. 1976); 2nd, 1979, David Mills; one *s* one *d*. *Educ:* St Margaret's Sch., Aberdeen; Aberdeen Univ. (MA); Edinburgh Univ. (DSA). Child Care Officer, Lambeth, 1969–71; psychiatric social worker training, Goldsmiths' Coll., London Univ., 1971–72; Psychiatric Social Worker, Maudsley Hosp., 1972–74; Asst Dir, Mind, 1974–86; Dir, Community Care Special Action Project, Birmingham, and Sen. Vis. Fellow, PSI, 1986–90; Dir, Community Care Prog., Joseph Rowntree Foundn, and Vis Fellow, King's Fund Inst., 1990–92. Councillor, Camden, 1971–86. Chair, Social Services Cttee, AMA, 1984–86; Mem., Mental Health Act Commn, 1985–90. An Opposition Whip, 1994–. *Publications:* articles and contribs in social work and social policy jls. *Recreations:* gardening, reading, music, Italy. *Address:* House of Commons, Westminster, SW1A 0AA.

JOWETT, Very Rev. Alfred, CBE 1972; Dean of Manchester, 1964–83; *b* 29 May 1914; *s* of Alfred Edmund Jowett; *m* 1939, Margaret, *d* of St Clair Benford; one *s* three *d*. *Educ:* High Storrs Grammar Sch., Sheffield; St Catharine's Coll., Cambridge; Lincoln Theological Coll. BA 1935; Certif. Educn 1936; MA 1959. Deacon 1944; Priest 1945. Curate of St John the Evangelist, Goole, 1944–47; Sec., Sheffield Anglican and Free Church Council and Marriage Guidance Council, 1947–51; Vicar of St George with St Stephen, Sheffield, 1951–60; Part-time Lecturer, Sheffield Univ. Dept of Education, 1950–60; Vicar of Doncaster, 1960–64; Hon. Canon of Sheffield Cathedral, 1960–64. Select Preacher, Oxford Univ., 1964 and 1979. Mem., Community Relations Commn, 1968–77 (Dep. Chm., 1972–77). A Church Comr, 1978–80. Hon. Fellow, Manchester Polytechnic, 1972. OStJ 1979. Hon. LittD Sheffield, 1982. Hon. Freeman, City of Manchester, 1984. *Publication:* (part-author) The English Church: a New Look, 1966. *Recreations:* theatre, music, walking. *Address:* 37 Stone Delf, Sheffield S10 3QX. *T:* Sheffield (0114) 230 5455.

JOWITT, Hon. Sir Edwin (Frank), Kt 1988; **Hon. Mr Justice Jowitt;** a Justice of the High Court, Queen's Bench Division, since 1988; *b* 1 Oct. 1929; *s* of Frank and Winifred Jowitt; *m* 1959, Anne Barbara Dyson; three *s* two *d*. *Educ:* Swanwick Hall Grammar Sch.; London Sch. of Economics. LLB London 1950. Called to Bar, Middle Temple, 1951, Bencher 1977; Member Midland and Oxford Circuit, 1952–80. Dep. Chm. Quarter Sessions: Rutland, 1967–71; Derbyshire, 1970–71; QC 1969; a Recorder of the Crown Court, 1972–80; a Circuit Judge, 1980–88; a Sen. Circuit Judge, 1987–88; Hon. Recorder, Birmingham, 1987–88. *Recreations:* fell walking, cycling. *Address:* Royal Courts of Justice, Strand, WC2A 2LL.

JOWITT, Juliet Diana Margaret, (Mrs Thomas Jowitt); Member, Independent Broadcasting Authority, 1981–86; Director, Yorkshire Television, since 1987; *b* 24 Aug. 1940; *yr d* of late Lt-Col Robert Henry Langton Brackenbury, OBE and Eleanor Trewlove (*née* Springman); *m* 1963, Frederick Thomas Benson Jowitt; one *s* one *d*. *Educ:* Hatherop Castle; Switzerland and Spain. Associate Shopping Editor, House and Garden and Vogue, 1966–69; Proprietor, Wood House Design (Interior Design) (formerly Colour Go Round), 1971–. Member: Interior Decorators and Designers Assoc., 1985– (Mem. Council, 1989); Domestic Coal Consumers' Council, 1985–; Potato Marketing Bd, 1986–90. Mem., RTS, 1986–. JP North Yorkshire, 1973–89. *Address:* Thorpe Lodge, Littlethorpe, Ripon, N Yorkshire HG4 3LU; 11 St George's Square, SW1V 2HX.

JOXE, Pierre Daniel, Hon. KBE; Auditor General, Audit Office, Paris, since 1993; *b* 28 Nov. 1934; *s* of Louis Joxe and Françoise-Hélène Joxe (*née* Halévy); *m* 3rd, 1981, Valérie Cayeux; two *s*, and two *d* from a previous marr. *Educ:* Lycée Henri-IV; Faculté de droit de Paris; Ecole Nat. d'Administration. Started career in Audit Office, 1962; elected Deputy for Saône-et-Loire, 1973, 1978, 1981, 1986, 1988; Mem., European Parlt, 1977–79; Minister of Industry, 1981; Minister of the Interior, 1984–86, 1988–91; Minister of Defence, 1991–93. Mem. Exec., Socialist Party, 1971–. *Publications:* Parti socialiste, 1973; Atlas du socialisme, 1973. *Address:* (office) 13 rue Cambon, 75001 Paris, France.

JOY, David, CBE 1983; HM Diplomatic Service, retired; *b* 9 Dec. 1932; *s* of Harold Oliver Joy and late Doris Kate Buxton; *m* 1957, Montserrat Morancho Saumench, *o d* of Angel Morancho Garreta and Josefa Saumench Castells, Zaragoza, Spain; one *s* one *d*. *Educ:* Hulme Grammar Sch., Oldham, Lancs; St Catharine's Coll., Cambridge (MA). FBIM. HMOCS, Northern Rhodesia, 1956–64; Zambia, 1964–70: Cabinet Office, 1964; Under Sec. (Cabinet), 1968; Under Sec., Min. of Commerce and Industry, 1970; Ashridge Management Coll., 1970; joined HM Diplomatic Service, 1971; FCO, 1971–73; First Sec. (Inf.), Caracas, 1973–75; Head of Chancery, Caracas, 1975–77; Asst Head, Mexican and Caribbean Dept, FCO, 1977–78; Counsellor and Head of Chancery, Warsaw, 1978–82; Counsellor and Hd of British Interests Section, Buenos Aires, 1982–84; Head of Mexico and Central America Dept, FCO, 1984–87; Ambassador to Honduras and El Salvador, 1987–89; Consul Gen. Barcelona, 1989–92. *Recreations:* family-life, reading, tennis, golf, music. *Clubs:* United Oxford & Cambridge University; Circulo del Liceu (Barcelona).

JOY, Peter, OBE 1969; HM Diplomatic Service, retired; *b* 16 Jan. 1926; *s* of late Neville Holt Joy and Marguerite Mary Duff Beith; *m* 1953, Rosemary Joan Hebden; two *s* two *d*. *Educ:* Downhouse Sch., Pembridge; New Coll., Oxford. Served with RAF, 1944–47. Entered Foreign (subseq. Diplomatic) Service, 1952; 1st Sec., Ankara, 1959; 1st Sec., New Delhi, 1962; FO, 1965; 1st Sec., Beirut, 1968; FCO, 1973; Counsellor, Kuala Lumpur, 1979–80; Counsellor, FCO, 1980–86. *Recreations:* shooting, fishing. *Address:* The Old Rectory, Stoke Bliss, near Tenbury, Worcs WR15 8QJ. *T:* Kyre (01885) 410342; Carrick House, Eday, Orkney KW17 2AB.

JOY, Thomas Alfred, LVO 1979; President, Hatchards Ltd, 1985 (Managing Director, 1965–85); *b* 30 Dec. 1904; *s* of Alfred Joy and Annie Carpenter; *m* 1932, Edith Ellis. *Educ:* privately; Bedford House Sch., Oxford. Jun. Assistant, Bodleian Library, Oxford, 1919; indentured apprentice, 1919–25, buyer and cataloguer, 1925–35, J. Thornton & Son, University Booksellers, Oxford; Manager, Circulating Library, 1935–45, and Manager, Book Dept, 1942–45, Harrods; Army & Navy Stores: Manager, Book Dept, and founder of Library, 1945–56; Merchandise Manager, 1956; Dep. Managing Dir, 1956–65. Began Hatchards Authors of the Year parties, 1966. Employers' rep., Bookselling and Stationery Trade Wages Council, 1946–79, leader of employers' side, 1957; Member: Nat. Chamber of Trade, 1946–51; Wholesale Trades Adv. Cttee, 1946–51; 1948 Book Trade Cttee; Arts Council working party on obscene pubns, 1968–69, and sub-cttee on Public Lending Rights, 1970. President: Booksellers Assoc. of GB and Ire, 1957–58 (Hon. Life Pres., 1989); Book Trade Benevolent Soc., 1974–86 (Patron, 1986). Inaugurated Nat. Book Sale (first Chm. of Cttee, 1954–65). Hon. Life Mem., Soc. of Bookmen. FRSA 1967. Jubilee Medal, 1977. *Publications:* The Right Way to Run a Library Business, 1949; Bookselling, 1953; The Truth about Bookselling, 1964; Mostly Joy (autobiog.), 1971; The Bookselling Business, 1974; contribs to Bookseller and other trade jls. *Recreations:* reading, gardening, walking, motoring. *Address:* 13 Cole Park Gardens, Twickenham, Middlesex TW1 1JB. *T:* 0181–892 5660.

JOYCE, Robert John H.; *see* Hayman-Joyce.

JOYCE, William R., Jr; lawyer, since 1951; Director and Secretary-Treasurer, Battle of Britain Museum Foundation (USA), since 1976; President, Canterbury Institute Trust (USA), since 1989; *b* 18 May 1921; *s* of William R. Joyce and Winifred Lowery; *m* 1956, Mary-Hoyt Sherman; one *s* two *d*. *Educ:* Loyola Univ. (BA); New York and Harvard Law Schs. JD. Lawyer, in private practice, New York City and Washington, DC; member of firm, Vance Joyce & Carbaugh, 1977–; Consul General *ad hon.*, Republic of Bolivia (Washington, DC), 1963–. Pres., Consular Corps of Washington, DC, 1982–. FRGS. Kt 1973, Kt Comdr (pro Merito Melitensi), Order of Malta, 1977; Kt, Equestrian Order of Holy Sepulchre, Jerusalem, 1976; Kt Comdr of Grace, Order of Constantine and S George (Borbon-Two Sicilies), Naples, 1977; Order of Condor of the Andes, Bolivia, 1978; Order of Simon Bolivar the Liberator, Bolivia, 1988. *Recreations:* sailing, golf. *Address:* (residence) 4339 Garfield Street NW, Washington, DC 20007, USA. *T:* (202) 2447648; (office) 1701 Pennsylvania Avenue NW, Washington, DC 20006. *T:* (202) 2987133. *Clubs:* Squash Racquets Association, Middlesex CC; The Brook, India House, Union, New York Yacht (New York City); Metropolitan, Chevy Chase (Washington); Cooperstown Country (New York); Royal Malta Yacht (Malta).

JOYNSON-HICKS, family name of **Viscount Brentford.**

JOYNT, Rt. Rev. Michael Charles S.; *see* Scott-Joynt.

JUDD, family name of **Baron Judd.**

JUDD, Baron *cr* 1991 (Life Peer), of Portsea in the County of Hampshire; **Frank Ashcroft Judd;** consultant on international affairs, Third World issues, conflict resolution and arms control; Director, Oxfam, 1985–91; *b* 28 March 1935; *s* of late Charles Judd, CBE and Helen Judd, JP; *m* 1961, Christine Elizabeth Willington; two *d*. *Educ:* City of London Sch.; London Sch. of Economics. Sec.-Gen., IVS, 1960–66. Contested (Lab): Sutton and Cheam, 1959; Portsmouth West, 1964; MP (Lab) Portsmouth W, 1966–74, Portsmouth N, 1974–79; PPS: to Minister of Housing, 1967–70; to the Leader of the Opposition, 1970–72; Mem., Opposition's Front Bench Defence Team, 1972–74; Parliamentary Under-Secretary of State: for Defence (Navy), MoD, 1974–76; ODM 1976; Minister of State: for Overseas Develt, 1976–77; FCO, 1977–79; Mem., British Parly Delegn to Council of Europe and WEU, 1970–73; Opposition front bench spokesperson, H of L, on for. affairs, 1991–92, on educn, 1992–94, on overseas develt co-operation, 1994–. Indep. Advr to UK Delegn to UN Special Session on Disarmament, 1982. Associate Dir, Internat. Defence Aid Fund for Southern Africa, 1979–80; Dir, VSO, 1980–85. Chairman: Centre for World Development Educn, 1980–85; Internat. Council of Voluntary Agencies, 1985–90; World Econ. Forum Conf., Geneva, on the future of S Africa, 1990 and 1991; Member: Steering Cttee, World Bank—NGO Cttee, 1989–91; Internat. Commn on Global Governance, 1992–; WHO Task Force on Health and Develt. Past Chm., Fabian Soc. Chm., Oxford Diocesan Bd for Social Responsibility, 1992–. Member: Council, Overseas Development Inst.; ASTMS; Governing Body, Queen Elizabeth House, Oxford Univ., 1989–94; Council for Charitable Support, 1991–94; Trustee, Internat. Alert, 1994–. Chm. Council, Selly Oak Colls, Birmingham; Governor: LSE, 1982–; Westminster Coll., Oxford, 1991–. Freeman, City of Portsmouth, 1995. Hon. Fellow, Univ. of Portsmouth (formerly Portsmouth Poly.), 1978–. Hon. DLitt Bradford Univ., 1987. FRSA 1988. *Publications:* (jtly) Radical Future, 1967; Fabian International Essays, 1970; Purpose in Socialism, 1973; (jtly) Our Global Neighbourhood, 1995; various papers and articles on current affairs. *Recreations:* walking, family holidays. *Address:* House of Lords, SW1A 0PW. *Club:* Commonwealth Trust.

JUDD, Clifford Harold Alfred, CB 1987; Under Secretary, HM Treasury, 1981–87; *b* 27 June 1927; *s* of Alfred Ernest and Florence Louisa Judd; *m* 1951, Elizabeth Margaret Holmes; two *d*. *Educ:* Christ's Hospital; Keble Coll., Oxford. National Service, RA, 1946–48 (to 2/Lt). HM Treasury: Executive Officer, 1948, through ranks to Principal, 1964, Sen. Prin., 1969, Asst Sec., 1973. *Recreations:* cricket, golf, do-it-yourself. *Address:* 4 Colets Orchard, Otford, Kent TN14 5RA. *T:* Otford (01959) 522398. *Clubs:* Sevenoaks Vine; Knole Park Golf.

JUDD, Eric Campbell, CBE 1974; LVO 1956; Chairman, West Africa Committee, 1976–85 (Vice-Chairman, 1963–76); *b* St Thomas, Ont, 10 Aug. 1918; *s* of Frederick William Judd, PhmB (Canada), and Marjorie Katherine (*née* Bell); *m* 1947, Janet Creswell (*née* Fish); two *s* one *d*. *Educ:* Wellington, Canada; St Thomas Collegiate; Toronto Univ. Trainee Manager, Cities Service Oil Co., Canada, 1937–40. RCAF and RAF, 1940–45: Canada, N Atlantic Ferry Comd, Europe, Malta, Middle East, Far East, W Indies; retd Sqdn Ldr RCAF Reserve, 1945. Joined Unilever Ltd, 1946; United Africa Co. Ltd, Nigeria, 1946–60, Chm., 1957–60; Dir, UAC Ltd London, 1960, Man. Dir, 1968; Dep. Chm. and Jt Man. Dir, UAC International, 1969–77. Mem. House of Assembly, Western Nigeria, 1955–56; Chm., BNEC Africa, 1969–72; Chm., Adv. Gp Africa BOTB, 1972–74. Mem. Council, 1975–88, a Vice-Pres., 1983–88, Royal African Soc. *Recreations:* golf, tennis, theatre, music, reading. *Address:* 2 Gerard Court, Hitherfield Lane, Lydekker Park, Harpenden, Herts AL5 4JA. *T:* Harpenden (01582) 712617. *Clubs:* MCC; Mid-Herts Golf.

JUDD, Nadine; *see* Nerina, Nadia.

JUDGE, Harry George, MA Oxon, PhD London; Fellow of Brasenose College, Oxford, since 1973; Senior Research Associate, University of Oxford Department of Educational Studies, since 1988 (Director, 1973–88); *b* 1 Aug. 1928; *s* of George Arthur and Winifred Mary Judge; *m* 1956, Elizabeth Mary Patrick; one *s* two *d*. *Educ:* Cardiff High Sch.; Brasenose Coll., Oxford. Asst Master, Emanuel Sch. and Wallington County Grammar Sch., 1954–59; Dir of Studies, Cumberland Lodge, Windsor, 1959–62; Head Master, Banbury Grammar Sch., 1962–67; Principal, Banbury Sch., 1967–73. Visiting Professor: MIT, 1977 and 1980–82; Carnegie-Mellon Univ., 1984–86; Univ. of Virginia, 1987; Michigan State Univ., 1988–93; Pennsylvania State Univ., 1995–; Vis. Schol., Harvard Univ., 1985–87; Sachs Lectr, Teachers' Coll., Columbia Univ., 1993. Member: Public Schools Commission, 1966–70; James Cttee of Inquiry into Teacher Training, 1971–72; Educn Sub-Cttee, UGC, 1976–80; Oxon Educn Cttee, 1982–87. Chairman: School Broadcasting Council, 1977–81; RCN Commn on Education, 1984–85. Gen. Editor, Oxford Illus. Encyclopedia, 1985–. *Publications:* Louis XIV, 1965; School Is Not Yet Dead, 1974; Graduate Schools of Education in the US, 1982; A Generation of Schooling:

English secondary schools since 1944, 1984; The University and the Teachers: France, the United States, England, 1994; contribs on educational and historical subjects to collective works and learned jls. *Recreation:* canals. *Address:* Brasenose College, Oxford OX1 4AJ.

JUDGE, Ian; theatre director; *b* 21 July 1946; *s* of Jack and Marjorie Judge. *Educ:* King George V Grammar Sch., Southport; GSMD. Joined RSC as an asst dir, 1975; recent productions include: The Wizard of Oz, 1987; The Comedy of Errors, 1990; Love's Labour's Lost, 1993; Twelfth Night, 1994; A Christmas Carol, 1994; The Relapse, 1995; *opera:* English National Opera: Faust, 1985; Cavalleria Rusticana and Pagliacci, 1987; Don Quichotte, 1994; Opera North: Macbeth, 1987; Tosca, 1988; Boris Godunov, 1989; Attila, 1990; Show Boat, 1990 (also at London Palladium); Scottish Opera: Falstaff, 1991; Norma, 1993; Los Angeles: Tosca, 1989; Madama Butterfly, 1991; Melbourne: Faust, 1990; Tales of Hoffman, 1992 (and Australian tour); West Side Story, 1994; Macbeth, Cologne, 1992; The Flying Dutchman, Royal Opera House, 1992; *theatre:* Chichester: Oh! Kay, 1984; A Little Night Music, 1990 (also Piccadilly Theatre); Henry VIII, 1991. *Address:* c/o Simpson Fox Associates, 52 Shaftesbury Avenue, W1V 7DE. *T:* 0171–434 9167.

JUDGE, Hon. Sir Igor, Kt 1988; **Hon. Mr Justice Judge;** a Judge of the High Court, Queen's Bench Division, since 1988; *b* 19 May 1941; *s* of Raymond and Rosa Judge; *m* 1965, Judith Mary Robinson; one *s* two *d. Educ:* Oratory Sch., Woodcote; Magdalene Coll., Cambridge (Exhbnr, MA). Harmsworth Exhbnr and Astbury Scholar, Middle Temple. Called to the Bar, Middle Temple, 1963, Bencher, 1987; QC 1979. A Recorder, 1976–88; Prosecuting Counsel to Inland Revenue, 1977–79, Leader, 1988, Presiding Judge, 1993–, Midland and Oxford Circuit. Member: Senate, Inns of Court and the Bar, 1980–83, 1984–86; Bar Council, 1987–88; Judicial Studies Bd, 1984–88, 1991–94 (Chm. Criminal Cttee, 1991–93). *Recreations:* history, music, cricket. *Address:* Royal Courts of Justice, Strand, WC2A 2LL.

JUDGE, Paul Rupert; Director General, Conservative Party, since 1992; *b* 25 April 1949; *s* of late Rupert Cyril Judge and of Betty Rosa Muriel Judge (*née* Daniels), Forest Hill; *m* 1983, Anne Marie, *d* of late John James Foff and Anne Marie Foff (*née* Brown), Philadelphia; two *s. Educ:* St Dunstan's Coll.; Trinity Coll., Cambridge (MA, Open Scholar); Wharton Business Sch., Univ. of Pennsylvania (MBA, Thouron Schol.). Cadbury Schweppes, 1973–86 (Group Planning Dir, 1984–86); Premier Brands: Man. Dir, 1986–87; Chm., 1987–89; Chairman: Isoworth, 1989–; Food from Britain, 1989–92; Director of WPP plc and other cos. Chm., Adv. Bd, Cambridge Univ. Inst. of Management Studies, 1991–; Trustee, Cambridge Foundn, 1991–; Mem. Council, Assoc. of MBAs, 1992–. Gov., Bromsgrove Sch., 1990–. FInstD; FIGD; Fellow, Marketing Soc.; FRSA. Freeman, City of London; Liveryman, Marketors' Co., 1993. *Recreations:* family, travel. *Address:* Conservative Central Office, 32 Smith Square, SW1P 3HH. *T:* 0171–222 9000. *Clubs:* Athenæum, Carlton, St Stephen's Constitutional; Mombasa (Kenya).

JUGNAUTH, Rt. Hon. Sir Aneerood, KCMG 1988; PC 1987; QC (Mauritius) 1980; Prime Minister of Mauritius, since 1982; concurrently Minister of Defence and Internal Security, Minister of Information and Minister of Internal and External Communications and the Outer Islands; *b* 29 March 1930; *m* Sarojini Devi Ballah; one *s* one *d. Educ:* Church of England School, Palma, Mauritius; Regent Coll., Quatre Bornes. Called to the Bar, Lincoln's Inn, 1954. Teacher, New Eton Coll., 1948; worked in Civil Service, 1949. MLA Rivière du Rempart, 1963–67, Piton-Rivière du Rempart, 1976, 1982, 1983, 1987 and 1991–; Town Councillor, Vacoas-Phoenix, 1964; Minister of State for Develt, 1965–67; Minister of Labour, 1967; Leader of the Opposition, 1976–82; Minister of Finance, 1983–84 and 1990–91; Dist Magistrate, 1967–69, Crown Counsel, 1969; Sen. Crown Counsel, 1971. Attended London Constitutional Conf., 1965. Leader, Mouvement Socialist Militant, 1983–. Dr *hc* Aix-en-Provence, 1985; Hon. DCL Mauritius, 1985. Order of Rising Sun (1st cl.) (Japan), 1988; Grand Officier, Ordre de la Légion d'Honneur (France), 1990. *Address:* Office of the Prime Minister, Government House, Port Louis, Mauritius.

JUKES, Rt. Rev. John, OFMConv; STL; VG; an Auxiliary Bishop in Southwark, (RC), since 1980; Titular Bishop of Strathearn, since 1980; *b* 7 Aug. 1923; *s* of Francis Bernard Jukes and Florence Jukes (*née* Stampton). *Educ:* Blackheath; Rome. Professed in Order of Friars Minor Conventual, 1948; Priest, 1952. Lectr in Canon Law, Franciscan Study Centre, Univ. of Kent at Canterbury; Minister Provincial, English Province, 1979. Episcopal Vicar for Religious, Southwark; Area Bishop with special responsibility for Deaneries of Canterbury, Chatham, Dover, Gravesend, Maidstone, Ramsgate and Tunbridge Wells. Chm., World of Work Cttee, RC Bishops' Conf. of England and Wales, 1983–. Chm. Governors, St Mary's UC, Sussex Univ. *Publications:* contribs to Misc. Francescana, Studia Canonica, New Life, Clergy Rev., etc. *Recreation:* mountain walking and climbing. *Address:* The Hermitage, More Park, West Malling, Kent ME19 6HN.

JUKES, John Andrew, CB 1968; *b* 19 May 1917; *s* of Captain A. M. Jukes, MD, IMS, and Mrs Gertrude E. Jukes (*née* King); *m* 1943, Muriel Child; two *s* two *d. Educ:* Shrewsbury Sch.; St John's Coll., Cambridge; London Sch. of Economics. MA in physics Cambridge, BSc (Econ.) London. Cavendish Laboratory, Cambridge, 1939; Radar and Operational Research, 1939–46; Research Dept, LMS Railway, 1946–48; Economic Adviser, Cabinet Office and Treasury, 1948–54; British Embassy, Washington, DC, 1949–51; Economic Adviser to UK Atomic Energy Authority, 1954–64 and Principal Economics and Programming Office, UKAEA, 1957–64; Dep. Dir Gen., DEA, 1964; Dep. Under-Sec. of State, Dept of Economic Affairs, 1967; Dir Gen., Research and Economic Planning, MoT, 1969–70; Dir Gen., Economics and Resources, DoE, 1970–72; Dep. Sec. (Environmental Protection), DoE, 1972–74; Chm., Steering Gp on Water Authority Econ. and Financial Objectives, 1973–74; Dir-Gen., Highways, DoE, 1974–76, Dept of Transport, 1976–77. Mem., CEGB, 1977–80. Mem., Merton and Sutton DHA, 1986–90. Alliance (SDP) Councillor, London Borough of Sutton, 1986–90 (Chm., Finance Sub-Cttee, 1986–90). Rep. Sutton SDP on Council for Social Democracy, 1982–86; Pres., Sutton Lib Dems, 1990–93. *Recreations:* gardening, travelling, sometime orienteer and Himalayan trekker. *Address:* 38 Albion Road, Sutton, Surrey SM2 5TF. *T:* 0181–642 5018.

JULIAN, Prof. Desmond Gareth, CBE 1993; MD, FRCP; Consultant Medical Director, British Heart Foundation, 1987–93; *b* 24 April 1926; *s* of Frederick Bennett Julian and Jane Frances Julian (*née* Galbraith); *m* 1st, 1956, Mary Ruth Jessup (decd); one *s* one *d*; 2nd, 1988, Claire Marley. *Educ:* Leighton Park Sch.; St John's Coll., Cambridge; Middlesex Hosp. MB BChir (Cantab) 1948; MA 1953; MD 1954; FRCPE 1967; FRCP 1970; FRACP 1970; FACC 1985. Surgeon Lieut, RNVR, 1949–51. Med. Registrar, Nat. Heart Hosp., 1955–56; Res. Fellow, Peter Bent Brigham Hosp., Boston, 1957–58; Sen. Reg., Royal Inf., Edinburgh, 1958–61; Cons. Cardiologist, Sydney Hosp., 1961–64, Royal Inf., Edinburgh, 1964–74; Prof. of Cardiology, Univ. of Newcastle upon Tyne, 1975–86. Mem., MRC Systems Bd, 1980–84. Pres., British Cardiac Soc., 1985–87; Second Vice-Pres., RCP, 1990–91. Hon. MD Gothenburg, 1987. Editor, European Heart Jl, 1980–88. *Publications:* Cardiology, 1972, 6th edn 1992; (ed) Angina Pectoris, 1975, 2nd edn 1984; Acute Myocardial Infarction, 1967; (ed) Diseases of the Heart, 1989, 2nd edn 1995; Coronary Heart Disease: the facts, 1991; contribs to med. jls, particularly on coronary disease and arrhythmias. *Recreations:* walking, ski-ing, writing. *Address:* Flat 1, 7 Netherhall Gardens, NW3 5RN. *T:* 0171–435 8254. *Clubs:* Athenæum, Garrick.

JULIEN, Michael Frederick, FCA; FCT; Chairman, First Choice Holidays PLC (formerly Owners Abroad Group plc), since 1993; *b* 22 March 1938; *s* of late Robert Auguste François and Olive Rita (*née* Evans); *m* 1963, Ellen Martinsen; one *s* two *d. Educ:* St Edward's Sch., Oxford. Price Waterhouse & Co., 1958–67; other commercial appts, 1967–76; Gp Finance Dir, BICC, 1976–83; Exec. Dir, Finance and Planning, Midland Bank, 1983–86; Man. Dir, Finance and Administration, Guinness PLC, 1987–88; Gp Chief Exec., Storehouse PLC, 1988–92. Director (non-executive): Guinness PLC; Medeva PLC; Chiltern Financial Services PLC. *Recreations:* family, travel. *Address:* Bendochy, Ellesmere Road, Weybridge, Surrey KT13 0HQ. *T:* Weybridge (01932) 844999. *Club:* Athenæum.

JUNCKER, Dr Jean-Claude; Prime Minister, Minister of State, Minister of Finance and Minister of Labour and Employment, Luxembourg, since 1995; *b* Redange-Attert, 9 Dec. 1954; *m* 1979, Christiane Frising. *Educ:* Secondary Sch., Clairefontaine, Belgium; Univ. of Strasbourg (Dr Public Law 1979). Parly Sec., Christian Social Party, 1979–82; State Sec. for Labour and Social Affairs, 1982–84; Minister of: Labour and Minister i/c Budget, 1984–89; Labour and of Finance, 1989–95. Pres., Christian Social Party, 1990–95. *Address:* Hôtel de Bourgogne, 4 rue de la Congrégation, 2910 Luxembourg. *T:* 4782101, *Fax:* 461720.

JUNGELS, Dr Pierre Jean Marie Henri, Hon. CBE 1989; Executive Director, Exploration and Production, Petrofina Group, since 1992; *b* 18 Feb. 1944; *s* of Henri and Jeanne Jungels; *m* 1988, Caroline Benc; one *s* one *d* from former marriage. *Educ:* Univ. of Liège; California Inst. of Technology (PhD 1973). Petroleum Engr, Shell, 1973–74; Dist Manager, 1975–77, General Manager and Chief Exec., 1977–80, Petrangol (Angola); Man. Dir and Chief Exec., Petrofina UK, 1980–89; Exec. Dir, Downstream, Petrofina Gp, 1989–92. Director: Fina SA, Belgium; Fina Italiana; Fina plc; Fina Inc.; Petrofina Delaware Inc.; Fina Explo. Norway; American Petrofina; Fina Marine; Fina Research. Past Pres., Inst. of Petroleum. *Recreation:* shooting. *Address:* Petrofina SA, 52 rue de l'Industrie, 1040 Brussels, Belgium. *T:* (2) 2883455, *Telex:* 21556, *Fax:* (2) 2883150.

JUNGIUS, Vice-Adm. Sir James (George), KBE 1977; Supreme Allied Commander Atlantic's Representative in Europe, 1978–80, retired; Vice Lord-Lieutenant of Cornwall, since 1994; *b* 15 Nov. 1923; *s* of Major E. J. T. Jungius, MC; *m* 1949, Rosemary Frances Turquand Matthey; three *s. Educ:* RNC, Dartmouth. Served War of 1939–45 in Atlantic and Mediterranean; Commando Ops in Adriatic (despatches). Specialised in Navigation in 1946, followed by series of appts as Navigating Officer at sea and instructing ashore. Comdr, Dec. 1955; CO, HMS Wizard, 1956–57; Admlty, 1958–59; Exec. Officer, HMS Centaur, 1960–61; Captain, 1963; Naval Staff, 1964–65; CO, HMS Lynx, 1966–67; Asst Naval Attaché, Washington, DC, 1968–70; CO, HMS Albion, 1971–72; Rear-Adm., 1972; Asst Chief of Naval Staff (Operational Requirements), 1972–74; Vice-Adm., 1974; Dep. Supreme Allied Comdr Atlantic, 1975–77. County Pres., Cornwall, RBL, 1995–. Fellow, Woodard Corp., 1988. Gov., Grenville Coll., 1981–. CIMgt. DL Cornwall, 1982. CStJ 1995 (Chm., St John Council for Cornwall, 1987–95). *Address:* c/o National Westminster Bank, Wadebridge, Cornwall PL27 7DL. *Clubs:* Royal Navy Club of 1765 and 1785; Pilgrims; Royal Cornwall Yacht.

JUNOR, Sir John, Kt 1980; Editor, Sunday Express, 1954–86; *b* 15 Jan. 1919; *s* of Alexander Junor, Black Isle, Ross and Cromarty; *m* 1942, Pamela Mary Welsh; one *s* one *d. Educ:* Glasgow Univ. (MA Hons English). Lt (A) RNVR, 1939–45. Contested (L) Kincardine and West Aberdeen, 1945, East Edinburgh, 1948, Dundee West, 1951; Asst Editor, Daily Express, 1951–53; Dep. Editor, Evening Standard, 1953–54; Director: Beaverbrook (later Express) Newspapers, 1960–86; Fleet Hldgs, 1981–85. Columnist: Sunday Express, 1973–89; Mail on Sunday, 1990–. Hon. LLD New Brunswick, 1973. *Publications:* The Best of JJ, 1981; Listening for a Midnight Tram (memoirs), 1990. *Recreations:* golf, tennis. *Address:* c/o Associated Newspapers, Northcliffe House, 2 Derry Street, W8 5AT. *Clubs:* Royal and Ancient; Walton Heath.

JUPE, George Percival; Under Secretary, Ministry of Agriculture, Fisheries and Food, 1979–90; *b* 6 April 1930; *s* of Frederick Stuart Jupe and Elizabeth (*née* Clayton); unmarried. *Educ:* Sandown Grammar Sch., IoW; Hertford Coll., Oxford. Ministry of Agriculture, Fisheries and Food: Asst Principal, 1955; Principal, 1960; Asst Sec., 1970–79: Eggs and Poultry, and Potatoes Divs, 1970–74; Internat. Fisheries Div., 1975–78; Emergencies, Food Quality and Pest Controls Gp, 1979–85; Dir, ADAS Admin, 1985–88; Horticulture, Seeds, Plant Health and Flood Defence Gp, 1988–90. *Recreations:* hill walking, gardening, music. *Address:* Briar Cottages, Brook, Isle of Wight PO30 4EU.

JUPP, Sir Kenneth Graham, Kt 1975; MC 1943; a Judge of the High Court, Queen's Bench Division, 1975–90; *b* 2 June 1917; *s* of Albert Leonard and Marguerite Isabel Jupp; *m* 1947, Kathleen Elizabeth (*née* Richards); two *s* two *d. Educ:* Perse Sch., Cambridge; University Coll., Oxford (Sen. Class. Schol., 1936; 1st Cl. Hon. Mods (Classics) 1938; College Prize for Greek, 1939; MA Oxon (War Degree), 1945); Lincoln's Inn (Cholmeley Schol., 1939; Cassel Schol., 1946). Regimental Service in France, Belgium, N Africa and Italy, 1939–43; War Office Selection Board, 1943–46. Called to Bar, Lincoln's Inn, 1945, Bencher, 1973; QC 1966; Dep. Chm., Cambridge and Isle of Ely QS, 1965–71; a Recorder of the Crown Court, 1972–75; Presiding Judge, NE Circuit, 1977–81. Chm., Independent Schs Tribunal, 1964–67; conducted MAFF inquiry into Wool Marketing Scheme, 1965; Chm., Public Inquiry into Fire at Fairfield Home, Nottingham, 1975. *Recreations:* playing and singing, language. *Address:* Farrar's Building, Temple, EC4Y 7BD. *Club:* Garrick.

JUPPÉ, Alain Marie; Prime Minister of France, since 1995; *b* 15 Aug. 1945; *s* of Robert Juppé and Marie Darroze; *m* 1st, 1965, Christine Leblond (marr. diss.); one *s* one *d*; 2nd, 1993, Isabelle Bodin. *Educ:* Lycées Victor-Duruy, Mont-de-Marsan and Louis-le-Grand, Paris; Ecole Normale Superieure (Dr in Classical Langs); Inst. of Political Studies; Nat. Sch. of Admin. Finance Inspector, 1972; Asst to Prime Minister Jacques Chirac, 1976; Advr to Minister for Co-operation, 1976–78; MEP, 1984–86; Minister of Foreign Affairs, France, 1993–95. Rassemblement pour la République: Nat. Deleg., 1976–78; Nat. Sec., 1984–86; Dep. Minister of Finance, Govt Spokesman, 1986–88; Gen. Sec., 1988–; Deputy for Paris, 1988–93. Adviser to Mayor of Paris, 1978; Dir of Finance and Economic Affairs, City of Paris, 1980–81; Mem., Paris City Council, 1983–; Dep. Mayor of Paris, i/c Finance, 1983–95. *Publication:* La Tentation de Venise, 1993. *Address:* Hôtel Matignon, 57 rue de Varenne, 75700 Paris, France; Hôtel de Ville, 75196 Paris, France.

JURINAC, (Srebrenka) Sena; opera singer; Member of Vienna State Opera, 1944–82, now Honorary; retired from stage, 1982; *b* Travnik, Yugoslavia, 24 Oct. 1921; *d* of Ludwig Jurinac, MD, and Christine Cerv. *Educ:* High Sch.; Musical Academy. Made first appearance on stage as Mimi with Zagreb Opera, 1942. Frequent appearances at Glyndebourne Festivals, 1949–56, as well as at the Salzburg Festivals. Guest appearances at

La Scala, Covent Garden, San Francisco, Teatro Colón. Principal parts include: Donna Anna and Donna Elvira in Don Giovanni; Elisabeth in Tannhauser; Tosca; Jenufa; Marie in Wozzeck; Marschallin in Der Rosenkavalier; Composer in Ariadne auf Naxos; Elisabeth in Don Carlos; Desdemona in Othello. *Film:* Der Rosenkavalier, 1962. Singing teacher; frequent appearances as mem. of jury in singing competitions. Kammersängerin award, 1951; Ehrenkreuz für Wissenschaft und Kunst, 1961; Grosses Ehrenzeichen für Verdienste um die Republik Oesterreich, 1967. *Address:* c/o Vienna State Opera, 1010 Vienna, Austria.

JURY, Archibald George, CBE 1961; FRIBA; FRIAS; City Architect, Glasgow, 1951–72, retired; *b* 23 June 1907; *s* of late George John Jury and Mabel Sophie Jury (*née* Fisher); *m* 1931, Amy Beatrice Maw (MBE 1983); one *d*. *Educ:* Mount Radford, Exeter; SW School of Art. Architect to Council, Taunton, 1938–40, and 1945. Served War, 1940–45, with Corps of Royal Engineers (rank of Major). Chief Housing Architect, Liverpool, 1946–49; Dir of Housing, Glasgow, 1949–51; Dir of Planning, Glasgow, 1951–66. Organised the building of 100,000 houses, 100,000 school places and numerous civic buildings; responsible for the Glasgow Devpt Plan, 1960–80, and implementation of urban renewal programme and official architecture. Several Saltire Soc. awards for best-designed flats in Scotland. Chairman: Technical Panel, Scottish Local Authorities Special Housing Group, 1965–72; Technical Panel, Clyde Valley Planning Adv. Cttee, 1960–70; Pres., Glasgow Inst. of Architects, 1970–72. *Publications:* contrib. professional and technical journals. *Recreations:* fishing, gardening, painting. *Address:* Redcliffe, Annan Road, Dumfries DG1 3HE.

K

KABERRY, Hon. Sir Christopher Donald, (Hon. Sir Kit), 2nd Bt *cr* 1960, of Adel cum Eccup, City of Leeds; management consultant, since 1991; *b* 14 March 1943; *s* of Lord Kaberry of Adel (Life Peer) and Lily Margaret (*d* 1992), *d* of Edmund Scott; *S* to baronetcy of father, 1991; *m* 1967, Gaenor Elizabeth Vowe, *d* of C. V. Peake; two *s* one *d*. *Educ:* Repton Sch. FCA 1967. Various overseas positions, Costain Group PLC, 1969–80; Financial Manager, United Buildings Factories, Bahrain, 1980–82; Resources Manager, Balfour Beatty Group, Indonesia and Bahamas, 1983–90. *Recreations:* walking, gardening, Land Rover driving. *Heir: s* James Christopher Kaberry [*b* 1 April 1970; *m* 1989, Juliet Clare Hill; two *s* one *d*]. *Address:* Rock View, Chiddingstone Hoath, Kent TN8 7BT.

KADRI, Sibghatullah; QC 1989; barrister-at-law; President, Standing Conference of Pakistani Organisations in UK, 1978–90 (Secretary General, 1975–78); Member, Race Relations Committee, Senate, since 1983; *b* 23 April 1937; *s* of Haji Maulana Firasat Ullah Kadri and Begum Tanwir Fatima Kadri; *m* 1963, Carita Elisabeth Idman; one *s* one *d*. *Educ:* S. M. Coll., Karachi; Karachi Univ. Called to the Bar, Inner Temple, 1969. Sec. Gen., Karachi Univ. Students Union, 1957–58; jailed without trial, for opposing military regime of Ayub Khan, 1958–59; triple winner, All Pakistan Students Debates, 1960; Gen. Sec., Pakistan Students' Fedn in Britain, 1961–62, Vice Pres., 1962–63; Pres., Inner Temple Students Assoc., 1969–70. Producer and broadcaster, BBC Ext. Urdu Service, 1965–68, and Presenter, BBC Home Service Asian Prog., 1968–70. In practice at the Bar, 1969– (Head of Chambers, 6 King's Bench Walk). Chm., Soc. of Afro-Asian and Caribbean Lawyers, UK, 1979–83. Vis. Lectr in Urdu, Holborn Coll., London, 1967–70. Org. Pakistani Def. Cttees during wave of 'Paki-bashing', 1970; active in immigrant and race-relations activities, 1970–; led Asian delegn to Prime Minister, June 1976; attended UN Conf., Migrant Workers in Europe, Geneva, 1975; led Pakistan delegn to 3rd Internat. Conf., Migrant Workers in Europe, Turin, 1977. Gen. Sec., Pakistan Action Cttee, 1973; Convenor, Asian Action Cttee, 1976. Vice Chm., All Party Jt Cttee Against Racism, 1978–80. Publisher, Scopo News, London, until 1984. FRSA 1991. *Publications:* articles in ethnic minority press on immigration and race relations. *Recreations:* family and reading. *Address:* 6 King's Bench Walk, Temple, EC4Y 7EQ. *T:* 0171–353 4931/2.

KAFITY, Most Rev. Samir; President Bishop of the Episcopal Church in Jerusalem and the Middle East, since 1986; Anglican Bishop of Jerusalem, since 1984; *b* 21 Sept. 1933; *s* of Hanna and Nazha Kafity; *m* 1963, Najat Abed; two *d*. *Educ:* American Univ., Beirut (BA); Near East Sch. of Theol. (DipTh). Ordained deacon, 1957, priest, 1958; Parish priest: to the Arab congregation at St George's Cathedral, Jerusalem, 1957–59; St Andrew's Ramallah, 1959–64; St Peter's, Beir Zeit, then All Saints, Beirut, 1964–77; Lectr, Beir Zeit Univ.; Archdeacon of Jerusalem, 1977–82; Coadjutor Bp in Jerusalem, 1982. Member: Standing Cttee, ACC, 1965; Bd of Managers and Exec. Cttee, Near East Sch. of Theol., 1965; Council of Evangelical Community in Syria and Lebanon, 1965–77. Sec., ME Council of Churches, 1974–94 (Pres., 1985). Hon. Canon, Cathedral Church of St John the Divine, NY, 1988. Hon. STD Dickenson Coll., Pa, 1985; Hon. DD Virginia Theol Seminary, 1986. KHS. *Publications:* articles in Anglican and ecumenical jls. *Recreation:* travel. *Address:* PO Box 19122, Jerusalem, Israel. *T:* (2) 287708, *Fax:* (2) 273847. *Club:* YMCA (Jerusalem).

KAHAN, Barbara Joan, OBE 1990; Vice President, National Children's Bureau, since 1994 (Chair, 1985–94); consultant in child care, since 1988; *b* 18 March 1920; *d* of Alfred George Langridge and Emily Kathleen (*née* Bromley); *m* 1955, Dr Vladimir Leon Kahan. *Educ:* Cambridge Univ. (MA); LSE (Post-grad. Dip. in Social Sci.). HMI of Factories, 1943–48; Children's Officer, 1948–70; Dep. Chief Inspector, Children's Dept, Home Office, 1970–71, DHSS, 1971–80. Mem., Finer Cttee on One Parent Families, 1969–73; Dir, Gatsby Project, 1980–91; Professional Advr to H of C Select Cttee on Social Services, 1983–90; jtly with A. Levy, QC, investigation into Staffs "Pindown" abuse, 1990. Chair, Wagner Develt Children's Gp, 1990–93. Pres., Assoc. of Children's Officers, 1964; Hon. Mem., Assoc. of Dirs of Social Services, 1983. MUniv Open, 1987; Hon. LLD Victoria, BC, 1994. *Publications:* (with G. Banner) Residential Task in Child Care, 1968; Growing Up in Care: ten people talking, 1979; (with G. Banner and D. Lane) Staff: finding them, choosing them, keeping them, 1986; (ed) Child Care Research, Policy and Practice, 1989; (with A. Levy) The Pindown Experience and the Protection of Children, 1991; Growing up in Groups, 1994. *Recreations:* reading, writing, music, cooking. *Address:* Hampton House, The Green, Cassington, Witney, Oxon OX8 1DW. *T:* Oxford (01865) 881265. *Club:* Reform.

KAHAN, George; Director of Conciliation and Arbitration, Advisory, Conciliation and Arbitration Service, 1988–91; *b* 11 June 1931; *er s* of late Joseph Kahan and of Xenia (*née* Kirschner); *m* 1959, Avril Pamela Cooper; one *s*. *Educ:* St Paul's Sch. Nat. Service, RAF, 1950–51. Park Royal Woodworkers Ltd, 1951–74 (Dir, 1960–74); Principal: Dept. of Employment, 1975–76; Health and Safety Executive, Health and Safety Commn, 1976–80; Asst Sec., Dept of Employment, 1980–88. *Recreations:* lazing in the sun, reading, listening to music. *Address:* Half Timbers, The Thatchway, Rustington, Sussex BN16 2BN. *T:* Rustington (01903) 784070.

KAHN, Prof. Franz Daniel, DPhil; FRS 1993; Professor of Astronomy, University of Manchester, 1966–93, now Emeritus; *b* 13 May 1926; *s* of Siegfried and Grete Kahn; *m* 1951, Carla Copeland (*d* 1981); two *s* two *d*. *Educ:* St Paul's Sch.; Queen's and Balliol Colls, Oxford Univ. MA, DPhil (Oxon). University of Manchester: Asst Lectr in Mathematics, 1949–52; Turner Newall Fellow, 1952–55; Lectr in Astronomy, 1955–58; Sen. Lectr, 1958–62; Reader, 1962–66. Jt Winner, Prize Essay Comp. on Star Formation, German Soc. of Scientists and Physicians, 1958. Asteroid Kahnia named by Internat. Astronomical Union, 1991. *Publications:* (with H. P. Palmer) Quasars, 1966; scientific papers in Monthly Notices, Astronomy and Astrophysics and other astronomical jls. *Recreations:* food and drink, with special interest in processes involving fermentation, eg baking bread and visiting distilleries. *Address:* 27 Ballbrook Avenue, Manchester M20 3JG. *T:* 0161–445 3648.

KAHN, Paula; Chief Executive and Chairman, Longman Group Ltd, 1990–94; *b* 15 Nov. 1940; *d* of Cyril Maurice Kahn and Stella Roscoe. *Educ:* Chiswick County High Sch.; Bristol Univ. (BA Hons). Teacher, administrator, 1962–66; Longman Group, 1966–94: editor, publisher, Publishing Director, Divl Man. Dir, 1966–79; Managing Director: ELT Div., Dictionaries Div. and Trade and Ref. Div., 1980–85; Internat. Sector, 1986–88; Chief Exec. (Publishing), 1988–89. Member: English Teaching Adv. Cttee, British Council, 1990–; Educn and Training Sector Gp, DTI, 1993–; Bd, Inst. of Internat. Visual Arts, 1994–. Founder Mem., Bentick Gp, 1994–. Vice-Pres., Publishers Assoc., 1994–95. Mem., Governing Body, SOAS, 1993–. FRSA 1993; CIMgt 1992. *Recreations:* cinema, theatre, France, books. *Address:* 4 Mica House, Barnsbury Square, N1 1RN.

KAHN-ACKERMANN, Georg; Secretary General, Council of Europe, 1974–79; *b* 4 Jan. 1918; *m* 1945, Rosmarie Müller-Diefenbach; one *s* three *d*. *Educ:* in Germany and Switzerland. Served in Armed Forces, 1939–45. Press Reporter and Editor from 1946; Commentator with Radio Bavaria and wrote for newspaper, Abendzeitung, 1950. Author of several books, a publisher's reader, and mem. Exec. Cttee of Bavarian Assoc. of Journalists. Dir, VG WORT, Munich, 1972–74; Vice-Chm., Bd of Deutschlandfunk (Cologne). Mem., Social Democratic Party (SDP), from 1946, and of the German Federal Parliament, 1953–57, 1962–69 and 1970–74. Previous appts include: Vice-Pres., Western European Union Assembly, 1967–70; Chm., Political Commn of Western European Union, 1971–74; Vice-Pres., Consultative Assembly of Council of Europe until elected Secretary General in 1974. Vice-Pres., Deutsche Welthunger hilfe; Pres., VG WORT. *Recreation:* ski-ing. *Address:* Sterzenweg 3, 82541 Ammerland, Bayern, Germany.

KAHURANANGA, Rt. Rev. Musa; *b* 1921; *s* of Samweli and Mariamu Kahurananga; *m* 1941, Raheli Lutozi; three *s* four *d* (and one *s* decd). *Educ:* Teachers' Training College, Katoke Bukoba. Teacher; Deacon 1952, Priest 1953; Asst Bishop in Diocese of Central Tanganyika, 1962; Archbishop of Tanzania, 1979–83; Bishop of Western Tanganyika, 1966–83. *Recreation:* farming. *Address:* PO Box 234, Kasulu, Tanzania.

KAIN, Prof. Roger James Peter, PhD; FSA; FBA 1990; Montefiore Professor of Geography, Exeter University, since 1991; *b* 12 Nov. 1944; *s* of Peter Albert Kain and Ivy Kain; *m* 1970, Annmaree Wallington; two *s*. *Educ:* Harrow Weald County Grammar Sch.; University College London (BA, PhD). FSA 1992. Tutor, Bedford Coll., London, 1971–72; Exeter University: Lectr, 1972–88; Montefiore Reader in Geography, 1988–91. Gill Meml Medal, RGS, 1990; Kenneth Nebenzahl Prize, Newberry Liby, Chicago, 1991. *Publications:* Planning for Conservation: an international perspective, 1984; The Tithe Surveys of England and Wales, 1985; An Atlas and Index of the Tithe Files of Mid-Nineteenth-Century England and Wales, 1986; (jtly) Cadastral Mapping in the Service of the State: a history of property mapping, 1992; (jtly) The Tithe Maps of England and Wales: a cartographic analysis and county-by-county catalogue, 1995. *Recreations:* mountain walking, gardening, fishing. *Address:* Department of Geography, Exeter University, Exeter EX4 4RJ. *T:* Exeter (01392) 263333.

KAISER, Philip M.; political and economic consultant; *b* 12 July 1913; *s* of Morris Kaiser and Temma Kaiser (*née* Sloven); *m* 1939, Hannah Greeley; three *s*. *Educ:* University of Wisconsin; Balliol Coll., Oxford (Rhodes Scholar). Economist, Bd of Governors, Fed. Reserve System, 1939–42; Chief, Project Ops Staff, also Chief, Planning Staff, Bd Economic Warfare and Foreign Econ. Admin., 1942–46; Expert on Internat. Organization Affairs, US State Dept., 1946; Exec. Asst to Asst Sec. of Labor in charge of internat. labor affairs, US Dept of Labor, 1947–49; Asst Sec. of Labor for Internat. Labor Affairs, 1949–53; mem., US Govt Bd of Foreign Service, Dept of State, 1948–53; US Govt mem., Governing Body of ILO, 1948–53; Chief, US delegn to ILO Confs, 1949–53; Special Asst to Governor of New York, 1954–58; Prof. of Internat. Relations and Dir, Program for Overseas Labor and Industrial Relations, Sch. of Internat. Service, American Univ., 1958–61; US Ambassador, Republic of Senegal and Islamic Republic of Mauritania, 1961–64; Minister, Amer. Embassy, London, 1964–69. Chm., Encyclopaedia Britannica International Ltd, 1969–75; Dir, Guinness Mahon Holdings Ltd, 1975–77. US Ambassador to Hungary, 1977–80, to Austria, 1980–81. Member: US Govt Interdepartmental Cttee on Marshall Plan, 1947–48; Interdepartmental Cttee on Greek-Turkish aid and Point 4 Technical Assistance progs, 1947–49. Sen. Consultant, SRI International, 1981–. Professorial Lectr, Johns Hopkins Sch. of Adv. Internat. Studies, 1983–84; Woodrow Wilson Vis. Fellow, Hartford Univ. of W Hartford, Connecticut, 1983. Board Member: Soros Hungarian Foundn; Amer. Ditchley Foundn; Council of Amer. Ambassadors; Inst. for Diplomatic Studies; Partners for Democratic Change; Member: Council on Foreign Relations; Washington Inst. of Foreign Affairs; IISS; Amer. Acad. of Diplomacy. *Publication:* Journeying Far and Wide: a political and diplomatic memoir, 1993. *Recreations:* tennis, swimming, music. *Address:* 2101 Connecticut Avenue NW, Washington, DC 20008, USA.

KAKKAR, Prof. Vijay Vir, FRCS, FRCSE; Professor of Surgical Science, King's College School of Medicine and Dentistry, since 1975, and National Heart and Lung Institute, since 1990, University of London; Director, Thrombosis Research Institute, since 1990; *b* 22 March 1937; *s* of Dr H. B. and Mrs L. W. Kakkar; *m* 1962, Dr Savitri Karnani; two *s*. *Educ:* Vikram Univ., Ujjain, India (MB, BS 1960). FRCS 1964; FRCSE 1964. Junior staff appts, 1960–64; Lectr, Nuffield Dept of Surgery, Univ. of Oxford, 1964–65; Dept of Surgery, King's Coll. Hosp., London: Pfizer Res. Fellow and Hon. Sen. Registrar, 1965–68; Sen. Registrar, 1968–69; Lectr and Hon. Sen. Registrar, 1969–71; Sen. Lectr and Hon. Consultant Surgeon, 1972–76; Dir, Thrombosis Res. Unit, 1975–; Hon.

Consultant Surgeon: King's Coll. Hosp. Gp, 1972–; Mayday Hosp., Croydon, 1984–; Hon. Cons. Vascular Surgeon, Royal Brompton Nat. Heart and Lung Hosps, 1990–. Vis. Prof., Harvard Univ. Med. Sch., Boston, 1972. Pres., British Soc. for Haemostasis and Thrombosis, 1984– (Founder Mem., 1980, Sec., 1982–83); Member: Eur. Thrombosis Res. Orgn; Concerted Action Cttee on Thrombosis, EEC; Internat. Soc. on Thrombosis and Haemostasis (Chm., Cttee on Venous Thromboembolism); Internat. Surg. Soc.; Assoc. of Surgeons of GB and NI; Vascular Surg. Soc. of GB; Pan-Pacific Surg. Assoc.; Internat. Soc. for Haematology; Internat. Soc. for Angiology; Surg. Res. Soc. of GB; Hon. Mem., Assoc. of Surgeons of India; Hon. Fellow, Acad. of Medicine of Singapore. Hunterian Prof., RCS, 1969; Lectures: Gunnar Bauer Meml, Copenhagen, 1971; James Finlayson Meml, RCPGlas, 1975; Cross Meml, RCS, 1977; Wright-Schulte, Internat. Soc. on Thrombosis and Haemostasis, 1977; Freyer Meml, RCSI, 1981. David Patey Prize, Surg. Soc. of GB and Ireland, 1971. Member Editorial Board: Haemostasis, 1982–; Clinical Findings, 1982–; Internat. Angiology, 1982–; Thrombosis Research, 1990–. *Publications:* (jtly) Vascular Disease, 1969; (jtly) Thromboembolism: diagnosis and treatment, 1972; (jtly) Heparin: chemistry and clinical usage, 1976; (jtly) Chromogenic Peptide Substrates: chemistry and clinical usage, 1979; Atheroma and Thrombosis, 1983; 500 pubns in jls on thromboembolism and vascular disease. *Recreations:* golf, skiing, cricket. *Address:* Thrombosis Research Institute, Emmanuel Kaye Building, Manresa Road, Chelsea, SW3 6LR. *T:* 0171–351 8301. *Clubs:* Athenæum; Sundridge Park Golf (Bromley, Kent).

KALETSKY, Anatole; Associate Editor, since 1992, Economics Editor, since 1990, The Times; *b* Moscow, 1 June 1952; *s* of Jacob and Esther Kaletsky; *m* 1985, Fiona Murphy; two *s* one *d*. *Educ:* Melbourne High Sch., Australia; Westminster City Sch.; King's Coll., Cambridge (BA Maths); Harvard Univ. (MA Econs). Financial Writer, The Economist, 1976–79; Financial Times: Leader Writer, 1979–81; Washington Corresp., 1981–83; Internat. Econs Corresp., 1984–86; NY Bureau Chief, 1986–90; Moscow Assignment, 1990. Hon. Sen. Scholar, King's Coll., Cambridge, 1973–74; Kennedy Scholar, Harvard Univ., 1974–76. Mem., Adv. Bd, UK Know-How Fund for E Europe and former Soviet Union, 1991–. Specialist Writer of Year, British Press Awards, 1980, 1992. *Publications:* The Costs of Default, 1985; In the Shadow of Debt, 1992. *Recreations:* playing the violin, cinema, family life. *Address:* The Times, 1 Pennington Street, E1 9XN. *T:* 0171–782 5000.

KALISHER, Michael David Lionel; QC 1984; a Recorder, since 1985; *b* 24 Feb. 1941; *s* of Samuel and Rose Kalisher; *m* 1967, Helen; one *s* two *d*. *Educ:* Hove County Grammar Sch.; Bristol Univ. (LLB Hons 1962). Articled as solicitor to Gates & Co., Sussex, 1962–64; admitted as solicitor, 1965; practised as solicitor in London with Avery Midgen & Co., 1965–69, Partner from 1966; called to the Bar, Inner Temple, 1970, Bencher, 1989; practised first from 9 King's Bench Walk, until 1976; then at 1 Hare Court, Temple. Chm., Criminal Bar Assoc., 1991–93; Mem., Bar Council, 1994–. Member: Crown Court Rules Cttee, 1989–; Lord Chancellor's Efficiency Commn, 1989–. *Recreations:* tennis, reading. *Address:* 1 Hare Court, Temple, EC4Y 7BE. *Clubs:* Athenæum; Roehampton.

KALLIPETIS, Michel Louis; QC 1989; a Recorder, since 1989; *b* 29 Aug. 1941; *s* of late Takis George Kallipetis and of Sheila Gallally; *m* 1984, Dr Esther Inge Seidel. *Educ:* Cardinal Vaughan Sch.; University Coll., London. Exchequer and Audit Dept, 1960–63. Called to the Bar, Gray's Inn, 1968. *Recreations:* opera, cooking, travel. *Address:* 3 King's Bench Walk North, Temple, EC4Y 7HR. *T:* 0171–797 8600. *Club:* Reform.

KALMS, Stanley; Founder and Chairman, since 1972, Dixons Group plc; *b* 21 Nov. 1931; *s* of Charles and Cissie Kalms; *m* 1953, Pamela Jimack; three *s*. *Educ:* Christ's College, Finchley. Whole career with Dixons Group: started in 1948 in one store owned by father; went public, 1962; Man. Dir, 1962–72; Dir, British Gas, 1987–. Chm., King's Healthcare NHS Trust, 1993–. Dir, Centre for Policy Studies, 1991–. Vis. Prof., Business Sch., Univ. (formerly Poly.) of N London, 1991–. Mem., Funding Agency for Schs, 1994–. Gov., Dixons Bradford City Technol. Coll., 1988–. Trustee, Industry in Educn, 1993–. Hon. FCGI. Hon. DLitt CNAA, 1991; DUniv Univ. of N London, 1994. *Recreations:* aft decking, opera, ballet. *Address:* Dixons Group plc, 29 Farm Street, W1X 7RD. *T:* 0171–499 3494.

KALMUS, Prof. George Ernest, FRS 1988; Director, Particle Physics, Rutherford Appleton Laboratory, since 1986; Visiting Professor, Physics and Astronomy Department, University College London, since 1984; *b* 21 April 1935; *s* of Hans Kalmus and Anna Kalmus; *m* 1957, Ann Christine Harland; three *d*. *Educ:* St Albans County Grammar Sch.; University Coll. London (BSc Hons, PhD). Res. Asst, Bubble Chamber Gp, UCL, 1959–62; Research Associate, Powell-Birge Bubble Chamber Gp, Lawrence Radiation Lab., Univ. of California, Berkeley, 1962–63 and 1964–67; Lectr, Physics Dept, UCL, 1963–64; Sen. Physicist, Lawrence Rad. Lab., 1967–71; Gp Leader, Bubble Chamber and Delphi Gps, Rutherford Appleton Lab., 1971–86. Mem., various Programme Cttees at CERN, 1974–; Mem., CERN Scientific Policy Cttee, 1990–. *Publications:* numerous articles on experimental particle physics in Phys. Rev., Phys. Rev. Letters, Nuclear Phys., etc. *Recreations:* ski-ing, cycling, reading. *Address:* 16 South Avenue, Abingdon, Oxon OX14 1QH. *T:* Abingdon (01235) 523340.

See also P. I. P. Kalmus.

KALMUS, Prof. Peter Ignaz Paul, PhD; CPhys, FInstP; Professor of Physics, since 1978, and Head of Physics Department, since 1992, Queen Mary and Westfield (formerly Queen Mary) College, University of London; *b* 25 Jan. 1933; *s* of Hans and Anna Kalmus; *m* 1957, Felicity (Trixie) Barker; one *s* one *d*. *Educ:* University Coll. London (BSc, PhD). CPhys, FInstP 1967. Res. Associate, University Coll. London, 1957–60; Lectr (part-time), Northern Poly. and Chelsea Poly., 1955–60; Physicist, Argonne Nat. Lab., USA, 1960–64; Queen Mary College, University of London: Lectr, 1964–66; Reader, 1966–78. Visiting Scientist: CERN, Geneva, 1961–62, 1970–71, 1981–82; Univ. of Chicago, 1965. Scientific Advr, UK Delegn to CERN, 1978–81; Member: SERC Nuclear Physics Bd, 1979–82, 1989–93; SERC Astronomy and Planetary Sci. Bd, 1990–93. Mem. Council, Inst. of Physics, 1993– (Chm., High Energy Physics Gp, 1989–93); MRI 1989; Member: Amer. Phys. Soc., 1963; European Phys. Soc., 1970 (Mem., High Energy Particle Physics Bd, 1994–); BAAS, 1986 (Pres., Physics Sect., 1990–91); Commn on Particles and Fields, IUPAP, 1994–. Rutherford Medal and Prize, Inst. Physics, 1988. *Publications:* numerous papers in scientific jls. *Recreations:* photography, swimming, listening to jazz. *Address:* Department of Physics, Queen Mary and Westfield College, Mile End Road, E1 4NS. *T:* 0171–975 5042.

See also G. E. Kalmus.

KALO, Sir Kwamala, Kt 1983; MBE 1975; Director of Administrative College, Port Moresby, 1987–89; *b* 28 Feb. 1929; *s* of Kalo Navu and Navuga Kila; *m* 1951, Gimaralai Samuel; two *s* two *d*. *Educ:* up to secondary level in Papua New Guinea. Govt Primary School teacher, 1949; served in Dept of Education as classroom teacher, Headmaster, Inspector, Supt of Schools, Asst Sec. of Technical Educn, until 1979; represented Papua New Guinea in Trusteeship Council Meeting of UN, 1963; seconded to Public Services Commn as a Comr, 1979; High Comr for Papua New Guinea in New Zealand, 1983–86. Hon. Award, PNG Trng and Develt Soc., 1991. *Publication:* Sam Ila' Apa Gena Mari (Hymns by Sam Ila' Apa), 1989. *Address:* PO Box 6572, Boroko, Papua New Guinea.

KAMBA, Prof. Walter Joseph; Vice-Chancellor, 1981–91 (Vice-Principal, 1980–81), Professor of Law, 1980–91, University of Zimbabwe; *b* 6 Sept. 1931; *s* of Joseph Mafara and Hilda Kamba; *m* 1960, Angeline Saziso Dube; three *s*. *Educ:* University of Cape Town (BA, LLB); Yale Law School (LLM). Attorney of the High Court of Rhodesia (now Zimbabwe), 1963–66; Research Fellow, Institute of Advanced Legal Studies, London Univ., 1967–68; Lecturer, then Sen. Lectr, in Comparative Law and Jurisprudence, 1969–80, Dean of the Faculty of Law, 1977–80, Univ. of Dundee. Chm., Kingstons (booksellers and distributors) (Zimbabwe), 1984–. Chm., Bd of Governors, Zimbabwe Broadcasting Corp., 1987 (Vice-Chm., 1980–87); Member: Public Service Professional Qualifications Panel, Harare, 1981–83; Council, ACU, 1981–83 (Member: Working Party on future policy, 1981; Budget Review Cttee, 1982–83); Commonwealth Standing Cttee on student mobility, 1981–88; Exec. Bd, Assoc. of African Univs, 1984 (Chm., Finance and Admin. Cttee, 1985); Nat. Commn, Law and Popn Studies Project, Zimbabwe, 1986–; Chm., Assoc. of Eastern and Southern African Univs, 1984–87; Vice-President: Internat. Assoc. of Univs, 1985–90; ACP-EEC Foundn for Cultural Co-op., Brussels, 1986–88; Mem., Zimbabwe Nat. Commn for UNESCO, 1987–. Mem., Univ. of Swaziland Commn on Planning, 1986. Legal Adviser, ZANU (Patriotic Front), until 1980; Chm., Electoral Supervisory Commn, 1984–. Trustee: Zimbabwe Mass Media Trust, 1981–; Conservation Trust of Zimbabwe, 1981–87; Legal Resources Foundn, Zimbabwe, 1984–90; African-American Inst., NY, 1985–; Zimbabwe Cambridge Trust, 1987–; Member: Bd of Trustees, Michael Gelfand Med. Res. Foundn, Zimbabwe, 1986–; Internat. Bd, United World Colls, 1985–87; Mem. Council: Univ. for Peace, Costa Rica, 1981–86; Univ. of Zambia, 1981–86; United Nations Univ., Tokyo, 1983–89 (Chm., Council, 1985–86; Mem., Cttee on Institutional and Programmatic Develt); Univ. of Lesotho, 1987–; Mem., Internat. Adv. Cttee, Synergos Inst., NY, 1987–; Patron, Commonwealth Legal Educn Assoc., 1986–; Governor, Ranche House Coll., Harare, 1980–; Member Board of Governors: Zimbabwe Inst. of Development Studies, 1981– (Chm. Bd, 1986–); Internat. Develt Res. Centre, Canada, 1986–; Commonwealth of Learning, 1988– (Vice-Chm., 1989–); Member: Nat. St John's Ambulance Council for Republic of Zimbabwe, 1982–87; Indep. Internat. Commn on Health Res. for Develt, 1987–; Bd, Internat. Cttee for Study of Educnl Exchange, 1988–; Exec. Cttee, Internat. Develt Res. Centre, Canada, 1989–. Hon. LLD Dundee, 1982. Officier dans l'Ordre des Palmes Académiques (France). *Publications:* articles in Internat. and Comparative Law Quarterly, Juridical Review. *Recreation:* tennis. *Address:* c/o University of Zimbabwe, PO Box MP 167, Mount Pleasant, Harare, Zimbabwe. *T:* (4) 303211, *Telex:* 26580, *Fax:* (4) 303292.

KAMIL, Geoffrey Harvey; His Honour Judge Kamil; a Circuit Judge, since 1993; *b* 17 Aug. 1942; *s* of Peter and Sadie Kamil; *m* 1968, Andrea Pauline Kamil (*née* Ellis); two *d*. *Educ:* Leeds Grammar Sch.; Leeds University (LLB). Admitted as Solicitor of the Supreme Court, 1968; Partner with J. Levi & Co., solicitors, Leeds, 1968–87; Asst Stipendiary Magistrate, 1985–87; Stipendiary Magistrate, W Midlands, 1987–90, W Yorks, 1990–93; Asst Crown Court Recorder, 1986–91; Recorder, 1991–93. Member: Magisterial Cttee, Judicial Studies Bd, 1991–93; Centre for Criminal Justice Studies, Leeds Univ., 1992–. Leeds Law Society: Mem. Cttee, 1983–87; Chm., Courts Cttee, 1983–87; Mem., Duty Solicitor Cttee, 1986–87; Mem., Leeds Bar/Law Soc. Liaison Cttee, 1983–87. Sec., Kirkstall Lodge Hostal for Ex-Offenders, 1976–87. *Recreations:* golf, swimming, sailing, tennis, the Lake District, classic cars, TV soap addict. *Address:* Bradford Court Centre, The Law Courts, Exchange Square, Drake Street, Bradford BD1 1JA. *Club:* Moor Allerton Golf (Leeds).

KAN, Prof. Yuet Wai, FRCP 1983; FRS 1981; Louis K. Diamond Professor of Hematology, since 1984, Investigator, Howard Hughes Medical Institute Laboratory, since 1976, and Head, Division of Molecular Medicine and Diagnostics, Department of Laboratory Medicine, since 1989, University of California, San Francisco; *b* 11 June 1936; *s* of Kan Tong Po and Kan Li Lai Wan; *m* 1964, Alvera L. Limauro; two *d*. *Educ:* Univ. of Hong Kong (MB, BS, DSc). Research Associate, Children's Hosp. Medical Center, Dept of Pediatrics, Harvard Medical Sch., Boston, Mass; Asst Prof. of Pediatrics, Harvard Medical Sch., 1970–72; Associate Prof. of Medicine, Depts of Medicine and Laboratory Medicine, Univ. of California, San Francisco, 1972–77; Chief, Hematology Service, San Francisco General Hospital, 1972–79; Prof. of Lab. Medicine and Medicine, Univ. of California, 1977–. Dir, Molecular Biology Inst., Univ. of Hong Kong, 1990–94 (Hon. Dir, 1988–90). Trustee, Croucher Foundn, 1992–. Member: Nat. Acad. of Scis, USA, 1986; Academia Sinica, Taiwan, 1988. Hon. MD Univ. of Cagliari, Sardinia, 1981; Hon. DSc: Chinese Univ. of Hong Kong, 1981; Univ. of Hong Kong, 1987. *Publications:* contribs to: Nature, Proc. of Nat. Academy of Sciences, Jl of Clinical Investigation, Blood, British Jl of Haematology, and others. *Recreations:* tennis, skiing. *Address:* U426, University of California San Francisco, San Francisco, CA 94143–0724, USA. *T:* (415) 4765841, *Fax:* (415) 5664969.

See also Sir Kan Yuet-Keung.

KAN Yuet-Keung, Sir, GBE 1979 (CBE 1967; OBE 1959); Kt 1972; JP; Chairman, Hong Kong Trade Development Council, 1979–83; Chairman, Bank of East Asia Ltd, 1963–83; *b* 26 July 1913; *s* of late Kan Tong Po, JP; *m* 1940, Ida; two *s* one *d*. *Educ:* Hong Kong Univ.; London Univ. BA Hong Kong 1934. Solicitor and Notary Public. Sen. Unofficial MLC 1968–72, Sen. Unofficial MEC 1974–80, Hong Kong. Pro-Chancellor, Chinese Univ. of Hong Kong, 1983– (Chm., Council, 1973–83). Hon. Fellow, LSE, 1980. Hon. LLD: Chinese Univ. of Hong Kong, 1968; Univ. of Hong Kong, 1973. Order of Sacred Treasure, 3rd Class, Japan; Officier de l'Ordre National du Mérite (France), 1978; Officer's Cross, Order of Merit 1st class (Germany), 1983; Grand Decoration of Honour in Gold with Star (Austria), 1983; Order of Sacred Treasure, 2nd class (Japan), 1983; Knight Grand Cross, Royal Order of Northern Pole Star (Sweden), 1983. *Recreations:* tennis, swimming, golf. *Address:* Swire House, 11th Floor, Chater Road, Hong Kong. *T:* Hong Kong 238181.

See also Yuet Wai Kan.

KANE, Professor George, FBA 1968; Professor of English Language and Medieval Literature, 1965–76 and Head of English Department, 1968–76, King's College, London, Professor Emeritus, University of London, since 1975; *b* 4 July 1916; *o s* of George Michael and Clara Kane; *m* 1946, Katherine Bridget, *o d* of Lt-Col R. V. Montgomery, MC; one *s* one *d*. *Educ:* St Peter's Coll.; British Columbia University; Toronto Univ.; University Coll., London. BA (University of BC), 1936; Research Fellow, University of Toronto, 1936–37; MA (Toronto), 1937; Research Fellow, Northwestern Univ., 1937–38; IODE Schol., for BC, 1938–39. Served War of 1939–45: Artists' Rifles, 1939–40; Rifle Bde, 1940–46 (despatches). PhD (London), 1946; Asst Lecturer in English, University Coll., London, 1946, Lecturer, 1948, Reader in English, 1953, Fellow, 1971; Prof. of English Language and Literature and Head of English Dept, Royal Holloway College, London Univ., 1955–65; William Rand Kenan Jr Prof. of English in Univ. of N Carolina at

Chapel Hill, 1976–87, Chm. of Div. of Humanities, 1980–83, Prof. Emeritus, 1987–. Fellow, KCL, 1976. Vis. Prof., Medieval Acad. of America, 1970, 1982, Corresp. Fellow, 1975, Fellow, 1978; Fellow: Amer. Acad. of Arts and Scis, 1977–91 (resigned); Nat. Humanities Center, 1987–88; Sen. Fellow, Southeastern Inst. of Medieval and Renaissance Studies, 1978. Member: Council, Early English Text Soc., 1969–88; Governing Body, SOAS, 1970–76; Council, British Acad., 1974–76; Governing Body, Univ. of N Carolina Press, 1979–84. Sir Israel Gollancz Memorial Prize, British Acad., 1963; Haskins Medallist, Med. Acad. of Amer., 1978. Lectures: Chambers Meml, UCL, 1965; Accademia Nazionale dei Lincei, Rome, 1976; John Coffin Meml, Univ. of London, 1979; M. W. Bloomfield Meml, Harvard, 1989; Tucker-Cruse Meml, Bristol Univ., 1991; Public Orator, Univ. of London, 1962–66; Annual Chaucer Lectr, New Chaucer Soc., 1980. Gen. editor of London Edn of Piers Plowman. *Publications:* Middle English Literature, 1951; Piers Plowman, the A Version, 1960; Piers Plowman: The Evidence for Authorship, 1965; Piers Plowman: the B version, 1975; Geoffrey Chaucer, 1984; Chaucer and Langland, 1989; articles and reviews. *Recreation:* fishing. *Clubs:* Athenæum, Flyfishers'.

KANE, Jack, OBE 1969; DL; JP; Hon. Vice President, Age Concern, Scotland, since 1987 (Chairman, 1983–86); Lord Provost of the City of Edinburgh and Lord Lieutenant of the County of the City of Edinburgh, 1972–75; *b* 1 April 1911; *m* 1940, Anne Murphy; one *s* two *d*. *Educ:* Bathgate Academy. Served War, 1940–46. Librarian, 1936–55. Pres., SE of Scotland Dist, Workers' Educnl Assoc., 1983– (Sec., 1955–76). Chm., Board of Trustees for Nat. Galls of Scotland, 1975–80; Mem., South of Scotland Electricity Bd, 1975–81, Chm., Consultative Council, 1977–81. JP Edinburgh, 1945; DL City of Edinburgh, 1976. Dr *hc* Edinburgh, 1976. Grand Officer, Order of the Oaken Crown (Luxembourg), 1972; Grand Cross of Merit (W Germany). *Recreations:* reading, walking. *Address:* 42 Palmerston Place, Edinburgh EH12 5BJ. *Club:* Newcraighall Miners' Welfare Inst.

KANTOROWICH, Prof. Roy Herman, BArch (Witwatersrand), MA (Manchester), RIBA, FRTPI; Professor of Town and Country Planning, 1961–84, Professor Emeritus, since 1984, Dean of the Faculty of Arts, 1975–76 and Director of Wolfson Design Unit, 1981–84, University of Manchester; *b* Johannesburg, 24 Nov. 1916; *s* of George Kantorowich and Deborah (*née* Baranov); *m* 1943, Petronella Sophie Wissema (violinist, as Nella Wissema); one *s* two *d*. *Educ:* King Edward VII Sch., Johannesburg; University of Witwatersrand. BArch 1939; ARIBA 1940; MTPI 1965 (AMTPI 1946). Post-grad. studies in Housing and Planning, MIT and Columbia Univ., 1939–41; Planning Officer: Vanderbijl Park New Town, 1942–45; directing Cape Town Foreshore Scheme, 1945–48; private practice in Cape Town, in architecture and town planning, 1948–61. Pres., S African Inst. Town and Regional Planners, 1960. Formerly Town Planning Consultant to Cape Provincial Admin., and for many cities and towns in S Africa incl. Durban, Pretoria and Port Elizabeth; Cons. for New Town of Ashkelon, Israel, 1950–56. Member: NW Econ. Planning Coun. 1965–79; Council (Chm., Educn Cttee), RTPI, 1965–70; Planning Cttee, SSRC, 1969–73; Construction and Environment Bd, and Chm., Town Planning Panel, CNAA, 1971–75; Natal Building Soc. Fellowship, 1980. Buildings include: Civic Centre, Welkom, OFS; Baxter Hall, University of Cape Town; Sea Point Telephone Exchange (Cape Province Inst. of Architects Bronze Medal Award); Architecture and Planning Building, Univ. of Manchester. FRSA 1972. *Publications:* Cape Town Foreshore Plan, 1948; (with Lord Holford) Durban 1985, a plan for central Durban in its Regional Setting, 1968; Three Perspectives on planning for the 'eighties, 1981; contribs to SAArch. Record, Jl RTPI and other professional jls. *Recreations:* music, tennis. *Address:* 3 Winster Avenue, West Didsbury, Manchester M20 2YG. *T:* 0161–445 9417. *Club:* Northern Lawn Tennis.

KAPI, Hon. Sir Mari, Kt 1988; CBE 1983; Deputy Chief Justice of Papua New Guinea, since 1982, a Justice of the Court of Appeal: Solomon Islands, since 1982; Fiji, since 1992; *b* 12 Dec. 1950; *s* of Kapi 'Ila and Mea Numa; *m* 1973, Tegana Kapi; two *s* three *d*. *Educ:* Univ. of Papua New Guinea (LLB); SOAS, Univ. of London (LLM). Admitted to practice in PNG and Australia, 1974. Dep. Public Solicitor, 1976; Associate Public Solicitor, 1977; Public Solicitor, 1978; a Judge of Nat. and Supreme Courts of PNG, 1979. Cross of Solomon Islands, 1994. *Recreations:* tennis, touch Rugby. *Address:* PO Box 7018, Boroko, Papua New Guinea. *T:* 259273.

KAPLAN, Neil Trevor; QC (Hong Kong) 1982; arbitrator, mediator; Chairman, Disputes Review Board, new Hong Kong airport; special counsel, Deberoise & Plimpton; *b* 1 Sept. 1942; *s* of Leslie Henry Kaplan and Sybil Sylvia Kaplan (*née* Gasson); *m* 1971, Barbara Jane Spector; one *s* one *d*. *Educ:* St Paul's Sch.; King's College London (LLB). FCIArb. Called to the Bar, Inner Temple, 1965, Bencher 1991; practised London, 1965–80; Dep. Principal Crown Counsel, Hong Kong, 1980, Principal Crown Counsel, 1982; private practice, Hong Kong Bar, 1984–90; Solicitor-barrister, Victoria, NSW, 1983; NY Bar, 1986; High Court Judge, Hong Kong, 1990–94; Judge in charge of Construction and Arbitration List, 1990–94. Vis. Prof., City Univ. of Hong Kong, 1995–. Chm., Hong Kong Internat. Arbitration Centre, 1991–; Vice-Pres., CIArb, 1992– (Chm., Hong Kong Branch, 1984–87 and 1989–90); Dep. Chm., Justice, Hong Kong, 1988–90; Mem., Judicial Studies Bd, 1994–. Liveryman, Arbitrators' Co., 1982–. JP Hong Kong, 1984. *Publications:* (jtly) Hong Kong Arbitration—Cases and Materials, 1991; (jtly) Arbitration in Hong Kong and China, 1994; articles on arbitration. *Recreations:* tennis, travel, food and wine, films, theatre, walking. *Address:* 7F Pearl Gardens, 7 Conduit Road, Hong Kong. *T:* 28696301, *Fax:* 28696372. *Clubs:* Athenæum, Royal Automobile, Old Pauline; Hong Kong, Royal Hong Kong Jockey, Hong Kong Cricket.

KAPOOR, Anish; artist and sculptor; *b* Bombay, 12 March 1954; *s* of Rear Adm. D. C. Kapoor and Mrs H. Kapoor. *Educ:* Hornsey Coll. Art; Chelsea Sch. Art. Lectr, Wolverhampton Polytechnic, 1979–83. Artist in Residence, Walker Art Gall., Liverpool, 1982–83. One-man exhibitions include: Lisson Gall., London, 1982, 1984, 1985, 1988, 1989–90, 1993; Walker Art Gall., Liverpool, 1982, 1983; Barbara Gladstone Gall., NY, 1984, 1986, 1989, 1990; Tate Gall., London, 1990–91; San Diego Mus. Contemporary Art, 1992; Tel Aviv Mus. of Art, 1993; Nat. Gall. of Canada, Ottawa, 1993; and others in Europe, USA, Australia and Japan; contrib. numerous group exhibns in Britain, Europe, USA, Canada, Australia and Japan, incl. Tate Gall., London, 1983, 1991; Art Inst., Chicago, 1990; Expo '92, Seville, 1992. Turner Prize, 1991. *Address:* c/o Lisson Gallery, 67 Lisson Street, NW1 5DA.

KARAMANLIS, Konstantinos; President of Greece, 1980–85 and 1990–95; *b* 8 March 1907; *m* Amalia Kanelopoulos (marr. diss.). *Educ:* Univ. of Athens. Lawyer, 1932; MP, 1935–67, 1974–80 (Deputy for Serres, Populist Party, 1935; founded National Radical Union Party, 1955; reformed as New Democracy Party, 1974). Minister of: Labour, 1946; of Transport, 1947; Social Welfare, 1948–50; Nat. Defence, 1950–52; Public Works, 1952–54; Communications and Public Works, 1954–55; Prime Minister, 1955–63; self-imposed exile in France, 1963–74; Leader of New Democratic Party and Prime Minister, 1974–80. Gold Medal, Onassis Foundn, 1981; Gold Medal, European Parlt. *Address:* c/o Office of the President, Athens, Greece.

KARK, (Arthur) Leslie; MA (Oxon); FRSA; author, barrister; Chairman: Lucie Clayton Secretarial College; Lucie Clayton Ltd; Founder, Lucie Clayton College of Nursery Training, 1993; *b* 12 July 1910; *s* of Victor and Helena Kark, Johannesburg; *m* 1st, 1935, Joan Tetley (marr. diss., 1956); two *d*; 2nd, 1956, Evelyn Gordine (*see* E. F. Kark); one *s* one *d*. *Educ:* Clayesmore; St John's Coll., Oxford. Called to Bar, Inner Temple, 1932; Features Editor of World's Press News, 1933; Editor of Photography, 1934; Public Relations Officer to Advertising Association, 1935; Features Editor News Review, 1936–39; London Theatre Critic, New York Herald Tribune; News Editor, Ministry of Information, 1940. Served War of 1939–45, RAF, 1940–46; Air-gunner; Wing Commander in Command of Public Relations (Overseas) Unit; author, Air Ministry's official book on Air War, Far East. Associate Editor, Courier Magazine Gp, 1947–51; Dir of Public Relations for Australian Trade Comr, 1959–63. Short stories and novels translated into French, Swedish, German, Polish, etc. *Publications:* The Fire Was Bright, 1944; Red Rain, 1946; An Owl in the Sun, 1948; Wings of the Phœnix, 1949; On the Haycock, 1957. *Recreations:* fly-fishing, golf. *Address:* 9 Clareville Grove, SW7 5AU. *T:* 0171–373 2621; Roche House, Sheep Street, Burford, Oxon OX18 4LS. *T:* Burford (0199382) 3007. *Club:* United Oxford & Cambridge University.

KARK, Austen Steven, CBE 1987; Managing Director, External Broadcasting (now World Service), BBC, 1985–86; *b* 20 Oct. 1926; *s* of Major Norman Kark and late Ethel Kark, formerly of Eaton Place, London, and Johannesburg; *m* 1st, 1949, Margaret Solomon (marr. diss. 1954); two *d*; 2nd, 1954, Nina Mary Bawden, *qv*; one *d* one step *s* (and one step *s* decd). *Educ:* Upper Canada Coll., Toronto; Nautical Coll., Pangbourne; RNC; Magdalen Coll., Oxford (MA). Served RN and RIN, 1943–46. Directed first prodn in UK of Sartre's The Flies, Oxford, 1948; trained in journalism, Belfast Telegraph, L'Illustré, Zofingen, Switzerland; Courier, Bandwagon, London Mystery Magazine; free-lance journalist and broadcaster, London and New York, 1952–54; joined BBC, 1954; scriptwriter; Producer, External Services; Head of S European Service, 1964; Head of E European (and Russian) Service, 1972; Editor, World Service, 1973; Controller, English Services, and Editor, World Service, 1974; advised Lord Soames on election broadcasting, Rhodesia, and chaired, for Prime Minister Mugabe, enquiry into future of radio and television in Zimbabwe, 1980; Dep. Man. Dir, External Broadcasting, BBC, 1981–85. Broadcasting consultant, 1987–; Chm., CPC Guidebooks, 1988–. Mem. UK Delegn, CSCE London Information Forum, 1989. Trustee, Commonwealth Journalists Assoc. Trust., 1992–. *Publication:* Attic in Greece, 1994. *Recreations:* Real tennis, mosaics, Greece, grandchildren. *Address:* 22 Noel Road, N1 8HA; 19 Kapodistriou, Nauplion 21100, Greece. *Clubs:* Oriental, MCC, Queen's, Royal Tennis Court, Bushmen (ex-Chairman).

KARK, Mrs Evelyn Florence, (*nom de plume* **Lucie Clayton**); Director; *b* 5 Dec. 1928; *d* of Emily and William Gordine; *m* 1956 (Arthur) Leslie Kark, *qv*; one *s* one *d*. *Educ:* privately and inconspicuously. Asst to Editor, Courier Magazine, 1950; became Head of model school and agency (assuming name of Lucie Clayton), 1952; founded Lucie Clayton Sch. of Fashion Design and Dressmaking, 1961, and Lucie Clayton Secretarial College, 1966. *Publications:* The World of Modelling, 1968; Modelling and Beauty Care, 1985. *Recreations:* talking, tapestry, cooking. *Address:* 9 Clareville Grove, SW7 5AU. *T:* 0171–373 2621; Roche House, Burford, Oxfordshire OX18 4LS. *T:* Burford (0199382) 3007.

KARK, Leslie; *see* Kark, A. L.

KARK, Nina Mary, (Mrs A. S. Kark); *see* Bawden, N. M.

KARLE, Jerome, PhD; Chief Scientist, Laboratory for the Structure of Matter, since 1968; *b* NY, 18 June 1918; *s* of Louis Karfunkle and Sadie Helen Kun; *m* 1942, Isabella, *d* of Zygmunt and Elizabeth Lugoski; three *d*. *Educ:* Abraham Lincoln High Sch., City Coll. of NY (BS 1937); Harvard Univ. (AM 1938); Univ. of Michigan (MS 1942, PhD 1943). Research Associate, Manhattan Project, Chicago, 1943–44; US Navy Project, Michigan, 1944–46; Head, Electron Diffraction Section, Naval Res. Lab., 1946–58, Head of Diffraction Branch, 1958–68. Prof. (part-time), Univ. of Maryland, 1951–70. Pres., Amer. Crystallographic Assoc., 1972; Chm., US Nat. Cttee for Crystallography, NAS and Nat. Res. Council, 1973–75, Pres., Internat. Union of Crystallography, 1981–84. Fellow, Amer. Phys. Soc.; Mem., NAS. Nobel Prize for Chemistry, 1985 (jtly). *Publications:* articles in learned jls on study of atoms, molecules, crystals and solid surfaces by diffraction methods. *Recreations:* stereo-photography, swimming, ice skating. *Address:* Laboratory for the Structure of Matter, Code 6030, Naval Research Laboratory, Washington, DC 20375–5341, USA. *T:* (202) 7672665.

KARMEL, His Honour Alexander D., QC 1954; an Additional Judge, Central Criminal Court, later a Circuit Judge, 1968–79; *b* 16 May 1904; *s* of Elias Karmel and Adeline (*née* Freedman); *m* 1937, Mary, *widow* of Arthur Lee and *d* of Newman Lipton; one *s*. *Educ:* Newcastle upon Tyne Royal Grammar Sch. Barrister-at-law, Middle Temple, 1932; Master of the Bench, 1962; Leader of Northern Circuit, 1966; Comr of Assize, Stafford, summer 1967; Recorder of Bolton, 1962–68. Mem., Bar Council, 1950–53, 1961–64. *Recreations:* croquet, golf. *Address:* 171 Rivermead Court, Ranelagh Gardens, SW6 3SF. *T:* 0171–736 4609. *Club:* Hurlingham.

KARMEL, Emeritus Prof. Peter Henry, AC 1976; CBE 1967; Chairman, Australian National University Institute of the Arts, since 1992; *b* 9 May 1922; *s* of Simeon Karmel; *m* 1946, Lena Garrett; one *s* five *d*. *Educ:* Caulfield Grammar Sch.; Univ. of Melbourne (BA); Trinity Coll., Cambridge (PhD). Research Officer, Commonwealth Bureau of Census and Statistics, 1943–45; Lectr in Econs, Univ. of Melbourne, 1946; Rouse Ball Res. Student, Trinity Coll., Cambridge, 1947–48; Sen. Lectr in Econs, Univ. of Melbourne, 1949; Prof. of Econs, 1950–62, Emeritus, 1965, Univ. of Adelaide; Principal-designate, Univ. of Adelaide at Bedford Park (subseq. Flinders Univ. of SA), 1961–66; Vice-Chancellor, Flinders Univ. of SA, 1966–71; Chancellor, Univ. of Papua and New Guinea, 1969–70 (Chm., Interim Council, 1965–69); Chairman: Univs Commn, 1971–77; Commonwealth Tertiary Educn Commn, 1977–82; Vice-Chancellor, ANU, 1982–87. Chairman: Aust. Inst. of Health, 1987–92; Nat. Council on AIDS, 1988–92. Mem. Council, Univ. of Adelaide, 1955–69; Vis. Prof. of Econs, Queen's Univ., Belfast, 1957–58; Mem. Commonwealth Cttee: on Future of Tertiary Educn, 1961–65; of Economic Enquiry, 1963–65; Mem., Australian Council for Educn Research, 1968– (Pres., 1979–); Chairman: Cttee of Enquiry into Educn in SA, 1969–70; Interim Cttee for Aust. Schools Commn, 1972–73; Cttee of Enquiry on Med. Schs, 1972–73; Cttee of Enquiry on Open Univ., 1973–74; Australia Council, 1974–77; Cttee on Post-Secondary Educn in Tasmania, 1975–76; Quality of Educn Review Cttee, 1984–85; Member: Commonwealth Govt Cttee to Review Efficiency and Effectiveness in Higher Educn, 1985–86; Adv. Cttee of Cities Commn, 1972–74; CSIRO Adv. Council, 1979–82; Australian Stats Adv. Council, 1988–. Leader, OECD Review of US Educn Policy, 1978–79 and NZ Educn Policy, 1982. Pres., Acad. of Social Sciences in Australia, 1987–90 (FASSA 1952); Chm., Canberra Inst. of the Arts, 1988–91. Mem. Council, Chinese Univ. of Hong Kong, 1990–94. FACE 1969. Hon. LLD: Univ. of Papua and New Guinea, 1970; Univ. of Melbourne, 1975; Univ. of Queensland, 1985; Hon. LittD Flinders Univ. of SA, 1971; Hon. DLit Murdoch Univ., 1975; Hon. DLitt Macquarie, 1992; DU Newcastle, NSW, 1978. Mackie Medal, 1975; Aust. Coll. of Educn Medal, 1981. *Publications:* Applied Statistics for Economists, 1957, 1962 (1970 edn with M. Polasek, 4th edn 1977), Portuguese edn, 1972; (with M. Brunt) Structure of the Australian Economy,

1962, repr. 1963, 1966; (with G. C. Harcourt and R. H. Wallace) Economic Activity, 1967 (Italian edn 1969); articles in Economic Record, Population Studies, Jl Royal Statistical Assoc., Australian Jl of Education, and other learned jls. *Address:* 4/127 Hopetoun Circuit, Canberra, ACT 2600, Australia.

KARMILOFF-SMITH, Prof. Annette Dionne, FBA 1993; Senior Research Scientist (with Special Appointment status), MRC Cognitive Development Unit, since 1982; Visiting Professor of Psychology, University College London, since 1982; *b* 18 July 1938; *d* of late Jack Smith and Doris Ellen Ruth Smith (*née* Findlay); *m* 1966, Igor Alexander Karmiloff (marr. diss. 1991); two *d. Educ:* Edmonton County GS; Inst Français de Londres; Holborn Coll. of Law and Langs (Dip. Internat. Conf. Interpreting); Geneva Univ. (Dr of exptl and genetic psychol.). Internat. Conf. Interpreter, UN, 1966–70; Res. Consultant, UNWRA-UNESCO Inst. of Educn, Beirut, 1970–72; Res. Collaborator, Internat. Centre for Genetic Epistemiol., Geneva, 1972–76; Vis. Res. Associate, Max Planck Inst. for Psycholinguistics, Nijmegen, 1978–83. Vis. Prof., Univs of Sussex, Brussels, Munich, Chicago, Tel-Aviv and Barcelona, 1979–88. Sloan Fellow: Yale Univ., 1978; Univ. of Berkeley, 1981. MAE 1991. *Publications:* A Functional Approach to Child Language, 1979, 2nd edn 1981; (jtly) Child Language Research in ESF Countries, 1981; Beyond Modularity: a developmental perspective on cognitive science, 1992; Baby It's You, 1994; (jtly) Rethinking Innateness: connectionism in a developmental framework, 1994; many chapters, and articles in learned jls. *Recreations:* writing/reading poetry, working out, going on multiple diets, writing a satire (Powerful Minds in Flabby Bodies). *Address:* 1 Lutton Terrace, Flask Walk, Hampstead, NW3 1HB. *T:* 0171–431 5009; (work) 0171–387 4692.

KARN, Prof. Valerie Ann; Professor of Housing Studies, University of Manchester, since 1994; *b* 17 May 1939; *d* of Arthur and Winnifred Karn; one *d. Educ:* Newquay County Grammar School; Lady Margaret Hall, Oxford (BA Geography); Univ. of the Punjab, Lahore (Commonwealth scholar); Graduate Sch. of Design, Harvard Univ.; PhD Birmingham (Urban Studies). Res. Officer, ODI, 1963; Res. Fellow, Inst. of Social and Economic Res., Univ. of York, 1964–66; Res. Associate, Lectr, Sen. Lectr, Centre for Urban and Regional Studies, Univ. of Birmingham, 1966–84; Prof. of Envmtl Health and Housing, Univ. of Salford, 1984–94; Co-Dir, Salford Centre for Housing Studies, 1986–94. Res. Officer, Central Housing Adv. Cttee, Sub-Cttee on Housing Management, 1967–69; Chair, Hulme Study, 1989–91; Member: Housing Services Adv. Gp, 1976–79; Inquiry into British Housing, 1984–86 and 1990–91; Inquiry into Glasgow's Housing, 1985–86; ESRC Social Affairs Cttee, 1985–87; Co-ordinating Cttee, Eur. Network for Housing Res.; Special Comr, CRE, 1987–89. Mem. Bd, Nat. Housing and Tenant Resource Centre; Mem. Adv. Panel, Housing Assoc. Tenants Ombudsman Service, 1994–. BAAS Lister Lectr, 1979; Vis. Fellow, Urban Inst., Washington DC, 1979–80. MIH. Gov., Peabody Trust, 1993–. *Publications:* Retiring to the Seaside, 1977 (Oddfellows Social Concern Book Prize); (jtly) Housing in Retirement, 1973; (ed jtly) The Consumers' Experience of Housing, 1980; (jtly) Home-ownership in the Inner City, Salvation or Despair, 1985; (jtly) Race, Class, and Public Housing, 1987; (jtly) Comparing Housing Systems Performance and Housing Policy in the United States and Britain, 1992; (jtly) Neighbour Disputes: responses by social landlords, 1993; (jtly) New Homes in the 1990s, 1994; (jtly) Choosing Your Home, 1995; (jtly) The Settlement of Refugees in Britain, 1995; (jtly) Housing Quality: a practical guide for tenants and their representatives, 1995; *chapters in:* The Future of Council Housing, 1982; Family Matters, 1983; Ethnic Pluralism and Public Policy, 1983; Between Centre and Locality, 1986; Low Cost Home Ownership, 1986; The Housing Crisis, 1986; The Property Owing Democracy, 1987; Urban Housing Segregation of Minorities in Western Europe and the United States, 1991; Implementing Housing Policy, 1992; res. reports and articles in jls. *Recreation:* gardening. *Address:* 4 Harricroft Farm Cottages, Smithills Dean Road, Bolton BL1 7NS. *T:* Bolton (01204) 300203.

KARP, David; novelist; *b* New York City, 5 May 1922; *s* of Abraham Karp and Rebecca Levin; *m* 1st, 1944, Lillian Klass (*d* 1987); two *s*; 2nd, 1988, Claire Leighton. *Educ:* College of The City of New York. US Army, 1943–46, S Pacific, Japan; College, 1946–48; Continuity Dir, Station WNYC, New York, 1948–49; free-lance motion picture-television writer and motion picture producer, 1949–; President: Leda Productions Inc., 1968–; Television-Radio Branch, Writers Guild of America West, 1969–71; Member: Editorial Bd, Television Quarterly, 1966–71, 1972–77; Council, Writers Guild of America, 1966–73; Bd of Trustees, Producer-Writers Guild of America Pension Plan, 1968– (Chm., 1978, 1988, 1996; Sec., 1987, 1995); Bd of Trustees, Writers Guild-Industry Health Fund, 1973– (Chm., 1980, 1988, 1996; Sec., 1987, 1995). Guggenheim Fellow, 1956–57. *Publications:* One, 1953; The Day of the Monkey, 1955; All Honorable Men, 1956; Leave Me Alone, 1957; The Sleepwalkers, 1960; Vice-President in Charge of Revolution (with Murray D. Lincoln), 1960; The Last Believers, 1964; short stories in Saturday Eve. Post, Collier's, Esquire, Argosy, The American, etc; articles and reviews in NY Times, Los Angeles Times, Saturday Review, Nation, etc. *Recreations:* photography, reading. *Address:* 300 East 56th Street #3C, New York, NY 10022, USA. *Club:* PEN (New York).

KARRAN, Graham, QFSM 1985; Managing Director, Able Fire Advisory Service, since 1991; *b* 28 Nov. 1939; *s* of Joseph Karran and Muriel Benson; *m* 1960, Thelma Gott; one *s* one *d. Educ:* Bootle Grammar Sch.; Liverpool College of Building. Estate Management, 1958–60; Southport Fire Bde, 1960–63; Lancashire County Fire Bde, 1963–74; Greater Manchester Fire Service, 1974–78; Cheshire County Fire Service, 1978–80; Derbyshire Fire Service, 1980–83; Chief Fire Officer, W Yorks Fire Service, 1983–90. *Publications:* articles in English and Amer. Fire jls. *Recreations:* music, beachcombing. *T:* (business) Huddersfield (01484) 607212, *Fax:* Huddersfield (01484) 608736.

KARSH, Yousuf, CC 1990 (OC 1968); Portrait Photographer since 1932; *b* Mardin, Armenia-in-Turkey, 23 Dec. 1908; parents Armenian; Canadian Citizen; *m* 1939, Solange Gauthier (*d* 1961); *m* 1962, Estrellita Maria Nachbar. *Educ:* Sherbrooke, PQ Canada; studied photography in Boston, Mass., USA. Portrayed Winston Churchill in Canada's Houses of Parliament, 1941; King George VI, 1943; HM Queen (then Princess) Elizabeth and the Duke of Edinburgh, 1951; HH Pope Pius XII, 1951; also portrayed, among many others: Shaw, Wells, Einstein, Sibelius, Somerset Maugham, Picasso, Eden, Eisenhower, Tito, Eleanor Roosevelt, Thomas Mann, Bertrand Russell, Attlee, Nehru, Ingrid Bergmann, Lord Mountbatten of Burma, Augustus John, Pope John Paul II; 14 portraits used on postage stamps of 15 countries. One man exhibitions: Men Who Make our World, Pav. of Canada, Expo. 67; Montreal Mus. of Fine Arts, 1968; Boston Mus. of Fine Arts, 1968; Corning Mus., 1968; Detroit Inst. of Arts, 1969; Corcoran Gall. of Art, Washington, 1969; Macdonald House, London, 1969; Seattle Art Museum; Japan (country-wide), and Honolulu, 1970, in Europe and USA annually, 1971–; exhibn acquired in toto by: Museum of Modern Art, Tokyo; Nat. Gall. of Australia; Province of Alberta, Canada, 1975–76; numerous exhibns throughout US, 1971–75, 1976–77; Ulrich Museum, Wichita, Kansas, 1978; Museum of Science and Industry, Chicago, 1978; Evansville Museum, Ind., 1979; Palm Springs Desert Museum, 1980; inaugural exhibn, Museum of Photography, Film and TV, Bradford, 1983; NY, 1983; Nat. Portrait Gall., 1983, 1991; Edinburgh, 1984; Internat. Center of Photography, NY, 1983; Helsinki, 1984; Minneapolis Museum, 1985; Syracuse Museum, 1985; Sarasota (Florida) Museum, 1986; 80th birthday gala exhibn, Barbican, London, and in France, Germany, Spain, Switzerland, 1988; Muscarelle Mus. of Art, William and Mary Coll., Williamsburg, Virginia, 1987; Castle Buda Palace, Budapest, 1989; Nat. Gall. of Canada, 1989; Gulbenkian Foundn, Lisbon, 1989; Copenhagen, Brussels, Zurich, 1989; Vancouver Art Mus., 1990; Vero Beach, Fla, 1991; Montreal Mus. of Fine Arts, 1992; Internat. Centre of Photography, NY, 1992; Corcoran Gall., Washington, 1993; Minton Mus., Charlotte, NC, 1993; Tribute Exhibn, Bradford, 1993; Canadian Embassy, Washington, 1994. Visiting Professor: Ohio Univ., 1967–69; Emerson Coll., Boston, 1972–73, 1973–74; Photographic Advisor, Internat. Exhibn, Expo '70, Osaka, Japan; Judge, UN 40th anniversary internat. poster contest, 1985. Trustee, Photographic Arts and Scis Foundn, 1970. FRPS; Fellow Rochester Sci. Mus. RCA 1975. Holds 27 hon. degrees. Canada Council Medal, 1965; Centennial Medal, 1967; Master of Photographic Arts, Prof. Photogrs of Canada, 1970; First Gold Medal, Nat. Assoc. Photog. Art, 1974; Life Achievement Award, Encyclopaedia Britannica, 1980; Silver Shingle Award, Law Sch., Boston Univ., 1983; Lotos Medal of Merit, Lotos Club of NY, 1989; first Creative Edge Award, NY Univ., 1989; Gold Medal, Americas Soc., 1989; Master Photographer, Internat. Center of Photography, 1990. *Publications:* Faces of Destiny, 1947; (co-author) This is the Mass, 1958; Portraits of Greatness, 1959; (co-author) This is Rome, 1960; (co-author) This is the Holy Land, 1961; (autobiog.) In Search of Greatness, 1962; (co-author) These are the Sacraments, 1963; (co-author) The Warren Court; Karsh Portfolio, 1967; Faces of our Time, 1971; Karsh Portraits, 1976; Karsh Canadians, 1979; Karsh: a fifty year retrospective, 1983; American Legends, 1992. *Recreations:* tennis, bird-watching, archæology, music. *Address:* Chateau Laurier Hotel, Ottawa K1N 8S7, Canada. *T:* (613) 2417272. *Clubs:* Garrick; Rideau (Ottawa); Century, Dutch Treat (NY).

KARSTEN, Ian George Francis; QC 1990; a Recorder, since 1994; *b* 27 July 1944; *s* of Dr Frederick Karsten and Edith Karsten; *m* 1984, Moira Elizabeth Ann O'Hara; one *s* two *d. Educ:* William Ellis School, Highgate; Magdalen College, Oxford (MA, BCL); Diplômé, Hague Acad. of Internat. Law. Called to the Bar, Gray's Inn, 1967; Midland and Oxford Circuit; commenced practice 1970; Lectr in Law, Southampton Univ., 1966–70, LSE, 1970–88. UK Deleg. to Hague Conf. on Private Internat. Law (Convention on the Law Applicable to Agency) (Rapporteur), 1973–77; Leader, UK Delegn to Unidroit Conf. on Agency in Internat. Sale of Goods, Bucharest, 1979, Geneva, 1983; Legal Assessor, UK Council for Nursing, Midwifery and Health Visiting, 1989–. *Publications:* Conflict of Laws, Halsbury's Laws of England, 4th edn (jtly), 1974; Report on the Convention on the Law Applicable to Agency (Hague Conf.), 1979; articles and notes in legal jls. *Recreations:* opera, travel, chess. *Address:* Queen Elizabeth Building, Temple, EC4Y 9BS. *T:* 0171–797 7837.

KASER, Michael Charles, MA; General Editor, International Economic Association, since 1986; Reader in Economics, University of Oxford, and Professorial Fellow of St Antony's College, 1972–93 (Sub-Warden, 1986–87), now Reader Emeritus; *b* 2 May 1926; *er s* of Charles Joseph Kaser and Mabel Blunden; *m* 1954, Elisabeth Anne Mary, *er d* of Cyril Gascoigne Piggford; four *s* one *d. Educ:* King's Coll., Cambridge (Exhibr). DLitt. Foreign Service, London and Moscow, 1947–51; UN Secretariat, Econ. Commn for Europe, Geneva, 1951–63; Faculty Fellow, St Antony's Coll., Oxford, 1963–72; Dir, Inst. of Russian, Soviet and E European Studies, Univ. of Oxford, 1988–93; Associate Fellow, Templeton Coll., Oxford, 1983–; Principal, Charlemagne Inst., Edinburgh, 1993–94. Hon. Fellow, Divinity Faculty, Univ. of Edinburgh, 1993; Hon. Prof., Univ. of Birmingham, 1994–. Visiting Professor of Economics: Inst. Universitaire des Hautes Etudes Internats, Geneva, 1959–63; Univ. of Michigan, 1966; Vis. Fellow, Henley Management Coll., 1987–; Vis. Lectr, Cambridge Univ., 1967–68, 1977–78 and 1978–79; Vis. Lectr, INSEAD, Fontainebleau, 1959–82, 1988–92. Specialist Advr, Foreign Affairs Cttee, H of C, 1985–87. Oxford Univ. Latin Preacher, 1982. Convenor/Chm., Nat. Assoc. for Soviet and East European Studies, 1965–73, Chm., Jt Cttee with BUAS, 1980–84; Vice-Chm., Internat. Activities Cttee (Vice-Chm., Area Studies Panel, SSRC) ESRC, 1980–84; Chm., Co-ordinating Council, Area Studies Assocs, 1986–88 (Mem., 1980–93; Sec., 1980–84, Vice-Chm., 1984–86); Governor, Plater Coll., Oxford, 1968–; Chairman: Acad. Council, Wilton Park (FCO), 1986–92 (Mem., 1985–); Acad. Cttee, St Catharine's, Cumberland Lodge, 1991–; Sir Heinz Koeppler Trust, 1992– (Mem., 1987–). President: British Assoc. for Slavonic and East European Studies, 1988–91 (Vice-Pres., 1991–93); British Assoc. of Former UN Civil Servants, 1994–; Chairman: Standing Cttee on E European Affairs, European Econ. Assoc., 1990–93; Keston Inst., 1994–. Member: Council, Royal Econ. Soc., 1976–86, 1987–90; Council, RIIA, 1979–85, 1986–92; Internat. Soc. Sci. Council, UNESCO, 1980–; Council, SSEES, 1981–87; Sec., British Acad. Cttee for SE European Studies, 1988–93 (Mem., 1970–75, 1983–93). Steering Cttee, Königswinter Anglo-German Confs, 1969–90 (Chm., Oxford Organizing Cttee, 1975–78). Pres., Albania Soc. of Britain, 1992–; Trustee, King George VI and Queen Elizabeth Foundn, 1987–. Missions for various internat. agencies, 1953–, incl. EC to Moscow, 1991 and UNICEF to Albania, 1991, Turkmenistan and Uzbekistan, 1992. Editorial Boards: Member: Energy Econs; Central Asian Review; former Member: Econ. Jl; Jl of Industrial Econs; Soviet Studies; Oxford Rev. of Educn; CUP E European Monograph Series; World Develt; European Econ Rev. Hon. DSocSc Birmingham, 1994. KSG 1990. *Publications:* Comecon: Integration Problems of the Planned Economies, 1965, 2nd edn 1967; (ed) Economic Development for Eastern Europe, 1968; (with J. Zieliński) Planning in East Europe, 1970; Soviet Economics, 1970; (ed, with R. Portes) Planning and Market Relations, 1971; (ed, with H. Höhmann and K. Thalheim) The New Economic Systems of Eastern Europe, 1975; (ed, with A. Brown) The Soviet Union since the Fall of Khrushchev, 1975, 2nd edn 1978; Health Care in the Soviet Union and Eastern Europe, 1976; (ed with A. Brown) Soviet Policy for the 1980s, 1982; (ed jtly) The Cambridge Encyclopaedia of Russia and the Former Soviet Union, 1982, revd edn as The Cambridge Encyclopaedia of Russia and the Former Soviet Union, 1994; Gen. Ed., The Economic History of Eastern Europe 1919–1975, vols I and II (1919–49), vol. III (1949–75), 1985–86; (ed with E. A. G. Robinson) Early Steps in Comparing East-West Economies, 1992; (ed with D. Phillips) Education and Economic Change in Eastern Europe and the Former Soviet Union, 1992; (with S. Mehrotra) The Central Asian Economies after Independence, 1992; papers in economic jls and symposia. *Address:* 7 Chadlington Road, Oxford OX2 6SY. *T:* Oxford (01865) 515581. *Club:* Reform.

KASMIN, John; art dealer, since 1960; *b* 24 Sept. 1934; *s* of Vera D'Olzewski and David Kosminsky (known as Kaye); *m* 1959, Jane Nicholson (marr. diss.); two *s. Educ:* Magdalen College School, Oxford. Adventurous and varied jobs in New Zealand, 1952–56; art gallery assistant, London, 1956–60; Founder Director: Kasmin Ltd, 1961– (in partnership with late Marquess of Dufferin and Ava); Knoedler Kasmin Ltd, 1977–92. *Recreation:* study of art and literature. *Address:* c/o Kasmin Ltd, 34 Warwick Avenue, W9 2PT. *Fax:* 0171–289 0746. *Club:* Groucho.

KASPAROV, Garry Kimovich; chess player; *b* Azerbaidzhan, 13 April 1963; *né* Harry Weinstein; *s* of Kim Moiseyevich Weinstein and Klara Kasparian; *m* 1989, Maria Arapova; one *d.* Youngest world chess champion, 1985; retained title, 1986, 1987, 1990, 1992. Resigned from FIDE and formed Professional Chess Assoc. (with Nigel Short); won first title, 1993; rejoined FIDE, 1994. *Publications:* New World Chess Champion; London-Leningrad Championship Games; The Test of Time; (with Donald Trelford) Child of

Change, 1987. *Address:* c/o Russian Chess Federation, Luzhnetskaya 8, Moscow 119270, Russia.

KASTNER, Prof. Leslie James, MA, ScD Cantab, FIMechE; Professor of Mechanical Engineering, King's College, University of London, 1955–76, now Emeritus; Dean of Faculty of Engineering, University of London, 1974–76; *b* 10 Dec. 1911; *o s* of late Professor Leon E. Kastner, sometime Prof. of French Language and Literature, University of Manchester, and of Elsie E. Kastner; *m* 1958, Joyce, *o d* of Lt-Col Edward Lillingston, DSO, Belstone, Devon. *Educ:* Dreghorn Castle Sch.; Colinton, Midlothian; Highgate Sch.; Clare Coll., Cambridge (Mechanical Science Tripos). Apprenticeship with Davies and Metcalfe, Ltd, Locomotive Engineers, of Romiley, Stockport, 1930–31 and 1934–36; Development Engineer, 1936–38; Osborne Reynolds Research Fellowship, University of Manchester, 1938; Lectr in Engineering, University of Manchester, 1941–46; Senior Lectr, 1946–48; Prof. of Engineering, University Coll. of Swansea, University of Wales, 1948–55. Mem. of Council, Institution of Mechanical Engineers, 1954. FKC 1974. Graduates' Prize, InstMechE, 1939; Herbert Ackroyd Stuart Prize, 1943; Dugald Clerk Prize, 1956. *Publications:* various research papers in applied thermodynamics and fluid flow. *Address:* 37 St Anne's Road, Eastbourne BN21 2HP.

KATCHALSKI-KATZIR, Prof. Ephraim; *see* Katzir, Prof. E.

KATENGA-KAUNDA, Reid Willie; Malaŵi Independence Medal, 1964; Malaŵi Republic Medal, 1966; business executive; *b* 20 Aug. 1929; *s* of Gibson Amon Katenga Kaunda and Maggie Talengeske Nyabanda; *m* 1951, Elsie Nyabanda; one *s* three *d* (and one *s* one *d* decd). *Educ:* Ndola Govt Sch., Zambia; Inst. of Public Administration, Malaŵi; Trinity Coll., Oxford Univ.; Administrative Staff Coll., Henley. Sec., Nkhota Kota Rice Co-op. Soc. Ltd, 1952–62; Dist. Comr, Karonga, Malaŵi, 1964–65; Sen. Asst Sec., Min. of External Affairs, Zomba, Malaŵi, 1966; MP and Parly Sec., Office of the President and Cabinet, Malaŵi, 1966–68; Dep. Regional Chm., MCP, Northern Region, 1967–68; Under Sec., Office of the President and Cabinet, 1968–69; High Comr in London, 1969–70; Perm. Sec., Min. of Trade, Industry and Tourism, 1971–72; High Comr in London, 1972–73, and concurrently to the Holy See, Portugal, Belgium, Holland and France. Dep. Chm., Ncheu and Mchinji Inquiry Commn, 1967. *Recreations:* reading, walking, cinema, Association football. *Address:* c/o PO Box 511, Blantyre, Malaŵi.

KATIN, Peter Roy; concert pianist; Professor, Royal College of Music, since 1992; *b* 14 Nov. 1930; *m* 1954, Eva Zweig; two *s*. *Educ:* Henry Thornton Sch.; Westminster Abbey; Royal Academy of Music. First London appearance at Wigmore Hall, 1948. A leading Chopin interpreter. Performances abroad include most European countries, West and East, S and E Africa, Japan, Canada, USA, Hong Kong, India, New Zealand, Singapore, Malaysia. Many recordings, incl. complete sonatas of Mozart, complete nocturnes and impromptus of Chopin, complete preludes of Rachmaninov, complete lyric pieces of Grieg, and major works by Brahms, Mendelssohn, Scarlatti, Schubert, Schumann and Tchaikovsky. Prof., Royal Acad. of Music, 1956–59. Vis. Prof. in piano, Univ. of Western Ontario, 1978–84. Founder, Katin Centre for Advanced Piano Studies, 1991. Mem. Incorporated Soc. of Musicians (ISM). FRAM, ARCM. Hon. DMus De Montfort, 1994. Chopin Arts Award, NY, 1977. *Recreations:* reading, writing, theatre, tape recording, photography. *Address:* c/o Maureen Lunn Management, Top Farm, Parish Lane, Hedgerley, Bucks SL2 3JH. *T:* Farnham Common (01753) 645008, *Fax:* (01753) 647431.

KATO, Tadao, Hon. KBE 1988; 1st Class Order of Sacred Treasure, 1988; Counsellor, Suntory, Long-Term Credit Bank, since 1980; *b* 13 May 1916; *m* 1946, Yoko; two *s*. *Educ:* Tokyo Univ.; Cambridge Univ. Joined Japanese Diplomatic Service 1939; Singapore, 1952; London, 1953; Counsellor, Economic Affairs Bureau, Min. of Foreign Affairs, 1956–69; Counsellor, Washington, 1959–63 (Vis. Fellow, Harvard, 1959–60); Dep. Dir, Econ. Affairs Bureau, Min. of Foreign Affairs, 1963–66, Dir, 1966–67; Ambassador to OECD, 1967–70, to Mexico, 1970–74, to UK, 1975–79. Advisor: NI Development Bd, 1981–; Hotel Okura; Nitto Kogyo Enterprise. Vice-Pres., Japan British Soc., 1988– (Chm., 1981–88); Mem., UK-Japan 2000 Gp, 1988– (Japanese Chm., 1985–88). 1st Class Order of Aztec Star, Mexico, 1972. *Recreations:* golf, goh. *Address:* 3–10–22, Shimo-Ochiai, Shinjuku-Ku, Tokyo, Japan. *Clubs:* Tokyo (Tokyo); Oxfordshire Golf (Hon. Mem., 1993); Royal Co. Down Golf; Koganei Golf, Abiko Golf, Karuizawa Golf, Hamano Golf (Chm., 1984–), Mito Golf (Chm., 1988–), Shinyo Golf (Chm., 1989–) (Japan); Green Academy Country (Chm., 1985–) (Fukushima).

KATRITZKY, Prof. Alan Roy, DPhil, PhD, ScD; FRS 1980; FRSC; Kenan Professor of Chemistry, since 1980, and Director, Center for Heterocyclic Compounds, since 1986, University of Florida; *b* 18 Aug. 1928; *s* of Frederick Charles Katritzky and Emily Catherine (*née* Lane); *m* 1952, Agnes Juliane Dietlinde Kilian; one *s* three *d*. *Educ:* Oxford Univ. (BA, BSc, MA, DPhil); Cambridge Univ. (PhD, ScD). FRIC 1963. Lectr, Cambridge Univ., 1958–63; Fellow of Churchill Coll., Cambridge, 1960–63; Prof. of Chemistry, Univ. of E Anglia, 1963–80, Dean, Sch. of Chem. Sciences, UEA, 1963–70 and 1976–80. For. Mem., Polish Acad. of Sci., 1991. Foreign Fellow, RACI, 1983; Hon. Fellow: Italian Chem. Soc., 1978; Polish Chem. Soc., 1985. Hon. Prof., Beijing Inst. of Tech., China, 1995. Dr *hc*: Univ. Nacional, Madrid, 1986; Univ. Poznan, Poland, 1990; Medical Acad., Gdansk, 1994; Univ. of E Anglia, 1995. Tilden Medal, Chem. Soc., 1975–76. Heterocyclic Award, RSC, 1983; Medals of Tartu State Univ., Estonia, USSR, 1986, 1992; Golden Tiger award, Exxon Corp., 1989; Inernat. Soc. of Heterocyclic Chemistry Award, 1993; Medal of Univ. of Thessaloniki, 1993. Cavaliere ufficiale, Order Al Merito Della Repubblica Italiana, 1975. *Publications:* (ed) Advances in Heterocyclic Chemistry, Vols 1–55, 1963–; (ed) Physical Methods in Heterocyclic Chemistry, Vols 1–6, 1963–72; Principles of Heterocyclic Chemistry, 1968 (trans. into French, German, Italian, Japanese, Russian, Polish and Spanish); Chemistry of Heterocyclic N-Oxides (monograph), 1970; Heteroaromatic Tautomerism (monograph), 1975; Handbook of Heterocyclic Chemistry, 1985; Chm. Editorial Bd, Comprehensive Heterocyclic Chemistry (8 vols), 1985; Chm. Editorial Bd, Comprehensive Organic Functional Group Transformations (7 vols), 1995; scientific papers in Heterocylic Chem. *Recreations:* walking, travel, windsurfing. *Address:* Department of Chemistry, University of Florida, Gainesville, FL 32611, USA. *T:* (904) 3920554, *Fax:* (904) 3929199. *Club:* United Oxford & Cambridge University.

KATZ, Sir Bernard, Kt 1969; FRS 1952; Professor and Head of Biophysics Department, University College, London, 1952–78, now Emeritus, Hon. Research Fellow, 1978; *b* Leipzig, 26 March 1911; *s* of M. N. Katz; *m* 1945, Marguerite, *d* of W. Penly, Sydney, Australia; two *s*. *Educ:* University of Leipzig (MD 1934). Biophysical research, University Coll., London, 1935–39; PhD London, and Beit Memorial Research Fellow, 1938; Carnegie Research Fellow, Sydney Hospital, Sydney, 1939–42; DSc London, 1943. Served War of 1939–45 in Pacific with RAAF, 1942–45; Flt-Lt, 1943. Asst Dir of Research, Biophysics Research Unit, University Coll., London, and Henry Head Research Fellow (Royal Society), 1946–50; Reader in Physiology, 1950–51. Lectures: Herter, Johns Hopkins Univ., 1958; Dunham, Harvard Coll., 1961; Croonian, Royal Society, 1961; Sherrington, Liverpool Univ., 1967. A Vice-Pres., Royal Society, 1965, Biological Secretary and Vice-President, 1968–76. Mem., Agric. Research Coun., 1967–77. For. Member: Royal Danish Academy Science and Letters, 1968; Accad. Naz. Lincei, 1968; Amer. Acad. of Arts and Sciences, 1969; For. Assoc., Nat. Acad. of Scis, USA, 1976; Hon. Member: Japanese Pharmacol. Soc., 1977; American Physiolog. Soc., 1985; Assoc. Mem., European Molecular Biol. Orgn, 1978; Corresp. Mem., Australian Acad. of Science, 1987. Fellow of University Coll., London. FRCP, 1968. Hon. FIBiol, 1978. Hon. DSc: Southampton, 1971; Melbourne, 1971; Cambridge, 1980; Hon. PhD Weizmann Inst., Israel, 1979; Hon. MD Leipzig, 1990. Feldberg Foundation Award, 1965; Baly Medal, RCP, 1967; Copley Medal, Royal Society, 1967; Nobel Prize (jtly) for Physiology and Medicine, 1970; Cothenius Medal, Deutsche Akademie der Wissenschaften, Leopoldina, 1989. Foreign Mem., Orden Pour le Mérite für Wissenschaften und Künste, 1982. *Publications:* Electric Excitation of Nerve, 1939; Nerve, Muscle and Synapse, 1966; The Release of Neural Transmitter Substances, 1969; papers on nerve and muscle physiology in Jl of Physiol., Proc. Royal Society, etc. *Recreation:* chess. *Address:* University College, WC1E 6BT.

KATZIR, Prof. Ephraim (Katchalski), PhD; Institute Professor, Weizmann Institute of Science, since 1978; President, State of Israel, 1973–78; *b* Kiev, Ukraine, 16 May 1916; *s* of Yehuda and Tsila Katchalski; *m* 1938, Nina Gotlieb (decd); one *s* one *d*. *Educ:* Rehavia High Sch., Jerusalem; Hebrew Univ., Jerusalem (chemistry, botany, zool., bacteriol.; MSc *summa cum laude* 1937; PhD 1941). Settled in Israel with parents, 1922; involved in Labour youth movement; Inf. Comdr, Jewish Self-Defence Forces (Hagana). Asst, Dept of Theoretical and Macromolecular Chem., Hebrew Univ., 1941–45; Res. Fellow, Polytechnic Inst., and Columbia Univ., NY, 1946–48; Actg Head, Dept of Biophys., Weizmann Inst. of Science, Rehovot, Israel, 1949–51, Head 1951–73 (mem. founding faculty of Inst.); Chief Scientist, Israel Def. Min., 1966–68; Head, Dept of Biotechnology, Tel Aviv Univ., 1980–88. Vis. Prof. of Biophys., Hebrew Univ., 1953–61; Guest Scientist, Harvard Univ., 1957–59; Vis. Prof., Rockefeller Univ., NY, and Univ. of Mich, Ann Arbor, 1961–65; Sen. Foreign Scientist Fellowship, UCLA, 1964; Battelle Seattle Res. Center, Washington, 1971; Regents Prof., Univ. of Calif., San Diego, 1979; First Herman F. Mark Chair in Polymer Sci., Poly. Inst., NY, 1979. President: World ORT Union, 1986–90; Cobiotech, 1989–. Member: Biochem. Soc. of Israel; Israel Acad. of Sciences and Humanities; Israel Chem. Soc.; Council, Internat. Union of Biochem.; AAAS; Assoc. of Harvard Chemists; Leopoldina Acad. of Science, Germany; World Acad. of Art and Science; New York Acad. of Science (Life Mem.). Centennial Foreign Fellow, Amer. Chem. Soc.; For. Associate, Nat. Acad. of Sciences of USA. For. Member: The Royal Soc.; Amer. Philosoph. Soc.; Acad. des Scis, France, 1989. Hon. Fellow, Scientific Acad. of Argentina, 1986; Hon. Member: Amer. Acad. of Arts and Sciences; Amer. Soc. of Biol Chemists; Harvey Soc.; Romanian Acad. of Scis, 1991; Hon. MRI 1989. Hon. Prof., Polytechnic Inst. of New York, 1975. Hon. Dr: Hebrew Univ., 1973; Brandeis Univ., Univ. of Mich, and Hebrew Union Coll., 1975; Weizmann Inst. of Science, 1976; Northwestern Univ., Evanston, 1978; Harvard, 1978; McGill, 1980; ETH Zurich, 1980; Thomas Jefferson, 1981; Oxford, 1981; Miami, 1983; Technion, Israel Inst. of Technology, 1983; Univ. of Buenos Aires, 1986. Tchernikhovski Prize, 1948; Weizmann Prize, 1950; Israel Prize in Nat. Sciences, 1959; Rothschild Prize in Nat. Sciences, 1961; Linderstrøm Lang Gold Medal, 1969; Hans Krebs Medal, 1972; Alpha Omega Achievement Medal, 1979; Underwood Prescott Award, MIT, 1982; first Japan Prize, Science and Technol. Foundn of Japan, 1985; Internat. Enzyme Engineering Award, 1987. Ephraim Katzir Chair of Biophysics, Bar Ilan Univ., Israel, founded 1976. Hon. Founding Editor, Biopolymers, 1986– (Mem., Editorial Bd, 1963–86). Comdr, Legion of Honour (France), 1990. *Address:* Weizmann Institute of Science, Rehovot 76100, Israel.

KAUFFMANN, Prof. C. Michael, MA, PhD; FBA 1987; FMA; FSA; Professor of History of Art and Director, Courtauld Institute of Art, University of London, 1985–95, now Professor Emeritus; *b* 5 Feb. 1931; *s* of late Arthur and late Tamara Kauffmann; *m* 1954, Dorothea (*née* Hill); two *s*. *Educ:* St Paul's Sch.; Merton Coll., Oxford (Postmaster); Warburg Inst., London Univ. (Jun. Research Fellow). Asst Curator, Photographic Collection, Warburg Inst., 1957–58; Keeper, Manchester City Art Gall., 1958–60; Victoria and Albert Museum: Asst Keeper, 1960–75, Keeper, 1975–85, Dept of Prints & Drawings and Paintings; Asst to the Director, 1963–66; Visiting Associate Prof., Univ. of Chicago, 1969. Mem. Exec. Cttee, NACF, 1987–; Trustee, Nat. Museums and Galls on Merseyside, 1986–. *Publications:* The Baths of Pozzuoli: medieval illuminations of Peter of Eboli's poem, 1959; An Altar-piece of the Apocalypse, 1968; Victoria & Albert Museum: catalogue of foreign paintings, 1973; British Romanesque Manuscripts 1066–1190, 1975; Catalogue of Paintings in the Wellington Museum, 1982; John Varley, 1984; Studies in Medieval Art, 1992.

KAUFMAN, Rt. Hon. Gerald (Bernard); PC 1978; MP (Lab) Manchester, Gorton, since 1983 (Manchester, Ardwick, 1970–83); *b* 21 June 1930; *s* of Louis and Jane Kaufman. *Educ:* Leeds Grammar Sch.; The Queen's Coll., Oxford. Asst Gen.-Sec., Fabian Soc., 1954–55; Political Staff, Daily Mirror, 1955–64; Political Correspondent, New Statesman, 1964–65; Parly Press Liaison Officer, Labour Party, 1965–70. Parly Under-Sec. of State, DoE, 1974–75, Dept of Industry, 1975; Minister of State, Dept of Industry, 1975–79; Parly Cttee of PLP, 1980–92; Shadow Home Sec., 1983–87; Shadow Foreign Sec., 1987–92. Chm., Select Cttee on Nat. Heritage, 1992–. Mem., Labour Party NEC, 1991–92. *Publications:* (jtly) How to Live Under Labour, 1964; (ed) The Left, 1966; To Build the Promised Land, 1973; How to be a Minister, 1980; (ed) Renewal: Labour's Britain in the 1980s, 1983; My Life in the Silver Screen, 1985; Inside the Promised Land, 1986; Meet Me in St Louis, 1994. *Recreations:* travel, going to the pictures. *Address:* 87 Charlbert Court, Eamont Street, NW8 7DA. *T:* (office) 0171–219 3000.

KAUFMAN, Prof. Matthew Howard, PhD, DSc; Professor of Anatomy and Head of Department of Anatomy, University of Edinburgh, since 1985; *b* 29 Sept. 1942; *s* of Benjamin and Dora Kaufman; *m* 1973, Claire Lesley Kaufman (*née* Farrow); two *s*. *Educ:* Westminster City Sch.; Univ. of Edinburgh (MB ChB 1967; DSc 1984); Univ. of Cambridge (PhD 1973; MA 1975; ScD 1994). Pre- and post-registration clinical posts, 1967–69; Research Associate, Inst. of Animal Genetics, Edinburgh, 1970; MRC Jun. Research Fellow, Physiol Lab., Cambridge, 1970–73; Royal Soc./Israel Acad. of Scis Research Fellow, and MRC Travelling Fellow, Weizmann Inst. of Science, 1973–75; University of Cambridge: Univ. Demonstrator, 1975–77; Lectr in Anatomy, 1977–85; Fellow and College Lectr in Anatomy, King's Coll., 1980–85. *Publications:* Early Mammalian Development: parthenogenetic studies, 1983; The Atlas of Mouse Development, 1992; research papers in the fields of experimental and descriptive embryology, cytogenetics, developmental biology and teratology. *Recreations:* history of medicine, particularly of anatomy; the artefacts of phrenology. *Address:* Department of Anatomy, University Medical School, Teviot Place, Edinburgh EH8 9AG. *T:* 0131–650 3114.

KAUL, Mahendra Nath, OBE 1975; Managing Director, Viceroy of India (Restaurants) Ltd, since 1982; UK correspondent, Daily Jagran, since 1983; *b* 28 July 1922; *s* of Dina Nath Kaul and Gauri Kaul; *m* 1955, Rajni Kapur, MA, MLS; one *d*. *Educ:* Univ. of the Punjab, India (BA). Joined Radio Kashmir of All India Radio, as news reader, actor and producer of dramas, 1949; appeared in two feature films and assisted in producing several documentaries, 1950–52; news reader and actor in three languages, also drama producer, All India Radio, New Delhi, 1952–55; joined Indian service of Voice of America, Washington DC, 1955, later becoming Editor of the service; joined external service of BBC, as newscaster, producer and dir of radio plays; producer/presenter, BBC TV prog. for Asian Viewers in UK, 1966–82. Director: Hotels & Restaurants Suppliers Ltd (formerly SK Giftware), 1985–; Arts and Crafts Emporium Ltd, 1985–; Bokhara Cuisine Ltd, 1985–. OBE awarded for services to race relations in Gt Britain. Received The Green Pennant from HRH The Duke of Edinburgh, awarded by Commonwealth Expedition (COMEX 10), 1980. *Recreations:* golf, cooking, boating, classical and light classical music, reading political works. *Address:* 50 Grove Court, Grove End Road, St John's Wood, NW8 9EP. *T:* 0171–286 8131.

KAULBACK, Ronald John Henry, OBE 1946; *b* 23 July 1909; *er s* of late Lieutenant-Colonel Henry Albert Kaulback, OBE, and Alice Mary, *d* of late Rev. A. J. Townend, CF; *m* 1st, 1940, Audrey Elizabeth (marr. diss. 1984; she *d* 1994), 3rd *d* of late Major H. R. M. Howard-Sneyd, OBE; two *s* two *d*; 2nd, 1984, Joyce Nora, *widow* of Capt. H. S. Woolley, MC. *Educ:* Rugby; Pembroke Coll., Cambridge. In 1933 journeyed through Assam and Eastern Tibet with Kingdon Ward; returned to Tibet, 1935, accompanied by John Hanbury-Tracy, spending eighteen months there in an attempt to discover source of Salween River; 1938 spent eighteen months in Upper Burma hunting and collecting zoological specimens for the British Museum (Natural History); Murchison Grant of Royal Geog. Society, 1937. *Publications:* Tibetan Trek, 1934; Salween, 1938. *Address:* Altbough, Hoarwithy, Hereford HR2 6QE. *T:* Carey (01432) 840676.

KAUNDA, Kenneth David; President of Zambia, Oct. 1964–1991 (Prime Minister, N Rhodesia, Jan.–Oct. 1964); Chancellor of the University of Zambia, 1966; *b* 28 April 1924; *s* of late David Julizgia and Hellen Kaunda, Missionaries; *m* 1946, Betty Banda; six *s* two *d* one adopted *s* (and one *s* decd). *Educ:* Lubwa Training Sch.; Munali Secondary Sch. Teacher, Lubwa Training Sch., 1943–44, Headmaster, 1944–47; Boarding Master, Mufulira Upper Sch., 1948–49. African National Congress: District Sec., 1950–52; Provincial Organising Sec., 1952–53; Sec.-Gen., 1953–58; Nat. Pres., Zambia African Nat. Congress, 1958–59; founded United Nat. Independence Party, 1958, Nat. Pres., 1960–91, re-elected, 1995; Chm., Pan-African Freedom Movement for East, Central and South Africa, 1962; Minister of Local Government and Social Welfare, N Rhodesia, 1962–63. Chairman: Organization of African Unity, 1970, 1987; Non-aligned Countries, 1970. Hon. Doctor of Laws: Fordham Univ., USA, 1963; Dublin Univ., 1964; University of Sussex, 1965; Windsor Univ., Canada, 1966; University of Chile, 1966; Univ. of Zambia, 1974; Univ. of Humboldt, 1980; DUniv York, 1966. *Publications:* Black Government, 1961; Zambia Shall Be Free, 1962; Humanist in Africa, 1966; Humanism in Zambia and its implementation, 1967; Letter to My Children; Kaunda on Violence, 1980. *Recreations:* golf, music, table tennis, football, draughts, gardening and reading. *Address:* c/o UNIP, POB 30302, Lusaka, Zambia.

KAUNDA, Reid Willie K.; *see* Katenga-Kaunda.

KAUNTZE, Ralph, MBE 1944; MD; FRCP; Physician to Guy's Hospital, 1948–71, Consultant Physician Emeritus since 1971; *b* 5 June 1911; *s* of Charles Kauntze and Edith, *d* of Ralph Bagley; *m* 1st, 1935, Katharine Margaret (*d* 1993), *yr d* of late Ramsay Moodie; two *s* one *d*; 2nd, 1994, Enid M., *widow* of Lt-Col F. J. P. Dewhurst, RTR. *Educ:* Canford Sch.; Emmanuel Coll., Cambridge; St George's Hosp., London. William Brown Sen. Schol., St George's Hosp. 1932; MRCS, LRCP 1935; MA, MB, BCh Cantab 1937; MRCP 1939; MD Cantab 1946; FRCP 1950. Served, 1939–45, RAMC, chiefly Mediterranean area, Lt-Col O i/c Med. Div. Asst Dir of Dept of Med., Guy's Hosp., 1947–48, Physician to Cardiac Dept, 1956–71; Cons. Phys. to High Wycombe War Memorial Hosp., 1948–50; Dir Asthma Clinic, 1948–52, and of Dept of Student Health, 1950–63, Guy's Hosp.; Physician to Royal Masonic Hospital, 1963–76. Former Senior Cons. Phys. to: Commercial Union Assurance Co. Ltd; British & European Assurance Co.; European Assurance Co. Ltd. Hon. Vis. Phys., Johns Hopkins Hosp., Baltimore, 1958. Examiner in Medicine: RCP; London Univ. Mem. Brit. Cardiac Soc.; Mem. Assoc. of Physicians. *Publications:* contrib. med. jls. *Recreations:* farming, walking. *Address:* Arran House, rue de la Forge, St Martin, Jersey JE3 6BD. *T:* Jersey (01543) 854162.

KAVANAGH, P. J., (Patrick Joseph Gregory Kavanagh), FRSL; writer; columnist, The Spectator, since 1983; *b* 6 Jan. 1931; *s* of H. E. (Ted) Kavanagh and Agnes O'Keefe; *m* 1st, 1956, Sally Philipps (*d* 1958); 2nd, 1965, Catherine Ward; two *s*. *Educ:* Douai Sch.; Lycee Jaccard, Lausanne; Merton Coll., Oxford (MA). British Council, 1957–59. Actor, 1959–70. Mem., Kingman Cttee of Inquiry into English Lang., 1986–88. *Publications: poems:* One and One, 1960; On the Way to the Depot, 1967; About Time, 1970; Edward Thomas in Heaven, 1974; Life before Death, 1979; Selected Poems, 1982; Presences (new and selected poems), 1987; An Enchantment, 1991; Collected Poems, 1992; *novels:* A Song and Dance, 1968 (Guardian Fiction Prize, 1968); A Happy Man, 1972; People and Weather, 1979; Only by Mistake, 1986; *essays:* People and Places, 1988; *autobiography:* The Perfect Stranger, 1966 (Richard Hillary Prize, 1966); *travel autobiography:* Finding Connections, 1990; *for children:* Scarf Jack, 1978; Rebel for Good, 1980; *edited:* Collected Poems of Ivor Gurney, 1982; (with James Michie) Oxford Book of Short Poems, 1985; The Bodley Head G. K. Chesterton, 1985; Selected Poems of Ivor Gurney, 1990; A Book of Consolations, 1992; Voices in Ireland: a traveller's literary companion, 1994. *Recreation:* walking. *Address:* c/o Peters, Fraser, Dunlop, The Chambers, Chelsea Harbour, SW10 0XF.

KAVANAGH, Patrick Bernard, CBE 1977; QPM 1974; Deputy Commissioner, Metropolitan Police, 1977–83; *b* 18 March 1923; *s* of late Michael Kavanagh and late Violet Kavanagh (*née* Duncan); *m* Beryl (*d* 1984), *er d* of late Lt-Comdr Richard Owen Williams, RNR and Annie (*née* McShiells); one *s* two *d*. *Educ:* St Aloysius Coll., Glasgow. Rifle Bde, 1941–43; Para. Regt, 1943–46 (Lieut). Manchester City Police (Constable to Supt), 1946–64; Asst Chief Constable, Cardiff City Police, 1964–69; Asst and Dep. Chief Constable, S Wales Constabulary, 1969–73; Asst Comr (Traffic), Metropolitan Police, 1974–77. Attended Administrative Staff Coll., Henley-on-Thames, 1961. Mem., Gaming Bd for GB, 1983–91. *Recreations:* walking, bird watching, music, crosswords. *Address:* c/o Metropolitan Police, 2 Bessborough Street, SW1V 2JF. *Club:* Royal Automobile.

KAWHARU, Prof. Sir (Ian) Hugh, Kt 1989; FRSNZ 1995; Professor, Maori Studies, and Head of Department of Anthropology, 1985–93, Professor Emeritus, and Director, James Henare Maori Research Centre, since 1993, University of Auckland; *b* 18 Feb. 1927; *s* of Wiremu and Janet Paora Kawharu; *m* 1st, 1957, Nina; three *d*; 2nd, 1970, Freda; two *d*. *Educ:* Univ. of New Zealand (BSc); Univ. of Cambridge (MA); Univ. of Oxford (DPhil); Hon. Fellow, Exeter Coll., Oxford, 1993. Dept of Maori Affairs, housing welfare and trust admin, variously, 1953–65; Lectr, Dept of Anthropology, Univ. of Auckland, 1965–70; Prof. (personal chair), Social Anthropology and Maori Studies, Massey Univ., 1970–84. Consultant: FAO, 1961–63; NZ Govt, 1968–; Unesco, 1974–76; NZ Council for Educnl Res., 1976–89; NZ Maori Council, 1981–. Member: NZ Nat. Commn for Unesco, 1969–73; Royal Commn on the Courts, 1976–78; Waitangi Tribunal, 1986–; Bd of Maori Affairs, 1987–90; Council, Auckland Inst. and Mus., 1986–. Pres., Polynesian Soc., 1993– (Mem. Council, 1965–68). Patron, Pitt-Rivers Mus. Soc., Oxford, 1991–. *Publications:* Orakei, a Ngati Whatua Community, 1975; Maori Land Tenure, 1977; (ed. and co-author): Administration in New Zealand's Multiracial Society, 1967; Conflict and Compromise, 1975; Trends in Ethnic Group Relations in Asia and Oceania, 1979; Waitangi: Maori and Pakeha Perspectives of the Treaty of Waitangi, 1989; contrib. to numerous government reports on Maori people. *Recreation:* music. *Address:* University of Auckland, Private Bag 92019, Auckland, New Zealand. *T:* (9) 3737999.

KAY, Sir Andrew Watt, Kt 1973; retired; Regius Professor of Surgery, University of Glasgow, 1964–81; part-time Chief Scientist, Scottish Home and Health Department, 1973–81; *b* 14 Aug. 1916; of Scottish parentage; *m* 1st, 1943, Janetta M. Roxburgh (*d* 1990); two *s* two *d*; 2nd, 1992, Phyllis Gillies. *Educ:* Ayr Academy; Glasgow Univ. MB, ChB (Hons) with Brunton Memorial Prize, 1939; FRCSEd 1942; FRFPSG 1956 (Pres. 1972–); FRCS 1960; FRCSGlas 1967; FRSE 1971; MD (Hons) with Bellahouston Gold Medal, 1944; Major Royal Army Medical Corps i/c Surgical Div., Millbank Military Hospital, 1946–48; ChM (Hons) 1949; Consultant Surgeon in charge of Wards, Western Infirmary, Glasgow, 1956–58; Asst to Regius Prof. of Surgery, Glasgow Univ., 1942–56; Prof. of Surgery, University of Sheffield, 1958–64. Sims Travelling Prof., Australasia, 1969; McLaughlin Foundn Edward Gallie Vis. Prof., Canada, 1970. Rock Carling Fellowship, 1977. Pres., Surgical Research Soc., 1969–71. Member: Royal Commission on Medical Education, 1965–68; MRC, 1967–71; Chm., Scottish Hosps Endowment Research Trust, 1983–89; Hon. Mem., The N Pacific Surgical Assoc. FRACS 1970; FRCSCan 1972; FCS(SoAf) 1972; Hon. Fellow: Norwegian Surgical Assoc., Belgian Surgical Soc.; Amer. Surg. Assoc., 1972; Hon. FACS, 1973; Hon. FRCSI, 1979. Hon. DSc: Leicester, 1973; Sheffield, 1975; Manchester, 1981; Nebraska, 1981; Hon. MD Edinburgh, 1981. Cecil Joll Prize, RCS, 1969; Gordon-Taylor Lectureship and Medal, 1970. *Publications:* (with R. A. Jamieson, FRCS) Textbook of Surgical Physiology, 1959 (2nd edn 1964); Research in Medicine: problems and prospects, 1977; several papers in medical and surgical jls on gastroenterological subjects. *Recreation:* gardening. *Address:* 5 Loch Road, Milngavie, Glasgow G62 8BB.

KAY, Prof. Anthony Barrington, PhD, DSc; FRCPE, FRCP, FRCPath; Professor of Clinical Immunology and Director, Department of Allergy and Clinical Immunology and Hon. Consultant Physician, Royal Brompton Hospital and National Heart and Lung Institute, London, since 1980; *b* 23 June 1939; *s* of Anthony Chambers and Eva Gertrude (*née* Pearcey; she *m* 2nd H. Kay; now Mrs E. G. Reuben); *m* 1966, Rosemary Margaret Johnstone; three *d*. *Educ:* King's Sch., Peterborough; Edinburgh Univ. (MB, ChB 1963; DSc 1976); Jesus Coll., Cambridge (MA 1966; PhD 1970); Harvard Med. Sch. FRCPE 1975; FRCP 1980; FRCPath 1989. T. K. Stubbins Res. Fellow, RCP, 1969; Res. Fellow, Harvard Med. Sch., 1970–71; Lectr in Respiratory Diseases, Univ. of Edinburgh, 1972–74; Dep. Dir and Consultant, Immunology Div., Blood Transfusion Service, Royal Infirmary, Edinburgh, 1974–76; Sen. Lectr, then Reader, in Exptl Pathology, Dept of Pathology, Univ. of Edinburgh, 1977–79. President: European Acad. of Allergology and Clinical Immunology, 1989–92; Brit. Soc. of Allergy and Clinical Immunology, 1993–. Jt Editor, Clinical and Exptl Allergy, 1984–. FRSE 1993. Hon. Fellow, Amer. Coll. of Allergy, 1986; Hon. Member: Amer. Assoc. of Physicians, 1988; Hungarian Soc. of Allergology and Clinical Immunology, 1990; Swiss Soc. of Allergology and Clinical Immunology, 1991. Scientific Achievement Award, Internat. Assoc. of Allergology and Clinical Immunology, 1991. *Publications:* edited: Asthma: clinical pharmacology and therapeutic progress, 1986; Allergy and Inflammation, 1987; Allergic Basis of Asthma, 1988; Allergy and Asthma: new trends and approaches to therapy, 1989; Eosinophils, Allergy and Asthma, 1990; Eosinophils in Allergy and Inflammation, 1993; numerous scientific articles on allergy and asthma. *Recreations:* Baroque and modern bassoon, tennis, country walks. *Address:* Stamford Brook House, 12 Stamford Brook Avenue, W6 0YD. *T:* 0181–741 5899. *Club:* Hurlingham.

KAY, Bernard Hubert Gerard; HM Diplomatic Service, retired; *b* 7 July 1925; *s* of William and Alice Kay; *m* 1957, Teresa Jean Dyer; three *d*. *Educ:* St Bede's, Bradford; Wadham Coll., Oxford (MA, MLitt). Royal Navy, 1943–46. Foreign Office, 1955; served: Hong Kong, 1958–62; Singapore, 1964; Manila, 1965; New Delhi, 1967; Vientiane, 1968; Dacca, 1972; Ulan Bator, 1973; FCO, 1973–80. *Recreations:* Asia, books, mountains, the sea. *Address:* 6 Savona Close, Wimbledon, SW19 4HT. *Club:* United Oxford & Cambridge University.

KAY, Brian Christopher; broadcaster and musician; *b* 12 May 1944; *s* of Noel Bancroft Kay and Gwendoline Mary (*née* Sutton); *m* 1st, 1970, Sally Lyne; one *s* one *d*; 2nd, 1983, Gillian Fisher. *Educ:* Rydal Sch.; King's Coll., Cambridge (MA 1966); New Coll., Oxford (DipEd 1967). Bass Singer: Westminster Abbey Choir, 1968–71; King's Singers, 1968–82; Chorus Master, Huddersfield Choral Soc., 1983–93; Conductor: Cecilian Singers of Leicester, 1984–92; Cheltenham Bach Choir, 1989–; Principal Guest Conductor and Pres., Harrogate Choral Soc., 1992–. Presenter: Music in Mind, Radio 4, 1989–; Brian Kay's Sunday Morning, Radio 3, 1992–; The Tingle Factor, Radio 2. President: Nottingham Choral Trust; Market Harborough Singers; Derbys Singers; Bristol Bach Choir; Friends of Llangollen Internat. Music Eisteddfod. Vice-Pres., Assoc. of British Choral Dirs; Stars Orgn for Spastics; Vice-Chm., Young Persons Concert Foundn. *Recreations:* gardening, reading. *Address:* c/o BBC Radio 3, Broadcasting House, W1A 1AA.

KAY, Brian Wilfrid; Consultant, Culham College Institute, since 1989 (Senior Research Fellow, 1982–89); *b* 30 July 1921; *s* of Wilfrid and Jessie Kay; *m* 1st, 1947, Dorothea Sheppard Lawson (*d* 1993); two *d*; 2nd, 1994, Anthea Grace Barrett. *Educ:* King's Sch., Chester; University Coll., Oxford (exhibnr). Classics Master, Birkenhead Sch., 1947–59; Head of Classics, Liverpool Collegiate Sch., 1959–64; HM Inspector of Schs (Wales), 1964–71; Staff Inspector, Classics, Secondary Educn, 1971–74; Head of Assessment of Performance Unit, DES, 1974–77; Chief Inspector, Res. and Planning, DES, 1977–79; Chief Inspector, Teacher Trng and Res., DES, 1979–81, retired. Co-ordinator, Hulme Project, Dept Educnl Studies, Oxford Univ., 1982–87. *Recreations:* gardening, music, architecture. *Address:* Pond Cottage, Botolph Claydon, Buckingham MK18 2NG. *T:* Winslow (01296) 713477.

KAY, Prof. Harry, CBE 1981; PhD; Vice-Chancellor, University of Exeter, 1973–84 (Hon. Professor, 1984); *b* 22 March 1919; *s* of late Williamson T. Kay; *m* 1941, Gwendolen Diana, *d* of Charles Edward Maude; one *s* one *d*. *Educ:* Rotherham Grammar Sch.; Trinity Hall, Cambridge (1938–39, 1946–51). Served War of 1939–45 with Royal Artillery. Research with Nuffield Unit into Problems of Ageing, Cambridge, 1948–51; Psychologist of Naval Arctic Expedition, 1949. Lecturer in Experimental Psychology, Univ. of Oxford, 1951–59; Prof. of Psychology, Univ. of Sheffield, 1960–73. Visiting Scientist, National Institutes of Health, Washington, DC, 1957–58. Pro-Vice-Chancellor, University of Sheffield, 1967–71. Pres., British Psychological Soc., 1971–72. Hon. Director: MRC Unit, Dept of Psychology, Sheffield; Nat. Centre of Programmed Instruction for Industry, Sheffield. Member: SSRC, 1970–73; MRC, 1975–77 (Chm., Environmental Medicine Res. Policy Cttee, 1975–77); CNAA, 1974–79; Open Univ. Acad. Adv. Cttee; BBC Continuing Educn Adv. Cttee; Southern Univs Jt Bd (Chm., 1978–80); UCCA (Chm.,

1978–84); NATO Human Factors Panel, 1972–75; GMC, 1984–89. Chairman: Central Council for Educn and Trng in Social Work, 1980–84; Bd of Management, Northcott Theatre, 1973–84. Hon. DSc: Sheffield, 1981; Exeter, 1985. Vernon Prize, 1962. *Publication:* (with B. Dodd and M. Sime) Teaching Machines and Programmed Instruction, 1968. *Recreations:* listening, Sir Walter Raleigh. *Address:* Coastguard House, 18 Coastguard Road, Budleigh Salterton EX9 6NU.

KAY, Prof. Humphrey Edward Melville, MD, FRCP, FRCPath; Haematologist, Royal Marsden Hospital, 1956–84; Professor of Haematology, University of London, 1982–84 (Professor Emeritus, since 1984); *b* 10 Oct. 1923; *s* of late Rev. Arnold Innes and Winifred Julia Kay; *m* 1950, April Grace Lavinia Powlett (*d* 1990); one *s* two *d*. *Educ:* Bryanston Sch.; St Thomas's Hospital. MB, BS 1945. RAFVR, 1947–49; junior appts at St Thomas's Hosp., 1950–56. Sec., MRC Cttee on Leukaemia, 1968–84; Dean, Inst. of Cancer Research, 1970–72. Editor, Jl Clinical Pathology, 1972–80. Member: Council, Wiltshire Wildlife Trust (formerly Wiltshire Trust for Nature Conservation), 1983–; Nat. Badger Adv. Panel, 1988–. *Publications:* papers and chapters on blood diseases, etc; occasional poetry. *Recreation:* natural history including gardening. *Address:* New Mill Cottage, Pewsey, Wilts SN9 5LD.

KAY, John Menzies, MA, PhD; CEng, FIMechE, FIChemE; engineering consultant; Director, GSK Steel Developments Ltd, 1976–83; *b* 4 Sept. 1920; *s* of John Aiton Kay and Isabel Kay (*née* Menzies). *Educ:* Sherborne Sch.; Trinity Hall Cambridge. University Demonstrator in Chemical Engineering, Cambridge University, 1948; Chief Technical Engineer, Division of Atomic Energy Production, Risley, 1952; Prof. of Nuclear Power, Imperial Coll. of Science and Technology, University of London, 1956; Dir of Engineering Development, Tube Investments Ltd, 1961; Chief Engineer, Richard Thomas & Baldwins Ltd, 1965; Dir-in-charge, Planning Div., BSC, 1968–70; Dir of Engrng, Strip Mills Div., BSC, 1970–76. Mem., Nuclear Safety Adv. Cttee, 1960–76; Chm., Radioactive Waste Study Gp, 1974–81; Mem., Adv. Cttee on Safety of Nuclear Installations, 1980–83. *Publications:* Introduction to Fluid Mechanics and Heat Transfer, 1957, 3rd edn 1974; Fluid Mechanics and Transfer Processes, 1985; contribs to Proc. of Institution of Mechanical Engineers. *Recreations:* hill-walking, tree planting, music. *Address:* Church Farm, St Briavels, near Lydney, Glos GL15 6QE. *Clubs:* Alpine, United Oxford & Cambridge University.

KAY, Hon. Sir John (William), Kt 1992; **Hon. Mr Justice Kay;** a Judge of the High Court of Justice, Queen's Bench Division, since 1992; *b* 13 Sept. 1943; *y s* of late C. Herbert Kay and Ida Kay; *m* 1966, Jeffa Connell; one *s* two *d*. *Educ:* Denstone; Christ's Coll., Cambridge (MA). Called to Bar, Gray's Inn, 1968, Bencher, 1992. Tutor in Law, Liverpool Univ., 1968–69; in practice on Northern Circuit, 1968–92; a Recorder, 1982–92; QC 1984; Presiding Judge, Northern Circuit, 1994–. Mem., Gen. Council of Bar, 1988–92. *Recreations:* Rugby, genealogy, horse racing. *Address:* c/o Royal Courts of Justice, Strand, WC2A 2LL. *Club:* Waterloo Football.

KAY, Jolyon Christopher; HM Diplomatic Service, retired; consultant on Gulf affairs; *b* 19 Sept. 1930; *s* of Colin Mardall Kay and Gertrude Fanny Kay; *m* 1956, Shirley Mary Clarke; two *s* two *d*. *Educ:* Charterhouse; St John's Coll., Cambridge (BA). MEng 1993. Chemical Engr, Albright and Wilson, 1954; UKAEA, Harwell, 1958; Battelle Inst., Geneva, 1961; Foreign Office, London, 1964; MECAS, 1965; British Interests Section, Swiss Embassy, Algiers, 1967; Head of Chancery and Information Adviser, Political Residency, Bahrain, 1968; FCO, 1970; Economic Counsellor, Jedda, 1974–77; Consul-Gen., Casablanca, 1977–80; Science, later Commercial, Counsellor, Paris, 1980–84; Counsellor and Consul-Gen., Dubai, 1985–90. Convenor, Transport Campaign Gp, Oxfordshire CPRE. *Recreations:* acting, skiing, croquet. *Address:* 3 Manor Cottages, Blewbury, Oxfordshire OX11 9QG. *T:* Blewbury (01235) 850010, *Fax:* (01235) 851770.

KAY, Hon. Sir Maurice (Ralph), Kt 1995; **Hon. Mr Maurice Justice Kay;** a Judge of the High Court of Justice, Queen's Bench Division, since 1995; *b* 6 Dec. 1942; *s* of Ralph and Hylda Kay; *m* 1968, Margaret Angela Alcock; four *s*. *Educ:* William Hulme's Grammar Sch., Manchester; Sheffield Univ. (LLB, PhD). Called to the Bar, Gray's Inn, 1975; Bencher, 1995. Lecturer in Law: Hull Univ., 1967–72; Manchester Univ., 1972–73; Prof. of Law, Keele Univ., 1973–82. Practising barrister, 1975–95; an Asst Recorder, 1987–88; a Recorder, 1988–95; QC 1988. *Publications:* (author, contributor) numerous legal books and jls. *Recreations:* music, theatre, sport. *Address:* Royal Courts of Justice, Strand, WC2A 2LL. *Club:* Reform.

KAY, Neil Vincent; Director of Social Services, Sheffield, 1979–90 (Deputy Director, 1971–79); *b* 24 May 1936; *s* of Charles Vincent Kay and Emma Kay; *m* 1961, Maureen (*née* Flemons); one *s* two *d*. *Educ:* Woodhouse Grammar Sch.; Downing Coll., Cambridge (MA); Birmingham Univ. (Prof. Social Work Qual.). Social Worker (Child Care), Oxford CC, and Sheffield CC, 1960–66; Lectr and Tutor in Social Work, Extramural Dept, Sheffield Univ., 1966–71. *Address:* 22 Westwood Road, Sheffield S11 7EY. *T:* Sheffield (0114) 230 1934.

KAY, Maj.-Gen. Patrick Richard, CB 1972; MBE 1945; RM retired; *b* 1 Aug. 1921; *y s* of late Dr and Mrs A. R. Kay, Blakeney, Norfolk; *m* 1944, Muriel Austen Smith; three *s* one *d*. *Educ:* Eastbourne Coll. Commissioned in Royal Marines, 1940; HMS Renown, 1941–43; 4 Commando Bde, 1944–45; Combined Ops HQ, 1945–48; Staff of Commandant-Gen., Royal Marines, 1948–50 and 1952–54; Staff Coll., Camberley, 1951; 40 Commando, RM, 1954–57; Joint Services Amphibious Warfare Centre, 1957–59; Plans Div., Naval Staff, 1959–62; CO, 43 Commando, RM, 1963–65; CO, Amphibious Training Unit, RM, 1965–66; Asst Dir (Jt Warfare) Naval Staff, 1966–67; Asst Chief of Staff to Comdt-Gen. RM, 1968; IDC, 1969; C of S to Comdt-Gen., RM, 1970–74, retired 1974. Dir of Naval Security, 1974–81. Sec., Defence, Press and Broadcasting Cttee, 1984–86. *Recreations:* gardening, golf. *Address:* c/o Barclays Bank, Fleet, Hants GU13 8BS.

KAY-SHUTTLEWORTH, family name of **Baron Shuttleworth.**

KAYE, Rev. Dr Bruce Norman; General Secretary, The Anglican Church of Australia General Synod, since 1994; *b* 30 June 1939; *s* of John Harold Kaye and Elsie Evelyn Kaye; *m* 1st, 1965, Rosemary Jeanette Hutchison (*d* 1979); one *s* one *d*; 2nd, 1983, Margaret Louise Mathieson. *Educ:* Sydney Boys' High Sch.; Moore Theol Coll. (ThL 1963); Univ. of London (BD 1964); Univ. of Sydney (BA 1966); Univ. of Basel (Dr Theol 1976). Professional Officer, Sydney Water Bd, NSW, 1955–60. Deacon 1964, priest 1965; Curate, St Jude's, Dural, NSW, 1964–66; St John's College, University of Durham: Asst Tutor, 1968; Tutor, 1969; Tutor-Librarian, 1970–75; Sen. Tutor, 1975–82; Vice-Principal, 1979–82; Lectr, Faculty of Divinity, Univ. of Durham, 1970–82; Master, New Coll., Univ. of NSW, 1983–94; Dir, New Coll. Inst. for Values Research, 1987–92. Vis. Fellow, Deutsche Akademische Austauschdienst, Freiberg, 1974; Vis. Fellow, Sch. of Sci. and Technol. Studies, Univ. of NSW, 1984–94; Fellow Commoner, Churchill Coll., and Vis. Schol., Faculty of Divinity, Univ. of Cambridge, 1991–92. *Publications:* Using the Bible in Ethics, 1976; The Supernatural in the New Testament, 1977; (ed) Obeying Christ in a Changing World, 1977; (ed) Law, Morality and the Bible, 1978; The Argument of Romans with Special Reference to Chapter 6, 1979; (ed) Immigration: what kind of Australia do we want?, 1989; A Church Without Walls: being Anglican in Australia, 1995; contrib. numerous articles to theological and other learned jls. *Recreations:* ballet, golf, walking, reading. *Address:* The Anglican Church of Australia, General Synod Office, PO Box Q190, Queen Victoria Building, Sydney, NSW 2000, Australia. *Club:* Australian (Sydney).

KAYE, Sir David Alexander Gordon, 4th Bt *cr* 1923, of Huddersfield; *b* 26 July 1919; *s* of Sir Henry Gordon Kaye, 2nd Bt and Winifred (*d* 1971), *d* of Walter H. Scales, Verwood, Bradford; *S* brother, 1983; *m* 1st, 1942, Elizabeth (marr. diss. 1950), *o d* of Captain Malcolm Hurtley; 2nd, 1955, Adelle, *d* of Denis Thomas, Brisbane, Queensland; two *s* four *d*. *Educ:* Stowe; Cambridge Univ. (BA). MRCS Eng., LRCP London 1943. *Heir: s* Paul Henry Gordon Kaye [*b* 19 Feb. 1958; *m* 1984, Sally Ann Louise].

KAYE, Col Douglas Robert Beaumont, DSO 1942 (Bar 1945); DL; JP; *b* 18 Nov. 1909; *s* of late Robert Walter Kaye, JP, Great Glenn Manor, Leics; *m* 1946, Florence Audrey Emma, *d* of late Henry Archibald Bellville, Tedstone Court, Bromyard, Herefordshire; one *s* one *d*. *Educ:* Harrow. 2nd Lieut Leicestershire Yeo., 1928; 2nd Lieut 10th Royal Hussars, 1931. Served War of 1939–45: Jerusalem, 1939–41; Cairo and HQ 30 Corps, 1941–42; Lieut-Col comdg 10th Royal Hussars, Africa and Italy, 1943–46 (despatches twice; wounded). Bde Major, 30 Lowland Armd Bde (TA), 1947–49; Lieut-Col comdg 16th/5th Queen's Royal Lancers, 1949–51; AA & QMG 56 London Armd Div. (TA), 1952–54; Col Comdt and Chief Instructor, Gunnery Sch., RAC Centre, 1954–56; retd 1956. Master of Newmarket and Thurlow Foxhounds, 1957–59. DL 1963, JP 1961, High Sheriff 1971, Cambridgeshire and Isle of Ely. Mem., Newmarket RDC, 1958–74 (Chm., 1972–74), E Cambridgeshire DC, 1974–84. *Recreations:* hunting, shooting. *Address:* Brinkley Hall, near Newmarket, Suffolk CB8 0SB. *T:* Stetchworth (01638) 507202. *Club:* Cavalry and Guards.

KAYE, Dr Elaine Hilda; Headmistress, Oxford High School, GPDST, 1972–81; *b* 21 Jan. 1930; *d* of late Rev. Harold Sutcliffe Kaye and Kathleen Mary (*née* White). *Educ:* Bradford Girls' Grammar Sch.; Milton Mount Coll.; St Anne's Coll., Oxford. Assistant Mistress: Leyton County High Sch., 1952–54; Queen's Coll., Harley Street, 1954–59; South Hampstead High Sch., GPDST, 1959–65; Part-time Tutor, Westminster Tutors, 1965–67; Dep. Warden, Missenden Abbey Adult Coll., 1967–72. Project Dir, Oxford Project for Peace Studies, 1989–92 (Vice-Chair and Editor, 1984–89); College Historian, Mansfield Coll., Oxford, 1990–. *Publications:* History of the King's Weigh House Church, 1968; History of Queen's College, Harley St, 1972; Short History of Missenden Abbey, 1973, 2nd edn 1992; (contrib.) Biographical Dictionary of Modern Peace Leaders, 1985; (ed) Peace Studies: the hard questions, 1987; C. J. Cadoux: theologian, scholar and pacifist, 1988; (with Ross Mackenzie) W. E. Orchard: a study in Christian exploration, 1990. *Recreations:* music, walking, conversation. *Address:* 31 Rowland Close, Wolvercote, Oxford OX2 8PW.

KAYE, Sir Emmanuel, Kt 1974; CBE 1967; Founder and Chairman: The Kaye Organisation Ltd, 1966–89; Kaye Enterprises Ltd, since 1989; Thrombosis Research Institute, since 1990; *b* 29 Nov. 1914; *m* 1946, Elizabeth Cutler; one *s* two *d*. *Educ:* Richmond Hill Sch.; Twickenham Technical Coll. Founded jtly with J. R. Sharp (*d* 1965), J. E. Shay Ltd, Precision Gauge, Tool and Instrument Makers, and took over Lansing Bagnall & Co. of Isleworth, 1943; then founded Lansing Bagnall Ltd, 1943–89; transf. to Basingstoke, 1949 (from being smallest manufr of electric lift trucks, became largest in Europe). Royal Warrant as supplier of Industrial Trucks to Royal Household, 1971; Queen's Awards for Export Achievement in 1969, 1970, 1971, 1979, 1980 and only co. to win Queen's Awards for both Export Achievement and Technological Innovation, 1972; Design Council Awards, 1974, 1980; winners of Gold and other Continental Awards. Chairmanships include: Elvetham Hall Ltd, 1965–; Lansing GmbH, Germany, 1966–91; Pool & Sons (Hartley Wintney) Ltd, 1967–90; Kaye Steel Stockholders, 1978–95; Kaye Office Supplies Ltd, 1983–89; Hart Ventures, 1989–; Industrial Modernisation, 1991–; Pres., Lansing Linde Ltd, 1989–. Founded Unquoted Companies' Gp, 1968. Confederation of British Industry: Member: Taxation Cttee, 1970–77; Wealth Tax Panel, 1974–77; President's Cttee, 1976–85; Council, 1976–89; Econ. and Financial Policy Cttee, 1985–92. Member: Council of Industry for Management Educn, 1970–87; Export Credit Guarantees Adv. Council, 1971–74; Inflation Accounting Cttee, 1974–75; Queen's Award Review Cttee, 1975; Reviewing Cttee on Export of Works of Art, 1977–80. Visiting Fellow, Univ. of Lancaster, 1970–87. Governor: Girls' High Sch., Basingstoke, 1955–70; Queen Mary's Coll., Basingstoke, 1971–75. Trustee, Glyndebourne, 1977–84. Chairman: Thrombosis Research Trust, 1985– (Vice Chm., 1981–85); Vice President: Natural Medicines Soc., 1986–; Nat. Pure Water Assoc.; Patron, British Homœopathic Assoc. Fellow, Psionic Medical Soc., 1977–. Liveryman, Farriers' Co., 1953; Freeman, City of London, 1954. FIMgt (FBIM 1975); FRSA 1978. Hon. Mem., Emmanuel Coll., Cambridge, 1994. *Recreations:* chess, music, walking. *Club:* Brooks's.

KAYE, Geoffrey John; President, Allied Automotive Inc., since 1992; *b* 14 Aug. 1935; *s* of Michael and Golda Kaye; two *d*. *Educ:* Christ College, Finchley. Started with Pricerite Ltd when business was a small private company controlling six shops, 1951; apptd Manager (aged 18) of one of Pricerite Ltd stores, 1953; Supervisor, Pricerite Ltd, 1955; Controller of all stores in Pricerite Ltd Gp, 1958; Director, 1963; Chairman and Man. Dir, 1966–73. *Recreations:* tennis, golf. *Address:* 10175 East Bayview Drive, Scottsdale, AZ 85258, USA. *Club:* Desert Highlands (Arizona).

KAYE, Sir John Phillip Lister L.; *see* Lister-Kaye.

KAYE, Lindsey Joy, (Mrs D. N. Kaye); *see* Kushner, L. J.

KAYE, Mary Margaret, (Mrs G. J. Hamilton), FRSL; authoress and illustrator; *d* of late Sir Cecil Kaye, CSI, CIE, CBE, and Lady Kaye; *m* Maj.-Gen. G. J. Hamilton, CB, CBE, DSO (*d* 1985); two *d*. *Publications: historical novels:* Shadow of the Moon, 1957, rev. edn 1979; Trade Wind, 1963, revd edn 1981; The Far Pavilions, 1978 (televised 1984); *detective novels:* Six Bars at Seven, 1940; Death Walks in Kashmir, 1953 (republished as Death in Kashmir, 1984); Death Walks in Berlin, 1955; Death Walks in Cyprus, 1956 (republished as Death in Cyprus, 1984); Later Than You Think, 1958 (republished as Death in Kenya, 1983); House of Shade, 1959 (republished as Death in Zanzibar, 1983); Night on the Island, 1960 (republished as Death in the Andamans, 1985); Death in Berlin, 1985; *for children:* The Potter Pinner Books (series), 1937–41; The Ordinary Princess, 1980, US 1984 (shown on BBC TV Jackanory, 1983, 1984); Thistledown, 1981; *autobiography:* Vol. I, The Sun in the Morning, 1990; *edited:* The Golden Calm, 1980; Moon of Other Days, a personal choice of Kipling's verse, 1988; *illustrated:* The Story of St Francis; Children of Galilee; Adventures in a Caravan. *Recreation:* painting. *Club:* Army and Navy.

KAYE, Michael, OBE 1991; General Administrator, Young Concert Artists Trust, 1983–92; Festival Director, City of London Festival, 1984–94; *b* 27 Feb. 1925; *s* of Harry Kaye and Annie Steinberg; *m* 1st, 1950, Muriel Greenberg (marr. diss. 1959); one *d*; 2nd, 1962, Fay Bercovitch. *Educ:* Malmesbury Road, Bow; Cave Road, Plaistow; Water Lane, Stratford; West Ham Secondary Sch., E15. Served in Army, REME and Intelligence

Corps, 1943–47. Journalism and Public Relations, 1947–53; Marketing and Public Relations in tobacco industry, 1953–61; PR Manager, later PR Director, Carreras-Rothmans, 1961–76; Director, Peter Stuyvesant Foundation, 1963–76; General Administrator, Rupert Foundn, 1972–76; Man. Dir, London Symphony Orchestra, 1976–80; Arts Dir, GLC, and Gen. Administrator, S Bank Concert Halls, 1980–83. Chm., Educn Cttee, British Assoc. of Concert Agents, 1989–92; Member: Exec. Cttee, Carl Flesch Internat. Violin Competition, 1984–95; Council, Centre for Study of Judaism and Jewish/Christian Relations, 1989–94. Trustee: Whitechapel Art Gallery, 1964–75; Youth & Music, 1970–78; Bath Mozartfest, 1994–. *Recreations:* photography, music (clarinet). *Address:* 3 Coppice Way, E18 2DU. *T:* 0181–989 1281.

KAYE, Roger Godfrey, TD 1980 and Bar 1985; QC 1989; a Recorder, since 1994; *b* 21 Sept. 1946; *s* of late Anthony Harmsworth Kaye and Heidi Alice (*née* Jordy); *m* 1974, Melloney Rose, *d* of Rev. H. M. Westall. *Educ:* King's Sch., Canterbury; Birmingham Univ. (LLB 1968). Lectr in Law, Kingston Poly., 1968–73. Called to the Bar, Lincoln's Inn, 1970; Jun. Treasury Counsel in Insolvency Matters, 1978–89; Dep. High Court Registrar in Bankruptcy, 1985–; Dep. High Court Judge, Chancery Div., 1990–. Chairman: Fees Collection Cttee, Bar Council, 1991–93 (Dep. Chm., 1990–91); Bristol & Cardiff Chancery Bar Assoc., 1990–. Varied TA service in Europe, 1967–87. *Recreation:* going home. *Address:* 24 Old Buildings, Lincoln's Inn, WC2A 3UJ. *T:* 0171–404 0946. *Clubs:* Army and Navy, Royal Automobile, Special Forces.

KAYE, Rosalind Anne, (Mrs J. A. Kaye); *see* Plowright, R. A.

KAYLL, Wing Commander Joseph Robert, DSO 1940; OBE 1946; DFC 1940; DL; JP; *b* 12 April 1914; *s* of late J. P. Kayll, MBE, The Elms, Sunderland; *m* 1940, Annette Lindsay Nisbet; two *s*. *Educ:* Aysgarth; Stowe. Timber trader; joined 607 Sqdn AAF, 1934; mobilised Sept. 1939; Commanding Officer 615 Squadron, 1940; (prisoner) 1941; OC 607 Sqdn AAF 1946. DL Durham, 1956; JP Sunderland, 1962. Mem., Wear Boating Assoc. *Recreation:* yachting. *Address:* Hillside House, Hillside, Sunderland, Tyne and Wear SR3 1YN. *T:* 0191–528 3282. *Club:* Sunderland Yacht.

KAYSEN, Prof. Carl; David W. Skinner Professor of Political Economy, Massachusetts Institute of Technology, 1977–90, now Emeritus (Director, Program in Science, Technology, and Society, 1981–87); *b* 5 March 1920; *s* of Samuel and Elizabeth Kaysen; *m* 1st, 1940, Annette Neutra (*d* 1990); two *d*; 2nd, 1994, Ruth Butler. *Educ:* Philadelphia Public Schs; Overbrook High Sch., Philadelphia; Pennsylvania, Columbia and Harvard Univs. AB Pa 1940; MA 1947, PhD 1954, Harvard. Nat. Bureau of Economic Research, 1940–42; Office of Strategic Services, Washington, 1942–43; Intelligence Officer, US Army Air Force, 1943–45; State Dept, Washington, 1945. Dep. Special Asst to President, 1961–63. Harvard University, 1947–66: Teaching Fellow in Econs, 1947; Asst Prof. of Economics, 1950–55; Assoc. Prof. of Economics 1955–57; Prof. of Economics, 1957–66; Assoc. Dean, Graduate Sch. of Public Administration, 1960–66; Lucius N. Littauer Prof. of Political Economy, 1964–66; Jr Fellow, Soc. of Fellows, 1947–50, Actg Sen. Fellow, 1957–58, 1964–65; Syndic, Harvard Univ. Press, 1964–66; Dir, Inst. for Advanced Study, Princeton, NJ, 1966–76, Dir Emeritus, 1976; Vice Chm., and Dir of Research, Sloan Commn on Govt and Higher Educn, 1977–79. Sen. Fulbright Res. Schol., LSE, 1955–56. Trustee: Pennsylvania Univ., 1967–; Russell Sage Foundn, 1979–89. *Publications:* United States *v* United Shoe Machinery Corporation, an Economic Analysis of an Anti-Trust Case, 1956; The American Business Creed (with others), 1956; Anti-Trust Policy (with D. F. Turner), 1959; The Demand for Electricity in the United States (with F. M. Fisher), 1962; The Higher Learning, The Universities, and The Public, 1969; (contrib.) Nuclear Energy Issues and Choices, 1979; A Program for Renewed Partnership (Sloan Commn on Govt and Higher Educn Report), 1980; (ed jtly and contrib.) Emerging Norms of Justified Intervention, 1995; numerous articles on economic theory, applied economics, higher education, military strategy and arms control. *Address:* E38–603, Massachusetts Institute of Technology, Cambridge, MA 02139, USA.

KAZAN, Elia; author; independent producer and director of plays and films; *b* Constantinople, 7 Sept. 1909; *s* of George Kazan and Athena Sismanoglou; *m* 1st, 1932, Molly Thacher (*d* 1963); two *s* two *d*; 2nd, 1967, Barbara Loden (*d* 1980); one *s*; 3rd, 1982, Frances Rudge. *Educ:* Williams Coll. (AB); 2 years postgraduate work in Drama at Yale. Actor, Group Theatre, 1932–39; first London appearance as Eddie Fuseli in Golden Boy, St James, 1938. Directed *plays:* Skin of Our Teeth, 1942; All My Sons, A Streetcar Named Desire, 1947; Death of a Salesman, 1949; Camino Real, Tea and Sympathy, 1953; Cat on a Hot Tin Roof, 1955; Dark at Top of the Stairs, JB, 1958; Sweet Bird of Youth, 1959; After the Fall, 1964; But For Whom Charlie, 1964; The Changeling, 1964; Four times won best stage Director of Year, 1942, 1947, 1948, 1949. Directed *films:* Streetcar named Desire, 1951; Viva Zapata, 1952; Pinky, 1949; Gentleman's Agreement, 1948 (won Oscar, best Dir); Boomerang, 1947; A Tree Grows in Brooklyn, 1945; On the Waterfront, 1954 (won Oscar, best Dir); East of Eden, 1954; Baby Doll, 1956; A Face in the Crowd, 1957; Wild River, 1960; Splendour in the Grass, 1962; America, America, 1964; The Arrangement, 1969; The Visitors, 1972; The Last Tycoon, 1977. Three times won Best Picture of Year from New York Film Critics, 1948, 1952, 1955. *Publications:* America, America (novel), 1963; The Arrangement (novel), 1967; The Assassins, 1972; The Understudy, 1974; Acts of Love, 1978; The Anatolian, 1982; Elia Kazan, A Life (autobiog.), 1988; Beyond the Aegean, 1994; magazine articles in New York Times, Theatre Arts, etc. *Recreation:* tennis.

KEABLE-ELLIOTT, Dr (Robert) Anthony, OBE 1988; FRCGP; general practitioner, 1948–87; *b* 14 Nov. 1924; *s* of Robert Keable and Jolie Buck; *m* 1953, Gilian Mary Hutchison; four *s*. *Educ:* Sherborne Sch., Dorset; Guy's Hosp., London, 1943–48 (MB BS London). Founder Mem., Chiltern Medical Soc., 1956, Vice-Pres. 1958, Pres. 1964; Member, Faculty Board of Thames Valley, Faculty of Royal Coll. of General Practitioners, 1960; Upjohn Travelling Fellowship, 1962; Member: Bucks Local Med. Cttee, 1958–75 (Chm., 1964–68; Hon. Life Mem., 1975–); GMC, 1989–94. British Medical Association: Mem., 1948–; Mem. Council, 1974–94; Treasurer, 1981–87; Chm., Journal Cttee, 1987–93; Chm., Gen. Med. Services Cttee, 1966–72. Mem., Finance Corp. of General Practice, 1974–79. Mem., Soc. of Apothecaries, 1985–; Freeman, City of London, 1986. Asst Editor, Guy's Hospital Gazette, 1947–48. BMA Gold Medal, 1994. *Recreations:* sailing, golf, gardening. *Address:* Peels, Ibstone, near High Wycombe, Bucks HP14 3XX. *T:* Turville Heath (01491) 638385.

KEAL, Dr Edwin Ernest Frederick, FRCP; Honorary Consulting Physician, St Mary's and Brompton Hospitals, London; *b* 21 Aug. 1921; *s* of Frederick Archibald Keal and Mabel Orange Keal; *m* 1945, Constance Mary Gilliams; one *s*. *Educ:* Kingston High Sch., Hull; London Hospital Med. Coll. MB BS London 1952, DCH 1954, MD London 1971; FRCP 1973 (MRCP 1957). Service in RNVR (Exec. Lieut), 1939–46. Junior hosp. posts, London Hosp., 1952–59; Sen. Medical Registrar, Brompton Hosp., 1959–63; Consultant Physician: St Charles Hosp., London, 1963–77; Kensington Chest Clinic, 1963–86; Brompton Hosp., 1966–86; St Mary's Hosp., London, 1977–86; Cardiothoracic Institute: Sen. Lectr, 1972–77; Hon. Sen. Lectr, 1978–86; Dean, 1979–84. Hon. Consultant in Chest Diseases to the Army, 1979–86. Member: Bd of Governors, National Heart and Chest Hosps, 1975–85; Cttee of Management, Cardiothoracic Inst., 1978–84. *Publications:* chapters in various books, and articles, mainly related to diseases of the chest. *Recreations:* gardening, travel. *Address:* 55 Church Street, Orford, Woodbridge, Suffolk IP12 2NT. *T:* Woodbridge (01394) 450515.

KEALEY, Gavin Sean James; QC 1994; *b* 2 Sept. 1953; *m* 1981, Karen Elizabeth Nowak; three *d*. *Educ:* Charterhouse; University Coll., Oxford (BA Jurisp.). Lectr in Law, King's Coll. London, 1976–77; called to the Bar, Inner Temple, 1977; Commercial Barrister, 1978–. *Address:* 7 King's Bench Walk, Temple, EC4Y 7DS. *T:* 0171–583 0404.

KEALY, Robin Andrew, CMG 1991; HM Diplomatic Service; Head, Aviation and Maritime Department, Foreign and Commonwealth Office, since 1995; *b* 7 Oct. 1944; *s* of Lt-Col H. L. B. Kealy, Royal Signals and Mrs B. E. Kealy; *m* 1987, Annabel Jane Hood; two *s*. *Educ:* Harrow Sch.; Oriel Coll., Oxford (Open Scholar; BA Lit. Hum. (1st Cl. Hons Mods); MA). Joined HM Diplomatic Service, 1967; FO, 1967; MECAS, 1968; Tripoli, 1970; Kuwait, 1972; ME Dept, FCO, 1975; Port of Spain, 1978; Commercial Sec., Prague, 1982; Asst, Aid Policy Dept, FCO, 1985; Counsellor and Consul Gen., Baghdad, 1987–90; Dir of Trade Promotion and Investment, Paris, 1990–95. *Recreations:* music, theatre, ski-ing, cooking, gardening. *Address:* c/o Foreign and Commonwealth Office, King Charles Street, SW1A 2AH. *Club:* Travellers'.

KEAN, Arnold Wilfred Geoffrey, CBE 1977; FRAeS; Member, UN Administrative Tribunal, 1980–92 (Vice-President, 1982–88; President, 1988–89; Hon. President, since 1992); *b* 29 Sept. 1914; *s* of Martin Kean; *m* 1939, Sonja Irene, *d* of Josef Andersson, Copenhagen; two *d*. *Educ:* Blackpool Gram. Sch.; Queens' Coll., Cambridge (Schol.). 1st cl. 1st div. Law Tripos, Pts I and II; Pres., Cambridge Union, 1935; Wallenberg (Scandinavian) Prize; Commonwealth Fund Fellow, Harvard Law Sch., 1936–38; Yarborough-Anderson Schol., Inner Temple. Called to the Bar (studentship, certif. of honour, 1939). Wartime service on legal staff of British Purchasing Commn and UK Treas. Delegn in N America. HM Treasury Solicitor's Dept, 1945; Princ. Asst Solicitor, 1964–72; Sec. and Legal Adviser, CAA, 1972–79. Mem., Legal Cttee, ICAO, 1954–92 (Chm., 1978–83). Visiting Lecturer: Univ. of Auckland, NZ, 1980; Univ. of Sydney, NSW, 1982; UCL, 1983–88 (Hon. Fellow). Air Law Editor, Jl of Business Law, 1970–94. Edward Warner award, ICAO, 1993. King Christian X Liberation Medal (Denmark), 1945. *Publications:* (ed) Essays in Air Law, 1982; articles in legal periodicals. *Recreations:* music, stamps, gardening. *Address:* Tall Trees, South Hill Avenue, Harrow HA1 3NU. *T:* 0181–422 5791.

KEANE, Desmond St John; QC 1981; QC (Hong Kong) 1982; QC (NSW) 1986; a Recorder of the Crown Court, 1979–91; *b* 21 Aug. 1941; *er s* of late Henry Keane, MB, BCh, and of Patricia Keane; *m* 1968, Susan Mary Little (marr. diss. 1987); two *s* two *d*. *Educ:* Downside Sch.; Wadham Coll., Oxford (Schol.; MA Mod. Hist.); Harmsworth Law Schol., 1964. Called to the Bar, Middle Temple, 1964. Dep. Judge, High Court of Hong Kong, 1983 and 1986. Hon. Lectr, Faculty of Law, Univ. of Hong Kong, 1982–88. *Recreation:* cricket. *Address:* 2 Paper Buildings, Temple, EC4Y 7ET. *T:* 0171–936 2611. *Clubs:* United Oxford & Cambridge University; Kildare Street and University (Dublin); Hong Kong (Hong Kong).

KEANE, Francis Joseph; Sheriff of Lothian and Borders at Edinburgh, since 1993; *b* 5 Jan. 1936; *s* of Thomas and Helen Keane; *m* 1960, Lucia Corio Morrison; two *s* one *d*. *Educ:* Blairs Coll., Aberdeen; Gregorian Univ., Rome (PhL); Univ. of Edinburgh (LLB). Solicitor; Partner, McCluskey, Keane & Co., 1959; Depute Procurator Fiscal, Perth, 1961, Edinburgh, 1963; Senior Depute PF, Edinburgh, 1971; Senior Legal Asst, Crown Office, Edinburgh, 1972; PF, Airdrie, 1976; Regional PF, S Strathclyde, Dumfries and Galloway, 1980; Sheriff of Glasgow and Strathkelvin, 1984–93. Pres., PF Soc., 1982–84. *Recreations:* music, painting, tennis. *Address:* Sheriff Court House, 27 Chambers Street, Edinburgh EH1 1LB.

KEANE, Mary Nesta, (Molly), (Mrs Robert Keane); (*nom de plume:* **M. J. Farrell**); *b* 20 July 1904; *d* of Walter Clarmont Skrine and Agnes Shakespeare Higginson; *m* 1938, Robert Lumley Keane; two *d*. *Educ:* privately. Author of plays: (with John Perry) Spring Meeting (play perf. Ambassadors Theatre and New York, 1938); Ducks and Drakes (play perf. Apollo Theatre, 1941); Guardian Angel (play perf. Gate Theatre, Dublin, 1944); Treasure Hunt (play perf. Apollo Theatre, 1949); Dazzling Prospects. *Publications: as M. J. Farrell:* The Knight of Cheerful Countenance; This Angel Knight, Young Entry; Taking Chances; Mad Puppettstown; Conversation Piece; Devoted Ladies, 1934; Full House, 1935; The Rising Tide, 1937; Two Days in Aragon, 1941; Loving Without Tears, 1951; Treasure Hunt, 1952; *as Molly Keane:* Good Behaviour, 1981 (televised 1983); Time After Time, 1983 (televised 1986); Nursery Cooking, 1985; Loving and Giving, 1988. *Address:* Dysert, Ardmore, Co. Waterford, Ireland. *TA:* Ardmore. *T:* Youghal (24) 4225. *Clubs:* Lansdowne, Groucho.

KEANE, Major Sir Richard (Michael), 6th Bt *cr* 1801; farmer; *b* 29 Jan. 1909; *s* of Sir John Keane, 5th Bart, DSO, and Lady Eleanor Hicks-Beach (*d* 1960), *e d* of 1st Earl St Aldwyn; *S* father, 1956; *m* 1939, Olivia Dorothy Hawkshaw; two *s* one *d*. *Educ:* Sherborne Sch.; Christ Church, Oxford. Diplomatic Correspondent to Reuters 1935–37; Diplomatic Corresp. and Asst to Editor, Sunday Times, 1937–39. Served with County of London Yeomanry and 10th Royal Hussars, 1939–44; Liaison Officer (Major) with HQ Vojvodina, Yugoslav Partisans, 1944; attached British Military Mission, Belgrade, 1944–45. Publicity Consultant to Imperial Chemical Industries Ltd, 1950–62. *Publications:* Germany: What Next?, (Penguin Special), 1939; Modern Marvels of Science (editor), 1961. *Recreation:* fishing. *Heir:* *s* John Charles Keane [*b* 16 Sept. 1941; *m* 1977, Corinne, *d* of Jean Everard de Harzir; two *s* one *d*]. *Address:* Cappoquin House, Cappoquin, County Waterford, Ireland. *T:* (58) 54004. *Club:* Kildare Street and University (Dublin).

KEAR, Graham Francis; Under-Secretary, Department of Energy, 1974–80; *b* 9 Oct. 1928; *s* of Richard Walter Kear and Eva Davies; *m* 1978, Joyce Eileen Parks. *Educ:* Newport (St Julian's) High Sch., Mon; Balliol Coll., Oxford (BA). Min. of Supply, 1951–52 and 1954–57; UK Delegn to ECSC, 1953–54; Min. of Aviation, 1957–59 and 1960–63; NATO Maintenance Supply Agency, Paris, 1959–60; MoD, 1963–65; Cabinet Office, 1968–71; Min. of Aviation Supply/DTI, 1971–72; Fellow, Harvard Univ. Center for Internat. Affairs, 1972–73. Asst Sec., 1984–92, volunteer mem., 1992–, Abbeyfield Richmond Soc. *Recreation:* music. *Address:* 28 Eastbourne Road, Brentford, Mddx TW8 9PE. *T:* 0181–560 4746.

KEAR, Dr Janet, (Mrs J. V. N. Turner), OBE 1993; ornithologist; Director of Centres, Wildfowl and Wetlands Trust, 1991–93, retired; *b* 13 Jan. 1933; *d* of Harold Kear and Constance May Kear (*née* Betteridge); *m* 1st, 1963, Geoffrey Vernon Matthews, *qv* (marr. diss. 1977); 2nd, 1993, John V. N. Turner. *Educ:* Walthamstow Hall, Sevenoaks; Caspar Jun. Coll., Caspar, Wyoming; King's Coll., London (BSc 1956); Girton Coll., Cambridge (PhD 1959). Wildfowl and Wetlands Trust: Research Scientist, 1959–74; PSO 1974; Avicultural Co-ordinator, 1974–77; Curator, Martin Mere Centre, 1977–90; Asst Dir, 1978–90; Mem., Mgt Cttee, 1988–93. Fellow, Zool Dept, Liverpool Univ., 1978–92. Wildlife Inspector, Scientific Authy for Animals, DoE, 1977–81. Council Mem., NCC, later NCCE, 1990– (Mem., Animal Cttee, 1981–). Mem. Council, 1965–76, Sec., 1966–73, Assoc, for Study of Animal Behaviour; Zoological Society of London International Zoo Yearbook: Mem., Editl Bd, 1974–79 and 1989–; Chm., 1980–88; Mem. 1974, Chm. 1975–83, Breeding and Conservation Sub-cttee, Zoo Fedn; Member: Avicl Soc. Council, 1975–77; British Trust for Ornithology Council, 1983–86; Res. Adv. Cttee, 1977–83, Council 1994–, RSPB; International Union for Conservation of Nature: Chm., Endangered Waterfowl Gp, 1976–87; Mem., Captive Breeding Specialist Gp, 1979–92; Jersey Wildlife Preservation Trust: Mem., Scientific Adv. Cttee, 1979–; Dir, Summer Sch., 1993; Council Mem., 1994–; British Ornithologists' Union: Mem. Council, 1980–88; Vice-Pres., 1989–91; Pres., 1991–95; Mem., Internat. Ornithol Cttee, 1982–; Pres., Devon Bird Watching and Preservation Soc., 1995. Editor: Ibis, BOU Jl, 1980–88; Wildfowl, Jl of Wildfowl and Wetlands Trust, 1989–. Hon. Fellow, Manchester Metropolitan Univ. (formerly Manchester Poly.), 1983; Hon. Prof., Liverpool John Moores Univ. (formerly Liverpool Poly.), 1990–. Hon. DSc Liverpool Poly., 1990. *Publications:* (ed with N. Duplaix-Hall) Flamingos, 1975; (with A. J. Berger) The Hawaiian Goose, 1980; Eric Hosking's Wildfowl, 1985; The Mute Swan, 1989; Man and Wildfowl (Natural World's Book of the Year), 1990; Swans, 1990; Ducks of the World, 1991. *Recreations:* reading, gardening, walking. *Address:* Jewells Lodge Cottage, Umberleigh, Devon EX37 9EY. *T:* South Molton (01769) 580057. *Club:* Naval and Military.

KEARLEY, family name of **Viscount Devonport.**

KEARNEY, Brian; Sheriff of Glasgow and Strathkelvin, since 1977; *b* 25 Aug. 1935; *s* of late James Samuel and Agnes Olive Kearney; *m* 1965, Elizabeth Mary Chambers; three *s* one *d. Educ:* Largs Higher Grade; Greenock Academy; Glasgow Univ. (MA, LLB). Qualified solicitor, 1960; Partner, Biggart, Lumsden & Co., Solicitors, Glasgow, 1965–74. Sheriff of N Strathclyde at Dumbarton (floating sheriff), 1974–77. Sometime tutor in Jurisprudence, and external examnr in legal subjects, Glasgow Univ.; Hon. Lectr, Social Work Dept, Dundee Univ., 1995–. Chm., Inquiry into Child Care Policies in Fife, 1989–92 (report published, 1992). Pres., Glasgow Juridical Soc., 1964–65; Chm., Glasgow Marriage Guidance Council, 1977–90; Hon. Pres., Glasgow Marriage Counselling Service, 1990–. *Publications:* An Introduction to Ordinary Civil Procedure in the Sheriff Court, 1982; Children's Hearings and the Sheriff Court, 1987; articles in legal jls. *Recreations:* cutting sandwiches for family picnics, listening to music, reading, writing and resting. *Address:* Sheriff's Chambers, Sheriff Court House, 1 Carlton Place, Glasgow G5 9DA.

KEARNEY, Hon. Sir William (John Francis), Kt 1982; CBE 1976; Judge of the Supreme Court of the Northern Territory, since 1982; *b* 8 Jan. 1935; *s* of William John Kilbeg Kearney and Gertrude Ivylene Kearney; *m* 1959, Jessie Alice Elizabeth Yung; three *d. Educ:* Univ. of Sydney (BA, LLB); University Coll. London (LLM). Legal Service of Papua New Guinea, 1963–75; Sec. for Law, 1972–75; dormant Commn as Administrator, 1972–73, and as High Comr, 1973–75; Judge, Supreme Ct of PNG, 1976–80; Dep. Chief Justice, 1980–82. Aboriginal Land Comr, 1982–89. *Recreations:* travelling, literature. *Address:* Judges' Chambers, Supreme Court, Darwin, NT 0800, Australia.

KEARNS, David Todd; Chairman since 1985, and Chief Executive since 1982, Xerox Corp.; *b* 11 Aug. 1930; *m* 1954, Shirley Cox; two *s* four *d. Educ:* Univ. of Rochester (BA). Served US Navy; IBM, 1954–71; Xerox Corp.: Corporate Vice Pres., 1971; Group Vice Pres. and Board of Dirs, 1976; Pres. and Chief Operating Officer, 1977. Mem. Boards of Directors: Chase Manhattan Corp.; Time Inc.; Dayton Hudson Corp; Ryder System. Member: Council on Foreign Relations; Business Roundtable; Business Council; President's Commn on Executive Exchange. Trustee: Cttee for Economic Develt; Nat. Urban League. Member: Bd of Dirs, Junior Achievement; Bd of Visitors, Fuqua Sch. of Business Administration, Duke Univ.; Mem. Exec. Adv. Commn, William E. Simon Sch. of Business, and Trustee, Univ. of Rochester. *Address:* Xerox Corporation, PO Box 1600, Stamford, CT 06904, USA. *T:* (203) 9683201.

KEARNS, Dr William Edward, FFPHM; consultant in health policy and public health, since 1993; *b* 10 July 1934, *s* of William Edward Kearns and Kathleen Wolfenden; *m* 1954, Beryl Cross; four *s* one *d* (and one *s* decd). *Educ:* Liverpool Coll.; Univ. of Liverpool (MB ChB); Univ. of London (MSc). MRCS, LRCP. Hosp. posts in cardiorespiratory physiology, gen. medicine and pathology, United Liverpool Hosps, 1958–70; NW Metropolitan Regional Hospital Board: Asst SMO, 1970–73; Regional Sci. Officer, 1973–74; Dist Community Physician, Kensington and Chelsea and Westminster AHA (Teaching), 1974–82; Hon. Sen. Lectr in Community Medicine, St Mary's Hosp. Med. Sch., 1975–86; Dist MO, Paddington and N Kensington HA, 1982–86; Regional MO and Dir of Health Care Policy, 1986–90, Dir of Public Health, 1990–92, CMO, 1990–93, NE Thames RHA. Reader, Neasden Parish Church (S Catherine); regular volunteer driver for Gateway Clubs in Brent. *Publications:* The Health Report, North East Thames Health Region, 1990, 1991; contribs to med. jls. *Recreation:* gardening for wild life conservation. *Address:* Five Midholm, Barn Hill, Wembley Park, Middx HA9 9LJ. *T:* 0181–908 1511, *Fax:* 0181–904 3884. *Club:* Royal Society of Medicine.

KEATING, Frank; Sports Columnist, The Guardian, since 1976; *b* 4 Oct. 1937; *s* of Bryan Keating and Monica Marsh; *m* 1987, Jane Sinclair; one *s* one *d. Educ:* Belmont Abbey; Douai. Local newspapers, Stroud, Hereford, Guildford, Bristol, Southern Rhodesia, Gloucester and Slough, 1956–63; Editor, Outside Broadcasts, Rediffusion Television, 1963–67; Editor, Features, and Head of Special Projs, Thames Television, 1968–72; columnist: The Guardian, 1972–; Punch, 1979–90; The Spectator, 1990–. Astroturf Sportswriter of the Year, 1978; 'What the Papers Say' Sportswriter of the Year, 1979; Sports Council Magazine Writer of the Year, 1987; Specialist Writer of Year, Magazine Publishers Awards, 1988; Sports Journalist of the Year, British Press Awards, 1988. *Television series:* Maestro, BBC, 1981–85. *Publications:* Caught by Keating, 1979; Bowled Over, 1980; Another Bloody Day in Paradise, 1981; Up and Under, 1983; Long Days, Late Nights, 1984; High, Wide and Handsome, 1986; Gents and Players, 1986; Passing Shots, 1988; Sportswriter's Eye, 1989; Half-Time Whistle, 1992; (with Graham Gooch) Gooch: My Autobiography, 1995; contrib. New Statesman, BBC. *Recreations:* bad gardening, worse weeding. *Address:* Church House, Marden, near Hereford HR1 3EN. *T:* Sutton St Nicholas (01432880) 213. *Club:* Chelsea Arts.

KEATING, Henry Reymond Fitzwalter; author; *b* 31 Oct. 1926; *s* of John Hervey Keating and Muriel Marguerita Keating (*née* Clews); *m* 1953, Sheila Mary Mitchell; three *s* one *d. Educ:* Merchant Taylors' Sch.; Trinity Coll., Dublin. Journalism, 1952–60; Crime Reviewer for The Times, 1967–83. Chairman: Crime Writers' Assoc., 1970–71; Society of Authors, 1983–84; Pres., Detection Club, 1985. FRSL 1990. *Publications:* Death and the Visiting Firemen, 1959; Zen there was Murder, 1960; A Rush on the Ultimate, 1961; The Dog it was that Died, 1962; Death of a Fat God, 1963; The Perfect Murder, 1964 (filmed 1988); Is Skin-Deep, Is Fatal, 1965; Inspector Ghote's Good Crusade, 1966; Inspector Ghote Caught in Meshes, 1967; Inspector Ghote Hunts the Peacock, 1968; Inspector Ghote Plays a Joker, 1969; Inspector Ghote Breaks an Egg, 1970; Inspector Ghote goes by Train, 1971; The Strong Man, 1971; (ed) Blood on My Mind, 1972; Inspector Ghote Trusts the Heart, 1972; The Underside, 1974; Bats Fly Up for Inspector Ghote, 1974; A Remarkable Case of Burglary, 1975; Filmi, Filmi, Inspector Ghote, 1976; Murder Must Appetize, 1976; (ed) Agatha Christie: First Lady of Crime, 1977; A Long Walk to Wimbledon, 1978; Inspector Ghote Draws a Line, 1979; Sherlock Holmes: the man and his world, 1979; The Murder of the Maharajah, 1980; Go West, Inspector Ghote, 1981; (ed) Whodunit, 1982; The Lucky Alphonse, 1982; The Sheriff of Bombay, 1984; Mrs Craggs, Crimes Cleaned Up, 1985; Under a Monsoon Cloud, 1986; Writing Crime Fiction, 1986; The Body in the Billiard Room, 1987; Crime and Mystery: the 100 best books, 1987; Dead on Time, 1988; Inspector Ghote, His Life and Crimes, 1989; (ed) Bedside Companion to Crime, 1989; The Iciest Sin, 1990; (ed) Crime Wave 1, 1991; Cheating Death, 1992; (ed) The Man Who, 1992; The Rich Detective, 1993; Doing Wrong, 1994; The Good Detective, 1995. *Recreation:* popping round to the post. *Address:* 35 Northumberland Place, W2 5AS. *T:* 0171–229 1100.

KEATING, Kay Rosamond Blundell; Metropolitan Stipendiary Magistrate, since 1987; *b* 3 Oct. 1943; *d* of Geoffrey Blundell Jones and Avis Blundell Jones; *m* 1st, 1965, Edmund Deighton (decd); one *d* decd; 2nd, 1978, Donald Norman Keating, QC (*d* 1995); one *s. Educ:* St Hugh's College, Oxford (BA Jurisp. 1965; MA 1968). Called to the Bar, Gray's Inn, 1966. *Recreations:* travel, walking, tennis, riding, opera. *Address:* Horseferry Road Magistrates' Court, 70 Horseferry Road, SW1P 2AX. *T:* 0181–761 8102.

KEATING, Dr Michael Stockton, AO 1990; Secretary, Department of the Prime Minister and Cabinet, Australia, since 1991; *b* 25 Jan. 1940; *s* of Russell James Keating and Alice (*née* Skinner); *m* 1962, Rosemary Gardner; four *s. Educ:* Geelong Coll.; Univ. of Melbourne (BCom Hons); ANU (PhD). Hd, Growth Studies and Resource Allocation Div., OECD, 1976–78; First Asst Sec., Econ. Div., Dept of Prime Minister and Cabinet, 1979–82; Dep. Sec., Dept of Finance, 1982–83; Secretary: Dept of Employment and Industrial Relns, 1983–86; Dept of Finance, 1986–91. *Publications:* The Australian Workforce 1910–1911 to 1960–61, 1973; (jtly) The Making of Australian Economic Policy: 1983–88, 1989. *Recreations:* tennis, sail-boarding, bushwalking, reading. *Address:* 5/11 Broinowski Place, Isaacs, ACT 2607, Australia. *T:* (6) 2715111; Department of the Prime Minister and Cabinet, 3–5 National Circuit, Barton, ACT 2600.

KEATING, Hon. Paul John; Prime Minister of Australia, since 1991; MP (Lab) for Blaxland, NSW, since 1969; *b* 18 Jan. 1944; *s* of Matthew and Minnie Keating; *m* 1975, Anita Johanna Maria Van Iersel; one *s* three *d. Educ:* De La Salle College, Bankstown, NSW. Research Officer, Federated Municipal and Shire Council Employees Union of Australia, 1967. Minister for Northern Australia, Oct.-Nov. 1975; Shadow Minister for Agriculture, Jan.-March 1976, for Minerals and Energy, 1976–80, for Resources and Energy, 1980–83; Shadow Treasurer, Jan.-March 1983; Federal Treas. of Australia, 1983–91; Dep. Prime Minister, 1990–91. Member: Cabinet Expenditure Review Cttee (Dep. Chm.), 1987–91; Parly Structural Adjustment Cttee, 1987; Parly Social and Family Policy Cttee, 1983. Chm., Australian Loan Council, 1983–91. *Address:* Office of the Prime Minister, Parliament House, Canberra, ACT 2600, Australia. *T:* (6) 2777700.

KEATINGE, Sir Edgar (Mayne), Kt 1960; CBE 1954; *b* Bombay, 3 Feb. 1905; *s* of late Gerald Francis Keatinge, CIE; *m* 1930, Katharine Lucile Burrell (*d* 1990); one *s* one *d. Educ:* Rugby Sch.; School of Agriculture, S Africa. Diploma in Agriculture, 1925. S African Dept of Agriculture, 1926–29. Served War of 1939–45 with RA. Resigned with rank of Lieut-Col. West African Frontier Force, 1941–43; Commandant Sch. of Artillery, West Africa, 1942–43; CC West Suffolk, 1933–45. Parliamentary Candidate, Isle of Ely, 1938–44; MP (C) Bury St Edmunds, 1944–45; JP Wilts 1946; Chm. Wessex Area Nat. Union of Conservative Assocs, 1950–53; Mem. Panel, Land Tribunal, SW Area. Director: St Madeleine Sugar Co., 1944–62; Caroni Ltd, 1962–66. Governor, Sherborne Sch., 1951–74. Mem. Council, Royal African Soc., 1970–80. *Recreations:* travel, shooting. *Address:* Rose Cottage, Teffont, Salisbury, Wilts SP3 5RG. *T:* Teffont (0172276) 224. *Clubs:* Carlton, Boodle's.

See also Prof. W. R. Keatinge.

KEATINGE, Prof. William Richard; MA; PhD; Professor of Physiology, Queen Mary and Westfield College, since 1990; *b* 18 May 1931; *s* of Sir Edgar Keatinge, *qv*; *m* 1955, M. E. Annette Hegarty; one *s* two *d. Educ:* Upper Canada Coll.; Rugby Sch.; Cambridge Univ.; St Thomas's Hospital. MB BChir; FRCP 1991. House Phys., St Thomas's Hospital, 1955–56; Surg.-Lt RN (Nat. Service), 1956–58; Jun. Research Fellow and Dir of Studies in Medicine, Pembroke Coll., Cambridge, 1958–60; Fellow, Cardiovascular Research Inst., San Francisco, 1960–61; MRC appt Radcliffe Infirmary, Oxford, 1961–68; Fellow of Pembroke Coll., Oxford, 1965–68; Reader in Physiology, 1968–71, Prof. of Physiol., 1971–90, London Hosp. Med. Coll. *Publications:* Survival in Cold Water, 1969; Local Mechanisms Controlling Blood Vessels, 1980; chapters in textbooks of physiology and medicine; papers in physiological and medical jls on temperature regulation and on control of blood vessels. *Recreations:* ski-ing, archaeology. *Address:* Queen Mary and Westfield College, Mile End Road, E1 4NS.

KEAY, Ronald William John, CBE 1977 (OBE 1966); DPhil; Executive Secretary, The Royal Society, 1977–85; *b* 20 May 1920; *s* of Harold John Keay and Marion Lucy (*née* Flick); *m* 1944, Joan Mary Walden; one *s* two *d. Educ:* King's College Sch., Wimbledon; St John's Coll., Oxford (BSc, MA, DPhil). Colonial Forest Service, Nigeria, 1942–62. Seconded to Royal Botanic Gardens, Kew, 1951–57; Dir, Federal Dept of Forest Research, Nigeria, 1960–62; Dep. Exec. Sec., The Royal Society, 1962–77. Leverhulme Emeritus Fellow, 1987–88; Vis. Prof., Univ. of Essex, 1991–93. Pres., Science Assoc. of Nigeria, 1961–62; Vice-President: Linnean Soc., 1965–67, 1971–73, 1974–76 (Treas., 1989–95); Nigerian Field Soc., 1987–; President: African Studies Assoc., 1971–72; Inst. of Biology, 1988–90. Chairman: Finance Cttee, Internat. Biological Programme, 1964–74; UK Br., Nigerian Field Soc., 1985–91; Treasurer, Scientific Cttee for Problems of the Environment, 1976–77; Scientific Advr, Earthwatch Europe, 1991–; Member: Lawes Agricl Trust Cttee, 1978–90; RHS Review Cttee, 1984–85 (Chm., RHS Liby Rev. Cttee, 1988–89); Council, Roehampton Inst. of Higher Educn, 1986–89; Council, British Initiative Against Avoidable Disablement (IMPACT Foundn), 1985–92. Church Warden, St Martin-in-the-Fields, 1981–87. Hon. FIBiol 1985; Hon. FRHS 1986. *Publications:* Flora of West Tropical Africa, Vol. 1, pt 1 1954, pt 2 1958; Nigerian Trees, part 1 1960, part 2 1964, rev. and shortened edn as Trees of Nigeria, 1989; papers on tropical African plant ecology and taxonomy, and science policy. *Recreations:* gardening, walking, natural history. *Address:* 38 Birch Grove, Cobham, Surrey KT11 2HR. *T:* Cobham (01932) 865677. *Club:* Athenæum.

KEE, Robert; author and broadcaster; *b* 5 Oct. 1919; *s* of late Robert and Dorothy Kee; *m* 1st, 1948, Janetta (marr. diss. 1950), *d* of Rev. G. H. Woolley, VC; one *d*; 2nd, 1960, Cynthia (marr. diss. 1989), *d* of Edward Judah; one *s* one *d* (and one *s* decd); 3rd, 1990, Catherine Mary, *yr d* of Humphrey Trevelyan. *Educ:* Stowe Sch.; Magdalen Coll., Oxford (Exhibr, MA). RAF, 1940–46. Atlantic Award for Literature, 1946. Picture Post, 1948–51; Picture Editor, WHO, 1953; Special Corresp., Observer, 1956–57; Literary Editor, Spectator, 1957; Special Corresp., Sunday Times, 1957–58; BBC TV (Panorama, etc), 1958–62; Television Reporters International, 1963–64; ITV (Rediffusion, Thames, London Week-End, ITN, Yorkshire), 1964–78, Presenter, First Report, ITN's first lunch-time news prog., 1972–74; BBC, 1978–82; Presenter: Panorama, BBC1, 1982; TV-am,

1983; Channel 4's Seven Days, 1984–88. *Television series:* Ireland: a television history (13 parts), 1980; *radio series:* A Century Remembered, 1991–94; Foreign Postings, 1995. Alistair Horne Research Fellow, St Antony's Coll., Oxford, 1972–73. BAFTA Richard Dimbleby Award, 1976. *Publications:* A Crowd Is Not Company, 1947, repr. 1982; The Impossible Shore, 1949; A Sign of the Times, 1955; Broadstrop In Season, 1959; Refugee World, 1961; The Green Flag, 1972; Ireland: a history, 1980, revd edn 1995; The World We Left Behind, 1984; The World We Fought For, 1985; Trial and Error, 1986; Munich: the eleventh hour, 1988; The Picture Post Album, 1989; The Laurel and the Ivy: Parnell and Irish nationalism, 1993; many translations from German. *Recreations:* swimming, listening to music.

See also William Kee.

KEE, His Honour William; a Circuit Judge, 1972–90; *b* 15 Oct. 1921; *yr s* of Robert and Dorothy Kee; *m* 1953, Helga Wessel Eckhoff; one *s* three *d*. *Educ:* Rottingdean Sch.; Stowe Sch. Served War, Army, 1941–46: attached 9th Gurkha Rifles, Dehra Dun, 1943; Staff Captain, Area HQ, 1945–46. Called to Bar, Inner Temple, 1948. Principal Judge for County Courts in Kent, 1985–90. Jt Chm., Independent Schools' Tribunal, 1971–72. *Publications:* (jt) Divorce Case Book, 1950; contributor to: titles in Atkin's Encyclopaedia of Court Forms; Halsbury's Laws of England. *Recreations:* listening to music, walking.

See also Robert Kee.

KEEBLE, Sir (Herbert Ben) Curtis, GCMG 1982 (KCMG 1978; CMG 1970); HM Diplomatic Service, retired; Ambassador at Moscow, 1978–82; *b* 18 Sept. 1922; *s* of Herbert Keeble and Gertrude Keeble, BEM; *m* 1947, Margaret Fraser; three *d*. *Educ:* Clacton County High Sch.; London University. Served HM Forces, 1942–47. Entered HM Foreign (subsequently Diplomatic) Service, 1947; served in Jakarta, 1947–49; Foreign Office, 1949–51; Berlin, 1951–54; Washington, 1954–58; Foreign Office, 1958–63; Counsellor and Head of European Economic Organisations Dept, 1963–65; Counsellor (Commercial), Berne, 1965–68; Minister, Canberra, 1968–71; Asst Under-Sec. of State, FCO, 1971–73; HM Ambassador, German Democratic Republic, 1974–76; Dep. Under Sec. of State (Chief Clerk), FCO, 1976–78. Special Adviser, H of C Foreign Affairs Cttee, 1985–86. A Governor, BBC, 1985–90. Chairman: Britain-Russia Centre (formerly GB-USSR Assoc.), 1985–95; Foundn for Accountancy and Financial Management, 1993–; Member Council: RIIA, 1985–90; SSEES, 1985–. *Publications:* (ed) The Soviet State, 1985; Britain and The Soviet Union, 1917–1989, 1990. *Recreations:* sailing, ski-ing. *Address:* Dormers, St Leonards Road, Thames Ditton, Surrey KT7 0RR. *T:* 0181–398 7778. *Club:* Travellers.

KEEBLE, Major Robert, DSO 1940; MC 1945; TD 1946; Director: Associated Portland Cement Manufacturers Ltd, 1970–74; Aberthaw & Bristol Channel Portland Cement Co. Ltd, 1970–74; engaged in cement manufacture; *b* 20 Feb. 1911; *s* of late Edwin Percy and Alice Elizabeth Keeble; unmarried. *Educ:* King Henry VIII's Sch., Coventry. Commanded Royal Engineer Field Company; Territorial Army Commission, passed Staff Coll., Camberley, 1939; served in War of 1939–45 (despatches twice, twice wounded, DSO, MC, 1939–45 Star, African Star, France-Germany Star and Defence Medal, TD). Mem., Inst. Quarrying. Governor, Hull Univ. Hon. Brother, Hull Trinity House. Freeman of City of London and Liveryman of Company of Fanmakers. *Recreation:* fishing. *Address:* 15 Fernhill Close, Kenilworth CV8 1AN. *T:* Kenilworth (01926) 55668. *Club:* Army and Navy.

KEEFFE, Barrie Colin; dramatist; *b* 31 Oct. 1945; *s* of Edward Thomas Keeffe and Constance Beatrice Keeffe (*née* Marsh); *m* 1st, 1969, Dee Sarah Truman (marr. diss. 1979); 2nd, 1981, Verity Eileen Proud (*née* Bargate) (*d* 1981); Guardian of her two *s*; 3rd, 1983, Julia Lindsay (marr. diss. 1993). *Educ:* East Ham Grammar School. Formerly actor with Nat. Youth Theatre; began writing career as journalist; Thames Television Award writer-in-residence, Shaw Theatre, 1977; Resident playwright, Royal Shakespeare Co., 1978; Associate Writer, Theatre Royal, Stratford East, 1986–91. Member: Board of Directors: Soho Theatre Co., 1978–; Theatre Royal, Stratford E, 1988–91. UN Ambassador, 1995. French Critics Prix Revelation, 1978; Giles Cooper Best Radio Plays, 1980; Mystery Writers of America Edgar Allan Poe Award, 1982. *Theatre plays:* Only a Game, 1973; A Sight of Glory, 1975; Scribes, 1975; Here Comes the Sun, 1976; Gimme Shelter, 1977; A Mad World My Masters, 1977, 1984; Barbarians, 1977; Frozen Assets, 1978; Sus, 1979; Bastard Angel, 1980; She's So Modern, 1980; Black Lear, 1980; Chorus Girls, 1981; Better Times, 1985; King of England, 1988; My Girl, 1989; Not Fade Away, 1990; Wild Justice, 1990; *television plays:* Substitute, 1972; Not Quite Cricket, 1977; Gotcha, 1977; Nipper, 1977; Champions, 1978; Hanging Around, 1978; Waterloo Sunset, 1979; King, 1984; *television series:* No Excuses, 1983; *film:* The Long Good Friday, 1981; also radio plays. *Publications: novels:* Gadabout, 1969; No Excuses, 1983; *plays:* Gimme Shelter, 1977; A Mad World My Masters, 1977; Barbarians, 1977; Here Comes the Sun, 1978; Frozen Assets, 1978; Sus, 1979; Bastard Angel, 1980; The Long Good Friday, 1984; Better Times, 1985; King of England, 1988; My Girl, 1989; Wild Justice, Not Fade Away, Gimme Shelter, 1990. *Recreation:* origami. *Address:* 110 Annandale Road, SE10 0JZ.

KEEGAN, John Desmond Patrick, OBE 1991; FRSL; FRHistS; military historian; Defence Editor, The Daily Telegraph, since 1986; *b* 15 May 1934; *e s* of Francis Joseph Keegan and Eileen Mary Keegan (*née* Bridgman); *m* 1960, Susanne Ingeborg Everett; two *s* two *d*. *Educ:* King's Coll., Taunton; Wimbledon Coll.; Balliol Coll., Oxford (BA 1957; MA 1962). Political Analyst, US Embassy, London, 1958–60; Sen. Lectr in Mil. Hist., RMA Sandhurst, 1960–86; corresp. from numerous countries, incl. Gulf, 1991. Vis. Fellow, Princeton, 1984; Lectures: Lees Knowles, Cambridge, 1986; Eisenhower Meml, Kansas State, 1986; Brown Meml, Brown Univ., 1989; Whidden Meml, McMaster, 1990; Frum Meml, Toronto, 1994. Visitor, Hugh Sexey's Hosp., 1986–; Dir, E Somerset NHS Trust, 1991–. Trustee: Nat. Heritage Meml Fund, 1994–; Heritage Lottery Fund, 1994–. Contributing Editor: The New Republic, 1980–90; US News and World Report, 1986–. *Publications:* The Face of Battle, 1976; World Armies, 1978; Six Armies in Normandy, 1982; The Mask of Command, 1987; The Price of Admiralty, 1988, reissued as Battle at Sea, 1993; The Second World War, 1989; (ed) The Times Atlas of the Second World War, 1989; (ed) Churchill's General's, 1991; A History of Warfare, 1993 (Duff Cooper Prize, 1994); Warpaths: travels of a military historian in North America, 1995; contribs to DNB, Encyclopaedia Britannica. *Address:* The Manor House, Kilmington, near Warminster, Wilts BA12 6RD. *T:* Warminster (01985) 844856. *Clubs:* Garrick, Beefsteak; Brook (NY).

KEEGAN, (Joseph) Kevin, OBE 1982; professional footballer, 1966–84; Manager of Newcastle United Football Club, since 1992; *b* 14 Feb. 1951; *s* of late Joseph Keegan; *m* 1974, Jean Woodhouse; two *d*. Professional footballer with: Scunthorpe Utd, 1966–71; Liverpool, 1971–77; Hamburg, 1977–80; Southampton, 1980–82; Newcastle Utd, 1982–84. Internat. appearances for England, 1973–82, Captain, 1976–82. Football expert, Thames TV. Winners' medals: League Championships, 1973, 1976; UEFA Cup, 1973, 1976; FA Cup, 1974; European Cup, 1977. European Footballer of the Year, 1978, 1979. *Publications:* Kevin Keegan, 1978; Against the World: playing for England, 1979. *Address:* Newcastle United Football Club, St James' Park, Newcastle upon Tyne NE1 4ST.

KEEGAN, William James Gregory; Economics Editor, since 1977, and Associate Editor, since 1983, The Observer; *b* 3 July 1938; *s* of William Patrick Keegan and Sheila Julia Keegan (*née* Buckley); *m* 1st, 1967, Tessa (*née* Young, *widow* of John Ashton) (marr. diss. 1982); two *s* two *d*; 2nd, 1992, Hilary, *d* of Maurice Stonefrost, *qv*; one *d*. *Educ:* Wimbledon Coll.; Trinity Coll., Cambridge (MA). National Service (Army), 1957–59 (commissioned). Journalist, Financial Times, Daily Mail and News Chronicle, 1963–67; Economics Correspondent, Financial Times, 1967–76; Economic Intell. Dept, Bank of England, 1976–77; Asst Editor and Business Editor, The Observer, 1981–83. Member: BBC Adv. Cttee on Business and Indust. Affairs, 1981–88; Council, Employment Inst., 1987–; Adv. Bd, Dept of Applied Economics, Cambridge, 1988–92; Cttee for Soc. Scis., CNAA, 1991–92. Vis. Prof. of Journalism, 1989–, Hon. Res. Fellow, 1990, Sheffield Univ. *Publications:* Consulting Father Wintergreen, 1974; A Real Killing, 1976; (jtly) Who Runs the Economy?, 1978; Mrs Thatcher's Economic Experiment, 1984; Britain Without Oil, 1985; Mr Lawson's Gamble, 1989; The Spectre of Capitalism, 1992; contribs to The Tablet. *Address:* 9 Compton Road, Islington, N1. *T:* 0171–359 6824; The Observer, 119 Farringdon Road, EC1R 3ER. *T:* 0171–278 2332. *Clubs:* Garrick, MCC.

KEELING, Maj.-Gen. Andrew Myles, CB 1994; CBE 1992 (OBE 1988); Director of Humanitarian Affairs, AMAR International Charitable Foundation, since 1995; *b* 4 July 1943; *s* of Richard George Maynard Keeling and Audrey Stuart Baxter (*née* Frederick); *m* 1965, Ann Margaret Grey Dudley; one *s* two *d*. *Educ:* Rugby School. Infantry Training Centre, Royal Marines; Commissioned 2nd Lieut RM, 1961; served 41, 42 and 45 Commandos, and training jobs at BRNC and RMA, 1963–75; student, Canadian Forces Command and Staff Coll., 1975–76; HQ 3 Cdo Bde RM, 1976–78; 41 Cdo, 1978–80; Bde Major, HQ 3 Cdo Bde, 1980–81; Directing Staff, NDC and JSDC, 1982–83; Jt Force HQ, 1984–85; CO 45 Cdo, 1985–87; MoD, 1987–89; Comd, 3 Cdo Bde, 1990–92; COS to Comdt-Gen. RM, 1992–93; Maj.-Gen., RM, 1992–94; retired RM, 1995. Naval Vice-Pres., CCF Assoc., 1995–; Mem. Council, St Dunstan's, 1995–. Freeman, City of London, 1993. *Recreations:* sailing, walking. *Clubs:* Special Forces; Royal Marines Sailing (Hon. Life-Commodore); Royal Marines Squash (President).

KEELING, Surgeon Rear-Adm. John, CBE 1978; retired; Director of Medical Policy and Plans, Ministry of Defence, 1980–83; Chairman, NATO Joint Civil/Military Medical Group, 1981–83; *b* 28 Oct. 1921; *s* of John and Grace Keeling; *m* 1948, Olwen Anne Dix; one *s* (and one *s* decd). *Educ:* Queen Elizabeth's Sch., Hartlebury; Birmingham Univ. MRCS, LRCP; MFOM. Entered RN as Surg. Lieut, 1946; served with Fleet Air Arm, 1947–75: Pres., Central Air Med. Bd, 1954–56 and 1960–63; SMO, HMS Albion, 1956–57, HMS Victorious, 1965–67, and several Royal Naval Air Stns; Staff MO to Flag Officer Sea Trng, 1970–73; Dir of Environmental Medicine and Dep. MO i/c Inst. of Naval Medicine, 1975–77; Dep. Med. Dir-Gen. (Naval), 1977–80. Surg. Captain 1970, Surg. Cdre 1977, Surg. Rear-Adm. 1980. QHP, 1977–83. Member: Fleet Air Arm Officers' Assoc., 1973–; Soc. of Occupational Medicine, 1976–. Membership Sec., Herefordshire Nature Trust, 1988–. *Recreations:* music, gardening, micro-computing, caravanning. *Address:* Merlin Cottage, Brockhampton, Hereford HR1 4TQ. *T:* How Caple (01989) 740649. *Club:* Army and Navy.

KEELING, Robert William Maynard; a Recorder of the Crown Court, 1980–89; *b* 16 Dec. 1917; *s* of Dr George Sydney Keeling, MD, and Florence Amy Keeling (*née* Maynard); *m* 1942, Kathleen Busill-Jones; one *s* two *d*. *Educ:* Uppingham; Corpus Christi Coll., Cambridge (BA 1939). Served War, RASC, 1939–46: Western Desert, Italy, Greece (despatches 1944), Berlin. FO, 1946–47. Solicitor 1950; Partner in Monier-Williams & Keeling, 1956–80; Solicitor to Vintners Company, 1953–79. Director, Sherry Producers Committee Ltd, 1967–80, Chairman 1980–. Diplôme de Grande Médaille d'Argent, Corporation des Vignerons de Champagne, 1988. Knight Comdr, Order of Civil Merit (Spain), 1967; Chevalier de la Légion d'Honneur (France), 1993. *Recreations:* travel, painting, music. *Address:* Vale Bank, Chadlington, Chipping Norton, Oxon OX7 3LZ.

KEEMER, Peter John Charles; Assistant Auditor General, National Audit Office, 1989–93; *b* 27 Jan. 1932; *s* of late Frederick and Queenie Keemer; *m* 1954, Yvonne Griffin; one *s* one *d* (and one *s* decd). *Educ:* Price's Sch., Fareham; Univ. of Bath (MPhil). Exchequer and Audit Department: Asst Auditor and Auditor, 1950–62; Private Sec. to Comptroller and Auditor Gen., 1962–65; seconded to Parly Comr for Administration as Chief Exec. Officer, 1966–70; Chief Auditor, 1970; Dep. Dir, 1973; Dir, 1978–89 (seconded to European Court of Auditors as Director, 1978–86). External Auditor, European Univ. Inst., Florence, 1994–; Member: CIPFA, 1982; Council, Inst. of Cancer Res., 1994–. *Address:* How Green Cottage, How Lane, Chipstead, Surrey CR5 3LL. *T:* Downland (01737) 553711. *Club:* Royal Anglo-Belgian.

KEEN, (David) Alan; MP (Lab) Feltham and Heston, since 1992; *b* 25 Nov. 1937; *m* 1980, Ann Lloyd; one *s* one *d*. *Educ:* Sir William Turner's Sch., Redcar. Various posts as systems analyst, accountant and manager, 1963–92. Mem. (Lab) Hounslow BC, 1986–90. *Address:* House of Commons, SW1A 0AA.

KEEN, Kenneth Roger; QC 1991; *b* 13 May 1946; *s* of Kenneth Henry Keen and Joan Megan Keen (*née* Weetman); *m* 1969, Hilary Jane Wood; one *s* one *d*. *Educ:* Doncaster Grammar School. Qualified Solicitor, 1968; called to the Bar, Gray's Inn, 1976; practice on NE circuit; a Recorder, 1989. *Recreations:* everything Italian, food, drink. *Address:* 12 Paradise Square, Sheffield S1 2DE. *T:* Sheffield (0114) 273 8951.

KEEN, Maurice Hugh, FSA; FBA 1990; Fellow of Balliol College, Oxford, since 1961; *b* 30 Oct. 1933; *e s* of Harold Hugh Keen and Catherine Eleanor Lyle Keen (*née* Cummins); *m* 1968, Mary Agnes Keegan; three *d*. *Educ:* Winchester College; Balliol College, Oxford (BA 1st Cl. Mod. Hist. 1957). FSA 1987. Nat. Service 1952–54, commissioned Royal Ulster Rifles. Junior Res. Fellow, The Queen's Coll., Oxford, 1957–61; Tutor in Medieval History, Balliol Coll., Oxford, 1961–. External examr, Nat. Univ. of Ireland, 1971–78. Fellow, Winchester Coll., 1989–. Alexander Prize, RHistS, 1962. *Publications:* The Outlaws of Medieval Legend, 1961; The Laws of War in the Later Middle Ages, 1965; A History of Medieval Europe, 1968; England in the Later Middle Ages, 1973; Chivalry, 1984 (Wolfson Lit. Award for History, 1985); English Society in the later Middle Ages, 1990. *Recreations:* fishing, shooting. *Address:* Balliol College, Oxford OX1 3BJ. *T:* Oxford (01865) 277735. *Club:* United Oxford & Cambridge University.

See also G. L. Norman.

KEEN, Prof. Peter Marley, PhD; Professor of Pre-Clinical Veterinary Studies, Department of Pharmacology, University of Bristol, 1988–95, now Professor Emeritus; *b* 14 May 1930; *s* of Ernest Keen and Kathleen (*née* Marley); *m* 1956, Pauline Helen Franklin; four *d*. *Educ:* Wellington Sch., Somerset; Univ. of Bristol (BVSc); PhD London Univ. 1964. MRCVS 1955. Nat. Service, RAF, 1948–50. Veterinary practice, 1955–59; Lectr in Vet. Pharmacol., RVC, London, 1959–64; University of Bristol: Lectr, then Reader, in Vet. Pharmacol., 1964–88; Head of Vet. Sch., 1988–93; Dean of Medicine, 1993–95. *Publications:* articles in learned jls. *Recreations:* oil painting, pub walks, local architecture. *Address:* Old Orchard, Winscombe Hill, Winscombe, Avon BS25 1DF. *T:* Weston-super-Mare (01934) 842026.

KEEN, Richard Sanderson; QC (Scot) 1993; *b* 29 March 1954; *s* of Derek Michael Keen and Jean Sanderson Keen; *m* 1978, Jane Carolyn Anderson; one *s* one *d*. *Educ:* King's Sch., Rochester; Dollar Acad.; Edinburgh Univ. (LLB Hons 1976). Bar Apprentice with Balfour & Manson, Edinburgh, 1976–78; pupil, 1979, admitted 1980, Faculty of Advocates; Standing Jun. Counsel in Scotland to DTI, 1986–93. *Recreations:* golf, ski-ing, shooting, opera. *Address:* 18 India Street, Edinburgh EH3 6EZ. *T:* 0131–225 8340; Advocates' Library, Parliament House, Edinburgh EH1 1RF. *T:* 0131–226 5071. *Clubs:* New (Edinburgh); Bruntsfield Links Golfing Society, Grange (Edinburgh).

KEENE, Hon. Sir David (Wolfe), Kt 1994; **Hon. Mr Justice Keene;** a Judge of the High Court of Justice, Queen's Bench Division, since 1994; *b* 15 April 1941; *s* of Edward Henry Wolfe Keene and Lilian Marjorie Keene; *m* 1965, Gillian Margaret Lawrance; one *s* one *d*. *Educ:* Hampton Grammar Sch.; Balliol Coll., Oxford (Winter Williams Prizewinner, 1962; BA 1st Cl. Hons Law, 1962; BCL 1963). Called to the Bar, Inner Temple, 1964, Bencher, 1987; Eldon Law Scholar, 1965; QC 1980; a Recorder, 1989–94; a Deputy High Court Judge, 1993–94. Chm. of Panel, Cumbria Structure Plan Examination in Public, 1980; conducted County Hall, London, Inquiry, 1987. Vice-Chm., Local Govt and Planning Bar Assoc., 1990–. *Recreations:* walking, opera, jazz. *Address:* Royal Courts of Justice, Strand, WC2A 2LL. *Club:* Athenæum.

KEENE, Dr Derek John; Director, Centre for Metropolitan History, Institute of Historical Research, since 1987; *b* 27 Dec. 1942; *s* of Charles Henry Keene and Edith Anne Keene (*née* Swanston); *m* 1969, Suzanne Victoria Forbes; one *s* one *d*. *Educ:* Ealing Grammar Sch.; Oriel Coll., Oxford (MA, DPhil). FRHistS. Researcher, 1968–74, Asst Dir, 1974–78, Winchester Research Unit; Dir, Social and Economic Study of Medieval London, Inst. of Historical Research, 1979–87. Member: RCHM, 1987–; Commn internat. pour l'histoire de villes, 1990–; Fabric Adv. Cttee, St Paul's Cathedral, 1991–. *Publications:* Winchester in the Early Middle Ages (jtly), 1976; Survey of Medieval Winchester, 1985; Cheapside Before the Great Fire, 1985; (with V. Harding) A survey of documentary sources for property holding in London before the Great Fire, 1985; (with V. Harding) Historical Gazetteer of London before the Great Fire, 1987; (ed with P. J. Corfield) Work in Towns 850–1850, 1990; contribs to learned jls and to collections of essays. *Recreations:* metropolises, walking uphill, making and repairing things. *Address:* 162 Erlanger Road, SE14 5TJ. *T:* 0171–639 5371.

KEENE, John Robert R.; *see* Ruck Keene.

KEEP, Charles Reuben; Chairman and Managing Director, Resource Management Associates Ltd, since 1992; Chairman and Chief Executive, Bellair Holdings Ltd (formerly Bellair Cosmetics plc), since 1984; *b* 1932; *m*; one *d*. *Educ:* HCS, Hampstead. Joined Lloyds & Scottish Finance Ltd, 1956, Director, 1969; Man. Dir, International Factors Ltd, 1970; Group Man. Dir, Tozer Kemsley & Millbourn (Holdings) Ltd, 1973–77; Chm., Tozer Kemsley & Millbourn Trading Ltd, 1978–80; Director: Tozer Standard & Chartered Ltd, 1973–77; Barclays Tozer Ltd, 1974–77; Manufacturers Hanover Credit Corp., 1977–80; Chm., Export Leasing Ltd, Bermuda 1974–77; Pres., France Motors sa Paris, 1974–81. *Address:* The Oaks, 20 Forest Lane, Chigwell, Essex IG7 5AE. *T:* 0181–504 3897. *Club:* Chigwell Golf.

KEIGHLEY, Prof. Michael Robert Burch, FRCS, FRCSE; Barling Professor of Surgery, University of Birmingham, since 1988; *b* 12 Oct. 1943; *s* of late Dr Robert Arthur Spink Keighley and of Dr Jacqueline Vivian Keighley; *m* Dr Dorothy Margaret; one *s* one *d*. *Educ:* Monkton Combe Sch.; St Bartholomew's Hosp., Univ. of London (MB BS 1967; MS 1976). FRCS 1970; FRCSE 1970. Prof. of Surgery, General and Dental Hosps, Univ. of Birmingham, 1984–88. Boerhaave Prof. of Surgery, Univ. of Leiden, 1985; Eyber's Vis. Prof., Univ. of OFS, 1987; Vis. Prof., Harvard Univ., 1990; Penman Vis. Prof., Univ. of Cape Town, 1992. Mem., Christian Med. Fellowship, 1967–. Hon. Fellow, Brazilian Coll. of Surgeons, 1991. Jacksonian Prize, RCS, 1979; Hunterian Prof., RCS, 1979. *Publications:* Antimicrobial Prophylaxis in Surgery, 1979; Inflammatory Bowel Diseases, 1981, 3rd edn 1995; Gastrointestinal Haemorrhage, 1983; Textbook of Gastroenterology, 1985, 2nd edn 1994; Surgery of the Anus, Rectum and Colon, 1994. *Recreations:* painting, music, sailing, climbing. *Address:* University of Birmingham, Department of Surgery, Queen Elizabeth Hospital, Edgbaston, Birmingham B15 2TH. *T:* 0121–627 2274, *Fax:* 0121–472 1230. *Club:* Royal Society of Medicine.

KEIGHLEY, Thomas Christopher; Regional Director of Nursing, Yorkshire Health, since 1990; Director, Institute of Nursing, University of Leeds, since 1993; *b* 4 May 1951; *s* of late John Charles Keighley and of Frances Louise Keighley (*née* Leary); *m* 1st, 1974, Anne Gibson (marr. diss. 1978); 2nd, 1979, Elizabeth Redfern (marr. diss. 1989); 3rd, 1990, Amanda Gunner; one step *s* one step *d*. *Educ:* St Michael's Coll., Kirkby Lonsdale; Preston Sch. of Nursing (SRN 1974; RMN 1976); Charles Frear Sch. of Nursing (NDN Cert. 1976); Huddersfield Polytechnic (RCNT 1979); Dip. Nursing, London Univ., 1981; BA Hons Open Univ. 1985. Aux. Nurse, Deepdale Hosp., Preston, 1970; Staff Nurse, Preston Royal Infirmary, 1974; Community Charge Nurse, NW Leics, 1976; Clinical Teacher: Maidstone, 1977; Cambridge HA, 1979; RCN Adviser, Research, 1982; Dist Dir of Nursing, 1986, of Nursing and Quality, 1988, Waltham Forest. Mem., EC Adv. Cttee on Training for Nursing, 1990–. Winifred Raphael Meml Lecture, RCN Res. Soc., 1988. *Publications:* articles on nursing and health care. *Recreations:* opera, art, walking, rug making. *Address:* Institute of Nursing, University of Leeds, 18 Blenheim Terrace, Leeds LS2 9HD. *T:* Leeds (0113) 242 2411.

KEIGHTLEY, Maj.-Gen. Richard Charles, CB 1987; Chairman, Dorset (formerly West Dorset) Health Authority, since 1988; *b* 2 July 1933; *s* of General Sir Charles Keightley, GCB, GBE, DSO, and Lady (Joan) Keightley (*née* Smyth-Osbourne); *m* 1958, Caroline Rosemary Butler, *er d* of Sir Thomas Butler, 12th Bt, CVO, DSO, OBE; three *d*. *Educ:* Marlborough Coll.; RMA, Sandhurst. Commissioned into 5th Royal Inniskilling Dragoon Guards, 1953; served Canal Zone, BAOR, N Africa, Singapore, Cyprus; sc Camberley, 1963; comd 5th Royal Inniskilling Dragoon Guards, 1972–75; Task Force Comdr, 3 Armd Div., 1978–79; RCDS 1980; Brigadier General Staff HQ UKLF, 1981; GOC Western Dist, 1982–83; Comdt, RMA Sandhurst, 1983–87. Col, 5th Royal Inniskilling Dragoon Guards, 1986–91. Defence Consultant, Portescap (UK), 1987–92. Pres., Dorset Br., Royal British Legion, 1990–. Chm., Combined Services Polo Assoc., 1982–86. *Recreations:* field sports, cricket, farming. *Address:* Kennels Cottage, Tarrant Gunville, Blandford, Dorset DT11 8JQ.

KEIR, James Dewar; QC 1980; Director, Open University Educational Enterprises Ltd, 1983–88; Chairman, City and East London Family Practitioner Committee, 1985–89; part-time Member, Monopolies and Mergers Commission, 1987–92; *b* 30 Nov. 1921; *s* of David Robert Keir and Elizabeth Lunan (*née* Ross); *m* 1948, Jean Mary, *e d* of Rev. and Mrs E. P. Orr; two *s* two *d*. *Educ:* Edinburgh Acad.; Christ Church, Oxford (MA 1948). Served War, 1941–46: ME, Italy; Captain, The Black Watch (RHR). Called to the Bar, Inner Temple, 1949; Yarborough-Anderson Scholar, Inner Temple, 1950. Legal Adviser, United Africa Co. Ltd, 1954–66, Sec., 1966; Dep. Head of Legal Services, Unilever Ltd, 1973; Jt Sec., Unilever PLC and Unilever NV, 1976–84; Dir, UAC Internat. Ltd, 1973–77. Chm., 1969–72, Pres., 1980–82, Bar Assoc. for Commerce, Finance and Industry; Member: Bar Council, 1971–73; Senate of Inns of Ct and Bar, 1973–78. Chairman: Pharmacists Rev. Panel, 1986–; Professional Cttee, Coll. of Speech and Language Therapists, 1993–. *Recreations:* ski-ing, Rugby, opera, reading. *Address:* The Crossways, 1 High Street, Dormansland, Lingfield, Surrey RH7 6PU. *T:* Lingfield (01342) 834621. *Club:* Caledonian.

KEITH, family name of **Barons Keith of Castleacre** and **Keith of Kinkel** and of **Earl of Kintore.**

KEITH OF CASTLEACRE, Baron *cr* 1980 (Life Peer), of Swaffham in the County of Norfolk; **Kenneth Alexander Keith;** Kt 1969; merchant banker and industrialist; *b* 30 Aug. 1916; *er s* of late Edward Charles Keith, Swanton Morley House, Norfolk; *m* 1st, 1946, Lady Ariel Olivia Winifred Baird (marr. diss., 1958), 2nd *d* of 1st Viscount Stonehaven, PC, GCMG, DSO, and Countess of Kintore; one *s* one *d*; 2nd, 1962, Mrs Nancy Hayward (marr. diss. 1972; she *d* 1990), Manhasset, New York; 3rd, 1973, Mrs Marie Hanbury, Burley-on-the-Hill, Rutland. *Educ:* Rugby Sch. Trained as a Chartered Accountant. 2nd Lt Welsh Guards, 1939; Lt-Col 1945; served in North Africa, Italy, France and Germany (despatches, Croix de Guerre with Silver Star). Asst to Dir Gen. Political Intelligence Dept, Foreign Office, 1945–46. Partner, 1946, Man. Dir, 1951, Philip Hill; Chairman: Philip Hill Investment Trust Ltd, 1967–87; Hill Samuel Group Ltd, 1970–80; Chm. and Chief Exec., Rolls Royce Ltd, 1972–80; Vice-Chm., BEA, 1964–71; Director: Beecham Gp Ltd, 1949–87 (Vice-Chm., 1970–87, Chm., 1986–87); Eagle Star Insurance Co., 1955–75; Nat. Provincial Bank, 1967–69; Times Newspapers Ltd, 1967–81; British Airways, 1971–72; Standard Telephones and Cables, subseq. STC, 1977–89 (Chm., 1985–89); Bank of Nova Scotia Ltd, 1978–87. Member: NEDC, 1964–71; CBI/NEDC Liaison Cttee, 1974–78; Pres., BSI, 1989–94; Vice-Pres., EEF. Chairman: Economic Planning Council for East Anglia, 1965–70; Governor, Nat. Inst. of Economic and Social Research. Council Mem. and Dir, Manchester Business Sch. President: Royal Norfolk Agricl Assoc., 1989; RoSPA, 1989–93. FIMgt; FRSA. Hon. Companion, RAeS. *Recreations:* farming, shooting, golf. *Address:* 9 Eaton Square, SW1 9DB. *T:* 0171–730 4000; The Wicken House, Castle Acre, Norfolk. *T:* Swaffham (01760) 755225. *Clubs:* White's; Links (New York).

KEITH OF KINKEL, Baron *cr* 1977 (Life Peer), of Strathtummel; **Henry Shanks Keith,** PC 1976; a Lord of Appeal in Ordinary, since 1977; *b* 7 Feb. 1922; *s* of late Baron Keith of Avonholm, PC (Life Peer); *m* 1955, Alison Hope Alan Brown, JP, MA; four *s* (including twin *s*) one *d*. *Educ:* Edinburgh Academy; Magdalen Coll., Oxford (MA; Hon. Fellow 1977); Edinburgh Univ. (LLB). War of 1939–45 (despatches); commnd Scots Guards, Nov. 1941; served N Africa and Italy, 1943–45; released, 1945 (Capt.). Advocate, Scottish Bar, 1950; Barrister, Gray's Inn, 1951, Bencher 1976; QC (Scotland), 1962. Standing Counsel to Dept of Health for Scotland, 1957–62; Sheriff Principal of Roxburgh, Berwick and Selkirk, 1970–71; Senator of Coll. of Justice in Scotland, 1971–77. Chairman: Scottish Valuation Adv. Coun., 1972–76 (Mem., 1957–70); Cttee on Powers of Revenue Depts, 1980–83; Dep. Chm., Parly Boundary Commn for Scotland, 1976; Member: Law Reform Cttee for Scotland, 1964–70; Cttee on Law of Defamation, 1971–74; Mem. Panel of Arbiters: European Fisheries Convention, 1964–71; Convention for Settlement of Investment Disputes, 1968–71. *Address:* House of Lords, SW1A 0PW. *Club:* Flyfishers'.

KEITH, Hon. Brian Richard; Hon. Mr Justice Keith; a Judge of the Supreme Court of Hong Kong, since 1991; *b* 14 April 1944; *s* of Alan Keith, OBE, broadcaster, and Pearl Keith (*née* Rebuck); *m* 1978, Gilly, *d* of late Air Cdre Ivan de la Plain, CBE; one *s* one *d*. *Educ:* University College School, Hampstead; Lincoln College, Oxford (MA). John F. Kennedy Fellow, Harvard Law School, 1966–67; called to the Bar, Inner Temple, 1968, in practice, 1969–91; Assistant Recorder, 1988; QC 1989; a Recorder, 1993–. Hon. Lectr, Univ. of Hong Kong, 1994–. Mem., Judicial Studies Bd, Hong Kong, 1994–. *Recreations:* stamp collecting, playing tennis. *Address:* The Supreme Court, Queensway, Hong Kong. *Club:* Hong Kong.

KEITH, Sir Kenneth (James), KBE 1988; QC (NZ) 1994; Professor of Law, Victoria University of Wellington, 1974–91, now Professor Emeritus; President, New Zealand Law Commission, since 1991; *b* 19 Nov. 1937; *s* of Patrick James Keith and Amy Irene Keith (*née* Witheridge); *m* 1961, Jocelyn Margaret Buckett; two *s* two *d*. *Educ:* Auckland Grammar Sch.; Auckland Univ.; Victoria Univ. of Wellington (LLM); Harvard Law Sch. Barrister and Solicitor, High Court of New Zealand. NZ Dept of External Affairs, 1960–62; Victoria Univ., 1962–64, 1966–91; UN Secretariat, NY, 1968–70; NZ Inst. of Internat. Affairs, 1972–74. Judge: Western Samoan Court of Appeal, 1982–; Cook Is Court of Appeal, 1982–. Mem., Internat. Fact Finding Commn (Geneva Conventions), 1991–. *Publications:* (ed) Human Rights in New Zealand, 1968; The Extent of the Advisory Jurisdiction of the International Court, 1971; contrib. to Amer. Jl of Internat. Law, Internat. and Comparative Law Qly, NZ Univs Law Rev., etc. *Recreations:* walking, reading, music. *Address:* 70 Raroa Road, Wellington 6005, New Zealand. *T:* (4) 4757108.

KEITH, Penelope Anne Constance, (Mrs Rodney Timson), OBE 1989; *b* 2 April; *d* of Frederick A. W. Hatfield and Constance Mary Keith; *m* 1978, Rodney Timson. *Educ:* Annecy Convent, Seaford, Sussex; Webber Douglas Sch., London. First prof. appearance, Civic Theatre, Chesterfield, 1959; repertory, Lincoln, Salisbury and Manchester, 1960–63; RSC, Stratford, 1963, and Aldwych, 1965; rep., Cheltenham, 1967; Maggie Howard in Suddenly at Home, Fortune Theatre, 1971; Sarah in The Norman Conquests, Greenwich, then Globe Theatre, 1974; Lady Driver in Donkey's Years, 1976; Orinthia in The Apple Cart, Chichester, then Phoenix Theatre, 1977; Epifania in The Millionairess, Haymarket, 1978; Sarah in Moving, Queen's Theatre, 1981; Maggie in Hobson's Choice, Haymarket, 1982; Lady Cicely Waynflete in Captain Brassbound's Conversion, Haymarket, 1982; Judith Bliss in Hay Fever, Queen's, 1983; The Dragon's Tail, Apollo, 1985; Miranda, Chichester, 1987; The Deep Blue Sea, Haymarket, 1988; Dear Charles, Yvonne Arnaud, Guildford, 1990; The Merry Wives of Windsor, Chichester, 1990; Lady Bracknell in The Importance of Being Earnest, UK tour, 1991; On Approval, UK tour, 1992; (dir) Relatively Speaking, nat. tour, 1992; *film:* The Priest of Love, 1980. Television plays and series include: The Good Life, 1974–77; The Norman Conquests, 1977; To the Manor Born, 1979, 1980 and 1981; Sweet Sixteen, 1983; Moving, 1985; Executive Stress, 1986–88; No Job for a Lady, 1990–92; presenter: What's My Line?, 1988; Growing Places, 1989. Mem., HFEA, 1990–. Pres., Actors Benevolent Fund, 1990–. Governor: Queen Elizabeth's Foundn for the Disabled, 1989–; Guildford Sch. of Acting, 1991–. Trustee, Yvonne Arnaud Theatre, 1992–. Awards: BAFTA, 1976 and 1977; SWET, 1976; Variety Club of GB, 1976 and 1979. *Recreations:* gardening, theatre-going. *Address:* c/o London Management, 235/241 Regent Street, W1A 2JT. *T:* 0171–493 1610.

KEITH-LUCAS, Prof. Bryan, CBE 1983; Professor of Government, University of Kent at Canterbury, 1965–77, now Emeritus (Master of Darwin College, 1970–74); *b* 1 Aug. 1912; *y s* of late Keith Lucas, ScD, FRS, and Alys (*née* Hubbard); *m* 1946, Mary Hardwicke (MBE 1982; Sheriff of Canterbury, 1971); one *s* two *d*. *Educ:* Gresham's Sch., Holt; Pembroke Coll., Cambridge. MA Cantab 1937, MA Oxon 1948; DLitt Kent, 1980. Solicitor, 1937. Asst Solicitor: Kensington Council, 1938–46; Nottingham, 1946–48. Served 1939–45 in Buffs and Sherwood Foresters, N Africa and Italy (Major, despatches);

DAAG Cyprus, 1945–46. Sen. Lectr in Local Govt, Oxford, 1948–65; Faculty Fellow of Nuffield Coll., 1950–65, Domestic Bursar, 1957–65. Leverhulme Emeritus Fellow, 1983. Part-time Asst Master, King's Sch., Canterbury, 1978–83. Chm., Commn on Electoral System, Sierra Leone, 1954; Commn on local govt elections, Mauritius, 1955–56. Member: Roberts Cttee on Public Libraries, 1957–59; Commn on Administration of Lagos, 1963; Mallaby Cttee on Staffing of Local Govt, 1964–67; Local Govt Commn for England, 1965–66; Royal Commn on Elections in Fiji, 1975. Vice-Chm., Hansard Soc., 1976–80. Chairman: Nat. Assoc. of Parish Councils, 1964–70 (Vice-Pres., 1970–; Pres., Kent Assoc., 1972–81); Canterbury Soc., 1972–75; President: Kent Fedn of Amenity Socs, 1976–81; Wye Historical Soc., 1986–. City Councillor, Oxford, 1950–65. Hon. Fellow, Inst. of Local Govt Studies, Birmingham Univ., 1973. *Publications:* The English Local Government Franchise, 1952; The Mayor, Aldermen and Councillors, 1961; English Local Government in the 19th and 20th Centuries, 1977; (with P. G. Richards) A History of Local Government in the 20th Century, 1978; The Unreformed Local Government System, 1980; Parish Affairs, 1986; (with Dr G. M. Ditchfield) A Kentish Parson, 1991; (with K. P. Poole) Parish Government 1894–1994, 1994; various articles on local govt. *Address:* 7 Church Street, Wye, Kent TN25 5BN. *T:* Wye (01233) 812621. *Club:* National Liberal.

See also David Keith-Lucas.

KEITH-LUCAS, Prof. David, CBE 1973; MA; FEng, FIMechE, Hon. FRAeS; Chairman, Airworthiness Requirements Board, 1972–82; *b* 25 March 1911; *s* of late Keith Lucas, ScD, FRS, and Alys (*née* Hubbard); *m* 1st, 1942, Dorothy De Bauduy Robertson (*d* 1979); two *s* one *d*; 2nd, 1981, Phyllis Marion Everard (*née* Whurr). *Educ:* Gresham's Sch., Holt; Gonville and Caius Coll., Cambridge. BA (Mech Sci Tripos, 2nd Class Hons) 1933; MA 1956; FRAeS 1948, Hon. FRAeS 1979; FIMechE 1949; FAIAA 1973, Hon. FAIAA 1974; FEng 1978. Apprenticed 1933–35, design team 1935–39, C. A. Parsons & Co. Ltd; Chief Aerodynamicist, Short Bros Ltd, 1940–49; Short Bros & Harland Ltd: Chief Designer, 1949–58; Technical Dir, 1958–64; Dir of Research, 1964–65; Dir, John Brown & Co., 1970–77; Cranfield Inst. of Technology: Prof. of Aircraft Design, 1965–72; Pro-Vice-Chancellor, 1970–73; Prof. of Aeronautics and Chm. College of Aeronautics, 1972–76, now Emeritus Prof. Member: Senate, Queen's Univ., Belfast, 1955–65; Council, Air Registration Board, 1967–72; Commn on Third London Airport, 1968–70; Civil Aviation Authority, 1972–80. President: RAeS, 1968; Engrg Section, British Assoc. for the Advancement of Science, 1972. Hon. DSc: Queen's Univ., Belfast, 1968; Cranfield Inst. of Technology, 1975. Gold Medal, RAeS, 1975. *Publications:* The Shape of Wings to Come, 1952; The Challenge of Vertical Take-Off (lects IMechE), 1961–62; The Role of Jet Lift (lect. RAeS), 1962; Design Council report on design educn; papers on aircraft design, vertical take-off, engrg economics, in engrg jls. *Recreation:* small boats. *Address:* Manor Close, Emberton, Olney, Bucks MK46 5BX. *T:* Bedford (01234) 711552.

See also B. Keith-Lucas.

KEKEDO, Dame Mary (Angela), DBE 1987 (CBE); BEM; formerly Headmistress and Manageress of schools in Kokoda; retired from active public service, 1981; *b* 12 July 1919; *d* of Alphonse Natera and Lucy Silva; *m* 1939, Walter Gill Kekedo; two *s* six *d* (and two *s* decd). *Educ:* St Patrick's Sch., Yule Island, PNG. Certificated teacher. Began first sch. in Kokoda, in own private home, and first women's club in Kokoda, 1949; Headmistress of Kokoda Sch. (first female apptd in PNG), 1956; founded first Vocational Sch. in Kokoda, 1974, Manageress, 1976. Member: Kokoda Area Authority, 1975–; (first) Interim Northern Province Provincial Assembly, 1978–. Cross Pro Ecclesia et Pontifice (Holy See), 1987. *Address:* Post Office Box 10, Kokoda, Northern Province, Papua New Guinea.

KEKWICK, Prof. Ralph Ambrose, FRS 1966; Professor of Biophysics, University of London, 1966–71, now Emeritus; Member Staff, Lister Institute, 1940–71 (Head, Division of Biophysics, 1943–71); *b* 11 Nov. 1908; 2nd *s* of late Oliver A. and Mary Kekwick; *m* 1st, 1933, Barbara (*d* 1973), 3rd *d* of W. S. Stone, DD, New York; one *d*; 2nd, 1974, Dr Margaret Mackay (*d* 1982), *er d* of J. G. Mackay, MB, BS, Adelaide, Australia. *Educ:* Leyton County High Sch.; University Coll., London (Fellow, 1971). BSc 1928; MSc 1936; DSc 1941. Bayliss-Starling Scholar, University Coll. London, 1930–31; Commonwealth Fund Fellow, New York and Princeton Univs, 1931–33; Lectr in Biochemistry University Coll. London, 1933–37; Rockefeller Fellow, University of Uppsala, Sweden, 1935; MRC Fellow, Lister Inst., 1937–40; Reader in Chemical Biophysics, University of London, 1954–66. Vice-Chm., Wanstead-Woodford Assoc. for Welfare of Blind, 1982–94. Oliver Memorial Award for Blood Transfusion, 1957. *Publications:* (with M. E. Mackay) Separation of protein fractions from human plasma (MRC Special Report), 1954; papers on physical biochemistry and hæmatology, mostly in Biochemical Jl and Brit. Jl of Hæmatology. *Recreations:* music, gardening and bird watching. *Address:* 31 Woodside Road, Woodford Wells, Essex IG8 0TW. *T:* 0181–504 4264.

KELBIE, Sheriff David; Sheriff of Grampian, Highland and Islands, at Aberdeen, and Stonehaven, since 1986; *b* 28 Feb. 1945; *s* of Robert Kelbie and Monica Eileen Pearn; *m* 1966, Helen Mary Smith; one *s* one *d*. *Educ:* Inverurie Acad.; Aberdeen Univ. (LLB Hons). Advocate; called to the Scottish Bar, 1968; Sheriff of N Strathclyde, 1979–86. Associate Lectr, Heriot-Watt Univ., 1971–75; Hon. Sec., Scottish Congregational Coll., 1975–82; Mem., Christian Aid UK/Ireland Cttee, 1986–90. *Publications:* Small Claims Procedure in the Sheriff Court, 1994; articles in legal jls. *Recreations:* sailing, music, reading. *Address:* 38 Earlspark Drive, Bieldside, Aberdeen AB1 9AH. *T:* Aberdeen (01224) 868237.

KELBURN, Viscount of; David Michael Douglas Boyle; *b* 15 Oct. 1978; *s* and *heir* of 10th Earl of Glasgow, *qv*.

KELLAND, Gilbert James, CBE 1978; QPM 1975; Assistant Commissioner (Crime), Metropolitan Police, 1977–84, retired; *b* 17 March 1924; *m* 1950, Edith Ellen Marshall; two *d*. *Educ:* Georgeham Church Sch.; Braunton Secondary Modern Sch.; National Police Coll. Served RN, Fleet Air Arm, 1942–46. Metropolitan Police, 1946–84: Police Coll. Jun. Comd (Insp.) Course, 1955, Sen. Comd Course, 1964; Chm., London Dist of Supts' Assoc. of England & Wales and Mem. Police Council of GB and of Police Adv. Bd, 1966–69; Pres., Supts' Assoc. of England & Wales, 1968; Ford (Dagenham Trust) Fellowship studying Fed. Law Enforcement in USA, 1969; Hon. Sec., London Reg. Assoc. of Chief Police Officers, 1971–77; Brit. rep., INTERPOL, 1977–84, and Mem. Exec. Cttee, 1978–81. Stated Cases: Kelland *v* de Frietas, 1961 and Kelland *v* Raymond, 1964. Member: Parole Bd, 1986–89; AAA Cttee of Enquiry into Drug Abuse, 1988. Chairman: Met. Pol. Athletic Club, 1964–84; UK Pol. Athletic Assoc. and Met. Pol. Athletic Assoc., 1977–84; Life Vice Pres., Pol. AA, and Hon. Life Mem., Met. Pol. AA, 1984. Freeman, City of London, 1983. *Publication:* Crime in London, 1986, 1987. *Recreations:* following athletics, walking, gardening, reading. *Address:* c/o Metropolitan Police Athletic Association, Wellington House, 67 Buckingham Gate, SW1E 6BE.

KELLAND, John William, LVO 1977; QPM 1975; Overseas Police Adviser and Inspector General of Dependent Territories' Police, Foreign and Commonwealth Office, 1985–91; *b* 18 Aug. 1929; *s* of William John Kelland and Violet Ethel (*née* Olsen); *m* 1st, 1960, Brenda Nancy (*née* Foulsham) (decd); two *s*; 2nd, 1986, Frances Elizabeth (*née* Byrne); one step *d*. *Educ:* Sutton High Sch.; Plymouth Polytechnic. FIMgt. Pilot Officer, RAF, 1947–49. Constable, later Insp., Plymouth City Police, 1950–67; Insp., later Supt, Devon & Cornwall Constabulary, 1968–72; Asst Chief Constable, Cumbria Constabulary, 1972–74; Dir, Sen. Comd Courses, Nat. Police Coll., Bramshill, 1974–75 and 1978–80; Comr, Royal Fiji Police, 1975–78; 1981–85: Management Consultant and Chm., CSSBs; Sen. Consultant, RIPA; Sen. Lectr, Cornwall Coll.; Facilitator, Interpersonal Skills, Cornwall CC Seminars. Mem., Cornwall & Isles of Scilly FHSA, 1992–93. *Publications:* various articles in learned jls. *Recreations:* Rugby football, choral singing, wildlife. *Address:* Casuarina, 3 Oak Avenue, St Mellion Park, Saltash, Cornwall PL12 6UF. *Clubs:* Civil Service; St Mellion Golf and Country; Royal Western Yacht.

KELLAS, Arthur Roy Handasyde, CMG 1964; HM Diplomatic Service, retired; High Commissioner in Tanzania, 1972–74; *b* 6 May 1915; *s* of Henry Kellas and Mary Kellas (*née* Brown); *m* 1952, Katharine Bridget, *d* of Sir John Le Rougetel, KCMG, MC; two *s* one *d*. *Educ:* Aberdeen Grammar Sch.; Aberdeen Univ.; Oxford Univ.; Ecole des Sciences Politiques. Passed into Diplomatic Service, Sept. 1939. Commissioned into Border Regt, Nov. 1939. War of 1939–45: Active Service with 1st Bn Parachute Regt and Special Ops, Af. and Gr, 1941–44 (despatches twice). Third Sec. at HM Embassy, Tehran, 1944–47; First Sec. at HM Legation, Helsingfors, 1948–50; First Sec. (press) at HM Embassy, Cairo, 1951–52; First Sec. at HM Embassy, Baghdad, 1954–58; Counsellor, HM Embassy, Tehran, 1958–62; Imperial Defence Coll., 1963–64; Counsellor, HM Embassy and Consul-Gen., Tel Aviv, 1964–65; Ambassador to Nepal, 1966–70, to Democratic Yemen, 1970–72. Pres., Britain-Nepal Soc., 1975–79. *Publication:* Down to Earth (war memoir of parachute subaltern), 1990. *Recreations:* reading, reviewing books. *Address:* Inverockle, Achateny, Acharacle, Argyll PH36 4LG. *T:* Kilchoan (019723) 265. *Club:* United Oxford & Cambridge University.

KELLAWAY, (Charles) William; Secretary and Librarian, Institute of Historical Research, University of London, 1971–84; *b* 9 March 1926; *s* of late Charles Halliley Kellaway, FRS; *m* 1952, Deborah, *d* of late Sir Hibbert Alan Stephen Newton; one *s* two *d*. *Educ:* Geelong Grammar Sch.; Lincoln Coll., Oxford. BA Modern History, 1949, MA 1955. FLA, FRHistS, FSA. Asst Librarian, Guildhall Library, 1950–60; Sub-Librarian, Inst. of Historical Research, 1960–71. Hon. General Editor, London Record Society, 1964–83. *Publications:* The New England Company, 1649–1776, 1961; (ed jtly) Studies in London History, 1969; Bibliography of Historical Works Issued in UK, 1957–70, 3 vols, 1962, 1967, 1972; (ed jtly) The London Assize of Nuisance 1301–1431, 1973. *Address:* 18 Canonbury Square, N1 2AL. *T:* 0171–354 0349.

KELLEHER, Dame Joan, (Joanna), DBE 1965; Hon. ADC to the Queen, 1964–67; Director, Women's Royal Army Corps, 1964–67; *b* 24 Dec. 1915; *d* of late Kenneth George Henderson, barrister-at-law, Stonehaven; *m* 1970, Brig. M. F. H. Kelleher, OBE, MC, late RAMC. *Educ:* privately at home and abroad. Joined ATS, 1941; commissioned ATS, 1941; WRAC, 1949. *Recreations:* golf, gardening.

KELLER, Prof. Andrew, FRS 1972; Research Professor in Polymer Science, Department of Physics, University of Bristol, 1969–91, Professor Emeritus, since 1991; *b* 22 Aug. 1925; *s* of Imre Keller and Margit Klein; *m* 1951, Eva Bulhack; one *s* one *d*. *Educ:* Budapest Univ. (BSc); Bristol Univ. (PhD). FInstP. Techn. Officer, ICI Ltd, Manchester, 1948–55; Bristol Univ.: Min. of Supply res. appt, 1955–57; Res. Asst, 1957–63; Lectr, 1963–65; Reader, 1965–69. MAE 1994. High Polymer Prize, Amer. Phys. Soc., 1964; Swinburne Award, Plastics Inst., 1974; Max Born Medal, Inst. Physics and Deutsche Physik Gesellschaft, 1983; Rumford Medal, Royal Soc., 1994; Medal, Collège de France, 1994. *Publications:* numerous papers in Jl Polymer Science, Progress Reports in Physics, Proc. Royal Soc., Macromol. Chem., etc. *Recreations:* outdoor sports, mountain walking, skiing, travel, reading, opera, concerts. *Address:* 41 Westbury Road, Bristol BS9 3AU. *T:* Bristol (0117) 962 9767.

KELLER, René Jacques; Ambassador of Switzerland to Austria, 1976–79, retired; *b* 19 May 1914; *s* of Jacques Keller and Marie (*née* Geiser); *m* 1942, Marion (*née* Werder); one *s* two *d*. *Educ:* Geneva; Trinity Coll., Cambridge. Vice-Consul, Prague, 1941–45; 2nd Sec. of Legation, The Hague, 1947–50; 1st Sec., London, 1950–54; Head of News Dept, Berne, 1954–56; 1st Counsellor, Swiss Embassy, Paris, 1957–60; Ambassador to Ghana, Guinea, Liberia, Mali and Togo, 1960–62; Ambassador to Turkey, 1962–65; Head of Perm. Mission of Switzerland to Office of UN and Internat. Organisations, Geneva, 1966–68; Ambassador of Switzerland to UK, 1968–71; Head of Direction for International Organisation, Foreign Ministry of Switzerland, 1971–75. *Address:* 1 Promenade du Pin, 1204 Geneva, Switzerland. *Club:* Cercle de la Terrase (Geneva).

KELLER, Prof. Rudolf Ernst, MA Manchester; DrPhil Zürich; Professor of German Language and Medieval German Literature, University of Manchester, 1960–82, now Emeritus; *b* 3 Feb. 1920; *m* 1947, Ivy Sparrow; two *d*. *Educ:* Kantonsschule Winterthur, Switzerland; University of Zürich. Teacher at Kantonsschule Winterthur, 1944–46; Asst, 1946–47, Asst Lecturer, 1947–49, University of Manchester; Lecturer in German, Royal Holloway College, University of London, 1949–52; Sen. Lecturer, 1952–59, Reader in German, 1959–60, Dean of Faculty of Arts, 1968–70, Pro-Vice-Chancellor, 1976–79, University of Manchester. Corresp. Mem., Inst. für deutsche Sprache, 1969; Goethe Medal, 1981. *Publications:* Die Ellipse in der neuenglischen Sprache als semantisch-syntaktisches Problem, 1944; Die Sprachen der Welt, 1955 (trans. Bodmer: The Loom of Language); German Dialects, Phonology and Morphology with Selected Texts, 1961; The German Language, 1978; articles in learned periodicals. *Recreations:* reading, travel. *Address:* 8 Wadham Way, Hale, Altrincham, Cheshire WA15 9LJ. *T:* 0161–980 5237.

KELLETT, Alfred Henry, CBE 1965; Chairman, South Western Areas, National Coal Board, 1967–69, retired; *b* 2 Aug. 1904; British; *m* 1934, Astrid Elizabeth (*née* Hunter); one *s* three *d*. *Educ:* Rossall Sch.; Universities of Cambridge and Birmingham. Man. Dir, Washington Coal Co. Ltd, 1940–47; Area Gen. Man., NCB Durham Div., 1950–59; Dep. Chm., Durham Div., 1960; Chm., South Western Div., NCB, 1961–67. CStJ. *Recreation:* travel. *Address:* Pent House, Benenden, Cranbrook, Kent TN17 4EH.

KELLETT, Sir Stanley Charles, 7th Bt *cr* 1801; *b* 5 March 1940; *s* of Sir Stanley Everard Kellett, 6th Bt, and of Audrey Margaret Phillips; *S* father, 1983; *m* 1st, 1962, Lorraine May (marr. diss. 1968), *d* of F. Winspear; 2nd, 1968, Margaret Ann (marr. diss. 1974), *d* of James W. Bofinger; 3rd, 1982, Catherine Lorna, *d* of W. J. C. Orr; one *d*. *Heir:* *uncle* Charles Rex Kellett [*b* 1916; *m* 1940, Florence Helen Bellamy (*d* 1984); two *s* one *d*]. *Address:* 58 Glad Gunson Drive, Eleebana, Newcastle, NSW 2280, Australia.

KELLETT-BOWMAN, Edward Thomas, JP; Member (C) European Parliament, Itchen, Test and Avon, since 1994 (Hampshire Central, Dec. 1988–1994); business and management consultant in private practice, since 1974; *b* 25 Feb. 1931; *s* of late R. E. Bowman and of M. Bowman (*née* Mathers); *m* 1st, 1960, Margaret Patricia Blakemore (*d* 1970); three *s* one *d*; 2nd, 1971, (Mary) Elaine Kellett (*see* Dame Elaine Kellett-Bowman). *Educ:* Reed's Sch.; Cranfield Inst. of Technol. MBA, DMS, FIMgt. Technical and management trng in textiles, 1951–53; textile management, 1953–55; pharmaceutical man., 1955–72. Mem. (C) Lancs East, European Parlt, 1979–84; contested same seat,

1984. Liveryman, Worshipful Co. of Wheelwrights, 1979; Freeman, City of London, 1978; Hon. Citizen, New Orleans, 1960. JP Mddx, 1966. *Recreations:* shooting, tennis, swimming. *Address:* (office) 18A Bargates, Christchurch, Dorset BH23 1QL. *T:* Christchurch (01202) 475548.

KELLETT-BOWMAN, Dame (Mary) Elaine, DBE 1988; MA; MP (C) Lancaster, since 1970; *b* 8 July 1924; *d* of late Walter Kay; *m* 1st, 1945, Charles Norman Kellett (decd); three *s* one *d*; 2nd, 1971, Edward Thomas Kellett-Bowman, *qv*. *Educ:* Queen Mary Sch., Lytham; The Mount, York; St Anne's Coll., Oxford; Barnett House, Oxford (post-graduate distinction in welfare diploma). Contested (C): Nelson and Colne, 1955; South-West Norfolk, March and Oct. 1959; Buckingham, 1964, 1966. Mem. (C) European Parlt, 1975–84 (Mem. for Cumbria, 1979–84); Mem. Social Affairs, Regional Policy and Development Cttees, Europ. Parlt, 1975–84. Camden Borough Council: Alderman, 1968–74; Vice-Chm., Housing Cttee, 1968; Chm., Welfare Cttee, 1969. Called to Bar, Middle Temple, 1964. Lay Mem., Press Council, 1964–68. Governor, Culford Sch., 1963; Mem. Union European Women, 1956; Delegate to Luxemburg, 1958. No 1 Country Housewife, 1960; Christal MacMillan Law Prize, 1963. *Recreations:* gardening, collecting and repairing antiques. *Address:* House of Commons, SW1A 0AA.

KELLEY, Joan, CB 1987; Member, Official Side Panel, Civil Service Appeal Board, since 1987; *b* 8 Dec. 1926; *er d* of late George William Kelley and Dora Kelley. *Educ:* Whalley Range High Sch. for Girls, Manchester; London Sch. of Econs and Polit. Science (BScEcon 1947). Europa Publications Ltd, 1948; Pritchard, Wood & Partners Ltd, 1949; joined Civil Service as Econ. Asst in Cabinet Office, 1949; admin. work in Treasury, 1954; Principal, 1956; Asst Sec., 1968; Under Sec., 1979; on secondment to NI Office, 1979–81; Under Sec., 1979–86, Principal Estabt Officer and Principal Finance Officer, 1984–86, HM Treasury. Mem. Council, Univ. of London Inst. of Educn, 1992–. *Recreations:* gardening, map reading, drinking wine, foreign travel. *Address:* 21 Langland Gardens, NW3 6QE.

KELLEY, Mrs Joanna Elizabeth, OBE 1973; Assistant Director of Prisons (Women), 1967–74; *b* 23 May 1910; *d* of late Lt-Col William Beadon, 51st Sikhs; *m* 1934, Harper Kelley (*d* 1962); no *c*. *Educ:* Hayes Court; Girton Coll., Cambridge (MA). Souschargé, Dept of Pre-History, Musée de l'Homme, Paris, 1934–39; Mixed Youth Club Leader, YWCA, 1939–42; Welfare Officer, Admiralty, Bath, 1942–47; Prison Service, 1947–74; Governor of HM Prison, Holloway, 1959–66. Member: Council, St George's House, Windsor, 1971–77; Redundant Churches Cttee, 1974–79; Scott Holland Trust, 1978–86; Sponsor, YWCA of GB, 1979–. FSA. Hon. Fellow Girton Coll., Cambridge, 1968. Hon. LLD Hull Univ., 1960. *Publications:* When the Gates Shut, 1967; Who Casts the First Stone, 1978. *Recreation:* reading. *Address:* 31 Westmoreland Terrace, SW1V 4AQ.

KELLGREN, Prof. Jonas Henrik, FRCS, FRCP; Professor of Rheumatology, University of Manchester, 1953–76, now Emeritus; Dean, 1970–73; *b* 11 Sept. 1911; *s* of Dr Harry Kellgren and Vera (*née* Dumelunksen); *m* 1942, Thelma Marian Reynolds; four *d*. *Educ:* Bedales Sch.; University Coll., London. MB, BS, 1934; FRCS 1936; FRCP 1951. Junior clinical appointments, University Coll. Hosp., 1934–42 (Beit Memorial Fellow 1938–39); served War, 1942–46, as surgical and orthopædic specialist, RAMC; Mem. Scientific Staff, Med. Research Council, Wingfield Morris Orthopædic Hosp., Oxford, Chronic Rheumatism, University of Manchester, 1947. Pres. Heberden Soc., 1958–59. *Publications:* numerous articles in medical and scientific jls. *Recreation:* landscape painting. *Address:* Beckside Cottage, Rusland, Ulverston, Cumbria LA12 8JY. *T:* Ulverston (01229) 84244.

KELLOCK, Jane Ursula, JP; Member, Council on Tribunals, 1987–93; *b* 21 Oct. 1925; *d* of late Arthur George Symonds and late Gertrude Frances Symonds; *m* 1967, His Honour Thomas Oslaf Kellock (*d* 1993). *Educ:* Priors Field Sch., Godalming. WRNS, 1943–45. Sec., Africa Bureau, London, 1957–67; Editor, Africa Digest, 1957–75; Member: Bd, Commonwealth Development Corporation, 1965–73; Police Complaints Board, 1977–85. Former Mem., S Metropolitan Conciliation Cttee, Race Relations Bd. JP: Inner London, 1968–77; Nottingham City Bench, 1977–91; Inner London (N Westminster), 1992. Editor, Commonwealth Judicial Jl, 1985–89. *Recreation:* travel. *Address:* 1 Paper Buildings, Temple, EC4Y 7EP; 4 Pound Lane, Dorchester DT1 1LP.

KELLY, Prof. Anthony, CBE 1988; DL; FRS 1973; FEng; Extraordinary Fellow, Churchill College, Cambridge, 1985; *b* 25 Jan. 1929; *s* of late Group Captain Vincent Gerald French and Mrs Violet Kelly; *m* 1956, Christina Margaret Dunleavie, BA; three *s* one *d*. *Educ:* Presentation Coll., Reading; Univ. of Reading (Schol.); Trinity Coll., Cambridge. BSc Reading 1949; PhD 1953, ScD 1968, Cantab. Research Assoc., Univ. of Illinois, 1953–55; ICI Fellow, Univ. of Birmingham, 1955; Asst, Associate Prof., Northwestern Univ., 1956–59; Univ. Lectr, Cambridge, 1959–67; Founding Fellow, Churchill Coll., 1960; Dir of Studies, Churchill Coll., 1960–67; Supt, Div. of Inorganic and Metallic Structure, 1967–69, Dep. Dir, 1969–75, Nat. Physical Lab. (seconded to ICI, 1973–75); Vice-Chancellor, Univ. of Surrey, 1975–94. Univ. Prof., Univ. of Surrey, 1987. Director: Johnson Wax Ltd, 1981–; QUO-TEC Ltd, 1984–; Chm., Surrey Satellite Technology, 1985–. Vis. Fellow, Univ. of Göttingen, 1960; Vis. Prof., Carnegie Inst. of Technol., 1967; Prof. invité, Ecole Polytechnique Fédérale de Lausanne, 1977. Chm., Jt Standing Cttee on Structural Safety, Instns of Civil and Structural Engrs, 1988–; Member: SRC Cttee, 1967–72; Council, Inst. of Metals, 1969–74; Council, British Non-Ferrous Metals Res. Assoc., 1970–73; Engrg Materials Requirements Bd, DoI, 1973–75 (Chm., 1976–80); Adv. Cttee, Community Ref. Bureau of EEC, 1973–75. Mem., Academia Europaea, 1990; Foreign Associate, Nat. Acad. of Engrg of USA, 1986. FRSA 1992. DL Surrey, 1993. Hon. FIL 1988. DUniv Surrey, 1994. William Hopkins Prize, Cambridge Philosophical Soc., 1967; Beilby Medal, RIC, 1967; A. A. Griffith Medal, 1974, Platinum Medal, 1992, Inst. of Materials; Medal of Excellence, Univ. of Delaware, 1984; Internat. Gold Medal, Amer. Soc. for Materials, 1991. KSG 1992. *Publications:* Strong Solids, 1966, 3rd edn (with N. H. Macmillan) 1986; (with G. W. Groves) Crystallography and Crystal Defects, 1970; many papers in jls of physical sciences. *Recreations:* science of materials, sailing. *Address:* 10 Wootton Way, Cambridge CB3 9LX. *Club:* Island Sailing (Cowes).

KELLY, Barbara Mary, CBE 1992; President, Rural Forum, since 1992 (Chairman, 1988–92); *b* 27 Feb. 1940; *d* of John Maxwell Prentice and Barbara Bain Adam; *m* 1960, Kenneth Archibald Kelly; one *s* two *d* (and two *s* decd). *Educ:* Dalbeattie High Sch.; Kirkcudbright Academy; Moray House Coll., Edinburgh. DipEd. Partner in mixed dairy farming enterprise. Dir, Clydesdale Bank, 1994–; Mem., Scottish Adv. Bd, BP, 1990–. Chairman: Area Manpower Bd, MSC, 1987–88; Scottish Consumer Council, 1985–90; Training 2000, 1991–; Member: Nat. Consumer Council, 1985–90; Scottish Enterprise Bd, 1990–; Priorities Bd, MAFF, 1990–; Scottish Econ. Council, 1991–; Scottish Tourist Bd, 1993–; Comr, EOC, 1991–; Community Industry Bd, 1993–. Nat. Vice-Chm., Scottish Women's Rural Insts, 1983–86. Chm., Scottish Adv. Cttee, and Mem., Nat. Adv. Cttee, Duke of Edinburgh's Award Scheme, 1980–85. Trustee: Scottish Silver Jubilee Trust; Scottish Children's Bursary Fund, 1986–. *Recreations:* home and family, music, painting, the pursuit of real food, gardening of necessity. *Address:* Barncleugh, Irongray, Dumfries DG2 9SE. *T:* Dumfries (01387) 730210.

KELLY, Rt. Hon. Sir Basil; *see* Kelly, Rt Hon. Sir J. W. B.

KELLY, Brian; *see* Kelly, H. B.

KELLY, Charles Henry, CBE 1986; QPM 1978; DL; Chief Constable of Staffordshire, since 1977; *b* 15 July 1930; *s* of Charles Henry Kelly and Phoebe Jane Kelly; *m* 1952, Doris (*née* Kewley); one *s* one *d*. *Educ:* Douglas High Sch. for Boys, IOM; London Univ. LLB (Hons). Asst Chief Constable of Essex, 1972; Dep. Chief Constable of Staffordshire, 1976. Associate Prof., Criminal Justice Dept, Michigan State Univ., 1990–. Pres., Staffordshire Small Bore Rifle Assoc.; Chairman: Staffordshire Police St John Special Centre; ACPO Communications Cttee, 1982–92; No 3 Region, ACPO Cttee, 1985–93. Mem. Court, Keele Univ., 1990–. DL Stafford, 1979. MUniv Keele, 1991. KStJ 1991. *Recreations:* cricket, reading, walking. *Address:* Chief Constable's Office, Cannock Road, Stafford ST17 0QG. *T:* Stafford (01785) 57717. *Club:* Special Forces.

KELLY, Christopher William; Director of Budget and Public Finances, HM Treasury, since 1995; *b* 18 Aug. 1946; *s* of late Reginald and of Peggy Kelly; *m* 1970, Alison Mary Collens Durant; two *s* one *d*. *Educ:* Beaumont College; Trinity College, Cambridge (MA); Manchester University (MA (Econ)). HM Treasury, 1970; Private Sec. to Financial Sec., 1971–73; Sec. to Wilson Cttee of Inquiry into Financial Instns, 1978–80; Under Sec., 1987–; Dir of Fiscal and Monetary Policy, 1994. Mem. Bd, Public Finance Foundn, 1994–. Gov., Acland Burghley Sch., 1991–. *Recreations:* narrow-boating, swimming. *Address:* 22 Croftdown Road, NW5 1EH.

KELLY, David Robert Corbett, CBE 1991; Chairman, Kelly Packaging Limited, since 1962 (Managing Director, 1962–85); President, National Union of Conservative and Unionist Associations, 1995–March 1996 (Vice President, 1992–95); *b* 10 Dec. 1936; *s* of late Col R. C. Kelly, TD, DL, JP and of Jean Haswell Kelly (*née* Bowran), JP; *m* 1969, Angela Frances Taylor; four *d*. *Educ:* Sedbergh; St John's Coll., Cambridge (Lamor Award; MA). Farm labourer, 1955–56; Nat. Service, 2nd Lt, 2nd Bn, 7th DEO Gurkha Rifles, 1960–61; 17th (later 4th) Bn, Parachute Regt (9 DLI), TA, 1962–69 (Major); Mil. Mem., TA&VRA for N of England, 1969–75. Board Member: Regl Bd, Brit. Technol. Gp, 1980–84; Northumbrian Water Authy, 1983–89; Washington Develt Corp., 1984–88; NE Industrial Develt Bd, 1989–. Chm., NE Reg., 1966–67, Industrial Relns Cttee, 1968–71, British Box and Packaging Assoc. Confederation of British Industry: Member: Smaller Firms Council, 1977–83; Regl Council, 1979–86; Council, 1981–83; Industrial Policy Cttee, 1981–83; Mem., Lord Chancellor's Adv. Cttee on Tax Comrs, Tyne and Wear, 1981–93. Hon. Advr, Govt-Enterprise Communications Unit, Dept of Politics, Newcastle Univ., 1991–93. Contested (C) Gateshead W, 1979. Chm., Northern Area Conservatives, 1990–93. Mem., Gateshead CHC, 1975–77. President: Gateshead Dispensary Housing Assoc., 1992– (Chm., 1982–92 and 1993–); Craigielea Community Nursing Home, 1992– (Chm., 1988–92, 1993–). Trustee: Gateshead Dispensary Trust, 1965–; Northbrian Educnl Trust, 1981– (Chm., 1983–93). Chm. Govs, Westfield Sch., 1983–93. *Recreations:* country pursuits, wine, theatre, light adventure (Mount Kilimanjaro, 1994). *Address:* Stanton Fence, Morpeth, Northumberland NE65 8PP. *T:* Hartburn (01670) 722236. *Club:* Northern Counties (Newcastle upon Tyne).

KELLY, Edward Ronald; journalist and trout farmer; *b* 14 Oct. 1928; *s* of late William Walter Kelly and of Millicent Kelly; *m* 1954, Storm Massada. *Educ:* Honiton Sch. Journalist: Bath Evening Chronicle, 1952; East African Standard, 1953; Sunday Post, Kenya, 1954; Reuters, 1956; Central Office of Information, 1958–: Editor in Chief, Overseas Press Services Div., 1964; Asst Overseas Controller, 1968; Dir, Publications and Design Services Div., 1970; Home Controller, 1976; Overseas Controller, 1978–84. Chm., Assoc. of Stillwater Game Fishery Managers, 1993–95. *Recreations:* fishing, fly-tying, carpentry. *Address:* Duncton Mill, near Petworth, West Sussex GU28 0LF. *T:* Petworth (01798) 42294. *Club:* Flyfishers'.

KELLY, Prof. Francis Patrick, FRS 1989; Professor of the Mathematics of Systems, University of Cambridge, since 1990; Fellow of Christ's College, Cambridge, since 1976; *b* 28 Dec. 1950; *s* of Francis Kelly and Margaret Kelly (*née* McFadden); *m* 1972, Jacqueline Pullin; two *s*. *Educ:* Cardinal Vaughan Sch.; Van Mildert Coll., Durham (BSc 1971); Emmanuel Coll., Cambridge (Knight Prize 1975; PhD 1976). Operational Research Analyst, Scicon, 1971–72; Cambridge University: Asst Lectr in Op. Res., Faculty of Engineering, 1976–78; Lectr in Statistical Lab., 1978–86; Reader in Faculty of Maths, 1986–90; Dir, Statistical Lab., 1991–93; variously Research Fellow, Dir of Studies, Tutor, Mem. College Council and Investments Cttee, Christ's Coll., 1976–. Nuffield Foundn Sci. Res. Fellow, 1986–87. Chm., Lyndewode Research Ltd, 1987–. Rollo Davidson Prize, Cambridge Univ., 1979; Guy Medal in Silver, Royal Statistical Soc., 1989; Lanchester Prize, ORS of Amer., 1992. *Publications:* Reversibility and Stochastic Networks, 1979; articles in math. and stat. jls. *Recreations:* rewiring old houses, ski-ing, football with children. *Address:* Statistical Laboratory, 16 Mill Lane, Cambridge CB2 1SB. *T:* Cambridge (01223) 337963, 312708.

KELLY, Graham; *see* Kelly, R. H. G.

KELLY, Air Vice-Marshal (Herbert) Brian, CB 1983; LVO 1960; MD, FRCP; RAF, retired; *b* 12 Aug. 1921; *s* of late Surg. Captain James Cecil Kelly and of Meta Matheson (*née* Fraser). *Educ:* Epsom Coll.; St Thomas' Hosp. (MB, BS 1943, MD 1948). MRCP 1945, FRCP 1968; DCH 1966; MFOM 1982. House appts, St Thomas' Hosp., and St Luke's Hosp., Guildford, 1943–45; RNVR, Med. Specialist, RNH Hong Kong, 1945–48; Med. Registrar and Lectr in Medicine, St Thomas' Hosp., 1948–53; joined RAF Medical Br., 1953; Consultant in Medicine at RAF Hosps, Aden, Ely, Nocton Hall, Singapore, Cyprus, Germany, 1953–83; Consultant Adviser in Medicine to RAF, 1974, Senior Consultant, 1979–83. QHS 1978–83. Consultant, CAA, 1974–93. FRSocMed; Fellow, Med. Soc. London. Liveryman, Worshipful Soc. of Apothecaries, 1978; Freeman, City of London, 1978. *Publications:* papers in BMJ, Lancet, Brit. Heart Jl, and Internat. Jl of Epidemiology. *Recreation:* choir singing. *Address:* 32 Chiswick Quay, Hartington Road, W4 3UR. *T:* 0181–995 5042. *Club:* Royal Air Force.

KELLY, Rev. Dr John Norman Davidson, FBA 1965; Principal of St Edmund Hall, Oxford, 1951–79, Honorary Fellow 1979; Vice-Chancellor, Oxford University, Sept.–Oct. 1966 (Pro-Vice-Chancellor, 1964–66, 1972–79); *b* 13 April 1909; *s* of John and Ann Davidson Kelly. *Educ:* privately; Glasgow Univ.; The Queen's Coll., Oxford (Ferguson Scholar; Hertford Scholar; 1st Cl. Hon. Mods, Greats and Theology; Hon. Fellow, 1963); St Stephen's House; DD Oxon 1951. Deacon, 1934; priest, 1935; Curate, St Lawrence's, Northampton, 1934; St Edmund Hall, Oxford: Chaplain, 1935; Vice-Principal and Trustee, 1937; Dean of Degrees, 1982–89; Oxford University: Speaker's Lectr in Biblical Studies, 1945–48; Lecturer in Patristic Studies, 1948–76. Select Preacher: Oxford, 1944–46, 1959, 1961, 1962; Cambridge, 1953; Chm. Cttee of Second Internat. Conf. on Patristic Studies, Oxford, 1955; Proctor in Convocation of Canterbury representing Oxford University, 1958–64; Chm. Archbishop's Commn on Roman Catholic Relations, 1964–68; accompanied Archbishop of Canterbury on his visit to Pope Paul VI, 1966; Mem., Academic Council, Ecumenical Theological Inst., Jerusalem, 1966–. In the War of 1939–45 did part-time work at Chatham House and collaborated in organizing the Oxford Leave Courses for United States, Allied, and Dominions Forces. Canon of Chichester and Prebendary of Wightring, 1948, Highleigh, 1964–93. Took lead in obtaining Royal

Charter, new statutes and full collegiate status for St Edmund Hall, 1957. Mem. Governing Body: Royal Holloway Coll., London, 1959–69; King's Sch., Canterbury. Lectures: Paddock, General Theological Seminary, NY, 1963; Birkbeck, Cambridge, 1973; Hensley Henson, Oxford, 1979–80. Hon. DD: Glasgow, 1958; Wales, 1971. *Publications:* Early Christian Creeds, 1950, 3rd edn 1972; Rufinus, a Commentary on the Apostles' Creed, 1955; Early Christian Doctrines, 1958, 5th edn 1977; The Pastoral Epistles, 1963; The Athanasian Creed, 1964; The Epistles of Peter and of Jude, 1969; Aspects of the Passion, 1970; Jerome, 1975; The Oxford Dictionary of Popes, 1986; St Edmund Hall: almost seven hundred years, 1989; Golden Mouth, 1995. *Recreations:* videos of films, chatting with young people. *Address:* 7 Crick Road, Oxford OX2 6QJ. *T:* Oxford (01865) 512907. *Clubs:* Athenæum; Vincent's (Oxford).

KELLY, Rt. Hon. Sir (John William) Basil, Kt 1984; PC 1984; PC (NI) 1969; **Rt. Hon. Lord Justice Kelly;** Lord Justice of Appeal, Supreme Court of Judicature, Northern Ireland, since 1984; a Judge of the High Court of Justice in Northern Ireland, 1973–84; *b* 1920; *o s* of late Thomas William Kelly and late Emily Frances (*née* Donaldson); *m* 1957, Pamela, *o d* of late Thomas Colmer and Marjorie Colthurst. *Educ:* Methodist Coll., Belfast; Trinity Coll., Dublin. BA (Mod.) Legal Science, 1943; LLB (Hons) 1944. Called to Bar: of Northern Ireland, 1944; Middle Temple, 1970; QC (N Ireland) 1958. MP (U) Mid-Down, Parliament of Northern Ireland, 1964–72; Attorney-Gen. for Northern Ireland, 1968–72. Chairman: Council of Legal Educn, NI, 1989–93; Judicial Studies Bd, NI, 1993–; Mem., Law Adv. Cttee, British Council, 1982–92. *Recreations:* golf, music. *Address:* Royal Courts of Justice, Belfast.

KELLY, Laurence Charles Kevin; non-executive Director, 1972–93, and Vice-Chairman, 1988–93, Helical Bar PLC (Deputy Chairman, 1981–84; Chairman, 1984–88); *b* 11 April 1933; *s* of late Sir David Kelly, GCMG, MC, and Lady Kelly (*née* Jourda de Vaux); *m* 1963, (Alison) Linda McNair Scott; one *s* two *d. Educ:* Downside Sch.; New Coll., Oxford (Beresford Hope Schol.; MA Hons); Harvard Business Sch. Lieut, The Life Guards, 1949–52; served (temp.) Foreign Office, 1955–56; Guest, Keen and Nettlefolds, 1956–72; Director: GKN International Trading Ltd, 1972–77; Morganite International Ltd, 1984–91; KAE, subseq. Mintel, Ltd, 1980–; Chm., Queenborough Steel Co., 1980–89. Member: Northern Ireland Development Agency, 1972–78; Monopolies and Mergers Commn, 1982–89. Chairman, Opera da Camera Ltd (charity), 1981–87. Vice-Chm., British Iron and Steel Consumers' Council, 1976–85. Sen. Associate Mem., St Antony's Coll., Oxford, 1985–91. FRGS 1972. *Publications:* Lermontov, Tragedy in the Caucasus (biog.), 1978 (Cheltenham Literary Prize, 1979); St Petersburg, a Travellers' Anthology, 1981; Moscow, a Travellers' Anthology, 1983; Istanbul, a Travellers' Anthology, 1987; (with Linda Kelly) Proposals, 1989; reviews, TLS, etc. *Recreation:* opera-going. *Address:* 44 Ladbroke Grove, W11 2PA. *T:* 0171–727 4663; Lorton Hall, Low Lorton, near Cockermouth, Cumbria CA13 9UP. *T:* Cockermouth (01900) 85252. *Clubs:* Beefsteak, Brooks's, Turf; Kildare Street and University (Dublin).

KELLY, Dr Michael, CBE 1983; JP; DL; Managing Director, Michael Kelly Associates, since 1984; Chairman, Royal Scottish Society for the Prevention of Cruelty to Children, since 1987; *b* 1 Nov. 1940; *s* of David and Marguerite Kelly; *m* 1965, Zita Harkins; one *s* two *d. Educ:* Univ. of Strathclyde (BSc(Econ), PhD). FCIM (FInstM 1988). Asst Lectr in Economics, Univ. of Aberdeen, 1965–67; Lectr in Economics, Univ. of Strathclyde, 1967–84. Councillor: Anderston Ward Corp. of Glasgow, 1971–75 (Convener, Schools and Sch. Welfare; Vice-Convener, Transport); Hillington Ward, Glasgow Dist, 1977–84 (Chairman: General Purposes Cttee; Buildings and Property Cttee); Lord Provost of Glasgow, 1980–84 (masterminded "Glasgow's Miles Better" Campaign); Campaign Dir, Edinburgh—Count Me In, 1987–89. Rector, Univ. of Glasgow, 1984–87. Dir, Celtic Football Club, 1990–94. Mem., Scottish Cttee, NACF, 1990–93. BBC Radio Scotland News Quiz Champion, 1986, 1987. Hon. Mem., Clan Donald, USA; Hon. Mayor, Tombstone, Ariz; Hon. Citizen: Illinois; San José; St Petersburg; Kansas City; Dallas; Fort Worth; Winnipeg. JP Glasgow 1973; DL Glasgow 1984. Hon. LLD Glasgow, 1984. Glasgow Herald Scot of the Year, 1983. OStJ 1983. Founding Editor, Jl Economic Studies. *Publications:* Studies in the British Coal Industry, 1970; Paradise Lost: the struggle for Celtic's soul, 1994. *Recreations:* photography, ski-ing, golf, philately. *Address:* 50 Aytoun Road, Glasgow G41 5HE. *T:* 0141–427 1627.

KELLY, Prof. Michael Joseph, FRS 1993; FInstP, FIEE; Professor of Physics and Electronics, University of Surrey, since 1992; *b* New Plymouth, NZ, 14 May 1949; *s* of late Steve and Mary Constance Kelly; *m* 1991, Ann Elizabeth Taylor, BA, *d* of Dr Daniel Brumhall Cochrane Taylor, *qv*; one *d. Educ:* Francis Douglas Meml Coll., New Plymouth, NZ; Victoria Univ. of Wellington (BSc Hons 1970; MSc 1971); Gonville and Caius Coll., Univ. of Cambridge (PhD 1974); Trinity Hall, Cambridge (MA 1975; ScD 1994). FInstP 1988; FIEE 1989. Fellow, Trinity Hall, Cambridge, 1974–81, 1989–92; IBM Res. Fellow, Univ. of Calif., Berkeley, 1975–76; SRC Advanced Fellow, Cavendish Lab., 1977–81; Mem., Research Staff, GEC Hirst Res. Centre, 1981–92, Co-ordinator, GEC Superlattice Res., 1984–92. Vis. Scientist, Cavendish Lab., 1988–92; Royal Soc./SERC Industrial Fellow, 1989–91. Paterson Medal and Prize, Inst. of Physics, 1989; GEC Nelson Gold Medal, 1991. *Publications:* (ed jtly) The Physics and Fabrication of Microstructures and Microdevices, 1986; numerous papers and review articles on semiconductor physics-for-devices in scientific jls. *Recreations:* music, literature. *Address:* Department of Physics, University of Surrey, Guildford, Surrey GU2 5XH. *T:* Guildford (01483) 259410.

KELLY, Owen, QPM 1987; Commissioner of Police for City of London, 1985–93; *b* 10 April 1932; *s* of Owen Kelly and Anna Maria (*née* Hamill); *m* 1957, Sheila Ann (*née* McCarthy); five *s. Educ:* St Modan's High School, St Ninians, Stirlingshire. National Service, RAF, 1950–52; Metropolitan Police in all ranks from Police Constable to Commander, 1953–82; Asst and Dep. to Comr of Police for City of London, 1982–85; by use of traffic management, created secure zone in City of London for prevention of terrorist activity, July 1993, and scheme continues for envmtl reasons. 18th Senior Command Course, Nat. Police Coll., 1981; Mem., 14th Session of Nat. Exec. Inst., FBI, USA, 1991. Mem., Police Disciplinary Appeals Bd, Home Office, 1994–. Hon. Sec., Chief Constables' Club, 1989–93. Chm., City of London Br., Leukaemia Res. Fund, 1985–93. CStJ 1987 (OStJ 1986). Commendation, Order of Civil Merit, Spain, 1986; Ordre du Wissam Alouite Class III, Morocco, 1987; Ordre du Mérite, Senegal, 1988; Ordem do Merito, Class III (Portugal), 1993. *Recreations:* enjoying the society of a large family, do-it-yourself house and car maintenance, reading, horse riding.

KELLY, Rt. Rev. Patrick A.; *see* Salford, Bishop of, (RC).

KELLY, Peter (John); Under-Secretary for Atomic Energy, United Kingdom Department of Energy, 1980–82; *b* 26 Nov. 1922; *s* of Thomas and Lucy Kelly; *m* 1949, Gudrun Kelly (*née* Falck); two *s* three *d* (and one *s* decd). *Educ:* Downside; Oxford Univ. (BA). RNVR, 1942–46. 3rd Secretary, Moscow Embassy, 1948–49; journalism, 1950; rejoined public service, 1956; posts in Foreign Office, Defence Dept, Dept of Trade and Industry; Asst Secretary for Internat. Atomic Affairs, 1969–71; Counsellor, Office of UK Permanent Representative to the European Communities, Brussels, 1972–75; Director, Internat. Energy Agency, 1976–79. Trustee, Trust of St Francis and St Sergius. *Publication:* Safeguards in Europe, 1985. *Recreations:* walking, music. *Address:* 2 The Crouch, Seaford, Sussex BN25 1PX. *T:* Seaford (01323) 896881.

KELLY, Philip Charles; Director of Resources and Chief Finance Officer (formerly City Treasurer), Liverpool City Council, since 1986; Treasurer, Merseyside Fire and Civil Defence Authority; *b* 23 Aug. 1948; *s* of late Charles and of Irene May Kelly; *m* 1971, Pamela (*née* Fagan); one *s* two *d. Educ:* Inst. of Science and Technology, Univ. of Wales (BSc Econ). DipM; CIPFA. Market Research, British Steel Corp., 1970–72; Economist, Coventry City Council, 1972–74; Technical Officer, 1974–78, Asst Dir of Finance, 1978–82, Kirklees MDC; Dep. City Treasurer, Liverpool CC, 1982–86. *Recreation:* family. *Address:* c/o Municipal Buildings, PO Box 1, Dale Street, Liverpool L69 2DQ. *T:* 0151–225 2347.

KELLY, Philip John; journalist and political consultant; *b* 18 Sept. 1946; *s* of late William Kelly and of Mary Winifred Kelly; *m* 1988, Dorothy Margaret Jones; two *s. Educ:* St Mary's Coll., Crosby; Leeds Univ. (BA Hons Politics). Freelance journalist and PR consultant, 1970–87; Editor, Tribune, 1987–91; Press Officer to Michael Meacher, MP, 1991–92. Co-Founder: Leveller, 1976; State Research, 1977; Chair, London Freelance Br., NUJ, 1983. Councillor (Lab) London Borough of Islington, 1984–86, 1990– (Chm., Educn Cttee, 1993–). Contested (Lab) Surrey SW, 1992. *Recreations:* railways, model railways, Arsenal FC. *Address:* 56 Windsor Road, N7 6JL. *Club:* Red Rose.

KELLY, (Robert Henry) Graham, FCIS; Chief Executive/General Secretary of the Football Association, since 1989; *b* 23 Dec. 1945; *s* of Thomas John Kelly and Emmie Kelly; *m* 1970, Elizabeth Anne Wilkinson; one *s* one *d. Educ:* Baines Grammar Sch., Poulton-le-Fylde. FCIS 1973. Barclays Bank, 1964–68; Football League, 1968–88, Sec., 1979–88. Trustee, Football Grounds Improvement Trust, 1985–88. *Address:* The Football Association, 16 Lancaster Gate, W2 3LW.

KELLY, Rosaline; publishing and industrial relations consultant; Visiting Lecturer in Journalism, London College of Printing, since 1981; *b* 27 Nov. 1922; *d* of Laurence Kelly and Ellen (*née* Fogarty), Drogheda, Co. Louth, Eire. *Educ:* St Louis Convent, Carrickmacross; University Coll., Dublin, NUI. Journalist with Woman magazine, 1958–77; local management, IPC Magazines Ltd, 1977–80. Active in NUJ, 1958–: Mem., National Exec. Council, 1972–78; first woman Pres., 1975–77; Membership of Honour, 1979; Member: NUJ Appeals Tribunal, 1978–; NUJ Standing Orders Cttee, 1978–; Trustee, NUJ Provident Fund Management Cttee, 1977– (Chairperson, 1980–82). Mem., Press Council, 1977–80 (first woman to represent Press side). Has been rejected as a catalogue holder by Empire Stores. *Recreations:* language and languages, music, compulsive reader. *Address:* c/o Robert Fleming & Co. Ltd, Hexagon House, 28 Western Road, Romford RM1 3LB; Arash Areesh, 7 Lakeview Road, Wicklow, Eire. *T:* (404) 69596.

KELLY, Susan; *see* Hamilton, S.

KELLY, Sir Theo, (William Theodore), Kt 1966; OBE 1958; JP; Chairman, Woolworths Ltd, Australia, 1963–80, retired (Managing Director, 1945–71), and its subsidiary and associated companies; Chairman: Woolworths (NZ) Ltd, 1963–79 (Director and General Manager, 1934–71); Woolworths Properties Limited, 1963–80; retired 1980; *b* 27 June 1907; *s* of W. T. Kelly; *m* 1944, Nancy Margaret, *d* of W. E. Williams, NZ; two *s* two *d.* War of 1939–45; RAAF, 1942–44, Wing Comdr. Chm., RAAF Canteen Services Bd, 1944–59. General Manager: Woolworths Ltd (NZ), 1932; Woolworths (Australia and NZ), 1945. Mem. Board, Reserve Bank of Australia, 1961–75; Dep. Chm., Australian Mutual Provident Soc., 1972–79 (Dir, 1967–79); Chm., Aust. Mutual Provident Fire and Gen. Insurance Pty Ltd, 1967–79. Life Governor, Royal Life Saving Soc.; Vice-Pres., Royal Hort. Soc., NSW; Trustee, National Parks and Wildlife Foundn, 1969–. Mem. Board, Royal North Shore Hosp., 1969–77. Fellow, Univ. of Sydney Senate, 1968–75. FAIM 1967. JP NSW, 1946. *Recreations:* golf, boating. *Address:* 8/73 Yarranabbe Road, Darling Point, Sydney, NSW 2027, Australia. *Clubs:* Sydney Rotary, American National, 18ft Sailing (Sydney).

KELLY, Sir William Theodore; *see* Kelly, Sir Theo.

KELSALL, John Arthur Brooks, MA; Headmaster, Brentwood School, Essex, since 1993; *b* 18 June 1943; *o s* of Joseph Brooks Kelsall and Dorothy Kelsall (*née* Bee); *m* 1965, Dianne Scott Woodward, *o d* of Rev. William James Vaughan Woodward and Jean Ewart Woodward; one *s* one *d. Educ:* Royal Grammar Sch., Lancaster; Emmanuel Coll., Cambridge (BA 1965; MA 1969). Head of Economics, King Edward VII Sch., Lytham St Annes, 1965–68; Head of Geography, Whitgift Sch., Croydon, 1968–78; Dep. Headmaster, 1978–81, Headmaster, 1981–87, Bournemouth Sch.; Headmaster, Arnold Sch., Blackpool, 1987–93. Vis. Headmaster, RAF Scholarship Board, RAF Cranwell, 1990–. *Recreations:* golf, fell-walking, opera, ornithology. *Address:* Brentwood School, Essex CM15 8AS. *T:* Brentwood (01277) 212271. *Clubs:* East India; Royal Lytham St Annes Golf.

KELSALL, William, OBE 1971; QPM 1969; DL; Chief Constable of Cheshire, 1974–77; retired; *b* 10 Jan. 1914. DL Cheshire, 1979. CStJ 1983. *Address:* Three Keys Cottage, Quarry Bank, Utkinton, Tarporley, Cheshire CW6 0LA.

KELSEY, Maj.-Gen. John, CBE 1968; Director, Wild Heerbrugg (UK) Ltd, 1978–87; Director of Military Survey, 1972–77; *b* 1 Nov. 1920; *s* of Benjamin Richard Kelsey and Daisy (*née* Powell); *m* 1944, Phyllis Margaret (*d* 1995), *d* of Henry Ernest Smith, Chingford; one *s* one *d. Educ:* Royal Masonic Sch.; Emmanuel Coll., Cambridge; Royal Mil. Coll. of Science. BSc. Commnd in RE, 1940; war service in N Africa and Europe; Lt-Col 1961; Col 1965; Dep. Dir Mil. Survey; Brig. Dir Field Survey, Ordnance Survey, 1968; Dir of Mil. Survey, Brig. 1972; Maj.-Gen. 1974. *Recreations:* Rugby football (played for Cambridge Univ., Richmond, Dorset, Wilts; Mem. RFU, 1965–66); sailing.

KELSEY, Linda; Editor, She magazine, since 1989; *b* 15 April 1952; *d* of Samuel Cohen and Rhona (*née* Fox); *m* 1972 (marr. diss. 1980); one *s* by Christian Testorf. *Educ:* Woodhouse Grammar Sch., N12. Sub-editor, Good Housekeeping, 1970–72; Features Editor, Cosmopolitan, 1975–78; Deputy Editor: Company, 1978–81; Options, 1981–82; Cosmopolitan, 1983–85, Editor, 1985–89. Editor of the Year Award: PPA, 1989, for Cosmopolitan; Brit. Soc. Mag. Editors, 1990, for She. *Recreations:* reading, theatre, film, family. *Address:* National Magazine House, 72 Broadwick Street, W1V 2BP. *Clubs:* Groucho, Royal Automobile.

KELSICK, Osmund Randolph, DFC 1944; Chairman and Managing Director, Carib Holdings Ltd (owning and operating The Blue Waters Beach Hotel), 1979–85, retired; Director: Caribbean Consultants Ltd; T. H. Kelsick Ltd (Montserrat); Caribbean Hotel Association; Antigua Hotel Association; *b* 21 July 1922; *s* of T. H. Kelsick; *m* 1950, Doreen Avis Hodge; one *s* (and one *s* decd); two step *d. Educ:* private preparatory sch.; Montserrat Grammar Sch.; Oxford Univ. (Devonshire Course). RAF, Fighter Pilot, 1940–46. ADC and Personal Sec. to Governor of the Leeward Islands, 1946–47; District Commissioner, Carriacou, 1947–51; Asst Chief Sec., Governor's Office, Grenada, 1951–52; Asst Administrator and Administrator, St Vincent, 1952–57. In 1956 seconded for short periods as Asst Trade Commissioner for British West Indies, British Guiana and British Honduras in UK, and Executive Sec. of Regional Economic Cttee in Barbados. Chief Sec., Leeward Islands, 1957–60. Past Pres., Caribbean Hotel Assoc. FRSA 1973. *Recreations:* fishing, gardening, tennis. *Address:* PO Box 454, Antigua, Leeward Islands, West Indies. *Clubs:* Commonwealth Trust; New (Antigua).

KEMBALL, Prof. Charles, CBE 1991; MA, ScD Cantab; FRS 1965; MRIA; FRSE; Hon. Fellow, Edinburgh University, since 1988 (Professor of Chemistry, 1966–83; Dean of the Faculty of Science, 1975–78); *b* 27 March 1923; *s* of late Charles Henry and Janet Kemball; *m* 1956, Kathleen Purvis, *o d* of late Dr and Mrs W. S. Lynd, Alsager, Cheshire; one *s* two *d. Educ:* Edinburgh Academy; Trinity Coll., Cambridge (Sen. Schol.). First Class Hons in Natural Sciences Tripos, Pt I, 1942, Pt II, 1943. Employed by Ministry of Aircraft Production in Dept of Colloid Science, University of Cambridge, 1943–46; Commonwealth Fund Fellow, Princeton Univ., 1946–47; Fellow of Trinity Coll., Cambridge, 1946–54 (Junior Bursar, 1949–51; Asst Lectr, 1951–54); Univ. Demonstrator in Physical Chemistry, 1951–54; Professor of Physical Chemistry, Queen's Univ., Belfast, 1954–66 (Dean of the Faculty of Science, 1957–60, Vice-Pres., 1962–65). President: RIC, 1974–76 (Vice-Pres., 1959–61); British Assoc. Section B (Chem.), 1976–77; RSE, 1988–91 (Vice-Pres., 1971–74, 1982–85); Vice-Pres., Faraday Soc., 1970–73; Chm., Publications Bd, Chem. Soc./RSC, 1973–81. Governor, East of Scotland Coll. of Agriculture, 1977–84. Hon. DSc: Heriot-Watt, 1980; QUB, 1983. Meldola Medal, 1951, Royal Inst. of Chemistry; Corday-Morgan Medal, 1958, Tilden Lectr, 1960, Surface and Colloid Chem. Award, 1972, Chemical Soc.; Ipatieff Prize, American Chemical Soc., 1962; Gunning Victoria Jubilee Prize, RSE, 1981; Award for Service to RSC, 1985. *Publications:* contributions to various scientific jls. *Recreations:* walking, gardening, genealogy. *Address:* 24 Main Street, Tyninghame, Dunbar, East Lothian EH42 1XL. *T:* East Linton (01620) 860710. *Clubs:* English-Speaking Union; New (Edinburgh).

KEMBALL, Brig. Humphrey Gurdon, CBE 1971 (OBE 1966); MC 1940; *b* 6 Nov. 1919; *s* of late Brig.-Gen. Alick Gurdon Kemball (late IA) and late Evelyn Mary (*née* Synge); *m* 1945, Ella Margery Emmeline (*née* Bickham); no *c. Educ:* Trinity Coll., Glenalmond; RMC, Sandhurst. Commissioned 1939, 1st Bn The Prince of Wales's Volunteers. Served War of 1939–45 (MC); Staff Coll., 1943. JSSC, 1956; commanded 1st Bn The Lancashire Regt (PWV), 1961–63; i/c Administration, HQ Federal Regular Army, Aden, 1964–66; Asst Dir, MoD, 1966–68; Mil. Attaché, Moscow, 1968–71; HQ British Forces, Near East, 1971–73; Dep. Comdr, SW District, 1973–74, retired. *Recreations:* fishing, travelling. *Address:* 28 Windsor End, Beaconsfield, Bucks HP9 2JW. *T:* Beaconsfield (01494) 671698. *Club:* Naval and Military.

KEMBALL, Air Marshal Sir (Richard) John, KCB 1990; CBE 1981; BA; Chairman, Essex Rivers Healthcare NHS Trust, since 1993; *b* 31 Jan. 1939; *s* of Richard and Margaret Kemball; *m* 1962, Valerie Geraldine Webster; two *d. Educ:* Uppingham; Open Univ. (BA 1991). Commissioned RAF, 1957; OC No 54 Squadron, 1977; OC RAF Laarbruch, 1979; Commandant, CFS, 1983–85; Comdr, British Forces, Falkland Islands, 1985–86; COS and Dep. C-in-C, Strike Command and UK Air Forces, 1989–93. ADC to HM The Queen, 1984–85. Hon. Col, 77 Engr Regt (V), 1993–. Vice-Pres., RAFA, 1993–; Gov., Corps of Commissionaires, 1993–. *Recreations:* country pursuits, tennis, cricket, gardening. *Address:* c/o Midland Bank plc, 46 Market Hill, Sudbury, Suffolk CO10 6ES. *Club:* Royal Air Force.

KEMBALL-COOK, Brian Hartley, MA Oxon; Headmaster, Bedford Modern School, 1965–77; *b* 12 Dec. 1912; *s* of Sir Basil Alfred Kemball-Cook, KCMG, CB, and Lady (Nancy Annie) Kemball-Cook (*née* Pavitt); *m* 1947, Marian, *d* of R. C. R. Richards, OBE; three *s* one *d. Educ:* Shrewsbury Sch. (Sidney Gold Medal for Classics); Balliol Coll., Oxford (Scholar). First Class Classical Honour Mods, 1933; First Class, Litt. Hum., 1935. Sixth Form Classics Master, Repton Sch., 1936–40. Intelligence Corps, 1940–46 (despatches); Regional Intelligence Officer and Political Adviser to Regional Comr, Hanover, 1946; Principal, Min. of Transport, 1946–47. Sen. Classics Master, Repton Sch., 1947–56; Headmaster, Queen Elizabeth's Grammar Sch., Blackburn, 1956–65. Chm., Bedfordshire Musical Festival, 1967–77. Croix de Guerre with Palm, 1946. *Publications:* Ed. Shakespeare, Coriolanus, 1954; trans., Homer, Odyssey, 1994; (contrib.) Education: Threatened Standards, 1972. *Recreations:* mountaineering, music. *Address:* 12 Francis Close, Hitchin, Herts SG4 9EJ. *T:* Hitchin (01462) 438862. *Club:* Climbers.

KEMBER, Anthony Joseph, MA; Communications Adviser, Department of Health, 1989–95; *b* 1 Nov. 1931; *s* of Thomas Kingsley Kember and May Lena (*née* Pryor); *m* 1957, Drusilla Mary (*née* Boyce); one *s* two *d. Educ:* St Edmund Hall, Oxford (MA). Associate, Inst. of Health Services Management (AHSM). Deputy House Governor and Secretary to Bd of Governors, Westminster Hospital, 1961–69; Gp Secretary, Hillingdon Gp Hospital Management Cttee, 1969–73; Area Administrator, Kensington and Chelsea and Westminster AHA(T), 1973–78; Administrator, 1978–84, Gen. Man., 1984–89, SW Thames RHA. Mem., SW London Area Adv. Cttee on Appointment of JPs, 1994–. Trustee, Disabled Living Foundn, 1981– (Chm., 1993–). Chm., Richmond Art Soc., 1995– (Sec., 1992–95). CIMgt (CBIM 1988). *Publications:* The NHS—a Kaleidoscope of Care, 1993; various articles for professional jls. *Recreations:* painting, inside and out; tennis, royal and common-or-garden. *Address:* 16 Orchard Rise, Richmond, Surrey TW10 5BX. *Clubs:* Roehampton; Royal Tennis Court (Hampton Court).

KEMBER, William Percy, FCA; FCT; Group Financial Controller, British Telecommunications, 1981–92; *b* 12 May 1932; *s* of late Percy Kember, Purley, and Mrs Q. A. Kember, Oxted, Surrey; *m* 1982, Lynn Kirkham. *Educ:* Uppingham. Chartered Accountant; Corporate Treasurer. Various posts with Royal Dutch/Shell Group in Venezuela, 1958–63; British Oxygen Co., 1963–67; Coopers & Lybrand, 1967–72; Post Office (Telecommunications), 1972–81. Director: Centel Financial Systems Inc., 1983–86; Marshalls Finance, 1991–. Visitor, Royal Institution, 1977, Chm., 1979. *Recreations:* golf, ski-ing. *Address:* 83 Hillway, N6 6AB. *Clubs:* Royal Automobile; Highgate Golf, Royal Dornoch Golf, Ski Club of Great Britain.

KEMMER, Prof. Nicholas, FRS 1956; FRSE 1954; MA Cantab, DrPhil Zürich; Tait Professor of Mathematical Physics, University of Edinburgh, 1953–79, now Professor Emeritus; *b* St Petersburg, 7 Dec. 1911; *o s* of late Nicholas P. Kemmer and of late Barbara Kemmer (*née* Stutzer; later Mrs Barbara Classen); *m* 1947, Margaret, *o d* of late George Wragg and late Nellie (who *m* 2nd, C. Rodway); two *s* one *d. Educ:* Bismarckschule, Hanover; Universities of Göttingen and Zürich. DrPhil Zürich, 1935; Imperial Coll., London: Beit Scientific Research Fellow, 1936–38; Demonstrator, 1938; Fellow 1971. Mem. of UK Govt Atomic Energy Research teams in Cambridge and Montreal, 1940–46; University Lecturer in Mathematics, Cambridge, 1946–53 (Stokes Lecturer since 1950). Hon. FInstP 1988. Hughes Medal, Royal Society, 1966; J. Robert Oppenheimer Meml Prize (Univ. of Miami), 1975; Max Planck Medal, German Physical Soc., 1983; Gunning Victoria Jubilee Prize, RSE, 1985. *Publications:* The Theory of Space, Time and Gravitation, 1959 (trans. from the Russian of V. Fock, 1955); What is Relativity?, 1960 (trans from the Russian, What is the theory of Relativity?, by Prof. L. D. Landau and Prof. G. B. Rumer, 1959); Vector Analysis, 1977; papers in scientific jls on theory of nuclear forces and elementary particles. *Address:* 35 Salisbury Road, Edinburgh EH16 5AA. *T:* 0131–667 2893.

KEMP, family name of **Viscount Rochdale.**

KEMP, Arnold; Consultant Editor, Caledonian Publishing, since 1994; *b* 15 Feb. 1939; *s* of Robert Kemp and Meta Strachan; *m* 1963, Sandra Elizabeth Shand (marr. diss.); two *d. Educ:* Edinburgh Academy; Edinburgh Univ. (MA). Sub-Editor, Scotsman, 1959–62, Guardian, 1962–65; Production Editor, Scotsman, 1965–70, London Editor, 1970–72, Dep. Editor, 1972–81; Editor, Glasgow Herald, subseq. The Herald, 1981–94. Dr *hc* Edinburgh, 1992. *Publication:* The Hollow Drum: Scotland since the war, 1993. *Recreations:* jazz, reading, theatre. *Address:* 8 Buckingham Gate, 2 Queen Margaret Drive, Glasgow G12 8DQ. *Clubs:* Caledonian; Glasgow Art.

KEMP, Rear-Adm. Cuthbert Francis, CB 1967; Chief Service Manager, Westland Helicopters, 1968–69; *b* 15 Sept. 1913; *s* of A. E. Kemp, Willingdon; *m* 1947, Margaret Law, *d* of L. S. Law, New York; two *s. Educ:* Victoria Coll., Jersey. Joined RN, 1931; RN Engrg Coll., 1936. Served in HMS Ajax and Hood; Pilot, 1939. Served War of 1939–45: carriers and air stations at home and abroad; Naval Staff, Washington, 1945–47; Fleet Engr Officer, E Indies, 1950–52; qual. Staff Coll., 1956; Admty, 1957–59; qual. Canadian Nat. Defence Coll., 1962; Supt RN Aircraft Yard, Belfast, 1962–65; ADC 1965; Rear-Adm., Engineering, Staff of Flag Officer, Naval Air Command, 1965, retd 1967. *Recreations:* cricket, gardening, shooting. *Address:* Beech House, Marston Magna, Som BA22 8DQ. *T:* Marston Magna (01935) 850563. *Club:* Army and Navy.

KEMP, David Ashton McIntyre, QC 1973; a Recorder of the Crown Court, since 1976; *b* 14 Oct. 1921; *s* of late Sir Kenneth McIntyre Kemp and Margaret Caroline Clare Kemp; *m* 1st, 1949, Margaret Sylvia Jones (*d* 1971); 2nd, 1972, Maureen Ann Frances Stevens, *widow. Educ:* Winchester Coll.; Corpus Christi Coll., Cambridge. 1st cl. hons Law Cantab. Called to Bar, Inner Temple, 1948, Bencher, 1980. *Publications:* (with M. S. Kemp) The Quantum of Damages, Personal Injuries Claims, 1954 (4th edn 1975); (with M. S. Kemp) The Quantum of Damages, Fatal Accident Claims, 1956 (4th edn 1975). *Recreations:* ski-ing, tennis, gardening. *Address:* 63 Brixton Water Lane, SW2 1PH. *T:* 0171–733 9735. *Clubs:* Hurlingham, Ski Club of Great Britain; Kandahar Ski.

KEMP, Sir (Edward) Peter, KCB 1991 (CB 1988); Executive, Foundation for Accountancy and Financial Management, since 1993; *b* 10 Oct. 1934; *s* of late Thomas Kemp and Nancie (*née* Sargent); *m* 1961, Enid van Popta; three *s* one *d. Educ:* Millfield Sch.; Royal Naval Coll., Dartmouth. FCA (ACA 1959). Principal, later Asst Sec., Min. of Transport, 1967–73; HM Treasury, 1973, Under-Sec., 1978, Dep. Sec., 1983; Second Perm. Sec. and Next Steps Project Manager, Cabinet Office (OMCS, subseq. Office of Public Service and Sci.), 1988–92. Comr, Audit Commission, 1993–. *Publications:* Beyond Next Steps: a civil service for the twenty-first century, 1993; articles and pieces. *Address:* 2 Longton Avenue, SE26 6QJ. *Club:* Reform.

KEMP, Rt. Rev. Eric Waldram; *see* Chichester, Bishop of.

KEMP, Air Vice-Marshal George John, CB 1976; *b* 14 July 1921; *m* 1943, Elspeth Beatrice Peacock; one *s* two *d.* Commnd RAF, 1941; served in night fighter sqdns with spell on ferrying aircraft to Middle East; served in Iraq, 1953–54 and Far East, 1960–61; Stn Comdr RAF Upwood, 1968–69; Dir of Manning RAF, 1970–71; Dir of Personnel (Policy and Plans) RAF, 1972; Dir-Gen. of Personnel Management, RAF, 1973–75. *Recreations:* many and various. *Address:* Old Court, Woolley Street, Bradford on Avon, Wilts BA15 1AE. *T:* Bradford on Avon (01225) 867832. *Club:* Royal Air Force.

KEMP, Hubert Bond Stafford, MS; FRCS, FRCSE; Hon. Consultant Orthopaedic Surgeon, since 1992; Consultant Orthopaedic Surgeon: Royal National Orthopaedic Hospital, London and Stanmore, 1974–92; The Middlesex Hospital, 1984–90; Hon. Consultant Orthopaedic Surgeon, St Luke's Hospital for the Clergy, 1975–90, University Teacher in Orthopaedics; *b* 25 March 1925; *s* of John Stafford Kemp and Cecilia Isabel (*née* Bond); *m* 1967, Moyra Ann Margaret Odgers; three *d. Educ:* Cardiff High Sch.; Univ. of South Wales; St Thomas' Hosp., Univ. of London (MB, BS 1949; MS 1969); MRCS, LRCP 1947; FRCSE 1960; FRCS 1970. Robert Jones Gold Medal and Assoc. Prize, 1969 (Proxime Accessit, 1964); Hunterian Prof., RCS, 1969; Hon. Consultant, Royal Nat. Orthopaedic Hosp., London and Stanmore, 1965–74; Sen. Lectr, Inst. of Orthopaedics, 1965–74, Hon. Sen. Lectr, 1974–90. Vis. Professor, VII Congress of Soc. Latino Amer. de Orthopedia y Traumatologica, 1971. Member: MRC Working Party on Tuberculosis of the Spine, 1974–; MRC Working Party on Osteosarcoma, 1985–94. Fellow, Brit. Orthopaedic Assoc., 1972–; Chm., London Bone Tumour Unit, 1985–91; Member: Brit. Orthopaedic Research Soc., 1967–; Internat. Skeletal Soc., 1977–. *Publications:* (jtly) Orthopaedic Diagnosis, 1984; chapter in: A Postgraduate Textbook of Clinical Orthopaedics, 1983, 2nd edn 1995; Baillière's Clinical Oncology, Bone Tumours, 1987; (contrib.) Essential Surgical Practice, 3rd edn, 1995; papers on diseases of the spine, the hip, bone tumours. *Recreations:* fishing, painting. *Address:* 55 Loom Lane, Radlett, Herts WD7 8NX. *T:* Radlett (01923) 854265; 45 Bolsover Street, W1P 8AQ. *T:* 0171–383 5656, 0171–387 5070.

See also G. D. W. Odgers.

KEMP, Prof. Kenneth Oliver, FEng 1988; Emeritus Professor of Civil Engineering and Fellow, University College London, 1984; *b* 19 Oct. 1926; *s* of Eric Austen Kemp; *m* 1952, Josephine Gloria (*née* Donovan); no *c. Educ:* University College London. BSc(Eng), PhD; FICE, FIStructE. Surveyor, Directorate of Colonial Surveys, 1947–49; Asst Engr, Collins and Mason, Consulting Engrs, 1949–54. University College London: Lectr, Sen. Lectr, Dept of Civil Engrg, 1954–69; Reader in Structural Engrg, 1969–70; Chadwick Prof. of Civil Engrg and Hd of Civil Engrg Dept, 1970–84. *Publications:* papers in: Proc. Instn of Civil Engrs; The Structural Engr; Magazine of Concrete Research; Internat. Assoc. of Bridge and Structural Engrg. *Address:* Rowan Cottage, Brinton, Melton Constable, Norfolk NR24 2QF. *T:* Melton Constable (01263) 860631.

KEMP, Kenneth Reginald; Director, since 1962, and Hon. Life President, 1990, Smith & Nephew plc (Chairman, 1976–90); *b* 13 Nov. 1921; *s* of Philip R. Kemp and Siew Pukalanan of Thailand; *m* 1949, Florence M. Hetherington. *Educ:* Bradfield College, Berks. FCA. Joined Leeds Rifles, 1939; commissioned Royal Artillery, 1940–46; served in France, Germany, India, Far East (Captain). Peat, Marwick Mitchell & Co., 1947; qualified CA, 1950; Smith & Nephew: Company Sec., 1953, later Finance Dir; Chief Exec., 1968–76. *Recreations:* unlimited. *Address:* Smith & Nephew, 2 Temple Place, WC2R 3BP. *T:* 0171–836 7922.

KEMP, Leslie Charles, CBE 1982; FCIArb; Chairman, Griffiths McGee Ltd, Demolition Contractors, 1982–87; Proprietor, Leslie Kemp Associates, since 1976; *b* 10 Oct. 1920; *s* of Thomas and Violet Kemp. *Educ:* Hawkhurst Moor Boys' School. Apprentice blacksmith, 1934–39; served War, 1939–46: Infantry, N Africa and Italy. Civil Engrg Equipment Operator, 1947–51; District Organiser, 1951–57, Regional Organiser, 1958–63, Nat. Sec. (Construction), TGWU, 1963–76. Jt Registrar, 1975–76, Dep. Chm., 1976–81, Demolition and Dismantling Industry Registration Council. Member, Nat. Jt Council for

Building Industry, 1957–76; Operatives Sec., Civil Engrg Construction Conciliation Bd for GB, 1963–76; Mem., 1964–73, Dep. Chm., 1973–76, Chm., 1976–85, Construction Industry Trng Bd (Chm., Civil Engrg Cttee, 1964–76); Member: EDC for Civil Engrg, 1964–76; Construction Ind. Liaison Gp, 1974–76; Construction Ind. Manpower Bd, 1976–; Bragg Adv. Cttee on Falsework, 1973–75; Vice-Pres., Construction Health and Safety Gp. Chm., Corby Develt Corp., 1976–80; Dep. Chm., Peterborough Develt Corp., 1974–82. Member, Outward Bound Trust, 1977–88; Pres., W Norfolk Outward Bound Assoc., 1983–88. Chm., Syderstone Parish Council, 1983–87. Construction News Man of the Year Award, 1973; in recognition of services to trng, Leslie Kemp Europ. Prize for Civil Engrg trainees to study in France, instituted 1973. CompICE; FIMgt. *Recreations:* travel, bird-watching, fishing. *Address:* Lamberts Yard, Syderstone, King's Lynn, Norfolk PE31 8SF. *Clubs:* Lighthouse; Fakenham Golf (Pres., 1985–88).

KEMP, Lindsay; Founder, Artistic Director and Principal Performer, Lindsay Kemp Co., since 1962; painter, designer, teacher; *b* 3 May 1938; *s* of Norman Kemp and Marie (*née* Gilmour). *Educ:* Sunshine Sch. of Dancing, Bradford; Royal Merchant Navy Sch., Bearwood; Bradford Coll. of Art; Sigurd Leeder Sch. of Modern Dance; Ballet Rambert Sch.; studied with Marcel Marceau. Lindsay Kemp Co. productions include: Illuminations, Lyric, Hammersmith, 1965; Turquoise Pantomime; Woyzeck; Salomé; Legends; Flowers, West End, 1974, later Broadway and world tour, 1974–94; Mr Punch's Pantomime; A Midsummer Night's Dream; Duende; Nijinsky; Façade; The Big Parade; Alice; Onnagata; Cinderella: a gothic operetta. Dir, David Bowie's Ziggy Stardust concerts, 1972; created for Ballet Rambert: The Parade's Gone By, 1975; Cruel Garden, 1978; film appearances include: Savage Messiah, 1971; The Lindsay Kemp Circus, 1971; Wicker Man, 1972; Sebastian, 1974; Jubilee, 1977; Italian Postcards, 1986; Travelling Light, 1993. *Publication:* (with D. Haughton) Drawing and Dancing, 1988; *relevant publications:* Lindsay Kemp, by David Haughton, 1982; Flowers, 1987. *Recreation:* interior decorating. *Address:* Via del Tempio 1A, Interno 13, 00186 Rome, Italy; Ex Monastero S Maria, Rosceto, Fraz. Colvalenza, Todi, Umbria, Italy.

KEMP, Prof. Martin John, FBA 1991; Professor of the History of Art, and Fellow of Trinity College, Oxford University, since 1995; British Academy Wolfson Research Professor, since 1993; *b* 5 March 1942; *s* of Frederick Maurice Kemp and Violet Anne Tull; *m* 1966, Jill Lightfoot, *d* of Dennis William Lightfoot and Joan Betteridge; one *s* one *d. Educ:* Windsor Grammar Sch.; Cambridge Univ. (MA Nat. Scis and Art History); Courtauld Inst. of Art, London Univ. (Academic Dip.). Lectr in History of Art, Dalhousie Univ., Halifax, NS, Canada, 1965–66; Lectr in History of Fine Art, Univ. of Glasgow, 1966–81; Fellow, Inst. for Advanced Study, Princeton, 1984–85; University of St Andrews: Prof. of Fine Arts, subseq. of Hist. and Theory of Art, 1981–95; Associate Dean of Graduate Studies, Faculty of Arts, 1983–87; Mem. Court, 1988–91; Provost of St Leonard's Coll., 1991–95. Prof. of History and Hon. Mem., Royal Scottish Acad., 1985–; Slade Prof. of Fine Art, Cambridge Univ., 1987–88; Visiting Professor: Benjamin Sonnenberg, Inst. of Fine Arts, New York Univ., 1988; Wiley, Univ. of N Carolina, Chapel Hill, 1993. Chair, Assoc. of Art Historians, 1989–92; Member: Board, Scottish Museums Council, 1990–95; Res. Awards Adv. Cttee, Leverhulme Trust, 1991–; Board, Mus. Trng Inst., 1993–; Board, Interalia, 1993–; Council, British Soc. for History of Sci., 1994–. Pres., Leonardo da Vinci Soc., 1987–. Trustee: National Gall. of Scotland, 1982–87; V&A Museum, 1985–89. FRSA 1983; FRSE 1992. Hon. FRIAS 1988. Broadcasts, Radio 3 and TV. Hon. DLitt Heriot-Watt, 1995. Mitchell Prize for best first book in English on Art History, 1981; Armand Hammer Prize for Leonardo Studies, 1992. *Publications:* Leonardo da Vinci, The Marvellous Works of Nature and Man, 1981; (jtly) Leonardo da Vinci, 1989; (jtly) Leonardo on Painting, 1989; The Science of Art, 1990; articles in Jl of Warburg and Courtauld Insts, Burlington Magazine, Art History, Art Bull., Connoisseur, Procs of British Acad., Jl of RSA, L'Arte, Bibliothèque d'Humanisme et Renaissance, Med. History, TLS, London Rev. of Books, Guardian, Sunday Times, etc. *Recreations:* hockey, running, gardening, avoiding academics. *Address:* Trinity College, Oxford OX1 3BH.

KEMP, Oliver, CMG 1969; OBE 1960; HM Diplomatic Service, retired; *b* 12 Sept. 1916; *s* of Walter Kemp; *m* 1940, Henrietta Taylor; two *s. Educ:* Wakefield Grammar Sch.; Queen's Coll., Oxford. MA Oxon (Lit. Hum.), 1939. Served in HM Forces, 1939–45. Apptd Officer in HM Foreign Service, 1945; served in Moscow, Egypt, Indonesia, Yemen, Laos, Mongolia and Foreign Office. HM Chargé d'Affaires in Yemen, 1957–58; First Secretary and Head of Chancery in Laos, 1958–60; Ambassador to Togo (and Consul-General), 1962–64; Deputy Head of the United Kingdom Delegation to the European Communities, Luxembourg, 1964–67; Ambassador to Mongolia, 1967–68; FCO, 1968–70 and 1971–73 (European affairs). Dir, BSC Office, Brussels, 1973–81. *Recreations:* music, reading, gardening. *Address:* 16 The Oval, Scarborough, N Yorks YO11 3AP. *T:* Scarborough (01723) 373354.

KEMP, Sir Peter; *see* Kemp, Sir E. P.

KEMP, Robert Thayer; export credit consultant; non-executive Director, Sedgwick Credit Ltd, since 1989; *b* 18 June 1928; *s* of Robert Kemp and Ada Kemp (*née* Thayer); *m* 1951, Gwendolyn Mabel Minty; three *s. Educ:* Bromley Grammar Sch.; London Univ. (BA (Hons) Medieval and Mod. History). Export Credits Guarantee Department: Asst Sec., 1970; Under-Sec., 1975; Head of Project Underwriting Gp, 1981–85; Dir, Internat. Gp, 1985–88, retd. *Publication:* Review of Future Status Options (ECGD), 1989. *Recreations:* cricket, music, theatre. *Address:* 294 Tubbenden Lane South, Farnborough, Orpington, Kent BR6 7DN. *T:* Orpington (01689) 53924.

KEMP, Thomas Arthur, MD; FRCP; Physician, St Mary's Hospital, 1947–75, Paddington General Hospital 1950–75; *b* 12 Aug. 1915; *s* of Fred Kemp and Edith Peters; *m* 1942, Ruth May Scott-Keat; one *s* one *d. Educ:* Denstone Coll.; St Catharine's Coll., Cambridge (Exhibitioner); St Mary's Hospital, London (Scholar). MB, BChir 1940; MRCP 1941; FRCP 1949; MD 1953. Examiner in Medicine, Universities of London and Glasgow. FRSM (Jt Hon. Sec., 1961–67). Served in Middle East, 1944–47; Lt-Col RAMC Officer i/c Medical Division; Hon. Cons. Physician to the Army, 1972–75. Pres. Brit. Student Health Assoc., 1962–63; Chm. Brit. Student Tuberculosis Foundation, 1963–65. Fellow, Midland Div., Woodard Schs, 1962–85; Commonwealth Travelling Fellowship, 1967. *Publications:* papers in medical journals. *Recreations:* games, especially Rugby football (played for Cambridge, 1936, for Barbarians, 1936–49, for St Mary's Hosp., 1937–43, for England, 1937–48 (Captain, 1948, Selector, 1954–61); President: Rugby Football Union, 1971–72; Students' RFU, 1980–). *Address:* 2 Woodside Road, Northwood, Mddx HA6 3QE. *T:* Northwood (01923) 821068. *Club:* Hawks (Cambridge).

KEMP-WELCH, John; Chairman, London Stock Exchange, since 1994 (Director, since 1991); *b* 31 March 1936; *s* of Peter Wellesbourne Kemp-Welch and Peggy Penelope Kemp-Welch; *m* 1964, Diana Elisabeth Leishman; one *s* three *d. Educ:* Winchester Coll. CIMgt (CBIM 1984). Hoare & Co., 1954–58; Cazenove & Co., 1959–94 (Jt Sen. Partner, 1980–94). Chairman: Scottish Eastern Investment Trust, 1994– (Dir, 1993–); Lowland Investment Co., 1993– (Dir, 1963–); Claridge's Hotel, 1995–; Director: Savoy Hotel PLC, 1985–; SunAlliance Gp, 1994–; British Invisibles, 1994–; Pro Share, 1995–. Dep. Chm., Financial Reporting Council, 1994–; Dir, SFA, 1994–. Member: City Capital Markets Cttee, 1989–94; Panel on Takeovers and Mergers, 1994–. Governor: Ditchley Foundn, 1980–; North Foreland Lodge Sch., 1980–92; Chm., King's Med. Res. Trust, 1991– (Trustee, 1984–); Trustee and Mem. Council, Game Conservancy Trust, 1990–; Trustee: Sandford St Martin Trust, 1994–; Dulverton Trust, 1994–. MSI 1992; FRSA 1989. Joseph Nickerson Heather Award, Joseph Nickerson Heather Improvement Foundn, 1988. *Recreations:* the hills of Perthshire, country life, cricket, champagne and claret, Impressionist paintings, heather moorland management. *Address:* 12 Tokenhouse Yard, EC2R 7AN. *Clubs:* White's, City of London, Pilgrims, MCC.

KEMPE, John William Rolfe, CVO 1980; Headmaster of Gordonstoun, 1968–78; *b* 29 Oct. 1917; *s* of late William Alfred Kempe and Kunigunda Neville-Rolfe; *m* 1957, Barbara Nan Stephen, *d* of late Dr C. R. Huxtable, MC, FRCS and of Mrs Huxtable, OAM, Sydney, Australia; two *s* one *d. Educ:* Stowe; Clare Coll., Cambridge (Exhibitioner in Mathematics). Served war of 1939–45, RAFVR Training and Fighter Command; CO 153 and 255 Night Fighter Squadrons. Board of Trade, 1945; Firth-Brown (Overseas) Ltd, 1946–47; Head of Maths Dept, Gordonstoun, 1948–51; Principal, Hyderabad Public Sch., Deccan, India, 1951–54; Headmaster, Corby Grammar School, Northants, 1955–67. Chm., Round Square Internat. Service Cttee, 1979–87; Vice-Chm., The European Atlantic Movement, 1982–. Exploration and mountaineering, Himalayas, Peru, 1952–56; Member: Cttee, Mount Everest Foundation, 1956–62; Cttee, Brathay Exploration Group, 1964–73; Foundn Trustee, Univ. of Cambridge Kurt Hahn Trust, 1986–89; Trustee: Thornton Smith Trust, 1981–; Plevins Charity, 1987–. FRGS. *Publications:* articles in Alpine Jl, Geographical Jl, Sociological Review. *Address:* Maple Tree Cottage, 24 Old Leicester Road, Wansford, near Peterborough PE8 6JR. *Club:* Alpine.

KEMPNER, Prof. Thomas; Hon. Professor, Brunel University, 1990–91, now Professor Emeritus (Professor of Management Studies and Director of Business Studies, 1972–90); Professor Emeritus, Henley The Management College (formerly Administrative Staff College), since 1990 (Principal and Professor of Management Studies, 1972–90); Director, Henley Centre for Forecasting, since 1974 (Chairman, 1974–95); Chairman, Henley Distance Learning Ltd, 1985–95; *b* 28 Feb. 1930; *s* of late Martin and Rosa Kempner; *m* 1st, 1958, June Maton (*d* 1980); two *d* (and one *d* decd); 2nd, 1981, Mrs Veronica Ann Vere-Sharp; one step *s* two step *d. Educ:* University Coll. London (BSc (Econ)). Asst Administrator, Hyelm Youth Hostels, 1948–49, and part-time, 1951–55; Research Officer, Administrative Staff Coll., Henley, 1954–59; Lectr (later Sen. Tutor) in Business Studies, Sheffield Univ., 1959–63; Prof. of Management Studies, Founder, and Dir of Management Centre, Univ. of Bradford, 1963–72. Member of various cttees, including: Social Studies and Business Management Cttees of University Grants Cttee, 1966–76; Management, Education and Training Cttee of NEDO, 1969–72 (Chm. of its Student Grants Sub-Cttee); Chm., Food Industry Manpower Cttee of NEDO, 1968–71; Jt Chm., Conf. of Univ. Management Schools, 1973–75. Vice-Chm., Council, Brunel Univ., 1992–. CIMgt (FBIM 1971). Hon. DSc Cranfield, 1976; Hon. LLD Birmingham, 1983; DUniv Brunel, 1990. Burnham Gold Medal, 1970. *Publications:* editor, author, and contributor to several books, including: Bradford Exercises in Management (with G. Wills), 1966; Is Corporate Planning Necessary? (with J. Hewkin), 1968; A Guide to the Study of Management, 1969; Management Thinkers (with J. Tillet and G. Wills), 1970; Handbook of Management, 1971, 4th edn 1987; (with K. Macmillan and K. H. Hawkins) Business and Society, 1974; Models for Participation, 1976; numerous articles in Management jls. *Recreation:* travel. *Address:* Garden House, Maidensgrove, Henley-on-Thames, Oxon RG9 6EZ. *T:* Henley-on-Thames (01491) 638597.

KEMPSON, Rachel, (Lady Redgrave); actress; *b* Devon, 28 May 1910; *d* of Eric William Edward Kempson and Beatrice Hamilton Ashwell Kempson; *m* 1935, Sir Michael Redgrave, CBE (*d* 1985); one *s* two *d. Educ:* St Agnes Convent, East Grinstead; Colchester County High Sch.; Oaklea, Buckhurst Hill; RADA. First stage appearance in Much Ado About Nothing, Stratford, 1933; first London appearance in The Lady from Alfaqueque, Westminster, 1933; Stratford season, 1934; Liverpool Playhouse, 1935–36; Love's Labour's Lost, Old Vic, 1936; Volpone, Westminster, 1937; Twelfth Night, Oxford, 1937; The School for Scandal, Queen's, 1937; The Shoemaker's Holiday, Playhouse, 1938; Under One Roof, Richmond, 1940; The Wingless Victory, Phoenix, 1943; Uncle Harry, Garrick, 1944; Jacobowsky and the Colonel, Piccadilly, 1945; Fatal Curiosity, Arts, 1946; The Paragon, Fortune, 1948; The Return of the Prodigal, Globe, 1948; Candida, Oxford, 1949; Venus Observed, Top of the Ladder, St James's, 1950; The Happy Time, St James's, 1952; Shakespeare Meml Theatre Co., 1953; English Stage Co., 1956; The Seagull, St Joan of the Stockyards, Queen's, 1964; Samson Agonistes, Lionel and Clarissa, Guildford, 1965; A Sense of Detachment, Royal Court, 1972; The Freeway, National Theatre, 1974; A Family and a Fortune, Apollo, 1975; The Old Country, Queen's, 1977; Savannah Bay, Royal Court, 1983; Chekhov's Women, Queen's, 1986; The Cocktail Party, Phoenix, 1986; Uncle Vanya, Vaudeville, 1988; Coriolanus, Young Vic, 1989. *Films* include: The Captive Heart, 1945; Georgy Girl; The Jokers; Charge of the Light Brigade; The Virgin Soldiers; Jane Eyre; Out of Africa, 1985; The Understanding, 1985. Frequent *television* appearances include series and serials: Elizabeth R; Jennie; Love for Lydia; The Bell, 1981; The Jewel in the Crown, 1984; The Black Tower, 1985; Small World, 1988; plays: Winter Ladies, Sweet Wine of Youth, 1979; Kate, the Good Neighbour, Getting On, The Best of Everything, and Jude, 1980; Blunt Instrument, Bosom Friends, and The Boxwallah, 1981; World's Beyond, 1986; Boon, She's been away, 1989; Lorna Doone, For the Greater Good, Uncle Vanya, 1990; *radio:* Hester, in The Forsyte Saga, 1990. *Publication:* A Family and its Fortunes (autobiog.), 1986. *Recreations:* gardening, letter writing. *Address:* c/o Philip Shaw, Creative Artists Management, 11–15 Betterton Street, Covent Garden, WC2H 9BF.

See also Lynn Redgrave, Vanessa Redgrave.

KEMPSON, Prof. Ruth Margaret, (Mrs M. J. Pinner), FBA 1989; Professor of General Linguistics, since 1987 and Head of Linguistics Department, since 1992, University of London, at School of Oriental and African Studies; *b* 26 June 1944; *d* of Edwin Garnett Hone Kempson and Margaret Cecilia Kempson; *m* 1973, Michael John Pinner; two *s. Educ:* Univ. of Birmingham (BA (2 ii) Music and English); Univ. of London (MA (with dist.) Mod. English Language 1969; PhD Linguistics 1972). Res. Asst to Survey of English Usage, UCL, 1969–70; Lectr in Linguistics, SOAS, 1971–85; Reader in Gen. Linguistics, Univ. of London, 1985–87. Vis. Prof. in Semantics, Univ. of Massachusetts, 1982–83. Pres., Linguistics Assoc. of GB, 1986–91. *Publications:* Presupposition and the Delimitation of Semantics, 1975; Semantic Theory, 1977; Mental Representations: the interface between language and reality, 1988; articles in Linguistics and Philosophy, Jl of Linguistics and edited collections. *Address:* Linguistics Department, School of Oriental and African Studies, Thornhaugh Street, Russell Square, WC1H 0XG. *T:* 0171–637 2388.

KEMPSTER, Hon. Michael Edmund Ivor, CBE 1993; a Justice of Appeal, Court of Appeal, Bermuda, since 1993; a Justice of Appeal, 1984–93, Vice-President, 1993, of the Supreme Court of Hong Kong (a Judge of the Supreme Court, 1982–84); Commissioner, Supreme Court of Brunei, since 1983; *b* 21 June 1923; *s* of late Rev. Ivor T. Kempster, DSO; *m* 1949, Sheila, *d* of late Dr T. Chalmers, KiH, Inverness; two *s* two *d. Educ:* Mill

Hill Sch.; Brasenose Coll., Oxford (Scholar, MA, BCL). Royal Signals, 1943–46; commissioned in India, served 14th Army. Called to Bar, Inner Temple, 1949; Profumo Prize; Bencher 1977. QC 1969; a Recorder of the Crown Court, 1972–81. Mem., Govt Cttee on Privacy, 1971; apptd to report to Gov. of Hong Kong on an incident in a Vietnamese Detention Centre, 1992; Comr to report to Gov. of Hong Kong on Witness Protection, 1993. Chm., Court of Governors, Mill Hill School, 1979–82. FCIArb, 1982. *Recreations:* fishing, hare-hunting, travel. *Address:* 5 King's Bench Walk, Temple, EC4Y 7DN; Knapp House, Gillingham, Dorset SP8 4NQ. *Clubs:* Travellers, Pilgrims; Hong Kong (Hong Kong).

KEMSLEY, 2nd Viscount *cr* 1945, of Dropmore; **(Geoffrey) Lionel Berry,** DL; Bt 1928; Baron 1936; *b* 29 June 1909; *e s* of 1st Viscount Kemsley, GBE and Mary Lilian (*d* 1928), *d* of Horace George Holmes; *S* father, 1968; *m* 1933, Lady Helen Hay, DStJ, *e d* of 11th Marquess of Tweeddale; four *d. Educ:* Marlborough; Magdalen Coll., Oxford. Served War of 1939–45. Capt. Grenadier Guards; invalided out of Army, 1942. MP (C) Buckingham Div. of Bucks, 1943–45. Dep. Chm., Kemsley Newspapers Ltd, 1938–59. Chm., St Andrew's Hospital, Northampton, 1973–84; Pres., Assoc. of Independent Hospitals, 1976–83. Mem. Chapter General, Order of St John. Master of Spectacle Makers' Co., 1949–51, 1959–61. CC Northants, 1964–70; High Sheriff of Leicestershire, 1967, DL 1972. FRSA; KStJ. *Heir: nephew* Richard Gomer Berry [*b* 17 April 1951; *m* 1981, Tana-Marie, *e d* of Clive Lester]. *Address:* Field House, Thorpe Lubenham, Market Harborough, Leics LE16 9TR. *T:* Market Harborough (01858) 462816. *Clubs:* Pratt's, Royal Over-Seas League.

See also Sir G. N. Mobbs.

KENDAL, Felicity Ann, CBE 1995; actress; *d* of Geoffrey and late Laura Kendal; *m* (marr. diss.); one *s*; *m* 1983, Michael Rudman (marr. diss. 1994), *qv*; one *s. Educ:* six convents in India. First appeared on stage at age of 9 months, when carried on as the Changeling boy in A Midsummer Night's Dream; grew up touring India and Far East with parents' theatre co., playing pageboys at age of eight and graduating through Puck, at nine, to parts such as Viola in Twelfth Night, Jessica in The Merchant of Venice, and Ophelia in Hamlet; returned to England, 1965; made London debut, Carla in Minor Murder, Savoy, 1967; Katherine in Henry V, and Lika in The Promise, Leicester, 1968; Amaryllis in Back to Methuselah, Nat. Theatre, 1969; Hermia in A Midsummer Night's Dream, and Hero in Much Ado About Nothing, Regent's Park, 1970; Anne Danby in Kean, Oxford, 1970, London, 1971; Romeo and Juliet, 'Tis Pity She's A Whore, and The Three Arrows, 1972; The Norman Conquests, Globe, 1974; Viktosha in Once Upon a Time, Bristol, 1976; Arms and The Man, Greenwich, 1978; Mara in Clouds, Duke of York's, 1978; Constance Mozart in Amadeus, NT, 1979; Desdemona in Othello, NT, 1980; Christopher in On the Razzle, NT, 1981; Paula in The Second Mrs Tanqueray, NT, 1981; The Real Thing, Strand, 1982; Jumpers, Aldwych, 1985; Made in Bangkok, Aldwych, 1986; Hapgood, Aldwych, 1988; Ivanov, and Much Ado About Nothing, Strand, 1989 (Best Actress Award, Evening Standard); Hidden Laughter, Vaudeville, 1990; Tartuffe, Playhouse, 1991; Heartbreak House, Haymarket, 1992; Arcadia, NT, 1993; An Absolute Turkey, Globe, 1994; Indian Ink, Aldwych, 1995. *Television:* four series of The Good Life, 1975–77; Viola in Twelfth Night, 1979; Solo, 1980, 2nd series 1982; The Mistress, 1985, 2nd series 1986; The Camomile Lawn, 1992; Honey for Tea, 1994; plays and serials. *Films:* Shakespeare Wallah, 1965; Valentino, 1976. Variety Club Most Promising Newcomer, 1974, Best Actress, 1979; Clarence Derwent Award, 1980; Variety Club Woman of the Year Best Actress Award, 1984. *Recreation:* reading, working. *Address:* c/o Chatto & Linnit, Prince of Wales Theatre, Coventry Street, W1V 7FE. *T:* 0171–930 6677.

KENDALL, Prof. David George, DSc; ScD; FRS 1964; Professor of Mathematical Statistics, University of Cambridge, 1962–85 and Fellow of Churchill College, since 1962; *b* 15 Jan. 1918; *s* of Fritz Ernest Kendall and Emmie Taylor, Ripon, Yorks; *m* 1952, Diana Louise Fletcher; two *s* four *d. Educ:* Ripon GS; Queen's Coll., Oxford (MA, 1943; Hon. Fellow 1985); DSc Oxford, 1977; ScD Cambridge, 1988. Fellow Magdalen Coll., Oxford, and Lectr in Mathematics, 1946–62 (Emeritus Fellow, 1989). Visiting Lecturer: Princeton Univ., USA, 1952–53 (Wilks Prize, 1980); Zhong-shan Univ., Guangzhou; Xiangtan Univ.; Changsha Inst. Rlwys; Jiaotong Univ., Xi'an, 1983. Lectures: Larmor, Cambridge Philos. Soc., 1980; Milne, Wadham Coll., Oxford, 1983; Hotelling, Univ. of N Carolina, 1985; Rietz, Inst. of Math. Stats, 1989; Kolmogorov, Bernoulli Soc., 1990. Member: Internat. Statistical Inst.; Academia Europaea, 1991; Council, Royal Society, 1967–69, 1982–83; President: London Mathematical Soc., 1972–74; Internat. Assoc. Statist. in Phys. Sci., 1973–75; Bernoulli Soc. for Mathematical Stats and Probability, 1975; Section A (Math.) and Section P (Physics), BAAS, 1982. Chm. Parish Reg. Sect., Yorks Archaeol. Soc., 1974–79. Hon. Mem., Romanian Acad., 1992. Hon. D. de l'U Paris (René Descartes), 1976; Hon. DSc Bath, 1986. Guy Medal in Silver, Royal Statistical Soc., 1955; Weldon Meml Prize and Medal for Biometric Science, 1974; Sylvester Medal, Royal Soc., 1976; Whitehead Prize, London Math. Soc., 1980; Guy Medal in Gold, Royal Statistical Soc., 1981; De Morgan Medal, London Math. Soc., 1989. *Publications:* (jt ed) Mathematics in the Archaeological and Historical Sciences, 1971; (jt ed) Stochastic Analysis, 1973; (jt ed) Stochastic Geometry, 1974; (ed) Analytic and Geometric Stochastics, 1986. *Address:* 37 Barrow Road, Cambridge CB2 2AR.

KENDALL, David William; Chairman: Ruberoid plc, since 1993; Whitecroft plc, since 1993; Blagden Industries plc, since 1994; Celtic Energy Ltd, since 1994; *b* 8 May 1935; *s* of William Jack Kendall and Alma May Kendall; *m* 1st, 1960, Delphine Hitchcock (marr. diss.); one *s* one *d*; 2nd, 1973, Elisabeth Rollison; one *s* one *d. Educ:* Enfield Grammar School; Southend High School. FCA. Elles Reeve, Shell-Mex & BP, Irish Shell & BP, 1955–70; British Petroleum Co.: Crude Oil Sales Manager, 1971–72; Manager, Bulk Trading Div., 1973–74; Organisation Planning Cttee, 1975; BP New Zealand: Gen. Manager, 1976–79; Man. Dir and Chief Exec., 1979–82; Chm., BP SW Pacific, 1979–82; BP Oil: Finance and Planning Dir, 1982–85; Man. Dir and Chief Exec., 1985–88; Director: BP Chemicals Internat., 1985–88; BP Oil Internat., 1985–88; Associated Octel Co., 1985–88. Chairman: Bunzl, 1990–93 (Dir, 1988–93); Meyer Internat., 1994–95; Dep. Chm., British Coal Corp., 1989–91; Director: STC plc, 1988–90; Danka Business Systems plc, 1993–; Gowrings plc, 1993–; South Wales Electricity plc, 1993–. President: UK Petroleum Industries Assoc., 1987–88; Oil Industries Club, 1988. *Recreations:* golf, music, family. *Address:* 41 Albion Street, W2 2AU. *T:* 0171–258 1955. *Clubs:* Athenæum; Rye Golf, Royal Mid Surrey Golf.

KENDALL, Rev. Frank; Inspector of Schools, since 1993; Consultant, SOLACE International, since 1995; Licensed Priest, Diocese of Liverpool, since 1989; *b* 15 Dec. 1940; *s* of Norman and Violet Kendall; *m* 1965, Brenda Pickin; one *s* one *d. Educ:* Bradford Grammar School; Corpus Christi College, Cambridge (MA Classics); Southwark Ordination Course (London Univ. Dip. in Religious Studies). MPBW, 1962; DEA, 1967–68; MPBW, DoE and Dept of Transport, 1969–89; Under Secretary 1984; Chief Exec., St Helens MBC, 1989–91; Venue Develt Manager, British Olympic Bid, 1992. Ordained deacon, 1974, priest, 1975. Hon. Curate: Lingfield, dio. Southwark, 1974–75 and 1978–82; Sketty, dio. Swansea and Brecon, 1975–78; Limpsfield, dio. Southwark, 1982–84; Licensed Preacher, dio. of Manchester, 1984–89. FRSA 1990. *Recreations:* painting: (i) pictures, (ii) decorating. *Address:* Cromwell Villa, 260 Prescot Road, St Helens WA10 3HR. *T:* St Helens (01744) 27626.

KENDALL, Graham; Chief Executive, Sheffield Development Corporation (on secondment), since 1990; *b* 24 Sept. 1943; *s* of Robert David Kendall and Phillis Margaret Moreton; *m* 1968, Helen Sheila Blackburn; two *s* two *d. Educ:* Helsby Grammar Sch.; Leicester Univ. (BSc); Liverpool Univ. (Post-grad. CertEd). Entered Civil Service as Asst Principal, 1966; DTI; Dept of Employment, 1981–; Grade 3, 1990–. *Recreations:* running, gardening, family. *Address:* 56 Blackamoor Road, Dore, Sheffield S17 3GJ. *T:* Sheffield (0114) 236 4533.

KENDALL, Prof. Henry W., PhD; J. A. Stratton Professor of Physics, Massachusetts Institute of Technology, since 1991; *b* Boston, 9 Dec. 1926. *Educ:* Amherst Coll. (BA Maths 1950; Hon. ScD 1975); MIT (PhD Nuclear and Atomic Physics 1954). Nat. Sci. Foundn Postdoctoral Fellow, Brookhaven Nat. Lab. and MIT, 1954–56; Res. Associate, Lectr, Asst Prof., Physics Dept, Stanford Univ., 1956–61; Prof. of Physics, Physics Dept, MIT, 1967–91. Consultant: Dept of Defense, as Mem. Jason Gp, Inst. for Defense Analysis, 1960–71; classified Dept of Defense project, 1966–70; Dir and Founding Mem., Union for Concerned Scientists, 1969–, Chm., 1973–. Member: Jason Div., Inst. Defense Analysis, 1960–73; Subcttee on Nuclear Constants, Nat. Acad. Scis, 1961; Scientific Adv. Panel, Defense Communications Planning Gp, US Dept of Defense, 1966–70; Port of NY Authy Steering and Rev. Cttee NAS-PONYA Jamaica Bay Study, Nat. Acad. Scis, 1970–71; Energy Study Planning Cttee, APS, 1973–76; Public Participation Panel, Congressional Office of Technology Assessment, 1977; Director: Bulletin of Atomic Scientists, 1975–84; Arms Control Assoc., 1979–. Fellow: Amer. Acad. of Arts and Scis, 1982; APS, 1985; AAAS, 1988. Public Service Award, Fedn Amer. Scientists, 1976; (jtly) Leo Szilard Award, APS, 1981; Bertrand Russell Soc. Award, 1982; (jtly) W. K. H. Panofsky Prize, APS, 1989; (jtly) Nobel Prize in Physics, 1990; Envmtl Leadership Award, Tufts Univ., Lincoln Filene Center, 1991. *Publications:* (jtly) Nuclear Fuel Cycle: a survey of the public health environmental and national security effects of nuclear power, 1975; (with S. Nadis) Strategies: toward a solar future, 1980; (with S. Nadis and D. Ford) The Freeze, 1982; (jtly) Fallacy of Star Wars, 1985; (jtly) Crisis Stability and Nuclear War, 1988; numerous articles on nuclear power, nuclear safety and effects of nuclear war in Nuclear News, Environment, Trial, Bull. Atomic Scientists, Think, Scientific American, etc. *Address:* Room 24–519, Laboratory for Nuclear Sciences, Massachusetts Institute of Technology, Cambridge, MA 02139, USA.

KENDALL, Henry Walter George, OBE 1979; Director, British Printing Industries Federation, 1972–81; *b* 21 Dec. 1916; *s* of Henry Kendall and Beatrice (Kerry) Kendall; *m* 1945, Audrey Alison Woodward; two *s* one *d. Educ:* Archbishop Temple's Sch., Lambeth. FCMA. Training with Blades, East & Blades Ltd, 1933–40. War service, RAOC; special duties, War Office, London, 1941; Mil. Coll. of Science, Inspecting Ordnance Officer Western Comd, HQ Allied Land Forces SE Asia, 1940–46. Cost accountant, British Fedn of Master Printers, 1947–55; Chief Cost Accountant, 1955; Head of Management Services, 1967. Mem. Council: CBI, 1972–81; Printing Industry Research Assoc., 1972–81; Inst. of Printing, 1972–81. *Recreations:* theatre, gardening, travel. *Address:* 28 Foxgrove Avenue, Beckenham, Kent BR3 2BA. *Clubs:* Royal Automobile, Wig and Pen.

KENDALL, Prof. Kevin, FRS 1993; Professor of Materials Science, Keele University, since 1993; *b* 2 Dec. 1943; *s* of Cyril Kendall and Margaret (*née* Swarbrick); *m* 1969, Patricia Jennifer Heyes; one *s* one *d. Educ:* London Univ. (BSc Physics External); PhD Cantab. Joseph Lucas, 1961–66; Cavendish Lab., 1966–69; British Rail Research, 1969–71; Monash Univ., 1972–74 (QEII fellowship); Akron Univ., 1974; ICI Runcorn, 1974–93. *Publications:* papers in learned jls on adhesion, fracture, ceramics, material properties. *Recreation:* squash. *Address:* Wycherley, Tower Road, Ashley Heath, Market Drayton, Shropshire TF9 4PY. *T:* Market Drayton (01630) 672665.

KENDALL, Raymond Edward, QPM 1984; Secretary General, International Criminal Police Organization (Interpol), since 1985; *b* 5 Oct. 1933; *m* Antoinette Marie. *Educ:* Simon Langton School, Canterbury; Exeter College, Oxford (MA Hons). RAF, 1951–53 (principally Malaya). Asst Supt of Police, Uganda Police, 1956–62; Metropolitan Police, New Scotland Yard, 1962–86 (principally Special Branch). *Recreations:* shooting, golf. *Address:* ICPO-Interpol, 50 Quai Achille Lignon, 69006 Lyon, France. *T:* 72447000. *Club:* Special Forces.

KENDALL, William Leslie, CBE 1983; Secretary General, Council of Civil Service Unions (formerly Civil Service National Whitley Council, Staff Side), 1976–83; *b* 10 March 1923; *m* 1943, Irene Canham; one *s* one *d.* Clerk, S Shields Insurance Cttee, 1937–41. RAF 1941–46. Entered Civil Service, 1947; Civil Service Clerical Association: Asst Sec., 1952; Dep. Gen. Sec., 1963; Gen. Sec., CPSA (formerly CSCA), 1967–76. Sec., Civil Service Alliance, 1967; Governor, Ruskin Coll., 1967–76. Member: CS Nat. Whitley Council (Chm. Staff Side, 1973–75); Advisory Council, Civil Service Coll., 1976–83; Civil Service Pay Bd, 1978–81; Vice Pres., Civil Service Council Further Educn, 1978–83. Member: Employment Appeal Tribunal, 1976–87; CS Appeal Bd, 1985–93; ACAS Indep. Panel on Teachers' Dispute, 1986–87. Dir, Civil Service Building Soc., 1980–87; Mem., Management Cttee, CS Housing Assoc., 1984–87; Trustee, CS Benevolent Fund, 1987–93. *Recreations:* reading, music, pottering. *Address:* 38 The Glade, Shirley, Croydon CR0 7QD. *T:* 0181–654 8612.

KENDELL, Dr Robert Evan, CBE 1992; FRCP, FRCPE, FRCPsych, FRSE; Chief Medical Officer, Scottish Office Home and Health Department, since 1991; *b* 28 March 1935; *s* of Robert Owen Kendell and Joan Evans; *m* 1961, Ann Whitfield; two *s* two *d. Educ:* Mill Hill School; Peterhouse, Cambridge. MA, MD. FRCP 1974; FRCPE 1977; FRCPsych 1979; FRSE 1993. KCH Med. School, 1956–59; Maudsley Hosp., 1962–68; Vis. Prof., Univ. of Vermont Coll. of Medicine, 1969–70; Reader in Psychiatry, Inst. of Psychiatry, 1970–74; Prof. of Psychiatry, 1974–91, Dean, Faculty of Medicine, 1986–90, Univ. of Edinburgh. Chm., WHO Expert Cttee on Alcohol Consumption, 1979; Mem., MRC, 1984–88, 1991–. Gaskell Medal, RCPsych, 1967; Paul Hoch Medal, Amer. Psychopathol Assoc., 1988; Medal, Marcé Soc., 1994. *Publications:* The Classification of Depressive Illnesses, 1968; The Role of Diagnosis in Psychiatry, 1975; (ed) Companion to Psychiatric Studies, 3rd edn 1983, 5th edn 1993. *Recreations:* overeating and walking up hills. *Address:* 3 West Castle Road, Edinburgh EH10 5AT. *T:* 0131–229 4966. *Club:* Climbers'.

KENDREW, Sir John (Cowdery), Kt 1974; CBE 1963; ScD; FRS 1960; President of St John's College, Oxford, 1981–87, Hon. Fellow, since 1987; *b* 24 March 1917; *s* of late Wilfrid George Kendrew, MA, and Evelyn May Graham Sandberg. *Educ:* Dragon Sch., Oxford; Clifton Coll., Bristol; Trinity Coll., Cambridge (Hon. Fellow, 1972). Scholar of Trinity Coll., Cambridge, 1936; BA 1939; MA 1943; PhD 1949; ScD 1962. Min. of Aircraft Production, 1940–45; Hon. Wing Comdr, RAF, 1944. Fellow, Peterhouse, Cambridge, 1947–75 (Hon. Fellow, 1975); Dep. Chm., MRC Lab. for Molecular Biology, Cambridge, 1946–75; Dir Gen., European Molecular Biology Lab., 1975–82. Reader at Davy-Faraday Laboratory at Royal Instn, London, 1954–68. Mem., Council for Scientific

Policy, 1965–72 (Dep. Chm., 1970–72); Sec.-Gen., European Molecular Biology Conf., 1970–74. Chm., Defence Scientific Adv. Council, 1971–74; Pres., British Assoc. for Advancement of Science, 1973–74; Trustee, British Museum, 1974–79. President: Internat. Union for Pure and Applied Biophysics, 1969–72; Confedn of Science and Technology Orgns for Develt, 1981–85; Sec. Gen, ICSU, 1974–80, first Vice-Pres., 1982–83, Pres., 1983–88, Past Pres., 1988–90; Trustee, Internat. Foundn for Science, 1975–78; Mem. Council, UN Univ., 1980–86, (Chm., 1983–85); Chm., Bd of Governors, Joint Research Centre, EEC, 1985–92. Hon. MRIA 1981; Hon. Member: American Soc. of Biological Chemists, 1962; British Biophysical Soc.; Chilean Acad. of Scis, 1992; Foreign Hon. Mem., Amer. Acad. of Arts and Sciences, 1964; Leopoldina Academy, 1965; Foreign Assoc., Amer. Nat. Acad. of Sciences, 1972; Hon. Fellow: Inst. of Biology, 1966; Weizmann Inst., 1970; Corresp. Mem., Heidelberg Acad. of Scis, 1978; Foreign Mem., Bulgarian Acad. of Scis, 1979; Foreign Fellow, Indian Nat. Science Acad., 1989. Lectures: Herbert Spencer, Univ. of Oxford, 1965; Crookshank, Faculty of Radiologists, 1967; Procter, Internat. Soc. of Leather Chemists, 1969; Fison Meml, Guy's Hosp., 1971; Mgr de Brún, Univ. Coll. of Galway, 1979; Saha Meml, Univ. of Calcutta, 1980. Hon. Prof., Univ. of Heidelberg, 1982. Hon. DSc: Univ. of Reading, 1968; Univ. of Keele, 1968; Exeter, 1982; Univ. of Buckingham, 1983; DUniv Stirling, 1974; Dr *honoris causa:* Pécs, Hungary, 1975; Madrid, 1987; Siena, 1991; Santiago, 1992. (Jointly) Nobel Prize for Chemistry, 1962; Royal Medal of Royal Society, 1965; William Procter Prize, Sigma xi, 1988. Order of Madara Horseman, 1st degree, Bulgaria, 1980. Editor in Chief, Jl of Molecular Biology, 1959–87. *Publications:* The Thread of Life, 1966; (Ed. in Chief) The Encyclopedia of Molecular Biology, 1994; scientific papers in Proceedings of Royal Society, etc. *Address:* The Old Guildhall, 4 Church Lane, Linton, Cambridge CB1 6JX. *T:* Cambridge (01223) 891545. *Club:* Athenæum.

KENDRICK, John Bebbington Bernard; Chief Inspector of Audit, Ministry of Housing and Local Government, 1958–65, retired; *b* 12 March 1905; 3rd *s* of late John Baker Kendrick and Lenora Teague, Leominster, Herefordshire; *m* 1932, Amelia Ruth, 4th *d* of late James Kendall, Grange-over-Sands; two *s*. *Educ:* Leominster Grammar Sch.; King's Sch., Chester; Queen's Coll., Oxford (MA). Called to Bar, Middle Temple. Asst District Auditor, 1926; Deputy District Auditor, 1946; District Auditor, 1953; Deputy Chief Inspector of Audit, 1958. *Recreation:* fell walking. *Address:* Green Acres, Old Hall Road, Troutbeck Bridge, Windermere, Cumbria LA23 1HF. *T:* Windermere (019662) 3705.

KENEALLY, Thomas Michael, AO 1983; FRSL; FAAAS; author; *b* 7 Oct. 1935; *s* of Edmond Thomas Keneally; *m* 1965, Judith Mary Martin; two *d*. Studied for NSW Bar. Schoolteacher until 1965; Commonwealth Literary Fellowship, 1966, 1968, 1972; Lectr in Drama, Univ. of New England, 1968–69. Vis. Prof., Dept of English, Univ. of California, Irvine, 1985; Berg Prof., Dept of English, New York Univ., 1988; Distinguished Prof., Dept of English and Comparative Lit., Univ. of Calif, Irvine, 1991–. Chm., Australian Republican Movement, 1991–94. Member: (inaugural) Australia–China Council, 1978–83; Adv. Panel, Australian Constitutional Commn, 1985–88; Literary Arts Bd, Australia, 1985–88; Chm., Aust. Soc. Authors, 1987–90 (Mem. Council, 1985–); Pres., Nat. Book Council Australia, 1985–89. FRSL 1973. Silver City (screenplay, with Sophia Turkiewicz), 1985. Hon. DLitt: Queensland, 1993; NUI, 1994; Fairleigh Dickinson, NJ, 1994. *Publications:* The Place at Whitton, 1964; The Fear, 1965, 2nd edn 1973; Bring Larks and Heroes, 1967, 2nd edn 1973; Three Cheers for the Paraclete, 1968; The Survivor, 1969; A Dutiful Daughter, 1971; The Chant of Jimmie Blacksmith, 1972 (filmed 1978); Blood Red, Sister Rose, 1974; Gossip from the Forest, 1975 (TV film, 1979); The Lawgiver, 1975; Season in Purgatory, 1976; A Victim of the Aurora, 1977; Ned Kelly and the City of the Bees, 1978; Passenger, 1979; Confederates, 1979; Schindler's Ark, 1982, reissued as Schindler's List, 1994 (Booker Prize; LA Times Fiction Prize; filmed as Schindler's List, 1994); Outback, 1983; The Cut-Rate Kingdom, 1984; A Family Madness, 1985; The Playmaker, 1987 (stage adaptation, perf. Royal Court, 1988); Towards Asmara, 1989; Flying Hero Class, 1991 (also screenplay); The Place where Souls are born, 1992; Now and in Time to be, 1992; Woman of the Inner Sea, 1992 (also screenplay); Memoirs from a Young Republic, 1993; Jacko, 1993; The Utility Player (biog.), 1994; A River Town, 1995. *Recreations:* swimming, crosswords, hiking, cross-country ski-ing. *Address:* c/o Deborah Rogers, 20 Powis Mews, W11 1JN.

KENILOREA, Rt. Hon. Sir Peter (Kauona Keninaraiso'ona), KBE 1982; PC 1979; MP (formerly MLA), East Are-Are, Solomon Islands, since 1976; Minister for Foreign Affairs and Trade Relations, since 1990; Prime Minister of the Solomon Islands, 1978–81 and 1984–86; *b* Takataka, Malaita, 23 May 1943; *m* 1971, Margaret Kwanairara; two *s* two *d*. *Educ:* Univ. and Teachers' Coll., NZ (Dip. Ed.). Teacher, King George VI Secondary Sch., 1968–70. Asst Sec., Finance, 1971; Admin. Officer, Dist Admin, 1971–73; Lands Officer, 1973–74; Dep. Sec. to Cabinet and to Chief Minister, 1974–75; Dist Comr, Eastern Solomon Is, 1975–76; Chief Minister, 1976–78; Leader of the Opposition, 1981–84; Dep. Prime Minister and Minister of Foreign Affairs, 1987–88. Queen's Silver Jubilee Medal, 1977; Solomon Is Indep. Medal, 1978. *Publications:* political and scientific, numerous articles. *Address:* c/o Legislative Assembly, Honiara, Guadalcanal, Solomon Islands.

KENILWORTH, 4th Baron *cr* 1937, of Kenilworth; **(John) Randle Siddeley;** Managing Director, Siddeley Landscapes, since 1976; Director, John Siddeley International Ltd; *b* 16 June 1954; *s* of John Tennant Davenport Siddeley (3rd Baron Kenilworth) and of Jacqueline Paulette, *d* of late Robert Gelpi; *S* father, 1981; *m* 1st, 1983, Kim (marr. diss. 1989), *o d* of Danie Serfontein, Newcastle upon Tyne; 2nd, 1991, Mrs Kiki McDonough; two *s*. *Educ:* Northease Manor, near Lewes, Sussex; West Dean College (studied Restoration of Antique Furniture); London College of Furniture. Worked at John Siddeley International as interior designer/draughtsman, 1975; formed own company, Siddeley Landscapes, as landscape gardener, 1976; formed Randle Siddeley Associates, as landscape designer, 1994. *Recreation:* ski-ing. *Heir: s* Hon. William Randle John Siddeley, *b* 24 Jan. 1992. *Address:* Randle Siddeley Associates, 2 Palmerston Court, Palmerston Way, SW8 4AJ. *Clubs:* St James's, Annabel's.

KENLIS, Lord; Thomas Rupert Charles Christopher Taylour; *b* 18 June 1989; *s* and *heir* of Earl of Bective, *qv*.

KENNAN, Prof. George Frost; Professor, Institute for Advanced Study, Princeton, NJ, 1956–74, now Professor Emeritus; *b* 16 Feb. 1904; *m* 1931, Annelise Sorensen; one *s* three *d*. *Educ:* Princeton Univ. (AB); Seminary for Oriental Languages, Berlin. Foreign Service of the USA; many posts from 1926–52; US Ambassador to the USSR, 1952–53; Institute for Advanced Study, Princeton, 1953–61; US Ambassador to Yugoslavia, 1961–63. George Eastman Vis. Prof., Oxford, 1957–58; Reith Lectr, BBC, 1957; Prof., Princeton Univ., 1963 and 1964. Hon. LLD: Dartmouth and Yale, 1950; Colgate, 1951; Notre Dame, 1953; Kenyon Coll., 1954; New School for Social Research, 1955; Princeton, 1956; University of Michigan and Northwestern, 1957; Brandeis, 1958; Wisconsin, 1963; Harvard, 1963; Denison, 1966; Rutgers, 1966; Marquette, 1972; Catholic Univ. of America, 1976; Duke, 1977; Ripon Coll., 1978; Dickinson Coll., 1979; Lake Forest Coll., 1982; Clark Univ., 1983; Oberlin Coll., 1983; Brown Univ., 1983; New York Univ., 1985; William and Mary Coll., and Columbia Univ., 1986; Rider Coll., 1988; Hon. DCL Oxford, 1969; Dr of Politics *hc* Univ. of Helsinki, 1986. Benjamin Franklin Fellow RSA, 1968. President: Nat. Inst. of Arts and Letters, 1965–68; Amer. Acad. of Arts and Letters, 1968–72; Corresp. FBA, 1983. Pour le Mérite (Germany), 1976. Albert Einstein Peace Prize, Albert Einstein Peace Prize Foundn of Chicago, 1981; Grenville Clark Prize, Grenville Clark Fund at Dartmouth Coll., Inc., 1981; Börsenverein Peace Prize, Frankfurt, 1982; Gold Medal for History, AAIL, 1984; Creative Arts Award for Nonfiction, Brandeis Univ., 1986; Freedom from Fear Award, FDR Foundn, 1987; Physicians for Social Responsibility Award, 1988; Toynbee Prize, 1988; Encyclopaedia Britannica Award 1989; Presidential Medal of Freedom, 1989; Governor's Award of NJ, 1990. *Publications:* American Diplomacy, 1900–50, 1951 (US); Realities of American Foreign Policy, 1954 (US); Amerikanisch Russische Verhältnis, 1954 (Germany); Soviet-American Relations, 1917–20; Vol. I, Russia Leaves the War, 1956 (National Book Award; Pulitzer Prize 1957); Vol. II, The Decision to Intervene, 1958; Russia, the Atom and the West, 1958; Soviet Foreign Policy, 1917–1941, 1960; Russia and the West under Lenin and Stalin, 1961; On Dealing with the Communist World, 1964; Memoirs, vol. 1, 1925–1950, 1967 (National Book Award 1968; Pulitzer Prize 1968); Memoirs, vol. 2, 1950–1963, 1973; From Prague after Munich: Diplomatic Papers 1938–1940, 1968; Democracy and the Student Left, 1968; The Marquis de Custine and his 'Russie en 1839', 1972; The Cloud of Danger, 1977; The Decline of Bismarck's European Order, 1979; The Nuclear Delusion, 1982; The Fateful Alliance: France, Russia and the coming of the First World War, 1985; Sketches from a Life, 1989; Around the Cragged Hill: a personal and political philosophy, 1993. *Club:* Century (New York City).

KENNARD, Sir George Arnold Ford, 3rd Bt *cr* 1891; *b* 27 April 1915; *s* of Sir Coleridge Kennard, 1st Bt; *S* brother, 1967; *m* 1st, 1940, Cecilia Violet Cokayne Maunsel (marr. diss. 1958); one *d*; 2nd, 1958, Jesse Rudd Miskin (marr. diss. 1974), *d* of Hugh Wyllie; 3rd, 1985, Nichola (marr. diss. 1992), *o d* of late Peter Carew, Tiverton; 4th, 1992, Mrs Georgina Phillips. *Educ:* Eton. Commissioned 4th Queen's Own Hussars, 1939; served War of 1939–45 (despatches twice), Egypt, Greece (POW Greece); comd Regt, 1955–58; retired, 1958. Joined Cement Marketing Co., 1967, becoming Midland Representative; retired 1979. *Recreations:* hunting, shooting, fishing. *Publication:* Loopy (autobiog.), 1990. *Heir:* none. *Address:* 13 Burton Court, Franklin's Row, SW3 4TA. *Club:* Cavalry and Guards.

KENNARD, Dr Olga, (Lady Burgen), OBE 1988; ScD; FRS 1987; Scientific Director, Cambridge Crystallographic Data Centre, since 1965; *b* 23 March 1924; *d* of Joir and Catherina Weisz; *m* 1st, 1948, David William Kennard (marr. diss. 1961); two *d*; 2nd, 1993, Sir Arnold Burgen, *qv*. *Educ:* Cambridge University (MA 1948; ScD 1973). Res. Asst, Cavendish Laboratory, Cambridge, 1944–48; MRC Scientific Staff: Inst. of Ophthalmology, London, 1948–51; Nat. Inst. for Med. Res., London, 1951–61; seconded to University Chemical Laboratory, Cambridge, 1961–71; MRC special appt, 1974–89. *Publications:* about 200 pubns in field of X-ray structure determination of organic and bioactive molecules and correlation between structure, chemical properties and biological activity, and technical innovations in X-ray crystallography; ed 20 standard reference books. *Recreations:* music, swimming, architecture, friendship and interaction with people of wit and intelligence. *Address:* (office) 12 Union Road, Cambridge CB2 1EZ. *T:* Cambridge (01223) 336408.

KENNAWAY, Prof. Alexander, MA; Eur Ing, CEng, FIM; Senior Researcher and Lecturer, Conflict Studies Research Centre, Royal Military Academy, Sandhurst, since 1993; *b* 14 Aug. 1923; *s* of late Dr and Mrs Barou; *m* 1st, 1947, Xenia Rebel (marr. diss. 1970); one *s* one *d*; 2nd, 1973, Jean Simpson. *Educ:* Downsend Sch., Leatherhead; St Paul's Sch., London; Pembroke Coll., Cambridge (MA). CEng, FIMechE 1962; FIM (FPRI 1968). Engr Officer, RN: active list, 1942–47; reserve, 1970. Imperial Chemical Industries Ltd, 1947–58; Metal Box Co., 1958–60; Director: BTR Industries, 1960–66; Allied Polymer Gp, 1972–78; Thomas Jourdan, 1976–83; Imperial Polymer Technology, 1984–86. Chm., Terrafix, 1983–90. Mem. Bd, CAA, 1979–83. Hon. medical engrg consultant, various hosps and charities, 1950–. Mem., Standing Adv. Cttee on artificial limbs, DHSS, 1964–70. Vis. Prof. of Mech. Engrg, Imp. Coll. of Science and Technology, 1976–. Interim Sec., Nat. Fedn of Zool Gardens of GB and Ireland, 1984–86. Pres., English Chess Assoc., 1988–. For. Mem., Ukrainian Acad. of Transport, 1994. *Publications:* (contrib.) Advances in Surgical Materials, 1956; (contrib.) Polythene—technology and uses, 1958, 2nd edn 1960; Engineers in Industry, 1981; (contrib.) The British Malaise, 1982; some 30 papers on biomechanics, technology of use and production of rubbers and plastics, and on design of specific aids for disabled living; 10 papers on Soviet economy and conversion of its defence industries. *Recreations:* sailing, chess, music, trying to do less, applying thought to the solution of useful problems. *Address:* 12 Fairholme Crescent, Ashtead, Surrey KT21 2HN. *T:* Ashtead (01372) 277678.

See also L. Archibald.

KENNAWAY, Sir John (Lawrence), 5th Bt, *cr* 1791; *b* 7 Sept. 1933; *s* of Sir John Kennaway, 4th Bt and Mary Felicity (*d* 1991), *yr d* of late Rev. Chancellor Ponsonby; *S* father, 1956; *m* 1961, Christina Veronica Urszenyi, MB, ChB (Cape Town); one *s* two *d*. *Educ:* Harrow; Trinity Coll., Cambridge. *Heir: s* John Michael Kennaway [*b* 17 Feb. 1962; *m* 1988, Lucy Frances, *yr d* of Dr Jeremy Houlton Bradshaw-Smith; two *d*]. *Address:* Escot, Ottery St Mary, Devon EX11 1LU.

KENNEDY, family name of **Marquess of Ailsa.**

KENNEDY, A(lfred) James, CBE 1979; DSc (London), PhD (London), FEng, MIEE, FIM, FInstP; consultant; *b* 6 Nov. 1921; *m* 1950, Anna Jordan (*d* 1986); no *c*. *Educ:* Haberdashers' Aske's Hatcham Sch.; University Coll., London (Fellow 1976). BSc (Physics) 1943. Commissioned R Signals, 1944; Staff Major (Telecommunications) Central Comd, Agra, India, 1945–46 and at Northern Comd, Rawalpindi, 1946–47; Asst Lectr in Physics, UCL 1947–50; Res. Fellow, Davy-Faraday Lab. of Royal Institution, London, 1950–51; Royal Society, Armourers' and Brasiers' Research Fellow in Metallurgy (at Royal Institution), 1951–54; Head of Metal Physics Sect., BISRA, 1954–57; Prof. of Materials and Head of Dept. of Materials, Coll. of Aeronautics, Cranfield, 1957–66; Dir, British Non-Ferrous Metals Res. Assoc., later BNF Metals Technol. Centre, Wantage, 1966–78; Dir of Research, Delta Metal Co., and Man. Dir, Delta Materials Research Ltd, 1978–81; Dep. Dir, Technical Change Centre, 1981–86; Dir, BL Technology Ltd, 1979–83. Vis. Prof. in Metallurgy, Imperial Coll. of Science and Technol., London, 1981–86. Institution of Metallurgists: Pres., 1976–77; a Vice Pres., 1971–74, 1975–76; Mem. Council, 1968–76. President: Inst. of Metals, 1970–71 (Mem. Council, 1968–73; Fellow, 1973); Engrg Section, BAAS, 1983; Member: Metallurgy Cttee, CNAA, 1965–71; ARC, 1967–70, 1971–74, 1977–80 (also Mem., ARC cttees); Adv. Council on Materials, 1970–71; Council, The Metals Soc., 1974–84 (Platinum Medallist, 1977); Inst. of Physics, 1968–71; SRC, 1974–78; Metall. and Mat. Cttee, SRC, 1970–75 (Chm. 1973–74); Engrg Bd, 1973–78; Council of Env. Sci. and Eng., 1973–78; Adv. Council for Applied R&D, 1976–80; Mat. and Chem. Res. Requirements Bd, DoI, 1981–83 (Chm., Non-Ferrous Metals Cttee); Chm., Council of Sci. and Tech. Insts, 1983–84. Fellow, Amer. Soc. Met., 1972. Pres., Brit. Soc. of Rheology, 1964–66; a Governor, Nat. Inst. for Agric. Engrg, 1966–74. Hon. DSc Aston, 1980. *Publications:* Processes of Creep and Fatigue in Metals,

1962; The Materials Background to Space Technology, 1964; Creep and Stress Relaxation in Metals (English edn), 1965; (ed) High Temperature Materials, 1968; research papers and articles, mainly on physical aspects of deformation and fracture in crystalline materials, particularly metals. *Recreations:* music, painting. *Address:* Woodhill, Milton under Wychwood, Chipping Norton, Oxford OX7 6EP. *T:* Chipping Norton (01993) 830334. *Club:* Athenæum.

KENNEDY, Anthony McLeod; Associate Justice of the Supreme Court of the United States, since 1988; *b* 23 July 1936; *s* of Anthony J. Kennedy and Gladys Kennedy; *m* Mary Davis; two *s* one *d*. *Educ:* Stanford Univ. (AB 1958); LSE; Harvard Univ. (LLB 1961). Mem., Calif. Bar, 1962, US Tax Court Bar, 1971. Associate, Thelen Marrin John & Bridges, San Francisco, 1961–63; sole practice, 1963–67; partner Evans, Jackson & Kennedy, 1967–75. Prof. of Constitutional Law, McGeorge Sch. of Law, Univ. of Pacific, 1965–88; Judge, US Court of Appeals, 9th Circuit, Sacramento, 1976–88. *Address:* Supreme Court Building, 1 First Street NE, Washington, DC 20543, USA.

KENNEDY, Prof. Arthur Colville, CBE 1992; FRCPE, FRCPGlas, FRCP; FRSE 1984; Muirhead Professor of Medicine, Glasgow University, 1978–88; *b* 23 Oct. 1922; *s* of Thomas and Johanna Kennedy; *m* 1947, Agnes White Taylor; two *d* (one *s* decd). *Educ:* Whitehill Sch., Glasgow; Univ. of Glasgow. MB ChB 1945; MD 1956. FRCPE 1960; FRCPGlas 1964; FRCP 1977; FRCPI 1988. Hon. Consultant in Medicine, Royal Infirmary, Glasgow, 1959–88; Titular Professor, Univ. of Glasgow, 1969–78. Member: Greater Glasgow Health Bd, 1985–89; GMC, 1989–92 (Chm., Professional and Linguistic Bd, 1987–89). President: RCPSG, 1986–88; BMA, 1991–92; Royal Medico-Chirurgical Soc. of Glasgow, 1971–72; Europ. Dialysis and Transplant Assoc., 1972–75; Scottish Soc. of Physicians, 1983–84; Harveian Soc. of Edinburgh, 1985. Hon. FACP 1987; Hon. FRACP 1988. *Publications:* various papers on renal disease. *Recreations:* gardening, walking, reading, photography. *Address:* 16 Boclair Crescent, Bearsden, Glasgow G61 2AG. *T:* 0141–942 5326. *Clubs:* Athenæum; Royal Scottish Automobile (Glasgow).

KENNEDY, Charles Peter; MP Ross, Cromarty and Skye, since 1983 (SDP 1983–88, Lib Dem since 1988); President, Liberal Democrats, 1990–94; *b* Inverness, 25 Nov. 1959; *yr s* of Ian Kennedy, crofter, and Mary McVarish MacEachen. *Educ:* Lochaber High Sch., Fort William; Univ. of Glasgow (joint MA Hons Philosophy and Politics). President, Glasgow Univ. Union, 1980–81; winner, British Observer Mace for Univ. Debating, 1982. Journalist, BBC Highland, Inverness, 1982; Fulbright Schol. and Associate Instructor in Dept of Speech Communication, Indiana Univ., Bloomington Campus, 1982–83. SDP spokesman on health, social services, social security and Scottish issues, 1983–87; SDP-Liberal Alliance spokesman on social security, 1987; Lib Dem spokesman on trade and industry, 1988–89, on health, 1989–92, on Europe and East-West relations, 1992–. Member: Select Cttee on Social Services, 1986–87; Select Cttee on Televising of H of C, 1988–. Chm., SDP Council for Scotland, 1986–88. Occasional journalist, broadcaster and lecturer. *Address:* House of Commons, SW1A 0AA. *T:* 0171–219 5090. *Club:* National Liberal.

KENNEDY, Sir Clyde (David Allen), Kt 1973; Chairman of Sydney (New South Wales) Turf Club, 1972–77 and 1980–83 (Vice-Chairman, 1967–72); company director; *b* 20 Nov. 1912; *s* of late D. H. Kennedy; *m* 1937, Sarah Stacpoole; two *s* one *d*. Member, NSW Totalisator Agency Board, 1965–82; Chairman, Spinal Research Foundation, 1977–. *Address:* 13A/23 Thornton Street, Darling Point, NSW 2027, Australia. *Clubs:* Australian Jockey, Sydney Turf; Rugby, Tattersalls (all NSW).

KENNEDY, David; Director-General, Commonwealth War Graves Commission, since 1993; *b* 7 Nov. 1940; *s* of Lilian Alice Kennedy; *m* 1964, Peta Jennifer Hatton; two *d*. *Educ:* Ryhope Robert Richardson Grammar Sch., Co. Durham; City of London Coll. Exchequer and Audit Dept, 1959–69; Commonwealth War Graves Commission: Higher Exec. Officer, 1969–71; Sen. Exec. Officer, 1971–74; Principal: Dir of Management Services, 1975–79; Dir, Outer Area, 1979–84; Senior Principal: Dir, France Area, 1984–86; Dir of Personnel, 1986–87; Dep. Dir-Gen., Admin, 1987–92; rcds 1992. *Recreations:* tennis, badminton, ski-ing, photography, hill-walking, travel. *Address:* Commonwealth War Graves Commission, 2 Marlow Road, Maidenhead, Berks SL6 7DX. *T:* Maidenhead (01628) 34221; March House, Blands Close, Burghfield Common, Berks RG7 3JY. *T:* Reading (01734) 832941.

KENNEDY, David Matthew; American Banker; Special Representative of the First Presidency of The Church of Jesus Christ of Latter-day Saints; *b* Randolph, Utah, 21 July 1905; *s* of George Kennedy and Katherine Kennedy (*née* Johnson); *m* 1925, Lenora Bingham; four *d*. *Educ:* Weber Coll., Ogden, Utah (AB); George Washington Univ., Washington, DC (MA, LLB); Stonier Grad. Sch. of Banking, Rutgers Univ. (grad.). Special Asst to Chm. of Bd, Federal Reserve System, 1930–46; Vice-Pres. in charge of bond dept, Continental Illinois Bank and Trust Co., Chicago, 1946–53, full Vice-Pres., 1951, Pres., 1956–58, Chm. Bd and Chief Exec. Officer, 1959– (temp. resigned, Oct. 1953–Dec. 1954, to act as special Asst to Sec. of Treas., in Republican Admin.); after return to Continental Illinois Bank, still advised Treasury (also under Democrat Admin). Appointed by President Kennedy as incorporator and dir of Communication Satellite Corp.; Chm. of Commn (apptd by President Johnson) to improve drafting of Federal budget, 1967; Chm of Cttee (apptd by Mayor of Chicago) for Economic and Cultural Develt of Chicago, 1967. Again in Govt, when nominated to Nixon Cabinet, Dec. 1968; Secretary of the Treasury, 1969–70; Ambassador-at-large, USA, and Mem. President Nixon's Cabinet, 1970–73; US Ambassador to NATO, 1972. Director (past or present) of many corporations and companies including: Internat. Harvester Corp.; Abbott Laboratories; Swift & Co.; Pullman Co.; Nauvoo Restoration Inc.; Member of numerous organizations; Trustee: Univ. of Chicago; George Washington Univ.; Brookings Instn, etc. Holds hon. doctorates. *Address:* 3793 Parkview Drive, Salt Lake City, UT 84124, USA. *Clubs:* Union League, Commercial Executives (Chicago); Old Elm Country (Fort Sheridan, Ill); Glenview Country, etc.

KENNEDY, Eamon, MA, BComm, PhD; Special Adviser, with rank of Ambassador, Permanent Mission of Ireland, United Nations, New York, since 1987; *b* 13 Dec. 1921; *s* of Luke William Kennedy and Ellen (*née* Stafford); *m* 1960, Barbara Jane Black, New York; one *s* one *d*. *Educ:* O'Connell Schools, Dublin; University Coll., Dublin (MA, BComm); National University of Ireland (PhD 1970). Entered Irish Diplomatic Service, 1943; 2nd Sec., Ottawa, 1947–49; 1st Sec., Washington, 1949–50; 1st Sec., Paris, 1950–54; Chief of Protocol, Dublin, 1954–56; Counsellor, UN Mission, New York, 1956–61; Ambassador to: Nigeria, 1961–64; Federal Republic of Germany, 1964–70; France, OECD and UNESCO, 1970–74; UN, 1974–78; UK, 1978–83; Italy, Turkey, Libya, and FAO Rome, 1983–86. Grand Cross: German Order of Merit, 1970; French Order of Merit, 1974. *Recreations:* golf, theatre, music. *Address:* 525 East 86th Street, Apartment 17-D, New York, NY 10028, USA; 6730 Nassau Point Road, Cutchogue, NY 11935, USA. *Club:* North Fork Country (Long Island, NY).

KENNEDY, Edward Arthur Gilbert; retired; *b* Dublin, 5 May 1920; *s* of Captain Edward H. N. Kennedy, RN, and Frances A. Gosling, Bermuda; *m* 1944, Margarita Dagmara Hofstra; two *s* two *d*. *Educ:* Oundle; Pembroke Coll., Cambridge (BA Mod Langs). Served War, RNVR, 1941–46. Joined Northern Ireland Civil Service, 1947; served mainly in Dept of Commerce until 1970, then in Office of NI Ombudsman (Sen. Dir, 1973–83). Vice-Chm., Music Cttee, N Ireland Arts Council, 1978–83; Hon. Pres., Belfast Ballet Club, 1970–82; Chm., Belfast Picture Borrowing Gp, 1970–84. *Recreation:* interest in the arts. *Address:* 29 Tweskard Park, Belfast BT4 2JZ. *T:* Belfast (01232) 763638.

KENNEDY, Edward Moore; US Senator (Democrat) from Massachusetts, since 1962; *b* Boston, Mass, 22 Feb. 1932; *y s* of late Joseph Patrick Kennedy and Rose Kennedy (*née* Fitzgerald); *m*; two *s* one *d*; *m* 1992, Victoria Anne Reggie. *Educ:* Milton Acad.; Harvard Univ. (BA 1956); Internat. Law Inst., The Hague; Univ. of Virginia Law Sch. (LLB 1959). Served US Army, 1951–53. Called to Massachusetts Bar, 1959; Asst Dist Attorney, Suffolk County, Mass, 1961–62. Senate majority whip, 1969–71; Chairman: Judiciary Cttee, 1979–81; Labor and Human Resources Cttee, 1987– (Ranking Democrat, 1981–86); Member: Senate Armed Forces Cttee; Senate Jt Economic Cttee; Bd, Office of Technology Assessment. Pres., Joseph P. Kennedy Jr Foundn, 1961–; Trustee: John F. Kennedy Lib.; John F. Kennedy Center for the Performing Arts; Robert F. Kennedy Meml Foundn. Holds numerous hon. degrees, foreign decorations and awards. *Publications:* Decisions for a Decade, 1968; In Critical Condition, 1972; Our Day and Generation, 1979; (with Senator Mark Hatfield) Freeze: how you can help prevent nuclear war, 1982. *Address:* United States Senate, Washington, DC 20510, USA.

KENNEDY, Sir Francis, KCMG 1986; CBE 1977 (MBE 1958); HM Diplomatic Service, retired; Special Adviser to the Chairman and Board, British Airways, since 1986 (Director, since 1987); Chairman, British Airways Regional, since 1993; *b* 9 May 1926; *s* of late James Kennedy and Alice (*née* Bentham); *m* 1957, Anne O'Malley; two *s* two *d*. *Educ:* Univs of Manchester and London. RN, 1944–46. Min. of Supply, 1951–52; HM Colonial Service, Nigeria, 1953–63; Asst Dist Officer, 1953–56; Dist Officer, 1956–59; Principal Asst Sec. to Premier E Nigeria, 1961–62; Provincial Sec., Port Harcourt, 1962–63; HM Diplomatic Service, 1964; First Sec., Commercial and Economic, Dar-es-Salaam, 1965; First Sec. and Head of Post, Kuching, 1967–69; Consul, Commercial, Istanbul, 1970–73; Consul-Gen., Atlanta, 1973–78; Counsellor later Minister Lagos, 1978–81; Ambassador to Angola, 1981–83; Dir-Gen., British Trade and Investment, and Consul-Gen., NY, 1983–86. Chm., Fluor Daniel Ltd, 1989 (Dir, 1986–); Director: Leslie & Godwin Ltd, 1986–91; Global Analysis Systems, 1986–88; Hambourne Development Co., 1987–94; Smith & Nephew, 1988–; Fleming Overseas Investment Trust, 1988–; Brunner Mond Hldgs, 1992–; Mem. Bd and Council, Inward, 1986–90. Mem. Bd, Univ. of Central Lancs (formerly Lancashire Polytechnic), 1989–. Governor, British Liver Foundn, 1990–93. *Clubs:* Brooks's; Shaw Hill Golf and Country; Lancashire County Cricket.

See also Rt Rev. Mgr J. Kennedy.

KENNEDY, (George) Michael (Sinclair), OBE 1981; Chief Music Critic, The Sunday Telegraph, since 1989; Staff Music Critic, The Daily Telegraph, since 1950 (Joint Chief Critic, 1987–89); *b* 19 Feb. 1926; *s* of Hew Gilbert Kennedy and Marian Florence Sinclair; *m* 1947, Eslyn Durdle; no *c*. *Educ:* Berkhamsted School. Joined Daily Telegraph, Manchester, 1941; served Royal Navy (BPF), 1943–46; rejoined Daily Telegraph, Manchester, serving in various capacities on editorial staff; Asst Northern Editor, 1958; Northern Ed., 1960–86. Gov., Royal Northern Coll. of Music; Mem. Cttee, Vaughan Williams Trust, 1965– (Chm., 1977–); Vice-Pres., Elgar Foundn and Elgar Soc. Hon. Mem., Royal Manchester Coll. of Music, 1971. Hon. MA Manchester, 1975. FJI 1967; FRNCM 1981. *Publications:* The Hallé Tradition, 1960; The Works of Ralph Vaughan Williams, 1964, 2nd edn 1980; Portrait of Elgar, 1968, 4th edn 1993; Portrait of Manchester, 1970; Elgar Orchestral Works, 1970; History of Royal Manchester College of Music, 1971; Barbirolli: Conductor Laureate, 1971; (ed) The Autobiography of Charles Hallé, 1973; Mahler, 1974, 2nd edn 1990 (Japanese edn 1978); Richard Strauss, 1976, 2nd edn 1995; (ed) Concise Oxford Dictionary of Music, 3rd edn, 1980, 4th edn 1995; Britten, 1981, 2nd edn 1993; The Hallé, 1858–1983, 1983; Strauss Tone Poems, 1984; Oxford Dictionary of Music, 1985, 2nd edn 1994; Adrian Boult, 1987; Portrait of Walton, 1989; Music Enriches All: 21 years of the Royal Northern College of Music, 1994; scripts for BBC, contrib. musical jls. *Recreations:* listening to music, watching cricket. *Address:* 3 Moorwood Drive, Sale, Cheshire M33 4QB. *T:* 0161–973 7225. *Clubs:* Athenæum; Lancashire CC, Middlesex CC.

KENNEDY, Graham Norbert, CVO 1993; Director, James Capel & Co., since 1990; *b* 21 Oct. 1936; *s* of Ernest Norbert Kennedy and Joan Foster Kennedy; *m* 1960, Dinah Mary Berrill. *Educ:* St Andrews Coll., Grahamstown, S Africa; Millfield. Union Acceptances Ltd, 1964–70; James Capel & Co., 1971–: Partner, 1974–86; Consultant, 1993–. Chairman: Anglo Pacific Resources, 1989–; Dwyer plc, 1993–. Mem., Council and Bd, London Stock Exchange, 1980–92. *Recreations:* shooting, golf, bridge, ski-ing, music. *Address:* Hatchetts, Church Lane, Worting, Basingstoke, Hants RG23 8PX. *Clubs:* Boodle's, City of London; Rand (Johannesburg); Berkshire Golf.

KENNEDY, Helena Ann; QC 1991; *b* 12 May 1950; *d* of Joshua Patrick Kennedy and Mary Veronica (*née* Jones); partner, 1978–84, (Roger) Iain Mitchell; one *s*; *m* 1986, Dr Iain Louis Hutchison; one *s* one *d*. *Educ:* Holyrood Secondary Sch., Glasgow; Council of Legal Educn. Called to the Bar, Gray's Inn, 1972; established chambers at: Garden Court, 1974; Tooks Court, 1984; Doughty St, 1990. Member: Bar Council, 1990–93; Cttee, Assoc. of Women Barristers, 1991–; Nat. Bd, Women's Legal Defence Fund, 1989–91; Council, Howard League for Penal Reform, 1989– (Chm., commn of inquiry into violence in penal instns for children, 1994–); CIBA Commn into Child Sexual Abuse, 1981–83; Exec. Cttee, NCCL, 1983–85; Bd, Minority Access to Legal Profession Project, Poly. of South Bank, 1984–85. Chancellor, Oxford Brookes Univ., 1994–. Chairman: Haldane Soc., 1983–86 (Vice-Pres., 1986–); Charter '88, 1992–; Standing Cttee for Youth Justice, NACRO, 1993–; Leader of inquiry into health, envmtl and safety aspects of Atomic Weapons Establishment, Aldermaston (report, 1993); Patron: Civil Liberties Trust, 1991–; Victims Helpline; Clean Break Theatre Co. (for ex-prisoners); Fleet Counselling; Prisoners of Conscience; S Essex Rape and Incest Crisis Centre; Bishops Simeon Trust; Trustee, Anti-Racist Alliance Educn Trust; Commissioner: BAFTA inquiry into future of BBC, 1990; Hamlyn Nat. Commn on Educn, 1991–. Chm., London Internat. Fest. of Theatre, 1993. Vis. Lectr on Criminal Law, BPMF, 1991–; Advr, Mannheim Inst. on Criminology, LSE, 1992–. Member Board: City Limits Magazine, 1982–84; New Statesman, 1990–; Counsel Magazine, 1990–; Hampstead Theatre, 1989–. Broadcaster: first female moderator, Hypotheticals (Granada) on surrogate motherhood and artificial insemination; presenter: Heart of the Matter, BBC, 1987; Putting Women in the Picture, BBC2, 1987; The Trial of Lady Chatterley's Lover, Radio 4, 1990; Raw Deal, series of progs on med. negligence, BBC2, 1990; co-producer, Women Behind Bars, Channel 4, 1990; presenter, The Maguires: forensic evidence on trial, BBC2, 1991; creator, drama series, Blind Justice, BBC, 1988; host, After Dark, Channel 4, 1988–; presenter, Time Gentlemen Please, BBC Scotland, 1994. FRSA. Hon. LLD: Strathclyde, 1992; Teesside, 1993; Keele, 1994; Lancaster, 1994. *Publications:* (jtly) The Bar on Trial, 1978; (jtly) Child Abuse Within the Family, 1984; (jtly) Balancing Acts, 1989; Eve was Framed, 1992; lectures; contribs on issues connected with law, civil liberties and women. *Recreations:* theatre, spending time with family and friends. *Address:* 11 Doughty Street, WC1N 2PG.

T: 0171–404 1313; c/o Hilary Hard, 12 Athelstan Close, Harold Wood, Essex RM3 0QJ. *T* and *Fax:* Romford (01708) 379482.

KENNEDY, Horas Tristram, OBE 1966; HM Diplomatic Service, retired; *b* 29 May 1917; *s* of George Lawrence Kennedy and Mary Dow; *m* 1953, Maureen Beatrice Jeanne Holmes (formerly Stevens) (*d* 1976); three *d* (one *s* decd). *Educ:* Oundle; King's Coll., Cambridge. History and Mod Langs, MA. Entered HM Consular Service, 1939; Vice-Consul, Valparaiso, Chile, 1939–46; Foreign Office, 1946–48; 1st Secretary: Belgrade, 1949–52; Buenos Aires, 1952–56; Berne, 1956–61; Santiago de Chile, 1961–67; Commercial Counsellor, Warsaw, 1967–70; Consul-Gen., Barcelona, 1971–73. *Recreations:* country walking, painting, carpentry. *Address:* Borea Farm, Nancledra, Penzance, Cornwall TR20 8AY. *T:* Penzance (01736) 62722.

KENNEDY, Hon. Sir Ian (Alexander), Kt 1986; **Hon. Mr Justice Ian Kennedy;** Judge of the High Court of Justice, Queen's Bench Division, since 1986; *b* 7 Sept. 1930; *s* of late Gerald Donald Kennedy, OBE, and Elizabeth Jane (*née* McBeth); *m* 1962, Susan Margaret, *d* of late Lt-Col Edward John Hatfield, OBE, DL, and of Eileen (*née* Menneer); three *s* one *d. Educ:* Wellington Coll., Berks; Pembroke Coll., Cambridge (BA). Called to the Bar, Middle Temple, 1953. Dep. Chm., IoW QS, 1971; a Recorder of the Crown Court, 1972; QC 1974. Judge, Employment Appeal Tribunal, 1990–. *Recreations:* sailing, theatre, walking, gardening. *Address:* Royal Courts of Justice, Strand, WC2A 2LL.

KENNEDY, Prof. Ian McColl; Professor of Medical Law and Ethics, since 1983, President, Centre of Medical Law and Ethics, since 1993, King's College London; *b* 14 Sept. 1941; *s* of Robert Charles Kennedy and late Dorothy Elizabeth Kennedy; *m* 1980, Andrea, *d* of Frederick and Barbara Gage, Ventura, Calif; two *s. Educ:* King Edward VI Sch., Stourbridge; University Coll. London (1st Cl. Hons LLB); Univ. of Calif, Berkeley (LLM); LLD London. Called to the Bar, Inner Temple, 1974. Fulbright Fellow, 1963–65; Lectr in Law, UCL, 1965–71; Ford Foundn Fellow, Yale Univ. and Univ. of Mexico, 1966–67; Vis. Prof., Univ. of Calif, LA, 1971–72; King's College, London: Lectr in Law, 1973–78; Reader in English Law 1978–83; British Acad. Res. Fellow, 1978; Dir, Centre of Law, Medicine and Ethics, subseq. Centre of Med. Law and Ethics, 1978–93; Hd, Dept of Laws, 1986–89; Hd and Dean of Sch. of Law, 1989–92 and 1993–. FKC 1988. Member: Medicines Commn, 1984–91; GMC, 1984–93; Expert Adv. Gp on AIDS, DHSS, later Dept of Health, 1987–94; Gen. Adv. Council, BBC, 1987–91; Med. Ethics Cttee, BMA, 1990–; Nuffield Council on Bioethics, 1991–. Mem., Council, Open Section, RSM, 1978–88 (Vice-Pres., 1981–86; FRSM 1985). Reith Lectr, 1980. Editor, Medical Law Review, 1993–; Mem. Editorial Bd, Jl of Medical Ethics, 1978–. *Publications:* The Unmasking of Medicine, 1981, rev. edn 1983; Treat Me Right, 1988; (with A. Grubb) Medical Law: cases and materials, 1989, 2nd edn as Medical Law: text with materials, 1994. *Address:* 10 Dartmouth Park Road, NW5 1SY.

KENNEDY, James; *see* Kennedy, A. J.

KENNEDY, Jane Elizabeth; MP (Lab) Liverpool, Broadgreen, since 1992; *b* 4 May 1958; *d* of Clifford and Barbara Hodgson; *m* 1977, Robert Malcolm Kennedy; two *s. Educ:* Haughton Comprehensive Sch.; Darlington; Queen Elizabeth Sixth Form Coll.; Liverpool Univ. Child care residential worker 1979–84, Care Assistant 1984–88, Liverpool Social Services; Area Organiser, NUPE, 1988–92. Mem., Social Security Select Cttee, 1992–94. *Recreations:* rambling, dogs. *Address:* House of Commons, SW1A 0AA. *T:* 0171–219 4523; 302–304 Kensington, Liverpool L7 2RS. *T:* 0151–261 0007.

KENNEDY, Joanna Alicia Gore, OBE 1995; CEng; FICE; Associate Director, Ove Arup and Partners, since 1994; *b* 22 July 1950; *d* of late Captain G. A. G. Ormsby, DSO, DSC, RN and Susan Ormsby; *m* 1979, Richard Paul Kennedy, *qv*; two *s. Educ:* Queen Anne's School, Caversham; Lady Margaret Hall, Oxford (Scholar, 1969; BA 1st cl. Hons Eng. Sci. 1972; MA 1976; Hon. Mem., Senior Common Room, 1985–87). MICE 1979, FICE 1992; ACIArb 1983. Ove Arup and Partners, consulting engineers: Design Engineer, 1972; Asst Resident Engineer (Runnymede Bridge), 1977; Sen. Engr, 1979; Arup Associates, 1987; Project Management Services, 1990; Associate, 1992. Member: Engineering Council, 1984–86 and 1987–90; Council, ICE, 1984–87; Adv. Council, RNEC Manadon, 1988–94; Engrg and Technol. Prog. Adv. Gp, PCFC, 1989–91; Engrg, later Engrg and Technol. Bd, SERC, 1990–94; Tech. Opportunities Panel, EPSRC, 1994–. Trustee, Science Mus., 1992–; Fellow, Smallpeice Trust, 1994. Gov., Channing Sch., 1991–. Hon. DSc Salford, 1994. FRSA 1986. *Address:* Ove Arup & Partners, 13 Fitzroy Street, W1P 6BQ. *T:* 0171–636 1531.

KENNEDY, Rt. Rev. Mgr John; Parish Priest, Holy Family, Southport, since 1991; *b* 31 Dec. 1930; *s* of James Kennedy and Alice Kennedy (*née* Bentham). *Educ:* St Joseph's College, Upholland; Gregorian University, Rome (STL); Oxford University (MPhil). Curate: St John's, Wigan, 1956–63; St Austin's, St Helens, 1963–65; St Edmund's, Liverpool, 1965–68; Lectr in Theology, Christ's College, Liverpool, 1968–84 (Head of Dept, 1976–84); Rector, Ven. English Coll., Rome, 1984–91; Asst Lectr in Theol., Gregorian Univ., Rome, 1984–91. *Recreations:* golf, squash. *Address:* Holy Family Presbytery, 1 Brompton Road, Southport, Merseyside PR8 6AS.

See also Sir Francis Kennedy.

KENNEDY, John Maxwell; Senior Partner, Allen & Overy, 1986–94; *b* 9 July 1934; *s* of George and Betty Gertrude Kennedy; *m* 1958, Margaret Joan (*née* Davies); four *s. Educ:* University Coll., London (LLB). Admitted Solicitor, 1957; Partner, Allen & Overy, 1962. Chm., Law Debenture Corp., 1994–; Dir, Angerstein Underwriting Trust, 1993–. Mem., SIB, 1993–. *Recreations:* sport, music, reading. *Address:* 16 Kensington Park Road, W11 3BU. *T:* 0171–727 6929. *Clubs:* City of London, Bankers, City Law, Hurlingham; Royal Wimbledon Golf.

KENNEDY, Kevin; Chairman and Chief Executive, Domestic Appliances and Personal Care Division, and Member, Group Management Committee, Philips Electronics NV, since 1993; *b* 1 May 1937; *s* of John and Catherine Kennedy; *m* 1962, Ann Larkin; three *s. Educ:* Our Lady's High Sch., Motherwell. Dir and Gen. Man., Honeywell Information Systems Ltd, 1983–86; Group Man. Dir, Philips, 1986–89; Chm. and Sen. Man. Dir, Philips Information Systems, 1989–91; Chm. and Man. Dir, Philips Electronics and Associated Industries, 1991–93. CIMgt; FInstD. Freeman, City of London, 1988. *Recreations:* golf, music. *Address:* Hill House, Bute Avenue, Petersham, Richmond, Surrey TW10 7AX.

KENNEDY, Sir Ludovic (Henry Coverley), Kt 1994; writer and broadcaster; *b* Edinburgh, 3 Nov. 1919; *o s* of Captain E. C. Kennedy, RN (killed in action, 1939, while commanding HMS Rawalpindi against German battle-cruisers Scharnhorst and Gneisenau), and Rosalind, *d* of Sir Ludovic Grant, 11th Bt of Dalvey; *m* 1950, Moira Shearer King (*see* Moira Shearer); one *s* three *d. Educ:* Eton; Christ Church, Oxford (MA). Served War, 1939–46, RNVR. Priv. Sec. and ADC to Gov. of Newfoundland, 1943–44. Librarian, Ashridge (Adult Education) Coll., 1949; Rockefeller Foundation Atlantic Award in Literature, 1950; Winner, Open Finals Contest, English Festival of Spoken Poetry, 1953; Editor, feature, First Reading (BBC Third Prog.), 1953–54; Lecturer for British Council, Sweden, Finland and Denmark, 1955; Belgium and Luxembourg, 1956. Lectures: Voltaire Meml, 1985; Stevens, RSocMed, 1993. Mem. Council, Navy Records Soc., 1957–60. Contested (L) Rochdale, by-elec., 1958 and Gen. elec., 1959; Pres., Nat. League of Young Liberals, 1959–61; Mem., Lib. Party Council, 1965–67. Pres., Sir Walter Scott Club, Edinburgh, 1968–69; Patron, Russian Convoy Club, 1989–. Columnist: Newsweek International, 1974–75; Sunday Standard, 1981–82. Chm., Royal Lyceum Theatre Co. of Edinburgh, 1977–84. Dir, The Spectator, 1988–90. Chm. of Judges, NCR Book Award, 1990–91. FRSA 1974–76. Hon. LLD: Strathclyde, 1985; Southampton, 1993; Dr *hc* Edinburgh, 1990; DUniv Stirling, 1991. Richard Dimbleby BAFTA Award, 1988. Cross, First Class, Order of Merit, Fed. Repub. of Germany, 1979. *TV and radio:* Introd. Profile, ATV, 1955–56; Newscaster, Independent Television News, 1956–58; Introducer of AR's feature On Stage, 1957; Introducer of AR's, This Week, 1958–59; Chm. BBC features: Your Verdict, 1962; Your Witness, 1967–70; Commentator: BBC's Panorama, 1960–63; Television Reporters Internat., 1963–64 (also Prod.); Introducer, BBC's Time Out, 1964–65, World at One, 1965–66; Presenter: Lib. Party's Gen. Election Television Broadcasts, 1966; The Middle Years, ABC, 1967; The Nature of Prejudice, ATV, 1968; Face the Press, Tyne-Tees, 1968–69, 1970–72; Against the Tide, Yorkshire TV, 1969; Living and Growing, Grampian TV, 1969–70; 24 Hours, BBC, 1969–72; Ad Lib, BBC, 1970–72; Midweek, BBC, 1973–75; Newsday, BBC, 1975–76; Tonight, BBC, 1976–78; A Life with Crime, BBC, 1979; Change of Direction, BBC, 1979; Lord Mountbatten Remembers, 1980; Did You See?, 1980–88; Timewatch, 1984; Indelible Evidence, 1987 and 1990; A Gift of the Gab, 1989; Portrait, 1989. *Television films include:* The Sleeping Ballerina; The Singers and the Songs; Scapa Flow; Battleship Bismarck; Life and Death of the Scharnhorst; U-Boat War; Target Tirpitz; The Rise of the Red Navy; Lord Haw-Haw; Coast to Coast; Who Killed the Lindbergh Baby; Elizabeth: the first thirty years; Happy Birthday, dear Ma'am; Consider The End. *Publications:* Sub-Lieutenant, 1942; Nelson's Band of Brothers, 1951; One Man's Meat, 1953; Murder Story (play, with essay on Capital Punishment), 1956; play: Murder Story (Cambridge Theatre), 1954; Ten Rillington Place, 1961; The Trial of Stephen Ward, 1964; Very Lovely People, 1969; Pursuit: the chase and sinking of the Bismarck, 1974; A Presumption of Innocence: the Amazing Case of Patrick Meehan, 1975; Menace: the life and death of the Tirpitz, 1979; The Portland Spy Case, 1979; Wicked Beyond Belief, 1980; (ed) A Book of Railway Journeys, 1980; (ed) A Book of Sea Journeys, 1981; (ed) A Book of Air Journeys, 1982; The Airman and the Carpenter, 1985; On My Way to the Club (autobiog.), 1989; Euthanasia: the good death, 1990; Truth to Tell (collected writings), 1991; Gen. Editor, The British at War, 1973–77. *Address:* c/o Rogers, Coleridge and White, 20 Powis Mews, W11 1JN. *Clubs:* Brooks's, Army and Navy.

KENNEDY, Dr Malcolm William, FEng 1985; FIEE; Executive Chairman, Merz and McLellan, since 1995; *b* 13 March 1935; *s* of William and Lily Kennedy; *m* 1962, Patricia Ann Forster; one *d*. Educ: Durham Univ. (BSc 1961); Univ. of Newcastle upon Tyne (PhD 1964). CEng; FIEE 1974. Apprentice, C. A. Parsons, 1951–56; Merz and McLellan, 1964–: Power Systems Design Engr, 1964; Head, Electrical Div., 1976; Sen. Partner, 1988–91; Chm. and Man. Dir, 1991–95. Head, Northern Engrg Centre. Mem. Electricity Panel, Monopolies and Mergers Commn. Dir, Port of Tyne Authority. Vice-Pres., IEE, 1989, 1994 (Henry Nimmo Premium, 1961; Chm., Power Div., 1986–87). CIMgt 1992. Methodist local preacher. *Publications:* papers on electricity industry, UK and overseas. *Recreations:* cricket, railways. *Address:* Merz and McLellan, Amber Court, William Armstrong Drive, Newcastle upon Tyne NE4 7YQ. *T:* 0191–226 1899. *Club:* National.

KENNEDY, Michael; *see* Kennedy, G. M. S.

KENNEDY, Michael Denis; QC 1979; **His Honour Judge Kennedy;** a Circuit Judge, since 1984; *b* 29 April 1937; *s* of Denis George and Clementina Catherine (*née* MacGregor); *m* 1964, Elizabeth June Curtiss; two *s* two *d. Educ:* Downside School; Gonville and Caius College, Cambridge (open Schol., Mod. Langs; MA). 15/19 King's Royal Hussars, 1955–57. Called to the Bar, Inner Temple, 1961; a Recorder, 1979–84. *Address:* c/o Brighton County Court, William Street, Brighton, E Sussex BN2 2LG. *T:* Brighton (01273) 670868.

KENNEDY, Sir Michael Edward, 8th Bt *cr* 1836, of Johnstown Kennedy, Co. Dublin; *b* 12 April 1956; *s* of Sir (George) Ronald Derrick Kennedy, 7th Bt and of Noelle Mona, *d* of Charles Henry Green; *S* father, 1988; *m* 1984, Helen Christine Jennifer, *d* of Patrick Lancelot Rae; one *s* two *d. Heir: s* George Mathew Rae Kennedy, *b* 9 Dec. 1993. *Address:* 48 Telston Lane, Otford, Kent TN14 5LA.

KENNEDY, Moira, (Lady Kennedy); *see* Shearer, M.

KENNEDY, Nigel Paul; solo concert violinist; *b* 28 Dec. 1956; *s* of John Kennedy and Scylla Stoner. *Educ:* Yehudi Menuhin School; Juilliard School of Performing Arts, NY. ARCM. Début at Festival Hall with Philharmonia Orch., 1977; regular appearances with London and provincial orchestras, 1978–; Berlin début with Berlin Philharmonic, 1980; Henry Wood Promenade début, 1981; New York début with BBC SO, 1987; tour of Hong Kong and Australia, with Hallé Orch., 1981; foreign tours, 1978–: India, Japan, S Korea, Turkey, USA; many appearances as jazz violinist with Stephane Grappelli, incl. Edinburgh Fest., 1974 and Carnegie Hall, 1976; many TV and radio appearances, incl. Vivaldi's Four Seasons with ECO (Golden Rose of Montreux, 1990), and two documentaries; pop, jazz and classical recordings; Best Classical Record, 1985, British Record Industry Awards, for recording of Elgar Violin Concerto; Guinness Book of Records, 1990, for sustaining Vivaldi's Four Seasons at No 1 in UK Classical Chart for over one yr; Variety Club Showbusiness Personality of the Year, 1991. Sen. Vice-Pres., Aston Villa FC, 1990–. Hon. DLitt Bath, 1991. *Publication:* Always Playing (autobiog.), 1991. *Recreations:* golf, football (watching and playing), cricket. *Address:* c/o Pamela Esterson, 81 Landor Road, SW9 9RT. *T:* 0171–924 0402, *Fax:* 0171–274 3243.

KENNEDY, Rt. Hon. Sir Paul (Joseph Morrow), Kt 1983; PC 1992; **Rt. Hon. Lord Justice Kennedy;** a Lord Justice of Appeal, since 1992; *b* 12 June 1935; *o s* of late Dr J. M. Kennedy, Sheffield; *m* 1965, Virginia, twin *d* of Baron Devlin, FBA and of Madeleine, *yr d* of Sir Bernard Oppenheimer, 1st Bt; two *s* two *d. Educ:* Ampleforth Coll.; Gonville and Caius Coll., Cambridge (MA, LLB). Called to Bar, Gray's Inn, 1960, Bencher, 1982; a Recorder, 1972–83; QC 1973; Judge, High Court of Justice, QBD, 1983–92; Presiding Judge, N Eastern Circuit, 1985–89. Chm., Criminal Cttee, 1993; Mem., Judicial Studies Bd, 1993–. *Address:* Royal Courts of Justice, Strand, WC2A 2LL.

KENNEDY, Prof. Peter Graham Edward, MD, DSc; FRCP; Burton Professor of Neurology, University of Glasgow and Consultant Neurologist, Institute of Neurological Sciences, Southern General Hospital, Glasgow, since 1987; *b* 28 March 1951; *s* of Philip Kennedy and Gertrude Sylvia Kennedy (*née* Summer); *m* 1983, Catherine Ann King; one *s* one *d. Educ:* University Coll. Sch.; University College London and UCH Med. Sch. (MB BS, MPhil, MD, PhD, DSc). MRCPath. FRSE. Med. Registrar, UCH and Whittington Hosps, 1976–78; Hon. Res. Asst, MRC Neuroimmunology Project, UCL, 1978–80; Registrar and Res. Fellow, Univ. of Glasgow, 1981; Registrar then Sen. Registrar, Nat. Hosp. for Nervous Diseases, 1982–84; Asst Prof. of Neurology, Johns Hopkins Univ. Hosp., 1985; New Blood Sen. Lectr in Neurology and Virology, Univ. of Glasgow, 1986–87. Vis. Fellow in Medicine, Jesus Coll., Cambridge, 1992; Fogarty

Internat. Scholar, NIH, 1993–94. BUPA Med. Foundn Doctor of the Year Res. Award, 1990; Linacre Medal and Lectr, RCP, 1991; T. S. Srinivasan Gold Medal and Endowment Lectr, 1993. *Publications:* (with R. T. Johnson) Infections of the Nervous System, 1987; numerous papers on neurology, neurobiology and neurovirology. *Recreations:* philosophy, tennis, music, astronomy, walking in the country. *Address:* Glasgow University Department of Neurology, Institute of Neurological Sciences, Southern General Hospital, Glasgow G51 4TF. *T:* 0141–201 2474, *Fax:* 0141–201 2993.

KENNEDY, Richard Paul; Head Master of Highgate School, since 1989; *b* 17 Feb. 1949; *e s* of David Clifton Kennedy and Evelyn Mary Hall (*née* Tindale); *m* 1979, Joanna Alicia Gore Ormsby (*see* J. A. G. Kennedy); two *s*. *Educ:* Charterhouse; New College, Oxford (BA Maths and Phil. 1970; MA 1977). Assistant Master, Shrewsbury Sch., 1971–77, Westminster Sch., 1977–84; Dep. Headmaster, Bishop's Stortford Coll., 1984–89 (Acting Headmaster 1989). Headmasters' Conference: Mem., Sports Cttee, 1992–; Mem., Cttee, 1995–; Chm., London Div., 1996. Governor: The Hall Sch., Hampstead, 1989–; Wycombe Abbey Sch., 1992–. GB internat. athlete (sprints), 1973–76. Mem., Acad. of St Martin-in-the-Fields Chorus, 1977–. *Recreations:* reading biographies, choral music. *Address:* 12 Bishopswood Road, N6 4NY. *T:* 0181–340 7626.

KENNEDY, Thomas Alexander; economist; *b* 11 July 1920; *s* of late Rt Hon. Thomas Kennedy, PC, and Annie S. Kennedy (*née* Michie); *m* 1947, Audrey (*née* Plunkett) (*d* 1991); one *s* two *d*. *Educ:* Alleyn's Sch., Dulwich; Durham Univ. (BA). Economist: Bd of Trade, 1950–52; Colonial Office, 1952–55; Lecturer in Economics at Makerere Coll., Uganda, 1955–61; Economist: Treasury, Foreign Office, DEA, 1961–67; Economic Director, NEDO, 1967–70; Under-Sec.: DTI, 1970–74; Dept of Energy, 1974–80, resigned. Chief Tech. Adviser (Economist Planner), Min. of Petroleum and Mineral Resources, Bangladesh, 1980–81. Vis. Fellow, Clare Hall, Cambridge, 1981–82. Consultant, World Bank: Uganda, Zambia, Swaziland, 1983–86, retired 1987. *Address:* 1 Beckside Mews, Staindrop, Darlington, Co. Durham DL2 3PG. *T:* Staindrop (01833) 660616.

KENNEDY, Air Chief Marshal Sir Thomas (Lawrie), GCB 1985 (KCB 1980; CB 1978); AFC 1953 and Bar 1960; DL; Royal Air Force, retired; Controller, RAF Benevolent Fund, 1988–93; *b* 19 May 1928; *s* of James Domoné Kennedy and Margaret Henderson Lawrie; *m* 1959, Margaret Ann Parker; one *s* two *d*. *Educ:* Hawick High Sch. RAF Coll., Cranwell, 1946–49; commissioned, 1949. Sqdn service, 1949–53; exchange service, RAAF, 1953–55; returned to UK, 1955; 27 Sqdn (Canberra), 1955–57; Radar Research Estabt, 1957–60; RAF Coll. Selection Bd, 1960–62; RN Staff Coll., Greenwich, 1962; HQ Middle East, 1962–64; CO, No 99 (Britannia) Sqdn, 1965–67; HQ Air Support Comd, 1967–69; CO, RAF Brize Norton, 1970–71; Dep. Comdt, RAF Staff Coll., 1971–73; Dir of Ops (AS) MoD, 1973–75; Royal Coll. of Defence Studies, 1976; Comdr, Northern Maritime Air Region, 1977–79; Deputy C-in-C, RAF Strike Command, 1979–81; C-in-C, RAF Germany, and Comdr, 2nd Allied Tactical Air Force, 1981–83; Air Mem. for Personnel, 1983–86; Air ADC to the Queen, 1983–86. Dir, Dowty Group, 1987–92. Freeman, City of London, 1987; Hon. Liveryman, Fruiterers' Co., 1987. DL Leics, 1989. *Recreations:* golf, sailing. *Address:* c/o Lloyds Bank, Cox's & King's Branch, PO Box 1190, SW1Y 5NA. *Club:* Royal Air Force.

KENNEDY, William Andrew; Metropolitan Stipendiary Magistrate, since 1991; Chairman, Youth Courts, since 1992; *b* 13 Feb. 1948; *s* of Sidney Herbert and Kathleen Blanche Kennedy; *m* 1st, 1974, Alice Steen Wilkie (*d* 1987); 2nd, 1988, Lindsey Jane Sheridan; one *s* one *d*. *Educ:* Buckhurst Hill County High Sch., College of Law, Lancaster Gate. Articled Clerk, Trotter Chapman & Whisker, Epping, Essex, 1966–72, admitted Solicitor, 1972; Partner 1972–75, Jt Sen. Partner 1975–91, Trotter Chapman & Whisker, later Whiskers. Notary Public, 1981. Pres., W Essex Law Soc., 1983–84. *Recreations:* golf, gentle domestic pursuits. *Address:* c/o Greenwich Magistrates' Court, Blackheath Road, SE10 8PG. *T:* 0181–694 0033. *Club:* Chigwell Golf.

KENNEDY-GOOD, Sir John, KBE 1983; QSO 1977; JP; Mayor of Lower Hutt, 1970–86; *b* Goulburn, NSW, 8 Aug. 1915; *s* of Charles Kennedy-Good; *m* 1940, June, *d* of Charles Mackay; four *s* three *d*. *Educ:* Southland Boys' High Sch.; Otago Univ. (BDS). Practised as dentist, 1942–72. Mem., Lower Hutt City Council, 1962–. Dir, Hutt Milk Corp., 1970–71, 1974–; Chairman: Hutt Valley Underground Water Authy, 1970–72 (Mem., 1962–72); Wellington Regl Council, 1980– (Dep. Chm., 1980–83); NZ Council of Social Services, 1975–82; Member: Wellington Harbour Bd, 1971–80; Hutt Valley Energy Bd, 1970–. Past Mem., NZ Catchment Authorities' Exec. Pres., NZ Sister Cities Inc. Chm., Dowse Art Mus. Bd, 1971–; Dep. Chm., Nat. Art Gall. and Mus. Trust Bd (Mem., 1971). Mem., NZ Acad. Fine Arts, 1948. Founder Chm., John Kennedy-Good Human Resources Centre; Chm., Wellington Paraplegic Trust Bd (Vice-Pres., NZ Fed.); past Chm., Council for Dental Health, and past Pres., Wellington Br., NZ Dental Assoc.; Life Patron and Mem. Bd, Hutt Valley Disabled Resources Trust; Pres., Wellington Div., Order of St John; Patron, Wellington Reg. Centre, NZ Red Cross Soc.; patron, pres. or vice-pres. of numerous charity, cultural and sporting orgns. Trustee, Waiwhetu Marae, 1970–; Hon. Elder, Te Atiawa Tribe. JP Lower Hutt, 1970. *Clubs:* Hutt, Hutt Rotary (past Pres.), Hutt Golf.

KENNEDY MARTIN, (Francis) Troy; writer; *b* 15 Feb. 1932; *s* of Frank Martin and Kathleen Flanagan; *m* 1967, Diana Aubrey; one *s* one *d*. *Educ:* Finchley Catholic Grammar Sch.; Trinity Coll., Dublin (BA (Hons) History). Following nat. service with Gordon Highlanders in Cyprus, wrote Incident at Echo Six, a TV play, 1959; *BBC TV:* originated: Storyboard, and The Interrogator, 1961; Z Cars, 1962; Diary of a Young Man, 1964; Man Without Papers, 1965; Edge of Darkness, 1985; *Thames TV:* Reilly, Ace of Spies, 1983; *films:* The Italian Job, 1969; Kelly's Heroes, 1970. Jt Screenwriters' Guild Award, 1962; BAFTA Scriptwriter's Award, 1962. *Publication:* Beat on a Damask Drum, 1961. *Recreation:* collecting marine models. *Address:* 6 Ladbroke Gardens, W11 2PT.

KENNERLEY, Prof. (James) Anthony (Machell), CEng, MIMechE; Chairman, West Surrey Health Commission; Tutor to Senior Management Courses in the Public Sector; *b* 24 Oct. 1933; *s* of William James Kennerley and late Vida May (*née* Machell); *m* 1978, Dorothy Mary (*née* Simpson); one *s* one *d* (twins). *Educ:* Universities of Manchester (BSc; Silver Medallist, 1955) and London (MSc; IMechE James Clayton Fellow). AFIMA, AFRAeS. Fourth Engr, Blue Funnel Line, Alfred Holt, 1954; Engineer, A. V. Roe, Manchester, 1955–58; Aerodynamicist, Pratt & Whitney, Montreal, Canada, 1958–59; Jet Pilot, RCAF, 1959–62; Asst Professor of Mathematics, Univ. of New Brunswick, Canada, 1962–67; Director of Graduate Studies, Manchester Business Sch., 1967–69; Associate Professor of Business Studies, Columbia Univ., New York, 1969–70; Director, Executive Programme, London Business Sch., 1970–73; Prof. of Business Admin, and Dir, Strathclyde Business Sch., 1973–83; Dir, InterMatrix Ltd, Management Consultants, 1984–92; Vis. Prof. of Management, 1984–93, Prof. of Health Care Management, 1993–, Univ. of Surrey. Chm., W Surrey and NE Hants, then NW Surrey, HA, 1986–95. Chairman: Management Res. Gp, Scotland, 1981–82; Scottish Milk Marketing Scheme Arbitration Panel, 1981–83; Council for Professions Supplementary to Medicine, 1990–. Member: South of Scotland Electricity Bd, 1977–84; Management Studies Bd, CNAA, 1977–84; BIM Educn Cttee, 1982–92; Monopolies and Mergers Commn, 1992–; Adv. Bd, Meta Generics, Cambridge, 1992–95; Chm., Conf. of Univ. Management Schs, 1981–83; Director: Business Graduates Assoc., 1983–86; First Step Housing Co., Waverley BC, 1990–. Arbitrator, ACAS, 1976–. Mem., Trans-Turkey Highway World Bank Mission, 1982–83. Founder Mem., Bridgegate Trust, Glasgow, 1982–85. *Publications:* Guide to Business Schools, 1985; Arbitration: cases in industrial relations, 1994; articles, papers on business studies, on Public Sector management, and on applied mathematics. *Recreations:* flying, travelling. *Address:* The Ridgewood Centre, Old Bisley Road, Frimley, Camberley, Surrey GU16 5QE; 5 Old Rectory Gardens, Busbridge, Godalming, Surrey GU7 1XB. *T:* Godalming (01483) 428108. *Clubs:* Reform, Caledonian.

KENNET, 2nd Baron *cr* 1935; **Wayland Hilton Young;** author and politician; *b* 2 Aug. 1923; *s* of 1st Baron Kennet, PC, GBE, DSO, DSC, and of Kathleen Bruce (who *m* 1st, Captain Robert Falcon Scott, CVO, RN, and died 1947); *S* father 1960; *m* 1948, Elizabeth Ann, *d* of late Captain Bryan Fullerton Adams, DSO, RN; one *s* five *d*. *Educ:* Stowe; Trinity Coll., Cambridge. Served in RN, 1942–45. Foreign Office, 1946–47, and 1949–51. Deleg., Parliamentary Assemblies, WEU and Council of Europe, 1962–65; Parly Sec., Min. of Housing and Local Govt, 1966–70; Opposition Spokesman on Foreign Affairs and Science Policy, 1971–74; SDP Chief Whip in H of L, 1981–83; SDP spokesman in H of L on foreign affairs and defence, 1981–90. Chairman: Adv. Cttee on Oil Pollution of the Sea, 1970–74; CPRE, 1971–72; Internat. Parly Confs on the Environment, 1972–78; Dir, Europe Plus Thirty, 1974–75; Mem., European Parlt, 1978–79; Vice Pres., Parly and Scientific Cttee, 1989–. Chm., Architecture Club, 1983–94. Hon. FRIBA 1970. Editor of Disarmament and Arms Control, 1962–65. *Publications:* (as Wayland Young): The Italian Left, 1949; The Deadweight, 1952; Now or Never, 1953; Old London Churches (with Elizabeth Young), 1956; The Montesi Scandal, 1957; Still Alive Tomorrow, 1958; Strategy for Survival, 1959; The Profumo Affair, 1963; Eros Denied, 1965; Thirty-Four Articles, 1965; (ed) Existing Mechanisms of Arms Control, 1965; (as Wayland Kennet) Preservation, 1972; The Futures of Europe, 1976; The Rebirth of Britain, 1982; (with Elizabeth Young) London's Churches, 1986; (with Elizabeth Young) Northern Lazio, 1990; Parliaments and Screening, 1995; Fabian and SDP pamphlets on defence, disarmament, environment, multinational companies, etc. *Heir:* *s* Hon. William Aldus Thoby Young [*b* 24 May 1957; *m* 1987, Hon. Josephine, *yr d* of Baron Keyes, *qv*; one *s* one *d*]. *Address:* House of Lords, SW1A 0PW.

KENNETT, Hon. Jeffrey (Gibb); MLA (L) Burwood, since 1976; Premier of Victoria, since 1992; *b* 2 March 1948; *m* 1972, Felicity; three *s* one *d*. Founder, KNF Advertising Pty Ltd. Minister for Aboriginal Affairs, Immigration, Ethnic Affairs and Housing, 1981–82; Leader of the Opposition, 1982–89, 1991–92. *Address:* Office of the Premier, 3/55 Collins Street, Melbourne, Vic 3000, Australia; Parliament House, Melbourne, Vic 3002, Australia.

KENNETT, Ronald John, FRAeS; Director, Royal Aeronautical Society, since 1988; *b* 25 March 1935; *s* of William John and Phyllis Gertrude Kennett; *m* 1957, Sylvia Barstow; one *s* three *d*. *Educ:* Bradford Technical College. Lucas Aerospace: joined 1956; Chief Engineer, 1978–86; Quality Assurance Manager, 1986–88. FIMgt; FInstD; FCIT; AFAIAA; FRSA. *Recreations:* reading, writing, music, country recreation. *Address:* Royal Aeronautical Society, 4 Hamilton Place, W1V 0BQ. *T:* 0171–499 3515.

KENNETT BROWN, David, JP; FCIArb; a Metropolitan Stipendiary Magistrate, since 1982; a Recorder, since 1989 (authorised in County Courts, since 1992); *b* 29 Jan. 1938; *s* of late Thomas Kennett Brown, solicitor, and Vanda Brown; *m* 1966, Wendy Margaret Evans; one *s* two *d*. *Educ:* Monkton Combe Sch.; Lincoln Coll., Oxford. FCIArb 1982. Admitted Solicitor, 1965. Partner, Kennett Brown & Co., 1965–82. Chm., Family Proceedings and Youth Courts, 1983–. Chm., London Rent Assessment Panel, 1979–82; Pres., Central and S Mddx Law Soc., 1982. JP Willesden, 1975–82. *Recreations:* escaping to Cornwall, gardening. *Address:* c/o Marylebone Magistrates' Court, 181 Marylebone Road, NW1 5QJ.

KENNEY, Anthony, FRCS; FRCOG; Consultant Obstetrician and Gynaecologist, St Thomas' Hospital, since 1980; *b* 17 Jan. 1942; *s* of Eric Alfred Allen Kenney and Doris Winifred Kenney; *m* 1973, Patricia Clare Newbery; four *s* one *d*. *Educ:* Brentwood School; Gonville and Caius College, Cambridge (MA 1967); London Hosp. Med. Coll. MB BChir 1966; FRCS 1970; MRCOG 1972, FRCOG 1987. House appts, London Hosp., Queen Charlotte's Hosp. and Chelsea Hosp. for Women, 1966–72; Registrar and Sen. Registrar, Westminster and Kingston Hosps, 1972–79. Examiner in Obstetrics and Gynaecology: Univs of London, Liverpool and Cambridge; RCOG. *Publications:* contribs to med. jls. *Recreations:* canal cruising, foreign travel. *Address:* 92 Coombe Lane West, Kingston upon Thames, Surrey KT2 7DB. *T:* 0181–942 0440. *Clubs:* Royal Society of Medicine, Medical Society of London.

KENNEY, Prof. Edward John, FBA 1968; Kennedy Professor of Latin, University of Cambridge, 1974–82; Fellow of Peterhouse, Cambridge, 1953–91; *b* 29 Feb. 1924; *s* of George Kenney and Emmie Carlina Elfrida Schwenke; *m* 1955, Gwyneth Anne, *d* of late Prof. Henry Albert Harris. *Educ:* Christ's Hospital; Trinity Coll., Cambridge. BA 1949, MA 1953. Served War of 1939–45: Royal Signals, UK and India, 1943–46; commissioned 1944, Lieut 1945. Porson Schol., 1948; Craven Schol., 1949; Craven Student, 1949; Chancellor's Medallist, 1950. Asst Lectr, Univ. of Leeds, 1951–52; University of Cambridge: Research Fellow, Trinity Coll., 1952–53; Asst Lectr, 1955–60, Lectr, 1966–70; Reader in Latin Literature and Textual Criticism, 1970–74; Peterhouse: Director of Studies in Classics, 1953–74; Librarian, 1953–82, Perne Librarian, 1987–91; Tutor, 1956–62; Senior Tutor, 1962–65; Domestic Bursar, 1987–88. James C. Loeb Fellow in Classical Philology, Harvard Univ., 1967–68; Sather Prof. of Classical Literature, Univ. of California, Berkeley, 1968; Carl Newell Jackson Lectr, Harvard Univ., 1980. President: Jt Assoc. of Classical Teachers, 1977–79; Classical Assoc., 1982–83. For. Mem., Royal Netherlands Acad. of Arts and Scis, 1976. Treasurer and Chm., Council of Almoners, Christ's Hosp., 1984–86. Jt Editor, Classical Qly, 1959–65; Jt Gen. Ed., Cambridge Greek and Latin Classics, 1966–. *Publications:* P. Ouidi Nasonis Amores etc (ed), 1961, 2nd edn 1994; (with Mrs P. E. Easterling) Ovidiana Graeca (ed), 1965; (with W. V. Clausen, F. R. D. Goodyear, J. A. Richmond) Appendix Vergiliana (ed), 1966; Lucretius, De Rerum Natura III (ed), 1971; The Classical Text, 1974 (trans. Italian, 1995); (with W. V. Clausen) Latin Literature (ed and contrib.) (Cambridge History of Classical Literature II), 1982; The Ploughman's Lunch (*Moretum*), 1984; introd. and notes to Ovid, Metamorphoses, trans. A. D. Melville, 1986; Ovid, The Love Poems, 1990; Apuleius, Cupid & Psyche (ed), 1990; introd. and notes to Ovid, Sorrows of an Exile (*Tristia*), trans A. D. Melville, 1992; articles and reviews in classical jls. *Recreations:* cats and books. *Address:* Peterhouse, Cambridge CB2 1RD.

KENNY, Sir Anthony (John Patrick), Kt 1992; FBA 1974; Warden, Rhodes House, since 1989; Professorial Fellow, St John's College, Oxford, since 1989; Master of Balliol College, Oxford, 1978–89 (Fellow, 1964–78; Senior Tutor, 1971–72 and 1976–78); President, British Academy, 1989–93; *b* Liverpool, 16 March 1931; *s* of John Kenny and Margaret Jones; *m* 1966, Nancy Caroline, *d* of Henry T. Gayley, Jr, Swarthmore, Pa; two *s. Educ:* Gregorian Univ., Rome (STL); St Benet's Hall, Oxford; DPhil 1961, DLitt 1980. Ordained priest, Rome, 1955; Curate in Liverpool, 1959–63; returned to lay state, 1963. Asst Lectr, Univ. of Liverpool, 1961–63; University of Oxford: Lectr in Philosophy, Exeter and Trinity Colls, 1963–64; University Lectr, 1965–78; Wilde Lectr in Natural and Comparative Religion, 1969–72; Speaker's Lectureship in Biblical Studies, 1980–83; Mem., Hebdomadal Council, 1981–93; Pro-Vice-Chancellor, 1984–95; Vice-Chm., Libraries Bd, 1985–88; Curator, Bodleian Library, 1985–88; Deleg., and Mem., Finance Cttee, OUP, 1986–93. Jt Gifford Lectr, Univ. of Edinburgh, 1972–73; Stanton Lectr, Univ. of Cambridge, 1980–83; Bampton Lectr, Columbia Univ., 1983. Visiting Professor: Univs of Chicago, Washington, Michigan, Minnesota and Cornell, Stanford and Rockefeller Univs. Mem. Council, British Acad., 1985–88 (Vice-Pres., 1986–88). Chairman: British Liby Bd, 1993– (Mem., 1991–); Soc. for Protection of Science and Learning, 1989–93; British Nat. Corpus Adv. Bd, 1990–95; British Irish Assoc., 1990–94. Hon. DLitt: Bristol, 1982; Liverpool, 1988; Glasgow, 1990; TCD, 1992; Hull, 1993; Sheffield, Warwick, 1995; Hon. DHumLitt: Denison Univ., Ohio, 1986; Lafayette Univ., Penn, 1990; Hon. DCL: Oxon, 1987; QUB, 1994. Editor, The Oxford Magazine, 1972–73. *Publications:* Action, Emotion and Will, 1963; Responsa Alumnorum of English College, Rome, 2 vols, 1963; Descartes, 1968; The Five Ways, 1969; Wittgenstein, 1973; The Anatomy of the Soul, 1974; Will, Freedom and Power, 1975; The Aristotelian Ethics, 1978; Freewill and Responsibility, 1978; Aristotle's Theory of the Will, 1979; The God of the Philosophers, 1979; Aquinas, 1980; The Computation of Style, 1982; Faith and Reason, 1983; Thomas More, 1983; The Legacy of Wittgenstein, 1984; A Path from Rome (autobiog.), 1985; Wyclif, 1985; The Logic of Deterrence, 1985; The Ivory Tower, 1985; A Stylometric Study of the New Testament, 1986; The Road to Hillsborough, 1987; Reason and Religion, 1987; The Heritage of Wisdom, 1987; God and Two Poets, 1988; The Metaphysics of Mind, 1989; The Oxford Diaries of Arthur Hugh Clough, 1990; Mountains: an anthology, 1991; Aristotle on the Perfect Life, 1992; What is Faith?, 1992; Aquinas on Mind, 1993; (ed) Oxford Illustrated History of Western Philosophy, 1994; Frege, 1995. *Address:* Rhodes House, Oxford OX1 3RG. *Club:* Athenæum.

KENNY, Anthony Marriott; His Honour Judge Kenny; a Circuit Judge, since 1987; Principal Judge in Civil Matters for Berkshire and Buckinghamshire; designated Family Judge, Reading; *b* 24 May 1939; *o s* of late Noel Edgar Edward Marriott Kenny, OBE, and Cynthia Margaret Seton Kenny (*née* Melville); *m* 1969, Monica Grant Mackenzie, *yr d* of late H. B. Grant Mackenzie, Pretoria; three *s. Educ:* St Andrew's Coll., Grahamstown, Cape Province; Christ's Coll., Cambridge (MA). Called to the Bar, Gray's Inn, 1963; South Eastern Circuit. A Recorder, 1980–87. *Recreations:* music, reading, tennis, skiing. *Address:* Winchendon Hill Farm, Nether Winchendon, Bucks HP18 0DX.

KENNY, Arthur William, CBE 1977; CChem, FRSC; Director in the Directorate General of Environmental Protection of the Department of the Environment, 1974–79; *b* 31 May 1918; *s* of Ernest James Kenny and Gladys Margaret Kenny; *m* 1947, Olive Edna West; one *s* two *d. Educ:* Canton High Sch., Cardiff; Jesus Coll., Oxford (schol.). BA (1st Cl. Hons Natural Sci.), MA, BSc, Oxon. Min. of Supply, 1941; Min. of Health, 1950; Min. of Housing and Local Govt, 1951; DoE, 1971. *Publications:* papers on disposal of radioactive and toxic wastes and on quality of drinking water. *Address:* 134 Manor Green Road, Epsom, Surrey KT19 8LL. *T:* Epsom (01372) 724850.

KENNY, Gen. Sir Brian (Leslie Graham), GCB 1991 (KCB 1985); CBE 1979; Governor, Royal Hospital, Chelsea, since 1993; *b* 18 June 1934; *s* of late Brig. James Wolfenden Kenny, CBE, and of Aileen Anne Georgina Kenny (*née* Swan); *m* 1958, Diana Catherine Jane Mathew; two *s. Educ:* Canford School. Commissioned into 4th Hussars (later Queen's Royal Irish Hussars), 1954; served BAOR, Aden, Malaya and Borneo; Pilot's course, 1961; Comd 16 Recce Flt QRIH; psc 1965; MA/VCGS, MoD, 1966–68; Instructor, Staff Coll., 1971–73; CO QRIH, BAOR and UN Cyprus, 1974–76; Col GS 4 Armd Div., 1977–78; Comd 12 Armd Bde (Task Force D), 1979–80; RCDS 1981; Comdr 1st Armoured Div., 1982–83; Dir, Army Staff Duties, MoD, 1983–85; Comdr 1st (British) Corps, BAOR, 1985–87; Comdr, Northern Army Gp, and C-in-C, BAOR, 1987–89; Dep. SACEUR, 1990–93. Col QRIH, 1985–93; Colonel Commandant: RAVC, 1983–95; RAC, 1988–93. Chm., Army Benevolent Fund, 1993–. Governor, Canford Sch., 1983–. *Recreations:* ski-ing, cricket, shooting, racing. *Address:* c/o Lloyds Bank plc, Camberley, Surrey GU15 3SE. *Clubs:* Cavalry and Guards, MCC, I Zingari, Free Foresters.

KENNY, David John, CBE 1991; Regional General Manager, North West Thames Regional Health Authority, 1984–91 (Regional Administrator, 1982–84); *b* 2 Dec. 1940; *s* of late Gerald Henry Kenny and Ellen Veronica (*née* Crosse); *m* 1964, Elisabeth Ann, *d* of late Robert and of Jean Ferris; three *s. Educ:* Royal Belfast Academical Instn; Queen's Univ., Belfast (LLB). FHSM. Dep. House Governor, Bd of Governors, London Hosp., 1972; Dist Administrator, Tower Hamlets Health Dist, 1974; Area Administrator, Kensington and Chelsea and Westminster AHA, 1978. Mem. Nat. Council, Inst. of Health Service Managers, 1975–86 and 1988– (Pres. 1981–82); Chm., Gen. Managers of RHAs, 1989–. Chm., Data Protection Working Gp, Internat. Med. Informatics Assoc., 1979–87. *Publications:* (jtly) Data Protection in Health Information Systems, 1980; articles on management topics, data protection and ethics. *Recreations:* cinema, theatre, athletics, rugby football. *Address:* 131 Maze Hill, SE3 7UB. *T:* 0181–858 1545. *Club:* Athenæum.

KENNY, Douglas Timothy, MA, PhD; psychologist, educator; President and Vice Chancellor, University of British Columbia, 1975–83, President Emeritus, since 1989; *b* Victoria, BC, 20 Oct. 1923; *s* of John Ernest Kenny and Margaret Julia (*née* Collins); *m* 1st, 1950, Lucille Rabowski (decd); one *s* one *d*; 2nd, 1976, Margaret Lindsay Little. *Educ:* Victoria Coll.; Univ. of British Columbia (BA 1945, MA 1947); Univ. of Washington (PhD 1952). University of British Columbia: Lectr, 1950–54; Asst Prof., 1954–57; Associate Prof., 1957–64; Prof., 1965; Pres., Faculty Assoc., 1961–62; Head, Dept of Psychology, 1965–69; Acting Dean, Faculty of Arts, 1969–70, Dean, 1970–75; Hon. Pres., Alumni Assoc., 1975–83. Vis. Associate Prof., Harvard Univ., 1963–65. Member: Internat. Assoc. of Univ. Presidents, 1975–83; Social Science and Humanities Res. Council, 1978–83; BC Res. Council, 1975–; Canada Council, 1975–78; Monterey Inst. of Internat. Studies, 1980–83; Discovery Foundn, BC, 1979–83; Amer. Psychol Assoc.; Amer. Psychol Soc.; Bd of Trustees, Vancouver Gen. Hosp., 1976–78; Bd of Governors, Arts, Sciences and Technol. Centre, Vancouver, 1980 (Founder Mem.); President: BC Psychol Assoc., 1951–52; Vancouver Inst., 1973–75 (Hon. Pres., 1975–83). Hon. Patron, Internat. Foundn of Learning, 1983–. Hon. LLD Univ. of BC, 1983. Park O. Davidson Meml Award for outstanding contribn to develt of psychol., 1984. Silver Jubilee Medal, 1977. *Publications:* articles in professional jls. *Address:* 4810 Crown Crescent, Vancouver, BC V6R 2A9, Canada; (office) 2136 West Mall, Vancouver, BC V6T 1Y7. *Clubs:* Vancouver, University, Faculty (Vancouver).

KENNY, Michael, RA 1986 (ARA 1976); FRBS 1992; sculptor; Head of Fine Art Department, later Director of Fine Art Studies, Goldsmiths' College, University of London, 1983–88; *b* 10 June 1941; *s* of James Kenny and Helen (*née* Gordon); *m* Rosemary Flood (marr. diss. 1988); one *s* one *d* and one step *d*; *m* Angela Helen (*née* Smith) (marr. diss. 1992); *m* 1993, Susan (*née* Rowland). *Educ:* St Francis Xavier's Coll., Liverpool; Liverpool Coll. of Art; Slade Sch. of Fine Art (DFA London). Works in public collections of: Arts Council; V&A; British Council; British Museum; Borough of Camden; Contemporary Arts Soc.; Tate Gall.; Leicestershire Education Cttee; North West Arts Assoc.; Wilhelm Lehmbruck Museum, Duisburg; Staatsgalerie, Stuttgart; Unilever Collection, London; Hara Mus. of Contemporary Tokyo; Leeds City Art Gall.; Hat Hill Sculpture Foundn, Goodwood; Walker Art Gall.; Dulwich Gall.; Nat. Gall., Bucharest; public works sited at: Lumsden, Aberdeenshire; Addenbrooke's Hosp., Cambridge; Le Parc de la Courneuve, St Denis, Paris; Yokohama Business Park, Yokohama; public commissioned work: Muraoka-cho, Japan, 1992; London Docklands, 1993; works in private collections in England, Europe, Japan and America. Numerous one-man and mixed exhibitions in GB, Europe, S America, Canada, Japan, Australia and USA. Chairman, Faculty of Sculpture, British School at Rome, 1982–87. *Relevant publications:* Contemporary Artists, 1977, 3rd edn 1989; Contemporary British Artists, 1979; British Art in 20th Century, 1991; exhibition catalogues. *Recreations:* ornithology, physics, cosmology. *Address:* 71 Stepney Green, E1 3LE. *Club:* Chelsea Arts.

KENNY, Yvonne Denise, AM 1989; international opera singer; *b* Australia, 25 Nov. 1950; *d* of late Arthur Raymond Kenny and of Doris Jean (*née* Campbell). *Educ:* Sydney Univ. (BSc). Operatic début in Donizetti's Rosmonda d'Inghilterra, Queen Elizabeth Hall, 1975; joined Royal Opera House, Covent Garden as a principal soprano, 1976; roles include: Pamina in Die Zauberflöte; Ilia in Idomeneo; Marzelline in Fidelio; Susanna in Le Nozze di Figaro; Adina in L'Elisir d'Amore; Liu in Turandot; Aspasia in Mitridate; international appearances include: Berlin Staatsoper; Vienna State Opera; La Scala, Milan; La Fenice, Venice; Paris; Hamburg; Zurich; Australian Opera, Sydney, etc; regular concert appearances with major orchs and conductors in Europe and USA. Has made numerous recordings. *Recreations:* swimming, walking, gardening. *Address:* c/o Diane Mulgan, IMG Artists Management, Media House, 3 Burlington Lane, Chiswick, W4 2TH.

KENSINGTON, 8th Baron *cr* 1776 (Ire.); **Hugh Ivor Edwardes;** Baron Kensington (UK) 1886; *b* 24 Nov. 1933; *s* of Hon. Hugh Owen Edwardes (*d* 1937) (2nd *s* of 6th Baron) and of Angela Dorothea (who *m* 1951, Lt Comdr John Hamilton, RN retd), *d* of late Lt-Col Eustace Shearman, 10th Hussars; *S* uncle, 1981; *m* 1961, Juliet Elizabeth Massy Anderson; two *s* one *d. Educ:* Eton. *Heir: s* Hon. William Owen Alexander Edwardes [*b* 21 July 1964; *m* 1991, Marie Hélène Anne Véronique, *d* of Jean-Alain Lalouette; one *s*]. *Address:* Friar Tuck, PO Box 549, Mooi River, Natal, 3300, Republic of S Africa. *Clubs:* Boodle's; Durban (Durban).

KENSINGTON, Area Bishop of; *no new appointment at time of going to press.*

KENSWOOD, 2nd Baron, *cr* 1951; **John Michael Howard Whitfield;** *b* 6 April 1930; *o s* of 1st Baron Kenswood; *S* father, 1963; *m* 1951, Deirdre Anna Louise, *d* of Colin Malcolm Methven, Errol, Perthshire; four *s* one *d. Educ:* Trinity Coll. Sch., Ontario; Harrow; Grenoble Univ.; Emmanuel Coll., Cambridge (BA). *Heir: s* Hon. Michael Christopher Whitfield, *b* 3 July 1955.

KENT, Arthur William, CMG 1966; OBE 1950; Chairman, United Transport Overseas Ltd, 1980–82 (Deputy Chairman, 1978–80, Joint Managing Director, 1977–80); Managing Director, United Transport Co., 1980–82; *b* 22 March 1913; *s* of Howard and Eliza Kent; *m* 1st, 1944, Doris Jane (*née* Crowe; marr. diss., 1958); one *s* one *d*; 2nd, 1958, Mary (*née* Martin). Deputy City Treasurer, Nairobi, 1946–48, City Treasurer, 1948–65. Chief Executive: United Transport Overseas Ltd, Nairobi, 1966–69; Transport Holdings of Zambia Ltd, 1969–71; Chief Exec., United Transport Holdings (Pty) Ltd, Johannesburg, 1971–76; Dir of a number of cos owned by United Transport Overseas Ltd and other BET cos. IPFA; FCA; FCIT. *Address:* Muthaiga, Beechwood Road, Combe Down, Bath, Avon BA2 5JS. *T:* Bath (01225) 834940.

KENT, Brian Hamilton, FEng 1995; FIEE, FIMechE; Chairman, Wellington Holdings plc, since 1993; President, Institution of Mechanical Engineers, 1994–95; *b* 29 Sept. 1931; *s* of Clarence Kent and Edyth (*née* Mitchell); *m* 1954, Margery Foulds; one *s* two *d. Educ:* Hyde Grammar Sch.; Salford Coll. of Technology (BSc Eng). Instructor Lieut, RN Short Service Commn, 1954–57. Mather & Platt Ltd: graduate apprentice, 1952–54; Asst Technical Manager, Electrical Gp, then Gen. Manager, Mather & Platt Contracting Ltd, 1957–65; Morgan Crucible Co. Ltd, London, 1965–69; Man. Dir and Chief Exec., Alfa-Laval Ltd, 1969–78; Dir, Staveley Industries Ltd, 1978–80; Staveley Industries plc: Chief Exec., 1980–87; Chm., 1987–93; non-exec. Chm., 1993–94. Mem., Engrg Council (Chm., Bd of Engrg Profession); Chm., Management Cttee, Industry and Parlt Trust, 1988–90. MInstD; FRSA. Hon. DSc Salford, 1995. *Recreation:* sailing. *Address:* Wellington Holdings plc, 130 Oldfield Road, Hampton, Middx TW12 2HT. *T:* 0181–941 3774. *Club:* Royal Automobile.

KENT, Bruce; campaigner for nuclear disarmament; Chairman, Campaign for Nuclear Disarmament, 1987–90 (General Secretary, 1980–85; Vice-Chairman, 1985–87; Hon. Vice President, 1985); *b* 22 June 1929; *s* of Kenneth Kent and Rosemary Kent (*née* Marion); *m* 1988, Valerie Flessati. *Educ:* Lower Canada Coll., Montreal; Stonyhurst Coll.; Brasenose Coll., Univ. of Oxford. LLB. Ordination, Westminster, 1958; Curate, Kensington, North and South, 1958–63; Sec., Archbishop's House, Westminster, 1963–64; Chm., Diocesan Schools Commn, 1964–66; Catholic Chaplain to Univ. of London, 1966–74; Chaplain, Pax Christi, 1974–77; Parish Priest, Somers Town, NW1, 1977–80; resigned Ministry, Feb. 1987. Pres., Internat. Peace Bureau, 1985–92; Mem., Nat. Exec., UNA, 1993–. Contested (Lab) Oxford West and Abingdon, 1992. Hon LLD Manchester, 1987. *Publications:* Undiscovered Ends (autobiog.), 1992; essays and pamphlets on disarmament, Christians and peace. *Recreations:* friends, walking. *Address:* 11 Venetia Road, N4 1EJ.

KENT, Sir Harold Simcox, GCB 1963 (KCB 1954; CB 1946); QC 1973; Commissary to Dean and Chapter of St Paul's Cathedral, since 1976; *b* 11 Nov. 1903; *s* of late P. H. B. Kent, OBE, MC; *m* 1930, Zillah Lloyd (*d* 1987); one *s* (one *d* decd). *Educ:* Rugby School; Merton Coll., Oxford. Barrister-at-law, 1928; Parliamentary Counsel to the Treasury, 1940–53; HM Procurator-General and Treasury Solicitor, 1953–63; Solicitor to Vassall Tribunal, 1963; Mem., Security Commn, 1965–71; Standing Counsel to Church Assembly and General Synod, 1964–72; Vicar-General of the Province of Canterbury, 1971–76; Dean of the Arches Court of Canterbury and Auditor of the Chancery Court of York, 1972–76. Mem., Departmental Cttee to examine operation of Section 2 of Official Secrets Act, 1911, 1971–72. DCL Lambeth, 1977. *Publication:* In On the Act, 1979. *Address:* Alderley, Calf Lane, Chipping Campden, Glos GL55 6UQ. *T:* Evesham (01386) 840421. *Club:* United Oxford & Cambridge University.

KENT, John Philip Cozens, PhD; FSA; FMA; FBA 1986; Keeper, Department of Coins and Medals, British Museum, 1983–90; *b* 28 Sept. 1928; *s* of late John Cozens Kent, DCM and Lucy Ella Kent; *m* 1961, Patricia Eleanor Bunford; one *s* one *d. Educ:* Minchenden County Grammar Sch.; University Coll. London (BA 1949; PhD 1951). FSA 1961; FMA 1988. Nat. Service, 1951–53. Asst Keeper, 1953, Dep. Keeper, 1974, Dept of Coins and Medals, BM. Hon. Lectr in Numismatics, Birmingham Univ., 1993. President: British Assoc. of Numismatic Socs, 1974–78; Royal Numismatic Soc., 1984–89; London and

Middlesex Archaeological Soc., 1985–88. Member: Instituto de Sintra, 1986; Internat. Numismatic Commn, 1986–91 (Hon. Mem., 1991). Medallist: RNS, 1990; Amer. Numismatic Soc., 1994. *Publications:* (jtly) Late Roman Bronze Coinage, 1960; (with K. S. Painter) Wealth of the Roman World, 1977; Roman Coins, 1978; 2000 Years of British Coins and Medals, 1978 (Lhotka Meml Prize, RNS); Roman Imperial Coinage: vol. VIII, the family of Constantine I 337–364, 1981; vol. X, the divided Empire and the fall of the western parts 395–491, 1994; A Selection of Byzantine Coins in the Barber Institute of Fine Arts, 1985; (ed with M. R. Mays) Catalogue of the Celtic Coins in the British Museum, vol. I, 1987, vol. II, 1990; contribs to Festschriften, congress procs, and Numismatic Chronicle, British Numismatic Jl etc. *Recreations:* local history and archaeology, early (mediaeval) music, railway history and model railways, monumental brasses. *Address:* 16 Newmans Way, Hadley Wood, Barnet, Herts EN4 0LR. *T:* 0181–449 8072.

KENT, Paul Welberry, DSc; FRSC; JP; Student Emeritus of Christ Church, Oxford; *b* Doncaster, 19 April 1923; *s* of Thomas William Kent and Marion (*née* Cox); *m* 1952, Rosemary Elizabeth Boutflower, *y d* of Major C. H. B. Shepherd, MC; three *s* one *d*. *Educ:* Doncaster Grammar Sch.; Birmingham Univ. (BSc 1944, PhD 1947); Jesus Coll., Oxford (MA 1951, DPhil 1953, DSc 1966). Asst Lectr, subseq. ICI Fellow, Birmingham Univ., 1946–50; Vis. Fellow, Princeton Univ., 1948–49; Univ. Demonstrator in Biochem., Oxford, 1950–72; Lectr, subseq. Student, Tutor and Dr Lees Reader in Chem., Christ Church, Oxford, 1955–72; Durham University: Master of Van Mildert Coll. and Dir, Glycoprotein Res. Unit, 1972–82; Mem. of Senate, 1972–82; Mem. of Council, 1976–80. Research Assoc., Harvard, 1967; Vis. Prof., Windsor Univ., Ont, 1971, 1980. Bodleian Orator, 1959. Mem., Oxford City Council, 1964–72; Governor: Oxford Coll. of Technology, subseq. Oxford Polytechnic, 1964–72, 1983–89 (Vice-Chm. 1966–69, Chm. 1969–70); Oxford Polytechnic Higher Educn Corp., 1988–92 (Dep. Chm., 1988–92); Oxford Brookes Univ., 1992– (Vice-Chm., 1992–94). Member: Cttee, Biochemical Soc., 1963–67; Chemical Council, 1965–70; Res. Adv. Cttee, Cystic Fibrosis Res. Trust, 1977–82; Commn on Religious Educn in School. Sec., Foster and Wills Scholarships Bd, 1960–72; Pres., Soc. for Maintenance of the Faith, 1974–; Governor, Pusey House, 1983–. JP Oxford, 1972. Hon. Fellow, Canterbury Coll., Ont, 1976. Hon. DLitt Drury Coll., 1973; Hon. DSc CNAA, 1991. Rolleston Prize, 1952; Medal of Société de Chemie Biologique, 1969; Verdienstkreuz (Bundesrepublik), 1970. *Publications:* Biochemistry of Amino-sugars, 1955; (ed) Membrane-Mediated Information, Vols I and II, 1972; (ed) International Aspects of the Provision of Medical Care, 1976; (ed) New Approaches to Genetics, 1978; (ed with W. B. Fisher) Resources, Environment and the Future, 1982; articles in sci. and other jls. *Recreations:* music, travel. *Address:* 18 Arnolds Way, Cumnor Hill, Oxford OX2 9JB. *T:* Oxford (01865) 862087; Briscoe Gate, Cotherstone, Barnard Castle, Co. Durham. *Club:* Athenæum.

KENT, Pendarell Hugh; Executive Director, Bank of England, since 1994; *b* 18 Aug. 1937; *s* of Hugh and Ann Kent; *m* 1960, Jill George; one *s* one *d*. *Educ:* University College Sch.; Jesus Coll., Oxford (MA Hons). Served Intelligence Corps, 2nd Lieut, 1959–61. Bank of England, 1961–: UK Alternate Exec. Dir, IMF, 1976–79; Head: of Inf. Div., 1984–85; of Internat. Div. (Internat. Financial Instns and Developing Countries), 1985–88; Associate Dir, Finance and Industry, 1988–94. Dir (non-exec.), BR Southern Region, 1986–92 (Chm., 1989–92). Trustee, Blind in Business, 1992–; Vice Patron, Missing Persons Helpline, 1994–. *Publication:* Nursery Schools for All (with Jill Kent), 1970. *Recreations:* art, jazz, ski-ing. *Address:* c/o Bank of England, Threadneedle Street, EC2R 8AH. *T:* 0171–601 4221.

KENT, Ronald Clive, CB 1965; Deputy Under-Secretary of State, MoD, 1967–76; *b* 3 Aug. 1916; *s* of Dr Hugh Braund Kent and Margaret Mary Kent; *m* 1965, Mary Moyles Havell; one step-*s* one step-*d*. *Educ:* Rugby Sch.; Brasenose Coll., Oxford. Air Ministry, 1939; Royal Artillery, 1940–45; Air Ministry, 1945–58; Asst Under-Sec. of State, Air Min., 1958–63, MoD, 1963–67. Dir (Admin), ICE, 1976–79, Consultant and Council Sec., 1980–85. *Address:* 21 Heathside Court, Tadworth Street, Tadworth, Surrey KT20 5RY.

KENT, Brig. Sidney Harcourt, OBE 1944; *b* 22 April 1915; *s* of Major Geoffrey Harcourt Kent, Hindhead; *m* 1945, Nina Ruth, *d* of Gen. Sir Geoffry Scoones, KCB, KBE, CSI, DSO, MC; one *s* one *d*. *Educ:* Wellington Coll.; RMC Sandhurst. 2nd Lieut KOYLI, 1935; Lt-Col 1944; Brig. 1944; GSO1 Eighth Army, 1944; BGS Allied Land Forces, SE Asia, 1944. Comd 128 Inf. Bde (TA), 1960–63. Manager and Sec., Turf Board, 1965; Gen. Manager, 1969, Chief Executive, 1973–76, The Jockey Club; Racing Adviser, Royal Horse Soc., Iran, 1978; Consultant Steward, Jamaica Racing Commn, 1984–86; Dir of Racing, 1989–91, Racing consultant, 1991–92, Macau Jockey Club. *Recreations:* farming, travel. *Address:* The Old Vicarage, Kingsey, Aylesbury, Bucks HP17 8LT. *T:* Haddenham (01844) 291411; Maroni Village, Larnaca District, Cyprus. *T:* (4) 332614.

KENT, Thomas George, CBE 1979; CEng, MIMechE, FRAeS; aerospace and defence consultant; Director: Grosvenor Technology Ltd, since 1984; Third Grosvenor Ltd, since 1987; Grosvenor Development Capital, since 1993; *b* 13 Aug. 1925. *Educ:* Borden Grammar School; Medway College of Technology. Joined English Electric Co., 1951; Special Director, British Aircraft Corp., 1967; Dep. Managing Director, 1974; Director, Hatfield/Lostock Division and Stevenage/Bristol Div. of Dynamics Group, British Aerospace, 1977–79; Gp Dep. Chief Exec., BAe Dynamics Gp, 1980–85; Bd Mem., BAe, 1981–85; Director: BAe Australia Ltd, 1980–86 (Chm., 1984–86); Arab British Dynamics, 1980–85; BAJ Vickers Ltd, 1982–87 (non.-exec.). *Address:* Weeamara, Grove Park, Hampton on the Hill, Warwick CV35 8QR.

KENT-JONES, Trevor David, TD; **His Honour Judge Kent-Jones;** a Circuit Judge, since 1991; *b* 31 July 1940; *s* of late David Sandford Kent-Jones and of Madeline Mary Kent-Jones (*née* Russell-Pavier); one *s* one *d*. *Educ:* Bedford Sch.; Liverpool Univ. (LLB; DipIntLaw). Called to the Bar, Gray's Inn, 1962; Mem., NE Circuit, 1963–91, Junior, 1969; a Recorder, 1985–91. Commnd KOYLI TA, 1959; served 4th Bn KOYLI, 5th Bn Light Infantry, HQ NE Dist, 1959–85; Lt-Col 1977. *Recreations:* cricket, travel, fell-walking. *Address:* Leeds Combined Court Centre, 1 Oxford Row, Leeds LS1 3BG. *Club:* Naval and Military.

KENTFIELD, Graham Edward Alfred; Deputy Director, since 1994, and Chief Cashier, since 1991, Bank of England; *b* 3 Sept. 1940; *s* of late E. L. H. Kentfield and F. E. M. Kentfield (*née* Tucker); *m* 1965, Ann Dwelley Hewetson; two *d*. *Educ:* Bancroft's Sch., Woodford Green, Essex; St Edmund Hall, Oxford (BA 1st cl. Lit.Hum.). Entered Bank of England, 1963; seconded to Dept of Applied Econs, Cambridge, 1966–67; Editor, Bank of England Qly Bull., 1977–80; Adviser: Financial Stats Div., 1980–84; Banking Dept, 1984–85; Dep. Chief of Banking Dept and Dep. Chief Cashier, 1985–91; Chief of Banking Dept, 1991–94. Mem., Financial Law Panel, 1994–. Hon. Treas., Soc. for Promotion of Roman Studies, 1991–. *Recreations:* Roman history, genealogy, philately. *Address:* Bank of England, Threadneedle Street, EC2R 8AH. *T:* 0171–601 4444.

KENTRIDGE, Sydney; QC 1984; a Judge of the Courts of Appeal of Jersey and Guernsey, 1988–92; *b* Johannesburg, 5 Nov. 1922; *s* of Morris and May Kentridge; *m* 1952, Felicia Geffen; two *s* two *d*. *Educ:* King Edward VII Sch., Johannesburg; Univ. of the Witwatersrand (BA); Exeter Coll., Oxford Univ. (MA; Hon. Fellow, 1986). War service with S African forces, 1942–46. Advocate 1949, Senior Counsel 1965, South Africa; called to the English Bar, Lincoln's Inn, 1977, Bencher, 1986. Mem., Ct of Appeal, Botswana, 1981–. Roberts Lectr, Univ. of Pennsylvania, 1979. Hon. LLD: Seton Hall Univ., NJ, 1978; Leicester, 1985; Cape Town, 1987; Natal, 1989. Granville Clark Prize, USA, 1978. *Recreation:* opera-going. *Address:* Brick Court Chambers, 15–19 Devereux Court, WC2R 3JJ. *T:* 0171–583 0777. *Club:* Athenæum.

KENWARD, Michael Ronald John, OBE 1990; science writer and editorial consultant; *b* 12 July 1945; *s* of late Ronald Kenward and of Phyllis Kenward; *m* 1969, Elizabeth Rice. *Educ:* Wolverstone Hall; Sussex Univ. Res. scientist, UKAEA, Culham Laboratory, 1966–68; Technical editor, Scientific Instrument Res. Assoc., 1969; various editorial posts, New Scientist, 1969–79, Editor, 1979–90; Science Consultant, The Sunday Times, 1990. Member: Royal Soc. COPUS, 1986–90; Public Affairs Cttee, 1989–93, Sci. and Industry Cttee, 1994–, BAAS; Bd, Assoc. of British Editors, 1986–90. Internat. Rep., Assoc. of British Sci. Writers, 1993–. Mem. Editl Cttee, Science and Public Affairs, 1994–. *Publications:* Potential Energy, 1976; articles on science and technology and energy in particular. *Recreations:* photography, collecting 'middle-aged' books, listening to Requiems and Texas rock-and-roll, reconfigurating my operating system. *Address:* Grange Cottage, Staplefield, W Sussex RH17 6EL.

KENWORTHY, family name of **Baron Strabolgi.**

KENWORTHY, Cecil; Registrar of Family Division (formerly Probate and Divorce Division), of High Court of Justice, 1968–83; *b* 22 Jan. 1918; *s* of John T. and Lucy Kenworthy; *m* 1944, Beryl Joan Willis; no *c*. *Educ:* Manchester and Bristol Grammar Schools. Entered Principal Probate Registry, 1936. *Publications:* (co-editor) supplements to Rayden on Divorce, 1967, 1968; (co-editor) Tolstoy on Divorce, 7th edn, 1971. *Address:* Gable Lodge, 2 Zetland Road, Malvern, Worcs WR14 2JJ.

KENWORTHY, Frederick John; Management Consultant, ICL (International), since 1993; *b* 6 Dec. 1943; *s* of late Rev. Fred Kenworthy and of Mrs Ethel Kenworthy; *m* 1968, Diana Flintham; one *d*. *Educ:* William Hulme's Grammar Sch., Manchester; Manchester Univ. (BA Econ Hons, Politics). Entered Admin. Class, Home Civil Service, as Asst Principal, MoD (Navy), 1966; Treasury Centre for Admin. Studies, 1968–69; joined BSC, Sheffield, 1969; Principal, MoD, 1972; Royal Commn on the Press Secretariat, 1974; Asst Sec., Dir, Weapons Resources and Progs (Naval), MoD, 1979–83; Head of Resources and Progs (Navy) (formerly DS4), RN Size and Shape Policy, MoD, 1983–86; Dir of Ops (Grade 4), Disablement Services Authy (formerly Div.), DHSS, 1986–88; Dir, IT Systems Directorate (Under Sec.), 1989–90, Chief Exec., IT Services Agency, 1990–93, Dept of Social Security. MInstD. Freeman, Co. of Information Technologists, 1992. *Recreations:* music, sport, photography. *Address:* c/o ICL International, ICL House, SW15 1SW. *T:* 0181–788 7272. *Clubs:* Lansdown Lawn Tennis and Squash Racquets (Bath); Hendon Golf.

KENWORTHY, Joan Margaret, BLitt, MA; Principal, St Mary's College, University of Durham, since 1977; *b* Oldham, Lancs, 10 Dec. 1933; *o d* of late Albert Kenworthy and Amy (*née* Cobbold). *Educ:* Girls Grammar Sch., Barrow-in-Furness; St Hilda's Coll., Oxford (BLitt, MA). Henry Oliver Beckit Prize, Oxford, 1955; Leverhulme Overseas Res. Scholar, Makerere Coll., Uganda, and E African Agriculture and Forestry Res. Org., Kenya, 1956–58; Actg Tutor, St Hugh's Coll., Oxford, 1958–59; Tutorial Res. Fellow, Bedford Coll., London, 1959–60; Univ. of Liverpool: Asst Lectr in Geography, 1960–63; Lectr, 1963–73; Sen. Lectr, 1973–77; Warden of Salisbury Hall, 1966–77 and of Morton House, 1974–77. IUC short-term Vis. Lectr, Univ. of Sierra Leone, 1975; Vis. Lectr, Univ. of Fort Hare, Ciskei, 1983. Mem., NE England, Churches Regl Broadcasting Council, 1978–82; Bishop's Selector for ACCM, 1982–87. Member: Council, African Studies Assoc. of UK, 1969–71, 1994–, Standing Cttee on Univ. Studies of Africa, 1994; Council, Inst. of Brit. Geographers, 1976–78; Cttee, Merseyside Conf. for Overseas Students Ltd, 1976–77; Council, RMetS, 1980–83; Treasurer, Assoc. of Brit. Climatologists, 1976–79; Northern Chm., Durham Univ. Soc., 1979–82. Gov., St Anne's Sch., Windermere, 1992–. *Publications:* (contrib.) Geographers and the Tropics, ed R. W. Steel and R. M. Prothero, 1964; (contrib.) Oxford Regional Economic Atlas for Africa, 1965; (contrib.) Studies in East African Geography and Development, ed S. Ominde, 1971; (contrib.) An Advanced Geography of Africa, ed J. I. Clarke, 1975; (contrib.) Rangeland Management and Ecology in East Africa, ed D. J. Pratt and M. D. Gwynne, 1977; (contrib.) The Climatic Scene: essays in honour of Emeritus Prof. Gordon Manley, ed M. J. Tooley and G. Sheail, 1985; (ed with B. D. Giles) Observatories and Climatological Research, 1994; articles in jls, encycs and reports of symposia. *Address:* 1 Elvet Garth, South Road, Durham DH1 3TP. *T:* Durham (091) 3843865. *Clubs:* Commonwealth Trust, Royal Over-Seas League.

KENWORTHY-BROWNE, (Bernard) Peter (Francis); a District Judge (formerly Registrar) of the High Court (Family Division), since 1982; *b* 11 May 1930; *s* of late Bernard Elelyn Kenworthy-Browne and Margaret Sibylla Kenworthy-Browne; *m* 1975, Jane Elizabeth Arthur (marr. diss. 1982); *m* 1989, Elizabeth, *o d* of late Dr J. A. Bowen-Jones. *Educ:* Ampleforth; Oriel Coll., Oxford. MA. 2nd Lieut, Irish Guards, 1949–50. Called to the Bar, Lincoln's Inn, 1955; Oxford, and Midland and Oxford Circuit, 1957–82; a Recorder of the Crown Court, 1981–82. *Recreations:* music, hunting, shooting. *Address:* 30 Dewhurst Road, W14 0ES. *T:* 0171–602 9580.

KENWRIGHT, Prof. John, MD; FRCS; Nuffield Professor of Orthopaedic Surgery, Oxford University, since 1992; Professorial Fellow, Worcester College, Oxford, since 1992; *b* 2 May 1936; *s* of Cecil Kenwright and Norah (*née* Langley); *m* 1960, Vivien Mary Curtis; two *s*. *Educ:* University College Sch.; Nottingham High Sch.; St John's Coll., Oxford; University College Hosp. MA Oxon; BM, BCh; MD Stockholm 1972. FRCS 1966. Nuffield Surgical Res. Fellow, Oxford, 1968; Res. Fellow, Karolinska Inst., Stockholm, 1971; Consultant Orthopaedic Surgeon, Nuffield Orthopaedic Centre and John Radcliffe Hosp., Oxford, 1973–92. Hunterian Prof., RCS, 1991–92. *Publications:* articles in scientific jls on factors which control fracture and soft tissue healing; also on leg lengthening and correction of post traumatic deformity. *Recreation:* sailing. *Address:* Nuffield Orthopaedic Centre, Headington, Oxford OX3 7LD. *T:* Oxford (01865) 741155, *Fax:* (01865) 742348. *Club:* Oxford and Cambridge Sailing Society.

KENYON, family name of **Baron Kenyon.**

KENYON, 6th Baron *cr* 1788; **Lloyd Tyrell-Kenyon;** Bt 1784; Baron of Gredington, 1788; *b* 13 July 1947; *s* of 5th Baron Kenyon, CBE and of Leila Mary, *d* of Comdr John Wyndham Cookson, RN and *widow* of Hugh William Jardine Ethelston Peel; *S* father, 1993; *m* 1971, Sally Carolyn, *e d* of J. F. P. Matthews; two *s*. *Educ:* Eton; Magdalene Coll., Cambridge (BA). Mem., Wrexham Maelor BC, 1991–. Mem., EU Cttee of the Regions, 1994–. High Sheriff, Clwyd, 1986. *Heir:* *s* Hon. Lloyd Nicholas Tyrell-Kenyon, *b* 9 April 1972. *Address:* Gredington, Whitchurch, Shropshire SY13 3DH.

KENYON, Sir George (Henry), Kt 1976; DL; JP; LLD; *b* 10 July 1912; *s* of George Henry Kenyon and Edith (*née* Hill); *m* 1938, Christine Dorey (*née* Brentnall); two *s* one *d*.

Educ: Radley; Manchester Univ. Director: William Kenyon & Sons Ltd, 1942–92 (Chm., 1961–82); Tootal Ltd, 1971–79 (Chm., 1976–79); Manchester Ship Canal, 1972–86; Williams & Glyn's Bank, 1972–83 (Chm., 1978–83); Royal Bank of Scotland, 1978–83; Chm., Vuman Ltd, 1982–88. Gen. Comr, Inland Revenue, 1957–73. Manchester University: Chm. Bldgs Cttee, 1962–70; Treas., 1970–72, 1980–82; Chm. Council, 1972–80. Hon. Treas., Civic Trust, NW, 1962–78, Vice Pres., 1978; Member: NW Adv. Cttee, Civil Aviation, 1967–72; Manchester Reg. Hosp. Bd, 1962–68; NW Reg. Econ. Planning Council, 1970–73. Pres., Arkwright Soc., Cromford, 1995 (Vice-Pres., 1988–94). JP Cheshire, 1959; Chm., S Tameside Bench, 1974–82; DL Chester, 1969, Greater Manchester, 1983. High Sheriff, Cheshire, 1973–74. Hon. LLD Manchester, 1980. *Recreations:* reading, talking, travel. *Address:* Limefield House, Hyde, Cheshire SK14 1DN. *T:* 0161–368 2012.

KENYON, Ian Roy; Executive Secretary, Preparatory Commission for Organisation for Prohibition of Chemical Weapons, The Hague, since 1993 (on leave from HM Diplomatic Service); *b* 13 June 1939; *s* of late S. R. Kenyon and of Mrs E. M. Kenyon; *m* 1962, Griselda Rintoul; one *s* one *d*. *Educ:* Lancaster Royal Grammar School; Edinburgh University. BSc Hons. CEng, MIChemE. Lever Bros, 1962–68; Birds Eye Foods, 1968–74; First Secretary, FCO, 1974–76; Geneva, 1976–78; Head of Chancery, Bogota, 1979–81; FCO, 1982–83; Head of Nuclear Energy Dept, FCO, 1983–85; Overseas Inspectorate, 1986–88; Dep. Leader, UK Delegn to Conf. on Disarmament, Geneva, 1988–92. *Recreations:* riding, carriage driving. *Address:* c/o Provisional Technical Secretariat for OPCW, Laan van Meerdervoort 51, 2517 AE Den Haag, Netherlands. *Club:* Travellers.

KENYON, Prof. John Philipps, FBA 1981; Joyce and Elizabeth Hall Distinguished Professor in Early Modern British History, University of Kansas, 1987–94, now Professor Emeritus; *b* 18 June 1927; *s* of William Houston Kenyon and Edna Grace Philipps; *m* 1962, Angela Jane Ewert (*née* Venables); one *s* two *d*. *Educ:* King Edward VII Sch., Sheffield; Univ. of Sheffield (BA 1948; Hon. LittD 1980); Christ's Coll., Cambridge (PhD). Fellow of Christ's Coll., Cambridge, 1954–62; Lectr in Hist., Cambridge, 1955–62; G. F. Grant Prof. of History, Univ. of Hull, 1962–81; Prof. of Modern History, Univ. of St Andrews, 1981–87. Visiting Prof., Columbia Univ., New York, 1959–60; Junior Proctor, Cambridge, 1961–62; John U. Nef Lectr, Univ. of Chicago, 1972; Ford's Lectr in English Hist., Oxford, 1975–76; Andrew W. Mellon Fellow, Huntington Library, Calif, 1985. *Publications:* Robert Spencer Earl of Sunderland, 1958; The Stuarts, 1958, 2nd edn 1970; The Stuart Constitution, 1966, 2nd edn 1986; The Popish Plot, 1972; Revolution Principles, 1977, 2nd edn 1990; Stuart England, 1978, 2nd edn 1985; The History Men, 1983, 2nd edn 1993; The Civil Wars of England, 1988; contribs to various learned jls. *Recreation:* bridge. *Address:* Breck House, Church Lane, Mattishall Burgh, Dereham, Norfolk NR20 3QZ. *T:* Mattishall (01362) 858364.

KENYON, Margaret; Headmistress, Withington Girls' School, Manchester, since 1986; *b* 19 June 1940; *d* of Hugh Richard Parry and Aileen Cole (*née* Morgan); *m* 1962, Christopher George Kenyon; two *s*. *Educ:* Merchant Taylors' Sch. for Girls, Crosby; Somerville Coll., Oxford (MA). Asst French Mistress, Cheadle Hulme Sch., 1962–63 and 1974–83; Hd of French, Withington Girls Sch., 1983–85. Girls' School Association: Chm., NW Region, 1989–91; Pres., 1993–94. Mem. Adv. Council, Granada Foundn, 1986–. Mem. Court, Univ. of Manchester, 1991–. *Recreations:* reading, talking. *Address:* Withington Girls' School, Wellington Road, Fallowfield, Manchester M14 6SL. *T:* 0161–224 1077.

KENYON, Nicholas Roger; Controller, BBC Radio 3, since 1992; Director, BBC Promenade Concerts, since 1995; *b* 23 Feb. 1951; *s* of Thomas Kenyon and Kathleen Holmes; *m* 1976, Marie-Ghislaine Latham-Koenig; three *s* one *d*. *Educ:* Balliol College, Oxford (BA Hons 1972). English Bach Festival, 1973–76; BBC Music Div., 1976–79; music critic: The New Yorker, 1979–82; The Times, 1982–85; The Observer, 1985–87; Music Editor, The Listener, 1982–87; Chief Music Critic, Observer, 1987–92. Programme Advr, Mozart Now Fest., South Bank Centre, 1991. Editor, Early Music, 1983–92. *Publications:* The BBC Symphony Orchestra 1930–80, 1981; Simon Rattle, 1987; (ed) Authenticity and Early Music, 1988; (ed jtly) The Viking Opera Guide, 1993. *Recreation:* family. *Address:* BBC, 16 Langham Street, W1A 1AA. *T:* 0171–928 4928.

KEOHANE, Desmond John, OBE 1991; FIMgt; consultant in education and training, since 1991; *b* 5 July 1928; *s* of William Patrick Keohane and Mabel Margaret Keohane; *m* 1960, Mary Kelliher; two *s* two *d*. *Educ:* Borden Grammar Sch., Sittingbourne; Univ. of Birmingham (BA and Baxter Prize in History, 1949); London Univ. (Postgrad. Cert. in Educn). FIMgt (FBIM 1981). Postgrad. res., 1949–50; Nat. Service, Educn Officer, RAF, 1950–52; sch. teacher and coll. lectr, 1953–64; Head, Dept of Social and Academic Studies, 1964–68, and Vice-Principal, 1969–71, Havering Technical Coll.; Principal, Northampton Coll. of Further Educn, 1971–76; Principal, Oxford Coll. of Further Educn, 1976–90. Part-time Lectr in Educnl Management, Univ. of Leicester, 1990–93; Vis. Fellow (Educn), Oxford Brookes Univ. (formerly Oxford Polytechnic), 1991–94. Pt-time Inspector, FEFC, 1994–. Member: Council, Southern Regional Council for Further Educn, 1977–90; Secondary Exams Council, 1983–86; Berks and Oxon Area Manpower Board, 1985–88; Special Employment Measures Adv. Gp, MSC, 1986–89; Northampton RC Diocesan Educn Commn, 1991–. Chm. Management Cttee, Stress at Work, 1992–. Formerly governor of various educnl instns; Chm. of Govs, Thomas Becket Sch., Northampton, 1983–. Gen. Ed., series Managing Colleges Effectively, 1994–. *Recreations:* enjoying family and friends, watching cricket. *Address:* 14 Abington Park Crescent, Northampton NN3 3AD. *T:* Northampton (01604) 38829.

See also K. W. Keohane.

KEOHANE, Dr Kevin William, CBE 1976; Rector, Roehampton Institute of Higher Education, 1976–88, Hon. Fellow, 1988; *b* 28 Feb. 1923; *s* of William Patrick and Mabel Margaret Keohane; *m* 1949, Mary Margaret (Patricia) Ashford; one *s* three *d*. *Educ:* Borden Grammar Sch., Sittingbourne, Kent; Univ. of Bristol (BSc; PhD). FInstP. War service, RAF, Radar Br, Flt Lt. Research appts and Lectr in Anatomy, Univ. of Bristol, 1947–59; Chelsea College, London: Reader in Biophysics, 1959; Prof. of Physics and Head of Dept of Physics, 1965; Prof. of Science Educn and Dir, Centre for Science Educn, 1967–76; Vice-Principal, 1966–76. Royal Society Leverhulme Prof., Fed. Univ. of Bahia, Brazil, 1971; Visiting Professor: Chelsea College, 1977–82; KCL, 1989; Vis. Prof. of Science Educn, KCL, 1990–. Member: Academic Adv. Cttee, Open Univ., 1970–81 (Chm., 1978–81); Court, Univ. of Bristol, 1968–76; Court, 1982–92, Council, 1988–92, Univ. of Surrey; Court, Brunel Univ., 1993–; University of London: Member: Academic Council, 1974–76; Extra-Mural Council, 1974–76; School Examinations Council, 1975–76. Dir, Nuffield Foundn Science Projects, 1966–79; Chairman: DES Study Gp on Cert. of Extended Educn, 1978–79; Education Cttee, Commonwealth Inst., 1978–85; Nuffield-Chelsea Curriculum Trust, 1979–; Southwark Archdiocesan Educn Cttee, 1989–; Vice Chm., Internat. Adv. Panel for Provincial Univs in China, 1986–; Member: Nat. Programme Cttee for Computers in Educn, 1974–78; Royal Society/Inst. of Physics Educn Cttee, 1970–73; SSRC Educn Bd, 1971–74; BBC Further Educn Adv. Cttee, 1972–75; TEAC, RAF, 1977–79; Gen. Optical Council, 1979–84; Bd of Educn, Royal Coll. of Nursing, 1980–84; National Adv. Bd for Higher Educn, 1983–86; Froebel Council, 1992–; Merton Educn Authy, 1986–90; Richmond, Twickenham and Roehampton DHA, 1987–90. Dir, 1972–, and Vice-Chm., 1978–, Taylor & Francis, Scientific Pubns. Manager, Royal Instn, 1972–75. Mem. Delegacy, Goldsmiths' Coll., 1974–76; Chairman of Governors: Garnett Coll., 1974–78; St Francis Xavier VIth Form Coll., 1985–; Governor: Philippa Fawcett and Digby Stuart Colls, 1973–76; Ursuline Convent Sch., Wimbledon, 1967–; Heythrop Coll., Univ. of London, 1977–86; Wimbledon Coll., 1982–; Commonwealth Inst., 1977–85; W London Inst. of Higher Educn, 1990–94. Numerous overseas consultancies and visiting professorships; Academic Mem., British Assoc. of Science Writers, 1971–; Editor, Jl of Physics Educn, 1966–69; Mem., Editorial Bd, Jl Curriculum Studies, and Studies in Sci. Educn. DUniv Surrey, 1987. Bragg Medal, Inst. of Physics, 1991. KSG 1983. *Recreations:* Rugby (spectator), railways, bee-keeping. *Address:* 3 Thetford Road, New Malden, Surrey KT3 5DN. *T:* 0181–942 6861. *Club:* Athenæum.

See also D. J. Keohane.

KEPA, Sailosi Wai; Judge of the High Court, Fiji, since 1992; *b* 4 Nov. 1938; *m* Adi Teimumu Tuisawau; four *c*. *Educ:* Draiba Fijian Sch.; Lelean Memorial Sch.; Nasinu Training Coll.; Sydney Univ. (Dip. in Teaching of English, 1966). Called to the Bar, Middle Temple, 1972; Barrister and Solicitor, Fiji, 1974. Joined Judicial Dept, as Magistrate, 1969; served Suva, Northern Div., Sigatoka, Nadi; Chief Magistrate, July 1980; Dir of Public Prosecutions, Nov. 1980; High Comr for Fiji in London, 1985–88; Attorney-Gen. and Minister for Justice, Fiji, 1988–92. Rugby player (rep. Fiji, Australia 1961), coach, manager, administrator; Chm., Fiji Rugby Union, 1983–85; Pres., Suva Rugby Union, 1989–. *Address:* High Court, Government Buildings, Suva, Fiji. *T:* 211491.

KEPPEL, family name of **Earl of Albemarle.**

KER; *see* Innes-Ker, family name of Duke of Roxburghe.

KERBY, John Vyvyan; Under Secretary, Asia and Pacific Division, Overseas Development Administration, Foreign and Commonwealth Office, since 1993; *b* 14 Dec. 1942; *s* of Theo Rosser Fred Kerby and Constance Mary (*née* Newell); *m* 1978, Shirley Elizabeth Pope; one step *s* one step *d*. *Educ:* Eton Coll.; Christ Church, Oxford (MA). Temp. Asst Principal, CO, 1965; Asst Principal, ODM, 1967; Pvte Sec. to Parly Under-Sec. of State, FCO, 1970; Principal, ODA, 1971–74, 1975–77; CSSB, 1974–75; Asst Sec., ODA, 1977; Head of British Develt Div. in Southern Africa, 1983; Under Sec. and Prin. Establishment Officer, ODA, 1986–93. *Recreations:* gardening, cricket, music, entomology. *Address:* c/o Overseas Development Administration, 94 Victoria Street, SW1E 5JL. *T:* 0171–917 0352.

KERDEL-VEGAS, Francisco, Hon. CBE 1973; MD; Venezuelan Ambassador to the Court of St James's, 1987–92; *b* 3 Jan. 1928; *s* of Oswaldo F. Kerdel y Sofia Vegas de Kerdel; *m* 1977, Martha Ramos de Kerdel; two *s* four *d*. *Educ:* Liceo Andrés Bello, Caracas (BSc); Univ. Central de Venezuela (MD); Harvard; New York Univ. (MSc). Prof. of Dermatology, Central Univ. of Venezuela, 1954–77; Vis. Scientist, Dept of Experimental Pathology, ARC Inst. of Animal Physiology, Cambridge, 1966–67; Mem., Trinity Coll, Cambridge, 1966–67; Scientific Attaché, Venezuelan Embassy, London, 1966–67; Vice-Chancellor, Simón Bolívar Univ., 1969–70; Mem. Board, Univ. Metropolitana, Caracas, 1970–. Vis. Prof. of Dermatol., UMDS of Guy's and St Thomas' Hosps, 1990. Prosser White Oration, RCP, 1972. A Dir, Internat. Foundn of Dermatol., 1987–. Fellow, Venezuelan Acads of Medicine, 1967–, of Sciences, 1971–; Mem., Nat. Res. Council, Venezuela, 1969–79; President: FUDENA (Nat. chapter of WWF), 1974; Internat. Soc. of Dermatol., 1985–90. Fellow: Amer. Coll. of Physicians; Philadelphia Coll. of Physicians; Amer. Acad. of Dermatology. Foreign Mem., Nat. Academies of Medicine of Brazil, Chile and Paraguay; Hon. Member: RSM; British Assoc. of Dermatologists; German Assoc. of Dermatologists; Socs of Dermatology of France, Austria, Spain, Portugal, Brazil, Argentina, Mexico, Colombia, Ecuador, Peru, Central America, Cuba, Israel, S Africa. Hon. DSc: California Coll. of Podiatric Medicine, 1975; Cranfield, 1991. Venezuelan Orders of: Andrés Bello, 1970; Cecilio Acosta, 1976; Francisco de Miranda, 1978; Diego de Losada, 1985; El Libertador, 1986; Chevalier de la Legion d'Honneur (France), 1972. *Publications:* Tratado de Dermatologia, 1959, 4th edn 1986; chapters of textbooks of Dermatology, UK, USA, Canada, Spain, Mexico. *Recreations:* travelling, swimming, photography. *Address:* Flat 14, 76 Jermyn Street, St James's, SW1Y 6NY. *Clubs:* United Oxford & Cambridge University, White's; Caracas Country, Camurí Grande (Venezuela).

KERLE, Rt. Rev. Ronald Clive; Rector of St Swithun's, Pymble, Diocese of Sydney, 1976–82; *b* 28 Dec. 1915; *s* of William Alfred Ronald Kerle and Isabel Ada (*née* Turner); *m* 1940, Helen Marshall Jackson; one *s* one *d*. *Educ:* Univ. of Sydney (BA); Moore Theological Coll., Sydney. Sydney ACT, ThL 1937; BA 1942. Deacon 1939; Priest, 1940; Curate, St Paul's, Sydney, 1939; St Anne, Ryde, 1939–41; Rector, Kangaroo Valley, 1941–43; St Stephen, Port Kembla, 1943–47; Chaplain, AIF, 1945–47; Gen. Sec., NSW Branch, Church Missionary Society, 1947–54; Rector of Summer Hill, 1954–56; Archdeacon of Cumberland, 1954–60; Bishop Co-adjutor of Sydney, 1956–65; Bishop of Armidale, 1965–76. *Address:* Gowrie Retirement Village, 10 Edward Street, Gordon, NSW 2072, Australia.

KERMACK, Stuart Ogilvy; Sheriff of Tayside, Central and Fife: at Forfar, 1971–93; at Perth, 1971–75; at Arbroath, 1975–91; at Dundee, 1991–93; *b* 9 July 1934; *s* of late Stuart Grace Kermack, CBE and of Nell P., *y d* of Thomas White, SSC; *m* 1961, Barbara Mackenzie, BSc; three *s* one *d*. *Educ:* Glasgow Academy; Jesus Coll., Oxford; Glasgow Univ.; Edinburgh Univ. BA Oxon (Jurisprudence), 1956; LLB Glasgow, 1959. Called to Scots Bar, 1959. Sheriff Substitute of Inverness, Moray, Nairn and Ross, at Elgin and Nairn, 1965–71. *Publications:* articles in legal journals. *Address:* 23 South Learmonth Gardens, Edinburgh EH4 1EZ. *T:* 0131–337 1898.

KERMAN, Prof. Joseph Wilfred; Professor of Music, University of California at Berkeley, since 1974 (Chambers Professor of Music, 1986–89); *b* 3 April 1924; *m* 1945, Vivian Shaviro; two *s* one *d*. *Educ:* New York Univ. (AB); Princeton Univ. (PhD). Dir of Graduate Studies, Westminster Choir Coll., Princeton, NJ, USA, 1949–51; Music Faculty, Univ. of California at Berkeley, 1951–72, 1974– (Dep. Chm., 1960–63, 1991–93); Heather Prof. of Music, Oxford Univ., and Fellow of Wadham Coll., Oxford, 1972–74. Co-editor, 19th Century Music, 1977–88. Guggenheim, Fulbright and NEH Fellowships; Visiting Fellow: All Souls Coll., Oxford, 1966; Society for the Humanities, Cornell Univ., USA, 1970; Clare Hall, Cambridge, 1971; Walker-Ames Vis. Prof., Univ. of Washington, 1986; Valentine Vis. Prof., Amherst Coll., 1988; Gauss Lectr, Princeton Univ., 1988; Phi Beta Kappa Scholar, 1993. Fellow, American Academy of Arts and Sciences; Corresp. FBA 1984. Hon. FRAM. Hon. DHL Fairfield Univ., 1970. *Publications:* Opera as Drama, 1956, rev. edn 1988; The Elizabethan Madrigal, 1962; The Beethoven Quartets, 1967; A History of Art and Music (with H. W. Janson), 1968; (ed) Ludwig van Beethoven: Autograph Miscellany, 1786–99 (Kafka Sketchbook), 2 vols, 1970 (Kinkeldey Award); Listen, 1972; The Masses and Motets of William Byrd, 1981 (Kinkeldey Award; Deems Taylor Award); The New Grove Beethoven (with A. Tyson), 1983; (co-ed) Beethoven Studies, vol. 1 1973, vol 2 1977, vol. 3 1982; Musicology, 1985; (ed) Music at the Turn of the Century, 1990; Write All These Down, 1994; essays, in music criticism and musicology, in: Hudson Review, New York Review, San Francisco Chronicle, etc. *Address:* Music Department, University of California, Berkeley, CA 94720, USA; 107 Southampton Avenue, Berkeley, CA 94707.

KERMODE, Sir (John) Frank, Kt 1991; MA; FBA 1973; *b* 29 Nov. 1919; *s* of late John Pritchard Kermode and late Doris Pearl Kermode; *m* 1947, Maureen Eccles (marr. diss. 1970); twin *s* and *d*. *Educ:* Douglas High Sch.; Liverpool Univ. BA 1940; War Service (Navy), 1940–46; MA 1947; Lecturer, King's Coll., Newcastle, in the University of Durham, 1947–49; Lecturer in the University of Reading, 1949–58; John Edward Taylor Prof. of English Literature in the University of Manchester, 1958–65; Winterstoke Prof. of English in the University of Bristol, 1965–67; Lord Northcliffe Prof. of Modern English Lit., UCL, 1967–74; King Edward VII Prof. of English Literature, Cambridge Univ., 1974–82; Fellow, King's Coll., Cambridge, 1974–87, Hon. Fellow, 1988. Charles Eliot Norton Prof. of Poetry at Harvard, 1977–78. Co-editor, Encounter, 1966–67. Editor: Fontana Masterguides and Modern Masters series; Oxford Authors. FRSL 1958. Mem. Arts Council, 1968–71; Chm., Poetry Book Soc., 1968–76. For. Hon. Mem., Amer. Acad. of Arts and Scis. Hon. DHL Chicago, 1975; Hon. DLitt: Liverpool, 1981; Newcastle, 1993; Hon Dr. Amsterdam, 1988. Officier de l'Ordre des Arts et des Sciences. *Publications:* (ed) Shakespeare, The Tempest (Arden Edition), 1954; Romantic Image, 1957; John Donne, 1957; The Living Milton, 1960; Wallace Stevens, 1960; Puzzles & Epiphanies, 1962; The Sense of an Ending, 1967; Continuities, 1968; Shakespeare, Spenser, Donne, 1971; Modern Essays, 1971; Lawrence, 1973; (ed, with John Hollander) Oxford Anthology of English Literature, 1973; The Classic, 1975; (ed) Selected Prose of T. S. Eliot, 1975; The Genesis of Secrecy, 1979; Essays on Fiction, 1971–82, 1983; Forms of Attention, 1985; (ed jtly) The Literary Guide to the Bible, 1987; History and Value, 1988; An Appetite for Poetry, 1989; Poetry, Narrative, History, 1990; (ed with Keith Walker) Andrew Marvell, 1990; Uses of Error, 1991; (ed with Anita Kermode) The Oxford Book of Letters, 1995; Not Entitled (memoirs), 1995; contrib. New Republic, Partisan Review, New York Review, New Statesman, London Rev. of Books, etc. *Address:* 27 Luard Road, Cambridge CB2 2PJ. *T:* Cambridge (01223) 247398. *Club:* Savile.

KERMODE, Hon. Sir Ronald (Graham Quayle), KBE 1986 (CBE 1975); Judge of the Court of Appeal, Republic of Fiji, 1988–91; *b* 26 June 1919; *s* of George Graham Kermode and Linda Margaret (*née* McInnis); *m* 1945, Amy Rivett Marr; two *s* two *d*. *Educ:* Whangarei High Sch., NZ; Auckland University Coll. (LLB). Served with NZ and Fiji Mil. Forces, 1939–45. In private legal practice, 1945–75; Puisne Judge, Supreme Court of Fiji, 1976–86; Judge of the Court of Appeal: Kiribati, 1983–86; Fiji, 1985–87. Tribunal, Fiji Sugar Industry, 1985–92. Elected European MLC, Fiji, 1958, and served for 15 years as Mem. of Council and Parliament; first elected Speaker of the House of Representatives, 1968–73. *Recreations:* fishing, contract bridge, reading, gardening, bird watching. *Address:* 44A Cook Street, Howick, Auckland, New Zealand. *T:* 5375102.

KERN, Karl-Heinz; Head of Arms Control Department, Ministry of Foreign Affairs, German Democratic Republic, 1987–90; *b* 18 Feb. 1930; *m* 1952, Ursula Bennmann; one *s*. *Educ:* King George Gymnasium, Dresden; Techn. Coll., Dresden (chem. engrg); Acad. for Polit. Science and Law (Dipl. jur., post-grad. History). Leading posts in diff. regional authorities of GDR until 1959; foreign policy, GDR, 1959–62; Head of GDR Mission in Ghana, 1962–66; Head of African Dept, Min. of For. Affairs, 1966–71; Minister and Chargé d'Affaires, Gt Britain, 1973; Ambassador to UK, 1973–80; Dep. Head of Western European Dept, Min. of Foreign Affairs, 1980–82; Ambassador to N Korea, 1982–86. Holds Order of Merit of the Fatherland, etc. *Recreations:* sport, reading, music. *Address:* Karl-Marx-Allee 70a, 10243 Berlin, Germany.

KERNOHAN, Thomas Hugh, CBE 1978 (OBE 1955); Founder, 1959, and Chairman, 1961–80 and 1987–93, Kernohans Joinery Works Ltd (family joinery and plastic firm); *b* 11 May 1922; *s* of Thomas Watson Kernohan and Caroline Kernohan; *m* 1948, Margaret Moore; one *s* one *d*. *Educ:* Carrickfergus Model Sch.; Carrickfergus Technical Sch. On staff (admin), Harland & Wolff Ltd, Belfast, 1940–44; Engineering Employers' NI Association: Asst Sec., 1945; Sec., 1953; Dir, 1966–80; Parly Comr for Admin and Comr for Complaints, NI, 1980–87. *Address:* Beach House, Island Park, Greenisland, Carrickfergus, N Ireland BT38 8TW. *T:* Belfast (01232) 862030.

KERR, family name of **Marquess of Lothian** and **Baron Teviot.**

KERR, Alan Grainger, FRCS, FRCSE; Consultant Otolaryngologist, Royal Victoria and Belfast City Hospitals, since 1968; *b* 15 April 1935; *s* of Joseph William and Eileen Kerr; *m* 1962, Patricia Margaret M'Neill; two *s* one *d*. *Educ:* Methodist College, Belfast; Queen's Univ., Belfast (MB). DObst RCOG. Clinical and Res. Fellow, Harvard Med. Sch., 1967; Prof. of Otorhinolaryngology, QUB, 1979–81. Otolaryngology Mem. Council, RCS, 1987–92. Lectures, UK, Europe and USA. Prizes: Jobson Horne, BMA; Harrison, RSocMed; Howells, Univ. of London. Gen. Editor, Scott-Brown's Otolaryngology, 1987–. *Publications:* papers on ear surgery. *Recreations:* squash, tennis, ski-ing. *Address:* 6 Cranmore Gardens, Belfast BT9 6JL. *T:* Belfast (01232) 669181. *Club:* Royal Society of Medicine.

KERR, Prof. Allen, AO 1992; FRS 1986; FAA; Professor of Plant Pathology, University of Adelaide, 1980–91, Professor Emeritus, since 1992; *b* 21 May 1926; *s* of A. B. Kerr and J. T. Kerr (*née* White); *m* 1951, Rosemary Sheila Strachan; two *s* one *d*. *Educ:* George Heriot's Sch., Edinburgh; Univ. of Edinburgh. North of Scotland Coll. of Agric., 1947–51; University of Adelaide: Lectr, 1951–59; Sen. Lectr, 1959–67 (seconded to Tea Research Inst., Ceylon, 1963–66); Reader, 1968–80. For. Associate, Nat. Acad. of Scis, USA, 1991. *Recreation:* golf. *Address:* 419 Carrington Street, Adelaide, SA 5000, Australia. *T:* (8) 2322325.

KERR, Andrew Mark; Senior Partner, Bell & Scott, WS, Edinburgh, since 1987 (Partner, since 1969); Clerk to Society of Writers to HM Signet, since 1983; *b* Edinburgh 17 Jan. 1940; *s* of William Mark Kerr and Katharine Marjorie Anne Stevenson; *m* 1967, Jane Susanna Robertson; one *d*. *Educ:* Edinburgh Acad.; Cambridge Univ. (BA); Edinburgh Univ. (LLB). Served RNR, 1961–76. British Petroleum, 1961–62. Vice-Chm., Edinburgh New Town Conservation Cttee, 1972–76; Chm., Edinburgh Solicitors' Property Centre, 1976–81. Member: Council, Edinburgh Internat. Fest., 1978–82; Scottish Arts Council, 1988–94 (Chm., Drama Cttee, 1988–91, and 1993–94); Sec., Edinburgh Fest. Fringe Soc. Ltd, 1969–. Mem. Council, St George's Sch. for Girls, Edinburgh, 1985–93. *Recreations:* architecture, hill walking, music, ships, ski-ing, theatre. *Address:* 16 Ann Street, Edinburgh EH4 1PJ. *T:* (home) 0131–332 9857; (office) 0131–226 6703. *Club:* New (Edinburgh).

KERR, Hon. Sir Brian (Francis), Kt 1993; **Hon. Mr Justice Kerr;** a Judge of the High Court of Justice, Northern Ireland, since 1993; *b* 22 Feb. 1948; *s* of late James William Kerr and of Kathleen Rose Kerr; *m* 1970, Gillian Rosemary Owen Widdowson; two *s*. *Educ:* St Colman's College, Newry, Co. Down; Queen's Univ., Belfast (LLB 1969). Called to NI Bar, 1970, to the Bar of England and Wales, Gray's Inn, 1974; QC (NI) 1983; Bencher, Inn of Court of NI, 1990; Junior Crown Counsel (Common Law), 1978–83; Sen. Crown Counsel, 1988–93. Chm., Mental Health Commn for NI, 1988. *Recreations:* France, accepting defeat by sons at tennis. *Address:* Royal Courts of Justice, Belfast BT1 3JY.

KERR, Clark; educator; *b* 17 May 1911; *s* of Samuel W. and Caroline Clark Kerr; *m* 1934, Catherine Spaulding; two *s* one *d*. *Educ:* Swarthmore Coll. (AB); Stanford Univ. (MA); Univ. of Calif., Berkeley (PhD). Actg Asst Prof., Stanford Univ., 1939–40; Asst Prof., later Assoc. Prof., Univ. of Washington, 1940–45; Prof., Dir, Inst. of Industrial Relations, Univ. of Calif, Berkeley, 1945–52; Chancellor, Univ. of Calif at Berkeley, 1952–58; Pres., Univ. of Calif, 1958–67, now Emeritus President. Chairman: Carnegie Commn on Higher Educn, 1967–74; Carnegie Council on Policy Studies in Higher Educn, 1974–80; Bd, Work in America Inst., 1975–; Bd, Global Perspectives in Educn, 1976–85, now Chm. Emeritus. Govt service with US War Labor Board, 1942–45. Mem. Pres. Eisenhower's Commn on Nat. Goals, President Kennedy and President Johnson Cttee on Labor-Management Policy; Program Dir, Strengthening Presidential Leadership Project, Assoc. of Governing Bds of Univs and Colls, 1982–85; Contract Arbitrator for: Boeing Aircraft Co. and Internat. Assoc. of Machinists, 1944–45; Armour & Co. and United Packinghouse Workers, 1945–47, 1949–52; Waterfront Employers' Assoc. and Internat. Longshoremen's and Warehousemen's Union, 1946–47, etc. Member: Amer. Acad. of Arts and Sciences; Royal Economic Society; Amer. Econ. Assoc.; Nat. Acad. of Arbitrators, etc. Phi Beta Kappa, Kappa Sigma. Trustee, Rockefeller Foundation, 1960–75; Chm., Armour Automation Cttee, 1959–79. Hon. Fellow, LSE, 1977. Hon. LLD: Swarthmore, 1952; Harvard, 1958; Princeton, 1959; Notre Dame, 1964; Chinese Univ. of Hong Kong, 1964; Rochester, 1967; Hon. DLitt, Strathclyde, 1965; Hon. Dr, Bordeaux, 1962, etc. Harold W. McGraw, Jr, Prize in Educn, 1990. *Publications:* (jtly) Unions, Management and the Public, 1948, rev. edns 1960, 1967; (jtly) Industrialism and Industrial Man, 1960, rev. edns 1964, 1973; The Uses of the University, 1963, 4th edn 1995; Labor and Management in Industrial Society, 1964, rev. edn 1972; Marshall, Marx and Modern Times, 1969; (jtly) Industrialism and Industrial Man Reconsidered, 1975; Labor Markets and Wage Determination, 1977; Education and National Development, 1979; The Future of Industrial Societies, 1983; (jtly) The Many Lives of Academic Presidents, 1986; (ed jtly) Industrial Relations in a New Age, 1986; (ed jtly) Economics of Labor in Industrial Society, 1986; (jtly) How Labor Markets Work, 1988; (jtly) The Guardians: boards of trustees of American colleges and universities, 1989; The Great Transformation in Higher Education 1960–1980, 1991; Troubled Times for American Higher Education, 1993; Higher Education Cannot Escape History: issues for the twenty-first century, 1993; (ed jtly) Labor Economics and Industrial Relations: markets and institutions, 1994; contribs to American Economic Review, Review of Economics and Statistics, Quarterly Jl of Economics, etc. *Recreation:* gardening. *Address:* 8300 Buckingham Drive, El Cerrito, CA 94530, USA. *T:* (510) 2239651; (office) Institute of Industrial Relations, University of California, Berkeley, CA 94720-5555, USA. *T:* (510) 6428106, *Fax:* (510) 6435528.

KERR, Dr David Leigh; *b* 25 March 1923; *s* of Myer Woolf Kerr and Paula (*née* Horowitz); *m* 1st, 1944, Aileen Saddington (marr. diss. 1969); two *s* one *d*; 2nd, 1970, Margaret Dunlop; one *s* two *d*. *Educ:* Whitgift Sch., Croydon; Middlesex Hosp. Med. Sch., London. Hon. Sec., Socialist Medical Assoc., 1957–63; Hon. Vice-Pres., 1963–72. LCC (Wandsworth, Central), 1958–65, and Coun., London Borough of Wandsworth, 1964–68; Mem., Herts CC (Welwyn Garden City S), 1989–. Contested (Lab) Wandsworth, Streatham (for Parlt), 1959; MP (Lab) Wandsworth Central, 1964–70; PPS to Minister of State, FCO, 1967–69. Vis. Lectr in Medicine, Chelsea Coll., 1972–82. War on Want: Dir, 1970–77; Vice-Chm., 1973–74; Chm., 1974–77. Family Doctor, Tooting, 1946–82; Chief Exec., Manor House Hosp., London, 1982–87. Member: Inter-departmental Cttee on Death Certification and Coroners, E Herts CHC, 1992–; Med. Assessor, Registered Homes Tribunals, 1986–. Hon. Vice Pres. and Trustee, Health Visitors' Assoc., 1969–. FRSM. Governor, British Film Inst., 1966–71. *Recreations:* reading other people's biographies, refusing to write own. *Address:* 19 Calder Avenue, Brookmans Park, Herts AL9 7AH. *T:* Potters Bar (01707) 653954.

KERR, Prof. David Nicol Sharp, CBE 1992; MSc; FRCP, FRCPE; Professor of Renal Medicine, Royal Postgraduate Medical School, University of London, 1987–93 (Dean, 1984–91); *b* 27 Dec. 1927; *s* of William Kerr and Elsie (Ransted) Kerr; *m* 1960, Eleanor Jones; two *s* one *d*. *Educ:* George Watson's Boys' College; Edinburgh University (MB ChB); University of Wisconsin (MSc); FRCPE 1966; FRCP 1967; House Physician and Surgeon, Royal Infirmary, Edinburgh, 1951–52; Exchange scholar, Univ. of Wisconsin, 1952–53; Surgeon Lieut, RNVR, 1953–55; Asst Lectr, Univ. of Edinburgh, 1956–57; Registrar, Hammersmith Hosp., 1957–59; Lectr, Univ. of Durham, 1959–63; Consultant Physician, Royal Victoria Infirmary, Newcastle upon Tyne, 1962–83; Senior Lectr, 1963–68, Prof. of Medicine, 1968–83, Univ. of Newcastle upon Tyne. Postgrad. Med. Advr, NW Thames RHA, 1991–. Med. Awards Administrator, Commonwealth Scholarships Commn, 1993–. Member: Council, Internat. Soc. of Nephrology, 1984–93; Council, British Heart Foundn, 1989–; NW Thames RHA, 1989–91; Hammersmith and Queen Charlotte's SHA, 1984–91; Ealing Hosp. NHS Trust, 1991–; Standing Med. Adv. Cttee, DHSS, 1979–90. Sen. Censor and First Vice Pres., RCP, 1990–91. Hon. Fellow, SA Coll. of Medicine, 1992; Hon. Mem., Spanish Soc. of Nephrology, 1992. Editor, Jl of RCP, 1994–. *Publications:* Short Textbook of Renal Disease, 1968; (ed) Oxford Textbook of Clinical Nephrology, 1992; chapters in numerous books incl. Cecil-Loeb Textbook of Medicine and Oxford Textbook of Medicine; articles on renal disease in med. jls. *Recreation:* fell walking. *Address:* 22 Carbery Avenue, W3 9AL. *T* and *Fax:* 0181–992 3231. *Club:* Athenæum.

KERR, Deborah Jane, (Deborah Kerr Viertel); actress; *b* 30 Sept. 1921; *d* of Capt. Arthur Kerr-Trimmer; *m* 1st, 1945, Sqdn Ldr A. C. Bartley (marr. diss., 1959); two *d*; 2nd, 1960, Peter Viertel. *Educ:* Northumberland House, Clifton, Bristol. Open Air Theatre, Regent's Park, 1939, Oxford Repertory, 1939–40; after an interval of acting in films, appeared on West End Stage; Ellie Dunn in Heartbreak House, Cambridge Theatre, 1943; went to France, Belgium, and Holland for ENSA, playing in Gaslight, 1945. *Films:* Major Barbara, 1940; Love on the Dole, 1940–41; Penn of Pennsylvania, 1941; Hatter's Castle, 1942; The Day Will Dawn, 1942; Life and Death of Colonel Blimp, 1942–43; Perfect Strangers, 1944; I See a Dark Stranger, 1945; Black Narcissus, 1946; The Hucksters and If Winter Comes, 1947 (MGM, Hollywood); Edward My Son, 1948; Please Believe Me, 1949 (MGM, Hollywood); King Solomon's Mines, 1950; Quo Vadis, 1952; Prisoner of Zenda, Julius Caesar, Dream Wife, Young Bess (MGM), 1952; From Here to Eternity, 1953; The End of the Affair, 1955; The Proud and Profane, The King and I, 1956; Heaven Knows, Mr Allison, An Affair to Remember, Tea and Sympathy, 1957; Bonjour Tristesse, 1958; Separate Tables, The Journey, Count Your Blessings, 1959; The Sundowners, The Grass is Greener, The Naked Edge, The Innocents, 1961; The Chalk Garden, The Night of the Iguana, 1964; Casino Royale, 1967; Eye of the Devil, Prudence and the Pill, 1968; The Arrangement, 1970; The Assam Garden, 1985. *Stage:* Tea and Sympathy, NY, 1953; The Day After the Fair, London, 1972, tour of US, 1973–74; Seascape, NY, 1975; Candida, London, 1977; The Last of Mrs Cheyney, tour of US, 1978–79; The Day After the Fair, Melbourne and Sydney, 1979; Overheard, Haymarket, 1981; The Corn is Green, Old Vic, 1985. BAFTA Special Award, 1991; Hon. Oscar, Acad. of Motion Picture Arts and Scis, 1994. *Address:* Klosters, 7250 Grisons, Switzerland.

KERR, Desmond Moore, OBE 1970; HM Diplomatic Service, retired; *b* 23 Jan. 1930; *s* of late Robert John Kerr and Mary Elizabeth Kerr; *m* 1956, Evelyn Patricia South; one *s* two *d*. *Educ:* Methodist Coll., Belfast; Queen's Univ., Belfast. BA Hons (Classics and Ancient History). CRO, 1952; British High Commn, Karachi, 1956–59, Lagos, 1959–62; Second Sec., 1960; Commonwealth Office, 1962–66; First Sec., 1965; Dep. British Govt Rep., West Indies Associated States, 1966–70; FCO, 1970–76; Dep. High Comr, Dacca, 1976–79; High Comr, Swaziland, 1979–83; Head of Claims Dept, FCO, 1983–87. Mem. Exec. Council, CS Pensioners' Alliance, 1991–. *Address:* c/o Foreign and Commonwealth Office, SW1A 2AH.
See also E. Kerr.

KERR, Donald Frederick, CVO 1961; OBE 1960; Manager, Government Press Centre, Foreign and Commonwealth Office, 1976–77, retired; *b* 20 April 1915; *s* of Dr David Kerr, Cheshire; *m* 1942, Elizabeth Hayward (*d* 1978); two *s* one *d*. *Educ:* Sydney High Sch.; University of Sydney (BEcon). Served RAF (Navigator), SEAC, 1942–46. Deputy Director: British Information Services, New Delhi, 1947–53; UK Information Service, Ottawa, 1953–55; UK Information Service, Toronto, 1955–56; Dir, UK Information Service in Canada, Ottawa, 1956–59; Dir, British Information Services in India, New Delhi, 1959–63; Controller (Overseas), COI, 1963–76; on secondment, Dir of Information, Commonwealth Secretariat, Sept. 1969–Sept. 1970. *Recreation:* golf. *Address:* 4 Southdown House, 11 Lansdowne Road, Wimbledon, SW20 8AN. *Club:* Royal Wimbledon Golf.

KERR, Dr Edwin, CBE 1986; Chief Executive, College for Financial Planning, since 1988; *b* 1 July 1926; *e s* of late Robert John Kerr and Mary Elizabeth Kerr (*née* Ferguson); *m* 1949, Gertrude Elizabeth (*née* Turbitt); one *s* two *d*. *Educ:* Royal Belfast Academical Instn; Queen's Univ., Belfast (BSc, PhD). FIMA, FBCS. Asst Lectr in Maths, QUB, 1948–52; Lectr in Maths, Coll. of Technology, Birmingham (now Univ. of Aston in Birmingham), 1952–55; Lectr in Maths, Coll. of Science and Technology, Manchester (now Univ. of Manchester Inst. of Science and Technology), 1956–58; Head of Maths Dept, Royal Coll. of Advanced Technology, Salford (now Univ. of Salford), 1958–66; Principal, Paisley Coll. of Technology, 1966–72; Chief Officer, CNAA, 1972–86; Chm. and Chief Exec., Exam. Bd for Financial Planning, 1987–89. Member: Adv. Cttee on Supply and Training of Teachers, 1973–78; Adv. Cttee on Supply and Educn of Teachers, 1980–85; Bd for Local Authority Higher Educn, 1982–85; Bd for Public Sector Higher Educn, 1985–86; Mem. and Vice-Chm., Continuing Educn Standing Cttee, 1985–88. President: Soc. for Res. into Higher Educn, 1974–77; The Mathematical Assoc., 1976–77. Hon. FCP 1984; Hon. Fellow: Coventry Lanchester, Newcastle upon Tyne, Portsmouth and Sheffield Polytechnics, 1986; Huddersfield Polytechnic, and Paisley Coll. of Technol., 1987; Goldsmiths' Coll., London, 1991. DUniv: Open, 1977; Paisley, 1993; Hon. DSc Ulster, 1986; Hon. DEd CNAA, 1989. *Publications:* (with R. Butler) An Introduction to Numerical Methods, 1962; various mathematical and educational. *Recreation:* gardening. *Address:* 59 Craigdarragh Road, Helen's Bay, Co. Down BT19 1UB. *Club:* Travellers'.
See also D. M. Kerr.

KERR, Francis Robert Newsam, OBE 1962; MC 1940; JP; farmer, 1949–85, retired; Vice Lord-Lieutenant of Berwickshire, 1970–90; *b* 12 Sept. 1916; *s* of late Henry Francis Hobart Kerr and Gertrude Mary Kerr (*née* Anthony); *m* 1941, Anne Frederica Kitson; two *s* one *d*. *Educ:* Ampleforth College. Regular Officer, The Royal Scots, 1937–49; TA 1952–63; retired as Lt-Col. Member: Berwickshire County Council, 1964–75; SE Scotland Regional Hosp. Bd, 1971–74; Borders Area Health Bd, 1973–81 (Vice-Chm.); Borders Reg. Council, 1974–78; Post Office Users Nat. Council, 1972–73; Whitley Council, 1970–81; Council, Multiple Sclerosis Soc., 1971–93. Sheriff of Berwick upon Tweed, 1974; JP Berwickshire, 1975. *Recreations:* country pursuits. *Address:* The Coach House, Howden, Jedburgh, Roxburghshire TD8 6QP. *T:* Jedburgh (01835) 64193.

KERR, Hugh; Member (Lab) Essex West and Hertfordshire East, European Parliament, since 1994; *m*; one *s*. Former Sen. Lectr, Univ. of North London. Former Mem. (Lab) Harlow DC. *Address:* European Parliament, 97 Rue Belliard, 1040 Brussels, Belgium.

KERR, James, QPM 1979; Chief Constable, Lincolnshire Police, 1977–83; *b* 19 Nov. 1928; *s* of William and Margaret Jane Kerr; *m* 1952, Jean Coupland; one *d*. *Educ:* Carlisle Grammar School. Cadet and Navigating Officer, Merchant Navy, 1945–52 (Union Castle Line, 1949–52). Carlisle City Police and Cumbria Constabulary, 1952–74; Asst Director of Command Courses, Police Staff Coll., Bramshill, 1974; Asst Chief Constable (Operations), North Yorkshire Police, 1975; Deputy Chief Constable, Lincs, 1976. Officer Brother, OStJ, 1980. *Recreations:* music, squash. *Address:* 15 Kelvin Court, North Ringwood, Vic 3134, Australia. *Clubs:* Royal Automobile (Victoria); Heathmont Bowling (Heathmont).

KERR, Adm. Sir John (Beverley), GCB 1993 (KCB 1989); Commander-in-Chief, Naval Home Command, 1991–94; Flag Aide-de-Camp to the Queen, 1991–94; *b* 27 Oct. 1937; *s* of late Wilfred Kerr and of Vera Kerr (*née* Sproule); *m* 1964, Elizabeth Anne, *d* of late Dr and Mrs C. R. G. Howard, Burley, Hants; three *s*. *Educ:* Moseley Hall County Grammar Sch., Cheadle; Britannia Royal Naval Coll., Dartmouth. Served in various ships, 1958–65 (specialized in navigation, 1964); Staff, BRNC, Dartmouth, 1965–67; HMS Cleopatra, 1967–69; Staff, US Naval Acad., Annapolis, 1969–71; NDC, Latimer, 1971–72; i/c HMS Achilles, 1972–74; Naval Plans, MoD, 1974–75; Defence Policy Staff, MoD, 1975–77; RCDS, 1978; i/c HMS Birmingham, 1979–81; Dir of Naval Plans, MoD, 1981–83; i/c HMS Illustrious, 1983–84; ACNS (Op. Requirements), 1984; ACDS (Op. Requirements) (Sea Systems), 1985–86; Flag Officer First Flotilla/Flotilla One, 1986–88; MoD, 1988–91. Mem., Indep. Rev. of Armed Forces' Manpower, Career and Remuneration Structures, 1994–95. Mem., Museums and Galls Commn, 1994–. Mem., CWGC, 1994–. Cdre, RNSA, 1992–95; Member: Cttee of Management, RNLI, 1993–; Audit Cttee, Lancaster Univ., 1994–; Cttee, Manchester Mus., 1994–. CIMgt 1993. *Recreations:* music, sailing, hill walking, history. *Club:* Army and Navy.

KERR, Sir John (Olav), KCMG 1991 (CMG 1987); HM Diplomatic Service; Ambassador to the United States of America, since 1995; *b* 22 Feb. 1942; *s* of late Dr and Mrs J. D. O. Kerr; *m* 1965, Elizabeth, *d* of Mr and Mrs W. G. Kalaugher; two *s* three *d*. *Educ:* Glasgow Academy; Pembroke Coll., Oxford (Hon. Fellow, 1991). Entered Diplomatic Service, 1966; served FO, Moscow, Rawalpindi, FCO; Private Sec. to Permanent Under Secretary, FCO, 1974–79; Head of DM1 Division, HM Treasury, 1979–81; Principal Private Sec. to Chancellor of the Exchequer, 1981–84; Hd of Chancery, Washington, 1984–87; Asst Under-Sec. of State, FCO, 1987–90; Ambassador and UK Perm. Rep. to the EU, Brussels, 1990–95. *Address:* c/o Foreign and Commonwealth Office, King Charles Street, SW1A 2AH.

KERR, Rt. Hon. Sir Michael (Robert Emanuel), Kt 1972; PC 1981; a Lord Justice of Appeal, 1981–89; *b* 1 March 1921; *s* of Alfred Kerr; *m* 1st, 1952, Julia (marr. diss. 1982), *d* of Joseph Braddock; two *s* one *d*; 2nd, 1983, Diana, *yr d* of H. Neville Sneezum; one *s* one *d*. *Educ:* Aldenham Sch.; Clare Coll., Cambridge (Hon. Fellow, 1986). Served War, 1941–45 (Pilot; Flt-Lt). BA Cantab (1st cl. Hons Law) 1947, MA 1952; called to Bar, Lincoln's Inn, 1948, Bencher 1968, Treas., 1989; QC 1961. Member: Bar Council, 1968–72; Senate, 1969–72. Dep. Chm., Hants QS, 1961–71; Mem. Vehicle and General Enquiry Tribunal, 1971–72; a Judge of the High Court of Justice, Queen's Bench Div., and of the Commercial and Admiralty Cts, 1972–78; Chm., Law Commn of England and Wales, 1978–81. Pres., London Court of Internat. Arbitration, 1985–94, Hon. Pres., 1994. Mem. Council of Management: British Inst. of Internat. and Comparative Law, 1973–; Inst. of Advanced Legal Studies, 1979–85; Chairman: Lord Chancellor's interdeptl cttee on Foreign Judgments, 1974–81; Cttee of Management, Centre of Commercial Law Studies, QMC, 1980–89; Supreme Court Procedure Cttee, 1982–86; Mem., Internat. Adv. Cttee, British Columbia Internat. Arbitration Centre, 1986–. Vice-Pres., British Maritime Law Assoc., 1977–; President: CIArb, 1983–86; British-German Jurists Assoc., 1986–91. Hon. Mem., Amer. Law Inst., 1985; Hon. Life Mem., Amer. and Canadian Bar Assocs, 1976. Chorley Lectr, LSE, 1977; Alexander Lectr, CIArb, 1984. Governor, Aldenham Sch., 1959–87. Hon. Fellow, QMC, 1986. Knight Comdr, Grand Cross of Order of Merit (Germany), 1991. *Publications:* McNair's Law of the Air, 1953, 1965; articles and lectures on commercial law and arbitration. *Recreations:* travel, music, trying not to work, a second edition of children. *Address:* 10 Peterborough Villas, SW6 2AT. *T:* 0171–736 2144/6655. *Clubs:* Garrick, Pilgrims.

KERR, Robert Reid, TD; MA (Oxon), LLB; Sheriff of Tayside, Central and Fife (formerly Stirling, Dumbarton and Clackmannan) at Falkirk, 1969–83; *b* 7 May 1914; *s* of James Reid Kerr, sugar refiner, and Olive Rodger; *m* 1942, Mona Kerr; three *d*. *Educ:* Cargilfield; Trinity Coll., Glenalmond; Oxford Univ.; Glasgow Univ. Sheriff-Substitute: of Inverness, Moray, Nairn and Ross and Cromarty at Fort William, 1952–61; of Aberdeen, Kincardine and Banff at Banff, 1961–69. OStJ. *Address:* Bagatelle, 14 Rennie Street, Falkirk FK1 5QW.
See also J. K. G. Watson.

KERR, Rose; Curator of the Far Eastern Collections, Victoria and Albert Museum, since 1990; *b* 23 Feb. 1953; *d* of William Antony Kerr and Elizabeth Rendell; *m* 1990. *Educ:* SOAS, Univ. of London (BA Hons 1st Cl., Art and Archaeology of China); Languages Inst., Beijing. Fellow, Percival David Foundn of Chinese Art, 1976–78; joined Far Eastern Dept, V&A, 1978, Keeper, 1987–90. Member: Council, Oriental Ceramic Soc., 1987–; Exec. Cttee, GB-China Centre, 1989–. *Publications:* (with P. Hughes-Stanton) Kiln Sites of Ancient China, 1980; (with John Larson) Guanyin: a masterpiece revealed, 1985; Chinese Ceramics: porcelain of the Qing Dynasty 1644–1911, 1986; Later Chinese Bronzes, 1990; (ed and contrib.) Chinese Art and Design: the T. T. Tsui Gallery of Chinese Art, 1991; (with Rosemary Scott) Ceramic Evolution in the Middle Ming Period, 1994; articles in Oriental Art, Orientations, Apollo, Craft Magazine, V&A Album. *Recreations:* gardening, writing, sleeping. *Address:* Garrison House, Church Street, Presteigne, Powys LD8 2BU.

KERR, Thomas Henry, CB 1983; Director, Royal Aircraft Establishment, 1980–84; retired; *b* 18 June 1924; *s* of late Albert Edward Kerr and Mrs Francis Jane Kerr (*née* Simpson); *m* 1946, Myrnie Evelyn Martin Hughes; two *d*. *Educ:* Magnus Grammar, Newark; University Coll., Durham Univ. BSc 1949; CEng, FRAeS; Diplôme Paul Tissendier 1957. RAFVR pilot, 1942–46. Aero Flight, RAE, 1949–55; Head of Supersonic Flight Group, 1955–59; Scientific Adviser to C-in-C Bomber Comd, High Wycombe, 1960–64; Head of Assessment Div., Weapons Dept, RAE, 1964–66; Dep. Dir and Dir of Defence Operational Analysis Estabt, 1966–70; Head of Weapons Research Gp, Weapons Dept, RAE, 1970–72; Dir Gen. Establishments Resources Programmes (C), MoD (PE), 1972–74; Dir, Nat. Gas Turbine Estabt, 1974–80; R&D Dir, Royal Ordnance plc, 1984–86; Dir, Hunting Engineering, 1986–94 (Technical Dir, 1986–88). Consultant, Systems Designers Scientific, 1985–88. Mem. Council, RAeS, 1979, Pres., 1985–86. *Publications:* reports and memoranda of Aeronautical Research Council, lectures to RAeS and RUSI. *Recreations:* bridge, water ski-ing, tennis, badminton. *Address:* Bundu, 013 Kingsley Avenue, Camberley, Surrey GU15 2NA. *T:* Camberley (01276) 25961.

KERR, William Francis Kennedy, OBE 1984; PhD, CEng, FIMechE; Principal, Belfast College of Technology, 1969–84; *b* 1 Aug. 1923; *m* 1953, H. Adams; two *s*. *Educ:* Portadown Technical Coll. and Queen's Univ., Belfast. BSc (Hons) in Mech. Engineering, MSc, PhD. Teacher of Mathematics, Portadown Techn. Coll., 1947–48; Teacher and Sen. Lectr in Mech. Eng, Coll. of Techn., Belfast, 1948–55; Lectr and Adviser of Studies in Mech. Eng, Queen's Univ. of Belfast, 1955–62; Head of Dept of Mech., Civil, and Prod. Eng, Dundee Coll. of Techn., 1962–67; Vice-Principal, Coll. of Techn., Belfast, 1967–69. Chm., NI Cttee for Educnl Technology, 1973–79; Member: Mech. and Prodn Engrg Subject Panel, CNAA, 1964–67; Council for Educnl Technology, 1973–79; Belfast Educn and Library Bd, 1977–81; NI Council for Educnl Develt, 1980–84; NI Manpower Council, 1981–84; Chm., Assoc. of Principals of Colleges (NI Branch), 1982; Governor, Royal Belfast Academical Instn, 1969–84; Mem. Court, Ulster Univ., 1985–92. *Publications:* contribs on environmental testing of metals, etc. *Recreations:* golf, motoring, reading. *Address:* 27 Maxwell Road, Bangor, Co. Down, Northern Ireland BT20 3SG. *T:* Bangor (01247) 465303.

KERRIGAN, Greer Sandra; Under Secretary and Principal Assistant Solicitor, Department of Social Security, since 1991; *b* Port of Spain, Trinidad, 7 Aug. 1948; *d* of Wilfred M. Robinson and Rosina Robinson (*née* Ali); *m* 1974, Donal Brian Mathew Kerrigan; one *s* one *d*. *Educ:* Bishop Anstey High Sch., Trinidad; Coll. of Law, Inns of Court. Called to the Bar, Middle Temple, 1971. Legal Advr, Public Utilities Commn, Trinidad, 1972–74; Department of Health and Social Security, subseq. Department of Social Security, 1974–: Legal Assistant, 1974–77; Sen. Legal Assistant, 1977–85; Asst Solicitor, 1985–91. *Recreations:* reading, music, squash, bridge. *Address:* Department of Social Security, New Court, 48 Carey Street, WC2A 2LS. *T:* 0171–412 1341.

KERRIGAN, Herbert Aird; QC (Scot) 1992; *b* 2 Aug. 1945; *s* of Herbert Kerrigan and Mary Agnes Wallace Hamilton or Kerrigan; one adopted *s*. *Educ:* Whitehill, Glasgow; Univ. of Aberdeen (LLB Hons 1968); Hague Acad. of Internat. Law; Keele Univ. (MA 1970). Admitted Faculty of Advocates, 1970; Lectr in Criminal Law and Criminology, 1969–73, in Scots Law, 1973–74, Edinburgh Univ.; called to the Bar, Middle Temple, 1990; in practice, 1991–. Vis. Prof., Univ. of Southern Calif., 1979–. Mem., Longford Commn, 1972. Church of Scotland: Elder, 1967– (now at Greyfriars Tolbooth and Highland Kirk, Edinburgh); Reader, 1969; Mem., Assembly Council, 1981–85. Pres., Edinburgh Royal Infirmary Samaritan Soc., 1992– (Vice-Pres., 1989–92). *Publications:* An Introduction to Criminal Procedure in Scotland, 1970; (contrib.) Ministers for the 1980s, 1979; (contributing ed.) The Law of Contempt, 1982; (contrib.) Sport and the Law, 2nd edn 1994. *Recreation:* travel. *Address:* c/o Advocates' Library, Parliament House, Edinburgh EH1 4RF. *T:* 0131–226 5071; 4 Paper Buildings, Temple, EC4Y 7EX. *T:* 0171–583 7765; (home) 20 Edinburgh Road, Dalkeith, Midlothian EH22 1JY. *T:* 0131–660 3307; 2 Plowden Buildings, Middle Temple Lane, Temple, EC4Y 7AT. *T:* 0171–936 2105.

KERRUISH, Sir (Henry) Charles, Kt 1979; OBE 1964; President of Tynwald and of Legislative Council, Isle of Man, since 1990; Speaker, House of Keys, 1962–90; *b* 23 July 1917; *m* 1st, 1944, Margaret Gell; one *s* three *d*; 2nd, 1975, Kay Warriner. *Educ:* Ramsey Grammar Sch. Farmer. Member, House of Keys, 1946–90; Ex-Officio MLC, 1990–. Pres., CPA, 1983–84 (Regional Councillor for British Isles and Mediterranean, 1975–77).

Mem. Court, Liverpool Univ., 1974–90. Hon. LLD Lancaster, 1990. *Recreations:* horse breeding, motor cycling. *Address:* Ballafayle, Maughold, Isle of Man. *T:* Ramsey (01624) 812293. *Club:* Farmers'.

KERRY, Knight of; *see* FitzGerald, Sir G. P. M.

KERRY, Sir Michael (James), KCB 1983 (CB 1976); QC 1984; *b* 5 Aug. 1923; *s* of Russell Kerry and Marjorie (*née* Kensington); *m* 1951, Sidney Rosetta Elizabeth (*née* Foster); one *s* two *d. Educ:* Rugby Sch.; St John's Coll., Oxford (MA; Hon. Fellow 1986). Served with RAF, 1942–46. Called to Bar, Lincoln's Inn, 1949, Bencher 1984. Joined BoT as Legal Asst, 1951; Sen. Legal Asst, 1959; Asst Solicitor, 1964; Principal Asst Solicitor, Dept of Trade and Industry, 1972, Solicitor, 1973–80; HM Procurator Gen. and Treasury Solicitor, 1980–84. Dep. Chm., LAUTRO, 1988–91. *Recreations:* golf, gardening. *Address:* South Bedales, Lewes Road, Haywards Heath, W Sussex RH17 7TE. *T:* Scaynes Hill (01444) 831303. *Club:* Piltdown Golf.

KERSE, Christopher Stephen; Second Counsel to Chairman of Committees and Legal Adviser to European Communities Committee, House of Lords, since 1995; *b* 12 Dec. 1946; *s* of late William Harold Kerse and of Maude Kerse; *m* 1971, Gillian Hanks; one *s* one *d. Educ:* King George V Sch., Southport; Univ. of Hull (LLB). Admitted Solicitor, 1972. Lecturer in Law: Univ. of Bristol, 1968–72; Univ. of Manchester, 1972–76; Asst Prof., Faculty of Law, Univ. of British Columbia, 1974–75; Sen. Legal Asst, OFT, 1976–81; Department of Trade and Industry: Sen. Legal Asst, 1981–82; Asst Solicitor, 1982–88; Head, Consumer Affairs Div., 1991–93; Under-Sec. (Legal), 1988–95. Vis. Prof., KCL, 1992–. *Publications:* The Law Relating to Noise, 1975; EEC Antitrust Procedure, 1981, 3rd edn 1994; (with J. C. Cook) EEC Merger Control, 1991; articles in various legal jls. *Recreations:* the horn, the double bass, the Vendée.

KERSFELT, Anita Ingegerd, (Fru Bertil Kersfelt); *see* Gradin, A. I.

KERSHAW, family name of **Baron Kershaw.**

KERSHAW, 4th Baron, *cr* 1947; **Edward John Kershaw;** JP; Chartered Accountant; Partner in Kidsons Impey, Chartered Accountants, 3 Beaufort Buildings, Spa Road, Gloucester; *b* 12 May 1936; *s* of 3rd Baron and Katharine Dorothea Kershaw (*née* Staines); *S* father, 1962; *m* 1963, Rosalind Lilian Rutherford; one *s* two *d. Educ:* Selhurst Grammar Sch., Surrey. Entered RAF Nov. 1955, demobilised Nov. 1957. Admitted to Inst. of Chartered Accountants in England and Wales, Oct. 1964. Mem., Acad. of Experts, 1995. Lay Governor, The King's Sch., Gloucester, 1986–. JP Gloucester, 1982. *Heir: s* Hon. John Charles Edward Kershaw, *b* 23 Dec. 1971.

KERSHAW, Sir Anthony; *see* Kershaw, Sir J. A.

KERSHAW, Betty; *see* Kershaw, J. E. M.

KERSHAW, His Honour Henry Aidan; a Circuit Judge, 1976–92; *b* 11 May 1927; *s* of late Rev. H. Kershaw, Bolton; *m* 1960, Daphne Patricia, *widow* of Dr. C. R. Cowan; four *s. Educ:* St John's, Leatherhead; Brasenose Coll., Oxford (BA). Served RN, 1946–48. Called to Bar, Inner Temple, 1953. Councillor, Bolton CBC, 1954–57. Asst Recorder of Oldham, 1970–71; a Recorder of the Crown Court, 1972–76. Dep. Chm., Agricultural Land Tribunal, 1972–76. Chm., Lancs Schs Golf Assoc., 1981–84; Vice-Pres., English Schs Golf Assoc., 1984–. *Recreations:* golf, ski-ing, oil-painting. *Address:* Broadhaven, St Andrew's Road, Lostock, Bolton, Lancs BL6 4AB. *Clubs:* Royal and Ancient Golf (St Andrews); Bolton Golf; West Hill Golf.

KERSHAW, Prof. Ian, DPhil; FBA 1991; Professor of Modern History, University of Sheffield, since 1989; *b* Oldham, 29 April 1943; *s* of late Joseph Kershaw and of Alice (*née* Robinson); *m* 1966, Janet Elizabeth Murray Gammie (*see* J. E. M. Kershaw); two *s. Educ:* St Bede's Coll., Manchester; Univ. of Liverpool (BA 1965); Merton Coll., Oxford (DPhil 1969). FRHistS, 1972–74, 1991. University of Manchester: Asst Lectr in Medieval Hist., 1968–70, Lectr, 1970–74; Lectr in Modern Hist., 1974–79, Sen. Lectr, 1979–87, Reader elect, 1987; Prof. of Modern History, Univ. of Nottingham, 1987–89. Vis. Prof. of Contemporary Hist., Ruhr-Univ., Bochum, 1983–84. Fellow: Alexander von Humboldt-Stiftung, 1976; Wissenschaftskolleg zu Berlin, 1989–90. Bundesverdienstkreuz (Germany), 1995. *Publications:* (ed) Rentals and Ministers' Accounts of Bolton Priory 1473–1539, 1969; Bolton Priory: the economy of a Northern monastery, 1973; Der Hitler-Mythos: Volksmeinung und Propaganda im Dritten Reich, 1980, Eng. trans. 1987; Popular Opinion and Political Dissent in the Third Reich: Bavaria 1933–1945, 1983; The Nazi Dictatorship: problems and perspectives of interpretation, 1985, 3rd edn 1993; (ed) Weimar: why did German democracy fail?, 1990; Hitler: a profile in power, 1991; articles in learned jls. *Recreations:* Rugby League, cricket, music, real ale, outings in the Yorkshire dales. *Address:* Department of History, University of Sheffield, Sheffield S10 2TN. *T:* Sheffield (0114) 276 8555.

KERSHAW, Janet Elizabeth Murray, (Betty); President, Royal College of Nursing, since 1995; Director of Nurse Education, College of Midwifery and Nursing, Manchester, since 1994; *b* 11 Dec. 1945; *d* of Ian U. Gammie and Janet Gammie; *m* 1966, Ian Kershaw, *qv*; two *s. Educ:* Crossley and Porter Grammar Sch., Halifax; United Manchester Hosps (SRN; OND); Manchester Univ. (MSc Nursing; RNT). Dir of Educn, Royal Marsden Hosp., 1984–87; Principal, Stockport, Tameside and Glossop Coll. of Nursing, 1987–94. Hon. LLD Manchester, 1995. *Publications:* (with J. Salvage) Models For Nursing, 1986; (with J. Salvage) Models for Nursing 2, 1990; (with Bob Price) The Riehl Model of Care, 1993. *Recreations:* theatre, music, travel. *Address:* Royal College of Nursing, 20 Cavendish Square, W1M 0AB.

KERSHAW, Sir (John) Anthony, Kt 1981; MC 1943; DL; Barrister-at-Law; *b* 14 Dec. 1915; *s* of Judge J. F. Kershaw, Cairo and London, and of Anne Kershaw, Kentucky, USA; *m* 1939, Barbara, *d* of Harry Crookenden; two *s* two *d. Educ:* Eton; Balliol Coll., Oxford (BA). Called to the Bar 1939. Served War, 1940–46: 16th/5th Lancers. Mem. LCC, 1946–49; Westminster City Council, 1947–48. MP (C) Stroud Div. of Gloucestershire, 1955–87. Parly Sec., Min. of Public Building and Works, June–Oct. 1970; Parliamentary Under-Secretary of State: FCO, 1970–73; for Defence (RAF), 1973–74; Chm., H of C Select Cttee on Foreign Affairs, 1979–87; Mem. Exec., 1922 Cttee, 1983–87. Vice-Chm., British Council, 1974–87. DL 1989, Vice Lord-Lieut, 1990–93, Glos. *Address:* West Barn, Didmarton, Badminton, Avon GL9 1DT. *Club:* White's.

KERSHAW, Joseph Anthony; *b* 26 Nov. 1935; *s* of Henry and Catherine Kershaw, Preston; *m* 1959, Ann Whittle; three *s* two *d. Educ:* Ushaw Coll., Durham; Preston Catholic Coll., SJ. Short service commn, RAOC, 1955–58; Unilever Ltd, 1958–67; Gp Marketing Manager, CWS, 1967–69; Managing Director: Underline Ltd, 1969–71; Merchant Div., Reed International Ltd, 1971–73; Head of Marketing, Non-Foods, CWS, 1973–74; (first) Director, Nat. Consumer Council, 1975; independent management consultant, 1975–91. Chairman: Antonian Investments Ltd, 1985–87; Organised Business Data Ltd, 1987–89; Director: John Stork & Partners Ltd, 1980–85; Allia (Holdings) Ltd, 1984–88; Associate Director: Foote, Cone & Belding Ltd, 1979–84; Phoenix Advertising, 1984–86. *Recreations:* turning and woodcarving, fishing, cooking, CPRE. *Address:* Westmead, Meins Road, Blackburn, Lancs BB2 6QF. *T:* Blackburn (01254) 55915.

KERSHAW, Michael; *see* Kershaw, P. M.

KERSHAW, (Philip) Michael, QC 1980; **His Honour Judge Michael Kershaw;** a Circuit Mercantile Judge (formerly a Circuit Commercial Judge), since 1990; *b* 23 April 1941; *s* of His Honour Philip Kershaw; *m* 1980, Anne (*née* Williams); one *s. Educ:* Ampleforth Coll.; St John's Coll., Oxford (MA). FCIArb 1991. Called to the Bar, Gray's Inn, 1963; in practice, 1963–90; a Recorder, 1980–90. *Publications:* Fraud and Misrepresentation, and, Injunctions, in Atkins Court Forms, 1991; (contrib.) Interests in Goods, 1993. *Address:* Crown Court, Crown Square, Manchester M60 9DJ.

KERSHAW, Mrs W. J. S.; *see* Paling, Helen Elizabeth.

KERSHAW, Prof. William Edgar, CMG 1971; VRD; Professor of Biology, University of Salford, 1966–76, now Emeritus Professor; *b* 9 Feb. 1911; *m* 1st, 1941, Mary Alexa Clayton Cowell, MD (marr. diss.); one *s* one *d*; 2nd, 1961, Lois Freeland. *Educ:* Stand Grammar Sch., Manchester; Manchester University. MB, ChB, 1935; MRCS, LRCP, 1936; DTM&H Eng. 1946; MD 1949; DSc 1956. FIBiol; FIFM. Surgeon Captain, RNR. Formerly: Demonstrator in Morbid Anatomy, Manchester Univ.; Leverhulme Senior Lectr in Med. Parasitology, Liverpool Sch. of Trop. Med. and Liverpool Univ.; Walter Myers and Everett Dutton Prof. of Parasitology and Entomology, Liverpool Univ., 1958–66. Hon. Lectr, Dept of Bacteriology, Univ. of Manchester, 1977–. Scientific Advisor: Ribble Fisheries Assoc.; Humane Res. Trust; formerly Advr in Tropical Medicine, Manchester AHA; Hon. MO, Manchester, Salford and Liverpool Univs Naval Units; formerly: Cons. in Parasitology, WHO; Cons. to UN Envmt Prog., SE Asia; Chm., Tsetse Fly and Trypanosomiasis Cttee, ODM; Mem., Tropical Medicine Res. Bd, MRC (Chm., Helminthiasis Cttee). Vice-Pres., RSTM&H (Chalmers Meml Gold Medal, 1955); Hon. Fellow, British Soc. of Parasitology. Non-exec. Chm., Mayor's Boatyard, Tarlton. Vice-Chm., W Lancs Victims Support; Mem., Dunkirk Veterans' Assoc. Hon. Freeman, City of Rangoon, 1961. *Recreation:* work. *Address:* Mill Farm, Hesketh Bank, Preston PR4 6RA. *T:* Hesketh Bank (01772) 814299. *Clubs:* East India, Naval.

KERSS, William; Chief Executive, National Grid Company plc, 1990–94; *b* 8 March 1931; *s* of William Kerss and Josephine Kerss (*née* Rankin); *m* 1959, Amy Murrey; two *d. Educ:* Durham Univ. (BSc Hons Elec. Eng). Student apprentice, NE Electricity Bd, 1948–53; power stations, research, planning and ops, transmission system design, system ops, CEGB, 1957–77; management appts, CEGB, 1963–77; Chief Engineer, SE Electricity Bd, 1977–83; Dep. Chm., S Wales Electricity Bd, 1983–88. *Recreations:* golf, gardening. *Address:* Veddw Farm, Devauden, Gwent NP6 6PH. *T:* Chepstow (01291) 650321.

KERWIN, Prof. Larkin, CC 1980 (OC 1977); FRSC; Professor Emeritus, Laval University, since 1991; *b* 22 June 1924; *s* of T. J. Kerwin and Catherine Lonergan-Kerwin; *m* 1950, Maria Guadalupe Turcot; five *s* three *d. Educ:* St Francis Xavier Univ. (BSc 1944); MIT (MSc 1946); Université Laval (DSc 1949). Laval University: Asst Prof., 1946; full Prof. of Physics, 1956; Dir, Dept of Physics, 1961–67; Vice-Dean, Faculty of Sciences, 1967–68; Vice-Rector, Academic, 1969–72; Rector, 1972–77. President: Royal Soc. of Canada, 1976–77; National Res. Council of Canada, 1980–89; Canadian Space Agency, 1989–92; IUPAP, 1987–90 (Sec.-Gen., 1972–84; First Vice-Pres., 1984–87). Hon. LLD: St Francis Xavier, 1970; Toronto, 1973; Concordia, 1976; Alberta, 1983; Dalhousie, 1983; Hon. DSc: British Columbia, 1973; McGill, 1974; Memorial, 1978; Ottawa, 1981; Royal Military Coll., Canada, 1982; Hon. DCL Bishop's, 1978; DSc (*hc*): Winnipeg, 1983; Windsor, 1984; Moncton, 1985; Montreal, 1991. Médaille du Centenaire, 1967; Médaille de l'Assoc. Canadienne des Physiciens, 1969; Médaille Pariseau, 1965; Medal of Centenary of Roumania, 1977; Jubilee Medal, 1977; Laval Alumni Medal, 1978; Gold Medal, Canadian Council of Professional Engineers, 1982; Rousseau Medal, l'ACFAS, 1983. Kt Comdr with star, Holy Sepulchre of Jerusalem, 1974; Officier de la Légion d'Honneur, 1989. *Publications:* Atomic Physics, 1963 (trans. French, 1964, Spanish, 1970); papers in jls. *Recreation:* sailing. *Address:* 2166 Parc Bourbonnière, Sillery, Quebec G1T 1B4, Canada. *T:* (418) 527–7949.

KESSEL, Prof. William Ivor Neil, MD; FRCP, FRCPE, FRCPsych; Professor of Psychiatry, 1965–90, and Dean of Postgraduate Studies, Faculty of Medicine, 1982–90, University of Manchester; *b* 10 Feb. 1925; *s* of Barney Kessel and Rachel Isabel Kessel; *m* 1958, Pamela Veronica Joyce (*née* Boswell); one *s* one *d. Educ:* Highgate Sch.; Trinity Coll., Cambridge (MA, MD); UCH Med. Sch.; Inst. of Psychiatry. MSc Manchester. FRCP 1967; FRCPE 1968; FRCPsych 1972. Staff, Inst. of Psych., 1960; scientific staff, MRC Unit for Epidemiol. of Psych. Illness, 1961, Asst Dir 1963; Hon. Sen. Lectr, Edinburgh Univ., 1964; Dean, Faculty of Med., Univ. of Manchester, 1974–76. Member: NW RHA, 1974–77; GMC, 1974–95; Adv. Council on Misuse of Drugs, 1972–80; Health Educn Council, 1979–86; Chm., Adv. Cttee on Alcoholism, DHSS, 1975–78; Cons. Adviser on alcoholism to DHSS, 1972–81, 1983–86. *Publications:* Alcoholism (with Prof. H. J. Walton), 1965, 3rd edn 1975, rev. edn 1989; articles on suicide and self-poisoning, alcoholism, psych. in gen. practice, psychosomatic disorders, psych. epidemiol., genius and mental illness *Address:* 24 Lees Road, Bramhall, Stockport, Cheshire SK7 1BT. *T:* 0161–439 5121. *Club:* Athenæum.

KESWICK, Sir Chippendale; *see* Keswick, Sir J. C. L.

KESWICK, Henry Neville Lindley; Chairman: Matheson & Co. Ltd, since 1975; Jardine, Matheson Holdings Ltd, Hong Kong, 1972–75 and since 1989 (Director, since 1967); Jardine Strategic Holdings, since 1989 (Director, since 1988); *b* 29 Sept. 1938; *e s* of Sir William Keswick and of Mary, *d* of Rt Hon. Sir Francis Lindley, PC, GCMG; *m* 1985, Tessa, Lady Reay, *y d* of 17th Baron Lovat, *qv. Educ:* Eton Coll.; Trinity Coll., Cambridge. BA Hons Econs and Law; MA. Commnd Scots Guards, Nat. Service, 1956–58. Director: Sun Alliance and London Insurance, 1975–; Robert Fleming Holdings Ltd; Rothmans Internat., 1988–94; Hongkong Land Co., 1988–; Mandarin Oriental Internat., 1988–; Dairy Farm Internat. Hldgs, 1988–; Sun Alliance Group, 1989– (Dep. Chm., 1993–); The Daily Telegraph, 1990–. Member: London Adv. Cttee, Hongkong and Shanghai Banking Corp., 1975–92; 21st Century Trust, 1987–. Proprietor, The Spectator, 1975–81. Trustee, Nat. Portrait Gall., 1982– (Chm., 1994–). Chm., Hong Kong Assoc, 1988–. *Recreation:* country pursuits. *Address:* 3 Lombard Street, EC3V 9AQ. *Clubs:* White's, Turf; Third Guards.

See also Sir J. C. L. Keswick, S. L. Keswick.

KESWICK, Sir (John) Chippendale (Lindley), Kt 1993; Chairman, Hambros Bank Ltd, since 1986; a Director, Bank of England, since 1993; *b* 2 Feb.1940; 2nd *s* of Sir William Keswick and of Mary, *d* of Rt Hon. Sir Francis Lindley, PC, GCMG; *m* 1966, Lady Sarah Ramsay, *d* of 16th Earl of Dalhousie, *qv*; three *s. Educ:* Eton; Univ. of Aix/Marseilles. Glyn Mills & Co., 1961–65; Jt Vice Chm., 1986, Jt Dep. Chm., 1990–, Hambros PLC. Director: Persimmon Plc; De Beers Consolidated Mines Ltd; Edinburgh Investment Trust plc; IMI plc; Anglo Amer. Corp. of SA Ltd; De Beers Centenary AG. Vice Counsellor, Cancer Research Campaign; Hon. Treas., Children's Country Holidays Fund. Mem., Queen's Body Guard for Scotland, Royal Company of Archers. *Recreations:* bridge,

country pursuits. *Address:* Hambros Bank, 41 Tower Hill, EC3N 4HA. *T:* 0171–480 5000. *Clubs:* White's, Portland.
See also H. N. L. Keswick, S. L. Keswick.

KESWICK, Simon Lindley; Director: Jardine Matheson Holdings Ltd, since 1972 (Chairman, 1983–89); Jardine Strategic Holdings Ltd, since 1987 (Chairman, 1987–89); Matheson & Co. Ltd, since 1982; Chairman: Hongkong Land Holdings Ltd, since 1983; Mandarin Oriental International Ltd, since 1984; Dairy Farm International Holdings Ltd, since 1984; Fleming Mercantile Investment Trust, since 1990 (Director, since 1988); Jardine International Motor Holdings Ltd, since 1990; Trafalgar House plc, since 1993; *b* 20 May 1942; *s* of Sir William Keswick and of Mary, *d* of Rt Hon. Sir Francis Lindley, PC, GCMG; *m* 1971, Emma, *d* of Major David Chetwode; two *s* two *d*. *Educ:* Eton Coll. Dir, Hanson plc, 1991–. Trustee, British Museum, 1989–. Ordinary Gov., London Hosp. Med. Coll., 1989–. Mem., the Queen's Body Guard for Scotland, Royal Co. of Archers, 1982. FRSA 1989. *Recreations:* country pursuits, Tottenham Hotspurs. *Address:* No 9, Shek O, Hong Kong; Rockcliffe, Upper Slaughter, Cheltenham, Glos GL54 2JW. *Clubs:* White's, Portland; Union (Sydney); Shek O (Hong Kong).
See also H. N. L. Keswick, Sir J. C. L. Keswick.

KETTLE, Captain Alan Stafford Howard, CB 1984; Royal Navy (retired); General Manager, HM Dockyard, Chatham, 1977–84; *b* 6 Aug. 1925; *s* of Arthur Stafford Kettle and Marjorie Constance (*née* Clough); *m* 1952, Patricia Rosemary (*née* Gander); two *s*. *Educ:* Rugby School. CEng, FIMechE. Joined RN, 1943; Comdr, Dec. 1959; Captain, Dec. 1968; retired, Sept. 1977. Entered Civil Service as Asst Under-Sec., Sept. 1977. *Address:* 3 Leather Tor Close, Grangelands, Yelverton PL20 6EQ. *T:* Yelverton (01822) 854249.

KETTLE, Roy Henry Richard; Group Deputy Chairman, Evered Bardon plc, 1991; *b* 2 May 1924; *s* of Arthur Charles Edwin and Emily Grace Kettle; *m* 1956, Jean Croudace; one *s* three *d*. *Educ:* Wolverhampton Grammar School. Tarmac Roadstone Ltd: Accountancy Asst, 1947; Management Acct, 1960; Chief Management Acct, 1964; Dir of Admin, 1967; Man. Dir, 1976; Tarmac plc: Dir, 1977; Gp Man. Dir, 1982–86, retd. Chm., CI Gp plc (formerly Cooper Industries), 1985–89; Dir, Evered Hldgs, subseq. Evered Bardon, 1985–91; Chief Exec., Evered Hldgs, 1989–91; Dir, London and Northern Gp, 1987–91. Mem., Black Country Develt Corp., 1987–92. *Recreations:* walking, gardening. *Address:* Hilbre, Watling Street South, Church Stretton, Shropshire SY6 7BG. *T:* Church Stretton (01694) 722445.

KETTLEWELL, Comdt Dame Marion M., DBE 1970 (CBE 1964); General Secretary, Girls' Friendly Society, 1971–78; *b* 20 Feb. 1914; *d* of late George Wildman Kettlewell, Bramling, Virginia Water, Surrey, and of Mildred Frances (*née* Atkinson), Belford, Northumberland. *Educ:* Godolphin Sch., Salisbury; St Christopher's Coll., Blackheath. Worked for Fellowship of Maple Leaf, Alta, Canada, 1935–38; worked for Local Council, 1939–41; joined WRNS as MT driver, 1941; commnd as Third Officer WRNS, 1942; Supt WRNS on Staff of Flag Officer Air (Home), 1961–64; Supt WRNS Training and Drafting, 1964–67; Director, WRNS, 1967–70. Pres., Assoc. of Wrens, 1981–92. *Recreations:* needlework, walking, and country life. *Address:* Flat 2, 9 John Islip Street, SW1P 4PU.

KEVILL-DAVIES, Christopher Evelyn, CBE 1973; JP; DL; *b* 12 July 1913; 3rd *s* of William A. S. H. Kevill-Davies, JP, Croft Castle, Herefordshire; *m* 1938, Virginia, *d* of Adm. Ronald A. Hopwood, CB; one *s* one *d*. *Educ:* Radley College. Served with Suffolk Yeomanry, 1939–43 and Grenadier Gds, 1943–45, France, Belgium and Germany. Mem., Gt Yarmouth Borough Council, 1946–53; Chm., Norfolk Mental Deficiency HMC, 1950–69; Mem., East Anglian Regional Hosp. Bd, 1962 (Vice-Chm. 1967); Vice-Chm., E Anglian RHA, 1974–82. JP 1954, DL 1974–83, Norfolk; High Sheriff of Norfolk, 1965. *Address:* 11 Hale House, 34 De Vere Gardens, Kensington, W8 5AQ. *T:* 0171–937 5066. *Clubs:* Cavalry and Guards, Royal Automobile; Norfolk (Norwich).

KEY, Brian Michael; Member (Lab) Yorkshire South, European Parliament, 1979–84; *b* 20 Sept. 1947; *s* of Leslie Granville Key and Nora Alice (*née* Haylett); *m* 1974, Lynn Joyce Ambler. *Educ:* Darfield County Primary Sch.; Wath upon Dearne Grammar Sch.; Liverpool Univ. (BA Hons). Careers Officer, West Riding County Council, 1970–73; Sen. Administrative Officer, South Yorkshire CC, 1973–79. *Address:* 25 Cliff Road, Darfield, Barnsley S73 9HR. *Clubs:* Darfield Working Men's; Trades and Labour (Doncaster).

KEY, (Simon) Robert; MP (C) Salisbury, since 1983; *b* 22 April 1945; *s* of late Rt Rev. J. M. Key; *m* 1968, Susan Priscilla Bright Irvine, 2nd *d* of late Rev. T. T. Irvine; one *s* two *d* (and one *s* decd). *Educ:* Salisbury Cathedral Sch.; Forres Sch., Swanage; Sherborne Sch.; Clare Coll., Cambridge. MA; CertEd. Assistant Master: Loretto Sch., Edinburgh, 1967; Harrow Sch., 1969–83. Warden, Nanoose Field Studies Centre, Wool, Dorset, 1972–78; Governor: Sir William Collins Sch., NW1, 1976–81; Special Sch. at Gt Ormond Street Hosp. for Sick Children, 1976–81; Roxeth Sch., Harrow, 1979–82. Founder Chm., ALICE Trust for Autistic Children, 1977–82; Council Mem., GAP Activity Projects, 1975–84. Vice-Chm., Wembley Br., ASTMS, 1976–80. Contested (C) Camden, Holborn and St Pancras South, 1979. Political Sec. to Rt Hon. Edward Heath, 1984–85; PPS to: Minister of State for Energy, 1985–87; Minister for Overseas Develt, 1987–89; Sec. of State for the Envmt, 1989–90; Parly Under-Sec. of State, DoE, 1990–92, Dept of Nat. Heritage, 1992–93, Dept of Transport, 1993–94. Mem., Select Cttee on Educn, Science and the Arts, 1983–86, on Health, 1994–95, on Defence, 1995–; Sec., Cons. Parly Backbench Cttee on Arts and Heritage, 1983–84; Jt Parly Chm., Council for Educn in the Commonwealth, 1984–87; Vice-Chm., All-Party Gp on AIDS, 1988–90. Chm., Harrow Central Cons. Assoc., 1980–82; Vice-Chm., Central London Cons. Euro-Constit., 1980–82; Mem., Cons. Party Nat. Union Exec., 1981–83. Member: UK Nat. Commn for UNESCO, 1984–85; MRC, 1989–90 (Mem., AIDS Cttee, 1988–90). Vice-Pres., Haemophilia Soc., 1988–90. Hon. FCollP, 1989. *Recreations:* singing, cooking, country life. *Address:* House of Commons, SW1A 0AA. *T:* 0171–219 3000.

KEYES, family name of **Baron Keyes.**

KEYES, 2nd Baron, *cr* 1943, of Zeebrugge and of Dover; **Roger George Bowlby Keyes;** Bt, *cr* 1919; RN, retired; *b* 14 March 1919; 2nd *s* of Admiral of the Fleet Baron Keyes, GCB, KCVO, CMG, DSO and Eva Mary Salvin Bowlby (*d* 1973), Red Cross Order of Queen Elisabeth of Belgium, *d* of late Edward Salvin Bowlby, DL, of Gilston Park, Herts, and Knoydart, Inverness-shire; *S* father 1945; *m* 1947, Grizelda Mary (*d* 1993), 2nd *d* of late Lieut-Col William Packe, DSO; three *s* two *d*. *Educ:* King's Mead Sch., Seaford; RNC, Dartmouth. *Publication:* Outrageous Fortune, 1984 (SE Arts Literary Prize). *Heir: s* Hon. Charles William Packe Keyes, *b* 8 Dec. 1951. *Address:* East Farleigh House, Lower Road, East Farleigh, near Maidstone, Kent ME15 0JW. *T:* Maidstone (01622) 726295, *Fax:* (01622) 721471.
See also Baron Kennet.

KEYNES, Prof. Richard Darwin, CBE 1984; MA, PhD, ScD Cantab; FRS 1959; Professor of Physiology, University of Cambridge, 1973–87; Fellow of Churchill College, since 1961; *b* 14 Aug. 1919; *e s* of Sir Geoffrey Keynes, MD, FRCP, FRCS, FRCOG, and late Margaret Elizabeth, *d* of Sir George Darwin, KCB; *m* 1945, Anne Pinsent Adrian, *e d* of 1st Baron Adrian, OM, FRS, and Dame Hester Agnes Adrian, DBE, *o d* of Hume C. and Dame Ellen Pinsent, DBE; three *s* (and one *s* decd). *Educ:* Oundle Sch. (Scholar); Trinity Coll., Cambridge (Scholar). Temporary experimental officer, HM Anti-Submarine Establishment and Admiralty Signals Establishment, 1940–45. 1st Class, Nat. Sci. Tripos Part II, 1946; Michael Foster and G. H. Lewes Studentships, 1946; Research Fellow of Trinity Coll., 1948–52; Gedge Prize, 1948; Rolleston Memorial Prize, 1950. Demonstrator in Physiology, University of Cambridge, 1949–53; Lecturer, 1953–60; Fellow of Peterhouse, 1952–60 (Hon. Fellow, 1989); Head of Physiology Dept and Dep. Dir, 1960–64, Dir, 1965–73, ARC Inst. of Animal Physiology. Sec.-Gen., Internat. Union for Pure and Applied Biophysics, 1972–78, Vice-Pres., 1978–81, Pres., 1981–84; Chairman: Internat. Cell Research Orgn, 1981–83; ICSU/Unesco Internat. Biosciences Networks, 1982–93; Pres., Eur. Fedn of Physiol Socs, 1991–; a Vice-Pres., Royal Society, 1965–68, Croonian Lectr, 1983. Fellow of Eton, 1963–78. For. Member: Royal Danish Acad., 1971; American Philosophical Soc., 1977; Amer. Acad. of Arts and Scis, 1978; Amer. Physiolog. Soc., 1994. Dr *hc* Brazil, 1968; Rouen, 1995. *Publications:* The Beagle Record, 1979; (with D. J. Aidley) Nerve and Muscle, 1981, 2nd edn 1991; (ed) Charles Darwin's Beagle Diary, 1988; (ed jtly) Lydia and Maynard: the letters of Lydia Lopokova and John Maynard Keynes, 1989; papers in Journal of Physiology, Proceedings of Royal Soc., etc. *Recreations:* writing, pre-Columbian antiquities. *Address:* 4 Herschel Road, Cambridge CB3 9AG. *T:* Cambridge (01223) 353107; Primrose Farm, Wiveton, Norfolk NR25 7TQ. *T:* Cley (01263) 740317.
See also S. J. Keynes.

KEYNES, Stephen John, OBE 1993; Chief Executive, SK Productions, since 1991; *b* 19 Oct. 1927; 4th *s* of Sir Geoffrey Keynes, MD, FRCP, FRCS, FRCOG, and late Margaret Elizabeth, *d* of Sir George Darwin, KCB; *m* 1955, Mary, *o d* of late Senator the Hon. Adrian Knatchbull-Hugessen, QC (Canada), and late Margaret, *o d* of G. H. Duggan; three *s* two *d*. *Educ:* Oundle Sch.; King's Coll., Cambridge (Foundn Scholar; MA). Royal Artillery, 1949–51. Partner, J. F. Thomasson & Co., Private Bankers, 1961–65; Director: Charterhouse Japhet Ltd and Charterhouse Finance Corp., 1965–72; Arbuthnot Latham Holdings Ltd, 1973–80; Sun Life Assce Soc. plc, 1965–89; Premier Oil plc, 1976–; PK English Trust Co. Ltd, 1980–90; Hawkshead Ltd, 1987–91. Member: IBA (formerly ITA), 1969–74; Cttee and Treas., Islington and North London Family Service Unit, 1956–68; Adv. Cttee, Geffrye Museum, 1964–87; Trustee: Centerprise Community Project, 1971–75; Needham Research Inst. (E Asian Hist. of Science Trust), 1984–; Chairman of Trustees: Whitechapel Art Gallery, 1979–; English Chamber Theatre; William Blake Trust, 1981–. *Recreations:* medieval manuscripts, painting, gardening, travelling. *Address:* 16 Canonbury Park South, Islington, N1. *T:* 0171–226 8170; Lammas House, Brinkley, Newmarket, Suffolk CB8 0SB. *T:* Newmarket (01638) 507268; Gunnerside, near Richmond, Yorks; (office) 24 Baltic Street, EC1Y 0TB. *T:* 0171–251 9111, *Fax:* 0171–251 2609. *Clubs:* Cranium, Roxburghe.
See also R. D. Keynes.

KEYS, Sir (Alexander George) William, AC 1988; Kt 1980; OBE 1969; MC 1951; Director: FAI Insurance Group, since 1984; Pembroke Financial Planners, since 1990; Australian Overseas Mining, since 1978; National President, Returned Services League of Australia, 1978–88; *b* 2 Feb. 1923; *s* of John Alexander Binnie Keys and Irene Daisy Keys; *m* 1950, Dulcie Beryl (*née* Stinton); three *d*. *Educ:* Hurlstone Agricultural High Sch. National Secretary, RSL, 1961–78 (Life Member); Nat. President, Korea and SE Asia Forces Assoc. of Australia, 1964–90; World Pres., Internat. Fedn of Korean War Veterans Assoc., 1978–; Member: Fed. Govt adv. cttees; Council, Aust. War Memorial, 1975–94; ACT Churchill Fellows Assoc. Korean Order of National Security Merit, 1980. *Address:* Glenlee, Post Office Box 455, Queanbeyan, NSW 2620, Australia. *T:* (home) (6) 2975440; (office) (6) 2977000. *Clubs:* Commonwealth, National Press (Canberra); Returned Services League (Queanbeyan).

KEYS, Derek Lyle; Minister of Finance, South Africa, 1992–94; *b* 30 Aug. 1931; *m* Silma. *Educ:* King Edward's Sch., Johannesburg; Univ. of Witwatersrand (BComm). CA (SA); FIB (SA). Auditing, 1951–56; Industrial Development Corp. of South Africa, 1956–65; financial, later management, consultant; former Dir, Malbak, National Discount House, ASEA, Price Forbes, Sandvik, Samancor, Sappi; Exec. Chm., Gencor, 1986–91. Minister of Trade and Industry, 1992–94. *Address:* PO Box 29, Cape Town 8000, South Africa.

KEYS, Sir William; *see* Keys, Sir A. G. W.

KHABRA, Piara Singh, JP; MP (Lab) Ealing, Southall, since 1992; *b* Punjab, India, 20 Nov. 1924. *Educ:* Punjab Univ., India (BA Social Scis, BEd); Whitelands Coll., London (DipEd). Chm., Co-op. Bank and Sarpanch of village Panchayat, Dist Hoshiarpur, Punjab; sch. teacher and later Head of a middle sch.; arrived in UK, 1959; factory work, 1959–61; clerical work, British Oxygen, 1961–64; teacher, ILEA, 1964–78; community worker, 1978–86. Councillor (Lab), London Borough of Ealing, 1978–82; Gen. Cttee Delegate, Ealing/Southall CLP, 1989–90; Member: Exec. Cttee, Ealing, 1989; Local Govt Cttee, Ealing, 1989–90. Founder Mem. and Treas., Ealing CRC (Chm., Finance Cttee); Chairman: Southall Community Law Centre, 1982–; Community Prog. Agency, Southall, 1984–88; Member: Unified Community Action; Community Action Policy Gp, Ealing; Indian Workers' Association, Southall: Educn Sec., 1959–63; Gen. Sec., 1963–65 and 1977–79; Chm., 1979–. Trustee, Dominion Centre, Southall (Vice-Chm., Management Cttee). Gov., various schs in Ealing, incl. Featherstone High Sch. JP Ealing. *Address:* House of Commons, SW1A 0AA; 25 Frensham Close, Southall, Mddx UB1 2QZ. *T:* 0181–578 6139.

KHAIR-UD-DIN, Rt. Rev.; *see* Ud-Din.

KHAMENEI, Ayatollah Sayyed Ali; Leader of the Islamic Revolution, since 1989; *b* 1940; *m* 1964; four *s* two *d*. *Educ:* Qom; studied under Iman Khomeini, 1956–64. Imprisoned six times, 1964–78; once exiled, 1978; Mem., Revolutionary Council, 1978 until its dissolution, 1979 (Rep. in Iranian Army and Assistant of Revolutionary Affairs in Min. of Defence); Rep. of First Islamic Consultative Assembly, and of Iman Khomeini in the Supreme Council of Defence, 1980; Comdr, Revolutionary Guards, 1980; Friday Prayer Leader, Teheran, 1980–; Sec. Gen., Islamic Republic Party, 1980–87; Pres., Islamic Republic of Iran, 1981–89. *Recreations:* reading, arts, literature. *Address:* Office of Leadership, Teheran, Islamic Republic of Iran.

KHAN, Ghulam Ishaq; President of Pakistan, 1988–93; *b* 20 Jan. 1915; *m* 1950; one *s* five *d*. *Educ:* Islamia Coll., Peshawar; Punjab Univ. Indian Civil Service, 1940–47; NWFP service, 1947–56; Government of West Pakistan: Sec. for Devlt and Irrigation, 1956–58; Chm., Water and Power Develt Authy, 1961–66; Chm., Land Reforms Commn, 1978; Sec., Finance, 1966–70; Cabinet Sec., 1970; Sec.-Gen., Ministry of Defence, 1975–77; Sec.-Gen.-in-Chief, Adviser for Planning and Co-ordination, 1977–78; Adviser to Chief Martial Law Administrator, 1978; Minister for Finance and Co-ordination, 1978–79, for Finance, Econ. Affairs, Commerce and Co-ordination, 1979–85; Chairman of Senate, 1985–88. Governor, State Bank of Pakistan, 1971–75; Chm., Jt Ministerial Cttee, Board of Governors of World Bank and IMF, 1982–88. Life Pres., Soc. for Promotion of Engrg Scis and Technology in Pakistan, 1988–; Pres., Bd of Govs, Gulam Ishaq Khan Inst. of Engrg Scis and Technology, 1988–. *Address:* 3–B Jamrud Road, University Town, Peshawar, NWFP, Pakistan.

KHAN, Humayun; Director, Commonwealth Foundation, since 1993; *b* 31 Aug. 1932; *s* of K. B. Safdar Khan and Mumtaz Safdar; *m* 1961, Munawar; three *d*. *Educ:* Bishop Cotton Sch., Simla; Trinity College, Cambridge (MA); Univ. of Southern California (MPA, Dr PA). Called to the Bar, Lincoln's Inn, 1954; joined Pakistan CS, 1955; Sec. to Govt of NWPP, 1970–73; Jt Sec., Pakistan Govt, 1973–74; Minister, Pakistan Embassy, Moscow, 1974–77; Dep. Perm. Rep., UNO, Geneva, 1977–79; Ambassador to Bangladesh, 1979–82; Additional Sec., Min. of Foreign Affairs, Pakistan, 1982–84; Ambassador to India, 1984–88; Foreign Sec. of Pakistan, 1988–89; High Comr in UK, 1990–92. *Recreations:* golf, cricket, shooting, fishing. *Address:* Commonwealth Foundation, Marlborough House, Pall Mall, SW1Y 5HY. *Clubs:* Royal Over-Seas League, Travellers'; Islamabad.

KHAN NIAZI, Imran Ahmad; *see* Imran Khan.

KHAW, Prof. Kay-Tee, (Mrs Kay-Tee Fawcett), FRCP; Professor of Clinical Gerontology, University of Cambridge, since 1989; Fellow, Gonville and Caius College, Cambridge, since 1991; *b* 14 Oct. 1950; *d* of Khaw Kai Boh and Tan Chwee Geok; *m* 1980, Dr James William Fawcett; one *s* one *d*. *Educ:* Girton Coll., Cambridge (BA, MA; MB BChir); St Mary's Hosp. Med. Sch., London; London Sch. of Hygiene and Tropical Med. (MSc). MRCP 1977, FRCP 1993; DCH 1978; MFPHM 1993. LTCL 1969. Wellcome Trust Research Fellow, LSHTM, St Mary's Hosp. and Univ. of California San Diego, 1979–84; Asst Adjunct Prof., Univ. of California Sch. of Med., San Diego, 1985; Sen. Registrar in Community Medicine, Univ. of Cambridge Sch. of Clinical Medicine, 1986–89. Member: NHS Central R&D Cttee, 1991–; HEFCE, 1992–. Daland Fellow, Amer. Philosophical Soc., 1984. Trustee, Help the Aged, 1993–. *Publications:* contribs to scientific jls on chronic disease epidemiology. *Recreation:* piano. *Address:* Clinical Gerontology Unit, University of Cambridge School of Clinical Medicine, Addenbrooke's Hospital, Cambridge CB2 2QQ.

KHAYAT, Georges Mario; QC 1992; a Recorder, since 1987; *b* 15 Aug. 1941; *s* of Fred Khayat and Julie Germain. *Educ:* Terra Sancta Coll., Nazareth; Prior Park Coll., Bath. Called to the Bar, Lincoln's Inn, 1967. *Recreations:* horse riding, reading, boating, music. *Address:* 10 King's Bench Walk, Temple, EC4Y 7EB. *T:* 0171–353 2501.

KHOO, Francis Kah Siang; writer; General Secretary (Director), War on Want, 1988–89; *b* 23 Oct. 1947; *s* of late Teng Eng Khoo and of Swee Neo Chew; *m* 1977, Dr Swee Chai Ang, MB BS, MSc, FRCS. *Educ:* Univ. of Singapore (LLB (Hons) 1970); Univ. of London (MA 1980). Advocate and Solicitor, Singapore, 1971. Lawyer, Singapore, 1971–77; journalist, South magazine, and Mem., NUJ (UK), 1980–87. Founding Mem. and Vice-Chm. of British charity, Medical Aid for Palestinians, 1984–. *Publications:* And Bungaraya Blooms All Day: collection of songs, poems and cartoons in exile, UK, 1978; Hang On Tight, No Surrender: tape of songs, 1984. *Recreations:* photography, hill-walking, song-writing, camera designing and inventions, swimming. *Address:* 17 Knollys House, 39 Tavistock Place, WC1H 9SA. *T:* 0171–380 0648.

KHORANA, Prof. Har Gobind; Sloan Professor of Chemistry and Biology, Massachusetts Institute of Technology, since 1970; *b* Raipur, India, 9 Jan. 1922; *s* of Shri Ganpat Rai and Shrimata Krishna (Devi); *m* 1952, Esther Elizabeth Sibler; one *s* two *d*. *Educ:* Punjab Univ. (BSc 1943; MSc 1945); Liverpool Univ. (PhD 1948; Govt of India Student). Post-doctoral Fellow of Govt of India, Federal Inst. of Techn., Zurich, 1948–49; Nuffield Fellow, Cambridge Univ., 1950–52; Head, Organic Chemistry Group, BC Research Council, 1952–60. Univ. of Wisconsin: Prof. and Co-Dir, Inst. for Enzyme Research, 1960–70; Prof., Dept of Biochemistry, 1962–70, Conrad A. Elvehjem Prof. in the Life Sciences, 1964–70. Visiting Professor: Rockefeller Inst., NY, 1958–60; Stanford Univ., 1964; Harvard Med. Sch., 1966; Andrew D. White Prof.-at-large, Cornell Univ., 1974–80. Has given special or memorial lectures in USA, Poland, Canada, Switzerland, UK and Japan. Fellow: Chem. Inst. of Canada, 1959; Amer. Assoc. for Advancement of Science, 1966; Amer. Acad. of Arts and Sciences, 1967. Overseas Fellow, Churchill Coll., Cambridge, 1967. Member: Nat. Acad. of Sciences; Deutsche Akademie der Naturforscher Leopoldina; Pontifical Acad. of Scis, Rome; Foreign Member: Indian Acad. of Scis, 1976; Royal Society, 1978; RSE, 1982. Various hon. degrees. Merck Award, Chem. Inst. Canada, 1958; Gold Medal for 1960, Professional Inst. of Public Service of Canada; Dannie-Heinneman Preiz, Germany, 1967; Remsen Award, Johns Hopkins Univ., ACS Award for Creative Work in Synthetic Organic Chemistry, Louisa Gross Horwitz Award, Lasker Foundn Award for Basic Med. Research, Nobel Prize for Medicine (jtly), 1968. US Nat. Medal of Science, 1987. Order of San Carlos (Columbia), 1986. *Publications:* Some Recent Developments in the Chemistry of Phosphate Esters of Biological Interest, 1961; numerous papers in Biochemistry, Jl Amer. Chem. Soc., etc. *Recreations:* hiking, swimming. *Address:* Department of Biology and Chemistry, Massachusetts Institute of Technology, Cambridge, MA 02139, USA.

KHUSH, Dr Gurdev Singh, FRS 1995; Head, Division of Plant Breeding, Genetics and Biochemistry, International Rice Research Institute, Philippines, since 1989; *b* 22 Aug. 1935; *s* of Kartar Singh and Pritam Kaur; *m* 1961, Harwant Kaur Grewal; one *s* three *d*. *Educ:* Punjab Univ., Chandigarh, India (BScAgr); Univ. of Calif, Davis (PhD Genetics 1960). University of California, Davis: Research Asst, 1957–60; Asst Geneticist, 1960–67; International Rice Research Institute, Philippines: Plant Breeder, 1967–72; Head, Dept of Plant Breeding, 1972–89. Hon. DSc Punjab Agricl, 1987. Borlaug Award in Plant Breeding, Coromandel Fertilizers Ltd, India, 1977; Japan Prize, Japan Sci. and Technol. Foundn, 1987; Fellows Award 1989, Internat. Agronomy Award 1990, Amer. Soc. of Agronomy; Emil M. Mrak Internat. Award, Univ. of California, Davis, 1990. *Publications:* Cytogenetics of Aneuploids, 1973; Host Plant Resistance to Insects, 1995; *edited:* Rice Biotechnology, 1991; Nodulation and Nitrogen Fixation in Rice, 1992; Apomix: exploiting hybrid vigor in rice, 1994; Rice Genetics III, 1996; contrib. chapters in books; numerous papers in jls. *Recreation:* reading world history. *Address:* International Rice Research Institute, PO Box 933, 1099 Manila, Philippines. *T:* (2) 8181926.

KIBBEY, Sidney Basil; Under-Secretary, Department of Health and Social Security, 1971–76; *b* 3 Dec. 1916; *y s* of late Percy Edwin Kibbey and Winifred Kibbey, Mickleover, Derby; *m* 1939, Violet Gertrude, (Jane), Eyre; (twin) *s* and *d*. *Educ:* Derby Sch. Executive Officer, Min. of Health, 1936; Principal, Min. of National Insurance, 1951; Sec., Nat. Insurance Adv. Cttee, 1960–62; Asst Sec., Min. of Pensions and Nat. Insurance, 1962. *Address:* 29 Beaulieu Close, Datchet, Berks SL3 9DD. *T:* Slough (01753) 549101.

KIBBLE, Prof. Thomas Walter Bannerman, PhD; FRS 1980; Professor of Theoretical Physics, since 1970, and Head of the Department of Physics, 1983–91, Imperial College, London; *b* 1932; *s* of Walter Frederick Kibble and Janet Cowan Watson (*née* Bannerman); *m* 1957, Anne Richmond Allan; one *s* two *d*. *Educ:* Doveton-Corrie Sch., Madras; Melville Coll., Edinburgh; Univ. of Edinburgh (MA, BSc, PhD). Commonwealth Fund Fellow, California Inst. of Technology, 1958–59; Imperial College, London: NATO Fellow, 1959–60; Lecturer, 1961; Sen. Lectr, 1965; Reader in Theoretical Physics, 1966. Sen. Visiting Research Associate, Univ. of Rochester, New York, 1967–68. Member: Nuclear Physics Bd, SERC, 1982–86; Astronomy, Space and Radio Bd, 1984–86; Physical Sciences Sub-cttee, UGC, 1985–89. Chairman: Scientists Against Nuclear Arms, 1985–91 (Vice-Chm., 1981–85); Martin Ryle Trust, 1985–. Mem. Council, Royal Soc., 1987–89 (Vice-Pres., 1988–89). (Jtly) Hughes Medal, Royal Soc., 1981; (jtly) Rutherford Medal, 1984, Guthrie Medal, 1993, Inst. of Physics. *Publications:* Classical Mechanics, 1966, 3rd edn 1985; papers in Phys. Rev., Proc. Royal Soc., Nuclear Physics, Nuovo Cimento, Jl Physics, and others. *Recreations:* cycling, destructive gardening. *Address:* Blackett Laboratory, Imperial College, Prince Consort Road, SW7 2BZ. *T:* 0171–594 7845.

KIDD, Prof. Cecil; Regius Professor of Physiology, Marischal College, University of Aberdeen, since 1984; *b* 28 April 1933; *s* of Herbert Cecil and Elizabeth Kidd; *m* 1956, Margaret Winifred Goodwill; three *s*. *Educ:* Queen Elizabeth Grammar School, Darlington; King's College, Newcastle upon Tyne, Univ. of Durham (BSc, PhD). FIBiol; FRSA. Research Fellow then Demonstrator in Physiology, King's Coll., Univ. of Durham, 1954–58; Asst Lectr then Lectr in Physiol., Univ. of Leeds, 1958–68; Res. Fellow in Physiol., Johns Hopkins Univ., 1962–63; Sen. Lectr then Reader in Physiol., 1968–84, Sen. Res. Associate in Cardiovascular Studies, 1973–84, Univ. of Leeds. *Publications:* scientific papers in physiological jls. *Recreations:* squash, gardening. *Address:* Department of Biomedical Sciences, Marischal College, University of Aberdeen, Aberdeen AB9 1AS. *T:* Aberdeen (01224) 273006.

KIDD, Charles William; Editor of Debrett's Peerage, since 1980; *b* 23 May 1952; *yr s* of Charles Vincent Kidd and Marian Kidd, BEM (*née* Foster), Kirkbymoorside. *Educ:* St Peter's Sch., York; Bede Coll., Durham. Assistant Editor: Burke's Peerage, 1972–77; Debrett's Peerage, 1977–80. *Publications:* Debrett's Book of Royal Children (jtly), 1982; Debrett Goes to Hollywood, 1986. *Recreations:* cinema, researching film and theatre dynasties, tennis. *Address:* Debrett's Peerage, 73–77 Britannia Road, SW6 2JR.

KIDD, Prof. Frank Forrest; Partner, Coopers & Lybrand, Chartered Accountants, since 1979; *b* 4 May 1938; *s* of Frank F. Kidd and Constance Mary Kidd (*née* Godman); *m* 1961, Beryl Ann (*née* Gillespie); two *s* two *d*. *Educ:* George Heriot's Sch., Ballards. CA; Mem. Inst. of Taxation. CA apprentice, 1955–60; Partner, Wylie & Hutton, 1962–79; Partner, Coopers & Lybrand, 1979– (following merger of Coopers & Lybrand with Wylie & Hutton in 1979). Pres., Inst. of Chartered Accountants of Scotland, 1988–89. Hon. Prof., Dept of Accountancy and Business Law, Univ. of Stirling, 1987–. *Recreations:* squash, golf, walking. *Address:* (home) 17 Merchiston Park, Edinburgh EH10 4PW. *T:* 0131–229 3577; (business) Coopers & Lybrand, PO Box 90, Erskine House, 68–73 Queen Street, Edinburgh EH2 4NH. *T:* 0131–226 4488. *Club:* Luffness New Golf (Gullane).

KIDD, Prof. Ian Gray, FBA 1993; Emeritus Professor of Greek, since 1987, Chancellor's Assessor, since 1989, University of St Andrews; *b* 6 March 1922; *s* of A. H. Kidd and I. Gray; *m* 1949, Sheila Elizabeth Dow; three *s*. *Educ:* Dundee High Sch.; Univ. of St Andrews (MA, Miller Prize 1947); Queen's Coll., Oxford (BA Greats, MA). Served War of 1939–45: commnd Argyll and Sutherland Highlanders; Sicily, Italy, 1943–44; POW, 1944–45. St Andrews University: Lectr in Greek, 1949–65; Sen. Lectr, 1965–73; Professor: of Ancient Philosophy, 1973–76; of Greek, 1976–87; Provost, St Leonard's Coll., 1978–83 (Hon. Fellow, 1987). Vis. Prof. of Classics, Univ. of Texas at Austin, 1965–66; Mem., Inst. for Advanced Study, Princeton, 1971–72 and 1979–80. General Comr of Inland Revenue, 1982–. Chm., E Fife Educnl Trust, 1977–89. Gov., Dollar Acad., 1982–91. Hon. Fellow, Inst. for Res. in Classical Philosophy and Sci., Princeton, 1989–. *Publications:* (with L. Edelstein) Posidonius, The Fragments, 1972, 2nd edn 1989; Posidonius, The Commentary, 1988; (with R. Waterfield) Plutarch, Essays, 1992; contributions to: Concise Encyclopedia of Western Philosophy and Philosophers, 1960; The Encyclopedia of Philosophy, ed P. Edwards, 1967; Problems in Stoicism, 1971; The Stoics, 1978; Les Stoiciens et leur Logique, 1978; Stoic and Peripatetic Ethics, 1983; Aspects de la Philosophie Hellénistique, 1986; The Criterion of Truth, 1989; Philosophia Togata, 1989; Theophrastus, 1992; articles in learned jls. *Recreations:* music, reading, thinking, looking at pictures, night-walking. *Address:* Ladebury, Lade Braes Lane, St Andrews, Fife KY16 9EP. *T:* St Andrews (01334) 74367.

KIDD, Sir Robert (Hill), KBE 1979; CB 1975; Head of Northern Ireland Civil Service, 1976–79; *b* 3 Feb. 1918; *s* of Andrew Kidd and Florence Hill, Belfast; *m* 1942, Harriet Moore Williamson; three *s* two *d*. *Educ:* Royal Belfast Academical Instn; Trinity Coll., Dublin. BA 1940, BLitt 1941. Army, 1941–46: commnd 1942, Royal Ulster Rifles, later seconded to Intell. Corps. Entered Northern Ireland Civil Service, 1947; Second Sec., Dept of Finance, NI, 1969–76. Allied Irish Banks: Dir, 1979–85; Mem., NI Local Bd, 1979–85 (Chm., 1980–85); Mem., NI Adv. Bd, 1985–88. Chairman: Ireland Co-operation North (UK) Ltd, 1982–85 (Bd Mem., 1985–89); Belfast Car Ferries Ltd, 1983–88. Board Mem., Irish Amer. Partnership, 1988–91. Governor, Royal Belfast Academical Inst., 1967–76, 1979–83; a Pro-Chancellor and Chm. Council, New Univ. of Ulster, 1980–84; Pres., TCD Assoc. of NI, 1981–83; Trustee: Scotch-Irish Trust of Ulster, 1980–; Ulster Historical Foundn, 1981– (Chm., 1987–93). Hon. DLitt Ulster, 1985. *Recreation:* gardening. *Address:* 24 Massey Court, Belfast BT4 3GJ. *T:* Belfast (01232) 768694.

KIDD, Ronald Alexander; HM Diplomatic Service, retired; *b* 19 June 1926; *s* of Alexander and Jean Kidd; *m* 1st, 1954, Agnes Japp Harrower (marr. diss. 1985); two *d*; 2nd, 1985, Pamela Dempster. *Educ:* Robert Gordon's College, Aberdeen; Queens' College, Cambridge; BA Hons 1951, MA 1956. Royal Air Force, 1944–48; Foreign Office, 1951; served at Singapore, Djakarta, Osaka and Macau, 1952–56; FO, 1956–60; Second, later First Sec., Seoul, 1961–62; Djakarta, 1962–63; Tokyo, 1964–68; FCO, 1968–71; Dar Es Salaam, 1971–72; Tokyo, 1972–77; Counsellor, FCO, 1977–81. Jubilee Medal, 1977. *Recreation:* golf. *Address:* 41 Princess Road, NW1 8JS. *T:* 0171–722 8406. *Club:* Royal Air Force.

KIDGELL, John Earle; Head of Economic Accounts Division, Central Statistical Office, since 1994 (Grade 3, since 1988); *b* 18 Nov. 1943; *s* of Gilbert James Kidgell and Cicely Alice (*née* Earle); *m* 1968, Penelope Jane Tarry; one *s* two *d*. *Educ:* Eton House Sch., Southend-on-Sea; Univ. of St Andrews (MA); London School of Economics and Political Science (MSc). NIESR, 1967–70; Gallup Poll, 1970–72; Statistician, CSO and Treasury, 1972–79; Chief Statistician, DoE, 1979–86; Hd of Finance Div., PSA, 1986–88; Head of Directorate D, Central Statistical Office, 1989–91. *Publications:* articles in Nat. Inst. Econ. Rev., Econ. Trends, etc. *Recreations:* hill walking, tennis, reading. *Address:* Central Statistical Office, Great George Street, SW1P 3AQ. *T:* 0171–270 6040.

KIDMAN, Thomas Walter, ERD 1954; Regional Administrator, East Anglian Regional Health Authority, 1973–75, retired; *b* 28 Aug. 1915; *s* of Walter James Kidman and Elizabeth Alice Kidman (*née* Littlejohns); *m* 1939, Lilian Rose Souton (*d* 1988); one *s* two *d*. *Educ:* Cambridge Central Sch.; Cambs Techn. Coll. FHSM, 1972–88. War service, 1939–46: Warrant Officer, RAMC, BEF France, 1940; Major, Suffolk Regt, seconded Corps of Mil. Police, MEF Egypt and Palestine, 1943–46; served in TA/AER, 1939–67.

Local Govt Officer, Health and Educn, Cambridgeshire CC, 1930–48; East Anglian Regional Hosp. Bd: Admin. Officer, 1948; Asst Sec., 1952; Dep. Sec., 1957; Sec. of Bd, 1972. Mem., NHS Advisory Service, 1976–83; Chm., Cambs Mental Welfare Assoc., 1977–86. *Recreations:* photography, walking, gardening, swimming. *Address:* Alwoodley, 225 Arbury Road, Cambridge CB4 2JJ. *T:* Cambridge (01223) 357384.

KIDWELL, Raymond Incledon, QC 1968; a Recorder, since 1972; a Deputy High Court Judge, since 1976; *b* 8 Aug. 1926; *s* of late Montague and Dorothy Kidwell; *m* 1st, 1951, Enid Rowe (marr. diss. 1975); two *s*; 2nd, 1976, Carol Evelyn Beryl Maddison, *d* of late Warren G. Hopkins, Ontario. *Educ:* Whitgift Sch.; Magdalen Coll., Oxford. RAFVR, 1944–48. BA (Law) 1st cl. 1950; MA 1951; BCL 1st cl. 1951; Vinerian Law Schol., 1951; Eldon Law Schol., 1951; Arden Law Schol., Gray's Inn, 1952; Birkenhead Law Schol., Gray's Inn, 1955. Called to Bar, 1951; Bencher, 1978. Lectr in Law, Oriel Coll., Oxford, 1952–55; Mem., Winn Commn on Personal Injuries, 1966–68. Member: Bar Council, 1967–71; Senate, 1981–85. *Address:* Sanderstead House, Rectory Park, Sanderstead, Surrey CR2 9JR. *T:* 0181–657 4161; 2 Crown Office Row, Temple, EC4Y 7HJ. *T:* 0171–797 8100, *Fax:* 0171–797 8101.

KIELY, Dr David George; Chief Naval Weapons Systems Engineer (Under Secretary), Ministry of Defence, Procurement Executive, 1983–84; consultant engineer; *b* 23 July 1925; *o s* of late George Thomas and Susan Kiely, Ballynahinch, Co. Down; *m* 1956, Dr Ann Wilhelmina (*née* Kilpatrick), MB, BCh, BAO, DCH, DPH, MFCM, Hillsborough, Co. Down; one *s* one *d*. *Educ:* Down High Sch., Downpatrick; Queen's Univ., Belfast (BSc, MSc); Sorbonne (DSci). CEng, FIEE; CPhys, FInstP; psc 1961. Appts in RN Scientific Service from 1944; Naval Staff Coll., 1961–62; Head of Electronic Warfare Div., ASWE, 1965–68; Head of Communications and Sensor Dept, ASWE, 1968–72; Dir-Gen., Telecommunications, 1972–74, Dir-Gen., Strategic Electronic Systems, 1974–76, Dir-Gen., Electronics Res., 1976–78, Exec. Officer, Electronics Research Council, 1976–78, Dir, Naval Surface Weapons, ASWE, 1978–83, MoD, PE. Gp Chief Exec. and Dir, Chemring PLC, 1984–85. Chm., R&D Policy Cttee, Gen. Lights Authorities of UK and Eire, 1974–89. Governor: Portsmouth Coll. of Technology, 1965–69; Springfield Sch., Portsmouth, 1993–. Mem., 1982–89, Chm., 1985–89, Council, Chichester Cathedral. *Publications:* Dielectric Aerials, 1953; Marine Navigational Aids for Coastal Waters of the British Isles, 1987; Naval Electronic Warfare, 1988; Naval Surface Weapons, 1988; Defence Procurement, 1990; The Future for the Defence Industry, 1990; chapter: in Progress in Dielectrics, 1961; in Fundamentals of Microwave Electronics, 1963; in Naval Command and Control, 1989; papers in Proc. IEE and other learned jls, etc. *Recreations:* fly fishing, gardening. *Address:* Cranleigh, 107 Havant Road, Emsworth, Hants PO10 7LF. *T:* Emsworth (01243) 372250. *Club:* Naval and Military.

KIERNAN, Prof. Christopher Charles; Professor of Behavioural Studies in Mental Handicap, Director of the Hester Adrian Research Centre, University of Manchester, since 1984; *b* 3 June 1936; *s* of Christopher J. and Mary L. Kiernan; *m* 1962, Diana Elizabeth Maynard; two *s* one *d*. *Educ:* Nottingham Univ. (BA); London Univ. (PhD); ABPsS. Lecturer in Psychology, Birkbeck Coll., London Univ., 1961–70; Sen. Lectr, Child Development, Univ. of London Inst. of Education, 1970–74; Dep. Director, Thomas Coram Research Unit, Univ. of London Inst. of Education, 1975–84. *Publications:* Behaviour Assessment Battery, 1977, 2nd edn 1982; Starting Off, 1978; Behaviour Modification with the Severely Retarded, 1975; Analysis of Programmes for Teaching, 1981; Signs and Symbols, 1982. *Recreation:* survival. *Address:* 29 Edge Lane, Chorlton-cum-Hardy, Manchester M21 1JH.

KILBRACKEN, 3rd Baron, *cr* 1909, of Killegar; **John Raymond Godley,** DSC 1945; journalist and author; *b* 17 Oct. 1920; *er s* of 2nd Baron, CB, KC, and Elizabeth Helen Monteith, *d* of Vereker Hamilton and *widow* of Wing Commander N. F. Usborne, RNAS; *S* father 1950; *m* 1st, 1943, Penelope Anne (marr. diss., 1949), *y d* of Rear-Adm. Sir C. N. Reyne, KBE; one *s* (and one *s* decd); 2nd, 1981, Susan Lee (marr. diss. 1989), *yr d* of N. F. Heazlewood, Melbourne, Australia; one *s*. *Educ:* Eton; Balliol Coll., Oxford (MA). Served in RNVR (Fleet Air Arm), as pilot, 1940–46; commissioned 1941; Lieut-Comdr (A) 1945; commanded Nos 835 and 714 Naval Air Sqdns. A reporter for: Daily Mirror, 1947–49; Sunday Express, 1949–51; freelance contributor to UK and US jls, incl. New Yorker, Punch, Vogue, Time-Life, Tatler and Evening Standard, 1951–. Joined Parly Liberal Party, 1960; transferred to Labour, 1966. Hon. Sec., Connacht Hereford Breeders' Assoc., 1973–76. Pres., British-Kurdish Friendship Soc., 1975–90. *Publications:* Even For An Hour (poems), 1940; Tell Me The Next One, 1950; The Master Forger, 1951; (ed) Letters From Early New Zealand, 1951; Living Like a Lord, 1955; A Peer Behind the Curtain, 1959; Shamrocks and Unicorns, 1962; Van Meegeren, 1967; Bring Back My Stringbag, 1979; The Easy Way to Bird Recognition, 1982 (TES Sen. Information Book Award, 1983); The Easy Way to Tree Recognition, 1983; The Easy Way to Wild Flower Recognition, 1984. TV documentaries: The Yemen, 1965; Morgan's Treasure, 1965; Kurdistan, 1966. *Recreations:* bird-watching, chess. *Heir: s* Hon. Christopher John Godley, Countertrade Manager, Zeneca Plant Protection Div. [*b* 1 Jan. 1945; *m* 1969, Gillian Christine, *yr d* of late Lt-Comdr S. W. Birse OBE, DSC, RN retd, Alverstoke; one *s* one *d*. *Educ:* Rugby; Reading Univ. (BSc Agric.)]. *Address:* Killegar, Co. Leitrim, Ireland. *T:* (49) 34309.

See also Hon. W. A. H. Godley.

KILBURN, Prof. Tom, CBE 1973; FRS 1965; FEng 1976; Professor of Computer Science, University of Manchester, 1964–81, now Emeritus; *b* 11 Aug. 1921; *o s* of John W. and Ivy Kilburn, Dewsbury; *m* 1943, Irene (*née* Marsden); one *s* one *d*. *Educ:* Wheelwright Grammar Sch., Dewsbury; Sidney Sussex Coll., Cambridge (MA 1944); Manchester Univ. (PhD 1948; DSc 1953). FIEE; FBCS 1970 (Distinguished Fellow, 1974). Telecommunications Research Estab., Malvern, 1942–46. Manchester Univ., 1947–81; Lecturer, 1949; Senior Lecturer, 1951; Reader in Electronics, 1955; Prof. of Computer Engineering, 1960. Foreign Associate, Nat. Acad. of Engrg, USA, 1980. Hon. Fellow, UMIST, 1984; DU Essex, 1968; DUniv Brunel, 1977; Hon. DSc Bath, 1979; Hon. DTech CNAA, 1981. McDowell Award, 1971, Computer Pioneer Award, 1982, IEEE; John Player Award, BCS, 1973; Royal Medal, Royal Society, 1978; Eckert Mauchly Award, ACM-IEEE, 1983. Mancunian of the year, Manchester Junior Chamber of Commerce, 1982. *Publications:* papers in Jl of Instn of Electrical Engineers, etc. *Address:* 11 Carlton Crescent, Urmston, Greater Manchester M31 1HZ. *T:* Urmston (01617) 483846.

KILBY, Michael Leopold; *b* 3 Sept. 1924; *s* of Guy and Grace Kilby; *m* 1952, Mary Sanders; three *s*. *Educ:* Luton College of Technology. General Motors, 1942–80: Apprentice; European Planning and Govt and Trade Regulations Manager; European Sales, Marketing and Service Ops Manager; Plant Manager; internat. management consultant, 1980–84. Mayor of Dunstable, 1963–64. MEP (C) Nottingham, 1984–89; contested (C) Nottingham, Eur. parly elecn, 1989. Member: SE Economic Planning Council; Industry and Economic Cttee, British Assoc. of Chambers of Commerce. *Publications:* The Man at the Sharp End, 1983, 2nd edn 1991; Mammon's Ladder, 1993; technical and political papers. *Recreations:* all sports; first love cricket; former Minor Counties cricketer. *Address:* Grange Barn, Haversham Village, Milton Keynes, Bucks MK19 7DX. *T:* Milton Keynes (01908) 313613.

KILDARE, Marquess of; Maurice FitzGerald; landscape and contract gardener; *b* 7 April 1948; *s* and *heir* of 8th Duke of Leinster, *qv*; *m* 1972, Fiona Mary Francesca, *d* of Harry Hollick; one *s* two *d*. *Educ:* Millfield School. Pres., Oxfordshire Dyslexia Assoc. *Heir: s* Earl of Offaly, *qv*. *Address:* Courtyard House, Oakley Park, Frilford Heath, Oxon OX13 6QW.

KILDARE AND LEIGHLIN, Bishop of, (RC), since 1987; **Most Rev. Laurence Ryan,** DD; *b* 13 May 1931; *s* of Michael Ryan and Brigid Foley. *Educ:* St Patrick's Coll., Maynooth (BA, DD). Lectr in Theology, St Patrick's Coll., Carlow, 1958–80, Pres. 1974–80; Parish Priest of Naas, Co. Kildare, 1980–85; Vicar General of Kildare and Leighlin, 1975–87; Coadjutor Bishop of Kildare and Leighlin, 1984–87. Sec. 1966–71, Pres. 1974–76, Irish Theological Assoc.; Pres., Nat. Conf. of Priests of Ireland, 1976–82. *Publications:* contribs to Irish Theological Qly, The Furrow, Irish Ecclesiastical Record, Christus Rex. *Recreation:* walking. *Address:* Bishop's House, Carlow, Ireland. *T:* 0503 31102.

KILÉNYI, Edward A.; Adjunct Professor of Music, Florida State University, since 1982 (Professor of Music, 1953–82); *b* 7 May 1911; *s* of Edward Kilényi and Ethel Frater; *m* 1945, Kathleen Mary Jones; two *d*. *Educ:* Budapest; since childhood studied piano with Ernö Dohnányi; Theory and conducting Royal Academy of Music. First concert tour with Dohnányi (Schubert Centenary Festivals), 1928; concert tours, recitals, and soloist with Principal Symphony Orchestras, 1930–39, in Holland, Germany, Hungary, Roumania, France, Scandinavia, North Africa, Portugal, Belgium; English debut, 1935, with Sir Thomas Beecham in Liverpool, Manchester, London; tours, 1940–42, and 1946–, US, Canada, Cuba. Columbia, Remington and records internationally distributed. Hon. Mem., Franz Liszt Soc., Hungary, 1987. Liszt Commemorative Medal awarded by Hungarian Govt, 1986; named Florida Ambassador of the Arts by Sec. of State for Florida, 1990. Served War of 1939–45, Capt. US Army, European theatre of operations. *Address:* 2206 Ellicott Drive, Tallahassee, FL 32312, USA.

KILFOIL, Geoffrey Everard; His Honour Judge Kilfoil; a Circuit Judge, since 1987; *b* 15 March 1939; *s* of Thomas Albert and Hilda Alice Kilfoil; *m* 1962, Llinos Mai Morris; one *s* one *d*. *Educ:* Acrefair Jun. Sch.; Ruabon Grammar Sch.; Jesus Coll., Oxford (Lord Chancellor Sankey Bar Scholar, 1960). Called to the Bar, Gray's Inn, 1966 (Holker Sen. Scholar); practised on Wales and Chester Circuit (Circuit Jun., 1980); Dep. Circuit Judge, 1976–80; a Recorder, 1980–87. *Address:* Plas y Garth, Glyn Ceiriog, Llangollen, Clwyd.

KILFOYLE, Peter; MP (Lab) Walton Division of Liverpool, since July 1991; *b* 9 June 1946; *s* of Edward and Ellen Kilfoyle; *m* 1968, Bernadette (*née* Slater); two *s* three *d*. *Educ:* St Edward's Coll., Liverpool; Durham Univ.; Christ's Coll., Liverpool. Building labourer, 1965–70; student, 1970–73; building labourer, 1973–75; teacher/youth worker, 1975–85; Labour Party Organiser, 1985–91. *Recreations:* reading, music, spectator sport. *Address:* 24 Brockholme Road, Mossley Hill, Liverpool L18 4QQ. *T:* 0171–219 3000.

KILGOUR, Dr John Lowell, CB 1987; Medical Examiner, Benefits Agency, Department of Social Security; Chairman, Industrial Injuries and War Pensions Medical Boards; Consultant to various commercial firms; *b* 26 July 1924; *s* of Ormonde John Lowell Kilgour and Catherine (*née* MacInnes); *m* 1955, Daphne (*née* Tully); two *s*. *Educ:* St Christopher's Prep. Sch., Hove; Aberdeen Grammar Sch.; Aberdeen Univ. MB, ChB 1947, MRCGP, FFCM. Joined RAMC, 1948; served in: Korea, 1950–52; Cyprus, 1956; Suez, 1956; Singapore, 1961–64 (Brunei, Sarawak); comd 23 Para. Field Amb., 1954–57; psc 1959; ADMS GHQ FARELF, 1961–64; jssc 1964; Comdt, Field Trng Sch., RAMC, 1965–66. Joined Min. of Health, 1968, Med. Manpower and Postgrad. Educn Divs; Head of Internat. Health Div., DHSS, 1971–78; Under-Sec. and Chief Med. Advr, Min. of Overseas Develt, 1973–78; Dir of Co-ordination, WHO, 1978–83; Dir, Prison Medical Services, Home Office, 1983–89; Chm., CS Commn Recruitment Bds, 1989–91. UK Deleg. to WHO and to Council of Europe Public Health Cttees; Chm., European Public Health Cttee, 1976; Mem. WHO Expert Panel on Communicable Diseases, 1972–78, 1983–; Chm., Cttee for Internat. Surveillance of Communicable Diseases, 1976; Consultant, WHO Special Programme on AIDS, 1987–. Vis. Lectr, 1976–89, Governor, 1987–89, LSHTM; Mem. Governing Council, Liverpool Sch. of Tropical Medicine, 1973–87; Mem. Council, 1983–89, Mem. Exec. Cttee, 1987–90, Royal Commonwealth Society for the Blind. Winner, Cons. Constituency Speakers' Competition for London and the SE, 1968. *Publications:* chapter in, Migration of Medical Manpower, 1971; chapter in, The Global Impact of AIDS, 1988; contrib. The Lancet, BMJ, Hospital Medicine, Health Trends and other med. jls. *Recreations:* horse racing, reading, gardening, travel. *Address:* Stoke House, 22 Amersham Road, Chesham Bois, Bucks HP6 5PE. *Clubs:* Athenæum, Hurlingham; Royal Windsor Racing.

KILLALOE, Bishop of, (RC), since 1967; **Most Rev. Michael Harty;** *b* Feb. 1922; *s* of Patrick Harty, Lismore, Toomevara, Co. Tipperary, Ireland. *Educ:* St Flannan's Coll., Ennis, Ire.; St Patrick's Coll., Maynooth, Ire.; University Coll., Galway. Priest, 1946; Prof., St Flannan's Coll., Ennis, 1948; Dean, St Patrick's Coll., Maynooth, 1949, 1955–67; Asst Priest, dio. Los Angeles, 1954. BA, BD, LCL, DD (Hon.); HDiplEduc. *Address:* Westbourne, Ennis, Co. Clare, Ireland. *T:* (065) 28638.

KILLANIN, 3rd Baron, *cr* 1900; **Michael Morris;** Bt *cr* 1885; MBE 1945; TD 1945; MA; Author, Film Producer; President, International Olympic Committee, 1972–80, now Honorary Life President; *b* 30 July 1914; *o s* of late Lieut-Col Hon. George Henry Morris, Irish Guards, 2nd *s* of 1st Baron, and Dora Maryan (who *m* 2nd, 1918, Lieut-Col Gerard Tharp, Rifle Brigade (*d* 1934)), *d* of late James Wesley Hall, Mount Morgan and Melbourne, Australia; *S* uncle, 1927; *m* 1945, Mary Sheila Cathcart, MBE 1946, *o d* of late Rev. Canon Douglas L. C. Dunlop, MA, Kilcummin, Galway; three *s* one *d*. *Educ:* Eton; Sorbonne, Paris; Magdalene Coll., Cambridge. BA 1935; MA 1939. Formerly on Editorial Staff, Daily Express; Daily Mail, 1935–39; Special Daily Mail War Correspondent Japanese-Chinese War, 1937–38. Political Columnist Sunday Dispatch, 1938–39. Served War of 1939–45 (MBE, TD), KRRC (Queen's Westminsters); Brigade Maj. 30 Armd Bde, 1943–45. Past Director: Chubb (Ireland) Ltd (Chm.); Northern Telecom (Ireland) Ltd (Chm.); Gallahers (Dublin) Ltd (Chm.); Irish Shell Ltd; Hibernian Life Association Ltd (Chm.); Ulster Investment Bank (Chm.); Lombard & Ulster Banking Ireland Ltd (Chm.); Dir, Syntex Ireland Ltd. International Olympic Committee: Mem., 1952; Mem., Exec. Bd, 1967; Vice-Pres., 1968–72; President: Olympic Council of Ireland, 1950–73; Incorporated Sales Managers' Association (Ireland), 1955–58; Galway Chamber of Commerce, 1952–53; Chm. of the Dublin Theatre Festival, 1958–70. Mem., Irish Govt Commn on Film Industry, 1957; Chairman: Irish Govt Commn on Thoroughbred Horse Breeding, 1982; Nat. Heritage Council, 1988–. Member: Council Irish Red Cross Soc., 1947–72; Cttee RNLI (a Life Vice-Pres.); Cultural Adv. Cttee to Minister for External Affairs, 1947–72; Nat. Monuments of Ireland Advisory Council, 1947–80 (Chm., 1961–65); RIA, 1952; Irish Nat. Sports Council, 1970–72; Irish Turf Club (Steward 1971–73, 1981–83); Irish National Hunt Steeplechase Cttee; first President, Irish Club, London, 1947–65; Hon. Life Mem., Royal Dublin Soc., 1982; Trustee, Irish Sailors and

Soldiers Land Trust, 1955–. Fellow, Irish Management Inst., 1987. Hon. LLD NUI, 1975; Hon. DLitt New Univ. of Ulster, 1977. Mem., French Acad. of Sport, 1974. Knight of Honour and Devotion, SMO, Malta, 1943; Comdr, Order of Olympic Merit (Finland), 1952; Star of Solidarity 1st Class (Italy), 1957; Comdr, Order of the Grimaldis, 1961; Medal, Miroslav Tyrš (Czechoslovakia), 1970; Commander, Order of Merit (German Federal Republic), 1972; Star of the Sacred Treasure (Japan), 1972; Order of the Madara Rider (Bulgaria), 1973; Grand Officer, Order of Merit of Rep. of Italy, 1973; Grand Cross, Order of Civil Merit (Spain), 1976; Grand Officer, Order of Republic (Tunis), 1976; Grand Officer, Order of the Phoenix of Greece, 1976; Commander, Order of Sports Merit (Ivory Coast), 1977; Chevalier, Order of Duarte Sanchez y Mella (Dominican Rep.), 1977; Commander's Order of Merit with Star (Poland), 1979; Comdr, Legion of Honour (France), 1980; Olympic Order of Merit (gold), 1980; Yugo Slav Flag with ribbon, 1984; Commander, Order of Merit (Congo), 1978; decorations from Austria, Brazil, China, Columbia, USSR etc. *Films:* (with John Ford) The Quiet Man; The Rising of the Moon; Gideon's Day; Young Cassidy; also, Playboy of the Western World; Alfred the Great; Connemara and its Pony (scriptwriter). *Publications:* contributions to: British, American and European Press; Four Days; Sir Godfrey Kneller; Shell Guide to Ireland, 1975 (with Prof. M. V. Duignan); (ed with J. Rodda) The Olympic Games, 1976; Olympic Games Moscow-Lake Placid, 1979; My Olympic Years (autobiog.), 1983; (ed with J. Rodda) Olympic Games—Los Angeles and Sarajevo, 1984; My Ireland, 1987. *Heir: s* Hon. (George) Redmond (Fitzpatrick) Morris, film producer [*b* 26 Jan. 1947; *m* 1972, Pauline, *o d* of late Geoffrey Horton, Dublin; one *s* one *d. Educ:* Ampleforth; Trinity Coll., Dublin]. *Address:* 9 Lower Mount Pleasant Avenue, Dublin 6. *T:* Dublin 4972114; St Annins, Spiddal, County Galway. *T:* Galway 83103. *Clubs:* Garrick; Stephen's Green (Dublin); County (Galway).

See also W. C. R. Bryden.

KILLEARN, 2nd Baron, *cr* 1943; **Graham Curtis Lampson;** 4th Bt *cr* 1866; *b* 28 Oct. 1919; *er s* of 1st Baron Killearn, PC, GCMG, CB, MVO, and his 1st wife (*née* Rachel Mary Hele Phipps) (*d* 1930), *d* of W. W. Phipps; *S* father as 2nd Baron, 1964, and kinsman as 4th Bt, 1971; *m* 1946, Nadine Marie Cathryn, *o d* of late Vice-Adm. Cecil Horace Pilcher, DSO; two *d. Educ:* Eton Coll.; Magdalen Coll., Oxford (MA). Served war of 1939–45, Scots Guards (Major): served ME and N Africa with 2nd Bn, and Italy on staff of HQs 5th US and 8th British Armies, and 15th Allied Army Gp. US Bronze Star. *Heir: half-b* Hon. Victor Miles George Aldous Lampson, Captain RARO, Scots Guards [*b* 9 Sept. 1941; *m* 1971, Melita Amaryllis Pamela Astrid, *d* of Rear-Adm. Sir Morgan Morgan-Giles, *qv*; two *s* two *d*]. *Address:* 58 Melton Court, Old Brompton Road, SW7 3JJ. *T:* 0171–584 7700.

See also Sir N. C. Bonsor, Bt, Earl of St Germans.

KILLEN, Hon. Sir (Denis) James, KCMG 1982; LLB; MP (Lib) for Moreton, Queensland, 1955–83; *b* 23 Nov. 1925; *s* of James W. Killen, Melbourne; *m* 1949, Joyce Claire; two *d. Educ:* Brisbane Grammar Sch.; Univ. of Queensland. Barrister-at-Law. Jackaroo; RAAF (Flight Serjeant); Mem. staff, Rheem (Aust.) Pty Ltd. Minister for the Navy, 1969–71; Opposition Spokesman: on Educn, 1973–74; on Defence, 1975; Minister for Defence, 1975–82; Vice-Pres. of Exec. Council and Leader, House of Representatives, Commonwealth of Australia, 1982–83. Foundn Pres., Young Liberals Movement (Qld); Vice-Pres., Lib. Party, Qld Div., 1953–56. *Recreations:* horseracing, golf. *Address:* 253 Chapel Hill Road, Chapel Hill, Qld 4069, Australia. *Clubs:* Tattersall's, Irish Association, QTC (Brisbane).

KILLEN, John Tyrrell, PhD, FBA 1995; Reader in Mycenaean Greek, Cambridge University, since 1990; Fellow, Jesus College, Cambridge, since 1969; *b* 19 July 1937; *e s* of John Killen and Muriel Caroline Elliott Killen (*née* Bolton); *m* 1964, Elizabeth Ann Ross; one *s* two *d. Educ:* High Sch., Dublin; Trinity Coll., Dublin (1st Foundn Schol. in Classics 1957; 1st Vice-Chancellor's Latin Medallist 1959; BA 1st Cl. 1960); St John's Coll., Cambridge (Gardiner Meml Schol. 1959; PhD 1964). Cambridge University: Asst Lectr in Classics and Lectr, 1967–90; Chm., Faculty Bd of Classics, 1985–86; Churchill College: Gulbenkian Res. Fellow, 1961–62; Fellow and Librarian, 1962–69; Jesus College: Lectr, 1965–; acting Bursar, 1973; Sen. Bursar, 1979–89; Dir, Quincentenary Develt Appeal, 1987–90. *Publications:* (jtly) Corpus of Mycenaean Inscriptions from Knossos, 1985–; (with J.-P. Olivier) The Knossos Tablets, 1989; articles in learned jls. *Recreations:* golf, watching sport on television, reading the FT, music. *Address:* Jesus College, Cambridge CB5 8BL. *T:* Cambridge (01223) 339424. *Club:* Gog Magog Golf.

KILLICK, Anthony John, (Tony); Senior Research Fellow, Overseas Development Institute, since 1987 (Director, 1982–87); *b* 25 June 1934; *s* of William and Edith Killick; *m* 1958, Ingeborg Nitzsche; two *d. Educ:* Ruskin and Wadham Colls, Oxford (BA Hons PPE). Lectr in Econs, Univ. of Ghana, 1961–65; Tutor in Econs, Ruskin Coll., Oxford, 1965–67; Sen. Econ. Adviser, Min. of Overseas Develt, 1967–69; Econ. Adviser to Govt of Ghana, 1969–72; Res. Fellow, Harvard Univ., 1972–73; Ford Foundn Vis. Prof., Econs Dept, Univ. of Nairobi, 1973–79; Res. Officer, Overseas Develt Inst., 1979–82. Vis. Fellow, Wolfson Coll., and Vis. Scholar, Dept of Applied Economics, Cambridge Univ., 1987–88. Vis. Prof., Dept of Economics, Univ. of Surrey, 1988–. Member: Commn of Inquiry into Fiscal System of Zimbabwe, 1984–86; Council, Royal Africa Soc. Chm. Bd of Dirs, African Econ. Res. Consortium, 1995–. Former consultant: Govt of Sierra Leone; Govt of Kenya; Govt of Republic of Dominica; Govt of Nepal; Govt of Ethiopia; various internat. orgns. Associate, Inst. of Develt Studies, Univ. of Sussex, 1986–94. Pres., Develt Studies Assoc., 1986–88. Hon. Res. Fellow, Dept of Political Economy, UCL, 1985–. Editorial adviser: Journal of Economic Studies; Eastern Africa Economic Review, Jl of Internat. Develt; World Develt. *Publications:* The Economies of East Africa, 1976; Development Economics in Action: a study of economic policies in Ghana, 1978; Policy Economics: a textbook of applied economics on developing countries, 1981; (ed) Papers on the Kenyan Economy: structure, problems and policies, 1981; (ed) Adjustment and Financing in the Developing World: the role of the IMF, 1982; The Quest for Economic Stabilisation: the IMF and the Third World, 1984; The IMF and Stabilisation: developing country experiences, 1984; The Economies of East Africa: a bibliography 1974–80, 1984; A Reaction Too Far: the role of the state in developing countries, 1989; The Adaptive Economy: adjustment policies in low income countries, 1993; The Flexible Economy: causes and consequences of the adaptability of national economies, 1995; learned articles and contribs to books on Third World develt and economics. *Recreations:* gardening, music. *Address:* Karibu, 64 Thundridge Hill, Cold Christmas Lane, Ware, Herts SG12 0UF. *T:* Ware (01920) 465493.

KILLICK, Sir John (Edward), GCMG 1979 (KCMG 1971; CMG 1966); HM Diplomatic Service, retired; *b* 18 Nov. 1919; *s* of late Edward William James Killick and Doris Marjorie (*née* Stokes); *m* 1st, 1949, Lynette du Preez (*née* Leach) (*d* 1984); no *c*; 2nd, 1985, I. M. H. Easton, OBE. *Educ:* Latymer Upper Sch.; University Coll., London, Fellow 1973; Bonn Univ. Served with HM Forces, 1939–46: Suffolk Regt, W Africa Force and Airborne Forces. Foreign Office, 1946–48; Control Commn and High Commn for Germany (Berlin, Frankfurt and Bonn), 1948–51; Private Sec. to Parly Under-Sec., Foreign Office, 1951–54; British Embassy, Addis Ababa, 1954–57; Canadian Nat. Def. Coll., 1957–58; Western Dept, Foreign Office, 1958–62; Imp. Def. Coll., 1962; Counsellor and Head of Chancery, British Embassy, Washington, 1963–68; Asst Under-Sec. of State, FCO, 1968–71; Ambassador to USSR, 1971–73; Dep. Under-Sec. of State, FCO and Permanent Rep. on Council of WEU, 1973–75; Ambassador and UK Permanent Rep. to NATO, 1975–79. Dir, Dunlop South Africa, 1980–85. Pres., 1985–92, Vice-Pres., 1992–93, GB Atlantic Cttee; Vice-Pres., Atlantic Treaty Assoc., 1992–94. *Recreations:* golf. *Address:* Challoner's Cottage, 2 Birchwood Avenue, Southborough, Kent TN4 0UE. *Clubs:* East India, Brooks's, Garrick.

KILLICK, Paul Victor St John, OBE 1969; HM Diplomatic Service, retired; Ambassador to the Dominican Republic, 1972–75; *b* 8 Jan. 1916; *s* of C. St John Killick and Beatrice (*née* Simpson); *m* 1947, Sylva Augusta Leva; one *s* two *d. Educ:* St Paul's School. Served with Army, N Africa and Italy, 1939–46 (despatches 1944). Diplomatic Service: Singapore, 1946–47; Tokyo, 1947–49; Katmandu, 1950–53; FO, 1953–55; Oslo, 1955–58; San Francisco, 1958–60; Djakarta, 1960–61; Rome, 1962–66; Pretoria/Cape Town, 1966–70; Tangier, 1971–72. *Recreations:* walking, gardening. *Address:* c/o Barclays Business Centre, Knightsbridge Group of Branches, PO Box 40, SW3 1QB.

KILLICK, Tony; *see* Killick, A. J.

KILMAINE, 7th Baron *cr* 1789; **John David Henry Browne;** Bt 1636; Director of Fusion (Bickenhill) Ltd, since 1969; Director of Whale Tankers Ltd, since 1974; *b* 2 April 1948; *s* of 6th Baron Kilmaine, CBE, and of Wilhelmina Phyllis, *o d* of Scott Arnott, Brasted, Kent; *S* father, 1978; *m* 1982, Linda, *yr d* of Dennis Robinson; one *s* one *d. Educ:* Eton. *Heir: s* Hon. John Francis Sandford Browne, *b* 4 April 1983.

KILMARNOCK, 7th Baron *cr* 1831; **Alastair Ivor Gilbert Boyd;** Chief of the Clan Boyd; *b* 11 May 1927; *s* of 6th Baron Kilmarnock, MBE, TD, and Hon. Rosemary Guest (*d* 1971), *er d* of 1st Viscount Wimborne; *S* father, 1975; *m* 1st, 1954, Diana Mary (marr. diss. 1970, she *d* 1975), *o d* of D. Grant Gibson; 2nd, 1977, Hilary Ann, *yr d* of Leonard Sidney and Margery Bardwell; one *s. Educ:* Bradfield; King's Coll., Cambridge. Lieutenant, Irish Guards, 1946; served Palestine, 1947–48. Mem. SDP, 1981–92; Chief SDP Whip, House of Lords, 1983–86; Dep. Leader, SDP Peers, 1986–87. Chm., All-Party Parly Gp on AIDS, 1987–. Gen. Sec., European Public Health Foundn, 1994–. Editl Consultant, The Social Market Foundn, 1992– (Exec. Dir, 1989–92). *Publications:* Sabbatical Year, 1958; The Road from Ronda, 1969; The Companion Guide to Madrid and Central Spain, 1974, revised edn 1987; (ed) The Radical Challenge: the response of social democracy, 1987; The Essence of Catalonia, 1988; The Sierras of the South, 1992. *Heir: b* Dr the Hon. Robin Jordan Boyd, MB BS, MRCP, MRCPEd, DCH, *b* 6 June 1941. *Address:* House of Lords, SW1A 0PW.

KILMISTER, (Claude Alaric) Anthony; Chairman, Prayer Book Society, since 1989; *b* 22 July 1931; *s* of late Dr Claude E. Kilmister and of Margaret E. Mogford, *d* of Ernest Gee; *m* 1958, Sheila, *d* of Lawrence Harwood. *Educ:* Shrewsbury Sch. National Service (army officer), 1950–52. NCB, 1952–54; Conservative Party Org., 1954–60; Asst Sec. 1960–61, Gen. Sec. 1962–72, Cinema & Television Benevolent Fund; Sec., Royal Film Performance Exec. Cttee, 1961–72; Exec. Dir, Parkinson's Disease Soc. of UK, 1972–91. Founding Cttee Mem., Action for Neurological Diseases, 1987–91; Founder, Prostate Res. Campaign UK, 1994. Founding Mem. and Dep. Chm., Prayer Book Soc. (and its forerunner, BCP Action Gp), 1972–89; Member: Internat. Council for Apostolic Faith, 1987–93; Steering Cttee, Assoc. for Apostolic Ministry, 1989–. *Publications:* The Good Church Guide, 1982; When Will Ye be Wise? 1983; My Favourite Betjeman, 1985; contribs to jls, etc. *Recreations:* walking, writing. *Address:* 36 The Drive, Northwood, Middlesex HA6 1HP. *T:* Northwood (01923) 824278. *Club:* Athenæum.

KILMISTER, Prof. Clive William; Professor of Mathematics, King's College, London, 1966–84; *b* 3 Jan. 1924; *s* of William and Doris Kilmister; *m* 1955, Peggy Joyce Hutchins; one *s* two *d. Educ:* Queen Mary Coll., Univ. of London. BSc 1944, MSc 1946, PhD 1950. King's Coll. London: Asst Lectr, 1950; Lectr, 1953; Reader, 1959; FKC 1983. Gresham Prof. of Geometry, 1972–88. President: British Soc. for History of Mathematics, 1973–76; Mathematical Assoc., 1979–80; British Soc. for Philos. of Science, 1981–83. *Publications:* Special Relativity for Physicists (with G. Stephenson), 1958; Eddington's Statistical Theory (with B. O. J. Tupper), 1962; Hamiltonian Dynamics, 1964; The Environment in Modern Physics, 1965; Rational Mechanics (with J. E. Reeve), 1966; Men of Physics: Sir Arthur Eddington, 1966; Language, Logic and Mathematics, 1967; Lagrangian Dynamics, 1967; Special Theory of Relativity, 1970; The Nature of the Universe, 1972; General Theory of Relativity, 1973; Philosophers in Context: Russell, 1984; (ed) Schrödinger: centenary celebration of a polymath, 1987; Eddington's search for a fundamental theory, 1995. *Recreation:* opera going. *Address:* Red Tiles Cottage, High Street, Barcombe, Lewes, East Sussex BN8 5DH.

KILMORE, Bishop of, (RC), since 1972; **Most Rev. Francis J. McKiernan,** DD; *b* 3 Feb. 1926; *s* of Joseph McKiernan and Ellen McTague. *Educ:* Aughawillan National School; St Patrick's Coll., Cavan; University College, Dublin; St Patrick's Coll., Maynooth. BA, BD, HDE. St. Malachy's Coll., Belfast, 1951–52; St Patrick's Coll., Cavan, 1952–53; University Coll., Dublin, 1953–54; St Patrick's Coll., Cavan, 1954–62; Pres., St Felim's Coll., Ballinamore, Co. Leitrim, 1962–72. Editor of Breifne (Journal of Breifne Historical Society), 1958–72. *Address:* Bishop's House, Cullies, Cavan. *T:* (49) 31496.

KILMORE, ELPHIN AND ARDAGH, Bishop of, since 1993; **Rt. Rev. Michael Hugh Gunton Mayes;** *b* 31 Aug. 1941; *s* of Thomas David Dougan Mayes and Hilary Gunton; *m* 1966, Elizabeth Annie Eleanor Irwin; one *s* two *d. Educ:* The Royal Sch., Armagh; Trinity Coll., Dublin (BA); Univ. of London (BD). Ordained, 1964; Assistant Curate: St Mark's, Portadown, 1964–67; St Columba's, Portadown, 1967–68; Missionary, Japan, 1968–74; Incumbent: St Michael's, Cork, 1975–86; Moviddy, Cork, 1986–88; Rathcooney, Cork, 1988–93; Archdeacon of Cork, Cloyne and Ross, 1986–93. *Recreations:* reading, music, photography, walking. *Address:* The See House, Kilmore, Cavan, Irish Republic. *T:* Cavan (049) 31336.

KILMOREY, 6th Earl of; *see* Needham, Rt Hon. Richard Francis.

KILNER BROWN, Hon. Sir Ralph; *see* Brown.

KILPATRICK, Francesca; *see* Greenoak, F.

KILPATRICK, Prof. (George) Stewart, OBE 1986; MD; FRCP, FRCPE; retired; David Davies Chair of Tuberculosis and Chest Diseases and Head of Department, 1968–92, Vice-Provost, 1987–90, University of Wales College of Medicine, Cardiff; Senior Hon. Consultant Physician to South Glamorgan Health Authority, 1963–90; *b* 26 June 1925; *s* of Hugh Kilpatrick and Annie Merricks Johnstone Stewart; *m* 1954, Joan Askew. *Educ:* George Watson's Coll., Edinburgh; Edinburgh Univ. Med. Sch. (MB ChB 1947, MD 1954). MRCPE 1952, FRCPE 1966; MRCP 1971, FRCP 1975. Medical posts in Edinburgh; Captain RAMC, 1949–51; Mem., Scientific Staff, MRC Pneumoconiosis Research Unit, 1952–54; med. and res. posts, London, Edinburgh and Cardiff; Dean of Clin. Studies, Univ. of Wales Coll. of Medicine, 1970–87. Formerly

Chm., Sci. Cttees, Internat. Union Against Tuberculosis (formerly Chm., Treatment Cttee); Chm. Council, Assoc. for Study of Med. Educn, 1981–86; Chm., Assoc. of Medical Deans in Europe, 1982–85. Ext. Examr in Medicine, Queen's Univ. Belfast, 1986–88. Marc Daniels Lectr, RCP 1987. Pres., Cardiff Medical Soc., 1990–91. FRSocMed. Silver Jubilee Medal, 1977. *Publications:* numerous papers to med. and sci. jls; chapters in books on chest diseases, tuberculosis, heart disease, anaemia and med. educn. *Recreations:* travel, reading, photography. *Address:* Millfield, 14 Millbrook Road, Dinas Powys, South Glamorgan CF64 4DA. *T:* Cardiff (01222) 513149.

KILPATRICK, Sir Robert, Kt 1986; CBE 1979; President, General Medical Council, 1989–95 (Member, 1972–76 and since 1979); *b* 29 July 1926; *s* of Robert Kilpatrick and Catherine Sharp Glover; *m* 1950, Elizabeth Gibson Page Forbes; two *s* one *d*. *Educ:* Buckhaven High Sch.; Edinburgh Univ. MB, ChB (Hons) 1949; Ettles Schol.; Leslie Gold Medallist; MD 1960; FRCP(Ed) 1963; FRCP 1975; FRCPSGlas 1991. Med. Registrar, Edinburgh, 1951–54; Lectr, Univ. of Sheffield, 1955–66; Rockefeller Trav. Fellowship, MRC, Harvard Univ., 1961–62; Commonwealth Trav. Fellowship, 1962; Prof. of Clin. Pharmacology and Therapeutics, Univ. of Sheffield, 1966–75; Dean, Faculty of Medicine, Univ. of Sheffield, 1970–73; Univ. of Leicester: Prof. and Head of Dept of Clinical Pharmacology and Therapeutics, 1975–83; Dean, Faculty of Medicine, 1975–89; Prof. of Medicine, 1984–89. Chairman: Adv. Cttee on Pesticides, 1975–87; Soc. of Endocrinology, 1975–78. Hon. FRCS 1995. Dr *hc* Edinburgh, 1987; Hon. LLD Dundee, 1992; Hon. DSc: Hull, 1994; Leicester, 1994. *Publications:* articles in med. and sci. jls. *Recreation:* golf. *Address:* 12 Wester Coates Gardens, Edinburgh EH12 5LT. *Clubs:* Reform; Royal and Ancient (St Andrews).

KILPATRICK, Stewart; *see* Kilpatrick, G. S.

KILROY, Dame Alix; *see* Meynell, Dame Alix.

KILROY-SILK, Robert; Television Presenter, Kilroy, BBC, since 1987 (Day to Day, 1986–87); Chairman, The Kilroy Television Co., since 1989; *b* 19 May 1942; *m* 1963, Jan Beech; one *s* one *d*. *Educ:* Saltley Grammar Sch., Birmingham; LSE (BScEcon). Lectr, Dept of Political Theory and Institutions, Liverpool Univ., 1966–74. Contested (Lab) Ormskirk, 1970. MP (Lab): Ormskirk, Feb. 1974–1983; Knowsley N, 1983–86; PPS to Minister for the Arts, 1974–75; opposition frontbench spokesman on Home Office, 1984–85. Vice-Chairman: Merseyside Gp of MPs, 1974–75; PLP Home Affairs Gp, 1976–86; Chairman: Parly All-Party Penal Affairs Gp, 1979–86; PLP Civil Liberties Gp, 1979–84; Parly Alcohol Policy and Services Group, 1982–83; Mem., Home Affairs Select Cttee, 1979–84. Member: Council, Howard League for Penal Reform, 1979–; Adv. Council, Inst. of Criminology, Cambridge Univ., 1984–; Sponsor, Radical Alternatives to Prison, 1977–; Patron, APEX Trust; Chm., FARE, 1981–84. Governor, National Heart and Chest Hospital, 1974–77. Political columnist: Time Out, 1985–86; Police Review, 1983–; columnist: The Times, 1987–90; Today, 1988–90; Daily Express, 1990–. *Publications:* Socialism since Marx, 1972; (contrib.) The Role of Commissions in Policy Making, 1973; The Ceremony of Innocence: a novel of 1984, 1984; Hard Labour: the political diary of Robert Kilroy-Silk, 1986; articles in Political Studies, Manchester School of Economic and Social Science, Political Quarterly, Industrial and Labor Relations Review, Parliamentary Affairs, etc. *Recreation:* gardening. *Address:* Kilroy, Kilroy Television Company Ltd, Teddington Studios, Teddington Lock, Mddx TW11 9NT. *T:* 0181–943 3555.

KILVINGTON, Frank Ian; Headmaster of St Albans School, 1964–84; *b* West Hartlepool, 26 June 1924; *e s* of H. H. Kilvington; *m* 1949, Jane Mary, *d* of late Very Rev. Michael Clarke and of Katharine Beryl (*née* Girling); one *s* one *d*. *Educ:* Repton (entrance and foundn scholar); Corpus Christi, Oxford (open class. scholar). 2nd cl. Lit Hum, 1948; MA 1950. Served War of 1939–45: RNVR, 1943–46 (Lt); West Africa Station, 1943–45; RN Intelligence, Germany, 1945–46. Westminster School: Asst Master, 1949–64; Housemaster of Rigaud's House, 1957–64. Chairman: St Albans Marriage Guidance Council, 1968–74; St Albans CAB, 1981–86; Herts Record Soc., 1985–90; St Albans Hospice Care Team, 1988–93. Pres., St Albans and Herts Architectural and Archæological Soc., 1974–77. *Publication:* A Short History of St Albans School, 1970. *Recreations:* music, local history. *Address:* 122 Marshalswick Lane, St Albans, Herts AL1 4XD.

KIMBALL, family name of **Baron Kimball.**

KIMBALL, Baron *cr* 1985 (Life Peer), of Easton in the County of Leicestershire; **Marcus Richard Kimball,** Kt 1981; DL; *b* 18 Oct. 1928; *s* of late Major Lawrence Kimball; *m* 1956, June Mary Fenwick; two *d*. *Educ:* Eton; Trinity Coll., Cambridge. Contested (C) Derby South, 1955; MP (C) Lincs, Gainsborough, Feb. 1956–1983. Privy Council Rep., Council of RCVS, 1969–82, Hon. ARCVS 1982. External Mem. Council, Lloyd's, 1982–90. Jt Master and Huntsman: Fitzwilliam Hounds, 1950–51 and 1951–52; Cottesmore Hounds, 1952–53, 1953–54, 1955–56 (Jt Master, 1956–58). Chm., British Field Sports Soc., 1966–82. Chairman: River Naver Fishing Bd, 1964–92; Firearms Consultative Cttee, 1989–94. President: Hunters Improvement Soc., 1990; Olympia Internat. Showjumping, 1991–; British Inst. of Innkeeping, 1992–; Chairman: Cambridge Univ. Vet. Sch. Trust, 1989–; British Greyhound Racing Fund, 1993. Lt Leics Yeo. (TA), 1947; Capt., 1951. Mem. Rutland CC, 1955. DL Leics, 1984. *Address:* Great Easton Manor, Market Harborough, Leics LE16 8TB. *T:* Rockingham (01536) 770333. *Clubs:* White's, Pratt's.

KIMBER, Sir Charles Dixon, 3rd Bt, *cr* 1904; *b* 7 Jan. 1912; *o* surv. *s* of Sir Henry Dixon Kimber, 2nd Bt, and Lucy Ellen, *y d* of late G. W. Crookes; *S* father 1950; *m* 1st, 1933, Ursula (marr. diss., 1949; she *d* 1981), *er d* of late Ernest Roy Bird, MP; three *s*; 2nd, 1950, Margaret Bonham (marr. diss., 1965), writer; one *d* (and one *s* decd). *Educ:* Eton; Balliol Coll., Oxford (BA). Co Founder and Gen. Sec., Federal Union, 1938–41; Market Gardener, 1941–47; Diploma in Social Anthropology, 1948; collaborated in survey of Banbury, 1949–52; small holder, 1952–60; Landlord, Three Pigeons, Drayton St Leonard, 1962–65; apptd to undertake review of Parish Charities in Oxfordshire for Oxfordshire CC, 1967–77. *Heir: s* Timothy Roy Henry Kimber [*b* 3 June 1936; *m* 1960, Antonia Kathleen Brenda (marr. diss. 1974), *d* of Sir Francis Williams, 8th Bt; two *s*; *m* 1979, Susan, *widow* of Richard North, Newton Hall, near Carnforth]. *Address:* No 2 Duxford, Hinton Waldrist, near Faringdon, Oxon SN7 8SQ. *T:* Longworth (01865) 820004.

KIMBER, Derek Barton, OBE 1945; FEng 1976; Chairman: London & Overseas Freighters Ltd, since 1984; London & Overseas Freighters (UK) Ltd, since 1992; Short Sea Europe Plc, since 1989; *b* 2 May 1917; *s* of George Kimber and Marion Kimber (*née* Barton); *m* 1943, Gwendoline Margaret Maude Brotherton; two *s* two *d*. *Educ:* Bedford Sch.; Imperial Coll., London Univ; Royal Naval Coll., Greenwich. MSc(Eng), FCGI, DIC; FRINA, FIMechE, FIMarE, FNECInst, FRSA. Royal Corps of Naval Constructors, 1939–49; Consultant, Urwick, Orr & Partners Ltd, 1950–54; Fairfield Shipbuilding & Engineering Co. Ltd: Manager, 1954; Dir, 1961; Dep. Man. Dir, 1963–65; Dir, Harland & Wolff Ltd, 1966–69; Dir Gen., Chemical Industries Assoc., 1970–73; Chairman: Austin & Pickersgill, 1973–83; Bartram & Sons, 1973–83; Sunderland Shipbuilders, 1980–83; Govan Shipbuilders, 1980–83; Smith's Dock, 1980–83; Director: A. & P. Appledore International Ltd, 1974–77; British Ship Research Assoc. (Trustees) Ltd, 1973–81; R. S. Dalgliesh Ltd, 1978–80; Equity Capital for Industry Ltd, 1977–86; Eggar Forrester (Hldgs), 1983–93; Wilks Shipping Co. Ltd, 1986–93; AMARC (TES) Ltd, subseq. Community Industry Ltd, then Rathbone CI, 1986–; Community Industry Ltd, 1990–. Dir, Glasgow Chamber of Commerce, 1962–65. Chm., C. & G. Jt Adv. Cttee for Shipbuilding, 1968–70; Pres., Clyde Shipbuilders Assoc., 1964–65; Lloyds Register of Shipping: Member: Scottish Cttee, 1964–65; Gen. Cttee, 1973–90; Technical Cttee, 1976–80; Exec. Bd, 1978–84; Member: Shipbuilding Industry Trng Bd, 1964–69; Research Council, British Ship Res. Assoc., 1973–81; Brit. Tech. Cttee, Amer. Bureau of Shipping, 1976– (Chm., 1989–94); Standing Cttee, Assoc. of W European Shipbuilders, 1976–89 (Chm., 1983–84); Cttee of EEC Shipbuilders' Assoc., 1985–89; Underwriting Mem., Lloyd's, 1985–; Chm., Management Bd, Shipbuilders & Repairers Nat. Assoc., 1974–76, Vice-Pres., 1976–77; Mem., Jt Industry Cons. Cttee, (SRNA/CSEU), 1966–76. Member: EDC for Chem. Industry, 1970–72; Process Plant Working Party (NEDO), 1970–72; CBI Central Council, 1970–72, 1975–84; CBI Northern Reg. Council, 1973–80 (Chm. 1975–77); Steering Cttee, Internat. Maritime Industries Forum, 1981–. Member: Council, RINA, 1961– (Chm., 1973–75, Pres. RINA 1977–81); Council, Welding Inst., 1959–74, 1976–82; Bd, CEI, 1977–81, Exec. Cttee, 1978–80; C. & G. Senior Awards Cttee, 1970–81; Council, NE Coast Inst. of Engrs and Shipbuilders, 1974–92 (Pres., 1982–84); Vice-Pres., British Maritime League, 1985–87; Life Gov., Marine Soc., 1987. Mem., City of London Br., Royal Soc. of St George, 1985–. Liveryman: Worshipful Co. of Shipwrights, 1967 (Asst to Court 1974–, Prime Warden, 1986–87); Worshipful Co. of Engineers, 1984–. Mem., Smeatonion Soc., 1984–; Pres., Old Centralians, 1985–86. Mem., Propeller Club of US. Mem. Court, City Univ., 1984–; Governor, Imperial Coll., London Univ., 1967–87. Hon. FRINA 1981. RINA Gold Medallist, 1977. *Publications:* papers on shipbuilding subjects in learned soc. trans. *Recreations:* DIY, golf, rough gardening. *Address:* Broughton, Monk's Road, Virginia Water, Surrey GU25 4RR. *T:* Wentworth (01344) 844274. *Clubs:* Brooks's, Caledonian, City Livery, Aldgate Ward, United Wards, Anchorites, MCC; Den Norske; Yacht of Greece.

KIMBER, Herbert Frederick Sidney; Director, Southern Newspapers Ltd, 1975–82 (Chief Executive, 1980–81); *b* 3 April 1917; *s* of H. G. Kimber; *m* Patricia Boulton (*née* Forfar); one *s*. *Educ:* elementary sch., Southampton. Southern Newspapers Ltd, office boy, 1931. Served War, Royal Navy, 1939–46: commissioned Lieut RNVR, 1941. Manager, Dorset Evening Echo, 1960; Advertisement Manager-in-Chief, Southern Newspapers Ltd, 1961; then Dep. Gen. and Advertisement Manager, 1972; Gen. Manager, 1974. Chairman: Bird Bros, Basingstoke, 1976–81; W. H. Hallett, 1981–82; Southtel, 1981–82. Dir, Regl Newspaper Advertising Bureau, 1980–81. Member: Press Council, 1977–81; Council, Newspaper Soc., 1974–81 (Mem., Industrial Relations Cttee, 1975–81). *Recreations:* reading, travel, gardening under protest. *Address:* Apartment B6, Residence Les Rampes du Loch, Auray 56400, Brittany, France.

KIMBERLEY, 4th Earl of, *cr* 1866; **John Wodehouse;** Bt, 1611; Baron Wodehouse, 1797; Lt Grenadier Guards; *b* 12 May 1924; *o s* of 3rd Earl and Margaret (*d* 1950), *d* of late Col Leonard Howard Irby; *S* father 1941; *m* 1st, 1945; 2nd, 1949; one *s*; 3rd, 1953; two *s*; 4th, 1961; one *s*; 5th, 1970; 6th, 1982, Sarah Jane Hope Consett, *e d* of Colonel Christopher D'Arcy Preston Consett, DSO, MC. *Educ:* Eton; Cambridge. Lieut, Grenadier Guards, 1942–45; Active Service NW Europe. Chm., J & P Security Services Ltd, 1994–. Member: House of Lords All Party Defence Study Gp, 1976– (Sec., 1978–92; Pres., 1992–); House of Lords All Party UFO Study Gp, 1979–; former Liberal Spokesman on: aviation and aerospace; defence; voluntary community services; left Liberal Party, May 1979, joined Cons. Party. Chm., Foreign Affairs Cttee, Monday Club, 1979–82; Mem. Exec. Cttee, Assoc. of Cons. Peers, 1981–84; Pres., Cricklade and Latton Cons. Assoc., 1988– (Chm., 1986–88). Member: Council, The Air League; Council, British Maritime League; RUSI; IISS; British Atlantic Cttee. Delegate to N Atlantic Assembly, 1981–93. Vice-Pres., World Council on Alcoholism; Chm., Nat. Council on Alcoholism, 1982–85. Mem., British Bobsleigh Team, 1949–58. ARAeS 1977. *Recreations:* shooting, fishing, all field sports, gardening, bridge. *Heir: s* Lord Wodehouse, *qv*. *Address:* House of Lords, Westminster, SW1A 0PW; Hailstone House, Cricklade, Swindon, Wilts SN6 6JP. *T:* Swindon (01793) 750344. *Clubs:* White's, Naval and Military, MCC; House of Lords' Yacht; Falmouth Shark Angling (Pres.).

KIMBLE, Dr David (Bryant), OBE 1962; Editor, Journal of Modern African Studies, since 1972; *b* 12 May 1921; *s* of John H. and Minnie Jane Kimble; *m* 1st, 1949, Helen Rankin (marr. diss.); three *d* (and one *d* decd); 2nd, 1977, Margareta Westin. *Educ:* Eastbourne Grammar Sch.; Reading Univ. (BA 1942, DipEd 1943, Pres. Students Union, 1942–43); London Univ. (PhD 1961). Lieut RNVR, 1943–46. Oxford Univ. Staff Tutor in Berks, 1946–48, and Resident Tutor in the Gold Coast, 1948–49; Dir, Inst. of Extra-Mural Studies, Univ. of Ghana, 1949–62, and Master of Akuafo Hall, 1960–62; Prof. of Political Science, Univ. Coll., Dar es Salaam, Univ. of E Africa, and Dir, Inst. of Public Admin, Tanzania, 1962–68; Research Advr in Public Admin and Social Sciences, Centre africain de formation et de recherche administratives pour le développement, Tanger, Morocco, 1968–70, and Dir of Research, 1970–71; Prof. of Govt and Admin, Univ. of Botswana, Lesotho, and Swaziland, 1971–75, and Nat. Univ. of Lesotho, 1975–77, Prof. Emeritus, 1978; Tutor in Politics to King Moshoeshoe II, 1975, and Queen 'MaMohato, 1977; Vice-Chancellor, Univ. of Malaŵi, and Chm., Malaŵi Certificate Exam. and Testing Bd, 1977–86. Founder and Joint Editor (with Helen Kimble), West African Affairs, 1949–51, Penguin African Series, 1953–61, and Jl of Modern African Studies, 1963–71; Officier, Ordre des Palmes Académiques, 1982. *Publications:* The Machinery of Self-Government, 1953; (with Helen Kimble) Adult Education in a Changing Africa, 1955; A Political History of Ghana, Vol. I, The Rise of Nationalism in the Gold Coast, 1850–1928, 1963; nine University Congregation Addresses, 1978–86. *Recreations:* cricket, editing. *Address:* Huish, Chagford, Devon TQ13 8AR.

See also G. H. T. Kimble.

KIMBLE, George (Herbert Tinley), PhD; retired; *b* 2 Aug. 1908; *s* of John H. and Minnie Jane Kimble; *m* 1935, Dorothy Stevens Berry; one *s* one *d*. *Educ:* Eastbourne Grammar Sch.; King's Coll., London (MA); University of Montreal (PhD). Asst Lecturer in Geography, University of Hull, 1931–36; Lecturer in Geography, University of Reading, 1936–39. Served War as Lt and Lt-Comdr, British Naval Meteorological Service, 1939–44. Prof. of Geography and Chm. Dept of Geography, McGill Univ., 1945–50; Sec.-Treasurer, Internat. Geographical Union, 1949–56; Chm., Commn on Humid Tropics, Internat. Geog. Union, 1956–61. Dir, Amer. Geog. Soc., 1950–53; Dir, Survey of Tropical Africa, Twentieth Century Fund, NY, 1953–60. Chm., Dept of Geography, Indiana Univ., 1957–62; Prof. of Geography, Indiana Univ., 1957–66; Research Dir, US Geography Project, Twentieth Century Fund, 1962–68. Rushton Lecturer, 1952; Borah Lecturer, University of Idaho, 1956; Haynes Foundn Lectr, University of Redlands, 1966; Visiting Prof., University of Calif. (Berkeley), 1948–49; Stanford Univ., 1961; Stockholm Sch. of Economics, 1961. Governor, Eastbourne Sixth Form Coll., 1980–81. FRGS 1931. Hon. Mem., Inst. British Geographers. Editor, Weather Res. Bulletin, 1957–60. *Publications:* Geography in the Middle Ages, 1938; The World's Open Spaces, 1939; The Shepherd of Banbury, 1941; (with Raymond Bush) The

Weather, 1943 (Eng.), 1946 (Amer.), (author) 2nd (Eng.) edn, 1951; Military Geography of Canada, 1949; (with Sir Dudley Stamp) An Introduction to Economic Geography, 1949; (with Sir Dudley Stamp) The World: a general geography, 1950; The Way of the World, 1953; Our American Weather, 1955; Le Temps, 1957; Tropical Africa (2 vols), 1960; Ghana, 1960; Tropical Africa (abridged edition), 1962; (with Ronald Steel) Tropical Africa Today, 1966; Hunters and Collectors, 1970; Man and his World, 1972; Herdsmen, 1973; From the Four Winds, 1974; This is our World, 1981; (ed for Hakluyt Soc.) Esmeraldo de Situ Orbis, 1937; (ed for American Geographical Soc. with Dorothy Good) Geography of the Northlands, 1955; articles in: Geog. Jl, Magazine, Review; Canadian Geog. Jl; Bulletin Amer. Meteorological Soc.; The Reporter; Los Angeles Times; The New York Times Magazine. *Recreations:* music, gardening. *Address:* 2 Dymock's Manor, Ditchling, E Sussex BN6 8SX. *T:* Hassocks (01273) 843157.

See also Dr D. B. Kimble.

KIMMANCE, Peter Frederick, CB 1981; Chief Inspector of Audit, Department of the Environment, 1979–82; Member, Audit Commission for Local Authorities in England and Wales, 1983–87; *b* 14 Dec. 1922; *s* of Frederick Edward Kimmance, BEM, and Louisa Kimmance; *m* 1944, Helen Mary Mercer Cooke. *Educ:* Raines Foundation, Stepney; University of London. Post Office Engineering Dept, 1939; served Royal Signals, 1943; District Audit Service, 1949; District Auditor, 1973; Controller (Finance), British Council, 1973–75; Dep. Chief Inspector of Audit, DoE, 1978. Mem. Council, CIPFA, 1979–83; Hon. Mem., British Council, 1975. *Recreations:* sailing, books, music. *Address:* Herons, School Road, Saltwood, Hythe, Kent CT21 4PP. *T:* Hythe (01303) 267921. *Clubs:* Royal Over-Seas League; Medway Yacht (Lower Upnor).

KIMMINS, Simon Edward Anthony, VRD 1967; Lt-Comdr RNR; *b* 26 May 1930; *s* of late Captain Anthony Kimmins, OBE, RN, and Elizabeth Kimmins; *m* 1976, Jonkvrouwe Irma de Jonge; one *s* one *d*. *Educ:* Horris Hill; Charterhouse. Man. Dir, London American Finance Corpn Ltd (originally BOECC Ltd), 1957–73; Dir (non-exec.), Balfour Williamson, 1971–74; Chief Exec., Thomas Cook Gp, 1973–75; Director: Debenhams Ltd, 1972–85; TKM International Trade Finance, 1978–80; Delfinance SA Geneva, 1984–; Aurelian Futures Fund, 1985–87; Chm., Associated Retail Develt Internat. SA Geneva, 1980–85; Pres., Piquet Internat. SA Geneva, 1986–91. Vice-Pres., British Export Houses Assoc., 1974–80 (Chm., 1970–72). Governor, Royal Shakespeare Theatre, 1975–. *Recreations:* cricket (played for Kent), golf, shooting. *Address:* 37 Chemin de Grange Canal, Geneva 1208, Switzerland. *T:* (22) 7356657. *Clubs:* Garrick, MCC, The Pilgrims; Haagseclub.

KINAHAN, Maj.-Gen. Oliver John, CB 1981; Paymaster-in-Chief and Inspector of Army Pay Services, 1979–83; *b* 17 Nov. 1923; *m* 1950, Margery Ellis Fisher (*née* Hill); one *s* two *d*. Commissioned Royal Irish Fusiliers, 1942; served with Nigeria Regt, RWAFF, Sierra Leone, Nigeria, India, Burma, 1943–46; Instr, Sch. of Signals, 1947–49, Sch. of Infantry, 1950–51; transf. to RAPC, 1951; Japan and Korea, 1952–53; psc 1957; Comdt, RAPC Trng Centre, 1974–75; Chief Paymaster, HQ UKLF, 1975–76, Dep. Paymaster-in-Chief (Army), 1977–78. Col Comdt RAPC, 1984–87. FIMgt. *Recreations:* country pursuits. *Address:* c/o Drummonds Branch, Royal Bank of Scotland, 49 Charing Cross, SW1A 2DX.

KINAHAN, Sir Robert (George Caldwell), (Sir Robin Kinahan), Kt 1961; ERD 1946; JP; Lord-Lieutenant, County Borough of Belfast, 1985–91 (Vice Lord-Lieutenant, 1976–85); *b* 24 Sept. 1916; *s* of Henry Kinahan, Lowwood, Belfast; *m* 1950, Coralie I., *d* of late Capt. C. de Burgh, DSO, RN; two *s* three *d*. *Educ:* Stowe Sch., Buckingham Vintners' Scholar (London), 1937. Served Royal Artillery, 1939–45, Capt. Chairman: Inglis & Co. Ltd, 1962–82; E. T. Green Ltd, 1964–82; Ulster Bank Ltd, 1970–82 (Dir, 1963–85); Director: Bass Ireland, 1958–78; Gallaher Ltd, 1967–82; NI Bd, Eagle Star, 1970–81; Nat. Westminster Bank, 1973–82, Abbey Life, 1981–87; STC, 1984–87; Abbeyfield Belfast Soc., 1983–; Cheshire House (NI), 1983–. Mem., NI Adv. Commn, 1972–73. MP (NI) Clifton, 1958–59. Councillor, Belfast Corporation, 1948; Lord Mayor of Belfast, 1959–61. JP Co. Antrim, 1950, DL 1962; High Sheriff: Belfast, 1956; Co. Antrim, 1969. Hon. LLD (Belfast) 1962. *Recreations:* gardening, family life. *Address:* Castle Upton, Templepatrick, Co. Antrim BT39 0BE. *T:* Templepatrick (018494) 32466.

See also Sir P. A. Neave, Bt.

KINCADE, James, CBE 1988; MA, PhD; *b* 4 Jan. 1925; *s* of George and Rebecca Jane Kincade; *m* 1952, Elizabeth Fay, 2nd *d* of J. Anderson Piggot, OBE, DL, JP; one *s* one *d*. *Educ:* Foyle Coll.; Magee University Coll.; Trinity Coll. Dublin (Schol. and Gold Medallist, MA, Stein Research Prize); Oriel Coll., Oxford (MA, BLitt); Edinburgh Univ. (PhD). Served RAF, India and Burma, 1943–47 (commnd, 1944). Senior English Master, Merchiston Castle Sch., 1952–61; Vis. Professor of Philosophy, Indiana Univ., 1959; Headmaster: Royal Sch., Dungannon, 1961–74; Methodist Coll., Belfast, 1974–88. Dir, Design Council, NI, 1990–93; Mem., Design Council, UK, 1993–94; Chm., Fashion Business Centre, NI, 1992–94. Nat. Gov. for NI, BBC, 1985–91. President, Ulster Headmasters' Assoc., 1975–77; Vice Pres., Assoc. for Art and Design Educn, 1991–; Mem., Council for Catholic Maintained Schools, 1987–90. Mem. of Senate, Chm. External Relations Cttee, and Mem. Standing Cttee, QUB, 1982–. Trustee: Save the Homeless Fund, 1990–; Pantridge Foundn, NI, 1993–. *Publications:* articles in Mind, Hermathena, Jl of Religion. *Recreations:* reading, writing and arithmetic. *Address:* 10A Harry's Road, Hillsborough BT26 6HJ. *T:* Hillsborough (01846) 683865.

KINCH, Anthony Alec, CBE 1987; counsellor for European Community affairs; Member, since 1988, Hon. Leader, since 1993, Speakers Panel, Commission of the European Communities; *b* 13 Dec. 1926; *s* of late Edward Alec Kinch, OBE, former Polit. Adviser, Iraq Petroleum Co. Ltd, and Catherine Teresa Kinch (*née* Cassidy); *m* 1952, Barbara Patricia (*née* Paton Walsh) (*d* 1992); four *s* one *d* (and one *d* decd). *Educ:* Ampleforth; Christ Church, Oxford (MA). Practised at Bar, 1951–57; Contracts Man., Electronics Div., Plessey Co. Ltd, 1957–60; Legal Adviser and Insce Consultant, R. & H. Green and Silley Weir Ltd, 1960–66; Dir, Fedn of Bakers, 1966–73; Head of Foodstuffs Div., Commn of EEC, 1973–82; Head of Div. for Project Ops, European Regl Develt Fund ops, EEC, 1982–86. Chm., Brussels Area, SDP, 1981–84; Vice Chm., SDP Europe, 1989; Mem., Council for Social Democracy, 1982–90. Contested (SDP) Kent E, 1984, London SE, 1989, European Parly elecns. Chef de Division Honoraire, EEC, 1987. *Recreation:* living. *Address:* 36 Greenways, Beckenham, Kent BR3 3NG. *T:* 0181–658 2298, *Fax:* 0181–663 0737.

KINCHEN, Richard, MVO 1976; HM Diplomatic Service; Head of Regional Secretariat for the British Dependent Territories in the Caribbean, Bridgetown, since 1993; *b* 12 Feb. 1948; *s* of Victor and Margaret Kinchen; *m* 1972, Cheryl Vivienne Abayasekera; one *s* two *d* (and one *d* decd). *Educ:* King Edward VI Sch., Southampton; Trinity Hall, Cambridge (BA). Entered FCO, 1970; attached British Commn on Rhodesian Opinion, 1972; MECAS, 1972; Kuwait, 1973; FCO, 1974; Luxembourg, 1975; Paris, 1977; FCO, 1980; Pvte Sec. to Parly Under-Sec. of State, 1982; Rabat, 1984; Counsellor, UK Mission to UN, 1988–93. Member: UN Adv. Cttee on Admin. and Budgetary Questions, 1991–93; UN Jt Staff Pension Bd, 1992–93. *Address:* c/o Foreign and Commonwealth Office, SW1A 2AH. *T:* Barbados 4366694.

KINCHIN SMITH, Michael, OBE 1987; Chairman: Diocesan Trustees (Oxford) Ltd, since 1991; Banburyshire Community Transport Association Ltd, since 1993; *b* 8 May 1921; *s* of Francis John Kinchin Smith, Lectr in Classics, Inst. of Educn, London, and Dione Jean Elizabeth, *d* of Sir Francis Henry May, GCMG, sometime Governor of Hong Kong; *m* 1947, Rachel Frances, *er d* of Rt Hon. Sir Henry Urmston Willink, Bt, MC, QC, Master of Magdalene Coll., Cambridge; four *s* two *d*. *Educ:* Westminster Sch. (King's Schol.); Christ Church, Oxford (Schol.). 1st cl. hons Mod. History; Pres. Oxford Union, 1941. Served with 2nd and 3rd Bns, Coldstream Guards in Italian Campaign (Captain; despatches). Commercial and Admin. Trainee, ICI Ltd, 1947; admin. posts with BBC, 1950–78: Asst, Staff Admin, 1950; Admin Officer, Talks (Sound), 1954; Asst Estabt Officer, TV, 1955; Estabt Officer, Programmes, TV, 1961; Staff Admin Officer, 1962; Asst Controller, Staff Admin, 1964; Controller, Staff Admin, 1967; Controller, Development, Personnel, 1976. Lay Assistant to Archbishop of Canterbury, 1979–84; Appointments' Sec. to Archbishops of Canterbury and York, and Sec., Crown Appts Commn, 1984–87. Chm. Exec. Council, RIPA, 1975–77; CIPM; Vice Pres. (Pay and Employment Conditions), IPM, 1978–80; Lay Selector, ACCM, 1963–73 (Mem. Candidates Cttee, 1966–69); Lay Chm., Richmond and Barnes Deanery Synod, 1970–76; Mem. General Synod, C of E, 1975–78. 1st Chm., Mortlake with East Sheen Soc., 1969–71; Chm., Assoc. of Amenity Societies in Richmond-upon-Thames, 1973–77. *Publication:* (jtly) Forward from Victory, 1943. *Recreations:* walking, local history. *Address:* The Old Bakery, Epwell, Banbury, Oxon OX15 6LA. *T:* Swalcliffe (01295) 780773. *Club:* United Oxford & Cambridge University.

KINCRAIG, Hon. Lord; Robert Smith Johnston; a Senator of the College of Justice in Scotland, 1972–87; Chairman, Review of Parole and related matters in Scotland, since 1988; *b* 10 Oct. 1918; *s* of W. T. Johnston, iron merchant, Glasgow; *m* 1943, Joan (decd), *d* of late Col A. G. Graham, Glasgow; one *s* one *d*. *Educ:* Strathallan, Perthshire; St John's Coll., Cambridge; Glasgow Univ. BA (Hons) Cantab, 1939; LLB (with distinction) Glasgow, 1942. Mem. of Faculty of Advocates, 1942; Advocate-Depute, Crown Office, 1953–55; QC (Scotland) 1955; Home Advocate Depute, 1959–62; Sheriff Principal of Roxburgh, Berwick and Selkirk, 1964–70; Dean of the Faculty of Advocates of Scotland, 1970–72. Contested (U) Stirling and Falkirk Burghs General Election, 1959. *Recreation:* gardening. *Address:* Westwood Cottage, Longniddry, East Lothian EH32 0PL. *T:* Longniddry (01875) 853583. *Clubs:* Hon. Company of Edinburgh Golfers (Edinburgh); Royal Scottish Automobile (Glasgow).

See also A. G. Johnston.

KINDER, Eric; Chairman: Smith & Nephew, since 1990; Brunner Mond Holdings, since 1992; Merchant Retail Group, since 1992; *b* 26 Dec. 1927; *s* of William and Amy Kinder; *m* 1954, Isobel Margaret Barnes; one *s* one *d*. *Educ:* Ashton-under-Lyne and Accrington Grammar Schs, ATI. Joined Textile Div., Smith & Nephew plc, 1957; Divisional Man. Dir, 1969–72; Dir, 1972–; Chief Exec., 1982–90. Non-exec. Dir, Christie Hosp. NHS Trust, Manchester, 1993–. *Recreations:* tennis, angling, golf, music. *Address:* Smith & Nephew plc, 2 Temple Place, Victoria Embankment, WC2R 3BP. *T:* 0171–836 7922. *Club:* Queen's.

KINDERSLEY, family name of **Baron Kindersley.**

KINDERSLEY, 3rd Baron *cr* 1941; **Robert Hugh Molesworth Kindersley,** DL; Chairman: Commonwealth Development Corporation, 1980–89; Siam Selective Growth Fund, since 1990; *b* 18 Aug. 1929; *s* of 2nd Baron Kindersley, CBE, MC, and Nancy Farnsworth (*d* 1977), *d* of Dr Geoffrey Boyd, Toronto; *S* father, 1976; *m* 1st, 1954, Venice Marigold (Rosie) (marr. diss. 1989), *d* of late Captain Lord (Arthur) Francis Henry Hill; two *s* one *d* (and one *s* decd); 2nd, 1989, Patricia Margaret Crichton-Stuart, *d* of late Hugh Norman. *Educ:* Eton, Trinity Coll., Oxford; Harvard Business Sch., USA. Lt Scots Guards; served Malaya, 1948–49. Chm., Brent Walker Gp, 1991–92; Director: London Assurance, 1957–; Witan Investment Co. Ltd, 1958–85; Steel Company of Wales, 1959–67; Lazard Bros & Co. Ltd, 1960–90 (a Vice-Chm, 1981–85); Marconi Co. Ltd, 1963–68; Sun Alliance & London Insurance Gp, 1965–; English Electric Co. Ltd, 1966–68; Gen. Electric Co. Ltd, 1968–70; British Match Corp. Ltd, 1969–73; Swedish Match Co., 1973–85; Maersk Co. Ltd, 1986–. Financial Adviser to Export Gp for the Constructional Industries, 1961–86; Mem., Adv. Panel, Overseas Projects Gp, 1975–77; Dep. Chm., ECGD Adv. Council, 1975–80; Chm., Exec. Cttee, BBA, 1976–78; Pres., Anglo-Taiwan Trade Cttee, 1976–86. Hon. Treasurer, YWCA, 1965–76. Mem., Institut International d'Etudes Bancaires, 1971–85. Chm., Smith's Charity, 1990–. Mem. Ct, Fishmongers' Co., 1973–, Prime Warden, 1989–90. DL Kent, 1986. *Recreations:* all country pursuits, including tennis and ski-ing. *Heir: s* Hon. Rupert John Molesworth Kindersley [*b* 11 March 1955; *m* 1975, Sarah, *d* of late John D. Warde; one *s* one *d*]. *Address:* West Green Farm, Shipbourne, Kent TN11 9PU. *T:* Plaxtol (01732) 810293. *Clubs:* Pratt's, MCC, All England Lawn Tennis and Croquet, Queen's.

KINDERSLEY, Peter David; Chairman, Dorling Kindersley, publishers, since 1974; *b* 13 July 1941; *s* of late David Kindersley, MBE and of Christine Kindersley; *m* 1965, Juliet Elizabeth Martyn; one *s* one *d*. *Educ:* King Edward VI School, Norwich; Camberwell School of Arts and Crafts. Founding Art Director, Mitchell Beazley, 1969–74. *Recreations:* philosophy, art, science. *Address:* Dorling Kindersley Holdings plc, 9 Henrietta Street, WC2E 8PS.

KING, family name of **Baron King of Wartnaby** and **Earl of Lovelace.**

KING OF WARTNABY, Baron *cr* 1983 (Life Peer), of Wartnaby in the County of Leicestershire; **John Leonard King;** Kt 1979; President: British Airways Plc, since 1993 (Chairman, 1981–93); Babcock International Group plc, since 1994 (Chairman, 1970–94); *yr s* of Albert John King and Kathleen King; *m* 1st 1941, Lorna Kathleen Sykes (*d* 1969); three *s* one *d*; 2nd, 1970, Hon. Isabel Monckton, *y d* of 8th Viscount Galway. Founded Ferrybridge Industries Ltd and Whitehouse Industries Ltd, subseq. Pollard Ball & Roller Bearing Co. Ltd, 1945 (Man. Dir 1945, Chm., 1961–69); Chairman: Dennis Motor Hldgs Ltd, 1970–72; Babcock & Wilcox Ltd, subseq. Babcock International plc, later FKI Babcock plc, then Babcock Internat. Gp, 1970–94; Dir, David Brown Corp. Ltd, 1971–75. Current chairmanships and directorships include: The Daily Telegraph plc; Short Brothers plc; Aerostructures Hamble Ltd; Norman Broadbent International; Wide Range Engineering Services Ltd; York Trust; former directorships include: Dick Corp. (USA); Royal Ordnance plc (Dep. Chm.); Clogau Gold Mines; National Nuclear Corp.; British Nuclear Associates Ltd; Tyneham Investments; Babcock (Plant Leasing); 1928 Investment Trust; SKF (UK); Sabena World Airlines; First Union Corp. (USA). Member: Engineering Industries Council, 1975; NEDC Cttee on Finance for Investment, 1976–78; Grand Council and Financial Policy Cttee, CBI, 1976–78; Chairman: City and Industrial Liaison Council, 1973–85; Review Bd for Govt Contracts, 1975–78; British Olympic Appeals Cttee, 1975–78; Macmillan Appeal for Continuing Care, 1977–78; NEB, 1980–81 (Dep. Chm., 1979–80); Alexandra Rose Day Foundn, 1980–85; Mem. Cttee, Ranfurly Library Service; Vice-Pres., Cancer Relief Macmillan Fund (formerly Nat. Soc. for Cancer Relief),

1988; Trustee, Liver Res. Unit Trust, 1988–. Dir, Royal Opera Trust. MFH: Badsworth Foxhounds, 1949–58; Duke of Rutland's Foxhounds (Belvoir), 1958–72; Chm., Belvoir Hunt, 1972. Freeman, City of London, 1984. FBIM 1978; FCIT 1982. Hon. CRAeS, 1986. Hon. Dr Gardner-Webb Coll., USA, 1980; Hon. DSc Cranfield Inst. of Technology, 1989. Comdr, Royal Order of Polar Star (Sweden), 1983. Nat. Free Enterprise Award, 1987. *Recreations:* hunting, field sports, racing, painting. *Address:* Berkeley Square House, Berkeley Square, W1X 6BA. *T:* 0171–930 4915. *Clubs:* White's, Pratts'; Brook (New York).

See also M. Marckus.

KING, Sir Albert, Kt 1974; OBE 1958; Leader, Labour Group, Leeds Metropolitan District Council, 1975–78, retired (Leader of the Council with one break, 1958–75); *b* 20 Aug. 1905; *s* of George and Ann King; *m* 1928, Pauline Riley; one *d. Educ:* Primrose Hill, Leeds. Full-time officer, engrg, 1942–70, retd. Hon. Freedom of the City of Leeds, 1976. *Recreations:* walking, reading. *Address:* 25 Brook Hill Avenue, Leeds LS17 8QA. *T:* Leeds (0113) 268 4684. *Clubs:* Beeston Working Men's, East Leeds Labour (Leeds).

KING, Albert Leslie, MBE 1945; *b* 28 Aug. 1911; *s* of late William John King and late Elizabeth Mary Amelia King; *m* 1938, Constance Eileen Stroud (*d* 1989); two *d. Educ:* University Coll. Sch., Hampstead. Joined Shell-Mex and BP Statistical Dept, 1928. Joined Territorial Army, 1939; Major, RA, 1944. Manager, Secretariat, Petroleum Board, 1947; Manager, Trade Relations Dept, Shell-Mex and BP Ltd, 1948; Gen. Manager: Administration, 1954; Sales, 1957; Operations, 1961; apptd Dir, 1962, Managing Dir, 1963–66. Dep. Dir-Gen., BIM, 1966–68. FCCA; FSS; CBIM; Hon. JDipMA. Barrister (called to the Bar 1980). *Address:* Highlands, 50 Waggon Road, Hadley Wood, Barnet, Herts EN4 0PP. *T:* 0181–449 6424. *Clubs:* MCC; Saracens.

KING, Alexander, CMG 1975; CBE 1948; Co-Founder, 1968, and Hon. President, Club of Rome (President, 1984–91); *b* Glasgow, 26 Jan. 1909; *s* of J. M. King; *m* 1933, Sarah Maskell Thompson; three *d. Educ:* Highgate Sch.; Royal College of Science, London (DSc; FIC 1992); University of Munich. Demonstrator, 1932, and later Senior Lecturer, until 1940, in physical chemistry, Imperial Coll. of Science (FIC 1992); Dep. Scientific Adviser, Min. of Production, 1942; Head of UK Scientific Mission, Washington, and Scientific Attaché, British Embassy 1943–47; Head of Lord President's Scientific Secretariat, 1947–50; Chief Scientific Officer, Dept of Scientific and Industrial Research, 1950–56; Dep. Dir, European Productivity Agency, 1956–61; Dir for Scientific Affairs, OECD, 1961–68, Dir-Gen., 1968–74; Chm., Internat. Federation of Insts for Advanced Study, 1974–84. Adviser, Govt of Ontario. Assoc. Fellow, Center for the Study of Democratic Institutions, Santa Barbara, Calif; Vis. Professor: Brandeis Univ., 1978; Univ. of Montréal, 1979. Hon. Sec. Chemical Soc., 1948–50. Leader Imperial Coll. Expedition to Jan Mayen, 1938; Harrison Prize of Chemical Soc., 1938; Gill Memorial Prize, Royal Geographical Society, 1938 (Mem. Council, 1939–41); Erasmus Prize, 1987; Great Medal of Paris, 1988. DSc (hc): Ireland, 1974; Guelph, 1987; Bucharest, 1993; DUniv Open, 1976; Hon. LLD Strathclyde, 1982. *Publications:* The International Stimulus, 1974; The State of the Planet, 1980; The First Global Revolution, 1991; various chemistry textbooks, and papers in Journal of The Chemical Soc., Faraday Soc.; numerous articles on education, science policy and management. *Address:* 5 Chartwell House, 12 Ladbroke Terrace, W11 3PG; La Negronne, Callion, 83440 Fayence, France. *Club:* Athenæum.

See also C. S. Peckham.

KING, Prof. Anthony Stephen; Professor of Government, University of Essex, since 1969; *b* 17 Nov. 1934; *o s* of late Harold and Marjorie King; *m* 1st, 1965, Vera Korte (*d* 1971); 2nd, 1980, Jan Reece. *Educ:* Queen's Univ., Kingston Ont. (1st Cl. Hons, Hist. 1956); Magdalen Coll., Oxford (Rhodes Schol.; 1st Cl. Hons, PPE, 1958). Student, Nuffield Coll., Oxford, 1958–61; DPhil (Oxon) 1962. Fellow of Magdalen Coll., Oxford, 1961–65; Sen. Lectr, 1966–68, Reader, 1968–69, Essex Univ. ACLS Fellow, Columbia Univ., NY, 1962–63; Fellow, Center for Advanced Study in the Behavioral Scis, Stanford, Calif., 1977–78; Visiting Professor: Wisconsin Univ., 1967; Princeton Univ., 1984. Elections Commentator: BBC; Daily Telegraph. Mem., Cttee on Standards in Public Life, 1994–. Hon. Foreign Mem., Amer. Acad. of Arts and Scis, 1993–. *Publications:* (with D. E. Butler) The British General Election of 1964, 1965; (with D. E. Butler) The British General Election of 1966, 1966; (ed) British Politics: People, Parties and Parliament, 1966; (ed) The British Prime Minister, 1969, 2nd edn 1985; (with Anne Sloman) Westminster and Beyond, 1973; British Members of Parliament: a self-portrait, 1974; (ed) Why is Britain becoming Harder to Govern?, 1976; Britain Says Yes: the 1975 referendum on the Common Market, 1977; (ed) The New American Political System, 1978, 2nd edn 1990; (ed) Both Ends of the Avenue: the Presidency, the Executive Branch and Congress in the 1980s, 1983; (ed) Britain at the Polls 1992, 1992; (with Ivor Crewe) SDP: the birth, life and death of the British Social Democratic Party, 1995; frequent contributor to British and American jls and periodicals. *Recreations:* music, theatre, holidays, walking. *Address:* Department of Government, University of Essex, Wivenhoe Park, Colchester, Essex CO4 3SQ. *T:* Colchester (01206) 873393; The Mill House, Middle Green, Wakes Colne, Colchester, Essex CO6 2BP. *T:* Earls Colne (01787) 222497.

KING, Prof. Bernard, PhD; FIWSc; CBiol, FIBiol; Vice-Chancellor, University of Abertay Dundee, since 1994 (Principal, Dundee Institute of Technology, 1992–94); *b* 4 May 1946; *s* of Bernard and Cathleen King; *m* 1970, Maura Antoinette Collinge; two *d. Educ:* Synge St Christian Brothers Sch., Dublin; Coll. of Technology, Dublin; Univ. of Aston in Birmingham (MSc 1972; PhD 1975). FIWSc 1975; CBiol, FBiol 1987. Research Fellow, Univ. of Aston in Birmingham, 1972–76; Dundee Institute of Technology: Lectr, 1976–79; Sen. Lectr, 1979–83; Head, Dept of Molecular Life Scis, 1983–91; Dean, Faculty of Sci., 1987–89; Asst Principal, Robert Gordon Inst. of Technol., 1991–92. Chm., Conf. of Scottish Centrally-Funded Colls. Dir, Dundee Enterprise Trust; Gov., Unicorn Preservation Soc. *Publications:* numerous scientific and tech. papers on biodeterioration with particular ref. to biodeterioration and preservation of wood. *Recreations:* reading, music, sailing, family life. *Address:* 11 Dalhousie Place, Arbroath, Angus DD11 2BT.

KING, Billie Jean; tennis player; Chief Executive Officer, Team Tennis, since 1981; *b* 22 Nov. 1943; *d* of Willard J. Moffitt; *m* 1965, Larry King. *Educ:* Los Cerritos Sch.; Long Beach High Sch.; Los Angeles State Coll. Played first tennis match at age of eleven; won first championship, Southern California, 1958; coached by Clyde Walker, Alice Marble, Frank Brennan and Mervyn Rose; won first All England Championship, 1966, and five times subseq., and in 1979 achieved record of 20 Wimbledon titles (six Singles, ten Doubles, four Mixed Doubles); has won all other major titles inc. US Singles and Doubles Championships on all four surfaces, and 24 US national titles in all. Pres., Women's Tennis Assoc., 1980–81. *Publications:* Tennis to Win, 1970; Billie Jean, 1974; (with Joe Hyams) Secrets of Winning Tennis, 1975; Tennis Love (illus. Charles Schulz), 1978; (with Frank Deford) Billie Jean King, 1982; (with Cynthia Starr) We Have Come a Long Way: the story of women's tennis, 1989. *Address:* c/o TeamTennis, 445 N Wells #404, Chicago, Ill 60610, USA.

KING, Dr Brian Edmund; owner manager, King Innovations, since 1994; *b* 25 May 1928; *s* of Albert Theodore King and Gladys Johnson; *m* 1952 (marr. diss.); two *s*; *m* 1972, Eunice Wolstenholme; one *d. Educ:* Pocklington Sch.; Leeds Univ. TMM (Research) Ltd, 1952–57; British Oxygen, 1957–67; Dir, 1967–87, and Chief Exec., 1977–87, Wira Technology Group Ltd (formerly Wool Industries Research Assoc.); Dir and Chief Exec., Barnsley Business and Innovation Centre, 1987–93. *Recreations:* bridge, swimming, tennis.

KING, Rt. Rev. Brian Franklin Vernon; Bishop in Parramatta for Western Sydney and an Assistant Bishop of Sydney, since 1993; *b* 3 Jan. 1938; *s* of Francis Brindley King and Merle Florence King; *m* 1965, Pamela Diane Gifford; three *s. Educ:* Sydney Boys' High Sch.; Univ. of NSW (BComm); Univ. of London (BDiv); DMin, Fuller; Diploma, Moore Coll., NSW; DipRe, Aust. Coll. of Theol. ACA (Sydney). Chartered Accountant, 1959–61; theolog. student, 1961–64; Curate, Manly Anglican Church, 1964–67; Rector: Dural, 1967–73; Wahroonga, 1973–87; Manly, 1987–93; Canon, St Andrew's Cathedral, 1989–93. *Recreations:* travel, gardening, sport, family. *Address:* PO Box 1443, Paramatta, NSW 2124, Australia. *T:* (2) 6353186. *Clubs:* Gordon Rugby (Chatswood, Sydney); City Tattersalls (Sydney).

KING, Charles Andrew Buchanan, CMG 1961; MBE 1944; HM Diplomatic Service, retired; *b* 25 July 1915; *s* of late Major Andrew Buchanan King, 7th Argyll and Sutherland Highlanders and of Evelyn Nina (*née* Sharpe). *Educ:* Wellington Coll.; Magdalene Coll., Cambridge (MA). Vice-Consul: Zürich, 1940, Geneva, 1941; Attaché, HM Legation, Berne, 1942; transf. to FO, 1946; 2nd Sec., Vienna, 1950; transf. to FO 1953; to Hong Kong, 1958; to FO 1961; retired, 1967; Head of W European Div., Overseas Dept, London Chamber of Commerce, 1968–70. *Recreation:* travel. *Club:* Naval and Military.

KING, Charles Martin M. ; *see* Meade-King.

KING, Colin Sainthill W.; *see* Wallis-King.

KING, Prof. David Anthony, FRS 1991; FRSC, FInstP; Master of Downing College, Cambridge, since 1995; 1920 Professor of Physical Chemistry, since 1988, and Head of Department of Chemistry, since 1993, University of Cambridge; *b* 12 Aug. 1939; *s* of Arnold King and Patricia (*née* Vardy), Durban; *m* Jane Lichtenstein; one *s* one *d*, and two *s* by previous marriage. *Educ:* St John's Coll., Johannesburg; Univ. of the Witwatersrand, Johannesburg. BSc, PhD (Rand), ScD (E Anglia). Shell Scholar, Imperial Coll., 1963–66; Lectr in Chemical Physics, Univ. of E Anglia, Norwich, 1966–74; Brunner Prof. of Physical Chemistry, Univ. of Liverpool, 1974–88; Fellow, St John's College, Cambridge, 1988–95. Member: Comité de Direction of Centre de Cinétique Physique et Chimique, Nancy, 1974–81; Nat. Exec., Assoc. of Univ. Teachers, 1970–78 (Nat. Pres., 1976–77); British Vacuum Council, 1978–87 (Chm., 1982–85); Internat. Union for Vacuum Science and Technology, 1978–86; Faraday Div., Council, Chem. Soc., 1979–82; Scientific Adv. Panel, Daresbury Lab., 1980–82; Res. Adv. Cttee, Leverhulme Trust, 1980–92 (Chm., 1995–); Beirat, Fritz Haber Inst., West Berlin, 1981–93. Chairman: Gallery Cttee, Bluecoat Soc. of Arts, 1986–88; Kettle's Yard Gall., Cambridge, 1989–. Moller Vis. Res. Prof., Berkeley, 1996. Lectures: Tilden, Chem. Soc., 1989; Frontiers, Texas A & M Univ., 1993; Dupont Distinguished, Indianapolis Univ., 1993; Dow Chemical Canada, Univ. W Ont, 1994. Member Editorial Board: Jl of Physics C, 1977–80; Surface Science Reports, 1983–; Editor, Chemical Physics Letters, 1989–. Chem. Soc. Award for surface and colloid chemistry, 1978; British Vacuum Council medal and prize for research, 1991. *Publications:* papers on the physics and chemistry of solid surfaces in: Proc. Royal Soc., Surface Science, Jl Chem. Soc., Jl of Physics, etc. *Recreations:* photography, art. *Address:* The Master's Lodge, Downing College, Cambridge CB2 1DQ. *T:* Cambridge (01223) 334806.

KING, David E., FCCA; Chief Executive, London Metal Exchange Ltd, since 1989; *b* 18 Aug. 1945; *m* 1972, Jenny Hall; four *s. Educ:* Manchester Poly.; Cranfield Sch. of Mgt (MBA 1984). FCCA 1976. Qualified as Certified Accountant, 1976; sen. financial positions both overseas and in UK, 1976–; joined London Metal Exchange, 1987. *Address:* London Metal Exchange Ltd, 56 Leadenhall Street, EC3A 2JB.

KING, (Denys) Michael (Gwilym), CVO 1989; CEng, FICE, MIMechE; Director, 1986–91, Assistant Chief Executive, 1991, BAA plc, retired (Member, British Airports Authority, 1980–86); *b* 29 May 1929; *s* of William James King, FCIS, and Hilda May King; *m* 1st, 1956, Monica Helen (marr. diss. 1973); three *d*; 2nd, 1985, Ann Elizabeth. *Educ:* St Edmund's Sch., Canterbury; Simon Langton Sch., Canterbury; Battersea Polytechnic, London (BScEng Hons London, 1949). MIMechE 1966; FICE 1977. Engr, J. Laing Construction Ltd, 1961–71, Dir, 1971–74; Engrg Dir, BAA, 1974–77; Dir, 1977–86, Man. Dir, 1986–88, Heathrow Airport; Man. Dir, Airports Div., BAA, 1988–91. *Recreations:* yachting, golf.

KING, Prof. Edmund James, MA, PhD, DLit; Professor of Education, University of London King's College, 1975–79, now Emeritus Professor; *b* 19 June 1914; *s* of James and Mary Alice King; *m* 1939, Margaret Mary Breakell; one *s* three *d. Educ:* Univ. of Manchester (BA, MA); Univ. of London (PhD, DLit). Taught in grammar schs, 1936–47; Asst, then Sen. Asst to Dir of Extra-Mural Studies, Univ. of London, 1947–53; Lectr, subseq. Reader, Univ. of London King's Coll., 1953–75, also Dir, Comparative Research Unit, King's Coll., 1970–73. Visiting appts at Amer., Can. and Chinese univs; also in Melbourne, Tokyo, Tehran, etc; lecturing and adv. assignments in many countries. Editor, Comparative Education, 1978–92. *Publications:* Other Schools and Ours, 1958, 5th edn 1979; World Perspectives in Education, 1962, 2nd edn 1965; (ed) Communist Education, 1963; Society, Schools and Progress in the USA, 1965; Education and Social Change, 1966; Comparative Studies and Educational Decision, 1968; Education and Development in Western Europe, 1969; (ed) The Teacher and the Needs of Society, 1970; The Education of Teachers: a comparative analysis, 1970; (with W. Boyd) A History of Western Education, 1972; Post-compulsory Education, vol. I: a new analysis in Western Europe, 1974; vol. II: the way ahead, 1975 (both with C. H. Moor and J. A. Mundy); (ed) Reorganizing Education, 1977; (ed) Education for Uncertainty, 1979; Technological/occupational Challenge, Social Transformation and Educational Response, 1986. *Recreations:* gardening, music, writing. *Address:* 40 Alexandra Road, Epsom, Surrey KT17 4BT.

KING, Very Rev. Edward Laurie; Dean of Cape Town, 1958–88, Dean Emeritus since 1988; *b* 30 Jan. 1920; *s* of William Henry and Norah Alice King; *m* 1950, Helen Stuart Mathers, MB, BCh, MMed; one *s* three *d. Educ:* King's Coll., Taunton; University of Wales (BA). Deacon, 1945; priest, 1946, Monmouth; Associate in Theology (S Af.). Curate of Risca, 1945–48; Diocese of Johannesburg, 1948–50; Rector of Robertson, Cape, 1950–53; Rector of Stellenbosch, 1953–58. *Recreations:* cricket, reading. *Address:* 30 6th Avenue, Rondebosch East, 7700, South Africa. *T:* (21) 6868204. *Club:* City and Civil Service.

KING, Francis Henry, CBE 1985 (OBE 1979); FRSL 1948; author; Drama Critic, Sunday Telegraph, 1978–88; *b* 4 March 1923; *o s* of late Eustace Arthur Cecil King and Faith Mina Read. *Educ:* Shrewsbury; Balliol Coll., Oxford. British Council, 1950–63 (Asst Rep., Helsinki, 1957–58; Regl Dir, Kyoto, 1958–63). Chm., Soc. of Authors, 1975–77; Internat. Vice-Pres., PEN, 1989– (Pres., English PEN, 1978–86; Vice-Pres., 1977; Internat. Pres., 1986–89). *Publications: novels:* To the Dark Tower, 1946; Never Again, 1947; An Air That Kills, 1948; The Dividing Stream, 1951 (Somerset Maugham Award,

1952); The Dark Glasses, 1954; The Widow, 1957; The Man on the Rock, 1957; The Custom House, 1961; The Last of the Pleasure Gardens, 1965; The Waves Behind the Boat, 1967; A Domestic Animal, 1970; Flights (two short novels), 1973; A Game of Patience, 1974; The Needle, 1975; Danny Hill, 1977; The Action, 1978; Act of Darkness, 1983; Voices in an Empty Room, 1984; Frozen Music, 1987; The Woman Who Was God, 1988; Punishments, 1989; Visiting Cards, 1990; The Ant Colony, 1991; (with Tom Wakefield and Patrick Gale) Secret Lives, 1991; The One and Only, 1994; *short stories:* So Hurt and Humiliated, 1959; The Japanese Umbrella, 1964 (Katherine Mansfield Short Story Prize, 1965); The Brighton Belle, 1968; Hard Feelings, 1976; Indirect Method, 1980; One is a Wanderer, 1985; *poetry:* Rod of Incantation, 1952; *biography:* E. M. Forster and His World, 1978; (ed) My Sister and Myself: the diaries of J. R. Ackerley, 1982; Yesterday Came Suddenly (autobiog.), 1993; *general:* (ed) Introducing Greece, 1956; Japan, 1970; Florence, 1982; (ed) Lafcadio Hearn: Writings from Japan, 1984; Florence: A Literary Companion, 1991. *Address:* 19 Gordon Place, W8 4JE. *T:* 0171–937 5715. *Club:* PEN.

KING, Gen. Sir Frank (Douglas), GCB 1976 (KCB 1972; CB 1971); MBE 1953; Director, 1978–92: Kilton Properties; Springthorpe Property Co.; *b* 9 March 1919; *s* of Arthur King, Farmer, and Kate Eliza (*née* Sheard), Brightwell, Berks; *m* 1947, Joy Emily Ellen Taylor-Lane; one *s* two *d*. *Educ:* Wallingford Gram. Sch. Joined Army, 1939; commnd into Royal Fusiliers, 1940; Parachute Regt, 1943; dropped Arnhem, Sept. 1944; Royal Military College of Science (ptsc), 1946; Staff Coll., Camberley (psc), 1950; comd 2 Parachute Bn, Middle East, 1960–62; comd 11 Infantry Bde Gp, Germany, 1963–64; Military Adviser (Overseas Equipment), 1965–66; Dir, Land/Air Warfare, MoD, 1967–68; Dir, Military Assistance Overseas, MoD, 1968–69; Comdt, RMCS, 1969–71; GOC-in-C, Army Strategic Comd, 1971–72; Dep. C-in-C UK Land Forces, 1972–73; GOC and Dir of Ops, N Ireland, 1973–75; Comdr, Northern Army Gp, and C-in-C BAOR, 1976–78; ADC Gen. to the Queen, 1977–78. Col Comdt, Army Air Corps, 1974–79. Mil. Advr, Short Bros Ltd, 1979–85. Chairman: Assets Protection Internat. Ltd, 1981–86; John Taylor Trust, 1978–88; Director: Control Risks Ltd, 1979–86; Plaza Fish, 1978–91; Director 1978–88: John Taylor Ltd; John Taylor (Worksop); Leicester Frozen Foods. Trustee, Airborne Forces Security Trust, 1981–; Mem. Council, Air League, 1982–90; Dir, Airborne Forces Charitable Trust, 1988–; Pres., Arnheim Veterans Club, 1988–. Kermit Roosevelt Lectr, 1977. *Recreation:* gardening. *Address:* c/o Royal Bank of Scotland, Columbia House, 69 Aldwych, WC2B 4JJ.

KING, Frederick Ernest, FRS 1954; MA, DPhil, DSc Oxon; PhD London; Scientific Adviser to British Petroleum Co. Ltd, 1959–71, retired; *er s* of late Frederick and Elizabeth King, Bexhill, Sussex. *Educ:* Bancroft's Sch.; University of London; Oriel Coll., Oxford. Ramsay Memorial Fellow, 1930–31; Demonstrator, Dyson Perrins Laboratory, 1931–34; University Lecturer and Demonstrator in Chemistry, Oxford Univ., 1934–48, and sometime lecturer in Organic Chemistry, Magdalen Coll. and Balliol Coll.; Sir Jesse Boot Prof. of Chemistry, University of Nottingham, 1948–55; Dir in charge of research, British Celanese Ltd, 1955–59. Fellow Queen Mary Coll., 1955. Tilden Lectr, Chem. Soc., 1948. *Publications:* scientific papers mainly in Jl of Chem. Soc. *Recreation:* gardening. *Address:* 9 Saffrons Court, Compton Place Road, Eastbourne, East Sussex BN21 1DX.

KING, Henry Edward St Leger; Chairman: Denton Hall, Solicitors, since 1993; Rentokil Group PLC, since 1994 (Director, since 1985); *b* 11 Oct. 1936; *s* of Robert James King and Dorothy Louisa Marie (*née* Wickert); *m* 1st, 1964, Kathleen Bridget Wilcock (marr. diss. 1989); one *d* (one *s* decd); 2nd, 1990, Susan Amy Goldsmith (marr. diss. 1994). *Educ:* Whitgift Middle Sch., Fitzwilliam Coll., Cambridge (MA, LLB). Solicitor, England, 1964 and Hong Kong, 1977. Nat. Service, 1955–57. Joined Denton Hall, 1964: solicitor, 1964–67; Partner, 1967–. Director: City Centre Restaurants PLC, 1986–; Brambles Investments PLC, 1988–. *Recreations:* travel, theatre, music. *Address:* 5 Chancery Lane, Clifford's Inn, EC4A 1BU. *T:* 0171–320 6327. *Club:* Riverside Racquet.

KING, Hilary William, CBE 1964; HM Diplomatic Service, retired; *b* 10 March 1919; *s* of Dr W. H. King, Fowey, Cornwall; *m* 1947, Dr Margaret Helen Grierson Borrowman; one *s* three *d*. *Educ:* Sherborne; Corpus Christi Coll. Cambridge. Served War of 1939–45; Signals Officer, mission to Yugoslav Partizan GHQ, 1943–45 (MBE 1944). Apptd Mem. Foreign (subseq. Diplomatic) Service, Nov. 1946. A Vice-Consul in Yugoslavia, 1947–48; transferred to Foreign Office, 1949; promoted 1st Sec., 1950; transf. to Vienna as a Russian Sec., 1951; Washington, 1953; transf. Foreign Office, 1958; Commercial Counsellor, Moscow, 1959; acted as Chargé d'Affaires, 1960; Ambassador (and Consul-Gen.) to Guinea, 1962–65; St Antony's Coll., Oxford, Oct. 1965–June 1966; Counsellor of Embassy, Warsaw, 1966–67; Head of UN (Economic and Social) Dept, FCO, 1968–71; Consul-Gen., Hamburg, 1971–74. *Recreations:* sailing, amateur radio. *Address:* Fuaim an Sruth, South Cuan, Oban, Argyll PA34 4TU.

KING, Isobel Wilson; *see* Buchanan, I. W.

KING, Prof. James Lawrence; Regius Professor of Engineering, 1968–83, University Fellow, 1983–87, Edinburgh University; *b* 14 Feb. 1922; *s* of Lawrence Aubrey King and Wilhelmina Young McLeish; *m* 1951, Pamela Mary Ward Hitchcock; one *s* one *d*. *Educ:* Latymer Upper Sch.; Jesus Coll., Cambridge; Imperial Coll., London. Min. of Defence (Navy), 1942–68. *Recreation:* gardening. *Address:* 16 Lyne Park, West Linton, Peeblesshire EH46 7HP. *T:* West Linton (01968) 660038.

KING, John Arthur Charles; Chairman, Analysys Ltd, since 1991; *b* 7 April 1933; *s* of late Charles William King and of Doris Frances King; *m* 1958, Ina Solavici; two *s*. *Educ:* Univ. of Bristol. BSc. IBM UK, 1956–70; Managing Director, Telex Computer Products UK Ltd, 1970–73; Dir, DP Div., Metra Consulting Gp, 1974–75; Marketing Dir, UK, later Europe (Brussels), ITT Business Systems, 1976–81; Commercial Dir, Business Communications Systems, Philips (Hilversum), 1981–83; Dir, Marketing and Corporate Strategy, subseq. Corporate Dir and Man. Dir, Overseas Div., BT plc, 1984–88; Man. Dir, Citicorp Information Business Internat., 1988–91; Chm., Quotron Internat., 1988–91; Director: Olivetti UK Ltd, 1991–; Leeds Permanent Building Society, 1991–95 (Vice-Chm., 1994–95). Sec. Gen., Eur. Foundn for Quality Management, 1993–94. Mem., Restrictive Practices Ct, 1995–. Freeman, City of London, 1987; Liveryman, Co. of Information Technologists, 1992. FBCS 1968; CIMgt (CBIM 1986); FInstD 1986; FRSA 1993. *Recreations:* tennis, bridge, music. *Address:* Analysys Ltd, St Giles Court, 24 Castle Street, Cambridge CB3 0AJ. *T:* Cambridge (01223) 460600.

KING, Sir John (Christopher), 4th Bt *cr* 1888, of Campsie, Stirlingshire; *b* 31 March 1933; *s* of Sir James Granville Le Neve King, 3rd Bt, TD and of Penelope Charlotte, *d* of late Capt. E. Cooper-Key, CB, MVO, RN; *S* father, 1989; *m* 1st, 1958, Patricia Foster (marr. diss. 1972); one *s* one *d*; 2nd, 1984, Aline Jane Holley (*née* Brett). *Educ:* Eton. Sub Lt, RNVR, 1952–54; Lt, Berks Yeomanry, 1955–60. Mem., Stock Exchange, 1961–73. *Recreations:* sailing, shooting, travelling. *Heir:* *s* James Henry Rupert King [*b* 24 May 1961; *m* 1995, Elizabeth, *y d* of Richard Ellingworth, *qv*]. *Address:* Stillwater, Mathews, Va 23109, USA. *Club:* Brooks's.

KING, John Edward; Principal Establishment Officer and Under Secretary, Welsh Office, 1977–82; President, Friends of the Welsh College of Music and Drama, since 1992 (Chairman, 1990–92); *b* 30 May 1922; *s* of late Albert Edward and of Margaret King; *m* 1st, 1948, Pamela White (marr. diss.); one *d*; 2nd, 1956, Mary Margaret Beaton; two *d*. *Educ:* Penarth County Sch.; Sch. of Oriental and African Studies, London Univ. Served with Rifle Bde, RWF and Nigeria Regt, 1941–47; Chindit campaign, Burma (despatches). Cadet, Colonial Admin. Service, N Nigeria, 1947; Permanent Sec., Fed. Govt of Nigeria, 1960; retired from HMOCS, 1963. Principal, CRO, 1963; Navy Dept, MoD, 1966–69; Private Sec. to Sec. of State for Wales, 1969–71; Asst Sec., Welsh Office, 1971–77. CS Mem., 1977–82, External Mem., 1982–86, Final Selection Bd, CS Commn. Consultant, Dept of Educn and Dir, China Studies Centre, UC, Cardiff, 1984–87. *Recreations:* books, swimming, tennis, watercolour painting. *Address:* Fairfields, Fairwater Road, Llandaff, Cardiff CF5 2LF. *T:* Cardiff (01222) 562825. *Clubs:* Civil Service; Cardiff Lawn Tennis.

KING, Prof. (John) Oliver (Letts), FRCVS; FIBiol; Professor of Animal Husbandry, University of Liverpool, 1969–82, now Emeritus; *b* 21 Dec. 1914; *s* of Richard Oliver King and Helen Mary (*née* Letts); *m* 1942, Helen Marion Gudgin; one *s* one *d*. *Educ:* Berkhamsted Grammar Sch.; Royal Veterinary Coll. (MRCVS); Univ. of Reading (BScAgric); Univ. of Liverpool (MVSc, PhD); FRCVS 1969. Assistant in veterinary practice, 1937; Ho. Surg., Royal Veterinary Coll., 1938; Lectr in Animal Husbandry, 1941, Sen. Lectr 1948, Reader 1961, Univ. of Liverpool. Mem. Council, British Veterinary Assoc., 1953–68; Chairman: British Council Agric. and Vet. Adv. Panel, 1978–84; Council, UFAW, 1987–90 (a Vice-Pres., 1990–); Member: Medicines Commn, 1969–71; Horserace Anti-Doping Cttee, 1973–86, Horserace Scientific Adv. Cttee, 1986–89; Farm Animal Welfare Council, 1979–84; a Vice-President: N of England Zoological Soc., 1987– (Chm. Council, 1972–86); BVA Animal Welfare Foundn, 1989–; President: Assoc. of Veterinary Teachers and Research Workers, 1961; Lancashire Veterinary Assoc., 1967; British Veterinary Zoological Soc., 1971–74; Royal Coll. of Veterinary Surgeons, 1980. Dalrymple-Champneys Cup, 1976; Bledisloe Vet. Award, 1983. *Publications:* Veterinary Dietetics, 1961; An Introduction to Animal Husbandry, 1978; papers on animal husbandry in various scientific pubns. *Recreation:* gardening. *Address:* 6 Ashtree Farm Court, Willaston, South Wirral L64 2XL. *T:* 0151–327 4850. *Club:* Athenæum.

KING, Dr John William Beaufoy; Director, Advanced Breeders Ltd, since 1988; Head of AFRC Animal Breeding Liaison Group, 1982–87, retired; *b* 28 June 1927; *s* of late John Victor Beaufoy and Gwendoleen Freda King; *m* 1951, Pauline Margaret Coldicott; four *s*. *Educ:* Marling Sch., Stroud; St Catharine's Coll., Cambridge; Edinburgh Univ. BA Cantab 1947, MA Cantab 1952; PhD Edinburgh 1951; FIBiol 1974; FRSE 1975. ARC Animal Breeding Res. Organisation, 1951–82. Kellogg Foundn Schol. to USA, 1954; Genetics Cons. to Pig Industry Develt Authority, 1959; David Black Award (services to pig industry), 1966; Nuffield Foundn Fellowship to Canada, 1970; Vis. Lectr, Göttingen Univ., 1973. *Publications:* papers in scientific jls. *Recreations:* gardening, shooting, dog training. *Address:* Cottage Farm, West Linton, Peeblesshire EH46 7AS. *T:* West Linton (01968) 660448. *Club:* Farmers'.

KING, Leonard James, AC 1987; Chief Justice of South Australia, 1978–95; *b* 1 May 1925; *s* of Michael Owen and Mary Ann King; *m* 1953, Sheila Therese (*née* Keane); two *s* three *d*. *Educ:* Marist Brothers Sch., Norwood, S Aust; Univ. of Adelaide, S Aust (LLB). Admitted to Bar, 1950; QC 1967. Member, House of Assembly, Parlt of S Australia, 1970; Attorney-General and Minister of Community Welfare, 1970; additionally, Minister of Prices and Consumer Affairs, 1972. Judge of Supreme Court of S Aust, 1975. *Address:* 105 Alexandra Avenue, Toorak Gardens, Adelaide, SA 5000, Australia. *T:* (8) 2040390.

KING, Prof. Mervyn Allister, FBA 1992; Director, since 1990, and Chief Economist, since 1991, Bank of England; *b* 30 March 1948; *s* of Eric Frank King and Kathleen Alice Passingham. *Educ:* Wolverhampton Grammar School; King's College, Cambridge (BA 1st cl. hons 1969, MA 1973). Research Officer, Dept of Applied Economics, Cambridge, 1969–76; Kennedy Schol., Harvard Univ., 1971–72; Fellow, St John's Coll., Cambridge, 1972–77; Lectr, Faculty of Economics, Cambridge, 1976–77; Esmée Fairbairn Prof. of Investment, Univ. of Birmingham, 1977–84; Prof. of Economics, LSE, 1984–95. Vis. Professor of Economics: Harvard Univ., 1982, 1990; MIT, 1983–84. Co-Dir, LSE Financial Markets Gp, 1987–91. Mem., City Capital Markets Cttee, 1989–91. Pres., Eur. Econ. Assoc., 1993; Member: Meade Cttee, 1978; Council and Exec., Royal Economic Soc., 1981–86, 1992–; Fellow, Econometric Soc., 1982. Managing Editor, Review of Economic Studies, 1978–83; Associate Editor: Jl of Public Economics, 1983–; Amer. Economic Review, 1985–88. Indep. Dir, The Securities Assoc., 1987–89. Trustee, Kennedy Meml Trust, 1990–. Helsinki Univ. Medal, 1982. *Publications:* Public Policy and the Corporation, 1977; (with J. A. Kay) The British Tax System, 1978, 6th edn 1995; (with D. Fullerton) The Taxation of Income from Capital, 1984; numerous articles in economics jls. *Address:* Bank of England, Threadneedle Street, EC2R 8AH.

KING, Michael; *see* King, D. M. G.

KING, His Honour Michael Gardner; a Circuit Judge, 1972–87; *b* 4 Dec. 1920; *s* of late David Thomson King and late Winifred Mary King, Bournemouth; *m* 1951, Yvonne Mary Lilian, *d* of late Lt-Col M. J. Ambler; two *s* one *d*. *Educ:* Sherborne Sch.; Wadham Coll., Oxford (MA). Served in RN, Lieut RNVR, 1940–46. Called to Bar, Gray's Inn, 1949. Dep. Chm., IoW QS, 1966–72; Dep. Chm., Hants QS, 1968–72. *Recreations:* sailing, shooting, golf. *Clubs:* Royal Naval Sailing Association, Royal Lymington Yacht (Cdre, 1986–88).

KING, Vice-Adm. Sir Norman (Ross Dutton), KBE 1989; Chairman, Buckinghamshire Health Authority, since 1993; Chairman, Safety Centre (Milton Keynes) Ltd, since 1992; *b* 19 March 1933; *s* of Sir Norman King, KCMG and Lady (Mona) King (*née* Dutton); *m* 1967, Patricia Rosemary, *d* of Dr L. B. Furber; two *d*. *Educ:* Fonthill School; RNC Dartmouth; graduate, Naval Command College, Newport, USA, 1969; RCDS 1978. RN Cadet, 1946; served HM Ships Indefatigable, Tintagel Castle, Ceylon, Wild Goose, Hickleton, 1951–57, and Corunna, 1957–59; long TAS course, 1960; BRNC Dartmouth, 1961–63; CO HMS Fiskerton, 1963–64; Jun. Seaman Appointer, Naval Sec's Dept, 1965–66; CO HMS Leopard, 1967–68; Staff Officer (TAS) to CBNS (Washington), 1969–71; XO HMS Intrepid, 1972–73; Staff Warfare TAS Officer, to Dir Naval Warfare, 1974–75; Naval Asst to Second Sea Lord, 1975–77; CO HMS Newcastle and Capt. 3rd Destroyer Sqn, 1979–80; CSO to CBNS (Washington), 1981–82; Dir of Naval Officer Appts (Seaman Officers), 1983–84; Comdr, British Navy Staff and British Naval Attaché, Washington, and UK Nat. Liaison Rep. to SACLANT, 1984–86; Naval Sec., 1987–88; COS to Comdr Allied Naval Forces Southern Europe, 1988–91. *Publications:* (jointly) All The Queen's Men, 1967, paperback edn as Strictly Personal, 1972. *Recreations:* tennis, golf, music, chess. *Address:* c/o Lloyd's Bank, Faversham, Kent ME13 7AP. *Club:* Royal Navy Club of 1765 and 1785.

KING, Oliver; *see* King, J. O. L.

KING, Dr Paul Frederick; Group Managing Director, North & West, British Railways Board, since 1994; *b* 4 Jan. 1946; *s* of Cedric Marcus King and Theresa Mary King; *m* 1980, Bertha Ines Avila de King; two *s*. *Educ:* Charterhouse Sch.; Queens' Coll., Cambridge (MA); Univ. of London (MSc, PhD). Lectr, Management Studies, Cambridge Univ., 1970–75; Dir, Special Assignments, TI Group, 1975–79; Sales and Marketing Dir, TI Raleigh, 1979–87; Planning and Marketing Dir, British Shoe Corp, 1987–90; Regional Railways: Planning and Marketing Dir, 1990–93; Man. Dir, 1993–94. *Recreation:* canal cruising. *Address:* The Homestead, 65 Swithland Lane, Rothley, Leics LE7 7SG. *T:* Leicester (0116) 237 4670.

KING, Paul William; Agent General for British Columbia in the United Kingdom and Europe, since 1995; *b* Srinagar, Kashmir, 6 Sept. 1943; *s* of late Rev. Canon Roderick King and of Kathleen King; *m* 1969, Susan Jane Glenny; two *s*. *Educ:* Exeter Sch.; Univ. of Alberta (BA). With E. I. du Pont de Nemours, USA, 1964; Kodak Canada Ltd, 1965–77; Dir responsible for trade with Pacific Rim countries, Govt of Alberta, 1977–81; Director: European Ops, Alberta House, London, 1982–90; Trade and Investment, BC House, London, 1990–95. MInstD. *Recreations:* gardening, travel, motor-racing. *Address:* British Columbia House, 1 Regent Street, SW1Y 4NS. *T:* 0171–930 6857. *Club:* East India.

KING, Air Vice-Marshal Peter Francis, CB 1987; OBE (mil.) 1964; FRCSE; The Senior Consultant, RAF, 1985–87; Air Vice-Marshal, Princess Mary's RAF Hospital, Halton, 1983–87; Consultant Otorhinolaryngologist, King Edward VII Hospital, Midhurst, since 1988; *b* 17 Sept. 1922; *s* of William George King, RAF, and Florence Margaret King (*née* Sell); *m* 1945, Doreen Maxwell Aaröe, 2nd *d* of Jorgen Hansen-Aaröe; one *s* one *d*. *Educ:* Framlingham Coll.; King's Coll. London, 1940–42; Charing Cross Hosp., 1942–45; Univ. of Edinburgh, 1947. DLO; MRCS, LRCP; MFOM. Kitchener Med. Services Schol. for RAF, 1941; Ho. Phys., Ho. Surg., Charing Cross Hosp., 1945; commnd RAF, 1945; specialist in Otorhinolaryngology, employed Cosford, Ely, Fayid, Halton, CME; Cons. in Otorhinolaryngology, 1955; Hunterian Prof., RCS, 1964; Cons. Adviser in Otorhinolaryngology, 1966; Air Cdre 1976; Reader in Aviation Med., Inst. of Aviation Med., 1977; Whittingham Prof. in Aviation Med., IAM and RCP, 1979; QHS 1979–87; Dean of Air Force Medicine, 1983. Cons. to Herts HA, 1963, and CAA, 1973; Examiner for Dip. in Aviation Med., RCP, 1980. Pres., Sect. of Otology, RSocMed, 1977–78 (Sec., 1972–74); Chm., Brit. Soc. of Audiology, 1979–81; Vice-Pres., RNID, 1990 (Vice-Chm., 1980–88); Member: BMA, 1945–; Scottish Otological Soc., 1955–90; Royal Aeronaut. Soc., 1976–; Council, Brit. Assoc. of Otorhinolaryngologists, 1960–89; Editorial Bd, British Jl of Audiology, 1980–88. Fellow, Inst. of Acoustics, 1977. FRSM. CStJ 1987. Lady Cade Medal, RCS, 1967; (jtly) Howells Meml Prize, Univ. of London, 1992. *Publications:* Noise and Vibration in Aviation (with J. C. Guignard), 1972; (with John Ernsting) Aviation Medicine, 1988; (jtly) Assessment of Hearing Disability, 1992; numerous articles, chapters, lectures and papers, in books and relevant jls on aviation otolaryngology, noise deafness, hearing conservation, tympanoplasty, facial paralysis, otic barotrauma, etc. *Recreations:* sculpture, looking at prints. *Address:* 5 Churchill Gate, Oxford Road, Woodstock, Oxon OX20 1QW. *T:* Woodstock (01993) 813115. *Club:* Royal Air Force.

KING, Rev. Canon Philip David; Secretary, Board of Mission, General Synod of the Church of England, since 1991 (Secretary, Board for Mission and Unity, 1989–91); *b* 6 May 1935; *s* of Frank Harman King and Gladys Winifred King; *m* 1963, Margaret Naomi Rivers Pitt; two *s* two *d*. *Educ:* Keble College, Oxford (MA Jurisp.); Tyndale Hall, Bristol. Curate, Holy Trinity, Redhill, 1960–63; Minister in charge, St Patrick's, Wallington, 1963–68; Vicar, Christ Church, Fulham, 1968–74; Gen. Sec., S American Missionary Soc., 1974–86; Vicar, Christ Church and St Peter, Harrow, 1986–89. *Publications:* Leadership Explosion, 1987; Making Christ Known, 1992. *Recreation:* hill-walking. *Address:* Board of Mission, Church House, Great Smith Street, SW1P 3NZ. *T:* 0171–222 9011.

KING, Phillip, CBE 1975; RA 1991 (ARA 1977); sculptor; Professor of Sculpture, Royal College of Art, 1980–90, Emeritus since 1991; *b* 1 May 1934; *s* of Thomas John King and of Gabrielle (*née* Liautard); *m* 1957, Lilian Odelle (marr. diss. 1987); one *s* decd. *Educ:* Mill Hill Sch.; Christ's Coll., Cambridge Univ. (languages); St Martin's Sch. of Art (sculpture). Teacher at St Martin's Sch. of Art, 1959–78; Asst to Henry Moore, 1959–60. Trustee, Tate Gallery, 1967–69; Mem. Art Panel, Arts Council, 1977–79. Vis. Prof., Berlin Sch. of Art, 1979–81. *One-man Exhibitions include:* British Pavilion, Venice Biennale, 1968; European Mus. Tour, 1974–75 (Kroller-Muller Nat. Mus., Holland; Kunsthalle, Düsseldorf; Kunsthalle, Bern; Musée Galliera, Paris; Ulster Mus., Belfast); UK Touring Exhib., 1975–76 (Sheffield, Cumbria, Aberdeen, Glasgow, Newcastle, Portsmouth); Hayward Gall. (retrospective), 1981. Commissions include: Cross Bend, European Patent Office, Munich, 1978; Hiroshima Mus. of Art, 1989. First Prize, Socha Piestanskych Parkov, Piestany, Czechoslovakia, 1969. *Address:* c/o New Rowan Gallery, 25 Dover Street, W1X 3PA.

KING, Ralph Malcolm MacDonald, OBE 1968; Colonial Service, retired; *b* 8 Feb. 1911; *s* of Dr James Malcolm King and Mrs Norah King; *m* 1948, Rita Elizabeth Herring; two *s* one *d*. *Educ:* Tonbridge Sch. Solicitor (Hons) 1934. Asst to Johnson, Stokes and Master, Solicitors, Hong Kong, 1936–41. Commissioned Middx Regt, 1941; prisoner of war, 1941–45; demobilised, 1946. Colonial Legal Service, 1947; Legal Officer, Somaliland, 1947; Crown Counsel, Somaliland, 1950. Called to Bar, Gray's Inn, 1950. Solicitor-General, Nyasaland, 1953; Attorney-General, Nyasaland, 1957–61. Disbarred at his own request and since restored to Roll of Solicitors, in April 1961. Legal Draftsman to Government of Northern Nigeria, 1963–67, and to Northern States of Nigeria, 1967–73; Dir, Legislative Drafting Courses, Commonwealth Secretariat, Jamaica, 1974–75, Trinidad, 1976, and Barbados, 1977. *Recreations:* watching cricket, walking. *Address:* 36 Mill View Close, Woodbridge, Suffolk IP12 4HR. *T:* Woodbridge (01394) 385417.

KING, Sir Richard (Brian Meredith), KCB 1976 (CB 1969); MC 1944; Trustee, Simon Population Trust, since 1985; Director, Rural Investment Overseas, since 1987; *b* 2 Aug. 1920; *s* of late Bernard and Dorothy King; *m* 1944, Blanche Phyllis Roberts; two *s* one *d*. *Educ:* King's Coll. Sch., Wimbledon. Air Ministry, 1939; Min. of Aircraft Prod., 1940. Army 1940–46: Major, N Irish Horse; N Af. and Ital. campaigns (MC, Cassino). Min. of Supply, 1946; Asst Principal, Ministry of Works, 1948; Principal, 1949; Asst Regional Dir (Leeds), 1949–52; seconded Treas., 1953–54; Prin. Priv. Sec. to Minister of Works, 1956–57; Asst Sec., 1957; seconded Cabinet Off., 1958 (Sec. of Commonwealth Educn. Conf. (Oxford), 1959; Constitutional Confs: Kenya, 1960; N Rhodesia, Nyasaland and Fed. Review, 1960; WI Fedn, 1961); Dept of Tech. Co-op., on its formation, 1961; Min. of Overseas Develt, on its formation, 1964: Under-Sec., 1964; Dep. Sec., 1968; Permanent Sec., 1973–76; Exec. Sec., IMF/World Bank Develt Cttee, 1976–80; Senior Advr to S. G. Warburg & Co. Ltd, 1980–85. *Publications:* The Planning of the British Aid Programme, 1971; Criteria for Europe's Development Policy to the Third World, 1974. *Recreations:* music, lawn tennis, gardening, doing-it-himself. *Address:* Woodlands Farm House, Woodlands Lane, Stoke D'Abernon, Cobham, Surrey KT11 3PY. *T:* Oxshott (01372) 843491. *Club:* All England Lawn Tennis.

KING, Robert George Cecil; Chairman, Social Security Appeal Tribunals, since 1987; Under Secretary (Legal), HM Customs and Excise, 1985–87; *b* 21 Jan. 1927; *s* of Stanley Cecil and Kathleen Mary King; *m* 1952, Mary Marshall. *Educ:* Nunthorpe Grammar School, York. Called to the Bar, Lincolns Inn, 1965. Army, 1945–48; British Rail, 1948–53; Judicial Dept, Kenya, 1954–61; East African Common Services Organisation, 1962–64; Solicitor's Office, HM Customs and Excise, 1965–87. *Recreations:* golf, bowls, gardening, watching cricket, watching television. *Address:* 181 Greenshaw Drive, Wigginton, York YO3 3SD. *T:* York (01904) 765039. *Clubs:* MCC; Yorkshire (York); Wigginton Bowling; York Golf, Royal Nairobi Golf.

KING, Robert John Stephen; conductor; harpsichordist; Artistic Director, The King's Consort, since 1980; *b* 27 June 1960; *s* of Stephen King and Margaret Digby. *Educ:* Radley Coll.; St John's Coll., Cambridge (MA). Writer; Editor of much music *pre* 1750; conductor, orchestras and choirs, incl. Orq. Sinfonica Euskadi, Orq. di Madrid, Orebro Chamber Orch., Netherlands Chamber Orch. and Chamber Choir, RTL Symphony Orch., Orch. d'Auvergne. *Publications:* Henry Purcell, 1994; numerous musical edns. *Recreations:* ski-ing, cricket, graphic design. *Address:* 2 Salisbury Road, Ealing, W13 9TX. *T:* 0181–579 6283.

KING, Robert Shirley; Under Secretary, Department of Health and Social Security, 1976–80; *b* 12 July 1920; *s* of late Rev. William Henry King, MC, TD, MA, and Dorothy King (*née* Sharpe); *m* 1st, 1947, Margaret Siddall (*d* 1956); two *d*; 2nd, 1958, Mary Rowell; one *s* two *d*. *Educ:* Alexandra Road Sch., Oldham; Manchester Grammar Sch.; Trinity Coll., Cambridge (Schol., MA). Served War, RAF, 1940–45. Colonial Service, Tanganyika, 1949–62 (Dist Comr, Bukoba, 1956–58, Geita, 1959–62); Home Office: Principal, 1962–69 (seconded to Civil Service Dept, 1968–69); Asst Sec., 1969–70; transf., with Children's Dept, to DHSS, 1971; Asst Sec., DHSS, 1971–76; Sec., Wkg Party on Role and Tasks of Social Workers, Nat. Inst. for Social Work, 1980–82; part-time Asst Sec., Home Office, 1985–86. Sec., Health Promotion Res, Trust, 1984–89. Member Council: British and Foreign Sch. Soc., 1982–89; Shape, 1982–89. Governor: Cheshunt Foundn, 1976–83; Bell Educnl Trust, 1984–89. *Recreations:* walking, cycling, gardening, African affairs. *Address:* 3 Nightingale Avenue, Cambridge CB1 4SG. *T:* Cambridge (01223) 248965.

KING, Roger Douglas; Director of Public Affairs, Society of Motor Manufacturers and Traders, since 1992; *b* 26 Oct. 1943; *s* of Douglas and Cecilie King; *m* 1976, Jennifer Susan (*née* Sharpe); twin *s* one *d*. *Educ:* Solihull Sch. Served automobile engrg apprenticeship with British Motor Corp., 1960–66; sales rep., 1966–74; own manufg business, 1974–81; self-employed car product distributor, 1982–83. Dir (non-exec.), Nat. Express Hldgs, 1988–91. MP (C) Birmingham, Northfield, 1983–92. PPS to Minister for Local Govt, 1987–88, for Water and Planning, 1988, DoE, to Sec. of State for Employment, 1989–92. Mem., H of C Transport Select Cttee, 1984–87; Vice-Chm., All Party Motor Industry Gp, 1985–92; Jt Sec., Cons. Tourism Cttee, 1985–87. FIMI 1986. *Recreations:* swimming, motoring. *Address:* 241 Tessall Lane, Northfield, Birmingham B31 5EQ. *T:* 0121–476 6649.

KING, Prof. Roger Patrick; Vice-Chancellor, University of Humberside, since 1992; *b* 31 May 1945; *s* of Timothy Francis King and Vera May King; *m* 1966, Susan Winifred Ashworth; one *d*. *Educ:* Wimbledon Coll.; Univ. of London (BSc Hons Econ.); Univ. of Birmingham (MSocSci). HM Civil Service, 1963; Sales Management Trainee, United Glass, 1964; Sales Manager, Marley Tiles, 1965; Lectr and Sen. Lectr in Social Scis, Manchester Polytechnic, 1970–75; Principal Lectr, later Head of Dept of Behavioural Scis, Huddersfield Poly., 1976–85; Dep. Dir, 1985–89, Dir and Chief Exec., 1989–92, Humberside Poly. *Publications:* (with N. Nugent) The British Right, 1977; (with N. Nugent) Respectable Rebels, 1979; The Middle Class, 1981; Capital and Politics, 1983; The State in Modern Society, 1986; (with J. Simmie) The State in Action, 1990. *Recreations:* reading, running, music, Rugby League. *Address:* Rydon House, 14 St John's Square, Wakefield, West Yorks WF1 2RA. *T:* Wakefield (01924) 386970. *Club:* Reform.

KING, Dame Ruth; *see* Railton, Dame R.

KING, Thea, (Mrs T. Thurston), OBE 1985; FRCM, FGSM; freelance musician; Professor, Guildhall School of Music, since 1988; *b* 26 Dec. 1925; *m* Jan. 1953, Frederick John Thurston (*d* Dec. 1953). *Educ:* Bedford High Sch.; Royal College of Music (FRCM 1975; ARCM 1944 and 1947). FGSM 1992. Prof. of Clarinet, RCM, 1961–87. Sadler's Wells Orchestra, 1950–52; Portia Wind Ensemble, 1955–68; London Mozart Players, 1956–84; Member: English Chamber Orchestra, Vesuvius Ensemble, Robles Ensemble. Frequent soloist, broadcaster, recitalist; recordings include Mozart, Brahms, Spohr, Finzi, Bruch, Mendelssohn, Stanford and 20th Century British music. *Publications:* clarinet solos, Chester Woodwind series, 1977; arrangement of J. S. Bach, Duets for 2 Clarinets, 1979; Schumann for the Clarinet, 1991; Mendelssohn for the Clarinet, 1993; The Romantic Clarinet, Vol. 1, 1994. *Recreations:* cows, pillow lace, painting, ski-ing, piano-playing. *Address:* 16 Milverton Road, NW6 7AS. *T:* 0181–459 3453.

KING, Rt. Hon. Thomas Jeremy, (Tom), CH 1992; PC 1979; MP (C) Bridgwater since March 1970; *b* 13 June 1933; *s* of late J. H. King, JP; *m* 1960, Jane, *d* of late Brig. Robert Tilney, CBE, DSO, TD; one *s* one *d*. *Educ:* Rugby; Emmanuel Coll., Cambridge (MA). National service, 1951–53: commnd Somerset Light Inf., 1952; seconded to KAR; served Tanganyika and Kenya; Actg Captain 1953. Cambridge, 1953–56. Joined E.S. & A. Robinson Ltd, Bristol, 1956; various positions up to Divisional Gen. Man., 1964–69; Chm., Sale, Tilney Co Ltd, 1971–79 (Dir 1965–79). Mem., Cttee on Standards in Public Life, 1994–. PPS to: Minister for Posts and Telecommunications, 1970–72; Minister for Industrial Develt, 1972–74; Front Bench spokesman for: Industry, 1975–76; Energy, 1976–79; Minister for Local Govt and Environmental Services, DoE, 1979–83; Sec. of State for the Environment, Jan.–June 1983, for Transport, June–Oct. 1983, for Employment, 1983–85, for NI, 1985–89, for Defence, 1989–92. Chm., Parly Intelligence and Security Cttee, 1994–. *Recreations:* cricket, ski-ing. *Address:* House of Commons, SW1A 0AA.
See also Mrs S. R. Clarke.

KING, Timothy Roger Alan; QC 1991; a Recorder, since 1991; *b* 5 April 1949; *s* of late Harold Bonsall King and of Dorothy King; *m* 1986, Bernadette Goodman. *Educ:* Booker Avenue County Primary Sch., Liverpool; Liverpool Inst. High Sch.; Lincoln Coll., Oxford (MA, BCL). Called to the Bar, Lincoln's Inn, 1973; Mem., Northern Circuit, 1973. *Recreations:* travel, Association football. *Address:* 25 Byrom Street, Manchester M3 4PF. *T:* 0161–834 5238. *Clubs:* Athenæum (Liverpool); Liverpool Cricket.

KING, Prof. Ursula, PhD; Professor and Head of Department of Theology and Religious Studies, University of Bristol, since 1989; *b* 2 Sept. 1938; *d* of Hedwig and Adolf Brenke; *m* 1963, Prof. Anthony Douglas King; four *d*. *Educ:* Univs of Bonn, Munich, Paris (STL), Delhi (MA) and London (PhD). Lectr in Divinity, Coloma Coll. of Educn, 1963–65; Visiting Lecturer, 1965–70: Dept of Philosophy, Univ. of Delhi; Indian Inst. of Technology; Indian Social Inst.; Lectr and Sen. Lectr, Dept of Theology and Religious Studies, Univ. of Leeds, 1971–89; S. A. Cook Bye-Fellow, Newnham Coll. and Gonville and Caius Coll., Cambridge, 1976–77. FRSA. Student awards from Germany and France;

Indian Philosophical Congress Gold Medal, 1969. *Publications:* Towards a New Mysticism, 1980; The Spirit of One Earth, 1989; Women and Spirituality, 1989; (ed) Turning Points in Religious Studies, 1990; (ed) Feminist Theology from the Third World, 1994; (ed) Religion and Gender, 1995; contribs to acad. jls. *Recreations:* walking, reading, travelling. *Address:* Department of Theology and Religious Studies, University of Bristol, Bristol BS8 1PL. *T:* Bristol (0117) 928 7760.

KING, Air Vice-Marshal Walter MacIan, CB 1961; CBE 1957; retired, 1967; *b* 10 March 1910; *s* of Alexander King, MB, ChB, DPH, and Hughberta Blannin King (*née* Pearson); *m* 1946, Anne Clare Hicks (*d* 1991); two *s*. *Educ:* St Mary's Coll., Castries, St Lucia, BWI; Blundell's Sch., Tiverton, Devon. Aircraft Engineering (Messers Westland Aircraft Ltd, Handley-Page Ltd, Saunders-Roe Ltd), 1927–33; joined Royal Air Force, 1934; Overseas Service: No 8 Sqdn, Aden, 1935–37; South-east Asia, 1945–47; Middle East (Egypt and Cyprus), 1955–57. Student: RAF Staff Coll., 1944; Joint Services Staff Coll., 1947; IDC, 1954. Senior Air Staff Officer, RAF Maintenance Command, 1964–67. Joined Hooker Craigmyle & Co. Ltd, 1967; Gen. Manager, Hooker Craigmyle (Scotland) Ltd, 1969–72; Dir, Craigmyle & Co. (Scotland) Ltd, 1972–76. *Recreations:* gardening, making small models. *Address:* 24 Arthur's Avenue, Harrogate HG2 0DX.

KING, Sir Wayne Alexander, 8th Bt *cr* 1815; self-employed entrepreneur; *b* 2 Feb. 1962; *s* of Sir Peter Alexander King, 7th Bt, and of Jean Margaret (who *m* 2nd, 1978, Rev. Richard Graham Mackenzie), *d* of Christopher Thomas Cavell, Deal; *S* father, 1973; *m* 1984, Laura Ellen, *d* of Donald James Lea, Almonte, Ontario; one *s*. *Educ:* Sir Roger Manwood's Sch., Sandwich, Kent; Algonquin Coll., Ottawa, Ont (majored in Accounting and Retail Management). Coach and Head Referee, Almonte Soccer (Canadian Soccer Assoc. Coaching Level I designation); Referee-in-chief, Almonte/Pakenham Minor Ice Hockey Assoc. *Recreations:* all sports. *Heir:* *s* Peter Richard Donald King, *b* 4 May 1988. *Address:* 146 High Street, Almonte, Ont K0A 1A0, Canada.

KING-HAMILTON, His Honour (Myer) Alan (Barry), QC 1954; an additional Judge of the Central Criminal Court, 1964–79; a Deputy Circuit Judge, 1979–83; *b* 9 Dec. 1904; *o s* of Alfred King-Hamilton; *m* 1935, Rosalind Irene Ellis (*d* 1991); two *d*. *Educ:* Bishop's Stortford Grammar Sch.; Trinity Hall, Cambridge (BA 1927, MA 1929; Pres. Cambridge Union Soc., 1927). Called to Bar, Middle Temple, 1929; served War of 1939–45, RAF, finishing with rank of Squadron Leader; served on Finchley Borough Council, 1938–39 and 1945–50. Recorder of Hereford, 1955–56; Recorder of Gloucester, 1956–61; Recorder of Wolverhampton, 1961–64; Dep. Chm. Oxford County Quarter Sessions, 1955–64, 1966–71; Leader of Oxford Circuit, 1961–64. Elected Bencher, Middle Temple, 1961. Elected to General Council of Bar, 1958. President: West London Reform Synagogue, 1967–75, 1977–83 (Hon. Life Pres.); Westlon Housing Assoc., 1975–95 (Hon. Life Pres.); Vice-Pres., World Congress of Faiths, 1967–. Legal Member: Med. Practices Cttee, Min. of Health, 1961–64; ABTA Appeal Bd, 1980–95; Member: Cttee, Birnbeck Housing Assoc., 1982–95; Arts and Library Cttee, MCC, 1985–89; Chm., Pornography and Violence Res. Trust (formerly Mary Whitehouse Res. and Educn Trust), 1986–. Trustee, Barnet Community Trust, 1986–89. Freeman of City of London, Master, Needlemakers Co., 1969. *Publication:* And Nothing But the Truth (autobiog.), 1982. *Recreations:* cricket, gardening, the theatre. *Clubs:* Royal Air Force, MCC.

KING-HELE, Desmond George, FRS 1966; author; Deputy Chief Scientific Officer, Space Department, Royal Aircraft Establishment, Farnborough, 1968–88, retired; *b* 3 Nov. 1927; *s* of late S. G. and of B. King-Hele, Seaford, Sussex; *m* 1954, Marie Thérèse Newman (separated 1992); two *d*. *Educ:* Epsom Coll.; Trinity Coll., Cambridge. BA (1st cl. hons Mathematics) 1948; MA 1952. At RAE, Farnborough, 1948–88, working on space research from 1955. Mem., International Academy of Astronautics, 1961. Chairman: Satellite Optical Tracking Cttee, Royal Soc., 1972–95; History of Science Grants Cttee, Royal Soc., 1990–93; British Nat. Cttee for History of Science, Medicine and Technol., 1985–89. Lectures: Symons, RMetS, 1961; Duke of Edinburgh's, Royal Inst. of Navigation, 1964; Jeffreys, RAS, 1971; Halley, Oxford, 1974; Bakerian, Royal Soc., 1974; Sydenham, Soc. of Apothecaries, 1981; H. L. Welsh, Univ. of Toronto, 1982; Milne, Oxford, 1984. FIMA; FRAS. Hon. DSc Aston, 1979; DUniv Surrey, 1986. Eddington Medal, RAS, 1971; Charles Chree Medal, Inst. of Physics, 1971; Lagrange Prize, Acad. Royale de Belgique, 1972; Nordberg Medal, Internat. Cttee on Space Res., 1990. Editor, Notes and Records of Royal Soc., 1989–. *Publications:* Shelley: His Thought and Work, 1960, 3rd edn 1984; Satellites and Scientific Research, 1960; Erasmus Darwin, 1963; Theory of Satellite Orbits in an Atmosphere, 1964; (ed) Space Research V, 1965; Observing Earth Satellites, 1966, 2nd edn 1983; (ed) Essential Writings of Erasmus Darwin, 1968; The End of the Twentieth Century?, 1970; Poems and Trixies, 1972; Doctor of Revolution, 1977; (ed) The Letters of Erasmus Darwin, 1981; (ed) The RAE Table of Earth Satellites, 1981, 4th edn 1990; Animal Spirits, 1983; Erasmus Darwin and the Romantic Poets, 1986; Satellite Orbits in an Atmosphere: theory and applications, 1987; A Tapestry of Orbits, 1992; (ed) John Herschel, 1992; (ed) A Concordance to the Botanic Garden, 1994; *radio drama scripts:* A Mind of Universal Sympathy, 1973; The Lunaticks, 1978; 250 papers in Proc. Royal Society, Nature, Keats-Shelley Memor. Bull., New Scientist, Planetary and Space Science, and other scientific and literary jls. *Recreations:* tennis, reading, cross-country running. *Address:* 7 Hilltops Court, 65 North Lane, Buriton, Hants GU31 5RS. *T:* Petersfield (01730) 261646.

KING MURRAY, Ronald; *see* Murray.

KING-REYNOLDS, Guy Edwin; Head Master, Dauntsey's School, West Lavington, 1969–85; *b* 9 July 1923; *er s* of late Dr H. E. King Reynolds, York; *m* 1st, 1947, Norma Lansdowne Russell (*d* 1949); 2nd, 1950, Jeanne Nancy Perris Rhodes; one *d*. *Educ:* St Peter's Sch., York; Emmanuel Coll., Cambridge (1944–47). Served RAF, 1942–44. BA 1946, MA 1951. Asst Master, Glenhow Prep. Sch., 1947–48; Head of Geography Dept, Solihull Sch., Warwickshire, 1948–54; family business, 1954–55; Head of Geography, Portsmouth Grammar Sch., 1955–57; Solihull School: Housemaster, 1957–63, Second Master, 1963–69. Part-time Lecturer in International Affairs, Extra-Mural Dept, Birmingham Univ.; Chm., Solihull WEA. Mem., BBC Regl Adv. Council, 1970–73. LRAM (speech and drama) 1968. Governor: St Peter's Sch., York, 1984–; Dean Close Sch., Cheltenham, 1985–94 (Vice Pres., 1994); La Retraite, Salisbury, 1985–88. Mem. Cttee, GBA, 1986–89, 1990–. JP: Solihull, 1965–69; Wiltshire, 1970–91 (Chm., 1982–85, Vice-Chm., 1985–91, Devizes Bench); Avon (Bath), 1991–93. Freeman, City of London, 1988. *Recreations:* drama (director and actor); travel. *Address:* 14 Pulteney Mews, Great Pulteney Street, Bath, Avon BA2 4DS.

KING-TENISON, family name of **Earl of Kingston.**

KINGDON, Roger Taylor, CBE 1990; FIMechE, FIM; Chief Executive, Davy Corporation, 1987–90; *b* 27 June 1930; *s* of late Fletcher Munroe Kingdon and Laetitia May Kingdon (*née* Wissler); *m* 1956, Gaynor Mary Downs; two *s* one *d*. *Educ:* Christ's Hospital; Pembroke College, Cambridge (MA). CEng. Graduate trainee, Woodall Duckham Construction Co., 1954–58; Ashmore Benson Pease & Co., 1958–68 (Dir, 1964–68); Managing Director: Newell Dunford Group, 1968–80; Herbert Morris (Davy Group), 1980–83; Chm., Davy McKee (Stockton), 1983–87; Director: Dunford & Elliot, 1971–80; Peugeot Talbot Motor Co., 1979–92; Davy Corp., 1986–90; Teesside Develt Corp., 1987–; Hopkinson Group, 1992–. President: Process Plant Assoc., 1979–80; NE Engineering Employers' Assoc., 1986–89; Chairman: British Metallurgical Plant Constructors' Assoc., 1985–87; Latin American Trade Adv. Group, 1989–90. Vice Chm., South Tees Acute NHS Trust, 1992–. CIMgt. *Recreations:* fell walking, tennis, sailing. *Address:* West End Farm, The Green, Borrowby, Thirsk, North Yorks Y07 4QL. *T:* Thirsk (01845) 537663. *Club:* Army and Navy.

KINGHORN, Squadron Leader Ernest; *b* 1 Nov. 1907; *s* of A. Kinghorn, Leeds; *m* 1942, Eileen Mary Lambert Russell (*d* 1980); one *s* (and one *s* one *d* decd). *Educ:* Leeds, Basel and Lille Universities. Languages Master Ashville Coll., Doncaster Grammar Sch. and Roundhay Sch., Leeds. Served in Intelligence Branch, RAF. British Officer for Control of Manpower, SHAEF, and Staff Officer CCG. MP (Lab) Yarmouth Division of Norfolk, 1950–51, Great Yarmouth, 1945–50. *Address:* 59 Queens Avenue, Hanworth, Middx TW13 7NT.

KINGHORN, William Oliver; Chief Agricultural Officer, Department of Agriculture and Fisheries for Scotland, 1971–75; *b* 17 May 1913; *s* of Thomas Kinghorn, Duns, and Elizabeth Oliver; *m* 1943, Edith Johnstone; one *s* two *d*. *Educ:* Berwickshire High Sch.; Edinburgh Univ. BSc (Agr) Hons, BSc Hons. Senior Inspector, 1946; Technical Develt Officer, 1959; Chief Inspector, 1970. SBStJ. *Publication:* contrib. Annals of Applied Biology, 1936. *Address:* 23 Cumlodden Avenue, Edinburgh EH12 6DR. *T:* 0131–337 1435.

KINGMAN, Sir John (Frank Charles), Kt 1985; FRS 1971; Vice-Chancellor, University of Bristol, since 1985; *b* 28 Aug. 1939; *er s* of late Dr F. E. T. Kingman, FRSC; *m* 1964, Valerie, *d* of late F. Cromwell, OBE, ISO; one *s* one *d*. *Educ:* Christ's Coll., Finchley; Pembroke Coll., Cambridge. MA, ScD Cantab; Smith's Prize, 1962. CStat 1993. Fellow of Pembroke Coll., Cambridge, 1961–65, Hon. Fellow, 1988; Asst Lectr in Mathematics, 1962–64, Lectr, 1964–65, Univ. of Cambridge; Reader in Mathematics and Statistics, 1965–66, Prof. 1966–69, Univ. of Sussex; Prof. of Maths, Univ. of Oxford, 1969–85; Fellow, St Anne's Coll., Oxford, 1978–85, Hon. Fellow, 1985. Visiting appointments: Univ. of Western Australia, 1963, 1974; Stanford Univ., USA, 1968; ANU, 1978. Chairman: Science Bd, SRC, 1979–81; SERC, 1981–85; Vice-Pres., Parly and Scientific Cttee, 1986–89 (Vice-Chm., 1983–86); Mem. Bd, British Council, 1986–91. Chm., Cttee of Inquiry into the Teaching of English Language, 1987–88; Director: IBM UK Holdings Ltd, 1985–; Beecham Group plc, 1986–89; SmithKline Beecham plc, 1989–90; British Technology Group plc, 1992 (Mem. Council, British Technol. Gp, 1984–92). Chm., 1973–76, Vice-Pres., 1976–92, Inst. of Statisticians; President: Royal Statistical Soc., 1987–89 (Vice-Pres., 1977–79, Guy Medal in Silver, 1981); London Math. Soc., 1990–92. Mem., Brighton Co. Borough Council, 1968–71; Chm., Regency Soc. of Brighton and Hove, 1975–81. Hon. Senator, Univ. of Hanover, 1991. Hon. DSc: Sussex, 1983; Southampton, 1985; West of England, 1993; Hon. LLD Bristol, 1989. Royal Medal, Royal Soc., 1983. Officier des Palmes Académiques, 1989. *Publications:* Introduction to Measure and Probability (with S. J. Taylor), 1966; The Algebra of Queues, 1966; Regenerative Phenomena, 1972; Mathematics of Genetic Diversity, 1980; Poisson Processes, 1993; papers in mathematical and statistical jls. *Address:* Senate House, Tyndall Avenue, Bristol BS8 1TH. *Club:* Lansdowne.

KINGS NORTON, Baron *cr* 1965, of Wotton Underwood (Life Peer); **Harold Roxbee Cox,** Kt 1953; PhD, DIC; FEng 1976; FIMechE, Hon. FRAeS; Chairman: Landspeed Ltd, since 1975; Cotswold Research Ltd, since 1978; President: Campden and Chorleywood Food Research Association (formerly Campden Food Preservation Research Association), since 1961; British Balloon Museum and Library, since 1980; Chancellor, Cranfield University (formerly Cranfield Institute of Technology), since 1969; *b* 6 June 1902; *s* of late William John Roxbee Cox, Birmingham, and Amelia Stern; *m* 1st, 1927, Marjorie (*d* 1980), *e d* of late E. E. Withers, Northwood; two *s*; 2nd, 1982, Joan Ruth Pascoe, *d* of late W. G. Pack, Torquay. *Educ:* Kings Norton Grammar Sch.; Imperial Coll. of Science and Technology (Schol.). Engineer on construction of Airship R101, 1924–29; Chief Technical Officer, Royal Airship Works, 1931; Investigations in wing flutter and stability of structures, RAE, 1931–35; Lectr in Aircraft Structures, Imperial Coll., 1932–38; Principal Scientific Officer. Aerodynamics Dept, RAE, 1935–36; Head of Air Defence Dept, RAE, 1936–38; Chief Technical Officer, Air Registration Board, 1938–39; Supt of Scientific Research, RAE, 1939–40; Dep. Dir of Scientific Research, Ministry of Aircraft Production, 1940–43; Dir of Special Projects Ministry of Aircraft Production, 1943–44; Chm. and Man. Dir Power Jets (Research and Development) Ltd, 1944–46; Dir National Gas Turbine Establishment, 1946–48; Chief Scientist, Min. of Fuel and Power, 1948–54. Chairman: Metal Box Co., 1961–67 (Dir, 1957–67, Dep. Chm., 1959–60); Berger Jenson & Nicholson Ltd, 1967–75; Applied Photophysics, 1974–81; Withers Estates, 1976–81; Director: Ricardo & Co. (Engrs) 1927 Ltd, 1965–77; Dowty Rotol, 1968–75; British Printing Corp., 1968–77; Hoechst UK, 1970–75. Chm. Gas Turbine Collaboration Cttee, 1941–44, 1946–48; Mem. Aeronautical Research Council, 1944–48, 1958–60; Chairman: Coun. for Scientific and Industrial Research, 1961–65; Council for National Academic Awards, 1964–71; Air Registration Bd, 1966–72; President: Royal Aeronautical Soc., 1947–49; Royal Instn, 1969–76. Fellow of Imperial Coll. of Science and Technology, 1960; FCGI 1976; Hon. FIFST 1992. Membre Correspondant, Faculté Polytechnique de Mons, 1946–. R38 Memorial Prize, 1928; Busk Memorial Prize, 1934; Wilbur Wright Lecturer, 1940; Wright Brothers Lecturer (USA), 1945; Hawksley Lecturer, 1951; James Clayton Prize, 1952; Thornton Lectr, 1954; Parsons Memorial Lectr, 1955; Handley Page Memorial Lectr, 1969. Freeman, City of London, 1987; Liveryman, GAPAN, 1987. Hon. DSc: Birmingham, 1954; Cranfield Inst. of Technology, 1970; Warwick, 1986; Hon. DTech Brunel, 1966; Hon. LLD CNAA, 1969. Bronze Medal, Univ. of Louvain, 1946; Medal of Freedom with Silver Palm, USA, 1947. *Publications:* numerous papers on theory of structures, wing flutter, gas turbines, civil aviation and airships. *Address:* Westcote House, Chipping Campden, Glos GL55 6AG. *T:* Evesham (01386) 840440. *Club:* Athenæum.

KINGSALE, 35th Baron *cr* 1223 (by some reckonings 30th Baron); **John de Courcy;** Baron Courcy and Baron of Ringrone; Premier Baron of Ireland; President, Impex Consultants Ltd, since 1988; Director: Marquis de Verneuil Trust, since 1971; de Courcy, Daunt Professional & Executive Agencies (Australia), since 1987; Kinsale Development Co., since 1989; Chairman, National Association for Service to the Realm; *b* 27 Jan. 1941; *s* of Lieutenant-Commander the Hon. Michael John Rancé de Courcy, RN (killed on active service, 1940), and Joan (*d* 1967), *d* of Robert Reid; *S* grandfather, 1969. *Educ:* Stowe; Universities of Paris and Salzburg. Short service commission, Irish Guards, 1962–65. At various times before and since: law student, property developer, film extra, white hunter, bingo caller, etc. Patron, L'Orchestre du Monde, 1988–. *Recreations:* shooting, food and drink, palaeontology, venery. *Heir:* *cousin* Nevinson Russell de Courcy [*b* 21 July 1920; *m* 1954, Nora Lydia, *yr d* of James Arnold Plint; one *s* one *d*]. *Address:* 15 Dallimore Mead, Nunney, Frome, Somerset BA11 4NB. *Club:* Cavalry and Guards.

KINGSBOROUGH, Viscount; Robert Charles Henry King-Tenison; *b* 20 March 1969; *s* and *heir* of 11th Earl of Kingston, *qv*.

KINGSBURY, Derek John, CBE 1988; FEng 1991; FIEE; Chairman: Fairey Group plc, since 1987 (Group Chief Executive, 1982–91); David Brown Group plc, since 1992; Goode Durrant plc, since 1992; *b* 10 July 1926; *s* of late Major Arthur Kingsbury, BEM, Virginia Water and Gwendoline Mary Kingsbury; *m* 1st, 1959, Muriel June Drake; one *s* (and one *s* decd); 2nd, 1980, Sarah Muriel Morgan; one *s*. *Educ:* Strode's Secondary Sch., City and Guilds Coll. BScEng Hons; DIC. FIEE 1968, FCGI 1977. 2nd Lieut, REME, 1947–49. Apprentice, Metropolitan Vickers, 1949–51; Exch. Schol., Univ. of Pennsylvania, 1952–53; Associated Electrical Industries: Manager, E Canada, 1954–61; PA to Chm., 1961–63; Gen. Manager, AEI Distribution Transformers, 1963–66; Gen. Manager, Overseas Manufacturing Develt, 1966–69; Thorn Electrical Industries: Man. Dir, Foster Transformers, 1969–76; Man. Dir, Elect. & Hydr. Div., 1972–76, Exec. Dir, 1973–76; Dowty Group: Dep. Chief Exec., 1976–82. Chm., Ultra Electronics, 1977–82; non-executive Director: Vickers, 1981–91; ACAL plc, 1991–94. Institution of Electrical Engineers: Dir Peter Peregrinus, 1976–81; Mem., Finance Cttee, 1978–80; Confederation of British Industry: Mem. Council, 1980–86; Chm., Overseas Cttee, 1980–84; missions to Japan 1981, 1983, 1985; Defence Manufacturers Association: Mem. Council, 1985–92; Chm., 1987–90; Chm., F and GP Cttee, 1990–92; Vice-Pres., 1993–; Member: Review Bd for Govt Contracts, 1986–94; Engineering Council, 1990–93 (Chm., CET Pilot Scheme Steering Cttee, 1988–90); Council, BEAMA, 1973–75. Freeman, City of London, 1994; Liveryman, Scientific Instrument Makers' Co., 1994. CIMgt; FRSA 1994. President: BHF Horse Show, 1977–; Aircraft Golfing Soc., 1995–. *Recreations:* golf, swimming, walking. *Address:* Fairey Group plc, Station Road, Egham, Surrey TW20 9NP. *T:* Egham (01784) 470470. *Clubs:* Royal Automobile, MCC, Lord's Taverners; Beaconsfield Golf, St Enodoc Golf.

KINGSDOWN, Baron *cr* 1993 (Life Peer), of Pemberton in the County of Lancashire; **Robert Leigh-Pemberton, (Robin),** KG 1994; PC 1987; Governor, Bank of England, 1983–93; Lord-Lieutenant of Kent, since 1982 (Vice Lord-Lieutenant, 1972–82); *b* 5 Jan. 1927; *e s* of late Robert Douglas Leigh-Pemberton, MBE, MC, Sittingbourne, Kent; *m* 1953, Rosemary Davina, OBE, *d* of late Lt-Col D. W. A. W. Forbes, MC, and late Dowager Marchioness of Exeter; four *s* (and one *s* decd). *Educ:* St Peter's Court, Broadstairs; Eton; Trinity Coll., Oxford (MA; Hon. Fellow, 1984). Grenadier Guards, 1945–48. Called to Bar, Inner Temple, 1954 (Hon. Bencher, 1983); practised in London and SE Circuit until 1960. National Westminster Bank: Dir, 1972–83; Dep. Chm., 1974; Chm., 1977–83. Director: Birmid Qualcast, 1966–83 (Dep. Chm., 1970; Chm., 1975–77); University Life Assce Soc., 1967–78; Redland Ltd, 1972–83, 1993–; Equitable Life Assce Soc., 1979–83 (Vice-Pres., 1982–83); Glaxo-Wellcome (formerly Glaxo Holdings), 1993–; Foreign and Colonial Investment Trust, 1993–; Hambros, 1993–; Chm., Green Arrow, 1995–. County Councillor (Chm. Council, 1972–75), 1961–77, CA 1965, Kent. Member: SE Econ. Planning Council, 1972–74; Medway Ports Authority, 1974–76; NEDC, 1982–92; Prime Minister's Cttee on Local Govt Rules of Conduct, 1973–74; Cttee of Enquiry into Teachers' Pay, 1974; Cttee on Police Pay, 1977–79. Chm., Cttee of London Clearing Bankers, 1982–83. Trustee: Glyndebourne Arts Trust, 1978–83; RA Trust, 1982–88 (Hon. Trustee Emeritus, 1988–). Pro-Chancellor, Univ. of Kent at Canterbury, 1977–83; Seneschal, Canterbury Cathedral, 1983–. Hon. Colonel: Kent and Sharpshooters Yeomanry Sqn, 1979–92; 265 (Kent and Co. of London Yeo.) Signal Sqn (V), 1979–92; 5th (Volunteer) Bn, The Queen's Regt, 1987–92. Gov., Ditchley Foundn, 1987–. Hon. DCL Kent, 1983; Hon. DLitt: City, 1988; Loughborough, 1990. FRSA 1977; FIMgt (FBIM 1977). JP 1961–75, DL 1970, Kent. KStJ 1983. *Recreation:* country life. *Address:* Torry Hill, Sittingbourne, Kent ME9 0SP; Hambros PLC, 41 Tower Hill, EC3N 4HA. *T:* 0171–865 3955. *Clubs:* Brooks's, Cavalry and Guards.

KINGSHOTT, (Albert) Leonard; Director: International Banking Division, Lloyds Bank Plc, 1985–89; Mutual Management Services, since 1993; Member, Monopolies and Mergers Commission, since 1990; *b* 16 Sept. 1930; *s* of A. L. Kingshott and Mrs K. Kingshott; *m* 1958, Valerie Simpson; two *s* one *d*. *Educ:* London Sch. of Economics (BSc); ACIS 1958, FCIS 1983. Flying Officer, RAF, 1952–55; Economist, British Petroleum, 1955–60; Economist, British Nylon Spinners, 1960–62; Financial Manager, Iraq Petroleum Co., 1963–65; Chief Economist, Ford of Britain, 1965; Treas., Ford of Britain, 1966–67; Treas., Ford of Europe, 1968–70; Finance Dir, Whitbread & Co., 1972; Man. Dir, Finance, BSC, 1972–77; Dir, Lloyds Bank International, responsible for Merchant Banking activities, 1977–80, for European Div., 1980–82, for Marketing and Planning Div., 1983–84; Dep. Chief Exec., Lloyds Bank International, 1985. Exec. Dir, The Private Bank & Trust Co., 1989–91; Director: Bank of London and South America Ltd, 1977–89; Lloyds Bank International, 1977–89; Lloyds Bank (France) Ltd, 1980–89; Lloyd's Bank California, 1985–88; Rosehaugh plc, 1991–92 (Chm.); Shandwick plc, 1993–; Newmarket Foods Ltd, 1994–. Mem. Bd, Crown Agents for Oversea Govts and Admin, and Crown Agents Hldg and Realisation Bd, 1989–92. Associate Mem. of Faculty, 1978, Governor, 1980–91, Ashridge Management Coll. Chm., Oakbridge Counselling, 1990–. FCIS. *Publication:* Investment Appraisal, 1967. *Recreations:* golf, chess. *Address:* 4 Delamas, Beggar Hill, Fryerning, Ingatestone, Essex CM4 0PW. *T:* Ingatestone (01277) 352077.

KINGSHOTT, Air Vice-Marshal Kenneth, CBE 1972; DFC 1953; Royal Air Force, retired 1980; *b* 8 July 1924; *s* of Walter James Kingshott and Eliza Ann Kingshott; *m* 1st, 1948, Dorrie Marie (*née* Dent) (*d* 1978); two *s*; 2nd, 1990, Valerie Rosemary Brigden. Joined RAF, 1943; served: Singapore and Korea, 1950; Aden, 1960; Malta, 1965; MoD, London, 1968; OC RAF Cottesmore, 1971; HQ 2 Allied Tactical Air Force, 1973; HQ Strike Command, 1975; Dep. Chief of Staff Operations and Intelligence, HQ Allied Air Forces Central Europe, 1977–79. *Recreations:* golf, fishing, music. *Address:* Tall Trees, Manor Road, Penn, Bucks HP10 8HY. *Club:* Royal Air Force.

KINGSHOTT, Leonard; *see* Kingshott, A. L.

KINGSLAND, Baron *cr* 1994 (Life Peer), of Shrewsbury in the County of Shropshire; **Christopher James Prout,** Kt 1990; TD 1987; PC 1994; QC 1988; barrister-at-law; *b* 1 Jan. 1942; *s* of late Frank Yabsley Prout, MC and bar, and Doris Lucy Prout (*née* Osborne). *Educ:* Sevenoaks Sch.; Manchester Univ. (BA); The Queen's Coll., Oxford (Scholar; BPhil, DPhil). TA Officer (Major): OU OTC, 1966–74; 16/5 The Queen's Royal Lancers, 1974–82; 3rd Armoured Div., 1982–88; RARO, 1988–. Called to the Bar, Middle Temple, 1972. English-Speaking Union Fellow, Columbia Univ., NYC, 1963–64; Staff Mem., IBRD (UN), Washington DC, 1966–69; Leverhulme Fellow and Lectr in Law, Sussex Univ., 1969–79. MEP (C) Shropshire and Stafford, 1979–94; contested (C) Herefordshire and Shropshire, Eur. parly elecns, 1994. Leader, British Cons. MEPs, 1987–94; Dep. Whip, 1979–82, Chief Whip, 1983–87, Chairman and Leader, 1987–92, EDG; Vice Chm., Eur. People's Party Parly Gp, 1992–94; Chm., Parlt Cttee on Legal Affairs, 1987. Rapporteur, Revision of Europ. Parlt's Rules of Procedure, 1987 and 1993. Pres., Shropshire and W Midlands Agricl Show, 1993. Master, Shrewsbury Drapers' Co., 1995. Grande Médaille de la Ville de Paris, 1988; Schuman Medal, 1995. *Publications:* Market Socialism in Yugoslavia, 1985; (contrib.) vols 51 and 52, Halsbury's Laws of England, 1986; various lectures, pamphlets, chapters and articles. *Recreations:* riding, sailing, gardening. *Address:* c/o House of Lords, SW1A 0PW. *Clubs:* Pratt's, Beefsteak, Royal Ocean Racing; Royal Yacht Squadron.

KINGSLAND, Sir Richard, Kt 1978; AO 1989; CBE 1967; DFC 1940; idc; psa; Chairman, ACT Health Promotion Fund, 1990–94; *b* Moree, NSW, 19 Oct. 1916; *m* 1943, Kathleen Jewel, *d* of late R. B. Adams; one *s* two *d*. *Educ:* Sydney High Sch., NSW. Served War: No 10 Sqdn, Eng., 1939–41; commanded: No 11 Sqdn, New Guinea, 1941–42; RAAF Stn, Rathmines, NSW, 1942–43; Gp Captain 1943; Dir, Intell., RAAF, 1944–45. Director: Trng, 1946; Org. RAAF HQ, 1946–48; Manager, Sydney Airport, 1948–49; Airline Pilot, 1949–50; SA Reg. 1950–51, NT Reg. 1951–52, Dept of Civil Aviation; Chief Admin. Asst to CAS, RAAF, 1952–53; IDC 1955. Asst Sec., Dept of Air, Melb., 1954–58; First Asst Sec., Dept of Defence, 1958–63; Secretary: Dept of Interior, 1963–70; Dept of Repatriation, 1970–74; Repatriation and Compensation, 1974–76; Dept of Veterans' Affairs, Canberra, 1976–81. Chairman: Repatriation Commn, 1970–81; ACT Arts Develt Bd (first Chm.), 1981–83; Commonwealth Films Bd of Review, 1982–86; Uranium Adv. Council, 1982–84. Member-at-Large, Nat. Heart Foundn, 1990– (Hon. Nat. Sec., 1976–90). A Dir, Arts Council of Aust., 1970–72; first Chairman Council: Canberra Sch. of Music, 1970–74; Canberra Sch. of Art, 1976–83; Mem. Original Council, Australian Conservation Foundn, 1967–69; Member: Canberra Theatre Trust, 1965–75; Aust. Opera Nat. Council, 1983–; Canberra Festival Cttee, 1988–92; Mem. Bd of Trustees, Aust. War Meml, Canberra, 1966–76; a Dir, Aust. Bicentennial Authority, 1983–89. Pres., Bd of Management, Goodwin Retirement Villages, 1984–88. Vice Pres., Australia Day in the National Capital Cttee, 1987–91. *Recreations:* reading, writing. *Address:* 36 Vasey Crescent, Campbell, ACT 2601, Australia. *Clubs:* Commonwealth, National Press (Canberra).

KINGSLEY, Ben; actor; *b* 31 Dec. 1943; *s* of Rahimtulla Harji Bhanji and Anna Leina Mary Bhanji; *m*; three *s* one *d*. *Educ:* Manchester Grammar Sch. Associate artist, Royal Shakespeare Co.; work with RSC includes, 1970–80; 1985–86: Peter Brook's Midsummer Night's Dream, Stratford, London, Broadway, NY; Gramsci in Occupations; Ariel in The Tempest; title role, Hamlet; Ford in Merry Wives of Windsor; title role, Baal; Squeers and Mr Wagstaff in Nicholas Nickleby; title rôle, Othello, Melons; National Theatre, 1977–78: Mosca in Volponë; Trofimov in The Cherry Orchard; Sparkish in The Country Wife; Vukhov in Judgement; additional theatre work includes: Johnny in Hello and Goodbye (Fugard), King's Head, 1973; Errol Philander in Statements After An Arrest (Fugard), Royal Court, 1974; Edmund Kean, Harrogate, 1981, Haymarket, 1983 (also televised); title role, Dr Faustus, Manchester Royal Exchange, 1981; *television* 1974–, includes The Love School (series), 1974; Silas Marner (film), 1985, Murderers Amongst Us (mini-series), 1989, and several plays; *films:* title role, Gandhi, 1980 (2 Hollywood Golden Globe awards, 1982; NY Film Critics' Award, 2 BAFTA awards, Oscar, LA Film Critics Award, 1983, Variety Club of GB Best Film Actor award, 1983); Betrayal, 1982; Turtle Diary, 1985; Harem, 1986; Testimony, 1987; Maurice, 1987; Pascali's Island, The Train, 1988; Without a Clue, 1989; Bugsy, 1992; Sneakers, 1992; Dave, 1992; Schindler's List, 1993; Innocent Moves, 1994; Death and the Maiden, 1995; Species, 1995. Best Film Actor, London Standard Award, 1983; Medici Soc. Award, 1989; Simon Wiesenthal Humanitarian Award, 1989; Berlin Golden Camera Award, 1990. Hon. MA Salford, 1984. Padma Shri (India), 1984. *Address:* c/o ICM Ltd, 76 Oxford Street, W1R 1RB.

KINGSLEY, David John; consultant in management, marketing and communications, since 1975; Director: Kirloskar Multimedia (India), since 1992; Francis Kyle Gallery Ltd, since 1978; Integrated Communication Projects, since 1995; *b* 10 July 1929; *s* of Walter John Kingsley and Margery Kingsley; *m* 1st, 1954, Enid Sophia Jones; two *d*; 2nd, 1968, Gillian Leech; two *s*; 3rd, 1988, Gisela Reichardt. *Educ:* Southend High Sch.; London School of Economics (BScEcon; Hon. Fellow, 1992). Pres., Students' Union, LSE, 1952; Vice-Pres., Nat. Union of Students, 1953. Served RAF, Personnel Selection, commnd 1948. Prospective Parly Candidate (Lab) E Grinstead, 1952–54; founded Kingsley, Manton and Palmer, advertising agency, 1964; Publicity Advisor to Labour Party and Govt, 1962–70; Publicity and Election advisor to President of Republic of Zambia, 1974–82; Election and Broadcasting advisor to Govt of Mauritius, 1976–81; Publicity advisor to SDP, 1981–87. Mem. Boards, CNAA, 1970–82; Mem., Central Religious Adv. Cttee for BBC and IBA, 1974–82; Governor, LSE, 1966–. Pres., Worldaware, 1992–; Director: World Forum (1995), 1994–; Bristol 2000; Chairman: Inter-Action Trust, 1981–90; Deisgn and Industries Assoc., 1994–. Trustee, Royal Philharmonic Orch., 1993– (Vice-Chm., 1972–77); Dir, Wren Orch., 1990–. Mem., Develt Cttee, RCM, 1985–; Chm., Schumacher Coll. Foundn, 1991–; Chm., LSE Ext. Affairs Cttee, 1995–; Trustee, British American Arts Assoc., 1980–; Chm., Cartoon Arts Trust, 1994–. FIPA; FRSA; MCSD. Hon. RCM. Hon. Fellow, Soka Univ., Tokyo, 1990. *Publications:* Albion in China, 1979; contribs to learned jls; various articles. *Recreations:* politics, creating happy national events, music, travel, art and any books. *Address:* 81 Mortimer Road, N1 5AR. *Club:* Reform.

KINGSLEY, Sir Patrick (Graham Toler), KCVO 1962 (CVO 1950); Secretary and Keeper of the Records of the Duchy of Cornwall, 1954–72 (Assistant Secretary, 1930–54); *b* 1908; *s* of late Gerald Kingsley; *m* 1947, Priscilla Rosemary, *o d* of late Capt. Archibald A. Lovett Cameron, RN; three *s* one *d*. *Educ:* Winchester; New Coll., Oxford. OUCC 1928–30 (Capt. 1930), OUAFC 1927 and 1929. Served War of 1939–45 with Queen's Royal Regt. *Address:* West Hill Farm, West Knoyle, Warminster, Wilts BA12 6AL.

KINGSLEY, Roger James, OBE 1992; FEng, FIChemE; Chairman: LMK Engineering; UMIST Ventures Ltd; CAPCIS Ltd; Freeman Process Systems Ltd; Director, Kingsley Process & Management; *b* 2 Feb. 1922; *s* of Felix and Helene Loewenstein; changed name to Kingsley, 1942; *m* 1949, Valerie Marguerite Mary (*née* Hanna); one *s* two *d*. *Educ:* Manchester Grammar Sch.; Faculty of Technol., Manchester Univ. (BScTech); Harvard Business Sch. (Internat. Sen. Managers Program). Served War, Royal Fusiliers, 1940–46; Commando service, 1942–45; Captain; mentioned in despatches, 1946. Chemical Engr, Petrocarbon Ltd, 1949–51; technical appts, ultimately Tech. Dir, Lankro Chemicals Ltd, 1952–62; gen. management appts, Lankro Chemicals Group Ltd, 1962–77; Man. Dir, Lankro Chemicals Group Ltd, 1972–77; Director: ICI-Lankro Plasticisers Ltd, 1972–77; Fallek-Lankro Corp., Tuscaloosa, Ala, 1976–77. Dep. Chm., Diamond Shamrock Europe, 1977–82; Chm., Duolite Internat., 1978–84. Pres., IChemE, 1974–75. Member: Court of Governors, UMIST, 1969–79, 1985–. *Publications:* contrib. Chem. Engr, and Proc. IMechE. *Recreations:* skiing, riding, music. *Address:* Fallows End, Wicker Lane, Hale Barns, Cheshire WA15 0HQ. *T:* 0161–980 6253. *Club:* Royal Anglo-Belgian.

KINGSMILL, Denise Patricia Byrne; with Denton Hall, since 1994; Chairman, Optimum Health Services NHS Trust, since 1991; *b* 24 April 1947; *d* of Patrick Henry Byrne and Hester Jean Byrne; *m* 1970, David Gordon Kingsmill; one *s* one *d*. *Educ:* Girton Coll., Cambridge. Admitted Solicitor, 1980. With ICI Fibres, then Internat. Wool Secretariat, 1968–75; Robin Thompson & Partners, 1979–82; Russell Jones and Walker, 1982–85; Denise Kingsmill & Co., 1985–90; Partner, D. J. Freeman, 1990–93. *Recreation:* working out. *Address:* c/o Denton Hall, 5 Chancery Lane, EC4A 1BU. *Club:* Riverside Racquet.

KINGSTON, 11th Earl of, *cr* 1768; **Barclay Robert Edwin King-Tenison,** Bt 1682; Baron Kingston, 1764; Viscount Kingsborough, 1766; Baron Erris, 1800; Viscount Lorton, 1806; formerly Lieutenant, Royal Scots Greys; *b* 23 Sept. 1943; *o s* of 10th Earl of Kingston and Gwyneth, *d* of William Howard Evans (who *m* 1951, Brig. E. M. Tyler, DSO, MC, late RA; she *m* 1963, Robert Woodford); *S* father 1948; *m* 1st, 1965, Patricia Mary (marr. diss. 1974), *o d* of E. C. Killip, Llanfairfechan, N Wales; one *s* one *d*; 2nd, 1974, Victoria (marr. diss. 1979), *d* of D. C. Edmonds; 3rd, 1990, Corleen Jennifer Rathbone. *Educ:* Winchester. *Heir: s* Viscount Kingsborough, *qv*.

KINGSTON (Ontario), Archbishop of, (RC), since 1982; **Most Rev. Francis John Spence;** *b* Perth, Ont., 3 June 1926; *s* of William John Spence and Rose Anna Spence (*née* Jordan). *Educ:* St Michael's Coll., Toronto (BA 1946); St Augustine's Seminary, Toronto; St Thomas Univ., Rome (JCD 1955). Ordained priest, 1950; Bishop, 1967; Auxiliary to Mil. Vicar, Canadian Forces, 1967–82; Bishop of Charlottetown, PEI, 1970–82; Mil. Vicar, 1982–88. *Address:* 390 Palace Road, Kingston, Ont K7L 4T3, Canada.

KINGSTON, (William) Martin; QC 1992; a Recorder, since 1991; *b* 9 July 1949; *s* of William Robin Kingston and Iris Edith Kingston; *m* 1972, Jill Mary Bache; one *s* two *d*. *Educ:* Middlewich Secondary Modern Sch.; Hartford Coll. of Further Educn; Liverpool Univ. (LLB). Called to the Bar, Middle Temple, 1972; Asst Recorder, 1987. Dep. Chm., Agricl Lands Tribunal, 1985–. Asst Comr, Parly Boundary Commn for England, 1992–. *Recreations:* ski-ing, fishing, sheep, reading, going on holiday. *Address:* (chambers) 5 Fountain Court, Steelhouse Lane, Birmingham B4 6DR; Bevere Green, Bevere, Worcester WR3 7RG; 5 Old Pye Street, SW1P 2LD.

KINGSTON-UPON-THAMES, Area Bishop of, since 1992; **Rt. Rev. (John) Martin Wharton;** *b* 6 Aug. 1944; *s* of John and Marjorie Wharton; *m* 1970, Marlene Olive Duckett; two *s* one *d*. *Educ:* Van Mildert Coll., Durham (BA 1969); Linacre Coll., Oxford (BA 1971; MA 1976); Ripon Hall, Oxford, 1969. Ordained: deacon, 1972, priest, 1973; Assistant Curate: St Peter, Birmingham, 1972–75; St John the Baptist, Croydon, 1975–77; Dir of Pastoral Studies, Ripon Coll., Cuddesdon, 1977–83; Asst Curate, Cuddesdon, 1979–83; Exec. Sec., Bd of Ministry and Training, dio. of Bradford, 1983–91; Bishop's Officer for Ministry and Training, 1992. Hon. Canon, 1984, Residentiary Canon, 1992, Bradford Cathedral. *Recreation:* sport. *Address:* 24 Albert Drive, SW19 6LS. *T:* 0181–789 3218.

KINGTON, Miles Beresford; humorous columnist; *b* 13 May 1941; *s* of William Beresford Nairn Kington and Jean Anne Kington; *m* 1st, 1964, Sarah Paine (marr. diss. 1987); one *s* one *d*; 2nd, 1987, Mrs Hilary Caroline Maynard; one *s*. *Educ:* Trinity College, Glenalmond; Trinity College, Oxford (BAMod Langs). Plunged into free-lance writing, 1963; took up part-time gardening while starving to death, 1964; jazz reviewer, The Times, 1965; joined staff of Punch, 1967, Literary Editor, 1973, left 1980; free-lance, 1980–; regular Let's Parler Franglais column in Punch, 1977–; daily Moreover column in The Times, 1981–86; columnist, The Independent, 1986–; member, musical group Instant Sunshine on double bass; jazz player, 1970–; *television:* various programmes incl. Three Miles High (Great Railway Journeys of the World series), 1980, Steam Days, 1986, and The Burma Road, 1989. Stage play, Waiting for Stoppard, Bristol New Vic, 1995. *Publications:* World of Alphonse Allais, 1977, repr. as A Wolf in Frog's Clothing, 1983; 4 Franglais books, 1979–82; Moreover, 1982; Miles and Miles, 1982; Nature Made Ridiculously Simple, 1983; Moreover, Too . . ., 1985; The Franglais Lieutenant's Woman, 1986; Welcome to Kington, 1989; Steaming Through Britain, 1990; (ed) Jazz: an anthology, 1992. *Recreations:* mending punctures, rehabilitating Clementi's piano works, falsifying personal records to mystify potential biographers. *Address:* Lower Hayze, Limpley Stoke, Bath BA3 6HR. *T:* Bath (01225) 722262. *Clubs:* 100, Ronnie Scott's.

KINKEAD-WEEKES, Prof. Mark, FBA 1992; Professor of English and American Literature, University of Kent at Canterbury, 1974–84, now Professor Emeritus; *b* 26 April 1931; *s* of Lt-Col Alfred Bernard Kinkead-Weekes, MC and Vida May Kinkead-Weekes; *m* 1959, Margaret Joan Irvine; two *s*. *Educ:* Potchefstroom Boys' High Sch.; Univ. of Cape Town (BA), Brasenose Coll., Oxford (BA, MA). University of Edinburgh. Asst Lectr in English, 1956–58; Lectr, 1958–65; University of Kent at Canterbury: Lectr, 1965–66; Sen. Lectr, 1966–74; Pro-Vice-Chancellor, 1974–77. Rhodes Scholarship (Cape Province), 1951. *Publications:* William Golding, a Critical Study (with Ian Gregor), 1967, 2nd edn 1984; Samuel Richardson: dramatic novelist, 1973; (ed) D. H. Lawrence: The Rainbow, 1989; articles, mainly on fiction. *Recreations:* walking, sometimes after golf balls; music, travel. *Address:* 5 Albion Place, Ramsgate, Kent CT11 8HQ. *T:* Thanet (01843) 593168.

KINKEL, Klaus; Minister of Foreign Affairs, Germany, since 1992; *b* 17 Dec. 1936; *m* 1961, Ursula Vogel; one *s* three *d*. *Educ:* Bonn, Cologne and Tubingen univs. LLD. State Sec., Ministry of Justice, 1982–83, and 1987–91; Head of External Intelligence Service, 1983–87; Minister of Justice, 1991–92. Leader, FDP, 1993–95. *Address:* Ministry of Foreign Affairs, Adenauerallee 99-103, 53113 Bonn, Germany.

KINLOCH, Sir David, 13th Bt *cr* 1686, of Gilmerton; *b* 5 Aug. 1951; *s* of Sir Alexander Davenport Kinloch, 12th Bt and of Anna, *d* of late Thomas Walker, Edinburgh; *S* father, 1982; *m* 1st, 1976, Susan Middlewood (marr. diss. 1986); one *s* one *d*; 2nd, 1987, Maureen Carswell; two *s*. *Educ:* Gordonstoun. Career in research into, and recovery and replacement of underground services. *Recreation:* treasure hunting. *Heir: s* Alexander Kinloch, *b* 31 May 1978. *Address:* Gilmerton House, North Berwick, East Lothian EH39 5LQ. *T:* Athelstaneford (0162088) 207.

KINLOCH, Sir David Oliphant, 5th Bt *cr* 1873, of Kinloch, co. Perth; CA; Director, Caledonia Investments PLC, since 1988; *b* 15 Jan. 1942; *s* of Sir John Kinloch, 4th Bt and of Doris Ellaline, *e d* of C. J. Head; *S* father, 1992; *m* 1st, 1968, Susan Minette Urquhart (marr. diss. 1979), *y d* of Maj.-Gen. R. E. Urquhart, CB, DSO; three *d*; 2nd, 1983, Sabine Irene, *o d* of Philippe de Loës; one *s* one *d*. *Educ:* Charterhouse. *Heir: s* Alexander Peter Kinloch, *b* 30 June 1986. *Address:* House of Aldie, Kinross KY13 7QH; 29 Walpole Street, SW3 4QS. *Clubs:* Boodle's; Hong Kong (Hong Kong).

KINLOCH, Henry, (Harry); Chairman: Quartermaine & Co., since 1989; BDL Systems Ltd, since 1995; Speyside Glenlivet Water Co. Ltd, since 1995; Helm Investments Ltd, since 1995; *b* 7 June 1937; *s* of William Shearer Kinloch and Alexina Alice Quartermaine Kinloch; *m* 1st, 1966, Gillian Anne Ashley (marr. diss. 1979); one *s* one *d*; 2nd, 1987, Catherine Elizabeth Hossack. *Educ:* Queen's Park Sch., Glasgow; Univs of Strathclyde, Birmingham and Glasgow. MSc, PhD, ARCST, CEng, FIMechE. Lecturer in Engineering: Univ. of Strathclyde, 1962–65; Univ. of Liverpool, 1966; Vis. Associate Prof. of Engrg, MIT, 1967; Sen. Design Engr, CEGB, 1968–70; PA Management Consultants, 1970–73; Chief Exec., Antony Gibbs (PFP) Ltd, 1973–74; Chm. and Chief Exec., Antony Gibbs Financial Services Ltd, 1975–77; Man. Dir, British Shipbuilders, 1978–80; Dep. Man. Dir and Chief Exec., Liberty Life Assce Co., 1980–83; Chm. and Chief Exec., Ætna Internat. (UK), 1984–89. Dir, Slade & Kempton, 1990–. *Publications:* many publications on theoretical and applied mechanics, financial and business studies. *Recreations:* piano music, opera, political biography, ostling. *Address:* Slade & Kempton Ltd, 1 Benjamin Street, EC1M 5QN. *Club:* Athenæum.

KINLOSS, Lady (12th in line, of the Lordship *cr* 1602); **Beatrice Mary Grenville Freeman-Grenville** (surname changed by Lord Lyon King of Arms, 1950); *b* 1922; *e d* of late Rev. Hon. Luis Chandos Francis Temple Morgan-Grenville, Master of Kinloss; *S* grandmother, 1944; *m* 1950, Dr Greville Stewart Parker Freeman-Grenville, FSA, FRAS (name changed from Freeman by Lord Lyon King of Arms, 1950), Capt. late Royal Berks Regt, *er s* of late Rev. E. C. Freeman; one *s* two *d*. Cross-bencher; Mem., EC Sub-Cttee C (Social and Consumer Affairs); has served on numerous select cttees. *Heir: s* Master of Kinloss, *qv*. *Address:* North View House, Sheriff Hutton, York YO6 1PT. *T:* Sheriff Hutton (01347) 878447. *Club:* Civil Service.

KINLOSS, Master of; Hon. Bevil David Stewart Chandos Freeman-Grenville; *b* 20 June 1953; *s* of Dr Greville Stewart Parker Freeman-Grenville, FSA, Capt. late Royal Berks Regt, and of Lady Kinloss, *qv*. *Educ:* Redrice Sch. *Address:* North View House, Sheriff Hutton, York YO6 1PT.

KINNAIRD, family name of **Lord Kinnaird.**

KINNAIRD, 13th Lord *cr* 1682, of Inchture; **Graham Charles Kinnaird;** Baron Kinnaird of Rossie (UK), 1860; Flying Officer RAFVR; *b* 15 Sept. 1912; *e s* of 12th Lord Kinnaird, KT, KBE, and Frances Victoria (*d* 1960), *y d* of late T. H. Clifton, Lytham Hall, Lancs; *S* father, 1972; *m* 1st, 1938, Nadia (who obtained a decree of divorce, 1940), *o c* of H. A. Fortington, OBE, Isle of Jethou, Channel Islands; 2nd, 1940, Diana, *yr d* of R. S. Copeman, Roydon Hall, Diss, Norfolk; four *d* (one *s* decd). *Educ:* Eton. Demobilised RAF, 1945. *Address:* The Garden House, Rossie Estate, Inchture, Perthshire; Durham House, Durham Place, SW3 4ET. *Clubs:* Brooks's, Pratt's.

KINNEAR, Ian Albert Clark, CMG 1974; HM Diplomatic Service, retired; *b* 23 Dec. 1924; *s* of late George Kinnear, CBE and Georgina Lilian (*née* Stephenson), Nairobi; *m* 1966, Rosemary, *d* of Dr K. W. D. Hartley, Cobham; two *d*. *Educ:* Marlborough Coll.; Lincoln Coll., Oxford (MA). HM Forces, 1943–46 (1st E Africa Reconnaissance Regt). Colonial Service (later HMOCS): Malayan Civil Service, 1951–56: District Officer, Bentong, then Alor Gajah, Asst Sec. Econ. Planning Unit; Kenya, 1956–63: Asst Sec., then Sen. Asst Sec., Min. of Commerce and Industry; 1st Sec., CRO, later Commonwealth Office, 1963–66; 1st Sec. (Commercial), British Embassy, Djakarta, 1966–68; 1st Sec. and Head of Chancery, British High Commn, Dar-es-Salaam, 1969–71; Chief Sec., later Dep. Governor, Bermuda, 1971–74; Senior British Trade Comr, Hong Kong, 1974–77; Consul-Gen., San Francisco, 1977–82. *Recreation:* painting. *Address:* Castle Hill Cottages, Castle Hill, Brenchley, Tonbridge, Kent TN12 7BS. *T:* Brenchley (01892) 723782.

KINNEAR, Nigel Alexander, FRCSI; Surgeon to Federated Dublin Voluntary Hospitals until 1974, retired; *b* 3 April 1907; *s* of James and Margaret Kinnear; *m* 1947, Frances Gardner; one *d*. *Educ:* Mill Hill Sch.; Trinity Coll., Dublin (MA, MB). Surgeon to Adelaide Hosp., Dublin, 1936; Regius Prof. of Surgery, TCD, 1967–72. President: RCSI, 1961; Royal Academy of Medicine of Ireland, 1968 (Hon. Fellow, 1983); James IV Surgical Assoc. Hon. FRCSGlas. *Publications:* articles in surgical jls. *Recreations:* salmon fishing, gardening. *Address:* Summerseat Cottage, Clonee, Co. Meath. *T:* Dunboyne 8255353. *Club:* Kildare Street and University (Dublin).

KINNELL, Ian; QC 1987; professional arbitrator; part-time Chairman, Immigration Appeal Tribunal, since 1991; *b* 23 May 1943; *o s* of Brian Kinnell and Grace Madeline Kinnell; *m* 1970, Elizabeth Jane Ritchie; one *s* one *d*. *Educ:* Sevenoaks Sch., Kent. Called to the Bar, Gray's Inn, 1967. A Recorder, 1987–89; Immigration Appeal Adjudicator, 1990–91. Mem., London Maritime Arbitrator's Assoc., 1991–. *Recreations:* horticulture, equestrian and rural pursuits. *Address:* The Old Rectory, Little Birch, Hereford HR2 8BB. *T:* Golden Valley (01981) 540224, *Fax:* (01981) 540184.

KINNOCK, Glenys Elizabeth; Member (Lab) South Wales East, European Parliament, since 1994; *b* 7 July 1944; *m* 1967, Rt Hon. Neil Kinnock, *qv*; one *s* one *d*. *Educ:* Holyhead Comprehensive Sch.; University College of Wales, Cardiff. Teacher in secondary and primary schools, and special sch., 1966–93. Vice-Pres., Univ. of Wales, Cardiff. 1988–. Chm., One World Action, Board of Unicef UK, 1989–. *Publications:* Eritrea: images of war and peace, 1988; Namibia: birth of a nation, 1990; (ed) Voices for One World, 1988; By Faith and Daring, 1993. *Recreations:* reading, cinema, theatre. *Address:* 1 Bridge View, Cwmfelinfach, Ynysddu, Newport, Gwent NP1 7HG. *T:* Ynysddu (01495) 201201, *Fax:* (01495) 201030.

KINNOCK, Rt. Hon. Neil Gordon; PC 1983; Member, European Commission, since 1995; *b* 28 March 1942; *s* of Gordon Kinnock, labourer, and Mary Kinnock (*née* Howells), nurse; *m* 1967, Glenys Elizabeth Parry (*see* G. E. Kinnock); one *s* one *d*. *Educ:* Lewis Sch., Pengam; University Coll., Cardiff. BA in Industrial Relations and History, UC, Cardiff (Chm. Socialist Soc., 1963–66; Pres. Students' Union, 1965–66; Hon. Fellow, 1982). Tutor Organiser in Industrial and Trade Union Studies, WEA, 1966–70; Mem., Welsh Hosp. Bd, 1969–71. MP (Lab) Bedwellty, 1970–83, Islwyn, 1983–95. PPS to Sec. of State for Employment, 1974–75; Chief Opposition spokesman on educn, 1979–83; Leader of the Labour Party, and Leader of the Opposition, 1983–92. Member: Nat. Exec. Cttee, Labour Party, 1978–94 (Chm., 1987–88); Parly Cttee of PLP, 1979–92. Chm. Internat. Cttee, Labour Party, 1993–94; Vice-Pres., Socialist Internat., 1984–. Director (unpaid): Tribune Publications, 1974–82; 7:84 Theatre Co. (England) Ltd, 1979–83. Hon. Prof., Thames Valley Univ., 1993–. Hon. LLD Wales, 1992. *Publications:* Making Our Way, 1986; Thorns and Roses, 1992; contribs to Tribune, Guardian, New Statesman, etc. *Recreations:* music esp. opera and male choral, Rugby football, theatre, being with family. *Address:* European Commission, Rue de la Loi 200, 1049 Brussels, Belgium.

KINNOULL, 15th Earl of, *cr* 1633; **Arthur William George Patrick Hay;** Viscount Dupplin and Lord Hay, 1627, 1633, 1697; Baron Hay (Great Britain), 1711; *b* 26 March 1935; *o surv. s* of 14th Earl and Mary Ethel Isobel Meyrick (*d* 1938); *S* father 1938; *m* 1961, Gay Ann, *er d* of Sir Denys Lowson, 1st Bt; one *s* three *d*. *Educ:* Eton. Chartered Land Agent, 1960; Mem., Agricultural Valuers' Assoc., 1962. Fellow, Chartered Land Agents' Soc., 1964. Pres., National Council on Inland Transport, 1964–76. Mem. of Queen's Body Guard for Scotland (Royal Company of Archers), 1965. Junior Cons. Whip, House of Lords, 1966–68; Cons. Opposition Spokesman on Aviation, House of Lords, 1968–70. Mem., British Delegn, Council of Europe, 1985–. Chairman: Property Owners' Building Soc., 1976–87 (Dir, 1971–87); Woolwich Homes, 1994–; Dir, Woolwich Equitable Building Soc., 1987–. Mem., Air League Council, 1972; Council Mem., Deep Sea Fishermen's Mission, 1977. Vice-Pres., Nat. Assoc. of Local Councils (formerly Nat. Assoc. of Parish Councils), 1970–80. FRICS 1970. *Heir: s* Viscount Dupplin, *qv*. *Address:* 15 Carlyle Square, SW3 6EX; Pier House, Seaview, Isle of Wight. *Clubs:* Turf, Pratt's, White's, MCC.

KINROSS, 5th Baron *cr* 1902; **Christopher Patrick Balfour;** Partner in Shepherd & Wedderburn, WS, Solicitors, since 1977; *b* 1 Oct. 1949; *s* of 4th Baron Kinross, OBE, TD, and Helen Anne (*d* 1969), *d* of A. W. Hog; *S* father, 1985; *m* 1974, Susan Jane, *d* of I. R. Pitman, WS; two *s*. *Educ:* Belhaven Hill School, Dunbar; Eton College; Edinburgh Univ. (LLB). Mem., Law Soc. of Scotland, 1975; WS 1975. UK Treas., James IV Assoc. of Surgeons, 1981– (Hon. Mem., 1985–); Treas., Edinburgh Gastro-intestinal Res. Fund, 1981–. Member, Queen's Body Guard for Scotland, Royal Company of Archers, 1980–. Member: Mil. Vehicle Trust; Scottish Land Rover Owners' Club. *Recreations:* pistol, rifle and shotgun shooting, stalking, motorsport. *Heir:* *s* Hon. Alan Ian Balfour, *b* 4 April 1978. *Address:* 11 Belford Place, Edinburgh EH4 3DH. *T:* 0131–332 9704. *Club:* New (Edinburgh).

KINSELLA, Thomas; poet; Professor of English, Temple University, Philadelphia, 1970–90; *b* 4 May 1928; *m* 1955, Eleanor Walsh; one *s* two *d.* Entered Irish Civil Service, 1946; resigned from Dept of Finance, 1965. Artist-in-residence, 1965–67, Prof. of English, 1967–70, Southern Illinois Univ. Elected to Irish Academy of Letters, 1965. J. S. Guggenheim Meml Fellow, 1968–69, 1971–72. Hon. PhD NUI, 1984. *Publications: poetry:* Poems, 1956; Another September, 1958; Downstream, 1962; Nightwalker and other poems, 1968; Notes from the Land of the Dead, 1972; Butcher's Dozen, 1972, 2nd edn 1992; A Selected Life, 1972; Finistère, 1972; New Poems, 1973; Selected Poems 1956 to 1968, 1973; Vertical Man and The Good Fight, 1973; One, 1974; A Technical Supplement, 1976; Song of the Night and Other Poems, 1978; The Messenger, 1978; Fifteen Dead, 1979; One and Other Poems, 1979; Poems 1956–73, 1980; Peppercanister Poems 1972–78, 1980; One Fond Embrace, 1981 (complete) 1988; Songs of the Psyche, 1985; Her Vertical Smile, 1985; St Catherine's Clock, 1987; Out of Ireland, 1987; Blood and Family, 1988; Personal Places, 1990; Poems from Centre City, 1990; Madonna, 1991; Open Court, 1991; From Centre City, 1994; *translations and general:* (trans.) The Táin, 1969; contrib. essay in Davis, Mangan, Ferguson, 1970; (ed) Selected Poems of Austin Clarke, 1976; An Duanaire—Poems of the Dispossessed (trans. Gaelic poetry, 1600–1900), 1981; (ed) Our Musical Heritage: lectures on Irish traditional music by Seán Ó Riada, 1982; (ed, with translations) The New Oxford Book of Irish Verse, 1986; The Dual Tradition: an essay on poetry and politics in Ireland, 1995.

KINSEY, Thomas Richard Moseley, FEng 1982; Chairman, Delcam International (formerly Deltacam Systems), since 1989; *b* 13 Oct. 1929; *s* of late Richard Moseley Kinsey and Dorothy Elizabeth Kinsey; *m* 1953, Ruth (*née* Owen-Jones); two *s.* *Educ:* Newtown Sch.; Trinity Hall, Cambridge (MA). FIMechE; CIMgt. ICI Ltd, 1952–57; Tube Investments,1957–65; joined Delta plc, 1965: Director, 1973–77; Jt Man. Dir, 1977–82; Dir, 1980, Dep. Chief Exec., 1982–87, Mitchell Cotts plc, 1980–87. Chm., Birmingham Battery & Metal Co., 1984–89; Director: Gower Internat., 1984–89; Telcon, 1984–89; Unistrut Europe, 1989–92. *Recreations:* golf, travel. *Address:* Sutton Lodge, Solihull, W Midlands B91 1NB. *T:* 0121–704 2592. *Clubs:* Athenæum; Edgbaston Golf.

KINSMAN, Surgeon Rear-Adm. Francis Michael, CBE 1982 (OBE 1972); Surgeon Rear Admiral (Ships and Establishments), 1980–82, retired; *b* 5 May 1925; *s* of Oscar Edward Kinsman and Margaret Vera Kinsman; *m* 1st, 1949, Catherine Forsyth Barr; one *s*; 2nd, 1955, Margaret Emily Hillier; two *s.* *Educ:* Rydal Sch., Colwyn Bay; St Bartholomew's Hosp. MRCS, LRCP, MFCM; DA. Joined RN, 1952; served, 1952–66: HMS Comus, HMS Tamar, HMS Centaur; RN Hosp. Malta, RN Air Med. Sch., RNAS Lossiemouth; Pres., Central Air Med. Bd, 1966–69; Jt Services Staff Coll., 1969; Staff, Med. Dir Gen. (Naval), 1970–73; Dir, Naval Med. Staff Trng, 1973–76; Comd MO to C-in-C Naval Home Comd, 1976–79; MO i/c RN Hosp. Gibraltar, 1979–80. QHP 1980–82. OStJ 1977. *Recreations:* music, painting, fishing, woodwork. *Address:* Pound House, Meonstoke, Southampton, Hants SO32 3NP.

KINSMAN, Rodney William, RDI 1990; FCSD; Managing Director, OMK Design, since 1966; *b* 9 April 1943; *s* of John Thomas Kinsman and Lilian Kinsman (*née* Bradshaw); *m* 1966, Lisa Sai Yuk; one *s* two *d.* *Educ:* Mellow Lane Grammar Sch.; Central Sch. of Art (NDD 1965). FCSD 1983. Founded: OMK Design Ltd, 1966; Kinsman Associates, 1981. Mem., British Furniture Council, 1995 (Exec. Mem., RDI Cttee). Numerous internat. exhibns; work in permanent collections incl. Omstak Chair and other designs, in V&A, museums in USA, Spain, Germany. Broadcasts on TV and radio. Former Vis. Prof. and Ext. Examr, RCA. Hon. FRCA 1988; FRSA. Many internat. awards. *Recreations:* polo, ski-ing. *Address:* OMK Design, Stephen Building, 30 Stephen Street, W1P 1PN. *T:* 0171–631 1335. *Clubs:* Reform, Institute of Directors, Groucho, Chelsea Arts, Royal Berkshire.

KINTORE, 13th Earl of, *cr* 1677 (Scot.); **Michael Canning William John Keith;** Lord Keith of Inverurie and Keith Hall, 1677 (Scot.); Bt 1897; Baron 1925; Viscount Stonehaven 1938; *b* 22 Feb. 1939; *s* of 12th Earl of Kintore, and of Delia Virginia, *d* of William Loyd; assumed surname of Keith in lieu of Baird, 1967; *S* father, 1989; *m* 1972, Mary Plum, *d* of late Sqdn Leader E. G. Plum, Rumson, NJ, and of Mrs Roy Hudson; one *s* one *d.* *Educ:* Eton; RMA Sandhurst. Lately Lieutenant, Coldstream Guards. ACII. Pres., Internat. Assoc. of Book-Keepers, 1994–. Hon. LLD Aberdeen, 1993. *Heir:* *s* Lord Inverurie, Master of Kintore, *qv.* *Address:* The Stables, Keith Hall, Inverurie, Aberdeenshire AB51 0LD. *T:* Inverurie (01467) 620495.

KINVIG, Maj.-Gen. Clifford Arthur; Director, Educational and Training Services (Army) (formerly Director of Army Education, Ministry of Defence), 1990–93, retired; *b* 22 Nov. 1934; *s* of Frank Arthur Kinvig and Dorothy Maud (*née* Hankinson); *m* 1954, Shirley Acklam; two *s* one *d.* *Educ:* Waterloo Grammar Sch., Liverpool; Durham Univ. (BA 1956); King's Coll., London (MA War Studies 1969). Commnd, RAEC, 1957; educnl and staff appts in Lichfield, Beaconsfield and York, 1957–65; served FE, 1965–68; Sen. Lectr, RMA, Sandhurst, 1969–73; SO2 Educn, UKLF, 1973–75; Chief Educn Officer, W Midland Dist, 1976–79; SO1 Educn, MoD, 1979–82; Sen. Lectr and Head of Econs, Politics and Social Studies Br., RMCS, Shrivenham, 1982–86; Col AEd1, MoD, 1986; Comdt, RAEC Centre, 1986–90. Mem., Management Bd, NFER, 1990–93. Trustee and Sec., Gallipoli Meml Lect. Trust, 1990–92. *Publications:* Death Railway, 1973; River Kwai Railway, 1992; (contrib.) The Forgotten War, 1992; Scapegoat: General Percival of Singapore, 1996; contribs to jls on mil. hist. topics. *Recreations:* writing, gardening, reading, walking. *Address:* c/o Lloyds Bank, Gorse Hill, Swindon SN2 6AE.

KIPKULEI, Benjamin Kipkech; Permanent Secretary, Ministry of Education, Kenya, since 1987; *b* 5 Jan. 1946; *s* of Mr and Mrs Kipkulei Chesoro; *m* 1972, Miriam; three *s* two *d.* *Educ:* BAEd Nairobi; DipEd Scotland; MEd London. Local Government, 1964 and 1965; Teacher, 1970; Education Officer, 1974; Under Secretary, 1982; High Comr in UK, and Ambassador to Italy and Switzerland, 1984–86. *Recreations:* swimming, photography. *Address:* Ministry of Education, Joogoo House B, POB 30040, Nairobi, Kenya.

KIRALFY, Prof. Albert Kenneth Roland; Professor of Law, King's College, London, 1964–81, now Emeritus Professor; *b* Toronto, 5 Dec. 1915; *s* of Bolossy Kiralfy, Theatrical Impresario, and Helen Dawnay; *m* 1960, Roberta Ann Routledge. *Educ:* Streatham Grammar Sch.; King's Coll., London Univ. LLB 1935, LLM 1936, PhD 1949. Served War of 1939–45. Called to the Bar, Gray's Inn, 1947. King's Coll., London: Asst Lectr, 1937–39 and 1947–48; Lectr, 1948–51; Reader, 1951–64; Dean of College Law Faculty, 1974–77; FKC 1971. Chm., Bd of Studies in Laws, London Univ., 1971–74; Dean of Univ. Law Faculty, 1980–81. Vis. Prof., Osgoode Hall Law Sch., Toronto, 1961–62; Exchange Scholar, Leningrad Law Sch., Spring 1964, Moscow Law Sch., April 1970; Prague Acad. of Sciences, April 1975. Dir, Comparative Law Course, Luxembourg, Aug. 1968. Chm., Council of Hughes Parry Hall, London Univ., 1970–82. Editor, Journal of Legal History, 1980–90; Mem. Editorial Bd, Internat. and Comparative Law Quarterly, 1956–86; Reviser, English trans., Polish Civil Code, 1981. *Publications:* The Action on the Case, 1951; The English Legal System, 1954 (and later edns; 8th edn 1990); A Source Book of English Law, 1957; Potter's Historical Introduction to English Law, (4th edn) 1958; (with Prof. G. Jones) Guide to Selden Society Publications, 1960 reissued as part of Selden Soc. Centenary Guide, 1987; Translation of Russian Civil Codes, 1966; chapter, English Law, in Derrett, Introduction to Legal Systems, 1968; (with Miss R. A. Routledge) Guide to Additional MSS at Gray's Inn Library, 1971; General Editor, Comparative Law of Matrimonial Property, 1972; (ed jtly): New Perspectives in Scottish Legal History, 1984; Custom, Courts and Counsel, 1985; The Burden of Proof, 1987; contributed: Encyclopædia of Soviet Law (Leiden), 1973; Contemporary Soviet Law, 1974; East-West Business Transactions, 1974; Common Law, Encyclopædia Britannica, 1974; Codification in the Communist World, 1975; Russian Law: Historical Perspectives, 1977; Le Nuove Frontiere del Diritto, 1979; André Loeber Festschrift, 1988; Nuovi Moti per la Formazione del Diritto, 1988; International Encyclopedia of Comparative Law, 1989; Macerata Conference Papers, 1989 (Italy); Jean Bodin Soc., vol. 52, 1990, vol. 60, 1993; History of Law—Russia and England, 1990 (Moscow); Il Processo Civile Inglese, ed L. Moccia, 1991; European Current Law, 1992; Il Diritto Privato Europeo: problemi e prospettive, 1993; Studi in Memoria di Gino Gorla, 1994; Jl of Legal History; NY Jl of Internat. and Comparative Law; Review of Socialist Laws; *Rapporteur,* The Child without Family Ties, Congress of Jean Bodin Soc., Strasbourg, 1972. *Recreations:* history, languages. *Address:* Law School, King's College, Strand, WC2R 2LS; 58 Cheriton Square, SW17 8AE.

KIRBY, Prof. Anthony John, PhD; FRS 1987; CChem, FRSC; Professor of Bioorganic Chemistry, since 1995, and Fellow, Gonville and Caius College, since 1962, Cambridge University; *b* 18 Aug. 1935; *s* of Samuel Arthur Kirby and Gladys Rosina Kirby (*née* Welch); *m* 1962, Sara Sophia Benjamina Nieweg; one *s* two *d.* *Educ:* Eton College; Gonville and Caius College, Cambridge (MA, PhD 1962). NATO postdoctoral Fellow: Cambridge, 1962–63; Brandeis Univ., 1963–64; Cambridge University: Demonstrator, 1964–68, Lectr, 1968–85, Reader, 1985–95, in Organic Chemistry; Gonville and Caius College: Dir of Studies in Natural Scis and Coll. Lectr, 1968–; Tutor, 1966–74. Visiting Professor/Scholar: Paris (Orsay), 1970; Groningen, 1973; Cape Town, 1987; Paris VI, 1987; Haifa, 1991. Co-ordinator, European Network on Catalytic Antibodies, 1993–. Fellow, Japan Soc. for Promotion of Science, 1986; Royal Society of Chemistry: Fellow, 1980; Award in Organic Reaction Mechanisms, 1983; Tilden Lectr, 1987; Chm., Organic Reaction Mechanisms Gp, 1986–90. *Publications:* The Organic Chemistry of Phosphorus (with S. G. Warren), 1967; The Anomeric Effect and Related Stereoelectronic Effects at Oxygen, 1983; Stereoelectronic effects, 1995; papers in Jls of RSC and Amer. Chem. Soc. *Recreations:* chamber music, walking. *Address:* University Chemical Laboratory, Cambridge CB2 1EW. *T:* Cambridge (01223) 336370; 14 Tenison Avenue, Cambridge CB1 2DY. *T:* Cambridge (01223) 359343.

KIRBY, David Donald, CBE 1988; Consultant, since 1990, Chairman, since 1994, Transmark; *b* 12 May 1933; *s* of Walter Donald Kirby and Margaret Irene (*née* Halstead); *m* 1955, Joan Florence (*née* Dickins); one *s* one *d.* *Educ:* Royal Grammar Sch., High Wycombe; Jesus Coll., Oxford (MA). FCIT. British Rail and its subsidiaries: Divisional Shipping Manager, Dover, 1964; Operations Manager, Shipping and Continental, 1965; Asst Gen. Man., Shipping and International Services, 1966; Continental Traffic Man., BR, 1968; Gen. Man., Shipping and Internat. Services, 1974; Man. Dir, Sealink UK Ltd, 1979; Dir, London and SE, 1982–85; Mem., 1985–89, Jt Man. Dir (Rlys), 1985–87, Vice-Chm., 1987–89, BRB. *Recreations:* painting, choral singing. *Address:* Penrose, Tresarrett, Blisland, Bodmin, Cornwall PL30 4QY.

KIRBY, Dennis, MVO 1961; MBE 1955; Hon. Manager, European Investment Bank, Luxembourg; *b* 5 April 1923; *s* of William Ewart Kirby and Hannah Kirby; *m* 1st, 1943, Mary Elizabeth Kilby (*d* 1994); 2nd, 1994, Ava Robertson. *Educ:* Hull Grammar Sch.; Queens' Coll., Cambridge. Lt (A) RNVR (fighter pilot), 1940–46. Colonial Service, Sierra Leone, 1946–62 (District Comr, 1950; Perm. Sec., 1961–62); 1st Sec., UK Diplomatic Service, 1962; Managing Director: East Kilbride Development Corp., 1963–68; Irvine Development Corp., 1967–72; Industrial Dir, Scotland, DTI, 1972–74; European Investment Bank, 1974–87: Conseiller Principal, 1974; Dir Adjoint, 1976; Dir Associé, 1984; Dir, NM UK Ltd, 1988–93. MInstD 1970. *Recreations:* shooting, golf. *Address:* Queenscourt, Westcott Street, Westcott, Dorking, Surrey RH4 3NX. *T:* Dorking (01306) 889631. *Clubs:* United Oxford & Cambridge University, Commonwealth Trust; Betchworth Park Golf, Wisley Golf (Dir, 1991–95).

KIRBY, Dame Georgina (Kamiria), DBE 1994; QSO 1981; JP; Director, Maori Women's Development Fund, since 1978; *b* 31 Jan. 1936; *d* of William Tawhiri Matea Smith and Tuhe Nga Tukemata Christie (*née* Thompson); *m* 1961, Brian Ian Kirby; two *s* one *d.* *Educ:* Horohoro Sch., Rotorua; Rotorua High Sch.; Auckland Univ. Cert. Book-keeping; Cert. Practical Accounting. Jun. Asst Teacher, Rotorua, 1953–55; NZ PO Trng Officer, 1955–63; managed and partnered husband in service businesses, 1966–70; Personnel Officer, Stock & Station, 1971–76. Estabd Te Taumata Art Gall., 1991. Mem., Maori Women's Welfare League Inc., 1976– (Nat. Pres., 1983–87). NZ Vice Pres., Commonwealth Countries League, London, 1988–. JP NZ, 1987. Commemoration Medal (NZ), 1988; Women's Suffrage Medal (NZ), 1993. *Publications:* Liberated Learning, 1993; Vision Aotearoa Kaupapa New Zealand, 1994; contrib. NZ Maori Artists and Writers Mag., Koru. *Recreations:* reading, badminton, horse-riding. *Address:* 11A Northland Street, Grey Lynn, Auckland 1, New Zealand. *T:* (9) 3767032; (office) *T* and *Fax:* (9) 3760901. *Club:* Zonta International (Auckland).

KIRBY, Prof. Gordon William, ScD, PhD; FRSC; FRSE; Regius Professor of Chemistry, University of Glasgow, since 1972; *b* 20 June 1934; *s* of William Admiral Kirby and Frances Teresa Kirby (*née* Townson); *m* 1964, Audrey Jean Rusbridge (marr. diss. 1983), *d* of Col C. E. Rusbridge; two *s.* *Educ:* Liverpool Inst. High Sch.; Gonville and Caius Coll., Cambridge (Schuldham Plate 1956; MA, PhD, ScD); FRIC 1970; FRSE 1975. 1851 Exhibn Senior Student, 1958–60, Asst Lectr, 1960–61, Lectr, 1961–67, Imperial Coll. of Science and Technology; Prof. of Organic Chemistry, Univ. of Technology, Loughborough, 1967–72; Mem., Chem. Cttee, SRC, 1971–75. Chm., Jls Cttee, Royal Soc. of Chemistry, 1981–84. Corday-Morgan Medal, Chem. Soc., 1969; Tilden Lectr, Chem. Soc., 1974–75. *Publications:* Co-editor: Elucidation of Organic Structures by Physical and Chemical Methods, vol. IV, parts I, II, and III, 1972; Fortschritte der Chemie organischer Naturstoffe, subseq. entitled Progress in the Chemistry of Organic Natural Products, 1971–; (ed) Comprehensive Organic Functional Group Transformations, vol. IV, 1996; contributor to Jl Chem. Soc., etc. *Address:* Chemistry Department, The University, Glasgow G12 8QQ. *T:* 0141–339 8855, *Fax:* 0141–330 4888.

KIRBY, Gwendolen Maud, LVO 1969; Matron, The Hospital for Sick Children, Great Ormond Street, 1951–69; *b* 17 Dec. 1911; 3rd *d* of late Frank M. Kirby, Gravesend, Kent. *Educ:* St Mary's Sch., Calne, Wilts. State Registered Nurse: trained at Nightingale Training Sch., St Thomas' Hosp., SE1. 1933–36; The Mothercraft Training Soc., Cromwell House, Highgate, 1936; State Certified Midwife: trained at General Lying-in Hosp., York Road, Lambeth, 1938–39; Registered Sick Children's Nurse: trained at the Hospital for Sick Children, Great Ormond Street, WC1, 1942–44. Awarded Nightingale Fund Travelling

Scholarship, 1948–49, and spent 1 year in Canada and United States. Member: RCN, 1936–; Gen. Nursing Council, 1955–65. *Address:* Brackenfield, Winsford, Minehead, Som TA24 7JL.

KIRBY, Louis; Editor, UK Mail, since 1993; *b* 30 Nov. 1928; 2nd *s* of late William Kirby and Anne Kirby; *m* 1st, 1952, Marcia Teresa Lloyd (marr. diss. 1976); two *s* three *d*; 2nd, 1976, Heather Veronica (*née* Nicholson); one *s* one *d*; 3rd, 1983, Heather McGlone; two *d*. *Educ:* Coalbrookdale High Sch. Daily Mail: Gen. Reporter, subseq. Courts Corresp., and Polit. Corresp., 1953–62; Daily Sketch: Chief Reporter, subseq. Leader Writer and Polit. Editor, Asst Editor, Exec. Editor, and, Actg Editor, 1962–71; Daily Mail (when relaunched): Dep. Editor, 1971–74; Editor, Evening News, 1974–80; Vice-Chm., Evening News Ltd, 1975–80; Editor, Evening Standard, 1980–86; Editl Dir, Mail Newspapers plc, 1986–88; Political Consultant, Daily Mail, 1988–93. *Recreations:* theatre, reading. *Address:* Northcliffe House, Derry Street, W8 5TT. *Clubs:* Reform, Special Forces.

KIRBY, Michael Donald, AC 1991; CMG 1983; **Hon. Justice Kirby;** President, Court of Appeal, Supreme Court of New South Wales, Sydney, since 1984; *b* 18 March 1939; *s* of Donald Kirby and Jean Langmore Kirby. *Educ:* Fort Street Boys' High Sch.; Univ. of Sydney (BA, LLM, BEc). Admitted Solicitor, 1962; called to the Bar of NSW, 1967; Mem., NSW Bar Council, 1974; Judge, Federal Court of Australia, 1983–84; Actg Chief Justice of NSW, 1988, 1990, 1993. Dep. Pres., Aust. Conciliation and Arbitration Commn, 1974–83; Chairman: Australian Law Reform Commn, 1975–84; OECD Inter-govtl Gp on Privacy and Internat. Data Flows, 1978–80; OECD Inter-govtl Gp on Security of Information Systems, 1991–92; Member: Admin. Review Council of Australia, 1976–84; Council of Aust. Acad. of Forensic Scis, 1978–89 (Pres., 1987–89); Aust. National Commn for Unesco, 1980–83; Aust. Inst. of Multi-cultural Affairs, 1981–84; Exec., CSIRO, 1983–86. Deleg., Unesco Gen. Conf., Paris, 1983; Chm., Unesco Expert Gp on Rights of Peoples, 1989 (Rapporteur, Budapest, 1991); Member: Unesco Expert Gps on Self-Determination and Rights of Peoples, 1984, 1991, 1992; Perm. Tribunal of Peoples, Rome, 1992–; ILO Fact Finding and Conciliation Commn on S Africa, 1991–92; Special Rep. of UN Sec.-Gen., for Human Rights in Cambodia, 1993–; Indep. Chm., Malaŵi Constitl Conf., 1994. International Commission of Jurists: Comr, 1984–; Mem. Exec. Cttee, 1989–, Chm., 1992–; Pres., Aust. Section, 1989–. Internat. Consultant, Commn for Transborder Data Flow Develt, Intergovtl Bureau of Informatics, Rome, 1985–86; Mem., Bd, Internat. Trustees, Internat. Inst. for Inf. and Communication, Montreal, 1986–; President: Criminology Sect., ANZAAS, 1981– 82; Law Sect., ANZAAS, 1984–85. Granada Guildhall Lectr, 1985; Acting Prof., Fac. of Salzburg Seminar, Salzburg, 1985. Pres., Nat. Book Council of Australia, 1980–83; Member: Library Council of NSW, 1976–85; NSW Ministerial Adv. Cttee on AIDS, 1987; Trustee, AIDS Trust of Australia, 1987–93; Comr, Global Commn on AIDS, WHO, Geneva, 1989–91. Mem. Council, Australian Opera, 1983–89; Patron, RSPCA, Australia. Fellow, Senate, Sydney Univ., 1964–69; Dep. Chancellor, Univ. of Newcastle, NSW, 1978–83; Chancellor, Macquarie Univ., Sydney, 1984–93. Mem. Bd of Governors, Internat. Council for Computer Communications, Washington, 1984–. Hon. DLitt Newcastle, NSW, 1987; Hon. LLD Macquarie Univ., 1994. Sen. Anzac Fellow, NZ Govt, 1981; Fellow, NZ Legal Res. Foundn, 1985. Australian Human Rights Medal, 1991. *Publications:* Industrial Index to Australian Labour Law, 1978, 2nd edn 1983; Reform the Law, 1983; The Judges (Boyer Lectures), 1983; (ed jtly) A Touch of Healing, 1986; essays and articles in legal and other jls. *Recreation:* work. *Address:* 2C Dumaresq Road, Rose Bay, NSW 2029, Australia. *T:* (2) 2308202, *Fax:* (2) 2351006.

KIRBY, Maj.-Gen. Norman George, OBE 1971; FRCS; Consultant Accident and Emergency Surgeon, Guy's Hospital, since 1982; Director, Clinical Services, Accidents and Emergencies, 1985–93; *b* 19 Dec. 1926; *s* of George William Kirby and Laura Kirby; *m* 1949, Cynthia Bradley; one *s* one *d*. *Educ:* King Henry VIII Sch., Coventry; Univ. of Birmingham (MB, ChB). FRCS 1964, FRCSE 1980; FICS 1980; FFAEM 1993. Surgical Registrar: Plastic Surg. Unit, Stoke Mandeville Hosp., 1950–51; Birmingham Accident Hosp., 1953–55; Postgraduate Med. Sch., Hammersmith, 1964. Regt MO 10 Parachute Regt, 1950–51; OC 5 Parachute Surgical Team, 1956–59 (Suez Landing, 5 Nov. 1956); Officer i/c Surg. Div., BMH Rinteln, 1959–60; OC and Surg. Specialist, BMH Tripoli, 1960–62; OC and Consultant Surgeon, BMH Dhekelia, 1967–70; Chief Cons. Surgeon, Cambridge Mil. Hosp., 1970–72; Cons. Surg. HQ BAOR, 1973–78; Dir of Army Surgery, Cons. Surg. to the Army and Hon. Surgeon to the Queen, 1978–82; Hon. Cons. Surgeon, Westminster Hosp., 1979–. Examnr in Anatomy, RCSE, 1982–90; Mem., Court of Examiners, RCS, 1988–94. Chm., Army Med. Dept Working Party Surgical Support for BAOR, 1978–80; Mem., Med. Cttee, Defence Scientific Adv. Council, 1979–82. Hon. Colonel: 308 (Co. of London) Gen. Hosp. RAMC, TA, 1982–87; 144 Para Field Sqdn (formerly Field Ambulance) RAMC (Volunteers), TA, 1985–; Col Comdt, RAMC, 1987–92. Member: Council, Internat. Coll. of Surgeons; Airborne Med. Soc.; British Assoc. for Accident and Emergency Medicine (formerly Casualty Surgeons Assoc.), 1981–94 (Vice-Pres., 1988; Pres., 1990–93); Pres., Med. Soc. of London, 1992–93 (FMS 1981); Vice-Pres., British Assoc. of Trauma in Sport, 1982–88; Chm., Accidents & Emergencies Cttee, SE Thames RHA, 1984–88. Mem. Council, TAVRA, Gtr London, 1990–. Liveryman, Soc. of Apothecaries of London, 1983–; Mem., HAC, 1988. Hon. Fellow, Amer. Coll. of Emergency Physicians, 1993. McCombe Lectr, RCSE, 1979. Mem., Editl Bd, Brit. Jl Surg. and Injury, 1979–82. Mem., Surgical Travellers Club, 1979–. OStJ 1977 (Mem. Council, London, 1990–). Mitchener Medal, RCS, 1982. *Publications:* (ed) Field Surgery Pocket Book, 1981; Pocket Reference, Accidents and Emergencies, 1988, 2nd edn 1991; contrib. Brit. Jl Surg., Proc. RSocMed, etc. *Recreations:* travel, motoring, reading, archaeology. *Address:* 12 Woodsyre, Sydenham Hill, Dulwich, SE26 6SS. *T:* 0181–670 5327.

KIRBY, Hon. Sir Richard (Clarence), Kt 1961; AC 1985; Chairman, Advertising Standards Council, 1973–88; *b* 22 Sept. 1904; *s* of Samuel Enoch Kirby and Agnes Mary Kirby, N Queensland; *m* 1937, Hilda Marie Ryan; two *d*. *Educ:* The King's Sch., Parramatta; University of Sydney (LLB). Solicitor, NSW, 1928; called to Bar, 1933; served AIF, 1942–44; Mem. Adult Adv. Educl Council to NSW Govt, 1944–46; Judge, Dist Court, NSW, 1944–47; Mem. Austr. War Crimes Commn, 1945, visiting New Guinea, Morotai, Singapore, taking evidence on war crimes; Australia Rep. on War Crimes, Lord Mountbatten's HQ, Ceylon, 1945; Royal Commissioner on various occasions for Federal, NSW and Tasmanian Govts, 1945–47; Acting Judge Supreme Court of NSW, 1947; Chief Judge, Commonwealth Court of Conciliation and Arbitration, 1956–73; Austr. Rep., UN Security Council's Cttee on Good Offices on Indonesian Question, 1947–48, participating in Security Council Debates, Lake Success, USA; Chm. Stevedoring Industry Commn, 1947–49; (first) Pres., Commonwealth Conciliation and Arbitration Commn, 1956–73. Chm., Nat. Stevedoring Conf., 1976–77. Pres., H. V. Evatt Meml Foundn, 1979–85. Mem. Council, Wollongong Univ., 1979–84. Hon. DLitt Wollongong Univ., 1984. *Recreation:* encouraging good will in industry. *Address:* The White House, Berrara, NSW 2540, Australia. *T:* (44) 412171. *Club:* Athenæum (Melbourne).

KIRCHNER, Prof. Emil Joseph, PhD; Professor of European Studies, Department of Government, University of Essex, since 1992; *b* 19 March 1942; *m* 1975, Joanna Bartlett; two *s*. *Educ:* Case Western Reserve Univ. (BA Econ 1970; MA 1971; PhD 1976, Pol. Sci.). Essex University: Lectr and Sen. Lectr, Dept of Govt, 1974–92; Mem., Senate, 1992–. Dir, Inst. for European Community Policy Making, Brussels, 1981–86. Vis. Prof., Dept of Pol. Sci., Univ. of Connecticut, 1986–87; External Assessor, Poly. of W London, 1991. Member: Human Rights Steering Gp, Helsinki Conf. on Security Co-operation in Europe, 1991; Exec. Cttee, Univ. Assoc. for Contemporary European Studies, 1989; Exec. Cttee, Assoc. for Study of German Politics, 1989–90. Gen. Series Editor, Europe in Change (Manchester Univ. Press), 1993. *Publications:* Decision Making in the European Community, 1992; (jtly) Britain and Germany in the New Europe, 1994; (jtly) The Future of European Security, 1994. *Recreations:* music, sports, travel. *Address:* University of Essex, Centre for European Studies, Wivenhoe Park, Colchester CO4 3SQ. *T:* Colchester (01206) 872749.

KIRCHNER, Peter James, MBE 1970; HM Diplomatic Service, retired; Consul General, Berlin, 1978–79; *b* 17 Sept. 1920; *s* of late William John Kirchner and Winifred Emily Homer (*née* Adams); *m* 1952, Barbro Sarah Margareta (*née* Klockhoff); one *s* two *d*. *Educ:* St Brendan's Coll., Clifton, Bristol. BA Open, 1991. Served War, RA, 1939–41. Timber production, UK and Germany, 1941–48; FO, Germany, 1948; Home Office Immigration Dept, 1952–64; Head of UK Refugee Missions in Europe, 1960–63; FCO (formerly FO): Barbados, 1965; Nairobi, 1968; Ankara, 1970; Vienna, 1973; Jerusalem, 1976. Freeman, City of London, 1963. *Recreations:* golf, croquet, modern European history, northern baroque architecture, travel in Europe, trying to write. *Address:* 86 York Mansions, Prince of Wales Drive, SW11 4BN. *T:* 0171–622 7068.

KIRK, Prof. Geoffrey Stephen, DSC 1945; LittD; FBA 1959; Regius Professor of Greek, University of Cambridge, 1974–82, now Emeritus; Fellow of Trinity College, Cambridge, 1974–82; *b* 3 Dec. 1921; *s* of Frederic Tilzey Kirk, MC, and Enid Hilda (*née* Pentecost); *m* 1st, 1950, Barbara Helen Traill (marr. diss. 1975); one *d*; 2nd, 1975, Kirsten Jensen (Ricks). *Educ:* Rossall Sch.; Clare Coll., Cambridge. LittD Cambridge, 1965. Served War in Royal Navy, 1941–45; commissioned 1942; Temp. Lt, RNVR, 1945. Took Degree at Cambridge, 1946; Research Fellow, Trinity Hall, 1946–49; Student, Brit. Sch. at Athens, 1947; Commonwealth Fund Fellow, Harvard Univ., 1949–50; Fellow, Trinity Hall, 1950–70; Cambridge University: Asst Lecturer in Classics, 1951; Lecturer in Classics, 1952–61; Reader in Greek, 1961–65; Prof. of Classics, Yale Univ., 1965–70; Prof. of Classics, Bristol Univ., 1971–73. Visiting Lecturer, Harvard Univ., 1958; Sather Prof. of Classical Literature, University of California, Berkeley, 1968–69; Mellon Prof., Tulane Univ., 1979. Pres., Soc. for Promotion of Hellenic Studies, 1977–80. Corresp. Mem., Acad. of Athens, 1993. MA (Yale) 1965. *Publications:* Heraclitus, the Cosmic Fragments, 1954; (with J. E. Raven) The Presocratic Philosophers, 1958; The Songs of Homer, 1962 (abbrev., as Homer and the Epic, 1965); Euripides, Bacchae, 1970; Myth, 1970; The Nature of Greek Myths, 1974; Homer and the Oral Tradition, 1977; The Iliad: a commentary, Vol.1, books 1–4, 1985, Vol. 2, books 5–8, 1990; articles in classical, archæological and philosophical journals. *Recreations:* writing, a little sailing. *Address:* 9 Guillards Oak, Midhurst, West Sussex GU29 9JZ.

KIRK, Grayson Louis; President Emeritus, Columbia University; *b* 12 Oct. 1903; *s* of Traine Caldwell Kirk and Nora Eichelberger; *m* 1925, Marion Louise Sands; one *s*. *Educ:* Miami Univ. (AB); Clark Univ. (AM); Ecole Libre des Sciences Politiques, Paris, 1928–29. PhD University of Wisconsin, 1930. Prof. of History, Lamar Coll., Beaumont, Tex, 1925–27; Social Science Research Coun. Fellowship (chiefly spent at London Sch. of Economics), 1936–37; Instructor in Political Science, 1929–30, Asst Prof., 1930–36, Associate Prof., 1936–38, Prof., 1938–40, University of Wisconsin; Associate Prof. of Government, Columbia Univ., 1940–43; Head, Security Section, Div. of Political Studies, US Dept of State, 1942–43; Mem. US Delegn Staff, Dumbarton Oaks, 1944; Exec. Officer, Third Commn, San Francisco Conf., 1945. Research Associate, Yale Inst. of Internat. Studies, 1943–44; Prof. of Government, Columbia Univ., 1943–47; Prof. of Internat Relations, Acting Dir of Sch. of Internat. Affairs, and Dir of European Inst., 1947–49. Appointed Provost in Nov. 1949, and also Vice-Pres in July 1950; became acting head of Columbia in President Eisenhower's absence on leave, March 1951; Pres. and Trustee of Columbia Univ., 1953–68; Bryce Prof. of History of Internat. Relations, Columbia, 1959–72, Emeritus Prof., 1972. Trustee Emeritus, The Asia Foundation; Trustee: American Philosophical Soc.; Pilgrims of the US (Vice-Pres.); Council on Foreign Relations; Amer. Acad. of Arts and Sciences; Amer. Soc. of French Legion of Honour. Hon. LLD: Miami, 1950; Waynesburg Coll., Brown Univ., Union Coll, 1951; Puerto Rico, Clark, Princeton, New York, Wisconsin, Columbia, Jewish Theol. Seminary of America, 1953; Syracuse, Williams Coll., Pennsylvania, Harvard, Washington, St Louis, Central Univ., Caracas, Univ. of the Andes, Merida, Venezuela, Univ. of Zulia, Maracaibo, Venezuela, Univ. of Delhi, India, Thamasset Univ., Bangkok, 1954; Johns Hopkins Univ., Baltimore, Amherst, 1956; Dartmouth Coll., Northwestern Univ., 1958; Tennessee, 1960; St Lawrence, 1963; Denver, Notre Dame, Bates Coll., 1964; Waseda (Japan), Michigan, 1965; Sussex, 1966; Hon. LHD N Dakota, 1958; Hon. PhD Bologna, 1951; Dr of Civil Law King's Coll., Halifax, Nova Scotia, 1958. Associate KStJ 1959. Comdr, Order of Orange-Nassau, 1952; Hon. KBE, 1955; Grand Officer, Order of Merit, of the Republic, Italy, 1956; Grand Officier Légion d'Honneur, France, 1973. Medal of the Order of Taj, Iran, 1961; Grand Cross, Order of George I (Greece), 1965; Order of the Sacred Treasure, 1st Class (Japan), 1965; Comdr, Ordre des Palmes Académiques (France), 1966. *Publications:* Philippine Independence, 1936; Contemporary International Politics (with W. R. Sharp), 1940; (with R. P. Stebbins) War and National Policy, Syllabus, 1941; The Study of International Relations in American Colleges and Universities, 1947. *Address:* 28 Sunnybrook Road, Bronxville, NY 10708, USA. *T:* (914) 7930808.

KIRK, Rt. Hon. Herbert Victor, PC (N Ireland) 1962; Member (U) for South Belfast, Northern Ireland Assembly, 1973–75; *b* 5 June 1912; *s* of Alexander and Mary A. Kirk; *m* 1944, Gladys A. Dunn; three *s*. *Educ:* Queen's Univ., Belfast (BComSc). MP Windsor Div. of Belfast, NI Parlt, 1956–72; Minister of Labour and Nat. Insce, Govt of N Ireland, 1962–64; Minister of Education, 1964–65; Minister of Finance, 1965–72, Jan.–May 1974, resigned. FCA 1940. *Recreation:* golf. *Address:* 38 Massey Avenue, Belfast BT4 2JT, Northern Ireland. *Clubs:* Royal Portrush Golf, Belvoir Park Golf.

KIRK, John Henry, CBE 1957; Emeritus Professor of Marketing (with special reference to horticulture), University of London; *b* 11 April 1907; *s* of William Kirk, solicitor; *m* 1946, Wilfrida Margaret Booth; two *s*. *Educ:* Durban High Sch., S Africa; Universities of S Africa, Cambridge, North Carolina and Chicago. Ministry of Agriculture (from 1934, as economist and administrator); Under-Sec., 1959–65; Prof. of Marketing, Wye Coll., 1965–72. *Publications:* Economic Aspects of Native Segregation, 1929; Agriculture and the Trade Cycle, 1933; United Kingdom Agricultural Policy 1870–1970, 1982; contributions to journals of sociology, economics and agricultural economics. *Recreation:* gardening. *Address:* Yallands Farmhouse, Staplegrove, Taunton, Som TA2 6PZ. *T:* Taunton (01823) 278979.

KIRK, Dame (Lucy) Ruth, DBE 1975; *m* 1941, Norman Eric Kirk (later, Rt Hon. Norman Kirk, PC, Prime Minister of New Zealand; *d* 1974); three *s* two *d*. Former Patron, SPUC. Awarded title, Dame of the Order of the British Empire, for public services. *Address:* Flat 1, 8(A) Ansonby Street, Avonhead, Christchurch, S Island, New Zealand.

KIRK, Raymond Maurice, FRCS; Consulting Surgeon, Royal Free Hospital, since 1989; part-time Lecturer in Anatomy, Royal Free Hospital School of Medicine, since 1989; *b* 31 Oct. 1923; *m* 1952, Margaret Schafran; one *s* two *d*. *Educ:* Mundella Sch., Nottingham; County Secondary Sch., West Bridgford; King's College London; Charing Cross Hosp. MB BS, MS, London; LRCP. RN 1942–46; Lieut RNVR. Charing Cross Hosp., 1952–53; Lectr in Anatomy, King's Coll. London, 1953–54; Hammersmith Hosp., 1954–56; Charing Cross Hosp., 1956–60; Senior Surgical Registrar, Royal Free Hosp., 1961; Consultant Surgeon, Willesden Gen. Hosp., 1962–74, Royal Free Hosp. Group, 1964–89. Dir, Overseas Doctors' Trng Scheme, RCS, 1990–; Examiner: Univ. of London; formerly Mem. Court of Examrs, RCS; formerly Examr to RCPSG, Univs of Liverpool, Bristol, Khartoum, Colombo; Mem. Council, RCS, 1983–91; Pres., Medical Soc. of London, 1988; FRSocMed (Pres., Surgical Section, 1986–87). Member: British Soc. of Gastroenterol.; Surg. Res. Soc.; BMA; Med. Soc. of London; Hunterian Soc. (Pres., 1995–June 1996); RSL; Soc. of Authors. Hon. Editor, Annals of RCS, 1983–92. *Publications:* Manual of Abdominal Operations, 1967; Basic Surgical Techniques, 1973, 4th edn 1995; (jtly) Surgery, 1974; General Surgical Operations, 1978, 3rd edn 1994; Complications of Upper Gastrointestinal Tract Surgery, 1987; (jtly) Clinical Surgery in General, 1993; papers in sci. jls and chapters in books on peptic ulcer, oesophageal, gastric and general abdominal surgery. *Recreations:* opera, theatre, squash, cycling. *Address:* 10 Southwood Lane, Highgate Village, N6 5EE. *T:* 0181–340 8575. *Club:* Royal Society of Medicine.

KIRK, Richard Stanley; Managing Director, Iceland Group PLC, since 1986; *b* 16 Nov. 1945; *s* of Charles Kirk and Margaret (*née* Green); *m* 1969 (marr. diss. 1988); two *s*. *Educ:* Chesterfield Grammar Sch. Store Manager, then Area Manager, F. W. Woolworth, 1966–77; Iceland Frozen Foods, subseq. Iceland Gp, PLC, 1977–; Stores Dir, 1982–86. *Recreations:* ski-ing, shooting, travel. *Address:* Faddiley Hall, Lardon Green, Faddiley, Nantwich, Cheshire CW5 8JW.

KIRK, Dame Ruth; *see* Kirk, Dame L. R.

KIRKBY, Emma; free-lance classical concert singer; soprano; *b* 26 Feb. 1949; *d* of Geoffrey and Daphne Kirkby; one *s* by Anthony Rooley, *qv*. *Educ:* Hanford School; Sherborne School for Girls; Somerville College, Oxford (BA Classics). FGSM 1991. Private singing lessons with Jessica Cash. Regular appearances with Taverner Choir and Players, 1972–; Member: Consort of Musicke, 1973–; Academy of Ancient Music, 1975–; numerous radio broadcasts, gramophone recordings, appearances at the Proms, 1977–. Hon. DLitt Salford, 1985; Hon. DMus Bath, 1994.

KIRKE, Rear-Adm. David Walter, CB 1967; CBE 1962 (OBE 1945), retired; *b* 13 March 1915; *s* of late Percy St George Kirke and late Alice Gertrude, *d* of Sir James Gibson Craig, 3rd Bt; *m* 1st, 1936, Tessa O'Connor (marr. diss., 1950); one *s*; 2nd, 1956, Marion Margaret Gibb; one *s* one *d*. *Educ:* RN Coll., Dartmouth. China Station, 1933–35; Pilot Training, 1937; served War of 1939–45, Russian Convoys, Fighter Sqdns; loaned RAN, 1949–50; Chief of Naval Aviation, Indian Navy, New Delhi, 1959–62; Rear-Adm. 1965; Flag Officer, Naval Flying Training, 1965–68. MBIM 1967. *Recreation:* golf. *Address:* Lismore House, Pluckley, Kent TN27 0QZ. *T:* Pluckley (01233) 840439. *Club:* Army and Navy.

KIRKHAM, family name of **Baroness Berners.**

KIRKHAM, Donald Herbert, FCIS, FCIB; Group Chief Executive, Woolwich Building Society, 1991–95 (Chief Executive, 1986–90); *b* 1 Jan. 1936; *s* of Herbert and Hettie Kirkham; *m* 1960, Kathleen Mary Lond; one *s* one *d*. *Educ:* Grimsby Technical College. Woolwich Equitable Building Society, later Woolwich Building Society: Representative, 1959; Branch Manager, 1963; Gen. Manager's Asst, 1967; Business Planning Manager, 1970; Asst Gen. Manager, 1972; Gen. Manager, 1976; Mem. Local Board, 1979; Dep. Chief Gen. Manager, 1981; Mem. Board, 1982. Chartered Building Societies Institute: Mem. Council, 1976; Dep. Pres., 1980; Pres., 1981; Vice-Pres., 1986–93, then Vice-Pres., CIB, 1993–; Institute of Chartered Secretaries and Administrators: Mem. Council, 1979; Vice-Pres., 1985; Sen. Vice-Pres., 1990; Pres., 1991; Building Societies Assocation: Mem. Council, 1991–95; Dep. Chm., 1993–94; Chm., 1994–95. Hon. DBA Thames Poly., 1991. CIMgt. *Recreation:* boating. *Address:* 2 Chaundrye Close, The Court Yard, Eltham, SE9 5QB. *T:* 0181–850 6144.

KIRKHAM, Rt. Rev. John Dudley Galtrey; *see* Sherborne, Area Bishop of.

KIRKHAM, Keith Edwin, OBE 1987; PhD; Administrative Director, Clinical Research Centre, Medical Research Council, 1988–94; *b* 20 Oct. 1929; *s* of Thomas Kirkham and Clara Prestwich Willacy; *m* 1953, Dorothea Mary Fisher; two *s*. *Educ:* Kirkham Grammar Sch.; Birmingham Univ. (BSc); Fitzwilliam House, Cambridge (DipAgSci; T. H. Middleton Prize); MA, PhD Cantab. National Service, 2nd Lieut RA, 1955–57. Asst in Res., Cambridge, 1951–54; Univ. Demonstr, Cambridge, 1954–60; Sci. Staff, Clin. Endocrinology Res. Unit, MRC, 1960–73; Asst Dir (Admin), Clin. Res. Centre, MRC, 1973–88. Sec., Soc. for Endocrinology, 1975–79. Governor: Harrow Coll. of Higher Educn, 1983–90 (Chm. of Govs, 1986–90); Univ. of Westminster (formerly Poly. of Central London), 1990–. *Publications:* contribs to sci. jls on endocrinology. *Recreations:* cruising, sport (watching). *Address:* Spring Drive, Eastcote, Pinner, Mddx HA5 2ES.

KIRKHILL, Baron *cr* 1975 (Life Peer), of Kirkhill, Aberdeen; **John Farquharson Smith;** *b* 7 May 1930; *s* of Alexander F. Smith and Ann T. Farquharson; *m* 1965, Frances Mary Walker Reid; one step-*d*. Lord Provost of the City and Royal Burgh of Aberdeen, 1971–75. Minister of State, Scottish Office, 1975–78. Chm., N of Scotland Hydro-Electric Bd, 1979–82. Deleg. to Parly Assembly of Council of Europe, 1987– (Chm., Cttee on Legal Affairs and Human Rights, 1991–95). Hon. LLD Aberdeen, 1974. *Address:* 3 Rubislaw Den North, Aberdeen AB2 4AL. *T:* Aberdeen (01224) 314167.

KIRKHOPE, Timothy John Robert; MP (C) Leeds North East, since 1987; Vice-Chamberlain of HM Household, since 1995; *b* 29 April 1945; *s* of late John Thomas Kirkhope and Dorothy Buemann Kirkhope (*née* Bolt); *m* 1969, Caroline (*née* Maling); four *s*. *Educ:* Royal Grammar School, Newcastle upon Tyne; College of Law, Guildford. Solicitor. Conservative Party: joined 1961 (N Area Vice-Chm of YC and Mem., Nat. Cttee); contested Durham, 1974 and Darlington, 1979; Hexham Treasurer, 1982–85; Exec., N Area, 1975–87; Mem., Nat. Exec., 1985–87. County Councillor, Northumberland, 1981–85. Mem., Newcastle Airport Bd, 1982–85; Mem., Northern RHA, 1982–86; Founder Lawyer Mem., Mental Health Act Commn, 1983–86. PPS to Minister of State for the Envmt and Countryside, 1989–90; an Asst Govt Whip, 1990–92; a Lord Comr of HM Treasury (Govt Whip), 1992–95. Mem., Select Cttee on Statutory Instruments, 1987–90; Vice Chm., Backbench Legal Cttee, 1988–89; Jt Hon. Sec., Cons. Backbench Envmt Cttee, 1988–89. *Recreations:* flying (holds private pilot's licence), tennis, swimming, watching TV quiz shows. *Address:* House of Commons, SW1A 0AA. *T:* 0171–219 4417. *Clubs:* Northern Counties (Newcastle upon Tyne); Dunstanburgh Castle Golf.

KIRKLAND, Joseph Lane; President, American Federation of Labor & Congress of Industrial Organizations, since 1979; *b* Camden, SC, 12 March 1922; *s* of Randolph Withers Kirkland and Louise Richardson; *m* Irena Neumann; five *d*. *Educ:* US Merchant Marine Academy, Kings Point, NY (grad. 1942); Georgetown Univ. Sch. of Foreign Service (BS 1948). Deck officer, various merchant ships, 1942–46; master mariner; Staff Scientist, US Navy Hydrographic Office, 1946–48; Staff Representative, AFL-CIO, 1948–58; Research and Educn Dir, Internat. Union of Operating Engrs, 1958–60; Exec. Asst to President, AFL-CIO, 1960–69; Sec.-Treasurer, AFL-CIO, 1969–79. Pres., Trade Union Adv. Cttee, OECD; Vice-Pres., Internat. Confedn of Free Trade Unions. Member: Blue Ribbon Defense Panel, 1969–70; Commn on CIA Activities Within the US, 1975; Commn on Foundns and Private Philanthropy, 1969–70; Gen. Adv. Cttee on Arms Control and Disarmament, 1974–78; Nat. Commn on Productivity, 1971–74; Presidential Commn on Financial Structure and Regulation, 1970–72; President's Maritime Adv. Cttee, 1964–66; President's Missile Sites Labor Commn (Alternate), 1961–67; Commn on Exec., Legislative and Judicial Salaries; Cttee on Selection of Fed. Judicial Officers; President's Commn on Social Security, 1982–83; Bipartisan Commn on Central America, 1983–84; Bd for Internat. Broadcasting; Polish American Enterprise Fund (Dir, 1990); Citizens Democracy Corps; Nat. Endowment for Democracy, 1983–93. Director: Amer. Arbitration Assoc.; Afr.-Amer. Labor Center (Pres., 1980–); Asian-Amer. Free Labor Inst. (Pres., 1980–); Free Trade Union Inst. (Pres., 1983–); Amer. Inst. for Free Labor Develt (Pres., 1980–). Mem., Internat. Org. of Masters, Mates and Pilots. Presidential Citizen's Medal; Distinguished Public Service Medal, Dept of Defense. Comdr, Order of Merit (Poland); Order of Merit (Hungary); Order of Francisco de Miranda (Venezuela). *Recreation:* archaeology. *Address:* (office) 815 16th Street NW, Washington, DC 20006, USA. *T:* (202) 6375000.

KIRKMAN, William Patrick, MBE 1993; Secretary: University of Cambridge Careers Service, 1968–92; Cambridge Society, since 1992; Fellow, Wolfson College, Cambridge (formerly University College), since 1968; *b* 23 Oct. 1932; *s* of late Geoffrey Charles Aylward Kirkman and Bertha Winifred Kirkman; *m* 1959, Anne Teasdale Fawcett; two *s* one *d*. *Educ:* Churcher's Coll., Petersfield, Hants; Oriel Coll., Oxford. 2nd cl. hons, mod. langs, 1955; MA 1959; MA (Cantab) by incorporation, 1968. National Service, 1950–52, RASC (L/Cpl); TA, 1952–59, Intell. Corps (Lieut). Editorial staff: Express & Star, Wolverhampton, 1955–57; The Times, 1957–64 (Commonwealth staff, 1960–64, Africa Correspondent, 1962–64). Asst Sec., Oxford Univ. Appointments Cttee, 1964–68. Chm., Standing Conf. of University Appointments Services, 1971–73; Member: Management Cttee, Central Services Unit for Univ. Careers and Appointments Services, 1971–74, 1985–87; British Cttee, Journalists in Europe, 1985–; Cambridge Univ. PR Co-ordinating Cttee, 1987–; Trng Bd, ESRC, 1990–93; BBC South and East Regl Adv. Council, 1990–92, Midlands and E Regl Adv. Council, 1992–93, E Regl Adv. Council, 1994–; Chm., BBC Radio Cambridgeshire Adv. Council, 1992–. Wolfson College: Vice-Pres., 1980–84; Mem. Council, 1969–73, 1976–80, 1988–92, 1994–; Dir, Press Fellowship Programme, 1982–. Churchwarden, St Mary and All Saints Willingham, 1978–85. Trustee: Sir Halley Stewart Trust, 1969– (Hon. Sec., 1978–82); Willingham British Sch. Trust, 1974–91; Homerton Coll., 1980–89; Lucy Cavendish Coll., 1989–; Mem. Cttee, Cambridge Soc., 1979–83. Editor, Cambridge, 1992–. *Publications:* Unscrambling an Empire, 1966; contrib.: Policing and Social Policy, 1984; Models of Police/Public Consultation in Europe, 1985; Managing Recruitment, 4th edn 1988; Graduate Recruitment: a 25-year retrospective, 1993; contributor to journals incl.: Commonwealth, International Affairs, Africa Contemporary Record, Financial Times, Cambridge Rev., The Higher, Cambridge, The Hindu (Madras), and to BBC. *Recreations:* broadcasting, gardening, church activities, writing. *Address:* 19 High Street, Willingham, Cambridge CB4 5ES. *T:* Willingham (01954) 260393. *Club:* Commonwealth Trust.

KIRKNESS, Donald James, CB 1980; Deputy Secretary, Overseas Development Administration, 1977–80; *b* 29 Sept 1919; *s* of Charles Stephen and Elsie Winifred Kirkness; *m* 1947, Monica Mary Douch; one *d*. *Educ:* Harvey Grammar Sch., Folkestone. Exchequer and Audit Dept, 1938. Served War: RA and Royal Berkshire Regt, 1939–46. Colonial Office, 1947 (Asst Principal); Financial and Economic Adviser, Windward I, 1955–57; Dept of Economic Affairs, 1966; Civil Service Dept, 1970–73; ODA/ODM, 1973. UK Governor, Internat. Fund for Agricultural Develt, 1977–81; Mem., Exec. Bd, UNESCO, 1978–83.

KIRKPATRICK, Gavin Alexander Yvone, FIPD, FBCS; Chief Executive, The British Computer Society, 1991–95; *b* 8 July 1938; *s* of late Yvone Kirkpatrick, OBE, TD, MA and Margaret (*née* Sclanders); *m* 1961, Susan Ann Frances Parselle; two *s* one *d*. *Educ:* Cheltenham Coll. Nat. Service, RN, 1957–59. John Trundell & Partners, Publishers, 1959–61; International Computers Ltd: Technical Sales, Personnel Officer, 1961–67; Personnel Manager Internat., 1967–70; Sperry Univac Division of Sperry Rand Corporation: Personnel Dir, Europe, 1970–76; Dir, Worldwide Personnel, Planning and Develt (USA), 1976–78; International Computers Plc, 1978–91: Gp Personnel Manager, 1978–81; Ops Personnel Manager, HQ, 1981–92; on secondment to Brit. Computer Soc. as Programme Dir, Europe, 1989–91. Member: European Movement, 1990– (Vice Chm., Outer London Europe Gp, 1994–); Anglo-German Assoc., 1992–. Mem., London Bach Soc., 1989–. MInstD 1970. FRSA 1992. Liveryman, Co. of Information Technologists, 1994–. *Recreations:* music, sailing, travel, photography, contemporary European developments. *Address:* West Walks House, Dorchester, Dorset DT1 1RE.

KIRKPATRICK, Sir Ivone Elliott, 11th Bt, *cr* 1685; *b* 1 Oct. 1942; *s* of Sir James Alexander Kirkpatrick, 10th Bt and Ellen Gertrude, *o d* of Captain R. P. Elliott, late RNR; *S* father 1954. *Educ:* Wellington Coll., Berks; St Mark's Coll., University of Adelaide. *Heir: b* Robin Alexander Kirkpatrick, *b* 19 March 1944. *Address:* c/o ANZ Bank, 81 King William Street, Adelaide, SA 5000, Australia.

KIRKPATRICK, John Lister, CBE 1981; chartered accountant, retired; *b* 27 June 1927; *s* of late Dr Henry Joseph Rodway Kirkpatrick and Dr Nora Kirkpatrick (*née* Lister); *m* 1977, Gay Elmslie (*née* Goudielock) (*d* 1995); one *s* one *d* of former marriage. *Educ:* Inverness Royal Acad. Served RNVR, 1944–47. Thomson McLintock & Co., subseq. KMG Thomson McLintock and Peat Marwick McLintock: apprentice, 1948; qual. CA 1952; Partner, 1958; Joint Senior Partner, Glasgow and Edinburgh, 1974–80; Co-Chm., UK Policy Council, 1974–83; Sen. Partner, Scotland, 1980–87; UK Dep. Chm., 1983–87; Consultant, 1987–90; McLintock Main Lafrenz (MML), subseq. Klynveld Main Goerdeler (KMG): Partner, 1974–87; Mem. Bd of Mgt, and Chm., Eastern Hemisphere Exec. Cttee, 1974–79; Mem., Central Mgt Cttee, and Chm., Region 1 (Europe, Africa, ME, India, Pakistan), 1979–85; Chm., ME, 1985–87. Institute of Chartered Accountants of Scotland: Vice Pres., 1975–77; Pres., 1977–78; Member: Examg Bd, Parly and Law Cttee (Chm.), Acctg and Auditing Standards Cttee (Chm.), and F and GP Cttee, 1964–75; Council, 1970–75. Mem. (rep. UK and Ireland), 1978–85, Chm., 1985–87, Internat. Acctg Standards Cttee; Lay Mem., Scottish Solicitors' Discipline Tribunal, 1981–. Member: BoT Accountants' Adv. Cttee, 1967–72; Exam. Supervisory Bd, Arab Soc. of Certified

Accountants, 1988–; Rev. Body on Doctors' and Dentists' Remuneration, 1983–89; Panel for Financial Services Tribunal, 1988–; Audits Jt Cttee, Securities Assoc., 1990–. Member: Royal Glasgow Inst. of Fine Arts; Merchants House of Glasgow; RSPB; Saints and Sinners Club of Scotland. Trustee, Highland Fund Foundn, 1983–90. FRSA 1989. Addresses and TV presentations to nat. and internat. audiences. *Publications:* various prof. papers and articles. *Recreations:* fishing, gardening, painting (watercolour), protection of precious environment of rural and island Scotland. *Address:* 1 Letham Drive, Newlands, Glasgow G43 2SL. *T:* 0141–633 1407. *Clubs:* New (Edinburgh); Eaglesham Angling.

KIRKPATRICK, William Brown; Member: Gaming Board for Great Britain; National Lottery Charities Board; *b* 27 April 1934; *s* of late Joseph and Mary Kirkpatrick, Thornhill, Dumfriesshire; *m* 1990, Joan L. Millar. *Educ:* Morton Acad., Thornhill; George Watson's Coll., Edinburgh; Univ. of Strathclyde (BScEcon); Columbia Business Sch., NY (MS and McKinsey Scholar); Stanford Executive Program. After three years in manufacturing industry in Glasgow, Dundee and London, served 3i, 1960–85, latterly at director level, and worked in London, Scotland and Australia in investment capital, corporate finance, fixed interest capital markets, on secondment as Industrial Director of Industry Department for Scotland, in shipping finance and as a nominee director; company dir and corporate advr with various cos, 1985–95 (incl. appt within DoE on water privatisation). JP Inner London, 1985–92. *Recreations:* Scottish paintings, porcelain pigs, shooting, current affairs. *Address:* Marchmount, Golf Hill, Moffat, Dumfriesshire DG10 9ST. *T:* Moffat (01683) 20459; 20 Abbotsbury House, Abbotsbury Road, W14 8EN. *T:* 0171–603 3087. *Club:* Caledonian.

KIRKUP, James; travel writer, poet, novelist, playwright, translator, broadcaster; *b* 23 April 1923; *o s* of James Harold Kirkup and Mary Johnson. *Educ:* South Shields High Sch.; Durham Univ. (BA; Hon. Fellow, Grey Coll., 1992). FRSL 1962. Gregory Fellow in Poetry, University of Leeds, 1950–52; Visiting Poet and Head of English Dept, Bath Academy of Art, Corsham Court, Wilts, 1953–56; Lectr in English, Swedish Ministry of Education, Stockholm, 1956–57; Prof. of Eng. Lang. and Lit., University of Salamanca, 1957–58, of English, Tohoku Univ., Sendai, Japan, 1958–61; Lecturer in English Literature, University of Malaya in Kuala Lumpur, 1961–62; Literary Editor, Orient/West Magazine, Tokyo, 1963–64; Prof., Japan Women's Univ., 1964–; Poet in Residence and Visiting Prof., Amherst Coll., Mass, 1968–; Prof. of English Literature, Nagoya Univ., 1969–72; Arts Council Fellowship in Creative Writing, Univ. of Sheffield, 1974–75; Morton Vis. Prof. of Internat. Literature, Ohio Univ., 1975–76; Playwright in Residence, Sherman Theatre, University Coll., Cardiff, 1976–77; Prof. of English Lit., Kyoto Univ. of Foreign Studies, Kyoto, Japan, 1977–. President: Poets' Soc. of Japan, 1969; British Haiku Soc., 1990; Sponsor, Inst. of Psychophysical Res., 1970. Atlantic Award in Literature (Rockefeller Foundn), 1950; Mabel Batchelder Award, 1968; Keats Prize for Poetry, 1974. *Plays performed:* Upon this Rock (perf. Peterborough Cathedral), 1955; Masque, The Triumph of Harmony (perf. Albert Hall), 1955; The True Mistery of the Nativity, 1957; Dürrenmatt, The Physicists (Eng. trans.), 1963; Dürrenmatt, The Meteor (Eng. trans.); Dürrenmatt, Play Strindberg (Eng. trans.), 1972; The Magic Drum, children's play, 1972, children's musical, 1977; Dürrenmatt, Portrait of a Planet, 1972; Dürrenmatt, The Conformer, 1974; Schiller, Don Carlos, 1975; Cyrano de Bergerac, 1975; *operas:* An Actor's Revenge, 1979; Friends in Arms, 1980; The Damask Drum, 1982; *television plays performed:* The Peach Garden, Two Pigeons Flying High, etc. Contributor to BBC, The Listener, The Spectator, Times Literary Supplement, The Independent, Modern Poetry in Translation, Time and Tide, New Yorker, Botteghe Oscure, London Magazine, Japan Qly, English Teachers' Magazine (Tokyo), etc. *Publications:* The Drowned Sailor, 1948; The Cosmic Shape, 1947; The Creation, 1950; The Submerged Village, 1951; A Correct Compassion, 1952; A Spring Journey, 1954; Upon This Rock, 1955; The True Mistery of the Nativity, 1957; The Descent into the Cave, 1957; Sorrows, Passions and Alarms, 1959; These Horned Islands, A Journal of Japan, 1962; frères Gréban, The True Mistery of the Passion, 1962; Refusal to Conform, 1963; Tropic Temper: a Memoir of Malaya, 1963; Japan Industrial, 1964–65 (2 vols); Daily Life in the French Revolution, 1964; Tokyo, 1965; England, Now, 1965; Japan, Now, 1966; Frankly Speaking, I-II, 1968; Bangkok, 1968; One Man's Russia, 1968; Filipinescas, 1968; Streets of Asia, 1969; Japan Physical, 1969; Aspects of the Short Story, 1969; Hong Kong, 1970; Japan Behind the Fan, 1970; Heaven, Hell and Hara-Kiri, 1974; (with Birgit Skiöld) Zen Gardens, 1974; Scenes from Sesshu, 1977; Zen Contemplations, 1979; (with Birgit Skiöld) The Tao of Water, 1980; Folktales Japanesque, 1982; Modern American Myths, 1982; I Am Count Dracula, 1982; I Am Frankenstein's Monster, 1983; Miniature Masterpieces of Kawabata Yasunari, 1983; When I was a Child: a study of nursery-rhymes, 1983; My Way-USA, 1984; The Glory that was Greece, 1984; The Mystery & Magic of Symbols, 1987; The Cry of the Owl: Native Folktales & Legends, 1987; (ed) A Certain State of Mind: an anthology of modern and contemporary Japanese haiku poets, 1995; (ed) Modern and Contemporary Japanese Poets, 1995; *poems:* The Prodigal Son, 1959; Paper Windows: Poems from Japan, 1968; Shepherding Winds (anthol.), 1969; Songs and Dreams (anthol.), 1970; White Shadows, Black Shadows: Poems of Peace and War, 1970; The Body Servant; poems of exile, 1971; A Bewick Bestiary, 1971; Modern Japanese Poetry (anthol.), 1978; Dengonban Messages (one-line poems), 1980; To the Ancestral North: poems for an autobiography, 1983; The Sense of the Visit: new poems, 1984; The Guitar-Player of Zuiganji, 1985; Fellow Feelings, 1986; Shooting Stars (haiku), 1992; First Fireworks (haiku), 1992; Short Takes (one-line poems), 1993; Words for Contemplation, 1993; Look at it this way! (for children), 1993; Blue Bamboo: haiku, senryu and tanka, 1994; Formulas for Chaos, 1994; Strange Attractors, 1995; Collected Longer Poems, 1995; Selected Shorter Poems, 1995; Noems, Koans and a Navel Display, 1995; Counting to 9,999: haiku and tanka, 1995; *poems and translations:* Ecce Homo: My Pasolini, 1982; No More Hiroshimas, 1982; *autobiography:* vol. 1, The Only Child, 1957 (trans. Japanese, 1986); vol. 2, Sorrows, Passions and Alarms, 1987 (trans. Japanese); vol. 3, I, of All People: an Autobiography of Youth, 1990; vol. 4, A Poet could not But be Gay: some Legends of my Lost Youth, 1991; vol. 5, Me All Over: memoirs of a misfit, 1993; Throwback: poems towards an autobiography, 1992; *novels:* The Love of Others, 1962; Insect Summer (for children), 1971; The Magic Drum (for children), 1973; Gaijin on the Ginza, 1991; Queens have Died Young and Fair, 1993; *essays:* Eibungaku Saiken, 1980; The Joys of Japan, 1985; Lafcadio Hearn (biog.), 1985; James Kirkup's International Movie Theatre, 1985; Trends and Traditions, 1986; Portraits & Souvenirs (biog.), 1987; *opera:* The Damask Drum, 1982; An Actor's Revenge, 1989; The Genius of Haiku: essays on R. H. Blyth, 1994; *translations:* Camara Laye, The Dark Child, 1955; Ancestral Voices, 1956; Camara Laye, The Radiance of the King, 1956; Simone de Beauvoir, Memoirs of a Dutiful Daughter, 1958; The Girl from Nowhere, 1958; It Began in Babel, 1961; The Captive, 1962; Sins of the Fathers, 1962; The Gates of Paradise, 1962; The Heavenly Mandate, 1964; Daily Life of the Etruscans, 1964; Erich Kästner, The Little Man, 1966; Erich Kästner, The Little Man and The Little Miss, 1969; Heinrich von Kleist, Michael Kohlhaas, 1966; E. T. A. Hoffmann, Tales of Hoffmann, 1966; Camara Laye, A Dream of Africa, 1967; The Eternal Virgin (Eng. trans. of Valéry's La Jeune Parque), 1970; (with C. Fry) The Oxford Ibsen, vol III, Brand and Peer Gynt, 1972; Selected Poems of Takagi Kyozo, 1973; Camara Laye, The Guardian of the Word, 1980; Cold Mountain Poems (trans. Han Shan), 1980; Petru Dimitriu, To the Unknown God, 1982; Michel Kpomassié, An African in Greenland, 1982; Tierno Monénembo, The Bush Toads, 1982; Margherita Guidacci, This Little Measure, 1990; Patrick Drevet, A Room in the Woods, 1991; Marc Rigaudis, Ito-san, 1991; Jean-Baptiste Niel, Painted Shadows, 1991; Jean-Noël Pancrazi, Vagabond Winter, 1992; Pascal Quignard, All the World's Mornings, 1992; Patrick Drevet, My Micheline, 1993; Hervé Guibert, The Man in the Red Hat, The Compassion Protocol, 1993; Georges-Arthur Goldschmidt, Worlds of Difference, 1993; Hervé Guibert, Being Blind, Paradise, 1995; Tahar Ben Jelloun, State of Absence, 1995; Marcelle Lagesse, Isabelle, 1995. *Recreation:* standing in shafts of moonlight. *Address:* British Monomarks-Box 2780, London WC1N 3XX.

KIRKWOOD, family name of **Baron Kirkwood.**

KIRKWOOD, 3rd Baron *cr* 1951, of Bearsden; **David Harvie Kirkwood;** Senior Lecturer in Metallurgy, 1976–87, Hon. Senior Lecturer and Metallurgical Consultant, since 1987, Sheffield University; *b* 24 Nov. 1931; *s* of 2nd Baron Kirkwood and of Eileen Grace, *d* of Thomas Henry Boalch; *S* father, 1970; *m* 1965, Judith Rosalie, *d* of late John Hunt; three *d. Educ:* Rugby; Trinity Hall, Cambridge (MA, PhD); CEng. Lectr in Metallurgy, Sheffield Univ., 1962; Warden of Stephenson Hall, Sheffield Univ., 1974–80. Mem., Select Cttee on Sci. and Technology, H of L, 1987–92. *Heir: b* Hon. James Stuart Kirkwood [*b* 19 June 1937; *m* 1965, Alexandra Mary, *d* of late Alec Dyson; two *d*]. *Address:* 56 Endcliffe Hall Avenue, Sheffield S10 3EL. *T:* Sheffield (0114) 266 3107.

KIRKWOOD, Hon. Lord; Ian Candlish Kirkwood; a Senator of the College of Justice in Scotland, since 1987; *b* 8 June 1932; *o s* of late John Brown Kirkwood, OBE, and Mrs Constance Kirkwood, Edinburgh; *m* 1970, Jill Ingram Scott; two *s. Educ:* George Watson's Boys' Coll., Edinburgh; Edinburgh Univ.; Univ. of Michigan, USA. MA (Edin) 1952; LLB (Edin) 1954; LLM (Mich) 1956. Called to Scottish Bar, 1957; apptd Standing Junior Counsel to Scottish Home and Health Dept, 1963; QC (Scot.) 1970. Member: Rules Council (Court of Session); Parole Bd for Scotland. Formerly Pres., Wireless Telegraphy Appeal Tribunal in Scotland. Chm., Med. Appeal Tribunal in Scotland. *Recreations:* fishing, golf, chess, tennis. *Address:* 58 Murrayfield Avenue, Edinburgh EH12 6AY. *T:* 0131–477 1994; Knockbrex House, near Borgue, Kirkcudbrightshire. *Club:* New (Edinburgh).

KIRKWOOD, Hon. Sir Andrew (Tristram Hammett), Kt 1993; **Hon. Mr Justice Kirkwood;** a Judge of the High Court of Justice, Family Division, since 1993; *b* 5 June 1944; *s* of Maj. T. G. H. Kirkwood, RE (killed in action, 1944) and late Lady Faulks; *m* 1968, Penelope Jane (*née* Eaton); two *s* one *d. Educ:* Radley Coll., Abingdon, Oxon; Christ Church, Oxford (MA). Called to the Bar, Inner Temple, 1966, Bencher, 1993; QC 1989; a Recorder, 1987–93. Chm., Leics Inquiry, 1992. Mem., Judicial Studies Bd, 1994– (Co-Chm., Civil and Family Cttee, 1994–). *Address:* Royal Courts of Justice, Strand, WC2A 2LL. *Club:* MCC.

KIRKWOOD, Archy, (Archibald Johnstone Kirkwood); MP Roxburgh and Berwickshire, since 1983 (L/Alliance 1983–88, Lib Dem since 1988); *b* 22 April 1946; *s* of David Kirkwood and Jessie Barclay Kirkwood; *m* 1972, Rosemary Chester; one *d* one *s. Educ:* Cranhill School; Heriot-Watt University. BSc Pharmacy. Notary Public; Solicitor. Lib Dem convenor and spokesman on welfare, 1988–92, on social security, 1992–94, on community care, 1994–; Chief Whip, 1992–. Trustee, Joseph Rowntree Reform Trust, 1985–. *Address:* House of Commons, SW1A 0AA. *T:* 0171–219 3000.

KIRKWOOD, Ian Candlish; *see* Kirkwood, Hon. Lord.

KIRKWOOD, Prof. Kenneth, MA; Rhodes Professor of Race Relations, University of Oxford, 1954–86, Professor Emeritus, since 1986; Fellow of St Antony's College, 1954–86, Emeritus Fellow, since 1986, and Sub-Warden, 1968–71; *b* Benoni, Transvaal, 1919; *s* of late Thomas Dorman Kirkwood and Lily Kirkwood (*née* Bewley); *m* 1942, Deborah Burton, *d* of late Burton Ireland Collings and Emily Frances Collings (*née* Loram); three *s* three *d.* BA; BSc Rand. Captain, South African Engineer Corps, War of 1939–45; served in East Africa, North Africa and Italy (despatches). Lecturer, University of the Witwatersrand, 1947; Lecturer, University of Natal, 1948–51; Fellowship, University of London (Inst. of Commonwealth Studies, 1952); Carnegie Travelling Fellowship, USA, 1953; Senior Research Officer, Inst. of Colonial Studies, Oxford Univ., 1953; Organiser of Institute for Social Research, University of Natal, 1954. Chm. Regional Cttee, S African Inst. of Race Relations in Natal, 1954; UK Rep. SA Inst. of Race Relations, 1955–86. Investigation on behalf UNESCO into trends in race relations in British Non-Self-Governing Territories of Africa, 1958; Visiting Prof. of Race Relations (UNESCO), University Coll. of Rhodesia and Nyasaland, 1964; composed memorandum on meaning, and procedure for further study of 'racial discrimination,' for UN Div. of Human Rights, 1966–67; Mem., Africa Educational Trust, Oxfam, etc, 1955–. Chm., UK Standing Cttee on University Studies of Africa, 1975–78; Chm. of Trustees, Oxford Project for Peace Studies, 1983–; Hon. Pres., Oxford Br., UNA, 1986–. UK Official Observer, Rhodesian Elections, March 1980. *Publications:* The Proposed Federation of the Central African Territories, 1952; (contrib.) Lord Hailey's An African Survey, rev. edn 1957; (ed) St Antony's Papers: African Affairs, number 1, 1961; number 2, 1963; number 3, 1969; (contrib.) Vol. VIII, Cambridge History of the British Empire, 2nd edn 1963; (ed with E. E. Sabben-Clare and D. J. Bradley) Health in Tropical Africa during the Colonial Period, 1980; (ed and contrib.) Biosocial Aspects of Ethnic Minorities, 1983; Peace within States, Ethnic, Cultural and Racial Issues (lecture), 1989; booklets and articles on race relations and internat. affairs; *relevant publication:* Ethnicity, Empire and Race Relations: essays in honour of Kenneth Kirkwood, ed Anthony Kirk-Greene and John Stone, 1986. *Address:* St Antony's College, Oxford; 233 Woodstock Road, Oxford OX2 7AD. *T:* Oxford (01865) 515867.

See also T. B. L. Kirkwood.

KIRKWOOD, Prof. Thomas Burton Loram, PhD; Professor of Biological Gerontology, University of Manchester, since 1993; *b* 6 July 1951; *s* of Kenneth Kirkwood, *qv*; *m* 1973, Betty Rosamund Bartlett (marr. diss. 1995); one *s* one *d. Educ:* Dragon Sch., Oxford; Magdalen Coll. Sch., Oxford; St Catharine's Coll., Cambridge (MA; PhD 1983); Worcester Coll., Oxford (MSc). Scientist, Nat. Inst. for Biol Standards and Control, 1973–81; National Institute for Medical Research: Sen. Scientist, 1981–88; Head, Lab. of Mathematical Biol., 1988–93. Various distinguished lectures. Chm., Brit. Soc. for Research on Ageing, 1992–; mem., various scientific cttees and editl bds. Heinz Kargar Prize, 1983. *Publications:* (jtly) Accuracy in Molecular Processes: its control and relevance to living systems, 1986; many scientific articles. *Recreations:* hill-walking, running, pottery, Nefyn. *Address:* University of Manchester, 3.239 Stopford Building, Oxford Road, Manchester M13 9PT. *T:* 0161–275 6851.

KIRNER, Hon. Joan Elizabeth, AM 1980; Chairman: Employment Services Regulatory Authority, 1994–96; Advisory Committee, Centenary of Federation, 1994–96; *b* 20 June 1938; *d* of J. K. and B. E. Hood; *m* 1960, Ronald Kirner; two *s* one *d. Educ:* University High Sch.; Melbourne Univ. (BA, Dip. Educn). English and Social Studies Teacher, Ballarat Tech. Sch., 1959–60; positions with Vic. Fedn of State Schs Parents' Clubs, Aust. Council of State Schs Orgns and Tech. and Further Educn Councils, to 1982. Joined ALP 1979; MLC Melbourne West, 1982–88; MLA (ALP) Williamstown, Victoria, 1988–94;

Minister for: Conservation, Forests and Lands, 1985–88; Education, 1988–90; Ethnic Affairs, 1990–91; Women's Affairs, 1990–92; Dep. Premier, 1989–90; Premier of Victoria, 1990–92; Leader of the Opposition, 1992–94; Shadow Minister for Ethnic Affairs, and for Women's Affairs, 1992–93. Fellow, Aust. Coll. of Educn, 1983. *Recreations:* films, walking, music. *Address:* ESRA, 24th Floor, Casselden Place, 2 Lonsdale Street, Melbourne, Vic 3001, Australia. *T:* (3) 2857310, *Fax:* (3) 2857300.

KIRSHBAUM, Ralph; cellist; *b* Texas, 4 March 1946; *m* 1982, Antoinette Reynolds; one *s*. Founder and Artistic Dir, RNCM Manchester Internat. Cello Fest., 1988–. Has performed with major orchestras including: BBC Symphony; Boston Symphony; Cleveland Orch.; London Symphony; Orchestre de Paris; Pittsburgh Symphony; San Francisco Symphony; Chicago Symphony. Festival appearances at Aspen, Bath, Edinburgh, Lucerne, New York and Ravinia. Chamber music collaboration with Gyorgy Pauk, Peter Frankl and Pinchas Zukerman. Recordings include: concertos: Barber; Elgar; Haydn D major; Tippett Triple; Walton; Ravel, Shostakovich and Brahms Trios, complete Bach suites. *Address:* c/o Ingpen & Williams, 14 Kensington Court, W8 5DN.

KIRSTEIN, Lincoln Edward; Founder, 1934, former Director, now President Emeritus, School of American Ballet; former General Director, New York City Ballet; *b* Rochester, NY, 4 May 1907; *s* of Louis E. Kirstein and Rose Stein; *m* 1941, Fidelma Cadmus; no *c*. *Educ:* Harvard Coll.; BS 1930. Edited Hound & Horn, 1927–34; founded and directed American Ballet Caravan, 1936–41; Third US Army (Arts, Monuments and Archives Section), 1943–45. Editor, The Dance Index, 1941–47. Benjamin Franklin Medal, RSA, 1981; Governor's Arts Award, NY State, 1984; US Presidential Medal of Freedom, 1984; Nat. Medal of Arts, 1985; Municipal Art Soc. Award, 1985. *Publications:* Flesh is Heir, 1932, repr. 1975; Dance, A Short History of Theatrical Dancing, 1935; Blast at Ballet, 1938; Ballet Alphabet, 1940; Drawings of Pavel Tchelitchew, 1947; Elie Nadelman Drawings, 1949; The Dry Points of Elie Nadelman, 1952; What Ballet is About, 1959; Three Pamphlets Collected, 1967; The Hampton Institute Album, 1968; Movement and Metaphor: four centuries of ballet, 1970; Lay This Laurel, 1974; Nijinsky, Dancing, 1975; Ballet: bias and belief, 1983; *verse:* Rhymes of a PFC (Private First Class), 1964; *monographs:* Gaston Lachaise, 1935; Walker Evans, 1938; Latin American Art, 1942; American Battle Art, 1945; Henri Cartier-Bresson, 1946; Dr William Rimmer, 1946; Elie Nadelman, 1948; Pavel Tchelitchew, 1964; W. Eugene Smith, 1970; George Tooker, 1983; Paul Cadmus, 1983; *edited:* The Classic Dance, Technique and Terminology, 1951; William Shakespeare: A Catalogue of the Works of Art in the American Shakespeare Festival Theater, 1964; Elie Nadelman, 1973; New York City Ballet, 1973; Thirty Years: the New York City Ballet, 1978; A. Hyatt Mayor: collected writings, 1983; Quarry: a collection in lieu of memoirs, 1986; The Poems of Lincoln Kirstein, 1987. *Address:* School of American Ballet, 144 West 66th Street, New York, NY 10023–6547, USA. *T:* 8770600.

KIRTON, Col Hugh, TD 1952; Vice Lord-Lieutenant, County Durham, 1978–87; *b* Plawsworth, Co. Durham, 7 Aug. 1910; 2nd *s* of late Hugh Kirton and Margaretta Kirton (*née* Darling). *Educ:* Durham Sch. Chartered Accountant, 1933. Army Service: commnd in Tyne Electrical Engrs (TA), 1937; RE(TA), 1937–40; RA(TA), 1940–45 and 1951–56, Lt Col 1945; Dep. Comdr, 31AA Bde(TA), 1959–61, Col 1959; Hon. Col 439 (Tyne) Lt AD Regt RA(TA), 1961–67. With Procter & Gamble Ltd, Newcastle upon Tyne, 1934–70, Dir, 1963–70; retired 1970. Mem., North Regional Health Authority, 1973–76; General Comr of Taxes (Newcastle upon Tyne), 1965–85. Mem. Council, Inst. of Chartered Accountants in England and Wales, 1966–70; Pres., Northern Soc. of Chartered Accountants, 1968–69. Mem., St John Council for Co. Durham, 1970–, Chm., 1974–86. DL: Northumberland 1961; Durham 1974; High Sheriff Co. Durham 1973–74. KStJ 1983. *Recreations:* golf, gardening. *Address:* Ovington, Plawsworth, Chester-le-Street, Co. Durham DH2 3LE. *T:* Durham (0191) 3710261. *Clubs:* Northern Counties (Newcastle upon Tyne); Brancepeth Castle Golf (Captain 1969–71).

KIRWAN, Sir (Archibald) Laurence (Patrick), KCMG 1972 (CMG 1958); TD; MLitt Oxon; Hon. Vice-President, Royal Geographical Society, since 1981 (Director and Secretary, 1945–75); *b* 13 May 1907; 2nd *s* of Patrick Kirwan, Cregg, County Galway, Ireland, and Mabel Norton; *m* 1st, 1932, Joan Elizabeth Chetwynd; one *d*; 2nd, 1949, Stella Mary Monck. *Educ:* Wimbledon Coll.; Merton Coll., Oxford. Asst Dir of the Archaeological Survey of Nubia, Egyptian Dept of Antiquities, 1929–34; Field Dir, Oxford Univ. Expeditions to Sudan, 1934–37; Tweedie Fellowship in Archæology and Anthropology, Edinburgh Univ., 1937–39. Boston and Philadelphia Museums, 1937; Exploratory journeys, Eastern Sudan and Aden Protectorate, 1938–39. TARO Capt., General Staff, 1939; Major, 1941; Lieut-Col 1943; Joint Staffs, Offices of Cabinet and Ministry of Defence, 1942–45; Hon. Lt-Col, 1957. Editor, Geographical Journal, 1945–78; Pres., Brit. Inst. in Eastern Africa, 1961–81, Hon. Life Pres. and Hon. Mem., 1981. Pres. (Section E), British Assoc. for the Advancement of Science, 1961–62; Member: Court of Arbitration, Argentine-Chile Frontier Case, 1965–68 (Leader, Field Mission, 1966); Sec. of State for Transport's Adv. Cttee on Landscape Treatment of Trunk Roads, 1968–81 (Dep. Chm., 1970–80); UN Register of fact-finding experts, 1968–; Court, Exeter Univ., 1969–80; a Governor, Imperial Coll. of Science and Technology, 1962–81; British Academy/Leverhulme Vis. Prof., Cairo, 1976; Mortimer Wheeler Lectr, Brit. Acad., 1977. Hon. Pres., Sudan Archaeol Res. Soc., 1992. Fellow: University Coll. London; Imperial College of Science and Technology; Hon. Fellow: SOAS; Amer. Geographical Soc.; Hon. Member: Geographical Societies of Paris, Vienna, Washington; Royal Inst. of Navigation; Institut d'Egypte; Internat. Soc. for Nubian Studies (Patron). Founder's Medal, RGS, 1975. Knight Cross of the Order of St Olav, Norway; Jubilee Medal, 1977. *Publications:* (with W. B. Emery) Excavations and Survey between Wadi-es-Sebua and Adindan, 1935; (with W. B. Emery) Royal Tombs of Ballana and Qustal, 1938; Oxford University Excavations at Firka, 1938; The White Road (polar exploration), 1959; papers on archæology, historical and political geography, exploration, in scientific and other publications. *Recreation:* travel. *Address:* c/o Royal Geographical Society, SW7 2AR. *Club:* Geographical.

KIRWAN, Sir Laurence; *see* Kirwan, Sir A. L. P.

KIRYA, Prof. George Barnabas; High Commissioner for Uganda in the United Kingdom, since 1990; *b* 9 Feb. 1939; *m*; five *s* one *d*. *Educ:* Univ. of E Africa (MB ChB 1966); Birmingham Univ. (MSc Gen. Virology 1971); Manchester Univ. (Dip. Bacteriology 1974). Med. House Officer, Mulago Hosp., Uganda, 1966–67; Sen. House Officer, Dept of Paediatrics and Child Health, Makerere Fac. of Medicine, 1967; East Africa Virus Res. Inst., Entebbe: Virologist, 1967; Sen. Med. Res. Officer, 1968; Principal Med. Res. Officer and Head, Dept of Arbovirology, 1969; Hon. Lectr, Dept of Med. Microbiol., Makerere Univ., 1970; Consultant on Yellow Fever Epidemics, WHO, 1970; Department of Microbiology, Faculty of Medicine, Makerere University: Sen. Lectr, 1973–75; Associate Prof. and Hd of Dept, 1975–78; Prof. and Hd of Dept, 1978; Makerere University: Mem. Senate, 1977–90; Mem. Univ. Council, 1981–90; Vice Chancellor, 1986–90. Mem., WHO Scientific and Technical Adv. Gp, serving as WHO Temp. Advr, 1990–93. Dir, Central Public Health Labs in Uganda supported by WHO, UNICEF and Min. of Health; Chm., Disease Surveillance Sub-Cttee, Min. of Health; Member: Nat. Cttee for Prevention of Blindness in Uganda; Adv. Cttee for Res. of Viruses in Uganda; E and Central African Physicians Assoc. Uganda Medical Association: Treas., 1978–82; Pres., 1982–86. Teaching and supervising undergrad. and post-grad. med. students, med. lab. technologists, nurses and midwives and health visitors. Internal examnr and external examnr for several univs incl. Univ. of Ibadan, Lagos Univ. and Univ. of Nairobi. Member, Editorial Bd: E African Jl for Med. Res.; Uganda Med. Jl. *Address:* Uganda House, 58/59 Trafalgar Square, WC2N 5DX. *T:* 0171–839 5783; 30 Ingram Avenue, Hampstead, NW11. *Club:* Africa Cricket (Kampala).

KISSIN, family name of **Baron Kissin.**

KISSIN, Baron *cr* 1974 (Life Peer), of Camden in Greater London; **Harry Kissin;** Life President: Guinness Peat Group plc, since 1979; Lewis & Peat Holdings Ltd, since 1987; Director: Tycon SPA Venice, since 1975, and of other public and private companies in the City of London, since 1934; *b* 23 Aug. 1912; *s* of Israel Kissin and Reusi Kissin (*née* Model), both of Russian nationality; *m* 1935, Ruth Deborah Samuel, London; one *s* one *d*. *Educ:* Danzig and Switzerland. Dr of Law, Basle, Swiss lawyer until 1933. Chairman: Lewis & Peat Ltd, 1961–72; Guinness Peat Group, 1973–79; Lewis & Peat Holdings Ltd, 1982–87; Linfood Holdings, 1974–81; Esperanza International Services plc, 1970–83; Dir, Transcontinental Services NV, 1982–86. Dir, Royal Opera Hse, Covent Gdn, 1973–84; Mem., Royal Opera House Trust, 1974–87 (Chm., 1974–80). Chm. Council, ICA, 1968–75. Governor: Bezalel Acad. of Arts and Design, 1975–87; Hebrew Univ. of Jerusalem, 1980. Comdr, Ordem Nacional do Cruzeiro do Sul (Brazil), 1977; Chevalier, Légion d'honneur, 1981; Bulgarian Commemorative Medal, 1300 Years Bulgaria Medal, 1982. *Address:* c/o House of Lords, SW1A 0PW. *Clubs:* Reform, East India, Devonshire, Sports and Public Schools.

KISSINGER, Henry Alfred; Hon. KCMG 1995; Bronze Star (US); Chairman, Kissinger Associates Inc., since 1982; Counselor to Center for Strategic and International Studies, since 1977 and Trustee, since 1987; *b* Germany, 27 May 1923; *s* of late Louis Kissinger and of Paula (*née* Stern); *m* 1st, 1949, Anne Fleischer (marr. diss. 1964); one *s* one *d*; 2nd, 1974, Nancy Maginnes. *Educ:* George Washington High Sch., NYC; Harvard Univ., Cambridge, Mass (BA 1950, MA 1952, PhD 1954). Emigrated to United States, 1938; naturalised, 1943. Served Army, 1943–46. Teaching Fellow, Harvard Univ., 1950–54; Study Director: Council on Foreign Relations, 1955–56: Rockefeller Bros Fund, 1956–58; Associate Professor of Govt, Harvard Univ., 1958–62, Prof. of Govt, 1962–71, and Faculty Mem., Center for Internat. Affairs, Harvard; Director: Harvard Internat. Seminar, 1951–69; Harvard Defense Studies Program, 1958–69; Asst to US President for Nat. Security Affairs, 1969–75; Secretary of State, USA, 1973–77. Chm., Nat. Bipartisan Commn on Central America, 1983–84; Member: President's Foreign Intelligence Adv. Bd, 1984–90; Commn on Integrated Long-Term Strategy of the National Security Council and Defense Dept, 1986–88; Dir, Internat. Rescue Cttee, 1987–; Hon. Gov., Foreign Policy Assoc., 1985–. Chm., Internat. Adv. Bd, American Internat. Group, Inc.; Mem., Internat. Adv. Cttee, Chase Manhattan Bank, 1977–; Director: American Express Co.; Continental Grain Co.; CBS Inc.; Revlon Gp Inc.; Freeport-McMoRan. Trustee, Metropolitan Mus. of Art, 1977–. Syndicated writer, Los Angeles Times, 1984–: (Jtly) Nobel Peace Prize, 1973; Presidential Medal of Freedom, 1977; Medal of Liberty, 1986. *Publications:* A World Restored: Castlereagh, Metternich and the Restoration of Peace, 1957; Nuclear Weapons and Foreign Policy, 1957 (Woodrow Wilson Prize, 1958; citation, Overseas Press Club, 1958); The Necessity for Choice: Prospects of American Foreign Policy, 1961; The Troubled Partnership: a reappraisal of the Atlantic Alliance, 1965; Problems of National Strategy: A Book of Readings (ed), 1965; American Foreign Policy: three essays, 1969, 3rd edn 1977; White House Years (memoirs), 1979; For the Record: selected statements 1977–1980, 1981; Years of Upheaval (memoirs), 1982; Observations: selected speeches and essays 1982–1984, 1985; Diplomacy, 1994. *Address:* Suite 400, 1800 K Street, NW, Washington, DC 20006, USA; 350 Park Avenue, New York, NY 10022, USA. *Clubs:* Century, River (New York); Metropolitan (Washington); Bohemian (San Francisco).

KITAJ, R. B., RA 1991 (ARA 1984); artist; *b* Ohio, 29 Oct. 1932; *m* (wife decd); two *c*; *m* 1983, Sandra Fisher (*d* 1994); one *s*. *Educ:* Cooper Union Inst., NY; Acad. of Fine Art, Vienna; Ruskin Sch. of Art, Oxford; RCA (ARCA). Part-time teacher: Camberwell Sch. of Art, 1961–63; Slade Sch., 1963–67; Visiting Professor: Univ. of Calif. at Berkeley, 1968; UCLA, 1970. Lives in London. *One-man Exhibitions:* Marlborough New London Gall., 1963, 1970; Marlborough Gall., NY, 1965, 1974; Los Angeles County Museum of Art, 1965; Stedelijk Mus., Amsterdam, 1967; Mus. of Art, Cleveland, 1967; Univ. of Calif, Berkeley, 1967; Kestner Gesellschaft, Hanover, 1970; Boymans-van-Beuningen Mus., Rotterdam, 1970; Cincinnati Art Mus., Ohio, 1973; Marlborough Fine Art, 1977, 1980, 1985. *Retrospective Exhibitions:* Hirshhorn Museum, Washington, 1981; Cleveland Museum of Art, Ohio, 1981; Kunsthalle, Düsseldorf, 1982; Tate Gall. and LA County Mus., 1994; Metropolitan Mus., NY, 1994–95. Member: US Acad. (formerly Inst.) of Arts and Letters, NY, 1982; Nat. Acad. of Design, NY, 1982. Hon. DLit London, 1982; Hon. Dr RCA, 1991. *Publication:* First Diasporist Manifesto, 1989; *relevant publication:* R. B. Kitaj by M. Livingstone, 1985. *Address:* c/o Marlborough Fine Art (London) Ltd, 6 Albemarle Street, W1X 3HF.

KITAMURA, Hiroshi; Japanese Ambassador to the Court of St James's, 1991–94; Corporate Advisor to Mitsubishi Corporation; *b* 20 Jan. 1929; *s* of Teiji and Fusako Kitamura; *m* 1953, Sachiko Ito; two *d*. *Educ:* Univ. of Tokyo (LLB 1951); Fletcher School of Law and Diplomacy, Medford, USA, 1952. Joined Min. of Foreign Affairs, Tokyo, 1953; postings to Washington DC, New York, New Delhi, London; Dir, Policy Planning Div., Res. and Planning Dept, Tokyo, 1974; Private Sec. to Prime Minister, 1974–76; Dep. Dir-Gen., Amer. Affairs Bureau, 1977–79; Consul-Gen., San Francisco, 1979–82; Dir-Gen., American Affairs Bureau, 1982–84; Dep. Vice Minister for Foreign Affairs, 1984–87; Dep. Minister, 1987–88; Ambassador to Canada, 1988–90. *Publication:* Psychological Dimensions of US-Japanese Relations, 1977. *Recreations:* traditional Japanese music, culinary arts, golf. *Address:* c/o Mitsubishi Corporation, 6–3 Marunouchi 2–chome, Chiyoda-ku, Tokyo 100–86, Japan.

KITCATT, Sir Peter (Julian), Kt 1992; CB 1986; Speaker's Secretary, House of Commons, 1986–93; *b* 5 Dec. 1927; *s* of late Horace Wilfred Kitcatt and Ellen Louise Kitcatt (*née* Julian); *m* 1952, Audrey Marian Aylen; three *s* two *d*. *Educ:* Borden Grammar Sch., Sittingbourne; King's Coll., Cambridge (Scholar). RASC (2nd Lt) 1948. Asst Principal, Colonial Office, 1950–53; Asst Private Sec. to Sec. of State for the Colonies, 1953–54; Principal, Colonial Office, 1954–64; Sec. to HRH The Princess Royal on Caribbean Tour, 1960; Sec., E African Econ. and Fiscal Commn, 1960; HM Treasury: Principal, 1964; Asst Sec., 1966; RCDS, 1972; Under Sec., 1973, seconded to DHSS, 1975–78. *Recreation:* golf. *Club:* Croham Hurst Golf (Croydon).

KITCHEN, Michael; actor; with Royal Shakespeare Co., since 1986; *b* 31 Oct. 1948; *s* of Arthur and Betty Kitchen; partner, Rowena Miller; one *s*. *Educ:* City of Leicester Boys' Grammar School. Entered acting profession, 1970; *stage includes:* seasons at Belgrade Theatre, Coventry, National Youth Theatre; Royal Court, 1971–73; Big Wolf, Magnificence, Skyvers; Young Vic, 1975: Othello, Macbeth, As You Like It, Charley's

Aunt; National Theatre: Spring Awakening, 1974; Romeo and Juliet, 1974; State of Revolution, 1977; Bedroom Farce, 1977; No Man's Land, 1977; The Homecoming, 1978; Family Voices, 1981; On the Razzle, 1981; The Provok'd Wife, 1981; Rough Crossing, 1984; Royal Shakespeare Co: Romeo and Juliet, Richard II, 1986; The Art of Success, 1987; *films include:* The Bunker; Breaking Glass; Towards the Morning; Out of Africa; Home Run; The Russia House; Fools of Fortune; The Dive; *television series:* Steven Hind; Divorce; Freud, 1983; The Justice Game, 1989; The Guilty, 1992; To Play the King, 1993; Dandelion Dead, 1994; *television films and plays include:* Caught on a Train; Benefactors; Ball-Trap; Pied Piper; The Enchanted April; Hostage; numerous other TV and radio performances. *Recreations:* piano, guitar, flying, writing, tennis, riding. *Address:* c/o ICM, Oxford House, 76 Oxford Street, W1R 1RB.

KITCHEN, Stanley, FCA; *b* 23 Aug. 1913; *s* of late Percy Inman Kitchen, OBE and Elizabeth Kitchen; *m* 1941, Jean Craig; two *d.* *Educ:* Rugby Sch. ACA 1937, FCA 1953. Army, 1939–46: Major, RASC. Sec., British Rollmakers Corp. Ltd, Wolverhampton, 1946–48; Partner, Foster & Stephens, later Touche Ross & Co., chartered accountants, Birmingham, 1948–81. Chm., STEP Management Services Ltd, 1978–85; Dir, Cobalt (UK) Ltd, 1986–92. Birmingham and West Midlands Soc. of Chartered Accountants: Mem. Cttee, 1951–81; Sec., 1953–55; Pres., 1957–58; Inst. of Chartered Accountants in England and Wales: Mem. Council, 1966–81; Vice-Pres., 1974–75; Dep. Pres., 1975–76; Pres., 1976–77. Liveryman, Chartered Accountants' Co., 1977– (Mem. Court, 1979–85). *Publications:* Learning to Live with Taxes on Capital Gains, 1967; Important Aspects of Professional Partnerships, 1974. *Recreations:* gardening, golf. *Address:* 1194 Warwick Road, Knowle, Solihull, West Midlands B93 9LL. *T:* Knowle (01564) 772360. *Clubs:* Lansdowne; Birmingham, Chamber of Commerce (Birmingham).

KITCHENER OF KHARTOUM, and of Broome; 3rd Earl, *cr* 1914; **Henry Herbert Kitchener,** TD; DL; Viscount, *cr* 1902, of Khartoum; of the Vaal, Transvaal, and Aspall, Suffolk; Viscount Broome, *cr* 1914, of Broome, Kent; Baron Denton, *cr* 1914, of Denton, Kent; late Major, Royal Corps of Signals; *b* 24 Feb. 1919; *er s* of Viscount Broome (*d* 1928) and Adela Mary Evelyn (*d* 1986), *e d* of late J. H. Monins, Ringwould House, near Dover; *S* grandfather, 1937. *Educ:* Sandroyd Sch.; Winchester Coll.; Trinity Coll., Cambridge. President: Lord Kitchener Nat. Meml Fund, 1950–; Henry Doubleday Res. Assoc. DL Cheshire 1972. *Heir:* none. *Address:* Westergate Wood, Eastergate, Chichester, W Sussex PO20 6SB. *T:* Eastergate (01243) 543061. *Club:* Brooks's.

KITCHIN, David James Tyson; QC 1994; *b* 30 April 1955; *s* of late Norman Tyson Kitchin and of Shirley Boyd Kitchin (*née* Simpson); *m* 1989, Charlotte Anne Cadbury, *d* of Comdr David Jones; one *s* one *d.* *Educ:* Oundle Sch. (schol.); Fitzwilliam Coll., Cambridge (MA). Called to the Bar, Gray's Inn, 1977; pupilled to Robin Jacob, 1978; entered chambers of Thomas Blanco White, 1979. Chm., Vet. Code of Practice Cttee, Nat. Office of Animal Health, 1995–. *Publications:* (ed jtly) Patent Law of Europe and the United Kingdom, 1979–; (ed jtly) Kerly's Law of Trade Marks and Trade Names, Supplement to 12th edn, 1994; (jtly) The Trade Marks Act 1994 (text and commentary), 1995. *Recreations:* golf, tennis. *Address:* 8 New Square, Lincoln's Inn, WC2A 3QP. *T:* 0171–405 4321. *Clubs:* Hawks (Cambridge); Leander (Henley); Walton Heath Golf.

KITCHIN, Prof. Laurence Tyson; university teacher, translator and critic; *b* 21 July 1913; *s* of James Tyson Kitchin, MD Edin, and Eliza Amelia Kitchin (*née* Hopps); *m* 1955, Hilary Owen, artist; one step *s.* *Educ:* Bootham Sch.; King's Coll., London Univ. (BA 1934); Central Sch. of Speech and Drama (Acting Cert., 1st cl.). Served War, RAMC and briefly, RAEC, 1941–46. Mem., univ. debates team, USA, 1933; acted in Housemaster on stage and screen, 1936, and in films, incl. Pimpernel Smith; wrote extensively for BBC Third Prog., 1948–55; The Times corresp. and drama critic, 1956–62; numerous BBC talks on literature and drama, 1962–66; UK rep., Théâtre dans le Monde, UNESCO, 1961–66; Lectr, Bristol Univ. and Tufts, London, 1966–70; Vis. Prof. of Drama, Stanford Univ., Calif, 1970–72; Vis. Prof. of Liberal Arts, City Univ. of NY, 1972–73, Prof., 1973–76; Vis. Prof. of Shakespeare Studies, Simon Fraser Univ., Canada, 1976–77. Renaissance verse translations from Italian, French and Spanish, BBC, 1978–79. Selected as one of Outstanding Educators of America, 1973. *Publications:* Len Hutton, 1953; Three on Trial: Byron, Bowdler and Machiavelli, 1959; Mid-Century Drama, 1960, 2nd edn 1962; Drama in the Sixties, 1966; Love Sonnets of the Renaissance (trans. from Italian, French, Spanish and Portuguese), 1990; radio scripts, incl.: The Trial of Lord Byron, 1948, Canada 1978; The Trial of Machiavelli, 1957; The Court Lady (trans. from Castiglione), 1954; The Elizabethan, Canada 1978; The Flaming Heart (Crashaw), 1981; contrib. Shakespeare Survey, Confronto Letterario, Mod. Lang. Rev., TLS, Encounter, Observer, Listener, THES. *Recreations:* tennis, televised soccer. *Address:* c/o National Westminster Bank, 1 St James's Square, SW1Y 4JT. *Club:* Athenæum.

KITCHING, Alan, RDI 1994; Art Director and Proprietor, The Typography Workshop, since 1989; *b* 29 Dec. 1940; *s* of Walter Kitching and Kathleen (*née* Davies); *m* 1962, Rita Haylett (*d* 1984); two *s.* Apprentice compositor, 1955–61; Asst, Exptl Printing Workshop, Watford Coll. of Technol. Sch. of Art, 1963–68; Vis. Tutor in Typography, Central Sch. of Art and Design, 1968–72; Established freelance design practice, working in magazine, book and exhibition design, 1971; Partner, Omnific Studios (Graphic Design), 1977–88; Vis. Tutor in Typography, RCA, 1988–. AGI 1994. *Publication:* Typography Manual, 1970. *Recreation:* snooker. *Address:* 31 Clerkenwell Close, EC1R 0AT. *T:* 0171–490 4386, *Fax:* 0171–490 0063. *Club:* Chelsea Arts.

KITCHING, Christopher John, PhD; FSA, FRHistS; Secretary, Royal Commission on Historical Manuscripts, since 1992; *b* 5 Aug. 1945; *s* of Donald Walton Kitching and Vera (*née* Mosley); *m* 1976, Hilary Mary Ruth Horwood; two *s.* *Educ:* Durham Univ. (BA Mod. Hist. 1967; PhD 1970). Registered Mem., Soc. of Archivists, 1987. Asst Keeper, PRO, 1970–82; Asst Sec., Royal Commn on Historical MSS, 1982–92. Asst Editor, Archivum, 1984–92. Hon. Treasurer, RHistS, 1980–85; Council Member: Canterbury and York Soc.; C of E Record Soc.; C of E Record Centre Adv. Gp (formerly General Synod Archives Gp). Mem. Editl Bd, Jl of Soc. of Archivists, 1992–. Alexander Prize, RHistS, 1973. *Publications:* The Royal Visitation of 1559, 1975; Survey of the Central Records of the Church of England, 1976; London and Middlesex Chantry Certificate 1548, 1980; Surveys of historical manuscripts in the United Kingdom: a select bibliography, 1989, 2nd edn 1994; The impact of computerisation on archival finding aids, 1990; Archive Buildings in the United Kingdom 1977–1992, 1993; articles and reviews. *Recreations:* singing, writing choral music, reading, cycling. *Address:* 11 Creighton Road, NW6 6EE. *T:* 0181–969 6408.

KITCHING, Maj.-Gen. George, CBE 1945; DSO 1943; Canadian Military Forces, retired; President, Duke of Edinburgh's Award in Canada, 1967–70, President, British Columbia and Yukon Division, 1979–82; *b* 1910; *m* 1946, Audrey Calhoun; one *s* one *d.* *Educ:* Cranleigh; Royal Military College. 2nd Lieut Glos Regt, 1930. Served War of 1939–45 with Royal Canadian Regt and Loyal Edmonton Regt, in Sicily, Italy and North-West Europe; commanding Canadian Infantry Brigade, 1943; actg Maj.-Gen. comdg an armoured div., 1944 (DSO, despatches 1945, CBE). Subseq. Vice-Chief of General Staff at Army Headquarters, Ottawa; Chairman of the Canadian Joint Staff in London, 1958–62; GOC Central Command, Canada, 1962–65, retd. Col Comdt of Infantry, 1974–78. Comr, Ont Pavilion, Osaka, Japan, for Expo 1970; Chief Comr, Liquor Control Bd of Ont, 1970–76. Chm. and Patron, Gurkha Welfare Appeal (Canada), 1974–; Patron: United World Colls, 1970 (Exec. Dir, Canadian Nat. Cttee, 1968–70); Sir Edmund Hillary Foundn (Canada), 1976–; Old Fort York, Toronto, 1975–. Lord of the Manor of Bluntisham, Cambs. Commander: Order of Orange Nassau (Netherlands); Military Order of Italy; Order of Merit (US). *Publication:* Mud and Green Fields (autobiog.), 1986. *Address:* 3434 Bonair Place, Victoria, BC V8P 4V4, Canada.

KITCHING, John Alwyne, OBE 1947; FRS 1960; ScD (Cambridge); PhD (London); Professor of Biology, University of East Anglia, 1963–74, now Emeritus Professor; Dean of School of Biological Sciences, 1967–70; Leverhulme Fellowship, 1974; *b* 24 Oct. 1908; *s* of John Nainby Kitching; *m* 1933, Evelyn Mary Oliver; one *s* three *d.* *Educ:* Cheltenham Coll.; Trinity Coll., Cambridge. BA 1930, MA 1934, ScD 1956; PhD London. Lecturer: Birkbeck Coll., London, 1931; Edinburgh Univ., 1936; Bristol Univ., 1937; Rockefeller Fellow, Princeton Univ., 1938; Research in aviation-medical problems under Canadian Nat. Research Council, 1939–45; Reader in Zoology, University of Bristol, 1948–63. Hon. DSc NUI, 1983. *Publications:* contrib. Jl of Experimental Biol., Jl of Ecology, Jl of Animal Ecology, etc. *Recreations:* travel, gardening. *Address:* Oakwood House, Old Watton Road, Colney, Norwich NR4 7TP. *T:* Norwich (01603) 250101.

KITSON, family name of **Baron Airedale.**

KITSON, Alexander Harper, JP; Chairman, Lothian Region Transport Board, since 1990 (Director, since 1986); *b* 21 Oct. 1921; *m* 1942, Ann Brown McLeod; two *d.* *Educ:* Kirknewton Sch., Midlothian, Scotland. Lorry Driver, 1935–45; Trade Union official, 1945–86: Gen. Sec., Scottish Commercial Motormens' Union, 1959–71; Dep. Gen. Sec., TGWU, 1980–86; Chm., Scottish TUC, 1966. Mem., Freight Integration Council, 1969–78. Mem. Nat. Exec. Cttee of Labour Party, 1968–86; Chm., Labour Party, 1980–81. Mem., War on Want Council, 1986–90. Member: Lothian Health Challenge Cttee, 1988–; Corstorphine Community Council, Edinburgh, 1989. Fellow, Scottish Council of Develt and Industry. *Address:* 47 Craigs Crescent, Edinburgh EH12 8HU.

KITSON, Gen. Sir Frank (Edward), GBE 1985; (CBE 1972; OBE 1968; MBE 1959); KCB 1980; MC 1955 and Bar 1958; DL; *b* 15 Dec. 1926; *s* of late Vice-Adm. Sir Henry Kitson, KBE, CB and Lady (Marjorie) Kitson (*née* de Pass); *m* 1962, Elizabeth Janet, *d* of late Col C. R. Spencer, OBE, DL; three *d.* *Educ:* Stowe. 2nd Lt Rifle Bde, 1946; served BAOR, 1946–53; Kenya, 1953–55; Malaya, 1957; Cyprus, 1962–64; CO 1st Bn, Royal Green Jackets, 1967–69; Defence Fellow, University Coll., Oxford, 1969–70; Comdr, 39 Inf. Bde, NI, 1970–72 (CBE for gallantry); Comdt, Sch. of Infantry, 1972–74; RCDS, 1975; GOC 2nd Division, later 2nd Armoured Division, 1976–78; Comdt, Staff College, 1978–80; Dep. C-in-C, UKLF, and Inspector-Gen., TA, 1980–82; C-in-C, UKLF, 1982–85. ADC Gen. to the Queen, 1983–85. 2nd Bn, The Royal Green Jackets: Col Comdt, 1979–87; Rep. Col Comdt, 1982–85; Hon. Col, Oxford Univ. OTC, 1982–87. DL 1989. *Publications:* Gangs and Counter Gangs, 1960; Low Intensity Operations, 1971; Bunch of Five, 1977; Warfare as a Whole, 1987; Directing Operations, 1989; Prince Rupert: portrait of a soldier, 1994. *Address:* c/o Lloyds Bank, Farnham, Surrey GU9 7LT. *Club:* Boodle's.

KITSON, George McCullough; Principal, Central School of Speech and Drama, London, 1978–87; *b* Castlegore, Ireland, 18 May 1922; *s* of George Kitson and Anna May McCullough-Kitson; *m* 1951, Jean Evelyn Tyte; four *s.* *Educ:* early educn in Ireland; London Univ. (Dip. in Child Develt, 1947); Trent Park Coll. (Teachers' Cert., 1949), Associate, Cambridge Inst. of Educn, 1956; MEd Leicester, 1960. Served War, RAF, 1940–45; Navigator, Coastal Comd. Asst Master, schs in Herts, 1949–54; Dep. Headmaster, Broadfield Sch., Hemel Hempstead, Herts, 1954–56; Lectr in Educn, Leicester Coll. of Educn, 1956–66; Tutor i/c Annexe for Mature Teachers, Northampton, 1966–71; Dep. Principal, Furzedown Coll., London, 1971–76; Vice Principal, Philippa Fawcett and Furzedown Coll., 1976–78. Member: Nat. Council of Drama Trng, 1978–88; Conference of Drama Schs, 1980– (Chm., 1980–87). *Publications:* (contrib.) Map of Educational Research, 1969; articles on educn, social psychol., and interprofessionalism in Forum, New Era, Educn for Teaching, and Brit. Jl of Educnl Psychol. *Recreations:* book collecting (first editions), sailing, walking, music, theatre. *Address:* 24 Dovercourt Road, Dulwich, SE22 8ST. *T:* 0181–299 4516. *Club:* Arts.

KITSON, Prof. Michael William Lely; Director of Studies, Paul Mellon Centre for Studies in British Art, 1986–92; *b* 30 Jan. 1926; *s* of Rev. Bernard Meredyth Kitson and Helen May (*née* Lely); *m* 1950, Annabella Leslie Cloudsley (separated 1971); two *s.* *Educ:* Gresham's School; King's Coll., Cambridge (BA 1950; MA 1953); Courtauld Inst. of Art, Univ. of London. Served Army, 1945–48; commd RE 1946 and attached SIME, Egypt. Asst Lectr in History of Art, Slade Sch. of Art, 1952–54; Courtauld Institute of Art: Lectr, 1955–67; Reader, 1967–78; Prof., 1978–85; Dep. Dir, 1980–85; Fellow, 1985. Adjunct Prof., Yale Univ., 1986–92. Vice-Chm., Turner Soc., 1984–93. Chm., Courtauld Assoc. of Former Students, 1992–. *Publications:* J. M. W. Turner, 1964; The Age of Baroque, 1966; Claude Lorrain: Landscape with the Nymph Egeria (Charlton Lecture), 1968; The Art of Claude Lorrain (exhibn catalogue), 1969; The Complete Paintings of Caravaggio, 1969; Rembrandt, 1969, 3rd rev. edn 1992; Turner Watercolours from the Collection of Stephen Courtauld, 1974; Claude Lorrain: Liber Veritatis, 1978; *edited exhibition catalogues:* La Peinture romantique anglaise et les préraphaélites, 1972; Salvator Rosa, 1973; British Painting 1600–1800, 1977; Zwei Jahrhunderte Englische Malerei, 1979; contrib. Burlington Magazine, Jl of Warburg and Courtauld Insts, Walpole Soc., Turner Studies, etc. *Address:* 72 Halton Road, N1 2AD. *T:* 0171–359 6757.

KITSON, Sir Timothy (Peter Geoffrey), Kt 1974; Chairman, Provident Financial plc (formerly Provident Financial Group), since 1983; *b* 28 Jan. 1931; *s* of late Geoffrey H. and of Kathleen Kitson; *m* 1959, Diana Mary Fattorini; one *s* two *d.* *Educ:* Charterhouse; Royal Agricultural College, Cirencester. Farmed in Australia, 1949–51. Member: Thirsk RDC, 1954–57; N Riding CC, 1957–61. MP (C) Richmond, Yorks, 1959–83; PPS to Parly Sec. to Minister of Agriculture, 1960–64; an Opposition Whip, 1967–70; PPS to the Prime Minister, 1970–74, to Leader of the Opposition, 1974–75. Chm., Defence Select Cttee, 1982–83. *Recreations:* shooting, hunting, racing. *Address:* White House Farm, Ulshaw, Middleham, Leyburn, N Yorks DL8 9XX.

KITZINGER, Sheila Helena Elizabeth, MBE 1982; author, social anthropologist and birth educator; teacher and tutor, National Childbirth Trust; *b* 29 March 1929; *d* of Alec and Clare Webster; *m* 1952, Uwe Kitzinger, *qv*; five *d.* *Educ:* Bishop Fox's Girls' Sch., Taunton; Ruskin Coll., Oxford; St Hugh's Coll., Oxford; motherhood; educn continuing. Res. Asst, Dept of Anthropology, Univ. of Edinburgh, 1952–53 (MLitt 1954; thesis on race relations in Britain). Course Team Chm., Open Univ., 1981–83. Mem. Editl Bd, Midwives Information and Resource Service; Chairperson, Foundation for Women's Health Res. and Develt, 1985–87; Consultant, Internat. Childbirth Educn Assoc.; Adviser: Baby Milk Coalition; Maternity Alliance. Pres., Oxford Br., Royal Coll. of Midwives; Patron, Seattle Sch. of Midwifery. Co-founder (with Uwe Kitzinger), Lentils for Dubrovnik, 1991 (relief agency sending aid to women and children in Croatia).

MRSocMed. Hon. Prof., Thames Valley Univ., 1994. Joost de Blank Award, to do research on problems facing West Indian mothers in Britain, 1971–73. *Publications:* The Experience of Childbirth, 1962, 6th edn 1987; Giving Birth, 1971, rev. and expanded edn 1987; Education and Counselling for Childbirth, 1977; Women as Mothers, 1978; (ed with John Davis) The Place of Birth, 1978; Birth at Home, 1979; The Good Birth Guide, 1979; The Experience of Breastfeeding, 1979, 2nd edn 1987; Pregnancy and Childbirth, 1980; Sheila Kitzinger's Birth Book, 1981; (with Rhiannon Walters) Some Women's Experiences of Episiotomy, 1981; Episiotomy: physical and emotional aspects, 1981; Birth over Thirty, 1982; The New Good Birth Guide, 1983; Woman's Experience of Sex, 1983; (ed with Penny Simkin) Episiotomy and the Second Stage of Labor, 1984; Being Born, 1986; Celebration of Birth, 1987; Freedom and Choice in Childbirth (US edn Your Baby Your Way), 1987; Giving Birth: how it really feels, 1987; Some Women's Experiences of Epidurals, 1987; (ed) The Midwife Challenge, 1988; The Crying Baby, 1989; The New Pregnancy and Childbirth, 1989; Breastfeeding Your Baby, 1989; (with Celia Kitzinger) Talking With Children About Things That Matter, 1989; (contrib.) Ethnography of Fertility and Birth, 1982; (contrib.) The Management of Labour, 1985; (contrib.) Effective Care in Pregnancy and Childbirth, 1989; (with Vicky Bailey) Pregnancy Day by Day, 1990; Homebirth, 1991; (contrib.) Women's Health Matters, 1991; Ourselves as Mothers, 1992; The Year After Childbirth, 1994; Birth Over Thirty-Five, 1994. *Recreations:* painting, talking. *Address:* The Manor, Standlake, Oxfordshire OX8 7RH. *T:* Oxford (01865) 300266.

See also David Webster.

KITZINGER, Uwe, CBE 1980; consultant to various national and international organisations; Visiting Scholar, Harvard University, since 1993; President, Templeton College, Oxford, 1984–91 (sabbatical, 1991–93); *b* 12 April 1928; *o s* of late Dr G. and Mrs L. Kitzinger, Abbots Langley, Herts; *m* 1952, Sheila Helena Elizabeth Webster (*see* S. H. E. Kitzinger); five *d. Educ:* Watford Grammar Sch.; Balliol Coll. and New Coll. (Foundn Schol.), Oxford. 1st in Philosophy, Politics and Economics, MA, MLitt; Pres., Oxford Union, 1950. Economic Section, Council of Europe, Strasbourg, 1951–58; Nuffield College, Oxford: Research Fellow, 1956–62, Official Fellow, 1962–76, Emeritus Fellow, 1976; Acting Investment Bursar, 1962–64; Investment Bursar, 1964–76; Mem., Investment Cttee, 1962–88; Assessor of Oxford University, 1967–68. Visiting Professor: of Internat. Relations, Univ. of the West Indies, 1964–65; of Government, at Harvard, 1969–70; at Univ. of Paris (VIII), 1970–73. Leave of absence as Adviser to Sir Christopher (later Lord) Soames, Vice-Pres. of the Commn of the European Communities, Brussels, 1973–75; Dean, INSEAD (European Inst. of Business Admin), Fontainebleau, 1976–80 (Mem. Board, 1976–83); Dir, Oxford Centre for Management Studies, 1980–84; Founding Pres., Templeton Coll., 1984. Sen. Res. Fellow, Atlantic Council, 1993–. Founding Pres., Internat. Assoc. of Macro-Engineering Societies Inc., 1987–92. Member: ODM Cttee for University Secondment, 1966–68; British Universities Cttee of Encyclopædia Britannica, 1967–; Nat. Council of European Movement, 1974–76; Council, RIIA, 1973–85; Court, Cranfield Inst. of Technology, 1984–85. Founding Chm., Cttee on Atlantic Studies, 1967–70. Co-Founder, Lentils for Dubrovnik, 1991–. Member: Oxfam Council, 1981–84; Major Projects Assoc., 1981–91 (Founding Chm., 1981–86); Adv. Bd, Pace Univ., NY, 1982–92; Berlin Science Centre, 1983–90; Acad. Adv. Bd, World Management Council, 1989–; Bd, Jean Monnet Foundn, Lausanne, 1990–. Trustee: European Foundn for Management Educn, Brussels, 1978–80; Oxford Trust for Music and the Arts, 1986–91; Fontainebleau Youth Foundn, 1991–; Hanover Trust, 1992–. Chm., Oxford Radio Consortium, 1988. Hon. LLD, Buena Vista, 1986. *Publications:* German Electoral Politics, 1960 (German edn, 1960); The Challenge of the Common Market, 1961 (Amer. edn, The Politics and Economics of European Integration, 1963, et al); Britain, Europe and Beyond, 1964; The Background to Jamaica's Foreign Policy, 1965; The European Common Market and Community, 1967; Commitment and Identity, 1968; The Second Try, 1968; Diplomacy and Persuasion, 1973 (French edn, 1974); Europe's Wider Horizons, 1975; (with D. E. Butler) The 1975 Referendum, 1976. Founding Editor, Jl of Common Market Studies, 1962–. *Recreations:* sailing, travel, old buildings. *Address:* Nuffield College, Oxford. *T:* Oxford (01865) 278500; Standlake Manor, near Witney, Oxon OX8 7RH. *T:* Oxford (01865) 300266, *Fax:* Oxford (01865) 300438; La Rivière, 11100 Bages, France. *T:* and *Fax:* 68417013. *Clubs:* Royal Thames Yacht, United Oxford & Cambridge University.

KLARE, Hugh John, CBE 1967; *b* Berndorf, Austria, 22 June 1916; *yr s* of F. A. Klare; *m* 1946, Eveline Alice Maria, *d* of Lieut-Col J. D. Rankin, MBE. *Educ:* privately. Came to England, 1932. Served war in Middle East and Europe; Major. Dep. Dir, Economic Organisation Br., Brit. Control Commn for Germany, 1946–48; Sec., Howard League for Penal Reform, 1950–71; seconded to Coun. of Europe as Dep. Head, Div. of Crime Problems, 1959–61; Head of Div., 1971–72; Member of Council: Internat. Soc. of Criminology, 1960–66; Inst. for Study and Treatment of Delinquency, 1964–66; Nat. Assoc. for Care and Resettlement of Offenders, 1966–71. Chm. Planning Cttee, Brit. Congress on Crime, 1966. Member: Bd of Visitors, Long Lartin Prison, 1972–76; Gloucestershire Probation and Aftercare Cttee, 1972–85; Parole Board, 1972–74. Founder and Trustee, Cheltenham and N Cotswold Eye Therapy Trust, 1976–; Chm. of Trustees, Gloucestershire Arthritis Trust, 1987– (Trustee, 1984). A Governor, British Inst. of Human Rights, 1974–80. *Publications:* Anatomy of Prison, 1960; (ed and introd) Changing Concepts of Crime and its Treatment, 1966; (ed jtly) Frontiers of Criminology, 1967; People in Prison, 1972; contribs on crime and penology to Justice of the Peace. *Address:* 34 Herriots Court, St George's Crescent, Droitwich, Worcs WR9 8HJ. *T:* Droitwich (01905) 776316.

KLAUS, Václav; Prime Minister of the Czech Republic, since 1992; *b* 19 June 1941; *s* of Václav Klaus and Marie Klausová; *m* 1968, Livia Klausová; two *s. Educ:* Prague Sch. of Economics (Hon. Dr 1994); Cornell Univ. Researcher, Inst. of Econs, Czechoslovak Acad of Scis, to 1970; Czechoslovak State Bank, 1971–86 (Head, Dept of Macroeconomic Policy); Inst. of Forecasting, Czechoslovak Acad. of Scis, 1987–; founder, Civic Forum Movement (Chm., 1990–91); Minister of Finance, 1989–92; Chm., Civic Democratic Party, 1991–; Dep. Prime Minister, 1991–92. Hon. doctorates from Univs in USA, Guatemala, Mexico, Argentina, France; numerous awards from USA, Germany, France, Denmark. *Publications:* A Road to Market Economy, 1991; Tomorrow's Challenge, 1991; Economic Theory and Economic Reform, 1991; I Do Not Like Catastrophic Scenarios, 1991; Dismantling Socialism, 1992; Why Am I a Conservative?, 1992; The Year: how much is it in the history of the country?, 1993; The Czech Way, 1994; Rebirth of a Country, 1994. *Recreations:* tennis, ski-ing. *Address:* Office of the Government of the Czech Republic, nábř Edvarda Beneše 4, 118 01 Prague 1, Czech Republic. *T:* (2) 24002297, *Fax:* (2) 2312358.

KLEEMAN, Harry, CBE 1984; Chairman: Kleeman Plastics group of companies, 1968–94; Kleeman Management Ltd; *b* 2 March 1928; *s* of Max Kleeman and Lottie Bernstein; *m* 1955, Avril Lees; two *s* two *d. Educ:* Westminster Sch.; Trinity Coll., Cambridge. FIM (FPRI 1980). Director, O. & M. Kleemann Ltd, 1951–65. President, British Plastics Fedn, 1979–80; Chairman: Polymer Engineering Directorate, SERC, 1980–84; Plastics Processing EDC, NEDO, 1980–85; Small Firms Cttee, OFTEL, 1985–88; Council, Plastics & Rubber Inst., 1985–87; Adv. Bd, London Sch. of Polymer Technology, 1988–94; Member: CBI Smaller Firms Council, 1982–91 (Vice-Chm., 1987–88, Chm., 1988–90); CBI Council, 1984–94. Chairman: Central British Fund for World Jewish Relief, 1991– (Treasurer, 1969–91); Hampstead and Highgate Conservative Parly Club, 1991–. Trustee, ORT Trust, 1990–. Member: Zoological Soc., 1950–; Royal Society of Arts, 1978–; Worshipful Co. of Horners, 1954– (Master, 1992). Prison Visitor. *Recreations:* horse riding, amateur radio. *Address:* 41 Frognal, NW3 6YD. *T:* 0171–794 3366.

KLEIN, Bernat, CBE 1973; FCSD (FSIAD 1974); Chairman and Managing Director, Bernat Klein Ltd, 1973–93; *b* 6 Nov. 1922; *s* of Lipot Klein and Serena Weiner; *m* 1951, Margaret Soper; one *s* two *d. Educ:* Senta, Yugoslavia; Bezalel Sch. of Arts and Crafts, Jerusalem; Leeds Univ. Designer to: Tootal, Broadhurst, Lee, 1948–49; Munrospun, Edinburgh, 1949–51; Chm. and Man. Dir, Colourcraft, 1952–62; Man. Dir of Bernat Klein Ltd, 1962–66; Chm. and Man. Dir, Bernat Klein Design Ltd, 1966–81. Member: Council of Industrial Design, Scottish Cttee, 1965–71; Royal Fine Art Commn for Scotland, 1980–87. Exhibitions of paintings: E-SU, 1965; Alwyn Gall., 1967; O'Hana Gall., 1969; Assoc. of Arts Gall., Capetown, Goodman Gall., Johannesburg, and O'Hana Gall., 1972; Laing Art Gall., Newcastle upon Tyne, 1977; Manchester Polytechnic, 1977. Hon. FRIAS, 1990. *Publications:* Eye for Colour, 1965; Design Matters, 1976. *Recreations:* reading, tennis, walking. *Address:* High Sunderland, Galashiels, Selkirkshire TD1 3PL. *T:* Selkirk (01750) 20730.

KLEIN, Calvin Richard; fashion designer; *b* 19 Nov. 1942; *s* of Leo Klein and Flore (*née* Stern); *m* 1st, 1964, Jayne Centre (marr. diss. 1974); one *d*; 2nd, 1986, Kelly Rector. *Educ:* Fashion Inst. of Technology, NY; High Sch. of Art and Design. Started own fashion business, 1968; Pres. and Designer, Calvin Klein Ltd, 1969–; Dir, Fashion Inst. of Technology, 1975–. Numerous awards. *Address:* Calvin Klein Industries Inc., 205 West 39th Street, New York, NY 10018, USA.

KLEIN, Prof. Lawrence Robert; economist; Benjamin Franklin Professor, University of Pennsylvania, 1968–91, Emeritus 1991; *b* Omaha, 14 Sept. 1920; *s* of Leo Byron Klein and Blanche Monheit; *m* 1947, Sonia Adelson; one *s* three *d. Educ:* Univ. of Calif at Berkeley (BA); MIT (PhD 1944); Lincoln Coll., Oxford (MA 1957). Chicago Univ., 1944–47; Nat. Bureau of Econ. Res., NY, 1948–50; Michigan Univ., 1949–54; Oxford Inst. of Stats, 1954–58; Prof., 1958, University Prof., 1964, Univ. of Pennsylvania. Consultant: UNCTAD, 1966, 1967, 1975; UNIDO, 1973–75; Congressional Budget Office, 1977–; Council of Econ. Advisers, 1977–80. Mem., Commn on Prices, Fed. Res. Bd, 1968–70. Member: Adv. Bd, Strategic Studies Center, Stanford Res. Inst., 1974–76; Adv. Council, Inst. for Advanced Studies, Vienna, 1977–; Director: Nat. Bureau of Econ. Res., Inc., 1989–; Inst. for East-West Security Studies, 1989–; W. P. Carey & Co., 1984–. Corresp. FBA, 1991; Fellow: Econometric Soc. (past Pres.); Amer. Acad. of Arts and Scis; Member: Nat. Acad. of Scis; Amer. Philosophical Soc.; Amer. Economic Assoc. (Past Pres.; J. B. Clark Medal, 1959). William F. Butler Award, NY Assoc. of Business Economists, 1975; Nobel Prize for Economics, 1980. *Publications:* The Keynesian Revolution, 1947; Textbook of Econometrics, 1953; An Econometric Model of the United States 1929–52, 1955; Wharton Econometric Forecasting Model, 1967; Essay on the Theory of Economic Prediction, 1968; (ed) Econometric Model Performance, 1976; (ed) Comparative Performance of US Econometric Models, 1991. *Address:* 1317 Medford Road, Wynnewood, PA 19096, USA; University of Pennsylvania, Philadelphia, PA 19104, USA.

KLEIN, Hon. Ralph Phillip; Premier of Alberta, Canada, and Minister of Federal and Intergovernmental Affairs, since 1992; MLA (Progressive C) for Calgary-Elbow, since 1989; *b* Calgary, 1 Nov. 1942; *m* Colleen; one *d. Educ:* Calgary Business Coll. Teacher, later Principal, Calgary Business Coll.; PR with Alberta Div. of Red Cross and United Way of Calgary and Dist, 1963–69; Sen. Civic Affairs reporter, CFCN TV and Radio, 1969–80; Mayor of Calgary, 1980–89; Minister of Envmt, 1989–92; Leader, Progressive Cons. Party, 1992–. OStJ 1986. *Address:* Office of the Premier, 213 Legislature Building, Edmonton, Alberta T5K 2B6, Canada.

KLEIN, Prof. Rudolf Ewald; Professor of Social Policy, University of Bath, since 1978; *b* 26 Aug. 1930; *o s* of Robert and Martha Klein; *m* 1957, Josephine Parfitt; one *d. Educ:* Bristol Grammar Sch.; Merton Coll., Oxford (Postmaster) (Gibbs Schol. 1950; MA). Leader Writer, London Evening Standard, 1952–62; Editor, 'The Week', Leader Writer, Home Affairs Editor, The Observer, 1962–72; Research Associate, Organisation of Medical Care Unit, London Sch. of Hygiene and Tropical Medicine, 1972–73; Sen. Fellow, Centre for Studies in Social Policy, 1973–78. Member: Wiltshire AHA, 1980–82; Bath DHA, 1982–84. Jt Editor, Political Quarterly, 1981–87. *Publications:* Complaints Against Doctors, 1973; (ed) Social Policy and Public Expenditure, 1974; (ed) Inflation and Priorities, 1975; (with Janet Lewis) The Politics of Consumer Representation, 1976; The Politics of the NHS, 1983; (ed with Michael O'Higgins) The Future of Welfare, 1985; (with Patricia Day) Accountabilities, 1987; (with Linda Challis *et al*) Joint Approaches to Social Policy, 1988; (with Patricia Day) Inspecting the Inspectorates, 1990; (with Neil Carter and Patricia Day) How organisations measure success, 1991; (with Patricia Day and David Henderson) Home Rules, 1993; The New Politics of the NHS, 1995; papers on public policy, health policy and public expenditure in various jls. *Recreations:* opera, cooking, football. *Address:* 48 Springcroft Avenue, N2 9JE. *T:* 0181–442 1581.

KLEINDIENST, Richard Gordon; attorney; *b* 5 Aug. 1923; *s* of Alfred R. Kleindienst and late Gladys Love, Massachusetts; *m* 1948, Margaret Dunbar; two *s* two *d. Educ:* Harvard Coll. (*Phi Beta Kappa, magna cum laude*); Harvard Law Sch. Associate and Partner of Jennings, Strouss, Salmon & Trask, Phoenix, Arizona, 1950–57; Sen. Partner of Shimmel, Hill, Kleindienst & Bishop, 1958–Jan. 1969. Dep. Attorney-Gen. of the US, Jan. 1969–Feb. 1972; Actg Attorney-Gen. of the US, Feb. 1972–June 1972; Attorney-Gen. of the US, 1972–73, resigned 1973; private practice of law, Washington DC, 1973–75. Pres., Federal Bar Assoc., US, 1972– (was Pres. elect, Oct. 1971–72). Hon. Dr of Laws, Susquehanna Univ., 1973. *Publication:* Justice: the memoirs of Attorney General Richard G. Kleindienst, 1985. *Recreations:* golf, chess, classical music, art. *Address:* 3103 Crest View, Prescott, AZ 86303, USA.

KLEINPOPPEN, Prof. Hans Johann Willi, FRSE; Professor of Experimental Physics, since 1968, and Head, Unit of Atomic and Molecular Physics, University of Stirling; *b* Duisburg, Germany, 30 Sept. 1928; *m* 1958, Renate Schröder. *Educ:* Univ. of Giessen (Dipl. Physics); Univ. of Tübingen. Dr re.nat. 1961. Habilitation, Tübingen, 1967. Head, Physics Dept, 1971–73, Dir, Inst. of Atomic Physics, 1975–81, Univ. of Stirling. Vis. Fellow, Univ. Colorado, 1967–68; Vis. Associate Prof., Columbia Univ., 1968; Fellow, Center for Theoretical Studies, Univ. of Miami, 1972–73; Bielefeld University: Guest Prof., 1978–79; Vis. Fellow, Zentrum für interdisziplinäre Forschung, 1979–80; Sen. Res. Fellow, 1980–; Res. Visitor, Fritz Haber Inst., Berlin, 1991–. Chairman: Internat. Symposium on Physics of One- and Two-Electron Atoms (Arnold Sommerfeld Centennial Meml Meeting, Munich 1968); Internat. Symposium on Electron and Photon Interactions with Atoms, in honour of Ugo Fano, Stirling, 1974; Internat. Workshop on Coherence and Correlation in Atomic Collisions, dedicated to Sir Harrie Massey, UCL, 1978;

Internat. Symp. on Amplitudes and State Parameters in Atomic Collisions, Kyoto, 1979; Orgng Cttee on Workshops on Polarized Electron and Polarized Photon Physics, SERC, 1993, 1994; Co-Chm., Peter Farago Symposium on Electron Physics, RSE, 1995; Co-Dir, Advanced Study Inst. on Fundamental Processes in Energetic Atomic Collisions, Maratea, Italy, 1982; Dir, Advanced Study Inst. on Fundamental Processes in Atomic Collision Physics, S Flavia, Sicily, 1984; Co-Dir, Advanced Study Inst. on Fundamental Processes on Atomic Dynamics, Maratea, Italy, 1987. FInstP 1969; Fellow Amer. Physical Soc. 1969; FRAS 1974; FRSE 1987; FRSA 1990. *Publications:* edited: (with F. Bopp) Physics of the One- and Two-Electron Atoms, 1969; (with M. R. C. McDowell) Electron and Photon Interactions with Atoms, 1976; Progress in Atomic Spectroscopy, (with W. Hanle) Vol. A 1978 and Vol. B 1979, (with H.-J. Beyer) Vol. C 1984 and Vol. D 1987; (with J. F. Williams) Coherence and Correlations in Atomic Collisions, 1980; (with D. J. Fabian and L. H. Watson) Inner-Shell and X-Ray Physics of Atoms and Solids, 1981; (with J. S. Briggs and H. O. Lutz): Fundamental Processes in Energetic Atomic Collisions, 1983; Fundamental Processes in Atomic Collision Physics, 1985; Fundamental Processes in Atomic Dynamics, 1988; (with P. G. Burke) series editor, Physics of Atoms and Molecules; about 200 papers in Zeitschr. f. Physik, Z. f. Naturf., Z. f. Angew Physik, Physikalische Blätter, Physical Review, Physical Review Letters, Jl of Physics, Physics Letters, Internat. Jl of Quantum Chemistry; Physics Reports, Advances of Atomic and Molecular Physics, Applied Physics; *festschrift* (for 60th birthday): (ed H.-J. Beyer, K. Blum and R. Hippler) Coherence in Atomic Collision Physics, 1988. *Address:* 27 Kenningknowes Road, Stirling FK7 9JF.

KLEINWORT, Sir Richard (Drake), 4th Bt *cr* 1909, of Bolnore, Cuckfield, Sussex; Director, Cardew & Co., since 1994 (Partner, 1991); *b* 4 Nov. 1960; *s* of Sir Kenneth Drake Kleinwort, 3rd Bt and his 1st wife, Lady Davina Pepys (*d* 1973), *d* of 7th Earl of Cottenham; *S* father, 1994; *m* 1989, Lucinda, *d* of William Shand Kydd; one *s*. *Educ:* Stowe; Exeter Univ. (BA). Kleinwort Benson, Geneva, 1979; Banco General de Negocios, Buenos Aires, 1984; Deutsche Bank AG, Hamburg and Frankfurt, 1985–88; Biss Lancaster plc, 1988–89; Grandfield Rork Collins Financial 1989–91. President: Haywards Heath Hospital; The Little Black Bag Housing Assoc. Member: RHS; S of England Agricl Soc.; British Field Sports Soc.; WWF (1001) Club. Fellow, World Scout Foundn, Geneva. *Recreations:* travel, golf, tennis, shooting, gardening, farming. *Heir:* *s* Rufus Drake Kleinwort, *b* 16 Aug. 1994. *Clubs:* Turf, Royal Automobile, Groucho.

KLEMPERER, Prof. Paul David, PhD; Edgeworth Professor of Economics, University of Oxford, since 1995; Fellow, Nuffield College, Oxford, since 1995; *b* 15 Aug. 1956; *s* of late Hugh G. Klemperer and Ruth M. M. Klemperer (*née* Jordan); *m* 1989, Margaret Meyer. *Educ:* King Edward's Sch., Birmingham; Peterhouse, Cambridge (BA Engrg 1978); Stanford Univ. (MBA 1982; PhD Econs 1986). Consultant, Arthur Andersen & Co., 1978–80; Harkness Fellow, Commonwealth Fund, 1980–82; Oxford University: Univ. Lectr in Operations Res. and Mathematical Econs, 1985–90; Reader in Econs, 1990–95; John Thomson Fellow and Tutor, St Catharine's Coll., 1985–95. Visiting positions: MIT, 1987; Berkeley, 1991, 1993; Stanford, 1991, 1993; Yale, 1994. Fellow, Econometric Soc., 1994. Editor, RAND Jl of Econs, 1994–; Associate Editor or Member, Editorial Board: Rev. of Econ. Studies, 1989–; Jl of Industrial Econs, 1989–; Oxford Econ. Papers, 1986–; Internat. Jl of Industrial Orgn, 1993–. *Publications:* articles in econs jls on industrial organization and econ. theory. *Address:* Nuffield College, Oxford OX1 1NF. *T:* Oxford (01865) 271089.

KLEPSCH, Dr Egon Alfred; President, European Parliament, 1992–94; *b* 30 Jan. 1930; *m* 1952, Anita Wegehaupt; three *s* three *d*. *Educ:* Marburg Univ. (DPhil 1954). Mem., CDU, 1951 (Mem. of Bureau, 1977–94), Fed. Chm., Young Christian Democrats, 1963–69; Chm., European Young Christian Democrats, 1964–70; Mem. for Koblenz-St Goar, Bundestag, 1965–80; European Parliament: Member, 1973–79, elected Mem. (EPP/CDU), 1979–94; Vice-Pres., 1982–84; Mem., Political Affairs and other Cttees, 1989–92; Vice-Pres., EPP, 1977–92; Chm., EPP Gp, 1977–82, 1984–92; Mem. Bureau, EPP, 1992–94. Chm., Europa-Union Deutschland, 1989–; Vice-Chm., German Council of Eur. Movement, 1990–. Hon. LLD Sunderland; Dr *hc* Buenos Aires. Grosses Verdientstkreuz mit Stern und Schulterband (Germany), 1986; orders from Italy, Luxembourg, Argentina and Chile. *Publications:* Die Deutsche Russlandpolitik unter dem Reichsminister des Auswärtigen Dr Gustav Stresemann, 1955; Der Kommunismus in Deutschland, 1964; Der Europäische Abgeordnete, 1978; Programme für Europa, 1978; Die Abgeordneten Europas, 1984. *Address:* c/o European Parliament, 97–113 rue Belliard, 1047 Brussels, Belgium.

KLESTIL, Thomas; President of Austria, since 1992; *b* 4 Nov. 1932; *m*; two *s* one *d*. *Educ:* Economic Univ., Vienna. Mem., Austrian Delegn to OECD, Paris, 1959–62; with Austrian Embassy, Washington, 1962–66; Sec. to Chancellor, 1966–69; Consul-Gen., Los Angeles, 1969–74; Rep. of Austria to UN, 1978–82; Ambassador to Washington, 1982–87; Sec.-Gen. for Foreign Affairs, 1987–92. *Address:* Präsident-schaftskanzlei, Hofburg, 1014 Vienna, Austria.

KLEVAN, Rodney Conrad, QC 1984; a Recorder of the Crown Court, since 1980; Leader, Northern Circuit, since 1992; *b* 23 May 1940; *s* of Sidney Leopold Klevan and late Florence Klevan (*née* Eaton); *m* 1968, Susan Rebecca (*née* Lighthill) (*d* 1991); two *s* one *d*. *Educ:* Temple Primary School; Manchester Central Grammar School; Birmingham Univ. (LLB Hons 1962). Pres., Birmingham Univ. Guild of Undergraduates, 1962–63. Called to the Bar, Gray's Inn, 1966, Bencher, 1992; Deputy Circuit Judge, 1977. *Recreations:* theatre, art, following the fortunes of Lancashire CCC. *Address:* (chambers) 18 St John Street, Manchester M3 4EA; Beech House, 45 Manor Road, Bramhall, Stockport, Cheshire SK7 3LX. *T:* 0161–485 1847.

KLIBANSKY, Raymond, MA, PhD; FRSC; FRHistS; Frothingham Professor of Logic and Metaphysics, McGill University, Montreal, 1946–75, now Emeritus Professor; Fellow of Wolfson College, Oxford, 1981–95 (Hon. Fellow, 1995); *b* Paris, 15 Oct. 1905; *s* of late Hermann Klibansky. *Educ:* Paris; Odenwald Sch.; Univs of Kiel, Hamburg, Heidelberg. PhD, 1928; MA Oxon by decree, 1936. Asst, Heidelberg Acad., 1927–33; Lecturer in Philosophy: Heidelberg Univ., 1931–33; King's Coll., London, 1934–36; Oriel Coll., Oxford, 1936–48; Forwood Lectr in Philosophy of Religion, Univ. of Liverpool, 1938–39. Political Warfare Exec., FO, 1941–46. Dir of Studies, Warburg Inst., Univ. of London, 1947–48. Vis. Prof. of History of Philosophy, Université de Montréal, 1947–68; Mahlon Powell Prof., Indiana Univ., 1950; Cardinal Mercier Prof. of Philosophy, Univ. of Louvain, 1956; Vis. Prof. of Philosophy, Univ. of Rome, 1961, Univ. of Genoa, 1964, Univ. of Tokyo, 1971; Prof. Emeritus, Heidelberg Univ., 1975–, Hon. Senator, 1986–. President: Inst. Internat. de Philosophie, Paris, 1966–69 (Hon. Pres. 1969–); Société Internationale pour l'étude de la Philos. Médiévale, Louvain, 1968–72 (Hon. Pres., 1972–); Canadian Soc. for History and Philosophy of Science, 1959–72 (Pres. Emeritus, 1972–); Internat. Cttee for Anselm Studies, 1970–; Centro Studi di Civiltà del Medioevo e del Rinascimento, Parma 1990–. Fellow: Accademia Nazionale dei Lincei, Rome; Acad. of Athens; Académie Internationale d'Histoire des Sciences, Paris; Iranian Acad. of Philosophy, Teheran; Acad. dei Dafnici e degli Zelanti; Acireale; Corresponding Fellow: Mediaeval Acad. of America; Heidelberg Acad. of Scis; Deutsche Akad. für Sprache und Dichtung, Darmstadt; Braunschweigische Wissenschaftliche Gesellschaft. Hon. Member: Allgemeine Gesellsch. für Philosophie in Deutschland; Assoc. des Scientifiques de Roumanie, Bucarest; Hon. Foreign Mem., Amer. Acad. of Arts and Scis. Hon. Fellow: Oriel Coll., Oxford; Warburg Inst., Univ. of London; Accad. Ligure delle Scienze, Genoa; Canadian Mediterranean Inst., Athens, Rome, Cairo. Guggenheim Foundation Fellow, 1954 and 1965; Vis. Fellow, Wolfson Coll., Oxford, 1976–78. Dir, Canadian Academic Centre in Italy, Rome, 1980. Mem. Exec. Council, Union Académique Internationale, 1978–80. Comité Directeur, Fedn Internat. des Socs de Philosophie, 1958–83. DPhil *hc*: Bologna; Marburg; Ottawa; Reconnaissance de Mérite Scientifique, Québec à Montréal, 1991. Gauss Medal, Brunswick, 1990. Order of Merit (Germany), 1994. Gen. Editor, Corpus Platonicum Medii Aevi, (Plato Latinus and Plato Arabus), Union Académique Internat., 1937–; Joint Editor and contributor to: Magistri Eckardi Opera Latina, 1933–36; Philosophy and History, 1936; Mediaeval and Renaissance Studies, 1941–68; Editor: Philosophical Texts, 1951–62; Philosophy and World Community, 1957–90. Philosophy in the Mid-Century, 1958–59; Contemporary Philosophy, 1968–71; Dir, Bibliographie de la Philosophie, 41 vols, 1954–95. *Publications:* Ein Proklos-Fund und seine Bedeutung, 1929; Heidelberg Acad. edn of Opera Nicolai de Cusa, 5 vols, 1929–82; The Continuity of the Platonic Tradition, 1939, enlarged 4th edn incl. Plato's Parmenides in the Middle Ages and the Renaissance, 1982; (with E. Panofsky and F. Saxl) Saturn and Melancholy, 1964 (enlarged French, German and Spanish edns, 1989–92); (with F. Regen) Überlieferungsgeschichte der philosophischen Werke des Apuleius, 1993; (ed and contrib.) La Philosophie en Europe, 1993; articles in Jahresberichte d. Heidelberger Akademie, Proceedings of British Acad., Enciclopedia Italiana, and elsewhere. *Address:* Wolfson College, Oxford OX2 6UD; Leacock Building, McGill University, Montreal, Que H3A 2T7, Canada.

KLOOTWIJK, Jaap; Director, Grove Holdings Ltd, since 1991; *b* 16 Nov. 1932; *s* of J. L. Klootwijk and W. J. Boer; *Educ:* Rotterdam Grammar Sch.; Technological Univ., Delft (MSc Mech. Eng, 1956). Lieut Royal Netherlands Navy, 1956–58. Joined Royal Dutch/Shell Gp, 1958; worked in various capacities in Holland, UK, France, Switzerland, Sweden, Algeria, Kenya; Area Co-ordinator, SE Asia, 1976–79; Man. Dir, Shell Internat. Gas Ltd, 1979–82; Jt Man. Dir, Shell UK, 1983–88; Man. Dir, Shell UK Oil, 1983–88; Chm., UK Oil Pipelines, 1983–88. Dir, The Flyfishers' Co. Ltd, 1985–94. Pres., UK Petroleum Industry Assoc., 1985–87. FRSA 1986. *Recreations:* deer-stalking, shooting, fishing, reading. *Address:* 26 Manor House Court, Warwick Avenue, W9 2PZ. *T:* 0171–289 4276. *Club:* Flyfishers' (Pres., 1985–87).

KLOSE, Hans-Ulrich; Member (SPD), since 1983, Vice-President, since 1994, Bundestag, Germany; *b* 14 June 1937; *m* 1992, Dr Anne Steinbeck-Klose; two *s* two *d* by former marriages. *Educ:* Bielefeld; Clinton, Iowa; Freiburg Univ. (Law graduate 1965). Joined SDP 1964; Dep. Chm., Young Socialists, 1966; Dep. Chm., SPD, 1968; Mayor of Hamburg, 1974–81; Treasurer, SPD, 1987–91. Leader of the Opposition, Bundestag, 1991–94. *Publications:* Altern der Gesellschaft, 1993; Altern hat Zukunft, 1993. *Address:* c/o Bundeshaus, 53113 Bonn, Germany.

KLUG, Sir Aaron, Kt 1988; PhD (Cantab); FRS 1969; Director, Medical Research Council Laboratory of Molecular Biology, Cambridge, since 1986 (member of staff, since 1962, Joint Head, Division of Structural Studies, 1978–86); President, Royal Society, since 1995; Hon. Fellow of Peterhouse, since 1993 (Fellow, 1962–93); *b* 11 Aug. 1926; *s* of Lazar Klug and Bella Klug (*née* Silin); *m* 1948, Liebe Bobrow, Cape Town, SA; two *s*. *Educ:* Durban High Sch.; Univ. of the Witwatersrand (BSc); Univ. of Cape Town (MSc). Junior Lecturer, Cape Town, 1947–48; 1851 Exhibn Overseas Fellow from SA to Cambridge; Research Student, Cavendish Laboratory, Cambridge, 1949–52; Rouse-Ball Research Studentship, Trinity Coll., Cambridge, 1949–52; Colloid Science Dept, Cambridge, 1953; Nuffield Research Fellow, Birkbeck Coll., London, 1954–57; Head, Virus Structure Research Group, Birkbeck Coll., 1958–61. Mem., Council for Sci. and Technology, 1993–. Hon. Prof., Univ. of Cambridge, 1989. Lectures: Carter-Wallace, Princeton, 1972; Leeuwenhoek, Royal Soc., 1973; Dunham, Harvard Medical Sch., 1975; Harvey, NY, 1979; Lane, Stanford Univ., 1983; Silliman, Yale Univ., 1985; Nishina Meml, Tokyo, 1986; Pauli, ETH Zürich, 1986; Cetus, Univ. of California, Berkeley, 1987; Konrad Bloch, Harvard, 1988; Steenbock, Univ. of Wisconsin, 1989; National, US Biophysical Soc., Washington, 1993. For. Associate, Nat. Acad. of Scis, USA, 1984; For. Mem., Max Planck Soc., Germany, 1984; For. Hon. Mem., Amer. Acad. of Arts and Scis, 1969; For. Associate Acad. des Scis, Paris, 1989. Hon. FRCP 1987; Hon. FRCPath 1991. Hon. Fellow, Trinity Coll., Cambridge, 1983. Hon. DSc: Chicago, 1978; Columbia Univ., 1978; Dr *hc* Strasbourg, 1978; Hon. DSc: Witwatersrand, 1984; Hull, 1985; St Andrews, 1987; Western Ontario, 1991; Warwick, 1994; Hon. PhD Jerusalem, 1984; Hon. Dr Fil. Stockholm, 1980. Heineken Prize, Royal Netherlands Acad. of Science, 1979; Louisa Gross Horwitz Prize, Columbia Univ., 1981; Nobel Prize in Chemistry, 1982; Gold Medal of Merit, Univ. of Cape Town, 1983; Copley Medal, Royal Soc., 1985; Harden Medal, Biochem. Soc., 1985; Baly Medal, RCP, 1987. *Publications:* papers in scientific jls. *Recreations:* reading, ancient history. *Address:* MRC Laboratory of Molecular Biology, Hills Road, Cambridge CB2 2QH. *T:* Cambridge (01223) 248011.

KLYBERG, Rt. Rev. Charles John; *see* Fulham, Bishop Suffragan of.

KLYNE, Dame Barbara Evelyn; *see* Clayton, Dame B. E.

KNAGGS, Kenneth James, CMG 1971; OBE 1959; formerly overseas civil servant; *b* 3 July 1920; *e s* of late James Henry Knaggs and Elsie Knaggs (*née* Walton); *m* 1945, Barbara, *d* of late Ernest James Page; two *s*. *Educ:* St Paul's Sch., London. Served War, 1939–46 (Major). Northern Rhodesia Civil Service, 1946; Sec. to Govt, Seychelles, 1955 (Actg Governor, 1957–58); Northern Rhodesia: Asst Sec., 1960; Under Sec., 1961; Permanent Sec., Min. of Finance and subseq. the same in Zambia, 1964; retd 1970. European Rep. and Manager, Zambia Airways, 1970–72; Consultant, Commonwealth Devel Corp., 1974–87. *Recreations:* walking, gardening, cooking. *Address:* High House Farm, Earl Soham, near Framlingham, Suffolk IP13 7SN. *T:* Earl Soham (01728) 685416.

KNAPMAN, Dr Paul Anthony; HM Coroner for Westminster, since 1980 (Jurisdiction of Inner West London); *b* 5 Nov. 1944; *s* of Frederick Ethelbert and Myra Knapman; *m* 1970, Penelope Jane Cox; one *s* three *d*. *Educ:* Epsom Coll.; King's Coll., London; St George's Hosp. Med. Sch. (MB, BS 1968). MRCS, LRCP 1968; DMJ 1975. Called to the Bar, Gray's Inn, 1972. Dep. Coroner for Inner W London, 1975–80. Hon. Lectr in Med. Jurisprudence, St George's Hosp. Med. Sch., 1978–; Hon. Clinical Teacher (Forensic Medicine), Middlesex and UCH Med. Sch., 1981–; Hon. Sen. Lectr in Public Health Medicine, Westminster and Charing Cross Med. Sch., 1987–. President: S Eastern England Coroners' Soc., 1980; Sect. of Clinical Forensic Medicine, RSocMed, 1995–. Gov., London Nautical Sch., 1981–. Liveryman, 1982–, and Mem., Ct of Assistants, 1993–; Soc. of Apothecaries. Specialist Editor (Coroners Law), JP Reports, 1990–. *Publications:* (jtly) Coronership: the law and practice on coroners, 1985; Medicine and the Law, 1989; Casebook on Coroners, 1989; (contrib.) Medical Negligence, 1990; (contrib.) Atkins Court Forms, vol. 13, 1992; papers on medico-legal subjects. *Recreations:* boating, beagling.

Address: Westminster Coroner's Court, Horseferry Road, SW1P 2ED. *T:* 0171–834 6515. *Clubs:* Athenæum, Garrick; Royal Torbay Yacht.

KNAPMAN, Roger Maurice; MP (C) Stroud, since 1987; an Assistant Government Whip, since 1995; *b* 20 Feb. 1944; *m* 1967, Carolyn Trebell (*née* Eastman); one *s* one *d.* *Educ:* Royal Agricl Coll., Cirencester. FRICS 1967. PPS to Minister of State for Armed Forces, 1991–93. Vice-Chm., Cons. backbench European Affairs Cttee, 1989–90; Mem., Select Cttee on Agric., 1994–95. Mem., AFRC, 1991–94. *Address:* House of Commons, SW1A 0AA; (office) c/o Stroud Conservative Association, Carlton Gardens, London Road, Stroud, Glos GL5 2AH.

KNAPP, David; *see* Knapp, J. D.

KNAPP, Edward Ronald, CBE 1979; Managing Director, Timken Europe, 1973–85, retired; *b* 10 May 1919; *s* of Percy Charles and Elsie Maria Knapp; *m* 1942, Vera Mary Stephenson; two *s* two *d.* *Educ:* Cardiff High Sch.; St Catharine's Coll., Cambridge (MA 1940); Harvard Business Sch. (AMP 1954). Served RNVR, Special Branch, Lt-Comdr, 1940–46: HMS Aurora, 1941–44; US Naval Research, Anacostia, 1944–46. Joined British Timken, 1946, Man. Dir, 1969; Dir, Timken Co., USA, 1976. Technical and Management Educnl Governor, Nene Coll., 1953–. Pres., Northampton RFC, 1986–88. *Recreations:* gardening, golf; played Rugby for Wales, 1940, Captain of Cambridge Univ. 1940 and Northampton RFC, 1948. *Address:* The Elms, 1 Millway, Duston, Northampton NN5 6ER. *T:* Northampton (01604) 584737. *Clubs:* East India, Devonshire, Sports and Public Schools; Northants County Golf; Hawks (Cambridge).

KNAPP, James; General Secretary, Rail, Maritime and Transport Union, since 1990 (National Union of Railwaymen, 1983–90); *b* 29 Sept. 1940; *s* of James and Jean Knapp; *m* 1965, Sylvia Florence Yeomans; one *d.* *Educ:* Hurlford Primary Sch.; Kilmarnock Academy. British Rail employee (signalman), 1955–72; Hurlford NUR Branch Secretary, 1961–65; Sec., Amalgamated Kilmarnock and Hurlford NUR Br., 1965–72; Glasgow and W Scotland NUR Dist Council Sec., 1970–72; full time Divisional Officer, NUR, 1972–81; Headquarters Officer, NUR, 1981–82. Member: TUC Gen. Council, 1983–; ITF Exec. Bd, 1983–. Dir, Trade Union Unit Trust, 1984–; Pres., Unity Trust Bank, 1989– (Dir, 1984–). *Recreations:* walking, soccer, countryside. *Address:* (office) Unity House, 205 Euston Road, NW1 2BL.

KNAPP, (John) David, OBE 1986; Director of Conservative Political Centre, 1975–88; an Assistant Director, Conservative Research Department, 1979–88; *b* 27 Oct. 1926; *s* of late Eldred Arthur Knapp and Elizabeth Jane Knapp; *m* 1st, 1954, Dorothy Ellen May (*née* Squires) (marr. diss.); one *s*; 2nd, 1980, Daphne Monard, OBE, *widow* of Major S. H. Monard. *Educ:* Dauntsey's Sch., Wilts; King's Coll., London (BA Hons). Dir, Knapp and Bates Ltd, 1950–54. Vice-Chm., Fedn of University Conservative and Unionist Assoc., 1948–49; Conservative Publicity and Political Educn Officer, Northern Area, 1952–56; Political Educn Officer, NW Area, 1956–61, and Home Counties N Area, 1961; Dep. Dir, Conservative Political Centre, 1962–75. Member (C), Hampshire CC, 1989–93. *Recreations:* philately, walking cavalier spaniels. *Address:* 71 Kirby Road, Portsmouth, Hants PO2 0PF. *T:* Portsmouth (01705) 663709.

KNAPP, Trevor Frederick William Beresford; Assistant Under Secretary of State (Infrastructure and Logistics), Ministry of Defence, since 1992; *b* 26 May 1937; *s* of Frederick William Knapp and Linda Knapp (*née* Poffley); *m* 1964, Margaret Fry; one *s* one *d.* *Educ:* Christ's Hospital; King's College London (BSc 1958). ARIC 1960. Ministry of Aviation, 1961; Sec., Downey Cttee, 1965–66; Sec., British Defence Research and Supply Staff, Canberra, 1968–72; Asst Sec., MoD, 1974; GEC Turbine Generators Ltd, 1976; Central Policy Review Staff, 1977–79; Ministry of Defence: Under-Sec., 1983; Dir Gen. (Marketing), 1983–88; Asst Under Sec. of State (Supply and Organisation) (Air), 1988–91. *Address:* c/o Ministry of Defence, Main Building, Whitehall, SW1A 2HB.

KNAPP-FISHER, Rt. Rev. Edward George; Hon. Assistant Bishop, diocese of Chichester, since 1987; Custos of St Mary's Hospital, Chichester, since 1987; *b* 8 Jan. 1915; *s* of late Rev. George Edwin and Agatha Knapp-Fisher; *m* 1965, Joan, *d* of late R. V. Bradley. *Educ:* King's School, Worcester; Trinity College, Oxford (MA). Assistant Curate of Brighouse, Yorks, 1939; Chaplain, RNVR, 1942; Chaplain of Cuddesdon College, 1946; Chaplain of St John's College, Cambridge, 1949; Vicar of Cuddesdon and Principal of Cuddesdon Theological College, 1952–60; Bishop of Pretoria, 1960–75; Canon and Archdeacon of Westminster, 1975–87; Sub-Dean, 1982–87; Asst Bishop, Dio. Southwark 1975–87, Dio. London 1976–87. Member, Anglican Roman-Catholic Preparatory Commission, 1967–68; Member, Anglican-Roman Catholic Internat. Commn, 1969–81. *Publications:* The Churchman's Heritage, 1952; Belief and Prayer, 1964; To be or not to be, 1968; Where the Truth is Found, 1975; (ed jtly and contrib.) Towards Unity in Truth, 1981; Eucharist, Many-Sided Mystery, 1988. *Recreations:* walking, theatre, gardening. *Address:* 2 Vicars' Close, Canon Lane, Chichester, West Sussex PO19 1PT. *T:* Chichester (01243) 789219.

KNARESBOROUGH, Bishop Suffragan of, since 1986; **Rt. Rev. Malcolm James Menin;** *b* 26 Sept. 1932; *s* of Rev. James Nicholas Menin and Doreen Menin; *m* 1958, Jennifer Mary Cullen; one *s* three *d.* *Educ:* Dragon School; St Edward's School; University Coll., Oxford (MA); Cuddesdon Coll. Curate: Holy Spirit, Southsea, 1957–59; St Peter and St Paul, Fareham, 1959–62; Vicar of St James, Norwich, later St Mary Magdalene with St James, Norwich, 1962–86; RD Norwich East, 1981–86; Hon. Canon, Norwich Cathedral, 1982–86. *Recreations:* walking, photography, carpentry. *Address:* 16 Shaftesbury Avenue, Leeds LS8 1DT. *T:* Leeds (0113) 266 4800.

KNATCHBULL, family name of **Baron Brabourne** and **Countess Mountbatten of Burma.**

KNEALE, George Victor Harris, CBE 1989; Speaker, House of Keys, Isle of Man, 1990–91; retired; *b* 12 Jan. 1918; *s* of James Kneale and Ellen (*née* Harris); *m* 1940, Thelma Eugenie Creer; two *d.* *Educ:* Demesne Road Elementary Sch.; Douglas High Sch. for Boys. Served RHA, 1940–46, ME and Italy. Photo-process engraver, 1935–40 and 1946–57. Mem., IOM Educn Authy, 1951–62; Chm., Bd of Educn, 1962–72, 1981–86; Minister for Educn, 1986–90; Member: House of Keys, 1962–74, 1981–91; Legislative Council, 1974–81; Founder Chm., IOM PO Authy, 1972–81. President: IOM Art Soc.; IOM Br., Royal Artillery Assoc.; IOM Scout Assoc.; Manx Gateway Club. Hon. MA Salford, 1990. Boy Scouts Awards: Medal of Merit; Silver Acorn; Silver Wolf. *Recreations:* drawing, painting, photography, Boy Scouts. *Address:* Carrmyers, 15 Cronkbourne Avenue, Douglas, Isle of Man IM2 3LA. *T:* Douglas (0624) 676996.

KNEALE, (Robert) Bryan (Charles), RA 1974 (ARA 1970); sculptor; Professor of Drawing, Royal College of Art, 1990–95; *b* 19 June 1930; *m* 1956, Doreen Lister; one *s* one *d.* *Educ:* Douglas High Sch.; Douglas Sch. of Art, IOM; Royal Academy Schools: Rome prize, 1949–51; RA diploma. Tutor, RCA Sculpture Sch., 1964–; Head of Sculpture Sch., Hornsey, 1967; Assoc. Lectr, Chelsea Sch. of Art, 1970. Fellow RCA, 1972, Sen. Fellow, 1995; Head of Sculpture Dept, RCA, 1985–90 (Sen. Tutor, 1980–85); Prof. of Sculpture, RA, 1985–90 (Master of Sculpture, 1982–85). Member: Fine Art Panels, NCAD, 1964–71, Arts Council, 1971–73, CNAA, 1974–82; Chm., Air and Space, 1972–73. *Organised:* Sculpture '72, RA, 1972; Battersea Park Silver Jubilee Sculpture, 1977 (also exhibited); Sade Exhbn, Cork, 1982. *Exhibitions:* at Redfern Gallery, 1954, 1956, 1958, 1960, 1962, 1964, 1967, 1970, 1976, 1978, 1981; 1983; John Moores, 1961; Sixth Congress of Internat. Union of Architects, 1961; Art Aujourd'hui, Paris, 1963; Battersea Park Sculpture, 1963, 1966; Profile III Bochum, 1964; British Sculpture in the Sixties, Tate Gall., 1965; Whitechapel Gall. 1966 (retrospective), 1981; Structure, Cardiff Metamorphis Coventry, 1966; New British Painting and Sculpture, 1967–68; City of London Festival, 1968; Holland Park, Sculpture in the Cities, Southampton, and British Sculptors, RA, 1972; Holland Park, 1973; Royal Exchange Sculpture Exhibition, 1974; New Art, Hayward Gallery, 1975; Sculpture at Worksop, 1976; Taranman Gall., 1977, 1981; Serpentine Gall., 1978; Monumental Sculpture for Manx Millenium, Ronaldsway, Isle of Man, 1979; Compass Gall., Glasgow, 1981; 51 Gall., Edinburgh, 1981; Bath Art Fair, 1981; Henry Moore Gall., RCA (retrospective), 1986; Fitzwilliam Mus., 1987; Sala Uno, Rome, 1988; Chichester Fest., 1988; New Art Centre, 1990; Nat. History Mus., 1991. Arts Council Tours, 1966–71. *Collections:* Arts Council of Gt Britain; Contemp. Art Soc.; Manx Museum; Leics Educn Authority; Nat. Galls of Victoria, S Australia and New Zealand; City Art Galls, York, Nottingham, Manchester, Bradford and Leicester; Tate Gall.; Beaverbrook Foundn, Fredericton; Museum of Modern Art, Sao Paulo, Brazil; Bahia Museum, Brazil; Oriel Coll., Oxford; Museum of Modern Art, New York; City Galleries, Middlesbrough, Birmingham, Wakefield; Fitzwilliam Museum, Cambridge; W Riding Educn Authority; Unilever House Collection; Walker Art Gallery; Nat. History Mus., Taiwan; Nat. History Mus., London. *Address:* 10A Muswell Road, N10 2BG. *T:* 0181–444 7617.

KNEBWORTH, Viscount; Philip Anthony Scawen Lytton; *b* 7 March 1989; *s* and *heir* of Earl of Lytton, *qv.*

KNELLER, Alister Arthur; Hon. Mr Justice Kneller; Chief Justice of Gibraltar, since 1986; *b* 11 Nov. 1927; *s* of Arthur Kneller and Hester (*née* Farr). *Educ:* King's Sch., Canterbury; Corpus Christi Coll., Cambridge (MA 1954; LLM 1985). Kenya: Resident Magistrate, 1955; Sen. State Counsel, 1962; Registrar of the High Court, 1965; Puisne Judge, 1969; Judge of the Court of Appeal, 1982. *Recreations:* music, reading. *Address:* 2 Mount Road, Gibraltar. *T:* Gibraltar 75753. *Clubs:* United Oxford & Cambridge University; Mombasa (Kenya); Royal Yacht (Gibraltar).

KNIBB, Prof. Michael Anthony, PhD; FBA 1989; Professor of Old Testament Studies, since 1986, and Deputy Head, School of Humanities, since 1992, King's College London; *b* 14 Dec. 1938; third *s* of Leslie Charles Knibb and Christian Vera Knibb (*née* Hoggar); *m* 1972, Christine Mary Burrell. *Educ:* Wyggeston Sch., Leicester; King's Coll. London (BD, PhD; FKC 1991); Union Theol Seminary, NY (STM); Corpus Christi Coll., Oxford. King's College London: Lectr in OT Studies, 1964–82; Reader, 1982–86; Hd of Dept of Theology and Religious Studies, 1989–93. British Acad. Res. Reader, 1986–88; Mem., Humanities Res. Bd, 1995–. Editor: Book List of SOTS, 1980–86; Guides to the Apocrypha and Pseudepigrapha, 1995–. *Publications:* The Ethiopic Book of Enoch: a new edition in the light of the Aramaic Dead Sea Fragments, 2 vols, 1978; Het Boek Henoch, 1983; Cambridge Bible Commentary on 2 Esdras, 1979; (ed jtly) Israel's Prophetic Tradition: essays in honour of P. R. Ackroyd, 1982; The Qumran Community, 1987; (ed with P. W. van der Horst) Studies on the Testament of Job, 1989; articles in books and learned jls. *Recreation:* walking. *Address:* 6 Shootersway Park, Berkhamsted, Herts HP4 3NX. *T:* Berkhamsted (01442) 871459. *Club:* Athenæum.

KNIGHT, Prof. Alan Sydney, DPhil; Professor of the History of Latin America, and Fellow of St Antony's College, Oxford, since 1992; *b* 6 Nov. 1946; *s* of William Henry Knight and Eva Maud Crandon; *m* 1st, 1969, Carole Jones (marr. diss. 1979); one *d*; 2nd, 1985, Lidia Lozano; two *s.* *Educ:* Balliol Coll., Oxford (BA Modern Hist. 1968); Nuffield Coll., Oxford (DPhil 1974). Research Fellow, Nuffield Coll., Oxford, 1971–73; Lectr in Hist., Essex Univ., 1973–85; Worsham Centennial Prof. of History, Univ. of Texas at Austin, 1986–92. *Publications:* The Mexican Revolution (2 vols), 1986; US-Mexican Relations 1910–40, 1987; contrib. Jl of Latin American Studies, Bull. of Latin American Res., etc. *Recreation:* kayaking. *Address:* St Antony's College, Oxford OX2 6JF. *T:* Oxford (01865) 59651.

KNIGHT, Ven. Alexander Francis; Archdeacon of Basingstoke and Canon Residentiary of Winchester Cathedral, since 1990; *b* 24 July 1939; *s* of Benjamin Edward and Dorothy Mary Knight; *m* 1962, Sheelagh Elizabeth (*née* Faris); one *s* three *d.* *Educ:* Taunton Sch.; St Catharine's Coll., Cambridge (MA). Curate, Hemel Hempstead, 1963–68; Chaplain, Taunton Sch., 1968–74; Dir, Bloxham Project, 1975–81; Dir of Studies, Aston Training Scheme, 1981–83; Priest-in-charge, Easton and Martyr Worthy, 1983–90. *Publications:* contrib. SPCK Taleteller series. *Recreations:* hill walking, theatre, reading, gardening. *Address:* 1 The Close, Winchester, Hampshire SO23 9LS.

KNIGHT, Sir Allan Walton, Kt 1970; CMG 1960; Hon. FIE (Aust.); FTS; Commissioner, The Hydro-Electric Commission, Tasmania, 1946–77; Chief Commissioner, Tasman Bridge Restoration Commission, 1975–80; *b* 26 Feb. 1910; *s* of late Mr and Mrs G. W. Knight, Lindisfarne, Tasmania; *m* 1936, Margaret Janet Buchanan; two *s* one *d.* *Educ:* Hobart Technical Coll.; University of Tasmania. Diploma of Applied Science, 1929; BSc 1932; ME 1935; BCom 1946. Chief Engineer, Public Works Dept, Tasmania, 1937–46. Member: Australian Univs Commn, 1966–74; Council, Tasmanian Coll. of Advanced Education, 1968–75. Peter Nicol Russell Medal, Instn of Engrs of Australia, 1963; William Kernot Medal, Univ. of Melbourne, 1963; Wilfred Chapman Award, Inst. of Welding, Australia, 1974; John Storey Medal, Inst. of Management, Australia, 1975. Hon. DEng Tasmania, 1980. *Recreation:* royal tennis. *Address:* 64 Waimea Avenue, Sandy Bay, Hobart, Tasmania 7005, Australia. *T:* (02) 251498. *Club:* Tasmanian (Hobart).

KNIGHT, Andrew Stephen Bower; Chairman: News International plc, 1990–94; Times Newspapers Holdings, 1990–94; Director, The News Corporation Ltd, since 1991; *b* 1 Nov. 1939; *s* of late M. W. B. Knight and of S. E. F. Knight; *m* 1st, 1966, Victoria Catherine Brittain (marr. diss.); one *s*; 2nd, 1975, Sabiha Rumani Malik (marr. diss. 1991); two *d.* Editor, The Economist, 1974–86; Chief Exec., 1986–89, Editor-in-Chief, 1987–89, Daily Telegraph plc. Member: Steering Cttee, Bilderberg Meetings, 1980–; Adv. Bd, Center for Economic Policy Research, Stanford Univ., 1981–; Adv. Council, Inst. of Internat. Studies, Stanford Univ., 1990–. Trustee, Harlech Scholars' Trust. Governor and Mem. Council of Management, Ditchley Foundn, 1982–. *Clubs:* Brooks's, Royal Automobile.

KNIGHT, Angela Ann; MP (C) Erewash, since 1992; Economic Secretary to HM Treasury, since 1995; *b* 31 Oct. 1950; *d* of Andrew McTurk Cook and late Barbara Eve (*née* Gale); *m* 1981, David George Knight (marr. diss.); two *s.* *Educ:* Penrhos Coll., N Wales; Sheffield Girls' High Sch.; Bristol Univ. (BSc Hons Chem. 1972). Management posts with Air Products Ltd, 1972–77; Man. Dir and Chm., Cook & Knight (Metallurgical Processors) Ltd, 1977–84; Chief Exec., Cook & Knight (Process Plant), 1984–91. PPS to Minister for Industry, 1993–94, to Chancellor of the Exchequer, 1994–95. *Recreations:*

walking, ski-ing, music, books. *Address:* House of Commons, SW1A 0AA. *T:* 0171–219 3000. *Club:* Sheffield (Sheffield).

KNIGHT, Sir Arthur (William), Kt 1975; Chairman, National Enterprise Board, 1979–80; Chairman, Courtaulds Ltd, 1975–79; *b* 29 March 1917; *s* of Arthur Frederick Knight and Emily Scott; *m* 1st, 1945, Beatrice Joan Osborne (*née* Oppenheim) (*d* 1968); one *s* three *d*; 2nd, 1972, Sheila Elsie Whiteman. *Educ:* Tottenham County Sch.; London Sch. of Economics (evening student) (BCom; Hon. Fellow 1984). J. Sainsbury, Blackfriars, 1933–38; LSE, Dept of Business Admin (Leverhulme Studentship), 1938–39; Courtaulds, 1939. Served War, Army, 1940–46. Courtaulds, 1946–79: apptd Dir, 1958; Finance Dir, 1961. Non-exec. Director: Pye Holdings, 1972–75; Rolls-Royce (1971), 1973–78; Richard Thomas & Baldwin, 1966–67; Dunlop Holdings, 1981–84. Member: Council of Manchester Business Sch., 1964–71; Cttee for Arts and Social Studies of Council for Nat. Academic Awards, 1965–71; Commn of Enquiry into siting of Third London Airport, 1968–70; Council of Industry for Management Educn, 1970–73; Finance Cttee, RIIA, 1971–75; Council, RIIA, 1975–85; Court of Governors, London Sch. of Economics, 1971–94; Economic Cttee, CBI, 1965–72; Cairncross (Channel Tunnel) Cttee, 1974–75; NIESR Exec. Cttee, 1976–95; BOTB, 1978–79; The Queen's Award Adv. Cttee, 1981–86; Cttee on Fraud Trials, 1984–85. *Publications:* Private Enterprise and Public Intervention: the Courtauld experience, 1974; various papers. *Recreations:* walking, music, reading. *Address:* Charlton End, Singleton, West Sussex PO18 0HX. *Club:* Reform.

KNIGHT, Prof. Bernard Henry, CBE 1993; MD, FRCPath; Consultant Pathologist to Home Office, since 1965; Professor of Forensic Pathology, University of Wales College of Medicine, since 1980; *b* 3 May 1931; *s* of Harold Ivor Knight and Doris (*née* Lawes); *m* 1955, Jean Gwenllian Ogborne; one *s*. *Educ:* Univ. of Wales (BCh, MD); MRCPath 1964, FRCPath 1966; DMJ (Path) 1967; MRCP 1983. Called to the Bar, Gray's Inn, 1967. Captain RAMC, Malaya, 1956–59. Lecturer in Forensic Medicine: Univ. of London, 1959–61; Univ. of Wales, 1961–65; Sen. Lectr, Forensic Med., Univ. of Newcastle, 1965–68; Sen. Lectr, then Reader of Forensic Pathology, Univ. of Wales Coll. Med., 1968–80. Hon. Consultant Pathologist, Cardiff Royal Infirmary, 1968–. Vis. Prof., Univs of Hong Kong, Kuwait, Malaya and Guangzhou (China). Mem., Home Office Policy Adv. Cttee in Forensic Pathology; Chm., Forensic Sub-Cttee and Bd Examnrs, RCPath, 1990–93; Mem., GMC, 1979–. President: Brit. Assoc. Forensic Med., 1991–93; Forensic Science Soc., 1988–90; Vice-Pres., Internat. Acad. Legal Med., 1980–. Hon. FRSM 1994. Hon. Mem., German, Finnish and Hungarian Socs of Forensic Med. GSM Malaya, 1956. *Publications: fiction:* The Lately Deceased, 1961; The Thread of Evidence, 1963; Russian Roulette, 1968; Policeman's Progress, 1969; Tiger at Bay, 1970; Deg y Dragwyddoldeb (Welsh), 1972; Edyfyn Brau (Welsh), 1973; Lion Rampant, 1973; The Expert, 1975; Prince of America, 1977; *biography:* Autopsy: the memoirs of Milton Helpern, 1977; *non-fiction:* Murder, Suicide or Accident, 1965; Discovering the Human Body, 1980; *medical textbooks:* Legal Aspects of Medical Practice, 1972, 5th edn 1992; Forensic Radiology, 1982; Sudden Infant Death, 1982; Post-mortem Technician's Handbook, 1983; Forensic Medicine for Lawyers, 1984; Forensic Medicine, 1985; (ed) Simpson's Forensic Medicine, 9th edn 1985, 10th edn 1991; Coroner's Autopsy, 1985; Forensic Pathology, 1991; Estimation of the Time of Death, 1995. *Recreation:* writing. *Address:* Wales Institute of Forensic Medicine, University of Wales College of Medicine, Royal Infirmary, Cardiff CF2 1SZ. *T:* Cardiff (01222) 484358.

KNIGHT, Brian Joseph; QC 1981; practising barrister, since 1966; a Recorder, since 1991; *b* 5 May 1941; *s* of Joseph Knight and Vera Lorraine Knight (*née* Docksey); *m* 1967, Cristina Karen Wang Nobrega de Lima. *Educ:* Colbayns High Sch., Clacton; University Coll. London. LLB 1962, LLM 1963. FCIArb 1995. Called to the Bar, Gray's Inn, 1964; *ad eundem* Lincoln's Inn, 1979; called to the Bar of Hong Kong, 1978, of Northern Ireland, 1979. Asst Parly Boundary Comr, 1992. *Address:* 1 Atkin Building, Gray's Inn, WC1R 5BQ. *T:* 0171–404 0102. *Club:* Garrick.

KNIGHT, Edmund Alan; Commissioner of Customs and Excise, 1971–77; *b* 17 June 1919; *s* of Arthur Philip and Charlotte Knight; *m* 1953, Annette Ros Grimmitt; one *d*. *Educ:* Drayton Manor Sch.; London Sch. of Economics. Entered Exchequer and Audit Dept, 1938; HM Customs and Excise, 1948; Asst Sec., 1957; Sec. to Cttee on Turnover Taxation, 1963–64; seconded to Inland Revenue, 1969–71; returned to Customs and Excise, 1971; Eur. Affairs Adviser to BAT Co., 1978–85; consultant on indirect taxation, 1985–87. Member: SITPRO Bd, 1971–76; EDC for Internat. Freight Movement, 1971–76. *Recreations:* local history and environment, gardening. *Address:* 40 Park Avenue North, Harpenden, Herts AL5 2ED. *Club:* Commonwealth Trust.

KNIGHT, Geoffrey Egerton, CBE 1970; Chairman, Fenchurch Insurance Group Ltd, 1980–92 (Executive Vice-Chairman, 1975–80); *b* 25 Feb. 1921; *s* of Arthur Egerton Knight and Florence Gladys Knight (*née* Clarke); *m* 1947, Evelyn Bugle; two *d*. *Educ:* Stubbington House; Brighton Coll. Royal Marines, 1939–46. Joined Bristol Aeroplane Co. Ltd, 1953; Dir, Bristol Aircraft Ltd, 1956; Dir, BAC Ltd, 1964–77, Vice Chm., 1972–76. Director: Guinness Peat Group, later GPG plc, 1976–89 (Jt Dep. Chm., 1987–89; Chm., 1989); GPA Gp, 1977–93; Trafalgar House PLC, 1980–91. *Publication:* Concorde: the inside story, 1976. *Address:* 33 Smith Terrace, SW3 4DH. *T:* 0171–352 5391. *Clubs:* Boodle's, White's.

KNIGHT, Dr Geoffrey Wilfred; retired; Regional Medical Officer, North West Thames Regional Health Authority, 1973–76; *b* 10 Jan. 1920; *s* of Wilfred Knight and Ida Knight; *m* 1944, Christina Marion Collins Scott; one *s* one *d*. *Educ:* Leeds Univ. Med. Sch. MB, ChB, MD, DPH (Chadwick Gold Medal). County Med. Officer of Health, Herts, 1962–73. Formerly: Governor, Nat. Inst. of Social Work; Member: Personal Social Services Council; Central Midwives Bd; Exec. Cttee, Child Health Bureau; Adv. Panel, Soc. for Health Educn; formerly Mem., Govt Techn. and Sci. Cttee on Disposal of Toxic Wastes. *Recreations:* painting, golf. *Address:* 4947 197A Street, Langley, BC V3A 6W1, Canada.

KNIGHT, Rt Hon. Gregory; PC 1995; MP (C) Derby North, since 1983; Deputy Government Chief Whip and Treasurer of HM Household, since 1993; *b* 4 April 1949; *s* of George Knight and Isabella Knight (*née* Bell). *Educ:* Alderman Newton's Grammar School, Leicester; College of Law, Guildford. Self employed solicitor, 1973–83. Member: Leicester City Council, 1976–79; Leicestershire County Council, 1977–83 (Chm., Public Protection Cttee); PPS to the Minister of State: Home Office, 1987; Foreign Office, 1988–89; an Asst Govt Whip, 1989–90; a Lord Comr of HM Treasury, 1990–93. Dir, Leicester Theatre Trust, 1979–85 (Chm., Finance Cttee, 1982–83). *Publications:* (jtly) Westminster Words, 1988; Honourable Insults: a century of political insult, 1990; pamphlets and articles for law publications. *Recreations:* music, the arts, writing, film comedy, classic cars. *Address:* House of Commons, SW1A 0AA. *T:* 0171–219 5099. *Clubs:* Royal Automobile; Chaddesden Jubilee (Derby).

KNIGHT, Sir Harold (Murray), KBE 1980; DSC 1945; *b* 13 Aug. 1919; *s* of W. H. P. Knight, Melbourne; *m* 1951, Gwenyth Catherine Pennington; four *s* one *d*. *Educ:* Scotch Coll., Melbourne; Melbourne Univ. Commonwealth Bank of Australia, 1936–40. AIF (Lieut), 1940–43; RANVR (Lieut), 1943–45. Commonwealth Bank of Australia, 1946–55; Asst Chief, Statistics Div., Internat. Monetary Fund, 1957–59; Reserve Bank of Australia: Research Economist, 1960–62; Asst Manager, Investment Dept, 1962–64, Manager, 1964–68; Dep. Governor and Dep. Chm. of Board, 1968–75; Governor and Chm. of Bd, 1975–82. Chairman: Mercantile Mutual Hldgs, 1985–89; IBJ Australia Bank Ltd, 1985–92; Dir, Western Mining Corp., 1982–91. Mem., Police Bd of NSW, 1988–89, 1991–93. Mem. Council, Macquarie Univ., 1990–92. Pres., Scripture Union, NSW, 1983–. *Publication:* Introducción al Analisis Monetario (Spanish), 1959. *Address:* 76 Yarrara Road, West Pymble, NSW 2073, Australia.

KNIGHT, Jeffrey Russell, FCA; consultant; *b* 1 Oct. 1936; *s* of Thomas Edgar Knight and Ivy Cissie Knight (*née* Russell); *m* 1959, Judith Marion Delver Podger; four *d*. *Educ:* Bristol Cathedral Sch.; St Peter's Hall, Oxford (MA). Chartered Accountant, 1966; The Stock Exchange, subseq. Internat. Stock Exchange, 1967–90: Head of Quotations Dept, 1973; Dep. Chief Executive, 1975; Chief Exec., 1982–89. Member: City Company Law Cttee, 1974–80; Dept of Trade Panel on Company Law Revision, 1980–84; Accounting Standards Cttee, 1982–89; Special Adviser to Dept of Trade, 1975–81; Adviser to Council for the Securities Industry, 1978–85; UK Delegate: to EEC Working Parties; to Internat. Fedn of Stock Exchanges, 1973–90 (Chm., Task Force on Transnational Settlement, 1987–91); to Fedn of Stock Exchanges in EEC, 1974–90 (Chm., Wkng Cttee, 1980–90); to Internat. Orgn of Securities Commns, 1987–91 (Chm. Wkg Party on Capital Adequacy). *Recreations:* cricket, music. *Address:* Robin Haye, The Drive, Godalming, Surrey GU7 1PH. *T:* Godalming (01483) 424399. *Clubs:* Brooks's; Dorset Rangers (Cricket).

KNIGHT, Dame Joan Christabel Jill, (Dame Jill Knight), DBE 1985 (MBE 1964); MP (C) Birmingham, Edgbaston since 1966; *m* 1947, Montague Knight (*d* 1986); two *s*. *Educ:* Fairfield Sch., Bristol; King Edward Grammar Sch., Birmingham. Mem., Northampton County Borough Council, 1956–66. Member: Parly Select Cttee on Race Relations and Immigration, 1969–72; Council of Europe, 1977–88; WEU, 1977–88 (Chm., Cttee for Parly and Public Relations, 1984–88); Select Cttee for Home Affairs, 1980–83, 1992–; Chairman: Lords and Commons All-Party Child and Family Protection Gp, 1978–; Cons. Back Bench Health and Social Services Cttee, 1982–; Member: Exec. Cttee, 1922 Cttee, 1979– (Sec., 1983–87; Vice-Chm., 1987–88, 1992–); Exec. Cttee, IPU, 1991– (Chm., 1994–). Pres., West Midlands Conservative Political Centre, 1980–83. Vice-Pres., Townswomen's Guilds, 1986–. Dir, Computeach International plc, 1991–. Kentucky Colonel, USA, 1973; Nebraska Admiral, USA, 1980. *Recreations:* music, reading, tapestry work, theatre-going, antique-hunting. *Address:* House of Commons, SW1A 0AA.

KNIGHT, Maureen R.; *see* Rice-Knight.

KNIGHT, Sir Michael (William Patrick), KCB 1983 (CB 1980); AFC 1964; Chairman, Cobham plc, since 1995 (Deputy Chairman, 1994–95); *b* 23 Nov. 1932; *s* of William and Dorothy Knight; *m* 1967, Patricia Ann (*née* Davies); one *s* two *d*. *Educ:* Leek High Sch.; Univ. of Liverpool (BA Hons 1954; Hon. DLitt 1985). MBIM 1977; FRAeS 1984. Univ. of Liverpool Air Sqn, RAFVR, 1951–54; commnd RAF, 1954; served in Transport and Bomber Comds, and in Middle and Near East Air Forces, 1956–63; Comd No 32 Sqn, RAF Akrotiri, 1961–63; RAF Staff Coll., 1964; Min. of Aviation, 1965–66; Comd Far East Strike Wing, RAF Tengah, 1966–69; Head of Secretariat, HQ Strike Comd, 1969–70; Mil. Asst to Chm., NATO Mil. Cttee, 1970–73; Comd RAF Laarbruch, 1973–74; RCDS, 1975; Dir of Ops (Air Support), MoD, 1975–77; SASO, HQ Strike Command/DCS (Ops & Intelligence) HQ UK Air Forces, 1977–80; AOC No 1 Gp, 1980–82; Air Mem. for Supply and Organisation, 1983–86; UK Military Rep. to NATO, 1986–89. Air ADC to the Queen, 1986–89 (ADC, 1973–74). Ret'd Air Chief Marshal, 1989. Commnd Flying Officer, RAFVR (Trng Br.), 1989. Director: Craigwell Research, 1990–; RAFC Ltd, 1993–; non-executive Director: FR Group plc, 1990–94; Page Aerospace Ltd, 1991–; Smiths Industries Aerospace and Defence Systems Group, 1992–95; Chm., Northern Devon Healthcare NHS Trust, 1991–94; Mem., IISS, 1968–. Member Council: RUSI, 1984–87; The Air League, 1990– (Chm., 1992–); SBAC, 1995–; Vice-Pres., Atlantic Council of UK, 1994–. Chm., N Devon Family Support Service, Leonard Cheshire Foundn, 1989–91; Mem., Management Cttee, Westmead Cheshire Home, 1989–92; Devon County Rep., RAF Benev. Fund, 1990–; RAF Pres., Officers' Assoc., 1991–; President: Aircrew Assoc., 1992–; Buccaneer Assoc., 1994–; Vice-Pres., The Youth Trust, 1994–. Adjunct Prof., Internat. Peace and Security, Carnegie Mellon Univ., Pittsburgh, 1989–. Gov. and Council Mem., Taunton Sch., 1987–; Mem., Univ. of Liverpool Develt Team, 1986–. Rugby Football Union: Mem. Cttee, 1977–92; Mem. Exec. Cttee, 1989–92; Chm., Internat. Sub Cttee, 1987–90; Chm., Forward Planning Sub Cttee, 1990–92. President: RAF Rugby Union, 1985–89 (Chm., 1975–78); Combined Services RFC, 1987–89 (Chm., 1977–79); RAF Lawn Tennis Assoc., 1984–86. FRGS 1994 (Mem. Council, 1995–); FRSA 1994. Liveryman, GAPAN, 1993– (Upper Freeman, 1990–93); Freeman, City of London, 1989. *Publications:* (contrib.) War in the Third Dimension, 1986; Strategic Offensive Air Power and Technology, 1989; articles in prof. pubns, 1975–. *Recreations:* Rugby football, lesser sports, music, writing, after-dinner speaking. *Address:* c/o National Westminster Bank, Leek, Staffs. *Clubs:* Royal Air Force (Vice-Pres., 1983–), East India, Colonels (founder); Saunton Golf.

KNIGHT, Dr Peter Clayton, CBE 1995; Vice-Chancellor, University of Central England in Birmingham, since 1992 (Director, Birmingham Polytechnic, 1985–92); *b* 8 July 1947; *s* of Norman Clayton Knight and Vera Catherine Knight; *m* 1977, Catherine Mary (*née* Ward); one *s* one *d*. *Educ:* Bishop Vesey's Grammar Sch., Sutton Coldfield; Univ. of York (BA 1st cl. Hons Physics; DPhil). SRC Studentship, 1968; Asst Teacher, Plymstock Comprehensive Sch., 1971; Plymouth Polytechnic: Lectr, 1972; Sen. Lectr, 1974; Head of Combined Studies, 1981; Dep. Dir, Lancashire Polytechnic, 1982–85. Nat. Pres., NATFHE, 1977; Chm., SRHE, 1987–89; Member: Burnham Cttee of Further Educn, 1976–81; Working Party on Management of Higher Educn, 1977; Nat. Adv. Body on Public Sector Higher Educn, 1982–85; PCFC, 1989–93; Polytechnic and Colleges Employers Forum, 1989–; Focus Housing Assoc., 1991–; Teacher Training Agency, 1994–. DUniv York, 1991. *Publications:* articles, chapters and reviews in learned jls on educnl policy, with particular ref. to higher educn. *Recreations:* middle-distance running, flying light aircraft. *Address:* Sandy Lodge, Sandy Lane, Brewood, Staffs ST19 9ET. *T:* Brewood (01902) 851339.

KNIGHT, Prof. Peter Leonard, DPhil; Professor of Quantum Optics, since 1988, and Head of the Laser Optics and Spectroscopy Group, since 1992, Physics Department, Imperial College of Science, Technology and Medicine, University of London; *b* 12 Aug. 1947; *s* of Joseph and Eva Knight; *m* 1965, Christine Huckle; two *s* one *d*. *Educ:* Bedford Modern Sch.; Sussex Univ. (BSc, DPhil). Research Associate, Univ. of Rochester, NY, 1972–74; SRC Res. Fellow, Sussex Univ., 1974–76; Jubilee Res. Fellow, RHC, 1976–78; SERC Advanced Fellow: RHC, 1978–79; Imperial Coll., 1979–83; Lectr, 1983–87, Reader, 1987–88, Imperial Coll. Mem., SERC Atomic and Molecular Physics Sub Cttee, 1987–90; Co-ordinator, SERC Nonlinear Optics Initiative, 1989–92 (Chm., Prog. Adv. Gp, 1992–95). Chm., Quantum Electronics Div., European Physical Soc., 1988–92; Pres., Physics Sect., BAAS, 1994–; Sec., Commn 17 (Quantum Electronics), IUPAP, 1993–95. Parsons Meml Lectr, Royal Soc. and Inst. of Physics, 1991; Humboldt Res. Award, Alexander von Humboldt Foundn, 1993. Editor: Jl of Modern Optics, 1987–;

Contemporary Physics, 1993–. *Publications:* Concepts of Quantum Optics, 1983; papers in Phys. Rev., Phys. Rev. Letters and other jls. *Recreations:* traditional music, walking. *Address:* Blackett Laboratory, Imperial College of Science, Technology and Medicine, SW7 2BZ. *T:* 0171–594 7727.

KNIGHT, Richard James, MA; JP; *b* 19 July 1915; *s* of Richard William Knight; *m* 1953, Hilary Marian, *d* of Rev. F. W. Argyle; two *s* one *d. Educ:* Dulwich Coll. (Scholar); Trinity Coll., Cambridge (Scholar; 1st class Hons Classical Tripos Pt I, 1936, Part II, 1937); BA Open Univ., 1988. Asst Master, Fettes Coll., Edinburgh, 1938–39. Served War of 1939–45 in Gordon Highlanders, Capt. Asst Master and Housemaster, Marlborough Coll., 1945–56; Headmaster of Oundle Sch., 1956–68, of Monkton Combe Sch., 1968–78. Reader, Dio. Bath and Wells. JP Northants, 1960, Bath, 1970, Avon, 1974. Hon. Liveryman, Grocers' Co., 1989–. *Recreations:* cricket and other games. *Address:* 123 Midford Road, Bath BA2 5RX. *T:* Bath (01225) 832276.

KNIGHT, Roger David Verdon; Secretary, Marylebone Cricket Club, since 1994; *b* 6 Sept. 1946; *s* of David Verdon Knight and Thelma Patricia Knight; *m* 1971, Christine Ann McNab (*née* Miln); one *s* one *d. Educ:* Dulwich Coll.; St Catharine's Coll., Cambridge (BA Modern and Medieval Langs 1969; MA 1972; DipEd 1970). Assistant Master: Eastbourne Coll., 1970–78; Dulwich Coll., 1978–83; Housemaster, Cranleigh Sch., 1983–90; Headmaster, Worksop Coll., 1990–93. Professional cricketer (summers only): Gloucestershire, 1971–75; Sussex, 1976–77; Surrey, 1978–84 (Captain, 1978–83). Vice-Chm., SE Region, Sports Council, 1985–90; Chm. Management Cttee, SE Region, Centres of Excellence, 1987–90; Dep. Chm., Cricket Cttee, Surrey CCC, 1987–90; Member: MCC Cttee, 1989–92; HMC Sports Sub-Cttee, 1991–93. Gov., TVS Trust, 1987–92. *Recreations:* cricket, tennis, squash, bridge, piano music, 17th Century French literature. *Address:* MCC, Lord's Ground, NW8 8QN.

KNIGHT, Dr Roger John Beckett; Deputy Director, since 1993, Chief Curator, since 1988, National Maritime Museum; *b* 11 April 1944; *s* of John Beckett Knight and Alyson Knight (*née* Nunn); *m* 1968, Elizabeth Magowan (marr. diss. 1980); two *s. Educ:* Tonbridge Sch.; Trinity Coll., Dublin (MA); Sussex Univ. (PGCE); University Coll. London (PhD). Asst Master, Haberdashers' Aske's Sch., Elstree, 1972–73; National Maritime Museum: Dep. Custodian of Manuscripts, 1974–77, Custodian, 1977–80; Dep. Head, Printed Books and Manuscripts Dept, 1980–84; Head, Inf. Project Gp, 1984–86; Head, Documentation Div., 1986–88. Member: Council, Soc. for Nautical Research, 1977–81 (Vice-Pres., 1993–); Council, Navy Records Soc., 1974– (Vice-Pres., 1980–84). *Publications:* Guide to the Manuscripts in the National Maritime Museum, vol. 1, 1977, vol. 2, 1980; (with Alan Frost) The Journal of Daniel Paine 1794–1797, 1983; Portsmouth Dockyard Papers 1774–1783: the American War, 1987; (ed jtly) British Naval Documents 1204–1960, 1993; articles, reviews in jls. *Recreations:* sailing, cricket, music. *Address:* National Maritime Museum, Greenwich, SE10 9NF. *T:* 0181–858 4422. *Club:* West Wittering Sailing.

KNIGHT, Terence Gordon, FRICS; Senior Partner, Weatherall Green & Smith, since 1992; *b* 1 June 1944; *s* of Albert Henry and Eileen Doris Knight; *m* 1968, Gillian Susan West; two *s. Educ:* St Paul's Sch. Weatherall Green & Smith, Chartered Surveyors, 1962–. FRICS 1976. Liveryman, Chartered Surveyors' Co., 1988. *Recreations:* golf, walking. *Address:* Weatherall Green & Smith, 22 Chancery Lane, WC2A 1LT. *T:* 0171–405 6944. *Club:* Worplesdon Golf.

KNIGHT, Warburton Richard, CBE 1987; Director of Educational Services, Bradford Metropolitan District Council, 1974–91; *b* 2 July 1932; *s* of late Warburton Henry Johnston and Alice Gweneth Knight; *m* 1961, Pamela Ann (*née* Hearmon); two *s* one *d. Educ:* Trinity Coll., Cambridge (MA). Teaching in Secondary Modern and Grammar Schs in Middlesex and Huddersfield, 1956–62; joined West Riding in junior capacity, 1962; Asst Dir for Secondary Schs, Leics, 1967; Asst Educn Officer for Sec. Schs and later for Special and Social Educn in WR, 1970. Hon. DLitt Bradford, 1992. *Recreations:* walking, choral music, travel. *Address:* Thorner Grange, Sandhills, Thorner, Leeds LS14 3DE. *T:* Leeds (0113) 289 2356. *Club:* Royal Over-Seas League.

KNIGHT, William Arnold, CMG 1966; OBE 1954; Controller and Auditor-General of Uganda, 1962–68, retired; *b* 14 June 1915; *e s* of late William Knight, Llanfairfechan, and Clara Knight; *m* 1939, Bronwen Parry; one *s* one *d. Educ:* Friars' Sch., Bangor; University Coll. of North Wales (BA Hons). Entered Colonial Audit Dept as an Asst Auditor, 1938; service in Kenya, 1938–46; Mauritius, 1946–49; Sierra Leone, 1949–52; British Guiana, 1952–57; Uganda, 1957–68; Commissioner, inquiry into economy and efficiency, Uganda, 1969–70. *Recreations:* fishing and gardening. *Address:* Neopardy Mills, near Crediton, Devon EX17 5EP. *T:* Crediton (01363) 772513. *Club:* East India.

KNIGHT SMITH, Ian; HM Diplomatic Service; Counsellor and Deputy Head of Mission, Berne, since 1993; *b* 18 June 1938; *m* 1st, 1964, Glenys Audrey Hayter (*d* 1981); one *s*; 2nd, 1989, Ellen Ragnhild Sweet-Escott; one *s* one *d.* FCO, 1962; Mexico City, 1964; Second Secretary: Calcutta, 1967; Caracas, 1969; First Secretary: FCO, 1972; UKREP Brussels, 1982; FCO, 1987; on secondment as Counsellor to EEC, 1989, to DSS, 1991. *Address:* c/o Foreign and Commonwealth Office, SW1A 2AH.

KNIGHTLEY; *see* Finch-Knightley.

KNIGHTON, William Myles, CB 1981; Principal Establishment and Finance Officer, Department of Trade and Industry, 1986–91; *b* 8 Sept. 1931; *s* of late George Harry Knighton, OBE, and Ella Knighton (*née* Stroud); *m* 1957, Brigid Helen Carrothers; one *s* one *d. Educ:* Bedford School; Peterhouse, Cambridge (BA). Asst Principal, Min. of Supply, 1954; Principal, Min. of Aviation, 1959; Cabinet Office, 1962–64; Principal Private Sec. to Minister of Technology, 1966–68; Asst Sec., Min. of Technology, subseq. DTI and Dept of Trade, 1967–74; Under Sec., 1974–78, Dep. Sec., 1978–83, Dept of Trade; Dep. Sec., Dept of Transport, 1983–86. *Publication:* (with D. E. Rosenthal) National Laws and International Commerce, 1982. *Recreations:* gardening, hill-walking, listening to music. *Address:* Court Green, St Ann's Hill, Midhurst, W Sussex GU29 9NN. *T:* Midhurst (01730) 817860. *Club:* United Oxford & Cambridge University.

KNIGHTS, family name of **Baron Knights.**

KNIGHTS, Baron *cr* 1987 (Life Peer), of Edgbaston in the County of West Midlands; **Philip Douglas Knights;** Kt 1980; CBE 1976 (OBE 1971); QPM (Dist. Service) 1964; DL; Chief Constable, West Midlands Police, 1975–85; *b* 3 Oct. 1920; *s* of Thomas James Knights and Ethel Knights; *m* 1945, Jean Burman. *Educ:* King's Sch., Grantham. Lincolnshire Constabulary: Police Cadet, 1938–40; Constable, 1940. Served War, RAF, 1943–45. Sergeant, Lincs Constab., 1946; seconded to Home Office, 1946–50; Inspector, Lincs Constab., 1953, Supt 1955, Chief Supt 1957. Asst Chief Constable, Birmingham City Police, 1959; seconded to Home Office, Dep. Comdt, Police Coll., 1962–66; Dep. Chief Constable, Birmingham City Police, 1970; Chief Constable, Sheffield and Rotherham Constab., 1972–74; Chief Constable, South Yorks Police, 1974–75. Winner of Queen's Police Gold Medal Essay Competition, 1965. Mem. Lord Devlin's Cttee on Identification Procedures, 1974–75. Pres., Assoc. of Chief Police Officers, 1978–79. Member: Council, Univ. of Aston, 1985–; Adv. Council, Cambridge Univ. Inst. of Criminology, 1986–. CIMgt. DL W Midlands, 1985. *Recreations:* sport, gardening. *Address:* House of Lords, SW1A 0PW. *Club:* Royal Over-Seas League.

KNIGHTS, Lionel Charles, MA, PhD; King Edward VII Professor of English Literature, University of Cambridge, 1965–73, now Emeritus Professor; Fellow, Queens' College, Cambridge, 1965–73; *b* 15 May 1906; *s* of C. E. and Lois M. Knights; *m* 1936, Elizabeth M. Barnes; one *s* one *d. Educ:* grammar schs; Selwyn Coll. (Hon. Fellow, 1974), and Christ's Coll., Cambridge Univ.; Charles Oldham Shakespeare Scholar, 1928; Members' Prize, 1929. Lecturer in English Literature, Manchester Univ., 1933–34, 1935–47; Prof. of English Lit., Univ. of Sheffield, 1947–52; Winterstoke Prof. of English, Bristol Univ., 1953–64. Fellow, Kenyon Sch. of Letters, 1950; Andrew Mellon Vis. Prof., Univ. of Pittsburgh, 1961–62 and 1966; Mrs W. Beckman Vis. Prof., Berkeley, 1970. Mem. of editorial board of Scrutiny, a Quarterly Review, 1932–53. For. Hon. Mem., Amer. Acad. of Arts and Sciences, 1981. Docteur (*hc*) de l'Univ. de Bordeaux, 1964; Hon. DUniv York, 1969; Hon. DLitt: Manchester, 1974; Sheffield, 1978; Warwick, 1979; Bristol, 1984. *Publications:* Drama and Society in the Age of Jonson, 1937; Explorations: Essays in Literary Criticism, 1946; Shakespeare's Politics, Shakespeare Lecture, British Academy, 1957; Some Shakespearean Themes, 1959; An Approach to Hamlet, 1960; (ed with Basil Cottle), Metaphor and Symbol, 1961; Further Explorations, 1965; Public Voices: literature and politics (Clark Lectures), 1971; Explorations 3, 1976; Hamlet and other Shakespeare Essays, 1979; Selected Essays in Criticism, 1981. *Address:* 11 Summerville, Durham DH1 4QH.

KNIGHTS, Rosemary Margaret; Chief Executive, Warrington Hospital NHS Trust, since 1993; *b* 2 Nov. 1945; *d* of Donald and Margaret Robson; *m* 1983, Michael A. Knights. *Educ:* Houghton-le-Spring Grammar School; Coll. of Nursing, Sunderland AHA. RGN, OND. Clinical nursing career, 1962–75 (Ward Sister posts, Sunderland and Harrogate); Nursing Officer, Harrogate, 1975–78; Sen. Nursing Officer, North Tees, Stockton, 1978–80; Dir of Nursing, Central Manchester HA, 1981–85; Unit Gen. Manager and Dist Nursing Officer, Manchester Royal Eye Hosp., 1985–88; Regl Nursing Officer, 1988–90, Dep. Chief Exec., 1989–91, Mersey RHA; Exec. Dir, NHS Mgt Exec. Trust Monitoring Unit (NW), 1991–93. Mem., S Manchester HA, 1983–88; Sec. and Chief Exec., Ophthalmic Nursing Bd, 1983–88. *Publications:* articles in nursing and health service papers. *Recreations:* music (piano; Friends of Hallé); the NHS!! *Address:* (office) Warrington Hospital NHS Trust, Lovely Lane, Warrington WA5 1QG. *Club:* Soroptomist International (Manchester).

KNILL, Sir John Kenelm Stuart, 4th Bt *cr* 1893, of The Grove, Blackheath; *b* 8 April 1913; *s* of Sir John Stuart Knill, 3rd Bt and Lucy Emmeline (*d* 1952), *o d* of Captain Thomas Willis, MN, FRGS; *S* father, 1973; *m* 1951, Violette Maud Florence Martin Barnes (*d* 1983); two *s. Educ:* St Gregory's School, Downside. Served as Lieut, RNVR, 1940–45 (Atlantic Star, Italy, France and Germany Stars). Industrial management trainee, 1945–48; canal transport operator, 1948–54; pig farmer, 1954–63; civil servant, MoD, 1963–77. President: Avon Transport 2000; Commercial Narrowboat Operators' Assoc.; Vice-President: Cotswold Canals (formerly Thames Severn Canal) Trust; Hereford and Gloucester Canal Trust; Founder and Pres., Assoc. of Canal Enterprises, 1982–; Member: Great Western Soc.; Inland Waterways Assoc. *Recreations:* canal and railway restoration, scouting. *Heir: s* Thomas John Pugin Bartholomew Knill [*b* 24 Aug. 1952; *m* 1977, Kathleen Muszynski]. *Address:* 11 St Nicholas Court, Bathampton, Somerset BA2 6UZ. *T:* Bath (01225) 463603. *Club:* Victory Services.

KNILL, Sir John (Lawrence), Kt 1994; PhD, DSc; FEng, FICE; Director, Donaldson Associates, since 1993; Professor of Engineering Geology, Imperial College of Science, Technology and Medicine, University of London, 1973–93, now Emeritus, and Senior Research Fellow, since 1993; *b* 22 Nov. 1934; *s* of late William Cuthbert Knill and of Mary (*née* Dempsey); *m* 1957, Diane Constance Judge; one *s* one *d. Educ:* Whitgift Sch.; Imperial Coll. of Science and Technol. (BSc, ARCS 1955; PhD, DIC 1957; DSc 1981). FIGeol 1985; FICE 1981; FHKIE 1982; FEng 1991. Geologist, Sir Alexander Gibb & Partners, 1957; Imperial College, London: Asst Lectr, 1957; Lectr, 1959; Reader in Engrg Geology, 1965; Dean of Royal Sch. of Mines, 1980–83; Head of Dept of Geology, 1979–88; Chm., Centre for Remote Sensing, 1984–88; Chm., NERC, 1988–93. Member: Council, Nat. Stone Centre, 1984–91; Nature Conservancy Council, 1985–91; Jt Nature Conservation Cttee, 1991–; Radioactive Waste Management Adv. Cttee, 1985–95 (Chm., 1987–95); Univs Cttee for Non-Teaching Staffs, 1987–88; Resources Bd, BNSC, 1988–93; ABRC, 1988–93; Council, Royal Acad. of Engrg, 1992–95. President: Instn of Geologists, 1981–84; Geologists' Assoc., 1982–84 (Hon. Mem., 1990); Section C, BAAS, 1988–89. Chm., UK Coordinating Cttee for UN Decade for Natural Disaster Reduction, 1992–. Lectures: Manuel Rocha, Lisbon, 1991; F. H. Moore, Sheffield, 1991; Wilson Campbell, Newcastle, 1992; Royal Acad. of Engrg, Southampton, 1992. Membre Correspondant, Société Geologique de Belgique, 1976. Freeman, Engineers' Co., 1993. Hon. FCGI 1988. Hon. DSc: Kingston, 1992; Exeter, 1995. Whitaker Medal, IWEM, 1969; Aberconway Medal, Instn of Geologists, 1989; William Smith Medal, Geol Soc., 1995. *Publications:* Industrial Geology, 1978; Geological and Landscape Conservation, 1994; articles on geology of Scotland and engrg geology. *Recreation:* viticulture. *Address:* Highwood Farm, Shaw-cum-Donnington, Newbury, Berks RG16 9LB. *Clubs:* Athenæum, Chaps.

KNOLLYS, family name of **Viscount Knollys.**

KNOLLYS, 3rd Viscount, of Caversham, *cr* 1911; **David Francis Dudley Knollys;** Baron *cr* 1902; *b* 12 June 1931; *s* of 2nd Viscount Knollys, GCMG, MBE, DFC, and Margaret (*d* 1987), *o d* of Sir Stuart Coats, 2nd Bt; *S* father 1966; *m* 1959, Hon. Sheelin Virginia Maxwell (granted, 1959, title, rank and precedence of a baron's *d,* which would have been hers had her father survived to succeed to barony of Farnham), *d* of late Lt-Col Hon. Somerset Maxwell, MP and late Mrs Remington Hobbs; three *s* one *d. Educ:* Eton. Lt, Scots Guards, 1951. *Heir: s* Hon. Patrick Nicholas Mark Knollys, *b* 11 March 1962. *Address:* Bramerton Grange, Norwich NR14 7HF. *T:* Surlingham (015088) 266.

KNORPEL, Henry, CB 1982; QC 1988; Counsel to the Speaker, House of Commons, 1985–95; *b* 18 Aug. 1924; 2nd *s* of late Hyman Knorpel and Dora Knorpel; *m* 1953, Brenda Sterling; two *d. Educ:* City of London Sch.; Magdalen Coll., Oxford. BA 1945, BCL 1946, MA 1949. Called to Bar, Inner Temple, 1947, Entrance Scholar, 1947–50, Bencher, 1990; practised 1947–52; entered Legal Civil Service as Legal Asst, Min. of Nat. Insce, 1952; Sen. Legal Asst, Min. of Pensions and Nat. Insce, 1958; Law Commn, 1965; Min. of Social Security, 1967; Dept of Health and Social Security: Asst Solicitor, 1968; Principal Asst Solicitor (Under-Sec.), 1971; Solicitor (also to OPCS and Gen. Register Office), 1978–85. Vis. Lecturer: Kennington Coll. of Commerce and Law, 1950–58; Holborn Coll. of Law, Languages and Commerce, 1958–70; Univ. of Westminster (formerly Polytechnic of Central London), 1970–. *Publications:* articles on community law. *Recreation:* relaxing. *Address:* Conway, 32 Sunnybank, Epsom, Surrey KT18 7DX. *T:* Epsom (01372) 721394.

KNOTT, Prof. John Frederick, ScD; FRS 1990; FEng 1988; Feeney Professor of Metallurgy and Materials and Head of the School of Metallurgy and Materials, University of Birmingham, since 1990; *b* Bristol, 9 Dec. 1938; *s* of Fred Knott and Margaret (*née* Chesney); *m* 1st, 1963, Christine Mary Roberts (marr. diss. 1986); two *s*; 2nd, 1990, Susan Marilyn Cooke (*née* Jones); two step *s*. *Educ:* Queen Elizabeth's Hosp., Bristol; Sheffield Univ. (BMet 1st cl. Hons 1959); Cambridge Univ. (PhD 1963; ScD 1991). FIM 1974; FWeldI 1985; FIMechE 1994. Res. Officer, Central Electricity Res. Labs, Leatherhead, 1962–67; Cambridge University: Lectr, Dept of Metallurgy, 1967–81; Reader in Mechanical Metallurgy, 1981–90; Churchill College: Goldsmiths' Fellow, Coll. Lectr and Dir of Studies in Metallurgy and Materials Sci., 1967–90; Tutor, 1969–79; Tutor for Advanced Students, 1979–81; Vice-Master, 1988–90; Extra-Ordinary Fellow, 1991–. Pres., Internat. Congress on Fracture, 1993. FRSA. Hon. Prof., Beijing Univ. of Aeronautics and Astronautics, 1992. Foreign Mem., Acad. of Scis of the Ukraine, 1993. L.B. Pfeil Prize, 1973, Rosenhain Medal, 1978, Metals Soc.; Leslie Holliday Prize, Materials Sci. Club, 1978. *Publications:* Fundamentals of Fracture Mechanics, 1973, 2nd edn 1979; (with P. A. Withey) Fracture Mechanics: worked examples, 1993; many scientific papers in Acta Met., Metal Sci., Met. Trans, Engrg Fracture Mechanics, etc. *Recreations:* bridge, crosswords, traditional jazz, playing the tenor recorder rather badly. *Address:* 54 Evesham Road, Stratford-upon-Avon, Warwickshire CV37 9BA.

KNOTT, Sir John Laurence, AC 1981; Kt 1971; CBE 1960; *b* 6 July 1910; *s* of J. Knott, Kyneton, Victoria; *m* 1935, Jean R., *d* of C. W. Milnes; three *s* one *d*. *Educ:* Cobram State Sch.; Melbourne Univ. (Dip Com). Private Sec. to Minister for Trade Treaties, 1935–38; Sec., Aust. Delegn, Eastern Gp Supply Council, New Delhi, 1940; Exec. Officer, Secondary Industries Commn, 1943–45; Mem. Jt War Production Cttee; Dir, Defence Prod. Planning Br., Dept of Supply, 1950–52; Sec., Dept of Defence Prod., 1957–58; Mem., Aust. Defence Mission to US, 1957; Sec., Dept of Supply, Melb., 1959–65; Leader, Aust. Mission to ELDO Confs: London, 1961; Paris, 1965, 1966; Rome, 1967; Vice-Pres., ELDO Council, 1967–69. Dep. High Comr for Australia, London, 1966–68; Dir-Gen., Australian PO, 1968–72. Mem. Council, Melbourne Univ., 1973–76. Pres., ESU (Victoria); Chm., Epworth Hosp. Foundn; Chm., Salvation Army Red Shield Appeal, 1982–87. Freeman, City of London. AASA, FCIS, AFAIM, LCA; idc. *Recreations:* bowls (Vice-Pres., Royal Victorian Bowling Assoc., 1957–58; Chm., World Bowls (1980) Ltd), golf, gardening. *Address:* 3 Fenwick Street, Kew, Victoria 3101, Australia. *T:* (3) 98537777. *Clubs:* Melbourne, West Brighton (Melbourne).

KNOTT, Air Vice-Marshal Ronald George, CB 1967; DSO 1944; DFC 1943; AFC 1955 and Bar, 1958; retired 1972; *b* 19 Dec. 1917; *s* of late George and Edith Rose Knott; *m* 1941, Hermione Violet (*née* Phayre); three *s* one *d*. *Educ:* Borden Grammar Sch., Sittingbourne, Kent. No 20 Sqdn RAF, 1938–40; No 5 Flight IAFVR, 1940–41; HQ Coast Defence Wing, Bombay, 1942; No 179 Sqdn, 1943–44; No 524 Sqdn, 1944–45; RAF, Gatow (Ops), 1949–50; OC, RAF Eindhoven, 1950–51; HQ 2nd TAF, 1951–52; RAF Staff Coll., 1952; Flying Trng Comd, 1953–55; Chief Flying Instructor, Central Flying Sch., 1956–58; Air Plans, Air Min., 1959; OC, RAF Gutersloh, 1959–61; ACOS Plans, 2 ATAF, 1962–63; Defence Res. Policy Staff Min. of Def. 1963; DOR2 (RAF), Min. of Def., 1963–67; SASO, HQ NEAF Cyprus, 1967–70; AOA, HQ Air Support Comd, RAF, 1970–72. *Recreations:* gardening, wine growing. *Address:* Pilgrims Cottage, Charing, Kent TN27 0DR. *T:* Charing (0123371) 2723.

KNOWELDEN, Prof. John, CBE 1983; JP; MD, FRCP, FFCM, DPH; Professor of Community Medicine (formerly of Preventive Medicine and Public Health), University of Sheffield, 1960–84, retired; *b* 19 April 1919; *s* of Clarence Arthur Knowelden; *m* 1946, Mary Sweet; two *s*. *Educ:* Colfe's Grammar Sch., Lewisham; St George's Hosp. Med. Sch.; London Sch. of Hygiene and Trop. Med., Johns Hopkins Sch. of Public Health, Baltimore. Surg. Lt, RNVR, 1942–46. Rockefeller Fellowship in Preventive Med., 1947–49; Lectr in Med. Statistics and Mem., MRC Statistical Research Unit, 1949–60. Academic Registrar, FCM, 1977–83. Civil Consultant in Community Medicine to Royal Navy, 1977–84. Editor, Brit. Jl of Preventive and Social Medicine, 1959–69 and 1973–76. Formerly Hon. Sec., Sect. of Epidemiology, Royal Society Medicine and Chm., Soc. for Social Medicine; Mem., WHO Expert Advisory Panel on Health Statistics. *Publications:* (with Ian Taylor) Principles of Epidemiology, 2nd edn, 1964; papers on clinical and prophylactic trials and epidemiological topics. *Recreations:* photography, gardening. *Address:* 69 Esplanade, Scarborough, N Yorks YO11 2UZ. *T:* Scarborough (01723) 374502.

KNOWLAND, Raymond Reginald, CBE 1992; Managing Director, British Petroleum, 1990–92; *b* 18 Aug. 1930; *s* of Reginald George Knowland and Marjorie Doris Knowland (*née* Alvis); *m* 1956, Valerie Mary Higgs; three *s*. *Educ:* Bristol Grammar Sch.; Sir John Cass College London. FRSC 1972; CChem. BP Chemicals: specialty plastics and PVC Plant Management, Barry Works, 1957–69; Works Gen. Manager, Barry Works, 1969–75, Baglan Bay Works, 1975–78; Man. Dir, Belgium, 1978–80; Dir, London, 1980–90; Chief Exec. Officer, London, 1983–90. Non-executive Director: Laporte plc; BNFL plc; BSI. President: British Plastics Fedn, 1983–84; Assoc. of Petrochemical Producers in Europe, 1985–88; CIA, 1990–92; Chm., European Chemical Industry Ecology and Toxicology Centre, 1986–90. *Recreations:* sailing, photography, Rugby football (spectator). *Address:* Heron's Wake, Flowers Hill, Pangbourne, Reading RG8 7BD. *T:* Reading (01734) 844576. *Club:* Athenæum.

KNOWLES, Ann; *see* Knowles, P. A.

KNOWLES, Sir Charles (Francis), 7th Bt *cr* 1765; Senior Partner, Charles Knowles Design, architects, since 1984; *b* 20 Dec. 1951; *s* of Sir Francis Gerald William Knowles, 6th Bt, FRS, and of Ruth Jessie, *d* of late Rev. Arthur Brooke-Smith; *S* father, 1974; *m* 1979, Amanda Louise Margaret, *d* of Lance Bromley, *qv*; two *s*. *Educ:* Marlborough Coll.; Oxford Sch. of Architecture (DipArch 1977; RIBA 1979). FRSA. *Recreations:* shooting, travel, piloting light aircraft. *Heir:* *s* (Charles) William (Frederick Lance) Knowles, *b* 27 Aug. 1985. *Address:* Wyndham Croft, Turners Hill, W Sussex RH10 4PS.

KNOWLES, Colin George; company director; arbitrator and business consultant; Director of Development and Public Relations, University of Bophuthatswana, 1985–95; Secretary and Trustee, University of Bophuthatswana Foundation, 1985–95; *b* 11 April 1939; *s* of late George William Knowles, Tarleton, Lancs; *m* 1st, 1961, Mary B. D. Wickliffe, *e d* of William Wickliffe, Co. Antrim, NI; two *d*; 2nd, 1971 (marr. diss. 1980); 3rd, 1981, Mrs Carla Johannes (marr. diss. 1994); one *d*. *Educ:* King George V Grammar Sch., Southport; CEDEP, Fontainebleau. MInstM 1966; MIPR 1970; Mem. BAIE 1972; FIMgt (FBIM 1972); FPRISA 1993 (MPRISA 1983); APR 1987; AAArb 1991; MSAAIE 1993. Appointed Comr of Oaths, 1991. Joined John Player & Sons, 1960; sales and marketing management appts; Head of Public Relations, 1971–73; joined Imperial Tobacco Ltd, 1973; Hd of Public Affairs, 1973–80; Company Sec., 1979–80. Chairman: Griffin Associates Ltd, 1980–84; Concept Communications (Pty) Ltd (S Africa), 1983–84; Dir, TWS Public Relations (Pty) Ltd (S Africa), 1984–85. Mem. Council, Tobacco Trade Benevolent Assoc., 1975–80; Chm., Bophuthatswana Reg., PRISA, 1988–91. Dir, Bophuthatswana Council for Consumer Affairs, 1991–. Director: Nottingham Festival Assoc. Ltd, 1969–71; English Sinfonia Orchestra, 1972–80; Midland Sinfonia Concert Soc. Ltd, 1972–80; (also co-Founder) Assoc. for Business Sponsorship of The Arts Ltd, 1975–84 (Chm., 1975–80); Bristol Hippodrome Trust Ltd, 1977–81; Bath Archaeological Trust Ltd, 1978–81; The Palladian Trust Ltd, 1979–82; Mem., Chancellor of Duchy of Lancaster's Cttee of Honour on Business and the Arts, 1980–81. Arts sponsorship initiatives include responsibility for: Internat. Cello Competition (with Tortelier), Bristol, 1975 and 1977; Internat. Conductors Awards, 1978; Pompeii Exhibn, RA, 1976–77; new prodns at Royal Opera House, Covent Garden, at Glyndebourne, and at National Theatre. Governor: Manning Grammar Sch., Nottingham, 1972–73; Clayesmore Sch., Dorset, 1975–85. Chm., St John Ambulance Foundn in Bophuthatswana, 1989–94; Mem. Chapter, Priory of St John, S Africa, 1992–. Liveryman, Worshipful Co of Tobacco Pipe Makers and Tobacco Blenders, 1973; Freeman, City of London, 1974. FRSA 1975; FRCSoc 1976. KStJ 1995. *Recreations:* game watching, fishing, shooting, reading. *Address:* PO Box 1179, Stellenbosch 7599, South Africa. *Clubs:* Carlton, MCC.

KNOWLES, George Peter; Registrar of the Province and Diocese of York, and Archbishop of York's Legal Secretary, 1968–87; *b* 30 Dec. 1919; *s* of Geoffrey Knowles and Mabel Bowman; *m* 1948, Elizabeth Margaret Scott; one *s* two *d*. *Educ:* Clifton Coll., Bristol; Queens' Coll., Cambridge. MA, LLM. Served war, Royal Artillery, 1939–46 (Lieut). Admitted a solicitor, 1948; Chm., York Area Rent Tribunal, 1959; Mem., Mental Health Review Tribunal for Yorkshire Regional Health Authority Area, 1960. *Recreations:* gardening, fishing, wildlife. *Address:* 11 Lang Road, Bishopthorpe, York YO2 1QJ. *T:* York (01904) 706443. *Club:* Yorkshire (York).

KNOWLES, Ven. Graeme Paul; Archdeacon of Portsmouth, since 1993; *b* 25 Sept. 1951; *s* of Grace and Stanley Knowles; *m* 1973, Susan Gail Knowles. *Educ:* Dunstable Grammar Sch., 1963–70; King's Coll. London, 1970–73 (AKC). Ordained deacon, 1974, priest, 1975; Asst Curate, St Peter in Thanet, 1974–79; Precentor and Sen. Curate, Leeds Parish Church, 1979–81; Chaplain and Precentor, 1981–87, Chapter Clerk, 1985–87, Portsmouth Cathedral; Vicar of Leigh Park, 1987–93. Rural Dean of Havant, 1990–93. Mem., Council for the Care of Churches, 1991–. *Recreations:* Victorian and Edwardian songs, the books of E. F. Benson, wine and food. *Address:* Victoria Lodge, 36 Osborn Road, Fareham, Hampshire PO16 7DS. *T:* Fareham (01329) 280101. *Club:* Naval and Military.

KNOWLES, Prof. Jeremy Randall, CBE 1993; FRS 1977; Amory Houghton Professor of Chemistry and Biochemistry (formerly of Chemistry), since 1974, Dean of Faculty of Arts and Sciences, since 1991, Harvard University; *b* 28 April 1935; *s* of late Kenneth Guy Jack Charles Knowles and of Dorothy Helen Swingler; *m* 1960, Jane Sheldon Davis; three *s*. *Educ:* Magdalen College Sch.; Balliol Coll. (Hon. Fellow 1984), Merton Coll. and Christ Church, Oxford (MA, DPhil). Sir Louis Stuart Exhibr, Balliol Coll., Oxford, 1955–59; Harmsworth Schol., Merton Coll., Oxford, and Research Lectr, Christ Church, Oxford, 1960–62; Research Associate, Calif. Inst. of Technology, 1961–62; Fellow of Wadham Coll., Oxf., 1962–74 (Hon. Fellow 1990); Univ. Lectr, Univ. of Oxford, 1966–74. Visiting Prof., Yale Univ., 1969, 1971; Sloan Vis. Prof., Harvard Univ., 1973; Newton-Abraham Vis. Prof., Oxford Univ., 1983–84. Fellow, Amer. Acad. of Arts and Scis, 1982; Foreign Associate, Nat. Acad. of Scis, USA, 1988; Mem., Amer. Philosophical Soc., 1988. Charmian Medal, RSC, 1980; Prelog Medal, ETH, 1989; Davy Medal, Royal Soc., 1991. *Publications:* research papers and reviews in learned jls. *Address:* 7 Bryant Street, Cambridge, MA 02138, USA. *T:* (617) 8768469.

KNOWLES, Sir Leonard Joseph, Kt 1974; CBE 1963; barrister; Chief Justice of the Bahamas, 1973–78; *b* Nassau, 15 March 1916; *s* of late Samuel Joseph Knowles; *m* 1939, Harriet Hansen, *d* of John Hughes, Liverpool; two *s*. *Educ:* Queen's Coll., Nassau, Bahamas; King's Coll., Univ. of London (LLB); first Bahamian student to take and pass Higher Sch. Certif. in Bahamas, 1934; LLB Hons 1937, 1st cl. in Final Bar Examinations; BD London, 1985. Called to the Bar, Gray's Inn, London, 1939; Lord Justice Holker Scholar, Gray's Inn, 1940; practised law in Liverpool for some years. Served War of 1939–45, Royal Air Force (radar). Returned to Nassau, 1948, and was called to local Bar; Attorney-at-Law and Actg Attorney-Gen. of the Bahamas, 1949; Registrar-Gen., 1949–50. Past Stipendiary and Circuit Magistrate. Chm., Labour Board, Bahamas, 1953–63; MLC (Upper House of Legislature), 1960–63; President, Senate, 1964; re-elected, 1967, 1968, and continued to hold that office until 1972; returned to private law practice, 1978. Methodist local preacher. *Publications:* Elements of Bahamian Law, 1978, 2nd edn 1989; Financial Relief in Matrimonial Cases, 1980; Bahamian Real Property Law, 1989; My Life (autobiog.), 1989; Introduction to Bahamian Company Law, 1993; Law of Dower and Curtesy, 1994; Law of Executors and Administrators; compilations of Bahamian Statutes 1987–94. *Recreations:* music, motion photography, swimming. *Address:* PO Box SS 6378, Nassau, Bahamas. *Fax:* 3222085. *Club:* Commonwealth Trust.

KNOWLES, Michael; independent political consultant, since 1992; *b* 21 May 1942; *s* of Martin Christopher and Anne Knowles; *m* 1965, Margaret Isabel Thorburn; three *d*. *Educ:* Clapham Coll. RC Grammar Sch. Sales Manager, Export & Home Sales. Mem. (C), 1971–83, Leader, 1974–83, Kingston upon Thames Borough Council. MP (C) Nottingham East, 1983–92; PPS to Minister for Planning and Regional Affairs, DoT, 1986–92; Member: Select Cttee on European Legislation, 1984; Select Cttee on Defence, 1990. *Recreations:* walking, history. *Address:* 2 Ditton Reach, Portsmouth Road, Thames Ditton, Surrey KT7 0XB.

KNOWLES, Dr Michael Ernest, CChem, FRSC; FIFST; Director, Scientific Regulatory Affairs (Europe, Middle East and Africa), Coca Cola International, Brussels, since 1992; *b* 6 May 1942; *s* of late Ernest Frederick Walter Knowles and Lesley (*née* Lambert); *m* 1st, 1965, Rosalind Mary Griffiths (marr. diss. 1975); two *s*; 2nd, 1994, Alexandra Knowles (*née* Hadjiyianni). *Educ:* Nottingham Univ. (BPharm 1st cl. Hons; PhD). CChem 1969; FRSC 1982; FIFST 1983. ICI Postdoctoral Fellow, Nottingham Univ., 1967–69; Ministry of Agriculture, Fisheries and Food: Food Sci. Unit, Norwich, 1969–74; Scientific Advr, Food Sci. Div., 1974–79; Head, Food Sci. Lab., 1979–85; Head, Food Sci. Div., 1985–89; Chief Scientist (Fisheries and Food), 1989–91. *Publications:* series of papers on chemical aspects of food safety in learned jls. *Recreations:* target shooting, walking. *Address:* Avenue Winston Churchill 224, 1180 Brussels, Belgium. *T:* (2) 3462501. *Clubs:* Strangers (Norwich); Château St Ann (Brussels).

KNOWLES, (Patricia) Ann; Editor, The Universe, 1990–95; *b* 31 Oct. 1944; *d* of John and Margaret Miller; *m* 1964, Leslie John Knowles; two *s* one *d*. *Educ:* Our Lady's Prep. Sch., Barrow-in-Furness; Our Lady's Convent Sch.; Open Univ. (BA). Reporter: North Western Evening Mail, Barrow, 1962–68; North Somerset Mercury, Clevedon, 1969–70; Western Daily Press, Bristol, 1970–72; Theatre Critic, Evening Star, Burnley, 1973–77; Sub-Editor, Dep. Chief Sub-Editor, News Editor, Burnley Express, 1977–84; Asst Editor, Citizen Publications, Blackburn, 1985–87; Sub-Editor, Keighley News, 1987–89; Group Editor, Herald and Post, Burnley, 1989–90. Member: Nat. Assoc. of Tangent Clubs, 1984–; Soroptimists International, Burnley, 1990–92; Catholic Union of GB, 1991–. *Recreations:* gardening, interior decoration, family interests, travel. *Address:* The Rough, Castle Road, Colne, Lancs BB8 7DS.

KNOWLES, Peter Francis Arnold; Parliamentary Counsel, since 1991; *b* 10 July 1949; *s* of Sidney Francis Knowles and Patricia Anette Knowles (*née* New); *m* 1972, Patricia Katharine Clifford; two *s*. *Educ:* Whitgift School, Croydon; University College, Oxford (MA). Called to the Bar, Gray's Inn, 1971. In practice at Chancery Bar, 1973–75; joined

Parliamentary Counsel Office, 1975; with Law Commission, 1979–81, 1993–. *Recreations:* music, sailing, ski-ing, classic car restoration. *Address:* Law Commission, 37/38 John Street, Theobalds Road, WC1N 2BQ.

KNOWLES, Sir Richard (Marchant), Kt 1989; Lord Mayor of Birmingham, 1994–95; Member, Birmingham City Council, 1972–74 and since 1978 (Leader, 1984–93); *b* 20 May 1917; *s* of William and Charlotte Knowles; *m* 1st, 1941, Dorothy Forster (*d* 1979); one *s*; 2nd, 1981, Anne Little (*née* Macmenemey). *Educ:* village schools in Kent; WEA; technical school. Building industry, 1931–39; served RE, 1940; building and shipbuilding, 1941–50; Labour Organiser, Sevenoaks, Dover, Leeds and Birmingham, 1950–72; Nat. Organiser, Co-op Party, 1971–83. Mem., W Midlands County Council, 1973–77; Chm., Planning Cttee, Birmingham CC, 1972–74, 1980–82. Mem., Policy Cttee, 1974–77, 1984–, Sec., Lab Gp, 1992–94, AMA. Dir, Nat. Exhibition Centre Ltd, 1982–. *Publications:* UNIP Election Manual, 1964; ABC of Organisation, 1977; A Voice for your Neighbourhood, 1977; contribs to local govt jls, planning and political pamphlets. *Recreations:* cycling, travel, rough gardening. *Address:* 64 Woodgate Lane, Bartley Green, Birmingham B32 3QY. *T:* 0121–422 8061.

KNOWLES, Timothy; Director, Welsh Water plc, since 1989; *b* 17 May 1938; *s* of Cyril William Knowles and Winifred Alice Knowles (*née* Hood); *m* 1967, Gaynor Hallett; one *d*. *Educ:* Bishop Gore Grammar Sch., Swansea. Chartered Accountant. Company Sec./Accountant, Louis Marx & Co. Ltd, 1960–68; Controller, Modco Valenite, 1968–69; HTV Ltd: Company Sec., 1969–78; Financial Dir, 1975–81; Asst Man. Dir, 1981–86; HTV Group plc: Financial Dir, 1976–86; Gp Man. Dir., 1986–88; Finance Dir, Insurance Services Gp, ECGD (for privatisation), 1990–91; Financial Consultant, NCM (UK) Holdings Ltd, 1991–92. Dir, Frost & Reed (Holdings) Ltd, 1985–88. Member: S Wales Electricity Bd, 1981–82; Welsh Water Authority, 1982–89. Chm., CG90, 1994–. Contested (C) Swansea East, 1966. *Recreations:* travel, walking, watching cricket, golf. *Address:* Cae Ffynnon, 12 Ger-y-Llan, St Nicholas, Cardiff CF5 6SY. *T:* Peterston-super-Ely (01446) 760726. *Club:* Cardiff and County (Cardiff).

KNOWLES, Wyn; Editor, Woman's Hour, BBC, 1971–83; *b* 30 July 1923; *d* of Frederick Knowles and Dorothy Ellen Knowles (*née* Harrison). *Educ:* St Teresa's Convent, Effingham; Convents of FCJ in Ware and Switzerland; Polytechnic Sch. of Art, London. Cypher Clerk, War Office, 1941–45. Secretarial work, 1948–57; joined BBC, 1951; Asst Producer, Drama Dept, 1957–60; Woman's Hour: Producer, Talks Dept, 1960–65; Asst Editor, 1965–67; Dep. Editor, 1967–71. *Publication:* (ed with Kay Evans) The Woman's Hour Book, 1981. *Recreations:* travel, cooking, writing, painting, being a London Zoo Volunteer. *Address:* 80A Parkway, Regent's Park, NW1 7AN. *T:* 0171–485 8258.

KNOWLTON, Richard James, CBE 1983; QFSM 1977; HM Chief Inspector of Fire Services (Scotland), 1984–89; *b* 2 Jan. 1928; *s* of Richard John Knowlton and Florence May Humby; *m* 1949, Pamela Vera Horne; one *s*. *Educ:* Bishop Wordsworth's Sch., Salisbury. FIFE. Served 42 Commando RM, 1945. Southampton Fire Bde, 1948; Station Officer, Worcester City and County Fire Bde, 1959; London Fire Brigade: Asst Divl Officer, 1963; Divl Officer, 1965; Divl Comdr, 1967; Winston Churchill Travelling Fellowship, 1969; Firemaster: SW Area (Scotland) Fire Bde, 1971; Strathclyde Fire Bde, 1975–84. Mem., later Chm., Bds, Fire Service Coll. Extended Interview, 1970–81; Mem., Fire Service Coll. Bd, 1978–82; Mem., later Chm., Scottish Fire Services Examinations Panel, 1971–75; Mem., Scottish Fire Service Examinations Bd, 1974–75; Fire Adviser: to Scottish Assoc. of CCs, 1974; to Convention of Scottish Local Authorities, 1975–81; Sec. to Appliances and Equipment Cttee of Chief and Asst Chief Fire Officers Assoc., 1974–81, Pres. of the Assoc., 1980; Chm., Scottish Dist Chief and Asst Chief Fire Officers Assoc., 1977–81; Zone Fire Comdr (Designate), CD for Scotland, 1975–84; Member: Scottish Central Fire Bdes Adv. Council, 1977–81 (Uniform and Personal Equipment Cttee, 1974–82); Jt Cttee on Design and Develt, 1978–82; England and Wales Central Fire Bdes Adv. Council, 1979–81; Chairman: London Branch, Instn of Fire Engineers, 1969; Scottish Assoc., Winston Churchill Fellows, 1979–81; Hazfile Cttee, 1979–81; Vice-Pres., Fire Services Nat. Benevolent Fund, 1981– (Chm. 1980). Mem., Nat. Jt Council for Chief Fire Officers, 1980–82; Mem., later Chm., Management Structures Working Gp of Nat. Jt Council for Local Authority Fire Bdes, 1980–83; British Mem., Admin. Council of European Assoc. of Professional Fire Bde Officers, 1981–85 (Vice Pres., 1984–85). *Address:* 5 Potters Way, Laverstock, Salisbury, Wilts SP1 1PY. *T:* Salisbury (01722) 326487.

KNOX, family name of **Earl of Ranfurly.**

KNOX, (Alexander) David; CMG 1988; Vice President, International Bank for Reconstruction and Development, 1980–87, retired; *b* 15 Jan. 1925; *s* of James Knox and Elizabeth Maxwell Knox; *m* 1950, Beatrice Lily (*née* Dunell); one *s* two *d*. *Educ:* Univ. of Toronto (BA); London School of Economics and Political Science (Hon. Fellow, 1982). LSE, 1949–63, Reader in Economics, 1955–63; International Bank for Reconstruction and Development (World Bank), 1963–87: Vice President: W Africa, 1980–84; Latin America, 1984–87. *Publications:* Latin American Debt: facing facts, 1990; articles in Economica, OECF Res. Qly (Japan), etc. *Recreations:* opera, walking. *Address:* Knights Barn, Manor Farm Lane, East Hagbourne, Oxon OX11 9ND. *T:* Didcot (01235) 817792. *Club:* Reform.

KNOX, Bryce Harry, CB 1986; a Deputy Chairman, and Director General, Internal Taxation Group, Board of Customs and Excise, 1983–88, retired; *b* 21 Feb. 1929; *e s* of late Brice Henry Knox and of Rose Hetty Knox; *m* Norma, *d* of late George Thomas and of Rose Thomas; one *s*. *Educ:* Stratford Grammar Sch.; Nottingham Univ. BA(Econ). Asst Principal, HM Customs and Excise, 1953; Principal, 1958; on loan to HM Treasury, 1963–65; Asst Sec., HM Customs and Excise, 1966; seconded to HM Diplomatic Service, Counsellor, Office of UK Perm. Rep. to European Communities, 1972–74; Under-Sec., 1974, Comr, 1975, HM Customs and Excise. *Address:* 9 Manor Way, Blackheath, SE3 9EF. *T:* 0181–852 9404. *Clubs:* Reform; MCC.

KNOX, Col Sir Bryce (Muir), KCVO 1990; MC 1944 and Bar, 1944; TD 1947; Lord-Lieutenant of Ayrshire and Arran (formerly County of Ayr), 1974–91 (Vice-Lieutenant, 1970–74); Vice-Chairman, Lindustries Ltd, 1979 (Director, 1953–79); *b* 4 April 1916; *s* of late James Knox, Kilbirnie; *m* 1948, Patricia Mary Dunsmuir (*d* 1989); one *s* one *d*. *Educ:* Stowe; Trinity Coll., Cambridge. Served with Ayrshire (ECO) Yeomanry, 1939–45, N Africa and Italy; CO, 1953–56; Hon. Col, 1969–71; Hon. Col, The Ayrshire Yeomanry Sqdn, Queen's Own Yeomanry, T&AVR, 1971–77; Pres., Lowlands TA&VRA, 1978–83. Member, Queen's Body Guard for Scotland, Royal Company of Archers. Pres., RHAS, 1990–91. CStJ. *Publication:* The History of the Eglinton Hunt, 1984. *Recreation:* country sports. *Address:* Martnaham Lodge, By Ayr KA6 6ES. *T:* Dalrymple (0129256) 204.

KNOX, David; *see* Knox, A. D.

KNOX, Sir David (Laidlaw), Kt 1993; MP (C) Staffordshire Moorlands, since 1983 (Leek Division of Staffordshire, 1970–83); *b* 30 May 1933; *s* of late J. M. Knox, Lockerbie and Mrs C. H. C. Knox (*née* Laidlaw); *m* 1980, Mrs Margaret Eva Maxwell, *d* of late A. McKenzie. *Educ:* Lockerbie Academy; Dumfries Academy; London Univ. (BSc (Econ) Hons). Management Trainee, 1953–56; Printing Executive, 1956–62; O&M Consultant, 1962–70. Contested (C): Stechford, Birmingham, 1964 and 1966; Nuneaton, March 1967. PPS to Ian Gilmour, Minister of State for Defence, 1973, Sec. of State for Defence, 1974. Secretary: Cons. Finance Cttee, 1972–73; Cons. Trade Cttee, 1974; Vice-Chm., Cons. Employment Cttee, 1979–80; Member: Select Cttee on European Legislation, 1976–; House of Commons Chairmen's Panel, 1983–; Chairman: W Midlands Area Young Conservatives, 1963–64; W Midlands Area Cons. Political Centre, 1966–69; a Vice Chairman: Cons. Party Organisation, 1974–75; Cons. Gp for Europe, 1984–87. Editor, Young Conservatives National Policy Group, 1963–64. *Recreations:* watching association football, reading. *Address:* House of Commons, SW1A 0AA.

KNOX, Prof. Henry Macdonald; Professor of Education, The Queen's University of Belfast, 1951–82; *b* 26 Nov. 1916; *e s* of Rev. R. M. Knox, Edinburgh, and J. E. Church; *m* 1945, Marian, *yr d* of N. Starkie, Todmorden; one *s* one *d*. *Educ:* George Watson's Coll., Edinburgh; University of Edinburgh. MA 1938; MEd 1940; PhD 1949. Served as Captain, Intelligence Corps, commanding a wireless intelligence section, Arakan sector of Burma, and as instructor, War Office special wireless training wing, 1940–46. Lecturer in Education, University Coll. of Hull, 1946; Lecturer in Education, University of St Andrews, 1949; former Dean of Faculty of Education, and acting Dir, Inst. of Educn, 1968–69, QUB. Assessor in Educn, Univ. of Strathclyde, 1984–89; sometime Examiner in Educn, Universities of Durham, Leeds, Sheffield, Aberdeen, Glasgow, Strathclyde, Wales and Ireland (National); occasional Examiner, Universities of Edinburgh, Belfast, Dublin and Bristol. Chm., N Ireland Council for Educn Research, 1979–82; Member: Advisory Council on Educn for N Ireland, 1955–58, 1961–64; Senior Certificate Examination Cttee for N Ireland, 1962–65; Adv. Bd for Postgraduate Studentships in Arts Subjects, Ministry of Educn for N Ireland, 1962–74; Adv. Cttee on Supply and Training of Teachers for NI, 1976–82; NI Council for Educnl Develt, 1980–82. Mem. Governing Body: Stranmillis Coll. of Educn, Belfast, 1968–82 (Vice-Chm., 1975–82); St Joseph's Coll. of Educn, Belfast, 1968–82. *Publications:* Two Hundred and Fifty Years of Scottish Education, 1696–1946, 1953; John Dury's Reformed School, 1958; Introduction to Educational Method, 1961; Schools in Europe (ed W. Schultze): Northern Ireland, 1969; numerous articles in educational journals. *Address:* 9 Elliot Gardens, Colinton, Edinburgh EH14 1EH. *T:* 0131–441 6283.

KNOX, John; Under-Secretary, Department of Trade and Industry, retired, 1974; Head of Research Contractors Division, 1972–74; *b* 11 March 1913; *s* of William Knox and May Ferguson; *m* 1942, Mary Blackwood Johnston, *d* of late Rt Hon. Thomas Johnston, CH; one *s* one *d*. *Educ:* Lenzie Acad.; Glasgow Univ. (Kitchener's Schol.; MA). Business Management Trng, 1935–39; joined RAE, 1939; Op. Research with RAF, 1939–45; Asst Chief Scientific Adviser, Min. of Works, 1945–50; Dep. Dir and Dir, Intelligence Div., DSIR, 1950–58; Dep. Dir (Industry), DSIR, 1958–64; Min. of Technology, later DTI: Asst Controller, 1964–65; CSO, Head of External Research and Materials Div., 1965–68; Head of Materials Div., 1968–71; Head of Res. Div., 1971–73. *Publications:* occasional articles on management of research, development and industrial innovation. *Recreation:* golf. *Address:* 6 Mariners Court, Victoria Road, Aldeburgh, Suffolk IP15 5EH. *T:* Aldeburgh (01728) 453657.

KNOX, John, (Jack), RSA 1979 (ARSA 1972); RGI 1980; RSW 1987; Head of Painting Studios, Glasgow School of Art, 1981–92; *b* 16 Dec. 1936; *s* of Alexander and Jean Knox; *m* 1960, Margaret Kyle Sutherland; one *s* one *d*. *Educ:* Lenzie Acad.; Glasgow Sch. of Art (DA). On the Drawing and Painting Staff at Duncan of Jordanstone Coll. of Art, Dundee, 1965–81. Work in permanent collections: Scottish Nat. Gallery of Modern Art; Arts Council; Contemporary Arts Soc.; Scottish Arts Council; Otis Art Inst., Los Angeles; Olinda Museum, São Paulo; Aberdeen, Dundee and Manchester art galleries; Hunterian Museum, Glasgow; Scottish Nat. Portrait Gall.; Kelvingrove Art Galls and Mus. Retrospective exhibn, Knox 1960–83, Scottish Arts Council, 1983. Member: Scottish Arts Council, 1974–79; Trustees Cttee, Scottish Nat. Gallery of Modern Art, 1975–81; Bd of Trustees, Nat. Galls of Scotland, 1982–87. Sec., Royal Scottish Acad., 1990–91. Member: Bd of Governors, Duncan of Jordanstone Coll. of Art, Dundee, 1980–82; Bd of Governors, Glasgow Sch. of Art, 1985–88. *Address:* 31 North Erskine Park, Bearsden, Glasgow G61 4LY.

KNOX, John Andrew; Grade 3, since 1979, and Deputy Director, Serious Fraud Office, since 1990; *b* 22 July 1937; *s* of late James Telford Knox and Mary Knox; *m* 1964, Patricia Mary Martin; one *s* one *d*. *Educ:* Dame Allan's Sch., Newcastle upon Tyne; Merton Coll., Oxford (MA). ACA 1964, FCA 1974. Cooper Brothers & Co. Chartered Accountants, 1961–65; Vickers Ltd, 1966–72; entered CS as a Sen. Accountant, 1972; Chief Accountant, 1973; Asst Sec., 1976; Head of Accountancy Services Div., 1977–85; Hd of Industrial Financial Appraisal Div, DTI, 1985–87; Chief Accountant, Serious Fraud Office, 1987–90. Leonard Shaw Award for Management Accountancy, Leonard Shaw Meml Fund, 1973. *Address:* c/o Serious Fraud Office, Elm House, Elm Street, WC1X 0BJ.

KNOX, Prof. John Henderson, FRS 1984; FRSE 1971; University Fellow and Emeritus Professor of Physical Chemistry, University of Edinburgh, since 1984; *b* 21 Oct. 1927; *s* of John Knox and Elizabeth May Knox (*née* Henderson); *m* 1957, Josephine Anne Wissler; four *s*. *Educ:* George Watson's Boys' Coll.; Univ. of Edinburgh (BSc 1949, DSc 1963); Univ. of Cambridge (PhD 1953). University of Edinburgh: Lectr in Chemistry, 1953–66; Reader in Physical Chemistry, 1966–74; Director of Wolfson Liquid Chromatography Unit, 1972–92; Personal Prof. of Phys. Chem., 1974–84. Sen. Vis. Research Scientist Fellow, Univ. of Utah, 1963. *Publications:* Gas Chromatography, 1962; Molecular Thermodynamics, 1971, 2nd edn 1978; Applications of High Speed Liquid Chromatography, 1974; High Performance Liquid Chromatography, 1978, 3rd edn 1983. *Recreations:* skiing, sailing, hill walking. *Address:* 67 Morningside Park, Edinburgh EH10 5EZ. *T:* 0131–447 5057.

KNOX, Hon. Sir John (Leonard), Kt 1985; **Hon. Mr Justice Knox;** a Judge of the High Court of Justice, Chancery Division, since 1985; *b* 6 April 1925; *s* of Leonard Needham Knox and Berthe Hélène Knox; *m* 1st, 1953, Anne Jacqueline Mackintosh (*d* 1991); one *s* three *d*; 2nd, 1993, Benedicta Eugenie Cooksey. *Educ:* Radley Coll.; Worcester Coll., Oxford (Hon. Mods, 1st Cl.; Jurisprudence, 1st Cl.). Called to the Bar, Lincoln's Inn, 1953, Bencher, 1977; Member, Senate of the Inns of Court, 1975–78. QC 1979; Junior Treasury Counsel: in *bona vacantia*, 1971–79; in probate, 1978–79; Attorney-Gen., Duchy of Lancaster, 1984–85. Member: Lord Chancellor's Law Reform Cttee, 1978–; Council of Legal Educn, 1975–79; Chm., Chancery Bar Assoc., 1985. Dep. Chm., Parly Boundary Commn, 1987–. *Address:* Royal Courts of Justice, Strand, WC2A 2LL. *Club:* Beefsteak.

KNOX, Robert, MA, MD, FRCP, FRCPath; Emeritus Professor of Bacteriology, University of London (Professor of Bacteriology, Guy's Hospital Medical School, 1949–69); *b* 29 May 1904; *s* of Dr Robert Knox, radiologist; *m* 1936, Bessie Lynda Crust; three *d*. *Educ:* Highgate; Balliol Coll., Oxford (Classical Scholar); St Bartholomew's Hosp. 1st Class Hon. Mods, 1924, 2nd Class Lit Hum, 1926; BA Oxford, 1927; MB, BS London,

1932; MD 1934; MRCS 1932; LRCP 1932, MRCP 1934, FRCP 1953; FCPath, 1964. House Physician and Chief Asst St Bartholomew's Hosp., 1932–35; MA Cambridge 1935; Demonstrator in Pathology, University of Cambridge, 1935–37; Mem. of Scientific Staff, Imperial Cancer Research Fund, 1937–39; Dir of Public Health Laboratories (Med. Research Council) at Stamford, 1939, Leicester 1940, and Oxford, 1945; MA Oxford, 1945. Fellow Royal Society Medicine; Member: Pathological Soc.; Soc. of Gen. Microbiology; Assoc. of Clinical Pathologists. *Publications:* on bacteriological subjects in medical and scientific journals. *Recreations:* coxed Oxford Univ., 1925; golf. *Address:* Five Pines, The Marld, Ashtead, Surrey KT21 1RQ. *T:* Ashtead (01372) 275102.

KNOX, Hon. Sir William Edward, Kt 1979; FCIT, FAIM; MLA (Lib), Nundah, 1957–89; Leader of Parliamentary Liberal Party, Queensland, 1983–88; *b* 14 Dec. 1927; *s* of E. Knox, Turramurra; *m* 1956, Doris Ross; two *s* two *d*. *Educ:* Melbourne High School. State Pres., Qld Young Liberals, 1953–56; Vice-Pres., Qld Div., Liberal Party, 1956–57, Mem. Exec., 1953–58, 1962–65; Sec., Parly Lib. Party, 1960–65. Minister for Transport, Qld, 1965–72; Minister for Justice and Attorney-Gen., Qld, 1971–76; Dep. Premier and Treasurer of Qld, 1976–78; Leader, State Parly Liberal Party, 1976–78 and 1983–88; Minister for Health, Qld, 1978–80; Minister for Employment and Labour Relations, Qld, 1980–83. Chm., Qld Road Safety Council and Mem., Aust. Transport Adv. Council, 1965–72. Mem., Nat. Exec. Aust. Jnr Chamber of Commerce, 1961–62; Senator Jnr Chamber Internat., 1962–; State Pres., Father and Son Movement, 1965; Chm., St John Council for Qld, 1983–. Pres., Assoc. of Independent Schs, Qld, 1991–. CStJ. *Address:* 1621 Sandgate Road, Nundah, Queensland 4012, Australia.

KNOX-JOHNSTON, Sir William Robert Patrick, (Sir Robin), Kt 1995; CBE 1969; RD (and bar) 1983; Marina Consultant since 1974; *b* 17 March 1939; *s* of late David Robert Knox-Johnston and Elizabeth Mary Knox-Johnston (*née* Cree); *m* 1962, Suzanne (*née* Singer); one *d*. *Educ:* Berkhamsted School. Master Mariner; FRGS; MRIN. Merchant Navy, 1957–67. First person to sail single-handed non-stop Around the World 14 June 1968 to 22 April 1969, in yacht Suhaili; won Sunday Times Golden Globe, 1969; won Round Britain Race, Ocean Spirit, 1970; won round Britain Race, British Oxygen, 1974; set British transatlantic sailing record, from NY to the Lizard, 11 days 7 hours 45 mins, 1981; established new record of 10 days 14 hours 9 mins, 1986; set world sailing record for around Ireland, 76 hours 5 mins 34 secs, May 1986; World Class II Multihull Champion, 1985; completed Guardian Columbus voyage, 1989; with Peter Blake, set non-stop around the world sailing record, 74 days, 22 hours, 17 mins 22 secs, 1994. Man. Dir, St Katharine's Yacht Haven Ltd, 1975–76; Director: Mercury Yacht Harbours Ltd, 1970–73; Rank Marine International, 1973–75; Troon Marina Ltd, 1976–83; National Yacht Racing Centre Ltd, 1979–86; Knox-Johnston Insurance Brokers Ltd, 1983–; St Katherine's Dock, 1975– (Man. Dir, 1991–93). President: British Olympic Yachting Appeal, 1977–; STA, 1993; Member: Cttee of Management, RNLI, 1983–; Sports Council Lottery Panel, 1995. Trustee, Nat. Maritime Mus., Greenwich, 1993. Freeman, Borough of Bromley, Kent, 1969; Younger Brother, Trinity House, 1973. Freeman, City of London, 1992. Liveryman, Co. of Master Mariners, 1975. Lt-Comdr RNR 1971, retired. Hon. DSc Maine Maritime Acad., 1989; Hon. DTech Nottingham, 1993. Yachtsman of the Year, 1969; Silk Cut Seamanship Award, 1990; Seamanship Foundn Trophy, RYA, 1991; Gold Medal, RIN, 1992; Yachtsman of the Year, 1994; Internat. Yacht Racing Union Sailor of the Year, 1994. *Publications:* A World of my Own, 1969; Sailing, 1975; Twilight of Sail, 1978; Last but not Least, 1978; Bunkside Companion, 1982; Seamanship, 1986; The BOC Challenge 1986–1987, 1988; The Cape of Good Hope, 1989; History of Yachting, 1990; The Columbus Venture, 1991 (Book of the Sea Award); Sea, Ice and Rock, 1992; Cape Horn, 1994; Beyond Jules Verne, 1995. *Recreation:* sailing. *Address:* St Francis Cottage, Torbryan, Newton Abbot, Devon TQ12 5UR. *Clubs:* Royal Cruising, Royal Ocean Racing.

KNOX-LECKY, Maj.-Gen. Samuel, CB 1979; OBE 1967; BSc(Eng); CEng, FIMechE; Director-General, Agricultural Engineers Association, 1980–88; *b* 10 Feb. 1926; *s* of late J. D. Lecky, Coleraine; *m* 1947, Sheila Jones; one *s* two *d*. *Educ:* Coleraine Acad.; Queen's Univ., Belfast (BSc). Commnd REME, 1946; served Egypt, 1951–52; Kenya, 1953–54; jssc 1964; AA&QMG HQ 1(BR) Corps, 1965–66; CREME 4 Div., 1966–68; Sec., Principal Personnel Officers, MoD, 1968–70; RCDS, 1971; Comdt, SEME, 1972–74; DEME, BAOR, 1975; Dir, Military Assistance Office, MoD, 1976–77; Minister (DS), British Embassy, Tehran, 1977–79. Hon. Col, QUB OTC, 1978–83; Col Comdt, REME, 1980–86. *Recreations:* fishing, sailing.

KNOX-MAWER, Ronald; retired; *b* 3 Aug. 1925; *s* of George Robert Knox-Mawer and Clara Roberts; *m* 1951, June Ellis; one *s* one *d*. *Educ:* Grove Park Sch. (Denbighshire County Exhibnr); Emmanuel Coll., Cambridge (Exhibitioner; MA). Royal Artillery, 1943–47. Called to Bar, Middle Temple; Wales and Chester Circuit, 1947–52; Chief Magistrate and Actg Chief Justice, Aden, 1952–58; Sen. Magistrate, Puisne Judge, Justice of Appeal, Actg Chief Justice, Fiji, and conjointly Chief Justice, Nauru and Tonga, 1958–71; Northern Circuit, 1971–75; Metropolitan Stipendiary Magistrate, 1975–84; Dep. Circuit Judge, London, 1979–84. Various series of humorous reminiscences broadcast on BBC Radio: Tales from a Palm Court, 1984; Islands of Hope and Glory, 1985; Wretchedness in Wrexham, 1986; More Tales from a Palm Court, 1987–88; Tales of a Man called Father, 1989; The Queen Goes West, 1990; A Case of Bananas, 1992; Family Failings, 1994. *Publications:* Palm Court, 1979 (as Robert Overton); Tales from a Palm Court, 1986; Tales of a Man Called Father, 1989; A Case of Bananas and other South Sea Trials, 1992; Land of My Father, 1994; short stories and features (under different pseudonyms) in Punch, Cornhill, Argosy, The Times, Sunday Express, Blackwoods, Listener, Weekend Telegraph, Times Saturday Review, Sunday Telegraph; various contribs to legal jls. *Recreation:* countryside. *Address:* c/o Midland Bank, Ruabon, N Wales LL14 6AA.

KNUDSEN, Semon Emil; retired; Chairman and Chief Executive, White Motor Corporation, 1971–80; *b* 2 Oct. 1912; *o s* of William S. and Clara Euler Knudsen; *m* 1938, Florence Anne McConnell; one *s* three *d*. *Educ:* Dartmouth Coll.; Mass Inst. of Technology. Joined General Motors, 1939; series of supervisory posts; Gen. Man., Detroit Diesel Div., 1955; Gen. Man., Pontiac Motor Div., 1956; Gen. Man., Chevrolet Motor Div., 1961; Dir of General Motors and Gp Vice-Pres. i/c of all Canadian and overseas activities, 1965; Exec. Vice-Pres. with added responsibility for domestic non-automotive divs, 1966, also defense activities, 1967; resigned from Gen. Motors Corp., 1968; Pres., Ford Motor Co., 1968–69. Mem., MIT Corp. Mem. Bd of Dirs, Boys Clubs of Amer.; Trustee, Oakland (Mich) Univ. Foundn and Cleveland Clinic Fund. *Recreations:* golf, tennis, deepsea fishing, hunting. *Address:* 1965 N Woodward Avenue, Bloomfield Hills, MI 48304–2238, USA. *Clubs:* Detroit Athletic (Detroit); Bloomfield Hills Country (Mich); Everglades, Bath & Tennis (Fla).

KNUSSEN, (Stuart) Oliver, CBE 1994; composer and conductor; Co-Artistic Director, Aldeburgh Festival, since 1983; Co-ordinator of Contemporary Music Activities, Berkshire Music Center, Tanglewood, 1986–90; *b* Glasgow, 12 June 1952; *s* of Stuart Knussen and Ethelyn Jane Alexander; *m* 1972, Susan Freedman; one *d*. *Educ:* Watford Field Sch.; Watford Boys Grammar Sch.; Purcell Sch. Private composition study with John Lambert, 1963–68; Countess of Munster Awards, 1964, 1965, 1967; Peter Stuyvesant Foundn Award, 1965; début conducting Symph. no 1 with LSO, 1968; Watney-Sargent award for Young Conductors, 1969; Fellowships to Berkshire Music Center, Tanglewood, 1970, 1971, 1973; Caird Trav. Schol., 1971; Margaret Grant Composition Prize (Symph. no 2), Tanglewood, 1971; study with Gunther Schuller in USA, 1970–73; Koussevitzky Centennial Commn, 1974; Composer-in-residence: Aspen Fest., 1976; Arnolfini Gall., 1978; Instr in composition, RCM Jun. Dept, 1977–82; BBC commn for Proms 1979 (Symph. no 3); Berkshire Music Center, Tanglewood: Guest Teacher, 1981; Composer-in-residence, 1986. Arts Council Bursaries, 1979, 1981; winner, first Park Lane Gp Composer award (suite from Where the Wild Things Are), 1982; BBC commn for Glyndebourne Opera, 1983. Frequent guest conductor: London Sinfonietta, Philharmonia Orch., many other ensembles, UK and abroad, 1981–; Associate Guest Conductor, BBC SO, 1989–; Dir, Almeida Ensemble, 1986–. Mem. Executive Cttee, Soc. for Promotion of New Music, 1978–85; Member: Leopold Stokowski Soc.; International Alban Berg Soc., New York. *Publications:* Symphony no 1 op. 1, 1966–67; Symphony no 2 op. 7, 1970–71; Symphony no 3 op. 18, 1973–79; Where the Wild Things Are—opera (Maurice Sendak), op. 20, 1979–83 (staged, Glyndebourne at NT, 1984); Higglety Pigglety Pop!—opera (Sendak), op. 21, 1983–85 (staged Glyndebourne, 1984 and 1985); numerous orchestral, chamber, vocal works; articles in Tempo, The Listener, etc. *Recreations:* cinema, record collecting, record producing, visual arts. *Address:* c/o Faber Music Ltd, 3 Queen Square, WC1N 3AR.

KNUTSFORD, 6th Viscount *cr* 1895; **Michael Holland-Hibbert;** Bt 1853; Baron 1888; DL; *b* 27 Dec. 1926; *s* of Hon. Wilfrid Holland-Hibbert (*d* 1961) (2nd *s* of 3rd Viscount) and of Audrey, *d* of late Mark Fenwick; *S* cousin, 1986; *m* 1951, Hon. Sheila, *d* of 5th Viscount Portman; two *s* one *d*. *Educ:* Eton College; Trinity Coll., Cambridge (BA). Welsh Guards, 1945–48. SW Regional Director, Barclays Bank, 1956–86. National Trust: Chm. Cttee for Devon and Cornwall, 1973–86; Mem. Exec. Cttee, 1973–86; Mem. Council, 1979–85; Mem. Finance Cttee, 1986–. DL 1977, High Sheriff 1977–78, Devon. *Heir: er s* Hon. Henry Thurstan Holland-Hibbert [*b* 6 April 1959; *m* 1988, Katherine, *d* of Sir John Ropner, Bt, *qv*; one *s* two *d*]. *Address:* Broadclyst House, Exeter, Devon EX5 3EW. *T:* Exeter (01392) 461244. *Club:* Brooks's.

KNUTTON, Maj.-Gen. Harry, CB 1975; MSc, CEng, FIEE; Director-General, City and Guilds of London Institute, 1976–85; *b* Rawmarsh, Yorks, 26 April 1921; *m* 1958, Pamela Brackley, E Sheen, London; three *s* one *d*. *Educ:* Wath-upon-Dearne Grammar Sch.; RMCS. Commnd RA, 1943; served with 15th Scottish and 1st Airborne Divs, NW Europe, 1944–45; India, 1945–47; Instructor in Gunnery, 1946–49; Project Officer, Min. of Supply, 1949–51; served Middle East, 1953–55; Directing Staff, RMCS, 1955–58; jssc 1958; various staff appts, MoD, 1958–60, 1962–64, 1966–67; Comdr Missile Regt, BAOR, 1964–66; Comdr Air Defence Bde, 1967–69; Fellow, Loughborough Univ. of Technology, 1969–70; Dir-Gen. Weapons (Army), 1970–73; Dir, Royal Ordnance Factories and Dep. Master-Gen. of Ordnance, 1973–75. Col Comdt, RA, 1977–82. Teacher, Whitgift Foundn, 1975–76. Member: Associated Examining Bd, 1976–85; Dep. Chm., Standing Conf. on Schools' Science and Technology, 1983–90. Governor, Imperial Coll. of Science, Technology and Medicine (formerly Imperial Coll. of Science and Technology), 1976–91. CBIM 1978; FCollP 1983. FCGI 1985. Liveryman, Engineers' Co. *Address:* 43 Essendene Road, Caterham, Surrey CR3 5PB.

KOCH, Edward Irving; Partner, Robinson Silverman Pearce Aronsohn & Berman, New York, since 1990; Mayor, City of New York, 1978–89; *b* 12 Dec. 1924; *s* of Louis Koch and Joyce Silpe. *Educ:* Southside High School, Newark, NJ; City Coll. of NY; NY Univ. Law Sch. Served US Army, 1943–46, USA, France, Rhineland. Mem., NY State Bar, 1949; private law practice, 1949–64; Senior Partner, Koch, Lankenau, Schwartz & Kovner, 1965–69. Democratic dist. leader, Greenwich Village, 1963–65; Mem., NY City Council, 1967–68; NY Congressman, 1969–77. *Publications:* Mayor, 1983; Politics, 1985, (jtly) His Eminence and Hizzoner, 1989; All the Best, 1990; Citizen Koch, 1992; Ed Koch on Everything, 1994. *Address:* 2 Fifth Avenue, New York, NY 10011, USA.

KOECHLIN-SMYTHE, Patricia Rosemary, OBE 1956; President, 1983–86, Vice-President, since 1987, British Show Jumping Association; Member of British Show Jumping Team, 1947–64; *b* 22 Nov. 1928; *d* of late Capt. Eric Hamilton Smythe, MC, Légion d'Honneur, and late Frances Monica Smythe (*née* Curtoys); *m* 1963, Samuel Koechlin (*d* 1985), Switzerland; two *d*. *Educ:* St Michael's Sch., Cirencester; Talbot Heath, Bournemouth. Show Jumping: first went abroad with British Team, 1947; Leading Show Jumper of the Year, 1949, 1958 (with T. Edgar), and 1962; European Ladies' Championship: Spa, 1957; Deauville, 1961; Madrid, 1962; Hickstead, 1963; Harringay: BSJA Spurs, 1949, 1951, 1952, 1954 (Victor Ludorum Championship), 1953 and 1954; Harringay Spurs, 1953; Grand Prix, Brussels, 1949, 1952 and 1956. Ladies' record for high jump (2 m. 10 cm.) Paris, 1950; won in Madrid, 1951. White City: 1951 (Country Life Cup); 1953 (Selby Cup). Was Leading Rider and won Prix du Champion, Paris, 1952; Leading Rider, etc, Marseilles, 1953; Individual Championship, etc, Harrisburg, Penn, USA, 1953; Pres. of Mexico Championship, New York, 1953; Toronto (in team winning Nations Cup), 1953; Lisbon (won 2 events), Grand Prix, Madrid, and Championship, Vichy, 1954; Grand Prix de Paris and 3 other events, 1954; Bruxelles Puissance and new ladies' record for high jump (2m. 24 cm.), Leading Rider of Show, 1954; BHS Medal of Honour, Algiers Puissance and Grand Prix, 4 events in Paris, 4 events at White City including the Championship, 1955; Grand Prix and Leading Rider of Show and 4 other events, Brussels, 1956; Grand Prix Militaire and Puissance, Lucerne; Mem. British Equestrian Olympic Team, Stockholm (Show Jumping Bronze Medal), 1956; IHS National Championship, White City; Leading Rider and other events, Palermo, 1956; won 2 Puissance events, Paris, 1957; BSJA, 1957; Ladies' National Championship in 1954–59 and 1961 and 1962 (8 times); Daily Mail Cup, White City, 1955, 1957, 1960, 1962; Mem. winning British Team, White City: 1952, 1953, 1956, 1957; Amazon Prize, Aachen, 1958; Queen's Cup, Royal Internat. Horse Show, White City, 1958; Preis von Parsenn, Davos, 1957, 1958, 1959; Championship Cup, Brussels Internat. Horse Show, 1958; Lisbon Grand Prix, 1959; Olympic Trial, British Timken Show, and Prix de la Banque de Bruxelles at Brussels, 1959. Lucerne Grand Prix; Prince Hal Stakes, Country Life and Riding Cup, White City; Pembroke Stakes, Horse Show Cttee Cup, and Leading Rider, Dublin (all in 1960). Mem. British Olympic Team in Rome, 1960. Copenhagen Grand Prix; Amazon Prize, Aachen; John Player Trophy, White City; St Gall Ladies Championship (all in 1961); Saddle of Honour and Loriners' Cup, White City, 1962; British Jumping Derby, Hickstead, 1962. Member: Internat. Council, WWF; Nat. Council, WWF UK; Bd, Earthwatch Europe; Achievement Bd, ICBP. Hon. Freeman, Worshipful Co. of Farriers, 1955; Freeman of the City of London, 1956; Hon. Freeman, Worshipful Company of Loriners, 1962; Yeoman, Worshipful Company of Saddlers, 1963. *Publications:* (as Pat Smythe): Jump for Joy; Pat Smythe's Story, 1954; Pat Smythe's Book of Horses, 1955; One Jump Ahead, 1956; Jacqueline rides for a Fall, 1957; Three Jays against the Clock, 1957; Three Jays on Holiday, 1958; Three Jays go to Town, 1959; Horses and Places, 1959; Three Jays over the Border, 1960; Three Jays go to Rome, 1960; Three Jays Lend a Hand, 1961; Jumping Round the World, 1962; Florian's Farmyard, 1962; Flanagan My Friend, 1963; Bred to Jump, 1965; Show Jumping, 1967; (with Fiona

Hughes) A Pony for Pleasure, 1969; A Swiss Adventure, 1970; (with Fiona Hughes) Pony Problems, 1971; A Spanish Adventure, 1971; A Cotswold Adventure, 1972; Leaping Life's Fences, 1992. *Recreations:* swimming, music, sailing, all sports, languages. *Address:* Sudgrove House, Miserden, near Stroud, Glos GL6 7JD. *T:* Cirencester (01285) 821360.

KOENIGSBERGER, Prof. Helmut Georg, MA, PhD; FBA 1989; Professor of History, King's College London, 1973–84, now Emeritus; *b* 24 Oct. 1918; *s* of late Georg Felix Koenigsberger, chief architect, borough of Treptow, Berlin, Germany, and of late Käthe Koenigsberger (*née* Born); *m* 1961, Dorothy M. Romano; two *d* (twins). *Educ:* Adams' Grammar Sch., Newport, Shropshire; Gonville and Caius Coll., Cambridge. Asst Master: Brentwood Sch., Essex, 1941–42; Bedford Sch., 1942–44. Served War of 1939–45, Royal Navy, 1944–45. Lecturer in Economic History, QUB, 1948–51; Senior Lecturer in Economic History, University of Manchester, 1951–60; Prof. of Modern History, University of Nottingham, 1960–66; Prof. of Early Modern European History, Cornell, 1966–73. Visiting Lecturer: Brooklyn Coll., New York, 1957; University of Wisconsin, 1958; Columbia University, 1962; Cambridge Univ., 1963; Washington Univ., St Louis, 1964; Fellow, Historisches Kolleg, Munich, 1984–85. Sec., 1955–75, Vice-Pres., 1975–80, Pres., 1980–85, Internat. Commn for the History of Representative and Parliamentary Institutions; Vice-Pres., RHistS, 1982–85. *Publications:* The Government of Sicily under Philip II of Spain, 1951, new edn, as The Practice of Empire, 1969; The Empire of Charles V in Europe (in New Cambridge Modern History II), 1958; Western Europe and the Power of Spain (in New Cambridge Modern History III), 1968; Europe in the Sixteenth Century (with G. L. Mosse), 1968, 2nd edn (with G. L. Mosse and G. Q. Bowler) 1989; Estates and Revolutions, 1971; The Habsburgs and Europe, 1516–1660, 1971; (ed) Luther: a profile, 1972; Politicians and Virtuosi, 1986; Medieval Europe, 1987; Early Modern Europe, 1987; (ed) Republiken und Republikanismus im Europa der frühen Neuzeit, 1988; contrib. to historical journals. *Recreations:* playing chamber music, sailing, travel. *Address:* 116 Waterfall Road, N14 7JN. *T:* 0181–886 6416.

KOGAN, Prof. Maurice; Professor of Government and Social Administration, Brunel University, since 1969; Director, Centre for the Evaluation of Public Policy; *b* 10 April 1930; *s* of Barnett and Hetty Kogan; *m* 1960, Ulla Svensson; two *s*. *Educ:* Stratford Grammar Sch.; Christ's Coll., Cambridge (MA). Entered Civil Service, admin. cl. (1st in open examinations), 1953. Secretary: Secondary Sch. Exams Council, 1961; Central Advisory Council for Educn (England), 1963–66; Harkness Fellow of Commonwealth Fund, 1960–61; Asst Sec., DES, 1966. Brunel University: Head of Sch. of Social Scis, 1971–74; Dean, Faculty of Soc. Scis, 1987–89; Acting Vice-Chancellor, 1989–90. Member: Educn Sub-Cttee, Univ. Grants Cttee, 1972–75; SSRC, 1975–77; Davies Cttee on Hosp. Complaints' Procedure, 1971; Houghton Cttee on Teachers' Pay, 1974; Genetic Manipulation Adv. Gp, 1979–80; Chm., Adv. Gp, Cttee of award, Harkness Fellowship, 1989–. George A. Miller Vis. Prof., Univ. of Illinois, 1976; Vis. Scholar, Univ. of Calif, Berkeley, 1981. Hon. DSc (Econ) Hull, 1987; DUniv Brunel, 1991. *Publications:* The Organisation of a Social Services Department, 1971; Working Relationships within the British Hospital Service, 1971; The Government of Education, 1971; The Politics of Education, 1971; (ed) The Challenge of Change, 1973; County Hall, 1973; Advisory Councils and Committees in Education, 1974; Educational Policy-Making, 1975; The Politics of Educational Change, 1978; The Working of the National Health Service, 1978; (with T. Becher) Process and Structure in Higher Education, 1980, 2nd edn 1992; The Government's Commissioning of Research, 1980; (with T. Bush) Directors of Education, 1982; (with D. Kogan) The Battle for the Labour Party, 1982; (with M. Henkel) Government and Research, 1983; (with D. Kogan) The Attack on Higher Education, 1983; (with T. Husen) Educational Research and Policy: how do they relate?, 1984; (with D. Johnson and others) School Governing Bodies, 1984; Education Accountability, 1986; (jtly) The Use of Performance Indicators in Higher Education, 1988, 2nd edn 1990; (jtly) Higher Education and Employment, 1988; (ed) Evaluating Higher Education, 1989; (jtly) Directors of Education Facing Reform, 1989; (jtly) Evaluation as Policy Making, 1990; (jtly) Encyclopaedia of Government and Politics, 1992; (jtly) In Support of Education: the functioning of local government, 1993; (jtly) Graduate Education in Britain, 1994; contribs to TES, THES, Jl of Social Policy. *Recreations:* reading, listening to music. *Address:* 48 Duncan Terrace, Islington, N1 8AL. *T:* 0171–226 0038.

KOHL, Dr Helmut; Grosskreuz Verdienstorden, 1979; Chancellor, Federal Republic of Germany, since 1982, re-elected, 1991, as Chancellor of the Federal Republic of Germany (reunited Germany); Member, Bundestag, since 1976; *b* 3 April 1930; *s* of Hans and Cäcilie Kohl; *m* 1960, Hannelore Renner; two *s*. *Educ:* Frankfurt Univ.; Heidelberg Univ. (Dr phil 1958 Heidelberg). On staff of a Trade Assoc., 1958–59; Mem., Parlt of Rhineland Palatinate, 1959–76; Leader, CDU Party Party in Rhineland Palatinate Parlt, 1963–69; Mem., Federal Exec. Cttee of CDU at federal level, 1964–; Chairman: CDU, Rhineland Palatinate, 1966–74; CDU, 1973–; Minister-President, Rhineland Palatinate, 1969–76; Leader of the Opposition, Bundestag, 1976–82. Numerous foreign decorations. *Publications:* Die politische Entscheidung in der Pfalz und das Wiedererstehen der Parteien nach 1945, 1958; Hausputz hinter den Fassaden, 1971; Zwischen Ideologie und Pragmatismus, 1973; Die CDU: Porträt einer Volkspartei, 1981; Der Weg zur Wende, 1983; Reden 1982–1984, 1984; Die Deutsche Einheit, 1992; Der Kurs der CDU, 1993. *Address:* Bundeskanzleramt, Adenauerallee 139/141, 53106 Bonn, Germany. *T:* (228) 561; Marbacher Strasse 11, 67071 Ludwigshafen (Rhein), Germany.

KOHLER, Irene; pianist; Professor, Trinity College of Music, London, 1952–79; *b* London; *m* 1950, Dr Harry Waters, medical practitioner. *Educ:* Royal College of Music. Studied with Arthur Benjamin; Challen Medal, Danreuther Prize, etc; travelling scholarship to Vienna; studied there with Edward Steuermann and Egon Wellesz. BMus; Hon. FTCL, GRSM, LRAM, ARCM. First professional engagement, Bournemouth, 1933, resulting in engagement by BBC; played at first night of 40th Promenade Season, 1934. First foreign tour (recitals and broadcasts), Holland, 1938. During War of 1939–45 gave concerts for the Forces in this country and toured France and Belgium, also India and Burma, under auspices of ENSA; subsequently played in many countries of Europe and made tours. Eugene Goossens selected her for first European performance of his Phantasy Concerto; broadcast 1st performance of Sonata by Gunilla Lowenstein, Stockholm. She gave 3 concerts at the Festival Hall in Festival of Britain Year, 1951. Canadian American Tour, 1953; World Tour, 1955–56; African Tour, 1958; 2nd African Tour, 1959; Bulgarian Tour, 1959; 2nd World Tour, 1962; Czechoslovakian Tour, 1963; Scandinavian Tour, 1970; Far and Middle East Tour, 1972; recitals and master classes, Japan, 1979, 1981; Polish Tour, 1980. Film appearances include: Train of Events, Odette, Secret People, Lease of Life, and a documentary for the Ministry of Information. *Address:* 28 Castelnau, SW13 9RU. *T:* 0181–748 5512.

KOHLHAUSSEN, Martin; Chairman, Board of Managing Directors, Commerzbank AG, since 1991 (Member, Board of Managing Directors, since 1982); *b* 6 Nov. 1935; *m*; three *c*. *Educ:* Univs of Frankfurt (Main), Freiburg, Marburg (Law). Worked domestically in banking, Frankfurt and Hanan (Br. Man.), 1965–76; worked internationally in banking (Br. Man.), Tokyo and New York, 1976–81. *Address:* Commerzbank AG, PO Box 100505, 60005 Frankfurt, Germany. *T:* (69) 13620.

KOHNSTAM, George, PhD; Principal of the Graduate Society, University of Durham, 1981–86 (Deputy Principal, 1972–81); Reader in Physical Chemistry, University of Durham, 1962–86; *b* 25 Dec. 1920; *s* of Emil and Margaret Kohnstam; *m* 1953, Patricia Elizabeth, *d* of Rev. A. W. G. Duffield and Margaret Duffield; one *s* three *d*. *Educ:* Royal Grammar Sch., High Wycombe; University Coll. London (BSc 1940, PhD 1948). Tuffnel Scholar, Univ. of London, 1940 (postponed); applied chemical res., 1941–45; Temp. Asst Lectr in Chemistry, UCL, 1948–50; Lectr in Phys. Chem., Univ. of Durham, 1950–59, Sen. Lectr, 1959–62. *Publications:* papers and review articles in chemical jls. *Recreations:* dinghy sailing, gardening, bridge, travel. *Address:* 67 Hallgarth Street, Durham City DH1 3AY. *T:* Durham (0191) 3842018.

KOHNSTAMM, Max; Groot Officier, Order of Orange-Nassau, 1988; Comdr of the Order of House of Orange, 1949; Hon. Secretary-General, Action Committee for Europe, since 1989 (Sec.-Gen., 1985–88); Senior Fellow, Belmont European Policy Centre, Brussels, since 1991; *b* 22 May 1914; *s* of Dr Philip Abraham Kohnstamm and Johanna Hermana Kessler; *m* 1944, Kathleen Sillem; two *s* three *d*. *Educ:* Univ. of Amsterdam (Hist. Drs); American Univ., Washington. Private Sec. to Queen Wilhelmina, 1945–48; subseq. Head of German Bureau, then Dir of European Affairs, Netherlands FO; Sec. of High Authority, 1952–56; 1st Rep. of High Authority, London, 1956; Sec.-Gen. (later Vice-Pres.), Action Cttee for United States of Europe, 1956–75; Pres., European Community Inst. for Univ. Studies, 1958–75; Principal, Eur. Univ. Inst. of Florence, 1975–81. Co-Chm., Cttee on Soc. Develt and Peace, World Council of Churches and Pontifical Commn for Justice and Peace, 1967–75; European Pres., Trilateral Commn, 1973–75. Grande Ufficiale dell' Ordine Al Merito della Repubblica Italiana, 1981; Grosse Verdienstkreuz, 1982, mit Stern, 1989, Bundesrepublik Deutschland. *Publications:* The European Community and its Role in the World, 1963; (ed jtly) A Nation Writ Large?, 1972. *Recreations:* tennis, walking. *Address:* 20 Fenffe, 5560 Houyet, Belgium. *T:* (84) 377183.

KOHT, Paul; Ambassador of Norway to Denmark, 1975–82; *b* 7 Dec. 1913; *s* of Dr Halvdan Koht and Karen Elisabeth (*née* Grude); *m* 1938, Grete Sverdrup; two *s* one *d*. *Educ:* University of Oslo. Law degree, 1937. Entered Norwegian Foreign Service, 1938; held posts in: Bucharest, 1938–39; London, 1940–41; Tokyo, 1941–42; New York, 1942–46; Lisbon, 1950–51; Mem. Norwegian Delegn to OEEC and NATO, Paris, and Perm. Rep. to Coun. of Europe, 1951–53; Dir General of Dept for Econ. Affairs, Min. of For. Affairs, Oslo, 1953–56; Chargé d'Affaires, Copenhagen, 1956–58; Ambassador to USA, 1958–63; Ambassador to Fed. Republic of Germany, 1963–68; Ambassador to the Court of St James's, 1968–75. Comdr, Order of St Olav; Grand Cross, Order of Dannebrog; Grand Cross, Order of Merit (Federal Republic of Germany). *Address:* Lille Frogner Allé 4b, 0263 Oslo, Norway.

KOLAKOWSKI, Leszek, PhD; FBA 1980; Senior Research Fellow, All Souls College, Oxford, since 1970; *b* 23 Oct. 1927; *s* of Jerzy and Lucyna (*née* Pietrusiewicz); *m* 1949, Dr Tamara Kołakowska (*née* Dynenson); one *d*. *Educ:* Łódź Univ., Poland 1945–50; Warsaw Univ. (PhD 1953). Asst in Philosophy: Łódź Univ., 1947–49; Warsaw Univ., 1950–59; Prof. and Chm., Section of History of Philosophy, Warsaw Univ., 1959–68, expelled by authorities for political reasons; Visiting Professor: McGill Univ., 1968–69; Univ. of California, Berkeley, 1969–70; Yale Univ., Conn, 1975; Univ. of Chicago, 1981–. McArthur Fellowship, 1983. Mem. Internat. Inst. of Philosophy; Foreign Mem., Amer. Academy of Arts and Science; Mem.-correspondent, Bayerische Akademie des Künste. Hon. Dr Lit. Hum Bard Coll., 1984; Hon. LLD Reed Coll., 1985. Friedenpreis des Deutschen Buchhandels, 1977; Jurzykowski Foundn award, 1968; Charles Veillou Prix Européen d'Essai, 1980; (jtly) Erasmus Prize, 1984; Jefferson Award, 1986. *Publications:* about 30 books, some of them only in Polish; trans. of various books in 14 languages; *in English:* Marxism and Beyond, 1968; Conversations with the Devil, 1972; Positivist Philosophy, 1972; Husserl and the Search for Certitude, 1975; Main Currents of Marxism, 3 vols, 1978; Religion, 1982; Bergson, 1985; Metaphysical Horror, 1988; *in French:* Chrétiens sans Eglise, 1969; *in German:* Traktat über die Sterblichkeit der Vernunft, 1967; Geist und Ungeist christlicher Traditionen, 1971; Die Gegenwärtigkeit des Mythos, 1973; Der revolutionäre Geist, 1972; Leben trotz Geschichte Lesebuch, 1977; Zweifel und die Methode, 1977. *Address:* 77 Hamilton Road, Oxford OX2 7QA. *T:* Oxford (01865) 58790.

KOLANE, John Teboho, ODSM, OL; LLD; Director of Paliamentary Affairs, Lesotho, since 1990; *b* 22 Feb. 1926; *s* of Elizabeth and Zacharia Kolane; *m* 1955, Julia; two *s* three *d*. *Educ:* National University of Lesotho; Cambridge Univ. BA South Africa; attorney's admission, Pretoria. Interpreter, District Comr's Court and Judicial Comr's Court, 1950–59; Registrar of Births, Marriages and Deaths, 1959–63; Clerk of Senate, 1965–67; Permanent Secretary: Min. of Justice, 1967–69; Cabinet Office, 1969–70; Min. of Justice, 1970–73; Speaker, National Assembly, 1973–86; High Comr to UK, 1986–89; Speaker, National Constituent Assembly, 1990–. LLD 1985. *Recreations:* golf, gardening, walking. *Address:* National Assembly, PO Box 190, Maseru, Lesotho. *Club:* Maseru Golf.

KOLBERT, Colin Francis; His Honour Judge Kolbert; a Circuit Judge, since 1988; Fellow of Magdalene College, Cambridge, since 1968; *b* 3 June 1936; *s* of late Arthur Richard Alexander Kolbert and Dorothy Elizabeth Kolbert (*née* Fletcher); *m* 1959, Jean Fairgrieve Abson; two *d*. *Educ:* Queen Elizabeth's, Barnet; St Catharine's Coll., Cambridge (Harold Samuel Schol., 1959; BA 1959; PhD 1962; MA 1963). RA, 1954–56. Called to the Bar, Lincoln's Inn, 1961. A Recorder, SE Circuit, 1985–88. Oxford University: Fellow and Tutor in Jurisprudence, St Peter's Coll., 1964–68 (MA, DPhil (Oxon) by incorp., 1964); CUF Lectr, Faculty of Law, 1965–68; Cambridge University: Tutor, Magdalene Coll., 1969–88; Univ. Lectr in Law, Dept of Land Economy, 1969–88; Sec., Faculty of Music, 1969–75; Coll. Rugby Administrator, CURUFC, 1982–88 (Trustee, 1989–). Vis. Prof. and Moderator, Univs of Ife, Lagos, Enugu, and Ahmadu Bello, Nigeria, 1970–80. Mem., Cambridge City Council, 1970–74. Member: Istituto di Diritto Agrario Internazionale e Comparato, Florence, 1964–; Secretariat, World Conf. on Agrarian Reform and Rural Develt, FAO Rome, 1978–79 (Customary Land Tenure Consultant, 1974–80). Governor: Wellingborough Sch., 1970–80; Cranleigh Sch., 1970–88; Glenalmond Coll., 1978–89; Hurstpierpont Coll., 1978–89; Feoffee, Chetham's Hosp. and Library, 1993–. Violin music critic, Records and Recording, 1974–78. *Publications:* (trans. and ed) The Digest of Justinian, 1979, 4th edn 1993; various legal and musical. *Recreations:* music (especially playing the violin), cricket, Rugby, military history, cooking, walking in London and Yorkshire. *Address:* Magdalene College, Cambridge CB3 0AG; 35 Essex Street, Temple, WC2R 3AR. *Clubs:* MCC, Farmers'; Hawks (Cambridge); Cambridge University Rugby Union Football.

KOLO, Sule; Chairman, Alheri Enterprises; Consultant, NESCO Ltd; High Commissioner for Nigeria in London, 1970–75; *b* 1926; *m* 1957, Helen Patricia Kolo; two *s* four *d*. BSc (Econ); attended Imperial Defence College. Counsellor, Nigerian High Commn in London, 1962; Perm. Sec., Nigerian Min. of Defence, 1963; Perm. Sec., Nigerian Min. of Trade, 1966; Nigeria's Perm. Representative to European Office of UN and Ambassador to Switzerland, 1966; Chm. of GATT, 1969. Chm., Nigeria Section, Nigeria–US Business Council. Former Pres., Lions Club Internat. Dist 404, Nigeria. FREconS; FRSA 1973.

Franklin Peace Medal, 1969. *Recreations:* swimming, tennis. *Address:* PO Box 1453, Jos, Nigeria. *Clubs:* Travellers'; Island (Lagos).

KOLTAI, Ralph, CBE 1983; RDI 1985; freelance stage designer; designer for Drama, Opera and Dance, since 1950; Associate Designer, Royal Shakespeare Company, 1963–66 and since 1976; *b* 31 July 1924; Hungarian-German; *s* of Dr(med) Alfred Koltai and Charlotte Koltai (*née* Weinstein); *m* 1956, Annena Stubbs. *Educ:* Central Sch. of Art and Design (Dip. with Dist.). Early work entirely in field of opera. First production, Angelique, for London Opera Club, Fortune Theatre, 1950. Designs for The Royal Opera House, Sadler's Wells, Scottish Opera, National Welsh Opera, The English Opera Group. First of 7 ballets for Ballet Rambert, Two Brothers, 1958. Head , Sch. of Theatre Design, Central Sch. of Art & Design, 1965–72. *Productions:* RSC: The Caucasian Chalk Circle, 1962; The Representative, 1963; The Birthday Party; Endgame; The Jew of Malta, 1964; The Merchant of Venice; Timon of Athens, 1965; Little Murders, 1967; Major Barbara, 1970; Too True To Be Good, 1975; Old World, 1976; Wild Oats, 1977; The Tempest, Love's Labour's Lost, 1978; Hippolytus, Baal, 1979; Romeo and Juliet, Hamlet, 1980; The Love Girl and the Innocent, 1981 (London Drama Critics Award); Much Ado About Nothing, Molière, 1982; Custom of the Country, Cyrano de Bergerac (SWET Award), 1983; Troilus and Cressida, Othello, 1985; They Shoot Horses, Don't They?, 1987; for National Theatre: an "all male" As You Like It, 1967; Back to Methuselah, 1969; State of Revolution, 1977; Brand (SWET Award), The Guardsman, 1978; Richard III, The Wild Duck, 1979; Man and Superman, 1981; *other notable productions include: opera:* for Sadler's Wells/English National Opera: The Rise and Fall of the City of Mahagonny, 1963; From the House of the Dead, 1965; Bluebeard's Castle, 1972; Wagner's (complete) Ring Cycle, 1973; Seven Deadly Sins, 1978; Anna Karenina, 1981; Pacific Overtures, 1987; for The Royal Opera House: Taverner, 1972; The Ice Break, 1977; for Sydney Opera House: Tannhäuser, 1973; for Netherlands Opera: Wozzeck, 1973; Fidelio, Munich, 1974; Verdi's Macbeth, Edinburgh Festival, 1976; Les Soldats, Lyon Opera, 1983; Italian Girl in Algiers, 1984, Tannhäuser, 1986, Geneva; (also dir.) Flying Dutchman, Hong Kong, 1987, La Traviata, Hong Kong, 1990, Stockholm, 1993; The Makropulas Affair, Oslo, 1991; Otello, Essen, 1994; Madam Butterfly, Tokyo, 1995; *theatre:* Pack of Lies, Lyric, 1983; Across from the Garden of Allah, Comedy, 1986; for Aalborg Theatre, Denmark: Threepenny Opera, 1979; The Love Girl and the Innocent, 1980; Terra Nova, 1981; The Carmelites, 1981; Mahagonny, 1984; *musicals:* Billy, Drury Lane, 1974; Bugsy Malone, Her Majesty's, 1983; Dear Anyone, Cambridge Theatre, 1983; Carrie, Stratford, NY, 1988; Metropolis, Piccadilly, 1989; My Fair Lady, NY, 1993; *ballet:* The Planets, Royal Ballet, 1990; Cruel Garden, 1992; has worked in most countries in Western Europe, also Bulgaria, Argentine, USA, Canada, Australia. London Drama Critics Award, Designer of the Year, 1967 (for Little Murders and As You Like It); (jtly) Gold Medal, Internat. Exhibn of Stage Design, Prague Quadriennale, 1975, 1979; Individual Silver Medal, Prague Quadriennale, 1987. *Recreation:* wildlife photography. *Address:* c/o London Management, 2–4 Noel Street, W1V 3RB. *T:* 0171–287 9000.

KONSTANT, Rt. Rev. David Every; *see* Leeds, Bishop of, (RC).

KOOPS, Hon. Dame Mary Claire; *see* Hogg, Hon. Dame M. C.

KOOTENAY, Archbishop of, since 1994; **Most Rev. David Perry Crawley;** Metropolitan of British Columbia and Yukon, since 1994; *b* 26 July 1937; *s* of Rev. Canon George Antony Crawley, LTh and Lucy Lillian Crawley (*née* Ball); *m* 1st, 1959, Frances Mary Louise Wilmot; two *d*; 2nd, 1986, Joan Alice Bubbs; one *d* (and one *d* decd). *Educ:* Univ. of Manitoba (BA 1958); St John's Coll., Winnipeg (LTh 1961; DD 1990); Univ. of Kent at Canterbury (MA 1967). Ordained Deacon 1961, Priest 1962. Incumbent, St Thomas', Sherwood Park, Edmonton, 1961–66; Canon Missioner, All Saints Cathedral, Edmonton, 1967–70; Rector, St Matthew's, Winnipeg, 1971–77; Archdeacon of Winnipeg, 1974–77; Archdeacon of Rupert's Land, 1977–81; Lectr, St John's College, Winnipeg, 1981–82; Rector, St Michael and All Angels, Regina, 1982–85; Rector, St Paul's, Vancouver, 1985–90; Bishop of Kootenay, 1990–. *Recreations:* ski-ing, hiking. *Address:* 1876 Richter Street, Kelowna, BC V1Y 2M9, Canada.

KOPELOWITZ, Dr (Jacob) Lionel (Garstein), JP; General Medical Practitioner, since 1953; *b* 9 Dec. 1926; *s* of Maurice and Mabel Kopelowitz; *m* 1980, Sylvia Waksman (*née* Galler). *Educ:* Clifton Coll., Bristol; Trinity Coll., Cambridge (MA 1947); University Coll. Hosp. London. MRCS, LRCP 1951; MRCGP 1964. Resident MO, London Jewish Hosp., 1951–52; Flying Officer, RAF Med. Branch, 1952–53. Member: General Medical Council, 1984–; General Optical Council, 1979–93; Standing Med. Adv. Cttee, DHSS, 1974–78; British Medical Association: Fellow, 1980; Mem. Council, 1982–94; Chm., Newcastle Div., 1968–69; Pres., Northern Regional Council, 1984–88; Mem., Gen. Med. Services Cttee, 1971–90 (Past Chm., Maternity Services Sub-Cttee); Chm., Central Adv. Cttee, Deputising Services, 1980–; Dep. Chm., Private Practice Cttee, 1972–89; Chm., St Marylebone and Bloomsbury Div., 1992–. Chm., Newcastle upon Tyne FPC, 1979–85; Pres., Soc. of FPCs of England and Wales, 1978–79; Vice-Pres., Trades Adv. Council, 1988–. President: Board of Deputies of British Jews, 1985–90; Nat. Council for Soviet Jewry, 1985–91; European Jewish Congress, 1986–91; Vice President: Conf. on Jewish Material Claims Against Germany, 1988–; Conf. on Jewish Material Claims Against Austria, 1988–. Member: Exec. Cttee, Meml Foundn for Jewish Culture, 1988–; United Synagogue, 1991–. Mem., Chm., Pres., numerous med. bodies and Jewish organisations, UK and overseas. Vice-Pres., British Council, Share Zedek Med. Centre, 1990–. Mem. Bd of Govs, Clifton Coll., Bristol, 1988–; Pres., Old Cliftonian Soc., 1991–93. Liveryman, Apothecaries' Co., 1969. JP Northumberland, 1964. Grand Cross, Order of Merit (Germany), 1993. *Publications:* articles in med. jls; contrib. to Med. Annual. *Recreations:* foreign travel, contract bridge. *Address:* 10 Cumberland House, Clifton Gardens, W9 1DX. *T:* 0171–289 6375. *Club:* Athenæum.

KORALEK, Paul George, CBE 1984; RA 1991 (ARA 1986); RIBA; Partner in Ahrends Burton and Koralek, architects, since 1961; *b* 7 April 1933; *s* of late Ernest and Alice Koralek; *m* 1958, Jennifer Chadwick; one *s* two *d*. *Educ:* Aldenham School; Architectural Assoc. School of Architecture. RIBA 1957; AA Dip. Hons. Architect: with Powell & Moya, London, 1956–57; with Marcel Breuer, New York, 1959–60. Part-time teaching, Sch. of Arch., Leicester Polytechnic, 1982–84. *Major projects include: public buildings:* Redcar Library, 1971; Maidenhead Libr., 1972; Roman Catholic Chaplaincy, Oxford, 1972; Nucleus Low Energy Hosp., IoW, 1982; winning entry, Nat. Gall. Extension Hampton Site Comp., 1982; Dover Heritage Centre, 1988–90; *educational buildings:* Chichester Theol Coll., 1965; Berkeley Libr., TCD, 1967 (1st Prize, Internat. Comp., 1961); Templeton Coll., Oxford, 1967; Arts Faculty Bldg, TCD, 1975–79; Portsmouth Polytechnic Libr., 1975–79; Residential bldg, Keble Coll., Oxford, 1976 (RIBA Arch. Award, 1978); *residential buildings:* houses, Dunstan Rd, Oxford, 1969; Nebenzahl House, Jerusalem, 1972; Chalvedon Housing, 1975–77; Whitmore Court Housing, Basildon, 1975 (RIBA Good Design in Housing Award, 1977); Felmore Housing, 1975–80; *commercial/industrial buildings:* Habitat Warehouse, Showroom and Offices, Wallingford, 1974 (Financial Times Indust. Arch. Award, and Structl Steel Design Award (Warehouse), 1976); factory bldgs and refurbishment, Cummins Engine Co., Shotts, Scotland, 1975–83 (Structl Steel Design Award, 1980); J. Sainsbury supermarket, Canterbury, 1984 (Structl Steel Design Award, 1985; FT Arch. at Work Award Commendation, 1986); W. H. Smith Offices, Greenbridge, 1985 (FT Arch. at Work Award Commendation, 1987); John Lewis Dept Store, Kingston-upon-Thames, 1987 (Civic Trust Commendation, 1991); White Cliffs Experience, Dover, 1991 (Civic Trust Award, 1992). *Exhibitions of drawings and works:* RIBA Heinz Gall., 1980; Douglas Hyde Gall. Dublin, 1981; Technical Univ. of Braunschweig and Tech. Univ. of Hanover, Germany, Mus. of Finnish Arch., Helsinki, Univ. of Oulu, and Alvar Aalto Mus., Jvasklya, Finland, 1982; HQ of AA, Oslo, 1983. Member: Develt Adv. (formerly Design and Architectural Rev.) Panel, Cardiff Bay Develt Corp., 1988–; ARCUK Bd of Architectural Educn, 1987–93; Trustee, Bldg Industry Youth Trust, 1981–95. External Examiner: Sch. of Arch., Univ. of Manchester, 1981–85; Plymouth Poly, 1988–; Competition Assessor: RIBA; ABS Housing; Irish Dept of Educn Schs comp.; Assessor: Civic Trust Awards; Cardiff Bay Opera House, 1994–95. Papers and lectures, UK and abroad, 1964–. *Publications:* paper and articles in RIBA and other prof. jls. *Recreations:* drawing, walking, gardening. *Address:* Unit 1, 7 Chalcot Road, NW1 8LH. *T:* 0171–586 3311.

KORNBERG, Prof. Arthur; Professor of Biochemistry, Stanford University, since 1959; *b* Brooklyn, 3 March 1918; *m*; three *s*. *Educ:* College of the City of New York (BSc 1937); University of Rochester, NY (MD 1941). Strong Memorial Hospital, Rochester, 1941–42; National Insts of Health, Bethesda, Md, 1942–52; Professor of Microbiology, Washington Univ., and Head of Dept of Microbiology, 1953–59; Head of Dept of Biochemistry, Stanford Univ., 1959–69. MNAS; MAAS; Mem. Amer. Phil Soc. Foreign Mem., Royal Soc., 1970. Many honours and awards, including: Paul Lewis Award in Enzyme Chemistry, 1951; Nobel Prize (joint) in Medicine, 1959; Nat Medal of Science, 1979. *Publications:* DNA Synthesis, 1974; DNA Replication, 1980 (Suppl., 1982); articles in scientific jls. *Address:* Stanford University Medical Center, Palo Alto, CA 94305–5307, USA.

KORNBERG, Prof. Sir Hans (Leo), Kt 1978; MA, DSc, ScD, PhD; FRS 1965; FIBiol 1965; University Professor and Professor of Biology, Boston University, since 1995; Sir William Dunn Professor of Biochemistry, University of Cambridge, 1975–95, and Fellow of Christ's College, since 1975 (Master, 1982–95); *b* 14 Jan. 1928; *o s* of Max Kornberg and Margarete Kornberg (*née* Silberbach); *m* 1st, 1956, Monica Mary King (*d* 1989); twin *s* two *d*; 2nd, 1991, Donna, *d* of William B. Haber and Ruth Haber. *Educ:* Queen Elizabeth Grammar Sch., Wakefield; University of Sheffield (BSc, PhD). MA Cantab 1956; DSc Oxon 1961; ScD Cantab 1961. Commonwealth Fund Fellow of Harkness Foundation, at Yale University and Public Health Research Inst., New York, 1953–55; Mem. of scientific staff, MRC Cell Metabolism Res. Unit, University of Oxford, 1955–60; Lectr, Worcester Coll., Oxford, 1958–61 (Hon. Fellow 1980); Prof. of Biochemistry, Univ. of Leicester, 1960–75. Visiting Instructor, Marine Biological Lab., Woods Hole, Mass, 1964–66, 1981–, Trustee, 1982–93. Dir, UK Nirex Ltd, 1986–95. Member: SRC, 1967–72 (Chm., Science Bd, 1969–72); UGC Biol. Sci. Cttee, 1967–77; NATO Adv. Study Inst. Panel, 1970–76 (Chm., 1974–75); Kuratorium, Max-Planck Inst., Dortmund, 1979–90 (Chm., Sci. Adv. Cttee); AFRC (formerly ARC), 1980–84; Priorities Bd for R & D in Agriculture, 1984–90; BP Venture Res. Council, 1981–91; ACARD, 1982–85; Adv. Council on Public Records, 1984–86; UK Cttee on Eur. Year of the Environment, 1986–88; Vice-Chm., EMBO, 1978–81; Chairman: Royal Commn on Environmental Pollution, 1976–81; Adv. Cttee on Genetic Modification, 1986–95; Co-ordinating Cttee on Environmental Res., Res. Councils, 1986–88; Sci. Adv. Cttee, Inst. for Mol. Biol. and Medicine, Monash Univ., 1987–; President: BAAS, 1984–85; Biochemical Soc., 1990–95; IUBMB, 1991–94; Assoc. for Science Educn, 1991–92; Vice-Pres., Inst. of Biol., 1971–73. A Managing Trustee, Nuffield Foundn, 1973–93; Trustee, Wellcome Trust, 1990–95; Academic Governor, Hebrew Univ. of Jerusalem, 1976 ; Governor: Weizmann Inst., 1980–; Lister Inst., 1990–95. Hon. Fellow: Brasenose Coll., Oxford, 1983; Wolfson Coll., Cambridge, 1990. FRSA 1972. Fellow, Amer. Acad. of Microbiol., 1992. For. Associate: Nat. Acad. of Sciences, USA, 1986; Amer. Philosoph. Soc., 1993; Member: Leopoldina German Acad. of Scis, 1982; Acad. Europaea, 1989; Hon. Member: Amer. Soc. Biol Chem., 1972; Biochem. Soc., FRG, 1973; Japanese Biochem. Soc., 1981; Hon. For. Mem., Amer. Acad. of Arts & Scis, 1987. Hon. ScD Cincinnati, 1974; Hon. DSc: Warwick, 1975; Leicester, 1979; Sheffield, 1979; Bath, 1980; Strathclyde, 1985; South Bank, 1994; Leeds, 1995; DUniv Essex, 1979; Dr med Leipzig, 1984. Colworth Medal of Biochemical Soc., 1965; Otto Warburg Medal, Biochem. Soc. of Federal Republic of Germany, 1973. *Publications:* (with Sir Hans Krebs) Energy Transformations in Living Matter, 1957; articles in scientific jls. *Recreations:* cooking and conversation. *Address:* The University Professors, 745 Commonwealth Avenue, Boston, MA 02215, USA; (home) 134 Sewall Avenue, # 2, Brookline, MA 02146, USA.

KORNER, Joanna Christian Mary; QC 1993; a Recorder, since 1995; *b* 1 July 1951; *d* of John Hugh George Korner and Martha (*née* Tupay von Isertingen). *Educ:* Queensgate Sch.; Inns of Court Sch. of Law. Called to the Bar, Inner Temple, 1974. *Recreations:* collecting books and porcelain, cinema, tennis. *Address:* 6 King's Bench Walk, Temple, EC4Y 7DR. *T:* 0171–583 0410.

KÖRNER, Prof. Stephan, JurDr, PhD; FBA 1967; Professor of Philosophy, Bristol University, 1952–79, and Yale University, 1970–84; *b* Ostrava, Czechoslovakia, 26 Sept. 1913; *o s* of Emil Körner and Erna (*née* Maier); *m* 1944, Edith Laner, CBE, BSc, LLD, JP; one *s* one *d*. *Educ:* Classical Gymnasium; Charles' Univ., Prague; Trinity Hall, Cambridge (Hon. Fellow, 1991). Army Service, 1936–39, 1943–46. University of Bristol: Lectr in Philosophy, 1946; Dean, Faculty of Arts, 1965–66; Pro-Vice-Chancellor, 1968–71; Hon. Fellow, 1987. Visiting Prof. of Philosophy: Brown Univ., 1957; Yale Univ., 1960; Texas Univ., 1964; Indiana Univ., 1967; Graz Univ., 1980–86 (Hon. Prof., 1982). President: Brit. Soc. for Philosophy of Science, 1965; Aristotelian Soc., 1967; Internat. Union of History and Philosophy of Science, 1969; Mind Assoc., 1973. Editor, Ratio, 1961–80. Hon. DLitt Belfast, 1981; Hon. Phil. Dr Graz, 1984. *Publications:* Kant, 1955; Conceptual Thinking, 1955; (ed) Observation and Interpretation, 1957; The Philosophy of Mathematics, 1960; Experience and Theory, 1966; Kant's Conception of Freedom (British Acad. Lecture), 1967; What is Philosophy?, 1969; Categorial Frameworks, 1970; Abstraction in Science and Morals (Eddington Meml Lecture), 1971; (ed) Practical Reason, 1974; (ed) Explanation, 1976; Experience and Conduct, 1976; Metaphysics: its structure and function, 1984; contribs to philosophical periodicals. *Recreation:* walking. *Address:* 10 Belgrave Road, Bristol BS8 2AB.

KOSSOFF, David; actor; author; illustrator; *b* 24 Nov. 1919; *s* of Louis and Anne Kossoff, both Russian; *m* 1947, Margaret (Jennie) Jenkins; one *s* (and one *s* decd). *Educ:* elementary sch.; Northern Polytechnic. Commercial Artist, 1937; Draughtsman, 1937–38; Furniture Designer, 1938–39; Technical Illustrator, 1939–45. Began acting, 1943; working as actor and illustrator, 1945–52, as actor and designer, 1952–. BBC Repertory Company, 1945–51. Took over part of Colonel Alexander Ikonenko in the Love of Four Colonels, Wyndham's, 1952; Sam Tager in The Shrike, Prince's, 1953; Morry in The Bespoke Overcoat, and Tobit in Tobias and the Angel, Arts, 1953; Prof. Lodegger in No Sign of the Dove, Savoy, 1953; Nathan in The Boychik, Embassy, 1954 (and again Morry in The Bespoke Overcoat); Mendele in The World of Sholom Aleichem, Embassy, 1955, and Johannesburg, 1957; one-man show, One Eyebrow Up, The Arts, 1957; Man on Trial,

Lyric, 1959; Stars in Your Eyes, Palladium, 1960; The Tenth Man, Comedy, 1961; Come Blow Your Horn, Prince of Wales, 1962; one-man show, Kossoff at the Prince Charles, 1963, later called A Funny Kind of Evening (many countries); Enter Solly Gold, Mermaid, 1970; Cinderella, Palladium, 1971; Bunny, Criterion, 1972; own Bible storytelling programmes on radio and TV, as writer and teller, 1964–66; solo performance (stage), 'As According to Kossoff', 1970–. Has appeared in many films. Won British Acad. Award, 1956. Elected MSIA 1958. FRSA 1969. Hon. DLitt, Hatfield Poly., 1990. *Play:* Big Night for Shylock, 1968. *Publications:* Bible Stories retold by David Kossoff, 1968; The Book of Witnesses, 1971; The Three Donkeys, 1972; The Voices of Masada, 1973; The Little Book of Sylvanus, 1975; You Have a Minute, Lord?, 1977; A Small Town is a World, 1979; Sweet Nutcracker, 1985. *Recreations:* conversation, working with the hands. *Address:* 45 Roe Green Close, Hatfield, Herts AL10 9PD.

KOSTERLITZ, Hans Walter, MD, PhD, DSc; FRCPE 1981; FRS 1978; FRSE 1951; Director, Unit for Research on Addictive Drugs, University of Aberdeen, since 1973; *b* 27 April 1903; *s* of Bernhard and Selma Kosterlitz; *m* 1937, Johanna Maria Katherina Gresshöner; one *s*. *Educ:* Univs of Heidelberg, Freiburg and Berlin. MD Berlin 1929; PhD 1936, DSc 1944, Hon. LLD 1979, Aberdeen. Assistant, 1st Medical Dept, Univ. of Berlin, 1928–33; University of Aberdeen: Research Worker in Physiology, 1934–36; Asst and Carnegie Teaching Fellow, 1936–39; Lectr, 1939–45; Sen. Lectr, 1945–55; Reader in Physiology, 1955–68; Prof. of Pharmacology and Chm., 1968–73. Visiting Lecturer: in Pharmacology, Harvard Med. Sch., 1953–54; in Biology, Brown Univ., 1953; Vis. Prof. of Pharmacology, Harvard Med. Sch., 1977; Lectures: J. Y. Dent Meml, 1970; Otto Krayer, 1977; Scheele, 1977; Gen. Session, Fedn Amer. Socs for Experimental Biol., 1978; Sutcliffe Kerr, 1978; Charnock Bradley Meml, 1979; Arnold H. Maloney, 1979; Lister, 1980; Lita Annenberg Hazen, 1980; Lilly, 1980; Sherrington Meml, RSocMed, 1982; N. J. Giarman Meml, Yale Univ. Sch. of Med., 1982; Third Transatlantic, Endocrine Soc., 1982; Lorenzini, Milan, 1982; Sherrington, Univ. of Liverpool, 1989. Foreign Associate, National Acad. of Sciences, USA, 1985. Dr *hc* Liège, 1978; Hon. DSc St Andrews, 1982; Hon. LLD Dundee, 1988. Schmiedeberg Plakette, German Pharmacol Soc., 1976; Pacesetter Award, US Nat. Inst. on Drug Abuse, 1977; Nathan B. Eddy Award, US Cttee on Problems of Drug Dependence, 1978; (jtly) Albert Lasker Prize, 1978; Baly Medal, RCP, 1979; Royal Medal, 1979, Wellcome Foundn Prize, 1982, Royal Soc.; Makdougall-Brisbane Medal, RSE, 1980; Thudichum Medal, Biochem. Soc., 1980; Feldberg Foundn Prize, 1981; Harvey Prize, Technion, 1981; Prof. Lucien Dautrebande Prize, 1982; Wellcome Gold Medal, British Pharmacol Soc., 1987; Cameron Prize, Univ. of Edinburgh, 1988. *Publications:* (joint editor): Agonist and Antagonist Actions of Narcotic Analgesic Drugs, 1972; The Opiate Narcotics, 1975; Opiates and Endogenous Opioid Peptides, 1976; Pain and Society, 1980; Neuroactive Peptides, 1980; Opioids 1 and 2, 1993; articles in Nature, Jl of Physiol, Brit. Jl of Pharmacol. *Recreations:* music, walking, travelling. *Address:* Unit for Research on Addictive Drugs, University of Aberdeen, Aberdeen AB9 1AS. *T:* Aberdeen (01224) 273000; 16 Glendee Terrace, Cults, Aberdeen AB1 9HX. *T:* Aberdeen (01224) 867366. *Club:* Lansdowne.

KOTCH, Laurie, (Mrs J. K. Kotch); *see* Purden, R. L.

KOTSOKOANE, Hon. Joseph Riffat Larry; Commander, Order of Ramatseatsana, 1982; development consultant (human and natural resources), since 1986; Minister of Education, Sports and Culture, Lesotho, 1984–86; *b* 19 Oct. 1922; *s* of Basotho parents, living in Johannesburg, South Africa; *m* 1947, Elizabeth (*née* Molise); two *s* three *d*. BSc (SA); BSc Hons (Witwatersrand); Cert. Agric. (London). Development Officer, Dept of Agric., Basutoland, 1951–54; Agric. Educn Officer i/c of Agric. Sch. for junior field staff, 1955–62; Agric. Extension Officer i/c of all field staff of Min. of Agric., 1962–63; Prin. Agric. Off. (Dep. Dir), Min. of Agric., 1964–66; High Comr for Lesotho, in London, 1966–69; Ambassador to Germany, Holy See, Rome, France, and Austria, 1968–69; Permanent Sec. and Hd of Diplomatic Service, Lesotho, 1969–70; Permanent Sec. for Health, Educn and Social Welfare, Lesotho, 1970–71; High Comr for Lesotho in East Africa, Nigeria and Ghana, 1972–74; Minister: of Foreign Affairs, Lesotho, 1974–75; of Education, 1975–76; of Agriculture, 1976–78; Perm. Rep. to UN, 1978; Sec. to the Cabinet and Head of CS (Sen. Perm. Sec.), 1978–84. Guest of Min. of Agric., Netherlands, 1955; studied agric. educn, USA (financed by Carnegie Corp. of NY and Ford Foundn), 1960–61; FAO confs in Tunisia, Tanganyika and Uganda, 1962 and 1963; Mem. Lesotho delegn to 24th World Health Assembly, 1971; travelled extensively to study and observe methods of agric. administration, 1964; meetings on nutrition, Berlin and Hamburg, 1966; diplomatic trainee, Brit. Embassy, Bonn, 1966. *Recreations:* swimming, tennis, amateur dramatics, photography, debating, reading, travelling. *Address:* PO Box 1015, Maseru 100, Lesotho, Southern Africa.

KOVACEVICH, Stephen; pianist and conductor; *b* 17 Oct. 1940; *s* of Nicholas Kovacevich and Loreta (*née* Zuban, later Bishop). *Educ:* studied under Lev Shorr and Myra Hess. Solo and orchestral debut, San Francisco, USA 1951; London debut, Nov. 1961. First known professionally as Stephen Bishop, then as Stephen Bishop-Kovacevich, and since 1991 as Stephen Kovacevich. Concert tours: in England, Europe and USA, with many of the world's leading orchestras, incl. New York Philharmonic, Los Angeles Philharmonic, Israel Philharmonic, Amsterdam Concertgebouw, London Symphony, London Philharmonic, and BBC Symphony. Has appeared at Edinburgh, Bath, Berlin and San Sebastian Festivals. Gave 1st performance of Richard Rodney Bennett's Piano Concerto, 1969 (this work is dedicated to and has been recorded by him, under Alexander Gibson). Performed all Mozart Piano concertos, 1969–71. Principal Guest Conductor: Australian Chamber Orch., 1987–91; Zagreb Philharmonic Orch.; Music Dir, Irish Chamber Orch., 1990–93. Edison Award for his recording of Bartok's 2nd Piano Concerto and Stravinsky's Piano Concerto, with BBC Symphony Orchestra, under Colin Davis; Gramophone Award, 1993 and Stereo Review Record of the Year for Brahms' Piano Concerto No 1 with LPO, under Wolfgang Sawallisch. *Recreations:* snooker, chess, films, tennis. *Address:* c/o Van Walsum Management, 26 Wadham Road, SW15 2LR. *T:* 0181–874 6344.

KOWALSKI, Gregor; Scottish Parliamentary Counsel, since 1987 and Assistant Legal Secretary to Lord Advocate, since 1978; *b* 7 Oct. 1949; *s* of Mieczyslaw Kowalski and Jeanie Hutcheson Kowalski (*née* MacDonald); *m* 1974, Janet McFarlane Pillatt; two *s*. *Educ:* Airdrie Academy; Strathclyde Univ. (LLB 1971). Apprentice, then Asst Solicitor, Levy & McRae, Glasgow, 1971–74; Procurator Fiscal Depute, Glasgow, 1974–78; Asst, later Deputy Parly Draftsman for Scotland and Asst Legal Sec. to Lord Advocate, 1978–87; seconded to Govt of Seychelles as Legal Draftsman, 1982–83. Founding Mem. and Sec., Soc. of Scottish Lawyers in London, 1987–89 (Vice Pres., 1989–91; Pres., 1991–92). *Recreations:* singing, music. *Address:* Lord Advocate's Chambers, 2 Carlton Gardens, SW1Y 5AA. *T:* 0171–210 1053.

KRAEMER, (Thomas Whilhelm) Nicholas; conductor; *b* 7 March 1945; *s* of William Paul Kraemer and Helen Bartrum; *m* 1984, Elizabeth Mary Anderson; two *s* two *d* (and one *s* decd). *Educ:* Edinburgh Acad.; Lancing Coll.; Dartington Coll. of Arts; Nottingham Univ. (BMus 1967). ARCM. Harpsichordist with Acad. of St Martin in the Fields, 1972–80, with Monteverdi Choir and Orchestra, 1970–80; Musical Director: Unicorn Opera, Abingdon, 1971–75; West Eleven Children's Opera, 1971–88; Founder and Dir, Raglan Baroque Players, 1978–; Principal Conductor, Divertimenti, 1979–; Principal Guest Conductor, Manchester Camerata, 1995– (Principal Conductor, 1992–95); Conductor, Glyndebourne, 1980–82; Musical Dir, Opera 80, 1980–83; Associate Conductor, BBC Scottish SO, 1983–85; Artistic Director: London Bach Orch., 1985–; Irish Chamber Orch., 1985–90; Prog. Dir, Bath Fest., 1994. Recordings include: Vivaldi and Music from Versailles, and of Locatelli Concerti Op. 1 and 3, with Raglan Baroque Players; of Mozart piano concertos, with Linda Nicolson and Capella Coloniensis. *Recreations:* active fatherhood, keeping fit. *Address:* c/o Ron Gonsalves Management, 7 Old Town, Clapham, SW4 0JT. *T:* 0171–622 2244.

KRAFT, Rt. Rev. Richard Austin; *see* Pretoria, Bishop of.

KRAMER, Prof. Ivor Robert Horton, OBE 1984; MDS; DSc (Med); FDSRCS, FFDRCSI, Hon. FRACDS, FRCPath; Emeritus Professor of Oral Pathology, University of London; Hon. Consultant, Mount Vernon Hospital, Northwood; *b* 20 June 1923; *yr s* of late Alfred Bertie and Agnes Maud Kramer; *m* 1st, 1946, Elisabeth Dalley (*d* 1978); one *s*; 2nd, 1979, Mrs Dorothy Toller (*d* 1985); 3rd, 1991, Mrs Virginia Webster. *Educ:* Royal Dental Hosp. of London Sch. of Dental Surgery; MDS 1955; DSc (Med) London 1993. FDSRCS 1960 (LDSRCS 1944); FRCPath 1970 (MCRPath 1964); FFDRCSI 1973. Asst to Pathologist, Princess Louise (Kensington) Hosp. for Children, 1944–48; Wright Fleming Inst. of Microbiol., 1948–49; Instr in Dental Histology, Royal Dental Hosp. Sch. of Dental Surgery, 1944–50; Asst Pathologist, Royal Dental Hosp., 1950–56; Institute of Dental Surgery: Lectr in Dental Path., 1949–50, Sen. Lectr, 1950–57; Reader in Oral Path., 1957–62; Prof. of Oral Path., 1962–83; Sub-dean, 1950–70; Dean and Dir of Studies, 1970–83; Head, Dept of Path., Eastman Dental Hosp., 1950–83. Civilian Cons. in Dental Path., RN, 1967–83. Member: WHO Expert Adv. Panel on Dental Health, 1975–; Bd of Faculty of Dental Surgery, RCS, 1964–80, Council, RCS, 1977–80; GDC, 1973–84; Mem., Council for Postgrad. Med. Educn in Eng. and Wales, 1972–77 (Chm., Dental Cttee, 1972–77); Pres., Odontological Section, RSocMed, 1973–74; Pres., British Div., Internat. Assoc. for Dental Res., 1974–77. Hon. Pres. of the Assoc., 1974–75. Editor, Archives of Oral Biology, 1959–69. Lectures: Wilkinson, Manchester, 1962; Charles Tomes, 1969, Webb Johnson, 1981, RCS; Holme, UCH, 1969; Elwood Meml, QUB, 1970; Hutchinson, Edinburgh, 1971; Wilkinson, IDS, 1987. Hon. FRACDS 1978. Howard Mummery Prize, BDA, 1966; Maurice Down Award, Brit. Assoc. of Oral Surgeons, 1974; Colyer Gold Medal, FDS, RCS, 1985. *Publications:* (with R. B. Lucas) Bacteriology for Students of Dental Surgery, 1954, 3rd edn 1966; (with J. J. Pindborg and H. Torloni) World Health Organization International Histological Classification of Tumours: Odontogenic Tumours, Jaw Cysts and Allied Lesions, 1972 (2nd edn, with J. J. Pindborg and M. Shear, as World Health Organisation Histological Typing of Odontogenic Tumours, 1992); (with B. Cohen) Scientific Foundations of Dentistry, 1976; numerous papers in med. and dental jls. *Address:* 11 Sheepcote Close, Beaconsfield, Bucks HP9 1SX. *T:* Beaconsfield (01494) 680306.

KRAMER, Prof. Dame Leonie (Judith), AC 1993; DBE 1983 (OBE 1976); DPhil; Professor of Australian Literature, University of Sydney, 1968–89, now Professor Emeritus; Chancellor, University of Sydney Senate, since 1991 (Deputy Chancellor, 1989–91); Director: Australia and New Zealand Banking Group, since 1983; Western Mining Corporation Ltd, since 1984; Chairman, Quadrant Magazine Co. Ltd, since 1988; *b* 1 Oct. 1924; *d* of Alfred and Gertrude Gibson; *m* 1952, Harold Kramer; two *d*. *Educ:* Presbyterian Ladies Coll., Melbourne; Univ. of Melbourne (BA 1945); St Hugh's Coll., Oxford Univ. (DPhil 1953; Hon. Fellow, 1994); MA Sydney, 1989. FAHA; FACE. Tutor and Lectr, Univ. of Melb., 1945–49; Tutor and Postgrad. Student, St Hugh's Coll., Oxford, 1949–52; Lectr, Canberra University Coll., 1954–56; Lectr, subseq. Sen. Lectr and Associate Prof., Univ. of NSW, 1958–68. Member: Univs Council, 1977–; Bd of Studies, NSW, 1989–. Comr, Electricity Commn, NSW, 1988–. Chm., ABC, 1982–83; Dep. Chm. Bd of Dirs, Nat. Inst. of Dramatic Art, 1992– (Chm., 1987–92). Dir, St Vincent's Hosp., Sydney, 1988–93. Mem. Council, Nat. Roads & Motorists Assoc., 1984–; Nat. Pres., Australia–Britain Soc., 1984–93. Sen. Fellow, Inst. of Public Affairs, 1988–. Hon. DLitt: Tasmania, 1977; Queensland, 1991; New South Wales, 1992; Hon. LLD: Melbourne, 1983; ANU, 1984. Britannica Award, 1986. *Publications:* as L. J. Gibson: Henry Handel Richardson and Some of Her Sources, 1954; as Leonie Kramer: A Companion to Australia Felix, 1962; Myself when Laura: fact and fiction in Henry Handel Richardson's school career, 1966; Henry Handel Richardson, 1967, repr. as contrib. to Six Australian Writers, 1971; (with Robert D. Eagleson) Language and Literature: a synthesis, 1976; (with Robert D. Eagleson) A Guide to Language and Literature, 1977; A. D. Hope, 1979; (ed and introd) The Oxford History of Australian Literature, 1981; (ed with Adrian Mitchell) The Oxford Anthology of Australian Literature, 1985; (ed and introd) My Country: Australian poetry and short stories—two hundred years, 1985; (ed and introd) James McAuley, 1988; (ed) Collected Poems of David Campbell, 1989. *Recreations:* gardening, music. *Address:* 12 Vaucluse Road, Vaucluse, NSW 2030, Australia. *T:* 3719686.

KRAMER, Stephen Ernest; QC 1995; a Recorder, since 1991; *b* 12 Sept. 1947; *s* of Frederic Kramer and Lotte Karoline Kramer (*née* Weitheimer); *m* 1978, Miriam Leopold; one *s* one *d*. *Educ:* Hampton Grammar Sch.; Keble Coll., Oxford (BA 1969; MA 1987); Université de Nancy. Called to the Bar, Gray's Inn, 1970; Standing Counsel to HM Customs and Excise (Crime), S Eastern Circuit, 1989–95. Contested (L), Twickenham, Feb. and Oct. 1974. *Recreations:* swimming, walking, shouting at the children. *Address:* 1 Hare Court, Temple, EC4Y 7BE. *T:* 0171–353 5324.

KREBS, Prof. Edwin Gerhard, MD; Professor, Departments of Pharmacology and Biochemistry, University of Washington, Seattle, 1983–88, now Professor Emeritus (Professor and Chairman, Department of Pharmacology, 1977–83); *b* 6 June 1918, Iowa; *m* 1945, Virginia French; one *s* two *d*. *Educ:* Univ. of Illinois (AB Chem. 1940); Washington Univ. Sch. of Med., St Louis, Mo (MD 1943). Intern and Asst Resident in Internal Med., Barnes Hosp., St Louis, Mo, 1944–45; Res. Fellow, Washington Univ. Sch. of Med., St Louis, 1946–48; University of Washington, Seattle: Asst Prof. of Biochem., 1948–52; Associate Prof., 1952–57; Prof., 1957–68; Asst Dean for Planning, Sch. of Med., 1966–68; Prof. and Chm., Dept of Biol Chem., Sch. of Med., Univ. of Calif, Davis, 1968–76; Howard Hughes Medical Institute: Investigator, 1977–80; Sen. Investigator, 1980–90, Emeritus, 1991–. Member: Editl Bd, Jl Biol Chem., 1965–70 (Associate Ed., 1972–93); Editl Adv. Bd, Biochem., 1971–76; Editl and Adv. Bd, Molecular Pharmacol., 1972–77; Editl Advr, Molecular and Cellular Biochem., 1987–. Member: Amer. Soc. for Biochem. and Molecular Biol., 1951–; Amer. Acad. Arts and Scis, 1971–; Nat. Acad. Scis, 1973–; Amer. Soc. Pharmacology and Exptl Therapeutics, 1980–. Hon. DSc Geneva, 1979. Numerous awards; (jtly) Nobel Prize in Physiology or Medicine, 1992. *Address:* Department of Pharmacology and Biochemistry, University of Washington SL–15, Seattle, WA 98195, USA.

KREBS, Prof. John Richard, DPhil; FRS 1984; Chief Executive, Natural Environment Research Council, since 1994; Fellow, Pembroke College, Oxford, since 1981 (E. P. Abraham Fellow, 1981–88); *b* 11 April 1945; *s* of Sir Hans Adolf Krebs, FRCP, FRS and

Margaret Cicely Krebs; *m* 1968, Katherine Anne Fullerton; two *d*. *Educ:* City of Oxford High School; Pembroke College, Oxford. BA 1966; MA 1970; DPhil 1970. Asst Prof., Univ. of British Columbia, 1970–73; Lectr in Zoology, UCNW, 1973–75; Univ. Lectr in Zoology, Oxford Univ., 1976–88; Royal Soc. Res. Prof., Dept of Zoology, Oxford Univ., 1988–94. Dir, AFRC Unit of Ecology and Behaviour, NERC Unit of Behavioural Ecology, 1989–94. Storer Lectr, Univ. of Calif, 1985. Mem., AFRC, 1988–94 (Animals Res. Cttee, 1990–94; sen. scientific consultant, 1991–94). President: Internat. Soc. for Behavioral Ecology, 1988–90; Assoc. for the Study of Animal Behaviour, 1993–. Scientific Mem., Max Planck Soc., 1985–. Mem. Council, Zoological Soc. of London, 1991–92. Hon. DSc Sheffield, 1993. Scientific Medal, Zool. Soc., 1981; Bicentenary Medal, Linnaean Soc., 1983. *Publications:* Behavioural Ecology, 1978, 3rd edn 1991; Introduction to Behavioural Ecology, 1981, 3rd edn 1993; Foraging Theory, 1986; Behavioural and Neural Aspects of Learning and Memory, 1991; articles in Animal Behaviour, Jl of Animal Ecology. *Recreations:* gardening, violin, running. *Address:* Natural Environment Research Council, Polaris House, North Star Avenue, Swindon SN2 1EU. *T:* Swindon (01793) 411500.

KREISEL, Prof. Georg, FRS 1966; Professor Emeritus of Logic and the Foundations of Mathematics, Stanford University, Stanford, California, USA; *b* 15 Sept. 1923. *Address:* Institut für Wissenschaftstheorie, Internationales Forschungszentrum, Mönchsberg 2, 5020 Salzburg, Austria.

KREMER, Gidon; violinist; *b* 27 Feb. 1947. *Educ:* Riga Sch. of Music; Moscow Conservatory. First Prize, Internat. Tchaikovsky Competition, Moscow, 1970. Has played with most major internat. orchestras including: Berlin Philharmonic; Boston Symphony; Concertgebouw; London Philharmonic; LA Philharmonic; NY Philharmonic; Philadelphia; Royal Philharmonic; Vienna Philharmonic. Founded Lockenhaus Fest., Austria, 1981. *Address:* c/o ICM Artists, 40 West 57th Street, New York, NY 10019, USA.

KRETZMER, Herbert; journalist and lyricist; *b* Kroonstad, OFS, S Africa, 5 Oct. 1925; *s* of William and Tilly Kretzmer; *m* 1st, 1961, Elisabeth Margaret Wilson (marr. diss., 1973); one *s* one *d*; 2nd, 1988, Sybil Sever. *Educ:* Kroonstad High Sch.; Rhodes Univ., Grahamstown. Entered journalism, 1946, writing weekly cinema newsreel commentaries and documentary films for African Film Productions, Johannesburg. Reporter and entertainment columnist, Sunday Express, Johannesburg, 1951–54; feature writer and columnist, Daily Sketch, London, 1954–59; Columnist, Sunday Dispatch, London, 1959–61; theatre critic, Daily Express, 1962–78; TV critic, Daily Mail, 1979–87. TV Critic of the Year, Philips Industries Award, 1980; commended in British Press Awards, 1981. As lyric writer, contributed weekly songs to: That Was The Week . ., Not So Much A Programme . ., BBC 3, That's Life. Wrote lyrics of Goodness Gracious Me, 1960 (Ivor Novello Award) and Yesterday When I was Young, 1969 (ASCAP award); Gold record for She, 1974; Our Man Crichton, Shaftesbury Theatre, 1964 (book and lyrics); The Four Musketeers, Drury Lane, 1967 (lyrics); Les Misérables, RSC, 1985 (lyrics (Tony Award, 1987; Grammy Award, 1988)); *film:* Can Heironymus Merkin Ever Forget Mercy Humppe And Find True Happiness?, 1969 (lyrics); has also written lyrics for other films, and for TV programmes. Jimmy Kennedy Award, British Acad. of Songwriters, Composers and Authors, 1989. Chevalier de L'Ordre des Arts et des Lettres, 1988. *Publications:* Our Man Crichton, 1965; (jointly) Every Home Should Have One, 1970. *Address:* c/o London Management, 235/241 Regent Street, W1A 2JT. *Club:* Royal Automobile.

KRIKLER, Dennis Michael, MD; FRCP; Consultant Cardiologist, Hammersmith Hospital, and Senior Lecturer in Cardiology, Royal Postgraduate Medical School, 1973–94; *b* 10 Dec. 1928; *s* of late Barnet and Eva Krikler; *m* 1955, Anne (*née* Winterstein); one *s* one *d*. *Educ:* Muizenberg High Sch.; Univ. of Cape Town, S Africa. Ho. Phys. and Registrar, Groote Schuur Hosp., 1952–55; Fellow, Lahey Clinic, Boston, 1956; C. J Adams Meml Travelling Fellowship, 1956; Sen. Registrar, Groote Schuur Hosp., 1957–58; Consultant Physician: Salisbury Central Hosp., Rhodesia, 1958–66; Prince of Wales's Hosp., London, 1966–73; Consultant Cardiologist, Ealing Hosp., 1973–89. Expert Clinicien en Cardiologie, Ministère des Affaires Sociales, Santé, France, 1983. Visiting Professor: Baylor, Indiana and Birmingham Univs, 1985; Boston, Los Angeles and Kentucky, 1988; Lectures: Internat., Amer. Heart Assoc., 1984 (Paul Dudley White Citation for internat. achievement); George Burch Meml, Assoc. of Univ. Cardiologists, 1989; Joseph Welker Meml, Univ. of Kansas, 1989; Denolin, Eur. Soc. of Cardiology, 1990; Hideo Ueda, Japanese Soc. of Electrocardiology, 1990; Howard Burchell, Univ. of Minnesota, 1991. Member, British Cardiac Soc., 1971– (Treasurer, 1976–81); Hon. Member: Soc. Française de Cardiologie, 1981–; Soc. di Cultura Medica Vercellese, Italy; Soc. de Cardiologia de Levante, Spain. Editor, British Heart Journal, 1981–91; Member, Editorial Committee: Cardiovascular Res., 1975–91; Archives des Maladies du Coeur et des Vaisseaux, 1980–; Revista Latina de Cardiologia, 1980–; ACCEL Audiotape Jl, 1987–. Mem. Scientific Council, Revista Portuguesa de Cardiologia, 1982–. FACC 1971; Fellow, Eur. Soc. of Cardiology, 1989 (Medal of Honour, 1990). Hon. Fellow, Council on Clin. Cardiol., Amer. Heart Assoc., 1984. Freeman: Soc. of Apothecaries, 1989; City of London, 1990. McCullough Prize, 1949; Sir William Osler Award, Miami Univ., 1981. *Publications:* Cardiac Arrhythmias (with J. F. Goodwin), 1975; (with A. Zanchetti) Calcium antagonism in cardiovascular therapy, 1981; (with D. A. Chamberlain and W. J. McKenna) Amiodarone and arrhythmias, 1983; (with P. G. Hugenholtz) Workshop on calcium antagonists, 1984; papers on cardiology in British, American and French jls. *Recreations:* reading (and also writing), especially history (contemporary and cardiological); photography. *Address:* 55 Wimpole Street, W1M 7DF. *T:* 0171–935 2098.

KRIKLER, Leonard Gideon; His Honour Judge Krikler; a Circuit Judge, since 1984; *b* 23 May 1929; *s* of late Major James Harold Krikler, OBE, ED, and Tilly Krikler; *m* 1st, 1955, Dr Thilla Krikler (*d* 1973); four *s*; 2nd, 1975, Lily Appleson; one *s*, and one step *s* two step *d*. *Educ:* Milton Sch., Bulawayo, S Rhodesia (Zimbabwe). Called to Bar, Middle Temple, 1953. Crown Counsel, Court Martial Appeals Court, 1968; Dep. Circuit Judge, 1974; a Recorder, 1980–84. Head of Chambers, London and Cambridge, 1975–84. *Recreations:* cartooning, carpentry, painting. *Address:* Lamb Building, Temple, EC4Y 7AS. *T:* 0171–797 7788.

KRIKORIAN, Gregory, CB 1973; Solicitor for the Customs and Excise, 1971–78; *b* 23 Sept. 1913; *s* of late Kevork and late Christine Krikorian; *m* 1943, Seta Mary (*d* 1995), *d* of Souren Djirdjirian; one *d*. *Educ:* Polytechnic Secondary Sch.; Lincoln Coll., Oxford (BA). Called to Bar, Middle Temple, 1939; practised at Bar, 1939; BBC Overseas Intell. Dept, 1940; served in RAF as Intell. Officer, Fighter Comd, 1940–45 (despatches); practised at Bar, 1945–51, Junior Oxford Circuit, 1947; joined Solicitor's Office, HM Customs and Excise, 1951. *Publication:* (jtly) Customs and Excise, in Halsbury's Laws of England, 1975. *Recreations:* gardening, bird-watching. *Address:* The Coach House, Hawkchurch, Axminster, Devon EX13 5TX. *T:* Hawkchurch (01297) 678414. *Clubs:* Reform, Civil Service.

KRISH, Tanya, (Mrs Felix Krish); *see* Moiseiwitsch, T.

KRISTIANSEN, Erling (Engelbrecht), Grand Cross, Order of Dannebrog; Hon. GCVO 1974; Director, East Asiatic Co., 1978–90, and other companies; *b* 31 Dec. 1912; *s* of Kristian Engelbrecht Kristiansen, Chartered Surveyor, and Andrea Kirstine (*née* Madsen); *m* 1938, Annemarie Selinko (*d* 1986), novelist. *Educ:* Herning Gymnasium; University of Copenhagen (degree awarded equiv. of MA Econ). Postgraduate Studies, Economics and Internat. Relations, Geneva, Paris, London, 1935–37. Sec.-Gen., 1935, Pres. 1936, of the Fédération Universitaire Internationale pour la Société des Nations. Danish Civil Servant, 1941; served with: Free Danish Missions, Stockholm, 1943; Washington, 1944; London, 1945; joined Danish Diplomatic Service and stayed in London until 1947; Danish Foreign Ministry, 1947–48; Head of Denmark's Mission to OEEC, Paris, 1948–50; Sec. to Economic Cttee of Cabinet, 1950–51; Asst Under-Sec. of State, 1951; Dep. Under-Sec. of State (Economic Affairs), Danish For. Min., 1954–64; Ambassador to UK, 1964–77 (concurrently accredited to Republic of Ireland, 1964–73); Doyen of the Diplomatic Corps, 1973–77; retd 1977. Dir, S. G. Warburg & Co. International Holdings Ltd, 1980–84; Mem., Internat. Adv. Bd, S. G. Warburg & Co., 1984–86, Mercury Internat. Gp, 1986–90; Nordic Investment Bank: Dir, 1977–86; Vice-Chm., 1977–78; Chm., 1978–80. Co-founder and Bd Mem., CARE, Denmark, 1987–91. Grand Officier, Légion d'Honneur; Kt Comdr: Order of St Olav; Order of White Rose of Finland; Star of Ethiopia; Knight Grand Cross, Icelandic Falcon; Comdr, Order of Northern Star of Sweden. *Publication:* Folkeforbundet (The League of Nations), 1938. *Recreations:* ski-ing, fishing and other out-door sports, modern languages. *Address:* Kratkrogen 8, 2920, Charlottenlund, Denmark. *Clubs:* MCC; Special Forces *et al*.

KRIWET, Dr Heinz; Chairman, Executive Board, Thyssen AG, Düsseldorf, since 1991; *b* Bochum, 2 Nov. 1931. *Educ:* Univs of Köln and Freiburg (Masters degree 1957; Dr rer. pol. 1959). Trainee, German Iron and Steel Fedn, 1960–61; Hüttenwerk Rheinhausen (Krupp), 1962–67; Gen. Manager, Sales, 1968, Mem. Exec. Bd i/c Sales, Friedrich Krupp Hüttenwerke AG, Bochum, 1969–72; Mem. Exec. Bd i/c Sales, Thyssen AG, Düsseldorf, 1973–83; Chm. Exec. Bd, Thyssen Stahl AG, Duisburg, 1983–91. *Address:* Thyssen AG, August Thyssen-Strasse 1, 4000 Düsseldorf 1, Germany. *T:* (211) 8241.

KROHN, Dr Peter Leslie, FRS 1963; Professor of Endocrinology, University of Birmingham, 1962–66; *b* 8 Jan. 1916; *s* of Eric Leslie Krohn and Doris Ellen Krohn (*née* Wade); *m* 1941, Joanna Mary French; two *s*. *Educ:* Sedbergh; Balliol Coll., Oxford. BA 1st Cl. Hons Animal Physiol, 1937; BM, BCh Oxon, 1940. Wartime Research work for Min. of Home Security, 1940–45; Lectr, then Reader in Endocrinology, University of Birmingham, 1946–53; Nuffield Sen. Gerontological Research Fellow and Hon. Prof. in University, 1953–62. *Publications:* contrib. to scientific jls on physiology of reproduction, transplantation immunity and ageing. *Recreations:* scuba diving, mountain walking. *Address:* Coburg House, New St John's Road, St Helier, Jersey, Channel Islands JE2 3LD. *T:* Jersey (01534) 74870.

KROLL, Natasha, RDI 1966; FCSD; freelance television and film designer; *b* Moscow, 20 May 1914; *d* of Dr (phil.) Hermann Kroll and Sophie (*née* Rabinovich). *Educ:* Berlin. Teacher of window display, Reimann Sch. of Art, London, 1936–40; Display Manager: Messrs Rowntrees, Scarborough and York, 1940–42; Simpson Piccadilly Ltd, 1942–55; Sen. Designer, BBC TV, 1955–66: programmes include: Monitor, Panorama, science programmes, Lower Depths, Death of Danton, The Duel, Ring Round the Moon, La Traviata, Day by the Sea, The Sponge Room and many others; freelance designer, 1966–; TV designs include: The Seagull, 1966; Family Reunion, 1966; Eugene Onegin, 1967; The Soldier's Tale, 1968; La Vida Breve, 1968; Mary Stuart, 1968; Doll's House, 1969; Three Sisters, Cherry Orchard, Rasputin, Wild Duck, 1971, Summer and Smoke, Hedda Gabler, 1972; The Common, 1973; Lady from the Sea, 1974, Love's Labour's Lost, 1975; Very Like a Whale, 1980; production-designer of: The Music Lovers, 1970; The Hireling, 1973 (FTA Film award for best Art Direction); Summer Rag-time, 1976; Absolution, 1978. *Publication:* Window Display, 1954. *Recreations:* painting, family, entertaining. *Address:* 5 Ruvigny Gardens, SW15 1JR. *T:* 0181–788 1556.

KROLL, Rev. Dr Una (Margaret Patricia), CJC; writer and broadcaster, since 1970; Deacon of the Church in Wales, since 1988; *b* 15 Dec. 1925; *d* of George Hill, CBE, DSO, MC, and Hilda Hill; *m* 1957, Leopold Kroll (*d* 1987); one *s* three *d*. *Educ:* St Paul's Girls' Sch.; Malvern Girls' Coll.; Girton Coll., Cambridge; The London Hosp. MB, BChir (Cantab) 1951; MA 1969. MRCGP 1967. House Officer, 1951–53; Overseas service (Africa), 1953–60; General Practice, 1960–81; Clinical MO, 1981–85, Sen. Clinical MO, 1985–88, Hastings Health Dist. Theological trng, 1967–70; worker deaconess, 1970–88; Sister, Soc. of the Sacred Cross, 1991–94; political work as a feminist, with particular ref. to status of women in the churches in England and internationally, 1970–. Mem., Provincial Validating Bd, Church in Wales, 1989–. *Publications:* Transcendental Meditation: a signpost to the world, 1974; Flesh of My Flesh: a Christian view on sexism, 1975; Lament for a Lost Enemy: study of reconciliation, 1976; Sexual Counselling, 1980; The Spiritual Exercise Book, 1985; Growing Older, 1988; In Touch with Healing, 1991; Vocation to Resistance, 1995; contrib. Cervical Cytology (BMJ), 1969. *Recreation:* doing nothing. *Address:* St Mary's Lodge, Priory Street, Monmouth, Gwent NP5 3BR.

KROTO, Prof. Harold Walter, FRS 1990; Royal Society Research Professor, University of Sussex, since 1991 (Professor of Chemistry, 1985–91); *b* 7 Oct. 1939; *s* of Heinz and Edith Kroto; *m* 1963, Margaret Henrietta Hunter; two *s*. *Educ:* Bolton Sch.; Univ. of Sheffield (BSc, PhD). Res. in fullerenes spectroscopy, radioastronomy, clusters and nucleation; Res. student, Sheffield Univ., 1961–64; Postdoctoral Fellow, NRCC, 1964–66; Res. scientist, Bell Telephone Labs, NJ, 1966–67; Tutorial Fellow, 1967–68, Lectr, 1968–77, Reader, 1977–85, Univ. of Sussex. Visiting Professor: UBC 1973; USC 1981; UCLA, 1988–92. *Publications:* Molecular Rotation Spectra, 1975, 2nd edn 1983; 220 papers in chemistry, chem. physics and astronomy jls. *Recreations:* graphic design, tennis. *Address:* School of Chemistry and Molecular Sciences, University of Sussex, Brighton BN1 9QJ. *T:* Brighton (01273) 678329.

KRUGER, Prudence Margaret; *see* Leith, P. M.

KRUSIN, Sir Stanley (Marks), Kt 1973; CB 1963; Second Parliamentary Counsel, 1970–73; *b* 8 June 1908; *m* 1st, 1937 (she *d* 1972); one *s* one *d*; 2nd, 1976 (she *d* 1988). *Educ:* St Paul's Sch.; Balliol Coll., Oxford. Called to the Bar, Middle Temple, 1932. Served RAFVR, Wing Comdr, 1944. Dep. Sec., British Tabulating Machine Co. Ltd, 1945–47. Entered Parliamentary Counsel Office, 1947; Parliamentary Counsel, 1953–69. *Address:* 5 Coleridge Walk, NW11 6AT. *T:* 0181–458 1340. *Club:* Royal Air Force.

KUBELIK, Rafael; conductor and composer; Chief Conductor of Bayerischer Rundfunk, München, 1961–79; *b* Bychory, 29 June 1914; *s* of Jan Kubelik, violinist, and Marianne (*née* Szell); *m* 1942, Ludmila Bertlova (*decd*), violinist; one *s*; *m* 1963, Elsie Morison, soprano. *Educ:* Prague Conservatoire. Conductor, Czech Philharmonic Society, Prague, 1936–39; Musical Director of Opera, Brno, Czechoslovakia, 1939–41; Musical Dir, Czech Philharmonic Orchestra, 1941–48; Musical Dir, Chicago Symphony Orchestra, 1950–53; Musical Dir of the Covent Garden Opera Company, 1955–58; Music Dir, Metropolitan Opera, New York, 1973–74. *Compositions* include: 2 symphonies with chorus; a third symphony (in one movement); Orphikon, symphony for orch.; Sequences for orch.;

symphonic Peripeteia for organ and orch.; Invocation for tenor solo, boys' choir and orch.; 6 string quartets; 1 cantata; Cantata Without Words, for chorus and orch.; Inventions and Interludes, for children's chorus, oboes and trumpets; Children Ballades, Czech national poems for soprano solo and string sextet; Concerto in Modo Classico, for violin and strings; Trio Concertante, for piano, violin and cello; *operas:* Veronika; Daybreak; Cornelia Faroli; (after Hans Christian Anderson) Emperor's New Clothes; Flowers of Little Ida; *requiems:* Pro Memoria Uxoris; Libera Nos; Quattro Forme per Archi; songs; piano and violin music. Hon. RAM; Hon. Member: Bavarian Acad. of Fine Arts; Royal Swedish Acad. of Music; Italian Assoc. Anton Bruckner; Roy. Philharmonic Soc., London. Hon. Dr Amer. Conservatory of Music, Chicago; Hon. Dr Karls-Univ., Prague. Karl Amadeus Hartmann Gold Medal; Gold Medal, City of Munich; Gustav Mahler Gold Medal, Gustav Mahler Soc., Vienna; Carl Nielsen Gold Medal, Copenhagen; Medal of City of Amsterdam; Mahler Medal, Bruckner Soc. of Amer.; Hans von Bülow Medal, Berlin Phil. Orch.; Gold Medal, City of Lucerne; Medal of Dutch Bruckner Soc.; Grand Prix Nat. du Disque, Paris; Czechoslovak Soc. of Arts and Scis, Washington; Golden Book of the Jewish Nat. Fund; Golden Key, City of Cleveland. Hon. Citizen: Prague; Brno. Grosses Bundesverdienstkreuz (FRG); Bavarian Order of Merit; Chevalier, Order of the Dannebrog (Denmark); Comtur Istrucao Publica (Portugal); Commandeur de l'ordre des Arts et des Lettres (France); Thomas G. Masaryk Order, 1 (Czech and Slovak Fed. Republic), 1991. *Address:* 6047 Kastanienbaum, Haus im Sand, Switzerland.

KUBRICK, Stanley; producer, director, script writer; *b* 26 July 1928; *s* of Dr Jacques L. Kubrick and Gertrude Kubrick; *m* 1958, Suzanne Christiane Harlan; three *d*. *Educ:* William Howard Taft High Sch.; City Coll. of City of New York. Joined Look Magazine, 1946. At age of 21 made Documentary, Day of the Fight; made Short for RKO, Flying Padre. *Feature Films:* Fear and Desire, 1953 (at age of 24); Killer's Kiss, 1954; The Killing, 1956; Paths of Glory, 1957; Spartacus, 1960; Lolita, 1962; Dr Strangelove or How I Learned to Stop Worrying and Love the Bomb, 1964; 2001: A Space Odyssey, 1968; A Clockwork Orange, 1971; Barry Lyndon, 1975; The Shining, 1978; Full Metal Jacket, 1987. *Recreations:* literature, music, public affairs. *Address:* c/o Loeb & Loeb, 10100 Santa Monica Boulevard, Suite 2200, Los Angeles, CA 90067, USA.

KUENSSBERG, Ekkehard von, CBE 1969; FRCGP, 1967; FRCOG (*ae*) 1981; FRCPEd 1981; President, Royal College of General Practitioners, 1976–79; *b* 1913; *s* of Prof. Eberhard von Kuenssberg; *m* 1941, Dr Constance Ferrar Hardy; two *s* two *d*. *Educ:* Schloss Schule, Salem; Univs of Innsbruck, Heidelberg and Edinburgh. MB, ChB 1939. Gen. practice throughout (Edin.). RAMC, 1944–46 (Lt-Col, DADMS E Africa Comd). Mem., Safety of Drugs Cttee, 1964–71; Chm., Gen. Med. Services Cttee, Scotland; Mem., GMSC, UK, 1960–68; RCGP: Chm. Council, 1970–73; Hon. Treas., Research Foundn Bd, 1960–77; Mackenzie Lectr, 1970; Wolfson Travelling Prof., 1974. Mem., Lothian Area Health Bd, 1974–80; Member: Council, Queen's Nursing Inst., 1972–76; Court, Edinburgh Univ., 1971–79. Foundation Council Award, RCGP, 1967; Hippocrates Medal, 1974 (SIMG). FRSocMed. *Publications:* The Team in General Practice, 1966; An Opportunity to Learn, 1977. *Recreations:* music, history. *Address:* 2 St Martin's Close, Haddington, East Lothian EH41 4BN. *T:* Haddington (01620) 822529.
See also N. C. D. Kuenssberg.

KUENSSBERG, Nicholas Christopher Dwelly; Managing Director, Dawson International PLC, since 1994; *b* 28 Oct. 1942; *s* of Ekkehard von Kuenssberg, *qv*; *m* 1965, Sally Robertson; one *s* two *d*. *Educ:* Edinburgh Acad.; Wadham Coll., Oxford (BA Hons). FCIS; CIMgt. Worked overseas, 1965–78; Dir, J. & P. Coats Ltd, 1978–91; Chm., Dynacast International Ltd, 1978–91; Chief Exec., Dawson Premier Brands, 1991–94; Director: Coats Patons Plc, 1985–91; Coats Viyella plc, 1986–91. Director: Scottish Power plc (formerly S of Scotland Electricity Bd), 1984–; W of Scotland Bd, Bank of Scotland, 1984–88; Standard Life Assce Co., 1988–. Hon. Res. Fellow, 1986–88, Vis. Prof., 1988–91, Strathclyde Business Sch. Gov., Queen's Coll., Glasgow, 1989–91. *Recreations:* sport, travel, opera, languages. *Address:* Dawson International PLC, 9 Charlotte Square, Edinburgh EH2 4DR. *T:* 0131–220 1919.

KUHN, Prof. Karl Heinz, FBA 1987; Professor of Coptic, Durham University, 1982–84, now Emeritus Professor; *b* 2 Aug. 1919; *s* of Max Kuhn and Gertrud Kuhn (*née* Hiller); *m* 1949, Rachel Mary Wilkinson; one *s* one *d*. *Educ:* school in Germany; St John's Coll., Univ. of Durham (BA 1949, PhD 1952). Scarbrough Research Studentship, Durham Univ. and abroad, 1949–53; Univ. of Durham: Research Fellow in Arts, 1953–55; Lectr, later Sen. Lectr in Hebrew and Aramaic, 1955–77; Reader in Coptic, 1977–82; Prof. of Coptic, 1982–84. Mem., editl bd, Corpus Scriptorum Christianorum Orientalium, Louvain, 1970–. *Publications:* Letters and Sermons of Besa, 1956; Pseudo-Shenoute: on Christian behaviour, 1960; A Panegyric on John the Baptist attributed to Theodosius, Archbishop of Alexandria, 1966; A Panegyric on Apollo, Archimandrite of the Monastery of Isaac by Stephen, Bishop of Heracleopolis Magna, 1978; (contrib.) Sparks, The Apocryphal Old Testament, 1984; English trans of Foerster, Gnosis, 1974, and Rudolph, Gnosis, 1983; articles in Jl of Theol Studies, Le Muséon and other learned jls. *Recreations:* music. *Address:* 28 Nevilledale Terrace, Durham DH1 4QG. *T:* 0191–384 2993.

KÜHNL, Karel; Ambassador of the Czech Republic to the Court of St James's, since 1993; *b* 12 Sept. 1954; *s* of Karel Kühnl and Marie Kühnlova (*née* Větrovcová); *m* 1983, Daniela Kusin; one *s* one *d*. *Educ:* Charles Univ., Prague (BA Law 1978); Univ. of Vienna (BA Econs 1983). Left Czechoslovakia in 1980 for political reasons; free-lance journalist, Vienna and Munich, 1983–87; editor and analyst, Radio Free Europe, Munich (Czech and Slovak broadcasting), 1987–91; returned to Czechosovakia, 1991, after fall of communism in 1989; Sen. Lectr, Law Faculty, Charles Univ., Prague, 1991–93; Chief Advr to Prime Minister of Czech Republic, 1991–93. Hd of Bd, Czech TV, 1992–93. *Publications:* numerous articles in Czech, German and Austrian newspapers and jls. *Recreations:* family, history, archaeology, architecture. *Address:* Embassy of the Czech Republic, 26 Kensington Palace Gardens, W8 4QY. *T:* 0171–243 1115. *Clubs:* Athenæum (Hon. Mem.), Army and Navy (Hon. Mem.).

KUHRT, Ven. Gordon Wilfred; Archdeacon of Lewisham, since 1989; *b* 15 Feb. 1941; *s* of Wilfred and Doris Kuhrt; *m* 1963, Olive Margaret Powell; three *s*. *Educ:* Colfe's Grammar School; London Univ. (BD Hons); Oak Hill Theol Coll. Religious Education teacher, 1963–65; Curate: Illogan, Cornwall, 1967–70; Wallington, Surrey, 1970–74; Vicar: Shenstone, Staffs, 1974–79; Emmanuel, South Croydon, Surrey, 1979–89; RD, Croydon Central, 1981–86; Hon. Canon, Southwark Cathedral, 1987–. Mem., C of E Gen. Synod, 1986– (Mem., Bd of Ministry, 1991–). Mem. Council, Coll. of Preachers, 1992–. Theological Lectr, London Univ. Extra-Mural Dept, 1984–89. *Publications:* A Handbook for Council and Committee Members, 1985; Believing in Baptism, 1987; (contrib.) The Church and its Unity, 1992; (ed and contrib.) Doctrine Matters, 1993; Growing in Newness of Life; Christian initiation in Anglicanism today, 1993; (ed) To Proclaim Afresh, 1995. *Address:* 3A Court Farm Road, Mottingham, SE9 4JH. *T:* 0181–857 7982.

KUIPERS, John Melles; Chairman, ATT Ltd, 1984–91; *b* 7 July 1918; *s* of late Joh Kuipers and Anna (*née* Knoester); *m* 1947, Joan Lilian Morgan-Edwards; one *s* three *d*. *Educ:* Royal Masonic Sch., Bushey. Served RA, 1939–46 (Lt-Col). Ford Motor Co. Ltd, 1947–51; Treasurer, Canadian Chemical Co. Ltd, Montreal, 1951–55; Gp Manager, Halewood, and Dir, Stamping and Assembly Gp, Ford Motor Co. Ltd, 1955–67; EMI Ltd, 1967–80: Chief Exec. Electronic and Industrial Ops, 1969–72; Chm. and Chief Exec., EMI (Australia) Ltd, 1974–77; Man. Dir and Vice-Chm., 1977–79; Dir, Thames TV Ltd, 1977–81; Chm., Huntleigh Gp PLC, 1980–83. Dir, Gowrings, 1980–89. *Address:* 2 Bell Lane, Henley-on-Thames, Oxon RG9 2HP. *T:* Henley-on-Thames (01491) 574760.

KULUKUNDIS, Sir Eddie, Kt 1993; OBE 1988; Chairman, Knightsbridge Theatrical Productions Ltd, since 1970; Director: Rethymnis & Kulukundis Ltd, since 1964; London & Overseas Freighters, 1980–85 and since 1989; Member of Lloyd's, since 1964, Member Council, 1983–89; Member, Baltic Exchange, since 1959; *b* 20 April 1932; *s* of late George Elias Kulukundis and Eugénie (*née* Diacakis); *m* 1981, Susan Hampshire, *qv*. *Educ:* Collegiate Sch., New York; Salisbury Sch., Connecticut; Yale Univ. Chm., Sports Aid Foundn Ltd, 1988–93. Governor: The Raymond Mander and Joe Mitchenson Theatre Collection Ltd; Royal Shakespeare Theatre; Vice-President: Greenwich Theatre Ltd; Traverse Theatre Club; Director: Hampstead Theatre Ltd. Member, Councils of Management: Royal Shakespeare Theatre; Royal Shakespeare Theatre Trust (Vice-Chm., 1983–); pt owner, Duke of York's Theatre and Ambassadors Theatre. Mem. Exec. Council, SWET. Trustee: Salisbury Sch., Connecticut; Theatres Trust. FRSA. As Theatrical Producer, London productions include (some jtly): Enemy, 1969; The Happy Apple, Poor Horace, The Friends, How the Other Half Loves, Tea Party and The Basement (double bill), The Wild Duck, 1970; After Haggerty, Hamlet, Charley's Aunt, Straight Up, 1971; London Assurance, Journey's End, 1972; Small Craft Warnings, A Private Matter, Dandy Dick, 1973; The Waltz of the Toreadors, Life Class, Pygmalion, Play Mas, The Gentle Hook, 1974; A Little Night Music, Entertaining Mr Sloane, The Gay Lord Quex, What the Butler Saw, Travesties, Lies, The Sea Gull, A Month in the Country, A Room With a View, Too True to Be Good, The Bed Before Yesterday, 1975; Dimetos, Banana Ridge, Wild Oats, 1976; Candida, Man and Superman, Once A Catholic, 1977; Privates on Parade, Gloo Joo, 1978; Bent, Outside Edge, Last of the Red Hot Lovers, 1979; Beecham, Born in the Gardens, 1980; Tonight At 8.30, Steaming, Arms and the Man, 1981; Steafel's Variations, 1982; Messiah, Pack of Lies, 1983; Of Mice and Men, The Secret Diary of Adrian Mole Aged 13¾, 1984; Camille, 1985; The Cocktail Party, 1986; Curtains, 1987; Separation, South Pacific, Married Love, 1988; Over My Dead Body, 1989; Never the Sinner, 1990; The King and I, Carmen Jones, 1991; Noël and Gertie, A Slip of the Tongue, Shades, Making it Better, 1992; The Prime of Miss Jean Brodie, 1994; New York productions (jtly): How the Other Half Loves, 1971; Sherlock Holmes, London Assurance, 1974; Travesties, 1975; The Merchant, 1977; Players, 1978; Once a Catholic, 1979. *Address:* c/o Rethymnis & Kulukundis Ltd, 21 New Fetter Lane, EC4A 1JJ. *T:* 0171–583 2266; c/o Knightsbridge Theatrical Productions Ltd, 21 New Fetter Lane, EC4A 1JJ. *T:* 0171–583 8687. *Club:* Garrick.

KUMAR, Dr Ashok; Research Officer, British Steel Technical, since 1992; *b* 28 May 1956; *s* of Jagat Ram Saini and late Santosh Kumari. *Educ:* Univ. of Aston in Birmingham (BSc ChemEng 1978; MSc Process Control 1980; PhD Fluid Mechanics 1982). Res. Officer, British Steel Research, 1978–79; Res. Fellow, Imperial Coll. of Science and Technology, 1982–85; Sen. Res. Investigator, Teeside Labs, British Steel, 1985–91. MP (Lab) Langbaurgh, Nov. 1991–1992; contested (Lab) Langbaurgh, 1992. Chairman: Chem. Eng. Soc., 1981–82; Labour Club, Univ. of Aston, 1980–81. Mem., Middlesbrough BC, 1987–. *Publications:* articles in scientific and mathematical jls. *Recreations:* reading, listening to music, cricket, badminton. *Address:* 23 Canberra Road, Marton, Middlesbrough, Cleveland TS7 8ES. *T:* Middlesbrough (01642) 326629. *Clubs:* Easterside and Beechwood Social; Marton Cricket; Lingdale Working Men's.

KUME, Yutaka; President, since 1985, Chairman, since 1992, Nissan Motor Co.; *b* 20 May 1921; *s* of Kinzaburo Kume and Chiyo Kume; *m* 1947, Aya Yamamoto; one *s* one *d*. *Educ:* Univ. of Tokyo (BE aircraft engineering). Joined Nissan Motor Co., 1946; General Manager: Production control and Engineering Dept, Zama Plant, 1964; Yoshiwara Plant, 1971; Tochigi Plant, 1973–78; Dir and Mem. Bd, 1973; Managing Dir, 1977; Exec. Managing Dir, 1982; Exec. Vice-Pres. and Gen. Manager, Quality Admin Div., 1983. Blue Ribbon Medal from Emperor of Japan, 1986; Commander, Order of Orange Nassau (Holland), 1986; Order of Cruz de San Jordi (Catalonia, Spain), 1990; Commander, Order of the Crown (Belgium), 1991. *Recreations:* photography, haiku (Japanese short poems), reading. *Address:* Nissan Motor Co. Ltd, 17–1 Ginza 6-chome, Chuo-ku, Tokyo 104, Japan. *T:* (3) 5435523.

KUNCEWICZ, Eileen, (Mrs Witold Kuncewicz); *see* Herlie, E.

KUNDERA, Milan; writer; *b* Brno, 1 April 1929; *s* of Dr Ludvik Kundera and Milada Kunderova-Janosikova; *m* 1967, Věra Hrabánková. *Educ:* Film Faculty, Acad. of Music and Dramatic Arts, Prague, later Asst Prof. and Prof. there, 1958–69; Prof., Univ. of Rennes, 1975–80; Prof., Ecole des hautes études en sciences sociales, Paris, 1980–. Mem., Union of Czechoslovak Writers, 1963–69. Member: Editl Bd, Literární noviny, 1963–67, 1968; Editl Bd, Listy, 1968–69. Klement Lukes Prize, 1963; Czechoslovak Writers' Publishing House Prize, 1969; Commonwealth Award, 1981; Prix Europa-Littérature, 1982; Jerusalem Prize, 1985; Nelly Sachs Preis, 1987; Österreichische Staatspreis, 1988; London Independent Prize, 1991. Officier, Légion d'honneur (France), 1990. *Publications:* The Owners of the Keys (drama), 1962; The Joke, 1967; Laughable Loves (short stories), 1970; Jacques et son maître (drama), 1971–81; Life is Elsewhere, 1973 (Prix Médicis); The Farewell Party, 1976 (Prem. lett. Mondello); The Book of Laughter and Forgetting, 1979; The Unbearable Lightness of Being, 1984 (LA Times Prize); The Art of the Novel, 1987; Immortality, 1990; Les testaments trahis, 1993.

KUNERALP, Zeki, Hon. GCVO 1971; *b* Istanbul, 5 Oct. 1914; *s* of Ali Kemal and Sabiha, *d* of Mustafa Zeki Pasha; *m* 1943, Necla Ozdilci (*d* 1978); two *s*. *Educ:* Univ. of Berne. DrIuris 1938. Entered Diplomatic Service, 1940: served Bucharest, Prague, Paris, Nato Delegn and at Min. of Foreign Affairs, Ankara; Asst Sec.-Gen. 1957; Sec.-Gen. 1960; Ambassador to Berne, 1960, to Court of St James's, 1964–66; Sec.-Gen. at Min. of Foreign Affairs, Ankara, 1966–69; Ambassador to Court of St James's, 1969–72, to Spain, 1972–79, retired. Mem., Hon. Soc. of Knights of the Round Table. Holds German, Greek, Italian, Papal, Jordanian, Iranian and National Chinese orders. *Publication:* Sadece Diplomat (memoirs), 1981. *Recreations:* reading, ballet. *Address:* Fenerbahçe Cadessi 85/B, D4, Kiziltoprak, Istanbul 81030, Turkey.

KÜNG, Prof. Dr Hans; Ordinary Professor of Ecumenical Theology, since 1980 and Director of Institute for Ecumenical Research, since 1963, University of Tübingen; *b* Sursee, Lucerne, 19 March 1928. *Educ:* schools in Sursee and Lucerne; Papal Gregorian Univ., Rome (LPhil, LTh); Sorbonne; Inst. Catholique, Paris. DTheol 1957. Further studies in Amsterdam, Berlin, Madrid, London. Ordained priest, 1954. Pastoral work, Hofkirche, Lucerne, 1957–59; Asst for dogmatic theol., Univ. of Münster, 1959–60; Ord. Prof. of fundamental theol., 1960–63, Ord. Prof. of dogmatic and ecumenical theol., 1963–80, Univ. of Tübingen. Official theol. consultant (peritus) to 2nd Vatican Council, 1962–65; Guest Professor: Union Theol. Seminary, NYC, 1968; Univ. of Basle, 1969;

Univ. of Chicago Divinity Sch., 1981; Univ. of Michigan, 1983; Toronto Univ., 1985; guest lectures at univs in Europe, America, Asia and Australia; Hon. Pres., Edinburgh Univ. Theol Soc., 1982–83. Editor series, Theologische Meditationen; co-Editor series, Ökumenische Forschungen and Ökumenische Theologie; Associate Editor, Jl of Ecum. Studies. Mem., Amer. and German Pen Clubs. Holds hon. doctorates. *Publications:* (first publication in German) The Council and Reunion, 1961; That the World may Believe, 1963; The Living Church, 1963; The Changing Church, 1965; Justification: the doctrine of Karl Barth and a Catholic reflection, 1965; Structures of the Church, 1965; The Church, 1967; Truthfulness: the future of the Church, 1968; Infallible? an enquiry, 1971 (paperback 1972); Why Priests?, 1972; 20 Thesen zum Christsein, 1975; On Being a Christian, 1977 (abridged as The Christian Challenge, 1979); Was ist Firmung?, 1976; Jesus im Widerstreit: ein jüdisch-christlicher Dialog (with Pinchas Lapide), 1976; Brother or Lord?, 1977; Signposts for the Future, 1978; Freud and the Problem of God, 1979; The Church—Maintained in Truth?, 1980; Does God Exist?, 1980; Art and the Question of Meaning, 1981; Eternal Life?, 1984; (jtly) Christianity and World Religions, 1986; The Incarnation of God, 1986; Church and Change: the Irish experience, 1986; Why I am still a Christian, 1987; Theology for the Third Millennium: an ecumenical view, 1988; (with Julia Ching) Christianity and Chinese Religions, 1989; Reforming the Church Today: keeping hope alive, 1990; Global Responsibility: in search of a new world ethic, 1991; Judaism: the religious situation of our time, 1992; Mozart: traces of transcendence, 1992; Credo: the Apostles' Creed explained for today, 1993; Great Christian Thinkers, 1994; Christianity: essence and history, 1995; (contrib.) Theologische Meditationen, 1965 (Amer. edn as Freedom Today, 1966); (contrib.) Christian Revelation and World Religions, ed J. Neuner, 1967. *Address:* 72076 Tübingen, Waldhäuserstrasse 23, Germany.

KUNKEL, Edward Thomas; Director and Chief Executive Officer, Foster's Brewing Group Ltd, since 1992; *b* 22 May 1943; *s* of Francis James Kunkel and Doris Kunkel (*née* Baulcombe); *m* 1968, Dawn Ann Jucinsky; two *d.* *Educ:* Auckland Univ. (BSc Chem. and Zool.). Joined Carlton & United Breweries, Melbourne, 1968 as Asst Brewer; Gen. Manager, later Exec. Dir of Ops in NSW, 1985–87; Pres. and Chief Exec. Officer, Carling O'Keefe Breweries of Canada Ltd, 1987–89; Exec. Chm., Molson Breweries, N America, 1989–92. *Recreation:* golf. *Address:* Foster's Brewing Group Ltd, 1 Garden Street, S Yarra, Vic 3141, Australia. *T:* (3) 98282424. *Clubs:* Huntingdale Golf (Victoria); Killara Golf (NSW).

KUREISHI, Hanif; writer; *b* 5 Dec. 1954; *s* of Rafiushan Kureishi and Audrey Buss. *Educ:* King's College London. *Filmscripts:* My Beautiful Laundrette, 1984; Sammy and Rosie Get Laid, 1987; (also dir.) London Kills Me, 1991. *Publications:* Outskirts, 1981; Borderline, 1981; Birds of Passage, 1983; The Buddha of Suburbia, 1990 (televised, 1993); Outskirts and Other Plays, 1992; The Black Album, 1995; (ed jtly) The Faber Book of Pop, 1995. *Recreations:* pop music, cricket, sitting in pubs. *Address:* c/o Deborah Rogers Ltd, 20 Powis Mews, W11 1SN.

KURIA, Rt Rev. Manasses; Archbishop of Kenya and Bishop of Nairobi, 1980–94; *b* 22 July 1929; *s* of John Njoroge Kuria; *m* 1947, Mary Kuria; two *s* four *d.* *Educ:* locally. Teaching, 1944–53; Deacon, 1955; ordained Priest, 1957; Archdeacon of Eldoret, 1965–70; Asst Bishop of Nakuru, 1970–75; Bishop of Nakuru, 1976–79. *Publication:* Uwakili Katika Kristo (Stewardship of Christ), 1969. *Address:* c/o PO Box 40502, Nairobi, Kenya.

KURONGKU, Most Rev. Sir Peter; *see* Port Moresby, Archbishop of, (RC).

KUROSAWA, Akira; Japanese film director; *b* 23 March 1910; *m* 1945, Yoko Yaguchi (*d* 1985); one *s* one *d.* *Educ:* Keika Middle School. Assistant Director, Toho Film Co., 1936. Mem. Jury, Internat. Film Fest. of India, 1977. Directed first film, Sanshiro Sugata, 1943. *Films include:* Sanshiro Sugata; The Most Beautiful, 1944; Sanshiro Sugata II, 1945; They Who Step on the Tiger's Tail, 1945; No Regret for our Youth, 1946; One Wonderful Sunday, 1947; Drunken Angel, 1948; The Quiet Duel, 1949; Stray Dog, 1949; Scandal, 1950; Rashomon (1st prize, Venice Film Fest.), 1950; The Idiot, 1951; Ikuru, 1952; Seven Samurai, 1954; Record of a Living Being, 1955; The Throne of Blood, 1957; The Lower Depths, 1957; The Hidden Fortress, 1958; The Bad Sleep Well, 1960; Yojimbo, 1961; Sanjuro, 1962; High and Low, 1963; Red Beard, 1965; Dodes'kaden, 1970. Dersu Uzala (Oscar award), 1975; Kagemusha (Golden Palm Award, Cannes Film Festival), 1980; Ran, 1985; Dreams, 1990; Rhapsody in August, 1991. *Publication:* Something like an Autobiography (trans. Audie Bock), 1984.

KURTI, Prof. Nicholas, CBE 1973; FRS 1956; MA Oxon; DrPhil (Berlin); FInstP; Emeritus Professor of Physics, University of Oxford; Vice-President, Royal Society, 1965–67; *b* 14 May 1908; *s* of late Károly Kürti and Margit Pintér, Budapest; *m* 1946, Giana, *d* of late Brig.-Gen. and Mrs C. T. Shipley; two *d.* *Educ:* Minta-Gymnasium, Budapest; University of Paris (Licence ès sci. phys.); University of Berlin (DrPhil). Asst, Techn Hochschule Breslau, 1931–33; Research Position, Clarendon Laboratory, Oxford, 1933–40; UK Atomic Bomb Project, 1940–45; University Demonstrator in Physics, Oxford, 1945–60; Reader in Physics, Oxford, 1960–67; Prof. of Physics, Oxford, 1967–75; Senior Research Fellow, Brasenose Coll., 1947–67; Professorial Fellow, 1967–75, Emeritus Fellow, 1975–. Buell G. Gallagher Visiting Prof., City Coll., New York, 1963; Vis. Prof., Univ. of Calif, Berkeley, 1964; Dist. Vis. Prof., Amherst Coll., 1979. May Lecture, Inst. of Metals, 1963; Kelvin Lecture, IEE, 1971; Larmor Lecture, Queen's Univ., Belfast, 1975; James Scott Prize and Lecture, RSE, 1976; Cherwell-Simon Lecture, Oxford Univ., 1977; Tyndall Lecture, Inst. of Physics, Royal Dublin Soc., 1980. A Governor, College of Aeronautics, Cranfield, 1953–69. Member: Electricity Supply Research Council, 1960–79; Advisory Cttee for Scientific and Technical Information, 1966–68; Comité de Direction, Service Nat. des Champs Intenses, CNRS, 1973–75; Comité, Problèmes Socio-économique de l'Energie, CNRS, 1975–78; Chairman: Adv. Cttee for Research on Measurement and Standards, DTI, 1969–73; Jt Cttee on Scientific and Technol Records, Royal Soc./Royal Commn on Historical MSS, 1970–76. Member: Council, Royal Soc., 1964–67; Council, Soc. Française de Physique, 1957–60, 1970–73; Council, Inst. of Physics and Physical Soc., 1969–73; Treasurer, CODATA (Cttee on data for sci. and technol., ICSU), 1973–80; Chm., Cttee of Management, Science Policy Foundn, 1970–75. Gov., British Nutrition Foundn, 1986–. Editor-in-Chief, Europhysics Letters, 1985–89. Emeritus Mem., Acad. Europaea, 1990; Foreign Hon. Mem., Amer. Acad. Arts and Sciences, 1968; Hon. Member: Hungarian Acad. of Sciences, 1970; Société Française de Physique, 1974; Fachverband deutscher Köche, 1978; European Physical Soc., 1989; Foreign Member: Finnish Acad. of Sciences and Letters, 1974; Akad. der Wissenschaften der DDR, 1976–92. Holweck Prize (British and French Physical Socs), 1955; Fritz London Award, 1957; Hughes Medal, Royal Soc., 1969. Chevalier de la Légion d'Honneur, 1976; Hungarian Order of the Star, 1988. *Publications:* (jointly) Low Temperature Physics, 1952; (ed jtly) Experimental Cryophysics, 1961; (ed with Giana Kurti) But the Crackling is Superb, 1988; papers on cryophysics, magnetism, energy and culinary physics; articles in the New Chambers's Encyclopædia. *Recreations:* cooking, enjoying its results and judiciously applying physics to the noble art of cookery. *Address:* 38 Blandford Avenue, Oxford OX2 8DZ. *T:* Oxford (01865) 56176; Department of Engineering Science, Parks Road, Oxford OX1 3PJ. *T:* Oxford (01865) 273115, *Fax:* (01865) 272400. *Club:* Athenæum.

KUSHNER, Lindsey Joy; QC 1992; barrister; a Recorder, since 1993; *b* 16 April 1952; *d* of Harry Kushner and Rita Kushner (*née* Alexander); *m* 1976, David Norman Kaye; one *s* one *d.* *Educ:* Manchester High Sch. for Girls; Liverpool Univ. (LLB). Called to the Bar, Middle Temple, 1974; part time Chm., Medical Appeal Tribunal, 1989, Disablement Appeal Tribunal, 1992; Asst Recorder, 1989–93. *Recreations:* cooking, cinema. *Address:* 28 St John Street, Manchester M3 4DJ. *T:* 0161–834 8418.

KUSTOW, Michael David; writer, producer and director; *b* 18 Nov. 1939; *m* 1973, Orna, *d* of Jacob and Rivka Spector, Haifa, Israel. *Educ:* Haberdashers' Aske's; Wadham Coll., Oxford (BA Hons English). Festivals Organiser, Centre 42, 1962–63; Royal Shakespeare Theatre Company: Dir, RSC Club, Founder of Theatregoround, Editor of Flourish, 1963–67; Dir, Inst. of Contemporary Arts, 1967–70; Associate Dir, National Theatre, 1973–81; Commissioning Ed. for Arts progs, Channel Four TV, 1981–89; Dir, Michael Kustow Productions, 1990–; Co-Dir, The Greek Collection, 1990–. Lectr in Dramatic Arts, Harvard Univ., 1980–82. Chevalier de l'Ordre des Arts et des Lettres, République Française, 1980. *Productions:* Punch and Judas, Trafalgar Square, 1963; I Wonder, ICA, 1968; Nicholas Tomalin Reporting, 1975; Brecht Poetry and Songs, 1976; Larkinland, Groucho Letters, Robert Lowell, Audience, 1977–78; Miss South Africa, Catullus, A Nosegay of Light Verse, The Voice of Babel, Anatol, 1979; Iris Murdoch's Art and Eros, Shakespeare's Sonnets, Stravinsky's Soldier's Tale, 1980; Charles Wood's Has Washington Legs, Harold Pinter's Family Voices, 1981; The Mahabharata, 1989; The War that Never Ends, 1991; The Last Bolshevik, 1993; ABC of Democracy, 1994; A Maybe Day in Kazakhstan, 1994; Fireworks, 1994; Shakespeare Workshops, 1994; Everybody's Shakespeare Festival, 1994; Hiroshima, 1995. *Exhibitions:* Tout Terriblement Guillaume Apollinaire, ICA, 1968; AAARGH! A Celebration of Comics, ICA, 1971. *Publications:* Punch and Judas, 1964; The Book of US, 1968; Tank: an autobiographical fiction, 1975; One in Four, 1987. *Recreations:* painting, jazz. *Address:* 52 Shepherd's Hill, N6 5RR.

KWAPONG, Alexander Adum, MA, PhD Cantab; Director, African Programmes, Teacher Education, Research and Evaluation, The Commonwealth of Learning, Vancouver, 1991–93; *b* Akropong, Akwapim, 8 March 1927; *s* of E. A. Kwapong and Theophilia Kwapong; *m* 1956, Evelyn Teiko Caesar, Ada; six *d.* *Educ:* Presbyterian junior and middle schools, Akropong; Achimota Coll.; King's Coll., Cambridge (Exhibr, Minor Schol. and Foundn Schol.). BA 1951, MA 1954, PhD 1957, Cantab. 1st cl. prelims, Pts I and II, Classical Tripos, 1951; Sandys Res. Student, Cambridge Univ.; Richards Prize, Rann Kennedy Travel Fellowship, King's Coll., Cambridge. Lectr in Classics, UC Gold Coast, 1953, Sen. Lectr in Classics 1960; Vis. Prof., Princeton Univ., 1961–62; Prof. of Classics, Univ. of Ghana, 1962; Dean of Arts, Pro-Vice-Chancellor, Univ. of Ghana, 1962–65, Vice-Chancellor 1966–75; Vice-Rector for Instl Planning and Resource Develt, UN Univ., 1976–88 (Sen. Advr to Rector, 1988–); Lester B. Pearson Prof. in Develt Studies, Dalhousie Univ., Halifax, Canada, 1988–91. Chairman: Educn Review Cttee, Ghana Govt, 1966–67; Smithsonian Instn 3rd Internat. Symposium, 1969; Assoc. of Commonwealth Univs, 1971. Sir Samuel Manuwa Meml Lectr, W African Coll. of Surgeons, 1990. Member: Admin. Bd, Internat. Assoc. Univs, Paris, 1970–80; Exec. Bd, Assoc. African Univs, 1967–74; Bd of Trustees, Internat. Council for Educnl Develt, NY; Aspen Inst. for Humanistic Studies, 1972–85; Board of Directors: Internat. Assoc. for Cultural Freedom, Paris, 1967–75; Internat. Cttee for the Study of Educnl Exchange; Aspen Berlin Inst., 1975–; IDRC; Harold Macmillan Trust, 1986–; Internat. Foundn for Educn and Self Help, Phoenix, Arizona, 1988–; African Leadership Forum. Consultant, World Bank, 1988–89. Fellow, Ghana Academy of Arts and Sciences. Hon. DLitt: Warwick; Ife; Ghana; Hon. LLD Princeton. Order of Volta, Ghana. *Publications:* The Role of Classical Studies in Africa Today, 1969; Higher Education and Development in Africa Today: a reappraisal, 1979; Underdevelopment and the Challenges of the 1980's: the role of knowledge, 1980; The Relevance of the African Universities to the Development Needs of Africa, 1980; What Kind of Human Beings for the 21st Century—a second look, 1981; The Humanities and National Development: a second look, 1984; The Crisis of Development: education and identity, 1985; Medical Education and National Development, 1987; Culture, Development and African Unity, 1988; African Scientific and Technical Institution—Building and the Role of International Co-operation, 1988; The Challenge of Education in Africa, 1988; (ed with B. Lesser) Capacity Building and Human Resource Development in Africa, 1990; (ed with B. Lesser) Meeting the Challenge: the African Capacity Building Initiative, 1992; *contribs to:* Grecs et Barbars, 1962; Dawn of African History (ed R. Oliver); Man and Beast: Comparative Social Behaviour (ed J. F. Eisenberg and W. S. Dillon), 1971; Pearson Notes, 1988–89; The Role of Service-Learning in International Education (procs of Wingspread conf.) (ed S. W. Showalter), 1989; Culture, Development and Democracy: role of intellectuals in Africa, 1991; Recent Trends in Governance in African Universities: the challenge of scientific and intellectual leadership, 1992; various articles in classical jls, especially on Ancient and Greco-Roman Africa; various addresses and lectures on internat. higher educn in ICED pubns. *Recreations:* tennis, billiards, music and piano-playing, learning Japanese. *Address:* 19 Highfield Avenue, Golders Green, NW11 9EU. *T:* 0181–209 0878. *Club:* Athenæum.

KYLE, Barry Albert; freelance director, since 1991; Hon. Associate Director, Royal Shakespeare Company, since 1991 (Associate Director, 1978–91); *b* 25 March 1947; *s* of Albert Ernest Kyle and Edith Ivy Bessie Gaskin; *m* 1st, 1971, Christine Susan Iddon (marr. diss. 1988); two *s* one *d*; 2nd, 1990, Lucy Joy Maycock. *Educ:* Birmingham Univ. (BA, MA). Associate Dir, Liverpool Playhouse, 1970–72; joined RSC as Asst Dir, 1973; first Artistic Dir, Swan Theatre, Stratford-upon-Avon, 1987; numerous RSC productions and directing abroad, incl. Australia, Israel, USA, Czechoslovakia; founding Artistic Dir, Swine Palace Productions, La, USA; Dir, Theatre for a New Audience, NYC, 1995–96. Vis. Dir, Czechoslovak Nat. Theatre, Prague (first Briton to direct there). *Publications:* Sylvia Plath: a dramatic portrait, 1976; contribs to Literary Review. *Recreations:* foreign travel, reading, physical activities. *Address:* Flat 5, 20 Charing Cross Road, WC2H 0HR. *T:* 0171–836 5911.

KYLE, David William; Head of Headquarters Casework, Crown Prosecution Service, since 1993; *b* 30 March 1951; *s* of William and Judy Kyle; *m* 1975, Rosemary Elizabeth Bazire; two *d.* *Educ:* Monkton Combe Sch.; Queens' Coll., Cambridge (BA). Called to the Bar, Inner Temple, 1973; Office of Director of Public Prosecutions: Legal Asst, 1975–79; Sen. Legal Asst, 1979–86; Crown Prosecution Service: Branch Crown Prosecutor, 1986–89; Head of Div., HQ Casework, 1989–93. *Recreations:* music, walking, amateur dramatics. *Address:* Crown Prosecution Service, 50 Ludgate Hill, EC4M 7EX. *T:* 0171–273 1225.

KYLE, James, CBE 1989; FRCSE; FRCSI; FRCS; Chairman, Raigmore Hospital NHS Trust, since 1993; *b* 26 March 1925; *s* of John Kyle and Dorothy Frances Kyle; *m* 1950, Dorothy Elizabeth Galbraith; two *d.* *Educ:* Queen's Univ., Belfast. MB BCh BAO 1947 (Gold Medal in Surgery); MCh 1956 (Gold Medal); DSc 1972. FRCSI 1953; FRCS 1954; FRCSE 1964. Mayo Clinic, USA, 1950; Tutor in Surgery, QUB, 1952; Lectr in

Surgery, Univ. of Liverpool, 1957; Aberdeen University: Sen. Lectr, Surgery, 1959; Mem., Univ. Senatus, 1970; Consultant Surgeon, Aberdeen Royal Infirmary, 1959–89; Chm., Grampian Health Bd, 1989–93 (Mem., 1973). Mem., GMC, 1979–94; Chairman: Scottish Cttee for Hosp. Med. Services, 1977; Rep. Body, BMA, 1984–87; Scottish Jt Consultants' Cttee, 1984–89. Pres., Aberdeen Medico-Surgical Soc. Bicentenary, 1989–90. FRPSL. *Publications:* Peptic Ulceration, 1960; Pye's Surgical Handicraft, 21st edn, 1962; Scientific Foundations of Surgery, 3rd edn, 1967; Crohn's Disease, 1973; papers on surgery, history, philately. *Recreations:* amateur radio (callsign GM4 CHX), philately. *Address:* Grianan, 7 Fasaich, Gairloch, Ross-shire IV21 2BD. *T:* Gairloch (01445) 712398; 25 Gordondale Court, Aberdeen AB2 4GB. *T:* Aberdeen (01224) 636067. *Club:* Royal Northern (Aberdeen).

KYLE, Air Vice-Marshal Richard Henry, MBE 1977; Air Officer Commanding Maintenance Units, RAF Logistics Command, since 1993; *b* 4 Jan. 1943; *s* of Air Chief Marshal Sir Wallace Hart Kyle, GCB, KCVO, CBE, DSO, DFC and Lady (Molly) Kyle; *m* 1971, Anne Weatherup; two *s* two *d. Educ:* Cranbrook Sch., Kent; RAF Tech. College, Henlow; Southampton Univ. (BSc Eng 1964). CEng 1971. FRAeS 1993. Served RAF stations: Syerston, 1965–67; Acklington, 1967–68; Ternhill, 1968–69; Changi, 1969–71; MoD, 1971–73; No 1 (F) Sqn, RAF Wittering, 1973–76; MoD, 1976–78; RAF Staff Coll., 1978; RAF Gütersloh, 1979–81; MoD, 1982–84; RAF Halton, 1984–86; RCDS, 1987; MoD, 1988–89; RAF St Athan, 1990–92; Dir Gen. Support Services (RAF), 1992–93. *Recreations:* squash, orienteering, golf, offshore sailing, hill walking. *Club:* Royal Air Force.

KYME, Rt. Rev. Brian Robert; National Director, Australian Board of Missions, since 1993; *b* 22 June 1935; *s* of John Robert Kyme and Ida Eileen Benson; *m* 1961, Doreen Muriel Williams; one *s* one *d. Educ:* Melbourne High School; Ridley Theological Coll., Melbourne; WA Coll. of Advanced Educn. (BA 1989); Aust. Coll. of Theology (ThL 1956); Melbourne Coll. of Divinity (Dip RE 1958). MACE 1991. Deacon, 1958; priest, 1960; Curate: St John's, E Malvern, 1958–60; Glenroy and Broadmeadows, 1960–61; Morwell, 1961–63; Vicar, St Matthew's, Ashburton, 1963–69; Dean, Holy Cross Cathedral, Geraldton, WA, 1969–74; Rector, Christ Church, Claremont, Perth, 1974–82; Archdeacon of Stirling, 1977–82; Asst Bishop of Perth, 1982–93. ChLJ, WA, 1985–93. *Recreations:* golf, reading. *Address:* ABM House, 91 Bathurst Street, Sydney, NSW 2000, Australia. *T:* (office) (2) 2641021, (home) (2) 6603081, *Fax:* (2) 2613560. *Club:* Rotary.

KYNASTON, Nicolas; freelance organist, since 1971; Consultant Tutor, Birmingham Conservatoire (formerly Birmingham School of Music), since 1986; *b* 10 Dec. 1941; *s* of late Roger Tewkesbury Kynaston and Jessie Dearn Caecilia Kynaston (*née* Parkes); *m* 1st, 1961, Judith Felicity Heron (marr. diss. 1989); two *s* two *d*; 2nd, 1989, Susan Harwood Styles. *Educ:* Westminster Cathedral Choir Sch.; Downside; Accademia Musicale Chigiana, Siena; Conservatorio Santa Cecilia, Rome; Royal Coll. of Music. Organist of Westminster Cathedral, 1961–71; concert career, 1971–, travelling throughout Europe, North America, Asia and Africa; Organist, Athens Concert Hall, 1995–. Début recital, Royal Festival Hall, 1966; Recording début, 1968. Consultant, J. W. Walker & Sons Ltd, 1982–83 (Artistic Dir, 1978–82); Organ Consultant: Dean and Chapter, Bristol, 1986–91; Dean and Canons of Manchester, 1988–; Archbishop of Birmingham, 1989–94; Rector and PCC, Bath Abbey, 1993–; Vicar and PCC, Tewkesbury Abbey, 1993–; Christchurch Priory, 1994–. Jury member: Grand Prix de Chartres, 1971; St Albans Internat. Organ Festival, 1975. Pres., Incorp. Assoc. of Organists, 1983–85; Chm., Nat. Organ Teachers' Encouragement Scheme, 1993–. Hon. FRCO 1976. Records incl. 5 nominated Critic's Choice; EMI/CFP Sales Award, 1974; MTA nomination Best Solo Instrumental Record of the Year, 1977; Deutscher Schallplattenpreis, 1978; Preis der Deutschen Schallplattenkritik, 1988. *Recreations:* walking, church architecture. *Address:* 28 High Park Road, Kew Gardens, Richmond-upon-Thames, Surrey TW9 4BH. *T:* 0181–878 4455.

KYNOCH, George Alexander Bryson; MP (C) Kincardine and Deeside, since 1992; Parliamentary Under Secretary of State, Scottish Office (Minister for Industry and Local Government), since 1995; *b* 7 Oct. 1946; *s* of Lt Col Gordon Bryson Kynoch, CBE and Nesta Alicia Janet Thora (*née* Lyon); *m* 1971, Dr Rosslyn Margaret McDevitt; one *s* one *d. Educ:* Cargilfield Sch., Edinburgh; Glenalmond Coll., Perthshire; Univ. of Bristol (BSc Hons Mech. Engrg). Plant Engr Silicones Plant, ICI Ltd, Nobel Div., 1968–71; G. and G. Kynoch, subseq. Kynoch Group, 1971–92; Finance Dir, then Jt Man. Dir; Chief Exec., 1981–90; Gp Exec. Dir, 1990–92; Non-Exec. Dir, 1992–; Non-Exec. Dir, Aardvark Holdings Ltd, 1992–. Chm., Scottish Woollen Publicity Council, 1983–90; Pres., Scottish Woollen Industry, 1990–91; Mem., Aberdeen and Dist MMB, 1988–92; Dir, Moray Badenoch and Strathspey Local Enterprise Co. Ltd, 1991–92. Parliamentary Private Secretary: to Minister of State, FCO, 1992–94; to Sec. of State for Educn, 1994–95. Mem., Scottish Affairs Select Cttee, 1992–95. Chm., Moray and Banff Cons. and Unionist Assoc., 1990–92; Vice-Chm., Northern Area, Scottish Cons. and Unionist Assoc., 1991–92. *Recreations:* golf, ski-ing, travel. *Address:* House of Commons, SW1A 0AA. *T:* 0171–219 5808.

KYPRIANOU, Spyros; Grand Cross of the Order of George I of Greece, 1962; Grand Cross, Order of the Saviour, Greece, 1983; President of the Republic of Cyprus, 1977–88; President, Democratic Party of Cyprus, since 1976; *b* Limassol, 1932; *s* of Achilleas and Maria Kyprianou; *m* Mimi Kyprianou; two *s. Educ:* Greek Gymnasium, Limassol; City of London Coll. Called to the Bar, Gray's Inn, 1954 (Hon. Bencher, 1985); Dip. Comparative Law. Founded Cypriot Students' Union in England (first Pres. 1952–54). Sec. of Archbp Makarios, in London, 1952; Sec. of Cyprus Ethnarchy in London, 1954; left Britain for Greece, 1956, to work for world projection of Cyprus case; later in 1956, rep. Cyprus Ethnarchy, New York, until 1957; resumed London post until signing of Zürich and London Agreements, returning to Cyprus with the Archbp in 1959. On declaration of Independence, 16 Aug. 1960, following brief appt as Minister of Justice, became Foreign Minister, accompanying the Pres. on visits to countries world-wide, 1961–71; rep. Cyprus at UN Security Council and Gen. Assembly sessions, notably during debates on the Cyprus question; signed Agreement in Moscow for Soviet Military Aid to Cyprus, 1964; had several consultations with Greek Govt on Cyprus matter. Mem. Cttee of Ministers of Council of Europe at meetings in Strasburg and Paris (Pres. Cttee, April-Dec. 1967). Resigned post of Foreign Minister, 1972, after dispute with military régime in Athens. Practised law, withdrawing from politics until the coup and Turkish invasion of Cyprus, 1974; travelled between Athens, London and New York, where he led Cyprus delegn during debate on Cyprus in Gen. Assembly of UN, 1974; participated in talks between Greek Govt and Pres. Makarios, 1974; an *ad hoc* member of Cyprus delegn at Security meeting in New York, 1975. Announced estabt of Democratic Party in Cyprus, 1976, becoming Pres. of House of Reps on the party's victory in parly elections. On death of Archbp Makarios, Aug. 1977, became Actg Pres. of Republic, until elected Pres. in same month; re-elected Pres., unopposed, in Feb. 1978 for a full five-year term; re-elected for further five-year term, 1983. Holds numerous foreign decorations. *Recreations:* literature, music, sport. *Address:* Antistaseos 1, Engomi, Nicosia, Cyprus.

KYRIAZIDES, Nikos Panayis; Comdr, Order of George I of Greece; Deputy Minister, Ministry of Finance, Greece, since 1994; *b* 3 Sept. 1927; *m* 1960, Ellie Kyrou; one *s* one *d. Educ:* Exeter Coll., Oxford Univ. (MA); Chicago Univ. Min. of Co-ordination, 1949; Head, Monetary Policy Div., 1950–51; Dir, External Payments and Trade, 1951–54; Alternate Economic Advr, Bank of Greece, 1956–60; Mem., Greek Delegn, negotiations for EFTA and assoc. of Greece to EEC, 1957–61; seconded to Min. of Co-ordination as Dir Gen., relations with EEC, 1962–64; Economic Advr, Nat. Bank of Greece, 1964–67; Sen. Economist, IMF, 1968–70; Advr to Cyprus Govt, negotiations for assoc. of Cyprus to EEC, 1971–72; Dep. Governor, Bank of Greece, 1974–77; Head of Greek delegn to Accession negotiations to the EEC, 1974–77; Advr to Cyprus Govt on relations with EEC, 1979–82; Ambassador to UK, and to Republic of Ireland, 1982–85; Alternate Exec. Dir, IMF, 1986–92. Knight Commander: Order of Merit (Italy); Order of Leopold II (Belgium); Comdr, Order of Merit (FRG). *Address:* 2 Misthou Street, Athens 16121, Greece. *Club:* Athens (Athens).

KYRLE POPE, Rear-Adm. Michael Donald, CB 1969; MBE 1946; DL; *b* 1 Oct. 1916; *e s* of late Comdr R. K. C. Pope, DSO, OBE, RN retd, and of Mrs A. J. Pope (*née* Macdonald); *m* 1947, Angela Suzanne Layton; one *s* one *d. Educ:* Wellington Coll., Berks. Joined RN, 1934; Submarine Service, 1938; HMS Vanguard, 1946–47; BJSM, Washington, 1951–53; Naval Intelligence: Germany, 1955–57, FE, 1958–60; Sen. Naval Off., Persian Gulf, 1962–64; MoD (Naval Intell.), 1965–67; Chief of Staff to C-in-C Far East, 1967–69; retd 1970. Comdr 1951; Capt. 1958; Rear-Adm. 1967. Gen. Manager, Middle East Navigation Aids Service, Bahrain, 1971–77. Dean's Administrator, St Alban's Abbey, 1977–80. Dir, Jerusalem and East Mission Trust, 1978–92. County Pres., Royal British Legion, 1987–95. DL Herts 1983. *Recreations:* country pursuits, sailing. *Address:* Hopfields, Westmill, Buntingford, Herts SG9 9LB. *T:* Royston (01763) 271835. *Club:* Army and Navy.

See also Sir J. E. Pope.

L

LABOUCHERE, Sir George (Peter), GBE 1964; KCMG 1955 (CMG 1951); *b* 2 Dec. 1905; *s* of late F. A. Labouchere; *m* 1943, Rachel Katharine, *d* of Hon. Eustace Hamilton-Russell. *Educ:* Charterhouse Sch.; Sorbonne, Paris. Entered Diplomatic Service, 1929. Served in Madrid, Cairo, Rio de Janeiro, Stockholm, Nanking, Buenos Aires. UK Deputy-Commissioner for Austria, 1951–53; HM Minister, Hungary, 1953–55; Ambassador to Belgium, 1955–60; Ambassador to Spain, 1960–66. Retired, 1966. Member of Council, Friends of the Tate Gallery; Pres., Shropshire Br., CPRE; Mem., Dilettanti Society; FRSA. *Recreations:* shooting, fishing, Chinese ceramics, contemporary painting and sculpture. *Address:* Dudmaston, Bridgnorth, Salop WV15 6QN. *Clubs:* Brooks's, Pratt's, Beefsteak, White's.

LABOUISSE, Mrs H. R.; *see* Curie, Eve.

LABOVITCH, Neville, LVO 1993; MBE 1977; *b* Leeds; *s* of late Mark and Anne Labovitch; *m* 1958, Sonia Deborah Barney (marr. diss. 1986); two *d. Educ:* Brasenose College, Oxford (MA). Treasurer, Oxford Union, 1945. Dir, 1954–82, Man. Dir, 1966–82, Darley Mills. Chairman: Brenta Construction, 1987–91 (Dir, 1985–91); Brenta Cogifar-Impresit, 1990–91; Brenta AB, 1993–; CP Carpets, Kidderminster, 1991–93. Chairman: Trafalgar Square Assoc., 1974–76; Knightsbridge Assoc., 1978–; Cleaner London Campaign, 1978–; Piccadilly Tourist Trust, 1978–82; Great Children's Party for IYC, 1979; London Environmental Campaign, 1983; Westminster Quatercentenary Cttee, 1984; Prince of Wales Royal Parks Tree Appeal, 1987–; Mem., Royal Parks Adv. Cttee, 1993–; Mem., London Celebrations Cttee for Queen's Silver Jubilee, and Chm., Silver Jubilee Exhibn, Hyde Park, 1977; Vice-Chm., Jubilee Walkway Trust, 1978–; Chairman: Organizing Cttee, Queen's 60th Birthday Celebrations, 1986; Queen's Anniv. Cttee, Hampton Court Palace 1952–1992, 1992. Mem., Vis. Cttee, RCA, 1983–90. Director: Nat. Children's Charities Fund, 1979–; Spitalfields Market Opera Ltd, 1994–. Trustee, Albert Memorial Trust, 1994–. FRSA. Cavaliere Ufficiale, Order of Merit (Italy), 1991. *Recreations:* reading and ruminating. *Club:* Brooks's.

LACEY, Ven. Clifford George; Archdeacon of Lewisham, 1985–89, now Emeritus; *b* 1 April 1921; *s* of Edward and Annie Elizabeth Lacey; *m* 1944, Sylvia Lilian George; one *s* two *d. Educ:* King's College London (AKC); St Boniface Coll., Warminster. RAFVR, 1941–46. Curate: St Hilda, Crofton Park, 1950–53; Kingston-upon-Thames, 1953–56; Vicar: St James, Merton, 1956–66; Eltham, 1966–79 (Sub-dean, 1970–79); Borough Dean of Greenwich, 1979–85; Bp of Norwich's Officer for retired clergy and widows, 1991–. Hon. Canon of Southwark, 1974–. *Recreation:* photography. *Address:* 31 Kerridges, East Harling, Norwich NR16 2QA. *T:* East Harling (01953) 718458.

LACEY, Frank; Director, Metrication Board, 1976–79, retired; *b* 4 Feb. 1919; *s* of Frank Krauter and Maud Krauter (*née* Lacey); *m* 1944, Maggie Tyrrell Boyes, 2nd *d* of late Sydney Boyes; one *s* one *d. Educ:* St Ignatius Coll., N7. Served War, 1939–46, RAFVR. Tax Officer, Inland Revenue, 1936; joined Board of Trade, 1946, Regional Dir, E Region, 1967–70; Counsellor (Commercial), UK Mission, Geneva, 1973–76. *Recreation:* wood turning. *Address:* Alma Cottage, Whistley Green, Hurst, Berks RG10 0EH. *T:* Twyford (01734) 340880.

LACEY, George William Brian; Keeper, Department of Transport, Science Museum, London, 1971–86; *b* 15 Nov. 1926; *m* 1956, Lynette (*née* Hogg); two *s. Educ:* Brighton, Hove and Sussex Grammar Sch., 1938–44; Brighton Technical Coll., 1944–47. BSc(Eng) 2nd Cl. Hons (External, London). National Service, REME, 1947–49. Rolls-Royce Ltd, Derby: Grad. Apprentice, Tech. Asst, Mechanical Develt and Performance Analysis, 1949–54. Asst Keeper, Science Museum, London, SW7, 1954. Chm., Historical Gp, Royal Aeronautical Soc., 1971–78; Vice-Pres., Assoc. British Transport Museums, 1990– (Chm., 1973–83); Mem. Council, Transport Trust, 1978–89. *Recreation:* golf. *Address:* Hurst Grange Cottage, Albourne Road, Hurstpierpoint, W Sussex BN6 9ES. *T:* Hurstpierpoint (01273) 833914.

LACEY, Prof. Richard Westgarth, MD, PhD; FRCPath; Professor of Medical Microbiology, University of Leeds, since 1983; Consultant to Leeds Health Authority, since 1983; *b* 11 Oct. 1940; *s* of Jack and Sybil Lacey; *m* 1972, Fionna Margaret Stone; two *d. Educ:* Felsted Sch., Essex; Cambridge Univ. (BA, MB, BChir; MD 1969); London Hosp.; Univ. of Bristol (PhD 1974). FRCPath 1985; DCH 1966. House Officer, London and Eastbourne, 1964–66; Sen. House Officer, 1966–67, Registrar, 1967–68, Bristol Royal Infirmary; Lectr, 1968–73, Reader in Clinical Microbiology, 1973–74, Univ. of Bristol; Consultant in Microbiology, 1974–83, and Consultant in Chemical Pathology, 1975–83, Queen Elizabeth Hosp., King's Lynn; Consultant in Chem. Path., E Anglian RHA, 1974–83. Consultant, WHO, 1983–. Evian Health Award, 1989; Caroline Walker Award, 1989; Freedom of Information Award, 1990. *Publications:* Safe Shopping, Safe Cooking, Safe Eating, 1989; Unfit for Human Consumption, 1991; Hard to Swallow, 1994; Mad Cow Disease: a history of BSE in Britain, 1994; 210 contribs to learned scientific jls. *Recreations:* antique furniture, gardening, chess, sleeping, walking, eating (not recently). *Address:* Department of Microbiology, University of Leeds, Leeds LS2 9JT. *T:* Leeds (0113) 233 5596.

LACHMANN, Prof. Peter Julius, FRCP; FRCPath; FRS 1982; Sheila Joan Smith Professor of Immunology (formerly Tumour Immunology), since 1977, and Fellow of Christ's College, 1962–71 and since 1976, University of Cambridge; Hon. Director of MRC Molecular Immunopathology Unit (formerly MRC Mechanisms in Tumour Immunity Unit), since 1980; *b* 23 Dec. 1931; *s* of late Heinz Lachmann and Thea (*née* Heller); *m* 1962, Sylvia Mary, *d* of Alan Stephenson; two *s* one *d. Educ:* Christ's Coll., Finchley; Trinity Coll., Cambridge; University College Hosp. MA, MB BChir, PhD, ScD (Cantab). FRCP 1973; FRCPath 1981. John Lucas Walker Student, Dept of Pathology, Cambridge, 1958–60; Vis. Investigator, Rockefeller Univ., New York, 1960–61; Empire Rheumatism Council Res. Fellow, Dept of Pathology, Cambridge, 1962–64; Asst Dir of Res. in Pathology, Univ. of Cambridge, 1964–71; Prof. of Immunology, Royal Postgraduate Med. Sch., 1971–75; Hd, 1976–77, Hon. Hd, 1977–80, MRC Gp on Mechanisms in Tumour Immunity; Hon. Clin. Immunologist, Cambridge HA, 1976–. Member: Systems Bd, MRC, 1982–86; Med. Adv. Cttee, British Council, 1983–; Council, RCPath, 1982–85, 1989–93 (Pres., 1990–93); Gene Therapy Adv. Cttee, 1993–; UNESCO Internat. Bioethics Cttee, 1993–; Med. Educn Res. Co-ordinating Cttee, 1994–; Scientific Adv. Bd, SmithKline Beecham, 1995–. Chairman: Med. Res. Cttee, Muscular Dystrophy Gp, 1987–91; Sci. Cttee, Assoc. Medical Res. Charities, 1988–92. Trustee, Darwin Trust, 1991–. Vis. Investigator, Scripps Clinic and Research Foundn, La Jolla, 1966, 1975, 1980, 1986, 1989; Vis. Scientist, Basel Inst. of Immunology, 1971; RSM Vis. Prof. in USA (various centres), 1983; Smith Kline & French Vis. Prof. in Australia (various centres), 1987; Vis. Prof., Dept of Medicine, RPMS, London, 1986–89 (Fellow, 1995); Meyerhoff Vis. Prof., Weitzmann Inst. Rehovott, 1989; Prof., Collège de France, 1993; RCS Sir Arthur Sims Travelling Prof., India, 1994; Lectures: Foundn, RCPath, 1983; Langdon-Brown, RCP, 1986; first R. R. Porter Meml, 1986; Heberden Oration, 1986; Prathap Meml, Malaysia, 1991; Charnock Bradley Meml, Royal (Dick) Vet. Sch., Edinburgh, 1994; Frank May Med. Scis, Univ. of Leicester, 1994. Biological Sec., and a Vice-Pres., Royal Soc., 1993–. Foreign Member: Norwegian Acad. of Science and Letters, 1991; Academia Europea, 1992. Hon. Fellow, Faculty of Pathology, RCPI, 1993. Associate Editor, Clinical and Experimental Immunology, 1989–. *Publications:* co-ed, Clinical Aspects of Immunology, 3rd edn 1975, 4th edn 1982, 5th edn 1993; papers in sci. jls on complement and immunopathology. *Recreations:* walking in mountains, keeping bees. *Address:* Conduit Head, 36 Conduit Head Road, Cambridge CB3 0EY. *T:* Cambridge (01223) 354433. *Club:* Athenæum.

LACHS, Henry Lazarus; His Honour Judge Lachs; a Circuit Judge, since 1979; *b* 31 Dec. 1927; *s* of Samuel and Mania Lachs; *m* 1959, Edith Bergel; four *d. Educ:* Liverpool Institute High Sch.; Pembroke Coll., Cambridge (MA, LLB). Called to Bar, Middle Temple, 1951. A Recorder of the Crown Court, 1972–79. Chm., Merseyside Mental Health Review Tribunal, 1968–79. *Address:* 41 Menlove Gardens West, Liverpool L18 2ET. *T:* 0151–722 5936.

LACKEY, Rt. Rev. Edwin Keith; Archbishop and Metropolitan of Ontario, 1991–93; Bishop of Ontario, 1981–93. *Educ:* Bishop's Univ., Lennoxville (BA 1953). Deacon 1953, priest 1954, Ottawa; Curate of Cornwall, 1953–55; Incumbent of Russell, 1955–60, Vankleek Hill, 1960–63; Rector of St Michael and All Angels, Ottawa, 1963–72, Director of Programme, dio. Ottawa, 1972–78; Hon. Canon, 1972–78; Archdeacon of the Diocese, 1978–81. Hon. DCL Bishop's Univ., 1988. *Address:* Archbishop's Office, 71 Bronson Avenue, Ottawa, Ontario K1R 6G6, Canada.

LACKEY, Mary Josephine, CB 1985; OBE 1966; former Under Secretary, Department of Trade and Industry; *b* 11 Aug. 1925; *d* of William and Winifred Lackey. *Educ:* King Edward VI High Sch., Birmingham; Lady Margaret Hall, Oxford (MA). Board of Trade, 1946; Asst Principal, Central Land Bd, 1947–50; BoT, 1950–61; UK Delegn to EFTA and GATT, 1961–66; BoT, subseq. DTI and Dept of Trade, 1966–85; Asst Sec., 1968; Under Sec., 1974. *Club:* United Oxford & Cambridge University.

LACLOTTE, Michel René; Officier de la Légion d'honneur; Commandeur de l'ordre national du Mérite; Director, The Louvre Museum, Paris, 1987–94; *b* 27 Oct. 1929; *s* of Pierre Laclotte, advocate, and Huguette (*née* de Kermabon). *Educ:* Lycée Pasteur, Neuilly; Institut d'art et d'archéologie, l'Université de Paris; Ecole du Louvre. Inspector, Inspectorate General of provincial museums, 1955–66; Chief Conservator: Dept of Paintings, Louvre Mus., 1966–87; Collections of Musée d'Orsay, 1978–86. *Publications:* works on history of art, catalogues, articles in art reviews, esp. on Italian paintings of 14th and 15th centuries and French primitives. *Address:* 10 bis rue du Pré-aux-Clercs, 75007 Paris, France.

LACOME, Myer; professional artist/designer; Principal, Duncan of Jordanstone College of Art, Dundee, 1978–88; *b* 13 Nov. 1927; *s* of Colman Lacome and Sara (*née* Sholl); *m* 1954, Jacci Edgar; one *s* two *d. Educ:* Regional Coll. of Art, Liverpool. MSIAD, MSTD, MInstPkg; FRSA. National Service, RAF, 1946–48. Post-grad. course, 1948–49; designer, New York, 1949–51; consultant designer, London, 1951–59; Head of Sch. of Design, Duncan of Jordanstone Coll. of Art, Dundee, 1962–77. Vis. Fellow, Royal Melbourne Inst. of Technol., 1979. Chm., Fine Art Cttee, Scottish Arts Council, 1986–93; Member: Council, CNAA, 1979–84; Higher Educn Cttee, Scottish Design Council, 1984–86; Governor, Scottish Film Council, 1982–. *Publications:* papers on crafts in Scotland and on Scandinavian design and crafts. *Recreations:* enjoying: no longer sitting on committees or quangos, not wearing a tie, painting in my studio, listening to Bach, Glenn Gould, Miles Davis and Thelonius Monk. *Address:* 4 Campbells Close, off Royal Mile, Edinburgh EH8 8JJ.

LACON, Sir Edmund (Vere), 8th Bt *cr* 1818; Company Secretary, S.A.K. Ventures Ltd, since 1992; *b* 3 May 1936; *s* of Sir George Vere Francis Lacon, 7th Bt, and of Hilary Blanche (now Mrs J. D. Turner), *d* of late C. J. Scott, Adyar, Walberswick; *S* father, 1980; *m* 1963, Gillian, *d* of J. H. Middleditch, Wrentham, Suffolk; one *s* one *d. Educ:* Taverham Hall, Norfolk; Woodbridge School, Suffolk. RAF Regiment, 1955–59. Career in sales management and marketing, 1959–. *Recreations:* golf, water-skiing, being politically incorrect. *Heir: s* (Edmund) Richard (Vere) Lacon, *b* 2 Oct. 1967. *Club:* Naval and Military.

LACOSTE, Prof. Paul, OC 1977; DU Paris; Rector, Université de Montréal, 1975–85, Professor Emeritus since 1987; Chairman, Federal Environmental Assessment Review of the Great Whale Project, since 1991; *b* 24 April 1923; *s* of Emile Lacoste and Juliette

Boucher Lacoste; *m* 1973 (marr. diss.); one *s* two *d*. *Educ:* Univ. de Montréal (BA, MA, LPh, LLL). DUP 1948. Fellow, Univ. of Chicago, 1946–47; Univ. de Montréal: Prof., Faculty of Philosophy, 1948; Full Prof., 1958; Vice-Rector, 1968–75; Vis. Prof., Faculty of Law, 1962–70 and 1985–87. Practising lawyer, 1964–66. Pres., Assoc. des universités partiellement ou entièrement de langue française, 1978–81. Hon. LLD: McGill, 1975; Toronto, 1978; Hon Du Laval, 1986. Chevalier de la Légion d'Honneur, 1985. *Publications:* (jtly) Justice et paix scolaire, 1962; A Place of Liberty, 1964; Le Canada au seuil du siècle de l'abondance, 1969; Principes de gestion universitaire, 1970; (jtly) Education permanente et potentiel universitaire, 1977. *Address:* Université de Montréal, PO Box 6128, Montréal H3C 3J7, Canada. *T:* (514) 3437727; 2910 boulevard Edouard-Montpetit, Montréal.

LACROIX, Christian Marie Marc; Chevalier des Arts et des Lettres, France, 1991; designer; *b* 16 May 1951; *s* of Maxime Lacroix and Jeannette Bergier; *m* 1989, Françoise Roesenstiehl. *Educ:* Paul Valéry Univ., Montpellier; Sorbonne. History of Art degree. Assistant at Hermès, 1978; Asst for Guy Paulin, 1980; designer for Patou, 1981–86. Golden Thimble Award, 1986 and 1988; CFDA Award, NY, 1987. *Publication:* Pieces of a Pattern (autobiog.), 1992. *Address:* 73 Faubourg St Honoré, 75008 Paris, France. *T:* 42657908.

LACY, Sir Hugh Maurice Pierce, 3rd Bt, *cr* 1921; *b* 3 Sept 1943; *s* of Sir Maurice John Pierce Lacy, 2nd Bt, and of his 2nd wife, Nansi Jean, *d* of late Myrddin Evans, Bangor, Caernarvonshire; *S* father, 1965; *m* 1968, Deanna, *d* of Howard Bailey. *Educ:* Aiglon Coll., Switzerland. *Heir: b* Patrick Bryan Finucane Lacy [*b* 18 April 1948; *m* 1971, Phyllis Victoria, *d* of E. P. H. James; one *s* one *d*].

LACY, Sir John (Trend), Kt 1992; CBE 1983; General Director of Party Campaigning, Conservative Central Office, 1989–92; *b* 15 March 1928; *s* of Rev. Hubert Lacy and Mrs Gertrude Lacy (*née* Markham); *m* 1956, Pamela Guerin; one *s*. *Educ:* King's Sch., Ely, Cambs. Served RN, 1945–48. Harvey & Clark (Manufrs), 1948–50; Conservative Party: London, 1950–56; Aylesbury, 1956–61; W Midlands area, 1961–64; Northern area, 1964–71; S Eastern area, 1971–85; Dir of Campaigning, 1985–89. *Recreations:* racing, fishing, philately. *Address:* 18 Windmill Close, Milford-on-Sea, Hants SO41 0SX. *T:* Lymington (01590) 643984. *Clubs:* Carlton, St Stephen's Constitutional (Vice Chm., 1988–93).

LADAS, Mrs Diana Margaret; *b* 8 Feb. 1913; *er d* of late Bertram Hambro and late Mrs Charles Boyle; *m* 1945, Alexis Christopher Ladas (marr. diss. 1955); one *s*. *Educ:* Downe House Sch.; Girton Coll., Cambridge. Before the war, Sec. in Geneva, Malta and London. During War of 1939–45, worked as temp. asst Principal in Min. of Economic Warfare, Board of Trade and Political Warfare executive in Cairo. Transferred to UNRRA, worked in Athens, Washington and London; on the staff of British Information Services, in New York, 1948–50. Began teaching at Westminster Tutors, 1955; joined staff of Heathfield Sch., 1958; Dep. Head of Moira House Sch., 1959, Head Mistress, 1960; Vice-Principal of Queen's Gate Sch., 1962–65; Head Mistress, Heathfield Sch., 1965–72. Since retirement, occupied with voluntary social work and local politics. *Recreations:* gardening and travelling. *Address:* 154 Peckham Rye, SE22 9QH.

LADDIE, Hon. Sir Hugh Ian Lang, Kt 1995; **Hon. Mr Justice Laddie;** Judge of the High Court of Justice, Chancery Division, since 1995; *b* 15 April 1946; *s* of late Bertie Daniel Laddie and of Rachel Laddie; *m* 1970, Stecia Elizabeth (*née* Zamet); two *s* one *d*. *Educ:* Aldenham Sch.; St Catharine's Coll., Cambridge (MA). Called to the Bar, Middle Temple, 1969 (Blackstone Pupillage Award; Bencher, 1993); Jun. Counsel to HM Treasury in Patent Matters, 1981–86; QC 1986. Jun. Bar Rep., Patents Procedure Cttee, 1976. Sec., Patent Bar Assoc., 1971–75; Mem. Cttee, Chancery Bar Assoc., 1991–92. Chm., Vet. Code of Practice Cttee, Nat. Office of Animal Health. Asst Ed.-in-Chief, Annual of Industrial Property Law, 1975–79; UK Correspondent, European Law Rev., 1978–83. *Publications:* (jtly) Patent Law of Europe and the United Kingdom, 1978; (jtly) The Modern Law of Copyright, 1980. *Recreations:* music, gardening, fishing.

LADE, Hilary Jane; Director of Historic Properties, English Heritage, since 1993; *b* 11 June 1957; *d* of Herbert Alfred Lade and Margaret (*née* Clark). *Educ:* Selwyn Coll., Cambridge (MA Oriental Studies (Chinese)); Harvard Univ. (MA E Asian Langs and Civilisations); Univ. of Calif, Berkeley (MA Internat. Relns). Oil trader, Shell Internat., 1984–87; Man. Dir, Shell Gas Ltd, Shell UK, 1987–91; Estate Manager, Fountains Abbey and Studley Royal, NT, 1991–93. Winston Churchill Travelling Fellow, 1978; Harkness Fellow, 1980. *Recreations:* music (violin player), travel, ski-ing, mountaineering. *Address:* Keysign House, 429 Oxford Street, W1R 2HD. *T:* 0171–973 3486.

LAFITTE, Prof. François; Professor of Social Policy and Administration, University of Birmingham, 1959–80, now Emeritus; *b* 3 Aug. 1913; *s* of John Armistead Collier and Françoise Lafitte and adopted *s* of late Havelock Ellis; *m* 1938, Eileen (*née* Saville); (one *s* decd). *Educ:* Collège Municipal, Maubeuge; George Green's Sch., Poplar; St Olave's Grammar Sch., Southwark; Worcester Coll., Oxford. Research and translating for Miners' Internat. Fed., 1936–37; on research staff, and subseq. Dep. Sec., PEP, 1938–43; on editorial staff of The Times, as special writer on social questions, 1943–59; Chm. of PEP research groups on health services, 1943–46, on housing policy, 1948–51. Dean of Faculty of Commerce and Social Science, Birmingham, Univ., 1965–68. Member: Home Office Advisory Council on the Treatment of Offenders, 1961–64; Adv. Cttees Social Science Research Council, 1966–69; Redditch New Town Corp., 1964–75; Chm., British Pregnancy Adv. Service, 1968–88. *Publications:* The Internment of Aliens, 1940, repr. 1988; Britain's Way to Social Security, 1945; Family Planning in the Sixties, 1964; (part author) Socially Deprived Families in Britain, 1970; many PEP Planning monographs; many papers on abortion and related issues; contributed to British Journal of Delinquency, Eugenics Review, Chambers's Encyclopædia. etc. *Address:* 77 Oakfield Road, Birmingham B29 7HL. *T:* 0121–472 2709. *Club:* University Staff (Birmingham).

LA FRENAIS, Ian; writer, screenwriter and producer; *b* 7 Jan. 1937; *s* of Cyril and Gladys La Frenais; *m* 1984, Doris Vartan; one step *s*. *Educ:* Dame Allan's School, Northumberland. *Television:* writer or co-writer (with Dick Clement): The Likely Lads, 1965–68; The Adventures of Lucky Jim, 1968; Whatever Happened to the Likely Lads, 1971–73; Seven of One, 1973; Thick as Thieves, 1974; Comedy Playhouse, 1975; Porridge, 1974–77; Going Straight, 1978; Further Adventures of Lucky Jim, 1983; Auf Wiedersehen Pet, 1983–84; Mog, 1985; Lovejoy, 1986; Spender, 1990; Freddie and Max, 1990; Old Boy Network, 1991; Full Stretch, 1993; Over the Rainbow, 1993; *US television:* On The Rocks, 1976–77; Billy, 1979; Sunset Limousine, 1983; Tracy Ullman Special, 1993; *films:* writer or co-writer (with Dick Clement): The Jokers, 1967; The Touchables, 1968; Otley, 1968; Hannibal Brooks, 1969; The Virgin Soldiers, 1969; Villain, 1970; Catch Me a Spy, 1971; The Likely Lads, 1975; Porridge, 1979; To Russia with Elton, 1979; Prisoner of Zenda, 1981; Water, 1984; writer-producer (with Dick Clement), Vice Versa, 1987; The Commitments, 1991; *stage:* writer, Billy, 1974; co-producer, Anyone for Denis?, 1982. Partner (with Dick Clement and Allan McKeown), Witzend Productions; producer, co-producer, director, numerous productions. Awards from BAFTA, Broadcasting Guild, Evening News, Pye, Screen Writers' Guild, Soc. of TV Critics, Writers' Guild of America, London Film Critics' Circle. *Publications:* novelisations of The Likely Lads, Whatever Happened to the Likely Lads, Porridge, Auf Wiedersehen Pet. *Recreations:* music, films, sports, wine, driving. *Address:* 2557 Hutton Drive, Beverly Hills, CA 90210, USA.

LAGACOS, Eustace P.; Foreign Affairs Counsellor to the Leader of the Opposition, Greece, since 1985; *b* 4 June 1921; one *d*. *Educ:* Univ. of Athens (Graduate of Law). Embassy Attaché, 1949; served Athens, Paris, Istanbul, Nicosia, London; Minister, 1969; Foreign Ministry, Athens, 1970; Ambassador to Nicosia, 1972; Dir Gen., Economic Affairs, Foreign Ministry, Athens, 1974; Permanent Representative to NATO, Brussels, 1976; Ambassador to UK, 1979–82. Mem., Eur. Parlt, 1989–94. Grand Officer of Order of the Phoenix, Greece; Commander of Order of George I, Greece; Grand Cordon of Order of Manuel Amadoi Guerrero, Panama; Commander of Legion of Honour, France; Kt Commander of Order of Queen Isabella I, Spain; Grand Officer of Order of the Republic, Egypt. *Publication:* The Cyprus Question, 1987. *Address:* 7 Kapsali Street, Athens 10674, Greece.

LAGOS, Archbishop of, (RC), since 1973 (and Metropolitan); **Most Rev. Anthony Olubunmi Okogie,** DD; *b* Lagos, 16 June 1936. *Educ:* St Gregory's Coll., Lagos; St Theresa's Minor Seminary, Ibadan; St Peter and St Paul's Seminary, Ibadan; Urban Univ., Rome. Priest, 1966; appointments include: Acting Parish Priest, St Patrick's Church, Idumagbo, 1967–71; Asst Priest, and Master of Ceremonies, Holy Cross Cathedral, Lagos, 1967–71; Religious Instructor, King's Coll., Lagos, 1967–71; Director of Vocations, Archdiocese of Lagos, 1968–71; Manager, Holy Cross Group of Schools, Lagos, 1969–71; Auxiliary Bishop of Oyo, 1971–72; Auxiliary Bishop to Apostolic Administrator, Archdiocese of Lagos, 1972–73. Vice-Pres., 1983–88, Pres., 1988–94, Catholic Bishops Conf. of Nigeria; Roman Catholic Trustee of Christian Assoc. of Nigeria, 1974–; Member: State Community Relns Cttee, 1984–; Prerogative of Mercy, 1986–; Adv. Council on Religious Affairs, 1987–; Chm., Christian Assoc. of Nigeria, 1989–. *Address:* Holy Cross Cathedral, PO Box 8, Lagos, Nigeria. *T:* (1) 2635729 and (1) 2633841, *Fax:* 2633841.

LAGOS, Bishop of; *see* Nigeria, Metropolitan Archbishop and Primate of.

LAHNSTEIN, Manfred; Member of Executive Board, Bertelsmann Corporation, since 1983; President, Electronic-Media Division, since 1985; *b* 20 Dec. 1937; *s* of Walter and Hertha Lahnstein; one *s* one *d*. *Educ:* Cologne Univ. (Dipl. Kfm). German Trade Union Fedn, Dusseldorf, 1962–64; European Trade Union Office, Brussels, 1965–67; European Commn, 1967–73; German Govt service, 1973–82: served in Finance Min. and as Head of Chancellor's Office; Minister of Finance, April–Oct. 1982. Pres., Bertelsmann printing and manufacturing gp, 1983–85. *Publications:* various articles. *Recreation:* classical music. *Address:* c/o 4830 Gütersloh, Carl Bertelsmann Strasse 270, Germany. *T:* 05241801.

LAÏDI, Ahmed; Algerian Ambassador to Mexico, 1988–89; *b* 20 April 1934; *m* 1964, Aicha Chabbi-Lemsine; one *s* one *d* (and one *s* decd). *Educ:* Algiers Univ. (BA); Oran Univ. (LLB). Counsellor to Presidency of Council of Algerian Republic, 1963; Head of Cabinet of Presidency, 1963–64; Dir. Gen. of Political and Economic Affairs, Min. of Foreign Affairs, 1964–66; Chm., Prep. Cttee, second Afro-Asian Conf., 1964–65; Special Envoy to Heads of States, Senegal, Mali, Ivory Coast and Nigeria, 1966; Ambassador to Spain, 1966–70; Head, Delegn to Geneva Conf. of non-nuclear countries, 1968; Wali (Governor): province Médea, 1970–74; province Tlemcen, 1975–78; Ambassador to Jordan, 1978–84; Special Envoy to Heads of States and govts, Zambia, Malaŵi, Botswana, Zimbabwe, 1985; Ambassador to UK, 1984–88, and to Ireland, 1985–88. Member: Algerian Football Fedn, 1964–66; Algerian Nat. Olympic Cttee, 1965–72. Foreign Orders: Liberia, 1963; Bulgaria, 1964; Yugoslavia, 1964; Spain, 1970; Jordan, 1984. *Recreations:* theatre, cinema, football. *Address:* Villa Akram, Rue No 1, Parc Paradou, Hydra, Algiers, Algeria.

LAIDLAW, Sir Christopher (Charles Fraser), Kt 1982; Director: Daimler-Benz (UK) Ltd, since 1994; Amerada Hess Ltd, since 1986; *b* 9 Aug. 1922; *m* 1952, Nina Mary Prichard; one *s* three *d*. *Educ:* Rugby Sch.; St John's Coll., Cambridge (MA). Served War of 1939–45: Europe and Far East, Major on Gen. Staff; Intelligence Corps, 1941–46. Joined British Petroleum, 1948: BP Rep. in Hamburg, 1959–61; Gen. Manager, Marketing Dept, 1963–67; Dir, BP Trading, 1967; Dir (Ops), 1971–72; a Man. Dir, 1972–81, and Dep. Chm., BP, 1980–81; Dir, Soc. Française BP, 1964–85; President, BP: Belgium, 1967–71; Italiana, 1972–73; Deutsche BP, 1972–83; Chairman: BP Oil, 1977–81; BP Oil Internat., 1981; Boving & Co. Ltd, 1984–86. Chm., ICL plc, 1981–84; Pres., ICL France, 1983; Chm., Bridon, 1985–90. Director: Commercial Union Assurance, 1978–83; Barclays Bank International, 1980–87; Barclays Bank plc, 1981–88; Equity Capital for Industry Ltd, 1983–86; Amerada Hess Corp., 1983–94; Barclays Merchant Bank Ltd, 1984–86; Dalgety, 1984–92; Redland, 1984–92; TWIL Ltd, 1985–89; Mercedes-Benz (UK) Ltd, 1986–93. Pres., German Chamber of Industry and Commerce, 1983–86; Mem., Internat. Council, 1980–, Chm. UK Adv. Bd, 1984–91, Dir, INSEAD, 1987–94. Master, Tallow Chandlers' Co., 1988–89. *Address:* 49 Chelsea Square, SW3 6LH. *Clubs:* Buck's, Garrick.

LAIDLAW, (Henry) Renton; golf correspondent, Evening Standard, since 1973; *b* 6 July 1939; *s* of late Henry Renton Laidlaw and of Margaret McBeath Laidlaw (*née* Raiker). *Educ:* James Gillespie's Boys' School, Edinburgh; Daniel Stewart's College, Edinburgh. Golf corresp., Edinburgh Evening News, 1957–67; news presenter and reporter, Grampian Television, Aberdeen, 1968–69; BBC news presenter, Edinburgh, 1970–72; BBC Radio golf reporter, 1976–; presenter: BBC Radio Sport on 2, 1986, 1987; ITV Eurosport, 1988; golf presenter: BSB, 1989–91; Golf Channel, US, 1995–; Chief Commentator, PGA European Tour Prodns, 1988–. *Publications:* Play Golf (with Peter Alliss), 1977; Jacklin—the first 40 years, 1984; (ed) Johnnie Walker Ryder Cup '85, 1985; Play Better Golf, 1986; (ed) Johnnie Walker Ryder Cup '87, 1987; Ten Years—the history of the European Open, 1988; Golf Heroes, 1989; (ed) Johnnie Walker Ryder Cup '89, 1989; (with Bernard Gallacher) Captain at Kiawah, 1991; Wentworth: a host of happy memories, 1993. *Recreations:* theatre, golf. *Address:* c/o Evening Standard, Northcliffe House, 2 Derry Street, Kensington, W8 5EE. *Clubs:* Caledonian; Royal & Ancient (St Andrews); Sunningdale Golf, Wentworth, Royal Burgess Golf.

LAIGHT, Barry Pemberton, OBE 1970; Eur Ing; FEng, FIMechE, FRAeS; Consultant to: Design Council, since 1983; VAWT Ltd, since 1983; RES Ltd, since 1983; Production Engineering Research Association, since 1986; Department of Trade and Industry, 1988–90; *s* of Donald Norman Laight and Nora (*née* Pemberton); *m* 1951, Ruth Murton; one *s* one *d*. *Educ:* Johnston Sch., Durham; Birmingham Central Tech. Coll.; Merchant Venturers' Tech. Coll., Bristol; Bristol Univ. MSc. FEng 1981. SBAC Scholar, apprentice, Bristol Aeroplane Co., 1937; Chief Designer, 1952, Technical Dir, 1960, Blackburn & General Aircraft (develt of Beverley and design of Buccaneer, 1953, for RN service, 1960); Chief Engineer Kingston, 1963, Dir for Military Projects, 1968, Hawker Siddeley Aviation (Harrier develt to RAF service; introd. Hawk Trainer); Exec. Dir Engineering, Short Brothers, 1977–82 (develt SD360 and Blowpipe); Sec., RAeS, 1983–85. Mem. Council, RAeS, 1955–90 (Pres., 1974–75; British Silver Medal in Aeronautics, 1963); Chairman: Educn Cttee, SBAC, 1962–67; Tech. Board, SBAC, 1967–82; Member: Aircraft Res. Assoc. Board, 1972–77 (Chm., Tech. Cttee); ARC, 1973–76; Air Educn and Recreational Organisation Council, 1969–72; CBI: Mem., Res. and Tech. Cttee; Educn Cttee; Chm., Transport Technology Panel, SRC, 1969–73; Hon. Treasurer, Internat. Council of Aero. Scis, 1978–84; AGARD Nat. Delegate, 1968–73; Sec., Bristol Gliding Club, 1949–52;

Mem., Mensa, 1945; MAIAA; FInstD. *Publications:* papers in RAeS jls. *Recreations:* reading on any subject, house and car maintenance, music. *Address:* 5 Littlemead, Esher, Surrey KT10 9PE. *T:* Esher (01372) 463216.

LAINÉ, Christopher Norman; Partner, Coopers & Lybrand, since 1971; *b* 12 Oct. 1936; *s* of James Norman Balliol Lainé and Sybil Mary Lainé (*née* Fuge); *m* 1967, Sally Outhwaite; one *s* one *d*. *Educ:* King's Sch., Canterbury (Scholar); Trinity Coll., Oxford (Exhibnr; MA). FCA. Nat. Service, RA, 1955–57; commnd 1956. Cooper Brothers & Co., later Coopers & Lybrand: joined 1960; Partner i/c S Coast, 1971–90; Sen. Partner, S Coast, 1990–. Pres., Southern Soc. of Chartered Accountants, 1986–87; Institute of Chartered Accountants in England and Wales: Mem. Council, 1990–; Chm., Dist. Socs Cttee, 1991–95; Exec., 1993–; Vice-Pres., 1995–June 1996. Gov., Canford Sch., 1990–. *Recreations:* cricket, golf, classical music, painting. *Address:* Woodlands Cottage, Lower Common Road, West Wellow, Romsey, Hants SO51 6BT. *T:* Romsey (01794) 322247. *Clubs:* Hampshire CCC (Treasurer); Stoneham Golf; Hampshire Hogs Cricket, Forty.

LAINE, Cleo, (Mrs Clementine Dinah Dankworth), OBE 1979; vocalist; *b* 28 Oct. 1927; British; *m* 1st, 1947, George Langridge (marr. diss. 1957); one *s*; 2nd, 1958, John Philip William Dankworth, *qv*; one *s* one *d*. Joined Dankworth Orchestra, 1953. Melody Maker and New Musical Express Top Girl Singer Award, 1956; Moscow Arts Theatre Award for acting role in Flesh to a Tiger, 1958; Top place in Internat. Critics Poll by Amer. Jazz magazine, Downbeat, 1965. Lead, in Seven Deadly Sins, Edinburgh Festival and Sadler's Wells, 1961; acting roles in Edin. Fest., 1966, 1967, Cindy-Ella, Garrick, 1968. Many appearances with symphony orchestras performing Façade (Walton), Pierrot Lunaire and other compositions; played Julie in Show Boat, Adelphi, 1971; title role in Colette, Comedy, 1980; Hedda Gabler; Valmouth; A Time to Laugh; The Women of Troy; The Mystery of Edwin Drood, 1986; Into the Woods (US nat. tour), 1989; Noyes Fludde (Proms), 1990. Frequent TV appearances. Woman of the Year, 9th annual Golden Feather Awards, 1973; Edison Award, 1974; Variety Club of GB Show Business Personality Award (with John Dankworth), 1977; TV Times Viewers Award for Most Exciting Female Singer on TV, 1978; Grammy Award for Best Female Jazz Vocalist, 1985; Theatre World Award, 1986; NARM Presidential Lifetime Achievement Award, 1990; British Jazz Awards Vocalist of the Year, 1990; Gold Discs: Feel the Warm; I'm a Song; Live at Melbourne; Platinum Discs: Best Friends; Sometimes When We Touch. Hon. MA Open, 1975; Hon. DMus Berklee Sch. of Music, 1982; DUniv York, 1993. *Publication:* Cleo (autobiog.), 1994. *Recreation:* painting. *Address:* UK Management, Deke Arlon, D. & J. Arlon Enterprises Ltd, Pinewood Studios, Pinewood Road, Iver, Bucks SL0 0NH. *T:* Iver (01753) 650808, *Fax:* (01753) 650705.

LAING, family name of **Baron Laing of Dunphail**.

LAING OF DUNPHAIL, Baron *cr* 1991 (Life Peer), of Dunphail in the District of Moray; **Hector Laing,** Kt 1978; Life President, United Biscuits (Holdings) plc, 1990 (Director, 1953; Managing Director, 1964; Chairman, 1972–90); *b* 12 May 1923; *s* of Hector Laing and Margaret Norris Grant; *m* 1950, Marian Clare, *d* of Maj.-Gen. Sir John Laurie, 6th Bt, CBE, DSO; three *s*. *Educ:* Loretto Sch., Musselburgh, Scotland; Jesus Coll., Cambridge (Hon. Fellow, 1988). Served War, Scots Guards, 1942–47 (American Bronze Star, despatches, 1944); final rank, Captain. McVitie & Price: Dir, 1947; Chm., 1963. Mem. Bd, Royal Insurance Co., 1970–78; Director: Allied-Lyons, 1979–82; Exxon Corp. (USA), 1984–. A Dir, Bank of England, 1973–91. Chairman: Food and Drink Industries Council, 1977–79; Scottish Business in the Community, 1982–91; Business in the Community, 1987–91. Jt Treas., Cons. Party, 1988–93. Chm., Lambeth Fund, 1983–. Mem. Council, Wycombe Abbey Sch., 1981–94. FRSE 1989. DUniv Stirling, 1985; Hon. DLitt Heriot-Watt, 1986. Businessman of the Year Award, 1979; National Free Enterprise Award, 1980. *Recreations:* gardening, walking. *Address:* High Meadows, Windsor Road, Gerrards Cross, Bucks SL9 8ST. *T:* Gerrards Cross (01753) 885106. *Club:* White's.

LAING, Alastair Stuart, CBE 1980; MVO 1959; *b* 17 June 1920; *s* of Captain Arthur Henry Laing and Clare May Laing (*née* Ashworth); *m* 1946 Audrey Stella Hobbs, MCSP, *d* of Dr Frederick Hobbs and Gladys Marion Hobbs (*née* George); one *s* decd. *Educ:* Sedbergh School. Served Indian Army, 10th Gurkha Rifles, 1940–46, Captain; seconded to Civil Administration, Bengal, 1944–46. Commonwealth War Graves Commission, 1947–83 (Dep. Dir Gen., 1975–83). Chm., Vale of Aylesbury Hunt, 1981–87. *Publications:* various articles. *Recreations:* gardening, foxhunting, racing, history. *Address:* Wagtails, Lower Wood End, Marlow, Bucks SL7 2HN. *T:* Marlow (01628) 484481.

LAING, Dr Douglas Rees; Director General, CAB International, 1993; *b* 31 Aug. 1936; *s* of Douglas Harvey Laing and Jessie Hilda Laing; *m* 1st, 1966, Rosemary Isabel Whiting; one *s* one *d*; 2nd, 1992, Olga Lucia Villa. *Educ:* Univ. of Queensland (BAgrSc Hons); Iowa State Univ. (PhD 1966). Fulbright Scholar, 1962. Lectr, then Sen. Lectr, Dept of Agronomy, Univ. of Sydney, 1966–73; International Center for Tropical Agriculture, Colombia: Physiologist, 1974–79; Dir, Crop Research, 1979–84; Dep. Dir General, 1984–92. FAIAS 1993. *Publications:* contrib. chaps in books; numerous pubns and workshop and conference contribs on crop physiology, internat. agriculture and lately on intellectual property rights. *Recreations:* natural history, scuba diving, reading. *Address:* The Lime House, Ancastle Green, Henley-on-Thames, Oxon RG9 1TR.

LAING, Gerald O.; *see* Ogilvie-Laing.

LAING, James Findlay; Under Secretary, Scottish Office Environment Department (formerly Scottish Development Department), 1988–93; *b* 7 Nov. 1933; *s* of Alexander Findlay Laing and Jessie Ross; *m* 1969, Christine Joy Canaway; one *s*. *Educ:* Nairn Academy; Edinburgh Univ. MA (Hons History). Nat. Service, Seaforth Highlanders, 1955–57. Asst Principal and Principal, Scottish Office, 1957–68; Principal, HM Treasury, 1968–71; Asst Sec., Scottish Office, 1972–79; Under Sec., Scottish Econ. Planning Dept, later Industry Dept. for Scotland, 1979–88. *Recreations:* squash, chess. *Address:* 6 Barnton Park Place, Edinburgh EH4 6ET. *T:* 0131–336 5951. *Club:* Edinburgh Sports.

LAING, Prof. John Archibald, PhD; MRCVS; Professor Emeritus, University of London, since 1984 (Courtauld Professor of Animal Husbandry and Hygiene, at Royal Veterinary College, University of London, 1959–84); *b* 27 April 1919; *s* of late John and Alexandra Laing; *m* 1946, June Margaret Lindsay Smith, *d* of Hugh Lindsay Smith, Downham Market; one *s* two *d*. *Educ:* Johnston Sch., Durham; Royal (Dick) School of Veterinary Studies, Edinburgh University; Christ's Coll. Cambridge. BSc(Edinburgh); MRCVS; PhD (Cantab). FIBiol. Aleen Cust Scholar, Royal Coll. of Veterinary Surgeons. Research Officer, 1943–46, Asst Veterinary Investigation Officer, 1946–49, Ministry of Agriculture; Univ. of Bristol, 1949–59 (Reader in Veterinary Science, 1957–59). Anglo-Danish Churchill Fellowship, Univ. of Copenhagen, 1954; Visiting Professor, Univs of: Munich, 1967; Mexico, 1967; Queensland, 1970 (and John Thompson Memorial Lectr); Ankara, 1977; Assiut, 1980; Consultant to FAO, UN, 1955–57; Representative of FAO in Dominican Republic, 1957–58; Consultant to UNESCO in Central America, 1963–65; Mem., British Agricultural Mission to Peru, 1970. Member: EEC Veterinary Scientific Cttee, 1981–90; Dairy Product Quota Tribunal for England and Wales, 1984. Hon. Mem., Internat. Congress on Animal Reproduction, 1988 (Sec., 1961–80; Pres., 1980–84). Chm., Melrose Meml Trust, 1984–91; Member: Governing Body, Houghton Poultry Research Station, 1968–74; Council, Royal Veterinary Coll., 1975–84; Vice-Pres., University Fedn for Animal Welfare, 1977–84 (Treasurer, 1969–75; Chm., 1975–77). Chm., Steering Cttee, World Assoc. for Transport Animal Welfare Studies. Hon. Fellow Veterinary Acad., Madrid. Editor, British Veterinary Journal, 1960–84. *Publications:* Fertility and Infertility in the Domestic Animals, 1955, 4th edn 1988; papers on animal breeding and husbandry in various scientific journals. *Address:* Ayot St Lawrence, Herts AL6 9BW. *T:* Stevenage (01438) 820413. *Club:* Athenæum.

LAING, (John) Martin (Kirby), CBE 1991; DL; Chairman, John Laing, since 1985; *b* 18 Jan. 1942; *s* of Sir (William) Kirby Laing, *qv*; *m* 1965, Stephanie Stearn Worsdell; one *s* one *d*. *Educ:* St Lawrence College, Ramsgate; Emmanuel College, Cambridge (MA). FRICS. Joined Laing Group 1966; Dir, John Laing, 1980. Member: Building Employers' Confedn, 1981– (Chm., Nat. Contractors Gp, 1987); CBI Council, 1986–; CBI Overseas Cttee, 1983– (Chm., 1989–); CBI Task Force on Business and Urban Regeneration, 1987–88; Cttee for Middle East Trade, 1982–86; SE Asia Trade Adv. Group, 1985–89; UK Adv. Cttee, British American Chamber of Commerce, 1985–; Adv. Council, World Economic Forum, 1986–; NEDO Construction Industry Sector Gp, 1988–93; Business in the Community, 1986– (Dir, 1995–); Member: UK–Japan 2000 Gp, 1988–; Chm., British Urban Develt, 1988–90; Dep. Chm., Building Experience Trust, 1992–; Member: World Business Council for Sustainable Develt, 1991–; Council, London First, 1992–. Member: Home Office Parole Review Cttee, 1987–88; Archbishop's Council, Church Urban Fund, 1987–94; Trilateral Commn, 1994–. Dir, City of London Sinfonia, 1988–. Dir, Herts Groundwork Trust, 1986–91; Trustee: Nat. Energy Foundn, 1988–; WWF (UK), 1988– (Chm., 1990–); WWF Internat., 1991–. Crown Mem., Court of Univ. of London, 1987–95; Mem. Board of Governors, Papplewick School, Ascot, 1983–93; Gov., St Lawrence Coll., Ramsgate, 1988–. Master, Paviors' Co., 1995–March 1996. CIMgt (CBIM 1985); CIEx 1987; FCIM 1987; FRSA 1988; FICE 1993; FIHT 1995. DL Hertford, 1987. *Recreations:* gardening, music, travel. *Address:* John Laing plc, Page Street, NW7 2ER.

LAING, Sir (John) Maurice, Kt 1965; Director, 1939–88, and Life President, since 1988, John Laing plc (formerly John Laing & Son Ltd) (Deputy Chairman, 1966–76, Chairman, 1976–82); *b* 1 Feb. 1918; *s* of Sir John Laing, CBE, and late Beatrice Harland; *m* 1940, Hilda Violet Richards; one *s*. *Educ:* St Lawrence Coll., Ramsgate. RAF, 1941–45. Dir, Bank of England, 1963–80. Member: UK Trade Missions to Middle East, 1953, and to Egypt, Sudan and Ethiopia, 1955; Economic Planning Bd, 1961; Export Guarantees Adv. Council, 1959–63; Min. of Transport Cttee of Inquiry into Major Ports of Gt Brit. (Rochdale Cttee), 1961–62; NEDC, 1962–66. First Pres., CBI, 1965–66; President: British Employers Confederation, 1964–65; Export Group for the Constructional Industries, 1976–80; Fedn of Civil Engrg Contractors, 1977–80. Visiting Fellow, Nuffield Coll., 1965–70; A Governor: Administrative Staff Coll., 1966–72; Nat. Inst. of Economic and Social Research, 1964–82. Pres., London Bible Coll., 1993–. Admiral, Royal Ocean Racing Club, 1976–82; Rear-Cdre, Royal Yacht Squadron, 1982–86, Pres., Royal Yachting Assoc., 1983–87. Hon. FCGI 1978; Hon. FCIOB 1981. Hon. LLD University of Strathclyde, 1967. Winner, Aims of Industry Free Enterprise Award, 1979. Has keen interest in Church activities at home and abroad. *Recreations:* sailing, swimming. *Address:* John Laing plc, Page Street, NW7 2ER. *Clubs:* Royal Yacht Squadron, Royal Ocean Racing.

See also Sir W. K. Laing.

LAING, (John) Stuart, HM Diplomatic Service; Deputy Head of Mission and HM Consul General, British Embassy, Riyadh, since 1992; *b* 22 July 1948; *s* of late Dr Denys Laing and Dr Judy Laing (*née* Dods); *m* 1972, Sibella Dorman, *d* of Sir Maurice Dorman, GCMG, GCVO; one *s* two *d*. *Educ:* Rugby Sch.; Corpus Christi Coll., Cambridge. Joined HM Diplomatic Service, 1970; FCO, 1970–71; MECAS, Lebanon, 1971–72; 2nd Sec., Jedda, 1973–75; First Secretary: UK Perm. Rep. to EC, 1975–78; FCO, 1978–83; Cairo, 1983–87; FCO, 1987–89; Counsellor, Prague, 1989–92. *Recreations:* music, hill-walking, desert travel. *Address:* c/o Foreign and Commonwealth Office, King Charles Street, SW1A 2AH.

LAING, Sir Kirby; *see* Laing, Sir W. K.

LAING, Martin; *see* Laing, J. M. K.

LAING, Sir Maurice; *see* Laing, Sir J. M.

LAING, Peter Anthony Neville Pennethorne; Adviser, European Affairs, International Centre of Social Gerontology, since 1982; *b* 12 March 1922; *s* of late Lt-Col Neville Ogilvie Laing, DSO, 4th QO Hussars, and Zara Marcella (*née* Pennethorne), Fleet, Hants; *m* 1958, Penelope Lucinda, *d* of Sir William Pennington-Ramsden, 7th Bt; two *d*. *Educ:* Eton; Paris Univ. Served War: volunteer, French Army, 1939–40, Free French Forces, 1942–44; Grenadier Guards, 1944–46. Attaché, British Embassy, Madrid, 1946; internat. marketing consultant in Western Europe, USA, Caribbean and Latin America; UN, 1975–: Dir of ITC proj. for UNDP in the Congo; Dir, Help the Aged internat. charity, 1976–82. Creator, Mediterranean Retirement Inc. (wardened housing villages for ageing Europeans of ind. means), 1985–. *Recreations:* people, foreign travel, riding any horse, fine arts. *Address:* Northfields House, Turweston, near Brackley, Northants NN13 5JX. *T:* Brackley (01280) 700049, 703498. *Club:* Turf.

LAING, Stuart; *see* Laing, J. S.

LAING, (William James) Scott; special assignments for United Nations and other international agencies, since 1977; *b* 14 April 1914; *er s* of late William Irvine Laing and Jessie C. M. Laing (*née* Scott); *m* 1952, Isabelle Mary Durrant-Fox (*d* 1990); one *s*. *Educ:* George Watson's Coll., Edinburgh Univ. Appointed to Dept of Overseas Trade, 1937; Asst to Commercial Counsellor, British Embassy, Buenos Aires, 1938; Second Sec. (Commercial), Buenos Aires, 1944; First Sec. (Commercial), Helsinki, 1947; Consul, New York, 1950; Consul-Gen. (Commercial), New York, 1954; Counsellor (Commercial), Brussels and Luxembourg, 1955; Consultant to UN Secretariat, Financial Policies and Institutions Section, 1958, African Training Programme, 1960; Editor, UN Jl, 1964; Chief, Publications Sales Section, UN Secretariat, 1969–76; consultant to motor industry pubns, EIU, 1977–92. *Publications:* The US Market for Motor Vehicle Parts and Accessories, 1977; Concentration and Diversification of the Self-Propelled Heavy Machinery Industries in USA, 1979; (jtly) Financial Assessment of the US Automotive Industry, 1982; (jtly) Foreign Outsourcing by US Auto Manufacturers, 1983. *Address:* PO Box 384, Grand Central PO, New York, NY 10163, USA. *Club:* Caledonian.

LAING, Sir (William) Kirby, Kt 1968; JP; DL; MA; FEng, FICE; Chairman, Laing Properties plc, 1978–87, President, 1987–90; *b* 21 July 1916; *s* of late Sir John Laing, CBE, and late Lady Laing (*née* Beatrice Harland); *m* 1st, 1939, Joan Dorothy Bratt (*d* 1981); three *s*; 2nd, 1986, Dr (Mary) Isobel Lewis, *yr d* of late Edward C. Wray. *Educ:* St Lawrence Coll., Ramsgate; Emmanuel Coll., Cambridge (Hon. Fellow, 1983). Served with Royal Engineers, 1943–45. Dir John Laing plc (formerly John Laing & Son Ltd), 1939–80 (Chm., 1957–76). President: London Master Builders Assoc., 1957; Reinforced Concrete

Assoc., 1960; Nat. Fedn of Building Trades Employers (now Building Employers' Confedn) 1965, 1967 (Hon. Mem., 1975); ICE, 1973–74 (a Vice-Pres., 1970–73); Construction Industry Res. and Inf. Assoc., 1984–87 (Chm., 1978–81); Chm., Nat. Jt Council for Building Industry, 1968–74. Member, Board of Governors: St Lawrence Coll. (Chm., 1977–89, Pres., 1977–); Princess Helena Coll., 1984–87; Member: Court of Governors, The Polytechnic of Central London, 1963–82; Council, Royal Albert Hall, 1970–92 (Pres., 1979–92); Trustee, Inter-Varsity Fellowship. Hon. Mem., Amer. Assoc. of Civil Engineers. Master, Paviors' Co., 1987–88. DL Greater London, 1978–91. Hon. Fellow, UCNW, 1988. Hon. DTech, Poly. of Central London, 1990; Dr *hc* Edinburgh, 1991. *Publications:* papers in Proc. ICE and other jls concerned with construction. *Recreations:* flyfishing, travelling, listening to music. *Address:* 133 Page Street, NW7 2ER. *Clubs:* Naval and Military; Royal Fowey Yacht.

See also J. M. K. Laing.

LAINSON, Prof. Ralph, FRS 1982; Director, Wellcome Parasitology Unit, Instituto Evandro Chagas, Belém, Pará, Brazil, 1965–92; *b* 21 Feb. 1927; *s* of Charles Harry Lainson and Anne (*née* Denyer); *m* 1st, 1957, Anne Patricia Russell; one *s* two *d*; 2nd, 1974, Zeá Constante Lins. *Educ:* Steyning Grammar Sch., Sussex; London Univ. (BSc, PhD, DSc). Lecturer in Medical Protozoology, London Sch. of Hygiene and Tropical Medicine, London Univ., 1955–59; Officer-in-Charge, Dermal Leishmaniasis Unit, Baking-Pot, Cayo Dist, Belize, 1959–62; Attached Investigator, Dept of Medical Protozoology, London Sch. of Hygiene and Tropical Medicine, 1962–65. Career devoted to research in Medical Protozoology in the Tropics. Hon. Fellow, LSHTM, 1982; Hon. Professor, Federal Univ. of Pará, Brazil, 1982; Associate Fellow, Third World Acad. of Scis, 1989; Hon. Mem., British Soc. of Parasitology, 1984. Chalmer's Medal, Royal Soc. of Tropical Medicine and Hygiene, 1971; Oswaldo Cruz Medal, Conselho Estadual de Cultura do Pará, 1973; Manson Medal, Royal Soc. of Tropical Medicine and Hygiene, 1983; Commemorative medals: 10th anniv., Health Council for State of Pará, Brazil, 1983; 30th anniv., Fed. Univ. of Pará, Brazil, 1988. *Publications:* author, or co-author, of approximately 230 pubns in current scientific jls, on protozoal parasites of man and animals. *Recreations:* fishing, swimming, collecting South American Lepidoptera, music, philately. *Address:* Avenida Visconde de Souza Franco, 1237 (Edificio 'Visconti'), Apartamento 902, 66030 Belém, Pará, Brazil. *T:* (91) 2232382.

LAIRD, David Logan; JP, DL; solicitor; Partner, Thorntons WS, since 1985; chartered surveyor; Consultant, Smiths Gore, since 1989; *b* 13 April 1937; *s* of William Twaddle Laird and Janet Nicolson (*née* MacDonald); *m* 1965, Ann Ruth Thorley (marr. diss. 1995); two *s* one *d*. *Educ:* Bell Baxter Sch., Cupar. Chartered surveyor and land agent, 1963; Partner, Clark Oliver Dewar & Webster, SSC, 1971–85. Mem., and Chm. NE Region, NCC Scotland, now Scottish Natural Heritage, 1990–; Chm. Bd, Cairngorms Partnership, 1994–. JP 1968, DL 1989, Angus. *Recreations:* stalking, gardening, shooting, fishing. *Address:* West Memus, Forfar, Angus DD8 3TY. *T:* Forfar (01307) 86251. *Club:* New (Edinburgh).

LAIRD, Endell Johnston; Director and Editor in Chief, Scottish Daily Record and Sunday Mail, 1988–94; Editor in Chief, The Glaswegian, 1988–94; *m* 1958, June Keenan; one *s* two *d*. *Educ:* Forfar Academy. Served RAF, 1952–54. Journalist: Dundee Courier, 1954–56; Scottish Daily Express, 1956–58; Evening Times, 1958–60; Sunday Mail, 1960–71; Daily Record, 1971–81; Editor, Sunday Mail, 1981–88. Editl Dir (SDR), Mirror Gp Newspapers, 1991–94. Chm., Scottish Editors Cttee, 1986–88; Mem., D-Notice Cttee, 1986–94. *Recreations:* walking, golf, bridge. *Clubs:* Bishopbriggs Golf; Bishopbriggs Bridge.

LAIRD, Sir Gavin (Harry), Kt 1995; CBE 1988; General Secretary, AEU Section, Amalgamated Engineering and Electrical Union, 1992–95; Chairman, Greater Manchester Buses North, since 1994; *b* 14 March 1933; *s* of James and Frances Laird; *m* 1956, Catherine Gillies Campbell; one *d*. *Educ:* Clydebank High School. Full-time Trade Union Official, 1972–95; Mem. Exec. Council, 1975–95, Gen. Sec., 1982–94, AUEW, subseq. AEU, then AEEU. Mem., TUC Gen. Council, 1979–82; Mem. Exec., CSEU, 1975–. Director: BNOC, 1976–86; Bank of England, 1986–94; non-exec. Director: Scottish TV, 1986–; FS Assurance, then Brittania Life, 1988–; GEC Scotland, 1991–; Edinburgh Investment Trust, 1994–. Pt-time Mem., SDA, 1987–92. Member: Arts Council of GB, 1983–86; London Cttee, Scottish Council for Develt and Industry, 1984–; President's Cttee, Business in the Community, 1988–90; Forestry Commn, 1991–94; Envmtl Council, BNFL; Adv. Bd, Know How Fund. Chm., Trade Union Friends of Israel. Dir, Westminster Foundn for Democracy, 1992–. Mem. Governing Council, 1987–91, Gov., 1991–, Atlantic Coll.; Trustee, Anglo-German Foundn, 1994–. Fellow, Paisley Coll. of Technol., 1991. Hon. DLitt: Keele, 1994; Heriot-Watt, 1994. *Recreations:* hill walking, reading, music. *Address:* 35 Southlands Grove, Bromley BR1 2DA.

LAIRD, Margaret Heather; Third Church Estates Commissioner, since 1989; *b* 29 Jan. 1933; *d* of William Henry Polmear and Edith Polmear; *m* 1961, Rev. Canon John Charles Laird; two *s*. *Educ:* High Sch., Truro; Westfield College London (BA Hons Mediaeval History, 1954); King's College London (Cert. Rel. Know. 1955). Divinity Mistress: Grey Coat Hospital, SW1, 1955–59; Newquay Grammar Sch., 1959–60; St Albans High Sch., 1960–62; Head of Religious Studies, Dame Alice Harpur Sch., Bedford, 1969–89. Member: Gen. Synod of C of E, repr. Dio. St Albans, 1980–90 (ex officio, 1990–); Panel of Assessors, Dio. St Albans, 1988–. Vice-Pres., Soc. for Maintenance of the Faith, 1995–. Trustee, Lambeth Palace Library, 1993–. Governor, Pusey House, Oxford, 1993–. *Recreations:* mediaeval art, architecture, pilgrims' routes. *Address:* Church Commissioners, 1 Millbank, SW1P 3JZ. *T:* 0171–222 7010. *Club:* United Oxford & Cambridge University.

LAIRD, Hon. Melvin R.; Senior Counsellor for National and International Affairs, Reader's Digest Association, since 1974; *b* 1 Sept. 1922; *s* of Melvin R. Laird and Helen Laird (*née* Connor); *m* 1945, Barbara Masters (*d* 1992); two *s* one *d*. *Educ:* Carleton Coll., Northfield, Minn (BA 1944). Enlisted, US Navy, 1942, commissioned, 1944; served in Third Fleet and Task Force 58 (Purple Heart and other decorations). Elected: to Wisconsin State Senate, 1946 (re-elected, 1948); to US Congress, Nov. 1952 (83rd through 90th; Chm., House Republican Conf., 89th and 90th); Sec. of Defense, 1969–73; Counsellor to President of the US, 1973–74. Chm., Communications Satellite Corp., 1992– (Dir, 1974); Director: Metropolitan Life Insurance Co., 1974; Northwest Airlines, 1974–93; IDS Mutual Fund Gp Inc., 1974; Phillips Petroleum Co., 1976–93; Science Applications Internat. Corp., 1979; Martin Marietta Corp., 1981; Public Oversight Bd, 1984 (SEC Practice Sect., AICPA); DeWitt Wallace, and Lila Wallace, Reader's Digest Funds (for the promotion of the arts and humanities), 1990; Reader's Digest Assoc. Inc., 1990. Member Board of Trustees: George Washington Univ.; Kennedy Center. Various awards from Assocs, etc (for med. research, polit. science, public health, nat. educn); many hon. memberships and hon. degrees. *Publications:* A House Divided: America's Strategy Gap, 1962; Editor: The Conservative Papers, 1964; Republican Papers, 1968. *Recreations:* golf, fishing. *Address:* Suite 212, 1730 Rhode Island Avenue NW, Washington, DC 20036, USA. *Clubs:* Burning Tree (Washington, DC); Augusta National Golf.

LAISTER, Peter; company director; *b* 24 Jan. 1929; *s* of late Horace Laister and of Mrs I. L. Bates; *m* 1st, 1951, Barbara Cooke; one *s* one *d*; 2nd, 1958, Eileen Alice Goodchild (*née* Town); one *d*. *Educ:* King Edward's Sch., Birmingham; Manchester Univ., Coll. of Technology (BSc Tech, 1949; FUMIST, 1985). FInstPet, 1958; FIChemE, 1983; CEng; CIMgt. RAF, 1949–51. Esso Petroleum Co. Ltd, 1951–66: Process Engr to UK Refining Co-Ordinator, 1960; Gen. Manager, Marketing Ops, 1962–66; British Oxygen Co. Ltd (BOC Intl Ltd), 1966–75 (Gp Man Dir, 1969–75); Chm., BOC Financial Corp. (USA), 1974–75; Gp Man. Dir, Ellerman Lines Ltd, 1976–79; Chairman: Tollemache and Cobbold Breweries, 1977–79; London & Hull Insce Co., 1976–79; Oceonics plc, 1986–88; Group Man. Dir, Thorn Electrical Industries, later THORN EMI, 1979–84, Chm., 1984–85. Director: (non exec.) Inchcape plc, 1982–93; (non exec.) Fluor Daniel, 1985–90; Mirror Hldgs Ltd, 1985–90; Tower Maritime Gp Ltd, 1986–88; (non exec.) A&P Appledore, 1986–87; British Cable Services, 1987–89; Clyde Cable Vision, 1987–89; Metromode Ltd, 1987–90; Pergamon GED Internat. Ltd, 1987–90; Nimbus Records Ltd, 1987 (Chm., 1988–94); Pergamon Media plc, 1987–90; Tower Hotels (Management), 1987–89; VIP Marine and Aviation Ltd, 1987–90; Laister Dickson Ltd, 1988–; Chairman: Nimbus Manufacturing (UK) Ltd, 1985–94; Nimbus Communications Internat. Ltd, 1985–93; Park Hotels plc, 1985–91; SelecTV plc, 1987–94; MTV Europe, 1988–91; Tower Gp (formerly Finance, Land & General Hldgs), 1988–90; Maxwell Satellite Communications, 1988–91; Maxwell Communication Corp., 1991–92 (Dir, 1985–92). Industrial Society: Council Mem., 1971–86; Mem., Industrial Develt Adv. Bd, 1981–83; Mem., BIM Exec. Bd, 1983–88. Gov., BUPA, 1982–93; Chm., CICI, 1988–94. Vice-Pres., Research into Ageing, 1982–85. Mem., Council, UCL, 1978–88. *Recreations:* private flying, boating and angling, gardening, photography.

LAIT, Jacqui, (Mrs Peter Jones); MP (C) Hastings and Rye, since 1992; *b* 16 Dec. 1947; *d* of Graham Harkness Lait and Margaret Stewart (*née* Knight); *m* 1974, Peter Jones. *Educ:* Paisley Grammar Sch.; Univ. of Strathclyde. Public relations posts: jute trade, Dundee; Visnews, internat. TV news agency; with Govt Inf. Service, in Scottish Office, Privy Council Office and Dept of Employment, 1974–80; Parly Advr, Chemical Inds Assoc., 1980–84; Parly Consultancy, 1984–92. Chm., City and E London FHSA, 1988–91. Chm., British Section, European Union of Women, 1990–92; Vice-Chm., Cons. Women's Nat. Cttee, 1990–92. Contested (C): Strathclyde W, Euro-election, 1984; Tyne Bridge, Dec. 1985. *Recreations:* walking, theatre, food and wine. *Address:* House of Commons, SW1A 0AA. *T:* 0171–219 3000.

LAIT, Leonard Hugh Cecil, (Josh Lait); His Honour Judge Lait; a Circuit Judge, since 1987; *b* 15 Nov. 1930; *m* 1967, Cheah Phaik Teen; one *d*. *Educ:* John Lyon School, Harrow; Trinity Hall, Cambridge (BA). Called to the Bar, Inner Temple, 1959; Mem., SE circuit; a Recorder, 1985–87. *Recreations:* music, gardening.

LAITHWAITE, Prof. Eric Roberts; Professor of Heavy Electrical Engineering, Imperial College of Science and Technology, London, 1964–86, now Emeritus; *b* 14 June 1921; *s* of Herbert Laithwaite; *m* 1951, Sheila Margaret Gooddie; two *s* two *d*. *Educ:* Kirkham Gram. Sch.; Regent Street Polytechnic; Manchester Univ. (BSc 1949; MSc 1950; PhD 1957; DSc 1964). RAF, 1941–46 (at RAE Farnborough, 1943–46). Manchester University: Asst Lectr, 1950–53; Lectr, 1953–58; Sen. Lectr, 1958–64. Prof. of Royal Instn, 1967–76; Vis. Prof., Univ. of Sussex, 1990–. President: Assoc. for Science Educn, 1970; SEE 1991–. FIC 1990. Hon. FIEE 1993. S. G. Brown Award and Medal of Royal Society, 1966; Nikola Tesla Award, IEEE, 1986; Man of Achievement Award, IEE, 1992. *Publications:* Propulsion without Wheels, 1966; Induction Machines for Special Purposes, 1966; The Engineer in Wonderland, 1967; Linear Electric Motors, 1971; Exciting Electrical Machines, 1974; (with A. Watson and P. E. S. Whalley) The Dictionary of Butterflies and Moths, 1975; (ed) Transport without Wheels, 1977; (with M. W. Thring) How to Invent, 1977; Engineer through the Looking-Glass, 1980; (with L. L. Freris) Electric Energy: its Generation, Transmission and Use, 1980; Invitation to Engineering, 1984; A History of Linear Electric Motors, 1987; An Inventor in the Garden of Eden, 1994; many papers in Proc. IEE (7 premiums) and other learned jls. *Recreations:* entomology, gardening. *Address:* Department of Electrical Engineering, Imperial College, SW7 2BT. *T:* 0171–589 5111. *Club:* Athenæum.

LAITHWAITE, John, FIMechE, FInstPet; engineering consultant; Director, Capper Neill Ltd, 1965–83 (Vice-Chairman, 1972–82); *b* 29 Nov. 1920; *s* of Tom Prescott Laithwaite and Mary Anne Laithwaite; *m* 1943, Jean Chateris; one *s* two *d*. *Educ:* Manchester Univ. (BSc Hons Mech. Eng). FIMechE 1974; FInstPet 1960; MInstW 1950. Wm Neill & Son (St Helens) Ltd, 1942–43; Dartford Shipbuilding & Engineering Co., 1943–44; Dir, Wm Neill & Son (St Helens) Ltd, 1955–58, Man. Dir, 1958–64; Man. Dir, Capper Neill Ltd, 1968–72. Mem. Council, NW Regional Management Centre. Chm., Process Plant Assoc., 1975–77, Hon. Vice-Pres., 1980–. *Publications:* articles on process plant industry and pressure vessel standardisation. *Recreations:* shooting, golf. *Address:* Gwydd Gwyllt, Malltraeth, Gwynedd LL62 5AW. *T:* Bodorgan (01407) 840586. *Clubs:* Royal Automobile; Anglesey Golf.

LAKE, Sir (Atwell) Graham, 10th Bt *cr* 1711; Senior Technical Adviser, Ministry of Defence, retired 1983; *b* 6 Oct. 1923; *s* of Captain Sir Atwell Henry Lake, 9th Bt, CB, OBE, RN, and Kathleen Marion, *d* of late Alfred Morrison Turner; *S* father, 1972; *m* 1983, Mrs Katharine Margaret Lister, *d* of late D. W. Last and M. M. Last. *Educ:* Eton. British High Commission, Wellington, NZ, 1942; Gilbert and Ellice Military Forces, 1944; Colonial Administrative Service, 1945 (Secretary to Govt of Tonga, 1950–53); Norris Oakley Bros, 1957; Min. of Defence, 1959; British High Commission, New Delhi, 1966; attached Foreign and Commonwealth Office, 1969–72. Hon. Sec., Abbeyfield Epping Soc., 1987–. *Recreations:* golf, bridge, chess, skiing. *Heir:* *b* Edward Geoffrey Lake [*b* 17 July 1928; *m* 1965, Judith Ann, *d* of John Fox; one *s* one *d*]. *Address:* Magdalen Laver Hall, Chipping Ongar, Essex CM5 0EG. *Club:* Lansdowne.

LAKER, Sir Freddie, (Sir Frederick Alfred Laker), Kt 1978; Chairman and Managing Director, Laker Airways (Bahamas) Ltd, since 1992; *b* 6 Aug. 1922; British. *Educ:* Simon Langton Sch., Canterbury. Short Brothers, Rochester, 1938–40; General Aircraft, 1940–41; Air Transport Auxiliary, 1941–46; Aviation Traders, 1946–65; British United Airways, 1960–65; Chm. and Man. Dir, Laker Airways Ltd, 1966–82; Dir, Freddie Laker's Skytrain Ltd, 1982–83; creator of Skytrain Air Passenger Service to USA. Hon. Fellow Univ. of Manchester Inst. of Science and Technol., 1978; Hon. DSc: City, 1979; Cranfield Inst. of Technol., 1980; Hon. LLD Manchester, 1981. *Recreations:* horse breeding, racing, sailing. *Address:* Princess Tower, West Sunrise, Box F207, Freeport, Grand Bahama, Bahamas. *Clubs:* Eccentric, Little Ship, Jockey.

LAKES, Major Gordon Harry, CB 1987; MC 1951; Deputy Director General, Prison Service, 1985–88; *b* 27 Aug. 1928; *s* of Harry Lakes and Annie Lakes; *m* 1950, Nancy (*née* Smith) (*d* 1992); one *d*. *Educ:* Army Technical School, Arborfield; RMA Sandhurst. Commissioned RA 1948; service in Tripolitania, Korea, Japan, Hong Kong, Gold Coast (RWAFF), Ghana (Major), 1949–60. Middle Temple, 1960–61. Prison Service College, 1961–62; HM Borstal Feltham, 1962–65; Officers' Training Sch., Leyhill, 1965–68; Governor, HM Remand Centre, Thorp Arch, 1968–70; Prison Service HQ, 1970–74; HM Prisons: Pentonville, 1974–75; Gartree, 1975–77; Prison Service HQ, 1977–82; HM Dep. Chief Inspector of Prisons, 1982–85. Member: Council of Europe Cttee for Co-operation in Prison Affairs, 1986–91; Parole Bd, 1989–92. Chm., Nat. AIDS and Prisons Forum, 1989–. Consultant to 8th UN Congress on Prevention of Crime and Treatment of Offenders, 1989–90. Assessor to Lord Justice Woolf's Inquiry into Prison Disturbances, 1990–91. Comr, Mental Health Act, 1991–. *Recreations:* golf, photography.

LAKEY, Prof. John Richard Angwin, PhD; CEng, FINucE, FInstE; CPhys, FInstP; radiation protection and emergency planning consultant; founder John Lakey Associates, 1989; *b* 28 June 1929; *s* of late William Richard Lakey and Edith Lakey (*née* Hartley); *m* 1955, Dr Pamela Janet, *d* of late Eric Clifford Lancey and Florence Elsie Lancey; three *d*. *Educ:* Morley Grammar Sch.; Sheffield Univ. BSc (Physics) 1950, PhD (Fuel Technology) 1953. R&D posts with Simon Carves Ltd, secondment to AERE Harwell and GEC, 1953–60; Royal Naval College, Greenwich: Asst Prof., 1960–80; Prof. of Nuclear Sci. and Technol., 1980–89; Dean, 1984–86, 1988–89. Reactor Shielding Consultant, DG Ships, 1967–89; Radiation Consultant, WHO, 1973–74; Mem. and Vice-Chm., CNAA Physics Board, 1973–82; Mem., Medway Health Authy, 1981–90; Chm., UK Liaison Cttee for Scis Allied to Medicine and Biology, 1984–87. University of Surrey: External Examr, 1980–86; Hon. Vis. Prof., 1987–94; Vis. Lectr, Harvard Univ., 1984–. President: Internat. Radiation Protection Assoc., 1988–92 (Publications Dir, 1979–88); Instn of Nuclear Engrs, 1988–90 (Vice-Pres., 1983–87); Vice-President: London Internat. Youth Science Forum, 1988–; European Nuclear Soc., 1989–95. Liveryman, Engineers' Co., 1988–. Eur. Ing. 1989. Hon. FSRP 1992. Mem. Editorial Bd, Physics in Medicine and Biology, 1980–83; News Editor, Health Physics, 1980–88. *Publications:* Protection Against Radiation, 1961; Radiation Protection Measurement: philosophy and implementation, 1975; (ed) ALARA principles and practices, 1987; (ed) IRPA Guidelines on Protection Against Non-Ionizing Radiation, 1991; (ed) Off-site Emergency Response to Nuclear Accidents, 1993; (jtly) Radiation and Radiation Protection: a course for primary and secondary schools, 1995; papers on nuclear safety, radiological protection and management of emergencies. *Recreations:* yachting, photography, conversation. *Address:* John Lakey Associates, 5 Pine Rise, Meopham, Gravesend, Kent DA13 0JA. *T:* Meopham (01474) 812551. *Clubs:* Athenæum; Medway Yacht; Royal Naval Sailing Association.

LAKHANI, Kamlesh, (Mrs N. Lakhani); *see* Bahl, K.

LAKIN, Sir Michael, 4th Bt *cr* 1909; *b* 28 Oct. 1934; *s* of Sir Henry Lakin, 3rd Bt, and Bessie (*d* 1965), *d* of J. D. Anderson, Durban; *S* father, 1979; *m* 1965, Felicity Ann Murphy; one *s* one *d*. *Educ:* Stowe. *Heir:* *s* Richard Anthony Lakin, *b* 26 Nov. 1968. *Address:* Little Sherwood Hill, Tunley, near Cirencester, Glos GL7 6DN.

LAKIN, Peter Maurice; His Honour Judge Lakin; a Circuit Judge, since 1995; *b* 21 Oct. 1949; *s* of late Ronald Maurice Lakin and of Dorothy Kathleen Lakin (*née* Cowlishaw); *m* 1971, Jacqueline Jubb; one *s* one *d*. *Educ:* King Henry VIII Sch., Coventry; Manchester Univ. (LLB). Articled Clerk, Conn Goldberg, solicitors, Manchester, 1971–74; Goldberg Blackburn, solicitors, Manchester (later Pannone & Partners): Asst Solicitor, 1974–76; Partner i/c of Corporate Defence and Forensic Unit, 1976–95; Asst Recorder, 1989–93; Recorder, 1993–95. Hon. Sec., Manchester and Dist Medico-Legal Soc., 1989–95. *Recreations:* fell-walking, opera, gardening, local history. *Address:* Manchester Crown Court, Crown Square, Manchester M3 3FL.

LAKING, Sir George (Robert), KCMG 1985 (CMG 1969); Chief Ombudsman, New Zealand, 1977–84, retired; *b* Auckland, NZ, 15 Oct. 1912; *s* of R. G. Laking; *m* 1940, Patricia, *d* of H. Hogg; one *s* one *d*. *Educ:* Auckland Grammar Sch.; Auckland Univ.; Victoria Univ. of Wellington (LLB). Prime Minister's and Ext. Affairs Depts, 1940–49; New Zealand Embassy, Washington: Counsellor, 1949–54; Minister, 1954–56. Dep. Sec. of Ext. Affairs, Wellington, NZ, 1956–58; Acting High Comr for NZ, London, 1958–61, and NZ Ambassador to European Economic Community, 1960–61; New Zealand Ambassador, Washington, 1961–67; Sec. of Foreign Affairs and Permanent Head, Prime Minister's Dept, NZ, 1967–72; Ombudsman, 1975–77; Privacy Comr, 1977–78. Member: Human Rights Commn, 1978–84; Public and Administrative Law Reform Cttee, 1980–85. Chairman: NZ-US Educnl Foundn, 1976–78; NZ Oral History Archive Trust, 1985–90; Wellington Civic Trust, 1985–86; Legislation Adv. Cttee, 1986–91; Pres., NZ Inst. of Internat. Affairs, 1980–84. Mem. Internat. Council, Asia Soc., NY, 1985–92. *Address:* 3 Wesley Road, Wellington 1, New Zealand. *T:* (4) 4728454.

LAL, Prof. Devendra, PhD; FRS 1979; Professor, Geological Research Division, Scripps Institution of Oceanography, University of California, La Jolla, since 1967; Fellow, Physical Research Laboratory, Ahmedabad, since 1990 (Director, 1972–83; Senior Professor, 1983–89); *b* 14 Feb. 1929; *s* of Radhekrishna Lal and Sita Devi; *m* 1955, Aruna L. Damany. *Educ:* Banaras Hindu Univ. (MSc); Univ. of Bombay (PhD). Fellow, Indian Acad. of Sciences, 1964. Tata Inst. of Fundamental Research, Bombay: Res. Student, 1949–50; Res. Asst, 1950–53; Res. Fellow, 1953–57; Fellow, 1957–60; Associate Prof., 1960–63; Prof., 1963–70; Sen. Prof., 1970–72. Res. Geophysicist, UCLA-IGPP, 1965–66. Vis. Prof., UCLA, 1983–84. K. S. Krishnan Meml Lect., INSA, 1981. Foreign Sec., Indian Nat. Sci. Acad., 1981–84 (Fellow, 1971); Founder Mem., Third World Acad. of Scis, Trieste, 1983; President: Internat. Assoc. of Physical Scis of the Ocean, 1979–83; Internat. Union of Geodesy & Geophysics, 1983–87. Fellow, Nat. Acad. of Scis, Allahabad, 1988; Foreign Associate, Nat. Acad. of Sciences, USA, 1975; For. Mem., Amer. Acad. of Arts and Scis, 1989; Associate, RAS, 1984; Mem., Internat. Acad. Astronautics, 1985. Mem., Sigma Xi, USA, 1984. Hon. Fellow, Geol Soc. of India, 1992. Hon. DSc Banaras Hindu Univ., 1981. Krishnan Medal for Geochemistry and Geophysics, Indian Geophysical Union, Hyderabad, 1965; Shanti Swarup Bhatnagar Award for Physical Sciences, CSIR, 1967; Outstanding Scientist Award, Fedn of Indian Chambers of Commerce and Industry, 1974; Pandit Jawaharlal Nehru Award for Scis, Madhya Pradesh Govt, 1986. Padma Shri, 1971. *Publications:* (ed) Early Solar System Processes and the Present Solar System, 1980; *contributed:* Earth Science and Meteoritics, 1963; International Dictionary of Geophysics, 1968; The Encyclopedia of Earth Sciences: vol. IV, Geochemistry and Environmental Sciences, 1972; Further Advances in Lunar Research: Luna 16 and 20 samples, 1974; McGraw Hill Encyclopedia of Science and Technology, 1992; jt author of chapters in books; scientific papers to learned jls; proc. confs. *Recreations:* music, puzzles, painting, photography. *Address:* Scripps Institution of Oceanography, University of California at San Diego, La Jolla, CA 92093–0220, USA. *T:* (office) (619) 5342134, (home) (619) 5871535.

LALANDI-EMERY, Lina, (Mrs Ralph Emery), OBE 1975; Director, English Bach Festival, since 1962; *b* Athens; *d* of late Nikolas Kaloyeropoulos (former Dir of Byzantine Museum, Athens, and Dir of Beaux Arts, Min. of Educn, Athens) and Toula Gelekis. *Educ:* Athens Conservatoire (grad. with Hons in Music); privately, in England (harpsichord and singing studies). International career as harpsichordist in Concert, Radio and TV. Founded English Bach Festival Trust, 1962; now specialising in presentation of baroque opera perfs at ROH, Covent Gdn and numerous music fests. Officier, l'Ordre des Arts et des Lettres, 1978. *Recreations:* astrophysics, reading, knitting. *Address:* 15 South Eaton Place, SW1W 9ER. *T:* 0171–730 5925, *Fax:* 0171–730 1456.

LALANNE, Bernard Michel L.; *see* Loustau-Lalanne.

LALONDE, Hon. Marc; PC (Can.) 1972; OC 1989; QC 1971; Law Partner, Stikeman, Elliott, Montreal, since 1984; *b* 26 July 1929; *s* of late J. Albert Lalonde and Nora (*née* St Aubin); *m* 1955, Claire Tétreau; two *s* two *d*. *Educ:* St Laurent Coll., Montreal (BA 1950); Univ. of Montreal (LLL 1954; MA Law 1955); Oxford Univ. (Econ. and Pol. Science; MA 1957); Ottawa Univ. (Dip. of Superior Studies in Law, 1960). Prof. of Commercial Law and Econs, Univ. of Montreal, 1957–59; Special Asst to Minister of Justice, Ottawa, 1959–60; Partner, Gelinas, Bourque Lalonde & Benoit, Montreal, 1960–68; Lectr in Admin. Law for Doctorate Students, Univ. of Ottawa and Univ. of Montreal, 1961–62; Policy Advisor to Prime Minister, 1967; Principal Sec. to Prime Minister, 1968–72; MP (L) Montreal-Outremont, 1972–84; Minister of National Health and Welfare, 1972–77; Minister of State for Federal-Provincial Relations, 1977–78; Minister resp. for Status of Women, 1975–78; Minister of Justice and Attorney-Gen., 1978–79; Minister of Energy, Mines and Resources, 1980–82; Minister of Finance, 1982–84. Counsel before several Royal Commns inc. Royal Commn on Great Lakes Shipping and Royal Commn on Pilotage. Mem., Cttee on Broadcasting, 1964; Dir, Canadian Citizenship Council, 1960–65; Member, Bd of Directors: Inst. of Public Law, Univ. of Montréal, 1960–64; Citibank Canada, 1985–; Camder Corp., 1993–; Orleans Resources, 1994–; Cedar Group, 1995–; Chm. of Bd, Hotel-Dieu Hosp., Montreal, 1985–. Dr *hc* Univ. of Limburg, Maastricht, 1992. Dana Award, Amer. Public Health Assoc., 1978. *Publications:* The Changing Role of the Prime Minister's Office, 1971; New Perspectives on the Health of Canadians (working document), 1974. *Recreations:* tennis, squash, skiing, jogging, sailing, reading. *Address:* 5440 Légaré, Montréal, Québec H3T 1Z4, Canada.

LALUMIÈRE, Catherine; French politician; Secretary General, Council of Europe, since 1989; *b* Rennes, 3 Aug. 1935; *d* of Jacques and Andrée Bodin; *m* 1960, Pierre Lalumière. Specialist in public law; Asst Lectr, Univ. of Bordeaux and Bordeaux Inst. of Pol. Studies, 1960–71; Lectr, Univ. of Paris, 1971–81. Mem., Steering Cttee, Parti Socialiste, 1979–; Mem., National Assembly for Gironde, 1981, and 1986–June 1989 (resigned seat); Advr to Pres. on Civil Service; Sec. of State for the Civil and Admin. Reforms, May–June 1981; Minister for Consumer Affairs, 1981–83; Sec. of State, 1983–84; Minister for Europ. Affairs, 1984–86. *Recreation:* walking. *Address:* Council of Europe, 67075 Strasbourg Cedex, France; (permanent political) 54 rue Camille Pelletan, 33400 Talence, France.

LAM, Martin Philip; *b* 10 March 1920; *m* 1953, Lisa Lorenz; one *s* one *d*. *Educ:* University College Sch.; Gonville and Caius Coll., Cambridge (Scholar). Served War of 1939–45, Royal Signals. Asst Principal, Board of Trade, 1947; Nuffield Fellowship (Latin America), 1952–53; Asst Sec., 1960; Counsellor, UK Delegn to OECD, 1963–65, Advr, Commercial Policy, 1970–74, Leader UNCTAD Delegn, 1972; Under-Sec. (Computer Systems and Electronics), DoI, 1974–78; Associate of BIS Mackintosh, and of General Technology Systems, 1979–90; on contract to Directorate-Gen. XIII, European Commn, 1986–88; consultant: Scaneurope, 1989–90; KCL, 1991–92. *Publication:* (jtly) Kanji from the Start, 1995. *Address:* 22 The Avenue, Wembley, Middlesex HA9 9QJ. *T:* 0181–904 2584.

LAMB, family name of **Baron Rochester.**

LAMB, Sir Albert; *see* Lamb, Sir Larry.

LAMB, Sir Albert Thomas, (Sir Archie), KBE 1979 (MBE 1953); CMG 1974; DFC 1945; HM Diplomatic Service, retired; *b* 23 Oct. 1921; *s* of R. S. Lamb and Violet Lamb (*née* Haynes); *m* 1944, Christina Betty Wilkinson; one *s* two *d*. *Educ:* Swansea Grammar Sch. Served RAF 1941–46. FO 1938–41; Embassy, Rome, 1947–50; Consulate-General, Genoa, 1950; Embassy, Bucharest, 1950–53; FO 1953–55; Middle East Centre for Arabic Studies, 1955–57; Political Residency, Bahrain, 1957–61; FO 1961–65; Embassy, Kuwait, 1965; Political Agent in Abu Dhabi, 1965–68; Inspector, 1968–70, Sen. Inspector, 1970–73, Asst Under-Sec. of State and Chief Inspector, FCO, 1973–74; Ambassador to Kuwait, 1974–77; Ambassador to Norway, 1978–80. Mem., BNOC, 1981–82; Dir, Britoil plc, 1982–88, Member Board: British Shipbuilders, 1985–87; Nat. Bank of Kuwait (Internat.), 1994–; Sen. Associate, Conant and Associates Ltd, Washington DC, 1985–93; Adviser, Samuel Montagu and Co. Ltd, 1986–88. Clerk to Parish Councils of Zeals and Stourton with Gasper, 1991–. *Address:* White Cross Lodge, Zeals, Wilts BA12 6PF. *T:* Bourton (01747) 840321. *Club:* Royal Air Force.

LAMB, Air Vice-Marshal George Colin, CB 1977; CBE 1966; AFC 1947; Managing Director, Yonex (UK) Ltd, since 1990; *b* 23 July 1923; *s* of late George and Bessie Lamb, Hornby, Lancaster; *m* 1st, 1945, Nancy Mary Godsmark; two *s*; 2nd, 1981, Mrs Maureen Margaret Mepham. *Educ:* Lancaster Royal Grammar School. War of 1939–45: commissioned, RAF, 1942; flying duties, 1942–53; Staff Coll., 1953; Air Ministry, special duties, 1954–58; OC No 87 Sqdn, 1958–61; Dir Admin. Plans, MoD, 1961–64; Asst Comdt, RAF Coll., 1964–65; Dep. Comdr, Air Forces Borneo, 1965–66; Fighter Command, 1966; MoD (Dep. Command Structure Project Officer), 1967; HQ, Strike Command, 1967–69; OC, RAF Lyneham, 1969–71; RCDS, 1971–72; Dir of Control (Operations), NATS, 1972–74; Comdr, Southern Maritime Air Region, RAF Mount Batten, 1974–75; C of S, No 18 Gp Strike Comd, RAF, 1975–78. RAF Vice-Pres., Combined Cadet Forces Assoc., 1978–94. Chief Exec., Badminton Assoc. of England, 1978–89; Gen. Sec., London Inst. of Sports Medicine, 1989–90. Consultant, Television, Sport and Leisure Ltd, 1989–90. Chm., Lilleshall National Sports Centre, 1984–; Member: Sports Council, 1983–88 (Mem., Drug Abuse Adv. Gp, 1988–92); Sports Cttee, Prince's Trust, 1985–88; Privilege Mem. of RFU, 1985– (Mem., RFU Cttee, 1973–85); British Internat. Sports Cttee, 1989–. Pres., St George's Day Club, 1994–. FIMgt. *Recreations:* international Rugby football referee, cricket (former Pres., Adastrian Cricket Club). *Address:* Hambledon, 17 Meadway, Berkhamsted HP4 2PN. *T:* Berkhamsted (01442) 862583. *Club:* Royal Air Force.

LAMB, Harold Norman, CBE 1978; Regional Administrator, South East Thames Regional Health Authority, 1973–81; *b* 21 July 1922; *s* of Harold Alexander and Amelia Lamb; *m* 1946, Joyce Marian Hawkyard; one *s* one *d*. *Educ:* Saltley Grammar School. FHA. Served War, RAF, 1941–46. House Governor, Birmingham Gen. Hosp., 1958; Dep. Sec., United Birmingham Hosps, and House Governor, Queen Elizabeth Hosp., 1961; Sec., SE Metrop. RHB, 1968. Mem. Exec. Council, Royal Inst. of Public Admin, 1970–78. *Recreations:* golf, music. *Address:* 40 Windmill Way, Reigate, Surrey RH2 0JA. *T:* Reigate (01737) 221846. *Club:* Walton Heath Golf.

LAMB, Prof. Joseph Fairweather, PhD; FRCPE; FRSE; Chandos Professor of Physiology, St Leonard's College, University of St Andrews, 1969–93, now Professor Emeritus; *b* 18 July 1928; *s* of Joseph and Agnes May Lamb; *m* 1st, 1955, Olivia Janet Horne (marr. diss. 1989); three *s* one *d*; 2nd, 1989, Bridget Cecilia Cook; two *s*. *Educ:* Brechin High School; Edinburgh Univ. (MB ChB, BSc, PhD). FRCPE 1985. National Service, RAF, 1947–49. House Officer, Dumfries and Edinburgh, 1955–56; Hons Physiology Course, 1956–57; Univ. Junior Res. Fellow, 1957; Lectr in Physiology, Royal (Dick) Vet. Sch., 1958–61; Lectr, Sen. Lectr in Physiol., Glasgow, 1961–69. Sec., Physiol. Soc., 1984–87; Chm., Save British Science Soc., 1986–. Editor: Jl of Physiol., 1968–74; Amer. Jl of Physiol., 1985–88. FRSA; FRSE 1985. *Publications:* Essentials of Physiology, 1980, 3rd edn 1991; articles in learned jls. *Recreations:* sailing, boatbuilding, reading. *Address:* Kenbrae, Millbank, Cupar, Fife KY15 5DP. *T:* Cupar (01334) 52791. *Clubs:* Royal Society of Medicine; Little Ship.

LAMB, Sir Larry, Kt 1980; Editor, Daily Express, 1983–86; Chairman, Larry Lamb Associates, since 1986; *b* Fitzwilliam, Yorks, 15 July 1929; *m* Joan Mary Denise Grogan; two *s* one *d*. *Educ:* Rastrick Grammar Sch. Worked as journalist on Brighouse Echo, Shields Gazette, Newcastle Journal, London Evening Standard; Sub-Editor, Daily Mirror; Editor: (Manchester) Daily Mail, 1968–69; The Sun, 1969–72, 1975–81; Dir, 1970–81, Editorial Dir, 1971–81, News International Ltd; Dep. Chm., News Group, 1979–81; Dir, The News Corporation (Australia) Ltd, 1980–81; Dep. Chm. and Editor-in-Chief, Western Mail Ltd, Perth, Australia, 1981–82; Editor-in-Chief, The Australian, May 1982–Feb. 1983. *Publication:* Sunrise, 1989. *Recreations:* fell-walking, cricket, fishing. *Address:* Bracken Cottage, Bratton Fleming, N Devon EX31 4TG. *Club:* Royal Automobile.

LAMB, Timothy Robert; QC 1995; *b* 27 Nov. 1951; *s* of Stephen Falcon Lamb and Pamela Elizabeth Lamb (*née* Coombes); *m* 1978, Judith Anne Ryan; one *s* one *d*. *Educ:* Brentwood Sch.; Lincoln Coll., Oxford (MA Jurisp.). Called to the Bar, Gray's Inn, 1974. *Recreations:* family, travel, water sports. *Address:* 2 Temple Gardens, EC4Y 9AY. *T:* 0171–583 6041. *Club:* Booker Gliding.

LAMB, Prof. Trevor David, FRS 1993; Professor of Neuroscience, University of Cambridge, since 1994; Fellow, Darwin College, Cambridge, since 1985; *b* 20 Sept. 1948; *s* of Arthur and Margaret Lamb; *m* 1979, (Janet) Clare Conway; two *s* one *d*. *Educ:* Melbourne Grammar Sch.; Univ. of Melbourne (BE 1st Cl. Hons 1969); Univ. of Cambridge (PhD 1975; ScD 1988). Physiological Laboratory, University of Cambridge: Wellcome Sen. Res. Fellow, 1978–80; Royal Soc. Locke Res. Fellow, 1980–84; Univ. Lectr in Physiol., 1984–91; Reader in Neuroscience, 1991–94. *Publications:* articles on photoreceptors and sensory transduction in Jl Physiol. and other learned jls. *Recreation:* viticulture. *Address:* Physiological Laboratory, University of Cambridge, Downing Street, Cambridge CB2 3EG. *T:* Cambridge (01223) 333856.

LAMB, Prof. Willis E(ugene), Jr; Professor of Physics and Optical Sciences, University of Arizona, since 1974, and Regents' Professor, since 1990; *b* Los Angeles, California, USA, 12 July 1913; *s* of Willis Eugene Lamb and Marie Helen Metcalf; *m* Ursula Schaefer. *Educ:* Los Angeles High Sch.; University of California (BS, PhD). Columbia Univ.: Instructor in Physics, 1938–43, Associate, 1943–45, Assistant Professor, 1945–47, Associate Professor, 1947–48, Professor of Physics, 1948–52; Professor of Physics, Stanford Univ., California, 1951–56; Wykeham Prof. of Physics and Fellow of New Coll., University of Oxford, 1956–62; Yale University: Ford Prof. of Physics, 1962–72; Gibbs Prof. of Physics, 1972–74. Morris Loeb Lectr, Harvard Univ., 1953–54; Lectr, University of Colorado, Summer, 1959; Shrum Lectr, Simon Fraser Univ., 1972; Visiting Professor, Tata Institute of Fundamental Research, Bombay, 1960; Guggenheim Fellow, 1960–61; Visiting Professor, Columbia Univ., 1961; Fulbright Lecturer, University of Grenoble, Summer, 1964. MNAS, 1954. Hon. DSc: Pennsylvania, 1954; Gustavus Adolphus Coll., 1975; Columbia, 1990; MA (by decree), Oxford, 1956; Hon. MA Yale, 1961; Hon. LHD Yeshiva, 1965; Hon. Fellow: Institute of Physics and Physical Society, 1962; RSE, 1981; Res. Corp Award, 1954; Rumford Medal, American Academy of Arts and Sciences, 1953; (jointly) Nobel Prize in Physics, 1955; Guthrie Award, The Physical Society, 1958; Yeshiva University Award, 1962. *Publications:* (with M. Sargent and M. O. Scully) Laser Physics, 1974; contributions to The Physical Review, Physica, Science, Journal of Applied Physics, etc. *Address:* Optical Sciences Center, University of Arizona, Tucson, AZ 85721, USA.

LAMBART, family name of **Earl of Cavan.**

LAMBECK, Prof. Kurt, DPhil, DSc; FRS 1994; FAA; Professor of Geophysics, Australian National University, since 1977; *b* 20 Sept. 1941; *s* of Jacob and Johanna Lambeck; *m* 1967, Bridget Marguerite Nicholls; one *s* one *d*. *Educ:* Univ. of NSW (BSurv. Hons); Hertford Coll., Oxford (DPhil, DSc). Geodesist, Smithsonian Astrophysical Observatory and Harvard Coll. Observatory, Cambridge, Mass, 1967–70; Directeur Scientifique, Observatoire de Paris, 1970–73; Prof. of Geophysics, Univ. of Paris, 1973–77; Dir, Res. Sch. of Earth Scis, ANU, 1984–93. Fellow, Amer. Geophysical Union, 1976; FAA 1984. Foreign Member: Royal Netherlands Acad. of Arts and Scis, 1993; Norwegian Acad. of Science and Letters, 1994. Hon. Mem., European Geophysical Soc., 1987. Hon. DEng Nat. Tech. Univ., Athens, 1994. Mcelwane Medal, 1976, Whitten Medal, 1993, Amer. Geophysical Union. *Publications:* The Earth's Variable Rotation, 1980; Geophysical Geodesy: the slow deformations of the earth, 1988; numerous articles in fields of geodesy, geophysics and geology. *Address:* Research School of Earth Sciences, Australian National University, Canberra, ACT 0200, Australia; 31 Brand Street, Hughes, ACT 2605, Australia.

LAMBERT, family name of **Viscount Lambert.**

LAMBERT, 3rd Viscount *cr* 1945, of South Molton; **Michael John Lambert;** *b* 29 Sept. 1912; *s* of 1st Viscount Lambert, PC and Barbara (*d* 1963), *d* of George Stavers; *S* brother, 1989; *m* 1939, Florence Dolores, *d* of Nicholas Lechmere Cunningham Macaskie, QC; three *d*. *Educ:* Harrow; New College, Oxford (MA). *Heir:* none. *Address:* Casanuova di Barontoli, 53010 S Rocco a Pilli, Siena, Italy.

LAMBERT, Sir Anthony (Edward), KCMG 1964 (CMG 1955); HM Diplomatic Service, retired; *b* 7 March 1911; *o s* of late R. E. Lambert, Pensbury House, Shaftesbury, Dorset; *m* 1948, Ruth Mary, *d* of late Sir Arthur Fleming, CBE; two *d*. *Educ:* Harrow; Balliol Coll., Oxford (scholar). Entered HM Foreign (subseq. Diplomatic) Service, 1934, and served in: Brussels, 1937; Ankara, 1940; Beirut and Damascus, 1942; Brussels, 1944; Stockholm, 1949; Athens, 1952; HM Minister to Bulgaria, 1958–60; HM Ambassador to: Tunisia, 1960–63; Finland, 1963–66; Portugal, 1966–70.

LAMBERT, David Arthur Charles; General President, National Union of Knitwear, Footwear and Apparel Trades, 1991–94 (General Secretary, 1975–82, General President, 1982–90, National Union of Hosiery and Knitwear Workers); President, International Textile, Garment and Leather Workers' Federation, Brussels, since 1992 (Vice-President, 1984–92); *b* 2 Sept. 1933; *m* Beryl Ann (*née* Smith); two *s* one *d*. *Educ:* Hitchin Boys' Grammar Sch., Herts. Employed as production worker for major hosiery manufr; active as lay official within NUHKW; full-time official, NUHKW, 1964–90. Member: Employment Appeal Tribunal, 1978–; TUC Gen. Council, 1984–94; CRE, 1987–93. *Address:* (office) The Grange, 108 Northampton Road, Earls Barton, Northampton NN6 0JH.

LAMBERT, David George; Solicitor and Legal Adviser, Welsh Office, since 1991; Registrar of Diocese of Llandaff, since 1986; *b* 7 Aug. 1940; *s* of George and Elsie Lambert; *m* 1966, Diana Mary Ware; one *s* one *d*. *Educ:* Barry Grammar Sch.; UCW, Aberystwyth (LLB). Notary Public; Solicitor in private practice, 1965; Welsh Office: Legal Officer, 1966–74; Asst Legal Adviser, 1974–91. Tutor, Univ. of Wales Coll. of Cardiff (formerly UC, Cardiff), 1972–. *Recreations:* ecclesiastical law, Baroque music. *Address:* 9 The Chantry, Llandaff, Cardiff CF5 2NN. *T:* Cardiff (01222) 568154.

LAMBERT, Eric Thomas Drummond, CMG 1969; OBE 1946; KPM 1943; retd, 1968; *b* 3 Nov. 1909; *s* of late Septimus Drummond Lambert. *Educ:* Royal Sch., Dungannon; Trinity Coll., Dublin, 1928–29. Indian (Imperial) Police, 1929–47: Political Officer for Brahmaputra-Chindwin Survey, 1935–36, and Tirap Frontier Tract, 1942; District Comr, Naga Hills, 1938. Commnd General, Chinese Armed Forces, to find and evacuate Chinese Vth Army from Burma to Assam, India, June-Aug. 1942; Chief Civil Liaison Officer XIVth Army, 1944; FCO, 1947–68, with service in SE Asia, W Africa, S America, Nepal, Afghanistan. Pres., Republic of Ireland Br., Burma Star Assoc. Trustee, Nat. Library of Ireland, retired 1991. Corresp. Mem., Acad. of History, Venezuela. Chinese Armed Forces Distinguished Service, 1st Order, 1st class, 1942; Cruz Militar, Venezuela, 1983. *Publications:* Assam (jointly with Alban Ali), 1943; Carabobo 1821, 1974; Voluntarios Britanicos y Irlandeses en la Gesta Bolivariana, 1982; articles in jls of RGS and Royal Siam Soc.; Man in India; The Irish Sword. *Recreations:* historical research, lecturing a bit, golf just done with. *Address:* Drumkeen, Glenamuck Road, Dublin 18. *T:* 955887. *Club:* Stephen's Green (Dublin).

LAMBERT, Harold George; *b* 8 April 1910; *s* of late Rev. David Lambert; *m* 1934, Winifred Marthe, *d* of late Rev. H. E. Anderson, Farnham, Surrey; two *s*. *Educ:* King Edward's Sch., Birmingham; Corpus Christi Coll., Cambridge (MA); Imperial College of Science, London. Entered Ministry of Agriculture and Fisheries, 1933; Private Secretary to Parliamentary Secretary, 1938–39; Sec., Agricultural Machinery Develt Bd, 1942–45; Assistant Secretary, 1948; Under-Sec., MAFF, 1964–70, retired. Mem., panel of indep. inspectors for local enquiries, DoE and DoT, 1971–80. *Recreations:* music, art. *Address:* 74 Chichester Drive West, Saltdean, Brighton BN2 8SF.

LAMBERT, Henry Uvedale Antrobus; Chairman: Sun Alliance Insurance Group, 1985–93; Agricultural Mortgage Corporation PLC, 1985–93; *b* 9 Oct. 1925; *o s* of late Roger Uvedale Lambert and Muriel, *d* of Sir Reginald Antrobus, KCMG, CB; *m* 1951, Diana, *y d* of Captain H. E. Dumbell, Royal Fusiliers; two *s* one *d*. *Educ:* Winchester College (Scholar); New College, Oxford (Exhibitioner; MA). Served War of 1939–45, Royal Navy, in HM Ships Stockham and St Austell Bay in Western Approaches and Mediterranean, subseq. RNR; Lt-Comdr (retired). Entered Barclays Bank 1948; a Local Dir at Lombard Street, 1957, Southampton, 1959, Birmingham, 1969; Vice-Chm., Barclays Bank UK Ltd, 1972; Vice-Chm., Barclays Bank Ltd, 1973; Chm., Barclays Bank Internat., 1979–83; Dep. Chm., 1979–85, Dir, 1966–91, Barclays Bank PLC; Agricultural Mortgage Corporation: Dir, 1966; Dep. Chm., 1977–85; Sun Alliance Insurance Group: Dir, 1972; Vice-Chm., 1978–83; Dep. Chm., 1983–85. Dir, British Airways, 1985–89. Mem. Council, RASE, 1985– (Vice Pres., 1994–). Trustee: Imperial War Graves Endowment Fund, 1987–94 (Chm., 1989–94); Nat. Maritime Mus., 1990–95. Vice-Pres., Navy Records Soc., 1985–89, 1992– (Hon. Treas., 1974–85); Mem., Council, White Ensign Assoc., 1982– (Chm., 1992–). Fellow, Winchester Coll., 1979–91. Hon. Mem., RICS, 1993. *Recreations:* fishing, gardening, golf, naval history. *Address:* c/o Barclays Bank PLC, Jewry Street, Winchester, Hants SO23 8RG. *Clubs:* Brooks's, MCC.

LAMBERT, Jean Denise; Chair, Green Party Executive, since 1993; *b* 1 June 1950; *d* of Frederick John and Margaret Archer; *m* 1977, Stephen Lambert; one *s* one *d*. *Educ:* Palmers Grammar Sch. for Girls, Grays, Essex; University Coll., Cardiff (BA Modern Langs); St Paul's Coll., Cheltenham (PGCE). ADB(Ed). Secondary sch. teacher, Waltham Forest, 1972–89 (exmnr in spoken and written English, 1983–88). Green Party: joined 1977 (then Ecology Party); London Area Co-ordinator, 1977–81; Co-Chm. Council, 1982–85, 1986–87; Rep. to European Green Parties, 1985–86, 1988–89; UK rep. to Green Gp in European Parlt, 1989–94; Green Party Speaker, 1988–, Jt Principal Speaker, 1992–93. Contested (Green Party): GLC, 1981; local Council, 1986; London NE, European Parlt, 1984, 1989, 1994; Walthamstow, gen. elec., 1992. Founder Member: Ecology Building Soc., 1981 (Bd, 1981–84; Chm., 1982–83; now Patron); Play for Life, 1984; Council Mem., Charter 88, 1990–. Radio and TV broadcaster. *Publications:* (contrib.) Into the 21st Century, 1988; articles to magazines. *Recreations:* reading (esp. detective fiction), cooking, dance. *Address:* 3 Howard Road, E17 4SH. *T:* (home) 0181–520 0676; (office) 0181–673 0045.

LAMBERT, Sir John (Henry), KCVO 1980; CMG 1975; HM Diplomatic Service, retired; Director, Heritage of London Trust, since 1981; *b* 8 Jan. 1921; *s* of Col R. S. Lambert, MC, and Mrs H. J. F. Mills; *m* 1950, Jennifer Ann (*née* Urquhart); one *s* two *d*. *Educ:* Eton Coll.; Sorbonne; Trinity Coll., Cambridge. Grenadier Guards, 1940–45 (Captain). Appointed 3rd Secretary, HM Embassy, The Hague, 1945; Member of HM Foreign Service, 1947; FO, 1948; 2nd Secretary, Damascus, 1951; 1st Secretary, 1953; FO, 1954; Dep. to UK Representative on International Commn for Saar Referendum, 1955; Belgrade, 1956; Head of Chancery, Manila, 1958; UK Delegation to Disarmament Conference, Geneva, 1962; FO, 1963; Counsellor, Head of Chancery, Stockholm, 1964–67; Head of UN (Political) Dept, FCO, 1967–70; Commercial Counsellor and Consul-Gen. Vienna, 1971–74; Minister and Dep. Comdt, Berlin, 1974–77; Ambassador to Tunisia, 1977–81. Chm., Channel Tunnel Investment plc, 1986–92. *Recreations:* the arts, music, tennis, golf. *Address:* 103 Rivermead Court, SW6 3SB. *T:* 0171–731 5007. *Clubs:* MCC; Hurlingham, Royal St George's Golf.

LAMBERT, John Sinclair; Secretary (formerly Co-ordinator), Sheffield City Liaison Group, since 1993 (on secondment from Department of Employment); *b* 8 April 1948; *s* of late Norman Sinclair Lambert and of Doris May Lambert; *m* 1971, Ann Dowzell; two *s*. *Educ:* Denstone Coll.; Selwyn Coll., Cambridge (MA). Department of Employment, 1970–: Private Sec. to Perm. Sec., 1973–74; on secondment to Marconi Space and Defence Systems, 1977–78; Dep. Chief Conciliation Officer, ACAS, 1982–83; Head of European Communities Branch, 1983–85; Dir of Field Ops, MSC, 1987–90; Dir of Ops (N and W), 1990–92; Dir, Adult Learning Div., 1992–93. *Recreations:* birdwatching, music, reading, gardening. *Address:* City Liaison Group, c/o Town Hall, Sheffield S1 2HH.

LAMBERT, Patricia, OBE 1981; Public Interest Director, Life Assurance and Unit Trust Regulatory Organisation, 1986–94; *b* 16 March 1926; *d* of Frederick and Elsie Burrows; *m* 1949, George Richard Lambert (marr. diss. 1983); one *s* one *d*. *Educ:* Malet Lambert High Sch., Hull; West Bridgford Grammar Sch., Nottingham; Nottingham and Dist Technical Coll. Served Royal Signals, Germany, 1944–46; medical technician, 1946–49. British Standards Institution: Member: BSI Bd, 1980–86; Quality Assce Bd, 1986–91; Chm., Consumer Standards Adv. Council, 1980–86; chm. of several technical cttees. Member: National Consumer Council, 1978–82; National House Bldg Council, 1980–91; Consumer Affairs, Panel, Unit Trust Assoc., 1981–; Direct Mail Services Standards Bd, 1983–; Consumer Cttee, PIA, 1994–. Dir and Vice-Chm., Invest in Britain, 1983–94. Local Govt Councillor, 1959–78. *Recreations:* driving, music, theatre, glass engraving. *Address:* 100 Wolds Drive, Keyworth, Nottingham NG12 5FS.

LAMBERT, Sir Peter John Biddulph, 10th Bt *cr* 1711, of London; archaeological consultant; *b* 5 April 1952; *s* of John Hugh Lambert (*d* 1977) (*g s* of 5th Bt) and of Edith May, *d* of late James Bance; *S* kinsman, Sir Greville Foley Lambert, 9th Bt, 1988; *m* 1989, Leslie Anne, *d* of R. W. Lyne; one *d*. *Educ:* Upper Canada Coll., Toronto; Trent Univ.

(BSc 1975); Univ. of Manitoba (MA 1980). *Heir: uncle* Robert William Lambert [*b* 6 June 1911; *m* 1948, Margaret Daphne Harvey].

LAMBERT, Richard Peter; Editor, Financial Times, since 1991; *b* 23 Sept. 1944; *s* of Peter and Mary Lambert; *m* 1973, Harriet Murray-Browne; one *s* one *d*. *Educ:* Fettes Coll.; Balliol Coll., Oxford (BA). Staff of Financial Times, 1966–; Lex Column, 1972; Financial Editor, 1978; New York Correspondent, 1982; Dep. Editor, 1983. *Address:* c/o Financial Times, Number One, Southwark Bridge, SE1 9HL.

LAMBERT, Prof. Thomas Howard; Professor, 1967–91, and Kennedy Professor, 1983–91, now Emeritus, Department of Mechanical Engineering, University College London; *b* 28 Feb. 1926; *s* of Henry Thomas Lambert and Kate Lambert. *Educ:* Emanuel Sch.; Univ. of London (BSc (Eng), PhD). FIMechE. D. Napier & Sons: Graduate Apprentice, 1946–48; Develt Engr, 1948–51; University College London: Lectr, 1951–63; Sen. Lectr, 1963–65; Reader, 1965–67; Head of Mech. Engrg Dept, 1977–89; Hon. Fellow, 1991. Hon. RCNC. *Publications:* numerous articles in learned jls, principally in Stress Analysis, Medical Engrg and Automatic Control. *Recreations:* gardening, sailing, practical engineering. *Address:* Department of Mechanical Engineering, University College London, Gower Street, WC1E 6BT. *T:* 0171–387 7050.

LAMBERT, Verity Ann; independent film and television producer; Director, Cinema Verity Productions Ltd, since 1985; *b* 27 Nov.; *d* of Stanley Joseph Lambert and Ella Corona Goldburg. *Educ:* Roedean; La Sorbonne, Paris. Joined BBC Television as drama producer, 1963; first producer of Dr Who; also produced: The Newcomers, Somerset Maugham Short Stories (BAFTA Award, 1969), Adam Adamant, Detective; joined LWT as drama producer, 1970: produced Budgie and Between the Wars; returned to BBC, 1973: produced and co-created Shoulder to Shoulder; joined Thames Television as Controller of Drama Dept, 1974 (Dir of Drama, 1981–82; Dir, Thames Television, 1982–85): resp. for: Rock Follies, Rooms, Rumpole of the Bailey, Edward and Mrs Simpson, The Naked Civil Servant (many awards), Last Summer, The Case of Cruelty to Prawns, No Mama No; made creatively resp. for Euston Films Ltd, 1976 (Chief Executive, 1979–82): developed series which included Out and Danger UXB; resp. for: Minder (three series), Quatermass, Fox, The Flame Trees of Thika, Reilly: ace of spies; single films include: Charlie Muffin, Stainless Steel and the Star Spies, The Sailor's Return, The Knowledge; Dir of Prodn, THORN EMI Screen Entertainment, 1982–85: resp. for: Morons from Outer Space, Dreamchild, Restless Natives, Link, Clockwise. Executive Producer: American Roulette, 1987; May to December (5 series, 1989–); So Haunt Me (3 series), 1992–; Producer: A Cry in the Dark, 1988; Coasting, 1990; GBH, 1991; The Boys from the Bush, 1991, 1992; Sleepers, 1991; Comics, 1993; Class Act, 1994, Class Act II, 1995; She's Out, 1995. McTaggart Lect., Edinburgh TV Fest., 1990. Governor: BFI, 1981–86 (Chairperson, Prodn Bd, 1981–82); Nat. Film and Television Sch., 1984–. Hon. LLD Strathclyde, 1988. Veuve-Clicquot Businesswoman of 1982; Woman's Own Woman of Achievement, 1983. *Recreations:* reading, eating. *Address:* (office) The Mill House, Millers Way, 1A Shepherds Bush Road, W6 7NA.

LAMBETH, Archdeacon of; *see* Bird, Ven. C. R. B.

LAMBIE, David; *b* 13 July 1925; *m* 1954, Netta May Merrie; one *s* four *d*. *Educ:* Kyleshill Primary Sch.; Ardrossan Academy; Glasgow University; Geneva University. BSc, DipEd. Teacher, Glasgow Corp., 1950–70. Chm., Glasgow Local Assoc., Educnl Inst. for Scotland, 1958–59; Chm., Scottish Labour Party, 1964; Chief Negotiator on behalf of Scottish Teachers in STSC, 1969–70; Sec., Westminster Branch, Educnl Inst. for Scotland, 1985–88, 1991–92. MP (Lab) Ayrshire Central, 1970–83, Cunninghame South, 1983–92. Chm., Select Cttee on Scottish Affairs, 1981–87; Sec., Parly All Party Cttee for Energy Studies, 1980–92; Chm., PLP Aviation Cttee, 1990–92. Chm., Saltcoats Labour Party, 1993–; Mem., Cunninghame N Constituency Labour Party, 1993–. Chm. Develt Cttee, Cunninghame Housing Assoc., 1992–. Member: Council of Europe, 1987–92; WEU, 1987–92. FEIS 1970. *Recreation:* watching football. *Address:* 11 Ivanhoe Drive, Saltcoats, Ayrshire KA21 6LS. *T:* Saltcoats (01294) 464843. *Club:* Cunninghame North Constituency Labour Social (Saltcoats).

LAMBIE-NAIRN, Martin John, RDI 1987; FCSD; Chairman/Creative Director, Lambie-Nairn and Co. Ltd, Design Consultants (formerly Robinson Lambie-Nairn), since 1976; *b* 5 Aug. 1945; *s* of Stephen John and Joan Lois Lambie-Nairn; *m* 1970, Cordelia Margot Summers; one *s* two *d*. *Educ:* King Ethelbert Sch., Birchington, Kent; Canterbury Coll. of Art. NDD. Asst Designer, Graphic Design Dept, BBC, 1965; Designer, Rediffusion, 1966; freelance graphic designer, 1967; Art Dir, Conran Associates, 1968; Dep. to Sen. Designer, ITN, overseeing changeover from black and white to colour tv, 1968; Designer, LWT, working on light entertainment, drama and current affairs progs, 1970; formed Robinson Lambie-Nairn Ltd, design consultancy producing film and tv graphics, corporate identity, packaging and financial lit., 1976; renamed Lambie-Nairn and Co., 1990; work includes Channel 4 TV corporate identity, 1982, Anglia TV corporate identity, 1988, TFI (France) corporate identity, 1989, BSB 5 Channel identity, 1990, BBC1 and BBC2 channel identities, 1991, Carlton Television corporate identity, 1993, and design and prodn of tv commercials. Mem. Cttee, Design and Art Dirs Assoc. 1985– (Pres., 1990–91). Chm., Graphics Jury, BBC Design Awards, 1987. FCSD (FSIAD 1982). Hon. Fellow, Kent Inst. of Art and Design, 1994. Jt winner, BAFTA Craft Awards (for excellence in craft of graphics), 1991. *Recreations:* opera, family, playing bagpipes. *Address:* Lambie-Nairn and Co., 48 Beak Street, W1R 3DA.

LAMBO, Prof. Thomas Adeoye, NNOM 1979; CON 1979; OBE 1962; MD, DPM; FRCP; JP; Deputy Director-General, World Health Organization, 1973–88 (Assistant Director-General, 1971–73); Executive Director, Lambo Foundation, since 1988; *b* 29 March 1923; *s* of Chief D. B. Lambo, The Otunbade of Igbore, Abeokuta, and Madam F. B. Lambo, The Iyalode of Egba Christians; *m* 1945, Dinah Violet Adams; three *s*. *Educ:* Baptist Boys' High Sch., Abeokuta; Univs of Birmingham and London. From 1949, served as House Surg. and House Phys., Birmingham, England; Med. Officer, Lagos, Zaria and Gusau; Specialist, Western Region Min. of Health, 1957–60; Consultant Psychiatrist, UCH Ibadan, 1956–63; Sen. Specialist, Western Region Min. of Health, Neuro-Psychiatric Centre, 1960–63; Prof. of Psychiatry and Head of Dept of Psychiatry and Neurology, Univ. of Ibadan, 1963–71; Dean, Medical Faculty, Univ. of Ibadan, 1966–68; Vice-Chancellor, Univ. of Ibadan, 1968–71. Member: Scientific Council for Africa (Chm., 1965–70); Expert Adv. Panel on Mental Health, WHO, 1959–71; UN Perm. Adv. Cttee on Prevention of Crime and the Treatment of Offenders (Chm. 1968–71); Exec. Cttee, World Fedn for Mental Health, 1964–; Scientific Adv. Panel, Ciba Foundn, 1966–; WHO Adv. Cttee on Med. Research, 1970–71; Scientific Cttee on Advanced Study in Developmental Sciences, 1967–; Nigeria Medical Council, 1969–; Scientific Council of the World Future Studies Fedn, 1975–; World Soc. for Ekistics (Pres., 1979–81); Adv. Bd, Earthscan, 1975–; Bd of Dirs, Internat. Inst. for Envmt and Develt, 1986–; Vice-Chm., UN Adv. Cttee on Application of Science and Technology to Development, 1970–71; Co-Chm., Internat. Soc. for Study of Human Development, 1968–; Chairman: West African Examinations Council, 1969–71, co-ordinating Bd, African Chairs of Technology in Food Processing, Biotechnologies and Nutrition and Health, 1986–, etc. Founding Member: Third World Acad. of Scis, 1986–; African Acad. of Scis, 1986–. Member: Pontifical Acad. of Sciences, 1974– (first African Life Mem., 1982); Internat. Inst. for World Resources, Washington. Hon. Fellow: RCPsych, 1970 (Founding Fellow); Royal Australian and NZ Coll. of Psychiatrists. JP Western State, 1968. Hon. LLD: Kent State, Ohio, 1969; Birmingham 1971; Pennsylvania, Philadelphia; Hon. DSc: Ahmadu Bello, Nigeria; Long Island, NY, 1975; McGill, Canada, 1978; Jos, Nigeria, 1979; Nigeria, Nsukka, 1979; Hacettepe, Ankara, 1980; Hahnemann, Philadelphia, 1984; Dr *hc*: Benin, 1973; Aix-Marseille, France, 1974; Louvain, Belgium, 1976. Haile Selassie African Res. Award, 1970. *Publications:* (jtly) Psychiatric Disorders Among the Yorubas, 1963; monographs, and contribs to medical and other scientific jls. *Recreation:* tennis. *Address:* Lambo Foundation, 15 Olatunbosun Street, PO Box 702, Maryland Estate, Ikeja, Lagos State, Nigeria. *T:* (1) 961102, (home) (1) 4976111/4976110, *Fax:* (1) 962051/4936667.

LAMBTON, family name of **Earldom of Durham.**

LAMBTON, Viscount; Antony Claud Frederick Lambton; *b* 10 July 1922; *s* of 5th Earl of Durham (*d* 1970) and Diana (*d* 1924), *o d* of Granville Farquhar; disclaimed peerages for life, 1970 but allowed by Mr Speaker Lloyd to continue to sit in Parliament using courtesy title; *m* 1942, Belinda, *d* of Major D. H. Blew-Jones, Westward Ho!, North Devonshire; one *s* five *d*. MP (C) Berwick upon Tweed Div. of Northumberland, 1951–73; Parly Under-Sec. of State, MoD, 1970–May 1973; PPS to the Foreign Secretary, 1955–57. *Publications:* Snow and Other Stories, 1983; Elizabeth and Alexandra, 1985; The Abbey in the Wood, 1986; The Mountbattens, 1989; Pig and Other Stories, 1990. *Heir to disclaimed peerages: s* Hon. Edward Richard Lambton (Baron Durham) [*b* 19 Oct. 1961; *m* 1983, Christabel, *y d* of late Rory McEwen and of Mrs McEwen, Bardrochat; one *s*]. *Address:* Villa Cetinale, Sovicille, Siena, Italy; Biddick Hall, Chester-le-Street, Co. Durham.

See also Sir P. V. Naylor-Leyland, Bt, Sir P. G. Worsthorne.

LAMBTON, Prof. Ann Katharine Swynford, OBE 1942; FBA 1964; Professor of Persian, University of London, 1953–79, now Emeritus; *b* 8 Feb. 1912; *d* of late Hon. George Lambton. PhD London, 1939; DLit London, 1953. Press Attaché, British Embassy (formerly Legation), Tehran, 1939–45; Senior Lecturer in Persian, School of Oriental and African Studies, 1945–48; Reader in Persian, University of London, 1948–53. Hon. Fellow: New Hall, Cambridge, 1973; SOAS, Univ. of London, 1983. Hon. DLit Durham, 1971; Hon. LittD Cambridge, 1973. Reader Emeritus, dio. of Newcastle, 1988. *Publications:* Three Persian Dialects, 1938; Landlord and Peasant in Persia, 1953; Persian Grammar, 1953; Persian Vocabulary, 1964; The Persian Land Reform 1962–66, 1969; (ed, with others) The Cambridge History of Islam, vols 1–11, 1971; Theory and Practice in Medieval Persian Government, 1980; State and Government in Medieval Islam, 1981; Qajar Persia, 1987; Continuity and Change in Medieval Persia, 1988. *Address:* Gregory, Kirknewton, Wooler, Northumberland NE71 6XE.

LAMBURN, Patricia, (Mrs Donald Derrick), CBE 1985; Editorial Director, IPC Magazines Ltd, 1981–86; Director, IPC,1968–86; *er d* of Francis John Lamburn and Nell Winifred (*née* Kennedy); *m* 1949, Donald G. E. Douglas Derrick, DDS, LDSRCS, FRCD(Can.), FACD, FICD; one *s* one *d*. *Educ:* Queen's Gate Sch., S Kensington. Amalgamated Press, 1943–49; Curtis Publishing Co., USA, 1949–50; joined George Newnes Ltd, 1950; during ensuing yrs, edited, developed and was associated creatively with wide range of women's and teenage magazines; Dir, George Newnes Ltd, 1966–68; Gp Dir, Young Magazines Gp, 1968–71; Publishing Dir, Women's Magazines Gp, 1971–76, Asst Man. Dir (Editorial), 1976–81. Mem., Interim Licensing Authority for In Vitro Fertilisation and Embryology, 1986–91. Chm., Gen. Adv. Council, IBA, 1982–85 (Mem., 1980–82); Member: Health Educn Council, 1973–78; Editl Cttee, PPA, 1975–87; Information Cttee, British Nutrition Foundn, 1979–85; Periodical Publishing Trng Cttee, PPITB, 1980–82; Public Relations Cttee, RCP, 1981–88; Press Council, 1982–87; HFEA Inspectorate, 1991–94. Trustee, BACUP, 1993– (Mem. Exec. Cttee, 1986–93). Mem., Chelsea Crime Prevention Panel, 1990–. *Address:* Chelsea, London.

LAMER, Rt. Hon. Antonio, PC (Can.) 1990; Chief Justice of Canada, since 1990; *b* 8 July 1933; *m*; one *s*; *m* 1987, Danièle Tremblay; one step *s* one step *d*. *Educ;* Univ. of Montreal. Private practice, Cutler, Lamer, Bellemare & Associates; Prof., Faculty of Law, Univ. of Montreal; Judge, Superior Court and Queen's Bench, Province of Quebec, 1969; Chm., Law Reform Commn of Canada, 1976 (Vice-Chm., 1971); Justice, Quebec Court of Appeal, 1978; Justice, Supreme Court of Canada, 1980. KStJ. Order of Merit, Univ. of Montreal. *Address:* Supreme Court of Canada, Ottawa, Ontario K1A 0J1, Canada. *T:* (613) 9954330.

LAMERTON, Leonard Frederick, PhD, DSc, FInstP, FRCPath; Director, Institute of Cancer Research, London, 1977–80; Professor of Biophysics as Applied to Medicine, University of London, 1960–80; *b* 1 July 1915; *s* of Alfred Lamerton and Florence (*née* Mason); *m* 1965, Morag MacLeod. *Educ:* King Edward VI Sch., Southampton; University Coll., Southampton (PhD, DSc London). Staff member, Royal Cancer Hosp. and Inst. of Cancer Research, 1938–41 and 1946–80, Dean of the Inst., 1967–77; seconded to United Nations as a Scientific Sec. of First UN Conf. on Peaceful Uses of Atomic Energy, 1955. President: British Inst. of Radiology, 1957–58; Hosp. Physicists Assoc., 1961; Member: Bd of Governors, Royal Marsden Hosp., 1955–80; Bd of Governors, 1978–82, and Cttee of Management, 1978–82, Cardiothoracic Hosp. and Inst. Roentgen Award, 1950, Barclay Medal, 1961, British Inst. of Radiology. *Publications:* various papers on medical physics, radiation hazard, cell kinetics, experimental cancer therapy. *Recreations:* music, study of the development of Man. *Address:* 10 Burgh Mount, Banstead, Surrey SM7 1ER. *T:* Burgh Heath (01737) 353697.

LAMFALUSSY, Baron Alexandre; President, European Monetary Institute, since 1994; *b* 26 April 1929; *cr* Baron, 1993; *m* 1957, Anne-Marie Cochard; two *s* two *d*. *Educ:* Catholic Univ., Louvain (economics degree); Nuffield Coll., Oxford (PhD). Banque de Bruxelles: economist, 1955–61; Economic Advr, 1962; Exec. Dir, later Chm., Exec. Bd, 1965–76; Bank for International Settlements, Basle: Economic Advr, 1976–80; Asst Gen. Manager, 1981; Gen. Manager, 1985–93. Vis Lectr, Yale, 1961–62. Hon. doctorates: Univ. Lumière-Lyon, 1987; Inst. d'Etudes Politiques, Paris, 1993. *Publications:* Investment and Growth in Mature Economies, 1961; The UK and the Six, 1963; Les marchés financiers en Europe, 1968; The Restructuring of the Financial Industry, 1992; The Per Jacobsson Lecture, 1994. *Recreations:* hiking, sailing. *Address:* Eurotower, Kaiserstrasse 29, 60311 Frankfurt, Germany. *T:* (69) 272270.

LAMFORD, (Thomas) Gerald, OBE 1979; ASVU Representative, Cyprus, 1985–88; Commandant, Police Staff College, 1976–79; *b* Carmarthen, 3 April 1928; *s* of late Albert and Sarah Lamford; *m* 1952, Eira Hale; one *s* one *d*. *Educ:* Technical Coll., Swansea; London Univ. (LLB 1969); Police Coll. (Intermed. Comd Course, 1969; Sen. Comd Course, 1973). Radio Officer, Merchant Navy, 1945; Wireless Operator, RAF, 1946–48, Aden. Carmarthenshire Constab. (now Dyfed Powys Police), 1949; reached rank of Chief Inspector, CID, Crime Squad; Force Trng Officer, 1965–69; Supt, Haverfordwest, 1970; Chief Supt, Llanelli, 1971–74; Asst Chief Constable, Greater Manchester Police, 1974–79;

Investigating Officer, FCO, 1981–84. Vis. Prof. of Police Science, John Jay Coll. of Criminal Justice, City Univ. of New York, 1972; sometime Vis. Lecturer: Southern Police Inst., Univ. of Louisville, Ky; N Eastern Univ., Boston; NY Univ. Sch. of Law; Rutgers Univ., NJ; Mercy Coll., Detroit. County Comr, St John Amb. Bde, Pembrokeshire, 1970; SBStJ. Member: Rotary Club (Pres., 1991–92); Probus Club, Ammanford (Pres., 1996). *Publications:* articles in Police Studies, Internat. Rev. of Police Develt, Police Rev., Bramshill Jl, World Police. *Recreations:* photography, genealogy. *Address:* 11 Llwyn y Bryn, Ammanford, Dyfed SA18 2ES.

LAMING, (William) Herbert, CBE 1985; Chief Inspector, Social Services Inspectorate, Department of Health, since 1991; *b* 19 July 1936; *s* of William Angus Laming and Lillian Laming (*née* Robson); *m* 1962, Aileen Margaret Pollard. *Educ:* Univ. of Durham (Applied Social Scis); Rainer House (Home Office Probation Trng, 1960–61); LSE (Mental Health Course, 1965–66). Notts Probation Service: Probation Officer, 1961–66; Sen. Probation Officer, 1966–68; Asst Chief Probation Officer, Nottingham City and Co. Probation Service, 1968–71; Dep. Dir, 1971–75, Dir, 1975–91, Social Services, Herts CC. Pres., Assoc. of Dirs Social Services, 1982–83. *Publications:* Lessons from America: the balance of services in social care, 1985; contribs to professional jls. *Address:* Department of Health, Richmond House, 79 Whitehall, SW1A 2NS. *T:* 0171–210 5561.

LAMMIMAN, Surg. Rear Adm. David Askey, CB 1993; LVO 1978; FFARCS; Medical Director General (Naval), 1990–93; Deputy Surgeon General: Health Services, 1990–91; Operations and Plans, 1991–93; *b* 30 June 1932; *s* of Herbert Askey Lammiman and Lilian Elsie (*née* Park); *m* 1st, 1957, Sheila Mary Graham (marr. diss. 1984); three *s* one *d*; 2nd, 1984, Caroline Dale Brooks. *Educ:* Wyggeston Sch., Leicester; St Bartholomew's Hosp. (MB, BS 1957). DA 1962; DObstRCOG 1962; FFARCS 1969. Resident House Officer, Redhill County Hosp. and St Bartholomew's Hosp., 1957–58; joined RN, 1959; gen. service and hosp. appts at home and abroad; Clinical Asst, Southampton Gp of Hosps, Alder Hey Children's Hosp., Liverpool, and Radcliffe Infirmary, Oxford, 1966–69; served in: HMS Chaplet, 1959; HMS Eagle, 1967–68; HMY Britannia, 1976–78; Consultant Anaesthetist, RN Hospital: Malta, 1969–71; Haslar, 1971–73; Gibraltar, 1973–75; Plymouth, 1975–76; Haslar, 1978–82; Dir of Med. Personnel, MoD, 1982–84; Medical Officer i/c RN Hospital: Plymouth, 1984–86; Haslar, 1986–88; Surg. Rear Adm. (Support Med. Services), 1989–90. QHS 1987–93. *Recreations:* fly fishing, golf, tennis. *Clubs:* Naval and Military; Royal Naval Sailing Association (Portsmouth).

LAMOND, James Alexander, JP, DL; *b* Burrelton, Perthshire, 29 Nov. 1928; *s* of Alexander N. G. Lamond and Christina Lamond (*née* Craig); *m* 1954, June Rose Wellburn; three *d*. *Educ:* Burrelton Sch.; Coupar Angus Sch. Draughtsman. Mem., Aberdeen City Council, 1959–71; Lord Provost of Aberdeen, 1970–71; Lord Lieutenant of the County of the City of Aberdeen, 1970–71. MP (Lab) Oldham East, 1970–83, Oldham Central and Royton, 1983–92; Mem., Chairmen's Panel, 1979–92. Mem., Grampian Regl Council, 1994–. Mem., MSF (formerly TASS), 1944– (Chm., No 1 Divisional Council of DATA, 1965–70); Sec., Aberdeen Trades Council, 1994– (Pres., 1969). JP Aberdeen, DL Aberdeen, 1995. *Recreations:* golf, travel, reading, thinking. *Address:* 15 Belvidere Street, Aberdeen AB2 4QS. *T:* Aberdeen (01224) 638074.

LAMONT, Donald Alexander; HM Diplomatic Service; Head of Republic of Ireland Department, Foreign and Commonwealth Office, since 1994; *b* 13 Jan. 1947; *s* of Alexander Lamont and Alexa Lee Lamont (*née* Will); *m* 1981, Lynda Margaret Campbell; one *s* one *d*. *Educ:* Aberdeen Grammar Sch.; Aberdeen Univ. (MA Russian Studies). British Leyland Motor Corp., 1970; Second Sec., subseq. First Sec., FCO, 1974; First Sec., UNIDO/IAEA, Vienna, 1977; First Sec. (Commercial), Moscow, 1980; First Sec., FCO, 1982; Counsellor on secondment to IISS, 1988; Political Advr and Head of Chancery, British Mil. Govt, Berlin, 1988–91; Ambassador to Uruguay, 1991–94. *Address:* c/o Foreign and Commonwealth Office, SW1A 2AH. *Club:* Caledonian.

LAMONT, Rt. Hon. Norman Stewart Hughson, PC 1986; MP (C) Kingston-upon-Thames, since May 1972; non-executive Director, N. M. Rothschild & Sons, since 1993; *b* Lerwick, Shetland, 8 May 1942; *s* of late Daniel Lamont and of Helen Irene; *m* 1971, Alice Rosemary, *d* of Lt-Col Peter White; one *s* one *d*. *Educ:* Loretto Sch. (scholar); Fitzwilliam Coll., Cambridge (BA). Chm., Cambridge Univ. Conservative Assoc., 1963; Pres., Cambridge Union, 1964. PA to Rt Hon. Duncan Sandys, MP, 1965; Conservative Research Dept, 1966–68; Merchant Banker, N. M. Rothschild & Sons, 1968–79. Contested (C) East Hull, Gen. Election, 1970. PPS to Norman St John-Stevas, MP, Minister for the Arts, 1974; an Opposition Spokesman on: Prices and Consumer Affairs, 1975–76; Industry, 1976–79; Parly Under Sec. of State, Dept of Energy, 1979–81; Minister of State, DTI (formerly DoI), 1981–85; Minister of State for Defence Procurement, 1985–86; Financial Sec. to HM Treasury, 1986–89; Chief Sec. to HM Treasury, 1989–90; Chancellor of the Exchequer, 1990–93. Chairman: Coningsby Club, 1970–71; Bow Group, 1971–72. *Publications:* newspaper articles and Bow Group memoranda. *Recreations:* reading, ornithology. *Address:* House of Commons, SW1A 0AA. *Club:* Garrick.

LAMONTAGNE, Hon. (J.) Gilles, OC 1991; CD 1980; PC (Can.); Lieutenant-Governor of Quebec, 1984–90; *b* 17 April 1919; *s* of Trefflé Lamontagne and Anna Kieffer; *m* 1949, Mary Katherine Schaefer; three *s* one *d*. *Educ:* Collège Jean-de-Brébeuf, Montréal, Québec (BA). Served RCAF, 1941–45 (despatches, 1945). Businessman in Québec City, 1946–66. Alderman, Québec City, 1962–64, Mayor, 1965–77. MP (L) Langelier, 1977–84; Parly Sec. to Minister of Energy, Mines and Resources, 1977; Minister without Portfolio, Jan. 1978; Postmaster Gen., Feb. 1978; Actg Minister of Veterans Affairs, 1980–81; Minister of National Defence, 1980–83. Dir, Québec City Chamber of Commerce and Industry; Member: Econ. Council of Canada; Br. 260, Royal Canadian Legion. Hon. Col, Tactical Aviation Wing (Montreal), 1987. KStJ 1985. Hon. LLD Kingston Royal Mil. Coll., 1986; Hon. DAdmin St Jean Royal Mil. Coll., 1989. UN Medal 1987. Croix du Combattant de l'Europe. *Address:* 8 Jardins Mérici, # 1405, Quebec G1S 4N9, Canada. *Clubs:* Cercle de la Garrison de Québec, Royal Québec Golf.

LAMPARD, Martin Robert; *b* 21 Feb. 1926; *s* of Austin Hugo Lampard and late Edith Gertrude Lampard (formerly White); *m* 1957, Felice MacLean; three *d*. *Educ:* Radley College, Oxford; Christ Church, Oxford (MA). Served RNVR. Admitted solicitor, 1952; joined Ashurst Morris Crisp & Co., 1954, Partner, 1957, Sen. Partner, 1974–86. Farming in East Anglia, Simmental beef herd. Formerly Dir, Allied Lyons plc; dir of other companies. *Address:* Theberton House, Theberton, near Leiston, Suffolk IP16 4RL. *T:* Leiston (01728) 830510. *Clubs:* Royal Ocean Racing; Royal Yacht Squadron.

LAMPERT, Catherine Emily; Director, Whitechapel Art Gallery, since 1988; *b* 15 Oct. 1946; *d* of Emily F. Schubach and Chester G. Lampert; *m* 1971, Robert Keith Mason; one adopted *d*. *Educ:* Brown Univ. (BA); Temple Univ. (MFA). UCL, 1966–67; Asst Curator, RI Sch. of Design, Mus. of Art, 1968–69; Studio Internat., 1971–72; Sen. Exhibn Organiser, Hayward Gall., 1973–88. *Publications:* Rodin: sculpture and drawings, 1986; Lucian Freud: recent work, 1993; numerous catalogue essays on Frank Auerbach, Barry Flanagan, Tony Cragg and other subjects of Twentieth Century art. *Address:* 92 Lenthall Road, E8 3JN. *T:* 0171–249 7650.

LAMPL, Sir Frank (William), Kt 1990; Executive Director, Peninsular and Oriental Steam Navigation Company, since 1985; Chairman, Bovis Construction Group, since 1989; *b* 6 April 1926; adopted British nationality, 1974; *s* of Dr Otto Lampl and Olga (*née* Jelinek); *m* 1948, Blanka (*née* Kratochvílová); one *s*. *Educ:* Univ. of Brno, Czechoslovakia (Dip Eng, Faculty of Architecture and Engineering). FCIOB. Emigrated from Czechoslovakia to UK, 1968, after Russian invasion; Exec. Dir, Bovis Construction, 1974; Man. Dir, Bovis International, 1978; Dir, Bovis, 1979; Chm., Bovis Construction and Bovis International, 1985; Dep. Chm., Lehrer MacGovern-Bovis, NY, 1987. First Chancellor, Kingston Univ., 1994–. CIMgt. Hon. DEng Technical Univ., Brno, 1993; Dr *hc* Kingston. *Recreation:* reading. *Address:* Bovis, 127 Sloane Street, SW1X 9BA. *T:* 0181–422 3488. *Club:* Royal Automobile.

LAMPSON, family name of **Baron Killearn.**

LANCASTER, Bishop Suffragan of, since 1990; **Rt. Rev. John Nicholls;** *b* 16 July 1943; *s* of James William and late Nellie Nicholls; *m* 1969, Judith Dagnall; two *s* two *d*. *Educ:* Bacup and Rawtenstall Grammar School; King's Coll., London (AKC); St Boniface Coll., Warminster. Curate, St Clement with St Cyprian, Salford, 1967–69; Curate, 1969–72, Vicar 1972–78, All Saints and Martyrs, Langley, Manchester; Dir of Pastoral Studies, Coll. of the Resurrection, Mirfield, 1978–83; Canon Residentiary of Manchester Cathedral, 1983–90. *Recreations:* music (listening and singing), reading, films. *Address:* 7 Dallas Road, Lancaster LA1 1TN. *T:* Lancaster (01524) 32897.

LANCASTER, Bishop of, (RC), since 1985; **Rt. Rev. John Brewer;** *b* 24 Nov 1929; *s* of Eric W. Brewer and Laura H. Brewer (*née* Webster). *Educ:* Ushaw College, Durham; Ven. English College, Rome and Gregorian Univ. PhL, STL, JCL. Ordained priest, 1956; Parish Assistant, 1959–64; Vice-Rector, Ven. English Coll., Rome, 1964–71; Parish Priest of St Mary's, Middlewich, 1971–78; Auxiliary Bishop of Shrewsbury, 1971–83; Bishop Coadjutor of Lancaster, 1984. Officiating Chaplain, Royal Navy, 1966–71; Representative of RC Bishops of England and Wales in Rome, 1964–71. Chaplain to HH Pope Paul VI, 1965. *Recreations:* reading, travel. *Address:* Bishop's House, Cannon Hill, Lancaster LA1 5NG. *T:* Lancaster (01524) 32231.

LANCASTER, Archdeacon of; *see* Gibbons, Ven. K. H.

LANCASTER, Dame Jean, DBE 1963; *b* 11 Aug. 1909; *d* of late Richard C. Davies; *m* 1967, Roy Cavander Lancaster (*d* 1981). *Educ:* Merchant Taylors' Sch., Crosby, Lancashire. Director, Women's Royal Naval Service, 1961–64. *Address:* Warren Park Nursing Home, Warren Road, Blundellsands, Liverpool L23 6US.

LANCASTER, Patricia Margaret; Headmistress, Wycombe Abbey School, 1974–88; a Church Commissioner, since 1989; *b* 22 Feb. 1929; *d* of Vice-Adm. Sir John Lancaster, KBE, CB. *Educ:* Univs of London (BA) and Southampton (Certif. Educn). English Mistress, St Mary's Sch., Calne, 1951–58; Housemistress, St Swithun's Sch., Winchester, 1958–62; Headmistress, St Michael's, Burton Park, Petworth, 1962–73. Pres., Girls' Schools' Assoc., 1979–80. Governor: Berkhamsted Sch., 1989–; Marlborough Coll., 1989–; Repton Sch., 1989–95; St Mary's Sch., Calne, 1989–; St Swithun's Sch., Winchester, 1989–. *Recreations:* theatre, art galleries, gardening. *Address:* 8 Vectis Road, Alverstoke, near Gosport, Hants PO12 2QF.

LANCELOT, James Bennett, FRCO; Master of the Choristers and Organist, Durham Cathedral, since 1985; *b* 2 Dec. 1952; *s* of Rev. Roland Lancelot; *m* 1982, Sylvia Jane (*née* Hoare); two *d*. *Educ:* St Paul's Cathedral Choir Sch.; Ardingly Coll., Royal College of Music (ARCM); King's Coll., Cambridge (Dr Mann Organ Student; MA; BMus). Asst Organist, St Clement Danes and Hampstead Parish Ch., 1974–75; Sub-Organist, Winchester Cath., 1975–85; Asst Conductor, Winchester Music Club, 1983–85; Conductor, Durham Univ. Choral Soc., 1987–. Mem. Council, RCO, 1988–. Numerous recordings. *Publication:* (with R. Hird) Durham Cathedral Organs, 1991. *Recreations:* railways, the works of John Buchan. *Address:* 6 The College, Durham DH1 3EQ. *T:* Durham (0191) 3864766.

LANCHBERY, John Arthur, OBE 1990; FRAM; conductor; *b* London, 15 May 1923; *s* of William Lanchbery and Violet (*née* Mewett); *m* 1951, Elaine Fifield (divorced 1960); one *d*. *Educ:* Alleyn's Sch., Dulwich; Royal Academy of Music. Henry Smart Composition Scholarship, 1942. Served, Royal Armoured Corps, 1943–45. Royal Academy of Music, 1945–47; Musical Director, Metropolitan Ballet, 1948–50; Sadler's Wells Theatre Ballet, 1951–57; Royal Ballet, 1957–72 (Principal Conductor, 1959–72); Musical Director: Australian Ballet, 1972–77; American Ballet Theatre, 1978–80. ARAM 1953. Bolshoi Theatre Medal, Moscow, 1961; Queen Elizabeth II Coronation Award, Royal Acad. of Dancing, 1989; Carina Ari Medal, Stockholm, 1989. *Film scores* include: The Turning Point, 1977; Nijinsky, 1980; Evil Under the Sun, 1983; The Birth of a Nation, 1993; The Iron Horse, 1994. *Publications:* Arrangements and Compositions of Ballets include: Pleasuredrome, 1949; Eve of St Agnes (BBC commission), 1950; House of Birds, 1955; La Fille Mal Gardée, 1960; The Dream, 1964; Don Quixote, 1966; Giselle, 1968; La Sylphide, 1970; Tales of Beatrix Potter, 1971; Tales of Hoffman, 1972; Merry Widow, 1975; Month in the Country, 1976; Mayerling, 1978; Rosalinda, 1978; Papillon, 1979; La Bayadère, 1980; Peer Gynt, 1980; The Devil to Pay, 1982; The Sentimental Bloke, 1985; Le Chat Botté, 1985; Midsummer Night's Dream, 1985; Hunchback of Notre Dame, 1988; Figaro, 1992; Madame Butterfly, 1995. *Recreations:* walking, reading.

LANCHIN, Gerald; consultant; a Vice-President, National Federation of Consumer Groups, since 1984; Member, Data Protection Tribunal, since 1985; *b* 17 Oct. 1922; *o s* of late Samuel Lanchin, Kensington; *m* 1951, Valerie Sonia Lyons; one *s* two *d*. *Educ:* St Marylebone Grammar Sch.; London Sch. of Economics. BCom 1st cl. hons 1951; Leverhulme Schol. 1950–51. Min. of Labour, 1939–51; served with Army, RAOC and REME, 1942–46; Board of Trade (subseq. DTI and Dept of Trade): Asst Principal, 1952; Principal 1953; 1st Sec., UK Delegn to OEEC, Paris, 1955–59; Principal, Estabt and Commercial Relations and Exports Divs, 1959–66; Asst Sec., Finance and Civil Aviation Divs, 1966–71; Under-Sec., Tariff, Commercial Relations and Export, Shipping Policy, General and Consumer Affairs Divs, 1971–82. Chairman: Packaging Council, 1983–84; Direct Mail Services Standards Bd, 1983–89; Member: Council, Consumers' Assoc., 1983–88; Consumer Panel, PIA, 1994–. *Publication:* Government and the Consumer, 1985. *Recreations:* photography, reading, music. *Address:* 28 Priory Gardens, Berkhamsted, Herts HP4 2DS. *T:* Berkhamsted (01442) 875283.

LAND, Gillian; *see* Lynne, Gillian.

LAND, Prof. Michael Francis, FRS 1982; PhD; Professor of Neurobiology, University of Sussex, since 1984; *b* 12 April 1942; *s* of late Prof. Frank William Land and of Nora Beatrice Channon; *m* 1980, Rosemary (*née* Clarke); one *s* two *d*. *Educ:* Birkenhead Sch., Cheshire; Jesus Coll., Cambridge (MA); University Coll. London (PhD). Asst Lectr in Physiology, UCL, 1966–67; Miller Fellow, 1967–79, and Asst Prof. of Physiology-Anatomy, 1979–81, Univ. of Calif, Berkeley; Lectr in Biol Sciences, 1971–77, Reader, 1977–84, Univ. of Sussex. Vis. Prof., Univ. of Oregon, 1980; Sen. Res. Fellow, ANU, 1982–84. *Publications:* numerous papers on animal vision in learned jls. *Recreations:*

photography, music. *Address:* White House, Cuilfail, Lewes, East Sussex BN7 2BE. *T:* Lewes (01273) 476780.

LAND, Nicholas Charles Edward, FCA; Senior Partner, Ernst & Young, since 1995; *b* 6 Feb. 1948; *s* of Charles and Norma Land; *m* 1975, Sonia Tan; one *s*. *Educ:* Steyning Grammar Sch. FCA 1971. Articled Spain Brothers Dalling & Co., 1967–71; joined Turquand Young, later Ernst & Young, 1971: Partner, 1978–; Managing Partner, London Office, 1986–92; Managing Partner, 1992–95. *Recreations:* gardening, opera. *Address:* (office) Becket House, 1 Lambeth Palace Road, SE1 7EU. *T:* 0171–931 3002.

LANDA, Lynda; *see* Baroness Chalker of Wallasey.

LANDALE, Sir David (William Neil), KCVO 1993; DL; company director; *b* 7 May 1934; *s* of David Fortune Landale and Louisa (*née* Forbes); *m* 1961, Melanie Roper; three *s*. *Educ:* Eton Coll.; Balliol Coll., Oxford (MA Hist. 1958). Served Black Watch, RHR, 1952–54. Director: Jardine Matheson & Co. Ltd (served in Hong Kong, Thailand, Taiwan and Japan), 1959–75; Matheson & Co. Ltd, 1975–; Pinneys of Scotland, Annan, 1982–87; Duchy Originals Ltd, 1992–. Chm., T. C. Farries & Co. Ltd. 1982–. Regl Chm., Timber Growers, Scotland, 1983–85; Chm., Timber Growers UK Ltd, 1985–87. Member: Exec. Cttee and Council, NT for Scotland, 1980–85; Exec. Cttee, Scottish Landowners Fedn, 1980–87. Sec. and Keeper of Records, Duchy of Cornwall, 1987–93. Mem., Royal Co. of Archers, Queen's Body Guard for Scotland, 1966–. FRSA 1990. DL Nithsdale/Annandale Dumfries, 1988. *Recreations:* all countryside pursuits, theatre, reading, history. *Address:* Dalswinton, Dumfries DG2 0XZ. *T:* Dumfries (01387) 740208. *Clubs:* Boodle's, Pratt's; New (Edinburgh).

LANDAU, Sir Dennis (Marcus), Kt 1987; Chief Executive, Co-operative Wholesale Society Ltd, 1980–92 (Deputy Chief Executive Officer, 1974–80); *b* 18 June 1927; *s* of late Michael Landau, metallurgist; *m* 1992, Mrs Pamela Garlick. *Educ:* Haberdashers' Aske's Hampstead Sch. Schweppes Ltd, 1952; Man. Dir, Schweppes (East Africa) Ltd, 1958–62; Chivers-Hartley: Prodn Dir, 1963; Man. Dir, 1966–69; Chm., Schweppes Foods Div., 1969; Dep. Chm. and Man. Dir, Cadbury Schweppes Foods, 1970; Controller, Food Div., Co-operative Wholesale Society Ltd, 1971. Chairman: CWS (India) Ltd, 1980–92; Unity Trust Bank plc, 1992– (Dir, 1984–); Dep. Chm., Co-operative Bank plc, 1989–92; Vice-Chm., Lancashire Enterprises plc, 1989–; Director: Co-operative Retail Services Ltd, 1980–91; CWS (NZ Hldgs) Ltd, 1980–91; Co-operative Insce Soc. Ltd, 1980–92. Member: Metrication Bd, 1972–80; Exec. Cttee, Food & Drink Fedn (formerly Food Manufacturers' Fedn Inc.), 1972–92. Mem. Council, Manchester Business Sch., 1982–93 (Chm., 1991–93). FIGD 1977 (Pres. 1982–85); CIMgt (CBIM 1980). FRSA 1992. *Recreations:* Rugby, cricket, music. *Clubs:* Royal Over-Seas League; Lancashire CC.

LANDELS, William, (Willie); painter; *b* Venice, 14 June 1928; *s* of late Reynold Landels and Carla Manfredi; *m* 1958, Angela Ogden; two *d*. *Educ:* privately. Apprentice stage designer at La Scala, Milan, 1947; Art Director: J. Walter Thompson, 1950; Queen Magazine, 1965; Editor, Harpers & Queen, 1970–86; Art Dir, 1986–89, Editor, 1989–90, Departures. One-man Exhibitions: Hamburg, 1992; Rebecca Hossack Gall., London, 1993; Olsen-Carr Gall., Sydney, 1994. *Publication:* (with Alistair Burnet) The Best Years of Our Lives, 1981. *Recreation:* cooking. *Address:* 292 South Lambeth Road, SW8 1UJ.

LANDEN, Dinsdale (James); actor; *b* 4 Sept. 1932; *s* of Edward James Landen and Winifred Alice Landen; *m* 1959, Jennifer Daniel. *Educ:* King's Sch., Rochester; Hove County Grammar Sch. *Stage:* Dead Secret, Piccadilly, 1957; Auntie Mame, Adelphi; Provok'd Wife, Vaudeville; Philanthropist, May Fair, 1970; London Assurance, New, 1972, Alphabetical Order, May Fair, 1975; Bodies, Ambassadors, 1980; Taking Steps, Lyric, 1980, Loot, Lyric, 1984; Sufficient Carbohydrate, Albery, 1984; Wife Begins at Forty, Ambassadors, 1985; Selling the Sizzle, Hampstead, 1986; Dangerous Obsession, Apollo, then Fortune, 1987; Thark, Lyric, Hammersmith, 1989; Bookends, Apollo, 1990; Twelfth Night, Playhouse, 1991; Chatsky, Almeida, 1993; School for Scandal, Chichester Fest., 1995. *National Theatre:* Plunder; The Philanderer; On the Razzle, 1981, Uncle Vanya, 1982. *Films:* The Valiant; Every Home Should Have One; Digby the Biggest Dog in the World; Mosquito Squadron; Morons from Outer Space; The Steal; *television:* Great Expectations, Mickey Dunne, The Spies, Glittering Prizes, Devenish, Two Sundays, Fathers and Families, Pig in the Middle, Radio Pictures, Absent Friends, Events in a Museum; What the Butler Saw; Some Other Spring; Fighting Against Slavery; Arms and the Man; The Buccaneers. *Recreations:* walking, golf. *Address:* 90 Felsham Road, SW15 1DQ. *Club:* Stage Golfing Society.

LANDON, Prof. David Neil; Dean, Institute of Neurology, London, since 1987; Professor of Neurocytology, University of London, since 1991; *b* 15 May 1936; *er s* of Christopher Guy Landon and Isabella Catherine (*née* Campbell); *m* 1960, Karen Elizabeth, *yr d* of late John Copeland and Else Margrethe Poole, Bolney, Sussex; two *s* one *d*. *Educ:* Lancing Coll.; Guy's Hospital Med. Sch. (BSc Hons Anat.; MB BS 1960). LRCP, MRCS 1959. Ho. Officer, Guy's Hosp., 1959–60; Lectr in Anatomy, Guy's Hosp. Med. Sch., 1961–64; Lectr, later Sen. Lectr, in Neurobiology, MRC Res. Gp in Applied Neurobiology, 1964–77; Reader in Neurocytology, Inst. of Neurology, 1977–91. Hon. Cons. in Morbid Anatomy, National Hosps for Nervous Diseases, Queen Square, 1974–. Vis. Prof., Coll. of Medicine, Lagos, 1975. Gov., National Hosps for Nervous Diseases SHA, 1988–95; Appointed Mem., GMC, 1988–94. Member: Res. Cttee, World Fedn of Neurology, 1987–95; Cttees of Management, Inst. of Child Health, 1987–, Inst. of Neurology, 1987–, Inst. of Dental Surgery, 1993–; Chm., Med. Res. Ethics Cttee, Nat. Hosp. for Neurology and Neurosurgery, 1987–93. Mem., Senate and Academic Council, Univ. of London, 1992–94. Editorial Cttee, Jl of Anatomy, 1981–94; Associated Editor: Jl of Neurocytol., 1980–83; Neuromuscular Disorders, 1990–94. *Publications:* The Peripheral Nerve, 1976; contribs to learned jls on the fine structure, develt and pathology of nerve and muscle. *Recreations:* gardening, travel. *Address:* Woodmans, Wallcrouch, Wadhurst, East Sussex TN5 7JG. *T:* Ticehurst (01580) 200833.

LANDON, Howard Chandler Robbins; author and music historian; *b* 6 March 1926; *s* of late William Grinnell Landon and Dorothea LeBaron Robbins; *m* 1957, Else Radant. *Educ:* Aiken Preparatory Sch.; Lenox Sch.; Swarthmore Coll.; Boston Univ., USA (BMus). European rep. of Intercollegiate Broadcasting System, 1947; founded Haydn Soc. (which recorded and printed music of Joseph Haydn), 1949; became a Special Correspondent of The Times, 1957 and contrib. to that newspaper until 1961. Visiting Prof., Queen's Coll., NYC, 1969; Regents Prof. of Music, Univ. of California (Davis), 1970, 1975, 1979; John Bird Prof. of Music, UC Cardiff, 1978–; Christian Johnson Prof. of Music, Middlebury Coll., Vermont, USA, 1980–. Advr, Prague Mozart Foundn, 1992–. Hon. Professorial Fellow, University Coll., Cardiff, 1971–79; Hon. Fellow, Lady Margaret Hall, Oxford, 1979–. Hon. DMus: Boston Univ., 1969; Queen's Univ., Belfast, 1974; Bristol, 1982. Verdienstkreuz für Kunst und Wissenschaft from Austrian Govt, 1972; Gold Medal, City of Vienna, 1987; Haydn Prize, Govt of Burgenland, Austria, 1990. Co-editor, The Haydn Yearbook, 1962–. *Publications:* The Symphonies of Joseph Haydn, 1955; The Mozart Companion (co-ed with Donald Mitchell), 1956; The Collected Correspondence and London Notebooks of Joseph Haydn, 1959; Essays on Eighteenth-Century Music, 1969; Ludwig van Beethoven: a documentary study, 1970; critical edn of the 107 Haydn Symphonies, (completed) 1968; five-vol. biog. of Haydn: vol. 3, Haydn in England, 1976; vol. 4, Haydn: The Years of The Creation, 1977; vol. 5, Haydn: The Late Years, 1977; vol. 1, Haydn: The Early Years, and vol. 2, Haydn in Eszterhaza, 1978–80; Haydn: a documentary study, 1981; Mozart and the Masons, 1982; Handel and his World, 1984; 1791: Mozart's Last Year, 1988; (with David Wyn Jones) Haydn: his life and music, 1988; Mozart: the golden years, 1989; (ed) The Mozart Compendium, 1990; Mozart and Vienna, 1991; Five Centuries of Music in Venice, 1991; Vivaldi: voice of the Baroque, 1993; The Mozart Essays, 1995; scholarly edns of eighteenth-century music (various European publishing houses). *Recreations:* swimming, cooking, walking. *Address:* Anton Frankgasse 3, Vienna 1180, Austria. *T:* (1) 4796383; Château de Foncoussières, 81800 Rabastens (Tarn), France. *T:* 63406145.

LANDRETH, Rev. Canon Derek, TD 1963; Vicar of Icklesham, Diocese of Chichester, 1983–89 (Priest-in-charge, 1982–83), also Priest-in-charge of Fairlight, 1984–86; Chaplain to the Queen, 1980–90; Rural Dean of Rye, 1984–89; *b* 7 June 1920; *s* of Rev. Norman Landreth and Muriel Landreth; *m* 1st, 1943, Myra Joan Brown; one *s* three *d*; 2nd, 1986, Dss Mavis Isabella White. *Educ:* Kingswood School, Bath; King's College, Cambridge (MA); Bishops' College, Cheshunt. Commissioned, Royal Artillery, 1942–46 (service India and Burma); CF (TA), 1951–67, (TAVR) 1967–70; Asst Curate, St George, Camberwell, 1948–53; Vicar, St Mark, Battersea Rise, 1953–59; Deputy Chaplain, HM Prison, Wandsworth, 1954–59; Vicar of Richmond, Surrey, and Chaplain, Star and Garter Home for Disabled Soldiers, Sailors and Airmen, 1959–70; Rector of Sanderstead, Surrey, 1970–77; Hon. Chaplain to Bishop of Southwark, 1962–80; Hon. Canon of Southwark Cathedral, 1968–77; Canon Residentiary and Librarian, Southwark Cathedral, 1977–82; Canon Emeritus, 1982–. Proctor in Convocation, 1980–83. Indep. Mem., Richmond Borough Council, 1961–65. *Recreations:* gardening, fishing. *Address:* Gossamer Cottage, Slindon, near Arundel, W Sussex BN18 0QT. *T:* Slindon (01243) 814224.

LANDSHOFF, Prof. Peter Vincent, PhD; Professor of Mathematical Physics, since 1994, and Fellow of Christ's College, since 1963, University of Cambridge; *b* 22 March 1937; *m* 1962, Pamela Carmichael; three *s*. *Educ:* City of London Sch.; St John's Coll., Cambridge (MA, PhD). Cambridge University: Fellow, St John's Coll., 1961–63; Reader in Mathematical Physics, 1974–94. Instructor, Princeton Univ., 1961–62; Scientific Associate, CERN, Geneva, 1975–76, 1984–85, 1991–92. Editor, Physics Letters B (Elsevier Science), 1982–. *Publications:* (jtly) The Analytic S-matrix, 1966; (jtly) Simple Quantum Physics, 1979; research papers on theoretical high-energy physics. *Address:* Department of Applied Mathematics and Theoretical Physics, Silver Street, Cambridge CB3 9EW. *T:* Cambridge (01223) 337880.

LANE, family name of **Baron Lane** and **Baron Lane of Horsell.**

LANE, Baron *cr* 1979 (Life Peer), of St Ippollitts; **Geoffrey Dawson Lane;** PC 1974; Kt 1966; AFC 1943; Lord Chief Justice of England, 1980–92; *b* 17 July 1918; *s* of late Percy Albert Lane, Lincoln; *m* 1944, Jan, *d* of Donald Macdonald; one *s*. *Educ:* Shrewsbury; Trinity Coll., Cambridge (Hon. Fellow 1981). Served in RAF, 1939–45; Sqdn-Leader, 1942. Called to Bar, Gray's Inn, 1946; Bencher 1966. QC 1962. Dep. Chm., Beds. QS, 1960–66; Recorder of Bedford, 1963–66; a Judge of the High Court of Justice, Queen's Bench Div., 1966–74; a Lord Justice of Appeal, 1974–79; a Lord of Appeal in Ordinary, 1979–80. Mem., Parole Board, 1970–72 (Vice-Chm., 1972). Hon. Bencher, Inner Temple, 1980. Hon. LLD Cambridge, 1984. *Address:* Royal Courts of Justice, Strand, WC2A 2LL.

LANE OF HORSELL, Baron *cr* 1990 (Life Peer), of Woking in the County of Surrey; **Peter Stewart Lane,** Kt 1984; JP; FCA; Senior Partner, Binder Hamlyn, Chartered Accountants, 1979–92; Chairman, Automated Security (Holdings), since 1994; Deputy Chairman, More O'Ferrall, since 1985; *b* 29 Jan. 1925; *s* of late Leonard George Lane; *m* Doris Florence (*née* Botsford) (*d* 1969); two *d*. *Educ:* Sherborne Sch., Dorset. Served RNVR (Sub Lieut), 1943–46. Qualified as chartered accountant, 1948; Partner, Binder Hamlyn or predecessor firms, 1950–92. Chairman: Brent Internat., 1985–95; Elswick, 1993–94; Attwoods, 1994. National Union of Conservative Associations: Vice Chairman, 1981–83; Chairman, 1983–84; Chm., Exec. Cttee, 1986–91; Vice President, 1984–. Chm., Nuffield Hosps, 1993– (Dep. Chm., 1990–93). Chm., Action on Addiction, 1991–94. JP Surrey, 1976–; Freeman, City of London. *Address:* c/o House of Lords, SW1A 0PW. *Clubs:* Boodle's, MCC.
See also Baron Trefgarne.

LANE, Dr Anthony John, FRCP, FFPHM; Regional Medical Officer, North Western Regional Health Authority, 1974–86, retired; *b* 6 Feb. 1926; *s* of John Gill Lane and Marian (*née* Brumfield); *m* 1948, Hannah Holečková; one *s* two *d*. *Educ:* St Christopher's Sch., Letchworth; Emmanuel Coll., Cambridge. MA, MB, BChir. House posts in surgery, medicine, obstetrics and paediatrics, 1949–51; MO with Methodist Missionary Soc., Andhra State, India, 1951–57; Registrar: Tropical Diseases, UCH, 1958; Gen. Med., St James' Hosp., Balham, 1958–61; Infectious Diseases, Western Hosp., Fulham, 1961–63; MO (Trainee), Leeds RHB, 1963–64; Asst Sen. MO, Leeds RHB, 1964–66; Principal Asst Sen. MO, Leeds RHB, 1966–70; Dep. Sen. Admin. MO, SW Metrop. RHB, 1970–71; Sen. Admin. MO, Manchester RHB, 1971–74. Hon. MD Manchester, 1986. *Publications:* contrib. Positions, Movements and Directions in Health Services Research, 1974; contrib. Proc. Royal Soc. Med. *Recreations:* music, competitive indoor games, walking, gardening. *Address:* 4 Queens Road, Wilmslow, Cheshire SK9 5HS. *T:* Wilmslow (01625) 523889.

LANE, Anthony John, CB 1990; Deputy Secretary, Department of the Environment, since 1994; *b* 30 May 1939; *s* of late Eric Marshall Lane and Phyllis Mary Lane; *m* 1967, Judith Sheila (*née* Dodson); two *s* one *d*. *Educ:* Caterham Sch.; Balliol Coll., Oxford (BA PPE, MA). Investment Analyst, Joseph Sebag & Co., 1964–65; Asst Principal, Min. of Technology, 1965; Private Sec. to Parly Sec., 1968–69; Principal, 1969; Private Secretary: to Minister for Aerospace and Shipping, 1973–74; to Sec. of State for Prices and Consumer Protection, 1974–75; Asst Sec., Dept of Prices, 1975, Dept of Trade, 1979; Under Sec., Dept of Trade, then Dept of Transport, 1980–84; Under Sec., DTI, 1984–87, Dep. Sec., 1987–94; Dep. Dir Gen., OFT, 1987–90; DTI, 1990–94. *Recreations:* music, gardens, travel. *Address:* Department of Trade and Industry, 151 Buckingham Palace Road, SW1W 9SS.

LANE, Dr Anthony Milner, FRS 1975; Deputy Chief Scientific Officer, Atomic Energy Research Establishment, Harwell, 1976–89; *b* 27 July 1928; *s* of Herbert William Lane and Doris Ruby Lane (*née* Milner); *m* 1st, 1952, Anne Sophie Zissman (*d* 1980); two *s* one *d*; 2nd, 1983, Jill Valerie Parvin; five step *d*. *Educ:* Trowbridge Boys' High Sch.; Selwyn Coll., Cambridge. BA Maths, PhD Theoretical Physics. Joined Harwell, 1953. *Publications:* Nuclear Theory, 1963; numerous research articles in Review of Modern Physics, Phys. Review, Nuclear Physics, etc. *Recreations:* gardening, bird-watching. *Address:* 6 Walton Street, Oxford OX1 2HG. *T:* Oxford (01865) 56565.

LANE, Maj.-Gen. Barry Michael, CB 1984; OBE 1974 (MBE 1965); Chief Executive, Cardiff Bay Development Corporation, 1987–92; *b* 10 Aug. 1932; *m* 1st, 1956, Eveline

Jean (*d* 1986), *d* of Vice-Adm. Sir Harry Koelle, KCB and Enid (*née* Corbould-Ellis); one *s* one *d*; 2nd, 1987, Shirley Ann, *d* of E. V. Hawtin. *Educ:* Dover Coll. Commissioned, 1954; served Somerset LI, 1954–59, Somerset and Cornwall LI, 1959–68, LI, 1968–75; Instructor, Staff Coll. Camberley, 1970–72; CO, 1st Bn, LI, 1972–75; Comd, 11 Armoured Bde, 1977–78; RCDS, 1979; Dep. Dir, Army Staff Duties, MoD, 1980–81; Dir, Army Quartering, 1981–82; VQMG, 1982–83; GOC SW Dist, 1984–87. Col, The LI, 1982–87. Hon. Colonel: 6th Bn, LI, 1987; Bristol Univ., OTC, 1988. *Address:* c/o National Westminster Bank, Tadworth, Surrey KT20 5AF. *Club:* Army and Navy.

LANE, David Goodwin; QC 1991; a Recorder of the Crown Court, since 1987; *b* 8 Oct. 1945; *s* of James Cooper Lane and Joyce Lilian Lane; *m* 1991, Jacqueline Elizabeth Cocks. *Educ:* Crypt Sch., Gloucester; King's College London (LLB, AKC). Lord Justice Holker Junior Exhibnr; Lee Essay Prizeman, H. C. Richard Ecclesiastical Law Prizeman; Albion Richardson Scholar. Called to the Bar, Gray's Inn, 1968; Asst Recorder, 1982. Freeman, City of London. *Address:* 2 King's Bench Walk, Temple, EC4Y 7DE. *T:* 0171–353 1746; All Saints' Chambers, Holbeck House, 9/11 Broad Street, Bristol BS1 2HP. *T:* Bristol (0117) 921 1966.

LANE, Rev. David John; Principal, College of the Resurrection, Mirfield, since 1990; *b* 12 June 1935; *s* of late Rex Clayphen Fox Lane and Constance Mary Lane. *Educ:* Hurstpierpoint Coll. (Scholar); Magdalen Coll., Oxford (BA Theol 1958; Oriental Studies 1960; Pusey and Ellerton Schol., 1959; Hall Houghton Syriac Prize, 1961; MA 1962; BD 1989). Nat. Service, Royal Signals, 1953–55. Coll. of the Resurrection, Mirfield, 1960–61; Codrington Coll., Barbados, 1961–62. Deacon and Priest, Barbados, 1962; Lectr, 1961, Sen. Tutor, 1963, Codrington Coll., Barbados; Curate, St Peter's, Wolvercote, 1965–66; Associate Chaplain, and Kennicott Hebrew Fellow, 1966–68, Lectr in Theol., 1968–71, Pembroke Coll., Oxford; Lectr and Tutor, St Stephen's House, Oxford, 1968–71; Asst Prof., Near Eastern Studies, Univ. of Toronto, 1971, Associate Prof., 1974–83; Sen. Fellowship, Trinity Coll., Toronto, 1977–82; College of the Resurrection: Lectr and Tutor, 1983; Dir of Studies, 1984; Vice-Principal, 1987–90. Hon. Lectr, Dept of Theology and Religious Studies, Univ. of Leeds, 1983–. *Publications:* The Old Testament in Syriac: Part II, fasc. 5 ((ed) Ecclesiastes; (ed with J. A. Emerton) Wisdom of Solomon and Song of Songs), 1979, Part I, fasc. 2 ((ed) Leviticus), 1991; The Peshitta of Leviticus, 1994; articles in learned jls. *Recreations:* garden design and maintenance, domestic planning. *Address:* College of the Resurrection, Mirfield, West Yorks WF14 0BW. *T:* Mirfield (01924) 490441. *Club:* Royal Over-Seas League.

LANE, David Neil, CMG 1983; HM Diplomatic Service, retired; Assistant Secretary-General, 1989–92 and Secretary, 1990–92, Order of St John; *b* 16 April 1928; *er s* of late Clive and Hilda Lane, Bath; *m* 1968, Sara, *d* of late Cecil Nurcombe, MC; two *d*. *Educ:* Abbotsholme Sch.; Merton Coll., Oxford. Army, 1946–48; Foreign (later Foreign and Commonwealth) Office: 1951–53, 1955–58, 1963–68, 1972–74; British Embassy, Oslo, 1953–55; Ankara, 1959–61, 1975–78; Conakry, 1961–63; UK Mission to the United Nations, New York, 1968–72, 1979; High Comr in Trinidad and Tobago, 1980–85; Ambassador to the Holy See, 1985–88. Pres., UN Trusteeship Council, 1971–72; UK Delegate, Internat. Exhibns Bureau, 1973–74. OStJ 1990. *Recreation:* music. *Address:* 6 Montagu Square, W1H 1RA. *T:* 0171–486 1673. *Club:* Travellers'.

LANE, Prof. David Philip, PhD; FRSE; Professor of Molecular Oncology, University of Dundee, since 1990; *b* 1 July 1952; *s* of John Wallace Lane and Cecelia Frances Evelyn Lane (*née* Wright); *m* 1975, Ellen Birgitte Muldal; one *s* one *d*. *Educ:* John Fisher Sch., Purley; University College London (BSc, PhD). Res. Fellow, ICRF, 1976–77; Lectr, Imperial Coll., 1977–85; Staff Scientist, ICRF, 1985–90. Vis. Fellow, Cold Spring Harbor Labs, NY, 1978–80; Gibb Fellow, CRC, 1990–. Mem., EMBO, 1990–. Charles Rodolphe Brupbacher Prize, 1993; Joseph Steiner Prize, 1993; Howard Hughes Internat. Scholar, 1993; Yvette Mayent Prize, Inst. Curie, 1994; Medal, Swedish Soc. of Oncology, 1994. *Publications:* Antibodies: a laboratory manual, 1988; numerous papers in learned jls. *Recreations:* tennis, motor cycles, walking. *Address:* CRC Laboratories, Department of Biochemistry, The University, Dundee DD1 4HN. *T:* Dundee (01382) 344982.

LANE, David Stuart, PhD, DPhil; Reader in Sociology, since 1992, and Official Fellow of Emmanuel College, 1974–80 and since 1990, University of Cambridge; *b* Monmouthshire (now Gwent), 24 April 1933; *s* of Reginald and Mary Lane; *m* 1962, Christel Noritzsch; one *s* one *d*. *Educ:* Univ. of Birmingham (BSocSc); Univ. of Oxford (DPhil). PhD Cantab. Graduate student, Nuffield Coll., Oxford, 1961–62, 1964–65. Formerly engrg trainee, local authority employee, sch. teacher; univ. teacher, Birmingham, Essex (Reader in Sociology) and Cambridge Univs; Prof. of Sociology, Univ. of Birmingham, 1981–90; Lectr in Sociology, Cambridge Univ., 1990–92. Visiting Professor: Cornell Univ., 1987; Univ. of Graz, 1991; Harvard Univ., 1993. Mem. Exec. Cttee, British Sociol Assoc., 1987–92; Co-Chair, first European Conf. of Sociology, 1992. Vice-Chm., Birmingham Rathbone, 1986–90; Vice-Chm., Down's Children's Assoc., 1981–82; Chm., W Midlands Council for Disabled People, 1983–86. ESRC res. award to study Soviet and Russian political elites, 1991–. Member, Editorial Boards: Sociology, 1985–88; Disability, Handicap and Society, 1987–90. *Publications:* Roots of Russian Communism, 1969, 2nd edn 1975; Politics and Society in the USSR, 1970, 2nd edn 1978; The End of Inequality?, 1971; (with G. Kolankiewicz) Social Groups in Polish Society, 1973; The Socialist Industrial State, 1976; (with F. O'Dell) The Soviet Industrial Worker, 1978; The Work Needs of Mentally Handicapped Adults, 1980; Leninism: a sociological interpretation, 1981; The End of Social Inequality?: class status and power under state socialism, 1982; State and Politics in the USSR, 1985; Soviet Economy and Society, 1985; (ed jtly) Current Approaches to Down's Syndrome, 1985; (ed) Employment and Labour in the USSR, 1986; Soviet Labour and the Ethic of Communism, 1987; (ed) Political Power and Elites in the USSR, 1988; Soviet Society under Perestroika, 1990, 2nd edn 1992; (ed) Russia in Flux, 1992; (contrib.) Post-Soviet Leadership, ed T. Colton and R. Tucker, 1994; (ed and contrib.) Russia in Transition, 1995; contribs to jls incl. Communist and Post-Communist Studies, Europe-Asia Studies, Coexistence, and Jl of Communist and Transition Politics. *Recreations:* soccer, squash, films, TV. *Address:* Emmanuel College, Cambridge CB2 3AP. *T:* Cambridge (01223) 334202.

LANE, Sir David (William Stennis Stuart), Kt 1983; *b* 24 Sept. 1922; *s* of Hubert Samuel Lane, MC; *m* 1955, Lesley Anne Mary Clauson; two *s*. *Educ:* Eton; Trinity Coll., Cambridge; Yale Univ. Served War of 1939–45 (Navy). British Iron and Steel Federation, 1948 (Sec., 1956); Shell International Petroleum Co., 1959–67. Called to the Bar, Middle Temple, 1955. Chm., N Kensington Cons. Assoc., 1961–62. Contested (C) Lambeth (Vauxhall), 1964, Cambridge, 1966; MP (C) Cambridge, Sept. 1967–Nov. 1976; PPS to Sec. of State for Employment, 1970–72; Parly Under-Sec. of State, Home Office, 1972–74. Chairman: Commn for Racial Equality, 1977–82; NAYC, 1982–87. *Recreations:* walking, golf, travel. *Address:* 5 Spinney Drive, Great Shelford, Cambridge CB2 5LY. *Club:* MCC.

LANE, Denis Joseph; Editor in Chief, The Universe, since 1994; Managing Director and Editor in Chief, Gabriel Communications, since 1994; *b* 20 Nov. 1960; *s* of Richard and Annie Lane; *m* 1991, Fiona Fahey; one *s* one *d*. *Educ:* University Coll., Cork (BComm). Sen. Auditor, Peat Marwick Mitchell, 1981–83; Gp Accountant, James A. Barry, 1983–87; Manager of Finance, Princeton Gp, 1987–91; Financial Controller, 1991–93, Chief Exec., 1993–94, Gabriel Communications. Member: Grouse Shooting Ground Club, 1994–; British Assoc. for Shooting and Conservation, 1993–. *Recreations:* shooting, fell walking, chess. *Address:* Gabriel Communications, 1st Floor, St James's Buildings, Oxford Street, Manchester M1 6FP. *T:* 0161–236 8856.

LANE, Rev. John Ernest, OBE 1994; Director and Secretary, St Mungo Association Charitable Trust, since 1983; *b* 16 June 1939; *s* of Ernest William Lane and Winifred (*née* Lloyd); *m* 1958, Eileen Williams (marr. diss. 1988); three *d*. *Educ:* Burnley Grammar Sch.; Handsworth Coll., Birmingham; City of London Polytechnic (DMS); Cranfield Inst. of Technol. (MSc). MIMgt. Methodist Minister: Llanharan, 1962–64; Great Harwood, 1964–67; Lewisham and Peckham, 1967–72; Dir, Peckham Settlement, 1972–77; Nat. Public Relns Officer, YWCA of GB, 1977–80; Dir and Sec., St Mungo Community Housing Assoc. Ltd, 1980–94. Ordained deacon and priest, 1980; Hon. Curate, St John and St Andrew, Peckham, 1980–95; permission to officiate, dio. of Southwark, 1995–. Administrator, European Fedn of Nat. Orgns Working with the Homeless, 1991–. *Publication:* (ed) Homelessness in Industrialised Countries, 1987. *Recreations:* cooking, washing up, cricket, travel, arts. *Address:* (office) Atlantic House, 1–3 Rockley Road, W14 0DJ. *T:* 0181–600 3020; 24 Harcourt Road, SE4 2AJ. *Club:* City Livery.

LANE, Kenneth Frederick; mining consultant; Director, RTZ Consultants, since 1988; *b* 22 March 1928; British; *m* 1950, Kathleen Richards; one *s* two *d*. *Educ:* Emanuel Coll., Cambridge. Degree in Maths. Steel Industry in Sheffield, 1951–59; North America, 1959–61; Rio Tinto-Zinc Corp., 1961–65; Man. Dir, RTZ Consultants Ltd, 1965–70; Dir, RTZ Corp., 1970–75. Dir, Energy Management & Finance, 1988–89. Advisor to Civil Service, 1970–74. Vis. Prof., RSM, 1979–85. *Publication:* The Economic Definition of Ore, 1988. *Recreations:* bridge, boat building, sailing. *Address:* Down House, Lezant, Launceston, Cornwall PL15 9PR. *T:* Stoke Climsland (01579) 370495.

LANE, Hon. Mrs Miriam; *see* Rothschild, Hon. M. L.

LANE, Dr Richard Paul; Keeper of Entomology, Natural History Museum, since 1992; *b* 16 May 1951; *s* of Alfred George Lane and Patricia Ann Lane (*née* Trotter); *m* 1972, Maureen Anne Grogan; two *s* one *d*. *Educ:* Imperial Coll., Univ. of London (BSc, ARCS, DIC, PhD). Dept of Entomology, British Museum (Natural History), 1974–85, Head of Med. Insects Sect., 1983–85; Sen. Lectr, LSHTM, Univ. of London, 1985–92, Head of Vector Biology and Transmission Dynamics Unit, 1989–92. Member: Council, RSTM&H, 1985–89; Biological Council, 1985–89; Wellcome Trust Panels, 1986–; Expert Adv. Panel on Parasitic Diseases, WHO, 1988–; Steering Cttee on Leishmaniasis, WHO, 1988–93; Bd of Trustees, Biosis, Philadelphia, 1993–. Royal Entomological Society: Mem. Council, 1980–83, 1989–92; Vice-Pres., 1991–92; Pres., 1994–; Mem. Council, Internat. Congress of Entomology, 1992–. *Publications:* (ed jtly) Medical Insects and Arachnids, 1993; papers on insects of medical importance in sci. jls, esp. on sandflies and transmission of leishmaniasis. *Recreations:* sailing, beekeeping. *Address:* Department of Entomology, Natural History Museum, SW7 5BD. *T:* 0171–938 9474.

LANE, Ronald Anthony Stuart, CMG 1977; MC 1945; Deputy Chairman, Chartered Trust Ltd, 1979–83; *b* 8 Dec. 1917; 2nd *s* of late Wilmot Ernest Lane and F. E. Lane (*née* Blakey); *m* 1948, Anne Brenda, 2nd *d* of E. Walsh; one *s* one *d*. *Educ:* Lancing College. FIB. Served War, 1940–45, 7th Light Cavalry, Indian Army, India and Burma (Major). Joined Chartered Bank of India, Australia & China, 1937; served in Far East, 1939–60; Gen. Manager, 1961, Chief Gen. Manager, 1972, Man. Dir, 1973–77, Vice-Chm., 1977–83, Standard Chartered Bank Ltd. Mem., Export Guarantees Adv. Council, 1973–78 (Dep. Chm., 1977–78). *Recreations:* sailing, gardening. *Address:* West Hold, By the Church, West Mersea, Essex CO5 8QD. *T:* West Mersea (01206) 2563. *Clubs:* East India, MCC; West Mersea Yacht.

LANE FOX, Robin James, FRSL; Fellow, New College, Oxford, since 1977; Reader in Ancient History, Oxford, since 1990; *b* 5 Oct. 1946; *s* of James Henry Lane Fox and Anne (*née* Loyd); *m* 1970, Louisa Caroline Mary, *d* of Charles and Lady Katherine Farrell; one *s* one *d*. *Educ:* Eton; Magdalen Coll., Oxford (Craven and de Paravicini scholarships, 1966; Passmore Edwards and Chancellors' Latin Verse Prize, 1968). FRSL 1974. Fellow by examination, Magdalen Coll., Oxford, 1970–73; Lectr in Classical Lang. and Lit., 1973–76, Res. Fellow, Classical and Islamic Studies, 1976–77, Worcester Coll., Oxford; Lectr in Ancient Hist., Oxford Univ., 1977–90. Weekly gardening correspondent, Financial Times, 1970–. *Publications:* Alexander the Great, 1973, 3rd edn 1978 (James Tait Black, Duff Cooper, W. H. Heinemann Awards, 1973–74); Variations on a Garden, 1974, rev. edn 1986; Search for Alexander, 1980; Better Gardening, 1982; Pagans and Christians, 1986; The Unauthorized Version, 1991. *Recreations:* gardening, hunting, poetry, rough travel. *Address:* New College, Oxford OX1 3BN. *Club:* Beefsteak.

LANE-NOTT, Rear Adm. Roger Charles; Flag Officer Submarines, 1993–96; Commander Submarines (NATO), Eastern Atlantic and Northwest, 1993–96; Chief of Staff (Operations) to Commander-in-Chief Fleet, 1994–96; *b* 3 June 1945; *s* of John Henry Lane-Nott, MBE and Kathleen Mary Lane-Nott; *m* 1968, Roisin MacQuillan; one *s* two *d*. *Educ:* Pangbourne Coll.; BRNC, Dartmouth. Joined RN, 1963: qualified submarines, 1966; served in HM Submarines: Andrew, Opossum, Otus, Revenge (Starboard), Conqueror, Aeneas, 1966–74; commanded HM Submarines: Walrus, 1974–76; Swiftsure, 1979; Splendid, 1979–82 (mentioned in despatches, Falklands, 1982); US Naval War Coll., 1983; Captain SM, Third Submarine Sqdn, 1985–86; Asst Dir, Defence Concepts, MoD, 1986–89; RCDS 1989; Captain First Frigate Sqdn and in comd HMS Coventry, 1990–91; Sen. Naval Officer, ME, 1991; Chief of Staff to Flag Officer Submarines, 1992–93. MRIN 1976; MNI 1991; FIMgt 1983. *Recreations:* watching sport (Rugby, cricket, motor racing), unusual stationery, keeping my house up and my garden down.

LANESBOROUGH, 9th Earl of *cr* 1756; **Denis Anthony Brian Butler;** TD; DL; Baron of Newtown-Butler, 1715; Viscount Lanesborough, 1728; Major, Leicestershire Yeomanry (RA); *b* 28 Oct. 1918; *er s* of 8th Earl and Grace Lilian (*d* 1983), *d* of late Sir Anthony Abdy, 3rd Bt; *S* father 1950; *m* 1939, Bettyne Ione (marr. diss. 1950), *d* of late Sir Lindsay Everard; one *d* (and one *d* decd). *Educ:* Stowe. Leicestershire Yeomanry; Lieutenant, 1939; Major, RAC, TA, 1945. Member: Nat. Gas Consumers' Council, 1973–78; Trent RHA, 1974–82 (Vice-Chm., 1978–82). Chm., Loughborough and District Housing Assoc., 1978–85. Chm., 1953–64, Pres., 1964–86, Guide Dogs for the Blind Assoc. DL 1962, JP 1967, Leicester. *Heir:* none. *Address:* Allerly, Gattonside, Melrose, Roxburghshire TD6 9LT. *T:* Melrose (01896) 823482.

LANG, Prof. Andrew Richard, FRS 1975; Professor of Physics, University of Bristol, 1979–87, now Emeritus; Senior Research Fellow, University of Bristol, since 1995; *b* 9 Sept. 1924; *s* of late Ernest F. S. Lang and late Susannah (*née* Gueterbock); unmarried. *Educ:* University College of South-West, Exeter, (BSc Lond. 1944; MSc Lond. 1947); Univ. of Cambridge (PhD 1953). Research Dept, Lever Bros, Port Sunlight, 1945–47; Research Asst, Cavendish Laboratory, 1947–48; North American Philips, Irvington-on-

Hudson, NY, 1952–53; Instructor, Harvard Univ., 1953–54; Asst Professor, Harvard Univ., 1954–59; Lectr in Physics, 1960–66, Reader, 1966–79, Univ. of Bristol. FInstP. Mem. Geol Assoc.; Mem. Soc. Sigma Xi. Hon. DSc Exeter, 1994. Charles Vernon Boys Prize, Inst. of Physics, 1964. *Publications:* contribs to learned jls. *Address:* 1B Elton Road, Bristol BS8 1SJ. *T:* Bristol (0117) 973 9784.

LANG, Dr Brian Andrew; Chief Executive and Deputy Chairman, British Library, since 1991; *b* 2 Dec. 1945; *s* of Andrew Ballantyne Lang and Mary Bain Lang (*née* Smith); *m* 1st, 1975 (marr. diss. 1982); one *s*; 2nd, 1983, Caroline Susan, *e d* of David and Jean Purnell; one *s* one *d*. *Educ:* Royal High Sch., Edinburgh; Univ. of Edinburgh (MA, PhD). Social anthropological field research, Kenya, 1969–70; Lectr in social anthropology, Aarhus Univ., 1971–75; Scientific Staff, SSRC, 1976–79; Scottish Office (Sec., Historic Buildings Council for Scotland), 1979–80; Sec., Nat. Heritage Meml Fund, 1980–87; Dir of Public Affairs, Nat. Trust, 1987–91. Member: Liby and Inf. Services Council (England), 1991–94; Liby and Inf. Commn, 1995–. Pres., Inst. of Information Scientists, 1993–94 (Hon. Fellow, 1994). *Recreations:* music, museums and galleries, tennis. *Address:* British Library, 96 Euston Road, St Pancras, NW1 2DB. *T:* 0171–412 7262.

LANG, Lt-Gen. Sir Derek (Boileau), KCB 1967 (CB 1964); DSO 1944; MC 1941; DL; *b* 7 Oct. 1913; *s* of Lt-Col C. F. G. Lang and Mrs Lumsden Lang (*née* M. J. L. Forbes); *m* 1st, 1942, M. Massy Dawson (*d* 1953); one *s* one *d*; 2nd, 1953, A. L. S. Shields (marr. diss. 1969); 3rd, 1969, Mrs E. H. Balfour (*d* 1982); 4th, 1983, Mrs Maartje McQueen. *Educ:* Wellington Coll.; RMC Sandhurst. Commnd, The Queen's Own Cameron Highlanders, 1933; Adjutant, TA, 1938; active service in France, E and N Africa, 1940–42; Chief Instructor, Sch. of Infantry, 1943–44; Comdr, 5th Camerons, NW Europe, 1944–45; Comdt, Sch. of Infantry, BAOR, 1945–46; Directing Staff, Staff Coll., Camberley, 1947–48; Staff, Australia, 1949–51; GSO1, War Office, 1951–53; Chief Instructor, Sch. of Infantry, 1953–55; AAG, War Office, 1955–57; NDC, 1957–58; Comd Infty Bde (153–TA), 1958–60; Chief of Staff, Scottish Comd, 1960; Gen. Officer Commanding, 51st Highland Div. and District, Perth, 1962–64; Dir of Army Training, 1964–66; GOC-in-C, Scottish Command, 1966–69; Governor of Edinburgh Castle, 1966–69; Sec., Univ. of Stirling, 1970–73; Hon. Col, 153 (Highland) Regt, RCT (Volunteers), T&AVR, 1970–76; Pres., Army Cadet Force Assoc. (Scotland), 1975–85. Associate Consultant, PA Management Consultants Ltd, 1975–84. DL Edinburgh, 1978. OStJ. *Publication:* Return to St Valéry, 1974. *Recreations:* golf, fishing, shooting. *Address:* Templeland, Kirknewton, Midlothian EH27 8DJ. *T:* Mid Calder (01506) 883211. *Clubs:* New (Edinburgh); Senior Golfers' Society; Hon. Co. of Edinburgh Golfers (Muirfield).
See also J. M. Hunt.

LANG, Henry George, ONZ 1989; CB 1977; consultant and company director, since 1977; *b* 3 March 1919; *s* of Robert and Anna Lang; *m* 1942, Octavia Gwendolin (*née* Turton); one *s* four *d*. *Educ:* Victoria Univ., Wellington. DPA, BA, BCom. Private enterprise, 1939–44; RNZAF, 1944–46. NZ government service: various economic appointments, 1946–55; Economic Advisor to High Comr in London, 1955–58; Treasury, 1958–77, Sec. to Treasury, 1968–77. Vis. Prof. of Economics, Victoria Univ. of Wellington, 1977–82, consultant, 1982–. Director: Bayer NZ Ltd, 1977–; IBM Superannuation Fund, 1979–; Kleinwort Benson Australian Income Fund Inc., 1987–. Dir, NZ Press Council, 1984–. Hon. LLD Victoria Univ., Wellington, 1984. *Publications:* (with J. V. T. Baker) Economic Policy and National Income, in, NZ Official Year Book, 1950; articles in learned journals. *Recreations:* skiing, swimming, reading. *Address:* 81 Hatton Street, Wellington, NZ. *T:* (0) 4768788. *Club:* Wellington (Wellington, NZ).

LANG, Hugh Montgomerie, CBE 1978; Chairman: Brammer plc, since 1990; Manganese Bronze Holdings plc, since 1992; Victaulic plc, since 1995; *b* Glasgow, 7 Nov. 1932; *s* of John Montgomerie Lang and Janet Allan (*née* Smillie); *m* 1st, 1959, Marjorie Jean Armour (marr. diss. 1981); one *s* one *d*; 2nd, 1981, Susan Lynn Hartley (*née* Russell). *Educ:* Shawlands Acad., Glasgow; Glasgow Univ. (BSc). ARCST 1953; CEng 1967; FIEE (FIProdE 1976); FIMC 1970. Officer, REME, 1953–55 (National Service). Colvilles Ltd, 1955–56; Glacier Metal Co. Ltd, 1956–60; L. Sterne & Co. Ltd, 1960–61; P-E Consulting Group, 1961–92: Manager for ME, 1965–68; Scottish Reg. Manager, 1968–72; Man. Dir, 1974–77; Chm., P-E Internat., 1980–92 (Dir, 1972–92; Chief Exec., 1977–92). Director: Redman Heenan Internat., 1981–86 (Chm., 1982–86); Fairey Holdings Ltd, 1978–82; UKO International, 1985–86; B. Elliott, 1986–88; Siebe, 1987–91; Strong & Fisher (Hldgs), 1988–90; Co-ordinated Land and Estates, 1988–93; OGC International, 1993–94; Ericsson Ltd, 1993–. Chairman: Food, Drink and Packaging Machinery Sector Working Party, 1976–81; Technology Transfer Services Adv. Cttee, 1982–85 (Mem., 1978–85); Member: Business Educn Council, 1980–81; CBI Industrial Policy Cttee, 1980–83; Design Council, 1983–90 (Dep. Chm., 1986–90); Engrg Council, 1984–86. *Recreations:* fishing, gardening, golf, reading. *Address:* Welders Wood, Chalfont St Peter, Bucks SL9 8TT. *Clubs:* Brooks's; Denham Golf.

LANG, Rt Hon. Ian (Bruce), PC 1990; MP (C) Galloway and Upper Nithsdale, since 1983 (Galloway, 1979–83); President of the Board of Trade, since 1995; *b* 27 June 1940; *y s* of late James Fulton Lang, DSC, and of Maude Margaret (*née* Stewart); *m* 1971, Sandra Caroline *e d* of late John Alastair Montgomerie, DSC; two *d*. *Educ:* Lathallan Sch., Kincardineshire; Rugby Sch.; Sidney Sussex Coll., Cambridge (BA 1962). Director: Hutchison & Craft Ltd, 1975–81; Hutchison & Craft (Underwriting Agents) Ltd, Lloyd's, 1976–81; P. MacCallum & Sons Ltd, 1976–81; Rose, Thomson, Young & Co. (Glasgow) Ltd, 1966–75. Member, Queen's Body Guard for Scotland (Royal Company of Archers), 1974–. Dir, Glasgow Chamber of Commerce, 1978–81; Trustee: Savings Bank of Glasgow, 1969–74; West of Scotland Trustee Savings Bank, 1974–83. Contested (C): Central Ayrshire, 1970; Glasgow Pollok, Feb. 1974. An Asst Govt Whip, 1981–83; a Lord Comr of HM Treasury, 1983–86; Parliamentary Under Secretary of State: Dept of Employment, 1986; Scottish Office, 1986–87; Minister of State, Scottish Office, 1987–90; Sec. of State for Scotland and Lord Keeper of the Great Seal of Scotland, 1990–95. Mem., Select Cttee on Scottish Affairs, 1979–81. Vice-Chm., Conservative Party in Scotland, 1983–87. Pres., Scottish Young Conservatives, 1982–84. OStJ 1974. *Address:* House of Commons, SW1A 0AA. *Clubs:* Pratt's; Western (Glasgow); Prestwick Golf.

LANG, Jack Mathieu Emile, Chevalier de la Légion d'Honneur; Hon. GCVO 1992; Mayor of Blois, since 1989; *b* 2 Sept. 1939; *s* of Roger Lang and Marie-Luce Lang (*née* Bouchet); *m* 1961, Monique Buczynski; two *d*. *Educ:* Inst. d'Etudes Politiques; Dr of Public Law. Founder and Producer, World Fest. Univ. Theatre, Nancy, 1963–72; Dir, Nancy Univ. Theatre, 1963–72; Dir, Palais de Chaillot Théâtre, 1972–74; Prof. of Internat. Law, 1971–81; Dir, teaching and research unit in legal and econ. scis, Nancy, 1977–80; Prof., Univ. of Paris X, 1986–88. Paris councillor, 1977–89; nat. deleg. for cultural affairs, Socialist Party, 1979–81; Minister of Culture, 1981–83 and 1984–86; Deputy, Loir-et-Cher, 1986–88; Minister of Culture and Communication, 1988–92; Govt Spokesman, 1991–92; Minister of State, and Minister of Nat. Educn and Culture, 1992–93. Conseiller Général de Blois, 1992–. Order of Orange Nassau (Netherlands), 1991; Order of the Crown of Belgium, 1992. *Publications:* L'Etat et le Théâtre; Le plâteau continental de la mer du nord; Les politiques culturelles comparée en Europe; La jonction au fond des exceptions préliminaires devant la cour; contribs to newspapers. *Address:* La Mairie, 41000 Blois, France.

LANG, Very Rev. John Harley; Dean of Lichfield, 1980–93, now Emeritus; Chaplain to HM the Queen, 1976–80; Member, Broadcasting Standards Council, since 1994; *b* 27 Oct. 1927; *e s* of Frederick Henry Lang and Eileen Annie Lang (*née* Harley); *m* 1972, Frances Rosemary Widdowson; three *d*. *Educ:* Merchant Taylors' Sch.; King's Coll., London. MA Cantab, BD London, LRAM. Subaltern, XII Royal Lancers, 1951–52; Asst Curate, St Mary's Portsea, 1952–57; Priest Vicar, Southwark Cathedral, 1957–60; Chaplain, Emmanuel Coll., Cambridge, 1960–64; Asst Head of Religious Broadcasting, BBC, 1964–67; Head of Religious Programmes, Radio, 1967–71; Head of Religious Broadcasting, BBC, 1971–80. Mem., English Heritage Cathedrals and Churches Adv. Cttee, 1994–. Trustee, Historic Churches Preservation Trust, 1994. President: Staffordshire Soc., 1993–95; Lichfield Festival, 1994. Freeman, Goldsmiths' Co., 1994. Hon. DLitt Keele, 1988. *Recreations:* books, music. *Address:* South Barn, Stanton, Broadway, Worcs WR12 7NQ. *T:* Stanton (01386) 584251. *Club:* Brooks's.

LANG, Rear-Adm. John Stewart, FNI; Royal Navy, retired; *b* 18 July 1941; *s* of Comdr John Robert Lang, RN and Jennifer Douglas Lang; *m* 1971, Joanna Judith Pegler; two *d*. *Educ:* Cheltenham Coll. Jun. Sch.; Nautical Coll., Pangbourne. MRIN. Navigating Officer Apprentice, P&OSN Co., 1959–62; RN 1962; served HM Ships Chilcompton, Totem, Auriga, Oberon, Revenge, Opossum, 1964–71; qualified Submarine Command, 1971; commanded: HMS Walrus, 1971–72; HMS Renown, 1976–78; HMS Beaver, 1983–85; Captain, Royal Naval Presentation Team, 1986–87; ACOS (Ops) to C-in-C Fleet, 1987–89; Dir, Naval Ops and Trade, 1989–91; Def. Intell. Staff, 1992–95. *Recreations:* sailing, photography, oil painting, travel, pharology, international affairs. *Address:* Wangfield House, Martyr Worthy, Winchester, Hants SO21 1AT.

LANG, Rear-Adm. William Duncan, CB 1981; retired; *b* 1 April 1925; *s* of James Hardie Lang and Elizabeth Foggo Paterson Lang (*née* Storie); *m* 1947, Joyce Rose Weeks; one *s* one *d*. *Educ:* Edinburgh Acad. Entered Royal Navy, 1943; trained as Pilot; served in 800, 816 and 825 Sqdns and as Flying Instr and Test Pilot; comd 802 Sqdn, 1958–59; Commander (Air): RNAS Culdrose, 1962–63; HMS Eagle, 1964–65; Fleet Aviation Officer, Far East Fleet, 1966–68; Captain 1969; comd RNAS Lossiemouth, 1970–72; Dep. Comdt, Jt Warfare Estabt, 1973–74; COS to Flag Officer, Naval Air Comd, 1975–76; Mil. Dep. to Hd of Defence Sales, 1978–81; Dir, Naval Security, MoD, 1981–86. Naval ADC to the Queen, 1978; Rear-Adm. 1978. *Recreation:* golf (Pres., RN Golf Soc., 1979–85). *Address:* c/o Midland Bank, 19 High Street, Haslemere, Surrey GU27 2HQ. *Club:* Army and Navy.

LANGAN, Peter St John Hevey, QC 1983; **His Honour Judge Langan;** a Circuit Judge, since 1991; *b* 1 May 1942; *s* of late Frederick Hevey Langan and of Myrrha Langan (*née* Jephson), Mount Hevey, Hill of Down, Co. Meath; *m* 1976, Oonagh May Winifred McCarthy. *Educ:* Downside School; Trinity College, Dublin (MA, LLB); Christ's College, Cambridge (PhD). Lectr in Law, Durham Univ., 1966–69. In practice at the Bar, 1970–91; a Recorder, 1989–91. Legal Assessor: GMC, 1990–91; GDC, 1990–91. Mem., Legal Commn, Caritas Internationalis, Rome, 1991–93; Trustee, CAFOD, 1993– (Mem., Management Cttee, 1984–91). *Publications:* Maxwell on Interpretation of Statutes, 12th edn, 1969; Civil Procedure and Evidence, 1st edn, 1970, 3rd edn (with L. D. J. Henderson) as Civil Procedure, 1983; (with P. V. Baker) Snell's Principles of Equity, 28th edn, 1982, 29th edn, 1990. *Address:* Norwich Combined Court, Bishopgate, Norwich NR3 1UR. *T.* Norwich (01603) 761776.

LANGDALE, Simon John Bartholomew; Director of Educational and General Grants, The Rank Foundation, since 1988; *b* 26 Jan. 1937; *s* of late Geoffrey Ronald Langdale and Hilda Joan Langdale (*née* Bartholomew); *m* 1962, Diana Marjory Hall; two *s* one *d*. *Educ:* Tonbridge Sch.; St Catharine's Coll., Cambridge. Taught at Radley Coll., 1959–73 (Housemaster, 1968–73); Headmaster: Eastbourne Coll., 1973–80; Shrewsbury Sch., 1981–88. *Recreations:* reading, gardening, golf. *Address:* Park House, Culworth, Banbury, Oxon OX17 2AP. *T:* Sulgrave (01295760) 222. *Clubs:* East India; Hawks (Cambridge); Free Foresters, Jesters.
See also T. J. Langdale.

LANGDALE, Timothy James, QC 1992; *b* 3 Jan. 1940; *m* twice; two *d*. *Educ:* Sevenoaks Sch.; St Andrews Univ. (MA). Called to the Bar, Lincoln's Inn, 1966. Res. Assistant, Community Justice Center, Watts, Los Angeles, 1969–70; Jun. Prosecuting Counsel to the Crown, 1979–87, Sen. Prosecuting Counsel, 1987–92, CCC. *Recreations:* reading, opera, theatre, cinema. *Address:* Queen Elizabeth Building, Temple, EC4Y 9BS. *T:* 0171–583 5766.
See also S. J. B. Langdale.

LANGDON, Anthony James; Deputy Under Secretary of State, Home Office, 1989–95; *b* 5 June 1935; *s* of Dr James Norman Langdon and Maud Winifred Langdon; *m* 1969, Helen Josephine Drabble, *y d* of His Honour J. F. Drabble, QC; one *s* one *d*. *Educ:* Kingswood Sch., Bath; Christ's Coll., Cambridge. Entered Home Office, 1958; Office of Minister for Science, 1961–63; Treasury, 1967–69; Under Sec., Cabinet Office, 1985–89.

LANGDON, David, OBE 1988; FRSA; cartoonist, illustrator and caricaturist; regular contributor to Punch, 1937–92, and to The New Yorker, since 1952; *b* 24 Feb. 1914; *er s* of late Bennett and Bess Langdon; *m* 1955, April Sadler-Phillips; two *s* one *d*. *Educ:* Davenant Gram. Sch., London. Architect's Dept, LCC, 1931–39; Executive Officer, London Rescue Service, 1939–41; served in Royal Air Force, 1941–46; Squadron Leader, 1945. Editor, Royal Air Force Jl, 1945–46. Creator of Billy Brown of London Town for LPTB. Official Artist to Centre International Audio-Visuel d'Etudes et de Recherches, St Ghislain, Belgium, 1970–75. Cartoonist to Sunday Mirror, 1948–93. Caricatures of racing celebrities for Ladbrokes Racing Calendar, 1959–. Exhibitions: Ottawa, Oxford, New York, Lille, London. *Publications:* Home Front Lines, 1941; All Buttoned Up, 1944; Meet Me Inside, 1946; Slipstream (with R. B. Raymond), 1946; The Way I See It, 1947; Hold Tight There!, 1949; Let's Face It, 1951; Wake Up and Die (with David Clayton), 1952; Look at You, 1952; All in Fun, 1953; Laugh with Me, 1954; More in Fun, 1955; Funnier Still, 1956; A Banger for a Monkey, 1957; Langdon At Large, 1958; I'm Only Joking, 1960; Punch with Wings, 1961; How to Play Golf and Stay Happy, 1964; David Langdon's Casebook, 1969; How To Talk Golf, 1975; Punch in the Air, 1983. *Recreations:* golf, non-League soccer. *Address:* Greenlands, Honor End Lane, Great Missenden, Bucks HP16 9QY. *T:* Great Missenden (01494) 862475. *Club:* Royal Air Force.

LANGDON, Janet Mary; Director and Secretary, Water Services Association of England and Wales, since 1992; *b* 5 March 1940; *d* of late Geoffrey Harry Langdon and Iris Sarah Langdon. *Educ:* St Hilda's Coll., Oxford (BSc, MA). Asst Lectr, Wellesley Coll., Mass, 1962–63; Distillers' Co. Ltd, 1963–68; NEDO, 1968–71; Shell Chemicals UK Ltd and Shell Internat. Chemical Co. Ltd, 1971–82; Projects and Export Policy Div., DTI, 1982–85; Director: Asia, Gp Exports, GEC PLC, 1985–89; Export Div., GEC ALSTHOM Ltd, 1989–92. *Recreations:* walking, tennis, travel, theatre. *Address:* (office) 1 Queen Anne's Gate, SW1H 9BT. *T:* 0171–957 4500.

LANGDON, Jonathan Bertram Robert Louis; His Honour Judge Langdon; a Circuit Judge, since 1991; *b* 1 Nov. 1939; *s* of Captain John Edward Langdon, RN and Nancy Langdon; *m* 1962, Hilary Jean Fox Taylor; twin *s* one *d*. *Educ:* Hurstpierpoint Coll.; RNC Dartmouth. Entered RN, 1958; served HM Ships Bermuda, Lincoln and London, 1960–64; Supply Officer, HMS Daring, 1965–68; legal trng, 1968–70; called to the Bar, Gray's Inn, 1970; Lieut Comdr, 1970; Staff Legal Advr to FO Plymouth, 1970–73; RN FE Legal Advr, Hong Kong, 1973–75; Comdr, 1977; Supply Officer, HMS Norfolk, 1977–79; various MoD and staff appts, 1980–86; Captain, 1986; Chief Naval Judge Advocate, 1987–90; a Recorder, SE Circuit, 1989; Sec. to C-in-C Naval Home Command, 1990–91; retired voluntarily from RN, 1991. *Recreations:* sailing, gardening, croquet, travel. *Address:* The Law Courts, Chaucer Road, Canterbury, Kent CT1 1ZA.

LANGDON, Richard Norman Darbey, FCA; chairman and director of companies; *b* 19 June 1919; *s* of Norman Langdon and Dorothy Langdon; *m* 1944, June Dixon; two *s*. *Educ:* Shrewsbury Sch. Officer, RA, 1939–46. Admitted Mem. Inst. of Chartered Accountants in England and Wales, 1947; joined Spicer and Pegler, 1949, Partner 1953, Managing Partner, 1971–82, Senior Partner, 1978–84. Chairman: Hammond and Champness Ltd, 1966–89; Aspinall Hldg, 1983–89; Finlay Packaging PLC, 1984–93; First National Finance Corp., 1985–92; Beeson Gregory, 1989–95; Director: Time Products PLC, 1984–93 (Chm., 1984–92); Rockware Group PLC, 1985–91; Chemring Gp PLC, 1985– (Dep. Chm., 1985–92). Treasurer, CGLI, 1982–90. Mem. Council, Univ. of Surrey, 1988–90. *Recreations:* gardening, bricklaying. *Address:* Whitedale House, Hambledon, Hants PO7 4RZ. *T:* Hambledon (01705) 632457. *Club:* Old Salopian.

LANGDON-DOWN, Antony Turnbull; Part-time Chairman, Social Security Appeals Tribunal, since 1985; Clerk to Merchant Taylors Company, 1980–85; *b* 31 Dec. 1922; *s* of Dr Reginald Langdon-Down and Ruth Langdon-Down (*née* Turnbull); *m* 1954, Jill Elizabeth Style (*née* Caruth); one *s* one *d*. *Educ:* Harrow School. Member of Lincoln's Inn, 1940–60, called to the Bar, 1948; enrolled as a solicitor, 1960; practised as solicitor, 1961–80. Pilot, Royal Air Force, 1942–47 (finally Flt Lieut). Master of Merchant Taylors Company, 1979–80. *Recreations:* sailing, tennis, bridge, music, art. *Address:* Drumard, The Street, Plaxtol, Sevenoaks, Kent TN15 0QP. *T:* Plaxtol (01732) 810720. *Clubs:* Savile, MCC; Bough Beech Sailing.

LANGDON-DOWN, Barbara; *see* Littlewood, Lady (Barbara).

LANGE, Rt. Hon. David Russell, CH 1990; PC 1984; MP (Lab) Mangere, New Zealand, since 1977; Opposition Foreign Minister, since 1993; *b* 4 Aug. 1942; *s* of late Eric Roy Lange and Phoebe Fysh Lange; *m* 1st, 1968, Naomi Joy Crampton; two *s* one *d*; 2nd, 1992, Margaret Forsyth Pope. *Educ:* Univ. of Auckland (LLM Hons). Called to the Bar of NZ and admitted Solicitor, 1966; Dep. Leader of the Opposition, 1979–83, Leader 1983–84. Minister of Foreign Affairs, 1984–87; Prime Minister, and Minister in charge of Security Intelligence Service, 1984–89, and Minister of Education, 1987–89; Attorney Gen., and Minister of State, 1989–90. *Publications:* Nuclear-Free—the New Zealand Way, 1990; Broadsides, 1992; Cuttings, 1994. *Address:* Parliament House, Wellington, New Zealand. *T:* (4) 719998.

LANGER, Bernhard; golfer; *b* Germany, 27 Aug. 1957; *m* Vikki; two *c*. Major championships include: US Masters, 1985, 1993; German Open 5 times; 7 Ryder Cup appearances for Europe, 1981–94. *Publication:* (with Bill Elliott) While the Iron is Hot (autobiog.), 1988. *Address:* c/o Professional Golfers' Association, Apollo House, The Belfry, Sutton Coldfield, West Midlands B76 9PT

LANGFORD, 9th Baron, *cr* 1800; **Colonel Geoffrey Alexander Rowley-Conwy,** OBE 1943; DL; RA, retired; Constable of Rhuddlan Castle and Lord of the Manor of Rhuddlan; *b* 8 March 1912; *s* of late Major Geoffrey Seymour Rowley-Conwy (killed in action, Gallipoli, 1915), Bodrhyddan, Flints, and Bertha Gabrielle Rowley-Conwy, JP (*d* 1984), *d* of late Lieutenant Alexander Cochran, Royal Navy, Ashkirk, Selkirkshire; *S* kinsman 1953; *m* 1st, 1939, Ruth St John (marr. diss. 1956; she *d* 1991), *d* of late Albert St John Murphy, The Island House, Little Island, County Cork; 2nd, 1957, Grete (*d* 1973), *d* of late Col E. T. C. von Freiesleben, formerly Chief of the King's Adjutants Staff to the King of Denmark; three *s*; 3rd, 1975, Susan Winifred Denham, *d* of C. C. H. Denham, Chester; one *s* one *d*. *Educ:* Marlborough; RMA Woolwich. Served War of 1939–45, with RA (2nd Lieut, 1932; Lieut, 1935; Captain, 1939; Major 1941); Singapore, (POW escaped) and with Indian Mountain Artillery in Burma, 1941–45 (despatches, OBE); Staff Coll., Quetta, 1945; Berlin Airlift, Fassberg, 1948–49; GSOI 42 Inf. Div., TA, 1949–52; Lt-Col 1945; retired 1957; Colonel (Hon.), 1967. Freeman, City of London, 1986–. DL Clwyd, 1977. *Heir: s* Hon. Owain Grenville Rowley-Conwy, [*b* 27 Dec. 1958; *m* 1986, Joanna, *d* of Jack Featherstone; one *s* one *d*]. *Address:* Bodrhyddan, Rhuddlan, Clwyd LL18 5SB. *Club:* Army and Navy.

LANGFORD, Anthony John, FRICS; Chief Executive, Valuation Office Agency, since 1994; *b* 25 June 1936; *s* of Freeman and Ethel Langford; *m* 1958, Joan Winifred Barber; one *s* one *d*. *Educ:* Soham Grammar School. Joined Valuation Office, Inland Revenue, 1957; District Valuer, Camden, 1976; Superintending Valuer, Northern Region, 1981; Asst Chief Valuer, 1983; Dep. Chief Valuer, then Dep. Chief Exec., Valuation Office Agency, 1988–94. *Recreations:* walking, gardening, bowls. *Address:* New Court, Carey Street, WC2A 2JE.

LANGFORD, Paul, DPhil; FRHistS; FBA 1993; Reader in Modern History, Oxford University, since 1994; Fellow, and Tutor in Modern History, Lincoln College, Oxford, since 1970; *b* 20 Nov. 1945; *s* of Frederick Wade Langford and Olive Myrtle Langford (*née* Walters); *m* 1970, Margaret Veronica Edwards; one *s*. *Educ:* Monmouth Sch.; Hertford Coll., Oxford (MA, DPhil). FRHistS 1979. Jun. Res. Fellow, Lincoln Coll., Oxford, 1969–70. Ford's Lectr in English History, Oxford Univ., 1990. Gen. Editor, The Writings and Speeches of Edmund Burke, 1974–. *Publications:* The First Rockingham Administration 1765–66, 1973; The Excise Crisis: society and politics in the age of Walpole, 1975; (ed) Writings and Speeches of Edmund Burke, vol. II: Party, Parliament and The American Crisis 1766–74, 1981; A Polite and Commercial People 1727–83, 1989 (New Oxford History of England series); Public Life and the Propertied Englishman 1689–1789, 1991. *Recreation:* gardening. *Address:* Lincoln College, Oxford OX1 3DR; Valpys, Noakes Hill, Ashampstead, Berks RG8 8RY. *T:* Compton (01635) 578181.

LANGHAM, Sir James (Michael), 15th Bt *cr* 1660; TD 1965; *b* 24 May 1932; *s* of Sir John Charles Patrick Langham, 14th Bt, and Rosamond Christabel (MBE 1969) (*d* 1992), *d* of late Arthur Rashleigh; *S* father, 1972; *m* 1959, Marion Audrey Eleanor, *d* of O. H. Barratt, Gararagua Estate, Tanzania; two *s* one *d*. *Educ:* Rossall School, Fleetwood. Served as Captain, North Irish Horse, 1953–67. *Recreations:* shooting, skin-diving. *Heir: s* John Stephen Langham [*b* 14 Dec. 1960; *m* 1991, Sarah Jane, *d* of late J. D. Verschoyle-Greene]. *Address:* Claranagh, Tempo, Co. Fermanagh. *T:* Tempo (0136554) 247.

LANGHORNE, Richard Tristan Bailey; FRHistS; Director and Chief Executive, Wilton Park, Foreign and Commonwealth Office, since 1993; *b* 6 May 1940; *s* of late Eadward John Bailey Langhorne and of Rosemary Scott-Foster; *m* 1971, Helen Logue, *o d* of William Donaldson, CB and Mary Donaldson; one *s* one *d*. *Educ:* St Edward's Sch., Oxford; St John's Coll., Cambridge (Exhibr). BA Hist. Tripos, 1962; Certif. in Hist. Studies, 1963; MA 1965. Tutor in History, Univ. of Exeter, 1963–64; Research Student, St John's Coll., Cambridge, 1964–66; Lectr in History, 1966–74 and Master of Rutherford Coll., 1971–74, Univ. of Kent at Canterbury; St John's College, Cambridge: Steward, 1974–79; Junior Bursar, 1974–87; Fellow, 1974–93; Dir, Centre of Internat. Studies, Univ. of Cambridge, 1987–93. Visiting Professor: Univ. of Southern Calif, 1986; Sunway Coll., Kuala Lumpur, 1993; Hon. Prof. of Internat. Relns, Univ. of Kent at Canterbury, 1994. Freeland K. Abbott Meml Lectr, Tufts Univ., 1990. FRSA. *Publications:* The Collapse of the Concert of Europe, 1890–1914, 1980; (ed) Diplomacy and Intelligence during the Second World War, 1985; (with K. Hamilton) The Practice of Diplomacy, 1994; chapters in: The Twentieth Century Mind, 1971; British Foreign Policy under Sir Edward Grey, 1977; reviews and articles in Historical Jl, History, and Review of International Studies. *Recreations:* music, railways. *Address:* Wiston House, Steyning, W Sussex BN44 3DZ; 14 Love Lane, Canterbury, Kent CT1 1TZ. *Club:* Athenæum.

LANGLANDS, (Robert) Alan; Chief Executive, NHS Executive, since 1994 (Deputy Chief Executive, 1993–94); *b* 29 May 1952; *s* of James Langlands and May Langlands (*née* Rankin); *m* 1977, Elizabeth McDonald; one *s* one *d*. *Educ:* Allan Glen's Sch.; Univ. of Glasgow (BSc Pure Sci); MHSM, DipHSM. Grad. Trainee, NHS Scotland, 1974–76; Argyll and Clyde Health Bd, 1976–78; Simpson Meml Maternity Pavilion, Elsie Inglis Hosp., 1978–81; Unit Administrator, Middx and University Coll. Hosps and Hosp. for Women, Soho, 1981–85; Dist Gen. Manager, Harrow HA, 1985–89; Practice Leader, Health Care, Towers Perrin, 1989–91; Gen. Manager, NW Thames RHA, 1991–92. Member: King's Fund Coll. Management Cttee, 1992–94; Central R & D Cttee, NHS, 1991–92; Adv. Bd, Centre for Corporate Strategy and Change, Univ. of Warwick. Hon. FFPHM 1994; FRSM 1995. *Recreation:* walking in Scotland. *Address:* Department of Health, Richmond House, 79 Whitehall, SW1A 2NS.

LANGLANDS, Prof. Robert Phelan, FRS 1981; Professor of Mathematics, Institute for Advanced Study, Princeton, New Jersey, since 1972; *b* 6 Oct. 1936; *s* of Robert Langlands and Kathleen Johanna (*née* Phelan); *m* 1956, Charlotte Lorraine Cheverie; two *s* two *d*. *Educ:* Univ. of British Columbia (BA 1957, MA 1958); Yale Univ. (PhD 1960). FRSC 1972. Princeton University: Instructor, 1960–61; Lectr, 1961–62; Asst Prof., 1962–64; Associate Prof., 1964–67; Prof., Yale Univ., 1967–72. Associate Prof., Ortadoğu Teknik Universitesi, 1967–68; Gast Prof., Universität Bonn, 1980–81. Mem., Nat. Acad. of Scis, USA, 1993. Hon. DSc: British Columbia, 1985; McMaster, 1985; CUNY, 1985; Paris VII, 1989; McGill, 1991; Toronto, 1993; Hon. DMath Waterloo, 1988. Wilbur L. Cross Medal, Yale Univ., 1975; Cole Prize, Amer. Math. Sec., 1982; Common Wealth Award, Sigma Xi, 1984; Maths Award, Nat. Acad. of Scis, 1988. *Publications:* Automorphic Forms on GL(2) (with H. Jacquet), 1970; Euler Products, 1971; On the Functional Equations satisfied by Eisenstein Series, 1976; Base Change for GL(2), 1980; Les débuts d'une formule des traces stable, 1983; contrib. Canadian Jl Maths, Proc. Amer. Math. Soc. Symposia, Springer Lecture Notes. *Address:* Institute for Advanced Study, School of Mathematics, Princeton, NJ 08540, USA. *T:* (609) 7348106.

LANGLEY, Gordon Julian Hugh, QC 1983; a Recorder, since 1986; *b* 11 May 1943; *s* of late Gordon Thompson Langley and of Marjorie Langley; *m* 1968, Beatrice Jayanthi Langley; two *d*. *Educ:* Westminster School; Balliol College, Oxford (MA, BCL). Called to the Bar, Inner Temple, 1966. *Recreations:* music, sport. *Address:* 2 Bridgeman Road, Teddington, Mddx TW11 9AH. *T:* 0171–583 3335. *Club:* Travellers'.

LANGLEY, Maj.-Gen. Sir (Henry) Desmond (Allen), KCVO 1983; MBE 1967; Governor and Commander-in-Chief of Bermuda, 1988–92; *b* 16 May 1930; *s* of late Col Henry Langley, OBE, and Winsome Langley; *m* 1950, Felicity Joan, *d* of Lt-Col K. J. P. Oliphant, MC; one *s* one *d*. *Educ:* Eton; RMA Sandhurst. Commissioned The Life Guards, 1949; Adjt, Household Cavalry Regt, 1953–54; GSO3 HQ 10th Armoured Div., 1956–57; Regtl Adjt, Household Cavalry, 1959–60; psc 1961; GSO2(Ops) HQ Far East Land Forces, 1963–65; Bde Major, Household Bde, 1965–67; Comdg Officer, The Life Guards, 1969–71; Asst Sec., Chiefs of Staff Secretariat, 1971–72; Lt-Col Comdg Household Cavalry and Silver Stick-in-Waiting, 1972–75; Comdr 4th Guards Armoured Bde, 1976–77; RCDS 1978; BGS HQ UK Land Forces, 1979; GOC London District and Maj.-Gen. Comdg Household Div., 1979–83; Administrator, Sovereign Base Areas and Comdr, British Forces, Cyprus, 1983–85; retired, 1986. Gov., Church Lads' and Church Girls' Brigade, 1986–. Freeman, City of London, 1983. KStJ 1989.

LANGRIDGE, Philip Gordon, CBE 1994; FRAM; concert and opera singer (tenor), since 1964; *b* 16 Dec. 1939; *m* 1981, Ann Murray, *qv*; one *s* (and one *s* two *d* by former marriage). *Educ:* Maidstone Grammar Sch.; Royal Academy of Music, London. ARAM 1977; FRAM 1985. Glyndebourne Festival début, 1964; BBC Promenade Concerts, 1970–; Edinburgh Fest., 1970–; Netherlands Opera, Scottish Opera, Handel Opera etc. Covent Garden: L'Enfant et les Sortilèges, Rossignole, Boris, Jenufa, Idomeneo, Peter Grimes; Death in Venice; ENO: Turn of the Screw, Osud (Olivier Award, Outstanding Individual Performer in a New Opera Production, 1984), The Mask of Orpheus, Billy Budd, Beatrice and Benedict, Makropoulos Case; Peter Grimes; Glyndebourne, 1977–: Don Giovanni, Idomeneo, Fidelio, Jenufa, La Clemenza di Tito; The Second Mrs Kong; La Scala, 1979–: Rake's Progress, Wozzeck, Boris Godunov, Il Sosia, Idomeneo, Oberon; Frankfurt Opera: Castor and Pollux, Rigoletto, Die Entführung; Zurich Opera: Poppea, Lucio Silla; Don Giovanni; La Fenice: Janacek's Diary; Palermo: Otello (Rossini); Pesaro: La Donna del Lago; Aix en Provence: Alcina, Les Boriades; Metropolitan Opera, NY: Così fan Tutte, Boris Godunov, Das Rheingold; Vienna State Opera: Wozzeck; Salzburg Festival: Moses und Aron, Idomeneo, From the House of the Dead, Poppea, Boris Godunov; Amsterdam: Poppea, Idomeneo, Il Barbieri di Seviglia, Dorian Gray, Pelléas et Mélisande. Concerts with major, international orchestras and conductors including: Boston (Previn), Chicago (Solti, Abbado), Los Angeles (Christopher Hogwood), Sydney (Mackerras), Vienna Phil. (Previn), Orchestre de Paris (Barenboim, Mehta), and all major British orchestras. Many first performances of works, some dedicated to and written for him. Has made over 50 records of early, baroque, classical, romantic and modern music (Grammy Award for Schönberg's Moses und Aron, 1985). Mem., Music Panel, Arts Council of GB, 1983–86. Singer of the Year, RPS/Heidsieck Award, 1989. *Recreation:* collecting water colour paintings and Victorian postcards. *Address:* c/o Allied Artists Agency, 42 Montpelier Square, SW7 1JZ. *T:* 0171–589 6243.

LANGRIDGE, Richard James, CVO 1992; HM Diplomatic Service, retired; Consul-General, Bordeaux, 1990–92; *b* 29 Oct. 1932; *m* 1965, Jeannine Louise Joosen; one *d*. HM Forces, 1951–53; joined FO 1953; served NY, Leopoldville, Athens, Dakar, Paris and FCO; Ambassador to Madagascar, 1979–84; FCO, 1985; Dep. High Comr, Colombo, 1985–89.

LANGRISH, Rt. Rev. Michael Laurence; *see* Birkenhead, Bishop Suffragan of.

LANGRISHE, Sir Hercules (Ralph Hume), 7th Bt *cr* 1777; *b* 17 May 1927; *s* of Sir Terence Hume Langrishe, 6th Bt, and Joan Stuart (*d* 1976), *d* of late Major Ralph Stuart Grigg; *S* father, 1973; *m* 1955, Hon. Grania Sybil Enid Wingfield, *d* of 9th Viscount Powerscourt; one *s* three *d*. *Educ:* Summer Fields, St Leonards; Eton. 2nd Lieut, 9th

Queen's Royal Lancers, 1947; Lieut, 1948; retd 1953; *Recreations:* shooting, fishing. *Heir:* *s* James Hercules Langrishe [*b* 3 March 1957; *m* 1985, Gemma, *d* of Patrick O'Daly; one *s* one *d*]. *Address:* Arlonstown, Dunsany, Co. Meath. *T:* Navan (46) 25243. *Club:* Kildare Street and University (Dublin).

LANGSHAW, George Henry; Managing Director, UK Regions, British Gas, since 1992; *b* 6 Dec. 1939; *s* of George Henry and Florence Evelyn Langshaw; *m* 1962, Maureen Cosgrove; one *s* two *d*. *Educ:* Liverpool Inst. High Sch. FCMA; ACIS. Various accountancy appts, Wm Crawford & Sons, 1957–63, Littlewoods Orgn, 1963–67; British Gas: Accountant, NW, 1967–70; Develt Accountant, Southern, 1970–73; Prin. Financial Analyst, HQ, 1973–76; Chief Accountant, Wales, 1976–78; Dir of Finance, Southern, 1978–82; Dep, Chm., NW, 1982–87; Regional Chm., British Gas (Wales), 1987–89; Gp Dir of Personnel, 1989–90; Man. Dir, Global Gas, 1990–92. Chm., BG Corporate Ventures, 1990–. Director: British Gas Deutschland GmbH, 1991–; British Gas Holdings (Canada), 1992–; BG Holdings Inc., 1992–. Dir, Bd of Gas Consumers, Canada, 1990–. CIGasE 1988; CIMgt (CBIM 1991). *Recreations:* soccer, reading, golf. *Address:* British Gas, Rivermill House, 152 Grosvenor Road, SW1V 3JL.

LANGSLOW, Derek Robert, PhD; Chief Executive, English Nature, since 1990; *b* 7 Feb. 1945; *s* of Alexander Frederick Langslow and Beatrice Bibby Langslow (*née* Wright); *m* 1969, Helen Katherine (*née* Addison); one *s* one *d*. *Educ:* Ashville College, Harrogate; Queens' College, Cambridge (MA, PhD). Post-Doctoral Fellow, Cambridge and Univ. of Kansas; Lectr, Univ. of Edinburgh, 1972–78; Nature Conservancy Council: Senior Ornithologist, 1978–84; Asst Chief Scientist, 1984–87; Dir, Policy and Planning, 1987–90; Chief Scientist, 1990. Chm., Asia Wetland Bureau, 1994– (Dir, 1993–94). FRSA. *Publications:* numerous papers in learned jls. *Recreations:* badminton, walking, bird watching, music. *Address:* 4 Engaine, Orton Longueville, Peterborough PE2 7QA. *T:* Peterborough (01733) 232153.

LANGSTAFF, Brian Frederick James; QC 1994; a Recorder, since 1995; *b* 30 April 1948; *s* of Frederick Sidney Langstaff and Muriel Amy Maude Langstaff (*née* Griffin); *m* 1975, Deborah Elizabeth Weatherup; one *s* one *d*. *Educ:* George Heriot's Sch.; St Catharine's Coll., Cambridge (BA); Inns of Court Sch. of Law. VSO, Sri Lanka, 1966–67. Called to the Bar, Middle Temple, 1971 (Harmsworth Schol., 1975); Lectr and Sen. Lectr in Law, Mid-Essex Technical Coll. and Sch. of Art, Chelmsford, 1971–75; Asst Recorder, SE Circuit, 1991–95. Chm. of Govs, local primary sch., 1991–. *Publications:* Concise College Casenotes: equity and trusts, 1975; Health and Safety at Work: Halsbury's Laws vol. 20, 4th edn 1994; legal articles. *Recreations:* sport, politics, mowing the lawn, bell-ringing. *Address:* Cloisters, 1 Pump Court, Temple, EC4Y 7AA. *T:* 0171–583 0303.

LANGSTON, Group Captain John Antony S.; *see* Steff-Langston.

LANGTON; *see* Temple-Gore-Langton, family name of Earl Temple of Stowe.

LANGTON, Lord; James Grenville Temple-Gore-Langton; *b* 11 Sept. 1955; *er s* and *heir* of Earl Temple of Stowe, *qv*. *Educ:* Winchester.

LANGTON, Bryan David, CBE 1988; FHCIMA; Director, Bass plc, since 1985; Chairman and Chief Executive Officer, Holiday Inn Worldwide, since 1990; *b* 6 Dec. 1936; *s* of Thomas Langton and Doris (*née* Brown); *m* 1960, Sylva Degenhardt; two *d*. *Educ:* Accrington Grammar Sch.; Westminster Tech. Coll. (Hotel Operation Dip.); Ecole Hotelière de la SSA, Lausanne (Operations Dip.). Dep. Manager, Russell Hotel, London, 1959–63; General Manager: Victoria Hotel, Nottingham, 1961–66; Grand Hotel, Manchester, 1966–71; Crest Hotels: Divl Manager, 1971–73; Ops Dir UK, 1973–75; Ops Dir Europe, 1975–77; Divl Managing Dir, Europe, 1977–81; Managing Dir, Ops, 1981–82; Man. Dir, 1982–88; Chairman, 1985–90. Chairman: Holiday Inns International, 1988–90; Toby Restaurants, 1988–90. Vice Pres., Internat. Hotel Assoc., 1990–. Trustee, Educnl Inst., Amer. Hotel and Motel Assoc., 1990–. Member, Board of Trustees: Woodruff Arts Center, Atlanta, 1991–; Northside Hosp. Foundn Bd, 1991–. Trustee, Bd of Visitors, Emory Univ., 1991–. Hon. Fellow, Manchester Poly., 1986. *Recreations:* golf, cricket, reading, theatre. *Address:* 4185 Fairway Villas Drive, Alpharetta, GA 30202, USA. *T:* (404) 7409706.

LANGTON, Sir Henry Algernon; *see under* Calley, Sir H. A.

LANGTRY, (James) Ian; Education Officer, Association of County Councils, since 1988; *b* 2 Jan. 1939; *s* of late Rev. H. J. Langtry and I. M. Langtry (*née* Eagleson); *m* 1959, Eileen Roberta Beatrice (*née* Nesbitt); one *s* one *d*. *Educ:* Coleraine Academical Instn; Queen's Univ., Belfast (Sullivan Schol.; BSc 1st Cl., Physics). Assistant Master, Bangor Grammar Sch., 1960–61; Lectr, Belfast College of Technology, 1961–66; Asst Director of Examinations/Recruitment, Civil Service Commission, 1966–70; Principal, Dept of Educn and Science, 1970–76, Asst Sec., 1976–82, Under Sec., 1982–87; Under Sec., DHSS, 1987–88. *Recreations:* golf, sailing. *Clubs:* Royal Portrush Golf; West Kent Golf.

LA NIECE, Rear-Adm. Peter George, CB 1973; CBE 1967; *b* 23 July 1920; *s* of late George David Nelson La Niece and Gwynneth Mary (*née* Morgan); *m* 1948, Evelyn Mary Wrixon Babington (*d* 1982); two *s* one *d*. *Educ:* Whitgift Sch., Croydon. Entered RN, 1937; served War of 1939–45 in battleships, cruisers and destroyers; Gunnery Specialist 1945; Comdr 1953; Captain 1961; comd HMS Rame Head, 1962; Senior UK Polaris Rep., Washington, 1963–66; comd HMS Triumph, 1966–68; Cdre Clyde in Comd Clyde Submarine Base, 1969–71; Rear-Adm. 1971; Flag Officer Spithead and Port Admiral, Portsmouth, 1971–73; retired 1973. Dir in Exco Gp of Cos, 1976–85. *Recreation:* gardening. *Address:* Charltons, Yalding, Kent ME18 6DF. *T:* Maidstone (01622) 814161. *Club:* Army and Navy.

LANKESTER, Richard Shermer; Clerk of Select Committees, House of Commons, 1979–87; Registrar of Members' Interests, 1976–87; *b* 8 Feb. 1922; *s* of late Richard Ward Lankester; *m* 1950, Dorothy, *d* of late Raymond Jackson, Worsley; two *s* one *d* (and one *s* decd). *Educ:* Haberdashers' Aske's Hampstead Sch.; Jesus Coll., Oxford (MA). Served Royal Artillery, 1942–45. Entered Dept of Clerk of House of Commons, 1947; Clerk of Standing Cttees, 1973–75; Clerk of Expenditure Cttee, 1975–79. Co-Editor, The Table, 1962–67. *Address:* The Old Farmhouse, The Green, Boughton Monchelsea, Maidstone, Kent ME17 4LT. *T:* Maidstone (01622) 743749.

LANKESTER, Sir Timothy Patrick (Sir Tim), KCB 1994; Permanent Secretary, Department for Education, since 1994; *b* 15 April 1942; *s* of late Preb. Robin Prior Archibald Lankester and of Jean Dorothy (*née* Gilliat); *m* 1968, Patricia Cockcroft; three *d*. *Educ:* Monkton Combe Sch.; St John's Coll., Cambridge (BA); Jonathan Edwards Coll., Yale (Henry Fellow, MA). Teacher (VSO), St Michael's Coll., Belize, 1960–61; Fereday Fellow, St John's Coll., Oxford, 1965–66; Economist, World Bank, Washington DC, 1966–69; New Delhi, 1970–73; Principal 1973, Asst Sec. 1977, HM Treasury; Private Secretary to Rt Hon. James Callaghan, 1978–79; to Rt Hon. Margaret Thatcher, 1979–81; seconded to S. G. Warburg and Co. Ltd, 1981–83; Under Sec., HM Treasury, 1983–85; Economic Minister, Washington and Exec. Dir, IMF and World Bank, 1985–88; Dep. Sec., HM Treasury, 1988–89; Perm. Sec., ODA, FCO, 1989–94. *Address:* Department for Education, Sanctuary Buildings, Great Smith Street, SW1P 3BT.

LANSBURY, Angela Brigid, CBE 1994; actress; *b* London, England, 16 Oct. 1925; *d* of Edgar Lansbury and late Moyna Macgill (who *m* 1st, Reginald Denham); *m* 1st, Richard Cromwell; 2nd, 1949, Peter Shaw; one *s* one *d* and one step *s*. *Educ:* South Hampstead High Sch. for Girls; Webber Douglas Sch. of Singing and Dramatic Art, Kensington; Feagin Sch. of Drama and Radio, New York. With Metro-Goldwyn-Mayor, 1943–50; *films:* Gaslight, 1944; National Velvet, 1944; The Picture of Dorian Gray, 1945; The Harvey Girls, 1946; The Hoodlum Saint, 1946; Till the Clouds Roll By, 1946; The Private Affairs of Bel-Ami, 1947; If Winter Comes, 1948; Tenth Avenue Angel, 1948; State of the Union, 1948; The Three Musketeers, 1948; The Red Danube, or Storm over Vienna, or Vespers in Vienna, 1949; Samson and Delilah, 1949; Kind Lady, 1951; Mutiny, 1952; Remains to be Seen, 1953; A Life at Stake, or Key Man, 1955; The Purple Mask, 1956; The Court Jester, 1956; A Lawless Street, 1956; Please Murder Me, 1956; The Long Hot Summer, 1958; The Reluctant Debutante, 1958; Summer of the 17th Doll, 1959; Breath of Scandal, 1960; The Dark at the Top of the Stairs, 1960; Season of Passion, 1961; Blue Hawaii, 1961; All Fall Down, 1962; The Manchurian Candidate, 1962; In the Cool of the Day, 1963; The World of Henry Orient, 1964; The Out of Towners, 1964; Dear Heart, 1964; The Greatest Story Ever Told, 1965; Harlow, 1965; The Amorous Adventures of Moll Flanders, 1965; Mister Buddwing, or Woman Without a Face, 1966; Something for Everyone, or Black Flowers for the Bride, 1970; Bedknobs and Broomsticks, 1971; Death on the Nile, or Murder on the Nile, 1978; The Lady Vanishes, 1980; The Mirror Crack'd, 1980; The Last Unicorn, 1982; The Pirates of Penzance, 1982; The Company of Wolves, 1983; Beauty and the Beast, 1991; *plays:* appearances include: Hotel Paradiso (Broadway debut), 1957; Helen, in A Taste of Honey, Lyceum Theatre, New York, 1960; Anyone Can Whistle (Broadway musical), 1964; Mame (Tony Award for best actress in a Broadway musical), Winter Garden, NYC, 1966–68; Dear World (Broadway), 1969 (Tony Award); Gypsy (Broadway Musical), Piccadilly, 1973, US tour, 1974 (Tony Award; Chicago, Sarah Siddons Award, 1974); Gertrude, in Hamlet, Nat. Theatre, 1975; Anna, in The King and I (Broadway), 1978; Mrs Lovett, in Sweeney Todd (Broadway), 1979 (Tony Award). TV series, Murder She Wrote, 1984–95 (Golden Globe Award, 1984, 1986, 1991, 1992). NY Drama Desk Award, 1979; Sarah Siddons Award, 1980 and 1983; inducted Theatre Hall of Fame, 1982; Silver Mask for Lifetime Achievement, BAFTA, 1991. *Address:* Corymore Productions, 100 Universal City Plaza, Universal City, CA 91608, USA.

LANSDOWN, Gillian Elizabeth, (Mrs Richard Lansdown); *see* Tindall, G. E.

LANSDOWNE, 8th Marquess of (GB), *cr* 1784; **George John Charles Mercer Nairne Petty-Fitzmaurice;** 29th Baron of Kerry and Lixnaw, 1181; Earl of Kerry, Viscount Clanmaurice, 1723; Viscount FitzMaurice and Baron Dunkeron, 1751; Earl of Shelburne, 1753; Baron Wycombe, 1760; Earl of Wycombe and Viscount Calne, 1784; PC 1964; *b* 27 Nov. 1912; *o s* of Major Lord Charles George Francis Mercer Nairne, MVO (killed in action, 1914; 2nd *s* of 5th Marquess), and Lady Violet Mary Elliot (she *m* 2nd, 1916, 1st Baron Astor of Hever), *d* of 4th Earl of Minto; *S* cousin, 1944; *m* 1st, 1938, Barbara, (*d* 1965), *d* of Harold Stuart Chase, Santa Barbara; two *s* one *d* (and one *d* decd); 2nd, 1969, Mrs Polly Carnegie (marr. diss. 1978), *d* of Viscount Eccles, *qv*; 3rd, 1978, Gillian Ann, (*d* 1982), *d* of Alured Morgan; *m* 1995, Hon. Mrs John Astor. *Educ:* Eton; Christ Church, Oxford. Sec. Junior Unionist League for E Scotland, 1939. Served War of 1939–45, Capt. Royal Scots Greys 1940, formerly 2nd Lt Scottish Horse (TA); Major 1944; served with Free French Forces (Croix de Guerre, Légion D'Honneur), Private Sec. to HM Ambassador in Paris (Rt Hon. A. Duff Cooper), 1944–45. Lord-in-Waiting to the Queen, 1957–58; Joint Parliamentary Under-Sec. of State, Foreign Office, 1958–62; Minister of State for Colonial Affairs, 1962–64, and for Commonwealth Relations, 1963–64. Mem. Royal Company of Archers (Queen's Body Guard for Scotland); JP, Perthshire, 1950; DL Wilts, 1952–73. Patron of two livings. Chm., Victoria League in Scotland, 1952–56; Inter-Governmental Cttee on Malaysia, 1962. Chm., Franco-British Soc., 1972–83; Pres., Franco-Scottish Soc. President: Officers' Families Fund, 1946–89; Royal Surgical Aid Soc., 1985–. Prime Warden, Fishmongers' Company, 1967–68. Comdr, Légion d'Honneur, 1979. *Heir:* *s* Earl of Shelburne, *qv*. *Address:* Meikleour House, Perthshire PH2 6EA. *Clubs:* Turf; New (Edinburgh).
See also Lady Nairne.

LANSLEY, Andrew David; Director: Conservative Research Department, 1990–95; Public Policy Unit, 1995; *b* 11 Dec. 1956; *s* of Thomas and Irene Lansley; *m* 1985, Marilyn Jane Biggs; three *d*. *Educ:* Univ. of Exeter (BA). Administration trainee, Dept of Industry, 1979; Private Sec. to Sec. of State for Trade and Industry, 1984–85; Principal Private Sec. to Chancellor of Duchy of Lancaster, 1985–87; Dir, Policy, 1987, Dep. Dir-Gen., 1989–90, ABCC, 1987–89. *Publication:* A Private Route?, 1988. *Recreations:* travel, bridge, cricket, political biography. *Address:* Public Policy Unit, 50 Rochester Row, SW1P 2JU. *T:* 0171–828 6088.

LANYON, (Harry) Mark, CEng; Regional Director, Government Office for East Midlands, since 1994; *b* 15 July 1939; *s* of late Henry Lanyon and Heather Gordon (*née* Tyrrell); *m* 1975, Elizabeth Mary Morton; one *s* one *d*. *Educ:* Ardingly Coll.; St Andrews Univ. (BSc Hons 1962). CEng 1965; MIMechE 1965. Ministry of Aviation: Engr Cadet, 1963–65; Aeronautical Inspectorate, 1965–68; Concorde Div., Min. of Technol., 1968–75; Department of Trade and Industry: Shipbuilding Policy Div., 1975–77; Dep. Dir, SW Region, 1977–82; Regl Dir, W Midlands, 1982–85; Hd of Br., Mechanical and Electrical Engrg Div., 1985–90; Asst Dir, Consumer Affairs, OFT, 1990–93; Regl Dir, Yorks and Humberside, DTI, 1993–94. *Recreations:* caravanning, making things. *Address:* Government Office for East Midlands, Cranbrook House, Cranbrook Street, Nottingham NG1 1EY.
See also L. E. Lanyon.

LANYON, Prof. Lance Edward; Principal, Royal Veterinary College, since 1989; *b* 4 Jan. 1944; *s* of Harry Lanyon and Heather Gordon (*née* Tyrrell); *m* 1972, Mary Kear; one *s* one *d*. *Educ:* Christ's Hospital; Univ. of Bristol (BVSC, PhD, DSc). MRCVS. Lectr, 1967, Reader in Vet. Anatomy, 1967–79, Univ. of Bristol; Associate Prof., 1980–83, Prof., 1983–84, Tufts Sch. of Vet. Medicine, Boston, Mass; Prof. of Vet. Anatomy, Royal Vet. Coll., Univ. of London, 1984–89, personal title, 1989– (Head, Dept of Vet. Anatomy, 1984–87, of Vet. Basic Scis, 1987–88). *Publications:* chapters in books on orthopaedics, osteoporosis, and athletic training; articles in professional jls. *Recreations:* building, home improvements, sailing. *Address:* Royal Veterinary College, Royal College Street, NW1 0TU. *T:* 0171–387 2898.
See also H. M. Lanyon.

LANYON, Mark; *see* Lanyon, H. M.

LAPIDGE, Prof. Michael, PhD, LittD; FBA 1994; Elrington and Bosworth Professor of Anglo-Saxon, since 1991, and Fellow of Clare College, since 1990, Cambridge University; *b* 8 Feb. 1942; *s* of Rae H. Lapidge and Catherine Mary Lapidge (*née* Carruthers). *Educ:* Univ. of Calgary (BA 1962); Univ. of Alberta (MA 1965); Univ. of Toronto (PhD 1971);

LittD Cantab 1988. Cambridge University: Lectr, 1974–88; Reader in Insular Latin Literature, 1988–91. *Publications:* Aldhelm: the prose works, 1979; Alfred the Great, 1983; Aldhelm: the poetic works, 1985; A Bibliography of Celtic Latin Literature 400–1200, 1985; articles in learned jls. *Recreation:* mountaineering. *Address:* 9 West Road, Cambridge CB3 9DP. *T:* Cambridge (01223) 335085.

LAPOINTE, Paul André; Ambassador for Fisheries Conservation, Canada, since 1994; *b* 1 Nov. 1934; *s* of Henri and Regina Lapointe; *m* 1965, Iris Donati; one *d.* *Educ:* Université Laval. BA, LLL. Called to the Bar, Québec, 1958. Journalist, Le Soleil, 1959–60; joined Canadian Foreign Service, 1960; served Vietnam and Laos, 1961–62, NATO, Paris, 1962–64, Geneva, 1968–72, New Delhi, 1975–76, New York, 1976–79; Dep. Perm. Rep. to UN Security Council, 1977–78; Dep. High Comr in UK, 1981–85; Consul Gen., Marseille, France, 1985–87; Sen. Negotiator, Canada-France Maritime Affairs, Dept of External Affairs, Canada, 1987–90; Canadian Ambassador to Turkey, 1990–93. *Address:* Department of Foreign Affairs and International Trade, 125 Sussex Drive, Ottawa, Ontario K1A 0G2, Canada. *Club:* Travellers'.

LAPOTAIRE, Jane; actress; *b* 26 Dec. 1944; *d* of unknown father and Louise Elise Lapotaire; *m* 1st, 1965, Oliver Wood (marr. diss. 1967); 2nd, 1974, Roland Joffé (marr. diss. 1982); one *s.* *Educ:* Northgate Grammar Sch., Ipswich; Old Vic Theatre Sch., Bristol. Bristol Old Vic Co., 1965–67; Nat. Theatre Co., 1967–71, incl. Measure for Measure, Flea in Her Ear, Dance of Death, Way of the World, Merchant of Venice, Oedipus, The Taming of the Shrew; freelance films and TV, 1971–74; RSC, 1974–75 (roles included Viola in Twelfth Night, and Sonya in Uncle Vanya); Prospect Theatre Co., West End, 1975–76 (Vera in A Month in the Country, Lucy Honeychurch in A Room with a View); freelance films and TV, 1976–78; Rosalind in As You Like It, Edin. Fest., 1977; RSC, 1978–81: Rosaline in Love's Labours Lost, 1978–79; title role in Piaf, The Other Place 1978, Aldwych 1979, Wyndhams 1980, Broadway 1981 (SWET Award 1979, London Critics Award and Variety Club Award 1980, and Broadway Tony Award 1981); National Theatre: Eileen, Kick for Touch, 1983; Belvidera, Venice Preserv'd, Antigone, 1984; Saint Joan (title rôle), Compass Co., 1985; Double Double, Fortune Theatre, 1986; RSC, 1986–87: Misalliance, 1986; Archbishop's Ceiling, 1986; Greenland, Royal Court, 1988; Shadowlands, Queen's, 1989–90 (Variety Club Best Actress Award); RSC, 1992–94: Gertrude in Hamlet, 1992; Mrs Alving in Ghosts, 1993; *television:* Marie Curie (serial), 1977; Antony and Cleopatra, 1981; Macbeth, 1983; Seal Morning (series), 1985; Napoleon and Josephine, 1987; Blind Justice (serial), 1988 (British Press Guild Best Actress Award); The Dark Angel, 1989; Love Hurts (series), 1992, 1993; The Big Battalions (series), 1992; Johnny and the Dead, 1994; *films:* Eureka, 1983; Lady Jane, 1986. Vis. Fellow, Sussex Univ., 1986–. Mem., Marie Curie Meml Foundn Appeals Cttee, 1986–88. Pres., Bristol Old Vic Theatre Club, 1985–; Hon. Pres., Friends of Southwark Globe, 1986–. Hon. Associate Artist, RSC. *Publication:* Grace and Favour (autobiog.), 1989. *Recreation:* walking. *Address:* c/o London Management, 2–4 Noël Street, W1V 3RB. *T:* 0171–287 9000.

LAPPER, Maj.-Gen. John; Medical Director, International Hospitals Group, 1984–1988; *b* 24 July 1921; *s* of late Col Wilfred Mark Lapper, OBE, Legion of Merit (USA), late RE, and Agnes Lapper (*née* Powner); *m* 1948, Dorothy, *d* of late Roland John and Margaret Simpson (*née* Critchlow); three *s.* *Educ:* Wolverhampton Grammar Sch.; King Edward VI Sch., Birmingham; Birmingham Univ. MB, ChB 1946; DLO 1952. House appts, Queen Elizabeth and Children's Hosp., Birmingham, and Ronkswood Hosp. and Royal Infirm., Worcester; Registrar, Royal Berks Hosp., Reading. Commnd RAMC, 1950; ENT specialist, Mil. Hosps in UK, Libya, Egypt, Germany, Singapore, Malaya; CO 14 Field Amb., BAOR, 1958; CO BMH Rinteln, BAOR, 1964; Asst Comdt, Royal Army Med. Coll., 1965–68; ADMS Hong Kong, 1969–71; CO Queen Alexandra's Mil. Hosp., Millbank, 1971–73; ADMS 3 Div., 1973; DDMS HQ UKLF, 1974–77; Dir, Med. Supply, MoD, 1977; Dir, Med. Policy and Plans, MoD, 1978–80, retired; QHS 1977–80. Hospital and Medical Dir, Nat. Guard Saudi Arabia, 1981–83. Hudson-Evans Lectr, W Kent Medico-Chirurgical Soc., 1980; Mem. Sands Cox Med. Soc., Birmingham Univ. FFPHM (FFCM 1980); FIMgt (FBIM 1980); FRSocMed; FMedSoc London; Mem. BMA; Pres. Med. Soc., Hong Kong, 1970–71; Mem., RUSI; Chm. Council, Yateley Industries for the Disabled. OStJ 1959. *Publications:* articles in professional jls. *Recreations:* travel, militaria, DIY. *Address:* Holmbush, Old School Lane, Yateley, Camberley, Surrey GU17 7NG. *T:* Yateley (01252) 874180; Rocas Del Mar, Mijas Costa, (Malaga), Spain.

LAPPERT, Prof. Michael Franz, FRS 1979; Professor of Chemistry, University of Sussex, since 1969; *b* 31 Dec. 1928; *s* of Julius Lappert and Kornelie Lappert (*née* Beran); *m* 1980, Lorna McKenzie. *Educ:* Wilson's Grammar School; Northern Polytechnic, London. BSc, PhD, DSc (London). FRSC. Northern Polytechnic, London: Asst Lecturer, 1952–53; Lecturer, 1953–55; Sen. Lectr, 1955–59. UMIST: Lectr, 1959–61; Sen. Lectr, 1961–64; Reader, Univ. of Sussex, 1964–69. SERC Sen. Res. Fellow, 1980–85. Pres., Dalton Div., RSC, 1989–91. Tilden Lectr, Chem. Soc., 1972–73; Nyholm Lectr, RSC, 1994. Hon. Dr rer. nat. München, 1989. First recipient of (London) Chemical Soc. Award in Main Group Metal Chemistry, 1970; Award in Organometallic Chemistry, 1978; F. S. Kipping Award of American Chem. Soc., 1976. *Publications:* (ed jtly) Developments in Inorganic Polymer Chemistry, 1962; (jtly) Metal and Metalloid Amides, 1980; (jtly) Organo-zirconium and -hafnium Compounds, 1986; approx. 560 papers in Jl Chem. Soc., etc. *Recreations:* theatre, opera, tennis, walking. *Address:* 4 Varndean Gardens, Brighton BN1 6WL. *T:* Brighton (01273) 503661.

LAPPING, Anne Shirley Lucas; independent television producer, Brook Productions, since 1982; Director, North West London Mental Health NHS Trust, since 1992; *b* 10 June 1941; *d* of late Frederick Stone and of Dr Freda Lucas Stone; *m* 1963, Brian Michael Lapping; three *d.* *Educ:* City of London Sch. for Girls; London Sch. of Econs. New Society, 1964–68; London Weekend TV, 1970–73; writer on The Economist, 1974–82. Other writing and broadcasting. Director: Channel Four, 1989–94; Scott Trust, 1994–. Member: SSRC, 1977–79; Nat. Gas Consumers' Council, 1978–79. Gov., LSE, 1994–. *Recreations:* literature, housework. *Address:* 61 Eton Avenue, NW3 3ET. *T:* 0171–586 1047.

LAPPING, Peter Herbert; Headmaster of Sherborne, since 1988; *b* 8 Aug. 1941; *s* of late Dr Douglas James Lapping, MBE and Dorothy Lapping (*née* Horrocks) of Nhlangano, Swaziland; *m* 1967, Diana Dillworth, *d* of late Lt-Col E. S. G. Howard, MC, RA; one *s* one *d.* *Educ:* St John's College, Johannesburg; Univ. of Natal, Pietermaritzburg (BA Hons *cum laude*); Lincoln College, Oxford (MA). Asst Master, Reed's Sch., Cobham, 1966–67; Head of History, Loretto Sch., 1967–79 (Housemaster, Pinkie House, 1972–79); Headmaster, Shiplake Coll., Oxon, 1979–88. *Recreations:* cricket and other games, cooking, walking, travel. *Address:* Sherborne School, Dorset DT9 3AP. *T:* Sherborne (01935) 812249. *Clubs:* East India, Devonshire, Sports and Public Schools, MCC; Vincent's (Oxford).

LAPSLEY, Air Marshal Sir John (Hugh), KBE 1969 (OBE 1944); CB 1966; DFC 1940; AFC 1950; *b* 24 Sept. 1916; *s* of late Edward John Lapsley, Bank of Bengal, Dacca, and Norah Gladis Lapsley; *m* 1st, 1942, Jean Margaret MacIvor (*d* 1979); one *s* one *d*; 2nd, 1980, Millicent Rees (*née* Beadnell), *widow* of T. A Rees. *Educ:* Wolverhampton Sch.; Royal Air Force Coll., Cranwell. Served in Fighter Squadrons in UK, Egypt and Europe, 1938–45; psc 1946; Air Ministry Directorate of Policy, 1946–48; Commander No 74 Fighter Squadron and Air Fighting Development Squadron, 1949–52; HQ Fighter Command Staff, 1952–54; 2nd TAF Germany, 1954–58; Ministry of Defence Joint Planning Staff, 1958–60; Deputy Chief of Staff Air, 2nd Allied TAF, 1960–62; IDC, 1963; Secretary to Chiefs of Staff Cttee and Director of Defence Operations Staff, Ministry of Defence, 1964–66; No 19 Group, RAF Coastal Comd, 1967–68; AOC-in-C, RAF Coastal Comd, 1968–69; Head of British Defence Staff and Defence Attaché, Washington, 1970–73. Mem. Council, Officers' Pension Soc., 1976–87. Dir-Gen., Save the Children Fund, 1974–75. Dir, Falkland Is R&D Assoc. Ltd, 1978–83; Councillor, Suffolk Coastal District Council, 1979–87, Chm. 1983. Fellow RSPB. *Recreations:* golf, fishing, ornithology. *Address:* Milcroft, 149 Saxmundham Road, Aldeburgh, Suffolk IP15 5PB. *T:* Aldeburgh (01728) 453957. *Clubs:* Royal Air Force; Aldeburgh Golf; Suffolk Fly Fishers.

LAPUN, Sir Paul, Kt 1974; *b* 1923; *m* 1951, Lois; two *s* one *d.* *Educ:* Catholic Mission, Vunapope. Teacher, Catholic Mission, 1947–61. Under-Secretary for Forests, Papua and New Guinea, 1964–67. Founder Mem., for S Bougainville, PNG House of Assembly, 1964; Founder, Pangu Party, 1967 (Leader, 1967–68; Dep. Parly Leader, 1968); Minister: for Mines and Energy, 1972–75; for Health, 1975–77. Hon. Mem., Internat. Mark Twain Soc., USA. *Address:* Bougainville, N Solomons Province, Papua New Guinea.

LAQUEUR, Walter; Chairman, Research Council, Center for Strategic and International Studies, Georgetown University, since 1975; Director, Institute of Contemporary History and Wiener Library, London, 1964–92; *b* 26 May 1921; *s* of late Fritz Laqueur and late Else Laqueur; *m* 1941, Barbara (*née* Koch), *d* of Prof. Richard Koch and Maria Koch (*née* Rosenthal); two *d.* Agricultural labourer during War, 1939–44. Journalist, free lance author, 1944–55; Editor of Survey, 1955–65; Co-editor of Journal of Contemporary History, 1966–. Prof., History of Ideas, Brandeis Univ., 1967–71; Prof. of Contemporary History, Tel Aviv Univ., 1970–; Vis. Professor: Chicago Univ.; Johns Hopkins Univ.; Harvard Univ. Hon. Dr Hebrew Union Coll., NY, 1988. Grand Cross of Merit, FRG, 1986. *Publications:* Communism and Nationalism in the Middle East, 1956; Young Germany, 1961; Russia and Germany, 1965; The Road to War, 1968; Europe Since Hitler, 1970; Out of the Ruins of Europe, 1971; Zionism, a History, 1972; Confrontation: the Middle East War and World Politics, 1974; Weimar: a Cultural History, 1918–33, 1974; Guerrilla, 1976; Terrorism, 1977; The Missing Years, 1980; (ed jtly) A Reader's Guide to Contemporary History, 1972; (ed) Fascism: a reader's guide, 1978; The Terrible Secret, 1980; Farewell to Europe, 1981; Germany Today: a personal report, 1985; World of Secrets: the uses and limits of intelligence, 1986; The Long Road to Freedom, 1989; Stalin: the glasnost revelations, 1991; Europe in Our Time, 1992. *Recreations:* swimming, motor-boating.

LARCOM, Sir (Charles) Christopher (Royde), 5th Bt, *cr* 1868; *b* 11 Sept. 1926; *s* of Sir Philip Larcom, 4th Bt, and Aileen Monica Royde (*née* Colbeck); *S* father, 1967; *m* 1956, Barbara Elizabeth, *d* of Balfour Bowen; four *d.* *Educ:* Radley; Clare Coll., Cambridge. (Wrangler, 1947; BA, 1947; MA, 1951). Served RN (Lieutenant), 1947–50. Articled to Messrs Spicer and Pegler (Chartered Accountants), 1950–53; ACA 1954; FCA 1965; joined Grieveson, Grant and Co., 1955, Partner, 1960, retired, 1986. Member, The Stock Exchange, London, 1959 (Mem. Council, 1970–80). *Recreations:* sailing, music. *Address:* 8 The Postern, Barbican, Wood Street, EC2Y 8BJ. *T:* 0171–920 0388; 4 Village Cay Marina, PO Box 145, Roadtown, Tortola, BV1. *T:* Virgin Islands 42485.

LARGE, Andrew McLeod Brooks; Chairman, Securities and Investments Board, since 1992; *b* 7 Aug. 1942; *s* of late Maj.-Gen. Stanley Eyre Large, MBE and of Janet Mary Large (*née* Brooks); *m* 1967, Susan Mary Melville; two *s* one *d.* *Educ:* Winchester Coll.; Corpus Christi Coll., Cambridge (BA Hons Econ); INSEAD, Fontainebleau (MBA). BP, 1964–71; Orion Bank, 1971–79; Swiss Bank Corp., 1980–89; Large, Smith & Walter, 1990–92. Non-Executive Director: Nuclear Electric, 1990–94; Rank Hovis McDougall, 1990–92; Phoenix Securities, 1990–92; Dowty Gp, 1991–92; English China Clays, 1991–; London Fox, 1991–92 (Chm.); Luthy Baillie Dowsett Pethick, 1990–92 (Chm.). Chm., Securities Assoc., 1986–87; Member: Council, Stock Exchange, 1986–87; Panel on Takeovers and Mergers, 1987–88; Lloyds Council, 1992–93. Governor, Abingdon Sch., 1991–. *Recreations:* ski-ing, walking, photography, music. *Address:* Securities and Investments Board, Gavrelle House, 2–14 Bunhill Row, EC1Y 8RA. *Club:* Brooks's.

LARGE, Prof. John Barry; Professor of Applied Acoustics, University of Southampton, since 1969; Group Chief Executive, University of Southampton Holdings Ltd, since 1989; *b* 10 Oct. 1930; *s* of Thomas and Ada Large; *m* 1958, Barbara Alicia Nelson; two *s.* *Educ:* Queen Mary Coll., London Univ.; Purdue Univ., USA. BScEng (Hons), MS. Group Engr, EMI Ltd, Feltham, Mddx, 1954–56; Sen. Systems Engr, Link Aviation, Binghampton, NY, USA, 1956–58; Chief Aircraft Noise Unit, Boeing Co., Seattle, USA, 1958–69. Southampton University: Dir, Inst. of Sound and Vibration Res., 1978–82; Dean, Faculty of Engrg and Applied Sci., 1982–86; Dir of Industrial Affairs, 1986–92. Chm., Chilworth Centre Ltd; Chief Exec., Chilworth Manor Ltd; Director: Hants TEC; Southern Reg. Technol. Centre; Southampton Chamber of Commerce and Industry (Pres., 1992–94). Mem., Noise Adv. Council, 1976–80; Chm., Co-ordinating Cttee, BCAR-N (Noise), Air Registration Bd, 1973–; Pres., Assoc. Noise Consultants, 1985–. Mem., Southern Regl Council, CBI. Hon. Dep. Chief Scientific Officer, Defence Res. Estabt, 1974–. Corresp. Mem., Inst. Noise Control Engrg, USA, 1985–. *Publications:* contrib. (regarding aircraft noise, etc) to: Commn of European Communities, Eur 5398e, 1975; Proceedings of Internoise conferences include: Miami, 1980; San Francisco, 1982; Edinburgh, 1983; Hawaii, 1984; Hong Kong, 1985; The Development of Criteria for Environmental Noise Control (Proc. Royal Instn, vol. 52), 1979; Congress of Acoustics, 1983. *Recreations:* skiing, gardening. *Address:* Chinook, Southdown Road, Shawford, Hants. *T:* Twyford (01962) 712307.

LARGE, Sir Peter, Kt 1993; CBE 1987 (MBE 1974); Chairman, Joint Committee on Mobility for Disabled People (formerly Mobility for the Disabled), since 1971; *b* 16 Oct. 1931; *s* of Ethel May Walters and Rosslyn Victor Large; *m* 1st, 1962, Susy Fisher (*d* 1982); one step *s* two step *d*; *m* 2nd, 1992, Sheenah McCaffrey. *Educ:* Enfield Grammar Sch.; University Coll. London. BSc Civil Eng. 1953. National Service, HM Submarines, 1953–55 (Sub Lt (E)). Joined Shell International, 1956; West Africa, 1957; Ghana, 1957–60; South East Arabia, 1960–61; Indonesia, 1961–62; paralysed by poliomyelitis, 1962; Civil Service, 1966–91. Chm., Assoc. of Disabled Professionals, 1971–93; Governor, Motability, 1978–; Dep. Chm., Disabled Persons Transport Adv. Cttee, 1986–; Vice-Chm., Disablement Income Group, 1985–93 (Parly Advr, 1973–93); Member: Exec. Cttee, RADAR, 1977–; Nat. Adv. Council on Employment of People with Disabilities (formerly Disabled People), 1987–; Disability Living Allowance Adv. Bd, 1991–. *Recreation:* conversing with Siamese cats. *Address:* 14 Birch Way, Warlingham, Surrey CR6 9DA.

LARKEN, Comdt Anthea, CBE 1991; Director and Company Secretary, Operational Command Training Organisation Ltd, since 1991; *b* 23 Aug. 1938; *d* of Frederick William Savill and Nance (*née* Williams); *m* 1987, Rear Adm. Edmund Shackleton Jeremy Larken, *qv.* *Educ:* Stafford Girls' High Sch. Joined WRNS as Range Assessor, 1956; commnd,

1960; qualified: as Photographic Interpreter, 1961; as WRNS Secretarial Officer, 1967; Staff Officer in Singapore, 1964–66; i/c WRNS Officers' Training, BRNC Dartmouth, 1976–78; NATO Military Agency for Standardisation, Brussels, 1981–84; CSO (Admin) to Flag Officer Plymouth, 1985–86; RCDS, 1987; Dir, WRNS, 1988–91. ADC to the Queen, 1988–91. *Recreations:* theatre, music, reading, home, family and friends. *Club:* Commonwealth Trust.

LARKEN, Rear Adm. (Edmund Shackleton) Jeremy, DSO 1982; Managing Director, Operational Command Training Organisation Ltd, since 1991; advisory consultant to the offshore oil and gas and defence industries; *b* 14 Jan. 1939, *s* of Rear Adm. Edmund Thomas Larken, CB, OBE and Eileen Margaret (*née* Shackleton); *m* 1st, 1963, Wendy Nigella Hallett (marr. diss. 1987); two *d*; 2nd, 1987, Anthea Savill (*see* Comdt Anthea Larken). *Educ:* Bryanston Sch.; BRNC, Dartmouth. Joined RN as Cadet, 1957; qualified: in Submarines, 1960; in Navigation, 1965; in Submarine Comd, 1960; served HMS Tenby, Finwhale, Tudor, Ambush and Narwhal; Navigation Officer, HMS Valiant; First Lieut, HMS Otus; commanded HMS Osiris, Glamorgan and Valiant, Third Submarine Sqn, and HMS Fearless (including Falklands Campaign, 1982); exchange with USN (Submarines), 1971–73; Naval Plans; Dir, Naval Staff Duties, 1985; Cdre Amphibious Warfare, 1985–87; ACDS (Overseas), 1988–90. Governor, Bryanston Sch., 1988–. *Publications:* papers and articles in offshore and defence periodicals. *Recreations:* maritime and aviation interests, strategy, theatre, reading, home, family and friends. *Club:* Commonwealth Trust.

LARKIN, (John) Cuthbert, MA; Headmaster, Wyggeston School, Leicester, 1947–69, retired; *b* 15 Oct. 1906; *s* of J. W. Larkin; *m* 1933, Sylvia Elizabeth Pilsbury (*d* 1991); one *s* three *d*. *Educ:* King Edward VI Sch., Nuneaton; Downing Coll., Cambridge. Assistant Master, Shrewsbury Sch., 1928–45; Headmaster, Chesterfield Grammar Sch., 1946–47. *Recreations:* cricket, gardening. *Address:* The Old Farm, Hungarton, Leics LE7 9JR. *T:* Hungarton (0116) 259 5228.

LARMINIE, (Ferdinand) Geoffrey, OBE 1971; Director, British Geological Survey, 1987–90; *b* 23 June 1929; *s* of late Ferdinand Samuel Larminie and of Mary Larminie (*née* Willis); *m* 1956, Helena Elizabeth Woodside Carson; one *s* one *d*. *Educ:* St Andrews Coll., Dublin; Trinity Coll., Dublin (BA 1954, MA 1972; Hon. Fellow, 1989). Asst Lectr in Geology, Univ. of Glasgow, 1954–56; Lectr in Geology, Univ. of Sydney, 1956–60; joined British Petroleum Co. Ltd, 1960: Exploration Dept in Sudan, Greece, Canada, Libya, Kuwait, California, New York, Thailand and Alaska, 1960–74; Scientific Advr, Inf. Dept, London, 1974–75; Gen. Manager, Public Affairs and Inf. Dept, London, 1975–76; Gen. Manager, Environmental Control Centre, London, 1976–84; External Affairs Co-ordinator, Health, Safety and Environmental Services, BP plc, 1984–87. Vice-Chm., Cambridge Arctic Shelf Prog., 1993–. Member: Royal Commn on Environmental Pollution, 1979–83; NERC, 1983–87. Council Mem., RGS, 1984–90, Vice-Pres., 1987–90. President: Alaska Geol Soc., 1969; Soc. of Underwater Technol., 1987–89 (Hon. Fellow, 1992). Trustee, Bermuda Biological Station 1978–91, Life Trustee, 1991; Member: Bd of Management, Inst. of Offshore Engrg, Heriot-Watt Univ., 1981–90; Polar Res. Bd, Nat. Res. Council, Washington, DC, 1984–88. Mem., IBA Gen. Adv. Council, 1980–85. Mem. of numerous scientific and professional socs. *Publications:* papers in scientific and technical jls on oil ind., and occasional reviews. *Recreations:* archaeology, natural history, reading, shooting. *Address:* Lane End, Lanes End, Tring, Herts HP23 6LF. *T:* Wendover (01296) 624907.

LARMOUR, Sir Edward Noel, (Sir Nick Larmour), KCMG 1977 (CMG 1966); HM Diplomatic Service, retired; *b* 25 Dec. 1916; *s* of Edward and Maud Larmour, Belfast, N Ireland; *m* 1946, Nancy, 2nd *d* of Thomas Bill; one *s* two *d*. *Educ:* Royal Belfast Academical Institution (Kitchener Scholar); Trinity Coll., Dublin (Scholar) (1st Class Hons and University Studentship in Classics, 1939); Sydney Univ., NSW. Royal Inniskilling Fusiliers, 1940; Burma Civil Service, 1942; Indian Army, 1942–46 (Major); Dep. Secretary to Governor of Burma, 1947; Commonwealth Relations Office, 1948; served in New Zealand, Singapore, Australia and Nigeria, 1950–68; Asst Under-Secretary of State, 1964; Dep. Chief of Administration, FCO, 1968–70; High Comr, Jamaica, and non-resident Ambassador, Haiti, 1970–73; Asst Under Sec. of State, FCO, 1973–75; High Comr (non-resident) for New Hebrides, 1973–76; Dep. Under Sec. of State, FCO, 1975–76. Mem., Price Commn, 1977–80; Chm., Bermuda Constituency Boundaries Commn, 1979. *Recreations:* cricket, golf, music. *Address:* 68 Wood Vale, N10 3DN. *T:* 0181–444 9744. *Clubs:* Royal Over-Seas League, MCC.

LaROCQUE, Judith Anne, CVO 1992; Secretary to the Governor General of Canada, since 1990; Secretary General, Order of Canada and Order of Military Merit, and Herald Chancellor of Canada, since 1990; *b* Hawkesbury, Ontario, 27 Sept. 1956; *d* of Olier LaRocque and Elizabeth (*née* Murray); *m* 1991, André Roland Lavoie. *Educ:* Carleton Univ. (BA Pol Sci. 1979; MA Public Admin 1992). Admin. Asst, Internal Audit Directorate, Public Service Commn, 1979; writer/researcher, Prime Minister's Office, 1979; Special Asst, Office of Leader of Opposition, 1980–82; Cttee Clerk, Cttees and Private Legislation Br., H of C, 1982–84; Legislative Asst to Govt House Leader, 1984–85; Head of House Business, Office of Govt House Leader, Pres. Queen's Privy Council for Canada and Minister Responsible for Regulatory Affairs, 1985–86; Exec. Asst to Minister of Justice and Attorney Gen. of Canada, 1986–89; COS to Govt Leader in Senate and Minister of State for Federal-Provincial Relns, 1989–90. OStJ 1990. *Recreations:* gardening, cross-country ski-ing, fishing. *Address:* Government House, Rideau Hall, 1 Sussex Drive, Ottawa, Ont K1A 0A1, Canada, *T:* (613) 9938200.

LAROSIÈRE de CHAMPFEU, Jacques Martin Henri Marie de; *see* de Larosière de Champfeu.

LARRY; *see* Parkes, T.

LARSEN, Prof. Henning; architect; founder and owner, Henning Larsens Tegnestue, architectural practice; Professor of Architecture, Royal Academy of Fine Arts, Copenhagen; *b* 20 Aug. 1925; *s* of Erik Peter Larsen and Johanne Mary Gøbel; *m* Lone Backe. *Educ:* Royal Acad. of Fine Arts, Copenhagen (Dip. 1952); Sch. of Architecture, London; MIT, USA. Founder: architectural magazine Skala; Gallery Skala, 1986–94. Guest Professor: Yale, 1964, Princeton, 1965. Member: Royal Danish Acad. of Fine Arts; Royal Swedish Acad. of Fine Arts, Hon. mem. of Arch. Insts in England, Scotland, Germany, USA. Awards in competitions include: Min. of Foreign Affairs, Riyadh, 1980; Kammergericht, Berlin, 1979; Compton Verney Opera House, 1989; Conf. Centre, Cambridge, 1989; New Concert Hall, Copenhagen, 1993; Danish Design Centre, Copenhagen, 1994; architectural prizes: Aga Khan Award, 1989; Domino's 30 architects, 1988; Marble Architectural Award, Carrara, 1990; Internat. Design Award, UK, 1987. *Address:* Kronprinsessegade 46B, II, 1306 Copenhagen K, Denmark. *T:* 33135079.

LARSON, Frederick H., DFM 1943; General Manager, Business Development, Alberta Opportunity Co., Edmonton, Alberta (Alberta Crown Corporation), 1974–90; *b* 24 Nov. 1913; *s* of Herman B. and Martha C. Larson; *m* 1941, Dorothy A. Layng; one *s*. *Educ:* University of Saskatchewan. Observer, RCAF, 1941–43. Member for Kindersley, Parliament of Canada, 1949–53; Delegate to UN, Paris, 1952. Ten years in oil and gas business, production refining and sales, domestic and offshore; eight years in financial trust business, representing financial interests, Canada amd Jamaica; three years in construction and engineering; agricultural interests, Saskatchewan; Agent-Gen. for Province of Saskatchewan in London, 1967–73. *Recreation:* golf. *Address:* c/o Alberta Opportunity Co., PO Box 1860, Ponoka, Alberta T0C 2H0, Canada. *Clubs:* Ranchmen's (Calgary); Mayfair Golf (Edmonton, Alta).

LARSSON, Comr John; Territorial Commander in New Zealand and Fiji, Salvation Army, since 1993; *b* 2 April 1938; *s* of Sture and Flora Larsson; *m* 1969, Freda Turner; two *s*. *Educ:* London Univ. (BD). Commnd as Salvation Army Officer, 1957, in corps, youth and trng work; Chief Sec., S America West, 1980–84; Principal, William Booth Meml Trng Coll., 1984–88; Admin. Planning, 1988–90; Territorial Comdr in UK and Republic of Ireland, 1990–93. *Publications:* Doctrine Without Tears, 1974; Spiritual Breakthrough, 1983; The Man Perfectly Filled with the Spirit, 1986; How Your Corps can Grow, 1988. *Recreations:* music, walking. *Address:* Salvation Army Territorial Headquarters, PO Box 6015, Wellington, New Zealand.

LASCELLES, family name of **Earl of Harewood.**

LASCELLES, Viscount; David Henry George Lascelles; freelance film and television producer; *b* 21 Oct. 1950; *s* and *heir* of 7th Earl of Harewood, *qv*; *m* 1979, Margaret Rosalind Messenger; three *s* one *d*; *m* 1990, Diane Jane Howse. *Educ:* The Hall Sch.; Westminster; Bristol Univ. *Address:* Harewood House, Harewood, Leeds, West Yorks LS17 9LG.

LASCELLES, Maj.-Gen. Henry Anthony, CB 1967; CBE 1962 (OBE 1945); DSO 1944; Director-General, Winston Churchill Memorial Trust, 1967–80; *b* 10 Jan. 1912; *s* of Edward Lascelles and Leila Kennett-Barrington; *m* 1941, Ethne Hyde Ussher Charles. *Educ:* Winchester; Oriel Coll., Oxford (MA). Served War of 1939–45: Egypt, North Africa, Sicily and Italy, rising to second in command of an armoured brigade. Instructor, Staff Coll., Camberley, 1947–49; GSO 1, HQ 7th Armoured Div., BAOR, 1949–52; Comdg Officer 6th Royal Tank Regt, BAOR, 1952–55; Instructor NATO Defence Coll., 1955–56; Brigadier Royal Armoured Corps HQ 2nd Infantry Div., BAOR, 1956–57; National Defence Coll., Canada, 1958–59; BGS Military Operations, War Office, 1959–62; Chief of Staff, HQ Northern Ireland Command, 1962–63; Maj.-General, General Staff, Far East Land Forces, 1963–66. Pres., British Water Ski Fedn, 1980–. *Recreations:* squash, tennis, golf, music, gardening. *Address:* Manor Farm Cottage, Hedgerley Green, Bucks SL2 3XJ. *T:* Gerrards Cross (01753) 883582. *Club:* Naval and Military.

LASCELLES, Mary Madge, FBA 1962; Hon. Fellow, Somerville College, 1967; *b* 7 Feb. 1900; *d* of William Horace and Madeline Lascelles. *Educ:* Sherborne School for Girls; Lady Margaret Hall, Oxford. Research Studentship, Westfield Coll., 1923; Assistant Lecturer, Royal Holloway Coll., 1926; Somerville College: Tutor in English Language and Literature, 1931; Fellow, 1932–67; Vice-Principal, 1947–60; University Lecturer in English Literature, 1960–66; Reader, 1966–67. *Publications:* Jane Austen and her Art, 1939; Shakespeare's Measure for Measure, 1953; (ed) The Works of Samuel Johnson, Yale vol. ix, A Journey to the Western Islands of Scotland, 1971; The Adversaries and Other Poems, 1971; Notions and Facts, 1973; The Story-Teller Retrieves the Past, 1980; Further Poems, 1982; Selected Poems, 1990; contributions to learned journals, etc. *Address:* Valley House, Cley, Holt, Norfolk NR25 7TR. *T:* Cley (01263) 740413. *Club:* University Women's.

LASDUN, Sir Denys (Louis), CH 1995; Kt 1976; CBE 1965; RA 1991; RIBA; architect in private practice, since 1935; with Peter Softley & Associates, since 1986; *b* 8 Sept. 1914; *s* of Norman Lasdun and Julie Abrahams; *m* 1954, Susan Bendit; two *s* one *d*. *Educ:* Rugby Sch.; Architectural Assoc. Served with Royal Engineers, 1939–45 (MBE). Practised with Wells Coates, Tecton and Drake. Hoffman Wood Professor of Architecture, University of Leeds, 1962–63. Assessor, Competitions for Belgrade Opera Hse, 1971, and new Parly Bldg, London, 1971–72. Principal works: housing and schools for Bethnal Green and Paddington; London HQ, NSW Govt; flats at 26 St James's Place; Royal College of Physicians (RIBA Trustees' Medal, 1992); Fitzwilliam College, and Christ's College extension, Cambridge; new University of East Anglia and work for the Universities of London (SOAS, Inst. of Educn, Law Inst., project for Courtauld Inst.), Leicester and Liverpool; National Theatre and IBM, South Bank; EEC HQ for European Investment Bank, Luxembourg; design for new Hurva Synagogue, Old City, Jerusalem; Cannock Community Hosp.; Genoa Opera House competition; office buildings, Fenchurch Street, EC4 and Milton Gate, EC2. Trustee, BM, 1975–85; Member: CIAM and MARS Gp, 1935–59; Jerusalem Town Planning Cttee, 1970; V & A Adv. Cttee, 1973–83; Slade Cttee, 1976–92; Arts Panel, Arts Council of GB, 1980–84; Académie d'Architecture, Paris, 1984–; Accademia Nazionale di San Luca, Rome, 1984–; Academician, Internat. Acad. of Architecture, Bulgaria, 1986. Hon. Fellow, American Institute of Architects, 1966; Hon. FRCP, 1975; Hon. FRIAS, 1994; Hon. Dip. AA, 1994. Hon. DA, Manchester, 1966; Hon. DLitt: E Anglia, 1974; Sheffield, 1978. RIBA London Architecture Bronze Medallist, 1960 and 1964; Civic Trust Awards: Class I, 1967; Group A, 1969; Special Award, São Paulo Biennale, Brazil, 1969; Concrete Society Award, 1976; Royal Gold Medal for Architecture, RIBA, 1977; RIBA Architectural, Award for London Region, 1978; Wolf Prize in Arts (Architecture), Wolf Foundn, 1992; Centenary Medal, Architects' Jl, 1995. *Publications include:* An Architect's Approach to Architecture, 1965 (RIBA Jl); A Language and a Theme, 1976; Architecture in an Age of Scepticism, 1984. *Relevant publication:* Denys Lasdun: architecture, city, landscape, 1994, by William Curtis. *Address:* 146 Grosvenor Road, SW1V 3JY. *T:* 0171–630 8211.

LASH, Prof. Nicholas Langrishe Alleyne, DD; Norris-Hulse Professor of Divinity, University of Cambridge, since 1978; Fellow, Clare Hall, since 1988; *b* 6 April 1934; *s* of late Henry Alleyne Lash and Joan Mary Lash (*née* Moore); *m* 1976, Janet Angela Chalmers; one *s*. *Educ:* Downside Sch.; Oscott Coll.; St Edmund's House, Cambridge. MA, PhD, BD, DD. Served RE, 1952–57. Oscott Coll., 1957–63; Asst Priest, Slough, 1963–68; Fellow, 1969–85, Dean, 1971–75, St Edmund's House, Cambridge; Univ. Asst Lectr, Cambridge, 1974–78. *Publications:* His Presence in the World, 1968; Change in Focus, 1973; Newman on Development, 1975; Voices of Authority, 1976; Theology on Dover Beach, 1979; A Matter of Hope, 1982; Theology on the Way to Emmaus, 1986; Easter in Ordinary, 1988; Believing three ways in one God, 1992. *Address:* Faculty of Divinity, St John's Street, Cambridge CB2 1TW. *T:* Cambridge (01223) 332593; 4 Hertford Street, Cambridge CB4 3AG.

LASKEY, Prof. Ronald Alfred, FRS 1984; Charles Darwin Professor of Animal Embryology, since 1983 and Fellow of Darwin College, since 1982, University of Cambridge; *b* 26 Jan. 1945; *s* of Thomas Leslie and Bessie Laskey; *m* 1971, Margaret Ann Page; one *s* one *d*. *Educ:* High Wycombe Royal Grammar Sch.; Queen's Coll., Oxford. MA, DPhil 1970. Scientific Staff: Imperial Cancer Research Fund, 1970–73; MRC Lab. of Molecular Biology, 1973–83; Co-Dir, Molecular Embryology Group, Cancer Research Campaign, 1983–91; CRC Dir, Wellcome CRC Inst., 1991–. Mem., Academia Europaea,

1989. Colworth Medal, Biochem. Soc., 1979. *Publications:* articles on cell biology in scientific jls. *Recreations:* building, music, theatre. *Address:* Wellcome Trust/Cancer Research Campaign Institute for Cancer and Developmental Biology, Tennis Court Road, Cambridge CB2 1QR. *T:* Cambridge (01223) 334106.

LASKO, Prof. Peter Erik, CBE 1981; FSA; FBA 1978; Professor of the History of Art, Courtauld Institute, University of London, 1974–85; Director, Courtauld Institute, 1974–85; *b* 5 March 1924; *s* of Leo Lasko and Wally Lasko (*née* Seifert); *m* 1948, Gwendoline Joan Norman; three *d. Educ:* Courtauld Institute, Univ. of London. BA Hons 1949. Asst Keeper, British Museum, 1950–65; Prof. of the Visual Arts, Univ. of East Anglia, 1965–73. Member: Cathedrals Adv. Commn, 1981–91; Royal Commn on Historical Monuments (England), 1984–91; Cathedrals Fabric Commn, 1991–96; Trustee: British Mus., 1981–95; Royal Armouries, 1984–91. *Publication:* Ars Sacra 800–1200 (Pelican History of Art), 1972, 2nd edn 1994. *Address:* The Green, 17 Lower Street, Hoveton St John, Norwich NR12 8JG.

LASKY, Melvin Jonah, MA; Editor, Encounter Magazine, 1958–90; *b* New York City, 15 Jan. 1920; *s* of Samuel Lasky and Esther Lasky (*née* Kantrowitz); *m* 1947, Brigitte Newiger (marr. diss. 1974); one *s* one *d. Educ:* City Coll. of New York (BSS); Univ. of Michigan (MA); Columbia Univ. Literary Editor, The New Leader (NY), 1942–43; US Combat Historian in France and Germany, 1944–45; Capt., US Army, 1946; Foreign Correspondent, 1946–48; Editor and Publisher, Der Monat (Berlin), 1948–58 and 1978–83; Co-Editor, Encounter Magazine (London), 1958–90; Editorial Director, Library Press, NY, 1970–80; Publisher, Alcove Press, London, 1972–82. Regular television broadcaster, Cologne, Zürich and Vienna, 1955–. Fellow, Inst. of Advanced Study, Berlin, 1988–89. Hon. PhD York (Canada), 1990. Univ. of Michigan, Sesquicentennial Award, 1967; Distinguished Alumnus Award, City Univ., NY, 1978. *Publications:* Reisenotizen und Tagebücher, 1958; Africa for Beginners, 1962; Utopia and Revolution, 1976 (Spanish edn 1982; German edn 1989); On the Barricades, and Off, 1989; Voices in a Revolution, 1991 (also German edn); contributor to: America and Europe, 1951; New Paths in American History, 1965; Sprache und Politik, 1969; Festschrift for Raymond Aron, 1971; (ed) The Hungarian Revolution, 1957. *Address:* Mommsen Strasse 67, 10629 Berlin, Germany; 37 Godfrey Street, Chelsea, SW3 3SX. *Club:* Garrick.

LASLETT, (Thomas) Peter (Ruffell), FBA 1979; Reader in Politics and the History of Social Structure, Cambridge University, 1966–83; Co-Founder and Director, Cambridge Group for the History of Population and Social Structure, since 1964; Fellow of Trinity College, Cambridge, since 1953; *b* 18 Dec. 1915; *s* of Rev. G. H. R. Laslett and E. E. Laslett (*née* Alden); *m* 1947, Janet Crockett Clark; two *s. Educ:* Watford Grammar Sch.; St John's Coll., Cambridge. Served War, Royal Navy, 1940–45: Lieut RNVR, Japanese Naval Intelligence. Producer, BBC, 3rd Programme Talks, 1946–49; Fellow: St John's Coll., Cambridge, 1948–51; Inst. for Advanced Study, Princeton, 1959; Member, Working Party on Foundn of Open Univ., 1965; Founder (with Michael Young and others) University of the Third Age, 1981. Visiting Professor: Collège de France, Paris, 1976; Yale Univ., 1977. DUniv: Open, 1980; Keele, 1993. *Publications:* Locke's Two Treatises of Government, 1960, 3rd edn 1988; The World We Have Lost, 1965, 3rd edn 1983; (with R. Wall) Household and Family in Past Time, 1972; Family Life and Illicit Love in Earlier Generations, 1977; (with R. M. Smith and others) Bastardy and its Comparative History, 1980; A Fresh Map of Life, 1989, 2nd edn 1995; (with J. Fishkin) Justice between Age Groups and Generations, 1992; (with D. Kertzer) Ageing in the Past, 1995. *Recreations:* book collecting, gardening. *Address:* Trinity College, Cambridge CB2 1TQ; 27 Trumpington Street, Cambridge CB2 1QA. *T:* (Cambridge Group) Cambridge (01223) 333181.

LASOK, Prof. Dominik, QC 1982; PhD, LLD; Professor of European Law, 1973–86, and Director of Centre for European Legal Studies, 1972–86, University of Exeter; *b* 4 Jan. 1921; *s* of late Alojzy Lasok and Albina (*née* Przybyla); *m* 1952, Sheila May Corrigan; one *s* three *d* (and one *s* decd). *Educ:* secondary educn in Poland and Switzerland; Fribourg Univ. (Lic. en Droit); Univ. of Durham (LLM); Univ. of London (PhD, LLD); Universitas Polonorum in Exteris (Dr Juris). Called to the Bar, Middle Temple, 1954. Served Polish Army, Poland, France and Italy, 1939–46 (British, French and Polish mil. decorations). Industry, 1948–51; commerce, 1954–58; academic career, 1958–: Prof. of Law, Univ. of Exeter, 1968. Visiting Professor: William and Mary, Williamsburg, Va, 1966–67 and 1977; McGill, Montreal, 1976–77; Rennes, 1980–81; Fribourg, 1984; Coll. d'Europe, Bruges, 1984–86; Aix-Marseille, 1985; Marmara, Istanbul, 1987–94; Chukyo, Nagoya, 1990; Surugadi, Hanno-shi, 1990; Poznan, 1994–95. Dhc Aix/Marseille, 1987. Officier dans l'Ordre des Palmes Académiques, 1983. *Publications:* Polish Family Law, 1968; (jtly, also ed) Polish Civil Law, 4 vols, 1973–75; (with J. W. Bridge) Law and Institutions of the European Communities, 1973, 6th edn 1994; The Law of the Economy in the European Communities, 1980; (jtly, also ed) Les Communautés Européennes en Fonctionnement, 1981; Customs Law of the European Communities, 1983, 2nd edn 1990; Professions and Services in the European Community, 1986; (with P. A. Stone) Conflict of Laws in the European Community, 1987; (contrib.) Halsbury's Laws of England, 5th edn 1991; Turkey and the European Community, 1992; over 160 articles in British and foreign legal jls. *Address:* Reed, Barley Lane, Exeter EX4 1TA. *T:* Exeter (01392) 72582.

See also K. P. E. Lasok.

LASOK, Karol Paul Edward; QC 1994; *b* 16 July 1953; *s* of Prof. Dominik Lasok, *qv*; *m* 1991, Karen Bridget Morgan Griffith; one *d. Educ:* St Mary's Sch., Clyst St Mary; Jesus Coll., Cambridge (MA); Exeter Univ. (LLM, PhD). Called to the Bar, Middle Temple, 1977; Legal Sec., Court of Justice of the EC, 1980–84 and (*locum tenens*) 1985; private practice, 1985–. Consultant Editor, Butterworths European Court Practice. *Publications:* The European Court of Justice: practice and procedure, 1984, 2nd edn 1994; contribs to: Halsbury's Laws of England, 4th edn, vols 51 and 52; Law of European Communities (ed D. Vaughan); Lasok and Bridge's Law and Institutions of the European Union, 6th edn, 1994; (with J. Lever) Weinberg and Blank on Takeovers and Mergers; legal periodicals. *Recreation:* amusing daughter. *Address:* 4 Raymond Buildings, Gray's Inn, WC1R 5BP. *T:* 0171–405 7211.

LAST, Maj.-Gen. Christopher Neville, CB 1990; OBE 1976; Chief Executive, Clwyd Family Health Services Authority, since 1990; *b* 2 Sept. 1935; *s* of Jack Neville Last, MPS, FSMC, FBOA and Lorna (*née* Goodman), MPS; *m* 1961, Pauline Mary Lawton; two *d. Educ:* Culford Sch.; Brighton Tech. Coll. psc†, ndc. Commnd Royal Signals, 1956; Germany, Parachute Bde, Borneo, Singapore, 1956–67; OC 216 Para. Signal Sqdn, 1967; RMCS and Staff Coll., Logistics Staff 1 (BR) Corps, 1968–71; NDC, 1972; Lt-Col, Signal Staff HQ, BAOR, 1973; CO Royal Signals NI, 1974; Staff, MoD Combat Develt, 1976, Mil. Ops, 1977; Col, Project Manager MoD (PE) for Army ADP Comd and Control, 1977; CO (Col) 8 Signal Regt Trng, Royal Signals, 1980; Brig., Comd 1 Signal Bde 1 (BR) Corps, 1981; Dir, Mil. Comd and Control Projects, MoD (PE), 1984; Head of Defence Procurement Policy (Studies Team), on Chief of Defence Procurement Personal Staff, MoD (PE), 1985; Maj.-Gen. 1986; Vice Master Gen. of the Ordnance, 1986–88; Mil. Dep. to Head of Defence Export Services, 1988–90. Col Comdt, RCS, 1990–. Chm., Royal Signals Instn, 1994–. Dep. Pres., BRCS N Wales, 1993–. Liveryman, Co. of Information Technologists, 1988; Freeman, City of London, 1988. *Recreations:* travel, theatre, ballet, sailing, ski-ing, shooting and country pursuits, hockey (Army and Combined Services). *Address:* c/o National Westminster Bank, 34 North Street, Lancing, Sussex BN15 9AB. *Clubs:* Special Forces, Fadeaways.

LAST, John William, CBE 1989; Director, Public Affairs, North West Water Group, since 1993; Chairman, Museums Training Institute, since 1990; *b* 22 Jan. 1940; *s* of late Jack Last (sometime Dir of Finance, Metrop. Police) and Freda Last (*née* Evans); *m* 1967, Susan Josephine, *er d* of John and late Josephine Farmer; three *s. Educ:* Sutton Grammar Sch., Surrey; Trinity Coll., Oxford (MA 1965). Littlewoods Organisation, Liverpool, 1969–93. Director: Boom, 1990–93; Inward, investment agency for NW, 1992–. Mem., Merseyside CC, 1973–86 (Chm., Arts Cttee, 1977–81); contested (C) Liverpool, West Derby, Feb. and Oct. 1974, Stockport N, 1979. Vis. Prof., City Univ., London, 1987–. Bd Mem., Royal Liverpool Philharmonic Soc., 1973–93 (Chm., 1977–81, 1986–92); Founder Chairman: Merseyside Maritime Museum, 1977; Empire Theatre (Merseyside) Trust, 1979–81 (Bd Mem., 1986–); Chairman: Walker Art Gall., Liverpool, 1977–81; Library Assoc./Arts Council Wkg Party on Art in Libraries, 1982–84; Wkg Party to form Merseyside TEC, 1989–90; Nat. Chm., Area Museums Councils of GB, 1979–82; Vice-Pres., NW Museum and Art Gall. Service, 1992– (Chm., 1977–82, 1987–92); Vice-Chm., Merseyside Arts, 1985–88; Member: Museums Assoc. Council, 1978–86 (Vice-Pres., 1983); Arts Council of GB, 1980–84 (Chm., Housing the Arts Cttee, 1981–84; Chm., Regional Cttee, 1981–84); Museums and Galleries Commn, 1983– (Mem., Scottish Wkg Pty, 1984–85); Enquiry into Tyne and Wear Service, 1988–89; Chm., Enquiry into Local Authorities and Museums, 1989–91; Bd, Northern Ballet Theatre, 1986– (Vice Chm., 1986–88); Merseyside Tourism Bd, 1986–92; NW Industrial Council, 1985–; Court, Liverpool Univ., 1973– (Mem. Council, 1977–81, 1986–); Calcutt Cttee on Privacy and Intrusion by the Press, 1989–90; Lay Mem., Press Council, 1980–86; Advr on Local Govt to Arts Council, 1984–91; Chm., Arts, Initiative and Money Cttee, Gulbenkian Foundn, 1980–83. Mem. Bd, Charities Trust, 1990–; Trustee: Norton Priory Museum, 1983–87; V&A Museum, 1984–86 (Mem., Adv. Council, 1978–84; Mem., Theatre Museum Cttee, 1983–86); Nat. Museums and Galls on Merseyside, 1986–; Governor: NYO, 1985–93; Nat. Mus. of Wales, 1994–. Patron, N Wales Music Festival, 1994–. FRSA 1988. Hon. FMA, 1987. Hon. Fellow, Liverpool John Moores Univ. (formerly Liverpool Polytechnic), 1989. Freedom of City of London, 1985; Freeman, Barber Surgeons' Co., 1985; Liveryman 1987. Merseyside Gold Medal for Achievement, 1991. *Publications:* A Brief History of Museums and Galleries, 1986; The Last Report on Local Authorities and Museums, 1991; reports: (jtly) Arts: the way forward, 1978; (jtly) A Future for the Arts, 1987. *Recreations:* swimming, music, Victoriana. *Address:* 106 Waterloo Warehouse, Waterloo Dock, Liverpool L3 0BQ. *T:* 0151–236 6734; Llannerch Hall, near St Asaph, Clwyd LL17 6BD. *Club:* Royal Automobile.

LATEY, Rt. Hon. Sir John (Brinsmead), Kt 1965; MBE (mil.) 1943; PC 1986; Judge of the High Court of Justice, Family Division (formerly Probate, Divorce and Admiralty Division), 1965–89; *b* 7 March 1914; *s* of late William Latey, CBE, QC, and Anne Emily, *d* of late Horace G. Brinsmead; *m* 1938, Betty Margaret (*née* Beresford); one *s* one *d. Educ:* Westminster; Christ Church, Oxford. MA (Hon. Sch. Jurispr.). Called to the Bar, 1936; QC 1957. Served in Army during War, 1939–45, mainly in MEF (Lieut-Colonel, 1944–). General Council of the Bar, 1952–56, 1957–61 and 1964– (Hon. Treasurer, 1959–61). Master of the Bench of the Middle Temple, 1964. Chairman, Lord Chancellor's Cttee on Age of Majority, 1965–67. Dep. Chairman, Oxfordshire QS, 1966. *Publications:* (Asst Ed.) Latey on Divorce, 14th edn, 1952; Halsbury's Laws of England (Conflict of Laws: Husband and Wife), 1956. *Recreations:* golf, bridge, chess. *Address:* 16 Daylesford Avenue, Roehampton, SW15 5QR. *T:* 0181–876 6436. *Club:* United Oxford & Cambridge University.

LATHAM, family name of **Baron Latham.**

LATHAM, 2nd Baron *cr* 1942, of Hendon; **Dominic Charles Latham;** Senior Structural Engineer with Gerard Barry Associates, since 1992; *b* 20 Sept. 1954; *s* of Hon. Francis Charles Allman Latham (*d* 1959) and Gabrielle Monica (*d* 1987), *d* of Dr S. M. O'Riordan; *S* grandfather, 1970. *Educ:* Univ. of New South Wales, Australia (BEng (civil), 1977, Hons I; MEngSc 1981). Civil Engr, Electricity Commn, NSW, 1979–88; Structl Engr, Rankine & Hill, Consulting Engrs, 1988–91. Teacher, Rock around the Clock Dancing, 1993–. *Recreations:* rock-'n'-roll/ballroom dancing, electronics, personal computing, sailboarding. *Heir:* *yr* twin *b* Anthony Michael Latham, *b* 20 Sept. 1954. *Address:* PO Box 355, Kensington, NSW 2033, Australia.

LATHAM, Arthur Charles; Member (Lab), Havering Council (formerly Romford Borough Council), 1952–78 and since 1986, Leader, since 1990; *b* Leyton, 14 Aug. 1930; *m* 1951, Margaret Latham; one *s* one *d. Educ:* Romford Royal Liberty Sch.; Garnett Coll. of Educn. Lectr in Further Educn, Southgate Technical Coll., 1967–. Havering Council (formerly Romford Borough Council): Leader, Labour Gp, 1962–70 and 1986–; Leader of the Opposition, 1986–90; Alderman, 1962–78. Mem., NE Regional Metropolitan Hosp. Bd, 1966–72; part-time Mem., July-Nov. 1983, Mem., 1983–84, LTE. MP (Lab) Paddington N, Oct. 1969–1974, City of Westminster, Paddington, 1974–79; Founder, and Jt Chm., All Party Gp for Pensioners, 1971–79; Chm., Tribune Gp, 1975–76 (Treasurer, 1977–79). Contested (Lab): Woodford, 1959; Rushcliffe, Notts, 1964; City of Westminster, Paddington, 1979; Westminster N, 1983. Chm., Greater London Lab. Party, 1977–; Vice-Chm., Nat. Cttee, Labour League of Youth, 1949–53; Vice-President: Labour Action for Peace; AMA; Treasurer, Liberation (Movement for Colonial Freedom), 1969–79; Member: British Campaign for Peace in Vietnam; Campaign for Nuclear Disarmament. Vegetarian. *Recreations:* bridge, chess, cricket. *Address:* 17 Tudor Avenue, Gidea Park, Romford RM2 5LB.

LATHAM, Cecil Thomas, OBE 1976; Stipendiary Magistrate, Greater Manchester (sitting at Salford), 1976–94; *b* 11 March 1924; *s* of Cecil Frederick James Latham and Elsie Winifred Latham; *m* 1945, Ivy Frances (*née* Fowle); one *s* one *d. Educ:* Rochester Cathedral Choir Sch.; King's Sch., Rochester. Solicitor. War Service, 1942–45. Asst Clerk, Magistrates' Courts: Chatham, 1939–42; Maidstone, 1945; Leicester, 1948–54; Bromley, 1954–63; Dep. Justices' Clerk, Liverpool, 1963–65; Justices' Clerk, Manchester, 1965–76. Member: Magistrates' Courts Rule Cttee, 1966–94; Royal Commn on Criminal Procedure, 1978–81; Criminal Law Revision Cttee, 1981–94. Hon. MA Manchester, 1984. *Publications:* (ed) Stone's Justices' Manual, 101st-109th edns; How Much?: determining maintenance in magistrates' courts, 1976; Care Proceedings, 1989; (ed) Family Law Reports, 1980–86; specialist editor, Justice of the Peace Reports, 1986–; founder editor, Family Court Reporter, 1987–; contrib. Criminal Law Rev., Justice of Peace, Family Law. *Recreation:* music. *Address:* 59 Ravenoak Park Road, Cheadle Hulme, Cheshire SK8 7EH. *T:* 0161–485 1185.

LATHAM, Christopher George Arnot; Chairman, James Latham PLC, since 1987; *b* 4 June 1933; *s* of late Edward Bryan Latham and Anne Arnot Duncan; *m* 1963, Jacqueline Cabourdin; three *s. Educ:* Stowe Sch.; Clare Coll., Cambridge (MA). FCA. Articled Fitzpatrick Graham, chartered accountants, 1955; joined James Latham Ltd, timber importers, 1959, Dir 1963. A Forestry Comr, 1973–78. Dir, City and Inner London N TEC, 1991–. Pres., Inst. of Wood Sci., 1977–79; Chairman: Timber Res. and Develt Assoc., 1972–74; Commonwealth Forestry Assoc., 1975–77; Psychiatric Rehabilitation Assoc., 1983–91. Mem., Worshipful Co. of Builders Merchants, 1985–. FRGS 1995. *Recreations:* tennis, forestry. *Address:* 5 Canonbury Square, N1 2AU.

LATHAM, Hon. Sir David (Nicholas Ramsay), Kt 1992; **Hon. Mr Justice Latham;** a Judge of the High Court, Queen's Bench Division, since 1992; *b* 18 Sept. 1942; *s* of Robert Clifford Latham, CBE, FBA; *m* 1967, Margaret Elizabeth (*née* Forrest); three *d. Educ:* Bryanston Sch.; Queens' Coll., Cambridge (MA). Called to the Bar, Middle Temple, 1964, Bencher, 1989; QC 1985; one of the Junior Counsel to the Crown, Common Law, 1979–85; Junior Counsel to Dept of Trade in export credit matters, 1981–85; a Recorder, 1983–92; Presiding Judge, Midland and Oxford Circuit, 1995–. Vice-Chm., Council of Legal Educn, 1992– (Mem., 1988–); Member: Gen. Council of the Bar, 1987–92; Judicial Studies Bd, 1988–91. *Recreations:* reading, music. *Address:* Royal Courts of Justice, Strand WC2A 2LL. *Club:* Leander.

LATHAM, Sir Michael (Anthony), Kt 1993; DL; Chairman, Construction Industry Board, since 1995; Director, Ansoll Estates Ltd, since 1993; *b* 20 Nov. 1942; *m* 1969, Caroline Terry; two *s. Educ:* Marlborough Coll.; King's Coll., Cambridge; Dept of Educn, Oxford. BA Cantab 1964, MA Cantab 1968, CertEd Oxon 1965. Housing and Local Govt Officer, Conservative Research Dept, 1965–67; Parly Liaison Officer, Nat. Fedn of Building Trades Employers, 1967–73; Dir, House-builders Fedn, 1971–73. Westminster City Councillor, 1968–71. Contested (C) Liverpool, West Derby, 1970; MP (C) Melton, Feb. 1974–1983, Rutland and Melton, 1983–92. Vice-Chairman: Cons. Parly Housing Cttee, 1974–76; Cons. Parly Environment Cttee, 1979–83; Member: House of Commons Expenditure Cttee, 1974–79; Jt Cttee on Statutory Instruments, 1974–75; Jt Ecclesiastical Cttee of both Houses of Parliament, 1974–92; Select Cttee on Energy, 1979–82; Public Accounts Cttee, 1983–92; H of C Chairmen's Panel, 1987–92. Sec., British-Gibraltar Parly Gp, 1981–87; Chm., British-Israel Parly Gp, 1981–90; Vice President: Anglo-Israel Assoc., 1994– (Pres., 1990–94; Chm. Exec. Cttee, 1986–90); Cons. Friends of Israel, 1985– (Chm., 1982–85). Dir, Lovell Homes Ltd, 1975–85; Housing Adviser, Y. J. Lovell PLC, 1985–89; Dir, Lovell Partnerships, 1989–92; Dir, Building (Publications) Ltd, 1988–91; Corporate Affairs Dir, Builder Group, 1992–93; Public Affairs Consultant: Bldg Employers Confedn, 1992–93; House Builders Fedn, 1992–95. Chm., Jt Govt/Industry Rev. of Procurement and Contractual Problems in Construction Industry, 1993–94. Mem., Adv. Council on Public Records, 1985–91. Vice-Pres., Building Socs Assoc., 1981–91. Mem. Exec. Cttee, 1987–, Dir, 1992, CCJ. C of E Lay Reader, 1988–. Trustee, Oakham Sch., 1987–. FRSA 1992. Hon. FCIPS, 1994. DL Leics, 1994. *Publications:* articles on housing, land, town planning and building. *Recreations:* gardening, fencing, listening to classical music, cricket. *Address:* 508 Hood House, Dolphin Square, SW1V 3NH. *Club:* Carlton.

LATHAM, Air Vice-Marshal Peter Anthony, CB 1980; AFC 1960; *b* 18 June 1925; *s* of late Oscar Frederick Latham and Rhoda Latham; *m* 1953, Barbara Mary; two *s* six *d. Educ:* St Phillip's Grammar Sch., Birmingham; St Catharine's Coll., Cambridge. psa 1961. Joined RAF, 1944; 1946–69: served No 26, 263, 614, and 247 Sqdns; CFE; Air Min.; Comd No 111 Sqdn; RAF Formation Aerobatic Team (Leader of Black Arrows, 1959–60); MoD Jt Planning Staff; Comd NEAF Strike and PR Wing; Coll. of Air Warfare; Ops No 38 Gp; Comd RAF Tengah, 1969–71; MoD Central Staff, 1971–73; Comd Officer and Aircrew Selection Centre, Biggin Hill, 1973–74; SASO No 38 Gp, 1974–76; Dir Def. Ops, MoD Central Staff, 1976–77; AOC No 11 Group, 1977–81. Principal, Oxford Air Trng Sch., and Dir, CSE Aviation Ltd, 1982–85; Sen. Air Advr, Short Bros, 1985–90. Cdre, RAF Sailing Assoc., 1974–80; Pres., Assoc. of Service Yacht Clubs, 1978–81. Liveryman, Clockmakers' Co., 1987 (Mem., Ct of Assts, 1990–; Master, 1996). *Recreations:* sailing, horology. *Address:* c/o Lloyds Bank Ltd, 193 High Street, Deritend, Birmingham B12 0LJ. *Club:* Royal Air Force.

LATHAM, Richard Brunton; QC 1991; a Recorder, since 1987; *b* 16 March 1947; *s* of Frederick and Joan Catherine Latham; *m* 1972, Alison Mary Goodall; three *s. Educ:* Farnborough Grammar School; Univ. of Birmingham (LLB 1969). Called to the Bar, Gray's Inn, 1971; practice on Midland and Oxford Circuit; Standing Prosecuting Counsel to Inland Revenue, Midland and Oxford Circuit, 1987–91. Treas., Midland and Oxford Circuit, 1992–. *Recreations:* sailing, opera. *Address:* 9 Bedford Row, WC1R 4AZ. *T:* 0171–242 3555.

LATHAM, Sir Richard Thomas Paul, 3rd Bt, *cr* 1919, of Crow Clump; *b* 15 April 1934; *s* of Sir (Herbert) Paul Latham, 2nd Bt, and Lady Patricia Doreen Moore (*d* 1947), *o d* of 10th Earl of Drogheda; *S* father, 1955; *m* 1958, Marie-Louise Patricia, *d* of Frederick H. Russell, Vancouver, BC; two *d. Educ:* Eton; Trinity Coll., Cambridge. *Address:* 2125 Birnam Wood Drive, Santa Barbara, CA 93108, USA.

LATHAM, Roger Alan; County Treasurer, Nottinghamshire County Council, since 1991; *b* 3 May 1950; *s* of Edward and Florrie Latham; *m* 1973, Angela Judith Warwick (*née* Pearce); one *s. Educ:* Bristol Univ. (BSc Econs with Stats); Birmingham Univ. (MSocSc); Liverpool Polytechnic. IPFA. Economic Assistant, National Westminster Bank, 1972–76; Economist, 1976–85, Asst Chief Finance Officer, 1985–90, Dudley MBC; Dep. County Treasurer, Notts CC, 1990–91. Methodist Local Preacher. *Recreations:* photography, gardening, computers, reading, dinosaurs, Japanese films. *Address:* 25 Potters Lane, East Leake, Loughborough, Leics LE12 6NQ. *T:* Loughborough (01509) 856562.

LATHE, Prof. Grant Henry; Professor of Chemical Pathology, University of Leeds, 1957–77, now Emeritus Professor; *b* 27 July 1913; *s* of Frank Eugene and Annie Smith Lathe; *m* 1st, 1938, Margaret Eleanore Brown; one *s*; 2nd, 1950, Joan Frances Hamlin; one *s* two *d. Educ:* McGill Univ.; Oxford Univ. ICI Research Fellow: Dept. of Biochemistry, Oxford Univ., 1946; Dept. of Chemical Pathology, Post Graduate Medical School of London, 1948; Lecturer in Chemical Pathology, Guy's Hospital Medical School, 1948; Biochemist, The Bernhard Baron Memorial Research Laboratories, Queen Charlotte's Maternity Hospital, London, 1949. John Scott Award (with C. R. J. Ruthven), 1971, for invention of gel filtration. *Publications:* papers in medical and biochemical journals. *Recreations:* fell-walking, campaigning against nuclear weapons. *Address:* 12A The Avenue, Leeds LS8 1EH. *T:* Leeds (0113) 266 1507.

LATIMER, Sir (Courtenay) Robert, Kt 1966; CBE 1958 (OBE 1948); *b* 13 July 1911; *er s* of late Sir Courtenay Latimer, KCIE, CSI; *m* 1st, 1944, Elizabeth Jane Gordon (*née* Smail) (*d* 1989); one *s* one *d*; 2nd, 1990, Frederieka Jacoba Blankert (*née* Witteween). *Educ:* Rugby; Christ Church, Oxford. ICS, 1934 (Punjab); IPS, 1939; Vice-Consul, Bushire, 1940–41; Sec. Foreign Publicity Office, Delhi, 1941–42; Sec. Indian Agency Gen., Chungking, 1944; in NW Frontier Prov., as Asst Political Agent N Waziristan, Dir of Civil Supplies, Sec. to Governor and District Comr, Bannu, 1942–43 and 1945–47. HM Overseas Service, 1948; served in Swaziland, 1948–49; Bechuanaland Protectorate, 1951–54; Office of High Comr for Basutoland, the Bechuanaland Protectorate and Swaziland, as Asst Sec., 1949–51; Sec. for Finance, 1954–60; Chief Sec., 1960–64; Minister, British Embassy, Pretoria, 1965–66; Registrar, Kingston Polytechnic, 1967–76. *Recreations:* golf, photography. *Address:* Benedicts, Old Avenue, Weybridge, Surrey KT13 0PS.

LATIMER, Sir Graham (Stanley), KBE 1980; President, New Zealand Maori Council, since 1972 (Delegate, 1964; Vice-President, 1969–72); *b* Waiharara, N Auckland, 7 Feb. 1926; *s* of Graham Latimer and Lillian Edith Latimer (*née* Kenworthy); *m* 1948, Emily Patricia Moore; two *s* two *d. Educ:* Pukenui and Kaitaia District High School. Dairy farmer, 1961–. Chairman: Aotearoa Fisheries, 1991–; Crown Forestry Rental, 1991–; Moana Pacific, 1991–; Dep. Chm., Maori Fisheries Commn, 1989–90; Negotiator, NZ Maori Fisheries. Member: Tai Tokerau Dist Maori Council, 1962– (Sec. 1966–75; Chm., 1976–); Otamatea Maori Exec., 1959– (Sec. Treas. 1962–72, Chm. 1975–); Otamatea Maori Cttee, 1955–62; Arapaoa Maori Cttee, 1962– (Chm. 1962–69 and 1972–); N Auckland Power Bd, 1977–; Waitangi Tribunal, 1976–. Chairman: (since inception) Northland Community Coll.; Tai Tokerau Maori Trust Bd, 1979– (Mem., 1975–); Pacific Foundn, 1990–; Trustee: Kohanga Reo Nat. Trust, 1979–; Maori Education Foundn; Member: Ngatikahu Trust Bd, 1976–; Cttee, Nat. Art Gall. Museum and War Memorial; NZ Maori Arts and Crafts Inst., 1980–; Tourist Adv. Council; Northland Regional Develt Council, 1980–; Alcoholic Liquor Adv. Council, 1980–. Lay Canon, Auckland Anglican Cathedral, 1978; Mem. Gen. Synod. JP. *Recreations:* Rugby football, tennis. *Address:* RD1, Paparoa, Northland, New Zealand. *T:* (9) 4316837.

LATIMER, Sir Robert; *see* Latimer, Sir C. R.

LATOUR-ADRIEN, Hon. Sir (Jean François) Maurice, Kt 1971; Chief Justice of Mauritius, 1970–77; Chairman, Mauritius Union Assurance Co. Ltd, since 1982 (Director since 1978); *b* 4 March 1915; 2nd *s* of late Louis Constant Emile Adrien and late Maria Ella Latour. *Educ:* Royal Coll., Mauritius; Univ. Coll., London; Middle Temple, London. LLB 1940. Called to the Bar, Middle Temple, 1940. Mauritius: Dist Magistrate, 1947; Crown Counsel, 1950; Additl Subst. Procureur and Advocate-Gen., 1954; Sen. Crown Counsel, 1958; Asst Attorney-Gen., 1960; Solicitor-Gen., 1961; Dir of Public Prosecutions, 1964; Puisne Judge, 1966–70; Acting Governor-Gen., Feb. 1973, July–Aug. 1974, Jan.–Feb. and June–Aug. 1975, July–Sept. 1976. Pres., Mauritius Red Cross Soc., 1978–; Vice-Pres., Inst. Internat. de Droit d'Expression Française (IDEF). Pres., Mauritius Commercial Bank Ltd, 1993–94 (Dir, 1980–83, 1984–87, 1988–91, 1992–; Vice-Pres., 1992–93); Legal Consultant: Mauritius Commercial Bank Ltd, 1983–; Promotion and Development Ltd, 1985–; Mauritius Commercial Bank Finance Corp., 1991–94; Mauritius Commercial Bank Registry and Securities, 1991–; Caudan Development Co. Ltd, 1991–. President: Mental Health Assoc., 1985– (Vice-Pres., 1978–84); Mauritius Red Cross, 1978–. Mem., War Meml Bd of Trustees, 1978–84 (Vice Pres., 1985–). KLJ 1969. *Address:* Vacoas, Mauritius; c/o Mauritius Union Assurance Co. Ltd, 4 Léoville l'Homme Street, Port Louis, Mauritius.

LA TROBE-BATEMAN, Richard George Saumarez; structures designer/maker; *b* 17 Oct. 1938; *s* of John La Trobe-Bateman and Margaret (*née* Schmid); *m* 1969, Mary Elizabeth Jolly; one *s* two *d. Educ:* Westminster Sch.; St Martin's Sch. of Art; Royal Coll. of Art (MDesRCA). Set up workshop, 1968. Member: Council of Management, British Crafts Centre, 1975–86; Council, Contemporary Applied Arts, 1987–; Crafts Council: Mem., 1984–86; Index Selector, 1972–73; Chm., Index Selection Cttee, 1980–82. Work in: V&A Collection, 1979; Crafts Council Collection, 1981 and 1984; Keble Coll., Oxon, 1981; Temple Newsam Collection, 1983; Southern Arts Collection, 1983; Pembroke Coll., Oxon, 1984; Crafts Study Centre Collection, Bath, 1985; Northern Arts Collection 1988, work presented by Crafts Council to the Prince of Wales, 1982. Vis. Prof., San Diego State Univ., 1986–87. *Publications:* articles in Crafts, American Crafts. *Recreations:* listening to music, hill-walking. *Address:* Elm House, Batcombe, Shepton Mallet, Somerset BA4 6AB. *T:* Upton Noble (01749) 850442. *Club:* Contemporary Applied Arts.

LATTER, Leslie William; Director General, Merseyside Passenger Transport Executive, 1977–86; *b* 4 Nov. 1921; *s* of William Richard and Clara Maud Latter; *m* 1948, Pamela Jean Marsh; one *s* decd. *Educ:* Beckenham Grammar Sch., Kent. IPFA, FCIT. Served Royal Air Force, 1940–46. London County Council, 1947–62; Chief Asst, Beckenham Borough Council, 1962–64; Asst Borough Treasurer, Bromley, 1964–68; Dep. Borough Treasurer, Greenwich, 1968–74; Dir of Finance and Administration, Merseyside PTE, 1974–77. *Recreations:* gardening, music. *Address:* The Nursery, 19 Saxon Close, Seabrook Road, Hythe, Kent CT21 5QS. *T:* Hythe (01303) 264959.

LATTER, Michèle Brigitte; *see* Roberts, M. B.

LATTO, Dr Douglas; private medical practice; Chairman, British Safety Council, since 1971 (Vice-Chairman, 1968–71); *b* Dundee, Scotland, 13 Dec. 1913; *s* of late David Latto, Town Clerk of Dundee, and late Christina Latto; *m* 1945, Dr Edith Monica Druitt (*d* 1990); one *s* three *d. Educ:* Dundee High Sch.; St Andrews Univ. MB, ChB (St And.) 1939; DObst, RCOG 1944, MRCOG 1949, FRCOG 1989. During War: Ho. Surg., Dundee Royal Infirmary, 1939; Ho. Phys., Cornelia and East Dorset Hosp., Poole, 1940; Resident Obstetrician and Gynaecologist, Derbyshire Hosp. for Women, Derby, 1940; Res. Surgical Officer, Hereford Gen. Hosp., 1941; Res. Obst. and Gynaec., East End Maternity Hosp., London, 1942; Res. Obst. and Gynaec., City of London Maternity Hosp., 1943; Res. Surgical Officer, Birmingham Accident Hosp., 1944; Casualty Officer, Paddington Gen. Hosp., London, 1944; Asst Obst. and Gynaec., Mayday Hosp., Croydon, 1945. Res. Obst. and Gynaec., Southlands Hosp., Shoreham-by-Sea, Sussex, 1946–49; Asst, Nuffield Dept of Obstetrics and Gynaecology, Radcliffe Infirmary, Oxford, 1949–51. Member: BMA; Council, Soil Assoc.; Chm., Plantmilk Soc.; Vice-President: International Vegetarian Union; GB Philatelic Soc., 1986–. Governor, Internat. Inst. of Safety Management. Freeman, City of London, 1988; Liveryman, Worshipful Co. of Apothecaries. Mem., Order of the Cross. FRSocMed; FRPSL 1975. Estabd right to arms, 1995. Silver Jubilee Medal, 1977; Sword of Honour, British Safety Council, 1985. *Publications:* Smoking and Lung Cancer: a report to all Members of Parliament for the British Safety Council, May 1969; contribs to BMJ; Proc. Royal Soc. Med.; Philatelic Jl; etc. *Recreations:* squash, travelling, gardening, philately (Internat. Stamp Exhibns: Large Gold Medal, London, 1970; Gold Medal, Brussels, 1972, Munich, 1973, Basle, 1974; Large Gold Medals: Paris 1975; Copenhagen, 1976 (and Prix d'Honneur); London, 1980 (and GB Philatelic Soc. Award); Vienna, 1981. *Address:* Lethnot Lodge, 4 Derby Road, Caversham, Reading, Berks RG4 0EY. *T:* Reading (01734) 472282. *Clubs:* Royal Automobile, Rolls-Royce Enthusiasts' (Paulersbury).

LATYMER, 8th Baron *cr* 1431; **Hugo Nevill Money-Coutts;** *b* 1 March 1926; *s* of 7th Baron Latymer and Patience (*d* 1982), *d* of late William Courtenay-Thompson; *S* father, 1987; *m* 1st, 1951, Hon. Penelope Ann Clare (marr. diss. 1965), *yr d* of late T. A. Emmet and Baroness Emmet of Amberley; two *s* one *d*; 2nd 1965, Jinty, *d* of late Peter George Calvert; one *s* two *d. Educ:* Eton. *Heir: s* Hon. Crispin James Alan Nevill Money-Coutts [*b* 8 March 1955; *m* 1978, Hon. Lucy Rose, *y d* of Baron Deedes, *qv*; one *s* two *d*]. *Address:* Vivero Hortus, Santa Maria, Mallorca, Spain.

LAUDER, Sir Piers Robert Dick-, 13th Bt *cr* 1688; *S* father, 1981.

LAUDERDALE, 17th Earl of, *cr* 1624; **Patrick Francis Maitland;** Baron Maitland, 1590; Viscount Lauderdale, 1616; Viscount Maitland, Baron Thirlestane and Boltoun, 1624; Bt of Nova Scotia, 1680; Hereditary Bearer of the National Flag of Scotland, 1790 and 1952; Chief of the Clan Maitland; *b* 17 March 1911; *s* of Reverend Hon. Sydney G. W. Maitland and Ella Frances (*née* Richards); *S* brother, 1968; *m* 1936, Stanka, *d* of Professor Milivoje Lozanitch, Belgrade Univ.; two *s* two *d*. *Educ:* Lancing Coll., Sussex; Brasenose Coll., Oxford. BA Hons Oxon, 1933; Journalist 1933–59. Appts include: Balkans and Danubian Corresp., The Times, 1939–41; Special Corresp. Washington, News Chronicle, 1941; War Corresp., Pacific, Australia, New Zealand, News Chronicle, 1941–43. Foreign Office, 1943–45. MP (U) for Lanark Div. of Lanarks, 1951–Sept. 1959 (except for period May-Dec. 1957 when Ind. C). Founder and Chairman, Expanding Commonwealth Group, House of Commons, 1955–59; re-elected Chairman, Nov. 1959. Chm., Sub-Cttee on Energy, Transport and Res., House of Lords Select Cttee on EEC Affairs, 1974–79; Vice Chm. and Co-founder, Parly Gp for Energy Studies, 1980–. Dir, Elf Petroleum (UK). Editor of The Fleet Street Letter Service, and of The Whitehall Letter, 1945–58. Mem., Coll. of Guardians of National Shrine of Our Lady of Walsingham, Norfolk, 1955–82 (Guardian Emeritus, 1982–). President, The Church Union, 1956–61. FRGS. *Publications:* European Dateline, 1945; Task for Giants, 1957. *Heir: s* The Master of Lauderdale, Viscount Maitland, *qv*. *Address:* 10 Ovington Square, SW3 1LH. *T:* 0171–589 7451; 12 St Vincent Street, Edinburgh. *T:* 0131–556 5692. *Club:* New (Edinburgh).

See also R. W. P. H. Hay, Lady H. O. Maitland.

LAUDERDALE, Master of; *see* Maitland, Viscount.

LAUGHARNE, Albert, CBE 1983; QPM 1978; Deputy Commissioner, Metropolitan Police, 1983–85; *b* 20 Oct. 1931; *s* of Reginald Stanley Laugharne and Jessica Simpson Laugharne; *m* 1954, Barbara Thirlwall; two *d*. *Educ:* Baines' Grammar Sch., Poulton-le-Fylde; Manchester Univ. Detective Inspector, Manchester City Police, 1952–66; Supt, Cumbria Constab., 1966–70; Chief Supt, W Yorks Constab., 1970–73; Asst Chief Constable, Cheshire Constab., 1973–76; Chief Constable: Warwicks, 1977–78; Lancashire, 1978–83. RCDS, 1975. *Publication:* Seaford House Papers, 1975. *Recreations:* gardening, painting.

LAUGHLAND, (Graham Franklyn) Bruce, QC 1977; **His Honour Judge Laughland;** a Circuit Judge, since 1989, at the Central Criminal Court; *b* 18 Aug. 1931; 3rd *s* of late Andrew and late Constance Laughland; *m* 1969, Victoria Nicola Christina Jarman (*d* 1994); one *s*. *Educ:* King Edward's Sch., Birmingham; Christ Church, Oxford (MA). Stick of Honour, Mons Officer Cadet Sch., 1954; Lieut 8th RTR, 1954–56. Called to Bar, Inner Temple, 1958, Bencher, 1985; Dep. Chm., Bucks QS, 1971; Standing Counsel to the Queen's Proctor, 1968; a Recorder, 1972–89; First Prosecuting Counsel to the Inland Revenue (Midland and Oxford Circuit), 1973–77; actg Judge of the Supreme Court of the Falkland Is, 1985–. Mem., Gen. Council of the Bar, 1970; Treas., Midland and Oxford Circuit, 1986–89. Chm., Westminster Assoc. for Youth, 1984–89. Liveryman, Curriers' Co., 1992–. *Address:* Central Criminal Court, EC4M 7EH.

LAUGHTON, Sir Anthony Seymour, Kt 1987; FRS 1980; oceanographic consultant; Director, Institute of Oceanographic Sciences, 1978–88; *b* 29 April 1927; *s* of Sydney Thomas Laughton and Dorothy Laughton (*née* Chamberlain); m 1st, 1957, Juliet Ann Chapman (marr. diss. 1962); one *s*; 2nd, 1973, Barbara Clare Bosanquet; two *d*. *Educ:* Marlborough Coll.; King's Coll., Cambridge (MA, PhD). RNVR, 1945–48. John Murray Student, Columbia Univ., NY, 1954–55; Nat. Inst. of Oceanography, later Inst. of Oceanographic Sciences, 1955–88: research in marine geophysics in Atlantic and Indian Oceans, esp. in underwater photography, submarine morphology, ocean basin evolution, midocean ridge tectonics; Principal Scientist of deep sea expedns. Member: Co-ordinating Cttee for Marine Sci. and Technol., 1987–91; nat. and internat. cttees on oceanography and geophysics. President: Challenger Soc. for Marine Sci., 1988–90; Soc. for Underwater Technol., 1995–. Member Council: Royal Soc., 1986–87; Marine Biology Assoc., 1980–83, 1988–92; Soc. for Underwater Technology, 1986–92. Member: Governing Body, Charterhouse Sch., 1981– (Chm., 1995–); Council, University Coll. London, 1983–93; Adv. Council, Ocean Policy Inst., Hawaii, 1991–. Trustee, Natural Hist. Mus., 1990–94. Silver Medal, RSA, 1958; Cuthbert Peek grant, RGS, 1967; Prince Albert 1er Monaco Gold Medal for Oceanography, 1980; Founders Medal, RGS, 1987; Murchison Medal, Geol. Soc., 1989. *Publications:* papers on marine geophysics and oceanography. *Recreations:* music, gardening, sailing. *Address:* Okelands, Pickhurst Road, Chiddingfold, Surrey GU8 4TS. *T:* Wormley (01428) 683941.

LAUGHTON, Prof. Michael Arthur, PhD, DSc; FEng 1989; FIEE; Professor of Electrical Engineering, Queen Mary and Westfield (formerly Queen Mary) College, since 1977, and Dean of Engineering, since 1990, University of London; *b* 18 Dec. 1934; *s* of William Arthur Laughton and Laura (*née* Heap); *m* 1960, Margaret Mary Coleman; two *s* two *d*. *Educ:* King Edwards Five Ways Sch., Birmingham; Etobicoke Collegiate Inst., Toronto; Toronto Univ. (BASc 1957); Univ. of London (PhD 1965; DSc(Eng) 1976). CEng, FIEE 1977. GEC, Witton, 1957–61; Queen Mary, later Queen Mary and Westfield, College, London University: Res. Student, Dept of Elect. Engrg, 1961–64; Lectr, 1964–72; Reader, 1972–77; Dean, Faculty of Engrg, 1983–85; Pro-Principal, 1985–89. Visiting Professor: Purdue Univ., USA, 1966; Tokyo Univ., 1977. Sec. and Dir, Unicom Ltd, 1971–74; Dir, QMC Industrial Res. Ltd, 1979–91 (Chm., 1988–91); Chm., Tower Shakespeare Co. Ltd, 1985–93. Organising Sec., 1963–81, Chm., 1981–, Power Systems Computation Confs; Science and Engineering Research Council: Chm., Machines and Power Educn and Trng Cttee, 1983–86; Member: Elect. Engrg Cttee, 1982–84; Wind Energy Panel, 1985–86; Institution of Electrical Engineers: Chm., Wkg Gp on New Electronic Technol. in Publishing, 1983–87; Member: Council, 1990–; Governing Cttee, Benevolent Fund, 1990–93; Mem. Exec., Watt Cttee on Energy, 1986– (Chm., Wkg Gp on Renewable Energy Sources, 1986–88); Mem., Inf. Cttee, Royal Soc., 1988–. Specialist Advr, Sub-Cttee B (Energy, Transport and Technol.), H of L Select Cttee on Eur. Communities, 1987–89. Member: Fulbright Commn Scholarships Cttee, 1991–; Council, Cranfield Inst of Technol., 1991–. Freeman: City of London, 1990; Barbers' Co., 1990. Founder and Jt Ed., Internat. Jl of Electrical Power and Energy Systems, 1978–; Ed., Procs of Power System Computation Confs 5–8, 1975–84. *Publications:* edited: Energy Policy Planning, 1979; Electrical Engineers Reference Book, 14th edn 1985, 15th edn 1993; Renewable Energy Sources, 1990; Expert System Applications in Power Systems, 1990; many papers and contribs to learned jls. *Recreations:* music, cricket, Rugby. *Address:* Department of Electronic Engineering, Queen Mary and Westfield College, Mile End Road, E1 4NS. *T:* 0171–975 5331, *Fax:* 0181–981 0259. *Club:* Athenæum.

LAUNDER, Prof. Brian Edward, FRS 1994; FEng 1994; FIMechE; Professor of Mechanical Engineering, University of Manchester Institute of Science and Technology, since 1980 (Head of Department, 1983–85 and 1993–95); *b* 20 July 1939; *s* of Harry Edward Launder and Elizabeth Ann Launder (*née* Ayers); *m* 1967, Dagny Simonsen; one *s* one *d*. *Educ:* Enfield Grammar Sch.; Imperial Coll., London (BScEng Mech Engrg 1961); MIT (SM 1963; ScD 1965 Mech Engrg). Res. Asst, MIT, 1961–64; Lectr, 1964–71, Reader in Fluid Mechanics, 1971–76, Imperial Coll.; Prof. of Mech. Engrg, Univ. of California, Davis, 1976–80; Head, Thermo-Fluids Div., UMIST, 1980–90. Hon. Prof., Nanjing Aeronautics Inst., 1993. FASME. *Publications:* (with D. B. Spalding) Mathematical Models of Turbulence, 1972; (ed) Turbulent Shear Flows, vol. 1, 1978–vol. 9, 1994; numerous articles on turbulent flow in learned jls. *Recreations:* vacationing in France, photography, country walking, gentle bicycling. *Address:* Department of Mechanical Engineering, UMIST, PO Box 88, Manchester M60 2RD. *T:* 0161–200 3701.

LAURENCE, Ven. Christopher; *see* Laurence, Ven. J. H. C.

LAURENCE, Dan Hyman; Literary and Dramatic Advisor, Estate of George Bernard Shaw, 1973–90; *b* 28 March 1920. *Educ:* New York City public schs; Hofstra Univ. (BA 1946); New York Univ. (MA 1950). First went on the stage as child actor, 1932; radar specialist with Fifth Air Force, USA, in S Pacific, 1942–45; wrote and performed for Armed Forces Radio Service in New Guinea and the Philippines during World War II, and subseq. for radio and television in USA and Australia; began teaching in 1950 as graduate asst, New York Univ.; Instr of English, Hofstra Univ., 1953–58; Editor, Readex Microprint Corp., 1959–60; Associate Prof. of English, New York Univ., 1962–67, Prof., 1967–70. Vis. Professor: Indiana Univ., 1969; Univ. of Texas at Austin, 1974–75; Tulane Univ., 1981 (Mellon Prof. in the Humanities); Univ. of BC, Vancouver, 1984; Adjunct Prof. of Drama, Univ. of Guelph, 1986–91 (Dist. Vis. Prof. of Drama, 1983); Vis. Fellow, Inst. for Arts and Humanistic Studies, Pennsylvania State Univ., 1976. John Simon Guggenheim Meml Fellow, 1960, 1961 and 1972; Montgomery Fellow, Dartmouth Coll., 1982. Literary Advr, 1982–90, Associate Dir, 1987–, Shaw Fest., Ont. Associate Mem., RADA, 1979. Phi Beta Kappa (hon.), 1967. President's Medal, Hofstra Univ., 1990. *Publications:* Henry James: a bibliography (with Leon Edel), 1957 (3rd edn 1981); Robert Nathan: a bibliography, 1960; (ed) Collected Letters of Bernard Shaw, vol. 1, 1874–1897, 1965, vol. 2, 1898–1910, 1972, vol. 3, 1911–1925, 1985, Vol. 4, 1926–1950, 1988; (ed) Bernard Shaw, Collected Plays with their Prefaces, 1970–74; Shaw, Books, and Libraries, 1976; Shaw: an exhibit, 1977; (dramatization) The Black Girl in Search of God, 1977; (ed) Shaw's Music, 1981, 2nd edn 1989; Bernard Shaw: a bibliography, 1983; A Portrait of the Author as a Bibliography (Engelhard Lecture on the Book, L of C, 1982), 1983; (Uncollected Writings of Shaw): How to Become a Musical Critic, 1960 (2nd edn 1968); Platform and Pulpit, 1961; (ed with David H. Greene) The Matter with Ireland, 1962; (ed with Daniel J. Leary) Flyleaves, 1977; (Gen. Editor) Bernard Shaw: Early Texts, Play Manuscripts in Facsimile, 12 vols, 1981; (with James Rambeau) Agitations: letters to the Press 1875–1950, 1985; (with Martin Quinn) Shaw on Dickens, 1985; (with Nicholas Grene) Shaw, Lady Gregory, and the Abbey, 1993; (ed with Daniel J. Leary) Shaw, Complete Prefaces, vol. I, 1993, vol. II, 1995; Bernard Shaw, Theatrics, 1995. *Recreations:* theatre-going, music, mountain climbing. *Address:* 102 Rampart Drive (P-213), San Antonio, TX 78216, USA.

LAURENCE, George Frederick; QC 1991; *b* 15 Jan. 1947; *s* of Dr George Bester Laurence and Anna Margaretha Laurence; *m* 1976, Ann Jessica Chenevix Trench; one *s* one *d* and one step *s*. *Educ:* Pretoria High Sch. for Boys; Univ. of Cape Town (Smuts Meml Scholarship; BA); University College, Oxford (Rhodes Scholar; MA). Called to the Bar, Middle Temple, 1972 (Harmsworth Law Scholar); Asst Recorder, 1993–. *Publications:* articles in Rights of Way Law Review (Byways and Bridleways Trust). *Recreations:* communication, access to the countryside, cricket, tennis. *Address:* 12 New Square, Lincoln's Inn, WC2A 3SW. *T:* 0171–405 3808.

LAURENCE, Ven. (John Harvard) Christopher; Archdeacon of Lindsey, Diocese of Lincoln, 1985–94, now Archdeacon Emeritus; *b* 15 April 1929; *s* of Canon H. P. Laurence and Mrs E. Laurence; *m* 1952, E. Margaret E. Chappell; one *s* one *d*. *Educ:* Christ's Hospital; Trinity Hall, Cambridge (MA); Westcott House, Cambridge. Nat. service commn, Royal Lincolnshire Regt, 1948–50. Asst Curate, St Nicholas, Lincoln, 1955–59; Vicar, Crosby St George, Scunthorpe, 1959–73; St Hugh's Missioner, Lincoln Diocese, 1974–79; Bishops' Director of Clergy Training, London Diocese, 1979–85. *Recreation:* sculpture. *Address:* 5 Haffenden Road, Lincoln LN2 1RP. *T:* Lincoln (01522) 531444.

LAURENCE, Sir Peter (Harold), KCMG 1981 (CMG 1976); MC 1944; DL; HM Diplomatic Service, retired; Vice-President of Council, British Institute of Archaelogy, Ankara, since 1995 (Chairman, 1984–95); *b* 18 Feb. 1923; *s* of late Ven. George Laurence, MA, BD and late Alice (*née* Jackson); *m* 1948, Elizabeth Aïda Way; two *s* one *d*. *Educ:* Radley Coll.; Christ Church, Oxford. 60th Rifles, 1941–46 (Major). Entered Foreign Service, 1948; Western Dept, FO, 1948–50; Athens, 1950–53; Asst Political Adviser, Trieste, 1953–55; 1st Sec., Levant Dept, FO, 1955–57; Prague, 1957–60; Cairo, 1960–62; North and East African Dept, FO, 1962–65; Personnel Dept, DSAO, 1965–67; Counsellor, 1965; Political Adviser, Berlin, 1967–69; Visiting Fellow, All Souls Coll., 1969–70; Counsellor (Commercial), Paris, 1970–74; Chief Inspector, HM Diplomatic Service (Asst Under-Sec. of State), 1974–78; Ambassador to Ankara, 1980–83. Chairman: Foreign Anglican Church and Educnl Assoc. Ltd, 1976–; Community Council of Devon, 1986–92; Fellow, Woodard Corp. (W Div.), 1985. Mem. Council, Univ. of Exeter, 1989–. Chm. of Governors, Grenville Coll., Bideford, 1988–95. DL Devon, 1989. *Address:* Trevilla, Beaford, Winkleigh, N Devon EX19 8NS. *Club:* Army and Navy.

LAURENCE, Captain Timothy James Hamilton, MVO 1989; RN; Captain, HMS Cumberland, since 1995; *b* 1 March 1955; *s* of Guy Stewart Laurence and Barbara Alison Laurence (*née* Symons); *m* 1992, HRH The Princess Royal. *Educ:* Sevenoaks Sch.; Durham Univ. (BSc Geog.). Joined RN, 1973; in command: HMS Cygnet, 1979–80; HMS Boxer, 1989–91; MoD, 1992–95. *Recreations:* most sporting and outdoor activities. *Address:* c/o Buckingham Palace, SW1A 1AA.

See also under Royal Family.

LAURENS, André; Editor-in-Chief of Le Monde, 1982–84; *b* 7 Dec. 1934; unmarried. Journalist: L'Eclaireur méridional, Montpellier, 1953–55; l'Agence centrale de la presse, Paris, 1958–62; joined Le Monde, 1963; Home Affairs reporter, 1969; Associate Editor, Home Affairs, 1979. Vice-Pres., Société des Rédacteurs. *Publications:* Les nouveaux communistes, 1972; D'une France à l'autre, 1974; Le métier politique, 1980. *Address:* 34 rue de Clichy, 75009 Paris, France.

LAURENSON, James Tait; *b* 15 March 1941; *s* of James Tait Laurenson, FRCS and Vera Dorothy Kidd; *m* 1969, Hilary Josephine Thompson; one *s* three *d*. *Educ:* Eton; Magdalene College, Cambridge (MA). FCA. Ivory & Sime, investment managers, 1968–83, Partner 1970, Dir 1975; Tayburn Design Group: Man. Dir, 1983–84; Chm., 1984–89. Adam & Company Group: founder Dir and Dep. Chm., 1983; first Man. Dir, 1984–93. Director: Alvis (formerly United Scientific Holdings), 1971–; I & S UK Smaller Companies Trust (formerly First Charlotte Assets Trust), 1983–; Japan Assets Trust, 1983–88; The Life Association of Scotland, 1991–93; Hiscox Hldgs, 1992–; NSM plc, 1994–; Fidelity Special Values, 1994–; Chm., Nippon Assets Investments, 1984–. Chm. Governing Council, Erskine Stewart's Melville, 1994– (Dep. Chm., 1989–94). *Recreations:* spending time with the family, gardening. *Address:* Hill House, Kirknewton, Midlothian EH27 8DR. *T:* Mid Calder (01506) 883947. *Clubs:* New (Edinburgh); Hon. Company of Edinburgh Golfers.

LAURIE, Sir (Robert) Bayley (Emilius), 7th Bt *cr* 1834; *b* 8 March 1931; *s* of Maj.-Gen. Sir John Emilius Laurie, 6th Bt, CBE, DSO, and Evelyn Clare, (*d* 1987), *d* of late Lt-Col Lionel James Richardson-Gardner; *S* father, 1983; *m* 1968, Laurelie, *d* of Sir Reginald Lawrence William Williams, 7th Bt, MBE, ED; two *d*. *Educ:* Eton. National Service, 1st Bn Seaforth Highlanders, 1949–51; Captain, 11th Bn Seaforth Highlanders (TA), 1951–67. Member of Lloyd's, 1955. *Heir: cousin* Andrew Ronald Emilius Laurie [*b* 20 Oct. 1944; *m* 1970, Sarah Anne, *e d* of C. D. Patterson; two *s*]. *Address:* The Old Rectory, Little Tey, Colchester, Essex CO6 1JA. *T:* Colchester (01206) 210410.

LAURIE, Robert Peter, OBE 1994; JP; farmer, 1958–89, retired; Vice-Lord Lieutenant, Essex, 1985–92; *b* 20 Aug. 1925; *s* of late Col Vernon Stewart Laurie, CBE, TD, DL, and Mary, 2nd *d* of Selwyn Robert Pryor; *m* 1952, Oonagh Margaret Faber Wild, 3rd *d* of W. P. Wild, Warcop Hall, Westmorland; three *s* one *d*. *Educ:* Eton College. Served Coldstream Guards, 1943–47, Hon. Captain. Member of Stock Exchange, 1953; Partner, Heseltine, Powell & Co., then Heseltine, Moss & Co., 1953–80, Consultant, 1980–86; Director, British Empire Securites & General Trust Ltd, 1954– (Chm., 1973–84). Governor: Brentwood Sch., 1974–95; Alleyn's Sch., 1984–95; Chm., 1977–86, Pres., 1986–, Essex Assoc. of Boys' Clubs; a Vice-Pres., Nat. Assoc. of Boys' Clubs, 1986–; President: Essex Agricl Soc., 1986–87; Essex Shire Horse Assoc., 1987–; Essex Home Workers, 1986–; Chelmsford and Mid Essex Samaritans, 1986–92. Member: Ct, Essex Univ., 1979–; Council, CGLI, 1984–. Master, Saddlers' Co., 1981–82. Chm., Essex Co. Cttee, TAVRA, 1987–91; Hon. Col. Essex, ACF, 1994–. JP 1974, High Sheriff 1978–79, DL 1979, Essex. *Recreations:* foxhunting and field sports, gardening, reading. *Address:* Heatley's, Ingrave, Brentwood, Essex CM13 3QW. *T:* Brentwood (01277) 810224. *Club:* City Livery.

LAURIE, Robin; His Honour Judge Laurie; a Circuit Judge, South Eastern Circuit, since 1986; *b* 26 Jan. 1938; *s* of J. R. Laurie and Dr W. Metzner; *m* 1965, Susan Jane (*neé* Snelling); two *d*. *Educ:* Fettes Coll.; Geneva Univ.; Jesus Coll., Oxford (MA). Called to the Bar, Inner Temple, 1961; practice at the Bar (South Eastern Circuit), 1961–86. *Recreations:* mountaineering, mycology. *Address:* c/o 4 Paper Buildings, Temple, EC4Y 7EX. *Club:* Alpine.

LAURISTON, His Honour Alexander Clifford, QC 1972; a Circuit Judge, 1976–93; Chairman, Registered Homes Appeals Tribunal, since 1994; *b* 2 Oct. 1927; *s* of Alexander Lauriston and Nellie Lauriston (*née* Ainsworth); *m* 1954, Inga Louise Cameron; two *d*. *Educ:* Coatham Sch., Redcar, Yorks; Trinity Coll., Cambridge (MA). National Service: Army, Green Howards and RAPC, 2nd Lieut, 1948–50. Called to Bar, Inner Temple, 1952. A Recorder of the Crown Court, 1972–76. Mem., Loriners' Co., 1969; Freeman, City of London, 1969. *Recreations:* outdoor activities, painting, music. *Address:* 199 Strand, WC2R 1DR. *Clubs:* United Oxford & Cambridge University; Berkshire Golf.
See also R. B. Lauriston.

LAURISTON, Richard Basil; a Permanent Chairman of Industrial Tribunals, 1976–89; formerly Senior Partner, Alex Lauriston & Son, Solicitors, Middlesbrough; *b* 26 Jan. 1917; *s* of Alexander Lauriston, MBE, and Nellie Lauriston; *m* 1944, Monica, *d* of Wilfred Leslie Deacon, BA, Tonbridge, and Dorothy Louise Deacon; three *s*. *Educ:* Sir William Turner's Sch., Redcar; St John's Coll., Cambridge (MA, LLM). Solicitor, 1948; a Recorder of the Crown Court, 1974–82. Commnd and served in War of 1939–45, Royal Corps of Signals. *Recreations:* fishing, travelling. *Address:* 26 Easby Lane, Great Ayton, North Yorks TS9 6JZ. *T:* Great Ayton (01642) 722429.
See also A. C. Lauriston.

LAUTERPACHT, Elihu, CBE 1989; QC 1970; Fellow of Trinity College, Cambridge, since 1953; Director, Research Centre for International Law, since 1983, and Hon. Professor of International Law, since 1994, University of Cambridge; *b* 13 July 1928; *o s* of late Sir Hersch Lauterpacht, QC and Rachel Steinberg; *m* 1955, Judith Maria (*d* 1970), *er d* of Harold Hettinger; one *s* two *d*; *m* 1973, Catherine Daly; one *s*. *Educ:* Phillips Acad., Andover, Mass; Harrow; Trinity Coll., Cambridge (Entrance Schol.). 1st cl. Pt II of Law Tripos and LLB; Whewell Schol. in Internat. Law, 1950; Holt Schol. 1948 and Birkenhead Schol. 1950, Gray's Inn; called to Bar, 1950, Bencher, 1983. Joint Sec., Interdepartmental Cttee on State Immunity, 1950–52; Cambridge University: Asst Lectr in Law, 1953; Lecturer, 1958–81; Reader in Internat. Law, 1981–88. Sec., Internat. Law Fund, 1955–85; Dir of Research, Hague Academy of Internat. Law, 1959–60; Vis. Prof. of Internat. Law, Univ. of Delhi, 1960. Chm., East African Common Market Tribunal, 1972–75; Consultant to Central Policy Review Staff, 1972–74, 1978–81; Legal Adviser, Australian Dept of Foreign Affairs, 1975–77; Consultant on Internat. Law, UN Inst. for Training and Res., 1978–79; mem. arbitration panel, Internat. Centre for Settlement of Investment Disputes; Deputy Leader: Australian Delegn to UN Law of the Sea Conf., 1975–77; Australian Delegn to UN Gen. Assembly, 1975–77. Pres., Eastern Reg., UNA, 1991–; Vice-Pres., World Bank Admin. Tribunal, 1991– (Mem., 1980–); Chm., Asian Develt Bank Admin. Tribunal, 1991–95; Member: Social Sciences Adv. Cttee, UK Nat. Commn for Unesco, 1980–84; Panel of Arbitrators, Internat. Energy Agency Dispute Settlement Centre; Inst. of Internat. Law; Trustee, Internat. Law Fund, 1983. Editor: British Practice in International Law, 1955–68; International Law Reports, 1960–. Hon. Fellow, Hebrew Univ. of Jerusalem, 1989. Hon. Mem., Amer. Soc. of Internat. Law, 1993. Comdr, Order of Merit, Chile, 1969; awarded Annual Cert. of Merit, Amer. Soc. Internat. Law, 1972. *Publications:* Jerusalem and the Holy Places, 1968; (ed) International Law: the collected papers of Sir Hersch Lauterpacht, vol I, 1970, vol. II, 1975, vol. III, 1977, vol. IV, 1978; The Development of the Law of International Organization, 1976; (ed) Individual Rights and the State in Foreign Affairs, 1977; Aspects of the Administration of International Justice, 1991; various articles on international law. *Address:* Research Centre for International Law, 5 Cranmer Road, Cambridge CB3 9BL. *T:* Cambridge (01223) 335358; 20 Essex Street, WC2R 3AL. *T:* 0171–583 9294, *Fax:* 0171–583 1341. *Club:* Garrick.

LAUTI, Rt. Hon. Sir Toaripi, GCMG 1990; PC 1979; MP; Governor-General of Tuvalu, since 1990; *b* Papua New Guinea, 28 Nov. 1928; *m*; three *s* two *d*. *Educ:* Tuvalu; Fiji; Wesley Coll., Paerata, NZ; St Andrew's Coll., Christchurch, NZ; Christchurch Teachers' Coll., NZ. Taught in KGV, Tarawa, Kiribati, 1953–62; Labour Relations and Trng Officer, Nauru and Ocean Islands, engaged by British Phosphate Comrs; returned to Tuvalu, 1974, and entered politics; elected unopposed to House of Assembly, May 1975; elected Chief Minister, Tuvalu, upon separation of Ellice Islands (Tuvalu) from Kiribati, Oct. 1975, re-elected Chief Minister in Sept. 1977; First Prime Minister, Tuvalu, 1978–81; Leader of the Opposition, 1981–90. Chm., 18th South Pacific Conference, Noumea, Oct. 1978. *Address:* PO Box 84, Funafuti, Tuvalu, Central Pacific.

LAVAN, Hon. Sir John Martin, Kt 1981; retired 1981 as Senior Puisne Judge of the Supreme Court of Western Australia; *b* 5 Sept. 1911; *s* of late M. G. Lavan, KC; *m* 1st, 1939, Leith Harford (decd); one *s* three *d*; 2nd, 1984, Dorothy Bell. *Educ:* Aquinas Coll., Perth; Xavier Coll., Melbourne. Barrister in private practice, 1934–69; a Judge of the Supreme Court of WA, 1969–81. Chm., Parole Bd, WA, 1969–79. Mem., Barristers' Bd, WA, 1960–69; Pres., Law Soc. of WA, 1964–66. KStJ. *Address:* 165 Victoria Avenue, Dalkeith, WA 6009, Australia. *Club:* Weld (Perth).

LAVELLE, Roger Garnett, CB 1989; Director, European Bank for Reconstruction and Development, since 1993; Hon. Vice-President, European Investment Bank, since 1993 (Vice-President, 1989–93); *b* 23 Aug. 1932; *s* of Henry Allman Lavelle and Evelyn Alice Garnett; *m* 1956, Elsa Gunilla Odeberg; three *s* one *d*. *Educ:* Leighton Park; Trinity Hall, Cambridge (BA, LLB). Asst Principal, Min. of Health, 1955; Principal, HM Treasury, 1961; Special Assistant (Common Market) to Lord Privy Seal, 1961–63; Private Sec. to Chancellor of the Exchequer, 1965–68; Asst Secretary, 1968, Under Sec., 1975, Dep. Sec., 1985, HM Treasury; Dep. Sec., Cabinet Office, 1987. *Recreations:* music and gardening. *Address:* 36 Cholmeley Crescent, Highgate, N6 5HA. *T:* 0181–340 4845.

LAVENDER, Rt. Rev. Mgr Gerard; Parish Priest, Holy Family, Darlington, since 1993; *b* 20 Sept. 1943; *s* of Joseph and Mary Lavender. *Educ:* Ushaw Coll., Durham. Ordained, 1969; Asst Priest, St Mary Cath., Newcastle upon Tyne, 1969–75; loaned to Royal Navy as Chaplain, 1975; completed All Arms Commando Course, 1976; served with RM, 1976–79; sea going, 1979–80, 1987–89; Exchange Chaplain to San Diego, with US Navy, 1981–83; Chaplain in: Scotland (Rosyth), 1983–85; Portsmouth, 1985–87; Plymouth, 1989–90. GSM, NI, 4 visits 1977–79; Prin. RC Chaplain (Navy), MoD, 1990–93, retired. *Recreations:* golf, tennis, hill walking. *Address:* Holy Family Presbytery, 60 Cockerton Green, Darlington, Co. Durham DL3 9EU.

LAVER, Frederick John Murray, CBE 1971; Member, Post Office Corporation, 1969–73, retired; *b* 11 March 1915; *er s* of late Clifton F. Laver and Elsie Elizabeth Palmer, Bridgwater; *m* 1948, Kathleen Amy Blythe; one *s* two *d*. *Educ:* Plymouth Coll. BSc London. Entered PO Engrg Dept, 1935; PO Research Stn, 1935–51; Radio Planning, 1951–57; Organization and Efficiency, 1957–63; Asst Sec., HM Treasury, 1963–65; Chief Scientific Officer, Min. of Technology, 1965–68; Director, National Data Processing Service, 1968–70; Mem., NRDC, 1974–80. Vis. Prof., Computing Lab., Univ. of Newcastle upon Tyne, 1975–79. Mem. Council: IEE, 1966–69, 1972–73; British Computer Soc., 1969–72; Nat. Computing Centre, 1966–68, 1970–73; IEE Electronic Divl Bd, 1966–69, 1970–73. Mem. Council, 1979–87, Chm., 1985–87, Pro-Chancellor, 1981–87, Exeter Univ. Pres., Devonshire Assoc., 1990–91. CEng, FIEE; Hon. FBCS. Hon. DSc Exeter, 1988. *Publications:* nine introductory books on physics and computing; several scientific papers. *Recreations:* reading, writing, and watching the sea. *Address:* 2 Park Lane, Budleigh Salterton, Devon EX9 6QT.

LAVER, Prof. John David Michael Henry, FBA 1990; FRSE; Professor of Phonetics, since 1985, and Vice-Principal, since 1994, University of Edinburgh; *b* 20 Jan. 1938; *s* of Harry Frank Laver and Mary Laver (*née* Brearley); *m* 1st, 1961, Avril Morna Anel Macqueen Gibson; two *s* one *d*; 2nd, 1974, Sandra Traill; one *s*. *Educ:* Churcher's Coll., Petersfield; Univ. of Edinburgh (MA Hons; Postgrad. Dip. in Phonetics; PhD). Asst Lectr and Lectr in Phonetics, Univ. of Ibadan, 1963–66; University of Edinburgh: Lectr, Sen. Lectr, Reader in Phonetics, 1966–85; Dir, 1984–89, Chm., 1989–94, Centre for Speech Technology Research; Associate Dean, Faculty of Arts, 1989–92. Pres., Internat. Phonetic Assoc., 1991–95 (Mem. Council, 1986–); Member: Board, European Speech Communication Assoc., 1988–92; Council, Philological Soc., 1994–; Chm., Humanities Res. Bd, British Acad., 1994–. FRSE 1994; Fellow, Inst. of Acoustics, 1988. *Publications:* Communication in face to face interaction, 1972; Phonetics in Linguistics, 1973; The Phonetic Description of Voice Quality, 1980; The Cognitive Representation of Speech, 1981; Aspects of Speech Technology, 1988; The Gift of Speech, 1991; Principles of Phonetics, 1994. *Recreations:* travel, reading. *Address:* Humanities Research Board, Playfair Library, Old College, University of Edinburgh, South Bridge, Edinburgh EH8 9YL. *T:* 0131–650 2088. *Club:* Athenæum.

LAVER, Patrick Martin; HM Diplomatic Service, retired; Director of Research, Foreign and Commonwealth Office, 1980–83; *b* 3 Feb. 1932; *s* of late James Laver, CBE, RE, FRSL, and late Veronica Turleigh; *m* 1st, 1966, Marianne Ford (marr. annulled); one *d*; 2nd, 1979, Dr Elke Maria Schmitz, *d* of Thomas and Anneliese Schmitz. *Educ:* Ampleforth Coll., Yorks; New Coll., Oxford. Third Sec., Foreign Office, 1954; Second Sec., Djakarta, 1956; FO, 1957; Paris, 1958; Yaoundé, 1961; UK Delegn to Brussels Conf., 1962; First Sec., FO, 1963; UK Mission to UN, New York, 1964; Diplomatic Service Admin., 1965; Commercial Sec., Nairobi, 1968; FCO, 1970; Counsellor (Economic), Pretoria, 1973; UK Delegn to Conf. on Security and Co-operation in Europe, Geneva, 1974; Head of Rhodesia Dept, FCO, 1975–78; Counsellor, Paris, 1979–80. *Address:* Cheruskerstrasse 2 D, 53175, Bonn, Germany. *Club:* Athenæum.

LAVER, William Graeme, PhD; FRS 1987; Head, Influenza Research Unit, Australian National University, since 1983; *b* 3 June 1929; *s* of Lawrence and Madge Laver; *m* 1954, Judith Garrard Cahn; one *s* two *d*. *Educ:* Ivanhoe Grammar Sch., Melbourne; Univ. of Melbourne (BSc, MSc); Univ. of London (PhD). Technical Asst, Walter & Eliza Hall Inst. of Med. Res., Melbourne, 1947–52; Res. Asst, Dept of Biochemistry, Melbourne Univ., 1954–55; Res. Fellow, 1958–62, Fellow, 1962–64, Senior Fellow, 1964–90, Special Prof., 1990–, John Curtin Sch. of Med. Res., ANU. International Meetings: Rougemont, Switzerland, 1976; Baden, Vienna, 1977; Thredbo, Australia, 1979; Beijing, China, 1982; Banbury Center, Cold Spring Harbor, NY, 1985; Kona, Hawaii, 1989. *Publications:* papers on structure of influenza virus antigens and molecular mechanisms of antigenic shift and drift in type A influenza viruses; numerous research articles. *Recreations:* raising beef cattle, viticulture, wine-making, ski-ing, climbing volcanoes. *Address:* John Curtin School of Medical Research, PO Box 334, Canberra, ACT 2601, Australia. *T:* (62) 492397; Barton Highway, Murrumbateman, NSW 2582, Australia. *T:* (62) 275633.

LAVERICK, Elizabeth, OBE 1993; PhD, CEng, FIEE; CPhys, FInstP, FIEEE (US); Project Director, Advanced Manufacturing in Electronics, 1985–88; *b* 25 Nov. 1925; *d* of William Rayner and Alice Garland; *m* 1946 (marr. diss. 1960); no *c*. *Educ:* Dr Challoner's Grammar Sch., Amersham; Durham Univ. Research at Durham Univ., 1946–50; Section Leader at GEC, 1950–53; Microwave Engineer at Elliott Bros, 1954; Head of Radar Research Laboratory of Elliott-Automation Radar Systems Ltd, 1959; Jt Gen. Manager, Elliott-Automation Radar Systems Ltd, 1968–69, Technical Dir, 1969–71; Dep. Sec., IEE, 1971–85; Electronics CADMAT (Computer Aided Design, Manufacture and Test) Project Dir, 1982–85. Mem. Electronics Divisional Bd, 1967–70, Mem. Council, 1969–70, IEE. Chm., Engrg Careers Co-ordinating Cttee, 1983–85; Member: DE Adv. Cttee on Women's Employment, 1970–82; Adv. Cttee for Electronic and Electrical Engrg, Sheffield Univ., 1984–87; Nat. Electronics Council, 1986–; Chm., Ninth Internat. Conf. of Women Engrs and Scientists, 1989–91; Hon. Sec., Women's Engrg Soc., 1991–95 (Pres., 1967–69). Member Council: Inst. of Physics, 1970–73 (Chm., Women in Physics Cttee, 1985–90); City and Guilds of London Inst., 1984–87 (Hon. Mem., 1991); Member Court: Brunel Univ., 1985–88; City Univ., 1991–. Mem. Ct of Govs, IEE Benevolent Fund, 1991–. Liveryman, Worshipful Co. of Engrs, 1985. Hon. Fellow, UMIST, 1969; FRSA 1991. Editor, Woman Engr (Jl of Women's Engrg Soc.), 1984–90. *Publications:* contribs to IEE and IEEE Jls. *Recreations:* music, gardening, careers talks, tapestry, sailing. *Address:* Lynwood, Brays Lane, Hyde Heath, Amersham, Bucks HP6 5RU.

LAVERS, Patricia Mae, (Mrs H. J. Lavers); Executive Director, Bond Street Association, 1961–76, and Regent Street Association, 1972–76; *b* 12 April 1919; *d* of Edric Allan Jordan and May Holdcraft; *m* 1st, 1945, Frederick Handel Hayward (*d* 1965); one *s*; 2nd, 1966, John Harold Ellen; 3rd, 1976, Lt-Comdr Herbert James Lavers. *Educ:* Sydenham High School. Clerk, Securities Dept, National Provincial Bank, 1938–45; Export Dir, Perth Radios, 1955–60. Alderman, St Pancras Council, 1960–66 (Libraries/Public Health). Elected to Executive of Westminster Chamber of Commerce, 1971, Chm. City Affairs Cttee, 1971–75. Chm., Sandwich Soc., 1983–. FZS. *Recreations:* swimming, collecting first editions and press books, walking. *Address:* Horse Pond Sluice, Delf Street, Sandwich, Kent CT13 9HD. *Clubs:* Arts, Lansdowne, Players Theatre.

LAVERS, Richard Douglas; HM Diplomatic Service; Ambassador to Ecuador, since 1993; *b* Nairobi, 10 May 1947; *s* of Douglas Arthur Lavers and Edith Agnes (*née* Williams); *m* 1986, Brigitte Anne Julia Maria Moers, *e d* of late Robert Moers, Turnhout, Belgium; two *s*. *Educ:* Hurstpierpoint Coll.; Exeter Coll., Oxford (MA). Joined HM Diplomatic Service, 1969; Third Sec., Buenos Aires, 1970–72; Second, later First Sec., Wellington, 1973–76; FCO, 1976–81; First Sec., Pol and Econ., Brussels, 1981–85; on secondment to Guinness Mahon, 1985–87; FCO, 1987–89; NATO Defence Coll., Rome, 1989; Dep. Hd of Mission and HM Consul General, Santiago, 1990–93. *Recreations:* books, pictures, travel, fishing. *Address:* c/o Foreign and Commonwealth Office, King Charles Street, SW1A 2AH. *Clubs:* United Oxford & Cambridge University; Unión (Guayaquil).

LAVERTY, Ashley; *see* Page, A.

LAVIN, Deborah Margaret; Principal-elect of new college, and Co-Director, Howlands Institute for the Study of Change, Durham University, since 1995; Director, Howlands Trust, University of Durham, since 1993; *b* 22 Sept. 1939. *Educ:* Roedean Sch., Johannesburg, SA; Rhodes Univ., Grahamstown, SA; Lady Margaret Hall, Oxford (MA, DipEd). Asst Lectr, Dept of History, Univ. of the Witwatersrand, 1962–64; Lectr, Dept of Mod. Hist., The Queen's Univ. of Belfast, 1965–78, Sen. Lectr, 1978; Principal, Trevelyan College, Durham Univ., 1980–95. *Publications:* South African Memories, 1979; The Making of the Sudanese State, 1990; The Transformation of the Old Order in the Sudan, 1993; From Empire to International Commonwealth: a biography of Lionel Curtis, 1995; articles in learned jls. *Recreations:* broadcasting; the arts; passionate but unsuccessful tennis player. *Address:* (until Aug. 1996) The Principal's House, Trevelyan College, Elvet Hill Road, Durham DH1 3LN. *T:* Durham (0191) 3743761; (office) *T:* Durham (0191) 374 4690; Hickmans Cottages, Cat Street, East Hendred, Oxon OX12 8JT. *T:* Abingdon (01235) 833408. *Club:* Reform.

LAVIN, Mary, (Mrs M. MacDonald Scott); writer; *b* East Walpole, Mass, USA, 11 June 1912; *m* 1st, 1942, William Walsh (*d* 1954), MA, NUI; three *d*; 2nd, 1969, Michael MacDonald Scott (*d* 1990), MA, MSc. *Educ:* National Univ. of Ireland, Dublin (Graduate, MA; Hon DLitt, 1968). Member: Irish Academy of Letters (President, 1971); Aosdána, 1992. Guggenheim Fellow 1959, 1962 and 1972. Katherine Mansfield Prize, 1961; Ella Lynam Cabot Award, 1971; Eire Soc. Gold Medal, Boston, 1974; Arts Award, Royal Meath Assoc., 1975; Gregory Medal, Dublin, 1975; Amer. Irish Foundn Literary Award, 1979; Allied Irish Bank Award, 1981; Irish Arts Council Award, 1993. Personality of the Year, Royal Meath Assoc., 1976. *Publications:* Tales from Bective Bridge (short stories, awarded James Tait Black Memorial Prize), 1942 (London, 1943); The Long Ago (short stories), 1944; The House in Clewe Street (novel), 1945, repr. 1987; At Sally Gap (Boston), 1946; The Becker Wives, 1946; Mary O'Grady (novel), 1950, repr. 1986; Patriot Son (short stories), 1956; A Single Lady (short stories); A Likely Story (short novel), 1957; Selected Stories, 1959 (New York); The Great Wave (short stories), 1961; Stories of Mary Lavin, 1964; In the Middle of the Fields (short stories), 1966; Happiness (short stories), 1969; Collected Stories, 1971; A Memory and other Stories, 1972; The Second Best Children in the World, 1972; The Stories of Mary Lavin, vol. II, 1973; The Shrine and other stories, 1976; A Family Likeness, 1985; The Stories of Mary Lavin, vol. III, 1985; The House in Clewe Street, 1987. *Address:* Apt 5 Gilford Pines, Gilford Road, Sandymount, Dublin 4, Ireland. *T:* 2692402.

LAVOIE, Judith Anne, (Mrs A. R. Lavoie); *see* LaRocque, J. A.

LAW, family name of **Barons Coleraine** and **Ellenborough.**

LAW, Prof. Colin Nigel, PhD; Head of Laboratory, Cambridge Laboratory, Institute of Plant Science Research, John Innes Centre, Norwich, 1989–92; *b* 18 Nov. 1932; *s* of Joseph and Dorothy Mildred Law; *m* 1964, Angela Patricia Williams; three *d*. *Educ:* Queen Elizabeth's Grammar Sch., Blackburn; Univ. of Birmingham (BSc Hons Genetics); UCW, Aberystwyth (PhD). Nat. Service, RA, 1955–57. Res. worker, Plant Breeding Inst., Cambridge, 1960–87, Head of Cytogenetics Dept, 1972–87; Divl Head, Plant Genetics and Breeding, Inst. of Plant Sci. Res., 1987–89. Sen. Foreign Res. Fellow, Nat. Sci. Foundn, N Dakota State Univ., 1969. Hon. Prof., Univ. of East Anglia, 1990–. Prix Assinsel, Assoc. Internationale des Sélectionneurs, 1982. *Publications:* papers and articles on chromosome manipulation techniques to identify genes of agric. importance in crop plants, esp. wheat; genetic control of cereal plant responses to envmtl stress, particularly salinity. *Recreations:* fishing, painting. *Address:* 41 Thornton Close, Girton, Cambridge CB3 0NF. *T:* Cambridge (01223) 276554.

LAW, Francis Stephen, (Frank Law), CBE 1981; Chairman, Varta Group UK, since 1971; Director: Milupa Ltd, since 1978; NFC International Holdings Ltd, since 1985; *b* 31 Dec. 1916; *s* of Henry and Ann Law-Lowensberg; *m* 1959, Nicole Vigne (*née* Fesch); one *s* (one *d* by previous *m*). *Educ:* on the Continent. War service, 1939–45. Wills Law & Co., 1947; Truvox Engrg, 1960, subseq. Dir of Controls and Communications; Dep. Chm., NFC, 1982–85 (Dir, Consortium and its predecessors, 1969–87). Chairman: Rubis Investment & Cie, 1990–; Aegis (formerly WRCS Gp) plc, 1992– (Dir, 1988–); Director: B. Elliott Plc, 1968–86; BMW (GB) Ltd, 1978–88; Siemens, 1984–; Mem. Adv. Bd, Berliner Bank, 1988–92. Chm., Social Responsibilities Council, NFC, 1988–92; Member: Org. Cttee, NFC, 1968; Economic and Social Cttee, EEC, 1978–86. Governor, RSC, 1985–. Trustee, Nat. AIDS Trust, 1989–. *Recreations:* music, reading, theatre, skiing, riding, swimming. *Address:* 43 Lennox Gardens, SW1X 0DF. *T:* 0171–225 2142. *Clubs:* Boodle's; Pilgrims.

LAW, George Llewellyn; Vice Chairman, Morgan Grenfell Group plc, 1987–89; *b* 8 July 1929; *s* of late George Edward Law and Margaret Dorothy Law, OBE (*née* Evans); *m* 1960, Anne Stewart, *d* of late Arthur Wilkinson and Ness Wilkinson (*née* Muir); one *d*. *Educ:* Westminster Sch. (Schol.); Clare Coll., Cambridge (Schol.; BA). ACIArb. Solicitor. Slaughter and May, Solicitors, 1952–67, Partner 1961–67; Dir, Morgan Grenfell & Co. Ltd, 1968–91; Dir, Morgan Grenfell Gp plc, 1971–89. Deputy Chairman: Baker Perkins plc, 1986–87 (Dir, 1981–87); Blackwood Hodge plc, 1988–90 (Dir, 1968–90); Director: Bernard Sunley Investment Trust, 1968–75; Sidlaw Group, 1974–82; APV, 1987–90. Mem., Arbitration Panel, SFA Consumer Arbitration Scheme, 1988–. Member of Council: Furniture Hist. Soc., 1978–85; Ancient Monuments Soc., 1992–; British-Italian Soc., 1994–. Mem. Council of Management, and Chm. Patrons' Cttee, Spitalfields Fest., 1995–. FRSA. *Recreations:* history of furniture and decorative arts, opera, reading, swimming, cricket. *Address:* 6 Phillimore Gardens Close, W8 7QA. *T:* 0171–937 3061. *Clubs:* Brooks's, MCC, Surrey County Cricket.

LAW, Graham Couper, RSA 1995 (ARSA 1980); RIBA, FRIAS; Consultant, Law and Dunbar-Nasmith, Architects (Partner, 1957–89); *b* 28 Sept. 1923; *s* of William Ramsay Law and Eliza Templeton Hammond Couper; *m* 1951, Isobel Evelyn Alexander Drysdale; one *s* three *d*. *Educ:* Merchiston Castle Sch.; King's Coll., Cambridge (Exhibn and Book Prize; MA). ARIBA 1951 (Dist. in Thesis). Royal Engineers, QVO Madras Sappers and Miners, 1941–46. Member: Council, Edinburgh Arch. Assoc., 1964–69; RIAS, 1965–67 (Mem., Investigation Cttee, 1979–85); Architects' Registration Council, 1967–75; ARCUK Professional Purposes Cttee, 1967–75. Chm., Workshop and Artists' Studio Provision Scotland Ltd, 1977–81. Theatre designs include: Eden Court, Inverness; Festival Theatre, Pitlochry; exhibitions include: Epstein, Shakespeare, Scottish Treasures, Barbara Hepworth. *Publication:* Greek Thomson, 1954. *Recreations:* music, particularly opera, reading, painting. *Address:* Easter Society, Hopetoun, South Queensferry EH30 9SL. *T:* 0131–331 1268. *Club:* New (Edinburgh).

LAW, Adm. Sir Horace (Rochfort), GCB 1972 (KCB 1967; CB 1963); OBE 1950; DSC 1941; retired 1972; Chairman, R. & W. Hawthorn Leslie & Co., 1973–81; *b* 23 June 1911; *s* of S. Horace Law, MD, FRCSI, and Sybil Mary (*née* Clay); *m* 1941, Heather Valerie Coryton; two *s* two *d*. *Educ:* Sherborne Sch. Entered Royal Navy, 1929; gunnery specialist, 1937. Served War of 1939–45 (DSC): AA Cruisers: Cairo, 1939; Coventry, 1940; Cruiser Nigeria, 1942; Comdr 1946; Capt. 1952; comd HMS Centaur, 1958 and Britannia, RN Coll., 1960; Rear-Adm. 1961; Vice-Adm. 1965; Flag Officer Sea Training, 1961–63; Flag Officer, Submarines, 1963–65; Controller of the Navy, 1965–70; C-in-C, Naval Home Comd, and Flag Officer, Portsmouth Area, 1970–72; First and Principal Naval Aide-de-Camp to the Queen, 1970–72. Mem., Security Commn, 1973–82. President: RINA, 1975–77; Officers' Christian Union, 1976–86; Chm., Church Army Bd, 1980–87. Grand Cross, Order of the Crown (Netherlands), 1972. *Recreations:* sailing, gardening. *Address:* West Harting, Petersfield, Hants GU13 5NT.

LAW, James; QC (Scot.) 1971; *b* 7 June 1926; *s* of late George Law, MA, and late Isabella Rebecca Lamb (or Law), MA; *m* 1956, Kathleen Margaret, *d* of late Alexander Gibson; two *s* one *d*. *Educ:* Kilmarnock Academy; Girvan High Sch.; Univ. of Glasgow (MA 1948, LLB 1950). Admitted to Faculty of Advocates, 1951; Advocate-Depute, 1957–64. Mem., Criminal Injuries Compensation Bd, 1970–. *Address:* 7 Gloucester Place, Edinburgh EH3 6EE. *T:* 0131–225 2974. *Clubs:* New, Caledonian (Edinburgh).

LAW, Phillip Garth, AC 1995 (AO 1975); CBE 1961; MSc, FAIP, FTS, FAA; *b* 21 April 1912; *s* of Arthur James Law and Lillie Lena Chapman; *m* 1941, Nellie Isabel Allan; no *c*. *Educ:* Hamilton High Sch.; Ballarat Teachers' Coll.; Melbourne Univ. Science master, State secondary schs, Vic., 1933–38; Tutor in Physics, Newman Coll., Melbourne Univ., 1940–47; Lectr in Physics, 1943–48. Research Physicist and Asst Sec. of Scientific Instrument and Optical Panel of Austr. Min. of Munitions, 1940–45. Sen. Scientific Officer, ANARE, 1947–48; cosmic ray measurements in Antarctica and Japan, 1948; Dir, Antarctic Div., Dept of External Affairs, Aust., and Leader, ANARE, 1949–66; Expedition relief voyages to Heard I. and Macquarie I., 1949, 1951, 1952, 1954. Australian observer with Norwegian-British-Swedish Antarctic Exped., 1950; Leader of expedition: to establish first permanent Australian station in Antarctica at Mawson, MacRobertson Land, 1954; which established second continental station at Davis, Princess Elizabeth Land, 1957; which took over Wilkes station from USA, 1959; to relieve ANARE stations and to explore coast of Australian Antarctic Territory, annually, 1955–66. Chm., Australian Nat. Cttee for Antarctic Research, 1966–80. Exec. Vice-Pres., Victoria Inst. of Colls, 1966–77; Pres., Victorian Inst. of Marine Scis, 1978–80. Member: Council of Melbourne Univ., 1959–78; Council, La Trobe Univ., 1964–74; Chm., RMIT Foundn, 1995–; President: Royal Soc. of Victoria, 1967, 1968; Aust. and NZ Schs Exploring Soc., 1977–82. Dep. Pres., Science Museum of Victoria, Melbourne, 1979–82 (Trustee, 1968–83). Pres., Grad. Union, Melbourne Univ., 1972–77. Patron, British Schs Exploring Soc. Fellow: Australian Acad. of Technological Sciences; Aust. Acad. of Sci.; Aust. Inst. of Physics; ANZAAS. Hon. Fellow, Royal Melbourne Inst. of Technology. Hon. DAppSc (Melbourne); Hon. DEd (Victoria Inst. of Colls). Founder's Gold Medal, RGS, 1960; Gold Medal, Aust. Geographic Soc., 1988. *Publications:* (with John Béchervaise) ANARE, 1957; Antarctic Odyssey, 1983; The Antarctic Voyage of HMAS Wyatt Earp, 1995; chapters in: It's People that Matter, ed Donald McLean, 1969; Search for Human Understanding, ed M. Merbaum and G. Stricker, 1971; ed series of ANARE scientific reports; numerous papers on Antarctica and education. *Recreations:* tennis, ski-ing, skin diving, music, photography. *Address:* 16 Stanley Grove, Canterbury, Vic 3126, Australia. *Clubs:* Melbourne, Kelvin, Melbourne Cricket, Royal South Yarra Lawn Tennis (Melbourne).

LAW, Roger; Creative Director, Spitting Image Productions Ltd, since 1984; *b* 6 Sept. 1941; *m* 1959, Deirdre Amsden; one *s* one *d*. *Educ:* Littleport Secondary Mod. Sch.; Cambridge Sch. of Art (expelled 1960). Acquitted of malicious damage, 1959; fined £5 for rioting, 1960; cartoonist and illustrator, The Observer, 1962–65; voluntary probation for assault, 1963; illustrator, Sunday Times, 1965–67; probation for theft, 1967; Artist in Residence, Reed Coll., Oregon, and first puppet film, 1967; freelance illustrator, Pushpin Studios, NY, 1968–69; deported voluntarily from USA, 1969; caricaturist and features editor, Sunday Times, 1971–75; with Peter Fluck: formed Luck & Flaw, 1976; founder, Spitting Image, 1982 (first series on air, 1984, 17th series, 1995); first American show for NBC TV, 1986; TV series, The Winjin' Pom, 1991. Major installation for Barbican art gall., 1992; ceramic exhibn with Janice Tchalenko, V&A, 1993. D & AD Award, 1967; Assoc. of Illustrators Award (to Luck & Flaw), 1982; BPG TV Award for Best Light Entertainment Prog., 1984; D & AD Award (to Luck and Flaw), 1984; Internat. Emmy Award, 1986, and 1994 (for Peter & the Wolf); Grammy Award, 1987. *Publications:* The Appallingly Disrespectful Spitting Image Book, 1985; Spitting Images, 1987; The Spitting Image Giant Komic Book, 1988; (with L. Chester) A Nasty Piece of Work, 1992; Goodbye, 1992; Thatcha: The real Maggie memoirs, 1993; illustrator with Peter Fluck: A Christmas Carol, 1979; Treasure Island, 1986. *Recreation:* Heineken. *Address:* Cairo Studios, 4 Nile Street, N1 7ZZ. *T:* 0171–251 2626, *Fax:* 0171–251 2066.

LAW, Sylvia, OBE 1977; *b* 29 March 1931; *d* of late Reginald Howard Law and late Dorothy Margaret Law. *Educ:* Lowther Coll.; Girton Coll., Cambridge (MA); Regent Street Polytechnic (DipTP). MRTPI. Teaching, Benenden Sch., 1952–55; market research, Unilever Ltd, 1955–58; town and country planning and policy studies and research, Kent CC and GLC, 1959–86. Royal Town Planning Institute: Mem. Council, 1965–78; Chm. of Educn Cttee, 1970–73; Vice-Pres., 1972–74; Pres., 1974–75. Mem. Planning Cttee, SSRC, 1977–79. Volunteer Advr, CAB, 1986–. *Publications:* (contrib.) Recreational Economics and Analysis, 1974; (ed) Planning and the Future, 1976; articles in RTPI Jl, Official Architecture and Planning, Planning Outlook, Town Planning Rev., Greater London Intelligence Qly, etc. *Recreations:* music, photography, gardening.

LAWES, Glenville Richard; Chief Executive, Ironbridge Gorge Museum Trust, since 1991; *b* 28 May 1945; *s* of Eric Lawes and Phyllis (*née* Witchalls); *m* 1969, Isobel Prescott Thomas; one *s* two *d*. *Educ:* Univ. of Birmingham (BSc Eng). Technol. Editor, New

Scientist, 1967–70; HM Diplomatic Service, 1970–80: served Moscow, Geneva and Paris; First Sec., FCO, 1976; with British Petroleum Co. plc, 1980–91; Sen. Analyst, BP Internat., 1980–86; Gen. Manager, BP Middle East, 1986–90; Regl Manager, BP Oil Internat., 1990–91. *Recreations:* music, reading, theatre, renovating old houses. *Address:* c/o The Wharfage, Ironbridge, Telford, Shropshire TF8 7AW. *T:* Telford (01952) 433522.

LAWLER, Geoffrey John; Managing Director, The Public Affairs Company (formerly Lawler Associates), since 1987; Vice-President, International Access Inc., since 1987; *b* 30 Oct. 1954; *s* of Major Ernest Lawler (RAEC retd) and Enid Lawler; *m* 1989, Christine, *d* of Carl Roth, Cheyenne, Wyoming. *Educ:* Richmond Sch., N Yorks; Hull Univ. (BSc (Econ); Pres., Students' Union, 1976–77). Trainee chartered accountant, 1977–78. Community Affairs Dept, 1978–80, Research Dept, 1980–82, Cons. Central Office; Public Relations Exec., 1982–83; Dir, publicity co., 1983. Contested (C) Bradford N, 1987. MP (C) Bradford N, 1983–87. EC Observer for Russian elections, 1993; UN Observer for S African elections, 1994. Dir, Democracy Internat. Ltd, 1995–. Mem. Council, UKIAS, 1987–93. Hon. Pres., British Youth Council, 1983–87; Pres., W Yorks Youth Assoc., 1995– (Vice-Pres., 1986–95). *Recreations:* cricket, music, travel. *Address:* 1 Moorland Leys, Leeds LS17 5BD. *T:* Leeds (0113) 266 0583.

LAWLER, Sir Peter (James), Kt 1981; OBE 1965; retired 1987; Australian Ambassador to Ireland and the Holy See, 1983–86; *b* 23 March 1921; *m*; six *s* two *d*. *Educ:* Univ. of Sydney (BEc). Prime Minister's Dept, Canberra, 1949–68 (British Cabinet Office, London, 1952–53); Dep. Secretary: Dept of the Cabinet Office, 1968–71; Dept of the Prime Minister and Cabinet, 1972–73; Secretary: Dept of the Special Minister of State, 1973–75; Dept of Admin. Services, Canberra, 1975–83. *Recreation:* farming. *Address:* 6 Tennyson Crescent, Forrest, ACT 2603, Australia. *T:* (6) 2951946. *Clubs:* Melbourne (Melbourne); University House, Wine and Food (Canberra).

LAWLER, Simon William; QC 1993; a Recorder, since 1989; *b* 26 March 1949; *s* of Maurice Rupert Lawler and Daphne Lawler (*née* Elkins); *m* 1985, Josephine Sallie Day; two *s*. *Educ:* Winchester County Secondary Sch.; Peter Symonds, Winchester; Univ. of Hull (LLB Hons). Called to the Bar, Inner Temple, 1971; in practice at the Bar, 1972–; Asst Recorder, 1983–89. *Recreations:* cricket, gardening, opera, wine. *Address:* 6 Park Square, Leeds LS1 2LW. *T:* Leeds (0113) 245 9763; 11 King's Bench Walk, Temple, EC4Y 7EQ. *T:* 0171–535 3337.

LAWLEY, Dr Leonard Edward; Director of Kingston Polytechnic, 1969–82; *b* 13 March 1922; *yr s* of late Albert Lawley; *m* 1944, Dorothy Beryl Round; one *s* two *d*. *Educ:* King Edward VI Sch., Stourbridge; Univs of Wales and Newcastle upon Tyne. BSc, PhD; FInstP, CPhys. Served with RAF, 1941–46; Lectr, Univ. of Newcastle upon Tyne, 1947–53; Sen. Lectr, The Polytechnic, Regent Street, 1953–57; Kingston Coll. of Technology: Head of Dept of Physics and Maths, 1957–64; Vice-Principal, 1960–64; Principal, 1964–69. *Publications:* various papers in scientific jls on transmission ultrasonic sound waves through gases and liquids and on acoustic methods for gas analysis.

LAWLEY, Susan, (Sue); broadcaster, since 1970; *b* 14 July 1946; *d* of Thomas Clifford and Margaret Jane Lawley; *m* 1st, 1975, David Ashby (marr. diss. 1985); one *s* one *d*; 2nd, 1987, Hugh Williams. *Educ:* Dudley Girls' High Sch., Worcs; Bristol Univ. (BA Hons Modern Languages). Thomson Newspapers' graduate trainee, Western Mail and South Wales Echo, Cardiff, 1967–70; BBC Plymouth: sub-editor/reporter/presenter, 1970–72; presenter, BBC Television: Nationwide, 1972–75; Tonight, 1975–76; Nationwide, 1977–83; Nine O'Clock News, 1983–84; Six O'Clock News, 1984–88; Presenter, Desert Island Discs, BBC Radio Four, 1988–; other programmes, 1977–92, including: general elections; budgets; Wogan, Royal tours; interviews. Hon. LLD Bristol, 1989; Hon. MA Birmingham, 1989; Hon. DLitt CNAA, 1991. *Publication:* Desert Island Discussions, 1989. *Recreations:* family, walking, ski-ing, kettle-polishing. *Address:* c/o Noel Gay Ltd, 76 Oxford Street, W1R 1RB.

LAWLOR, Prof. John James, MA, DLitt, FSA; Professor of English Language and Literature, University of Keele, 1950–80, now Emeritus; *b* 5 Jan. 1918; *o s* of Albert John Lawlor, Chief Armourer, RN, and Teresa Anne Clare Lawlor, Plymouth; *m* 1st, 1941, Thelma Joan Weeks, singer (marr. diss. 1979); one *s* three *d*; 2nd, 1984, Kimie Imura, Prof. Meisei Univ., Tokyo. *Educ:* Ryder's; Magdalen Coll., Oxford. BA Hons English Cl. I, 1939. Service in Devonshire Regt, 1940–45; Asst Chief Instructor, 163 Artists' Rifles OCTU, 1943–44; CMF, 1944–45; AMG Austria. Sen. Mackinnon Scholar, Magdalen Coll., 1946; Sen. Demy, 1947; Lectr in English, Brasenose and Trinity Colls, 1947–50; University Lectr in Eng. Lit., Oxford, 1949–50. Fellow of Folger Shakespeare Library, Washington, DC, 1962. Toured Australian and NZ Univs and visited Japan, 1964. Ziskind Visiting Prof., Brandeis Univ., Mass, 1966; Vis. Professor: Univ. of Hawaii, 1972; Univ. of Maryland, 1981–82; Univ. of Arizona, 1983–84. Sec.-Gen. and Treasurer, Internat. Assoc. of University Profs of English, 1971–95; Contrib. Mem. Medieval Academy of America; Gov., Oswestry Sch.; Pres., N Staffs Drama Assoc.; Mem. Western Area Cttee, Brit. Drama League; Vice-Pres., The Navy League. *Publications:* The Tragic Sense in Shakespeare, 1960; Piers Plowman, an Essay in Criticism, 1962; The Chester Mystery Plays (with Rosemary Sisson), perf. Chester, 1962; The Vision of Piers Plowman, commnd, Malvern, 1964; (ed) Patterns of Love and Courtesy, 1966; (with W. H. Auden) To Nevill Coghill from Friends, 1966; Chaucer, 1968; (ed) The New University, 1968; (ed) Higher Education: patterns of change in the seventies, 1972; Elysium Revisited, 1978; (as James Dundonald): Letters to a Vice-Chancellor, 1962; La Vita Nuova, 1976; articles on medieval and modern literature in various journals and symposia. *Recreations:* travel, book-collecting, any sort of sea-faring. *Address:* Penwithian, Higher Fore Street, Marazion, Cornwall TR17 0BQ. *T:* Penzance (01736) 711180; 2-45-13 Misawa, Hinoshi, Tokyo 191, Japan. *T:* (0425) 944177. *Clubs:* Athenæum; Royal Fleet (Devonport).

LAWRANCE, John Ernest; Under Secretary, Director, Technical Division 1, Inland Revenue, 1982–88, retired; *b* 25 Jan. 1928; *s* of Ernest William and Emily Lewa Lawrance; *m* 1956, Margaret Elsie Ann Dodwell; two *s* one *d*. *Educ:* High School for Boys, Worthing; Southampton Univ. (BA Hons Modern History). Entered Inland Revenue as Inspector of Taxes, 1951; Principal Inspector, 1968; Senior Principal Inspector on specialist technical duties, 1974. *Address:* 71A Alderton Hill, Loughton, Essex IG10 3JD. *T:* 0181–508 7562.

LAWRANCE, Mrs June Cynthia; Headmistress of Harrogate Ladies' College, 1974–93; *b* 3 June 1933; *d* of late Albert Isherwood and of Ida Emmett; *m* 1957, Rev. David Lawrance, MA, BD; three *d*. *Educ:* St Anne's Coll., Oxford (MA). Teaching appts: Univ. of Paris, 1954–57; Cyprus, 1957–58; Jordan, 1958–61; Oldham, Lancs, 1962–70; Headmistress, Broughton High Sch., Salford, 1971–73. *Recreations:* music, French literature, chess. *Address:* Kinver House, The Green, Kirklington, Bedale DL8 2NQ.

LAWRANCE, Keith Cantwell; Deputy Chairman, Civil Service Appeal Board, 1981–89 (Member 1980–89); Vice-President, Civil Service Retirement Fellowship, since 1988 (Chairman, 1982–88); *b* 1 Feb. 1923; *s* of P. J. Lawrance; *m* 1952, Margaret Joan (*née* Scott); no *c*. *Educ:* Latymer Sch., N9. Clerical Officer, Admiralty, 1939. Served War, RNVR, 1942–46; Sub-Lt (A), 1945. Exec. Officer, Treasury, 1947; Asst Principal, Post Office, 1954; Principal, Post Office, 1959; Asst Sec., Dept of Economic Affairs, Dec. 1966; Under-Sec., Civil Service Dept, 1971–79. Vice-Chm., Inst. of Cancer Research, 1989–95. *Recreations:* model engineering, music. *Address:* White Gables, 35 Fairmile Avenue, Cobham, Surrey KT11 2JA. *T:* Cobham (01932) 863689.

LAWRENCE, family name of **Baron Lawrence** and of **Baron Trevethin and Oaksey.**

LAWRENCE, 5th Baron *cr* 1869; **David John Downer Lawrence;** Bt 1858; *b* 4 Sept. 1937; *s* of 4th Baron Lawrence and Margaret Jean (*d* 1977), *d* of Arthur Downer, Kirdford, Sussex; *S* father, 1968. *Educ:* Bradfield College. *Address:* c/o Bird & Bird, 90 Fetter Lane, EC4A 1JP.

LAWRENCE, Prof. Andrew, PhD; FRAS; Regius Professor of Astronomy, University of Edinburgh, since 1994; Head, Institute for Astronomy, Edinburgh, since 1994; *b* 23 April 1954; *s* of Jack Lawrence and Louisa Minnie (*née* Sandison); partner, Debbie Ann Capel; one *s* one *d*. *Educ:* Chatham House Grammar Sch., Ramsgate; Univ. of Edinburgh (BSc Hons 1976); Univ. of Leicester ((PhD 1980). FRAS 1983. Exchange scientist, MIT, 1980–81; Sen. Res. Fellow, Royal Greenwich Observatory, 1981–84; PDRA, QMC, 1984–87; Queen Mary and Westfield College, London: SERC Advanced Fellow, 1987–89; Lectr, 1989–94. Mem., various res. councils and internat. cttees, panels, etc, 1983–94. *Publications:* (ed) Comets to Cosmology, 1987; numerous contribs to professional astronomy jls. *Recreations:* acting, painting electrons, teasing publishers. *Address:* Edinburgh Institute for Astronomy, University of Edinburgh, Royal Observatory Edinburgh, Blackford Hill, Edinburgh EH9 3HJ. *T:* 0131–668 8346.

LAWRENCE, Rt. Rev. Caleb James; *see* Moosonee, Bishop of.

LAWRENCE, Hon. Carmen (Mary), PhD; MP (ALP) Fremantle, since 1994; Minister for Human Services and Health and Minister assisting the Prime Minister for the Status of Women, Australia, since 1994; *b* 2 March 1948; *d* of Ern and Mary Lawrence; *m* (marr. diss.); one *s*. *Educ:* Univ. of Western Australia (BPsych 1st cl. Hons 1968; PhD 1983). Univ. lectr, tutor, researcher, consultant, 1968–83; Research Psychologist, Psychiatric Services Unit, Health Dept, 1983–86. MLA (ALP): Subiaco, WA, 1986–89; Glendalough, WA, 1989–94; Minister for Education, 1988–90; Premier of WA, 1990–93; Leader of the Opposition, WA, 1993–94. *Publications:* psychological papers. *Recreations:* literature, theatre, music. *Address:* Parliament House, Canberra, ACT 2600, Australia; 11/18 John Street, Fremantle, WA 6159, Australia.

LAWRENCE, Christopher Nigel, NDD, FTC; FIPG; goldsmith, silversmith; modeller, medallist, industrial and graphic designer; *b* 23 Dec. 1936; *s* of late Rev. William W. Lawrence and Millicent Lawrence; *m* 1958, Valerie Betty Bergman; two *s* two *d*. *Educ:* Westborough High Sch.; Central School of Arts and Crafts. Apprenticed, C. J. Vander Ltd; started own workshops, 1968. *One man exhibitions:* Galerie Jean Renet, 1970, 1971; Hamburg, 1972; Goldsmiths' Hall, 1973; Ghent, 1975; Hasselt, 1977. Major commissions from British Govt, City Livery cos, banks, manufacturing cos; official silversmith to Bank of England. Judge and external assessor for leading art colleges; specialist in symbolic presentation pieces and limited edns of decorative pieces, *eg* silver mushrooms (creator of Capricious Mushrooms for John Hine Ltd). Chm., Goldsmiths, Silversmiths and Jewellers Art Council, 1976–77; Liveryman, Goldsmiths' Co., 1978–; television and radio broadcaster. Jacques Cartier Meml award for Craftsman of the Year, 1960, 1963, 1967 (unique achievement). *Recreations:* badminton, tennis, bowls, carpentry, painting. *Address:* 20 St Vincent's Road, Westcliff-on-Sea, Essex SS0 7PR. *T:* Southend-on-Sea (01702) 338443, (workshop) (01702) 344897.

LAWRENCE, Prof. Clifford Hugh; Professor of Medieval History, 1970–87, now Emeritus (Head of the Department of History, Bedford College, Royal Holloway and Bedford New College (formerly at Bedford College), University of London, 1981–85); *b* 28 Dec. 1921; *s* of Ernest William Lawrence and Dorothy Estelle; *m* 1953, Helen Maud Curran; one *s* five *d*. *Educ:* Stationers' Co.'s Sch.; Lincoln Coll., Oxford. BA 1st Cl. Hons Mod. Hist. 1948, MA 1953, DPhil 1956. War service in RA and Beds and Herts: 2nd Lieut 1942, Captain 1944, Major 1945. Asst Archivist to Co. of Gloucester, 1949. Bedford Coll., London: Asst Lectr in History, 1951; Lectr, 1953–63; Reader in Med. History, 1963–70. External Examr, Univ. of Newcastle upon Tyne, 1972–74, Univ. of Bristol, 1975–77, Univ. of Reading, 1977–79; Chm., Bd of Examnrs in History, London Univ., 1981–83. Mem., Press Council, 1976–80; Vice-Chm. of Govs, Governing Body, Heythrop Coll., Univ. of London; Mem. Council, Westfield Coll., Univ. of London, 1981–86. FRHistS 1960; FSA 1984. *Publications:* St Edmund of Abingdon, History and Hagiography, 1960; The English Church and the Papacy in the Middle Ages, 1965; Medieval Monasticism, 1984, 2nd edn 1989; The Friars: the impact of the early mendicant movement on western society, 1994; contribs to: Pre-Reformation English Spirituality, 1967; The Christian Community, 1971; The History of the University of Oxford, Vol. I, 1984; articles and reviews in Eng. Hist. Review, History, Jl Eccles. Hist., Oxoniensia, Encycl. Brit., Lexicon für Theol u Kirche, etc. *Recreations:* gardening, painting. *Address:* 11 Durham Road, SW20 0QH. *T:* 0181–946 3820. *Club:* Reform.

LAWRENCE, Sir David (Roland Walter), 3rd Bt, *cr* 1906; late Captain, Coldstream Guards, 1951; *b* 8 May 1929; *er s* of Sir Roland Lawrence, 2nd Bt, MC, and Susan, 3rd *d* of late Sir Charles Addis, KCMG; *S* father 1950; *m* 1955, Audrey, Duchess of Leeds, *yr d* of Brig. Desmond Young, OBE, MC. *Educ:* Radley; RMC Sandhurst. *Heir:* *b* Clive Wyndham Lawrence [*b* 6 Oct. 1939; *m* 1966, Sophia Annabel Stuart, *d* of late (Ian) Hervey Stuart Black, TD; three *s*]. *Address:* 28 High Town Road, Maidenhead, Berks SL6 1PB.

LAWRENCE, Dennis George Charles, OBE 1963; Director, 1978–82, Board Member, 1981–84, Cooperative Development Agency; retired; *b* 15 Aug. 1918; *s* of George Herbert and Amy Frances Lawrence; *m* 1946, Alida Jantine, *d* of Willem van den Berg, The Netherlands. *Educ:* Haberdashers' Aske's Hatcham School. Entered Civil Service as Clerical Officer, Min. of Transport, 1936; served RA, 1939–46; Exec. Officer 1946; Asst Principal, Central Land Board, 1947; Principal, 1949; GPO, 1953; Asst Sec. 1960; Sec., Cttee on Broadcasting, 1960–62; Asst Sec., GPO, 1962; Under-Secretary: GPO, 1969; Min. of Posts and Telecommunications, 1969–74; Dept of Industry, 1974–78. Chm., Working Group on a Cooperative Develt Agency, 1977. *Publications:* Democracy and Broadcasting (pamphlet), 1986; The Third Way, 1988. *Recreations:* walking, painting, travel. *Address:* Little London Farmhouse, Cann, Shaftesbury, Dorset SP7 0PZ.

LAWRENCE, Sir Guy Kempton, Kt 1976; DSO 1943; OBE 1945; DFC 1941; retired; Chairman, Eggs Authority, 1978–81; *b* 5 Nov. 1914; *s* of Albert Edward and Bianca Lawrence; *m* 1947, Marcia Virginia Powell; two *s* one *d*. *Educ:* Marlborough Coll. FBIM, FIGD. RAFO, 1934–45; War of 1939–45: Bomber Pilot (48 sorties), Sqdn Comdr, 78 Sqdn, Gp Captain Trng, HQ Bomber Command (DFC DSO, despatches, OBE). Contested (L) Colne Valley, 1945. Man. Dir, Chartair Ltd-Airtech Ltd, 1945–48; Chairman: Glacier Foods Ltd, 1948–75; Findus (UK) Ltd, 1967–75; Dep. Chairman: J. Lyons & Co. Ltd, 1950–75; Spillers French Holdings Ltd, 1972–75; Vice-Chm., DCA Food Industries Inc., 1973–75; Dir, Eagle Aircraft Services, 1977–81. Chm., Food and Drink Industries Council, 1973–77. Member of Stock Exchange, London, 1937–45. British Ski Team, FIS, 1937–38. *Recreations:* farming, carpentry, squash, tennis. *Address:*

Courtlands, Kier Park, Ascot, Berks SL5 7DS. *T:* Ascot (01344) 21074. *Club:* Royal Air Force.

LAWRENCE, (Henry) Richard (George); writer on music; Editor, Early Music News, since 1995 (Acting Editor, 1994–95); *b* 16 April 1946; *s* of late George Napier Lawrence, OBE, and of Peggy Neave (*née* Breay). *Educ:* Westminster Abbey Choir Sch.; Haileybury (music schol.); Worcester Coll., Oxford (Hadow Schol.; BA 1967). Overseas Dept, Ginn & Co., educational publishers, 1968–73; Music Officer, 1973–83, Music Dir, 1983–88, Arts Council of GB; Chief Exec., RSCM, 1990–94. Reviewer, Jl of RAS, 1991–. Occasional broadcaster, 1989–. Chm., Arts Council Staff Assoc., 1974–76. Voluntary work, Friends of the Earth Trust, 1989–90. *Recreations:* travelling in Asia, pre-1914 Baedekers. *Address:* 115 Camberwell Grove, SE5 8JH. *T:* 0171–701 1896.

LAWRENCE, Sir Ivan (John), Kt 1992; QC 1981; Barrister-at-law; MP (C) Burton, since Feb. 1974; a Recorder, since 1987; *b* 24 Dec. 1936; *o s* of late Leslie Lawrence, Brighton; *m* 1966, Gloria Hélène, *d* of Charles Crankshaw, Newcastle; one *d. Educ:* Brighton, Hove and Sussex Grammar Sch.; Christ Church, Oxford (MA). Nat. Service with RAF, 1955–57. Called to Bar, Inner Temple, 1962, Hon. Bencher, 1991; S Eastern Circuit; Asst Recorder, 1983–87. Contested (C) Peckham (Camberwell), 1966 and 1970. Mem., Select Cttee on Foreign Affairs, 1983–92; Chm., Select Cttee on Home Affairs, 1992–; Chairman: Cons. Parly Legal Cttee, 1987 (Vice Chm., 1979–87); Cons. Parly Home Affairs Cttee, 1988– (Vice Chm., 1982–88); All-Party Parly Anti-Fluoridation Cttee; All-Party Parly Barristers Gp, 1987–; Member: Parly Expenditure Select Sub-Cttee, 1974–79; Jt Parly Cttee on Consolidation of Statutes, 1974–87. Mem. Exec., 1922 Cttee, 1988–89, 1992–. Chm., Exec. Cttee, UK CPA, 1994– (Mem., 1989–). Member: Council of Justice, 1989–95; Council, Statute Law Soc., 1985–95; Exec., Soc. of Conservative Lawyers, 1989–. Vice-Pres., Fed. of Cons. Students, 1980–82; Mem., W Midlands Cons. Council, 1985–. Vice Chm., Cons. Friends of Israel, 1994–. Chm., Burton Breweries Charitable Trust, 1982–. *Publications:* pamphlets (jointly): Correcting the Scales; The Conviction of the Guilty; Towards a New Nationality; Financing Strikes; newspaper articles on law and order topics and foreign affairs. *Recreations:* piano, squash, football, travel. *Address:* 1 Essex Court, Temple, EC4Y 9AR. *T:* 0171–583 7759; House of Commons, SW1A 0AA. *T:* 0171–219 5054.

LAWRENCE, John, OBE 1974; Director, Africa and Middle East Division, British Council, 1990–93; *b* 22 April 1933; *s* of William and Nellie Lawrence. *Educ:* Queens' College, Cambridge (BA 1956, Cert. Ed. 1957, MA 1961); Indiana University (MA 1959). Teaching posts in USA and UK, 1957–60; British Council headquarters appts, 1961; Regional Representative, Sabah, 1965; Representative, Zambia, 1968, Sudan, 1974, Malaysia, 1976; Dir, South Asia Dept, 1980; Controller, America, Pacific and S Asia Div., 1982–87; Rep., Brazil, 1987–90. *Recreations:* walking and talking, simultaneously or otherwise. *Address:* Swinkle House, Longsleddale, Kendal, Cumbria LA8 9BD.

LAWRENCE, Sir (John) Patrick (Grosvenor), Kt 1988; CBE 1983; DL; Chairman, Kidderminster Healthcare NHS Trust, since 1993; *b* 29 March 1928; *s* of Ernest Victor Lawrence and Norah Grosvenor Lawrence (*née* Hill); *m* 1954, Anne Patricia (*née* Auld); one *d* (one *s* decd). *Educ:* Denstone Coll., Staffs. Served RNVR, 1945–48. Admitted Solicitor 1954; Partner, Wragge & Co., Solicitors, Birmingham 1959–93 (Sen. Partner, 1982–93). Chm., Midland Rent Assessment Panels, 1971–. Mem., Bromsgrove RDC, 1967–74. Vice-Pres., Nat. Union of Conservative and Unionist Assocs (Chm., 1986–87); Pres., W Midlands Conservative Council, 1988–91 (Chm., 1979–82). Vice-Chm., British Shooting Sports Council, 1985–. Member of Council: Denstone Coll., Staffs, 1989–; Birmingham Chamber of Industry and Commerce, 1989–93; ABCC, 1990–93; Aston Univ., 1990–. Chm., Birmingham Cathedral in Need Appeal, 1990. Freeman, City of London, 1991; Liveryman, Gunmakers' Co., 1991. DL West Midlands, 1993. *T:* 0121–454 1093. *Clubs:* Carlton, Royal Over-Seas League; Bean (Birmingham); Law Society's Yacht.

LAWRENCE, Air Vice-Marshal John Thornett, CB 1975; CBE (mil.) 1967 (OBE (mil.) 1961); AFC 1945; *b* 16 April 1920; *s* of late T. L. Lawrence, JP, and Mrs B. M. Lawrence; *m* 1951, Hilary Jean (*née* Owen); three *s* one *d. Educ:* The Crypt School, Gloucester. RAFVR 1938. Served War of 1939–45 in Coastal Command (235, 202 and 86 Squadrons); Directing staff, RAF Flying Coll., 1949–53; CO 14 Squadron, 1953–55; Group Captain Operations, HQ AFME, 1962–64; CO RAF Wittering, 1964–66; AOC, 3 Group, Bomber Command, 1967; Student, IDC, 1968; Dir of Organisation and Admin Plans (RAF), 1969–71; Dir-Gen. Personnel Management (RAF), 1971–73; Comdr N Maritime Air Region and AOC Scotland and NI, 1973–75, retired 1975. Corporate Mem., Cheltenham Ladies' Coll., 1977–. Vice-Pres., Glos County SSAFA, 1990– (Chm., 1980–90); Mem., Nat. Council, SSAFA, 1987–90. Order of Leopold II, Belgium, 1945; Croix de Guerre, Belgium, 1945. *Recreations:* golf, bridge. *Address:* The Coach House, Wightfield Manor, Apperley, Glos GL19 4DP. *Club:* Royal Air Force.

LAWRENCE, Sir John (Waldemar), 6th Bt, *cr* 1858; OBE 1945; freelance writer; Editor of Frontier, 1957–75; *b* 27 May 1907; *s* of Sir Alexander Waldemar Lawrence, 4th Bt, and Anne Elizabeth Le Poer (*née* Wynne); *S* brother, Sir Henry Eustace Waldemar Lawrence, 5th Bt, 1967; *m* 1948, Jacynth Mary (*née* Ellerton) (*d* 1987); no *c*; *m* 1988, Audrey Viola, *widow* of John Woodiwiss. *Educ:* Eton; New Coll., Oxford (MA, Lit. Hum.). Personal Asst to Dir of German Jewish Aid Cttee, 1938–39; with BBC as European Intelligence Officer and European Services Organiser, 1939–42; Press Attaché, HM Embassy, USSR, 1942–45; became freelance writer, 1946. Pres., Keston Inst. (formerly Centre for Study of Religion and Communism), 1984– (Chm., 1969–83); Chm., GB USSR Assoc., 1970–85. Officer, Order of Orange Nassau, 1950. *Publications:* Life in Russia, 1947; Russia in the Making, 1957; A History of Russia, 1960, 7th edn 1993; The Hard Facts of Unity, 1961; Russia (Methuen's Outlines), 1965; Soviet Russia, 1967; Russians Observed, 1969; Take Hold of Change, 1976; The Journals of Honoria Lawrence, 1980; The Hammer and the Cross, 1986; Lawrence of Lucknow, 1990. *Recreations:* travelling, reading in ten languages. *Heir: b* George Alexander Waldemar Lawrence [*b* 22 Sept. 1910; *m* 1949, Olga, *d* of late Peter Schilovsky; one *s* two *d*]. *Address:* 24 St Leonard's Terrace, SW3 4QG. *T:* 0171–730 8033; 1 Naishes Cottages, Northstoke, Bath BA1 9AT. *Club:* Athenæum.

LAWRENCE, John Wilfred, RE 1987; book illustrator and wood engraver; *b* 15 Sept. 1933; *s* of Wilfred James Lawrence and Audrey Constance (*née* Thomas); *m* 1957, Myra Gillian Bell; two *d. Educ:* Salesian Coll., Cowley, Oxford; Hastings Sch. of Art; Central Sch. of Art. Visiting Lecturer in Illustration: Brighton Polytech., 1960–68; Camberwell Sch. of Art, 1960–; Vis. Prof. in Illustration, London Inst., 1994–; External Assessor in Illustration: Bristol Polytech., 1978–81; Brighton Polytech., 1982–85; Duncan of Jordanstone Coll. of Art, 1986–89; Exeter Coll. of Art, 1986–89; Kingston Polytechnic, 1989–93; Edinburgh Coll. of Art, 1991–94. Member: Art Workers Guild, 1972 (Master, 1990); Soc. of Wood Engravers, 1984. Work represented in Ashmolean Mus., V&A Mus., Nat. Mus. of Wales, and collections abroad. *Publications:* The Giant of Grabbist, 1968; Pope Leo's Elephant, 1969; Rabbit and Pork Rhyming Talk, 1975 (Francis Williams Book Illustration Award, 1977); Tongue Twisters, 1976; George, His Elephant and Castle, 1983; A Selection of Wood Engravings, 1986; Good Babies, Bad Babies, 1987; *illustrated:* more than 100 books, incl.: Colonel Jack, 1967 (Francis Williams Book Illustration Award, 1971); Diary of a Nobody, 1969; The Blue Fairy Book, 1975; The Illustrated Watership Down, 1976; Everyman's Book of English Folk Tales, 1981; The Magic Apple Tree, 1982; Mabel's Story, 1984; Entertaining with Cranks, 1985; Emily's Own Elephant, 1987; Christmas in Exeter Street, 1989; A New Treasury of Poetry, 1990; The Sword of Honour trilogy, 1990; Treasure Island, 1990; Shades of Green, 1991 (Signal Prize for Poetry); Poems for the Young, 1992; King of King's, 1993; The Twelve Days of Christmas, 1994; The Christmas Collection, 1994; Memoirs of a Georgian Rake, 1995; Robin Hood, 1995; Poems for Christmas, 1995. *Address:* 22A Castlewood Road, N16 6DW. *T:* 0181–809 3482.

LAWRENCE, Michael Hugh, CMG 1972; Head of the Administration Department, House of Commons, 1972–80; retired 1980; *b* 9 July 1920; *s* of late Hugh Moxon Lawrence and Mrs. L. N. Lawrence; *m* 1948, Rachel Mary (MA Cantab), *d* of late Humphrey Gamon, Gt Barrow, Cheshire; one *s* two *d. Educ:* Highgate (Scholar); St Catharine's Coll., Cambridge (Exhibnr; MA). Served Indian Army, 1940–45. Indian Civil Service, 1945–46; Asst Clerk, House of Commons, 1947; Senior Clerk, 1948; Deputy Principal Clerk, 1962; Clerk of the Overseas Office, 1967–72; Clerk Administrator, H of C Services Cttee, 1972–76; Mem., Bd of Management, House of Commons, 1979–80. Sec., History of Parliament Trust, 1959–66. *Recreations:* beagling, looking at churches, gardening. *Address:* 22 Stradbroke Road, Southwold, Suffolk IP18 6LQ. *T:* Southwold (01502) 722794.

LAWRENCE, Michael John, PhD; FCA; Chief Executive, London Stock Exchange, since 1994; *b* 25 Oct. 1943; *s* of Geoffrey Frederick Lawrence and Kathleen Bridge Lawrence; *m* 1967, Maureen Joy Blennerhasset; two *s* one *d. Educ:* Exeter Univ. (BSc 1st Cl. Hons Physics); Bristol Univ. (PhD Mathematical Physics). FCA 1972. With Price Waterhouse, 1969–87, Partner 1978; Finance Dir, Prudential Corp., 1988–93. Non-executive Director: PLA, 1983–89; London Transport, 1994–. Ext. Mem., Council, DRA, 1990–. Chm., 100 Gp of Finance Dirs, 1991–93. Freeman, City of London, 1974; Liveryman Tin Plate Workers' Co., 1974–. *Recreations:* flying, sailing, bridge, tennis, opera. *Address:* London Stock Exchange, EC2N 1HP.

LAWRENCE, Murray; *see* Lawrence, W. N. M.

LAWRENCE, Sir Patrick; *see* Lawrence, Sir J. P. G.

LAWRENCE, Peter Anthony, PhD; FRS 1983; Staff Scientist, Medical Research Council Laboratory of Molecular Biology, Cambridge, since 1969; *b* 23 June 1941; *s* of Ivor Douglas Lawrence and Joy Lawrence (*née* Liebert); *m* 1971, Birgitta Haraldson. *Educ:* Wennington Sch., Wetherby, Yorks; Cambridge Univ. (MA, PhD). Harkness Fellowship, 1965–67; Dept of Genetics, Univ. of Cambridge, 1967–69. *Publications:* Insect Development (ed), 1976; The Making of a Fly, 1992; scientific papers. *Recreations:* Ascalaphidae, fungi, gardening, golf, theatre, trees. *Address:* MRC Laboratory of Molecular Biology, Hills Road, Cambridge CB2 2QH.

LAWRENCE, Richard; *see* Lawrence, H. R. G.

LAWRENCE, Timothy; His Honour Judge Lawrence; a Circuit Judge, since 1986; President of Industrial Tribunals for England and Wales, since 1991; *b* 29 April 1942; *s* of A. Whiteman Lawrence, MBE, and Phyllis G. Lawrence (*née* Lloyd-Jones). *Educ:* Bedford School. Admitted Solicitor, 1967; with Solicitor's Dept, New Scotland Yard, 1967–70; Partner with Claude Hornby & Cox, Solicitors, 1970–86 (Sen. Partner, 1977–86). An Asst Recorder, 1980; a Recorder, 1983–86. Pres., London Criminal Courts Solicitors' Assoc., 1984–86 (Sec., 1974–84); Chm., No 14 Area, Regional Duty Solicitor Cttee, 1984–86; Legal Mem., Mental Health Review Tribunals, 1989–; Member: No 13 Area, Legal Aid Cttee, 1983–86; Law Society's Criminal Law Cttee, 1980–86; Council, Westminster Law Soc., 1979–82; Judicial Studies Bd, 1984–88, 1991–; British Academy of Forensic Sciences, 1972– (Pres., 1992–93). Legal Assessor: Professions Supplementary to Medicine, 1976–86; Insurance Brokers Registration Council, 1983–86. FRSA 1991. *Publications:* various articles in legal jls. *Recreations:* walking, wine, travel. *Address:* 8 Slaidburn Street, SW10 0JP; Hill Cottage, Great Walsingham, Norfolk NR22 6DR. *Club:* Hurlingham.

LAWRENCE, Vernon John; Managing Director, MAI Productions, since 1995; *b* 30 April 1940; *m* 1960, Jennifer Mary Drewe; two *s* one *d. Educ:* Dulwich Coll.; Kelham Coll. BBC Studio Manager, 1958; BBC Radio Producer, 1964; BBC TV Producer and Dir, 1967; Yorkshire Television: Exec. Producer, 1973; Controller, Entertainment, 1985; Controller, Network Drama and Entertainment, ITV, 1993–95. FRTS. *Recreations:* oil painting, fishing, walking, gardening. *Address:* MAI Productions, 49 Leicester Square, WC2H 7LY. *T:* 0171–389 8651.

LAWRENCE, (Walter Nicholas) Murray; Chairman of Lloyd's, 1988–90 (a Deputy Chairman 1982, 1984–87; Member: Committee of Lloyd's, 1979–82; Council of Lloyd's, annually since 1984); Chairman, Murray Lawrence Holdings Ltd, since 1988; *b* 8 Feb. 1935; *s* of Henry Walter Neville Lawrence and Sarah Schuyler Lawrence (*née* Butler); *m* 1961, Sally Louise O'Dwyer; two *d. Educ:* Winchester Coll.; Trinity Coll., Oxford (BA, MA). C. T. Bowring & Co. (Ins.) Ltd, 1957–62; Asst Underwriter, H. Bowring & Others, 1962–70, Underwriter, 1970–84; Director: C. T. Bowring (Underwriting Agencies) Ltd, 1973–84; C. T. Bowring & Co. Ltd, 1976–84; Murray Lawrence Members Agency Ltd, 1988– (Chm., 1988–93); Murray Lawrence & Partners Ltd, 1989– (Sen. Partner, 1985–89; Chm., 1989–92); Chm., Fairway (Underwriting Agencies) Ltd, 1979–85. Mem., Lloyd's Underwriters Non-Marine Assoc., 1970–84 (Dep. Chm., 1977; Chm., 1978). *Recreations:* golf, opera, travelling. *Clubs:* Boodle's, MCC; Royal & Ancient (St Andrews), Woking, Swinley, Royal St George's (Sandwich), Rye.

LAWRENCE, Sir William (Fettiplace), 5th Bt *cr* 1867, of Ealing Park, Middlesex; General Manager, Newdawn & Sun Ltd, since 1981; *b* 23 Aug. 1954; *s* of Sir William Lawrence, 4th Bt and of Pamela, *yr d* of J. E. Gordon; *S* father, 1986. *Educ:* King Edward VI School, Stratford-upon-Avon. Assistant Accountant, Wilmot Breeden Ltd/W. B. Bumpers Ltd, 1973–81. Member: Stratford-on-Avon District Council, 1982– (Chm., 1990–91); S Warwickshire CHC, 1983–84; S Warwickshire HA, 1984–92; S Warwickshire Gen. Hosps NHS Trust, 1993–; Dir, S Warwickshire Business Partnership, 1995–. Chm., Heart of England Tourist Bd, 1991– (Mem. Bd, 1989–); Mem., W Midlands Arts, 1989–91 (Mem., Management Council, 1984–89). President: Stratford and District Mencap, 1990–; Stratford-upon-Avon Chamber Music Soc., 1991–; Stratford Town FC, 1992–94; Pres., and Chm. of Trustees, Action Unlimited Trust, 1991– (Trustee, 1988–). Mem. Court, Univ. of Birmingham, 1990–. Gov., Royal Shakespeare Theatre, 1991–. *Heir: cousin* Peter Stafford Hayden Lawrence [*b* 9 Feb. 1913; *m* 1940, Helena Francis, *d* of late Hon. George William Lyttelton; two *s* four *d*]. *Address:* The Knoll, Walcote, near Alcester, Warwickshire B49 6LZ. *T:* Great Alne (01789) 488303.

LAWRENCE, William Robert, QPM 1991; Chief Constable, South Wales Constabulary, since 1989; *b* 21 Sept. 1942; *s* of William Thomas and Norah Lawrence; *m* 1965, Kathleen Ann Lawrence; one *s* one *d. Educ:* Maesydderwen Grammar Sch. BA Open Univ., 1988. Joined Mid Wales, then Dyfed Powys Constabulary, 1961; Sergeant, 1970; Inspector,

1972; Chief Inspector, 1975; transf. to W Mercia as Supt, 1978; Chief Supt, 1982; Asst Chief Constable 1983, Dep. Chief Constable 1985, Staffordshire Police. SBStJ 1986. *Recreations:* golf, fly fishing, Rugby, amateur boxing. *Address:* Chief Constable's Office, South Wales Constabulary, Police Headquarters, Bridgend, Mid Glamorgan CF31 3SU. *T:* Bridgend (01656) 655555.

LAWRENCE-JONES, Sir Christopher, 6th Bt *cr* 1831; *b* 19 Jan. 1940; *S* uncle, 1969; *m* 1967, Gail Pittar, Auckland, NZ; two *s. Educ:* Sherborne; Gonville and Caius Coll., Cambridge; St Thomas' Hospital. MA Cantab 1964; MB, BChir Cantab 1964; DIH Eng. 1968. MFOM 1979, FFOM 1987; FRCP 1991. Medical adviser to various orgns, 1967–94; CMO, ICI, 1985–93; Chm., Medichem, 1986–92. Pres., Section of Occupational Medicine, RSM, 1990–91; Mem. Management Cttee, British Occupational Health Res. Foundn, 1991–94. *Recreation:* cruising under sail (yacht Mermerus). *Heir: s* Mark Christopher Lawrence-Jones, *b* 28 Dec. 1968. *Club:* Royal Cruising.

LAWRENSON, Prof. Peter John, DSc; FRS 1982; FEng, FIEE, FIEEE; Founder and Chairman, Switched Reluctance Drives Ltd, since 1981; Professor of Electrical Engineering, Leeds University, 1966–91, now Emeritus; *b* 12 March 1933; *s* of John Lawrenson and Emily (*née* Houghton); *m* 1958, Shirley Hannah Foster; one *s* three *d. Educ:* Prescot Grammar Sch.; Manchester Univ. (BSc, MSc; DSc 1971). FEng 1980; FIEE 1974; FIEEE 1975. Duddell Scholar, IEE, 1951–54; Res. Engr, Associated Electrical Industries, 1956–61; University of Leeds: Lectr, 1961–65; Reader, 1965–66; Head, Dept of Electrical and Electronic Engrg, 1974–84; Chm., Faculty of Science and Applied Science, 1978–80; Chm., Shadow Faculty of Engrg, 1981. Science and Engineering Research Council: Mem., Electrical and Systems Cttee, 1971–77; Chm., Electrical Engrg Sub-Cttee, 1981–84; Mem., Machines and Power Cttee, 1981–84; Mem., Engrg Bd, 1984–87; Organiser, National Initiative, Integrated Drive Systems, 1984–86. Director: Allenwest Ltd, 1988–91; Dale Electric Internat., 1988–94. Institution of Electrical Engineers: Mem. Council, 1966–69 and 1981–; Chm., Accreditation Cttee, 1979–83; Chm., Power Divisional Bd, 1985–86; Dep. Pres., 1990–92; Pres., 1992–93. Mem. of cttees, Engrg Council, 1983–89. Mem. Council, Buckingham Univ., 1987–93. IEE Awards: Premia-Crompton, 1957 and 1967; John Hopkinson, 1965; The Instn, 1981; Faraday Medal, 1990. James Alfred Ewing Medal, ICE and Royal Soc., 1983; Royal Soc. Esso Energy Award, 1985. *Publications:* (with K. J. Binns) Analysis and Computation of Electromagnetic Field Problems, 1963, 2nd edn 1973; (with M. R. Harris and J. M. Stephenson) Per Unit Systems, 1970; (with K. J. Binns and C. W. Trowbridge) The Analytical and Numerical Solution of Electric and Magnetic Fields, 1992; papers and patents in areas of electromagnetism, electromechanics and control. *Recreations:* lawn tennis, squash, chess, bridge, jewelry making. *Address:* Spen Watch, 318 Spen Lane, Leeds LS16 5BA. *T:* Leeds (0113) 275 5849.

LAWREY, Keith, JP; Headmaster, Cannock School, since 1992; *b* 21 Aug. 1940; *s* of George William Bishop Lawrey and Edna Muriel (*née* Gass); *m* 1969, Helen Jane Marriott, BA; two *s* two *d. Educ:* Colfe's Sch.; Birkbeck Coll., Univ. of London (MSc Econ; LLB). Barrister-at-Law; called to Bar, Gray's Inn, 1972. Education Officer, Plastics and Rubber Inst., 1960–68; Lectr and Sen. Lectr, Bucks Coll. of Higher Educn, 1968–74; Head of Dept of Business Studies, Mid-Kent Coll. of Higher and Further Educn, 1974–78; Sec.-Gen., Library Assoc., 1978–84; Dean, Faculty of Business and Management, Harrow Coll. of Higher Educn, subseq. Head, Sch. of Business and Management, Polytechnic of Central London/Harrow Coll., 1984–90; Sec. and Registrar, RCVS, 1990–91. FCollP (Hon. Treas., 1987–); FCIS. Gov., Cannock Sch., 1976–92. Mem., Orpington Rotary Club. Mem., Worshipful Co. of Chartered Secretaries and Administrators. JP Inner London, 1974. *Publications:* papers in Jl, Coll. of Preceptors, Jl Assoc. of Law Teachers, Trans and Jl of Plastics Inst. *Recreations:* preaching, sailing, swimming, theatre, gardening. *Address:* Cannock School, Chelsfield, Orpington, Kent BR6 7PH. *Clubs:* Old Colfeians; Dell Quay Sailing.

LAWS, Courtney Alexander, OBE 1987; OD 1978; Director, Brixton Neighbourhood Community Association, since 1971; *b* Morant Bay, St Thomas, Jamaica, 16 June 1934; *s* of Ezekiel Laws and Agatha Laws; *m* 1955, Wilhel, (Rubie), Brown, JP; one *s* two *d. Educ:* Morant Bay Elem. Sch.; Jones Pen and Rollington Town Elem. Sch.; Lincoln Coll.; Nat. Coll. for Youth Workers, Leicester; Cranfield Coll., Bedford. Rep., Works Cttee, Peak Freans Biscuit Co., 1960–69; Shop Steward, TGWU, 1960–70. Member: Lambeth Council for Community Relations, 1964–; Consortium of Ethnic Minorities, Lambeth, 1978–; W Indian Standing Conf., 1959–; Campaign against Racial Discrimination, 1960–; NCCI, 1960–; Commn for Racial Equality, 1977–80; Central Cttee, British Caribbean Assoc. (Exec. Mem.), 1960–; Assoc. of Jamaicans (Founder Mem.), 1965; Geneva and Somerleyton Community Assoc., 1966–; Consultative Cttee, ILEA, Lambeth, 1975–; Consultative Council, City and E London Coll., 1975–; South Eastern Gas Consumers' Council, 1980–; Governor, Brixton Coll. of Further and Higher Educn, 1970–; Member: W Indian Sen. Citizens' Assoc. (Pres.), 1973–; St John's Interracial Club, 1958–; Brixton United Cricket Club, 1968– (Pres.); Brixton Domino Club (Chm.); Oasis Sports and Social Club, 1969–. Medal of Appreciation, Prime Minister of Jamaica, 1987; Community of Brixton Award, 1987. *Recreations:* reading, music. *Address:* 71 Atlantic Road, SW9 8PU. *T:* 0171–274 0011.

LAWS, Frederick Geoffrey; Vice-Chairman, Commission for Local Administration in England, 1984–94; *b* Blackpool, 1 Aug. 1928; *s* of Frederick and Annetta Laws. *Educ:* Arnold School; Manchester Univ.; London Univ. (LLB); solicitor 1952. Asst Solicitor, Blackpool Corp., 1952–54, Bournemouth Corp., 1954–59; Southend-on-Sea Corporation: Asst Sol., 1959–62; Dep. Town Clerk and Clerk of the Peace, 1962–71; Town Clerk, 1971–74; Chief Exec., Southend-on-Sea Borough Council, 1974–84. Pres., Southend-on-Sea Law Soc., 1981. Hon. Freeman, Southend-on-Sea Borough Council, 1985.

LAWS, Hon. Sir John (Grant McKenzie), Kt 1992; **Hon. Mr Justice Laws;** a Judge of the High Court of Justice, Queen's Bench Division, since 1992; *b* 10 May 1945; *s* of late Dr Frederic Laws and Dr Margaret Ross Laws, *d* of Prof. John Grant McKenzie; *m* 1973, Sophie Susan Sydenham Cole Marshall, BLitt, MA; one *d. Educ:* Durham Cathedral Choir Sch.; Durham Sch. (King's Scholar); Exeter Coll., Oxford (Sen. Open Classical Scholar; BA 1967, Hon. Sch. of Lit. Hum. 1st Cl.; MA 1976). Called to the Bar, Inner Temple, 1970, Bencher, 1985; practice at Common Law Bar, 1971–92; First Junior Treasury Counsel, Common Law, 1984–92; Asst Recorder, 1983–85; Recorder, 1985–92; admitted to Bar: New South Wales, 1987; Gibraltar, 1988. Pres., Bar European Gp, 1994. An Hon. Vice-Pres., Administrative Law Bar Assoc., 1992. Hon. Fellow, Robinson Coll., Cambridge, 1992. *Publications:* (contrib.) Halsbury's Laws of England, 4th edn 1973; (contrib.) Dict. of Medical Ethics, 1977; (contrib.) Supperstone and Goudie, Judicial Review, 1992; reviews for Theology, Law & Justice; contribs to legal jls. *Recreations:* Greece, living in London, philosophy. *Address:* Royal Courts of Justice, WC2A 2LL. *Club:* Garrick.

LAWS, John William, CBE 1982; FRCP; FRCR; formerly consultant diagnostic radiologist; Director of Radiology, King's College Hospital, and Director of Radiological Studies, King's College Hospital Medical School, 1967–86; *b* 25 Oct. 1921; *s* of Robert Montgomery Laws and Lucy Ibbotson; *m* 1st, 1945, Dr Pamela King, MRCS, LRCP (*d* 1985); one *s* one *d*; 2nd, 1986, Dr Diana Brinkley (*née* Rawlence), FRCR. *Educ:* The Leys Sch., Cambridge; Sheffield Univ. Med. Sch. MB ChB 1944; DMRD 1952; MRCP 1951; FRCR (FFR 1955); FRCP 1967. Nat. service, 1947–49 (Captain RAMC). House Physician and House Surg., Royal Hosp., Sheffield, 1944–45; Res. Surgical Officer, Salisbury Gen. Infirmary, 1945–47; Med. Registrar, 1949–51, Radiology Registrar and Sen. Registrar, 1951–55, United Sheffield Hosps; Consultant Radiologist, Dep. Dir, Hammersmith Hosp., and Hon. Lectr, RPMS, 1955–67. Consultant Civilian Advr to Army, 1976–86; Med. Dir, King's Centre for Assessment of Radiol Equipment, 1979–86. Chm., Radiol Equipment Sub-Cttee, DHSS, 1972–81; Member: Central Adv. Cttee on Hosp. Med. Records, DHSS, 1969–74; Radiol Adv. Cttee, DHSS, 1972–86; Consultant Advr in Radiol., DHSS, 1982–86. Chm., British Delegn, XV Internat. Congress of Radiol., 1981. Royal College (formerly Faculty) of Radiologists: Mem. Fellowship Bd, 1966–71; Hon. Sec., 1974–75; Registrar, 1975–76; Warden of Fellowship, 1976–80; Pres., 1980–83; Knox Lectr, 1984. Mem. Council, RCS, 1981–84. Vis Prof. and Lectr at academic instns and congresses worldwide. Member Editorial Board: Clin. Radiol., 1960–63; Gut, 1970–74; Gastrointestinal Radiol., 1975–85; Asst, later Hon., Editor, British Jl of Radiol., 1961–71. Hon. FACR 1973; Hon. FFR RCSI 1975; Hon. FRACR 1979. Barclay Prize, British Inst. of Radiol., 1964. *Publications:* numerous papers and pubns on various aspects of clinical radiology, particularly gastrointestinal and hepatic radiology and the radiology of pulmonary disease, in medical journals and books. *Recreations:* listening to music, sculpting. *Address:* 5 Frank Dixon Way, Dulwich, SE21 7BB. *T:* 0181–693 4815.

LAWS, Richard Maitland, CBE 1983; PhD, ScD; FRS 1980; Director, British Antarctic Survey, 1973–87; Master, St Edmund's College, Cambridge, since 1985; *b* 23 April 1926; *s* of Percy Malcolm Laws and Florence May (*née* Heslop); *m* 1954, Maureen Isobel Winifred (*née* Holmes); three *s. Educ:* Dame Allan's Sch., Newcastle-on-Tyne; St Catharine's Coll., Cambridge (Open Scholar, 1944; Res. Scholar, 1952–53; Hon. Fellow, 1982). BA Cantab 1947, MA 1952, PhD 1953; ScD 1994; FIBiol 1973. Biologist and Base Leader, Falkland Is Dependencies Survey, 1947–53; Biologist and Whaling Inspector, F/F Balaena, 1953–54; Principal Sci. Officer, Nat. Inst. of Oceanography, 1954–61; Dir, Nuffield Unit of Tropical Animal Ecology, Uganda, 1961–67; Dir, Tsavo Research Project, Kenya, 1967–68; Smuts Meml Fund Fellowship, 1968–69; Leverhulme Research Fellowship, 1969; Head, Life Sciences Div., British Antarctic Survey, 1969–73. Dir, NERC Sea Mammal Res. Unit, 1977–87; Scientific Committee for Antarctic Research: Member: Gp of Specialists on Seals, 1972– (Convener, 1972–88); Biology Working Gp, 1972–90 (Chm., 1980–86); UK Delegate, 1984–93; Pres., 1990–94. Food and Agriculture Organization: Mem., 1974–77, Chm., 1976–77, Working Party on Marine Mammals; Chm., Scientific Consultation on Conservation and Management of Marine Mammals and their Environment, 1976. Zoological Society of London: Mem. Council, 1982–84; Vice-Pres., 1983–84; Sec., 1984–88. University of Cambridge: Mem., Financial Bd, 1988–91; Mem., Council of Senate, 1989–92; Chm., Local Examinations Syndicate, 1990–94. Vice-Pres., Inst. Biol., 1984–85. Hon. Lectr, Makerere Univ., 1962–66; 36th annual Lectr, CIBA Foundn, 1984. Hon. DSc Bath, 1991. Bruce Medal, RSE, 1954; Scientific Medal, Zool Soc. London, 1965; Polar Medal, 1976. *Publications:* (with I. S. C. Parker and R. C. B. Johnstone) Elephants and their Habitats, 1975; (ed) Scientific Research in Antarctica, 1977; (ed) Antarctic Ecology, 1984; (ed jtly) Antarctic Nutrient Cycles and Food Webs, 1985; Antarctica: the last frontier, 1989; (ed jtly) Life at Low Temperatures, 1990; (ed jtly) Antarctica and Environmental Change, 1992; (ed) Antarctic Seals: research methods and techniques, 1993; (ed jtly) Elephant Seals: aspects of population, ecology, behaviour and physiology, 1994; papers in biol jls. *Recreations:* walking, photography, painting. *Address:* St Edmund's College, Cambridge CB3 0BN. *T:* Cambridge (01223) 336250; 3 The Footpath, Coton, Cambridge CB3 7PX. *T:* Madingley (01954) 210567.

LAWS, Stephen Charles; Parliamentary Counsel, since 1991; *b* 28 Jan. 1950; *s* of late Dennis Arthur Laws and of Beryl Elizabeth Laws (*née* Roe); *m* 1972, Angela Mary Deardon; two *s* three *d. Educ:* St Dunstan's College, Catford; Bristol Univ. (LLB Hons 1972). Called to the Bar, Middle Temple, 1973. Asst Lectr, Univ. of Bristol, 1972; Legal Asst, Home Office, 1975; Asst, Sen. Asst, then Dep. Parly Counsel, 1976–91. *Publications:* (with Peter Knowles) Statutes title in Halsbury's Laws of England, 4th edn, 1983. *Address:* Office of the Parliamentary Counsel, 36 Whitehall, SW1A 2AY. *T:* 0171–210 6611.

LAWSON, family name of **Barons Burnham** and **Lawson of Blaby**.

LAWSON OF BLABY, Baron *cr* 1992 (Life Peer), of Newnham in the County of Northamptonshire; **Nigel Lawson**, PC 1981; *b* 11 March 1932; *o s* of late Ralph Lawson and of Joan Elisabeth Lawson (*née* Davis); *m* 1st, 1955, Vanessa Salmon (marr. diss. 1980; she *d* 1985); one *s* two *d* (and one *d* decd); 2nd, 1980, Thérèse Mary Maclear; one *s* one *d. Educ:* Westminster; Christ Church, Oxford (Scholar). 1st class hons PPE, 1954. Served with Royal Navy (Sub-Lt RNVR), 1954–56. Mem. Editorial Staff, Financial Times, 1956–60; City Editor, Sunday Telegraph, 1961–63; Special Assistant to Prime Minister (Sir Alec Douglas-Home), 1963–64; Financial Times columnist and BBC broadcaster, 1965; Editor of the Spectator, 1966–70; regular contributor to: Sunday Times and Evening Standard, 1970–71; The Times, 1971–72; Fellow, Nuffield Coll., Oxford, 1972–73; Special Pol Advr, Cons. Party HQ, 1973–74. Contested (C) Eton and Slough, 1970; MP (C) Blaby, Leics, Feb. 1974–1992; An Opposition Whip, 1976–77; an Opposition Spokesman on Treasury and Economic Affairs, 1977–79; Financial Sec. to the Treasury, 1979–81; Sec. of State for Energy, 1981–83; Chancellor of the Exchequer, 1983–89. Chm., Coningsby Club, 1963–64. Vice-Chm., Cons. Political Centre Nat. Adv. Cttee, 1972–75. Chm., Central Europe Trust Co., 1990–; Dir, Barclays Bank, 1990–; Member, International Advisory Board: Creditanstalt Bankverein, 1991–; Total SA, 1994–. Mem., Bd of Dirs, Inst. for Internat. Econs, Washington, 1991–; Pres., British Inst. of Energy Econs, 1995–. *Publications:* (with Jock Bruce-Gardyne) The Power Game, 1976; The View from No 11: memoirs of a Tory radical, 1992. *Address:* House of Lords, SW1P 0AW. *Clubs:* Garrick, Pratt's, Political Economy.

See also Hon. D. R. C. Lawson.

LAWSON, Sir Christopher (Donald), Kt 1984; management consultant; Director, Communications Centre, since 1984; *b* 31 Oct. 1922; *s* of James Lawson and Ellen de Verrine; *m* 1945, Marjorie Bristow; two *s* one *d. Educ:* Magdalen Coll., Oxford. Served RAF, 1941–49: Pilot, Sqdn Leader. Thomas Hedley (Proctor and Gamble), 1949–57; Cooper McDougal Robertson, 1958–61; Managing Dir, TMC, 1961–63; Director: Mars Ltd, 1965–81; Mars Inc., USA, 1975–82; Pres., Mars Snackmaster, USA, 1977–82; Chm. and Man. Dir, Goodblue Ltd, 1981–; Chm., Spearhead Ltd, 1983–; Dir of Marketing, 1982–83, Dir of Special Services, 1986–87, Cons. and Unionist Party. *Recreations:* collecting antiques and new artists' work; all sport, particularly golf, cricket, hockey. *Address:* Church Cottage, Great Witcombe, Glos GL3 4TT. *Clubs:* Royal Air Force, Carlton, MCC; Lillybrook Golf (Cheltenham); Doublegate Country (Ga, USA).

LAWSON, Prof. David Hamilton, CBE 1993; Consultant Physician, Glasgow Royal Infirmary, since 1973; *b* 27 May 1939; *s* of David Lawson and Margaret Harvey Lawson (*née* White); *m* 1963, Alison Diamond; three *s*. *Educ:* High Sch. of Glasgow; Univ. of Glasgow. MB, ChB 1962; MD 1973. FRCPE 1975; FRCPGlas 1986; FFPM 1989. Junior medical posts in Royal Infirmary and Western Infirmary, Glasgow; Boston Collaborative Drug Surveillance Prog., Boston, Mass, 1970–72; Attending Physician, Lemuel Shattuck Hosp., Boston, 1971; Adviser on Adverse Drug Reactions, Wellcome Foundn, 1975–87; Vis. Prof., Faculty of Sci., Univ. of Strathclyde, 1976–. Chm., Medicines Commn, 1994–; Member: Health Services Res. Cttee of Chief Scientist Office, SHHD, 1984–88; Cttee on Safety of Medicines, Dept of Health (formerly DHSS), 1987–93; Mem., 1979–91, Chm., 1987–91, Cttee on Review of Medicines, Dept of Health (formerly DHSS). Mem. Council, RCPE, 1992–. Examiner, Final MB, Univs of Glasgow, Dundee, Birmingham, London, Kuala Lumpur, Malaysia. *Publications:* Clinical Pharmacy and Hospital Drug Management (ed with R. M. E. Richards), 1982; Current Medicine 2, 1990; (ed jtly) Risk Factors for Adverse Drug Reactions: epidemiological approaches, 1990; Current Medicine 3, 1991; Current Medicine 4, 1994; papers on clinical pharmacol, haematol and renal topics. *Recreations:* hill-walking, photography, bird-watching. *Address:* 25 Kirkland Avenue, Blanefield, Glasgow G63 9BY. *T:* Blanefield (01360) 770081. *Club:* Commonwealth Trust.

LAWSON, Hon. Dominic Ralph Campden; Editor, The Spectator, since 1990; *b* 17 Dec. 1956; *s* of Baron Lawson of Blaby, *qv* and late Vanessa Mary Addison Lawson (*née* Salmon); *m* 1st, 1982, Jane Whytehead (marr. diss.); 2nd, 1991, Hon. Rosamond Mary, *o d* of Viscount Monckton of Brenchley, *qv*; two *d*. *Educ:* Westminster Sch.; Christ Church, Oxford (exhibnr; Hons PPE). Researcher, BBC TV and radio, 1979–81; Financial Times: joined 1981; energy corresp., 1983–86; columnist (Lex), 1986–87; Dep. Editor, The Spectator, 1987–90; columnist: Sunday Correspondent, 1990; Financial Times, 1991–94; Daily Telegraph, 1994–. Mem., Wing's Head Chess Club. FRSA 1993. Harold Wincott Prize for financial journalism, 1987. *Publications:* (with Raymond Keene) Kasparov-Korchnoi, the London Contest, 1983; (jtly) Britain in the Eighties, 1989; The Inner Game, 1993. *Recreations:* cricket, chess. *Address:* The Spectator, 56 Doughty Street, WC1N 2LL. *Clubs:* Garrick, Beefsteak, Academy, MCC.

LAWSON, Prof. Donald Douglas; Professor of Veterinary Surgery, University of Glasgow, 1974–86; *b* 25 May 1924; *s* of Alexander Lawson and Jessie Macnaughton; *m* 1949, Barbara Ness; two *s* two *d*. *Educ:* Whitehill Sch., Glasgow; Glasgow Veterinary Coll. MRCVS, BSc, DVR. Asst in Veterinary Practice, 1946–47; Asst, Surgery Dept, Glasgow Vet. Coll., 1947–49; Glasgow Univ.: Lectr, Vet. Surgery, 1949–57; Sen. Lectr, 1957–66; Reader, 1966–71; Titular Prof., 1971–74. *Publications:* many articles in Veterinary Record and Jl of Small Animal Practice. *Recreations:* gardening, motoring. *Address:* The Cottage, Mill of Lumphart, Oldmeldrum, Aberdeenshire AB51 0EA. *T:* Oldmeldrum (01651) 872688.

LAWSON, Edmund James, QC 1988; *b* 17 April 1948; *s* of Donald and Veronica Lawson; *m* 1973, Jennifer Cleary; three *s*. *Educ:* City of Norwich Sch.; Trinity Hall, Cambridge (BA Hons, Law). Called to the Bar, Gray's Inn, 1971; in chambers of: Dr F. Hallis, 1971–76; Sir Arthur Irvine, QC, subseq. Gilbert Gray, QC, 1976–; Head of Chambers, 1990–. *Recreations:* music, family. *Address:* 4 Paper Buildings, Temple, EC4Y 7EX. *T:* 0171–583 7765.

LAWSON, Elizabeth Ann; QC 1989; *b* 29 April 1947; *d* of Alexander Edward Lawson, FCA, and Helen Jane Lawson (*née* Currie). *Educ:* Croydon High School for Girls (GPDST); Nottingham Univ. (LLB). Called to Bar, Gray's Inn, 1969. Chm., Leeways Enquiry for London Borough of Lewisham, 1985; Chm., Liam Johnson Review for Islington Area Child Protection Cttee, 1989. *Recreations:* knitting, reading, cake decoration. *Address:* Cloisters, Temple, EC4Y 7AA. *T:* 0171–583 0303.

LAWSON, Rear-Adm. Frederick Charles William, CB 1971; DSC 1942 and Bar, 1945; Chief Executive, Royal Dockyards, Ministry of Defence, 1972–75; *b* 20 April 1917; *s* of M. L. Lawson, formerly of Public Works Dept, Punjab, India; *m* 1945, Dorothy (*née* Norman) (*d* 1986), Eastbourne; one *s* three *d*. *Educ:* Eastbourne Coll.; RNEC. Joined RN, 1935; specialised in engrg; Cmdr 1949; Captain 1960; Cdre Supt Singapore, 1965–69; Rear-Adm. 1969; Flag Officer, Medway and Adm. Supt, HM Dockyard, Chatham, 1969–71, retired. *Recreation:* golf. *Address:* Weaverhoult, Woolley Street, Bradford-on-Avon, Wilts BA15 1AF.

See also Vice-Adm. M. A. C. Moore.

LAWSON, Prof. Gerald Hartley; Professor of Business Finance, Manchester Business School, University of Manchester, 1969–88, now Emeritus; financial and economic consultant; *b* 6 July 1933; of English parents; *m* 1957, Helga Elisabeth Anna Heine; three *s*. *Educ:* King's Coll., Univ. of Durham. BA (Econ), MA (Econ); MBA, PhD Manchester; FCCA. Accountant in industry, 1957–59; Lectr in Accountancy and Applied Economics, Univ. of Sheffield, 1959–66; Prof. of Business Studies, Univ. of Liverpool, 1966–69. Prof., Univ. of Augsburg, Germany, 1971–72; Prof., Univ. of Texas, 1977, 1981; Prof., Ruhr Univ., Bochum, 1980; British Council Scholar, Hochschule für Welthandel, Vienna, 1967, and Univ. of Louvain, 1978. Visiting Professor: Southern Methodist Univ., Dallas, 1989–93; Nanyang Technological Univ., Singapore, 1989; Martin Luther Univ., Halle-Wittenberg, 1993–96. Dir, Dietsmann (UK), 1984–89. *Publications:* (with D. W. Windle): Tables for Discounted Cash Flow, etc, Calculations, 1965 (5th repr. 1978); Capital Budgeting in the Corporation Tax Regime, 1967; (with M. Schweitzer and E. Trossman) Break-Even Analyses: basic model, variants, extensions, 1991; Studies in Cash Flow Accounting, 1992; many articles and translations. *Recreations:* cricket, skiing. *Address:* 1702 Woodcreek Drive, Richardson, TX 75082, USA. *Club:* Manchester Business School.

LAWSON, Hugh McDowall, BScEng London; CEng, FICE; Director of Leisure Services, Nottingham City Council, 1973–76; *b* Leeds, 13 Feb. 1912; *s* of late John Lawson, Pharmaceutical Chemist; *m* 1st, 1937, Dorothy (*d* 1982), *d* of late Rev. T. H. Mallinson, BA; two *s*; 2nd, 1988, Eva (*d* 1991), *widow* of Richard Koch, *d* of late Prof. David Holde, Berlin. *Educ:* Nottingham High Sch.; University Coll., Nottingham. Served in Royal Engineers, 1940–44. MP (Common Wealth) Skipton Div. of Yorks, 1944–45. Contested (Common Wealth) Harrow West Div., 1945; (Lab) Rushcliffe Div., 1950; (Lab) King's Lynn Div., 1955. Dep. City Engr, Nottingham, 1948–73. Mem. Council, ICE, 1972–75. *Address:* 68 Marshall Hill Drive, Mapperley, Nottingham NG3 6FS. *T:* Nottingham (0115) 960 5241.

LAWSON, Air Vice-Marshal Ian Douglas Napier, CB 1965; CBE 1961; DFC 1941, Bar 1943; AE 1945; RAF, retired; *b* 11 Nov. 1917; *y s* of late J. L. Lawson and Ethel Mary Lawson (*née* Ludgate); *m* 1945, Dorothy Joyce Graham Nash; one *s* one *d*. *Educ:* Brondesbury Coll.; Polytechnic, Regent Street. Aircraft Industry, 1934–39. Joined RAFVR 1938. Served War of 1939–45 (despatches thrice): Bomber Comd, 1940–41; Middle East Comd, 1941–45. Permanent Commission, 1945. Bomber Comd, 1945–46; Staff Coll., 1946; Air Ministry, 1946–49; Transport Comd, 1949–50; Middle East Comd, 1950–52; JSSC, 1953; Ministry of Defence, 1953–56; Flying Coll., Manby, 1956–57; Transport Comd, 1957–62; Air Forces Middle East, 1962–64; Commandant, RAF Coll., Cranwell, 1964–67; Asst Chief Adviser (Personnel and Logistics), MoD, 1967–69. Joined BAC, 1969, Chief Sales Exec., Weybridge, Bristol Div., 1974–79; Gen. Marketing Manager (civil), BAe, 1979–81; non-exec. Dir, Glos Air (Holdings) Ltd, 1981–82. FIMgt (FBIM 1974). US Legion of Merit. *Recreations:* gardening, motor sport. *Address:* The Dower Cottage, Bewley Lane, Lacock, Wilts SN15 2PG. *T:* Lacock (01249) 730307. *Club:* Royal Air Force.

LAWSON, James Robert; Regional Nursing Officer, Mersey, 1985–89; *b* 29 Dec. 1939; *s* of James and Grace Lawson; *m* 1962, Jean; two *d*. *Educ:* Keswick High School; Royal Albert Hosp. (Registered Nurse of Mentally Handicapped); Cumberland Infirmary (Registered Gen. Nurse). Chief Nurse, 1972; Area Nurse, Personnel, 1974; Divl Nursing Officer, 1976; District Nursing Officer, 1982–85. *Recreations:* fellwalking, caravaning, active sports. *Address:* Browside Cottage, Tanhouse Lane, Burtonwood, Warrington, Cheshire WA5 4BY. *T:* Warrington (01925) 632735.

LAWSON, John Alexander Reid, OBE 1979; FRCGP; General Medical Practitioner, 1948–86, retired; Regional Adviser in General Practice, Tayside Region, 1972–82; *b* 30 Aug. 1920; *s* of Thomas Reid Lawson and Helen Scrimgour Lawson; *m* 1944, Pat Kirk; two *s* two *d*. *Educ:* High Sch. of Dundee; Univ. of St Andrews (MB, ChB). RAMC, 1944–47 (Major). Surgical Registrar, Royal Infirmary, Dundee, 1947–48. Royal College of General Practitioners: Mem., 1952; Fellow, 1967; Chm. Council, 1973–76; Pres., 1982–85. Mem. Cttee of Enquiry into Competence to Practice, 1974–76; Chairman: Jt Cttee on Postgraduate Training for General Practice, 1975–78; Armed Service Gen. Practice Approval Bd, 1979–87. *Recreations:* shooting, fishing, golf, gardening. *Address:* The Ridges, 458 Perth Road, Dundee. *T:* Dundee (01382) 66675. *Clubs:* New (Edinburgh); Royal and Ancient Golf (St Andrews).

LAWSON, Col Sir John Charles Arthur Digby, 3rd Bt, *cr* 1900; DSO 1943; MC 1940; Colonel 11th Hussars, retired; former Chairman, Fairbairn Lawson Ltd, Leeds; *b* 24 Oct. 1912; *e s* of Sir Digby Lawson, Bt, TD, JP, and late Mrs Gerald Wallis (*née* Iris Mary Fitzgerald); *S* father 1959; *m* 1st, 1945, Rose (marr. diss., 1950; she *d* 1972), *widow* of Pilot Officer William Fiske, RAF, and *er d* of late D. C. Bingham and late Lady Rosabelle Brand; 2nd, 1954, Tresilla Ann Elinor (de Pret Roose) (*d* 1985), *d* of late Major E. Buller Leyborne Popham, MC; one *s*. *Educ:* Stowe; RMC, Sandhurst; commissioned 11th Hussars (PAO), 1933; Palestine, 1936–37; Transjordan Frontier Force, 1938; Western Desert, 1940–43 (despatches twice, MC, DSO); Armoured Adviser to Gen. Patton, N Africa, 1943; Staff Coll., 1943; US Marines Staff Course, 1944; Special Liaison Officer to Gen. Montgomery, NW Europe, 1944; Comd Inns of Court Regt, 1945–47; retired, 1947. Colonel, 11th Hussars (PAO), 1965–69; Col, The Royal Hussars (PWO), 1969–73. Legion of Merit (US). *Heir:* *s* Charles John Patrick Lawson [*b* 19 May 1959; *m* 1987, Lady Caroline Lowther, *d* of Earl of Lonsdale, *qv*; two *s* one *d*. *Educ:* Harrow; Royal Agricl Coll., Cirencester. With Jackson-Stops & Staff]. *Clubs:* Cavalry and Guards, MCC.

LAWSON, John David, ScD; FRS 1983; Deputy Chief Scientific Officer, Rutherford Appleton Laboratory, Science and Engineering Research Council, Chilton, Oxon, 1978–87, retired, now Hon. Scientist; *b* 4 April 1923; *s* of Ronald L. Lawson and Ruth (*née* Houseman); *m* 1949, Kathleen (*née* Wyllie); two *s* one *d*. *Educ:* Wolverhampton Grammar Sch.; St John's Coll., Cambridge (BA, ScD). FInstP. TRE Malvern, Aerials group, 1943; AERE Malvern Br., Accelerator gp, 1947; AERE Harwell, Gen. Physics Div., 1951–62; Microwave Laboratory, Stanford, USA, 1959–60; Rutherford Laboratory (later Rutherford Appleton Laboratory), Applied Phys. Div., and later Technology Div., 1962–87, except, Vis. Prof., Dept of Physics and Astronomy, Univ. of Maryland, USA, 1971; Culham Lab., Technology Div., 1975–76. *Publications:* The Physics of Charged Particle Beams, 1977, 2nd edn 1988; papers on various topics in applied physics in several jls. *Recreations:* travel, walking, collecting old books, bookbinding. *Address:* 7 Clifton Drive, Abingdon, Oxon OX14 1ET. *T:* Abingdon (01235) 521516.

LAWSON, Sir John Philip H; *see* Howard-Lawson.

LAWSON, Lesley, (Twiggy); actress and singer; *b* 19 Sept. 1949; *y d* of (William) Norman Hornby and Nell (Helen) Hornby (*née* Reeman); *m* 1st, 1977, Michael Whitney Armstrong (*d* 1983); one *d*; 2nd, 1988, Leigh Lawson. Started modelling in London, 1966; toured USA and Canada, 1967; world's most famous model, 1966–71. *Films:* The Boy Friend, 1971; W, 1973; There Goes the Bride, 1979; Blues Brothers, 1981; The Doctor and the Devils, 1986; Club Paradise, 1986; Madame Sousatzka, 1989; Harem Hotel, Istanbul, 1989; *stage:* Cinderella, 1976; Captain Beaky, 1982; My One and Only, 1983, 1984; *television:* numerous appearances and series, UK and USA; numerous recordings. Many awards and honours including Hon. Col, Tennessee Army, 1977. *Publications:* Twiggy, 1975; An Open Look, 1985. *Recreations:* daughter Carly, music, design. *Address:* c/o ICM, Oxford House, 76 Oxford Street, W1R 1RB.

LAWSON, Michael Henry; QC 1991; a Recorder, since 1987; *b* 3 Feb. 1946; *s* of Dr Richard Pike Lawson, MC and late Margaret Haines (*née* Knight); *m* 1969, Ann Pleasance Symons Brisker; two *d*. *Educ:* Monkton Combe School, Bath; London Univ. (LLB). Called to the Bar, Inner Temple, 1969, Bencher, 1993. *Publications:* (jtly) Professional Conduct (Inns of Court School of Law Manual), annually, 1989–; (contrib.) Refocus on Child Abuse, 1994. *Recreations:* opera, music, tennis, sailing, food and wine. *Address:* 36 Essex Street, WC2R 3AS. *T:* 0171–413 0353.

LAWSON, Hon. Sir Neil, Kt 1971; Judge of High Court of Justice, Queen's Bench Division, 1971–83; *b* 8 April 1908; *s* of late Robb Lawson and Edith Marion Lawson (*née* Usherwood); *m* 1933, Gweneth Clare (*née* Wilby); one *s* one *d*. Called to Bar, Inner Temple, 1929; QC 1955; Recorder of Folkestone, 1962–71; a Law Commissioner, 1965–71. RAFVR, 1940–45. Hon. Fellow, LSE, 1974. Foreign decorations: DK (Dato' Peduka Kerubat), 1959, DSN (Dato' Setia Negara), 1962, PSMB (Dato' Sri Mahota), 1969, Brunei. *Recreations:* literature, music, the country. *Address:* 30a Heath Drive, Hampstead, NW3 7SB.

LAWSON, Gen. Sir Richard (George), KCB 1980; DSO 1962; OBE 1968; Commander-in-Chief, Allied Forces Northern Europe, 1982–86; *b* 24 Nov. 1927; *s* of John Lawson and Florence Rebecca Lawson; *m* 1956, Ingrid Lawson; one *s*. *Educ:* St Alban's Sch.; Birmingham Univ. CO, Independent Squadron, RTR (Berlin), 1963–64; GSO2 MoD, 1965–66; CofS, South Arabian Army, 1967; CO, 5th RTR, 1968–69; Comdr, 20th Armoured Bde, 1972–73; Asst Military Deputy to Head of Defence Sales, 1975–77; GOC 1st Armoured Div., 1977–79; GOC Northern Ireland, 1980–82. Col Comdt, RTR, 1980–82. Leopold Cross (Belgium), 1963; Knight Commander, Order of St Sylvester (Vatican), 1964. *Publications:* Strange Soldiering, 1963; All the Queen's Men, 1967; Strictly Personal, 1972. *Address:* c/o Drummonds, 45 Charing Cross, SW1A 2DX. *Club:* Army and Navy.

LAWSON, Richard Henry, CBE 1994; Chairman: Greenwell Montagu, Stockbrokers, 1987–91; Securities and Futures Authority, 1991; *b* 16 Feb. 1932; *s* of Sir Henry Brailsford Lawson, MC, and Lady (Mona) Lawson; *m* 1958, Janet Elizabeth Govier; three *s* (one *d* decd). *Educ:* Lancing College. ICI, 1952–54; W. Greenwell & Co. (now Greenwell Montagu & Co.), 1954–91; Jt Sen. Partner, 1980–86. Deputy Chairman: Stock Exchange, 1985–86; Securities Assoc., 1986–91. Chm., Investors Compensation Scheme, 1993–

(Dir, 1989–); Dir, Securities Institute, 1992–93. *Recreations:* golf, tennis, walking, birdwatching, skiing. *Club:* Naval and Military.

LAWSON, Roger Hardman; Director, 3i plc, since 1987; *b* 3 Sept. 1945; *s* of Harold Hardman Lawson and Mary Doreen Lawson (*née* Buckley); *m* 1974, Jenniferjane Grey; three *d*. *Educ:* Bedford School. CA 1967; FCA. Articled Wilson de Zouche & Mackenzie, 1963–67; joined ICFC, subseq. 3i, 1968; Manager, Regions, 1968–84; Dir, 3i International (USA, Asia and Pacific), 1984–92; Special Dir Resource (handling substantial investments), 3i plc, 1993–; Dir, several unquoted trading cos. Mem., Takeover Panel, 1994–95. Chairman: London Soc. of Chartered Accountants, 1985–86; Bd for Chartered Accountants in Business, 1990–91; CCAB Ltd; Pres., ICAEW, 1994–95 (Vice-Pres., 1992–93; Dep.-Pres., 1993–94). *Recreation:* golf. *Address:* 3i plc, 91 Waterloo Road, SE1 8XP. *T:* 0171–928 3131. *Club:* Royal Wimbledon Golf.

LAWSON, Sonia, RA 1991 (ARA 1982); RWS 1988 (ARWS 1985); artist; Tutor, Royal Academy Schools; Visiting Tutor, Royal College of Art; *b* 2 June 1934; *d* of Frederick Lawson and Muriel (*née* Metcalfe), artists; *m* 1969, C. W. Congo; one *d*. *Educ:* Leyburn; Southwick Girls' Sch.; Doncaster Sch. of Art; Royal Coll. of Art (ARCA 1st cl. 1959). Postgraduate year, RCA; Travelling Scholarship, France, 1960. *Solo exhibitions:* Zwemmer, London, 1960; New Arts Centre, London, 1963; Queen's Sq. Gall., Leeds, 1964; Trafford Gall., London, 1967; Bradford New Liby, 1972; Middlesbrough and Billingham, 1977; Open Univ., Darlington and Harrogate Art Galls, 1979; Harrogate Northern Artists, 1980; Manchester City Art Gall., 1987; Wakefield City Art Gall., 1988; Cartwright Hall, Bradford, 1989; Boundary Gall., London, 1989 and 1995; Galerie zur alten deutschen schule, Thun, Switzerland, 1990; Univ. of Birmingham, 1994; retrospective exhibn, Shrines of Life, toured 1982–83, Sheffield (Mappin), Hull (Ferens), Bradford (Cartwright), Leicester Poly., Milton Keynes (Exhibn Gall); *mixed exhibitions:* Arts Council of GB Touring Exhibns (Fragments against Ruin, The Subjective Eye); Tolly Cobbold National Exhibns; Moira Kelly Fine Art; Hayward Annual; Green Street, New York (8 in the 80s); Fruitmarket Gall., Edinburgh; Royal Acad. Annual; London Gp; RCA (Exhibition Road, to celebrate 150 years of RCA), 1988; Smith Gall., London, 1988, 1989; Olympia Fest., London, 1988, 1989; Bath Fest., 1989; Faces of Britain, China (British Council Touring Exhibn), 1989–90; Glasgow Royal Inst. of Fine Art, 1990; Royal Academy (The Infernal Method, etchings by Academicians), 1991; John Moores, Liverpool, 1991. Works in public collections: Arts Council of GB; Graves Art Gall., Sheffield; Huddersfield, Bolton, Carlisle, Belfast, Middlesbrough, Bradford, Dewsbury, Rochdale, Wakefield, and Harrogate Art Galls; Imperial War Mus.; Min. of Educn; Min. of Works; Leeds Univ.; Open Univ.; Cranfield Inst. of Technol.; RCA; St Peter's Coll., Oxford; Nuffield Foundn; Augustine (commissioned), presented by Archbishop of Canterbury to Pope John Paul II, Vatican Collection, Rome, 1989; private collections in UK, Germany, Australia, USA. BBC TV, Monitor, 1960, John Schlesinger's doc. "Private View". Visual records of preparations for Exercise Lionheart, BAOR, 1984 (Imperial War Mus. commn). Rowney Prize, Royal Acad., 1984; Gainsborough House Drawing Prize, Eastern Arts, 1984; Lorne Scholarship, Slade Sch. of Fine Art, 1986; Lady Evershed Drawing Prize, Eastern Arts Open, 1990. *Address:* c/o Royal Academy of Arts, Burlington House, Piccadilly, W1V 0DS. *T:* 0171–439 7438. *Clubs:* Royal Over-Seas League, Chelsea Arts.

LAWSON JOHNSTON, family name of **Baron Luke.**

LAWSON JOHNSTON, Hon. Hugh de Beauchamp, TD 1951; DL; *b* 7 April 1914; *yr s* of 1st Baron Luke of Pavenham, KBE, and *b* of 2nd Baron Luke, *qv*; *m* 1946, Audrey Warren, *d* of late Colonel F. Warren Pearl and late Mrs A. L. Pearl; three *d*. *Educ:* Eton; Chillon Coll.; Corpus Christi, Cambridge. BA 1934, MA (Cantab), 1938. With Bovril Ltd, 1935–71, finally as Chm. Territorial Service with 5th Bn Beds and Herts Regt, 1935–; Captain, 1939, and throughout War. Chm., Tribune Investment Trust Ltd, 1951–86; Chm., Pitman Ltd, 1973–81. Chm. of Cttees, United Soc. for Christian Literature, 1949–82. High Sheriff of Bedfordshire, 1961–62; DL Beds, 1964. *Recreations:* walking, gardening, photography. *Address:* Woodleys Farm House, Melchbourne, Bedfordshire MK44 1AG. *T:* Bedford (01234) 708282.

LAWSON-ROGERS, (George) Stuart; QC 1994; a Recorder, since 1990; *b* 23 March 1946; *s* of late George Henry Roland Rogers, CBE, sometime MP and Mary Lawson; *m* 1969, Rosalind Denise Leach; one *s* one *d*. *Educ:* LSE (LLB Hons). Called to the Bar, Gray's Inn, 1969; Asst Recorder, 1987–89. Asst Comr, Parly and Local Govt Boundary Commns, 1981, 1983; Chm., Structure Plan Exams in Public, DoE, 1984; Legal Assessor, GMC and GDC, 1988–; Standing Counsel (Crime, SE Circuit) to HM Customs and Excise, 1989–94; DTI Inspector, Insider Dealing, 1989; Dept of Transport Inspector, Merchant Shipping Act 1988, 1989–90. Dir. Watford AFC Ltd, 1990–. *Recreations:* theatre, music, opera, reading, gardening. *Address:* 36 Essex Street, WC2R 3AS. *T:* 0171–413 0353, 0171–353 3533, *Fax:* 0171–413 0374.

LAWSON-TANCRED, Sir Henry, 10th Bt, *cr* 1662; JP; *b* 12 Feb. 1924; *e surv. s* of Major Sir Thomas Lawson-Tancred, 9th Bt, and Margery Elinor (*d* 1961), *d* of late A. S. Lawson, Aldborough Manor; *S* father, 1945; *m* 1st, 1950, Jean Veronica (*d* 1970), 4th and *y d* of late G. R. Foster, Stockeld Park, Wetherby, Yorks; five *s* one *d*; 2nd, 1978, Mrs Susan Drummond, *d* of Sir Kenelm Cayley, 10th Bt. *Educ:* Stowe; Jesus Coll., Cambridge. Served as Pilot in RAFVR, 1942–46. JP West Riding, 1967. *Heir: s* Andrew Peter Lawson-Tancred, *b* 18 Feb. 1952. *Address:* Aldborough Manor, Boroughbridge, Yorks YO5 9EP. *T:* Boroughbridge (01423) 322716.

LAWTHER, Prof. Patrick Joseph, CBE 1978; DSc; FRCP; Professor of Environmental and Preventive Medicine, University of London, at St Bartholomew's Hospital Medical College, 1968–81, also at London Hospital Medical College, 1976–81, now Professor Emeritus; Member, Medical Research Council Scientific Staff, 1955–81; *b* 9 March 1921; *s* of Joseph and Winefride Lawther; *m* 1944, Kathleen May Wilkowski, MB BS; two *s* one *d*. *Educ:* Carlisle and Morecambe Grammar Schs; King's Coll., London; St Bartholomew's Hosp. Med. Coll. MB BS 1950; DSc London 1971. FRCP 1963 (MRCP 1954); FFOM 1981 (MFOM 1980). St Bartholomew's Hospital: Ho. Phys., Med. Professorial Unit, 1950; Cooper & Coventson Res. Schol., 1951–53; Associate Chief Asst, 1952–62; Hon. Cons. and Phys.-in-Charge, Dept of Envir. and Prev. Med., 1962–81; Consulting Physician, 1981–. Director, MRC Air Pollution Unit (later Envir. Hazards Unit), 1955–77; Head of Clinical Sect., MRC Toxicology Unit, 1977–81. Cons. Expert, WHO, 1960–; Civilian Cons. in Envir. Medicine, RN, 1975–90, now Emeritus. Chairman: DHSS Cttee on Med. Aspects of Contamination of Air and Soil, 1973–83; DHSS Working Party on Lead and Health, 1978–80; Environmental Dirs Gp, MRC, 1981–85; Cttee on Environmental and Occupational Health, MRC, 1985–89; Assessor, Inquiry on Lorries, People and Environment, (Armitage Inquiry), 1979–80. Pres., Nat. Soc. for Clean Air, 1975–77. Sir Arthur Thomson Vis. Prof., Univ. of Birmingham, 1975–76; RCP Marc Daniels Lectr, 1970; Harben Lectr, RIPH&H, 1970; Guymer Meml Lectr, St Thomas' Hosp., 1979. RSA Silver Medal, 1964; Acad. Nat. de Médecine Bronze Medal, 1972; RCP Bissett Hawkins Medal, 1974; RSM Edwin Stevens Gold Medal, 1975. *Publications:* various papers and chapters in books relating to environmental and occupational medicine. *Recreations:* almost everything. *Address:* Apple Trees, Church Road, Purley, Surrey CR2 3QQ. *T:* 0181–660 6398. *Club:* Surrey CC.

LAWTON, Alistair; *see* Lawton, J. A.

LAWTON, Prof. Denis; Chairman, University of London School Examinations and Assessment Council, since 1984; *b* 5 April 1931; *s* of William Benedict Lawton and Ruby (*née* Evans); *m* 1953, Joan Weston; two *s*. *Educ:* St Ignatius Coll.; Univ. of London Goldsmiths' Coll. (BA); Univ. of London Inst. of Education (PhD). Asst Master, Erith Grammar Sch., 1958–61; Head of English/Housemaster, Bacon's Sch., SE1, 1961–63; University of London Institute of Education: Research Officer, 1963–64; Lectr in Sociology, 1964–67; Sen. Lectr in Curriculum Studies, 1967–72; Reader in Education, 1972–74; Professor of Education, 1974; Dep. Dir, 1978–83; Dir, 1983–89. Chm., Consortium for Assessment and Testing in Schools, 1989–91. Hon. Fellow, College of Preceptors, 1983. *Publications:* Social Class, Language and Education, 1968; Social Change, Education Theory and Curriculum Planning, 1973; Class, Culture and the Curriculum, 1975; Social Justice and Education, 1977; The Politics of the School Curriculum, 1980; An Introduction to Teaching and Learning, 1981; Curriculum Studies and Educational Planning, 1983; (with P. Gordon) HMI, 1987; Education, Culture and the National Curriculum, 1989; Education and Politics in the 1990s, 1992; The Tory Mind on Education, 1994. *Recreations:* walking German Shepherd dogs, photographing bench-ends, sampling real ale, music. *Address:* Laun House, Laundry Lane, Nazeing, Essex EN9 2DY.

LAWTON, Prof. Sir Frank (Ewart), Kt 1981; DDS; FDSRCS; Professor of Operative Dental Surgery, University of Liverpool, 1956–80, now Emeritus Professor; *b* 23 Oct. 1915; *s* of Hubert Ralph Lawton and Agnes Elizabeth (*née* Heath); *m* 1943, Muriel Leonora Bacon; one *s* one *d*. *Educ:* Univ. of Liverpool (BDS 1937); Northwestern Univ., Chicago (DDS 1948). FDSRCS 1948. Lectr, 1939, and Dir of Dental Educn, 1957–80, Univ. of Liverpool. President: BDA, 1973–74; GDC, 1979–89. Editor, Internat. Dental Jl, 1963–81. Hon. DDSc Newcastle, 1981; Hon. DDS Birmingham, 1982; Hon. DSc Manchester, 1984. *Publications:* (ed with Ed Farmer) Stones Oral and Dental Diseases, 1966; contrib. scientific and prof. jls. *Recreation:* music. *Address:* Newcroft, Castle Bolton, Leyburn, N Yorks DL8 4EX. *T:* Wensleydale (01969) 22802.

LAWTON, Rt. Hon. Sir Frederick (Horace), PC 1972; Kt 1961; a Lord Justice of Appeal, 1972–86; *b* 21 Dec. 1911; *o s* of William John Lawton, OBE; *m* 1937, Doreen (*née* Wilton) (*d* 1979); two *s*. *Educ:* Battersea Grammar Sch.; Corpus Christi Coll., Cambridge (Hon. Fellow, 1968). Barrister, Inner Temple, 1935; Bencher, 1961. Served with London Irish Rifles, 1939–41; invalided out of Army, 1941, and returned to practice at the Bar. QC 1957; Judge of the High Court of Justice, Queen's Bench Div., 1961–72. Recorder of City of Cambridge, 1957–61; Dep. Chm., Cornwall QS, 1968–71. Member: Bar Council, 1957–61; Departmental Cttee on Proceedings before Examining Justices, 1957–58; Standing Cttee on Criminal Law Revision, 1959–86 (Chm., 1977–86); Inter-departmental Cttee on Court of Criminal Appeal, 1964–65; Chm., Adv. Cttee on Legal Educn, 1976–86. Presiding Judge, Western Circuit, 1970–72. President, British Academy of Forensic Sciences, 1964. *Address:* 1 The Village, Skelton, York YO3 6XX. *T:* York (01904) 470441. *Clubs:* Garrick; Yorkshire (York).

LAWTON, Harold Walter, MA; Docteur de l'Université de Paris; Officier d'Académie; Emeritus Professor, University of Sheffield, since 1964; *b* Stoke-on-Trent, 27 July 1899; *y s* of late William T. C. and Alice Lawton; *m* 1933, Bessie (*d* 1991), *y d* of T. C. Pate; one *s* one *d* (and one *s* decd). *Educ:* Middle Sch., Newcastle under Lyme; Rhyl Grammar Sch.; Universities of Wales and Paris. BA Hons (Wales) 1921; MA (Wales) 1923; Fellow University of Wales, 1923–26; Docteur de l'Univ. de Paris, 1926. University College, Southampton: Lecturer in French, 1926–37; Professor of French, 1937–50; Dean of Faculty of Arts, 1945–49; first Warden of New, later Connaught, Hall, 1930–33; University of Sheffield: Professor of French, 1950–64; Warden of Ranmoor House, 1957–63; Deputy Pro-Vice-Chancellor, 1958–61; Pro-Vice-Chancellor, 1961–64. Transcriber, the Gladstone Diaries, 1933–36. Médaille d'Argent de la Reconnaissance Française, 1946; Officier d'Académie, 1948. *Publications:* Térence en France au XVIe Siècle: éditions et traductions (Paris), 1926; repr. 1970; Handbook of French Renaissance Dramatic Theory, 1950, repr. 1972; J. du Bellay, Poems, selected with introduction and notes, 1961; Térence en France au XVIe Siècle: imitation et influence, 1972; articles and reviews to British and French periodicals. *Address:* 1 The Pastures, Toll Bar, Cottesmore, near Oakham, Leics LE15 7DZ. *T:* Oakham (01572) 812265.

LAWTON, (John) Alistair, CBE 1981; DL; with Sea Properties Ltd, since 1955; *b* 1 Oct. 1929; *s* of Richard Geoffrey Lawton and Emma Lawton; *m* 1952, Iris Lilian Barthorpe; one *s* two *d*. *Educ:* Crewkerne Sch., Somerset. Southern Rhodesia Govt, 1946–55. Member: Deal Borough Council, 1956–74 (Mayor, 1966–68); Kent County Council, 1966–89 (Chm., 1977–79; Chm., Educn Cttee, 1973–77); Chairman: Kent Police Authority, 1987–89; SE Kent HA, 1988–94; S Kent Community Healthcare Trust, 1994–. Comr, Manpower Services Commn, 1983–85. Treas., Kent CCC, 1988–92. DL Kent, 1983. Hon. DCL Kent, 1982. *Recreations:* cricket, Rugby (non-participating now). *Address:* The Sett, 1 Badgers Rise, Walmer, Deal, Kent CT14 7QW. *T:* Deal (01304) 375060.

LAWTON, Prof. John Hartley, FRS 1989; Professor of Community Ecology, and Director, NERC Centre for Population Biology, Imperial College of Science, Technology and Medicine, University of London, since 1989; *b* 24 Sept. 1943; *s* of Frank Hartley Lawton and Mary Lawton; *m* 1966, Dorothy (*née* Grimshaw); one *s* one *d*. *Educ:* Balshaw's Grammar Sch., Leyland, Lancs; University Coll. and Dept of Zoology, Univ. of Durham (BSc, PhD). Res. Student, Univ. of Durham, 1965–68; Deptl Demonstrator in Animal Ecology, Oxford Univ., 1968–71; College Lectr in Zoology, St Anne's and Lincoln Colls, Oxford, 1970–71; University of York: Lectr, 1971–78; Sen. Lectr, 1978–82; Reader, 1982–85; Personal Chair, 1985–89. Mem., Royal Commn on Envmtl Pollution, 1989–. Hon. Vis. Res. Fellow, Nat. Hist. Mus., 1990–; Adjunct Scientist, Inst. of Ecosystem Studies, NY Botanic Garden, 1991–. Chm. Council, RSPB, 1993–. Hon. DSc Lancaster, 1993. *Publications:* Insects on Plants: community patterns and mechanisms (with D. R. Strong and T. R. E. Southwood), 1984; (ed jtly) The Evolutionary Interactions of Animals and Plants, 1991; (ed jtly) Extinction Rates, 1995; (ed jtly) Linking Species and Ecosystems, 1995; over 200 sci. papers in specialist jls. *Recreations:* bird watching, natural history photography, travel, gardening, walking. *Address:* 21 Lime Avenue, York YO3 0BT. *T:* York (01904) 424873; 17 Course Road, Ascot, Berks SL5 7HQ. *T:* Ascot (01344) 26819.

LAXNESS, Halldór Kiljan; Icelandic writer; *b* 23 April 1902; *s* of Gudjon Helgason and Sigridur Halldorsdottir, Iceland; one *d*; *m* 1st, Ingibjörg Einarsdottir; one *s*; 2nd, Audur Sveinsdottir; two *d*. Hon. PhD: Aabo Univ., 1968; Eberhard-Karls Univ., Tübingen, 1982; Hon. DLitt Univ. of Iceland, 1972; Hon. Dr Edinburgh Univ., 1977. Nobel Prize for Literature, 1955; Nexö Prize for Literature, 1955; Sonning Prize, 1969. *Publications* include over 50 titles (originally published in Icelandic, trans. into over 40 langs): *novels:* Barn náttúrunnar, 1919; Undir Helgahnúk (Under the Holy Mountain), 1924; Vefarinn mikli frá Kasmir (The Great Weaver from Kashmir), 1927; Salka Valka, 1934 (first published as þu vínviður hreini, 1931, and Fuglinn í fjörunni, 1932; filmed, 1954); Sjálfstætt fólk (Independent People), 2 vols, 1934–35; Ljós heimsins, 1937, Höll sumarlandsins, 1938, Hús skáldsins, 1939, Fegurð himinsins, 1940 (these four republished as Heimsljos (The Light of the World), 2 vols, 1955); Íslandsklukkan, 1943; Hið ljósa man, 1944; Eldur í Kaupinhafn, 1946; Atómstöðin (The Atom Station), 1948; Gerpla (Happy Warriors), 1952; Brekkukotsannáll (Fish Can Sing), 1957 (filmed, 1973); Paradísarheimt (Paradise Reclaimed), 1960; Kristnihald undir Jökli (Christianity at Glacier), 1968 (filmed, 1989); Innansveitarkronika, 1970; Guðsgjafathula, 1972; *autobiography:* Skáldatími, 1963; Íslendíngaspjall, 1967; Í túninu heima, 1975; Úngur eg var, 1976; Sjömeistarasagan, 1978; Grikklandsárið, 1980; Dagar hjá múnkum, 1987; collections of short stories, essays, poems and plays; translations into Icelandic include: Farewell to Arms, and A Moveable Feast, by Ernest Hemingway; Candide by Voltaire. *Address:* Gljúfrasteinn, 270 Mosfellsbær, Iceland; Vaka-Helgafell, Síðumúli 6, 108 Reykjavík, Iceland.

LAY, Richard Neville; Chairman: Debenham Tewson & Chinnocks Holdings plc, since 1987; DTZ Debenham Thorpe, since 1993; *b* 18 Oct. 1938; *s* of Edward John Lay and late Nellie Lay; *m* 1st, 1964; one *s* one *d*; 2nd, 1991, Pauline Alison Margarita Pringle (*née* Howard Dorchy). *Educ:* Whitgift School. FRICS. Partner, Debenham Tewson & Chinnocks, 1965–87. Vice Chm., West End Central London Board, Sun Alliance and London Insurance Group, 1992–. Surveyor, Armourers' and Brasiers' Co., 1983–. Chairman: cttee advising RICS on market requirements of the profession, 1991; Commercial Property Panel, RICS, 1992–; Member: Council, British Property Fedn, 1992–; General Council, RICS 1994–; Bank of England Property Forum, 1994–. Trustee, Tate Gall. Foundn, 1989–94. Governor, Belmont Sch., Surrey, 1983–88. *Recreations:* gardening, walking. *Address:* 15 Clareville Grove, SW7 5AU. *T:* 0171–408 1161. *Club:* Royal Automobile.

LAYARD, Adm. Sir Michael (Henry Gordon), KCB 1993; CBE 1982; Second Sea Lord, and Chief of Naval Personnel (Member of Admiralty Board, Defence Council), 1993–95; Commander-in-Chief Naval Home Command, 1994–95; Flag Aide-de-Camp to the Queen, 1994–95; *b* Sri Lanka, 3 Jan. 1936; *s* of late Edwin Henry Frederick and Doris Christian Gordon (*née* Spence); *m* 1966, Elspeth Horsley Fisher; two *s*. *Educ:* Pangbourne Coll.; RN Coll., Dartmouth. Joined RN, 1954; specialised in aviation, 1958; Fighter Pilot, 1960–72; Air Warfare Instructor, 1964; Commanded: 899 Naval Air Sqn, in HMS Eagle, 1970–71; HMS Lincoln, 1971–72; ndc, 1974–75; Directorate, Naval Air Warfare, MoD, 1975–77; Comdr (Air), HMS Ark Royal, 1977–78; CSO (Air), FONAC, 1979–82; Sen. Naval Officer, SS Atlantic Conveyor, Falklands conflict, 1982 (CBE); Commanded: RNAS Culdrose, 1982–84; HMS Cardiff, 1984–85; Task Gp Comdr, Persian Gulf, 1984; Dep. Dir, Naval Warfare (Air), MoD, 1985–88; Flag Officer Naval Aviation (formerly Air Comd), 1988–90; Dir Gen., Naval Manpower and Trng, 1990–92; Leader of RN Officers Study Gp, MoD, 1992–93; Adm. Pres., RNC, Greenwich, 1993–94. Chm. of Trustees, FAA Mus., 1988–90. Mem., FAA Officers' Assoc. CIMgt 1994; MInstD. Chevalier Bretvin, 1984. Freeman, City of London, 1994. *Recreations:* painting, sailing, music, history, collecting experiences. *Address:* c/o Lloyds Bank plc, Cheapside, Langport, Somerset. *Clubs:* Royal Navy of 1765 and 1785; Royal Naval Sailing Association; Royal Navy Golfing Society (Pres, 1988–94.).

LAYARD, Prof. (Peter) Richard (Grenville); Professor of Economics, London School of Economics, since 1980, and Director, Centre for Economic Performance, since 1990; *b* 15 March 1934; *s* of Dr John Layard and Doris Layard; *m* 1991, Molly Meacher. *Educ:* Eton Coll.; King's Coll., Cambridge (BA); London School of Economics (MScEcon). History Master: Woodberry Down Sch., 1959–60; Forest Hill Sch., 1960–61; Senior Research Officer, Robbins Cttee on Higher Educn, 1961–63; London School of Economics: Dep. Director, Higher Educn Research Unit, 1964–74 (part-time from 1968); Lectr in Economics, 1968–75; Reader in the Economics of Labour, 1975–80; Hd, Centre for Labour Econs, 1974–90. Chm., Employment Inst., 1987–92. Mem., UGC, 1985–89. Econ. Consultant to Russian Govt, 1991–. *Publications:* (jtly) The Causes of Graduate Unemployment in India, 1969; (jtly) The Impact of Robbins: Expansion in Higher Education, 1969; (jtly) Qualified Manpower and Economic Performance: An Inter-Plant Study in the Electrical Engineering Industry, 1971; (ed) Cost-Benefit Analysis, 1973, 2nd edn 1994; (jtly) Microeconomic Theory, 1978; (jtly) The Causes of Poverty, 1978; More Jobs, Less Inflation, 1982; How to Beat Unemployment, 1986; (jtly) Handbook of Labour Economics, 1986; (jtly) The Performance of the British Economy, 1988; (jtly) Unemployment: Macroeconomic Performance and the Labour Market, 1991; (jtly) Reform in Eastern Europe, 1991; (jtly) East-West Migration: the alternatives, 1992; (jtly) Post-Communist Reform: pain and progress, 1993. *Recreations:* walking, tennis, the clarinet. *Address:* 45 Cholmeley Park, N6 5EL. *T:* 0171–955 7281.

LAYCRAFT, Hon. James Herbert; Chief Justice of Alberta, 1985–92; *b* 5 Jan. 1924; *s* of George Edward Laycraft and Hattie Cogswell Laycraft; *m* 1948, Helen Elizabeth Bradley; one *s* one *d*. *Educ:* University of Alberta (BA, LLB 1951). Admitted to Bar, 1952; law practice, 1952–75; Trial Div. Judge, Supreme Court of Alberta, 1975; Judge, Court of Appeal, Alberta, 1979–85. Hon. LLD Calgary, 1986. *Publications:* articles in Canadian Bar Review and Alberta Law Review. *Recreations:* outdoor activities. *Address:* 8952 Bayridge Drive SW, Calgary, Alberta, Canada. *Club:* Ranchman's (Calgary).

LAYDEN, Anthony Michael; HM Diplomatic Service; Counsellor (Economic and Commercial), since 1991, and Deputy Head of Mission, since 1994, Copenhagen; *b* 27 July 1946; *s* of Sheriff Michael Layden, SSC, TD and Eileen Mary Layden; *m* 1969, Josephine Mary McGhee; three *s* one *d*. *Educ:* Holy Cross Academy, Edinburgh; Edinburgh Univ. (LLB Hons Law and Econ. 1968). Lieut, 15th (Scottish Volunteer) Bn, Parachute Regt, 1966–69. Foreign Office, 1968; MECAS, Lebanon, 1969; Jedda, 1971; Rome, 1973; FCO, Middle East, Rhodesia, Personnel Ops Depts, 1977–82; Head of Chancery, Jedda, 1982–85; Hong Kong Dept, FCO, 1985–87; Counsellor and Head of Chancery, Muscat, 1987–91. *Recreations:* sailing, walking, music, bridge. *Address:* c/o Foreign and Commonwealth Office, SW1A 2AH. *Clubs:* Travellers'; Royal Danish Yacht.
See also P. J. Layden.

LAYDEN, Sir John, Kt 1988; JP; miner; Councillor, Rotherham Metropolitan Borough Council, since 1974, Leader since 1974; *b* 16 Jan. 1926; *m* 1949, Dorothy Brenda McLean; two *s*. Joined Labour Party, 1944. Elected to Maltby UDC, 1953 (Chm., 1959–60 and 1970–71). Chm., Assoc. of Metropolitan Authorities, 1984–91; Vice-Chm., British Section, IULA/CEM, 1974–; Mem., Bd of Trustees, Municipal Mutual Insurance Co., 1983–. Freeman, City of London, 1988. JP Rotherham Borough, 1965. Hon. Citizen of Indiannapolis, 1985. *Recreations:* music, sport (particularly football). *Address:* 9 Lilac Grove, Maltby, Rotherham, South Yorkshire S66 8BX. *T:* Rotherham (01709) 812481.

LAYDEN, Patrick John, TD 1981; Scottish Parliamentary Counsel and Senior Assistant Legal Secretary, Lord Advocate's Department, since 1987; *b* 27 June 1949; *s* of Sheriff Michael Layden, SSC, TD and Eileen Mary Layden; *m* 1984, Patricia Mary Bonnar; three *s* one *d*. *Educ:* Holy Cross Acad., Edinburgh; Edinburgh Univ. (LLB Hons). Called to the Scottish Bar, 1973; Dep. Scottish Parly Counsel and Asst Legal Sec., Lord Advocate's Dept, 1977–87. Univ. of Edinburgh OTC, 1967–71; 2/52 Lowland Vol., TA, 1971–77; 1/51 Highland Vol., 1977–81 (OC London Scottish, 1978–81); OC 73 Ord. Co. (V), 1981–84. *Recreations:* reading, walking.
See also A. M. Layden.

LAYE, Evelyn, CBE 1973; actress; singer; *b* London, 10 July 1900; *o d* of Gilbert Laye and Evelyn Froud; *m* 1st, 1926, Sonnie Hale (from whom she obtained a divorce, 1931); 2nd, 1934, Frank Lawton (*d* 1969). *Educ:* Folkestone; Brighton. Made first appearance on stage, Theatre Royal, Brighton, 1915, in Mr Wu. First London appearance in The Beauty Spot, Gaiety, 1918; first big success in title-role of The Merry Widow, Daly's, 1923; subsequently starred in London in Madame Pompadour, Daly's, 1923; The Dollar Princess, Daly's, 1925; Cleopatra, Daly's, 1925; Betty in Mayfair, Adelphi, 1925; Merely Molly, Adelphi, 1926; Princess Charming, Palace, 1927; Lilac Time, Daly's, 1927; Blue Eyes, Piccadilly, 1928; The New Moon, Drury Lane, 1929; Bitter Sweet, His Majesty's, 1930; Helen!, Adelphi, 1932; Give Me A Ring, Hippodrome, 1933; Paganini, Lyceum, 1937; Lights Up, Savoy, 1940; The Belle of New York, Coliseum, 1942; Sunny River, Piccadilly, 1943; Cinderella, His Majesty's, 1943; Three Waltzes, Prince's, 1945; Cinderella, Palladium, 1948; Two Dozen Red Roses, Lyric, 1949; Peter Pan, Scala, 1953; Wedding in Paris, Hippodrome, 1954–56; Silver Wedding, Cambridge, 1957; The Amorous Prawn, Saville/Piccadilly, 1959–62; Never Too Late, Prince of Wales, 1964; The Circle, Savoy, 1965; Strike A Light!, Piccadilly, 1966; Let's All Go Down the Strand, Phoenix, 1967; Charlie Girl, Adelphi, 1969; Phil the Fluter, Palace, 1969; No Sex, Please-We're British, Strand, 1971–73; A Little Night Music (revival), Exeter, 1979, 1981, on tour, 1979, Nottingham, 1980–81, 1982; one woman show, 1983; Babes in the Wood, Chichester, 1984, Richmond, 1985; A Glamorous Night with Evelyn Laye and Friends, tour and London Palladium, 1992. First New York appearance in Bitter Sweet, Ziegfeld Theatre, 1929; subsequently on Broadway in Sweet Aloes, Booth, 1936; Between the Devil, Majestic, 1937. Film début in silent production, The Luck of the Navy, 1927. Films include: One Heavenly Night (Hollywood), 1932; Waltz Time, 1933; Princess Charming, 1934; Evensong, 1935; The Night is Young (Hollywood), 1936; Make Mine A Million, 1959; Theatre of Death, 1967; Within and Without, 1969; Say Hello to Yesterday, 1971. Numerous broadcasts and television appearances incl. rôles in Dizzy, Tales of the Unexpected, The Gay Lord Quex, 1983; My Family and Other Animals, 1987. *Publication:* Boo, to my Friends (autobiography), 1958. *Address:* c/o Mary-Jane Burcher, Flat 6, Oak House, 6 Carlton Drive, Putney, SW15 2BZ.

LAYFIELD, Sir Frank (Henry Burland Willoughby), Kt 1976; QC 1967; *b* Toronto, 9 Aug. 1921; *s* of late H. D. Layfield; *m* 1965, Irene Patricia, *d* of late Captain J. D. Harvey, RN (retired); one *s* one *d*. *Educ:* Sevenoaks Sch. Army, 1940–46. Called to the Bar, Gray's Inn, 1954, Bencher, 1974; a Recorder, 1979–82. Chairman: Inquiry into Greater London Development Plan, 1970–73; Cttee of Inquiry into Local Government Finance, 1974–76; Inspector, Inquiry into Sizewell B Nuclear Power Station, 1983–85. Associate, RICS, 1977; Hon. FSVA 1978; Hon. Fellow, Coll. of Estate Management, 1982. Gold Medal, Lincoln Inst. of Land Policy, 1984. *Publications:* (with A. E. Telling) Planning Applications, Appeals and Inquiries, 1953; (with A. E. Telling) Applications for Planning Payments, 1955; Engineering Contracts, 1956. *Recreations:* walking, tennis. *Address:* 2 Mitre Court Buildings, Temple, EC4Y 7BX. *T:* 0171–583 1355. *Clubs:* Garrick, United Oxford & Cambridge University.

LAYMAN, Rear-Adm. Christopher Hope, CB 1991; DSO 1982; LVO 1977; Consultant in Communications and Information Systems and Maritime Affairs, since 1991; *b* 9 March 1938; *s* of late Captain H. F. H. Layman, DSO, RN and Elizabeth Hughes; *m* 1964, Katharine Romer Ascherson; one *s* one *d*. *Educ:* Winchester. Joined Royal Navy, 1956; specialised Communications and Electronic Warfare, 1966; commanded HM Ships: Hubberston, 1968–70; Lynx, 1972–74; Exec. Officer, HM Yacht Britannia, 1976–78; Captain, 7th Frigate Sqn, 1981–83; commanded HM Ships: Argonaut, 1981–82; Cleopatra, 1982–83; Invincible, 1984–86; Commander, British Forces Falkland Islands, 1986–87; Asst Dir (Communications and Information Systems), IMS, NATO HQ, Brussels, 1988–91, retd. *Publications:* Man of Letters, 1990; The Falklands and the Dwarf, 1995. *Recreations:* fishing, archaeology. *Club:* New (Edinburgh).

LAYTON, family name of **Baron Layton.**

LAYTON, 3rd Baron *cr* 1947, of Danehill; **Geoffrey Michael Layton;** Director: The Toxbox Co. Ltd, since 1986; Westminster and Whitehall Environmental Consultants Ltd, since 1990; *b* 18 July 1947; *s* of 2nd Baron Layton and Dorothy Rose (*d* 1994), *d* of Albert Luther Cross; *S* father, 1989; *m* 1st, 1969, Viviane Cracco (marr. diss. 1971); 2nd, 1989, Caroline Jane Soulis. *Educ:* St Paul's School; Stanford Univ., California; Univ. of Southern California. *Recreation:* riding. *Heir: uncle* Hon. David Layton, MBE [*b* 5 July 1914; *m* 1st, 1939, Elizabeth (marr. diss. 1972), *d* of Robert Gray; two *s* one *d*; 2nd, 1972, Joy Parkinson].
See also Hon. C. W. Layton.

LAYTON, Alexander William; QC 1995; *b* 23 Feb. 1952; *s* of Paul Henry Layton and Frances Evelyn Layton (*née* Weekes); *m* 1988, Sandy Forshaw (*née* Matheson); two *d*. *Educ:* Marlborough Coll.; Brasenose Coll., Oxford (MA); Ludwig-Maximillian Univ., Munich. Called to the Bar, Middle Temple, 1976. Chm., British-German Jurists Assoc., 1988–93. *Publications:* (contrib.) The Bar on Trial, 1977; (jtly) European Civil Practice, 1989. *Address:* 2 Temple Gardens, Temple, EC4Y 9AY. *T:* 0171–583 6041.

LAYTON, Hon. Christopher Walter; Founder Member, Grimstone Community, since 1990; *b* 31 Dec. 1929; *s* of 1st Baron Layton; *m* 1st, 1952, Anneliese Margaret, *d* of Joachim von Thadden, Hanover (marr. diss. 1957); one *s* one *d*; 2nd, 1961, Margaret Ann, *d* of Leslie Moon, Molesey, Surrey; three *d*. *Educ:* Oundle; King's Coll., Cambridge. Intelligence Corps, 1948–49; ICI Ltd, 1952; The Economist Intelligence Unit, 1953–54; Editorial writer, European affairs, The Economist, 1954–62; Economic Adviser to Liberal Party, 1962–69; Dir, Centre for European Industrial Studies, Bath Univ., 1968–71; Commission of European Communities: Chef de Cabinet to Commissioner Spinelli, 1971–73; Dir, Computer Electronics, Telecomms and Air Transp. Equipment Manufg, Directorate-Gen. of Internal Market and Industrial Affairs, 1973–81, now Hon. Dir-Gen.; Editor, Alliance, 1982–83, Associate Editor, New Democrat, 1983–85. Dir, World Order Project, Federal Trust, 1987–90. Contested (SDP) London W, European Parly Elecn, 1984. *Publications:* Transatlantic Investment, 1966; European Advanced Technology, 1968; Cross-frontier Mergers in Europe 1970; (jtly) Industry and Europe, 1971; (jtly) Ten Innovations: International Study on Development Technology and the Use of Qualified Scientists and Engineers in Ten Industries, 1972; Europe and the Global Crisis, 1987; A Step Beyond Fear, 1989; The Healing of Europe, 1990. *Recreations:* painting, sculpture, healing. *Address:* Grimstone Manor, Jordan Lane, Horrabridge, near Yelverton, Devon PL20 7QY.

LAZARIDIS, Stefanos; Associate Artist, English National Opera; freelance opera, ballet and theatre designer and opera director in UK and abroad, since 1967; *b* Ethiopia, 28 July 1942; *s* of Nicholas Lazaridis and Alexandra Cardovillis. *Educ:* Greek Sch., Addis Ababa; Ecole Internationale, Geneva; Byam Shaw Sch. of Art; Central Sch. of Speech and Drama. Professional début, Eccentricities of a Nightingale, Yvonne Arnaud Theatre, Guildford, 1967; *ballet:* Royal Ballet, Covent Garden, 1969 and 1975; *theatre:* London (Almeida, Barbican and West End), Stratford-upon-Avon, Chichester Fest., Oxford, Guildford, Watford, Milan, Bologna, Paris, 1967–91; *opera:* numerous prodns for major UK opera houses, 1970–, incl. Carmen, Earls Court, 1989; prodns for ENO incl. award-winning Doctor Faust, The Mikado, Hansel and Gretel, and Lady Macbeth of Mtsensk; directed and designed: Oedipus Rex, Opera North; Bluebeard's Castle, Scottish Opera; Orphée et Eurydice, Australian Opera, 1994; designs for opera houses of Paris, Berlin, Frankfurt, Munich, Stuttgart, La Scala Milan, Florence, Bologna, Venice, Bregenz Fest., Amsterdam, Moscow, St Petersburg, Tokyo, Vancouver, Sydney, Melbourne, Houston, LA and San Francisco. Lawrence Olivier and Evening Standard Awards for Most Outstanding Achievement in Opera, 1987. *Recreations:* reading, travel. *Address:* c/o English National Opera, London Coliseum, St Martin's Lane, WC2N 4ES. *T:* 0171–836 0111.

LAZARUS, Sir Peter (Esmond), KCB 1985 (CB 1975); FCIT; Director, Manchester Ship Canal Co., 1986–93; Member, Civil Aviation Authority, 1986–92; *b* 2 April 1926; *er s* of late Kenneth M. Lazarus and Mary R. Lazarus (*née* Halsted); *m* 1950, Elizabeth Anne Marjorie Atwell, *e d* of late Leslie H. Atwell, OBE; three *s*. *Educ:* Westminster Sch.; Wadham Coll., Oxford (Open Exhibition). Served RA, 1945–48. Entered Ministry of Transport, 1949: Secretary, London and Home Counties Traffic Advisory Cttee, 1953–57; Private Secretary to Minister, 1961–62; Asst Sec., 1962; Under-Sec., 1968–70; Under-Sec., Treasury, 1970–72; Deputy Secretary: DoE, 1973–76; Dept of Transport, 1976–82; Perm. Sec., Dept of Transport, 1982–85. Chairman: Assoc. of First Div. Civil Servants, 1969–71; Cttee for Monitoring Agreements on Tobacco Advertising and Sponsorship, 1986–91. Pres., Liberal Jewish Synagogue, St John's Wood, 1994– (Chm. Council, 1972–75, 1987–92); Chm., Jews' Temporary Shelter, 1993–; Comdt, Jewish Lads' and Girls' Brigade, 1987–95. FRSA 1981. *Recreations:* music, reading. *Address:* 28 Woodside Avenue, N6 4SS. *T:* 0181–883 3186. *Club:* Athenæum.

LAZENBY, Prof. Alec, AO 1988; FTS, FIBiol, FAIAS; Principal Consultant, International Development Program of Australian Universities (consultant on agricultural research and development and higher education), since 1991; *b* 4 March 1927; *s* of G. and E. Lazenby; *m* 1957, Ann Jennifer, *d* of R. A. Hayward; one *s* two *d*. *Educ:* Wath on Dearne Grammar Sch.; University Coll. of Wales, Aberystwyth. BSc 1949, MSc 1952, Wales; MA 1954, PhD 1959, ScD 1985, Cantab. Scientific Officer, Welsh Plant Breeding Station, 1949–53; Demonstr in Agricultural Botany, 1953–58, Lectr in Agricultural Botany, 1958–65, Univ. of Cambridge; Fellow and Asst Tutor, Fitzwilliam Coll., Cambridge, 1962–65; Foundation Prof. of Agronomy, Univ. of New England, NSW, 1965–70, now Professor Emeritus; Vice-Chancellor, Univ. of New England, Armidale, NSW, 1970–77; Dir, Grassland Res. Inst., 1977–82; Vice-Chancellor, Univ. of Tasmania, 1982–91. Vis. Prof., Reading Univ., 1978; Hon. Professorial Fellow, Univ. of Wales, 1979; Hon. Prof., Victoria Univ. of Technol., 1992–. Hon DRurSci New England, NSW, 1981; Hon. LLD Tasmania, 1992. *Publications:* (jt Editor) Intensive Pasture Production, 1972; (jt Editor) Australian Field Crops, vol. I, 1975, vol. II, 1979; Australia's Plant Breeding Needs, 1986; (jt Editor) The Grass Crop, 1988; papers on: pasture plant breeding; agronomy; weed ecology, in various scientific jls. *Recreation:* golf. *Address:* International Development Program, GPO Box 2006, Canberra, ACT 2601, Australia.

LEA, Rev. His Honour Christopher Gerald, MC; Assistant Curate (non-stipendiary), parish of Stratfield Mortimer, since 1992; a Circuit Judge, 1972–90; *b* 27 Nov. 1917; *y s* of late George Percy Lea, Franche, Kidderminster, Worcs; *m* 1952, Susan Elizabeth Dorrien Smith, *d* of Major Edward Pendarves Dorrien Smith, Greatwood, Restronguet, Falmouth, Cornwall; two *s* one *d* (and one *d* decd). *Educ:* Charterhouse; RMC, Sandhurst; St Stephen's House, Oxford. Commissioned into XX The Lancashire Fusiliers, 1937, and served with Regt in UK until 1939. Served War of 1939–45 (despatches, MC): with Lancashire Fusiliers, No 2 Commando, 11th SAS Bn, and Parachute Regt in France, Italy and Malaya. Post-war service in Indonesia, Austria and UK; retired, 1948. Called to Bar, Inner Temple, 1948; Oxford Circuit. Mem. Nat. Assistance Bd Appeal Tribunal (Oxford Area), 1961–63; Mem. Mental Health Review Tribunal (Oxford Region), 1962–68, 1983–92. A Metropolitan Magistrate, 1968–72; Dep. Chm., Berks QS, 1968–71. Ordained deacon, 1992, priest, 1993. *Address:* Simms Farm House, Mortimer, Berks RG7 2JP. *T:* Mortimer (01734) 332360. *Club:* English-Speaking Union.

See also J. A. Harvie.

LEA, David Edward, OBE 1978; Assistant General Secretary of the Trades Union Congress, since 1977; *b* 2 Nov. 1937; *s* of Edward Cunliffe Lea and Lilian May Lea. *Educ:* Farnham Grammar Sch.; Christ's Coll., Cambridge. Inaugural Chair, Cambridge Univ. Students' Representative Council, 1961. Economist Intelligence Unit, 1961; Economic Dept, TUC, 1964, Asst Sec., 1967, Sec. 1970. Jt Sec., TUC-Labour Party Liaison Cttee, 1972–86; Secretary: TUC Cttee on European Strategy, 1989–; Envmt Action Gp, 1989–; Task Force on Representation at Work, 1994–; Chm., Econ. Cttee, 1980–91, Mem. Steering Cttee, 1991–, ETUC; Member: Royal Commn on the Distribution of Income and Wealth, 1974–79; Adv. Gp on Channel Tunnel and Cross-Channel Services, 1974–75; Cttee of Inquiry on Industrial Democracy, 1975–77; Energy Commn, 1977–79; Retail Prices Index Adv. Cttee, 1977–; Delors Cttee on Economic and Social Concepts in the Community, 1977–79; NEDC Cttee on Finance for Investment, 1978–; Kreisky Commn on Unemployment in Europe, 1986–89; Franco-British Council, 1982–; EU Steering Cttee on Social Dialogue, 1992–; UK Round Table on Sustainable Develt, 1995–; Expert Adviser, UN Commn on Transnational Corporations, 1977–81; Hon. Mem., UK Delgn, earth summit on envmt and develt, Rio, 1992. Governor, NIESR, 1981–; Trustee, Employment Policy Inst., 1992–. Patron, Third Age (formerly Reaction) Trust, 1991–. FRSA 1993. Mem. Editl Bd, New Economy, Inst. of Public Policy Res. review, 1993–. *Publications:* Trade Unionism, 1966; contrib. The Multinational Enterprise, 1971; Industrial Democracy (TUC), 1974; Keynes Plus: a participatory economy (ETUC), 1979. *Address:* 17 Ormonde Mansions, 106 Southampton Row, WC1B 4BP. *T:* 0171–405 6237; South Court, Crondall, near Farnham, Surrey GU10 5QF. *T:* Farnham (01252) 850711.

LEA, Vice-Adm. Sir John (Stuart Crosbie), KBE 1979; retired; Director General, Naval Manpower and Training, 1977–80; *b* 4 June 1923; *m* 1947, Patricia Anne Thoseby; one *s* two *d*. *Educ:* Boxgrove Sch., Guildford; Shrewsbury Sch.; RNEC, Keyham. Entered RN, 1941; Cruisers Sheffield and Glasgow, 1943; RNEC, 1942–45; HMS Birmingham, 1945; entered Submarines, 1946; HMS/Ms Talent, Tireless, Aurochs, Explorer; Sen. Engr, HMS Forth (Depot Ship), 1952–53; on Staff, RNEC, 1954–57; psc 1958; Sqdn Engr Officer, 2nd Destroyer Sqdn and HMS Daring, 1959–61; Staff of CinC Portsmouth, 1961–62; Naval Staff in Ops Div., 1963–65; Engr Officer, HMS Centaur, 1966; Staff of Flag Officer Submarines; Dep. Supt, Clyde Submarine Base, 1967–68; idc 1969; Dir of Naval Admin. Planning, 1970–71; Cdre HMS Nelson, 1972–75; Asst Chief of Fleet Support, 1976–77. Comdr 1957; Captain 1966; Rear-Adm. 1976; Vice-Adm. 1978. Chm., 1980–86, Dir, 1986–88, GEC Marine & Industrial Gears Ltd. Chairman: Portsmouth Naval Heritage Trust, 1983–87; Regular Forces Employment Assoc., 1986–89; RN and RM Br. and Special Duties Officers Benevolent Fund, 1993–. President: Hayling Island Horticultural Soc., 1994– (Chm., 1980–94); Hants Autistic Soc., 1988–95. Trustee: Hayling Island Community Centre, 1981–; Plumbers Museum and Workshop, Singleton, 1993–. Master, Worshipful Co. of Plumbers, 1988–89. *Recreations:* walking, woodwork, gardening. *Address:* Springfield, Brights Lane, Hayling Island, Hants PO11 0JX.

LEA, Ruth Jane; Head of Policy Unit, Institute of Directors, since 1995; *b* 22 Sept. 1947; *d* of Thomas Lea and Jane (*née* Brown). *Educ:* Lymm Grammar Sch.; York Univ. (BA); Bristol Univ. (MSc). Asst Statistician, later Sen. Economic Assistant, HM Treasury, 1970–73; Lectr in Econs, Thames Poly., 1973–74; Statistician: CS Coll., 1974–77; HM Treasury, 1977–78; CSO, 1978–84; Statistician, 1984–87, Dep. Dir, Invest in Britain Bureau, 1987–88, DTI; Sen. Economist, 1988–90, Chief Economist, 1990–93, Mitsubishi Bank; Chief UK Economist, Lehman Bros, 1993–94; Econs Ed., ITN, 1994–95. Member: Retail Prices Adv. Cttee, 1992–94; NCC, 1993–; Nurses' Pay Rev. Body, 1994–. Mem., Oxford and Cambridge Musical Club. *Recreations:* music (singing), philately. *Address:* 25 Redbourne Avenue, N3 2BP. *T:* 0181–346 3482. *Club:* Reform.

LEA, Sir Thomas (William), 5th Bt *cr* 1892, of The Larches, Kidderminster and Sea Grove, Dawlish; *b* 6 Sept. 1973; *s* of Sir Julian Lea, 4th Bt and of Gerry Valerie, *d* of late Captain Gibson C. Fahnestock; *S* father, 1990. *Educ:* Uppingham Sch. *Heir: b* Alexander Julian Lea, *b* 28 Oct. 1978.

LEACH, Allan William, FLA; Director-General and Librarian, National Library for the Blind, since 1982; *b* 9 May 1931; *yr s* of Frank Leach, MBE and Margaret Ann Bennett; *m* 1962, Betty, *e d* of William George Gadsby and Doris Cree; one *s* one *d*. *Educ:* Watford Grammar Sch.; Loughborough Coll. BA Open; DPA London. Various posts with Hertfordshire County Library, 1948–59; Librarian, RAF Sch. of Educn, 1949–51; Regional Librarian, Warwickshire County Libr., 1959–65; County Librarian, Bute County Libr., 1965–71; Librarian and Curator, Ayr Burgh, 1971–74; Dir of Library Services, Kyle and Carrick District, 1974–82. Vice-Chm., UK Assoc. of Braille Producers, 1994– (Chm., 1991–94); Member: Standing Cttee, Section of Libraries for the Blind, IFLA, 1983– (Chm., 1985–87; Ed., Newsletter, 1985–92); Nat. Steering Cttee, Share the Vision, 1992–. Trustee, Ulverscroft Foundn, 1993–. Editor: Rickmansworth Historian, 1961–66; Ayrshire Collections, 1973–82. *Publications:* Begin Here, 1966; Rothesay Tramways, a brief history, 1969; Round old Ayr (with R. Brash and G. S. Copeland), 1972; Libraries in Ayr, 1975; Looking Ahead, 1987; articles on libraries, local history, literature, braille and educn. *Recreations:* music, the countryside, books, people. *Address:* 4 Windsor Road, Hazel Grove, Stockport, Cheshire SK7 4SW. *T:* 0161–483 6418.

LEACH, (Charles Guy) Rodney, MA; Director, Jardine Matheson Holdings Ltd, since 1984; Chairman, JIB Group plc (formerly Jardine Insurance Brokers), since 1984; *b* 1 June 1934; *s* of late Charles Harold Leach and Nora Eunice Ashworth; *m* 1993, Mrs Jessica Douglas Home; two *s* three *d* from a previous marriage. *Educ:* Harrow; Balliol Coll., Oxford (1st Cl. Hon. Mods, 1st Cl. Lit. Hum.). N. M. Rothschild & Sons, 1963–76: Partner, 1968; Dir, 1970; Director: Rothschild Investment Trust, 1970–76; Trade Development Bank, 1976–83; Matheson & Co., 1983–; Hong Kong Land, 1985–; Dairy Farm, 1987–; Mandarin Oriental, 1987–; Kwik Save Gp, 1987–; Safra Republic Hldgs, 1988–; Trafalgar House, 1992–. Trustee, PO Staff Superannuation Fund, 1976–; Chm., Res. Cttee, Mental Health Foundn, 1984–. *Recreations:* the humanities, tennis, bridge, golf. *Address:* 3 Lombard Street, EC3V 9AQ. *T:* 0171–528 4000. *Clubs:* White's, Portland, Queen's, Vanderbilt; Wisley Golf.

LEACH, Clive William; Chairman, Butler Advertising and Marketing Ltd, since 1994; *b* 4 Dec. 1934; *s* of Stanley and Laura Leach; *m* 1st, 1958, Audrey (*née* Parker) (*d* 1978); three *s*; 2nd, 1980, Stephanie (*née* McGinn); one *s*. *Educ:* Sir John Leman Grammar Sch., Beccles, Suffolk. DipM. Gen. Sales Manager, Tyne Tees Television, 1968–74; Sales Dir, 1974–79, Dir of Sales and Marketing, 1979–82, Trident Television; Man. Dir, Link Television, 1982–85; Dir of Sales and Marketing, 1985–88, Man. Dir, 1988–93, Yorkshire Television; Man. Dir, 1985–88, Chm., 1988–93, Yorkshire Television Enterprises. Chairman: Yorkshire Television Internat., 1988–93; Yorkshire–Tyne Tees Television Holdings, 1993 (Gp Chief Exec., 1992–93); Dir, ITN, 1988–93. Dir, Opera North Ltd. Chm., Leeds TEC, 1991–. FRSA; MCIM. *Recreations:* golf, cricket, travel. *Address:* The White House, Barkston Ash, Tadcaster, N Yorks LS24 9PJ. *Clubs:* Reform, MCC, Alwoodley Golf.

LEACH, David Andrew, OBE 1987; potter, designer, lecturer; *b* 7 May 1911; *e s* of Bernard Leach, CH, CBE, and Edith Muriel, *o d* of Dr William Evans Hoyle; *m* 1938, Mary Elizabeth Facey; three *s*. *Educ:* Prep. Sch., Bristol; Dauntsey's Sch., Wilts; Blundell's Sch., Devon. At age of 19, began to work in his father's pottery at St Ives, Cornwall (tuition from him and associates); Manager and Partner, 1946–55; took Manager's course, N Staffs Technical Coll., Stoke-on-Trent, to 1937; taught pottery at Dartington Hall Progressive Sch., 1933. Served War, DCLI, 1941–45. Taught at Penzance Sch. of Art and St Ives, 1945. Designed and made David Leach Electric Kiln, 1950; helped to start a pottery in Norway, 1951; in charge of Ceramic Dept, and taught, at Loughborough Coll. of Art, 1953 (later Vis. Lectr). Started workshop at Bovey Tracey, 1956; researched into glazes and changed from slipware to stoneware, 1961; now makes a large percentage of porcelain. Late Mem. Council, Craftsmen Potters Assoc. of GB (Past Chm.), late Mem. Grants Cttee of the Crafts Adv. Commn; Mem. Council, Crafts Council, 1977; Chm., Devon Guild of Craftsmen, 1986–87; Adviser, Dartington Pottery Trng Workshop. Has exhibited in Europe, USA and Far East; first major one-man show, CPA, 1966; Internat. Ceramics Exhibn, 1972, and Craftsmen's Art, 1973, V&A Mus., 1973; major one-man show, NY, 1978; exhibitions in Germany (Darmstadt, Munich, Deidesheim, Sandhausen-bei-Heidelberg, and Hanover), Holland (Amsterdam), Belgium (Brussels), USA (San Francisco), Japan (Osaka) and Norway (Oslo); Joint Exhibitions: New Ashgate Gall., Farnham, 1982, 1983, (3 Generations Leach) 1986; Beaux Arts Gall., Bath, 1984; (with John Leach) Peter Dingley Gall., Stratford, 1985; Solus Exhibitions: NY, and lecture tour, USA, 1978; Washington DC, and 2nd lecture tour, USA, 1979; British Crafts Centre, London, 1979. Galerie St Martin, Cologne, 1982; St Paul's Sch., Barnes, 1982; Robert Welch Gall., Chipping Campden, 1982; Frontroom Gall., Dallas, 1983; Chestnut Gall., Bourton-on-the-Water, 1984; Century Gall., Henley-on-Thames, 1984; Castle Mus., Norwich, 1985; Galerie F15, Oslo, 1986; Elaine Potter Gall., San Francisco, 1986; Greenwich House Gall., NY, 1987; New Ashgate Gall., Farnham, 1988; Lecture at Setagaya Mus., Tokyo, 1989; Lecture demonstration tours: in USA, 1985, 1986, 1987 and 1988; in Caracas, Venezuela, 1987, 1991 (with exhbn). Craft of the Potter, BBC, 1976. Gold Medal, Istanbul, 1967. *Publications:* David Leach: A Potter's Life, with Workshop Notes (introd. by Bernard Leach), 1977. *Address:* Lowerdown Pottery, Bovey Tracey, Devon TQ13 9LE. *T:* Bovey Tracey (01626) 833408.

LEACH, Prof. Donald Frederick; Principal since 1985, and Vice Patron, since 1993, Queen Margaret College, Edinburgh; *b* 24 June 1931; *s* of Frederick John Mansell Leach and Annie Ivy Foster; *m* 1952, June Valentine Reid; two *s* one *d*. *Educ:* John Ruskin Grammar Sch., Croydon; Norwood Tech. Coll.; Dundee Tech. Coll.; Univ. of London (Ext. Student, BSc); Jordanhill Coll. of Educn, MInstP, CPhys, 1960; FIMA, CMath, 1969; MBCS, CEng, 1968. Pilot Officer, RAF, 1951–53. Physicist, British Jute Trade Res. Assoc., Dundee, 1954–65; Tech. Dir, A. R. Bolton & Co., 1965–66; Napier College: Lectr and Sen. Lectr in Maths, 1966–68; Head, Dept of Maths and Computing, 1968–74; Asst Principal/Dean, Faculty of Science, 1974–85. Member: Council for Professions Supplementary to Medicine, 1985–; Exec. Cttee, Scottish Council Develt and Indust., 1987–; Boards of: Edinburgh Chamber of Commerce and Manufactures, 1991–; Leith

Chamber of Commerce, 1991– (Pres., 1994–); Higher Educn Quality Council, 1992–; The Capital Enterprise Trust, 1993–. Contested: (L) W Edinburgh, 1959; (L) E Fife by-election, 1961; (Lab) Kinross and W Perthshire, 1970. Hon. Prof., Queen Margaret Coll., 1993. Hon. Fellow, Soc. of Chiropodists and Podiatrists, 1994. FRSA. *Publications:* Future Employment and Technological Change (jtly), 1986; papers in sci., tech. and eductl jls on textile physics, electronic instrumentation, maths and statistics, higher educn. *Recreations:* badminton, walking, ski-ing, cooking. *Address:* Queen Margaret College, Clerwood Terrace, Edinburgh EH12 8TS. *T:* 0131–317 3202.

LEACH, Admiral of the Fleet Sir Henry (Conyers), GCB 1978 (KCB 1977); DL; Chairman, St Dunstan's, since 1983; *b* 18 Nov. 1923; 3rd *s* of Captain John Catterall Leach, MVO, DSO, RN and Evelyn Burrell Leach (*née* Lee), Yarner, Bovey Tracey, Devon; *m* 1958, Mary Jean (*d* 1991), *yr d* of Adm. Sir Henry McCall, KCVO, KBE, CB, DSO; two *d. Educ:* St Peter's Court, Broadstairs; RNC Dartmouth. Cadet 1937; served in: cruiser Mauritius, S Atlantic and Indian Ocean, 1941–42; battleship Duke of York, incl. Scharnhorst action, 1943–45; destroyers in Mediterranean, 1945–46; spec. Gunnery, 1947; various gunnery appts, 1948–51; Gunnery Officer, cruiser Newcastle, Far East, 1953–55; staff appts, 1955–59; comd destroyer Dunkirk, 1959–61; comd frigate Galatea as Captain (D) 27th Sqdn and Mediterranean, 1965–67; Dir of Naval Plans, 1968–70; comd Commando Ship Albion, 1970; Asst Chief of Naval Staff (Policy), 1971–73; Flag Officer First Flotilla, 1974–75; Vice-Chief of Defence Staff, 1976–77; C-in-C, Fleet, and Allied C-in-C, Channel and Eastern Atlantic, 1977–79; Chief of Naval Staff and First Sea Lord, 1979–82. First and Principal Naval ADC to the Queen, 1979–82. psc 1952; jssc 1961. President: RN Benevolent Soc., 1983–95; Sea Cadet Assoc., 1984–93; Royal Bath and West of England Soc., 1993 (Vice-Pres., 1994–); Patron: Meridian Trust Assoc., 1993–; Hampshire RBL, 1994–. Chm. Council, King Edward VII Hosp., 1987–. Gov., Cranleigh Sch., 1983–93. Freeman: City of London; Shipwrights' Co.; Hon. Freeman, Merchant Taylors' Co. DL Hampshire, 1992. *Recreations:* fishing, shooting, gardening, antique furniture repair. *Address:* Wonston Lea, Wonston, Winchester, Hants SO21 3LS.

LEACH, Norman, CMG 1964; Under-Secretary, Foreign and Commonwealth Office (Overseas Development Administration), 1970–72; *b* 8 March 1912; *s* of W. M. Leach. *Educ:* Ermysted's Gram. Sch., Skipton in Craven, Yorks; St Catharine's Coll., Cambridge (Scholar). 1st Class Hons, Pts I and II English Tripos, 1933 and 1934; Charles Oldham Shakespeare Schol., 1933. Asst Principal, Inland Revenue Dept, 1935; Under-Secretary: Ministry of Pensions and National Insurance, 1958–61; Dept of Technical Co-operation, 1961–64; ODM, 1964–70. *Address:* Low Bank, 81 Gargrave Road, Skipton in Craven, North Yorks BD23 1QN. *T:* Skipton (01756) 793719.

LEACH, Paul Arthur; General Consultant to The Law Society, 1980–81, retired; *b* 10 July 1915; *s* of Rev. Edward Leach and Edith Swannell Leach; *m* 1st, 1949, Daphne Copeland (marr. diss. 1957); one *s* one *d*; 2nd, 1958, Rachel Renée Lachmann. *Educ:* Marlborough Coll.; Keble Coll., Oxford (1st Cl. Hons BA Mod. Hist., 1937; MA 1945); Birmingham Univ. (2nd Cl. Hons LLB 1940). Law Soc. Finals, 1940; admitted Solicitor, 1946. Served War, RA, 1940–45: Staff Captain 1st AA Bde; attached SO II, RAEC, 1945–46. Private practice as solicitor, 1946–48; Talks Producer, BBC Home Talks, 1949; joined Law Soc. staff, 1950; Clerk and later Sec., Professional Purposes Cttee, 1950–71; Secretary: Future of the Profession Cttee, 1971–80; Internat. Relations Cttee, 1975–80; Dep. Sec.-Gen., 1975–80; removed from Roll of Solicitors, at own request, 1991. Secretary: UK Delegn to Commn Consultative des Barreaux de la Communauté Européenne, 1975–81; Inter-Professional Gp, 1978–81; UK Vice-Pres., Union Internationale des Avocats, 1978–81. *Publications:* (ed) Guide to Professional Conduct of Solicitors, 1974; articles in Law Society's Gazette. *Recreations:* foreign travel, gardening, history, listening to classical music. *Address:* 19 Lavant Court, Charles Street, Petersfield, Hants GU32 3EQ; 5333 Myrtlewood, The Meadows, Sarasota, FL 34235, USA.

LEACH, Penelope, PhD; psychologist and writer on childcare; *b* 19 Nov. 1937; *d* of late Nigel Marlin Balchin and Elisabeth Balchin; *m* 1963, Gerald Leach; one *s* one *d. Educ:* Newnham Coll., Cambridge (BA Hons 1959); LSE (Dip. in Soc. Sci. Admin 1960; MA Psychol. 1962; PhD Psychol. 1964). Home Office, 1960–61; Lectr in Psychol., LSE, 1965–67; Res. Officer and Res. Fellow, MRC, 1967–76; Ext Med. Ed., Penguin Books, 1970–78; Founder and Dir, Lifetime Productions (childcare videos), 1985–87; Res. Consultant, Internat. Centre for Child Studies, 1984–90. Mem., Voluntary Licensing Authy on IVF, 1985–89; Comr, Commn on Social Justice, 1993–. Founder and Parent-Educn Co-ordinator, End Physical Punishment for Children, 1989–; Chm., Child Develt Soc., 1993– (Pres., 1992–93); Vice-President: Pre-School Playgroups Assoc., 1977; Health Visitors Assoc., 1982–. Mem. Adv. Council, Amer. Inst. for Child, Adolescent and Family Studies, 1993–. Mem., professional socs and assocs; FBPsS 1988; Hon. Fellow, Dept of Mental Health, Bristol Univ., 1988. *Publications:* Babyhood, 1974; Baby and Child, 1977, 1989; Who Cares?, 1979; The Parents' A–Z, 1984; The First Six Months, 1987; The Babypack, 1990; Children First, 1994. *Recreations:* cooking, family and friends, gardening, travel. *Address:* 3 Tanza Road, NW3 2UA. *T:* 0171–435 9025.

LEACH, Rodney; *see* Leach, C. G. R.

LEACH, Rodney, PhD; CEng; FRINA; FIIM; FCIM; company director; Chief Executive and Managing Director, VSEL Consortium plc, 1986–88; Chief Executive, 1985–88, and Chairman, 1986–88, Vickers Shipbuilding and Engineering Ltd; Chairman, Cammell Laird Shipbuilders Ltd, 1985–88; *b* 3 March 1932; *s* of Edward and Alice Leach; *m* 1958, Eira Mary (*née* Tuck); three *s* one *d. Educ:* Baines Grammar Sch., Poulton Le Fylde, Lancs; Birmingham Univ. (BSc, PhD). CEng, FRINA 1987; FCIM (FInstM 1972); FIMgt (FIIM 1987). Radiation Physicist, Nuclear Power Plant Co. Ltd, 1957; Physicist, UKAEA, 1960; Sen. Physicist, South of Scotland Electricity Board, 1963; Associate, McKinsey & Co. Inc., 1965, Partner, 1970; Peninsular & Oriental Steam Navigation Co.: Hd of European and Air Transport Div., 1974; Dir, 1978–85; Chairman: P&O European Transport Services Ltd, 1979–83; P&O Cruises Ltd, 1980–85. Director: Jasmin plc, 1989–; North West Water Group plc, 1989–; Mem., NW Water Authority, 1989; Vice-Chm. and Dir, S Cumbria Community and Mental Health Services NHS Trust, 1993–. Member: Gen. Council, Cumbria Tourist Bd, 1986–92; Northern Council for Sport and Recreation, 1991–. Dir, 1989–93, Vice-Chm., 1991–94, Renaissance Arts Theatre Trust Ltd. Conseiller Spécial, Chambre de Commerce et d'Industrie de Boulogne-sur-Mer et de Montreuil, 1989–94. Mem., RYA, 1977–. Gov., St Anne's Sch., Windermere, 1991–. Liveryman: Worshipful Company of Carmen, 1976; Worshipful Company of Shipwrights, 1988–; Freeman, City of London, 1976. FRSA 1989. *Publications:* (jtly) Containerization: the key to low cost transport, 1965; frequent papers in scientific and technical jls, 1965–72. *Recreations:* fell-walking, sailing, gardening, literature. *Address:* Dockwray Cottage, Grasmere, Cumbria LA22 9QD. *T:* Grasmere (015394) 35288. *Club:* Royal Automobile.

LEACH, Sir Ronald (George), GBE 1976 (CBE 1944); Kt 1970; FCA; Chairman: Standard Chartered Bank(CI), since 1980; Standard Chartered Trust (CI) Ltd, since 1980; *b* 21 Aug. 1907; *s* of William T. Leach, 14 Furze Croft, Hove; *m* Margaret Alice Binns (*d* 1994). *Educ:* Alleyn's. Dep. Financial Sec. to Ministry of Food, Sept. 1939–June 1946. Sen. Partner in firm of Peat, Marwick, Mitchell & Co., Chartered Accountants, 1966–77; Dir, Samuel Montagu & Co., 1977–80. Director: Internat. Investment Trust of Jersey, 1980–93; Ann Street Brewery, 1981–; Barrington Management (CI), 1984–87; Berkeley Australian Develt Capital, 1985–90; Govett American Endeavour Fund Ltd. Member: Cttee on Coastal Flooding, 1953; Inquiry into Shipping, 1967–70; National Theatre Board, 1972–79; Chairman: Consumer Cttee for GB (Agricultural Marketing Acts, 1931–49), 1958–67; Accounting Standards Steering Cttee, 1970–76. Pres. Inst. of Chartered Accountants in England and Wales, 1969–70. Hon. LLD Lancaster, 1977. *Publication:* (with Prof. Edward Stamp) British Accounting Standards: the first ten years, 1981. *Address:* La Rosière, St Saviour, Jersey, CI. *T:* Jersey (01534) 77039 or 78427.

LEADBEATER, Howell; Under/Deputy Secretary, Department of the Environment, retired 1976; *b* 22 Oct. 1919; *s* of late Thomas and Mary Ann Leadbeater; *m* 1946, Mary Elizabeth Roberts; two *s* one *d. Educ:* Pontardawe Secondary Sch.; University College, Swansea. Army Service, 1940–46: Adjt 11th E African Div. Signals. Min. of Works, later MPBW and Dept of Environment: Asst Principal, 1948; Asst Sec., 1958; Under Sec., 1968; Under/Dep. Sec., 1973. Design Coordinator for Caernarfon Castle, Investiture of Prince of Wales, 1969. Mem., Crafts Adv. Cttee, 1978–80. FRSA 1968. *Address:* 1 Parsons Mead, East Molesey, Surrey KT8 9DT. *T:* 0181–979 6160.

LEADBETTER, Alan James, CBE 1994; DSc; Directeur Adjoint, Institut Laue Langevin, Grenoble, France, since 1994; *b* 28 March 1934; *s* of Robert and Edna Leadbetter; *m* 1957, Jean Brenda Williams; one *s* one *d. Educ:* Liverpool Univ. (BSc 1954; PhD 1957); Bristol Univ. (DSc 1971). CPhys 1972; FInstP 1972; CChem 1980; FRSC 1980. Fellow, NRCC, 1957–59; Res. Asst, Lectr and Reader, Univ. of Bristol, 1959–74; Prof. of Phys. Chem., Univ. of Exeter, 1975–82; Associate Dir, Science, Rutherford Appleton Lab., SERC, 1982–88; Dir, Daresbury Lab., SERC, 1988–94. Hon. Professor: Univ. of Hull, 1992–; Univ. of Manchester, 1989–94; Vis. Prof., De Montfort Univ., 1994–. *Publications:* res. papers in chem. and phys in learned jls. *Recreations:* gardening, walking, cooking. *Address:* Institut Laue Langevin, BP 156, 38042 Grenoble Cedex 9, France. *T:* 76207100.

See also M. Leadbetter.

LEADBETTER, David Hulse, CB 1958; Assistant Under-Secretary of State, Department of Education and Science, 1964–68 (Under Secretary, Ministry of Education, 1953–64); *b* 14 Aug. 1908; *s* of late Harold Leadbetter; *m* 1933, Marion, *d* of late Horatio Ballantyne, FRIC, FCS; two *s* two *d* (and one *d* decd.). *Educ:* Whitgift; Merton Coll., Oxford (Classical Postmaster). Entered Board of Education, 1933. *Recreations:* photography, gardening. *Address:* 5 Coverdale Court, Preston Road, Yeovil, Somerset BA21 3AQ. *T:* Yeovil (01935) 73442.

LEADBETTER, Michael; Director of Social Services, Essex, since 1993; *b* 25 July 1946; *s* of Robert Leadbetter and Edna (*née* Garlic); partner, Pamela Corti; two *s. Educ:* Ladybarn Secondary Mod. Sch.; Manchester Coll. of Sci. and Technol.; Manchester Coll., of Art and Design (DA); Manchester Univ. Extra Mural Dept (CQSW); MA (Econ) Manchester Univ. 1982. Works and prodn manager, 1971–72; Manchester Social Services: Social Worker, then Sen. Social Worker, 1972–82; Residential and Day Care Services Manager, 1982–86; Dir of Social Services, Tameside, 1986–92. NW Association of Directors of Social Services: Chm., Gtr Manchester Dirs Gp, 1987–92; Chm., Regl Trng Unit, 1987–92; Chm., 1989–90. Founder Mem., British Inst. of Transactional Analysis, 1974. FIMgt (FBIM 1990). England International, Rugby Union, 1970; 35 appearances for Lancs, 1968–74; Rugby League professional, Rochdale Hornets, 1974–76. *Recreations:* weight training, ski-ing, food, wine, lager, opera, reading. *Address:* Essex County Council, Social Services Department, PO Box 297, County Hall, Chelmsford, Essex CM1 1YS. *T:* Chelmsford (01245) 492211; The Laurels, Station Road, Wakes Colne, Essex CO6 2DS. *Club:* England Internationals.

See also A. J. Leadbetter.

LEADBITTER, Edward; *b* 18 June 1919; *s* of Edward Leadbitter, Easington, Durham; *m* 1940, Phyllis Irene Mellin, Bristol; one *s* one *d. Educ:* State Schs; Teachers' Training Coll. Served War, 1939–45, with RA; commissioned 1943; War Office Instructor in Gunnery. Became a teacher. Joined Labour Party, 1938; Pres., Hartlepools Labour Party, 1958–62; Mem., West Hartlepool Borough Council, 1954–67 (sometime Mem., Town Planning, Finance, Housing, Industrial Develt, and Educn Cttees). MP (Lab) The Hartlepools, 1964–92. Member: Estimates Cttee, 1966–69; Select Cttee on Science and Technology, 1970–80; Select Cttee on Energy, 1980–92; Chairmens' Panel, House of Commons, 1980–92; Chm., Anglo-Tunisian Parly Group, 1974–92. Sponsored Children's Homes Registration Bill, 1982. Mem. NUPE, 1963–. Organizer of Exhibition on History of Labour Movement, 1956. Pres., Hartlepool Football Club, 1983–. First Hon. Freeman, Co. Borough of Hartlepool, 1981; Freeman of City of London, 1986. *Address:* 32 Brimston Close, Hartlepool, Cleveland TS26 0QA. *T:* Hartlepool (01429) 263404.

LEAHY, Sir John (Henry Gladstone), KCMG 1981 (CMG 1973); HM Diplomatic Service, retired; *b* 7 Feb. 1928; *s* of late William Henry Gladstone and late Ethel Leahy; *m* 1954, Elizabeth Anne, *d* of J. H. Pitchford, CBE; two *s* two *d. Educ:* Tonbridge Sch.; Clare Coll., Cambridge; Yale University. RAF, 1950–52; FO, 1952–54 (Asst Private Sec. to Minister of State, 1953–54); 3rd, later 2nd Sec., Singapore, 1955–57; FO, 1957–58; 2nd, later 1st Sec., Paris, 1958–62; FO, 1962–65; Head of Chancery, Tehran, 1965–68; Counsellor, FCO, 1969; Head of Personnel Services Dept, 1969–70; Head of News Dept, FCO, 1971–73; Counsellor and Head of Chancery, Paris, 1973–75; seconded as Under Sec., NI Office, 1975–76; Asst Under-Sec. of State, FCO, 1977–79; Ambassador to South Africa, 1979–82; Dep. Under- Sec. of State, FCO, 1982–84; High Comr, Australia, 1984–88. Chm., Lonrho, 1994– (Dir, 1993–; Vice-Chm, 1994); Dir, The Observer, 1989–93. Chm., Urban Foundn (London), 1991–94 (Exec. Dir, 1989–91). Pro-Chancellor, City Univ., 1991–. Chm., British-Australia Soc., 1994–. Member: Franco-British Council (Chm., 1989–93); Maritime Trust (Vice-Chm., 1990–93); Gov., ESU, 1989–. Master, Skinners' Co., 1993–94. *Recreations:* tennis, golf. *Address:* Manor Stables, Bishopstone, near Seaford, East Sussex BN25 2UD. *T:* Seaford (01323) 898898. *Club:* United Oxford & Cambridge University.

LEAKE, Prof. Bernard Elgey, PhD, DSc, FRSE, FGS; Professor of Geology, Department of Geology and Applied Geology, and Keeper of Geological Collections in Hunterian Museum, University of Glasgow, since 1974 (Head, Department of Geology and Applied Geology, 1974–92); *b* 29 July 1932; *s* of late Norman Sidney Leake and Clare Evelyn (*née* Walgate); *m* 1955, Gillian Dorothy Dobinson; five *s. Educ:* Wirral Grammar Sch., Bebington, Cheshire; Liverpool Univ. (1st Cl. Hons BSc, PhD); Bristol Univ. (DSc 1974). Leverhulme post-doctoral Res. Fellow, Liverpool Univ., 1955–57; Asst Lectr, subseq. Lectr in Geology, Bristol Univ., 1957–68, Reader in Geol., 1968–74. Res. Associate, Berkeley, Calif, 1966; Gledden Sen. Vis. Fellow, Univ. of W Australia, 1986. Chm., Cttee on amphibole nomenclature, Internat. Mineral Assoc., 1982– (Sec., 1968–79); Member: NERC, 1978–84 (Chm., Vis. Gp to Brit. Geol Survey, formerly Inst. of Geological Sciences, 1982–84; Chm., Isotope Facilities Prog. Cttee, 1987–91); Council, Mineral Soc., 1965–68, 1978–80 (Vice-Pres., 1979–80); Council, Geol Soc., 1971–74, 1979–85, 1989– (Vice-Pres., 1980, Treasurer, 1981–85, 1989–, Pres., 1986–88; Lyell Medal, 1977); Council, RSE, 1988–90; publication cttees, Mineral Soc., 1970–85, Geol Soc., 1970–85, and 1986–; Chm., Geol Soc. Publication Bd, 1987–. FRSE 1978. Sodic amphibole mineral, leakeite, named by Internat. Mineral Assoc., 1992. Editor: Mineralogical Magazine, 1970–83; Jl of Geol Soc., 1973 and 1974. *Publications:* A Catalogue of analysed calciferous and sub-calciferous amphiboles, 1968; The Geology of South Mayo, 1989; The Geology of the Dalradian and associated rocks of Connemara, W Ireland, 1994; over 100 papers in geol, mineral and geochem. jls on geol. of Connemara, study of amphiboles, X-ray fluorescence anal. of rocks and use of geochem. in identifying origins of highly metamorphosed rocks; geological maps: Connemara, 1982; South Mayo, 1985; Slyne Head, 1985; Errismore, 1990. *Recreations:* walking, reading, theatre, gardening, museums, genealogy, study of railway and agricultural development. *Address:* Geology and Applied Geology Department, The University, Glasgow G12 8QQ. *T:* 0141–339 8855, ext. 5435; 2 Garngaber Avenue, Lenzie, Kirkintilloch, Dunbartonshire. *Club:* Geological Society.

LEAKE, Rt. Rev. David; *see* Argentina, Bishop of.

LEAKEY, Maj.-Gen. Arundell Rea, CB 1967; DSO 1945; MC 1941 (Bar 1942); retired; General Officer Commanding British and Maltese Troops in Malta and Libya, 1967–68; *b* 30 Dec. 1915; parents British; *m* 1994, Joan Morant. *Educ:* Weymouth Coll.; Royal Military Coll., Sandhurst. Command of 5th Royal Tank Regt, 1944; Instructor at Staff Coll., Camberley, 1951–52; Comdr, 1st Arab Legion Armoured Car Regt, 1954–56; Instructor (Col), Staff Coll., Camberley, 1958–60; Comdr, 7th Armoured Brigade, 1961–63; Dir-Gen. of Fighting Vehicles, 1964–66; declared redundant, 1968. Dir and Sec., Wolfson Foundn, 1968–80; fund raiser for St Swithun's Girls' Sch., Winchester, 1980–82. Mem., Houghton Br., Royal British Legion, 1984–87. Czechoslovakian Military Cross, 1944. *Recreations:* gardening, enjoying retirement. *Address:* Ladymead Cottage, Houghton, Stockbridge, Hants SO20 6LU. *T:* Romsey (01794) 388396. *Club:* Victory Services.

LEAKEY, Dr David Martin, FEng 1979; Group Technical Adviser, British Telecom, 1990–92; independent consultant, David Leakey Consultancy in telecommunication services, systems and networks, since 1992; *b* 23 July 1932; *s* of Reginald Edward and Edith Doris Leakey; *m* 1957, Shirley May Webster; one *s* one *d*. *Educ:* Imperial College, Univ. of London (BScEng, PhD, DIC). FCGI 1976; FIEE 1969. GEC Coventry, 1953–57; GEC Hirst Research Centre, 1957–63; Tech. Manager, Public Exchange Div., GEC Coventry, 1963–66; Head, Elect. Eng. Dept, Lanchester Polytechnic, 1966–67; Advanced Product Planning Manager, 1967–69, Technical Dir, 1969–84, GEC Coventry; Dep. E-in-C, 1984–86, Chief Scientist, 1986–90, British Telecom. Director: Fulcrum Ltd, 1985–92; Mitel Inc., 1986–92. Vis. Prof., Univ. of Bristol, 1987–. Vice-Pres., IEE, 1984–87. Liveryman, Worshipful Co. of Engineers, 1985–. *Publications:* papers to professional journals. *Recreations:* horticulture, wine. *Address:* Rocheberie, Grassy Lane, Sevenoaks, Kent TN13 1PW.

LEAKEY, Prof. Felix William; author; *b* 29 June 1922; *s* of Hugh Leakey and Kathleen Leakey (*née* March); *m* 1947, Daphne Joan Sleep (*née* Salter); one *s* two *d*. *Educ:* St Christopher Sch., Letchworth; Queen Mary Coll., London. BA, PhD (London). Asst Lectr, then Lectr in French, Univ. of Sheffield, 1948–54; Univ. of Glasgow: Lectr in French, 1954–64; Sen. Lectr, 1964–68; Reader, 1968–70; Prof. of French, Univ. of Reading, 1970–73; Prof. of French Lang. and Lit., Bedford Coll., London, 1973–84 (Head of Department, 1973–79 and 1982–84). Carnegie Research Fellow, 1961–62; Leverhulme Research Fellow, 1971–72. Assoc. of University Profs of French: Hon. Sec., 1972–73; Jt Hon. Sec., 1973–75; Vice-Chm., 1975–76; Chm., 1976–77. Public performances as poetry speaker: Baudelaire's Les Fleurs du Mal, French Inst., London, 1984, and Glasgow Univ., 1985; bilingual recital, Chants/Songs, univ. centres in Britain France and W. Germany, 1976–84. *Publications:* Baudelaire and Nature, 1969; (ed jtly) The French Renaissance and its Heritage: essays presented to Alan Boase, 1968; Sound and Sense in French Poetry (Inaugural Lecture, with readings on disc), 1975; (ed jtly) Samuel Beckett, Drunken Boat, 1977; Baudelaire: Love Poems (videotape), 1989; Baudelaire: Selected Poems from Les Fleurs du Mal (audiotape), 1989; Baudelaire: collected essays 1953–1988, 1990, Baudelaire: Les Fleurs du Mal, 1992; (trans. into English verse) Selected Poems from Baudelaire's Les Fleurs du Mal, 1994; contribs to: French Studies; Rev. d'hist. litt. de la France; Rev. de litt. comparée; Rev. des sciences humaines; Etudes baudelairiennes; etc. *Recreations:* foxhunting, beagling, riding, poetry, art, music, especially opera.

LEAKEY, Mary Douglas, FBA 1973; FRAI; former Director, Olduvai Gorge Excavations; *b* 6 Feb. 1913; *d* of Erskine Edward Nicol and Cecilia Marion Frere; *m* 1936, Louis Seymour Bazett Leakey, FBA (*d* 1972); three *s*. *Educ:* privately. Hon. Mem., American Assoc. for Arts and Sciences, 1979–; Foreign Associate, Amer. Nat. Acad. of Science, 1987; For. Mem., Royal Swedish Acad. of Scis., 1978. Hon. FSA. Geological Soc. of London, Prestwich Medal and Nat. Geographic Soc. Hubbard Medal (jointly with late L. S. B. Leakey); Gold Medal, Soc. of Women Geographers, USA; Linneus Gold Medal, Royal Swedish Acad., 1978. Elizabeth Blackwell Award, Mary Washington Coll., 1980; Bradford Washburn Award, Boston, 1980. Hon. DSc: Witwatersrand, 1968; Western Michigan, 1980; Chicago, 1981; Cambridge, 1982; Emory, 1988; Massachusetts, Amherst, 1988; Brown, 1990; Columbia, 1991; Hon. DSSc Yale, 1976; Hon. DLitt Oxford, 1981. *Publications:* Olduvai Gorge: vol. 3, Excavation in Beds I and II, 1971; vol. 5, Excavations in Beds III, IV and the Masek Beds, 1994; Africa's Vanishing Art: the rock paintings of Tanzania, 1983; Disclosing the Past (autobiog.), 1984; various papers in Nature and other scientific jls. *Recreations:* reading, game watching. *Address:* c/o National Museum, Box 30239, Nairobi, Kenya.

See also R. E. F. Leakey.

LEAKEY, Richard Erskine Frere; Managing Director, Richard Leakey and Associates, wildlife consultancy, since 1994; *b* 19 Dec. 1944; *s* of late Louis Seymour Bazett Leakey, FBA, and of Mary Leakey, *qv*; *m* 1970, Dr Meave (*née* Epps); three *d*. *Educ:* Nairobi Primary Sch.; Lenana (formerly Duke of York) Sch., Nairobi. Self employed tour guide and animal trapper, 1961–65; Dir, Photographic Safaris in E Africa, 1965–68; Administrative Dir, 1968–74, Dir, 1974–89, Nat. Museums of Kenya; Dir, Wildlife and Conservation Management Service, Kenya, 1989–90; Chm., 1989–93, Dir, 1993–94, Kenya Wildlife Service. Co-leader, palaeontol expedn to Lake Natron, Tanzania, 1963–64; expedn to Lake Baringo, Kenya, in search of early man, 1966; Co-leader, Internation Omo River Expedn, Ethiopia, in search of early man, 1967; Leader, E Turkana (formerly E Rudolf) Res. Proj. (multi-nat., interdisciplinary sci. consortium investigation of Plio/Pleistocene, Kenya's northern Rift Valley), 1968–. Chairman: Bd of Govs, Nat. Museums of Kenya; Bd of Trustees, Kenya Wildlife Service. Chairman: Foundn for Res. into Origin of Man (FROM), 1974–81; E African Wild Life Soc., 1984–89 (Vice-Chm., 1978–84); Kenya Cttee, United World Colls, 1987; Bd of Governors and Council, Regent's Coll., London, 1985–90; Trustee: Nat. Fund for the Disabled; Wildlife Clubs of Kenya, 1980–; Rockford Coll., Illinois, 1983–85. Presenter: The Making of Mankind, BBC TV series, 1981; Earth Journal, US TV series, 1991. Mem., Selection Cttee, Beyond War Award, 1985–; Juror: Kalinga Prize, Unesco, 1986–88; Rolex Awards, 1990. Hon. Mem., Bd of Dirs, Thunderbird Res. Corp., USA, 1988–. Hon. degrees from Wooster Coll., Rochford Coll. and Univ. of Kent. Golden Ark Medal for Conservation, 1989. *Publications:* (contrib.) General History of Africa, vol. 1, 1976; (with R. Lewin) Origins, 1978; (with R. Lewin) People of the Lake, 1979; (with M. G. Leakey) Koobi Fora Research Project, vol. I, 1979; The Making of Mankind, 1981; Human Origins, 1982; One Life, 1984; (with R. Lewin) Origins Reconsidered, 1992; articles on palaeontol. in Nature, Jl of World Hist., Science, Amer. Jl of Phys. and Anthropol. *Address:* PO Box 24926, Nairobi, Kenya.

LEANING, Very Rev. David; Provost and Rector of Southwell, since 1991; *b* 18 Aug. 1936. *Educ:* Keble Coll., Oxford, 1957–58; Lichfield Theological Coll. Deacon 1960, priest 1961, dio. Lincoln; Curate of Gainsborough, 1960–65; Rector of Warsop with Sookholme, 1965–76; Vicar of Kington and Rector of Huntington, Diocese of Hereford, 1976–80; RD of Kington and Weobley, 1976–80; Archdeacon of Newark, 1980–91; Warden, Community of St Laurence, Belper, 1984–. Mem., Bd of Selectors, ACCM, 1988–. *Address:* The Residence, Southwell, Notts NG25 0HP. *T:* Southwell (01636) 812593.

LEAPER, Prof. Robert Anthony Bernard, CBE 1975; Professor of Social Administration, University of Exeter, 1970–86, Professor Emeritus 1987; *b* 7 June 1921; *s* of William Bambrick Leaper and Gertrude Elizabeth (*née* Taylor); *m* 1950, Elizabeth Arno; two *s* one *d*. *Educ:* Ratcliffe Coll., Leicester; St John's Coll., Cambridge (MA); Balliol Coll., Oxford (MA). Dipl. Public and Social Admin. (Oxon). Coal miner, 1941–44. Warden, St John Bosco Youth Centre, Stepney, 1945–47; Cadet officer, Civil Service, 1949–50; Co-operative Coll., Stanford Hall, 1950–56; Principal, Social Welfare Trng Centre, Zambia, 1956–59; Lectr, then Sen. Lectr, then Acting Dir, Social Admin., UC, Swansea, 1960–70. Vis. Lectr, Roehampton Inst., Univ. of Surrey, 1986–94. Exec., later Vice-Chm., Nat. Council of Social Service, 1964–80; Pres., European Region, Internat. Council on Social Welfare, 1971–79; Chm., Area Bd, MSC, 1975–86; Governor, Centre for Policy on Ageing, 1982–88. Editor, Social Policy and Administration, 1973–93. DUniv Surrey, 1992; Dr *hc* Univ. de Rennes, 1987. Médaille de l'Ecole Nationale de Santé, France, 1975. *Publications:* Communities and Social Change, 1966; Community Work, 1969, 2nd edn 1972; Health, Wealth and Housing, 1980; Change and Continuity, 1984; At Home in Devon, 1986; Age Speaks for Itself, 1988; Age Speaks for Itself in Europe, 1993. *Recreations:* walking, railways, wine. *Address:* Birchcote, New North Road, Exeter EX4 4AD. *T:* Exeter (01392) 72565.

LEAR, Joyce, (Mrs W. J. Lear); *see* Hopkirk, J.

LEARMONT, Gen. Sir John (Hartley), KCB 1989; CBE 1980 (OBE 1975); Quarter Master General, Ministry of Defence, 1991–94, retired; *b* 10 March 1934; *s* of Captain Percy Hewitt Learmont, CIE, RIN and Doris Orynthia Learmont; *m* 1957, Susan (*née* Thornborrow); three *s*. *Educ:* Fettes College; RMA Sandhurst. Commissioned RA, 1954; Instructor, RMA, 1960–63; student, Staff Coll., 1964; served 14 Field Regt, Staff Coll. and 3 RHA, 1965–70; MA to C-in-C BAOR, 1971–73; CO 1 RHA, 1974–75 (despatches 1974); HQ BAOR, 1976–78; Comdr, 8 Field Force, 1979–81; Dep. Comdr, Commonwealth Monitoring Force, Rhodesia, Nov. 1979–March 1980; student RCDS, 1981; Chief of Mission, British Cs-in-C Mission to Soviet Forces in Germany, 1982–84; Comdr Artillery, 1 (British) Corps, 1985–87; COS, HQ UKLF, 1987–88; Comdt, Staff Coll. Camberley, 1988–89; Mil. Sec., MoD, 1989–91. Colonel Commandant: Army Air Corps, 1988–94; RA, 1989–; RHA, 1990–; Hon. Col, 2nd Bn Wessex Regt (Vols), 1990–95. Pres., Army Athletics Assoc., 1989–94. *Recreations:* fell walking, golf, theatre. *Club:* Naval and Military.

LEAROYD, Wing Comdr Roderick Alastair Brook, VC 1940; RAF; *b* 5 Feb. 1913; *s* of late Major Reginald Brook Learoyd and Marjorie Scott Boadle. *Educ:* Wellington Coll. *Address:* 12 Fittleworth Garden, Rustington, W Sussex BN16 3EW.

LEARY, Brian Leonard; QC 1978; *b* 1 Jan. 1929; *o s* of late A. T. Leary; *m* 1965, Myriam Ann Bannister, *d* of Kenneth Bannister, CBE, Mexico City. *Educ:* King's Sch. Canterbury; Wadham Coll., Oxford. MA Oxon. Called to the Bar, Middle Temple, 1953; Harmsworth Scholar; Bencher, 1986. Senior Prosecuting Counsel to the Crown at Central Criminal Court, 1971–78. Chm., British-Mexican Soc., 1989–92. *Recreations:* travel, sailing, growing herbs. *Address:* 5 Paper Buildings, Temple, EC4Y 7HB. *T:* 0171–353 7811.

LEASK, Lt-Gen. Sir Henry (Lowther Ewart Clark), KCB 1970 (CB 1967); DSO 1945; OBE 1957 (MBE 1945); GOC Scotland and Governor of Edinburgh Castle, 1969–72, retired; *b* 30 June 1913; *s* of Rev. James Leask, MA; *m* Zoë de Camborne, *d* of Col W. P. Paynter, DSO, RHA; one *s* two *d*. 2nd Lt Royal Scots Fusiliers, 1936. Served War of 1939–45 in Mediterranean and Italy; Staff College Camberley, 1942; GSO 1942; Bde Major Inf. Bde 1943; 2nd in Comd and CO, 8 Bn Argyll and Sutherland Highlanders, 1944–45; Comd 1st Bn London Scottish, 1946–47; RAF Staff College, 1947; Gen. Staff Mil. Ops, WO, 1947–49; Instr Staff Coll., 1949–51; Comd 1st Bn The Parachute Regt, 1952–54; Asst Military Sec. to Sec. of State for War, 1955–57; Comdt, Tactical Wing Sch. of Inf., 1957–58; Comd Infantry Bde, 1958–61; idc 1961; Dep. Mil. Sec. to Sec. of State for War, 1962–64; GOC 52 Lowland Div., 1964–66; Dir of Army Training, MoD (Army), 1966–69. Brig. 1961, Maj.-Gen. 1964, Lt-Gen. 1969. Col of the Royal Highland Fusiliers, 1964–69; Col Comdt, Scottish Div. of Infantry, 1968–72. Chm., Army Benevolent Fund, Scotland, 1972–88. *Recreation:* field sports. *Clubs:* Carlton, Hurlingham.

LEASOR, (Thomas) James; author; *b* 20 Dec. 1923; *s* of late Richard and Christine Leasor, Erith, Kent; *m* 1951, Joan Margaret Bevan, LLB, Barrister-at-law, *o d* of late Roland S. Bevan, Crowcombe, Somerset; three *s*. *Educ:* City of London Sch.; Oriel Coll., Oxford. Kentish Times, 1941–42. Served in Army in Burma, India, Malaya, 1942–46, Capt. Royal Berks Regt. Oriel Coll., Oxford, 1946–48, BA 1948; MA 1952; edited The Isis. On staff Daily Express, London, 1948–55, as reporter, foreign correspondent, feature writer. Contrib. to many American and British magazines, newspapers and periodicals; scriptwriter for TV series The Michaels in Africa. FRSA. OStJ. *Publications: novels:* Not Such a Bad Day, 1946; The Strong Delusion, 1951; NTR–Nothing to Report, 1955; Passport to Oblivion, 1964; Spylight, 1966; Passport in Suspense, 1967; Passport for a Pilgrim, 1968; They Don't Make Them Like That Any More, 1969; A Week of Love, 1969; Never had a Spanner on Her, 1970; Love-all, 1971; Follow the Drum, 1972; Host of Extras, 1973; Mandarin Gold, 1973; The Chinese Widow, 1974; Jade Gate, 1976; Love and the Land Beyond, 1979; Open Secret, 1982; Ship of Gold, 1984; Tank of Serpents, 1986; Frozen Assets, 1989; Love Down Under, 1991; *as Andrew MacAllan:* Succession, 1989; Generation, 1990; Diamond-Hard, 1991; Fanfare, 1992; Speculator, 1993; Traders, 1994; *non-fiction:* Author by Profession, The Monday Story, 1951; Wheels to Fortune, The Serjeant Major, 1954; The Red Fort; (with Kendal Burt) The One That Got Away, 1956; The Millionth Chance, 1957; War at the Top, 1959; (with Peter Eton) Conspiracy of Silence, 1959; Bring Out Your Dead, 1961; Rudolf Hess: The Uninvited Envoy, 1961; Singapore: The Battle that Changed the World, 1968; Green Beach, 1975; Boarding Party, 1977; The Unknown Warrior, 1980; Who Killed Sir Harry Oakes?, 1983; The Marine from Mandalay, 1988. *Recreation:* vintage sports cars. *Address:* Swallowcliffe Manor, Salisbury, Wilts SP3 5PB; Casa do Zimbro, Praia da Luz, Lagos, Algarve, Portugal. *Club:* Garrick.

LEATES, Margaret; parliamentary consultant, since 1990; *d* of Henry Arthur Sargent Rayner and Alice (*née* Baker); *m* 1973, Timothy Philip Leates; one *s* one *d*. *Educ:* Lilley and Stone Girls' High Sch., Newark; King's Coll., London (LLB, LLM; undergrad. and postgrad. entrance schol.; AKC). Admitted Solicitor, 1975; joined Office of Parliamentary Counsel, 1976; seconded to Law Commn, 1981–83 and 1987–89; Dep. Parly Counsel, 1987–90. *Recreations:* hermeneutics, junk, other people's gardens. *Address:* Crofton Farm, 161 Crofton Lane, Orpington, Kent BR6 0BP. *T:* Orpington (01689) 820192; Nyanza, 87 Bennell's Avenue, Whitstable, Kent CT5 2HR. *T:* Whitstable (01227) 272335. *Club:* Whitstable Yacht.

LEATHAM, Dr Aubrey (Gerald), FRCP; cardiologist; Hon. Consulting Physician: St George's Hospital, London; National Heart Hospital; King Edward VII Hospital, London; *b* 23 Aug. 1920; *s* of Dr H. W. Leatham (*d* 1973), Godalming and Kathleen Pelham Burn (*d* 1971), Nosely Hall, Leicester; *m* 1954, Judith Augustine Savile Freer; one *s* three *d*. *Educ:* Charterhouse; Trinity Hall, Cambridge; St Thomas' Hospital. BA Cambridge 1941; MB, BChir 1944; MRCP 1945; FRCP 1957. House Phys., St Thomas' Hosp., 1944; RMO, Nat. Heart Hosp., 1945; Phys., RAMC, 1946–47; Sherbrook Research Fellow, Cardiac Dept, and Sen. Registrar, London Hosp., 1948–50; Asst Dir, Inst. of Cardiology, 1951–54, Dean, 1962–69. Goulstonian Lectr, RCP, 1958. R. T. Hall Travelling Prof., Australia and NZ, 1963. Member: Brit. Cardiac Soc.; Sociedad Peruana de Cardiologia, 1966; Sociedad Colombiana de Cardiologia, 1966. Hon. FACC 1986. Royal Order of Bhutan, 1966. *Publications:* Auscultation of the Heart and Phonocardiography, 1970; (jtly) Lecture Notes in Cardiology, 1990; articles in Lancet, British Heart Jl, etc, on auscultation of the heart and phonocardiography, artificial pacemakers, coronary artery disease, etc. *Recreations:* ski-ing and ski-touring, mountain walking, tennis, racquets, gardening, photography. *Address:* 27 Sulivan Road, SW6 3DT. *T:* 0171–736 2237; Fitzroy-Nuffield Hospital, 10–12 Bryanston Square, W1H 8BB; Rookwood Farmhouse, West Wittering, Sussex PO20 8QH. *T:* Birdham (01243) 514649.

LEATHART, Air Cdre James Anthony, CB 1960; DSO 1940; *b* 5 Jan. 1915; *s* of P. W. Leathart, BSc, MD, Ear, Nose and Throat Specialist, Liverpool; *m* 1939, E. L. Radcliffe, Birkenhead; two *s* one *d*. *Educ:* St Edward's, Oxford; Liverpool Univ. Joined Auxiliary Air Force (610 County of Chester Squadron), 1936; transferred RAF, 1937, CO 54 Sqn, Battle of Britain, 1940; Chief of Staff Headquarters, 12 Group, RAF, 1959–61; Dir of Operational Requirements, Air Ministry, 1961–62, retd. Oct. 1962. *Recreations:* fly-fishing, motoring, ornithology, gardening. *Address:* Wortley Farmhouse, Wotton-under-Edge, Glos GL12 7QP. *T:* Dursley (01453) 842312.

LEATHER, Sir Edwin (Hartley Cameron), KCMG 1974; KCVO 1975; Kt 1962; Governor and C-in-C of Bermuda, 1973–77; writer and broadcaster; *b* 22 May 1919; *s* of Harold H. Leather, MBE, Hamilton, Canada, and Grace C. Leather (*née* Holmes); *m* 1940, Sheila A. A. (CStJ) (*d* 1994), *d* of Major A. H. Greenlees, Hamilton; two *d*. *Educ:* Trinity College Sch., Canada; Royal Military Coll., Kingston, Canada (BMilSc 1994). Commnd RCHA; served War of 1939–45 with Canadian Army, UK and in Europe, 1940–45. Contested (C) South Bristol, 1945; MP (C) N Somerset, 1950–64. Mem., Exec. Cttee, British Commonwealth Producers Organisation, 1960–63; Chairman: Bath Festival Soc., 1960–65; Horder Centre for Arthritics, 1962–65; Cons. and Unionist Assocs, 1969–70 (Mem. Nat. Exec. Cttee, 1963–70); Mem. Cons. Party Bd of Finance, 1963–67; Mem., Bd of Dirs, Yehudi Menuhin Sch., 1967–; Dir, N. M. Rothschild (Bermuda), 1978–91, and other cos. Canadian Legion rep. on Exec. Cttee of Brit. Commonwealth Ex-Servicemen's League, 1954–63; Pres., Institute of Marketing, 1963–67. Lay Reader, in Anglican Church, 1950–. Chm., Bermuda Cttee, United World Colls, 1975–91; Mem. Council, Imp. Soc. of Knights Bachelor, 1969–; Nat. Gov., Shaw Fest., Niagara-on-the-Lake, Ontario, 1990–; Trustee, Menuhin Foundn of Bermuda, 1975–; Hon. Patron, Bermuda Fest., 1975–; Hon. Mem. Cttee, Canada Meml Foundn, 1991–; Grand Senechal Confrerie des Chevaliers du Tastevin, 1990. FRSA 1969; Hon. LLD Bath, 1975. KStJ 1974. Hon. Citizen, Kansas City, USA, 1957; Gold Medal, Nat. Inst. Social Sciences, NY, 1977. Medal of Merit, Royal Canadian Legion, 1963. *Publications:* The Vienna Elephant, 1977; The Mozart Score, 1978; The Duveen Letter, 1980. *Address:* Chelsea, Inwood Close, Paget, Bermuda PG05. *Clubs:* Carlton; York (Toronto); Hamilton (Ontario); Royal Bermuda Yacht.

LEATHER, Ted; *see* Leather, Sir E. H. C.

LEATHERS, family name of **Viscount Leathers.**

LEATHERS, 2nd Viscount, *cr* 1954; **Frederick Alan Leathers;** Baron Leathers, 1941; *b* 4 April 1908; *er s* of 1st Viscount Leathers, PC, CH, LLD; *S* father, 1965; *m* 1st, 1940, Elspeth Graeme (marr. diss. 1983; she *d* 1985), *yr d* of late Sir Thomas (Alexander) Stewart; two *s* two *d*; 2nd, 1983, Mrs Lorna M. Barnett. *Educ:* Brighton Coll.; Emmanuel Coll., Cambridge (MA (hons) in Economics). Mem. of Baltic Exchange. Director: Wm Cory & Son Ltd, 1929–72 (Chm.); Cory Mann George Ltd, 1941–72 (Chm.); Cory Ship Towage Ltd, 1941–72 (Chm.); Smit & Cory International Port Towage Ltd, 1970–72 (Chm.); Hull Blyth & Co. Ltd, 1949–72 (Chm.); Rea Ltd, 1941–72 (Chm.); St Denis Shipping Co. Ltd, 1957–72 (Chm.); Laporte Industries Ltd, 1959–71; Laporte Industries (Holdings) Ltd, 1959–71; Tunnel Cement Ltd, 1960–74; Guardian Cement Co. Ltd, 1963–71; New Zealand Cement Holdings Ltd, 1963–71; National Westminster Bank, Outer London Region, 1968–78. Member: Court of Worshipful Company of Shipwrights; Court of Watermen's and Lightermen's Company; Fellow Institute of Chartered Shipbrokers; MInstPet. *Heir: s* Hon. Christopher Graeme Leathers [*b* 31 Aug. 1941; *m* 1964, Maria Philomena, *yr d* of Michael Merriman, Charlestown, Co. Mayo; one *s* one *d*]. *Address:* Park House, Chiddingfold, Surrey GU8 4TS. *T:* Wormley (01428) 683222. *Club:* Royal Automobile.

LEATHWOOD, Barry; National Secretary, Rural, Agricultural and Allied Workers National Trade Group, Transport and General Workers' Union, since 1987; *b* 11 April 1941; *s* of Charles and Dorothy Leathwood; *m* 1963, Veronica Ann Clarke; one *d*. Apprentice Toolmaker, 1956–62; Toolmaker/Fitter, 1962–73; District Organiser, Nat. Union of Agric. and Allied Workers, 1973–83; Regional Officer, TGWU Agric. Group, 1983–87. *Recreations:* socialist politics, reading, photography. *Address:* Transport House, Smith Square, SW1P 3JB. *T:* 0171–828 7788.

LEAVER, Sir Christopher, GBE 1981; JP; director of private and public companies; Vice Chairman, Thames Water Plc, since 1994 (Deputy Chairman, 1989–93; Chairman, 1993–94); *b* 3 Nov. 1937; *s* of Dr Robert Leaver and Mrs Audrey Kerpen; *m* 1975, Helen Mireille Molyneux Benton; one *s* two *d*. *Educ:* Eastbourne Coll. Commissioned (Army), RAOC, 1956–58. Member, Retail Foods Trades Wages Council, 1963–64. JP Inner London, 1970–83, City, 1974–; Member: Council, Royal Borough of Kensington and Chelsea, 1970–73; Court of Common Council (Ward of Dowgate), City of London, 1973; Alderman (Ward of Dowgate), City of London, 1974; Sheriff of the City of London, 1979–80; Lord Mayor of London, 1981–82; one of HM Lieutenants, City of London, 1982–. Chm., London Tourist Bd, 1983–89; Dep. Chm., Thames Water Authority, 1983–89; Chm., Thames Line Plc, 1987–89; Director: Bath & Portland Gp, 1983–85; Thermal Scientific plc, 1986–88; Unionamerica Holdings Plc, 1994–. Advr on Royal Parks to Sec. of State for Nat. Heritage, 1993–. Member: Bd of Brixton Prison, 1975–78; Court, City Univ., 1978– (Chancellor, 1981–82); Council of the Missions to Seamen, 1983–; Council, Wine and Spirit Benevolent Soc., 1983–88; Finance Cttee, London Diocesan Fund, 1983–86; Trustee: Chichester Festival Theatre, 1982–; LSO, 1983–91; Vice-President: Bridewell Royal Hosp., 1982–89; NPFA, 1983–; Governor: Christ's Hospital Sch., 1975–; City of London Girls' Sch., 1975–78; City of London Freemen's Sch., 1980–81; Chm., Council, Eastbourne Coll., 1989– (Mem., 1988–); Almoner Trustee, St Paul's Cathedral Choir Sch. Foundn, 1986–90. Trustee, Music Therapy Trust, 1981–89; Chairman, Young Musicians' Symphony Orch. Trust, 1979–81; Hon. Mem., Guildhall Sch. of Music and Drama, 1982–. Church Warden, St Olave's, Hart Street, 1975–90 (Patronage Trust, 1990–); Church Comr, 1982–93. Mem., Ct of Assistants, Carmen's Co., 1973 (Master, 1987–88); Hon. Liveryman, Farmers' Company, 1980; Freeman, Co. of Watermen and Lightermen, 1988; Hon. Freeman, Co. of Water Conservators, 1995; Hon. Mem., Co. of Environmental Cleaners, 1983–; Hon. Col, 151 (Greater London) Tpt Regt RCT (V), 1983–88; Hon. Col Comdt, RCT, 1988–91. Hon. DMus City, 1981. KStJ 1982. Order of Oman Class II. *Recreations:* gardening, music. *Address:* 381 Kennington Road, SE11 4PT. *T:* 0171–735 0385.

LEAVER, Prof. Christopher John, FRS 1986; FRSE; Sibthorpian Professor of Plant Sciences, since 1990, and Head, Department of Plant Sciences, since 1991, University of Oxford; Fellow, St John's College, since 1989; *b* 31 May 1942; *s* of Douglas Percy Leaver and Elizabeth Constance Leaver; *m* 1971, Anne (*née* Huggins); one *s* one *d*. *Educ:* Imperial College, University of London (BSc, ARCS, DIC, PhD); MA (Oxon) 1990. Fulbright Scholar, Purdue Univ., 1966–68; Scientific Officer, ARC Plant Physiology Unit, Imperial Coll., 1968–69; University of Edinburgh: Lectr, Dept of Botany, 1969–80; Reader, 1980–86; SERC Sen. Res. Fellow, 1985–89; Prof. of Plant Molecular Biol., 1986–89. Member: AFRC, 1990–94; Priorities Bd for R&D to advise MAFF, 1990–94 (Chm., Arable Crops Adv. Sectoral Gp, 1990–94); Council, EMBO, 1991–; ACOST, 1992–93; Council, Royal Soc., 1992–94; Chm., Adv. Bd, IACR, Rothamstead. Curator, Oxford Botanic Garden, 1991–. Trustee, John Innes Foundn, 1987–. Mem., Academia Europaea, 1988. T. H. Huxley Gold Medal, Imperial Coll., 1970; Tate & Lyle Award, Phytochem. Soc. of Europe, 1984. *Publications:* numerous papers in internat. sci. jls. *Recreations:* walking and talking in Upper Coquetdale. *Address:* Department of Plant Sciences, University of Oxford, South Parks Road, Oxford OX1 3RB. *T:* Oxford (01865) 275143, *Fax:* Oxford (01865) 275144.

LEAVER, Peter Lawrence Oppenheim; QC 1987; a Recorder, since 1994; *b* 28 Nov. 1944; *er s* of Marcus Isaac Leaver and Lena Leaver (*née* Oppenheim); *m* 1969, Jane Rachel, *o d* of Leonard and Rivka Pearl; three *s* one *d*. *Educ:* Aldenham Sch., Elstree; Trinity Coll., Dublin. Called to the Bar, Lincoln's Inn, 1967, Bencher, 1995. Chairman: Bar Cttee, 1989; Internat. Practice Cttee, 1990. Member: Gen. Council of the Bar, 1987–90; Cttee on the Future of the Legal Profession, 1986–88; Council of Legal Educn, 1986–91. Dir, IMRO Ltd. *Recreations:* sport, theatre, wine. *Address:* 1 Essex Court, Temple, EC4Y 9AR. *T:* 0171–583 2000; 5 Hamilton Terrace, NW8 9RE. *T:* 0171–286 0208. *Clubs:* Athenæum, MCC.

LEAVETT, Alan; Member, Woodspring District Council, 1986–95; *b* 4 May 1924; *s* of George and Mabel Dorothy Leavett; *m* 1948, Jean Mary Wanford; three *d*. *Educ:* Gosport County Sch.; UC, Southampton. BA Hons 1943. MAP (RAE), 1943; HM Customs and Excise, 1947; HM Foreign Service, 1949; Rio de Janeiro, 1950–53; Bangkok, 1955–59; UK Perm. Delegate to ECAFE, 1958; Cabinet Office, 1961; Min. of Housing and Local Govt, 1963; Sec., Noise Adv. Council, 1970; Under-Sec., Civil Service Selection Bd, 1973, Dept of Environment, 1974–81. Gen. Sec., Avon Wildlife Trust, 1981–84; Member: Rural Develt Commn, 1982–91; Council, World Wildlife Fund UK, 1983–86; Clifton Suspension Bridge Trust, 1991–95; Vice-Pres., ACRE, 1987–92; Vice-Chm., Avon Community Council, 1981–89. *Publication:* Historic Sevenoaks, 1969. *Recreations:* book-collecting, music. *Address:* Darenth House, St Martins, Long Ashton, Som BS18 9HP. *T:* Long Ashton (01275) 392876.

LEAVEY, John Anthony, BA; *b* 3 March 1915; *s* of George Edwin Leavey and Marion Louise Warnock; *m* 1952, Lesley Doreen, *d* of Rt Hon. Sir Benjamin Ormerod. *Educ:* Mill Hill Sch.; Trinity Hall, Cambridge. Served War, 1939–46; 5th Royal Inniskilling Dragoon Guards. MP (C) Heywood and Royton Div. of Lancashire, 1955–64. PPS to Minister of Defence, 1956–57, to Chancellor of Exchequer, 1959–60. Chairman: Wilson (Connolly) Hldgs, 1966–82 (Dir, 1966–85); Robert Moss, 1981–82 (Dir, 1981–86); Edward Barber & Co., 1982–88; Director: Smith & Nephew, 1948–80 (Dep. Chm., 1962–72); BIA, 1976–85; Fläkt, 1976–85; CSE Aviation, 1986–88. Panel Mem., SE London Indust. Tribunal, 1978–84. Mem. Council, Outward Bound Trust, 1974–92; Trustee, Kurt Hahn Trust, 1987–92. *Recreation:* fishing. *Address:* 30 Pembroke Gardens Close, W8 6HR. *Club:* Army and Navy.

LEAVEY, Thomas Edward, PhD; Director General, International Bureau of Universal Postal Union, since 1995; *b* Kansas City, 10 Nov. 1934; *s* of Leonard J. Leavey and Mary (*née* Horgan); *m* 1968, Anne Roland. *Educ:* Josephinium Coll., Columbus, Ohio (BA 1957); Institut Catholique, Paris; Princeton Univ. (MA 1967; PhD 1968). Sch. administrator and teacher, Kansas City, Mo, 1957–63; Prof., Fairleigh Dickinson Univ., NJ and George Washington Univ., Washington, 1968–70; United States Postal Service: Prof., Trng and Develt Inst., Bethesda, Md, 1970–72; Dir, Postal Service Trng and Develt Mgt Trng Center, LA, 1973–75; Gen. Manager, Employment and Placement Div., HQ, 1976–78; Dir, Postal Career Exec. Service, HQ, 1979; Postmaster/Sectional Manager, Charlottesville, Va, 1980; Regl Dir of Human Resources, Central Reg., Chicago, 1981; Controller, HQ, 1982; Gen. Manager, Internat. Mail Processing Div., HQ, 1982–87; Asst PMG and Sen. Dir, Internat. Postal Affairs, HQ, 1987–94. Universal Postal Union: Chairman: Customs Co-operation Council Contact Cttee, 1987–89; Private Operators Contact Cttee, 1991–94; Postal Develt Action Gp, 1991–94; Provident Scheme Mgt Bd, Internat. Bureau, 1989–94; Exec. Council, 1989–94. USPS Special Achievement Awards for Distinguished Service, 1970–90; John Wanamaker Award, USPS, 1991. *Publications:* numerous articles on business and postal matters in postal and trade jls. *Recreations:* golf, tennis, ski-ing. *Address:* International Bureau of the Universal Postal Union, Weltpoststrasse 4, 3000 Berne 15, Switzerland. *T:* (31) 3503101.

LE BAILLY, Vice-Adm. Sir Louis (Edward Stewart Holland), KBE 1972 (OBE 1952); CB 1969; DL; Director-General of Intelligence, Ministry of Defence, 1972–75; *b* 18 July 1915; *s* of Robert Francis Le Bailly and Ida Gaskell Le Bailly (*née* Holland); *m* 1946, Pamela Ruth Berthon; three *d*. *Educ:* RNC Dartmouth. HMS Hood, 1932; RNEC, 1933–37; HMS Hood, 1937–40; HMS Naiad, 1940–42; RNEC, 1942–44; HMS Duke of York, 1944–46; Admiralty, 1946–50; HMS Bermuda, 1950–52; RNEC, 1955–58; Admiralty: Staff Officer to Dartmouth Review Cttee, 1958; Asst Engineer-in-Chief, 1958–60; Naval Asst to Controller of the Navy, 1960–63; IDC, 1963; Dep. Dir of Marine Engineering, 1963–67; Naval Attaché, Washington, DC, and Comdr, British Navy Staff, 1967–69; Min. of Defence, 1970–72; Vice-Adm. 1970, retired 1972. Mem. Council, Research Inst. for Study of Conflict and Terrorism, 1976–. DL Cornwall, 1982. FIMechE; FInstPet; MIMarE. Hon DSc. *Publications:* The Man Around the Engine, 1990; From

Fisher to the Falklands, 1991; Old Loves Return, 1993. *Address:* Garlands House, St Tudy, Bodmin, Cornwall PL30 3NN. *Club:* Naval.

LeBLANC, Rt Hon. Roméo, PC (Can.) 1974; CC 1995; CMM 1995; CD 1995; Governor General and Commander-in-Chief of Canada, since 1995; *b* 18 Dec. 1927; *s* of Philias and Lucie LeBlanc; *m* Diana Fowler. *Educ:* Université St-Joseph, Memramcook (BA 1948; BEd 1951); Paris Univ. Teacher, New Brunswick, 1951–59; corresp. for Radio-Canada, in Ottawa, UK and US, 1960–67; Press Sec. to Prime Minister of Canada, 1967–71; Asst to Pres. and Dir of Public Relns, Moncton Univ., 1971–72. MP (L) Westmorland-Kent, 1972–84; Minister of State, Fisheries, 1974–76; Minister of: Fisheries and the Envmt, 1976–79; Fisheries and Oceans, 1980–82; Public Works, 1982–84; served on various Cabinet cttees; Mem., Senate, 1984–94; served on various Senate cttees; Speaker, 1993–94. Hon. DCL Mt Allison, 1977; Hon. Dr in Public Admin Moncton, 1979. *Address:* Rideau Hall, 1 Sussex Drive, Ottawa, Ontario K1A 0A1, Canada. *T:* (613) 9938200.

LEBLOND, Prof. C(harles) P(hilippe), OC 1977; MD, PhD, DSc; FRSC 1951; FRS 1965; Professor of Anatomy, McGill University, Canada, since 1948; *b* 5 Feb. 1910; *s* of Oscar Leblond and Jeanne Desmarchelier; *m* 1936, Gertrude Elinor Sternschuss; three *s* one *d*. *Educ:* Sch. St Joseph, Lille, France; Univs. of Lille, Nancy, Paris, Montreal. L-ès-S, Nancy 1932; MD Paris 1934; PhD Montreal 1942; DSc Sorbonne 1945. Asst in Histology, Med. School, Univ. of Paris, 1934–35; Rockefeller Fell., Sch. of Med., Yale Univ., 1936–37; Asst, Laboratoire de Synthése Atomique, Paris, 1938–40; McGill Univ.: Lectr in Histology and Embryology, 1941–42; Asst Prof. of Anatomy, 1942–43; Assoc. Prof. of Anatomy, 1946–48; Prof. of Anatomy, 1948–; Chm. of Dept of Anatomy, 1957–75. Mem. Amer. Assoc. of Anatomists; Fellow, Amer. Acad. of Arts and Scis. Hon. DSc: Acadia, 1972; McGill, 1982; Montreal, 1985; York, 1986. *Publications:* over 300 articles, mainly on radio-autography and cell dynamics, in anatomical journals. *Recreation:* country. *Address:* (home) 68 Chesterfield Avenue, Westmount, Montreal, Quebec H3Y 2M5, Canada. *T:* (514) 4864837; (office) Department of Anatomy, McGill University, 3640 University Street, Montreal, Quebec H3A 2B2, Canada. *T:* (514) 3986340

LE BRETON, David Francis Battye, CBE 1978; HM Diplomatic Service, retired; Secretary, Overseas Service Pensioners Association and Benevolent Society, since 1992; *b* 2 March 1931; *e s* of late Lt-Col F. H. Le Breton, MC, and Elisabeth, (Peter), Le Breton (*née* Trevor-Battye), Endebess, Kenya; *m* 1961, Patricia June Byrne; one *s* two *d*. *Educ:* Winchester; New Coll., Oxford. Colonial Administrative Service, Tanganyika, 1954; Private Sec. to Governor, 1959–60; Magistrate, 1962; Principal, CRO, 1963; HM Diplomatic Service, 1965; First Sec., Zanzibar, 1964; Lusaka, 1964–68; FCO, 1968–71; Head of Chancery, Budapest, 1971–74; HM Comr in Anguilla, 1974–78; Counsellor and Head of Chancery, Nairobi, 1978–81; High Comr in The Gambia, 1981–84; Head of Commonwealth Co-ordination Dept, FCO, 1984–86; Head of Nationality and Treaty Dept, FCO, 1986–87. Financial Advr/Sales Associate, Allied Dunbar Assurance, 1987–91. *Recreations:* country living, garden-clearing, African and colonial affairs. *Address:* Brackenwood, French Street, near Westerham, Kent TN16 1PN.

le BROCQUY, Louis, FCSD (FSIAD 1960); HRHA 1983; painter since 1939; *b* Dublin, 10 Nov. 1916; *s* of late Albert le Brocquy, MA, and late Sybil Staunton; *m* 1st, 1938, Jean Stoney (marr. diss., 1948); one *d*; 2nd, 1958, Anne Madden Simpson; two *s*. *Educ:* St Gerard's Sch., Wicklow, Ireland. Self-taught. Founder-mem. of Irish Exhibn of Living Art, 1943; Visiting Instructor, Central Sch. of Arts and Crafts, London, 1947–54; Visiting Tutor, Royal Coll. of Art, London, 1955–58. Member: Irish Council of Design, 1963–65; Adv. Council, Guinness Peat Awards, 1980–85. Director: Kilkenny Design Workshops, 1965–77; Irish Mus. of Modern Art, 1989–. Represented Ireland, Venice Biennale (awarded internat. prize), 1956. Work exhibited in: "50 Ans d'Art Moderne", Brussels, 1958; Painting since World War II, Guggenheim Mus., New York, 1987–88; Olympiad of Art, Seoul, 1988; L'Europe des Grands Maîtres 1870–1970, Inst. de France, 1989; Internat. Art Fest., Seoul, 1991; Premiers Chefs d'Oeuvres des Grands Maîtres, Museums of Art, Tokyo, Osaka, Kyoto, 1992. One Man Shows: Leicester Galleries, London, 1948; Gimpel Fils, London, 1947, 1949, 1951, 1955, 1956, 1957, 1959, 1961, 1966, 1968, 1971, 1974, 1978, 1983, 1988, 1991, 1993; Waddington, Dublin, 1951; Robles Gallery, Los Angeles, 1960; Gallery Lienhard, Zürich, 1961; Dawson/Taylor Gallery, Dublin, 1962, 1966, 1969, 1971, 1973, 1974, 1975, 1981, 1985, 1986, 1988, 1991, 1992, 1993; Municipal Gallery of Modern Art, Dublin, 1966, 1978; Ulster Mus., Belfast, (retrospective) 1967, 1987, 1993; Gimpel-Hanover, Emmerich Zürich, 1969, 1978 1983; Gimpel, NY, 1971, 1978, 1983; Fondation Maeght, 1973; Bussola, Turin, 1974; Arts Council, Belfast, 1975, 1978; Musée d'Art Moderne, Paris, 1976; Giustiniani, Genoa, 1977; Waddington, Montreal, Toronto, 1978; Maeght, Barcelona, Madrid, Granada, 1978–79; Jeanne Bucher, Paris, 1979, 1982; NY State Mus., 1981; Boston Coll. 1982; Westfield Coll., Mass, 1982; Palais des Beaux Arts, Charleroi, 1982; Art 13, Internat. Basel (Börjeson), 1982; Chicago Internat. Expo (Brownstone Gall.), 1986; Arts Council, Dublin, 1987; Nat. Gall. of Vic, Melbourne, Festival Centre, Adelaide, and Mus. of Contemp. Art, Brisbane, 1988; Musée Picasso, Antibes, 1989; Kerlin, Dublin, 1991; Mus. of Modern Art, Kamakura, 1991; Itami City Mus. of Art, Osaka, 1991; City Mus. of Contemp. Art, Hiroshima, 1991; Irish Mus. of Modern Art, 1996. Public Collections possessing work include: Albright Museum, Buffalo; Arts Council, London; Carnegie Inst., Pittsburgh; l'Etat Français; Chicago Arts Club; Columbus Mus., Ohio; Detroit Inst. of Art; Dublin Municipal Gallery; Fort Worth Center, Texas; Foundation of Brazil Museum, Bahia; Gulbenkian Mus., Lisbon; Guggenheim Museum, NY; J. H. Hirshhorn Foundation, Washington; Ho-Am Mus., Seoul; Itami Mus., Osaka; Kunsthaus, Zürich; Fondation Maeght, St Paul; Leeds City Art Gallery; Musée d'Art Moderne, Paris; Musée Picasso, Antibes; Mus. of Contemp. Art, Hiroshima; Mus. of Modern Art, Kamakura; NY State Mus.; San Diego Mus., Calif.; Tate Gallery; Uffizi, Florence; Ulster Museum, Belfast; Vatican Mus.; V&A Museum. RHA 1950–69. Film, An Other Way of Knowing, RTE, 1986. Chevalier de la Légion d'Honneur, 1975. Hon. DLitt Dublin, 1962; Hon. LLD NUI, 1988. Saoi, Aosdána, Irish Arts Council, 1993. Commandeur du Bontemps de Médoc et des Graves, 1969. *Illustrated work:* The Táin, trans. Thomas Kinsella, 1969; The Playboy of the Western World, Synge, 1970; The Gododdin O'Grady, 1978; Dubliners, Joyce, 1986; Stirrings Still, Samuel Beckett, 1988. *Relevant publication:* Louis le Brocquy by D. Walker, introd. John Russell, Ireland 1981, UK 1982. *Address:* c/o Gimpel Fils, 30 Davies Street, W1Y 1LG.

LE BRUN, Christopher Mark; artist; Trustee, Tate Gallery, 1990–95; *b* 20 Dec. 1951; *s* of late John Le Brun and of Eileen Betty (*née* Miles); *m* 1979, Charlotte Eleanor Verity; two *s* one *d*. *Educ:* Portsmouth Southern Grammar Sch.; Slade Sch. of Fine Art (DFA); Chelsea Sch. of Art (MA). Lecturer: Brighton Coll. of Art, 1975–82; Wimbledon Coll. of Art, 1982–84; Vis. Lectr, Slade Sch. of Fine Art, 1984–90. Deutsche Akademische Austauschdienste Fellowship, Berlin, 1987–88. Designer, Ballet Imperial, Royal Opera Hse, Covent Gdn, 1984. One man exhibitions include: Nigel Greenwood Gall., London, 1980, 1982, 1985, 1989; Gillespie-Laage-Salomon, Paris, 1981; Sperone Westwater, NY, 1983, 1986, 1988; Fruitmarket Gall., Edinburgh, 1985; Arnolfini Gall., Bristol, 1985; Kunsthalle, Basel, 1986; Daadgalerie, Berlin, 1988; Galerie Rudolf Zwirner, Cologne, 1988; Art Center, Pasadena, Calif, 1992; LA Louver Gall., Venice, Calif, 1992; Marlborough Fine Art, 1994, 1995; Galerie Fortlaan 17, Ghent, 1994; Astrup Fearnley Mus. of Modern Art, Oslo, 1995; group exhibitions include: Milan, 1980; Berlin, 1982; Tate Gall., 1983; Mus. Modern Art, NY, 1984; The British Show, toured Australia and NZ, 1985; Oxford, Budapest, Prague, Warsaw, 1987; LA County Mus., 1987; Cincinatti Mus. and American tour, 1988–89; Setagaya Art Mus. and Japanese tour, 1990–91; Scottish Nat. Gall. Modern Art, 1995; Yale Center for British Art, New Haven, 1995; work in public collections includes: Arts Council of GB, British Council, BM, NY Mus. Modern Art, Scottish Nat. Gall. Modern Art, Tate Gall., Walker Art Gall., Liverpool, Whitworth Art Gall., Manchester and Fitzwilliam Mus., Cambridge. Prizewinner, John Moores Liverpool Exhibns, 1978 and 1980; Gulbenkian Foundn Printmakers Award, 1983. *Address:* c/o Marlborough Fine Art, 6 Albemarle Street, W1X 4BY. *T:* 0171–629 5161.

LE CARRÉ, John; *see* Cornwell, David John Moore.

LE CHEMINANT, Peter, CB 1976; Director-General, General Council of British Shipping, 1985–91; consultant, UK Know-How Fund, to government of Lithuania, since 1993; *b* 29 April 1926; *s* of William Arthur Le Cheminant and Agnes Ann Le Cheminant (*née* Wilson); *m* 1959, Suzanne Elisabeth Horny; three *s*. *Educ:* Holloway Sch.; London Sch. of Economics. Sub-Lt, RNVR, 1944–47. Min. of Power, 1949; Cabinet Office, 1950–52 and 1964–65; UK Delegn to ECSC, 1962–63; Private Sec. to Prime Minister, 1965–68; Min. of Power, later Min. of Technology, 1968–71; Under-Sec., DTI, 1971–74; Deputy Secretary: Dept of Energy, 1974–77; Cabinet Office, 1978–81; CSD, subseq. HM Treas., 1981–83; Second Perm. Sec., Cabinet Office (MPO), 1983–84. Member, Council: Inst. of Employment Studies, 1983–; King George's Fund for Sailors, 1987–. Freeman, City of London, 1987; Liveryman, Worshipful Co. of Shipwrights, 1987. CIMgt (CBIM 1984); FCIT 1987. *Recreations:* reading, walking, history. *Club:* Reform.

LE CHEMINANT, Air Chief Marshal Sir Peter (de Lacey), GBE 1978; KCB 1972 (CB 1968); DFC 1943, and Bar, 1951; Lieutenant-Governor and Commander-in-Chief of Guernsey, 1980–85; *b* 17 June 1920; *s* of Lieut-Colonel Keith Le Cheminant and Blanche Etheldred Wake Le Cheminant (*née* Clark); *m* 1940, Sylvia, *d* of J. van Bodegom; one *s* two *d*. *Educ:* Elizabeth Coll., Guernsey; RAF Coll., Cranwell. Flying posts in France, UK, N Africa, Malta, Sicily and Italy, 1940–44; comd No 223 Squadron, 1943–44; Staff and Staff Coll. Instructor, 1945–48; Far East, 1949–53; comd No 209 Sqn, 1949–51; Jt Planning Staff, 1953–55; Wing Comdr, Flying, Kuala Lumpur, 1955–57; jssc 1958; Dep. Dir of Air Staff Plans, 1958–61; comd RAF Geilenkirchen, 1961–63; Dir of Air Staff Briefing, 1964–66; SASO, HQ FEAF, 1966–67, C of S, 1967–68; Comdt Joint Warfare Estabt, MoD, 1968–70; Asst Chief of Air Staff (Policy), MoD, 1971–72; UK Mem., Perm. Mil. Deputies Gp, CENTO, Ankara, 1972–73; Vice-Chief of Defence Staff, 1974–76; Dep. C-in-C, Allied Forces, Central Europe, 1976–79. KStJ 1980. *Recreations:* golf, sailing, reading. *Address:* La Madeleine De Bas, Ruette de la Madeleine, St Pierre du Bois, Guernsey, CI. *Club:* Royal Air Force.

LECHÍN-SUÁREZ, General Juan; Condor de los Andes (Bolivia), 1966; *b* 8 March 1921; *s* of Juan Alfredo Lechín and Julia Suárez; *m* 1947, Ruth Varela; one *s* three *d*. *Educ:* Bolivian Military College. Chief of Ops, Bolivian Army HQ, 1960–61; Military and Air Attaché, Bolivian Embassy, Bonn, 1962–63; Comdr, Bolivian Army Fifth Inf. Div., 1964; Pres., Bolivian State Mining Corp. (with rank of Minister of State), 1964–68; Comdr, Bolivian Army Third Inf. Div., 1969; Bolivian Ambassador to the UK and to the Netherlands, 1970–74; Minister for Planning and Co-ordination, 1974–78; Chm., Nat. Adv. and Legislation Council, 1980–81. Guerrillero José Miguel Lanza, Mérito Aeronautico, and Mérito Naval, 1966, Bolivia. Das Grosse Verdienstkreuz (FRG), 1975. *Publications:* La Estrategia del Altiplano Boliviano, 1975; La Batalla de Villa Montes, 1989. *Recreations:* tennis, swimming. *Address:* Casilla 4405, La Paz, Bolivia.

LECHMERE, Sir Berwick (Hungerford), 6th Bt, *cr* 1818; JP; Vice Lord-Lieutenant, Hereford and Worcester, 1977–92; Land Agent; *b* 21 Sept. 1917; *s* of Sir Ronald Berwick Hungerford Lechmere, 5th Bt, and Constance Marguerite (*née* Long) (*d* 1981); *S* father, 1965; *m* 1954, Norah Garrett Elkington; no *c*. *Educ:* Charterhouse; Magdalene Coll., Cambridge. High Sheriff of Worcs, 1962, JP, 1966, DL 1972. FRICS. CStJ. *Heir: cousin* Reginald Anthony Hungerford Lechmere [*b* 24 Dec. 1920; *m* 1956, Anne Jennifer Dind; three *s* one *d*]. *Address:* Church End House, Hanley Castle, Worcester WR8 0BL. *T:* Upton-on-Severn (01684) 592130.

LECKY, (Arthur) Terence, CMG 1968; HM Diplomatic Service, retired; *b* 10 June 1919; *s* of late Lieut-Colonel M. D. Lecky, DSO, late RA, and late Bertha Lecky (*née* Goss); *m* 1946, Jacqualine (*d* 1974), *d* of late Dr A. G. Element; three *s*. *Educ:* Winchester Coll.; Clare Coll., Cambridge (1938–39). Served RA, 1939–46. FO (Control Commission for Germany), 1946–49; FO, 1950–54; Vice-Consul, Zürich, 1954–56; FO, 1957–61; First Secretary, The Hague, 1962–64, FCO (formerly FO), 1964–70, retired. Mem., Hants CC, 1981–89. Vice-Chm., Hants Police Authority, 1988–89. *Address:* 1 Old Blackmore Museum, St Ann Place, Salisbury, Wilts SP1 2SU. *T:* Salisbury (01722) 338937.

LECKY, Maj.-Gen. Samuel K.; *see* Knox-Lecky.

LECKY, Terence; *See* Lecky, A. T.

LECONFIELD, Baron; *see* Egremont.

LECOURT, Robert; Commandeur, Legion of Honour; Croix de Guerre; Rosette de la Résistance; Member, Constitutional Council of the French Republic, 1979–89; *b* 19 Sept. 1908; *s* of Léon Lecourt and Angéle Lépron; *m* 1932, Marguerite Chabrerie; one *d*. *Educ:* Rouen; Univ. de Caen (DenDroit). Advocate, Court of Appeal: Rouen, 1928; Paris, 1932. Served with French Air Force, 1939–40; Mem. Resistance Movt, 1942–44; Deputy for Paris, 1945–58 and for Hautes Alpes, 1958–61, National Assembly; Pres., Parly Gp, MRP, 1945–48 and 1952–57; Minister of Justice, 1948–49 and 1957–58; Minister of State responsible for co-operation with Africa, 1958–61. Judge, Court of Justice, European Community, 1962, President 1967–76; Hon. Bencher, Gray's Inn, 1972; DUniv Exeter, 1975. Holds numerous foreign decorations. *Publications:* Nature juridique de l'action en réintégrande, 1931; Code pratique du travail, Responsabilité des architectes et entrepreneurs, etc, 1932–39; Le Juge devant le marché commun, 1970; L'Europe des juges, 1976; Concorde sans concordat 1952–57, 1978. *Address:* 11 Boulevard Suchet, 75016 Paris, France.

LEDERBERG, Prof. Joshua, PhD; University Professor, Rockefeller University, since 1990; consultant; *b* Montclair, NJ, USA, 23 May 1925; *s* of Zwi H. and Esther Lederberg (*née* Goldenbaum); *m* 1968, Marguerite Stein Kirsch, MD; one *d*, one step *s*. *Educ:* Stuyvesant High Sch., NYC; Columbia Coll. (BA); Yale Univ. (PhD). Assistant Professor of Genetics, University of Wisconsin, 1947; Associate Professor, 1950; Professor, 1954; Fulbright Vis. Prof. of Bacteriology, Univ. of Melbourne, Aust., 1957; Prof. and Exec. Head, Dept of Genetics, Sch. of Medicine, Stanford Univ., 1959–78; Pres., Rockefeller Univ., 1978–90. Consultant, Affymax Co., Palo Alto, Calif, 1990–. Shared in discoveries concerning genetic re-combination, and organization of genetic material of bacteria, contributing to cancer research; discovered a method of artificially introducing new genes into bacteria in investigation of hereditary substance. Chm., President's Cancer Panel (US), 1980–81. Member: Defense Sci. Bd, USA, 1979–; Chief of Naval Ops Exec. Panel, USN, 1981–; Council of Scholars, US Library of Congress, 1985–; Tech. Assessment Adv. Cttee, Office of Technology Assessment, US Congress, 1988–; Adv. Cttee to Dir, NIH, 1993–; Adv. Cttee for Med. Res., WHO, 1971–76; Member Board: Chemical Industry Inst. for Toxicology, 1980–; Dreyfus Foundn, 1983–; Revson Foundn, 1986–93; Trustee, Carnegie Corp., NYC, 1985–93. Columnist, Science and Man (Washington Post Syndicate), 1966–71. Mem., National Academy of Sciences, United States, 1957. For. Mem., Royal Society, 1979. ScD (*hc*): Yale Univ.; Columbia Univ.; Univ. of Wisconsin; Mt Sinai Sch. of Medicine; Rutgers; New York Univ.; MD (*hc*): Tufts Univ.; Univ. of Turin; LittD (*hc*) Jewish Theol Seminary; LLD (*hc*) Univ. of Pennsylvania. (Jointly) Nobel Prize in Medicine, 1958. US Nat. Medal of Science, 1989. *Publications:* contribs to learned journals on genetics, bacteria and general biological problems. *Address:* Rockefeller University, 1230 York Avenue, New York, NY 10021, USA. *T:* (212) 3277809.

LEDERMAN, David; QC 1990; a Recorder, since 1987; *b* 8 Feb. 1942; *s* of Eric Kurt Lederman and Marjorie Alice Lederman; *m* 1974, Georgina Anne Rubin; one *s* two *d.* *Educ:* Clayesmore School, Dorset; Gonville and Caius College, Cambridge. Called to the Bar, Inner Temple, 1966; general common law practice, particularly crime. *Recreations:* tennis, squash, horses, France, family.

LEDERMAN, Dr Leon Max; Director, Fermi National Accelerator Laboratory, 1979–89, Director Emeritus, since 1989; Pritzker Professor of Science, Illinois Institute of Technology, since 1992; *b* 15 July 1922; *s* of Minnie Rosenberg and Morris Lederman; *m* 1st, Florence Gordon; one *s* two *d*; 2nd, 1981, Ellen. *Educ:* City College of New York (BS 1943); Columbia Univ. (AM 1948; PhD 1951). US Army, 1943–46. Columbia University: Research Associate, Asst Prof., Associate Prof., 1951–58; Prof. of Physics, 1958–89; Associate Dir, Nevis Labs, 1953, Director, 1962–79. Ford Foundn Fellow, 1958–59; John Simon Guggenheim Foundn Fellow, 1958–59; Ernest Kempton Adams Fellow, 1961. Fellow, Amer. Physical Soc.; Mem., Nat. Acad. of Scis, 1965. Numerous hon. degrees. Nat. Medal of Science, 1965; (jtly) Nobel Prize in Physics, 1988; Enrico Fermi Prize, DOE, US, 1992. *Publications:* From Quartz to the Cosmos, 1989; The God Particle, 1992; papers and contribs to learned jls on high energy physics. *Recreations:* mountain hiking, ski-ing, jogging, piano, riding, gardening. *Address:* Fermi National Accelerator Laboratory, PO Box 500, Batavia, IL 60510, USA. *T:* (312) 8402856; (312) 5678920.

LEDGER, Frank, CBE 1992 (OBE 1985); FEng 1990; consultant; Deputy Chairman, Nuclear Electric plc, 1990–92, retired; *b* 16 June 1929; *s* of Harry and Doris Ledger; *m* 1953, Alma Moverley; two *s.* *Educ:* Leeds College of Technology (BSc Eng). FIMechE; FIEE; CBIM. Student Apprentice, Leeds Corp. Elect. Dept, 1947; appts in power station construction and generation operation in CEA then CEGB, 1955–65; Station Manager, Cottam Power Station, 1965; Central Electricity Generating Board: Group Manager, Midlands Region, 1968; System Operation Engineer, 1971; Dir, Resource Planning, Midlands Region, 1975; Dir of Computing, 1980; Dir of Operations, 1981; Exec. Bd Mem. for Prodn, 1986. Member: Council, IEE, 1987–92; British Nat. Cttee, UNIPEDE, 1981–90; Council, British Energy Assoc., 1990–92; Vice-Pres., Energy Industries Club, 1988–92. *Publication:* (jtly) Crisis Management in the Power Industry: an inside story, 1994. *Recreations:* music, photography, gardening, walking. *Address:* 3 Barns Dene, Harpenden, Herts AL5 2HH. *T:* Harpenden (01582) 762188.

LEDGER, Philip (Stevens), CBE 1985; Principal, Royal Scottish Academy of Music and Drama, since 1982; *b* 12 Dec. 1937; *s* of Walter Stephen Ledger and Winifred Kathleen (*née* Stevens); *m* 1963, Mary Erryl (*née* Wells); one *s* one *d.* *Educ:* Bexhill Grammar Sch.; King's Coll., Cambridge (Maj. Schol.); John Stewart of Rannoch Schol. in Sacred Music; 1st Cl. Hons in Pt I and Pt II, of Music Tripos; MA, MusB. FRCO (Limpus and Read prizes); FRCM 1983; FRNCM 1989; FRSE 1990. Master of the Music, Chelmsford Cathedral, 1962–65; Dir of Music, Univ. of East Anglia, 1965–73 (Dean of Sch. of Fine Arts and Music, 1968–71); Dir of Music and Organist, King's Coll., Cambridge, 1974–82; Conductor, CU Musical Soc., 1973–82. Artistic Dir, 1968–89, Vice-Pres., 1989–, Aldeburgh Festival of Music and the Arts. Hon. Prof., Univ. of Glasgow, 1993–. President: RCO, 1992–94; ISM, 1994–95. Hon. RAM 1984; Hon. GSM 1989. Hon. LLD Strathclyde, 1987. *Publications:* (ed) Anthems for Choirs 2 and 3, 1973; (ed) The Oxford Book of English Madrigals, 1978; other edns of Byrd, Handel and Purcell; carol arrangements. *Recreations:* swimming, theatre, membership of Sette of Odd Volumes. *Address:* 322 Albert Drive, Pollokshields, Glasgow G41 5DZ. *T:* 0141–429 0967.

LEDGER, Ronald Joseph; Casino Proprietor and Manager; *b* 7 Nov. 1920; *s* of Arthur and Florence Ledger; brought up by Dr Barnardo's, 1923–37; *m* 1946, Madeleine Odette de Villeneuve; three *s* one *d.* *Educ:* Skinners Grammar Sch., Tunbridge Wells; Nottingham Univ. Toolroom Engineer, 1938–42. Served RAF, 1942–47, fitter, Leading Aircraftsman; India three years. Univ. of Nottingham, 1947–49 (Diploma in Social Science); Staff Training Officer, Enfield Highway Co-op. Society, 1949; Business Partner, 1950, Company Director, 1953, Employment Specialists. Mem. Herts CC, 1952–54. Contested (Lab) Rushcliffe Div. of Nottingham, 1951; MP (Lab and Co-op) Romford, 1955–70. Director: Enfield Electronics (CRT) Ltd, 1958; London Co-operative Society Ltd, 1961. Chairman, Hairdressing Council, 1966–79. *Recreations:* tennis, cricket, golf, snooker. *Address:* 19 St Paul's Crescent, Shanklin, Isle of Wight PO37 7AN. *Club:* Shanklin and Sandown Golf.

LEDINGHAM, Prof. John Gerard Garvin, DM; FRCP; May Reader in Medicine, 1974–95, Professor of Clinical Medicine, 1989–95, and Director of Clinical Studies, 1977–82 and 1991–95, University of Oxford; Fellow of New College, Oxford, 1974–95, now Emeritus; Hon. Clinical Director, Biochemical and Clinical NMR Unit, Medical Research Council, Oxford, since 1988; *b* 1929; *s* of late John Ledingham, MB BCh, DPH, and late Una Ledingham, MD, FRCP, *d* of J. L. Garvin, CH, Editor of The Observer; *m* 1961, Elaine Mary, *d* of late R. G. Maliphant, MD, FRCOG, and of Dilys Maliphant, Cardiff; four *d.* *Educ:* Rugby Sch.; New Coll., Oxford; Middlesex Hosp. Med. Sch. (1st Cl. Physiol.; BM BCh; DM 1966). FRCP 1971 (MRCP 1959). Junior appts, Middlesex, London Chest, Whittington, and Westminster Hospitals, London, 1957–64; Travelling Fellow, British Postgraduate Med. Fedn, Columbia Univ., New York, 1965–66; Consultant Physician, Oxford AHA(T), 1966–82, Hon. Consultant Physician, Oxfordshire HA, 1982–. Chm., Medical Staff Council, United Oxford Hosps, 1970–72. Chm., Medical Res. Soc., 1988–92; Hon. Sec., Assoc. of Physicians of Gt Britain and Ireland 1977–82, Hon. Treas., 1982–88; Pro-Censor, RCP, 1983–84, Censor, 1984–85. Mem., Commonwealth Scholarship Commn, ACU, 1993. Governing Trustee, Nuffield Provincial Hosps Trust, 1978–; Trustee, Beit Trust, 1989–. *Publications:* (ed jtly) Oxford Textbook of Medicine, 1982, 3rd edn 1995; contribs to med. books and scientific jls in the field of hypertension and renal diseases. *Recreations:* music, golf. *Address:* 22 Hid's Copse Road, Cumnor Hill, Oxford OX2 9JJ. *T:* Oxford (01865) 862023. *Club:* Vincent's (Oxford).

LEDLIE, John Kenneth, CB 1994; OBE 1977; Deputy Under Secretary (Personnel and Logistics), Ministry of Defence, since 1993; *b* 19 March 1942; *s* of late Reginald Cyril Bell Ledlie and Elspeth Mary Kaye; *m* 1965, Rosemary Julia Allan; three *d.* *Educ:* Westminster School (Hon. Schol.); Brasenose Coll., Oxford (Triplett Exbnr; MA Lit Hum). Solicitor of the High Court; articles with Coward Chance, 1964–67; Min. of Defence, 1967; Asst Private Sec. to Minister of State for Equipment and Sec. of State for Defence, 1969–70; First Sec., UK Delegn to NATO, Brussels, 1973–76; Dep. Chief, Public Relations, 1977–79; NI Office and Cabinet Office, 1979–81; Procurement Exec., MoD, 1981–83; Head, Defence Secretariat 19, MoD, 1983; Regional Marketing Dir, Defence Sales Orgn, 1983–85; Chief of PR, MoD, 1985–87; Fellow, Center for Internat. Affairs, Harvard Univ., 1987–88; Asst Under-Sec. of State, MoD, 1988–90; Dep. Sec., NI Office, 1990–93. *Recreations:* ornithology, cricket, tennis, golf, theatre, opera. *Address:* Ministry of Defence, Main Building, Whitehall SW1A 2HB. *T:* 0171–218 9000. *Club:* United Oxford & Cambridge University.

LEDSOME, Neville Frank, CB 1988; Deputy Chairman, Civil Service Appeal Board, since 1994; Under Secretary, Personnel Management Division, Department of Trade and Industry, 1983–89, retired; *b* 29 Nov. 1929; *s* of late Charles Percy Ledsome and Florence Ledsome; *m* 1953, Isabel Mary Lindsay; three *s.* *Educ:* Birkenhead Sch. Exec. Officer, BoT, 1948; Monopolies Commn, 1957; Higher Exec. Officer, BoT, 1961; Principal, 1964; DEA, 1967; HM Treasury, 1969; DTI, 1970; Asst Sec., 1973; Under Sec., 1980. *Recreations:* gardening, theatre.

LEDWIDGE, Sir (William) Bernard (John), KCMG 1974 (CMG 1964); writer; HM Diplomatic Service, retired; Chairman, United Kingdom Committee for UNICEF, 1976–89; *b* 9 Nov. 1915; *s* of late Charles Ledwidge and Eileen O'Sullivan; *m* 1st, 1948, Anne Kingsley (marr. diss. 1970); one *s* one *d*; 2nd, 1970, Flora Groult. *Educ:* Cardinal Vaughan Sch.; King's Coll., Cambridge; Princeton Univ., USA. Commonwealth Fund Fellow, 1937–39; served War of 1939–45: RA 1940; Indian Army, 1941–45. Private Secretary to Permanent Under-Secretary, India Office, 1946; Secretary, Frontier Areas Cttee of Enquiry, Burma, 1947; Foreign Office, 1947–49; British Consul, St Louis, USA, 1949–52; First Secretary, British Embassy, Kabul, 1952–56; Political Adviser British Military Govt, Berlin, 1956–61; Foreign Office, 1961–65; Minister, Paris, 1965–69; Ambassador to Finland, 1969–72; Ambassador to Israel, 1972–75. Mem., Police Complaints Bd, 1977–82. *Publications:* Frontiers (novel), 1979; (jtly) Nouvelles de la Famille (short stories), 1980; De Gaulle, 1982; De Gaulle et les Américains, 1984; Sappho, La première voix de femme, 1987. *Recreation:* drinking and talking. *Address:* 54 rue de Bourgogne, 75007 Paris, France. *T:* 47058026; 19 Queen's Gate Terrace, SW7 5PR. *T:* 071–584 4132. *Clubs:* Travellers', MCC.

LEDWITH, Dr Anthony, CBE 1995; FRS 1995; Director, Group Research, Pilkington plc, since 1988; *b* 14 Aug. 1933; *s* of Thomas Ledwith and Mary (*née* Coghlan); *m* 1960, Mary Clare Ryan; one *s* three *d.* *Educ:* BSc (external) London 1954; PhD 1957, DSc 1970, Liverpool Univ. FRSC 1986. Liverpool University: Lectr, 1959, Prof., 1976, Campbell Brown Prof. of Industrial Chem., 1980, Dept of Inorganic Physical and Industrial Chem.; Dean, Faculty of Sci., 1980–83; Dep. Dir, Group R&D, Pilkington plc, 1984–88. Member: DSAC, 1988–; SERC, 1990–94; EPSRC, 1994–. *Publications:* (with A. D. Jenkins) Reactivity, Mechanism and Structure in Polymer Chemistry, 1974; (with A. M. North) Molecular Behaviour and the Development of Polymeric Materials, 1975; (with S. J. Moss) The Chemistry of the Semiconductor Industry, 1987; (ed jtly) Comprehensive Polymer Science, 7 vols, 1989. *Recreations:* squash, tennis, golf. *Address:* Pilkington Group Research, Hall Lane, Lathom, near Ormskirk L40 5UF. *T:* Skelmersdale (01695) 54230.

LEE, Alan Peter; cricket correspondent, The Times, since 1988; *b* 13 June 1954; *s* of Peter Alexander Lee and Christina Carmichael; *m* 1980, Patricia Drury; one *s* one *d.* *Educ:* Cavendish Grammar Sch., Hemel Hempstead. With Watford Observer, 1970–74; Hayters Agency, 1974–78; freelance, 1978–82; cricket corresp., Mail on Sunday, 1982–87. *Publications:* A Pitch in Both Camps, 1979; Diary of a Cricket Season, 1980; Lambourn, Village of Racing, 1983; *biographies:* (with Tony Greig) My Story, 1978; (with David Gower) With Time to Spare, 1980; (with Graham Gooch) Out of the Wilderness, 1985; Fred (biog. of Fred Winter), 1991; (with Pat Eddery) To Be A Champion, 1992. *Recreations:* National Hunt racing (has owned six horses), tennis, wine. *Address:* 8 The Courtyard, Montpellier Street, Cheltenham, Glos GL50 1SR. *T:* Cheltenham (01242) 572637. *Club:* Cricketers'.

LEE, Hon. Allen; *see* Lee Peng-Fei, A.

LEE, Dr Anne Mary Linda; Headmistress, Malvern Girls' College, since 1994; *b* 14 Oct. 1953; *d* of Cecil and Eugenie Covell; *m* 1973, Anthony M. Lee; one *s* one *d.* *Educ:* Shenfield High Sch.; Open Univ. (BA); Univ. of Surrey (PhD). FIPD. Inf. Officer, Unilever, 1972–74; Trng Officer, G. D. Searle & Co., 1974–76; Management and Trng Advr, Industrial Soc., 1976–78; Head of Trng, Morgan Guaranty Trust Co., 1978–81; Dir, Anne M. Lee (Training) Ltd, 1983–94. *Publications:* contribs to personnel and management jls. *Recreations:* singing, walking, friendship, words and music. *Address:* Malvern Girls' College, Avenue Road, Malvern, Worcs WR14 3BA. *T:* Malvern (01684) 892288. *Club:* Reform.

LEE, Sir Arthur (James), KBE 1966 (CBE 1959); MC and Bar (1939–45); Company Director; National President, Returned Services League, Australia, 1960–74 (State President, 1954–60); *b* 30 July 1912; *s* of Arthur James and Kathleen Maud Lee; *m* 1945, Valerie Ann Scanlan; three *s* one *d.* *Educ:* Collegiate School of St Peter, Adelaide. Chm., War Veterans Home, SA, 1967–91. Trustee, Aust. War Meml, 1960–74. *Recreation:* golf. *Address:* 2 Arthur Street, Toorak Gardens, SA 5065, Australia. *T:* 35106. *Clubs:* Naval and Military, Royal Adelaide Golf (Adelaide).

LEE, Christopher Frank Carandini; actor; entered film industry, 1947; *b* 27 May 1922; *s* of Geoffrey Trollope Lee (Lt-Col 60th KRRC), and Estelle Marie Carandini; *m* 1961, Birgit, *d* of Richard Emil Kroencke; one *d.* *Educ:* Wellington Coll. RAFVR, 1941–46 (Flt Lieut; mentioned in despatches, 1944). Films include: Moulin Rouge; Tale of Two Cities; Dracula; Rasputin; The Devil Rides Out; Private Life of Sherlock Holmes; The Wicker Man; The Three Musketeers; The Four Musketeers; The Man with the Golden Gun; To the Devil, a Daughter; Airport '77; The Passage; Bear Island; 1941; The Serial; The Last Unicorn; Safari 3000, The Salamander; Goliath Awaits; An Eye for an Eye; Charles and Diana; The Return of Captain Invincible; The House of the Long Shadows; The Far Pavilions; The Disputation; Mio My Mio; The Return of the Musketeers; The French Revolution; Gremlins II; Treasure Island; The Rainbow Thief; Sherlock Holmes—the Golden Years; Young Indy (TV); Death Train; A Feast at Midnight. OStJ 1986. Officier des Arts et des Lettres, France, 1973. *Publications:* Christopher Lee's 'X' Certificate, 1975 (2nd edn 1976); Christopher Lee's Archives of Evil, USA 1975 (2nd edn 1976); (autobiog.) Tall, Dark and Gruesome, 1977. *Recreations:* travel, opera, golf, cricket. *Address:* c/o James Sharkey & Associates, 21 Golden Square, W1; c/o DSA Inc., Garden Office Building, #345 15301 Ventura Boulevard, Sherman Oaks, CA 91403, USA. *Clubs:* Buck's, MCC; Honourable Company of Edinburgh Golfers; Travellers' (Paris).

LEE, David John, CBE 1989; FEng 1980; Chairman: G. Maunsell and Partners, Consulting Engineers, since 1984 (Partner since 1966); Maunsell Structural Plastics Ltd; Director of

Maunsell Group cos; *b* 28 Aug. 1930; *s* of Douglas and Mildred Lee; *m* 1957, Helga Bass; one *s* one *d*. *Educ:* Manchester Univ. (BSc Tech 1950); Imperial Coll. of Science and Technol. (DIC 1954). MICE 1957, FICE 1966; MIStructE 1960, FIStructE 1968. National Service, RE, 1950–52. Engr, Reinforced Concrete Steel Co. Ltd, 1952–53 and 1954–55; G. Maunsell and Partners, Consulting Engineers: Resident Engr, 1955–59; Sen. Engr, 1960–65; Associate, 1965–66. Vis. Prof., Imperial College, London, 1987–. OC Engr and Transport Staff Corps, RE (TA), 1977– (Col). Member: General Cttee, Parly and Scientific Cttee; Standing Cttee on Structural Safety. Mem. Council, IStructE, 1974–77, 1978–, Pres., 1985–86; Mem. Council, Concrete Soc., 1968–71, Vice Pres. 1977–78. Chm., Council, CIRIA, 1989–92; Member: Overseas Project Bd, DTI, 1989–; British Nat. Cttee for Internat. Engrg Affairs, 1989–. George Stephenson Medal, ICE, 1969; Medal, Fedn Internationale de la Précontrainte, 1974. *Publications:* The Theory and Practice of Bearings and Expansion Joints for Bridges, 1971, 2nd edn as Bridge Bearings and Expansion Joints, 1993; (contrib. chapter on bridges) The Civil Engineer's Reference Book, 3rd edn 1975, 4th edn 1989; (contrib. chapter on bridges) Developments in Prestressed Concrete, vol. 2 1978; papers in Proc. ICE and Proc. IStructE. *Recreations:* art, music, simple barbecuing. *Address:* G. Maunsell and Partners, Maunsell House, 154–160 Croydon Road, Beckenham, Kent BR3 4DE. *T:* 0181–663 6565, *Telex:* 946171, *Fax:* 0181–663 6723. *Club:* East India.

LEE, Air Chief Marshal Sir David (John Pryer), GBE 1969 (KBE 1965; CBE 1947; OBE 1943); CB 1953; retired, 1971; *b* 4 Sept. 1912; *s* of late John Lee, Byron Crescent, Bedford; *m* 1938, Denise, *d* of late Louis Hartoch; one *s* one *d*. *Educ:* Bedford Sch.; RAF Coll., Cranwell. NWFP, India, 1933–36; Central Flying Sch., Upavon, 1937; RAF Examining Officer, Supt. of Reserve, 1938–39; Bomber Command, Hemswell, 1939–40; RAF Staff Coll. (student), 1942; Deputy Director Plans, Air Ministry, 1943–44; OC 904 Fighter Wing, Batavia, Java, 1945–46; Directing Staff, RAF Staff Coll., 1948–50; Deputy Director Policy, Air Ministry, 1951–53; OC RAF Scampton, Lincs, 1953–55; Secretary, Chiefs of Staff Cttee, Ministry of Defence, 1956–59; AOC, AFME (Aden), 1959–61; Comdt, RAF Staff Coll., 1962–65; Air Member for Personnel, MoD, 1965–68; UK Military Rep. to NATO, 1968–71. Vice-Pres., RAF Benevolent Fund, 1988–; Chm., Governing Trustees, Nuffield Trust for Armed Forces, 1975–; Dir, Utd Services Trustee, 1971–88; Pres., Corps of Commissionaires, 1984–88. *Publications:* Flight from the Middle East, 1981; Never Stop the Engine When It's Hot, 1983; Eastward: a history of the Royal Air Force in the Far East 1945–1972, 1984; Wings in the Sun, 1989; And We Thought the War was Over, 1990. *Address:* The Garden House, Catherine Close, Shrivenham, Swindon SN6 8ER. *T:* Swindon (01793) 784624. *Club:* Royal Air Force.

LEE, Edward, MSc, PhD; Director, Admiralty Research Laboratory, Teddington, 1971–74, retired; *b* 2 March 1914; *s* of Thomas and Florence Lee; *m* 1942, Joan Pearson; three *d*. *Educ:* Consett Grammar Sch.; Manchester Univ.; Pembroke Coll., Cambridge. Admiralty Research Laboratory, 1939–46; Ministry of Defence, 1946–48; Dept of Physical Research, Admiralty, 1948–51; Admiralty Research Laboratory, 1951–55; Dir of Operational Research, Admty, 1955–58; Dep. Dir, Nat. Physical Laboratory, 1958–60; Director, Stations and Industry Div., DSIR, 1960–65; Dep. Controller (R), Min. of Technology, 1965–70; Head of Res. Services, Dept of Trade and Industry, 1970–71. *Publications:* scientific papers. *Address:* 17 Farington Acres, Vale Road, Weybridge, Surrey KT13 9NH. *T:* Weybridge (01932) 841114.

LEE, (Edward) Stanley, FRCS; Consulting Surgeon Westminster Hospital; formerly Civilian Consultant in Surgery of Neoplastic Diseases, Queen Alexandra Military Hospital; Surgeon Emeritus, Guildford Radiotherapy Centre; *b* 1907. *Educ:* Westminster Hospital. MB, BS 1931; FRCS, 1933; MS London, 1936. Past Member of Court of Examiners, Royal College of Surgeons, England, 1953–59, Past Member: Grand Council British Empire Cancer Campaign; Internat. Union against Cancer; Assoc. of Head and Neck Oncologists of GB. FRSM; Sen. Fellow, Assoc. of Surgeons. Hon. Mem. Royal College of Radiologists. *Publications:* contributions to medical literature, etc. *Address:* Ingram, The Grand, Folkestone, Kent CT20 2LR.

LEE, George Ranson, CVO 1980; CBE 1983; HM Diplomatic Service, retired; *b* 26 Sept. 1925; *s* of late Wilfred Lee and Janet (*née* Ranson); *m* 1955, Anne Christine Black; one *d*. Served Indian Army, 6th Gurkha Rifles, NW Frontier Prov., 1945–47; TA, W Yorks Regt, 1948–53. Employed in Trng Dept, Min. of Food, 1948–53; joined CRO, 1954; Karachi, 1955–58; First Sec., Madras, 1959–63; CRO, 1964; Head of Chancery: Singapore, 1965–69; Santiago, 1969–72; FCO, 1972–74; Dep. UK Perm. Rep. to Council of Europe, Strasbourg, 1974–78; Counsellor, Berne, 1978–83. Council of Europe Medal, *pro merito*, 1978. *Address:* Garthmynd, Trevor Hill, Church Stretton, Shropshire SY6 6JH. *Club:* Commonwealth Trust.

LEE, George Russell, CMG 1970; Acting Assistant Director, Ministry of Defence, 1967–78, retired; *b* 11 Nov. 1912; *s* of Ernest Harry Lee and Alice Mary Lee (*née* Russell); *m* 1947, Annabella Evelyn (*née* Dargie); one *s* one *d*. *Educ:* Birkenhead Sch., Cheshire. WO and MoD, 1940–78. *Address:* 13 Abberbury Road, Iffley, Oxford OX4 4ET.

LEE, Brig. Sir Henry; *see* Lee, Brig. Sir L. H.

LEE, Prof. Hermione, FRSL; Professor of English Literature, University of York, since 1993; *b* 29 Feb. 1948; *d* of Dr Benjamin Lee and Josephine Lee (*née* Anderson); *m* 1991, Prof. John Michael Barnard, *qv*. *Educ:* St Hilda's Coll., Oxford (BA); St Cross Coll., Oxford (BPhil). Instructor, Coll. of William and Mary, Williamsburg, Va, 1970–71; Lectr, Dept of English, Univ. of Liverpool, 1971–77; Department of English and Related Literature, University of York: Lectr. 1977–87; Sen. Lectr, 1987–90; Reader, 1990–93. Presenter, Book Four, Channel 4, 1982–86. FRSL 1992. *Publications:* The Novels of Virginia Woolf, 1977; Elizabeth Bowen: an estimation, 1981; Philip Roth, 1982; (ed) The Mulberry Tree: writings of Elizabeth Bowen, 1986; Willa Cather: a life saved up, 1989, US edn as Willa Cather: double lives, 1991; (ed) The Selected Stories of Willa Cather, 1989. *Recreations:* reading, music, countryside. *Address:* Department of English, University of York, Heslington, York YO1 5DD. *Club:* Academy.

LEE, Dr Hongkoo; Chairman, Seoul Forum for International Afairs, 1986–88 and since 1993; *b* 9 May 1934; *s* of Bong-Hoon Lee and In-Im Choo Lee; *m* 1969, Hanock Park; one *s* two *d*. *Educ:* Seoul Nat. Univ.; Emory Univ. (BA, LittD); Yale Univ. (MA, PhD). Asst Prof. of Political Science: Emory Univ., 1963–64; Case Western Reserve Univ., 1964–68; Prof. of Political Sci., Seoul Nat. Univ., 1968–88 (Dir, Inst. of Social Sci., 1979–83); Minister of Nat. Unification, 1988–90; Special Adviser to the President for Political Affairs, 1990–91; Ambassador to UK, 1991–93. Fellow: Woodrow Wilson Internat. Center, Smithsonian Instn, 1973–74; Harvard Law Sch., 1974–75. President: Korean Assoc. for Communist Studies, 1983–85; Korean Political Sci. Assoc., 1985–86; Mem., Exec. Cttee, Internat. Political Sci. Assoc., 1985–88. *Publications:* Social Conservation and Political Development, 1968; Modern Political Thought, 1973; Introduction to Political Science, 1975; Modernization, 1978; One Hundred Years of Marxism, 1982. *Recreations:* tennis, golf. *Address:* Seoul Forum for International Affairs, Asiana Building, 10-1 Hoehyun-dong 2-ka, Chung-ku, Seoul, Republic of Korea.

LEE, James Giles; Principal, Lee & Company, since 1992; non-executive Director, Pearson Television, since 1993; *b* 23 Dec. 1942; *s* of John Lee, CBE and Muriel Giles; *m* 1966, Linn Macdonald; one *s* two *d*. *Educ:* Trinity Coll., Glenalmond; Glasgow Univ.; Harvard Univ., USA. Consultant, McKinsey & Co., 1969–80; Mem., Central Policy Review Staff, 1972. Dep. Chm. and Chief Exec., Pearson Longman, 1980–83; Chairman: Penguin Publishing Co., 1980–84; Longman Gp, 1980–84; Direct Broadcasting by Satellite Consortium, 1986–87; Deputy Chairman: Westminster Press, 1980–84; Financial Times, 1980–84; Yorkshire TV, 1982–85; Dir, S. Pearson & Son, 1981–84; Chm., 1981–85, Chief Exec., 1983–85, Goldcrest Films and Television; Dir, Boston Consulting Gp, 1987–92. Chm., Performing Arts Labs Trust. *Publications:* Planning for the Social Services, 1978; The Investment Challenge, 1979. *Recreations:* photography, travelling, sailing. *Address:* Meadow Wood, Penshurst, Kent TN11 8AD. *T:* Penshurst (01892) 870309. *Clubs:* Reform; Harvard (New York, USA).

LEE, Hon. James Matthew, PC 1982; MLA; Leader, Progressive Conservative Party, Prince Edward Island, since 1981; Commissioner, Canadian Pension Commission, since 1986; *b* Charlottetown, 26 March 1937; *s* of late James Matthew Lee and of Catherine Blanchard Lee; *m* 1960, Patricia, *d* of late Ivan Laurie; one *s* two *d*. *Educ:* Queen's Square Sch.; St Dunstan's Univ. Architectural draftsman. First elected MLA (PC) for 5th Queens Riding, by-election, 1975; re-elected since; former Minister: of Health and Social Services; of Tourism, Parks and Conservation; Premier and Pres. Exec. Council, PEI, 1981–86. Jaycee Internat. Senator, 1983. *Address:* Stanhope Bay Road, York RR1, Prince Edward Island, C0A IP0, Canada. *T:* (902) 6722870.

LEE, Maj.-Gen. James Stuart, CB 1990; MBE 1970; Director of Army Education, 1987–90; *b* 26 Dec. 1934; *s* of George Lee and Elizabeth (*née* Hawkins); *m* 1960, Alice Lorna; one *s*. *Educ:* Normanton Grammar Sch.; Leeds Univ. (BA Hons); King's Coll., London (MA War Studies, 1976). Pres., Leeds Univ. Union, 1958–59. Educn Officer in UK Trng Units, Catterick, Taunton, Bovington, 1959–64; Mil. Trng Officer, Beaconsfield, 1964; RMCS and Staff Coll., 1964–65; DAQMG HQ Cyprus Dist, 1966 and HQ NEARELF, 1967; SO2 MoD (Army Educn 1), 1968–70; DAA&QMG HQ FARELF, 1970 and GSO2 HQ FARELF, 1970–71; OC Officer Wing, Beaconsfield, 1971–74; Gp Educn Officer, 34 AEC, Rheindahlen, 1974–75; Chief Educn Officer, HQ NE Dist, 1976–78; Hd, Officer Educn Br., 1978–79; SO1 Trng HQ UKLF, 1979; Chief Inspector of Army Educn and Col Res., 1980–82; Res. Associate, IISS, 1982–83; Comdr Educn, HQ BAOR, 1983–87. Dep. Col Comdt, AGC, 1993–. Pres., RAEC Assoc., 1993–. Dep. Comr, British Scouts Western Europe, 1983–87; Mem., Management Bd, NFER, 1987–90. Non-Exec. Dir, Exhibition Consultants Ltd, 1990–. Member: Nat Adv. Bd, Duke of Edinburgh Award Scheme, 1987–90; Council, Scout Assoc., 1988–; Council, CGLI, 1989– (Chm., Sen. Awards Cttee, 1990–; Jt Hon. Sec., 1993–). Trustee and Sec., Gallipoli Meml Lecture Trust, 1987–90. Gov., Imperial Coll., 1991–; Mem. Court, Univ. of Leeds, 1994–. FRSA 1987; FIPD (FITD 1991). *Publication:* contrib. Arms Transfers in Third World Development, 1984. *Recreations:* theatre, boats. *Address:* c/o Royal Bank of Scotland, London Drummonds Branch, Charing Cross, SW1A 2DX.

LEE, John Michael Hubert; Barrister-at-Law; *b* 13 Aug. 1927; *s* of late Victor Lee, Wentworth, Surrey, and late Renee Lee; *m* 1960, Margaret Ann, *d* of James Russell, ICS, retired, and late Kathleen Russell; one *s* one *d*. *Educ:* Reading Sch.; Christ's Coll., Cambridge (Open Exhibnr Modern Hist.; 2nd Cl. Hons Pts I and II of Hist. Tripos; MA). Colonial Service: Administrative Officer, Ghana, 1951–58; Principal Assistant Secretary, Min. of Communications, Ghana, 1958. On staff of BBC, 1959–65. Called to the Bar, Middle Temple, 1960; practising, Midland and Oxford Circuit, 1966–; Dep. Circuit Judge, 1978–81; Assistant Recorder, 1981–87. MP (Lab) Reading, 1966–70; MP (Lab) Birmingham, Handsworth, Feb. 1974–1979; Chm., W Midland Gp of Labour MPs, 1974–75. *Recreations:* watching tennis, watching cricket, walking, studying philosophy. *Address:* 2 Dr Johnson's Buildings, EC4Y 7AY. *Club:* Royal Over-Seas League.

LEE, John Robert Louis; Chairman, Christie Hospital NHS Trust; *b* 21 June 1942; *s* of late Basil and Miriam Lee; *m* 1975, Anne Monique Bakirgian; two *d*. *Educ:* William Hulme's Grammar Sch., Manchester. FCA. Accountancy Articles, 1959–64; Henry Cooke, Lumsden & Co., Manchester, Stockbrokers, 1964–66; Founding Dir, Chancery Consolidated Ltd, Investment Bankers; Director: Paterson Zochonis (UK) Ltd, 1974–75, 1990–; P. S. Turner (Hldgs); MS International plc; Paterson Zochonis PLC; Investment Consultant, Refuge Group PLC. Vice-Chm., NW Conciliation Cttee, Race Relations Bd, 1976–77; Chm. Council, Nat. Youth Bureau, 1980–83. Contested (C) Manchester, Moss Side, Oct. 1974; MP (C) Nelson and Colne, 1979–83, Pendle, 1983–92; contested (C) Pendle, 1992. PPS to Minister of State for Industry, 1981–83, to Sec. of State for Trade and Industry, 1983; Parly Under Sec. of State, MoD, 1983–86, Dept of Employment, 1986–89 (Minister for Tourism, 1987–89). Chm., All-Party Tourism Cttee, 1991–92. Jt Sec., Conservative Back Benchers' Industry Cttee, 1979–80. Chairman: ALVA, 1990–; Mus. of Sci. and Industry in Manchester; Mem., English Tourist Bd. *Recreations:* golf, fly fishing, collecting. *Address:* Bowdon Old Hall, 49 Langham Road, Bowdon, Altrincham, Cheshire WA14 3NS.

LEE, His Honour John (Thomas Cyril); Circuit Judge (attached Midland Oxford Circuit), 1972–93; *b* 14 Jan. 1927; *s* of Cyril and Dorothy Lee; *m* 1956, Beryl Lee (*née* Haden); one *s* three *d*. *Educ:* Holly Lodge Grammar Sch., Staffs; Emmanuel Coll., Cambridge (MA, LLB). Called to Bar, Gray's Inn, 1952. Practised, Oxford Circuit, 1952–72. Chairman various Tribunals. *Recreation:* golf. *Address:* The Red House, Upper Colwall, Malvern, Worcs WR13 6PX. *T:* Colwall (01684) 540645. *Clubs:* Union and County (Worcester); Worcester Golf and Country.

LEE KUAN YEW; Prime Minister, Singapore, 1959–90; Senior Minister, Prime Minister's Office, since 1990; *b* 16 Sept. 1923; *s* of Lee Chin Koon and Chua Jim Neo; *m* 1950, Kwa Geok Choo; two *s* one *d*. *Educ:* Raffles Coll., Singapore; Fitzwilliam Coll., Cambridge (class 1 both parts of Law Tripos). Called to Bar, Middle Temple, 1950, Hon. Bencher, 1969. Advocate and Solicitor, Singapore, 1951. Formed People's Action Party, 1954, Sec.-Gen., 1954–92; People's Action Party won elections, 1959; became PM, 1959, re-elected 1963, 1968, 1972, 1976, 1980, 1984, 1988; MP Fed. Parlt of Malaysia, 1963–65. Hon. Freeman, City of London, 1982. Hon. CH 1970; Hon. GCMG 1972. Hon. FRCPE 1988. Bintang Republik Indonesia Adi Pradana, 1973; Order of Sikatuna, The Philippines, 1974; Most Honourable Order of Crown of Johore (1st Cl.), Malaysia, 1984. *Recreations:* jogging, swimming. *Address:* Prime Minister's Office, Istana Annexe, Singapore 0922.

LEE, Laurie, MBE 1952; FRSL; poet and author; *m* 1950, Catherine Francesca Polge; one *d*. *Educ:* Slad Village Sch.; Stroud Central Sch. Travelled Mediterranean, 1935–39; GPO Film Unit, 1939–40; Crown Film Unit, 1941–43; Publications Editor, Ministry of Information, 1944–46; Green Park Film Unit, 1946–47; Caption Writer-in-Chief, Festival of Britain, 1950–51. Freeman of City of London, 1982. Hon. DLitt Cheltenham and Gloucester Coll. of Higher Educn, 1992. *Publications:* The Sun My Monument (Poems), 1944; Land at War (HMSO), 1945; (with Ralph Keene) A Film in Cyprus, 1947; The Bloom of Candles (Poems), 1947; The Voyage of Magellan, 1948; My Many-Coated Man (Poems), 1955; A Rose for Winter, 1955; Pocket Poets (Selection), 1960; The Firstborn,

1964; I Can't Stay Long, 1975; Selected Poems, 1983; Two Women, 1983; *autobiography:* Cider With Rosie, 1959; As I Walked Out One Midsummer Morning, 1969; A Moment of War, 1991 (trilogy reprinted as Red Sky At Sunrise, 1992). *Recreations:* indoor sports, music, travel. *Address:* 9/40 Elm Park Gardens, SW10 9NZ. *T:* 0171–352 2197. *Clubs:* Chelsea Arts, Garrick.

LEE, Brig. Sir (Leonard) Henry, Kt 1983; CBE 1964 (OBE 1960); Deputy Director, Conservative Board of Finance, 1970–92; *b* 21 April 1914; *s* of late Henry Robert Lee and Nellie Lee; *m* 1949, Peggy Metham. *Educ:* Portsmouth Grammar Sch.; Southampton Univ. (Law). Served War, 1939–45; with BEF in France, ME and NW Europe (despatches, 1945); Royal Scots Greys, Major; Staff Lt-Col 1954: Chief of Intelligence to Dir of Ops, Malaya, 1957–60; Mil. and Naval Attaché, Saigon, S Vietnam, 1961–64; Chief of Personnel and Admin, Allied Land Forces Central Europe, France, 1964–66; Chief of Intelligence, Allied Forces Central Europe, Netherlands, 1966–69; retd 1969. *Recreations:* gardening, golf. *Address:* Fairways, Sandy Lane, Kingswood, Surrey KT20 6ND. *T:* Mogador (01737) 832577. *Club:* Kingswood Golf.

LEE, Malcolm Kenneth, QC 1983; **His Honour Judge Malcolm Lee;** a Circuit Judge, and Designated Circuit Mercantile Judge in the Mercantile Court in Birmingham, since 1993; *b* 2 Jan. 1943; 2nd *s* of late Thomas Marston Lee, solicitor, Birmingham, and of Fiona Margaret Lee, JP (*née* Mackenzie); *m* 1970, Phyllis Anne Brunton Speed, *er d* of Andrew Watson Speed, Worcs; three *s* three *d* (and one *d* decd). *Educ:* King Edward's Sch., Birmingham (Foundation Schol.); Worcester Coll., Oxford (Schol.; MA Class. Hon. Mods and Lit.Hum.). Assistant Master: Marlborough Coll., 1965; King Edward's Sch., Birmingham, 1966; Major Schol., Inner Temple, 1967; called to the Bar, Inner Temple, 1967; practised on Midland Circuit, 1968–71, Midland and Oxford Circuit, 1972–93; a Recorder, 1980–93. Dep. Chm., Agricl Land Tribunal, E Midland Area, 1979–82, Midland Area, 1982–94; Chm., Agricl Land Tribunal, Midland Area, 1994–; Prosecuting Counsel to DHSS, Midland and Oxford Circuit, 1979–83. *Recreations:* squash, tennis, walking, reading. *Address:* The Priory Courts, 33 Bull Street, Birmingham B4 6DW. *T:* 0121–681 3134. *Club:* Edgbaston Priory (Birmingham).

LEE, Michael Charles M.; *see* Malone-Lee.

LEE, Maj.-Gen. Patrick Herbert, CB 1982; MBE 1964; CEng, FIMechE; Chairman, Road Haulage Association, since 1994 (Director, since 1988; Vice-Chairman, 1990–94); Director, Wincanton Ltd (formerly Wincanton Transport, subseq. Wincanton Distribution Services, Ltd), since 1983; *b* 15 March 1929; *s* of Percy Herbert and Mary Dorothea Lee; *m* 1952, Peggy Eveline Chapman; one *s* one *d*. *Educ:* King's Sch., Canterbury; London Univ. (BSc (Gen.), BSc (Special Physics)). Commnd RMA Sandhurst, 1948; Staff Coll., 1960; WO Staff Duties, 1961–63; CO, Parachute Workshop, 1964–65; JSSC, 1966; Military Asst to Master General of Ordnance, 1966–67; Directing Staff, Staff Coll., 1968–69; Commander, REME 2nd Div., 1970–71; Col AQ 1 British Corps, 1972–75; Dep. Comdt, Sch. of Electrical and Mechanical Engrg, 1975–77; Comdt, REME Trng Centre, 1977–79; Dir Gen., Electrical and Mechanical Engrg (Army), 1979–83. Col Comdt, REME, 1983–89. Mem., Wessex Water Authy, 1983–88. Confederation of British Industry: Mem. Council, 1991–; Vice-Chm., 1992–94, Chm., 1994–, SW Region. Gov., Wellington Sch., Som, 1992–. FIMgt; FInstD. *Recreations:* gardening, railways, Roman history, industrial archaeology. *Club:* Army and Navy.

LEE, Rt Rev. Patrick Vaughan; *see* Rupert's Land, Bishop of.

LEE, Rt. Rev. Paul Chun Hwan, Hon. CBE 1974; Bishop of Seoul, 1965–83; *b* 5 April 1922; unmarried. *Educ:* St Michael's Theological Seminary, Seoul; St Augustine's College, Canterbury. Deacon, 1952 (Pusan Parish); Priest, 1953 (Sangju and Choungju Parish). Director of Yonsei University, Seoul, 1960–, Chm., Bd of Trustees, 1972–, Hon. DD 1971. Chairman: Christian Council of Korea, 1966–67; Christian Literature Soc. of Korea, 1968–83; Korean Bible Soc., 1972–83 (Vice-Pres., 1969–72); Nat. Council of Churches in Korea, 1976–78. Hon. LLD Korea, 1978. *Recreation:* reading. *Address:* 104–410 Dae Woo Apt, Bang Bae 3 Dong, 981, So'cho-Ku, Seoul 137–063, Korea.

LEE, Peter Gavin; DL; FRICS; Senior Partner, Strutt & Parker, since 1979; *b* 4 July 1934; *s* of Mr and late Mrs J. G. Lee; *m* 1963, Caroline Green; two *s* one *d*. *Educ:* Midhurst Grammar School; College of Estate Management; Wye College. FRICS 1966. Joined Strutt & Parker, 1957; became full partner, 1972. Essex: High Sheriff, 1990; DL 1991. *Recreations:* the restoration and enjoyment of vintage cars and aircraft, flying, country pursuits. *Address:* Fanners, Great Waltham, Chelmsford, Essex CM3 1EA. *T:* Chelmsford (01245) 360470. *Club:* Boodle's.

LEE, Rowland Thomas Lovell; a Recorder of the Crown Court, 1979–92; *b* 7 March 1920; *s* of late Ronald Lovell Lee and of Jessie Maude Lee; *m* 1944, Marjorie Betty, *d* of late William Holmes and Clare Johnston Braid Holmes; two *d*. *Educ:* Bedford Modern School. Served Royal Navy, 1939–48; POW, Sept. 1942–March 1943. Bedfordshire Constabulary, 1948–52; Articles with E. A. S. Barnard, Dunstable, 1954; qualified as solicitor, 1957; Principal, Wynter Davies & Lee, Hertford, 1959–89, Consultant, 1989–. Chairman: Medical Services Cttee, Hertfordshire Family Practitioners Cttee, 1970–77; N Herts HA (formerly Herts AHA), 1977–84. *Address:* Culpepers, 5 Letty Green, Hertford, Herts SG14 2NZ. *T:* Hatfield (01707) 261445.

LEE, Stanley; *see* Lee, (Edward) S.

LEE, Tsung-Dao; Enrico Fermi Professor of Physics, since 1964, and University Professor, since 1984, Columbia University, USA; *b* 25 Nov. 1926; 3rd *s* of C. K. and M. C. Lee; *m* 1950, Jeannette H. C. Chin; two *s*. *Educ:* National Chekiang Univ., Kweichow, China; National Southwest Associated Univ., Kunming, China; University of Chicago, USA. Research Associate: University of Chicago, 1950; University of California, 1950–51; Member, Inst. for Advanced Study, Princeton, 1951–53. Columbia University: Asst Professor, 1953–55; Associate Professor, 1955–56; Professor, 1956–60; Member, Institute for Advanced Study, Princeton, 1960–63; Columbia Univ.: Adjunct Professor, 1960–62; Visiting Professor, 1962–63; Professor, 1963–. Hon. Professor: Univ. of Sci and Technol. of China, 1981; Jinan Univ., China, 1982; Fudan Univ., China, 1982; Qinghua Univ., 1984; Peking Univ., 1985; Nanjing Univ., 1985; Nankai Univ., 1986; Shanghai Jiao Tong and Suzhou Univs, 1987; Zhejiang Univ., 1988; Northwest Univ., Xian, 1993. Member: Acad. Sinica, 1957; Amer. Acad. of Arts and Scis, 1959; Nat. Acad of Scis, 1964; Amer. Philosophical Soc., 1972; Acad. Nazionale dei Lincei, Rome, 1982; Chinese Acad. of Scis, Beijing, 1994. Hon. DSc: Princeton, 1958; City Coll., City Univ. of NY, 1978; Bard Coll., 1984; Peking, 1985; Bologna, 1988; Columbia, 1990; Adelphi, 1991; Tsukuba, 1992; Rockefeller, 1994; Hon. LLD Chinese Univ. of Hong Kong, 1969; Hon. LittD Drexel Univ., 1986; Dip. di Perfezionamento in Physics, Scuola Normale Superiore, Pisa, 1982. Nobel Prize for the non-conservation of parity (with C. N. Yang), 1957; Albert Einstein Award in Science, 1957; Ettore Majorana-Erice Sci. for Peace Prize, 1990. Grand'Ufficiale, Order of Merit (Italy), 1986. *Publications:* Particle Physics: an introduction to field theory, 1981; papers mostly in Physical Review, and Nuclear Physics. *Address:* Department of Physics, Columbia University, New York, NY 10027, USA.

LEE, Sir William (Allison), Kt 1975; OBE 1945; TD 1948; DL; Chairman, Northern Regional Health Authority, 1973–78; *b* 31 May 1907; *s* of Samuel Percy and Florence Ada Lee, Darlington; *m* 1st, 1933, Elsa Norah (*d* 1966), *d* of late Thomas Hanning, Darlington; 2nd, 1967, Mollie Clifford (*d* 1989), *d* of late Sir Cuthbert Whiteside, Knysna, S Africa; no *c*. *Educ:* Queen Elizabeth Grammar Sch., Darlington. Insurance Branch Manager, retd. Served R Signals, 1935–53; Dep. Comdr, 151 Inf. Bde (TA), 1953–58; County Comdt, Durham ACF, 1962–70. Mem., Darlington RDC, 1949–61, Chm. 1957–60. Chairman: Winterton HMC, 1967–70 (Mem., 1954–70); Newcastle Reg. Hosp. Bd, 1973–74 (Mem., 1956–74). Pres., Darlington Div., SSAFA. DL County of Durham, 1965; High Sheriff, Durham, 1978. *Recreation:* gardening. *Address:* Whiteside, 23 Low Green, Gainford, Co. Durham DL2 3DS. *T:* Darlington (01325) 730564.

LEE YONG LENG, Dr; Professor of Geography, National University of Singapore, 1977–90, retired; *b* 26 March 1930; *m* Wong Loon Meng; one *d*. *Educ:* Univs of Oxford, Malaya and Singapore. BLitt (Oxon), MA (Malaya), PhD (Singapore). Research Asst, Univ. of Malaya, 1954–56; University Lectr/Sen. Lectr, Univ. of Singapore, 1956–70; Associate Prof., Univ. of Singapore, 1970–71; High Comr for Singapore in London, 1971–75; Ambassador to Denmark, 1974–75, and Ireland, 1975; Min. of Foreign Affairs, Singapore, 1975–76. Mem., Govt Parly Cttee on Defence and For. Affairs, 1987–90. Chm., Singapore Nat. Library Bd, 1978–80. Dir, Centre for Advanced Studies, National Univ. of Singapore, 1983–85. *Publications:* North Borneo, 1965; Sarawak, 1970; Southeast Asia and the Law of the Sea, 1978; The Razor's Edge: boundaries and boundary disputes in Southeast Asia, 1980; Southeast Asia: essays in political geography, 1982; articles in: Population Studies; Geog. Jl; Erdkunde; Jl Trop. Geog., etc. *Recreations:* swimming, tennis, travelling, reading.

LEE, Prof. Yuan Tseh; Professor of Chemistry, University of California, Berkeley, since 1974; *b* 29 Nov. 1936; *s* of Tse Fan Lee and Pei Tsai; *m* 1963, Bernice Chinli Wi; two *s* one *d*. *Educ:* Nat. Taiwan Univ. (BSc 1959); Nat. Tsinghua Univ., Taiwan (MSc 1961); Univ. of California (PhD 1965). Military service, 1961–62. University of California, Berkeley: Postdoctoral Fellow, 1965–67; Research Fellow, 1967–68; James Franck Inst. and Dept of Chemistry, Univ. of Chicago: Asst Prof. of Chemistry, 1968–71; Associate Prof. of Chemistry, 1971–72; Prof. of Chemistry, 1973–74. Principal Investigator, Materials and Molecular Research Div., Lawrence Berkeley Lab., 1974–. Vis Lectr, US and overseas univs. Mem., editl boards, chem. and sci. jls. Mem., Nat. Acad. of Sciences, 1979, and other learned bodies. Nobel Prize in Chemistry (jtly), 1986; numerous awards from US and foreign instns. *Publications:* papers on molecular chemistry and related subjects. *Recreations:* sports (baseball, ping pong, tennis), classical music. *Address:* Department of Chemistry, University of California, Berkeley, CA 94720, USA. *T:* (415) 4866154, 6423861.

LEE-BARBER, Rear-Adm. John, CB 1959; DSO 1940 and Bar 1941; Admiral Superintendent, HM Dockyard, Malta, 1957–59, retired; *b* 16 April 1905; *s* of Richard Lee-Barber, Herringfleet, near Great Yarmouth; *m* 1939, Suzanne (*d* 1976), *d* of Colonel Le Gallais, ADC, MC, La Moye, Jersey, CI; two *d*. *Educ:* Royal Naval Colleges, Osborne and Dartmouth. Service in destroyers and in Yangtze gunboat until 1937; CO Witch, 1937–38; CO Griffin, 1939–40–41; Commander, 1941; CO Opportune, 1942–44; 2nd in Command, HMS King Alfred, 1945; CO, HMS St James, 1946–47; Captain, 1947; Senior Officer Reserve Fleet, Harwich, 1948–49; Naval Attaché, Chile, 1950–52; CO Agincourt and Captain D4, 1952–54; Commodore, Inshore Flotilla, 1954–56; Rear-Admiral, 1957. Polish Cross of Valour, 1940. *Recreation:* sailing. *Address:* Ferry House, The Quay, Wivenhoe, Essex. *T:* Wivenhoe (01206) 822592.
See also D. R. W. Harrison.

LEE CHU-MING, Martin; QC (Hong Kong) 1979; JP; *b* 8 June 1938; *m* 1969, Amelia Lee; one *s*. *Educ:* Wah Yan College, Kowloon; Univ. of Hong Kong (BA 1960). Called to the Bar, Lincoln's Inn, 1966. Member: Hong Kong Legislative Council, 1985–95; Hong Kong Law Reform Commn, 1985–91; Hong Kong Fight Crime Cttee, 1986–; Basic Law Drafting Cttee, 1985–90; numerous groups and cttees advising on Govt, law, nationality and community matters. JP Hong Kong, 1980. *Publication:* The Basic Law: some basic flaws (with Szeto Wah), 1988. *Address:* Admiralty Centre, Room 704A, Tower I, 18 Harcourt Road, Hong Kong. *T:* 5290864. *Clubs:* Hong Kong; Royal Hong Kong Golf, Royal Hong Kong Jockey.

LEE PENG-FEI, Hon. Allen, (Hon. Allen Lee), CBE 1988 (OBE 1982); JP; Member, Hong Kong Legislative Council, since 1978; President, Meadville, since 1984; *b* 24 April 1940; *m* Maria Lee; two *s* one *d*. *Educ:* Univ. of Michigan (BSc Engineering Maths). Test Engineer Supervisor, Lockheed Aircraft International, 1966–67; Engineering Ops Manager, Fabri-teck, 1967; Test Engineer Manager, Lockheed Aircraft International, 1968–70; Test Manager, Ampex Ferrotec, 1970–72; Gen. Manager, Dataproducts HK, 1972–74; Managing Dir, Ampex Ferrotec, 1974–79; Gen. Manager, Ampex World Operations, 1979–83; Managing Dir, Ampex Far East Operations, 1983–84. MEC, Hong Kong, 1985–92. Chm., Bd of Overseers, Hong Kong Inst. of Biotechnol., 1990–. JP Hong Kong, 1980. FHKIE, 1985. Hon. DEng Hong Kong Poly., 1990; Hon. LLD Chinese Univ. of Hong Kong, 1990. Nat. Award, Asian Productivity Organization, 1986; Outstanding Young Persons Award, Hong Kong, 1977. *Recreations:* swimming, tennis. *Address:* 1604 Hong Kong Club Building, 3A Chater Road, Central, Hong Kong. *T:* 8452929. *Clubs:* Royal Hong Kong Jockey; Dynasty (Hong Kong).

LEE-POTTER, Jeremy Patrick, FRCPath; Consultant Haematologist, Poole General Hospital, 1969–95; *b* 30 Aug. 1934; *s* of Air Marshal Sir Patrick Lee Potter, KBE, MD, QHS and Audrey Mary (*née* Pollock); *m* 1957, Lynda Higginson; one *s* two *d*. *Educ:* Epsom Coll.; Guy's Hosp. Med. Sch. MB BS 1958; MRCS, LRCP 1958; DTM&H 1963; DCP 1965; FRCPath 1979. Specialist in Pathology, 1960, Sen. Specialist, 1965, RAF (Sqn Ldr); in charge of Haematology Dept, RAF Inst. of Pathology and Tropical Medicine; Lectr in Haematology, St George's Hosp. Med. Sch., 1968–69. British Medical Association: Dep. Chm., Central Consultants and Specialists Cttee, 1988–90; Mem. Council, 1988– (Chm., 1990–93). Member: Standing Med. Adv. Cttee, 1990–93; GMC, 1994–. Consultant Surveyor, King's Fund Orgnl Audit, 1993–. Mem., Editl Adv. Bd, Healthy Alliance Jl, 1994–. *Recreations:* printing, printmaking, visual arts. *Address:* Icen House, Stoborough, Wareham, Dorset BH20 5AN. *T:* Wareham (01929) 556307; 23 Palmerston House, Kensington Place, W8 7PU. *T:* 0171–727 9393. *Clubs:* Athenæum; Parkstone Golf.

LEE-STEERE, Sir Ernest (Henry), KBE 1977 (CBE 1963); JP; Lord Mayor of Perth, Western Australia, 1972–78; company director, pastoralist and grazier; *b* Perth, 22 Dec. 1912; *s* of Sir Ernest Lee-Steere, JP, KStJ; *m* 1942, Jessica Margaret, *d* of Frank Venn; two *s* three *d*. *Educ:* Hale Sch., Perth; St Peter's Coll., Adelaide. Served War: Captain Army/Air Liaison Group, AIF; SW Pacific Area, 1944–45. President (for WA): Pastoralists and Graziers Assoc., 1959–72; Boy Scout Assoc., 1957–64; National Trust, 1969–72. Vice-Pres., Council of Royal Flying Doctor Service of WA, 1954–59 and 1962–74. Chairman: State Adv. Cttee, CSIRO, 1962–71 (Councillor, Fed. Adv. Council, 1960–71); WA Soil Conservation Adv. Cttee, 1955–72; Aust. Capital Cities Secretariat, 1975–76; WA Turf

Club, 1963–84 (Vice-Chm., 1959–63). Member: Nat. Council of Aust. Boy Scouts Assoc., 1959–64; Exec. Cttee of WA State Cttee, Freedom from Hunger Campaign; WA State Adv. Cttee, Aust. Broadcasting Commn, 1961–64; Aust. Jubilee Cttee for the Queen's Silver Jubilee Appeal for Young Australians, 1977; Aust. Wool Industry Conf., 1971–74 (also Mem. Exec. Cttee). Councillor: Aust. Wool Growers and Graziers Council (Pres., 1972–73); St George's Coll., Univ. of WA, 1945–81. Chm. and dir of several cos. Leader, Trade Mission to India, 1962. JP Perth, 1965. *Recreation:* polo (played in WA Polo Team in Australasian Gold Cup). *Address:* Dardanup, 26 Odern Crescent, Swanbourne, WA 6010, Australia. *T:* (9) 3842929. *Club:* Weld (Perth).

LEECH, Prof. Geoffrey Neil, FBA 1987; Professor of Linguistics and Modern English Language, University of Lancaster, since 1974; *b* 16 Jan. 1936; *s* of Charles Richard Leech and Dorothy Eileen Leech; *m* 1961, Frances Anne Berman; one *s* one *d. Educ:* Tewkesbury Grammar School; University College London (BA 1959; MA 1963; PhD 1968). Asst Lectr, UCL, 1962–64; Harkness Fellow, MIT, 1964–65; Lectr, UCL, 1965–69; Reader, Univ. of Lancaster, 1969–74. Visiting Professor: Brown Univ., 1972; Kobe Univ., 1984. Hon. Fil Dr Lund, 1987. *Publications:* English in Advertising, 1966; A Linguistic Guide to English Poetry, 1969; Towards a Semantic Description of English, 1969; Meaning and the English Verb, 1971, 2nd edn 1987; (with R. Quirk, S. Greenbaum and J. Svartvik) A Grammar of Contemporary English, 1972; Semantics, 1974, 2nd edn 1981; (with J. Svartvik) A Communicative Grammar of English, 1975, 2nd edn 1994; Explorations in Semantics and Pragmatics, 1980; (ed with S. Greenbaum and J. Svartvik) Studies in English Linguistics: for Randolph Quirk, 1980; (with M. Short) Style in Fiction, 1981; (with R. Hoogenraad and M. Deuchar) English Grammar for Today, 1982; Principles of Pragmatics, 1983; (with R. Quirk, S. Greenbaum, and J. Svartvik) A Comprehensive Grammar of the English Language, 1985; (ed with C. N. Candlin) Computers in English Language Teaching and Research, 1986; (ed with R. Garside and G. Sampson) The Computational Analysis of English: a corpus-based approach, 1987; An A–Z of English Grammar and Usage, 1989; Introducing English Grammar, 1992; (ed with E. Black and R. Garside) Statistically-driven Computer Grammars of English, 1993; (ed with G. Myers and J. Thomas) Spoken English on Computer, 1995. *Recreations:* music, esp. playing the piano in chamber music groups. *Address:* Department of Linguistics, University of Lancaster, Bailrigg, Lancaster LA1 4YT.

LEECH, John, (Hans-Joachim Freiherr von Reitzenstein); Head of External Relations and Member of Management Board, Commonwealth Development Corporation, 1981–85; Chairman, Farm Services Co. BV, since 1988; Deputy Chairman, Rural Investment Overseas Ltd, since 1990 (Chairman, 1985–90); *b* 21 April 1925; *s* of Hans-Joachim and Josefine von Reitzenstein; *m* 1st, 1949, Mair Eiluned Davies (marr. diss. 1958); one *d*; 2nd, 1963, Noretta Conci, concert pianist. *Educ:* Bismarck Gymnasium, Berlin; Whitgift, Croydon. L. G. Mouchel & Partners, Consulting Civil Engineers, 1942–52; Bird & Co. Ltd, Calcutta, 1953–57; Dir, Europe House, London, and Exec. Mem. Council, Britain in Europe Ltd, 1958–63; Pres., Internat. Fedn of Europe Houses, 1961–65; Dir, Joint Industrial Exports Ltd, 1963–65; with Commonwealth Develt Corp., London and overseas, 1965–85; Co-ordinator, Interact Gp of European develt finance instns, 1973–85; Europ. Co-ordinator, West-West Agenda, 1987–. Asst Dir, NATO Parliamentarians' Conf., 1959–60. Vice-Chm., Indian Concrete Soc., 1953–57; Member: Council, Federal Trust for Educn and Research, 1985–; Adv. Council (formerly Exec. Cttee), London Symphony Orch., 1979–; Council, Royal Commonwealth Soc. for the Blind, 1983– (Exec. Cttee, 1988–); Internat. Council, Duke of Edinburgh's Award Internat. Assoc., 1993–. Chm., Keyboard Charitable Trust for Young Professional Performers, 1991–. Liveryman, Worshipful Co. of Paviors, 1968– (Mem. Court of Assts, 1992–). FRSA. *Publications:* The NATO Parliamentarians' Conference 1955–59, 1960; Europe and the Commonwealth, 1961; Aid and the Community, 1972; Halt! Who Goes Where?: the future of NATO in the new Europe, 1991; contrib. to jls on aspects of overseas develt, European matters and arts subjects. *Recreations:* music, travel, Italy. *Address:* 8 Chester Square Mews, SW1W 9DS. *T:* 0171–730 2307. *Club:* Travellers'.

LEECH, Rev. Kenneth; M. B. Reckitt Urban Fellow, St Botolph's Church, Aldgate, since 1991; *b* 15 June 1939; *s* of late John and Annie Leech; *m* 1970, Rheta Wall; one *s. Educ:* King's College London (BA Hons Mod. History, AKC 1961); Trinity Coll., Oxford (BA Hons Theol. 1961, MA 1968); St Stephen's House, Oxford. Deacon 1964, priest 1965; Curate: Holy Trinity, Hoxton, N1, 1964–67; St Anne, Soho, W1, 1967–71; Sec., Soho Drugs Group, 1967–71; Dir, Centrepoint, Soho, 1969–71; Chaplain and Tutor, St Augustine's Coll., Canterbury, 1971–74; Rector of St Matthew, Bethnal Green, 1974–80; Field Work Sec., BCC, 1980; Race Relations Field Officer, C of E Bd for Social Responsibility, 1981–87; Dir, Runnymede Trust, 1987–90. Visiting Lecturer: St Stephen's House, Chicago, 1978–90; Brent House, Chicago, 1990–. *Publications:* Pastoral Care and the Drug Scene, 1970; A Practical Guide to the Drug Scene, 1972; Keep the Faith, Baby, 1972; Youthquake, 1973; Soul Friend, 1977; True Prayer, 1980; The Social God, 1981; True God, 1984; Spirituality and Pastoral Care, 1986; Struggle in Babylon: Racism in the Cities and Churches of Britain, 1988; Care and Conflict, 1990; Subversive Orthodoxy, 1992; The Eye of the Storm, 1992 (HarperCollins Religious Book Award, 1993); We Preach Christ Crucified, 1994. *Recreations:* cartoon drawing, Lancashire dialect poetry, pubs. *Address:* St Botolph's Crypt, Aldgate, EC3N 1AB. *T:* 0171–377 0721.

LEECH, Prof. Rachel Mary, DPhil; Professor of Biology, University of York, since 1978; *b* 3 June 1936; *d* of Alfred Jack Leech and Frances Mary Ruth Leech (*née* Cowley). *Educ:* Prince Henry's Grammar Sch., Otley, W Yorks; St Hilda's Coll., Oxford (MA, DPhil 1961). Christopher Welch and Naples Biol Scholar, 1957–60. Professorial Res. Fellow, 1960–63, Lectr in Analytical Cytology, 1963–66, Imperial Coll., London; University of York: Lectr in Biology, 1966–69; Sen. Lectr, 1969–75; Reader, 1975–78. Mem., BBSRC, 1994–. *Publications:* (with R. A. Reid) The Biochemistry and Structure of Subcellular Organelles, 1980; articles in Plant Physiology, Nature, The Biochemical Jl, The Plant Jl. *Recreations:* gardening, walking, enjoying the company of friends. *Address:* Department of Biology, University of York, Heslington, York YO1 5DD. *T:* York (01904) 430000.

LEECH, His Honour Robert Radcliffe; a Circuit Judge (formerly Judge of County Courts), 1970–86; *b* 5 Dec. 1919; *s* of late Edwin Radcliffe Leech; *m* 1951, Vivienne Ruth, *d* of A. J. Rickerby, Carlisle; two *d. Educ:* Monmouth Sch.; Worcester Coll., Oxford (Open Classics Exhibnr 1938). Served War, 1940–44, Border Regt (despatches twice). Called to Bar, Middle Temple, 1949 (Harmsworth Law Scholar); Dep. Chm., Cumberland QS, 1966–71; Hon. Recorder of Carlisle, 1985–86. *Recreations:* sailing, golf. *Address:* Scaur House, Cavendish Terrace, Stanwix, Carlisle, Cumbria CA3 9ND. *Clubs:* Oriental; County and Border (Carlisle).

LEEDS, Bishop of, (RC), since 1985; **Rt Rev. David Every Konstant;** *b* 16 June 1930; *s* of Antoine Konstant and Dulcie Marion Beresford Konstant (*née* Leggatt). *Educ:* St Edmund's College, Old Hall Green, Ware; Christ's College, Cambridge (MA); Univ. of London Inst. of Education (PGCE). Priest, dio. Westminster, 1954; Cardinal Vaughan School, Kensington, 1959; Diocesan Adviser on Religious Education, 1966; St Michael's School, Stevenage, 1968; Director, Westminster Religious Education Centre, 1970; Auxiliary Bishop of Westminster (Bishop in Central London) and Titular Bishop of Betagbara, 1977–85. Chm., Dept for Catholic Education and Formation (formerly Dept for Christian Doctrine and Formation), Bishops' Conf. of Eng. and Wales, 1984–. *Publications:* various books on religious education and liturgy. *Recreation:* music. *Address:* Bishop's House, 13 North Grange Road, Headingley, Leeds LS6 2BR. *T:* Leeds (0113) 230 4533, *Fax:* (0113) 278 9890.

LEEDS, Archdeacon of; *see* Oliver, Ven. J. M.

LEEDS, Sir Christopher (Anthony), 8th Bt *cr* 1812; Senior Lecturer, University of Nancy II; *b* 31 Aug. 1935; *s* of Geoffrey Hugh Anthony Leeds (*d* 1962) (*b* of 6th Bt) and Yoland Thérèse Barré (*d* 1944), *d* of James Alexander Mitchell; *S* cousin, 1983; *m* 1974, Elaine Joyce (marr. diss. 1981), *d* of late Sqdn Ldr C. H. A. Mullins. *Educ:* King's School, Bruton; LSE, Univ. of London (BSc Econ. 1958); Univ. of Southern California (Sen. Herman Fellow in Internat. Relations, MA 1966). Assistant Master: Merchant Taylors' School, Northwood, 1966–68; Christ's Hospital, 1972–75; Stowe School, 1978–81. Publisher, 1975–78. Vis. Lectr, Univ. of Strasbourg I, 1983–87. *Publications include:* Political Studies, 1968, 3rd edn 1981; European History 1789–1914, 1971, 2nd edn 1980; Italy under Mussolini, 1972; Unification of Italy, 1974; Historical Guide to England, 1976; (with R. S. Stainton and C. Jones) Management and Business Studies, 1974, 3rd edn 1983; Basic Economics Revision, 1982; Politics in Action, 1986; World History—1900 to the present day, 1987; Peace and War, 1987; English Humour, 1989. *Recreations:* hill-walking, modern art, travel. *Heir: cousin* Antony Hildyard Leeds [*b* 15 Dec. 1937; *m* 1966, Elizabeth Helen Cornell (marr. diss. 1973)]. *Address:* 6 Hurlingham, 14 Manor Road, Eastcliff, Bournemouth BH1 3EY; 7 rue de Turique, 54000 Nancy, France. *Club:* Lansdowne.

LEEMING, Cheryl Elise Kendall, (Mrs J. C. Leeming); *see* Gillan, C. E. K.

LEEMING, Geraldine Margaret; *see* Coleridge, G. M.

LEEMING, Ian; QC 1988; a Recorder, since 1989; *b* Preston, Lancs, 10 April 1948; *s* of late Thomas Leeming (Bombing Leader, RAF), and of Lilian (*née* Male); *m* 1973, Linda Barbara Cook; one *s* two *d. Educ:* The Catholic Coll., Preston; Manchester Univ. (LLB 1970). Called to the Bar: Gray's Inn, 1970; Lincoln's Inn (*ad eundem*), 1981. In practice at Chancery and Commercial Bars, 1971–; Lectr in Law (part-time), Manchester Univ., 1971–75. Dir of limited cos. Vice-Chm., Northern Soc. of Cons. Lawyers, 1985–88. *Publications:* (with James Bonney) Observations upon the Insolvency Bill, 1985; articles, notes and reviews in legal jls and specialist periodicals. *Recreations:* squash, real tennis. *Address:* Lamb Chambers, Lamb Building, Temple EC4Y 7AS. *T:* 0171–797 8300. *Club:* Athenæum.

LEEMING, John Coates; space consultant; Director General, British National Space Centre, 1987–88 (Director, Policy and Programmes, 1985–87); *b* 3 May 1927; *s* of late James Arthur Leeming and Harriet Leeming; *m* 1st, 1949 (marr. diss. 1974); two *s*; 2nd, 1985, Cheryl Elise Kendall Gillan, *qv. Educ:* Chadderton Grammar Sch., Lancs; St John's Coll., Cambridge (Schol.). Teaching, Hyde Grammar Sch., Cheshire, 1948. Asst Principal, HM Customs and Excise, 1950 (Private Sec. to Chm.); Principal: HM Customs and Excise, 1954; HM Treasury, 1956; HM Customs and Excise, 1958; Asst Sec., HM Customs and Excise, 1965; IBRD (World Bank), Washington, DC, 1967; Asst Sec., 1970, Under Sec., 1972, CSD; a Comr of Customs and Excise, 1975–79; Dept of Industry (later DTI), 1979–85. *Recreation:* golf. *Club:* Royal Automobile.

LEES, Sir Antony; *see* Lees, Sir W. A. C.

LEES, C(harles) Norman; His Honour Judge Lees; a Circuit Judge since 1980; *b* 4 Oct. 1929; *s* of late Charles Lees, Bramhall, Cheshire; *m* 1961, Stella (*d* 1987), *d* of late Hubert Swann, Stockport; one *d. Educ:* Stockport Sch.; Univ. of Leeds. LLB 1950. Called to Bar, Lincoln's Inn, 1951. Dep. Chm., Cumberland County QS, 1969–71; a Recorder of the Crown Court, 1972–80; Chm., Mental Health Review Tribunal, Manchester Region, 1977–80 (Mem., 1971–80). *Recreations:* squash rackets, music, history. *Address:* 1 Deans Court, Crown Square, Manchester M3 3JL. *T:* 0161–834 4097. *Clubs:* Lansdowne; Northern Lawn Tennis.

LEES, Sir David (Bryan) Kt 1991; FCA; Chairman, GKN plc, since 1988; a Director: Bank of England, since 1991; Courtaulds, since 1991; *b* 23 Nov. 1936; *s* of late Rear-Adm. D. M. Lees, CB, DSO, and C. D. M. Lees; *m* 1961, Edith Mary Bernard; two *s* one *d. Educ:* Charterhouse. Qualified as a chartered accountant, 1962. Chief Accountant, Handley Page Ltd, 1964–68; GKN Sankey Ltd: Chief Accountant, 1970–72; Dep. Controller, 1972–73; Director and Controller, 1973–76; Guest Keen and Nettlefolds, later GKN plc: Group Finance Executive, 1976–77; General Manager Finance, 1977–82; Finance Dir, 1982–87; Man. Dir, 1987–88. Mem. Council, CBI, 1988– (Chm., Economic Affairs (formerly Economic and Financial Policy) Cttee, 1988–94); Pres., EEF, 1990–92; Member: Audit Commission, 1983–90; Listed Cos Adv. Cttee, 1990–; European Round Table, 1995–; Nat. Defence Industries Council, 1995–. Mem. Governing Body, Shrewsbury Sch., 1986–. *Recreations:* walking, golf, opera, music. *Address:* GKN plc, PO Box 55, Redditch, Worcs B98 0TL. *Club:* MCC.

See also Rear-Adm. R. B. Lees.

LEES, Prof. Dennis Samuel, CBE 1980; Emeritus Professor of Industrial Economics, University of Nottingham, since 1983 (Professor, 1968–82); *b* 20 July 1924; *s* of late Samuel Lees and Evelyn Lees (*née* Withers), Borrowash, Derbyshire; *m* 1950, Elizabeth Bretisch, London (*d* 1992); two *s* one *d. Educ:* Derby Technical Coll.; Nottingham Univ. BSc(Econ), PhD. Lecturer and Reader in Economics, Keele Univ., 1951–65; Prof. of Economics, University Coll., Swansea, 1965–67. Exchange Lectr, Reed Coll., Portland, Ore, 1958–59; Visiting Prof. of Economics: Univ. of Chicago, 1963–64; Univ. of California, Berkeley, 1971; Univ. of Sydney, 1975. Chairman: Nat. Ins. Advisory Committee, 1972–80; Industrial Injuries Advisory Council, 1973–78; Mem., Adv. Council, Inst. of Econ. Affairs, 1974–93 (Hon. Fellow, 1994). Freeman, City of London, 1973. *Publications:* Local Expenditure and Exchequer Grants, 1956; Health Thru Choice, 1961; Economic Consequences of the Professions, 1966; Economics of Advertising, 1967; Financial Facilities for Small Firms, 1971; Impairment, Disability, Handicap, 1974; Economics of Personal Injury, 1976; Solicitors' Remuneration in Ireland, 1977; articles on industrial and social policy in: Economica, Jl of Political Economy, Amer. Econ. Rev., Jl of Law and Econ., Jl Industrial Econ., Jl Public Finance. *Recreations:* cricket and pottering. *Address:* 8 Middleton Crescent, Beeston, Nottingham NG9 2TH. *T:* Nottingham (0115) 925 8730.

LEES, Geoffrey William; Headmaster, St Bees School, 1963–80; *b* 1 July 1920; *o s* of late Mr and Mrs F. T. Lees, Manchester; *m* 1949, Joan Needham, *yr d* of late Mr and Mrs J. Needham, Moseley, Birmingham. *Educ:* King's Sch., Rochester; Downing Coll., Cambridge. Royal Signals, 1940–46 (despatches): commissioned 1941; served in NW Europe and Middle East, Captain. 2nd Class Hons English Tripos, Pt I, 1947; History Tripos, Part II, 1948; Asst Master, Brighton Coll., 1948–63. Leave of absence in Australia, Asst Master, Melbourne Church of England Gram. Sch., 1961–62. *Recreations:* reading, lepidoptera, walking. *Address:* 10 Merlin Close, Upper Drive, Hove, Sussex BN3 6NU. *Clubs:* MCC; Hawks, Union (Cambridge).

LEES, Capt. Nicholas Ernest Samuel; Clerk of the Course and Managing Director, Leicester Racecourse, since 1972 (Assistant Manager, 1970–71); Chief Executive and Clerk of the Course, Newmarket, since 1974; *b* 3 May 1939; *s* of Ernest William Lees and Marjorie May Lees; *m* 1st, 1969, Elizabeth Helen Spink (marr. diss. 1985); one *d*; 2nd, 1985, Jocelyn Kosina; one *d*. *Educ:* Abbotsholme Sch., Rocester, Staffs. Shell Oil, 1956–59; commnd 17/21 Lancers, 1959; retd from Army, 1967; studied for Chartered Surveyors exams, 1967–69 (passed final exams but never practised); auctioneer, Warner, Sheppard & Wade Ltd, Leicester, 1969–73; Clerk of the Course: Teesside Park, 1972–73; Great Yarmouth, 1977–91. Director: Racecourse Assoc. Ltd, 1988–93; Stratford-on-Avon Racecourse Co. Ltd, 1990–. *Recreations:* horse racing, point to pointing, antique furniture, silver, sporting art. *Address:* Capers End, Bradfield St George, Bury St Edmunds, Suffolk IP30 0AY. *T:* Bury St Edmunds (01284) 386651.

LEES, Norman; *see* Lees, C. N.

LEES, Robert Ferguson; Regional Procurator Fiscal for Lothian and Borders, since 1991; *b* 15 Sept. 1938; *s* of William Lees and Martha Lees (*née* McAlpine); *m* 1966, Elizabeth (Elsie) Loughridge. *Educ:* Bellshill Acad.; Strathclyde Univ. (LLB). Joined Procurator Fiscal Service, 1972; Legal Asst, Paisley, 1972–75; Legal Asst, 1975–76, Sen. Legal Asst, 1976–78, and Sen. Depute Fiscal, 1978–81, Glasgow; Asst Procurator Fiscal, Dundee, 1982–88; Regl Procurator Fiscal for N Strathclyde, 1989–91. *Publication:* (jtly) Criminal Procedure, 1990. *Recreations:* music, travel, languages, photography. *Address:* The Sheriff Courthouse, Chambers Street, Edinburgh EH1 1LB.

LEES, Air Vice-Marshal Robin Lowther, CB 1985; MBE 1962; FIPM, FBIM; RAF retired; Chief Executive, British Hospitality Association (formerly British Hotels, Restaurants and Caterers Association), since 1986; *b* 27 Feb. 1931; *e s* of late Air Marshal Sir Alan Lees, KCB, CBE, DSO, AFC, and Norah Elizabeth (*née* Thompson); *m* 1966, Alison Mary Benson, *o d* of late Col C. B. Carrick, MC, TD, JP; three *s*. *Educ:* Wellington Coll.; RAF Coll., Cranwell. Commissioned RAF, 1952; served AAFCE Fontainebleau, 1953–56; Waterbeach, 1956–58; UKSLS Ottawa, 1958–61; DGPS(RAF) Staff MoD, 1962–66; Wyton, 1966–68; HQ Far East Comd, 1968–70; Directing Staff RAF Staff Coll., 1971–74; RAF PMC, 1974–76; Dir of Personnel (Ground) MoD, 1976; Dir of Personal Services (2) (RAF) MoD, 1976–80; RCDS 1980; Dir of Personnel Management (Policy and Plans) (RAF) MoD, 1981–82; AOA RAF Support Comd, 1982–85, and Head of Admin. Br., RAF, 1983–85. Mem. Council, CBI, 1990–93. Vice-Pres., HOTREC, 1991–93. Gov., Wellington Coll., 1990–. *Recreations:* real tennis, lawn tennis, squash, golf. *Address:* c/o Barclays Bank, 6 Market Place, Newbury, Berks RG14 5AY. *Clubs:* Royal Air Force (Chairman, 1977–82); Jesters', All England Lawn Tennis and Croquet.

LEES, Rear-Adm. Rodney Burnett; Director General Naval Personnel Strategy and Plans, since 1995; *b* 31 Dec. 1944; *s* of Rear-Adm. Dennis Maresceaux Lees, CB, DSO and Daphne Lees; *m* 1st, 1969, Rosemary Elizabeth Blake (marr. diss. 1978); two *s*; 2nd, 1982, Molly McEwen. *Educ:* Charterhouse; Gray's Inn. Joined RN 1962; HMS Devonshire, 1966–68; Captain SM10, 1968–70; HMS Apollo, 1972–74; legal training, 1974–77; Staff Legal Adviser to FO Portsmouth and Command Legal Adviser to C-in-C Naval Home Comd, 1977–79; Dep. Supply Officer, HM Yacht Britannia, 1980; DCSO (Pay), MoD 1980–82; Supply Officer, HMS Illustrious, 1982–83; Fleet Legal and Admin Officer, 1984–86; Sec. to Chief of Fleet Support, 1986–88; Dep. Comd Sec. to C-in-C Fleet, 1988–90; Sec. to First Sea Lord, 1990–92; Dir, Defence Personnel, 1992–95. *Recreations:* horse racing, soccer, golf, country and folk music. *Address:* Victory Building, HM Naval Base, Portsmouth, Hants PO1 3LS. *T:* Portsmouth (01705) 727100. *Clubs:* Army and Navy, Institute of Directors.

See also Sir D. B. Lees.

LEES, Sir Thomas (Edward), 4th Bt, *cr* 1897; landowner; *b* 31 Jan. 1925; 2nd *s* of Sir John Victor Elliott Lees, 3rd Bt, DSO, MC, and Madeline A. P. (*d* 1967), *d* of Sir Harold Pelly, 4th Bt; *S* father 1955; *m* 1949, Faith Justin, *d* of G. G. Jessiman, OBE, Great Durnford, Wilts; one *s* three *d*. *Educ:* Eton; Magdalene Coll., Cambridge. Served War in RAF; discharged 1945, after losing eye. Magdalene, Cambridge, 1945–47; BA Cantab 1947 (Agriculture). Since then has farmed at and managed South Lytchett estate. Chm., Post Green Community Trust Ltd. Mem., General Synod of C of E, 1970–90. JP 1951, CC 1952–74, High Sheriff 1960, Dorset. Hon. DLitt Bournemouth, 1992. *Recreation:* sailing. *Heir:* *s* Christopher James Lees [*b* 4 Nov. 1952; *m* 1st, 1977, Jennifer (marr. diss. 1987), *d* of John Wyllie; 2nd, 1989, Clare, *d* of Austen Young, FRCS, Aberystwyth; one *s* two *d*]. *Address:* Post Green, Lytchett Minster, Poole, Dorset BH16 6AP. *T:* Lytchett Minster (01202) 622048. *Club:* Royal Cruising.

LEES, Sir Thomas Harcourt Ivor, 8th Bt *cr* (UK) 1804, of Black Rock, County Dublin; *b* 6 Nov. 1941; *s* of Sir Charles Archibald Edward Ivor Lees, 7th Bt, and Lily, *d* of Arthur Williams, Manchester; *S* father, 1963. *Heir: kinsman* John Cathcart d'Olier-Lees [*b* 12 Nov. 1927; *m* 1957, Wendy Garrold, *yr d* of late Brian Garrold Groom; two *s*].

LEES, Dr William, CBE 1970; TD 1962; FRCOG; Medical Manpower Consultant to South West Thames Regional Health Authority, 1981–87, retired; *b* 18 May 1924; *s* of William Lees and Elizabeth Lees (*née* Massey); *m* 1947, Winifred Elizabeth (*née* Hanford); three *s*. *Educ:* Queen Elizabeth's, Blackburn; Victoria Univ., Manchester. MB ChB; LRCP; MRCS; MRCOG, FRCOG; DPH; MFCM. Obstetrics and Gynaecology, St Mary's Hosps, Manchester, 1947–58; Min. of Health, later DHSS, 1959–81; Under Sec., (SPMO) 1977–81. QHP, 1969–72. Col, 10th, later no 257, Gen. Hosp., TAVR RAMC, 1966–71; Col Comdt, NW London Sector, ACF, 1971–76; Mem. for Greater London, TA&VRA, 1966–. OStJ 1967. *Publications:* numerous contribs on: intensive therapy, progressive patient care, perinatal mortality, day surgery, district general hospital. *Recreations:* music, golf, travel. *Address:* 13 Hall Park Hill, Berkhamsted, Herts HP4 2NH. *T:* Berkhamsted (014427) 3010. *Clubs:* Athenæum, St John's.

LEES, Sir (William) Antony Clare, 3rd Bt *cr* 1937; *b* 14 June 1935; *s* of Sir (William) Hereward Clare Lees, 2nd Bt, and of Lady (Dorothy Gertrude) Lees, *d* of F. A. Lauder; *S* father, 1976; *m* 1986, Joanna Olive Crane. *Educ:* Eton; Magdalene Coll., Cambridge (MA). *Heir:* none.

LEES-MILNE, James; *b* 6 Aug. 1908; *er s* of George Crompton Lees-Milne, Crompton Hall, Lancs and Wickhamford Manor, Worcs; *m* 1951, Alvilde (*d* 1994), formerly wife of 3rd Viscount Chaplin and *d* of late Lt-Gen. Sir Tom Molesworth Bridges, KCB, KCMG, DSO; no *c*. *Educ:* Eton Coll.; Magdalen Coll., Oxford. Private Sec. to 1st Baron Lloyd, 1931–35; on staff, Reuters, 1935–36; on staff, National Trust, 1936–66; Adviser on Historic Buildings to National Trust, 1951–66. 2nd Lieut Irish Guards, 1940–41 (invalided). FRSL 1957; FSA 1974. *Publications:* The National Trust (ed), 1945; The Age of Adam, 1947; National Trust Guide: Buildings, 1948; Tudor Renaissance, 1951; The Age of Inigo Jones, 1953; Roman Mornings, 1956 (Heinemann Award, 1956); Baroque in Italy, 1959; Baroque in Spain and Portugal, 1960; Earls of Creation, 1962; Worcestershire: A Shell Guide, 1964; St Peter's, 1967; English Country Houses: Baroque 1685–1714, 1970; Another Self, 1970; Heretics in Love, 1973; Ancestral Voices, 1975; William Beckford, 1976; Prophesying Peace, 1977; Round the Clock, 1978; Harold Nicolson, vol. I, 1980, vol. II, 1981 (Heinemann Award, RSL, 1982); (with David Ford) Images of Bath, 1982; The Country House (anthology), 1982; Caves of Ice, 1983; The Last Stuarts, 1983; Midway on the Waves, 1985; The Enigmatic Edwardian, 1986; Some Cotswold Country Houses, 1987; Venetian Evenings, 1988; The Fool of Love, 1990; The Bachelor Duke, 1991; People and Places, 1992; A Mingled Measure, 1994. *Address:* Essex House, Badminton, Avon GL9 1DD. *T:* Badminton (01454) 218288. *Club:* Brooks's.

LEES-SPALDING, Rear-Adm. Ian Jaffery, (Tim), CB 1973; RN retd; Joint Editor, Macmillan and Silk Cut Yachtsman's Handbook, since 1984; *b* London, 16 June 1920; *s* of Frank Souter Lees-Spalding and Joan (*née* Bodilly); *m* 1946, June Sandys Lyster Sparkes; two *d*. *Educ:* Blundells Sch.; RNEC. Served War of 1939–45 (King's Commendation for Bravery, 1941; Royal Lifesaving Inst. medal, 1942); served in HMS Sirius, HM S/Ms Trespasser, Teredo, Truculent and Andrew, HMS Cleopatra and Tiger; Chief of Staff to C-in-C Naval Home Comd, 1969; CSO (Technical) to C-in-C Fleet, 1971; retd 1974. Administrator, London Internat. Film Sch., 1975–79. Jt Editor, Macmillan and Silk Cut Nautical Almanac, 1981–92. *Recreations:* music, travelling. *Address:* St Olaf's, Wonston, Winchester, Hants S021 3LP. *T:* Winchester (01962) 760249. *Club:* Army and Navy.

LEESE, Sir John Henry Vernon, 5th Bt *cr* 1908; *b* 7 Aug. 1901; *s* of Vernon Francis Leese, OBE (*d* 1927) and Edythe Gwendoline (*d* 1929), *d* of Charles Frederick Stevenson; *g s* of Sir Joseph Francis Leese, 1st Bt; *S* cousin, 1979. *Heir:* none.

LE FANU, Sir (George) Victor (Sheridan), KCVO 1987; Serjeant at Arms, House of Commons, 1982–89; *b* 1925; *s* of late Maj.-Gen. Roland Le Fanu, DSO, MC, and Marguerite (*née* Lumsden); *m* 1956, Elizabeth, *d* of late Major Herbert Hall and Kitty (*née* Gauvain); three *s*. *Educ:* Shrewsbury School. Served Coldstream Guards, 1943–63; Asst-Adjt, Royal Military Academy, Sandhurst, 1949–52; Adjt 2nd Bn Coldstream Guards, 1952–55; sc Camberley, 1959; Staff Captain to Vice-Quartermaster-General to the Forces, War Office, 1960–61; GSO2, Headquarters London District, 1961–63; Dep. Asst Serjeant at Arms, House of Commons, 1963–76; Asst Serjeant at Arms, 1976–81; Deputy Serjeant at Arms, 1981–82. Chm., Morley Coll., 1993–. Trustee, Wall Trust, 1991–. *Address:* 29 Cranmer Court, Whitehead's Grove, SW3 3HN.

LE FANU, Mark, OBE 1994; General Secretary, The Society of Authors, since 1982; *b* 14 Nov. 1946; *s* of Admiral of the Fleet Sir Michael Le Fanu, GCB, DSC and Prudence, *d* of Admiral Sir Vaughan Morgan, KBE, CB, MVO, DSC; *m* 1976, Lucy Cowen; three *s* one *d*. *Educ:* Winchester; Univ. of Sussex. Admitted Solicitor, 1976. Served RN, 1964–73; McKenna & Co., 1973–78; The Society of Authors, 1979–. Vice Chm., British Copyright Council, 1992–; Mem., Literature Adv. Cttee, British Council, 1989–. *Recreations:* sailing, travel, golf, coping with children. *Address:* 25 St James's Gardens, W11 4RE. *T:* 0171–603 4119; The Society of Authors, 84 Drayton Gardens, SW10 9SB. *T:* 0171–373 6642. *Clubs:* PEN; Thorney Island Sailing.

LeFANU, Prof. Nicola Frances; composer; Professor and Head of Department of Music, University of York, since 1994; *b* 28 April 1947; *d* of late William Richard LeFanu and Dame Elizabeth Violet Maconchy, DBE; *m* 1979, David Newton Lumsdaine; one *s*. *Educ:* St Mary's Sch., Calne; St Hilda's Coll., Oxford (BA Hons 1968, MA 1972; Hon. Fellow, 1993); Royal Coll. of Music; DMus London, 1988. Cobbett Prize for chamber music, 1968; BBC Composers' Competition, 1st Prize, 1971; Mendelssohn Scholarship, 1972; Harkness Fellowship for composition study, Harvard, 1973–74. Dir of Music, St Paul's Girls' Sch., 1975–77; Composer in Residence (jtly with David Lumsdaine), NSW Conservatorium of Music, Sydney, 1979; Sen Lectr in Music, 1977–93, Prof. of Musical Composition, KCL, 1993–94. Deleg. to Moscow Internat. New Music Festival, 1984. Hon. DMus Durham, 1995. Leverhulme Res. Award, 1989. *Publications:* numerous compositions, incl. opera, orchestral works, chamber music with and without voice, choral music and solo pieces; *major works include:* The Same Day Dawns (for soprano and ensemble), 1974; Columbia Falls (for symphony orch.), 1975; Dawnpath (chamber opera), 1977; The Old Woman of Beare (for soprano and ensemble), 1981; The Story of Mary O'Neill (radio opera), 1986; The Green Children (children's opera), 1990; Blood Wedding (opera), 1992; The Wildman (opera), 1995. *Recreations:* natural history, and therefore conservation; peace movement, women's movement. *Address:* 5 Holly Terrace, York YO1 4DS. *T:* York (01904) 651759, *Fax:* (01904) 610467.

LE FANU, Sir Victor; *see* Le Fanu, Sir G. V. S.

LEFEBVRE, Prof. Arthur Henry, FEng 1994; Distinguished Reilly Professor of Combustion Engineering, School of Mechanical Engineering, Purdue University, 1979–93, now Emeritus Professor (Professor and Head of School, 1976–80); *b* 14 March 1923; *s* of Henri and May Lefebvre; *m* 1952, Elizabeth Marcella Betts; two *s* one *d*. *Educ:* Long Eaton Grammar Sch; Nottingham Univ.; Imperial Coll., London. DSc (Eng), DIC, PhD, CEng, FIMechE, FRAeS. Ericssons Telephones Ltd: Engrg apprentice, 1938–41; Prodn Engr, 1941–47; res. work on combustion and heat transfer in gas turbines, Rolls Royce, Derby, 1952–61; Prof. of Aircraft Propulsion, Coll. of Aeronautics, 1961–71; Prof. and Hd of Sch. of Mechanical Engrg, Cranfield Inst. of Technol., 1971–76. Mem., AGARD Combustion and Propulsion Panel, 1957–61; Mem., AGARD Propulsion and Energetics Panel, 1970–76; Chm., Combustion Cttee, Aeronautical Res. Council, 1970–74. Hon. DSc Cranfield Inst. of Technology, 1989. Gas Turbine Award, ASME, 1982; R. Tom Sawyer Award, ASME, 1984; inaugural AIAA Propellants and Combustion Award, 1990; Marshall Award, Instn for Liquid Atomization and Spray Systems, 1993. *Publications:* Gas Turbine Combustion, 1983; Selected Papers on Fundamentals of Gas Turbine Combustion, 1988; Atomization and Sprays, 1989; papers on combustion and heat transfer in Proc. Royal Soc., internat. symposium vols on combustion, combustion and flame, combustion science and technology. *Recreations:* music, reading, golf. *Address:* Low Furrow, Pebworth, Stratford-upon-Avon, Warwicks CV37 8XW. *T:* Stratford-upon-Avon (01789) 721429. *Club:* Athenæum.

LEFEVER, Kenneth Ernest, CB 1974; Deputy Chairman, Civil Service Appeal Board, 1978–80 (Official Side Member, 1976–78); *b* 22 Feb. 1915; *s* of E. S. Lefever and Mrs E. E. Lefever; *m* 1939, Margaret Ellen Bowley; one *s* one *d*. *Educ:* County High Sch., Ilford. Board of Customs and Excise: joined Dept as Officer, 1935; War Service, 1942–46 (Captain, RE); Principal Inspector, 1966; Dep. Chief Inspector, 1969; Collector, London Port, 1971; Chief Inspector, 1972; Dir of Organisation and Chief Inspector, 1974; Comr, Bd of Customs and Excise, 1972–75, retd. *Recreations:* gardening, walking, cricket. *Address:* Trebarwith, 37 Surman Crescent, Hutton Burses, Brentwood, Essex CM13 2PW. *T:* Brentwood (01277) 212110. *Clubs:* MCC, Civil Service.

LEFF, Prof. Gordon; Professor of History, University of York, 1969–88, now Emeritus; *b* 9 May 1926; *m* 1953, Rosemary Kathleen (*née* Fox) (marr. diss 1980); one *s*. *Educ:* Summerhill Sch.; King's Coll., Cambridge. BA 1st Cl. Hons, PhD, LittD. Fellow, King's Coll., Cambridge, 1955–59; Asst Lectr, Lectr, Sen. Lectr, in History, Manchester Univ., 1956–65; Reader in History, Univ. of York, 1965–69. Carlyle Vis. Lectr, Univ. of Oxford, 1983. *Publications:* Bradwardine and the Pelagians, 1957; Medieval Thought, 1958; Gregory of Rimini, 1961; The Tyranny of Concepts, 1961; Richard Fitzralph,

1963; Heresy in the Later Middle Ages, 2 vols, 1967; Paris and Oxford Universities in 13th and 14th Centuries, 1968; History and Social Theory, 1969; William of Ockham: the metamorphosis of scholastic discourse, 1975; The Dissolution of the Medieval Outlook, 1976. *Recreations:* walking, gardening, watching cricket, listening to music. *Address:* The Sycamores, 12 The Village, Strensall, York Y03 5XS. *T:* York (01904) 490358.

LEFF, Prof. Julian Paul, MD; FRCPsych; Professor of Social and Cultural Psychiatry, Institute of Psychiatry, University of London, since 1987; *b* 4 July 1938; *s* of Samuel Leff and Vera Miriam (*née* Levy); *m* 1975, Joan Lillian Raphael; three *s* one *d*. *Educ:* University Coll. London (BSc, MB BS); MD London 1972. FRCPsych 1979; MRCP; MFPHM. House Officer: University Coll. Hosp., 1961–62; Whittington Hosp., 1962–63; career scientist, MRC, 1972–; Dir, Team for Assessment of Psychiatric Services, 1985–; Dir, MRC Social and Community Psychiatry Unit, 1989–95. Starkey Prize, Royal Coll. of Health, 1976. *Publications:* Psychiatric Examination in Clinical Practice, 1978, 3rd edn 1990; Expressed Emotion in Families, 1985; Psychiatry around the Globe, 1981, 2nd edn 1988; Family Work for Schizophrenia, 1992; Principles of Social Psychiatry, 1993. *Recreations:* piano, squash, croquet, swimming. *Address:* Institute of Psychiatry, De Crespigny Park, SE5 8AF. *T:* 0171–708 3235.

le FLEMING, Morris John; DL; Chief Executive, Hertfordshire County Council, and Clerk to the Lieutenancy, Hertfordshire, 1979–90; *b* 19 Aug. 1932; *s* of late Morris Ralph le Fleming and Mabel le Fleming; *m* 1960, Jenny Rose Weeks; one *s* three *d*. *Educ:* Tonbridge Sch.; Magdalene Coll., Cambridge (BA). Admitted Solicitor, 1958. Junior Solicitor, Worcester CC, 1958–59; Asst Solicitor: Middlesex CC, 1959; Nottinghamshire CC, 1959–63; Asst Clerk, Lindsey (Lincolnshire) CC, 1963–69; Hertfordshire CC: Second Dep. Clerk, 1969–74; County Secretary, 1974–79; Clerk, Magistrates' Courts Cttee, 1979–90; Sec., Probation Care Cttee, 1979–90. Dir, Herts TEC, 1989–90. Chm., Stansted Airport Consultative Cttee, 1991–. Dir, Herts Groundwork Trust, 1990–; Trustee, Herts Community Trust, 1991–. Chm., Herts Scouts, 1991–. DL Herts, 1991. Hon. LLD Hertfordshire, 1994. *Address:* Swangleys Lane, Knebworth, Herts SG3 6AA. *T:* Stevenage (01438) 813152. *Club:* Royal Over-Seas League.

LE FLEMING, Peter Henry John; health management consultant, since 1988; Regional General Manager, South East Thames Regional Health Authority, 1984–88; *b* 25 Oct. 1923; *s* of late Edward Ralph Le Fleming and Irene Louise Le Fleming (*née* Adams); *m* 1st, 1949, Gudrun Svendsen (marr. diss. 1981); two *s*; 2nd, 1987, Jean, *yr d* of Edgar and Alice Price, Llangenny, Wales. *Educ:* Addison Gardens Sch., Hammersmith; Pembroke Coll., Cambridge. MA; FHSM. Served 1942–47, RTR and Parachute Regt, MEF, CMF, Palestine; commnd 1943. Sudan Political Service, Equatoria, Kassala, Blue Nile Provinces, 1949–55; NHS, 1955–: Redevelt Sec., St Thomas's Hosp., London, 1955–57; Hosp. Sec., The London Hosp., 1957–61; Dep. Clerk to the Governors, Guy's Hosp., 1961–69; Gp Sec., Exeter and Mid Devon Hosp. Management Cttee, 1969–74; Area Administrator, Kent AHA, 1974–81; Regional Administrator, SE Thames RHA, 1981–84. Mem., Health Service Supply Council, 1982–86. Clerk to Special Trustees, Guy's Hosp., 1988–. Freeman, City of London, 1992. *Recreations:* long distance fell walking, horse riding, trad jazz and serious music. *Address:* Lilacs, Leys Road, Tostock, near Bury St Edmunds, Suffolk IP30 9PN. *T:* Beyton (01359) 271015.

le FLEMING, Sir Quentin (John), 12th Bt *cr* 1705, of Rydal, Westmorland; Taxi Proprietor, Palmerston North Taxis Ltd, since 1982; *b* 27 June 1949; *s* of Sir William Kelland le Fleming, 11th Bt and of Noveen Avis, *d* of C. C. Sharpe; *S* father, 1988; *m* 1971, Judith Ann, *d* of C. J. Peck; two *s* one *d*. *Recreations:* flying modern and vintage aircraft (private pilot), Scouting, caravanning, restoration of vintage cars. *Heir: s* David Kelland le Fleming, *b* 12 Jan. 1976. *Address:* 147 Stanford Street, Ashhurst, Manawatu, New Zealand. *T:* (63) 268406.

LEGARD, Sir Charles Thomas, 15th Bt *cr* 1660; *S* father, 1984. *Heir: s* Christopher John Charles Legard [*b* 19 April 1964; *m* 1986, Miranda, *d* of Maj. Fane Gaffney; one *s*].

LEGG, Allan Aubrey R.; *see* Rowan-Legg.

LEGG, Barry Charles, FCCA; MP (C) Milton Keynes South West, since 1992; *b* 30 May 1949; *s* of Henry and Elfreda Legg; *m* 1974, Margaret Rose; one *s* two *d*. *Educ:* Sir Thomas Rich's Grammar Sch., Gloucester; Manchester Univ. (BA Hons Hist.). ATII. Courtaulds Ltd, 1971–76; Coopers & Lybrand, 1976–78; Hillsdown Holdings plc, 1978–92. Mem., Treasury and Civil Service Select Cttee, 1992–. *Publication:* Maintaining Momentum: a radical tax agenda for the 1990s, 1992. *Recreation:* watching cricket. *Address:* House of Commons, SW1A 0AA. *T:* 0171–219 4022. *Clubs:* United and Cecil; Gloucestershire CC; Bletchley and Stony Stratford Cricket.

LEGG, Prof. Brian James, FEng 1994; Director, Silsoe Research Institute, Biotechnology and Biological Sciences Research Council (formerly Agricultural and Food Research Council), since 1990; *b* 20 July 1945; *s* of Walter and Mary Legg; *m* 1972, Philippa Whitehead; one *s* one *d*. *Educ:* Balliol Coll., Oxford (BA Physics 1966); Imperial Coll. London (PhD 1972). FInstP, FIAgrE, CPhys, CEng. Voluntary Service Overseas, The Gambia, 1966–67; Res. Scientist, Rothamsted Exptl Station, 1967–83; Head, Res. Divs, Silsoe Res. Inst., 1983–90. Vis. Scientist, CSIRO Div. of Envtl Mechanics, Canberra, 1980–82; Vis. Prof., Silsoe Coll., Cranfield Inst. of Technology, 1990–. *Publications:* contribs to learned jls. *Recreations:* sailing, ski-ing, music. *Address:* Silsoe Research Institute, Wrest Park, Silsoe, Bedford MK45 4HS. *T:* Silsoe (01525) 860000.

LEGG, Cyrus Julian Edmund; Secretary, The Natural History Museum (formerly British Museum (Natural History)), since 1987; *b* 5 Sept. 1946; *s* of Cyrus and Eileen Legg; *m* 1967, Maureen Jean (*née* Lodge); two *s*. *Educ:* Tiffin School. Agricultural and Food Research Council, 1967–83; HM Treasury, 1983–87. *Recreation:* gardening. *Address:* The Natural History Museum, Cromwell Road, SW7 5DB. *T:* 0171–938 8733.

LEGG, Keith (Leonard Charles), OBE 1981; PhD, MSc (Eng); CEng, FIMechE, FRAeS, FCIT; FHKIE; Hon. Professor and Advisor to Xian Jiaotung University, Shanghai Polytechnic University and South China Institute of Technology, China; consultant on aerospace engineering and on higher education; *b* 24 Oct. 1924; *s* of E. H. J. Legg; *m* 1947, Joan, *d* of H. E. Green; two *s*. *Educ:* London Univ. (External); Cranfield Inst. of Technology. Engineering apprenticeship, 1940–45; Dep. Chief Research and Test Engr, Asst Chief Designer, Chief Project and Structural Engr, Short Bros & Harland Ltd, Belfast, 1942–56; Chief Designer and Prof., Brazilian Aeronautical Centre, São Paulo, 1956–60; Head of Dept, 1960–72, and Prof., 1965–72, Loughborough Univ. of Technology (Sen. Pro Vice-Chancellor, 1967–70); Dir, Lanchester Polytechnic, 1972–75; Dir, Hong Kong Polytechnic, 1975–84. Chm., Internat. Directing Cttee, CERI/OECD Higher Educn Institutional Management, 1973–75; Member: Road Transport Industrial Trng Bd, 1966–75 (former Chm.); Bd of Educn, 1975–84; World Council for Co-operative Educn, 1979–; Adv. Cttee on Environmental Protection, 1977–84; Hong Kong Management Assoc. Council, 1982–84; Environmental and Pollution Council of Hong Kong; Indust. Develt Bd, 1982–84. Royal Aeronautical Society: Member: Council, 1967–75; Educn Cttee, 1990–; Grading Cttee, 1991–. Adviser to OECD in Paris; mem. various nat. and professional cttees. Member: Council of City Polytechnic of Hong Kong, 1984; Court, Cranfield Inst. of Technology, 1987– (Hon. Vice-Pres. of Convocation, 1987–); Court, Loughborough Univ., 1993–. JP Hong Kong, 1978–84. Fellow, Hong Kong Management Assoc. Hon. DTech Loughborough, 1982; Hon. LLD: Hong Kong Univ., 1984, Hong Kong Poly., 1992. *Publications:* numerous: on aerospace structures and design, transport systems, higher educn, educnl analytical models and on Hong Kong/China. *Recreations:* most sports, classical music, theatre, walking, aid to the handicapped. *Address:* 19 Broom Park, Broom Road, Teddington, Middx TW11 9RS. *T:* 0181–977 8215.

LEGG, Sir Thomas (Stuart), KCB 1993 (CB 1985); QC 1990; Permanent Secretary, Lord Chancellor's Department, and Clerk of the Crown in Chancery, since 1989; *b* 13 Aug. 1935; *e s* of Stuart Legg and Margaret Legg (*née* Amos); *m* 1st, 1961, Patricia Irene Dowie (marr. diss.); two *d*; 2nd, 1983, Dr Marie-Louise Clarke, *e d* of late Humphrey Jennings. *Educ:* Horace Mann-Lincoln Sch., New York; Frensham Heights Sch., Surrey; St John's Coll., Cambridge (MA, LLM). Royal Marines, 1953–55. Called to the Bar, Inner Temple, 1960, Bencher, 1984; joined Lord Chancellor's Dept, 1962; Private Secretary to Lord Chancellor, 1965–68; Asst Solicitor, 1975; Under Sec., 1977–82; SE Circuit Administrator, 1980–82; Dep. Sec., 1982–89; Dep. Clerk of the Crown in Chancery, 1986–89; Sec. of Commns, 1989. Chm., CS Benevolent Fund, 1993–. Member: Inst. of Advanced Legal Studies, 1989–; Council, Brunel Univ., 1993–. Hon. Mem., SPTL, 1991. *Address:* Lord Chancellor's Department, House of Lords, SW1A 0PW. *Club:* Garrick.

LEGGATT, Rt. Hon. Sir Andrew (Peter), Kt 1982; PC 1990; **Rt. Hon. Lord Justice Leggatt;** a Lord Justice of Appeal, since 1990; *b* 8 Nov. 1930; *er s* of late Captain William Ronald Christopher Leggatt, DSO, RN and Dorothea Joy Leggatt (*née* Dreyer); *m* 1953, Gillian Barbara Newton; one *s* one *d*. *Educ:* Eton; King's Coll., Cambridge (Exhibr). MA 1957. Commn in Rifle Bde, 1949–50; TA, 1950–59. Called to the Bar, Inner Temple, 1954, Bencher, 1976. QC 1972; a Recorder of the Crown Court, 1974–82; Judge, High Court of Justice, QBD, 1982–90. Mem., Judges' Council, 1988–. Pres., Council of Inns of Court, 1995–; Member: Bar Council, 1971–82; Senate, 1974–83; Chm. of the Bar, 1981–82. Hon. Member: American Bar Assoc.; Canadian Bar Assoc.; non-resident mem., American Law Inst.; Mem., Top Salaries Review Body, 1979–82. *Recreations:* listening to music, personal computers. *Address:* Royal Courts of Justice, Strand, WC2A 2LL. *Clubs:* MCC, Pilgrims.

LEGGATT, Sir Hugh (Frank John), Kt 1988; art dealer, retired; *b* 27 Feb. 1925; 2nd *s* of late Henry and Beatrice Leggatt; *m* 1st, 1953, Jennifer Hepworth (marr. diss. 1990); two *s*; 2nd, 1991, Gaynor, *yr d* of late W. L. Tregoning, CBE and D. M. E. Tregoning. *Educ:* Eton; New Coll., Oxford. RAF, 1943–46. Joined Leggatt Bros, 1946; Partner, 1952; Sen. Partner, 1962–92. Chm., Soc. of London Art Dealers, 1966–70; Mem., Museums and Galleries Commn, 1983–92. Hon. Sec., Heritage in Danger, 1974–. *Address:* 21 Rue du Lac, 1800 Vevey, Switzerland. *T:* and *Fax:* (21) 9236810.

LEGGE, family name of **Earl of Dartmouth.**

LEGGE, (John) Michael, CMG 1994; Deputy Under-Secretary of State, Northern Ireland Office, since 1993; *b* 14 March 1944; *s* of Alfred John Legge and Marion Frances Legge (*née* James); *m* 1971, Linda (*née* Bagley); two *s*. *Educ:* Royal Grammar Sch., Guildford; Christ Church Oxford (BA, MA). Ministry of Defence: Asst Principal, 1966; Asst Private Sec. to Sec. of State for Defence, 1970; Principal, 1971; 1st Sec., UK Delegn to NATO, 1974–77; Asst Sec., MoD, 1979–87; Rand Corp., Santa Monica, California, 1982; Asst Under Sec. of State (Policy), MoD, 1987–88; Asst Sec. Gen. for Defence Planning and Policy, NATO, 1988–93. *Publication:* Theatre Nuclear Weapons and the NATO Strategy of Flexible Response, 1983. *Recreations:* golf, gardening. *Address:* Northern Ireland Office, Whitehall, SW1A 2AZ. *Club:* Puttenham Golf.

LEGGE, Rt. Rev. William Gordon, DD; *b* 20 Jan. 1913; *s* of Thomas Legge and Jane (*née* Gill); *m* 1941, Hyacinth Florence Richards; one *s* one *d*. *Educ:* Bishop Feild and Queen's Colls, St John's, Newfoundland. Deacon 1938, priest 1939; Curate, Channel, 1938–41; Incumbent of Botwood, 1941–44; Rector, Bell Island, 1944–55; Sec., Diocesan Synod, 1955–68; Archdeacon of Avalon, 1955–68; Canon of Cathedral, 1955–76; Diocesan Registrar, 1957–68; Suffragan Bishop, 1968; Bishop of Western Newfoundland, 1976–78. DD *hc*, Univ. of King's College, Halifax, NS, 1973. *Address:* 52 Glenhaven Boulevard, Corner Brook, Newfoundland A2H 4P6, Canada.

LEGGE-SCHWARZKOPF, Dame Elisabeth; *see* Schwarzkopf.

LEGGETT, Sir Clarence (Arthur Campbell), Kt 1980; MBE (mil.) 1943; FRACS, FACS; Surgeon; Hon. Consulting Surgeon, Princess Alexandra Hospital, Brisbane, since 1968; *b* 24 July 1911; *s* of late A. J. Leggett; *m* 1939, Avril, *d* of late R. L. Bailey; one *s* two *d*. *Educ:* Sydney Univ. (MA, MB BS; 1st cl. Hons, Univ. Medallist, 1936); Queensland Univ. (MS). RMO, Royal Prince Alfred Hosp., Sydney, 1937–38; Asst Dep. Med. Supt, 1939. Major, AAMC, 1941–46. Asst Surgeon, Royal Brisbane Hosp., 1941–51; Junior Surg., 1951–56; Senior Surg., Princess Alexandra Hosp., Brisbane, 1956–68. University of Queensland: Hon. Demonstrator and Examiner, Anatomy Dept, 1941–47; Chief Asst, Dept of Surgery, 1947–51; Mem. Faculty Bd, 1947–51; Special Lectr, 1951–68. Member of Council: Queensland Inst. for Med. Research, 1948–65; RACS, 1966–75 (Gordon Craig Schol.; Chm. Court of Examiners, 1971–75; Junior Vice-Pres., 1973–75; Mem. Ct of Honour). FAMA 1985; Hon. FRCS 1983. *Publications:* numerous surgical and historical papers, orations and theses. *Recreations:* breeding Arabian horses and Hereford cattle; univ. blue, and mem., Australian hockey team, 1934. *Address:* Craigston, 217 Wickham Terrace, Brisbane, Queensland 4000, Australia. *T:* (7) 38310031. *Club:* Queensland (Brisbane).

LEGH; *see* Cornwall-Legh, family name of Baron Grey of Codnor.

LEGH, family name of **Baron Newton.**

LEGH-JONES, (Piers) Nicholas; QC 1987; *b* 2 Feb. 1943; *s* of late John Herbert Legh-Jones and of Elizabeth Anne (*née* Halford). *Educ:* Winchester College; New College, Oxford (MA Hist. 1964, Jurisp. 1966). Legal Instructor, Univ. of Pennsylvania, 1966–67; Lectr in Law, New College, Oxford, 1967–71; Eldon Law Scholar, Univ. of Oxford, 1968. Called to the Bar, Lincoln's Inn, 1968. *Publications:* (ed) MacGillivray and Parkington on Insurance Law, 6th edn, to 8th edn 1988; contribs to Modern Law Review and Cambridge Law Jl. *Recreations:* vintage motorcars, cycling, modern history. *Address:* 20 Essex Street, WC2R 3AL. *T:* 0171–583 9294. *Club:* Travellers'.

LEGHARI, Farooq Ahmed Khan; President of Pakistan, since 1993; *b* 2 May 1940; *s* of Nawab Sardar Muhammad Khan Leghari; *m*; two *s* two *d*. *Educ:* Aitchison Coll., Lahore; Punjab Univ. (BA Hons); St Catherine's Coll., Oxford (BA Hons, MA, PPE). Civil Servant, 1964–73; Mem., Pakistan People's Party, 1973–93; Senate of Pakistan, 1975; Mem. for Dera Ghazi Khan, Nat. Assembly, 1977; Minister for Production, 1977; jailed on numerous occasions, 1977–88; Sec.-Gen. and Mem. Exec. Cttee, Pakistan People's Party, 1978–83; Mem., Nat. Assembly, and Minister for Water and Power, 1989–90; re-elected 1990 and 1993; Dep. Leader of Opposition, 1990–93; Finance Minister, later

Minister for Foreign Affairs, 1993. Chief, Baluchi Leghari Tribe. *Address:* President's Office, Aiwan-e-Sadr, Islamabad, Pakistan.

LE GOY, Raymond Edgar Michel, FCIT; a Director General, Commission of the European Communities, now European Union, since 1981; *b* 1919; *e s* of J. A. S. M. N. and May Le Goy; *m* 1960, Ernestine Burnett, Trelawny, Jamaica; two *s.* *Educ:* William Ellis Sch.; Gonville and Caius Coll., Cambridge (MA). 1st cl. hons Hist. Tripos, 1939, 1940. Sec. Cambridge Union; Chm., Union Univ. Liberal Socs. Served Army, 1940–46: Staff Captain, HQ E Africa, 1944; Actg Major, 1945. LPTB, 1947; Min. of Transport, 1947; UK Shipping Adviser, Japan, 1949–51; Far East and SE Asia, 1951; Dir, Goeland Co., 1952; Asst Secretary: MoT, 1958; Min. of Aviation, 1959; BoT and DEA, 1966; Under-Sec., 1968, BoT, later DTI; Dir Gen. for Transport, EEC, 1973–81. *Publication:* The Victorian Burletta, 1953. *Recreations:* theatre, music, race relations. *Address:* Villa Mirliton, Avenue des Eglantiers, Woluwe, Brussels 1050 Belgium.

LEHANE, Maureen, (Mrs Peter Wishart); concert and opera singer; *d* of Christopher Lehane and Honor Millar; *m* 1966, Peter Wishart (*d* 1984), composer. *Educ:* Queen Elizabeth's Girls' Grammar Sch., Barnet; Guildhall Sch. of Music and Drama. Studied under Hermann Weissenborn, Berlin (teacher of Fischer Dieskau); also under John and Aida Dickens (Australian teachers of Joan Sutherland); gained Arts Council award to study in Berlin. Speciality is Handel; has sung numerous leading roles (operas inc. Ezio, Ariadne and Pharamondo) with Handel opera societies of England and America, in London, and in Carnegie Hall, New York, also in Poland, Sweden and Germany; gave a number of master classes on the interpretation of Handel's vocal music (notably at s'Hertogenbosch Festival, Holland, July 1972; invited to repeat them in 1973); masterclasses on Handel and Purcell, The Hague and Maastricht, 1991. Debut at Glyndebourne, 1967. Festival appearances include: Stravinsky Festival, Cologne; City of London; Aldeburgh; Cheltenham; Three Choirs; Bath; Oxford Bach; Göttingen Handel Festival, etc; has toured N America; also 3–month tour of Australia at invitation of ABC and 2–month tour of Far East and ME, 1971; sang in Holland, and for Belgian TV, 1978; visits also to Berlin, Lisbon, Poland and Rome, 1979–80, to Warsaw, 1981. Title rôle in: Handel's Ariodante, Sadler's Wells, 1974; (her husband's 4th opera) Clytemnaestra, London, 1974; Purcell's Dido and Aeneas, Netherlands Opera, 1976; castrato lead in J. C. Bach's Adriano in Siria, London, 1982; female lead in Hugo Cole's The Falcon, Somerset, 1983; Peter Wishart's The Lady of the Inn, Reading Univ., 1983. Cyrus in first complete recording of Handel's Belshazzar. Appeared regularly on BBC; also in promenade concerts. Has made numerous recordings (Bach, Haydn, Mozart, Handel, etc). Mem. Jury, Internat. Singing Comp., s'Hertogenbosch Fest., Holland, 1982–; Adjudicator, Llangollen Internat. Eisteddfod 1991–93. Musical Dir and Founder, Great Elm Music Festival, 1987–; Founder, Jackdaws Educnl Trust, 1993. *Publication:* (ed with Peter Wishart) Songs of Purcell. *Recreations:* cooking, gardening, reading. *Address:* Bridge House, Great Elm, Frome, Somerset BA11 3NY. *T:* Mells (01373) 812383.

LEHMAN, Prof. Meir, (Manny), DSc, PhD; FEng, FBCS, FIEE, FIEEE, FACM; Managing and Technical Director, Lehman Software Technology Associates Ltd, since 1985; Professor of Computing Science, Imperial College of Science and Technology, University of London, 1972–84, now Emeritus Professor; *b* 24 Jan. 1925; *s* of late Benno and Theresa Lehman; *m* 1953, Chava Robinson; three *s* two *d.* *Educ:* Letchworth Grammar Sch.; Imperial Coll. of Science and Technol. (BSc Hons, PhD, ARCS, DIC); DSc (London) 1987. FIEE 1972; FBCS 1968; FACM 1993 (MACM 1955); FIEEE 1985; FEng 1989. Murphy Radio, 1941–50; Imperial Coll., 1950–56; London Labs, Ferranti, 1956–57; Scientific Dept, Israeli Defence Min., 1957–64; Res. Div., IBM, 1964–72; Dept of Computing, Imperial Coll., 1972–84 (part-time 1984–87), Hd of Dept, 1979–84, Sen. Res. Fellow, 1989–; Imperial Software Technology Ltd: Founder, 1982; Chm., 1982–84; Dir, 1984–87; Exec. Dir, 1987–88. Vice-Chm. of Exec., Kisharon Day Sch. for Special Educn, 1976–. *Publications:* Software Evolution—Processes of Program Change, 1985; over 130 refereed pubns and some 6 book chapters. *Recreations:* family, Talmudic studies, classical orchestral music, gardening, DIY. *Address:* 5 Elm Close, NW4 2PH; Department of Computing, Imperial College of Science, Technology and Medicine, SW7 2BZ. *T:* (office) 0171–594 8214.

LEHMANN, Prof. Andrew George; Emeritus Professor, University of Buckingham; *b* 17 Feb. 1922; *m* 1942, Alastine Mary, *d* of late K. N. Bell; two *s* one *d.* *Educ:* Dulwich Coll.; The Queen's Coll., Oxford. MA, DPhil Oxon. Served with RCS and Indian Army, 6th Rajputana Rifles. Fenced for England (Sabre), 1939. Asst lecturer and lecturer, Manchester Univ., 1945–51; Prof. of French Studies, 1951–68, Dean of Faculty of Letters and Soc. Scis, Univ. of Reading, 1960–66. Hon. Prof., Univ. of Warwick, 1968–78; various industry posts, 1968–78; Dir, Inst. of European Studies, Hull Univ., 1978–83; Rank Foundn Prof. of European Studies, and Dean, Sch. of Humanities, Univ. of Buckingham, 1983–88. Mem., Hale Cttee on University Teaching Methods, 1961–63; Chm., Industrial Council for Educnl and Trng Technology, 1974–76 (Pres., 1979–81, Vice-Pres., 1981–85); Mem., Anglo-French Permanent Mixed Cultural Commission, 1963–68. Adviser: Chinese Univ. of Hong Kong, 1964; Haile Selassie I Univ., Ethiopia, 1965. Member: Hong Kong Univ. Grants Cttee, 1966–73; Academic Planning Board and Academic Adv. Cttee, New Univ. of Ulster, 1966–77; Planning Bd, 1970–72, Acad. Adv. Cttee, 1974–83, UC at Buckingham; Court and Council, Bedford Coll., London Univ., 1971–78; British Library Adv. Cttee (Reference), 1975–78; Princeton Univ. Academic Adv. Council, 1975–81. Shakespeare Prize Cttee, FVS Foundn, Hamburg, 1984–90. Governor, Ealing Tech. Coll., 1974. *Publications:* The Symbolist Aesthetic in France, 1950 and 1967; Sainte-Beuve, a portrait of the Critic, 1962; The European Heritage, 1984; articles in various periodicals and learned reviews. *Recreations:* music, travel, gardening. *Address:* Westway Cottage, West Adderbury, Banbury, Oxon OX17 3EU. *T:* Banbury (01295) 810272.

LEHN, Prof. Jean-Marie; Officier, Ordre National du Mérite, 1993 (Chevalier, 1976); Officier, Légion d'Honneur, 1988 (Chevalier, 1983); Professor of Chemistry, Collège de France, Paris, since 1979; *b* Rosheim, Bas-Rhin, 30 Sept. 1939; *s* of Pierre Lehn and Marie Lehn (*née* Salomon); *m* 1965, Sylvie Lederer; two *s.* *Educ:* Univ. of Strasbourg (PhD); Research Fellow, Harvard, 1964. CNRS, 1960–66; Asst Prof., Univ. of Strasbourg, 1966–69; University Louis Pasteur, Strasbourg: Associate Prof., 1970; Prof. of Chemistry, 1970–79. Visiting Professor, 1972–: Harvard, Zürich, Cambridge, Barcelona, Frankfurt. Mem. or Associate, and hon. degrees from professional bodies in Europe and USA; Hon. FRSC 1987; For. Mem., Royal Soc., 1993. Nobel Prize for Chemistry (jtly), 1987, and numerous awards from sci. instns. Orden pour le mérite für Wissenchaften und Künste (FRG), 1990. *Publications:* many chapters in books and contribs to learned jls on supramolecular chemistry, physical organic chemistry and photochemistry. *Recreation:* music. *Address:* Institut le Bel, Université Louis Pasteur, 4 rue Blaise Pascal, 67000 Strasbourg, France. *T:* 88416056; Collège de France, 11 place Marcelin Berthelot, 75005 Paris, France. *T:* 44271360.

LEHRER, Thomas Andrew; writer of songs since 1943; *b* 9 April 1928; *s* of James Lehrer and Anna Lehrer (*née* Waller). *Educ:* Harvard Univ. (AB 1946, MA 1947); Columbia Univ.; Harvard Univ. Student (mathematics, especially probability and statistics) till 1953. Part-time teaching at Harvard, 1947–51. Theoretical physicist at Baird-Atomic, Inc., Cambridge, Massachusetts, 1953–54. Entertainer, 1953–55, 1957–60. US Army, 1955–57. Lecturer in Business Administration, Harvard Business Sch., 1961; Lecturer: in Education, Harvard Univ., 1963–66; in Psychology, Wellesley Coll., 1966; in Political Science, MIT, 1962–71; Vis. Lectr, Univ. of Calif, Santa Cruz, 1972–. *Publications:* Tom Lehrer Song Book, 1954; Tom Lehrer's Second Song Book, 1968; Too Many Songs by Tom Lehrer, 1981; contrib. to Annals of Mathematical Statistics, Journal of Soc. of Industrial and Applied Maths. *Recreation:* piano. *Address:* PO Box 121, Cambridge, MA 02138, USA. *T:* (617) 3547708.

LEICESTER, 7th Earl of, *cr* 1837; **Edward Douglas Coke;** Viscount Coke 1837; *b* 6 May 1936; *er s* of 6th Earl of Leicester and his 1st wife, Moyra Joan (*d* 1987), *d* of Douglas Crossley; *S* father, 1994; *m* 1st, 1962, Valeria Phyllis (marr. diss. 1985), *e d* of late L. A. Potter; two *s* one *d*; 2nd, 1986, Mrs Sarah de Chair. *Educ:* St Andrew's, Grahamstown, CP, S Africa. *Heir: s* Viscount Coke, *qv.* *Address:* Holkham, Wells-next-the-Sea, Norfolk NR23 1AB. *Clubs:* Brooks's, White's, Farmers'.

LEICESTER, Bishop of, since 1991; **Rt. Rev. Thomas Frederick Butler;** *b* 5 March 1940; *s* of Thomas John Butler and Elsie Butler (*née* Bainbridge); *m* 1964, Barbara Joan Clark; one *s* one *d.* *Educ:* Univ. of Leeds (BSc 1st Cl. Hons, MSc, PhD); Leicester Univ. (LLD). CEng; MIEE. College of the Resurruection, Mirfield, 1962–64; Curate: St Augustine's, Wisbech, 1964–66; St Saviour's, Folkestone, 1966–68; Lecturer and Chaplain, Univ. of Zambia, 1968–73; Acting Dean of Holy Cross Cathedral, Lusaka, Zambia, 1973; Chaplain to Univ. of Kent at Canterbury, 1973–80; Archdeacon of Northolt, 1980–85; Area Bishop of Willesden, 1985–91. Chm., Bd of Mission, Gen. Synod of C of E, 1995–. Six Preacher, Canterbury Cathedral, 1979–84. *Publication:* (with B. J. Butler) Just Mission. *Recreations:* reading, mountain walking, marathon running. *Address:* Bishop's Lodge, 10 Springfield Road, Leicester LE2 3BD. *T:* Leicester (0116) 270 8985.

LEICESTER, Provost of; *see* Hole, Very Rev. D. N.

LEICESTER, Archdeacon of; *see* Edson, Ven. M.

LEIFLAND, Leif, Hon. GCVO 1983; Ambassador of Sweden to the Court of St James's, 1982–90; *b* 30 Dec. 1925; *s* of Sigfrid and Elna Leifland; *m* 1954, Karin Abard; one *s* two *d.* *Educ:* Univ. of Lund (LLB 1950). Joined Ministry of Foreign Affairs, 1952; served: Athens, 1953; Bonn, 1955; Stockholm, 1958; Washington, 1961; Stockholm, 1964; Washington, 1970; Stockholm, 1975. Secretary, Foreign Relations Cttee, Swedish Parliament, 1966–70; Under Secretary for Political Affairs, 1975–77; Permanent Under-Secretary of State for Foreign Affairs, 1977–82; Chm. Bd, Swedish Inst. of Internat. Affairs, 1991–. *Publications:* books and articles on foreign policy and national security questions. *Address:* Nybrogatan 77, 11440 Stockholm, Sweden.

LEIGH, family name of **Baron Leigh.**

LEIGH, 5th Baron *cr* 1839; **John Piers Leigh;** *b* 11 Sept. 1935; *s* of 4th Baron Leigh, TD and Anne (*d* 1977), *d* of Ellis Hicks Beach; *S* father, 1979; *m* 1st, 1957, Cecilia Poppy (marr. diss. 1974), *y d* of late Robert Cecil Jackson; one *s* one *d* (and one *d* decd); 2nd, 1976, Susan (marr. diss. 1982), *d* of John Cleave, Whitnash, Leamington Spa; one *s*; 3rd, 1982, Mrs Lea Hamilton-Russell, *o d* of Col Noel Wild, OBE. *Educ:* Eton; Oxford and London Universities. *Recreations:* horses, hunting, racing, sport, country pursuits. *Heir: s* Hon. Christopher Dudley Piers Leigh [*b* 20 Oct. 1960; *m* 1990, Sophy-Ann, *d* of Richard Burrows]. *Address:* House of Lords, SW1A 0PW.

LEIGH, (Archibald) Denis, MD, FRCP; Consultant Physician, Bethlem Royal and Maudsley Hospitals, 1949–80, now Emeritus; Secretary-General, World Psychiatric Association, 1966–78; Hon. Consultant in Psychiatry to the British Army, 1969–80; Lecturer, Institute of Psychiatry; *b* 11 Oct. 1915; *o s* of Archibald Leigh and Rose Rushworth; *m* 1941, Pamela Parish; two *s* three *d.* *Educ:* Hulme Grammar Sch.; Manchester Univ.; University of Budapest. Manchester City Schol. in Medicine, 1932; BSc 1936; MB, ChB (1st class hons) 1939; Dauntesey Med. Sen. Schol., Prof. Tom Jones Exhibitioner in Anatomy; Sidney Renshaw Jun. Prize in Physiol.; Turner Med. Prize; John Henry Agnew Prize; Stephen Lewis Prize; Prize in Midwifery; MRCP 1941; MD (Manchester), 1947; FRCP, 1955. RAMC, 1940–45 (Lt-Col); Adviser in Neurology, Eastern Army, India. 1st Assistant, Dept of Neurology, London Hospital; Nuffield Fellow, 1947–48; Clinical Fellow, Harvard Univ., 1948. Recognised Clinical Teacher, London Univ.; Founder European Society of Psychosomatic Research; Editor-in-Chief and Founder, Journal of Psychosomatic Res.; Editorial Bd, Japanese Journal of Psychosomatic Medicine, Medicina Psychosomatica, Psychosomatic Medicine, Behaviour Therapy; Examiner in Psychological Med., Edinburgh Univ., 1958–65; Beattie Smith Lectr, Melbourne Univ., 1967. Governor, Bethlem Royal and Maudsley Hospitals, 1956–62; President Sect. of Psychiatry, Royal Society Med., 1967–68. Hon. Member: Deutschen Gesellschaft für Psychiatrie und Nervenheilkunde; Italian Psychosomatic Soc.; Assoc. Brasileira de Psiquiatria; Sociedad Argentina de Medicina Psicosomática; Polish Psychiatric Assoc.; Corresp. Mem., Pavlovian Soc. of N America; Hon. Corresp. Mem., Austn Acad. of Forensic Scis; Hon Fellow: Swedish Soc. of Med. Scis; Soc. Colombiana de Psiquiatría; Soviet Soc. of Neurologists and Psychiatrists; Czechoslovak Psychiatric Soc.; Finnish Psychiatric Soc. Distinguished Fellow: Amer. Psychiatric Assoc.; Hong Kong Psychiatric Assoc. *Publications:* (trans. from French) Psychosomatic Methods of Painless Childbirth, 1959; The Historical Development of British Psychiatry, Vol. I, 1961; Bronchial Asthma, 1967; A Concise Encyclopaedia of Psychiatry, 1977; chapters in various books; papers on neurology, psychiatry, history of psychiatry and psychosomatic medicine. *Recreations:* fishing, collecting. *Address:* 152 Harley Street, W1N 1HH. *T:* 0171–935 8868; The Grange, Otford, Kent TN14 5PL. *T:* Otford (01959) 523427.

LEIGH, Christopher Humphrey de Verd; QC 1989; a Recorder of the Crown Court, since 1985; *b* 12 July 1943; *s* of late Wing Commander Humphrey de Verd Leigh and of Johanna Leigh; *m* 1970, Frances Powell. *Educ:* Harrow. Called to the Bar, Lincoln's Inn, 1967. *Recreations:* fishing, travel. *Address:* 1 Paper Buildings, Temple, EC4Y 7EP. *T:* 0171–353 3728. *Club:* Hampshire (Winchester).

LEIGH, Edward Julian Egerton; MP (C) Gainsborough and Horncastle, since 1983; *b* 20 July 1950; *s* of Sir Neville Egerton Leigh, KCVO; *m* 1984, Mary Goodman; two *s* three *d.* *Educ:* St Philip's Sch., Kensington; Oratory Sch., Berks; French Lycée, London; UC, Durham Univ. (BA Hons). Called to the Bar, Inner Temple, 1977. Mem., Cons. Res. Dept, seconded to office of Leader of Opposition, GLC, 1973–75; Prin. Correspondence Sec. to Rt Hon. Margaret Thatcher, MP, 1975–76. Member (C): Richmond Borough Council, 1974–78; GLC, 1977–81. Contested (C) Teesside, Middlesbrough, Oct. 1974. PPS to Minister of State, Home Office, 1990; Parly Under-Sec. of State, DTI, 1990–93. Sec., Conservative Backbench Cttees on agric., defence and employment, 1983–90. Chm., Nat. Council for Civil Defence, 1980–82; Dir, Coalition for Peace Through Security, 1982–83. Kt of Honour and Devotion, SMO Malta. *Publications:* Right Thinking, 1979; Responsible Individualism, 1994. *Recreations:* walking, reading. *Address:* House of Commons, SW1A 0AA.

LEIGH, Sir Geoffrey (Norman), Kt 1990; Chairman, Allied London Properties, since 1987 (Managing Director, 1970–87); *b* 23 March 1933; *s* of late Rose Leigh and of Morris Leigh; *m* 1st, 1955, Valerie Lennard (marr. diss. 1975; she *d* 1976); one *s* two *d*; 2nd, 1976, Sylvia Pell; one *s* one *d*. *Educ:* Haberdashers' Aske's Hampstead Sch.; Univ. of Michigan. Man. Dir, 1965, Chm., 1980, Sterling Homes. Founder and First Pres., Westminster Junior Chamber of Commerce, 1959–63; Underwriting Mem., Lloyd's, 1973. Special Advisor, Land Agency Bd, Commn for the New Towns, 1994; Member: Cttee, Good Design in Housing for Disabled, 1977; Cttee, Good Design in Housing, 1978–79; British ORT Council, 1979–80; Internat. Adv. Bd, American Univ., Washington, 1983–; Adv. Council, Prince's Youth Business Trust, 1985–; Main Finance Bd, NSPCC, 1985– (Hon. Mem. Council, 1995); Royal Vet. Coll. Appeal Cttee, 1985–88; London Historic House Museums Trust, 1987–; Governing Council, Business in the Community, 1987–; Somerville Coll. Appeal, 1987–; Royal Fine Art Commn Art and Arch. Educn Trust, 1988–; Per Cent Club, 1988–; Council, City Technology Colls Trust, 1988–; City Appeal Cttee, Royal Marsden Hosp., 1990–93; Review Body on Doctors' and Dentists' Remuneration, 1990–93; Wellbeing Council, 1994–; Chancellor's Ct of Benefactors, Oxford Univ., 1991–; Emmanuel Coll., Cambridge, Develt Campaign, 1994– (Hon. Mem., Emmanuel Coll., 1994); Chm., St Mary's Hosp. 150th Anniversary Appeal, 1995–. Comr and Trustee, Fulbright Commn, 1991– (Chm., Internat. Adv. Bd, 1995); Sponsor, Leigh City Technology Coll., Dartford (Chm. of Govs, 1988–); Founder/Sponsor, Friends of British Liby, 1987–; Founder, Margaret Thatcher Centre, Somerville Coll., Oxford, 1991; Treasurer: Commonwealth Jewish Council, 1983–89; Commonwealth Jewish Trust, 1983–89; a Treas., Cons. Party, 1995–; Pres., Hampstead and Highgate Cons. Assoc., 1994– (Patron, 1991–94); Vice Pres., Conservatives Abroad, 1995–; Treas. and Trustee, Action on Addiction, 1991–; Trustee: Margaret Thatcher Foundn, 1991–; Industry in Educn, 1993–; Philharmonia, 1992–. Governor: Royal Sch., Hampstead, 1991–; City Lit. Inst., 1991–. Freeman, City of London, 1976; Liveryman: Haberdashers' Co., 1992–; Furniture Makers' Co., 1987 (Mem., Court of Assistants, 1992–94). FRSA. Presidential Citation, The American Univ., 1987. *Recreations:* photography, reading, golf. *Address:* 26 Manchester Square, W1A 2HU. *T:* 0171–486 6080. *Clubs:* Carlton, United and Cecil, Pilgrims, Royal Automobile, Savile.

LEIGH, Jonathan; Head Master, Blundell's School, since 1992; *b* 17 June 1952; *s* of Rupert M. Leigh and Isabel A. Leigh (*née* Villiers); *m* 1976, Emma Mary Kyrle-Pope; one *s* one *d*. *Educ:* Eton Coll.; Corpus Christi Coll., Cambridge (MA History). Cranleigh School: Asst Master, 1976–82; Housemaster, 1982–88; Head of History, 1987; Second Master, 1988–92. Indep. Schs Rep., Devon County Residential Care Standards Adv. Cttee, 1993–. Member: Cttee, ISIS South-West, 1995–; Cttee, Belgian Sect., Assoc. Européen des Enseignants, 1994–; Admiralty Interview Bd, 1994–. FRSA 1994. Gov., St Petroc's Sch., Bude, 1993–. *Recreations:* singing, horse racing, opera, labradors, late 19th century African history. *Address:* Blundell House, Blundell's Avenue, Tiverton, Devon EX16 4DL. *T:* Tiverton (01884) 252543. *Club:* East India.

LEIGH, Prof. Leonard Herschel; Professor of Criminal Law in the University of London, at the London School of Economics and Political Science, since 1982; *b* 19 Sept. 1935; *s* of Leonard William and Lillian Mavis Leigh; *m* 1960, Jill Diane Gale; one *s* one *d*. *Educ:* Univ. of Alberta (BA, LLB); Univ. of London (PhD 1966). Admitted to Bar: Alberta, 1959; NW Territories, 1961; Inner Temple, 1993. Private practice, Province of Alberta, 1958–60; Dept of Justice, Canada, 1960–62; London School of Economics: Asst Lectr in Law, 1964–65; Lectr, 1965–71; Reader, 1971–82. Vis. Prof., Queen's Univ., Kingston, Ont, 1973–74; British Council Lecturer: Univ. of Strasbourg, 1978; National Univ. of Mexico, 1980; UN Asia and Far East Inst., Tokyo, 1986; South India, 1989, 1991. Mem. Canadian Govt Securities Regulation Task Force, 1974–78; UK Convenor, Université de l'Europe Steering Cttee, 1987–90; Chm., English Nat. Section, 1988–, Mem., Conseil de Direction, 1989–, Internat. Assoc. of Penal Law. Mem., Exec. Cttee, Canada-UK Colloquia, 1993–. Member, Council of Europe Training Missions: Hungary, 1990; Poland, 1991; Albania, 1992; Mem., Wkg Party on Reform of Russian Penal Law, 1994–95. *Publications:* The Criminal Liability of Corporations in English Law, 1969; (jtly) Northey and Leigh's Introduction to Company Law, 1970, 4th edn 1987; Police Powers in England and Wales, 1975, 2nd edn 1986; Economic Crime in Europe, 1980; (jtly) The Companies Act 1981, 1981; (jtly) The Management of the Prosecution Process in Denmark, Sweden and the Netherlands, 1981; The Control of Commercial Fraud, 1982; Strict and Vicarious Liability, 1982; (jtly) A Guide to the Financial Services Act, 1986; articles in British, European, Amer. and Canadian jls. *Recreations:* music, walking. *Address:* London School of Economics and Political Science, Houghton Street, WC2A 2AE. *T:* 0171–405 7686; (chambers) 2 Pump Court, Temple, EC4. *T:* 0171–353 5597.

LEIGH, Mike, OBE 1993; dramatist; theatre and film director; *b* 20 Feb. 1943; *s* of late Alfred Abraham Leigh, MRCS, LRCP and of Phyllis Pauline Leigh (*née* Cousin); *m* 1973, Alison Steadman; two *s*. *Educ:* North Grecian Street County Primary Sch.; Salford Grammar Sch.; RADA; Camberwell Sch. of Arts and Crafts; Central Sch. of Art and Design (Theatre Design Dept); London Film Sch. Sometime actor, incl. Victoria Theatre, Stoke-on-Trent, 1966; Assoc. Dir, Midlands Arts Centre for Young People, 1965–66; Asst Dir, RSC, 1967–68; Drama Lectr, Sedgley Park and De La Salle Colls, Manchester, 1968–69; Lectr, London Film Sch., 1970–73. Arts Council of GB: Member: Drama Panel, 1975–77; Dirs' Working Party and Specialist Allocations Bd, 1976–84; Member: Accreditation Panel, Nat. Council for Drama Trng, 1978–91; Gen. Adv. Council, IBA, 1980–82. NFT Retrospective, 1979; BBC TV Retrospective (incl. Arena: Mike Leigh Making Plays), 1982. Hon. MA Salford, 1991. George Devine Award, 1973. Productions of own plays and films; *stage plays:* The Box Play, 1965, My Parents Have Gone To Carlisle, The Last Crusade Of The Five Little Nuns, 1966, Midlands Arts Centre; Nenaa, RSC Studio, Stratford-upon-Avon, 1967; Individual Fruit Pies, E15 Acting Sch., 1968; Down Here And Up There, Royal Ct Th. Upstairs, 1968; Big Basil, 1968, Glum Victoria And The Lad With Specs, Manchester Youth Theatre, 1969; Epilogue, Manchester, 1969; Bleak Moments, Open Space, 1970; A Rancid Pong, Basement, 1971; Wholesome Glory, Dick Whittington and his Cat, Royal Ct Th. Upstairs, 1973; The Jaws of Death, Traverse, Edinburgh Fest., 1973; Babies Grow Old, Other Place, 1974, ICA, 1975; The Silent Majority, Bush, 1974; Abigail's Party, Hampstead, 1977; Ecstasy, Hampstead, 1979; Goose-Pimples, Hampstead, Garrick, 1981 (Standard Best Comedy Award); Smelling a Rat, Hampstead, 1988; Greek Tragedy, Sydney, 1989, Edinburgh Fest. and Theatre Royal, Stratford East, 1990; It's A Great Big Shame!, Theatre Royal, Stratford East, 1993. *BBC radio play:* Too Much Of A Good Thing, 1979; *feature films:* Bleak Moments, 1971 (Golden Hugo, Chicago Film Fest., 1972; Golden Leopard, Locarno Film Fest., 1972); High Hopes, 1989 (Critics' Award, Venice Film Fest., 1988; Evening Standard Peter Sellers Comedy Award, 1989); Life is Sweet, 1991; Naked, 1993 (Best Dir, Cannes Film Festival, 1993); *BBC TV plays and films:* A Mug's Game, 1972; Hard Labour, 1973; The Permissive Society, Afternoon, A Light Snack, Probation, Old Chums, The Birth Of The 2001 FA Cup Final Goalie, 1975; Nuts in May, Knock For Knock, 1976; The Kiss Of Death, Abigail's Party, 1977; Who's Who, 1978; Grown-Ups, 1980; Home Sweet Home, 1982; Four Days In July, 1984; *Channel Four films:* Meantime, 1983; The Short and Curlies, 1987. *Relevant publication:* The Improvised Play: the work of Mike Leigh, by Paul Clements, 1983. *Address:* c/o Peters, Fraser & Dunlop, 503 The Chambers, Chelsea Harbour, Lots Road, SW10 0XF.

LEIGH, Peter William John, FRICS; chartered surveyor and property consultant; *b* 29 June 1929; *s* of John Charles Leigh and Dorothy Grace Leigh; *m* 1956, Mary Frances (*née* Smith); two *s* one *d*. *Educ:* Harrow Weald County Grammar Sch.; Coll. of Estate Management (ext.). National Service, Royal Signals, 1947–49. Private surveying practice, 1949–53; Valuation Asst, Mddx CC, 1953–60; Commercial Estates Officer, Bracknell Develt Corp., 1960–66; sen. appts, Valuation and Estates Dept, GLC, 1966–81; Dir of Valuation and Estates, GLC, 1981–84; Dir of Property Services, Royal County of Berks, 1984–88. Member: Gen. Council, RICS, 1984–86 (Mem., Gen. Practice Divl Council, 1993–); Govt Property Adv. Gp, 1984–88. Exec. Mem., Local Authority Valuers Assoc. (formerly Assoc. of Local Authority Valuers and Estate Surveyors), 1981–88. Editor, Old Wealden Newsletter, 1978–. *Recreations:* exploring Cornwall, drawing, gardening (therapy). *Address:* 41 Sandy Lane, Wokingham, Berks RG11 4SS. *T:* Wokingham (01734) 782732.

LEIGH, Sir Richard (Henry), 3rd Bt *cr* 1918, of Altrincham, Cheshire; *b* 11 Nov. 1936; *s* of Eric Leigh (*d* 1982), 2nd *s* of Sir John Leigh, 1st Bt, and his 1st wife, Joan Lane Fitzgerald (*d* 1973), *e d* of M. C. L. Freer, South Africa; *S* uncle, 1992; *m* 1st, 1962, Barbro Anna Elizabeth (marr. diss. 1977), *e d* of late Stig Carl Sebastian Tham, Sweden; 2nd, 1977, Cherie Rosalind, *e d* D. D. Dale, Cherval, France and *widow* of Alan Reece, RMS. *Educ:* England and Switzerland. *Recreations:* fishing, gardening. *Heir:* step *b* Christopher John Leigh [*b* 6 April 1941; *m* 1963, Gillian Ismay, *o d* of W. K. Lowe; one *s* one *d*]. *Address:* Trythall Vean, Madron, Cornwall TR20 8SY. *T:* Penzance (01736) 66606; 0171–794 9203.

LEIGH-PEMBERTON, family name of **Baron Kingsdown**.

LEIGH-PEMBERTON, John, AFC 1945; artist painter; *b* 18 Oct. 1911; *s* of Cyril Leigh-Pemberton and Mary Evelyn Megaw; *m* 1948, Doreen Beatrice Townshend-Webster (*d* 1992). *Educ:* Eton. Studied Art, London, 1928–31. Past Member Royal Institute of Painters in Oils and other Societies. Served 1940–45 with RAF as Flying Instructor. Series of pictures for Coldstream Guards, 1950. Festival Almanack, 1951, for Messrs Whitbread; Royal Progress, 1953, for Shell Mex & BP Ltd. Works in public and private collections, UK and America; decorations for ships: City of York, City of Exeter, Britannic, Caledonia, Corfu, Carthage, Kenya, Uganda. Many series of paintings, chiefly of natural history subjects, for Midland Bank Ltd. *Publications:* A Book of Garden Flowers, 1960; A Book of Butterflies, Moths and other Insects, 1963; British Wildlife, Rarities and Introductions, 1966; Garden Birds, 1967; Sea and Estuary Birds, 1967; Heath and Woodland Birds, 1968; Vanishing Wild Animals of the World, 1968; Pond and River Birds, 1969; African Mammals, 1969; Australian Mammals, 1970; North American Mammals, 1970; Birds of Prey, 1970; European Mammals, 1971; Asian Mammals, 1971; South American Mammals, 1972; Sea and Air Mammals, 1972; Wild Life in Britain, 1972; Disappearing Mammals, 1973; Ducks and Swans, 1973; Lions and Tigers, 1974; Baby Animals, 1974; Song Birds, 1974; Leaves, 1974; Big Animals, 1975; Apes and Monkeys, 1975; Reptiles, 1976; Seals and Whales, 1976; Butterflies and Moths, 1978; Hedges, 1979; Birds of Britain and Northern Europe, 1979; Bears and Pandas, 1979. *Address:* 5 Roehampton Gate, Roehampton, SW15 5JR. *T:* 0181–876 3332.

LEIGHTON OF ST MELLONS, 2nd Baron, *cr* 1962; **John Leighton Seager;** Bt 1952; *b* 11 Jan. 1922; *er s* of 1st Baron Leighton of St Mellons, CBE, JP, and Marjorie (*d* 1992), *d* of William Henry Gimson, Breconshire; *S* father, 1963; *m* 1st, 1953, Elizabeth Rosita (*d* 1979), *o d* of late Henry Hopgood, Cardiff; two *s* one *d* (and one *d* decd); 2nd, 1982, Ruth Elizabeth Hopwood. *Educ:* Caldicott Sch.; The Leys Sch., Cambridge. Formerly Partner, Probity Industrial Maintenance Services. Past Chm., Bristol Channel Shipowners Assoc. *Heir:* *s* Hon. Robert William Henry Leighton Seager, *b* 28 Sept. 1955. *Address:* 24 Clwyd, Northcliffe, Penarth CF64 1DZ.

LEIGHTON, Leonard Horace; Under Secretary, Department of Energy, 1974–80; *b* 7 Oct. 1920; *e s* of Leonard and Pearl Leighton, Bermuda; *m* 1945, Mary Burrowes; two *s*. *Educ:* Rossall Sch.; Magdalen Coll., Oxford (MA). FInstF. Royal Engrs, 1940–46; Nat. Coal Bd, 1950–62; Min. of Power, 1962–67; Min. of Technology, 1967–70; Dept of Trade and Industry, 1970–74. *Publications:* papers in various technical jls. *Address:* Hither Mickley, Lower Grinsty Lane, Callow Hill, Worcs B97 5PJ.

LEIGHTON, Sir Michael (John Bryan), 11th Bt, *cr* 1693; *b* 8 March 1935; *o s* of Colonel Sir Richard Tihel Leighton, 10th Bt, and Kathleen Irene Linda (*d* 1993), *o d* of Major A. E. Lees, Rowton Castle, Shrewsbury; *S* father 1957; *m* 1st, 1974 (marr. diss. 1980); 2nd, 1991, Diana Mary Gamble; one *d*. *Educ:* Stowe; Tabley House Agricultural Sch.; Cirencester Coll. *Address:* Loton Park, Shrewsbury, Salop SY5 9AJ.

LEIGHTON WILLIAMS, John; *see* Williams.

LEINSTER, 8th Duke of, *cr* 1766; **Gerald FitzGerald;** Baron of Offaly, 1205; Earl of Kildare, 1316; Viscount Leinster (Great Britain), 1747; Marquess of Kildare, 1761; Earl of Offaly, 1761; Baron Kildare, 1870; Premier Duke, Marquess, and Earl, of Ireland; Major late 5th Royal Inniskilling Dragoon Guards; *b* 27 May 1914; *o s* of 7th Duke of Leinster and May (*d* 1935), *d* of late Jesse Etheridge; *S* father, 1976; *m* 1st, 1936, Joane (who obtained a divorce, 1946), *e d* of late Major McMorrough Kavanagh, MC, Borris House, Co. Carlow; two *d*; 2nd, 1946, Anne Eustace Smith; two *s*. *Educ:* Eton; Sandhurst. *Heir:* *s* Marquess of Kildare, *qv*. *Recreations:* fishing, shooting. *Address:* Kilkea House, Ramsden, Chipping Norton, Oxfordshire OX7 3BA.

LEISER, Helen; Head of Industrial Relations Policy, Department of Trade and Industry, since 1995; *b* 3 July 1947; *d* of George and Audrey Leiser. *Educ:* Twickenham County Grammar Sch.; LSE (BScEcon). Economic Dept, TUC, 1968–73; Employment Dept, 1974; seconded to Cabinet Office, Machinery of Govt Div., 1983–85; Asst Sec., HSE, 1986–93; seconded to Dept of Energy, Offshore Safety Directorate, 1991; Dir of Business Develt and Mem., Exec. Bd, Employment Service, 1993; Head, Industrial Relations Div., Dept of Employment, 1994. *Recreations:* reading, travel, gardening, keeping fit. *Address:* Department of Trade and Industry, Caxton House, Tothill Street, SW1H 9NF.

LEISHMAN, Frederick John, CVO 1957; MBE 1944; *b* 21 Jan. 1919; *s* of Alexander Leishman and Freda Mabel (*née* Hood); *m* 1945, Frances Webb, Evanston, Illinois, USA; two *d*. *Educ:* Oundle; Corpus Christi, Cambridge. Served RE, 1940–46, and with Military Government, Germany, 1945–46; Regular Commission, 1945; resigned 1946. Joined Foreign Service, 1946; FO, 1946–48; Copenhagen, 1948–51; CSSB, 1951; Asst Private Sec. to Foreign Sec., 1951–53; First Sec., Washington, 1953–58; First Sec. and Head of Chancery, Teheran, 1959–61; Counsellor, 1961; HM Consul-General, Hamburg, 1961–62; FO, 1962–63. Dir, Hill Samuel & Co. Ltd, 1965–80; Dep. Chm. and Chief Exec., Hill Samuel Gp (SA) Ltd, 1969–72; Partner and Chm., Hill Samuel & Co. oHG, Germany, 1975–77; Dir and Exec. Vice-Pres., Saehan Merchant Banking Corp., Seoul, 1977–80. Vice-Pres., The Friends of the Bowes Museum, 1992– (Chm., 1985–90). FRSA. *Recreations:* golf, fishing, hill walking. *Address:* Saltoun House, Cotherstone, Barnard Castle, Co. Durham DL12 9PF. *T:* Teesdale (01833) 650671. *Clubs:* Hawks (Cambridge); Cambridge University Rugby Union Football; London Scottish Football; Barnard Castle Rugby (Pres.); Royal Ashdown Forest Golf, Barnard Castle Golf.

LEITCH, David Alexander; Under Secretary, Social Work Services Group, Scottish Education Department, 1983–89; *b* 4 April 1931; *s* of Alexander and Eileen Leitch; *m* 1954, Marie (*née* Tain); two *s* one *d*. *Educ:* St Mungo's Acad., Glasgow. Min. of Supply, 1948–58; Dept of Agriculture and Fisheries for Scotland: Asst Principal, 1959; Principal, 1963; Asst Sec., 1971; Asst Sec., Local Govt Finance, Scottish Office (Central Services), 1976–81, Under Sec., 1981–83. Part-time Mem., Scottish Legal Aid Bd, 1989–. *Recreations:* climbing, hill-walking. *Address:* 3 The Glebe, Cramond, Edinburgh EH4 6NW.

LEITCH, Sir George, KCB 1975 (CB 1963); OBE 1945; retired; *b* 5 June 1915; *er s* of late James Simpson and Margaret Leitch; *m* 1942, Edith Marjorie Maughan; one *d*. *Educ:* Wallsend Grammar Sch.; King's Coll., University of Durham. Research and teaching in mathematics, 1937–39. War Service in Army (from TA), 1939–46 (despatches, OBE): Lieut-Colonel in charge of Operational Research in Eastern, then Fourteenth Army, 1943–45; Brigadier (Dep. Scientific Adviser, War Office), 1945–46; entered Civil Service, as Principal, 1947; Ministry of Supply, 1947–59 (Under-Secretary, 1959); War Office, 1959–64; Ministry of Defence: Asst Under-Secretary of State, 1964–65; Dep. Under-Sec. of State, 1965–72; Procurement Executive, MoD: Controller (Policy), 1971–72; 2nd Permanent Sec., 1972–74; Chief Exec. (Permanent Sec.), 1974–75; Chm., Short Brothers Ltd, 1976–83. Chm., Adv. Cttee on Trunk Rd Assessment, 1977–80. Commonwealth Fund Fellow, 1953–54. Hon. DSc Durham, 1946. *Address:* 10 Elmfield Road, Gosforth, Newcastle upon Tyne NE3 4AY. *T:* Tyneside (0191) 2846559.

LEITCH, William Andrew, CB 1963; Law Reform Consultant, Government of Northern Ireland, 1973–78; Examiner of Statutory Rules, Northern Ireland Assembly, 1974–78, retired; *b* 16 July 1915; *e s* of Andrew Leitch, MD, DPH, Castlederg, Co. Tyrone, and May, *d* of W. H. Todd, JP, Fyfin, Strabane, Co. Tyrone; *m* 1939, Edna Margaret, *d* of David McIlvennan, Solicitor, Belfast; one *s* two *d*. *Educ:* Methodist Coll., Belfast; Queen's Univ., Belfast; London Univ. (LLB). Admitted Solicitor, NI, 1937; Asst Solicitors Dept, Ministry of Finance, NI, 1937–43; Asst Parly Draftsman, 1944–56; First Parly Draftsman, 1956–74. Hon. LLM, Queen's Univ., Belfast, 1967. *Publications:* A Handbook on the Administration of Estates Act (NI), 1955, 1957; (jointly) A Commentary on the Interpretation Act (Northern Ireland) 1954, 1955; articles in various legal publications. *Recreations:* fishing, golf, reading. *Address:* 53 Kensington Road, Belfast BT5 6NL. *T:* Belfast (01232) 794784.

LEITH, family name of **Baron Burgh.**

LEITH, Sir Andrew George F.; *see* Forbes-Leith.

LEITH, Prudence Margaret, (Mrs Rayne Kruger), OBE 1989; Managing Director, Prudence Leith Ltd (parent company of the Leith's Group), since 1972; *b* 18 Feb. 1940; *d* of late Sam Leith and of Margaret Inglis; *m* Rayne Kruger; one *s* one *d*. *Educ:* Hayward's Heath, Sussex; St Mary's, Johannesburg; Cape Town Univ.; Sorbonne, Paris; Cordon Bleu, London. French studies at Sorbonne, and preliminary cooking apprenticeship with French families; Cordon Bleu sch. course; small outside catering service from bedsitter in London, 1960–65; started Leith's Good Food (commercial catering co.), 1965, and Leith's (restaurant), 1969 (Michelin star, 1994); Cookery Corresp., Daily Mail, 1969–73; opened Leith's Sch. of Food and Wine, 1975; added Leith's Farm, 1976; Cookery Corresp., Sunday Express, 1976–80; Cookery Editor, 1980–85, Columnist, 1986–90, The Guardian. Board Member: British Transport Hotels, 1977–83; Halifax (formerly Leeds Permanent) BS, 1992–; pt-time Mem., BRB, 1980–85. Member: Food from Britain Council, 1983–86; Leisure Industries EDC, NEDO, 1986–90; Nat. Trng Task Force, 1989–90; NCVQ, 1992–; Bd, UK Skills, 1993–. Chm., Restaurateurs' Assoc. of GB, 1990–; Mem. Council, Museum of Modern Art, Oxford, 1984–90. Governor: Ashridge Management Coll., 1992–; City Technology Coll., 1994–. FRSA 1984–90 (Mem. Council, 1992–; Chm., 1995–); FCGI 1992. Business Woman of the Year, 1990. *Publications:* Leith's All-Party Cook Book, 1969; Parkinson's Pie (in aid of World Wild Life Fund), 1972; Cooking For Friends, 1978; The Best of Prue Leith, 1979; (with J. B. Reynaud) Leith's Cookery Course (3–part paperback), 1979–80, (comp. hardback with C. Waldegrave), 1980; The Cook's Handbook, 1981; Prue Leith's Pocket Book of Dinner Parties, 1983; Dinner Parties, 1984; (with Polly Tyrer) Entertaining with Style, 1986; Confident Cooking (52 issue part-work), 1989–90; (with Caroline Waldegrave): Leith's Cookery School, 1985; Leith's Cookery Bible, 1991; Leith's Complete Christmas, 1992; Leith's Book of Baking, 1993; Leith's Vegetarian Cookery, 1993. *Recreations:* riding, tennis, walking, old cookbooks and kitchen antiques. *Address:* 94 Kensington Park Road, W11 2PN. *T:* 0171–221 5282.

LEITH-BUCHANAN, Sir Charles (Alexander James), 7th Bt *cr* 1775; President, United Business Machines Inc., Alexandria, Va, since 1978; *b* 1 Sept. 1939; *s* of John Wellesley MacDonald Leith-Buchanan (*g s* of 4th Bt) (*d* 1956) and Jane Elizabeth McNicol (*d* 1955), *d* of Ronald McNicol; *S* cousin, 1973; *m* 1962, Mary Anne Kelly (marr. diss. 1987); one *s* one *d*; *m* 1988, Janice J., *d* of Robert Granger Jenkins. *Heir: s* Gordon Kelly McNicol Leith-Buchanan, *b* 18 Oct. 1974. *Address:* 7510 Clifton Road, Clifton, VA 22024, USA.

LEITHEAD, James Douglas; *b* 4 Oct. 1911; *s* of late William Leithead, Berwick-on-Tweed; *m* 1936, Alice (*d* 1989), *d* of late Thomas Wylie, Stirling, Scotland; one *s*. *Educ:* Bradford Grammar Sch. Accountant, 1927–32; ACA 1932; FCA 1960; Chartered Accountant, 1932–39. Lecturer Bradford Technical Coll., 1934–39; Secretarial Assistant, Midland (Amalgamated) District (Coal Mines) Scheme, 1939–42; Ministry of Supply, 1942–45; BoT, 1945–64; HM Diplomatic Service, 1965–68; BoT, later DTI, 1968–72, retired. British Trade Commissioner: Australia, 1950–63; New Zealand, 1963–67. Vice-Pres., W Australian Branch of Royal Commonwealth Soc., 1957–63. *Recreation:* chess. *Address:* 48 Eaton Road, Appleton, Oxon OX13 5JH.

LELLO, Walter Barrington, (Barry); Deputy Director, North-West Region, Department of Trade and Industry, 1988–91; *b* 29 Sept. 1931; *o s* of Walter Joseph Lello and Louisa (*née* McGarrigle); *m* 1959, Margaret, *o d* of Alexander and Alice McGregor. *Educ:* Liverpool Institute High School. Nat. Service, RN, 1950–52. Open Exec. Comp. to Civil Service, 1949; Min. of Supply, later Aviation, 1952–64; Asst British Civil Aviation Rep., Far East, Hong Kong, 1964–67; BoT, later Dept of Trade, 1967–71; Civil Air Attaché, Middle East, Beirut, 1971–76; DTI, 1976–78; Dir Gen., Saudi-British Economic Co-operation Office, Riyadh, 1978–81; seconded to British Electricity International as Dir, Middle East Ops, 1981–83; DTI, 1983; Commercial Counsellor, Cairo, 1984–88. *Recreations:* mountaineering, reading, theatre, furniture restoration. *Address:* 15 Long Meadow, Gayton, Wirral, Merseyside L60 8QQ.

LE MARCHANT, Sir Francis (Arthur), 6th Bt *cr* 1841, of Chobham Place, Surrey; *b* 6 Oct. 1939; *s* of Sir Denis Le Marchant, 5th Bt and of Elizabeth Rowena, *y d* of late Arthur Hovenden Worth; *S* father, 1987. *Educ:* Gordonstoun; Royal Academy Schools. *Heir: cousin* Michael Le Marchant [*b* 28 July 1937; *m* 1st, 1963, Philippa Nancy (marr. diss.), *er d* of late R. B. Denby; two *s* two *d*; 2nd, 1981, Sandra Elisabeth Champion (*née* Kirby)]. *Address:* c/o Midland Bank, 88 Westgate, Grantham, Lincs NG31 6LF.

LE MARECHAL, Robert Norford, CB 1994; Deputy Comptroller and Auditor General, National Audit Office, since 1989; *b* 29 May 1939; *s* of late Reginald Le Marechal and of Margaret Le Marechal; *m* 1963, Linda Mary (*née* Williams); two *d*. *Educ:* Tauntons School, Southampton. Joined Exchequer and Audit Dept, 1957; Nat. Service, RAEC, 1958–60; Senior Auditor, Exchequer and Audit Dept, 1971; Chief Auditor, 1976; Dep. Dir of Audit, 1980; Dir of Audit, 1983; Dir of Policy and Planning, 1984–86, Asst Auditor General, 1986–89, Nat. Audit Office. *Recreations:* reading, gardening. *Address:* 62 Woodcote Hurst, Epsom, Surrey KT18 7DT. *T:* Epsom (0372) 721291.

LE MASURIER, Sir Robert (Hugh), Kt 1966; DSC 1942; Bailiff of Jersey, 1962–74; *b* 29 Dec. 1913; *s* of William Smythe Le Masurier and Mabel Harriet Briard; *m* 1941, Helen Sophia Sheringham; one *s* two *d*. *Educ:* Victoria Coll., Jersey. MA 1935; BCL 1936. Sub-Lieut RNVR, 1939; Lieut RNVR, 1943; Lieut-Commander RNVR, 1944. Solicitor-General, Jersey, 1955; Attorney-General, Jersey, 1958. *Recreations:* sailing, carpentry. *Address:* Flat 8, Oaklands, Mont de la Rosière, St Saviour, Jersey JE2 7XL. *T:* Jersey (01534) 865234. *Clubs:* St Helier Yacht, United (Jersey).

LEMIEUX, Prof. Raymond Urgel, CC (Canada) 1994 (OC 1968); FRS 1967; Professor of Organic Chemistry, University of Alberta, 1961–80, University Professor, 1980–85, now Emeritus; *b* 16 June 1920; *s* of Octave Lemieux; *m* 1948, Virginia Marie McConaghie; one *s* five *d* (and one *s* decd). *Educ:* Edmonton, Alberta. BSc Hons (Chem.) Alta, 1943; PhD (Chem.) McGill, 1946. Research Fellow, Ohio State Univ., 1947; Asst Professor, Saskatchewan Univ., 1948–49; Senior Research Officer, National Research Council, Canada, 1949–54; Member, 1976–81; Professor, Ottawa Univ., 1954–61. Pres., Chem. Inst. of Canada, 1984–85. Rhône-Poulenc Lectr, RSC, 1989. FRSC 1955. Hon. Mem., Canadian Soc. for Chemistry, 1986; Hon. Fellow, CIC, 1992. Hon. DSc: New Brunswick Univ., 1967; Laval Univ., 1970; Univ. de Provence, 1973; Univ. of Ottawa, 1975; Waterloo Univ., 1980; Meml Univ., Newfoundland, 1981; Quebec, 1982; Queen's Univ., Kingston, Ont, 1983; McGill, 1984; McMaster, 1986; Sherbrooke, 1986; Alberta, 1991; Hon. LLD: Calgary, 1979; Saskatchewan, 1993; Hon. PhD Stockholm, 1988. Chem. Inst. of Canada Medal, 1964; C. S. Hudson Award, Amer. Chem. Soc., 1966; W. N. Haworth Medal, Chem. Soc., 1978; Izaak Walton Killam Award, Canada Council, 1981; Diplôme d'Honneur, Groupe Français des Glucides, 1981; Sir Frederick Haultain Prize, Alberta, 1982; Tischler Award, Harvard Univ., 1983; Medal of Honor, CMA, 1985; Gairdner Foundn Internat. Award in Medical Science, 1985; LeSueur Award, SCI, 1989; King Faisal Internat. Prize for Science, 1990; Alberta Order of Excellence, 1990; Canada Gold Medal for Science and Engrg, 1991; E.C. Manning Nat. Award of Distinction, 1992; Medal of Honour, Pharmaceutical Manufacturers Assoc. of Canada Health Res. Foundn, 1992; Albert Einstein World Award of Sci., 1992; Alberta Sci. and Technol. Foundn Award, Alberta Pioneer, 1993; Great Canadian Award, 1993. Eponymous lectures inaugurated at Ottawa Univ., 1972, and Alberta Univ., 1987; R.U. Lemieux Award for Organic Chm., Canadian Soc. for Chem., inaug. 1992. *Publications:* over 200 research papers mainly in area of carbohydrate chemistry in Canadian Journal of Chemistry, etc. *Recreations:* golf, curling, fishing. *Address:* 7602, 119th Street, Edmonton, Alberta T6G 1W3, Canada. *T:* (403) 4365167. *Clubs:* University of Alberta Faculty (Edmonton); Lake Edith Golf (Jasper).

LEMKIN, James Anthony, CBE 1986; Consultant, Field Fisher Waterhouse, Solicitors, 1990–91 (Senior Partner, 1985–90); *b* 21 Dec. 1926; *s* of late William Lemkin, CBE, and Rachel Irene (*née* Faith); *m* 1960, Joan Dorothy Anne Casserley, FFARCS, MRCPsych; two *s* two *d*. *Educ:* Charterhouse; Merton Coll., Oxford (MA). Admitted solicitor, 1953; RN, 1945–47. Greater London Council: Additional Mem., 1970–73, Mem. for Hillingdon, Uxbridge, 1973–86; Chm., Legal and Parly Cttee, 1977–78; Chm., Scrutiny Cttee, 1978–81; Cons. spokesman on police, 1981–82; Opposition Chief Whip, 1982–86. Contested: (C and NL) Chesterfield, 1959; (L) Cheltenham, 1964. Chm., Bow Gp, 1952, 1956, 1957 (Founder Chm., Crossbow, 1957–60); Vice-Chm., Soc. of Cons. Lawyers, 1990–92. Member: N London Hosp. Management Cttee, 1971–74; NW Thames RHA, 1980–84; Royal Marsden Hosp. SHA, 1982–89; Appeal Cttee, Cancer Res. Campaign, 1967–81; Chm., Barnet FPC, 1985–90. Governor: Westfield Coll., London Univ., 1970–83; Commonwealth Inst., 1985–92. Trustee, Whitechapel Art Gall., 1983–93. Co-founder, Africa Confidential, 1960. High Sheriff, Gtr London, 1992–93. *Publication:* (ed) Race and Power, 1956. *Recreation:* umpiring cricket. *Address:* 4 Frognal Close, NW3 6YB. *T:* 0171–435 6499. *Clubs:* Athenæum, Carlton.

LEMLEY, Jack Kenneth; Chairman and Chief Executive Officer, American Ecology Corporation, Houston, Texas; *b* 2 Jan. 1935; *s* of Kenneth Clyde Lemley and Dorothy Whitsitte; *m* 1st, 1961, Georgia Marshall (marr. diss. 1978); two *s* one *d*; 2nd, 1983, Pamela (*née* Hroza). *Educ:* Coeur d'Alene High Sch., Idaho; Univ. of Idaho (BA Architecture 1960). Asst Project Engineer, Guy F. Atkinson Co., 1960–69; Pres., Healthcare, 1969–70; Manager, Indust. and Power Construction Div., Guy F. Atkinson Co., 1971–77; Sen. Vice-Pres., Constr. Div., Morrison-Knudsen Co., 1977–87; Pres. and Chief Exec., Blount Construction Gp, 1987–88; Management Consultant, Lemley & Associates, 1988–89; Chief Exec. Officer, Transmanche-Link, Channel tunnel contractors, 1989. *Publications:* numerous papers on underground construction projects and international tunnelling. *Recreations:* snow ski-ing, sailing, white water rafting, reading. *Address:* 1508 N 13th Street, Boise, ID 83702, USA. *T:* (208) 3455226; 2045 Table Rock Road, Boise, Idaho, ID 83712, USA. *T:* (208) 3839253. *Club:* Arid (Boise, Idaho).

LEMMON, David Hector; writer; *b* 4 April 1931; *s* of Frederick Robert Lemmon and Sophie Elizabeth Lemmon (*née* Beadle); *m* 1958, (Jean) Valerie Fletcher; two *s*. *Educ:* Southgate Grammar Sch.; Coll. of St Mark and St John, Chelsea. Teacher's Cert., 1953; BA Hons London 1968. ACP 1968. Shell Mex & BP Co., 1947–49; RAF, 1949–51; Master, Bound's Green Sch., 1953–57; Ankara Coll., Turkey, 1957–60 (Dir, Amer. Little Theatre, 1958–59); Head of English: Kingsbury High Sch., Warwicks, 1960–63; Torells Girls Sch., Thurrock, 1963–68; Nicholas Sch., Basildon, 1968–73 (and Dir of Studies, 1973–83); full-time writer, 1983–. Examnr, Advanced Level Theatre Studies Practical, 1980–93. Mem. Editl Bd, Cricket World, 1991–92. (Jtly) J. M. Kilburn Meml Award, Cricket Writer of the Year, 1994. *Publications:* Summer of Success, 1980; Great One-Day Cricket Matches, 1982, 1984; Tich Freeman, 1982; Wisden Book of Cricket Quotations, 1, 1982, 2, 1990; The Book of One-Day Internationals, 1983; Johnny Won't Hit Today, 1983; The Great Wicket-Keepers, 1984; Percy Chapman, 1985; Ken McEwan, 1985; (with Ted Dexter) A Walk to the Wicket, 1984; (ed) Cricket Heroes, 1984; (with Ken Kelly) Cricket Reflections, 1985; Cricket Mercenaries, 1987; (with Mike Marshall) The Official History of Essex CCC, 1987; The Crisis of Captaincy, 1988; One-Day Cricket, 1988; The Official History of Middlesex CCC, 1988, of Worcestershire CCC, 1989, of Surrey CCC, 1989; (with Chris Cowdrey) Know Your Sport—Cricket, 1989; British Theatre Yearbook, 1989, 2nd edn 1990, then Benson and Hedges British Theatre Yearbook, annually 1992; Len Hutton, a Pictorial Biography, 1990; Cricket's Champion Counties, 1991; The Cricketing Greigs, 1991; The Guinness Book of Test Cricket Captains, 1992; For Love of the Game, 1993; The Book of Essex Cricketers, 1994; Pelham Cricket Year, then Benson and Hedges Cricket Year, annually 1979–. *Recreations:* work—theatre, Arsenal FC and sport; music, literature, art, people, entertaining. *Address:* 26 Leigh Road, Leigh-on-Sea, Essex SS9 1LD. *T:* Southend-on-Sea (01702) 79640. *Clubs:* MCC, Cricket Writers'; Essex County Cricket.

LEMMON, Rt. Rev. George Colborne; *see* Fredericton, Bishop of.

LEMON, Sir (Richard) Dawnay, Kt 1970; CBE 1958; QPM 1964; Chief Constable of Kent, 1962–74; *b* 1912; *o s* of late Lieut-Colonel F. J. Lemon, CBE, DSO, and of Mrs Laura Lemon; *m* 1939, Sylvia Marie Kentish; one *s* one *d* (and one *d* decd). *Educ:* Uppingham Sch.; RMC, Sandhurst. Joined West Yorks Regt, 1932; retired 1934. Metropolitan Police, 1934–37; Leicestershire Constabulary, 1937–39; Chief Constable of East Riding of Yorkshire, 1939–42; Chief Constable of Hampshire and Isle of Wight, 1942–62. *Recreations:* cricket, golf, shooting. *Address:* Rosecroft, Ringwould, Deal, Kent CT14 8HR. *T:* Deal (01304) 367554. *Clubs:* Royal Yacht Squadron (Cowes (hon.)); Royal St Georges Golf (Sandwich).

LENG, Christopher Anthony William, OBE; Vice Lord-Lieutenant, Tweeddale, since 1994; *b* 5 April 1922; *s* of Douglas Christopher Leng and Marcia Mary Leng (*née* Maxwell Stuart); *m* 1953, Patricia Lillywhite; two *s* two *d. Educ:* Downside Sch.; Hertford Coll., Oxford (MA); Royal Agricl Coll. (MRAC). Royal Armoured Corps, 1940–43; Special Ops Executive, 1943–46. Overseas Develt Corp., 1947–50; farmer, 1952–91. *Recreations:* gardening, fishing, reading. *Address:* Juniper Bank, Walkerburn, Peeblesshire EH43 6DE. *T:* Walkerburn (01896) 870230. *Club:* Special Forces.

LENG, Gen. Sir Peter (John Hall), KCB 1978 (CB 1975); MBE 1962; MC 1945; Master-General of the Ordnance, 1981–83, retired; *b* 9 May 1925; *s* of J. Leng; *m* 1st, Virginia Rosemary Pearson (marr. diss. 1981); three *s* two *d*; 2nd, 1981, Mrs Flavia Tower, *d* of late Gen. Sir Frederick Browning and Lady Browning (Dame Daphne du Maurier, DBE). *Educ:* Bradfield Coll. Served War of 1939–45: commissioned in Scots Guards, 1944; Guards Armoured Div., Germany (MC). Various post-war appts; Guards Independent Parachute Company, 1949–51; commanded: 3rd Bn Royal Anglian Regt, in Berlin, United Kingdom and Aden, 1964–66; 24th Airportable Bde, 1968–70; Dep. Military Sec., Min. of Defence, 1971–73; Comdr Land Forces, N Ireland, 1973–75; Dir, Mil. Operations, MoD, 1975–78; Comdr 1 (Br) Corps, 1978–80. Colonel Commandant: RAVC, 1976–83; RMP, 1976–83. Fund Raising Dir, Jubilee Sailing Trust, 1984–85. Chm., Racecourse Assoc., 1985–89. Patron, Natural Therapeutic and Osteopathic Soc., 1989–93. *Recreations:* fishing, gardening. *Address:* c/o Barclays Bank, 1 Brompton Road, SW3 1EB. *Club:* Naval and Military.

See also V. H. A. Elliot.

LENG, Virginia Helen Antoinette; *see* Elliot, V. H. A.

LENIHAN, Brian Joseph; Teachta Dala (TD) for Dublin West, Parliament of Ireland, since 1981 (TD for Roscommon/Leitrim, 1961–73), for Dublin (West County), 1977–81); *b* 17 Nov. 1930; *s* of Patrick Lenihan (TD Longford-Westmeath, 1965–70); *m* 1958, Ann Devine; four *s* one *d. Educ:* St Mary's Coll. (Marist Brothers), Athlone; University Coll., Dublin. Member: Roscommon CC, 1955–61; Seanad Eireann (FF), 1957–61 and (as Leader in Seanad, Fianna Fáil), 1973–77; Parly Sec. to Minister for Lands, 1961–64; Minister for: Justice, 1964–68; Educn, 1968–69; Transport and Power, 1969–73; Foreign Affairs, 1973; Fisheries and Forestry, 1977–79; Foreign Affairs, 1979–81; Agriculture, 1982; Foreign Affairs, 1987–89; Defence, 1989–90; Tánaiste (Dep. Prime Minister), 1987–90; Chm., All Party Foreign Affairs Cttee, 1993–. Mem., European Parlt, 1973–77. Dep. Leader, Fianna Fáil Party, 1983–. Contested (FF), Presidency of Ireland, 1990. *Publication:* For the Record, 1991. *Address:* Leinster House, Dublin 2, Eire.

LENNARD, Rev. Sir Hugh Dacre B.; *see* Barrett-Lennard.

LENNIE, Douglas; *b* 30 March 1910, *e s* of Magnus S. Lennie; *m* 1941, Rhona Young Ponsonby; two *s. Educ:* Berkhamsted Sch., Guy's Hospital, LDS, RCS, 1934; Northwestern University, Chicago, DDS, 1938. Served War of 1939–45, Temporary Surg. Lt-Comdr (D) RNVR; formerly Surgeon Dentist to Queen Mary. *Address:* 72 Chiltley Way, Liphook, Hants GU30 7HE.

LENNON, Prof. (George) Gordon; retired gynæcologist; Professor Emeritus, University of Western Australia, Perth, 1974; *b* 7 Oct. 1911; *s* of late J. Lennon; *m* 1940, Barbara Brynhild (*née* Buckle); two *s. Educ:* Aberdeen Academy; Aberdeen Univ. MB, ChB Aberdeen, 1934; served in hospital posts in Aberdeen, Glasgow, London, Birmingham; MRCOG 1939; FRCOG 1952; MMSA 1943; ChM (Hons) Aberdeen, 1945. Served War of 1939–45, Sqdn-Ldr in charge of Surgical Div., RAFVR, 1942–46. First Asst, Nuffield Dept of Obstetrics and Gynæcology, Radcliffe Infirmary (University of Oxford), 1946–51; Prof. of Obstetrics and Gynæcology, Univ. of Bristol, 1951–67; Dean, Faculty of Med., Univ. of WA, Perth, 1967–74. Visiting Professor: Iraq and Turkey, 1956; South Africa and Uganda, 1958; Iran, 1965. *Publications:* Diagnosis in Clinical Obstetrics; articles in British Medical Journal, Proceedings of the Royal Society of Medicine, Journal of Obstetrics and Gynæcology of the British Empire, etc. *Recreation:* golf. *Address:* 3 Brouncker House, Canon's Court, Church Street, Melksham, Wilts SN12 6UR. *T:* Melksham (01225) 700291.

LENNOX; *see* Gordon-Lennox and Gordon Lennox.

LENNOX, Lionel Patrick Madill; Registrar of the Province and Diocese of York, and Registrar of the Convocation of York, since 1987; *b* 5 April 1949; *s* of Rev. James Lennox and Mrs May Lennox; *m* 1979, Barbara Helen Firth; two *s* one *d. Educ:* St John's Sch., Leatherhead; Univ. of Birmingham (LLB). Admitted Solicitor, 1973; Ecclesiastical Notary, 1987; Notary Public, 1992. Solicitor in private practice, 1973–81; Asst Legal Advr to Gen. Synod, 1981–87. Secretary: Archbishop of Canterbury's Gp on Affinity, 1982–84; Legal Adv. Commn, Gen. Synod of C of E, 1986–. Sec., Yorks Mus. of Farming, 1991–94. Trustee, Yorks Historic Churches Trust, 1988–. *Address:* 1 Peckitt Street, York YO1 1SG. *T:* York (01904) 623487.

LENNOX, Robert Smith, CBE 1978; JP; Lord Provost of Aberdeen, 1967–70 and 1975–77; *b* 8 June 1909; *m* 1963, Evelyn Margaret; no *c. Educ:* St Clement Sch., Aberdeen. Hon. LLD Aberdeen, 1970. JP Aberdeen. *Address:* 7 Gillespie Crescent, Ashgrove, Aberdeen AB2 5AX. *T:* Aberdeen (01224) 483862.

LENNOX-BOYD, family name of **Viscount Boyd of Merton.**

LENNOX-BOYD, Hon. Sir Mark (Alexander), Kt 1994; MP (C) Morecambe and Lunesdale, since 1983 (Morecambe and Lonsdale, 1979–83); *b* 4 May 1943; 3rd *s* of 1st Viscount Boyd of Merton, CH, PC and of Lady Patricia Guinness, 2nd *d* of 2nd Earl of Iveagh, KG, CB, CMG, FRS; *m* 1974, Arabella Lacloche; one *d. Educ:* Eton Coll.; Christ Church, Oxford. Called to the Bar, Inner Temple, 1968. Parliamentary Private Secretary: to Sec. of State for Energy, 1981–83; to the Chancellor of the Exchequer, 1983–84; Asst Govt Whip, 1984–86; a Lord Comr of HM Treasury (Govt Whip), 1986–88; PPS to Prime Minister, 1988–90; Parly Under-Sec. of State, FCO, 1990–94. *Recreation:* travel. *Address:* House of Commons, SW1A 0AA. *Clubs:* White's, Pratt's, Beefsteak.

LEON, Sir John (Ronald), 4th Bt, *cr* 1911; actor (stage name, **John Standing**); *b* 16 Aug. 1934; *er s* of 3rd Bt and late Kay Hammond; *S* father, 1964; *m* 1961, Jill (marr. diss. 1972), *d* of Jack Melford; one *s*; *m* 1984, Sarah, *d* of Bryan Forbes, *qv*; one *s* two *d. Educ:* Eton. Late 2nd Lt, KRRC. *Plays include:* Darling Buds of May, Saville, 1959; leading man, season, Bristol Old Vic, 1960; The Irregular Verb to Love, Criterion, 1961; Norman, Duchess, 1963; So Much to Remember, Vaudeville, 1963; The Three Sisters, Oxford Playhouse, 1964; See How They Run, Vaudeville, 1964; Seasons at Chichester Theatre, 1966, 1967; The Importance of Being Earnest, Haymarket 1968; Ring Round the Moon, Haymarket, 1968; The Alchemist, and Arms and the Man, Chichester, 1970; Popkiss, Globe, 1972; A Sense of Detachment, Royal Court, 1972; Private Lives, Queen's and Globe, 1973, NY and tour of USA, 1974; Jingo, Aldwych, 1975; Plunder, The Philanderer, NT, 1978; Close of Play, NT, 1979; Tonight at 8.30, Lyric, 1981; The Biko Inquest, Riverside, 1984; Rough Crossing, National, 1984; Hay Fever, Albery, 1992. *Films:* The Wild and the Willing, 1962; Iron Maiden, 1962; King Rat, 1964; Walk, Don't Run, 1965; Zee and Co., 1973; The Eagle has Landed, 1976; The Class of Miss MacMichael, 1977; The Legacy, 1977; The Elephant Man, 1979; The Sea Wolves, 1980; (TV film) The Young Visiters, 1984; Nightflyers. Television appearances incl.: for British TV: Arms and the Man; The First Churchills; Charley's Aunt; Rogue Male; The Sinking of HMS Victoria; Home and Beauty; Tinker, Tailor, Soldier, Spy; The Other 'Arf; Old Boy Network; Tonight at 8.30; Count of Solar; for American TV: Lime Street; Hotel; Flap Jack Floozie; Visitors; Murphy's Law; The Endless Game; Murder She Wrote; LA Law; Windmills of the Gods. *Recreation:* painting. *Heir: s* Alexander John Leon, *b* 3 May 1965. *Address:* c/o James Sharkey, 21 Golden Square, W1R 3AG; c/o Agency for Performing Arts, 9000 Sunset Boulevard, Los Angeles, Calif., USA.

LEONARD, Brian Henry; Regional Director, Government Office for the South West; *b* 6 Jan. 1948; *s* of William Henry Leonard and Bertha Florence Leonard (*née* Thomas); *m* 1975, Margaret Meade-King; two *s. Educ:* Dr Challoner's Grammar Sch., Amersham; LSE (BSc Econ 1969). Heal & Son, 1969–73; Price Commn, 1973–74; Department of the Environment, 1974–: Circle 33 Housing Trust, 1982–83; Fellow, Hubert H. Humphrey Inst., Minneapolis, 1987–88; Regl Dir, N Reg., 1993–94, SW, 1994, DoE and Dept of Transport. *Recreations:* friends, games, pottering about. *Address:* The Pithay, Bristol BS1 2NQ. *Club:* MCC.

LEONARD, David John; Hon. Mr Justice Leonard, TD 1974; Judge, Supreme Court of Hong Kong, since 1991; *b* 18 Sept. 1937; *s* of Jeremiah Leonard and Rosaleen Oonagh Leonard (*née* Mellett); *m* 1966, Frances Helen Good; two *s. Educ:* Hendon Grammar Sch.; Magdalene Coll., Cambridge (MA). FCIArb 1995. Admitted solicitor, 1967; admitted solicitor and barrister, Victoria, Australia, 1982. Solicitors' Dept, New Scotland Yard, 1966–71; Batten & Co., Solicitors, Yeovil, 1971–77; Hong Kong: Permanent Magistrate, 1977–81; Dist Judge, 1981–91. Chm., Judicial Studies Bd, Hong Kong, 1994–. Served in TA: HAC, RA, Intelligence Corps, 1960–77, Maj. (retd) Intelligence Corps; Royal Hong Kong Regt (Volunteers), 1977–91, Maj. (retd). *Recreations:* travel, reading, walking. *Address:* Supreme Court, Hong Kong. *Clubs:* Cavalry and Guards; Hong Kong (Hong Kong).

LEONARD, Dick; *see* Leonard, Richard Lawrence.

LEONARD, Rev. and Rt. Hon. Graham Douglas, KCVO 1991; PC 1981; *b* 8 May 1921; *s* of late Rev. Douglas Leonard, MA; *m* 1943, Vivien Priscilla, *d* of late M. B. R. Swann, MD, Fellow of Gonville and Caius Coll., Cambridge; two *s. Educ:* Monkton Combe Sch.; Balliol Coll., Oxford (Hon. Fellow, 1986). Hon. Sch. Nat. Science, shortened course. BA 1943, MA 1947. Served War, 1941–45; Captain, Oxford and Bucks Light Infantry; Army Operational Research Group (Ministry of Supply), 1944–45. Westcott House, Cambridge, 1946–47. Deacon 1947, Priest 1948; Vicar of Ardleigh, Essex, 1952–55; Director of Religious Education, Diocese of St Albans, 1955–58; Hon. Canon of St Albans, 1955–57; Canon Residentiary, 1957–58; Canon Emeritus, 1958; General Secretary, Nat. Society, and Secretary, C of E Schools Council, 1958–62; Archdeacon of Hampstead, Exam. Chaplain to Bishop of London, and Rector of St Andrew Undershaft with St Mary Axe, City of London, 1962–64; Bishop Suffragan of Willesden, 1964–73; Bishop of Truro, 1973–81; Bishop of London, 1981–91; received into RC Ch. and ordained priest *sub conditione*, 1994. Dean of the Chapels Royal, 1981–91; Prelate of the Order of the British Empire, 1981–91; Prelate of the Imperial Soc. of Knights Bachelor, 1986–91. Chairman: C of E Cttee for Social Work and the Social Services, 1967–76; C of E Board for Social Responsibility, 1976–83; Churches Main Cttee, 1981–91; C of E Board of Education, 1983–88; BBC and IBA Central Religious Adv. Cttee, 1984–89. Member: Churches Unity Commn, 1977–78, Consultant 1978; Churches Council for Covenanting, 1978–82; PCFC, 1989–93. An Anglican Mem., Commn for Anglican Orthodox Jt Doctrinal Discussions, 1974–81; one of Archbp of Canterbury's Counsellors on Foreign Relations, 1974–81. Elected delegate, 5th Assembly WCC, Nairobi, 1975. House of Lords, 1977–91. Select Preacher to University of Oxford, 1968, 1984 and 1989; Hensley Henson Lectr, Univ. of Oxford, 1991–92. Lectures: John Findley Green Foundn, Fulton, Missouri, 1987; Earl Mountbatten Meml, Cambridge Union, 1990. Freeman, City of London, 1970. President: Middlesex Assoc., 1970–73; Corporation of SS Mary and Nicholas (Woodard Schools), 1973–78, Hon. Fellow, 1978. Fellow, Sion Coll., 1991–. Member Court of City Univ., 1981–91. Hon. DD: Episcopal Seminary, Kentucky, 1974; Westminster Coll., Fulton, Missouri, 1987; Hon. DCnL Nashotah, USA, 1983; STD Siena Coll., USA, 1984; Hon. LLD, Simon Greenleaf Sch. of Law, USA, 1987; Hon. DLitt CNAA, 1989. Episcopal Canon of Jerusalem, 1982–91; Hon. Bencher, Middle Temple, 1982. *Publications:* Growing into Union (Jt author), 1970; The Gospel is for Everyone, 1971; God Alive: Priorities in Pastoral Theology, 1981; Firmly I Believe and Truly, 1985; Life in Christ, 1986; (jtly) Let God be God, 1990; contrib. to: The Christian Religion Explained, 1960; Retreats Today, 1962; Communicating the Faith, 1969; A Critique of Eucharistic Agreement, 1975; Is Christianity Credible?, 1981; The Price of Peace, 1983; The Cross and the Bomb, 1983; Unholy Warfare, 1983; Synod of Westminster, 1986; After the Deluge, 1987; (ed) Faith and the Future, 1988; Tradition and Unity, 1991; Families for the Future, 1991. *Recreations:* reading, especially biographies; music. *Address:* 25 Woodlands Road, Witney, Oxon OX8 6DR. *Club:* Garrick.

LEONARD, Sir (Hamilton) John, Kt 1981; a Judge of the High Court, Queen's Bench Division, 1981–93; Presiding Judge, Wales and Chester Circuit, 1982–86; *b* 28 April 1926; *s* of late Arthur and Jean Leonard, Poole, Dorset; *m* 1948, Doreen Enid, *yr d* of late Lt-Col Sidney James Parker, OBE, and May Florence Parker, Sanderstead, Surrey; one *s* one *d. Educ:* Dean Close Sch., Cheltenham; Brasenose Coll., Oxford (MA). Coldstream Guards (Captain), 1944–47. Called to Bar, Inner Temple, 1951; Master of the Bench, 1977; practised on South-Eastern Circuit; 2nd Junior Prosecuting Counsel to the Crown at Central Criminal Court, 1964–69; QC 1969; Dep. Chm., Surrey QS, 1969–71; Comr, CCC, 1969–71; a Recorder of the Crown Court, 1972–78; a Circuit Judge, 1978–81; Common Serjeant in the City of London, 1979–81. Member: General Council of the Bar, 1970–74, Senate, 1971–74, Senate of Four Inns and the Bar, 1974–77. Chm., Criminal Bar Assoc., 1975–77. Member: Home Sec.'s Adv. Bd on Restricted Patients, 1973–78; Deptl Cttee to Review Laws on Obscenity, Indecency and Censorship, 1977–79; Judicial Studies Bd, 1979–82. Mem. Council, Hurstpierpoint Coll., 1975–83; Gov., Dean Close Sch., Cheltenham, 1986–. Liveryman, Plaisterers' Co.; HM Lieutenant, City of London,

1980–81. *Recreations:* books, music, painting. *Address:* Royal Courts of Justice, WC2A 2LL. *Club:* Garrick.

LEONARD, Hugh, (John Keyes Byrne); playwright since 1959; Programme Director, Dublin Theatre Festival, since 1978; Literary Editor, Abbey Theatre, 1976–77; *b* 9 Nov. 1926; *m* 1955, Paule Jacquet; one *d*. *Educ:* Presentation College, Dun Laoghaire. Hon. DHL Rhode Island, 1980; Hon. DLitt TCD, 1988. *Stage plays:* The Big Birthday, 1956; A Leap in the Dark, 1957; Madigan's Lock, 1958; A Walk on the Water, 1960; The Passion of Peter Ginty, 1961; Stephen D, 1962; The Poker Session, and Dublin 1, 1963; The Saints Go Cycling In, 1965; Mick and Mick, 1966; The Quick and the Dead, 1967; The Au Pair Man, 1968; The Barracks, 1969; The Patrick Pearse Motel, 1971; Da, 1973; Thieves, 1973; Summer, 1974; Times of Wolves and Tigers, 1974; Irishmen, 1975; Time Was, 1976; A Life, 1977; Kill, 1982; Scorpions (3 stage plays), 1983; The Mask of Moriarty, 1985; Moving, 1991; Senna for Sonny, 1994; The Lily Lally Show, 1994; Chamber Music (2 plays), 1994; *adaptation:* Great Expectations, 1995. *TV plays:* Silent Song (Italia Award, 1967); The Last Campaign, 1978; The Ring and the Rose, 1978; A Life, 1986; Hunted Down, 1989; The Celadon Cup, 1993. *TV serials:* Nicholas Nickleby, 1977; London Belongs to Me, 1977; Wuthering Heights, 1978; Strumpet City, 1979; The Little World of Don Camillo, 1980; Good Behaviour, 1983; O'Neill, 1983; The Irish RM, 1985; Troubles, 1987; Parnell and the Englishwoman, 1991. *Films:* Herself Surprised, 1977; Da, 1988; Widows' Peak, 1994; Banjaxed, 1995. *Publications:* Home Before Night (autobiog.), 1979; Out After Dark (autobiog.), 1988; Parnell and the Englishwoman (novel), 1990; Rover and other cats (memoir), 1992; The Off-Off-Shore Island (novel), 1993; The Mogs (for children), 1995. *Recreations:* travel (esp. French canals and waterways), vintage films, lunch, dinner, friendships. *Address:* 6 Rossaun, Pilot View, Dalkey, Co. Dublin. *T:* Dublin 280–9590.

LEONARD, His Honour James Charles Beresford Whyte, MA Oxon; a Circuit Judge (formerly Deputy Chairman of Quarter Sessions, Inner London and Middlesex), 1965–79; Judge of the Mayor's and City of London Court, 1972–79; *b* 1905; *s* of Hon. J. W. Leonard, Middle Temple, KC (S Africa); *m* 1939, Barbara Helen (*d* 1989), *d* of late Capt. William Incledon-Webber; two *s* one *d*. *Educ:* Clifton Coll.; Christ Church, Oxford. Called to the Bar, Inner Temple, 1928, Bencher 1961. Served 1940–45, with RAF (Sqdn Ldr). Recorder of Walsall, Staffs, 1951–64; Junior Counsel to Ministry of Agriculture, Fisheries and Food, Forestry Commission and Tithe Redemption Commission, 1959–64; Deputy Chairman of QS: Co. of London, 1964–65; Oxfordshire, 1962–71. Chairman: Disciplinary Cttee, Pharmaceutical Soc. of GB, 1960–64; Adv. Cttee dealing with internment under Civil Authorities (Special Powers) Act (NI) 1962, April–Nov. 1972; Comr under Terrorism (N Ireland) Order 1972, 1972–74; Dep. Chm., Appeal Tribunal, 1974–75. *Address:* Cross Trees, Sutton Courtenay, Oxon OX14 4AD. *T:* Abingdon (01235) 848230.

See also Earl of Westmeath.

LEONARD, Hon. Sir John; *see* Leonard, Hon. Sir H. J.

LEONARD, Michael William, CVO 1984; BSc(Eng), FEng, FICE, MIMechE, FCIArb; Consultant; Founder Secretary, The Fellowship of Engineering, 1976–83; Founder Clerk to the Worshipful Company of Engineers, 1983–86; *b* 25 Dec. 1916; *e s* of late Frank Leonard and Marguerite Leonard (*née* Holborow); *m* 1945, Rosalinna Cushnir; three *s*. *Educ:* Haberdashers' Aske's; Pupilage in Mechanical Engineering, Messrs Fraser & Chalmers Ltd, Erith; University College London (Pres., Union Society, 1939). Civil Engineer, Mowlem Group of Companies, to 1968; Dir, later Chief Exec., Soil Mechanics Ltd; Dir, Soil Mechanics-Soletanche Ltd; Chm., Engineering Laboratory Equipment Ltd. Mem., BSI Code of Practice Cttee on Site Investigations; Mem., later Chm., Tip Safety Cttee (post Aberfan); Sec., Council of Engineering Institutions, 1969–82; Chm., BSI Code of Practice Cttee on Foundations; Member: Design Council Engineering Design, later Industrial, Adv. Cttee; DoI Cttee for Industrial Technologies. Parliamentary and Scientific Committee: Hon. Treasurer, 1984; Hon. Sec., 1987; Vice-Pres., 1990–; Mem. Council, 1991. Vice Pres., Fédération Européenne d'Associations Nationales d'Ingenieurs; Sec., Commonwealth Engineers' Council; Mem., Executive Cttee, World Fedn of Engineering Organizations (Vice-Pres., 1987–). Hon. Prof., Dept of Civil and Structural Engrg, Sheffield Univ., 1974. FEng 1983. *Publications:* papers and articles on Foundation and Geotechnical Engineering, and on Professional Engineering, for jls and confs. *Recreations:* touring, golf, fishing. *Address:* 5 Havelock Road, Croydon CR0 6QQ. *T:* 0181–654 4493. *Club:* Athenæum.

LEONARD, Richard Lawrence, (Dick Leonard); writer and political consultant; *b* 12 Dec. 1930; *s* of late Cyril Leonard, Pinner, Mddx, and Kate Leonard (*née* Whyte); *m* 1963, Irène, *d* of late Dr Ernst Heidelberger and Dr Gertrud Heidelberger, Bad Godesberg, Germany; one *s* one *d*. *Educ:* Ealing Grammar Sch.; Inst. of Education, London Univ.; Essex Univ. (MA). School teacher, 1953–55; Dep. Gen. Sec., Fabian Society, 1955–60; journalist and broadcaster, 1960–68; Sen. Research Fellow (Social Science Research Council), Essex Univ., 1968–70. Mem., Exec. Cttee, Fabian Soc., 1972–80 (Chm., 1977–78); Chm., Library Adv. Council, 1978–81. Trustee, Assoc. of London Housing Estates, 1973–78. Vis. Prof., Free Univ. of Brussels, 1988–. European Advr, Publishers Assoc., 1987–94; Sen. Advr, Centre for European Policy Studies, 1994–. Contested (Lab) Harrow W, 1955; MP (Lab) Romford, 1970–Feb. 1974; PPS to Rt Hon. Anthony Crosland, 1970–74; Mem., Speaker's Conf. on Electoral Law, 1972–74. Introduced Council Housing Bill, 1971; Life Peers Bill, 1973. Asst Editor, The Economist, 1974–85; Brussels and EC correspondent, The Observer, 1989–. *Publications:* Guide to the General Election, 1964; Elections in Britain, 1968; (ed jtly) The Backbencher and Parliament, 1972; Paying for Party Politics, 1975; BBC Guide to Parliament, 1979; (ed jtly) The Socialist Agenda, 1981; (jtly) World Atlas of Elections, 1986; Pocket Guide to the EEC, 1988; Elections in Britain Today, 1991; The Economist Guide to the European Community, 1992, 2nd edn 1994 (French, German, Spanish and Portuguese edns); Replacing the Lords, 1995; contrib.: Guardian, Financial Times, TLS, The Bulletin, Encounter and leading newspapers in USA, Canada, Japan, India, Australia and New Zealand. *Recreations:* walking, book-reviewing, family pursuits. *Address:* 32 rue des Bégonias, 1170 Brussels, Belgium. *T:* (2) 6602662. *Club:* Reform.

LEONTIEF, Prof. Wassily; Economist, New York University, since 1975 (Founder, 1978, Director, 1978–85, Institute for Economic Analysis; Member of Research Staff, since 1986); *b* Leningrad, Russia, 5 Aug. 1906; *s* of Wassily Leontief and Eugenia Leontief (*née* Bekker); *m* 1932, Estelle Helena Marks; one *d*. *Educ:* Univ. of Leningrad (Learned Economist, 1925; MA); Univ. of Berlin (PhD 1928). Research Associate, Inst. of World Econs, Univ. of Kiel, Germany, 1927–28; Economic Adviser to Chinese Govt, Nanking, 1928–29; Res. Associate, Nat. Bureau of Econ. Res., NY, 1931; Harvard University: Instr Economics, 1932–33; Asst Prof., 1933–39; Associate Prof., 1939–46; Prof. of Econs, 1946–53; Henry Lee Prof. of Pol. Econ., 1953–75; Sen. Fellow, Soc. of Fellows, 1956–75 (Chm., 1965–75); Dir, Harvard Economic Research Project, 1948–72; Guggenheim Fellow, 1940, 1950. Gen. Consultant: US Dept of Labor, 1941–47 and 1961–65; US Dept of Commerce, 1966–82; Office of Technology Assessment, 1980–; Econ. Consultant, Russian Econs Sub-Div., Office of Strategic Services, 1943–45; Consultant: UN Sec.-Gen.'s Consultative Gp of Econ. and Social Consequences of Disarmament, 1961–62; UN Develt Prog., 1980–; Mem., Exec. Bd, Science Adv. Council, Environmental Protection Agency, 1975–80. President: Amer. Econ. Assoc., 1970; Sect. F, BAAS, 1976; Mem., Nat. Acad. of Sciences, 1974; FAAAS 1977; Foreign Mem., USSR Acad. of Sciences, 1988; Mem., Soc. of the Optimate, Italian Cultural Inst., NY, 1989; Corr. Mem., Institut de France, 1968; Corr. FBA, 1970; Hon. MRIA, 1976. Dr *hc*: Brussels, 1962; York, 1967; Louvain, 1971; Paris (Sorbonne), 1972; Pennsylvania, 1976; Lancaster, 1976; Toulouse, Louisville, Vermont, Long Island, 1980; Karl Marx Univ., Budapest, 1981; Adelphi Coll., 1988; Cordoba, 1990; Hon. DHL Rensselaer Polytechnic Inst., 1988. Nobel Prize in Economic Science, 1973; Takemi Meml Award, Inst. of Seizon and Life Scis, Japan, 1991. Order of the Cherubim, Univ. of Pisa, 1953. Officier, Légion d'Honneur, 1968; Order of the Rising Sun, Japan, 1984; Commandeur des Arts et des Lettres, France, 1985. *Publications:* The Structure of the American Economy 1919–29, 1941, 2nd edn 1953; Studies in the Structure of the American Economy, 1953; Input-Output Economics, 1966, 2nd edn, 1986; Essays in Economics, vol. I 1966, vol. II 1977; The Future of the World Economy, 1977; (with F. Duchin) Military Spending: facts and figures, worldwide implications and future outlook, 1983; (jtly) The Future of Non-Fuel Minerals in the US and World Economy, 1983; (with F. Duchin) The Impact of Automation on Workers, 1986; contribs to learned jls. *Recreation:* fly fishing. *Address:* Institute for Economic Analysis, 269 Mercer Street, 2nd floor, New York, NY 10003, USA.

LEORO-FRANCO, Dr Galo; Gran Cruz, National Order Al Mérito of Ecuador, 1970; Minister of Foreign Affairs, Ecuador, since 1994; *s* of José Miguel Leoro and Albertina Franco de Leoro; *m* 1957, Aglae Monroy de Leoro; one *s* two *d*. *Educ:* Central Univ., Quito. Licenciado in Political and Soc. Scis, 1949; Dr in Jurisprudence, Faculty of Law, 1951. Third Sec., Washington, 1955–56, Second Sec., 1956–58; First Sec., Ministry of Foreign Affairs, 1960; Counsellor, Mexico, 1961, Chargé d'Affaires, 1962; Counsellor, Alternate Rep. of Ecuador to OAS, Washington, DC, 1962–64, Minister, 1964–68; Ambassador, 1968–; Chief Legal Advisor to Ministry of Foreign Affairs, 1969–70; Undersec. Gen., Ministry of Foreign Affairs, 1970–71; Ambassador to the Dominican Republic, 1971–72; Perm. Rep. of Ecuador to OAS, 1972–79; Advisor on Internat. Orgns, Ministry of Foreign Affairs, 1979–81; Advisor on Nat. Sovereignty, Ministry of Foreign Affairs, and Rep. of the Ministry in Nat. Congress, 1981–83; Ambassador to UK, 1983–84; Ambassador and Permanent Rep. to Office of UN, Geneva, 1984–91; Chief Legal Advr, Ministry of Foreign Affairs, 1991–92; Ambassador to Holy See, 1993–94. Chairman: OAS Permanent Council, 1972–78 (Chm. of several Cttees of OAS Council and Gen. Assembly); Cttee II, Special Commn for Study of Interamerican System, Economic Co-operation problems, Washington, DC, 1973–75; INTELSAT Panel of Jurisexperts, Washington, DC, 1983–85; Rapporteur, Interamerican Conf. for Revision of TIAR; elected mem., Interamerican Juridical Cttee, Rio de Janeiro, 1981–84, Vice-Chm., 1982–83, Chm., 1984–95; Conciliator, Internat. Center for Settlement of Investment Disputes, IMF, Washington, DC, 1986–; Ecuadorian Mem., National Gp of Arbiters, Internat. Court of Arbitration, The Hague, 1987. Representative of Ecuador at over 90 internat. conferences and Chm. of the Delegation at various of them. Gran Cruz: Iron Cross, Fed. Repub. of Germany, 1970; Order of Duarte, Sánchez and Mella, Dominican Repub., 1972; Order of the Sun, Perú, 1976; 1st Class, Order of Francisco de Miranda, Venezuela, 1976. *Publications:* contrib. Interamerican Law Year Book and Courses of Internat. Law of the OAS, Washington; various papers for Ecuadorean Year Book of Internat. Law. *Recreations:* chess, tennis. *Address:* Ministry of Foreign Affairs, Avenida 10 de Agosto y Carrión, Quito, Ecuador. *Club:* Quito Tennis and Golf.

LÉOTARD, François Gérard Marie; Minister of Defence, France, 1993–95; *b* Cannes, 26 March 1942; *s* of André Léotard and Antoinette (*née* Tomasi); *m* 1992, Isabelle Duret. *Educ:* Paris Law Univ.; Institut d'Etudes Politiques de Paris; Ecole Nationale d'Administration. Various appts in French admin, 1968–76; Mayor of Fréjus, 1977–; Mem., Nat. Assembly, 1978–86 and 1988–92; Minister of Culture and Communication, 1986–88; Mem., General Council, Var, 1980–88. Republican Party (Parti Républicain): Gen. Sec., 1982–89; Pres., 1989–90; Hon. Pres., 1990–95; Pres., 1995–. *Publications:* A Mots Découverts, 1987; Culture: les chemins de printemps, 1988; La Ville Aimée: mes chemins de Fréjus, 1989; Pendant la Crise, la Spectacle Continue, 1989; Adresse au Président des Républiques Françaises, 1991; Place de la République, 1992. *Address:* c/o Parti Républicain, 105 rue de l'Université, 75007 Paris, France.

LE POER, Baron; Richard John Beresford; *b* 19 Aug. 1987; *s* and *heir* of Earl of Tyrone, *qv*.

LE POER TRENCH, family name of **Earl of Clancarty.**

LE PORTZ, Yves; Comdr Légion d'Honneur 1978; Grand Officier de l'Ordre National du Mérite; French financial executive; Inspector-General of Finances, 1971; *b* Hennebont, 30 Aug. 1920; *m* 1946, Bernadette Champetier de Ribes; five *c*. *Educ:* Univ. de Paris à la Sorbonne; Ecole des Hautes Etudes Commerciales; Ecole Libre des Sciences Politiques. Attached to Inspection Générale des Finances, 1943; Directeur Adjoint du Cabinet, Président du Conseil, 1948–49; Sous-Directeur, then Chef de Service, Min. of Finance and Economic Affairs, 1949–51; Directeur du Cabinet: Sec. of State for Finance and Economic Affairs, 1951–52; Minister for Posts, Telegraphs and Telephones (PTT), 1952–55; Minister for Reconstruction and Housing, 1955–57; French Delegate to UN Economic and Social Council, 1957–58; Dir-Gén., Finance, Algeria, 1958–62; Administrateur-Gén., Development Bank of Algeria, 1959–62. European Investment Bank: Vice-Pres. and Vice-Chm., Bd of Dirs, 1962–70; Pres. and Chm. Bd of Dirs, 1970–84; Hon. Pres., 1984. Chairman: Commn des Opérations de Bourse, Paris, 1984–88; Investment Funds Supervisory Cttee, Principality of Monaco, 1988–. *Address:* 127 avenue de Wagram, 75017 Paris, France.

LEPPARD, Captain Keith André, CBE 1977; RN; Secretary, Institute of Brewing, 1977–90; Director Public Relations (Royal Navy), 1974–77; *b* 29 July 1924; *s* of Wilfred Ernest Leppard and Dora Gilmore Keith; *m* 1954, Betty Rachel Smith; one *s* one *d*. *Educ:* Purley Grammar Sch. MRAeS 1973; FBIM 1973; FSAE 1985. Entered RN, FAA pilot duties, 1943; Opnl Wartime Service, Fighter Pilot, N Atlantic/Indian Oceans, 1944–45; Fighter Pilot/Flying Instr, Aircraft Carriers and Air Stns, 1946–57; CO 807 Naval Air Sqdn (Aerobatic Display Team, Farnborough), 1958–59; Air Org./Flying Trng Staff appts, 1959–63; Comdr (Air), HMS Victorious, 1963–64; Jt Services Staff Coll., 1964–65; Dir, Naval Officer Appts (Air), 1965–67; Chief Staff Officer (Air), Flag Officer Naval Air Comd, 1967–69; Chief Staff Officer (Ops/Trng), Far East Fleet, 1969–71; CO, Royal Naval Air Stn, Yeovilton, and Flag Captain to Flag Officer Naval Air Comd, 1972–74. Naval ADC to the Queen, 1976–77. *Recreations:* country life, tennis, golf. *Address:* Little Holt, Kingsley Green, Haslemere, Surrey GU27 3LW. *T:* Haslemere (01428) 642797.

LEPPARD, Raymond John, CBE 1983; conductor, harpsichordist, composer; Music Director, Indianapolis Symphony Orchestra, since 1987; *b* 11 Aug. 1927; *s* of A. V. Leppard. *Educ:* Trinity Coll., Cambridge. Fellow of Trin. Coll., Cambridge, Univ. Lecturer in Music, 1958–68. Hon. Keeper of the Music, Fitzwilliam Museum, 1963–82.

Conductor: Covent Garden, Sadler's Wells, Glyndebourne, and abroad; Principal Conductor, BBC Northern Symphony Orchestra, 1972–80; Prin. Guest Conductor, St Louis SO, 1984–93. Hon. RAM 1972; Hon. GSM 1983; Hon. FRCM 1984. Hon. DLitt Univ. of Bath, 1972. Commendatore al Merito della Repúbblica Italiana, 1974. *Publications:* realisations of Monteverdi: Il Ballo delle Ingrate, 1958; L'Incoronazione di Poppea, 1962; L'Orfeo, 1965; Il Ritorno d'Ulisse, 1972; realisations of Francesco Cavalli: Messa Concertata, 1966; L'Ormindo, 1967; La Calisto, 1969; Magnificat, 1970; L'Egisto, 1974; L'Orione, 1983; realisation of Rameau's Dardanus, 1980; British Academy Italian Lecture, 1969, Procs Royal Musical Assoc. *Recreations:* music, theatre, books, friends. *Address:* c/o Colbert Artists Management, 111 West 57th Street, New York, NY 10019, USA.

LEPPING, Sir George (Geria Dennis), GCMG 1988; MBE 1981; Governor-General of the Solomon Islands, 1988–94; *b* 22 Nov. 1947; *e s* of Chief Dionisio Tanutanu, BEM and Regina Suluki; *m* 1972, Margaret Kwalea Teioli; two *s* four *d* (incl. twins) and one adopted *d. Educ:* St John's and St Peter's Primary Schs; King George VI Secondary Sch.; Agricl Coll., Vudal, PNG (Dip. Tropical Agric.); Reading Univ. (Dip. Agric.; MSc). Joined Solomon Is Public Service as Field Officer, Dept of Agric. and Rural Economy, 1968; Sen. Field Officer, then Under-Sec. (Agricl), Min. of Agric., 1979–80; Permanent Secretary: Min. of Home Affairs and Nat. Develt, 1981–84; Special Duties, as Project Dir, Rural Services Project (Develt), 1984–87; Min. of Finance, 1988. Sometime Dir, Chm. or Mem., various govt cos and authorities; Chm., Nat. Disaster Council, 1981–84. Pres., Solomon Is Amateur Athletics Union, 1970–73, 1981–82 (first Solomon Is athlete to win internat. sports medals). KStJ 1991. *Recreations:* reading, swimming, lawn tennis, snooker, snorkelling, high-speed boat driving, fishing. *Address:* Faisi Island, c/o Postal Agency, Nila, Shortland Island, Western Province, Solomon Islands.

LEPSCHY, Prof. Giulio Ciro, FBA 1987; Professor of Italian, University of Reading, since 1975; *b* 14 Jan. 1935; *s* of Emilio Lepschy and Sara Castelfranchi; *m* 1962, Anna Laura Momigliano. *Educ:* Univ. of Pisa (Dott. Lett.); Scuola Normale Superiore, Pisa (Dip. Lic. and Perf.). Lib. Doc., Italy. Research, 1957–64, at Univs of Zurich, Oxford, Paris, London, Reading; Lectr 1964, Reader 1967, Univ. of Reading. Mem. Council, Philological Soc., 1984–89, 1992–. Corr. Mem., Accademia della Crusca, 1991. Member editorial boards: The Italianist; Rivista di Grammatica Generativa; Rivista di Linguistica; Romance Philology; Spunti e Ricerche; Studi Linguistici e Semiologici. *Publications:* A Survey of Structural Linguistics, 1970, new edn 1982; (jtly) The Italian Language Today, 1977, 2nd edn 1988; Saggi di linguistica italiana, 1978; Intorno a Saussure, 1979; Mutamenti di prospettiva nella linguistica, 1981; Nuovi saggi di linguistica italiana, 1989; Sulla linguistica moderna, 1989; Storia della linguistica, 1990; La linguistica del Novecento, 1992; History of Linguistics, 1994; contribs to learned jls. *Address:* Department of Italian Studies, The University, Whiteknights, Reading RG6 2AA. *T:* Reading (01734) 316501.

LE QUESNE, Sir (Charles) Martin, KCMG 1974 (CMG 1963); HM Diplomatic Service, retired; *b* 10 June 1917; *s* of C. T. Le Quesne, QC; *m* 1948; three *s. Educ:* Shrewsbury; Exeter Coll., Oxford (Hon. Fellow, 1990). Served in Royal Artillery, 1940–45. Apptd HM Foreign Service, 1946; 2nd Sec. at HM Embassy, Baghdad, 1947–48; 1st Secretary: Foreign Office, 1948–51, HM Political Residency, Bahrain, 1951–54; attended course at NATO Defence Coll., Paris, 1954–55; HM Embassy, Rome, 1955–58; Foreign Office, 1958–60; apptd HM Chargé d'Affaires, Republic of Mali, 1960, subsequently Ambassador there, 1961–64; Foreign Office, 1964–68; Ambassador to Algeria, 1968–71; Dep. Under-Sec. of State, FCO, 1971–74; High Comr in Nigeria, 1974–76. Mem., States of Jersey, 1978–90 (Dep. for St Saviour's parish). Hon. Vice-Pres., Royal African Soc. Mem. Council, Southampton Univ. *Recreations:* gardening, books. *Address:* Beau Désert, St Saviour, Jersey, Channel Islands. *T:* Jersey (01534) 22076. *Clubs:* Reform (Chairman 1973–74), MCC; United (Jersey); Royal Channel Islands Yacht.

See also Sir J. G. Le Quesne, L. P. Le Quesne.

LE QUESNE, Sir (John) Godfray, Kt 1980; QC 1962; Judge of Courts of Appeal of Jersey and Guernsey, since 1964; a Recorder, since 1972; *b* 1924; 3rd *s* of late C. T. Le Quesne, QC; *m* 1963, Susan Mary Gill; two *s* one *d. Educ:* Shrewsbury Sch.; Exeter Coll., Oxford (MA). Pres. of Oxford Union, 1943. Called to Bar, Inner Temple, 1947; Master of the Bench, Inner Temple, 1969, Reader, 1988, Treasurer, 1989; admitted to bar of St Helena, 1959. Dep. Chm., Lincs (Kesteven) QS, 1963–71. Chm., Monopolies and Mergers Commn, 1975–87 (a part-time Mem., 1974–75). Chm. of Council, Regent's Park Coll., Oxford, 1958–87. *Publication:* Jersey and Whitehall in the Mid-Nineteenth Century, 1992. *Recreations:* music, walking. *Address:* 1 Crown Office Row, Temple, EC4Y 7HH. *T:* 0171–583 9292.

See also Sir C. M. Le Quesne, L. P. Le Quesne.

LE QUESNE, Prof. Leslie Philip, CBE 1984; DM, MCh, FRCS; Medical Administrator, Commonwealth Scholarship Commission, 1984–91; *b* 24 Aug. 1919; *s* of late C. T. Le Quesne, QC; *m* 1969, Pamela Margaret, *o d* of late Dr A. Fullerton, Batley, Yorks; two *s. Educ:* Rugby; Exeter Coll., Oxford; Middlesex Hosp. Med. Sch. Jun. Demonstrator, Path. and Anat., 1943–45; House Surgeon, Southend Hosp. and St Mark's Hosp., 1945–47; Appointments at Middlesex Hospital: Asst, Surgical Professorial Unit, 1947–52; Asst Dir, Dept of Surgical Studies, 1952–63; Surgeon, 1960–63; Prof. of Surgery, Med. Sch., and Dir, Dept of Surgical Studies, 1963–84; Dep. Vice-Chancellor and Dean, Fac. of Medicine, Univ. of London, 1980–84. Sir Arthur Sims Commonwealth Travelling Prof., 1975. Mem. GMC, 1979–84. Editor, Post Graduate Med. Jl, 1951–52. Arris and Gale Lectr, RCS, 1952; Baxter Lectr, Amer. Coll. Surgs, 1960. Mem., Ct of Examrs, RCS, 1971–77. Formerly Chm., Assoc. of Profs of Surgery; Pres., Surgical Res. Soc. Chm., The British Jl of Surgery. Hon. FRACS, 1975; Hon. FACS, 1982; Hon. Fellow RPMS, 1985. Moynihan Medal, 1953. *Publications:* medical articles and contribs to text books; Fluid Balance in Surgical Practice, 2nd edn, 1957. *Recreations:* fishing, reading. *Address:* 8 Eton Villas, NW3 4SX.

See also Sir C. M. Le Quesne, Sir J. G. Le Quesne.

LE QUESNE, Sir Martin; *see* Le Quesne, Sir C. M.

LEREGO, Michael John; QC 1995; *b* 6 May 1949; *s* of Leslie Ivor Lerego and late Gwendolen Frances Lerego; *m* 1972, Susan Northover; three *d* (one *s* decd). *Educ:* Manchester Grammar Sch.; Haberdashers' Aske's Sch., Elstree; Keble Coll., Oxford (Open Schol.; Dist. Law Mods 1968; Gibbs Prize in Law 1969; BA Jurisp. 1st Cl. 1970; BCL 1st Cl. 1971; MA Oxon 1978). Called to the Bar, Inner Temple, 1972; in practice, 1972–. Weekender, Queen's Coll., Oxford, 1972–78. Member: Jt Working Party of Law Soc. and Bar on Banking Law, 1987–91; Law Soc's Sub-Cttee on Banking Law, 1991–; an Arbitrator: Lloyd's Modified Arbitration Scheme, 1988–92; Lloyd's Arbitration Scheme, 1993–. Governor: Wroxham Sch., Potters Bar, 1985–. *Recreation:* watching sport. *Address:* Fountain Court, Temple, EC4Y 9DH. *T:* 0171–583 3335.

LE ROY LADURIE, Prof. Emmanuel Bernard; Officier de la Légion d'Honneur; Professor of History of Modern Civilisation, Collège de France, since 1973; General Administrator, Bibliothèque Nationale, since 1987; *b* 19 July 1929; *s* of Jacques Le Roy Ladurie and Léontine (*née* Dauger); *m* 1955, Madeleine Pupponi; one *s* one *d. Educ:* Univ. of Sorbonne (agrégé d'histoire); DèsL 1952. Teacher, Lycée de Montpellier, 1953–57; Res. Assistant, CNRS, 1957–60; Assistant, Faculté des Lettres de Montpellier, 1960–63; Asst Lectr, 1963, Dir of Studies, 1965–, Ecole Pratique des Hautes Etudes; Lectr, Faculté des Lettres de Paris, 1969; UER Prof. of Geography and Social Sci., Univ. de Paris VII, 1970–. Hon. FBA 1985. Hon. Dr: Michigan; Geneva; Leeds; Hull; Leicester; Hon. DLitt Oxford, 1993. *Publications:* Les Paysans du Languedoc, 1966; Histoire du climat depuis l'an mil, 1967; Le Territoire de l'historien, vol. 1 1973, vol. 2 1978; Montaillou: village occitan 1294–1324, 1975; (jtly) Histoire économique et sociale de la France, vol. 1 1450–1660, vol. 2 Paysannerie et Croissance, 1976; Le Carnaval de Romans (Prix Pierre Lafue), 1979; L'Argent, l'Amour et la Mort en pays d'Oc, 1980; (jtly) Inventaire des campagnes, 1980; (jtly) L'Histoire urbaine de la France, vol. 3, 1981; Parmi les historiens, 1983; Pierre Prion: scribe, 1987; L'Histoire de France: l'état royal 1460–1610, 1987; (ed) Monarchies, 1987; L'Ancien Régime, 1991; Le siècle des Platter, 1995. *Address:* Collège de France, 11 place Marcelin Berthelot, 75231 Paris cedex 05, France; (home) 88 rue d'Alleray, 75015 Paris, France.

LeROY-LEWIS, David Henry, FCA; Director, Touche, Remnant & Co., 1974–88 (Deputy Chairman, 1981–88); Chairman, Henry Ansbacher Holdings plc, 1982–88; *b* 14 June 1918; *er s* of late Stuyvesant Henry LeRoy-Lewis and late Bettye LeRoy-Lewis; *m* 1953, Cynthia Madeleine, *er d* of late Comdr John C. Boldero, DSC, RN (Retd); three *d. Educ:* Eton. FCA 1947. Chairman: TR North America Trust PLC (formerly Continental Union Trust Ltd) 1974–88 (Dir, 1948–88); R. P. Martin plc, 1981–85; Hill Martin, 1989–93; Director: TR Industrial & General Trust PLC, 1967–88; Akroyd & Smithers Ltd, 1970–81 (Chm., 1976–81); TR Trustees Corp. PLC, 1973–88; TR Energy PLC, 1981–88. Mem., 1961–81, a Dep. Chm., 1973–76, Stock Exchange Council. *Recreation:* fishing. *Address:* Stoke House, Stoke, Andover, Hants SP11 0NP. *T:* St Mary Bourne (01264) 738548. *Club:* MCC.

LESCHLY, Jan; Chief Executive, SmithKline Beecham, since 1994; *m* 1963, Lotte Engelbredt; four *s. Educ:* Coll. of Pharmacy and Sch. of Econ. and Business Admin., Copenhagen. Pharmaceutical industry, 1972–; Novo Industries A/S, Denmark, 1972–79; Squibb Corporation: joined 1979; Vice-Pres., Commercial Develt, 1979; US Pres., 1981; Gp Vice-Pres. and Dir, 1984; Exec. Vice-Pres., 1986; Pres. and Chief Operating Officer, 1988; Chm., SmithKline Beecham Pharmaceuticals, 1990. Chm., British Pharma Group; mem., pharm. assocs and educnl bodies. *Address:* SmithKline Beecham, One New Horizons Court, Brentford, Middx TW8 9EP. *T:* 0181–975 2600.

LESITER, Ven. Malcolm Leslie; Archdeacon of Bedford, since 1993; *b* 31 Jan. 1937; *m*; four *d. Educ:* Cranleigh Sch.; Selwyn Coll., Cambridge (BA 1961; MA 1965); Cuddeson Coll., Oxford. Ordained deacon, 1963, priest, 1964; Curate, Eastney, 1963–66; Curate, 1966–71, Team Vicar, 1971–73, St Paul, Hemel Hempstead; Vicar: All Saints, Leavesden, 1973–88; Radlett, 1988–93. RD, Watford, 1981–88. *Address:* 17 Lansdowne Road, Luton, Beds LU3 1EE. *T:* Luton (01582) 30722.

LESLIE, family name of **Earl of Rothes.**

LESLIE, Lord; James Malcolm David Leslie; *b* 4 June 1958; *s* and *heir* of 21st Earl of Rothes, *qv. Educ:* Eton. Graduated Parnham House, 1990. *Address:* Littlecroft, West Milton, Bridport, Dorset DT6 3SL.

LESLIE, Sir Alan; *see* Leslie, Sir C. A. B.

LESLIE, Ann Elizabeth Mary, (Mrs Michael Fletcher); journalist and broadcaster; *b* Pakistan; *d* of Norman Leslie and Theodora (*née* McDonald); *m* 1969, Michael Fletcher, one *d. Educ:* Presentation Convent, Matlock, Derbyshire; Convent of the Holy Child, Mayfield, Sussex; Lady Margaret Hall, Oxford (BA). Daily Express, 1962–67; freelance, 1967–: regular contributor to Daily Mail. Variety Club Women of the Year Award for journalism and broadcasting, 1981; British Press Awards Feature Writer of the Year, 1981, 1989; British Press Awards Commendation, 1980, 1983, 1985, 1987, 1991; Feature Writer of the Year Award, What the Papers Say, Granada Television, 1991. *Recreation:* family life. *Address:* c/o Daily Mail, Northcliffe House, 2 Derry Street, Kensington, W8 5TS. *T:* 0171–938 6000, *Fax:* 0171–937 3251.

LESLIE, Sir (Colin) Alan (Bettridge), Kt 1986; Commissioner, Foreign Compensation Commission, 1986–90; *b* 10 April 1922; *s* of Rupert Colin Leslie and Gladys Hannah Leslie (*née* Bettridge); *m* 1st, 1953, Anne Barbara (*née* Coates) (*d* 1982); two *d*; 2nd, 1983, Jean Margaret (Sally), widow of Dr Alan Cheatle. *Educ:* King Edward VII School, Lytham; Merton College, Oxford (MA Law). Solicitor. Commissioned, The Royal Scots Fusiliers, 1941–46. Legal practice, Stafford Clark & Co., Solicitors, 1948–60; Head of Legal Dept and Company Secretary, British Oxygen Co., later BOC International, then BOC Group, 1960–83. Law Society: Vice-Pres., 1984–85; Pres., 1985–86. Adjudicator, Immigration Appeals, 1990–94. *Recreation:* fishing. *Address:* Tile Barn Cottage, Alfriston, E Sussex BN26 5TT. *T:* Alfriston (01323) 870388; 36 Abingdon Road, W8 6AS. *T:* 0171–937 2874. *Club:* United Oxford & Cambridge University.

LESLIE, Rt. Rev. (Ernest) Kenneth, OBE 1972; *b* 14 May 1911; *s* of Rev. Ernest Thomas Leslie and Margaret Jane Leslie; *m* 1941, Isabel Daisy Wilson; two *s* one *d* (and one *s* decd). *Educ:* Trinity Gram. Sch., Kew, Vict.; Trinity Coll., University of Melbourne (BA). Aust. Coll. of Theology. ThL, 2nd Cl. 1933, Th Schol. 1951, 2nd Cl. 1952. Deacon, 1934; Priest, 1935; Asst Curate, Holy Trinity, Coburg, 1934–37; Priest-in-Charge, Tennant Creek, Dio. Carpentaria, 1937–38; Alice Springs with Tennant Creek, 1938–40; Rector of Christ Church, Darwin, 1940–44; Chaplain, AIF, 1942–45; Rector of Alice Springs with Tennant Creek, 1945–46; Vice-Warden, St John's Coll., Morpeth, NSW, 1947–52; Chap. Geelong Church of Eng. Gram. Sch., Timbertop Branch, 1953–58; Bishop of Bathurst, 1959–81. *Recreations:* walking, woodwork, cycling. *Address:* 54 Alcheringa Road, Kelso, NSW 2795, Australia.

LESLIE, Prof. Frank Matthews, JP; DSc; PhD; FRS 1995; FRSE; Professor of Mathematics, Strathclyde University, since 1982; *b* 8 March 1935; *s* of late William Ogilvy Leslie and Catherine Pitkethly Leslie (*née* Matthews); *m* 1965, Ellen Leitch Reoch; one *s* one *d. Educ:* Queen's Coll., Dundee, Univ. of St Andrews (BSc; DSc 1995); Manchester Univ. (PhD 1961). FRSE 1980. Asst Lectr in Maths, Manchester Univ., 1959–61; Res. Associate in Maths, MIT, 1961–62; Lectr in Maths, Newcastle Univ., 1962–68; Strathclyde University: Sen. Lectr, 1968–71; Reader, 1971–79; Personal Prof., 1979–82. Vis. Asst Prof. in Mechanics, Johns Hopkins Univ., 1966–67. Chm., Brit. Liquid Crystal Soc., 1987–91. JP Bearsden and Milngavie, 1984. Annual Award, Brit. Soc. Rheology, 1982; Mem., Johns Hopkins Soc. Scholars, 1982. *Publications:* res. papers in scientific jls mostly on theory of liquid crystals. *Recreations:* golf, hill-walking, gardening. *Address:* Department of Mathematics, Strathclyde University, Livingstone Tower, Richmond Street, Glasgow G1 1XH. *T:* 0141–552 4400.

LESLIE, James Bolton, AC 1993 (AO 1984); MC 1944; ED 1966; Chairman, Christies Australia Ltd, since 1990; director of companies; Chancellor, Deakin University, since 1987; *b* 27 Nov. 1922; *s* of Stuart Deacon Leslie and Dorothy Clare (*née* Murphy); *m* 1955, Alison Baker three *s* one *d. Educ:* Trinity Grammar Sch., Melbourne; Harvard Business Sch., Boston, USA. Served war, Australian Infantry, Pacific Theatre, 1941–46.

Mobil Oil Australia Ltd: joined, 1946; Manager, Fiji, 1947–50; various postings, Australia, 1950–59; Mobil Corp., New York, 1959–61; Gen. Manager, New South Wales, 1961–66; Director, Mobil Australia, 1966–68; Chm. and Chief Exec., Mobil New Zealand, 1968–72; Chairman: Mobil Australia and Pacific, 1972–80; Qantas Airways, 1980–89; Boral Ltd, 1991–94. Chm., Corps of Commissionaires Aust Ltd, 1991–; Dep. Chm., Equity Trustees, 1990–. *Recreations:* farming, horse breeding. *Address:* 42 Grey Street, East Melbourne, Victoria 3002, Australia. *T:* (3) 94196149. *Clubs:* Melbourne, Melbourne Cricket, Beefsteak, Victoria Racing (Melbourne).

LESLIE, Sir John (Norman Ide), 4th Bt *cr* 1876; *b* 6 Dec. 1916; *s* of Sir (John Randolph) Shane Leslie, 3rd Bt and Marjorie (*d* 1951), *y d* of Henry C. Ide, Vermont, USA; *S* father, 1971. *Educ:* Downside; Magdalene College, Cambridge (BA 1938). Captain, Irish Guards; served War of 1939–45 (prisoner-of-war). Kt of Honour and Devotion, SMO Malta, 1947; KCSG 1958. *Recreations:* ornithology, ecology. *Heir: b* Desmond Arthur Peter Leslie [*b* 29 June 1921; *m* 1st, 1945, Agnes Elizabeth, *o d* of late Rudolph Bernauer, Budapest; two *s* one *d*; 2nd, 1970, Helen Jennifer, *d* of late Lt-Col E. I. E. Strong; two *d*]. *Address:* Glaslough, Co. Monaghan, Ireland. *Clubs:* Travellers'; Circolo della Caccia (Rome).

LESLIE, Rt. Rev. Kenneth; *see* Leslie, Rt Rev. E. K.

LESLIE, (Percy) Theodore; retired British Aerospace engineer; *b* 19 Nov. 1915; *s* of Frank Harvey Leslie (*d* 1965) (*g g s* of 4th Bt), Christ's Hospital, and Amelia Caroline (*d* 1918), *d* of Alexander Russon; *heir* to the Leslie of Wardis and Findrassie baronetcy (*cr* 1625). *Educ:* London and privately. FSA Scot 1983. Freeman, City of London, 1978. Mem. Knightly Assoc. of St George (USA), 1983. *Recreations:* chess, gardening and visiting places of historic interest. *Address:* c/o National Westminster Bank, 5 Market Place, Kingston upon Thames, Surrey.

LESLIE, Sir Peter (Evelyn), Kt 1991; Chairman, Commonwealth Development Corporation, 1989–95; *b* 24 March 1931; *s* of late Patrick Holt Leslie, DSc and Evelyn (*née* de Berry); *m* 1975, Charlotte, former wife of W. N. Wenban-Smith, *qv* and *d* of Sir Edwin Chapman-Andrews, KCMG, OBE and of Lady Chapman-Andrews; two step *s* two step *d*. *Educ:* Dragon Sch., Oxford; Stowe Sch.; New Coll., Oxford (Exhibnr; MA). Commnd Argyll and Sutherland Highlanders, 1951; served 7th Bn (TA), 1952–56. Entered Barclays Bank DCO, 1955; served in Sudan, Algeria, Zaire, Kenya and the Bahamas, 1956–71; Gen. Manager, Barclays Bank and Barclays Bank Internat., 1973–81, Sen. Gen. Manager, 1981–84; Dir, 1980–91, Chief Gen. Man., 1985–87, Man. Dir, 1987–88, Dep. Chm., 1987–91, Barclays Bank plc. Dep. Chm., Midland Bank plc, 1991–92; Chm., NCM Credit Insurance Ltd, 1995–. Mem., Bd of Banking Supervision, Bank of England, 1989–94. Chm., Export Guarantees Adv. Council, 1987–92 (Mem., 1978–81, Dep. Chm., 1986–87); Mem., Matthews Cttee on ECGD, 1983. Chairman: Exec. Cttee, British Bankers Assoc., 1978–79; Cttee, London and Scottish Clearing Bankers, 1986–88; Overseas Develt Inst., 1988–. Member: Council for Ind. and Higher Educn, 1987–91; CARE Britain Bd, 1988–; Council, RIIA, 1991–; Ranfurly Liby Service, 1991–94. Chm. Council, Queen's Coll., London, 1989–94; Curator of Univ. Chest, Oxford, 1990–95; Chm., Audit Cttee, Oxford Univ., 1992–. Governor: Stowe Sch., 1983– (Chm., 1994–); National Inst. of Social Work, 1973–83. *Recreations:* natural history, historical research. *Address:* 153 Sutherland Avenue, W9 1ES.

LESLIE, Stephen Windsor; QC 1993; *b* 21 April 1947; *s* of Leslie Leonard Leslie and Celia Leslie (*née* Schulsinger); *m* 1st, 1974, Bridget Caroline Oldham (marr. diss. 1989); two *d*; 2nd, 1989, Amrit Kumari Mangra; one *s*. *Educ:* Brighton Coll.; King's Coll. London (LLB). Called to the Bar, Lincoln's Inn, 1971. *Publications:* articles in The Times and New Law Jl. *Recreations:* travelling, gardening, haggling for a bargain, the telephone. *Address:* 1 Crown Office Row, Temple, EC4Y 7HH. *T:* 0171–797 7111. *Clubs:* Carlton; Thunderers'.

LESLIE, Theodore; *see* Leslie, P. T.

LESLIE MELVILLE, family name of **Earl of Leven and Melville.**

LESOURNE, Jacques François; Officier de la Légion d'Honneur, 1993; Commandeur de l'ordre National de Mérite, 1981; Chevalier des Palmes Académiques, 1980; Directeur-gérant, Le Monde, 1991–94; Professor of Economics, Conservatoire National des Arts et Métiers, since 1974; *b* 26 Dec. 1928; *s* of André Lesourne and Simone Guille; *m* 1961, Odile Melin; one *s* two *d* (and one *s* decd). *Educ:* Ecole Polytechnique; Ecole Nationale Supérieure des Mines, Paris. Head, Econ. Dept, French Coal Mines, 1954–57; Directeur général, later Pres., Société d'Ingeniérie en Informatique, 1958–75; Dir, Interfutures Project, OECD, 1976–79. Pres., Internat. Fedn of OR Socs, 1986–88; Vice-President: Internat. Inst. for Applied Systems Analysis, 1973–79; Centre for European Policy Studies, 1987–; Member Council: Inst. of Management Science, 1976–79; Eur. Econ. Assoc., 1984–89. Harold Lander Prize, Canadian OR Soc., 1991. *Publications:* Technique économique et gestion industrielle, 1958 (Economic Technique and Industrial Management, 1962); Le Calcul économique, 1964; Du bon usage de l'étude économique dans l'entreprise, 1966; (jtly) Matière grise année O, 1970 (The Management Revolution, 1971); Le Calcul économique, théorie et applications, 1972 (Cost-Benefit Analysis and Economic Theory, 1975); Modèles économiques de croissance de l'entreprise, 1972; (jtly) Une Nouvelle industrie: la matière grise, 1973; Les Systèmes de destin, 1976; A Theory of the Individual for Economic Analysis, 1977; (jtly) L'Analyse des décisions d'aménagement regional, 1979; Demain la France dans le monde, 1980; Les Mille Sentiers de l'avenir, 1982 (World Perspectives—a European Assessment, 1982); (jtly) Facilitating Development in a Changing Third World, 1983; Soirs et lendemains de fête: journal d'un homme tranquille, 1981–84 (autobiog.), 1984; (jtly) La gestion des villes, analyse des décisions d'économie urbaine, 1985; (jtly) La Fin des habitudes, 1985; L'Entreprise et ses futurs, 1985; L'après-Communisme, de l'Atlantique à l'Oural, 1990 (After-communism, from the Atlantic to the Urals, 1991); L'economie de l'ordre et du désordre, 1991 (The Economics of Order and Disorder, 1992); Vérités et mensonges sur le chômage, 1995. *Recreation:* piano. *Address:* 52 rue de Vaugirard, 75006 Paris, France.

LESSELS, Norman, CBE 1993; Senior Partner, Chiene & Tait, CA, since 1993 (Partner, 1980–93); Chairman, Standard Life Assurance Co., since 1988 (Deputy Chairman, 1982–88); *b* 2 Sept. 1938; *s* of John Clark Lessels and Gertrude Margaret Ellen Lessels (*née* Jack); *m* 1st, 1960, Gillian Durward Lessels (*née* Clark) (*d* 1979); one *s* (and one *s* one *d* decd); 2nd, 1981, Christine Stevenson Lessels (*née* Hitchman). *Educ:* Melville Coll.; Edinburgh Acad. CA (Scotland) 1961. CA apprentice with Graham Smart & Annan, Edinburgh, 1955–60; with Thomson McLintock & Co., London, 1960–61; Partner, Wallace & Somerville, Edinburgh, merged with Whinney Murray & Co., 1969, latterly Ernst & Whinney, 1962–80. Director: Standard Life Assurance Co., 1978–; Scottish Eastern Investment Trust, 1980–; Bank of Scotland, 1988–; Cairn Energy, 1988– (Chm., 1991–); Havelock Europa, 1989– (Chm., 1993–); NWS Bank, 1989–; Robert Wiseman Dairies, 1994–. Pres., Inst. of Chartered Accountants of Scotland, 1987–88. *Recreations:* golf, bridge, music. *Address:* 11 Forres Street, Edinburgh EH3 6BJ. *T:* 0131–225 5596. *Clubs:* New (Edinburgh); Hon. Company of Edinburgh Golfers, Royal & Ancient Golf.

LESSING, Charlotte; Editor of Good Housekeeping, 1973–87; freelance writer; *b* 14 May; *m* 1948, Walter B. Lessing (*d* 1989); three *d*. *Educ:* Henrietta Barnet Sch.; evening classes. Univ. of London Dipl. Eng. Lit. Journalism and public relations: New Statesman and Nation; Royal Society of Medicine; Lilliput (Hulton Press); Notley Public Relations; Good Housekeeping: Dep. Editor, 1964–73; Editor, 1973–87; Editor-in-Chief, Country Living, 1985–86. *Publications:* short stories, travel and feature articles; monthly wine page in The Lady. *Address:* 2 Roseneath Road, SW11 6AH.

LESSING, Mrs Doris (May); author; *b* Persia, 22 Oct. 1919; *d* of Captain Alfred Cook Tayler and Emily Maude McVeagh; lived in Southern Rhodesia, 1924–49; *m* 1st, 1939, Frank Charles Wisdom (marr. diss. 1943); one *s* one *d*; 2nd, 1945, Gottfried Anton Nicholas Lessing (marr. diss. 1949); one *s*. Associate Member: AAAL, 1974; Nat. Inst. of Arts and Letters (US), 1974. Mem., Inst. for Cultural Res., 1974. Hon. Fellow, MLA (Amer.), 1974. Hon. DLitt Princeton, 1989. Austrian State Prize for European Literature, 1981; Shakespeare Prize, 1982; Grinzane Cavour Award, Italy, 1989. *Publications:* The Grass is Singing, 1950 (filmed 1981); This Was the Old Chief's Country, 1951; Martha Quest, 1952; Five, 1953 (Somerset Maugham Award, Soc. of Authors, 1954); A Proper Marriage, 1954; Retreat to Innocence, 1956; Going Home, 1957; The Habit of Loving (short stories), 1957; A Ripple from the Storm, 1958; Fourteen Poems, 1959; In Pursuit of the English, 1960 (adapted for stage, 1990); The Golden Notebook, 1962 (Prix Médicis 1976 for French trans., Carnet d'or); A Man and Two Women (short stories), 1963; African Stories, 1964; Landlocked, 1965; The Four-Gated City, 1969; Briefing for a Descent into Hell, 1971; The Story of a Non-Marrying Man (short stories), 1972; The Summer Before the Dark, 1973; The Memoirs of a Survivor, 1975 (filmed 1981); Collected Stories: Vol. I, To Room Nineteen, 1978; Vol. II, The Temptation of Jack Orkney, 1978; Canopus in Argos: Archives: Re Planet 5, Shikasta, 1979; The Marriages Between Zones Three, Four and Five, 1980; The Sirian Experiments, 1981; The Making of the Representative for Planet 8, 1982 (libretto, 1988); The Sentimental Agents in the Volyen Empire, 1983; The Diaries of Jane Somers, 1984 (Diary of a Good Neighbour, 1983; If the Old Could . . . ., 1984; published under pseudonym Jane Somers); The Good Terrorist, 1985 (W. H. Smith Literary Award, 1986; Palermo Prize and Premio Internazionale Mondello, 1987); The Fifth Child, 1988; Doris Lessing Reader, 1990; London Observed (short stories), 1992; *non-fiction:* Going Home, 1957; Particularly Cats, 1966, rev. edn as Particularly Cats and More Cats, 1990; Prisons We Choose to Live Inside, 1986; The Wind Blows Away Our Words, 1987; African Laughter: four visits to Zimbabwe, 1992; Under My Skin (autobiog.), 1994; A Small Personal Voice, 1994; *play:* play with a Tiger, 1962. *Address:* c/o Jonathan Clowes Ltd, Iron Bridge House, Bridge Approach, NW1 8BD.

LESSOF, Prof. Maurice Hart, FRCP; Professor of Medicine, University of London at United Medical and Dental Schools (Guy's Hospital), 1971–89, now Emeritus; *b* 4 June 1924; *s* of Noah and Fanny Lessof; *m* 1960, Leila Liebster; one *s* two *d*. *Educ:* City of London Sch.; King's Coll., Cambridge. Appts on junior staff of Guy's Hosp., Canadian Red Cross Memorial Hosp., Johns Hopkins Hosp., etc; Clinical Immunologist and Physician, Guy's Hosp., 1967. Chairman: SE Thames Regl Med. Audit Cttee, 1990–91; Lewisham NHS Trust, 1993– (Dep. Chm., Guy's and Lewisham NHS Trust, 1991–93). Adviser on Allergy, DHSS, 1982–91. Vice-Pres. and Sen. Censor, RCP, 1987–88; Past Pres., British Soc. for Allergy. Mem. Senate, London Univ., 1981–85. *Publications:* (ed) Immunological Aspects of Cardiovascular Diseases, 1981; (ed) Immunological and Clinical Aspects of Allergy, 1984 (Spanish and Portuguese edns, 1987); (ed) Clinical Reactions to Food, 1983; (ed) Allergy: an international textbook, 1987; Food Intolerance, 1992 (Spanish edn 1995). *Recreation:* painting. *Address:* 8 John Spencer Square, Canonbury, N1 2LZ. *T:* 0171–226 0919, *Fax:* 0171–354 8913. *Club:* Athenæum.

LESTER, family name of **Baron Lester of Herne Hill**.

LESTER OF HERNE HILL, Baron *cr* 1993 (Life Peer), of Herne Hill in the London Borough of Southwark; **Anthony Paul Lester;** QC 1975; QC (NI); a Recorder, 1987–93; *b* 3 July 1936; *e s* of Harry and Kate Lester; *m* 1971, Catherine Elizabeth Debora Wassey; one *s* one *d*. *Educ:* City of London Sch.; Trinity Coll., Cambridge (Exhibnr) (BA); Harvard Law Sch. (Harkness Commonwealth Fund Fellowship) (LLM). Served RA, 1955–57, 2nd Lieut. Called to Bar, Lincoln's Inn, 1963 (Mansfield scholar), Bencher, 1985; called to Bar of N Ireland, 1984; Irish Bar, 1983. Special Adviser to: Home Secretary, 1974–76; Standing Adv. Commn on Human Rights, 1975–77. Hon. Vis. Prof., UCL, 1983–. Lectures: Owen J. Roberts, Univ. of Pennsylvania Law Sch., 1976; F. A. Mann, London, 1983; Rubin, Columbia Law Sch., 1988; Street, 1993. Member: Bd of Overseers, Univ. of Pennsylvania Law Sch., 1978–89; Court of Governors, LSE. Pres., Interights, 1991–; Chm., Runnymede Trust, 1991–93 (Trustee, 1969–); Member: Internat. Law Assoc. Cttee on Human Rights; Amer. Law Inst., 1985–; Council, PSI; Council, Inst. of Advanced Legal Studies. Governor, British Inst. of Human Rights. Mem., Bd of Govs, James Allen's Girls' Sch., 1984–94 (Chm., 1987–91). *Publications:* Justice in the American South, 1964 (Amnesty Internat.); (co-ed.) Shawcross and Beaumont on Air Law, 3rd edn, 1964; (co-author) Race and Law, 1972; contributor to: British Nationality, Immigration and Race Relations, in Halsbury's Laws of England, 4th edn, 1973, repr. 1992; The Changing Constitution (ed Jowell and Oliver), 1985, 3rd edn 1994. *Address:* 2 Hare Court, Temple, EC4Y 7BH. *T:* 0171–583 1770.

LESTER, James Theodore; MP (C) Broxtowe, since 1983 (Beeston, Feb. 1974–1983); *b* 23 May 1932; *s* of Arthur Ernest and Marjorie Lester; *m* (marr. diss. 1989); two *s*; *m* 1989. *Educ:* Nottingham High School. Mem. Notts CC, 1967–74. An Opposition Whip, 1976–79; Parly Under-Sec. of State, Dept of Employment, 1979–81. Mem., Select Cttee on Foreign affairs, 1982–; Vice-Chm., All Party Gp on overseas devel, 1983–. Deleg. to Council of Europe and WEU, 1975–76. *Recreations:* reading, music, motor racing, travelling. *Address:* House of Commons, SW1A 0AA.

LESTER, Richard; film director; *b* 19 Jan. 1932; *s* of Elliott and Ella Young Lester; *m* 1956, Deirdre Vivian Smith; one *s* one *d*. *Educ:* Wm Penn Charter Sch.; University of Pennsylvania (BSc). Television Director: CBS (USA), 1951–54; AR (Dir TV Goon Shows), 1956. Directed The Running, Jumping and Standing Still Film (Acad. Award nomination; 1st prize San Francisco Festival, 1960). *Feature Films directed:* It's Trad, Dad, 1962; Mouse on the Moon, 1963; A Hard Day's Night, 1964; The Knack, 1964 (Grand Prix, Cannes Film Festival); Help, 1965 (Best Film Award and Best Dir Award, Rio de Janeiro Festival); A Funny Thing Happened on the Way to the Forum, 1966; How I won the War, 1967; Petulia, 1968; The Bed Sitting Room, 1969 (Gandhi Peace Prize, Berlin Film Festival); The Three Musketeers, 1973; Juggernaut, 1974 (Best Dir award, Teheran Film Fest.); The Four Musketeers, 1974; Royal Flash, 1975; Robin and Marian, 1976; The Ritz, 1976; Butch and Sundance: the early days, 1979; Cuba, 1979; Superman II, 1981; Superman III, 1983; Finders Keepers, 1984; The Return of the Musketeers, 1989; Get Back, 1991. *Recreations:* music, tennis. *Address:* Twickenham Film Studios, St Margaret's, Twickenham, Mddx TW1 2AW.

LESTER SMITH, Ernest; *see* Smith, E. L.

LESTOR, Joan; MP (Lab) Eccles, since 1987; freelance lecturer; *b* Vancouver, British Columbia, Canada; one *s* one *d* (both adopted). *Educ:* Blaenavon Secondary Sch., Monmouth; William Morris Secondary Sch., Walthamstow; London Univ. Diploma in Sociology. Nursery Sch. Teacher, 1959–66. Chairman: Council, Nat. Soc. of Children's Nurseries, 1969–70; UK Branch, Defence for Children International; Member: Wandsworth Borough Council, 1958–68; LCC, 1962–64; Exec. Cttee of the London Labour Party, 1962–65; Nat. Exec., Labour Party, 1967–82 (Chm., 1977–78) and 1987–; Chm., Internat. Cttee, Labour Party, 1978–. MP (Lab) Eton and Slough, 1966–83; Parliamentary Under-Secretary: Dept of Educn and Science, Oct. 1969–June 1970; FCO, 1974–75; DES, 1975–76; resigned from Labour Govt on cuts policy, 1976; frontbench spokesperson on overseas aid and develt co-operation, 1988–89, on children's affairs, young offenders and race relations, 1989–92, on children and the family, 1993–. Contested (Lab): Lewisham W, 1964; Slough, 1983. Dir, Trade Unions Child Care Project, 1986–87. Co-Chm., Jt Cttee against Racialism, 1978–; Mem., CND Nat. Council, 1983–. *Recreations:* theatre, reading, playing with children and animals.

L'ETANG, Hugh Joseph Charles James; medical editor and writer; *b* 23 Nov. 1917; *s* of Dr J. G. L'Etang and Frances L'Etang; *m* 1951, Cecily Margaret Tinker, MD, MRCP; one *s* one *d*. *Educ:* Haileybury Coll.; St John's Coll., Oxford; St Bartholomew's Hosp.; Harvard Sch. of Public Health. BA 1939, BM, BCh 1942, DIH 1952. War Service, 1943–46, RMO 5th Bn Royal Berks Regt; TA from 1947, RAMC; Lt-Col 1953–56. Medical Adviser: North Thames Gas Bd, 1948–56; British European Airways, 1956–58; John Wyeth & Brother Ltd, 1958–69; Asst and Dep. Editor, The Practitioner, 1969–72, Editor 1973–82. Hira S. Chouké Lectr, Coll. of Physicians of Philadelphia, 1972 (Hon. Fellow, 1985); Henry Cohen Hist. of Medicine Lectr, Univ. of Liverpool, 1986. Member: RUSI; IISS; Military Commentators' Circle; Amer. Civil War Round Table, London. Editor, Travel Medicine International, 1983–; Consultant Editor, The Physician, 1983–91; Editor-in-Chief: RSM International Congress and Symposium Series, 1983–89; RSM Round Table Series, 1989–; Section Editor, Jl of Med. Biography, 1992–. *Publications:* The Pathology of Leadership, 1969; Fit to Lead?, 1980; (ed) Regulation and Restraint in Contemporary Medicine in the UK and USA, 1983; (Consultant Editor) Fontana Dictionary of Modern Thought, 1988; (Specialist Corresp.) Chronicle of the 20th Century, 1988; (ed) Health Care Provision under Financial Constraint: a decade of change, 1990; Ailing Leaders in Power 1914–1994, 1995; articles in Practitioner, Jl RAMC, Jl RUSI, Army Qly, Brassey's Annual, Navy Internat., NATO's Fifteen Nations, Politics and the Life Sciences, Dictionary of Literary Biography Yearbook 1994. *Recreation:* medical aspects of military and foreign affairs. *Address:* 27 Sispara Gardens, West Hill Road, SW18 1LG. *T:* 0181–870 3836. *Club:* United Oxford & Cambridge University.

LETHBRIDGE, Sir Thomas (Periam Hector Noel), 7th Bt *cr* 1804; *b* 17 July 1950; *s* of Sir Hector Wroth Lethbridge, 6th Bt, and of Evelyn Diana, *d* of late Lt-Col Francis Arthur Gerard Noel, OBE; *S* father, 1978; *m* 1976, Susan Elizabeth Rocke; four *s* two *d*. *Educ:* Milton Abbey. Studied farming, Cirencester Agricultural Coll., 1969–70; Man. Dir, Art Gallery, Dorset and London, 1972–77; also fine art specialist in sporting paintings and engravings. *Recreations:* shooting, swimming, hunting. *Heir: s* John Francis Buckler Noel Lethbridge, *b* 10 March 1977. *Address:* Lloyds House, Honeymead, Simonsbath, Minehead, Somerset TA24 7JX. *Clubs:* Farmers'; Naval and Military.

LE TOCQ, Eric George, CMG 1975; HM Diplomatic Service, retired; British Government Representative in the West Indies Associated States, 1975–78; *b* 20 April 1918; *s* of Eugene Charles Le Tocq; *m* 1946, Betty Esdaile; two *s* one *d*. *Educ:* Elizabeth Coll., Guernsey; Exeter Coll., Oxford (MA). Served War of 1939–45, commissioned in Royal Engineers, 1939; North Africa, 1942–43; Italy, 1943, Austria and Greece; major. Taught Modern Languages and Mathematics at Monmouth Sch., 1946–48; Assistant Principal, Commonwealth Relations Office, 1948; Karachi, 1948–50; Principal, 1950; Dublin, 1953–55; Accra, 1957–59; Assistant Secretary, 1962; Adviser on Commonwealth and External Affairs, Entebbe, 1962; Deputy High Commissioner, Uganda, 1962–64; Counsellor, British High Commission, Canberra, 1964–67; Head of E African Dept, FCO, 1968–71; High Comr in Swaziland, 1972–75. *Address:* Forest Edge, May Lane, Pilley, Hants SO41 5QR.

LETTS, Anthony Ashworth; President, Charles Letts Group, since 1994 (Chairman, Charles Letts Holdings Ltd, 1977–94); *b* 3 July 1935; *s* of Leslie Charles Letts and Elizabeth Mary (*née* Gibson); *m* 1962, Rosa Maria Ciarrapico; one *s* one *d*. *Educ:* Marlborough Coll.; Cambridge Univ. (MAEcon); Yale Univ. (Industrial Admin). National Service, RE, 2 Lieut, 1954–56. Joined Charles Letts & Co. Ltd, 1960; Man. Dir, 1965 (Charles Letts family business founded by John Letts (g g g grandfather), 1796). Dir, Cambridge Market Intelligence, 1994–. Gov., Westminster Coll., 1993–. *Recreations:* tennis, sailing, hill walking, theatre. *Address:* 56 Eaton Place, SW1X 8AT. *T:* 0171–235 7337. *Club:* Hurlingham.

LETTS, Charles Trevor; Underwriting Member of Lloyd's, since 1944; Deputy Chairman of Lloyd's, 1966 (entered Lloyd's, 1924; Member, 1941; Committee, 1964–67); *b* 2 July 1905; *o s* of late Charles Hubert and Gertrude Letts; *m* 1942, Mary R. (Judy), *o d* of late Sir Stanley and late Lady (Hilda) Woodwark; two *s* one *d*. *Educ:* Marlborough Coll. Served RNVR, Lieut-Commander, 1940–45. Member: Cttee, Lloyd's Underwriters' Assoc., 1960–70 (Chairman, 1963–64); Council, Lloyd's Register of Shipping, 1964–77 (Chairman, Yacht Sub-Cttee, 1967–75); Salvage Association, 1963–70. Dir, Greig Fester (Agencies) Ltd, 1980–85. *Recreations:* sailing, golf. *Address:* Bearwood, Holtye, Edenbridge, Kent TN8 7EG. *T:* Cowden (01342) 850472. *Club:* Royal Ocean Racing.

LETTS, Melinda Jane Frances; Chief Executive (formerly Executive Director), National Asthma Campaign, since 1992; *b* 6 April 1956; *d* of Richard Letts and Jocelyn (*née* Adami); *m* 1991, Neil Scott Wishart McIntosh, *qv*; one *s* one *d*. *Educ:* Wycombe Abbey; Cheltenham Coll.; St Anne's Coll., Oxford (BA Hons, Lit Hum Cl. I). Theatre Jobs, 1978–80; Res. Asst, Brunel Univ., 1980–81; Head of Admin, CND, 1982–84, VSO, 1985–87; Prog. Funding Manager, 1987, Regl Prog. Manager, ME and S Asia, 1987–89, VSO; Staffing Manager, McKinsey & Co., 1989–91; Dep. Dir, Nat. Asthma Campaign, 1991–92. Mem. Council, Cheltenham Coll., 1990–93; Governor, Oakley Hall Sch., Cirencester, 1993–94. MIMgt; FRSA. *Recreations:* reading, knitting, tapestry, photography. *Address:* c/o National Asthma Campaign, Providence House, Providence Place, London N1 0NT. *T:* 0171–226 2260.

LETWIN, Prof. William; Professor Emeritus, London School of Economics, since 1988; Senior Advisor, Putnam, Hayes & Bartlett, since 1988; *b* 14 Dec. 1922; *s* of Lazar and Bessie Letwin; *m* 1944, Shirley Robin (*d* 1993); one *s*. *Educ:* Univ. of Chicago (BA 1943, PhD 1951); London Sch. of Economics (1948–50). Served US Army, 1943–46. Postdoctoral Fellow, Economics Dept, Univ. of Chicago, 1951–52; Research Associate, Law Sch., Univ. of Chicago, 1953–55; Asst. Prof. of Industrial History, MIT, 1955–60; Associate Prof. of Economic History, MIT, 1960–67; Reader in Political Science, 1966–76, Prof. of Pol Science, 1976–88, LSE. Chm., Bd of Studies in Economics, Univ. of London, 1971–73. *Publications:* (ed) Frank Knight, on The History and Method of Economics, 1956; Sir Josiah Child, 1959; Documentary History of American Economic Policy, 1961, 2nd edn 1972; Origins of Scientific Economics 1660–1776, 1963; Law and Economic Policy in America, 1965; (ed) Against Equality, 1983; Freeing the Phones, 1991; articles in learned jls. *Address:* 15 Arlington Road, NW1 7ER. *T:* 0171–387 6715.

LEUCHARS, Maj.-Gen. Peter Raymond, CBE 1966; Chief Commander, St John Ambulance, 1980–89 (Commissioner-in-Chief, 1978–80 and 1985–86); *b* 29 Oct. 1921; *s* of late Raymond Leuchars and Helen Inez Leuchars (*née* Copland-Griffiths); *m* 1953, Hon. Gillian Wightman Nivison, *d* of 2nd Baron Glendyne; one *s*. *Educ:* Bradfield College. Commnd in Welsh Guards, 1941; served in NW Europe and Italy, 1944–45; Adjt, 1st Bn Welsh Guards, Palestine, 1945–48; Bde Major, 4 Guards Bde, Germany, 1952–54; GSO1 (Instr.), Staff Coll., Camberley, 1956–59; GSO1 HQ 4 Div. BAOR, 1960–63; comd 1st Bn Welsh Guards, 1963–65; Principal Staff Off. to Dir of Ops, Borneo, 1965–66; comd 11 Armd Bde BAOR, 1966–68; comd Jt Operational Computer Projects Team, 1969–71; Dep. Comdt Staff Coll., Camberley, 1972–73; GOC Wales, 1973–76. Col, The Royal Welch Fusiliers, 1974–84. Pres., Guards' Golfing Soc., 1977. Chairman: St John Fellowship, 1989–95; Lady Grover's Fund for Officers' Families, 1991–. BGCStJ 1989. Order of Istiqlal (Jordan), 1946. *Recreations:* golf, shooting, travel, photography. *Address:* 5 Chelsea Square, SW3 6LF. *T:* 0171–352 6187. *Clubs:* Royal and Ancient Golf; Royal Wimbledon Golf; Sunningdale Golf (Captain 1975).

LEUPENA, Sir Tupua, GCMG 1986; MBE 1977; Governor General of Tuvalu, 1986–90; *b* 2 Aug. 1922; *s* of Leupena Vaisua, Vaitupu, and Tolotea Vaisua (*née* Tavita), Niutao; *m* 1947, Annie Nitz, Vaitupu; four *s* three *d* (and one *s* decd). *Educ:* Ellice Is Govt Sch., Vaitupu; King George V Secondary Sch., Tarawa, Gilbert Is (now Republic of Kiribati). Clerk, Gilbert and Ellice Is Colony, 1941; Sgt, GEIC Labour Corps, 1944; Clerk 1945, Chief Clerk 1953, Resident Comr's office; transf. to Dist Admin as Asst Admin Officer, 1957, frequently serving in Gilbert Is and Ellice Is Dists, 1958–64 and 1967–69; District Commissioner: Phoenix Is Dist, 1965–66; Ocean Is, 1970–72; Dist Officer, Ellice Is District, 1973–75; acted as Sec. to Govt on Separation of Tuvalu from Kiribati in 1976 and retired from service same year; re-employed on contract as Sec. Reserved Subjects in Queen's Comr's Office, 1977; Speaker of Tuvalu Parlt, 1978; Man., Vaitupu's Private Commercial Enterprise, 1979–81; Chm., Tuvalu's Public Service Commn, 1982–86. *Recreations:* fishing, gardening, cricket, football. *Address:* Vaiaku, Funafuti Island, Tuvalu. *T:* 714.

LEUTWILER, Fritz, PhD; Chairman, Leutwiler & Partners Ltd, Zürich, since 1992; *b* 30 July 1924; *m* 1951, Andrée Cottier; one *s* one *d*. *Educ:* Univ. of Zürich (PhD 1948). Sec., Assoc. for a Sound Currency, 1948–52; Swiss National Bank, Zürich: Econ. Scientist, 1952–59; Manager, 1959–66; Dep. Gen. Man., 1966–68; Mem., Governing Bd, and Head, Dept III, 1968–74; Chm., Governing Bd, and Head, Dept I, 1974–84; Chm. and Pres., BIS, Basle, 1982–84; Chm., Bd of Dirs, BBC Brown, Boveri Ltd, Baden, 1985–92; Co-Chm., Bd of Dirs, ABB Asea Brown Boveri Ltd, Zürich, 1988–92. Hon. Dr: Berne, 1978; Zürich, 1983; Lausanne, 1984. *Recreations:* golf; collector of rare books (Helvetica, Economica). *Address:* Zumikon, Switzerland. *Club:* Golf and Country (Zumikon).

LEVEN, 14th Earl of, **AND MELVILLE,** 13th Earl of, *cr* 1641; **Alexander Robert Leslie Melville;** Baron Melville, 1616; Baron Balgonie, 1641; Earl of Melville, Viscount Kirkcaldie, 1690; Lord-Lieutenant of Nairn since 1969; *b* 13 May 1924; *e s* of 13th Earl and Lady Rosamond Sylvia Diana Mary Foljambe (*d* 1974), *d* of 1st Earl of Liverpool; *S* father, 1947; *m* 1953, Susan, *er d* of Lieut-Colonel R. Steuart-Menzies of Culdares, Arndilly House, Craigellachie, Banffshire; two *s* one *d*. *Educ:* Eton. ADC to Governor General of New Zealand, 1951–52. Formerly Capt. Coldstream Guards; retired, 1952. Vice Pres., Highland Dist TA. Pres., British Ski Fedn, 1981–85. DL, County of Nairn, 1961; Convener, Nairn CC, 1970–74. Chm. Governors, Gordonstoun Sch., 1971–89. *Heir: s* Lord Balgonie, *qv*. *Address:* Glenferness House, Nairn IV12 5VP. *T:* Glenferness (01309) 651202. *Club:* New (Edinburgh)

LEVENE, Ben, RA 1986 (ARA 1975); painter; *b* 23 Dec. 1938; *s* of Mark and Charlotte Levene. *Educ:* Slade School (DFA). Boise Scholarship, 1961; lived in Spain, 1961–62. Exhibited at: Thackeray Gall., 1973–81 (one man shows, 1973, 1975, 1978, 1981); Browse & Darby, London, 1986– (one man shows, 1986, 1988, 1993). Works in private and public collections. *Address:* c/o Royal Academy of Arts, Piccadilly, W1V 0DS.

LEVENE, Prof. Malcolm Irvin, MD; FRCP; Professor of Paediatrics and Child Health, University of Leeds, since 1989; *b* 2 Jan. 1951; *s* of Maurice Levene and Helen Levene (*née* Kutner); *m* 1st, 1972, Miriam Bentley (marr. diss. 1990); three *d*; 2nd, 1991, Susan Anne Cave; one *s* one *d*. *Educ:* Varndean Grammar Sch., Brighton; Guy's Hosp. Med. Sch., London Univ. (MB BS 1972); MD 1981. MRCS, LRCP, 1972; MRCP 1978; FRCP 1988. Junior posts at Royal Sussex, Northampton General and Charing Cross Hosps, 1974–77; Registrar, Derby Children's and Charing Cross Hosps, 1977–79; Res. Lectr, RPMS, Hammersmith Hosp., 1979–82; Sen. Lectr and Reader, Dept of Paediatrics, Univ. of Leicester, 1982–88. Mem., DoH Nat. Adv. Body, Confidential Enquiry into Stillbirths and Deaths in Infancy, 1991. Chm., Scientific Adv. Cttee, Action Res., 1994–. Hancock Prize, RCS, 1974; British Paediatric Association: Donald Paterson Prize, 1982; Michael Blecklow Meml Prize, 1982; Guthrie Medal, 1987; Ronnie MacKeith Prize, British Paed. Neurology Assoc., 1984; BUPA Res. Prize, 1988. *Publications:* (with H. Nutbeam) A Handbook for Examinations in Paediatrics, 1981; (jtly) Ultrasound of the Infant Brain, 1985; (jtly) Essentials of Neonatal Medicine, 1987, 2nd edn 1993; (ed jtly) Fetal and Neonatal Neurology and Neurosurgery, 1988, 2nd edn 1995; Diseases of Children, 6th edn, 1990; chapters in books and articles in learned jls on paed. topics, esp. neurology of new-born. *Recreations:* music, occasional gentle golf and gardening. *Address:* Acacia House, Acacia Park Drive, Apperley Bridge, W Yorks BD10 0PH. *T:* Leeds (0113) 240 9959.

LEVENE, Sir Peter (Keith), KBE 1989; JP; Chairman and Chief Executive, Canary Wharf Ltd, since 1993; Adviser to Prime Minister on Efficiency and Effectiveness, since 1992; *b* 8 Dec. 1941; *s* of late Maurice Levene and Rose Levene; *m* 1966, Wendy Ann (*née* Fraiman); two *s* one *d*. *Educ:* City of London School; Univ. of Manchester (BA Econ). Joined United Scientific Holdings, 1963; Man. Dir, 1968–85; Chm., 1982–85; Chief of Defence Procurement, MoD, 1985–91; UK Nat. Armaments Dir, 1988–91; Chm., European Nat. Armaments Dirs, 1989–90. Member: SE Asia Trade Adv. Group, 1979–83; Council, Defence Manufacturers' Assoc., 1982–85 (Vice-Chm., 1983–84; Chm., 1984–85); Citizen's Charter Adv. Panel, 1992–93; Personal Adviser to Sec. of State for Defence, 1984; Special Adviser to: Sec. of State for the Envmt, 1991–92; Chancellor of the Exchequer on Competition and Purchasing, 1992; Personal Advr to Pres. of BoT, 1992–95. Chm., Docklands Light Railway Ltd, 1991–94; Dep. Chm., Wasserstein Perella & Co. Internat., subseq. Wasserstein Perella & Co. Ltd, 1991–94. Mem., Bd of Management, London Homes for the Elderly, 1984–93 (Chm., 1990–93). Governor: City of London Sch. for Girls, 1984–85; City of London Sch., 1986–; Sir John Cass Primary Sch., 1985–93 (Dep. Chm., 1990–93). Mem. Court, HAC, 1984–; Mem., Court of Common Council, City of London, 1983–84 (Ward of Candlewick); Alderman (Ward of Portsoken), 1984–; Sheriff, City of London, 1995–96; Liveryman, Carmen's Co., 1984– (Master, 1992–93). Hon. Col Comdt, RCT, 1991–93, RLC, 1993–. Fellow, QMW,

1995. CIMgt, FRSA; FCIT; FCIPS. JP City of London, 1984. *Recreations:* ski-ing, watching association football, travel. *Address:* One Canada Square, Canary Wharf, E14 5AB. *Clubs:* Guildhall, City Livery, Royal Automobile.

LEVENTHAL, Colin David; Director of Acquisition, Channel Four Television Corporation, since 1993 (Director of Acquisition and Sales, Channel Four Television Co., 1987–92); Managing Director, Channel Four International Ltd, since 1993; *b* 2 Nov. 1946; *s* of Morris and Olga Leventhal. *Educ:* Carmel Coll., Wallingford, Berks; King's Coll., Univ. of London (BA Philosophy). Solicitor of Supreme Court of England and Wales. Admitted Solicitor, 1971; BBC, 1974–81: Asst Head of Programme Contracts, 1977; Head of Copyright, 1978; Head of Prog. Acquisition, Channel Four TV, 1981–87; Dir, Channel Four TV Co., 1988–92. *Recreations:* theatre, film. *Address:* (office) 124 Horseferry Road, SW1P 2TX. *T:* 0171–396 4444.

LEVER, family name of **Viscount Leverhulme.**

LEVER, Sir Christopher; *see* Lever, Sir T. C. A. L.

LEVER, Jeremy Frederick; QC 1972; QC (NI) 1988; *b* 23 June 1933; *s* of late A. Lever. *Educ:* Bradfield Coll.; University Coll., Oxford; Nuffield Coll., Oxford. Served RA, 1951–53. 1st cl. Jurisprudence, 1956, MA Oxon; Pres., Oxford Union Soc., 1957, Trustee, 1972–77 and 1988–. Fellow, All Souls Coll., Oxford, 1957– (Sub-Warden, 1982–84; Sen. Dean, 1988–). Called to Bar, Gray's Inn, 1957, Bencher, 1985. Mem. Council, British Inst. of Internat. and Comparative Law, 1987–. Director (non-exec.): Dunlop Holdings Ltd, 1973–80; Wellcome plc, 1983–94. Mem., Arbitral Tribunal, US/UK Arbitration concerning Heathrow Airport User Charges, 1989–94. Hamlyn Lectr, Hamlyn Trust, 1991. Governor, Berkhamsted Schs, 1985–. *Publications:* The Law of Restrictive Practices, 1964; other legal works. *Recreations:* ceramics, music. *Address:* 4 Raymond Buildings, Gray's Inn, WC1R 5BP. *T:* 0171–405 7211, *Fax:* 0171–405 2084. *Club:* Garrick.

LEVER, John Darcy, MA; Headmaster, Canford School, since 1992; *b* 14 Jan. 1952; *s* of Prof. Jeffrey Darcy Lever; *m* 1981, Alisoun Margaret Yule; one *s* two *d*. *Educ:* Westminster Sch.; Trinity Coll., Cambridge (MA); Christ Church, Oxford (Cert Ed). St Edward's Sch., Oxford, 1974–76; Winchester Coll., 1976–92. *Recreations:* walking, coaching rowing, visiting country houses. *Address:* Canford School, Wimborne, Dorset BH21 3AD. *T:* Wimborne (01202) 882411.

LEVER, (John) Michael, QC 1977; **His Honour Judge Lever;** a Circuit Judge, since 1981; *b* 12 Aug. 1928; *s* of late John and Ida Donaldson Lever; *m* 1964, Elizabeth Marr; two *s*. *Educ:* Bolton Sch.; Gonville and Caius Coll., Cambridge (Schol.). BA (1st cl. hons Law Tripos), 1949. Flying Officer, RAF, 1950–52. Called to Bar, Middle Temple, 1951 (Blackstone Schol.); practised Northern Circuit from 1952; Asst Recorder, Salford, 1969–71; a Recorder of the Crown Court, 1972–81. Governor, Bolton Sch. *Recreations:* theatre, fell-walking. *Address:* Lakelands, Rivington, near Bolton, Lancs BL6 7RT.

LEVER, Paul, CMG 1991; HM Diplomatic Service; Deputy Secretary, Cabinet Office, and Chairman, Joint Intelligence Committee, since 1994; *b* 31 March 1944; *s* of John Morrison Lever and Doris Grace (*née* Battey); *m* 1990, Patricia Anne, *d* of John and Anne Ramsey. *Educ:* St Paul's Sch.; The Queen's Coll., Oxford (MA). 3rd Secretary, Foreign and Commonwealth Office, 1966–67; 3rd, later 2nd Secretary, Helsinki, 1967–71; 2nd, later 1st Secretary, UK Delegn to NATO, 1971–73; FCO, 1973–81; Asst Private Sec. to Sec. of State for Foreign and Commonwealth Affairs, 1978–81; Chef de Cabinet to Christopher Tugendhat, Vice-Pres. of EEC, 1982–84; Head of UN Dept, FCO, 1985–86; Head of Defence Dept, 1986–87; Head of Security Policy Dept, FCO, 1987–90; Ambassador and Hd, UK Delegn to Conventional Arms Control Negotiations, Vienna, 1990–92; Asst Under-Sec. of State, FCO, 1992–94. *Recreations:* walking, art deco pottery. *Address:* c/o Cabinet Office, SW1A 2AH.

LEVER, Sir (Tresham) Christopher (Arthur Lindsay), 3rd Bt *cr* 1911; *b* 9 Jan. 1932; *s* of Sir Tresham Joseph Philip Lever, FRSL, 2nd Bt, and Frances Yowart (*d* 1959), *d* of Lindsay Hamilton Goodwin; step *s* of Pamela Lady Lever, *d* of late Lt-Col Hon. Malcolm Bowes Lyon; *S* father, 1975; *m* 1st, 1970; 2nd, 1975, Linda Weightman McDowell, *d* of late James Jepson Goulden, Tennessee, USA. *Educ:* Eton; Trinity Coll., Cambridge (BA 1954, MA 1957). FLS. Commissioned, 17th/21st Lancers, 1950. Peat, Marwick, Mitchell & Co., 1954–55; Kitcat & Aitken, 1955–56; Dir, John Barran & Sons Ltd, 1956–64. Consultant: Zoo Check Charitable Trust, 1984–91; Born Free Foundn, 1991–; Chairman: African Fund for Endangered Wildlife (UK), 1987–90; UK Elephant Gp, 1991–92; Mem., IUCN Species Survival Commn, 1988–; Trustee: Internat. Trust for Nature Conservation, 1980–92 (Vice-Pres. 1986–91; Pres., 1991–92); Migraine Trust, 1983–89; Rhino Rescue Trust, 1986–91 (Patron 1985–); Nat. Eczema Soc., 1989–92 (Council, 1992–94); Chm. and Patron, Tusk Trust, 1990–; Chm., Ruaha Trust, 1990–95; Member Council: Soc. for Protection of Animals in N Africa, 1986–88; British Trust for Ornithology, 1988–91 (Chm., Nat. Centre Appeal, 1987–92); Patron: British Broadleaf Heritage, 1989–; Lynx Educnl Trust for Animal Welfare, 1991–; Respect for Animals, 1995–. Hon. Life Mem., Brontë Soc., 1988. *Publications:* Goldsmiths and Silversmiths of England, 1975; The Naturalized Animals of the British Isles, 1977; (contrib.) Wildlife '80: the world conservation yearbook, 1980; (contrib.) Evolution of Domesticated Animals, 1984; Naturalized Mammals of the World, 1985; Naturalized Birds of the World, 1987; (contrib.) Beyond the Bars: the zoo dilemma, 1987; (contrib.) For the Love of Animals, 1989; The Mandarin Duck, 1990; They Dined on Eland: the story of the acclimatisation societies, 1992; (contrib.) The New Atlas of Breeding Birds in Britain and Ireland: 1988–1991, 1993; Naturalized Animals: the ecology of successfully introduced species, 1994; contribs to fine art, scientific and general publications. *Recreations:* watching and photographing wildlife, golf, fishing. *Heir:* none. *Address:* Newell House, Winkfield, Berks SL4 4SE. *T:* Winkfield Row (01344) 882604. *Club:* Boodle's.

LEVERHULME, 3rd Viscount, *cr* 1922, of the Western Isles; **Philip William Bryce Lever,** KG 1988; TD; Baron, *cr* 1917; Bt, *cr* 1911; Knight of Order of St John of Jerusalem; Major, Cheshire Yeomanry; Lord-Lieutenant of City and County of Chester, 1949–90; Advisory Director of Unilever Ltd; Chancellor of Liverpool University, 1980–94; *b* 1 July 1915; *s* of 2nd Viscount and Marion, *d* of late Bryce Smith of Manchester; *S* father, 1949; *m* 1937, Margaret Ann (*d* 1973), *o c* of John Moon, Tiverton; three *d*. *Educ:* Eton; Trinity Coll., Cambridge. Hon. Air Commodore 663 Air OP Squadron, RAuxAF; Hon. Air Commodore 610 (County of Chester) Squadron, Royal Auxiliary Air Force; Dep. Hon. Col, Cheshire Yeomanry, T&AVR, 1971–72, Hon. Col, 1972–81; Hon. Col, The Queen's Own Yeomanry, 1979–81. Pres. Council, Liverpool Univ., 1957–63, Sen. Pro-Chancellor, 1963–66. Member: National Hunt Cttee, 1961 (Steward, 1965–68); Deputy Senior Steward, Jockey Club, 1970–73, Senior Steward, 1973–76; Council of King George's Jubilee Trust; Chairman, Exec. Cttee Animal Health Trust, 1964. Hon. FRCS 1970; Hon. ARCVS 1975. Hon. LLD Liverpool, 1967. *Recreations:* shooting, fishing. *Heir:* none. *Address:* Thornton Manor, Thornton Hough, Wirral, Merseyside L63 1JB; Badanloch, Kinbrace, Sutherland KW11 6UE; Flat 6, Kingston House East, Prince's Gate, Kensington, SW7 1LJ. *Clubs:* Boodle's, Jockey.

LEVERSEDGE, Leslie Frank, CMG 1955; MA Cantab; Economic Secretary to Northern Rhodesia Government, 1956–60, retired; *b* 29 May 1904; *s* of F. E. Leversedge, UP, India; *m* 1945, Eileen Melegueta Spencer Payne; two *s* three *d*. *Educ:* St Paul's Sch., Darjeeling, India; St Peter's Sch., York; St John's Coll., Cambridge; Inner Temple, London. Cadet in Colonial Administrative Service, Northern Rhodesia, Dec. 1926; District Officer, Dec. 1928; Provincial Commissioner, Jan. 1947; Senior Provincial Commissioner, Dec. 1948. Development Secretary to Northern Rhodesia Government, 1951–56. MLC 1951; MEC 1951. British Council Local Correspondent for Kent, 1963–75. FRSA 1973. *Recreations:* walking, overseas travelling. *Address:* 24 Ashley Brake, West Hill, Ottery St Mary, Devon EX11 1TW. *T:* Ottery St Mary (01404) 813956.

LEVERTON, Colin Allen H.; *see* Hart-Leverton.

LEVERTON, Roger Frank, FCA; Chief Executive, Pilkington plc, since 1992; *b* 22 April 1939; *s* of Frank Arthur Leverton and Lucia Jean Leverton (*née* Harden); *m* 1st, 1962, Patricia Jones (marr. diss.); one *s* one *d* (and one *d* decd); 2nd, 1992, Marilyn Williams. *Educ:* Haberdashers' Askes Sch. FCA 1962. Black & Decker Manufacturing Co., 1968–84: European Dir and Gen. Manager, France, 1978–81; Gp Vice-Pres., Southern Europe, 1981–84; Chief Exec., MK Electric Gp, subseq. Pillar Electrical plc, 1984–89; Pres. and Chief Exec., Indal Ltd (RTZ Corp. plc), 1989–92. Non-exec. Dir, Smiths Industries, 1994–. *Recreations:* tennis, golf, ski-ing, theatre. *Address:* Pilkington plc, Prescot Road, St Helens, Merseyside WA10 3TT. *T:* St Helens (01744) 28882.

LEVESON, Lord; Granville George Fergus Leveson Gower; *b* 10 Sept. 1959; *s* and *heir* of 5th Earl Granville, *qv*.

LEVESON, Brian Henry; QC 1986; a Recorder, since 1988; *b* 22 June 1949; *er s* of late Dr Ivan Leveson and Elaine Leveson, Liverpool; *m* 1981, Lynne Rose (*née* Fishel); two *s* one *d*. *Educ:* Liverpool College, Liverpool; Merton College, Oxford (MA). Called to the Bar, Middle Temple, 1970, Bencher, 1995; Harmsworth Scholar, 1970; practised Northern Circuit, 1971; University of Liverpool: Lectr in Law, 1971–81; Mem. Council, 1983–92. Mem., Parole Bd, 1992–. *Recreation:* golf. *Address:* 61 Fleet Street, EC4Y 1JU. *T:* 0171–353 4363; 25 Byrom Street, Manchester M3 4PF. *T:* 0161–834 5238.

LEVESON GOWER, family name of **Earl Granville.**

LEVESQUE, Most Rev. Louis, ThD; Archbishop Emeritus of Rimouski, since 1973; *b* 27 May 1908; *s* of Philippe Levesque and Catherine Levesque (*née* Beaulieu). *Educ:* Laval Univ. Priest, 1932; Bishop of Hearst, Ontario, 1952–64; Archbishop of Rimouski, 1967–73. Chm., Canadian Cath. Conf., 1965–67; Mem. Congregation Bishops, Rome, 1968–73. *Address:* 300 avenue du Rosaire, Rimouski, PQ G5L 3E3, Canada.

LEVEY, Sir Michael (Vincent), Kt 1981; LVO 1965; MA Oxon and Cantab; FRSL; FBA 1983; Director of the National Gallery, 1973–87 (Deputy Director, 1970–73); *b* 8 June 1927; *s* of O. L. H. Levey and Gladys Mary Milestone; *m* 1954, Brigid Brophy, FRSL; one *d*. *Educ:* Oratory Sch.; Exeter Coll., Oxford, Hon. Fellow, 1973. Served with Army, 1945–48; commissioned, KSLI, 1946, and attached RAEC, Egypt. National Gallery: Asst Keeper, 1951–66, Dep. Keeper, 1966–68, Keeper, 1968–73. Slade Professor of Fine Art, Cambridge, 1963–64; Supernumerary Fellow, King's Coll., Cambridge, 1963–64; Slade Professor of Fine Art, Oxford, 1994–95; Hon. Fellow, Royal Acad., 1986; Foreign Mem., Ateneo Veneto, 1986. Hon. DLitt Manchester, 1989. *Publications:* Six Great Painters, 1956; National Gallery Catalogues: 18th Century Italian Schools, 1956; The German School, 1959; Painting in 18th Century Venice, 1959, 3rd. edn 1994; From Giotto to Cézanne, 1962; Dürer, 1964; The Later Italian Paintings in the Collection of HM The Queen, 1964, rev. edn 1991; Canaletto Paintings in the Royal Collection, 1964; Tiepolo's Banquet of Cleopatra (Charlton Lecture, 1962), 1966; Rococo to Revolution, 1966; Bronzino (The Masters), 1967; Early Renaissance, 1967 (Hawthornden Prize, 1968); Fifty Works of English Literature We Could Do Without (co-author), 1967; Holbein's Christina of Denmark, Duchess of Milan, 1968; A History of Western Art, 1968; Painting at Court (Wrightsman Lectures), 1971; 17th and 18th Century Italian Schools (Nat. Gall. catalogue), 1971; The Life and Death of Mozart, 1971, 2nd edn 1988; The Nude: Themes and Painters in the National Gallery, 1972; (co-author) Art and Architecture in 18th Century France, 1972; The Venetian Scene (Themes and Painters Series), 1973; Botticelli (Themes and Painters Series), 1974; High Renaissance, 1975; The World of Ottoman Art, 1976; Jacob van Ruisdael (Themes and Painters Series), 1977; The Case of Walter Pater, 1978; Sir Thomas Lawrence (Nat. Portrait Gall. exhibn), 1979; The Painter Depicted (Neurath Lect.), 1981; Tempting Fate (fiction), 1982; An Affair on the Appian Way (fiction), 1984; (ed) Pater's Marius the Epicurean, 1985; Giambattista Tiepolo, 1986 (Banister Fletcher Prize, 1987); The National Gallery Collection: a selection, 1987; Men at Work (fiction), 1989; (ed) The Soul of the Eye: anthology of painters and painting, 1990; Painting and Sculpture in France 1700–1789, 1992; Florence: a portrait, 1995; contributions Burlington Magazine, etc. *Address:* 36 Little Lane, Louth, Lincs LN11 9DU.

LEVI, Prof. Edward Hirsch; Glen A. Lloyd Distinguished Service Professor, University of Chicago, 1977–84, now Emeritus; *b* 26 June 1911; *s* of Gerson B. Levi and Elsa B. Levi (*née* Hirsch); *m* 1946, Kate Sulzberger; three *s*. *Educ:* Univ. of Chicago; Yale Univ. Law Sch. Univ. of Chicago: Asst Prof. of Law, 1936–40; Prof. of Law, 1945–75; Dean of the Law School, 1950–62; Provost, 1962–68; President, 1968–75; Pres. emeritus, 1975; Attorney-Gen. of US, 1975–77. Public Dir, Chicago Bd of Trade, 1977–80. Herman Phleger Vis. Prof., Stanford Law Soc., 1978. Special Asst to Attorney-Gen., Washington, DC, 1940–45; 1st Asst, War Div., Dept of Justice, 1943; 1st Asst, Anti-trust Div., 1944–45; Chm., Interdeptl Cttee on Monopolies and Cartels, 1944; Counsel, Subcttee on Monopoly Power Judiciary Cttee, 81st Congress, 1950; Chm., Council on Educn in Professional Responsibility, 1965–69; Member: Nat. Council on Legal Clinics, 1960–76; White House Task Force on Educn, 1966–67; President's Task Force on Priorities in Higher Educn, 1969–70; White House Central Gp in Domestic Affairs, 1964; Citizens Commn on Graduate Medical Educn, 1963–66; Sloan Commn on Cable Communications, 1970–71; Nat. Commn on Productivity, 1970–75; Commn on Foundations and Private Philanthropy, 1969–70; Martin Luther King, Jr, Federal Holiday Commn, 1985–86. Mem. Council, American Law Inst., 1965–; American Bar; Illinois Bar; Chicago Bar; Supreme Court, 1945–; Amer. Judicature Soc.; Council on Legal Educn for Profl. Responsibility, 1968–74; Order of Coif; Phi Beta Kappa; res. adv. bd, Commn Econ. Develt, 1951–54; bd Dirs, SSRC, 1959–62; Nat. Commn on Productivity, 1970–75; Nat. Council on the Humanities, 1974–75. Dir Emeritus, MacArthur Foundn, 1984– (Dir, 1979–84); Trustee: Internat. Legal Center; Museum of Science and Industry, 1971–75; Russell Sage Foundn, 1971–75; Aspen Inst. for Humanist Studies, 1970–75, 1977–79; Univ. Chicago, 1966; Woodrow Wilson Nat. Fellowship Foundn, 1972–75, 1977–79; Inst. Psycho-analysis, Chicago, 1961–75; Skadden Fellowship Foundn, 1988–94; Member Board of Trustees: Nat. Humanities Center, 1978– (Chm., 1979–83); The Aerospace Corp., 1978–80 (Life Trustee, 1989); William Benton Foundn, 1980–92; Mem. Bd of Dirs, Continental Illinois Holding Corp., 1985–. Salzburg Seminar in Amer. Studies, 1980; Mem. Bd of Overseers, Univ. of Pennsylvania Law Sch., 1978–82; Mem. Bd of Governors, Univ. of Calif Humanities Res. Inst., 1988–91; Pres., Amer. Acad. of Arts and

Scis, 1986–89; Hon. Trustee: Inst. of Internat. Educn; Univ. of Chicago, 1975. Fellow: Amer. Bar Foundn; Amer. Acad. Arts and Scis; Amer. Philos. Soc. (Vice-Pres., 1991–94). Chubb Fellow, Yale, 1977. Hon. degrees: LHD: Hebrew Union Coll.; Loyola Univ.; DePaul Univ.; Kenyon Coll.; Univ. of Chicago; Bard Coll.; Beloit Coll.; LLD: Univ. of Michigan; Univ. of California at Santa Cruz; Univ. of Iowa; Jewish Theological Seminary of America; Brandeis Univ.; Lake Forest Coll.; Univ. of Rochester; Univ. of Toronto; Yale Univ.; Notre Dame; Denison Univ., Nebraska Univ. Law Sch.; Univ. of Miami; Boston Coll.; Ben N. Cardozo Sch. of Law, Yeshiva Univ., NYC; Columbia Univ., Dropsie Univ., Pa; Univ. of Pa Law Sch.; Brigham Young Univ.; Duke Univ.; Ripon Coll.; Georgetown Univ.; Claremont Univ. Center and Grad. Sch.; Indiana Univ.; DCL NY Univ. Legion of Honour (France); Chicago Bar Assoc. Centennial Award, 1975; Distinguished Citizen Award, Ill St Andrews Soc., 1976; Herbert H. Lehman Ethics Medal, Jewish Theol. Seminary, 1976; Learned Hand Medal, Fedn Bar Council, NYC, 1976; Wallace Award, Amer.-Scottish Foundn, 1976; Morris J. Kaplun Meml Prize, Dropsie, 1976; Laureate of Lincoln, Acad. of Illinois, 1976; Fed. Bar Assoc. Award, 1977; Fordham–Stein Prize, Fordham, 1977; Citation of Merit, Yale, 1977; Louis Dembitz Brandeis Award, 1978; Award of Honor, Illinois Bar Assoc, 1990; Dist. Service Award, Illinois Bar Foundn, 1990; Constitutional Rights Award, Constitutional Rights Foundn, 1992. *Publications:* Introduction to Legal Reasoning, 1949; Four Talks on Legal Education, 1952; Point of View, 1969; The Crisis in the Nature of Law, 1969; Elements of the Law (ed, with Roscoe Steffen), 1936; Gilbert's Collier on Bankruptcy (ed, with James W. Moore), 1936; Member, editorial board: Jl Legal Educn, 1956–68; Encyclopaedia Britannica, 1968–75. *Address:* (office) 1116 East 59th Street, Chicago, IL 60637, USA. *T:* (312) 7028588; (home) 4950 Chicago Beach Drive, Chicago, IL 60615. *Clubs:* Quadrangle, Columbia Yacht, Mid-America (Chicago); Chicago (DC).

LEVI, Peter Chad Tigar, FSA; FRSL; Professor of Poetry, University of Oxford, 1984–89; Fellow of St Catherine's College, Oxford, 1977–91, Emeritus Fellow, since 1993; *b* 16 May 1931; *s* of Herbert Simon Levi and Edith Mary Tigar; *m* 1977, Deirdre, *o d* of Hon. Dennis Craig, MBE, and *widow* of Cyril Connolly, CBE, CLit. *Educ:* Beaumont; Oxford Univ. (MA). FSA 1976; FRSL 1985. Society of Jesus, 1948–77: priest, 1964; resigned priesthood, 1977. Tutor and Lectr in Classics, Campion Hall, Oxford, 1965–77; student, Brit. Sch. of Archaeol., Athens, 1965–68; Lectr in Classics, Christ Church, Oxford, 1979–82. The Times Archaeol Correspondent, 1977–78. Mem., Kingman Cttee on English, 1987–88. Pres., Virgil Soc., 1993–95; Corres. mem., Soc. of Greek Writers, 1983. Television films: Ruined Abbeys, 1966; Foxes have holes, 1967; Seven black years, 1975; presenter of TV series, Art, Faith and Vision, 1989. *Publications: poetry:* The Gravel Ponds, 1960; Water, Rock and Sand, 1962; The Shearwaters, 1965; Fresh Water, Sea Water, 1966; Ruined Abbeys, 1968; Pancakes for the Queen of Babylon, 1968; Life is a Platform, 1971; Death is a Pulpit, 1971; Collected Poems, 1976; Five Ages, 1978; Private Ground, 1981; The Echoing Green, 1983; Shakespeare's Birthday, 1985; Shadow and Bone, 1989; Goodbye to the Art of Poetry, 1989; (with Alan Powers) The Marches, 1989; Rags of Time, 1994; *edited:* The Penguin Book of English Christian Verse, 1985; New Verses by Shakespeare, 1988; *prose:* Beaumont, 1961; Ὁ τόνος τῆς φωνῆς τοῦ Σεφέρη (Mr Seferis' Tone of Voice), 1970; The Lightgarden of the Angel King, 1973; The English Bible (1534–1859), 1974; In Memory of David Jones, 1975; John Clare and Thomas Hardy, 1975; The Noise made by Poems, 1976; The Hill of Kronos, 1980; Atlas of the Greek World, 1980; The Flutes of Autumn, 1983; (ed) Johnson and Boswell, Western Islands, 1984; The Lamentation of the Dead, 1984; A History of Greek Literature, 1985; The Frontiers of Paradise: a study of monks and monasteries, 1987; Life and Times of Shakespeare, 1988; To the Goat (novella), 1988; Boris Pasternak, 1990; The Art of Poetry (lectures), 1991; Life of Lord Tennyson, 1993; Edward Lear, 1994; *thrillers:* The Head in the Soup, 1979; Grave Witness, 1985; Knit One, Drop One, 1987; (with Cyril Connolly) Shade Those Laurels, 1990; *translations:* Yevtushenko, 1962; Pausanias, 1971; Pavlopoulos, The Cellar, 1976; The Psalms, 1976; Marko the Prince (Serbo-Croat heroic verse), 1983; Papadiamantis, The Murderess, 1983; The Holy Gospel of John, a New Translation, 1985; Revelation, 1992. *Recreations:* elderly. *Address:* Prospect Cottage, The Green, Frampton on Severn, Glos GL2 7DY.

LEVI, Renato, (Sonny), RDI 1987; freelance powerboat designer; *b* 3 Sept. 1926; *s* of Mario Levi and Eleonora Ciravegna; *m* 1954, Ann Watson; two *s* one *d*. *Educ:* Collège de Cannes; St Paul's, Darjeeling. Over 30 years contributing to development of fast planing craft. *Publications:* Dhows to Deltas, 1971; Milestones in my Designs, 1992. *Recreation:* the Far East. *Address:* Sandhills, Porchfield, Isle of Wight PO30 4LH.

LEVI-MONTALCINI, Prof. Rita; research scientist; *b* 22 April 1909; *d* of Adamo Levi and Adele Montalcini; *Educ:* Turin Univ. Med. Sch. Neurological research, Turin and Brussels, 1936–41, Piemonte, 1941–43; in hiding in Florence, 1943–44; worked among war refugees, Florence, 1944–45; Univ. of Turin, 1945; with Prof. Viktor Hamburger, St Louis, USA, at Washington Univ., 1947–77 (Associate Prof., 1956, Prof., 1958–77); Dir, Inst. of Cell Biology, Italian Nat. Council of Research, Rome, 1969–79, Guest Prof., 1979–. For. Mem., Royal Soc., 1995. (Jtly) Nobel Prize for Physiology or Medicine, 1986. *Publications:* In Praise of Imperfection: my life and work (autobiog.), 1988; articles in learned jls on chemical growth factors controlling growth and development of different cell lines. *Address:* Institute of Neurobiology, CNR, Viale Marx 15, 00137 Rome, Italy.

LÉVI-STRAUSS, Claude; Grand Croix de la Légion d'Honneur, 1991; Commandeur, Ordre Nationale du Mérite, 1971; Member of French Academy, since 1973; Professor, Collège de France, 1959–82, Hon. Professor, since 1983; *b* 28 Nov. 1908; *s* of Raymond Lévi-Strauss and Emma Lévy; *m* 1st, 1932, Dina Dreyfus; 2nd, 1946, Rose-Marie Ullmo; one *s*; 3rd, 1954, Monique Roman; one *s*. *Educ:* Lycée Janson-de-Sailly, Paris; Sorbonne. Prof., Univ. of São Paulo, Brazil, 1935–39; Vis. Prof., New School for Social Research, NY, 1941–45; Cultural Counsellor, French Embassy, Washington, 1946–47; Associate Curator, Musée de l'Homme, Paris, 1948–49. Corresp. Member: Royal Acad. of Netherlands; Norwegian Acad.; British Acad.; Nat. Acad. of Sciences, USA; Amer. Acad. and Inst. of Arts and Letters; Amer. Philos. Soc.; Royal Anthrop. Inst. of Great Britain; London Sch. of African and Oriental Studies. Hon. Dr: Brussels, 1962; Oxford, 1964; Yale, 1965; Chicago, 1967; Columbia, 1971; Stirling, 1972; Univ. Nat. du Zaïre, 1973; Uppsala, 1977; Johns Hopkins, 1978; Laval, 1979; Mexico, 1979; Visva Bharati, India, 1980; Harvard, 1986. *Publications:* La Vie familiale et sociale des Indiens Nambikwara, 1948; Les Structures élémentaires de la parenté, 1949 (The Elementary Structures of Kinship, 1969); Race et histoire, 1952; Tristes Tropiques, 1955 (A World on the Wane, 1961; complete English edn as Tristes Tropiques, 1973); Anthropologie structurale, Vol. 1, 1958, Vol. 2, 1973 (Structural Anthropology, Vol. 1, 1964, Vol. 2, 1977); Le Totémisme aujourd'hui, 1962 (Totemism, 1963); La Pensée sauvage, 1962 (The Savage Mind, 1966); Le Cru et le cuit, 1964 (The Raw and the Cooked, 1970); Du Miel aux cendres, 1967 (From Honey to Ashes, 1973); L'Origine des manières de table, 1968 (The Origin of Table Manners, 1978); L'Homme nu, 1971 (The Naked Man, 1981); La Voie des masques, 1975 (The Way of the Masks, 1982); Le Regard éloigné, 1983 (The View from Afar, 1985); Paroles Données, 1984 (Anthropology and Myth, 1987); La Potière Jalouse, 1985 (The Jealous Potter, 1988); (with D. Eribon) De Près et de loin, 1988 (Conversations with Claude Lévi-Strauss, 1991); Regarder écouter lire, 1993; Saudades do Brasil, 1994; *relevant publications:* Entretiens avec Lévi-Strauss (ed G. Charbonnier), 1962; by Octavio Paz: On Lévi-Strauss, 1970; Claude Lévi-Strauss: an introduction, 1972. *Address:* 2 rue des Marronniers, 75016 Paris, France. *T:* 42883471.

LEVICK, William Russell, FRS 1982; FAA; Professor, John Curtin School of Medical Research, Australian National University, since 1983; *b* 5 Dec. 1931; *s* of Russell L. S. Levick and Elsie E. I. (*née* Nance); *m* 1961, Patricia Jane Lathwell; two *s* one *d*. *Educ:* Univ. of Sydney (BSc 1st Cl. Hons, MSc, MB, BS 1st Cl. Hons). Registered Medical Practitioner, State of NSW. FAA 1973. RMO, Royal Prince Alfred Hosp., Sydney, 1957–58; National Health and Med. Res. Council Fellow, Univ. of Sydney, 1959–62; C. J. Martin Travelling Fellow, Cambridge Univ. and Univ. of Calif, Berkeley, 1963–64; Associate Res. Physiologist, Univ. of Calif, Berkeley, 1965–66; Sen. Lectr in Physiol., Univ. of Sydney, 1967; Professorial Fellow of Physiology, John Curtin Sch. of Medicine, ANU, 1967–83. Fellow, Optical Soc. of America, 1977. *Publications:* articles on neurophysiology of the visual system in internat. scientific jls. *Address:* John Curtin School of Medical Research, Australian National University, Canberra, ACT 2601, Australia. *T:* (6)2492525.

LEVIN, David Roger; Headmaster, Royal Grammar School, High Wycombe, since 1993; *b* 2 Oct. 1949; *s* of Jack Levin, Cape Town and Isobel Elizabeth Levin (*née* Robinson), Norfolk, England; *m* 1977, Jean Isobel, *d* of Major J. A. P. Hall. *Educ:* Kearsney Coll., Natal; Univ. of Natal (BEcon); Univ. of Sussex (MA). Gen. Manager, Cutty Sark Hotel, Scottburgh, S Africa (family business), 1972–73; Asst Master, Whitgift Sch., Croydon, 1974–75; Articled Clerk, Radcliffes & Co., Solicitors, 1976–78; Asst Master, Portsmouth Grammar Sch., 1978–80; Head of Economics, 1980–93 and Second Master, 1987–93, Cheltenham Coll. Mem., Economic Res. Council, 1991. FRSA. Gov., Canford School, 1995–. *Recreations:* long distance swimming, Rugby football coaching, theatre, hill walking, opera, economic history. *Address:* Malden Court, Cheltenham, Glos GL52 2BL. *T:* Cheltenham (01242) 521692; Old Stores Cottage, Elm Road, Penn, Bucks HP10 8LB. *T:* Penn (01494) 815268.

LEVIN, (Henry) Bernard, CBE 1990; journalist and author; *b* 19 Aug. 1928; *s* of late Phillip Levin and Rose (*née* Racklin). *Educ:* Christ's Hospital; LSE, Univ. of London. BSc (Econ.). Has written regularly or irregularly for many newspapers and magazines in Britain and abroad, 1953–, principally The Times, Sunday Times, Observer, Manchester Guardian, Truth, Spectator, Daily Express, Daily Mail, Newsweek, International Herald-Tribune; has written and broadcast for radio and television, 1952–, incl. BBC and most ITV cos. Sir Dorab Tata Trust Lectr, India, 1990. Pres., English Assoc., 1984–85, Vice-Pres., 1985–88. Various awards for journalism. Hon. Fellow, LSE, 1977–. Mem., Order of Polonia Restituta (by Polish Government-in-Exile), 1976. *Publications:* The Pendulum Years, 1971; Taking Sides, 1979; Conducted Tour, 1981; Speaking Up, 1982; Enthusiasms, 1983; The Way We Live Now, 1984; A Shakespeare Mystery (English Assoc. Presidential address), 1985; Hannibal's Footsteps, 1985; In These Times, 1986; To The End Of The Rhine, 1987; All Things Considered, 1988; A Walk Up Fifth Avenue, 1989; Now Read On, 1990; If You Want My Opinion, 1992; A World Elsewhere, 1994; I should say so, 1995. *Address:* The Times, 1 Pennington Street, E1 9XN.

LEVIN, Richard, OBE 1952; RDI 1971; photographer, since 1975; *b* 31 Dec. 1910; *s* of Henry Levin and Margaret Sanders; *m* 1st, 1932, Evelyn Alexander; two *d*; 2nd, 1960, Patricia Foy, Producer, BBC TV. *Educ:* Clayesmore; Slade, UC London. Assistant Art Director, Gaumont British, 1928; private practice: exhibition; graphic and industrial designer working for BBC, C. C. Wakefield Ltd, Bakelite Ltd, LEB, etc, 1931–39; Camouflage Officer, Air Ministry, 1940; MOI Exhibn Div.; Designer, British Army Exhibns, UK and Paris, 1943; private practice, 1946; Designer, Festival of Britain, Land Travelling Exhibn, 1951; Head of Design, BBC Television, 1953–71. FSIAD 1955. Silver Medal, RTS, 1972; Judge's Award, RTS Design Awards, 1992. *Publications:* Television by Design, 1960; Design for Television (BBC lunch-time lecture), 1968. *Recreation:* fishing. *Address:* Sandells House, West Amesbury, Wilts SP4 7BH. *T:* Amesbury (01980) 623857; 2 Nothe Parade, The Old Harbour, Weymouth, Dorset DT4 8TX.

LEVIN, Prof. Richard Charles, PhD; Frederick William Beinecke Professor of Economics, since 1992, President, since 1993, Yale University; *b* San Francisco, 7 April 1947; *s* of D. Derek Levin and Phylys (*née* Goldstein); *m* 1968, Jane Ellen Aries; two *s* two *d*. *Educ:* Stanford Univ. (BA 1968); Univ. of Oxford (LittB 1971); Yale Univ. (PhD 1974). Yale University, 1974–: Chm., Econs Dept, 1987–92; Dean, Grad. Sch., 1992–93; Res. Associate, Nat. Bureau of Econ. Res., Cambridge, Mass, 1985–90; Program Dir, Internat. Inst. Applied System Analysis, Vienna, 1990–92. Consultant, numerous law and business firms. Member: Univs Res. Assoc., 1994–; Amer. Econ. Assoc.; Econometric Soc. Hon. LLD: Princeton, 1993; Harvard, 1994. *Recreations:* hiking, basket-ball. *Address:* Yale University, 105 Wall Street, New Haven, CT 06511, USA.

LEVINE, Sir Montague (Bernard), Kt 1979; FRCGP; general practitioner, 1956–87; HM Coroner, Inner South District, Greater London, since 1987; Clinical Tutor in General Practice, St Thomas' Hospital, since 1972; *b* 15 May 1922; *s* of late Philip Levine and of Bessie Levine; *m* 1959, Dr Rose Gold; one *s* one *d*. *Educ:* Royal Coll. of Surgeons in Ireland (LRCSI); Royal Coll. of Physicians in Ireland (MRCPI, LRCPI, LM). DMJ Clin.; FRCGP 1988. Licentiate of Rubber Industry, 1944. Industrial physicist, rubber industry, 1939–45; House Surgeon: Royal Victoria Hosp., Bournemouth, 1955; Meath Hosp., Dublin, 1955; Metrop. Police Surg., 1960–66; Asst Dep. Coroner, Inner South London, 1974. Hon. Lectr in Coroners' Law, St Thomas' Hosp. and Guy's Hosp., 1987–. Pres., British Assoc. of Forensic Scientists, 1993–94. Fellow, Hunterian Soc., 1990. Royal Coll. of Surgeons in Ireland: Stoney Meml Gold Medal in Anatomy, 1951; Silver Medallist, Medicine, 1953, Pathology, 1953, and Medical Jurisprudence, 1954; Macnaughton Gold Medal in Obs and Gynae., 1955; Lectr in Anat., 1956. *Publication:* Inter-parental Violence and its Effect on Children, 1975. *Recreations:* fishing, photography, painting. *Address:* Gainsborough House, 120 Ferndene Road, Herne Hill, SE24 0AA. *T:* 0171–274 9196. *Club:* Organon.

LEVINE, Sydney; a Recorder, North-Eastern Circuit, since 1975; *b* 4 Sept. 1923; *s* of Rev. Isaac Levine and Mrs Miriam Levine; *m* 1959, Cécile Rona Rubinstein; three *s* one *d*. *Educ:* Bradford Grammar Sch.; Univ. of Leeds (LLB). Called to the Bar, Inner Temple, 1952; Chambers in Bradford, 1953–. *Recreations:* music, gardening, amateur theatre, marathon running. *Address:* 2A Primley Park Road, Leeds LS17 7HS. *T:* Leeds (0113) 268 3769.

LEVINGE, Sir Richard (George Robin), 12th Bt *cr* 1704; farming since 1968; *b* 18 Dec. 1946; *s* of Sir Richard Vere Henry Levinge, 11th Bt, MBE, TD, and of Barbara Mary, *d* of late George Jardine Kidston, CMG; *S* father, 1984; *m* 1st, 1969, Hilary (marr. diss. 1978), *d* of Dr Derek Mark; one *s*; 2nd, 1978, Donna Maria d'Ardia Caracciolo; one *s* one *d*. *Educ:* Brook House, Bray, Co. Wicklow; Hawkhurst Court, West Sussex; Mahwah High School, New York; Craibstone Agricultural Coll. *Heir:* *s* Richard Mark Levinge, *b* 15 May 1970. *Address:* Clohamon House, Bunclody, Co. Wexford, Ireland. *T:* (54) 77253.

LEVINSON, Dr Stephen Curtis, FBA 1988; Director, since 1994, and Head of Research Group for Cognitive Anthropology, since 1991, Max Planck Institute for Psycholinguistics; *b* 6 Dec. 1947; *s* of Dr Gordon A. Levinson and Dr Mary C. Levinson; *m* 1976, Dr Penelope Brown; one *s*. *Educ:* Bedales Sch.; King's Coll., Cambridge (Sen. Schol.; 1st Cl. Hons. Archaeology and Anthropology Tripos 1970); PhD Linguistics Anthropology, Calif., 1977. Asst Lectr, 1975–78, Lectr, 1978–91, Reader, 1991–94, Linguistics Dept, Cambridge. Vis. Res. Fellow, ANU, 1980–82; Vis. Associate Prof., Stanford Univ., 1987–88. *Publications:* Pragmatics, 1983; (with Dr P. Brown) Politeness, 1987; articles in books and jls. *Recreations:* Sunday painting, hiking. *Address:* Payensweg 7, 6523 MB Nijmegen, The Netherlands; Research Group for Cognitive Anthropology, Max Planck Institute for Psycholinguistics, PB 310, 6500 AH Nijmegen, The Netherlands.

LEVISON, Rev. Mary Irene; an Extra Chaplain to the Queen in Scotland, since 1993 (Chaplain, 1991–93); *b* 8 Jan. 1923; *d* of late Rev. David Colville Lusk and Mary Theodora Lusk (*née* Colville); *m* 1965, Rev. Frederick Levison. *Educ:* St Leonard's Sch., St Andrews; Lady Margaret Hall, Oxford (BA); Univ. of Edinburgh (BD). Deaconess in the parish of Inveresk, Musselburgh, 1954–58; Tutor, St Colm's Coll., Edinburgh, 1958–61; Asst Chaplain, Univ. of Edinburgh, 1961–64; Asst Minister, St Andrew's and St George's Church, Edinburgh and Chaplain to the retail trade, 1978–83. Moderator of the Presbytery of Edinburgh, 1988. Hon. DD Edinburgh, 1994. *Publication:* Wrestling with the Church, 1992. *Recreations:* music, gardening, golf. *Address:* 2 Gillsland Road, Edinburgh EH10 5BW. *T:* 0131–228 3118.

LEVY, Allan Edward; QC 1989; a Recorder, since 1993 (an Assistant Recorder, 1990–93); barrister; author; *b* 17 Aug. 1942; *s* of Sidney Levy and Mabel (*née* Lewis). *Educ:* Bury Grammar Sch.; Hull Univ. (LLB Hons); Inns of Court Law School. Called to the Bar, Inner Temple, 1969, Bencher, 1993. Member: Family Law Bar Assoc. Cttee, 1987–; Council, Justice, 1988–; Bar Council Law Reform Cttee, 1989–90; Council, Medico-Legal Soc., 1990–. Speaker at seventh Internat. Congress on Child Abuse, Rio de Janeiro, 1988; Chm., Staffs Child Care Inquiry, 1990; Member: Gulbenkian Foundn Commn on children and violence, 1994–95; Howard League Commn of Inquiry into violence in penal instns for young people, 1994–95. Hon. Legal Advr, Nat. Children's Bureau, 1990–. Chm., Intercountry Adoption Lawyers' Assoc., 1991–. Internat. Bar Assoc. Observer, Hague Conf. on Private Internat. Law (special commn on intercountry adoption), 1992. Fellow, Internat. Acad. of Matrimonial Lawyers, 1992. FRSocMed 1993. Broadcaster on legal topics. *Publications:* Wardship Proceedings, 1982, 2nd edn 1987; Custody and Access, 1983; (with J. F. Josling) Adoption of Children, 10th edn 1985; (ed and contrib.) Focus on Child Abuse, 1989; (with B. Kahan) The Pindown Experience and the Protection of Children, 1991; (contrib.) One Scandal Too Many: the case for comprehensive protection for children in all settings, 1993; (ed and contrib.) Re-Focus on Child Abuse, 1994; contrib. legal jls and nat. newspapers. *Recreations:* travel, writing, watching sport. *Address:* 17 Bedford Row, WC1R 4EB. *T:* 0171–831 7314, *Fax:* 0171–831 0061. *Club:* Reform.

LEVY, Dennis Martyn; QC 1982; **His Honour Judge Levy;** a Circuit Judge, since 1991; *b* 20 Feb. 1936; *s* of Conrad Levy and late Tillie (*née* Swift); *m* 1967, Rachel Jonah; one *s* one *d*. *Educ:* Clifton Coll.; Gonville and Caius Coll., Cambridge (MA). Called to the Bar, Gray's Inn, 1960, Hong Kong, 1985, Turks and Caicos Is, 1987. Granada Group Ltd, 1960–63; Time Products Ltd, 1963–67; in practice at the Bar, 1967–91; a Recorder, 1989–91. *Recreations:* living in London and travelling abroad. *Address:* c/o 24 Old Buildings, Lincoln's Inn, WC2A 3UJ. *T:* 0171–404 0946, *Fax:* 0171–289 2079.

LEVY, Sir Ewart Maurice, 2nd Bt *cr* 1913; *b* 10 May 1897; *o s* of Sir Maurice Levy, 1st Bt; *S* father, 1933; *m* 1932, Hylda (*d* 1970), *e d* of late Sir Albert Levy; one *d*. *Educ:* Harrow. High Sheriff of Leicestershire, 1937; served, 1940–45, Royal Pioneer Corps, Lieut-Colonel, 1944; BLA, 1944–45 (despatches). JP Co. Leicester. *Heir:* none. *Address:* Welland House, Weston-by-Welland, Market Harborough, Leicestershire LE16 8HS. *Club:* Reform.

LEVY, George Joseph, MBE 1992; Chairman, H. Blairman & Sons Ltd, since 1965; *b* 21 May 1927; *s* of Percy and Maude Levy; *m* 1952, Wendy Yetta Blairman; one *s* three *d*. *Educ:* Oundle Sch. Joined H. Blairman & Sons Ltd (Antique Dealers), 1950, Dir, 1955. Pres., British Antique Dealers Assoc., 1974–76. Chairman: Grosvenor House Antiques Fair, 1978–79; Somerset Hse Art Treasures Exhibn, 1979; Burlington Hse Fair, 1980–82; Friends of the Iveagh Bequest, Kenwood, 1978–; London Historic House Museums Liaison Gp, English Heritage, 1985–; Mem. Council, Jewish Museum, 1980–. FRSA 1993. *Recreations:* theatre, visiting museums, photography. *Address:* Apartment 4, 6 Aldford Street, W1Y 5PS. *T:* 0171–495 1730.

LEVY, Prof. John Court, (Jack), OBE 1984; FEng 1988; FIMechE, FRAeS; FCGI; engineering consultant, since 1990; Director, Engineering Profession, Engineering Council, 1983–90; *b* London, 16 Feb. 1926; *s* of Alfred and Lily Levy; *m* 1952, Sheila Frances Krisman; two *s* one *d*. *Educ:* Owens Sch., London; Imperial Coll., Univ. of London (BScEng, ACGI, PhD); Univ. of Illinois, USA (MS). Stressman, Boulton-Paul Aircraft, 1945–47; Asst to Chief Engr, Fullers Ltd, 1947–51. Asst Lectr, Northampton Polytechnic, London, 1951–53; Fulbright Award to Univ. of Illinois, for research into metal fatigue, 1953–54; Lectr, Sen. Lectr, Reader, Northampton Polytechnic (later City Univ.), 1954–66; also a Recognised Teacher of the Univ. of London, 1958–66; Head of Department of Mechanical Engineering, 1966–83 (now Prof. Emeritus), and Pro-Vice-Chancellor, 1975–81, City Univ. Consultant to Shell International Marine, 1963–85; Chairman, 1st Panel on Marine Technology, SRC, 1971–73; Chm., Chartered Engr Section, Engineers Registration Bd, CEI, 1978–82; non-exec. Dir, City Technology Ltd, 1980–91. Freeman, City of London, 1991; Liveryman, Co. of Engineers, 1991. Hon. DTech CNAA, 1990; DUniv Leeds Metropolitan, 1992; Hon DSc City, 1994. *Publications:* The Engineering Dimension in Europe, 1991; papers on metal fatigue, marine technology, engrg educn, IMechE, RAeS, etc. *Recreations:* theatre, chess, exploring cities. *Address:* 18 Woodberry Way, Finchley, N12 0HG. *T:* 0181–445 5227. *Club:* Island Sailing (Cowes, IoW).

LEVY, Paul, PhD; FRSL; author and broadcaster; Contributing Editor, Europe, Wall Street Journal, since 1993; Wine Editor, You Magazine, The Mail on Sunday, since 1993; Contributing Editor, Travel & Leisure (USA), since 1993; *b* 26 Feb. 1941; *er s* of late H. S. Levy and Mrs Shirley Meyers (*née* Singer), Lexington, Ky, USA; *m* 1977, Penelope, *o c* of late Clifford and of Ruby Marcus; two *d*. *Educ:* Univ. of Chicago (AB); University Coll. London; Harvard Univ. (PhD 1979); Nuffield Coll., Oxford. FRSL 1980. Teaching Fellow, Harvard, 1966–68; lapsed academic, 1971–; freelance journalist, 1974–80; Food Correspondent, 1980–82, Food and Wine Ed., 1982–92, The Observer; frequent radio and television broadcasting. Member: Soc. of Authors; PEN; Location Register of Manuscripts Panel, SCONUL. Trustee: Strachey Trust, 1972–; Jane Grigson Trust, 1990–. Corning Award for food writing, 1980, 1981; Glenfiddich Food Writer of the Year, 1980, 1983; Glenfiddich Restaurant Critic of the Year, 1983; Specialist Writer Commendation, British Press Awards, 1985, 1987; Wine Journalist of the Year, Wine Guild of the UK, 1986. Confrèrie des Mousquetaires, 1981; Chevalier du Tastevin, 1987; Chevalier de l'ordre des Dames du Vin et de la Table, 1989; Chevalier de la Commanderie des Dindes de Lique, 1991. *Publications:* (ed) Lytton Strachey: the really interesting question, 1972; The Bloomsbury Group, in Essays on John Maynard Keynes, ed Milo Keynes, 1975; G. E. Moore and the Cambridge Apostles, 1979, 3rd edn 1989; (ed with Michael Holroyd) The Shorter Strachey, 1980, 2nd edn 1989; (with Ann Barr) The Official Foodie Handbook, 1984; Out to Lunch, 1986 (Seagrams/Internat. Assoc. of Cookery Professionals Award, USA, 1988); Finger-Lickin' Good: a Kentucky childhood (autobiog.), 1990; The Feast of Christmas, 1992 (also TV series); contribs to New York Times, TLS, Petits Propos Culinaires, Independent. *Recreations:* being cooked for, drinking better wine. *Address:* PO Box 35, Witney, Oxon OX8 8BF. *T:* Freeland (01993) 883477. *Club:* Groucho.

LEVY, Prof. Philip Marcus, PhD; CPsychol, FBPsS; Professor of Psychology, University of Lancaster, 1972–94, now Professor Emeritus; *b* 4 Feb. 1934; *s* of late Rupert Hyam Levy and of Sarah Beatrice Levy; *m* 1958, Gillian Mary (*née* Harker); two *d*. *Educ:* Leeds Modern School; Univ. of Leeds (BA 1955); Univ. of Birmingham (PhD 1960). Res. Fellow, Birmingham Univ., 1955–59; Psychologist, RAF, 1959–62; Sen. Res. Fellow, Lectr, Sen. Lectr, Birmingham Univ., 1962–72. Economic and Social Research Council (formerly Social Science Research Council): Mem. Council, 1983–86; Mem., Psychol. Cttee, 1976–82 (Chm., 1979–82); Chm., Educn and Human Develt Cttee, 1982–87; Chm., Human Behaviour and Develt R&D Gp, 1987–89 (Mem. Council, 1987–89). British Psychological Society: Mem. Council, 1973–80; Pres., 1978–79. Editor, Brit. Jl of Mathematical and Statistical Psychology, 1975–80. *Publications:* (jtly) Tests in Education, 1984; (jtly) Cognition in Action, 1987; numerous in psychol jls. *Address:* Department of Psychology, University of Lancaster, Lancaster LA1 4YF. *T:* Lancaster (01524) 65201.

LEVY, Prof. Raymond, FRCPE, FRCPsych; Professor of Old Age Psychiatry, University of London at Institute of Psychiatry, since 1984; Hon. Consultant, Bethlem Royal and Maudsley Hospitals, since 1984; *b* 23 June 1933; *o s* of late Gaston Levy and Esther Levy (*née* Bigio); *m* 1956, Katherine Margaret Logie (marr. diss. 1982); two *d*. *Educ:* Victoria Coll., Cairo; Edinburgh Univ. (MB, ChB 1957; PhD 1961); Univ. of London (DPM 1964). Jun. hosp. appts, Royal Infirmary, Northern Gen., Leith, Bethlem Royal and Maudsley Hosps, to 1966; Sen. Lectr and Hon. Consultant Psychiatrist, Middx Hosp. Med. Sch., 1966–71; Consultant Psychiatrist, Bethlem Royal and Maudsley Hosps, 1971–84. Mem., Med. Adv. Commn on Res. into Ageing. Pres., Internat. Psychogeriatric Assoc., 1995–; Vice-Pres., Eur. Assoc. Geriatric Psych.; Foundn Mem., RCPsych, 1971. Asst Editor, Internat. Jl Geriatric Psych. *Publications:* (all jtly) The Psychiatry of Late Life, 1982; Diagnostic and Therapeutic Assessment in Alzheimer's Disease, 1991; Delusions and Hallucinations in Old Age, 1992; Clinical diversity in late onset of Alzheimer's Disease, 1992; Treatment and Care in Old Age Psychiatry, 1993; Dementia, 1993; contribs to learned jls. *Recreations:* looking at pictures, drinking good wine, travelling, playing tennis. *Address:* Institute of Psychiatry, de Crespigny Park, Denmark Hill, SE5 8AF. *T:* 0171–703 5411; 52 Westminster Palace Gardens, Artillery Row, SW1P 1RR. *Clubs:* Reform; Campden Hill Lawn Tennis.

LEVY-LANG, André; Légion d'Honneur; Chairman: Compagnie Financière de Paribas, since 1990; Banque-Paribas, since 1991; *b* 26 Nov. 1937. *Educ:* Ecole Polytechnique; Stanford Univ. (PhD Business Admin; Harkness Fellow, 1963–65). Res. physicist, French Atomic Energy Commn, 1960–62; Schlumberger Gp, 1962–74; Compagnie Bancaire: joined 1974; Mem. Bd, 1979; Chm., 1982; Chm., Adv. Bd, 1993. Director: Cie de Navigation Mixte; Crédit National; Péchiney; Schneider; Power Corp., Canada; CLT; Schlumberger; Co. Belge de Participation Paribas; Eurasia Holding; Mem. Exec. Cttee, Pargesa Holding. Bd mem., banking and employers' assocs. *Address:* Cie Financière de Paribas, 5 rue d'Antin, 75002 Paris, France.

LEW, Jonathan Michael; Chief Executive, United Synagogue, since 1986; *b* 23 Nov. 1937; *s* of Rabbi Maurice A. Lew and Rachel Lew; *m* 1963, Linda Samad; one *s* one *d*. *Educ:* Univ. of Witwatersrand (BCom). ACMA. Finance Director: Dorland Advertising, 1973–79; Dancer Fitzgerald Sample Internat., 1979–83; MWK Advertising, 1984–85. Hon. Officer, United Synagogue, 1984–86. Lay Mem., Marylebone Duty Solicitors' Cttee, 1987–; Gen. Comr for Income Taxes, 1992–. *Recreations:* bridge, travel, family. *Address:* 41 Eyre Court, St John's Wood, NW8 9TU.

LEWANDO, Sir Jan (Alfred), Kt 1974; CBE 1968; *b* 31 May 1909; *s* of Maurice Lewando and Eugenie Lewando (*née* Goldsmid); *m* 1948, Nora Slavouski; three *d*. *Educ:* Manchester Grammar Sch.; Manchester University. Served War of 1939–45, British Army: British Army Staff, Washington DC and British Min. of Supply Mission, 1941–45 (Lt-Col, 1943). Marks & Spencer Ltd, 1929–70 (Dir 1954–70); Chairman: Carrington Viyella Ltd, 1970–75; Consolidated Textile Mills Ltd, Canada, 1972–75; Penn Consultants Ltd, 1975–; Pres., Carrington Viyella Inc. (USA), 1971–75; Director: Carrington Tesit (Italy), 1971–75; Heal and Son Holdings, 1975–82 (Dep. Chm., 1977–82); Bunzl PLC (formerly Bunzl Pulp & Paper Ltd), 1976–86; W. A. Baxter & Sons Ltd, 1975–; Johnston Group Inc. (USA) (formerly Johnston Industries Inc.), 1976–85; Edgars Stores Ltd (South Africa), 1976–82; Royal Worcester Spode Ltd, 1978–79; Bunzl and Biach AG (Austria), 1979–80; Johnston Industries Ltd, 1980–85; Chm., Gelvenor Textiles Ltd, S Africa, 1973–75. Vice Chm., Clothing Export Council, 1966–70; Pres., British Textile Confedn, 1972–73; Vice Pres., Comitextil, Brussels, 1972–73; Member: British Overseas Trade Bd, 1972–77 (Mem., European Trade Cttee, 1973–83); British Overseas Trade Adv. Council, 1975–77; BNEC, 1969–71; Council, UK-S Africa Trade Assoc., 1973–92; Export Council for Europe, 1965–69; European Steering Cttee, CBI, 1968–71; Grand Council, CBI, 1971–75. Pres., Transport Trust, 1989–91 (Vice Pres., 1973–88). Chm., Appeal Cttee, British Inst. of Radiology, 1979–84. CIMgt (CBIM 1980; FBIM 1972); FRSA 1973. Companion, Textile Inst., 1972. Order of Legion of Merit (USA), 1946. *Address:* Langham House, Drews Park, Beaconsfield, Bucks HP9 2TT. *T:* Beaconsfield (01494) 674987. *Clubs:* Carlton, Royal Automobile, Pilgrims, Institute of Directors, MCC; Wentworth, Beaconsfield Golf, Stoke Poges Golf.

LEWEN, John Henry, CMG 1977; HM Diplomatic Service, retired; Ambassador to the People's Republic of Mozambique, 1975–79; *b* 6 July 1920; *s* of Carl Henry Lewen and Alice (*née* Mundy); *m* 1945, Emilienne Alette Julie Alida Galant; three *s*. *Educ:* Christ's Hospital; King's Coll., Cambridge. Royal Signals, 1940–45. HM Foreign (subseq. Diplomatic) Service, 1946; HM Embassy: Lisbon, 1947–50; Rangoon, 1950–53; FO, 1953–55; HM Embassy: Rio de Janeiro, 1955–59; Warsaw, 1959–61; FO, 1961–63; Head of Chancery, HM Embassy, Rabat, 1963–67; Consul-General, Jerusalem, 1967–70; Inspector of HM Diplomatic Estabts, 1970–73; Dir, Admin and Budget, Secretariat-Gen. of Council of Ministers of European Communities, 1973–75. OStJ 1969. *Recreations:* singing, history. *Address:* 1 Brimley Road, Cambridge CB4 2DQ. *T:* Cambridge (01223) 359101.

LEWER, Michael Edward; QC 1983; a Recorder of the Crown Court, since 1983; *b* 1 Dec. 1933; *s* of late Stanley Gordon Lewer and Jeanie Mary Lewer; *m* 1965, Bridget Mary Gill; two *s* two *d*. *Educ:* Tonbridge Sch.; Oriel Coll., Oxford (MA). Called to Bar, Gray's Inn, 1958, Bencher, 1992. Territorial Army: Captain, 300 LAA Regt, RA, 1955–64; APIS, Intelligence Corps, 1964–67. Chm., Home Secretary's Adv. Cttee on Local Govt Electoral Arrangements for England, 1971–73; Asst Comr, Parly Boundary Commn for

England, 1965–69, 1976–88, 1992–. Chm., Criminal Injuries Compensation Appeals Panel, 1994–; Mem., Criminal Injuries Compensation Bd, 1986–. Mem., European Parly Constituency Cttee for England, 1993–94. Mem., Bar Council, 1978–81. *Address:* Farrar's Building, Temple, EC4Y 7BD. *T:* 0171–583 9241. *Club:* Western (Glasgow).

LEWERS, Very Rev. Benjamin Hugh; Provost of Derby, since 1981; *b* 25 March 1932; *s* of late Hugh Bunnett Lewers, DSO, OBE and Coral Helen Lewers; *m* 1957, Sara Blagden; three *s. Educ:* Sherborne School; Selwyn Coll., Cambridge (MA); Lincoln Theological Coll. Employee, Dunlop Rubber Co., 1953–57. Curate, St Mary, Northampton, 1962–65; Priest-in-charge, Church of the Good Shepherd, Hounslow, 1965–68; Industrial Chaplain, Heathrow Airport, 1968–75; Vicar of Newark, 1975–80, Rector 1980–81. A Church Commissioner, 1985–. *Recreations:* cricket, music, gardening, wine and rug making, photography. *Address:* The Provost's House, 9 Highfield Road, Derby DE22 1GX. *T:* Derby (01332) 342971.

LEWES, Suffragan Bishop of, since 1992; **Rt. Rev. Ian Patrick Martyn Cundy;** *b* 23 April 1945; *s* of Henry Martyn Cundy and Kathleen Ethel Cundy; *m* 1969, Josephine Katherine Boyd; two *s* one *d. Educ:* Monkton Combe Sch., 1958–63; Trinity Coll., Cambridge, 1964–67 (BA 1967; MA 1971); Tyndale Hall, Bristol, 1967–69. Ordained: deacon, 1969; priest, 1970; Asst curate, Christ Church, New Malden, 1969–73; Tutor and Lectr in Church History, Oak Hill Coll., London, 1973–77; Team Rector, Mortlake with East Sheen, 1978–83; Warden, Cranmer Hall, St John's Coll., Durham, 1983–92. *Publication:* Ephesians—2 Thessalonians, 1981. *Recreations:* walking, music, photography, vintage cars. *Address:* Beacon View, Berwick, Polegate, East Sussex BN26 6ST. *T:* Alfriston (01323) 870387, *Fax:* (01323) 870967.

LEWES AND HASTINGS, Archdeacon of; *see* Glaisyer, Ven. H.

LEWIN, family name of **Baron Lewin.**

LEWIN, Baron *cr* 1982 (Life Peer), of Greenwich in Greater London; **Admiral of the Fleet Terence Thornton Lewin,** KG 1983; GCB 1976 (KCB 1973); LVO 1958; DSC 1942; Chief of the Defence Staff, 1979–82; *b* Dover, 19 Nov. 1920; *m* 1944, Jane Branch-Evans; two *s* one *d. Educ:* The Judd Sch., Tonbridge. Joined RN, 1939; War Service in Home and Mediterranean Fleets in HMS Valiant, HMS Ashanti in Malta Convoys, N Russian Convoys, invasion N Africa and Channel (despatches); comd HMS Corunna, 1955–56; Comdr HM Yacht Britannia, 1957–58; Captain (F) Dartmouth Training Squadron and HM Ships Urchin and Tenby, 1961–63; Director, Naval Tactical and Weapons Policy Division, MoD, 1964–65; comd HMS Hermes, 1966–67; Asst Chief of Naval Staff (Policy), 1968–69; Flag Officer, Second-in-Comd, Far East Fleet, 1969–70; Vice-Chief of the Naval Staff, 1971–73; C-in-C Fleet, 1973–75; C-in-C Naval Home Command, 1975–77; Chief of Naval Staff and First Sea Lord, 1977–79. Flag ADC to the Queen, 1975–77; First and Principal ADC to the Queen, 1977–79. Life Col Comdt, RM, 1995. Mem. Council, White Ensign Assoc. Ltd, 1982– (Chm. Council and Assoc., 1983–87); Chm., Trustees, National Maritime Museum, 1987–95 (Trustee, 1981–; Dep. Chm., 1986–87); Mem., Museums and Galleries Commn, 1983–87; President: Shipwrecked Fishermen and Mariners' Royal Benevolent Soc., 1984–; British Schools Exploring Soc., 1985–; George Cross Island Assoc., 1988–; Soc. for Nautical Res., 1989–. Elder Brother of Trinity House, 1975; Hon. Freeman: Skinners' Co., 1976; Shipwrights' Co., 1978. Hon. DSc City, 1977; Hon. DLitt Greenwich, 1993. *Address:* House of Lords, SW1A 0PW.

LEWINTON, Sir Christopher, Kt 1993; FEng 1994; Chief Executive since 1986, and Chairman since 1989, TI Group plc (Deputy Chairman, 1986–89); Chairman, Dowty Group PLC, since 1992; *b* 6 Jan. 1932; *s* of Joseph and Elizabeth Lewinton; *m* 1st, Jennifer Alcock (marr. diss.); two *s*; 2nd, 1979, Louise Head; two step *s. Educ:* Acton Technical College; Univ. of London. CEng, FIMechE; FRAeS. Army Service, Lieut REME. Pres., Wilkinson Sword, N America, 1960–70; Chm., Wilkinson Sword Group, 1970–85; Pres., Internat. Gp, Allegheny International, 1976–85 (Exec. Vice-Pres., Mem. Board). Director: Reed Internat., 1990–; Reed Elsevier, 1993–. *Recreations:* golf, tennis, travel, reading. *Address:* TI Group, 50 Curzon Street, W1Y 7PN. *T:* 0171–499 9131. *Clubs:* Buck's; Sunningdale Golf; University (New York); Key Biscayne Yacht (Florida).

LEWIS; *see* Day-Lewis.

LEWIS, family name of **Baron Lewis of Newnham** and of **Barony of Merthyr.**

LEWIS OF NEWNHAM, Baron *cr* 1989 (Life Peer), of Newnham in the County of Cambridgeshire; **Jack Lewis;** Kt 1982; FRS 1973; FRSC; (first) Warden of Robinson College, Cambridge, since 1975; Professor of Chemistry, University of Cambridge, 1970–95; Hon. Fellow of Sidney Sussex College (Fellow, 1970–77); *b* 13 Feb. 1928; *m* 1951, Elfreida Mabel (*née* Lamb); one *s* one *d. Educ:* Barrow Grammar Sch. BSc London 1949; PhD Nottingham 1952; DSc London 1961; MSc Manchester 1964; MA Cantab 1970; ScD Cantab 1977. Lecturer: Univ. of Sheffield, 1953–56; Imperial Coll., London, 1956–57; Lecturer-Reader, University Coll., London, 1957–62; Prof. of Chemistry: Univ. of Manchester, 1962–67; UCL, 1967–70. Firth Vis. Prof., Univ. of Sheffield, 1969; Lectures: Frontiers of Science, Case/Western Reserve, 1963; Tilden, RIC, 1966; Miller, Univ. of Illinois, 1966; Shell, Stanford Univ., 1968; Venables, Univ. of N Carolina, 1968; A. D. Little, MIT, 1970; Boomer, Univ. of Alberta, 1971; AM, Princeton, 1972; Baker, Cornell, 1974; Nyholm, Chem. Soc., 1974; Chini, Italian Chem. Soc., 1981; Bailar, Illinois Univ., 1982; Dwyer, NSW Inst. of Tech., 1982; Powell, Queensland Univ., 1982; Mond, Chem. Soc., 1984; Leeumaker, Wesleyan Univ., 1984; Pettit May, Texas, 1985; Wheeler, Dublin, 1986; Bakerian, Roy. Soc., 1989. Member: CNAA Cttee, 1964–70; Exec. Cttee, Standing Cttee on Univ. Entry, 1966–76; Schs Council, 1966–76; SERC (formerly SRC): Polytechnics Cttee, 1973–; Chemistry Cttee (Chm., 1975–82); Science Bd, 1975–82; Council, 1980–; SERC/SSRC Jt Cttee, 1981–84; UGC (Phy. Sci.), 1975–81; Council, Royal Soc., 1982–84 (a Vice-Pres., 1984); Vis. Cttee, Cranfield Inst. of Tech., 1983– (Chm., 1985–93); Royal Commn on Environmental Pollution, 1985– (Chm., 1986–93). Mem., H of L European Communities Select Cttee, 1993– (Chm. Sub-Cttee C, 1993–). Pres., Royal Soc. of Chemistry, 1986–88; Sci. Rep. for UK on NATO Sci. Cttee, 1985–. Trustee, Crocker Foundn, 1989–. Dir, BOC Foundn, 1990–. Patron, Student Community Action Develt Unit, 1985–. For. Mem., Amer. Acad. of Arts and Science, 1984; For. Associate, Nat. Acad. of Sciences, USA, 1987. FNA 1980 (For. Fellow 1986); Fellow, Amer. Philos. Soc., 1994. Hon. Fellow: UCL, 1990; UMIST, 1990; Central Lancs, 1993; Edinburgh, 1994. Dr *hc* Rennes, 1980; DUniv: Open, 1982; Kingston, 1993; Hon. DSc: Nottingham, 1983; Keele, 1984; Leicester, 1988; Birmingham, 1988; Waterloo, Canada, 1988; Manchester, 1990; Wales (Swansea), 1990; Sheffield, 1992; Cranfield, 1993; Hon. ScD East Anglia, 1983. American Chem. Soc. Award in Inorganic Chemistry, 1970; Transition Metal Award, Chem. Soc., 1973; Davy Medal, Royal Soc., 1985; Mallinckrodt Award in Inorganic Chemistry, American Chem. Soc., 1986. Chevalier, Ordre des Palmes Académiques, 1993. *Publications:* papers, mainly in Jl of Chem. Soc. *Address:* Robinson College, Grange Road, Cambridge CB3 9AN. *Club:* United Oxford & Cambridge University.

LEWIS, Adam Anthony Murless, FRCS, FRCSE; Surgeon to the Royal Household, since 1991; Consultant Surgeon, Royal Free Hospital, since 1975; Surgeon: St John and Elizabeth Hospital, London; King Edward VII Hospital for Officers, London; *s* of Bernard S. Lewis and Mary Lewis (*née* Murless); *m* 1964, Margaret Catherine Ann Surgey; two *s* two *d. Educ:* St Bartholomew's Hosp. Med. Coll. (MB, BS London 1963); FRCSE 1968; FRCS 1969. Formerly: Sen. Registrar (Surg.), Royal Free Hosp.; Post Doctoral Fellow, Stanford Univ.; Sen. Lectr (Surg.), Univ. of Benin. *Publications:* papers on general and gastro-intestinal surgery. *Address:* 8 Upper Wimpole Street, W1M 7TD. *T:* 0171–935 1956.

LEWIS, Maj.-Gen. Alfred George, CBE 1969; *b* 23 July 1920; *s* of Louis Lewis; *m* 1946, Daye Neville, *d* of Neville Greaves Hunt; two *s* two *d. Educ:* St Dunstan's Coll.; King's Coll., London. Served War of 1939–45, India and Burma. Commanded 15th/19th Hussars, 1961–63; Dir, Defence Operational Requirements Staff, MoD, 1967–68; Dep. Comdt, Royal Mil. Coll. of Science, 1968–70; Dir Gen., Fighting Vehicles and Engineer Equipment, 1970–72, retired 1973. Man. Dir, 1973–80, Dep. Chm., 1980–81, Alvis Ltd; Dep. Chm., Self Changing Gears Ltd, 1976–81; Company Secretary: Leyland Vehicles, 1980–81; Bus Manufacturers (Hldgs), 1980–84; Staff Dir, BL plc, 1981–84. Hon. Col, Queen's Own Mercian Yeomanry, 1977–82. Mem., St John Council for Warwickshire, 1973–; SBStJ 1989. *Recreations:* gardening, writing, making things, croquet.

LEWIS, (Alun) Kynric, QC 1978; QC (NI) 1988; a Recorder of the Crown Court, since 1979; *b* Harlech, 23 May 1928; 3rd *s* of late Rev. Cadwaladr O. Lewis and Ursula Lewis; *m* 1955, Bethan, *er d* of late Prof. Edgar Thomas, CBE, and Eurwen Thomas; one *s* two *d. Educ:* The Grammar School, Beaumaris; University Coll. of N Wales (BSc); London School of Economics (LLB). Barrister, Middle Temple, 1954, Bencher, 1988; Gray's Inn, 1961; in practice in intellectual property law chambers, 1955–. Member: Cttees of Investigation for GB and England and Wales under Agricl Marketing Act, 1979–88; Parole Bd, 1982–85; Welsh Arts Council, 1986–92. Hon. Counsel: Welsh Books Council, 1989–; Ymddiriedolaeth Nant Gwtheyrn, 1992–. *Recreations:* walking, fishing, tending vines. *Address:* Penrallt, Llys-faen, Caerdydd CF4 5TG; 8 New Square, Lincoln's Inn, WC2A 3QP. *Club:* Reform.

LEWIS, Anthony; *see* Lewis, J. A.

LEWIS, Anthony Meredith; Joint Senior Partner, Taylor Joynson Garrett, Solicitors, since 1989; *b* 15 Nov. 1940; *s* of Col Glyndwr Vivian Lancelot Lewis and Gillian Lewis (*née* Fraser); *m* 1970, Mrs Ewa Maria Anna Strawinska; one *s* one *d. Educ:* Rugby School; St Edmund Hall, Oxford (MA Law). Freshfields, 1964–70; Partner, Joynson-Hicks, 1970–86, Senior Partner, 1986–89. *Recreations:* opera, tennis, ski-ing, shooting, cricket. *Address:* Hampnett House, Northleach, Glos GL54 3NN.

LEWIS, Anthony Robert, (Tony Lewis); DL; Chairman, Wales Tourist Board, since 1992; Board Member, British Tourist Authority, since 1992; writer and broadcaster; BBC TV presenter of cricket and commentator, since 1974; *b* 6 July 1938; *s* of Wilfrid Llewellyn Lewis and Florence Marjorie Lewis (*née* Flower); *m* 1962, Joan (*née* Pritchard); two *d. Educ:* Neath Grammar Sch.; Christ's Coll., Cambridge (MA). Double Blue, Rugby football, 1959, cricket, 1960–62, Captain of cricket, 1962, Cambridge Univ. Glamorgan CCC: cricketer, 1955–74; Captain, 1967–72; Chm., 1988–; 9 Tests for England, 1972–73 (Captain of 8); Captained MCC to India, Ceylon and Pakistan, 1972–73. Presenter: sports and arts magazine programmes, HTV, 1971–82; Sport on Four, BBC Radio, 1977–86. Cricket Correspondent, Sunday Telegraph, 1974–93; freelance sports contributor, Daily Telegraph, 1993–. Chm. Cttee, Assoc. of Business Sponsorship of the Arts (Wales), 1988–; Member: Welsh Economic Council, 1994–; Tourism Action Gp, CBI, 1994–. DL Mid Glam, 1994. Hon. Fellow: St David's, Lampeter; Glamorgan Univ. *Publications:* A Summer of Cricket, 1976; Playing Days, 1985; Double Century, 1987; Cricket in Many Lands, 1991; MCC Masterclass, 1994. *Recreations:* classical music, golf. *Address:* Castellau, near Llantrisant, Mid Glamorgan CF7 8LP. *Clubs:* East India, MCC; Cardiff and County; Royal Porthcawl Golf, Royal Worlington & Newmarket Golf, Royal & Ancient Golf.

LEWIS, Arthur William John; ex-Trade Union Official (National Union of General and Municipal Workers); *b* 21 Feb. 1917; *s* of late J. Lewis; *m* 1940, Lucy Ethel Clack; one *d. Educ:* Elementary Sch.; Borough Polytechnic. Shop steward of his Dept of City of London Corporation at 17; Vice-Chairman of TU branch (City of London NUGMW) at 18; full-time London district official NUGMW 1938–48; Member of London Trades Council and Holborn City Trades Council, various joint industrial councils, Government cttees, etc; Member: ASTMS; APEX; G&MWU. MP (Lab): West Ham, Upton, 1945–50; W Ham N, 1950–74; Newham NW, 1974–83; contested (Ind. Lab) Newham NW, 1983. Mem., Expenditure Cttee. Formerly Member Exec. Cttee, London Labour Party; Chairman Eastern Regional Group of Labour MPs, 1950–83; Member Eastern Regional Council of Labour Party and Exec. Cttee of that body, 1950–83. Served in the Army. *Recreations:* swimming, motoring, boxing, general athletics.

LEWIS, Prof. Barry, MD, PhD; FRCP; FRCPath; Consultant Physician and Professor Emeritus, University of London; *b* 16 March 1929; *s* of George Lewis and Pearl Lewis; *m* 1972, Eve Simone Rothschild; three *c. Educ:* Rondebosch School, Cape Town; University of Cape Town. PhD, MD. Training posts, Groote Schuur Hosp., Cape Town, 1953; lectureship and fellowships, St George's Hosp., 1959; MRC, 1963; Consultant Pathologist, St Mark's Hosp., 1967; Sen. Lectr in Chemical Pathology, hon. consultant chem. pathologist and physician, Hammersmith Hosp., 1971; Chm., Dept of Chem. Path. and Metabolic Disorders, St Thomas' Hosp., and Dir of Lipid Clinic, 1976–88. Present research interests: causes, prevention and regression of atherosclerosis. Chm., Internat. Taskforce for Prevention of Coronary Heart Disease, 1987–94. Heinrich Wieland Prize, 1980. *Publications:* The Hyperlipidaemias: clinical and laboratory practice, 1976; (with Eve Lewis) The Heart Book, 1980; (with N. Miller) Lipoproteins, Atherosclerosis and Coronary Heart Disease, 1981; (jtly) Metabolic and Molecular Bases of Acquired Disease, 1990; Handbook on Prevention of Coronary Heart Disease, 1990; (with G. Assmann) Social and Economic Contexts of Coronary Disease Prevention, 1990; (jtly) Prevention of Coronary Heart Disease in the Elderly, 1991; (jtly) Prevention of Coronary Heart Disease: scientific background and clinical guidelines, 1993; (jtly) Low Blood Cholesterol: health implications, 1993; numerous papers on heart disease, nutrition and lipoproteins in med. and sci. jls. *Recreations:* music, travel, reading. *Address:* York House, Westminster Bridge Road, SE1 7UT. *T:* 0171–928 5485.

LEWIS, Bernard, BA, PhD; FBA 1963; FRHistS; Cleveland E. Dodge Professor of Near Eastern Studies, Princeton University, 1974–86, now Emeritus; Director of Annenberg Research Institute, Philadelphia, 1986–90; *b* London, 31 May 1916; *s* of H. Lewis, London; *m* 1947, Ruth Hélène (marr. diss. 1974), *d* of late Overretsagfrer M. Oppenhejm, Copenhagen; one *s* one *d. Educ:* Wilson Coll.; The Polytechnic; Universities of London and Paris (Fellow UCL 1976). Derby Student, 1936. Asst Lecturer in Islamic History, Sch. of Oriental Studies, University of London, 1938; Prof. of History of Near and Middle East, SOAS, London Univ., 1949–74 (Hon. Fellow, 1986). Served RAC and Intelligence Corps, 1940–41; attached to a dept of Foreign Office, 1941–45. Visiting Professor: UCLA, 1955–56; Columbia Univ., 1960; Indiana Univ., 1963; Collège de France, 1980; Ecoles des Hautes Etudes, Paris 1983–86; A. D. White Prof.-at-Large, Cornell Univ., 1984–90; Hon. Incumbent, Kemal Atatürk Chair in Ottoman and Turkish Studies, 1992–93. Vis. Mem., 1969, Long-term Mem., 1974–86, Inst. for Advanced Study, Princeton, New Jersey; Lectures: Class of 1932, Princeton Univ., 1964; Gottesman, Yeshiva Univ., 1974; Exxon Foundn, Chicago, 1986; Tanner, Brasenose Coll., Oxford, 1990; Jefferson, NEH, 1990; Il Mulino, Bologna, 1991; Weizman, Rehovot, Israel, 1991; Henry M. Jackson Meml, Seattle, 1992; Merle Curti, Wisconsin, 1993. Mem., Amer. Acad. of Arts and Scis, 1983; Membre Associe, Institut d'Egypte, Cairo, 1969; For. Mem., Amer. Philosophical Soc., 1973. Hon. Fellow, Turkish Historical Soc., Ankara, 1972; Hon. Dr: Hebrew Univ., Jerusalem, 1974; Tel Aviv Univ., 1979; State Univ. of NY, Univ. of Penn, Hebrew Union Coll., 1987; Haifa, 1991; Yeshiva, 1991; Bar-Ilan, 1992. Brandeis, 1993. Certificate of Merit for services to Turkish Culture, Turkish Govt, 1973. Harvey Prizewinner, 1978. *Publications:* The Origins of Ismā'īlism, 1940; Turkey Today, 1940; British contributions to Arabic Studies, 1941; Handbook of Diplomatic and Political Arabic, 1947, 1956; (ed) Land of Enchanters, 1948; The Arabs in History, 1950, 6th rev. edn 1993; Notes and Documents from the Turkish Archives, 1952; The Emergence of Modern Turkey, 1961 (rev. edn, 1968); The Kingly Crown (translated from Ibn Gabirol), 1961; co-ed. with P. M. Holt, Historians of the Middle East, 1962; Istanbul and the Civilization of the Ottoman Empire, 1963; The Middle East and the West, 1964; The Assassins, 1967; Race and Colour in Islam, 1971; Islam in History, 1973, rev. edn 1993; Islam from the Prophet Muhammad to the Capture of Constantinople, 2 vols, 1974; History, Remembered, Recovered, Invented, 1975; (ed) The World of Islam: Faith, People, Culture, 1976; Studies in Classical and Ottoman Islam, 7th-16th centuries, 1976; (with Amnon Cohen) Population and Revenue in the Towns of Palestine in the Sixteenth Century, 1978; The Muslim Discovery of Europe, 1982; The Jews of Islam, 1984; Le Retour de l'Islam, 1985; (ed, with others) As Others See Us: mutual perceptions East and West, 1985; Semites and Anti-Semites, 1986; The Political Language of Islam, 1988; Race and Slavery in the Middle East, 1990; (ed jtly) Musulmans en Europe, 1992; (ed jtly) Religionsgerspräche im Mittelalter, 1992; Islam and the West, 1993; The Shaping of the Modern Middle East, 1994; Cultures in Conflict: Christians, Muslims and Jews in the Age of Discovery, 1994; co-ed, Encyclopaedia of Islam, 1956–87; (ed, with others) The Cambridge History of Islam, vols 1–11, 1971; articles in learned journals. *Address:* Near Eastern Studies Department, Jones Hall, Princeton University, Princeton, NJ 08540, USA. *Club:* Athenæum.

LEWIS, His Honour Bernard; a Circuit Judge (formerly a County Court Judge), 1966–80; *b* 1 Feb. 1905; 3rd *s* of late Solomon and Jeannette Lewis, London; *m* 1934, Harriette, *d* of late I. A. Waine, Dublin, London and Nice; one *s*. *Educ:* Trinity Hall, Cambridge (MA). Called to the Bar, Lincoln's Inn, 1929. Mem. S-E Circuit. Hon. Mem., Central Criminal Court Bar Mess. *Recreations:* revolver shooting, bricklaying. *Address:* Trevelyan House, Arlington Road, Twickenham, Middx TW1 2AS. *T:* 0181–892 1841. *Clubs:* Reform, Aula; Cambridge Society; Ham and Petersham Rifle and Pistol.

LEWIS, Very Rev. Bertie; Vicar of Nevern with Eglwyswrw, Meline, Eglwyswen and Llanfair Nant-gwyn, since 1994; *b* 24 Aug. 1931; *m* 1958, Rayann Pryce; one *s* three *d*. *Educ:* St David's Coll., Lampeter (BA); St Catherine's Coll., Oxford (MA); Wycliffe Hall, Oxford. Deacon 1957; priest 1958; Curate: Cwmaman, 1957–60; Aberystwyth St Michael, 1960–62; Vicar: Llanddewibrefi, 1962–65; Henfynyw with Aberaeron, 1965–75; Lampeter, 1975–80; Canon, St Davids Cathedral, 1978–86; Rector, Rectorial Benefice of Aberystwyth, 1980–88; Archdeacon of Cardigan, 1986–90; Vicar of Nevern, 1988–90; Dean of St David's Cathedral, 1990–94, Hon. Canon, 1994–. *Recreations:* rugby, music, books. *Address:* The Vicarage, Nevern, Newport, Dyfed SY42 0NF. *T:* Newport (01239) 820427.

LEWIS, Cecil Arthur, MC; author; *b* Birkenhead, 29 March 1898; *m* 1921 (marr. diss. 1940); one *s* one *d*; *m* 1942 (marr. diss. 1950); no *c*; *m* 1960. *Educ:* Dulwich Coll.; University Coll. Sch.; Oundle. Royal Flying Corps, 1915 (MC, despatches twice); Manager Civil Aviation, Vickers, Ltd, 1919; Flying Instructor to Chinese Government, Peking, 1920, 1921; one of four founders of BBC, Chm. of Programme Board, 1922–26; Varied Literary Activities: stage, screen (first two adaptations of Bernard Shaw's plays to screen, 1930–32), and television plays (Nativity, Crucifixion and Patience of Job, 1956–59) and production connected therewith. RAF, 1939–45. Sheep farming, South Africa, 1947–50. United Nations Secretariat, New York, radio and television, 1953–55. Commercial television, London, 1955–56. Daily Mail, 1956–66; retd. Compiled and presented, Between Ourselves, (radio play), 1991. *Publications:* Broadcasting From Within, 1924; The Unknown Warrior, trans. from French of Paul Raynal, 1928; Sagittarius Rising (autobiog.), 1936, 5th edn 1993; The Trumpet is Mine, 1938; Challenge to the Night, 1938; Self Portrait: Letters and Journals of the late Charles Ricketts, RA (Editor), 1939 (filmed for TV, 1979); Pathfinders, 1943, rev. edn 1986; Yesterday's Evening, 1946; Farewell to Wings, 1964; Turn Right for Corfu, 1972; Never Look Back (autobiog.), 1974 (filmed for TV, 1978); A Way to Be, 1977; Gemini to Joburg, 1984; The Gospel According to Judas, 1989; The Dark Sands of Shambala, 1990; Sagittarius Surviving, 1991; (Introd.) Wind, Sand and Stars by Antoine De St Exupéry, 1991; All My Yesterdays (autobiog.), 1993; A Wish to Be, 1994. *Address:* c/o National Westminster Bank, 34 Henrietta Street, WC2E 8NL.

LEWIS, Very Rev. Christopher Andrew, PhD; Dean of St Albans, since 1994; *b* 4 Feb. 1944; *s* of Adm. Sir Andrew Lewis, KCB and late Rachel Elizabeth (*née* Leatham); *m* 1970, Rhona Jane Martindale; two *s* one *d*. *Educ:* Marlborough Coll.; Bristol Univ. (BA 1969); Corpus Christi Coll., Cambridge (PhD 1974); Westcott House, Cambridge. Served RN, 1961–66; ordained deacon, 1973, priest, 1974; Asst Curate, Barnard Castle, 1973–76; Tutor, Ripon Coll., Cuddesdon, 1976–81; Dir, Oxford Inst. for Church and Soc., 1976–79; Priest-in-charge, Aston Rowant and Crowell, 1978–81; Vice Principal, Ripon Coll., Cuddesdon, 1981–82; Vicar of Spalding, 1982–87; Canon Residentiary, Canterbury Cathedral, 1987–94; Dir of Ministerial Trng, dio. of Canterbury, 1989–94. *Address:* The Deanery, St Albans, Herts AL1 1BY. *T:* St Albans (01727) 852120.

LEWIS, Clive Hewitt, FRICS, FSVA; Joint Chairman, Colliers Erdman Lewis (formerly Erdman Lewis International), since 1992; President, Royal Institution of Chartered Surveyors, 1993–94; *b* 29 March 1936; *s* of Thomas Jonathan Lewis, OBE and Marguerite Eileen Lewis; *m* 1961, Jane Penelope White; two *s* one *d*. *Educ:* St Peter's Sch., York. FRICS 1963; FSVA 1979. With Goddard & Smith, 1957–62; Founder and Sen. Partner, Clive Lewis & Partners, 1963–92, when merged with Edward Erdman. Director: St Modwen Properties, 1983 ; Town Centre Securities, 1994–. Dep. Chm., Merseyside Develt Corp., 1989–. Chm., Bank of England Property Forum, 1994–. Mem. Council, Internat. Year of Shelter for the Homeless, 1985–88. Mem., Gen. Council, RICS, 1987–95 (Pres., Gen. Practice Div., 1989–90); President: Eur. Council of Real Estate Professionals, 1990; UK, 1976–77, World, 1984–85, Internat. Real Estate Fedn (Mem. Exec. Cttee, 1977–92). Pres., Land Aid Charitable Trust, 1986. Freeman, City of London, 1983; Liveryman, Chartered Surveyors' Co., 1983–. Hon. DLitt S Bank, 1993. *Recreations:* bridge, dogs, golf, cricket. *Address:* Colliers Erdman Lewis, 6 Grosvenor Street, W1X 0AD. *T:* 0171–629 8191. *Club:* MCC.

LEWIS, Prof. Dan, PhD; DSc; FRS 1955; Quain Professor of Botany, London University, 1957–78, now Emeritus; Hon. Research Fellow, University College, London, since 1978; *b* 30 Dec. 1910; *s* of Ernest Albert and Edith J. Lewis; *m* 1933, Mary Phœbe Eleanor Burry; one *d*. *Educ:* High Sch., Newcastle-under-Lyme, Staffs; Reading University (BSc); PhD, DSc (London). Research Scholar, Reading Univ., 1935–36; Scientific Officer, Pomology Dept, John Innes Hort. Inst., 1935–48; Head of Genetics Dept, John Innes Horticultural Institution, Bayfordbury, Hertford, Herts, 1948–57. Rockefeller Foundation Special Fellowship, California Inst. of Technology, 1955–56; Visiting Prof. of Genetics, University of Calif, Berkeley, 1961–62; Royal Society Leverhulme Visiting Professor: University of Delhi, 1965–66; Singapore, 1970; Vis. Prof., QMC, 1978–. Pres., Genetical Soc., 1968–71; Mem., UGC, 1969–74. *Publications:* Sexual Incompatibility in Plants, 1979; Editor, Science Progress; scientific papers on Genetics and Plant Physiology. *Recreations:* swimming, gardening, music. *Address:* 56/57 Myddelton Square, EC1R 1YA. *T:* 0171–278 6948.

LEWIS, Sir David Courtenay M.; *see* Mansel Lewis.

LEWIS, Very Rev. David Gareth; Dean of Monmouth, since 1990; *b* 13 Aug. 1931; *s* of Mordecai Lewis and Bronwen May Lewis (*née* Evans). *Educ:* Cyfarthfa Grammar Sch., Merthyr Tydfil; Bangor Coll., Univ. of Wales (BA); Oriel Coll., Oxford (MA); St Michael's Coll., Llandaff. Deacon 1960, priest 1961; Curate of Neath, 1960–63; Vice-Principal, Salisbury Theol Coll., 1963–69; Dean of Belize, 1969–78; Vicar of St Mark, Newport, 1978–82; Canon Residentiary of Monmouth, 1982–90. The Church in Wales: Clerical Sec., Governing Body, 1986–; Chairman: Provincial Stewardship Council, 1985–87; Provincial Evangelism and Adult Educn Council, 1987–95. Mem., BCC, 1985–90. *Publication:* The History of St John's Cathedral, Belize, 1976. *Recreations:* swimming, travelling. *Address:* The Deanery, Stow Hill, Newport, Gwent NP9 4ED. *T:* Newport (01633) 263338.

LEWIS, David Henry L.; *see* LeRoy-Lewis.

LEWIS, David Robert; Secretary, Royal Commission on Environmental Pollution, since 1992, on secondment from Department of the Environment; *b* 27 Nov. 1940; *o c* of William Lewis, Pembroke Dock and Kate Lewis (*née* Sperring); *m* 1965, Christine, *o d* of Leslie and Maud Tye; three *s*. *Educ:* Stoneleigh W Co. Primary Sch.; Tiffin Sch.; New Coll., Oxford (Classical Exhibn; MA; DPhil 1970). Editor: Breakthrough, 1960–61; New Directions, 1964–66; joined Min. of Housing and Local Govt, 1965; Sec., Central Adv. Water Cttee, 1969–73; HM Treasury, 1973–75; Asst Sec., Central Unit on Envmtl Pollution, 1975–77; Dir, Public Admin and Social Policy, CS Coll., 1978–80; Asst Sec., DoE, 1981–; Hd, Water Services Div., DoE, 1990–92. Chm. Govs, Ernest Bevin Sch., 1988–. *Publications:* Electricity Before Nationalisation, 1979; (ed jtly) Policies into Practice, 1984. *Recreations:* exploring new places, 17th and 18th century literature. *Address:* Royal Commission on Environmental Pollution, Church House, Great Smith Street, SW1P 3BZ. *T:* 0171–276 2109. *Clubs:* London Welsh Rugby Football; Powysland (Welshpool).

LEWIS, Dr Dennis Aubrey, BSc; Director, Aslib, the Association for Information Management, 1981–89; *b* 1 Oct. 1928; *s* of Joseph and Minnie Lewis; *m* 1956, Gillian Mary Bratby; two *s*. *Educ:* Latymer Upper Sch.; Univ. of London (BSc 1st Cl. Hons Chemistry, 1953; PhD 1956). FIInfSc 1984. Res. Chemist, 1956–68, Intelligence Manager, 1968–81, ICI Plastics Div. Member: Adv. Council, British Library, 1976–81; Library Adv. Cttee, British Council, 1981–. Member: Welwyn Garden UDC, 1968–74; Welwyn Hatfield DC, 1974– (Chm., 1976–77). *Publications:* Index of Reviews in Organic Chemistry, annually 1963–; (ed jtly) Great Information Disasters, 1991; pubns on information management in Aslib Procs and other journals. *Recreations:* music, old churches, 'futurology'. *Address:* c/o National Westminster Bank, Welwyn Garden City, Herts.

LEWIS, Derek (Compton); Chief Executive and Director General, HM Prison Service, since 1993; Chairman, UK Gold Television Ltd, since 1992; *b* 9 July 1946; *s* of Kenneth Compton Lewis and Marjorie Lewis; *m* 1969, Louise (*née* Wharton); two *d*. *Educ:* Wrekin Coll., Telford; Queens' Coll., Cambridge (MA); London Business Sch. (MSc). Ford Motor Co., 1968–82, Dir of Finance, Ford of Europe, 1978–82; Dir of Corporate Develt and Gp Planning Man., Imperial Gp, 1982–84; Granada Group: Finance Dir, 1984–87; Man. Dir, 1988–89; Gp Chief Exec., 1990–91. Dir, Courtaulds Textiles, 1990–93. *Address:* Cleland House, Page Street, SW1P 4LN. *Club:* Caledonian.

LEWIS, (Derek) Trevor; Joint Senior Partner, Hammond Suddards, Solicitors, since 1987; *b* 21 Oct. 1936; *s* of Lionel Lewis and Mabel (*née* Clare); *m* 1961, Pamela Jean Ratcliffe; one *s* one *d*. *Educ:* Bradford Grammar Sch.; Leeds Univ. (LLB); 2nd Cl. Hons Solicitors' Final Exam., 1960. With A. V. Hammond & Co., subseq. Hammond Suddards: articled to Sir Richard Denby, 1955–60; Asst Solicitor, 1960–63; Partner 1964–87. Director: W Yorks Independent Hosp., 1979–85 (Chm., 1985–88); Bradford & Bingley Building Soc., 1990–. *Address:* 2 Park Lane, Leeds, W Yorks LS3 1ES. *T:* Leeds (0113) 234 3500.

LEWIS, Donald Gordon, OBE 1988; Director, National Exhibition Centre, 1982–84; *b* 12 Sept. 1926; *s* of late Albert Francis Lewis and Nellie Elizabeth Lewis; *m* 1950, Doreen Mary (*née* Gardner); one *d*. *Educ:* King Edward's Sch., Birmingham; Liverpool Univ. Dairy Industry, 1947–91; Gen. Sales Manager, Birmingham Dairies, 1961–91. Councillor (C) Birmingham CC, Selly Oak Ward, 1959, Alderman 1971–74; past Chairman, Transport and Airport Committees; West Midlands County Council: Mem., 1974–81; Chm., 1980–81; Chairman, Airport Cttee, 1974–80; Sec., Conservative Group, 1974–80; City of Birmingham District Council: Mem., 1982–; Chm., Nat. Exhibn Centre Cttee, 1982–84; Chm., Birmingham Housing Cttee, 1983–84. Dir, Birmingham International Airport plc. Chm., Selly Oak (Birmingham) Constituency Conservative Assoc., 1975–80, Pres., 1980–; Vice-Pres., Birmingham Cons. Assoc., 1987– (Chm., 1984–87). Mem., West Midlands Passenger Transport Authority, 1984–. Governor: Dame Elizabeth Cadbury Sch., 1979–; Selly Park Girls' Sch. *Recreation:* eating out. *Address:* 8 Pavenham Drive, Edgbaston, Birmingham B5 7TW. *T:* 0121–471 3139.

LEWIS, Ernest Gordon, (Toby), CMG 1972; OBE 1958; HM Diplomatic Service, retired; *b* New Zealand, 26 Sept. 1918; *s* of George Henry Lewis; *m* 1949, Jean Margaret, *d* of late A. H. Smyth. *Educ:* Otago Boys' High Sch.; Otago Univ., NZ. Served War, Army, with 2nd NZ Div., Middle East, 1939–46 (Lt-Col; despatches, MBE). Joined Colonial Service, Nigeria, 1947; Administrator, Turks and Caicos Is, 1955–59; Permanent Sec., to Federal Govt of Nigeria, 1960–62; First Sec., Pakistan, 1963–66; Foreign and Commonwealth Office, 1966–69; Kuching, Sarawak, 1969–70; Governor and C-in-C, Falkland Islands, and High Comr, British Antarctic Territory, 1971–75; Head of Gibraltar and General Dept, FCO, 1975–77. *Address:* 5 Smith Street, Chelsea, SW3 4EE. *Club:* Army and Navy.

LEWIS, Esyr ap Gwilym; QC 1971; **His Honour Judge Esyr Lewis;** a Circuit Judge (Official Referee), since 1984; Senior Official Referee, since 1994; *b* 11 Jan. 1926; *s* of late Rev. T. W. Lewis, BA, and Mary Jane May Lewis (*née* Selway); *m* 1957, Elizabeth Anne Vidler Hoffmann, 2nd *d* of O. W. Hoffmann, Bassett, Southampton; four *d*. *Educ:* Salford Grammar Sch.; Mill Hill Sch.; Trinity Hall, Cambridge (MA, LLM). Served in Intelligence

Corps, 1944–47. Exhibitioner, 1944, Scholar, 1948, at Trinity Hall (Dr Cooper's Law Studentship, 1950); 1st cl. hons, Law Tripos II, 1949, 1st cl. LLB, 1950, Cambridge. Holker Sen. Schol., Gray's Inn, 1950; Called to Bar, Gray's Inn, 1951; Bencher, 1978. Law Supervisor, Trinity Hall, 1950–55; Law Lectr, Cambridgeshire Technical Coll., 1949–50. A Recorder, 1972–84; Leader, Wales and Chester Circuit, 1978–81. Member: Bar Council, 1965–68; Council of Legal Education, 1967–73; Criminal Injuries Compensation Bd, 1977–84. Contested (L) Llanelli, 1964. *Publication:* contributor to Newnes Family Lawyer, 1963. *Recreations:* reading, gardening, watching Rugby football. *Address:* 2 South Square, Gray's Inn, WC1R 5HP. *T:* 0171–405 5918; The High Court of Justice, Official Referees' Courts, St Dunstan's House, 133–137 Fetter Lane, EC4A 1HD. *T:* 0171–936 6466. *Clubs:* Garrick; Old Millhillians.

See also M. ap G. Lewis.

LEWIS, Prof. Geoffrey Lewis, FBA 1979; Professor of Turkish, University of Oxford, 1986, now Emeritus; Fellow, St Antony's College, Oxford, 1961, now Emeritus; *b* 19 June 1920; *s* of Ashley Lewis and Jeanne Muriel (*née* Sintrop); *m* 1941, Raphaela Rhoda Bale Seideman; one *s* (one *d* decd). *Educ:* University Coll. Sch.; St John's Coll., Oxford (MA 1945, DPhil 1950; James Mew Arabic Scholar, 1947). Lectr in Turkish, 1950–54, Sen. Lectr in Islamic Studies, 1954–64, Sen. Lectr in Turkish, 1964–86, Oxford Univ. Vis. Professor: Robert Coll., Istanbul, 1959–68; Princeton Univ., 1970–71, 1974; UCLA, 1975; British Acad. Leverhulme Vis. Prof., Turkey, 1984. Vice-Pres., Anglo-Turkish Soc., 1972–; Mem., British-Turkish Mixed Commn, 1975–; Pres., British Soc. for Middle Eastern Studies, 1981–83. Corresp. Mem., Turkish Language Soc., 1953–. DUniv: Univ. of the Bosphorus, Istanbul, 1986; Univ. of Istanbul, 1992. Turkish Govt Cert. of Merit, 1973; Turkish Min. of For. Affairs Exceptional Service Plaque 1991. *Publications:* Teach Yourself Turkish, 1953, rev. edn 1989; Modern Turkey, 1955, 4th edn 1974; (trans., with annotations) Katib Chelebi, The Balance of Truth, 1957; Plotiniana Arabica, 1959; (with Barbara Hodge) A Study in Education for International Misunderstanding (Cyprus School History Textbooks), 1966; Turkish Grammar, 1967, rev. edn 1988; (with M. S. Spink) Albucasis on Surgery and Instruments, 1973; The Book of Dede Korkut, 1974; The Atatürk I Knew, 1981; Thickhead and other Turkish Stories, 1988; Just a Diplomat, 1992; articles on Turkish language, history and politics, and on Arab alchemy. *Recreations:* bodging, etymology. *Address:* St Antony's College, Oxford OX2 6JF; 25 Warnborough Road, Oxford OX2 6JA. *T:* Oxford (01865) 57150.

LEWIS, Gillian Marjorie, FMA, FIIC; heritage consultant; *b* 10 Oct. 1945; *d* of late William Lewis and of Marjorie Lewis (*née* Pargeter). *Educ:* Tiffin Sch., Kingston upon Thames; Univ. of Newcastle upon Tyne (BA 1967); DCP, Gateshead Tech. Coll., 1969; Birkbeck Coll., London. FIIC 1977; FMA 1988. Shipley Art Gallery, Co. Durham, 1967–69; free-lance conservator, 1969–73; Nat. Maritime Mus., 1973–94; Keeper of Conservation, 1978; Hd, Div. of Conservation and Technical Services, 1978–88; Asst Dep. Dir, 1982–86; Hd of Conservation and Registration, 1988–91; Head of Collection Projects, 1991–92; Head of External Affairs, 1992–94. Vice-Chm., UK Inst. for Conservation, 1983–84 (Mem. Cttee, 1978–80). Member: Cttee, Dulwich Picture Gall., 1983–92; Wallpaintings Conservation Panel, Council for Care of Churches, 1985–88; Volunteer Steering Cttee, Office of Arts and Libraries, 1988–90; Trng Standards Panel, Museums and Galleries Commn Museums Trng Inst., 1990–93; Council, Leather Conservation Centre, 1991–92; Visitor, City and Guilds of London Sch. of Art, 1981–90; Trustee, Whatmore Trust, 1988–. Examiner, London Inst., Camberwell Sch. of Art, 1991–93. FRSA 1987. *Publications:* official publications of the National Maritime Museum. *Address:* 28 Trinity Church Square, SE1 4HY. *Clubs:* Architecture, Arts; Civil Service Riding.

LEWIS, Graham D., *see* Dixon-Lewis.

LEWIS, Prof. Graham Pritchard; Dean, Hunterian Institute (formerly Institute of Basic Medical Sciences), 1982–89, Vandervell Professor of Pharmacology, 1974–89, now Emeritus, Royal College of Surgeons; *b* 5 Aug. 1927; *s* of George Henry and Ruth Lewis; *m* Averil Priscilla Myrtle; two *s* two *d*. *Educ:* Monkton House School, Cardiff; University College Cardiff (BPharm, PhD). Mem., Scientific Staff, Nat. Inst. for Med. Research, MRC, 1953–63; Dep. Dir, Research, and Dir, Biological Research, Ciba-Geigy Pharmaceuticals, 1964–73. *Publications:* 5-Hydroxytryptamine, 1958; The Role of Prostaglandins in Inflammation, 1976; Mechanisms of Steroid Action, 1981; Mediators of Inflammation, 1986; numerous contribs to British and overseas sci. jls, esp. Jl Physiol., BJ Pharmacol. *Recreations:* writing unfathomable stories, painting indescribable paintings and cooking excruciating dishes.

LEWIS, Henry Nathan; director of companies; *b* 29 Jan. 1926; *m* 1953, Jenny Cohen; one *s* two *d*. *Educ:* Hollywood Park Council Sch., Stockport; Stockport Sch.; Manchester Univ. (BA Com); LSE. Served RAF (Flt Lt), 1944–48. Joined Marks & Spencer, 1950; Dir, 1965; Jt Man. Dir responsible for textiles, 1973–76, 1983–85, for foods, 1976–83; retired 1985. Chm., Primrose Care Ltd, 1992–; Dep. Chm., S&W Berisford, subseq. Berisford Internat., 1987–90; Director: Dixons Group, 1985–95; Hunter Saphir, 1987–91; Porter Chadburn (formerly LDH Group), 1987–; Delta Galil, 1988–; Gabicci, 1992–93; Oasis, 1994–. Mem. Adv. Bd, Bank of Hapoalim BM, 1973–. *Address:* Flat 1, 28 Eton Avenue, NW3 3HL.

LEWIS, H(erbert) J(ohn) Whitfield, CB 1968; *b* 9 April 1911; *s* of Herbert and Mary Lewis; *m* 1963, Pamela (*née* Leaford); one *s* three *d*. *Educ:* Monmouth Sch.; Welsh Sch. of Architecture. Associate with Norman & Dawbarn, Architects and Consulting Engineers; in charge of housing work, 1945–50; Principal Housing Architect, Architects Dept, London County Council, 1950–59; County Architect, Middlesex County Council, 1959–64; Chief Architect, Ministry of Housing and Local Govt, 1964–71. FRIBA; DisTP 1957. *Recreations:* music, electronics. *Address:* 8 St John's Wood Road, NW8 8RE.

LEWIS, Rt Rev. Hurtle John, AM; Bishop of North Queensland, 1971–96; *b* 2 Jan. 1926; *s* of late Hurtle John Lewis and late Hilda Lewis. *Educ:* Prince Alfred Coll.; London Univ. (BD). ThL of ACT. Royal Australian Navy, 1943–46; Student, St Michael's House, S Aust., 1946–51; Member, SSM, 1951–; Provincial Australia, SSM, 1962–68; Prior, Kobe Priory, Japan, 1969–71. *Recreations:* rowing, horse riding. *Address:* Unit 1, 4 Stuart Street, North Ward, Townsville 4810, Australia.

LEWIS, Ian Talbot; Under Secretary (Legal), Treasury Solicitor's Office, 1982–90; *b* 7 July 1929; *s* of late Cyril Frederick Lewis, CBE and Marjorie (*née* Talbot); *m* 1st, 1962, Patricia Anne (*née* Hardy) (marr. diss. 1978); two *s*; 2nd, 1986, Susan Lydia Sargant. *Educ:* Marlborough Coll. Admitted Solicitor, 1951. National Service, 3rd The King's Own Hussars, 1952–53. Solicitor, private practice, London, 1954–57; Treasury Solicitor's Office: Legal Asst, 1957; Sen. Legal Asst, 1963; Asst Treasury Solicitor, 1977. Liveryman, Merchant Taylors' Co., 1966–. Chm., Panshurst Parish Council, 1994–. Chm., Fordcombe Soc., 1990–94; Pres., Fordcombe Village Hall, 1989–. Gov., Fordcombe C of E Primary Sch., 1991–93. *Recreations:* sport, the countryside, reading, theatre, cinema. *Address:* Gables, Fordcombe, near Tunbridge Wells, Kent TN3 0RY. *T:* Fordcombe (01892) 740413. *Clubs:* MCC; Blackheath Football (Rugby Union) (Past Pres.); Blackheath Cricket (Hon. Vice Pres.); Piltdown Golf.

LEWIS, Prof. Ioan Myrddin, DPhil; FBA 1986; Professor of Anthropology, London School of Economics and Political Science, 1969–93, now Emeritus; Consultative Director, International African Institute, since 1988 (Hon. Director, 1981–88); *b* 30 Jan. 1930; *s* of John Daniel Lewis and Mary Stevenson Scott (*née* Brown); *m* 1954, Ann Elizabeth Keir; one *s* three *d*. *Educ:* Glasgow High Sch.; Glasgow Univ. (BSc 1951); Oxford Univ. (Dip. in Anthrop., 1952; BLitt 1953; DPhil 1957). Res. Asst to Lord Hailey, Chatham House, 1954–55; Colonial SSRC Fellow, 1955–57; Lectr in African Studies, University Coll. of Rhodesia and Nyasaland, 1957–60; Lectr in Social Anthrop., Glasgow Univ., 1960–63; Lectr, then Reader in Anthrop., UCL, 1963–69. Hitchcock Prof., Univ. of Calif at Berkeley, 1977; Vis. Professor: Univ. of Helsinki, Finland, 1982; Univ. of Rome, 1983; Univ. of Malaya, 1986; Univ. of Kyoto, 1986; Univ. of Naples, 1989; Univ. of Addis Ababa, 1992; CNRS, Marseille, 1993. Malinowski Meml Lectr, London, 1966. Hon. Sec., Assoc. of Social Anthropologists of the Commonwealth, 1964–67; Member: Council and Standing Cttee of Council, Royal Anthropol Inst., 1965–67 and 1981–84 (Vice-Pres., 1992–); Court of Governors and Standing Cttee, LSE, 1984–88; Internat. Cttee, Centro di Ricerca e Documentazione Febbraio '74, 1980–; Chm., African Educn Trust, 1993 (Trustee, 1992). Editor, Man (Jl of RAI), 1969–72. *Publications:* Peoples of the Horn of Africa, 1955, 3rd edn 1994; A Pastoral Democracy: pastoralism and politics among the Northern Somali of the Horn of Africa, 1961, 2nd edn 1982 (trans. Italian); (with B. W. Andrzejewski) Somali Poetry, 1964, 2nd edn 1968; The Modern History of Somaliland: from nation to state, 1965, 3rd rev. edn 1988; Ecstatic Religion, 1971, 4th rev. edn 1989 (trans. Dutch, Italian, French, Portuguese and Japanese); Social Anthropology in Perspective, 1976, 4th edn 1990 (trans. Italian and Chinese); Religion in Context: cults and charisma, 1986 (trans. German and Italian); (ed and introd): Islam in Tropical Africa, 1966, 3rd edn 1980; History and Anthropology, 1968 (trans. Spanish); Symbols and Sentiments: cross-cultural studies in symbolism, 1977; (co-ed with Fred Eggan and C. von Fürer-Haimendorf), Atlas of Mankind, 1982; Nationalism and Self-Determination in the Horn of Africa, 1983; (co-ed with Gustav Jahoda) Acquiring Culture: cross cultural studies in child development, 1988; (ed jtly) Women's Medicine: the Zar-Bori Cult in Africa and beyond, 1991; Understanding Somalia, 1993; Blood and Bone: the call of Kinship in Somali society, 1994; contrib. learned jls. *Recreations:* travel, fishing. *Address:* 26 Bramshill Gardens, NW5 1JH. *T:* 0171–272 1722.

LEWIS, Ven. John Arthur; Archdeacon of Cheltenham, since 1988; *b* 4 Oct. 1934; *s* of Lt-Col Harry Arthur Lewis and Evaline Helen Ross Lewis; *m* 1959, Hazel Helen Jane Morris; one *s* one *d*. *Educ:* Jesus College, Oxford (MA); Cuddesdon College. Assistant Curate: St Mary, Prestbury, Glos, 1960–63; Wimborne Minster, 1963–66; Rector, Eastington with Frocester, 1966–70; Vicar of Nailsworth, 1970–78; Vicar of Cirencester, 1978–88; RD of Cirencester, 1984–88. Hon. Canon, 1985–88, Canon, 1988–, Gloucester Cathedral. Hon. Chaplain, Glos Constabulary, 1988–. Chairman: Diocesan Stewardship Cttee, 1988–; Diocesan Redundant Church Uses Cttee, 1988–; Diocesan Bd of Educn, 1990–. Mem. Council, Cheltenham Ladies' Coll., 1992–. *Recreations:* travel, music, walking, gardening. *Address:* Westbourne, 283 Gloucester Road, Cheltenham, Glos GL51 7AD. *T:* Cheltenham (01242) 522923.

LEWIS, John Elliott, MA; Head Master, Eton College, since 1994; *b* 23 Feb. 1942; *s* of John Derek Lewis and Margaret Helen (*née* Shaw); *m* 1968, Vibeke Lewis (*née* Johansson). *Educ:* King's College, Auckland, NZ; Corpus Christi Coll., Cambridge (Girdlers' Company Schol.; MA Classics). Assistant Master, King's Coll., Auckland, 1964, 1966–70; Jun. Lecturer in Classics, Auckland Univ., 1965; Asst Master, 1971–80, Master in College, 1975–80, Eton College; Head Master, Geelong Grammar Sch., Australia, 1980–94. *Address:* Eton College, Windsor, Berks SL4 6DL.

LEWIS, Rt. Rev. (John Hubert) Richard; *see* Taunton, Bishop Suffragan of.

LEWIS, Maj.-Gen. (Retd) John Michael Hardwicke, CBE 1970 (OBE 1955); *b* 5 April 1919; *s* of late Brig. Sir Clinton Lewis, OBE, and Lilian Eyre (*née* Wace); *m* 1942, Barbara Dorothy (*née* Wright), three *s*. *Educ:* Oundle; RMA, Woolwich. Commissioned, 2nd Lieut, RE, 1939. Served War: in 18 Div. and Special Force (Chindits), in Far East, 1940–45. Staff Coll., Camberley, 1949; CRE, Gibraltar, 1959–61; Instr, JSSC, 1961–63; IDC, 1966; Asst Chief of Staff (Ops), HQ Northern Army Gp, 1967–69; Brig. GS (Intell.), MoD, 1970–72; ACOS (Intelligence), SHAPE, 1972–75. *Publications:* Michiel Marieschi: Venetian artist, 1967; J. F. Lewis, RA (1805–1876): a monograph, 1978; The Lewis Family—Art and Travel: a family history, 1992. *Recreations:* English water-colours, Swiss painters, picture framing. *Address:* Bedford's Farm, Frimley Green, Surrey GU16 6HE. *T:* Deepcut (01252) 835188.

LEWIS, (Joseph) Anthony; Chief London Correspondent, New York Times, 1965–72, editorial columnist, since 1969; Lecturer in Law, Harvard Law School, 1974–89; James Madison Visiting Professor, Columbia University, since 1983; *b* 27 March 1927; *s* of Kassel Lewis and Sylvia Lewis (*née* Surut), NYC; *m* 1st, 1951, Linda (marr. diss. 1982), *d* of John Rannells, NYC; one *s* two *d*; 2nd, 1984, Margaret, *d* of Bernard Charles Marshall, Osterville, Mass. *Educ:* Horace Mann Sch., NY; Harvard Coll. (BA). Sunday Dept, New York Times, 1948–52; Reporter, Washington Daily News, 1952–55; Legal Corresp., Washington Bureau, NY Times, 1955–64; Nieman Fellow, Harvard Law Sch., 1956–57. Governor, Ditchley Foundation, 1965–72. Mem., Amer. Acad. of Arts and Scis, 1991. Pulitzer Prize for Nat. Correspondence, 1955 and 1963; Heywood Broun Award, 1955; Overseas Press Club Award, 1970. Hon. DLitt: Adelphi Univ. (NY), 1964; Rutgers Univ., NJ, 1973; NY Med. Coll., 1976; Williams Coll., Mass, 1978; Clark Univ., Mass, 1982; Hon. LLD: Syracuse, 1979; Colby Coll., 1983; Northeastern Univ., Mass, 1987. *Publications:* Gideon's Trumpet, 1964; Portrait of a Decade: The Second American Revolution, 1964; Make No Law: the Sullivan case and the First Amendment, 1991; articles in American law reviews. *Recreation:* dinghy sailing. *Address:* 2 Faneuil Hall Marketplace, Boston, MA 02109, USA. *Club:* Tavern (Boston).

LEWIS, Keith William, AO 1994; CB 1981; Deputy Chairman, Electricity Trust of South Australia, since 1994; *b* 10 Nov. 1927; *s* of Ernest John and Alinda Myrtle Lewis; *m* 1958, Alison Bothwell Fleming; two *d*. *Educ:* Adelaide High Sch.; Univ. of Adelaide (BE Civil); Imperial Coll., Univ. of London (DIC). FTS; FIE(Aust). Engineer for Water and Sewage Treatment, E and WS Dept, 1968–74; Dir Gen. and Engr in Chief, Engrg and Water Supply Dept, SA, 1974–87; Chm., Pipelines Authy of SA, 1987–94. Chairman: S Australian Water Resources Council, 1976–87; Australian Water Res. Adv. Council, 1985–90; Murray-Darling Basin Freshwater Res. Centre, 1986–91; Energy Planning Exec., 1987–93; SA Urban Land Trust, 1990–94; Member: Standing Cttee, Australian Water Resources Council, 1974–87; Electricity Trust of S Australia, 1974–84; State Planning Authority 1974–82; Golden Grove Jt Venture Cttee, 1984–; Bd, Amdel Ltd, 1987–94. River Murray Commissioner, representing SA, 1982–87. Silver Jubilee Medal, 1977. *Recreations:* reading, ornithology, golf, tennis. *Address:* 24 Delamere Avenue, Netherby, SA 5062, Australia. *T:* (home) (8) 3381507; (office) (8) 3381507. *Clubs:* Adelaide, Kooyonga Golf (South Australia).

LEWIS, Sir Kenneth, Kt 1983; DL; *b* 1 July 1916; *s* of William and Agnes Lewis, Jarrow; *m* 1948, Jane (*d* 1991), *d* of Samuel Pearson, of Adderstone Mains, Belford,

Northumberland; one *s* one *d*. *Educ:* Jarrow; Edinburgh Univ. Served War of 1939–45. RAF, 1941–46; Flt Lt. Contested (C) Newton-le-Willows, 1945 and 1950, Ashton-under-Lyne, 1951. MP (C): Rutland and Stamford, 1959–83; Stamford and Spalding, 1983–87. Chm., Cons. Back Bench Labour Cttee, 1962–64. CC Middx, 1949–51; Mem., NW Metropolitan Hosp. Management Cttee, 1949–62. DL Rutland 1973. *Recreations:* music, travel. *Address:* Redlands, Preston, Oakham, Rutland. *T:* Oakham (01572) 737320. *Clubs:* Carlton, Royal Air Force.

LEWIS, Kynric; *see* Lewis, A. K.

LEWIS, Leigh Warren; Director of Finance, Department for Education and Employment, since 1995; *b* 17 March 1951; *s* of Harold and Ray Rene Lewis; *m* 1973, Susan Evelyn Gold; two *s*. *Educ:* Harrow County Grammar Sch. for Boys; Liverpool Univ. (BA Hons 1973). MIPD. Dept of Employment, 1973; Private Sec. to Parly Under Sec. of State, 1975–76; Incomes and Indust. Relations Divs, 1978–84; Principal Private Sec. to Minister without Portfolio and Sec. of State for Employment, 1984–86; Asst Sec., EC Br., 1986–87; Dir of Ops, Unemployment Benefit Service, 1987–88; Group Dir of Personnel, Cable and Wireless plc, 1988–91 (on secondment); Dir, Internat. Div., 1991–94; Dir, Finance and Resource Mgt Div., 1994–95. *Recreations:* tennis, Watford Football Club. *Address:* Department for Education and Employment, Sanctuary Buildings, Great Smith Street, SW1P 3BT. *T:* 0171–925 6513.

LEWIS, Prof. Leonard John, CMG 1969; BSc; DipEd; Professor of Education, with special reference to Education in Tropical Areas, in the University of London, 1958–73, now Emeritus; *b* 28 Aug. 1909; of Welsh-English parentage; *s* of Thomas James Lewis and Rhoda Lewis (*née* Gardiner); *m* 1940, Nora Brisdon (marr. diss. 1976); one *s* (and one *s* decd); *m* 1982, Gwenda Black (decd). *Educ:* Lewis Sch., Pengam; University Coll., of South Wales and Monmouth (BSc); University of London Institute of Education (DipEd). Lecturer, St Andrew's Coll., Oyo, Nigeria, 1935–36; Headmaster, CMS Gram. Sch., Lagos, Nigeria, 1936–41; Education Sec., CMS Yoruba Mission, 1941–44; Lectr, University of London Institute of Education, 1944–48; Editorial staff, Oxford Univ. Press, 1948–49; Prof. of Educn and Dir of Institute of Educn, University Coll. of Ghana, 1949–58. Principal and Vice-Chancellor, Univ. of Zimbabwe, 1980–81; Vice-Chancellor, PNG Univ. of Technology, 1982–83. Nuffield Visiting Prof., University of Ibadan, 1966. Hon. Professorial Fellow, University Coll., Cardiff, 1973; Hon. FCP 1974. Coronation Medal, 1953; Zimbabwe Independence Medal, 1980. *Publications:* Equipping Africa, 1948; Henry Carr (Memoir), 1948; Education Policy and Practice in British Tropical Areas, 1954; (ed and contrib.) Perspectives in Mass Education and Community Development, 1957; Days of Learning, 1961; Education and Political Independence in Africa, 1962; Schools, Society and Progress in Nigeria, 1965; the Management of Education (with A. J. Loveridge), 1965. *Address:* Flat 1, 6 Stanwell Road, Penarth, S Glamorgan CF6 2EA. *T:* Cardiff (01222) 702299.

LEWIS, Martyn John Dudley; journalist and broadcaster; Presenter, BBC Television Six O'Clock News, since 1994; *b* 7 April 1945; *s* of late Thomas John Dudley Lewis and of Doris (*née* Jones); *m* 1970, Elizabeth Anne Carse; two *d*. *Educ:* Dalriada High Sch., Ballymoney, NI; Trinity Coll., Dublin (BA 1967). Reporter: BBC, Belfast, 1967–68; HTV, Cardiff, 1968–70; Independent Television News; reporter, 1970–86; Head, Northern Bureau, 1971–78; presenter, News at Ten, 1981–86; Presenter: BBC One O'Clock News, 1986–87; BBC Nine O'Clock News, 1987–94; Today's the Day, BB2, 1993–. Documentaries include: Battle for the Falklands; The Secret Hunters; Fight Cancer; Living with Dying; Great Ormond Street—a Fighting Chance; Health UK. Dir, Drive for Youth, 1986– (Chm., 1990–); Chm. and Founder, Youthnet UK, 1995–. Mem., Policy Adv. Cttee, Tidy Britain Gp, 1988–; Director: Hospice Arts, 1989–; CLIC UK, 1990–; Cities in Schools, 1989–; Adopt-A-Student, 1988–; Inst. for Citizenship Studies, 1993–; Pres., United Response, 1989–; Vice-President: Cancer Relief Macmillan Fund, 1988– (Dir, 1990–); Marie Curie Cancer Care, 1990–; Help the Hospices, 1990–; British Soviet Hospice Soc., 1990–; Patron: Cambridge Children's Hospice, 1989–; SW Children's Hospice, 1991–; London Lighthouse, 1990–; Internat. Sch. for Cancer Care, 1991–; Hope House Children's Hospice, 1992–. Freeman, City of London, 1989; Liveryman, Pattenmakers' Co., 1989–. FRSA 1990. Hon. DLitt Ulster, 1994. *Publications:* And Finally, 1983; Tears and Smiles—the Hospice Handbook, 1989; Cats in the News, 1991 (trans. Japanese, 1994); Dogs in the News, 1992; Go For It: Martyn Lewis's essential guide to opportunities for young people, annually, 1993–. *Recreations:* tennis, photography, piano, good food. *Address:* c/o BBC Television News, BBC Television Centre, Wood Lane, W12 7RJ. *T:* 0181–743 8000. *Clubs:* Annabel's, Vanderbilt.

LEWIS, Michael ap Gwilym; QC 1975; a Recorder of the Crown Court, since 1976; *b* 9 May 1930; *s* of Rev. Thomas William Lewis and Mary Jane May Selway; *m* 1988, Sarah Turvill; two *d*, and one *d* three *s* by a previous marriage. *Educ:* Mill Hill; Jesus Coll., Oxford (Scholar). MA (Mod. History). 2nd Royal Tank Regt, 1952–53. Called to Bar, Gray's Inn, 1956, Bencher, 1986; Mem., Senate, 1979–82; South Eastern Circuit. Mem., Criminal Injuries Compensation Bd, 1993–. *Address:* 3 Hare Court, Temple, EC4Y 7BJ. *T:* 0171–353 7561.

See also E. ap G. Lewis.

LEWIS, Michael David; Deputy Controller, and Commissioning Editor, Sport, BBC Radio 5 Live, since 1994; *b* 5 June 1947; *s* of late David Lloyd Lewis and of Gwendoline Lewis; *m* 1992, Hilary Anne East; two *d*. *Educ:* Erith Grammar Sch., Kent. Dartford Reporter newspaper, 1966–70; Brighton Evening Argus, 1970–73; LBC/Independent Radio News, 1973–82; BBC Radio Sport: Duty Editor, 1982–83; Dep. Editor, 1983–84; Editor, 1984–91; Head of Sport and Outside Broadcasts, 1991–93. *Recreations:* watching Arsenal, bringing up two daughters, reading newspapers. *Address:* BBC Radio 5 Live, Broadcasting House, Portland Place, W1A 1AA. *T:* 0171–765 3756.

LEWIS, Naomi, FRSL; author, critic and broadcaster; *b* coastal Norfolk. Contributor at various times to Observer, New Statesman, New York Times, Listener, Encounter, TLS, TES, etc. *Publications:* A Visit to Mrs Wilcox, 1957; A Peculiar Music, 1971; The Silent Playmate, 1979; Leaves, 1980; Come With Us (poems), 1982; Once upon a Rainbow, 1981; A Footprint on the Air (poems), 1983; Messages (poems), 1985; A School Bewitched, 1985; Arabian Nights, 1987; Cry Wolf!, 1988; Proud Knight, Fair Lady, 1989; Johnny Longnese, 1989; *translations:* Hans Andersen's Fairy Tales, 1981; The Snow Queen, 1988; The Frog Prince, 1990. *Recreation:* trying in practical ways to alleviate the lot of pigeons, wolves, camels, horses and other ill-used fellow mortals in a human world. *Address:* 13 Red Lion Square, WC1R 4QF. *T:* 0171–405 8657.

LEWIS, Norman; author; *s* of Richard and Louise Lewis. *Educ:* Enfield Grammar Sch. Served War of 1939–45, in Intelligence Corps. *Publications:* Sand and Sea in Arabia, 1938; Samara, 1949; Within the Labyrinth, 1950, new edn 1985; A Dragon Apparent, 1951, new edn 1982; Golden Earth, 1952, repr. 1983; A Single Pilgrim, 1953; The Day of the Fox, 1955, new edn 1985; The Volcanoes Above Us, 1957; The Changing Sky, 1959, repr. 1984; Darkness Visible, 1960; The Tenth Year of the Ship, 1962; The Honoured Society, 1964, rev. edn 1984; A Small War Made to Order, 1966; Every Man's Brother, 1967; Flight from a Dark Equator, 1972; The Sicilian Specialist, 1974, new edn 1985; The German Company, 1979; Cuban Passage, 1982; A Suitable Case for Corruption, 1984; A View of the World, 1986; The March of the Long Shadows, 1987; To Run Across the Sea, 1989; A Goddess in the Stones: travels in India, 1991; An Empire of the East, 1993; The Norman Lewis Omnibus, 1995; *autobiography:* Naples '44, 1978, repr. 1983; Voices of the Old Sea, 1984, new edn 1985; Jackdaw Cake, 1985, revd edn as I Came, I Saw, 1994; The Missionaries, 1988. *Address:* c/o Jonathan Cape, 20 Vauxhall Bridge Road, SW1V 2SA.

LEWIS, Peter; Director, Company Tax Division, since 1991, and Policy Co-ordination Unit, since 1994, Inland Revenue; *b* 24 June 1937; *s* of Reginald George and Edith Lewis; *m* 1962, Ursula Brigitte Kilian; one *s* one *d*. *Educ:* Ealing Grammar School; St Peter's Hall, Oxford. Royal Navy, 1955–57. Inland Revenue Inspector of Taxes, 1960–69; Inland Revenue Policy and Central Divs, 1969–85; Dir, Personal Tax Div., 1986–91. *Address:* Inland Revenue, West Wing, Somerset House, Strand, WC2R 1LB. *T:* 0171–438 6371.

LEWIS, Peter Ronald; Director General, Bibliographic Services, British Library, 1980–89; *b* 28 Sept. 1926; *s* of Charles Lewis and Florence Mary (née Kirk); *m* 1952, June Ashley; one *s* one *d*. *Educ:* Royal Masonic Sch.; Belfast Univ. (MA). FLA; Hon. FLA 1989. Brighton, Plymouth, Chester public libraries, 1948–55; Head, Bibliographic Services, BoT Library, 1955–65; Lectr in Library Studies, QUB, 1965–69; Librarian: City Univ., 1969–72; Univ. of Sussex, 1972–80. Vice-Pres., 1979–85 and Hon. Treasurer, 1980–82, Library Assoc. (Chm., Bd of Fellowship, 1979–87); Mem., IFLA Professional Bd, 1985–87. Chm., LA Publishing Co., 1983–85. *Publications:* The Literature of the Social Sciences, 1960; The Fall and Rise of National Bibliography (Bangalore), 1982; numerous papers on librarianship and bibliography, 1963–. *Recreation:* wild life photography. *Address:* Wyvern, Blackheath Road, Wenhaston, Suffolk IP19 9HD.

LEWIS, Peter Tyndale; Chairman, John Lewis Partnership, 1972–93; *b* 26 Sept. 1929; *s* of Oswald Lewis and Frances Merriman Lewis (*née* Cooper); *m* 1961, Deborah Anne, *d* of late Sir William (Alexander Roy) Collins, CBE and Priscilla Marian, *d* of late S. J. Lloyd; one *s* one *d*. *Educ:* Eton; Christ Church, Oxford. National service, Coldstream Guards, 1948–49; MA (Oxford) 1953; called to Bar (Middle Temple) 1956; joined John Lewis Partnership, 1959. Member: Council, Industrial Soc., 1968–79; Design Council, 1971–74; Chm., Retail Distributors' Assoc., 1972. Member: Southampton Univ. Develt Trust, 1994–; Council, Queen's Coll., Harley St, 1994–. Trustee, Jt Educnl Trust, 1985–87. Governor: NIESR, 1983; Windlesham Hse Sch., 1979–95; The Bell Educnl Trust, 1987–. CIMgt; FRSA. *Address:* 34 Victoria Road, W8 5RG.

LEWIS, Rt. Rev. Richard; *see* Lewis, Rt Rev. J. H. R., Bishop Suffragan of Taunton.

LEWIS, Very Rev. Richard; Dean of Wells, since 1990; *b* 24 Dec. 1935; *m* 1959, Jill Diane Wilford; two *s*. *Educ:* Royal Masonic Sch.; Fitzwilliam House, Cambridge (BA 1958; MA 1961); Ripon Hall, Oxford. Asst Curate, Hinckley, Leicester, 1960–63; Priest-in-Charge, St Edmund, Riddlesdown, 1963–66; Vicar: All Saints, South Merstham, 1966–72; Holy Trinity and St Peter, Wimbeldon, 1972–79; St Barnabas, Dulwich and Foundation Chaplain of Alleyn's College of God's Gift at Dulwich, 1979–90. *Recreations:* music of all sorts, walking, gardening, reading. *Address:* The Dean's Lodging, 25 The Liberty, Wells, Somerset BA5 2SZ. *T:* Wells (01749) 72192.

LEWIS, Rev. Canon Robert Hugh Cecil; Chaplain to the Queen, 1987–95; *b* 23 Feb. 1925; *s* of Herbert Cecil and Olive Frances Lewis; *m* 1948, Joan Dorothy Hickman; one *s* one *d*. *Educ:* Manchester Grammar School; New Coll., Oxford (BA 1950, MA 1950); Westcott House, Cambridge. Deacon 1952, priest 1953; Curate: St Mary, Crumpsall, 1952–54; New Bury, 1954–56; Incumbent, Bury St Peter, 1956–63; Vicar, Poynton, dio. of Chester, 1963–91; RD of Stockport, 1972–85, of Cheadle, 1985–87. Diocesan Ecumenical Officer, 1987–91; County Ecumenical Officer for Cheshire, 1987–91; Hon. Canon, Chester Cathedral, 1975–91, Canon Emeritus, 1991–. *Recreations:* gardening, poetry. *Address:* 78 Dean Drive, Wilmslow, Cheshire SK9 2EY. *T:* Wilmslow (01625) 524761.

LEWIS, Roland Swaine, FRCS; Honorary Consultant Surgeon to the ENT Department, King's College Hospital, since 1973 (Consultant Surgeon, 1946–65, Senior Consultant Surgeon, 1965–73); Honorary Consultant ENT Surgeon: to Mount Vernon Hospital and The Radium Institute; to Norwood and District Hospital; *b* 23 Nov. 1908; *s* of Dr William James Lewis, MOH, and Constance Mary Lewis, Tyrwaun, Ystalyfera; *m* 1936, Mary Christianna Milne (Christianna Brand) (*d* 1988); one adopted *d*. *Educ:* Epsom Coll.; St John's Coll., Cambridge; St George's Hospital. BA Cantab 1929; FRCS 1934; MA Cantab 1945; MB BCh Cantab 1945. Surgical Chief Asst, St George's Hospital, 1935. Major, RAMC (ENT Specialist), 1939–45. *Publications:* papers to medical journals. *Recreations:* ornithology, fishing. *Address:* 88 Maida Vale, W9 1PR. *T:* 0171–624 6253; Aberdar, Cwrt y Cadno, Llanwrda, Dyfed.

LEWIS, Terence; MP (Lab) Worsley, since 1983; *b* 29 Dec. 1935; *s* of Andrew Lewis; *m* 1958, Audrey, *d* of William Clarke; one *s*. *Educ:* Mt Carmel Sch., Salford. Nat. service, RAMC, 1954–56. Personnel Officer. Sponsored by TGWU. Member: Kearsley UDC, 1971–74; Bolton BC, 1975– (Chm., Educn Cttee, 1982–83). *Address:* House of Commons, SW1; 54 Greenmount Park, Kearsley, Bolton, Lancs BL4 8NS. *Labour Clubs:* Astley, Higher Folds, Mosley Common, Little Hulton, Armitage, Walkden, Cadishead.

LEWIS, Sir Terence (Murray), Kt 1986; OBE 1979; GM 1960; QPM 1977; Commissioner of Police, Queensland, 1976–89; *b* 29 Feb. 1928; *s* of late George Murray Lewis and of Monica Ellen Lewis (*née* Hanlon); *m* 1952, Hazel Catherine Lewis (*née* Gould); three *s* two *d*. *Educ:* Univ. of Queensland (DPA 1974; BA 1978). Queensland Police Force, 1948; Criminal Investigation Br., 1950–63; Juvenile Aid Bureau, 1963–73; Inspector of Police, 1973. Member: Royal Aust. Inst. of Public Admin, 1964; Internat. Police Assoc., 1968; Internat. Assoc. of Chiefs of Police, 1977. Churchill Fellow, 1968; FAIM 1978. Hon. Correspondent for Royal Humane Soc. of Australasia, 1981. Patron, Vice-Patron, Pres., Trustee, or Mem., numerous Qld organisations. Queensland Father of the Year, 1980. Silver Jubilee Medal, 1977. *Recreation:* reading. *Address:* 12 Garfield Drive, Paddington Heights, Qld 4064, Australia.

LEWIS, Thomas Loftus Townshend, CBE 1979; FRCS; Consultant Obstetric and Gynæcological Surgeon at Guy's Hospital, Queen Charlotte's Maternity Hospital and Chelsea Hospital for Women, 1948–83; Hon. Consultant in Obstetrics and Gynaecology, to the Army, 1973–83; *b* 27 May 1918; *e s* of late Neville Lewis and his first wife, Theodosia Townshend; *m* 1946, Kathleen Alexandra Ponsonby Moore; five *s*. *Educ:* Diocesan Coll., Rondebosch, S Africa; St Paul's Sch.; Cambridge Univ.; Guy's Hospital. BA Cantab (hons in Nat. Sci. Tripos), 1939; MB, BChir Cantab, 1942. FRCS 1946; MRCOG 1948; FRCOG 1961. House Appointments Guy's Hospital, 1942–43; Gold Medal and Prize in Obstetrics, Guy's Hospital, 1942. Volunteered to join South African Medical Corps, 1944; seconded to RAMC and served as Capt. in Italy and Greece, 1944–45. Returned to Guy's Hospital; Registrar in Obstetrics and Gynæcology, 1946, Obstetric Surgeon, 1948; Surgeon, Chelsea Hosp. for Women, 1950; Surgeon, Queen Charlotte's Maternity Hosp., 1952. Examiner in Obstetrics and Gynæcology: University of Cambridge, 1950; University of London, 1954; Royal College of Obstetricians and

Gynæcologists, 1952; London Soc. of Apothecaries, 1955; University of St Andrews, 1960. Hon. Sec. and Mem. Council, Royal College of Obstetricians and Gynæcologists, 1955–68, 1971–, Vice-Pres., 1976–78; Mem. Council Obstetric Section, Royal Society of Med., 1953– (Pres. 1981); co-opted Mem. Council, RCS, 1978–81. Guest Prof. to Brisbane, Australia, Auckland, New Zealand, 1959, Johns Hopkins Hosp., Baltimore, 1966; Litchfield Lectr, University of Oxford, 1968; Sims-Black Prof. to Australia, NZ and Rhodesia, 1970. *Publications:* Progress in Clinical Obstetrics and Gynæcology, 2nd edn 1964; (ed jtly and contrib.) Obstetrics by Ten Teachers, 11th edn 1966 to 15th edn 1990; (jtly) Queen Charlotte's Textbook of Obstetrics, 12th edn 1970; (ed jtly and contrib.) Gynaecology by Ten Teachers, 12th edn 1970 to 15th edn 1990; (contrib.) French's Index of Differential Diagnosis, 10th edn 1973 to 12th edn 1984; contributions to: Lancet, BMJ, Practitioner, Proc. Roy. Soc. Med., Encyclopædia Britannica Book of the Year (annual contrib.), etc. *Recreations:* ski-ing, sailing, tennis, golf, croquet, wind-surfing, underwater swimming, photography, viniculture on the Isle of Elba. *Address:* 13 Copse Hill, Wimbledon, SW20 0NB. *T:* 0181–946 5089. *Clubs:* Old Pauline; Royal Wimbledon Golf; Guy's Hospital Rugby Football (ex-Pres.).

LEWIS, Tony; *see* Lewis, A. R.

LEWIS, Trevor; *see* Lewis, D. T.

LEWIS, Dr Trevor, CBE 1992; Director, AFRC Institute of Arable Crops Research, 1989–93; Head, 1987–93, Lawes Trust Senior Fellow, since 1993, Rothamsted Experimental Station; Visiting Professor in Invertebrate Zoology, University of Nottingham, since 1977; *b* 8 July 1933; *s* of Harold and Maggie Lewis; *m* 1959, Margaret Edith Wells; one *s* one *d*. *Educ:* Univ. of Nottingham (DSc 1986); Imperial Coll. of Science and Technol., Univ. of London (PhD, DIC 1958); MA Cambridge, 1960. University Demonstr in Agricl Zoology, Sch. of Agriculture, Cambridge, 1958–61; scientific staff, Rothamsted Experimental Station, 1961–; seconded to ODA as Sen. Res. Fellow, Univ. of WI, Trinidad, 1970–73; Head, Entomology Dept, 1976–83; Dep. Dir, 1983–87; Hd of Crop and Envmt Protection Div., 1983–89. Special Lectr in Invertebrate Zool., Univ. of Nottingham, 1968–69 and 1973–75. AFRC Assessor to MAFF Adv. Cttee on Pesticides, 1984–89; Member: Management Bd, British Crop Protection Council, 1985–94; Bd, British Crop Protection Enterprises, 1994–; R&D Cttee, Potato Marketing Bd, 1985–89. Mem. Council, British Ecological Soc., 1982–84; Pres., Royal Entomol Soc. of London, 1985–87. Huxley Gold Medal, Imperial Coll. of Science and Technol., Univ. of London, 1977. *Publications:* (with L. R. Taylor) Introduction to Experimental Ecology, 1967; Thrips—their biology, ecology and economic importance, 1973; (ed) Insect Communication, 1984; contribs to scientific jls on topics in entomology. *Recreations:* music, gardening. *Address:* 41 Tennyson Road, Harpenden, Herts AL5 4BD. *T:* Harpenden (01582) 715861.

LEWIS, Trevor Oswin, CBE 1983; DL; *b* 29 Nov. 1935; *s* of 3rd Baron Merthyr, PC, KBE, TD, and of Violet, *y d* of Brig.-Gen. Sir Frederick Charlton Meyrick, 2nd Bt, CB, CMG; *S* father, 1977, as 4th Baron Merthyr, but disclaimed his peerage for life; also as 4th Bt (*cr* 1896) but does not use the title; *m* 1964, Susan Jane, *yr d* of A. J. Birt-Llewellin; one *s* three *d*. *Educ:* Downs Sch.; Eton; Magdalen Coll., Oxford; Magdalene Coll., Cambridge. Member: Landscape Adv. Cttee, Dept of Transport, 1968–92 (Chm., 1991–92); Countryside Commn, 1973–83 (Dep. Chm., 1980–83); Chm., Countryside Commn's Cttee for Wales, 1973–80. JP Pembs, then Dyfed, 1969–94; DL Dyfed, 1994. *Heir* (*to disclaimed peerage*): *s* David Trevor Lewis, *b* 21 Feb. 1977. *Address:* Hean Castle, Saundersfoot, Dyfed SA69 9AL. *T:* Saundersfoot (01834) 812222.

LEWIS, Dame Vera Margaret; *see* Lynn, Dame Vera.

LEWIS-BOWEN, Thomas Edward Ifor, His Honour Judge Lewis-Bowen; a Circuit Judge, since 1980; *b* 20 June 1933; *s* of late Lt-Col J. W. Lewis-Bowen and K. M. Lewis-Bowen (*née* Rice); *m* 1965, Gillian, *d* of late Reginald Brett, Puckington, Som; one *s* two *d*. *Educ:* Ampleforth; St Edmund Hall, Oxford. Called to Bar, Middle Temple, 1958. A Recorder of the Crown Court, 1974–80. *Address:* Flat 4, Asquith Court, Eaton Crescent, Swansea, West Glamorgan SA1 4QL. *T:* Swansea (01792) 473736; Clynfyw, Boncath, Dyfed SA37 0HF. *T:* Boncath (01239) 841236.

LEWIS-JONES, Captain (Robert) Gwilym, CBE 1969; RN retired; President, Meirionydd Citizens' Advice Bureau, since 1992 (Chairman, 1988–92); Member, Clwyd Social Security Appeals Tribunal, since 1988; *b* 22 Feb. 1922; *s* of Captain David Lewis Jones and Olwen Lewis Jones (*née* Evans), Corris and Dolgellau; *m* 1946, Ann Mary, *d* of David and Margaret Owen, Dolgellau; two *s*. *Educ:* Tywyn Grammar Sch.; Gonville and Caius Coll., Cambridge. CEng, MRAeS, FBIM. FAA Observers Course, 1942–43; 842 Sqdn in HM Ships Indefatigable, Furious and Fencer on Murmansk and Atlantic convoys, 1943–45; Long Air Communications Course, 1945–46; Long Air Electronics/Electrical Course, 1946–47; RRE Malvern, 1947–49; Long Ships Electrical Course, 1950; RAE Farnborough, 1950–53; Sen. Aircraft Engr Off., HMS Albion, 1953–56; Dep. Comd Engr Off., Staff of Flag Officer Naval Air Comd, 1956–58; Head of Air Electrical Comd, RN Air Stn Brawdy, 1958–61; Sqdn Weapons Off., HMS Caesar and 8th Destroyer Sqdn, 1961–63; Exec. Off. and 2nd in Comd, HMS Condor, 1963–65; Gen. Man., RN Aircraft Yard, Belfast, 1965–67; Dir of Aircraft Armament, MoD (N), 1967–68; Jt Services Planning and Co-ordinating Off. responsible for Armed Forces participation in Investiture of Prince of Wales, 1967–69; Sen. Officers War Course, RNC Greenwich, 1969–70; Staff of Dir Gen. Ships (Directorate Naval Ship Production), 1970–72; Dir, Fleet Management Services, 1973–75; Dir, Naval Management and Orgn, 1975–76. ADC to HM the Queen, 1976. Lt-Comdr 1952; Comdr 1958; Captain 1967. Member: (C) for Carshalton, GLC, 1977–81; Mayor of Dolgellau and Chm., Dolgellau Town Council, 1987–88 (Dep. Mayor, 1986–87). Chm., Merioneth SSAFA, 1984–93; Dep. Chm., 1984–88, Chm., 1988–89, Gwynedd Valuation Panel; Pres., Gwynedd Valuation and Community Charge Tribunal, 1989–93; Member: Snowdonia Nat. Park Cttee, 1982–88; Prince of Wales' Cttee (Mid Wales Gp), 1988–93. Deacon, Welsh Presbyterian Church, 1983–. JP SE London, 1979–81. High Sheriff of Gwynedd, 1991–92. *Recreations:* golf, choral music, Welsh culture. *Address:* Mansiriol, Dolgellau, Gwynedd LL40 2YS. *T:* Dolgellau (01341) 422526.

LEWISHAM, Viscount; William Legge; Chartered Accountant; *b* 23 Sept. 1949; *e s* and *heir* of 9th Earl of Dartmouth, *qv* and of Comtesse de Chambrun, *qv*. *Educ:* Eton; Christ Church, Oxford; Harvard Business Sch. Secretary, Oxford Union Soc., 1969. Contested (C): Leigh, Lancs, Feb. 1974; Stockport South, Oct. 1974. Chm. and Founder, Kirklees Cable. *Recreations:* squash, supporting American football. *Address:* Blakelea House, Marsden, near Huddersfield, W Yorks HD7 5AU. *Clubs:* Turf; Harvard (New York); Stockport County Football.

LEWISHAM, Archdeacon of; *see* Kuhrt, Ven. G. W.

LEWISOHN, His Honour Anthony Clive Leopold; a Circuit Judge, 1974–90; *b* 1 Aug. 1925; *s* of John Lewisohn and Gladys (*née* Solomon); *m* 1957, Lone Ruthwen Jurgensen; two *s*. *Educ:* Stowe; Trinity Coll., Oxford (MA). Royal Marines, 1944–45; Lieut, Oxf. and Bucks LI, 1946–47. Called to Bar, Middle Temple, 1951; S Eastern Circuit.

LEWISOHN, Neville Joseph; Director of Dockyard Manpower and Productivity (Under Secretary), Ministry of Defence, 1979–82; *b* 28 May 1922; *s* of Victor and Ruth Lewisohn; *m* 1944, Patricia Zeffertt; two *d* (and one *d* decd). *Educ:* Sutton County Sch., Surrey. Entered Admiralty as Clerical Officer, 1939; promoted through intervening grades to Principal, 1964; Dir of Resources and Progs (Ships), 1972 (Asst Sec.); Head of Civilian Management (Specialists), 2 Div., 1976. *Recreations:* music, drama. *Address:* 20 Ragleth Grove, Trowbridge, Wilts BA14 7LE. *T:* Trowbridge (01225) 776046.

LEWISON, Kim Martin Jordan; QC 1991; *b* 1 May 1952; *s* of Anthony Frederick Lewison and Dinora Lewison (*née* Pines); *m* 1979, Helen Mary Janecek; one *s* one *d*. *Educ:* St Paul's Sch., London; Downing Coll., Cambridge (MA 1973); Council of Legal Education. Called to the Bar, Lincoln's Inn, 1975; Asst Recorder, 1994–. Mem. Council, Liberal Jewish Synagogue, 1990–96. *Publications:* Development Land Tax, 1978; Drafting Business Leases, 1979, 4th edn 1993; Lease or Licence, 1985; The Interpretation of Contracts, 1989; (Gen. Editor) Woodfall on Landlord and Tenant, 1990–. *Recreations:* visiting France, avoiding tsores. *Address:* Falcon Chambers, Falcon Court, EC4Y 1AA. *T:* 0171–353 2484.

LEWITTER, Prof. Lucjan Ryszard; Professor of Slavonic Studies, University of Cambridge, 1968–84; *b* 1922. *Educ:* schools in Poland; Perse Sch., Cambridge; Christ's Coll., Cambridge. PhD 1951. Univ. Asst Lectr in Polish, 1948; Fellow of Christ's Coll., 1951; Dir of Studies in Modern Languages, 1951–64; Tutor, 1960–68; Vice-Master, 1977–80; Univ. Lectr in Slavonic Studies (Polish), 1953–68. *Publications:* (ed, with A. P. Vlasto) Ivan Pososhkov, The Book of Poverty and Wealth, 1987; articles, mostly on Russo-Polish relations, in learned jls. *Address:* Christ's College, Cambridge CB2 3BU. *T:* Cambridge (01223) 357320. *Club:* United Oxford & Cambridge University.

LEWTHWAITE, Brig. Sir Rainald Gilfrid, 4th Bt *cr* 1927, of Broadgate, Thwaites, Co. Cumberland; CVO 1975; OBE 1974; MC 1943; *b* 21 July 1913; 2nd *s* of Sir William Lewthwaite, 2nd Bt of Broadgate, Cumberland, and Beryl Mary Stopford Hickman; *S* brother, 1993; *m* 1936, Margaret Elizabeth Edmonds, MBE 1942 (*d* 1990), 2nd *d* of late Harry Edmonds and Florence Jane Moncrieffe Bolton, High Green, Redding, Conn, USA; one *s* (and one *s* two *d* decd). *Educ:* Rugby Sch.; Trinity Coll., Cambridge. BA (Hons) Law 1934. Joined Scots Guards, 1934. Served War of 1939–45 (MC, despatches twice). Retired as Defence and Military Attaché, British Embassy, Paris, 1968. Dir of Protocol, Hong Kong, 1969–76. French Croix-de-Guerre with Palm, 1945. *Recreation:* country life. *Heir:* *s* David Rainald Lewthwaite [*b* 26 March 1940; *m* 1969, Diana Helena, twin *d* of W. R. Tomkinson, TD; two *d*]. *Address:* Broadgate, Millom, Cumbria LA18 5JY. *T:* Broughton-in-Furness (01229) 716295. *Club:* Cavalry and Guards.

LEY, Sir Ian (Francis), 5th Bt *cr* 1905, of Epperstone, Nottingham; *b* 12 June 1934; *o s* of Sir Francis Douglas Ley, 4th Bt, MBE and Violet Geraldine Ley (*née* Johnson) (*d* 1991); *S* father, 1995; *m* 1957, Caroline Margaret (*née* Errington); one *s* one *d*. *Educ:* Eton Coll. Dep. Chm., 1972–80, Chm., 1981–82, Ley's Foundries and Engineering plc. High Sheriff, Derbyshire, 1985. *Recreation:* shooting. *Heir:* *s* Christopher Ian Ley, *b* 2 Dec. 1962. *Address:* Fauld Hall, Tutbury, Staffordshire DE13 9HR. *T:* Tutbury (01283) 812266. *Club:* White's.

LEY, Prof. Steven Victor, FRS 1990; Professor of Organic Chemistry, and Fellow of Trinity College, University of Cambridge, since 1992; *b* 10 Dec. 1945; *s* of Mary Ley (*née* Hall) and Ralph Gilbert Ley; *m* 1970, Rosemary Ann Jameson; one *d*. *Educ:* Loughborough Univ. of Technology (BSc (BTech 1st cl. Hons 1969); DIS 1969; PhD 1972); DSc London 1983. Res. Fellow, Ohio State Univ., 1972–74; Imperial College, London: Res. Asst, 1974–75; Lectr, 1975–83; Prof. of Organic Chemistry, 1983–92; Head of Chemistry Dept, 1989–92. Vis. Lectr and Vis. Prof., overseas estabts. Chm., Organic Chem. Cttee, SERC, 1985–89. Hon. DSc Loughborough, 1994. Royal Society of Chemistry: Hickinbottom Res. Fellow, 1981–83 (1st recipient); Corday Morgan Medal and Prize, 1982; Tilden Lectr and Medal, 1988; Award for Synthetic Chem., 1989; Pedlar Lectr and Medal, 1992; Simonsen Lectr and Medal, 1993; Award for Natural Products Chemistry, 1994. Pfizer Res. Award, 1983 (1st recipient); Adolf Windaus Medal, German Chem. Soc. *Publications:* over 300 papers in internat. jls of chemistry. *Recreations:* walking, ski-ing, listening to music. *Address:* Department of Chemistry, Lensfield Road, Cambridge CB2 1EW.

LEYLAND, Sir Philip Vyvian N.; *see* Naylor-Leyland.

LEYLAND, Ronald Arthur; Chief Executive, North Yorkshire County Council, 1990–94; *b* 23 Aug. 1940; *s* of Arthur and Lucy Leyland; *m* 1962, Joan Virginia Sinclair; three *s*. *Educ:* Merchant Taylors' Sch., Crosby; Liverpool Univ. (LLB Hons 1961). Solicitor (Hons 1964). Assistant Solicitor: Bootle CBC, 1964–65; Nottingham City Council, 1965–68; Sen. Asst Solicitor, then Dir of Admin, Leeds MDC, 1968–75; County Sec., Hampshire CC., 1975–90. Dir, N Yorks TEC, 1990–94. Chm., Soc. of County Secretaries, 1986–87. *Recreation:* walking. *Address:* White House, Maunby, near Thirsk YO7 4HG.

LI, David Kwok Po, OBE 1990; FCIB; FCA; Director and Chief Executive, Bank of East Asia Ltd, since 1981; *b* 13 March 1939; *s* of Li Fook Shu and Woo Tze Ha; *m* 1971, Penny Poon; two *s*. *Educ:* Univ. of Cambridge (MA). FCIB 1988; FCA 1977. Bank of East Asia Ltd: Chief Accountant, 1969–72; Asst Chief Manager, 1973–76; Dep. Chief Manager, 1977–81. Hon. Fellow: Robinson Coll., Univ. of Cambridge, 1989; Selwyn Coll., Cambridge, 1992. Hon. LLD: Cantab, 1993; Warwick, 1994. *Recreations:* tennis, art, antiques, reading. *Address:* Bank of East Asia Ltd, 22nd Floor, 10 Des Voeux Road Central, Hong Kong. *T:* 28423206. *Clubs:* Wentworth; Hong Kong Country, Royal Hong Kong Golf, Royal Hong Kong Yacht (Hong Kong); Waialae Country (Hawaii).

LI, Fook Kow, CMG 1975; JP; Chairman, Public Service Commission, Hong Kong, 1980–87, retired; *b* 15 June 1922; *s* of Tse Fong Li; *m* 1946, Edith Kwong Li; four *c*. *Educ:* Massachusetts Inst. of Technology (BSc,MSc). Mem. Hong Kong Admin. Service; Teacher, 1948–54; various departmental posts and posts in the Government Secretariat, 1955–60; Asst Financial Sec., Asst Estabt Officer, Dep. Financial Sec. and Estabt Officer, 1961–69; Dep. Dir of Commerce and Industry, 1970; Dep. Sec. for Home Affairs, 1971–72; Dir of Social Welfare, 1972; Sec. for Social Services, 1973; Sec. for Home Affairs, 1977–80. JP Hong Kong, 1959. *Address:* D21 Carolina Garden, 32 Coombe Road, Hong Kong. *Clubs:* Royal Hong Kong Jockey, Hong Kong Country.

LI, Simon Fook Sean; Director, The Bank of East Asia Ltd, Hong Kong, since 1987; *b* 19 April 1922; 3rd *s* of late Koon Chun Li and Tam Doy Hing Li; *m* Marie Veronica Lillian Yang; four *s* one *d*. *Educ:* King's Coll., Hong Kong; Hong Kong Univ.; Nat. Kwangsi Univ.; University Coll., London Univ. (LLB 1950; Fellow, 1991). Barrister-at-Law, Lincoln's Inn, 1951. Crown Counsel, Attorney-General's Chambers, Hong Kong, 1953; Senior Crown Counsel, 1962; District Judge, 1966–71, Puisne Judge, 1971–80, Justice of Appeal, 1980–84, Vice-Pres., Court of Appeal, 1984–87, Hong Kong. Chm., Insce Claims Complaints Bd, 1990–; Mem., Hong Kong Special Admin. Region Basic Law Drafting Cttee, 1985–90. PR China: Hong Kong Affairs Advr, 1992; Dep Dir, Preliminary Working Cttee, HKSAR Prep. Cttee, 1993. Hon. LLD Chinese Univ., Hong Kong,

1986. *Recreations:* hiking, swimming. *Address:* Room 1104/5, Hing Wai Building, 36 Queen's Road, Central, Hong Kong. *T:* 5232541. *Clubs:* Commonwealth Trust; Hong Kong, Chinese, Royal Hong Kong Jockey (Hon. Steward) (Hong Kong).

LIANG, Prof. Wei Yao, PhD; Professor of Superconductivity, University of Cambridge, since 1994; Official Fellow and Lecturer, Gonville and Caius College, Cambridge, since 1971; *b* 23 Sept. 1940; *s* of Tien Fu Liang and Po Seng Nio Lie; *m* 1968, Lian Choo (*née* Choong); three *d. Educ:* Pah Chung Chinese High Sch., Jakarta; Portsmouth Coll. of Technology; Imperial Coll., London (BSc, ARCS 1st Class Hons Theoretical Physics); Univ. of Cambridge (PhD). Gonville and Caius College, Cambridge: Research Fellow, 1969–71; Dir of Studies in Natural Scis, 1975–89; University of Cambridge: Demonstrator, 1971–75; Lectr in Physics, 1975–92; Reader in high temperature superconductivity, 1992–93; Co-Dir, 1988–89, Dir, 1989–, Interdisciplinary Res. Centre in Superconductivity. Vis. Scientist, Xerox Palo Alto Res. Centre, 1975, 1976; Visiting Professor: EPF Lausanne, 1978; Inst. of Semiconductors, Beijing, 1983. *Publication:* (ed with A. S. Alexandrov and E. K. H. Salje) Polarons and Bipolarons in High Tc Superconductors and Related Materials, 1995. *Recreations:* music, photography. *Address:* Gonville and Caius College, Cambridge CB2 1TA. *T:* Cambridge (01223) 337077.

LIAO Poon-Huai, Donald, CBE 1983 (OBE 1972); company director; *b* 29 Oct. 1929; *s* of late Liao Huk-Koon and Yeo Tsai-Hoon; *m* 1963, Christine Yuen Ching-Me; two *s* one *d. Educ:* Univ. of Hong Kong (BArch Hons); Univ. of Durham (Dip. Landscape Design). Architect, Hong Kong Housing Authority, 1960, Housing Architect, 1966; Commissioner for Housing and Member, Town Planning Board, 1968; Director of Housing and Vice-Chm., Hong Kong Housing Authority, 1973; Sec. for Housing and Chm., Hong Kong Housing Authority, 1980; Sec. for Dist Admin, Hong Kong, 1985. Chm., HSBC China Fund; Director: Shun Hing Gp, Hong Kong, 1990–; Morgan Crucible Co., 1991–; CNT Gp, 1991–; Stock Exchange of Hong Kong Ltd, 1991–. MLC, Hong Kong, 1980; MEC, 1985. Mem., Sino-British Jt Liaison Gp, 1987. Mem. Council, Hong Kong Univ., 1991–. Fellow, Hong Kong Inst. of Architects. Hon. FIH. *Recreations:* golf, skiing, riding. *Address:* (residence) 95A Kadoorie Avenue, Kowloon, Hong Kong. *T:* 27155822; (office) 1515 Ocean Centre, Canton Road, Kowloon, Hong Kong. *T:* 23020820. *Clubs:* Athenæum; Royal Hong Kong Golf, Royal Hong Kong Jockey (Hong Kong).

LIARDET, Rear-Adm. Guy Francis, CB 1990; CBE 1985; *b* 6 Dec. 1934; *s* of Maj.-Gen. Henry Maughan Liardet, *qv*; *m* 1962, Jennifer Anne O'Hagan; one *s* two *d. Educ:* Royal Naval Coll., Dartmouth. Trng Comdr, BRNC, Dartmouth, 1969–70; comd HMS Aurora, 1970–72; Exec. Officer, HMS Bristol, 1974–76; Defence Policy Staff, MoD, 1978–79; RCDS, 1980; CSO (Trng), C-in-C Naval Home Comd, 1981–82; comd HMS Cleopatra and Seventh Frigate Sqn, 1983–84; Dir of Public Relations (Navy), MoD, 1984–86; Flag Officer Second Flotilla, 1986–88; Comdt, JSDC, 1988–90, retd. Dir of Public Affairs, CIA, 1990–93. Mem., RNSA, 1970–. *Publications:* contrib. Naval Review. *Recreation:* sailing. *Address:* The Downs Cottage, New Road, Meonstoke, Southampton SO32 3NN. *Club:* Royal Yacht Squadron (Cowes).

LIARDET, Maj.-Gen. Henry Maughan, CB 1960; CBE 1945 (OBE 1942); DSO 1945; DL; *b* 27 Oct. 1906; *s* of late Maj.-Gen. Sir Claude Liardet, KBE, CB, DSO, TD, DL; *m* 1st, 1933, Joan Sefton (*d* 1991), *d* of Major G. S. Constable, MC, JP; three *s*; 2nd, 1994, Mrs Barbara Corcoran. *Educ:* Bedford School. 1st Commission for Territorial Army, 1924, Royal Artillery; Regular Commission, Royal Tank Corps, 1927; service UK, India, Egypt, 1927–38; Staff Coll., Camberley, 1939; War of 1939–45: War Office, 1939–41; active service in Egypt, N Africa, Italy, 1941–45; General Staff appointments, command of 6th RTR, 1942–44; GSO1, 10th Armoured Div., Alamein; Comdr, 1st Armoured Replacement Gp, 1944; 2nd in Comd, 25th Tank Brigade (later Assault Brigade), 1944–45; Commander: 25th Armoured Engr Brigade, April–Sept. 1945 (despatches twice); Detachment, 1st Armoured Div., Palestine, 1947; Brig., RAC, MELF, 1947–49; Comdr, 8th RTR, 1949–50; Dep. Dir, Manpower Planning, War Office, 1950–52; Comdr, 23 Armd Bde, 1953–54; idc, 1955; Chief of Staff, British Joint Services Mission (Army Staff), Washington, DC, 1956–58; ADC to the Queen, 1956–58; Director-General of Fighting Vehicles, WO, 1958–61; Deputy Master-General of the Ordnance, War Office, 1961–64, retired. Colonel Comdt, Royal Tank Regt, 1961–67. Dir, British Sailors' Soc., 1961–78; Chm., SS&AFA W Sussex Cttee, 1966–85. DL, Sussex, 1964–74, W Sussex 1974–. W Sussex CC, 1964–74; Alderman, 1970–74. Pres. Sussex Council, Royal British Legion, 1975–81. *Recreations:* shooting, gardening. *Address:* 44 Martlets Court, Arundel, West Sussex BN18 9NZ. *T:* Arundel (01903) 882533. *Clubs:* Army and Navy; Sussex.

See also G. F. Liardet.

LIBBY, Donald Gerald, PhD; Adviser, Logica UK Ltd, since 1995; *b* 2 July 1934; *s* of late Herbert Lionel Libby and Minnie Libby; *m* 1st, 1961, Margaret Elizabeth Dunlop McLatchie (*d* 1979); one *d*; 2nd, 1982, June Belcher. *Educ:* RMA, Sandhurst; London Univ. (BSc, PhD Physics). CEng, FIEE. Department of Education and Science: Principal Scientific Officer, 1967–72; Principal, 1972–74; Asst Sec., 1974–80; Under Sec., 1980–92 (Planning and Internat. Relations Br., 1980–82, Architects, Bldg and Schs Br., 1982–86, Further and Higher Educn Br. 2, 1986–91); Under Sec., OST, Cabinet Office, and Sec., ABRC, 1991–94. FRSA; Mem., NY Acad. of Scis. *Recreations:* music, rowing, golf. *Address:* Lygon Cottage, 26 Wayneflete Tower Avenue, Esher, Surrey KT10 8QG.

LICHFIELD, 5th Earl of, *cr* 1831; **Thomas Patrick John Anson;** Viscount Anson and Baron Soberton, 1806; *b* 25 April 1939; *s* of Viscount Anson (Thomas William Arnold) (*d* 1958) and Princess Anne of Denmark (*née* Anne Fenella Ferelith Bowes-Lyon) (*d* 1980); *S* grandfather, 1960; *m* 1975, Lady Leonora Grosvenor (marr. diss. 1986), *d* of 5th Duke of Westminster, TD; one *s* two *d. Educ:* Harrow Sch.; RMA, Sandhurst. Joined Regular Army, Sept. 1957, as Officer Cadet; Grenadier Guards, 1959–62 (Lieut). Now photographer (known professionally as Patrick Lichfield). FBIPP; FRPS. Freeman, City of London, 1981. *Publications:* The Most Beautiful Women, 1981; Lichfield on Photography (also video cassettes), 1981; A Royal Album, 1982; Patrick Lichfield's Unipart Calendar Book, 1982; Patrick Lichfield Creating the Unipart Calendar, 1983; Hot Foot to Zabriskie Point, 1985; Lichfield on Travel Photography, 1986; Not the Whole Truth (autobiog.), 1986; (ed) Courvoisier's Book of the Best, 1986, 5th edn 1994; Lichfield in Retrospect, 1988; (ed) Queen Mother: the Lichfield selection, 1990; (ed) Elizabeth R: a photographic celebration of 40 years, 1991. *Heir: s* Viscount Anson, *qv*. *Address:* Lichfield Studios, 133 Oxford Gardens, W10 6NE. *T:* 0181–969 6161; (seat) Shugborough Hall, Stafford. *T:* Little Haywood (01889) 881454. *Club:* White's.

LICHFIELD, Bishop of, since 1983; **Rt. Rev. Keith Norman Sutton;** *b* 23 June 1934; *s* of Norman and Irene Sutton; *m* 1963, Edith Mary Jean Geldard; three *s* one *d. Educ:* Jesus College, Cambridge (MA 1959). Curate, St Andrew's, Plymouth, 1959–62; Chaplain, St John's Coll., Cambridge, 1962–67; Tutor and Chaplain, Bishop Tucker Coll., Mukono, Uganda, 1968–73; Principal of Ridley Hall, Cambridge, 1973–78; Bishop Suffragan of Kingston-upon-Thames, 1978–83. General Synod: Chairman: Bd for Mission and Unity, 1989–91; Bd of Mission, 1991–94; Member: Standing Cttee, 1989–94; Theol Gp, House of Bishops, 1989–. Select Preacher, Univ. of Cambridge, 1987. Pres., Queen's Coll., Birmingham, 1986–. Entered House of Lords, 1989. Episcopal Visitor, Simon of Cyrene Theol Inst., 1992–. DUniv Keele, 1992; Hon. DLitt Wolverhampton, 1994. *Publication:* The People of God, 1983. *Recreations:* Russian literature, third world issues, music. *Address:* Bishop's House, 22 The Close, Lichfield, Staffs WS13 7LG.

LICHFIELD, Dean of; *see* Wright, Very Rev. N. T.

LICHFIELD, Archdeacon of; *see* Ninis, Ven. R. B.

LICHFIELD, Prof. Nathaniel; Professor Emeritus, University of London, since 1978; Partner, Dalia and Nathaniel Lichfield Associates, urban and environmental planners and economists, since 1992; *b* 29 Feb. 1916; 2nd *s* of Hyman Lichman and Fanny (*née* Grecht); *m* 1st, 1942, Rachel Goulden (*d* 1968); two *d*; 2nd, 1970, Dalia Kadury; one *s* one *d. Educ:* Raines Foundn Sch.; University of London. BSc (EstMan), PhD (Econ), PPRTPI, FRICS, CEng, MICE. Sen. Partner, 1962–89, Chm., 1989–92, Nathaniel Lichfield & Partners Ltd, planning, develt, urban design and econ. consultants; from 1945 has worked continuously in urban and regional planning, specialising in econs of planning from 1950, with particular reference to social cost-benefit in planning, land policy and urban conservation; worked in local and central govt depts and private offices. Consultant commns in UK and all continents. Special Lectr, UCL, 1950; Prof. of Econs of Environmental Planning, UCL, 1966–79. Visiting Professor: Univ. of California, 1976–78; Univ. of Tel Aviv, 1959–60, 1966; Technion—Israel Inst. of Technol., 1972–74; Hebrew Univ., Jerusalem, 1980–; Univ. of Naples, 1986–; Special Prof., Univ. of Nottingham, 1989–. Chm., Econs Cttee, Internat. Council for Monuments and Sites, 1988–; Member: Exec. Cttee, Internat. Centre for Land Policy Studies, 1975–85; Council, Tavistock Inst. of Human Relations, 1968–93 (Vice Pres., 1993–); formerly Member: SSRC; CNAA; SE Econ. Planning Council. Hon. Fellow, Centre for Social and Econ. Res. on Global Envmt, 1992. *Publications:* Economics of Planned Development, 1956; Cost Benefit Analysis in Urban Redevelopment, 1962; Cost Benefit Analysis in Town Planning: A Case Study of Cambridge, 1966; Israel's New Towns: A Development Strategy, 1971; (with Prof. A. Proudlove) Conservation and Traffic: a case study of York, 1975; (with Peter Kettle and Michael Whitbread) Evaluation in the Planning Process, 1975; (with Haim Darin-Drabkin) Land Policy in Planning, 1980; (with Leslie Lintott) Period Buildings: evaluation of development–conservation options, 1985; (with Prof. J. Schweid) Conservation of the Built Heritage, 1986; Economics in Urban Conservation, 1988; Land Policy in Israel, 1993; Community Impact Evaluation, 1994; papers in Urban Studies, Regional Studies, Land Economics, Town Planning Review, Restauro, Built Environment. *Recreations:* finding out less and less about more and more, countering advancing age, singing. *Address:* 13 Chalcot Gardens, Englands Lane, NW3 4YB. *T:* 0171–483 0724. *Club:* Reform.

LICHINE, Mme David; *see* Riabouchinska, Tatiana.

LICHTENSTEIN, Roy; American painter and sculptor; *b* 27 Oct. 1923; *s* of Milton Lichtenstein and Beatrice (*née* Werner); *m* 1st, 1949, Isabel Wilson (marr. diss.); two *s*; 2nd, 1968, Dorothy Herzka. *Educ:* Art Students League, NY; Ohio State Univ. (BFA 1946; MFA 1949). Cartographical draughtsman, US Army, 1943–46; Instructor, Fine Arts Dept, Ohio State Univ., 1946–51; product designer for various cos, Cleveland, 1951–57; Asst Prof., Fine Arts Dept, NY State Univ., 1957–60, Rutgers Univ., 1960–63. Mem., Amer. Acad. and Inst. of Arts and Letters, 1979. Hon. RA 1994. Hon. degrees in Fine Arts. Skowhegan Medal for Painting, 1977. Works in Pop Art and other themes derived from comic strip techniques. One-man shows include: Carlebach Gall., NY, 1951; Leo Castelli Gall., NY, 1962, 1963, 1965, 1967, 1971–75, 1977, 1979, 1981, 1983, 1985, 1986, 1987; Galerie Illeana Sonnabend, Paris, 1963, 1965, 1970, 1975; Venice Biennale, 1966; Pasadena Art Museum, 1967; Walker Art Center, Minneapolis, 1967, 1986; Stedelijk Museum, Amsterdam, 1967; Tate Gall., London, 1968; Guggenheim Museum, NY, 1969; Nelson Gall., Kansas City, 1969; Museum of Contemporary Art, Chicago, 1970; Centre Nat. d'Art Contemporain, Paris, 1975, travelling to Berlin; Seattle Art Museum, 1976; Inst. of Contemp. Art, Boston, 1979; Portland Center for Visual Arts, 1980; St Louis Art Museum, 1981; Fundación Juan March, Madrid, 1982; Seibu Mus., Takanawa, 1983; Mus. of Modern Art, NY, 1987, travelling to Amsterdam and Tel Aviv, 1987, to Frankfurt, Oxford and Washington, 1988. Group shows include: Nat. Collection of Fine Art, Washington, 1966; Venice Biennale, 1966; 36th Biennial Exhibn of Contemp. Amer. Painting, Corcoran Gall., Washington, DC, 1979; Nat. Mus. of Amer. Art, Smithsonian Instn, Washington, 1984. Created outside wall for Circarama of NY State Pavilion, NY World's Fair, 1963; large painting for Expo '67, Montreal, 1967; brushstroke murals for Düsseldorf Univ. Med. Centre, 1970; public sculpture, Mermaid, for Theater of Performing Arts, Miami, 1979; Brushstrokes in Flight, Port Columbus Airport, Columbus, Ohio, 1984; Mural with Blue Brushstrokes, Equitable Life Tower, NY, 1985; Coups de Pinceau, Caisse des Dépôts et Consignations, Paris, 1988; Tel Aviv Mural, Tel Aviv Mus. of Art, 1989. Retrospectives: Guggenheim Mus., NY, and Tate Gall., Liverpool, 1993. Represented in permanent collections: Albright Knox Gall., Buffalo; Chicago Art Inst.; Corcoran Gall. of Art, Washington; Hirschorn Mus. and Sculpture Garden, Washington; Liby of Congress, Washington; Ludwig Mus., Cologne; Mus. of Modern Art, NY; Nat. Gall. of Art, Washington; Norton Simon Mus., Pasedena; San Francisco Mus. of Modern Art; Seibu Art Mus., Tokyo; Smithsonian Instn, Washington; Stedelijk Mus., Amsterdam; Tate Gall.; V&A Mus.; Walker Art Center, Minneapolis; Whitney Mus. of Amer. Art, NY; Yale Univ.

LICKISS, Sir Michael (Gillam), Kt 1993; Senior Partner, Grant Thornton, 1989–94; *b* 18 Feb. 1934; *s* of Frank Gillam and Elaine Rheta Lickiss; *m* 1st, 1959, Anita (marr. diss. 1979); two *s* two *d*; 2nd, 1987, Anne; one *s. Educ:* Bournemouth Grammar Sch.; LSE, London Univ. (BSc Econ 1955). FCA. Articled, Bournemouth, 1955–58; commissioned, Army, 1959–62; practised Bournemouth, 1962–68; Partner, Thornton Baker, Bournemouth, 1968–73, London, 1973–94: Exec. Partner, 1975; Managing Partner, 1985–89; firm's name changed to Grant Thornton, 1986. DTI Inspector, jtly with Hugh Carlisle, QC, 1986–88; Lectr, UK and overseas. Chairman: Accountancy Television Ltd, 1992–94; Somerset Economic Partnership, 1994–; West of England Develt Agency, 1994–; Dir, MAI plc, 1994–, and other cos. Institute of Chartered Accountants: Mem. Council, 1971–81, 1983–; Vice-Pres., 1988–89; Dep. Pres., 1989–90; Pres., 1990–91; Past Chairman: Educn and Training, Tech. Cttee and Ethics Cttee; Professional Conduct Directorate. Chm., CCAB, 1990–91; Dep. Chm., Financial Reporting Council, 1990–91; Member: Council, BTEC (Chm., Finance Cttee, 1985–93; Chm., 1994–); FEFCE, 1992–. Founder President, Assoc. of Accounting Technicians, 1980–82. Trustee, Parnham Trust, 1992–. Mem., Court of Govs, LSE, 1992–. *Publications:* articles in learned jls. *Recreations:* gardening in Somerset, walking in the Lake District. *Address:* Old Vicarage, Drayton, near Langport, Som TA10 0JX. *Club:* Royal Automobile.

LICKLEY, Sir Robert (Lang), Kt 1984; CBE 1973; BSc; DIC; FRSE; FEng; Hon. FIMechE; FRAeS; FIEE; consultant; *b* Dundee, 19 Jan. 1912. *Educ:* Dundee High Sch.; Edinburgh Univ. (Hon. DSc 1972); Imperial Coll. (Fellow, 1973); FCGI 1976. Formerly: Professor of Aircraft Design, College of Aeronautics, Cranfield; Managing Director, Fairey Aviation Ltd; Hawker Siddeley Aviation Ltd, 1960–76 (Asst Man. Dir, 1965–76); Head,

Rolls Royce Support Staff, NEB, 1976–79. President: IMechE, 1971; IProdE, 1981–82. FRSE 1977. Hon. FIMechE 1982; Hon. MIED. Hon. DSc: Edinburgh, 1973; Strathclyde, 1987. *Address:* Moorlands, Midway, Walton-on-Thames, Surrey KT12 3HY.

LICKORISH, Leonard John, CBE 1975; *b* 10 Aug. 1921; *s* of Adrian J. and Josephine Lickorish; *m* 1945, Eileen Maris Wright (*d* 1983); one *s. Educ:* St George's Coll., Weybridge; University Coll., London (BA). Served RAF, 1941–46. British Travel Assoc., 1946–70; Dir-Gen., BTA, 1970–86. Vis. Prof., Univ. of Strathclyde, 1989–. Chm., European Travel Commn, 1984–86 (Hon. Vice-Chm., 1986); Vice-Pres., Exhibition Industry Federation, 1989– (Chm., 1987–89); Sec., European Tourism Action Group, 1986. Officer of Crown of Belgium, 1967. *Publications:* The Travel Trade, 1955; The Statistics of Tourism, 1975; Tourism Marketing, 1989; Developing Tourism Destinations, 1991; numerous for nat. and internat. organisations on internat. travel. *Recreation:* gardening. *Address:* 46 Hillway, Highgate, N6 6EP. *Club:* Royal Over-Seas League.

LIDDELL, family name of **Baron Ravensworth.**

LIDDELL, Alasdair Donald MacDuff; Director of Planning, NHS Executive, since 1994; *b* 15 Jan. 1949; *s* of late Donald Liddell and of Barbara Liddell (*née* Dixon); *m* 1976, Jennifer Abramsky, *qv*; one *s* one *d. Educ:* Balliol College, Oxford (BA Hons Jurisp. 1970); DMS Thames Polytechnic; LHA. King's College and Royal Free Hosps, 1972–77; Administrator (Planning and Policy), Tower Hamlets HA, 1977–79; Area Gen. Administrator, Kensington and Chelsea and Westminster AHA (T), 1979–82; District Administrator, Hammersmith and Fulham HA, 1982–84; District Administrator later District Gen. Manager, Bloomsbury HA, 1984–88; Regl Gen. Manager, E Anglian RHA, 1988–94. King's Fund Internat. Fellow, 1987–88. Mem., NHS Central R&D Cttee, 1991–94. Chm. Trustees, Public Management Foundn, 1990–94; Jt Chm. and Founder, Assoc. for Public Health, 1992–94. *Publication:* contrib. to In Dreams Begins Responsibility: a tribute to Tom Evans, 1987; Towards an Effective NHS, 1993. *Recreations:* ski-ing, playing with computers, buying French wine. *Address:* NHS Executive, Quarry House, Quarry Hill, Leeds LS2 7UE. *T:* Leeds (0113) 254 5807. *Club:* Royal Society of Medicine.

LIDDELL, Dr Donald Woollven, FRCP 1964; FRCPsych; Head of Department of Psychological Medicine, King's College Hospital, 1961–79; *b* 31 Dec. 1917; *m* 1954, Emily (*née* Horsfall) (marr. diss. 1977); one *s* one *d. Educ:* Aldenham Sch.; London Hospital. MRCP 1941; Neurological training as RMO, The National Hospital, Queen Square, 1942–45; Psychiatric training, Edinburgh and Maudsley Hospital. Medical Superintendent, St Francis Hospital, Haywards Heath, 1957–61; retired as Physician to Bethlem and Maudsley Hosps, 1968. Examr to RCP and RCPsych. Founder FRCPsych, 1971. *Publications:* contrib. Journal of Mental Science, Journal of Neurology, Psychiatry and Neuro-surgery, American Journal of Mental Diseases, Journal of Social Psychology. *Address:* 8 Newmarket Street, Usk, Gwent NP5 1AT.

LIDDELL, Helen Lawrie; MP (Lab) Monklands East, since July 1994; *b* 6 Dec. 1950; *d* of Hugh Reilly and Bridget Lawrie Reilly; *m* 1972, Dr Alistair Henderson Liddell; one *s* one *d. Educ:* St Patrick's High Sch., Coatbridge; Strathclyde Univ. Head, Econ. Dept, 1971–75, and Asst Sec., 1975–76, Scottish TUC; Econ. Correspondent, BBC Scotland, 1976–77; Scottish Sec., Labour Party, 1977–88; Dir, Personnel and Public Affairs, Scottish Daily Record and Sunday Mail (1986) Ltd, 1988–92; Chief Exec., Business Venture Prog., 1993–94. Contested (Lab) Fife E, Oct. 1974. *Publication:* Elite, 1990. *Recreations:* cooking, hill-walking, music, writing. *Address:* House of Commons, SW1A 0AA.

LIDDELL, Jennifer, (Mrs Alasdair Liddell); *see* Abramsky, Jennifer.

LIDDERDALE, Sir David (William Shuckburgh), KCB 1975 (CB 1963); TD; Clerk of the House of Commons, 1974–76; *b* 30 Sept. 1910; *s* of late Edward Wadsworth and Florence Amy Lidderdale; *m* 1943, Lola, *d* of late Rev. Thomas Alexander Beckett, Tubbercurry and Ballinew; one *s. Educ:* Winchester; King's Coll., Cambridge (MA). Assistant Clerk, House of Commons, 1934. Served War of 1939–45, The Rifle Brigade (TA); active service, N Africa and Italy. Senior Clerk, 1946, Fourth Clerk at the Table, 1953, Second Clerk Assistant, 1959, Clerk Assistant, 1962, House of Commons. Joint Secretary, Assoc. of Secretaries-General of Parliaments (Inter-Parliamentary Union), 1946–54, Mem., 1954–76, Vice-Pres., 1973–76, Hon. Vice-Pres., 1976. *Publications:* The Parliament of France, 1951; (with Lord Campion) European Parliamentary Procedure, 1953; (ed) Erskine May's Parliamentary Practice, 19th edn, 1976. *Recreation:* walking. *Address:* 46 Cheyne Walk, SW3 5LP. *Club:* Travellers'.

LIDDIARD, Ronald; social work, financial and management consultant, flying instructor and airline pilot; *b* 26 July 1932; *s* of Tom and Gladys Liddiard; *m* 1957, June Alexandra (*née* Ford); two *d. Educ:* Canton High Sch., Cardiff; Colleges of Commerce and Technology, Cardiff; Inst. of Local Govt Studies, Birmingham Univ. Dip. Municipal Admin, Certif. Social Work. Health Administrator, 1958–60; Social Worker, 1960–64; Sen. Welfare Administrator, 1964–70; Dir of Social Services: Bath, 1971–74; Birmingham, 1974–85. Hon. Kentucky Col, 1977. *Publications:* How to Become an Airline Pilot, 1989; chapters in: Innovations in the Care of the Elderly, 1984; Self-Care and Health in Old Age, 1986; articles in social work, aviation, management and health jls. *Recreations:* travel, freelance journalism, wines. *Address:* Whitefriars, Portway, Worcs B48 7HP. *T:* Wythall (01564) 826235.

LIDINGTON, David Roy, PhD; MP (C) Aylesbury, since 1992; *b* 30 June 1956; *s* of Roy N. and Rosa Lidington; *m* 1989, Helen Mary Farquhar Parry; two *s. Educ:* Haberdashers' Aske's Sch., Elstree; Sidney Sussex Coll., Cambridge (MA, PhD). British Petroleum plc, 1983–86; RTZ plc, 1986–87; Special Adviser to: Home Sec., 1987–89; Foreign Sec., 1989–90; Consultant, PPU Ltd, 1991–92. *Publications:* articles on Tudor history. *Recreations:* history, choral singing. *Address:* House of Commons, SW1A 0AA. *T:* 0171–219 3000; 100 Walton Street, Aylesbury, Bucks HP21 7QP.

LIEBESCHUETZ, Prof. (John Hugo) Wolfgang (Gideon), PhD; FBA 1991; Professor of Classical and Archaeological Studies, Nottingham University, 1979–92, now Professor Emeritus; *b* Hamburg, 22 June 1927; *s* of Prof. H. Liebeschuetz and Dr E. A. R. Liebeschuetz (*née* Plaut); *m* 1955, Margaret Rosa Taylor; one *s* three *d. Educ:* UCL (BA 1951); PhD London 1957. Schoolteacher, 1957–63; Leicester University: Lectr in Classics, 1963–74; Sen. Lectr, 1974–78; Reader, 1978–79. Mem., Princeton Inst. for Advanced Study, 1993. Corresp. Mem., German Archaeol Inst., 1994. *Publications:* Antioch: city and imperial administration in the later Roman Empire, 1972; Continuity and Change in Roman Religion, 1979; Barbarians and Bishops: army, church and state in the age of Arcadius and Chrysostom, 1990; From Diocletian to the Arab Conquest: change in the late Roman Empire, 1990; contribs to learned jls. *Address:* 1 Clare Valley, The Park, Nottingham NG7 1BU.

LIESNER, Hans Hubertus, CB 1980; Member, Monopolies and Mergers Commission, since 1989 (Deputy Chairman, 1989–95); *b* 30 March 1929; *e s* of Curt Liesner, lawyer, and Edith L. (*née* Neumann); *m* 1968, Thelma Seward; one *s* one *d. Educ:* German grammar schs; Bristol Univ. (BA); Nuffield Coll., Oxford; MA Cantab. Asst Lectr, later Lectr, in Economics, London Sch. of Economics, 1955–59; Lectr in Economics, Univ. of Cambridge; Fellow, Dir of Studies in Economics and some time Asst Bursar, Emmanuel Coll., Cambridge, 1959–70; Under-Sec. (Economics), HM Treasury, 1970–76; Dep. Sec., and Chief Econ. Advr, DTI (formerly Industry, Trade and Prices and Consumer Protection), 1976–89, retd. *Publications:* The Import Dependence of Britain and Western Germany, 1957; Case Studies in European Economic Union: the mechanics of integration (with J. E. Meade and S. J. Wells), 1962; Atlantic Harmonisation: making free trade work, 1968; Britain and the Common Market: the effect of entry on the pattern of manufacturing production (with S. S. Han), 1971; articles in jls, etc. *Recreations:* ski-ing, walking, gardening. *Address:* Monopolies and Mergers Commission, New Court, 48 Carey Street, WC2A 2JT. *Club:* Reform.

LIFFORD, 9th Viscount *cr* 1781 (Ire.); **Edward James Wingfield Hewitt;** Director, Neilson Cobbold, Stockbrokers, since 1991; *b* 27 Jan. 1949; *s* of 8th Viscount Lifford and of Alison Mary Patricia, *d* of T. W. Ashton; *S* father, 1987; *m* 1976, Alison Mary, *d* of Robert Law; one *s* two *d. Educ:* The Old Malthouse, Dorset; Aiglon College, Switzerland. Mem., Stock Exchange; Director: City of Winchester Assured Tenancies; Winchester Cottage Improvement Soc. plc. *Recreations:* country sports. *Heir: s* Hon. James Thomas Wingfield Hewitt, *b* 29 Sept. 1979. *Address:* Field House, Hursley, Hants SO21 2LE. *T:* Hursley (01962) 775203. *Clubs:* Boodle's, Pratt's; Hampshire (Winchester).

LIGETI, Prof. György Sándor; Member, Order of Merit, Germany, 1975; music composer; Professor for Composition, Hamburg Academy of Music, 1973–89; *b* 28 May 1923; *s* of Dr Sándor Ligeti and Dr Ilona Somogyi; *m* 1957, Dr Vera Spitz; one *s. Educ:* Budapest Academy of Music (Dipl. in composition). Lecturer for harmony and counterpoint, Budapest Acad. of Music, 1950–56; Guest Prof., Stockholm Acad. of Music, 1961–71; composer in residence, Stanford Univ., Calif, 1972. Member: Swedish Royal Acad. of Music, 1964; Acad. of Arts, Berlin, 1968; Free Acad. of Arts, Hamburg, 1971; Bavarian Acad. of Fine Arts, Munich, 1978. Hon. Mem., Amer. Acad. and Inst. of Arts and Letters, 1984. Dr *hc* Hamburg, 1988. Grawemeyer Award, 1986. *Main compositions:* Apparitions, for orch., 1959; Atmosphères, for orch., 1961; Aventures, for 3 singers and 7 instrumentalists, 1962; Requiem, for 2 soli, chorus and orch., 1965; Cello concerto, 1966; Chamber concerto, 1970; Melodien, for orch., 1971; Le Grand Macabre, opera, 1977; Trio, for violin, horn, piano, 1982; Piano études, 1985; Piano concerto, 1986; Nonsense madrigals, 1988; Violin concerto, 1991. *Address:* Himmelhofgasse 34, 1130 Vienna, Austria; Mövenstrasse 3, 2000 Hamburg 60, Germany.

LIGGINS, Sir Graham (Collingwood), Kt 1991; CBE 1983; FRCSE, FRACS, FRCOG; FRS 1980; FRSNZ 1976; Professor of Obstetrics and Gynaecological Endocrinology, University of Auckland, New Zealand, 1968–87, now Professor Emeritus (formerly Senior Lecturer); Consultant to National Women's Hospital, Auckland. *Educ:* Univ. of NZ. MB, ChB, Univ. NZ, 1949; PhD, Univ. of Auckland, 1969. MRCOG Lond. 1956; FRCSE 1958; FRACS 1960. Is distinguished for his work on the role of foetal hormones in the control of parturition. Hon. FAGS, 1976; Hon. FACOG, 1978. Hon. MD Lund, 1983. Hector Medal, RSNZ, 1980. *Publications:* approx. 200 published papers. *Recreations:* forestry, sailing, fishing. *Address:* Postgraduate School of Obstetrics and Gynaecology, National Women's Hospital, Claude Road, Auckland 3, New Zealand. *T:* (9) 3775127; 3/38 Awatea Road, Parnell, Auckland 1, New Zealand.

LIGHT, (Sidney) David; a Civil Service Commissioner, 1978–79; Member, Civil Service Commission's Panel of Selection Board Chairmen, 1980–89; *b* 9 Dec. 1919; *s* of late William Light; *m* Edna Margaret Honey; one *s. Educ:* King Edward VI Sch., Southampton. RAF, 1940–46. HM Customs and Excise, 1938; HM Treasury, 1948–60, Asst Sec., CS Commn, 1969–75; Under Sec., CSD, 1975–78. *Recreations:* bricolage, watching cricket, travel. *Address:* Oakhanger, Vicarage Hill, Farnham, Surrey GU9 8HJ. *T:* Farnham (01252) 721522. *Clubs:* Commonwealth Trust; Hampshire Cricket.

LIGHTBODY, Ian (Macdonald), CMG 1974; Chairman, Public Services Commission, Hong Kong, 1978–80; *b* 19 Aug. 1921; *s* of Thomas Paul Lightbody and Dorothy Marie Louise Lightbody (*née* Cooper); *m* 1954, Noreen, *d* of late Captain T. H. Wallace, Dromore, Co. Down; three *s* one *d. Educ:* Queens Park Sch., Glasgow; Glasgow Univ. (MA). War service, Indian Army, India and Far East, 1942–46 (Captain); Colonial Admin. Service, Hong Kong, 1945; various admin. posts; District Comr, New Territories, 1967–68; Defence Sec., 1968–69; Coordinator, Festival of Hong Kong, 1969; Comr for Resettlement, 1971; Sec. for Housing and Chm., Hong Kong Housing Authority, 1973–77; Sec. for Admin, Hong Kong, 1977–78. MLC 1971; MEC 1977; retd from Hong Kong, 1980. Mem., Arun DC, 1983–91. *Recreations:* walking, politics, tennis. *Address:* Two Stacks, Lake Lane, Barnham, Sussex PO22 0AD. *Clubs:* Hong Kong, Royal Hong Kong Jockey.

LIGHTBOWN, Sir David Lincoln, Kt 1995; MP (C) Staffordshire South East, since 1983; *b* 30 Nov. 1932; *m* Margaret Ann. Former Engrg Dir, a public limited co. in West Midlands. Member: Lichfield Dist Council, 1975–86 (Leader of Council, 1977–83); Staffs CC, 1977–85 (formerly Chm., Educn and Finance Cttees). An Assistant Govt Whip, 1986–87; a Lord Comr of HM Treasury (Govt Whip), 1987–90; Vice-Chamberlain, HM Household, 1990; Comptroller of HM Household, 1990–95. *Address:* House of Commons, SW1A 0AA. *T:* 0171–219 6241/4212.

LIGHTBOWN, Ronald William, MA; FSA, FRAS; art historian and author; Keeper of the Department of Metalwork, Victoria and Albert Museum, 1985–89; *b* Darwen, Lancs, 2 June 1932; *s* of late Vincent Lightbown and of Helen Anderson Lightbown (*née* Burness); *m* 1962, Mary Dorothy Webster; one *s. Educ:* St Catharine's Coll., Cambridge (MA). FSA, FRAS. Victoria and Albert Museum: Asst Keeper, Library, 1958–64; Asst Keeper, Dept of Metalwork, 1964–73; Dep. Keeper, 1973–76, Keeper, 1976–85, Library. Fellow, Inst. for Res. in the Humanities, Wisconsin Univ., 1974. Pres., Jewellery History Soc., 1990–93; a Vice-Pres., Soc. of Antiquaries, 1986–90 (Sec., 1979–86); Associate Trustee, Soane Mus., 1981–. Socio dell' Ateneo Veneto, for contrib. to study of culture of Venice and the Veneto, 1987; Socio dell' Accademia Clementina, Bologna, for contribns to study of Italian art, 1988. *Publications:* French Secular Goldsmith's work of the Middle Ages, 1978; Sandro Botticelli, 1978, 2nd edn, 1989 (Prix Vasari, 1990); (with M. Corbett) The Comely Frontispiece, 1978; (ed and trans. with A. Caiger-Smith) Piccolpasso: the art of the potter, 1980; Donatello and Michelozzo, 1980; Andrea Mantegna, 1986; Piero della Francesca, 1992 (Prix de Mai des Libraires de France, 1992); Viaggio in un capolavoro di Piero della Francesca, 1992; (ed and introd) History of Art in 18th Century England (series of source-books on 18th century British art), 14 vols, 1970–71; V&A Museum catalogues and publications: (pt author) Italian Sculpture, 1964; Tudor Domestic Silver, 1970; Scandinavian and Baltic Silver, 1975; French Silver, 1979; (with M. Archer) India Observed, 1982; Medieval European Jewellery, 1992; many articles in learned jls, incl. Burlington Magazine, Warburg Jl and Art Bulletin. *Recreations:* reading, travel, music, conversation. *Address:* Barrowmount House, Goresbridge, Co. Kilkenny, Ireland.

LIGHTFOOT, George Michael; His Honour Judge Lightfoot; a Circuit Judge, since 1986; *b* 9 March 1936; *s* of Charles Herbert Lightfoot and Mary Lightfoot (*née* Potter); *m* 1963, Dorothy (*née* Miller); two *s* two *d. Educ:* St Michael's Catholic College, Leeds; Exeter College, Oxford (MA). Schoolmaster, 1962–66. Called to the Bar, Inner Temple,

1966; practised on NE circuit. A Recorder, 1985–86. Mem., Home Farm Trust, 1980–; President: Leeds Friends of Home Farm Trust, 1987–; Mencap, Leeds, 1987–. *Recreations:* cricket and sport in general, gardening (labourer), learning to listen to music, reading. *Address:* Leeds Combined Court Centre, Oxford Row, Leeds. *Clubs:* Catenian Association (City of Leeds Circle); Yorkshire CC.

LIGHTHILL, Sir (Michael) James, Kt 1971; FRS 1953; FRAeS; Provost of University College London, 1979–89, Hon. Fellow, 1982, Hon. Research Fellow, 1989; *b* 23 Jan. 1924; *s* of E. B. Lighthill; *m* 1945, Nancy Alice Dumaresq; one *s* four *d*. *Educ:* Winchester Coll.; Trinity Coll., Cambridge (Hon. Fellow, 1986). Aerodynamics Division, National Physical Laboratory, 1943–45; Fellow, Trinity Coll., Cambridge, 1945–49; Sen. Lectr in Maths, Univ. of Manchester, 1946–50; Beyer Prof. of Applied Mathematics, Univ. of Manchester, 1950–59; Dir, RAE, Farnborough, 1959–64; Royal Soc. Res. Prof., Imperial Coll., 1964–69; Lucasian Prof. of Mathematics, Univ. of Cambridge, 1969–79. Chairman: Academic Adv. Cttee, Univ. of Surrey, 1964; ICSU Special Cttee on Natural Disaster Reduction, 1990–95; Member: Adv. Council on Technology, 1964; NERC, 1965–70; Shipbuilding Inquiry Cttee, 1965; (part-time) Post Office Bd, 1972–74; First Pres., Inst. of Mathematics and its Applications, 1964–66; a Sec. and Vice-Pres., Royal Soc., 1965–69; President: Internat. Commn on Mathematical Instruction, 1971–74; Internat. Union of Theoretical and Applied Mechanics, 1984–88. FRAeS 1961, Hon. FRAeS 1990. Foreign Member: American Academy of Arts and Sciences, 1958; American Philosophical Soc., 1970; US Nat. Acad. of Sciences, 1976; US Nat. Acad. of Engineering, 1977. Associate Mem., French Acad. of Sciences, 1976. FIC 1991; Hon. Fellow American Inst. of Aeronautics and Astronautics, 1961. Hon. DSc: Liverpool, 1961; Leicester, 1965; Strathclyde, 1966; Essex, Princeton, 1967; East Anglia, Manchester, 1968; Bath, St Andrews, Surrey, 1969; Cranfield, 1974; Paris, Aachen, 1975; Rensselaer, 1980; Leeds, 1983; Brown, Southern California, 1984; Lisbon, 1986; Rehovot, 1987; London, 1993; Compiègne, Kiev, 1994. Royal Medal, Royal Society, 1964; Gold Medal, Royal Aeronautical Society, 1965; Harvey Prize for Science and Technol., Israeli Inst. of Technol., 1981; Gold Medal, Inst. of Maths and Its Applications, 1982; Ludwig-Prandtl-Ring, 1984. Comdr Order of Léopold, 1963. *Publications:* Introduction to Fourier Analysis and Generalised Functions, 1958; Mathematical Biofluiddynamics, 1975; Newer Uses of Mathematics, 1977; Waves in Fluids, 1978; An Informal Introduction to Theoretical Fluid Mechanics, 1986; articles in Royal Soc. Proc. and Trans, Qly Jl of Mechanics and Applied Maths, Philosophical Magazine, Jl of Aeronautical Scis, Qly Jl of Maths, Aeronautical Qly, Communications on Pure and Applied Maths, Proc. Cambridge Philosophical Soc., Jl of Fluid Mechanics, Reports and Memoranda of ARC; contrib. to Modern Developments in Fluid Dynamics: High Speed Flow; High Speed Aerodynamics and Jet Propulsion; Surveys in Mechanics; Laminar Boundary Layers. *Recreations:* music and swimming. *Address:* Department of Mathematics, University College London, Gower Street, WC1E 6BT. *Club:* Athenæum.

LIGHTMAN, Hon. Sir Gavin (Anthony), Kt 1994; **Hon. Mr Justice Lightman;** a Judge of the High Court of Justice, Chancery Division, since 1994; *b* 20 Dec. 1939; *s* of Harold Lightman, *qv*; *m* 1965, Naomi Ann Claff; one *s* two *d*. *Educ:* Univ. of London (LLB); Univ. of Michigan (LLM). Called to the Bar, Lincoln's Inn, 1963, Bencher 1987; QC 1980. Vice Pres., Anglo Jewish Assoc., 1995– (Dep. Pres., 1986–92); Chairman: Educn Cttee, Anglo Jewish Assoc., 1986–94; Educn Cttee, Hillel House, 1992–; Legal Friends, Haifa Univ., 1990– (Gov., 1994). Patron, Jewish Commonwealth Council, 1994–. *Publications:* (with G. Battersby) Cases and Statutes on Real Property, 1965; (with G. Moss) The Law Relating to the Receivers of Companies, 1986, 2nd edn 1994; A Report on the National Union of Miners, 1990. *Recreations:* reading, cricket, walking, travel. *Address:* Royal Courts of Justice, Strand, WC2A 2LL. *Club:* Royal Automobile.
See also S. L. Lightman.

LIGHTMAN, Harold, QC 1955; Master of the Bench of Lincoln's Inn; *b* 8 April 1906; *s* of Louis Lightman, Leeds; *m* 1936, Gwendoline Joan, *d* of David Ostrer, London; three *s*. *Educ:* City of Leeds Sch.; privately. Accountant, 1927–29. Barrister, Lincoln's Inn, 1932. Home Guard, 1940–45. Defence Medal, 1946. Liveryman, Company of Glovers, 1960. *Publication:* (ed) 40th edn, Gore Browne, Company Law and Emergency War Legislation, 1945. *Recreation:* reading. *Address:* Stone Buildings, Lincoln's Inn, WC2A 3XT. *T:* 0171–242 3840. *Club:* Royal Automobile.
See also Hon. Sir G. A. Lightman, S. L. Lightman.

LIGHTMAN, Ivor Harry, CB 1984; Hon. Lecturer, Cardiff Business School, since 1992; Member, Parole Board, 1990–94; *b* 23 Aug. 1928; *s* of late Abraham Lightman, OBE and Mary (*née* Goldschneider); *m* 1950, Stella Doris Blend; one *s*. *Educ:* Abergele Grammar Sch. Clerical Officer, Min. of Food, 1946; Officer of Customs and Excise, 1949–56; Asst Principal, then Principal, Ministry of Works, 1957–65; HM Treasury, 1965–67; Assistant Secretary: MPBW, 1967–70; CSD, 1970–73; Under Secretary: Price Commn, 1973–76; Dept of Prices and Consumer Protection, 1976–78; Dept of Industry, 1978–81; Dep. Sec., Welsh Office, 1981–88, retd. Chairman: First Choice Housing Assoc., 1989–94; All-Wales Adv. Panel on Services for Mentally Handicapped People, 1990–. *Address:* 6 Clos Coedydafarn, Lisvane, Cardiff CF4 5ER.

LIGHTMAN, Lionel; Lay Observer attached to Lord Chancellor's Department, 1986–90; *b* 26 July 1928; *s* of late Abner Lightman and late Gitli Lightman (*née* Szmul); *m* 1952, Helen, *y d* of late Rev. A. Shechter and late Mrs Shechter; two *d*. *Educ:* City of London Sch.; Wadham Coll., Oxford (MA). Nat. Service, RAEC, 1951–53 (Temp. Captain). Asst Principal, BoT, 1953; Private Sec. to Perm. Sec., 1957; Principal 1958; Trade Comr, Ottawa, 1960–64; Asst Sec. 1967; Asst Dir, Office of Fair Trading, 1973–75; Under Sec., Dept of Trade, 1975–78, DoI, 1978–81; Dir of Competition Policy, OFT, 1981–84. *Address:* 73 Greenhill, NW3 5TZ. *T:* 0171–435 3427.

LIGHTMAN, Prof. Stafford Louis, PhD; FRCP; Professor of Medicine, University of Bristol, since 1993; *b* 7 Sept. 1948; *s* of Harold Lightman, *qv*; *m* 1977, Susan Louise Stubbs; three *s* one *d*. *Educ:* Repton Sch.; Gonville and Caius Coll., Cambridge (MA, MB BChir, PhD); Middlesex Hosp. Med. Sch. Vis. Sen. Scientist, MRC Neuro. Pharm. Unit, Cambridge, 1980–81; Wellcome Trust Sen. Lectr, St Mary's Hosp. Med. Sch. and Hon. Consultant Physician and Endocrinologist, St Mary's Hosp., 1981–82; Charing Cross and Westminster Medical School: Reader in Medicine, 1982–88; Prof. of Clinical Neuroendocrinology, 1988–92; Consultant Physician and Endocrinologist to Charing Cross and Westminster Hosps, 1988–92; Hon. Sen. Res. Fellow, Inst. of Neurology and Consultant Endocrinologist to Nat. Hosp. for Neurology and Neurosurgery, 1988–. Editor-in-Chief, Jl of Neuroendocrinology, 1989–. *Publications:* (ed with B. J. Everitt) Neuroendocrinology, 1986; (with Michael Powell) Pituitary Tumours: a handbook on management, 1995. *Recreations:* squash, hill walking, scuba diving, music, theatre, anthropology. *Address:* University of Bristol, Department of Medicine, Marlborough Street, Bristol BS2 8HW. *T:* Bristol (0117) 928 2871; 3 Worcester Crescent, Clifton, Bristol BS8 3JA.
See also Hon. Sir G. A. Lightman.

LIGHTON, Sir Thomas (Hamilton), 9th Bt *cr* 1791 (Ire.), of Merville, Dublin; Chairman, Society of London Art Dealers, 1993–95; *b* 4 Nov. 1954; *o s* of Sir Christopher Robert Lighton, 8th Bt, MBE and his 2nd wife, Horatia Edith (*d* 1981), *d* of A. T. Powlett; *S* father, 1993; *m* 1990, Belinda, *d* of John Fergusson; twin *s* one *d* (and one *s* decd). *Educ:* Eton. *Heir: s* James Christopher Hamilton Lighton, *b* 20 Oct. 1992. *Address:* c/o Waddington Galleries, 11 Cork Street, W1X 1PD.

LIKIERMAN, Prof. (John) Andrew; Professor of Accounting and Financial Control, London Business School, since 1987; on secondment as Head of Government Accountancy Service and Chief Accountancy Adviser to HM Treasury, since 1993; Director, Financial Management Reporting and Audit, and Principal Finance Officer, HM Treasury, since 1995; *b* 30 Dec. 1943; *s* of Dolek and Olga Likierman; *m* 1987, Meira, *d* of Joshua and Miriam Gruenspan; one step *s* one step *d*. *Educ:* Stowe Sch.; Univ. of Vienna; Balliol Coll., Oxford (MA). FCMA, FCCA. Divl Management Accountant, Tootal Ltd, 1965–68; Asst Lectr, 1968–69, Lectr, 1972–74, Dept of Management Studies, Leeds Univ.; Qualitex Ltd, 1969–72 (Man. Dir, Overseas Div., 1971–72); Vis. Fellow, Oxford Centre for Management Studies, 1972–74; Chm., Ex Libris Ltd, 1973–74; London Business Sch., 1974–76 and 1979–: Dir, Part-time Masters Programme, 1981–85; Dir, Inst. of Public Sector Management, 1983–88; Chm., Faculty Bd, 1986–89; Dean of External Affairs, 1989–92; Dep. Principal, 1990–92; Elected Governor, 1986–89, Governor, 1990–93. Asst Sec., Cabinet Office (Mem., Central Policy Review Staff), 1976–79, Advr, 1979–82; Advisor, H of C Select Committees: Treasury and CS, 1981–90; Employment, 1985–89; Transport, 1981, 1987–90; Social Services, 1988; Social Security, 1991; Mem., various govt inquiries including: North Sea Oil Costs, 1975; Power Plant Industry, 1976; Post Office Internat. Comparisons, 1981; Accounting for Econ. Costs (Byatt Cttee), 1986; Professional Liability (Chm.), 1989. Member: Finance Cttee, Oxfam, 1974–84; Cttee on med. costs, London Univ., 1980–81; Current Affairs Adv. Gp, Channel 4, 1986–87; Acad. Adv. Panel, Accounting Standards Cttee, 1987–90 (Mem., Public Sector Liaison Gp, 1984–86); Audit Commn, 1988–91; Financial Reporting Council, 1990– (Observer, 1993–); Exec. Cttee, British Acad. of Management, 1988–90; Consultative Cttee of Accountancy Bodies, 1989–92; Auditing Practices Bd, 1991–92; Cttee on Financial Aspects of Corporate Governance (Cadbury Cttee), 1991–95 (Chm., Monitoring Cttee, 1993–95); Council: RIPA, 1982–88; Consumers' Assoc., 1983–85; Chartered Inst. of Management Accountants, 1985–94 (Pres., 1991–92); Civil Service Coll., 1989–94; Scientific Council, Eur. Inst. of Public Admin, 1990–93; Defence Operational Analysis Centre, 1992–93. Chm. Editl Bd, Public Money and Management, 1988–93; non-exec. Dir, Economists' Bookshop, 1981–91 (non-exec. Chm., 1987–91). *Publications:* The Reports and Accounts of Nationalised Industries, 1979; Cash Limits and External Financing Limits, 1981; (jtly) Public Sector Accounting and Financial Control, 1983, 4th edn 1992; (with P. Vass) Structure and Form of Government Expenditure Reports, 1984; Public Expenditure, 1988; (jtly) Accounting for Brands, 1989; contribs to academic and professional jls. *Recreations:* tennis, cycling, choral singing, architecture, wine. *Address:* 5 Downshire Hill, NW3 1NR. *T:* 0171–435 9888. *Club:* Reform.

LILFORD, 7th Baron, *cr* 1797; **George Vernon Powys;** *b* 8 Jan. 1931; *s* of late Robert Horace Powys (*g g grandson* of 2nd Baron) and of Vera Grace Bryant, Rosebank, Cape, SA; *S* kinsman, 1949; *m* 1st, 1954, Mrs Eve Bird (marr. diss.); 2nd, 1957, Anuta Merritt (marr. diss., 1958); 3rd, 1958, Norma Yvonne Shell (marr. diss., 1961); 4th, 1961, Mrs Muriel Spottiswoode (marr. diss., 1969); two *d*; 5th, 1969, Margaret Penman; one *s* two *d*. *Educ:* St Aidan's Coll., Grahamstown, SA; Stonyhurst Coll. *Recreations:* golf, cricket. *Heir: s* Hon. Mark Vernon Powys, *b* 16 Nov. 1975. *Address:* Le Grand Câtelet, St John, Jersey, Channel Islands JE3 4FL.

LILL, John Richard, OBE 1978; concert pianist; Professor at Royal College of Music; *b* 17 March 1944; *s* of George and Margery Lill. *Educ:* Leyton County High Sch.; Royal College of Music. FRCM; Hon. FTCL; FLCM; Hon. RAM 1988. Gulbenkian Fellowship, 1967. First concert at age of 9; Royal Festival Hall debut, 1963; Promenade Concert debut, 1969. Numerous broadcasts on radio and TV; has appeared as soloist with all leading British orchestras. Recitals and concertos throughout Great Britain, Europe, USA, Canada, Scandinavia, USSR, Japan and Far East, Australia, New Zealand, etc. Overseas tours as soloist with many orchestras including London Symphony Orchestra and London Philharmonic Orchestra. Complete recordings of Beethoven sonatas and concertos; complete Beethoven cycle, London, 1982, 1986, and Tokyo, 1988. Chappell Gold Medal; Pauer Prize; 1st Prize, Royal Over-Seas League Music Competition, 1963; Dinu Lipatti Medal in Harriet Cohen Internat. Awards; 1st Prize, Internat. Tchaikovsky Competition, Moscow, 1970. Hon. DSc Aston, 1978; Hon. DMus Exeter, 1979. *Recreations:* amateur radio, chess, walking. *Address:* c/o Harold Holt Ltd, 31 Sinclair Road, W14 0NS. *T:* 0171–603 4600.

LILLEY, Prof. Geoffrey Michael, OBE 1981; CEng, FRSA, FRAeS, MIMechE, FIMA; Professor of Aeronautics and Astronautics, University of Southampton, 1964–82, now Emeritus Professor (Head of Department of Aeronautics and Astronautics, 1963–82); Director and Deputy Chairman, Hampshire Technology Centre, since 1985; *b* Isleworth, Mddx, 16 Nov. 1919; *m* 1948, Leslie Marion Wheeler; one *s* two *d*. *Educ:* Isleworth Grammar Sch.; Battersea and Northampton Polytechnics; Imperial Coll. BSc(Eng) 1944, MSc(Eng) 1945, DIC 1945. RAF, 1935–36. Gen. engrg trg, Benham and Kodak, 1936–40; Drawing Office and Wind Tunnel Dept, Vickers Armstrong Ltd, Weybridge, 1940–46; Coll. of Aeronautics: Lectr, 1946–51; Sen. Lectr, 1951–55; Dep. Head of Dept of Aerodynamics, 1955, and Prof. of Experimental Fluid Mechanics, 1962–64. Visiting Professor: Stanford Univ., 1977–78; ME Technical Univ., Ankara, Turkey, 1983–90; Univ. of the Witwatersrand, 1990; Vis. Scientist, Inst. of Computer Applications in Sci. and Engrg, NASA Langley Res. Center, 1992–93. Past Member: Aeronautical Res. Council (past Mem. Council and Chm. Aerodynamics, Applied Aerodynamics, Noise Res., Fluid Motion and Performance Cttees); Noise Advisory Council (Chm., Noise from Air Traffic Working Group); Past Chm., Aerodynamics Cttee, Engrg Sci. Data Unit. Consultant to: Rolls Royce, 1959–61, 1967–84; AGARD, 1959–63 and 1988–89; OECD, 1969–71. Gold Medal for Aeronautics, RAeS, 1983; Aerodynamic Noise Medal, AIAA, 1985. *Publications:* (jt editor) Proc. Stanford Conf. on Complex Turbulent Flows; articles in reports and memoranda of: Aeronautical Research Council; Royal Aeronautical Soc., and other jls. *Recreations:* music, chess, walking. *Address:* Highbury, Pine Walk, Chilworth, Southampton SO16 7HQ. *T:* Southampton (01703) 769109. *Club:* Athenæum.

LILLEY, Rt. Hon. Peter Bruce, PC 1990; MP (C) St Albans, since 1983; Secretary of State for Social Security, since 1992; *b* 23 Aug. 1943; *s* of Arnold Francis Lilley and Lillian (*née* Elliott); *m* 1979, Gail Ansell. *Educ:* Dulwich Coll.; Clare Coll., Cambridge. MA; FInstPet 1978. Economic consultant in underdeveloped countries, 1966–72; investment advisor on energy industries, 1972–84. Chm., London Oil Analysts Gp, 1979–80; Partner, 1980–86, Dir, 1986–87, W. Greenwell & Co., later Greenwell Montagu. Consultant Dir, Cons. Res. Dept, 1979–83. Chm., Bow Group, 1972–75. Contested (C) Tottenham, Oct. 1974. PPS to Ministers for Local Govt, Jan.–Oct. 1984, to Chancellor of the Exchequer, 1984–87; Economic Sec. to HM Treasury, 1987–89, Financial Sec., 1989–90; Sec. of State for Trade and Industry, 1990–92. *Publications:* Do You Sincerely Want to Win?, 1972, 2nd edn 1973; Lessons for Power, 1974; (with S. Brittan) Delusion of Incomes Policy, 1977; (contrib.) Skidelsky: End of the Keynesian Era, 1980; Thatcherism:

the next generation, 1990. *Address:* House of Commons, SW1A 0AA. *T:* 0171–219 3000. *Club:* Carlton.

LILLICRAP, Harry George, CBE 1976; Chairman, Cable and Wireless, 1972–76; *b* 29 June 1913; *s* of late Herbert Percy Lillicrap; *m* 1938, Kathleen Mary Charnock; two *s.* *Educ:* Erith County Sch.; University College London. BSc (Eng) 1934. Post Office Telecommunications, 1936–72; Sen. Dir Planning, Sen. Dir Customer Services, 1967–72. Dir, Telephone Rentals Ltd, 1976–84. *Address:* Lower Flat, Leysters, Highfield Road, East Grinstead, West Sussex RH19 2DX. *T:* East Grinstead (01342) 325811.

LILLINGSTON, George David I. I.; *see* Inge-Innes-Lillingston.

LILLY, Prof. Malcolm Douglas, FRS 1991; FEng 1982; Professor of Biochemical Engineering, University College London, since 1979; *b* 9 Aug. 1936; *s* of Charles Victor Lilly and Amy Gardiner; *m* 1959, Sheila Elizabeth Stuart; two *s.* *Educ:* St Olave's Grammar Sch.; University College London (BSc, PhD, DSc). FIChemE, FIBiotech. University College London: Lecturer in Biochemical Engrg, 1963–72; Reader in Enzyme Technology, 1972–79; Dir, Centre for Biochem. Engrg and Biotechnol., 1982–89; Fellow, 1988. Director, Whatman Biochemicals, 1968–71. Vis. Prof., Univ. of Pennsylvania, 1969; Vis. Engrg Fellow, Merck & Co., USA, 1987 (Vice-Dean, Faculty of Engrg, 1987). Past Chm., Internat. Orgn for Biotechnology and Bioengineering, 1980– (Chm, 1972–80); Dir, Internat. Inst. of Biotechnology, 1989–; Member: Council, Soc. for Gen. Microbiol., 1979–83; Research Cttee, British Gas, 1982–94; Bd of Management and Executive Cttee, Inst. for Biotechnological Studies, 1983–89; Bd, PHLS, 1988–94; Biotechnology Jt Adv. Bd, 1992–94; Chairman: Advanced Centre for Biochemical Engrg, UCL, 1991–; AFRC Engrg Res. Bd, 1992–94. Hartley Lecture, Royal Soc., 1988; Danckwerts Lecture, IChemE, 1993. Food, Pharmaceutical and Bioengrg Award, Amer. Inst. of Chem. Engrs, 1976; Enzyme Engrg Award, Engrg Foundn, 1993. *Publications:* (jtly) Fermentation and Enzyme Technology, 1979; (jtly) OECD Report, Biotechnology: international trends and perspectives, 1982; numerous papers on biochemical engrg, fermentation and biotransformation. *Recreations:* sailing, advanced motoring (IAM Observer), volunteer countryside ranger. *Address:* 8 Tower Road, Orpington, Kent BR6 0SQ. *T:* Orpington (01689) 821762.

LIM FAT, Sir (Maxime) Edouard (Lim Man), Kt 1991; Professor Emeritus, University of Mauritius, since 1975; company director; *s* of V. Lim Fat and S. Lifo; *m* 1952, Y. H. Chan Wah Hak; two *s* one *d.* *Educ:* Univ. of London (BSc Chem. Eng.); Univ. of Newcastle (MSc Agric. Eng.). AEE Harwell, 1950–51; Engineer, Min. of Agriculture, Mauritius, 1951–63; Principal, Mauritius Coll. of Agriculture, 1963–68; Head, Sch. of Industrial Technology, Univ. of Mauritius, 1968–80; Director: Bank of Mauritius, 1980–92; NEDC, 1991–; two factories; Chm., Mauritius Freeport, 1992–. *Publications:* numerous articles, mainly on industrial develt and educn. *Recreations:* golf, economics, music. *Address:* 19 Rev. Lebrun Street, Rose-hill, Mauritius. *T:* (home) 4547680, (office) 2110738, *Fax:* 2110728. *Clubs:* Gymkhana, Vacoas.

LIM PIN, Professor, MD; FRCP, FRCPE, FRACP, FACP; Vice-Chancellor, National University of Singapore, since 1981; *b* 12 Jan. 1936; *s* of late Lim Lu Yeh and of Choo Siew Kooi; *m* 1964, Shirley Loo; two *s* one *d.* *Educ:* Univ. of Cambridge (MA; MD 1970). FRCP 1976; FRCPE 1981; FRACP 1978; FACP 1981. MO, Min. of Health, Singapore, 1965–66; Univ. of Singapore: Lectr in Medicine, 1966–70; Sen. Lectr in Medicine, 1971–73; Associate Prof. of Medicine, 1974–77; Prof. and Head, Dept of Medicine, 1978–81; Dep. Vice-Chancellor, 1979–81. Eisenhower Fellow, USA, 1982. Chm., Applied Res. Corp., 1982–; Director: Neptune Orient Lines, 1981–; Nat. Univ. Hosp., 1985–. Dep. Chm., Econ. Develt Bd, 1995–; Mem., Nat. IT Cttee, 1992–; Founder Pres., Endocrine and Metabolic Soc. of Singapore. Chm., Bd of Govs, Raffles Instn, 1988–; Member, Board of Governors: Inst. of E. Asian Political Economy (formerly E Asian Philosophies), 1987–; Inst. of Policy Studies, 1988–, Singapore Inst. of Labour Studies, 1990–; Singapore Internat. Foundn, 1991–; Member: Bd of Dirs, Overseas Union Bank, 1991–; Bd of Dirs, Lee Kuan Yew Exchange Fellowship, 1991–. Queen's Schol., 1957; Hon. Fellow, Coll. of Gen. Practitioners of Singapore, 1982. Public Administration Medal (Gold), Singapore, 1984; Meritorious Service Medal, Singapore, 1990. Officier, Ordre des Palmes Académiques (France), 1988. *Publications:* articles in New England Jl of Medicine, Med. Jl of Australia, BMJ, Qly Jl of Medicine, and Tissue Antigens. *Recreations:* swimming, badminton. *Address:* National University of Singapore, 10 Kent Ridge Crescent, Singapore 0511, Republic of Singapore. *T:* 7756666. *Club:* Singapore Island Country.

LIMANN, Dr Hilla, Hon. GCMG 1981; President of Ghana, 1979–81; *b* 1934; *m*; five *c.* *Educ:* Lawra Primary Boarding Sch.; Tamale Middle Boarding Sch.; Govt Teacher Trng Coll.; London Sch. of Economics (Hon. Fellow, 1982); Sorbonne; Univ. of London; Faculty of Law and Econ. Sciences, Univ. of Paris. BSc(Econ.) 1960; BA Hons (Hist.), 1964; PhD (Polit. Sci. and Law), 1965. Teacher, 1952–55; examiner for Civil Service grad. entry, W African Exams Council. Councillor, Tumu Dist Council, 1952 (Chm., 1953–55); contested (Indep.) Constituency, Party Elec., 1954. Head of Chancery and Official Sec., Ghana Embassy, Lomé, Togo, 1968–77; Mem., Constitutional Commn on 1969 Constitution for Ghana; Mem. Govt Delegns for opening of borders of Ghana with the Ivory Coast/Upper Volta; Mem./Sec. to Ghana delegns, OAU and Non-aligned States, Confs of ILO, WHO, Internat. Atomic Energy Agency. Leader, People's National Party.

LIMBU; *see* Rambahadur Limbu.

LIMERICK, 6th Earl of, *cr* 1803 (Ire.); **Patrick Edmund Pery,** KBE 1983; DL; MA, CA; Baron Glentworth, 1790 (Ire.); Viscount Limerick, 1800 (Ire.); Baron Foxford, 1815 (UK); Chairman: Pirelli UK, since 1989; AMP Asset Management plc, since 1992; De La Rue plc, since 1993 (Director, since 1983); *b* 12 April 1930; *e s* of 5th Earl of Limerick, GBE, CH, KCB, DSO, TD, and Angela Olivia, Dowager Countess of Limerick, GBE, CH (*d* 1981); *S* father, 1967; *m* 1961, Sylvia Rosalind Lush (*see* Countess of Limerick); two *s* one *d.* *Educ:* Eton; New Coll., Oxford. CA 1957. Chairman: Mallinson–Denny Ltd, 1979–81; Polymeters Response Internat., 1988–93; Director: Kleinwort Benson Ltd, 1967–87 (Vice Chm., 1983–85; Dep Chm., 1985–87); Kleinwort Benson Gp, 1982–90; Kleinwort Benson Australian Income Fund Inc., 1986–; Commercial Bank of Australia Ltd (London Adv. Bd), 1969–72; TR Pacific Investment Trust, 1987–92; Brooke Bond Gp, 1981–84. Parly Under-Sec. of State for Trade, DTI, 1972–74; Chairman: BOTB, 1979–83 (Mem., 1975–91); BIEC, subseq. British Invisibles, 1984–91; Pres., Inst. of Export, 1983–; Vice-Pres., Assoc. of British Chambers of Commerce, 1977– (Pres., 1974–77); Member: Cttee for ME Trade, 1968– (Chm., 1975–79); Council, London Chamber of Commerce, 1968–79. Pres., Canning House, 1994–. Chairman: Ct of Govs, London Guildhall Univ. (formerly City of London Poly.), 1984–; Cttee of Univ. Chairmen, 1995–; Trustees, City Parochial Foundn, 1992– (Trustee, 1971–). Pres., South of England Agricl Soc., 1993. Master, Guild of World Traders, 1991. President: Anglo-Swiss Soc., 1984–; Ski Club of GB, 1974–81; Alpine Ski Club, 1985–87 (Vice-Pres., 1975–77); Vice-Pres., Alpine Club, 1989–91. Hon. Col 71st (Yeomanry) Signal Regt (Volunteers), 1993–. DL W Sussex, 1988. *Recreations:* skiing, mountaineering. *Heir: s* Viscount Glentworth, *qv.* *Address:* Chiddinglye, West Hoathly, East Grinstead, West Sussex RH19 4QT. *T:* Sharpthorne (01342) 810214; 30 Victoria Road, W8 5RG. *T:* 0171–937 0573.

LIMERICK, Countess of; Sylvia Rosalind Pery, CBE 1991; Chairman, British Red Cross Society, 1985–95, now Chairman Emeritus; President, Health Visitors' Association, since 1984 (a Vice President, 1978–84); Vice-Chairman, Foundation for the Study of Infant Deaths, since 1971; *b* 7 Dec. 1935; *e d* of Maurice Stanley Lush, CB, CBE, MC; *m* 1961, Viscount Glentworth (now 6th Earl of Limerick, *qv*); two *s* one *d.* *Educ:* St Swithun's, Winchester; Lady Margaret Hall, Oxford (MA). Research Asst, Foreign Office, 1959–62. Mem., Bd of Governors, St Bartholomew's Hosp., 1970–74; Vice-Chm., Community Health Council, S District of Kensington, Chelsea, Westminster Area, 1974–77; Mem., Kensington, Chelsea and Westminster AHA, 1977–82. British Red Cross Society: Nat. HQ Staff, 1962–66; Pres., Kensington and Chelsea Div., 1966–72; a Vice-Pres., London Br., 1972–85; a Vice-Pres., Internat. Fedn of Red Cross Red Crescent Socs, 1993–; Vice President: UK Cttee for UN Children's Fund, 1979– (Pres., 1972–79); Nat. Assoc. for Maternal and Child Welfare, 1985–90 (Pres., 1973–84). Member: Cttee of Management, Inst. of Child Health, 1976–; Council, King Edward's Hospital Fund (Mem., Cttee of Management, 1977–81, 1985–89); Maternity Services Adv. Cttee, DHSS, 1981–84; CS Occupational Health Service Adv. Bd, 1989–92; Eastman Dental Hosp., SHA, 1990–. Trustee, Child Accident Prevention Trust, 1979–87. Reviewed National Association of Citizens Advice Bureaux, 1983. FRSocMed 1977. Hon. FRCP 1994 (Hon. MRCP 1990); Hon. Mem., BPA, 1986. Hon. DLitt CNAA, 1990. Hon. Freeman, Salters' Co., 1992. *Publication:* (jtly) Sudden Infant Death: patterns, puzzles and problems, 1985. *Recreations:* music, mountaineering, ski-ing. *Address:* 30 Victoria Road, W8 5RG. *T:* 0171–937 0573; Chiddinglye, West Hoathly, East Grinstead, W Sussex RH19 4QT. *T:* Sharpthorne (01342) 810214.

LIMERICK AND KILLALOE, Bishop of, since 1985; **Rt. Rev. Edward Flewett Darling;** *b* 24 July 1933; *s* of late Ven. Vivian W. Darling and Honor F. G. Darling; *m* 1958, E. E. Patricia Mann; three *s* two *d.* *Educ:* Cork Grammar School; Midleton Coll., Co. Cork; St John's School, Leatherhead, Surrey; Trinity Coll., Dublin (MA). Curate: St Luke's, Belfast, 1956–59; St John's, Orangefield, Belfast, 1959–62; Incumbent, St Gall's, Carnalea, Co. Down, 1962–72; Chaplain, Bangor Hosp., Co. Down, 1963–72; Rector, St John's, Malone, Belfast, 1972–85; Chaplain, Ulster Independent Clinic, Belfast, 1981–85. *Publications:* Choosing the Hymns, 1984; (ed) Irish Church Praise, 1990. *Recreations:* music, gardening. *Address:* Bishop's House, North Circular Road, Limerick, Ireland. *T* and *Fax:* (61) 451532.

LIMON, Donald William, CB 1993; Clerk of the House of Commons, since 1994; *b* 29 Oct. 1932; *s* of late Arthur and Dora Limon; *m* 1987, Joyce Beatrice Clifton. *Educ:* Durham Cathedral Chorister Sch.; Durham Sch.; Lincoln Coll., Oxford (MA). A Clerk in the House of Commons, 1956–: Sec. to House of Commons Commn, 1979–81; Clerk of Financial Cttees, 1981–84; Principal Clerk, Table Office, 1985–89; Clerk of Cttees, 1989–90; Clerk Asst, 1990–94. *Recreations:* cricket, golf, singing. *Address:* Wicket Gate, Churt, Farnham, Surrey GU10 2HY. *T:* Headley Down (01428) 714350.

LINACRE, Sir (John) Gordon (Seymour), Kt 1986; CBE 1979; AFC 1943; DFM 1941; CIMgt; Deputy Chairman, United Newspapers plc, 1981–91 (Director, 1969–91; Joint Managing Director, 1981–83; Chief Executive, 1983–88); President, Yorkshire Post Newspapers Ltd, since 1990 (Managing Director, 1965–83; Deputy Chairman, 1981–83; Chairman, 1983–90); *b* 23 Sept. 1920; *s* of John James Linacre and Beatrice Barber Linacre; *m* 1943, Irene Amy (*née* Gordon); two *d.* *Educ:* Firth Park Grammar Sch., Sheffield. CIMgt (FBIM 1973). Served War, RAF, 1939–46, Sqdn Ldr. Journalistic appts, Sheffield Telegraph/Star, 1937–47; Kemsley News Service, 1947–50; Dep. Editor: Newcastle Journal, 1950–56; Newcastle Evening Chronicle, 1956–57; Editor, Sheffield Star, 1958–61; Asst Gen. Man., Sheffield Newspapers Ltd, 1961–63; Exec. Dir, Thomson Regional Newspapers Ltd, London, 1963–65. Chairman: United Provincial Newspapers Ltd, 1983–88; Sheffield Newspapers Ltd, 1981–88; Lancashire Evening Post Ltd, 1982–88; Northampton Mercury Co. Ltd, 1983–88; The Reporter Ltd, 1970–88; Blackpool Gazette & Herald Ltd, 1984–88; Chameleon Television, 1992–; Dep. Chm., Express Newspapers, 1985–88; Director: United Newspapers (Publications) Ltd, 1969–88; Trident Television Ltd, 1970–84; Yorkshire Television Ltd, 1967–90. Dir, INCA/FIEJ Res. Assoc., Darmstadt, Germany, 1971–79 (Pres., 1974–77); Pres. FIEJ, 1984–88 (Mem. Bd, 1971–90). Chm., ASA, 1991–94; Member: Newspaper Soc. Council, 1966–90 (Pres., Newspaper Soc., 1978–79); Press Assoc., 1967–74 (Chm., 1970–71); Reuters Ltd, 1970–74 (Trustee, 1974–); Evening Newspaper Advertising Bureau Ltd, 1966–78 (Chm., 1975–76); English National Opera, 1978–81; Opera North (formerly English National Opera North), 1978– (Chm.); N Eastern Postal Bd, 1974–80; Adv. Bd, Yorks and Lincs, BIM, 1973–75; Health Educn Council, 1973–77; Leeds TEC, 1989–91 (Chm.). Governor, Harrogate Festival of Arts and Sciences Ltd, 1973– (Pres., 1992–). Trustee, Yorks and Lincs Trustee Savings Bank, 1972–78; Mem. Council, 1985–93, and Court, 1985–, Chm. Foundation, 1989–, Leeds Univ. Kt, Order of White Rose (Finland), 1987; Grande Ufficiale al Merito della Repubblica Italiana, 1988 (Commendatore, 1973). *Recreations:* golf, fishing, walking. *Address:* White Windows, Staircase Lane, Bramhope, Leeds LS16 9JD. *T:* Arthington (0113) 284 2751. *Clubs:* Alwoodley Golf; Kilnsey Angling; Yorkshire Fly; Huby Angling.

LINAKER, Lawrence Edward, (Paddy); Chairman, Fisons, since 1994; *b* 22 July 1934; *s* of late Lawrence Wignall and Rose Linaker; *m* 1963, Elizabeth Susan Elam; one *s.* *Educ:* Malvern College. FCA. Esso Petroleum, 1957–63; joined M&G Group, 1963; Dep. Chm. and Chief Exec., 1987–94; Man. Dir, 1972, Chm., 1987–94, M&G Investment Management. Director: Fleming Mercantile Investment Trust, 1994–; TSB Gp, 1994–. Chm., Institutional Fund Managers' Assoc., 1992; Dir, Securities Inst., 1992. Trustee, TSB Foundn for Eng. and Wales; Life Trustee, Carnegie UK Trust, 1995. Chm., YMCA Nat. Coll., 1992; Treas., Childline, 1994–; Member: Council, RPMS, 1977–88; Governing Body, SPCK, 1976–; Council, Malvern College, 1988– (Treas., 1993–); Governing Body, Canterbury Christ Church Coll., 1993–. *Recreations:* music, wine, gardening. *Club:* Athenæum.

LINCOLN, 18th Earl of, *cr* 1572; **Edward Horace Fiennes-Clinton;** retired; *b* 23 Feb. 1913; *s* of Edward Henry Fiennes-Clinton (killed in action, 1916) and Edith Annie (*née* Guest) (*d* 1965); *S* to earldom of 10th Duke of Newcastle, 1988; *m* 1st, 1940, Leila Ruth Millen (*d* 1947); one *s* one *d*; 2nd, 1953, Linda Alice O'Brien. *Educ:* Hale School; Govt Schools; Junior Technical Coll., Perth. In goldmining industry, Kalgoorlie, 1935–53; Public Works Dept (water supply) and farming (mainly wheatbelt), 1956–76. *Publication:* Memoirs of an embryo Earl (family edn). *Recreations:* boating, gardening. *Heir: s* Hon. Edward Gordon Fiennes-Clinton [*b* 7 Feb. 1943; *m* 1970, Julia, *d* of William Howson; two *s* one *d*]. *Address:* Flat 45, Elanora Villas, 37 Hastie Street, Bunbury, WA 6230, Australia. *T:* 211223.

LINCOLN, Bishop of, since 1986; **Rt. Rev. Robert Maynard Hardy;** Bishop to HM Prisons, since 1985; *b* 5 Oct. 1936; *s* of Harold and Monica Mavie Hardy; *m* 1970, Isobel

Mary, *d* of Charles and Ella Burch; two *s* one *d*. *Educ:* Queen Elizabeth Grammar School, Wakefield; Clare College, Cambridge (MA). Deacon 1962, priest 1963; Assistant Curate, All Saints and Martyrs, Langley, Manchester, 1962; Fellow and Chaplain, Selwyn College, Cambridge, 1965 (Hon. Fellow, 1986); Vicar of All Saints, Borehamwood, 1972; Priest-in-charge, Aspley Guise, 1975; Course Director, St Albans Diocese Ministerial Training Scheme, 1975; Incumbent of United Benefice of Aspley Guise with Husborne Crawley and Ridgmont, 1980; Bishop Suffragan of Maidstone, 1980–86. Hon. DD Hull, 1992. *Recreations:* walking, gardening, reading. *Address:* Bishop's House, Eastgate, Lincoln LN2 1QQ. *T:* Lincoln (01522) 534701.

LINCOLN, Dean of; *see* Jackson, Very Rev. B. D.

LINCOLN, Archdeacon of; *see* Hawes, Ven. A. J.

LINCOLN, Prof. Dennis William, FRSE; Director, Medical Research Council Reproductive Biology Unit, Edinburgh, since 1982; *b* 21 July 1939; *s* of late Ernest Edward Lincoln and Gertrude Emma Holmes; one *s* one *d*. *Educ:* Bracondale Sch., Norwich; Essex Inst. of Agriculture; Univ. of Nottingham (BSc 1964); Univ. of Cambridge (MA 1966; PhD 1967); Univ. of Bristol (DSc 1974). FRSE 1992. Agricl labourer, 1955–57; Research Technician, Univ. of Nottingham, 1957–59; Res. Fellow, Corpus Christi Coll., Cambridge, 1966–67; Lectr, 1967–74, Reader, 1974–81, Prof., 1981–82, Univ. of Bristol. Short-term appts in Switzerland, The Netherlands, USA, Australia; numerous nat. and internat. duties related to promotion of reproductive health. Hon. Prof., Univ. of Edinburgh, 1984. *Publications:* papers on reproductive biology, esp. on neural mechanisms in control of lactation and fertility. *Recreations:* ornithology, international travel, wildlife photography. *Address:* Centre for Reproductive Biology, 37 Chalmers Street, Edinburgh EH3 9EW. *T:* Edinburgh 0131–229 2575, *Fax:* 0131–228 5571.

LINCOLN, F(redman) Ashe, QC 1947; MA, BCL; Captain RNVR; a Recorder, 1972–79 (Recorder of Gravesend, 1967–71); Master of the Bench, Inner Temple, since 1955; Master of the Moots, 1955–64, and 1968–70; *s* of Reuben and Fanny Lincoln; *m* 1933, Sybil Eileen Cohen; one *s* one *d*. *Educ:* Hoe Gram. Sch., Plymouth; Haberdashers' Aske's Sch.; Exeter Coll., Oxford. Called to Bar, Inner Temple, Nov. 1929. Joined RNV(S)R, 1937; served in Royal Navy (RNVR), Sept. 1939–May 1946: Admiralty, 1940–42; in parties to render mines safe, May 1940; rendered safe first type G magnetic mine (King's Commendation for bravery); Mediterranean, 1943, with commandos in Sicily and Italy at Salerno landings, 1943; Seine Bay (D-day) Landings, 1944; assault crossing of Rhine, March 1945 (despatches twice). Dep. World Pres., Internat. Assoc. of Jewish Lawyers and Jurists, 1973–. Renter Warden of Worshipful Company of Plaisterers, 1946–47, Master, 1949–50; Freeman and Liveryman of City of London; fought general election 1945 (C) Harrow East Div. (Middx.); Chm. Administrative Law Cttee of Inns of Court Conservative Association, 1951; Mem. Exec., Gen. Council of the Bar, 1957–61. Associate MNI, 1976; Pres., RNR Officers' Club, 1981–; Member: Council, British Maritime League, 1983–92; Exec., London Flotilla, 1984– (Vice-Pres., 1994). Mem., RNSA. Pres., Royal Masonic Hosp., 1993–; Chm., London Devonian Assoc., 1965–85, Pres., 1985–; Nat. Chm., Maritime Volunteer Service, 1994–. Trustee: British Maritime Charitable Fund, 1983; Associated Marine and Related Charities (Trng, Educn and Safety), 1985–91. KStJ 1980. *Publications:* The Starra, 1939; Secret Naval Investigator, 1961. *Recreation:* yachting. *Address:* 9 King's Bench Walk, Temple, EC4Y 7DX. *T:* 0171–353 7202. *Clubs:* Athenæum, Royal Automobile, MCC, Naval, City Livery; Royal Corinthian Yacht (Burnham-on-Crouch and Cowes); Bar Yacht; RNVR Yacht.

LIND, Per; Swedish Ambassador to the Court of St James's, 1979–82, retired; *b* 8 Jan. 1916; *s* of Erik and Elisabeth Lind; *m* 1942, Eva Sandström; two *s* two *d*. *Educ:* Univ. of Uppsala. LLB 1939. Entered Swedish Foreign Service as Attaché, 1939; served in Helsinki, 1939–41; Berlin, 1942–44; Second Sec., Stockholm Foreign Ministry, 1944–47; First Sec., Swedish Embassy, Washington, 1947–51; Personal Asst to Sec.-General of UN, 1953–56; re-posted to Swedish Foreign Ministry: Chief of Div. of Internat. Organisations, 1956–59; Dep. Dir Political Affairs, 1959–64; Ambassador with special duties (*ie* disarmament questions) and actg Chm., Swedish Delegation in Geneva, 1964–66; Ambassador to Canada, 1966–69; Under-Sec. of State for Administration at Foreign Ministry, Stockholm, 1969–75; Chm. Special Political Cttee of 29th Session of Gen. Assembly of UN, 1974; Ambassador to Australia, 1975–79. *Recreation:* golf. *Address:* Gyllenstiernsgatan 7, 11526 Stockholm, Sweden.

LINDAHL, Tomas Robert, MD; FRS 1988; Director, Clare Hall Laboratories, Imperial Cancer Research Fund, since 1983; *b* 28 Jan. 1938; *s* of Robert and Ethel Lindahl; *m* 1967, Alice Adams (marr. diss. 1979); one *s* one *d*. *Educ:* Karolinska Inst., Stockholm (MD). Research Fellow, Princeton Univ., 1964–67; Helen Hay Whitney Fellow, 1967–69, Asst Prof., 1968–69, Rockefeller Univ.; Asst Prof., 1969–75, Associate Prof., 1975–77, Karolinska Inst.; Prof. of Medical Biochemistry, Univ. of Gothenburg, 1978–81; Imperial Cancer Research Fund: Staff Scientist, 1981–83; Asst Dir of Research, 1985–89; Associate Dir of Research, 1989–91; Dep Dir, Res., 1991–. Member: EMBO; Royal Swedish Acad. of Scis; Academia Europaea. *Publications:* res. papers in biochem. and molecular biol. *Recreations:* piano, wine, modern art. *Address:* ICRF Clare Hall Laboratories, South Mimms, Herts EN6 3LD.

LINDBERGH, Anne Spencer Morrow; author, United States; *b* 1906; *d* of Dwight Whitney Morrow and Elizabeth Reeve Morrow (*née* Cutter); *m* 1929, Col Charles Augustus Lindbergh, AFC, DFC (*d* 1974); three *s* one *d* (and one *s* one *d* decd). *Educ:* Miss Chapin's Sch., New York City; Smith Coll., Northampton, Mass (two prizes for literature). Received Cross of Honour of United States Flag Association for her part in survey of air route across Atlantic, 1933; received Hubbard Gold Medal of National Geographical Soc. for work as co-pilot and radio operator in flight of 40,000 miles over five continents, 1934. Hon. MA, Smith Coll., Mass., 1935. *Publications:* North to the Orient, 1935; Listen, the Wind, 1938; The Wave of the Future, 1940; The Steep Ascent, 1944; Gift from the Sea, 1955; The Unicorn and other Poems, 1935–55, 1958; Dearly Beloved, 1963; Earth Shine, 1970; Bring Me a Unicorn (autobiog.), 1972; Hour of Gold, Hour of Lead (autobiog.), 1973; Locked Rooms and Open Doors: diaries and letters 1933–35, 1974; The Flower and the Nettle: diaries and letters 1936–39, 1976; War Within and Without: diaries and letters 1939–44, 1980.

LINDEN, Anya, (Lady Sainsbury of Preston Candover); Ballerina, Royal Ballet, 1958–65, retired; *b* 3 Jan. 1933; English; *d* of George Charles and Ada Dorothea Eltenton; *m* 1963, John Davan Sainsbury (*see* Baron Sainsbury of Preston Candover); two *s* one *d*. *Educ:* Berkeley, Calif; Sadler's Wells Sch., 1947. Entered Sadler's Wells Co. at Covent Garden, 1951; promoted Soloist, 1952; Ballerina, 1958. Principal rôles in the ballets: Coppelia; Sylvia; Prince of Pagodas; Sleeping Beauty; Swan Lake; Giselle; Cinderella; Agon; Solitaire; Noctambules; Fête Etrange; Symphonic Variations; The Invitation; Firebird; Lady and the Fool; Antigone; Ondine; Seven Deadly Sins. Ballet coach: Royal Ballet Sch., 1989–; Rambert Sch., 1989–. Member: Nat. Council for One-Parent Families, 1978–90 (Hon. Vice-Pres., 1985–90; Mem. Appeal Cttee, 1966–87); Adv. Council, British Theatre Museum, 1975–83; Drama and Dance Adv. Cttee, British Council, 1981–83; Theatre Museum Assoc., 1984–86. Dep.-Chm. and Dir, Rambert Dance Co. (formerly Ballet Rambert), 1975–89; Governor: Royal Ballet Sch., 1977–; Rambert Sch. of Ballet Charitable Trust Ltd, 1983–; Dep. Chm. and Mem. Council of Management, Benesh Inst. of Choreology (formerly Benesh Inst. of Movement Notation), 1986–. Chm., Linbury Prize for Theatre Design, 1987–. Dir, Anvil Trust, 1992–; Trustee, Galitzine—St Petersburg Trust, 1993–; Patron, Landlife 1993–. *Recreations:* gardening, painting, photography. *Address:* c/o Stamford House, Stamford Street, SE1.

LINDESAY-BETHUNE, family name of **Earl of Lindsay.**

LINDISFARNE, Archdeacon of; *see* Bowering, Ven. M. E.

LINDLEY, Bryan Charles, CBE 1982; Chairman, North Lakeland Healthcare NHS Trust, since 1993; Chairman and Chief Executive, Lord Lindley Associates, since 1990; *b* 30 Aug. 1932; *m* 1987; one *s* by former *m*. *Educ:* Reading Sch.; University Coll., London (Fellow 1979). BSc (Eng) 1954; PhD 1960; FIMechE 1968; FIEE 1968; FInstP 1968; FInstD 1968; FPRI 1984. National Gas Turbine Establishment, Pyestock, 1954–57; Hawker Siddeley Nuclear Power Co. Ltd, 1957–59; C. A. Parsons & Co. Ltd, Nuclear Research Centre, Newcastle upon Tyne, 1959–61; International Research and Development Co. Ltd, Newcastle upon Tyne, 1962–65; Man., R&D Div., C. A. Parsons & Co. Ltd, Newcastle upon Tyne, 1965–68; Electrical Research Assoc. Ltd: Dir, 1968–73; Chief Exec. and Man. Dir, ERA Technology Ltd, 1973–79; Dir, ERA Patents Ltd, 1968–79; Chm. and Man. Dir, ERA Autotrack Systems Ltd, 1971–79. Director: Dunlop Ltd, 1982–85; Soil-Less Cultivation Systems, 1980–85; Chm. and Dir, Thermal Conversions (UK), 1982–85; Dir of Technology, Dunlop Holdings, 1979–85; Director: BICC Cables Ltd, 1985–88; BICC Research and Engineering Ltd, 1985–88; Thomas Bolton & Johnson Ltd, 1986–88; Settle-Carlisle Railway Develt Co., 1992–; Chairman: Optical Fibres, 1985–87; Linktronic Systems Ltd, 1990–92; Wetheriggs Pottery Ltd, 1992–; Chief Exec., Nat. Advanced Robotics Res. Centre, 1989–90. Vis. Prof., Univ. of Liverpool, 1989–. Chairman: Materials, Chemicals and Vehicles Requirements Bd, DTI, 1982–85; RAPRA Council, 1984–85; Dir, RAPRA Technology Ltd, 1985–; Member: Nat. Electronics Council, 1969–79; Res. and Technol. Cttee, CBI, 1974–80; Design Council, 1980–86 (Mem., Design Adv. Cttee, 1980–86); Cttee of Inquiry into Engineering Profession, 1977–80; Adv. Council for Applied Research and Develt, 1980–86; Adv. Cttee for Safety of Nuclear Installations, 1987–; Chm., Sci. Educn and Management Div., IEE, 1974–75; Dep. Chm., Watt Cttee on Energy Ltd, 1976–80. Mem., SAE, 1984. *Publications:* articles on plasma physics, electrical and mechanical engineering, management science, impact of technological innovation, etc, in learned jls. *Recreations:* music, ski-ing, walking, sailing. *Address:* Lindenthwaite, Beacon Edge, Penrith, Cumbria CA11 8BN.

LINDLEY, Prof. Dennis Victor; Professor and Head of Department of Statistics and Computer Science, University College London, 1967–77; *b* 25 July 1923; *s* of Albert Edward and Florence Louisa Lindley; *m* 1947, Joan Armitage; one *s* two *d*. *Educ:* Tiffin Boys' Sch., Kingston-on-Thames; Trinity Coll., Cambridge. MA Cantab 1948. Min. of Supply, 1943–45; Nat. Physical Lab., 1945–46 and 1947–48; Statistical Lab., Cambridge Univ., 1948–60 (Dir, 1957–60); Prof. and Head of Dept of Statistics, UCW, Aberystwyth, 1960–67, Hon. Professorial Fellow, 1978–. Hon. Prof., Univ. of Warwick, 1978–. Vis. Professor: Chicago and Stanford Univs, 1954–55; Harvard Business Sch., 1963; Univ. of Iowa, 1974–75; Univ. of Bath, 1978–81. Wald Lectr, Inst. Math. Statistics, 1988. Guy Medal (Silver), Royal Statistical Soc., 1968. Fellow, Inst. Math. Statistics; Fellow, American Statistical Assoc. *Publications:* (with J. C. P. Miller) Cambridge Elementary Statistical Tables, 1953; Introduction to Probability and Statistics (2 vols), 1965; Making Decisions, 1971, rev. edn 1985; Bayesian Statistics, 1971; (with W. F. Scott) New Cambridge Elementary Statistical Tables, 1985; contribs to Royal Statistical Soc., Biometrika, Annals of Math. Statistics. *Address:* 2 Periton Lane, Minehead, Somerset TA24 8AQ. *T:* Minehead (01643) 705189.

LINDLEY, Simon Geoffrey; Master of the Music, Leeds Parish Church, since 1975; Leeds City Organist, since 1976; Senior Assistant Music Officer (formerly Music and Special Projects Officer), Leeds Leisure Services Department, since 1988; *b* 10 Oct. 1948; *s* of Rev. Geoffrey Lindley and Jeanne Lindley (*née* Cammaerts); *m* 1974, Carel Louise McMiram (separated); three *s* one *d*. *Educ:* Magdalen Coll. Sch., Oxford; Royal Coll. of Music. FRCO(CHM), FTCL, GRSM (Lond), ARCM, LRAM, ARSCM 1987. Studies with Richard Silk, David Carver, Dr Bernard Rose, Vincent Packford, Dr Philip Wilkinson and Dr John Birch. Dir of Music, St Anne & St Agnes and St Olave, London, 1968–70; Asst Master of Music, St Alban's Abbey, 1970–75; Dir of Music, St Alban's Sch., 1971–75; Sen. Lectr, Leeds Poly., 1976–88. Chorus Master: Leeds Phil. Soc., 1975–83; Halifax Choral Soc., 1975–87 (Vice-Pres., 1988–); Conductor, St Peter's Singers and Chamber Orch., 1977–; Organist, London Festival Players; Special Comr, RSCM, 1975–; Centre Chm., ISM, 1976–82; Mem. Council, RCO, 1977–; Sec., Church Music Soc., 1991–. Advr, Yorks TV Religious and Educl Progs, 1981–; Artistic Advr, Leeds Summer Heritage Festivals, biennially, 1989–. Concert Organist début, Westminster Cathedral, 1969; tours of USA, France, Germany, Far East, USSR. Numerous recordings as organist and as conductor. *Compositions:* Come, sing and dance (carol), 1977; Anthems for Unison and 2 part singing, vol. 2, 1979; Ave Maria, 1980; Matthew, Mark, Luke and John, 1986. *Publications:* contribs to Musical Times, Organists' Review, The Dalesman. *Recreations:* churches, cathedrals, Victorian architecture, food. *Address:* 8 The Chandlers, The Calls, Leeds LS2 7EZ. *T:* Leeds (0113) 234 1146; Leeds Leisure Services, Leeds Town Hall, The Headrow, Leeds LS1 3AD. *T:* (0113) 247 8334. *Club:* Leeds (Leeds).

LINDOP, Sir Norman, Kt 1973; DL; MSc; CChem, FRSC; Director, Hatfield Polytechnic, 1969–82; *b* 9 March 1921; *s* of Thomas Cox Lindop and May Lindop, Stockport, Cheshire; *m* 1974, Jenny C. Quass; one *s*. *Educ:* Northgate Sch., Ipswich; Queen Mary Coll., Univ. of London (BSc, MSc). Various industrial posts, 1942–46; Lectr in Chemistry, Queen Mary Coll., 1946; Asst Dir of Examinations, Civil Service Commn, 1951; Sen. Lectr in Chemistry, Kingston Coll. of Technology, 1953; Head of Dept of Chemistry and Geology, Kingston Coll. of Technology, 1957; Principal: SW Essex Technical Coll. and Sch. of Art, 1963; Hatfield Coll. of Technology, 1966; Principal, British Sch. of Osteopathy, 1982–90. Mem. (Lab), Herts CC, 1993–. Chairman: Cttee of Dirs of Polytechnics, 1972–74; Council for Professions Supplementary to Medicine, 1973–81; Home Office Data Protection Cttee, 1976–78; Cttee of Enquiry into Public Sector Validation, DES, 1984–85; British Library Adv. Council, 1986–94; Herts Area Manpower Bd, 1986–88; Res. Council for Complementary Medicine, 1989–90; Member: CNAA, 1974–81; US-UK Educn (Fulbright) Commn, 1971–81; SRC, 1974–78; GMC, 1979–84. Chm. Council, Westfield Coll., London Univ., 1983–89. FCP 1980; Fellow: QMC, 1976; Hatfield Polytechnic, 1983; Hon. Fellow, Brighton Polytechnic, 1990. FRSA. DL Hertford, 1989. Hon. DEd CNAA, 1982; Hon. DSc Ulster, 1994. *Recreations:* mountain walking, music (especially opera). *Address:* 36 Queens Road, Hertford, Herts SG13 8AZ. *Club:* Athenæum.

LINDOP, Prof. Patricia Joyce, (Mrs G. P. R. Esdale); Professor of Radiation Biology, University of London, 1970–84, now Emeritus; Chairman, Thames Liquid Fuels (Holdings) Ltd, since 1992; *b* 21 June 1930; 2nd *c* of Elliot D. Lindop and Dorothy Jones; *m* 1957, Gerald Paton Rivett Esdale (*d* 1992); one *s* one *d*. *Educ:* Malvern Girls' Coll.; St

Bartholomew's Hospital Med. Coll.; BSc (1st cl. Hons), MB, BS, PhD; DSc London 1974; MRCP 1956; FRCP 1977. Registered GP, 1954. Research and teaching in physiology and medical radiobiology at Med. Coll. of St Bartholomew's Hosp., 1955–84. UK Mem., Council of Pugwash Confs on Science and World Affairs, 1982–87 (Asst Sec. Gen., 1961–71); Mem., Royal Commn on Environmental Pollution, 1974–79; Chm. and Trustee, Soc. for Education in the Applications of Science, 1968–91; Member: Cttee 10 of ICRU, 1972–79; ESRO-NASA, 1970–74; Soc. for Radiol Protection, 1987–. Member Council: Science and Society, 1975–90; Soc. for Protection of Science and Learning, 1974–86; formerly Mem. Council, British Inst. of Radiology; Chairman: Univ. of London Bd of Studies in Radiation Biology, 1979–81; Interdisciplinary Special Cttee for the Environment, 1979–81. Governor, St Bartholomew's Hosp. Med. Coll., 1984–. Hon. Member: RCR, 1972; ARR, 1984. Ciba Award, 1957; Leverhulme Res. Award, 1984. *Publications:* in field of radiation effects. *Address:* 58 Wildwood Road, NW11 6UP. *T:* 0181–455 5860. *Club:* Royal Society of Medicine.

LINDSAY, family name of **Earl of Crawford** and **Baron Lindsay of Birker.**

LINDSAY, 16th Earl of, *cr* 1633 (Scot.); **James Randolph Lindesay-Bethune;** Lord Lindsay of The Byres, 1445; Lord Parbroath, 1633; Viscount of Garnock, Lord Kilburnie, Kingsburn and Drumry, 1703; landscape architect and environmental consultant; Parliamentary Under-Secretary of State, Scottish Office, since 1995; *b* 19 Nov. 1955; *s* of 15th Earl of Lindsay and of Hon. Mary Clare Douglas-Scott-Montagu, *y d* of 2nd Baron Montagu of Beaulieu; *S* father, 1989; *m* 1982, Diana, *er d* of Major Nigel Chamberlayne-Macdonald, Cranbury Park, Winchester; two *s* three *d* (of whom one *s* one *d* are twins). *Educ:* Eton; Univ. of Edinburgh (MA Hons); Univ. of Calif, Davis. A Lord in Waiting (Govt Whip), 1995. Trustee, Gardens for the Disabled Trust, 1984–; Mem. Council, London Gardens Soc., 1985– (Trustee, 1989–). Pres., Brighter Kensington and Chelsea Scheme, 1989–. Chm., Landscape Foundn, 1991–; Vice-Pres., Internat. Tree Foundn, 1994–; Mem., Adv. Council, World Resource Foundn, 1994–. *Publications:* (jtly) Garden Ornament, 1989; Trellis, 1991. *Heir: s* Viscount Garnock, *qv*. *Address:* Lahill, Upper Largo, Fife KY8 6JE.

See also Sir G. R. B. Wrey, Bt.

LINDSAY OF BIRKER, 3rd Baron *cr* 1945, of Low Ground, Co. Cumberland; **James Francis Lindsay;** Deputy High Commissioner, Australian High Commission, Islamabad, Pakistan, since 1993; *b* 29 Jan. 1945; *s* of 2nd Baron Lindsay of Birker and of Li Hsiao-li, *d* of Col Li Wen-chi; *S* father, 1994; *m* 1969 (marr. diss. 1985); no *c*. *Educ:* Univ. of Keele (BSc 1966); Univ. of Liverpool (Post-grad. Dip. in transport design). Lectr in physics, Tunghai Univ., Taichung, Taiwan, 1967–68; exploration geophysicist, Darwin, Australia, 1969–70; Australian Foreign Service, 1972–; served in Chile, 1973–76; Laos, 1980–81; Bangladesh, 1982–84; Venezuela, 1987–90. *Recreations:* hiking, tennis. *Heir: uncle* Hon. Thomas Martin Lindsay, MBE [*b* 5 March 1915; *m* 1st, 1939, Denise Theresa Vaughan (marr. diss. 1951); two *s* one *d*; 2nd, 1951, Felicitas Lange (marr. diss. 1961); two *s*; 3rd, 1961, Erica, *d* of Major Eric Thirkell-Cooper; two *s*]. *Address:* Box 1046, Islamabad, Pakistan. *T:* (51) 214902, *Fax:* (51) 214763.

LINDSAY, Master of; Alexander Thomas Lindsay; *b* 5 Aug. 1991; *s* and *heir* of Lord Balniel, *qv*.

LINDSAY, Maj.-Gen. Courtenay Traice David, CB 1963; Director-General of Artillery, War Office, 1961–64, retired; *b* 28 Sept. 1910; *s* of late Courtenay Traice Lindsay and Charlotte Editha (*née* Wetenhall); *m* 1934, Margaret Elizabeth, *d* of late William Pease Theakston, Huntingdon; two *s*. *Educ:* Rugby Sch.; RMA Woolwich. 2nd Lt RA, 1930. Mem., Ordnance Board (Col), 1952; Dir of Munitions, British Staff (Brig.), Washington, 1959; Maj.-Gen. 1961. *Address:* Huggits Farm, Stone-in-Oxney, Tenterden, Kent TN30 7JT. *Club:* Rye Golf.

LINDSAY, Crawford Callum Douglas; QC 1987; barrister; a Recorder of the Crown Court, since 1982; *b* 5 Feb. 1939; *s* of Douglas Marshall Lindsay, FRCOG and Eileen Mary Lindsay; *m* 1963, Rosemary Gough; one *s* one *d*. *Educ:* Whitgift Sch., Croydon; St John's Coll., Oxford. Called to the Bar, Lincoln's Inn, 1961, Bencher, 1994. Mem., Criminal Injuries Compensation Bd, 1988–. *Address:* 1 Serjeant's Inn, Fleet Street, EC4Y 1LL. *Clubs:* Garrick, MCC.

LINDSAY, Donald Dunrod, CBE 1972; *b* 27 Sept. 1910; *s* of Dr Colin Dunrod Lindsay, Pres. BMA 1938, and Mrs Isabel Baynton Lindsay; *m* 1936, Violet Geraldine Fox; one *s* one *d*. *Educ:* Clifton Coll., Bristol; Trinity Coll., Oxford. Asst Master, Manchester Gram. Sch., 1932; Asst Master, Repton Sch., 1935; temp. seconded to Bristol Univ. Dept of Education as lecturer in History, 1938; Senior History Master, Repton Sch., 1938–42; Headmaster: Portsmouth Gram. Sch., 1942–53; Malvern Coll., 1953–71. Dir, Independent Schs Information Service, 1972–77. Chm., Headmasters' Conference, 1968. Governor, Harrow Sch., 1977–82. *Publications:* A Portrait of Britain Between the Exhibitions, 1952; A Portrait of Britain, 1688–1851, 1954; A Portrait of Britain Before 1066, 1962; Authority and Challenge, Europe 1300–1600, 1975; Europe and the World, 1979; Friends for Life: a portrait of Launcelot Fleming, 1981; Forgotten General, 1986; Sir Edmund Bacon: a Norfolk life, 1988; A Form of Gratitude: the life of Angela Limerick, 1992. *Recreations:* walking, theatre, music. *Address:* 29 Teme Avenue, Malvern, Worcs WR14 2XA.

LINDSAY, Rt. Rev. Hugh; Bishop (RC) of Hexham and Newcastle, 1974–92; *b* 20 June 1927; *s* of William Stanley Lindsay and Mary Ann Lindsay (*née* Warren). *Educ:* St Cuthbert's Grammar Sch., Newcastle upon Tyne; Ushaw Coll., Durham. Priest 1953. Asst Priest; St Lawrence's, Newcastle upon Tyne, 1953; St Matthew's, Ponteland, 1954; Asst Diocesan Sec., 1953–59; Diocesan Sec., 1959–69; Chaplain, St Vincent's Home, West Denton, 1959–69; Auxiliary Bishop of Hexham and Newcastle and Titular Bishop of Chester-le-Street, 1969–74. *Recreations:* walking, swimming. *Address:* Boarbank Hall, Grange-over-Sands, Cumbria LA11 7NH. *T:* Grange-over-Sands (015395) 35591.

LINDSAY, Sir James Harvey Kincaid Stewart, Kt 1966; Board Member, Institute of Cultural Affairs International, Brussels, 1982–89; *b* 31 May 1915; *s* of Arthur Harvey Lindsay and Doris Kincaid Lindsay; *m* Marguerite Phyllis Boudville (one *s* one *d* by previous marriage). *Educ:* Highgate Sch. Joined Metal Box Co. Ltd, 1934; joined Metal Box Co. of India Ltd, 1937; Man. Dir, 1961; Chm., 1967–69; Dir of Internat. Programmes, Admin. Staff Coll., Henley-on-Thames, 1970–79. Vis. Lectr, Univ. of Buckingham, 1984–89. President: Bengal Chamber of Commerce and Industry; Associated Chambers of Commerce and Industry of India, 1965; Rotary Club of Calcutta, 1965. Director: Indian Oxygen Co., 1966; Westinghouse, Saxby Farmer Ltd, Hindusthan Pilkington, 1966. Pres., Calcutta Management Association, 1964; Pres. (and elected Life Mem., 1984), All India Management Assoc., 1964–69; Mem. of Governing Body: Indian Inst. of Management, Calcutta, 1964; Administrative Staff Coll. of India, 1965; Indian Institutes of Technology, 1966; National Council of Applied Economic Research, 1966; All-India Board of Management Studies, 1964; Indian Inst. of Foreign Trade, 1965; Member: BoT, Central Adv. Council of Industries, Direct Taxes Adv. Cttee, 1966; National Council on Vocational and Allied Trades, 1963. Convener, Internat. Exposition of Rural Develt, 1980–86; Trustee, Inst. of Family and Environmental Research, 1971–92. Mem. Council, Inst. of Organizational Mgt, 1988–. FCIM (FInstM 1975); CIMgt (FBIM 1971). *Recreations:* music, computing. *Address:* Christmas Cottage, Lower Shiplake, near Henley-on-Thames, Oxon RG9 3JT. *T:* Wargrave (01734) 402859. *Club:* East India, Devonshire, Sports and Public Schools.

LINDSAY, Hon. James Louis; *b* 16 Dec. 1906; *yr s* of 27th Earl of Crawford and Balcarres; *m* 1933, Bronwen Mary, *d* of 8th Baron Howard de Walden; three *s* one *d*. *Educ:* Eton; Magdalen Coll., Oxford. Served 1939–45 war, Major KRRC. Contested (C) Bristol South-East, 1950 and 1951; MP (C) N Devon, 1955–Sept. 1959. *Address:* Pound House, Nether Cerne, Dorchester, Dorset DT2 7AJ.

LINDSAY, Hon. Sir John (Edmund Fredric), Kt 1992; **Hon. Mr Justice Lindsay;** a Judge of the High Court of Justice, Chancery Division, since 1992; *b* 16 Oct. 1935; *s* of late George Fredric Lindsay and Constance Mary Lindsay (*née* Wright); *m* 1967, Patricia Anne Bolton; three *d*. *Educ:* Ellesmere Coll.; Sidney Sussex Coll., Cambridge (BA 1959; MA). Fleet Air Arm, 1954–56; Sub-Lt, RNVR. Called to the Bar, Middle Temple, 1961, Bencher, 1987; joined Lincoln's Inn (*ad eundem*); Junior Treasury Counsel, *bona vacantia*, 1979–81; QC 1981. Chm., Employed Barristers' Registration Cttee, 1982–89; Member: Senate of Inns of Court and Bar, 1979–82; Legal Panel, Insolvency Law Review Cttee (Cork Report), 1980–82; Insolvency Rules Adv. Cttee, 1985–92. *Address:* Royal Courts of Justice, Strand, WC2A 2LL.

LINDSAY, (John) Maurice, CBE 1979; TD 1946; Consultant, The Scottish Civic Trust, since 1983 (Director, 1967–83); *b* 21 July 1918; *s* of Matthew Lindsay and Eileen Frances Brock; *m* 1946, Aileen Joyce Gordon; one *s* three *d*. *Educ:* Glasgow Acad.; Scottish National Acad. of Music (now Royal Scottish Acad. of Music, Glasgow). Drama Critic, Scottish Daily Mail, Edinburgh, 1946–47; Music Critic, The Bulletin, Glasgow, 1946–60; Prog. Controller, 1961–62, Prodn Controller, 1962–64, and Features Exec. and Chief Interviewer, 1964–67, Border Television, Carlisle. Mem., Historic Buildings Council for Scotland, 1976–87; Pres., Assoc. for Scottish Literary Studies, 1988–91; Trustee: National Heritage Meml Fund, 1980–84; New Lanark Conservation Trust, 1987–94; Hon. Vice-Pres., Scottish Envmtl Educn Council, 1984–; Hon. Sec.-Gen., Europa Nostra, 1983–91. Hon. FRIAS 1985. Hon. DLitt Glasgow, 1982. Atlantic Rockefeller Award, 1946. Editor: Scots Review, 1949–50; The Scottish Review, 1975–85. *Publications: poetry:* The Advancing Day, 1940; Perhaps To-morrow, 1941; Predicament, 1942; No Crown for Laughter: Poems, 1943; The Enemies of Love: Poems 1941–1945, 1946; Selected Poems, 1947; Hurlygush: Poems in Scots, 1948; At the Wood's Edge, 1950; Ode for St Andrews Night and Other Poems, 1951; The Exiled Heart: Poems 1941–1956, 1957; Snow Warning and Other Poems, 1962; One Later Day and Other Poems, 1964; This Business of Living, 1969; Comings and Goings: Poems, 1971; Selected Poems 1942–1972, 1973; The Run from Life, 1975; Walking Without an Overcoat, Poems 1972–76, 1977; Collected Poems, 1979; A Net to Catch the Winds and Other Poems, 1981; The French Mosquitoes' Woman and Other Diversions and Poems, 1985; Requiem for a Sexual Athlete and Other Poems and Diversions, 1988; Collected Poems 1940–1990, 1990; On the Face of It: Collected Poems, vol. 2, 1993; News of the World: last poems, 1995; *prose:* A Pocket Guide to Scottish Culture, 1947; The Scottish Renaissance, 1949; The Lowlands of Scotland: Glasgow and the North, 1953, 3rd edn, 1979; Robert Burns: The Man, His Work, The Legend, 3rd edn, 1980; Dunoon: The Gem of the Clyde Coast, 1954; The Lowlands of Scotland: Edinburgh and the South, 1956, 3rd edn, 1979; Clyde Waters: Variations and Diversions on a Theme of Pleasure, 1958; The Burns Encyclopedia, 1959, 3rd edn, 1980; Killochan Castle, 1960; By Yon Bonnie Banks: A Gallimaufry, 1961; Environment: A Basic Human Right, 1968; Portrait of Glasgow, 1972, rev. edn, 1981; Robin Philipson, 1977; History of Scottish Literature, 1977, rev. edn 1992; Lowland Scottish Villages, 1980; Francis George Scott and the Scottish Renaissance, 1980; (with Anthony F. Kersting) The Buildings of Edinburgh, 1981, 2nd edn 1987; Thank You For Having Me: a personal memoir, 1983; (with Dennis Hardley) Unknown Scotland, 1984; The Castles of Scotland, 1986, rev. edn 1994; Count All Men Mortal—A History of Scottish Provident 1837–1987, 1987; Victorian and Edwardian Glasgow, 1987; Glasgow 1837, 1989; (with David Bruce) Edinburgh Past and Present, 1990; (with Joyce Lindsay) Chambers Guide to Good Scottish Gardens, 1995; *editor:* Poetry Scotland One, Two, Three, 1943, 1945, 1946, (with Hugh MacDiarmid) Scottish Poetry Four, 1949; Sailing Tomorrow's Seas: An Anthology of New Poems, 1944; Modern Scottish Poetry: An Anthology of the Scottish Renaissance 1920–1945, 1946, 4th edn, 1986; (with Fred Urquhart) No Scottish Twilight: New Scottish Stories, 1947; Selected Poems of Sir Alexander Gray, 1948; Poems, by Sir David Lyndsay, 1948; (with Hugh MacDiarmid) Poetry Scotland Four, 1949; (with Helen Cruickshank) Selected Poems of Marion Angus, 1950; John Davidson: A Selection of His Poems, 1961; (with Edwin Morgan and George Bruce) Scottish Poetry One to Six 1966–72; (with Alexander Scott and Roderick Watson) Scottish Poetry Seven to Nine, 1974, 1976, 1977; (with R. L. Mackie) A Book of Scottish Verse, 1967, 3rd edn 1983; The Discovery of Scotland: Based on Accounts of Foreign Travellers from the 13th to the 18th centuries, 1964, 2nd edn 1979; The Eye is Delighted: Some Romantic Travellers in Scotland, 1970; Scotland: An Anthology, 1974, 2nd edn 1989; As I Remember, 1979; Scottish Comic Verse 1425–1980, 1980; (with Alexander Scott) The Comic Poems of William Tennant, 1990; Thomas Hamilton, The Youth and Manhood of Cyril Thornton, 1991; with Joyce Lindsay: The Scottish Dog, 1989; The Scottish Quotation Book, 1991; A Pleasure of Gardens, 1991; The Music Quotation Book, 1992; The Theatre and Opera Lovers' Quotation Book, 1993; A Mini-Guide to Scottish Gardens, 1994; The Robert Burns Quotation Book, 1994. *Recreations:* enjoying and adding to compact disc collection, walking. *Address:* 7 Milton Hill, Milton, Dumbarton G82 2TS. *T:* Dumbarton (01389) 762655.

LINDSAY, John Vliet; Of Counsel, Mudge Rose Guthrie Alexander & Ferdon, New York City, since 1991; *b* 24 Nov. 1921; *s* of George Nelson and Eleanor (Vliet) Lindsay; *m* 1949, Mary Harrison; one *s* three *d*. *Educ:* St Paul's Sch., Concord, NH; Yale Univ. BA 1944; LLB 1948. Lt US Navy, 1943–46. Admitted to: NY Bar, 1949; Fed. Bar, Southern Dist NY, 1950; US Supreme Court, 1955; DC Bar, 1957. Mem., law firm of Webster & Sheffield, NYC, 1949–55, 1957–61, 1974–91 (Presiding Partner, 1989–91). Exec. Asst to US Attorney Gen., 1955–57; Mem., 86th-89th Congresses, 17th Dist, NY, 1959–66. Mayor of NYC, 1965–73 (elected as Republican-Liberal, Nov. 1965, re-elected as Liberal-Independent, Nov. 1969). Bd Mem. Emeritus, Lincoln Center for Performing Arts; Chm. Emeritus, Bd of Dirs, Lincoln Center Theatre Co. Hon. LLD: Williams Coll., 1968; Harvard, 1969. *Publications:* Journey into Politics, 1967; The City, 1970; The Edge, 1976. *Address:* Mudge Rose Guthrie Alexander & Ferdon, 180 Maiden Lane, New York, NY 10038, USA.

LINDSAY, Maurice; *see* Lindsay, J. M.

LINDSAY, Most Rev. Orland Ugham; *see* West Indies, Archbishop of.

LINDSAY of Dowhill, Sir Ronald Alexander, 2nd Bt *cr* 1962, of Dowhill; 23rd Representer of Baronial House of Dowhill; *b* 6 Dec. 1933; *er s* of Sir Martin Lindsay of Dowhill, 1st Bt, CBE, DSO, and of Joyce Lady Lindsay, *d* of late Major Hon. Robert Lindsay, Royal Scots Greys; *S* father, 1981; *m* 1968, Nicoletta, *yr d* of late Captain Edgar

Storich, Royal Italian Navy and late Mrs Storich; three *s* one *d*. *Educ:* Eton College; Worcester Coll., Oxford (MA). National service in Grenadier Guards (Lieut), 1952–54. Insurance broker, 1958– (chiefly Hogg Robinson and Minets); Lloyd's Members' Agent, 1984–; Dir, Sturge Hldgs members' agencies, 1989–93. Mem., Standing Council of the Baronetage, 1978– (Chm., 1987–89); Trustee, Baronets Charitable Trust, 1986– (Chm., 1990–92); Vice-Pres., Anglo-Spanish Soc., 1993– (Vice-Chm., 1985–93). Member of Queen's Body Guard for Scotland (Royal Company of Archers), 1963. FCII 1963. Encomienda, Orden de Isabel la Católica (Spain), 1988. *Heir: s* James Martin Evelyn Lindsay, *b* 11 Oct. 1968. *Address:* 104 Edith Road, W14 9AP. *T:* 0171–603 0278.

LINDSAY-HOGG, Sir Edward William, 4th Bt *cr* 1905, of Rotherfield Hall, Sussex; Hereditary Cavaliere d'Italia; dramatist and scriptwriter; *b* 23 May 1910; *s* of William Lindsay Lindsay-Hogg (*d* 1918) (1st *s* of 1st Bt) and Nora Cicely (*d* 1929), *d* of John James Barrow; *S* nephew, 1988; *m* 1st, 1936, Geraldine (marr. diss. 1946), *d* of E. M. Fitzgerald; one *s*; 2nd, 1957, Kathleen Mary, *widow* of Captain Maurice Cadell, MC and *d* of James Cooney. *Educ:* Eton. Former racehorse trainer and amateur jockey when living at the Curragh. *Publications:* contrib. to literary periodicals, mainly in Ireland. *Recreations:* gardening, reading, walking. *Club:* Stephen's Green (Dublin). *Heir: s* Michael Edward Lindsay-Hogg [*b* 5 May 1940; *m* 1967, Lucy Mary (marr. diss. 1971), *o d* of Donald Davies].

LINDSAY-SMITH, Iain-Mór; Chief Executive and Managing Director, Lloyd's of London Press Ltd, since 1991 (Executive Director, 1984–87; Deputy Managing Director, 1987–90); Publisher, since 1984, and Chairman, since 1990, Lloyds List Ltd; Chairman and Chief Executive, Lloyd's Information Services Ltd, since 1990; Chairman, LLP Business Publishing Ltd, since 1990; *b* 18 Sept. 1934; *s* of Edward Duncanson Lindsay-Smith and Margaret Anderson; *m* 1960, Carol Sara (*née* Paxman); one *s*. *Educ:* High Sch. of Glasgow; London Univ. (diploma course on Internat. Affairs). Scottish Daily Record, 1951–57; Commissioned 1st Bn Cameronians (Scottish Rifles), 1953–55; Daily Mirror, 1957–60; Foreign Editor, subseq. Features Editor, Daily Mail, 1960–71; Dep. Editor, Yorkshire Post, 1971–74; Editor, Glasgow Herald, 1974–77; Exec. Editor, The Observer, 1977–84. Chm., Lloyd's Aviation Ltd, 1993–; Director: Lloyd's of London Press Incorporated, USA, 1985– (Chm., 1992–); Lloyd's of London Press (Far East) Ltd, Hong Kong, 1989–; Lloyd's of London Press GmbH, Germany, 1989–; Lloyd's Maritime Information Services Ltd, 1990– (Chm., 1993–); Lloyd's Maritime Information Services Inc., USA, 1990– (Chm., 1992–); Lutine Publications Ltd, 1984– (Chm., 1992–); Internat. Art & Antique Loss Register Ltd, 1990–; Colchester Mercury Theatre Ltd, 1985–; PPA, 1992–; Dyp Gp, 1995–. Member: Little Horkesley Parish Council, 1987–91; PCC, 1985–92. FRSA 1992. *Publication:* article in Electronics and Power. *Recreations:* shooting (game and clay), playing Highland bagpipe, the outdoors. *Address:* Lloyd's of London Press, One Singer Street, EC2A 4LQ; Sheepen Place, Colchester, Essex CO3 3LP. *Club:* Travellers'.

LINDSEY, 14th Earl of, *cr* 1626, **AND ABINGDON,** 9th Earl of, *cr* 1682; **Richard Henry Rupert Bertie;** Baron Norreys, of Rycote, 1572; *b* 28 June 1931; *o s* of Lt-Col Hon. Arthur Michael Bertie, DSO, MC (*d* 1957) and Aline Rose (*d* 1948), *er d* of George Arbuthnot-Leslie, Warthill, Co. Aberdeen, and *widow* of Hon. Charles Fox Maule Ramsay, MC; *S* cousin, 1963; *m* 1957, Norah Elizabeth Farquhar-Oliver, *yr d* of late Mark Oliver, OBE; two *s* one *d*. *Educ:* Ampleforth. Lieut, late Royal Norfolk Regt. Insurance broker and underwriting agent at Lloyd's, 1958–92. Chm., Anglo-Ivory-Coast Soc., 1974–77. High Steward of Abingdon, 1963–. *Heir: s* Lord Norreys, *qv*. *Address:* Gilmilnscroft, Sorn, Mauchline, Ayrshire KA5 6ND; 3 Westgate Terrace, SW10 9BT. *Clubs:* White's, Turf, Pratt's.

LINDT, Auguste Rudolph, LLD; retired as Swiss Ambassador; *b* Berne, Switzerland, 5 Aug. 1905. Studied law at Universities of Geneva and Berne. Special correspondent of several European newspapers, in Manchuria, Liberia, Palestine, Jordan, the Persian Gulf, Tunisia, Roumania and Finland, 1932–40. Served in Swiss Army, 1940–45. Special delegate of International Cttee of the Red Cross at Berlin, 1945–46. Counsellor, and Press Attaché, 1946, Swiss Legation in London. Switzerland's Permanent Observer to the United Nations (appointed 1953) and subseq. Minister plenipotentiary (1954); appointments connected with work of the United Nations: Chairman Exec. Board of UNICEF, 1953 and 1954; President, UN Opium Conference, 1953; Head of Swiss Delegation to Conference on Statute of International Atomic Energy Agency, held in New York, 1956. United Nations High Commissioner for Refugees (elected by acclamation), Dec. 1956–60; Swiss Ambassador to USA, 1960–63; Delegate, Swiss Fed. Council for Technical Co-operation, 1963–66; Swiss Amassador to Soviet Union and Mongolia, 1966–69, on leave as International Red Cross Comr-Gen. for Nigeria-Biafra relief operation, 1968–69; Swiss Ambassador to India and Nepal, 1969–70. Adviser to Pres. of Republic of Rwanda, 1972–75. Pres., Internat. Union for Child Welfare, Geneva, 1971–77. Hon. DrUniv Geneva, 1960; Hon. Dr, Coll. of Wilmington, Ohio, 1961. *Publications:* Special Correspondent with Bandits and Generals in Manchuria, 1933; Generäle hungern nie: Geschichte einer Hilfsaktion in Afrika, 1983; Die Schweiz: das kleine Staehelschwein, 1992. *Address:* Jolimontstrasse 2, 3006 Bern, Switzerland.

LINE, Frances Mary, (Mrs James Lloyd); Controller, BBC Radio 2, 1990–Feb. 1996; *b* 22 Feb. 1940; *d* of Charles Edward Line and Leoni Lucy Line (*née* Hendriks); *m* 1972, James Richard Beilby Lloyd. *Educ:* James Allen's Girls' Sch., Dulwich. Joined BBC as clerk/typist, 1957; Sec. in TV and Radio, 1959–67; Radio 2 producer, 1967–73; senior producer, 1973–79; Chief Assistant: Radio 2, 1979–83; Radio 4, 1983–85; Head, Radio 2 Music Dept, 1985–89. *Recreations:* theatre, Sussex, happy-snaps. *Address:* c/o BBC, Broadcasting House, W1A 1AA. *T:* 0171–580 4468.

LINE, Maurice Bernard, MA; FRSA; FLA, FIInfSc; CIMgt; Director General (Science, Technology and Industry), British Library, 1985–88 (Deputy Director General, 1973–74, Director General, 1974–85, Lending Division); *b* 21 June 1928; *s* of Bernard Cyril and Ruth Florence Line; *m* 1954, Joyce Gilchrist; one *s* one *d*. *Educ:* Bedford Sch.; Exeter Coll., Oxford (MA). Library Trainee, Bodleian Library, 1950–51; Library Asst, Glasgow Univ., 1951–53; Sub-Librarian, Southampton Univ., 1954–65; Dep. Librarian, Univ. of Newcastle upon Tyne, 1965–68; Librarian, Univ. of Bath, 1968–71; Librarian, Nat. Central Library, 1971–73; Project Head, DES Nat. Libraries ADP Study, 1970–71. Prof. Associate, Sheffield Univ., 1977–; External Prof., Loughborough Univ., 1986–92. Member: Library Adv. Council for England, 1972–75; British Library Board, 1974–88; Pres., Library Assoc., 1990. Editor, Alexandria, 1988–; Gen. Editor, Librarianship and Information Work Worldwide, 1990–. Fellow, Birmingham Polytech., 1992. Hon. DLitt Heriot Watt, 1980; Hon. DSc Southampton, 1988. *Publications:* A Bibliography of Russian Literature in English Translation to 1900, 1963; Library Surveys, 1967, 2nd edn 1982; (ed jtly) Essays on Information and Libraries, 1975; (ed with Joyce Line) National Libraries, 1979; (jtly) Universal Availability of Publications, 1983; (jtly) Improving the Availability of Publications, 1984; (ed) The World of Books and Information, 1987; (ed with Joyce Line) National Libraries II, 1987; (jtly) The Impact of New Technology on Document Availability and Access, 1988; Line on Interlending, 1988; A Little Off Line, 1988; (ed)Academic Library Management, 1990; contribs to: Jl of Documentation; Aslib Proc.; Jl of Librarianship and Information Science, etc. *Recreations:* music, walking, other people. *Address:* 10 Blackthorn Lane, Burn Bridge, Harrogate, North Yorks HG3 1NZ. *T:* Harrogate (01423) 872984.

LINEHAN, Anthony John; Director, Hinton & Higgs, since 1992; *b* 27 June 1931; *s* of Daniel and Ada Linehan; *m* 1955, Oonagh Patricia FitzPatrick; two *s* two *d*. *Educ:* Bristol Univ. (BA Hons 1952). Short Service Commission, RN, 1953–57. HM Factory Inspectorate: joined 1958; HM District Inspector, 1969; Labour Adviser, Hong Kong Govt, 1973–76; Health and Safety Executive: HQ, 1976–79; Area Dir, Wales, 1979–84; HM Dep. Chief Inspector of Factories, 1984–88; Chief Inspector of Factories, 1988–92; Dir of Field Ops, 1990–92. *Recreations:* walking, reading, watching Rugby. *Address:* 2 Brookside Manor, Leigh Road, Wimborne, Dorset BH21 2BZ. *T:* Wimborne (01202) 848597.

LINEHAN, Stephen; QC 1993; a Recorder, since 1990; *b* 12 March 1947; *s* of Maurice Gerald Linehan and Mary Joyce (*née* Norrish); *m* 1976, Victoria Maria Rössler; one *s*. *Educ:* Mount St Mary's Coll., Spinkhill, Derbys; King's Coll., London (LLB Hons). Called to the Bar, Lincoln's Inn, 1970. *Address:* 5 Fountain Court, Steelhouse Lane, Birmingham B4 6DR. *T:* 0121–606 0500.

LINEKER, Gary Winston, OBE 1992; journalist and broadcaster; professional footballer, 1976–94; *b* 30 Nov. 1960; *s* of Barry and Margaret Lineker; *m* 1986, Michelle Cockayne; two *s*. Football Clubs played for: Leicester City, 1976–85; Everton, 1985–86; Barcelona, 1986–89; Tottenham Hotspur, 1989–92; Nagoya Grampus 8, 1993–94; England team, 1984–92: Captain, 1990–92; 80 appearances, 48 goals. Mem., Sports Council, 1995–. Hon. MA: Loughborough; Leicester 1992. *Recreations:* golf, cricket, snooker. *Address:* c/o Park Associates, 6 George Street, Nottingham NG1 3BE. *T:* Nottingham (0115) 948 3206. *Clubs:* Groucho, MCC.

LINES, (Walter) Moray, CBE 1969; Chairman, Lines Brothers Ltd, 1962–71 (Joint Managing Director, 1962–70); *b* 26 Jan. 1922; *er s* of late Walter Lines; *m* 1955, Fiona Margaret Denton; three *s* one *d*. *Educ:* Gresham Sch. Joined Board of Lines Bros Ltd, 1946; Chm., British Toy Manufacturers Assoc., 1968–70. *Address:* Stable Cottage, Shirwell, near Barnstaple, N Devon EX31 4JU. *T:* Shirwell (01271) 850265.

LINFORD, Alan C.; *see* Carr Linford.

LING, Arthur George, FRIBA; PPRTPI; architect and town planner in practice with Arthur Ling and Associates; *b* 20 Sept. 1913; *s* of George Frederick Ling and Elsie Emily (*née* Wisbey); *m* 1939, Marjorie Tall; one *s* three *d*. *Educ:* Christ's Hospital; University College, London (Bartlett School of Architecture). BA (Architecture), London. Architect in Office of E. Maxwell Fry and Walter Gropius, 1937–39; Structural Engineer with Corporation of City of London (Air raid shelters and War debris clearance), 1939–41; Member town planning team responsible for preparation of County of London Plan, 1943, under direction of J. H. Forshaw and Sir Patrick Abercrombie, 1941–45; Chief Planning Officer, London County Council, 1945–55; Head of Department of Town Planning, University College, London Univ., 1947–48; Sen. Lecturer in Town Planning, 1948–55; City Architect and Planning Officer, Coventry, 1955–64; Prof. and Head of Dept of Architecture and Civic Planning, Univ. of Nottingham, 1964–69, Special Prof. of Environmental Design, 1969–72. Visiting Professor: University of Santiago, Chile, 1963; Univ. of NSW, Australia, 1969; Chancellor Lectures, Univ. of Wellington, NZ, 1969. Joint Architect for Development Plan for University of Warwick. Cons. Architect Planner, Runcorn New Town Corporation. UN (Habitat) Project Manager, Physical Perspective Plan, 1981–2000, Libyan Jamahiriya, 1977–80. Former Chairman, Board of Chief Officers, Midlands Housing Consortium; Past Vice-Pres., RIBA; President: RTPI, 1968–69; Commonwealth Assoc. of Planners, 1968–76. Mem., Sports Council, 1968–71; Vice-Chm., E Midlands Sports Council, 1968–76. Pres., Heckington Village Trust, 1974–84. RIBA Dist. in Town Planning, 1956; Silver Medallist (Essay), 1937; Hunt Bursary, 1939. Fellow University College, London, 1967. *Publications:* Urban and Regional Planning and Development in the Commonwealth, 1988; contrib. to professional journals on architecture and town planning. *Address:* The Old Barn, 11 Luke's Close, Helmdon, Northants NN13 5UQ.

LING, Jeffrey, CMG 1991; HM Diplomatic Service; Assistant Under-Secretary of State and Director of Information Systems, Foreign and Commonwealth Office, since 1989; *b* 9 Sept. 1939; *s* of Frank Cecil Ling and Mary Irene Nixon; *m* 1967, Margaret Anne Tatton; one *s*. *Educ:* Bristol Univ. BSc (Hons); FInstP; FIMgt; FBCS. FCO, 1966–69; Private Sec. to HM Ambassador, Washington, 1969–71; First Sec., Washington, 1971–73; Perm. Delegn to OECD, Paris, 1973–77; FCO, 1977–79; on secondment as Special Adviser to HM the Sultan of Brunei, 1979–82; Counsellor (Technology), Paris, 1982–86; Dir of Res., FCO, 1986–89; Asst Under-Sec. of State and Dir of Communications, 1989. Dir (non-exec.), RTZ Borax and Minerals, 1991–. *Recreations:* travel, old cars. *Address:* c/o Foreign and Commonwealth Office, SW1A 2AH.

LING, John de Courcy; *see* de Courcy Ling.

LINGARD, (Peter) Anthony, CBE 1977; TD; Director General, St John Ambulance Association, 1978–82; *b* 29 Feb. 1916; *s* of late Herbert Arthur Lingard and Kate Augusta Burdett; *m* 1946, Enid Nora Argile; two *d*. *Educ:* Berkhamsted Sch.; London Univ. (BCom). Served RA, 1939–46; Major, 1941 (despatches twice). Co. of London Electric Supply Gp, 1936; Area Manager Lambeth and Camberwell, County Group, 1947; Commercial Officer, S Western Sub-Area, 1948, Chief Commercial Officer, 1959–62, London Electricity Board; Commercial and Development Adviser, Electricity Council, 1962–65; Mem., Electricity Council, 1965–77; Chm., E Midlands Electricity Bd, 1972–77. Member: CEGB, 1972–75; Directing Cttee, Internat. Union of Producers and Distributors of Electrical Energy, 1973–77. County Dir, Suffolk, St John Ambulance, 1982–85. Member until 1977: Ct of Governors, Admin. Staff Coll.; Council, IEE; Council of Industrial Soc.; E Midlands Econ. Planning Council; Mem. Nottingham Univ. Ct, 1975–77. CompIEE 1967. FBIM 1973. KStJ. *Recreations:* photography, painting, sailing, golf, fly-fishing, reading. *Address:* The Dumble, High Street, Orford, Woodbridge, Suffolk IP12 2NW. *T:* Orford (01394) 450622. *Clubs:* Army and Navy; Aldeburgh Yacht, Aldeburgh Golf.

LINGARD, Robin Anthony; Director of Highlands and Islands University Project, Highlands and Islands Enterprise, since 1993; *b* 19 July 1941; *s* of late Cecil Lingard and Lucy Lingard; *m* 1968, Margaret Lucy Virginia Elsden; two *d*. *Educ:* Felsted School; Emmanuel College, Cambridge (Exhibnr, MA). Min. of Aviation, 1963–66; Min. of Technology, 1966–70 (Private Sec. to Jt Parly Sec., 1966–68); DTI, 1971–74; DoI, 1974–83, Asst Sec., 1976; Under Sec., DTI, 1984, Cabinet Office (Enterprise Unit), 1984–85; Hd, Small Firms and Tourism Div., Dept of Employment, 1985–87; Mem. Bd, Highlands and Islands Develt Bd, 1988–91; Dir of Trng and Social Develt, Highlands and Islands Enterprise, 1991–93. Member: NEDC Sector Gp for Tourism and Leisure Industries, 1987–92; Scottish Tourist Bd, 1988–92; Management Bd, Prince's Trust and Royal Jubilee Trusts, 1989–; Chm., Highlands, Orkney and Western Isles Cttee, Prince's

Trust, 1992–. FTS 1988. *Recreations:* reading, walking, watching birds, aviation history. *Address:* Kinnairdie House, Dingwall, Ross-shire IV15 9LL. *T:* Dingwall (01349) 861044.

LINGS, Dr Martin; Keeper Emeritus of Oriental Manuscripts and Printed Books, British Library; *b* 24 Jan. 1909; *e s* of late George Herbert Lings and late Gladys Mary Lings (*née* Greenhalgh), Burnage, Lancs; *m* 1944, Lesley, 3rd *d* of late Edgar Smalley. *Educ:* Clifton Coll.; Magdalen Coll., Oxford; Sch. of Oriental and African Studies, Univ. of London. Class. Mods 1930, BA English 1932, MA 1937, Oxon; BA Arabic 1954, PhD 1959, London. Lectr in Anglo-Saxon and Middle English, Univ. of Kaunas, 1935–39; Lectr in English Lit., Univ. of Cairo, 1940–51; Asst Keeper, Dept of Oriental Printed Books and Manuscripts, British Museum, 1955–70; Deputy Keeper, 1970; Keeper, 1971; seconded to the British Library, 1973. FRAS. *Publications:* The Book of Certainty, 1952 (trans. Spanish, Turkish and French); (with A. S. Fulton) Second Supplementary Catalogue of Arabic Printed Books in the British Museum, 1959; A Moslem Saint of the Twentieth Century, 1961 (trans. French and Arabic); Ancient Beliefs and Modern Superstitions, 1965 (trans. Turkish, Portuguese, French, German and Greek); Shakespeare in the Light of Sacred Art, 1966; The Elements and Other Poems, 1967; The Heralds and Other Poems, 1970; A Sufi Saint of the Twentieth Century, 1971 (trans. Urdu, Persian, Spanish, Turkish and French); What is Sufism?, (trans. French, Italian, Spanish, German, Portuguese and Bosnian); (with Y. H. Safadi) Third Supplementary Catalogue of Arabic Printed Books in the British Library, 1976; (with Y. H. Safadi) The Qur'ān, Catalogue of an Exhibition at the British Library, 1976; The Quranic Art of Calligraphy and Illumination, 1977; Muhammad: his life based on the earliest sources, 1983 (trans. French, Urdu, Tamil, Spanish, Arabic, Dutch, Bosnian and Italian); The Secret of Shakespeare, 1984 (trans. Italian, Spanish, Persian, Greek and French); The Eleventh Hour, 1987 (trans. German and French); Collected Poems, 1987; Symbol and Archetype: studies in the meaning of existence, 1990 (trans. French); contrib. Encycl. Britannica, Encycl. Islam, Studies in Comparative Religion, Cambridge History of Arabic Literature, etc. *Recreations:* walking, gardening, music. *Address:* 3 French Street, Westerham, Kent TN16 1PN. *T:* Westerham (01959) 562855.

LINKIE, William Sinclair, CBE 1989; Controller, Inland Revenue (Scotland), 1983–90; *b* 9 March 1931; *s* of late Peter Linkie and of Janet Black Linkie (*née* Sinclair; she *m* 2nd, John McBryde); *m* 1955, Elizabeth Primrose Marion (*née* Reid); one *s* one *d*. *Educ:* George Heriot's Sch., Edinburgh. Dept of Agriculture and Fisheries for Scotland, 1948; Inland Revenue (Scotland), 1952–90: HM Inspector of Taxes, 1961; Dist Inspector, Edinburgh 6, 1964; Principal Inspector i/c Centre I, 1975; Dist Inspector, Edinburgh 5, 1982. Pres., Inland Revenue Sports Assoc. (Scotland), 1983–90. Elder, Church of Scotland. *Recreations:* golf, painting, choral singing.

LINKLATER, Magnus Duncan; journalist; *b* 21 Feb. 1942; *s* of late Eric Robert Linklater, CBE, TD, and of Marjorie MacIntyre; *m* 1967, Veronica Lyle; two *s* one *d*. *Educ:* Eton Coll.; Freiburg Univ.; Sorbonne; Trinity Hall, Cambridge (BA 2nd Cl. Hons (Mod. Lang.)). Reporter, Daily Express, Manchester, 1965–66; Diary Reporter, London Evening Standard, 1966–67; Editor: Londoner's Diary, Evening Standard, 1967–69; 'Spectrum', Sunday Times, 1969–72; Sunday Times Colour Magazine, 1972–75; Assistant Editor: News, Sunday Times, 1975–79; Features, Sunday Times, 1979–81; Exec. Editor (Features), Sunday Times, 1981–83; Man. Editor (News), The Observer, 1983–86; Editor: London Daily News, 1987; The Scotsman, 1988–94; columnist, The Times; broadcaster, Radio Scotland, 1994–. Chm., Edinburgh Book Fest. Hon. DArts Napier. *Publications:* (with Stephen Fay and Lewis Chester) Hoax—The Inside Story of the Howard Hughes/Clifford Irving Affair, 1972; (with Lewis Chester and David May) Jeremy Thorpe: a secret life, 1979; Massacre: the story of Glencoe, 1982; (with the Sunday Times Insight Team) The Falklands War, 1982; (with Isabel Hilton and Neal Ascherson) The Fourth Reich—Klaus Barbie and the Neo-Fascist Connection, 1984; (with Douglas Corrance) Scotland, 1981; (contrib.) A Scottish Childhood, 1985; (with David Leigh) Not With Honour: inside story of the Westland Scandal, 1986; (with Christian Hesketh) For King and Conscience: the life of John Graham of Claverhouse, Viscount Dundee, 1989; (ed jtly) Anatomy of Scotland, 1992; (with Colin Prior) Highland Wilderness, 1993. *Recreations:* cricket, fishing, book-collecting. *Address:* 5 Drummond Place, Edinburgh EH3 6PH. *T.* 0131–557 5705. *Clubs:* Caledonian, MCC.

LINKLATER, Nelson Valdemar, CBE 1974 (OBE 1967); Drama Director, Arts Council of Great Britain, 1970–77; *b* 15 Aug. 1918; *s* of Captain Arthur David Linklater and Elsie May Linklater; *m* 1944, Margaret Lilian Boissard; two *s*. *Educ:* Imperial Service Coll.; RADA. RNVR, 1939–46 (final rank Lieut (S)). Professional theatre as actor and business manager, 1937–39. Documentary Films Manager, Army Kinema Corp., 1946–48; Arts Council of Great Britain: Asst Regional Dir (Nottingham), 1948–52; Asst and Dep. Drama Dir (London), 1952–70. Mem., Southern Arts Gen. Council and Exec. Cttee, 1978–89. Chm., CPRE, Wallingford Area Cttee, 1977–80. Member: Bd, Anvil Productions (Oxford Playhouse), 1977–88; Trent Polytechnic Theatre Design Adv. Cttee, 1980–83; Develt Panel, Cheek by Jowl Theatre Co., 1988–93. Mem., London Inst. Formation Cttee, 1985; Governor: Central Sch. of Art and Design, London, 1978–87; Wyvern Arts Trust (Swindon), 1978–91; Theatre Design Trust, 1988–91; Trustee, Arts Council Trust for Special Funds, 1981–. *Publication:* (contrib.) The State and the Arts, 1980. *Recreations:* painting, reading, gardening. *Address:* 1 Church Close, East Hagbourne, Oxon OX11 9LP. *T:* Didcot (01235) 813340.

LINKS, Mary, (Mrs J. G. Links); *see* Lutyens, Mary.

LINLEY, Viscount; David Albert Charles Armstrong-Jones; *b* 3 Nov. 1961; *s* and *heir* of 1st Earl of Snowdon, *qv*, and *s* of HRH the Princess Margaret; *m* 1993, Hon. Serena Alleyne Stanhope, *o d* of Viscount Petersham, *qv*. *Educ:* Bedales; Parnham School for Craftsmen in Wood. Designer and Cabinet maker; Chairman: David Linley Furniture Ltd, 1985–; David Linley Company Ltd, 1985–; Dir, Lachmead Group, 1988–. Vogue—Sotheby's Cecil Beaton Award for portrait photograph, 1983. *Publication:* Classical Furniture, 1993. *Address:* David Linley Furniture Ltd, 60 Pimlico Road, SW1W 8LP.
See under Royal Family.

LINLITHGOW, 4th Marquess of, *cr* 1902; **Adrian John Charles Hope;** Bt (NS) 1698; Baron Hope, Viscount Aithrie, Earl of Hopetoun 1703 (Scot.); Baron Hopetoun 1809 (UK); Baron Niddry 1814 (UK); Stockbroker; *b* 1 July 1946; *s* of 3rd Marquess of Linlithgow, MC, TD, and Vivienne (*d* 1963), *d* of Capt. R. O. R. Kenyon-Slaney and of Lady Mary Gilmour; *S* father, 1987; *m* 1st, 1968, Anne (marr. diss. 1978), *e d* of A. Leveson, Hall Place, Hants; two *s*; 2nd, 1980, Peta C. Binding; one *s* one *d*. *Educ:* Eton. Joined HM Navy, 1965. *Heir: s* Earl of Hopetoun, *qv*. *Address:* Hopetoun House, South Queensferry, West Lothian EH30 9SL. *T:* 0131–331 1169. *Club:* White's.
See also Baron Glendevon.

LINNANE, Prof. Anthony William, FAA; FRS 1980; Director, Centre for Molecular Biology and Medicine, Monash University, Australia, since 1983 (Professor of Biochemistry, 1965–94); *b* 17 July 1930; *s* of late W. Linnane, Sydney; *m* 1956, Judith Neil (marr. diss. 1980); one *s* one *d*; *m* 1980, Daryl, *d* of A. Skurrie. *Educ:* Sydney Boys' High School; Sydney Univ. (PhD, DSc); Univ. of Wisconsin, USA. Lecturer, then Senior Lectr, Sydney Univ., 1958–62; Reader, Monash Univ., Aust., 1962. Visiting Prof., Univ. of Wisconsin, 1967–68. President: Aust. Biochemical Soc., 1974–76; Fedn of Asian and Oceanic Biochemical Socs, 1975–77; 12th Internat. Congress of Biochemistry, 1982; Treasurer, Internat. Union of Biochemistry and Molecular Biol., 1988–. Work concerned especially with the biogenesis and genetics of mitochondria, mucinous cancers and the human ageing process. Editor-in-Chief, Biochemistry and Molecular Biol. Internat. *Publications:* Autonomy and Biogenesis of Mitochondria and Chloroplasts, 1971; over 240 contributions to learned journals. *Address:* Centre for Molecular Biology and Medicine, Monash University, Clayton, Victoria 3168, Australia. *T:* (3) 9053727, *Fax:* (3) 9051418; 15 Chaucer Crescent, Canterbury, Vic 3126, Australia. *Clubs:* Athenæum; Moonee Valley Race; VRC; VATC.

LINNELL, David George Thomas, CBE 1987; Chairman: Birkdale Group PLC, 1987–95; Hiscox Dedicated Insurance Fund plc, since 1993; Kendell plc, since 1994; *b* 28 May 1930; *s* of George and Marguerite Linnell; *m* 1953, Margaret Mary Paterson; one *s* one *d*. *Educ:* Leighton Park School, Reading. Managing Dir, Thomas Linnell & Sons, 1964–75; Chief Exec., Linfood Holdings, 1975–79; Chm., Spar Food Holdings, 1975–81. Pres., Inst. of Grocery Distribution, 1980–82; Chm., Eggs Authority, 1981–86; Chm., Neighbourhood Stores, 1983–87. *Address:* The Old Rectory, Titchmarsh, Kettering, Northants NN14 3DG. *Club:* Carlton.

LINNETT, Dr Michael Joseph, OBE 1975; FRCGP; Apothecary to the Prince and Princess of Wales, 1983–90; general medical practitioner, 1957–90, retired; *b* 14 July 1926; *s* of Joseph Linnett and Dora Alice (*née* Eabry); *m* 1950, Marianne Patricia, *d* of Aubrey Dibdin, CIE; two *d* (and one *s* decd). *Educ:* Wyggeston Grammar School for Boys, Leicester; St Bartholomew's Hosp. Med. Coll., London (MB BS 1949; Wix Prize Essay 1947). FRCGP 1970 (MRCGP 1957). House Physician, 1949, Demonstrator in Pharmacology, 1954, Jun. Registrar, 1955, St Bartholomew's Hosp., London; Ho. Phys., Evelina Children's Hosp., 1950; RAF Medical Br., Sqdn Ldr, 1950–54. Chm. Council, RCGP, 1976–79; Member: Cttee on Safety of Medicines, 1970–75; Medicines Commn, 1976–92 (Vice-Chm., 1984–92); Med. Adv. Panel, IBA, 1979–92; Pres., Chelsea Clinical Soc., 1987–88; Governor: National Hosp. for Nervous Diseases, 1974–82; Sutton's Hosp., Charterhouse, 1985–. Freeman, City of London, 1980; Chm., Livery Cttee, Worshipful Soc. of Apothecaries, 1982–84, Mem., Ct of Assts, 1985–92, Asst Emeritus, 1992. Chm., Editorial Bd, Prescribers' Jl, 1973–74. FRSocMed 1958. *Publications:* chapter, People with Epilepsy—the Burden of Epilepsy, in A Textbook of Epilepsy, ed Laidlaw & Richens, 1976; chapter, Ethics in General Practice, in Doctors' Decisions—Ethical Conflicts in Medical Practice, ed Dunstan and Shinebourne, 1989; contrib. BMJ (jtly) Drug Treatment of Intractable Pain, 1960. *Recreation:* music. *Address:* The Ground Floor Flat, 11 Astley Avenue, NW2 4AD. *T:* 0181–452 9263.

LINSTEAD, Stephen Guy; Director, Department of Trade and Industry, West Midlands Region, 1990–94; *b* 23 June 1941; *s* of late George Frederick Linstead and of May Dorothy Linstead (*née* Griffiths); *m* 1st, 1971 (marr. diss.); two *s*; 2nd, 1982, Rachael Marian Feldman; two *d*. *Educ:* King Edward VII Sch., Sheffield; Corpus Christi Coll., Oxford (MA Mod. Hist.; Dip. Public and Social Admin.); Carleton Univ., Ottawa (MA Political Sci.). Board of Trade, 1964–76 (Private Sec. to Minister of State, 1967–69); Principal, 1969; Asst Sec., Dept of Prices and Consumer Protection, 1976–79; Dept of Trade, 1979–82; Office of Fair Trading, 1982–90; Under-Sec., DTI, 1990–94. Mem. Steering Gp, Industry '96, 1994–. Vice-Chm., Assoc. of First Div. Civil Servants, 1982–84. Reader, dio. of Birmingham,. 1991–. *Publication:* contrib. Ottawa Law Review. *Recreations:* biblical criticism, swimming, travel, entertainment, building a replica Roman villa. *Address:* 20 Silhill Hall Road, Solihull, W Midlands B91 1JH. *T:* and *Fax:* 0121–705 1376. *Club:* Royal Over-Seas League.

LINTON, Alan Henry Spencer, LVO 1969; HM Diplomatic Service, retired; Consul-General, Detroit, USA, 1976–79; *b* Nottingham, 24 July 1919; *s* of Rt Rev. James Henry Linton, DD and Alicia Pears (*née* Aldous); *m* 1959, Kaethe Krebs (*d* 1990); four *d*. *Educ:* St Lawrence, Ramsgate, Magdalen Coll., Oxford (MA). Served War, RA, 1940–46. HM Overseas Civil Service, Tanganyika, 1947–62; FO, 1963–65; First Sec. (Inf.), Vienna, 1965–69; Head of Chancery, Lusaka, Zambia, 1970–73; First Sec. (Commercial), Kingston, Jamaica, 1973–75; Dep. High Comr, Kingston, 1975–76. *Recreations:* walking, photography. *Address:* 29 The Avenue, Poole BH13 6LH. *Club:* Royal Over-Seas League.

LINTOTT, Robert Edward, FInstPet; Chief Executive, Coverdale Organisation, 1987–91; *b* 14 Jan. 1932; *s* of Charles Edward and Doris Mary Lintott; *m* 1958, Mary Alice Scott; three *s*. *Educ:* Cambridgeshire High School; Trinity College, Cambridge. BA Nat. Scis 1955, MA. Served RAF, 1950–52 (Flying Officer); joined Esso Petroleum Co. Ltd, 1955; Corporate Planning Dept, Exxon Corp., 1975–78; Exec. Asst to Chm., Exxon Corp., 1978–79; Director: Esso Petroleum Co. Ltd, 1979–84; Esso Pension Trust, 1979–87; Esso Exploration & Production UK, 1984–87; Esso UK plc, Esso Petroleum, 1984–87 (Man. Dir, 1984–86); Matthew Hall Engineering Holdings Ltd, 1987–89; Chairman: Irish Refining Co., 1979–82; Esso Teoranta, 1982–84. Vice-Pres., UK Petroleum Industry Assoc., 1985–86; Pres., Oil Industries Club, 1986–88. Mem., Standards Bd, BSI, 1991–. Council Mem., 1979–, and Chm. Exec. Cttee, 1987–, Foundn for Management Educn; Member: Council for Management Educn and Develt, 1989–; Steering Cttee, Oxford Summer Business Sch., 1979–94 (Chm., 1987–91); Council, Manchester Business Sch., 1985–92. Councillor, Royal Bor. of Windsor and Maidenhead, 1987–91. Chm. of Govs, Queen's Coll. Taunton, 1994–. *Recreations:* cricket, vintage and modern motoring. *Address:* Huish Barton, Watchet, Somerset TA23 0LU. *T:* Watchet (01894) 40208. *Clubs:* Royal Air Force, MCC.

LION, Jacques Kenneth, OBE 1979; President, The London Metal Exchange Ltd, 1987–91; *b* 18 Dec. 1922; *s* of Felix J. Lion and Ethel (*née* Myers); *m* 1947, Jean Elphinstone (*née* Mackenzie); two *s* one *d*. *Educ:* St Paul's Sch. Pres., Non-Ferrous Div., Bureau Internationale de la Récupération, 1970–74; Mem. Council, British Secondary Metals Assoc., 1956–77 (Pres., 1959 and 1964). Dir, 1972, Chm., 1984–91, Metal Market & Exchange Co. Ltd. *Recreations:* music, gardening, golf. *Club:* City of London.

LIPFRIEND, His Honour Alan; Circuit Judge, 1974–91; *b* 6 Oct. 1916; 2nd *s* of I. and S. Lipfriend; *m* 1948, Adèle Burke (*d* 1986); one *s*. *Educ:* Central Foundation Sch., London, Queen Mary Coll., London (BSc(Eng) (Hons) 1938; Pres. Union Soc., 1938–39; Fellow, 1987). Design Staff, Hawker Aircraft Ltd, 1939–48. Called to Bar, Middle Temple, 1948; Pres., Appeal Tribunal, under Wireless and Telegraphy Act, 1949, 1971–73; Mem. Parole Bd, 1978–81. A Governor, Queen Mary Coll., Univ. of London, 1981–89; Trustee and Gov., Central Foundation School for Boys, 1985–. *Recreations:* theatre and all sport. *Address:* 27 Edmunds Walk, N2 0HU. *T:* 0181–883 4420. *Club:* Royal Automobile.

LIPKIN, Miles Henry J.; *see* Jackson-Lipkin.

LIPMAN, Maureen Diane, (Mrs J. M. Rosenthal); actress; *b* 10 May 1946; *d* of Maurice and Zelma Lipman; *m* 1973, Jack Morris Rosenthal, *qv*; one *s* one *d*. *Educ:* Newland High Sch. for Girls, Hull; London Acad. of Music and Dramatic Art. Professional début in The Knack, Watford, 1969; Stables Theatre, Manchester, 1970; National Theatre (Old Vic),

1971–73: Molly, in The Front Page; Long Day's Journey into Night; The Good Natur'd Man; *West End*: Candida, 1976; Maggie, in Outside Edge, 1978; Meg, in Meg and Mog, 1982; Messiah, 1983; Miss Skillen, in See How They Run, 1984 (Laurence Olivier Award; Variety Club of GB Award); Wonderful Town, Queen's, 1986; Re: Joyce!, Fortune, 1988, Vaudeville, 1989 and 1991, Long Wharf, Conn, USA, 1990; The Cabinet Minister, Albery, 1991; Lost in Yonkers, Strand, 1992 (Variety Club Best Stage Actress, 1993); other plays include: Celia, in As You Like It, RSC, 1974; Jenny, in Chapter Two, Hammersmith, 1981; Kitty McShane, in On Your Way, Riley, Stratford East, 1983; The Sisters Rosenweig, Greenwich, 1994; Dir, The Sunshine Boys, Royal Lyceum, Edinburgh, 1993; *television:* plays, series and serials include: The Evacuees; Smiley's People; The Knowledge; Rolling Home; Outside Edge; Princess of France, in Love's Labour's Lost; Absurd Person Singular; Shift Work; Absent Friends; Jane Lucas, in 4 series of Agony; All at No 20 (TV Times Award, 1989); About Face, 1989 and 1990; Re: Joyce; Enid Blyton, in Sunny Stories, 1992; *films:* Up the Junction, 1969; Educating Rita, 1983; Water, 1984. BAFTA Award, for BT Commercials, 1992. Magazine columnist: Options, 1983–88; She, 1988–91 (PPA Columnist of the Year, 1991); Good Housekeeping, 1993–. Hon. DLitt Hull, 1994. *Publications:* How Was it for You?, 1985; Something to Fall Back On, 1987; You Got an 'Ology?, 1989; Thank You for Having Me, 1990; When's It Coming Out?, 1992. *Recreations:* friends, food, films, seaside towns out of season.

LIPSCOMB, Prof. William Nunn; Abbott and James Lawrence Professor of Chemistry, Harvard University, 1971–90, now Emeritus; Nobel Laureate in Chemistry, 1976; *b* 9 Dec. 1919; *s* of late William Nunn Lipscomb Sr, and of Edna Patterson Porter; *m* 1983, Jean Craig Evans; one *s* one *d* by previous marriage. *Educ:* Univ. of Kentucky (BS); California Inst. of Technology (PhD). Univ. of Minnesota, Minneapolis: Asst Prof. of Physical Chem., 1946–50; Associate Prof., 1950–54; Actg Chief, Physical Chem. Div., 1952–54; Prof. and Chief of Physical Chem. Div., 1954–59; Harvard Univ.: Prof. of Chemistry, 1959–71 (Chm., Dept of Chem., 1962–65). Member: Bd of Dir's, Dow Chemical Co., USA, 1982–89; Scientific Adv. Bd, Robert A. Welch Foundn, 1982–. Member: Amer. Chemical Soc. (Chm., Minneapolis Section, 1949); Amer. Acad. of Arts and Sciences, 1959–; Nat. Acad. of Sciences, USA, 1961–; Internat. Acad. of Quantum Molecular Science, 1980; Académie Européenne des Scis, des Arts et des Lettres, Paris, 1980; Foreign Mem., Netherlands Acad. of Arts and Sciences, 1976; Hon. Member: Internat. Assoc. of Bioinorganic Scientists, 1979; RSC, 1983. MA (hon.) Harvard, 1959; Hon. DSc: Kentucky, 1963; Long Island, 1977; Rutgers, 1979; Gustavos Adolphus, 1980; Marietta, 1981; Miami, 1983; Dr *hc* Munich, 1976. *Publications:* Boron Hydrides, 1963 (New York); (with G. R. Eaton) Nuclear Magnetic Resonance Studies of Boron and Related Compounds, 1969 (New York); chapters in: The Aesthetic Dimensions of Science, ed D. W. Curtin, 1982; Crystallography in North America, ed D. Mchachlan and J. Glusker, 1983; contribs to scientific jls concerning structure and function of enzymes and natural products in inorganic chem. and theoretical chem. *Recreations:* tennis, chamber music. *Address:* Gibbs Chemical Laboratory, Harvard University, 12 Oxford Street, Cambridge, Mass 02138, USA. *T:* (617) 4954098.

LIPSEY, David Lawrence; journalist, since 1992, Political Editor, since 1994, The Economist; *b* 21 April 1948; *s* of Lawrence and Penelope Lipsey; *m* 1982, Margaret Robson; one *d*. *Educ:* Bryanston Sch.; Magdalen Coll., Oxford (1st Cl. Hons PPE). Research Asst, General and Municipal Workers' Union, 1970–72; Special Adviser to Anthony Crosland, MP, 1972–77 (Dept of the Environment, 1974–76; FCO, 1976–77); Prime Minister's Staff, 10 Downing Street, 1977–79; Journalist, New Society, 1979–80; Sunday Times: Political Staff, 1980–82; Economics Editor, 1982–86; Editor, New Society, 1986–88; Co-founder and Dep. Editor, The Sunday Correspondent, 1988–90; Associate Ed., The Times, 1990–92. Vis. Prof. in Public Policy, Univ. of Ulster. Secretary, Streatham Labour Party, 1970–72; Chm., Fabian Soc., 1981–82; Mem., Exec. Cttee, Charter for Jobs, 1984–86. A public interest Dir, PIA, 1994–. *Publications:* Labour and Land, 1972; (ed, with Dick Leonard) The Socialist Agenda: Crosland's Legacy, 1981; Making Government Work, 1982; The Name of the Rose, 1992. *Recreations:* golf, racing, opera, wine, sleeping. *Address:* 44 Drakefield Road, SW17 8RP. *T:* 0181–767 3268.

LIPSEY, Prof. Richard George, OC 1991; FRSC; Professor of Economics, Simon Fraser University, Burnaby, BC, since 1989; Fellow, Canadian Institute for Advanced Research, since 1989; *b* 28 Aug. 1928; *s* of R. A. Lipsey and F. T. Lipsey (*née* Ledingham); *m* 1960, Diana Louise Smart; one *s* two *d*. *Educ:* Univ. of British Columbia (BA 1st Cl. Hons 1950); Univ. of Toronto (MA 1953); LSE (PhD 1957). Dept of Trade and Industry, British Columbia Provincial Govt, 1950–53; LSE: Asst Lectr, 1955–58; Lectr, 1958–60; Reader, 1960–61; Prof. 1961–63; Univ. of Essex: Prof. of Economics, 1963–70; Dean of School of Social Studies, 1963–67; Sir Edward Peacock Prof. of Econs, Queen's Univ., Kingston, Ont, 1970–87. Vis. Prof., Univ. of California at Berkeley, 1963–64; Simeon Vis. Prof., Univ. of Manchester, 1973; Irving Fisher Vis. Prof., Yale Univ., 1979–80. Economic Consultant, NEDC, 1961–63; Sen. Econ. Advr, C. D. Howe Inst., Toronto, 1984–89. Member of Council: SSRC, 1966–69; Royal Economic Soc., 1968–71. President: Canadian Economics Assoc., 1980–81; Atlantic Economic Assoc., 1986–87. Editor, Review of Economic Studies, 1960–64. Fellow, Econometric Soc., 1972. FRSC 1980. Hon. LLD: McMaster, 1984; Victoria, 1985; Carleton, 1987; Queen's Univ. at Kingston, 1990; Guelph, 1993; Western Ontario, 1994; Hon. DSc Toronto, 1992. *Publications:* An Introduction to Positive Economics, 1963, 8th edn 1995; (with P. O. Steiner) Economics, 1966, 11th edn 1995; (with G. C. Archibald) An Introduction to a Mathematical Treatment of Economics, 1967, 3rd edn 1977; The Theory of Customs Unions: a general equilibrium analysis, 1971; (with G. C. Archibald) An Introduction to Mathematical Economics, 1975; (with C. Harbury) An Introduction to the UK Economy, 1983, 5th edn 1993; (with F. Flatters) Common Ground for the Canadian Common Market, 1984; (with M. Smith): Canada's Trade Options in a Turbulent World, 1985; Global Imbalance and US Policy Response, 1987; (with R. York) A Guided Tour through the Canada—US Free Trade Agreement, 1988; (with C. Harbury) First Principles of Economics, 1988, 2nd edn 1992; (jtly) The NAFTA: what's in, what's out, what's next; articles in learned jls on many branches of theoretical and applied economics. *Recreations:* skiing, sailing, film making. *Address:* Economic Growth and Policy Program, Simon Fraser University at Harbour Centre, 515 W Hastings Street, Vancouver, BC V6B 5K3, Canada.

LIPSTEIN, Prof. Kurt; Professor of Comparative Law, Cambridge University, 1973–76; Fellow of Clare College, Cambridge, since 1956; *b* 19 March 1909; *e s* of Alfred Lipstein, MD and Hilda (*née* Sulzbach); *m* 1944, Gwyneth Mary Herford; two *d*. *Educ:* Goethe Gymnasium, Frankfurt on Main; Univs of Grenoble and Berlin; Trinity Coll., Cambridge. Gerichtsreferendar 1931; PhD Cantab 1936; LLD 1977. Called to Bar, Middle Temple, 1950, Hon. Bencher, 1966. Univ. Lectr, Cambridge, 1946; Reader in Conflict of Laws, Cambridge Univ., 1962–73. Dir of Research, Internat. Assoc. Legal Science, 1954–59. Vis. Professor: Univ. of Pennsylvania, 1962; Northwestern Univ., Chicago, 1966, 1968; Paris I, 1977. Associate Mem., Inst. de Droit Internat., 1993. Hon. Dr jur. Würzburg, 1995. Humboldt Prize, Alexander von Humboldt Stiftung, Bonn, 1981. *Publications:* The Law of the EEC, 1974; Principles of the Conflict of Laws, National and International, 1981; joint editor and contributor: Dicey's Conflict of Laws, 6th edn, 1948—8th edn, 1967; Leske-Loewenfeld, Das Eherecht der europäischen Staaten, 1963; (ed) International Encyclopaedia of Comparative Law, vol. Private International Law, 1972; Harmonization of Private International Law by the EEC, 1978; contrib. English and foreign legal periodicals. *Address:* Clare College, Cambridge CB2 1TL. *T:* Cambridge (01223) 333200; 7 Barton Close, Cambridge CB3 9LQ. *T:* (01223) 357048; 13 Old Square, Lincoln's Inn, WC2A 3UA. *T:* 0171–404 4800.

LIPTON, Stuart Anthony; Chief Executive, Stanhope PLC, since 1995; Member, Royal Fine Art Commission, since 1988; *b* 9 Nov. 1942; *s* of Bertram Green and Jeanette Lipton; *m* 1966, Ruth Kathryn Marks; two *s* one *d*. *Educ:* Berkhamsted Sch. Director: Sterling Land Co., 1971–73; First Palace Securities Ltd, 1973–76; Man. Dir, Greycoat PLC, 1976–83; Chief Exec., Stanhope Properties PLC, 1983–95. Advr to Hampton Site Co. for Sainsbury Bldg, Nat. Gall., 1985–91; Advr, new Glyndebourne Opera House, 1988–94; Member: Adv. Bd, Dept of Construction Management, Reading Univ., 1983–91; Property Adv. Gp, DoE, 1986–; Mil. Bldgs Cttee, MoD, 1987–. Mem. Council, British Property Fedn, 1987–. Trustee: Whitechapel Art Gall., 1987–94; Architecture Foundn, 1992–; Member: Bd, Nat. Theatre, 1988–; Mem., Governing Body, Imperial Coll., 1987–. Hon. RIBA 1986. *Recreations:* architecture, crafts, art and technology, wine. *Address:* (office) 11 Bruton Street, W1X 7AG.

LIPWORTH, Sir (Maurice) Sydney, Kt 1991; Chairman: ZENECA Group plc, since 1995 (Director, since 1994); Financial Reporting Council, since 1993; a Deputy Chairman, National Westminster Bank, since 1993; *b* 13 May 1931; *s* of Isidore and Rae Lipworth; *m* 1957, Rosa Liwarek; two *s*. *Educ:* King Edward VII Sch., Johannesburg; Univ. of the Witwatersrand, Johannesburg (BCom, LLB). Admitted Solicitor, Johannesburg, 1955; called to the South African Bar, 1956; called to Bar, Inner Temple, 1991. Barrister, Johannesburg, 1956–64; Non-Exec. Dir, Liberty Life Assoc. of Africa Ltd, 1956–64; Director: private trading/financial gps, 1965–67; Abbey Life Assurance Gp, 1968–70; Allied Dunbar Assurance plc (formerly Hambro Life Assurance), 1971–88 (Jt Man. Dir, 1980–84; Dep. Chm., 1984–87); Chairman: Dunbar Bank, 1983–88; Allied Dunbar Unit Trusts, 1985–88 (Man. Dir, 1983–85); Director: J. Rothschild Holdings plc, 1984–87; BAT Industries plc, 1985–88; Carlton Communications plc, since 1993. Mem., 1981–93, Chm., 1988–93, Monopolies and Mergers Commn; Member: Sen. Salaries Review Body, 1994–; Cttee on Financial Aspects of Corporate Governance, 1994–95. Mem. Adv. Panel, BreakThrough Breast Cancer Res. Trust, 1990–; Trustee: Allied Dunbar Charitable Trust, 1971–; Philharmonia Orchestra, 1982– (Dep. Chm., 1986–93, Chm., 1993–, of Trustees); Royal Acad. Trust, 1988–; Governor: Contemp. Dance Trust, 1981–87; Sadler's Wells Foundn, 1987–90. Chm., Bar Assoc. for Commerce, Finance and Industry, 1991–92. Mem., Gen. Council of the Bar, 1992–94. Hon. Bencher, Inner Temple, 1989; Hon. QC 1993. *Publications:* chapters and articles on investment, life insurance, pensions and competition law. *Recreations:* tennis, music, theatre. *Address:* (office) 41 Lothbury, EC2P 2BP. *Clubs:* Reform, Queen's.

LISBURNE, 8th Earl of, *cr* 1776; **John David Malet Vaughan,** DL; Viscount Lisburne and Lord Vaughan, 1695; barrister-at-law; *b* 1 Sept. 1918; *o s* of 7th Earl of Lisburne; *S* father, 1965; *m* 1943, Shelagh, *er d* of late T. A. Macauley, 1266 Redpath Crescent, Montreal, Canada; three *s*. *Educ:* Eton; Magdalen Coll., Oxford (BA, MA). Called to Bar, Inner Temple, 1947. Captain, Welsh Guards. Director: British Home Stores Ltd, 1964–87; S Wales Regional Bd, Lloyds Bank Ltd, 1978–; Divisional Dir for Wales, Nationwide Building Soc., 1982–. Chm., Wales Council for Voluntary Action (formerly Council of Social Service for Wales), 1976–; Hon. Life Mem., AA (Mem. Exec. Cttee, 1981–88). DL Dyfed, 1992. *Heir:* *s* Viscount Vaughan, *qv*. *Address:* Cruglas, Ystrad Meurig, Dyfed SY25 6AN. *T:* Pontrhydfendigaid (019745) 230. *Clubs:* Pratt's, Turf.

LISHMAN, Prof. William Alwyn, MD, DSc; FRCP, FRCPsych; Professor of Neuropsychiatry, Institute of Psychiatry, University of London, 1979–93, now Professor Emeritus; Consultant Psychiatrist, Bethlem Royal and Maudsley Hospitals, 1967–93; *b* 16 May 1931; *s* of George Hackworth Lishman and Madge Scott (*née* Young); *m* 1966, Marjorie Loud; one *s* one *d*. *Educ:* Houghton-le-Spring Grammar Sch.; Univ. of Birmingham (BSc Hons Anatomy and Physiology, 1953; MB, ChB Hons 1956; MD 1965). DPM London, 1963; DSc London, 1985. MRCP 1958, FRCP 1972; FRCPsych 1972. House Phys. and House Surg., Queen Elizabeth Hosp., Birmingham, 1956–57; MO Wheatley Mil. Hosp., 1957–59 (Major, RAMC); Registrar, United Oxford Hosps, 1959–60; Registrar, later Sen. Registrar, Maudsley Hosp., London, 1960–66; Consultant in Psychol Medicine, Nat. Hosp. and Maida Vale Hosp., London, 1966–67; Sen. Lectr in Psychol Medicine, Hammersmith Hosp. and RPMS, 1967–69; Consultant Psychiatrist, Bethlem Royal and Maudsley Hosps, 1967–74; Reader in Neuropsychiatry, Inst. of Psychiatry, 1974–79. Vis. Fellow, Green Coll., Oxford, 1983. Advisor to Bermuda Hosps Bd, 1971; Scientific Advisor, DHSS, 1979–82; Civilian Consultant, RAF, 1987–. Member: Neurosciences Bd, MRC, 1976–78 (Dep. Chm., 1976–77); Scientific Adv. Panel, Brain Res. Trust, 1986–93; Adv. Cttee, Mason Med. Res. Trust, 1986–93. Examiner: Univ. of Oxford (also Mem. Bd of Examrs), 1975–79; Univ. of Birmingham, 1984–87; Nat. Univ. of Malaysia, 1989. Chm., British Neuropsychiatry Assoc., 1987–93; (Hon. Life Pres., 1993); Member: Experimental Psychology Soc., 1975–; Assoc. of British Neurologists, 1979–. Gaskell Gold Medal, Royal Medico-Psychol Assoc., 1965. Member, Editorial Boards: Psychological Medicine, 1970–93; Psychiatric Developments, 1983–; Neuropsychiatry, Neuropsychology and Behavioral Neurology, 1988–. Guarantor of Brain, 1984–. *Publications:* Organic Psychiatry: the psychological consequences of cerebral disorder, 1978, 2nd edn 1987; physiol and psychol papers on brain maturation, cerebral dominance, organisation of memory; clinical papers on head injury, dementia, epilepsy, neuroimaging, and alcoholic brain damage. *Recreations:* organ, piano, harpsichord, travelling. *Address:* 9 Elwill Way, Beckenham, Kent BR3 3AB.

LISLE; *see* Orchard-Lisle.

LISLE, 7th Baron, *cr* 1758; **John Nicholas Horace Lysaght;** *s* of late Hon. Horace G. Lysaght and Alice Elizabeth, *d* of Sir John Wrixon Becher, 3rd Bt; *b* 10 Aug. 1903; *S* grandfather, 1919; *m* 1st, 1928, Vivienne Brew (who obtained a divorce, 1939; she *died* 1948); 2nd, 1939, Mary Helen Purgold, Shropshire. *Heir:* *nephew* Patrick James Lysaght [*b* 1 May 1931; *m* 1957, Mrs Mary Louise Shaw-Stewart (marr. diss.); two *s* one *d*]. *Address:* The Chestnuts, Barge Farm, Taplow, Bucks.

LISS, Prof. Peter Simon, PhD; Professor, School of Environmental Sciences, University of East Anglia, since 1985; *b* 27 Oct. 1942; *s* of Michael and Gertrude Liss; *m* 1967, Ruth Adler; three *s*. *Educ:* University College, Durham (BSc); Marine Science Labs, Univ. of Wales (PhD). NERC Post-doctoral Res. Fellow, Dept. of Oceanography, Southampton Univ., 1967–69; Lectr, 1969–77, Reader, 1977–85, Sch. of Envmtl Scis, UEA. Vis. Prof., Univ. of Washington, Seattle, 1977; Visiting Scientist: Ocean Chem. Lab., Canada, 1975; Grad. Sch. of Oceanography, Univ. of Rhode Island, 1989, 1990. Scientific Advisor, CEGB, London, 1979–82. Mem., NERC, 1990–; Treasurer, 1990–93, Chm., 1993–, Sci. Cttee for Internat. Geosphere-Biosphere Prog. *Publications:* Estuarine Chemistry, 1976; Environmental Chemistry, 1980; Quimica Ambiental, 1983; Air-Sea Exchange of Gases and Particles, 1983; Power Generation and the Environment, 1990; The Sea Surface and Global Change, 1995. *Recreations:* reading, music, house renovation. *Address:* 6 Heigham Grove, Norwich, Norfolk NR2 3DQ. *T:* Norwich (01603) 623815.

LISSACK, Richard Antony; QC 1994; *b* 7 June 1956; *s* of late Victor Jack Lissack and of Antoinette Rosalind Lissack; *m* 1986, Carolyn Dare Arscott; twin *d*. *Educ:* UCS, Hampstead. Called to the Bar, Inner Temple, 1978; an Asst Recorder, 1993–. *Recreations:* breeding, competing and falling off thoroughbred horses, farming. *Address:* 2 King's Bench Walk, Temple, EC4Y 7DE. *T:* 0171–353 1746.

LISTER; *see* Cunliffe-Lister, family name of Earl of Swinton.

LISTER, Geoffrey Richard, CBE 1994; FCA; FCIB; Chief Executive, since 1985, Director, since 1988, Bradford & Bingley Building Society; *b* 14 May 1937; *s* of Walter and Margaret Lister; *m* 1962, Myrtle Margaret (*née* Cooper); one *s* two *d*. *Educ:* St Bede's Grammar Sch., Bradford. Articled clerk, J. Pearson & Son, 1955–60, qual. chartered accountant, 1960; Computer and Systems Sales, Burroughs Machines Ltd, 1961–63; Audit Man., Thos Gardner & Co., 1963–65; Bradford & Bingley Building Society: Asst Accountant, 1965–67; Computer Man., 1967–70; Chief Accountant, 1970–73; Asst Gen. Man., 1973–75; Dep. Gen. Man., 1975–80; Gen. Man., 1980–84; Dep. Chief Exec., 1984–85. Director: NHBC, 1992–94; PIA, 1994–95. Building Societies' Association: Mem. Council, 1984–; Dep. Chm., 1992–93; Chm., 1993–94. CIMgt. *Recreations:* walking, gardening. *Address:* Harbeck House, Harbeck Drive, Harden, Bingley, W Yorks BD16 1JG. *T:* Cullingworth (01535) 272350. *Clubs:* Carlton; Bradford and Bingley Rugby Union Football (Bingley).

LISTER, Prof. James, MD, FRCS; Professor of Paediatric Surgery, University of Liverpool, 1974–86, now Emeritus; *b* 1 March 1923; *s* of Thomas and Anna Rebecca Lister; *m* 1946, Greta Redpath; three *d*. *Educ:* St Paul's Sch., London; Edinburgh Univ. (MB, ChB 1945; MD 1972). FRCS 1975, FRCSE 1950, FRCSGlas 1969. Surg. Lieut, RNVR, 1945–48. Surgical training posts, Edinburgh and Dundee, 1948–58; Halstead Res. Fellow, Colorado Univ., 1959; Sen. Lectr in Paediatric Surgery and Consultant Surgeon, Hosp. for Sick Children, Great Ormond St, and Queen Elizabeth Hosp., Hackney Rd, 1960–63; Consultant Paediatric Surgeon, Sheffield Children's Hosp., 1963–74. Civil Consultant in Paediatric Surgery to RN, 1979–86. Past Examiner: Univs of Glasgow and Sheffield (in paediatric surgery); DCH London; Part I and Part II FRCSE. Mem. Council, RCSE, 1977–91 (Convenor of Examinations Cttee, 1986–90; a Vice-Pres., 1988–91); Mem., St Helens & Knowsley DHA, 1983–86. Chm., European Union of Paediatric Surgical Assocs, 1983–86; Hon. Member: British Assoc. of Paediatric Surgeons (Pres., 1975–76); Paediatric Surgical Assocs of Austria, Brazil, Chile, Germany, Greece, Hungary, Peru, Poland, Scandinavia, Yugoslavia. Hon. Fellow: Amer. Acad. of Paediatrics, 1976; Assoc. of Surgeons of India, 1985. Member of Editorial Board: Jl of RCSEd; Jl of Paediatric Surgery; Consultant editor, Annals of Tropical Paediatrics, 1985–. *Publications:* Neonatal Surgery, ed jtly 2nd edn 1978 and 3rd edn, 1990; Complications in Paediatric Surgery, 1986; papers on neonatal surgery and myelomeningocele. *Recreations:* gardening, hill walking. *Address:* Kailheugh, Hownam, Kelso, Roxburghshire TD5 8AL. *T:* Morebattle (01573) 440224.

LISTER, Very Rev. John Field, MA; *b* 19 Jan. 1916; *s* of Arthur and Florence Lister. *Educ:* King's Sch., Worcester; Keble Coll., Oxford; Cuddesdon Coll., Oxford. Asst Curate, St Nicholas, Radford, Coventry, 1939–44; Asst Curate, St John Baptist, Coventry, 1944–45; Vicar of St John's, Huddersfield, 1945–54; Asst Rural Dean of Halifax, 1955–61; Archdeacon of Halifax, 1961–72; Vicar of Brighouse, 1954–72; Provost of Wakefield, 1972–82. Examng Chaplain to Bishop of Wakefield, 1972–78. Hon. Canon of Wakefield Cathedral, 1961, Canon, 1968; RD of Wakefield, 1972–80. Chaplain to The Queen, 1966–72. *Address:* 5 Larkcliff Court, The Parade, Birchington, Kent CT7 9NB.

LISTER, Prof. (Margot) Ruth (Aline); Professor of Social Policy and Administration, University of Loughborough, since 1994; *b* 3 May 1949, *d* of Dr Werner Bernard Lister and Daphne (*née* Carter). *Educ:* Univ. of Essex (BA Hons Sociology); Univ. of Sussex (MA Multi-Racial Studies). Child Poverty Action Group: Legal Res. Officer, 1971–75; Asst Dir, 1975–77; Dep. Dir, 1977–79; Dir, 1979–87; Prof. of Applied Social Studies, Univ. of Bradford, 1987–93, Vice Chair, NCVO, 1991–93 Member: Opsahl Commn, 1992–93; Commn for Social Justice, 1992–94. Eleanor Rathbone Meml Lecture, Univ. of Leeds, 1989. Hon. LLD Manchester, 1987. *Publications:* Supplementary Benefit Rights, 1974; Welfare Benefits, 1981; The Exclusive Society, 1990; Women's Economic Dependency and Social Security, 1992; chapters in: Justice, Discretion and Poverty, 1975; Labour and Equality, 1980; The Economics of Prosperity, 1980; Taxation and Social Policy, 1981; Families in Britain, 1982; The New Politics of Welfare, 1989; The Social Economy and the Democratic State, 1989; The Economics of Social Security, 1989; Year Book of Social Work, 1989; Debating the Constitution, 1993; Social Security and Social Change, 1994; pamphlets and articles on poverty, social security and women's citizenship. *Recreations:* relaxing—with friends, music, and through walking, meditation and Tai Chi; reading. *Address:* University of Loughborough, Loughborough, Leics LE11 3TU; 45 Quayside Close, Nottingham NG2 3BP.

LISTER, Patrick; *see* Lister, R. P.

LISTER, Raymond (George), MA, LittD Cantab; President, Royal Society of Miniature Painters, Sculptors and Gravers, 1970–80; Chairman, Board of Governors, Federation of British Artists, 1976–80 (Governor, 1972–80); *b* 28 March 1919; *s* of late Horace Lister and Ellen Maud Mary Lister (*née* Arnold); *m* 1947, Pamela Helen, *d* of late Frank Bishop Brutnell; one *s* one *d*. *Educ:* St John's Coll. Choir Sch., Cambridge; Cambridge and County High Sch. for Boys. Served apprenticeship in family firm (architectural metalworking), 1934–39; specialised war service (engrg), 1939–45; Dir of family firm, 1941–94; Man. Editor, Golden Head Press, 1952–72; Dir, John P. Gray and Son, craft bookbinders, 1978–82. Hon. Senior Mem., University Coll., subseq. Wolfson Coll., Cambridge, 1971–75, Mem. Coll. Council, 1983–85, Emeritus Fellow, 1986 (Fellow, 1975–86); a Syndic, Fitzwilliam Mus., Cambridge, 1981–89. Liveryman, Blacksmiths' Co., 1957, Mem. Ct of Assistants, 1980, Prime Warden, 1989–90. Associate Mem. 1946, Mem. 1948, Royal Soc. of Miniature Painters; Pres., Private Libraries Assoc., 1971–74; Vice-Pres., Architectural Metalwork Assoc., 1970–75, Pres., 1975–77. *Publications:* Decorative Wrought Ironwork in Great Britain, 1957; Decorative Cast Ironwork in Great Britain, 1960; Edward Calvert, 1962; Beulah to Byzantium, 1965; Victorian Narrative Paintings, 1966; William Blake, 1968; Hammer and Hand, 1969; Samuel Palmer and his Etchings, 1969; A Title to Phoebe, 1972; British Romantic Art, 1973; Samuel Palmer: a biography, 1974; (ed) The Letters of Samuel Palmer, 1974; Infernal Methods: a Study of William Blake's art techniques, 1975; Apollo's Bird, 1975; For Love of Leda, 1977; Great Images of British Printmaking, 1978; (jtly) Samuel Palmer: a vision recaptured, 1978; Samuel Palmer in Palmer Country, 1980; George Richmond, 1981; Bergomask, 1982; There was a Star Danced, 1983; Prints and Printmaking, 1984; Samuel Palmer and 'The Ancients', (catalogue of exhibn at Fitzwilliam Mus., Cambridge, also selected by R. Lister), 1984; The Paintings of Samuel Palmer, 1985; The Paintings of William Blake, 1986; Samuel Palmer, his Life and Art, 1987; Catalogue Raisonné of the Works of Samuel Palmer, 1988; British Romantic Painting, 1989; trans., A. M. St Léon, Stenochoreography, 1992; With My Own Wings (autobiog.), 1994; contrib. Climbers' Club Jl, The Irish Book, Blake Studies, Blake Quarterly, Gazette des Beaux-arts, Connoisseur, Studies in Romanticism, Book Collector and TLS. *Recreations:* mountaineering in the fens, merels. *Address:* 9 Sylvester Road, Cambridge CB3 9AF. *T:* Cambridge (01223) 324443. *Club:* Sette of Odd Volumes (Pres. 1960, 1982).

LISTER, (Robert) Patrick, CBE 1993; retired; *b* 6 Jan. 1922; *s* of Robert B. Lister; *m* 1942, Daphne Rosamund, *d* of Prof. C. J. Sisson; three *s* one *d* (and one *s* decd). *Educ:* Marlborough College; Cambridge University (MA); Harvard Business School (MBA). Captain Royal Engineers, 1942–46; Massey Harris, Toronto, 1949–51; joined Coventry Climax Ltd, 1951, Managing Director, 1971–80, Deputy Chairman, 1980–81; Dir, Climax Fork Trucks, 1981–83; Dir and Chief Exec., Engrg Employers W Midlands Assoc., 1983–84. President: Fedn Européenne de la Manutention, 1978–80; Coventry and Dist Engineering Employers' Assoc., 1979–80 and 1983; British Indust. Truck Assoc., 1980–81; Vice-Pres., Inst. of Materials Handling, later Inst. of Materials Management, 1982–93 (FILog Emeritus, 1993). Chm., Bd of Governors, Coventry Univ. (formerly Poly.), 1986– (Mem., 1984–); Gov., Coventry Technical Coll., 1984–; Chm. Trustees, St Joseph's Sch., Kenilworth. KSS 1992. *Recreations:* pastoral work, travel, gardening, DIY. *Address:* 35 Warwick Avenue, Coventry CV5 6DJ. *T:* Coventry (01203) 673776.

LISTER, Ruth; *see* Lister, M. R. A.

LISTER, Tom, CBE 1978; QFSM 1977; Chief Fire Officer, West Midlands County Council, 1975–81, retired; *b* 14 May 1924; *s* of late T. Lister and of Mrs E. Lister; *m* 1954, Linda, *d* of late T. J. and Mrs H. Dodds; one *d*. *Educ:* Charter House, Hull. Hull Fire Service, 1947–60; divisional officer, Lancs, 1960–62; Asst Chief Fire Officer, Warwicks, 1962–68; Chief Fire Officer, Glos, 1968–71, Bristol and Avon, 1972–75.

LISTER, Dame Unity (Viola), DBE 1972 (OBE 1958); Member of Executive, European Union of Women, since 1971 (Vice-Chairman, 1963–69); Member: European Movement, since 1970; Conservative Group for Europe, since 1970; *b* 19 June 1913; *d* of Dr A. S. Webley; *m* 1940, Samuel William Lister. *Educ:* St Helen's, Blackheath; Sorbonne Univ. of Paris. Member, London County Council, 1949–65 (Dep.-Chm., 1963–64); Chairman: Women's Nat. Advisory Cttee, 1966–69; Nat. Union of Conservative and Unionist Assocs, 1970–71 (Mem. Exec); Mem., Inner London Adv. Cttee on Appt of Magistrates, 1966–. Vice-Chm., Horniman Museums (Chm., 1967–70); Governor: Royal Marsden Hosp., 1952–; various schools and colleges. *Recreations:* languages, travel, music, gardening, theatre, museums, reading, walking. *Address:* 32 The Court Yard, Eltham, SE9 5QE. *T:* 0181–850 7038. *Club:* St Stephen's Constitutional.

LISTER-KAYE, Sir John (Phillip Lister), 8th Bt *cr* 1812, of Grange, Yorks; Director of the Aigas Trust, since 1979; *b* 8 May 1946; *s* of Sir John Christopher Lister Lister-Kaye, 7th Bt and Audrey Helen (*d* 1979), *d* of E. J. Carter; *S* father, 1982; *m* 1st, 1972, Sorrel Deirdre Bentinck (marr. diss. 1987), *d* of Earl of Portland, *qv*; one *s* two *d*; 2nd, 1989, Lucinda Anne (formerly Hon. Mrs Evan Baillie), *d* of Robin Law, Withersfield; one *d*. *Educ:* Allhallows School. Naturalist, author, farmer, lecturer. Created first field studies centre in Highlands of Scotland, 1970; Founder Director of Scottish conservation charity, the Aigas Trust, 1979. Mem., Internat. Cttee, World Wilderness Foundn, 1983–; Chairman: Scottish Adv. Cttee, RSPB, 1986–92; Cttee for Scotland, NCC, 1989–91; NW Region, NCC for Scotland, 1991–92; NW Region, Scottish Natural Heritage, 1992–. *Publications:* The White Island, 1972; Seal Cull, 1979; The Seeing Eye, 1980; One for Sorrow, 1994. *Recreations:* breeding and showing pedigree highland cattle. *Heir:* *s* John Warwick Noel Lister-Kaye, *b* 10 Dec. 1974. *Address:* Aigas House, Beauly, Inverness-shire IV4 7AD. *T:* Beauly (01463) 782729. *Club:* Caledonian.

LISTON, James Malcolm, CMG 1958; Chief Medical Adviser, Foreign and Commonwealth Office, Overseas Development Administration, 1970–71; *b* 1909; *m* 1935, Isobel Prentice Meiklem, Edinburgh, one *s* one *d*. *Educ:* Glasgow High Sch.; Glasgow Univ. MB, ChB, Glasgow, 1932; DTM & H Eng., 1939; DPH University of London, 1947; FRCP Glasgow, 1963. Medical Officer, Kenya, 1935; Director of Medical and Health Services, Sarawak, 1947–52; Deputy Director of Medical Services, Hong Kong, 1952–55; Director of Medical Services, Tanganyika, 1955–59; Permanent Secretary to Ministry of Health, Tanganyika, 1959–60; Deputy Chief Medical Officer: Colonial Office, 1960–61; Dept of Tech. Co-op., 1961–62; Chief Medical Adviser, Dept of Tech. Co-op., 1962–64; Medical Adviser, Min. of Overseas Develt, 1964–70. *Address:* 6A Western Terrace, Murrayfield, Edinburgh EH12 5QF. *T:* 0131–337 4236.

LISTOWEL, 5th Earl of, *cr* 1822; **William Francis Hare,** PC 1946; GCMG 1957; Baron Ennismore, 1800; Viscount Ennismore, 1816; Baron Hare (UK), 1869; Chairman of Committees, House of Lords, 1965–76; *b* 28 Sept. 1906; *e s* of 4th Earl and Hon. Freda Vanden-Bempde-Johnstone (*d* 1968), *y d* of 2nd Baron Derwent; *S* father, 1931; *m* 1st, 1933, Judith (marr. diss., 1945), *o d* of R. de Marffy-Mantuano, Budapest; one *d*; 2nd, 1958, Stephanie Sandra Yvonne Wise (marr. diss., 1963), Toronto; one *d*; 3rd, 1963, Mrs Pamela Read; two *s* one *d*. *Educ:* Eton; Balliol Coll., Oxford. PhD London Univ. Lieut, Intelligence Corps; Whip of Labour Party in House of Lords, 1941–44; Parliamentary Under-Secretary of State, India Office, and Deputy Leader, House of Lords, 1944–45; Postmaster-General, 1945–47; Secretary of State for India, April–Aug 1947; for Burma, 1947–Jan. 1948; Minister of State for Colonial Affairs, 1948–50; Joint Parliamentary Secretary, Ministry of Agriculture and Fisheries, 1950–51; Member (Lab) LCC for East Lewisham, 1937–46, for Battersea North, 1952–57. Governor-General of Ghana, 1957–60. Jt Patron, British Tunisian Soc.; President: British-Cameroon Soc.; Council for Aid to African Students; Jt Pres., Anti-Slavery Soc. for Protection of Human Rights; Vice-Pres., European-Atlantic Gp. *Publications:* The Values of Life, 1931; A Critical History of Modern Æsthetics, 1933 (2nd edn, as Modern Æsthetics: an Historical Introduction, 1967). *Heir:* *s* Viscount Ennismore, *qv*. *Address:* 10 Downshire Hill, NW3 1NR.

See also Baron Grantley.

LITCHFIELD, Jack Watson, FRCP; retired; Consulting Physician, St Mary's Hospital, since 1972 (Physician, 1946–72 and Physician i/c Cardiac Department, 1947–72); *b* 7 May 1909; *s* of H. L. Litchfield, Ipswich; *m* 1941, Nan (*d* 1984), *d* of A. H. Hatherly, Shanghai; two *s* one *d*. *Educ:* Ipswich Sch.; Oriel Coll., Oxford (Scholar); St Mary's Hospital. Theodore Williams Schol. in Physiology, 1929, in Pathology, 1931; Radcliffe Schol. in Pharmacology, 1932; BA (2nd class hons) 1930; BM, BCh 1933; University schol. at St Mary's Hospital Medical Sch., 1931; MRCP 1936; FRCP 1947. Medical Registrar: St Mary's Hospital, 1936; Brompton Hospital, 1938; Physician, King Edward Memorial Hosp., W13, 1947–69. Served in RAMC in N Africa, Italy, etc (despatches), Lt-Col i/c Medical Div. *Publications:* papers on various subjects in medical journals. *Recreations:* gardening, conservation. *Address:* 2 Pound Cottages, The Green, Long Melford, Sudbury, Suffolk CO10 9DX. *T:* Sudbury (01787) 312730.

LITCHFIELD, Dame Ruby (Beatrice), DBE 1981 (OBE 1959); Director, Festival City Broadcasters Ltd, 1975–86, retired (first woman appointed); Trustee, Adelaide Festival Centre, 1971–82, retired (first woman to be appointed to this position) (Life Member, 1982); *b* 5 Sept. 1912; *d* of Alfred John Skinner and Eva Hanna (*née* Thomas); *m* 1940,

Kenneth Lyle Litchfield (*d* 1976); one *d*. *Educ:* North Adelaide Primary Sch.; Presbyterian Girls' Coll., Glen Osmond. Bd Mem., Kidney Foundn, 1968–; Chairperson: Carclew Youth Performing Arts Centre, 1972–88 (Life Patron, 1988); Families, Religion, Cultural Cttee, S Aust. Jubilee 150th, 1980–86. First woman Mem., Bd of S Aust. Housing Trust, 1962–70; Life Member: Queen Victoria Maternity Hosp., 1972 (Mem. Bd and Vice-Pres., 1953–72); Adelaide Rep. Th., 1967 (Mem. Bd, 1951–68); Hon. Life Mem., Spastic Paralysis Welfare Assoc. Inc. Mayoress of Prospect, 1954–57; Pres., Sportswomen's Assoc., 1969–74; Mem., Divl Council, Red Cross Soc., SA, 1955–71; Councillor, Royal Dist Bush Nursing Soc., 1957–64; Member: S Aust. Davis Cup Cttee, 1952, 1963, 1968; SA Cttee of Royal Acad. of Dancing, 1961–66; Bd, Telethon Channel 9, 1969–86; Mem. Cttee, Adelaide Festival of Arts, 1960 (Mem. Bd of Govs, 1966–90); Council, Sudden Infant Death Syndrome Res. Foundn, 1979–; Bd, Mary Potter Foundn (Chair, Hospice Appeal Cttee, 1988–; Life Mem., 1992); Mem. Bd, Crippled Children's Assoc., 1976–; First Life Mem., Telethon, 1992; Patron: Adelaide Chamber Orch., 1992–; State Theatre Co. Friends Cttee, 1993–; SA Div., Internat. AIDS Meml Fund, 1993–. Silver Jubilee Medal, 1977; Advance Australia Award, 1985; S Australia Great Award, 1987. *Recreation:* tennis (SA Hardcourt Champion, 1932–35). *Address:* 33 Hallett Road, Burnside, SA 5066, Australia. *Club:* Royal Commonwealth Society (Adelaide).

LITHERLAND, Prof. Albert Edward, FRS 1974; FRSC 1968; University Professor, 1979–93, now Emeritus, and Professor of Physics, 1966–93, University of Toronto; Director, Isotrace Laboratory, University of Toronto, since 1982; *b* 12 March 1928; *e s* of Albert Litherland and Ethel Clement; *m* 1956, (Elizabeth) Anne Allen; two *d*. *Educ:* Wallasey Grammar Sch.; Univ. of Liverpool (BSc, PhD). State Scholar to Liverpool Univ., 1946; Rutherford Memorial Scholar to Atomic Energy of Canada, Chalk River, Canada, 1953; Scientific Officer at Atomic Energy of Canada, 1955–66. Guggenheim Fellow, Toronto Univ., 1986–87. Canadian Assoc. of Physicists Gold Medal for Achievement in Physics, 1971; Rutherford Medal and Prize of Inst. of Physics (London), 1974; JARI Silver Medal, Pergamon Press, 1981; Henry Marshall Tory Medal, RSC, 1993. Izaac Walton Killam Memorial Scholarship, 1980. *Publications:* numerous, in scientific jls. *Address:* 3 Hawthorn Gardens, Toronto, Ontario M4W 1P4, Canada. *T:* (416) 9235616.

LITHERLAND, Robert Kenneth; MP (Lab) Manchester Central, since Sept. 1979; *b* 1930; *s* of Robert Litherland and Mary (*née* Parry); *m* 1953, Edna Litherland; one *s* one *d*. *Educ:* North Manchester High Sch. for Boys. Formerly sales representative for printing firm. Mem., Manchester City Council (Dep. Chm., Housing Cttee; former Chm., Manchester Direct Works Cttee); Dep. Chm., Public Works Cttee, Assoc. of Municipal Authorities. Member: Council of Europe, 1987–; WEU, 1987–. *Address:* House of Commons, SW1A 0AA; 32 Darley Avenue, Didsbury, Manchester M20 8YD.

LITHGOW, Sir William (James), 2nd Bt of Ormsary, *cr* 1925; DL; CEng; industrialist and farmer; Chairman, 1959–84 and since 1988, Director, since 1956, Lithgows Ltd; *b* 10 May 1934; *o s* of Colonel Sir James Lithgow, 1st Bt of Ormsary, GBE, CB, MC, TD, DL, JP, LLD, and Gwendolyn Amy, *d* of late John Robinson Harrison of Scalesceugh, Cumberland; *S* father, 1952; *m* 1964, Valerie Helen (*d* 1964), 2nd *d* of late Denis Scott, CBE and Mrs Laura Scott; *m* 1967, Mary Claire, *d* of Colonel F. M. Hill, CBE and Mrs Hill; two *s* one *d*. *Educ:* Winchester Coll. CEng; FRINA; CBIM 1980 (FBIM 1969). Chm., Lithgow Drydocks Ltd, 1967–78; Vice-Chm., Scott Lithgow Ltd, 1968–78; Chairman: Western Ferries (Argyll) Ltd, 1972–85; Hunterston Develt Co. Ltd, 1987– (Dir, 1971–); Director: Bank of Scotland, 1962–86; Campbeltown Shipyard Ltd, 1970–; Lithgows Pty Ltd, 1972–; Landcatch, 1981–. Member: Council, Shipbuilding Employers Fedn, 1961–62; British Cttee, Det Norske Veritas, 1966–92; Exec. Cttee, Scottish Council Develt and Industry, 1969–85; Scottish Regional Council of CBI, 1969–76; Clyde Port Authority, 1969–71; Bd, National Ports Council, 1971–78; West Central Scotland Plan Steering Cttee, 1970–74; General Board (Royal Soc. nominee), Nat. Physical Lab., 1963–66; Greenock Dist Hosp. Bd, 1961–66; Scottish Milk Marketing Bd, 1979–83. Chm., Iona Cathedral Trustees Management Bd, 1979–83; Mem. Council, Winston Churchill Meml Trust, 1979–83. Hon. Pres., Students Assoc., and Mem. Court, Univ. of Strathclyde, 1964–69. Petitioner in case of Lithgow and others *v* UK, at Eur. Court of Human Rights, 1986. Member, Queen's Body Guard for Scotland (Royal Company of Archers), 1964. Fellow, Scottish Council, 1988. FRSA 1990. DL Renfrewshire, 1970. Hon. LLD Strathclyde, 1979. *Publications:* lectures and papers. *Recreations:* rural life, invention, photography. *Heir:* *s* James Frank Lithgow, *b* 13 June 1970. *Address:* Ormsary House, by Lochgilphead, Argyllshire PA31 8PE. *T:* Ormsary (01880) 770252; Drums, Langbank, Renfrewshire PA14 6YH. *T:* Langbank (01475) 540606; RMB 125A, Karridale, WA 6288, Australia. *T:* 758–2297; (office) PO Box 7, Lochgilphead, Argyllshire PA31 8JH. *T:* Ormsary (01880) 770244. *Clubs:* Oriental; Western, Royal Scottish Automobile (Glasgow).

LITHIBY, John Grant; Chairman, Panmure Gordon & Co. Ltd, since 1987; *b* 1 Dec. 1930; *s* of John Stewart Lithiby and Dorothy (*née* Schwartz); *m* 1961, Sarah Branch; two *s* one *d*. *Educ:* Eton Coll. Nat. Service, 1950–53; commnd Life Guards, 1950. Carl M. Loeb Rhoades, 1953–57; joined Panmure Gordon & Co. Ltd, 1957. *Recreations;* bridge, gardening, tennis. *Address:* Panmure Gordon & Co. Ltd, New Broad Street House, New Broad Street, EC2M 1NH. *Clubs:* White's, Hurlingham.

LITTLE, Ian Malcolm David, AFC 1943; FBA 1973; *b* 18 Dec. 1918; *s* of Brig.-Gen. M. O. Little, CB, CBE, and Iris Hermione Little (*née* Brassey); *m* 1st, 1946, Doreen Hennessey (*d* 1984); one *s* one *d*; 2nd, 1991, Lydia Segrave. *Educ:* Eton; New Coll., Oxford (MA, DPhil). RAF Officer, 1939–46. Fellow: All Souls Coll., Oxford, 1948–50; Trinity Coll., Oxford, 1950–52; Nuffield Coll., Oxford, 1952–76, Emeritus Fellow, 1976. Dep. Dir, Economic Section, Treasury, 1953–55; Mem., MIT Centre for Internat. Studies, India, 1958–59 and 1965; Vice-Pres., OECD Develt Centre, Paris, 1965–67; Prof. of Economics of Underdeveloped Countries, Oxford Univ., 1971–76. Dir, Investing in Success Ltd, 1960–65; Bd Mem., British Airports Authority, 1969–74. Dir, Gen. Funds Investment Trust, 1974–76; Special Adviser, IBRD, 1976–78. Hon. DSc(SocSci) Edinburgh, 1976. *Publications:* A Critique of Welfare Economics, 1950; The Price of Fuel, 1953; (jtly) Concentration in British Industry, 1960; Aid to Africa, 1964; (jtly) International Aid, 1965; (jtly) Higgledy-Piggledy Growth Again, 1966; (jtly) Manual of Industrial Project Analysis in Developing Countries, 1969; (jtly) Industry and Trade in Some Developing Countries, 1970; (jtly) Project Analysis and Planning, 1974; Economic Development: theory, policy and international relations, 1982; (jtly) Small Manufacturing Enterprises, 1987; (jtly) Boom, Crisis and Adjustment, 1993; (jtly) India: macroeconomics and political economy 1964–1991, 1994; many articles in learned jls. *Address:* 25 Norham Road, Oxford OX2 6SF.

LITTLE, John Eric Russell, OBE 1961 (MBE 1943); HM Diplomatic Service, retired; *b* 29 Aug. 1913; *s* of William Little and Beatrice Little (*née* Biffen); *m* 1945, Christine Holt; one *s* one *d*. *Educ:* Strand Sch. Served in FO, 1930–40, and in Army, 1940–41. Transferred to Minister of State's Office, Cairo, 1941, and seconded to Treasury. Returned to FO and appointed to British Middle East Office, 1946. Transferred to FO, 1948; Consul, Milan, 1950 (acting Consul-General, 1951, 1952); Bahrain as Asst Political Agent, 1952 (acting Political Agent, 1953, 1954, 1955); 1st Secretary, Paris, 1956; Asst Finance Officer, Foreign Office, 1958; HM Consul-General: Basra, 1962–65; Salonika, 1965–70; Counsellor, British Embassy, Brussels, 1970–72. *Recreations:* walking, reading, music. *Address:* Golna, Stonestile Lane, Hastings, East Sussex TN35 4PE.

LITTLE, John Philip Brooke B.; *see* Brooke-Little.

LITTLE, Dr Robert Clement; Head of Chemistry Division, Agricultural Science Service, Ministry of Agriculture, Fisheries and Food, 1979–85; *b* 8 Nov. 1925; *s* of Ernest William Little and Hannah Little; *m* 1950, Margaret Isobel Wilson; two *d*. *Educ:* Carlisle Grammar Sch.; Manchester Univ. (BScTech); Glasgow Univ. (PhD). W of Scotland Agricultural Coll., 1946–55; Agricultural Develt and Adv. Service (formerly National Agricl Adv. Service), MAFF, 1955–85. *Recreations:* golf, gardening, fell walking. *Address:* 9 Ashcroft Close, Harpenden, Herts AL5 1JJ. *T:* Harpenden (01582) 715613.

LITTLE, Tasmin, (Mrs M. Hatch); violinist; *b* 13 May 1965; *d* of George Villiers Little and Gillian (*née* Morris); *m* 1993, Michael Hatch. *Educ:* Yehudi Menuhin Sch.; Guildhall Sch. of Music (DipGSM 1986). ARCM 1984. Has performed as soloist in UK, Europe, Scandinavia, S America, Hong Kong, Oman, Zimbabwe and SA. Concerto performances with leading orchestras including: Leipzig Gewandhaus; Berlin Symphony; LSO; Philharmonia; Royal Philharmonic; Halle; Bournemouth; Royal Liverpool Philharmonic; EC Chamber Orch.; Royal Danish; Stavanger Symphony; acknowledged interpreter of music of Delius. TV appearances, radio broadcasts; recordings. *Publication:* contrib. Delius Soc. Jl. *Recreations:* theatre, cinema, swimming, cooking, languages. *Address:* c/o Ingpen & Williams Ltd, 14 Kensington Court, W8 5DN. *T:* 0171–937 5158.

LITTLE, Most Rev. Thomas Francis; *see* Melbourne, Archbishop of, (RC).

LITTLE, Dr Thomas William Anthony, FIBiol; Director and Chief Executive, Central Veterinary Laboratory, Ministry of Agriculture, Fisheries and Food, since 1990; *b* 27 June 1940; *s* of Thomas Lowden Little and Marjorie Annie Little; *m* 1st, 1963 (marr. diss.); one *s* one *d*; 2nd, 1985, Sally Anne Headlam; two *s*. *Educ:* Dame Allan's Sch., Newcastle upon Tyne; Edinburgh Univ. (BVMS); London Univ. (Dip. Bact., PhD). MRCVS 1963. General veterinary practice, March, Cambs, 1963–66; joined MAFF, 1966; Central Vet. Lab., Weybridge, 1966–82, Sen. Res. Officer 1973–82; Dep. Regl Vet. Officer, 1982–85, Vet. Head of Section, 1985–86, Tolworth; Dep. Dir, Central Vet. Lab., 1986–90. *Publications:* contribs to veterinary jls and text books. *Recreations:* sailing, outdoor activities. *Address:* Central Veterinary Laboratory, Ministry of Agriculture, Fisheries and Food, New Haw, Weybridge, Surrey KT15 3NB.

LITTLECHILD, Prof. Stephen Charles; Director General of Electricity Supply, since 1989; Professor of Commerce and Head of Department of Industrial Economics and Business Studies, University of Birmingham, since 1975 (on leave of absence); *b* 27 Aug. 1943; *s* of Sidney F. Littlechild and Joyce M. Littlechild (*née* Sharpe); *m* 1974, Kate Crombie (*d* 1982); two *s* one *d*. *Educ:* Wisbech Grammar Sch.; Univ. of Birmingham (BCom); Univ. of Texas (PhD). Temp. Asst Lectr in Ind. Econs, Univ. of Birmingham, 1964–65; Harkness Fellow, Stanford Univ., 1965–66; Northwestern Univ., 1966–68; Univ. of Texas at Austin, 1968–69; ATT Post-doctoral Fellow, UCLA and Northwestern Univ., 1969; Sen. Res. Lectr in Econs, Graduate Centre for Management Studies, Birmingham, 1970–72; Prof. of Applied Econs and Head of Econs, Econometrics, Statistics and Marketing Subject Gp, Aston Management Centre, 1972–75; Vis. Scholar, Dept of Econs, Univ. of California at Los Angeles, 1975; Vis. Prof., New York, Stanford and Chicago Univs, and Virginia Polytechnic, 1979–80. Member: Monopolies and Mergers Commn, 1983–89; Sec. of State for Energy's Adv. Council on R&D, 1987–89. *Publications:* Operational Research for Managers, 1977, 2nd edn (with M. F. Shutler) as Operations Research in Management, 1991; The Fallacy of the Mixed Economy, 1978, 2nd edn 1986; Elements of Telecommunications Economics, 1979; Energy Strategies for the UK, 1982; Regulation of British Telecommunications' Profitability, 1983; Economic Regulation of Privatised Water Authorities, 1986; over 50 articles in econs and ops res. jls. *Recreations:* football, genealogy. *Address:* Office of Electricity Regulation, Hagley House, Hagley Road, Birmingham B16 8QG. *T:* 0121–456 2100.

LITTLEJOHN, Alan Morrison; Director, Shipbuilders and Shiprepairers Association (formerly Shiprepairers and Shipbuilders Independent Association), 1977–90; Secretary General, UK Land and Hydrographic Survey Association Limited, 1980–90; retired; *b* 17 Oct. 1925; *s* of Frank Littlejohn and (Ethel) Lucy (*née* Main); *m* 1955, Joy Dorothy Margaret (*née* Till); one *d*. *Educ:* Dame Allan's Boys' Sch., Newcastle upon Tyne; King's Coll., Durham Univ. (BScAgric); Lincoln Coll. and Agricultural Economics Res. Inst., Oxford Univ. (BLitt, DipAgEcon). Asst Agric. Economist: King's Coll., Durham Univ., 1945–47; Wye Coll., London Univ., 1950–51; Agric. Chemical Div., Shell Internat. Chemical Co., London, 1951–67; Economist, Agric. Engineers Assoc., 1968–73; Dir Gen., Clay Pipe Develt Assoc., 1973–77; Dir, Assoc. of High Pressure Water Jetting Contractors, 1980–87. Chm., Catherine Place Personnel Services Ltd, 1981–89. Member: Chorleywood Parish Council, 1979–91 (Chm., 1985–87); (C) Three Rivers Dist Council, 1988– (Chm., Resources Cttee, 1990–91; Dep. Leader, 1990–91, Leader, 1991–, Cons. Gp; Leader, Council, 1992–94). *Recreations:* current affairs, gardening, photography. *Address:* 5 The Readings, Chorleywood, Herts WD3 5SY. *T:* Chorleywood (01923) 284420.

LITTLEJOHN, Bel; *see* Brown, C. E. M.

LITTLEJOHN, Doris; President, Industrial Tribunals (Scotland), since 1991; *b* 19 March 1935; *m* 1958, Robert White Littlejohn; three *d*. *Address:* 125 Henderson Street, Bridge of Allan, Stirlingshire. *T:* Bridge of Allan (01786) 832032.

LITTLEJOHN, William Hunter, RSA 1973 (ARSA 1966); Head of Fine Art Department, 1982–85, Head of Drawing and Painting Department, 1970–85, Gray's School of Art, Aberdeen, (Lecturer, 1966–70); *b* Arbroath, 16 April 1929; *s* of late William Littlejohn and Alice Morton King. *Educ:* Arbroath High Sch.; Dundee Coll. of Art (DA). National Service, RAF, 1951–53; taught Art at Arbroath High Sch. until 1966. *One man exhibitions:* The Scottish Gallery, Edinburgh, 1962, 1967, 1972, 1977, 1984, 1989; Bohun Gall., Henley-on-Thames, 1991. Exhibits in RA, RSA, SSA, etc. *Address:* 16 Colvill Place, Arbroath, Angus, Scotland DD11 1RB. *T:* Arbroath (01241) 874402.

LITTLEJOHN COOK, George Steveni; HM Diplomatic Service, retired; *b* 29 Oct. 1919; *s* of late William Littlejohn Cook, OBE, and Xenia Steveni, BEM; *m* 1st, 1949, Marguerite Teresa Bonnaud; one *d*; 2nd, 1964, Thereza Nunes Campos; one *s*. *Educ:* Wellington Coll.; Trinity Hall, Cambridge. Served with 2nd Bn Cameronians (Scottish Rifles), 1939–46, rank of Capt.; POW Germany; Political Intelligence Dept, Foreign Office, 1945–46. Entered Foreign Service, 1946; Third Secretary, Foreign Office, 1946–47; Second Secretary, Stockholm, 1947–49; Santiago, Chile, 1949–52; First Secretary, 1950; Foreign Office, 1952–53; Chargé d'Affaires, Phnom-Penh, 1953–55; Berne, 1956–58; Director of British Information Service in Brazil, 1959–64; Head of Information Depts, FO (and FCO), 1964–69; Counsellor and Consul-General, Bangkok, 1969–71. Underwriting Mem. of Lloyd's, 1957–. *Recreations:* painting, sailing, ski-ing.

Address: Quinta da Madrugada, Apartado 30, 8600 Lagos, Algarve, Portugal. *Clubs:* Brooks's, Royal Automobile.

LITTLER, Sir (James) Geoffrey, KCB 1985 (CB 1981); Senior Adviser to BZW Ltd, since 1993; Chairman: TR European Growth Trust plc, since 1990; Israel Fund plc, since 1994; *b* 18 May 1930; *s* of late James Edward Littler and Evelyn Mary Littler (*née* Taylor); *m* 1958, Shirley Marsh (*see* Shirley Littler); one *s*. *Educ:* Manchester Grammar Sch.; Corpus Christi Coll., Cambridge (MA; Hon. Fellow, 1994). Asst Principal, Colonial Office, 1952–54; transf. to Treasury, 1954; Principal 1957; Asst Sec. 1966; Under-Sec. 1972; Dep. Sec., 1977; Second Permanent Sec. (Overseas Finance), 1983–88. Chairman: EC Monetary Cttee Deputies, 1974–77; Working Party 3, OECD, 1985–88; EC Monetary Cttee, 1987–88. Chm., County NatWest Group Ltd, 1991–92; Director: NatWest Investment Bank, 1989–91; National Westminster Bank PLC, 1991–92; Maritime Transport Services Ltd, 1990–93. *Recreation:* music. *Club:* Reform.

LITTLER, Shirley, (Lady Littler); Chairman, Gaming Board for Great Britain, since 1992; *b* 8 June 1932; *d* of late Sir Percy William Marsh, CSI, CIE, and late Joan Mary Beecroft; *m* 1958, Sir (James) Geoffrey Littler, *qv*; one *s*. *Educ:* Headington Sch., Oxford; Girton Coll., Cambridge (MA). Assistant Principal, HM Treasury, 1953; Principal: HM Treasury, 1960; Dept of Trade and Industry, 1964; HM Treasury, 1966; Asst Secretary, National Board for Prices and Incomes, 1969; Secretary, V&G Tribunal, 1971; transf. to Home Office, 1972, Asst Under-Sec. of State, 1978–83. Joined IBA, 1983; Dep. Dir Gen., 1986–89; Dir Gen., 1990. Chm., Nat. Adv. Body for Health Depts' Confidential Enquiry into Stillbirths and Deaths in Infancy, 1992–. Trustee, Police Foundn, 1992–. *Recreations:* history, reading.

LITTLER, William Brian, CB 1959; MSc, PhD; *b* 8 May 1908; *s* of William Littler, Tarporley, Ches; *m* 1937, Pearl Davies (*d* 1990), Wrexham; three *d*. *Educ:* Grove Park, Wrexham; Manchester Univ.; BSc (1st Class), Chemistry, 1929; MSc, 1930; PhD, 1932; Beyer Fellow, 1930–31. Joined Res. Dept, Woolwich, 1933; loaned by Min. of Supply to Defence Res. Bd, Canada; Chief Supt, Cdn Armament Research and Devel. Establishment, Valcartier, Quebec, 1947–49; Supt of Propellants Research, Explosives Research and Devel. Estab., Waltham Abbey, 1949–50; in industry (Glaxo Laboratories Ltd, Ulverston), 1950–52; Dir of Ordnance Factories (Explosives), Min. of Supply, 1952–55; Principal Dir of Scientific Research (Defence), Ministry of Supply, 1955–56; Dir-Gen. of Scientific Research (Munitions), Ministry of Supply, 1956–60; Dep. Chief Scientist, Min. of Defence (Army), 1960–65; Minister, and Head of Defence R&D Staff, British Embassy, Washington, DC, 1965–69; Chemist-in-Charge, Quality Assurance Directorate (Materials), Royal Ordnance Factory, Bridgwater, 1969–72. *Publications:* Papers on Flame and Combustion in Proc. Royal Society and Jour. Chem. Soc. *Recreations:* drawing and painting; supporting Manchester United; watching golf on television. *Address:* Gloucester House, Lansdowne Road, Sevenoaks, Kent TN13 3XU. *T:* Sevenoaks (01732) 741488.

See also Philip Attenborough, G. M. Fallows.

LITTLETON, family name of **Baron Hatherton.**

LITTLEWOOD, Lady (Barbara); Consultant with Barlows, Solicitors, of Guildford; *b* 7 Feb. 1909; *d* of Dr Percival Langdon-Down, Teddington; *m* 1934, Sir Sydney Littlewood (*d* 1967); one *s*. *Educ:* Summerleigh Sch., Teddington; King's Coll., London, (BSc). Admitted solicitor, 1936. Pres. West Surrey Law Soc., 1952–53; Mem. Home Office Departmental Committees on: the Summary Trial of Minor Offences, 1954–55; Matrimonial Proceedings in Magistrates' Courts, 1958–59; Financial Limits prescribed for Maintenance Orders made in Magistrates' Courts, 1966–68. Pres., Nat. Fedn of Business and Professional Women's Clubs of Gt Brit. and N Ire., 1958–60; Pres. Internat. Fedn of Business and Professional Women, 1965–68; Lay Member, Press Council, 1960–74. JP Middx, 1950–. *Recreation:* occasional golf. *Address:* 26 St Margarets, London Road, Guildford, Surrey GU1 1TJ. *T:* Guildford (01483) 504348.

LITTLEWOOD, James, CB 1973; Director of Savings, Department for National Savings, 1972–81; *b* Royton, Lancashire, 21 Oct. 1922; *s* of late Thomas and Sarah Littlewood; *m* 1950, Barbara Shaw; two *s* one *d*. *Educ:* Manchester Grammar Sch.; St John's Coll., Cambridge (Scholar, MA). Army (Captain), 1942–46. HM Treasury, 1947–67; Civil Service Selection Bd, 1951–52; Sec. to Cttee on Administrative Tribunals and Enquiries, 1955–57; Colombo Plan Conf. Secretariat, 1955 and 1959; Dept for Nat. Savings, 1967–81. *Recreations:* golf, bridge. *Address:* 3 Smugglers Lane South, Highcliffe, Christchurch, Dorset BH23 4NF.

LITTLEWOOD, Joan (Maud); theatre artist. *Educ:* London. Dir, Theatre of Action, Manchester (street theatre), 1931–37; founder, Theatre Union, Manchester, introducing individual work system, 1937–39; freelance writer, 1939–45 (banned from BBC and ENSA for political opinions); founded Theatre Workshop with Gerry Raffles, 1945; touring in GB, Germany, Norway, Sweden with original works, 1945–53; moved to Theatre Royal, Stratford, London, with classics, 1953; invited to Theatre of the Nations, Paris, 1955, then yearly (Best Production of the Year three times); Centre Culturel, Hammamet, Tunisia, 1965–67; Image India, Calcutta, 1968; creation of Children's Environments, Bubble Cities, learn and play areas around Theatre Royal, Stratford, 1968–75. Left England to work in France, 1975; Seminar Relais Culturel, Aix-en-Provence, 1976. Productions include: Lysistrata, 1958 (Gold Medal, East Berlin, 1958; Olympic Award, Taormina, 1959), transferred to London from Stratford, 1960–61; Sparrers Can't Sing (film), 1962; Oh What a Lovely War (with Gerry Raffles and the Company), 1963. Mem., French Academy of Writers, 1964. SWET Special Award, 1983. Women of Achievement in the Arts Award, Arts Council of GB, 1993. Dr *hc* Univ. of the Air, 1977; DUniv Flinders, SA, 1995. Commandeur de l'Ordre des Arts et des Lettres (France), 1986. *Publications:* Milady Vine: biography of Philippe de Rothschild, 1984; Joan's Book (autobiog.), 1994. *Recreation:* theatre. *Address:* c/o Theatre Royal Stratford East, Gerry Raffles Square, Newham, E15 1BN.

LITTMAN, Mark; QC 1961; Director: Granada Group PLC, 1977–93; Burton Group plc, 1983–93; *b* 4 Sept. 1920; *s* of Jack and Lilian Littman; *m* 1965, Marguerite Lamkin, USA. *Educ:* Owen's Sch.; London Sch. of Economics; The Queen's Coll., Oxford. BScEcon. (first class hons) 1939; MA Oxon 1941. Served RN, Lieut, 1941–46. Called to Bar, Middle Temple, 1947, Bencher, 1970, Treas., 1988; practised, as Barrister-at-law, 1947–67 and 1979–; Member: General Council of the Bar, 1968–72; Senate of Inns of Court and the Bar, 1968. Dep. Chm., BSC, 1970–79. Mem. Royal Commn on Legal Services, 1976–79. Director: Rio Tinto-Zinc Corp. PLC, 1968–91; Commercial Union Assurance Co. Ltd, 1970–81; Amerada Hess Corp. (US), 1973–86; British Enkalon Ltd, 1976–80; Envirotech Corp. (US), 1974–78. Mem., Internat. Council for Commercial Arbitration, 1978–. Mem., Ct of Governors, LSE, 1980–. *Address:* 79 Chester Square, SW1W 9DU. *Clubs:* Garrick, Reform, United Oxford & Cambridge University, Royal Automobile; Century Association (New York).

LITTON, Peter Stafford; Under Secretary, Department of Education and Science, 1978–81; a General Commissioner of Income Tax, Epsom Division, since 1983; *b* 26 Oct. 1921; *s* of late Leonard Litton and Louisa (*née* Horn); *m* 1942, Josephine Peggy Bale; one *d*. *Educ:* Barnstaple Grammar School. Clerical Officer, Board of Education, 1938. Served in Royal Corps of Signals, 1941–46. Min. of Education, 1946; Principal Private Sec. to Secretary of State for Educn and Science, 1965–66. *Recreations:* gardening, armchair astronomy. *Address:* 14 Guillards Oak, Midhurst, W Sussex GU29 9JZ. *T:* Midhurst (01730) 815491.

LIU, Tsz-Ming, Benjamin; Hon. Mr Justice Liu; a Justice of Appeal, Hong Kong, since 1994; *b* 17 May 1931; *s* of late Dr Y. T. Liu and of Dorothy Mei-Kow (*née* Kwok); *m* 1954, Annemarie Marent; one *s* one *d*. *Educ:* Wah Yan College. Called to the Bar, Lincoln's Inn, 1957, Hong Kong, 1959; QC (Hong Kong) 1973; Judge of the District Court, Hong Kong, 1973–79; Judicial Comr, Supreme Ct, State of Brunei, 1978–89; a Judge of the High Court, Hong Kong, 1980–94. Panel Mem., Inland Revenue Bd of Review, Hong Kong, 1972; Chairman: Sub-Cttee on Bail in Criminal Proceedings, Law Reform Commn, 1985–89; Working Party on appropriate safeguards for execution of Anton Piller Orders, 1992–94. Pres., Hong Kong Local Judicial Officers' Assoc., 1992–95. *Address:* Supreme Court, Hong Kong. *T:* 28498539. *Clubs:* Hong Kong, Chinese, Hong Kong Country (Hong Kong).

LIVELY, Penelope Margaret, OBE 1989; writer; *b* 17 March 1933; *d* of Roger Low and Vera Greer; *m* 1957, Jack Lively; one *s* one *d*. *Educ:* St Anne's Coll., Oxford (BA Mod. History). Member: Soc. of Authors, 1973–; PEN, 1985–. FRSL 1985. *Publications: children's books:* Astercote, 1970; The Whispering Knights, 1971; The Wild Hunt of Hagworthy, 1971; The Driftway, 1972; The Ghost of Thomas Kempe, 1973 (Carnegie Medal); The House in Norham Gardens, 1974; Going Back, 1975; Boy Without a Name, 1975; A Stitch in Time, 1976 (Whitbread Award); The Stained Glass Window, 1976; Fanny's Sister, 1976; The Voyage of QV66, 1978; Fanny and the Monsters, 1979; Fanny and the Battle of Potter's Piece, 1980; The Revenge of Samuel Stokes, 1981; Fanny and the Monsters (three stories), 1983; Uninvited Ghosts and other stories, 1984; Dragon Trouble, 1984; Debbie and the Little Devil, 1987; A House Inside Out, 1987; The Cat, the Crow and the Banyan Tree, 1994; *non-fiction:* The Presence of the Past: an introduction to landscape history, 1976; *fiction:* The Road to Lichfield, 1976; Nothing Missing but the Samovar and other stories, 1978 (Southern Arts Literature Prize); Treasures of Time, 1979 (National Book Award); Judgement Day, 1980; Next to Nature, Art, 1982; Perfect Happiness, 1983; Corruption and other stories, 1984; According to Mark, 1984; Pack of Cards, collected short stories 1978–86, 1986; Moon Tiger, 1987 (Booker Prize); Passing On, 1989; City of the Mind, 1991; Cleopatra's Sister, 1993; Oleander, Jacaranda: a childhood perceived, 1994; television and radio scripts. *Recreations:* gardening, landscape history, talking and listening. *Address:* c/o Murray Pollinger, 222 Old Brompton Road, SW5 0BZ. *T:* 0171–373 4711.

LIVERMAN, John Gordon, CB 1973; OBE 1956; Deputy Secretary, Department of Energy, 1974–80; *b* London, 21 Oct. 1920; *s* of late George Gordon Liverman and Hadassah Liverman. *Educ:* St Paul's Sch.; Trinity Coll., Cambridge (BA). Served with RA, 1940–46. Civil servant in various government departments, 1947–80. Mem., British Nat. Oil Corp., 1976–80. *Address:* 24 Graces Mews, Camberwell, SE5 8JF. *T:* 0171–708 5017.

LIVERPOOL, 5th Earl of, *cr* 1905 (2nd creation); **Edward Peter Bertram Savile Foljambe;** Baron Hawkesbury, 1893; Viscount Hawkesbury, 1905; Joint Chairman, Melbourns Brewery Ltd, since 1975 (Managing Director, 1970–87); Chairman and Managing Director, Rutland Properties Ltd, since 1987 (Director, since 1986); *b* posthumously, 14 Nov. 1944; *s* of Captain Peter George William Savile Foljambe (killed in action, 1944) and of Elizabeth Joan (who *m* 1947, Major Andrew Antony Gibbs, MBE, TD), *d* of late Major Eric Charles Montagu Flint, DSO; *S* great uncle, 1969; *m* 1970, Lady Juliana Noel, *e d* of Earl of Gainsborough, *qv*; two *s*. *Educ:* Shrewsbury School; Univ. for Foreigners, Perugia. Director: Rutland Properties Ltd, 1985–; Hart Hambleton Plc, 1986–92; J. W. Cameron & Co., 1987–90; Hilstone Developments Ltd, 1987–91; Rutland Management Ltd, 1989–; Naylor Automatics Ltd, 1988–92. *Heir: s* Viscount Hawkesbury, *qv*. *Address:* House of Lords, SW1A 0PW. *Clubs:* Turf, Pratt's, Air Squadron.

LIVERPOOL, Archbishop of, (RC), and Metropolitan of Northern Province with Suffragan Sees, Hallam, Hexham, Lancaster, Leeds, Middlesbrough and Salford, since 1976; **Most Rev. Derek John Harford Worlock;** *b* 4 Feb. 1920; 2nd *s* of Captain Harford Worlock and Dora (*née* Hoblyn). *Educ:* St Edmund's Coll., Ware, Herts. Ordained RC Priest, 1944. Curate, Our Lady of Victories, Kensington, 1944–45; Private Secretary to Archbishop of Westminster, 1945–64; Rector and Rural Dean, Church of SS Mary and Michael, London, E1, 1964–65; Bishop of Portsmouth, 1965–76. Privy Chamberlain to Pope Pius XII, 1949–53; Domestic Prelate of the Pope, 1953–65; *Peritus* at Vatican Council II, 1963–65; Consultor to Council of Laity, 1967–76; Episcopal Secretary to RC Bishops' Conference, 1967–76, Vice-Pres., 1979–. Member: Synod Council, 1976–77; Holy See's Laity Council, 1977– (formerly Mem., Cttee for the Family); English delegate to Internat. Synod of Bishops, 1974, 1977, 1980, 1983, 1987 and 1990. Chm., Nat. Pastoral Congress, 1980. Freedom, City of Liverpool, 1995. Hon. Fellow, Portsmouth Polytechnic, 1988. Hon. LLD Liverpool, 1981; Hon. DTech Liverpool Polytechnic, 1987; Hon. DD Cambridge, 1990. Knight Commander of Holy Sepulchre of Jerusalem, 1966. *Publications:* Seek Ye First (compiler), 1949; Take One at Bedtime (anthology), 1962; English Bishops at the Council, 1965; Turn and Turn Again, 1971; Give Me Your Hand, 1977; Bread Upon the Waters, 1991; with Rt Rev. D. Sheppard: Better Together, 1988; With Christ in the Wilderness, 1990; With Hope in Our Hearts, 1994. *Address:* Archbishop's House, 87 Green Lane, Mossley Hill, Liverpool L18 2EP. *T:* 0151–722 2379.

LIVERPOOL, Bishop of, since 1975; **Rt. Rev. David Stuart Sheppard;** *b* 6 March 1929; *s* of late Stuart Morton Winter Sheppard, Solicitor, and Barbara Sheppard; *m* 1957, Grace Isaac; one *d*. *Educ:* Sherborne; Trinity Hall, Cambridge (MA; Hon. Fellow, 1983); Ridley Hall Theological Coll. Asst Curate, St Mary's, Islington, 1955–57; Warden, Mayflower Family Centre, Canning Town, E16, 1957–69; Bishop Suffragan of Woolwich, 1969–75. Chairman: Evangelical Urban Training Project, 1968–75; Peckham Settlement, 1969–75; Martin Luther King Foundn, 1970–75; Urban Ministry Project, 1970–75; Area Bd for Merseyside, MSC, 1978–85; Central Religious Adv. Cttee for BBC and IBA, 1989–93; Gen. Synod Bd for Social Responsibility, 1991–; Vice-Chm., Archbishop of Canterbury's Commn on Urban Priority Areas, 1983–85. Nat. Pres., Family Service Units, 1987–. Cricket: Cambridge Univ., 1950–52 (Captain 1952); Sussex, 1947–62 (Captain 1953); England (played 22 times) 1950–63 (Captain 1954). Freedom, City of Liverpool, 1995. Hon. LLD Liverpool, 1981; Hon. DTech Liverpool Polytechnic, 1987; Hon. DD Cambridge, 1991. *Publications:* Parson's Pitch, 1964; Built as a City, 1974; Bias to the Poor, 1983; The Other Britain (Richard Dimbleby Lecture), 1984; with Most Rev. D. Worlock: Better Together, 1988; With Christ in the Wilderness, 1990; With Hope in Our Hearts, 1994. *Recreations:* family, reading, music, painting, visiting gardens, reading Wisden. *Address:* Bishop's Lodge, Woolton Park, Woolton, Liverpool L25 6DT.

LIVERPOOL, Auxiliary Bishops of, (RC); *see* Malone, Rt Rev. Vincent; Rawsthorne, Rt Rev. John.

LIVERPOOL, Dean of; *see* Walters, Very Rev. R. D. C.

LIVERPOOL, Archdeacon of; *see* Metcalf, Ven. R. L.

LIVERPOOL-BANKSTOWN, Bishop of; *See* Smith, Rt Rev. R. G.

LIVESAY, Adm. Sir Michael (Howard), KCB 1989; Chief of Naval Personnel, Second Sea Lord and Admiral President, Royal Naval College, Greenwich, 1991–93; *b* 5 April 1936; *s* of William Lindsay Livesay and Margaret Eleanor Chapman Steel; *m* 1959, Sara House; two *d. Educ:* Acklam Hall Grammar Sch.; Britannia Royal Naval Coll. Joined RN, 1952; training appts, 1954–57; commnd 1957; qual. Aircraft Direction Specialist, 1959; Direction Officer, HMS Hermes, HMS Aisne, Fighter Direction Sch., and 893 Sqdn, 1959–66; i/c HMS Hubberston, 1966–68, HMS Plymouth, 1970–72; Captain Fishery Protection/Captain Mine Counter Measures, 1975–77; 1st CO HMS Invincible, 1979–82; Dir of Naval Warfare, 1982–84; Flag Officer Sea Training, 1984–85; ACNS, 1986–88; Flag Officer Scotland and NI, 1989–91. Director: Scottish Nuclear, 1993–; Inter Exec Edinburgh, 1994–. Comr, Northern Lighthouse Bd, 1994–. *Recreations:* sailing, ski-ing, fishing, golf. *Address:* c/o The Naval Secretary, Victory Building, HM Naval Base, Portsmouth PO1 3LS. *Clubs:* Army and Navy, Royal Navy of 1765 and 1785; Royal Yacht Squadron.

LIVESEY, Bernard Joseph Edward; QC 1990; a Recorder, since 1987; *b* 21 Feb. 1944; *s* of Joseph Augustine Livesey and Marie Gabrielle Livesey (*née* Caulfield); *m* 1971, Penelope Jean Harper; two *d. Educ:* Cardinal Vaughan Sch., London; Peterhouse, Cambridge (MA, LLB). Called to the Bar, Lincoln's Inn, 1969. Fellow, Internat. Acad. of Trial Lawyers, 1993. *Recreations:* music, gardening, ski-ing, bellringing. *Address:* 2 Crown Office Row, Temple, EC4Y 7HJ. *T:* 0171–797 8000.

LIVESEY, Ronald John Dearden, QC 1981; **His Honour Judge Livesey;** a Circuit Judge, since 1992; Deputy Senior Judge, Sovereign Base Areas, Cyprus, since 1983; *b* 11 Sept. 1935; *s* of John William and Una Florence Livesey; *m* 1965, Elizabeth Jane Coutts; one *s* one *d. Educ:* Malvern Coll.; Lincoln Coll., Oxford (MA). Called to the Bar, Lincoln's Inn, 1962, Bencher, 1989; a Recorder, 1981–92. *Recreation:* golf. *Address:* 46A Grosvenor Road, Birkdale, Southport PR8 2ET. *T:* Southport (01704) 560561. *Club:* Union (Southport).

LIVESLEY, Prof. Brian, JP; MD; FRCP; Professor in the Care of the Elderly, University of London at Charing Cross and Westminster Medical School, since 1988; Director-General, St John Ambulance, since 1994; (Assistant Director-General, 1993–94); *b* 31 Aug. 1936; *s* of late Thomas Clement Livesley and Stella Livesley; *m* 1st, 1963, Beryl Hulme (*d* 1966); one *s*; 2nd, 1979, Valerie Anne Nuttall; two *d. Educ:* King George V Grammar Sch., Southport; Leeds Univ. Med. Sch. (MB, ChB 1960); Univ. of London (MD 1979). MRCP 1971, FRCP 1989. DHMSA 1973. Hospital appointments: Leeds Gen. Infirmary, 1961–62; Dist and Univ. Hosps, Leeds, Manchester and Liverpool, 1963–68; Harvey Res. Fellow, KCH, 1969–72; Cons. Physician in Geriatric Medicine, Lambeth, Southwark and Lewisham HA, 1973–87. Clinical Examnr in Medicine, Univ. of London, 1980–94 (Sen. Examnr, 1990–94); Examiner: for Dip. in Geriatric Medicine, RCP, 1987–93; in Medicine, Soc. of Apothecaries, 1987–93; Mem., United Examng Bd for England and Scotland, 1993–. NW Thames Regl Advr on Medicine for the Elderly, 1990–; Chm., N Thames Regl Trng Commn, 1993–. Mem., Med. Commn on Accident Prevention, 1984–89 (Chm., Home and Family Safety Commn, 1988–89). Freeman, City of London, 1975. Liveryman, Soc. of Apothecaries (Yeoman, 1975; Mem. Ct of Assts, 1990–) JP SE London, 1983. KStJ 1994. *Publications:* monographs and investigations on scientific, historical and educnl problems of medicine in our ageing soc. *Recreations:* family, Christian culture study, encouraging people to think, scuba-diving. *Address:* Chelsea and Westminster Hospital, Fulham Road, SW10 9NH. *T:* 0181–746 8063, Fax: 0181–746 8183; 4 Berger Close, Petts Wood, Kent BR5 1HR. *T:* Farnborough (01689) 876694, *Fax:* (01689) 896979.

LIVINGS, Henry; *b* 20 Sept. 1929; *m* 1957, Judith Francis Carter; one *s* one *d. Educ:* Park View Primary Sch.; Stand Grammar Sch.; Liverpool Univ. Served in RAF. Joined Puritex, Leicester. Theatre Royal Leicester, then many Repertories; Theatre Workshop, 1956. 1st TV play, 1961; 1st stage play, 1961. *Publications:* contribs to Penguin New English Dramatists 5 and 6; Kelly's Eye and Other Plays, 1964; Eh?, 1965; Good Grief!, 1968; The Little Mrs Foster Show, 1969; Honour and Offer, 1969; Pongo Plays 1–6, 1971; This Jockey Drives Late Nights, 1972; The Ffinest Ffamily in the Land, 1973; Jonah, 1974; Six More Pongo Plays, 1975; That the Medals and the Baton be Put on View, 1975; Cinderella, 1976; Pennine Tales, 1983; Flying Eggs and Things, 1986; The Rough Side of the Boards, 1993; trans., Lorca, The Public, 1994. *Recreations:* dominoes, walking. *Address:* 49 Grains Road, Delph, Oldham, Lancs OL3 5DS. *T:* Saddleworth (014577) 70854. *Clubs:* Dobcross Band, Delph Band.

LIVINGSTON, Air Vice-Marshal Graham; consultant occupational health physician: *b* 2 Aug. 1928; *s* of late Neil Livingston and Margaret Anderson (*née* Graham); *m* 1970, Carol Judith Palmer; one *s* one *d* (and one *s* one *d* (and one *d* decd) of former marriage). *Educ:* Bo'ness Academy; Edinburgh Univ. (MB ChB 1951, DPH 1963); DIH (Conjoint) 1963; MFPHM (MFCM 1974); MFOM 1981. Joined RAF 1952; served N Ireland and Egypt, 1952–55; civilian GP and obst., 1956–57; rejoined RAF 1958; served Lindholme and Honington, 1958–62; post grad. study in public and indust. health, Edinburgh Univ., 1962–63; SMO, RAF Laarbruch, 1963–66; RAF Coll., Cranwell, 1966–70; served Cosford, Halton and Akrotiri, 1970–74; OC RAF Hosps, Cosford, 1974–76, Wegberg, 1976–79; Dep. Dir. Med. Personnel and Dep. Dir Med. Orgn, MoD, 1979–80; Dep. PMO, Strike Command, 1981–83; Principal Medical Officer: RAF Germany, 1983–84; RAF Support Comd, 1984–89; QHS 1985–89. Consultant in community medicine, 1984; Consultant Occupational Health Physician: NW Herts HA, 1989–94; Wycombe HA, 1991–94. Freeman, City of London, 1982. FIMgt (FBIM 1986). *Recreations:* golf, ski-ing, caravanning. *Address:* c/o Lloyds Bank, Cox's and King's Branch, PO Box 1190, 7 Pall Mall, SW1Y 5NA. *Clubs:* Royal Air Force; Ashridge Golf.

LIVINGSTON BOOTH, John Dick, OBE 1976; Chairman, Legislation Monitoring Service for Charities, 1981–91; Patron, International Standing Conference on Philanthropy, since 1987 (President, 1975–87); *b* 7 July 1918; *o s* of late Julian Livingston Booth and late Grace Marion (*née* Swainson); *m* 1st, 1941, Joan Ashley Tabrum (d 1976), *d* of Ashley Tabrum, OBE, LLM, MA; two *s* one *d*; 2nd, 1979, Audrey Betty Hope Harvey, PhD, AcDipEd (Psych), DipHEd, DipSoc, SRN, FRSH, MIHE, *d* of Sqdn Leader John James Haslett, RAF. *Educ:* Melbourne Church of England Grammar Sch.; Sidney Sussex Coll., Cambridge (MA). Served War, 1940–43; T/Captain RA; RWAFF; Instructor, 121 HAC OCTU RHA. Nigerian Administrative Service, 1943–57; Perm. Sec., Min. of Local Govt, Eastern Nigeria, 1956–57; Dir, Charities Aid Foundn, 1957–81. Member: Exec. Cttee, Nat. Council for Voluntary Organisations, 1974–81; Exec. Cttee, Christian Orgs Research and Adv. Trust, 1975–88; Develt and Stewardship Cttee, Central Bd of Finance, 1977–80. Mem. of Lloyd's, 1979–89. Trustee, Europhil Trust, 1987–90 (Chm., 1986–87). Lay Reader, Church of England, 1955–83. *Publications:* Directory of Grant-Making Trusts, 1968, 7th edn 1981; Trusts and Foundations in Europe, 1971; Report on Foundation Activity, 1977; Charity Statistics (annual), 1978–81; articles and booklets on charity. *Recreations:* home-making, travel, philately. *Address:* Mullions, Trulls Hatch, Argos Hill, Rotherfield, Crowborough, E Sussex TN6 3QL. *T:* Rotherfield (01892) 853205. *Clubs:* Garrick, Commonwealth Trust.

LIVINGSTONE, Prof. David Noel, PhD; FBA 1995; Professor of Geography, Queen's University of Belfast, since 1993; *b* 15 March 1953; *s* of Robert Livingstone and Winifred (*née* Turkington); *m* 1977, Frances Allyson Haugh; one *s* one *d. Educ:* Queen's Univ. of Belfast (BA; PhD; DipEd). Curator of Maps, 1984–89; Lectr, 1989–91, Reader, 1991–93, QUB. *Publications:* Nathaniel Southgate Shaler and the Culture of American Science, 1987; Darwin's Forgotten Defenders, 1987; The Preadamite Theory, 1992; The Geographical Tradition, 1992; (ed jtly) The Behavioural Environment, 1989. *Recreations:* music, painting, photography. *Address:* School of Geosciences, Queen's University of Belfast, Belfast BT7 1NN. *T:* Belfast (01232) 335145.

LIVINGSTONE, Ian Lang, OBE 1993; Chairman: Lanarkshire Health Board, since 1993 (Member, since 1989); Lanarkshire Development Agency, since 1991; *b* 23 Feb. 1938; *s* of John Lang Livingstone and Margaret Steele Livingstone (*née* Barbour); *m* 1967, Diane Hales; two *s. Educ:* Hamilton Acad.; Glasgow Univ. (BL). NP 1960. Qualified as solicitor, 1960; apprentice, Alex L. Wright & Co., Solicitors, 1957–60, legal asst, 1960–62; Ballantyne & Copland, Solicitors: Partner, 1962–70; Sen. Partner, 1970–86; Consultant, 1986–89; Chm. and Dir, Bowmere Properties Ltd, 1967–. Chm., Motherwell Coll. Bd, 1991–. Chm., Motherwell FC, 1975–88. *Recreations:* football, walking, travelling, music. *Address:* Roath Park, 223 Manse Road, Motherwell, Strathclyde ML1 2PY. *T:* Motherwell (01698) 253750.

LIVINGSTONE, Ken; MP (Lab) Brent East, since 1987; *b* 17 June 1945; *s* of Robert Moffat Livingstone and Ethel Ada Livingstone; *m* 1973, Christine Pamela Chapman (marr. diss. 1982). *Educ:* Tulse Hill Comprehensive Sch.; Philippa Fawcett Coll. of Educn (Teacher's Cert.). Technician, Chester Beatty Cancer Res. Inst., 1962–70. Joined Labour Party, 1969; Reg. Exec., Greater London Lab. Party, 1974–86; Lambeth Borough Council: Councillor, 1971–78; Vice-Chm., Housing Cttee, 1971–73; Camden Borough Council: Councillor, 1978–82; Chm., Housing Cttee, 1978–80; Greater London Council: Mem. for Norwood, 1973–77, for Hackney N, 1977–81, for Paddington, 1981–86; Lab. Transport spokesman, 1980–81; Leader of Council and of Lab. Gp, 1981–86. Mem., NEC, Labour Party, 1987–89. Contested (Lab) Hampstead, gen. elec., 1979. *Publications:* If voting changed anything they'd abolish it, 1987; Livingstone's Labour, 1989. *Recreations:* cinema, science fiction, gardening, natural history. *Address:* House of Commons, SW1A 0AA.

LIVSEY, Richard Arthur Lloyd, CBE 1994; *b* 2 May 1935; *s* of Arthur Norman Livsey and Lilian Maisie (*née* James); *m* 1964, Irene Martin Earsman; two *s* one *d. Educ:* Talgarth County Primary Sch.; Bedales Sch.; Seale-Hayne Agricl Coll.; Reading Univ. (MSc Agric.). Develt Officer, Agric. Div., ICI, 1961–67; Farm Manager, Blairdrummond, 1967–71; farmer at Llanon; Sen. Lectr in Farm Management, Welsh Agricl Coll., Aberystwyth, 1971–85. Joined Liberal party, 1960; contested (L): Perth and E Perth, 1970; Pembroke, 1979; Brecon and Radnor, 1983; MP (L 1985–88, Lib Dem 1988–92) Brecon and Radnor. Liberal Parly spokesman on agric., 1985–87; Alliance spokesman on the countryside and on agric. in Wales, and on Wales, 1987; Leader, Welsh Liberal Democrats and Parly Spokesman on Wales, 1988–92. *Recreations:* cricket, fishing.

LLANDAFF, Bishop of, since 1985; **Rt. Rev. Roy Thomas Davies;** *b* 31 Jan. 1934; *s* of Hubert and Dilys Davies; unmarried. *Educ:* St David's Coll., Lampeter (BA); Jesus Coll., Oxford (BLitt); St Stephen's House, Oxford. Asst Curate, St Paul's, Llanelli, 1959–64; Vicar of Llanafan, 1964–67; Chaplain to Anglican Students, University Coll. of Wales, Aberystwyth, 1967–73; Sec., Provincial Council for Mission and Unity of Church in Wales, 1973–79; Vicar of St David's, Carmarthen, 1979–83; Vicar of Llanegwad, 1983–85; Archdeacon of Carmarthen, 1982–85; Clerical Sec., Governing Body of Church in Wales, 1983–85. ChStJ 1986. *Recreations:* walking, reading. *Address:* Llys Esgob, Llandaff, Cardiff CF5 2YE. *T:* Cardiff (01222) 562400.

LLANDAFF, Dean of; *see* Rogers, Very Rev. J.

LLEWELLIN, Rt. Rev. John Richard Allan; *see* Dover, Bishop Suffragan of.

LLEWELLYN, Bryan Henry; Director, Granada Travel PLC, 1989–92; *s* of Nora and Charles Llewellyn; *m* 1983, Joanna (*née* Campbell); two *s. Educ:* Charterhouse; Clare Coll., Cambridge (BA). Commissioned, The Queen's, 1946. Research Asst, Dept of Estate Management, Cambridge, 1954; joined Fisons Ltd, 1955; Marketing Manager, Greaves & Thomas Ltd, 1960; Regional Marketing Controller, Thomson Regional Newspapers Ltd, 1962; Marketing Dir, TRN Ltd, 1966; Managing Director: Thomson Holidays Ltd, 1969; Thomson Travel Ltd, 1972 (Chm., 1977–78); Exec. Dir, Thomson Organisation Ltd, 1972–80; Man. Dir and Chief Exec., Thomson Publications Ltd, 1977–80; Man. Dir, The Kitchenware Merchants Ltd, 1985–88. Non-Exec. Dir, Orion Insurance Ltd, 1976–92.

LLEWELLYN, Prof. David Thomas; Professor of Money and Banking, and Chairman of the Banking Centre, Loughborough University, since 1976; Public Interest Director, Personal Investment Authority, since 1994; *b* 3 March 1943; *s* of Alfred George Llewellyn and Elsie Alexandria Frith; *m* 1970, Wendy Elizabeth James; two *s. Educ:* William Ellis Grammar Sch., London; London Sch. of Econs and Pol Science (BSc Econ). FCIB. Economist: Unilever NV, Rotterdam, 1964; HM Treasury, London, 1965–67; Lectr in Econs, Nottingham Univ., 1967–73; Economist, IMF, Washington, 1973–76. Consultant Economist to Harlow Butler Ueda, 1981–; Mem., London Bd of Dirs, Halifax Building Soc., 1988–93; at various times Consultant to World Bank, Building Societies Assoc., bldg socs and banks in UK and overseas. Member: Bank of England Panel of Academic Consultants; Internat. Adv. Bd, Italian Bankers' Assoc., 1994–; Exec. Bd, European Financial Management Assoc., 1994–. TV and radio broadcasts on financial issues. FRSA. *Publications:* International Financial Integration, 1980; Framework of UK Monetary Policy, 1984; The Evolution of the British Financial System, 1985; Prudential Regulation and Supervision of Financial Institutions, 1986; Reflections on Money, 1989; (ed) Recent Developments in International Monetary Economics, 1991; (ed) Surveys in Monetary Economics, vols 1 and 2, 1991; Competition or Credit Controls?, 1991; articles in academic and professional jls and books on monetary policy and instns, and on internat. finance. *Recreations:* DIY, culinary arts, travel, boating. *Address:* 8 Landmere Lane, Ruddington, Notts NG11 6ND. *T:* Nottingham (0115) 921 6071.

LLEWELLYN, David Walter, CBE 1983; Director, Walter Llewellyn & Sons Ltd, and other Companies in the Llewellyn Group, since 1953; *b* 13 Jan. 1930; *s* of late Eric Gilbert and Florence May Llewellyn; *m* 1st, 1955, Josephine Margaret Buxton (marr. diss. 1985); three *s*; 2nd, 1986, Tessa Caroline Sandwith. *Educ:* Radley College. FCIOB. Commissioned Royal Engineers, 1952. Industrial Adviser to Minister of Housing and Local Govt, 1967–68; Mem., Housing Corp., 1975–77; Pres., Joinery and Timber Contractors' Assoc., 1976–77; Chm., Nat. Contractors' Gp of Nat. Fedn of Building Trades Employers (now Building Employers Confedn), 1977; Chm., Building Regulations Adv. Cttee, 1977–85 (Mem. 1966–74); Dep. Chm., Nat. Building Agency, 1977–82 (Dir. 1968–82). Pres., CIOB, 1986–87. Master, Worshipful Co. of Tin Plate Workers alias Wireworkers, 1985. Governor, St Andrew's Sch., Eastbourne, 1966–78; Trustee, Queen

Alexandra Cottage Homes, Eastbourne, 1973–94. Provincial Grand Master, Sussex, United Grand Lodge of Freemasons of England, 1989–. *Recreation:* the use, restoration and preservation of historic vehicles. *Address:* (office) 16/20 South Street, Eastbourne BN21 4XE; (home) Cooper's Cottage, Chiddingly, near Lewes, East Sussex BN8 6HD. *Clubs:* Reform; Devonshire (Eastbourne), Eastbourne.

LLEWELLYN, Dr Donald Rees, CBE 1992; JP; Foundation Vice-Chancellor, University of Waikato, 1964–85; *b* 20 Nov. 1919; *s* of late R. G. Llewellyn, Dursley; *m* 1943, Ruth Marian, *d* of late G. E. Blandford, Dursley; one *s* one *d*. *Educ:* Dursley Grammar Sch.; Univ. of Birmingham, 1939–41, BSc 1st cl. hons Chem. 1941, DSc 1957; Oxford 1941–44, DPhil 1943. Research Fellow, Cambridge Univ., 1944–46; Lectr in Chemistry, UC of N Wales, 1946–49; ICI Research Fellow, UCL, 1949–52; Lectr in Chemistry, UCL, 1952–57; Prof. of Chemistry and Dir of Labs, Univ. of Auckland, 1957–64; Asst Vice-Chancellor, Univ. of Auckland, 1962–64. Mem., NZ Atomic Energy Cttee, 1958–85. Pres., NZ Inst. Chemistry, 1967 and 1988 (Vice-Pres., 1965–67, 1986–88). Member: Council, Hamilton Teachers Coll., 1965–85; Council, Waikato Tech. Inst., 1968–85; Pres., NZ Nat. Fieldays Soc., 1969–75 and 1978–81 (Life Mem., 1981); Patron, Waikato Med. Res. Foundn, 1990–. Paul Harris Fellow, Rotary Foundn. JP Waikato, 1971. Freeman, City of Hamilton, 1985. CChem, FRSC (FRIC 1952); FNZIC 1957 (Hon. FNZIC 1985); FRSA 1960. Hon. Dr Waikato, 1985. Waikato Business Pioneer, 1990; Thomson Medal, Royal Soc. of NZ, 1994. *Publications:* numerous papers on application of stable isotopes in Jl Chem. Soc. and others. *Recreations:* badminton, showjumping (FEI Judge), photography, travel. *Address:* RD4, Hamilton, New Zealand. *T:* (7) 8569172. *Club:* Hamilton (NZ).

LLEWELLYN, Sir Henry Morton, (Sir Harry Llewellyn), 3rd Bt *cr* 1922; Kt 1977; CBE 1953 (OBE (mil.) 1944); MA; late Warwicks Yeomanry; President, Whitbread Wales Ltd, since 1972 (Chairman, 1958–72); Director, Chepstow Racecourse Co. Ltd; Vice-Chairman, Civic Trust for Wales, since 1960; *b* 18 July 1911; 2nd *s* of Sir David Llewellyn, 1st Bt, and Magdalene (*d* 1966), *d* of Dr H. Hiley Harries, DD, Porthcawl; *S* brother, 1978; *m* 1944, Hon. Christine Saumarez, 2nd *d* of 5th Baron de Saumarez; two *s* one *d*. *Educ:* Oundle; Trinity Coll., Cambridge (MA). Joined Warwickshire Yeo., Sept. 1939; Iraq-Syria Campaign, 1941; Middle East Staff Coll., Haifa, 1942; 8th Army from El Alamein to Tunis as GSO II Ops (Liaison) (despatches), 1942–43; Sicily, Italy (despatches), 1943; MA Chief of Staff HQ 21 Army Gp, 1943; NW Europe GSO I Ops (Liaison), 1943–44; OBE 1944; US Legion of Merit, 1945; Hon. Lt Col. Riding Ego, came 2nd in Grand National 'chase, 1936, 4th, 1937. Nat. Hunt Cttee, 1946– (Steward, 1948–50); The Jockey Club, 1969–. Jt Master Monmouthshire Hounds, 1952–57, 1963–65. Captain winning Brit. Olympic Show-Jumping Team, Helsinki (riding Foxhunter), 1952; Chm., Brit. Show Jumping Assoc., 1967–69; Pres./Chm., British Equestrian Fedn, 1976–81; Pres., Royal Internat. Horse Show, 1989–91. Chm., Welsh Sports Council, 1971–81; Mem., GB Sports Council, 1971–81. President: Inst. of Directors (Wales), 1963–65; Inst. of Marketing, Wales, 1965–67. Chm., C. L. Clay & Co. Ltd (Coal Exporters), 1936–47. Chairman: Wales Bd, Nationwide Building Soc., 1972–86; Eagle Star Assurance Co. (Wales Bd), 1963–81; formerly Director: North's Navigation Colliery Ltd; TWW Ltd; Rhigos Colliery Ltd; S Wales Reg. Bd, Lloyds Bank, 1963–82. Member: Wales Tourist Board, 1969–75; WWF Council, 1986–; Pres., Royal Welsh Agricl Show, 1985. Hon. Deleg., FEI, 1983. DL Monmouthshire, 1952, JP 1954–68, High Sheriff 1966. Royal Humane Soc. Medal for Life-saving, 1956; FEI Gold Medal, 1962. *Publications:* Foxhunter in Pictures, 1952; Passports to Life, 1980. *Recreations:* hunting, all sports, wild life photography. *Heir: s* David St Vincent Llewellyn [*b* 2 April 1946; *m* 1980, Vanessa Mary Theresa (marr. diss. 1987), *y d* of Lieut-Comdr Peregrine and Lady Miriam Hubbard; two *d*. *Educ:* Eton]. *Address:* Ty'r Nant, Llanarth, Raglan, Gwent NP5 2AR. *Clubs:* Cavalry and Guards; Shikar.

LLEWELLYN, Rear-Adm. Jack Rowbottom, CB 1974; Assistant Controller of the Navy, 1972–74; retired; *b* 14 Nov. 1919; *s* of Ernest and Harriet Llewellyn, Ashton under Lyne, Lancs; *m* 1944, Joan Isabel, *d* of Charles and Hilda Phillips, Yelverton, Devon; one *s*. *Educ:* Purley County Sch. Entered RN, 1938; RNEC, Keyham, 1939. Served War of 1939–45: HMS Bermuda, 1942; RNC, Greenwich, 1943; HMS Illustrious, 1945. Engr in Chief's Dept, Admlty, 1947, HMS Sluys, 1949; HMS Thunderer, 1951; HMS Diamond, 1953; Comdr, 1953; Asst Engr in Chief, on loan to Royal Canadian Navy, 1954; in charge Admty Fuel Experimental Station, Haslar, 1958; HMS Victorious, 1960; Asst Dir, Marine Engrg, MoD (N), 1963; Captain, 1963; in command, HMS Fisgard, 1966; Dep. Dir, Warship Design, MoD (N), 1969; Rear-Adm., 1972. *Recreations:* travel, gardening. *Address:* 3 Jubilee Terrace, Chichester, W Sussex PO19 1XL. *T:* Chichester (01243) 780180.

LLEWELLYN, His Honour John Desmond S.; *see* Seys-Llewellyn.

LLEWELLYN, Rev. Richard Morgan, CB 1992; OBE 1979 (MBE 1976); Chaplain, Christ College, Brecon, since 1995; *b* 22 Aug. 1937; *s* of Griffith Robert Poyntz Llewellyn and Bridget Margaret Lester Llewellyn (*née* Karslake); *m* 1964, Elizabeth Lamond (Polly) Sobey; three *s* one *d* (and one *d* decd). *Educ:* Haileybury; Imperial Service College; rcds, psc; Salisbury and Wells Theol Coll. Enlisted Royal Welch Fusiliers (Nat. Service), 1956; active service, Malaya and Cyprus, 1957–59; Instructor, Army Outward Bound Sch., 1962–63; Staff Coll., 1970; MA to CGS, 1971–72; Brigade Major, 1974–76; CO, 1st Bn RWF, 1976–79; Directing Staff, RCDS, 1979–81; Comdr, Gurkha Field Force, 1981–84; Dir, Army Staff Duties, 1985–87; GOC Wales, 1987–90; C of S, HQ UKLF, 1990–91; retired in rank of Maj.-Gen. Ordained deacon, 1993, priest, 1994; Minor Canon, Brecon Cathedral and Asst Curate, Brecon with Battle and Llandew, 1993–95. Regtl Col, Gurkha Transport Regt, subseq. Queen's Own Gurka Transport Regt, 1984–94; Col, RWF, 1990–. Chm., Army Mountaineering Assoc., 1988–91; Council Mem., Soldiers' and Airmen's Scripture Readers Assoc. FIMgt. *Recreations:* most outdoor pursuits, gardening, reading. *Address:* Christ College, Brecon, Powys LD3 8AG. *Club:* Army and Navy.

LLEWELLYN, Timothy David; Director, Henry Moore Foundation, since 1994; *b* 30 May 1947; *s* of Graham David Llewellyn and Dorothy Mary Driver; *m* 1st, 1970, Irene Sigrid Mercy Henriksen (marr. diss.); one *s*; 2nd, 1978, Elizabeth Hammond. *Educ:* St Dunstan's College; Magdalene College, Cambridge. Sotheby's: Old Master Painting Dept, 1969; Director, 1974; Man. Dir, 1984–91; Chief Exec., 1991–92; Dep. Chm., Europe, 1992–94. Chm., Friends of the Courtauld Inst. of Art, 1986–. Internat. Council Mem., Harvard Univ. Center for Italian Renaissance Studies, Villa I Tatti, 1990–. Trustee: Elgar Foundn, 1992–; Bd, Courtauld Inst. of Art, 1992–; Chm., Henry Moore Sculpture Trust, 1994–. Fellow, Ateneo Veneto, 1992–. Order of Cultural Merit, Min. of Culture and Fine Arts, Poland, 1986. *Recreations:* music, fishing, travel. *Address:* 3 Cranley Mansion, 160 Gloucester Road, SW7 4QF. *T:* 0171–373 2333, *Fax:* 0171–244 0126; Henry Moore Foundation, Dane Tree House, Perry Green, Much Hadham, Herts SG10 6EE. *T:* Much Hadham (01279) 843333, *Fax:* (01279) 843647. *Club:* Brooks's.

LLEWELLYN, Rt. Rev. William Somers; first Suffragan Bishop of Lynn, 1963–72; *b* 16 Aug. 1907; *s* of Owen John and Elizabeth Llewellyn; *m* 1947, Innis Mary, *d* of Major Arthur Dorrien Smith, Tresco Abbey, Isles of Scilly; three *s*. *Educ:* Eton; Balliol and Wycliffe Hall, Oxford. BA 1929; diploma in Theology (with dist.) 1934; MA 1937. Priest, 1936; Curate of Chiswick, 1935–37; Vicar of Badminton, with Acton Turville, 1937–49. CF 1940–46; served with Royal Gloucestershire Hussars in Egypt and Western Desert, and as Senior Chaplain with 8th Army HQ, Canal Area and East Africa; Vicar of Tetbury with Beverston, 1949–61; Rural Dean of Tetbury, 1955–61; Archdeacon of Lynn, 1961–72; Priest-in-charge of Boxwell with Leighterton, 1973–77; Asst Curate, Tetbury with Beverston, 1977–93; Hon. Asst Bishop, dio. of Gloucester, 1973–94. *Address:* Glebe House, Leighterton, Tetbury, Glos GL8 8UW. *T:* Leighterton (01666) 890236.

LLEWELLYN-JONES, Frank; *see* Jones, F. Ll.

LLEWELLYN JONES, His Honour Ilston Percival; a Circuit Judge, 1978–88; *b* 15 June 1916; *s* of Rev. L. Cyril F. Jones and Gertrude Anne Jones; *m* 1963, Mary Evelyn; one *s* (by a former *m*). *Educ:* Baswich House and Fonthill prep. schs; St John's Sch., Leatherhead. Admitted Solicitor, Nov. 1938; practised privately until served Sussex Yeomanry RA and 23rd Field Regt RA (commnd), 1939–42; Solicitors Dept, Metropolitan Police, New Scotland Yard, 1942–48; private practice, Torquay, 1948–52; Devon County Prosecuting Solicitor, 1952–56; Clerk to N Devon Justices, 1956–62; private practice, 1962–77; a Recorder of the Crown Court, 1972–78. *Recreations:* golf, swimming, learning a language; formerly Rugby football, tennis, squash, cross country running. *Address:* Calle Toni Llido, 3–4° pta. 11, 03730 Javea (Alicante), Spain. *T:* (96) 5795584.

LLEWELLYN SMITH, Prof. Christopher Hubert, DPhil; FRS 1984; Director-General, CERN (European Organisation for Nuclear Research), since 1994; Professor of Theoretical Physics, University of Oxford, since 1987 (on leave of absence); Fellow of St John's College, Oxford, since 1974; *b* 19 Nov. 1942; *s* of late J. C. and of M. E. F. Llewellyn Smith; *m* 1966, Virginia Grey; one *s* one *d*. *Educ:* Wellington College; New College, Oxford (Scholar). BA 1964, DPhil 1967; full Blue for cross-country running, 1961–63, Captain 1963; full Blue for Athletics, 1963. Royal Society Exchange Fellow, Lebedev Inst., Moscow, 1967; Fellow, CERN, Geneva, 1968; Research Associate, SLAC, Stanford, Calif, 1970; Staff Mem., CERN, 1972; Oxford University: Lectr, 1974; Reader in Theoretical Physics, 1980; Chm. of Physics, 1987–92. Mem. of various policy and programme cttees for CERN (Chm., Scientific Policy Cttee, 1990–92), SLAC, Deutsches Elektronen-Synchrotron Hamburg and SERC, 1972–92; Mem., ACOST, 1989–92. Maxwell Prize and Medal, Inst. of Physics, 1979. *Publications:* numerous articles in Nuclear Physics, Physics Letters, Phys. Rev., etc. *Recreations:* books, travel, opera. *Address:* CERN, 1211 Geneva 23, Switzerland.

See also E. M. Llewellyn-Smith, M. J. Llewellyn Smith.

LLEWELLYN-SMITH, Elizabeth Marion, CB 1985; Principal, St Hilda's College Oxford, since 1990; *b* 17 Aug. 1934; *d* of late John Clare Llewellyn Smith and of Margaret Emily Frances (*née* Crawford). *Educ:* Christ's Hospital, Hertford; Girton Coll., Cambridge (MA). Joined Board of Trade, 1956; various appointments in Board of Trade, Cabinet Office, Dept of Trade and Industry, Dept of Prices and Consumer Protection, 1956–76; Royal Coll. of Defence Studies, 1977; Under Sec., Companies Div., Dept of Trade, later DTI, 1978–82; Dep. Dir Gen., OFT, 1982–87; Dep. Sec., DTI, 1987–90. UK Dir, EIB, 1987–90. Member: Hebdomadal Council, Oxford Univ., 1993–; Res. Ethical Cttee, HSE, 1993–. Trustee, Jacqueline du Pré Meml Fund, 1991–. Mem., Governing Body, Rugby Sch., 1991–. *Recreations:* travel, books, entertaining. *Address:* The Principal's Lodgings, St Hilda's College, Oxford OX4 1DY. *T:* Oxford (01865) 276814; 1 Charlwood Road, Putney, SW15 1PJ. *T:* 0181–789 1572.

See also C. H. Llewellyn Smith, M. J. Llewellyn Smith

LLEWELLYN SMITH, Michael John, CMG 1989; HM Diplomatic Service; Ambassador to Poland, since 1991; *b* 25 April 1939; *s* of late J. C. Llewellyn Smith and of M. E. F. Crawford; *m* 1967, Colette Gaulier; one *s* one *d*. *Educ:* Wellington Coll.; New Coll., Oxford; St Antony's Coll., Oxford. BA, DPhil. FCO, 1970; Cultural Attaché, Moscow, 1973; Paris, 1976; Royal Coll. of Defence Studies, 1979; Counsellor and Consul Gen., Athens, 1980–83; Hd of Western European Dept, FCO, 1984–85; Hd of Soviet Dept, FCO, 1985–87; Minister, Paris, 1988–91. *Publications:* The Great Island: a study of Crete, 1965, 2nd edn 1973; Ionian Vision: Greece in Asia Minor 1919–22, 1973. *Recreations:* music, walking, wine. *Address:* c/o Foreign and Commonwealth Office, King Charles Street, SW1A 2AH. *Club:* United Oxford & Cambridge University.

See also C. H. Llewellyn Smith, E. M. Llewellyn-Smith.

LLEWELYN, Sir John Michael D. V.; *see* Venables-Llewelyn.

LLEWELYN-DAVIES, family name of **Baroness Llewelyn-Davies of Hastoe.**

LLEWELYN-DAVIES OF HASTOE, Baroness *cr* 1967 (Life Peer), of Hastoe; **Patricia Llewelyn-Davies,** PC 1975; Principal Deputy Chairman of Committees and Chairman, Select Committee on European Communities, House of Lords, 1982–87; *b* 16 July 1915; *d* of Charles Percy Parry and Sarah Gertrude Parry (*née* Hamilton); *m* 1943, Richard Llewelyn-Davies (later Baron Llewelyn-Davies) (*d* 1981); three *d*. *Educ:* Liverpool Coll., Huyton; Girton Coll., Cambridge (Hon. Fellow, 1979). Civil Servant, 1940–51 (Min. of War Transp., FO, Air Min., CRO). Contested (Lab) Wolverhampton S-W, 1951, Wandsworth Cent., 1955, 1959. A Baroness-in-Waiting (Govt Whip), 1969–70; Dep. Opposition Chief Whip, House of Lords, 1972–73; Opposition Chief Whip, 1973–74, 1979–82; Captain of the Gentlemen at Arms (Govt Chief Whip), 1974–79. Hon. Sec., Lab. Parly Assoc., 1960–69. Chm., Women's National Cancer Control Campaign, 1972–75; Member: Bd of Govs, Hosp. for Sick Children, Gt Ormond Street, 1955–67 (Chm. Bd, 1967–69); Court, Univ. of Sussex, 1967–69. Dir, Africa Educnl Trust, 1960–69. Co.-Chm., Women's Nat. Commn, 1976–79. *Address:* Flat 15, 9–11 Belsize Grove, NW3 4UU. *T:* 0171–586 4060.

LLOWARCH, Martin Edge, FCA; Chairman (part-time): Transport Development Group plc, since 1992; Johnson & Firth Brown plc, since 1993; Deputy Chairman, Abbey National plc, since 1994 (Director, since 1989); non-executive Director, Hickson International plc, since 1992; *b* 28 Dec. 1935; *s* of Wilfred and Olga Llowarch; *m* 1965, Ann Marion Buchanan; one *s* two *d*. *Educ:* Stowe Sch., Buckingham. Coopers & Lybrand, 1962–68; British Steel Corporation, subseq. British Steel plc: Hd of Special Projects, 1968; Man. Dir (S Africa), 1971; Dir, Finance and Admin (Internat.), 1973; Finance Dir, Tubes Div., 1975; Finance Controller, Strip Products Gp, 1980; Man. Dir, Finance, 1983; Mem., Main Bd, 1984–91; Dep. Chief Exec., 1986; Chief Exec., 1986–91. Mem., Accounting Standards Cttee, 1985–87. FCA 1973. CIMgt (CBIM 1985). *Recreations:* most forms of sport, music, gardening, reading.

LLOYD, family name of **Baron Lloyd of Berwick.**

LLOYD OF BERWICK, Baron *cr* 1993 (Life Peer), of Ludlay in the County of East Sussex; **Anthony John Leslie Lloyd,** Kt 1978; PC 1984; DL; a Lord of Appeal in Ordinary, since 1993; Chairman, Security Commission, since 1992 (Vice-Chairman, 1985–92); *b* 9 May 1929; *o s* of late Edward John Boydell Lloyd and Leslie Johnston Fleming; *m* 1960, Jane Helen Violet, *er d* of C. W. Shelford, Chailey Place, Lewes, Sussex. *Educ:* Eton (Schol.); Trinity Coll., Cambridge (Maj. Schol.). 1st cl. Classical Tripos Pt I;

1st cl. with distinction Law Tripos Pt II. National Service, 1st Bn Coldstream Guards, 1948. Montague Butler Prize, 1950; Sir William Browne Medal, 1951. Choate Fellow, Harvard, 1952; Fellow of Peterhouse, 1953 (Hon. Fellow, 1981); Fellow of Eton, 1974–86. Called to Bar, Inner Temple, 1955; QC 1967; Bencher, 1976. Attorney-General to HRH The Prince of Wales, 1969–77; Judge of the High Court of Justice, Queen's Bench Div., 1978–84; a Lord Justice of Appeal, 1984–93. Vice-Chm., Parole Bd, 1984–85 (Mem., 1983–); Mem., Criminal Law Revision Cttee, 1981–. Chm., Sussex Assoc. for Rehabilitation of Offenders, 1985–91; Vice-Pres., British Maritime Law Assoc., 1983–. Mem., Top Salaries Review Body, 1971–77. Trustee: Smiths Charity, 1971–; Glyndebourne Arts Trust, 1973–94 (Chm., 1975–94); Dir, RAM, 1979– (Hon. FRAM 1985); Chm., Chichester Diocesan Bd of Finance, and Mem., Bishop's Council, 1972–76. Hon. Mem., Salters' Co., 1988. DL E Sussex, 1983. *Recreations:* music, carpentry; formerly running (ran for Cambridge in Mile, White City, 1950). *Address:* 68 Strand-on-the-Green, Chiswick, W4 3PF. *T:* 0181–994 7790; Ludlay, Berwick, East Sussex BN26 6TE. *T:* Alfriston (01323) 870204. *Club:* Brooks's.

LLOYD, Rev. (Albert) Kingsley; President of the Conference of the Methodist Church, 1964; *b* 2 Nov. 1903; *s* of Rev. Albert Lloyd; *m* 1926, Ida Marian (*née* Cartledge) (*d* 1969); one *s* one *d*; 2nd, 1972, Katharine G., *d* of late A. G. L. Ives, CVO. *Educ:* Kingswood Sch., Bath; Richmond Coll., Surrey (University of London). Methodist Circuit Minister: London, Bedford, Cambridge, 1926–52; Chm., London N Dist, 1951–53. Secretary, Dept of Connexional Funds of the Methodist Church, 1952–69. Wesley Historical Soc. Lectr, 1968. *Recreation:* gardening. *Address:* 13 High Street, Orwell, Royston, Herts SG8 5QN.

LLOYD, Anthony Joseph; MP (Lab) Stretford, since 1983; *b* 25 Feb. 1950; *s* of late Sydney and Ciceley Beaumont Lloyd; *m* 1974, Judith Ann Tear; three *d* one *s*. *Educ:* Stretford Grammar Sch.; Nottingham Univ. (BSc Hons); Manchester Business Sch. (DipBA). Lectr, Dept of Business and Administration, Salford Univ., 1979–83. *Address:* House of Commons, SW1A 0AA.

LLOYD, Ven. (Bertram) Trevor; Archdeacon of Barnstaple, since 1989; *b* 15 Feb. 1938; *s* of Bertram and Gladys Lloyd; *m* 1962, Margaret Eldey; two *s* one *d* (and one *s* decd). *Educ:* Highgate School; Hertford Coll., Oxford (schol; BA History 1960, Theology 1962; MA 1962); Clifton Theol Coll., Bristol. Curate, Christ Church, Barnet, 1964–69; Vicar, Holy Trinity, Wealdstone, 1970–84; Priest-in-charge, St Michael and All Angels, Harrow Weald, 1980–84; Vicar, Trinity St Michael, Harrow, 1984–89; Area Dean of Harrow, 1977–82; Prebendary of Exeter Cathedral, 1991–. Member: C of E Liturgical Commn, 1981–; Gen. Synod of C of E, 1990–; Central Bd of Finance, C of E, 1990–; Council for the Care of Churches, 1992–. *Publications:* Informal Liturgy, 1972; Institutions and Inductions, 1973; The Agape, 1973; Liturgy and Death, 1974; Ministry and Death, 1974; Lay Presidency at the Eucharist?, 1977; Evangelicals, Obedience and Change, 1977; (ed) Anglican Worship Today, 1980; Ceremonial in Worship, 1981; Introducing Liturgical Change, 1984; Celebrating Lent, Holy Week and Easter, 1985; Celebrating the Agape today, 1986; The Future of Anglican Worship, 1987. *Recreations:* hill walking, photography, swimming, caravanning, making things from wood. *Address:* Stage Cross, Whitemoor Hill, Bishop's Tawton, Barnstaple, Devon EX32 0BE. *T:* Barnstaple (01271) 75475, *Fax:* (01271) 77934.

LLOYD, Dr Brian Beynon, CBE 1983; Director, International Nutrition Foundation, since 1990; Chairman of Directors, Oxford Gallery, since 1967; Chairman, Trumedia Study Oxford Ltd, since 1985; *b* 23 Sept. 1920; *s* of David John Lloyd, MA Oxon and Olwen (*née* Beynon); *m* 1949, Reinhild Johanna Engeroff; four *s* three *d* (inc. twin *s* and twin *d*). *Educ:* Newport High Sch.; Winchester Coll. (Schol.); Balliol Coll., Oxford (Domus and Frazer Schol.). Special Certif. for BA (War) Degree in Chem., 1940; took degrees BA and MA, 1946; Theodore Williams Schol. and cl. I in Physiology, 1948; DSc 1969. Joined Oxford Nutrition Survey after registration as conscientious objector, 1941; Pres., Jun. Common Room, Balliol, 1941–42; Chm., Undergraduate Rep. Coun., 1942; Biochemist: SHAEF Nutrition Survey Team, Leiden, 1945; Nutrition Survey Group, Düsseldorf, 1946. Fellow of Magdalen by exam. in Physiology, 1948–52, by special election, 1952–70; Senior Tutor, 1963–64; Vice-Pres., 1967 and 1968; Emeritus Fellow, 1970; Chemist, Laboratory of Human Nutrition, later Univ. Lectr in Physiology, Univ. of Oxford, 1948–70; Senior Proctor, 1960–61; Dir, Oxford Polytechnic, 1970–80 (Hon. Fellow, 1991; opened Lloyd Bldg, 1984). Chairman: CNAA Health and Med. Services Bd, 1975–80; Health Educn Council, 1979–82 (Mem., 1975–82); Mem., Adv. Council on Misuse of Drugs, 1978–81. Vis. Physiologist, New York, 1963. Pres., Section I, 1964–65, Section X, 1980, British Assoc. for the Advancement of Science. Chm. of Govs, Oxford Coll. of Technology, 1963–69. Chairman: Oxford-Bonn Soc., 1973–81; Oxford Management Club, 1979–80; Pullen's Lane Assoc., 1985–; Pres., Oxford Polytechnic Assoc., 1984–90 (Hon. Mem., 1992). *Publications:* Gas Analysis Apparatus, 1960; (jt ed) The Regulation of Human Respiration, 1962; Cerebrospinal Fluid and the Regulation of Respiration, 1965; (jt ed) Sinclair (biog.), 1990; articles in physiological and biochemical jls. *Recreations:* Klavarskribo, Correggio, round tables, the analysis of athletic records, slide rules, ready reckoners. *Address:* High Wall, Pullen's Lane, Oxford OX3 0BX. *T:* Oxford (01865) 63353.

See also Sir J. P. D. Lloyd.

LLOYD, Charles William, JP; MA; Master, Dulwich College, 1967–75; *b* 23 Sept. 1915; *s* of late Charles Lloyd and late Frances Ellen Lloyd, London; *m* 1939, Doris Ethel, *d* of late David Baker, Eastbourne; one *s* one *d* (and one *d* decd). *Educ:* St Olave's Sch.; Emmanuel Coll., Cambridge. Asst Master Buckhurst Hill Sch., 1938–40. War Service with RA, 1940–46 (despatches). Asst Master Gresham's Sch., Holt, 1946–51; Headmaster, Hutton Gram. Sch., near Preston, 1951–63; Headmaster, Alleyn's Sch., London, 1963–66. Trustee, Nat. Maritime Museum, 1974–86. JP Inner London, 1970. *Recreations:* reading, travel, golf. *Address:* 16 Tavistock, Devonshire Place, Eastbourne, E Sussex BN21 4AG. *T:* Eastbourne (01323) 720577.

LLOYD, Christopher, VMH 1979; MA, BSc (Hort.); writer on horticulture; regular gardening correspondent, Country Life, since 1963; *b* 2 March 1921; *s* of late Nathaniel Lloyd and Daisy (*née* Field). *Educ:* Wellesley House, Broadstairs, Kent; Rugby Sch.; King's Coll., Cambridge (MA Mod Langs); Wye Coll., Univ of London (BSc Hort.). Asst Lectr in Decorative Horticulture, Wye Coll., 1950–54. Then returned to family home at Great Dixter and started Nursery in clematis and uncommon plants. *Publications:* The Mixed Border, 1957; Clematis, 1965, rev. edn (with Tom Bennett), 1989; Shrubs and Trees for Small Gardens, 1965; Hardy Perennials, 1967; Gardening on Chalk and Lime, 1969; The Well-Tempered Garden, 1970, rev. edn 1985; Foliage Plants, 1973, rev. edn 1985; The Adventurous Gardener, 1983; The Well-Chosen Garden, 1984; The Year at Great Dixter, 1987; (with Richard Bird) The Cottage Garden, 1990; (with Graham Rice) Garden Flowers from Seed, 1991; Christopher Lloyd's Flower Garden, 1993; In My Garden, 1993; Other People's Gardens, 1995; regular gardening contributor to The Guardian, American Horticulture, Country Life. *Recreations:* walking, entertaining and cooking for friends. *Address:* Great Dixter, Northiam, Rye, East Sussex TN31 6PH. *T:* Northiam (01797) 253107.

LLOYD, Christopher Hamilton; Surveyor of The Queen's Pictures, since 1988; *b* 30 June 1945; *s* of Rev. Hamilton Lloyd and Suzanne Lloyd (*née* Moon); *m* 1967, Christine Joan Frances Newth; four *s*. *Educ:* Marlborough Coll.; Christ Church, Oxford (BA 1967; MA 1971; BLitt 1972). Asst Curator of Pictures, Christ Church, Oxford, 1967–68; Dept of Western Art, Ashmolean Museum, 1968–88. Fellow of Villa I Tatti, Florence (Harvard Univ.), 1972–73; Vis. Res. Curator of Early Italian Painting, Art Inst., Chicago, 1980–81. *Publications:* Art and its Images, 1975; Catalogue of Earlier Italian Paintings in the Ashmolean Museum, 1977; Camille Pissarro (cat. of retr. exhibn, 1980–81); (with Richard Brettell) Catalogue of Drawings by Camille Pissarro in the Ashmolean Museum, 1980; Camille Pissarro, 1981; (with Richard Thomson) Impressionist Drawings from British Collections, 1986; (introd. and ed) Catalogue of Old Master Drawings at Holkham Hall, by A. E. Popham, 1986; (ed) Studies on Camille Pissarro, 1986; (with Simon Thurley) Henry VIII—images of a Tudor King (cat. of exhibn, Hampton Court Palace, 1990–91); The Queen's Pictures: Royal collectors through the centuries (cat. of exhibn, Nat. Gall., 1991–92); The Royal Collection: a thematic exploration of the paintings in the collection of HM the Queen, 1992; (contrib.) Alfred Sisley, ed M. A. Stevens, 1992; Early Italian paintings in the Art Institute of Chicago (cat. of collection), 1993; Gainsborough and Reynolds: contrasts in Royal patronage (cat. of exhibn, The Queen's Gall., 1994); The Queen's Pictures: Old Masters from the Royal Collections (exhibn cat., 1994); reviews and contribs to learned jls. *Recreations:* books, theatre, cinema, music, real tennis. *Address:* Apartment 29B, St James's Palace, SW1A 1BG. *T:* 0171–839 5902. *Club:* Garrick.

LLOYD, Clive Hubert, AO 1985; CBE 1992; OJ 1985; OB 1986; Executive Promotion Officer, Project Fullemploy, since 1987; *b* Georgetown, Guyana, 31 Aug. 1944; *er s* of late Arthur Christopher Lloyd and of Sylvia Thelma Lloyd; *m* 1971, Waveney Benjamin; one *s* two *d*. *Educ:* Chatham High Sch., Georgetown (schol.). Clerk, Georgetown Hosp., 1960–66. Began cricket career, Demarara CC, Georgetown, 1959; début for Guyana, 1963; first Test Match, 1966; played for Haslingden, Lancs League, 1967; Lancashire County Cricket Club: Mem., 1968–86, capped 1969; Captain, 1981–84 and 1986; Captain, W1 cricket team, 1974–78 and 1979–85; World Series Cricket in Australia, 1977–79. Made first 1st class century, 1966; passed total of 25,000 runs (incl. 69 centuries), 1981; captained WI teams which won World Cup, 1975, 1979; Manager, WI cricket tour in Australia, 1988–89. First Pres., WI Players' Assoc., 1973. Former Dir, Red Rose Radio. Mem. (part-time), Commn for Racial Equality, 1987–90. Hon. Fellow: Manchester Polytechnic, 1986; Lancashire Polytechnic, 1986. Hon. MA: Manchester; Hull; Hon. Dr of Letters, Univ. of West Indies, Mona. Golden Arrow of Achievement (Guyana), 1975; Cacique Crown of Honours, Order of Rorima (Guyana), 1985. *Publications:* (with Tony Cozier) Living for Cricket, 1980; *relevant publication:* Clive Lloyd, by Trevor McDonald, 1985. *Address:* c/o Harefield, Harefield Drive, Wilmslow, Cheshire SK9 1NJ.

LLOYD, Air Vice-Marshal Darrell Clive Arthur, CB 1980; Commander, Northern Maritime Air Region, 1981–83; retired; *b* 5 Nov. 1928; *s* of Cecil James Lloyd and Doris Frances Lloyd; *m* 1957, Pamela (*née* Woodside); two *s*. *Educ:* Stowe; RAF Coll., Cranwell. Commnd 1950; ADC to C-in-C, ME Air Force, 1955–57; Instr, Central Flying Sch., 1958–60; Personal Air Sec. to Sec. of State for Air, 1961–63; CO, RAF Bruggen, 1968–70; RCDS, 1972; Dir of Defence Policy, UK Strategy Div., 1973–75; Dep. Comdr, RAF Germany, 1976–78; ACAS (Ops), 1978–81. FBIM 1972. *Recreations:* travel, golf, painting. *Address:* c/o Lloyds Bank, 7 Pall Mall, SW1Y 5NA. *Clubs:* Royal Air Force; Royal Cinque Ports Golf (Deal); Tandridge Golf (Oxted).

LLOYD, David Alan; Chairman, David Lloyd Leisure, since 1981; *b* 3 Jan. 1948; *s* of Dennis and Doris Lloyd; *m* 1972, Veronica Jardine; one *s* two *d*. *Educ:* Southend High Sch. Tennis player; mem., British Davis Cup team, 1973–82; ranked in Britain's top ten, 1970–81; semi-finalist, Wimbledon Championship doubles, 1973; British Wightman Cup coach, 1981; non-playing Captain, British Davis Cup team, 1995–. Freeman, City of London, 1985. Entrepreneur of the Year, PLC Awards, 1994. *Publications:* Improve Your Tennis Skills, 1989; Successful Tennis, 1989; Winning Tennis Fitness, 1991. *Recreations:* golf, swimming, tennis, football.*Address:* David Lloyd Leisure, Southall Lane, Hounslow, Middx TW5 9PE. *T:* 0181–573 9378. *Clubs:* All England Lawn Tennis; Wisley Golf.

LLOYD, David Bernard; Secretary, Royal College of Physicians, since 1986; *b* 14 Jan. 1938; *s* of George Edwards and Lilian Catherine Lloyd; *m* 1968, Christine Vass; three *d*. *Educ:* Presteigne Grammar Sch.; Hereford High Sch. FCCA. Early posts in local govt, UCL, UCH Med. Sch.; Royal College of Obstetricians and Gynaecologists: Accountant, 1971–76; Secretary, 1976–82; Secretary, Nat. Inst. of Agricultural Engineering, 1982–86. Chm., Management Cttee, St Albans CAB, 1990–94 (Mem., 1985–). Mem., Harpenden Town Council, 1992–. Vice Chm., Harpenden Trust, 1994–. Governor: Sir John Lawes Sen. Sch., 1986–87 (also Chm.); Roundwood Jun. Sch., 1980–89 (Chm., 1985–88). *Recreations:* local charity, garden. *Address:* 16 Hartwell Gardens, Harpenden, Herts AL5 2RW. *T:* Harpenden (01582) 761292.

LLOYD, David Graham, PhD; FRS 1992; FRSNZ; Professor of Plant Science, University of Canterbury, Christchurch, New Zealand, 1986–93, now Emeritus; *m* 1st, 1973, Jacqueline Mary Renouf (marr. diss. 1985); two adopted *s* one adopted *d*; 2nd, 1994, Linda Eileen Newstrom. *Educ:* Univ. of Canterbury, NZ (BSc 1st Cl. Hons 1959); Harvard Univ. (PhD 1964). University of Canterbury: Postdoctorate Fellow, 1964–67; Lectr, 1967–71; Sen. Lectr, 1971–75; Reader, 1975–86. FRSNZ 1984. Foreign Mem., Amer. Acad. of Arts and Scis, 1993. *Publications:* numerous res. papers. *Recreations:* reading, hiking.

LLOYD, David Mark; Senior Commissioning Editor, News and Current Affairs, Channel Four Television, since 1988; *b* 3 Feb. 1945; *s* of late Maurice Edward and Roma Doreen Lloyd; *m* 1982, Jana Tomas; one *s* one *d* and one step *s*. *Educ:* Felsted Sch.; Brentwood Sch.; Brasenose Coll., Oxford (MA 1967). Joined BBC as Gen. Trainee, 1967: Dep. Ed., Nationwide, 1978; Editor: Money Prog., 1980; Newsnight, 1982; Sixty Minutes, 1983; Breakfast Time, 1984. Shell Film and TV Award, 1982. *Recreations:* cricket, golf, music, travel. *Address:* Channel Four Television Co. Ltd, 124 Horseferry Road, SW1P 2TX. *T:* 0171–396 4444.

LLOYD, Rev. David Richard, (Rev. Denys Lloyd); Assistant Priest, St Mark's, Ipswich, since 1994; *b* 28 June 1939; *s* of Richard Norman Lloyd and Grace Enid Lloyd. *Educ:* Brighton College (George Long Scholar); Trinity Hall, Cambridge (Exhibitioner; BA 1961, MA 1965); Leeds Univ. (MA 1969). Asst Curate, St Martin's, Rough Hills, Wolverhampton, 1963–67; professed as Mem. of Community of Resurrection, 1969 (taking name Denys); Tutor, Coll. of Resurrection, 1970–75, Vice-Principal, 1975–84; Principal, 1984–90; Associate Lecturer, Dept of Theology and Religious Studies, Univ. of Leeds, 1972–90. Received into Roman Catholic Church at Quarr Abbey, 1990; Missionary Inst., London, 1993–94; ordained priest, 1994. *Publications:* contribs to theolog. jls. *Address:* St Mark's Presbytery, 180 Hawthorn Drive, Ipswich, Suffolk IP2 0QQ.

LLOYD, His Honour Denis Thelwall; a Circuit Judge, 1972–94; *b* 3 Jan. 1924; *s* of late Col Glyn Lloyd, DSO, FRCVS, Barrister-at-Law and Olga Victoria Lloyd (*née* Roberts); *m* 1st, 1950, Margaret Sheila (*d* 1976), *d* of Bernard Bushell, Wirral, Ches; one *s* two *d*; 2nd, 1983, Ann, *d* of John and Georgia Cunningham, Montana and Hawaii, USA. *Educ:*

Wellington College. Enlisted KRRC, 1942; commnd KRRC Dec. 1942; Central Mediterranean Force, (Italy, S France, Greece) 1943–45; attached 1st York and Lancaster Regt and then joined Parachute Regt, 1944 (wounded); Palestine, 1945–46; GSO3 (ops) HQ British Troops Austria, 1946; Staff Captain British Mil. Mission to Czechoslovakia, 1947. Called to the Bar, Gray's Inn, 1949; joined NE Circuit, 1950; Asst Recorder, Leeds, 1961–67; Recorder of Pontefract, 1971; Dep. Chm., WR Yorks QS, 1968–71; Sen. Resident Judge, Knightsbridge Crown Court, 1988–94. Dep. Chm., Agricultural Land Tribunal, Yorks and Lancs, 1968–71; Legal Chm., Mental Health Review Tribunal, 1983–86. Contested (L): York, 1964; Hallam Div. of Sheffield, 1966. Czech War Cross, 1946. *Recreations:* gardening, travel. *Address:* Flat 5, 37 Cadogan Square, SW1X 0HU. *T:* 071–235 7439.

LLOYD, Rev. Denys; *see* Lloyd, Rev. David Richard.

LLOYD, Eve, (Lady Lloyd); *see* Pollard, E.

LLOYD, Frances Mary, (Mrs James Lloyd); *see* Line, F. M.

LLOYD, Frederick John, CBE 1977; FIA; Chairman, Road Transport Industry Training Board, 1978–83; *b* 22 Jan. 1913; *m* 1942, Catherine Johnson (*née* Parker); one *s* one *d*. *Educ:* Ackworth Sch., Yorks; Liverpool Univ. (BSc). FIA 1947; FIS 1949; FCIT 1968. War Service, Operational Research, Bomber Comd, 1942–45. Royal Insurance Co., 1933–47; London Passenger Transport Bd, 1947–69: Staff Admin Officer, 1952; Divl Supt (South), 1957; Chief Operating Manager (Central Buses), 1961; Chief Commercial and Planning Officer, 1965–69; Dir Gen., West Midlands Passenger Transport Exec., 1969–78. *Publications:* contribs to actuarial and transport jls. *Recreations:* golf, gardening. *Address:* 8 Cliveden Coppice, Sutton Coldfield, West Midlands B74 2RG. *T:* 0121–308 5683. *Clubs:* Birmingham Rotary; Whittington Heath Golf (Lichfield, Staffs).

LLOYD, Prof. Geoffrey Ernest Richard, PhD; FBA 1983; Professor of Ancient Philosophy and Science, University of Cambridge, since 1983; Master of Darwin College, Cambridge, since 1989; *b* 25 Jan. 1933; *s* of William Ernest Lloyd and Olive Irene Neville Lloyd; *m* 1956, Janet Elizabeth Lloyd; three *s*. *Educ:* Charterhouse; King's Coll., Cambridge. BA 1954, MA 1958, PhD 1958. Cambridge University: Asst Lectr in Classics, 1965–67; Lectr, 1967–74; Reader in Ancient Philosophy and Science, 1974–83; Fellow, 1957–89 (Hon. Fellow, 1990), and Sen. Tutor, 1969–73, King's Coll. Bonsall Prof., Stanford Univ., 1981; Sather Prof., Berkeley, 1983–84; A. D. White Prof.-at-large, Cornell Univ., 1990–. Chm., E Asian Hist. of Sci. Trust, 1992–. Fellow, Japan Soc. for the Promotion of Science, 1981. Sarton Medal, History of Science Soc., USA, 1987. *Publications:* Polarity and Analogy, 1966; Aristotle: the growth and structure of his thought, 1968; Early Greek Science: Thales to Aristotle, 1970; Greek Science after Aristotle, 1973; (ed) Hippocratic Writings, 1978; (ed) Aristotle on Mind and the Senses, 1978; Magic, Reason and Experience, 1979; Science, Folklore and Ideology, 1983; Science and Morality in Greco-Roman Antiquity, 1985; The Revolutions of Wisdom, 1987; Demystifying Mentalities, 1990; Methods and Problems in Greek Science, 1991; contribs to classical and philosophical jls. *Recreation:* travel. *Address:* 2 Prospect Row, Cambridge CB1 1DU; Darwin College, Cambridge CB3 9EU.

LLOYD, (George) Peter, CMG 1965; CVO 1983; Governor, Cayman Islands, 1982–87, retired; *b* 23 Sept. 1926; *er s* of late Sir Thomas Ingram Kynaston Lloyd, GCMG, KCB; *m* 1957, Margaret Harvey; two *s* one *d*. *Educ:* Stowe Sch.; King's Coll., Cambridge. Lieut, KRRC, 1945–48; ADC to Governor of Kenya, 1948; Cambridge, 1948–51 (MA; athletics blue); District Officer, Kenya, 1951–60; Principal, Colonial Office, 1960–61; Colonial Secretary, Seychelles, 1961–66; Chief Sec., Fiji, 1966–70; Defence Sec., Hong Kong, 1971–74; Dep. Governor, Bermuda, 1974–81. Chm., Bermuda Fest., 1987 ; Trustee, Bermuda Maritime Mus., 1987–. *Address:* Watch house, 13 Fort Hamilton Drive, Pembroke HM 19, Bermuda.

LLOYD, George Walter Selwyn; composer and conductor; *b* 28 June 1913; *s* of William Alexander Charles Lloyd and Constance Priestley Rawson; *m* 1937, Nancy Kathleen Juvet. *Educ:* privately, and with Albert Sammons for violin, Harry Farjeon for composition. Works composed and conducted: Symphony No 1, Bournemouth, 1933; Symphony No 2, Eastbourne, 1935; opera Iernin, Lyceum, London, 1935; Symphony No 3, BBC Symph. Orch., 1935; composed 2nd opera The Serf, perf. Convent Garden, 1938; during 1939–45 war served in Royal Marines Band aboard HMS Trinidad, severely shell-shocked 1942, whilst on Arctic convoy; composed opera John Scoman, 1st perf. Bristol, 1951; due to poor health lived in Dorset growing carnations and mushrooms, only composing intermittently; health improved; subseq. composed many more symphonies, concertos (Symphonies No 11 and 12 commissioned and recorded by Albany Symph. Orch, NY; first perf. of No 11, 1986, of No 12, 1990); numerous recordings. Hon. DMus Salford, 1992. *Publications:* The Vigil of Venus, 1981; A Miniature Tryptich, 1981; Royal Parks, 1985; Diversions on a Bass Theme, 1986; Aubade, 1987; The Forest of Arden, 1988; English Heritage, 1990; A Symphonic Mass, 1993; Floating Cloud, 1993. *Recreation:* reading. *Address:* 199 Clarence Gate Gardens, Glentworth Street, NW1 6AU. *T:* 0171–262 7969.

LLOYD, Graham; *see* Lloyd, J. G.

LLOYD, Very Rev. Henry Morgan, DSO 1941; OBE 1959; MA; *b* 9 June 1911; *y s* of late Rev. David Lloyd, Weston-super-Mare, Somerset; *m* 1962, Rachel Katharine, *d* of late J. R. Wharton, Haffield, nr Ledbury; one *d*. *Educ:* Canford Sch.; Oriel Coll., Oxford; Cuddesdon Theological Coll. Deacon, 1935; priest, 1936; Curate of Hendon Parish Church, Middlesex, 1935–40. Served War as Chaplain RNVR, 1940–45. Principal of Old Rectory Coll., Hawarden, 1946–48; Secretary of Central Advisory Council of Training for the Ministry, 1948–50; Dean of Gibraltar, 1950–60; Dean of Truro and Rector of St Mary, Truro, 1960–81; Dean Emeritus, 1981. Hon. Citizen of the City of Truro, 1978. *Recreations:* walking, reading. *Address:* 3 Hill House, The Avenue, Sherborne, Dorset DT9 3AJ. *T:* Sherborne (01935) 812037. *Club:* Commonwealth Trust (Fellow).

LLOYD, Humphrey John; QC 1979; **His Honour Judge Humphrey Lloyd;** a Circuit Judge (Official Referee), since 1993; *b* 16 Nov. 1939; *s* of Rees Lewis Lloyd of the Inner Temple, barrister-at-law, and Dorothy Margaret Ferry (*née* Gibson); *m* 1969, Ann Findlay; one *s* one *d*. *Educ:* Westminster; Trinity Coll., Dublin (BA (Mod), LLB; MA). Called to the Bar, Inner Temple, 1963, Bencher, 1985. A Recorder, 1990–93. Pres., Soc. of Construction Law, 1985–88. Hon. Senior Vis. Fellow, QMC, 1987. Editor-in-chief: Building Law Reports, 1977–93 (Consultant Editor, 1993–); The Internat. Construction Law Rev., 1983–; Consultant Editor, Emden's Construction Law, 1993–. *Publications:* (ed) The Liability of Contractors, 1986; (contrib.) Halsbury's Laws of England, 4th edn, 1992. *Address:* St Dunstan's House, 133–137 Fetter Lane, EC4A 1HD. *Club:* Reform.

LLOYD, Sir Ian (Stewart), Kt 1986; *b* 30 May 1921; *s* of late Walter John Lloyd and Euphemia Craig Lloyd; *m* 1951, Frances Dorward Addison, *d* of late Hon. W. Addison, CMG, OBE, MC, DCM; three *s*. *Educ:* Michaelhouse; University of the Witwatersrand; King's Coll., Cambridge. President, Cambridge Union, and Leader, Cambridge tour of USA, 1947; MA 1951; MSc 1952. Econ. Adviser, Central Mining and Investment Corporation, 1949–52; Member, SA Board of Trade and Industries, 1952–55; Director, Acton Soc. Trust, 1956; Dir of Res., 1956–64, Economic Advr, 1956–83, British and Commonwealth Shipping. Chairman, UK Cttee and Vice-Chairman, International Exec., International Cargo Handling Co-ordination Assoc., 1961–64. MP (C): Portsmouth, Langstone, 1964–74; Havant and Waterloo, 1974–83; Havant, 1983–92. Chairman: Cons. Parly Shipping and Shipbuilding Cttee, 1974–77; Select Cttee on Sci. Sub-Cttee, 1975–77; Select Cttee on Sci. Sub-Cttee on Technological Innovation, 1977–79; Select Cttee on Energy, 1979–89; All-Party Cttee on Information Technology, 1979–87; Pres., Parly and Scientific Cttee, 1990–92 (Vice-Pres., 1983–87; Vice-Chm., 1988–90); Chm. Bd, Parly Office of Science and Technology. Member, UK Delegation, Council of Europe, Western European Union, 1968–72; UK rep., Internat. Parly Conf., Bucharest, 1975; Leader: UK Delegn, OECD Conf. on Energy, 1981; Parly and Scientific Cttee delegn to China, 1991. Member of Council: Save British Sci.; Sci. Policy Support Gp. Trustee: Kasanka Trust; New Era Schs Trust. *Publications:* Rolls-Royce, 3 vols, 1978; contribs to various journals on economics, politics and information technology. *Recreations:* yachting, ski-ing, good music. *Clubs:* Army and Navy, Royal Yacht Squadron.

LLOYD, Illtyd Rhys; HM Chief Inspector of Schools (Wales), 1982–90, retired; *b* 13 Aug. 1929; *s* of John and Melvina Lloyd; *m* 1955, Julia Lewis; one *s* one *d*. *Educ:* Port Talbot (Glan-Afan) County Grammar Sch.; Swansea UC (Hon. Fellow, Univ. of Wales, 1987). BSc, MSc; DipStat, DipEd. Commnd Educn Br., RAF, 1951–54 (Flt Lieut). Second Maths Master, Howardian High Sch. for Boys, Cardiff, 1954–57; Hd of Maths Dept, Pembroke Grammar Sch., 1957–59; Dep. Headmaster, Howardian High Sch., 1959–63; Welsh Office: HM Inspector of Schs, 1964–70; Staff Inspector (Secondary Educn), 1971–82. Chm., Educn Resources Centre, Aberystwyth Univ., 1991–; Vice-Chm., S Glam FHSA, 1993– (Mem., 1990–); Member: Indep. Schs Tribunal Educn Panel, 1990–; Council, Baptist Union of Wales, 1990– (Hon. Treas., 1992–); Council, Cardiff Theol Coll., 1990–; Council, Council for Educn in World Citizenship–Cymru, 1990–; Gov., Swansea Inst. of Higher Educn, 1990–. Hon. Mem., Gorsedd of Bards, 1990. *Recreation:* walking. *Address:* 134 Lake Road East, Roath Park, Cardiff CF2 5NQ. *T:* Cardiff (01222) 755296.

LLOYD, James Monteith, CD 1979; CMG 1961; Deputy Chairman, Industrial Disputes Tribunal, Jamaica, 1976–78; *b* 24 Nov. 1911; *s* of late Jethro and Frances Lloyd; *m* 1936, Mavis Anita Frankson; two *s* two *d*. *Educ:* Wolmer's High Sch., Jamaica. Called to Bar, Lincoln's Inn, 1948. Jamaica: entered Public Service as Asst, Registrar-General's Dept, 1931 (2nd Class Clerk, 1939, 1st Class Clerk, 1943, Asst Registrar-General, 1947); Asst Secretary, Secretariat, 1950; Principal Asst Secretary, Secretariat, 1953 (seconded to Grenada on special duty, Dec. 1955–May 1956); Permanent Secretary, Jamaica, 1956; Administrator, Grenada, 1957–62; Permanent Secretary, Jamaica, 1962–72; Chm., Ombudsman Working Party, Jamaica, 1972; retired from Civil Service, 1975. Chief Comr, Scouts, Jamaica, 1973–78. Coronation Medal, 1953; Jamaica Independence Medal, 1962. *Recreations:* cricket, tennis, golf. *Clubs:* Jamaica; Kingston CC; YMCA.

LLOYD, (John) Graham; consultant, since 1994; Director of Property Services, Commission for the New Towns, 1992–94; *b* Watford, 18 Feb. 1938; *s* of late Richard and Edith Lloyd; *m* 1st, 1960, Ann (*née* Plater) (marr. diss. 1989); three *s*; 2nd, 1989, Monica (*née* Barlow). *Educ:* City of London Sch.; College of Estate Management, London Univ. (BSc Estate Management). FRICS. In private practice, London and Leamington Spa, 1959–75. Commission for the New Towns: Commercial and Industrial Manager, 1975–78, Manager, 1978–81, Hemel Hempstead; Exec. Officer/Commercial Surveyor, Corby, 1981–91; Head of Estate Management Services, 1991–92. *Recreations:* soccer, motor racing, jazz and popular music, gardening. *Address:* 4 Fairway, Kibworth Beauchamp, Leics LE8 0LB.

LLOYD, John Nicol Fortune; journalist; Moscow Correspondent, Financial Times, since 1991; *b* 15 April 1946; *s* of Joan Adam Fortune and Christopher Lloyd; *m* 1983, Marcia Levy; one *s*. *Educ:* Waid Comprehensive School; Edinburgh Univ. (MA Hons). Editor, Time Out, 1972–73; Reporter, London Programme, 1974–76; Producer, Weekend World, 1976–77; industrial reporter, labour corresp., industrial and labour editor, Financial Times, 1977–86; Editor, New Statesman, 1986–87; with Financial Times, 1987–. Sen. Associate Fellow, Kennedy Sch., Harvard Univ., 1995. Journalist of the Year, Granada Awards, 1984; Specialist Writer of the Year, IPC Awards, 1985. *Publications:* (with Ian Benson) The Politics of Industrial Change, 1982; (with Martin Adeney) The Miners' Strike: loss without limit, 1986; (with Charles Leadbeater) In Search of Work, 1987; (contrib.) Counterblasts, 1989. *Recreations:* opera, hill walking, squash. *Address:* 14 Kutuzovsky Prospekt, Moscow, Russia. *T:* Moscow 2302267.

LLOYD, Sir (John) Peter (Daniel), Kt 1971; Chancellor, University of Tasmania, 1982–85; *b* 30 Aug. 1915; *s* of late David John Lloyd; *m* 1947, Gwendolen, *d* of late William Nassau Molesworth; two *s* four *d*. *Educ:* Rossall Sch.; Brasenose Coll., Oxford (MA). Royal Artillery, 1940–46 (despatches, Order of Leopold, Belgian Croix de Guerre). Joined Cadbury Bros Ltd, Birmingham, 1937; served in UK and Australia; Dir, Cadbury Fry Pascall Australia Ltd, 1949, Chm., 1953–71. Member: Council, Univ. of Tasmania, 1957–85; Council, Australian Admin. Staff Coll., 1959–71; Board, Commonwealth Banking Corp., 1967–82; Board, Goliath Cement Holdings, 1969–88; Board, Australian Mutual Provident Society, 1970–88. Member: Australian Taxation Review Cttee, 1972–74; Cttee of Inquiry into Educn and Training, 1976–78. Hon. LLD Tasmania, 1986. *Address:* 90 Carrington Street, Macedon, Vic 3440, Australia. *Club:* Australian (Sydney).

See also B. B. Lloyd.

LLOYD, Prof. John Raymond; *see under* Lloyd, M. R.

LLOYD, John Wilson, CB 1992; Deputy Secretary, Welsh Office, since 1988; *b* 24 Dec. 1940; *s* of late Dr Ellis Lloyd and of Mrs Dorothy Lloyd; *m* 1967, Buddug Roberts; two *s* one *d*. *Educ:* Swansea Grammar Sch.; Clifton Coll., Bristol; Christ's Coll., Cambridge (MA). Asst Principal, HM Treasury, 1962–67 (Private Sec. to Financial Sec., 1965–67); Principal, successively HM Treasury, CSD and Welsh Office, 1967–75 (Private Sec. to Sec. of State for Wales, 1974–75); Welsh Office: Asst Sec., 1975–82; Under Sec., 1982–88; Principal Establishment Officer, 1982–86; Hd, Housing, Health and Social Servs Policy Gp, 1986–88. *Recreations:* golf, walking, swimming. *Address:* c/o Welsh Office, Cathays Park, Cardiff CF1 3NQ. *T:* Cardiff (01222) 825111. *Club:* United Oxford & Cambridge University.

LLOYD, Dame June (Kathleen), DBE 1990; FRCP, FRCPE; FRCGP; Nuffield Professor of Child Health, British Postgraduate Medical Federation, London University, 1985–92, now Emeritus Professor; *b* 1 Jan. 1928; *d* of Arthur Cresswell Lloyd and Lucy Bevan Lloyd. *Educ:* Royal School, Bath; Bristol Univ. (MD); Durham Univ. (DPH). FRCP 1969; FRCPE 1989; FRCGP 1990. Junior Hosp. appts, Bristol, Oxford and Newcastle, 1951–57; Res. Fellow and Lectr in Child Health, Univ. of Birmingham, 1958–65; Sen. Lectr, Reader in Paediatrics, Inst. of Child Health, 1965–73; Prof. of Paediatrics, London Univ., 1973–75; Prof. of Child Health, St George's Hosp. Med. Sch., London Univ., 1975–85. Vis. Examr in Paediatrics in Univs in UK and abroad. Scientific

Advr, Assoc. Med. Res. Charities, 1992–. Chm., DoH Adv. Cttee on Gene Therapy, 1993–; Member: Council, RCP, 1982–85, 1986–88 (Paediatric Vice Pres., 1992–95); MRC, 1984–88; ABRC, 1989–90. Pres., British Paediatric Assoc., 1988–91; Mem., Finnish, French, Swiss, German, Amer. and Sri Lankan Paediatric Assocs; Hon. Mem., Paediatric Res. Soc. of Australia. Hon. DSc: Bristol, 1991; Birmingham, 1993. *Publications:* research articles, reviews and leading articles in sci. jls. *Recreations:* cooking, gardening, walking. *Address:* 37 Allingham Street, N1 8NX.

LLOYD, Rev. Kingsley; *see* Lloyd, Rev. A. K.

LLOYD, Leslie, CBE 1981; FCIT; General Manager, Western Region, British Rail, 1976–82; *b* 10 April 1924; *s* of Henry Lloyd and Lilian Wright; *m* 1953, Marie Snowden; one *s* two *d. Educ:* Hawarden Grammar Sch. RAF, 1943–47. British Rail: Management Trainee, Eastern Reg., 1949–52; Chief Controller, Manchester, 1953–56; Freight Officer, Sheffield, 1956–59; Modernisation Asst, King's Cross, 1959–61; Dist Manager, Marylebone, 1961–63; Movements Supt, Great Northern Line, 1963–64; Ops Officer, Eastern Reg., 1964–67; Man., Sundries Div., 1967; Movements Man., Western Reg., 1967–69; Chief Ops Man., British Rail HQ, 1969–76. *Recreations:* golf, gardening. *Address:* 73 The Fairway, Burnham, Bucks SL1 8DY. *Club:* Burnham Beeches Golf (Burnham).

LLOYD, Prof. Michael Raymond; Professor, Oslo School of Architecture, 1993; Executive Architect/Planner, Norconsult International, Oslo, 1981–93; *b* 20 Aug. 1927; *s* of W. R. Lloyd; *m* 1957, Berit Hansen; one *s* two *d. Educ:* Wellington Sch., Somerset; AA School of Architecture. AA Dipl. 1953; ARIBA 1954; MNAL 1960. Private practice and Teacher, State School of Arts and Crafts, Oslo, 1955–60 and 1962–63; First Year Master, AA School of Architecture, 1960–62; Dean, Faculty of Arch., and Prof. of Arch., Kumasi Univ. of Science and Technology, 1963–66; Principal, AA Sch. of Architecture, 1966–71; Consultant, Land Use Consultants (Internat.) Lausanne, 1971–72; Senior Partner, Sinar Associates, Tunbridge Wells, 1973–78; Consultant Head, Hull Sch. of Architecture, 1974–77; Technical Officer, ODA, Central America, 1979–81. Prof., Bergen Sch. of Architecture, 1986–92. Leverhulme Sen. Res. Fellow, UCL, 1976–78. *Publications:* (as J. R. Lloyd) Tegning og Skissing; ed World Architecture, Vol. I Norway, Vol. III Ghana; Norwegian Laftehus; Environmental Impact of Development Activities. *Recreations:* sailing, ski-ing. *Address:* Setravn 11B, 0390 Oslo 3, Norway.

LLOYD, Sir Nicholas (Markley), Kt 1990; MA; Editor, Daily Express, since 1986; *b* 9 June 1942; *s* of Walter and Sybil Lloyd; *m* 1st, 1968, Patricia Sholliker (marr. diss. 1978); two *s* one *d*; 2nd, 1979, Eve Pollard, *qv*; one *s. Educ:* Bedford Modern Sch.; St Edmund Hall, Oxford (MA Hons History); Harvard Univ., USA. Reporter, Daily Mail, 1964; Educn Correspondent, Sunday Times, 1966; Dep. News Editor, Sunday Times, 1968; News Editor, The Sun, 1970; Asst Editor, News of the World, 1972; Asst Editor, The Sun, 1976; Dep. Editor, Sunday Mirror, 1980; Editor: Sunday People, 1982–83; News of the World, 1984–85. *Recreations:* football, golf, tennis, cinema, theatre. *Address:* Ludgate House, 245 Blackfriars Road, SE1 9UX. *T:* 0171–928 8000.

LLOYD, Peter, CBE 1957; Director, Booth International Holdings Ltd, 1973–79 (Consultant, 1980–83); *b* 26 June 1907; *s* of late Godfrey I. H. Lloyd and late Constance L. A. Lloyd; *m* 1st, 1932, Nora K. E. Patten; one *s* one *d*; 2nd, 1951, Joyce Evelyn Campbell. *Educ:* Gresham's Sch.; Trinity Coll., Cambridge (MA). Industrial Research in Gas Light and Coke Co., London, 1931–41; Royal Aircraft Establishment, 1941–44; Power Jets (Research and Development), 1944–46. National Gas Turbine Establishment, Pyestock, 1946–60, Deputy Director, 1950; Dir-Gen. Engine R&D, Mins of Aviation and Technology, 1961–69; Head of British Defence Research and Supply Staff, Canberra, 1969–72. Chm., Gas Turbine Collaboration Cttee, 1961–68. CEng, FRAeS, SFInstE. Pres., Cambridge Univ. Mountaineering Club, 1928–29; Chm., Mount Everest Foundn, 1982–84 (Vice Chm., 1980–82). Himalayan expeditions: Nanda Devi, 1936; Everest, 1938; Langtang Himal, 1949; Kulu, 1977. *Publications:* various papers in scientific and technical journals. *Recreations:* mountaineering, fishing, gardening. *Address:* 121 Tourist Road, Toowoomba, Qld 4350, Australia. *Clubs:* Alpine (Vice-Pres., 1961–63, Pres., 1977–80); Queensland (Brisbane).
See also T. A. Evans.

LLOYD, Peter; *see* Lloyd, G. P.

LLOYD, Sir Peter; *see* Lloyd, Sir J. P. D.

LLOYD, Peter Gordon, CBE 1976 (OBE 1965); retired; British Council Representative, Greece, 1976–80; *b* 20 Feb. 1920; *s* of Peter Gleave Lloyd and Ellen Swift; *m* 1952, Edith Florence (*née* Flurey); two *s* one *d. Educ:* Royal Grammar Sch., Newcastle upon Tyne; Balliol Coll., Oxford (Horsley Exhibnr, 1939; BA, MA 1948). RA (Light Anti-Aircraft), subseq. DLI, 1940–46, Captain. British Council, 1949–: Brit. Council, Belgium and Hon. Lector in English, Brussels Univ., 1949–52; Reg. Dir, Mbale, Uganda, 1952–56; Dep. Dir Personnel, 1956–60; Representative: Ethiopia, 1960–68; Poland, 1969–72; Nigeria, 1972–76. *Publications:* (introd) Huysmans, A Rebours, 1940; The Story of British Democracy, 1959; Perspectives and Identities, 1989; critical essays on literature in periodicals. *Recreations:* literature, music, travel. *Address:* 111 Sussex Road, Petersfield, Hants GU31 4LB. *T:* Petersfield (01730) 262007. *Club:* United Oxford & Cambridge University.

LLOYD, Rt Hon. Sir Peter (Robert Cable), Kt 1995; PC 1994; MP (C) Fareham, since 1979; *b* 12 Nov. 1937; *s* of late David and Stella Lloyd; *m* 1967, Hilary Creighton; one *s* one *d. Educ:* Tonbridge Sch.; Pembroke Coll., Cambridge (MA). Formerly Marketing Manager, United Biscuits Ltd. Sec., Cons. Parly Employment Cttee, 1979–81; Vice-Chm., Cons. European Affairs Cttee, 1980–81; PPS to Minister of State, NI Office, 1981–82, to Sec. of State for Educn and Sci., Sir Keith Joseph, 1983–84; Asst Govt Whip, 1984–86; a Lord Comr of HM Treasury (Govt Whip), 1986–88; Parly Under-Sec. of State, Dept of Social Security, 1988–89, Home Office, 1989–92; Minister of State, Home Office, 1992–94. Chairman, Bow Group, 1972–73; Editor of Crossbow, 1974–76. *Recreations:* theatre, gardening. *Address:* House of Commons, SW1A 0AA.

LLOYD, Sir Richard (Ernest Butler), 2nd Bt *cr* 1960, of Rhu, Co. Dunbarton; Chairman: Vickers plc, since 1992 (Director, since 1978; Deputy Chairman, 1989–92); Argos plc, since 1995; Deputy Chairman, Hill Samuel & Co. Ltd, 1978–87 and since 1991 (Chief Executive, 1980–87, Chairman, 1987–91); *b* 6 Dec. 1928; *s* of Major Sir (Ernest) Guy Richard Lloyd, 1st Bt, DSO, and Helen Kynaston (*d* 1984), *yr d* of Col E. W. Greg, CB; *S* father, 1987; *m* 1955, Jennifer Susan Margaret, *e d* of Brigadier Ereld Cardiff, CB, CBE; three *s. Educ:* Wellington Coll.; Hertford Coll., Oxford (MA). Nat. Service (Captain, Black Watch), 1947–49. Joined Glyn, Mills & Co., 1952; Exec. Dir, 1964–70; Chief Executive, Williams & Glyn's Bank Ltd, 1970–78. Director: SIEBE, 1988–; Simon Engineering, 1988–. Member: CBI Council, 1978–; Industrial Develt Adv. Bd, 1972–77; Nat. Econ. Develt Council, 1973–77; Cttee to Review the Functioning of Financial Institutions, 1977–80; Overseas Projects Bd, 1981–85; Advisory Bd, Royal Coll. of Defence Studies, 1987–. Hon. Treas., British Heart Foundn, 1989–94; Gov., Ditchley Foundn, 1974. *Recreations:* walking, fly-fishing, gardening. *Heir: s* Richard Timothy Butler Lloyd [*b* 12 April 1956; *m* 1989, Wilhelmina, *d* of Henri Schut]. *Address:* Sundridge Place, Sundridge, Sevenoaks, Kent TN14 6DD. *T:* Westerham (01959) 563599. *Club:* Boodle's.

LLOYD, Richard Hey; *b* 25 June 1933; *s* of Charles Yates Lloyd and Ann Lloyd; *m* 1962, Teresa Morwenna Willmott; four *d. Educ:* Lichfield Cathedral Choir Sch.; Rugby Sch. (Music Scholar); Jesus Coll., Cambridge (Organ Scholar). MA, FRCO, ARCM. Asst Organist, Salisbury Cath., 1957–66; Organist and Master of the Choristers, Hereford Cath., 1966–74; Conductor, Three Choirs Festival, 1966–74 (Chief Conductor 1967, 1970, 1973); Organist and Master of the Choristers, Durham Cathedral, 1974–85; Dep. Headmaster, Salisbury Cathedral Choir Sch., 1985–88. Examiner, Associated Bd of Royal Schs of Music, 1967–. Mem. Council, RCO, 1974–93. *Publications:* church music. *Recreations:* cricket, theatre, travel, reading. *Address:* Refail Newydd, Pentraeth, Anglesey LL75 8YF. *T:* Pentraeth (01248) 450220.

LLOYD, Robert Andrew, CBE 1991; freelance opera singer, broadcaster and writer; *b* 2 March 1940; *s* of William Edward Lloyd and May (*née* Waples); *m* 1st, 1964, Sandra Dorothy Watkins (marr. diss. 1990); one *s* three *d*; 2nd, 1992, Lynda Anne Hazell (*née* Powell). *Educ:* Southend-on-Sea High Sch.; Keble Coll., Oxford (MA Hons Mod. History; Hon. Fellow, 1990). Instructor Lieut RN (HMS Collingwood), 1963–66; Civilian Tutor, Police Staff Coll., Bramshill, 1966–68; studied at London Opera Centre, 1968–69; début in Leonore, Collegiate Theatre, 1969; Principal Bass: Sadler's Wells Opera, Coliseum, 1969–72; Royal Opera House, 1972–82; Parsifal, Covent Garden, 1988; Flying Dutchman, La Scala, 1988; début at Metropolitan Opera, NY, in Barber of Seville, 1988; début at Vienna State Opera in La Forza del Destino. Guest appearances in Amsterdam, Berlin, Hamburg, Aix-en-Provence, Milan (La Scala), San Francisco, Florence, Paris, Munich, Nice, Boston, Toronto, Salzburg, Tokyo; soloist with major orchestras; over 60 recordings; associated with rôles of King Philip, Boris Godunov (first British bass to sing this rôle at Kirov Opera), Gurnemanz (opened 1991 season, La Scala), Fiesco, Banquo, King Henry; film, Parsifal; TV productions: Six Foot Cinderella, 1988; Bluebeard's Castle (opera), 1988. Pres., British Youth Opera, 1989–94; Mem., Exec. Cttee, Musicians Benevolent Fund, 1988–. *Publications:* contrib. miscellaneous jls. *Recreations:* sailing, straight theatre. *Address:* c/o Lies Askonas Ltd, 186 Drury Lane, WC2B 5RY. *Club:* Garrick.

LLOYD, Prof. Seton Howard Frederick, CBE 1958 (OBE 1949); FBA 1955; Archæologist; Professor of Western Asiatic Archæology, University of London, 1962–69, now Emeritus; *b* 30 May 1902; *s* of John Eliot Howard Lloyd and Florence Louise Lloyd (*née* Armstrong); *m* 1944, Margery Ulrica Fitzwilliams Hyde (*d* 1987); two *s* one *d. Educ:* Uppingham; Architectural Assoc. ARIBA 1926; Asst to Sir Edwin Lutyens, PRA, 1926–28; excavated with Egypt Exploration Society, 1928–30; excavated in Iraq for University of Chicago Oriental Institute, 1930–37; excavated in Turkey for University of Liverpool, 1937–39; FSA 1938 (Vice-Pres., 1965–69); Technical Adviser, Government of Iraq; Directorate-General of Antiquities, 1939–49; Director British Institute of Archæology, Ankara, Turkey, 1949–61. Hon. MA (Edinburgh), 1960. Lawrence of Arabia Meml Medal, RCAS, 1971; Gertrude Bell Meml Medal, British Sch. of Archaeology in Iraq, 1979. *Publications:* Mesopotamia (London), 1936; Sennacherib's Aqueduct at Jerwan (Chicago), 1935; The Gimilsin Temple (Chicago), 1940; Presargonid Temples (Chicago), 1942; Ruined Cities of Iraq (Oxford), 1942; Twin Rivers, (Oxford), 1942; Foundations in the Dust (London), 1947, rev. edn 1980; Early Anatolia (Pelican), 1956; Art of the Ancient Near East (London), 1961; Mounds of the Ancient Near East (Edinburgh) 1963; Highland Peoples of Anatolia (London), 1967; Archaeology of Mesopotamia (London), 1978; The Interval (London), 1986; Ancient Turkey, 1989; Excavation Reports and many articles in journals. *Recreation:* mnemonics. *Address:* Woolstone Lodge, Faringdon, Oxon SN7 7QL. *T:* Uffington (0136782) 248. *Club:* Chelsea Arts.

LLOYD, Timothy Andrew Wigram; QC 1986; Attorney General, Duchy of Lancaster, since 1993; *b* 30 Nov. 1946; *s* of late Thomas Wigram Lloyd and of Margo Adela Lloyd (*née* Beasley); *m* 1978, Theresa Sybil Margaret Holloway. *Educ:* Winchester College; Lincoln College, Oxford. MA. Called to the Bar, Middle Temple, 1970, Bencher, 1994; Mem., Middle Temple and Lincoln's Inn. *Publication:* (ed) Wurtzburg & Mills, Building Society Law, 15th edn 1989. *Recreations:* music, travel. *Address:* 11 Old Square, Lincoln's Inn, WC2A 3TS. *T:* 0171–430 0341.

LLOYD, Ven. Trevor; *see* Lloyd, Ven. B. T.

LLOYD DAVIES, J(ohn) Robert, CMG 1953; *b* 24 March 1913; *o s* of late J. R. and Mrs Davies, Muswell Hill; *m* 1st, 1943, Margery (*née* McClelland), Nottingham (*d* 1978); one *s* one *d*; 2nd, 1982, Grace, *widow* of Frederick Reynolds, Bethesda, Md, USA. *Educ:* Highgate Sch.; Oriel Coll., Oxford. Served War of 1939–45: Royal Navy; Lieut RNVR; Asst Sec., Dept of Employment; Labour Counsellor, Paris and Washington, FCO. Part-time Teacher, Working Men's Coll., London, 1970–94. *Recreations:* key-board music, reading. *Address:* 59 Elm Park Court, Pinner, Middlesex HA5 3LL. *Club:* United Oxford & Cambridge University.

LLOYD DAVIES, Trevor Arthur, MD; FRCP; *b* 8 April 1909; *s* of Arthur Lloyd Davies and Grace Margret (*née* Bull); *m* 1936, Joan (*d* 1972), *d* of John Keily, Co. Dublin; one *d*; *m* 1975, Margaret, *d* of Halliday Gracey, Woodford. *Educ:* Woking Grammar Sch.; St Thomas' Hospital, SE1. MRCS, LRCP 1932; MB, BS London (gold medal and hons in surgery, forensic med., obst. and gynæc.); MRCP 1933; MD London 1934; FRCP 1952. Resident Asst Physician, St Thomas' Hospital, 1934–36; MO, Boots Pure Drug Co., 1937–53; Prof. of Social Medicine, University of Malaya, 1953–61; Senior Medical Inspector of Factories, Min. of Labour and Dept of Employment and Productivity, 1961–70; Chief Med. Adviser, Dept of Employment, 1970–73. QHP 1968–71. *Publications:* The Practice of Industrial Medicine, 2nd edn, 1957; Respiratory Diseases in Foundrymen, 1971; Whither Occupational Medicine?, 1973; The Bible: medicine and myth, 1991; numerous papers on industrial and social medicine, in Lancet and Medical Journal of Malaya. *Recreations:* gardening, carpentry and bricklaying. *Address:* The Old Bakery, High Street, Elmdon, Saffron Walden, Essex CB11 4NL. *Club:* Athenæum.

LLOYD-EDWARDS, Captain Norman, RD 1971 and Bar 1980, RNR; JP; Lord-Lieutenant of South Glamorgan, since 1990 (Vice Lord-Lieutenant, 1986–90); *b* 13 June 1933; *s* of Evan Stanley Edwards and Mary Leah Edwards. *Educ:* Monmouth School for Boys; Quaker's Yard Grammar School; Univ. of Bristol (LLB). Joined RNVR 1952, RN 1958–60; RNR 1960–86; CO S Wales Div., RNR, 1981–84; Naval ADC to the Queen, 1984. Partner, Cartwrights, later Cartwrights, Adams & Black, Solicitors, Cardiff, 1960–93, Consultant, 1993–. Cardiff City Councillor, 1963–87; Dep. Lord Mayor, 1973–74; Lord Mayor, 1985–86. Member: Welsh Arts Council, 1983–89; BBC Adv. Council (Wales), 1987–90. Chapter Clerk, Llandaff Cathedral, 1975–90. Chm. of Wales, Duke of Edinburgh's Award, 1981–; Nat. Rescue Training Council, 1983–. Chm., Glamorgan TAVRA, 1987–90; President: S Glam Scouts, 1989–; Cardiff Assoc., National Trust, 1990–; King George's Fund for Sailors, 1990–; Christian Aid (Cardiff and Dist), 1992–; SE Wales Community Foundn, 1993–. Founder Master, Welsh Livery Guild, 1992–. Patron, British Red Cross (S Glam), 1991–. DL S Glamorgan 1978; JP 1990. KStJ 1988 (Prior of Wales, 1989–). *Recreations:* music, gardening, table talk. *Address:* Hafan Wen,

Llantrisant Road, Llandaff CF5 2PU. *Clubs:* Army and Navy; Cardiff and County, United Services Mess (Cardiff).

LLOYD-ELEY, John, QC 1970; a Recorder of the Crown Court, since 1972; *b* 23 April 1923; *s* of Edward John Eley; *m* 1946, Una Fraser Smith; two *s*. *Educ:* Xaverian Coll., Brighton; Exeter Coll., Oxford (MA). Served War, 1942–46, Lieut 50th Royal Tank Regt and 7th Hussars, N Africa, Sicily and Italy. Barrister, Middle Temple, 1951; South-Eastern Circuit; Mem., Bar Council, 1969. *Recreations:* farming, travel. *Address:* 1 Hare Court, Temple, EC4Y 7BE. *T:* 0171–353 5324; Luxfords Farm, East Grinstead. *T:* East Grinstead (01342) 21583.

LLOYD GEORGE, family name of **Earl Lloyd George of Dwyfor.**

LLOYD-GEORGE, family name of **Viscount Tenby.**

LLOYD GEORGE OF DWYFOR, 3rd Earl, *cr* 1945; **Owen Lloyd George;** Viscount Gwynedd, 1945; DL; *b* 28 April 1924; *s* of 2nd Earl Lloyd George of Dwyfor, and Roberta Ida Freeman, 5th *d* of Sir Robert McAlpine, 1st Bt; *S* father, 1968; *m* 1st, 1949, Ruth Margaret (marr. diss. 1982), *o d* of Richard Coit; two *s* one *d*; 2nd, 1982, Cecily Josephine, *d* of late Sir Alexander Gordon Cumming, 5th Bt, MC, and of Elizabeth Countess Cawdor, *widow* of 2nd Earl of Woolton and former wife of 3rd Baron Forres. *Educ:* Oundle. Welsh Guards, 1942–47. Italian Campaign, 1944–45. Formerly Captain Welsh Guards. An Underwriting Member of Lloyd's. Carried the Sword at Investiture of HRH the Prince of Wales, Caernarvon Castle, 1969. Mem., Historic Buildings Council for Wales, 1971. Mem. Court, Nat. Mus. of Wales, 1978. DL Dyfed 1993. *Heir: s* Viscount Gwynedd, *qv*. *Recreations:* shooting, gardening. *Address:* Ffynone, Boncath, Pembrokeshire SA37 0HQ; 47 Burton Court, SW3 4SZ. *Clubs:* White's, City of London, Pratt's.

LLOYD-HUGHES, Sir Trevor Denby, Kt 1970; author; former consultant in Government/industry relations, now retired; Chairman, Lloyd-Hughes Associates Ltd, International Consultants in Public Affairs, 1970–89; *b* 31 March 1922; *er s* of late Elwyn and Lucy Lloyd-Hughes, Bradford, Yorks; *m* 1st, 1950, Ethel Marguerite Durward (marr. diss., 1971), *o d* of late J. Ritchie, Dundee and Bradford; one *s* one *d*; 2nd, 1971, Marie-Jeanne, *d* of Marcel and late Helene Moreillon, Geneva; one *d* (and one adopted *d*— a Thai girl). *Educ:* Woodhouse Grove Sch., Yorks; Jesus Coll., Oxford (MA). Commissioned RA, 1941; served with 75th (Shropshire Yeomanry) Medium Regt, RA, in Western Desert, Sicily and Italy, 1941–45. Asst Inspector of Taxes, 1948; freelance journalist, 1949; joined staff of Liverpool Daily Post, 1949; Political Corresp., Liverpool Echo, 1950, Liverpool Daily Post, 1951. Press Secretary to the Prime Minister, 1964–69; Chief Information Adviser to Govt, 1969–70. Dir, Trinity International Holdings plc (formerly Liverpool Daily Post and Echo Ltd), 1978–91. Member of Circle of Wine Writers, 1961, Chm., 1972–73. *Recreations:* yoga, gardening, playing the Spanish guitar, golf, walking, travel. *Address:* Au Carmail, Labarrère, 32250 Montréal du Gers, France. *T:* 62294531. *Clubs:* Mosimann's, Wellington; Golf de Guinlet.

LLOYD-JACOB, David Oliver, CBE 1984; Executive Chairman, Butte Mining plc, since 1991; Chairman, Gem River Corp., since 1994; *b* 30 March 1938; *s* of Sir George and Lady Lloyd-Jacob; *m* 1st, 1961, Clare Bartlett; two *d*; 2nd, 1982, Carolyn Howard. *Educ:* Westminster; Christ Church, Oxford. Pres., Azcon Corp., USA, 1974–79; Man. Dir, Consolidated Gold Fields plc, 1979–81; Chm., Amcon Group Inc., USA, 1979–82; Chm. and Chief Exec. Officer, Levinson Steel Co., Pittsburgh, 1983–90. Chm., Britain Salutes NY, 1981–83. *Recreations:* opera, theatre, restoring old houses. *Address:* 3 Neal Street, WC2H 9PU. *T:* 0171–240 5776. *Clubs:* Garrick; Leander (Henley-on-Thames); River (New York).

LLOYD JONES, Charles Beynon; *see* Jones, C. B. L.

LLOYD-JONES, David Mathias, freelance conductor; *b* 19 Nov. 1934; *s* of late Sir Vincent Lloyd-Jones, and of Margaret Alwena, *d* of late G.H. Mathias; *m* 1964, Anne Carolyn Whitehead; two *s* one *d*. *Educ:* Westminster Sch.; Magdalen Coll., Oxford (BA). Repetiteur, Royal Opera House, Covent Garden, 1959–60; Chorus Master, New Opera Co., 1961–64; conductor: Bath Fest., 1966; City of London Fest., 1966; Wexford Fest., 1967–70; Scottish Opera, 1968; WNO, 1968; Royal Opera House, 1971; ENO (formerly Sadler's Wells Opera), 1969 (Asst Music Dir, 1972–78); Artistic Dir, Opera North, 1978–90; also conductor of BBC broadcasts, TV operas (Eugene Onegin, The Flying Dutchman, Hansel and Gretel), and operas in Amsterdam, Paris, Karlsruhe, Nice, Toronto, Tel Aviv, Santiago and Leningrad; has appeared with most British symph. orchs; recordings with LPO and English Northern Philharmonia (Founder Conductor). FGSM 1992. Hon. DMus Leeds, 1986. *Publications:* (trans.) Boris Godunov (vocal score), 1968; (trans.) Eugene Onegin (vocal score), 1971; Boris Godunov (critical edn of original full score), 1975; The Gondoliers (first ever pubn of a Gilbert and Sullivan full score), 1986; contrib. 6th edn Grove's Dictionary of Music and Musicians, 1981; contrib. Musik in Geschichte und Gegenwart, Music and Letters, and The Listener. *Recreations:* theatre, old shrub roses, French cuisine. *Address:* 9 Clarence Road, Leeds LS18 4LB; 94 Whitelands House, Cheltenham Terrace, SW3 4RA. *T:* 0171–730 8695.

LLOYD-JONES, His Honour David Trevor, VRD 1958; a Circuit Judge, 1972–88; *b* 6 March 1917; *s* of Trevor and Ann Lloyd-Jones, Holywell, Flints; *m* 1st, 1942, Mary Violet (marr. diss.; she *d* 1980), *d* of Frederick Barnardo, CIE, CBE, MD, London; one *d*; 2nd, 1958, Anstice Elizabeth, MB, BChir (*d* 1981), *d* of William Henry Perkins, Whitchurch; one *s* one *d*; 3rd, 1984, Florence Mary, *d* of William Fairclough, MM, Wallasey. *Educ:* Holywell Grammar School. Banking, 1934–39 and 1946–50. Called to the Bar, Gray's Inn, 1951; practised Wales and Chester Circuit, 1952–71; Prosecuting Counsel to Post Office (Wales and Chester Circuit), 1961–66; Dep. Recorder, Chester and Birkenhead, 1964–70; Dep. Chm., Caerns QS, 1966–70, Chm, 1970–71; Legal Mem., Mental Health Appeal Tribunal (Wales Area), 1960–72; Dep. Chm., Agricultural Land Tribunal (Wales Area), 1968–72. JP Gwynedd, 1966–71. Served War of 1939–45, RNVR, Atlantic, Mediterranean and Pacific; Lt-Comdr, RNR, 1952–60, retd. *Recreations:* golf, music. *Address:* 29 Curzon Park North, Chester. *T:* Chester (01244) 675144. *Clubs:* Army and Navy; Royal Dornoch Golf.

LLOYD-JONES, Sir (Peter) Hugh (Jefferd), Kt 1989; FBA 1966; Regius Professor of Greek in the University of Oxford and Student of Christ Church, 1960–89, now Emeritus Professor and Emeritus Student; *b* 21 Sept. 1922; *s* of Major W. Lloyd-Jones, DSO, and Norah Leila, *d* of F. H. Jefferd, Brent, Devon; *m* 1st, 1953, Frances Elisabeth Hedley (marr. diss. 1981); two *s* one *d*; 2nd, 1982, Mary Lefkowitz (Andrew W. Mellon Professor in the Humanities, Wellesley College, Mass), *d* of Harold and Mena Rosenthal, New York. *Educ:* Lycée Français du Royaume Uni, S Kensington; Westminster Sch.; Christ Church, Oxford. Served War of 1939–45, 2nd Lieut, Intelligence Corps, India, 1942; Temp. Captain, 1944. 1st Cl. Classics (Mods), 1941; MA 1947; 1st Cl., LitHum, 1948; Chancellor's Prize for Latin Prose, 1947; Ireland and Craven Schol., 1947; Fellow of Jesus Coll., Cambridge, 1948–54; Asst Lecturer in Classics, University of Cambridge, 1950–52, Lecturer, 1952–54; Fellow and E. P. Warren Praelector in Classics, Corpus Christi Coll., Oxford, 1954–60; J. H. Gray Lecturer, University of Cambridge, 1961; Visiting Prof., Yale Univ., 1964–65, 1967–68; Sather Prof. of Classical Literature, Univ. of California at Berkeley, 1969–70; Alexander White Vis. Prof., Chicago, 1972; Vis. Prof., Harvard Univ., 1976–77. Fellow, Morse Coll., Yale Univ. Hon. Mem., Greek Humanistic Soc., 1968; Corresponding Member: Acad. of Athens, 1978; Nordrhein-Westfälische Akad. der Wissenschaften, 1983; Accademia di Archeologia Lettere e Belle Arti, Naples, 1984; Bayerische Akad. der Wissenschaften, 1992; Hon. Foreign Mem., Amer. Acad. of Arts and Scis, 1978; Mem., Amer. Philos. Soc., 1992. Hon. DHL Chicago, 1970; Hon. DPhil Tel Aviv, 1984. *Publications:* Appendix to Loeb Classical Library edn of Aeschylus, 1957; Menandri Dyscolus (Oxford Classical Text), 1960; Greek Studies in Modern Oxford, 1961; (trans.) Paul Maas, Greek Metre, 1962; (ed) The Greeks, 1962; Tacitus (in series The Great Historians), 1964; (trans.) Aeschylus: Agamemnon, The Libation-Bearers, and The Eumenides, 1970, 2nd edn 1979; The Justice of Zeus, 1971, 2nd edn 1983; (ed) Maurice Bowra, 1974; Females of the Species: Semonides of Amorgos on Women, 1975; (with Marcelle Quinton) Myths of the Zodiac, 1978; (with Marcelle Quinton) Imaginary Animals, 1979; Blood for the Ghosts, 1982; Classical Survivals, 1982; (with P. J. Parsons) Supplementum Hellenisticum, 1983; (with N. G. Wilson) Sophoclis Fabulae, 1990; (with N. G. Wilson) Sophoclea, 1990; Academic Papers (2 vols), 1990; Greek in a Cold Climate, 1991; Sophocles I–II, 1994; contribs to periodicals. *Recreations:* cats, remembering past cricket. *Address:* 15 West Riding, Wellesley, MA 02181, USA. *T:* (617) 2372212, *Fax:* (617) 2372246; Christ Church, Oxford OX1 1DP. *T:* Oxford (01865) 791063. *Club:* United Oxford & Cambridge University.

LLOYD JONES, Sir Richard (Anthony), KCB 1988 (CB 1981); Permanent Secretary, Welsh Office, 1985–93; Chairman, Arts Council of Wales, since 1994; *b* 1 Aug. 1933; *s* of Robert and Anne Lloyd Jones; *m* 1955, Patricia Avril Mary Richmond; two *d*. *Educ:* Long Dene Sch., Edenbridge; Nottingham High Sch.; Balliol Coll., Oxford (MA). Entered Admiralty, 1957; Asst Private Sec. to First Lord of the Admiralty, 1959–62; Private Sec. to Secretary of the Cabinet, 1969–70; Asst Sec., Min. of Defence, 1970–74; Under Sec., 1974–78, Dep. Sec. 1978–85, Welsh Office. Chairman: Civil Service Benevolent Fund, 1987–93 (Trustee, 1993–); Adv. Cttee on local govt staff transfers (Wales), 1993–94; Local Govt Staff Commn for Wales, 1994–. Member: BBC Gen. Adv. Council, 1994–; Commn for Local Democracy, 1994–95. Pres., Welsh Council, Ramblers' Assoc., 1993–; Vice-Chm., Prince of Wales' Cttee, 1993–. Vice Pres., Univ. of Wales, Cardiff, 1993–; Mem. Ct, Univ. of Wales, 1995–. Hon. Fellow, UCW Aberystwyth, 1990. *Recreations:* music, railways, swimming, walking. *Address:* Radyr, Cardiff. *Club:* United Oxford & Cambridge University.

LLOYD-JONES, Robert; Director-General, Brick Development Association, since 1984; *b* 30 Jan. 1931; *s* of Robert and Edith Lloyd-Jones; *m* 1958, Morny Baggs-Thompson (marr. diss. 1977); two *s* one *d*. *Educ:* Wrekin Coll.; Queens' Coll., Univ. of Cambridge (MA Hons); Harvard Business School. Short Service Commission, RN, 1956; Shell International, 1959; BTR Industries Ltd, 1962; International Wool Secretariat, 1964; Schachenmayr, Germany, 1971; British Textile Employers Association, 1977–81; Dir-Gen., Retail Consortium, 1981–83. Chm., Nordic Country Gp, and Mem., European Trade Cttee, DTI. Governor, Coll. for Distributive Trades, 1982–84; Founder Chm., Nat. Retail Trng Council, 1982–84. Trustee, Building Crafts and Conservation Trust, 1990–. Mem., BFI. Member: RN Golf Soc. (Match Sec.); China Golfing Soc. Friend of Royal Acad. and of Tate Gall. FRSA. Freeman, City of London, 1986; Liveryman, Co. of Tylers and Bricklayers, 1986. *Recreations:* golf, squash, tennis, music, chess, art, and the general pursuit of pleasure. *Address:* Mill Cottage, 10 High Street, Odiham, Hants RG25 1LG. *T:* (office) Winkfield Row (01344) 885651. *Clubs:* Lansdowne, Institute of Directors; Dormy House (Rye); Royal Birkdale Golf, Rye Golf, Formby Golf, Liphook Golf, Royal Ascot Squash, Royal Ascot Tennis, Odiham Tennis.

LLOYD-MOSTYN, family name of **Baron Mostyn.**

LLOYD-NEWSTROM, Prof. David Graham; *see* Lloyd, D. G.

LLOYD OWEN, Maj.-Gen. David Lanyon, CB 1971; DSO 1945; OBE 1954; MC 1942; Chairman, Long Range Desert Group Association, since 1945; *b* 10 Oct. 1917; *s* of late Capt. Reginald Charles Lloyd Owen, OBE, RN; *m* 1947, Ursula Evelyn (MBE 1991), *d* of late Evelyn Hugh Barclay and Hon. Mrs Barclay, MBE; three *s*. *Educ:* Winchester; RMC, Sandhurst. 2nd Lieut, The Queen's Royal Regt, 1938. Comdr, Long Range Desert Group, 1943–45. Military Asst to High Commissioner in Malaya, 1952–53; Comdg 1st Queen's, 1957–59; Comdr 24 Infantry Bde Group, 1962–64; GOC Cyprus District, 1966–68; GOC Near East Land Forces, 1968–69. Pres., Regular Commns Bd, 1969–72, retd. Kt of Cross of Merit, SMO Malta, 1946. *Publications:* The Desert My Dwelling Place, 1957; Providence Their Guide, 1980. *Address:* Violet Bank, Swainsthorpe, Norwich NR14 8PR. *T:* Swainsthorpe (01508) 470468.

LLOYD WEBBER, Sir Andrew, Kt 1992; composer; *b* 22 March 1948; *s* of late William Southcombe Lloyd Webber, CBE, DMus, FRCM, FRCO, and Jean Hermione Johnstone; *m* 1st, 1971, Sarah Jane Tudor (*née* Hugill) (marr. diss. 1983); one *s* one *d*; 2nd, 1984, Sarah Brightman (marr. diss. 1990); 3rd, 1991, Madeleine Astrid Gurdon; two *s*. *Educ:* Westminster Sch.; Magdalen Coll., Oxford; Royal Coll. of Music (FRCM 1988). Composer: (with lyrics by Timothy Rice): Joseph and the Amazing Technicolor Dreamcoat, 1968 (rev. 1973 and 1991); Jesus Christ Superstar, 1970; Evita, 1976 (stage version, 1978); (with lyrics by Alan Ayckbourn) Jeeves, 1975; (with lyrics by Don Black) Tell Me on a Sunday, 1980; Cats, 1981 (based on poems by T. S. Eliot); (with lyrics by Don Black) Song and Dance, 1982; (with lyrics by Richard Stilgoe) Starlight Express, 1984; (with lyrics by Richard Stilgoe and Charles Hart) The Phantom of the Opera, 1986; (with lyrics by Don Black and Charles Hart) Aspects of Love, 1989; Sunset Boulevard (with lyrics by Christopher Hampton and Don Black), 1993. Producer: Joseph and the Amazing Technicolor Dreamcoat, 1973, 1974, 1978, 1980, 1991; Jeeves Takes Charge, 1975; Cats, 1981; Song and Dance, 1982; Daisy Pulls It Off, 1983; The Hired Man, 1984; Starlight Express, 1984; On Your Toes, 1984; The Phantom of the Opera, 1986; Cafe Puccini, 1986; The Resistable Rise of Arturo Ui, 1987; Lend Me a Tenor, 1988; Aspects of Love, 1989; Shirley Valentine, 1989 (Broadway); La Bête, 1992; Sunset Boulevard, 1993, and others. Film scores: Gumshoe, 1971; The Odessa File, 1974. Composed "Variations" (based on A minor Caprice No 24 by Paganini), 1977, symphonic version, 1986; Requiem Mass, 1985. Awards include Tony, Drama Desk, and Grammy. *Publications:* (with Timothy Rice) Evita, 1978; Cats: the book of the musical, 1981; (with Timothy Rice) Joseph and the Amazing Technicolor Dreamcoat, 1982; The Complete Phantom of the Opera, 1987; The Complete Aspects of Love, 1989; Sunset Boulevard: from movie to musical, 1993. *Recreations:* architecture, art. *Address:* 22 Tower Street, WC2H 9NS.
See also J. Lloyd Webber.

LLOYD WEBBER, Julian, FRCM; 'cellist; *b* 14 April 1951; *s* of late William Southcombe Lloyd Webber, CBE, DMus, FRCM, FRCO, and Jean Hermione Johnstone; *m* 1st, 1974, Celia Mary Ballantyne (marr. diss. 1989); 2nd, 1989, Princess Zohra Mahmud Ghazi; one *s*. *Educ:* University College Sch., London; Royal College of Music. ARCM. Studied 'cello with: Douglas Cameron, 1965–68; Pierre Fournier, Geneva, 1972. Début, Queen Elizabeth Hall, 1972; USA début, Lincoln Center, NY, 1980. Has performed with all major British orchestras; toured: USA, Germany, Holland, Africa, Bulgaria, S America,

Spain, Belgium, France, Scandinavia, Portugal, Denmark, Australasia, Singapore, Japan, Korea, Czechoslovakia, Austria, Canada, Hong Kong and Taiwan. Has made first recordings of works by Benjamin Britten, Frank Bridge, Delius, Rodrigo, Holst, Vaughan Williams, Haydn, Sullivan, John McCabe, Malcolm Arnold; recorded: Elgar Cello Concerto (cond. Menuhin), 1985 (British Phonographic Industry Award for Best Classical Recording, 1986); Dvořák Cello Concerto with Czech Philharmonic Orchestra, 1988; also concertos by Delius, Haydn, Honegger, Lalo, Miaskovsky, Saint-Saens and Tchaikovsky Rococo Variations. *Publications:* Travels with My Cello, 1984; Song of the Birds, 1985; edited: series, The Romantic 'Cello, 1978, The Classical 'Cello, 1980, The French 'Cello, 1981; Frank Bridge 'Cello Music, 1981; Young Cellist's Repertoire, Books 1, 2, 3, 1984; Holst, Invocation, 1984; Vaughan Williams, Fantasia on Sussex Folk Tunes, 1984; Recital Repertoire for Cellists, 1987; Short, Sharp Shocks, 1990; The Great 'Cello Solos, 1992; contribs to music jls and national Press in UK, US, Canada and Australia. *Recreations:* countryside (especially British), reading horror stories, Leyton Orient FC. *Address:* c/o Columbia Artists Management, 165 West 57th Street, New York, NY10019, USA.

See also Sir A. Lloyd Webber.

LLWYD, Elfyn; MP (Plaid Cymru) Meirionnydd Nant Conwy, since 1992; *b* 26 Sept. 1951; *s* of late Huw Meirion Hughes and of Hefina (*née* Roberts); surname Hughes abandoned by deed poll, 1970; *m* 1974, Eleri Llwyd; one *s* one *d*. *Educ:* Ysgol Dyffryn Conwy Llanrwst; Univ. of Wales, Aberystwyth (LLB Hons); Coll. of Law, Chester. Admitted solicitor, 1977. *Recreations:* pigeon breeding, Rugby, choral singing, fishing. *Address:* Bryn Meurig, Dolgellau, Gwynedd LL40 1DS. *T:* Dolgellau (01341) 422661; Glandwr, Llanuwchllyn, Y Bala, Gwynedd LL23 7TW.

LOACH, Kenneth; television and film director; *b* 17 June 1936; *s* of late John Loach and of Vivien Loach (*née* Hamlin); *m* 1962, Lesley Ashton; two *s* two *d* (and one *s* decd). *Educ:* King Edward VI School, Nuneaton; St Peter's Hall, Oxford (Hon. Fellow, St Peter's Coll., 1993). BBC Trainee, Drama Dept, 1963. *Television:* Diary of a Young Man, 1964; 3 Clear Sundays, 1965; The End of Arthur's Marriage, 1965; Up The Junction, 1965; Coming Out Party, 1965; Cathy Come Home, 1966; In Two Minds, 1966; The Golden Vision, 1969; The Big Flame, 1969; After A Lifetime, 1971; The Rank and File, 1972; Days of Hope, 1975; The Price of Coal, 1977; The Gamekeeper, 1979; Auditions, 1980; A Question of Leadership, 1981; Questions of Leadership, 1983 (banned from TV); The Red and the Blue, 1983; Which Side Are You On?, 1985; The View from the Woodpile, 1988; Dispatches, 1991. *Films:* Poor Cow, 1968; Kes, 1970; In Black and White, 1970; Family Life, 1972; Black Jack, 1979; Looks and Smiles, 1981; Fatherland, 1987; Hidden Agenda, 1990; Riff-Raff, 1991; Raining Stones, 1993; Ladybird, Ladybird, 1994; Land and Freedom, 1995. *Address:* c/o Parallax Pictures, 7 Denmark Street, WC2H 8LS.

LOADER, Sir Leslie (Thomas), Kt 1987; CBE 1980; retired company chairman; *b* 27 April 1923; *s* of Edward Robert Loader and Ethel May Loader (*née* Tiller); *m* 1957, Jennifer; three *d*. *Educ:* Bitterne Park; Bournemouth Municipal Coll.; London Sch. of Economics and Political Science (occasional student). Served War of 1939–45; commnd Hampshire Regt (now Royal Hampshire Regt); saw active service in Italy. Mem., Southampton Borough Council, 1947–59; contested (C) Southampton, Itchen, 1955; Chairman: Southampton Young Conservatives, 1947; Southampton Itchen Cons. Assoc., 1964–70; Wessex Area Cons. Party, 1972–75; Euro-Cons. Council for Wight and Hants E, 1979–82 (Hon. Treas., 1984–87); Mem. Exec., Nat. Union of Cons. and Unionist Assocs, 1967–76 (Mem., Standing Adv. Cttee on Parly Cands; Hon. Life Vice Pres., Wessex Area, 1990); Pres., Eastleigh Cons. Assoc., 1985–; Founder Chairman: Southern Parishes Cons. Club, Eastleigh; Cosham Cons. Club, Portsmouth N. Founded Rotary Club of Bitterne and Woolston Housing Assoc., 1962 (Chm., 1962–83; Pres., 1983–); Pres., Swaythling Housing Soc. Ltd, 1983–92 (Chm., 1976–83); Chm., Wessex Body Scanner Appeal, 1980–83; Member: Southampton Harbour Bd, 1951–56; Southampton and SW Hampshire HA, 1981–86; Trustee, Wessex Med. Sch. Trust, 1983–86. Formerly Mem. Ct of Governors, UC Southampton, later Univ. of Southampton. Founder, S Hampshire Aviation Historical Soc., 1980. Freeman, City of London; Liveryman, Painter-Stainers' Co. *Publications:* booklets and articles on housing and political matters. *Recreation:* social history research. *Club:* Carlton.

LOADES, Prof. Ann Lomas, PhD; Professor of Divinity, Durham University, since 1995; *b* 21 Sept. 1938; *d* of Gerard Joseph Glover and Amy Lomas. *Educ:* Durham Univ. (BA Theol. 1960; PhD 1975); McMaster Univ. (MA 1965). Durham University: Lectr in Theology, 1975–81; Sen. Lectr, 1981–90; Reader, 1990–95; Chm., Bd of Studies in Theol., 1989–91. Editor, Theology, 1991–. *Publications:* (ed) W. A. Whitehouse, The Authority of Grace, 1981; (ed with J. C. Eaton) For God and Clarity, 1983; Kant and Job's Comforters, 1985; Searching for Lost Coins (Scott Holland Lectures), 1987; (ed) Feminist Theology, 1990; (ed with M. McLain) Hermeneutics, the Bible and Literary Criticism, 1992; (ed with L. Rue) Contemporary Classics in Philosophy of Religion, 1991; (ed) Dorothy L. Sayers, Spiritual Writings, 1993; (ed with D. W. Brown) The Sense of the Sacramental, 1995. *Recreations:* going to the theatre, cooking, teaching classical ballet. *Address:* Theology Department, Abbey House, Palace Green, Durham DH1 3RS. *T:* 0191–374 2052.

LOADES, David Henry, FIA; Directing Actuary (Under Secretary), Government Actuary's Department, since 1983; *b* 16 Oct. 1937; *s* of John Henry Loades and Evelyn Clara Ralph; *m* 1962, Jennifer Glenys Stevens; one *s* two *d*. *Educ:* Beckenham and Penge County Grammar Sch. for Boys. BA. FIA 1961. Govt Actuary's Dept, 1956–. Medal of Merit for services to the Scout Assoc., 1986. *Publications:* papers in actuarial jls. *Recreations:* painting, visiting art galleries, supporting the Institute of Actuaries. *Address:* 22 Kingsway, WC2B 6LE.

LOANE, Most Rev. Marcus Lawrence, KBE 1976; DD; *b* 14 Oct. 1911; *s* of K. O. A. Loane; *m* 1937, Patricia Evelyn Jane Simpson Knox; two *s* two *d*. *Educ:* The King's School, Parramatta, NSW; Sydney University (MA). Moore Theological College, 1932–33; Australian College of Theology (ThL, 1st Class, 1933; Fellow, 1955). Ordained Deacon, 1935, Priest, 1936; Resident Tutor and Chaplain, Moore Theological College, 1935–38; Vice-Principal, 1939–53; Principal, 1954–59. Chaplain AIF, 1942–44. Canon, St Andrew's Cathedral, 1949–58; Bishop-Coadjutor, diocese of Sydney, 1958–66; Archbishop of Sydney and Metropolitan of Province of NSW, 1966–82; Primate of Australia, 1978–82. Hon. DD Wycliffe College, Toronto, 1958. *Publications:* Oxford and the Evangelical Succession, 1950; Cambridge and the Evangelical Succession, 1952; Masters of the English Reformation, 1955; Life of Archbishop Mowll, 1960; Makers of Religious Freedom, 1961; Pioneers of the Reformation in England, 1964; Makers of Our Heritage, 1966; The Hope of Glory, 1968; This Surpassing Excellence, 1969; They Were Pilgrims, 1970; Hewn from the Rock, 1976; Men to Remember, 1987. *Address:* 18 Harrington Avenue, Warrawee, NSW 2074, Australia.

LOASBY, Prof. Brian John, FBA 1994; Professor of Management Economics, University of Stirling, 1971–84, Emeritus and Hon. Professor of Economics, since 1984; *b* 2 Aug. 1930; *s* of Frederick Thomas Loasby and Mabel Phyllis Loasby; *m* 1957, Judith Ann Robinson; two *d*. *Educ:* Kettering GS; Emmanuel Coll., Cambridge (BA 1952; MLitt 1958). Assistant in Pol Economy, Aberdeen Univ., 1955–58; Bournville Res. Fellow, Birmingham Univ., 1958–61; Tutor in Management Studies, Bristol Univ., 1961–67; Stirling University: Lectr in Econs, 1967–68; Sen. Lectr, 1968–71. Management Fellow, Arthur D. Little Inc., Cambridge, Mass, 1965–66; Vis. Fellow, Oxford Centre for Management Studies, 1974. Pres., Scottish Economic Soc., 1987–90. *Publications:* The Swindon Project, 1973; Choice, Complexity and Ignorance, 1976; The Mind and Method of the Economist, 1989; Equilibrium and Evolution, 1991; contrib. books, and econs and management jls. *Recreation:* gardening. *Address:* Department of Economics, University of Stirling, Stirling FK9 4LA. *T:* Stirling (01786) 467470; 8 Melfort Drive, Stirling FK7 0BD. *T:* Stirling (01786) 472124.

LOBO, António C.; *see* Costa-Lobo.

LOBO, Sir Rogerio Hyndman, (Sir Roger Lobo), Kt 1985; CBE 1978 (OBE 1972); JP; Chairman, P. J. Lobo & Co. Ltd, Hong Kong, since 1960; Chairman, Broadcasting Authority of Hong Kong, since 1989; *b* 15 Sept. 1923; *s* of Dr P. J. Lobo and Branca Helena (*née* Hyndman); *m* 1947, Margaret Mary (*née* Choa); five *s* five *d*. *Educ:* Escola Central, Macao; Seminario de S Jose, Macao; Liceu Nacional Infante Dom Henrique, Macao; La Salle Coll., Hong Kong. Director: Associated Liquor Distributors, 1975–; Kjeldsen & Co. (HK) (formerly Danish Fancy Food Gp), 1982–; Shun Tak Hldgs Ltd, 1994–; dir of 14 other cos. Unofficial MLC, Hong Kong, 1972–85 (Sen. Mem., 1980–85); Unofficial MEC, 1978–85. Member: Urban Council, 1965–78; Housing Authority, 1967–83; Chm., Adv. Cttee on Post-Retirement Employment, 1987–; Comr, Civil Aid Services, 1977–92 (Mem., 1955–). Hon. LLD Univ. of Hong Kong, 1982. JP Hong Kong, 1963. Silver Jubilee Medal, 1977; Civil Aid Services Long Service Medal, 1970; Civil Defence Long Service Clasp, 1982. Comdr, Order of St Gregory the Great, The Vatican, 1969. *Recreation:* golf. *Address:* Woodland Heights, E1, 2 Wongneichong Gap Road, Hong Kong. *T:* 25740779; (business) 28/F Inchcape Insurance Tower, 3 Lockhart Road, Wanchai, Hong Kong. *T:* 25269418/25378697. *Clubs:* Dynasty, Hong Kong, Rotary, Royal Hong Kong Jockey, Royal Hong Kong Golf, Hong Kong Country, Shek O Country (Hong Kong).

LOCK, David Peter; Chief Planning Adviser, Department of the Environment, since 1994; Chairman, David Lock Associates Ltd, since 1988; *b* 12 March 1948; *s* of Arthur Lovering Lock and late Kathleen Barbara (*née* Nash); *m* 1970, Jeanette Anita Jones; three *d*. *Educ:* Sir Roger Manwood's Grammar Sch., Sandwich, Kent; Nottingham Coll. of Art and Design/Trent Poly. (DipT&CP). MRTPI 1975. Area Planning Officer, Leicester CC, 1970–73; Planning Aid Officer, TCPA, 1973–78; Planning Manager, Milton Keynes Develt Corp., 1978–81; Associate Dir, Conran Roche Ltd, 1981–88. Vis Prof., Univ. of Central England in Birmingham. *Publications:* (contrib.) People and their Settlements, 1976; (contrib.) Growth and Change in the Future City Region, 1976; (contrib.) New Towns in National Development, 1980; Riding the Tiger: planning the South of England, 1989; (jtly) Alternative Development Patterns: new settlements, 1993. *Recreations:* history, geography, reading, research. *Address:* Department of the Environment, Room C13/03, 2 Marsham Street, SW1P 3EB. *T:* 0171–276 3502; David Lock Associates Ltd, 50 North Thirteenth Street, Central Milton Keynes, Bucks MK9 3BP. *T:* Milton Keynes (01908) 666276.

LOCK, Lt-Comdr Sir Duncan; *see* Lock, Lt-Comdr Sir J. D.

LOCK, (George) David; Managing Director, Private Patients Plan Ltd, 1975–85; *b* 24 Sept. 1929; *s* of George Wilfred Lock and Phyllis Nita (*née* Hollingworth); *m* 1965, Ann Elizabeth Biggs; four *s* one *d*. *Educ:* Haileybury and ISC; Queens' Coll., Cambridge (MA). British Tabulating Machine Co. Ltd (now ICL), 1954–59; Save & Prosper Group Ltd, 1959–69; American Express, 1969–74; Dir, Plan for Active Retirement, Frizzell Insce and Financial Services Ltd (formerly New Business Ventures, Frizzell Consumer Services Ltd), 1986–89. Director: Priplan Investments Ltd, 1979–85; Priplan Services Ltd, 1979–85; PPP Medical Centre Ltd (incorp. Cavendish Medical Centre), 1981–85. Director: Home Concern for the Elderly, 1985–87, 1989–; The Hosp. Management Trust, 1985–92; Bd of Management, St Anthony's Hosp., Cheam, 1986–; HMT Hospitals Ltd, 1993– (Vice-Chm.); Sec., Frizzell Foundn, 1989–93. Sec., Friends of Children of Great Ormond Street, 1986. Trustee, Eynsham Trust, 1975–83; Gov., PPP Medical Trust Ltd (Dir, 1983–89). Member: Nuffield Nursing Homes Trust, 1979–; Exec. Cttee, Assoc. of Independent Hosps, 1981–87. Mem., RSocMed., 1979–92. Freeman, Barbers' Co., 1982–. *Recreations:* bridge, golf, music, family activities, entertaining. *Address:* Buckhurst Place, Horsted Keynes, Sussex RH17 7AH. *T:* Danehill (01825) 790599.

LOCK, Graham; *see* Lock, T. G.

LOCK, John Arthur, QPM 1975; Deputy Assistant Commissioner, Metropolitan Police, and National Co-ordinator, Regional Crime Squads of England and Wales, 1976–79, retired; *b* 20 Oct. 1922; *s* of Sidney George Lock and Minnie Louise Lock; *m* 1950, Patricia Joyce Lambert; two *d*. *Educ:* George Palmer Central School, Reading. Royal Air Force, 1941–46; Wireless Operator/Air Gunner; Flying Officer. Joined Metropolitan Police, 1946. *Recreation:* golf. *Club:* St Mellion Golf and Country.

LOCK, Lt-Comdr Sir (John) Duncan, Kt 1978; RN; Chairman, Association of District Councils of England and Wales, 1974–79 (Member, 1974–93); *b* 5 Feb. 1918; *s* of Brig. Gen. F. R. E. Lock, DSO, and Mary Elizabeth Lock; *m* 1947, Alice Aileen Smith (*d* 1982); three *d*. *Educ:* Royal Naval Coll., Dartmouth. Served as regular officer in Royal Navy (retiring at his own request), 1931–58: specialised in navigation and navigated Battleships HMS King George V and Howe, the Cruiser Superb, destroyers and minesweepers. Served War of 1939–45: took part in Battle of Atlantic, Norwegian and N African campaigns, Pacific War and Normandy and Anzio landings. Farmed family estate in Somerset, 1958–61. Admty Compass Observatory as specialist in magnetic compasses, 1962–83. Member of Lloyd's. Eton RDC, 1967–74; Chairman: Bucks Br., RDC Assoc., 1969–74; S Bucks Dist Council, 1985–87 (Mem., 1973–); Assoc. of Dist Councils of England and Wales Council and Policy Cttee, 1974–79 (Chm. Bucks Br., 1974–91); Rep. Body for England, 1977–89; Local Authorities Management Services and Computer Cttee, 1981–86; Mem., Adv. Cttee on Local Govt Audit, 1979–82; British Rep., Conference of Local and Reg. Authorities of Europe, 1979–94. Chm., Beaconsfield Constituency Conservative Assoc., 1972–75; Mem., S Bucks Housing Assoc., 1990– (Chm., 1990–91). *Recreations:* gardening, shooting. *Address:* Red Cottage, Ethorpe Close, Gerrards Cross, Bucks SL9 8PL. *T:* Gerrards Cross (01753) 882467.

LOCK, Stephen Penford, CBE 1991; MA, MD; FRCP; Research Associate, Wellcome Institute for the History of Medicine, since 1992; Editor, British Medical Journal, 1975–91; *b* 8 April 1929; *er s* of Wallace Henry Lock, Romford, Essex; *m* 1955, Shirley Gillian Walker, *d* of E. W. Walker, Bridlington, Yorks; one *d* (one *s* decd). *Educ:* City of London Sch.; Queens' Coll., Cambridge; St Bartholomew's Hosp., London. MA 1953; MB 1954; MD 1987; MRCP 1963; FRCP 1974; FACP 1989; FRCPE 1989. Jun. hosp. appts, 1954–63; Asst Editor, British Med. Jl, 1964–69, Sen. Asst Editor, 1969–74, Dep. Editor, 1974–75. Consulting Editor: Encyclopaedia Britannica Year Book of Medicine, 1992–;

Med. Jl of Australia, 1994–. Organiser and/or participant in numerous Postgrad. Courses in Med. Writing and confs in scientific editing worldwide, 1971–. Mem., Res. Ethics Cttee, KCH Medical Sch., 1992–. Mem. Council, Harveian Soc., 1992– (Pres., 1994); Founder Pres., 1982–85, Mem. Council, 1985–91, European Assoc. of Sci. Editors. Vis. Prof. in Medicine, McGill Univ., 1978; Visitor, Acad. Dept of Medicine, Monash Univ., 1982; Foundn Vis. Prof. in Medicine, RCSI, 1986; Vis. Prof. in Epidemiology and Biostatistics, McGill Univ., 1992; Vis. Lectr, Erasmus Summer Sch., Rotterdam, 1993–. Lectures: Wade, Keele Univ., 1980; Morgan, Royal Cornwall Hosp., 1984; Rock Carling, Nuffield Provincial Hosps Trust, 1985; Maurice Bloch, Glasgow Univ., 1986; Wolfson, Wolfson Coll., Oxford, 1986; Estelle Brodman, Washington Univ., St Louis, 1989; Sarah Davies, TCD, 1990; William Hey, Leeds Univ., 1990; George McGovern, Med. Library Assoc. of America, San Francisco, 1991. Chm., Friends of Dulwich Picture Gall., 1993–. Hon. FRCPI 1987; Hon. Fellow, Amer. Med. Writers Assoc., 1994; Hon. Mem., BPA, 1991. Hon. MSc Manchester, 1985. Donders Medal, Ned. Tijdsch. Geneesk, 1981; Internat. Medal, Finnish Med. Soc. Duodecim, 1981; Medal of Honour, Finnish Med. Jl, 1987; Fothergillian Medal, Med. Soc., London, 1992; Meritorious Award, Council of Biol. Eds, 1993. Officer, first cl., White Rose of Finland, 1982. *Publications:* An Introduction to Clinical Pathology, 1965; Health Centres and Group Practices, 1966; The Enemies of Man, 1968; Better Medical Writing, 1970; Family Health Guide, 1972; Medical Risks of Life, 1976; Thorne's Better Medical Writing, 2nd edn 1977; (ed) Adverse Drug Reactions, 1977; (ed) Remembering Henry, 1977; (contrib.) Oxford Companion to Medicine, 1983; A Difficult Balance: editorial peer review in medicine, 1985; (ed) The Future of Medical Journals, 1991; Medical Journals and Medical Progress, 1992; (ed) Fraud and Misconduct in Medical Research, 1993, 2nd edn 1996; (ed jtly) The Oxford Medical Companion, 1995; (contrib.) Oxford Illustrated History of Medicine, 1996. *Recreation:* reading reviews of operas I can't afford to see. *Address:* 3 Alde House, Alde House Drive, Aldeburgh, Suffolk IP15 5EE. *T:* Aldeburgh (01728) 452411; 110 Sedden House, Barbican, EC2Y 8BX. *T:* 0171–588 5503.

LOCK, (Thomas) Graham; Chief Executive, Amalgamated Metal Corporation plc, 1983–91; *b* 19 Oct. 1931; *s* of Robert Henry Lock and Morfydd Lock (*née* Thomas); *m* 1954, Janice Olive Baker Lock (*née* Jones) (marr. diss. 1992); two *d. Educ:* Whitchurch Grammar School; University College of South Wales and Monmouthshire (BSc Metall); College of Advanced Technology, Aston; Harvard Business School. CEng, FIM, CBIM. Instructor Lieut, RN, 1953–56; Lucas Industries and Lucas Electrical, 1956–61; Dir, Girling Bremsen GmbH, 1961–66; Gen. Man. and Overseas Ops Dir, Girling Ltd, 1966–73; Gen. Man. and Dir, Lucas Service Overseas Ltd, 1973–79; Man. Dir, Industrial Div., Amalgamated Metal Corp., 1979–83; non-exec. Director: Marshall's Universal plc, 1983–86; Evode Gp plc, 1985–91. Liveryman, Co. of Gold and Silver Wyre Drawers, 1988–. Freeman, City of London, 1987. *Recreations:* sailing, music, skiing. *Address:* Parolas Villa, Parekklisia, near Limassol, Cyprus. *Clubs:* Army and Navy; Royal Naval Sailing Association (Portsmouth), Royal Southern Yacht (Hamble).

LOCKE, John Christopher, FRICS; Chief Executive, NHS Estate Management and Health Building Agency (NHS Estates), since 1991; *b* 4 March 1947; *s* of Comdr Cyril Frederick Locke, RN (retd) and Marjorie Alice Batt Locke (*née* Collins); *m* 1st, 1969 (marr. diss.); two *s*; 2nd, 1990, Maria Patricia, *d* of Eileen Rogers. *Educ:* Pangbourne Coll.; Regent Street Poly.; Brixton Sch. of Building; Northern Poly. ARICS 1971, (Prizewinner), FRICS, 1981. Prudential Assurance Co. Ltd, 1964–88 (Dir, Estate Management, 1987–88); Divl Dir, Estate Management, Prudential Portfolio Managers Ltd, 1989–91; Director: Southbank Technopark Ltd, 1985–91 (Chm., 1989–90); City Aviation Insurance Tenancies Ltd, 1989–90; Chm., Briggait Co. Ltd, 1987–90; Surveyor, Watling Street Properties 1989–90, Mem., Commercial Property Cttee, RICS, 1983–89. Hon. FIHospE 1992. *Recreations:* opera, theatre, music, film, travel, family, home. *Address:* NHS Estates, 1 Trevelyan Square, Boar Lane, Leeds LS1 6AE. *T:* Leeds (0113) 254 7000.

LOCKE, John Howard, CB 1984; Chairman, National Examination Board in Occupational Safety and Health, 1986–92; *b* 26 Dec. 1923; *s* of Percy Locke and Josephine Locke (*née* Marshfield); *m* 1948, Eirene Sylvia Sykes; two *d. Educ:* Hymers Coll., Hull; Queen's Coll., Oxford. MIOSH. Ministry of Agriculture, Fisheries and Food, 1945–65; Under-Secretary: Cabinet Office, 1965–66; MoT, 1966–68; Dept of Employment and Productivity, 1968–71; Dep. Sec., Dept of Employment, 1971–74; Dir, Health and Safety Exec., 1975–83. *Address:* Box Trees, East Preston, Sussex BN16 1JP. *T:* Rustington (01903) 785154.

LOCKE, Patrick; Secretary to Church Commissioners, since 1992; *b* 17 March 1934; *s* of Roy Albert Locke and Nora Katherine Locke (*née* Taylor); *m* 1959, Iris Constance Cory; one *s* one *d. Educ:* Bristol Cathedral Sch.; Wadham Coll., Oxford (Schol.; MA). Nat. Service, 1952–54. Church Commissioners Office, 1957–: Dep. Sec., 1985–92. *Recreations:* 18th and 19th century literature, theatre, opera. *Address:* Romans, Beggars Lane, Winchester, Hants SO23 0HE. *T:* Winchester (01962) 866386. *Club:* Athenæum.

LOCKETT, Reginald; His Honour Judge Lockett; a Circuit Judge, since 1981; *b* 24 June 1933; *s* of George Alfred Lockett and Emma (*née* Singleton); *m* 1959, Edna (*née* Lowe); one *s* one *d. Educ:* Ashton-in-Makerfield Grammar Sch.; Manchester Univ.; London Univ. (LLB 1954). Solicitor, 1955. Asst Coroner for Wigan, 1963–70; Dist Registrar and County Court Registrar, Manchester, 1970–81; a Recorder of the Crown Court, 1978–81. Pres., Manchester Law Students' Soc., 1975–77. Vice Pres., The Boys' Bde, 1978– (Dist Pres., NW Dist, 1973–90). Reader, Anglican Church, 1970–. Editor, Butterworths Family Law Service, 1983–90; Consultant Editor, Sweet-Maxwell's High Court Litigation Manual, 1990. *Recreations:* music, photography. *Address:* c/o The Sessions House, Lancaster Road, Preston PR1 2PD. *T:* Preston (01772) 21451.

LOCKHART, Brian Alexander; Sheriff in Glasgow and Strathkelvin, since 1981 (in North Strathclyde, 1979–81); *b* 1 Oct. 1942; *s* of John Arthur Hay Lockhart and Norah Lockhart; *m* 1967, Christine Ross Clark; two *s* two *d. Educ:* Glasgow Academy; Glasgow Univ. (BL). Qualified as solicitor, 1964; Partner in Robertson Chalmers & Auld, Solicitors, Glasgow, 1966–79. *Recreations:* fishing, golf, family. *Address:* 18 Hamilton Avenue, Glasgow G41 4JF. *T:* 0141–427 1921.

LOCKHART, Frank Roper; His Honour Judge Lockhart; a Circuit Judge, since 1988; *b* 8 Dec. 1931; *s* of Clement and Betsy Lockhart; *m* 1958, Brenda Harriett Johnson; one *s* one *d. Educ:* King Edward VI Sch., Retford; Doncaster Grammar Sch.; Univ. of Leeds (LLB Hons). Asst Town Clerk, Southend-on-Sea, 1960–65; Partner, Jefferies, Solicitors, 1965–87. Chairman: Industrial Tribunal, 1983–87; Social Security Tribunal, 1970–87; a Recorder, 1985–88. *Recreations:* golf, tennis, Rack. *Address:* Southend Crown Court, The Court House, Southend SS2 6EG. *Clubs:* Thorpe Hall Golf, Hazards Golf, Chigwell Golf.

LOCKHART, Harry Eugene, (Gene), CPA; Chief Executive, MasterCard International, since 1994; *b* 4 Nov. 1949; *s* of Harry Eugene Lockhart, Sen., Austin, Texas, and Gladys Cummings Lockhart; *m* 1974, Terry Lockhart; one *s* three *d. Educ:* Univ. of Virginia (MechEng degree); Darden Graduate Bus. Sch. (MBA). CPA 1976. Sen. Cons., Arthur Anderson & Co., 1974–77; Man. Principal, Europe, Nolan Norton & Co., 1977–82; Gp Dir, Management Services, C. T. Bowring & Co., 1982–85; Vice Pres., First Manhattan Consulting Gp, 1985–87; Chief Exec., IT, 1987–88, Gp Ops, 1988–92, UK Banking, 1990–92, Midland Bank; Pres., First Manhattan Consulting Internat., 1992–94. *Recreations:* tennis, golf, running, ski-ing, photography, riding, classical music, ballet. *Clubs:* Royal Automobile, Annabel's.

LOCKHART, James Lawrence, FRCM, FRCO(CHM); Director of Opera, London Royal Schools' Vocal Faculty, since 1992 (Director of Opera, Royal College of Music, 1986–92); *b* 16 Oct. 1930; *s* of Archibald Campbell Lockhart and Mary Black Lawrence; *m* 1954, Sheila Margaret Grogan; two *s* one *d. Educ:* George Watson's Boys' College; Edinburgh Univ. (BMus); Royal College of Music (ARCM, FRCM). Yorkshire Symphony Orchestra, 1954–55; Münster City Opera, 1955–56; Bavarian State Opera, 1956–57; Glyndebourne Festival Opera, 1957, 1958, 1959; Opera Workshop, Univ. of Texas, 1957–59; Royal Opera House, Covent Garden, 1959–60; BBC Scottish Orchestra, 1960–61; Scottish Opera, 1960–61; Conductor, Sadler's Wells Opera, 1961–62; Conductor and Repetiteur, Royal Opera House, Covent Garden, 1962–68; Music Dir, Welsh National Opera, 1968–73; Generalmusikdirektor: Staatstheater, Kassel, 1972–80; Koblenz Opera, 1981–88; Rheinische Philharmonie, 1981–91 (Ehrendirigent, 1991). Hon. RAM 1993. *Recreations:* swimming, hill-walking, driving fast cars. *Address:* 105 Woodcock Hill, Harrow, Middx HA3 0JJ. *T:* 0181–907 2112. *Club:* Savage.

LOCKHART, Sir Simon John Edward Francis S.; *see* Sinclair-Lockhart.

LOCKHART-MUMMERY, Christopher John; QC 1986; a Recorder, since 1994; *b* 7 Aug. 1947; *s* of Sir Hugh Lockhart-Mummery, KCVO, MD, MChir, FRCS and late Elizabeth Jean Crerar, *d* of Sir James Crerar, KCSI, CIE; *m* 1st, 1971, Elizabeth Rosamund (marr. diss. 1992), *d* of N. P. M. Elles, *qv* and of Baroness Elles, *qv*; one *s* two *d*; 2nd, 1993, Mary Lou Putley. *Educ:* Stowe; Trinity College, Cambridge (BA). Called to the Bar, Inner Temple, 1971 (Bencher, 1991). Specialist Editor, Hill and Redman's Law of Landlord and Tenant, 1974–89. *Recreations:* fishing, listening to music, opera.

LOCKLEY, Andrew John Harold; Director, Legal Practice, The Law Society, since 1987; *b* 10 May 1951; *s* of Ven. Harold Lockley, *qv*; *m* 1974, Ruth Mary Vigor; two *s* one *d. Educ:* Marlborough Coll.; Oriel Coll., Oxford (BA Lit. Hum. 1973; MA 1982). Admitted a Solicitor, 1979. Res. Fellow, World Council of Churches, 1973–75; Solicitor in private practice, 1979–82; Asst Sec., 1982–85, Sec., 1985–87, Contentious Business Dept, The Law Soc. Mem., Commn on Efficiency in the Criminal Courts, 1986–93. Mem., IT and Courts Cttee, 1990–. Gov., William Austin Sch., Luton, 1992–. *Publications:* Christian Communes, 1976; (ed) The Pursuit of Quality: a guide for lawyers, 1993; contribs to legal periodicals. *Recreations:* growing fruit and vegetables, swimming, walking, cooking. *Address:* The Law Society, 113 Chancery Lane, WC2A 1PL. *T:* 0171–242 1222.

LOCKLEY, Ven. Harold; Archdeacon of Loughborough, 1963–86, Archdeacon Emeritus since 1986; *b* 16 July 1916; *s* of Harry and Sarah Elizabeth Lockley; *m* 1947, Ursula Margaret, JP (*d* 1990), *d* of Rev. Dr H. Wedell and Mrs G. Wedell (*née* Bonhoeffer); three *s. Educ:* Loughborough Coll. (Hons Dip. Physical Education); London University; Westcott House, Cambridge. BA Hons 1937, BD Hons 1943, MTh 1949, London Univ.; PhD 1955, Nottingham Univ.; MLitt Cantab 1990. Served RN, 1940–46. Chaplain and Tutor, Loughborough Coll., 1946–51; Vicar of Glen Parva and South Wigston, 1951–58; Canon Chancellor of Leicester Cathedral, 1958–63; Vicar of All Saints, Leicester, 1963–78. Postgrad. res student, Emmanuel Coll., Cambridge, 1986–88. OCF Royal Leics Regt, 1951–58; Chaplain, Leics Yeomanry Assoc., 1968–; Chaplain, Leicester Royal Infirmary Maternity Hospital, 1967–74; Proctor in Convocation of Canterbury, 1960–80. Sen. Examining Chaplain to Bishop of Leicester, 1951–79; part-time Lectr in Divinity, Univ. of Leicester, 1953–86; Mem., Leics Educn Cttee, 1973–85. Chm., Anglican Young People's Assoc., 1966–86. Founder Governor, Leicester Grammar Sch., 1981–. Editor, Leicester Cathedral Quarterly, 1960–63. *Publications:* Leicester Grammar School: the first ten years, 1992; Dietrich Bonhoeffer: his 'Ethics' and its value for today, 1993; numerous reviews and theological articles. *Recreations:* walking and foreign travel. *Address:* 21 Saxon Close, Market Harborough, Leics LE16 7PR; Emmanuel College, Cambridge. *Club:* Leicestershire (Leicester).

See also Prof. E. A. O. G. Wedell, A. J. H. Lockley.

LOCKLEY, Ronald Mathias; author and naturalist; *b* 8 Nov. 1903. Hon. MSc Wales, 1977. *Publications:* Dream Island, 1930, rev. 1988; The Island Dwellers, 1932; Island Days, 1934; The Sea's a Thief, 1936; Birds of the Green Belt, 1936; I Know an Island, 1938; Early Morning Island, 1939; A Pot of Smoke, 1940; The Way to an Island, 1941; Shearwaters, 1942; Dream Island Days, 1943; Inland Farm, 1943; Islands Round Britain, 1945; Birds of the Sea, 1946; The Island Farmers, 1947; Letters from Skokholm, 1947; The Golden Year, 1948; The Cinnamon Bird, 1948; Birds of Pembrokeshire, 1949; The Charm of the Channel Islands, 1950; (with John Buxton) Island of Skomer, 1951; Travels with a Tent in Western Europe, 1953; Puffins, 1953; (with Rosemary Russell) Bird Ringing, 1953; The Seals and the Curragh, 1954; Gilbert White, 1954; (with James Fisher) Sea-Birds, 1954; Pembrokeshire, 1957; The Pan Book of Cage Birds, 1961; Britain in Colour, 1964; The Private Life of the Rabbit, 1964; Wales, 1966; Grey Seal, Common Seal, 1966; Animal Navigation, 1967; The Book of Bird-Watching, 1968; The Channel Islands, 1968, rev. edn, A Traveller's Guide to the Channel Islands, 1971; The Island, 1969; The Naturalist in Wales, 1970; Man Against Nature, 1970; Seal Woman, 1974; Ocean Wanderers, 1974; Orielton, 1977; Myself when Young, 1979; Whales, Dolphins & Porpoises, 1979; (with Noel Cusa) New Zealand Endangered Species, 1980; The House Above the Sea, 1980; (with Richard Adams) Voyage Through the Antarctic, 1982; Flight of the Storm Petrel, 1983; (with Geoff Moon) New Zealand's Birds, 1983; The Lodge above the Waterfall, 1987; (with Betty Brownlie) Secrets of Natural New Zealand, 1987; Birds and Islands: travels in wild places, 1991; *edited:* Natural History of Selborne, by G. White, 1949, rev. edn 1976; Nature Lover's Anthology, 1951; The Bird-Lover's Bedside Book, 1958; *compiled:* In Praise of Islands, 1957. *Address:* Te Puke Country Lodge, No 1 Road, Te Puke, New Zealand.

LOCKLEY, Stephen Randolph, FCIT; Director General, Strathclyde Passenger Transport Executive, since 1986; Chairman, PTE Group, since 1993; *b* 19 June 1943; *s* of Randolph and Edith Lockley; *m* 1968, Angela; two *d. Educ:* Manchester Univ. (BScCivEng, 1st Cl. Hons). MICE; MIHT; FCIT 1987. Lancashire County Council: North West Road Construction Unit, Highway Engrg and Planning, 1964–72; Highway/Transportation Planning, 1972–75; Lanarkshire CC, Strathclyde Regional Council: Prin. Engr (Transportation), 1975–77; Depute Dir of Policy Planning, 1977–80; Prin. Exec. Officer, 1980–86. *Address:* 64 Townhead Street, Strathaven ML10 6DJ. *T:* Strathaven (01357) 21774.

LOCKWOOD, Baroness *cr* 1978 (Life Peer), of Dewsbury, W Yorks; **Betty Lockwood;** DL; President, Birkbeck College, London, 1983–89; a Deputy Speaker, House of Lords, since 1989; *b* 22 Jan. 1924; *d* of Arthur Lockwood and Edith Alice Lockwood; *m* 1978, Lt-Col Cedric Hall (*d* 1988). *Educ:* Eastbrough Girls' Sch., Dewsbury; Ruskin Coll., Oxford. Chief Woman Officer and Asst Nat. Agent of Labour Party, 1967–75; Chm., Equal Opportunities Commn, 1975–83. Vice-Chm., Internat. Council of Social Democratic Women, 1969–75; Chm., Adv. Cttee to European Commn on Equal

Opportunities for Women and Men, 1982–83. Chm., Mary Macarthur Educnl Trust, 1971–; Pres., Mary Macarthur Holiday Trust, 1990– (Chm., 1971–90). Member: Dept of Employment Adv. Cttee on Women's Employment, 1969–83; Adv. Council on Energy Conservation, 1977–80; Council, Advertising Standards Authority, 1983–93; Leeds Urban Develt Corp., 1988–95. Pres., Hillcroft Coll., 1987–. Member, Council: Bradford Univ., 1983– (a Pro-Chancellor, 1988–); Leeds Univ., 1985–91; Vice Pres., UMIST, 1992–95. Hon. Fellow: UMIST, 1986; Birkbeck Coll., 1987. Hon. DLitt Bradford, 1981; Hon. LLD Strathclyde, 1985. DL W Yorks, 1987. Editor, Labour Woman, 1967–71. *Recreations:* walking and country pursuits, music. *Address:* 6 Sycamore Drive, Addingham, Ilkley LS29 0NY. *Club:* Soroptomist.

LOCKWOOD, Prof. David, FBA 1976; Professor of Sociology, since 1968 (Pro-Vice-Chancellor, 1989–92); University of Essex; *b* 9 April 1929; *s* of Herbert Lockwood and Edith A. (*née* Lockwood); *m* 1954, Leonore Davidoff; three *s*. *Educ:* Honley Grammar Sch.; London Sch. of Economics. BSc(Econ) London, 1st Cl. Hons 1952; PhD London, 1957. Trainee, textile industry, 1944–47; Cpl, Intell. Corps, Austria, 1947–49. Asst Lectr and Lectr, London Sch. of Economics, 1953–60; Rockefeller Fellow, Univ. of California, Berkeley, 1958–59; Univ. Lectr, Faculty of Economics, and Fellow, St John's Coll., Cambridge, 1960–68. Visiting Professor: Dept of Sociology, Columbia Univ., 1966–67; Delhi Univ., 1975; Stockholm Univ., 1989; Vis. Fellow, ANU, 1993. Mem., SSRC (Chm., Sociol. and Soc. Admin Cttee), 1973–76; Chm., ESRC Rev. of OPCS Social Classifications, 1994–. Mem., Academia Europaea, 1990. *Publications:* The Blackcoated Worker, 1958, 2nd edn 1989; (jtly) The Affluent Worker in the Class Structure, 3 vols, 1968–69; Solidarity and Schism, 1992; numerous articles in jls and symposia. *Address:* 82 High Street, Wivenhoe, Essex CO7 9AB. *T:* Wivenhoe (01206282) 3530.

LOCKWOOD, Robert; General Director, Overseas Planning and Project Development, General Motors Corporation, 1982–85, retired; *b* 14 April 1920; *s* of Joseph A. Lockwood and Sylvia Lockwood; *m* 1947, Phyllis M. Laing; one *s* one *d*. *Educ:* Columbia Univ. (AB); Columbia Law Sch. (LLB). Attorney, Bar of New York, 1941; US Dist of New York and US Supreme Court, 1952. Pilot, USAAF (8th Air Force), 1944–45. Attorney: Ehrich, Royall, Wheeler & Holland, New York, 1941 and 1946–47; Sullivan & Cromwell, New York, 1947–54; Sec. and Counsel, Cluett, Peabody & Co., Inc., New York, 1955–57; Man. Dir, Cluett, Peabody & Co., Ltd, London, 1957–59; General Motors: Overseas Ops, Planning and Develt, 1960–61; Asst to Man. Dir, GM Argentina, Buenos Aires, 1962; Asst to Man. Dir, and Manager, Parts, Power and Appliances, GM Continental, Antwerp, 1964–66; Branch Man., Netherlands Br., GM Continental, Rotterdam, 1967–68; Man., Planning and Develt, GM Overseas Ops, New York, 1969–73; Vice Pres., GM Overseas Corp., and Gen. Man., Japan Br., 1974–76; Exec. Vice Pres., Isuzu Motors Ltd, Tokyo, 1976; Chm., GM European Adv. Council, 1977–82. Mem., Panel of Arbitrators, Amer. Arbitration Assoc., 1989–. *Recreations:* tennis, chess, reading. *Address:* 126 Littlefield Road, Monterey, CA 93940, USA. *Clubs:* Royal Air Force; Monterey Peninsula Country, Spanish Bay, Beach and Tennis (Pebble Beach).

LOCKYER, Rear-Adm. (Alfred) Austin, LVO 1973; Chief Staff Officer (Engineering) to Commander-in-Chief Fleet, 1982–84, retired; Director General, Timber Trade Federation, 1985–92; *b* 4 March 1929; *s* of late Austin Edmund Lockyer and Jane Russell (*née* Goldman); *m* 1965, Jennifer Ann Simmons; one *s*. *Educ:* Frome County School; Taunton School; Royal Naval Engineering College. Entered RN 1947; Comdr 1965; Staff of Commander Far East Fleet, 1965–67; jssc, 1968–69; Ship Dept, 1969–71; HMY Britannia, 1971–73; Captain 1973; sowc, 1973–74; Naval Ship Production Overseer, Scotland and NI, 1974–76; Dep. Dir, Fleet Maintenance, 1976–78; Dir, Naval Officers Appointments (Engrg), 1978–80; HMS Sultan in Comd, 1980–82; ADC to the Queen, 1981; Rear-Adm. 1982. Governor: Forres Sch., Swanage, 1980–92 (Chm., 1983–92); Sherborne Sch., 1981–. *Recreations:* gardening, listening to good music and watching sport. *Address:* 8 Darlington Place, Bath, Avon BA2 6BX. *Club:* Army and Navy.

LODER, family name of **Baron Wakehurst.**

LODER, Sir Giles Rolls, 3rd Bt, *cr* 1887; DL; *b* 10 Nov. 1914; *o s* of late Capt. Robert Egerton Loder, *s* of 2nd Bt, and late Muriel Rolls, *d* of J. Rolls-Hoare; *S* grandfather, 1920; *m* 1939, Marie, *o c* of Bertram Hanmer Bunbury Symons-Jeune; two *s*. *Educ:* Eton; Trinity Coll., Cambridge (MA). High Sheriff of Sussex, 1948–49; DL West Sussex, 1977. Vice-Pres., RHS, 1983–. VMH 1971. *Recreations:* sailing, horticulture. *Heir:* *s* Edmund Jeune Loder [*b* 26 June 1941; *m* 1st, 1966, Penelope Jane Forde (marr. diss. 1971); one *d*; 2nd, 1992, Susan Warren Pearl]. *Address:* Ockenden House, Cuckfield, Haywards Heath, West Sussex RH17 5LD; Leonardslee Gardens, Horsham, Sussex RH13 6PP. *Club:* Royal Yacht Squadron.

LODGE, Anton James Corduff; QC 1989; *b* 17 April 1944; *s* of Sir Thomas Lodge, *qv*. *Educ:* Ampleforth College; Gonville and Caius College, Cambridge (MA). Called to the Bar, Gray's Inn, 1966; a Recorder, 1985. *Recreations:* cricket, tennis, ski-ing, music, theatre. *Address:* Park Court Chambers, Park Cross Street, Leeds LS1 2QH. *T:* Leeds (0113) 243 3277. *Club:* Yorkshire (York).

LODGE, Prof. David John, MA, PhD; FRSL 1976; Professor 1976–87, Hon. Professor, since 1987, of Modern English Literature, University of Birmingham; *b* 28 Jan. 1935; *s* of William Frederick Lodge and Rosalie Marie Lodge (*née* Murphy); *m* 1959, Mary Frances Jacob; two *s* one *d*. *Educ:* St Joseph's Acad., Blackheath; University College, London (Hon. Fellow, 1982). BA hons, MA (London); PhD (Birm). National Service, RAC, 1955–57. British Council, London, 1959–60. Univ. of Birmingham: Asst Lectr in English, 1960–62; Lectr, 1963–71; Sen. Lectr, 1971–73; Reader in English, 1973–76. Harkness Commonwealth Fellow, 1964–65; Visiting Associate Prof., Univ. of California, Berkeley, 1969; Henfield Writing Fellow, Univ. of E Anglia, 1977. Hon. Fellow, Goldsmiths' Coll., London, 1992. Yorkshire Post Fiction Prize, 1975; Hawthornden Prize, 1976; Whitbread Book of the Year Award, 1980; Sunday Express Book of the Year Award, 1988. Stage play, The Writing Game, Birmingham Rep., 1990. Adaptation of Dickens, Martin Chuzzlewit, for television, 1994. *Publications: novels:* The Picturegoers, 1960; Ginger, You're Barmy, 1962; The British Museum is Falling Down, 1965; Out of the Shelter, 1970, rev. edn 1985; Changing Places, 1975; How Far Can You Go?, 1980; Small World, 1984 (televised 1988); Nice Work, 1988 (adapted for television, 1989); Paradise News, 1991; Therapy, 1995; *criticism:* Language of Fiction, 1966; The Novelist at the Crossroads, 1971; The Modes of Modern Writing, 1977; Working with Structuralism, 1981; Write On, 1986; After Bakhtin (essays), 1990; The Art of Fiction, 1992; *edited:* Jane Austen's Emma: a casebook, 1968; Twentieth Century Literary Criticism, 1972; Modern Criticism and Theory, 1988. *Recreations:* tennis, television, cinema, theatre. *Address:* c/o Department of English, University of Birmingham, Birmingham B15 2TT. *T:* 0121–414 3344.

LODGE, Prof. Geoffrey Arthur, BSc, PhD, FIBiol; FRSE 1986; Professor of Animal Science, Sultan Qaboos University, Muscat, 1986–90, retired; *b* 18 Feb. 1930; *m* 1956, Thelma (*née* Calder); one *s* two *d*. *Educ:* Durham University (BSc). PhD Aberdeen. Formerly Reader in Animal Production, Univ. of Nottingham School of Agriculture, and Principal Research Scientist, Animal Research Inst., Ottawa; Strathcona-Fordyce Prof. of Agriculture, Univ. of Aberdeen, and Principal, North of Scotland Coll. of Agriculture, 1978–86. *Publications:* (ed jointly) Growth and Development of Mammals, 1968; contribs to journals and books. *Recreations:* food, malt whisky, travelling, house restoration. *Address:* RR2, Iroquois, Ont K0E 1K0, Canada.

LODGE, Oliver Raymond William Wynlayne; Regional Chairman of Industrial Tribunals, London South Region, 1980–92; *b* Painswick, Glos, 2 Sept. 1922; *e s* of Oliver William Foster Lodge and Winifred, (Wynlayne), *o d* of Sir William Nicholas Atkinson, ISO, LLD; *m* 1953, Charlotte (*d* 1990), *o d* of Col Arthur Davidson Young, CMG; one *s* two *d*. *Educ:* Bryanston Sch.; King's Coll., Cambridge. BA 1943, MA 1947. Officer-cadet, Royal Fusiliers, 1942. Called to the Bar, Inner Temple, 1945; admitted *ad eundem*, Lincoln's Inn, 1949 (Bencher, 1973; Treas., 1995); practised at Chancery Bar, 1945–74; Permanent Chairman of Industrial Tribunals, 1975–92, part-time Chm., 1992–94. Member: Bar Council, 1952–56, 1967–71; Supreme Court Rules Cttee, 1968–71. Gen. Comr of Income Tax, Lincoln's Inn, 1983–91. *Publications:* (ed) Rivington's Epitome of Snell's Equity, 3rd edn, 1948; (ed) Fraudulent and Voidable Conveyances, article in Halsbury's Laws of England, 3rd edn, 1956; contribs to legal periodicals. *Recreations:* walking, bell-ringing, reading history, formerly sailing. *Address:* Southridge House, Hindon, Salisbury, Wilts. SP3 6ER. *T:* Hindon (01747) 820238; 8 Stone Buildings, Lincoln's Inn, WC2A 3TA. *T:* 0171–831 0555. *Clubs:* Garrick; Bar Yacht.

LODGE, Sir Thomas, Kt 1974; Consultant Radiologist, United Sheffield Hospitals, 1946–74, retired; Clinical Lecturer, Sheffield University, 1960–74; *b* 25 Nov. 1909; *s* of James Lodge and Margaret (*née* Lowery); *m* 1940, Aileen Corduff (*d* 1990); one *s* one *d*. *Educ:* Univ. of Sheffield. MB, ChB 1934, FFR 1945, FRCP 1967, FRCS 1967. Asst Radiologist: Sheffield Radium Centre, 1936; Manchester Royal Infirmary, 1937–38; 1st Asst in Radiology, United Sheffield Hosps, 1938–46; Cons. Adviser in Radiology, DHSS, 1965–74. Fellow, BMA, 1968; Hon. FRSocMed; Hon. FFR RCSI; Hon. FRACR 1963; Hon. FACR 1975; Hon. MSR 1975; Hon. Mem., British Inst. of Radiology, 1990. Twining Medal, 1945, Knox Lectr, 1962, Pres., 1963–66, Faculty of Radiologists. Gold Medal, RCR, 1986. Hon. Editor, Clinical Radiology, 1954–59. Hon. MD Sheffield, 1985. *Publications:* Recent Advances in Radiology, 3rd edn 1955, 4th edn 1964, 5th edn 1975, 6th edn 1979; articles in Brit. Jl Radiology, Clinical Radiology, etc. *Recreation:* gardening. *Address:* 46 Braemore Court, Kingsway, Hove, E Sussex BN3 4FG. *T:* Brighton (01273) 724371.

See also A. J. C. Lodge.

LOEHNIS, Anthony David, CMG 1988; Director: J. Rothschild International Assurance Holdings plc, since 1992; J. Rothschild Assurance Holdings plc, since 1993; St James's Place Capital plc, since 1993; *b* 12 March 1936; *s* of Sir Clive Loehnis, KCMG; *m* 1965, Jennifer Forsyth Anderson; three *s*. *Educ:* Eton; New Coll., Oxford (MA); Harvard Sch. of Public Administration. HM Diplomatic Service, 1960–66; J. Henry Schroder Wagg & Co. Ltd, 1967–80 (on secondment to Bank of England, 1977–79); Bank of England: Associate Dir (Overseas), 1980–81; Exec. Dir, 1981–89; Dir, S. G. Warburg Group plc, 1989–92; a Vice-Chm., S. G. Warburg & Co., 1989–92. Chairman: Baring Securities Emerging Markets Index Tracker Fund, 1993–; HTR Japanese Smaller Companies Trust, 1993–; Matheson Lloyd's Investment Trust, 1994–; Director: Bank of Tokyo Internat., 1994–; Alpha Bank London, 1994–. A Public Works Loan Comr, 1994–. Chm., Centre for Economic Policy Res., 1990–. Dir, UK–Japan 2000 Gp, 1990–. Member: Council: Ditchley Foundn, 1992– (Chm., F & G P Cttee, 1993–); Baring Foundn, 1994–. Gov., British Assoc. for Central and Eastern Europe, 1994–. *Address:* (office) 27 St James's Place, SW1A 1NR. *Club:* Garrick.

LOFTHOUSE, Sir Geoffrey, Kt 1995; JP; MP (Lab) Pontefract and Castleford, since Oct. 1978; Deputy Chairman of Ways and Means and Deputy Speaker, House of Commons, since 1992; *b* 18 Dec. 1925; *s* of Ernest and Emma Lofthouse; *m* 1946, Sarah Lofthouse (*d* 1985); one *d*. *Educ:* Featherstone Primary and Secondary Schs; Leeds Univ. MIPM 1984. Haulage hand in mining industry at age of 14. Personnel Manager, NCB Fryston, 1970–78. Member: Pontefract Borough Council, 1962–74 (Mayor, 1967–68); Wakefield Metropolitan District Council, 1974– (Chm., Housing Cttee). Mem., NUM, 1939–64, APEX, 1970–. JP Pontefract, 1970. *Publication:* A Very Miner MP (autobiog.), 1986. *Recreations:* Rugby League, cricket. *Address:* 67 Carleton Crest, Pontefract, West Yorkshire WF8 2QR.

LOFTHOUSE, John Alfred, (Jack), OBE 1967; Member, British National Oil Corporation, 1980–82; *b* 30 Dec. 1917; *s* of John Duncan Lofthouse and Clara Margaret Smith; *m* 1950, Patricia Ninette Mann (*d* 1956); one *d*. *Educ:* Rutlish Sch., Merton; St Catharine's Coll., Cambridge (BA Hons, MA). Joined ICI Ltd as engr, 1939; Engrg Manager, Petrochemicals Div., 1958; Technical Dir, Nobel Div., 1961; Chm., Petrochems Div., 1967; Dir, Main Bd of ICI Ltd, 1970–80: responsibilities included Personnel Dir, Petrochems, Oil, and Explosives businesses, and Chm., ICI Americas Ltd; Dir, Britoil, 1983–88. *Publications:* contrib. Geographical Jl and engrg jls. *Recreations:* gardening, hill-walking, music. *Address:* 10 Westley Court, Austcliffe Lane, Cookley, near Kidderminster, Worcs DY10 3RT.

LOFTHOUSE, Reginald George Alfred, FRICS; Member, Advisory Committee, Centre for Agricultural Strategy, Reading University, since 1980 (Chairman, 1982–92); Vice-Chairman, Standing Conference on Countryside Sports, since 1988 (Convener, 1978–88); *b* Workington, 30 Dec. 1916; *m* 1939, Ann Bernardine Bannan; two *d* (and one *d* decd). *Educ:* Workington Secondary Sch.; with private land agent, Cockermouth. Chartered Surveyor and Land Agent (Talbot-Ponsonby Prizeman). Asst District Officer, Penrith, 1941–42; District Officer, Carlisle, for Cumberland War Agric. Exec. Cttee, 1942–43; Asst Land Comr, West Riding, 1943–46; Land Commissioner: N and E Ridings, 1946–48; Derbs, Leics, Rutland, Northants, 1948–50; Somerset and Dorset, 1950–52; Regional Land Comr, Hdqtrs, 1952–59, and SE Region, 1959–71; Regional Officer, SE Region, Agric., Devel t and Adv. Service, 1971–73; Chief Surveyor, MAFF, 1973–76. Chairman: UK Jt Shelter Res. Cttee, 1958–71; Statutory Cttee on Agric1 Valuations, 1973–76. Mem., Farming and Wildlife Adv. Gp, 1966–81. Adviser to: Lord Porchester's Exmoor Study, 1977; Nature Conservancy Council, 1978–82; Council for Environmental Conservation, 1980–81. Vis. Lectr in Rural Estate Management and Forestry, Regent Street Polytechnic, 1954–62. Member: Bd of Governors, Coll. of Estate Management, 1963–85 (Chm., 1972–77; Research Fellow, 1982–85, Hon. Fellow 1985; Chm., Centre for Advanced Land Use Studies, 1972–81); Court and Council, Reading Univ., 1973–; Delegacy for Nat. Inst. for Res. in Dairying, Shinfield, 1974–80; Gen. Council, RICS, 1974–76; RICS Land Agency and Agric. Div. Council, 1974–77. Hon. Life Mem., Cambridge Univ. Land Soc.; Chm. Farm Bldgs Cttee 1973–80, Mem. Engrg and Bldgs Res. Bd 1973–80, Jt Consultative Organisation. Liveryman, Loriners' Co., 1976; Freeman, City of London, 1976. *Publications:* The Berwyn Mountains Area of Wales, 1979; contrib. professional, techn. and countryside jls. *Address:* c/o College of Estate Management, Whiteknights, Reading RG6 2AW. *Clubs:* Athenæum, MCC.

LOFTUS, Viscount; Charles John Tottenham; Head of French Department, Strathcona-Tweedsmuir School, Calgary; *b* 2 Feb. 1943; *e s* and *heir* of 8th Marquess of Ely, *qv*; *m* 1969, Judith Marvelle, *d* of Dr J. J. Porter, FRS, Calgary, Alberta; one *s* one *d*. *Educ:*

Trinity Coll. Sch., Port Hope, Ont; Ecole Internationale de Genève; Univ. of Toronto (MA). *Address:* 1424 Springfield Place SW, Calgary, Alberta T2W 0Y1, Canada.

LOGAN, David Brian Carleton, CMG 1991; HM Diplomatic Service; Minister, British Embassy, Washington, since 1995; *b* 11 Aug. 1943; *s* of late Captain Brian Ewen Weldon Logan, RN (Retd) and Mary Logan (*née* Fass); *m* 1967, Judith Margaret Walton Cole; one *s* one *d* (and one *s* decd). *Educ:* Charterhouse; University College, Oxford. MA. Foreign Office, 1965; served Istanbul, Ankara and FCO, 1965–70; Private Sec. to Parly Under Sec. of State for Foreign and Commonwealth Affairs, 1970–73; First Sec., 1972; UK Mission to UN, 1973–77; FCO, 1977–82; Counsellor, Hd of Chancery and Consul-Gen., Oslo, 1982–86; Hd of Personnel Ops Dept, FCO, 1986–88; Sen. Associate Mem., St Antony's Coll., Oxford, 1988–89; Minister and Dep. Head of Mission, Moscow, 1989–92; Asst Under Sec. of State (Central and Eastern Europe), 1992–94, (Defence Policy), 1994–95, FCO. *Recreations:* music, reading, sailing. *Address:* c/o Foreign and Commonwealth Office, King Charles Street, SW1A 2AH. *Clubs:* Royal Ocean Racing, Hurlingham.

LOGAN, Sir Donald (Arthur), KCMG 1977 (CMG 1965); HM Diplomatic Service, retired; *b* 25 Aug. 1917; *s* of late Arthur Alfred Logan and Louise Anne Bradley; *m* 1957, Irène Jocelyne Angèle, *d* of Robert Everts (Belgian Ambassador at Madrid, 1932–39) and Alexandra Comnène; one *s* two *d*. *Educ:* Solihull. Fellow, Chartered Insurance Institute, 1939. War of 1939–45: Major, RA; British Army Staff, Washington, 1942–43; Germany, 1945. Joined HM Foreign (subseq. Diplomatic) Service, Dec. 1945; Foreign Office, 1945–47; HM Embassy, Tehran, 1947–51; Foreign Office, 1951–53; Asst Political Agent, Kuwait, 1953–55; Asst Private Sec. to Sec. of State for Foreign Affairs, 1956–58; HM Embassy, Washington, 1958–60; HM Ambassador to Guinea, 1960–62; Foreign Office, 1962–64; Information Counsellor, British Embassy, Paris, 1964–70; Ambassador to Bulgaria, 1970–73; Dep. Permanent UK Rep. to NATO, 1973–75; Ambassador and Permanent Leader, UK Delegn to UN Conf. on Law of the Sea, 1976–77. Leader, UK delegn to Conf. on Marine Living Resources of Antarctica, Buenos Aires and Canberra, 1978–80. Dir, GB/E Europe Centre, 1980–87. Gov., St Clare's Coll., Oxford, 1982– (Chm., 1984–93). Chairman: Jerusalem and the East Mission Trust Ltd, 1981–93; Friends of Bulgaria, 1991–. Vice-Pres., Internat. Exhibitions Bureau, Paris, 1963–67. *Address:* 6 Thurloe Street, SW7 2ST. *Clubs:* Brooks's, Royal Automobile.

LOGAN, Sir Douglas; *see* Logan, Sir R. D.

LOGAN, Prof. Malcolm Ian, PhD; Vice-Chancellor, Monash University, since 1987; *b* 3 June 1931; *m* 1954, Antoinette, *d* of F. Lalich; one *d*. *Educ:* Univ. of Sydney (BA Hons 1951, DipEd 1952, PhD 1965). Lectr in Geography, Sydney Teachers Coll., 1956–58; Lectr in Geog., 1959–64, Sen. Lectr, 1965–67, Univ. of Sydney; Prof. of Geog. and of Urban and Regional Planning, Univ. of Wisconsin, Madison, USA, 1967–71; Monash University: Prof. of Geog., 1971–81; Pro Vice-Chancellor, 1982–85; Dep. Vice-Chancellor, 1986. Visiting Professor: Univ. of Ibadan, Nigeria, 1970–71; LSE, 1973; Nanyang Univ., Singapore, 1979. *Publications:* (jtly) New Viewpoints in Economic Geography, 1966; Studies in Australian Geography, 1968; New Viewpoints in Urban and Industrial Geography, 1971; Urban and Regional Australia, 1975; Urbanisation, the Australian Experience, 1980; (jtly) The Brittle Rim, 1989; contribs to Aust. Geographical Studies, Regional Studies, Land Econs, and Econ. Geography. *Address:* Vice Chancellor's Residence, Monash University, Clayton, Vic 3168, Australia. *T:* 5652000. *Club:* Athenæum (Melbourne).

LOGAN, Sir (Raymond) Douglas, Kt 1983; grazier (sheep and cattle), since 1944; *b* 31 March 1920; *s* of Raymond Hough Logan and Agnes Eleanor Logan; *m* 1944, Florence Pearl McGill (MBE 1975); one *s* one *d* (and one *s* decd). *Educ:* Thornburgh College, Charters Towers. Served RAAF, 1941–44 (Flying Officer, pilot; trained EATS, Australia, 1941–42; served with 66 Sqdn RAF, 1942–44). Member: Qld Govt Beef Cttee of Enquiry, 1975–77; Qld Meat Industry Orgn and Marketing Authority (now Livestock and Meat Authority of Qld), 1978–87; United Graziers Assoc. of Qld; Cattlemen's Union, Qld. *Recreations:* tennis, horse riding, sailing, flying. *Address:* PO Box 200, Dobson Road, Malanda, Qld 4885, Australia.

LOGAN, Rt. Rev. Vincent; *see* Dunkeld, Bishop of, (RC).

LOGAN, William Philip Dowie, MD, PhD, BSc, DPH, FRCP; epidemiological consultant to various national and international organisations, 1974–89; Director, Division of Health Statistics, WHO, 1961–74; *b* 2 Nov. 1914; *s* of late Frederick William Alexander Logan and late Elizabeth Jane Dowie; *m* 1st, Pearl (*née* Piper) (marr. diss.); four *s* two *d* (and one *s* decd); 2nd, Barbara (*née* Huneke). *Educ:* Queen's Park Sch., Glasgow; Universities of Glasgow and London. RAF Med. Branch, 1940–46 (Squadron Leader). Hospital appointments in Glasgow, 1939–40 and 1946. Gen. practice in Barking, Essex, 1947–48; General Register Office, 1948–60 (Chief Medical Statistician, Adviser on Statistics to Ministry of Health, Head of WHO Centre for Classification of Diseases, and Member, WHO panel of experts on Health Statistics). *Publications:* contribs on epidemiology, vital and health statistics in official reports and medical jls. *Address:* 164 Elmer Road, Bognor Regis, West Sussex PO22 6JA; 10 chemin de la Tourelle, 1209 Geneva, Switzerland.

LOGSDAIL, (Christopher) Nicholas (Roald); Managing Director, Lisson Gallery, since 1967; *b* 21 June 1945; *s* of late John Logsdail and of Else Logsdail (*née* Dahl); *m* 1st, 1968, Fiona McLean; one *s*; 2nd, 1985, Caroline Mockett; two *s* one *d*. *Educ:* Bryanston Sch.; Slade Sch., University College London. Opened Lisson Gallery, 1967; organised numerous exhibns, representing work of British and internat. artists; instrumental in introducing new generation of British sculptors, 1979–; Mem., Soc. of London Art Dealers. *Publications:* monographs and artists books, 1970–. *Recreations:* collecting 20th century art and furniture, sailing. *Address:* Lisson Gallery, 67 Lisson Street, NW1 5DA. *T:* 0171–724 2739.

LOGUE, Christopher; *b* 23 Nov. 1926; *s* of John Logue and Molly Logue (*née* Chapman); *m* 1985, Rosemary Hill. *Educ:* Prior Park Coll., Bath; Portsmouth Grammar Sch. Mem., Equity. *Plays:* The Story of Mary Frazer, 1962; trans. Brecht, Baal, 1985. *Screen plays:* Savage Messiah (dir Ken Russell), 1972; (with Walon Green) Crusoe (based on Defoe's novel), 1989. *Broadcast:* The Arrival of the Poet in the City: a melodrama for narrator and seven musicians (music by George Nicholson), 1985; Strings (melodrama for voice and 14 musicians, with music by Jason Osborn), 1988. *Recordings:* (with Tony Kinsey and Bill Le Sage) Red Bird (poetry and jazz), 1960; Songs from The Establishment (singer Annie Ross), 1962; The Death of Patroclus (with Vanessa Redgrave, Alan Dobie and others), 1963. *Film roles:* Swinburne, in Ken Russell's Dante's Inferno, 1966; John Ball, in John Irvin's The Peasants' Revolt, 1969; Cardinal Richelieu, in Ken Russell's The Devils, 1970; TV and stage roles. *Publications: verse:* Wand & Quadrant, 1953; Devil, Maggot & Son, 1956; Songs, 1959; Patrocleia, 1962; ABC, 1966; Pax, 1967; New Numbers, 1969; Twelve Cards, 1972; The Crocodile (illus. Binette Schroeder), 1976; Abecedary (illus. Bert Kitchen), 1977; War Music, 1981; Ode to the Dodo, 1981; Kings, 1991; The Husbands, 1995; *prose:* Ratsmagic (illus. Wayne Anderson), 1976; The Magic Circus (illus. Wayne Anderson), 1979; The Bumper Book of True Stories (illus. Bert Kitchen), 1980; *plays:* The Trial of Cob & Leach, 1959; (with Harry Cookson) The Lilywhite Boys, 1959; trans. Hugo Claus, Friday, 1971; trans. Brecht and Weill, The Seven Deadly Sins, 1986; *anthologies:* The Children's Book of Comic Verse, 1979; London in Verse, 1982; Sweet & Sour, 1983; The Oxford Book of Pseuds, 1983; The Children's Book of Children's Rhymes, 1986; contrib. Private Eye, The Times, The Sunday Times, etc; *as Count Palmiro Vicarion:* Lust, a pornographic novel, 1957; (ed) Count Palmiro Vicarion's Book of Limericks, 1957; (ed) Count Palmiro Vicarion's Book of Bawdy Ballads, 1957. *Address:* 41 Camberwell Grove, SE5 8JA.

LOISELLE, Hon. Gilles, PC 1990; Chief Executive and Adviser to the President, Power Corporation of Canada, since 1994; *b* 20 May 1929; *s* of Arthur Loiselle and Antoinette Lethiecq; *m* 1962, Lorraine Benoît; one *s* one *d*. *Educ:* Sacred-Heart Coll., Sudbury, Ont. BA Laval. Tafari Makonnen Sch., Addis Ababa, 1951–53; Journalist, Le Droit, Ottawa, 1953–56; Haile Selassie First Day Sch., Addis Ababa, 1956–62; Dir, Behrane Zarie Néo Inst., Addis Ababa, 1958–62; Canadian Broadcasting Corporation: Editor, TV French Network, 1962–63; Quebec and Paris correspondent, French Radio and TV Network, 1963–67; Counsellor, Quebec House, Paris, 1967–72; Dir Gen. of Quebec Govt Communications, 1972–76; Pres., Intergovtl Deptl Cttee for Olympic Year, 1976; Dir, Interparly Relations, Quebec Nat. Assembly, 1977; Agent General for Quebec in London, with responsibility for Scandinavian countries, Iceland, and Ireland, 1977–83; Dep. Minister for federal provincial relations, 1983–84, for Cultural Affairs, Quebec, 1984–85; Agent Gen. for Quebec in Rome, 1985–88. MP (PC) Langelier, 1988–93; Minister of State for Finance, 1989–93; Pres., Treasury Bd of Canada, 1990–93; Minister of Finance, 1993. Founder Mem., Assoc. France-Québec, 1969–72; Member: Council, Office franco-québécois pour la Jeunesse, 1973–76; Inst. of Public Admin; RIIA. *Recreations:* reading, gardening. *Address:* Power Corporation of Canada, 751 Victoria Square, Montreal, Quebec H2Y 2J3, Canada.

LOKOLOKO, Sir Tore, GCMG 1977; GCVO 1982; OBE; Chairman, Indosuez Niugini Bank, 1983–89; *b* 21 Sept. 1930; *s* of Loko Loko Tore and Kevau Sarufa; *m* 1950, Lalahaia Meakoro; four *s* six *d*. *Educ:* Sogeri High Sch., PNG. Dip. in Cooperative, India. Chm., PNG Cooperative Fedn, 1965–68; MP, 1968–77 (two terms); Minister for Health, and Dep. Chm. of National Exec. Council, 1968–72. Rep. PNG: Co-op. Conf., Australia, 1951; S Pacific Conf., Lae, 1964; attended UN Gen. Assembly, 1969, and Trusteeship Council, 1971. Governor-General of Papua New Guinea, 1977–82. KStJ 1979. *Address:* c/o Indosuez Niugini Bank, Burns House, Port Moresby, Papua New Guinea.

LOMAS, Alfred; Member (Lab) London North East, European Parliament, since 1979; Leader, British Labour Group, European Parliament, 1985–87; *b* 30 April 1928; *s* of Alfred and Florence Lomas; one *s* one *d*. *Educ:* St Paul's Elem. Sch., Stockport; various further educnl estabs. Solicitor's clerk, 1942–46; Radio Telephony Operator, RAF, 1946–49; various jobs, 1949–51; railway signalman, 1951–59; Labour Party Sec./Agent, 1959–65; Polit. Sec., London Co-op., 1965–79. *Publication:* The Common Market—why we should keep out, 1970. *Recreations:* chess, jogging, arts, sport. *Address:* 28 Brookway, SE3 9BJ. *T:* 0181–852 6689. *Club:* Hackney Labour.

LOMAS, Eric George; Managing Director, Gatwick Airport, since 1994; *b* 26 June 1938; *s* of Arthur Edward Lomas and Florence Lomas; *m* 1959, Carol Letitia Davies; two *d*. *Educ:* Willesden County Grammar School. FCIT. PLA, 1954–69; Associated Container Transportation, 1969–70; BAA, 1970–86, BAA plc, 1986–, Man. Dir, Stansted Airport, 1989–94. Dir, Sussex TEC, 1995–. Mem., SE Reg., CBI, 1995–. *Recreation:* motor boat cruising. *Address:* Gatwick Airport Ltd, London Gatwick Airport, W Sussex RH6 0NP. *Club:* British Motor Yacht.

LOMAS, Julia Carole; Public Trustee, and Chief Executive, Public Trust Office, since 1994; *b* 9 Dec. 1954; *d* of Charles James Lomas and Sadie Lomas; *m* (marr. diss.); one *s*. *Educ:* Coventry Poly. (BA Business Law). Admitted solicitor, 1980. Articled clerk, London Borough of Islington, 1977–80; Dep. Borough Solicitor, London Borough of Waltham Forest, 1980–89; Borough Solicitor, London Borough of Haringey, 1989–94. FIMgt 1994. *Recreations:* theatre, crosswords, dining out. *Address:* The Public Trust Office, 24 Kingsway, WC2B 6JX. *T:* 0171–269 7022.

LOMAX, (Janis) Rachel; Chief of Staff to the President of the World Bank, since 1995; *b* 15 July 1945; *d* of William and Dilys Salmon; *m* 1967, Michael Acworth Lomax (marr. diss. 1990); two *s*. *Educ:* Cheltenham Ladies' Coll.; Girton Coll., Cambridge (MA); LSE (MSc). HM Treasury: Econ. Assistant, 1968; Econ. Advr, 1972; Sen. Econ. Advr, 1978; Principal Pvte Sec. to Chancellor of the Exchequer, 1985–86; Under-Sec., 1986–90; Dep. Sec., 1990–94; Dep. Chief Econ. Advr, 1990–92; Dep. Sec. (Financial Instns and Markets), 1992–94; Dep. Sec., Cabinet Office, 1994–95. Chm., UK Selection Cttee, Harkness Fellowships, 1995–. Mem. Council, REconS, 1989–94. *Address:* World Bank, 1818 H Street NW, Washington, DC 20043, USA. *T:* (202) 4731383.

LOMAX, Rachel; *see* Lomax, J. R.

LOMBARD, Rt. Rev. Charles F.; *see* Fitzgerald-Lombard.

LOMBE, Hon. Sir Edward Christopher E.; *see* Evans-Lombe.

LOMER, Dennis Roy, CBE 1984; *b* 5 Oct. 1923; *s* of Bertie Cecil Lomer and Agnes Ellen Coward; *m* 1949, Audrey May Bick; one *s* one *d*. With Consulting Engineers, 1948–50; joined Electricity Supply Industry, 1950; Project Engr, Transmission Div., 1961; Asst Chief Transmission Engr, 1965; Generation Construction Div. (secondment at Dir level), 1972; Dep. Dir-Gen. (Projects), 1973; Dir-Gen., Transmission Div., 1975; Member: CEGB, 1977–83; Technical Review Gp for Eurotunnel, 1988–92. Dir, Davidson Gp Ltd, 1983–88. Pres., 1985–87, Non-Exec. Dir, 1988–94, Welding Inst; Hon. FWeldI. FIEE; CIMgt. *Recreations:* golf, sailing. *Address:* Henley House, Heathfield Close, Woking, Surrey GU22 7JQ. *T:* Woking (01483) 764656. *Club:* West Hill Golf (Surrey).

LOMER, Geoffrey John, CBE 1985; MA; FEng 1984; FIEE; Chairman, Satellite Information Services Ltd, since 1993; Director (non-executive), Vodafone Group plc, since 1992; *b* 5 Jan. 1932; *s* of Frederick John Lomer and Dorothy Lomer; *m* 1st, 1955, Pauline Helena May (*d* 1974); one *s* one *d*; 2nd, 1977, Antoinette Ryall; one step *s* one step *d*. *Educ:* St Austell Grammar School; Queens' College, Cambridge (MA). Research Engineer, EMI Research Laboratories, 1953–57; Head of Radio Frequency Div., Broadcast Equipment Dept, EMI Electronics, 1957–63; Head of Transmitter Lab., Racal Communications, 1963–68; Technical Dir, Racal Mobilcal, 1968–70; Dir in Charge, Racal Communications Equipment, 1970–76; Dep. Man. Dir, Racal Tacticom, 1976–77; Technical Dir, Racal Electronics plc, 1977–92. Vice Pres., IEE, 1991–94. *Recreations:* music, theatre. *Address:* Ladiko, Little Croft Road, Goring-on-Thames, Reading RG8 9ER.

See also W. M. Lomer.

LOMER, William Michael, PhD; Director, Culham Laboratory, United Kingdom Atomic Energy Authority, 1981–90, retired; *b* 2 March 1926; *s* of Frederick John Lomer and Dorothy Lomer; *m* 1952, Pamela Anne Wakelin; one *s* two *d*. *Educ:* St Austell County

School; University College of the South West, Exeter (MSc London); Queens' College, Cambridge (MA, PhD). Research Scientist, UKAEA, 1952; AERE Harwell: Divison Head, Theory Div., 1958–62; Division Head, Solid State Physics, 1962–68; Research Director, 1968–81; Dep. Dir, Inst. Laue Langevin, Grenoble, 1973–74. Hon. Treasurer, Inst. of Physics, 1980–82. Chm., Oxford CAB, 1994–. Trustee, Oxford Trust, 1991–. FInstP. *Publications:* papers in physics and metallurgical jls. *Recreations:* gardening, walking, painting. *Address:* 7 Hids Copse Road, Cumnor Hill, Oxford OX2 9JJ. *T:* Oxford (01865) 862173.

See also G. J. Lomer.

LONDESBOROUGH, 9th Baron, *cr* 1850; **Richard John Denison;** *b* 2 July 1959; *s* of John Albert Lister, 8th Baron Londesborough, TD, AMICE, and Elizabeth Ann (*d* 1994), *d* of late Edward Little Sale, ICS; *S* father, 1968; *m* 1987, Rikki Morris, *d* of J. E. Morris, Bayswater; one *s* one *d*. *Educ:* Wellington College; Exeter Univ. *Heir: s* Hon. James Frederick Denison, *b* 4 June 1990. *Address:* Edw Cottage, Aberedw, Builth Wells, Powys LD2 3UR.

LONDON, Bishop of, since 1995, **Rt Rev. and Rt Hon. Richard John Carew Chartres;** PC 1995; Prelate of the Order of the British Empire, since 1995; Dean of the Chapels Royal, since 1995; *b* 11 July 1947; *s* of Richard and Charlotte Chartres; *m* 1982, Caroline Mary (*née* McLintock); two *s* two *d*. *Educ:* Hertford Grammar Sch.; Trinity Coll., Cambridge (BA 1968; MA 1973); Cuddesdon Theol Coll., Oxford; Lincoln Theol Coll. Ordained: deacon, 1973; priest, 1974; Asst Curate, St Andrew's, Bedford, dio. of St Albans, 1973–75; Bishop's Domestic Chaplain, St Albans, 1975–80; Archbishop of Canterbury's Chaplain, 1980–84; Vicar, St Stephen with St John, Westminster, 1984–92; Director of Ordinands for London Area, 1985–92; Area Bishop of Stepney, 1992–95. Gresham Prof. of Divinity, 1986–92. Six Preacher, Canterbury Cathedral, 1991–. BD Lambeth, 1983. *Address:* c/o London Diocesan House, 36 Causton Street, SW1P 4AU.

LONDON, Archdeacon of; *see* Cassidy, Ven. G. H.

LONDON, EAST, Bishop in, (RC); *see* Guazzelli, Rt Rev. Victor.

LONDON, NORTH, Bishop in, (RC); *see* Harvey, Rt Rev. Philip.

LONDON, WEST, Bishop in, (RC); *see* O'Donoghue, Rt Rev. P.

LONDONDERRY, 9th Marquess of, *cr* 1816; **Alexander Charles Robert Vane-Tempest-Stewart;** Baron Londonderry, 1789; Viscount Castlereagh, 1795; Earl of Londonderry, 1796; Baron Stewart, 1814; Earl Vane, Viscount Seaham, 1823; *b* 7 Sept. 1937; *s* of 8th Marquess of Londonderry and Romaine (*d* 1951), *er d* of Major Boyce Combe, Great Holt, Dockenfield, Surrey; *S* father 1955; *m* 1st, 1958, Nicolette (marr. diss. 1971; she *d* 1993), *d* of Michael Harrison, Netherhampton, near Salisbury, Wilts; two *d*; 2nd, 1972, Doreen Patricia Wells, *qv*; two *s*. *Educ:* Eton. *Heir: s* Viscount Castlereagh, *qv*. *Address:* PO Box No 8, Shaftesbury, Dorset SP7 0LR.

LONDONDERRY, Marchioness of; *see* Wells, Doreen P.

LONG, family name of **Viscount Long.**

LONG, 4th Viscount, *cr* 1921, of Wraxall; **Richard Gerard Long,** CBE 1993; a Lord in Waiting (Government Whip), since 1979; *b* 30 Jan. 1929; *s* of 3rd Viscount and Gwendolyn (*d* 1959), *d* of Thomas Reginald Hague Cook; *S* father, 1967; *m* 1957, Margaret Frances (marr. diss. 1984), *d* of late Ninian B. Frazer; one *s* one *d* (and one *d* decd); *m* 1984, Catherine Patricia Elizabeth Mier-Woolf (marr. diss. 1990), *d* of C. T. Mills-Ede, S Africa; *m* 1990, Helen Fleming-Gibbons. *Educ:* Harrow. Wilts Regt, 1947–49. Opposition Whip, 1974–79. Vice-Pres. and formerly Vice-Chm., Wilts Royal British Legion; Pres., Bath Gliding Club. Freedom, City of London, 1991. *Heir: s* Hon. James Richard Long, *b* 31 Dec. 1960. *Address:* House of Lords, SW1A 0PW. *Club:* Pratt's.

LONG, Athelstan Charles Ethelwulf, CMG 1968; CBE 1964 (MBE 1959); President, United Bank International, Cayman Islands, since 1975; Chairman: International Management Group, since 1988; Casualty Underwriters Inc., since 1989; Chairman and Director of some twelve companies; Chairman, Public Service Commission, since 1987; Deputy Chairman, Public Service Pensions Board, since 1992; *b* 2 Jan. 1919; *s* of Arthur Leonard Long and Gabrielle Margaret Campbell (historical writer and novelist, Marjorie Bowen); *m* 1948, Edit Mäjken Zadie Harriet Krantz, *d* of late Erik Krantz, Stockholm; two *s*. *Educ:* Westminster Sch.; Brasenose Coll., Oxford. Served War of 1939–45: commnd into RA, 1940; seconded 7th (Bengal) Battery, 22nd Mountain Regt, IA, 1940; served Malaya; POW as Capt., 1942–45; appointed to Indian Political Service, 1946. Cadet, Burma Civil Service, 1947–48; Colonial Admin. Service (N Nigeria), 1948; Sen. District Officer, 1958; Resident, Zaria Province, 1959; Perm. Sec., Min. of Animal Health and Forestry, 1959; started new Min. of Information as Perm. Sec., 1960; Swaziland: appointed Govt Sec., 1961; Chief Sec., 1964; Leader of Govt business in Legislative Council and MEC, 1964–67; HM Dep. Comr, 1967–68; Administrator, later Governor, of the Cayman Is, 1968–71; Comr of Anguilla, March-July 1972; Admin. Sec., Inter-University Council, 1972–73. Man. Dir, Anegada Corp. Ltd, 1973–74; Dir and Chm., Cayman Airways, 1977–81. Chairman: Planning Appeals Tribunal, 1982–84; Coastal Works Adv. Cttee, 1986–91. Chm. Governing Council, Waterford Sch., Swaziland, 1963–68. FRAS; FRGS. *Recreations:* travel, tropical farming, reading. *Address:* Box 131, Savannah, Grand Cayman, Cayman Islands, West Indies.

LONG, Christopher William, CMG 1986; HM Diplomatic Service; Ambassador to Hungary, since 1995; *b* 9 April 1938; *s* of late Eric and May Long; *m* 1972, Patricia, *d* of late Dennis and May Stanbridge; two *s* one *d*. *Educ:* King Edward's Sch., Birmingham; Balliol Coll., Oxford (Deakin Scholar); Univ. of Münster, W Germany. Served RN, 1956–58. HM Diplomatic Service, 1963–: FO, 1963–64; Jedda, 1965–67; Caracas, 1967–69; FCO, 1969–74; Budapest, 1974–77; Belgrade (CSCE), 1977; Counsellor, Damascus, 1978–80; Counsellor and Dep. Perm. Rep., UKMIS, Geneva, 1980–83; Head, Near East and N Africa Dept, FCO, 1983–85; Asst Under-Sec. of State (Dep. Chief Clerk and Chief Inspector), FCO, 1985–88; Ambassador to Switzerland, 1988–92 and also to Liechtenstein, 1992; Ambassador to Egypt, 1992–95. *Address:* c/o Foreign and Commonwealth Office, King Charles Street, SW1A 2AH; British Embassy, Harmincad Utca 6, Budapest, Hungary. *T:* (1) 2662888. *Club:* Athenæum.

LONG, Gerald; *b* 22 Aug. 1923; *o s* of Fred Harold Long and Sabina Long (*née* Walsh); *m* 1951, Anne Hamilton Walker; two *s* three *d*. *Educ:* St Peter's Sch., York; Emmanuel Coll., Cambridge. Army Service, 1943–47. Joined Reuters, 1948: served as Reuter correspondent in Germany, France and Turkey, 1950–60; Asst General Manager, 1960; Chief Exec., 1963–81 (Gen. Manager, 1963–73; Man. Dir, 1973–81); Man. Dir, Times Newspapers Ltd, 1981–82; Dep. Chm., News International plc, 1982–84. Chairman: Visnews Ltd, 1968–79; Exec. Cttee, Internat. Inst. of Communications Ltd, 1973–78. Mem., Design Council, 1974–77; Council Mem., Journalists in Europe, 1974– (Exec. Dir, 1987–88). CBIM (FBIM 1978). Commander, Royal Order of the Phoenix, Greece, 1964; Grand Officer, Order of Merit, Italy, 1973; Commander, Order of the Lion of Finland, 1979; Chevalier de la Légion d'Honneur, France, 1979; Commander's Cross, Order of Merit, Federal Republic of Germany, 1983. *Recreation:* cooking. *Address:* 15 rue d'Aumale, BP5.09, 75421 Paris, France. *T:* 48746726; 15 rue W. K. Ferguson, 14400 St Martin-des-Entrees, France. *T:* 31924712.

LONG, Hubert Arthur, CBE 1970; Deputy Secretary, Exchequer and Audit Department, 1963–73; *b* 21 Jan. 1912; *s* of Arthur Albert Long; *m* 1937, Mary Louise Parker; three *s*. *Educ:* Taunton's Sch., Southampton. Entered Exchequer and Audit Department, 1930. *Address:* 2A Hawthorndene Road, Hayes, Kent BR2 7DY. *T:* 0181–462 4373.

LONG, John Richard, CBE 1987; freelance consultant on National Health Service management and state regulation of medicines; *b* 9 March 1931; *s* of late Thomas Kendall Long and Jane Long; *m* 1952, Margaret (*née* Thistlethwaite); one *s* two *d*. *Educ:* Kirkham Grammar School. Clerical Officer, Customs and Excise, 1947; Exec. Officer, Min. of Pensions, subseq. DHSS, 1949; various posts on health functions; Asst Sec., 1978 (posts on regulation and pricing of medicines, maternity and child health, and communicable diseases); Under Sec., 1987 (NHS Personnel Div.), resigned 1988; Associate Mem., Lambeth, Southwark and Lewisham FHSA, 1992–. *Publications:* co-author, articles on regulation of medicines. *Recreations:* vegetable growing, wild life, writing stories for children. *Address:* 77 Prospect Road, Farnborough, Hants GU14 8NT. *T:* Farnborough (01252) 548525.

LONG, Ven. John Sanderson, MA; Archdeacon of Ely, Hon. Canon of Ely and Rector of St Botolph's, Cambridge, 1970–81; Archdeacon Emeritus, 1981; *b* 21 July 1913; *s* of late Rev. Guy Stephenson Long and Ivy Marion Long; *m* 1948, Rosamond Mary, *d* of Arthur Temple Forman; one *s* three *d*. *Educ:* St Edmund's Sch., Canterbury; Queens' Coll., Cambridge; Cuddesdon Theological Coll. Deacon, 1936; Priest, 1937; Curate, St Mary and St Eanswythe, Folkestone, 1936–41. Chaplain, RNVR, 1941–46. Curate, St Peter-in-Thanet, 1946; Domestic Chaplain to the Archbishop of Canterbury, 1946–53; Vicar of: Bearsted, 1953–59; Petersfield with Sheet, 1959–70; Rural Dean of Petersfield, 1962–70. *Recreations:* walking, gardening. *Address:* 23 Thornton Road, Girton, Cambridge CB3 0NP. *T:* Cambridge (01223) 276421.

LONG, Olivier; Ambassador; President, Graduate Institute of Public Administration, Lausanne, 1981–89; *b* 1915; *s* of Dr Edouard Long and Dr Marie Landry; *m* 1946, Francine Roels; one *s* two *d*. *Educ:* Univ. de Paris, Faculté de Droit et Ecole des Sciences Politiques; Univ. de Genève. PhD Law, 1938; Rockefeller Foundn Fellow, 1938–39; PhD Pol. Sc., 1943. Swiss Armed Forces, 1939–43; International Red Cross, 1943–46; Swiss Foreign Affairs Dept, Berne, 1946–49; Washington Embassy, 1949–54; Govt Delegate for Trade Agreements, 1955–66; Head of Swiss Delegn to EFTA, 1960–66; Ambassador to UK and Malta, 1967–68; Dir-Gen., GATT, 1968–80. Prof., Graduate Inst. of Internat. Studies, Geneva, 1962–85. Mem., Internat. Red Cross Cttee, 1980–. Trustee, Foundn for Internat. Conciliation, Geneva, 1984–. *Publications:* Law and its Limitations in the GATT Multilateral Trade System, 1985; Le dossier secret des Accords d'Evian—une mission suisse pour la paix en Algérie, 1988. *Address:* 6 rue Constantin, 1206 Geneva, Switzerland.

LONG, Pamela Marjorie, (Mrs John Nichols); Metropolitan Stipendiary Magistrate, 1978–92; *b* 12 Sept. 1930; *d* of late John Holywell Long, AMICE, and Emily McNaughton; *m* 1966, Kenneth John Heastey Nichols, *qv*. *Educ:* Carlisle and County High School for Girls. Admitted Solicitor of Supreme Court, 1959; private practice, 1959–63; Solicitor's Dept, New Scotland Yard, 1963–77. Mem., Cttee of Magistrates for Inner London, 1984–90. *Address:* Flat 1, 36 Buckingham Gate, SW1E 6PB; Dolphin House, Porthgwarra, St Levan, Cornwall TR19 6JP.

LONG, Captain Rt. Hon. William Joseph, OBE 1985; PC (N Ireland) 1966; JP; Minister of Education, Northern Ireland, 1969–72; MP (Unionist) Ards, Parliament of Northern Ireland, 1962–72; *b* 23 April 1922; *s* of James William Long and Frederica (Walker); *m* 1942, Dr Elizabeth Doreen Mercer; one *s*. *Educ:* Friends' Sch., Great Ayton, Yorks; Edinburgh Univ.; RMC, Sandhurst. Served Royal Inniskilling Fusiliers, 1940–48. Secretary: NI Marriage Guidance Council, 1948–51; NI Chest and Heart Assoc., 1951–62. Parliamentary Secretary, Min. of Agriculture, NI, 1964–66; Sen. Parliamentary Secretary, Min. of Development, NI, Jan.-Oct. 1966; Minister of Educn, 1966–68; Minister of Home Affairs, Dec. 1968–March 1969; Minister of Develt, March 1969–May 1969. *Recreations:* cricket, horticulture, angling, sailing, model engineering, aviation. *Address:* Lisvarna, Warren Road, Donaghadee, Co. Down. *T:* Donaghadee (01247) 2538.

LONGAIR, Prof. Malcolm Sim, PhD; FRSE 1981; Jacksonian Professor of Natural Philosophy, University of Cambridge, since 1991; Professorial Fellow, Clare Hall, Cambridge, since 1991; *b* 18 May 1941; *s* of James Sim Longair and Lily Malcolm; *m* 1975, Dr Deborah Janet Howard; one *s* one *d*. *Educ:* Morgan Acad., Dundee; Queen's Coll., Dundee, Univ. of St Andrews (BSc Electronic Physics, 1963); Cavendish Lab., Univ. of Cambridge (MA, PhD 1967). Res. Fellow, Royal Commn for Exhibn of 1851, 1966–68; Royal Soc. Exchange Fellow to USSR, 1968–69; University of Cambridge: Res. Fellow, 1967–71, and Official Fellow, 1971–80, Clare Hall; Univ. Demonstrator in Phys., 1970–75; Univ. Lectr in Phys., 1975–80; Astronomer Royal for Scotland, Regius Prof. of Astronomy, Univ. of Edinburgh, and Dir, Royal Observatory, Edinburgh, 1980–90. Vis. Professor: of Radio Astronomy, Calif Inst. of Technol., 1972; of Astronomy, Inst. for Advanced Study, Princeton, 1978; Regents' Fellow, Carnegie Inst., Harvard Univ., 1990. Editor, Monthly Notices of RAS, 1974–78. Hon. LLD Dundee, 1982. Britannica Award, 1986. *Publications:* (ed) Confrontation of Cosmological Theories with Observational Data, 1974; (ed with J. Einasto) The Large-Scale Structure of the Universe, 1978; (with J. E. Gunn and M. J. Rees) Observational Cosmology, 1978; (ed with J. Warner) The Scientific Uses of the Space Telescope, 1980; High Energy Astrophysics: an informal introduction, 1980, rev. edn as High Energy Astrophysics, vol. 1: Particles, Photons and their Detection, 1992; High Energy Astrophysics, vol. 2: Stars, the Galaxy and the Interstellar Medium, 1994; (ed with H. A. Brück and G. Coyne) Astrophysical Cosmology, 1982; Theoretical Concepts in Physics, 1984; Alice and the Space Telescope, 1989; The Origins of Our Universe, 1991, rev. edn 1994; over 100 papers, mostly in Monthly Notices of RAS. *Recreations:* music, art, architecture. *Address:* c/o Cavendish Laboratory, Madingley Road, Cambridge CB3 0HE. *T:* Cambridge (01223) 337083.

LONGBOTTOM, Charles Brooke; Chairman, Acorn Christian Healing Trust, since 1988; *b* 22 July 1930; *s* of late William Ewart Longbottom, Forest Hill, Worksop; *m* 1962, Anita, *d* of G. Trapani and Mrs Basil Mavroleon; two *d*. *Educ:* Uppingham. Contested (C) Stockton-on-Tees, 1955; MP (C) York, 1959–66; Parly Private Secretary to Mr Iain Macleod, Leader of the House, 1961–63. Barrister, Inner Temple, 1958; Chairman: Austin & Pickersgill, Shipbuilders, Sunderland, 1966–72; A&P Appledore International Ltd, 1970–79; Seascope Holdings Ltd, 1970–82; Seascope Sale & Purchase, 1970–87; Seascope Shipping Ltd, 1982–87; Seascope Insurance Holdings Ltd, 1984–86; Seascope Insurance Services Ltd, 1984–87; Illingworth Morris Pension Trustees Ltd, 1990–94; Director: Henry Ansbacher Hldgs Ltd, 1982–87; Henry Ansbacher & Co., 1982–87; Ansbacher (Guernsey) Ltd, 1982–87; British Shipbuilders, 1986–; Kelt Energy plc, 1988–95; MC Shipping Inc., 1989–; Newman Martin & Buchan, 1992–. Member: General Advisory Council, BBC, 1965–75; Community Relations Commn, 1968–70. *Recreations:* shooting, golf and racing. *Address:* 66 Kingston House North, Princes Gate, SW7 1LN. *Clubs:* White's, Carlton; Wentworth; Berkshire.

LONGDEN, Sir Gilbert (James Morley), Kt 1972; MBE 1944; MA (Cantab), LLB; *b* 16 April 1902; *e s* of late Lieut-Colonel James Morley Longden, Castle Eden, Co. Durham, and of late Kathleen, *d* of George Blacker Morgan, JP; unmarried. *Educ:* Haileybury; Emmanuel Coll., Cambridge. Secretary ICI (India) Ltd, 1930–37; travelled throughout Asia (Middle and Far East) and in North and South America. Student at University of Paris, 1937. Called up from AOER into DLI, 1940; served with 2nd and 36th Divisions in Burma campaigns (MBE (mil.)). Adopted Parliamentary Candidate for Morpeth, 1938; contested (C) Morpeth, 1945; MP (C) SW Herts, 1950–Feb. 1974. UK Representative to Council of Europe, 1953–54; United Kingdom Delegate to 12th and 13th Sessions of United Nations; Past Chairman: British Atlantic Cttee; Conservative Gp for Europe; Great Britain-East Europe Centre. Vice-Chm., British Council. *Publications:* A Conservative Philosophy, 1947; and (jointly): One Nation, 1950; Change is our Ally, 1954; A Responsible Society, 1959; One Europe, 1969. *Recreations:* reading, writing, gardening. *Address:* 89 Cornwall Gardens, SW7 4AX. *T:* 0171–584 5666. *Club:* Brooks's.

LONGDEN, Henry Alfred, FEng, FICE, FIMinE; FGS; Director, Trafalgar House Investments Ltd, 1970–76; *b* 8 Sept. 1909; *s* of late Geoffrey Appleby Longden and late Marjorie Mullins; *m* 1935, Ruth, *d* of Arthur Gilliat, Leeds; one *s* four *d*. *Educ:* Oundle; Birmingham Univ. (BSc Hons). Served in Glass Houghton and Pontefract Collieries, 1930; Asst Gen. Manager, Stanton Ironworks Co., 1935; Gen. Manager, Briggs Colliers Ltd, 1940; Director: Blackwell Colliery Co., 1940; Briggs Collieries Co., 1941; New Hucknell Colliery Co., 1941; Area Gen. Manager, 1947, and Production Dir, 1948, NE Div., NCB; Dir-Gen., Production, NCB, 1955; Chm., W Midlands Div., NCB, 1960; Chm. and Chief Exec., Cementation Co. Ltd, 1963–70 (Dep. Chm. and Chief Exec, 1961–63). President: Instn of Mining Engineers, 1958; Engineering Industries Assoc., 1965–71; Member: Engineering Industry Trg Bd, 1967–70; Confedn of British Industry, 1968. Fellow, Fellowship of Engineering, 1977. *Publication:* Cadman Memorial Lecture, 1958. *Recreations:* Rugby football, cricket, tennis, shooting, fishing, sailing. *Address:* Raeburn, Northdown Road, Woldingham, Surrey CR3 7BB. *T:* Woldingham (01883) 852245.

LONGDEN, Wilson, JP; education and training consultant; *b* 26 May 1936; *s* of late Harold and Doris Longden; *m* 1st, 1966 (marr. diss. 1982); two *s*; 2nd, 1985, Olga Longden. *Educ:* Chesterfield Grammar Sch.; Univ. of Hull (BA Hons, Dip Ed); Univ. of Bradford (MSc). National service, RAF, 1955–57; Teacher, Northmount High Sch., Canada, 1961–62; Lecturer: Matthew Boulton Tech. Coll., Birmingham, 1962–66; Bingley Coll. of Educn, 1966–67; Margaret McMillan Coll. of Educn, 1967–68; Hatfield Polytechnic, 1968–69; Coventry (Lanchester) Polytechnic, 1969–73; Vice-Principal, Barnfield College, Luton, 1973–87. Sec., Assoc. of Vice-Principals of Colleges, 1986–87 (Pres., 1982–84). Comr, MSC, 1983–85. JP Luton, 1980. *Publications:* The School Manager's and the School Governor's Handbook, 1977; Meetings, 1977; Making Secondments Work, 1990. *Recreations:* music, playing the organ and the piano. *Address:* 311 Turnpike Drive, Luton LU3 3RE. *T:* Luton (01582) 573905.

LONGFIELD, Dr Michael David; Vice-Chancellor, University of Teesside, 1992 (Director, Teesside Polytechnic, 1980–92), retired; *b* 28 April 1928; *s* of late Edric Douglas Longfield and Dorothy Longfield (*née* Hennessey); *m* 1st, 1952, Ann McDonnell; two *s* two *d*; 2nd, 1970, June Shirley, *d* of late Levi and Esther Beman; two *s*. *Educ:* Prince Henry's Grammar Sch., Otley; Leeds Univ. BSc, PhD; CEng, MIMechE. Lectr in Mech. Engrg, Univ. of Leeds, 1960–68; Manager, Leeds Univ. Industrial Unit of Tribology, 1968–70; Head of Dept of Mech., Marine and Production Engrg, Liverpool Polytechnic, 1970–72; Asst Dir, Teesside Poly., 1972–80. *Recreation:* the genealogy of not only the Longfields but also the Langfields. *Address:* Plum Tree House, Thirlby, Thirsk, N Yorks YO7 2DJ.

LONGFORD, 7th Earl of, *cr* 1785, **Francis Aungier Pakenham,** KG 1971; PC 1948; Baron Longford, 1759; Baron Silchester (UK), 1821; Baron Pakenham (UK), 1945; *b* 5 Dec. 1905; 2nd *s* of 5th Earl of Longford, KP, MVO; *S* brother (6th Earl) 1961; *m* 1931, Elizabeth (*see* Countess of Longford); four *s* three *d* (and one *d* decd). *Educ:* Eton; New Coll., Oxford, MA. 1st Class in Modern Greats, 1927. Tutor, University Tutorial Courses, Stoke-on-Trent, 1929–31; Cons. Party Economic Res. Dept, 1930–32. Christ Church, Oxford: Lecturer in Politics, 1932; Student in Politics, 1934–46, and 1952–64. Prospective Parliamentary Labour Candidate for Oxford City, 1938. Enlisted Oxford and Bucks LI (TA), May 1939; resigned commission on account of ill-health, 1940. Personal assistant to Sir William Beveridge, 1941–44; a Lord-in-Waiting to the King, 1945–46; Parliamentary Under-Secretary of State, War Office, 1946–47; Chancellor of the Duchy of Lancaster, 1947–48; Minister of Civil Aviation, 1948–51; First Lord of the Admiralty, May-Oct. 1951; Lord Privy Seal, 1964–65; Secretary of State for the Colonies, 1965–66; Leader of the House of Lords, 1964–68; Lord Privy Seal, 1966–68; Chm., The National Bank Ltd, 1955–63; Dir, Sidgwick and Jackson, 1980–85 (Chm., 1970–80). Chm., Nat. Youth Employment Council, 1968–71; Joint Founder: New Horizon Youth Centre, 1964; New Bridge for Ex-Prisoners, 1956; (also Dir) The Help Charitable Trust, 1986. *Publications:* Peace by Ordeal (The Anglo-Irish Treaty of 1921), 1935 (repr. 1972); (autobiog.) Born to Believe, 1953; (with Roger Opie), Causes of Crime, 1958; The Idea of Punishment, 1961; (autobiog.) Five Lives, 1964; Humility, 1969; (with Thomas P. O'Neill) Eamon De Valera, 1970; (autobiog.) The Grain of Wheat, 1974; Abraham Lincoln, 1974; Jesus Christ, 1974; Kennedy, 1976; St Francis of Assisi, 1978; Nixon, 1980; (with Anne McHardy) Ulster, 1981; Pope John Paul II, 1982; Diary of a Year, 1982; Eleven at No. 10: a personal view of Prime Ministers, 1984; One Man's Faith, 1984; The Search for Peace, 1985; The Bishops, 1986; Saints, 1987; A History of the House of Lords, 1989; Suffering and Hope, 1990; Punishment and the Punished, 1991; Prisoner or Patient, 1992; Young Offenders, 1993; (autobiog.) Avowed Intent, 1994. *Heir: s* Thomas (Frank Dermot) Pakenham, *qv*. *Address:* Bernhurst, Hurst Green, East Sussex TN19 7QN. *T:* Hurst Green (0158086) 248; 18 Chesil Court, Chelsea Manor Street, SW3 5QP. *T:* 0171–352 7794.

See also Lady Rachel Billington, Lady Antonia Fraser, Hon. M. A. Pakenham, A. D. Powell.

LONGFORD, Countess of; Elizabeth Pakenham, CBE 1974; *b* 30 Aug. 1906; *d* of late N. B. Harman, FRCS, 108 Harley Street, W1, and of Katherine (*née* Chamberlain); *m* 1931, Hon. F. A. Pakenham (*see* 7th Earl of Longford); four *s* three *d* (and one *d* decd). *Educ:* Headington Sch., Oxford; Lady Margaret Hall, Oxford (MA). Lectr for WEA and Univ. Extension Lectr, 1929–35. Contested (Lab) Cheltenham, 1935, Oxford, 1950; candidate for King's Norton, Birmingham, 1935–43. Mem., Rent Tribunal, Paddington and St Pancras, 1947–54; Trustee, National Portrait Gall., 1968–78; Member: Adv. Council, V&A Museum, 1969–75; Adv. Bd, British Library, 1976–80; Hon. Life Pres., Women Writers and Journalists, 1979. Hon. DLitt Sussex 1970. *Publications:* (as Elizabeth Pakenham): Points for Parents, 1956; Catholic Approaches (ed), 1959; Jameson's Raid, 1960, new edn 1982; (as Elizabeth Longford) Victoria RI, 1964 (James Tait Black Memorial Prize for Non-Fiction, 1964); Wellington: Years of the Sword, 1969 (Yorkshire Post Prize); Wellington: Pillar of State, 1972; The Royal House of Windsor, 1974; Churchill, 1974; Byron's Greece, 1975; Life of Byron, 1976; A Pilgrimage of Passion: the life of Wilfrid Scawen Blunt, 1979; (ed) Louisa: Lady in Waiting, 1979; Images of Chelsea, 1980; The Queen Mother, a biography, 1981; Eminent Victorian Women, 1981; Elizabeth R, 1983; The Pebbled Shore (autobiog.), 1986; The Oxford Book of Royal Anecdotes, 1989; Darling Loosy; Letters to Princess Louise 1856–1939, 1991; Wellington (abridged), 1992; Poet's Corner: an anthology, 1992; Royal Throne: the future of the Monarchy, 1993. *Recreations:* gardening, reading. *Address:* Bernhurst, Hurst Green, East Sussex TN19 7QN. *T:* Hurst Green (0158086) 248; 18 Chesil Court, Chelsea Manor Street, SW3 5QP. *T:* 0171–352 7794.

See also Lady Rachel Billington, Lady Antonia Fraser, Hon. M. A. Pakenham, T. F. D. Pakenham.

LONGFORD, Elizabeth; *see* Longford, Countess of.

LONGHURST, Andrew Henry, FCIB; FBCS; Chief Executive, Cheltenham & Gloucester Building Society, since 1982; *b* 23 Aug. 1939; *s* of Henry and Connie Longhurst; *m* 1962, Margaret; one *s* two *d*. *Educ:* Nottingham University (BSc Hons). FBCS 1968; FCIB (FCBSI 1990); CIMgt (CBIM 1989). Computer systems consultancy, 1961; Cheltenham & Gloucester Building Society: Data Processing Manager, 1967; Asst Gen. Man. (Admin), 1970; Dep. Gen. Man., 1977. Mem. Exec. Cttee, Lloyds Bank, 1995–. Chm., Council of Mortgage Lenders, 1994. *Recreation:* golf. *Address:* Cheltenham & Gloucester Building Society, Chief Office, Barnett Way, Gloucester GL4 7RL. *T:* Gloucester (01452) 372372.

LONGLEY, Mrs Ann Rosamund; Head Mistress, Roedean School, since 1984; *b* 5 March 1942; *d* of late Jack Gilroy Dearlove and of Rhoda E.M. Dearlove (*née* Billing); *m* 1964, Stephen Roger Longley (*d* 1979); one *s* two *d*. *Educ:* Walthamstow Hall School, Sevenoaks; Edinburgh University (MA 1964); PGCE Bristol University, 1984. Wife and mother, 1964–; Teacher, Toorak Coll., Victoria, Australia, 1964–65; Asst Housemistress, Peninsula C of E Sch., Victoria, 1966–67; Residential Teacher, Choate School, Conn, USA, 1968–73; Teacher, Webb School, Calif, 1975–78; Headmistress, Vivian Webb School, Calif, 1981–84. DUniv Sussex, 1991. *Recreations:* tennis, swimming, fishing, walking. *Address:* Roedean House, Roedean School, Brighton, Sussex BN2 5RQ. *T:* Brighton (01273) 603181.

LONGMAN, Peter Martin; Director (formerly Secretary), Museums and Galleries Commission, 1984–95; *b* 2 March 1946; *s* of Denis Martin Longman and Mary Joy Longman (*née* Simmonds); *m* 1976, Sylvia June Prentice; two *d*. *Educ:* Huish's School, Taunton; University College, Cardiff; Univ. of Manchester. Finance Dept and Housing the Arts Officer, Arts Council, 1968–78; Dep. Dir, Crafts Council, 1978–83; Dep. Sec., Museums and Galleries Commn, 1983–84. Dir, Caryl Jenner Productions Ltd, 1983–87. A Dir, Scottish Museums Council, 1986–95; Mem. Council, Textile Conservation Centre Ltd, 1983– (Mem., Exec. Cttee, 1983–85); Mem., BTA Heritage Cttee, 1991–95. Trustee, Theatres Trust, 1991–. FRSA 1989. *Publications:* Working Party Reports: Training Arts Administrators, Arts Council, 1971; Area Museum Councils and Services, HMSO, 1984; Museums in Scotland, HMSO, 1986; articles on theatre, the arts, museums. *Recreations:* discovering Britain, listening to music. *Address:* 8 Eastbourne Road, Chiswick, W4 3EB. *T:* and *Fax:* 0181–987 9390.

LONGMORE, Hon. Sir Andrew (Centlivres), Kt 1993; **Hon. Mr Justice Longmore;** a Judge of the High Court, Queen's Bench Division, since 1993; *b* 25 Aug. 1944; *s* of John Bell Longmore and Virginia Longmore (*née* Centlivres); *m* 1979, Margaret Murray McNair; one *s*. *Educ:* Winchester College; Lincoln College, Oxford. MA. Called to the Bar, Middle Temple, 1966, Bencher, 1990. QC 1983; a Recorder, 1992–93. Chm., Law Reform Cttee, Bar Council, 1987–90. *Publications:* (co-editor) MacGillivray and Parkington, Law of Insurance, 6th edn 1975, 8th edn 1988. *Recreation:* fell-walking. *Address:* Royal Courts of Justice, Strand, WC2A 2LL.

LONGRIGG, Anthony James, CMG 1992; HM Diplomatic Service; Counsellor, Madrid, since 1991; *b* 21 April 1944; *m* 1967, Jane Rosa Cowlin; three *d*. Joined FCO, 1972; Second, later First, Sec., Moscow, 1975; FCO 1978; Brasilia, 1981; First Sec., FCO, 1985; Counsellor, Moscow, 1987. *Address:* c/o Foreign and Commonwealth Office, SW1A 2AH.

LONGRIGG, John Stephen, CMG 1973; OBE 1964; HM Diplomatic Service, retired; *b* 1 Oct. 1923; *s* of late Brig. Stephen Hemsley Longrigg, OBE; *m* 1st, 1953, Lydia Meynell (marr. diss. 1965); one *s* one *d*; 2nd, 1966, Ann O'Reilly; one *s* decd. *Educ:* Rugby Sch.; Magdalen Coll., Oxford (BA). War Service, Rifle Bde, 1942–45 (despatches). FO, 1948; Paris, 1948; Baghdad, 1951; FO, 1953; Berlin, 1955; Cabinet Office, 1957; FO, 1958; Dakar, 1960; Johannesburg, 1962; Pretoria, 1962; Washington, 1964; FO, 1965–67; Bahrain, 1967–69; FCO, 1969–73; seconded to HQ British Forces, Hong Kong, 1974–76; FCO, 1976–82; Administrator, Common Law Inst. of Intellectual Property, 1983–88. *Recreation:* golf. *Address:* 45A Blackheath Park, Blackheath, SE3 9SQ. *T:* 0181–852 4007. *Clubs:* Reform; Royal Blackheath Golf, Littlestone Golf.

See also R. E. Longrigg.

LONGRIGG, Roger Erskine; author; *b* 1 May 1929; *s* of Brig. S. H. Longrigg, OBE; *m* 1957, Jane Chichester; three *d*. *Educ:* Bryanston Sch.; Magdalen Coll., Oxford (BA Hons Mod. Hist.). *Publications:* A High Pitched Buzz, 1956; Switchboard, 1957; Wrong Number, 1959; Daughters of Mulberry, 1961; The Paper Boats, 1963; The Artless Gambler, 1964; Love among the Bottles, 1967; The Sun on the Water, 1969; The Desperate Criminals, 1971; The History of Horse Racing, 1972; The Jevington System, 1973; Their Pleasing Sport, 1975; The Turf, 1975; The History of Foxhunting, 1975; The Babe in the Wood, 1976; The English Squire and his Sport, 1977; Bad Bet, 1982; also 38 books under pseudonyms Megan Barker, Gloria Beckford, Laura Black, Ivor Drummond, Rosalind Erskine, Frank Parish, Domini Taylor. *Recreation:* painting. *Address:* Orchard House, Crookham, Hants. GU13 0SY. *T:* Aldershot (01252) 850333. *Clubs:* Brooks's, Pratt's.

See also J. S. Longrigg.

LONGSTRETH THOMPSON, Francis Michael; *see* Thompson, F. M. L.

LONGUET-HIGGINS, Prof. Hugh Christopher, DPhil (Oxon); FRS 1958; Professor Emeritus, University of Sussex, 1989 (Royal Society Research Professor, 1974–88); *b* 11 April 1923; *e s* of late Rev. H. H. L. Longuet-Higgins. *Educ:* Winchester (schol.); Balliol Coll., Oxford (schol., MA). Research Fellow of Balliol Coll., 1946–48; Lecturer and Reader in Theoretical Chemistry, University of Manchester, 1949–52; Prof. of Theoretical Physics, King's Coll., University of London, 1952–54; FRSE; John Humphrey Plummer Professor of Theoretical Chemistry, University of Cambridge, 1954–67; Royal Soc. Res. Prof., Univ. of Edinburgh, 1968–74; Fellow of Corpus Christi Coll., 1954–67, Life Fellow 1968; Hon. Fellow: Balliol Coll., Oxford, 1969; Wolfson Coll., Cambridge, 1977. A Governor, BBC, 1979–84. Warden, Leckhampton House, 1961–67. Editor of Molecular Physics, 1958–61. For. Mem., Amer. Acad. of Arts and Scis, 1961; Foreign Associate, US National Academy of Sciences, 1968. DUniv York, 1973; DU Essex, 1981; Hon. DSc: Bristol, 1983; Sussex, 1989; Hon. DMus Sheffield, 1995. Harrison Meml Prize, Chemical Soc., 1950; Naylor Prize, London Mathematical Soc., 1981. *Publications:* co-author, The

Nature of Mind (Gifford Lectures), 1972; Mental Processes, 1987; papers on theoretical physics, chemistry and biology in scientific journals. *Recreations:* music and arguing. *Address:* Centre for Research on Perception and Cognition, Laboratory of Experimental Psychology, University of Sussex, Falmer, Brighton BN1 9QY. *T:* Brighton (01273) 678341.

LONGUET-HIGGINS, Michael Selwyn, FRS 1963; Royal Society Research Professor, University of Cambridge, 1969–89; Fellow, Trinity College, Cambridge, since 1969; *b* 8 Dec. 1925; *s* of late Henry Hugh Longuet and Albinia Cecil Longuet-Higgins; *m* 1958, Joan Redmayne Tattersall; two *s* two *d*. *Educ:* Winchester Coll. (Schol.); Trinity Coll., Cambridge (Schol.). (BA). Admiralty Research Lab., Teddington, 1945–48; Res. Student, Cambridge, 1948–51; PhD Cambridge, 1951; Rayleigh Prize, 1951; Commonwealth Fund Fellowship, 1951–52; Res. Fellow, Trinity Coll., Cambridge, 1951–55; Nat. Inst. of Oceanography, 1954–69. Visiting Professor: MIT, 1958; Institute of Geophysics, University of California, 1961–62; Univ. of Adelaide, 1964. Prof. of Oceanography, Oregon State Univ., 1967–69. Foreign Associate, US Nat. Acad. of Sci., 1979. Hon. DTech Tech. Univ. of Denmark, 1979; Hon. LLD Glasgow, 1979. Sverdrup Gold Medal, Amer. Meteorolog. Soc., 1983; Internat. Coastal Engrg Award, Amer. Soc. of Civil Engineers, 1984; Oceanography Award, Soc. for Underwater Technol., 1990. *Publications:* papers in applied mathematics, esp. physical oceanography, dynamics of sea waves and currents. *Recreations:* music, mathematical toys. *Address:* Gage Farm, Comberton, Cambridge CB3 7DH.

LONGWORTH, Ian Heaps, CBE 1994; PhD; FSA, FSAScot; Keeper of Prehistoric and Romano-British Antiquities, British Museum, 1973–95; *b* 29 Sept. 1935; *yr s* of late Joseph Longworth and Alice (*née* Heaps); *m* 1967, Clare Marian Titford; one *s* one *d*. *Educ:* King Edward VII, Lytham; Peterhouse, Cambridge. Open and Sen. Scholar, Matthew Wren Student, 1957, MA, PhD, Cantab. Temp. Asst Keeper, Nat. Museum of Antiquities of Scotland, 1962–63; Asst Keeper, Dept of British and Medieval Antiquities, Brit. Mus., 1963–69; Asst Keeper, Dept of Prehistoric and Romano-British Antiquities, Brit. Mus., 1969–73. Member: Ancient Monuments Bd for England, 1977–84; Ancient Monuments Adv. Cttee, Historic Buildings and Monuments Commn, 1991–94. Chm., Area Archaeol. Adv. Cttee for NW England, 1978–79. Hon. Sec., Prehistoric Soc., 1966–74, Vice-Pres., 1976–80; Sec., Soc. of Antiquaries of London, 1974–79, Vice-Pres., 1985–89. *Publications:* Yorkshire (Regional Archaeologies Series), 1965; (with G. J. Wainwright) Durrington Walls—excavations 1966–68, 1971; Collared Urns of the Bronze Age in Great Britain and Ireland, 1984; Prehistoric Britain, 1985; (with I. A. Kinnes) Catalogue of the Excavated Prehistoric and Romano-British Material in the Greenwell Collection, 1985; (ed with J. Cherry) Archaeology in Britain since 1945, 1986; (with A. Ellison and V. Rigby) Excavations at Grimes Graves, Norfolk, 1972–76, Fasc. 2, 1988, (*et al.*) Fasc. 3, 1991, Fasc. 4, 1992; articles in various learned jls on topics of prehistory. *Address:* 2 Hurst View Road, South Croydon, Surrey CR2 7AG. *T:* 0181–688 4960. *Club:* MCC.

LONGWORTH, Peter; HM Diplomatic Service; Consul-General, Johannesburg, and Director of Trade Promotion, South Africa, since 1994; *b* 26 May 1942; *y s* of late Frank Longworth and of Edith E. (*née* Robinson); *m* 1975, Christina Margareta, *d* of late Folke Wallin and Gun Wallin, Växjö. *Educ:* Chislehurst and Sidcup Grammar Sch.; Univ. of Sheffield (BA). Journalist, 1963–74: Labour and Ind. Corresp., Bristol Evening Post, 1964–66; Lobby Corresp., Western Daily Press., 1966–68; Diplomatic Corresp., Westminster Press., 1968–74; joined FCO, 1974; First Secretary: FCO, 1974–77; (Econ.), Bonn, 1977–81; Head of Chancery and HM Consul, Sofia, 1981–84; FCO, 1984–87; Counsellor (Econ. and Commercial), Copenhagen, 1987–91; Dep. Hd of Mission, Counsellor (Econ. and Commercial) and Consul Gen., Seoul, 1991–94. *Address:* c/o Foreign and Commonwealth Office, King Charles Street, SW1A 2AH. *Club:* Seoul (Seoul).

LONGWORTH, Wilfred Roy, AM 1986; MSc, PhD; FRSC, FRACI, FACE; Principal Director (formerly Director), Swinburne Institute of Technology and College of Technical and Further Education, 1970–86, retired; *b* 13 Dec. 1923; *s* of Wilfred Arnold Longworth and Jessie Longworth; *m* 1951, Constance Elizabeth Dean; two *d*. *Educ:* Bolton Sch.; Manchester Univ. (BSc, MSc, PhD). FRIC 1963; FRACI 1970; FACE 1976. Works Manager and Chief Chemist, Blackburn & Oliver, 1948–56; postgrad. res., Univ. of Keele, 1956–59; Lectr in Physical Chemistry, Huddersfield Coll. of Technol., 1959–60; Sen. Lectr in Phys. Chem., Sunderland Technical Coll., 1960–64; Head, Dept of Chem. and Biol., Manchester Polytechnic, 1964–70. Pres., World Council on Co-op. Educn, 1983–85. *Publications:* articles on cationic polymerisation in learned jls. *Recreations:* lawn bowls, gardening. *Address:* Unit 28, Fountain Court Village, 100 Station Street, Burwood, Vic 3125, Australia. *T:* (3) 8080346. *Club:* Naval and Military (Melbourne).

LONSDALE, 7th Earl of (UK), *cr* 1807; **James Hugh William Lowther,** Viscount and Baron Lowther, 1797; Bt 1764; *b* 3 Nov. 1922; *er s* of Anthony Edward, Viscount Lowther (*d* 1949), and Muriel Frances, Viscountess Lowther (*d* 1968), 2nd *d* of late Sir George Farrar, Bt, DSO, and Lady Farrar; *S* grandfather, 1953; *m* 1975, Caroline, *y d* of Sir Gerald Ley, 3rd Bt, TD; one *s* one *d* (and three *s* three *d* of previous marriages). *Educ:* Eton. Armed Forces, 1941–46; RAC and East Riding Yeo. (despatches, Captain). Retired. CIMgt; FRSA 1984. *Heir:* *s* Viscount Lowther, *qv*. *Address:* Askham Hall, Penrith, Cumbria CA10 2PF. *T:* Hackthorpe (01931) 712208. *Clubs:* Brooks's, Turf.

LONSDALE, Anne Mary; President, New Hall, Cambridge, since 1996; *b* 16 Feb. 1941; *d* of Dr Alexander Menzies and Mabel Menzies; *m* 1st, 1962, Geoffrey Griffin (*d* 1962); 2nd, 1964, Roger Harrison Lonsdale, *qv* (marr. diss. 1994); one *s* one *d*. *Educ:* St Anne's Coll., Oxford (BA Hons Lit. Hum. 1962; BA Hons Chinese (Oriental Studies) 1965; MA 1965). Oxford University: Davis Sen. Schol. and Lectr in Chinese, St Anne's Coll., 1965–74; Univ. Adminr, 1974–90; Dir, External Relations, 1990–93; Sec.-Gen., Central European Univ., Budapest, Prague, and Warsaw, 1994–96. Chm., Conf. of Univ. Admin UK and Ireland, 1991–93; Jt Chm., Assoc. of Univ. Admin, 1993–94; Mem. Steering Cttee, COIMBRA Gp of Euro Univs, 1993–94; UK Rep., Commonwealth Univs Study Abroad Consortium; Trustee, Inter-Univ. Foundn, 1988–. Cavaliere, Order of Merit (Italy), 1988. *Publications:* Marco Polo, 1973; (contrib. and trans.) The Chinese Experience, 1978; Merchant Adventurers in the East, 1980; Merchant Adventurers, 1981; University Administration in China, 1983; The Government and Management of Indian Universities, 1987; contrib. on Chinese topics to encyclopaedias in UK and Italy. *Recreations:* travelling, walking, music. *Address:* New Hall, Cambridge CB3 0DF. *T:* Cambridge (01223) 351721, *Fax:* (01223) 352941.

LONSDALE, Maj.-Gen. Errol Henry Gerrard, CB 1969; MBE 1942; Transport Officer-in-Chief (Army) 1966–69; *b* 26 Feb. 1913; 2nd *s* of Rev. W. H. M. Lonsdale, Arlaw Banks, Barnard Castle; *m* 1944, Muriel Allison, *d* of E. R. Payne, Mugswell, Chipstead; one *s* one *d*. *Educ:* Westminster Sch.; St Catharine's Coll., Cambridge (MA). 2nd Lt, RASC, 1934; Bt Lt-Col 1952; Col 1957; Brig. 1961; Maj.-Gen. 1965. Sudan Defence Force, 1938–43 (despatches); Chief Instr, RASC Officers Trng Centre, 1944–45; AQMG FARELF, 1945–47; CRASC 16 Airborne Div., 1947–48; GSOI, 1948–51; AA & QMG, War Office, 1951–53; Korea, 1953–54; Malaya, 1954–56 (despatches); ACOS, G4 Northern Army Group, 1957–60; DDST, 1st Corps, 1960–62; Comdt RASC Trng Centre, 1962–64; Inspector, RASC, 1964–65; ADC to the Queen, 1964–66; Inspector, RCT, 1965–66; psc; jssc. Col Comdt, RCT, 1969–74. Hon. Colonel: 160 Regt RCT(V), 1967–74; 562 Para Sqdn RCT(V), 1969–78. FCIT (MInstT) 1966. Vice-President: Transport Trust, 1969; Internat. Union for Modern Pentathlon and Biathlon, 1976–80; Pres., Modern Pentathlon Assoc. of Great Britain, 1977–88, Hon. Pres., 1988– (Chm., 1967); Chm., Inst. of Advanced Motorists, 1971–79, Vice-Pres., 1979. *Recreations:* modern pentathlon, photography, driving. *Address:* Windleys, Podgers Lane, Ilton, Ilminster, Somerset TA19 9HE.

LONSDALE, Robert Henry H.; *see* Heywood-Lonsdale.

LONSDALE, Prof. Roger Harrison, DPhil; FBA 1991; Fellow and Tutor in English, Balliol College, Oxford, since 1963; Professor of English Literature, University of Oxford, since 1992; *b* 6 Aug. 1934; *s* of Arthur John Lonsdale and Phebe (*née* Harrison); *m* 1964, Anne Mary Menzies (*see* A. M. Lonsdale) (marr. diss. 1994); one *s* one *d*. *Educ:* Hymers Coll., Hull; Lincoln Coll., Oxford (BA 1st class Hons 1957); DPhil (Oxon) 1962. National Service, RAF, commnd as Navigator, 1952–54. English Dept, Yale Univ., 1958–60; Oxford University: Bradley Jun. Res. Fellow, Balliol Coll., 1960–63; Reader in English Literature, 1990–92. *Publications:* Dr Charles Burney: a literary biography, 1965; *edited:* The Poems of Gray, Collins and Goldsmith, 1969; Vathek, by William Beckford, 1970; Dryden to Johnson, 1971; The New Oxford Book of Eighteenth-century Verse, 1984; The Poems of John Bampfylde, 1988; Eighteenth-century Women Poets: an Oxford anthology, 1989. *Recreations:* music, book-collecting. *Address:* Balliol College, Oxford OX1 3BJ. *T:* Oxford (01865) 277777.

LOOP, Bernadine P., (Mrs Floyd Loop); *see* Healy, B. P.

LOOSLEY, Brian; Metropolitan Stipendiary Magistrate, since 1989; *b* 20 Dec. 1948; *s* of Bernard Allan Loosley and Barbara Clara Randle; *m* 1971, Christine Mary Batt; one *s* one *d*. *Educ:* Sir William Borlase Grammar Sch., Marlow; Leeds Univ. (LLB 1971). Admitted Solicitor 1974; Prosecuting Solicitor, Thames Valley Police, 1975–78; practised privately, 1978–89. *Recreations:* fishing, Russian history and literature, foreign travel. *Address:* Clerkenwell Magistrates' Court, 78 King's Cross Road, WC1X 9QJ. *T:* 0171–278 6541.

LOPES, family name of **Baron Roborough.**

LOPPERT, Max Jeremy; Chief Music Critic, Financial Times, since 1980; Associate Editor, Opera, since 1986; *b* Johannesburg, 24 Aug. 1946; *m* 1972, Delayne Aarons. *Educ:* Univ. of Witwatersrand, Johannesburg (BA 1966); Univ. of York (BA Music 1971). *Publications:* contrib. to: Opera on Record (ed Alan Blyth), 3 vols, 1979, 1983, 1984; The New Grove Dictionary of Music and Musicians, 1980; The New Grove Dictionary of Opera, 1992; Who's Who in Hollywood, 1993. *Recreations:* cinema, cooking, walking in Richmond Park. *Address:* c/o Financial Times, 1 Southwark Bridge, SE1 9HL.

LORAM, Vice-Adm. Sir David (Anning), KCB 1979; CVO 1994 (LVO 1957); Deputy Supreme Allied Commander Atlantic, 1977–80, retired; Gentleman Usher to The Queen, 1982–94, Extra Gentleman Usher, since 1994; *b* 24 July 1924; *o surv. s* of late Mr and Mrs John A. Loram; *m* 1st, 1958, Fiona Beloe (marr. diss. 1981); three *s*; 2nd, 1983, Diana Keigwin (marr. diss. 1990). *Educ:* Royal Naval Coll., Dartmouth (1938–41). Awarded King's Dirk. Served War: HMS Sheffield, Foresight, Anson, Zealous, 1941–45. ADC to Governor-Gen. of New Zealand, 1946–48; specialised in Signal Communications, 1949; served in HMS Chequers, 1951; Equerry to the Queen, 1954–57; qualified helicopter pilot, 1955; commanded HMS Loch Fada, 1957; Directing Staff, JSSC, 1959–60; served in HMS Belfast, 1961; Naval Attaché, Paris, 1964–67; commanded HMS Arethusa, 1967; Dir, Naval Ops and Trade, 1970–71; commanded HMS Antrim, 1971; ADC to The Queen, 1972–73; Comdr British Forces, FO Malta, and NATO Comdr SE Mediterranean, 1973–75; Comdt, Nat. Defence Coll., 1975–77. Mem., RN Cresta Team, 1954–59. *Recreation:* fishing. *Address:* Sparkford Hall, Sparkford, Yeovil, Somerset BA22 7LD. *T:* North Cadbury (01963) 40834. *Club:* Chesapeake.

LORANT, Stefan; *b* 22 Feb. 1901; *m* 1963, Laurie Robertson (marr. diss. 1978); one *s* (and one *s* decd). *Educ:* Evangelical Gymnasium, Budapest; Academy of Economics, Budapest; Harvard Univ. (MA 1961). Editor: Das Magazin, Leipzig, 1925; Bilder Courier, Berlin, 1926; Muenchner Illustrierte Presse, Munich, 1928–33; Editor, in England: Weekly Illustrated, 1934 (also Creator); Picture Post, 1938–48; Founding editor and creator of Lilliput, Editor, 1937–40. Hon. LLD, Knox Coll., Galesburg, Ill., 1958; DHL *hc* Syracuse Univ., NY, 1985; Hon. Dr Univ. of Bradford, 1989. *Publications:* Wir vom Film, 1928, repr. 1986; I Was Hitler's Prisoner, 1935 (trans. of Ich war Hitlers Gefangener, German edn first pubd 1985); Chamberlain and the Beautiful Llama, 1940; Lincoln, His Life in Photographs, 1941; The New World, 1946, rev. edn 1965; F.D.R., a pictorial biography, 1950; The Presidency, a pictorial history of presidential elections from Washington to Truman, 1951; Lincoln: a picture story of his life, 1952, rev. and enl. edns 1957, 1969; The Life of Abraham Lincoln, 1954; The Life and Times of Theodore Roosevelt, 1959; Pittsburgh, the story of an American city, 1964, rev. and enl. edns 1975, 1980, 1988; The Glorious Burden: the American Presidency, 1968, rev. and enl. edn, 1976; Sieg Heil: an illustrated history of Germany from Bismarck to Hitler, 1974 (German trans. 1976); Pete: the story of Peter F. Flaherty, 1978; My Years in England, fragments to an autobiography, 1995; Mark I Love You (a memorial to my son), 1995. *Address:* Farview, PO Box 803, Lenox, MA 01240, USA. *T:* (413) 6370666.

LORD, Alan, CB 1972; Deputy Chairman and Chief Executive, Lloyd's of London, 1986–92; *b* 12 April 1929; *er s* of Frederick Lord and Anne Lord (*née* Whitworth), Rochdale; *m* 1953, Joan Ogden; two *d*. *Educ:* Rochdale; St John's Coll., Cambridge (BA 1950 (1st Cl. Hons); MA 1987). Entered Inland Revenue, 1950; Private Sec. to Dep. Chm. and to Chm. of the Board, 1952–54; HM Treasury, 1959–62; Principal Private Sec. to First Secretary of State (then Rt Hon. R. A Butler), 1962–63; Comr of Inland Revenue, 1969–73, Dep. Chm. Bd, 1971–73; Principal Finance Officer to DTI, subseq. to Depts of Industry, Trade, and Prices and Consumer Protection, 1973–75; Second Permanent Sec. (Domestic Econ.), HM Treasury, 1975–77. Man. Dir, 1980, Chief Exec., 1982–84, Dunlop Hldgs plc; formerly: Exec. Dir, Dunlop Hldgs; Man. Dir, Dunlop Internat. Ltd, 1978. Director: Allied-Lyons plc, 1979–86; Bank of England, 1983–86; Johnson Matthey Bankers, 1985–86. Chm., CBI Taxation Cttee, 1979–81. Mem. Council of Management, Henley Centre for Forecasting, 1977–82. Governor, NIESR. Pres., Johnian Soc., 1985–86. *Publications:* A Strategy for Industry (Sir Ellis Hunter Meml Lecture, Univ. of York), 1976; Earning an Industrial Living (1985 Johnian Society Lecture). *Recreations:* reading, gardening, rough-shooting. *Address:* Mardens, Hildenborough, Tonbridge, Kent TN11 8PA. *T:* Hildenborough (01732) 832268. *Club:* Reform.

LORD, Geoffrey, OBE 1989; Founder Director, Adapt Trust, since 1989; *b* 24 Feb. 1928; *s* of Frank Lord and Edith Lord; *m* 1955, Jean; one *s* one *d*. *Educ:* Rochdale Grammar Sch.; Univ. of Bradford (MA Applied Social Studies). AIB. Midland Bank Ltd, 1946–58; Probation and After-Care Service, 1958–76: Dep. Chief Probation Officer, Greater Manchester, 1974–76; Sec. and Treas., Carnegie UK Trust, 1977–93. Chairman: Unemployed Voluntary Action Fund (Scotland), 1990–; Pollock Meml Missionary Trust, 1985–; Pres., Centre for Envmtl Interpretation, 1984–. Mem., Scottish Arts Lottery Bd,

1994–. Trustee, Home-Start (formerly Home-Start Consultancy) UK, 1993–. FRSA 1985. Hon. Fellow, Manchester Metropolitan Univ. (formerly, Manchester Poly.), 1987. *Publication:* The Arts and Disabilities, 1981. *Recreations:* philately, walking, appreciation of the arts. *Address:* 9 Craigleith View, Ravelston, Edinburgh EH4 3JZ. *T:* 0131–337 7623. *Club:* New (Edinburgh).

LORD, Michael Nicholson; MP (C) Suffolk Central, since 1983; *b* 17 Oct. 1938; *s* of John Lord and Jessie Lord (*née* Nicholson); *m* 1965, Jennifer Margaret (*née* Childs); one *s* one *d. Educ:* Christ's College, Cambridge. MA. FArborA. Arboricultural consultant. PPS: to Minister of State, MAFF, 1984–85; to Chief Secretary to the Treasury, 1985–87. Member: Select Cttee on Parly Comr for Admin, 1990–; Council of Europe, 1987–91; WEU, 1987–91. *Recreations:* golf, sailing, gardening, trees. *Address:* House of Commons, SW1A 0AA.

LORD, Peter Herent, OBE 1991; FRCS; Consultant Surgeon, Wycombe General Hospital, High Wycombe, 1964–90; *b* 23 Nov. 1925; *s* of Sir Frank Lord, KBE, JP, DL and Rosalie Jeanette Herent; *m* 1952, Florence Shirley Hirst; two *s* two *d. Educ:* Manchester Grammar Sch.; St John's Coll., Cambridge (MA, MChir). St George's Hosp., Salford Royal Hosp., Christie Hosp., Manchester, St Margaret's, Epping, St George's Hosp., 1949–63 (Captain, RAMC, 1952–53). Royal College of Surgeons: H. N. Smith Research Fellow, 1964; Penrose May Teacher, 1970; Mem. Council, 1978–90; Vice-Pres., 1986–87. *Publications:* Cardiac Pacemakers, 1964; Pilonidal Sinus, 1964; Wound Healing, 1966; Haemorrhoids, 1969; Hydrocoele, 1972, Surgery in Old Age, 1980. *Recreations:* sailing, fishing. *Address:* Holly Tree House, 39 Grove Road, Beaconsfield, Bucks HP9 1PE. *T:* Beaconsfield (01494) 674488, *Fax:* (01494) 675188.

LORD, William Burton Housley, CB 1979; scientist; *b* 22 March 1919; *s* of Arthur James Lord and Elsie Lord (*née* Housley); *m* 1942, Helena Headon Jaques; two *d. Educ:* King George V Sch., Southport; Manchester Univ.; London Univ. (External MSc); Trinity Coll., Cambridge (MA). Enlisted Royal Fusiliers, commn S Lancs Regt (served Middle East and N Africa), 1941–46. Cambridge Univ., 1946. Entered Civil Service, 1949; joined Atomic Weapons Res. Estab., 1952; Head of Metallurgy Div., AWRE, 1958; moved to MoD, 1964; Asst Chief Scientific Adviser (Research), 1965; Dep. Chief Scientist (Army), 1968–71; Dir Gen., Establishments, Resources and Programmes (B), MoD, 1971–76; Dir, RARDE, 1976–79. Award for wartime invention of radio proximity fuse, 1952. *Recreations:* amateur radio, hill-walking, swimming. *Address:* c/o Barclays Bank, 2 Victoria Street, SW1H 0ND.

LOREN, Sophia; film actress; *b* 20 Sept. 1934; *d* of Ricardo Scicolone and Romilda Villani; *m* 1957, Carlo Ponti, film producer (marriage annulled in Juarez, Mexico, Sept. 1962; marriage in Paris, France, April 1966); two *s. Educ:* parochial sch. and Teachers' Institute, Naples. First leading role in, Africa sotto i Mari, 1952; acted in many Italian films, 1952–55; subsequent films include: The Pride and the Passion; Boy on a Dolphin; Legend of the Lost; The Key; Desire under the Elms; Houseboat; The Black Orchid (Venice Film Festival Award, 1958); That Kind of Woman; It Started in Naples; Heller in Pink Tights; The Millionairess; Two Women (Cannes Film Festival Award, 1961); A Breath of Scandal; Madame sans Gêne; La Ciociara; El Cid; Boccaccio 70; Five Miles to Midnight; Yesterday, Today and Tomorrow; The Fall of the Roman Empire; Marriage, Italian Style; Operation Crossbow; Lady L; Judith; A Countess from Hong Kong; Arabesque; Sunflower; The Priest's Wife; The Man of La Mancha; The Verdict; The Voyage; Una Gionnata Particolare; Firepower; Blood Feud; Prêt-à-Porter. *Publications:* Eat with Me, 1972; Sophia Loren on Woman and Beauty, 1984; *relevant publication:* Sophia: living and loving, by A. E. Hotcher, 1979. *Address:* Chalet Daniel Burgenstock, Luzern, Switzerland.

LORIMER, Sir Desmond; *see* Lorimer, Sir T. D.

LORIMER, Dr George Huntly, FRS 1986; Dupont Fellow, Central Research Department, Dupont Co., Delaware, since 1991; *b* 14 Oct. 1942; *s* of Gordon and Ellen Lorimer; *m* 1970, Freia (*née* Schulz-Baldes); one *s* one *d. Educ:* George Watson's College, Edinburgh; Univ. of St Andrews (BSc); Univ. of Illinois (MS); Michigan State Univ. (PhD). Scientist, Max-Planck Society, Berlin, 1972–74; Research Fellow, Inst. for Advanced Studies, ANU, Canberra, 1974–77; Scientist, Society for Radiation and Environmental Research, Munich, 1977; Prin. Investigator, then Res. Leader, E. I. Du Pont de Nemours & Co., 1978–91. Adjunct Prof., Dept of Biochemistry, Univ. of Pennsylvania, 1992. Mem., Amer. Soc. of Biological Chemists; Amer. Soc. of Biochemistry and Molecular Biology. Mem. Adv, Bd, Res. Sch. of Biol Sci., ANU, 1992. Editor, Biochimica et Biophysica Acta, 1995. *Publications:* contribs to Biochemistry, Jl of Biological Chemistry, Nature, Science. *Recreation:* music. *Address:* 2025 Harwyn Road, Wilmington, DE 19810–3870, USA. *T:* (home) (302) 4756748; (office) (302) 6954584, *Fax:* (home) (302) 5291739; (office) (302) 6954509.

LORIMER, Sir (Thomas) Desmond, Kt 1976; Chairman, Northern Bank Ltd, since 1986 (Director, since 1983; Deputy Chairman, 1985); *b* 20 Oct. 1925; *s* of Thomas Berry Lorimer and Sarah Ann Lorimer; *m* 1957, Patricia Doris Samways; two *d. Educ:* Belfast Technical High Sch. Chartered Accountant, 1948; Fellow, Inst. of Chartered Accountants in Ireland, 1957. Practised as chartered accountant, 1952–74; Sen. Partner, Harmood, Banner, Smylie & Co., Belfast, Chartered Accountants, 1960–74; Chairman: Lamont Holdings PLC, 1973–; Northern Ireland Electricity, 1991–94; Dir, Irish Distillers PLC, 1986–. Chm., Industrial Develt Bd for NI, 1982–85; Pres., Inst. of Chartered Accountants in Ireland, 1968–69; Chairman: Ulster Soc. of Chartered Accountants, 1960; NI Housing Exec., 1971–75; Mem., Rev. Body on Local Govt in NI, 1970. *Recreations:* gardening and golf. *Address:* Windwhistle Cottage, 6A Circular Road West, Cultra, Holywood, Co. Down BT18 0AT. *T:* Holywood (01232) 423323. *Clubs:* Carlton; Royal Belfast Golf, Royal Co. Down Golf (Co. Down).

LORNE, Marquess of; Torquhil Ian Campbell; *b* 29 May 1968; *s* and *heir* of 12th Duke of Argyll, *qv. Educ:* Craigflower; Cargilfield; Glenalmond Coll. A Page of Honour to the Queen, 1981–83. *Address:* Inveraray Castle, Inveraray, Argyll PA32 8XF.

LOSINSKA, Kathleen Mary, (Kate), OBE 1986; Senior Vice-President, Civil and Public Services Association, 1986–88 (President, 1979–82 and 1983–86, a Vice-President, 1982–83); *b* Croydon, Surrey, 5 Oct. 1924; *d* of late James Henry Conway, Border Regt and Dorothea Marguerite Hill; *m* 1942, Stanislaw Losinski (formerly serving Officer, Polish Air Force, subseq. 301 Bomber Sqdn, RAF, retd with rank of Sqdn Leader; awarded Polish Virtuti Militari Cross, Croix de Guerre, Cross of Lorraine, Yugoslav Cross of Valour, etc); one *s. Educ:* Selhurst Grammar Sch., Croydon (matriculation); university of life generally. Entered Civil Service, 1939; with Office of Population Censuses and Surveys. Delegate Mem., Council of Civil Service Unions, 1970–87 (Chm. 1980–81); Vice-Chm., CS Retirement Fellowship, 1988–; Management Cttee, CS Benevolent Fund, 1991–. Commissioner: Trade Union TUC Nuclear Energy Review; CS Appeals BD, 1988–. Chairman: White Eagle Trust, 1985–; Solidarnosc Foundn. Has held all honorary positions, CPSA. Founder Mem., Resistance Internat., 1983–. Governor, Ruskin Coll., 1976, 1979–86. Silver Jubilee Medal, 1977. Kt Comdr, Order of Polonia Restituta, 1987. *Recreations:* journalism, reading, music, history, travel; work for the Christian Trade Union and Moderate Trade Union Movements. *Address:* Loretto, Baggottstown West, Bruff, , Co. Limerick, Ireland. *T:* Limerick (61) 82225. *Club:* Civil Service.

LOSOWSKY, Prof. Monty Seymour, FRCP; Professor of Medicine and Head of University Department of Medicine, St James's University Hospital, Leeds, since 1969; *b* 1 Aug. 1931; *s* of Dora and Myer Losowsky; *m* 1971, Barbara Malkin; one *s* one *d. Educ:* Coopers' Company's Sch., London; Univ. of Leeds (Hons MB, ChB; MD). House appts, Leeds Gen. Infirmary, 1955–56; Registrar in Medicine, Epping, 1957–59; Asst, Externe Hôpital St Antoine, Paris, 1960; Research Fellow, Harvard Med. Unit, 1961–62; Lectr, Sen. Lectr, Reader in Medicine, 1962–69, Dean, Faculty of Medicine, 1989–94, Univ. of Leeds. Member: Leeds Eastern Health Authy, 1981–89; Specialist Adv. Cttee on General (Internal) Medicine, 1984–88; Systems Bd Grants Cttee B, MRC, 1984–88; Panel of Studies Allied to Medicine, UGC, 1982–89; British Digestive Foundn Sci. and Res. Awards Cttee, 1987–90; Yorks RHA, 1989–90; Working Gp, France Steering Gp on Undergrad. Medical and Dental Educn, DoH, 1990–; Council, British Nutrition Foundn, 1991– (Mem. Scientific Adv. Cttee, 1987–91; Scientific Governor, 1991–); GMC, 1991–; CVCP Rep., Acad. and Res. Staff Cttee of DoH Jt Planning and Adv. Cttee, 1990–94 (Mem., General Purposes Working Gp, 1989–94); Chm., Other Studies and Professions Allied to Medicine Panel, HEFCE, 1995–. Pres., British Soc. of Gastroenterol., 1993–94. Chm., Coeliac Trust, 1983–. Examr for Membership, RCP, 1982–; Academic Observer and Ext. Examr, Utd Examining Bd, 1994–. *Publications:* (jtly) Malabsorption in Clinical Practice, 1974; (ed) The Gut and Systemic Disease, 1983; (ed jtly) Advanced Medicine, 1983; (jtly) The Liver and Biliary System, 1984; (jtly) Clinical Nutrition in Gastroenterology, 1986; (jtly) Gut Defences in Clinical Practice, 1986; (jtly) Gastroenterology, 1988; Consensus in Clinical Nutrition, 1994; papers relating to hepatology and gastroenterology. *Recreations:* table tennis, watching cricket, walking, DIY, medical biography. *Address:* Department of Medicine, St James's University Hospital, Leeds LS9 7TF. *T:* Leeds (0113) 243 3144. *Club:* Royal Society of Medicine.

LOSTY, Howard Harold Walter, FEng, FIEE; Secretary, Institution of Electrical Engineers, 1980–89; *b* 1 Aug. 1926; *s* of Patrick J. Losty and Edith E. Wilson; *m* 1950, Rosemary L. Everritt; two *d. Educ:* Harvey Grammar Sch, Folkestone; Sir John Cass Coll., London. BSc. GEC Research Laboratories, 1942–53; GEC Nuclear Power Programme, 1953–66; Head of Engineering Div., GEC Research Centre, 1966–71; Dir, GEC Hirst Research Centre, 1971–77; Man. Dir, GEC Electronic Devices Ltd, 1977–80. Hon. DEng Bradford, 1986. *Publications:* (co-author) Nuclear Graphite, 1962; some forty technical papers. *Recreations:* walking, listening to music (opera), reading history. *Address:* Shandon, 14 Wyatts Road, Chorleywood, Herts WD3 5TE. *T:* Chorleywood (01923) 283568.

LOTEN, Alexander William, CB 1984; FCIBSE; Under Secretary, Department of the Environment, and Director, Mechanical and Electrical Engineering Services, Property Services Agency, 1981–85, retired; *b* 11 Dec. 1925; *s* of late Alec Oliver Loten and Alice Maud Loten; *m* 1954, Mary Diana Flint; one *s* one *d. Educ:* Churcher's Coll., Petersfield; Corpus Christi Coll., Cambridge Univ. (BA). CEng, FIMechE 1980; FCIBSE 1970. Served War, RNVR, 1943–46 (Air Engr Officer). Engineer: Rolls-Royce Ltd, Derby, 1950–54; Benham & Sons, London, 1954–58; Air Min. Work Directorate, 1958–64; Sen. Engr, 1964–70, Superintending Engr (Mechanical Design), 1970–75, MPBW; Dir of Works, Civil Accommodation, PSA, 1975–81. Pres., CIBS, 1976–77. Lt-Col, Engr and Railway Staff Corps RE, T&AVR, 1979–. *Recreations:* walking, gardening. *Address:* Hockridge House, London Road, Maresfield, E Sussex TN22 2EH.

LOTHIAN, 12th Marquess of *cr* 1701; **Peter Francis Walter Kerr,** KCVO 1983; DL; Lord Newbattle, 1591; Earl of Lothian, 1606; Baron Jedburgh, 1622, Earl of Ancram, Baron Kerr of Nisbet, Baron Long-Newton and Dolphingston, 1633; Viscount of Brien, Baron Kerr of Newbattle, 1701; Baron Ker (UK), 1821; Lord Warden of the Stannaries and Keeper of the Privy Seal of the Duke of Cornwall, 1977–83; *b* 8 Sept. 1922; *s* of late Captain Andrew William Kerr, RN, and Marie Constance Annabel, *d* of Capt. William Walter Raleigh Kerr; *S* cousin, 1940; *m* 1943, Antonella, *d* of late Maj.-Gen. Sir Foster Newland, KCMG, CB, and Donna Agnese Carr; two *s* four *d. Educ:* Ampleforth; Christ Church, Oxford. Lieut, Scots Guards, 1943. Mem. Brit. Delegation: UN Gen. Assembly, 1956–57; European Parliament, 1973; UK Delegate, Council of Europe and WEU, 1959. PPS to Foreign Sec., 1960–63; a Lord in Waiting (Govt Whip, House of Lords), 1962–63, 1972–73; Joint Parliamentary Sec., Min. of Health, April-Oct. 1964; Parly Under-Sec. of State, FCO, 1970–72. Chm., Scottish Council, British Red Cross Soc., 1976–86. Mem., Queen's Body Guard for Scotland (Royal Company of Archers). Mem., Prince of Wales Council, 1976–83. DL, Roxburgh, 1962. Kt, SMO Malta. *Heir: s* Earl of Ancram, *qv. Address:* Ferniehirst Castle, Jedburgh, Roxburghshire TD8 6NX. *T:* Jedburgh (01835) 64021; 54 Upper Cheyne Row, SW3 5JJ. *Clubs:* Boodle's, Beefsteak; New (Edinburgh).

See also Col Sir D. H. Cameron of Lochiel, Earl of Dalkeith, Earl of Euston.

LOTHIAN, Prof. Niall; Professor of Accounting, Heriot-Watt University, since 1988; President, Institute of Chartered Accountants of Scotland, 1995–April 1996 (Senior Vice-President, 1994–95); *b* 27 Feb. 1948; *s* of Revd Thomas Lothian and Jean Morgan Lothian (*née* Henderson); *m* 1971, Carol Miller; one *s* one *d. Educ:* Daniel Stewart's Coll.; Heriot-Watt Univ. (BA 1971). CA 1972. Lectr, Sen. Lectr, 1973–88, Director, 1991–93, Business School, Heriot-Watt Univ. Visiting Professor: IMEDE, Lausanne, 1979–80; Univ. of Witwatersrand, 1984; Mem., internat. vis. faculty, INSEAD, Fontainebleau, 1984–; Consultant: UNIDO, China, 1980; NZ Soc. of Accountants, 1992. Mem., Internat. Exec. Adv. Bd, Coll. of Finance and Accountancy, Budapest; Gov., George Watson's Coll., 1991–. FRSA. *Publications:* How Companies Manage R&D, 1984; Measuring Corporate Performance, 1987; (jtly) Accounting, 1991; (contrib.) Ernst and Young Manager's Handbook, 2nd edn 1992; articles in professional jls. *Recreations:* graveyards, golf. *Address:* 30 Granby Road, Edinburgh EH16 5NL. *T:* 0131–667 4429. *Clubs:* New (Edinburgh); Luffness New Golf.

LOTON, Brian Thorley, AC 1989; FTS; Chairman, Broken Hill Proprietary Co. Ltd, since 1992; Director, National Australia Bank, since 1988; *b* Perth, WA, 17 May 1929; *s* of Sir (Ernest) Thorley Loton and Grace (*née* Smith); *m* 1956, Joan Kemelfield; two *s* two *d. Educ:* Hale Sch., Perth; Trinity Coll., Melbourne Univ. (BMetEng 1953). Joined BHP as Cadet 1954; Technical Asst, 1959; Asst Chief Engr, 1961; Gen. Manager Planning and Develt, 1969, Gen. Manager Newcastle Steel Works, 1970; Exec. Gen. Manager Steel Div., 1973; Dir, 1976; Chief Gen. Manager, 1977; Man. Dir, 1982; Chief Exec. Officer, 1984, Dep. Chm., 1991. President: Aust. Inst. of Mining and Metallurgy, 1982 (Mem. Council); Australian Mining Industry Council, 1983–84; Business Council of Aust., 1990–92; Vice-Chairman: Internat. Iron and Steel Inst., 1988–91, 1992– (Chm., 1991–92); Defence Industry Cttee, 1976–88; Member: Aust. Sci. and Tehnol. Council, 1977–80; Aust. Manufg Council, 1977–81; Vict. Govt Long Range Policy Planning Cttee, 1980–82; Aust. Council on Population and Ethnic Affairs, 1980–82. Internat. Counsellor, The Conf. Bd, 1984–. Mem. Faculty Engrg, Melbourne Univ., 1980–83. FIE (Aust) 1984

(Hon. Fellow); FAIM 1973; FIDA 1980. *Address:* c/o GPO Box 86A, Melbourne, Vic 3001, Australia. *Clubs:* Melbourne, Australian (Melbourne).

LOTT, Dr Bernard Maurice, OBE 1966; Research Fellow, University College London, since 1980; *b* 13 Aug. 1922; *s* of late William Lott and of Margaret Lott (*née* Smith); *m* 1949, Helena, *d* of late Clarence Winkup; one *s* one *d* (and one *s* decd). *Educ:* Bancroft's Sch.; Keble Coll., Oxford (MA); Univ. of London (MA Distinction, PhD); Univ. of Edinburgh (Dip, in Applied Linguistics, Dist.). RN, 1942–46. Brit. Council Lectr in English, Ankara Univ. and Gazi Inst. of Educn, Turkey, 1949–55; Brit. Council Asst Rep., Finland, 1955–57; Prof. of Eng. and Head of Dept, Univ. of Indonesia, 1958–61; Dir of Studies, Indian Central Inst. of Eng., 1961–66; Dep. Controller, Educn Div., Brit. Council, 1966–72; Controller, Eng. Teaching Div., Brit. Council, 1972–75; Brit. Council Representative, Poland, 1975–77; English Language Teaching Develt Adviser, British Council, 1977–79; Course Tutor, Open Univ., 1979–86; Lectr in Applied Linguistics, Poly. of Central London, 1989–90. *Publications:* A Course in English Language and Literature, 1986; Gen. Editor, New Swan Shakespeare series, and edited: Macbeth, 1958, Twelfth Night, 1959, Merchant of Venice, 1962, Hamlet, 1968 (also Open Univ. edn 1970), King Lear, 1974, Much Ado About Nothing, 1977; contribs on teaching of English as foreign lang. to Times Educnl Supp. and Eng. Lang. Teaching Jl. *Recreations:* local studies, music. *Address:* 8 Meadway, NW11 7JT. *T:* 0181–455 0918.

LOTT, Felicity Ann Emwhyla, CBE 1990; soprano; *b* 8 May 1947; *d* of John Albert Lott and Whyla (*née* Williams); *m* 1st, 1973, Robin Mavesyn Golding (marr. diss. 1982); 2nd, 1984, Gabriel Woolf; one *d*. *Educ:* Pate's Grammar Sch. for Girls, Cheltenham; Royal Holloway Coll., Univ. of London (BA Hons French; Hon. Fellow, 1995); Royal Acad. of Music (LRAM; ARAM 1976; FRAM 1986). Début: ENO, 1975; Covent Garden, 1976; Glyndebourne, 1977. Particularly associated with Mozart and Richard Strauss, whose operas she has sung in Glyndebourne, Covent Garden, Cologne, Hamburg, Brussels, Paris, Vienna, Munich, Dresden, Milan, NY, Chicago and Japan; gives recitals all over Europe; many recordings. Founder Mem., The Songmakers' Almanac. Dr *hc* Sussex, 1989. Chevalier, Ordre des Arts et des Lettres (France), 1993. *Recreations:* reading, sleeping. *Address:* c/o Lies Askonas, 6 Henrietta Street, WC2E 8LA. *T:* 0171–405 1808.

LOTZ, Prof. Dr Kurt; German business executive; *b* 18 Sept. 1912; *m* Elizabeth Lony; two *s* one *d*. *Educ:* August-Vilmar-Schule, Homberg. Joined Police Service, 1932; Lieut 1934. Served Luftwaffe (Gen. Staff; Major), 1942–45. Employed by Brown Boveri & Cie, Dortmund, 1946; Head of Business Div., Mannheim, 1954; Dir 1957; Chm. 1958–67; Mem. Board of Directors in parent company, Baden, Switzerland, 1961; Managing Director, 1963–67. Dep. Chm., 1967–68, Chm., 1968–71, Volkswagenwerk AG. Member: Deutscher Rat für Landespflege. Chm., World Wildlife Fund, Germany, 1980. Mem., Rotary Internat. Hon. Senator, Heidelberg Univ., 1963; Hon. Prof., Technische Universität Carolo Wilhelmina, Brunswick, 1970. Dr rer. pol. *hc* Mannheim, 1963. *Publication:* Lebenserfahrungen: Worüber man in Wirtschaft und Politik auch sprechen sollte, 1978. *Recreations:* hiking, hunting, golf. *Address:* W-6900 Heidelberg, Bergstrasse 110, Germany.

LOUDEN, Rt. Rev. Mgr. Stephen Henry; Principal Roman Catholic Chaplain and Vicar General (Army), since 1993; *b* 18 Nov. 1941; *s* of late Joseph Henry Louden and Sarah (*née* McNaughten). *Educ:* Upholland Coll. BA (Open) 1975; DipTh (CNAA) 1991; MTh (Oxon) 1993. Ordained priest, dio. Liverpool, 1968; Curate: All Saints, Anfield, 1968–73; St John's, Kirkdale, 1973–75; Our Lady's, Formby, 1975–78; Royal Army Chaplains' Department: TA Commn, 1973–78; Regular Army Commn, 1978; Dortmund Garrison, 1978–79; 8 Inf. Bde, 1979–80; Munster Garrison, 1980–82; Dhekelia Garrison, 1982–84; RC Chaplain, RMA Sandhurst, 1984–86; Berlin Inf. Bde, 1986–88; HQ NI, 1988; Hong Kong, 1988–90; Senior Chaplain RC: HQ BAOR, 1990–92; HQ NI, 1992–93. Prelate of Honour, 1993. *Recreations:* horology, photography, history. *Address:* Ministry of Defence Chaplains (Army), Bagshot Park, Bagshot, Surrey GU19 5PL. *T:* Bagshot (01276) 412825. *Club:* Army and Navy.

LOUDON, George Ernest; Chairman, Helix Associates Ltd, since 1993; Trustee, Tate Foundation, since 1992; Director: Arjo-Wiggins Appleton, since 1993; Global Asset Management, since 1994; *b* 19 Nov. 1942; *m* 1968, Angela Mary Goldsbrough; one *s* one *d*. *Educ:* Christelijk Lyceum, Zeist; Balliol Coll., Oxford (BA); Johns Hopkins Univ., Washington (MA). Lazard Frères & Cie, Paris, 1967–68; Ford Foundn, New York and Jakarta, 1968–71; McKinsey & Co., Amsterdam, 1971–76; Amro Bank, Amsterdam: Gen. Man., 1976–83; Mem., Bd of Man. Dirs, 1983–88; Dir, Midland Group, 1988–92; Chief Exec., 1988–92, Chm., 1991–92, Midland Montagu. Director: M&G Group, 1993–94; Harrison/Parrott Ltd, 1993–. *Address:* 154 Brompton Road, SW3 1HX.

LOUDON, John Duncan Ott, OBE 1988; FRCSE, FRCOG; retired; Consultant Obstetrician and Gynaecologist, Eastern General Hospital, Edinburgh, 1960–87; Senior Lecturer, University of Edinburgh, 1962–93; *b* 22 Aug. 1924; *s* of late James Alexander Law Loudon and Ursula (*née* Ott) *m* 1953, Nancy Beaton (*née* Mann); two *s*. *Educ:* John Watson's Sch., Edinburgh; Wyggeston Sch., Leicester; Univ. of Edinburgh (MB, ChB 1947). FRCSE 1954; FRCOG 1973 (MRCOG 1956). National Service, RAF, 1948–50. House appts, Edinburgh and Cambridge, 1948–52; Registrar, Sen. Registrar and Consultant Obstetrician and Gynaecologist, Simpson Maternity Pavilion and Royal Infirm., Edinburgh, 1954–66. Formerly Examiner in Obstetrics and Gynaecology: Univs of Cardiff, Manchester, Leeds, Dundee, Glasgow, Aberdeen, Newcastle upon Tyne, Cape Town, RCSI, RCSE, RCOG and RACOG. Adviser in Family Welfare to Govt of Malta, 1976–81. Vice Pres., RCOG, 1981–84 (Mem. Council, 1966–72 and 1976–81). Member: Interim Licensing Authority for IVF, 1985–91; GMC, 1986–92. *Publications:* papers to obstetric and gynaecol jls. *Recreations:* gardening, golf, travel, food and wine. *Address:* Ardbeg, 4 Kinnear Road, Edinburgh EH3 5PE. *T:* 0131–552 1327. *Clubs:* Royal Air Force; Bruntsfield Links Golfing Society (Edinburgh).

LOUDON, John Hugo; Jonkheer (Netherlands title); Knight in the Order of the Netherlands Lion, 1953; Grand Officer, Order of Orange-Nassau, 1965; KBE (Hon.) (Gt Brit.), 1960; Officer, Légion d'Honneur, 1963; holds other decorations; *b* 27 June 1905; *s* of Jonkheer Hugo Loudon and Anna Petronella Alida Loudon (*née* van Marken); *m* 1931, Baroness Marie Cornelie van Tuyll van Serooskerken (*d* 1988); three *s* (and one *s* decd). *Educ:* Netherlands Lyceum, The Hague; Utrecht Univ., Holland. Doctor of Law, 1929. Joined Royal Dutch/Shell Group of Cos, 1930; served in USA, 1932–38; Venezuela, 1938–47 (Gen. Man., 1944–47); Man. Dir, 1947–52, Pres., 1952–65, Chm., 1965–76, Royal Dutch Petroleum Co.; former Chm., Shell Oil Co. (New York); Vice-Chm. Bd, Royal Netherlands Blast-furnaces & Steelworks, NV, 1971–76; Director: Orion Bank Ltd, 1971–81; Chase Manhattan Corp., 1971–76; Estel NV Hoesch-Hoogovens, 1972–76; Russell Reynolds Assocs Inc., 1977–; Adv. Dir, Bd, Arrow Partners CV, NY, 1983–. Chairman: Internat. Adv. Cttee, Chase Manhattan Bank, 1965–77; Bd, Atlantic Inst., 1969–84; European Adv. Cttee, Ford Motor Co., 1976–83. Internat. Bd Mem., Institut Européen d'Administration des Affaires, 1971–; Mem., Rockefeller Univ. Council, NY, 1978–95; Mem. Bd Trustees, Ford Foundation, 1966–75; Internat. Pres., World Wildlife Fund, 1977–81. *Recreations:* golf, yachting. *Address:* Koekoeksduin, 5 Vogelenzangseweg, 2111 HP Aerdenhout, Netherlands. *T:* Haarlem 245924. *Clubs:* White's; Royal Yacht Squadron.

LOUDON, Prof. Rodney, FRS 1987; Professor of Physics, Essex University, since 1967; *b* 25 July 1934; *s* of Albert Loudon and Doris Helen (*née* Blane); *m* 1960, Mary Anne Philips; one *s* one *d*. *Educ:* Bury Grammar Sch.; Brasenose Coll., Oxford (MA, DPhil). Postdoctoral Fellow, Univ. of California, Berkeley, 1959–60; Scientific Civil Servant, RRE Malvern, 1960–65; Member, Technical Staff: Bell Labs, Murray Hill, NJ, 1965–66, 1970; RCA Labs, Zurich, 1975; Essex University: Reader in Physics, 1966–67; Dean of Sch. of Physical Scis, 1972–74; Chm. of Physics Dept, 1976–79 and 1988–89. Visiting Professor: Yale Univ., 1975; Univ. of California, Irvine, 1980; Ecole Polytechnique, Lausanne, 1985; Univ. of Rome, 1988. Chm., Bd of Editors of Optica Acta, 1984–87. Fellow, Optical Soc. of America, 1994. Thomas Young Medal and Prize, Inst. of Physics, 1987; Max Born Award, Optical Soc. of Amer., 1992. *Publications:* The Quantum Theory of Light, 1973, 2nd edn 1983; (with W. Hayes) Scattering of Light by Crystals, 1978; (ed with V. M. Agranovich) Surface Excitations, 1984; (with D. J. Barber) An Introduction to the Properties of Condensed Matter, 1989; papers in Nature, Phys. Rev., Optica Acta, Jl Phys., etc. *Recreation:* music, particularly choral singing and instrument making. *Address:* 3 Gaston Street, East Bergholt, Colchester, Essex CO7 6SD. *T:* Colchester (01206) 298550.

LOUDOUN, Countess of (13th in line) *cr* 1633; **Barbara Huddleston Abney-Hastings;** Lady Campbell Baroness of Loudoun, 1601; Lady Tarrinzean and Mauchline, 1638; the 3 English baronies of Botreaux 1368, Stanley 1456, and Hastings 1461, which were held by the late Countess, are abeyant, the Countess and her sisters being *co-heiresses*; *b* 3 July 1919; assumed by deed poll, 1955, the surname of Abney-Hastings in lieu of that of Griffiths; *S* mother, 1960; *m* 1st, 1939 (marr. diss., 1945), Capt. Walter Strickland Lord; one *s*; 2nd, 1945, Capt. Gilbert Frederick Greenwood (*d* 1951); one *s* one *d*; 3rd, 1954, Peter Griffiths (who assumed by deed poll the surname of Abney-Hastings in lieu of his patronymic, 1958); three *d*. *Heir:* *s* Lord Mauchline, *qv*. *Address:* Mount Walk, Ashby-de-la-Zouch, Leics LE65 1BG. *T:* Ashby-de-la-Zouch (01530) 415844.

LOUDOUN, Maj.-Gen. Robert Beverley, CB 1973; OBE 1965; Director, Mental Health Foundation, 1977–90; *b* 8 July 1922; *s* of Robert and Margaret Loudoun; *m* 1950, Audrey Stevens; two *s*. *Educ:* University College Sch., Hampstead. Served War of 1939–45 (despatches): enlisted Royal Marines, 1940; commissioned, 1941; 43 Commando, Central Mediterranean, 1943–45; 45 Commando, Hong Kong, Malta and Palestine, 1945–48. Instructor, RNC Greenwich, 1950–52; Staff of C-in-C America and West Indies, 1953–55; RN Staff Coll., 1956; Adjt, 40 Commando, Malta and Cyprus, 1958–59; USMC Sch., Quantico, Virginia, 1959–60; MoD, 1960–62; Second-in-Command, 42 Commando, Singapore and Borneo, 1963–64; CO, 40 Commando, Far East, 1967–69; Brig., UK Commandos, Plymouth, 1969–71; Maj.-Gen. RM Training Gp, Portsmouth, 1971–75, retired 1975. Representative Col Comdt, RM, 1983–84. Chairman: Jt Shooting Cttee for GB, 1977–82; British Southern Slav Soc. (formerly British Yugoslav Soc.), 1989–. Freeman, City of London, 1979. *Address:* The Heathers, Bathampton Lane, Bathampton, Avon BA2 6SU. *Club:* Army and Navy.

LOUGH, Prof. John, FBA 1975; Professor of French, University of Durham (late Durham Colleges), 1952–78; *b* 19 Feb. 1913; *s* of Wilfrid Gordon and Mary Turnbull Lough, Newcastle upon Tyne; *m* 1939, Muriel Barker; one *d*. *Educ:* Newcastle upon Tyne Royal Grammar Sch.; St John's Coll., Cambridge; Sorbonne. Major Schol., St John's Coll., 1931; BA, First Cl. Hons Parts I and II Mod. and Medieval Langs Tripos, 1934; Esmond Schol. at British Inst. in Paris, 1935; Jebb Studentship, Cambridge, 1936; PhD 1937, MA 1938, Cambridge. Asst (later Lectr), Univ. of Aberdeen, 1937; Lectr in French, Cambridge, 1946. Leverhulme Res. Fellow, 1973. Hon. Dr, Univ. of Clermont, 1967; Hon. DLitt Newcastle, 1972. Officier de l'Ordre National du Mérite, 1973. *Publications:* Locke's Travels in France, 1953; (ed) selected Philosophical Writings of Diderot, 1953; (ed) The Encyclopédie of Diderot and d'Alembert: selected articles, 1954; An Introduction to Seventeenth Century France, 1954; Paris Theatre Audiences in the 17th and 18th centuries, 1957; An Introduction to Eighteenth Century France, 1960; Essays on the Encyclopédie of Diderot and D'Alembert, 1968; The Encyclopédie in 18th Century England and other studies, 1970; The Encyclopédie, 1971; The Contributors to the Encyclopédie, 1973; (ed with J. Proust) Diderot: Œuvres complètes, vols V–VIII, 1977; (with M. Lough) An Introduction to Nineteenth Century France, 1978; Writer and Public in France, 1978; Seventeenth Century French Drama: the background, 1979; The Philosophes and Post-Revolutionary France, 1982; France Observed in the Seventeenth Century by British Travellers, 1985; France on the Eve of Revolution: observations by British travellers 1763–1788, 1987; (with E. Merson) John Graham Lough (1798–1876), a Northumbrian Sculptor, 1987; articles on French literature and ideas in 17th and 18th centuries in French and English learned jls. *Address:* 1 St Hild's Lane, Durham DH1 1QL. *T:* Durham (0191) 3848034.

LOUGHBOROUGH, Lord; Jamie William St Clair-Erskine; *b* 28 May 1986; *s* and *heir* of Earl of Rosslyn, *qv*.

LOUGHBOROUGH, Archdeacon of; *see* Stanes, Ven. I. T.

LOUGHEAD, Peter, DPhil; Under Secretary, Coal Division, Department of Trade and Industry, since 1994; *b* 26 Aug. 1950; *s* of Arnold George Loughead and Dora Loughead; *m* 1st, 1975, Kristien Wynants (marr. diss. 1989); 2nd, 1993, Virginia Pasqua Dias. *Educ:* Liverpool Inst.; Lincoln Coll., Oxford (MA, DPhil). Admin Trainee, Dept of Prices and Consumer Protection, 1975; Principal, DoI, 1980; on secondment as First Sec., UK Rep., Brussels, 1982; Asst Sec., DTI, 1985–92; HM Treasury, 1992; Under Sec., Coal Review Team, 1992–93, Coal Privatisation Unit, 1993–94, DTI. *Recreation:* Everton FC. *Address:* Department of Trade and Industry, 1 Palace Street, SW1E 5HE.

LOUGHEED, Hon. (Edgar) Peter, CC (Can.) 1987; PC (Can.) 1982; QC (Can.) 1972; Partner, Bennett Jones Verchere, barristers and solicitors, Calgary and Edmonton; *b* Calgary, 26 July 1928; *s* of late Edgar Donald Lougheed and Edna Bauld; *m* 1952, Jeanne Estelle Rogers, Edmonton; two *s* two *d*. *Educ:* public and secondary schs, Calgary; Univ. of Alberta (BA, LLB); Harvard Grad. Sch. of Business (MBA). Read law with Calgary firm of lawyers; called to Bar of Alberta, 1955, and practised law with same firm, 1955–56. Joined Mannix Co. Ltd, as Sec., 1956 (Gen. Counsel, 1958, Vice-Pres., 1959, Dir, 1960). Entered private legal practice, 1962. Chm., Quorum (Asia) Ltd. Director: ATCO Ltd; Luscar Ltd; Canadian Pacific; Royal Bank of Canada; Princeton Developments; Northern Telecom; Bombardier Inc.; Quorum Growth Inc. (formerly Quorum Capital Corp.); Reed Stenhouse Cos Ltd; Norcen Energy Resources Ltd; CFCN Telecommunications Ltd; PWA Corporation Ltd; Bechtel Canada Inc.; DMR Gp Inc.; Noranda Inc.; Encal Oil & Gas Ltd. Mem. Adv. Bd, Morgan Stanley Gp Inc. Elected: Provincial Leader of Progressive Conservative Party of Alberta, also Member for Calgary West, 1965; Leader of the Official Opposition, 1967; Premier of Alberta, 1971–85 (re-elected 1975, 1979 and 1982). Hon. LLD: St Francis Xavier, 1983; Alberta, 1986; Calgary, 1987; Windsor, Lethbridge, 1988. *Recreations:* golf, ski-ing. *Address:* (office) 4500 Bankers Hall East, 855 2nd Street SW, Calgary, Alberta T2P 4K7, Canada.

LOUGHRAN, James; Principal Conductor and Musical Adviser, Hallé Orchestra, 1971–83, Conductor Laureate, 1983–91; *b* 30 June 1931; *s* of James and Agnes Loughran; *m* 1st, 1961, Nancy Coggon (marr. diss. 1983); two *s*; 2nd, 1985, Ludmila (*née* Navratil). *Educ:* St Aloysius' Coll., Glasgow; Bonn, Amsterdam and Milan. FRNCM 1976; FRSAMD 1983. 1st Prize, Philharmonia Orchestra's Conducting Competition, 1961. Associate Conductor, Bournemouth Symphony Orchestra, 1962–65; Principal Conductor: BBC Scottish Symphony Orchestra, 1965–71; Bamberg Symphony Orchestra, 1979–83; Musical Dir, English Opera Gp, 1966 (Festivals of Drottningholm, Versailles and Aldeburgh). Guest conductor of principal orchestras of Europe, America, Australia and Japan; Permanent Guest Conductor, Japan Philharmonic Symphony Orch., 1993–. Internat. festivals and tours with Bamberg and Hallé orchestras, as well as Munich Philharmonic, BBC Symphony, Stockholm Philharmonic, London Philharmonic and Scottish Chamber orchestras. Many recordings, including complete Beethoven and Brahms symphonies. Gold Disc, EMI, 1983. Freeman, City of London, 1991; Liveryman, Musicians' Co., 1992. Hon. DMus Sheffield, 1983. *Address:* The Rookery, Bollington Cross, Macclesfield, Cheshire SK10 5EL.

LOUGHRAN, Rear-Adm. Terence William; Flag Officer, Naval Aviation, since 1995; *b* Newcastle-upon-Tyne, 27 March 1943; parents decd; *m* (marr. diss. 1988); one *s* two *d*. *Educ:* Devonport High Sch.; Britannia Royal Naval Coll. MNI 1993. Qualified as: rotary wing pilot, 1967; flying instructor, 1971; graduated Canadian Forces Comd and Staff Coll., 1976; i/c 706 Naval Air Sqdn, 1976–77; Comdr 1979; i/c HMS Phoebe, 1980–81; Executive Officer: HMS Bristol, 1983–84; HMS Intrepid, 1984–85; Captain 1986; i/c HMS Gloucester and Comdr Armilla Patrol, Arabian Gulf Task Unit, 1986–88; Dep. Dir, Internat. Affairs in Naval Staff Duties, 1988–90; Dir, Naval Manpower Planning, 1990–92; i/c HMS Ark Royal and Comdr, Grapple Adriatic Task Gp, 1993–94; Rear-Adm., 1995. *Publications:* (contrib.) Royal United Services Inst. Jl. *Recreations:* sailing, motor cycling, spinning yarns. *Address:* FONA Headquarters, Yeovilton, Yeovil, Som BA22 8HL. *Clubs:* Naval; Travellers' (Newcastle).

LOUGHREY, (Stephen) Patrick (Victor); Controller, BBC Northern Ireland, since 1994; *b* 29 Dec. 1955; *s* of Eddie Loughrey and Mary Loughrey (*née* Griffin); *m* 1978, Patricia Kelly; one *s* two *d*. *Educ:* Loretto Coll., Milford; Univ. of Ulster (BA); Queen's Univ. (MA). Res. student, Trent Univ., Canada, 1977; teacher, St Colm's Draperstown, 1978–84; BBC: Producer, Educn, 1984–88; Hd, Educnl Broadcasting, 1988–91; Hd of Progs, NI, 1991–94. Jt Editor, Ulster Local Studies, 1988–91. *Publication:* People of Ireland, 1988. *Recreations:* walking, talking. *Address:* 7 The Willows, Coolshinney Road, Magherafelt, Co. Derry, Northern Ireland. *T:* (office) Belfast (01232) 338200.

LOUIS, Prof. William Roger, DLitt; Kerr Professor of English History and Culture, Universtiy of Texas at Austin, since 1985; Supernumerary Fellow, St Antony's College, Oxford, since 1986; *b* 8 May 1936; *s* of Henry Edward and Bena May Louis; *m* 1st, 1960, Patricia Ann Leonard; one *s* one *d*; 2nd, 1981, Dagmar Cecilia Friedrich. *Educ:* Univ. of Oklahoma (BA 1959); Harvard (Woodrow Wilson Fellow; MA 1960); St Antony's Coll., Oxford (Marshall Scholar; DPhil 1962); DLitt Oxon 1979. FRHistS 1984; corresp. FBA 1993. Asst and Associate Prof., Yale, 1962–70; Humanities Research Center, University of Texas: Prof. of History and Curator, Historical Collections, 1970–85; Dir, British Studies, 1975–; Teaching Awards, 1984, 1992, 1993; National Endowment Humanities: Sen. Fellow, 1974–75; Dir, Seminars, 1985–91. Guggenheim Fellow, 1979–80; Vis. Fellow, 1979–80, Chichele Lectr, 1990, All Souls Coll., Oxford; Fellow/Lecturer: Churchill Coll., Cambridge, 1985; Brookings Instn, 1989; LSE, 1992; Woodrow Wilson Internat. Center for Scholars, 1994–95; Cust Lectr, Univ. of Nottingham, 1995. Editor, British Documents on the End of Empire, 1988–; Editor-in-Chief, Oxford History of the British Empire, 1993–. *Publications:* Ruanda-Urundi, 1963; Germany's Lost Colonies, 1967; (ed with P. Gifford) Britain and Germany in Africa, 1967; (with J. Stengers) Congo Reform Movement, 1968; British Strategy in the Far East, 1971; (ed with P. Gifford) France and Britain in Africa, 1971; (ed) Nationalism Security and International Trusteeship in the Pacific, 1972; (ed) A. J. P. Taylor and his Critics, 1972; (ed) Imperialism: the Robinson and Gallagher controversy, 1976; Imperialism at Bay, 1977; (ed with W. S. Livingston) Australia, New Zealand and the Pacific Islands, 1979; (ed with P. Gifford) The Transfer of Power in Africa, 1982; The British Empire in the Middle East 1945–51, 1984 (Amer. Hist. Assoc. Prize); (ed with R. Stookey) The End of the Palestine Mandate, 1986; (ed with H. Bull) The Special Relationship, 1986; (ed with P. Gifford) Decolonization in Africa, 1988; (ed with J. A. Bill) Musaddiq, Nationalism and Oil, 1988; (ed with R. Owen) Suez 1956, 1989; (ed with R. Fernea) The Iraqi Revolution, 1991; In the Name of God Go! Leo Amery and the British Empire, 1992; (ed with R. Blake) Churchill, 1993; (ed) Adventures with Britannia: personalities, politics and culture in Britain, 1995. *Recreation:* a German wife. *Address:* Department of History, University of Texas, Austin, TX 78712, USA. *Clubs:* Reform; Century (NY), Metropolitan (Washington).

LOUSTAU-LALANNE, Bernard Michel; Secretary-General, European Federation of Management Consulting Associations, 1991; *b* 20 June 1938; *s* of Joseph Antoine Michel Loustau-Lalanne, OBE, and Marie Therese Madeleine (*née* Boullé); *m* 1974, Debbie Elizabeth Temple-Brown (marr. diss. 1982); one *d*. *Educ:* Seychelles Coll.; St Mary's Coll., Southampton; Imperial Coll., London. Called to the Bar, Middle Temple, London, 1969. Assistant Inspector, Northern Rhodesia Police, 1962–64; Crown Counsel, Seychelles, 1970–72; Sen. State Counsel and Official Notary, 1972–76; Attorney-General, Seychelles, 1976–78; High Comr for Seychelles, in London, 1978–80; concurrently Seychelles Ambassador to USA, and Seychelles Perm. Rep. to UN; Internat. Rep., PRS, 1980–90. *Recreations:* international affairs, French literature, theatre, tennis, ski-ing. *Club:* Seychelles Yacht.

LOUTH, 16th Baron, *cr* 1541, **Otway Michael James Oliver Plunkett;** *b* 19 Aug. 1929; *o s* of Otway Randal Percy Oliver Plunkett, 15th Baron, and Ethel May, *d* of Walter John Gallichen, Jersey, Channel Islands; *S* father, 1950; *m* 1951, Angela Patricia Cullinane, Jersey; three *s* two *d*. *Heir:* *s* Hon. Jonathan Oliver Plunkett, BSc, AMIEE [*b* 4 Nov. 1952; *m* 1981, Jennifer, *d* of Norman Oliver Hodgetts, Weston-super-Mare; one *s* one *d*]. *Address:* Les Sercles, La Grande Pièce, St Peter, Jersey, Channel Islands JE3 7AE.

LOVAT, 18th Lord (S) *cr* 1458–1464 (*de facto* 16th Lord, 18th but for the attainder); **Simon Fraser;** Baron (UK) 1837; *b* 13 Feb. 1977; *er s* of Hon. Simon Augustine Fraser, Master of Lovat (*d* 1994) and of Virginia Fraser, *d* of David Grose; *S* grandfather, 1995. *Educ:* Harrow. *Heir:* *b* Jack Fraser, *b* 1984.

LOVAT, Sheriff Leonard Scott; Sheriff of South Strathclyde, Dumfries and Galloway at Hamilton, 1978–93; *b* 28 July 1926; *s* of late Charles Lovat and Alice (*née* Hunter); *m* 1960, Elinor Frances (decd), *d* of late J. A. McAlister and Mary McAlister; one *s* one *d*. *Educ:* St Aloysius Coll., Glasgow; Glasgow Univ. (BL 1947). Solicitor, 1948; in partnership, 1955–59. Asst to Prof. of Roman Law, Glasgow Univ., 1954–63; Cropwood Fellow, Inst. of Criminology, Univ. of Cambridge, 1971. Procurator Fiscal Depute, Glasgow, 1960; Sen. Asst Procurator Fiscal, Glasgow and Strathkelvin, 1976. Mem., CCJ. Hon. Member: Aloysian Assoc.; Sheriffs' Soc. *Publication:* Climbers' Guide to Glencoe and Ardgour, 2 vols, 1959, 1965. *Recreations:* music, hill-walking, bird-watching. *Address:* 38 Kelvin Court, Glasgow G12 0AE. *T:* 0141–357 0031.

LOVE, Prof. Andrew Henry Garmany, CBE 1995: MD; FRCP, FRCPI; Professor of Medicine since 1983, and Dean of Faculty of Medicine, 1981–86, Queen's University of Belfast; *b* 28 Sept. 1934; *s* of Andrew and Martha Love; *m* 1963, Margaret Jean Lennox; one *s*. *Educ:* Bangor Endowed Sch., NI; Queen's Univ. of Belfast (BSc Hons 1955; MD 1963). FRCP 1973; FRCPI 1972. Lectr in Physiology, 1960–63 and Lectr in Medicine, 1963–64, QUB; MRC Travelling Fellow, and Hon. Consultant, US Naval Med. Res. Unit-2, Taipei, Taiwan, 1964–65; Sen. Lectr in Medicine, 1966–73 and Prof. of Gastroenterology, 1973–83, QUB (on leave of absence, Res. Fellow, Boston City Hosp., Mass, 1966). Hon. Consultant, SEATO Cholera Labs, Pakistan, 1967–70. Mem., GMC, 1981–87; Chm., NI Council for Postgrad. Med. and Dental Educn. Pres., Assoc. of Medical Deans of Europe, 1988–91. FRSA. *Publications:* articles in learned jls on gen. medicine, intestinal function, trace element metabolism and nutrition. *Recreations:* golf, sailing. *Address:* The Glen Farm, Carrowdore Road, Greyabbey, Co. Down BT22 2LU. *T:* Greyabbey (0124774) 414. *Clubs:* East India, Devonshire, Sports and Public Schools; Royal Ulster Yacht (Bangor, Co. Down); Royal County Down Golf (Newcastle).

LOVE, Prof. Philip Noel, CBE 1983; Vice Chancellor, University of Liverpool, since 1992, Member, Scottish Law Commission, since 1986; *b* 25 Dec. 1939; *o s* of Thomas Isaac and Ethel Violet Love; *m* 1963, Isabel Leah (*d* 1993), *yr d* of Innes Taylor and Leah Wallace Mearns; three *s*; *m* 1995, Isobel, *widow* of David Pardey. *Educ:* Aberdeen Grammar Sch.; Aberdeen Univ. (MA 1961, LLB 1963). Admitted Solicitor in Scotland, 1963; Advocate in Aberdeen, 1963–; Partner, Campbell Connon, Solicitors, Aberdeen, 1963–74, Consultant, 1974–. University of Aberdeen: Prof. of Conveyancing and Professional Practice of Law, 1974–92; Dean, Faculty of Law, 1979–82, 1991–92; Vice Principal, 1986–90. Law Society of Scotland: Mem. Council, 1975–86; Examr, 1975–83 (Chm. Examrs, 1977–80); Vice-Pres., 1980–81; Pres., 1981–82. Local Chm., Rent Assessment Panel for Scotland, 1972–92; Chairman: Sec. of State for Scotland's Expert Cttee on house purchase and sale, 1982–84; Scottish Conveyancing and Executry Services Bd, 1991–; Vice-Pres., Scottish Law Agents Soc., 1970; Member: Jt Standing Cttee on Legal Educn in Scotland, 1976–85 (Chm., 1976–80); Rules Council, Court of Session, 1968–92; Council, Internat. Bar Assoc., 1983–87 (Vice-Chm., Legal Educn Div., 1983–87); Jt Ethical Cttee, Grampian Health Bd, 1984–92 (Vice-Chm., 1985; Chm., 1986–92). Chm., Aberdeen Home for Widowers' Children, 1971–92. Pres., Aberdeen Grammar Sch. Former Pupils' Club, 1987–88. Hon. Sheriff of Grampian, Highland and Islands, 1978–. Chm., Registers of Scotland Customer Adv. Gp, 1990–92. Trustee, Grampian and Islands Family Trust, 1988–92. Chm., Mersey Partnership, 1995–. Gov., Inst. of Occupational Medicine Ltd, 1990–. Mem., Editl Consultative Bd for Scotland, Butterworth & Co. (Publishers) Ltd, 1990–. *Recreations:* Rugby (Golden Oldies variety now), keep-fit (FRS Club, Aberdeen). *Address:* Vice-Chancellor's Lodge, 12 Sefton Park Road, Liverpool L8 3SL. *T:* 0151–794 2003. *Clubs:* Athenæum; New (Edinburgh); Racquet (Liverpool); Aberdeen Grammar School Former Pupils' Club Centre (Aberdeen).

LOVE, Sir Ralph; *see* Love, Sir M. R. R.

LOVEDAY, Alan (Raymond); solo violinist; *b* 29 Feb. 1928; *s* of Leslie and Margaret Loveday; *m* 1952, Ruth Stanfield; one *s* one *d*. *Educ:* privately; Royal College of Music (prizewinner). Made debut at age of 4; debut in England, 1946; has given many concerts, broadcasts, and made TV appearances, in this country and abroad, playing with all leading conductors and orchestras; repertoire ranges from Bach (which he likes to play on an unmodernised violin), to contemporary music. Prof., RCM, 1955–72. Full-time Mem. and Soloist, Acad. of St Martin-in-the-Fields. *Recreations:* chess, bridge.

LOVEDAY, Mark Antony; Senior Partner, Cazenove & Co., since 1994; *b* 22 Sept. 1943; *s* of George Arthur Loveday and Sylvia Mary Loveday; *m* 1981, Mary Elizabeth Tolmie; one *s* one *d*. *Educ:* Winchester Coll.; Magdalen Coll., Oxford (MA). Cazenove & Co., 1966–; Partner, 1974–. Trustee, Magdalen Coll. Develt Trust, 1982–. *Recreation:* golf. *Address:* 42 Royal Avenue, SW3 4QF. *T:* 0171–730 4031; (office) 12 Tokenhouse Yard, EC2R 7AN. *T:* 0171–588 2828. *Clubs:* Boodle's, Hurlingham, MCC.

LOVEGROVE, His Honour Geoffrey David, QC 1969; a Circuit Judge (formerly County Court Judge), 1971–92; *b* 22 Dec. 1919; *s* of late Gilbert Henry Lovegrove; *m* 1959, Janet, *d* of John Bourne; one *s* two *d*. *Educ:* Haileybury; New College, Oxford (MA). Army, 1940–46. Called to the Bar, Inner Temple, 1947; Dep. Chairman, W Sussex Quarter Sessions, 1965–71. Master, Innholders' Company, 1980–81.

LOVELACE, 5th Earl of, *cr* 1838; **Peter Axel William Locke King;** Baron King and Ockham, 1725; Viscount Ockham, 1838; *b* 26 Nov. 1951; *s* of 4th Earl of Lovelace and Manon Lis (*d* 1990), *d* of Axel Sigurd Transo, Copenhagen, Denmark; *S* father, 1964; *m* 1994, Kathleen Anne Smolders, Melbourne, Aust. *Address:* Torridon House, Torridon, Ross-shire IV22 2HA.

LOVELL, Sir (Alfred Charles) Bernard, Kt 1961; OBE 1946; FRS 1955; Director of Jodrell Bank Experimental Station, Cheshire, now Nuffield Radio Astronomy Laboratories, 1951–81; Professor of Radio Astronomy, University of Manchester, 1951–80, now Emeritus Professor; *b* 31 Aug. 1913; *s* of G. Lovell, Oldland Common, Gloucestershire; *m* 1937, Mary Joyce Chesterman (*d* 1993); two *s* three *d*. *Educ:* Kingswood Grammar Sch., Bristol; University of Bristol. Asst Lectr in Physics, Univ. of Manchester, 1936–39; Telecommunication Res. Establishment, 1939–45; Physical Laboratories, Univ. of Manchester and Jodrell Bank Experimental Station, Cheshire; Lectr, 1945, Sen. Lectr, 1947, Reader, 1949, in Physics. Reith Lectr, 1958; Lectures: Condon, 1962; Guthrie, 1962; Halley, 1964; Queen's, Berlin, 1970; Brockington, Kingston, Ont, 1970; Bickley, Oxford, 1977; Crookshank, RCR, 1977; Angel Meml, Newfoundland, 1977; Blackett Meml, Operational Res. Soc., 1987. Vis. Montague Burton Prof. of Internat. Relations, Univ. of Edinburgh, 1973. Member: Air Navigation Cttee, 1953–56 (Vice-Chm., 1955–56); Air Warfare Cttee, 1954–60; ARC, 1955–58; Radar & Signals Adv. Bd, 1956–59; Sci. Adv. Council, 1957–60; Guided Weapons Adv. Bd, 1958–60; SRC, 1965–70; Amer. Philosophical Soc., 1974–. Pres., RAS, 1969–71; Vice-Pres., Internat. Astronomical Union, 1970–76; Pres., British Assoc., 1975–76. Pres., Guild of Church Musicians, 1976–89; Jun. Warden, 1984–85, Sen. Warden, 1985–86, Master, 1986–87, Musicians' Co. Hon. Freeman, City of Manchester, 1977. Hon. Fellow, Society of Engineers, 1964; Hon. Foreign Member American Academy of Arts and Sciences, 1955; Hon. Life Member, New York Academy, 1960; Hon. Member: Royal Swedish Academy, 1962; RNCM, 1981; Manchester Lit. & Philos. Soc., 1988. Hon. LLD: Edinburgh, 1961; Calgary, 1966; Hon. DSc: Leicester, 1961; Leeds, 1966; London, 1967; Bath, 1967; Bristol, 1970; DUniv Stirling, 1974; DUniv Surrey, 1975; Hon. FIEE, 1967; Hon. FInstP, 1976. Duddell Medal, 1954; Royal Medal, 1960; Daniel and Florence Guggenheim International Astronautics Award, 1961; Ordre du Mérite pour la Recherche et l'Invention, 1962; Churchill Gold Medal, 1964; Maitland Lecturer and Silver Medallist, Institution of Structural Engineers, 1964; Second RSA American Exchange Lectr, Philadelphia, 1980; Benjamin Franklin Medal, RSA, 1980; Gold Medal, Royal Astronomical Soc., 1981; Rutherford Meml Lectr, Royal Soc., 1984. Commander's Order of Merit, Polish People's

Republic, 1975. *Publications:* Science and Civilisation, 1939; World Power Resources and Social Development, 1945; Radio Astronomy, 1951; Meteor Astronomy, 1954; The Exploration of Space by Radio, 1957; The Individual and The Universe, (BBC Reith Lectures, 1958); The Exploration of Outer Space (Gregynog Lectures, 1961); Discovering the Universe, 1963; Our Present Knowledge of the Universe, 1967; (ed with T. Margerison) The Explosion of Science: The Physical Universe, 1967; The Story of Jodrell Bank, 1968; The Origins and International Economics of Space Exploration, 1973; Out of the Zenith, 1973; Man's Relation to the Universe, 1975; P. M. S. Blackett: a biographical memoir, 1976; In the Centre of Immensities, 1978; Emerging Cosmology, 1981; The Jodrell Bank Telescopes, 1985; Voice of the Universe, 1987; (with Sir Francis Graham Smith) Pathways to the Universe, 1988; Astronomer by Chance (autobiog.), 1990; Echoes of War, 1991; many publications in Physical and Astronomical journals. *Recreations:* cricket, gardening, music. *Address:* The Quinta, Swettenham, Cheshire CW12 2LD. *T:* Lower Withington (01477) 571254. *Clubs:* Athenæum, MCC; Lancashire County Cricket (Pres., 1995–96).

LOVELL, Kenneth Ernest Walter; Treasurer to the Greater London Council, 1977–80, retired; *b* 25 Oct. 1919; *s* of Ernest John and Alice Lovell; *m* 1946, Vera Mary Pithouse; one *s* two *d.* *Educ:* Ashford County Grammar School. Mem. Chartered Inst. of Public Finance and Accountancy. Middlesex County Council (Finance Dept): Computer Manager, 1961; Asst County Treasurer, 1963. Greater London Council: Asst Treasurer, 1965; Finance Officer, ILEA, 1972. *Recreations:* gardening, cricket, hockey, photography; study of social and economic development of British Isles; study of landscape of British Isles. *Address:* 15 Meadway Close, Staines, Mddx TW18 2PR. *T:* Staines (01784) 452806.

LOVELL-DAVIS, family name of **Baron Lovell-Davis.**

LOVELL-DAVIS, Baron *cr* 1974 (Life Peer), of Highgate; **Peter Lovell Lovell-Davis;** Member: Commonwealth Development Corporation, 1978–84; London Consortium, 1978–88; *b* 8 July 1924; *s* of late William Lovell Davis and late Winifred Mary Davis; *m* 1950, Jean Graham; one *s* one *d.* *Educ:* Christ's Coll., Finchley; King Edward VI Sch., Stratford-on-Avon; Jesus Coll., Oxford. BA Hons English, MA. Served War, RAF (Pilot), to Flt-Lt, 1943–47. Oxford, 1947–50. Managing Dir, Central Press Features Ltd, 1952–70; Dir, various newspaper and printing cos. Chm., Colour Features Ltd; Chairman: Davis & Harrison Ltd, 1970–73; Features Syndicate, 1971–74; Lee Cooper Licensing Services, 1983–90; Pettifor, Morrow & Associates, 1986–. Mem., Islington DHA, 1982–85. A Lord in Waiting (Govt Whip), 1974–75; Parly Under-Sec. of State, Dept of Energy, 1975–76. Adviser to various Govt Cttees, Health Educn Council, Labour Party and Govt, on media. Vice-Pres., YHA, 1978–; Trustee, Whittington Hosp. Academic Centre, 1980–. *Recreations:* industrial archaeology, inland waterways, bird-watching, walking, sketching. *Address:* 80 North Road, Highgate, N6 4AA. *T:* 0181–348 3919.

LOVELL-PANK, Dorian Christopher; QC 1993; a Recorder, since 1989; *b* 15 Feb. 1946; *s* of late Christopher Edwin Lovell-Pank, Madrid and Jean Alston de Oliva-Day (*née* McPherson), Cape Town and Buenos Aires; *m* 1983, Diana, *d* of late Michael Cady Byford and of Sonia Byford, Claret Hall, Clare, Suffolk; one *s* one *d.* *Educ:* Downside; Colegio Sarmiento, Buenos Aires; LSE; Inns of Court Sch. of Law. Called to the Bar, Inner Temple, 1971; in practice SE Circuit; Asst Recorder, 1985–89. Member: Cttee, Criminal Bar Assoc., 1989–; Gen. Council of Bar, 1989–92; Internat. Bar Assoc., 1993–. Mem. Panel of Chairmen, Police Discipline Appeal Tribunals, 1991–. *Recreations:* travel, reading, things latin, swimming. *Address:* 6 King's Bench Walk, Temple, EC4Y 7DR. *T:* 0171–583 0410. *Clubs:* Garrick, Hurlingham, Riverside, Annabel's.

LOVELOCK, Sir Douglas (Arthur), KCB 1979 (CB 1974); First Church Estates Commissioner, 1983–93; Chairman, Central Board of Finance of the Church of England, 1983–92; *b* 7 Sept. 1923; *s* of late Walter and Irene Lovelock; *m* 1961, Valerie Margaret (*née* Lane); one *s* one *d.* *Educ:* Bec Sch., London. Entered Treasury, 1949; Min. of Supply, 1952; Private Sec. to Permanent Sec., 1953–54; Principal, 1954; Private Sec. to successive Ministers of Aviation (Rt Hon. Peter Thorneycroft and Rt Hon. Julian Amery), 1961–63; Asst Sec., 1963; Under-Sec. (Contracts), Min. of Technology, subseq. Min. of Aviation Supply, 1968–71; Asst Under-Sec. of State (Personnel), MoD, 1971–72; Dep. Sec., DTI, 1972–74, Depts of Trade, Industry, Prices and Consumer Protection, 1974–77; Chm., Bd of Customs and Excise, 1977–83. Chm., Civil Service Benevolent Fund, 1980–83. Chm., Review of Citizens' Advice Bureaux Service, 1983–84. Governor: Whitgift Foundn, 1986–; Whitgift Sch., 1986–; Trinity Sch., 1986– (Chm., 1993–); Old Palace Sch., 1995–. *Recreations:* walking, gardening, outdoor activities generally. *Address:* The Old House, 91 Coulsdon Road, Old Coulsdon, Surrey CR3 2LD. *T:* Downland (017375) 55211.

LOVELOCK, Prof. James Ephraim, CBE 1990; FRS 1974; independent scientist, since 1964; Visiting Fellow, Green College, Oxford, since 1994; *b* 26 July 1919; *s* of Tom Arthur Lovelock and Nellie Ann Elizabeth (*née* March); *m* 1st, 1942, Helen Mary Hyslop (*d* 1989); two *s* two *d;* 2nd, 1991, Sandra Jean Orchard. *Educ:* Strand Sch., London; Manchester and London Univs. BSc, PhD, DSc, ARIC. Staff Scientist, Nat. Inst. for Med. Research, 1941–61; Rockefeller Fellow, Harvard Univ., 1954–55; Yale Univ., 1958–59; Prof. of Chemistry, Baylor Univ. Coll. of Medicine, Texas, 1961–64. Vis. Prof., Univ. of Reading, 1967–90. Pres., Marine Biol Assoc., 1986–90. Mem. Sigma Xi, Yale Chapter, 1959. Hon. ScD East Anglia, 1982; Hon. DSc: Exeter, 1988; Plymouth Univ. (formerly Plymouth Poly.), 1988; Edinburgh, 1993; Hon. DSci Stockholm, 1991. Amsterdam Prize, Roy. Netherlands Acad. of Arts and Scis, 1990. *Publications:* Gaia, 1979; (with Michael Allaby) The Great Extinction, 1983; The Ages of Gaia, 1988; Gaia: the practical science of planetary medicine, 1991; numerous papers and patents. *Recreations:* walking, painting, computer programming, reading. *Address:* Coombe Mill, St Giles on the Heath, Launceston, Cornwall PL15 9RY.

LOVELUCK, Paul Edward, CBE 1993; JP; Chief Executive, Wales Tourist Board, since 1984; *b* 3 Feb. 1942; *s* of Edward Henry Loveluck and Elizabeth Loveluck (*née* Treharne); *m* 1965, Lynne Gronow; one *s* one *d.* *Educ:* Maesteg Grammar Sch.; UCW, Cardiff (BA). Board of Trade, 1963–69; Welsh Office, 1969–84 (Asst Sec., 1975–84). Vice-Pres., Nat. Welsh-American Foundn, 1989–. Chm., Governing Body, Whitchurch High Sch., 1988–. JP Cardiff, 1982. *Recreations:* hillwalking, music. *Address:* Wales Tourist Board, Brunel House, 2 Fitzalan Road, Cardiff CF2 1UY. *T:* Cardiff (01222) 475208; Tudor Cottage, 38 Rhiwbina Hill, Cardiff CF4 6UQ.

LOVEMAN, Stephen Charles Gardner; Under Secretary, Department for Education and Employment (formerly Department of Employment), since 1989; *b* 26 Dec. 1943; *s* of Charles Edward Loveman and Edith Mary Gardner; *m* 1972, Judith Pamela Roberts; one *s* one *d.* *Educ:* Arnold Sch., Blackpool; Emmanuel College, Cambridge (BA). Dept of Employment, 1967; Private Sec. to Minister of State for Employment, 1972–74; Health and Safety Exec., 1974–77; Dept of Employment, 1977–80; Manpower Services Commn, 1980–87; Dept of Employment, 1987–88; Cabinet Office, 1988–89. *Recreations:* walking, opera, reading, swimming. *Address:* 24 Brincliffe Crescent, Sheffield S11 9AW.

LOVERIDGE, Sir John (Warren), Kt 1988; JP; senior partner of family businesses in agriculture, education and property; *b* 9 Sept. 1925; *s* of C. W. Loveridge and Emily (Mickie), *d* of John Malone; *m* 1954, Jean Marguerite, *d* of E. J. Chivers; three *s* two *d.* *Educ:* St John's Coll., Cambridge (MA). Mem., Hampstead BC, 1953–59. Contested (C) Aberavon, 1951, Brixton (LCC), 1952. MP (C) Hornchurch, 1970–74, Upminster, 1974–83. Member: Parly Select Cttee on Expenditure (Mem. General Purposes Sub-Cttee); Procedure Cttee; Chm., Cons. Smaller Business Cttee, 1979–83). Treasurer/Trustee, Hampstead Conservative Assoc., 1959–74; President: Hampstead and Highgate Conservative Assoc., 1986–91; Upminster Conservative Assoc., 1992–; Greater London Area Conservatives, 1993– (Vice-Pres., 1984–93). Vice-Pres., Nat. Council for Civil Protection (formerly Civil Defence), 1980–. Chm., Dinosaurs Club (former Cons. MPs), 1993–. JP West Central Division, 1963. FRAS; FRAgS; MRIIA. Liveryman, Girdlers' Co. *Publications:* (jtly) Moving Forward: small businesses and the economy, 1983; *poems:* God Save the Queen: Sonnets of Elizabeth I, 1981; Hunter of the Moon, 1983; Hunter of the Sun, 1984. *Recreations:* painting, writing, historic houses, shooting. *Address:* c/o The Private Office, 2 Arkwright Road, NW3 6AD. *Clubs:* Buck's, Carlton, Hurlingham.

LOVERING, John David; Chief Operating Officer, Tarmac plc, 1993–95; *b* 11 Oct. 1949; *s* of John George and Ruby Beatrice Lovering; *m* 1971, Brenda Joan Wotherspoon; two *s* one *d.* *Educ:* Dulwich Coll.; Exeter Univ. (BA Hons); Manchester Business Sch. (MBA). Planning Manager, Spillers Internat. Div., 1975–78; Corporate Strategy Manager, Lex Service plc, 1978–83; Grand Metropolitan plc, Commercial Dir Express Dairy Ltd, 1983–85; Head of Gp Finance and Planning, Imperial Gp plc, 1985–86; Finance Dir, Sears plc, 1986–93. Trustee and Dir, SCF, 1990–. *Recreations:* sport, walking, opera. *Club:* Alleyn (Dulwich).

LOVERING, Prof. John Francis, AO 1993; FAA; FTS; President, Murray-Darling Basin Commission, since 1994; *b* 27 March 1930; *s* of George Francis Lovering and Dorothy Irene Mildwater; *m* 1954, Jennifer Kerry FitzGerald; two *s* one *d.* *Educ:* Canterbury High Sch., Sydney; Univ. of Sydney (MSc); Univ. of Melbourne (MSc); California Inst. of Technology (PhD). FAA 1982; FTS 1993. Asst Curator of Minerals, Australian Museum, 1951–55; Research Fellow, Fellow and Sen. Fellow, Dept of Geophysics and Geochemistry, ANU, 1956–69; University of Melbourne: Prof. of Geology, 1969–87; Dean of Science, 1983–85; Dep. Vice-Chancellor (Research), 1985–87; Vice-Chancellor and Prof. of Geology, Flinders Univ. of SA, 1987–95. Chairman of Directors: Comlabs Ltd, 1985–93; Geotrack International Pty Ltd, 1987–93; Open Learning Technology Corp., 1992–. Hon. DSc Flinders Univ. Chevalier des Palmes Académiques, 1981. *Publications:* Last of Lands: Antarctica (with J. R. V. Prescott), 1979; contribs to learned jls. *Recreations:* music, wine, food. *Address:* Flinders House, Flinders Road, Bellevue Heights, SA 5050, Australia. *T:* (8) 2782441. *Clubs:* Adelaide (Adelaide); Commonwealth (Canberra); Antarctic, Banool Ski, Melbourne, Wallaby (Melbourne).

LOVICK, Albert Ernest Fred; retired; Chairman, 1964–68, Director, 1950–68 and 1969–78, Co-operative Insurance Society Ltd; Chairman, Cumbrian Co-operative Society Ltd, Carlisle, 1972–86; Director: CWS Ltd, 1949–78; Shoefayre Ltd, 1975–78; *b* 19 Feb. 1912; *s* of late Arthur Alfred Lovick and late Mary Lovick (*née* Sharland); *m* 1934, Florence Ena Jewell; no *c.* *Educ:* Elementary Sch., Eastleigh, Hants; Peter Symonds, Winchester. Hearne & Partner, rating surveyors, 1928; Eastleigh Co-operative Society, 1929–33; Harwich, Dovercourt and Parkeston CS, 1933–35; Managing Secretary, Basingstoke CS, 1935–49. During War of 1939–45, government cttees. Member, Basingstoke Borough Council, 1946–49. Former Chm., Centratours Ltd. Member: Export Credits Guarantees Advisory Council, 1968–73; Bristol Rent Assessment Cttee, 1973–; Bristol Rent Tribunal, 1973–. Fellow, Co-operative Secretaries Assoc.; FCIS; FCIArb. *Recreations:* golf, gardening. *Address:* Coedway, Bristol Road, Stonehouse, Glos GL10 2BQ. *T:* Stonehouse (0145382) 3167. *Club:* Commonwealth Trust.

LOVILL, Sir John (Roger), Kt 1987; CBE 1983; DL; Chairman, Sloane Square Investments, since 1980 (Director since 1960); *b* 26 Sept. 1929; *s* of Walter Thomas Lovill and Elsie Lovill (*née* Page); *m* 1958, Jacqueline (*née* Parker); two *s* one *d.* *Educ:* Brighton Hove and Sussex Grammar School. S. G. Warburg, 1951–55; Dep. Gen. Manager, Securicor Ltd, 1955–60; Dir, Municipal Gen. Insce Co., 1984–95; Managing Trustee, Municipal Mutual Insce, 1988– (Chm., 1993–); Chm., Nationwide Small Business Property Trust, 1988–; Chm., Prime Health Ltd, 1992–94. Contested (C) Ebbw Vale, 1966; Mem., East Sussex CC, 1967–89, Leader, 1973–77; Chairman: Sussex Police Authority, 1976–79; Local Authority Conditions of Service Adv. Bd, 1978–83; ACC, 1983–86; Pres., Sussex Assoc. of Local Councils, 1987–; Vice Pres., Nat. Assoc. of Local Councils, 1991–93; Leader, Conservative Assoc. of County Councils, 1981–83. DL E Sussex 1983. *Recreations:* opera, politics, marine paintings. *Address:* Narroway, Beddingham, near Lewes, Sussex BN8 6JU. *T:* Glynde (01273) 858212.

LOW, family name of **Baron Aldington.**

LOW, Sir Alan (Roberts), Kt 1977; retired; Governor, Reserve Bank of New Zealand, 1967–77; *b* 11 Jan. 1916; 4th *s* of Benjamin H. Low and Sarah Low; *m* 1940, Kathleen Mary Harrow; one *s* two *d.* *Educ:* Timaru Main Sch.; Timaru Boys' High Sch.; Canterbury University College. MA 1937. Joined Reserve Bank of New Zealand, 1938; Economic Adviser, 1951; Asst Governor, 1960; Deputy Governor, 1962; Governor, 1967. Army Service, 1942–44; on loan to Economic Stabilisation Commission, 1944–46. Hon. Fellow, Bankers' Inst. of NZ, 1977. Hon. LLD Canterbury, 1977. *Publications:* No Free Lunch, 1983; Where DO We Go For Lunch, 1984; contributions to many economic and financial jls. *Recreations:* gardening, music, reading. *Address:* 171 Muritai Road, Eastbourne, Lower Hutt, New Zealand. *T:* 628861.

LOW, Brian Buik, CBE 1994; HM Diplomatic Service; High Commissioner to Papua New Guinea, since 1994; *b* 15 Nov. 1937; *s* of Robert James Low and Helen Duncan Low; *m* 1960, Anita Joan Allum; three *d.* *Educ:* Arbroath High Sch. Served RAF, 1956–61. Joined Diplomatic Service, 1962; FO, 1962–65; Sofia, 1965–67; Sydney, 1967–69; Kuala Lumpur, 1969–73; Moscow, 1973–74; FCO, 1974–78; Singapore, 1978–81; Commercial Consul, British Trade Develt Office, NY, 1981–84; First Sec., FCO, 1984–88; Head of Chancery, Lima, 1988–91; Ambassador to Estonia, 1991–94. *Recreations:* music, reading, golf, watching sport. *Address:* c/o Foreign and Commonwealth Office, SW1A 2AH. *Clubs:* Carnoustie Golf; Singapore Cricket.

LOW, Prof. Donald Anthony, DPhil; PhD; FAHA, FASSA; President of Clare Hall, 1987–94, Smuts Professor of the History of the British Commonwealth, 1983–87, and Deputy Vice-Chancellor, 1990–94, University of Cambridge; *b* 22 June 1927; *o s* of late Canon Donald Low and Winifred (*née* Edmunds); *m* 1952, Isobel Smails; one *s* two *d.* *Educ:* Haileybury and ISC; Univ. of Oxford (MA, DPhil); PhD Cantab 1983. Open Scholar in Modern History, 1944, Amelia Jackson Sen. Student, 1948, Hon. Fellow, 1992, Exeter Coll., Oxford; Lectr, subseq. Sen. Lectr, Makerere Coll., University Coll. of E Africa, 1951–58; Uganda corresp., The Times, 1952–58; Fellow, subseq. Sen. Fellow in History, Res. Sch. of Social Sciences, ANU, 1959–64; Founding Dean of Sch. of African and Asian Studies, and Prof. of Hist., Univ. of Sussex, 1964–72; Australian National University: Prof. of History, 1973–83; Dir, Res. Sch. of Pacific Studies, 1973–75; Vice Chancellor, 1975–82; University of Cambridge: Fellow, Churchill Coll., 1983–87; Dir,

Centre of Internat. Studies, 1985–87; Mem., Council of Senate, 1985–88. Sen. Visitor Nuffield Coll., Oxford, 1956–57; Smuts Fellow and Vis. Fellow, Clare Hall, Cambridge, 1971–72. Chm., Educn Adv. Cttee, Aust. Develt Assistance Bureau, 1979–82; Mem. Exec., 1976–82, Dep. Chm., 1980, Aust. Vice-Chancellors' Cttee; Member: Council, Univ. of Papua New Guinea, 1974–82; Standing Cttee, Aust. Univs Internat. Develt Program, 1975–82; Council, ACU, 1980–82; Cttee, Australian Studies Centre, London Univ., 1983–94; Governing Body: Inst. of Develt Studies, Sussex Univ., 1966–72 and 1984–91; SOAS, 1983–94; Haileybury, 1985–94; Chm., Cttee of Management, Inst. of Commonwealth Studies, London Univ., 1984–94. Hon. Fellow: Inst. of Develt Studies, UK, 1972; University House, ANU 1983. President: African Studies Assoc. of Aust. and Pacific, 1979–82; Asian Studies Assoc. of Aust., 1980–82; British Australian Studies Assoc., 1984–86; Chm., Co-ordinating Council, Area Studies Assoc., 1988–91. Chm., Round Table Moot, 1992–94. Commander of the Order of Civil Merit (Spain), 1984. *Publications:* Buganda and British Overrule, 1900–1955 (with R. C. Pratt), 1960; (ed) Soundings in Modern South Asian History, 1968; (with J. C. Iltis and M. D. Wainwright) Government Archives in South Asia, 1969; Buganda in Modern History, 1971; The Mind of Buganda, 1971; Lion Rampant, 1973; (ed) Congress and the Raj 1917–1947, 1977; Oxford History of East Africa: (contrib.) Vol. I, 1963 and Vol. II, 1965; (contrib. and ed jtly) Vol. III, 1976; (ed) Constitutional Heads and Political Crises, 1988; (ed) The Indian National Congress, 1988; (ed jtly) Sovereigns and Surrogates, 1990; Eclipse of Empire, 1991; (ed) Political Inheritance of Pakistan, 1991; articles on internat. history in jls. *Address:* 18/36 Shackleton Park, Mawson, Canberra, ACT 2607, Australia.

LOW, Dr (George) Graeme (Erick), CBE 1989; Member, 1986–91, Managing Director, Site Operations, 1990–91, United Kingdom Atomic Energy Authority; *b* Palmerston North, NZ, 29 Nov. 1928; *s* of George Eric Low and Evelyn Edith Low (*née* Gillman); *m* 1st, 1952, Marion Townsend (marr. diss. 1977); two *d*; 2nd, 1985, Joan Kathleen Swinburne. *Educ:* New Plymouth Boys' High Sch., NZ; Canterbury Coll., Univ. of NZ (BSc, MSc); Univ. of Reading (PhD, DSc). FInstP. Special Branch, RNZN, 1952–58; Research Scientist, 1958–68, Head of Materials Physics Div., 1968–70, AERE Harwell; Special Asst to Dir, UKAEA Research Gp, 1970–73; Programme Dir (Applied Nuclear), 1973–76, Research Dir (Industry), 1976–81, Dir of Environmental Research, 1981–83, AERE Harwell; Dir, AEE, Winfrith, 1983–86; Dir, AERE Harwell, 1986–87; Mem. for Estabts, UKAEA, 1987–90. Dir, UK Nirex Ltd, 1986–91. *Publications:* papers on semi-conductors, neutron beam studies of the solid state, magnetism and management. *Recreations:* reading, walking, family and friends. *Address:* 21 New Road, Reading RG1 5JD.

LOW, Sir James (Richard) Morrison-, 3rd Bt, *cr* 1908; DL; DFH, CEng, MIEE; Director, Osborne & Hunter Ltd, Glasgow, 1956–89 (Electrical Engineer with firm, since 1952); *b* 3 Aug. 1925; *s* of Sir Walter John Morrison-Low, 2nd Bt and Dorothy Ruth de Quincey Quincey (*d* 1946); *S* father 1955; *m* 1953, Ann Rawson Gordon; one *s* three *d*. *Educ:* Ardvreck; Harrow; Merchiston. Served Royal Corps of Signals, 1943–47; demobilised with rank of Captain. Faraday House Engineering Coll., 1948–52. Chm., Scottish Cttee, Nat. Inspection Council for Electrical Installation Contracting, 1982–88; Pres., Electrical Contractors Assoc. of Scotland, 1982–84. Chm., Fife Area Scout Council, 1966–84. Hon. Pipe-Major, Royal Scottish Pipers Soc., 1981–83. Eur Ing, 1990. DL Fife, 1978. *Recreations:* shooting, piping. *Heir: s* Richard Walter Morrison-Low, *b* 4 Aug. 1959. *Address:* Kilmaron Castle, Cupar, Fife KY15 4NE. *T:* Cupar (01334) 652248. *Clubs:* New, Royal Scottish Pipers Society (Edinburgh).

LOWDEN, Gordon Stuart; President, Institute of Chartered Accountants of Scotland, 1989–90 (Senior Vice-President, 1988–89); Chairman, Dundee Port Authority, 1979–92; *b* 22 May 1927; *s* of James Soutar Lowden and Jean Lowden; *m* 1953, Kathleen Arnot; two *s* one *d*. *Educ:* Dundee High Sch.; Strathallan Sch.; St John's Coll., Cambridge (MA); Univ. of St Andrews (LLB). CA. Moody Stuart & Robertson, later Peat Marwick McLintock: training, 1949–53; Partner, 1959; Office Managing Partner, 1985; retired 1988. University of Dundee: Lectr, Sen. Lectr, 1955–83; Hon. Vis. Prof., Dept of Accountancy and Business Finance, 1987. *Recreations:* golf, watching sport, bridge. *Address:* 169 Hamilton Street, Barnhill, Dundee DD5 2RE. *T:* Dundee (01382) 78360. *Clubs:* New (Edinburgh); Royal and Ancient Golf.

LOWDEN, Richard Purdie; His Honour Judge Lowden; a Circuit Judge, North Eastern Circuit, since 1994; *b* 23 April 1948; *s* of Thomas Geoffrey Lowden, FRCS and Margaret Lowden (*née* Purdie); *m* 1973, Patricia; one *s* two *d*. *Educ:* Sedbergh Sch.; Keble Coll., Oxford (MA). Called to the Bar, Inner Temple, 1971; a Recorder of the Crown Court, 1988–94. *Recreations:* fishing, fell walking, theatre. *Address:* Newcastle upon Tyne Combined Court Centre, Quayside, Newcastle upon Tyne NE1 2TH.

LOWE, David Alexander; QC 1984; *b* Kilbirnie, Ayrshire, 1 Nov. 1942; *o s* of late David Alexander Lowe and of Rea Sadie Aitchison Lowe (*née* Bridges); *m* 1972, Vivian Anne Langley; three *s* two *d*. *Educ:* Pocklington Sch., York; St John's Coll., Cambridge (schol.; MA; MacMahon Law Student). Called to Bar, Middle Temple, 1965 (Harmsworth Schol.; Bencher, 1992), *ad eundem*, Lincoln's Inn, 1975. In practice at the Chancery Bar, 1966–. *Address:* Wilberforce Chambers, 8 New Square, Lincoln's Inn, WC2A 3QP. *T:* 0171–306 0102.

LOWE, David Bruce Douglas; His Honour Judge Lowe; a Circuit Judge, since 1983; *b* 3 April 1935; *o s* of late Douglas Gordon Arthur Lowe, QC, and of Karen, *e d* of Surgeon Einar Thamsen; *m* 1978, Dagmar, *o d* of Horst and Anneliese Bosse; one *s* three *d* (and one *s* one *d* by a previous marriage). *Educ:* Winchester College; Pembroke Coll., Cambridge (MA). National service, RN, 1953–55. Profumo Scholar, Inner Temple. Called to the Bar, Inner Temple, 1960; Midland and Oxford Circuit (formerly Midland); Prosecuting Counsel to Dept of Trade, 1975–83; a Recorder of the Crown Court, 1980–83. *Recreations:* music, tennis, gardening (formerly rackets and real tennis). *Address:* Crown Court at Middlesex Guildhall, Broad Sanctuary, SW1P 3BB. *Club:* Hawks (Cambridge).

LOWE, David Nicoll, OBE 1946; MA, BSc; FRSE; Secretary, Carnegie United Kingdom Trust, 1954–70; *b* 9 Sept. 1909; *s* of George Black Lowe and Jane Nicoll, Arbroath, Angus; *m* 1939, Muriel Enid Bryer, CSP (*d* 1991); one *s* three *d*. *Educ:* Arbroath High Sch.; St Andrews Univ. (Kitchener Scholar). MA 1931; BSc (1st Class Hons Botany) 1934; President Union, 1933–34; President Students' Representative Council, 1934–35; Founder President, University Mountaineering Club; Asst Secretary British Assoc. for the Advancement of Science, 1935–40, Secretary 1946–54. War Cabinet Secretariat, 1940–42 and 1945–46; Ministry of Production, 1942–45. Joint Hon. Secretary, Society of Visiting Scientists, 1952–54; Member Executive Cttee: Scottish Council of Social Service, 1953–71; Nat. Trust for Scotland, 1971–81; Member, Countryside Commn for Scotland, 1968–78. Chairman: Scottish Congregational Coll., 1961–68; Pollock Meml Missionary Trust, 1973–84; Governor, Scottish Nat. Meml to David Livingstone, 1974–80. Contributor to Annual Register, 1947–59. Silver Jubilee Medal, 1977. *Recreations:* gardening, choral music, painting in watercolours. *Address:* 34 Strathearn Court, Crieff, Perthshire PH7 3DS.

LOWE, Hon. Douglas Ackley; Executive Officer, Tasmanian Branch, Australian Medical Association, since 1992; *b* 15 May 1942; *s* of Ackley Reginald Lowe and Dulcie Mary Lowe (*née* Kean); *m* 1963, Pamela June (*née* Grant); two *s* two *d*. *Educ:* St Virgil College, Hobart. Mem. Tasmanian House of Assembly, for Franklin, 1969–86: ALP, 1969–82; Ind., 1982–86. Minister for Housing, 1972; Chief Secretary, 1974; Deputy Premier, 1975–77; Chief Sec. and Minister for Planning and Reorganisation, 1975; Premier, 1977–81; Treasurer, 1980–81; Minister for: Industrial Relations, Planning and the Environment, 1976; Industrial Relations and Health, Aug. 1976; Industrial Relations and Manpower Planning, 1977–79; Economic Planning and Development, 1979–80; Energy, 1979–81; MLC (Ind.) Buckingham, Tas., 1986–92; Dep. Leader for Govt, Legislative Council, 1989–92. Australian Labor Party: State Sec. 1965–69, State Pres. 1974–75, Tasmanian Section. Tasmanian Deleg. to Aust. Constitutional Convention. Silver Jubilee Medal, 1977. *Publication:* The Price of Power, 1984. *Address:* (home) 1 Michele Court, Berriedale, Tas 7011, Australia; (office) AMA House, 2 Gore Street, Hobart, Tas 7001, Australia. *T:* (02) 232047.

LOWE, Air Chief Marshal Sir Douglas (Charles), GCB 1977 (KCB 1974; CB 1971); DFC 1943; AFC 1946; *b* 14 March 1922; *s* of John William Lowe; *m* 1944, Doreen Elizabeth (*née* Nichols); one *s* one *d*. *Educ:* Reading School. Joined RAF, 1940; No 75 (NZ) Sqdn, 1943; Bomber Comd Instructors' Sch., 1945; RAF Coll., Cranwell, 1947; Exam. Wing CFS, 1950; Air Min. Operational Requirements, 1955; OC No 148 Sqdn, 1959; Exchange Officer, HQ SAC, USAF, 1961; Stn Comdr Cranwell, 1963; idc 1966; DOR 2 (RAF), MoD (Air), 1967; SASO, NEAF, 1969–71; ACAS (Operational Requirements), 1971–73; AOC No 18 Group, RAF, 1973–75; Controller, Aircraft, MoD Procurement Executive, 1975–82; Chief of Defence Procurement, MoD, Sept. 1982–June 1983. Air ADC to the Queen, 1978–83. Chairman: Mercury Communications Ltd, 1984–85; Band III Hldgs, 1986–91; Director: Royal Ordnance plc, 1984–7; Rolls Royce, 1984–92. Mem. Council, St John's Sch., Leatherhead, 1984–94. CRAeS 1982; CBIM 1984. *Recreations:* gardening, domestic odd-jobbing, photography, theatre, music. *Address:* c/o Lloyds Bank, Byfleet, Surrey. *Club:* Royal Air Force.

See also Baron Glanusk.

LOWE, Duncan; *see* Lowe, J. D.

LOWE, Frank Budge; Founder, 1981, and Chairman of The Lowe Group; Director, Interpublic, USA, since 1990; *b* 23 Aug. 1941; *s* of Stephen and Marion Lowe; two *s* one *d*. *Educ:* Westminster School. *Recreations:* tennis, ski-ing, shooting. *Address:* The Lowe Group, Bowater House, Knightsbridge, SW1X 7LT.

LOWE, Geoffrey Colin; aviation consultant, 1980–88; *b* 7 Sept. 1920; *s* of late Colin Roderick and late Elsie Lowe; *m* 1948, Joan Stephen (*d* 1985); one *d*; *m* 1988, Jean Marion Bailey (*née* Wigginton). *Educ:* Reigate Grammar Sch. GPO, 1937; Exchequer and Audit Dept, 1939. Served War, RAFVR, 1941–46 (Flt-Lt). Asst Principal, Min. of Civil Aviation, 1947; Private Sec. to Permanent Sec., MCA, 1950; Principal, 1950; Colonial Office, 1954–57; Min. of Transport and Civil Aviation, 1957–61; Civil Air Attaché, SE Asia, 1961–64; Asst Sec., Overseas Policy Div., Min. of Aviation, 1964–68; Investment Grants Div., Bd of Trade, 1968–71; Counsellor (Civil Aviation), British Embassy, Washington, 1971–73, Counsellor (Civil Aviation and Shipping), Washington, 1973–74; Under Sec. (Management Services and Manpower), Depts of Industry and Trade, 1974–80. *Recreations:* theatre, crossword puzzles. *Address:* 13 Highwood, Sunset Avenue, Woodford Green, Essex IG8 0SZ. *T:* 0181–504 7035.

LOWE, Prof. Gordon, FRS 1984; CChem, FRSC; Professor of Biological Chemistry, University of Oxford, since 1989; Official Fellow and Tutor, Lincoln College, Oxford, since 1962; *b* 31 May 1933; *s* of Harry Lowe and Ethel (*née* Ibbetson); *m* 1956, Gwynneth Hunter; two *s*. *Educ:* Imperial Coll. of Science and Technol., Univ. of London (Governors Prize and Edmund White Prize, 1954; Edmund White Prize, 1957; BSc 1954; ARCS 1954, PhD 1957; DIC 1957). DSc Oxon 1985 (MA 1960). CChem, FRSC 1981. University of Oxford: Pressed Steel Res. Fellow, 1957–59; Deptl Demonstrator, 1959–65; Weir Jun. Res. Fellow, University Coll., 1959–61; Lectr, Organic Chemistry, 1965–88; Aldrichian Praelector in Chemistry, 1988–89; Sub-Rector, Lincoln Coll., 1986–89. Irvine Lectr, Univ. of St Andrews, 1984; Upper Rhine Lectr, Univs of Basle, Mulhouse, Strasbourg, Freiburg and Karlsruhe, 1989; Liversidge Lectr, Univ. of Sydney, 1990. Member: Biochemistry and Biophysics Cttee, SERC, 1979–82; Molecular Enzymology Cttee, Biochemical Soc., 1978–84; Editorial Adv. Panel, Biochemical Jl, 1981–; Editorial Bd, Bio-organic Chemistry, 1983–. FRSA 1986. Charmian Medal, 1983, Stereochemistry Medal, 1992, RSC. *Publications:* reports on the cysteine proteinases, β-Lactam antibiotics, and chiral phosphate and sulphate esters; articles in primary chemical and biochemical jls. *Address:* 17 Norman Avenue, Abingdon, Oxon OX14 2HQ. *T:* Abingdon (01235) 523029.

LOWE, Dr John; Head, Country Educational Policy Reviews, Education and Training Division, OECD, 1973–87; *b* 3 Aug. 1922; *s* of John Lowe and Ellen (*née* Webb); *m* 1949, Margaret James (*d* 1982); two *s* one *d*. *Educ:* Univ. of Liverpool (BA Hons 1950); Univ. of London (CertEd 1951, PhD 1960). Served War of 1939–45 and Control Commn for Germany, 1945–47 (Captain). Lectr, subseq. Sen. Lectr, Univ. of Liverpool, 1955–63; Dir, Extra-Mural Studies, Univ. of Singapore, 1963–64; Dir, Dept of Adult Educn and Extra-Mural Studies, subsequently Head, Dept of Educnl Studies, Univ. of Edinburgh, 1964–72; Consultant in field, 1964–. Sec./Treas., Internat. Congress of Univ. Adult Educn, 1972–76. Hon. Prof., Warwick Univ., 1990–. *Publications:* On Teaching Foreign Languages to Adults (ed jtly), 1965; Adult Education in England and Wales, 1970; (ed) Adult Education and Nation-Building, 1970; (ed) Education and Nation-Building in the Third World, 1971; The Education of Adults: a world perspective, 1975, rev. edn, 1982; (ed) The Clanricarde Letter Book, 1983; Compulsory Schooling in a Changing World, 1983; (jtly) Schools and Quality, 1989; (jtly) Reviews of National Policies for Education: Ireland, 1991; Educational Trends and Prospects in OECD Countries, 1991; articles in educnl and hist. jls. *Recreations:* reading, music, theatre, swimming. *Address:* 3 Rue Ribera, 75016 Paris, France. *T:* 45202515.

LOWE, (John) Duncan, CB 1995; Crown Agent for Scotland, since 1991; *b* 18 May 1948; *s* of John Duncan Lowe and Davina Lowe (*née* Hunter); *m* 1971, Jacqueline Egan; two *s*. *Educ:* Hamilton Acad.; Glasgow Univ. (MA, LLB). Procurator Fiscal Depute, Kilmarnock, 1974–76; Legal Asst, later Sen. Legal Asst, Crown Office, 1976–78; Sen. Procurator Fiscal Depute, 1978–79, Asst Procurator Fiscal, 1979–83, Glasgow; Asst Solicitor, Crown Office, 1983–84; Dep. Crown Agent, 1984–88; Regl Procurator Fiscal, Lothian and Borders, 1988–91. *Recreations:* golf, fishing. *Address:* Crown Office, 25 Chambers Street, Edinburgh EH1 1LA. *T:* 0131–226 2626.

LOWE, John Eric Charles, LVO 1965; MBE 1937; *b* 11 Aug. 1907; 6th *s* of late John Frederick Lowe; *m* 1935, Trudy (*née* Maybury); one *s* two *d*. *Educ:* Burghley Road Sch., Highgate. Vice-Consul, Jibuti, 1930–37, Harar, 1940; Political Officer, Aden Protectorate, 1940; served in HM Forces, Somaliland and Ethiopia, 1941–46; Senior Asst, Foreign Office, 1947–49; Acting Consul, Suez, 1949; Vice-Consul, Beira, 1950; Vice-Consul, Hamburg, 1951 and Frankfurt, 1953; 2nd Secretary, Helsinki, 1953; Political Agent's

Representative, Mina-Al-Ahmadi (Kuwait), 1956; Vice-Consul, Leopoldville, 1959; Consul, Khartoum, 1962; Consul-General, Basra, 1965–67; retired, Sept. 1967. Order of the Two Niles (Sudan), 1965. *Recreations:* gardening, golf, sailing. *Address:* Dunnocks, Turners Geen Lane, Wadhurst, E Sussex TN5 6TS. *T:* Wadhurst (01892) 784451.

LOWE, John Evelyn, MA, FSA, FRSA; cultural consultant and author, since 1978; foreign travel specialist, journalist and photographer; *b* 23 April 1928; *s* of late Arthur Holden Lowe; *m* 1st, 1956, Susan Helen Sanderson (marr. diss. 1981); two *s* one *d*; 2nd, 1989, Yukiko Nomura; one *d*. *Educ:* Wellington Coll., Berks; New Coll., Oxford. Served in RAEC, 1947–49 (Sgt Instructor). Victoria and Albert Museum, Dept of Woodwork, 1953–56; Deputy Story Editor, Pinewood Studios, 1956–57; Victoria and Albert Museum: Dept of Ceramics, 1957–61; Assistant to the Director, 1961–64; Dir, City Museum and Art Gall., Birmingham, 1964–69; Dir, Weald and Downland Open Air Museum, 1969–74; Principal, West Dean College, Chichester, West Sussex, 1972–78; Literary Editor, Kansai Time Out, 1983–88. Hofer-Hecksher Bibliographical Lectr, Harvard, 1974; Vis. Prof. in British Cultural Studies, Doshisha Univ., Japan, 1979–81. Pres., Midlands Fedn of Museums, 1967–69. Member: Exec. Cttee, Midland Arts Centre for Young People, 1964–69; Council of the British School at Rome, 1968–70; Crafts Adv. Cttee, 1973–78. Consultant to: Seibu Ltd, Tokyo, 1968–72; Specialtours, London, 1969–74. Trustee: Sanderson Art in Industry Fund, 1968–; Edward James Foundn, 1972–73; Idlewild Trust, 1972–78. Hon. Fellow, RCA, 1988. Asst Ed., Collins Crime Club, 1953–54; Founding Ed., Faber Furniture Series, 1954–56. *Publications:* Thomas Chippendale, 1955; Cream Coloured Earthenware, 1958; Japanese Crafts, 1983; Into Japan, 1985; Into China, 1986; Corsica: a traveller's guide, 1988; A Surrealist Life—Edward James—Poet, Patron & Eccentric, 1991; major contribs to Encylopædia Britannica and OUP Junior Encyclopedia; articles on applied arts, foreign travel, social history and Japan. *Recreations:* Japan, music, reading, book-collecting, travel. *Address:* Paillole-Basse, 47360 Prayssas, France. *T:* 53688645.

LOWE, Prof. Kenneth Gordon, CVO 1982; MD; FRCP, FRCPE, FRCPGlas; Physician to the Queen in Scotland, 1971–82; Formerly Consultant Physician, Royal Infirmary and Ninewells Hospital, Dundee; Hon. Professor of Medicine, Dundee University, since 1969; *b* 29 May 1917; *s* of Thomas J. Lowe, MA, BSc, Arbroath, and Flora MacDonald Gordon, Arbroath; *m* 1942, Nancy Young, MB, ChB, twin *d* of Stephen Young, Logie, Fife; two *s* one *d*. *Educ:* Arbroath High Sch.; St Andrews Univ. (MD Hons). Served with RAMC, 1942–46; Registrar, Hammersmith Hosp., Royal Postgrad. Med. Sch., 1947–52; Sen. Lectr in Medicine, St Andrews Univ., 1952–61. *Publications:* (jtly) Regional Anatomy Illustrated, 1983; contribs to med. and scientific jls, mainly on renal, metabolic and cardiac disorders. *Recreations:* reading, fishing. *Address:* 36 Dundee Road, West Ferry, Dundee DD5 1HY. *T:* Dundee (01382) 78787. *Club:* Flyfishers'.

LOWE, Philip Martin; Chef de Cabinet to Rt Hon. Neil Kinnock, Member of the European Commission, since 1995; *b* 29 April 1947; *s* of late Leonard Ernest Lowe and Marguerite Helen Lowe (*née* Childs); *m* 1st, 1967, Gillian Baynton Forge (marr. diss. 1980); two *s*; 2nd, 1984, Nora Mai O'Connell. *Educ:* Leeds Grammar Sch.; Reading Sch.; St John's Coll., Oxford (MA in PPE); London Business Sch. (MSc Business Studies). Tube Investments, 1968–73; Commission of the European Communities, later European Commission: Directorate-Gen. for Credit and Investments, Luxembourg, 1973–82; Mem., Cabinet of President Gaston Thorn, 1982–85, of Alois Pfeiffer, 1985–86; Directorate-Gen. for Co-ordination of Structural Instruments, 1986–89; Chef de Cabinet to Rt Hon. Bruce Millan, Comr for regl policy, 1989–91; Dir, Rural Develt, 1991–93; Dir, Merger Task Force, 1993–94. *Recreations:* music, running, hillwalking. *Address:* avenue Michel-Ange 18, 1040 Brussels, Belgium. *T:* (office) 2965040; (home) 7349665.
See also Ven. S. R. Lowe.

LOWE, Dr Robert David; Medical Research Consultant, National Heart Foundation of Australia, 1986–89, retired; *b* 23 Feb. 1930; *s* of John Lowe and Hilda Althea Mead; *m* 1952, Betty Irene Wheeler; one *s* three *d*. *Educ:* Leighton Park Sch.; Emmanuel Coll., Cambridge; UCH Medical School. BCh, MB, MA, MD, PhD Cantab; FRCP, LMSSA. Medical Specialist, RAMC, 1955–59; Research Asst, UCH Med. Sch., 1959–61; St George's Hosp. Med. Sch.: MRC Res. Fellow, 1961–62; Wellcome Sen. Res. Fellow in Clinical Science, 1963–64; Sen. Lectr in Medicine, St Thomas' Hosp. Med. Sch., 1964–70; Hon. Consultant to St Thomas' Hosp., 1966–70; Dean, St George's Hosp. Med. Sch., 1971–82. AUCAS: Exec. Mem., 1967–; Chm., 1972–78. *Publications:* (with B. F. Robinson) A Physiological Approach to Clinical Methods, 1970; papers on peripheral circulation, hypertension, adrenergic mechanisms, central action of angiotensin, control of cardiovascular system. *Recreations:* bridge, squash, hill-walking, sailing. *Address:* Te Uenga, RD4 Hikurangi, Northland, New Zealand. *T:* 0940 37416.

LOWE, Robson; philatelist, publisher, editor, author, auctioneer; *b* 7 Jan. 1905; *s* of John Lowe and Gertrude Lee; *m* 1928, Winifred Marie Denne (*d* 1973); two *d*. *Educ:* Fulham Central Sch. Started own business, 1920; worked on PO Records, 1926; purchased control of Woods of Perth (Printers), 1964; formed Australian co., 1967; joined bd of Christie, Manson & Woods, 1968; formed Italian co., 1969 (founded Il Piccolo for Italian collectors). Chm., Expert Cttee of British Philatelic Assoc., 1941–61; Past Pres., British Philatelic Fedn, 1979–81; Co-founder, Postal History Soc., 1935; Founder: Soc. of Postal Historians, 1950; annual British Philatelic Exhibn, 1965. Mem. jury at internat. philatelic exhibns: first, Durban, 1928; Chm., Cape Town, 1979. Over 1000 lectures. Took over Philatelic Jl of GB, 1958 (still the publisher); Editor, The Philatelist, 1934–74 (centenary, 1966), 1986–. *Publications:* Philatelic Encyclopaedia (ed), 1935; Handstruck Stamps of the Empire, 1937, 4th edn 1941; Sperati and his Craft, 1953; British Postage Stamps, 1968; (jtly) St Vincent, 1971; Encyclopaedia of Empire Stamps: Europe, 1947, 2nd edn 1951; Africa, 1949; Asia, 1951; Australia, 1962; North America, 1973; Leeward Islands, 1991; monographs (latest, US Military Mail, WW II); articles in philatelic pubns. *Recreations:* history, philately, study of forgers and forgery. *Address:* Robson Lowe, Premier House, Hinton Road, Bournemouth BH1 2EF. *T:* Bournemouth (01202) 299277. *Clubs:* East India; Collectors (New York).

LOWE, Ven. Stephen Richard; Archdeacon of Sheffield, since 1988; *b* 3 March 1944; *s* of Leonard Ernest Lowe and Marguerite Helen Lowe; *m* 1967; one *s* one *d*. *Educ:* Leeds Grammar School; Reading School; London Univ. (BSc Econs); Ripon Hall, Oxford. Curate, St Michael's Anglican Methodist Church, Gospel Lane, Birmingham, 1968–72; Minister-in-Charge, Woodgate Valley Conventional District, 1972–75; Team Rector of East Ham, 1975–88. Hon. Canon, Chelmsford Cathedral, 1985–88; Chelmsford Diocesan Urban Officer, 1986–88. Travelling Fellowship, Winston Churchill Meml Trust, 1980. A Church Comr, 1992–. Member: Gen. Synod of C of E, 1991–; Churches Council for Britain and Ire., 1991–; Exec., Central Bd of Finance, Gen. Synod, 1993–; Archbishop's Commn on Orgn of C of E; Bishops' Adv. Gp on urban priority areas, 1993–; Trustee, Church Urban Fund, 1991–. Chm., Sheffield Somalian Refugees Trust, 1990–94. Mem., Duke of Edinburgh Commonwealth Study Conf., 1989–. *Publication:* Churches' Role in Care of the Elderly, 1974. *Recreations:* watching football, music, cinema, theatre and travel. *Address:* 23 Hill Turrets Close, Ecclesall, Sheffield S11 9RE. *T:* Sheffield (0114) 235 0191, *fax:* Sheffield (0114) 235 2275.
See also P. M. Lowe.

LOWE, Sir Thomas (William Gordon), 4th Bt *cr* 1918, of Edgbaston, City of Birmingham; *b* 14 Aug. 1963; *s* of Sir Francis Reginald Gordon Lowe, 3rd Bt and of Franziska Cornelia, *d* of Siegfried Steinkopf; *S* father, 1986. *Educ:* Stowe School; London School of Economics (LLB 1984); Jesus Coll., Cambridge (LLM 1986). Called to the Bar, Inner Temple, 1985. *Publications:* articles in various legal periodicals. *Heir:* *b* Christopher Colin Francis Lowe, *b* 25 Dec. 1964. *Address:* 45 Limerston Street, SW10 0BL; 2 Gray's Inn Square, WC1R 5JH.

LOWE, Veronica Ann; Director, Solicitors Complaints Bureau, since 1990; *b* 29 June 1951; *d* of late Arthur Ernest Bagley and Agatha (*née* Blackham); *m* 1977, Ian Stanley Lowe; one *d*. *Educ:* King Edward VI Grammar Sch. for Girls, Handsworth, Birmingham; St Hugh's Coll., Oxford (MA); Oxford Polytechnic (MIL Exams); City of Birmingham Polytechnic. Articled Clerk, Ryland, Martineau & Co., Birmingham, 1976–78; Lectr in Labour Law, Univ. of Aston in Birmingham, 1978–80; admitted solicitor, 1979; solicitor in private practice, 1979–86; Asst Area Dir, Legal Aid Area No 8, 1986–88; Area Dir (W Midlands), Legal Aid Area No 6, 1988–89; Gp Manager (Midlands), Legal Aid Bd, 1989–90. *Publications:* contribs to publications on law for accountants and businessmen. *Recreations:* cooking, eating and drinking, reading, writing unfinished novels, listening to music, travel, talking, current affairs, being with my daughter, all historical subjects. *Address:* Phoenix Cottage, 6 Rugby Road, Dunchurch, Warwicks CV22 6PE.

LOWENSTEIN, Prof. Otto Egon, FRS 1955; FRSE; DSc (Glasgow); PhD (Birmingham); DrPhil (Munich); Honorary Senior Research Fellow, Pharmacology Department (formerly at Neurocommunications Research Unit), Birmingham University Medical School, since 1976 (Leverhulme Emeritus Research Fellow, 1974–76); *b* 24 Oct. 1906; *s* of Julius Lowenstein and Mathilde Heusinger; *m* 1st, Elsa Barbara, *d* of R. Ritter; two *s*; 2nd, Gunilla Marika (*d* 1981), *d* of Prof. Gösta Dohlman; one step *s*; 3rd, Maureen Josephine, *d* of K. McKernan. Educ: Neues Realgymnasium, Munich; Munich Univ. Asst, Munich Univ., 1931–33; Research Scholar, Birmingham Univ., 1933–37; Asst Lecturer, University College, Exeter, 1937–38; Senior Lecturer, Glasgow Univ., 1938–52; Mason Prof. of Zoology and Comparative Physiology, Birmingham Univ., 1952–74. President: Assoc. for the Study of Animal Behaviour, 1961–64; Section D, British Assoc., 1962; Institute of Biology, 1965–67; Member Council, Royal Society, 1968–69. *Publications:* Revision of 6th edn of A Textbook of Zoology (Parker and Haswell), Vol. I; The Senses, 1966; papers in various learned journals on Electrophysiology and Ultrastructure of Sense Organs, esp. inner ear of vertebrates. *Recreations:* music, mountain walking, painting. *Address:* 22 Estria Road, Birmingham B15 2LQ. *T:* 0121–440 2526.

LOWES, Peter Donald; Director, Anti-Slavery Society for Protection of Human Rights, 1987–89; *b* 13 Sept. 1926; *s* of Col J. H. Lowes and Queenie Frances Lowes (*née* Bowyer); *m* 1954, Linnea Newton (marr. diss. 1980); one *s* two *d*. *Educ:* Bradfield Coll.; Emmanuel Coll., Cambridge (MA); Univ. of British Columbia (LLB); Geneva Univ. (PhD). Served with Royal Engineers, 1946–48. Master, Wanganui Collegiate Sch., NZ, 1949; Upper Canada Coll., Toronto, 1950–51; practised law, Vancouver, 1953–55; UNRWA, Jordan, 1955–58; journalist, Canadian Broadcasting Corp., 1958; UN Narcotic Drugs, Geneva, 1959–65; External Aid, Canadian Govt, Ottawa, 1965–66; Resident Representative, United Nations Development Programme: Lesotho, 1966–68; Swaziland, 1968–71; Malaŵi, 1971–74; HQ, NY, 1974–75; Morocco, 1975–79; Co-ordinator, Internat. Drinking Water Supply and Sanitation Decade, Geneva, 1979–86. Mem. Bd, 1980–86, Consultant, 1987, Internat Reference Centre, The Hague; UNDP and World Bank Consultant, 1987–95. Adviser: CARE (UK), 1987–93; Help the Aged, 1987–93. *Publication:* The Genesis of International Narcotics Control, 1965. *Recreations:* walking, mountaineering, history. *Address:* Apartment 34, 4 Clos Belmont, Geneva 1208, Switzerland. *T:* 7350313. *Clubs:* Alpine, Climbers'.

LOWNIE, His Honour Ralph Hamilton; a Circuit Judge, 1986–95; *b* 27 Sept. 1924; *yr s* of James H. W. Lownie and Jesse H. Aitken; *m* 1960, Claudine Therese, *o d* of Pierre Lecrocq, Reims; one *s* one *d*. *Educ:* George Watson's Coll.; Edinburgh Univ. (MA, LLB, Dip. Admin. Law and Practice); Univ. of Kent (PhD). Royal Engineers, 1943–47, NW Europe. WS 1952; enrolled as solicitor, 1953; Mem. Faculty of Advocates 1959; called to Bar, Inner Temple, 1962. Dep. Registrar, Supreme Court of Kenya, 1954–56; Resident Magistrate, 1956–61, Sen. Resident Magistrate, 1961–63, Dep. Registrar-Gen., Kenya, 1963–65; Sen. Magistrate, Bermuda, 1965–72; a Metropolitan Stipendiary Magistrate, 1974–86; a Deputy Circuit Judge, 1976–82; a Recorder, 1983–86. Chm. of Juvenile Courts, 1976–85. Lectr, Kenya Sch. of Law, 1963–65. *Recreations:* hill-walking, military heraldry. *Address:* 57 Greenhill Road, Otford, Kent TN14 5RR.

LOWREY, Air Comdt Dame Alice, DBE 1960; RRC 1954; Matron-in-Chief, Princess Mary's Royal Air Force Nursing Service, 1959–63 (retired); *b* 8 April 1905; *d* of William John Lowrey and Agnes Lowrey (formerly Walters). *Educ:* Yorkshire; Training Sch., Sheffield Royal Hospital. Joined PMRAFNS, 1932; served in Iraq and Aden. Principal Matron: HQ, MEAF and FEAF, 1956–58; HQ, Home Command and Technical Training Command, 1958–59. Air Commandant, 1959. Officer Sister Order of St John, 1959. *Address:* c/o Midland Bank, Attleborough, Norfolk.

LOWRY, family name of **Baron Lowry.**

LOWRY, Baron *cr* 1979 (Life Peer), of Crossgar in the County of Down; **Robert Lynd Erskine Lowry;** PC 1974; PC (NI) 1971; Kt 1971; a Lord of Appeal in Ordinary, 1988–94; *b* 30 Jan. 1919; *o s* of late William Lowry (Rt Hon. Mr Justice Lowry) and Catherine Hughes Lowry, 3rd *d* of Rev. R. J. Lynd, DD; *m* 1st, 1945, Mary Audrey (*d* 1987), *o d* of John Martin, 12 Deramore Park, Belfast; three *d*; 2nd, 1994, Barbara Adamson Calvert, *qv*. *Educ:* Royal Belfast Academical Institution (Porter exhibnr, 1937); Jesus Coll., Cambridge (Hon. Fellow 1977). Entrance Exhibn (Classics); Scholar, 1939; 1st Class Classical Tripos, Part I, 1939, Part II 1940; MA 1944. Served HM Forces, 1940–46; enlisted Royal Inniskilling Fusilers, 1940; Tunisia, 1942–43 with 38 Irish Inf. Bde; commissioned Royal Irish Fusiliers, 1941; Major, 1945; Hon. Colonel: 7th Bn Royal Irish Fusiliers, 1969–71 (5th Bn, 1967–68); 5th Bn Royal Irish Rangers, 1971–76. Called to the Bar of N Ireland, 1947; Bencher of the Inn of Court, 1955–; Hon. Bencher, Middle Temple, 1973; Hon. Bencher, King's Inns, Dublin, 1973; QC (N Ireland), 1956. Counsel to HM Attorney-General, 1948–56; Judge of the High Court of Justice (NI), 1964–71; Lord Chief Justice of N Ireland, 1971–88. Member Departmental Cttees on Charities, Legal Aid and Registration of Title; Dep. Chm., Boundaries Commn (NI) 1964–71; Chairman: Interim Boundary Commn (NI Constituencies), 1967; Permanent Boundary Commn, 1969–71; Dep. Chm., Lord Chancellor's Cttee on NI Supreme Court; Member, Jt Law Enforcement Commn, 1974; Chairman: N Ireland Constitutional Convention, 1975; Council of Legal Educn (NI), 1976–79. Chm., SJAI Exec., 1969–72; Member: Nat. Equestrian Fedn, 1969–78; Judicial Cttee, FEI, 1991– (Chm., 1995–); Internat. Showjumping Judge, 1973, Official Internat. Judge, 1987–93. Governor, Royal Belfast Academical Instn, 1956–71, Chm., Richmond Lodge Sch., 1956–77; Chm. Governing Bodies Assoc. (NI), 1965; Visitor, Univ. of Ulster, 1989–. Hon. LLD QUB, 1980; Hon. DLitt NUU, 1981. *Recreations:* golf (Pres., Royal Portrush GC, 1974–); showjumping.

Address: House of Lords, SW1A 0PW; White Hill, Crossgar, Co. Down BT30 9HJ. *T:* Crossgar (01396) 830397. *Clubs:* Army and Navy, MCC; Royal and Ancient (St Andrews).

LOWRY, Sir (John) Patrick, (Sir Pat), Kt 1985; CBE 1978; President, Institute of Personnel Management, 1987–89; *b* 31 March 1920; *s* of John McArdle and Edith Mary Lowry; *m* 1952, Sheilagh Mary Davies; one *s* one *d*. *Educ:* Wyggeston Grammar Sch., Leicester; London Sch. of Economics (evening student). BCom London; CIPM, CBIM. Statistical Clerk, Engineering Employers' Fedn, 1938; served Army, 1939–46; various posts in EEF, 1946–70, Dir 1965–70; Dir of Industrial Relations, British Leyland Motor Corp., 1970, Board Dir 1972; Dir of Personnel, 1975–77, of Personnel and Admin, British Leyland Ltd, 1977–78, of Personnel and External Affairs, 1978–81; Chairman: ACAS, 1981–87; Nat. Jt Council for Engineering Construction Industry, 1987–; Univs Academic Salaries Cttee, 1987–. Hon. Prof., Sch. of Industrial and Business Studies, Warwick Univ., 1983. Member: UK Employers' Delegn, ILO, 1962, 1963, 1967; Court of Inquiry, Barbican and Horseferry Road Building Disputes, 1967; Court of Inquiry, Grunwick Dispute, 1977. Pres., Inst. of Supervisory Management, 1972–74. FRSA 1984. Hon. LLD Leicester, 1984. *Recreation:* theatre. *Address:* 31 Seaton Close, Lynden Gate, SW15 3TJ. *T:* 0181–785 6199.

LOWRY, Mrs Noreen Margaret, (Nina); Her Honour Judge Lowry; a Circuit Judge, since 1976; *b* 6 Sept. 1925; *er d* of late John Collins, MC, and Hilda Collins; *m* 1st, 1950, Edward Lucas Gardner, QC (marr. diss., 1962); one *s* one *d*; 2nd, 1963, Richard John Lowry, *qv*; one *d*. *Educ:* Bedford High Sch.; Birmingham Univ. LLB Birmingham, 1947. Called to the Bar, Gray's Inn, 1948. Criminal practice on S Eastern Circuit, Central Criminal Court, Inner London Sessions, etc., practising as Miss Nina Collins; Metropolitan Stipendiary Magistrate, 1967–76. Mem. Criminal Law Revision Cttee, 1975–. Hon. LLD Birmingham, 1992. *Recreations:* theatre, travel. *Address:* Central Criminal Court, EC4M 7EH.

LOWRY, Sir Pat; *see* Lowry, Sir J. P.

LOWRY, Richard John; QC 1968; **His Honour Judge Richard Lowry;** a Circuit Judge, since 1977; *b* 23 June 1924; *s* of late Geoffrey Charles Lowry, OBE, TD, and late Margaret Spencer Lowry; *m* 1963, Noreen Margaret Lowry, *qv*; one *d*. *Educ:* St Edward's Sch.; University College, Oxford. RAF, 1943; qualified as pilot and commnd, 1944; No 228 Group Staff Officer, India, 1945; Flt-Lieut, 1946. University College, Oxford, 1942–43 and 1946–48; BA, 1948, MA 1949. Called to Bar, Inner Temple, 1949; Bencher 1977; Member, General Council of Bar, 1965–69. Dep. Chm., Herts QS, 1968; a Recorder, 1972–77. Mem., Home Office Adv. Council on Penal System, 1972–78. *Recreations:* theatre, swimming, fossicking; formerly rowing (Oxford Univ. wartime VIII, 1943). *Address:* Central Criminal Court, EC4M 7EH. *Clubs:* Garrick; Leander (Henley-on-Thames).

LOWRY-CORRY, family name of **Earl of Belmore.**

LOWSON, Sir Ian (Patrick), 2nd Bt *cr* 1951; *b* 4 Sept. 1944; *s* of Sir Denys Colquhoun Flowerdew Lowson, 1st Bt and of Patricia, OStJ, *yr d* of 1st Baron Strathcarron, PC, KC; *S* father, 1975; *m* 1979, Mrs Tanya Du Boulay, *d* of R. F. A. Judge; one *s* one *d*. *Educ:* Eton; Duke Univ., USA. OStJ. *Heir: s* Henry William Lowson, *b* 10 Nov. 1980. *Address:* 23 Flood Street, SW3 5ST. *Clubs:* Boodle's, Pilgrims; Brook (NY).

LOWSON, Prof. Martin Vincent, FEng 1991; FRAeS; Sir George White Professor of Aerospace Engineering, University of Bristol, since 1986; *b* 5 Jan. 1938; *s* of Alfred Vincent Lowson and Irene Gertrude Lowson; *m* 1961, Ann Pennicutt; one *s* one *d*. *Educ:* King's Sch., Worcester; Univ. of Southampton (BScEng, PhD). CEng. Apprentice, Vickers Armstrong (Aircraft), 1955; Res. student and Assistant, Univ. of Southampton, 1960; Head, Applied Physics, Wyle Labs, Huntsville, USA, 1964; Rolls-Royce Reader, Loughborough Univ., 1969; Westland Helicopters: Chief Scientist, 1973; Div. Dir, Corporate Develt, 1979. Chm., Flow Solutions Ltd, 1986–. Fellow, Acoustical Soc. of America, 1969. *Publications:* numerous papers in learned jls, and patents. *Recreations:* research, squash, bluegrass music. *Address:* Alpentels, North Road, Leigh Woods, Bristol BS8 3PJ. *T:* Bristol (0117) 973 6497.

LOWTHER, family name of **Earl of Lonsdale** and **Viscount Ullswater.**

LOWTHER, Viscount; Hugh Clayton Lowther; *b* 27 May 1949; *s* and *heir* of 7th Earl of Lonsdale, *qv*, and Tuppina Cecily, *d* of late Captain G. H. Bennet; *m* 1971, Pamela Middleton; *m* 1986, Angela M., *d* of Captain Peter J. Wyatt, RN and Mrs Christine Wyatt; one *d*.

LOWTHER, Col Sir Charles (Douglas), 6th Bt *cr* 1824; farmer, company director; *b* 22 Jan. 1946; *s* of Lt-Col Sir William Guy Lowther, 5th Bt, OBE, and of Grania Suzanne, *d* of late Major A. J. H. Douglas Campbell, OBE; *S* father, 1982; *m* 1975, Florence Rose, *y d* of Colonel Alexander James Henry Cramsie, O'Harabrook, Ballymoney, Co. Antrim; one *s* one *d*. *Educ:* Winchester College. Commissioned, Queen's Royal Irish Hussars, 1966; Regimental Duty UK and BAOR, 1974–76; Army Staff College, Camberley, 1978–79; Staff appointment, 1981; CO, QRIH, 1986–89; Officer i/c, Household Cavalry and RAC Manning and Record Office, 1989–93. *Recreations:* fieldsports, travel. *Heir: s* Patrick William Lowther, *b* 15 July 1977. *Club:* Cavalry and Guards.

LOWTHER, John Luke, CBE 1983; JP; Lord Lieutenant for Northamptonshire, since 1984; *b* 17 Nov. 1923; *s* of Col J.G. Lowther, CBE, DSO, MC, TD and the Hon. Mrs Lowther; *m* 1952, Jennifer Jane Bevan; one *s* two *d*. *Educ:* Eton; Trinity College, Oxford. MA 1949. Served King's Royal Rifle Corps, 1942–47; worked for Singer Sewing Co., USA, 1949–51; Managing Dir, own manufacturing Co., 1951–60; farmer, 1960–. CC Northants, 1970–84 (Leader of Council, 1977–81); High Sheriff 1971, DL 1977, JP 1984, Northants. Hon. Colonel: Royal Anglian Regt (Northamptonshire), TA, 1986–89; Northants ACF. *Recreations:* shooting, countryman. *Address:* Guilsborough Court, Northampton NN6 8QW. *T:* Northampton (01604) 740289. *Club:* Boodle's.

LOXAM, John Gordon; Director of Veterinary Field Services, Ministry of Agriculture, Fisheries and Food, 1983–86, retired; *b* 26 April 1927; *s* of John Loxam and Mary Elizabeth Loxam (*née* Rigby); *m* 1950, Margaret Lorraine Smith; one *d* (and one *s* decd). *Educ:* Lancaster Royal Grammar Sch.; Royal (Dick) Veterinary Coll., Edinburgh. MRCVS. General veterinary practice: Marlborough, 1949–51; Carlisle, 1951–53; Vet. Officer, MAFF, Lincoln, 1953–63; Divisional Veterinary Officer: Tolworth, Surrey, 1963–66; Bury St Edmunds, 1966–71; Dep. Regl Vet. Officer, Leeds, 1971–76; Regl Vet. Officer, Tolworth, 1976–78; Asst Chief Vet. Officer, Tolworth, 1979–83. Hon. Sec., 1987–90, Pres., 1990–, Vet. Benevolent Fund. Life Mem., BVA, 1993. Churchwarden, All Saints, Chelsworth, 1990–; Chm., Chelsworth Parish Meeting, 1992–94. *Recreations:* gardening, spectator sports, particularly Rugby football and equestrian events. *Address:* Riverside, Chelsworth, Ipswich, Suffolk IP7 7HU. *T:* Bildeston (01449) 740619. *Club:* Farmers'.

LOY, Francis David Lindley; Stipendiary Magistrate at Leeds since 1974; a Recorder of the Crown Court, since 1983; *b* 7 Oct. 1927; *s* of late Archibald Loy and late Sarah Eleanor Loy; *m* 1954, Brenda Elizabeth Walker; three *d*. *Educ:* Repton Sch.; Corpus Christi Coll., Cambridge. BA Hons (Law) 1950. Royal Navy, 1946–48. Called to the Bar, Middle Temple, 1952; practised North-Eastern Circuit, 1952–72; Recorder (Northern Circuit), 1972; Stipendiary Magistrate of Leeds, 1972–74. Hon. Sec., Soc. of Provincial Stipendiary Magistrates, 1980–89, Chm., 1990–. *Recreations:* reading, English History, walking, travel. *Address:* 4 Wedgewood Drive, Roundhay, Leeds LS8 1EF; 14 The Avenue, Sheringham, Norfolk NR26 8DG. *T:* Sheringham (01263) 822697. *Club:* Leeds (Leeds).

LOYD, Christopher Lewis, MC 1943; *b* 1 June 1923; 3rd and *o* surv. *s* of late Arthur Thomas Loyd, OBE, JP, Lockinge, Wantage, Berks, and Dorothy, *d* of late Paul Ferdinand Willert, Headington, Oxford; *m* 1957, Joanna, *d* of Captain Arthur Turberville Smith-Bingham, Milburn Manor, Malmesbury, Wilts; two *s* one *d*. *Educ:* Eton; King's Coll., Cambridge (MA). Served 1942–46, with Coldstream Guards, Captain. ARICS 1952, FRICS 1955. Mem., Jockey Club. Trustee, Wallace Collection, 1973–90. JP 1950, DL 1954, Oxfordshire (formerly Berks); High Sheriff of Berkshire, 1961. *Address:* Lockinge, Wantage, Oxfordshire OX12 8QL. *T:* Abingdon (01235) 833265. *Club:* Boodle's.

LOYD, Sir Francis Alfred, KCMG 1965 (CMG 1961); OBE 1954 (MBE 1951); *b* 5 Sept. 1916; *s* of Major A. W. K. Loyd, Royal Sussex Regt; *m* 1st, 1946, Katharine Layzell (*d* 1981), *d* of Lt Col S. C. Layzell, MC, Mwatati, Kenya; two *d*; 2nd, 1984, Helen Monica, *widow* of Lt Col C. R. Murray Brown, DSO, Worlington, Suffolk. *Educ:* Eton; Trinity Coll., Oxford (MA). District Officer, Kenya, 1939; Mil. Service, E Africa, 1940–42; Private Secretary to Governor of Kenya, 1942–45; HM Consul, Mega, Ethiopia, 1945; District Comdr, Kenya, 1947–55; Commonwealth Fund Fellowship to USA, 1953–54; Provincial Commissioner, 1956; Permanent Secretary, Governor's Office, 1962–63; HM Commissioner for Swaziland, 1964–68. Dir, London House for Overseas Graduates, 1969–79; Chm., Oxfam Africa Cttee, 1979–85. *Recreations:* golf, gardening. *Address:* 53 Park Road, Aldeburgh, Suffolk IP15 5EN. *T:* Aldeburgh (01728) 452478. *Clubs:* Army and Navy; Vincent's (Oxford).

LOYD, John Anthony Thomas; QC 1981; **His Honour Judge Loyd;** a Circuit Judge, assigned to Official Referees' business, London, since 1990; *b* 18 July 1933; *e s* of Leslie William Loyd and Joan Louisa Loyd; *m* 1963, Rosaleen Iona Ward; one *d* (and one *d* decd). *Educ:* Wycliffe Coll.; Gonville and Caius Coll., Cambridge (BA 1956, MA 1959). RAF Regt, 1951–53. Called to the Bar, Gray's Inn, 1958, Bencher, 1994; a Recorder, 1985–90. *Recreations:* viticulture, sailing. *Address:* 9 Coldharbour, E14 9NS; Segos, Le Boulvé, Lot, France.

LOYD, Sir Julian (St John), KCVO 1991 (CVO 1979); DL; FRICS; Land Agent to HM The Queen, Sandringham Estate, 1964–91; *b* 25 May 1926; *s* of General Sir Charles Loyd, GCVO, KCB, DSO, MC and Lady Moyra Loyd; *m* 1960, Mary Emma, *d* of Sir Christopher Steel, GCMG, MVO and Lady Steel; one *s* two *d*. *Educ:* Eton Coll.; Magdalene Coll., Cambridge (MA). FRICS 1955. Coldstream Guards, 1944–45. Partner in Savills, Norwich, 1955–64. DL Norfolk, 1983. *Recreation:* fishing. *Address:* Perrystone Cottage, Burnham Market, King's Lynn PE31 8HA. *Club:* Army and Navy.

LOYDEN, Edward; MP (Lab) Liverpool, Garston, Feb. 1974–1979 and since 1983; *b* 3 May 1923; *s* of Patrick and Mary Loyden; *m* 1944, Rose Ann (*d* 1986); one *s* two *d* (and one *d* decd). *Educ:* Friary RC Elem. School. Shop boy, margarine factory, 1937; Able-Seaman, MN, 1938–46; Seaman Port Worker, Mersey Docks & Harbour Co., 1946–74. Member: Liverpool City Council, 1960 (Dep. Leader, 1983); Liverpool District Council, 1973; Merseyside Met. CC, 1973; Liverpool Met. Dist Council (St Mary's Ward), 1980–83. Shop Steward, TGWU, 1954, Branch Chm. 1959; Mem. District Cttee, Docks and Waterways, 1967; Mem. Nat. Cttee, TGWU, 1968; Vice-Chm., TGWU Parly Gp of MPs. Pres., Liverpool Trades Council, 1967; Pres., Merseyside Trades Council, 1974. Member: PLP Transport Cttee, For. Affairs Cttee, Health Cttee. *Recreations:* full-time political. *Address:* House of Commons, SW1A 0AA. *Clubs:* Gillmoss Labour, Woolton Labour.

LOYN, Prof. Henry Royston, DLitt; FSA, FRHistS; FBA 1979; Professor Emeritus, University of London; Professor of History, Westfield College, University of London, 1977–87 (Vice-Principal, 1980–86; Fellow, 1989); *b* 16 June 1922; *s* of late Henry George Loyn and Violet Monica Loyn; *m* 1950, Patricia Beatrice, *d* of late R. S. Haskew, OBE; three *s*. *Educ:* Cardiff High Sch.; University Coll., Cardiff (MA 1949, DLitt 1968). FRHistS 1958; FSA 1968. Dept of History, University Coll., Cardiff: Asst Lectr, 1946; Lectr, 1949; Sen. Lectr, 1961; Reader, 1966; Prof. of Medieval Hist., 1969–77; Dean of Students, 1968–70 and 1975–76; Fellow, 1981. President: Historical Assoc., 1976–79; Glam Hist. Soc., 1975–77; Cardiff Naturalists Soc., 1975–76; Soc. for Medieval Archaeol., 1983–86 (Vice-Pres., 1971–74); St Albans and Herts Architectural and Archaeolog. Soc., 1990–93; Vice-President: Soc. of Antiquaries, 1983–87; RHistS, 1983–86. Mem., Ancient Monuments Bd for England, 1982–84. W. N. Medlicott Medal for service to history, Historical Assoc., 1986. *Publications:* Anglo-Saxon England and the Norman Conquest, 1962, 2nd edn 1991; Norman Conquest, 1965; Norman Britain, 1966; Alfred The Great, 1967; A Wulfstan MS, Cotton, Nero Ai, 1971; (ed with H. Hearder) British Government and Administration, 1974; (with J. Percival) The Reign of Charlemagne, 1975; The Vikings in Britain, 1977; (with Alan and Richard Sorrell) Medieval Britain, 1977; The Governance of England, vol. 1, 1984; (introd.) facsimile edn, Domesday Book, 1987; (ed) The Middle Ages: a concise encyclopaedia, 1989; The Making of the English Nation, 1991; Society and Peoples: studies in the history of England and Wales *c* 600–1200, 1992; The Vikings in Britain, 1995; contribs to Eng. Hist. Rev., History, Antiquaries Jl, and Med. Archaeol. *Recreations:* natural history, gardening. *Address:* 4 Clinton Road, Penarth, S Glam CF64 3JB. *Club:* Athenæum.

LUBBOCK, family name of **Baron Avebury.**

LUBBOCK, Christopher William Stuart; a Master of the Supreme Court (Queen's Bench Division), 1970–90; *b* 4 Jan. 1920; 2nd *s* of late Captain Rupert Egerton Lubbock, Royal Navy; *m* 1947, Hazel Gordon, *d* of late Gordon Chapman; one *s* one *d*. *Educ:* Charterhouse; Brasenose Coll., Oxford. Served 1939–46, RNVR. Called to Bar, Inner Temple, 1947. *Address:* Great Horkesley, Essex.

LUCAN, 7th Earl of, *cr* 1795; **Richard John Bingham;** Bt 1632; Baron Lucan, 1776; Baron Bingham (UK), 1934; *b* 18 Dec. 1934; *e s* of 6th Earl of Lucan, MC; *S* father, 1964; *m* 1963, Veronica, *d* of late Major C. M. Duncan, MC, and of Mrs J. D. Margrie; one *s* two *d*. *Educ:* Eton. Lieut (Res. of Officers) Coldstream Guards. *Heir: s* Lord Bingham, *qv*.
[*The Earl has been missing since Nov. 1974.*]

LUCAS, family name of **Baron Lucas of Chilworth.**

LUCAS; *see* Keith-Lucas.

LUCAS OF CHILWORTH, 2nd Baron *cr* 1946, of Chilworth; **Michael William George Lucas;** *b* 26 April 1926; *er s* of 1st Baron and Sonia (*d* 1979), *d* of Marcus Finkelstein, Libau, Latvia; *S* father, 1967; *m* 1955, Ann-Marie, *o d* of Ronald Buck, Southampton; two *s* one *d*. *Educ:* Peter Symond's Sch., Winchester; Luton Technical Coll. Served with Royal

Tank Regt. A Lord in Waiting (Govt Whip), 1983–84; Parly Under-Sec. of State, DTI, 1984–87. Mem., House of Lords Select Cttee on Science and Technol., 1980–83, on European Communities, 1988–; UK deleg., N Atlantic Assembly, 1981–83, 1988–. TEng(CEI); FIMI (Mem. Council, 1972–76; Vice Pres., 1993–); FInstTA; LAE. President: League of Safe Drivers, 1976–80; Inst. of Transport Administration, 1980–83; Vice-Pres., RoSPA, 1980; Mem., Public Policy Cttee, RAC, 1981–83, 1988–. Governor, Churcher's Coll., Petersfield, 1985–. *Heir: s* Hon. Simon William Lucas, late Capt. RE [*b* 6 Feb. 1957; *m* 1993, Fiona, *yr d* of Thomas Mackintosh, Vancouver. *Educ:* Churcher's Coll., Petersfield; Leicester Univ. (BSc). Geophysicist, Canada]. *Address:* House of Lords, SW1A 0PW.

See also Hon. I. T. M. Lucas.

LUCAS OF CRUDWELL, 11th Baron *cr* 1663, **AND DINGWALL,** 14th Lord *cr* 1609; **Ralph Matthew Palmer;** a Lord in Waiting (Government Whip), since 1994; *b* 7 June 1951; *s* of 10th Baroness Lucas of Crudwell and 13th Lady Dingwall and of Maj. the Hon. Robert Jocelyn Palmer, MC, 3rd *s* of 3rd Earl of Selborne, PC, CH; *S* mother, 1991; *m* 1978, Clarissa Marie, *d* of George Vivian Lockett, TD; one *s* one *d*. *Educ:* Eton; Balliol Coll., Oxford (BA (Hons) Physics). BDO Binder Hamlyn, 1972–76; S. G. Warburg & Co. Ltd, 1976–88. *Heir: s* Hon. Lewis Edward Palmer, *b* 7 Dec. 1987. *Address:* The Old House, Wonston, Winchester, Hants SO21 3LS. *T:* Winchester (01962) 760323.

LUCAS, Prof. Arthur Maurice, PhD; Professor of Science Curriculum Studies, since 1980, and Principal, since 1993, King's College, London; *b* 26 Oct. 1941; *s* of Joseph Alfred Percival Lucas and May Queen Lucas (*née* Griffin); *m* 1970, Paula Jean Williams; one *s* one *d*. *Educ:* Univ. of Melbourne (BSc 1963; BEd 1968); Ohio State Univ. (PhD 1972; Fulbright Award). Appts at Yallourn and Newborough High Schs, 1964–66; Flinders Univ. of SA, 1967–70; Ohio State Univ., 1970–72; Warrnambool Inst. of Advanced Educn, 1973; Flinders University: Lectr in Sci. Educn, 1974–80; Sen. Lectr, 1976; Vice-Chm., 1976, Chm., 1977–79, Sch. of Educn; King's College, London: Asst Principal, 1987–89; Vice-Principal, 1991–93; Actg Principal, 1992. Chm., Bd of Educnl Studies, 1986–88, Mem. Council, 1995–, Univ. of London. Member, Council: Commonwealth Assoc. for Sci., Maths and Technol. Educn, 1981–89; Zoological Soc. of London, 1992–93 (Vice Pres., 1993); Mem., COPUS, 1993–. Mem., SE Thames RHA, 1993–94. *Publications:* Review of British Science Curriculum Projects (with D. G. Chisman), 1973; Environment and Environmental Education, 1979; (ed jtly) New Trends in Biology Education, 1987; (ed with P. J. Black) Children's Informal Ideas in Science, 1993; numerous articles in learned jls. *Recreation:* reading. *Address:* Principal's Office, King's College London, Cornwall House, Waterloo Road, SE1 8WA. *T:* 0171–872 3434. *Club:* Athenæum.

LUCAS, Ven. Brian Humphrey, CB 1993; Chaplain-in-Chief, Royal Air Force, 1991–95; *b* 20 Jan. 1940; *s* of Frederick George Humphrey Lucas and Edith Mary Lucas; *m* 1966, Joy Penn; two *s* one *d*. *Educ:* St David's Coll., Lampeter (BA); St Stephen's House, Oxford. Ordained deacon 1964, priest 1965; Curate: Llandaff Cathedral, 1964–67; Parish of Neath, 1967–70; Royal Air Force: Chaplain, 1970–87; Asst Chaplain-in-Chief, 1987–91. QHC, 1989–95. Canon and Prebendary of Lincoln Cathedral, 1991–95. Mem., Gen. Synod of C of E, 1991–95. Vice-Pres., Clergy Orphan Corp., 1991–95; Visitor, Soldiers' and Airmen's Scripture Readers Assoc., 1991–95; Mem. Council, Bible Reading Fellowship, 1992–95. Mem. Council, RAF Benevolent Fund, 1991–95. FRSA 1993. *Recreations:* archaeology of the Near East, travel (excluding tourist areas), watching Welsh Rugby football. *Address:* Pen-y-coed, 6 Arnhem Drive, Caythorpe, Lincs NG32 3DQ. *Club:* Royal Air Force.

LUCAS, (Charles) Vivian; Chief Executive, Devon County Council, 1974–79; solicitor; *b* 31 May 1914; *s* of Frank and Mary Renshaw Lucas, Malvern, Worcs; *m* 1941, Oonah Holderness; two *s* two *d*. *Educ:* Malvern Coll.; abroad; London Univ. (LLB). Clerk, Devon County Council, 1972–74; Clerk to the Lieutenancy of Devon, 1972–79. *Recreations:* sport, bridge. *Address:* Highfield Lodge, 7 Salterton Road, Exmouth EX8 2BR. *Club:* Golf and Country (Exeter).

LUCAS, Christopher Charles; Under Secretary, Community and International Policy Division, Department of Energy, 1977–80, retired; *b* 5 June 1920; *s* of Charles Edwin Lucas and Mabel Beatrice Read; *m* 1945, Beryl June Vincent; two *d*. *Educ:* Devonport High Sch.; Balliol Coll., Oxford (Newman Exhibnr). Min. of Fuel, 1946; Central Econ. Planning Staff, 1948; HM Treasury, 1950–70; Cabinet Office, 1970–72; Sec., NEDC, 1973–76; Under-Sec., Dept of Energy, 1976–. *Recreation:* riding. *Address:* Orchard Croft, Withycombe, near Minehead, Somerset TA24 6PT. *T:* Dunster (01643) 821551.

LUCAS, Christopher Tullis, CBE 1994; Acting Director, RSA 2001, since 1994; Director and Secretary, Royal Society for the encouragement of Arts, Manufactures & Commerce, 1977–94; *b* 20 Dec. 1937; *s* of late Philip Gaddesden Lucas, GM and Maise Lucas; *m* 1962, Tina Colville; two *d*. *Educ:* Winchester Coll. CA 1965. Articled, 1958; with Thomson McLintock & Co., 1958–66; Chief Exec., ICEM Ltd, 1966–72; Sen. Radio Officer, IBA, 1972–74; first Man. Dir, Radio Forth, Edinburgh, 1974–77. Dir, RSA Exams Bd, 1977–94; Sec., Faculty of Royal Designers for Industry, 1977–94. Mem., Tax Law Review Cttee, Inst. for Fiscal Studies, 1994–. Governor: Central Sch. of Art and Design, 1977–86; Design Dimension, Halifax, 1994–. *Recreations:* designer manqué, carpenter, walking, ski-ing, theatre. *Address:* 24 Montpelier Row, Twickenham TW1 2NQ. *T:* 0181–892 6584.

LUCAS, Prof. Colin Renshaw, DPhil; FRHistS; Master of Balliol College, Oxford, since 1994; *b* 25 Aug. 1940; *s* of Frank Renshaw Lucas and Janine (*née* Charpentier); *m* 1st, 1964, Christiane Berchon de Fontaine Goubert (marr. diss. 1975); one *s*; 2nd, 1990, Mary Louise Hume. *Educ:* Sherborne Sch.; Lincoln Coll., Oxford (MA, DPhil). FRHistS 1974. Asst Lectr, then Lectr, Sheffield Univ., 1965–69; Vis. Asst Prof., Indiana Univ., 1969–70; Lectr, Manchester Univ., 1970–73; Fellow, Balliol Coll., Oxford, and Lectr in Modern History, Oxford University, 1973–90; Prof., 1990–94, and Dean, Div. of Social Scis, 1993–94, Chicago Univ. Hon. DLitt Lyon, 1989. Officier, Ordre des Arts et des Lettres (France), 1989; Chevalier, Ordre du Mérite (France), 1994. *Publications:* The Structure of the Terror, 1973; (with G. Lewis) Beyond the Terror, 1983; (ed) The Political Culture of the French Revolution, 1988; contrib. Past and Present, Jl of Modern Hist., French Histl Studies. *Address:* c/o Balliol College, Oxford OX1 3BJ. *T:* Oxford (01865) 277777.

LUCAS, Sir Cyril (Edward), Kt 1976; CMG 1956; FRS 1966; Director of Fisheries Research, Scotland (Department of Agriculture and Fisheries for Scotland) and Director Marine Laboratory Aberdeen, 1948–70; *b* Hull, Yorks, 30 July 1909; *o s* of late Archibald and Edith Lucas, Hull; *m* 1934, Sarah Agnes (*d* 1974), *o d* of late Henry Alfred and Amy Rose; two *s* one *d*. *Educ:* Grammar Sch., Hull; University Coll., Hull. BSc (London) 1931, DSc (London) 1942. FRSE 1939; Vice-Pres., 1962–64; Neill Prize, 1960. Research Biologist, University Coll., Hull, 1931; Head of Dept of Oceanography, University Coll., Hull, 1942. UK Expert or Delegate to various internat. confs on Marine Fisheries and Conservation, 1948–, and Chm. of research cttees in connexion with these; Chm., Consultative and Liaison Cttees, Internat. Council for Exploration of Sea, 1962–67; Member: Adv. Cttee on Marine Resources Research, FAO, 1964–71 (Chm. 1966–71); Council for Scientific Policy, 1968–70; Nat. Environmental Res. Council, 1970–78. Hon. DSc Hull, 1975; Hon. LLD Aberdeen, 1977. *Publications:* various scientific, particularly on marine plankton and fisheries research in Bulletins of Marine Ecology (Joint Editor), Jl of Marine Biological Assoc., etc and various international jls. *Address:* 16 Albert Terrace, Aberdeen AB1 1XY. *T:* Aberdeen (01224) 645568.

LUCAS, George; film director, producer and screenwriter; Chairman, Lucasfilm, since 1974; *b* 14 May 1944; *s* of George and Dorothy Lucas. *Educ:* Univ. of Southern California (Bachelor of Fine Arts, 1966). Asst to Francis Ford Coppola on The Rain People, 1967 (winner, Grand Prize, Nat. Student Film Festival for short film, THX-1138, 1967); director, co-author of screenplays: THX-1138, 1970; American Graffiti, 1973; dir, author, Star Wars, 1977; executive producer, author: More American Graffiti, 1979; The Empire Strikes Back, 1980; Return of the Jedi, 1983; Indiana Jones and the Temple of Doom, 1984; Willow, 1988; The Young Indiana Jones Chronicles (TV series), 1992–93; co-executive producer: Raiders of the Lost Ark (and co-author), 1981; Land Before Time, 1988; Indiana Jones and the Last Crusade, 1989; executive producer: Mishima, 1985; Howard the Duck, 1986; Labyrinth, 1986; Tucker, the Man and his Dream, 1988; Radioland Murders, 1994. *Publication:* Star Wars, 1976. *Address:* Lucasfilm Ltd, PO Box 2009, San Rafael, CA 94912, USA. *T:* (415) 6621800.

LUCAS, Prof. Ian Albert McKenzie, CBE 1977; Principal of Wye College, 1977–88, Professor, 1988, University of London, now Professor Emeritus, and Fellow since 1992; *b* 10 July 1926; *s* of Percy John Lucas and Janie Inglis (*née* Hamilton); *m* 1950, Helen Louise Langerman; one *s* two *d*. *Educ:* Clayesmore Sch.; Reading Univ.; McGill Univ. BSc, MSc; FIBiol; FRAgS. Lectr, Harper Adams Agricl Coll., 1949–50; pig nutrition res., Rowett Res. Inst., Aberdeen, 1950–57 and 1958–61; Res. Fellow, Ruakura Res. Station, New Zealand, 1957–58; Prof. of Agriculture, UCNW, Bangor, 1961–77. Chm., Agricl and Vet. Cttee, British Council, 1978–87. Member: Jt Cttee on use of antibiotics in animal husbandry and vet. medicine, 1969; MAFF Adv. Council for Agric. and Hortic., 1969–79; Agric. and Vet. Sub-Cttee, UGC, 1972–77; CVCP, 1985–88; Cttee, Internat. Co-operation in Higher Educn, British Council, 1986–90. President: Sect. M, BAAS, 1983; Agricl Educn Assoc., 1987; Rural Educn and Develt Assoc., 1994. Member Governing Body: Grassland Res. Inst., 1970–79; Rydal Sch., 1975–77; RVC, 1978–88; E Malling Res. Station, 1978–87; Hadlow Agric. Coll., 1978–88; Inst. for Grassland and Animal Production Research, 1987–89. Hon. Life Mem., British Council, 1987. *Publications:* scientific papers in Jl Agricl Science, Animal Production, Brit. Jl Nutrition and others. *Recreations:* sailing. *Address:* Valley Downs, Brady Road, Lyminge, Folkestone, Kent CT18 8DU. *T:* Lyminge (01303) 863053. *Clubs:* Farmers'; Hollowshore Cruising (Oare, Kent).

LUCAS, Hon. Ivor Thomas Mark, CMG 1980; HM Diplomatic Service, retired; Assistant Secretary-General, Arab–British Chamber of Commerce, 1985–87; *b* 25 July 1927; 2nd *s* of George William Lucas, 1st Baron Lucas of Chilworth, and Sonia Lucas; *m* 1954, Christine Mallorie Coleman; three *s*. *Educ:* St Edward's Sch., Oxford; Trinity Coll., Oxford (MA). Served in Royal Artillery, 1945–48 (Captain). BA Oxon 1951. Entered Diplomatic Service, 1951; Middle East Centre for Arab Studies, Lebanon, 1952; 3rd, later 2nd Sec., Bahrain, Sharjah and Dubai, 1952–56; FO, 1956–59; 1st Sec., Karachi, 1959–62; 1st Sec. and Head of Chancery, Tripoli, 1962–66; FO, 1966–68; Counsellor, Aden, 1968–69 (Chargé d'Affaires, Aug. 1968–Feb. 1969); Dep. High Comr, Kaduna, Nigeria, 1969–71; Counsellor, Copenhagen, 1972–75; Head of Middle East Dept, FCO, 1975–79; Ambassador to Oman, 1979–81, to Syria, 1982–84. Fellow in Internat. Politics of ME, Centre of Internat. Studies, Cambridge, 1991–94. Mem., Central Council, Royal Over-Seas League, 1988–94; Chm., Anglo-Omani Soc., 1990–95; Mem. Council, RSAA, 1988–94. Chm. Adv. Bd, Centre of Near and Middle Eastern Studies, SOAS, 1987–90. *Publications:* chapters in: Politics and the Economy in Syria, 1987; The Middle East: a handbook, 1988; various articles and reviews. *Recreations:* music, crosswords, scrabble. *Clubs:* Royal Over-Seas League, Commonwealth Trust.

LUCAS, John Randolph, FBA 1988; Fellow and Tutor of Merton College, Oxford, since 1960; *b* 18 June 1929; *s* of late Rev. E. de G. Lucas, sometime Archdeacon of Durham and Joan Mary Lucas; *m* 1961, Morar Portal, *er d* of Sir Reginald Portal, KCB, DSC; two *s* two *d*. *Educ:* St Mary's Coll., Winchester; Balliol Coll., Oxford (John Locke Schol., 1952; MA). Jun. Res. Fellow, Merton Coll., Oxford, 1953–56; Fellow and Asst Tutor, Corpus Christi Coll., Cambridge, 1956–59; Reader in Philosophy, Oxford Univ., 1990–. Jane Eliza Procter Vis. Fellow, Princeton Univ., 1957–58; Leverhulme Res. Fellow, Leeds Univ., 1959–60. Chm., Oxford Consumers' Gp, 1961–63, 1965. Member: Archbishops' Commn on Christian Doctrine, 1967–76; Lichfield Commn on Divorce and Remarriage, 1975–78. Pres., British Soc. for the Philosophy of Sci., 1991–93. Lectures: (jtly) Gifford, Univ. of Edinburgh, 1971–73; Margaret Harris, Univ. of Dundee, 1981; Harry Jelema, Calvin Coll., Grand Rapids, 1987. *Publications:* Principles of Politics, 1966, 2nd edn 1985; The Concept of Probability, 1970; The Freedom of the Will, 1970; (jtly) The Nature of Mind, 1972; (jtly) The Development of Mind, 1973; A Treatise on Time and Space, 1973; Essays on Freedom and Grace, 1976; Democracy and Participation, 1976 (trans. Portuguese, 1985); On Justice, 1980; Space, Time and Causality, 1985; The Future, 1989; (jtly) Space, Time and Electromagnetism, 1990; Responsibility, 1993; various articles in learned jls. *Recreation:* walking and talking. *Address:* Merton College, Oxford OX1 4JD. *T:* Oxford (01865) 276327; Postmasters' Hall, Merton Street, Oxford OX1 4JE. *T:* Oxford (01865) 276321; Lambrook House, East Lambrook, South Petherton, Som TA13 5HW. *T:* South Petherton (01460) 240413.

LUCAS, Keith Stephen; artist and teacher; Head of Radio, Film and Televison Studies, Christ Church College, Canterbury, 1984–89; *b* 28 Aug. 1924; *m* 1969, Rona Stephanie Lucas (*née* Levy); two *s* one *d* (and two step *s*). *Educ:* Royal Coll. of Art (ARCA). London Press Exchange, 1956–64; Prof. of Film and Television, Royal Coll. of Art, 1964–72 (first holder of Chair); Dir, British Film Institute, 1972–78; Television Consultant, BFI, 1979–84. Artistic Dir, Commonwealth Film and TV Fest. and supporting arts prog., Cyprus, 1980. Chairman: Canterbury New Theatre Ltd, 1979–83; Canterbury Theatre and Festival Trust, 1983–86 (Pres., 1986); Vice-Pres., Centre Internat. de Liaison des Ecoles de Cinéma et de Télévision, 1970–72. Governor: North East London Poly., 1971–72; Canterbury Coll. of Art (formerly Canterbury Sch. of Art), 1971–74, 1981–87; Maidstone Coll. of Art, 1982–87; Kent Inst. of Art and Design, 1987–89. Exhibitions: retrospective 1956–86, Poor Priests Hosp., Canterbury, 1986; John Nevill Gall., Canterbury, 1988; Royal Mus., Canterbury, 1990; Anna Mei Chadwick Gall., 1993, 1995; Cleary Gall., Canterbury, 1993. Hon. Fellow, Royal Coll. of Art, 1972. *Recreations:* writing, listening to music. *Address:* The Old School House, Bishopsbourne, Canterbury, Kent CT4 5JB. *T:* Canterbury (01227) 830026. *Club:* Chelsea Arts.

LUCAS, Percy Belgrave, CBE 1981; DSO 1943 and Bar 1945; DFC 1942; Chairman: GRA Property Trust Ltd, 1965–75 (Managing Director, 1957–65); John Jacobs Golf Consultants Ltd, 1978–91; John Jacobs Golf Associates Ltd, 1985–94; *b* Sandwich Bay, Kent, 2 Sept. 1915; *y s* of late Percy Montagu Lucas, Prince's, Sandwich, form. of Filby House, Filby, Norfolk; *m* 1946, Jill Doreen, *d* of Lt-Col A. M. Addison, Ascot; two *s* (and one *s* decd). *Educ:* Stowe; Pembroke Coll., Cambridge. Editorial Staff, Express Newspapers, 1937–40. Joined RAFVR, 1939; Commanded: 249 (Fighter) Sqdn, Battle of Malta, 1942; 616 (Fighter) Sqdn, 1943; Coltishall Wing, Fighter Command, 1943; 613 (Mosquito)

Sqdn, 2 Gp, 2nd TAF, North-West Europe, 1944–45; Fighter Command, HQ Staff, 1942; Air Defence of Great Britain HQ Staff, 1944; demobilised with rank of Wing Comdr, 1946. Contested (C) West Fulham, 1945; MP (C) Brentford and Chiswick, 1950–59. Capt. Cambridge Univ. Golf team, 1937; Pres. Hawks Club, Cambridge, 1937; English International Golf team, 1936, 1948, 1949 (Capt. 1949); British Walker Cup team, 1936, 1947, 1949 (Capt. 1949); Capt., Walker Cup Society, 1986–88. Vice-President: Golf Foundation Ltd, 1983– (Mem. Council, 1966–83; Pres., 1963–66); Nat. Golf Clubs Advisory Assoc., 1969– (Pres., 1963–69); Assoc. of Golf Club Secretaries, 1974– (Pres., 1968–74). Member: General Advisory Council, BBC, 1962–67; Council, National Greyhound Racing Soc. of Great Britain, 1957–72; Policy Cttee, Nat. Greyhound Racing Club Ltd, 1972–77; AAA Cttee of Inquiry, 1967; Exec. Cttee, General Purposes and Finance Cttee; Central Council of Physical Recreation; Management Cttee, Crystal Palace Nat. Sports Centre, 1961–73; Sports Council, 1971–83 (Chm., Finance Cttee, 1978–82; Chm., Sports Trade Adv. Panel, 1972–83); Governor, Stowe Sch., 1964–79. Pres., Old Stoic Soc., 1979–81. Croix de Guerre avec Palme, 1945. *Publications:* Five-Up (autobiography), 1978, 2nd edn 1991; The Sport of Prince's (reflections of a golfer), 1980; Flying Colours: the epic story of Douglas Bader, 1981, 2nd edn 1990; Wings of War: airmen of all nations tell their stories 1939–1945, 1983; Out of the Blue: the role of luck in air warfare 1917–66, 1985; John Jacobs' Impact on Golf: the man and his methods, 1987; Thanks for the Memory: unforgettable characters in air warfare 1939–1945, 1989; Malta—the thorn in Rommel's side, 1992; with Air Vice-Marshal J. E. Johnson: Glorious Summer: the story of the Battle of Britain, 1990; Courage in the Skies: great air battles from the Somme to Desert Storm, 1992; Winged Victory: the recollections of two Royal Air Force leaders, 1995. *Recreations:* golf, photography. *Address:* 11 Onslow Square, SW7 3NJ. *T:* 0171–584 8373. *Clubs:* Naval and Military, Royal Air Force; Sandy Lodge Golf; Walton Heath Golf; Prince's Golf; Royal West Norfolk Golf.

LUCAS, Prof. Raleigh Barclay; Professor of Oral Pathology, University of London, 1954–79, now Emeritus; Consultant Pathologist, Royal Dental Hospital of London, 1950–79; *b* 3 June 1914; *s* of H. Lucas; *m* 1942, Violet Sorrell; one *d* (one *s* decd). *Educ:* George Watson's Coll.; Univ. of Edinburgh. MB, ChB (Edinburgh) 1937; DPH 1939; MD 1945; MRCP 1946; FRCPath 1963; FRCP 1974; FDS RCS 1974. Asst Bacteriologist, Edinburgh Royal Infirmary, 1939–40; Pathologist, Stoke Mandeville Hosp. and Royal Buckinghamshire Hospital, 1947–49; Reader in Pathology, University of London, 1950–54; Dean, Sch. of Dental Surgery, Royal Dental Hospital of London, 1958–73. Examiner in Pathology and Bacteriology for dental degrees, Univs of London, Glasgow, Birmingham, Sheffield, Liverpool and Wales. Served War of 1939–45, Major RAMC. FRSocMed; Fellow and Past Pres., Royal Medical Society; Mem. Pathological Soc. of Great Britain and Ireland; Mem. BMA. *Publications:* (jtly) Bacteriology for Students of Dental Surgery, 1954; Pathology of Tumours of the Oral Tissues, 1964; (jtly) Tumors of the Major Salivary Glands, 1974; (jtly) Atlas of Oral Pathology, 1985; various articles in medical and scientific journals.

LUCAS, Sir Thomas (Edward), 5th Bt *cr* 1887; MA; CEng; engineer, research analyst, healer; *b* 16 Sept. 1930; *s* of late Ralph John Scott Lucas (killed in action, Libya, 1941), and Dorothy (*d* 1985), *d* of late H. T. Timson, Tatchbury Mount, Hants; *S* cousin, 1980; *m* 1st, 1958, Charmian (*d* 1970), *d* of late Col J. S. Powell; one *s*; 2nd, 1980, Ann Graham Moore. *Educ:* Wellington College; Trinity Hall, Cambridge. External Consultant to DG XIII, Commn of EU (formerly EC), and to other orgns; Founder, Engrg Capacity Exchange, 1963; formerly Director: SGF Properties plc; Columbia Industrial Gp; Vacuum Metallizing Processes Inc., and other cos. FRSA; NFSH. *Publications:* Handbook of Vacuum Physics, Vol. 1, part 2, 1964; Patterns of World Social and Economic Change the next 15 years, 1984; articles in scientific and technical jls. *Heir: s* Stephen Ralph James Lucas, *b* 11 Dec. 1963. *Address:* c/o Drummonds, Admiralty Arch, SW1A 2DX. *Fax:* Dedham (01206) 322737.

LUCAS, Vivian; *see* Lucas, C. V.

LUCAS-TOOTH, Sir (Hugh) John, 2nd Bt *cr* 1920, of Bught; *b* 20 Aug. 1932; *s* of Sir Hugh Vere Huntly Duff Munro-Lucas-Tooth of Teananich, 1st Bt and Laetitia Florence, OBE (*d* 1978), *er d* of Sir John Ritchie Findlay, 1st Bt, KBE; *S* father, 1985; *m* 1955, Hon. Caroline, *e d* of 1st Baron Poole, PC, CBE, TD; three *d*. *Educ:* Eton College; Balliol Coll., Oxford. *Heir: cousin* James Lingen Warrand [*b* 6 Oct. 1936; *m* 1960, Juliet Rose, *yr d* of late T. A. Pearn; two *s* one *d*]. *Address:* Parsonage Farm, East Hagbourne, Didcot, Oxon OX11 9LN. *Clubs:* Brooks's, Beefsteak.

LUCE, Rt. Hon. Sir Richard (Napier), Kt 1991; PC 1986; DL; Vice Chancellor, University of Buckingham, since 1992; *b* 14 Oct. 1936; *s* of late Sir William Luce, GBE, KCMG, and Margaret, *d* of late Adm. Sir Trevylyan Napier, KCB; *m* 1961, Rose, *d* of Sir Godfrey Nicholson, 1st Bt; two *s*. *Educ:* Wellington Coll.; Christ's Coll., Cambridge. 2nd cl. History. Nat. Service officer, 1955–57, served in Cyprus. Overseas Civil Service, served as District Officer, Kenya, 1960–62; Brand Manager, Gallaher Ltd, 1963–65; Marketing Manager, Spirella Co. of GB; Dir, National Innovations Centre, 1968–71; Chairman: IFA Consultants Ltd, 1972–79; Selanex Ltd, 1973–79; Courtenay Stewart International Ltd, 1975–79; Mem. European Adv. Bd, Corning Glass International, 1975–79; Director: Booker Tate, 1991–; Meridian Broadcasting, 1991–. Chairman: Commonwealth Foundn, 1992–; Atlantic Council of the UK, 1993–. Contested (C) Hitchin, 1970. MP (C) Arundel and Shoreham, Apr. 1971–74, Shoreham, 1974–92. PPS to Minister for Trade and Consumer Affairs, 1972–74; an Opposition Whip, 1974–75; an Opposition spokesman on foreign and commonwealth affairs, 1977–79; Parly Under Sec. of State, 1979–81, Minister of State, 1981–82 and 1983–85, FCO; Minister of State, Privy Council Office (Minister for the Arts), 1985–90. Pres., Voluntary Art Network. Mem. Council, Open Univ.; Gov., RSC. Trustee, Geographers' A–Z Map Trust. DL W Sussex, 1991. *Recreations:* tennis, walking, reading, etc. *Address:* University of Buckingham, Buckingham MK18 1EG. *T:* Buckingham (01280) 820207, *Fax:* (01280) 820311.

LUCE, Thomas Richard Harman; Head of Social Care Policy, Department of Health, since 1995; *b* 11 July 1939; *s* of late Air Cdre Charles Luce, DSO, and Joyce Marjorie Elizabeth Luce (*née* Johnson); *m* 1991, Virginia Manson Hunt; two step *s*. *Educ:* Clifton Coll.; Christ's Coll., Cambridge (BA Hons); Indiana Univ., USA. HM Inspector of Taxes, 1965–67; Asst Principal, Ministries of Aviation and Technology, 1967–69; Principal, CSD, 1969–72; Department of Health and Social Security: Principal, 1972–75; Asst Sec., 1975–84; Under Sec., 1984–; seconded to HM Treasury (Head of Management Policy and Running Costs Gp), 1987–90; Dep. Dir, NHS Finance, 1990; Under Sec., Community Services Div., DoH, 1990–94. *Publications:* occasional music criticism. *Recreations:* music, reading, walking, swimming. *Address:* Department of Health, Wellington House, 133–155 Waterloo Road, SE1 8UG. *Clubs:* Athenæum, Royal Automobile.

LUCIE-SMITH, (John) Edward (McKenzie); poet and art critic; *b* Kingston, Jamaica, 27 Feb. 1933; *s* of John Dudley Lucie-Smith and Mary (*née* Lushington); unmarried. *Educ:* King's Sch., Canterbury; Merton Coll., Oxford (MA). Settled in England, 1946. Education Officer, RAF, 1954–56; subseq. worked in advertising and as free-lance journalist and broadcaster. FRSL. *Publications:* A Tropical Childhood and other poems, 1961 (jt winner, John Llewellyn Rhys Mem. Prize; winner, Arts Coun. Triennial Award); (ed, with Philip Hobsbaum) A Group Anthology, 1963; Confessions and Histories, 1964; (with Jack Clemo, George MacBeth) Penguin Modern Poets 6, 1964; (ed) Penguin Book of Elizabethan Verse, 1965; What is a Painting?, 1966; (ed) The Liverpool Scene, 1967; (ed) A Choice of Browning's Verse, 1967; (ed) Penguin Book of Satirical Verse, 1967; Thinking about Art, 1968; Towards Silence, 1968; Movements in Art since 1945, 1969; (ed) British Poetry Since 1945, 1970; (with Patricia White) Art in Britain 69–70, 1970; (ed) A Primer of Experimental Verse, 1971; (ed with S. W. Taylor) French Poetry: the last fifteen years, 1971; A Concise History of French Painting, 1971; Symbolist Art, 1972; Eroticism in Western Art, 1972; The First London Catalogue, 1974; The Well Wishers, 1974; The Burnt Child (autobiog.), 1975; The Invented Eye (early photography), 1975; World of the Makers, 1975; (with Celestine Dars) How the Rich Lived, 1976; Joan of Arc, 1976; (with Celestine Dars) Work and Struggle, 1977; Fantin-Latour, 1977; The Dark Pageant (novel), 1977; Art Today, 1977; A Concise History of Furniture, 1979; Super Realism, 1979; Cultural Calendar of the Twentieth Century, 1979; Art in the Seventies, 1980; The Story of Craft, 1981; The Body, 1981; A History of Industrial Design, 1983; Art Terms: an illustrated dictionary, 1984; Art in the Thirties, 1985; American Art Now, 1985; Lives of the Great Twentieth Century Artists, 1986; Sculpture since 1945, 1987; (ed) The Essential Osbert Lancaster, 1988; (with Carolyn Cohen, Judith Higgins) The New British Painting, 1988; Art in the Eighties, 1990; Art Deco Painting, 1990; Fletcher Benton, 1990; Jean Rustin, 1991; Harry Holland, 1992; Art and Civilisation, 1992; (ed) The Faber Book of Art Anecdotes, 1992; Andres Nagel, 1992; Wendy Taylor, 1992; Alexander, 1992; British Art Now, 1993; Race, Sex and Gender: issues in contemporary art, 1994; (with Elisabeth Frink) Elisabeth Frink: a portrait, 1994; American Realism, 1994; contribs to Times, Sunday Times, Independent, Mail-on-Sunday, Listener, Spectator, New Statesman, Evening Standard, Encounter, London Magazine, Illustrated London News, etc. *Recreation:* the Internet. *Address:* c/o Rogers, Coleridge & White, 20 Powis Mews, W11 1JN.

LUCKHOO, Hon. Sir Edward Victor, Kt 1970; QC (Guyana); Order of Roraima, 1979; attached to Luckhoo and Luckhoo, Guyana, 1949–66 and 1984–87; *b* Guyana (when Br. Guiana), 24 May 1912; *s* of late E. A. Luckhoo, OBE and *g s* of Moses Luckhoo, official interpreter to the courts; *m* 1981, Maureen Moxlow, Batley, Yorks. *Educ:* New Amsterdam Scots Sch.; Queen's Coll., Guyana; St Catherine's Coll., Oxford (BA). Called to Bar, Middle Temple, 1936; QC Guyana 1965. Began career in magistracy as acting Magistrate, Essequibo District, 1943; Magistrate, 1944–47; Judge of Appeal, 1966; Chancellor and President of Court of Appeal, Guyana, 1968–76; Actg Governor-General, 1969–70; Actg Pres. of Guyana, Feb.–March, 1970; High Comr in India and Sri Lanka, 1976–83. Chairman: Customs Tariff Tribunal, 1954–56; Judicial Service Commn, 1966–75; Honours Adv. Council, 1970–76. Mem. Exec. Bd, UNESCO, 1983–87. *Address:* 43 Penn Drive, Liversedge, W Yorks WF15 8DB.

See also Sir L. A. Luckhoo.

LUCKHOO, Sir Lionel (Alfred), KCMG 1969; Kt 1966; CBE 1962; QC (Guyana) 1954; Judge of Supreme Court, Guyana, 1980, retired; *b* 2 March 1914; 2nd *s* of late Edward Alfred Luckhoo, OBE, Solicitor, and Evelyn Luckhoo; *g s* of Moses Luckhoo, official interpreter to the Courts; *m* Sheila Chamberlin; two *s* three *d*. *Educ:* Queen's Coll., Georgetown, Brit. Guiana; Middle Temple, London. MLC, 1949–51; Mem. State Coun., 1952–53; Minister without Portfolio, 1954–57; Mem. Georgetown Town Council, 1950–64; Mayor, City of Georgetown, 1954, 1955, 1960, 1961 (Dep. Mayor three times), High Comr in UK, for Guyana, May 1966–70; for Barbados, Nov. 1966–70, Ambassador of Guyana and Barbados, to Paris, Bonn and The Hague, 1967–70. Pres., MPCA Trade Union, Brit. Guiana, 1949–52; Pres. of several Unions; has served on Commns of Enquiry, Public Cttees, Statutory Bodies, Legal Cttees, Drafting Cttees, Disciplinary Cttees, etc. Head of Luckhoo & Luckhoo, Legal Practitioners. Chm., Red Cross Soc., 1978. Pres., Guyana Olympic Assoc., 1974–79. Mem. of the Magic Circle. Listed in the Guinness Book of Records as the world's most successful advocate with 245 successful defences in murder cases. Has travelled more than four million miles around the world speaking of Jesus. *Publications:* (jtly) The Fitzluck Theory of Breeding Racehorses, 1960; I Believe, 1968; God is Love, 1975; Life After Death, 1975; The Xmas Story, 1975; Sense of Values, 1975; Dear Atheist, 1977; Dear Boys and Girls, 1978; Dear Adults, 1979; God and Science, 1980; Dear Muslims, 1980; The Question Answered, 1984; The Verdict is Yours, 1985; (jtly) Destiny of Guilt. *Recreation:* cricket. *Address:* Luckhoo Ministries, PO Box 815881, Dallas, TX 75381, USA; Lot 1, Croal Street, Georgetown, Guyana. *Club:* Commonwealth Trust.

See also Hon. Sir E. V. Luckhoo.

LUCY, Sir Edmund J. W. H. C. R. F.; *see* Fairfax-Lucy.

LUDDINGTON, Sir Donald (Collin Cumyn), KBE 1976; CMG 1973; CVO 1974; retired; *b* 18 Aug. 1920; *s* of late F. Norman John Luddington, Ceylon Civil Service, and late M. Myrtle Amethyst Payne; *m* 1945, Garry Brodie Johnston; one *s* one *d*. *Educ:* Dover Coll.; St Andrews Univ. (MA). Served War, Army, 1940–46, KOYLI and RAC, Captain. Hong Kong Govt, 1949–73; Sec. for Home Affairs, 1971–73; Governor, Solomon Islands, 1973–76. Chm., Public Services Commn, Hong Kong, 1977–78; Comr, Indep. Commn against Corruption, Hong Kong, 1978–80. *Recreation:* walking. *Address:* The Firs, Little Lane, Easingwold, York YO6 3AQ. *Clubs:* Commonwealth Trust; Hong Kong (Hong Kong).

LUDER, (Harold) Owen, CBE 1986; President, Royal Institute of British Architects, 1981–83 and since 1995; architect and construction industry consultant; Principal, Owen Luder Consultancy, Communication in Construction Ltd, since 1987; *b* London, 7 Aug. 1928; *s* of late Edward Charles and Ellen Clara Luder; *m* 1st, 1951, Rose Dorothy (Doris) Broadstock (marr. diss. 1988); four *d* (one *s* decd); 2nd, 1989, Jacqueline Ollerton. *Educ:* Deptford Park Primary Sch.; Peckham Sch. for Girls; Brixton Sch. of Building; Regent St Polytechnic Sch. of Architecture. ARIBA 1954, FRIBA 1967. Private practice in architecture, 1957–87; Founder and Sen. Partner, Owen Luder Partnership, 1958–78, when it became one of the first architectural partnerships to convert to an unlimited co., Chm. and Man. Dir, 1978–87; on withdrawal from architectural practice, set up Owen Luder Consultancy (specialising in communication in construction), 1987; Director: Communication in Construction Ltd, 1990–; Jarvis PLC, 1995–. Principal architectural works in commercial and industrial architecture and environmental and urban planning in UK and abroad; consultant: to NCB for Vale of Belvoir coal mining project, 1975–87; to BR for re-use of Engrg Works, Shildon and Swindon, 1985–86; Consultant Architect, RCS, 1974–87; Architect/Planning Consultant, Marine Soc., 1990–. Royal Institute of British Architects: Mem. Council, 1967–89, 1993–; Hon. Treasurer, 1975–78; Vice-Pres., Membership Communications, 1989–90; Hon. Sec./Treasurer, Commonwealth Assoc. of Architects, 1985–87; Chm. Organising Cttee, IUA Congress 1987. Pres., Norwood Soc., 1981–92. Columnist: Building magazine, 1969–78, 1983–90; Building Design magazine, 1978–81, 1994–95; Editor and Presenter, Architectural Practice Video Magazine, 1987–90; Consultant and Presenter: RIBA Technical Seminar Prog., 1985–93; Building

Design Update Seminars, 1994–. Occasional radio and TV broadcaster, UK and USA. British Kart Racer, 1961–63; survivor, Lakonia cruise-liner disaster, 1963. FRSA 1984. Mem., British Acad. of Experts, 1991. RIBA Architecture Bronze Medal (for Eros House, Catford), 1963; various Civic Trust architectural and housing awards and commendations; Silver Jubilee Medal, for Housing Strategy for the 80s, Town Planning Assoc., 1981; Business Columnist of the Year, Publisher magazine, 1985. Arkansas Traveller, USA, 1971. *Publications:* Sports Stadia after Hillsborough, 1990; contribs on architectural, planning and building matters to various jls. *Recreations:* writing, swimming, photography, theatre, playing golf badly, supporting Arsenal FC avidly. *Address:* 2 Smith Square, SW1P 3HS. *Club:* Royal Automobile.

LUDLOW, Bishop Suffragan of, since 1994; **Rt. Rev. John Charles Saxbee,** PhD; Archdeacon of Ludlow, since 1992; *b* 7 Jan. 1946; *s* of Charles Albert Saxbee and Florence Violet Saxbee (*née* Harris); *m* 1965, Jacqueline Margaret Carol Saxbee (*née* Skym); one *d. Educ:* Cotham Grammar Sch., Bristol; Bristol Univ. (BA 1968); Durham Univ. (DipTh 1969; PhD 1976); Cranmer Hall, Durham. Ordained deacon, 1972, priest, 1973; Asst Curate, Emmanuel with St Paul, Plymouth, 1972–77; Vicar of St Philip, Weston Mill, Plymouth, 1977–81; Team Vicar, Central Exeter Team Ministry, 1981–87; Dir, SW Ministry Training Course, 1981–92; Priest-in-Charge of Holy Trinity, Wistanstow with St Michael, Cwm Head and St Margaret, Acton Scott, 1992–94. Prebendary: of Exeter Cathedral, 1988–92; of Hereford Cathedral, 1992–. *Publication:* Liberal Evangelism: a flexible response to the decade, 1994. *Recreations:* Victorian novels, televised sport, most kinds of music. *Address:* Bishop's House, Halford, Craven Arms, Shropshire SY7 9BT. *T:* Craven Arms (01588) 673571.

LUDLOW, Archdeacon of; *see* Ludlow, Bishop Suffragan of.

LUDLOW, (Ernest John) Robin, TD 1979; Managing Consultant, Euro Management Search, since 1990; *b* 2 May 1931; *s* of late Donald Ernest Ludlow, Blandford, Dorset, and Buxted, Sussex; *m* 1970, Sonia Louise Hatfeild (marr. diss. 1993); one *s* one *d. Educ:* Framlingham Coll., Suffolk. RMA Sandhurst, 1949–52; commissioned RASC, 1952; Staff, RMA Sandhurst, 1954–57; retd 1957. J. Lyons & Co. Ltd, 1957–59; The Economist, 1959–72; Press Sec. to the Queen, 1972–73; Dep. Dir, Aims of Industry, 1973–77; Head of Publicity, Strutt and Parker, 1977; Man. Dir, Kiernan and Co. Ltd (Exec. Search), 1977–79; Partner, Boyden Internat. (Exec. Search), 1979–81; Managing Director: Robin Ludlow & Associates (Exec. Search), 1981–89; Management Search Internat., 1985–89. Governor: Clergy Orphan Corp., 1973–83; Royal Star and Garter Home for Disabled Servicemen, 1987–91; Chairman: The Yeomanry Benevolent Fund, 1981–90; Sharpshooters Yeomanry Assoc., 1973–83. Kent and Co. of London Yeomanry (Sharpshooters), TA, 1959–69; The Queen's Regt, TA, 1971–78 (Maj.). Vice Chm., SE, TA&VRA, 1988–91 (Mem., F and GP Cttee, 1973–86; Mem., 1973–86, Chm., 1988–91, Kent Cttee). *Recreations:* shooting, gardening, conservation. *Club:* Cavalry and Guards.

LUDMAN, Harold, FRCS; Consultant Surgeon in Neuro-otology, National Hospital for Neurology and Neurosurgery, since 1967; Consultant Surgeon to Ear, Nose and Throat Department, King's College Hospital, 1965–94; *b* 23 Feb. 1933; *s* of Nathan Ludman and Fanny Dinah Jerome; *m* 1957, Lorraine Israel; one *s* one *d. Educ:* Bradford Grammar Sch.; Sidney Sussex Coll., Cambridge (BA 1954; MB, BChir 1957; MA 1958). FRCS 1961. House Physician, UCH, 1957; House Surgeon: Royal Ear Hosp., UCH, 1957; Edgware Gen. Hosp., 1958; Royal Marsden Hosp., 1958–59; Registrar and Sen. Registrar, Ear, Nose and Throat Dept, KCH, 1960–65. President: British Assoc. Otolaryngology, 1990–93; Section of Otology, RSocMed, 1985; Chm., Soc. Audiology Technicians, 1967–75. Chm., Specialist Adv. Cttee in Otolaryngology, Jt Cttee Higher Surgical Trng, 1988–91; Mem., Intercollegiate Bd in Otolaryngology, RCS (formerly Mem. Court of Examiners); Chm., working party on deafness, MRC, 1973–77; formerly Mem., Hearing Aid Council. W. J. Harrison Prize, RSocMed, 1987; W. Jobson Horne Prize, BMA, 1990. *Publications:* (jtly) Diseases of the Ear, 1963, 5th edn 1988; (contrib.) Scott-Brown's Diseases of the Ear, Nose and Throat, 4th edn 1979, 5th edn 1987; contribs to books on ear diseases; numerous papers to learned jls on diseases of the ear. *Recreations:* computers, reading, theatre, walking on the flat. *Address:* 149 Harley Street, W1N 2DE. *T:* 0171–935 4444.

LUDWIG, Christa; singer; *b* Berlin, 16 March; *d* of Anton Ludwig, singer, stage director and opera general manager and Eugenie (*née* Besalla), singer; *m* 1st, 1957, Walter Berry (marr. diss. 1970), baritone; one *s*; 2nd, 1972, Paul-Emile Deiber, actor and stage-director. *Educ:* Matura. Staedtische Buehnen, Frankfurt; Landestheater Darmstadt; Landestheater, Hannover; Vienna State Opera; guest appearances in New York, Chicago, London, Berlin, Munich, Tokyo, Milan, Rome, Lucerne, Salzburg, Epidauros, Zürich, Holland, Los Angeles, Cleveland, Saratoga, Bayreuth, Copenhagen, Gent, Montreal, Prague, Budapest and others. Kammersängerin, Austria, 1962; Grand Prix du Disque, 1966; Mozart Medal, Mozartgemeinde, Vienna, 1969; First Class Art and Science, Austria, 1969; Deutscher Schallplattenpreis, 1970; Orphée d'Or, 1970; Prix des Affaires Culturelles, 1972; Vienna Philharmonic Silver Rose, 1980; Hugo Wolf Medal, 1980; Gustav Mahler Medal, 1980; Ehrenring, Staatsoper Vienna, 1980, Hon. Mem., 1981; Golden Medal, City of Salzburg, 1987, and Vienna, 1987; Echo Prize, Germany, 1994. Commandeur des Arts et des Lettres (France), 1988; Chevalier, Légion d'Honneur (France), 1989. *Recreations:* listening to music, theatre, concerts, reading. *Address:* c/o Heidrun Artmüller, Goethegasse 1, 1010 Wien, Austria; Rigistrasse 14, 6045 Meggen, Switzerland.

LUFF, Rev. Canon Alan Harold Frank; Canon Residentiary of Birmingham Cathedral, since 1992; *b* 6 Nov. 1928; *s* of Frank Luff and late Elsie Lilian Luff (*née* Down), Bristol; *m* 1956, Enid Meirion, *d* of late Robert Meirion Roberts and Daisy Harker Roberts; three *s* one *d. Educ:* Bristol Grammar School; University Coll., Oxford (BA 1951, Dip. Theol. 1952, MA 1954); Westcott House, Cambridge. ARCM 1977. Deacon, 1956; priest, 1957; Assistant Curate: St Mathew, Stretford, Manchester, 1956–59; St Peter, Swinton, Manchester (with charge of All Saints, Wardley), 1959–61; Precentor of Manchester Cathedral, 1961–68; Vicar of Dwygyfylchi (otherwise Penmaenmawr), Gwynedd, dio. Bangor, 1968–79; Precentor, 1979–92, also Sacrist, 1979–86, Westminster Abbey. Chm., Hymn Soc. of Great Britain and Ireland, 1987–93 (Hon. Sec., 1973–86). Hon. FGCM 1993. *Publications:* Hymns and Psalms (composer and author), 1981; Welsh Hymns and their tunes, 1990; (ed) Story Song, 1993; contribs to New Christian, Musical Times, Choir and Organ, etc. *Recreations:* singing, conducting, cooking. *Address:* 119 Selly Park Road, Birmingham B29 7HY. *T:* 0121–472 0146.

LUFF, Geoffrey Shadrack, IPFA; County Treasurer, Nottinghamshire County Council, 1984–91; *b* 12 July 1933; *s* of Shadrack Thomas Luff and Rosie Winifred Luff (*née* Lister); *m* 1956, Gloria Daphne Taylor; one *s* one *d. Educ:* Mundella Grammar Sch., Nottingham. Various posts in City Treasury, Nottingham CC, 1949–67; Sen. Technical Asst and Asst Bor. Treasurer, Derby CBC, 1967–73; Asst County Treasurer, Derbyshire CC, 1973–78; Dep. County Treasurer, Nottinghamshire CC, 1978–84. *Recreations:* bowls, gardening, birdwatching, photography.

LUFF, Peter James; MP (C) Worcester, since 1992; *b* 18 Feb. 1955; *s* of Thomas Luff and Joyce (*née* Mills); *m* 1982, Julia Jenks; one *s* one *d. Educ:* Windsor Grammar Sch.; Corpus Christi Coll., Cambridge (MA Econs). Research Asst to Rt Hon. Peter Walker, 1977–80; Head of Private Office to Rt Hon. Edward Heath, 1980–82; Dir, Good Relations Public Affairs, 1982–87; Special Advr to Rt Hon. Lord Young of Graffham, 1987–89; Sen. Consultant, Lowe Bell Communications, 1989–90; Asst Man. Dir, Good Relations Ltd, 1990–92. PPS to Minister for Industry and Energy, 1993–. Patron, Conservative Students, 1995–. *Recreations:* performing arts, steam railways. *Address:* House of Commons, SW1A 0AA. *T:* Worcester (01905) 763952. *Clubs:* Royal Automobile; Worcestershire CC.

LUFFINGHAM, Prof. John Kingley, FDSRCSE; Professor of Orthodontics, University of Glasgow, 1976–93; *b* 14 Aug. 1928; *s* of Alfred Hulbert Carr Luffingham and Frances Tugby; *m* 1968, Elizabeth Margaret Anderson; two *s* one *d. Educ:* Haileybury; London Hosp. Med. Coll. (BDS, PhD London); Dip. Orth RCSE. House Surgeon, London Hosp. Med. Coll., 1957–58; Registrar, KCH, 1959–61; Clinical Research Fellow, MRC, 1961–64; Sen. Registrar, Guy's Hosp., 1965–67; Sen. Lectr, Glasgow Univ., 1968–76; Consultant Orthodontist, Greater Glasgow Health Board, 1968–76. *Publications:* articles in dental jls, incl. British Jl of Orthodontics, European Jl of Orthodontics, Archives of Oral Biology. *Recreations:* sailing, skiing.

LUFT, His Honour Arthur Christian, CBE 1988; Member, Legislative Council, Isle of Man, since 1988; *b* 21 July 1915; *e s* of late Ernest Christian Luft and late Phoebe Luft; *m* 1950, Dorothy, *yr d* of late Francis Manley; two *s. Educ:* Bradbury Sch., Cheshire. Served Army, 1940–46. Admitted to Manx Bar, 1940; Attorney-Gen., IOM, 1972–74; Second Deemster, 1974–80; HM's First Deemster, Clerk of the Rolls, and Dep. Governor, IOM, 1980–88. Chairman: IOM Criminal Injuries Compensation Tribunal, 1974–80; Prevention of Fraud (Unit Trust) Tribunal, 1974–80; IOM Licensing Appeal Court, 1974–80; Wireless Telegraphy Appeal Bd for IOM, 1974–80; IOM Income Tax Appeal Comrs, 1980–88; IOM Gaming Control Comrs, 1988–90; Rivers Pollution Cttee, 1989–92; Data Protection Tribunal, 1990–92; IOM Arts Council, 1992–; Member: Dept of Local Govt and Envmt, IOM, 1988–93; Dept of Agric., Fisheries and Forestry, IOM, 1993–; Public Accounts Cttee, 1988–; Ecclesiastical Cttee of Tynwald, 1992–; Standing Orders Cttee of Legislative Council. Chm., Legislative Cttee, Diocesan Synod., 1989–. Pres., Youth Adv. Gp, 1991–94. Pres., Manx Deaf Soc., 1975–. Pres., IOM Cricket Club, 1980. *Recreations:* theatre, watching cricket, gardening. *Address:* Leyton, Victoria Road, Douglas, Isle of Man IM2 6AQ. *T:* Douglas (01624) 621048. *Clubs:* Ellan Vannin, Manx Automobile (Douglas).

LUKE, 2nd Baron *cr* 1929, of Pavenham; **Ian St John Lawson Johnston,** KCVO 1976; TD; DL; JP; *b* 7 June 1905; *e s* of 1st Baron and Hon. Edith Laura (*d* 1941), *d* of 16th Baron St John of Bletsoe; *S* father, 1943; *m* 1932, Barbara, *d* of Sir FitzRoy Hamilton Anstruther-Gough-Calthorpe, 1st Bt; four *s* one *d. Educ:* Eton; Trinity Coll., Cambridge, MA. Life President, Electrolux Ltd, 1978– (Chm., 1963–78); Chm., Gateway Building Society, 1978–86; Dir, Ashanti Goldfields Corporation Ltd and other companies; Chm., Bovril Ltd, 1943–70. One of HM Lieutenants, City of London, 1953–. Hon. Col 5th Bn Beds Regt, 1947–62; OC 9th Bn Beds and Herts Regt, 1940–43; Chairman: Area Cttee for National Fitness in Herts and Beds, 1937–39; London Hospitals Street Collections Cen. Cttee, 1943–45; Beds TAA, 1943–46; Duke of Gloucester's Red Cross and St John Fund, 1943–46; Nat. Vice-Pres., Royal British Legion; Chm., National Playing Fields Assoc., 1950–76 (a Vice-Pres., 1977–); an Hon. Sec., Assoc. of British Chambers of Commerce, 1944–52; Mem. of Church Assembly (House of Laity), 1935; Lay Reader, St Alban's dio., 1933–; Mem., International Olympic Cttee, 1951–88, Hon. Mem., 1988–; President: Incorporated Sales Managers Assoc., 1953–56; Advertising Assoc., 1955–58; Outdoor Advertising Council, 1957; Operation Britain Organisation, 1957–62; London Chamber of Commerce, 1952–55; Inst. of Export, 1973–83; Chm. Governors, Queen Mary Coll., Univ. of London, 1963–82, Fellow, 1980. MFH Oakley Hunt, 1947–49. CC, DL, JP, Bedfordshire. *Heir: s* Hon. Arthur Charles St John Lawson Johnston, DL [*b* 13 Jan. 1933; *m* 1st, 1959, Silvia Maria (marr. diss. 1971), *yr d* of Don Honorio Roigt and Doña Dorothy Goodall de Roigt; one *s* two *d*; 2nd, 1971, Sarah, *d* of Richard Hearne; one *s*]. *Address:* Odell Castle, Odell, Beds MK43 7BB. *T:* Bedford (01234) 720240. *Club:* Carlton.

See also Hon. H. de B. Lawson Johnston.

LUKES, Prof. Steven Michael, DPhil; FBA 1987; Professor of Political and Social Theory, European University Institute, Florence, since 1987; *b* 8 March 1941; *o s* of S. Lukes; *m* 1977, Nina Vera Mary Stanger; two *s* one *d. Educ:* Royal Grammar School, Newcastle upon Tyne; Balliol Coll., Oxford (MA 1965; DPhil 1968). Student, 1962–64, Res. Fellow, 1964–66, Nuffield Coll., Oxford; Fellow of Balliol Coll., Oxford, 1966–88; Lectr in Politics, Oxford Univ., 1967–88. *Publications:* (ed jtly) The Good Society, 1972; Emile Durkheim: his life and work, 1972; Individualism, 1973; Power: a radical view, 1974; Essays in Social Theory, 1976; (ed) Durkheim: Rules of Sociological Method, 1982; (ed jtly) Rationality and Relativism, 1982; (ed jtly) Durkheim and the Law, 1984; Marxism and Morality, 1985; (jtly) No Laughing Matter: a collection of political jokes, 1985; (ed) Power, 1986; Moral Conflict and Politics, 1991; The Curious Enlightenment of Professor Caritat: a comedy of ideas, 1995. *Recreation:* playing jazz piano. *Address:* European University Institute, Badia Fiesolana, Via dei Roccetini 9, 50016 San Domenico di Fiesole, Florence, Italy. *T:* (55) 50921.

LUMET, Sidney; film director; *b* Philadelphia, 25 June 1924; *o s* of Baruch and Eugenia Lumet; *m* Rita Gam (marr. diss.); *m* 1956, Gloria Vanderbilt (marr. diss. 1963); *m* 1963, Gail Jones (marr. diss. 1978); two *d*; *m* 1980, Mary Gimbel. *Educ:* Professional Children's Sch., NY; Columbia Univ. Served US Army, SE Asia, 1942–46. Appeared as child actor: Dead End; The Eternal Road; Sunup to Sunday; Schoolhouse on the Lot; My Heart's in the Highlands; Dir, Summer Stock, 1947–49; taught acting, High Sch. of Professional Arts; Associate Dir, CBS, 1950, Dir, 1951–57. *TV shows include:* Danger; Your Are There; Alcoa: The Sacco and Vanzetti Story; Goodyear Playhouse; Best of Broadway; Omnibus. *Films directed include:* Twelve Angry Men, 1957; Stage Struck, 1958; That Kind of Woman, 1959; The Fugitive Kind, 1960; A View from the Bridge, Long Day's Journey into Night, 1962; Fail Safe, 1964; The Pawnbroker, The Hill, 1965; The Group, 1966; The Deadly Affair, 1967; Bye Bye Braverman, Last of the Mobile Hot Shots, Child's Play, The Seagull, 1969; The Anderson Tapes, 1971; The Offence, 1973; Serpico, Murder on the Orient Express, 1974; Dog Day Afternoon, 1975; Network, 1977; Equus, 1977; The Wiz, 1979; Just Tell Me What You Want, 1979; Prince of the City, 1980; Deathtrap, 1981; The Verdict, 1982; Daniel, 1983; Garbo Talks, 1984; Power, 1985; The Morning After, 1987; Family Business, 1990; Q & A, 1991; A Stranger Among Us, 1992; Guilty as Sin, 1993; *play:* Caligula, 1960. *Address:* c/o Jeff Berg, ICM, 8899 Beverly Boulevard, Los Angeles, Calif 90048, USA.

LUMLEY, family name of **Earl of Scarbrough.**

LUMLEY, Viscount; Richard Osbert Lumley; *b* 18 May 1973; *s* and *heir* of 12th Earl of Scarbrough, *qv.*

LUMLEY-SAVILE, family name of **Baron Savile.**

LUMSDAINE, Nicola Frances; *see* LeFanu, N. F.

LUMSDEN, Prof. Andrew Gino, PhD; FRS 1994; Professor of Developmental Neurobiology, United Medical and Dental Schools of Guy's and St Thomas' Hospitals, London University, since 1989; *b* 22 Jan. 1947; *s* of Dr Edward Gilbert Sita-Lumsden, MD and Stella Pirie Lumsden; *m* 1970, Anne Farrington Roberg; two *d*. *Educ:* Kingswood Sch., Bath; St Catharine's Coll., Cambridge (BA 1968; MA 1972; Frank Smart Scholar); Yale Univ.; PhD London 1978. Fulbright Scholar, 1968–70; Lectr in Anatomy, 1973–87, Reader in Craniofacial Biology, 1987–89, Guy's Hosp. Med. Sch. Miller Foundn Vis. Prof., Univ. of California, Berkeley, 1994; Lectr, Coll. de France, Paris, 1991; Yntema Lectr, SUNY, 1993; Howard Hughes Internat. Res. Scholar, 1993–; Jenkinson Meml Lectr, Univ. of Oxford, 1994. Médaille de la Ville de Paris, 1986. *Publications:* reports in learned jls. *Recreations:* mechanical engineering, natural history, Lotus sevens. *Address:* 23 Coates Hill Road, Bickley, Kent BR1 2BJ.

LUMSDEN, Sir David (James), Kt 1985; Principal, Royal Academy of Music, 1982–93; *b* Newcastle upon Tyne, 19 March 1928; *m* 1951, Sheila Daniels; two *s* two *d*. *Educ:* Dame Allan's Sch., Newcastle upon Tyne; Selwyn Coll., Cambridge (Hon. Fellow, 1986). Organ scholar, Selwyn Coll., Cambridge, 1948–51; BA Class I, 1950; MusB (Barclay Squire Prize) 1951; MA 1955; DPhil 1957. Asst Organist, St John's Coll., Cambridge, 1951–53; Res. Student, 1951–54; Organist and Choirmaster, St Mary's, Nottingham, 1954–56; Founder and Conductor, Nottingham Bach Soc., 1954–59; Rector Chori, Southwell Minster, 1956–59; Dir of Music, Keele, 1958–59; Prof. of Harmony, Royal Academy of Music, 1959–61; Fellow and Organist, New Coll., Oxford, and Lectr in the Faculty of Music, Oxford Univ., 1959–76; Principal, RSAMD, Glasgow, 1976–82. Conductor: Oxford Harmonic Soc., 1961–63; Oxford Sinfonia, 1967–70; BBC Scottish Singers, 1977–80; Organist, Sheldonian Theatre, 1964–76; Choragus, Oxford Univ., 1968–72. Harpsichordist to London Virtuosi, 1972–75. Member of Board: Scottish Opera, 1977–83; ENO, 1983–88. President: Inc. Assoc. of Organists, 1966–68; ISM, 1984–85; RCO, 1986–88; Chairman: NYO, 1985–94; Early Music Soc., 1985–89. Hugh Porter Lectr, Union Theological Seminary, NY, 1967; Vis. Prof., Yale Univ., 1974–75. Hon. Editor, Church Music Soc., 1970–73. Hon. FRCO 1976; Hon. RAM 1978; FRCM 1980; FRNCM 1981; FRSAMD 1982; Hon. GSM 1984; FLCM 1985; FRSA 1985; FRSCM 1987; Hon. FTCL 1988; FKC 1991. Hon. DLitt Reading, 1990. *Publications:* An Anthology of English Lute Music, 1954; Thomas Robinson's Schoole of Musicke, 1603, 1971; Articles in: The Listener; The Score; Music and Letters: Galpin Soc. Jl; La Luth et sa Musique; La Musique de la Renaissance, etc. *Recreations:* reading, theatre, photography, travel, hill-walking, etc. *Address:* Melton House, Soham, Cambs CB7 5DB.

LUMSDEN, George Innes, FRSE; CGeol, FGS, consultant in geology and scientific staff recruitment, since 1991; *b* 27 June 1926; *s* of George Lumsden and Margaret Ann Frances Lumsden (*née* Cockburn); *m* 1958, Sheila Thomson; two *s* one *d*. *Educ:* Banchory Academy; Aberdeen University (Lyon Prize in Geol.; BSc). Geological Survey of GB, 1949; District Geologist S Scotland, 1970, Asst Dir and Sen. Officer Scotland, 1980, Inst. of Geol Scis; British Geological Survey: CSO and Dep Dir, 1982–85; Dir, 1985–87; Mem., CS Commn Sci. Div's Panel of Chairmen, 1988–91. Member: Council of Management, Macaulay Inst. for Soil Research, 1980–87; Engineering and Sci. Adv. Cttee, Derby Coll. of Higher Educn, 1983–87; Geol. Museum Adv. Panel, 1985–87; Chm., Dirs of Western European Geol Surveys' Standing Gp on Envmtl Geology, 1984–87, Hon. Pres., 1987–, Hon. Sec., 1988–. FRSA. *Publications:* (ed) Geology and the Environment in Western Europe, 1992, 2nd edn 1994; maps, papers and books on geol topics in official Geol Survey. *Recreations:* music, theatre, sport, gardening, word processing. *Address:* 3 Barn Close, Cumnor Hill, Oxford OX2 9JP. *T:* Oxford (01865) 864203.

LUMSDEN, James Alexander, MBE 1945; TD 1962; DL; Partner, Maclay, Murray & Spens, Solicitors, Glasgow and Edinburgh, 1947–82; *b* 24 Jan. 1915; *s* of late Sir James Robert Lumsden and Lady (Henrietta) Lumsden (*née* Macfarlane Reid); *m* 1947, Sheila, *d* of late Malcolm Cross and Evelyn Cross (*née* Newlands); three *s*. *Educ:* Rugby Sch.; Corpus Christi Coll., Cambridge (BA, MA 1995; LLB). Director: Bank of Scotland, 1958–85; Weir Group PLC, 1957–84; William Baird PLC, 1959–84; Murray Growth Trust PLC and other companies in Murray Johnstone Group, 1967–85 (Chm., 1971–84); Scottish Provident Instn, 1968–85 (Chm., 1977–83); Burmah Oil Co. Ltd, 1957–76 (Chm., 1971–75). Mem. Jenkins Cttee on Company Law. Mem., Queen's Body Guard for Scotland, Royal Company of Archers, 1963–. DL Dunbartonshire, 1966. *Recreations:* shooting and other country pursuits. *Address:* Bannachra, Helensburgh, Dunbartonshire G84 9EF. *T:* Arden (01389) 850653. *Clubs:* Caledonian; New (Edinburgh); Western (Glasgow).

LUMSDEN, Prof. Keith Grant, FRSE; Director, The Esmée Fairbairn Research Centre, Heriot-Watt University, since 1975; *b* 7 Jan. 1935; *s* of Robert Sclater Lumsden and Elizabeth Brow; *m* 1961, Jean Baillie Macdonald; one *s*. *Educ:* Univ. of Edinburgh (MA Hons Econ 1959); Stanford Univ., California (PhD 1968). FRSE 1992. Stanford University: Instructor, Dept of Econs, 1960–63; Asst Prof., Graduate Sch. of Business, 1964–67; Research Associate, Stanford Res. Inst., 1965–71; Associate Prof., Grad. Sch. of Business, 1968–75. Vis. Prof., Heriot-Watt Univ., 1969–70; Affiliate Prof. of Econs, INSEAD, 1975; Acad. Dir, Sea Transport Exec. Programme, 1979; Prof. of Econs, Advanced Management Coll., Stanford Univ., 1971. Director: Economic Educn Project, 1969–74; Behavioral Res. Labs, 1970–72; Capital Preservation Fund, 1971–75; Nielsen Engineering Research, 1972–75; Hewlett-Packard Ltd, 1981–92. *Publications:* The Free Enterprise System, 1963; The Gross National Product, 1964; International Trade, 1965; (jtly) Macroeconomics, 1966, 4th edn 1981; (jtly) Macroeconomics, 1966, 4th edn 1981; (ed) New Development in the Teaching of Economics, 1967; Excess Demand and Excess Supply in World Tramp Shipping Markets, 1968; (ed) Recent Research in Economics Education, 1970; (jtly) Basic Economics: theory and cases, 1973, 2nd edn 1977; (ed) Efficiency in Universities: the La Paz papers, 1974; (jtly) Division Management Simulation, 1978; (jtly) Economics Education in the UK, 1980; (jtly) Basic Macroeconomic Models, 1981; (jtly) Running the British Economy, 1981, 6th edn 1990; (jtly) Managing the Australian Economy, 1985; (jtly) Shipping Management Model—Stratship, 1983; (jtly) Macroeconomic Database, 1984; (jtly) Strategies for Life—Stratlife, 1988; Economics, 1991; articles in professional jls. *Recreations:* tennis, deep sea game fishing. *Address:* 40 Lauder Road, Edinburgh EH9 1UE. *Clubs:* New (Edinburgh); Waverley Lawn Tennis & Squash (Edinburgh); Dalmahoy Golf and Leisure (Kirknewton); Tantallon Golf (N Berwick).

LUNCH, John, CBE 1975; VRD 1965; FCA, FCIT; Director-General of the Port of London Authority, and Board Member, 1971–76; Chairman: Comprehensive Shipping Group, 1973–75; Transcontinental Air Ltd, 1973–75; *b* 11 Nov. 1919; *s* of late Percy Valentine Lunch and late Amy Lunch (*née* Somerville); *m* 1943, Joyce Barbara Clerke (*d* 1989); two *s*. *Educ:* Roborough Sch., Eastbourne. Served War, Lt RNVR, Medit. and Home Fleets, 1939–46 (N Atlantic convoys, Crete, N Africa, Malta convoys, Sicily D-Day landings; Torpedo specialist, 1944), subseq. Permanent RNVR, later RNR; Lt-Comdr RNR, retd list, 1969; Lt-Col RE (TA), Engr and Transport Staff Corps (formerly Engr and Railway Staff Corps), 1971, Col, 1976, retd list, 1994. In business in City, 1946–48: Asst Man. Dir, Tokenhouse Securities Corp. Ltd, 1947, and dir several cos; British Transport Commn, 1948–61: road and rail transport and ancillary businesses; PLA, 1961; Dir of Finance, also Dir of Commerce, 1966; Asst Dir-Gen., responsible docks and harbour, 1969; Chairman: (and founder) PLA Port Users Consultative Cttee, 1966–71; Internat. Port Develt Cttee, Internat. Assoc. of Ports and Harbors, 1972–76; Pres., Inst. of Freight Forwarders, 1972–73. Chm., London Industrial Chartered Accountants, 1971–72; Member Council: Inst. of Chartered Accountants, 1970–77; Chartered Inst. of Transport, 1973–76. Mem. Cttee of Management, 1977–94, a Vice-Pres., 1987–94, a Life Vice-Pres., 1994, RNLI; Founder Chm., RNLI Manhood Br., 1976–78; Pres., RNLI, Hayling Island Lifeboat Station, 1978–88; Hon. Art Adviser, RNLI, 1981–. Hon. Life Mem. Internat. Assoc. of Airport and Seaport Police, 1974. CIMgt (FBIM 1971); FCIM (FInstM 1973); FRSA (Council nominee) 1976; Hon. FIFF 1986. Freeman: City of London, 1970; Watermen & Lightermen's Co. of River Thames, 1970 (Court Mem., 1976–80, Hon. Court Mem., 1980–). ADC to Governor of Louisiana, with rank Adm., 1971–. Malta GC 50th Anniv. Medal, 1992. *Publications:* The Chartered Accountant in Top Management, 1965; A Plan for Britain's Ports, 1975. *Recreations:* sailing, art, opera, horse racing. *Address:* Martins, East Ashling, Chichester, West Sussex PO18 9AX. *T:* Bosham (01243) 575252; 97A York Mansions, Prince of Wales Drive, SW11 4BN. *T:* 0171–622 8100. *Clubs:* Army and Navy; Itchenor Sailing (West Sussex).

LUND, John Walter Guerrier, CBE 1975; FRS 1963; DSc, PhD; Botanist, at Windermere Laboratory of Freshwater Biological Association, 1945–78; Deputy Chief Scientific Officer; *b* 27 Nov. 1912; *s* of George E. Lund and Kate Lund (*née* Hardwick); *m* 1949, Hilda M. Canter; one *s* one *d*. *Educ:* Sedbergh Sch.; Univ. of Manchester; London Univ. (PhD 1939; DSc 1951). Demonstrator in Botany, Univ. of Manchester, also Queen Mary Coll. and Chelsea Polytechnic, Univ. of London, 1935–38; Temp. Lectr in Botany, Univ. of Sheffield, 1936; Staff Biologist, W Midland Forensic Science Laboratory, Birmingham, 1938–45. Hon. DSc Buckingham, 1988. *Publications:* papers and articles in scientific jls, symposium vols, etc. *Recreation:* gardening. *Address:* Ellerbeck, Ellerigg Road, Ambleside, Cumbria LA22 9EU. *T:* Ambleside (015394) 32369.

LUND, Prof. Raymond Douglas, PhD; FRS 1992; Duke-Elder Professor of Ophthalmology, Institute of Ophthalmology, London, since 1995; *b* 10 Feb. 1940; *s* of Henry Douglas Lund and Rose Lund; *m* 1963, Jennifer Sylvia Hawes; two *s*. *Educ:* University College London (BSc 1st cl. Hons, PhD). LRAM. Asst Lectr, then Lectr, Anatomy Dept, UCL, 1963–66; Res. Associate, Univ. of Pennsylvania, 1966–67; Asst Prof., Anatomy Dept, Univ. of Stanford, 1967–68; Asst Prof., then Prof., Depts of Biological Structure and Neurological Surgery, Univ. of Washington, 1968–79; Prof. and Chm., Dept of Anatomy, Univ. of S Carolina, 1979–83; Prof. and Chm., Dept of Neurobiology, Anatomy and Cell Sci., Univ. of Pittsburgh, 1983–91 (Dir, Centre for Neuroscience, 1984–87); Prof. and Head of Dept of Anatomy, and Fellow of Clare College, Cambridge, 1992–95. Chm. Scientific Cttee, Internat. Spinal Res. Trust, 1994–. NIH Merit Award, 1988. *Publications:* Development and Plasticity of the Brain, 1978; contribs to learned jls. *Recreation:* music. *Address:* Department of Patholgy, Institute of Ophthalmology, Bath Street, EC1V 9EL. *T:* 0171–608 6893.

LUND, Rodney Cookson; a Director: Short Brothers, since 1988 (Chairman, 1988–90); Hazlewood Foods, since 1991; *b* 16 June 1936; *s* of late Arthur and Doris Lund; *m* 1st, Lynda Brooks (marr. diss.); one *s*; 2nd, Hyacinth, (Miki), Wallace. *Educ:* Wallasey Grammar School; Liverpool University (BCom Hons). Served RAPC, 1957–59 (commissioned). Evans Medical, 1959; Carreras Rothmans, 1960–64; Partner, Urwick Orr & Partners, 1964–66 and 1969–73; Man. Dir, The Mace Voluntary Gp, 1966–69; Vice-Chm., Produce Importers Alliance, 1966–69; Exec. Director, Rank Radio International, 1973–75; British Sugar Corp., 1976–82; Woolworth Holdings, 1982–86; Chm., Nat. Bus Co., 1986–88 (Part-time Mem., 1989–92). Mem., Nationalised Industries Chairmen's Gp, 1986–88; Chm., The Enterprise Support Gp, 1991–94. CIMgt. *Recreations:* travel, opera, cooking. *Address:* 18 Billing Road, Chelsea, SW10 9UL. *T:* 0171–352 2641.

LUNN, Rt. Rev. David Ramsay; *see* Sheffield, Bishop of.

LUNN, Peter Northcote, CMG 1957; OBE 1951; Secret Intelligence Service, retired 1986; *b* 15 Nov. 1914; *e s* of late Sir Arnold Lunn; *m* 1939, Hon. (Eileen) Antoinette (*d* 1976), *d* of 15th Viscount Gormanston; three *s* two *d* (and one *d* decd). *Educ:* Eton. Joined SIS, 1941; Malta, 1941–44; Italy, 1944–45; W Germany, 1945–46; London, 1946–47; Vienna, 1948–50; Bern, 1950–53; Berlin, 1953–56; London, 1956–57; Bonn, 1957–62; Beirut, 1962–67; London, 1967–86. Mem., Brit. International Ski team, 1931–37, Capt. 1934–37; Capt. British Olympic Ski team, 1936; competitor, Inferno downhill ski race, 1978–86, 1988–89, 1995. *Publications:* High-Speed Skiing, 1935; Evil in High Places, 1947; A Skiing Primer, 1948, rev. edn 1951; The Guinness Book of Ski-ing, 1983. *Club:* Ski Club of Great Britain.

LUNNY, William Francis; Sheriff of South Strathclyde, Dumfries and Galloway, since 1984; *b* 10 Dec. 1938; *s* of James F. Lunny and Sarah Ann Crawford or Lunny; *m* 1967, Elizabeth McDermott; two *s* one *d*. *Educ:* Our Lady's High School, Motherwell; Glasgow Univ. (MA, LLB). Solicitor, 1961–67; Depute Procurator Fiscal, 1967–74; Crown Counsel/Legal Draftsman, Antigua, 1974–76; Advocate, 1977. Barrister, Antigua, 1981. KHS 1989. *Recreations:* walking, travelling. *Address:* Sheriff's Chambers, Sheriff Court, Hamilton, Lanarkshire ML3 6AA. *T:* Hamilton (01698) 282957.

LUNS, Dr Joseph Marie Antoine Hubert; Officer, Order of Orange-Nassau, 1947; Knight Grand Cross, Order of the Netherlands Lion, 1971; Hon. GCMG; Hon. CH 1971; Secretary-General of NATO, 1971–84; *b* 28 Aug. 1911; *m* Baroness E. C. van Heemstra (*d* 1990); one *s* one *d*. *Educ:* sec. schs, Amsterdam and Brussels; universities of Leyden, Amsterdam, London and Berlin. Attaché of Legation, 1938; 2nd Sec., 1942; 1st Sec., 1945; Counsellor, 1949. Served in: Min. for For. Affairs, 1938–40; Berne, 1940–41; Lisbon, 1941–43; London, at Netherlands Min. for For. Affairs, 1943–44, and at Netherlands Embassy, 1944–49; Netherlands Delegn to UN, NY, 1942–52; Minister of Foreign Affairs, The Netherlands, 1952–71. MP (Second Chamber, Netherlands), July-Oct. 1956 and March-June 1959. Hon. Fellow, London Sch. of Economics, 1969. Prix Charlemagne, Aachen, 1967; Gustav Stresemann Medal, 1968. Hon. DCL: Harvard, 1970; Oxon, 1972; Exeter, 1974; Dr Humanities, Hope Coll., USA, 1974. Holds numerous foreign orders. *Publications:* The Epic of The Royal Netherlands Navy; articles on Royal Netherlands Navy in Dutch and foreign jls, and articles on international affairs in International Affairs, La Revue Politique, and others. *Recreation:* swimming. *Address:* 117 Avenue Franklin Roosevelt, 1050 Brussels, Belgium. *Clubs:* Athenæum, Reform (Hon. Mem.); Haagsche, De Witte (Netherlands).

LUNT, Maj.-Gen. James Doiran, CBE 1964 (OBE 1958); MA (Oxon); FRGS; FRHistS; Domestic Bursar, and Fellow, Wadham College, Oxford, 1973–83, now Emeritus Fellow; *b* 13 Nov. 1917; *s* of late Brig. W. T. Lunt, MBE, Camberley, Surrey; *m* 1940, Muriel, *d* of late A. H. Byrt, CBE, Bournemouth; one *s* one *d*. *Educ:* King William's Coll., IOM; RMC, Sandhurst. 2nd Lieut, Duke of Wellington's Regt, 1937; served with 4th Bn Burma Rifles, 1939–41; Burma Campaign, 1942; transf. to 16/5th Queen's Royal Lancers, 1949; served with Arab Legion, 1952–55; comd 16/5th Queen's Royal Lancers, 1957–59; comd Fed. Regular Army, Aden, 1961–64; Dir of Admin. Planning (Army), MoD,

1964–66; Defence Adviser to British High Commissioner, India, 1966–68; Chief of Staff, Contingencies Planning, SHAPE, 1969–70; Vice-Adjt-Gen., MoD, 1970–72; Col, 16th/5th The Queen's Royal Lancers, 1975–80. Order of Independence (Jordan), 1956; Commander, Order of South Arabia, 1964. *Publications:* Charge to Glory, 1961; Scarlet Lancer, 1964; The Barren Rocks of Aden, 1966; Bokhara Burnes, 1969; From Sepoy to Subedar, 1970; The Duke of Wellington's Regiment, 1971; 16th/5th The Queen's Royal Lancers, 1973; John Burgoyne of Saratoga, 1975; Imperial Sunset, 1981; Glubb Pasha, 1984; A Hell of a Licking: the retreat from Burma 1941–42, 1986; Hussein of Jordan, 1989; The Scarlet Lancers, 1993; Jai Sixth!: story of the 6th Gurkha Rifles, 1994. *Recreations:* fly fishing, writing. *Address:* Hilltop House, Little Milton, Oxon OX9 7PU. *T:* Great Milton (01844) 279242. *Clubs:* Cavalry and Guards, Flyfishers'.

LUPTON, Prof. Thomas; Professor of Organisational Behaviour, University of Manchester, 1966–86; Visiting Professor, Instituto de Estudios Superiores de la Empresa, Barcelona, since 1987; Director of International Programmes, Escuela de Alta Dirección y Administración, Barcelona, since 1990; *b* 4 Nov. 1918; *s* of Thomas Lupton, blacksmith, and Jane Lupton (*née* Vowell); *m* 1st, 1942, Thelma Chesney; one *d*; 2nd, 1963, Dr Constance Shirley Wilson; one *s* one *d*; 3rd, 1987, Dorothy Joyce Meredith. *Educ:* Elem. and Central Sch.; Technical Coll.; Ruskin Coll.; Oriel Coll., Oxford; Univ. of Manchester. DipEconPolSci (Oxon), MA (Oxon), PhD (Manch.). Served War, HM Forces, 1939–41 and 1944–46; Marine Engr, 1932–39, 1941–44. Research Posts: Liverpool Univ., 1951–54; Manchester Univ., 1954–57; Lectr in Sociology, Manchester Univ., 1957–59; Head of Dept of Industrial Admin, Coll. of Advanced Techn., Birmingham, 1959–64; Montague Burton Prof. of Ind. Rel., Univ. of Leeds, 1964–66; Dir, Manchester Business Sch., 1977–83. Gen. Editor, Jl of Management Studies, 1966–76; Dir, Pirelli General Cables Ltd, 1970–77; Member: Civil Service Arbitration Tribunal, 1967–70; Arbitration Panel, Dept of Employment, 1969–; various official commns and tribunals, 1960–. Hon. DSc Aston, 1987. *Publications:* On the Shop Floor, 1963; Industrial Behaviour and Personnel Management, 1964; Management and the Social Sciences, 1966, 3rd edn, 1983; Selecting a Wage Payment System (with D. Gowler), 1969; Job and Pay Comparisons (with A. M. Bowey), 1973; Wages and Salaries (with A. M. Bowey), 1974, rev. edn 1983; Achieving Change (with I. R. Tanner), 1987; articles in Jl of Management Studies, Manchester Sch., Production Engineer, etc. *Recreations:* golf, Association Football.

LUPU, Radu; pianist; *b* 30 Nov. 1945; *s* of Mayer Lupu, lawyer, and Ana Gabor, teacher of languages; *Educ:* Moscow Conservatoire. Debut at age of twelve with complete programme of own music; studied with Florica Muzicescu, Cella Delavrancea, Heinrich Neuhaus and Stanislav Neuhaus. 1st prize: Van Cliburn Competition, 1966; Enescu Internat. Competition, 1967; Leeds Internat. Pianoforte Competition, 1969. Numerous recordings include complete Mozart violin and piano sonatas, complete Beethoven Piano Concertos, 1979. *Recreations:* history, art, sport. *Address:* c/o Terry Harrison Artists Management, The Orchard, Market Street, Charlbury, Oxon OX7 3PJ. *T:* Charlbury (01608) 810330.

LURIE, Prof. Alison; writer; Professor of English, Cornell University, since 1976; *b* 3 Sept. 1926; *d* of Harry Lurie and Bernice Stewart; *m* 1948, Jonathan Bishop (marr. diss. 1985); three *s*. *Educ:* Radcliffe Coll., Cambridge, Mass (AB). *Publications:* Love and Friendship, 1962; The Nowhere City, 1965; Imaginary Friends, 1967 (televised, 1987); Real People, 1969; The War Between the Tates, 1974; Only Children, 1979; Foreign Affairs, 1984 (Pulitzer Prize, 1985); The Truth About Lorin Jones, 1988; (ed) The Oxford Book of Modern Fairy Tales, 1993; Women and Ghosts (short stories), 1994; *non-fiction:* The Language of Clothes, 1981; Don't Tell the Grown-ups, 1990; *children's books:* Clever Gretchen, 1980; The Heavenly Zoo, 1980; Fabulous Beasts, 1981. *Address:* c/o English Department, Cornell University, Ithaca, NY 14853, USA.

LUSBY, John Martin; Executive Director, Lothian Health Board, 1991–95 (Member, 1990–91, General Manager, 1990–95); *b* 27 April 1943; *s* of late William Henry Lusby and of Florence Mary (*née* Wharam); *m* 1966, Clare, *d* of late John Gargan; one *s* one *d*. *Educ:* Marist Coll., Hull; Ushaw Coll., Durham. DipHSM 1972; MHSM (AHA 1972). Entered NHS, 1961; junior appointments: De la Pole Hosp., Hull, 1961–66; County Hosp., York, 1966–67; Kettering Gen. Hosp., 1967–68; Admin. Asst, United Sheffield Hosps, 1968–70; Dep. Hosp. Sec., E Birmingham Hosp, 1970–72; Hosp. Sec., Pontefract Gen. Infirmary and Headlands Hosp., Pontefract, 1972–74; Area Gen. Administrator, Kirklees AHA, 1974–76; Asst Dist Administrator (Patient Services), 1976–79, Dist Administrator, Wandsworth and E Merton Dist, 1979–81, Merton, Sutton and Wandsworth AHA(T); Area Administrator, Doncaster AHA, 1981; Dist Administrator, 1981–84, Dist. Gen. Man., 1984–90, Exec. Dir, 1990, Doncaster HA. Member: Scottish Council for Postgrad. Med. and Dental Educn, 1992–95; Health Services and Public Health Res. Cttee, Chief Scientist Orgn, SHHD, 1993–95. Trustee: Dementia Services Develt Centre, Univ. of Stirling, 1991–; Scottish Dementia Appeal Trust, 1994–95. *Recreations:* music, reading, walking. *Address:* 95/6 Grange Loan, Edinburgh EH9 2ED. *T:* 0131–668 4281.

LUSCOMBE, Prof. David Edward, LittD; FSA; FRHistS; FBA 1986; Professor of Medieval History, University of Sheffield, since 1972; *b* 22 July 1938; *s* of Edward Dominic and Nora Luscombe; *m* 1960, Megan Phillips; three *s* one *d*. *Educ:* St Michael's Sch., North Finchley; Finchley Catholic Grammar Sch.; King's Coll., Cambridge (BA, MA, PhD, LittD). Fellow, King's Coll., Cambridge, 1962–64; Fellow and Dir of Studies in History, Churchill Coll., Cambridge, 1964–72; Sheffield University: Head of Dept of History, 1973–76, 1979–84; Dep. Dean, 1983–85, Dean, 1985–87, Faculty of Arts; Pro-Vice-Chancellor, 1990–94. Vis. Prof., Univ. of Connecticut, 1993; Leverhulme European Fellow, 1973; British Acad./RSC Exchange Visitor to Canada, 1991. Raleigh Lectr, British Acad., 1988. External examiner for higher degrees in Univs. of Cambridge, Oxford, London, Liverpool, Bangor, ANU, Toronto, Groningen, for BA degrees at Bangor, Leicester and Leeds. Dir, Historical Assoc. Summer Vacation Sch., 1976 and 1992. Member: Governing Body, later Assoc. St Edmund's House, Cambridge, 1971–84; Cttee, Ecclesiastical History Soc., 1976–79; Council, RHistS, 1981–85; Council, British Acad., 1989– (Publications Sec., 1990–95; Member: Medieval Texts Cttee, 1982– (Chm., 1991–); Publications Cttee, 1987– (Chm., 1990–); Postgrad. Studies Cttee, 1988–90; Humanities Res. Bd, 1994–); Cttee on Acad. Res. Projects, 1990–; Commonwealth Scholarships Commn in UK, 1994–; Auditor, HEQC, 1994–; Vice-Pres., Soc. internat. pour l'étude de la philosophie médiévale, 1987–. Gen. Editor, Cambridge Studies in Medieval Life and Thought, 4th series, 1988– (Adv. Editor, 1983–88); Mem., Jt Supervisory Cttee, British Acad./OUP, for New DNB, 1992– (Associate Editor, 1993–). *Publications:* The School of Peter Abelard, 1969; Peter Abelard's Ethics, 1971 (trans. Italian, 1976); (ed jtly) Church and Government in the Middle Ages, 1976; (ed jtly) Petrus Abaelardus 1079–1142: Person, Werk und Wirkung, 1980; (jtly) David Knowles Remembered, 1991; articles in learned jls. *Recreations:* walking a spaniel, swimming, using libraries. *Address:* 4 Caxton Road, Broomhill, Sheffield S10 3DE. *T:* Sheffield (0114) 268 6355.

LUSCOMBE, Rt. Rev. Lawrence Edward; Bishop of Brechin, 1975–90; Primus of the Episcopal Church in Scotland, 1985–90; *b* 10 Nov. 1924; *s* of Reginald John and Winifred Luscombe; *m* 1946, Doris Carswell Morgan, BSc, MB, ChB (*d* 1992); one *d*. *Educ:* Torquay Grammar Sch.; Kelham Theological Coll.; King's Coll., London; MA, MPhil 1991, PhD 1993, Dundee. CA 1952, ASAA 1957. FSAScot 1980. Served Indian Army, 1942–47, Major. Partner, Galbraith, Dunlop & Co., Chartered Accountants, Glasgow, 1952–63. Ordained deacon, 1963; priest, 1964; Curate, St Margaret's, Glasgow, 1963–66; Rector, St Barnabas', Paisley, 1966–71; Provost of St Paul's Cathedral, Dundee, 1971–75. Hon. Canon, Trinity Cathedral, Davenport, Iowa, 1983. Hon. Res. Fellow, Dundee Univ., 1993–. Chm. of Council, Glenalmond Coll., 1987–94. FRSA 1987. Hon. DLitt Geneva Theological Coll., 1972; Hon. LLD Dundee, 1987. OStJ 1986. *Address:* Woodville, Kirkton of Tealing, by Dundee DD4 0RD. *T:* Tealing (01382) 380331.

LUSH, Christopher Duncan, CMG 1983; HM Diplomatic Service, retired; Governor, British Institute of Human Rights, since 1988; Editor, Human Rights Case Digest, since 1989; *b* 4 June 1928; *s* of late Eric Duncan Thomas Lush and Iris Leonora (*née* Greenfield); *m* 1967, Marguerite Lilian, *d* of Frederick Albert Bolden; one *s*. *Educ:* Sedbergh; Magdalen Coll., Oxford. Called to Bar, Gray's Inn, 1953. Asst Legal Adviser, FO, 1959–62; Legal Adviser, Berlin, 1962–65, Dep. Political Adviser, Berlin, 1965–66; FO (later FCO), 1966–69; Head of Chancery, Amman, 1969–71; Head of Aviation and Telecommunications Dept, FCO, 1971–73; Canadian Nat. Defence Coll., 1973–74; Counsellor, Paris, 1974–78; Counsellor, Vienna, 1978–82; Ambassador and UK Perm. Rep. to Council of Europe, Strasbourg, 1983–86. Médaille de Vermeil, Société d'Encouragement au Progrès, 1978. *Publications:* articles in Internat. and Compar. Law Qly, Connoisseur. *Club:* Travellers'.

LUSH, Hon. Sir George (Hermann), Kt 1979; Justice, Supreme Court of Victoria, 1966–83; *b* 5 Oct. 1912; *s* of John Fullarton Lush and Dora Louise Emma Lush; *m* 1943, Winifred Betty Wragge; three *d*. *Educ:* Carey Grammar Sch.; Ormond Coll., Melbourne Univ. (LLM). Admitted, Victorian Bar, 1935; served War, Australian Imperial Forces, 1940–45; Lecturer, Mercantile Law, Melbourne Univ., 1947–55; QC: Victoria 1957, Tasmania 1958. Chairman, Victorian Bar Council, 1964–66; President: Medico-Legal Soc., Victoria, 1962–63; Australian Bar Assoc., 1964–66; Commissioner, Overseas Telecommunications Commn, 1961–66. Chancellor, Monash Univ., 1983–92 (Mem. Council, 1969–74); Chm. Council, Ormond Coll., 1981–90. Hon. LLD Monash, 1993. *Recreations:* tennis, walking. *Address:* 37 Rochester Road, Canterbury, Victoria 3126, Australia. *Clubs:* Melbourne, Melbourne Cricket (Melbourne); Lorne Country (Lorne, Vic.).

LUSHINGTON, Sir John (Richard Castleman), 8th Bt *cr* 1791, of South Hill Park, Berkshire; *b* 28 Aug. 1938; *s* of Sir Henry Edmund Castleman Lushington, 7th Bt and of Pamela Elizabeth Daphne, *er d* of Major Archer Richard Hunter; *S* father, 1988; *m* 1966, Bridget Gillian Margaret, *d* of late Colonel John Foster Longfield; three *s*. *Educ:* Oundle. Partner, Management and Skills Trng Orgn. *Heir: s* Richard Douglas Longfield Lushington, BA, Flight Lieut RAF, *b* 29 March 1968. *Address:* The Glebe House, Henham, Bishops Stortford, Herts CM22 6AH.

LÜST, Prof. Reimar; President, Alexander von Humboldt Foundation, Bonn, since 1989; Director General, European Space Agency, 1984–90; *b* 23 March 1923; *s* of Hero Lüst and Grete (*née* Strunck); *m* 1986, Nina Grunenberg; two *s* by a previous marriage. *Educ:* Univ. of Frankfurt; Univ. of Göttingen (Dr rer. nat.). Max-Planck-Institut of Physics: Staff Scientist, 1950–60; Head of Astrophysics Dept, 1960–63; Dir, Max-Planck-Institut of Extraterrestrial Physics, 1963–72; Pres., Max-Planck-Gesellschaft zur Förderung der Wissenschaften, 1972–84. Vis. Prof., Univs of Princeton, Chicago, New York, MIT, CIT, 1955–63; Hon. Prof., Technical Univ. of Munich, 1965; Prof., Univ. of Hamburg, 1992. Chm., German Science Council, 1969–72. Mem. and Hon. Mem. of eight academies. Dr *hc:* Sofia, 1991; Birmingham 1993. Planet No 4386 named Lüst, 1991. Adenauer-de Gaulle Prize, 1994. Grand Cross, Order of Merit (FRG), 1984; Officier, Légion d'Honneur (France), 1984; Grand Cross of Merit with Star and Shoulderblade (FRG), 1990. *Publications:* Hydrodynamik, 1955; articles in scientific jls. *Recreations:* tennis, history, ski-ing. *Address:* Max-Planck-Institute of Meterology, Bundesstrasse 55, 20146 Hamburg, Germany. *T:* (40) 41173300.

LUSTIGER, His Eminence Cardinal Jean-Marie; Archbishop of Paris, since 1981; *b* Paris, 1926. *Educ:* Carmelite Seminary; Institut Catholique de Paris; Sorbonne (Lèsl, LenThéol). Ordained priest, 1954. Chaplain to students, Sorbonne, Paris; Dir, Centre d'étudiants Richelieu, Paris, 1959–69; Parish Pastor, Sainte Jeanne de Chantal, Paris, 1969–79; Bishop of Orléans, 1979–81. Cardinal, 1983. *Publications:* Sermons d'un curé de Paris, 1978; Pain de vie, peuple de Dieu, 1981; Osez croire, 1985 (trans. Dare to Believe, 1986); Osez vivre, 1985 (trans. Dare to Live, 1989); Freude der Weihnacht, 1985, revd and enlarged edn as Petites Paroles de Nuit de Noël, 1992; Premiers pas dans la prière, 1986 (trans. First Steps in Prayer, 1988); Six sermons aux élus de la nation, 1987; The Mass, 1987 (abridged edn of La Messe, 1988); Le choix de Dieu, 1987 (trans. Choosing God, Chosen by God, 1990); The Lord's Prayer, 1988; Le Sacrement de l'onction des malades, 1990; Dieu merci, les droits de l'homme, 1990; Dare to Rejoice, 1990; Nous avons rendez-vous avec l'Europe, 1991. *Address:* Maison diocésaine, 8 rue de la Ville-l'Evêque, 75008 Paris, France.

LUSZTIG, Prof. George, PhD; FRS 1983; Professor of Mathematics, Massachusetts Institute of Technology, Cambridge, USA, since 1978; *b* 20 May 1946; *s* of Akos and Erzsébet Lusztig; *m* 1972, Michal-Nina Abraham; two *d*. *Educ:* Univ. of Bucharest, Rumania; Princeton Univ. (MA, PhD). Asst, Univ. of Timisoara, Rumania, 1969; Mem., Inst. for Advanced Study Princeton, 1969–71; Univ. of Warwick: Res. Fellow, 1971–72; Lectr in Maths, 1972–74; Prof. of Maths, 1974–78. Mem., US Nat. Acad. of Scis, 1992. *Publications:* The Discrete Series of GL_n over a Finite Field, 1974; and Characters of Reductive Groups over a Finite Field, 1984; Introduction to Quantum Groups, 1993. *Address:* 106 Grant Avenue, Newton, MA 02159, USA. *T:* (617) 9648579.

LUTHER, Rt. Rev. Arthur William; retired; *b* 21 March 1919; *s* of William and Monica Luther; *m* 1946, Dr Kamal Luther; one *s* two *d*. *Educ:* Nagpur University; India (MA, BT); General Theological Seminary, New York (STD 1957). Deacon, 1943; Priest, 1944; in USA and Scotland for study and parish work, 1952–54; Chaplain to Bishop of Nagpur, 1954; Head Master, Bishop Cotton School, Nagpur, 1954–57; Bishop of Nasik, 1957–70; Bishop of Bombay, 1970–73; held charge of Kolhapur Diocese concurrently with Bombay Diocese, Dec. 1970–Feb. 1972; Bishop, Church of North India, and Reg. Sec. of the Leprosy Mission, 1973–80; Promotional Sec., 1980–84. *Address:* Convent of St Mary, 5 Guruwar Peth, Panchhowd, Pune 411 042, Maharashtra, India. *T:* 423897.

LUTON, Jean-Marie; Chevalier de la Légion d'Honneur, 1992; Officier de l'Ordre National du Mérite, 1989; Director General, European Space Agency, since 1990; *b* Chamalières, 4 Aug. 1942; *m* 1967, Cécile Robine; three *s*. *Educ:* Ecole Polytechnique. Centre National de la Recherche Scientifique: researcher, 1964–71; Chargé de Recherches, 1971–74; Chargé de Mission, Service des Programmes des Organismes de Recherche, Min. for Industrial and Scientific Develt, 1971–73; Centre National d'Etudes Spatiales: Hd, Res. Progs Div., Progs and Indust. Policy Directorate, 1974–75; Hd, Planning and Projs Div., Progs and Indust. Policy Directorate, 1975–78; Dir, Progs and Planning,

1978–84; Dep. Dir. Gen., 1984–87; Dir for Space Progs, Space Systems Div., Aérospatiale, 1987–89; Dir Gen., Centre National d' Etudes Spatiales, 1989–90. Mem., Internat. Acad. of Astronautics, 1986–. Astronautics Prize, French Assoc. for Aeronautics and Astronautics, 1985. *Recreations:* tennis, sailing. *Address:* European Space Agency, 8-10 rue Mario Nikis, 75738 Paris, France.

LUTTRELL, Col Sir (Geoffrey) Walter (Fownes), KCVO 1993; MC 1945; JP; Lord-Lieutenant of Somerset, 1978–94; *b* 2 Oct. 1919; *s* of late Geoffrey Fownes Luttrell of Dunster Castle, Somerset; *m* 1942, Hermione Hamilton, *er d* of late Capt. Cecil Gunston, MC, and Lady Doris Gunston. *Educ:* Eton; Exeter Coll., Oxford. Served War of 1939–45, with 15th/19th King's Royal Hussars, 1940–46; North Somerset Yeomanry, 1952–57; Lt-Col 1955; Hon. Col, 6th Bn LI, TAVR, 1977–87; Col 1987. Liaison Officer, Ministry of Agriculture, 1965–71. Regional Dir, Lloyds Bank, 1972–83. Member: National Parks Commn, 1962–66; Wessex Regional Cttee, Nat. Trust, 1970–85; SW Electricity Bd, 1969–78; UGC, 1973–76. Pres., Royal Bath and West and Southern Counties Soc., 1983. DL Somerset, 1958–68, Vice Lord-Lieutenant, 1968–78; High Sheriff of Somerset, 1960; JP 1961. Hon. Col Somerset ACF, 1982–89. KStJ. *Address:* Court House, East Quantoxhead, Bridgwater, Somerset TA5 1EJ. *T:* Holford (01278) 741242. *Club:* Cavalry and Guards.

LUTYENS, Mary, (Mrs J. G. Links), FRSL; writer since 1929; *b* 31 July 1908; *y d* of late Sir Edwin Lutyens, OM, KCIE, PRA, and late Lady Emily Lutyens; *m* 1st, 1930, Anthony Sewell (marr. diss. 1945; decd); one *d*; 2nd, 1945, J. G. Links, OBE. *Educ:* Queen's Coll., London; Sydney, Australia. FRSL 1976. *Publications: fiction:* Forthcoming Marriages, 1933; Perchance to Dream, 1935; Rose and Thorn, 1936; Spider's Silk, 1939; Family Colouring, 1940; A Path of Gold, 1941; Together and Alone, 1942; So Near to Heaven, 1943; And Now There is You, 1953; Week-End at Hurtmore, 1954; The Lucian Legend, 1955; Meeting in Venice, 1956; Cleo, 1973; *for children:* Julie and the Narrow Valley, 1944; *autobiography:* To Be Young, 1959, repr. 1989; *edited:* Lady Lytton's Court Diary, 1961; (for Krishnamurti) Freedom from the Known, 1969; The Only Revolution, 1970; The Penguin Krishnamurti Reader, 1970; The Urgency of Change, 1971; (with Malcolm Warner) Rainy Days at Brig O'Turk, 1983; *biography:* Effie in Venice, 1965; Millais and the Ruskins, 1967; The Ruskins and the Grays, 1972; Krishnamurti: the years of awakening, 1975; The Lyttons in India, 1979; Edwin Lutyens, 1980, repr. 1991; Krishnamurti: the years of fulfilment, 1982; Krishnamurti: the open door, 1988; The Life and Death of Krishnamurti, 1990, repr. 1991; also numerous serials, afterwards published, under pseudonym of Esther Wyndham; contribs to TLS, Apollo, The Cornhill, The Walpole Soc. Jl. *Recreations:* reading, cinema-going. *Address:* 8 Elizabeth Close, Randolph Avenue, W9 1BN. *T:* 0171–286 6674.

LUTZ, Marianne Christine, (Mrs C. A. Whittington-Smith); Headmistress, Sheffield High School for Girls (Girls' Public Day School Trust), 1959–83; *b* 9 Dec. 1922; *d* of Dr H. Lutz; *m* 1981, Charles Alexander Whittington-Smith, LLM, FCA. *Educ:* Wimbledon High Sch., GPDST; Girton Coll., Cambridge (Schol.; MA Historical Tripos); University of London (DipEd, DipTh). Asst Mistress (History) at: Clergy Daughters' Sch., Bristol, 1946–47; South Hampstead High Sch., GPDST, 1947–59. Former Member: History Textbooks Panel for W Germany (under auspices of FO and Unesco); Professional Cttee, Univ. of Sheffield; Historical Assoc.; Secondary Heads' Assoc.; Schnauzer Club of Great Britain. *Publications:* several in connection with Unesco work and Historical Assoc. *Recreations:* crosswords, opera, art, theatre. *Address:* Evona, Hydro Close, Baslow, Bakewell, Derbyshire DE45 1SH. *T:* Baslow (01246) 582152.

LUXMOORE, Rt. Rev. Christopher Charles; Bishop of Bermuda, 1984–89; Assistant Bishop and Canon Emeritus of Chichester, since 1991; *b* 9 April 1926; *s* of Rev. William Cyril Luxmoore and Constance Evelyn Luxmoore; *m* 1955, Judith, *d* of late Canon Verney Johnstone; four *s* one *d*. *Educ:* Sedbergh School, Yorks; Trinity Coll., Cambridge; Chichester Theol Coll. Deacon 1952, priest 1953; Asst Curate, St John the Baptist, Newcastle upon Tyne, 1952–55; Priest in Charge, St Bede's Ecclesiastical Dist, Newsham, 1955–57; Vicar of Newsham, 1957–58; Rector of Sangre Grande, Trinidad, 1958–66; Vicar of Headingley, Leeds, 1967–81; Proctor in Convocation and Mem. Gen. Synod, 1975–81; Hon. Canon of Ripon Cathedral, 1980–81; Precentor and Canon Residentiary of Chichester Cathedral, 1981–84; Dean of Bermuda Cathedral, 1984–89; Archdeacon of Lewes and Hastings, 1989–91. Commissary for Bishop of Trinidad and Tobago, 1968–84. Provost, Woodard Schools Southern Div., 1989–April 1996. *Recreations:* music, church history, winemaking. *Address:* 42 Willowbed Drive, Chichester, W Sussex PO19 2JB. *T:* Chichester (01243) 784680.

LUXON, Benjamin Matthew, CBE 1986; FGSM; baritone; *b* Camborne, Cornwall, 1937; *m* 1969, Sheila Amit; two *s* one *d*. *Educ:* Truro Sch.; Westminster Trng Coll.; Guildhall Sch. of Music. Teacher of Physical Education until becoming professional singer, 1963. Repertoire includes lieder, folk music, Victorian songs and duets, oratorio (Russian, French and English song), and operatic rôles at major opera houses at home and abroad. Major rôles include: Eugene Onegin, Don Giovanni, Wozzeck, Papageno, Julius Caesar, Posa, Gianni Schicchi, Falstaff. Numerous recordings. Appointed Bard of the Cornish Gorsedd, 1974. Third prize, Munich Internat. Festival, 1961; Gold Medal GSM, 1963. FGSM 1970; Hon. RAM, 1980; Hon. DMus Exeter, 1980. *Recreations:* collecting English water-colours and drawings; tennis, swimming. *Address:* Lower Cox Street Farm, Detling, Maidstone, Kent ME14 3HE.

LUZZATTO, Prof. Lucio, MD; FRCP, FRCPath; Chairman, Department of Human Genetics, Memorial Sloan-Kettering Cancer Center, since 1994; *b* 28 Sept. 1936; *s* of Aldo and Anna Luzzatto; *m* 1963, Paola Caboara; one *s* one *d*. *Educ:* Genoa Univ. (MD 1959); Pavia Univ. (Spec. Haematology 1962); Lib. Doc. Italy, 1965. FRCPath 1982; FRCP 1983. Research Fellow in Haematology, Columbia Univ., 1963–64; Lectr, then Prof. of Haematology, Univ. of Ibadan, 1964–74; Dir, Internat. Inst. of Genetics and Biophysics, Naples, 1974–81; Prof. of Haematology, RPMS, 1981–94; Hon Dir., MRC Leukaemia Res. Fund's Leukaemia Unit, 1987–93. Pius XI Medal, 1976; Laurea ad hon., Univ. of Urbino, 1990. *Publications:* numerous contribs to learned jls. *Address:* Department of Human Genetics, MSKCC, 1275 York Avenue, New York, NY 10021, USA. *T:* (212) 6396165.

LYALL, Andrew Gardiner, CMG 1976; Under Secretary, Department of Transport, 1981–86, retired; *b* 21 Dec. 1929; *s* of late William and Helen Lyall (*née* Gardiner); *m* 1953, Olive Leslie Gennoe White; one *s* one *d*. *Educ:* Kirkcaldy High Sch. Joined MoT, 1951; Asst Shipping Attaché, British Embassy, Washington, DC, 1961–64; Principal, Nationalised Industry Finance and Urban Transport Planning, 1965–70; Asst Sec., Railways Div., 1970–72; seconded to FCO as Counsellor, UK Representation to European Communities, 1972–75; Assistant Secretary: Land Use Planning, DoE, 1975–76; Central Unit on Environmental Pollution, 1976–77; Under Sec., PSA, 1978–81. *Recreations:* photography, travel, walking, countryside conservation. *Address:* 5 Barrowfield, Cuckfield, Haywards Heath, West Sussex RH17 5ER. *T:* Haywards Heath (01444) 454606. *Club:* Civil Service.

LYALL, Gavin Tudor; author; *b* 9 May 1932; *s* of J. T. and A. A. Lyall; *m* 1958, Katharine E. Whitehorn, *qv*; two *s*. *Educ:* King Edward VI Sch., Birmingham; Pembroke Coll., Cambridge (MA). RAF, 1951–53 (Pilot Officer, 1952). Journalist with: Picture Post, 1956–57; BBC, 1958–59; Sunday Times, 1959–63. Hon. Consultant, Air Transport Users' Cttee, CAA, 1985–94 (Mem., 1979–85); Mem., Air Travel Trust Cttee, 1986–. *Publications:* The Wrong Side of the Sky, 1961; The Most Dangerous Game, 1964; Midnight Plus One, 1965; Shooting Script, 1966; Venus with Pistol, 1969; Blame the Dead, 1972; Judas Country, 1975; Operation Warboard, 1976; The Secret Servant, 1980 (televised, 1984); The Conduct of Major Maxim, 1982; The Crocus List, 1985; Uncle Target, 1988; Spy's Honour, 1993; (as Editor) Freedom's Battle: The RAF in World War II, 1968. *Recreations:* cooking, military history, model making. *Address:* 14 Provost Road, NW3 4ST. *T:* 0171–722 2308. *Clubs:* Royal Air Force, Detection.

LYALL, Katharine Elizabeth; *see* Whitehorn, K.

LYALL, William Chalmers, MBE 1952; HM Diplomatic Service, retired; *b* 6 Aug. 1921; *s* of John Brown Lyall and Margaret Angus Leighton Stevenson Lyall; *m* 1948, Janet Lawson McKechnie; two *s* one *d*. *Educ:* Kelty Public and Beath Secondary schools. Min. of Labour, 1940–48; HM Forces, 1941–47; FO, 1948; Hankow, 1948–51; São Paulo, 1952–53; Manila, 1953–55; FO, 1955–57; Caracas, 1957–60; Bahrain, 1960–64; FO, 1964–65; DSAO, 1965–68; FCO, 1968–69; Consul-General, Genoa, 1969–73; FCO, 1973; Counsellor (Administration), Bonn, 1974–78. *Recreations:* music, photography.

LYALL GRANT, Maj.-Gen. Ian Hallam, MC 1944; CEng; Director General, Supply Co-ordination, Ministry of Defence, 1970–75; retired; *b* 4 June 1915; *s* of Col H. F. Lyall Grant, DSO and Lucy Ellinor (*née* Hardy); *m* 1951, Mary Jennifer Moore; one *s* two *d*. *Educ:* Cheltenham Coll.; RMA, Woolwich; Gonville and Caius Coll., Cambridge (MA). Regular Commission, RE, 1935; service in: India, Burma and Japan, 1938–46 (MC; twice mentioned in despatches); Cyprus and Egypt, 1951–52; CO 131 Para Engr Regt (TA), 1954–56; Imperial Defence Coll., 1961; Aden, 1962–63; Comdt, Royal School of Mil. Engineering, 1965–67; Maj.-Gen. 1966; Dep. QMG, 1967–70, retired 1970. Col Comdt, RE, 1972–77. Pres., Bengal Sappers Officers' Assoc., 1987–; Chm., Burma Campaign Fellowship Gp, 1991–. FGA. *Publication:* Burma: the turning point, 1993. *Recreations:* travel, flyfishing, paintings, gemmology. *Address:* Friary House, 6 St Martin's Square, Chichester, W Sussex PO19 1NT. *T:* Chichester (01243) 784214. *Club:* Naval and Military.

LYCETT GREEN, Candida; writer; *b* 22 Sept. 1942; *d* of Sir John Betjeman, CBE and Penelope, *d* of Field Marshal Lord Chetwode, GCB, OM, GCSI; *m* 1963, Rupert Lycett Green; two *s* three *d*. *Educ:* St Mary's, Wantage. TV documentary films: The Front Garden, 1979; The English Woman and the Horse, 1981; A Cottage in the Country, 1983. Mem., Historic Bldgs and Monuments Commn for England (English Heritage), 1992–. *Publications:* Hadrian the Hedgehog, 1969; Hadrian in the Orient, 1971; (with Christopher Booker) Goodbye London, 1972; The Front Garden, 1974; English Cottages, 1984; Brilliant Gardens, 1989; The Perfect English Country House, 1991; John Betjeman: Letters, Vol. I, 1994. *Recreation:* touring England by horse. *Address:* c/o Desmond Elliott, 38 Bury Street, St James's, SW1Y 6AU. *Club:* Academy.

LYDDON, (William) Derek (Collier), CB 1984; Chief Planning Officer, Scottish Development Department, 1967–85; *b* 17 Nov. 1925; *s* of late A. J. Lyddon, CBE, and E. E. Lyddon; *m* 1949, Marian Louise Kaye Charlesworth, *d* of late Prof. J. K. Charlesworth, CBE; two *d*. *Educ:* Wrekin Coll.; University Coll., London. BA (Arch.) 1952; ARIBA 1953; DipTP 1954; AMTPI 1963, FRTPI 1973. Depute Chief Architect and Planning Officer, Cumbernauld Development Corp., 1962; Chief Architect and Planning Officer, Skelmersdale Development Corp., 1963–67. Chairman: Edinburgh Sch. of Environmental Design, 1988–; Planning Exchange, 1991– (Vice-Chm., 1984–88); Vice-Chm., Edinburgh Old Town Renewal Trust, 1991–. Pres., Internat. Soc. of City and Regional Planners, 1981–84. Hon. Prof., Heriot-Watt Univ., 1986; Vis. Prof., Strathclyde Univ., 1986–89, Hon. Fellow: Univ. of Edinburgh, 1986–89; Duncan Jordanstone Coll. of Art, Dundee, 1986–. Hon. DLitt Heriot-Watt, 1981. *Recreations:* walking, reading. *Address:* 38 Dick Place, Edinburgh EH9 2JB. *T:* 0131–667 2266.

LYELL, family name of **Baron Lyell.**

LYELL, 3rd Baron *cr* 1914, of Kinnordy; **Charles Lyell;** Bt, 1894; DL; *b* 27 March 1939; *s* of 2nd Baron, VC (killed in action, 1943), and Sophie, *d* of Major S. W. and Lady Betty Trafford; *S* father, 1943. *Educ:* Eton; Christ Church, Oxford. 2nd Lieut Scots Guards, 1957–59. CA Scotland. An Opposition Whip, 1974–79; a Lord in Waiting (Govt Whip), 1979–84; Parly Under-Sec. of State, NI Office, 1984–89. Mem., Queen's Body Guard for Scotland (Royal Company of Archers). DL Angus, 1988. *Heir:* none. *Address:* Kinnordy House, Kirriemuir, Angus DD8 5ER. *T:* Kirriemuir (01575) 72848; 20 Petersham Mews, SW7 5NR. *T:* 0171–584 9419. *Clubs:* Turf, White's.

LYELL, Rt. Hon. Sir Nicholas (Walter), Kt 1987; PC 1990; QC 1980; MP (C) Mid Bedfordshire, since 1983 (Hemel Hempstead, 1979–83); Attorney General, since 1992; *b* 6 Dec. 1938; *s* of late Sir Maurice Legat Lyell and Veronica Mary Lyell; *m* 1967, Susanna Mary Fletcher; two *s* two *d*. *Educ:* Stowe Sch.; Christ Church, Oxford (MA Hons Mod. Hist.). National Service, commnd Royal Artillery, 1957–59; Walter Runciman & Co., 1962–64; called to the Bar, Inner Temple, 1965, Bencher, 1986; private practice, London (Commercial and Industrial Law), 1965–86; a Recorder, 1985–. Jt Sec., Constitutional Cttee, 1979; PPS to the Attorney General, 1979–86; Parly Under-Sec. of State (Social Security), DHSS, 1986–87; Solicitor General, 1987–92. Chm., Soc. of Cons. Lawyers, 1985–86 (Vice-Chm., 1982–85). Vice-Chm., BFSS, 1983–86. Governor, Stowe Sch., 1990–. *Recreations:* gardening, shooting, drawing. *Address:* House of Commons, SW1A 0AA. *Clubs:* Brooks's, Pratt's, Beefsteak.

LYGO, Adm. Sir Raymond (Derek), KCB 1977; CIMgt; aerospace, defence and industrial consultant; Chairman: Rutland Trust PLC, since 1992; TNT Europe Ltd and TNT Express (UK), since 1992; *b* 15 March 1924; *s* of late Edwin T. Lygo and of Ada E. Lygo; *m* 1950, Pepper Van Osten, USA; two *s* one *d*. *Educ:* Valentine's Sch., Ilford; Ilford County High Sch.; Clark's Coll., Bromley. The Times, 1940; Naval Airman, RN, 1942; Naval Pilot, 1943; CO, HMS Ark Royal, 1969–71; Vice Chief of Naval Staff, 1975–78 and Chief of Naval Staff, 1978. British Aerospace: Man. Dir, Hatfield/Lostock Div., 1978–79, Group Dep. Chm., 1980; Bd Mem., 1980–89; Chm. and Chief Exec., Dynamics Gp, 1980–82; Man. Dir, 1983–86; Chief Exec., 1986–89; Chairman: BAe Inc., 1983–88; Royal Ordnance, 1987–88; BAe Enterprises Ltd, BAe (Space Systems) Ltd, BAe Hldgs Inc., 1988–89; Mem., Supervisory Bd, Airbus Industrie, 1987–89. Director: James Capel Corporate Finance, 1990–92; LET, 1990–92. Dir, CBI Educn Foundn, 1985–92; Member: NEDC, 1989–91; Council, Foundn for Management Educn, 1992–. Conducted review of the management of prison service, 1991. Freeman, City of London, 1985; Liveryman: Coachmakers' and Coach Harness Makers' Co., 1986–; Shipwrights' Co., 1988–. Appeal Pres., SENSE (Nat. Deaf-Blind & Rubella Assoc.), 1983–; Appeal Chm., Industrial Soc., 1989–91. Pres., FAA Officers Assoc., 1990–; Patron, Nat. FAA Assoc., 1989–. Life Mem., Royal Soc. of St George, 1984. FRSA. Hon. FRAeS; Hon. Fellow, Univ. of Westminster (formerly Poly. of Central London), 1989. *Recreations:* flying, building, gardening, joinery. *Address:* c/o Barclays Premier Banking, 54 Lombard Street, EC3 9EX. *Clubs:* City Livery, Ambassadeurs; Royal Naval and Royal Albert Yacht (Portsmouth).

LYLE, Alexander Walter Barr, (Sandy), MBE 1987; professional golfer, since 1977; *b* 9 Feb. 1958; *s* of Alex and Agnes Lyle; *m* (marr. diss.); two *s*; *m* 1989, Brigitte Jolande Huurman; one *s* one *d*. *Educ:* Shrewsbury local sch. Rookie of the Year, 1978; 1st in European order of merit, 1979, 1980, 1985; Open Champion, Royal St George's, 1985; won US Masters, 1988. *Publication:* Learning Golf the Lyle Way, 1986. *Recreation:* cars. *Address:* c/o Advantage International, The Limes, 123 Mortlake High Street, Barnes, SW14 8SN.

LYLE, Lt-Col (Archibald) Michael, OBE 1994; JP; Vice Lord-Lieutenant, Perth and Kinross, since 1984; farmer and landowner; *b* 1 May 1919; 3rd *s* of Col Sir Archibald Lyle, 2nd Bt, MC, TD and Lady Lyle; *m* 1942, Hon. Elizabeth Sinclair (*d* 1994), *yr d* of 1st Viscount Thurso, KT, CMG, PC; three *d* (and one *d* decd). *Educ:* Eton College; Trinity College, Oxford (BA; MA). Hon. Attaché, Rome, 1938–39; served 1939–45 with The Black Watch, RHR (wounded Normandy, 1944 and discharged, 1945); Lt-Col, The Scottish Horse RAC (TA), 1953–56. Chm., T&AFA, 1959–64. Mem., Royal Company of Archers, Queen's Body Guard for Scotland. Member: Perth and Kinross CC, 1946–74; Tayside Regional Council, 1974–79. Chm., Perth Coll. of Further Educn, 1978–91. JP Perth 1950; DL Perthshire 1961. *Recreations:* fishing, shooting, music. *Address:* Riemore Lodge, Dunkeld, Perthshire PH8 0HP. *T:* Butterstone (01350) 724205. *Clubs:* Brooks's, MCC; Puffin's (Edinburgh); Royal Perth Golfing Society.

LYLE, Sir Gavin Archibald, 3rd Bt *cr* 1929; estate manager, farmer; company director; *b* 14 Oct. 1941; *s* of late Ian Archibald de Hoghton Lyle and of Hon. Lydia Yarde-Buller (who *m* 1947, as his 2nd wife, 13th Duke of Bedford; marr. diss. 1960; now Lydia Duchess of Bedford), *d* of 3rd Baron Churston; *S* grandfather, 1946; *m* 1967, Suzy Cooper (marr. diss. 1985); five *s* one *d*. *Heir:* *s* Ian Abram Lyle, *b* 25 Sept. 1968. *Address:* Glendelvine, Caputh, Perthshire PH1 4JN.

LYLE, Lt-Col Michael; *see* Lyle, Lt-Col A.M.

LYLE, Sandy; *see* Lyle, A. W. B.

LYLES, John, CBE 1987; JP; Lord-Lieutenant of West Yorkshire, since 1992; Chairman, S. Lyles plc, since 1972; *b* 8 May 1929; *yr s* of Percy George Lyles and Alice Maud Mary (*née* Robinson); *m* 1953, Yvonne Johnson; two *s* two *d*. *Educ:* Giggleswick Sch.; Leeds Univ. (BSc Textiles 1950). Non-exec. Dir, Hillards plc, 1983–87. Chairman: Assoc. of Yorks and Humberside Chambers of Commerce, 1975–76; Yorks and Humberside CBI, 1983–85; Industry Year 86: Yorks and Humberside Reg. CBI Mem., Commn on Citizenship, 1988–90; Mem., Nat. Employers' Liaison Cttee for Volunteer and Reserve Forces, 1986–92. Mem., Yorks Cttee, NT, 1988–. Mem. Council, Leeds Univ., 1988–. Chm., Shrievalty Assoc., 1993–95. Vice-Patron, Royal Nat. Rose Soc., 1993–. FRSA 1986. Hon. Col, 8th (Yorks) Bn, LI (Vols), 1993–. JP Batley and Dewsbury, 1967; High Sheriff, W Yorks, 1985–86, DL 1987, W Yorks. *Recreations:* gardening, photography, music, opera. *Address:* PO Box 777, Dewsbury, W Yorks WF12 8XX. *T:* Dewsbury (01924) 463161. *Club:* Lansdowne.

LYMBERY, His Honour Robert Davison; QC 1967; a Circuit Judge (formerly Judge of County Courts), 1971–93; Common Serjeant in the City of London, 1990–93; *b* 14 Nov. 1920; *s* of late Robert Smith Lymbery and late Louise Lymbery; *m* 1952, Pauline Anne, *d* of late John Reginald and of Kathleen Tuckett; three *d*. *Educ:* Gresham's Sch.; Pembroke Coll., Cambridge. Served Army, 1940–46; commissioned 17/21 Lancers, 1941; Middle East, Italy, Greece (Royal Tank Regt), 1942–46, Major. Pembroke Coll., 1939–40, 1946–48 (MA, LLB 1st class hons). Foundation Exhibn. 1948; called to Bar, Middle Temple, 1949, Bencher, 1990; Harmsworth Law Scholar, 1949; practice on Midland Circuit, 1949–71. Recorder of Grantham, 1965–71; Chairman: Rutland QS, 1966–71 (Dep. Chm., 1962–66); Bedfordshire QS, 1969–71 (Dep. Chm., 1961–69); Commissioner of Assize, 1971. Freeman, City of London, 1983; Liveryman, Cutlers' Co., 1992–. *Recreations:* various. *Address:* c/o Central Criminal Court, EC4M 7EH. *Club:* Hawks (Cambridge).

LYMINGTON, Viscount; Oliver Henry Rufus Wallop; *b* 22 Dec. 1981; *s* and *heir* of Earl of Portsmouth, *qv*.

LYMPANY, Dame Moura, DBE 1992 (CBE 1979); FRAM 1948; concert pianist; *b* Saltash, Cornwall, 18 Aug. 1916; British; *d* of John and Beatrice Johnstone; *m* 1944, Lt-Col Colin Defries (marr. diss. 1950); *m* 1951, Bennet H. Korn, American Television Executive (marr. diss. 1961); one *s* decd. *Educ:* Belgium, Austria, England. First public performance at age of 12, 1929, at Harrogate, playing Mendelssohn G Minor Concerto. Won second prize out of 79 competitors at Ysaye International Pianoforte Competition at Brussels, 1938. Has played in USA, Canada, South America, Australia, New Zealand, India, and all principal European countries. Records for HMV and Decca. Commander of the Order of the Crown, Belgium, 1980; Chevalier, Ordre des Arts et des Lettres (France), 1992. *Publication:* Moura Lympany: her autobiography, 1991. *Recreations:* gardening, tapestry, reading. *Address:* c/o Transart, 8 Bristol Gardens, W9 2JG.

LYNAM, Desmond Michael; sports broadcaster, BBC, since 1969; *b* 17 Sept. 1942; *s* of Edward Lynam and Gertrude Veronica Lynam (*née* Malone); *m* 1965, Susan Eleanor Skinner (marr. diss. 1974); one *s*. *Educ:* Varndean Grammar Sch., Brighton; Brighton Business Coll. ACII. Business career in insurance, until 1967; also freelance journalist; reporter for local radio, 1967–69; reporter, presenter and commentator, BBC Radio, 1969–78; presenter and commentator, BBC TV Sport, 1978–, incl. Grandstand, Sportsnight, Match of the Day, Commonwealth and Olympic Games, and World Cup; presenter: Holiday, BBC TV, 1988–; How Do They Do That?, BBC TV, 1994–. TV Sports Presenter of the Year, TV and Radio Industries Club, 1985, 1987, 1988, 1992; Radio Times Male TV Personality, 1989; RTS Sports Presenter of the Year, 1994; Richard Dimbleby Award, BAFTA, 1995. *Publications:* Guide to Commonwealth Games, 1986; The 1988 Olympics, 1988; The 1992 Olympics, 1992. *Recreations:* golf, tennis, Brighton and Hove Albion, reading, theatre. *Address:* c/o BBC, Richmond Way, Shepherds Bush, W14 0AX.

LYNCH, David; His Honour Judge Lynch; a Circuit Judge, since 1990; *b* 23 Aug. 1939; *s* of Henry and Edith Lynch; *m* 1974, Ann Knights; two *s*. *Educ:* Liverpool Collegiate Grammar School. LLB London. Called to the Bar, Middle Temple, 1968; a Recorder, 1988–90. Pres., Mental Health Review Tribunals (restricted patients), 1991–. *Recreations:* classical guitar, archery, golf. *Address:* The Queen Elizabeth II Law Courts, Derby Square, Liverpool L2 1XA. *T:* 0151–473 7373. *Clubs:* Caldy Golf; Neston Co. of Archers.

LYNCH, Rev. Prebendary Donald MacLeod, CBE 1972; MA; *b* 2 July 1911; *s* of Herbert and Margaret Lynch; *m* 1st, 1941, Ailsa Leslie Leask; three *s* one *d*; 2nd, 1963, Jean Wileman. *Educ:* City of London Sch.; Pembroke Coll., Cambridge; Wycliffe Hall, Oxford. Curate, Christ Church, Chelsea, 1935; Tutor, Oak Hill Theological Coll., 1938; Curate, St Michael's, Stonebridge Park, 1940; Minister, All Saints, Queensbury, 1942; Vicar, St Luke's, Tunbridge Wells, 1950; Principal, Church Army Training Coll., 1953; Chief Sec., Church Army, 1960–76; Preb. of Twiford, St Paul's Cathedral, 1964–76, now Emeritus; Priest-in-Charge of Seal, St Lawrence, dio. Rochester, 1974–85, also of Underriver, 1980–85; RD, Sevenoaks, 1979–84. Chaplain to the Queen, 1969–81. *Publications:* Action Stations, 1981; Chariots of the Gospel, 1982. *Recreation:* reading. *Address:* Flat 2, 20 Grassington Road, Eastbourne, Sussex BN20 7BJ. *T:* Eastbourne (01323) 720849.

LYNCH, John; *b* 15 Aug. 1917; *y s* of Daniel Lynch and Norah O'Donoghue; *m* 1946, Mairin O'Connor. *Educ:* Christian Brothers' Schools, N Monastery, Cork; University College, Cork; King's Inns, Dublin. Entered Civil Service (Dept of Justice), 1936; called to Bar, 1945; resigned from Civil Service, became Mem. Munster Bar and commenced practice in Cork Circuit, 1945. Teachta Dala (TD) for Cork, Parlt of Ireland, 1948–81; Parly Sec. to Govt and to Minister for Lands, 1951–54; Minister for: Education, 1957–59; Industry and Commerce, 1959–65; Finance, 1965–66; Leader of Fianna Fail, 1966–79; Taoiseach (Head of Government of Ireland), 1966–73 and 1977–79; Pres., European Council (EEC), July–Dec. 1979. Alderman, Co. Borough of Cork, 1950–57; Mem. Cork Sanatoria Board and Cttee of Management, N Infirmary, Cork, 1950–51 and 1955–57; Mem. Cork Harbour Comrs, 1956–57; Vice-Pres., Consultative Assembly of Council of Europe, 1958; Pres., Internat. Labour Conf., 1962. Freeman, City of Cork, 1980. Hon. LLD: Univ. of Dublin, 1967; Nat. Univ. of Ireland, 1969; Rhode Island Coll., USA, 1980; Hon. DCL N Carolina, 1971. Grand Cross, Order of the Crown (Belgium), 1968. Robert Schumann Gold Medal, 1973; Mérite Européen Gold Medal, 1981. *Address:* 21 Garville Avenue, Rathgar, Dublin 6, Ireland.

LYNCH, Prof. John; Director of Institute of Latin American Studies, 1974–87 and Professor of Latin American History, 1970–87, University of London, now Professor Emeritus; *b* 11 Jan. 1927; *s* of late John P. Lynch and Teresa M. Lynch, Boldon Colliery, Co. Durham; *m* 1960, Wendy Kathleen, *d* of late Frederick and Kathleen Norman; two *s* three *d*. *Educ:* Corby Sch. Sunderland; Univ. of Edinburgh; University College, London. MA Edinburgh 1952; PhD London 1955. FRHistS 1958. Army, 1945–48. Asst Lectr and Lectr in Modern History, Univ. of Liverpool, 1954–61; Lectr in Hispanic and Latin American History, 1961–64, Reader, 1964–70, UCL. Harrison Vis. Prof., Coll. of William and Mary, Williamsburg, 1991–92. Corresp. Member: Academia Nacional de la Historia, Argentina, 1963, Academia Nacional de la Historia, Venezuela, 1980; Academia Panameña de la Historia, 1981; Academia Chilena de la Historia, 1985; Real Academia de la Historia, Spain, 1986; Sociedad Boliviana de Historia, 1987. Dr *hc* Seville, 1990. Order of Andrés Bello (Venezuela), 1979; Comdr, Order of Isabel la Católica (Spain), 1988. *Publications:* Spanish Colonial Administration 1782–1810, 1958; Spain under the Habsburgs, vol. 1 1964, vol. 2 1969; (with R. A. Humphreys) The Origins of the Latin American Revolutions, 1808–1826, 1965; The Spanish American Revolutions 1808–1826, 1973; Argentine Dictator: Juan Manuel de Rosas, 1829–52, 1981; (ed) Andrés Bello: the London years, 1982; (ed) Past and Present in the Americas, 1984; Hispanoamérica 1750–1850, 1987; Bourbon Spain 1700–1808, 1989; Caudillos in Spanish America 1800–1850, 1992; Latin American Revolution 1808–1826: old and new world origins, 1994; (contrib.) Cambridge History of Latin America, vol. III 1985, vol. IV 1986. *Address:* 8 Templars Crescent, N3 3QS. *T:* 0181–346 1089.

LYNCH, Martin Patrick James; Under Secretary, Overseas Development Administration, Foreign and Commonwealth Office, 1975–83, retired; *b* 4 June 1924; 2nd *s* of late Frederick Lynch, DSM, and late Elizabeth Yeatman; *m* 1959, Anne, *d* of late Major Gerald McGorty, MC, RAMC; two *s* one *d* (and one *s* decd). *Educ:* London Oratory School. BA Hons London. RAF, 1942–49; Exec. Officer, HM Treasury, 1950; Asst Private Sec. to Financial Sec., 1953–54; Private Sec. to Minister Without Portfolio, 1954–55; Principal, 1958; Asst Sec., Min. of Overseas Develt, 1966 and 1971–75; Counsellor, UK Treasury and Supply Delegn, Washington, and UK Alternate Dir, World Bank, 1967–71. Asst Sec. (Admin), British Coll. of Optometrists (formerly British Coll of Ophthalmic Opticians), 1984–87; Asst to Gen. Optical Council, 1989–94; Project Man., British Coll. of Optometrists, 1993–; Sec., UK Inter Professional Gp, 1995–. FRSA 1973; Mem. Council, Assoc. for Latin Liturgy, 1973–92 (Chm., 1976–88). *Publication:* (contrib.) A Voice for All Time, 1993. *Address:* Hillside, Combe Hill, Combe St Nicholas, Chard, Somerset TA20 3NW. *T:* Chard (01460) 65029. *Club:* Reform.

LYNCH, Patrick, MA; MRIA; Professor of Political Economy (Applied Economics), University College, Dublin, 1975–80, now Emeritus; *b* 5 May 1917; *s* of Daniel and Brigid Lynch, Co. Tipperary and Dublin; *m* 1st, 1965, Mary Crotty (*née* Campbell), MA (*d* 1982); 2nd, 1991, Mary Moloney. *Educ:* Univ. Coll., Dublin. Fellow Commoner, Peterhouse, Cambridge, 1956. Entered Irish Civil Service, 1941; Asst Sec. to Govt, 1950; Univ. Lectr in Econs, UC Dublin, 1952, Associate Prof., 1966–75. Chm., Aer Lingus, 1954–75; Jt Dep. Chm., Allied Irish Banks, 1976–84. Has acted as economic consultant to OECD, Council of Europe, Dept of Finance, Dublin, Gulbenkian Inst., Lisbon. Directed surveys sponsored by Irish Govt with OECD into long-term Irish educnl needs, 1965, and into requirements of Irish economy in respect of scientific res., develt and technology, 1966; estab. Science Policy Res. Centre in Dept of Applied Econs, UC Dublin, 1969. Mem., various Irish Govt Commns and Cttees, 1952–; Member: Club of Rome, 1973; EEC Economic and Monetary Union 1980 Group, 1974; Nat. Science Council, 1968–78; Higher Educn Authority, 1968–72; Nat. Economic and Social Council, 1973–76; European Science Foundn, 1974–77; Chairman: Medico-Social Research Board, 1966–72; Public Service Adv. Council, 1973–77; Exec. Cttee, Econ. and Social Res. Inst., 1983–88; Editl Bd, Economic and Social Review; Mem. Editorial Bd, University Review. Chm., Nat. Library of Ireland Soc., 1969–72; Chm., Irish Anti-Apartheid Movement, 1972; Member: Irish Assoc. for Civil Liberty; Movement for Peace in Ireland. Chm., Inst. of Public Administration, 1973–77. Member: Governing Body UC Dublin, 1963–75; Senate NUI, 1972–77; Treasurer, RIA, 1972–80. Hon. DUniv Brunel, 1976; Hon. LLD: Dublin, 1979; NUI, 1985; Hon. DEconSc Limerick, 1994. *Publications:* Planning for Economic Development in Ireland, 1959; (with J. Vaizey) Guinness's Brewery in the Irish Economy, 1960; (jtly) Economics of Educational Costing, 1969; (with Brian Hillery) Ireland in the International Labour Organisation, 1969; (with B. Chubb) Economic Development Planning, 1969; Whither Science Policy, 1980; (ed with J. Meenan) Essays in Memory of Alexis Fitzgerald, 1987; essays in various symposia, etc; articles in Administration, The Bell, Encycl. Britannica, Econ. History Review, Irish Hist. Studies, Irish Jl of Educn, Statist, Studies, University Review, etc. *Address:* 79 Wellington Road, Dublin 4, Ireland.

LYNCH, Roderick Robertson; Managing Director Resources, BBC, since 1993; *b* 22 May 1949; *s* of Nanson Lynch and Catherine (*née* Robertson); *m* 1972, Christina Williams; two *s*. *Educ:* Perth Acad.; Dundee Univ. (MA 1971). Served RAC, 1966–67. British Airways, 1971–89: Gen. Manager, Southern Europe, 1983–84; Man. Dir, British Airtours, 1984–86; Head, Customer Service, 1986–89; Man. Dir, Air Europe, 1989–91; Dir, Forte Hotels, 1991–93. Bd Mem., CAA, 1993–. *Recreations:* Rugby football (watching), miltary history, music, aviation. *Address:* c/o BBC, 201 Wood Lane, W12 7TS. *T:* 0181–752 5000.

LYNCH-BLOSSE, Sir Richard Hely, 17th Bt *cr* 1622; RAMC, 1975–85, retired; general medical practioner, since 1985; *b* 26 Aug. 1953; *s* of Sir David Edward Lynch-Blosse, 16th Bt, and of Elizabeth, *er d* of Thomas Harold Payne, Welwyn Garden City; *S* father, 1971; *m* 1976, Cara, *o d* of George Sutherland, St Ives, Cambs; two *d*. *Educ:* Royal Free Hosp. Sch. of Medicine. Commnd RAMC, July 1975; LRCP MRCS 1978; MB BS 1979; DRCOG 1983; MRCGP 1984. *Publication:* contrib. to Jl of RAMC. *Heir: cousin* (Eric) Hugh Lynch-Blosse, OBE [*b* 30 July 1917; *m* 1946, Jean Evelyn, *d* of Commander Andrew Robertson Hair, RD, RNR; one *s* one *d* (and one *d* decd)]. *Address:* The Surgery, Watery Lane, Clifton Hampden, Oxon OX14 3EL.

LYNCH-ROBINSON, Sir Niall (Bryan), 3rd Bt *cr* 1920; DSC 1941; late Lieut RNVR; one time Chairman, Leo Burnett Ltd, 1969–78; *b* 24 Feb. 1918; *s* of Sir Christopher Henry Lynch-Robinson, 2nd Bt and Dorothy (*d* 1970), *d* of Henry Warren, Carrickmines, Co. Dublin; *S* father 1958; *m* 1940, Rosemary Seaton, *e d* of Mrs M. Seaton Eller; one *s* (one adopted *d* decd). *Educ:* Stowe. Sub-Lieut 1939, Lieut 1940, RNVR; served War of 1939–45 (DSC, Croix de Guerre). Mem. Exec. Cttee, Nat. Marriage Guidance Council, 1961–86. Chm. of Governors, Cranbourne Chase School, 1970–82. *Recreations:* fishing, gardening. *Heir: s* Dominick Christopher Lynch-Robinson [*b* 30 July 1948; *m* 1973, Victoria, *d* of Kenneth Weir; one *s* one *d*]. *Address:* Flat 25, Headbourne Worthy House, Headbourne Worthy, Winchester, Hants SO23 7JG.

LYNDEN-BELL, Prof. Donald, FRS 1978; Professor of Astrophysics, University of Cambridge, since 1972; Director, Institute of Astronomy, Cambridge, 1972–77, 1982–87, and 1992–94; *b* 5 April 1935; *s* of late Lt-Col L. A. Lynden-Bell, MC and M. R. Lynden-Bell (*née* Thring); *m* 1961, Ruth Marion Truscott, MA, PhD; one *s* one *d*. *Educ:* Marlborough; Clare Coll., Cambridge (MA, PhD). Harkness Fellow of the Commonwealth Fund, NY, at the California Inst. of Technology and Hale Observatories, 1960–62; Research Fellow and then Fellow and Dir of studies in mathematics, Clare Coll., Cambridge, 1960–65; Asst Lectr in applied mathematics, Univ. of Cambridge, 1962–65; Principal Scientific officer and later SPSO, Royal Greenwich Observatory, Herstmonceux, 1965–72. Visiting Associate, Calif. Inst. of Technology and Hale Observatories, 1969–70. Pres., RAS, 1985–87. FHMAAAS 1985. Foreign Associate: US NAS, 1990; RSSAf 1994. Hon. DSc Sussex, 1987. Eddington Medal, RAS, 1984; Brouwer Prize, AAS, 1990; Gold Medal, RAS, 1993. *Publications:* contrib. to Monthly Notices of Royal Astronomical Soc. *Recreations:* hill walking, golf, squash racquets. *Address:* Institute of Astronomy, The Observatories, Madingley Road, Cambridge CB3 0HA. *T:* Cambridge (01223) 337525.

LYNE, Prof. Andrew Geoffrey, PhD; FRAS; Professor of Radio Astronomy, University of Manchester at Jodrell Bank, since 1990; *b* 13 July 1942; *s* of Lionel Geoffrey Lyne and Kathleen Elizabeth Lyne; *m* 1st, Jennifer Anne Duckels; two *d*; 2nd, 1994, Diane Elizabeth Stanway; one step *s* one step *d*. *Educ:* Portsmouth GS; St John's Coll., Cambridge (MA); Manchester Univ. (PhD). Lectr in Radio Astronomy, 1969–79, Sen. Lectr, 1979–90, Manchester Univ. Vis. Scientist, CSIRO Div. of Radiophysics, Sydney, 1975–76; Leverhulme Fellow, Royal Soc., 1994. Herschel Medal, RAS, 1992; Sir George Thomson Gold Medal, Inst. of Measurement and Control, 1993. *Publications:* Pulsar Astronomy, 1990; contrib. Nature, Monthly Notes of RAS and other scientific jls. *Recreations:* tennis, golf, walking, sailing. *Address:* Nuffield Radio Astronomy Laboratories, Jodrell Bank, Macclesfield, Cheshire SK11 9DL; 6 Nether Lea, Goostrey, Cheshire CW4 8HX. *T:* Lower Withington (01477) 71321.

LYNE, Air Vice-Marshal Michaei Dillon, CB 1968; AFC (two Bars); DL; *b* 23 March 1919; *s* of late Robert John Lyne, Winchester; *m* 1943, Avril Joy Buckley, OStJ, *d* of late Lieut-Colonel Albert Buckley, CBE, DSO (and bar); two *s* two *d*. *Educ.* Imperial Service Coll.; RAF Coll., Cranwell. Fighter Comd and Middle East, 1939–46; Comdg No 54 Fighter Squadron, 1946–48; Comdg RAF Wildenrath, 1958–60; Air Attaché, Moscow, 1961–63; Commandant, Royal Air Force Coll., Cranwell, 1963–64; Air Officer Commanding No 23 Group, RAF Flying Training Command, 1965–67; Senior RAF Instructor, Imperial Defence Coll., 1968–69; Dir-Gen. Training, RAF, 1970–71; retired. Sec., Diocese of Lincoln, 1971–76. Vice-Chm. (Air), TAVR Assoc. for East Midlands, 1977–84. Vice Chm., Governing Body, Bishop Grosseteste Coll., 1976–86. Vice-President: RAF Gliding and Soaring Assoc.; RAF Motor Sport Assoc.; Old Cranwellian Assoc., 1982–. Founder and first Chm., Lincs Microprocessor Soc., 1979–83; Mem. Council, British Computer Soc., 1980–83. President: Lincoln Branch, SCF, 1977–89; Grantham Constituency Liberal Assoc., 1979–88; Grantham Constituency Liberal Democrats, 1990–93; No 54 Squadron Assoc., 1981–94. DL Lincs, 1973. *Recreations:* writing, gardening. *Address:* Far End, Far Lane, Coleby, Lincoln LN5 0AH. *T:* Lincoln (01522) 810468. *Club:* Royal Air Force.

See also R. M. J. Lyne.

LYNE, Roderic Michael John, CMG 1992; HM Diplomatic Service; on secondment as Private Secretary to the Prime Minister, since 1993; *b* 31 March 1948; *s* of Air Vice-Marshal Michael Dillon Lyne, *qv*; *m* 1969, Amanda Mary, *d* of Sir Howard Frank Trayton Smith, *qv*; two *s* one *d*. *Educ:* Legbourne County Primary Sch., Lincs; Highfield Sch., Hants; Eton Coll.; Leeds Univ. (BA Hist. 1970). FCO 1970; Army Sch. of Langs, 1971; Moscow, 1972–74; Dakar, 1974–76; Eastern European and Soviet Dept, FCO, 1976–79; Rhodesia Dept, FCO, 1979; Asst Pvte Sec. to Sec. of State for Foreign and Commonwealth Affairs, 1979–82; UK Mission to UN, NY, 1982–86; Vis. Res. Fellow, RIIA, 1986–87; Counsellor and Hd of Chancery, Moscow, 1987–90; Hd of Soviet Dept, 1990–92, Hd of Eastern Dept, 1992–93, FCO. *Recreation:* sport. *Address:* c/o Foreign and Commonwealth Office, SW1A 2AH.

LYNK, Roy, OBE 1990; National President, Union of Democratic Mineworkers, 1987–93; General Secretary, Nottingham Section, 1985–93; *b* 9 Nov. 1932; *s* of John Thomas Lynk and Ivy Lynk; *m* 1978, Sandra Ann; three *s* three *d*. *Educ:* Station Road Higher Sch. and Healdswood Sch., Sutton-in-Ashfield; Nottingham Univ. Cert. in Industrial Relations. Miner at Teversal Colliery, Nottingham, 1947; RN 1948; Miner at various collieries, Nottingham, 1950–79. National Union of Mineworkers: Branch Sec., Sutton Colliery, 1958–79; full time Area Official, Nottingham, 1979–83; Financial Sec., Nottingham Area, 1983–85, Gen. Sec., 1985; Union of Democratic Mineworkers: formed, Dec. 1985; Nat. Gen. Sec., 1985–86. Member: European Coal and Steel Community's Consultative Cttee, 1988–93; Employment Appeal Tribunal, Nottingham, 1993–; (part-time), Coal Authy, 1995–. *Recreation:* watching football. *Address:* Columbia House, 143 Huthwaite Road, Sutton-in-Ashfield, Notts NG17 2HB.

LYNN, Bishop Suffragan of, since 1994; **Rt. Rev. David John Conner;** *b* 6 April 1947; *s* of William Ernest Conner and Joan Millington Conner; *m* 1969, Jayne Maria Evans; two *s*. *Educ:* Erith Grammar School; Exeter College, Oxford (Symes Exhibnr; MA); St Stephen's House, Oxford. Asst Chaplain, St Edward's School, Oxford, 1971–73, Chaplain, 1973–80; Team Vicar, Wolvercote with Summertown, Oxford, 1976–80; Senior Chaplain, Winchester College, 1980–86; Vicar, St Mary the Great with St Michael, Cambridge, 1987–94; RD of Cambridge, 1989–94. Hon. Fellow, Girton Coll., Cambridge. *Address:* The Old Vicarage, Castle Acre, King's Lynn, Norfolk PE32 2AA. *T:* Swaffham (01760) 755553.

LYNN, Archdeacon of; *see* Foottit, Ven. A. C.

LYNN, Jonathan Adam; director, writer and actor; *b* 3 April 1943; *s* of Robin and Ruth Lynn; *m* 1967, Rita Merkelis; one *s*. *Educ:* Kingswood Sch., Bath; Pembroke Coll., Cambridge (MA). Acted in Cambridge Circus, New York, 1964; TV debut, Ed Sullivan Show, 1964; actor in repertory, Leicester, Edinburgh and Bristol Old Vic, and in London; performances include: Green Julia, 1965; Fiddler on the Roof, 1967–68; Blue Comedy, 1968; The Comedy of the Changing Years, 1969; When We Are Married, 1970; Dreyfus, 1982; actor in TV comedy programmes and plays, including: Barmitzvah Boy, 1975; The Knowledge, 1979; Outside Edge, 1982; Diana, 1984; actor in films including: Prudence and the Pill, 1967; Into the Night, 1984; Three Men and a Little Lady, 1990; Artistic Dir, Cambridge Theatre Co., 1977–81 (dir. 19 prodns); *director: London:* The Plotters of Cabbage Patch Corner, 1970; The Glass Menagerie, 1977; The Gingerbread Man, 1977 and 1978; The Unvarnished Truth, 1978; The Matchmaker, 1978; Songbook, 1979 (SWET Award, Best Musical, 1979); Tonight at 8.30, 1981; Arms and the Man, 1981; Pass the Butler, 1982; Loot, 1984; *National Theatre:* A Little Hotel on the Side, 1984; Jacobowski and the Colonel, 1986; Three Men on a Horse, 1987 (Olivier Award for Best Comedy); *RSC:* Anna Christie, Stratford 1979, London 1980; *Broadway:* The Moony Shapiro Songbook, 1981; *films:* Mick's People (also wrote), 1982; Clue (also wrote), 1984; Nuns on the Run (also wrote), 1990; My Cousin Vinny, 1991; The Distinguished Gentleman, 1992; Greedy, 1994. *TV scriptwriter:* situation comedies, including: My Brother's Keeper, 2 series, 1974 and 1975 (also co-starred); Yes, Minister (also radio scripts), 3 series, 1980, 1981 and 1982; Yes, Prime Minister, 1986, 1987; Life After Life, 1990; *film scriptwriter:* The Internecine Project, 1974. Writer's Award, BAFTA, 1987; Pye TV Writers Award (for Yes, Minister and Yes, Prime Minister), 1981, 1986; Broadcasting Press Guild Award, 1980, 1986; ACE Award for Amer. Cable TV Best Comedy Writing (for Yes, Prime Minister), 1988. Hon. MA Sheffield. *Publications:* A Proper Man (novel), 1976; with Antony Jay: Yes, Minister, The Diaries of a Cabinet Minister: Vol. I, 1981; Vol. II, 1982; Vol. III, 1983; The Complete Yes Minister, 1984; Yes, Prime Minister, the Diaries of the Rt Hon. James Hacker: Vol. I, 1986; Vol. II, 1987; The Complete Yes Prime Minister, 1989; Mayday (novel), 1993. *Recreation:* changing weight. *Address:* c/o Peters, Fraser & Dunlop, Ltd, The Chambers, Chelsea Harbour, Lots Road, SW10 0XF.

LYNN, Maurice Kenneth, MA; Assistant Master, Westminster School, since 1992; *b* 3 March 1951. *Educ:* Thornleigh Salesian College, Bolton; Magdalen College, Oxford (Open Scholar; BA Hons 1973; MA 1977). Asst Master, Oratory Sch., 1973–79; Asst Master, Radley Coll., 1979–83; Head of French, Westminster Sch., 1983–88; Headmaster, The Oratory Sch., 1989–91; Dir of Europ. interests for The Oratory Sch. Assoc., 1992. *Recreations:* English Catholic poetry, twentieth century French drama, soccer, ski-ing, cricket, acting and producing, cycling, travel. *Address:* 16a Vincent Square, SW1P 2NA. *T:* 0171–821 1959.

LYNN, Michael David; Controller and Chief Executive, HM Stationery Office, since 1995; *b* 18 July 1942; *s* of Martin and Dorothy Lynn; *m* 1965, Hilary Smyth; one *s* one *d*. *Educ:* Lincoln Sch. Joined HMSO 1960; Director: Publications Distribution, 1980; Finance, 1983; Print Procurement, 1984; Dir-Gen., Corporate Services, 1987; Dep. Chief Exec., 1989. *Recreations:* swimming, chess, crosswords, gardening. *Address:* HMSO, St Crispins, Duke Street, Norwich NR3 1PD. *T:* Norwich (01603) 694200.

LYNN, Prof. Richard; Professor of Psychology, University of Ulster, since 1972; *b* 20 Feb. 1930; *s* of Richard and Ann Lynn; *m* 1st, 1956, Susan Maher (marr. diss. 1978); one *s* two *d*; 2nd, 1990, Susan Hampson. *Educ:* Bristol Grammar Sch., King's Coll., Cambridge (Passingham prizeman). Lectr in Psychology, Univ. of Exeter, 1956–67; Prof. of Psychology, Dublin Economic and Social Res. Inst., 1967–72. US Mensa Award for Excellence, for work on intelligence, 1985, 1988. *Publications:* Attention, Arousal and the Orientation Reaction, 1966; The Irish Braindrain, 1969; The Universities and the Business Community, 1969; Personality and National Character, 1971; An Introduction to the Study of Personality, 1972; (ed) The Entrepreneur, 1974; (ed) Dimensions of Personality, 1981; Educational Achievement in Japan, 1987; The Secret of the Miracle Economy, 1991; articles on personality, intelligence and social psychology. *Recreation:* do-it-yourself house renovation. *Address:* Dunderg House, Coleraine, Co. Londonderry BT51 3QT. *Club:* Northern Counties (Londonderry).

LYNN, Dame Vera, (Dame Vera Margaret Lewis), DBE 1975 (OBE 1969); singer; *b* 20 March 1917; *d* of Bertram Samuel Welch and Annie Welch; *m* 1941, Harry Lewis; one *d*. *Educ:* Brampton Rd Sch., East Ham. First public appearance as singer, 1924; joined juvenile troupe, 1928; ran own dancing school, 1932; broadcast with Joe Loss and joined Charlie Kunz, 1935; singer with Ambrose Orch., 1937–40, then went solo; voted most popular singer, Daily Express comp., 1939, and named Forces Sweetheart; own radio show, Sincerely Yours, 1941–47; starred in Applesauce, London Palladium, 1941; sang to troops in Burma, etc, 1944 (Burma Star, 1985); subseq. Big Show (radio), USA; London Laughs, Adelphi; appeared at Flamingo Hotel, Las Vegas, and many TV shows, USA and Britain, including own TV series on Rediffusion, 1955; BBC TV, 1956; BBC 2, 1970; also appearances in Holland, Denmark, Sweden, Norway, Germany, Canada, NZ and Australia; in seven Command Performances, also films and own shows on radio. 14 Gold Records; records include Auf Wiederseh'n (over 12 million copies sold), became first British artiste to top American Hit Parade. Pres., Printers' Charitable Corp., 1980. Internat. Ambassador, Variety Club Internat., 1985. Hon. Citizen: Winnipeg, 1974; Nashville, Tennessee, 1977. Freedom: City of London, 1978; City of Corner Brook, Newfoundland, 1981. FInstD. Fellow, Univ. (formerly Poly.) of E London, 1990. Hon. LLD Memorial Univ. of Newfoundland, 1977 (founded Lynn Music Scholarship, first award, 1982); Hon. MMus City, 1992. Music Publishers' Award, 1975; Show Business Personality of the Year, Grand Order of Water Rats, 1975; Ivor Novello Award, 1975; Humanitarian Award, Variety Club Internat., 1985. Comdr, Order of Orange-Nassau, Holland. *Publications:* Vocal Refrain (autobiog.), 1975; (jtly) We'll Meet Again, 1989; Unsung Heroines, 1990. *Recreations:* gardening, painting, sewing, swimming.

LYNNE, Elizabeth; MP (Lib Dem) Rochdale, since 1992; *b* 22 Jan. 1948. *Educ:* Dorking Co. Grammar Sch. Started acting career, 1966; numerous theatre appearances in repertory and West End; speech consultant, 1989–92. Contested (L) Harwich, 1987. Lib Dem spokesperson: on health and community care, 1992–94; on social security and disability, 1994–. *Address:* House of Commons, SW1A 0AA.

LYNNE, Gillian, (Mrs Peter Land); director, choreographer, dancer, actress; *d* of late Leslie Pyrke and Barbara (*née* Hart); *m* 1980, Peter Land, actor. *Educ:* Baston Sch., Bromley, Kent; Arts Educnl Sch. Leading soloist, Sadler's Wells Ballet, 1944–51; star dancer, London Palladium, 1951–53; role in film, Master of Ballantrae, 1952; lead in Can-Can, Coliseum, 1954–55; Becky Sharp in Vanity Fair, Windsor, 1956; guest principal dancer: Samson and Delilah, Sadler's Wells, 1957; Aida, and Tannhauser, Covent Garden, 1957; Puck in A Midsummer Night's Dream, TV, 1958; star dancer in Chelsea at Nine (featured dance segments), TV, 1958; lead in New Cranks, Lyric, Hammersmith, 1959; roles in Wanda, Rose Marie, Cinderella, Out of My Mind, and lead in revue, 1960–61; leading lady, 5 Past Eight Show, Edinburgh, 1962; conceived, dir., chor. and starred in

Collages (mod. dance revue), Edinburgh Fest., 1963, transf. Savoy; *choreographed:* The Owl and the Pussycat (1st ballet), Western Theatre Ballet, 1962; Queen of the Cats, London Palladium, 1962–63; Wonderful Life (1st film), 1963–64; Every Day's a Holiday, and Three Hats for Lisa (musical films), 1964; The Roar of the Greasepaint, and Pickwick, Broadway, 1965; The Flying Dutchman, Covent Garden, 1966; Half a Sixpence (film), 1966–67 (also staged musical nos); How Now Dow Jones, Broadway, 1967; Midsummer Marriage, Covent Garden, 1968; The Trojans, Covent Garden, 1969, 1977; Breakaway (ballet), Scottish Theatre Ballet, 1969; Phil the Fluter, Palace, 1969; Ambassador, Her Majesty's, 1971; Man of La Mancha (film), 1972; The Card, Queen's, 1973; Hans Andersen, London Palladium, 1975; The Way of the World, Aldwych, 1978; My Fair Lady, national tour and Adelphi, 1979; Parsifal, Covent Garden, 1979; (also Associate Dir) Cats, New London, 1981 (Olivier Award, 1981), Broadway 1982, nat. tour, 1983, Los Angeles, Sydney, 1985, East Berlin, 1987, Canada, Japan, Australia, Holland, Paris, 1989 (Molière Award, Best Musical); Café Soir (ballet), Houston Ballet Co., 1985; Cabaret, Strand, 1986; The Phantom of the Opera, Her Majesty's, 1986, Broadway, Japan, Vienna, 1989, Stockholm, Chicago, Hamburg, Australia, Canada, 1990; A Simple Man (ballet), Sadler's Wells, 1988; The Brontës (ballet), Northern Ballet Theatre, 1995; *directed and choreographed* The Match Girls, Globe, 1966; Bluebeard, Sadler's Wells Opera, 1966, new prodn, Sadler's Wells Opera, Coliseum, 1969; Love on the Dole (musical), Nottingham Playhouse, 1970; Liberty Ranch, Greenwich, 1972; Once Upon a Time, Duke of York's, 1972; Jasperina, Amsterdam, 1978; Cats, Vienna, 1983 (1st proscenium arch prodn; Silver Order of Merit, Austria, 1984), Paris, 1989; Valentine's Day, Chichester, 1991; Dancing in the Dark, 1991; Valentine's Day, Globe, 1992; *directed:* Round Leicester Square (revue), Prince Charles, 1963; Tonight at Eight, Hampstead, 1970 and Fortune, 1971; Lillywhite Lies, Nottingham, 1971; A Midsummer Night's Dream (co-dir.), Stratford, 1977; Tomfoolery, Criterion, 1980; Jeeves Takes Charge, Fortune, 1980, off-Broadway, 1983, Los Angeles, 1985; To Those Born Later, New End, 1981; (Additional Dir) La Ronde, RSC, Aldwych, 1982; (also appeared in) Alone Plus One, Newcastle, 1982; The Rehearsal, Yvonne Arnaud, Guildford and tour, 1983; Cabaret, Strand, 1986; *staged:* England Our England (revue), Princes, 1961; 200 Motels (pop-opera film), 1971; musical nos in Quilp (film), 1974; A Comedy of Errors, Stratford, 1976 (TV musical, 1977); musical As You Like It, Stratford, 1977; Songbook, Globe, 1979; Once in a Lifetime, Aldwych, 1979; new stage act for Tommy Steele, 1979; wedding sequence in Yentl (film), 1982; European Vacation II (film); Pirelli Calendar, 1988; Pickwick, Chichester and Sadler's Wells, 1993; *choreographed for television:* Peter and the Wolf (narrated and mimed all 9 parts), 1958; At the Hawk's Well (ballet), 1975; There was a Girl, 1975; The Fool on the Hill (1st Colour Special for ABC), with Australian Ballet and Sydney Symph. Orch., staged Sydney Opera House, 1975; Muppet Show series, 1976–80; (also musical staging) Alice in Wonderland, 1985; shows and specials for Val Doonican, Perry Como, Petula Clark, Nana Mouskouri, John Curry, Harry Secombe, Ray Charles, and Mike Burstein; also produced and devised Noel Coward and Cleo Laine specials; *directed for television:* Mrs F's Friends, 1981; Easy Money, 1982; Le Morte d'Arthur (also devised), 1983; The Simple Man, 1987 (BAFTA award for direction and choreog.); The Look of Love, 1989. Patron: Indep. Dancers Resettlement Trust; Liverpool Inst. for Performing Arts; Nat. Orgn for Dance and Mime; Lang. of Dance Centre, Holland Pk; Doreen Bird Coll of Performing Arts. *Publications:* (contrib.) Cats, The Book of the Musical; articles in Dancing Times. *Address:* Lean Two Productions Ltd, 18 Rutland Street, SW7 1EF. *Club:* Pickwick.

LYNTON, Norbert Casper; Professor of the History of Art, 1975–89, and Dean of the School of European Studies, 1985–88, University of Sussex, now Professor Emeritus; *b* 22 Sept. 1927; *s* of Paul and Amalie Christiane Lynton; *m* 1st, 1949, Janet Irving; two *s*; 2nd, 1969, Sylvia Anne Towning; two *s*. *Educ:* Douai Sch.; Birkbeck Coll., Univ. of London (BA Gen.); Courtauld Inst., Univ. of London (BA Hons). Lectr in History of Art and Architecture, Leeds Coll. of Art, 1950–61; Sen. Lectr, then Head of Dept of Art History and Gen. Studies, Chelsea Sch. of Art, 1961–70. London Corresp. of Art International, 1961–66; Art Critic, The Guardian, 1965–70; Dir of Exhibitions, Arts Council of GB, 1970–75; Vis. Prof. of History of Art, Open Univ., 1975; Vis. Tutor in Painting, RCA, 1989–92. Trustee, National Portrait Gallery, 1985–. Responsible for many exhibns and catalogues, including: Marc Vaux, NY, 1989; Victor Pasmore, NY, 1959; Ben Nicholson, Tokyo and Japanese tour, 1992–93; for British Council: Henry Moore, Delhi, 1987; Picturing People, Kuala Lumpur, Hong Kong and Singapore, 1989–90; Henry Moore: The human dimension, Leningrad, Moscow, Helsinki, 1991–92. *Publications:* (jtly) Simpson's History of Architectural Development, vol. 4 (Renaissance), 1962; Kenneth Armitage, 1962; Paul Klee, 1964; The Modern World, 1968; The Story of Modern Art, 1980, 2nd edn 1989; Looking at Art, 1981; (jtly) Looking into Paintings, 1985; Victor Pasmore, paintings and graphics 1980–92, 1992; Ben Nicholson, 1993; articles in Burlington Mag., TLS, Studio International, Architectural Design, Art in America, Smithsonian, Leonardo, Modern Painters, etc. *Recreations:* art, people, music, travel. *Address:* 4/14 Clifton Terrace, Brighton BN1 3HA. *T:* Brighton (01273) 328078.

LYON; *see* Bowes Lyon.

LYON, Prof. Christina Margaret; Professor of Common Law and Head of the Department of Law, since 1993, and Dean of the Faculty of Law, since 1994, Liverpool University; *b* 12 Nov. 1952; *d* of Edward Arthur Harrison and Kathleen Joan Harrison; *m* 1976, Adrian Pirrie Lyon, LLB, Barrister; one *s* one *d*. *Educ:* Wallasey High Sch. for Girls; University Coll. London. LLB (1st Cl. Hons) 1974; admitted Solicitor, 1977. Tutor and sometime Lectr in Law, University Coll. London, 1974–75; Trainee and Asst Solicitor, Bell & Joynson, 1975–77; Liverpool University: part-time Tutor in Law, 1976–77; Lectr in Law, 1977–80; Manchester University: Lectr in Law and Law and Social Work, 1980–86; Sub-Dean, Law Faculty, 1986; Prof. of Law, Head of Dept and of Sch. of Law, Keele Univ., 1987–93. Member: ESRC Res. Grants Bd, 1988–91; Child Policy Review Gp, Nat. Children's Bureau, 1989–; Chm., Independent Representation for Children in Need, 1991–; Mem., Nat. Exec. Cttee and Fundraising Cttee, Relate, 1990– (Pres., N Staffs Relate, 1987–93); Vice Chm., Merseyside Panels of Guardians *ad Litem*, 1993–. Dr Barnardo's Research Fellow, 1987–. Jt Editor, Jl of Social Welfare and Family Law (formerly Jl of Social Welfare Law), 1984–. FRSA 1991. *Publications:* Matrimonial Jurisdiction of Magistrates' Courts, 1981; Cohabitation without Marriage, 1983; (ed) Butterworth's Family Law Service Encyclopaedia, 1983, rev. edn 1992; Law of Residential Homes and Day Care Establishments, 1984; Child Abuse, 1990, 2nd edn 1993; The Law Relating to Children in Principles and Practice of Forensic Psychiatry, 1990; (ed with A. P. Lyon) Butterworth's Family Law Handbook, 1991; Atkins Court Forms on Infants, vols I and II, 1992; The Law Relating to Children, 1993; Child Abuse, 1993; Legal Issues Arising from the Care and Control of Children with Learning Disabilities who also Present Severely Challenging Behaviour, vol. I, Policy Guidance, vol. II, A Guide for Parents and Carers, 1994; Child Protection and the Civil Legal Framework in The Child Protection Handbook, 1995; Children's Rights and The Children Act 1989 in Children's Rights, 1995; Working Together: an analysis of collaborative inter-agency responses to the problem of domestic violence in Law and Body Politics, 1995. *Recreations:* riding, swimming, foreign travel, reading, theatre, opera. *Address:* 54 Cromptons Lane, Calderstones, Liverpool L18 3EX.

LYON, Clare; *see* Short, C.

LYON, (Colin) Stewart (Sinclair), FIA; FSA, FRNS; General Manager (Finance), Group Actuary and Director, Legal & General Group Plc, 1980–87; company director; *b* 22 Nov. 1926; *s* of late Col Colin Sinclair Lyon, OBE, TD and Mrs Dorothy Winstanley Lyon (*née* Thomason); *m* 1958, Elizabeth Mary Fargus Richards; four *s* one *d*. *Educ:* Liverpool Coll.; Trinity Coll., Cambridge (MA). FIA 1954; FSA 1972; FRNS 1955. Chief Exec., Victory Insurance Co. Ltd, 1974–76; Chief Actuary, Legal & General Assurance Soc. Ltd, 1976–85. Director: Lautro Ltd, 1987–92; Cologne Reinsurance Co. Ltd, 1987–; City of Birmingham Touring Opera Ltd, 1987–90; Ætna Internat. (UK) Ltd, 1988–91; Pearl Gp PLC, 1991–; UK Bd, AMP and London Life, 1991–. Member: Occupational Pensions Bd, 1979–82; Inquiry into Provision for Retirement, 1983–85; Treasure Trove Reviewing Cttee, 1986–93. President: Inst. of Actuaries, 1982–84 (Gold Medal, 1991); British Numismatic Soc., 1966–70 (Sanford Saltus Gold Medal, 1974). Trustee, Disablement Income Gp Charitable Trust, 1967–84; Dir, Disablement Income Gp, 1984–94; Trustee, Independent Living Fund, 1988–93. *Publications:* (with C. E. Blunt and B. H. I. H. Stewart) Coinage in Tenth-Century England, 1989; papers on Anglo-Saxon coinage, particularly in British Numismatic Jl; contrib. Jl of Inst. of Actuaries and Trans Internat. Congress of Actuaries. *Recreations:* numismatics, music, amateur radio (call sign GW3EIZ). *Address:* Ardraeth, Malltraeth, Bodorgan, Gwynedd LL62 5AW. *T:* Bodorgan (01407) 840273. *Club:* Actuaries'.

LYON, (John) David (Richard); Chief Executive, Rexam plc (formerly Bowater Industries, then Bowater plc), 1987–June 1996; *b* 4 June 1936; *s* of John F. A. Lyon and Elizabeth Lyon (*née* Owen); *m* 1st, 1960, Nicola M. E. Bland (marr. diss. 1986); two *s* (and one *s* decd); 2nd, 1987, Lillis Lanphier. *Educ:* Wellington College; Magdalen College, Oxford (BA Modern History 1959); Harvard Business Sch. (Advanced Management Programme, 1973). 1st Bn The Rifle Brigade, Kenya and Malaya, 1954–56 (despatches). Courtaulds, 1959–70; Rank Organisation, 1970–71; Redland, 1971–87 (Dir 1976; Man. Dir, 1982); Dir, Smiths Industries, 1991–94. Mem., Adv. Cttee on Business and the Envmt, 1991–. *Recreations:* stalking, opera, old fashioned roses, bonfires, and much else. *Address:* c/o Rexam, 114 Knightsbridge, SW1X 7NN. *Club:* Special Forces.

LYON, John MacDonald; Head, Criminal Policy Department, Home Office, since 1994; *b* 12 April 1948; *m*; two *c*. *Educ:* Selwyn Coll., Cambridge (BA Hist., MA). Joined Home Office, 1969; Asst Sec., Cttee on Future of Broadcasting, 1974–77; Sec., Inquiry into Prison Disturbances, 1990–91. *Address:* Home Office, 50 Queen Anne's Gate, SW1H 9AT.

LYON, Mary Frances, ScD; FRS 1973; Deputy Director, Medical Research Council Radiobiology Unit, Harwell, 1982–90, retired; *b* 15 May 1925; *e d* of Clifford James Lyon and Louise Frances Lyon (*née* Kirby). *Educ:* King Edward's Sch., Birmingham; Woking Grammar Sch.; Girton Coll., Cambridge (ScD 1968; Hon. Fellow 1985). FIBiol. MRC Scientific Staff, Inst. of Animal Genetics, Edinburgh, 1950–55; MRC Radiobiology Unit, Harwell, 1955–90, Hd Genetics Div., 1962–87. Clothworkers Visiting Research Fellow, Girton Coll., Cambridge, 1970–71. Foreign Hon. Mem., Amer. Acad. Arts and Scis, 1980 (Amory Prize, 1977). Foreign Associate, US Nat. Acad. of Scis, 1979. Royal Medal, Royal Soc., 1984; Prize for Genetics, Sanremo, Italy, 1985; Gairdner Foundn Award, 1985; Allan Award, Amer. Soc. of Human Genetics, 1986. *Publications:* papers on genetics in scientific jls. *Address:* MRC Radiobiology Unit, Chilton, Oxon OX11 0RD. *T:* Abingdon (01235) 834393.

LYON, Maj.-Gen. Robert, CB 1976; OBE 1964 (MBE 1960); Bursar, Loretto School, Musselburgh, 1979–91; *b* Ayr, 24 Oct. 1923; *s* of David Murray Lyon and Bridget Lyon (*née* Smith); *m* 1st, 1951, Constance Margaret Gordon (*d* 1982); one *s* one *d*; 2nd, 1992, Rosemary Jane, *d* of G. H. Allchin, Torquay. *Educ:* Ayr Academy. Commissioned, Aug. 1943, Argyll and Sutherland Highlanders. Served Italy, Germany, Palestine, Greece; transf. to Regular Commn in RA, 1947; Regtl Service, 3 RHA in Libya and 19 Field in BAOR, 1948–56; Instr, Mons Officer Cadet Sch., 1953–55; Staff Coll., 1957; DAQMG, 3 Div., 1958–60; jssc, 1960; BC F (Sphinx) Bty 7 PARA, RHA, 1961–62 (Bt Lt-Col); GSO1, ASD2, MoD, 1962–65 (Lt-Col); CO 4 Lt Regt, RA, 1965–67, Borneo (despatches), UK and BAOR (Lt-Col); as Brig.: CRA 1 Div., 1967–69, BAOR; IDC, 1970; Dir Operational Requirements, MoD, 1971–73; DRA (Maj.-Gen.), 1973–75; GOC SW District, 1975–78; retired 1979. Pres., Army Hockey Assoc., 1974–76; Chm., Army Golf Assoc., 1977–78. Chm., RA Council of Scotland, 1984–90. Col Comdt RA. Director: Braemar Civic Amenities Trust, 1986–90; Edinburgh Military Tattoo Ltd, 1988–. HM Comr, Queen Victoria Sch., Dunblane, 1984–95. Pres., La Punta Urbanisation, Los Cristianos, 1995–. FIMgt (MBIM 1978). *Publication:* Irish Roulette, 1991. *Recreations:* golf, writing. *Address:* (Apr. to Nov.) Woodside, Braemar, Aberdeenshire AB3 5YB. *T:* Braemar (013397) 41667; (Nov. to Apr.) Appt 6 La Punta, Avenida de Suecia, Los Cristianos, Tenerife, Canary Is. *T:* (22) 794592. *Club:* New (Edinburgh); Hon. Company of Edinburgh Golfers; Craigendarroch Country.

LYON, Hon. Sterling Rufus Webster, PC 1982; **Hon. Mr Justice Lyon;** a Judge of the Manitoba Court of Appeal, since 1986; *b* 30 Jan. 1927; *s* of David Rufus Lyon and Ella May (*née* Cuthbert); *m* 1953, Barbara Jean Mayers; two *s* three *d*. *Educ:* Portage Collegiate (Governor-General's Medal); United College (BA 1948); Univ. of Manitoba Law Sch. (LLB 1953). Crown Attorney, Manitoba, 1953–57; QC (Canada) 1960. Member, Manitoba Legislative Assembly, and Executive Council, 1958–69; Attorney-General, 1958–63 and 1966–69; Minister of: Municipal Affairs, 1960–61; Public Utilities, 1961–63; Mines and Natural Resources, 1963–66; Tourism and Recreation, Commissioner of Northern Affairs, 1966–68; Govt House Leader, 1966–69; Leader, Progressive Cons. Party of Manitoba, 1975–83; MLA: for Fort Garry, 1958–69; for Souris-Killarney, 1976–77; for Charleswood, 1977–86; Leader of the Opposition, Manitoba, 1976–77 and 1981–83; Premier of Manitoba and Minister of Dominion-Provincial Affairs, 1977–81. *Recreations:* hunting, fishing. *Address:* Law Courts, Winnipeg, Manitoba R3C 0V8, Canada. *T:* (204) 9452050. *Club:* Albany (Toronto).

LYON, Stewart; *see* Lyon, C. S. S.

LYON-DALBERG-ACTON, family name of **Baron Acton.**

LYONS, Alastair David; Chief Executive, National & Provincial Building Society, since 1994; *b* 18 Oct. 1953; *o s* of late Alexander Lyons and of Elizabeth (*née* Eynon); *m* 1980, Judith Shauneen Rhodes; one *s* two *d*. *Educ:* Whitgift Sch.; Trinity Coll., Cambridge (Sen. Schol.; MA 2nd Cl. Hons). With Price Waterhouse & Co., 1974–79; N. M. Rothschild & Sons Ltd, 1979; H. P. Bulmer Holdings PLC, 1979–88: Gp Treas., 1979–82; Gp Financial Controller, 1983–88; Actg Gp Finance Dir, and Finance Dir, H. P. Bulmer Drinks Ltd, 1988–89; Divl Dir, Corporate Finance, Asda Gp PLC, 1989–90; Finance Director: ASDA Stores Ltd, 1990–91; Nat. & Provincial Building Soc., 1991–94. Non-exec. Dir, Benefits Agency, 1994–. Mem., Yorks Regl Cttee, NT, 1994–. Gov., Giggleswick Sch., 1994–. *Recreations:* cycling, running, riding, hill walking, collecting antiques. *Address:* c/o Provincial House, Bradford BD1 1NL.

LYONS, Bernard, CBE 1964; JP; DL; Chairman: UDS Group PLC, 1972–82 (Director, 1954–83; Joint Managing Director, 1966; Managing Director, 1972–79); Colmore Trust

Ltd, since 1984; *b* 30 March 1913; *m* 1938, Lucy Hurst; three *s* one *d*. *Educ:* Leeds Grammar Sch. Chairman: Yorkshire and City Properties Ltd, 1956–73; Glanfield Securities, 1958–74. Chm., Yorkshire and NE Conciliation Cttee, Race Relations Bd, 1968–70; Member: Leeds City Council, 1951–65; Community Relations Commn, 1970–72; Govt Adv. Cttee on Retail Distribution, 1970–76. Mem. Court and Council, Univ. of Leeds, 1953–58; Chm., Swarthmore Adult Educn Centre Appeal for Building Extensions, 1957–60. Chm., Leeds Judean Youth Club, 1955–70; Jt Chm., Leeds Br., CCJ, 1955–60; Life Pres., Leeds Jewish Representative Council, 1960–. JP Leeds, 1960; DL West Riding, Yorks, 1971. Hon. LLD Leeds, 1973. *Publications:* The Thread is Strong, 1981; The Narrow Edge, 1985. *Recreations:* farming, forestry, travel, writing. *Address:* Upton Wood, Fulmer, Bucks SL3 6JJ. *T:* Fulmer (01753) 662404.

See also S. R. Lyons.

LYONS, Charles Albert; General Secretary, Transport Salaried Staffs' Association, 1982–89, retired; *b* Liverpool, 13 Aug. 1929; *s* of Maurice Lyons and Catherine Jones; *m* 1958, Judith Mary Robinson; three *s*. *Educ:* St Mary's RC Secondary Modern Sch., Fleetwood. Wages Clerk, fishing industry, 1943–47; National Service, RAPC, 1947–49; Clerical Officer, British Rail, 1950–59; Transport Salaried Staffs' Association: Clerical Asst, 1959–64; Scottish Sec., 1965–68; London Midland Div. Officer, 1968–73; Asst Gen. Sec., 1973–77; Senior Asst Gen. Sec., 1977–82; Member: TUC Gen. Council, 1983–89 (Mem. Committees: Finance and Gen. Purposes; Equal Rights; Transport; Public Enterprise; Social Insurance and Indust. Welfare; Employment, Policy and Orgn); Hotels and Catering Industrial Training Bd, 1982–84; Railway Industry Adv. Cttee, 1982–86; Jt Council for Railways, EEC; Vice-Chm., ITF Travel Bureau Section, 1979–89; individual Mem., Labour Party, 1950–.

LYONS, Dennis John, CB 1972; CEng, FRAeS; Director General of Research, Department of the Environment, 1971–76; *b* 26 Aug. 1916; *s* of late John Sylvester Lyons and of Adela Maud Lyons; *m* 1939, Elisabeth, *d* of Arnold and Maria Friederika Müller Haefliger, Weggis, Switzerland; five *s* two *d*. *Educ:* Grocers' Company School; Queen Mary Coll., London Univ. (Fellow, 1969). Aerodynamics Dept, Royal Aircraft Estabt, 1937; RAFVR, 1935–41; Aerodynamics Flight Aero Dept, RAE, 1941–51; Head of Experimental Projects Div., Guided Missiles Dept, RAE, 1951; Head of Ballistic Missile Group, GW Dept, 1956; Head of Weapons Dept, RAE, 1962; Dir., Road Research Laboratory, 1965–71. Member: Adv. Board for Res. Councils, 1973–76; SRC, 1973–76; Engineering Bd, SRC, 1970–76; Natural Environment Res. Council, 1973–76. Pres. OECD Road Research Unit, 1968–72. Hon. Mem., Instn Highway Engineers. *Publications:* papers in scientific jls. *Recreations:* ski-ing, pottery-making, philately. *Address:* Summerhaven, Gough Road, Fleet, Hants GU13 8LJ. *T:* Fleet (01252) 4773.

LYONS, Edward; QC 1974; LLB; a Recorder of the Crown Court, since 1972; *b* 17 May 1926; *s* of late A. Lyons and of Mrs S. Taylor; *m* 1955, Barbara, *d* of Alfred Katz; one *s* one *d*. *Educ:* Roundhay High Sch.; Leeds Univ. LLB (Hons) 1951. Served Royal Artillery, 1944–48; Combined Services Russian Course, Cambridge Univ., 1946; Interpreter in Russian, Brit. CCG, 1946–48. Called to Bar, Lincoln's Inn, 1952, Bencher, 1983. MP (Lab 1966–81, SDP 1981–83) Bradford E, 1966–74, Bradford W, 1974–83; PPS at Treasury, 1969–70; SDP Parly spokesman: on home affairs, 1981–82; on legal affairs, 1982–83. Member: H of C Select Cttee on European Legislation, 1975–83; SDP Nat. Cttee, 1984–90; Chairman: PLP Legal and Judicial Gp, 1974–77; PLP Home Office Gp, 1974–79 (Dep. Chm., 1970–74). Contested: (Lab) Harrogate, 1964; (SDP) Bradford W, 1983; (SDP) Yorkshire West, European Parly Elecn, 1984. Mem., Exec. of Justice, 1974–89. *Recreations:* history, opera. *Address:* 4 Brick Court, Temple, EC4Y 9AD. *T:* 0171–797 8910; 59 Westminster Gardens, Marsham Street, SW1P 4JG. *T:* 0171–834 1960; 4 Primley Park Lane, Leeds LS17 7JR. *T:* Leeds (0113) 268 5351; 6 Park Square, Leeds LS1 2NG. *T:* Leeds (0113) 245 9763.

LYONS, Sir Edward Houghton, Kt 1977; FAIM; Chairman, Totalisator Administration Board, Queensland, 1981–85. Formerly Chairman, Katies Ltd, and Gen. Manager, Industrial Acceptance Corp. Ltd; Dir, Bruck (Australia) Ltd. Trustee, National Party. *Address:* 47 Kneale Street, Holland Park Heights, Queensland 4121, Australia. *T:* (7) 33496461.

LYONS, (Isidore) Jack; Chairman: J. E. London Properties Ltd, since 1986; Natural Nutrition Company Ltd, 1989–91; Advisor, Cranbury Group, 1981–89; Director of other companies; *b* 1 Feb. 1916; *s* of Samuel H. Lyons and Sophia Niman; *m* 1943, Roslyn Marion Rosenbaum; two *s* two *d*. *Educ:* Leeds Grammar Sch. Dir, UDS Gp, 1955–80. Chm., Leeds Musical Festival, 1955–72, Vice-Pres., 1973; Jt Founder, 1961, and former Chm., Leeds Internat. Pianoforte Competition; Chm., London Symphony Orchestra Trust, 1970–91 (Jt Chm., 1963–70), Trustee, 1970– (Hon. Mem., LSO, 1973); Jt Chm., Southwark Rehearsal Hall Trust, 1974–; Chm., Shakespeare Exhibn (quatercentenary celebrations Stratford-upon-Avon), 1964; Mem. Exec. Cttee, Royal Acad. of Dancing, 1964; Life Trustee, Shakespeare Birthplace Trust, 1967; Mem., Culture Adv. Cttee, UNESCO, 1973–, Dep. Chm., Fanfare for Europe, 1972–73; Chm., FCO US Bicentennial Cttee for the Arts, 1973–; Mem., Adv. Cttee of Honour, Britain's Salute to NY 1983 Bicentennial. Chairman: Sir Jack Lyons Charitable Trust; Musical Therapy Charity, 1984–85; Trustee, Heslington Foundn for Music and Associated Arts, 1987–; Dir, Wolf Trap Foundn, USA. Vice-Pres., Anglo-Italian Chamber of Commerce, 1977–. Vice-Pres., Jt Israel Appeal, 1972– (Dep. Chm. 1957); Chm., Fedn of Jewish Relief Organisations, 1958–86. Member: Canadian Veterans' Assoc., 1964; Pilgrims, 1965. Mem. Council, Internat. Triangle Res. Inst., 1983–. Patron, St Gemma's Hospice. Dep. Chm., Governors of Carmel Coll., 1961–69; Mem. Ct, York Univ., 1965. FRSA 1973. Hon. FRAM, 1972. DUniv York, 1975. *Recreations:* music, the arts and swimming.

LYONS, Sir James (Reginald), Kt 1969; JP; Chairman and Company Director, Park Lodge Property Company; Airport Manager, Cardiff Airport, 1955–75; *b* 15 March 1910; *s* of James Lyons; *m* 1937, Doreen Mary Fogg; one *s*. *Educ:* Howard Gardens High Sch.; Cardiff Technical Coll. Served War of 1939–45: Royal Tank Regt, 1940–46 (1939–45 Star, Africa Star, Italy Star, Defence Medal, War Medal of 1939–45). Civil Service, 1929–65: Post Office, Min. of Supply, Min. of Aviation. Mem., Wales Tourist Bd. Glamorgan CC, 1965–74; Cardiff City Council: Councillor, 1949–58; Alderman, 1958–74; Lord Mayor of Cardiff, 1968–69. Mem., Norfolk Cttee for investiture of Prince of Wales, 1968–69. Mem., BBC Broadcasting Council. Assessor under Race Relations Act, 1976. President: Welsh Games Council, 1985– (Life Vice-Pres., 1975); Cardiff Horticultural Soc., 1962–. Trustee, Wales and Border Counties TSB. Chairman of Governors: UC Cardiff, 1955–70; St Illtyd's Coll., 1956–; Governor, De La Salle Prep. Sch. JP Cardiff, 1966–. OStJ; KCSG. *Recreations:* Rugby football, swimming, tennis. *Address:* 101 Minehead Avenue, Sully, S Glam CF6 2TL. *T:* Sully (01222) 530403.

LYONS, Sir John, Kt 1987; FBA 1973; Master of Trinity Hall, Cambridge, since 1984; *b* 23 May 1932; *s* of Michael A. Lyons and Mary B. Lyons (*née* Sullivan); *m* 1959, Danielle J. Simonet; two *d*. *Educ:* St Bede's Coll., Manchester; Christ's Coll., Cambridge. MA; PhD 1961; LittD 1988. Lecturer: in Comparative Linguistics, SOAS, 1957–61; in General Linguistics, Univ. of Cambridge, 1961–64; Prof. of General Linguistics, Edinburgh Univ., 1964–76; Prof. of Linguistics, 1976–84, Pro-Vice-Chancellor, 1981–84, Sussex Univ. DèsL (*hc*) Univ. Catholique de Louvain, 1980; Hon. DLitt: Reading, 1986; Edinburgh, 1988; Sussex, 1990; Antwerp, 1992. *Publications:* Structural Semantics, 1964; Introduction to Theoretical Linguistics, 1968; New Horizons in Linguistics, 1970; Chomsky, 1970, 3rd edn 1991; Semantics, vols 1 and 2, 1977; Language and Linguistics, 1981; Language, Meaning and Context, 1981, 2nd edn 1991; Natural Language and Universal Grammar, 1991; Linguistic Semantics, 1995; articles and reviews in learned journals. *Address:* The Master's Lodge, Trinity Hall, Cambridge CB2 1TJ.

LYONS, John, CBE 1986; General Secretary, Engineers' and Managers' Association, 1977–91, and Electrical Power Engineers' Association, 1973–91; *b* 19 May 1926; *s* of Joseph and Hetty Lyons; *m* 1954, Molly McCall; two *s* two *d*. *Educ:* St Paul's Sch.; Polytechnic, Regent Street; Cambridge Univ. (BA Econ). RN 1944–46. Asst. to Manager of Market Research Dept, Vacuum Oil Co., 1950; Research Officer: Bureau of Current Affairs, 1951; Post Office Engineering Union, 1952–57; Asst. Sec., Instn of Professional Civil Servants 1957–66, Dep. Gen. Sec. 1966–73. Member: TUC Gen. Council, 1983–91 (Chm., Energy Cttee, 1988–91); Nat. Enterprise Bd, 1975–79; Exec. Cttee PEP, 1975–78; Council, PSI, 1978–80; Adv. Council for Applied R&D, 1978–81; Engrg Council, 1982–86; PO Bd, 1980–81, British Telecommunications Bd, 1981–83; Sec., Electricity Supply Trade Union Council (formerly Employees' Nat. Cttee for Electricity Supply Industry), 1976–91; Chm., NEDO Working Party on Industrial Trucks, 1977–80. A Vice-Pres., Industrial Participation Assoc., 1976–90; British rep., Econ. and Social Cttee, EU (formerly EC), 1990–. Governor, Kingsbury High School, 1974–86; Member: Court of Governors, LSE, 1978–84; Bd of Governors, London Business Sch., 1987–88. Hitachi Lectr, Sussex Univ., 1983; addresses to: British Assoc., 1973; IEE, 1977; Internat. Monetary Conference, 1984; Newcastle Univ., 1989. FRSA. Hon. Life Mem., EPEA, 1991; Hon. Fellow, IIEXE, 1992. *Publications:* various papers and articles. *Recreation:* family. *Address:* 305 Salmon Street, Kingsbury, NW9 8YA.

LYONS, Prof. Malcolm Cameron; Sir Thomas Adams's Professor of Arabic, University of Cambridge, 1985–Sept. 1996; Fellow, Pembroke College, Cambridge, since 1957 (President, 1989–93); *b* Indore, India, 11 Feb. 1929; *s* of Harold William Lyons and Florence Katharine (*née* Cameron); *m* 1961, Ursula Schedler. *Educ:* New Park Sch., St Andrews; Fettes Coll.; Pembroke Coll., Cambridge (Major Open Classical Schol., 1946; John Stewart of Rannoch Classical Schol. in Latin and Greek, 1948; Browne Medallist, 1948, 1949; 1st cl. hons Pts I and II, Classical Tripos, 1948, 1949; 1st cl. hons Pts I and II, Oriental Studies, Arabic and Persian, 1953; E. G. Browne Prize, 1953; MA 1954; PhD 1957). RAF, 1949–51, commissioned 1950. University of Cambridge: Asst Lectr in Arabic, 1954–59; Lectr, 1959–84; Reader in Medieval Islamic Studies, 1984–85. Seconded to FO as Principal Instructor, MECAS, Lebanon, 1961–62. Founder Editor: Arabic Technical and Scientific Texts, 1966–78; Jl of Arabic Literature, 1970–. *Publications:* Galen on Anatomical Procedures (with W. Duckworth and B. Towers), 1962; In Hippocratis de Officina Medici, 1963, and De Partibus Artis Medicativae, De Causis Contentivis, De Diaeta in Morbis Acutis (in Corpus Medicorum Graecorum), 1967; An Arabic Translation of Themistius' Commentary on Aristotle's De Anima, 1973; Aristotle's Ars Rhetorica, Arabic version, 1982; (with E. Maalouf) The Poetic Vocabulary of Michel Trad, 1968; (with J. Riley-Smith and U. Lyons) Ayyubids, Mamlukes and Crusaders, 1971; (with D. Jackson) Saladin, The Politics of the Holy War, 1982; (jtly) Meredith Dewey: diaries, letters, writings, 1992; The Arabian Epic, 1995; articles and reviews in learned jls. *Recreations:* golf, ski-ing, walking. *Address:* Pembroke College, Cambridge CB1 2RF. *T:* Cambridge (01223) 352241. *Club:* Royal and Ancient Golf (St Andrews).

LYONS, Michael Thomas; Chief Executive, Birmingham City Council, since 1994; *b* West Ham, 15 Sept. 1949; *s* of Thomas Lyons and Lillian Lyons (*née* Stafford); *m* 1976, Gwendolene Jane Calvert; two *s* one *d*. *Educ:* Stratford Grammar Sch.; Middlesex Polytechnic (BA Soc. Scis Hons); Queen Mary Coll., London (MSc Econ). Street market trader, 1970–72; Brand Manager, Crookes Anestan, 1971–72; Lectr and Res. Fellow, Dept of Industrial Econs, Univ. of Nottingham, 1973–75; Sen. Res. Officer, DoE, 1975–78; W Midlands County Council: Principal Economist, 1978–82; Dep. Dir and Dir, Economic Develt, 1982–85; Chief Executive: Wolverhampton MBC, 1985–90; Notts CC, 1990–94. Councillor, Birmingham City Council, 1980–83. FRSA. *Publications:* (ed with A. Johnson) The Winning Bid, 1992; contribs to professional jls. *Recreations:* the demands of a young and energetic family, developing my kitchen skills, cinema, walking. *Address:* The Council House, Victoria Square, Birmingham B1 1BB. *T:* 0121–235 2000.

LYONS, Roger Alan; General Secretary, Manufacturing Science and Finance Union, since 1992; *b* 14 Sept. 1942; *s* of late Morris and Phyllis Lyons; *m* 1971, Kitty Horvath; two *s* two *d*. *Educ:* Roe Green Junior Sch., Kingsbury; Christ's Coll., Finchley; University Coll. London (BSc Hons Econ.). Regional Officer, ASSET, then ASTMS, 1966–70; Nat. Officer 1970–87, Asst Gen. Sec. 1987–89, ASTMS; Asst Gen. Sec., MSF, 1989–92. Exec., European Metalworker Fedn, 1987–; Mem., Gen. Council, TUC, 1990–. Mem., Monopolies and Mergers Commn, 1995–. *Recreations:* family, take-aways, cinema, football (Arsenal in particular). *Address:* 22 Park Crescent, N3 2NJ. *T:* 0181–346 6843, *Fax:* 0181–349 9075.

LYONS, Sally; *see* Morgan, S.

LYONS, Shaun; His Honour Judge Lyons; a Circuit Judge, since 1992; Resident Judge, Wood Green Crown Court, since 1995; *b* 20 Dec. 1942; *s* of late Jeremiah Lyons and of Winifred Ruth Lyons; *m* 1970, Nicola Rosemary, *d* of late Capt. D. F. Chilton, DSO, RN; one *s* one *d*. *Educ:* Portsmouth Grammar Sch.; Inns of Court Sch. of Law. Joined RN, 1961; Lt 1966; Lt Comdr 1974; called to the Bar, Middle Temple, 1975; Comdr 1981; Captain 1988; Chief Naval Judge Advocate, 1989–92; retd RN, 1992. Asst Recorder and Recorder, 1988–92. *Club:* Army and Navy.

LYONS, Stuart Randolph, CBE 1993; Chief Executive, Royal Doulton, since 1985 (Chairman, 1987–93); Chairman: Lawleys Ltd; The Royal Crown Derby Porcelain Co. Ltd, Minton Ltd, Royal Doulton subsidiaries in UK, USA, Canada, Australia, Japan and Hong Kong; *b* 24 Oct. 1943; 3rd *s* of Bernard Lyons, *qv*; *m* 1969, Ellen Harriet Zion; two *s* one *d*. *Educ:* Rugby (Scholar); King's Coll., Cambridge (Major Scholar; 1st Cl. Hons Pt I Classical Tripos, Cl. II(I) Pt II Classical Tripos; BA 1965, MA 1969). Man. Dir, John Collier Tailoring Ltd, 1969–74 (Chm., 1975–83); Dir, UDS Group plc, 1974–83 (Man. Dir, 1979–83); Chairman: Wm Timpson, 1976–83; Richard Shops, 1982–83. Dir, British Ceramic Res. Ltd, 1987–94. Member: Leeds CC, 1970–74; Yorkshire and Humberside Econ. Planning Council, 1972–75; Clothing EDC, 1976–79; Ordnance Survey Review Cttee, 1978–79; Monopolies and Mergers Commn, 1981–85; Council, CBI, 1991–; Nat. Manufacturing Council, 1992–; Dir, Staffs TEC, 1990–93. Pres., BCMF, 1989–90; Chairman: British Ceramic Confedn, 1989–95; Staffs Devlt Assoc., 1992–95; W Midlands Develt Assoc., 1995–; Vice-Chm., Industry 96 (W Midlands Fest. of Industry and Enterprise), 1994–. Mem. Council, Keele Univ., 1989–; Gov., Staffs Univ. (formerly Staffs Poly.), 1991–. Contested (C) Halifax, Feb. and Oct. 1974. Hon. DLitt Keele, 1994. *Address:* Minton House, London Road, Stoke-on-Trent ST4 7QD. *T:* Stoke-on-Trent (01782) 292292. *Clubs:* Carlton, Hurlingham, Potters.

LYSAGHT, family name of **Baron Lisle.**

LYTHALL, Basil Wilfrid, CB 1966; MA; occasional research consultant; *b* 15 May 1919; *s* of Frank Herbert Lythall and Winifred Mary (*née* Carver); *m* 1942, Mary Olwen Dando; one *s*. *Educ:* King Edward's Sch., Stourbridge; Christ Church, Oxford. Joined Royal Naval Scientific Service, 1940; Admiralty Signal and Radar Establishment, 1940–53; Admiralty Research Laboratory, 1954–57; Asst Dir of Physical Research, Admty, 1957–58; a Dep. Chief Scientist, Admty Signal and Radar Estabt (later Admty Surface Weapons Estabt), 1958–60; first Chief Scientist of Admty Underwater Weapons Estabt, Portland, 1960–64; Member of Admiralty Bd of Defence Council and Chief Scientist (Royal Navy), 1964–78; Dep. Controller, R&D Estab., Procurement Exec., 1971–78; Dir, SACLANT Anti-Submarine Warfare Res. Centre, La Spezia, Italy, 1978–81. Chm., Policy Bd, Centre for Operational Res. and Defence Analysis, CAP Scientific Ltd, 1986–88. Technical Advr, Monopolies and Mergers Commn, 1989, 1990. Trustee, National Maritime Museum, 1974–80. UK Mem., Editorial Bd, Naval Forces, 1986–. *Publications:* occasional articles in learned jls. *Recreations:* gardening, sculpting, genealogy. *Address:* 48 Grove Way, Esher, Surrey KT10 8HL. *T:* 0181–398 2958.

LYTHGO, Wilbur Reginald, OBE 1964; HM Diplomatic Service, retired; *b* 7 June 1920; *yr s* of late Alfred and Marion Lythgo, Monkton, Ayrshire; *m* 1943, Patricia Frances Sylvia Smith; two *s*. *Educ:* Palmer's Sch., Grays, Essex. Joined Home Office, 1937. Served in RASC, 1939–41 and Indian Army, 1941–46. Rejoined Home Office, 1946; British Information Services, New Delhi, 1948–54; UK High Commn, New Delhi, 1956–59; British High Commn, Ottawa, 1962–66; Head of Office Services and Supply Dept, DSAO, 1966–68; Counsellor, British Embassy, and Consul-Gen., Washington DC, 1968–71; Consul-Gen., Cleveland, Ohio, 1971–73. Hon. Kentucky Col, 1971. *Recreations:* reading, gardening. *Address:* 200 Dovercourt Avenue, Ottawa, Ontario K1Z 7H2, Canada. *T:* (613) 7223242.

LYTHGOE, Prof. Basil, FRS 1958; Professor of Organic Chemistry, Leeds University, 1953–78, now Emeritus; *b* 18 Aug. 1913; 2nd *s* of Peter Whitaker and Agnes Lythgoe; *m* 1946, Kathleen Cameron, *er d* of H. J. Hallum, St Andrews; two *s*. *Educ:* Leigh Grammar Sch.; Manchester Univ. Asst Lectr, Manchester Univ., 1938; Univ. Lectr, Cambridge Univ., 1946. Fellow of King's Coll., Cambridge, 1950. *Publications:* papers on chemistry of natural products, in Jl of Chem. Soc. *Recreation:* mountaineering. *Address:* 113 Cookridge Lane, Leeds LS16 7NB. *T:* Leeds (0113) 267 8837.

LYTHGOE, Ian Gordon, CB 1975; company director, retired; *b* 30 Dec. 1914; *s* of John and Susan Lythgoe; *m* 1st, 1939, Marjory Elsie Fleming; three *s*; 2nd, 1971, Mary Margaret Pickard, CBE 1980. *Educ:* Southland Boys' High Sch., Invercargill; Victoria UC, Wellington. MComm (Hons); FCA(NZ). Private Sec., Ministers of Finance, 1944–53; Asst Sec., Treasury, 1962; State Services Commission: Mem., 1964–66; Dep. Chm., 1967–70; Chm., 1971–74. NZ Soc. of Accountants: Mem. Council, 1966–76; Vice-Pres., 1973–74; Pres., 1974–75; Chm., Disciplinary Cttee, 1982–87 (Mem., 1979–87). Mem. Council, Central Inst. of Technology, 1977–86 (Vice Chm., 1978–80, Chm., 1980–86). Member: Commn of Enquiry into Rescue and Fire Safety at Internat. Airports (NZ); Information Authority, 1982–88; Commn of Enquiry concerning Ian David Donaldson, 1983. Director: Fletcher Challenge Corp. Ltd (formerly Challenge Corp. Ltd), 1975–84; Philips Electrical Industries Ltd, 1975–87. *Recreations:* gardening, reading. *Address:* 6A/19 Cottleville Terrace, Wellington 6001, New Zealand. *Club:* Wellington (Wellington, NZ).

LYTLE, Maj.-Gen. Simon William St John, CB 1995; Director, Army Aviation (formerly Army Air Corps), since 1992; *b* 1 Oct. 1940; *s* of Dr W. D. F., (Bobby), Lytle, and Anne M. E. Lytle; *m* 1966, Pamela Mary O'Ferrall; three *s*. *Educ:* Sherborne; RMA Sandhurst. Commissioned RIrF, 1960; transf. AAC, 1969; Staff College, Camberley, 1973; CO 1 Regt AAC, 1980–83; MoD, 1984–87; Comd Avn, BAOR, 1987–89; RCDS, 1989; Dir, Army Recruiting, 1990–92. *Recreations:* sailing, bridge, tennis. *Clubs:* MCC, Royal Automobile; Leckford Golf.

LYTTELTON, family name of **Viscount Chandos** and of **Viscount Cobham.**

LYTTELTON, Humphrey Richard Adeane; musician; band-leader (specializing in Jazz); journalist; *b* Eton, Bucks, 23 May 1921; *s* of late Hon. George William Lyttelton; *m* 1st, 1948, Patricia Mary Braithwaite (marr. diss. 1952); one *d*; 2nd, 1952, Elizabeth Jill, *d* of Albert E. Richardson; two *s* one *d*. *Educ:* Sunningdale Sch.; Eton Coll.; Camberwell Sch. of Art; self-taught as regards musical educn. Served War of 1939–45: Grenadier Guards, 1941–46. Cartoonist, Daily Mail, 1949–53. Formed his own band, 1948; leader of Humphrey Lyttelton's Band, and free-lance journalist, 1953–; founded: own record label, Calligraph, 1984; own music publishers, Humph Music. Has composed over 150 original works for his band; numerous recordings and television appearances; jazz festival appearances, Nice, Bracknell, Zürich, Camden, Montreux, Newcastle, Warsaw. Compère, BBC radio jazz programmes: Jazz Scene, Jazz Club, The Best of Jazz, etc. Pres., Soc. for Italic Handwriting, 1990–. Hon. Prof. of Music, Keele Univ., 1993–. Hon. DLitt: Warwick, 1987; Loughborough, 1988; Hon. DMus: Durham, 1989; Keele, 1992. *Publications:* I Play as I Please, 1954; Second Chorus, 1958; Take It from the Top (autobiog.), 1975; The Best of Jazz: Basin Street to Harlem, 1978; Humphrey Lyttelton's Jazz and Big Band Quiz, 1979; The Best of Jazz 2—Enter the Giants, 1981; Why No Beethoven? the diary of a vagrant musician, 1984; contributor: Melody Maker, 1954–; Reynolds News, 1955–62; Sunday Citizen, 1962–67; Harper's & Queen's, Punch, The Field, High Life. *Recreations:* birdwatching, calligraphy. *Address:* BBC Light Music Department, Broadcasting House, Portland Place, W1A 4WW. *T:* 0171–580 4468; (home) Alyn Close, Barnet Road, Arkley, Herts.

LYTTLE, James Brian Chambers; Secretary, Probation Board for Northern Ireland, since 1987; *b* 22 Aug. 1932; *s* of late James Chambers Lyttle and Margaret Kirkwood Billingsley; *m* 1957, Mary Alma Davidson; four *d*. *Educ:* Bangor Grammar Sch.; Trinity Coll., Dublin (BA 1st Cl. Hons Classics). Entered NI Civil Service as Asst Principal, 1954; Private Sec. to Minister of Commerce, 1960–62; Chief Exec., Enterprise Ulster, 1972–75; Dir, Employment Service, Dept of Manpower Services, 1975–77; Dir, Industrial Develt Orgn, Dept of Commerce, 1977–81; Under Secretary, Dept of Commerce, later Dept of Economic Develt, 1977–84; Under Sec., Dept of Finance and Personnel, 1984–87. *Recreations:* reading, walking, music.

LYTTON, family name of **Earl of Lytton.**

LYTTON, 5th Earl of, *cr* 1880; **John Peter Michael Scawen Lytton;** Baron Wentworth, 1529; Bt 1838; Baron Lytton, 1866; Viscount Knebworth, 1880; Sole practitioner, John Lytton & Co., Chartered Surveyors and Valuers, since 1988; *b* 7 June 1950; *s* of 4th Earl of Lytton, OBE, and of Clarissa Mary, *d* of Brig.-Gen. C. E. Palmer, CB, CMG, DSO, RA; *S* father, 1985; *m* 1980, Ursula Alexandra (*née* Komoly); two *s* one *d*. *Educ:* Downside; Reading Univ. (BSc, Estate Management). FRICS 1987 (ARICS 1976); IRRV 1990. Chairman: Horsham Chamber of Trade and Commerce, 1993–95; Leasehold Enfranchisement Adv. Service, 1994–. Mem. Council, CLA, 1993– (Exec., 1994–). Pres., Newstead Abbey Byron Soc., 1988–. *Heir: s* Viscount Knebworth, *qv*. *Address:* (office) Estate Office, Newbuildings Place, Shipley, Horsham, West Sussex RH13 7JQ. *T:* Coolham (01403) 741650.

LYTTON COBBOLD, family name of **Baron Cobbold.**

LYVEDEN, 6th Baron *cr* 1859; **Ronald Cecil Vernon;** retired; *b* 10 April 1915; *s* of 5th Baron Lyveden and Ruby (*née* Shanley) (*d* 1932); *S* father 1973; *m* 1938, Queenie Constance, *d* of Howard Ardern; three *s*. *Educ:* Te Aroha College. *Heir: e s* Hon. Jack Leslie Vernon [*b* 10 Nov. 1938; *m* 1961, Lynette June, *d* of William Herbert Lilley; one *s* two *d*]. *Address:* 20 Farmer Street, Te Aroha, New Zealand. *T:* 410. *Club:* RSA (Te Aroha).

M

MA LIN, Hon. CBE 1983; PhD; JP; Emeritus Professor of Biochemistry, and Chairman of Board of Trustees of Shaw College, since 1986, The Chinese University of Hong Kong; *b* 8 Feb. 1925; *s* of late Prof. Ma Kiam and Sing-yu Cheng; *m* 1958, Dr Meng-Hua Chen; three *d*. *Educ:* West China Union Univ., China (BSc); Univ. of Leeds (PhD). Postdoctorate Fellow, University College Hosp. Med. Sch., London, and St James's Hosp., Leeds, 1955–56. Assistant Lectr, 1957–59, and Lectr, 1959–64, in Clinical Chemistry, Dept of Pathology, Univ. of Hong Kong; Chinese University of Hong Kong: part-time Lectr in Chemistry, 1964; Sen. Lectr, 1965–72, Reader, 1972–73, Prof., 1973–78, in Biochemistry; Dean of Faculty of Science, 1973–75; Vice-Chancellor, 1978–87. Visiting Biochemist, Hormone Research Laboratory, Univ. of California, San Francisco, 1969. FRSA 1982. Unofficial JP, 1978. Hon. DSc Sussex, 1984; Hon. DLit East Asia, 1987; Hon. LLD Chinese Univ. of Hong Kong, 1987; Hon. DHL SUNY, 1989. Order of the Rising Sun, Gold Rays, with neck ribbon (Japan), 1986; Commander's Cross, Order of Merit (FRG), 1988. *Publications:* various research papers in academic jls. *Recreations:* swimming, table-tennis. *Address:* Shaw College, The Chinese University of Hong Kong, Hong Kong.

MA, Yo-Yo; 'cellist; *b* Paris, 7 Oct. 1955 of Chinese parentage; *m* 1978, Jill A. Horner; one *s* one *d*. *Educ:* Harvard Univ.; Juilliard Sch. of Music, NY. First public recital at age of 5 years; winner Avery Fisher Prize, 1978; has performed under many distinguished conductors with all major world orchestras including: Berlin Philharmonic; Boston Symphony; Chicago Symphony; Israel Philharmonic; LSO; NY Philharmonic; also appears in chamber music ensembles; regular participant in festivals at Tanglewood, Edinburgh, Salzburg and other major European fests. Has made numerous recordings. Dr *hc*: Northeastern, USA, 1985; Harvard, 1991. Grammy Awards, 1984, 1985. *Address:* c/o Harold Holt Ltd, 31 Sinclair Road, W14 0NS. *T:* 0171–603 4600; c/o ICM Artists Ltd, 40 W 57th Street, New York, NY 10019, USA. *T:* (212) 5565600.

MA, Yuzhen; Chinese Ambassador to the Court of St James's, since 1991; *b* Sept. 1934; *s* of Ma Ziqiang and Li Jinghui; *m* 1961, Zou Jichun; one *s* one *d*. *Educ:* Beijing Inst. of Foreign Languages. Staff Mem., Inf. Dept, Min. of Foreign Affairs, People's Republic of China, 1951–63; Attaché and Third Sec., Burma, 1963–69; Dep. Div. Chief and Div. Chief, Inf. Dept, Min. of Foreign Affairs, 1969–80; First Sec. and Counsellor, Ghana, 1980–84; Dir, Inf. Dept, Min. of Foreign Affairs, 1984–88; Consul-Gen., Los Angeles, 1988–91. *Address:* Chinese Embassy, 49–51 Portland Place, W1N 4JL. *T:* 0171–636 5726.

MAAN, Bashir Ahmed, JP; DL; Chairman: Strathclyde Community Relations Council, 1987–93 and since 1994; Strathclyde Interpreting Services Advisory Committee, since 1988; Bailie, City of Glasgow, 1980–84; Judge, City of Glasgow District Courts; *b* Maan, Gujranwala, Pakistan, 22 Oct. 1926; *s* of Choudhry Sardar Khan Maan and late Mrs Hayat Begum Maan; *m*; one *s* three *d*. *Educ:* D. B. High Sch., Qila Didar Singh; Panjab Univ. MSc. Involved in struggle for creation of Pakistan, 1943–47; organised rehabilitation of refugees from India in Maan and surrounding areas, 1947–48; emigrated to UK and settled in Glasgow, 1953; Glasgow Founder Sec., Pakistan Social and Cultural Soc., 1955–65, Pres., 1966–69; Vice-Chm., Glasgow Community Relations Council, 1970–75; Pres., Standing Conf. of Pakistani Orgns in UK, 1974–77; a Dep. Chm., Commn for Racial Equality, 1977–80; Founder Chm., Scottish Pakistani Assoc., 1984–. Member: Immigrants Prog. Adv. Cttee, BBC, 1972–80; Gen. Adv. Cttee, BBC, 1991–; Scottish Selecting Panel, BBC, 1992–. Hon. Res. Fellow, Univ. of Glasgow, 1988–91. Councillor, Glasgow Corp., 1970–75, City of Glasgow Dist, 1974–84; Mem., Glasgow City Council, 1995–; Magistrate, City of Glasgow, 1971–74; Vice-Chm. 1971–74, Chm. 1974–75, Police Cttee, Glasgow Corp.; Police Judge, City of Glasgow, 1974–75; Mem. Exec. Cttee, Glasgow City Labour Party, 1969–70. Contested (Lab) East Fife, Feb. 1974. Convener, Pakistan Bill Action Cttee, 1973; Member: Nat. Road Safety Cttee, 1971–75; Scottish Accident Prevention Cttee, 1971–75; Scottish Gas Consumers' Council, 1978–81; Greater Glasgow Health Bd, 1981–91; Management Bd, Scottish Council for Voluntary Orgns, 1988–. Chm., Organising Cttee, Glasgow Internat. Sports Festival Co. Ltd, 1987–89. Mem. Bd of Governors, Jordanhill Coll. of Educn, Glasgow, 1987–91. JP 1968, DL 1982, Glasgow. *Publications:* The New Scots, 1992; articles, contrib. to press. *Recreations:* golf, reading. *Address:* 8 Riverview Gardens, Flat 6, Glasgow G5 8EL. *T:* 0141–429 7689. *Club:* Douglas Park Golf.

MAAZEL, Lorin; symphony conductor; Music Director: Pittsburgh Symphony Orchestra, 1988–Aug. 1996; Bayerischer Rundfunk Symphony Orchestra, Munich, since 1993; *b* 6 March 1930; *s* of Lincoln Maazel and Marie Varencove; *m* 3rd, 1986, Dietlinde Turban; two *s* one *d*, and one *s* three *d* by previous marriages. *Educ:* Pittsburgh University. FRCM 1981. Début as a conductor at age of 9, as violinist a few years later; by 1941 had conducted foremost US Orchestras, including Toscanini's NBC; European début as conductor, 1953; active as conductor in Europe, Latin America, Australia, Japan and USA, 1954–; performances at major festivals, including Edinburgh, Bayreuth, Salzburg and Lucerne; in USA: conducted Boston Symphony, New York Philharmonic, Philadelphia Orchestra, and at Metropolitan, 1960 and 1962; Covent Garden début, 1978. Artistic Director of Deutsche Oper Berlin, 1965–71; Chief Conductor, Radio Sinfonie Orchester, Berlin, 1965–75; Associate Principal Conductor, Philharmonia (formerly New Philharmonia) Orchestra, 1970–72, Principal Guest Conductor, 1976–80; Music Director, Cleveland Orchestra, 1972–82, Conductor Emeritus, 1982; Principal Guest Conductor, 1977–88, Music Director, 1988–90, Orchestre National de France; Director, Vienna State Opera, 1982–84. Has made over 300 recordings. Hon. Dr of Music Pittsburgh Univ., 1968; Hon. Dr of Humanities Beaver Coll., 1973; Hon. Dr of Fine Arts, Carnegie-Mellon Univ., Pennsylvania; Hon. Dr of Music, RCM, 1984; Hon. DCL Univ. of South, Sewanee, 1988; Hon. Dr Indiana Univ., 1988. Sibelius Medal, Finland, 1969. Commander's Cross of Order of Merit, Federal Republic of Germany, 1977; Officier, Légion d'Honneur, France, 1981. *Address:* (until Aug. 1996) c/o Pittsburgh Symphony Society, Heinz Hall, 600 Penn Avenue, Pittsburgh, PA 15222–3259, USA; c/o Bayerischer Rundfunk, Rundfunkplatz, 80300 Munich, Germany.

MABBS, Alfred Walter, CB 1982; Keeper of Public Records, 1978–82; *b* 12 April 1921; *e s* of James and Amelia Mabbs; *m* 1942, Dorothy Lowley; one *s*. *Educ:* Hackney Downs Sch. Served War, RAF, 1941–46. Asst Keeper, Public Record Office, 1950–66; Principal Asst Keeper, 1967–69; Records Admin. Officer, 1970–73; Dep. Keeper of Public Records, 1973–78. Pres., Internat. Council on Archives, 1980–82. FRHistS 1954. FSA 1979. *Publications:* Guild Stewards Book of the Borough of Calne (vol. vii, Wilts Arch. and Record Soc.), 1953; The Records of the Cabinet Office to 1922, 1966; Guide to the Contents of the Public Record Office, vol. iii (main contributor), 1968; Exchequer of the Jews, vol. iv (jt contrib.), 1972; The Organisation of Intermediate Records Storage (with Guy Duboscq), 1974; articles and reviews in various jls. *Recreations:* golf, reading. *Address:* 32 The Street, Wallington, Baldock, Herts SG7 6SW.

MABEY, Richard Thomas; writer and broadcaster; *b* 20 Feb. 1941; *s* of late Thomas Gustavus Mabey and Edna Nellie (*née* Moore). *Educ:* Berkhamsted Sch.; St Catherine's Coll., Oxford (BA Hons 1964, MA 1971). Lectr in Social Studies, Dacorum Coll. of Further Educn, 1963–65; Sen. Editor, Penguin Books, 1966–73; freelance writer, 1973–. Presenter, Tomorrow's World, BBC TV, 1995. Pres., London Wildlife Trust, 1982–92; Member: Nature Conservancy Council, 1982–86; Council, Botanical Soc. of the British Isles, 1981–83. Dir, Common Ground, 1988–; Mem., Adv. Council, Open Spaces Soc., 1992–. Patron, Thomas Bewick Trust, 1986–. Leverhulme Trust Res. Award, 1983–84; Leverhulme Res. Fellowship, 1993–94. *Publications:* (ed) Class, 1967; The Pop Process, 1969; Food for Free, 1972, 2nd edn 1989; Children in Primary School, 1972; The Unofficial Countryside, 1973; The Pollution Handbook, 1973; The Roadside Wildlife Book, 1974; Street Flowers, 1976 (TES Inf. Book Award); Plants with a Purpose, 1977; The Common Ground, 1980; The Flowering of Britain, 1980; (ed) Landscape with Figures, 1983; Oak and Company, 1983 (NY Acad. of Sci. Children's Book Award, 1984); In a Green Shade, 1983; Back to the Roots, 1983; (ed) Second Nature, 1984; The Frampton Flora, 1985; Gilbert White: a biography, 1986 (Whitbread Biography Award), Gen. Ed., The Journals of Gilbert White, 1986–89; (ed) The Gardener's Labyrinth, 1987; The Flowering of Kew, 1988; Home Country, 1990; (ed) The Flowers of May, 1990; A Nature Journal, 1991; Whistling in the Dark, 1993; Landlocked, 1994; (ed) The Oxford Book of Nature Writing, 1995; Flora Britannica, 1996. *Recreations:* food, woods, walking. *Address:* c/o Sheil Land Associates, 43 Doughty Street, WC1N 2LF. *Club:* Groucho.

MABON, Rt. Hon. (Jesse) Dickson, PC 1977; company director and physician; *b* 1 Nov. 1925; *s* of Jesse Dickson Mabon and Isabel Simpson Montgomery; *m* 1970, Elizabeth, *o d* of Maj. William Zinn; one *s*. *Educ:* Possilpark, Cumbrae, North Kelvinside Schools. Worked in coalmining industry before Army service, 1944–48. MB, ChB (Glasgow); DHMSA; MFHom; Visiting Physician, Manor House Hospital, London, 1958–64. Political columnist, Scottish Daily Record, 1955–64; studied under Dr Kissinger, Harvard, 1963. President: Glasgow University Union, 1951–52; Scottish Union of Students, 1954–55; Chairman: Glasgow Univ. Labour Club, 1948–50; National Assoc. of Labour Students, 1949–50. Contested: (Lab) Bute and N Ayrshire, 1951; (Lab and Co-op) W Renfrewshire, 1955; Renfrew W and Inverclyde (SDP) 1983, (SDP/Alliance) 1987; (SDP) Lothians, European Parly Election, 1984. MP (Lab and Co-op 1955–81, SDP 1981–83) Greenock, Dec. 1955–1974, Greenock and Port Glasgow, 1974–83; Joint Parly Under-Sec. of State for Scotland, 1964–67; Minister of State, Scottish Office, 1967–70; Dep. Opposition Spokesman on Scotland, 1970–72 (resigned over Labour's attitude to Common Mkt); Minister of State, Dept of Energy, 1976–79. Chairman: UK Labour Cttee for Europe, 1974–76; Scottish Parly Labour Party, 1972–73, 1975–76; Member: Council of Europe, 1970–72 and 1974–76; Assembly, WEU, 1970–72 and 1974–76; North Atlantic Assembly, 1980–82; Chm., European Movement, 1975–76, Dep. Chm., 1979–83. Founder Chm., Manifesto Gp, Parly Lab. Party, 1974–76. Founder Mem., SDP, 1981; Mem., SDP Nat. Cttee, 1984–88; rejoined Labour Party, 1991. Chm., Young Volunteer Force Foundn, 1974–76. Mem., Energy Saving Trust, 1992–. Fellow: Inst. of Petroleum; Inst. of Directors; Faculty of History of Medicine (Pres. 1990–94); Soc. of Apothecaries; FRSA. Freeman of City of London. *Recreations:* gardening, theatre. *Address:* 57 Hillway, N6 6AD. *T:* 0181–342 9583.

MABY, (Alfred) Cedric, CBE 1962; HM Diplomatic Service, retired; *b* 6 April 1915; 4th *s* of late Joseph Maby, Penrhos, Monmouthshire; *m* 1944, Anne-Charlotte, *d* of Envoyén Einar Modig, Stockholm; one *s* two *d*. *Educ:* Cheltenham; Keble Coll., Oxford. Joined HM Consular Service, 1939. Served at Peking, 1939, Chungking, 1940, Tsingtao, 1941, Istanbul, 1943, Angora, 1944, Buenos Aires, 1946, Caracas, 1949, Singapore, 1954; Counsellor and Consul-General, Peking, 1957–59 (Chargé d'Affaires, 1957 and 1958); Deputy Consul-General, New York, 1959–62; Counsellor (Commercial) at Vienna, 1962–64; Asst Sec., Min. of Overseas Development, 1964–67; Consul-General, Zürich and Liechtenstein, 1968–71; Dir, Trade Promotion for Switzerland, 1970–71. Member: Governing Body, Church in Wales, 1975–78; Church in Wales Adv. Commn on Church and Society, 1977–86. Fellow, Huguenot Soc. of GB and Ire., 1977. High Sheriff of Gwynedd, 1976. *Publications:* Dail Melyn o Tseina, 1983; Y Cocatŵ Coch, 1987; Looking Both Ways, 1995; contribs to Planet, Y Faner and other Welsh periodicals. *Address:* Cae Canol, Minffordd, Penrhyn-Deudraeth, Gwynedd LL48 6EN.

McADAM, Sir Ian (William James), Kt 1966; OBE 1957; FRCS, FRCSE; *b* 15 Feb. 1917; *s* of W. J. McAdam and Alice Culverwell; *m* 1st, 1939, Hrothgarde Gibson (marr. diss. 1961); one *s* two *d*; 2nd, 1967, Lady (Pamela) Hunt (*née* Medawar). *Educ:* Plumtree Sch., S Rhodesia; Edinburgh Univ. MB, ChB. Cambridge Anatomy Sch., 1940; Dept of Surgery, Edinburgh, 1942; Wilkie Surgical Research Fellow, 1942; Clinical Tutor, Royal

Infirmary, Edinburgh, 1942; Surgical Specialist, Uganda, 1946; Senior Consultant, Uganda, 1957; Prof. of Surgery, Makerere Univ., Univ. of E Africa, 1957–72, also Consultant Surgeon Uganda Govt and Kenyatta Hosp., Kenya; Consultant to Nat. Insts of Health, Bethesda, Md, 1973–74. *Publications:* various papers in medical jls. *Recreations:* golf, gardening. *Address:* 16 Middleton Park, Middleton Stoney, Oxon OX6 8SQ.
See also K. P. W. J. McAdam.

McADAM, James, CBE 1995; Chairman, Signet (formerly Ratners) Group plc, since 1992; *b* 10 Dec. 1930; *s* of John Robert McAdam and Helen McAdam (*née* Cormack); *m* 1955, Maisie Una Holmes; two *d. Educ:* Lenzie Academy. Joined J. & P. Coats Ltd, 1945; Finance Dir, Coats Chile, 1962–66, Coats India, 1966–70, Coats Patons UK, 1972–75; Dir, 1975, Chief Exec., 1985–86, Chm., 1986–91, Coats Patons plc; Dep. Chm. and Chief Operating Officer, Coats Viyella (merged co.), 1986–91. Chm., Bisley Office Equipment Co., 1991–; Dir, Scotia Hldgs, 1991–. Director: London Region Post Office, 1985–87; Textile Pensions Trust Ltd, 1985–94. Chairman: British Clothing Industry Assoc., 1991–; British Knitting and Clothing Confedn, 1991–; British Apparel and Textile Confedn, 1992–; Mem., Exec. Cttee, Scottish Council Develt and Industry, 1988–. FRSA; CIMgt; FInstD. *Recreations:* theatre, gardening, travel. *Address:* Signet Group plc, 15 Stratton Street, W1X 5FD. *Clubs:* Royal Automobile, Farmers.

McADAM, Prof. Keith Paul William James, FRCP; Wellcome Professor of Tropical Medicine, London School of Hygiene and Tropical Medicine, London University, since 1984 (Head of Department of Clinical Sciences, 1988–94); Consultant Physician, Hospital for Tropical Diseases, NW1, since 1984; *b* 13 Aug. 1945; *s* of Sir Ian William James McAdam, *qv*, and Mrs L. M. Hrothgaarde Bennett (*neé* Gibson); *m* 1968, Penelope Ann (*neé* Spencer); three *d. Educ:* Prince of Wales School, Nairobi; Millfield School, Som.; Clare Coll., Cambridge (MA, MB BChir); Middlesex Hosp. Med. Sch. FRSTM&H; Fellow, London Med. Soc.; Dip. Amer. Bd of Internal Medicine, Dip. Amer. Bd of Allergy and Clinical Immunology. Medical posts at Middlesex Hosp., Royal Northern Hosp., Brompton Hosp., Nat. Hosp. for Nervous Diseases, 1969–73; Lectr in Medicine, Inst. of Med. Research, Goroka, Papua New Guinea, 1973–75; MRC Travelling Fellow, 1975–76; Vis. Scientist, Immunology Branch, Nat. Cancer Inst., NIH, Bethesda, 1976–77; Asst Prof., Tufts Univ. Sch. of Medicine, 1977–82; Associate Prof., Divs of Allergy, Exptl Medicine and Geographic Medicine, Tufts Univ., 1982–84. *Publications:* scientific articles on immunology and tropical medicine, esp. on amyloidosis, acute phase proteins, leprosy, tuberculosis, AIDS, inflammation. *Recreations:* cricket, squash, tennis, golf, ski-ing. *Address:* Department of Clinical Sciences, London School of Hygiene and Tropical Medicine, Keppel Street, WC1E 7HT. *T:* 0171–927 2256. *Club:* MCC.

MACADAM, Sir Peter, Kt 1981; Chairman: BAT Industries plc, 1976–82; Libra Bank, 1984–90; *b* 9 Sept. 1921; *s* of late Francis Macadam and Marjorie Mary Macadam (*née* Browne); *m* 1949, Ann Musson; three *d. Educ:* Buenos Aires, Argentina; Stonyhurst Coll., Lancs. Served as Officer in Queen's Bays, 1941–46. Joined BAT Gp tobacco co., Argentina, 1946; Chm. and Gen. Man., gp co., Argentina, 1955–58; PA in London to Dir resp. for Africa, 1959–60 (travelled widely in Africa); Chm., BAT Hong Kong, 1960–62; BAT Main Bd, 1963 (resp. at times for interest in S and Central Africa, S and Central America and Caribbean); Mem., Chm.'s Policy Cttee with overall resp. for tobacco interests and special interest, USA, Canada and Mexico, 1970; Chm., Tobacco Div. Bd and Dir, Gp HQ Bd, 1973; Vice-Chm., 1975. Dir, National Westminster Bank, 1978–84. Chm., British Nat. Cttee, ICC, 1978–85; Mem. Exec. Cttee, ICC, Paris, 1982–85. Pres., Hispanic and Luso Brazilian Council, 1982–87; Chm., Anglo-Argentine Soc., 1987–92. Hon. FBIM; FRSA 1975. *Recreations:* golf, shooting. *Address:* Layham Hall, Layham, near Hadleigh, Suffolk IP7 5LE. *T:* Hadleigh (01473) 822137. *Club:* Canning.

McADAM CLARK, James; *see* Clark, James McAdam.

McADOO, Most Rev. Henry Robert, PhD, STD, DD; *b* 1916; *s* of James Arthur and Susan McAdoo; *m* 1940, Lesley Dalziel Weir; one *s* two *d. Educ:* Cork Grammar School; Mountjoy School, Dublin. Deacon, 1939; Priest, 1940; Curate of Holy Trinity Cathedral, Waterford, 1939–43; Incumbent of Castleventry with Ardfield, 1943–48 (with Kilmeen, 1947–48); Rector of Kilmocomogue, Diocese of Cork, 1948–52; Rural Dean of Glansalney West and Bere, 1948–52; Canon of Kilbrittain in Cork Cathedral, and Canon of Donoughmore in Cloyne Cathedral, 1949–52; Dean of Cork, 1952–62; Canon of St Patrick's Cathedral, Dublin, 1960–62; Bishop of Ossory, Ferns and Leighlin, 1962–77; Archbishop of Dublin and Primate of Ireland, 1977–85. Member, Anglican-Roman Catholic Preparatory Commission, 1967–68; Jt Chm., Anglican-Roman Catholic International Commission, 1969–81 (Canterbury Cross). Hon. Fellow, TCD, 1989. *Publications:* The Structure of Caroline Moral Theology, 1949; John Bramhall and Anglicanism, 1964; The Spirit of Anglicanism, 1965; Modern Eucharistic Agreement, 1973; Modern Ecumenical Documents on Ministry, 1975; Being an Anglican, 1977; Rome and the Anglicans, 1982; The Unity of Anglicanism: Catholic and Reformed, 1983; The Eucharistic Theology of Jeremy Taylor Today, 1989; Anglican Heritage: theology and spirituality, 1991; ; First of its Kind: Jeremy Taylor's life of Christ, 1994; The Mystery of the Eucharist in the Anglican Tradition, 1995; contribs to: Authority in the Anglican Communion, 1987; Christian Authority, 1988; The English Religious Tradition and the Genius of Anglicanism, 1992. *Address:* 2 The Paddocks, Dalkey, Co. Dublin. *Club:* Kildare Street and University (Dublin).

McAFEE, Maj.-Gen. Robert William Montgomery; Director General, Army Training, since 1993; *b* 8 Nov. 1944; *s* of Andrew Montgomery McAfee and Jane Beryl McAfee; *m* 1967, Erica-May MacLennan; one *s* one *d. Educ:* Inverness Royal Academy; Mons Officer Cadet Sch. Commnd, RTR, 1965; served Aden, BAOR, NI (despatches), Cyprus, Gulf; CO 2nd RTR, 1982–84; Instructor, Staff Coll., 1985–86; Col, Higher Command and Staff Course, 1987; Comdr 6 Armd Bde, 1988–89; ACOS (Land), HQ British Forces, ME, 1990; COS HQ 1 (BR) Corps, 1991–92; RCDS 1993. Rep. Col Comdt, RTR, 1995–; Comdt, APTC, Chm., Army Bobsleigh Assoc., 1992–; Dep. Pres., Army Rugby Union, 1994–. *Recreations:* golf, ski-ing, watching Rugby and motor racing. *Address:* c/o Clydesdale Bank, 15 Academy Street, Inverness IV1 7JN. *Clubs:* Army and Navy; St Fillans Golf.

McALEESE, Mary Patricia, (Mrs Martin McAleese); Director, Institute of Professional Legal Studies, Queen's University, Belfast, since 1987; *b* 27 June 1951; *d* of Patrick Leneghan and Claire (*née* McManus); *m* 1976, Martin McAleese; one *s* two *d. Educ:* QUB (LLB, MA). AIL. Called to the Bar: N Ireland, 1974; King's Inn, Dublin, 1978. Barrister, NI, 1974–75; Reid Prof. of Criminal Law, Criminology and Penology, TCD, 1975–79 and 1981–87; journalist and TV presenter, Radio Telefis Eireann, 1979–81. Director: Northern Ireland Electricity, 1991–; Channel 4 Television, 1992–. *Publications:* (jtly) Reports on Irish Penal System, 1981; Children in Custody (ed Stewart and Tutt), 1987; (jtly) Sectarianism: a discussion document, 1993; contrib. legal and religious jls. *Recreations:* hill-walking, set dancing, reading, theology. *Address:* Institute of Professional Legal Studies, Queen's University of Belfast, Belfast BT7 1NN. *T:* Belfast (01232) 245133.

McALISKEY, (Josephine) Bernadette, (Mrs Micheal McAliskey); Chairman, Independent Socialist Party, Ireland; *b* 23 April 1947; *d* of late John James Devlin and Elizabeth Devlin; *m* 1973, Micheal McAliskey; three *c. Educ:* St Patrick's Girls' Acad., Dungannon; psychology student at Queen's Univ., Belfast, 1966–69. Youngest MP in House of Commons when elected at age of 21; MP (Ind. Unity) Mid Ulster, Apr. 1969–Feb. 1974. Founder Member and Mem. Exec., Irish Republican Socialist Party, 1975–76. Contested: (Ind) N Ireland, European Parlt, 1979; (People's Democracy), Dublin N Central, Dáil Eireann, Feb. and Nov. 1982. *Publication:* The Price of my Soul (autobiog.), 1969. *Recreations:* walking, folk music, doing nothing, swimming.

McALISTER, Michael Ian, FCA; Director, Ionian Corporate Finance Ltd, since 1992; Executive Director, The Tam Programme, European Bank for Reconstruction and Development, since 1993; *b* Leeds, Yorkshire, 23 Aug. 1930; *s* of S. McAlister, CBE, and J. A. McAlister (*née* Smith); *m* 1st, 1953, Patricia (*née* Evans) (marr. diss. 1983); four *s* three *d*; 2nd, 1984, Elizabeth Anne, *o d* of Mr and Mrs Ludwig Hehn. *Educ:* Brazil; France; St John's Coll., Oxford (MA). National Service, Lieut, Intelligence Corps (MI8), 1950–51 (Acting Capt). Articled Clerk, Price Waterhouse, London, 1954–58; Private Sec. to the Duke of Windsor, 1959–61; Investment Manager, Ionian Bank Ltd, London, 1961–67; Managing Dir, Ionian Bank Trustee Co, London, 1967–68; Slater Walker Securities (Australia): Dep. Chm., 1969–70, Chm., 1970–72; Pres., Aust. Associated Stock Exchanges, 1972–74; Director: (Middle Est), Lester B. Knight and Associates, USA, 1975–79; Cluff Oil Holdings, subseq. Cluff Resources, 1979–89. Chm., Woking Cons. Assoc., 1967–68. *Recreations:* carpentry, DIY. *Address:* Two Berwick Cottages, Terling Hall Road, Hatfield Peveral, Chelmsford, Essex CM3 2EY. *T:* Chelmsford (01245) 380158, *Fax:* (01245) 382056. *Club:* Royal Automobile.

McALISTER, Maj.-Gen. Ronald William Lorne, CB 1977; OBE 1968 (MBE 1959); *b* 26 May 1923; 2nd *s* of late Col R. J. F. McAlister, OBE and Mrs T. M. Collins, Bath; *m* 1964, Sally Ewart Marshall; two *d. Educ:* Dreghorn Castle Sch., Edinburgh; Sedbergh School. Commnd 3rd QAO Gurkha Rifles, 1942; Adjt 1/3 GR Burma, 1945 (despatches); Adjt 2/10 GR Malaya, 1950–52 (despatches); Instructor, Sch. of Infantry, 1953–55; psc 1956; Bde Major 99 Gurkha Bde, Malaya, 1957–59 (MBE); jssc 1961–62; Asst Sec., Chiefs of Staff Cttee, 1962–64; 2nd in comd and CO 10th PMO Gurkha Rifles, Borneo, 1964–66 (despatches); Internal Security Duties, Hong Kong, 1967–68 (OBE); Instructor, Jt Services Staff Coll., 1968; comd Berlin Inf. Bde, 1968–71; ndc, Canada, 1971–72; Exercise Controller UK Cs-in-C Cttee, 1972–75; Dep. Commander Land Forces Hong Kong and Maj.-Gen. Brigade of Gurkhas, 1975–77; retired 1977. Col, 10th Princess Mary's Own Gurkha Rifles, 1977–85; Chm., Gurkha Brigade Assoc., 1980–90. Bursar, Wellesley House Sch., Broadstairs, 1977–88. Chm., Buckmaster Meml Home, Broadstairs, 1980–. *Publication:* (ed and contrib.) Bugle and Kukri, Vol. 2, 1986. *Recreations:* golf, gardening. *Address:* The Chalet, 41 Callis Court Road, Broadstairs, Kent CT10 3AU. *T:* Thanet (01843) 862351. *Clubs:* Army and Navy; Royal St George's Golf (Captain, 1989–90; Hon. Treas., 1991–), Senior Golfers' Society.

McALISTER, William Harle Nelson; Cultural Policy Adviser (formerly Programme Co-ordinator), Soros Foundations, since 1992; *b* 30 Aug. 1940; *s* of Flying Officer William Nelson (*d* 1940) and Marjorie Isobel (*née* McIntyre); adopted by William Edwyn McAlister (whom she *m* 2nd); *m* 1968 (marr. diss. 1985); two *s* two *d*; one *s. Educ:* Sorbonne, Paris; Univ. of Copenhagen; University Coll. London (BA Hons Psychology, 1967). Dir, Almost Free Theatre, 1968–72; Dep. Dir, Inter-Action Trust, 1968–72; Founder Dir, Islington Bus Co., 1972–77; Director: Battersea Arts Centre, 1976–77; ICA, 1977–90; Creative Research Ltd, 1989–91. Dir, Sense of Ireland Fest., 1980; Bd Dir, London International Theatre Fest., 1983; Chm. for the Arts, IT 82 Cttee, 1982. Chm., Recreational Trust, 1972–88; Co-Founder, Fair Play for Children, 1974–75; Advr, Task Force Trust, 1972–74; Trustee: Circle 33 Housing Trust, 1972–75; Moving Picture Mime Trust, 1978–80; Shape (Arts for the Disadvantaged), 1979–81. Trustee: International House, 1989–; Africa Centre, 1990–. Governor, Holloway Adult Educn Inst., 1974–76. Mem. Court, RCA, 1980–. British Deleg. to Ministerial Conf. on cultural policy, Bulgaria, 1980; British Cultural Deleg., China, 1982; CSCE British Deleg., Krakow, Poland, 1991. *Publications:* Community Psychology, 1975; EEC and the Arts, 1978; articles on Arts Policy. *Recreations:* angling, tennis, travel. *Address:* 151c Grosvenor Avenue, N5 2NH. *T:* 0171–226 0205.

MacALLAN, Andrew; *see* Leasor, T. J.

McALLION, John; MP (Lab) Dundee East, since 1987; *b* 13 Feb. 1948; *s* of Joseph and Norah McAllion; *m* 1971, Susan Jean Godlonton; two *s. Educ:* St Augustine's Comprehensive School, Glasgow; St Andrews Univ. (MA Hons 2nd cl. Modern and Medieval Hist. 1972); Dundee Coll. of Education. Civil Servant, Post Office, 1967–68; History Teacher, St Saviour's High Sch., Dundee, 1973–78; Social Studies Teacher, Balgowan Sch., Dundee, 1978–82; Research Asst to Bob McTaggart, 1982–86. Regional Councillor, 1984–87, Convener, 1986–87, Tayside Regional Council. *Recreations:* sport, reading, music. *Address:* 3 Haldane Street, Dundee DD3 0HP. *T:* Dundee (01382) 826678; House of Commons, SW1A 0AA. *T:* 0171–219 5048.

McALLISTER, Ian Gerald; Chairman, since 1992 and Managing Director, since 1991, Ford Motor Co.; *b* 17 Aug. 1943; *s* of Ian Thomas McAllister and Margaret Mary McAllister (*née* McNally); *m* 1968, Susan Margaret Frances Mitchell; three *s* one *d. Educ:* Thornleigh College, Bolton; University College London (BScEcon). Ford Motor Co.: analysis, operations and marketing appts, 1964–79; Gen. Field Manager, 1979; Director: Part Sales, 1980; Product and Marketing Parts Ops, 1981; Car Sales Ops, 1983; Marketing Plans and Programs, 1984; Sales, Ford Germany, 1987; Gen. Marketing Manager, Lincoln Mercury Div., USA, 1989. Pres., Essex Motor Project. Mem. Bd and Council, BITC. Mem. Adv. Bd, Victim Support. Member: Adv. Council, Imperial Coll., London; Bd, Anglia Univ.; Bd of Trustees, Nat. Motor Mus., Beaulieu. Hon. PhD E London, 1993. *Recreations:* gardening, golf, computer studies, running. *Address:* Ford Motor Co., Eagle Way, Brentwood, Essex CM13 3BW. *T:* Brentwood (01277) 253000.

McALLISTER, John Brian; Chief Executive, Craegmoor Healthcare, since 1994; *b* 11 June 1941; *s* of late Thomas McAllister and of Jane (*née* McCloughan); *m* 1966, Margaret Lindsay Walker; two *d. Educ:* Royal Belfast Academical Instn; Queen's Univ., Belfast (BA Hons). Joined NI Civil Service as Asst Principal, Dept of Educn, 1964; Dep. Principal, Higher Educn Div., 1968; Principal: Secondary Schs Br., 1969; Re-Organisation of Local Govt Br., 1970; Principal, Dept of Finance, 1971, Dept's Central Secretariat, 1972; Asst Sec. 1973, Sen. Asst Sec. 1976, Dep. Sec., 1978–80, Dept of Educn; Dep. Sec., later Under Sec., Dept of Finance, 1980–83; Under Sec., DoE, NI, 1983–84; Dep. Chief Exec., 1984–85, Chief Exec., 1985–88, Industrial Develt Bd for NI; Chief Exec., Crestacare (formerly Cresta Hldgs Ltd), 1990–93 (Gp Man. Dir, 1988–90); consultant, 1993–94. *Recreations:* watching sport of all kinds, reading. *Address:* Craegmoor Healthcare, Craegmoor House, 97 Friar Street, Droitwich, Worcs WR9 8EG.

McALPINE, family name of **Baron McAlpine of West Green.**

McALPINE OF WEST GREEN, Baron *cr* 1984 (Life Peer), of West Green in the County of Hampshire; **Robert Alistair McAlpine;** Director, Sir Robert McAlpine & Sons Ltd, 1963–95; *b* 14 May 1942; *s* of Lord McAlpine of Moffat and Ella Mary Gardner Garnett (*d* 1987); *m* 1964, Sarah Alexandra Baron (marr. diss. 1979); two *d*; *m* 1980, Romilly, *o d* of A. T. Hobbs, Cranleigh, Surrey; one *d*. *Educ:* Stowe. Joined Sir Robert McAlpine & Sons Ltd, 1958. Hon. Treasurer: Europ. Democratic Union, 1978–88; Europ. League for Econ. Co-operation, 1974–75 (Vice Pres., 1975–); Conservative and Unionist Party, 1975–90 (Dep. Chm., 1979–83). Director: George Weidenfeld Holdings Ltd, 1975–83; ICA, 1972–73. Mem., Arts Council of GB, 1981–82; Vice-President: Friends of Ashmolean Museum, 1969–; Greater London Arts Assoc., 1971–77; Vice-Chm., Contemporary Arts Soc., 1973–80. Pres., British Waterfowl Assoc., 1978–81, Patron 1981–. Member: Friends of V&A Museum, 1976–; Council, English Stage Co., 1973–75. Trustee, Royal Opera House Trust, 1974–80; Dir, Theatre Investment Fund, 1981–90 (Chm., 1985–90). Governor: Polytechnic of the South Bank, 1981–82; Stowe Sch., 1981–84; Pres., St Bartholomew's Hosp. Med. Coll., 1993–. *Publications:* The Servant, 1992; Journal of a Collector, 1994; Letters to a Young Politician, 1995. *Recreations:* the arts, horticulture, aviculture, agriculture. *Address:* House of Lords, SW1A 0PW. *Clubs:* Garrick, Carlton, Buck's, Pratt's, Beefsteak.

See also Hon. Sir W. H. McAlpine, Bt.

McALPINE, Christopher; *see* McAlpine, R. D. C.

McALPINE, Robert Douglas Christopher, CMG 1967; HM Diplomatic Service, retired; Director: Baring Brothers, 1969–79; H. Clarkson (Holdings) plc, 1980–87; *b* 14 June 1919; *s* of late Dr Douglas McAlpine, FRCP and late Elizabeth Meg Sidebottom; *m* 1943, Helen Margery Frances Cannan; two *s* one *d* (and one *d* decd). Educ: Winchester; New Coll., Oxford. RNVR, 1939–46. Entered Foreign Service, 1946. FO, 1946–47; Asst Private Sec. to Sec. of State, 1947–49; 2nd Sec. and later 1st Sec., UK High Commn at Bonn, 1949–52; FO, 1952–54; Lima, 1954–56; Moscow, 1956–59; FO, 1959–62; Dep. Consul-Gen. and Counsellor, New York, 1962–65; Counsellor, Mexico City, 1965–68. Town Councillor, Tetbury, 1987–91. *Recreations:* sailing, tennis, fishing. *Address:* Longtree House, Cutwell, Tetbury, Glos GL8 8EB. *Club:* United Oxford & Cambridge University.

McALPINE, Robert James, FCIOB; Director, Alfred McAlpine plc, 1957–94 (Chairman, 1983–92); *b* 6 May 1932; *s* of late Alfred James McAlpine and of Peggy (*née* Saunders); *m* 1st, Mary Jane Anton; two *s* one *d*; 2nd, Angela Bell (*née* Langford Brooke); one *d*. *Educ:* Harrow Sch. FCIOB. Director: Haynes Hanson & Clarke, 1978– (Chm., 1993–); Hall Engrg, 1985–. Chm., Export Gp for Constructional Industries, 1975–77. Mem., Jockey Club. High Sheriff, Cheshire, 1994–95. *Recreations:* racing, shooting, golf, bridge. *Address:* c/o Alfred McAlpine plc, Hooton, South Wirral, Cheshire L66 7ND. *T:* 0151–339 4141. *Clubs:* White's, Turf, Portland, MCC.

McALPINE, Hon. Sir William (Hepburn), 6th Bt *cr* 1918, of Knott Park; FRSE; FCIT; company director; *b* 12 Jan. 1936; *s* of Lord McAlpine of Moffat (Life Peer) and Ella Mary Gardner Garnett (*d* 1987); *S* to baronetcy of father, 1990; *m* 1959, Jill Benton, *o d* of Lt-Col Sir Peter Fawcett Benton Jones, 3rd Bt, OBE, ACA; one *s* one *d*. *Educ:* Charterhouse. Life Guards, 1954–56. Dir, Sir Robert McAlpine (formerly Sir Robert McAlpine & Sons Ltd), 1956–. FRSA. *Recreation:* railways. *Heir: s* Andrew William McAlpine [*b* 22 Nov. 1960; *m* 1991, Caroline Claire, *yr d* of Frederick Hodgson; two *s*]. *Address:* (office) 40 Bernard Street, WC1N 1LG. *Clubs:* Garrick, Caledonian; Western (Glasgow).

See also Baron McAlpine of West Green.

MACAN, Thomas Townley; HM Diplomatic Service; Ambassador to Lithuania, since 1994; *b* 14 Nov. 1946; only *s* of Thomas Townley Macan and Zaida Bindloss (*née* Boddington); *m* 1976, Janet Ellen Martin, Hollidaysburg, Penn; one *s* one *d*. *Educ:* Shrewsbury Sch.; Univ. of Sussex (BA Hons Econs; Pres., Students' Union, 1967–68). MIL 1992. Joined HM Diplomatic Service, 1969; UN Dept, FCO, 1969–71; Bonn, 1971–74; Brasilia, 1974–78; Maritime, Aviation and Envmt Dept, FCO, 1978–81; Press Sec., Bonn, 1981–86; Hd, Commonwealth Co-ordination Dept, FCO, 1986–88; Hd, Trng Dept, FCO, 1988–90; Counsellor, Lisbon, 1990–91. *Recreations:* steam boats, sailing, church architecture, walking. *Address:* c/o Foreign and Commonwealth Office, King Charles Street, SW1A 2AH. *Clubs:* Island Cruising (Salcombe); Royal British (Lisbon).

MacANDREW, family name of **Baron MacAndrew.**

MacANDREW, 3rd Baron *cr* 1959, of the Firth of Clyde; **Christopher Anthony Colin MacAndrew;** farmer; *b* 16 Feb. 1945; *s* of 2nd Baron MacAndrew and Ursula Beatrice (*d* 1986), *d* of Captain Joseph Steel; *S* father, 1989; *m* 1975, Sarah, *o d* of Lt-Col P. H. Brazier; one *s* two *d*. *Educ:* Malvern. *Heir: s* Hon. Oliver Charles Julian MacAndrew, *b* 3 Sept. 1983. *Recreations:* cricket, golf, tennis. *Address:* Hall Farm, Archdeacon Newton, Darlington, Co. Durham DL2 2YB.

McANDREW, Nicolas; Chairman, Murray Johnstone Ltd, since 1992; *b* 9 Dec. 1934; *s* of Robert Louis McAndrew and Anita Marian McAndrew (*née* Huband); *m* 1960, Diana Leonie Wood; two *s* one *d*. *Educ:* Winchester Coll. CA 1961. Commnd Black Watch, 1953–55. With Peat, Marwick, Mitchell & Co., 1955–61; S. G. Warburg & Co. Ltd, 1962–78: Dir, 1969–78; Chm., Warburg Investment Mgt, 1975–78; Dir, Mercury Securities Ltd, 1975–78; N. M. Rothschild & Sons Ltd, 1979–88 (Man. Dir, 1980–88); Murray Johnstone Ltd, 1988– (Man. Dir,1988–92). Board Mem., Highlands & Islands Enterprise, 1993–. Deputy Chairman: Moorgate Investment Trust PLC, 1985–; Moorgate Smaller Companies Income Trust PLC, 1990–; Burn Stewart Distillers PLC, 1991–. Master, Grocers' Co., 1978–79. *Recreations:* shooting, fishing, golf, bridge. *Address:* Kilcoy Castle, Killearnan, Muir of Ord, Ross-shire IV6 7RX. *T:* Inverness (01463) 871393. *Clubs:* White's, City of London.

MACARA, Dr Alexander Wiseman, FRCP, FRCGP, FFPHM; Consultant Senior Lecturer in Epidemiology and Public Health Medicine, University of Bristol and Hon. Visiting Consultant, Bristol Royal Infirmary, since 1976; Chairman of Council, British Medical Association, since 1993; *b* 4 May 1932; *s* of late Rev. Alexander Macara, MA Hons and Marion Wiseman Macara (*née* Mackay); *m* 1964, Sylvia May Williams, BSc Hons, DipEd, *d* of late Edward Brodbeck and Ellen Florence Williams; one *s* one *d*. *Educ:* Irvine Royal Acad.; Glasgow Univ. (Carnegie Bursar; MB ChB 1958); LSHTM. DPH (Hecht Prize) 1960; FFPHM 1989 (FFCM 1973; MFCM 1972); FRIPHH 1973; FRCGP (*ad eundem gradum*) 1983; FRCP 1991. House Physician and House Surgeon posts in Glasgow Teaching Hosps, 1958–59; General Practice experience, London and Glasgow, 1959–60; Asst MOH and Sch. MO, City and Co. of Bristol, 1960–63, then Hon. Community Physician, 1963–74; Lectr then Sen. Lectr, Univ. of Bristol, 1963–76 (Actg Head, Dept of Public Health, 1974–76). Sir Wilson Jameson Travelling Scholar, LSHTM, 1967; Vis. Prof., Univ. of Malaya, 1980; Vis. Prof. and Ext. Examnr for higher degrees, Univ. of Khartoum, 1983; Ext. Examnr, Inst. of Population Studies, Univ. of Exeter, 1993. Ext. Examnr in Community Med. (Human Ecology), Univ. of Glasgow, 1979–82. Jt Chm., Jt Wkg Party of Med. Profession and DoH on Med. Services for Children, 1991–92, and Chm., Jt Wkg Party on Child Protection, 1993–94. General Medical Council: Mem., 1979–; mem. various cttees. Faculty of Community Medicine (now of Public Health Medicine): Mem. Bd, 1973–79; Treasurer, 1979–84; Rep. on Jenner Trust, 1989–. British Medical Association: Chm., Med. Ethics Cttee, 1982–89; Dep. Chm., 1987–89, Chm., 1989–92, Representative Body; Rep. on Standing Cttee, Doctors in the EC, 1980–; Chm. or Mem., numerous working parties, incl. Bd of Science and Educn; Fellow, 1978. Sec.-Gen., World Fedn for Educn and Res. in Public Heath, 1988–; Dir, WHO Collaborating Centre in Envmtl Health Promotion and Ecology, 1989–; Advr and Consultant on Educn, Trng and Health Manpower Develt, WHO, 1970–; Sec., European Collaborative Health Services Studies, 1977–89. Hon. Member: Hungarian Soc. Social Medicine, 1989; Italian Soc. Hygiene, Preventive Medicine and Public Health (Gold Medallist), 1991; Hon. Life Fellow, Soc. Public Health, 1991. FRSA 1995. Hon. Dr Public Health and Gerasimos Alivizatos Award, Sch. of Public Health, Athens, 1992. James Preston Meml Award, Soc. of Public Health and BMA, 1993. *Publications:* (jtly) Personal Data Protection in Health and Social Services, 1988; chapters in various books and articles and reports in med. jls on epidemiology, public health, envmtl health and ethics in medicine. *Recreations:* gardening, reading, music, church activities, rusty golf and tennis. *Address:* Department of Social Medicine, University of Bristol, Canynge Hall, Whiteladies Road, Clifton, Bristol BS8 2PR. *T:* Bristol (0117) 930 3030; Elgon, 10 Cheyne Road, Stoke Bishop, Bristol BS9 2DH. *T:* Bristol (0117) 968 2838. *Club:* Athenæum.

MACARA, Sir Hugh Kenneth, 4th Bt *cr* 1911, of Ardmore, St Anne-on-the-Sea, Co. Lancaster; *b* 17 Jan. 1913; 4th *s* of Sir William Cowper Macara, 2nd Bt and Lilian Mary (*d* 1971), *d* of John Chapman; *S* brother, 1982. *Heir:* none.

McARDLE, Rear-Adm. Stanley Lawrence, CB 1975; LVO 1952; GM 1953; JP; Flag Officer, Portsmouth, and Port Admiral, Portsmouth, 1973–75; retired; *b* 1922; *s* of Theodore McArdle, Lochmaben, Dumfriesshire; *m* 1st, 1945, (Helen) Joyce, *d* of Owen Cummins, Wickham, Hants; one *d*; 2nd, 1962, Jennifer, *d* of Walter Talbot Goddard, Salisbury, Wilts; one *d*. *Educ:* Royal Hospital Sch., Holbrook, Suffolk. Joined RN, 1938; served War, 1939–45. Lieut 1945; Comdr 1956; Captain 1963. Directorate of Naval Operations and Trade, 1969; Comd HMS Glamorgan, 1970; Dir Naval Trng, Director General, Personal Services and Trng (Naval), 1971–73; Rear Admiral 1972. Dir, Endless Holdings Ltd, 1985–. JP Wilts, 1977. *Address:* Barn Ridge Cottage, Farley, Salisbury, Wilts SP5 1AH.

MACARTHUR, Rev. Arthur Leitch, OBE 1981; MA, MLitt; inducted, Christ Church, Marlow-on-Thames, 1980, retired 1986; *b* 9 Dec. 1913; *s* of Edwin Macarthur and Mary Macarthur (*née* Leitch); *m* 1950, Doreen Esmé Muir; three *s* one *d*. *Educ:* Rutherford Coll.; Armstrong Coll., Durham Univ. (MA, MLitt Dunelm); Westminster Coll., Cambridge. Ordained, 1937; inducted, Clayport, Alnwick, 1937; served with YMCA in France, 1940. Inducted: St Augustine's, New Barnet, 1944; St Columba's, North Shields, 1950. Gen. Sec., Presbyterian Church of England, 1960–72; Moderator, Presbyterian Church of England, 1971–72; Jt Gen.-Sec., URC, 1972–74; Moderator, URC, 1974–75; Gen. Sec., URC, 1975–80; Moderator, Free Church Federal Council, 1980–81. Vice-Pres., BCC, 1974–77 (Chm., Admin. Cttee, 1969–74). *Recreations:* gardening, golf, walking. *Address:* Haywards Corner, Randalls Green, Chalford Hill, near Stroud, Glos GL6 8LH. *T:* Brimscombe (01453) 883700.

MacARTHUR, Brian; Executive Editor (Features), The Times, since 1991; *b* 5 Feb. 1940; *o s* of late S. H. MacArthur and Mrs M. MacArthur; *m* 1966, Peta Deschampsneufs (*d* 1971); *m* 1975, Bridget Trahair (separated); two *d*. *Educ:* Brentwood Sch.; Helsby Grammar Sch.; Leeds Univ. (BA). Yorkshire Post, 1962–64; Daily Mail, 1964–66; The Guardian, 1966–67; The Times: Education Correspondent, 1967–70; Founder Editor, The Times Higher Educn Supplement, 1971–76; Home News Editor, 1976–78; Dep. Editor, Evening Standard, 1978–79; Chief Asst to the Editor, The Sunday Times, 1979–81; Exec. Editor (News), The Times, 1981–82; Jt Dep. Editor, The Sunday Times, 1982–84; Editor, Western Morning News, 1984–85; Editor-in-Chief, Today, 1986–87; Exec. Ed., The Sunday Times, 1987–91. Hon. MA, Open Univ., 1976. *Publications:* Eddy Shah: Today and the Newspaper Revolution, 1988; Deadline Sunday, 1991; Gulf War Despatches, 1991; (ed) The Penguin Book of Twentieth Century Speeches, 1992; (ed) The Penguin Book of Historic Speeches, 1995. *Recreations:* reading, travel. *Address:* (office) 1 Pennington Street, E1 9XN. *T:* 0171–782 5801. *Clubs:* Garrick, London Press.

MACARTHUR, Charles Ramsay, QC (Scot.) 1970; Sheriff of Tayside, Central and Fife, 1981–91; *s* of late Alastair and late Joan Macarthur; *m* 1973, Rosemary Valda Morgan (marr. diss. 1982), Edinburgh. *Educ:* Glasgow Univ. (MA, LLB). Served War of 1939–45: joined Royal Navy, 1942; demobilised as Lieut, RNVR, 1946. Solicitor, 1952–59; admitted Scottish Bar, 1960; Standing Junior Counsel, Highlands and Islands Development Board, 1968–70; Sheriff of the Lothians and Borders, 1974–76. *Recreations:* travel, talking. *Club:* New (Edinburgh).

MacARTHUR, Ian, OBE 1988; Hon. Treasurer, since 1991, and Vice-Chairman, since 1992, Texprint Ltd, charity; *b* 17 May 1925; *yr s* of late Lt-Gen. Sir William MacArthur, KCB, DSO, OBE, MD, DSc, FRCP, KHP; *m* 1957, Judith Mary, (RGN 1976), *d* of late Francis Gavin Douglas Miller; four *s* three *d*. *Educ:* Cheltenham Coll.; The Queen's Coll., Oxford (Scholar, MA). Served War of 1939–45, with RN (Ord. Seaman) and RNVR, 1943–46 (King's Badge; Flag Lieut to C-in-C Portsmouth, 1946). Contested (U), Greenock Gen. Election, May 1955, also by-election, Dec. 1955; MP (C) Perth and E Perthshire, 1959–Sept. 1974; an Asst Government Whip (unpaid), 1962–63; a Lord Comr of the Treasury and Govt Scottish Whip, 1963–64; Opposition Scottish Whip, 1964–65; an Opposition Spokesman on Scottish Affairs, 1965–70 (Opposition front bench, 1965–66, 1969–70). Former Member: Speaker's Conf. on Electoral Law; Select Cttees on European Legislation, on Scottish Affairs, and on Members' Interests. Chm., Scottish Cons. Mems' Cttee, 1972–73. Introduced, as Private Member's Bills: Law Reform (Damages and Solatium) (Scotland) Act, 1962; Interest on Damages (Scotland) Act, 1971; Social Work (Scotland) Act, 1972; Domicile and Matrimonial Proceedings Act, 1973. Personal Asst to the Prime Minister, Rt Hon. Sir Alec Douglas-Home, Kinross and W Perthshire By-Election, Nov. 1963. Hon. Pres., Scottish Young Unionists, 1962–65; Vice-Chm., Cons. Party in Scotland, 1972–75. Formerly Dir of Administration, J. Walter Thompson Co. Ltd. Dir, British Textile Confederation, 1977–89. FRSA 1984. Gold Cross of Merit, Polish Govt in Exile, 1971. *Address:* 15 Old Palace Lane, Richmond, Surrey TW9 1PG. *Club:* Naval.

See also R. A. G. Douglas Miller.

McARTHUR, Dr John Duncan, FRCPGlas; FRCPE; Consultant Physician and Cardiologist, Western Infirmary, Glasgow, since 1978; *b* 7 Jan. 1938; *s* of Neil McPhail McArthur and Elizabeth Duncan; *m* 1963, Elizabeth Agnew Bowie; two *s* one *d*. *Educ:* Univ. of Glasgow (BSc Hons 1960; MB ChB Hons 1963); DM Madras 1970. DObstRCOG 1965; MRCP 1966; MRCPG 1966; MRCPE 1967, FRCPE 1994; FRCPGlas 1980. Junior House Officer, Glasgow Royal Infirmary and Ayrshire Hosps, 1963–65; Senior House Officer and Registrar, Glasgow Royal Inf., 1965–67; Lectr, Sen. Lectr, Reader, Christian Med. Coll. Hosp., Vellore, India, as Missionary, Church of Scotland, 1968–73; Sen. Registrar, Medicine/Cardiology, Glasgow Teaching Hosps, 1973–78. *Publications:* articles on valvular heart disease and pacemakers. *Recreations:* DIY, gardening. *Address:* 8 Durness Avenue, Bearsden, Glasgow G61 2AQ. *T:* 0141–942 7330.

McARTHUR, Dr Thomas Burns, (Tom); English teacher, since 1959; feature writer, since 1962; lecturer and writer on yoga and Indian philosophy, since 1962; author and language consultant, since 1970; Editor: English Today, since 1984; Oxford Companion to the English Language, since 1987; *b* 23 Aug. 1938; *s* of Archibald McArthur and Margaret Burns; *m* 1963, Fereshteh Mottahedin (*d* 1993); one *s* two *d*. *Educ:* Glasgow Univ. (MA 1958); Edinburgh Univ. (MLitt 1970; PhD 1978). Officer-Instr, RAEC, 1959–61; Asst Master, Riland Bedford Sch., Warwicks, 1961–63; Head of English, Cathedral and John Connon Sch., Bombay, India, 1965–67; Vis. Prof. in the English of the Media, Rajendra Prasad College of Mass Communication (Bharatiya Vidya Bhavan), Univ. of Bombay, 1965–67; Dir of Extra-Mural English Language Courses, Univ. of Edinburgh, 1972–79; Associate Prof. of English, Université du Québec à Trois-Rivières, Canada, 1979–83; Recognised Teacher (pt-time), 1986–, Res. Fellow, 1992–, Exeter Univ. Co-founder (with Reinhard Hartmann), Internat. Lexicography Course, Univ. of Exeter, 1987–. Consultant: Min. of Educn, Quebec, 1980–81; Société pour la promotion de l'enseignement de l'anglais (langue seconde) au Québec, 1980–83; Henson International Television (the Muppets), 1985–86; Dictionary Res. Centre, Exeter Univ., 1987–90; BBC Policy Planning Unit, 1992; also on dictionaries, encyclopedias and ELT books published by Century Hutchinson, Chambers, Collins, CUP, Longman, OUP and Time-Life. The Story of English (BBC radio series with D. Crystal), 1987. Member, Editorial Board: Internat. Jl of Lexicography, 1988–; World Englishes, 1993–; Editl Advr, The Good Book Guide, 1992–; Mem., Internat. Adv. Bd, Logos, 1994–. *Publications:* Patterns of English series, 1972–74; English for Students of Economics, 1973; (with Beryl Atkins) Collins Dictionary of English Phrasal Verbs, 1974; (ed with A. J. Aitken) Languages of Scotland, 1979; Longman Lexicon of Contemporary English, 1981; A Foundation Course for Language Teachers, 1983; The Written Word, Books 1 and 2, 1984; Worlds of Reference, 1986; Yoga and the Bhagavad-Gita, 1986; Understanding Yoga, 1986; Unitive Thinking, 1988 (Beyond Logic and Mysticism, USA, 1990); The English Language as Used in Quebec: a survey, 1989; (ed) The Oxford Companion to the English Language, 1992. *Recreations:* reading, television, walking, cycling, travel. *Address:* 22–23 Ventress Farm Court, Cherry Hinton Road, Cambridge CB1 4HD. *T:* Cambridge (01223) 245934.

MACARTNEY, Allan; *see* Macartney, W. J. A.

MACARTNEY, Sir John Barrington, 6th Bt *cr* 1799, of Lish, Co. Armagh; dairy farmer, retired; *b* 21 Jan. 1917; *s* of John Barrington Macartney (3rd *s* of Sir John Macartney, 3rd Bt; he *d* 1951) and Selina Koch, Hampden, Mackay, Qld, Australia; *S* uncle, Sir Alexander Miller Macartney, 5th Bt, 1960; *m* 1944, Amy Isobel Reinke (*d* 1978); one *s*. *Heir: s* John Ralph Macartney [*b* 24 July 1945; *m* 1966, Suzanne Marie Fowler; four *d*]. *Address:* 37 Meadow Street, North Mackay, Qld 4740, Australia.

MACARTNEY, Dr (William John) Allan; Member (SNP) North East Scotland, European Parliament, since 1994; Deputy Leader, Scottish National Party, since 1992; *b* Accra, Ghana, 17 Feb. 1941; *s* of Rev. William M. Macartney and Jessie H. I. Macartney (*née* Low); *m* 1963, J. D. Anne Forsyth; two *s* one *d*. *Educ:* Elgin Acad., Moray; Univ. of Tübingen; Univ. of Marburg; Univ. of Edinburgh (MA; PhD 1978); Univ. of Glasgow (BLitt). Teacher, Eastern Nigeria, 1963–64; Lectr in Govt and Admin, Univ. of Botswana, Lesotho and Swaziland, 1966–74; Research Fellow, Univ. of Edinburgh, 1974–75; Staff Tutor in Politics, Open Univ., 1975–94. *Publications:* Readings in Boleswa Government, 1971; The Referendum Experience, 1981; Islands of Europe, 1984; Self-determination in the Commonwealth, 1987. *Recreations:* music, languages, walking, vexillology. *Address:* 70 Rosemount Place, Aberdeen AB2 4XJ. *T:* Aberdeen (01224) 623150, *Fax:* (01224) 623160.

MACAULAY OF BRAGAR, Baron *cr* 1989 (Life Peer), of Bragar in the county of Ross and Cromarty; **Donald Macaulay.** *Educ:* Univ. of Glasgow (MA, LLB). Admitted to Faculty of Advocates, 1963; QC (Scot.) 1975. *Address:* House of Lords, SW1.

MACAULAY, Janet Stewart Alison, MA; Headmistress of St Leonards and St Katharines Schools, St Andrews, 1956–70; *b* 20 Dec. 1909; 3rd *d* of late Rev. Prof. A. B. Macaulay, DD, of Trinity Coll., Glasgow. *Educ:* Laurel Bank Sch., Glasgow; Glasgow Univ.; Somerville Coll., Oxford. BA Oxon 1932; BLitt Oxon 1934; MA Oxon 1936. Asst Mistress, Wycombe Abbey Sch., Bucks, 1933–36; Sutton High Sch. (GPDST), Sutton, Surrey, 1937–45; Headmistress, Blackheath High Sch. (GPDST), 1945–Dec. 1955. Hon. LLD St Andrews, 1977. *Address:* 3 Drummond Place, Edinburgh EH3 6PH.

McAVOY, Sir (Francis) Joseph, Kt 1976; CBE 1969; Chairman: Queensland and Australian Canegrowers Councils, 1963–82 (Member, 1952–82); Australian Canegrowers Council, 1952–82; retired; *b* 26 Feb. 1910; *s* of William Henry McAvoy and Hanorah Catherine McAvoy; *m* 1936, Mary Irene Doolan; four *s* (one *d* decd). *Educ:* Nudgee Coll., Brisbane; Sacred Heart Convent, Innisfail, Qld. Member: Goondi Mill Suppliers Cttee, 1947–82; Innisfail Canegrowers Exec., 1949–82; Metric Conversion Bd (Aust.), 1970–78; Aust. Immigration Adv. Council, 1964–72; Exec. Council of Agriculture, 1963–82; Exec., Aust. Farmers Fedn, 1969–77, Nat. Farmers Fedn, 1977–82. Vice-Pres., Internat. Fedn of Agricultural Producers, 1968–74. Paul Harris Fellow, Rotary Internat., USA, 1986. *Recreation:* lawn bowls. *Address:* Unit 19, Wellington Close, 233 Wellington Road, East Brisbane, Qld 4169, Australia. *Clubs:* Rotary, IDB (Innisfail, Qld).

McAVOY, Thomas McLaughlin; MP (Lab and Co-op) Glasgow, Rutherglen, since 1987; *b* 14 Dec. 1943; *m* Eleanor Kerr; four *s*. Employee, Hoover, Cambuslang; shop steward, AEU. Mem., Strathclyde Regl Council, 1982–87; former Chm., Rutherglen Community Council. An Opposition Whip, 1990–93. *Address:* House of Commons, SW1A 0AA; 9 Douglas Avenue, Rutherglen, Glasgow G73 4RA.

McBAIN, (David) Malcolm, LVO 1972; HM Diplomatic Service, retired; Ambassador to Madagascar, 1984–87; *b* 19 Jan. 1928; *s* of David Walker McBain and Lilian J. McBain; *m* 1951, Audrey Yvonne Evison; one *s* three *d*. *Educ:* Sutton County School; London School of Economics (evening student). Min. of Civil Aviation appts in Tripoli, Libya, 1949–51, New Delhi, 1953–54; Diplomatic Service: New Delhi, 1958–61; Kenya, 1963–67; Thailand, 1968–75; Brunei, 1978–81; Texas, 1981–84. Order of Crown of Thailand, 1972. *Recreations:* golf, fishing. *Address:* Edmeads Cottage, Teffont Magna, Salisbury, Wilts SP3 5QY.

McBAIN, Ed; *see* Hunter, Evan.

McBAIN, Malcolm; *see* McBain, D. M.

MACBEATH, Prof. Alexander Murray, PhD (Princeton, NJ); MA (Cantab); Professor of Mathematics and Statistics, University of Pittsburgh, 1979–90; *b* 30 June 1923; *s* of late Prof. Alexander Macbeath, CBE; *m* 1951, Julie Ormrod, Lytham St Anne's; two *s*. *Educ:* Royal Belfast Academical Inst.; Queen's Univ., Belfast; Clare Coll., Cambridge. Entrance Schol., Dixon Prize in Maths, Purser Studentship, 1st class hons in Maths, BA, QUB. Temp. post with Foreign Office, 1943–45. Cambridge, 1945–48; Maj. Entrance Schol., Wrangler Math. Tripos, Part II, dist. Part III, BA, Owst Prize. Commonwealth Fund Fellowship, Princeton, NJ, 1948–50; Smith's Prize, 1949; PhD Princeton, 1950. Research Fellow, Clare Coll., Cambridge, 1950–51; MA Cambridge, 1951. Lectr in Maths, Univ. Coll. of North Staffordshire, 1951–53; Prof. of Maths, Queen's Coll., Dundee, 1953–62; Mason Prof. of Pure Maths, Univ. of Birmingham, 1962–79. Visiting Professor: California Inst. of Technology, 1966–67; Univ. of Pittsburgh, 1974–75. *Publications:* Elementary Vector Algebra, 1964; papers in: Jl London Mathematical Soc.; Proc. London Math. Soc.; Proc. Cambridge Philosophical Soc.; Quarterly Jl of Mathematics; Annals of Mathematics; Canadian Jl of Mathematics. *Recreation:* Scottish country dancing. *Address:* 1 Church Hill Court, Lighthorne, Warwickshire CV35 0AR.

McBRATNEY, George, CEng, FIMechE; Principal, College of Technology, Belfast, 1984–89; *b* 5 May 1927; *s* of George McBratney and Sarah Jane McBratney; *m* 1949, Margaret Rose Patricia, (Trissie), *d* of late John Robinson, Melbourne, Australia; one *s*. *Educ:* Coll. of Technology, Belfast (BSc(Eng) 1948); Northampton Coll. of Advanced Technol.; QUB (Dip Ed 1976). CEng, FIMechE 1971. Apprentice fitter/draughtsman, Harland and Wolff, Belfast, 1943–47; Teacher, Comber Trades Prep. Sch., 1947–54; College of Technology, Belfast: successively Asst Lectr, Lectr and Sen. Lectr, 1954–67; Asst to Principal, 1967–69; Vice-Principal, 1969–84. Council Member: IMechE, 1984–86 (Chm., NI Br., 1984–86); NI Manpower Council, 1984–; Lambeg Industrial Res. Assoc. (formerly Linen Industry Res. Assoc.), 1984–90; BTEC, 1986–89; Chm., Further Educn Adv. Cttee, Faculty of Educn, Univ. of Ulster, 1986–90. *Publications:* Mechanical Engineering Experiments, vols 1 and 2 (with W. R. Mitchell), 1962, vol. 3 (with T. G. J. Moag), 1964; (with T. G. J. Moag) Science for Mechanical Engineering Technicians, vol. 1, 1966. *Recreation:* gardening. *Address:* 16 Glencregagh Drive, Belfast BT6 0NL. *T:* Belfast (01232) 796123.

McBREARTY, Tony; Head of Policy, London Borough of Newham, since 1988; *b* 26 April 1946; *s* of Patrick and Mary McBrearty; *m* 1969, Heather McGowan, solicitor; one *s*. Councillor (Lab) London Borough of Haringey, 1975–86 (Chm. of Personnel Cttee, 1976–79; Chm. of Housing Cttee, 1979–82); Mem. (Lab) Enfield N, 1981–86, Chm., Housing Cttee, 1982–86, GLC. Contested (Lab) W Herts, 1987. Chm., Central Technical Unit, 1986–88. *Recreations:* politics, history. *Address:* 112 Inderwick Road, Hornsey, N8 9JY. *T:* 0181–348 8159.

McBRIDE, Commandant (Sara) Vonla (Adair), CB 1979; Director, City of London Region, Lloyds Bank Ltd, 1980–91; a Chairman, Civil Service Commissioners' Interview Panel, 1985–91; *b* 20 Jan. 1921; *d* of late Andrew Stewart McBride and Agnes McBride. *Educ:* Ballymena Acad., NI; TCD (Moderatorship in Mod. Lit; BA Hons). CBIM. Teacher of English and French, Ballymena Acad., 1942–45; Housemistress, Gardenhurst Sch., Burnham-on-Sea, Somerset, 1945–49. Dir, WRNS, 1976–79 (joined 1949); Hon. ADC to the Queen, 1976–79. Vice-President: Ex Services Mental Welfare Soc., 1983–; Officers' Pension Soc., 1989–; RNLI, 1992–. Freeman, City of London, 1978. Liveryman, Shipwrights' Co., 1983–. *Publication:* Never at Sea (autobiog.), 1966. *Recreations:* golf, theatre entertaining, continental travel. *Address:* Flat 11, 8 The Paragon, Blackheath, SE3 0NY. *T:* 0181–852 8673. *Club:* Naval.

McBRIDE, Vonla; *see* McBride, S. V. A.

McBRIDE, William Griffith, AO 1977; CBE 1969; Medical Director, Foundation 41 (for the study of congenital abnormalities and mental retardation), 1972–93; Consultant Obstetrician and Gynaecologist, St George Hospital, Sydney, 1957–93; *b* 25 May 1927; *s* of late John McBride, Sydney; *m* 1957, Patricia Mary, *d* of late Robert Louis Glover; two *s* two *d*. *Educ:* Canterbury High Sch., Sydney; Univ. of Sydney; Univ. of London. MB, BS Sydney 1950; MD Sydney 1962; FRCOG 1968 (MRCOG 1954); FRACOG 1979. Resident: St George Hosp., Sydney, 1950; Launceston Hosp., 1951; Med. Supt, Women's Hosp., Sydney, 1955–57; Cons. Gynaecologist, Bankstown Hosp., Sydney, 1957–66; Consultant Obstetrician and Gynaecologist: Women's Hosp., Sydney, 1966–83; Royal Hosp. for Women, 1983–88. Lectr in Obstetrics and Gynaecology, Univ. of Sydney, 1957; Examr in Obstetrics and Gynaecology, Univ. of Sydney, 1960. Vis. Prof. of Gynaecology, Univ. of Bangkok, 1968. Mem., WHO Sub-Cttee on safety of oral contraceptives, 1971. Pres. Sect. of Obstetrics and Gynæcology, AMA, 1966–73. Fellow, Senate of Univ. of Sydney, 1976–90; FRSM 1988; Mem., Amer. Coll. of Toxicology, 1985. Member: Soc. of Reproductive Biology; Endocrine Soc.; Teratology Soc.; Soc. for Risk Analysis; NY Acad. of Scis, 1987; AAAS, 1992. Mem. Council, Royal Agricl Soc. of NSW, 1987–; Delegate, Council meeting of Royal Agricl Socs, Calgary, 1992; breeder and judge of Hereford cattle; judged Shropshire and W Midlands Show, 1989. Member: Bd of Dirs, Australian Opera, 1979–82; Australian Opera Council, 1982–. BP Prize of Institut de la Vie, 1971 (for discovery of the teratogenic effects of the drug Thalidomide; first person to alert the world to the dangers of this drug and possibly other drugs). *Publications:* Drugs, 1960–70; Killing the Messenger, 1994; contrib. (on teratogenic effect of the drug Thalidomide), Lancet 1961 (London), (on mutagenic effect of Thalidomide), BMJ 1994; numerous papers in internat. med. jls and scientific jls. *Recreations:* tennis, swimming, riding, music, cattle breeding. *Address:* Foundation 41, 211 Bourke Street, E Sydney, NSW 2011, Australia. *Clubs:* Union, Australian Jockey, Palm Beach Surf, Royal Sydney Golf (all in Sydney).

McBURNEY, Air Vice-Marshal Ralph Edward, CBE 1945; CD; RCAF, retired; *b* Montreal, Quebec, 17 Aug. 1906; *s* of Irville Albert and Lilian McBurney, Saskatoon, Sask.; *m* 1931, Gertrude Elizabeth Bate, Saskatoon; two *s* one *d*. *Educ:* Univs of Saskatchewan and Manitoba. BSc (EE); Commenced flying training as a cadet in RCAF, 1924; Pilot Officer, 1926; employed on Forest Fire Patrols and photographic mapping; Course in RAF School of Army Co-operation and tour as Instructor in RCAF School of Army Co-operation, 1931; Course at RAF Wireless School, Cranwell, and tour as Signals Adviser at Air Force HQ, Ottawa, 1935–36; RAF Staff Coll., Andover, 1939; Dir of Signals, AFHQ, Ottawa, 1939–42; CO, RCAF Station, Trenton, Ont., 1943; CO, RCAF Station, Dishforth, Yorks, 1943; Air Cdre 1944; Base Comdr of 61 Training Base, and later, 64 Operational Base in No 6 (RCAF) Bomber Group of Bomber Comd; SASO of the Group, Dec. 1944; AOC RCAF Maintenance Comd, 1945–46; Senior Canadian Air Force Liaison Officer, London, 1946–48; AOC Air Materiel Comd, RCAF, Ottawa, 1948–52. Business Consultant, 1952–60; Chief, Technical Information Service, Nat. Research Council, Ottawa, 1960–72. Pres., Internat. Fedn for Documentation, 1968–72. *Address:* 2022 Sharon Avenue, Ottawa, Ontario K2A 1L8, Canada.

McBURNIE, Tony; Chairman: The Strategic Index, since 1994; The Strategic Marketing Index, since 1994; *b* 4 Aug. 1929; *s* of William McBurnie and Bessie McKenzie Harvey McBurnie; *m* 1954, René Keating; one *s* one *d*. *Educ:* Lanark Grammar Sch.; Glasgow Univ. (MA). FCIM (FInstM 1984). National Service, RAF (FO), 1951–53. Divisional Manager Mullard Ltd, 1958–65; Group Marketing Dir, United Glass Ltd, 1965–69; Chairman and Managing Director: Ravenhead Co. Ltd, 1970–79; United Glass Containers Ltd, 1979–82; Man. Dir, United Glass PT&D Gp, 1982–84; Dir, United Glass Holdings PLC, 1966–84; Dir Gen., Chartered Inst. of Marketing (formerly Inst. of Marketing), 1984–89; Managing Director: Coll. of Marketing Ltd, 1985–89; Marketing Training Ltd, 1984–89; Marketing House Publishers Ltd, 1985–89. Chairman: Reed QT Search, 1989–90; Marketing Quality Assurance, 1991–95. Director: Reed Executive plc, 1987–90; Beard Dove Ltd, 1988–. Pres., Assoc. of Glass Container Manufacturers, 1981–83; Chm.,

NJIC for Glass Industry, 1982–83; Dir, European Glass Fedn, 1979–83. *Publications:* (with David Clutterbuck) The Marketing Edge, 1987; Marketing Plus, 1989. *Recreations:* golf, swimming, theatre, the arts. *Address:* Craigwood Lodge, Prince Consort Drive, Ascot, Berks SL5 8AW. *Club:* Wentworth.

McCABE, Bernice Alda; Headmistress, Chelmsford County High School for Girls, since 1990; *b* 7 Oct. 1952; *d* of Alan Collis Wood and Eileen May Wood (*née* Bolton); *m* 1988, Thomas Patrick McCabe. *Educ:* Clifton High Sch. for Girls; Bristol Univ. (BA, PGCE); Leeds Metropolitan Univ. Asst English Teacher, Filton High Sch., Bristol, 1974–81; Head of English: Cotham Grammar Sch., Bristol, 1981–83; Collingwood Sch., Camberley, 1984–86; Dep. Headteacher, Heathland Sch., Hounslow, 1986–90. FRSA 1995. *Recreations:* travel, interior design and decoration, opera, running. *Address:* Chelmsford County High School, Broomfield Road, Chelmsford, Essex CM1 1RW. *T:* Chelmsford (01245) 352592; The Old Grammar School, Cavendish, Suffolk CO10 8BB.

MacCABE, Prof. Colin Myles Joseph; Head of Research, British Film Institute, since 1989; Professor of English, University of Pittsburgh, since 1987; *b* 9 Feb. 1949; *s* of Myles Joseph MacCabe and Ruth Ward MacCabe; two *s* one *d. Educ:* Trinity College, Cambridge (BA English and Moral Scis 1971, MA 1974, PhD 1976); Ecole Normale Supérieure, 1972–73 (pensionnaire anglais). University of Cambridge: Research Fellow, Emmanuel College, 1974–76; Fellow, King's College, 1976–81; Asst Lectr, Faculty of English, 1976–81; Prof. of English Studies, 1981–85, Vis. Prof., 1985–91, Strathclyde Univ.; Head of Production, BFI, 1985–89. Vis. Fellow, School of Humanities, Griffith Univ., 1981, 1984; Chm., John Logie Baird Centre for Research in Television and Film, 1985–91 (Dir, 1983–85); Mellon Vis. Prof., Univ. of Pittsburgh, 1985; Vis. Prof., Birkbeck Coll., Univ. of London, 1992–. Mem., Editl Bd, Screen, 1973–81; Editor, Critical Qly, 1990– (Critical Editor, 1987–90). *Publications:* James Joyce and the Revolution of the Word, 1979; Godard: Images, Sounds, Politics, 1980; (ed) The Talking Cure: essays in psychoanalysis and language, 1981; (ed) James Joyce: new perspectives, 1982; Theoretical Essays: film, linguistics, literature, 1985; (ed jtly) The BBC and Public Sector Broadcasting, 1986; (ed) High Theory/Low Culture: analysing popular television and film, 1986; (ed) Futures for English, 1987; (ed jtly) The Linguistics of Writing, 1987; (with Isaac Julien) Diary of a Young Soul Rebel, 1991. *Recreations:* eating, drinking, talking. *Address:* British Film Institute Research Division, 21 Stephen Street, W1P 1PL. *T:* 0171–255 1444.

McCABE, Eamonn Patrick; Picture Editor, The Guardian, since 1988; *b* 28 July 1948; *s* of James and Celia McCabe; *m* 1972, Ruth Calvert (marr. diss. 1993); one *s. Educ:* Challoner School, Finchley; San Francisco State Coll. FRPS 1990. Freelance photographer on local papers and with The Guardian for one year; staff photographer, The Observer, 1977–86 and 1987–88; official photographer for the Pope's visit to England, 1982; Picture Editor, Sportsweek, 1986–87. Hon. Prof., Thames Valley Univ., 1994. Fellow in Photography, Nat. Mus. of Photography and TV, Bradford, 1988. Sports photographer of the year, RPS and Sports Council, 1978, 1979, 1981, 1984; News photographer of the year, British Press Awards, 1985; Picture Editor of the Year, Nikon Press Awards, 1992 and 1993. *Publications:* Sports Photographer, 1981; Eamonn McCabe, Photographer, 1987. *Recreations:* tennis, squash, occasional jogging, cinema. *Address:* The Guardian, 119 Farringdon Road, EC1R 3ER. *Club:* Chelsea Arts.

McCABE, John, CBE 1985; professional musician; composer and pianist; *b* 21 April 1939; *s* of Frank and Elisabeth McCabe; *m* 1974, Monica Christine Smith. *Educ:* Liverpool Institute High Sch. for Boys; Manchester Univ. (MusBac); Royal Manchester Coll. of Music (ARMCM); Hochschule fur Musik, Munich. Pianist-in-residence, University Coll., Cardiff, 1965–68; freelance musical criticism, 1966–71. Career as composer and pianist: many broadcasts and recordings as well as concert appearances in various countries. Prizewinner in Gaudeamus Competition for Interpreters of Contemporary Music, Holland, 1969. Recordings incl. 12 CD set of complete piano music by Haydn, complete piano music of Nielsen (2 records). Awarded Special Citation by Koussevitsky Internat. Recording Foundn of USA, for recording of Symph. No 2 and Notturni ed Alba, 1974; Special Award by Composers' Guild of Gt Brit. (services to Brit. music), 1975; Ivor Novello Award (TV theme tune, Sam), 1977. Pres., ISM, 1983–84; Chm., Assoc. of Professional Composers, 1984–85. Hon. FRMCM; Hon. FLCM 1983; Hon. FRCM 1984; Hon. RAM 1985; Hon. FTCL 1989. *Compositions* include: three symphonies, two operas, ballets, concerti, orchestral works incl. The Chagall Windows and Hartmann Variations, Notturni ed Alba, for soprano and orch., Fire at Durilgai for orch., Cloudcatcher Fells for brass band, Edward II (ballet), chamber music, keyboard works, and vocal compositions. *Publications:* Rachmaninov (short biog.), 1974; Bartok's Orchestral Music (BBC Music Guide), 1974; Haydn Piano Sonatas (Ariel Music Guide), 1986. *Recreations:* cricket, snooker, books, films. *Address:* 49 Burns Avenue, Southall, Mddx UB1 2LR.

McCABE, Primrose Smith; Senior Partner, Primrose McCabe & Co., since 1987; President, Institute of Chartered Accountants of Scotland, 1994–95; *b* 21 Sept. 1940; *m* 1965, Ernest McCabe. *Educ:* Ayr Acad. Trained with Stewart Gilmour, Ayr; qualified as CA, 1963; joined Romanes & Munro, Edinburgh, 1963; progressed through manager ranks to Partner, Deloitte Haskins & Sells, 1981–87; set up own practice, Linlithgow, 1987. Mem., Accounts Commn, 1988–92. Non-Exec. Dir, Dunfermline Building Soc., 1990–. Institute of Chartered Accountants of Scotland: Mem. Council, 1988–; first Convener, GP Cttee, 1990; Vice-Pres., 1992–94. Hon. Treas., Hospitality Industry Trust Scotland, 1994. Fellow, SCOTVEC, 1994. *Recreation:* walking my two dogs. *Address:* Primrose McCabe & Co., Regent House, Regent Centre, Linlithgow EH49 7HU. *T:* Linlithgow (01506) 842466.

McCAFFER, Prof. Ronald, FEng; Professor of Construction Management, since 1986, and Dean of Engineering, since 1992, Loughborough University of Technology; Project Director, European Construction Institute, since 1990; *b* 8 Dec. 1943; *s* of late John Gegg McCaffer and Catherine Turner (*née* Gourlay); *m* 1966, Margaret Elizabeth, *d* of late Cyril Warner and of Mary Huntley (*née* Mason); one *s. Educ:* Albert Sch., Glasgow; Univ. of Strathclyde (BSc 1965); PhD Loughborough 1977. FICE 1988; FCIOB 1988; MIMgt (MBIM 1989); FEng 1991; Eur Ing 1990. Design Engr, Babtie, Shaw & Morton, 1965–67; Site Engineer: Nuclear Power Gp, 1967–69; Taylor Woodrow Construction Ltd, 1969–70; Loughborough University of Technology: Lectr, 1970–78; Sen. Lectr, 1978–83; Reader, 1983–86; Head of Civil Engrg, 1987–93. Editor, Engineering, Construction and Architectural Management, 1994–. *Publications:* Modern Construction Management, 1977, 4th edn 1995; Worked Examples in Construction Management, 1978, 2nd edn 1986; Estimating and Tendering for Civil Engineering Works, 1984, 2nd edn 1991; Management of Construction Equipment, 1982, 2nd edn 1991; International Bid Preparation, 1995; International Bidding Case Study, 1995. *Recreations:* bad golf, jogging, being patient with administrators. *Address:* Department of Civil Engineering, Loughborough University of Technology, Loughborough, Leics LE11 3TU. *T:* Loughborough 01509) 222600, *Fax:* (01509) 260852.

McCAFFREY, Sir Thos Daniel, (Sir Tom McCaffrey), Kt 1979; public affairs consultant; *b* 20 Feb. 1922; *s* of William P. and B. McCaffrey; *m* 1949, Agnes Campbell Douglas; two *s* four *d. Educ:* Hyndland Secondary Sch. and St Aloysius Coll., Glasgow. Served War, RAF, 1940–46. Scottish Office, 1948–61; Chief Information Officer, Home Office, 1966–71; Press Secretary, 10 Downing Street, 1971–72; Dir of Information Services, Home Office, 1972–74; Head of News Dept, FCO, 1974–76; Chief Press Sec. to Prime Minister, 1976–79; Chief of Staff to Rt Hon. James Callaghan, MP, 1979–80; Chief Asst to Rt Hon. Michael Foot, MP, 1980–83; Hd, Chief Executive's Office, BPCC, 1983–84; Dir, Public Affairs, and Special Advr to the Publisher, Mirror Gp Newspapers, 1984–85. *Address:* Balmaha, 2 The Park, Great Bookham, Surrey KT23 3JL. *T:* Bookham (01372) 454171.

MacCAIG, Norman (Alexander), OBE 1979; MA; FRSL; FRSE; ARSA; *b* 14 Nov. 1910; *s* of Robert McCaig and Joan MacLeod; *m* 1940, Isabel Munro (*d* 1990); one *s* one *d. Educ:* Edinburgh University. MA Hons Classics. FRSL 1965; ARSA 1981; FRSE 1983. Schoolteacher, 1932–67 and 1969–70; Fellow in Creative Writing, Univ. of Edinburgh, 1967–69; Lectr in English Studies, Univ. of Stirling, 1970–72, Reader in Poetry, 1972–77. Travelling Scholarship, Soc. of Authors, 1964; RSL Award (Heinemann Bequest), 1967; Cholmondeley Award, 1975; Scottish Arts Council Awards, 1954, 1966–67, 1970, 1971, 1978, 1980, 1986; Royal Bank of Scotland Saltire Award, 1985; Queen's Gold Medal for Poetry, 1986; Poetry Soc. Award, 1992. DUniv Stirling, 1981; Hon. DLitt Edinburgh, 1983; Hon. LLD Dundee, 1986. *Publications: poetry:* Far Cry, 1943; The Inward Eye, 1946; Riding Lights, 1955; The Sinai Sort, 1957; A Common Grace, 1960; A Round of Applause, 1962; Measures, 1965; Surroundings, 1966; Rings on a Tree, 1968; A Man in My Position, 1969; The White Bird, 1973; The World's Room, 1974; Tree of Strings, 1977; The Equal Skies, 1980; A World of Difference, 1983; Collected Poems, 1985; Voice-over, 1988; Collected Poems, a new edition, 1990; (ed anthology) Honour'd Shade, 1959; (with Alexander Scott, ed anthology) Contemporary Scottish Verse, 1970. *Recreations:* fishing, music. *Address:* 7 Leamington Terrace, Edinburgh EH10 4JW. *T:* 0131–229 1809. *Club:* Scottish Arts (Edinburgh).

McCALL, Sir (Charles) Patrick (Home), Kt 1971; MBE 1944; TD 1946; solicitor; Clerk of the County Council, 1960–72, Clerk of the Peace, 1960–71, and Clerk of the Lieutenancy, Lancashire, 1960–74; *b* 22 Nov. 1910; *s* of late Charles and Dorothy McCall; *m* 1934, Anne (*d* 1991), *d* of late Samuel Brown, Sedlescombe, Sussex; two *s* one *d. Educ:* St Edward's Sch., Oxford. Served 1939–45; Substantive Major TA. Hon. Lt-Col. Mem., Economic and Social Cttee, EEC, 1973–78. *Recreations:* travel, walking, swimming, gardening. *Address:* Auchenhay Lodge, Corsock, by Castle Douglas, Kirkcudbrightshire DG7 3HZ. *T:* Corsock (016444) 651.

McCALL, Christopher Hugh; QC 1987; *b* 3 March 1944; *yr s* of late Robin Home McCall, CBE and Joan Elizabeth (*née* Kingdon); *m* 1981, Henrietta Francesca Sharpe. *Educ:* Winchester (Scholar); Magdalen Coll., Oxford (Demy; BA Maths, 1964; Eldon Law Scholar, 1966). Called to the Bar, Lincoln's Inn, 1966, Bencher, 1993. Second Jun. Counsel to the Inland Revenue in chancery matters, 1977–87; Jun. Counsel to Attorney Gen. in charity matters, 1981–87. Mem, Bar Council, 1973–76; Jt Hon. Treas., Barristers Benevolent Assoc., 1981–86. *Recreations:* music, travel, Egyptomania. *Address:* 13 Old Square, Lincoln's Inn, WC2A 3UA. *T:* 0171–404 4800. *Clubs:* Royal Automobile, Alpine; Leander (Henley-on-Thames).

McCALL, David Slesser, CBE 1988; DL; Chairman: Anglia Television Group, since 1994 (Director, since 1970; Chief Executive, 1986–94); Anglia Television Ltd, since 1994 (Director, since 1970; Chief Executive, 1976–94); *b* 3 Dec. 1934; *s* of Patrick McCall and Florence Kate Mary Walker; *m* 1968, Lois Patricia Elder. *Educ:* Robert Gordon's Coll., Aberdeen. Mem., Inst. of Chartered Accountants of Scotland, 1958. National Service, 1959–61. Accountant, Grampian Television Ltd, 1961–68; Company Sec., Anglia Television Ltd, 1968–76. Chairman: Oxford Scientific Films Ltd, 1982–89; Greene King plc, 1995–; Director: ITN, 1978–86, 1991–; Ind. Television Publications Ltd, 1971–89; Ind. Television Assoc. Ltd, 1976–; Sodastream Holdings Ltd, 1976–85; Norwich City Football Club, 1979–85; Channel Four Television Co., 1981–85; Radio Broadland, 1984–91; Super Channel Ltd, 1986–88; British Satellite Broadcasting, 1987–90; E Adv. Bd, National Westminster Bank, 1988–92; TSMS Group Ltd, 1989–; Hodder & Stoughton Holdings Ltd, 1992–93. Chm., ITCA, subseq. Ind. Television Assoc., 1986–88. Pres., Norfolk and Norwich Chamber of Commerce, 1988–90 (Dep. Pres., 1986–88); Chm., Norwich Playhouse Theatre, 1992–. Treas., UEA, 1995–. FRTS 1988. CIMgt (CBIM 1988). DL Norfolk, 1992. *Recreations:* sport, travel. *Address:* Woodland Hall, Redenhall, Harleston, Norfolk IP20 9QW. *T:* Harleston (01379) 4442.

McCALL, John Armstrong Grice, CMG 1964; *b* 7 Jan. 1913; 2nd *s* of Rev. Canon J. G. McCall; *m* 1951, Kathleen Mary Clarke; no *c. Educ:* Glasgow Academy; Trinity Coll., Glenalmond; St Andrews Univ.; St John's Coll., Cambridge. MA 1st class hons Hist. St Andrews, 1935. Colonial Administrative Service (HMOCS), Nigeria, 1935–67; Cadet, 1936; Class I, 1956; Staff Grade, 1958. Chm., Mid-Western Nigeria Development Corp., Benin City, 1966–67, retired 1967. Asst Chief Admin. Officer, East Kilbride Develt Corp., 1967–76. Scottish Rep., Executive Cttee, Nigerian-British Chamber of Commerce, 1977–88. Mem. 1969, Vice-Chm. 1971, S Lanarkshire Local Employment Cttee; Mem. Panel, Industrial Tribunals (Scotland), 1972–74; Gen. Sec., Scotland, Royal Over-Seas League, 1978–80. Sec., West Linton Community Council, 1980–83. *Recreations:* golf, walking. *Address:* Burnside, West Linton, Peeblesshire EH46 7EW. *T:* West Linton (01968) 660488. *Clubs:* Caledonian, Royal Over-Seas League (Hon. Life Mem.); Old Glenalmond (Chm., 1978–81); Royal and Ancient (St Andrews).

McCALL, John Donald; Director, Consolidated Gold Fields Ltd, 1959–81 (Chairman, 1969–76); *b* 1 Feb. 1911; *s* of late Gilbert Kerr McCall; *m* 1942, Vere Stewart Gardner; one *s* one *d. Educ:* Clifton Coll.; Edinburgh Univ. Gold Mining industry, S Africa, 1930–39. Served War of 1939–45: commissioned, Gordon Highlanders. Joined Consolidated Gold Fields Ltd, London, 1946 (Dir, 1959; Jt Dep. Chm., 1968). Dir, Ultramar plc, 1965–79. *Address:* 64 Pont Street, SW1X 0AE. *Club:* Caledonian.

McCALL, Sir Patrick; *see* McCall, Sir C. P. H.

McCALL, William; General Secretary, Institution of Professional Civil Servants, 1963–89; *b* 6 July 1929; *s* of Alexander McCall and Jean Corbet Cunningham; *m* 1955, Olga Helen Brunton; one *s* one *d. Educ:* Dumfries Academy; Ruskin College, Oxford. Civil Service, 1946–52; Social Insurance Dept, TUC, 1954–58; Asst Sec., Instn of Professional Civil Servants, 1958–63; Mem., Civil Service Nat. Whitley Council (Staff Side), 1963–89, Chm. 1969–71, Vice-Chm. 1983. Hon. Treasurer, Parly and Scientific Cttee, 1976–80; Part-time Mem., Eastern Electricity Board, 1977–86; Member: Cttee of Inquiry into Engrg Profession, 1977–79; PO Arbitration Tribunal, 1980–90; TUC Gen. Council, 1984–89; Pay and Employment Policy Cttee, CVCP, 1990–94; Police Complaints Authority, 1991–94. Member Council: Univ. of London, 1994– (Mem. Ct, 1984–94); Goldsmiths' Coll., 1989–95. *Address:* Foothills, Gravel Path, Berkhamsted, Herts HP4 2PF. *T:* Berkhamsted (01442) 864974.

McCALL, Rt. Rev. William David Hair; *see* Willochra, Bishop of.

McCALLUM, Alastair Grindlay; His Honour Judge McCallum; a Circuit Judge, since 1992; *b* 28 Feb. 1947; *s* of William and Catherine McCallum; *m* 1969, Lindsay Sheila

Watkins; two *d*. *Educ:* Gilbert Rennie, Northern Rhodesia; Leeds Univ. (LLB, LLM (Com.)). Called to the Bar, Inner Temple, 1970; Asst Recorder, 1984; Recorder, 1989; Head of Chambers, 1990. *Recreations:* golf, travel, reading. *T:* Bradford (01274) 840274. *Club:* Bradford Golf (Hawksworth).

McCALLUM, Sir Donald (Murdo), Kt 1988; CBE 1976; FEng 1982; FRSE; DL; Chairman, Laser Ecosse Ltd, since 1990; General Manager, Scottish Group, 1968–85, and Director, 1970–87, Ferranti plc; *b* 6 Aug. 1922; *s* of Roderick McCallum and Lillian (*née* McPhee); *m* 1st, 1949, Barbara Black (*d* 1971); one *d*; 2nd, 1974, Mrs Margaret Illingworth (*née* Broadbent). *Educ:* George Watson's Boys' Coll.; Edinburgh Univ. (BSc). FIEE 1969; FRAeS 1986; FRSGS 1992; CIMgt (CBIM 1983). Admiralty Signal Establishment, 1942–46; Standard Telecommunication Laboratories, 1946; Ferranti Ltd, 1947: Chairman: Ferranti Defence Systems Ltd, 1984–87 (Hon. Pres., 1987–90); Ferranti Industrial Electronics, 1984–87 (Hon. Pres., 1987–90). Dir, Short Bros Ltd, 1981–89; Chairman: Scottish Tertiary Education Adv. Council, 1984–87; Scottish Council Develt & Industry, 1985–91 (Pres., 1991–93); Scottish Sub-Cttee, UGC, 1987–88; Member: UFC, 1989–91 (Chm., Scottish Cttee, 1989–91); Scottish Econ. Council, 1983–92. Member: Court, Heriot-Watt Univ., 1979–85; Governing Body, Napier Polytechnic, 1988–93; Court, Napier Univ., 1993–95; Governing Body, Edinburgh Coll. of Art, 1988–93. Hon. Life Mem., Edinburgh Univ. Students' Assoc., 1984. Liveryman, Company of Engineers, 1984; Freeman, City of London. DL City of Edinburgh, 1984. Hon. Fellow, Paisley Coll. of Technol., 1987; Fellow, SCOTVEC, 1988. DUniv Stirling, 1985; Hon. DSc: Heriot-Watt, 1986; Napier Coll. of Commerce and Technology, Edinburgh, 1986; Hon. LLD: Strathclyde, 1987; Aberdeen, 1989. British Gold Medal, RAeS, 1985. *Recreations:* photography, fishing. *Address:* 46 Heriot Row, Edinburgh EH3 6EX. *T:* 0131–225 9331. *Clubs:* Caledonian; New (Edinburgh).

McCALLUM, Googie; *see* Withers, Googie.

McCALLUM, Ian Stewart; Executive Sales Manager, Save & Prosper Sales Ltd, since 1989 (Sales Manager, 1985–87, Area Manager, 1987–89); *b* 24 Sept. 1936; *s* of late John Blair McCallum and Margaret Stewart McCallum; *m* 1st, 1957, Pamela Mary (*née* Shave) (marr. diss. 1984); one *s* two *d*; 2nd, 1984, Jean (*née* Lynch); two step *d*. *Educ:* Kingston Grammar Sch. Eagle Star Insurance Co. Ltd, 1953–54; National Service, Highland Light Infantry, 1954–56; Eagle Star Insce Co. Ltd, 1956–58; F. E. Wright and Co., Insurance Brokers, 1958–63; H. Clarkson (Home) Ltd, Insurance Brokers, 1963–68; Save & Prosper Group Ltd, 1968–. Leader, Woking Borough Council, 1972–76 and 1978–81, Dep. Leader, 1981–82; Mayor of Woking, 1976–77; Chm., Assoc. of Dist Councils, 1979–84 (Leader, 1974–79); Vice-Chairman: Standing Cttee on Local Authorities and Theatre, 1977–81; UK Steering Cttee on Local Authority Superannuation, 1974–84; Member: Local Authorities Conditions of Service Adv. Bd, 1973–84; Consultative Council on Local Govt Finance, 1975–84; Council for Business in the Community, 1981–84; Audit Commn, 1983–86; Health Promotion Res. Trust, 1983–. Vice-Chm., Sports Council, 1980–86. *Recreations:* swimming, jogging, walking, reading, badminton. *Address:* 5 Minters Orchard, Maidstone Road, St Marys Platt, near Sevenoaks, Kent TN15 8QJ. *T:* Borough Green (01732) 883653. *Club:* St Stephen's Constitutional.

McCALLUM, John Neil, AO 1992; CBE 1971; Chairman and Executive Producer, Fauna Films, Australia, since 1967, and John McCallum Productions, since 1976; actor and producer; *b* 14 March 1918; *s* of John Neil McCallum and Lilian Elsie (*née* Dyson); *m* 1948, Georgette Lizette Withers (*see* Googie Withers); one *s* two *d*. *Educ:* Oatlands Prep. Sch., Harrogate; Knox Grammar Sch., Sydney; C of E Grammar Sch., Brisbane; RADA. Served War, 2/5 Field Regt, AIF, 1941–45. Actor, English rep. theatres, 1937–39; Stratford-on-Avon Festival Theatre, 1939; Old Vic Theatre, 1940; British films and theatre, 1946–58; films include: It Always Rains On Sunday; Valley of Eagles; Miranda; London stage plays include: Roar Like a Dove; Janus; Waiting for Gillian; J. C. Williamson Theatres Ltd, Australia: Asst Man. Dir, 1958; Jt. Man. Dir, 1959–65; Man. Dir, 1966. Appeared in: (with Ingrid Bergman) The Constant Wife, London, 1973–74; (with Googie Withers) The Circle, London, 1976–77, Australia, 1982–83; (with Googie Withers) The Kingfisher, Australia, 1978–79; The Skin Game, The Cherry Orchard, and Dandy Dick, theatrical tour, England, 1981; The School for Scandal, British Council European tour, 1984; (with Googie Withers, and dir.) Stardust, tours England, 1984, Australia, 1984–85; The Chalk Garden, Chichester Fest., 1986; Hay Fever, Chichester Fest., 1988; The Royal Baccarat Scandal, Chichester Fest., 1988, Haymarket, 1989; (with Googie Withers) The Cocktail Hour, Australian and UK tour, 1989–90; (with Googie Withers) High Spirits, Australia, 1991; On Golden Pond, UK tour, 1992; The Chalk Garden, Sydney, 1995. Author of play, As It's Played Today, produced Melbourne, 1974. Produced television series, 1967–: Boney; Barrier Reef; Skippy; Bailey's Bird. Prod., Attack Force Z (feature film), 1980; Exec. Prod., The Highest Honor (feature film), 1982. Pres., Aust. Film Council, 1971–72. *Publication:* Life with Googie, 1979. *Recreation:* golf. *Address:* 1740 Pittwater Road, Bayview, NSW 2104, Australia. *T:* Sydney (2) 99976879. *Clubs:* Garrick, MCC; Melbourne (Melbourne); Australian, Elanora Country (Sydney).

McCALLUM, Prof. Robert Ian, CBE 1987; MD, DSc; FRCP, FRCPEd, FFOM; Hon. Consultant, Institute of Occupational Medicine, Edinburgh, since 1985; Emeritus Professor, University of Newcastle upon Tyne, since 1985; *b* 14 Sept. 1920; *s* of Charles Hunter McCallum and Janet Lyon Smith; *m* 1952, Jean Katherine Bundy Learmonth; two *s* two *d*. *Educ:* Dulwich Coll., London; Guy's Hosp., London Univ. (MD 1946; DSc 1971). FRCP 1970; FRCPEd 1985; FFOM 1979. Ho. phys., ho. surgeon, Guy's Hosp., 1943; ho. phys., Brompton Hosp., 1945. Rockefeller Travelling Fellowship in Medicine (MRC), USA, 1953–54. Reader in Industrial Health, 1962–81, Prof. of Occupational Health and Hygiene, 1981–85, Univ. of Newcastle upon Tyne. Hon. Physician, Industrial Medicine, Royal Victoria Infirmary, Newcastle upon Tyne, 1958–85; Hon. Consultant in Occ. Health to the Army, 1980–86. Mem., MRC Decompression Sickness Panel, 1962– (Chm., 1982–85); Chm., Health Adv. Cttee, CEGB, 1987–89. British Council: Vis. Consultant, USSR, 1977; Vis. Specialist, Istanbul, 1987; Vis. Lectr, Faculty of Medicine, Baghdad, 1987. Stanley Melville Meml Lectr, Coll. of Radiographers, 1983; Sydenham Lectr, Soc. of Apothecaries, London, 1983; Ernestine Henry Lectr, RCP, 1987. Dean, Faculty of Occ. Medicine, RCP, 1984–86; President: Sect. of Occ. Medicine, RSM, 1976–77; Soc. of Occ. Medicine, 1979–80; British Occ. Hygiene Soc., 1983–84; Mem., Adv. Cttee on Pesticides, 1975–87. Hon. Dir, North of England Industrial Health Service, 1975–84. Editor, British Jl of Industrial Medicine, 1973–79. *Publications:* papers on pneumoconiosis, decompression sickness, dysbaric bone necrosis, and antimony toxicology. *Recreations:* gardening, swimming, Scottish country dancing. *Address:* 4 Chessel's Court, Canongate, Edinburgh EH8 8AD. *T:* 0131–556 7977. *Clubs:* Royal Society of Medicine; University of Edinburgh Staff (Edinburgh).

McCAMLEY, Sir Graham (Edward), KBE 1986 (MBE 1981); owner, cattle properties, since 1954; Chairman, Beeflands Australia Pty Ltd, since 1994; *b* 24 Aug. 1932; *s* of Edward William George and Ivy McCamley; *m* 1956, Shirley Clarice Tindale; one *s* two *d*. *Educ:* Rockhampton Boys Grammar Sch. President: Aust. Brahman Breeders, 1971–74; Central Coastal Graziers, 1974–75; Cattlemen's Union of Australia, 1976–78. Mem. Producer of Australian Meat and Livestock Co., 1982–84. *Recreations:* tennis, flying helicopter and fixed wing aircraft. *Clubs:* Queensland (Brisbane); Rockhampton, Rockhampton and District Masonic.

MAC CANA, Prof. Proinsias; Senior Professor, School of Celtic Studies, Dublin Institute for Advanced Studies, since 1985; *b* 6 July 1926; *s* of George Mc Cann and Mary Catherine Mallon; *m* 1952, Réiltín (*née* Supple); one *s* one *d*. *Educ:* St Malachy's Coll., Belfast; The Queen's Univ., Belfast (BA, MA, PhD); Ecole des Hautes Etudes, Paris. Asst Lectr, Celtic Dept, QUB, 1951–54; University College Wales, Aberystwyth: Asst Lectr in Early Irish, 1955–57; Lectr, 1957–61; Prof., Sch. of Celtic Studies, Dublin Inst. for Advanced Studies, 1961–63; Prof. of Welsh, 1963–71, Prof. of Early (incl. Medieval) Irish, 1971–85, UC Dublin. Prof. of Celtic Langs and Lits (Fall semester), Harvard Univ., 1987–92. Co-editor, Ériu (RIA Jl of Irish Studies), 1973–; General editor, Medieval and Modern Welsh Series, Dublin Inst. for Advanced Studies, 1962–. Chm., Governing Bd, Sch. of Celtic Studies, Dublin Inst. for Advanced Studies, 1975–85. PRIA, 1979–82. Mem., Academia Europaea, 1989. Foreign Hon. Member: Amer. Acad. Arts and Scis, 1989; Royal Gustavus Adolphus Acad., Sweden, 1994. Hon. LittD Dublin, 1985; Hon. DLitt: Ulster, 1991; Wales, 1995. *Publications:* Scéalaíocht na Ríthe (collection of early Irish tales trans. into Modern Irish), 1956; Branwen Daughter of Llŷr: the second branch of the Mabinogi, 1958; Celtic Mythology, 1970; The Mabinogi, 1977; Regnum and Sacerdotium: notes on Irish Tradition (Rhŷs Meml Lecture, British Academy), 1979; The Learned Tales of Medieval Ireland, 1980; (ed jtly) Rencontres de Religions, 1986. *Address:* 9 Silchester Road, Glenageary, Co. Dublin, Ireland. *T:* Dublin 2805062. *Club:* Kildare Street and University (Dublin).

McCANN, Peter Toland McAree, CBE 1977; JP; DL; Lord Provost of the City of Glasgow and Lord-Lieutenant of the City of Glasgow, 1975–77; *b* 2 Aug. 1924; *s* of Peter McCann and Agnes (*née* Waddell); *m* 1958, Maura Eleanor (*née* Ferris); one *s*. *Educ:* St Mungo's Academy; Glasgow Univ. (BL). Solicitor and Notary Public. Pres., Glasgow Univ. Law Soc., 1946; Pres., St Thomas More Soc., 1959. Mem. Glasgow Corp., 1961. Chm., McCann Cttee (Secondary Educn for Physically Handicapped Children), 1971. DL Glasgow, 1978. OStJ 1977. Medal of King Faisal of Saudi Arabia, 1976. *Recreations:* music, history, model aeroplane making. *Address:* 31 Queen Mary Avenue, Glasgow G42 8DS.

McCARRAHER, His Honour David, VRD 1964; a Circuit Judge, 1984–95; *b* 6 Nov. 1922; *s* of Colin McCarraher and Vera Mabel McCarraher (*née* Hickley) *m* 1950, Betty Johnson (*née* Haywood) (*d* 1990); one *s* three *d* *Educ:* King Edward VI Sch., Southampton; Magdalene Coll., Cambridge (MA Law). RN, 1941–45. Called to the Bar, Lincoln's Inn, 1948; practised Western Circuit until 1952, disbarred at own request to be articled; admitted solicitor, 1955; Sen. Partner in private practice, 1960–84; a Recorder, 1979–84. Mem. Panel, Dep. Circuit Judges, 1973–79. Pres., Hampshire Incorporated Law Soc., 1982–83. Founder Mem. and Past Pres., Southampton Junior Chamber of Commerce. Governor, King Edward VI Sch., Southampton, 1961–84 (Chm., 1983–84; Fellow, 1986). Sub-Lieut, RNVR, 1943–45, RNVSR, 1946–52; served to Captain RNR, 1969; CO Solent Div., RNR, 1969–72; ADC to the Queen, 1972–73; retired 1975. Hon. Sec., RNR Benevolent Fund, 1973–84. *Recreations:* family, golf. *Clubs:* Naval; Stoneham Golf (Southampton); Chipping Sodbury Golf; Royal Naval Sailing Association (Portsmouth); Southampton Police (Hon. Mem.) (Southampton).

McCARTHY, family name of **Baron McCarthy.**

McCARTHY, Baron *cr* 1975 (Life Peer), of Headington; **William Edward John McCarthy,** DPhil; Emeritus Fellow of Nuffield College and Associate Fellow of Templeton College, Oxford; engaged in Industrial Arbitration and Chairman of Committees of Inquiry and Investigation, since 1968; *b* 30 July 1925; *s* of E. and H. McCarthy; *m* 1957, Margaret, *d* of Percival Godfrey. *Educ:* Holloway County; Ruskin Coll.; Merton Coll.; Nuffield Coll. MA (Oxon), DPhil (Oxon). Trade Union Scholarship to Ruskin Coll., 1953; Research Fellow of Nuffield Coll., 1959; Research Dir, Royal Commn on Trade Unions and Employers' Assocs, 1965–68; Sen. Economic Adviser, Dept of Employment, 1968–71. Chm., Railway Staff Nat. Tribunal, 1973–86; Special Advisor on Industrial Relations to Sec. of State for Social Services, 1975–77; Member: Houghton Cttee on Aid to Political Parties, 1975–76; TUC Independent Review Cttee, 1976; Pres., British Univ. Industrial Relations Assoc., 1975–78; Special Comr, Equal Opportunities Commn, 1977–80; Dep. Chm., Teachers' Nat. Conciliation Cttee, 1979–. Chairman: TUC Newspaper Feasibility Adv. Study Gp, 1981–83; Independent Inquiry into Rover Closure Proposals, 1989–90. Adjudicator, Nursing and Midwifery Staffs Negotiating Council, 1994–. Mem., H of L Select Cttee on Unemployment, 1980–82; Opposition front bench spokesman on employment, 1980–. Mem., All Party Motor Industry Gp, 1989–; Vice Chm., All Party Friends of Music Gp, 1992–. *Publications:* The Closed Shop in Britain, 1964; The Role of Shop Stewards in British Industrial Relations, 1966; (with V. L. Munns) Employers' Associations, 1967; (with A. I. Marsh) Disputes Procedures in Britain, 1968; The Reform of Collective Bargaining at Plant and Company Level, 1971; (ed) Trade Unions, 1972, 2nd edn, 1985; (with A. I. Collier) Coming to Terms with Trade Unions, 1973; (with N. D. Ellis) Management by Agreement, 1973; (with J. F. O'Brien and V. E. Dowd) Wage Inflation and Wage Leadership, 1975; Making Whitley Work, 1977; (jtly) Change in Trade Unions, 1981; (jtly) Strikes in Post-War Britain, 1983; Freedom at Work 1985; The Future of Industrial Democracy, 1988; (with C. Jennings and R. Undy) Employee Relations Audits, 1989; (ed) Legal Intervention in Industrial Relations, 1992; articles in: Brit. Jl of Industrial Relns; Industrial Relns Jl. *Recreations:* gardening, theatre, ballet, opera. *Address:* 4 William Orchard Close, Old Headington, Oxford OX3 9DR. *T:* Oxford (01865) 62016. *Club:* Reform.

McCARTHY, Adolf Charles; HM Diplomatic Service, retired; *b* 19 July 1922; *s* of Herbert Charles McCarthy and Anna Schnorf; *m* 1949, Ursula Vera Grimm; one *s* two *d*. *Educ:* London Univ. (BScEcon). Served War, RN, 1942–46. Min. of Agriculture, Fisheries and Food, 1939–64; Min. of Overseas Develt, 1964–66; HM Diplomatic Service, 1966; First Secretary: (Economic), Pretoria, 1968–70; (Commercial), Wellington, 1971–74; Asst Head of Western European Dept, FCO, 1974–77; Consul-Gen., Stuttgart, 1977–82; Hon. Consul at Freiburg, 1985–92. *Publication:* Robert Grimm: the Swiss revolutionary, 1990. *Recreations:* music, modern political history. *Address:* Engeriedweg 17, Bern 3012, Switzerland. *T:* (31) 3013440. *Club:* Rotary (Freiburg i. Br.).

McCARTHY, Arlene; Member (Lab) Peak District, European Parliament, since 1994; *b* 10 Oct. 1960; *d* of J. J. McCarthy and F. L. McCarthy. *Educ:* South Bank Poly. (BA Hons). Researcher and Press Officer to Leader of European PLP, 1990–91; Lectr in Politics, Freie Univ., Berlin, 1991–92; Head of European Affairs, Kirklees MBC, W Yorks, 1992–94. Socialist Gp and European PLP spokesperson on regl affairs. *Publications:* articles on European issues for local govt jls. *Recreations:* swimming, dancing, travel, foreign languages, music. *Address:* 16 North Road, Glossop, Derbys SK13 9AS. *T:* Glossop (01457) 857300/857090, *Fax:* (01457) 867339.

McCARTHY, David Laurence; His Honour Judge McCarthy; a Circuit Judge, since 1995; *b* 7 April 1947; *s* of Laurence Alphonsus McCarthy and Vera May McCarthy; *m* 1981, Rosalind Marguerite Stevenson; two *s*. *Educ:* St Philip's Grammar Sch., Birmingham;

Christ Church, Oxford (MA). Called to the Bar, Middle Temple, 1970; a Recorder, 1992; Midland and Oxford Circuit. *Recreations:* science fiction, playing the organ, preaching. *Address:* c/o Circuit Administrator, Midland and Oxford Circuit, The Priory Courts, Bull Street, Birmingham B4 6DW. *T:* 0121–681 3443.

McCARTHY, Donal John, CMG 1969; HM Diplomatic Service, retired; *b* 31 March 1922; *s* of Daniel and Kathleen McCarthy; *m* 1st, Rosanna Parbury (marr. diss.); three *s*; 2nd, Margaretha Luijke-Roskott. *Educ:* Holloway Sch.; London Univ. Served Royal Navy, 1942–46. Foreign Office, 1946; Middle East Centre for Arab Studies, 1947–48; 3rd and 2nd Sec., Brit. Embassy, Jedda, 1948–51; 2nd Sec., Political Div., Brit. Middle East Office, 1951–55; 1st Sec., FO, 1955–58; Asst Polit. Agent, Kuwait, 1958–60; Brit. High Commn, Ottawa, 1960–63; FO, 1963–64; Counsellor, Brit. High Commn, Aden, and Polit. Adviser to C-in-C Middle East, 1964–67; Head of Aden Dept, FO, 1967–68, of Arabian Dept, FCO, 1968–70; IDC, 1970–71; Minister (Economic and Social Affairs), UK Mission to UN, 1971–73; Ambassador to United Arab Emirates, 1973–77; FCO, 1978–79. *Recreations:* music, sailing, golf. *Address:* Church Farmhouse, Sudbourne, Suffolk IP12 2BP. *T:* Orford (01394) 450443. *Clubs:* Travellers', Royal Automobile; Aldeburgh Golf.

McCARTHY, Eugene Joseph; writer, since 1971; *b* 29 March 1916; *s* of Michael J. and Anna Baden McCarthy; *m* 1945, Abigail Quigley McCarthy; one *s* three *d*. *Educ:* St John's Univ., Collegeville (BA); Univ. of Minnesota (MA). Teacher in public schools, 1935–40; Coll. Prof. of Econs and Sociology, and civilian techn. Asst in Mil. Intell. for War Dept, 1940–48; US Representative in Congress of 4th District, Minnesota, 1949–58; US Senator from Minnesota, 1959–70. Independent. Holds hon. degrees. *Publications:* Frontiers in American Democracy, 1960; Dictionary of American Politics, 1962; A Liberal Answer to the Conservative Challenge, 1964; The Limits of Power, 1967; The Year of the People, 1969; Other Things and the Aardvark (poetry), 1970; The Hard Years, 1975; Mr Raccoon and his Friends (children's stories), 1977; (with James Kilpatrick) A Political Bestiary, 1978; Ground Fog and Night (poetry), 1978; America Revisited: 150 years after Tocqueville, 1978; The Ultimate Tyranny: the majority over the majority, 1980; Gene McCarthy's Minnesota, 1982; Complexities and Contraries, 1982; The View from Rappahannock, 1984; Up 'Til Now, 1987; Required Reading, 1988; The View from Rappahannock II, 1989; Colony of the World, 1993; contribs to Saturday Review, Commonweal, Harper's, New Republic, USA Today. *Address:* Box 22, Woodville, VA 22749, USA.

McCARTHY, Nicholas Melvyn, OBE 1983; HM Diplomatic Service; Ambassador to Cameroon, and also (non-resident) to Gabon, Equatorial Guinea and the Central African Republic, since 1995; *b* 4 April 1938; *s* of Daniel Alfred McCarthy and Florence Alice McCarthy; *m* 1961, Gillian Eileen Hill; three *s* one *d*. *Educ:* Queen Elizabeth's Sch., Faversham; London Univ. (BA Hons). Attaché, Saigon, 1961–64; Language Student, then Second Sec., Tokyo, 1964–69; FCO, 1969–73; First Sec., Brussels, 1973–78; FCO, 1978–80; Head of Chancery, Dakar, 1980–84; FCO, 1984–85; Consul-Gen., Osaka, 1985–90; Dep. Hd of Mission, Consul-Gen. and Counsellor, Brussels, 1990–94. *Recreations:* bridge, squash, tennis, Japanese pottery. *Address:* c/o Foreign and Commonwealth Office, King Charles Street, SW1A 2AH. *Club:* Sundridge Park Lawn Tennis.

McCARTHY, (Patrick) Peter; Regional Chairman, London North, Industrial Tribunals, 1987–90; Part-time Chairman, Industrial Tribunals, 1990–92; *b* 10 July 1919; *er s* of late William McCarthy and Mary McCarthy; *m* 1945, Isabel Mary (*d* 1994), *y d* of late Dr Joseph Unsworth, St Helens; two *s* three *d*. *Educ:* St Francis Xavier's Coll., Liverpool; Liverpool Univ. LLB 1940, LLM 1942. Admitted Solicitor, 1942; in private practice until 1974. Part-time Chm., 1972–74, full-time Chm., 1975–90, Regl Chm., Liverpool, 1977–87, Industrial Tribunals; part-time Chm., Rent Assessment Cttee, 1972–74. JP Liverpool, 1968–74. *Address:* Brook Cottage, Sham Castle Lane, Bath BA2 6JH.

McCARTHY, Rt. Hon. Sir Thaddeus (Pearcey), ONZ 1994; KBE 1974; Kt 1964; PC 1968; Justice of the Court of Appeal of New Zealand, 1963–76, President, 1973–76; Chairman, New Zealand Press Council, 1978–89; *b* 24 Aug. 1907; *s* of Walter McCarthy, Napier, merchant; *m* 1938, Joan Margaret Miller; one *s* two *d* (and one *d* decd). *Educ:* St Bede's Coll., Christchurch, New Zealand; Victoria Univ. Coll., Wellington. Master of Laws (1st Class Hons) 1931. Served War of 1939–45 in MEF with 22 Bn 2 NZEF, later as DJAG, 2 NZEF. Practised as Barrister and Solicitor until 1957 when appointed to Supreme Court. Chairman: Royal Commn on State Services, 1961–62; Winston Churchill Memorial Trust, 1966–76; Royal Commissions: on Salary and Wage Fixing Procedures in the State Services, 1968; on Social Security, 1969; on Horse Racing, Trotting and Dog Racing, 1969; on Salaries and Wages in the State Services, 1972; on Nuclear Power Generation, 1976–78; on Maori Land Courts, 1979–; Chm., Security Review Authority and Comr of Security Appeals, 1977–94. Chm. Adv. Cttee, NZ Computer Centre, 1977–86. Vice-Pres., NZ Sect., Internat. Commn of Jurists. Chm., Queen Elizabeth II Nat. Trust, 1978–84. Fellow, NZ Inst. of Public Admin, 1984. Hon. Bencher, Middle Temple, 1974. Hon. LLD Victoria Univ. of Wellington, 1978. *Recreations:* golf (Captain, Wellington Golf Club, 1952, Pres., 1973–77), sailing. *Address:* Wharenui, 274 Oriental Parade, Wellington, New Zealand. *Club:* Wellington (Wellington, NZ) (Pres., 1976–78).

McCARTIE, Rt. Rev. (Patrick) Leo; *see* Northampton, Bishop of, (RC).

McCARTNEY, Gordon Arthur; consultant; Managing Director, Gordon McCartney Associates, since 1991; Associate, Succession Planning Associates, since 1991; *b* 29 April 1937; *s* of Arthur and Hannah McCartney; *m* 1st, 1960, Ceris Ysobel Davies (marr. diss. 1987); two *d*; 2nd, 1988, Wendy Ann Vyvyan Titman. *Educ:* Grove Park Grammar Sch., Wrexham. Articled to Philip J. Walters, MBE (Town Clerk, Wrexham), 1954–59; admitted solicitor, 1959. Asst Solicitor, Birkenhead County Bor. Council, 1959–61; Asst Solicitor, 1961–63, Sen. Asst Solicitor, 1963–65, Bootle County Bor. Council; Dep. Clerk, Wrexham RDC, 1965–73; Clerk, Holywell RDC, 1973–74; Chief Exec., Delyn Bor. Council, 1974–81; Sec., Assoc. of Dist Councils, 1981–91. Dir, Nat. Transport Tokens Ltd, 1984–92. Secretary-General, British Section, IULA/CEMR, 1984–88; Chm., CEMR Individual Members Gp, 1992–; Co. Sec., Local Govt Internat. Bureau, 1988–91. Mem., Hansard Soc. Commn on Legislative Process, 1991–93. Dir, Leisure England Ltd, 1993–. *Recreations:* gardening, football, cricket, music. *Address:* 33 Duck Street, Elton, Peterborough PE8 6RQ. *T:* Oundle (01832) 280659; 108 Frobisher House, Dolphin Square, SW1. *T:* 0171–798 8777. *Clubs:* MCC; Northants CCC.

McCARTNEY, Hugh; *b* 3 Jan. 1920; *s* of John McCartney and Mary Wilson; *m* 1949, Margaret; one *s* two *d*. *Educ:* Royal Technical Coll., Glasgow; John Street Senior Secondary School. Apprentice in textile industry, 1934–39; entered aircraft engrg industry, Coventry, 1939; joined Rolls Royce, Glasgow, 1941; joined RAF as aero-engine fitter, 1942 and resumed employment with Rolls Royce, 1947; representative with company (later one of GKN group) specialising in manufacture of safety footware, 1951. Joined Ind. Labour Party, 1934; joined Labour Party, 1936. Town Councillor, 1955–70 and Magistrate, 1965–70, Kirkintilloch; Mem., Dunbarton CC, 1965–70. MP (Lab): Dunbartonshire E, 1970–74; Dunbartonshire Central, 1974–83; Clydebank and Milngavie, 1983–87. Scottish Regional Whip, 1979–83; Mem., Speaker's Panel of Chairmen, 1984–87. Chm., TGWU Parly Group, 1986–87. Mem., Rent Assessment Panel for Scotland, 1968–70. *Recreation:* spectating at football matches and athletic meetings (political activities permitting). *Address:* 23 Merkland Drive, Kirkintilloch G66 3PG.

See also I. McCartney.

McCARTNEY, Ian; MP (Lab) Makerfield, since 1987; *b* 25 April 1951; *s* of Hugh McCartney, *qv*; *m* (marr. diss.); one *s* two *d*; *m* 1988, Ann Parkes (*née* Kevan). *Educ:* State primary, secondary schools; Tech. Colls. Led paper boy strike, 1965; joined Labour Party, 1966; joined trade union, 1966; seaman, local govt manual worker, chef, 1966–71; unemployed, 1971–73; Labour Party Organiser, 1973–87. Councillor, Wigan Borough, 1982–87. Hon. Parly Adviser: to Greater Manchester Fire and Civil Defence Authy, 1987–92 (Mem., 1986); to Nat. Assoc. for Safety in the Home, 1989–. Opposition spokesperson on NHS, 1992–. Mem., Parly Select Cttee on Health and Social Security, 1991–92; Jt Sec., Parly Leasehold Reform Gp. All Party Chairman: Rugby League Gp; Home Safety Gp, 1988–; Child Abduction Gp, 1990–; Chm., T&GWU Parly Gp, 1989–91. Sponsored by TGWU. *Recreations:* Wigan Rugby League fanatic; head of McCartney family, a family of proud working class stock. *Address:* 95 Victoria Road, Platt Bridge, Wigan WN2 5ND. *T:* Wigan (01942) 861502. *Club:* Platt Bridge Labour.

McCARTNEY, (James) Paul, MBE 1965; musician, composer; *b* Allerton, Liverpool, 18 June 1942; *s* of James McCartney and Mary McCartney; *m* 1969, Linda Eastman; one *s* two *d*, and one step *d*. *Educ:* Liverpool Inst. Mem., skiffle group, The Quarry Men, 1957–59; toured Scotland with them and Stuart Sutcliffe as the Silver Beetles, 1960; first of five extended seasons in Hamburg, Aug. 1960; made 1st important appearance as the Beatles at Litherland Town Hall, nr Liverpool, Dec. 1960; appeared as mem. of Beatles: UK, Sweden, and Royal Variety perf., London, 1963; UK, Netherlands, Sweden, France, Denmark, Hong Kong, Australia, NZ, Canada, 1964; TV appearances, USA, and later, coast-to-coast tour, 1964; UK, France, Italy, Spain, USA, Canada, 1965; West Germany, Japan, Philippines, USA, Canada, 1966; Beatles disbanded 1970; formed MPL group of cos, 1970, and own group, Wings, 1971; toured: UK, Europe, 1972–73; UK, Australia, 1975; Europe, USA, Canada, 1976; UK, 1979; Wings disbanded 1981; Europe, UK, Canada, Japan, USA, Brazil, 1989/90. Wrote (with Carl Davis) Liverpool Oratorio, 1991. *Songs* with John Lennon include: Love Me Do; Please Please Me; From Me To You; She Loves You; Can't Buy Me Love; I Want to Hold Your Hand; I Saw Her Standing There; Eight Days a Week; All My Loving; Help!; Ticket to Ride; I Feel Fine; I'm A Loser; A Hard Day's Night; No Reply; I'll Follow The Sun; Yesterday; For No One; Here, There and Everywhere; Eleanor Rigby; Yellow Submarine; Penny Lane; All You Need Is Love; Lady Madonna; Hey Jude; We Can Work It Out; Day Tripper; Paperback Writer; When I'm Sixty-Four; A Day in the Life; Back in the USSR; Hello, Goodbye; Get Back; Let It Be; The Long and Winding Road; subseq. *songs* include: Maybe I'm Amazed; My Love; Band on the Run; Jet; Let 'Em In; Silly Love Songs; Mull of Kintyre; Coming Up; Ebony and Ivory; Tug of War; Pipes of Peace; No More Lonely Nights; My Brave Face. *Albums* with the Beatles: Please Please Me, 1963; With The Beatles, 1963; A Hard Day's Night, 1964; Beatles for Sale, 1964; Help!, 1965; Rubber Soul, 1965; Revolver, 1966; Sgt Pepper's Lonely Hearts Club Band, 1967; Magical Mystery Tour, 1967; The Beatles (White Album), 1968; Yellow Submarine, 1969; Abbey Road, 1969; Let it Be, 1970; subseq. *albums*: McCartney, 1970; Ram, 1971; Wild Life, 1971; Red Rose Speedway, 1973; Band on the Run, 1973; Venus and Mars, 1975; Wings at the Speed of Sound, 1976; Wings over America, 1976; London Town, 1978; Wings Greatest, 1978; Back to the Egg, 1979; McCartney II, 1980; Tug of War, 1982; Pipes of Peace, 1983; Give My Regards to Broad Street, 1984; Press to Play, 1986; All the Best!, 1987; CHOBA B CCCP, 1988; Flowers in the Dirt, 1989; Tripping the Live Fantastic, 1990, Unplugged. The Official Bootleg, 1991; Paul McCartney's Liverpool Oratorio, 1991; Off The Ground, 1993. *Films* (with the Beatles): A Hard Day's Night, 1964; Help!, 1965; Magical Mystery Tour (TV), 1967; Yellow Submarine, 1968; Let It Be, 1970; (with Wings) Rockshow, 1981; (wrote, composed score, and acted in) Give My Regards To Broad Street, 1984; (wrote, composed score and produced) Rupert and the Frog Song, 1984 (BAFTA award, Best Animated Film); Get Back, 1991. *Film scores:* The Family Way, 1966; Live and Let Die, 1973 (title song only); Twice In A Lifetime, 1984 (title song only); Spies Like Us, 1985 (title song only); *TV scores:* Thingumybob (series), 1968; The Zoo Gang (series), 1974. Live Russian 'phone link-up, BBC Russian Service, 1989. Numerous Grammy Awards, Nat. Acad. of Recording Arts and Scis, USA, incl. Lifetime Achievement Award, 1990; Ivor Novello Awards include: for Internat. Achievement, 1980; for Internat. Hit of the Year (Ebony and Ivory), 1982; for Outstanding Contrib. to Music, 1989; PRS special award for unique achievement in popular music, 1990. Freeman, City of Liverpool, 1984. DUniv Sussex, 1988. *Address:* c/o MPL Communications Ltd, 1 Soho Square, W1V 6BQ.

McCARTNEY, Robert Law; QC (NI) 1975; MP (UK Unionist) North Down, since June 1995; *b* 24 April 1936; *s* of William Martin McCartney and Elizabeth Jane (*née* McCartney); *m* 1960, Maureen Ann Bingham; one *s* three *d*. *Educ:* Grosvenor Grammar Sch., Belfast; Queen's Univ., Belfast (LLB Hons 1958). Admitted solicitor of Supreme Court of Judicature, NI, 1962; called to NI Bar, 1968. *Publication:* Liberty and Authority in Ireland, 1985. *Recreations:* reading (biography and military history), walking. *Address:* St Catherines, 2 Circular Road East, Cultra, Holywood, Co. Down, Northern Ireland BT18 0HA; House of Commons, SW1A 0AA.

McCAUGHEY, (John) Davis, AC 1987; Governor of Victoria, Australia, 1986–92; *b* 12 July 1914; *s* of John and Lizzie McCaughey; *m* 1940, Jean Middlemas Henderson; three *s* two *d*. *Educ:* Pembroke Coll., Cambridge (MA; Hon. Fellow, 1988); New Coll., Edinburgh; Presbyterian Coll., Belfast. Ordained in Presbyt. Ch. in Ireland, 1942; Study Sec., SCM, 1946–52; Prof. of NT Studies, Ormond Coll., Univ. of Melbourne, 1953–64, Master of the Coll. 1959–79; Dep. Chancellor, Univ. of Melbourne, 1978–79, 1982–85. Pres., Uniting Church in Australia, 1977–79. Hon. FRACP 1988; FAHA 1990. Hon. DD Edinburgh, 1966; Hon. LLD: Melbourne, 1982; QUB, 1987; Monash, 1993; Hon. DLitt La Trobe, 1992; Hon. STD Melbourne Coll. of Divinity, 1992. *Publications:* Christian Obedience in the University, 1958; Diversity and Unity in the New Testament Picture of Christ, 1969; Piecing Together a Shared Vision (Boyer Lectures), 1988; Victoria's Colonial Governors 1839–1900, 1993; articles in Colloquium, Aust. Biblical Rev., etc. *Recreations:* reading, listening, golf. *Address:* 36 Chapman Street, North Melbourne, Vic 3051, Australia. *Clubs:* Melbourne, Royal Melbourne Golf.

McCAUSLAND, Benedict Maurice Perronet T.; *see* Thompson-McCausland.

McCAVE, Prof. Ian Nicholas, FGS; Woodwardian Professor of Geology, since 1985, and Head of the Department of Earth Sciences, since 1988, University of Cambridge; Fellow, St John's College, Cambridge, since 1986; *b* 3 Feb. 1941; *s* of Thomas Theasby McCave and Gwendoline Marguerite McCave (*née* Langlois); *m* 1972, Susan Caroline Adams (*née* Bambridge); three *s* one *d*. *Educ:* Elizabeth Coll., Guernsey; Hertford Coll., Oxford (MA, DSc); Brown Univ., USA (PhD). FGS 1963. NATO Research Fellow, Netherlands Inst. for Sea Research, 1967–69; Lectr 1969–76, Reader 1976–84, UEA, Norwich. Vis. Prof., Oregon State Univ., 1974; Adjunct Scientist, Woods Hole Oceanographic Instn, 1978–87. Shepard Medal for Marine Geol., US Soc. for Sedimentary Geol., 1995. *Publications:* (ed) The Benthic Boundary Layer, 1976; over 100 papers in jls. *Recreations:* pottering about in the garden, rowing. *Address:* Marlborough House, 23 Victoria Street, Cambridge CB1 1JP.

McCLEAN, Prof. (John) David, CBE 1994; Professor of Law, since 1973, Pro-Vice-Chancellor, since 1991, Public Orator, 1988–91, and since 1994, University of Sheffield; *b* 4 July 1939; *s* of Major Harold McClean and Mrs Mabel McClean; *m* 1966, Pamela Ann Loader; one *s* one *d.* *Educ:* Queen Elizabeth's Grammar Sch., Blackburn; Magdalen Coll., Oxford (DCL, 1984). Called to the Bar, Gray's Inn, 1963. University of Sheffield: Asst Lectr 1961; Lectr 1963; Sen. Lectr 1968; Dean, Faculty of Law, 1978–81. Vis. Lectr in Law, Monash Univ., Melbourne, 1968, Vis Prof., 1978. Chancellor, dio. of Sheffield, 1992–. Vice-Chm., C of E Bd for Social Responsibility, 1978–80. Member: Gen. Synod of C of E, 1970– (Vice-Chm., House of Laity, 1979–85, Chm. 1985–95); Crown Appts Commn, 1977–87. Pres., Eur. Consortium for Church and State Res., 1995. Hon. QC 1995. *Publications:* Criminal Justice and the Treatment of Offenders (jtly), 1969; (contrib.) Halsbury's Laws of England, Vol. 8, 4th edn 1974, re-issue 1995, Vol. 2 (re-issue), 4th edn 1991; The Legal Context of Social Work, 1975, 2nd edn 1980; (jtly) Defendants in the Criminal Process, 1976; (ed jtly) Shawcross and Beaumont, Air Law, 4th edn 1977, reissue (new edn of one vol.) 1983; (jtly) Recognition and Enforcement of Judgments, etc, within the Commonwealth, 1977; (ed jtly) Dicey and Morris, Conflict of Laws, 10th edn 1980, to 12th edn 1993; Recognition of Family Judgments in the Commonwealth, 1983; International Judicial Assistance, 1992; (contrib.) Chitty, Contracts, 27th edn 1994. *Recreation:* detective fiction. *Address:* 6 Burnt Stones Close, Sheffield S10 5TS. *T:* Sheffield (0114) 230 5794. *Club:* Commonwealth Trust.

McCLEAN, Kathleen; *see* Hale, Kathleen.

McCLEARY, Ann Heron, (Mrs David McCleary); *see* Gloag, A. H.

McCLELLAN, Col Sir (Herbert) Gerard (Thomas), Kt 1986; CBE 1979 (OBE 1960); TD 1955; JP; DL; company director; *b* 24 Sept. 1913; *s* of late George McClellan and Lilian (*née* Fitzgerald); *m* 1939, Rebecca Ann (Nancy) Desforges (*d* 1982); one *s* three *d.* Served War of 1939–45, Loyal (N Lancs) Regt, RA, London Irish Rifles, in ME and Italy (wounded; despatches). Vernons of Liverpool, 1934–82: formerly: Vice Chm. and Man. Dir, Vernons Trust Corp., Vernons Finance Corp., and Vernons Insurance Brokers; Dir, Vernons Orgn; Man. Dir, Competition Management Services. Chm., Intro-Merseyside Ltd, 1988–94; Director: JS Mortgage Corp., 1986–93; Richmond Storage & Transit Co. (UK) Ltd, 1990–93; Richmond Freight Services Ltd, 1990–93. Commanded 626 HAA (Liverpool Irish) Regt and 470 LAA (3rd West Lancs) Regt, RA TA, 1955–60; County Comdt, W Lancs ACF, 1961–66; Member: W Lancs T&AVRA, 1955–66 (Vice-Chm., 1966–68); NW England and IoM T&AVRA, 1968–70 (Vice-Chm., 1970–75; Chm., 1975–79). Former Mem. (C) for Childwall, Liverpool City Council; Member: Liverpool Cons. Assoc., 1960– (Vice-Chm., 1966–75; Chm., 1975–85), NW Area Cons. Assoc., 1971–90; Exec. Cttee, Nat. Union of Cons. and Unionist Assocs, 1982–87; Chairman: Wavertree Cons. Assoc., 1962–67 (Pres., 1967–76); Liverpool European Cons. Constituency Council, 1978–84; Merseyside W European Cons. Constit. Council, 1984–85 (Pres., 1985–); President: Garston Cons. Assoc., 1979–90; Halewood Cons. Club, 1983–88; Crosby Cons. Assoc., 1986–89 (Chm., 1989–91); Vice-Pres. Woolton Ward Cons. Assoc., 1981–. Vice-President: Merseyside Co. SSAFA, 1975–; Incorp. Liverpool Sch. of Tropical Medicine, 1987–92. Governor: Archbp Whiteside Secondary Modern Sch. and St Brigid's High Sch., 1961–91; Mabel Fletcher Technical Coll., 1969– (Chm., 1971–86); Sandown Coll., Liverpool, 1989–91. FIAM. DL Lancs later Merseyside, 1967; JP Liverpool, 1968; High Sheriff of Merseyside, 1980–81. *Address:* Ince Blundell Hall, Ince Blundell, Liverpool, Merseyside L38 6JN. *T:* 0151-929 2269. *Clubs:* Army and Navy; Athenæum (Liverpool).

McCLELLAN, John Forrest; Under Secretary, Industry Department for Scotland (formerly Scottish Economic Planning Department), 1980–85, retired; *b* 15 Aug. 1932; *s* of John McClellan and Hester (*née* Niven); *m* 1956, Eva Maria Pressel; three *s* one *d.* *Educ:* Ferryhill Primary Sch., Aberdeen; Aberdeen Grammar Sch.; Aberdeen Univ. (MA). Served Army, 2nd Lieut, Gordon Highlanders and Nigeria Regt, RWAFF, 1954–56. Entered Civil Service, 1956; Asst Principal, Scottish Educn Dept, 1956–59; Private Sec. to Perm. Under Sec. of State, Scottish Office, 1959–60; Principal, Scottish Educn Dept, 1960–68; Civil Service Fellow, Glasgow Univ., 1968–69; Asst Sec., Scottish Educn Dept, 1969–77; Asst Under Sec. of State, Scottish Office, 1977–80. Dir, Scottish Internat. Educn Trust, 1986–; Mem., Management Cttee, Hanover (Scotland) Housing Assoc., 1986–. Hon. Fellow, Dundee Inst. of Technology, 1988. *Publication:* Then a Soldier, 1991. *Recreations:* gardening, walking. *Address:* Grangeneuk, West Linton, Peeblesshire EH46 7HG. *T:* West Linton (01968) 660502. *Club:* Royal Scots (Edinburgh).

McCLELLAND, Hon. Douglas, AC 1987; Chairman, Australian Political Exchange Council, since 1993; *s* of Alfred McClelland and Gertrude Amy Cooksley; *m* Lorna Belva McNeill; one *s* two *d.* Mem. NSW ALP Executive, 1956–62; Hon. Dir, St George Hosp., Sydney, 1957–68. Member, Australian Senate for NSW, 1962–87; Senate appointments: Minister for the Media, 1972–75; Manager, Govt Business, 1974–75; Special Minister of State, June–Nov. 1975; Opposition spokesman on Admin. Services, 1976–77; Manager, Opposition Business, 1976–77; Dep. Leader of Opposition, May–Dec. 1977; Dep. Pres. and Chm of Cttees, 1981–82; Pres. of the Australian Senate, 1983–87; High Commissioner in UK, 1987–91; Comr-Gen., Australian Pavilion, Expo '92, Seville, Spain, 1992. *Recreations:* No 1 supporter, St George Rugby League FC; reading, making friends. *Address:* c/o Department of Foreign Affairs, Sydney, NSW, Australia. *Clubs:* City Tattersalls (Life Mem.); St George Rugby League Football.

McCLELLAND, George Ewart, CB 1986; Solicitor, Department of Employment, 1982–87; *b* 27 March 1927; *s* of George Ewart McClelland and Winifred (*née* Robinson); *m* 1956, Ann Penelope, *yr d* of late Judge Arthur Henry Armstrong; one *s* two *d.* *Educ:* Stonyhurst Coll.; Merton Coll., Oxford (Classical Scholar; MA). Called to the Bar, Middle Temple, 1952. Entered Solicitor's Dept, Min. of Labour, 1953; Asst Solicitor, 1969; Principal Asst Solicitor, 1978.

McCLELLAND, Prof. (William) Grigor, CBE 1994; DL; MA; MBA; former business executive and academic; *b* 2 Jan. 1922; *o c* of Arthur and Jean McClelland, Gosforth, Newcastle upon Tyne; *m* 1946, Diana Avery Close; two *s* two *d.* *Educ:* Leighton Park; Balliol Coll., Oxford. First Class PPE, 1948. Friends' Ambulance Unit, 1941–46. Man. Dir, Laws Stores Ltd, 1949–65, 1978–85 (Chm., 1966–85); Sen. Res. Fellow in Management Studies, Balliol Coll., 1962–65; Dir, Manchester Business Sch., 1965–77, and Prof. of Business Administration, 1967–77, Univ. of Manchester; Dep. Chm., Nat. Computing Centre, 1966–68; Chm., Washington Develt Corp., 1977–88. Chm., EDC for the Distributive Trades, 1980–84 (Mem., 1965–70); Member: The Consumer Council, 1963–66; Economic Planning Council, Northern Region, 1965–66; IRC, 1966–71; NEDC, 1969–71; SSRC, 1971–74; North Eastern Industrial Develt Bd, 1977–86. Vis. Prof., Durham Univ. Business Sch., 1977–. Chairman: Tyne Tees Telethon Trust, 1987–93; Tyne and Wear Foundn, 1988–93. Trustee: Anglo-German Foundn for the Study of Industrial Soc., 1973–79; Millfield House Foundn, 1976–; Employment Inst., 1985–92; Governor: Nat. Inst. of Econ. and Social Research; Leighton Park Sch., 1952–60 and 1962–66; Trustee, 1956–94, and Chm., 1965–78, Joseph Rowntree Charitable Trust. CIMgt (CBIM 1966). Hon. DCL Dunelm, 1985. DL Tyne and Wear, 1988. Founding Editor, Jl of Management Studies, 1963–65. *Publications:* Studies in Retailing, 1963; Costs and Competition in Retailing, 1966; And a New Earth, 1976; Washington: over and out, 1988; (ed) Quakers Visit China, 1957. *Recreations:* tennis, ski-ing, walking. *Address:* 66 Elmfield Road, Gosforth, Newcastle upon Tyne NE3 4BD.

MACCLESFIELD, 9th Earl of *cr* 1721; **Richard Timothy George Mansfield Parker;** Baron Parker, 1716; Viscount Parker, 1721; *b* 31 May 1943; *s* of 8th Earl of Macclesfield and Hon. Valerie Mansfield (*d* 1994), *o d* of 4th Baron Sandhurst, OBE; *S* father, 1992; *m* 1967, Tatiana Cleone, *d* of Major Craig Wheaton-Smith; three *d* (including twins); *m* 1986, Mrs Sandra Hope Mead. *Educ:* Stowe; Worcester Coll., Oxford. *Heir:* *b* Hon. (Jonathan) David (Geoffrey) Parker [*b* 2 Jan. 1945; *m* 1968, Lynne Valerie Butler; one *s* two *d*]. *Address:* Shirburn Castle, Shirburn, Watlington, Oxon OX9 5DL.

MACCLESFIELD, Archdeacon of; *see* Gillings, Ven. R. J.

McCLEVERTY, Prof. Jon Armistice; Professor of Inorganic Chemistry, University of Bristol, since 1990; *b* 11 Nov. 1937; *s* of John and Nessie McCleverty; *m* 1963, Dianne Barrack; two *d.* *Educ:* Univ. of Aberdeen (BSc 1960); Imperial College, London (DIC, PhD 1963); Massachusetts Inst. of Technology. Asst Lectr, part-time, Acton Coll. of Technology, 1962–63; Asst Lectr, then Lectr, Sen. Lectr, and Reader, Univ. of Sheffield, 1964–80; Prof. of Inorganic Chem., 1980–90, and Head of Dept of Chem., 1984–90, Univ. of Birmingham. Chairman: Cttee of Heads of Univ. Chem. Depts, 1989–91; Internat. Cttee, RSC, 1994–; Chemistry Cttee, SERC, 1990–93; Member: Science Bd, SERC, 1990–93; Technical Cttee for Chemistry, COST, EU, 1990–96. Tilden Lectr, RSC, 1981. RSC Medal, for work on chem. and electrochem. of transition metals, 1985. Golden Order of Merit (Poland), 1990. *Publications:* numerous articles, principally in Jl of Chem. Soc. *Recreations:* gardening, DIY, travel, traditional jazz. *Address:* School of Chemistry, University of Bristol, Cantock's Close, Bristol BS8 1TS.

McCLINTOCK, Surg. Rear-Adm. Cyril Lawson Tait, CB 1974; OBE 1964; Medical Officer in Charge, Royal Naval Hospital, Haslar and Command Medical Adviser on staff of Commander-in-Chief Naval Home Command, 1972–75; retired 1975; *b* 2 Aug. 1916; *o* surv. *s* of late Lawson Tait McClintock, MB, ChB, Loddon, Norfolk; *m* 1966, Freda Margaret, *o d* of late Robert Jones, Caergwle, Denbighshire; two step *s.* *Educ:* St Michael's, Uckfield; Epsom; Guy's Hospital. MRCS, LRCP 1940; DLO 1955. Joined RN Medical Service, 1940; served War of 1939–45 in Western Approaches, N Africa, Eritrea, India and Singapore; Korea, 1950–51; ENT Specialist, RN Hosps, Port Edgar, Chatham, Hong Kong, Portland, Haslar, Malta and Russell Eve Building, Hamilton, Bermuda; MO i/c RN Hosp. Bighi, Malta, 1969; David Bruce RN Hosp. Mtarfa, Malta, 1970–71; Comd Med. Adviser to C-in-C Naval Forces Southern Europe, 1969–71. QHS 1971–75. FRSocMed 1948; MFCM 1974. CStJ 1973. *Recreations:* cricket, tennis, Rugby refereeing, history. *Address:* 5 Ambleside Court, Alverstoke, Hants PO12 2DJ. *Clubs:* Army and Navy, MCC.

McCLINTOCK, David, TD; writer, naturalist and plantsman; *b* 4 July 1913; *o s* of Rev. E. L. L. McClintock, Glendaragh, Crumlin, Co. Antrim, and Margaret McClintock, *d* of John Henry Buxton, Easneye, Ware, Herts; *m* Elizabeth Anne (*d* 1993), *d* of Maj. V. J. Dawson, Miserden, Glos; two *s* two *d.* *Educ:* West Downs Sch., Winchester; Harrow Sch.; Trinity Coll., Cambridge. BA 1934, MA 1940. FCA 1938; FLS 1953. 2nd Lieut, Herts Yeomanry RA TA, 1938; HQ 54 Div., Captain, 1941; Intelligence Trng Centre, 1941–43; Major, 1942; Civil Affairs Trng Centre, 1943–44; Lt-Col, 1944; BAOR, 1944–45. K-H Newsletter, 1938–46; Commercial Manager, Air Contractors Ltd, 1946–47; Chief Accountant and Admin. Officer, Coal Utilisation Council, 1951–73. Member: Wild Flower Soc., 1934– (Chm., 1981–93, Treasurer, 1978–82; Hon. Vice-Pres., 1994); Council, Botanical Soc. of British Isles, 1954–64 (Pres., 1971–73; Hon. Mem., 1994–); Council, Kent Trust for Nature Conservation, 1958–62 (Vice-Pres., 1963–); Council, Ray Soc., 1968–72, 1976–80 (Vice-Pres., 1972–76; Pres., 1980–83; Hon. Vice-Pres., 1983–); Council, Linnean Soc., 1970–78 (Vice-Pres., 1971–74; Editl Sec., 1974–78; Editor, Biological Jl, 1976); Plant Variety Rights Adv. Panel for heathers, 1973–; Royal Horticultural Society: Scientific Cttee, 1978–94 (Vice-Chm., 1983–92; Actg Chm. 66 times), Publications Cttee, 1982–87; Council, Internat. Dendrology Soc., 1979– (Editor, 1979–83; Vice-Pres., 1990–); Council, Nat. Trust, 1980–84; Heather Soc., 1963– (Vice-Pres., 1980–89; Pres., 1989–); Pres., Kent Field Club, 1978–80 (Hon. Mem., 1994–). Internat. Registrar for heather cultivars, 1970–; holder of national collection of Sasa bamboos, 1986–. Membre d'Honneur, Soc. Guernesiaise, 1968–. Veitch Meml Medal in gold, RHS, 1981; H. H. Bloomer Award, Linnean Soc., 1993. *Publications:* Pocket Guide to Wild Flowers (with R. S. R. Fitter), 1956; Supplement to the Pocket Guide to Wild Flowers, 1957; (jtly) Natural History of the Garden of Buckingham Palace, 1964; Companion to Flowers, 1966; Guide to the Naming of Plants, 1969, 2nd edn 1980; Wild Flowers of Guernsey, 1975, Supplement, 1987; (with J. Bichard) Wild Flowers of the Channel Islands, 1975; Joshua Gosselin of Guernsey, 1976; (with F. Perring and R. E. Randall) Picking Wild Flowers, 1977; (ed) H. J. van de Laar, The Heather Garden, 1978; Guernsey's Earliest Flora, 1982; contribs to 25 other books and over 90 periodicals, incl. over 2,300 book reviews. *Recreations:* anything to do with wild life and gardening, music, formerly shooting, fishing, tennis *etc.* *Address:* Bracken Hill, Platt, Sevenoaks, Kent TN15 8JH. *T:* Borough Green (01732) 884102. *Clubs:* Horticultural, Linnean Dining.

See also Baron Hazlerigg.

McCLINTOCK, Sir Eric (Paul), Kt 1981; *b* 13 Sept. 1918; *s* of Robert and Ada McClintock; *m* 1942, Eva Lawrence; two *s* one *d.* *Educ:* De La Salle Coll., Armidale; Sydney Univ. (DPA). Supply Dept, Dept of the Navy, Australia, 1935–47; served successively in Depts of Commerce, Agriculture, and Trade, in Washington, New York, Melbourne and Canberra, 1947–61 (1st Asst Sec. on resignation); investment banking, 1962–. Chairman: McClintock Associates Ltd; Aust. Overseas Projects Corp., 1978–84; Woolworths Ltd, 1982–87; AFT Ltd, 1984–87; Plutonic Resources Ltd, 1990–; Malaysia Mining Corp. Australia Pty Ltd, 1993–; Dep. Chm., Development Finance Corp. Ltd, 1980–87; Director: Philips Industries Holdings Ltd, 1978–85; O'Connell Street Associates Pty Ltd, 1978–; Ashton Mining Ltd, 1986–93. Chm., Trade Develt Council, 1970–74. Pres., Royal Life Saving Soc. (NSW). Governor, Sydney Inst., 1990–. *Recreations:* tennis, golf. *Address:* Floor 6, 2 O'Connell Street, Sydney, NSW 2000, Australia. *T:* (2) 2253244. *Clubs:* Australian (Sydney); Commonwealth (Canberra).

McCLINTOCK, Nicholas Cole, CBE 1979; Secretary-General of the Order of St John, 1968–81 (Deputy Secretary-General, 1963–68); *b* 10 Sept. 1916; *s* of late Col Robert Singleton McClintock, DSO (3rd *s* of Adm. Sir Leopold McClintock), and Mary Howard, *d* of Sir Howard Elphinstone, VC; *m* 1953, Pamela Sylvia, *d* of late Major Rhys Mansel, Smedmore, Dorset; two *s* two *d.* *Educ:* Stowe Sch.; Trinity Coll., Cambridge (MA; Capt., Univ. Fencing Team). Entered Colonial Admin. Service, N Nigeria, 1939 but went immediately on War Service with 18th and 28th Field Regts RA, Dunkirk 1940, India and Burma, 1942–45; commanded 1st Field Battery RA in final Burma campaign. Asst Principal, Appointments Dept, CO, Feb.-Oct. 1946; Asst Dist Officer, N Nigeria,

1946–49; Private Sec. to Governor (Sir John Macpherson), 1949–50; Clerk to Exec. Council and Clerk, Legislature, N Nigeria, 1951–53; Sen. Dist Officer and Actg Resident, Kano Province, 1955–59; Admin. Officer Grade 1 and Resident, Bornu Province, 1960–62. Chm., Aidis Trust, 1988–94. KStJ 1968. *Publication:* Kingdoms in the Sand and Sun, 1992. *Address:* Lower Westport, Wareham, Dorset BH20 4PR. *T:* Wareham (01929) 553252. *Club:* Army and Navy.

McCLINTOCK-BUNBURY, family name of **Baron Rathdonnell.**

McCLOSKEY, Bernard Mary; Deputy Director of Public Prosecutions for Northern Ireland, 1972–84; *b* 7 Aug. 1924; *s* of Felix and Josephine McCloskey; *m* 1952, Rosalie Donaghy; three *s* two *d. Educ:* St Malachy's Coll., Belfast; Queen's Univ., Belfast (LLB (Hons)). Admitted solicitor (Northern Ireland), 1947; private practice, 1947–72. Joint Solicitor to Scarman Tribunal of Enquiry, 1969–71. *Recreations:* swimming, golf. *Club:* Fortwilliam Golf (Hon. Mem.).

McCLOY, Dr Elizabeth Carol, FRCP, FFOM; Chief Executive and Director, Civil Service Occupational Health Service, and Medical Adviser to the Civil Service, since 1993; *b* 25 April 1945; *d* of Edward Bradley and Ada Entwisle; *m* 1969, Rory McCloy (marr. diss. 1989); two *s. Educ:* Guildford Grammar Sch.; University Coll. and UCH, London (BSc Hons 1966; MB BS Hons 1969). MFOM 1988, FFOM 1993; FRCP 1995. Clinical Asst, Medicine, W Middlesex Univ. Hosp., 1972–83; Manchester Royal Infirmary: Sen. Clinical MO, Occupational Health, 1984–88; Consultant in Occupational Medicine, 1988–93; Dir of Occupational Health and Safety, Central Manchester Healthcare Trust, 1988–93. Pres., Soc. of Occupational Medicine, 1993–94. FRSocMed; FRSA. *Publications:* (ed jtly) Practical Occupational Medicine, 1994; (contrib.) Hunters Diseases of Occupations, 7th edn 1987, 8th edn 1994; (contrib.) Oxford Textbook of Medicine, 1994; articles on hepatitis. *Recreations:* theatre, gardening, antiques. *Address:* Occupational Health Service, 18–20 Hill Street, Edinburgh EH2 3NB. *T:* 031–220 4177.

McCLUNE, Rear-Adm. (William) James, CB 1978; *b* Londonderry, 20 Nov. 1921; *s* of James McClune, MBE, Carrickmacross, Co. Monaghan, and Matilda (*née* Burns); *m* 1953, Elizabeth, *yr d* of A. E. D. Prideaux, LDS, Weymouth; one *s* one *d. Educ:* Model Sch. and Foyle Coll., Derry; QUB (BSc 1st Cl. Hons Elec. Eng, 1941); RN Staff Coll., Greenwich (1961); Univ. of Birmingham (Ratcliff Prizeman, MSc 1970); RN War Coll. (1971). Bronze Medal, CGLI, 1940; Belfast Assoc. of Engrs' Prize, 1940, 1941. CEng, MIEE; CIMgt. Radar Officer, RNVR, 1941–47; Eng Dept, GPO, 1947–49; RN, 1949–78; CSO (Engrg) to C-in-C Fleet, 1976–78. A Vice-Pres., RNLI. Chm., Christian Alliance Housing Assoc.; Life Governor, Monkton Combe Sch. *Recreation:* sailing. *Address:* Harlam Lodge, Lansdown, Bath; 7 Theed Street, SE1 8ST. *Clubs:* Commonwealth Trust; Royal Naval and Royal Albert Yacht (Portsmouth).

McCLUNEY, Ian, CMG 1990; HM Diplomatic Service; High Commissioner, Sierra Leone, since 1993; *b* 27 Feb. 1937; *e s* of John McCluney and Annie (*née* Currie); *m* 1962, Elizabeth Mary Walsh; two *s* one *d. Educ:* Orange Hill Grammar Sch.; Edinburgh Univ. (BSc). Served HM Forces, Lieut RASC, 1958–62. Joined FO, 1964; Commerical Attaché, Addis Ababa, 1964–67; Asst Private Sec. to Foreign and Commonwealth Sec., 1969–70; Head, British Interests Section, Baghdad, 1972–74; FCO, 1975–78; Head of Chancery, Kuwait, 1979–82; Consul-Gen., Alexandria, 1982–86; FCO, 1986–88; Ambassador to Somalia, 1989–90; Dep. High Comr, Calcutta, 1991–93. *Recreation:* sailing. *Address:* c/o Foreign and Commonwealth Office, King Charles Street, SW1A 2AH. *Club:* Little Ship.

McCLURE, David, RSA 1971 (ARSA 1963); RSW 1965; RGI 1990; SSA 1951; painter and printmaker; *b* 20 Feb. 1926; *s* of Robert McClure, MM, and Margaret Helena McClure (*née* Evans); *m* 1st, 1950, Joyce Dixon Flanigan (*d* 1988); two *s* one *d*; 2nd, 1991, Angela Bradbury. *Educ:* Queen's Park Sch., Glasgow; Glasgow Univ., 1943–44; (coal-miner, 1944–47); Edinburgh Univ., 1947–49; Edinburgh Coll. of Art, 1947–52 (DA). Travelled in Spain and Italy, 1952–53; on staff of Edinburgh Coll. of Art, 1953–55; one year painting in Italy and Sicily, 1956–57; Duncan of Jordanstone Coll. of Art, Dundee: Lectr, 1957–71, Sen. Lectr, 1971–83; Head of Drawing and Painting, 1983–85. *One man exhibitions:* Palermo, 1957; Edinburgh, 1957, 1961, 1962, 1966, 1969, 1989, 1994; 14 Scottish Painters, London, 1964; Univ. of Birmingham, 1965; Thackeray Gall., London, 1978, 1986, 1991; retrospective exhibn, Dundee Art Galls, 1984; Forty Years of Painting, Fine Art Soc., Glasgow, Edinburgh, 1988. *Work in public and private collections:* UK, USA, Canada, Italy. *Publication:* John Maxwell (monograph), 1976. *Recreations:* collecting Victorian china, gardening, the pianoforte, cooking. *Address:* 16 Strawberry Bank, Dundee, Scotland. *T:* Dundee (01382) 66959.

McCLURE, Prof. John, MD; FRCPath; Procter Professor of Pathology, University of Manchester, since 1987; *b* 2 May 1947; *s* of Richard Burns McClure and Isabella McClure (*née* Nelson); *m* 1970, Sheena Frances Tucker; three *d. Educ:* Queen's Univ. Belfast (BSc Hons, MB, BCh, BAO, MD, DMJPath). Training posts in Pathology, QUB, 1972–78; Clinical Sen. Lectr and Specialist/Sen. Specialist in Pathology, Univ. of Adelaide and Inst. of Med. and Vet. Sci., Adelaide, 1978–83; University of Manchester: Sen. Lectr and Hon. Consultant in Histopathology, 1983–87; Head of Pathological Scis, 1987–95; Associate Dean, Faculty of Medicine, 1955–. *Publications:* papers in med. and path. jls. *Recreation:* DIY. *Address:* Department of Pathological Sciences, University of Manchester, Oxford Road, Manchester M13 9PT. *T:* 0161–275 5300.

McCLURE, Joseph Robert; JP; Councillor, Tyne and Wear County Council, 1974–81 (Chairman, 1977–78); *b* 23 Oct. 1923; *s* of Thomas Render McClure and Catherine Bridget McClure; *m* 1943, Evelyn Joice; one *d. Educ:* Prior Street Sch.; Oakwellgate Sch., Gateshead. Served War, Royal Marines, 1941–46. Elected Councillor, County Borough of Gateshead, 1964, Dep. Mayor, 1973–74. President, Gateshead Royal British Legion, 1976–. JP Gateshead and Blaydon 1979. *Recreation:* bowls. *Address:* 170 Rectory Road, Gateshead, Tyne and Wear NE8 4RR. *T:* 0191–477 0709.

McCLURE, Dr Judith, FSAScot; Head of St George's School, Edinburgh, since 1994; *b* 22 Dec. 1945; *d* of James McClure and Vera (*née* Knight); *m* 1977, Roger John Howard Collins, DLitt, FRHistS, FSAScot. *Educ:* Newlands GS, Middlesbrough; Coll. of Law, London; Somerville Coll., Oxford (BA 1st Cl. Hons 1973; MA 1977; DPhil 1979). Canoness of St Augustine, Les Oiseaux, Westgate, Kent, 1964–70; Sir Maurice Powicke Meml Res. Fellow, LMH, Oxford, 1976–77; Lecturer: in Medieval Latin and Medieval History, Univ. of Liverpool, 1977–79; in History, Jesus, Somerville and Worcester Colls, Univ. of Oxford, 1979–81; School of St Helen and St Katherine, Abingdon: teacher of History and Politics, 1981–83; Head, History and Politics Dept, 1983–84; Dep. Head, Kingswood Sch., Bath, 1984–87, Dir of Studies, 1986–87; Head, Royal Sch., Bath, 1987–93. Mem. Governing Body, Scottish Council of Ind. Schs, 1995–. Member: Court, Bath Univ., 1989–92; Gen. Convocation, Heriot-Watt Univ., 1994–; Bd of Govs, Selwyn Sch., Gloucester, 1988–90; Bd of Govs, Clifton Hall Sch., Lothian, 1995–. *Publications:* Gregory the Great: exegesis and audience, 1979; Introduction and notes to Bede's Ecclesiastical History, 1994; articles in Jl Theol Studies, Peritia, Papers of Liverpool Latin Seminar, Prep. School and in Festschriften. *Recreations:* reading, travel, thinking about the early Middle Ages. *Address:* 12A Ravelston Park, Edinburgh EH4 3DX; 26 Haygarth Court, Lansdown Grove, Bath BA1 5ER.

McCLUSKEY, family name of **Baron McCluskey.**

McCLUSKEY, Baron *cr* 1976 (Life Peer), of Churchhill in the District of the City of Edinburgh; **John Herbert McCluskey,** a Senator of the College of Justice in Scotland, since 1984; *b* 12 June 1929; *s* of Francis John McCluskey, Solicitor, and Margaret McCluskey (*née* Doonan); *m* 1956, Ruth Friedland; two *s* one *d. Educ:* St Bede's Grammar Sch., Manchester; Holy Cross Acad., Edinburgh; Edinburgh Univ. Harry Dalgety Bursary, 1948; Vans Dunlop Schol., 1949; Muirhead Prize, 1949; MA 1950; LLB 1952. Sword of Honour, RAF Spitalgate, 1953. Admitted Faculty of Advocates, 1955; Standing Jun. Counsel to Min. of Power (Scotland), 1963; Advocate-Depute, 1964–71; QC (Scot.) 1967; Chm., Medical Appeal Tribunals for Scotland, 1972–74; Sheriff Principal of Dumfries and Galloway, 1973–74; Solicitor General for Scotland, 1974–79. Chm., Scottish Assoc. for Mental Health, 1985–94. Independent Chairman: Scottish Football League's Compensation Tribunal, 1988–; Scottish Football Association's Appeals Tribunal, 1990–. Reith Lectr, BBC, 1986. Editor, Butterworth's Scottish Criminal Law and Practice series, 1988–. Hon. LLD Dundee, 1989. *Publications:* Law, Justice and Democracy, 1987; Criminal Appeals, 1992. *Recreations:* tennis, pianoforte. *Address:* Court of Session, Parliament House, Edinburgh EH1 1RF. *T:* 0131–225 2595. *Clubs:* Royal Air Force; Edinburgh University Staff (Edinburgh).

McCLUSKEY, Len; National Secretary, Transport and General Workers' Union, since 1990; *b* 23 July 1950; *s* of Leonard and Margaret McCluskey. *Educ:* Cardinal Godfrey High Sch., Merseyside. Dockworker, 1968–79; Transport and General Workers' Union: District Official, Merseyside, 1979–89; Political Officer, NW Region, 1985–89. *Recreations:* football, sport, reading, politics, chess. *Address:* Transport and General Workers' Union, Transport House, Smith Square, SW1P 3JB.

McCLUSKIE, John Cameron; QC (Scot.) 1989; Legal Secretary to the Lord Advocate and First Scottish Parliamentary Counsel, since 1989; *b* 1 Feb. 1946; *s* of Thomas and Marjorie McCluskie; *m* 1970, Janis Mary Helen McArthur; one *s* one *d. Educ:* Hyndland Sch., Glasgow; Glasgow Univ. (LLB Hons 1967). Admitted Solicitor, Scotland, 1970; admitted Faculty of Advocates, 1974. Apprentice Solicitor, Boyds, Glasgow, 1967–69; Asst Town Clerk, Burgh of Cumbernauld, 1969–70; Legal Assistant: Macdonald, Jameson and Morris, Glasgow, 1970; SSEB, 1970–72; Asst, then Sen. Asst, Legal Sec. and Parly Draftsman, Lord Advocate's Dept, 1972–89. *Recreation:* growing vegetables. *Address:* Strathblane, Hearts Delight Road, Tunstall, Sittingbourne, Kent ME9 8JA. *T:* Sittingbourne (01795) 474453.

McCOLL, family name of **Baron McColl of Dulwich.**

McCOLL OF DULWICH, Baron *cr* 1989 (Life Peer), of Bermondsey in the London Borough of Southwark; **Ian McColl,** MS, FRCS, FACS, FRCSE; Professor of Surgery, University of London at the United Medical Schools of Guy's and St Thomas' Hospitals, since 1971; Director of Surgery, since 1985, and Consultant Surgeon, since 1971, Guy's Hospital; *b* 6 Jan. 1933; *s* of late Frederick George McColl and Winifred E. McColl, Dulwich; *m* 1960, Dr Jean Lennox, 2nd *d* of Arthur James McNair, FRCS, FRCOG; one *s* two *d. Educ:* Hutchesons' Grammar Sch., Glasgow; St Paul's Sch., London; Guy's Hosp., London. MB, BS 1957; FRCS 1962; FRCSE 1962; MS 1966; FACS 1975. Junior staff appts at St Bartholomew's, Putney, St Mark's, St Peter's, Great Ormond Street, Barnet, St Olave's and Guy's Hosps, 1957–67; Research Fellow, Harvard Med. Sch., and Moynihan Fellowship, Assoc. of Surgeons, 1967; Reader in Surgery, St Bartholomew's Hosp. Med. Coll., 1967 (Sub Dean, 1969); Dir of Surgical Unit, Guy's Hosp., 1971–. Visiting Professor: Univ. of South Carolina, 1974; Johns Hopkins Hosp., 1976. Consultant Surgeon: KCH, 1971–; Edenbridge Dist Meml Hosp., 1978–91; Lewisham Hosp., 1983–; Hon. Consultant in Surgery to the Army, 1982–. External examiner in Surgery to Univs of Newcastle upon Tyne and Cardiff, QUB, TCD and NUI. Royal College of Surgeons: Examr in Pathology, 1970–76; Regl Advr, SE Reg., 1975–80; Mem. Council, 1986–; Arris and Gale Lectr, 1964, 1965; Erasmus Wilson Lectr, 1972; Haig Gudenian Meml Lectr, 1988; Henry Cohen Meml Lectr, 1994; Lettsomian Lectr, Med. Soc. of London, 1993. Medical Advisor, BBC Television, 1976–92. A Dep. Speaker, H of L, 1994–; PPS to Prime Minister, 1994–. Member: Central Health Services Council, 1972–74; Standing Medical Adv. Cttee, 1972–82; Management Cttee, King Edward VII Hospital Fund (Chm., R&D Cttee), 1975–80; Council, Metrop. Hosp. Sunday Fund, 1986–91; Council, Imperial Cancer Res. Fund, 1986–; Exec. Council, British Limbless Ex-Service Men's Assoc., 1991–; Chairman: King's Fund Centre Cttee, 1976–86; Govt Wkg Pty on Artificial Limb and Appliance Centres in England, 1984–86; Vice Chm., SHA for Disablement Services, 1987–91. Hon. Sec., British Soc. of Gastroenterology, 1970–74. President: Soc. of Minimally Invasive Gen. Surgery, 1991–94; Limbless Assoc. (formerly Nat. Assoc. for Limbless Disabled), 1992– (Patron and Hon. Consultant, 1989–); Internat. Wheelchair Fedn, 1991–; Assoc. of Endoscopic Surgeons of GB and Ireland, 1994–; The Hospital Saving Assoc., 1994–; Vice-Pres., John Grooms Assoc. for Disabled People, 1990–. Governor-at-Large for England, Bd of Governors, Amer. Coll. of Surgeons, 1982–88. Pres., 1985–94, Chm. Bd of Govs, 1994–, Mildmay Mission Hosp.; Governor: Dulwich Coll. Prep. Sch., 1978–; James Allen's Girls' Sch., 1994–. *Publications:* (ed jtly) Intestinal Absorption in Man, 1975; Talking to Patients, 1982; NHS Data Book, 1984; med. articles, mainly on gastroenterology, rehabilitation and NHS management. *Recreation:* forestry. *Address:* Department of Surgery, Guy's Hospital, SE1 9RT. *Clubs:* Royal College of Surgeons Council, Royal Society of Medicine.

McCOLL, (Christopher) Miles; Provincial Stipendiary Magistrate for West Midlands Commission Area, since 1993; *b* 18 April 1946; *s* of John Parr McColl and Lilian McColl (*née* Oddy); *m* 1971, Susan Margaret Rathbone; three *d. Educ:* Liverpool Coll. Articled clerk in private practice, St Helens, 1965–69; admitted solicitor, 1969; trainee, Court Clerk, then Principal Court Clerk, Manchester City Magistrates' Court, 1969–74; Dep. Clerk to Stockport Justices, 1974–78; Clerk to Leigh Justices, 1978–93. Sec., Gtr Manchester Justices' Clerks and Courts Liaison Cttee, 1984–90; Member: Magistrates' Courts Rev. of Procedure Cttee, 1989–91; Magistrates' Courts Consultative Council, 1992–93; Children Act Procedure Adv. Gp, 1989–90; Pres. of Family Division's Cttee, 1990–92; Legal Aid Steering Cttee, 1992; Pre-trial Issues Steering Gp, 1992–93. Secretary: S Lancs Br., Magistrates' Assoc., 1979–85; British Juvenile and Family Courts' Soc., 1980–81; Justices' Clerks' Society: Mem. Council, 1988–93; Chm., Parly Cttee, 1989; Chm., Professional Purposes Cttee, 1989–93; Pre-trial Issues Nat. Action Manager, 1991–93; Vice-Pres., Duchy of Lancaster Br., 1993. Ed., 1979–87, Jt Ed., 1987–, Family Law. *Publications:* Court Teasers: practical situations arising in magistrates' courts, 1978; contrib. to legal jls. *Recreations:* sport, reading, music, British countryside. *Address:* Birmingham Magistrates' Court, Victoria Law Courts, Corporation Street, Birmingham B4 6QA. *T:* 0121–212 6600.

McCOLL, Sir Colin (Hugh Verel), KCMG 1990 (CMG 1983); HM Diplomatic Service, retired; Head of MI6, 1988–94; *b* 6 Sept. 1932; *s* of Dr Robert McColl and Julie McColl; *m* 1st, 1959, Shirley Curtis (*d* 1983); two *s* two *d*; 2nd, 1985, Sally Wyld; one *s. Educ:*

Shrewsbury School; The Queen's College, Oxford (BA). Foreign Office, 1956; Third Secretary, Bangkok, 1958, Vientiane, 1960; Second Secretary, FO, 1962; First Secretary, Warsaw, 1966; Consul and First Secretary (Disarmament), Geneva, 1973; Counsellor, FCO, 1977. *Recreations:* music, walks, cycling, tennis, classics. *Address:* PO Box 1105, SE1 1AG. *Club:* Commonwealth Trust.

McCOLL, Ian, CBE 1983; Chairman, Scottish Express Newspapers Ltd, 1975–82; *b* 22 Feb. 1915; *e s* of late John and Morag McColl, Glasgow and Bunessan, Isle of Mull; *m* 1968, Brenda, *e d* of late Thomas and Mary McKean, Glasgow; one *d*. *Educ:* Hillhead High Sch., Glasgow. Served in RAF, 1940–46 (despatches, 1945): Air Crew, Coastal Comd 202 Sqdn. Joined Scottish Daily Express as cub reporter, 1933; held various editorial executive posts; Editor, Scottish Daily Express, 1961–71; Editor, Daily Express, 1971–74; Dir, Express Newspapers Ltd, 1971–82. Contested (L): Dumfriesshire, 1945; Greenock, 1950. Mem., Presbytery of Glasgow and Synod of Clydesdale, 1953–71; Mem., General Assembly Publications Cttee, until 1971; Session Clerk, Sandyford-Henderson Memorial Church of Scotland, Glasgow, 1953–71. Mem., Press Council, 1975–78; a Vice-Pres., Newspaper Press Fund, 1981–. Mem., Gen. Assembly Bd of Communication, 1983–86. Chm. Media Div., XIII Commonwealth Games, Scotland 1986, 1983–86. Mem., Saints and Sinners Club of Scotland, Chm., 1981–82. Bank of Scotland Scottish Press Life Achievement Award, 1993. *Address:* 12 Newlands Road, Newlands, Glasgow G43 2JB.

McCOLL, Miles; *see* McColl, C. M.

McCOLLUM, Sir Liam; *see* McCollum, Sir W. P.

McCOLLUM, Sir William (Paschal), (Sir Liam), Kt 1988; **Hon. Mr Justice McCollum;** Judge of the High Court of Justice in Northern Ireland, since 1987; *b* 13 Jan. 1933; *s* of Patrick McCollum and Mary Ellen McCollum (*née* Strain); *m* 1958, Anne Bernadette Fitzpatrick (CBE 1995); six *s* two *d*. *Educ:* Waterside School; St Columb's Coll., Derry; University College Dublin (BA 1953; LLB 1954). Called to the Bar of N Ireland, 1955; called to Irish Bar, 1963; QC 1971. *Address:* Royal Courts of Justice, Chichester Street, Belfast BT1 3JF.

McCOMB, Leonard William Joseph, RA 1991 (ARA 1987); RE; artist; *b* 3 Aug. 1930; *s* of Archibald and Delia McComb, Glasgow; *m* 1st, 1955, Elizabeth Henstock (marr. diss. 1963); 2nd, 1966, Joan Allwork (*d* 1967); 3rd, 1975, Barbara Elenora. *Educ:* Manchester Art Sch.; Slade Sch. of Fine Art, Univ. of London (Dip. Fine Art, 1960). RE 1994. Teacher at art schools, Bristol, Oxford, RA schools, Slade, Goldsmiths', Sir John Cass, 1960–. *Exhibitions include:* Human Clay, Arts Council, 1976; British Painting 1952–77, RA, 1977; (one-man exhibn) Blossoms and Flowers, Coracle Press, 1979; Painters of the 80's, Venice, 1980; British Sculpture, Whitechapel, 1981; British Drawings and Watercolours, China, 1982; Arts Council Touring Exhibn, 1983; Hard Won Image, Tate, 1984; 50 Years of British Art, 1985; Representation Abroad, Washington, 1986; Large Watercolours and Drawings, Berlin, 1986; Museum of Modern Art, Brussels, 1987; Paintings from the South, London, 1989; School of London Drawings, London, 1989; (one-man exhibn) Recent Work, London, 1990; Twin Images, London, 1990; Recent Paintings, Pastels and Drawings, Rome, 1991; The Discerning Eye, Mall Galls, London, 1992; Paintings and Drawings, Browse & Darby Gall., London, 1993; Cambridge Centenary, Kettles Yard Gall., 1995; *work in public collections:* Arts Council; British Council; ICA; Cambridge Univ.; Tate; V&A; Art Galls of Birmingham, Manchester, Swindon, Worcester; *work includes:* commemorative plaque, Oxford Brookes Univ., 1994; tapestry (fishes and invertebrates in the sea), Edinburgh, 1994. Jubilee Prize, RA, 1977; Korn/Ferry Prize, RA, 1988. *Recreations:* travelling and walking in the countryside.

McCOMBE, Richard George Bramwell; QC 1989; *b* 23 Sept. 1952; *s* of Barbara Bramwell McCombe, MA, FCA; *m* 1st (marr. diss.); 2nd, 1986, Carolyn Sara Birrell; one *s* one *d*. *Educ:* Sedbergh Sch.; Downing Coll., Cambridge (MA). Called to the Bar, Lincoln's Inn, 1975; admitted (*ad hoc*) to Bars of Singapore, 1992, Cayman Is, 1993. Second Jun. Counsel to Dir-Gen. of Fair Trading, 1982–87, First Jun. Counsel, 1987–89; an Asst Recorder, 1993. Mem., Senate of Inns of Court and of Bar Council, 1981–86; Chm., Young Barristers' Cttee, Bar Council, 1983–84; Co-opted Mem., Bar Council Cttees, 1986–89; Mem., Gen. Council of the Bar, 1995– (Vice-Chm., Internat. Practice Cttee, 1995). Member: Singapore Acad. of Law, 1992–; Council, Bars and Law Socs of EC, 1994–95. Inspector into affairs of Norton Group PLC, 1991–92 (report, with J. K. Heywood, 1993). *Recreations:* cricket, Rugby (both as spectator), travel, karate, learning to fly light aircraft. *Address:* 13 Old Square, Lincoln's Inn, WC2A 3UA. *T:* 0171–404 4800. *Clubs:* Royal Automobile, MCC; London Scottish Football, Harlequin Football; Lancs CC.

McCOMBIE, John Alexander Fergusson, FRICS; General Manager, Glenrothes Development Corporation, since 1993; *b* 13 Sept. 1932; *s* of Alexander William McCombie and Charlotte Mary McCombie (*née* Fergusson); *m* 1959, Seana Joy Cameron Scott; two *s* one *d*. *Educ:* Perth Acad.; Coll. of Estate Management. ARICS 1968, FRICS 1982; IRRV 1969. Nat. service, RAF, 1955–57 (MEAF). E Kilbride Develt Corp., 1959–67; Irvine Develt Corp., 1968–70; Glenrothes Develt Corp., 1970–: Chief Estates Officer, 1970–74; Commercial Dir, 1975–93. Director: Glenrothes Enterprise Trust, 1983–94; Mid-Fife Business Trust, 1994–. *Recreations:* gardening, golf, philately, reading. *Address:* 13 Carnoustie Gardens, Glenrothes, Fife KY6 2QB. *T:* Glenrothes (01592) 755658.

McCONNELL, family name of **Baron McConnell.**

McCONNELL, Baron *cr* 1995 (Life Peer), of Lisburn in the County of Antrim; **Robert William Brian McConnell,** PC (N Ireland) 1964; Social Security (formerly National Insurance) Commissioner, Northern Ireland, 1968–87; *b* 25 Nov. 1922; *s* of late Alfred E. McConnell, Belfast; *m* 1951, Sylvia Elizabeth Joyce Agnew; two *s* one *d*. *Educ:* Sedbergh Sch.; Queen's Univ., Belfast (BA, LLB). Called to Bar of Northern Ireland, 1948. MP (U) for South Antrim, NI Parlt, 1951–68; Dep. Chm. of Ways and Means, NI Parlt, 1962; Parly Sec. to Min. of Health and Local Govt for N Ireland, 1963; Minister of Home Affairs for Northern Ireland, 1964–66; Minister of State, Min. of Develt, 1966–67; Leader of the House of Commons, NI, 1967–68. President: Industrial Court of NI, 1968–81; European Move in NI, 1992– (Vice-Chm., 1987–92). *Address:* 50A Glenavy Road, Knocknadona, Lisburn, Co. Antrim, Northern Ireland BT28 3UT. *T:* Lisburn (01846) 663432; House of Lords, SW1A 0PW. *Club:* Ulster Reform (Belfast).

McCONNELL, Prof. James Desmond Caldwell, FRS 1987; Professor of the Physics and Chemistry of Minerals, Department of Earth Sciences, University of Oxford, 1986–95, Head of Department, 1991–95; Fellow of St Hugh's College, Oxford, 1986–95; *b* 3 July 1930; *s* of Samuel D. and Cathleen McConnell; *m* 1956, Jean Elspeth Ironside; one *s* two *d*. *Educ.* Queen's Univ. of Belfast (BSc, MSc 1952); Univ. of Cambridge (MA 1955; PhD 1956); MA Oxon 1986. Univ. of Cambridge: Demonstrator, 1955; Lectr, 1960; Reader, 1972–82; Churchill College: Fellow, 1962–82; Extraordinary Fellow, 1983–88; Head of Dept of Rock Physics, Schlumberger Cambridge Research, 1983–86. *Publications:* Principles of Mineral Behaviour (with A. Putnis), 1980, Russian edn, 1983; papers in physics jls and mineralogical jls. *Recreations:* local history, hill walking, singing. *Address:* 8 The Croft, Old Headington, Oxford OX3 9BU. *T:* Oxford (01865) 69100.

McCONNELL, John, RDI 1987; FCSD; graphic designer; Director, Pentagram Design, since 1974; *b* 14 May 1939; *s* of Donald McConnell and Enid McConnell (*née* Dimberline); *m* 1963, Moira Rose Macgregor; one *s* one *d*. *Educ:* Borough Green Secondary Modern School; Maidstone College of Art (NDD). FCSD (FSIAD 1980). Employed in advertising and design, 1959–62; Lectr, Colchester College of Art, 1962–63; freelance design practice, 1963–74; co-founder, Face Photosetting, 1968. Member: Alliance Graphique Internat., 1976; Post Office Stamp Adv. Cttee, 1984; Pres., D&AD, 1986 (President's Award, 1985); served on design competition juries, D&AD. Gold medallist at Biennale, Warsaw. *Publications:* (jtly) Living by Design, 1978; (jtly) Ideas on Design, 1986; Editor, Pentagram Papers. *Recreations:* house restoration, cooking. *Address:* 11 Needham Road, W11 2RP. *T:* 0171–229 3477; 42 Bassett Road, W10 6JL. *Club:* Groucho.

McCONNELL, (Sir) Robert Shean, (4th Bt *cr* 1900); *S* father, 1987, but does not use the title. *Educ:* Stowe; Queen's Coll., Cambridge (MA Urban Estate Management); Regent St Polytech.; Univ. of BC (MSc Community and Regl Planning); DipTP. FRTPI; ARICS; MIMgt. Worked as a trainee surveyor in Belfast and as a town planner in UK, Canada and USA. Lectured in town planning and principles of management at univs in UK and Australia. Member: Bruce House Appeal Cttee; Peabody Trust. Governor, South Bank Univ. *Publications:* Theories for Planning, 1981; articles in professional jls on planning matters. *Recreations:* gardening, walking, the local community, travel. *Heir:* *b* James Angus McConnell.

McCONVILLE, Michael Anthony, MBE 1958; writer; *b* 3 Jan. 1925; *s* of late Lt-Col James McConville, MC and late Winifred (*née* Hanley); *m* 1952, Beryl Anne (*née* Jerrett); two *s* four *d*. *Educ:* Mayfield Coll.; Trinity Coll., Dublin. Royal Marines, 1943–46. Malayan Civil Service, 1950–61: served in Perak, Johore, Trengganu, Negri Sembilam, Pahang and Kedah; retd as Chm., Border War Exec. Cttee. CRO (later HM Diplomatic Service), 1961–77: Colombo, 1963–64; Kingston, Jamaica, 1966–67; Ottawa, 1967–71; Consul-Gen., Zagreb, 1974–77. Kesatria Mankgu Negara (Malaya), 1962. *Publications:* (as Anthony McCandless): Leap in the Dark, 1980; The Burke Foundation, 1985; (as Michael McConville) Ascendancy to Oblivion: the story of the Anglo-Irish, 1986; A Small War in the Balkans: the British in war time Yugoslavia, 1986; Nothing Much to Lose, 1993; (ed) Tell it to the Marines, 1994; (as Miles Noonan): Tales from the Mess, 1983; More Tales from the Mess, 1984; (as Patrick Plum): articles and short stories in Blackwoods, etc. *Recreations:* walking, gardening, watching Rugby. *Address:* 72 Friarn Street, Bridgwater, Som TA6 3LJ.

McCORD, Brig. Mervyn Noel Samuel, CBE 1978 (OBE 1974); MC 1951; retired; *b* 25 Dec. 1929; *s* of late Major G. McCord, MBE and Muriel (*née* King); *m* 1953, Annette Mary, *d* of C. R. W. Thomson; three *s*. *Educ:* Coleraine, NI; RMA Sandhurst. Commissioned Royal Ulster Rifles, 1949; Korea, 1950–51; School of Infantry, 1958–60; Staff Coll., Camberley, 1961–62; DAQMG, Eastern Command, Canada, 1963–65; BM, HQ 6 Infantry Brigade, 1967–69; JSSC, 1969; GSO1, HQNI, 1970–71; CO, 1st Bn The Royal Irish Rangers, 1971–74; Brig. 1975; Commander, Ulster Defence Regt, 1976–78; Dep. Comdr, Eastern Dist, 1978–81; Brig. King's Div., 1981–84. ADC to the Queen, 1981–84. Col, The Royal Irish Rangers, 1985–90 (Dep. Col, 1976–81). Chairman: SHAA, 1986–93; SHAA Retirement Homes plc, 1986–93. FIMgt (MBIM 1978). *Recreations:* cricket, athletics, country sports, gardening. *Address:* c/o Royal Bank of Scotland, Whitehall, SW1A 2DX. *Club:* Army and Navy.

McCORKELL, Col Sir Michael (William), KCVO 1994; OBE 1964; TD 1954; JP; Lord-Lieutenant, County Londonderry, since 1975; *b* 3 May 1925; *s* of late Captain B. F. McCorkell, Templeard, Culmore, Co. Londonderry and of Mrs E. M. McCorkell; *m* 1950, Aileen Allen, OBE 1975, 2nd *d* of late Lt-Col E. B. Booth, DSO, Darver Castle, Dundalk, Co. Louth, Eire; three *s* one *d*. *Educ:* Aldenham. Served with 16/5 Lancers, 1943–47; Major (TA) North Irish Horse, 1951; Lt-Col 1961; comd North Irish Horse (TA); retd, 1964. T&AVR Col, NI, 1971–74; Brevet Col, 1974; Pres., T&AVR, NI, 1977–88; ADC to the Queen, 1972. Hon. Col, N Irish Horse, 1975–81. Co. Londonderry: High Sheriff 1961; DL 1962; JP 1980. *Recreations:* fishing, shooting. *Address:* Ballyarnett, 50 Beragh Hill Road, Londonderry, Northern Ireland BT48 8LY. *T:* Londonderry (01504) 351239. *Club:* Cavalry and Guards.

MacCORMAC, Richard Cornelius, CBE 1994; RA 1993; PPRIBA; Partner, MacCormac, Jamieson, Prichard, Architects, since 1972; President, Royal Institute of British Architects, 1991–93; *b* 3 Sept. 1938; *s* of Henry MacCormac, CBE, MD, FRCP and Marion Maud, *d* of B. C. Broomhall, FRCS; *m* 1964, Susan Karin Landen; one *s* (and one *s* decd). *Educ:* Westminster Sch.; Trinity Coll., Cambridge (BA 1962); University College London (MA 1965). RIBA 1967. Served RN, 1957–59. Proj. Archt, London Bor. of Merton, 1967–69; estabd private practice, 1969; taught in Dept of Arch., Cambridge Univ., 1969–75 and 1979–81, Univ. Lectr, 1976–79; Vis. Prof., Univ. of Edinburgh (Dept of Architecture), 1982–85. Dir, Spitalfields Workspace, 1981–. Chm., Good Design in Housing Awards, RIBA London Region, 1977; Mem., Royal Fine Art Commn, 1983–. FRSA 1982. *Publications:* articles in Architectural Review and Archts Jl. *Recreations:* sailing, music, reading. *Address:* 9 Heneage Street, E1 5LJ. *T:* 0171–377 9262.

McCORMACK, Most Rev. John; Bishop of Meath (RC), 1968–90, now Emeritus; *b* 25 March 1921; *s* of Peter McCormack and Bridget Mulvany. *Educ:* St Finian's Coll., Mullingar; Maynooth Coll.; Lateran Univ., Rome. Priest, 1946. Ministered: Multyfarnham, 1950–52; St Loman's Hosp., 1952–58; Mullingar, 1958–68; Diocesan Sec., 1952–68. *Address:* Bishop's House, Dublin Road, Mullingar, Co. Westmeath, Ireland. *T:* Mullingar 48841/42038.

McCORMACK, John P(atrick); Vice President, in charge of Latin American and South African Operations, General Motors Corporation, 1983; *b* New York, 23 Nov. 1923; *s* of John McCormack and Margaret (*née* Bannon); *m* 1952, Mari Martha Luhrs; two *s*. *Educ:* St John's Univ., Jamaica, NY (Bachelor of Business Admin); NY Univ., NYC (LLB). Joined General Motors, 1949; Gen. Clerk, Accounting Dept, NY, 1949, Sen. Clerk 1950, Sen. Accountant 1952; Asst to Treas., Djakarta Br., 1953; Asst Treas., Karachi Br., 1956; Asst Treas., Gen. Motors South African (Pty) Ltd, Port Elizabeth, 1958, Treas. 1961; Asst Finance Man., Overseas Div., NY, 1966; Treas., subseq. Man. Dir, Gen. Motors Continental, Antwerp, 1968; Finance Man., Adam Opel, 1970, Man. Dir and Chm. Bd, 1974; Gen. Dir, European Ops, Gen. Motors Overseas Corp., 1976; Vice Pres. i/c joint ventures and African ops, 1980. *Recreations:* golf, photography. *Address:* c/o General Motors Corporation, General Motors Building, Detroit, Michigan 48202, USA; PO Box 1030, Pebble Beach, CA 93953-1030, USA.

McCORMACK, Mark Hume; Chairman and Chief Executive Officer, International Management Group; *b* 6 Nov. 1930; *s* of Ned Hume McCormack and late Grace Wolfe McCormack; *m* 1st, 1954, Nancy Breckenridge McCormack; two *s* one *d*; 2nd, 1986, Betsy Nagelsen. *Educ:* Princeton Univ.; William and Mary Coll. (BA); Yale Univ. (LLB). Admitted to Ohio Bar, 1957; Associate in Arter, Hadden, Wykoff & Van Duzer, 1957–63;

Partner, 1964–; started Internat. Management Gp, 1962. Commentator for televised golf, BBC. *Publications:* The World of Professional Golf, annually, 1967–; Arnie: the evolution of a legend, 1967; The Wonderful World of Professional Golf, 1973; What they don't teach you at Harvard Business School, 1984; The Terrible Truth about Lawyers, 1987; Success Secrets, 1989; What They Still Don't Teach You at Harvard Business School, 1989; The 110% Solution, 1991; Hit the Ground Running, 1993; monthly newsletters Success Secrets. *Recreations:* golf, tennis. *Address:* No 1300, One Erieview Plaza, Cleveland, OH 44114, USA. *T:* 216/522–1200. *Clubs:* Royal & Ancient Golf (St Andrews); Wentworth (Virginia Water); Sunningdale Golf (Berkshire, England); Old Prestwick (Prestwick); Royal Dornoch (Dornoch); Turnberry Hotel Golf; Deepdale (NY); Pepper Pike, Country Club of Cleveland (Ohio); Isleworth, Bay Hill (Florida); Ironwood Country (Calif).

MacCORMICK, Prof. (Donald) Neil, FBA 1986; Regius Professor of Public Law, University of Edinburgh, since 1972; *b* 27 May 1941; *yr s* of J. M. MacCormick, MA, LLD (Glasgow) and Margaret I. Miller, MA, BSc (Glasgow); *m* 1st, 1965, Caroline Rona Barr (marr. diss. 1992); three *d*; 2nd, 1992, Flora Margaret Britain (*née* Milne), Edinburgh. *Educ:* High School, Glasgow; Univ. of Glasgow (MA, 1st cl. Philos. and Eng. Lit.); Balliol Coll., Oxford (BA, 1st cl. Jurisprudence; MA); LLD Edinburgh, 1982. Pres., Oxford Union Soc., 1965. Called to the Bar, Inner Temple, 1971. Lecturer, St Andrew's Univ. (Queen's Coll., Dundee), 1965–67; Fellow and Tutor in Jurisprudence, Balliol Coll., Oxford, 1967–72, and CUF Lectr in Law, Oxford Univ., 1968–72; Pro-Proctor, Oxford Univ., 1971–72; University of Edinburgh: Dean of Faculty of Law, 1973–76 and 1985–88; Provost, Faculty Gp of Law and Social Scis, 1993–. Visiting Professor: Univ. of Sydney, 1981; Univ. of Uppsala, 1991; Anne Green Vis. Prof., Univ. of Texas, 1990; Higgins Visitor, NW Sch. of Law, Oregon, 1987. Lectures: Corry, Queen's Univ., Kingston, Ont, 1981; Dewey, NY Univ., 1982; Or Emet, Osgoode Hall, 1988; Chorley, LSE, 1992; Hart, Oxford, 1993; Stevenson, Glasgow, 1994. Contested (SNP): Edinburgh North, 1979; Edinburgh, Pentlands, 1983, 1987; Argyll and Bute, 1992–. President: Assoc. for Legal and Social Philosophy, 1974–76; Soc. of Public Teachers of Law, 1983–84; Vice-President: Internat. Assoc. for Phil. of Law and Social Phil., 1991–; RSE, 1991–. Member: Houghton Cttee on Financial Aid to Political Parties, 1975–76; Broadcasting Council for Scotland, 1985–89. For. Mem., Finnish Acad. of Scis, 1994. FRSE 1986. Hon. LLD: Uppsala, 1986; Saarland, 1994. *Publications:* (ed) The Scottish Debate: Essays on Scottish Nationalism, 1970; (ed) Lawyers in their Social Setting, 1976; Legal Reasoning and Legal Theory, 1978; H. L. A. Hart, 1981; Legal Right and Social Democracy: essays in legal and political philosophy, 1982; (with O. Weinberger) Grundlagen des Institutionalistischen Rechtspositivismus, 1985; An Institutional Theory of Law, 1986 (trans. Italian, 1991); (ed jtly) Enlightenment, Right and Revolution, 1989; (ed jtly) Interpreting Statutes, 1991; contribs to various symposia, jls on law, philosophy and politics. *Recreations:* hill walking, bagpiping, sailing. *Address:* The Old College, Edinburgh EH8 9YL.

See also I. S. MacD. MacCormick.

MacCORMICK, Iain Somerled MacDonald; Trade Consultant, The Bartering Co. Ltd, since 1993; *b* 28 Sept. 1939; *er s* of John MacDonald MacCormick, MA, LLB, LLD and Margaret Isobel MacCormick, MA, BSc; *m* 1st, 1964, Micky Trefusis Elsom (marr. diss.); two *s* three *d*; 2nd, 1988, Carole Burnett (*née* Story). *Educ:* Glasgow High Sch.; Glasgow Univ. (MA). Queen's Own Lowland Yeomanry, 1957–67 (Captain). Major Account Manager, 1982, Dir Liaison Manager, 1984, BT plc. Contested (SNP) Argyll, 1970; MP (SNP) Argyll, Feb. 1974–1979; introduced, as private member's bill, Divorce (Scotland) Act, 1976. Founder Mem., SDP, 1981. Mem., Argyll and Bute District Council, 1979–80. *Recreations:* Rugby football, sailing, local history. *Address:* 2 Dowanside Road, Glasgow G12 9DA. *T:* 0141–334 3367.

See also Prof. D. N. MacCormick.

McCORMICK, Prof. James Stevenson, FRCPI, FRCGP, FFCM, Professor of Community Health, Trinity College Dublin, 1973–91 (Dean of School of Physic, 1974–79); *b* 9 May 1926; *s* of Victor Ormsby McCormick and Margaretta Tate (*née* Stevenson); *m* 1954, Elizabeth Ann Dimond; three *s* one *d*. *Educ:* The Leys Sch., Cambridge; Clare Coll., Cambridge (BA, MB); St Mary's Hospital, W2. Served RAMC, 1960–62; St Mary's Hosp., 1963; general practice, 1964–73. Chairman: Eastern Health Board, 1970–72; Nat. Health Council, 1984–86. Pres., Irish Coll. of General Practitioners, 1986–87. Hon. MCFP 1982. *Publications:* The Doctor—Father Figure or Plumber, 1979; (with P. Skrabanek) Follies and Fallacies in Medicine, 1989; papers, espec. on General Practice and Ischaemic Heart Disease. *Recreations:* open air, patients. *Address:* The Barn, Windgates, Bray, Co. Wicklow, Ireland. *T:* Dublin 2874113.

McCORMICK, John; Controller of BBC Scotland, since 1992; *b* 24 June 1944; *s* of Joseph and Roseann McCormick; *m* 1973, Jean Frances Gibbons; one *s* one *d*. *Educ:* St Michael's Acad., Irvine; Univ. of Glasgow (MA Modern History with Econ. History 1967; MEd 1970). Teacher, St Gregory's Secondary Sch., Glasgow, 1968–70; Education Officer, BBC School Broadcasting Council, 1970–75; Senior Education Officer, Scotland, 1975–82; Sec., and Head of Information, BBC Scotland, 1982–87; The Sec. of the BBC, 1987–92. Jt Chm., Scotland, BAFTA; Mem. Bd, Edinburgh Film Fest. Member: Glasgow Children's Panel, 1972–77; Vis. Cttee, Glenochil Young Offenders' Instn, 1979–85; Vice-Chm., Youth-at-risk, (Scotland), 1985–92. *Recreation:* newspapers. *Address:* Broadcasting House, Queen Margaret Drive, Glasgow G12 8DG. *T:* 0141–339 8844.

McCORMICK, John Ormsby, CMG 1965; MC 1943; HM Diplomatic Service, retired; *b* Dublin, 7 Feb. 1916; *s* of Albert Victor McCormick and Sarah Beatty de Courcy; *m* 1955, Francine Guieu (*née* Pâris); one *d*, one step *s*. *Educ:* The Leys Sch., Cambridge; New Coll., Oxford. BA Hon. Mods and Greats (Oxford), 1938. Passed Competitive Exam. for Consular Service, 1939, and appointed Asst Officer, Dept of Overseas Trade. Served War of 1939–45, in Royal Corps of Signals, Africa, Sicily, Germany, 1940–45. 2nd Sec. (Commercial), British Embassy, Athens, 1945–47; FO, London, 1948–50; 1st Sec., UK High Commn, Karachi, 1950–52; Consul, New York, 1952–54; transferred to Washington, 1954–55; NATO Defence Coll., 1955; Asst Head, SE Asia Dept, FO, 1956–59; Foreign Service Officer, Grade 6, 1959; Counsellor (Commercial), British Embassy, Djakarta, 1959–62; Corps of Inspectors, FO, 1962–64; Counsellor (Commercial), British Embassy, Ankara, 1965–67; Consul-General, Lyons, 1967–72. *Address:* Oldfort, Newcastle, Co. Wicklow, Ireland.

MacCORMICK, Neil; *see* MacCormick, D. N.

McCORQUODALE, Dame Barbara (Hamilton); *see* Cartland, Dame B. H.

McCOWAN, Rt. Hon. Sir Anthony (James Denys), Kt 1981; PC 1989; **Rt. Hon. Lord Justice McCowan;** a Lord Justice of Appeal, since 1989; Senior Presiding Judge of England and Wales, since 1991; *b* 12 Jan. 1928; *yr s* of John Haines Smith McCowan, MBE, and Marguerite McCowan, Georgetown, British Guiana; *m* 1961, Sue Hazel Anne, *d* of late Reginald Harvey and of Mrs Harvey, Braiseworth Hall, Tannington, Suffolk; two *s* one *d*. *Educ:* Epsom Coll.; (Open Hist. schol.) Brasenose Coll., Oxford (MA, BCL). Called to Bar, Gray's Inn, 1951, Atkin Scholar; Bencher, 1980. Dep. Chm., E Sussex QS, 1969–71; a Recorder of the Crown Court, 1972–81; QC 1972; a Judge of the High Court, QBD, 1981–89. Leader, 1978–81, Presiding Judge, 1986–89, SE Circuit. Member: Parole Bd, 1982–84; Crown Court Rule Cttee, 1982–88. *Recreations:* sport, history, travel. *Address:* c/o Royal Courts of Justice, Strand, WC2A 2LL.

See also J. M. Archer.

McCOWAN, Sir Hew Cargill, 3rd Bt, *cr* 1934; *b* 26 July 1930; *s* of Sir David James Cargill McCowan, 2nd Bt and Muriel Emma Annie, *d* of W. C. Willmott; *S* father, 1965. *Heir: b* David William Cargill McCowan, [*b* 28 Feb. 1934; *m*; one *s* one *d*].

McCOWEN, Alec, (Alexander Duncan McCowen), CBE 1986 (OBE 1972); actor; *b* 26 May 1925; *s* of late Duncan McCowen and Hon. Mrs McCowen. *Educ:* Skinners' Sch., Tunbridge Wells; RADA, 1941. Repertory: York, Birmingham, etc, 1943–50; Escapade, St James's, 1952; The Matchmaker, Haymarket, 1954; The Count of Clérambard, Garrick, 1955; The Caine Mutiny Court Martial, Hippodrome, 1956; Look Back in Anger, Royal Court, 1956; The Elder Statesman, Cambridge, 1958; Old Vic Seasons, 1959–61: Touchstone, Ford, Richard II, Mercutio, Oberon, Malvolio; Dauphin in St Joan; Algy in The Importance of Being Earnest; Royal Shakespeare Company, 1962–63: Antipholus of Syracuse in The Comedy of Errors; Fool, in King Lear; Father Fontana in The Representative, Aldwych, 1963; Thark, Garrick, 1965; The Cavern, Strand, 1965; After the Rain, Duchess, 1967, Golden Theatre, NY, 1967; Hadrian VII, Birmingham, 1967, Mermaid, 1968, New York, 1969; Hamlet, Birmingham, 1970; The Philanthropist, Royal Court, 1970, NY, 1971; Butley, Criterion, 1972; The Misanthrope, NT, 1973, 1975, NY 1975; Equus, NT, 1973; Pygmalion, Albery, 1974; The Family Dance, Criterion, 1976; Antony and Cleopatra, Prospect Co., 1977; solo performance of St Mark's Gospel, Riverside Studios, Mermaid and Comedy, 1978, Globe, 1981, UK tour, 1985, Half Moon, 1990; Tishoo, Wyndham's, 1979; The Browning Version, and A Harlequinade, NT, 1980; The Portage to San Cristobal of A. H., Mermaid, 1982; Kipling (solo performance), Mermaid, 1984; The Cocktail Party, Phoenix, 1986; Fathers and Sons, Waiting for Godot, NT, 1987; Shakespeare, Cole & Co. (solo performance), UK tour, 1988; The Heiress, Chichester, 1989; Exclusive, Strand, 1989; A Single Man, Greenwich, 1990; Dancing at Lughnasa, NT, 1990, transf. Phoenix, 1991; Preserving Mr Panmure, Chichester, 1991; Caesar and Cleopatra, Greenwich, 1992; Someone Who'll Watch Over Me, Hampstead, 1992, transf. Vaudeville, NY, 1992; The Tempest, Elgar's Rondo, 1993, The Cherry Orchard, 1995, RSC, Stratford. Dir, Definitely the Bahamas, Orange Tree, Richmond, 1987. Films include: Frenzy, 1971; Travels with My Aunt, 1972; Stevie, 1978; Never Say Never Again, 1983; The Age of Innocence, 1994. TV series, Mr Palfrey of Westminster, 1984. Evening Standard (later Standard) Drama Award, 1968, 1973, 1982; Stage Actor of the Year, Variety Club, 1970. *Publications:* Young Gemini (autobiog.), 1979; Double Bill (autobiog.), 1980; Personal Mark, 1984. *Recreations:* music, gardening.

McCRACKEN, Philip Guy; Managing Director, Food Division, Marks & Spencer, since 1994; *b* 25 Nov. 1948; *m* 1972, Frances Elizabeth Addison; one *s* two *d*. *Educ:* Clee Numberston Foundn Sch., Cleethorpes; Nat. Coll. of Food and Technology, Reading Univ. (BSc 1st Class Hons Food Technology). Production Manager, Mars, 1972–73; Product Development Manager, Imperial Foods, 1973–75; Marks and Spencer, 1975–. *Recreations:* cricket, golf, tennis. *Address:* Marks & Spencer plc, 47 Baker Street, W1A 1DN.

McCRAE, Alister Geddes, CBE 1973; Chairman: Clyde Port Authority, 1966–77; British Ports Association, 1972–74; *b* 7 Aug. 1909; *s* of Alexander McCrae; *m* 1st, 1938, Margaret Montgomery Reid (*d* 1977); one *s*; 2nd, 1978, Norah Crawford Orr. *Educ:* Kelvinside Academy; High School of Glasgow. Joined: P. Henderson & Co., Shipowners, Glasgow, 1927; Irrawaddy Flotilla Co. Ltd (in Burma), 1933; Served War: Middle East and Burma, 1941–45; Lt-Col, Royal Indian Engrs (despatches). Irrawaddy Flotilla Co. Ltd, 1946–48 (Dep. Gen. Manager, in Burma); re-joined P. Henderson & Co., as Partner, 1948; Sen. Partner and Man. Dir, British & Burmese Steam Navigation Co. Ltd, 1963; retd 1972. Member: Nat. Dock Labour Bd, 1953–57; UK Chamber of Shipping Council, 1951–65; Clyde Navigation Trust, 1962–65; British Transport Docks Bd, 1963–65; Nat. Ports Council, 1967–71; Scottish Economic Council, 1969–74; Aldington/Jones Commn on Docks, 1972; Chm., Clyde Estuary Develt Gp, 1968–71; Dir, Hunterston Develt Co. Ltd, 1970–74. Chm., Glasgow Old People's Welfare Assoc. (Age Concern), 1969–79. Freeman, City of London, 1959; Liveryman, Worshipful Co. of Shipwrights, 1959. FRSA. *Publications:* Irrawaddy Flotilla, 1978; (jtly) Tales of Burma, 1981; Pioneers in Burma, 1986, new edn as Scots in Burma, 1990. *Recreation:* reading the classic novelists. *Address:* Belwood, Killearn, Stirlingshire G63 9LG.

McCRAITH, Col Patrick James Danvers, MC 1943; TD; DL; Solicitor and Notary Public; *b* 21 June 1916; *s* of late Sir Douglas McCraith; *m* 1946, Hon. Philippa Mary Ellis, *yr d* of 1st and last Baron Robins, KBE, DSO, of Rhodesia and Chelsea; one *s* one *d*. *Educ:* Harrow. 2nd Lieut, Sherwood Rangers Yeomanry, 1935; served War, 1939–45, N Africa and NW Europe (three times wounded); raised and commanded Yeomanry Patrol of Long Range Desert Group, 1940–41; commanded Sherwood Rangers Yeomanry, 1953–57; Bt Colonel, 1958. Hon. Col, B (Sherwood Rangers Yeomanry) Squadron, The Royal Yeomanry, 1968–79. High Sheriff of Nottinghamshire, 1963; DL Notts, 1965. *Address:* Cranfield House, Southwell, Notts NG25 0HQ. *T:* Southwell (01636) 812129. *Club:* Special Forces.

McCREA, Rev. Dr Robert Thomas William; MP (DUP) Mid Ulster, since 1983 (resigned seat Dec. 1985 in protest against Anglo-Irish Agreement; re-elected Jan. 1986); Minister, Free Presbyterian Church of Ulster, since 1967; *b* 6 Aug. 1948; *s* of Robert T. and Sarah J. McCrea; *m* 1971, Anne Shirley McKnight; two *s* three *d*. *Educ:* Cookstown Grammar Sch.; Theol Coll., Free Presbyterian Church of Ulster. Civil servant, 1966; Free Presbyterian Minister of the Gospel, 1967–. Dist Councillor, Magherafelt, 1973–; Mem. (DUP) Mid Ulster, NI Assembly, 1982–86. Dir, Daybreak Recording Co., 1981–. Gospel singer and recording artist; Silver, Gold and Platinum Discs for record sales. Hon. DD Marietta Bible Coll., Ohio, 1989. *Publication:* In His Pathway—the story of the Reverend William McCrea, 1980. *Recreations:* music, horse riding. *Address:* 10 Highfield Road, Magherafelt, Co. Londonderry BT45 5JD. *T:* Magherafelt (01648) 32664.

McCREA, Sir William (Hunter), Kt 1985; FRS 1952; MA; PhD, ScD (Cambridge); BSc (London); FRSE, FRAS, MRIA; Research Professor of Theoretical Astronomy, University of Sussex, 1966–72, now Emeritus; *b* Dublin, 13 Dec. 1904; *er s* of late Robert Hunter McCrea; *m* 1933, Marian Nicol Core (*d* 1995), 2nd *d* of late Thomas Webster, JP, Burdiehouse, Edinburgh; one *s* two *d*. *Educ:* Chesterfield Grammar Sch.; Trinity Coll., Cambridge (Scholar); University of Göttingen. Wrangler, Rayleigh Prizeman, Sheepshanks Exhibitioner, and Isaac Newton Student, of Cambridge Univ.; Rouse Ball Travelling Student, and Rouse Ball Senior Student, of Trinity Coll.; Comyns Berkeley Bye-Fellow, Gonville and Caius Coll., Cambridge, 1952–53. Lecturer in Mathematics, Univ. of Edinburgh, 1930–32; Reader in Mathematics, Univ. of London, and Assistant Prof., Imperial Coll. of Science, 1932–36; Prof. of Mathematics: Queen's Univ., Belfast, 1936–44; Royal Holloway Coll., Univ. of London, 1944–66 (Hon. Fellow, 1984). Visiting Prof. of Astronomy: Univ. of California, 1956; Case Inst. of Technology, 1964; Univ. of BC, Vancouver, 1975–76; Consulting Astronomer, Kitt Peak National Observatory,

Arizona, 1965, 1975; Royal Society Exchange Visitor: to USSR, 1960, 1968; to Mexico, 1971; to Argentina, 1971, 1983; to India, 1976; to Egypt, 1981; For. Visiting Prof. of American Astronomical Soc. and Vis. Prof., Berkeley Astronomy Dept, 1967; first occupant, Chaire Georges Lemaître, Louvain Univ., 1969; Royal Soc. Leverhulme Vis. Prof. of Astronomy, Cairo Univ., 1973; Vis. Prof., Istanbul Univ., 1977, 1978; William Evans Vis. Prof., Otago Univ., 1979. Visiting Lecturer: Univ. of Liège, 1960; Technische Hochschule, Aachen, 1962; various universities in Greece and Turkey (British Council), 1971; York Univ., 1965; Lectures: Harland, Univ. of Exeter, 1970; Larmor, QUB, 1970; Halley, Oxford, 1975; Milne, Oxford, 1985; R. H. Fowler Meml, Cambridge, 1989. Temp. Prin. Experimental Officer, Admty, 1943–45; commnd RAFVR (Training Branch), 1941–45. Mem., Governing Board of School of Theoretical Physics, Dublin Institute for Advanced Studies, 1940–50; Governor: Royal Holloway Coll., 1946–49; Ottershaw Sch., 1947–52; Barclay Sch. for Partially Sighted Girls, 1949–66; Mem. Adv. Council, Chelsea Coll. of Aeronautical and Automobile Engineering, 1958–86. Secretary of Section A of British Assoc., 1935–39, Pres. 1966; Pres., Mathematical Assoc., 1973–74 (Hon. Mem., 1985). Joint Editor of The Observatory, 1935–37. Pres., Royal Astronomical Soc., 1961–63 (Sec., 1946–49; Foreign Correspondent, 1968–71; Treasurer, 1976–79). Fellow, Imperial Coll., 1967–; Leverhulme Emeritus Fellow, 1973–75. Mem., Akademie Leopoldina, 1972–; Foreign Mem., Turin Acad. of Scis, 1990–. Freeman, City of London, 1988. Keith Prize, RSE, 1939–41; Gold Medal, RAS, 1976. Hon. DSc: National Univ., Ireland, 1954; QUB, 1970; Sussex, 1978; Dr *hc* National Univ., Cordoba, Argentina, 1971; Hon. ScD Dublin, 1972. *Publications:* Relativity Physics, 1935; Analytical Geometry of Three Dimensions, 1942; Physics of the Sun and Stars, 1950; trans. A. Unsöld's The New Cosmos, 1969; Royal Greenwich Observatory, 1975; (jtly) History of the Royal Astronomical Society 1920–1980, 1987; various papers and reviews in mathematical and astronomical journals. *Address:* 87 Houndean Rise, Lewes, East Sussex BN7 1EJ.

McCREERY, His Honour (Henry Edwin) Lewis, QC 1965; a Circuit Judge (formerly Judge of County Courts), 1971–90, retired; *b* 26 July 1920; *s* of late Rev. William John McCreery, BD, and late Anne Cullen McCreery; *m* 1945, Margaret Elizabeth Booth (*d* 1990); two *d. Educ:* St Andrew's Coll., Dublin; Trinity Coll., Dublin. RAF, 1942–47. Called: Irish Bar King's Inns, 1943; English Bar, Middle Temple, 1946 (Bencher, 1971). Dep. Chm., Quarter Sessions: Cornwall, 1966–71; Devon, 1967–71; Recorder of Salisbury, 1969–71. *Recreation:* gardening. *Address:* 110 Clare Park, Crondall, Farnham, Surrey GU10 5DT.

McCRICKARD, Donald Cecil; Chairman, London Town plc, since 1995; Chief Executive: TSB Group plc, 1990–92; TSB Bank plc, 1989–92; *b* 25 Dec. 1936; *s* of late Peter McCrickard and Gladys Mary McCrickard; *m* 1st, 1960, Stella May (marr. diss.), *d* of Walter Edward Buttle, RN retd; two *d*; 2nd, 1991, Angela Victoria Biddulph, *d* of late Robert Biddulph Mitchell and of Mary Buckley Mitchell. *Educ:* Hove Grammar Sch.; LSE; Univ. of Malaya. Financial, marketing and gen. management appts to 1975; Chief Exec., American Express Co. UK, 1975, American Express Co. Asia, Pacific, Australia, 1980; Dir, American Express Internat. Inc., 1978–83; Man. Dir, UDT Holdings, later TSB Commercial Holdings, 1983; Chairman: Swan National, 1983; UDT Bank, 1983; Dir, and Dep. Group Man. Dir, 1987, Chief Exec., Banking, 1988, TSB Group; Chm., Hill Samuel Bank, 1991–92. Non-executive Director: Carlisle Gp, 1993–; Nat. Counties Building Soc., 1995–. Chm., Barnet Enterprise Trust, 1985–88. Trustee: Crimestoppers (formerly Community Action) Trust, 1991–; Industry in Educn, 1993–. *Recreations:* golf, photography, ski-ing, theatre, writing, restaurants. *Club:* Royal Automobile.

MacCRINDLE, Robert Alexander, QC 1963; commercial lawyer; Partner, Shearman and Sterling; *b* 27 Jan. 1928; *s* of F. R. MacCrindle; *m* 1959, Pauline Dilys, *d* of Mark S. Morgan; one *s* one *d. Educ:* Girvan High Sch.; King's Coll., London; Gonville and Caius Coll., Cambridge. LLB London, 1948. Served RAF, 1948–50, Flt-Lt. LLM Cantab, Chancellor's Medal, 1951. Called to Bar, Gray's Inn, 1952 (Bencher, 1969); Junior Counsel to Board of Trade (Export Credits), 1961–63; Mem., Hong Kong Bar, 1967; Avocat, Barreau de Paris, 1991. Mem., Royal Commn on Civil Liability and Compensation for Personal Injury, 1973–78. Hon. Fellow, American Coll. of Trial Lawyers, 1974. *Publication:* McNair's Law of the Air, 1953. *Recreation:* golf. *Address:* Essex Court Chambers, 24 Lincoln's Inn Fields, WC2A 3ED. *T:* 0171–813 8000; 88 avenue de Breteuil, 75015 Paris, France. *T:* (1) 45671193. *Club:* University (New York).

McCRINDLE, Sir Robert (Arthur), Kt 1990; Public Affairs Consultant: Federation of Tour Operators; Board of Airline Representatives in UK; *b* 19 Sept. 1929; *o s* of Thomas Arthur and Isabella McCrindle; *m* 1953, Myra Anderson; two *s. Educ:* Allen Glen's Coll., Glasgow. Vice-Chm., Sausmarez, Carey & Harris, Financial Consultants, 1972–75; Director: Langham Life Assurance Co. Ltd, 1972–76; Worldmark Travel Ltd, 1978–82; Hogg Robinson PLC, 1987–; M & G Assurance Gp, 1988–; London and Edinburgh Insurance Group, 1991–; Bradford and Bingley Bldg Soc., 1991–; Chairman: Cometco Ltd, Commodity Brokers, 1972–78; Citybond Storage, 1975–91. Consultant, British Caledonian Airways, 1984–88. Contested: Dundee (East), 1959; Thurrock, 1964; MP (C) Billericay, 1970–74, Brentwood and Ongar, 1974–92. PPS to Minister of State, Home Office, 1974; Chm., All-Party Parly Aviation Cttee, 1980–92; Mem., Transport Select Cttee, 1988–92. Mem., UK Delegn to N Atlantic Assembly, 1977–92 (Chm., Economic Cttee, 1980–84). Parliamentary Consultant: British Transport Police Fedn, 1974–92; British Insurance and Investment Brokers' Assoc., 1976–92; Guild of Business Travel Agents, 1975–78. Nat. Vice-Pres., Corp. of Mortgage Brokers, 1970–76. Fellow, Corp. of Insurance Brokers; ACII. *Address:* 26 Ashburnham Gardens, Upminster, Essex RM14 1XA. *T:* Upminster (01708) 227152.

McCRIRRICK, (Thomas) Bryce, CBE 1987; FEng 1981; FIEE; Director of Engineering, BBC, 1978–87; *b* 19 July 1927; *s* of late Alexander McCrirrick and Janet McCrirrick (*née* Tweedie); *m* 1953, Margaret Phyllis Yates; three *s. Educ:* Galashiels Academy; Heriot Watt Coll., Edinburgh; Regent Street Polytechnic, London. BBC Radio, Studio Centres in Edinburgh, Glasgow and London, 1943–46; served RAF, 1946–49; BBC Television, 1949; Engineer-in-Charge Television Studios, 1963; Head of Engineering Television Recording, and of Studio Planning and Installation Dept, 1969; Chief Engineer, Radio Broadcasting, 1970; Asst Dir of Engrg, 1971; Dep. Dir of Engrg, 1976. Technical Assessor, Investigation into Clapham Junction Rly Accident, 1989. Pres., Soc. of Electronic and Radio Technicians, 1981–85 (Vice-Pres., 1979–80); Vice-Pres., IERE, 1985–88; Pres., IEE, 1988–89 (Dep. Pres., 1986–88, Vice-Pres., 1982–86; Hon. FIEE 1995); Mem. Council, Fellowship of Engrg, 1989–92. Gov., Imperial Coll., 1985–; Mem. Court, Heriot-Watt Univ., 1991–94; Mem. Senate, London Univ., 1992–94. FRTS 1980; FBKSTS 1982; FSMPTE 1989. Hon. DSc Heriot Watt, 1987. *Recreations:* skiing, theatre. *Address:* Surrey Place, Coach House Gardens, Fleet, Hants GU13 8QX. *T:* Fleet (01252) 623422.

McCRONE, Prof. Robert Gavin Loudon, CB 1983; FRSE 1983; Visiting Professor, Department of Business Studies, since 1994, and Hon. Fellow, Europa Institute, since 1992, University of Edinburgh; *b* 2 Feb. 1933; *s* of Robert Osborne Orr McCrone and Laura Margaret McCrone; *m* 1959, Alexandra Bruce Waddell; two *s* one *d. Educ:* St Catharine's Coll., Cambridge (Economics Tripos; MA); University Coll. of Wales, Aberystwyth (Milk Marketing Bd Research Schol. in agricl economics; MSc 1959); Univ. of Glasgow (PhD 1964). Fisons Ltd, 1959–60; Lectr in Applied Economics, Glasgow Univ., 1960–65; Economic Consultant to UNESCO and Mem. Educnl Planning Mission to Libya, 1964; Fellow of Brasenose Coll., Oxford, 1965–72; Mem. NEDC Working Party on Agricl Policy, 1967–68; Economic Adviser to House of Commons Select Cttee on Scottish Affairs, 1969–70; Special Economic Adviser to Sec. of State for Local Govt and Regional Planning, 1970; Sen. Economic Adviser and Head of Economics and Statistics Unit, 1970–72, Under-Sec. for Regional Develt, 1972–80, Scottish Office; Chief Econ. Advr to Sec. of State for Scotland, 1972–92; Secretary: Industry Dept for Scotland, 1980–87; Scottish Office Envmt Dept (formerly Scottish Develt Dept), 1987–92. Prof. of Applied Econs, Glasgow Univ., 1992–94. Mem., Inquiry into Implementation of Constitutional Reform, 1995–. Dep. Chm., Royal Infirmary of Edinburgh NHS Trust, 1994–. Member Council: Royal Economic Soc., 1977–82; Scottish Economic Soc., 1982–91; ESRC, 1986–89. Mem. Bd, Scottish Opera, 1992–. Trustee, Scottish Housing Assocs Charitable Trust, 1992–. Hon. LLD Glasgow 1986. *Publications:* The Economics of Subsidising Agriculture, 1962; Scotland's Economic Progress 1951–60, 1963; Agricultural Integration in Western Europe, 1963; Regional Policy in Britain, 1969; Scotland's Future, 1969; (with Mark Stephens) Housing Policy in Britain and Europe, 1995; contribs to various economic jls. *Recreations:* music, walking. *Address:* 28 Mansion House Road, Edinburgh EH9 2JD. *T:* 0131–667 6687. *Club:* United Oxford & Cambridge University.

McCRORIE, Linda Esther, (Mrs Peter McCrorie); *see* Gray, L. E.

McCRUM, (John) Robert; publisher and writer; Editor-in-Chief, Faber and Faber Ltd, since 1990; *b* 7 July 1953; *s* of Michael William McCrum, *qv* and Christine Mary Kathleen (*née* fforde); *m* 1st, 1979, Olivia Timbs (marr. diss. 1984); 2nd, 1995, Sarah Lyall. *Educ:* Sherborne Sch.; Corpus Christi Coll., Cambridge (Schol.; BA 1st Cl. Hons Hist.; MA); Univ. of Pennsylvania (Thornton Fellow; MA). House Reader, Chatto & Windus, 1977–79; Editl Dir, Faber and Faber Ltd, 1979–89. Scriptwriter and co-producer, The Story of Engish, BBC TV, 1980–86. Tony Godwin Prize, 1979; Peabody Award, 1986; Emmy Award, 1987. *Publications:* In the Secret State, 1980; A Loss of Heart, 1982; The Fabulous Englishman, 1984; The Story of English, 1986; The World is a Banana, 1988; Mainland, 1991; The Psychological Moment, 1993. *Recreation:* gardening. *Address:* Faber and Faber Ltd, 3 Queen Square, WC1N 3AU. *T:* 0171–465 0045, *Fax:* 0171–465 0034. *Clubs:* Royal Automobile, Groucho.

McCRUM, Michael William, MA; Master of Corpus Christi College, Cambridge, 1980–94; Chairman, Cathedrals Fabric Commission for England, since 1991; *b* 23 May 1924; 3rd *s* of late Captain C. R. McCrum, RN and Ivy Hilda Constance (*née* Nicholson); *m* 1952, Christine Mary Kathleen, *d* of Sir Arthur fforde, GBE; three *s* one *d. Educ:* Horris Hill, Newbury; Sherborne Sch.; Corpus Christi Coll., Cambridge (Hon. Fellow, 1994). Entrance Scholar to CCC, Dec. 1942. Served RN, 1943–45 (Sub-Lt RNVR, Dec. 1943). CCC, Cambridge, 1946–48; Part I, Class. Tripos, First Class, 1947; Part II, First Class, with distinction, 1948. Asst Master, Rugby School, Sept. 1948–July 1950 (Lower Bench Master, 1949–50); Fellow CCC, Cambridge, 1949; Second Tutor, 1950–51; Tutor, 1951–62; Headmaster, Tonbridge Sch. 1962–70; Head Master of Eton, 1970–80; Vice-Chancellor, Cambridge Univ., 1987–89. Lectures: Lansdowne, Univ. of Victoria, BC, 1985; Clayesmore, Blandford Forum, 1986; Lady Margaret's Preacher, Univ. of Cambridge, 1987. Member: Council of the Senate, University of Cambridge, 1955–58, 1981–89; General Board of Faculties, 1957–62, 1987–89; Financial Bd, 1985–89; Chairman: Faculty Bd of Educn, 1981–86, 1990–93; Bd of Extra-Mural Studies, 1982–86, Cambridge. Chairman: HMC, 1974; Joint Educnl Trust, 1984–87; GBA, 1989–94 (Dep. Chm., 1982–89); Member: Oxford and Cambridge Schs Exam. Bd, 1960–62, 1966–87 (Chm., 1981–87); BBC/IBA Central Religious Affairs Cttee, 1965–69; Governing Body, Schools Council, 1969–76 (also mem., various cttees); ISJC, 1982–94 (Dep. Chm., 1989–92; Chm., 1992–94). Governor: Bradfield Coll., 1956–62; Eastbourne Coll., 1960–62; King's Sch., Canterbury, 1980–94; Sherborne Sch., 1980–94; Oakham Sch., 1981–85; United World Coll. of the Atlantic, 1981–94; Rugby Sch., 1982–94. Pres., Cambridge Soc., 1989–. Trustee: King George VI and Queen Elizabeth Foundn of St Catharine's, Cumberland Lodge, 1983–; Nat. Heritage Meml Fund, 1984–90; Cambridge Foundn, 1989–; Henry Fund, 1994–95. Hon. Freeman, Skinners' Co., 1980. Hon. DEd Victoria, BC, 1989. Comendador de la Orden de Isabel la Católica (Spain), 1988. *Publications:* Select Documents of the Principates of the Flavian Emperors AD 68–96 (with A. G. Woodhead), 1961; Thomas Arnold, Head Master, 1989. *Address:* 32 Clarendon Street, Cambridge CB1 1JX. *T:* Cambridge (01223) 353303. *Clubs:* Athenæum, United Oxford & Cambridge University, East India, Devonshire, Sports and Public Schools; Hawks (Cambridge).

See also J. R. McCrum.

McCRUM, Robert; *see* McCrum, J. R.

McCUBBIN, Very Rev. David; Provost and Canon of Cumbrae Cathedral, 1987–94; *b* 2 Nov. 1929; *s* of late David McCubbin and late Annie Robertson Cram (*née* Young). *Educ:* Finnart School; Greenock Academy; King's Coll., London (AKC 1954); St Boniface Coll., Warminster. National service, RAF, 1948–50. Deacon 1955, priest 1956; Curate: Christ Church, Frome, 1955–57; Glastonbury Parish Church, 1957–60; Rector: Holy Trinity, Dunoon, 1960–63; St Peter's, Kirkcaldy, 1963–70; Wallsend (and Surrogate), 1970–79; St John's, Aberdeen, 1979–81; St Bride's, Kelvinside, 1981–87; St Andrew's, Millport, 1987–94; Canon of St John's Cathedral, Oban, 1987–94; Synod Clerk, Diocese of Argyll and The Isles, 1988–95; Hon. Canon, Cathedral of the Holy Spirit, Cumbrae, 1994–. Chm., Prayer Book Soc., Scotland, 1988–91. Trustee of Cumbrae Cathedral and Coll., 1994–. *Recreations:* music, reading, walking. *Address:* 137 Marlborough Avenue, Glasgow G11 7JE. *T:* Glasgow (0141) 357 1553. *Club:* Royal Scottish Automobile (Glasgow).

McCUBBIN, Henry Bell; *b* 15 July 1942; *s* of Henry McCubbin and Agnes (*née* Rankine); *m* 1967, Katie M. Campbell; three *d. Educ:* Allan Glen's Sch., Glasgow. BA Hons Open Univ. Film Cameraman: BBC TV, 1960–77; Grampian TV, 1977–89. MEP (Lab) Scotland NE, 1989–94; contested (Lab) Scotland NE, Eur. Parly elecns, 1994. *Recreations:* theatre, hill walking, politics.

McCULLAGH, Prof. Peter, PhD; FRS 1994; Professor, Department of Statistics, since 1985 and Chairman, Department of Statistics, since 1992, University of Chicago; *b* N Ireland, 8 Jan. 1952; *s* of John A. McCullagh and Rita McCullagh (*née* Devlin); *m* 1977, Rosa Bogues; one *s* three *d. Educ:* Univ. of Birmingham (BSc 1974); Imperial Coll., London, (PhD 1977). Vis. Asst Prof., Univ. of Chicago, 1977–79; Lectr, Imperial Coll., 1979–85. FIMS, FAAAS. President's Award, Cttee of Presidents of Statistical Socs of N Amer., 1990. *Publications:* Generalized Linear Models (with J. A. Nelder), 1983, 2nd edn 1989; Tensor Methods in Statistics, 1987. *Recreation:* swimming. *Address:* Department of Statistics, University of Chicago, 5734 University Avenue, Chicago, IL 60637, USA. *T:* (312) 7028340.

McCULLIN, Donald, CBE 1993; freelance photojournalist; *b* 9 Oct. 1935; *m* 1959 (marr. diss. 1987); two *s* one *d*; and one *s* by Laraine Ashton. *Educ:* Tollington Park Secondary Sch., Morden; Hammersmith Jun. Art Sch. Started work at 15 yrs of age after death of father; National Service (RAF), 1954–56; first pictures published by The Observer, 1958;

thereafter began photographic career; worked for The Sunday Times for 18 yrs, covering wars, revolutions and travel stories. Hon. FRPS 1977. DUniv Bradford, 1993; Hon. MA Open, 1994. *Publications:* Destruction Business, 1971; Is Anyone Taking Any Notice, 1971; The Palestinians, 1979; Homecoming, 1979; Hearts of Darkness, 1980; Battle Beirut, a City in Crisis, 1983; Perspectives, 1987; Skulduggery, 1987; Open Skies, 1989; (with Lewis Chester) Unreasonable Behaviour (autobiog.), 1990; Sleeping with Ghosts, 1995. *Recreations:* protecting the English countryside, travelling the world.

MacCULLOCH, Dr Malcolm John, MD; DPM; FRCPsych; Research Psychiatrist, Ashworth Hospital, Merseyside, since 1990; *b* 10 July 1936; *s* of William MacCulloch and Constance Martha MacCulloch; *m* 1962, Mary Louise Beton (marr. diss. 1975); one *s* one *d*; *m* 1975, Carolyn Mary Reid; two *d*. *Educ:* King Edward VII Sch., Macclesfield, Cheshire; Manchester Univ. (MB, ChB, DPM, MD). Consultant Child Psychiatrist, Cheshire Child Guidance Service, 1966–67; Director Univ. Dept, Child Psychiatry and Subnormality, Birmingham Univ., 1967–70; Sen. Lectr, Adult Psychiatry, Univ. of Liverpool, 1970–75; PMO, DHSS, 1975–78; SPMO, Mental Health Div., DHSS, 1979–80; Dir. Special Hosps Res. Unit, London, 1979–86; Med. Dir, Park Lane Hosp., Liverpool, 1979–89; Advr to Ontario Govt on Forensic Psychiatric Services, 1988–. Vis. Prof., Clarke Inst. of Psychiatry, Toronto, 1987–88. *Publications:* Homosexual Behaviour: therapy and assessment, 1971; Human Sexual Behaviour, 1980; numerous med. papers on aspects of psychiatry. *Recreations:* inventing, playing music. *Address:* Ashworth Hospital, Parkbourne, Merseyside L31 1HW. *T:* 0151–520 2244.

McCULLOCH, Rt. Rev. Nigel Simeon; *see* Wakefield, Bishop of.

McCULLOUGH, Hon. Sir Charles, Kt 1981; **Hon. Mr Justice McCullough;** a Judge of the High Court of Justice, Queen's Bench Division, since 1981; *b* 1931. Called to Bar, Middle Temple, 1956, Bencher, 1980. Midland Circuit, 1957–71, Midland and Oxford Circuit, 1972–81; Dep. Chm., Notts QS, 1969–71; QC 1971; a Recorder of the Crown Court, 1972–81. Member: Criminal Law Revision Cttee, 1973–; Parole Bd, 1984–86. *Address:* Royal Courts of Justice, Strand, WC2A 2LL.

McCURLEY, Anna Anderson; Head of Government Affairs, Corporate Communications Strategy, since 1990; *b* 18 Jan. 1943; *d* of George Gemmell and Mary (*née* Anderson); *m* (marr. diss.); one *d*. *Educ:* Glasgow High Sch. for Girls; Glasgow Univ. (MA); Jordanhill Coll. of Educn (Dip. in Secondary Educn); Strathclyde Univ. Secondary history teacher, 1966–72; College Methods Tutor, Jordanhill Coll. of Educn, 1972–74. Strathclyde Regional Councillor, Camphill/Pollokshaws Div., 1978–82. Sen. Exec., Dewe Rogerson, 1987–89. Contested (C) Renfrew W and Inverclyde, 1987. MP (C) Renfrew W and Inverclyde, 1983–87. Mem., Scottish Select Cttee, 1984–87. Mem., Horserace Betting Levy Bd, 1988–. *Recreations:* music, cookery, painting in oils. *Address:* Woodsley, 12 Shore Road, Skelmorlie PA17 5DY.

McCUSKER, Sir James (Alexander), Kt 1983; Founder, Town and Country Permanent Building Society, 1964, Foundation Chairman 1964–83; *b* Perth, WA, 2 Dec. 1913; *m* Mary Martindale McCusker; three *c*. *Educ:* Perth Modern Sch. Served War of 1939–45, 2½ years with 1st Armoured Div. (Sgt). 30 years with Commonwealth Bank of Aust.; resigned 1959, as Sen. Branch Manager in Perth. Chm., State Cttee of Inquiry into Rates and Taxes, 1980. Councillor: WA Permanent Building Socs Assoc., 1964–83 (former Pres.); Aust. Assoc. of Permanent Building Socs; Fellow, Aust. Inst. of Valuers; Member: Council of Rural and Allied Industries; WA Indicative Planning Cttee (Housing). Patron, Paraplegic Assoc. of WA. *Address:* 47 Birdwood Parade, Dalkeith, WA 6009, Australia.

McCUTCHEON, Prof. John Joseph, CBE 1994; PhD, DSc; FFA; FRSE; Professor of Actuarial Studies, Heriot-Watt University, since 1975; *b* 10 Sept. 1940; *s* of James Thomson McCutcheon and Margaret (*née* Hutchison); *m* 1978, Jean Sylvia Constable. *Educ:* Glasgow Acad.; St John's Coll., Cambridge (MA); Univ. of Liverpool (PhD, DSc). FFA 1965. Scottish Amicable Life Assce Soc., 1962–65; Consulting Actuary, Duncan C. Fraser and Co., 1965–66; Demonstrator in Pure Maths, Univ. of Liverpool, 1966–70; Associate Prof., Univ. of Manitoba, 1970–72; Sen. Lectr, Heriot-Watt Univ., 1972–75. Pres., Faculty of Actuaries in Scotland, 1992–94. FRSE 1993. *Publications:* (with W. F. Scott) An Introduction to the Mathematics of Finance, 1986; various papers on mathematics, actuarial science, mortality studies. *Recreations:* tennis, ski-ing, opera, reading, travel. *Address:* Department of Actuarial Mathematics and Statistics, Heriot-Watt University, Edinburgh EH14 4AS. *T:* 0131–451 3202.

McCUTCHEON, Dr William Alan, FSA, MRIA; author, lecturer and consultant; School Teacher (Geography Specialist), Ditcham Park School, Petersfield, 1986–93, retired; *b* 2 March 1934; *s* of late William John and Margaret Elizabeth McCutcheon; *m* 1956, Margaret Craig; three *s*. *Educ:* Royal Belfast Academical Instn; The Queen's University of Belfast (Hugh Wisnom Scholar, 1960; BA (Hons Geog.) 1955, MA 1958, PhD 1962). FRGS (1958–94); FSA 1970; MRIA 1983. School Teacher (Geography Specialist), Royal Belfast Academical Instn, 1956–62; Director, N Ireland Survey of Industrial Archaeology, 1962–68; Keeper of Technology and Local History, Ulster Museum, Belfast, 1968–77; Dir, Ulster Museum, 1977–82. Vis. Teacher, Glenalmond Coll., 1984, 1986. Chairman: Historic Monuments Council (NI), 1980–85; Jt Cttee on Industrial Archaeology (NI), 1981–85; Member: Malcolm Cttee on Regional Museums in Northern Ireland, 1977–78; Industrial Archaeol. Cttee, Council for British Archaeol., 1981–85. *Publications:* The Canals of the North of Ireland, 1965; Railway History in Pictures, Ireland: vol. 1 1970, vol. 2 1971; (contrib.) Travel and Transport in Ireland, 1973; (contrib.) Folk & Farm, 1976; Wheel and Spindle—Aspects of Irish Industrial History, 1977; The Industrial Archaeology of Northern Ireland, 1980 (Library Assoc. high commendation as an outstanding reference book); (contrib.) Some People and Places in Irish Science and Technology, 1985; (contrib.) An Economic and Social History of Ulster 1820–1939, 1985; numerous papers. *Recreations:* reading, classical music, photography, travel, gardening, swimming. *Address:* 11 The Meadow, Groomsport, Bangor, Co. Down BT19 6JH. *T:* Bangor (01247) 273018.

McDERMID, Ven. Norman George Lloyd Roberts; Archdeacon of Richmond, 1983–93, Emeritus since 1993; *b* 5 March 1927; *s* of Lloyd Roberts McDermid and Annie McDermid; *m* 1953, Vera Wood; one *s* three *d*. *Educ:* St Peter's School, York; St Edmund Hall, Oxford (MA); Wells Theological Coll. Deacon 1951, priest 1952; Curate of Leeds, 1951–56, in charge of St Mary, Quarry Hill, Leeds, 1953–56; Vicar of Bramley, Leeds, 1956–64; Rector of Kirkby Overblow, 1964–80; Stewardship Adviser, Ripon Diocese, 1964–76, Bradford and Wakefield, 1973–76; Vicar of Knaresborough, 1980–83. Hon. Canon of Ripon Cathedral, 1972–93, Emeritus 1993–; RD of Harrogate, 1977–83. Member: General Synod, 1970–93; Church of England Pensions Bd, 1972–78; Redundant Churches Fund, 1977–89; Central Bd of Finance of C of E, 1985–93. Church Commissioner, 1978–83. Chairman: Ripon Diocesan House of Clergy, 1981–93; Ripon Diocesan Bd of Finance, 1988–93. Mem., N Yorks County Educn Cttee, 1993–. *Recreations:* investment, historic churches, pedigree cattle, gardening. *Address:* Greystones, 10 North End, Bedale, N Yorks DL8 1AB. *T:* Bedale (01677) 422210. *Club:* National Liberal.

MacDERMOT, Brian (Charles), CBE 1966; LVO 1961; HM Diplomatic Service, retired; *b* 29 Jan. 1914; *m* 1949, Mary Arden Hunter; seven *s* two *d*. Probationer Vice-Consul, Peking, China, 1936; served at: Hankow, China, 1939–40; Kobe, Japan, 1940–41; Kunming, South China, 1942; Vice-Consul, Shiraz, Persia, 1943; Paris, 1944, promoted Consul, 1945; Foreign Office, 1946; Consul, Beirut, 1948; First Secretary, Belgrade, 1950; First Secretary, Berne, 1951, acted as Charge d'Affaires, 1951, 1952, 1953; transferred to Foreign Office, 1954; transferred to Holy See, 1955, acted as Chargé d'Affaires, 1958, 1959, 1960 and 1961; HM Consul-General, Oporto, 1962–68; Ambassador and Consul-Gen., Paraguay, 1968–72. *Address:* Little Orchard, Wetherden, Stowmarket, Suffolk IP14 3LY.

MACDERMOT, Niall, CBE 1991 (OBE (mil.) 1944); QC 1963; barrister-at-law; Secretary-General, International Commission of Jurists, 1970–90; *b* 10 Sept. 1916; *s* of late Henry MacDermot, KC, Dublin; *m* 1940, Violet Denise Maxwell (marr. diss.); one *s*; *m* 1966, Ludmila Benvenuto. *Educ:* Rugby Sch.; Corpus Christi Coll., Cambridge; Balliol Coll., Oxford. Served in Intelligence Corps, 1939–46; GSO1 HQ 21 Army Group, 1944–45. MP (Lab) Lewisham North, Feb. 1957–59, Derby North, April 1962–1970; Mem. Exec., London Labour Party, 1958–62. Dep. Chm., Beds QS, 1961–64, 1969–72; Recorder of Newark-on-Trent, 1963–64; a Recorder of the Crown Court, 1972–74. Master of the Bench, Inner Temple, 1970–. Financial Sec., Treasury, 1964–67; Minister of State, Min. of Housing and Local Govt, 1967–68. Hon. Treasurer, Justice, 1968–70. Member: Council, Internat. Inst. of Human Rights, Strasbourg, 1972–; Adv. Council, Interights, 1984–; Bd, Internat. Alert, 1985–; Pres., Special NGO Cttee on Human Rights, Geneva, 1973–86, Vice-Pres., 1986–. Founding Mem., Groupe de Bellerive, 1977–. Trustee of Tate Gall., 1969–76. *Address:* 34 avenue Weber, 1208 Geneva, Switzerland. *T:* (22) 354086.

MacDERMOTT, Edmond Geoffrey; Metropolitan Stipendiary Magistrate, 1972–84. Called to Bar, Gray's Inn, 1935; Dept of Dir of Public Prosecutions, 1946–72; Asst Dir of Public Prosecutions, 1968–72.

McDERMOTT, Sir Emmet; *see* McDermott, Sir L. E.

MacDERMOTT, Rt. Hon. Sir John Clarke, Kt 1987; PC 1987; **Rt. Hon. Lord Justice MacDermott;** a Lord Justice of Appeal, Supreme Court of Judicature, Northern Ireland, since 1987; *b* 1927; *s* of Baron MacDermott, PC, PC (NI), MC, and of Louise Palmer, *o d* of Rev. J. C. Johnston, DD; *m* 1953, Margaret Helen, *d* of late Hugh Dales, Belfast; four *d*. *Educ:* Campbell Coll., Belfast; Trinity Hall, Cambridge (BA); QUB. Called to Bar, Inner Temple and Northern Ireland, 1949; QC (NI) 1964. Judge, High Court of NI, 1973–87. *Address:* Royal Courts of Justice, Belfast, Northern Ireland BT1 3JF; 6 Tarawood, Holywood, Co. Down BT18 0HS.

McDERMOTT, Sir (Lawrence) Emmet, KBE 1972; Lord Mayor of Sydney, 1969–72; Alderman, Sydney, 1962–77; Dental Surgeon; *b* 6 Sept. 1911; *s* of O. J. McDermott; *m* 1st, 1939, Arline Beatrice Olga (*d* 1987); one *s* one *d*; 2nd, 1992, Eula Macdonald, *d* of Robert Murray Ross. *Educ:* St Ignatius Coll., Sydney; Univ. of Sydney; Northwestern Univ., Chicago. MDS Sydney; DDS Northwestern; FICD, FRACDS, FACD; FAIM 1983. Hon. Consultant Dental Surgeon: Royal Prince Alfred Hosp., 1942–; Eastern Suburbs Hosp., 1945–; Pres., Bd of Control, United Dental Hosp., Sydney, 1967–79; Mem., NSW Dental Bd, 1967–79; Pres., Australian Dental Assoc. (NSW Br.), 1960–61; Councillor, Australian Dental Assoc., 1962–66. Mem., Liberal Party State Council, 1969; Councillor, Sydney County Council, 1973–80, Dep. Chm., 1975–77, Chm., 1977–78. Dir, City Mutual Life Assce Soc. Ltd, 1970–85, Dep. Chm., 1976–85; Member: Sydney Cove Redevelopment Authority, 1971–76; Convocation, Macquarie Univ., 1966–94; Australia-Britain Soc. (NSW Br.), Vice-Pres., 1972–77. *Recreations:* golf, swimming (Sydney Univ. Blue), bowls. *Address:* 61 Fiddens Wharf Road, Killara, NSW 2071, Australia. *T:* (2) 4984382. *Clubs:* Royal Sydney Golf, Tattersall's, Chatswood Bowling, City Bowling (all Sydney).

McDERMOTT, Patrick Anthony, MVO 1972; HM Diplomatic Service; Counsellor, Paris, since 1990; *b* 8 Sept. 1941; *e s* of Patrick McDermott and Eileen (*née* Lyons); *m* 1976, Christa, *d* of Emil and Anne-Marie Herminghaus, Krefeld, W Germany; two *s*, and two *s* by previous *m*. *Educ:* Clapham College, London. FO 1960; Mexico City, 1963; Attaché, UK Delegn to UN, NY, 1966; Vice-Consul, Belgrade, 1971; FCO, 1973; Second Sec., Bonn, 1973; First Sec., Paris, 1976; FCO, 1979; Consul-Gen., and Econ. and Financial Advr to British Military Government, W Berlin, 1984; FCO, 1988. Freeman, City of London, 1986. *Address:* c/o Foreign and Commonwealth Office, SW1A 2AH.

MacDONAGH, Lesley Anne; Managing Partner, Lovell White Durrant, since 1995; *b* 19 April 1952; *d* of Arthur George Payne and Agnes Dowie Scott; *m* 1st, 1975, John Belton (marr. diss. 1985); one *d*; 2nd, 1987, Simon Michael Peter MacDonagh; two *s*. *Educ:* Queen Elizabeth I Sch., Wimborne; College of Law, Guildford and London. Admitted Solicitor, 1976; Partner, Lovell White Durrant, 1981–. Member: Council, Law Society, 1992– (Mem., Planning and Envtl Cttee, 1988–95); Lands Tribunal Consultative Cttee, 1991–95; Property Adv. Gp, 1993–. Trustee, Citizenship Foundn, 1991–. Vice-Chm., Envt Cttee, Knightsbridge Assoc., 1991–. Liveryman, Solicitors' Co. *Recreations:* family life, painting, drawing, dining. *Address:* Lovell White Durrant, 65 Holborn Viaduct, EC1A 2DY. *T:* 0171–236 0066.

MacDONAGH, Prof. Oliver Ormond Gerard; W. K. Hancock Professor of History, Australian National University, 1973, now Emeritus; *b* 23 Aug. 1924; *s* of Michael A. MacDonagh and Loretto (*née* Oliver); *m* 1952, Mary Carmel Hamilton; three *s* four *d*. *Educ:* Clongowes Wood Coll., Co. Kildare; University Coll. Dublin (MA); King's Inns, Dublin (BL); Univ. of Cambridge (PhD). Fellow, St Catharine's Coll., Cambridge, 1952–64, Vis. Fellow, 1986, Hon. Fellow, 1987; Foundn Prof. of History, Flinders Univ., SA, 1964–68; Prof. of Modern History, UC, Cork, 1968–73. Vis. Prof., Yale Univ., 1970; Overseas Schol., St John's Coll., Cambridge, 1981; Parnell Sen. Res. Fellow, Magdalene Coll., Cambridge, 1993–94; Res. Prof., Australian Catholic Univ., 1994–95. FASSA 1965; FAHA 1977; Corresp. FBA 1984; Hon. MRIA 1993. Hon. LittD: Flinders, 1982; Sydney, 1989; NUI, 1989. *Publications:* A Pattern of Government Growth, 1961, 2nd edn 1993; Ireland: the Union and its Aftermath, 1968, 2nd edn 1977; English Victorian Government, 1977; The Inspector-General, 1981; States of Mind, 1983, 2nd edn 1985; The Hereditary Bondsman: Daniel O'Connell 1775–1829, 1987; The Emancipist: Daniel O'Connell 1830–1847, 1989; Jane Austen: Real and Imagined Worlds, 1991; The Life of Daniel O'Connell 1775–1847, 1991. *Recreations:* watching Rugby, Nineteenth Century novels. *Address:* 9B Crescent Street, Fairlight, NSW 2094, Australia. *T:* Sydney (2) 9497824.

MACDONALD, family name of **Barons Macdonald** and **Macdonald of Gwaenysgor.**

MACDONALD, 8th Baron *cr* 1776; **Godfrey James Macdonald of Macdonald;** JP; DL; Chief of the Name and Arms of Macdonald; *b* 28 Nov. 1947; *s* of 7th Baron Macdonald, MBE, TD, and Anne (*d* 1988), *o d* of late Alfred Whitaker; *S* father, 1970; *m* 1969, Claire, *e d* of Captain T. N. Catlow, CBE, RN, Gabriel Cottage, Tunstall, Lancs; one *s* three *d*. JP Skye and Lochalsh, 1979; DL Ross and Cromarty, Skye and Lochalsh,

1986. *Heir: s* Hon. Godfrey Evan Hugo Thomas Macdonald of Macdonald, yr, *b* 24 Feb. 1982. *Address:* Kinloch Lodge, Isle of Skye. *Club:* New (Edinburgh).

McDONALD, Hon. Lord; Robert Howat McDonald, MC 1944; a Senator of the College of Justice in Scotland, 1973–89; *b* 15 May 1916; *s* of Robert Glassford McDonald, and Roberta May Howat, Paisley, Renfrewshire; *m* 1949, Barbara Mackenzie, *d* of John Mackenzie, Badcaul, Ross-shire; no *c. Educ:* John Neilson Institution, Paisley. MA (Glasgow) 1935; LLB (Glasgow) 1937; admitted Faculty of Advocates, 1946; QC (Scot.) 1957. Served with KOSB, 1939–46 (despatches, 1945). Sheriff Principal of Ayr and Bute, 1966–71. Mem., Criminal Injuries Compensation Board, 1964–71; Pres., Industrial Tribunals for Scotland, 1972–73; Chm., Gen. Nursing Council for Scotland, 1970–73; Chm., Mental Welfare Commn for Scotland, 1965–83; Mem., Employment Appeal Tribunal, 1976–86. Chm., Queen's Nursing Inst., Scotland, 1981–93. *Address:* 5 Doune Terrace, Edinburgh EH3 6EA. *Club:* New (Edinburgh).

MACDONALD OF GWAENYSGOR, 2nd Baron *cr* 1949, of Gwaenysgor, Flint; **Gordon Ramsay Macdonald;** business consultant; *b* 16 Oct. 1915; *er s* of 1st Baron Macdonald of Gwaenysgor, PC, KCMG; *S* father, 1966; *m* 1941, Leslie Margaret Taylor; three *d. Educ:* Manchester Univ. MA, Economics and Commerce. Served War, 1940–46; Army, Major, Artillery; GSO2 Operations and Intelligence (despatches, Burma). Board of Trade, 1946–53: Principal, 1946–47; UK Trade Comr, Canberra, ACT, 1947–53. With Tube Investments Ltd, and Man. Dir TI (Export) Ltd, 1953–64; Chief Exec., Telecommunications Group, Plessey Co., 1964–67; Chm., Hayek Engrg (UK) Ltd, 1967–76; Chm. and Chief Exec., Ferro Metal and Chemical Comp., and Satra Consultants (UK) Ltd, 1977. *Recreations:* golf, chess. *Heir:* none. *Address:* c/o House of Lords, SW1A 0PW.

MACDONALD of Sleat (Btcy); *see under* Bosville Macdonald.

MACDONALD, Alastair John Peter, CB 1989; Deputy Secretary, Department of Trade and Industry, since 1992; *b* 11 Aug. 1940; *s* of late Ewen Macdonald and Hettie Macdonald; *m* 1969, Jane, *d* of late T. R. Morris; one *s* two *d. Educ:* Wimbledon Coll.; Trinity Coll., Oxford. Editorial staff of Spectator, 1962; Financial Times, 1963–68: Washington DC, 1965–66; Features Editor, 1966–68; joined Home Civil Service as Asst Principal, DEA, 1968; Principal, DTI, 1971; Sec., Lord Devlin's Commn into Industrial and Commercial Representation, 1971–72; Asst Sec., DoI, 1975; RCDS, 1980; Under Sec., DTI, 1981. Dep. Sec., DTI, 1985–90; Dep. Under Sec. of State, MoD (PE), 1990–92. Non-exec. Dir, Rank Leisure Ltd (subsid. of Rank Organisation), 1981–85. *Address:* Department of Trade and Industry, 151 Buckingham Palace Road, SW1W 9SS.

McDONALD, Prof. Alexander John, MA (Cantab), LLB, WS; Professor of Conveyancing, University of Dundee (formerly Queen's College), 1955–82, now Emeritus (Dean of the Faculty of Law, 1958–62, 1965); Senior Partner, Thornton, Dickie & Brand, WS, Dundee, 1978–84, now Consultant to Thorntons, WS; *b* 15 March 1919; *o s* of late John McDonald, and Agnes Mary Stewart McDonald; *m* 1951, Doreen Mary, *o d* of late Frank Cook, OBE; two *s* two *d. Educ:* Cargilfield Sch.; Fettes Coll. (open scholar); Christ's Coll., Cambridge (Classical Exhibn, BA 1942); Edinburgh Univ. (Thow Schol. and John Robertson Prize in Conveyancing; LLB with dist., 1949). Admitted as Solicitor and Writer to the Signet, 1950; Lectr in Conveyancing, Edinburgh Univ., 1952–55. *Publications:* Conveyancing Case Notes, 1981, 2nd edn 1984; Conveyancing Manual, 1982, 5th edn 1993; Registration of Title Manual, 1986. *Address:* 1 Regent Place, Broughty Ferry, Dundee DD5 1AT. *T:* Dundee (01382) 477301.

McDONALD, Alistair; Economic Development Officer, Wandsworth Borough Council, 1983–89; *b* 13 March 1925; *e s* of late John Bell McDonald and Mary McDonald; *m* 1954, Isabel Margaret Milne; two *d. Educ:* Fraserburgh Academy; Aberdeen Univ. (BSc 1st Cl. Hons Natural Philosophy). Served RAF and Fleet Air Arm, 1943–46. Malayan Meteorological Service, 1950–56; ICI, 1956–66; Min. of Technology, 1966–70; Dept of Trade and Industry, 1970–74; Dept of Industry, 1974–77; Director, British Shipbuilders (on secondment), 1977–79; Regional Dir, NW Region, Dept of Industry, 1979–83. *Recreation:* golf.

MacDONALD, Alistair Archibald, MA, LLB; DL; Chairman, Social Security Appeal Tribunal and Medical Appeal Tribunal, since 1992; Sheriff of Grampian, Highland and Islands at Lerwick and Kirkwall, 1975–92; *b* 8 May 1927; *s* of James and Margaret MacDonald; *m* 1950, Jill Russell; one *s* one *d. Educ:* Broughton Sch.; Edinburgh Univ. Served in Army, 1945–48. Called to Scottish Bar, 1954. Formerly Sheriff Substitute, Caithness, Sutherland, Orkney and Zetland at Lerwick, 1961 and at Kirkwall, 1968. DL Shetland Islands, 1986. KHS 1988. *Address:* West Hall, Shetland Islands ZE1 0RN. *Club:* Royal Northern (Aberdeen).

MACDONALD, Alistair H.; Deputy Secretary, Equipment Leasing Association, 1971–87, retired; *b* 18 May 1925. *Educ:* Dulwich Coll.; Enfield Technical Coll.; Corpus Christi Coll., Cambridge. MP (Lab) Chislehurst, 1966–70. Councillor, Chislehurst and Sidcup UDC, 1958–62; Alderman, 1964–68, Councillor, 1971–90, London Borough of Bromley. *Address:* 1 Springbourne Court, The Avenue, Beckenham, Kent BR3 2ED. *T:* 0181–658 6953.

McDONALD, Allan Stuart; Headmaster, George Heriot's School, Edinburgh, 1970–83; *b* 20 Aug. 1922; *s* of Allan McDonald and Clementina Peebles (*née* Stuart), both of Edinburgh; *m* 1948, Margaret Wilson, *d* of late James Adams, Paisley and Stranraer, and of Margaret Wilson (*née* Ferguson); one *s* two *d. Educ:* Royal High Sch., Edinburgh; Giffnock and Eastwood Schs, Renfrewshire; Glasgow Univ.; Sorbonne. MA Hons 1944; DipEd 1948. Commnd, Royal Corps of Signals (21st Army Group Signals), 1943–45. Asst Master: Johnstone High Sch., 1948–50; Eastwood Sch., 1950–54; Principal Teacher: Modern Languages, Fortrose Acad., 1954–59; German, George Heriot's Sch., 1959–70; Depute Headmaster, George Heriot's Sch., 1967–70. *Recreations:* formerly Rugby, cricket; now gardening, photography. *Address:* 1 The Grove, Maxwell Park, Dalbeattie DG5 4LY. *T:* Dalbeattie (01556) 611231.

MACDONALD, Angus Cameron; His Honour Judge Macdonald; a Circuit Judge, since 1979; *b* 26 Aug. 1931; *o s* of late Hugh Macdonald, OBE, and of Margaret Cameron Macdonald (*née* Westley); *m* 1956, Deborah Anne, *d* of late John Denny Inglis, DSO, MC, JP, and of Deborah Margery Meiklem Inglis (*née* Thomson); three *d. Educ:* Bedford Sch.; Trinity Hall, Cambridge (BA 1954, MA 1960). Nat. service, 1950–51, commissioned, TA, 1951–57. Called to Bar, Gray's Inn, 1955; Resident Magistrate, then Crown Counsel, Nyasaland Govt, 1957–65; Sen. State Counsel, Malawi Govt, 1965–67; practised, NE Circuit, 1967–79; a Recorder of the Crown Court, 1974–79. *Recreations:* singing, fishing, shooting. *Address:* Newcastle upon Tyne Law Courts, Quayside, Newcastle upon Tyne NE1 2LA. *T:* 091–201 2000. *Club:* Northern Counties (Newcastle upon Tyne).

MACDONALD, Angus John, (Gus); Managing Director, Scottish Television, since 1990 (Director of Programmes, 1985–90); Visiting Professor, Film and Media Studies, Stirling University, since 1985; *b* 20 Aug. 1940; *s* of Colin Macdonald and Jean (*née* Livingstone); *m* 1963, Theresa McQuaid; two *d. Educ:* Allan Glen's Sch., Glasgow. Marine fitter, 1955–63; Circulation Manager, Tribune, 1963–65; feature writer, The Scotsman, 1965–66; Editor, Financial Scotsman, 1966–67; Granada Television: Editor/Exec. Producer, World in Action, 1969–75; successively Head of Current Affairs, Regl Progs, Features, 1975–82; presenter, variously, Camera, Devil's Advocate, Granada 500, Party conferences, What the Papers Say, World in Action, Union World; ombudsman, Right to Reply (viewers' complaints about independent television), Channel Four, 1982–88. Chairman: Scottish Television Enterprises, 1992–; TVMM Airtime Sales House, 1992–93; Time Exchange, 1993–94; Director: GMTV, 1991–; Pauline Hyde & Associates, 1990–95. Chairman: (Founder), Edinburgh Internat. Television Festival, 1976; Edinburgh Film Fest., 1994–; Council of Edinburgh Film and Television Festivals, 1993–; Co-Chm., BAFTA-Scotland, 1991–; Chm., ITV Broadcasting Bd, 1992–94; Mem., Press and Broadcasting Adv. Cttee, MoD, 1994–. Vice Pres., RTS, 1994–. Gov. Nat. Film and Television Sch., 1986–. FRSA 1989. DUniv Stirling, 1992. BAFTA Award, Best Factual Series (World In Action), 1973; Nat. Viewers and Listeners Assoc. Award for Services to Television, 1984; Scottish Business Elite Award, Services Sector, 1993. *Publications:* The Documentary Idea and Television Today, 1977; Camera: Victorian eyewitness, 1979. *Recreations:* stories, pictures, sports, hills. *Address:* Scottish Television, Cowcaddens, Glasgow G2 3PR. *T:* 0141–332 9999. *Clubs:* Reform, Royal Automobile.

MACDONALD, Angus Stewart, CBE 1985; DL; FRAgS; farmer; *b* 7 April 1935; *s* of Angus Macdonald and Mary Macdonald (*née* Anderson); *m* 1959, Janet Ann Somerville; three *s. Educ:* Conon Bridge School; Gordonstoun School. FRAgS 1982. Director: British Wool Marketing Board and Associated Cos, 1974–; Scottish English Welsh Wool Growers, 1974–; Grampian Television, 1980–. Chairman: Dingwall Auction Mart (formerly Reith & Anderson (Tain & Dingwall) Ltd), 1991–; SCOTVEC, Sector Bd 1, 1989–93. Chairman: RHAS, 1978–79; Scottish Agricl Develt Council, 1980–86; Member: Highlands & Islands Enterprise (formerly Develt Bd), 1980–; Panel of Agricl Arbiters, 1976–. Crown Estate Comr, 1990–. Mem. Queen's Body Guard for Scotland (Royal Co. of Archers), 1985–. Trustee: MacRobert Trust, 1982–; Moredun Animal Health Trust Fund, 1990–. Governor: Gordonstoun School (Chm., 1989–); Aberlour School, 1979–. DL Ross and Cromarty, 1984. *Recreations:* field sports. *Address:* Torgorm, Conon Bridge, Dingwall, Ross-shire IV7 8DN. *T:* Dingwall (01349) 61365. *Club:* Caledonian.

McDONALD, Air Marshal Sir Arthur (William Baynes), KCB 1958 (CB 1949); AFC 1938; CEng, FRAeS 1959; DL; retired; *b* 14 June 1903; *s* of late Dr Will McDonald, OBE, Antigua, BWI; *m* 1928, Mary Julia Gray, Hindhead, Surrey; two *s* two *d. Educ:* Antigua Grammar Sch.; Epsom Coll.; Peterhouse, Cambridge (MA). Joined RAF, 1924; served in Singapore, 1933–35; in Air Ministry, 1939–40; Fighter Command, 1941. Appointed Air Defence Commander, Ceylon, 1942; Air Officer Training, Air HQ, India, 1943–44; Air Officer Commanding No. 106 Group, 1945–46; Comdt RAF Staff Coll., Bulstrode and later Andover, 1947–48; Student Imperial Defence Coll., 1949; OC Aeroplane and Armament Experimental Establishment, under the Ministry of Supply, 1950–52; Director-General of Manning, Air Ministry, 1952–55; Commander-in-Chief, Royal Pakistan Air Force, 1955–57; AOC-in-C, RAF Technical Training Comd, 1958–59; Air Mem. for Personnel, Air Council, 1959–61, retired 1962. DL Hampshire, 1965. *Recreation:* sailing (rep. Great Britain in Olympic Games, 1948). *Clubs:* Royal Air Force; Royal Lymington Yacht; RAF Sailing Association (Adm.).

MACDONALD, Dr Calum Alasdair; MP (Lab) Western Isles, since 1987; *b* 7 May 1956; *s* of Malcolm and Donella Macdonald. *Educ:* Bayble Sch.; The Nicolson Inst.; Edinburgh Univ.; Univ. of California at Los Angeles (PhD). Member: TGWU; Crofters Union. *Address:* House of Commons, SW1A 0AA; 28 Francis Street, Stornoway, Isle of Lewis. *T:* Stornoway (01851) 704684.

MACDONALD, Charles Adam; QC 1992; *b* 31 Aug. 1949; *s* of Alasdair Cameron Macdonald, VRD, MB ChB, FRCP, FRCPGlas and Jessie Catherine Macdonald, BA; *m* 1978, Dinah Jane Manns; three *d. Educ:* Glasgow Academy; New Coll., Oxford (MA Hons Jurisp.). Called to the Bar, Lincoln's Inn, 1972. Gen. Editor, Internat. Maritime Law, 1994–. *Recreation:* family life. *Address:* 4 Essex Court, Temple, EC4Y 9AJ. *T:* 0171–797 7970.

MacDONALD, Colin Cameron; Under Secretary and Principal Establishment Officer, Scottish Office, since 1992; *b* 13 July 1943; *s* of Captain Colin D. C. MacDonald and Ann MacDonald (*née* Hough); *m* 1969, Kathryn Mary Campbell. *Educ:* Allan Glen's Sch., Glasgow; Univ. of Strathclyde (BA Hons Econ. 1967). Scottish Development Department, 1967–92: Asst Sec., Housing Div., 1988–91, Management Orgn, 1991–92. Non-exec. Dir, TSB Bank Scotland, 1994–. *Recreations:* tennis, fishing, music. *Address:* Scottish Office, 16 Waterloo Place, Edinburgh EH1 3DN; 51 Greenbank Crescent, Edinburgh EH10 5TD. *T:* 0131–447 6240.

McDONALD, David Arthur; Under-Secretary, Cities, Countryside and Private Finance Directorate, Department of the Environment, since 1994; *b* 16 Jan. 1940; *s* of late Campbell McDonald and Ethel McDonald; *m* 1st, 1963, Barbara MacCallum (marr. diss.); one *d*; 2nd, 1971, Mavis Lowe (*see* Mavis McDonald); one *s. Educ:* Campbell College, Belfast; Trinity College, Dublin. BA (Moderatorship) Classics. Asst Master, Classics, Methodist College, Belfast, 1963–66; Press Sec. to Minister of Education, N Ireland, 1967–68; joined Min. of Housing and Local Govt, later DoE, 1970; Asst Private Sec. to Sec. of State for the Envt, 1974–76; Asst Sec., Local Govt Finance Divs, 1977–82; Dir of Information, 1982–87; Under Sec., Construction Industry, and Sport and Recreation, Directorates, 1987–90; Dir of Information, 1990–92; Under Sec., Urban Develt and Relocation Directorate, 1992–94. Pres., Civil Service Men's Hockey Club, London. *Recreations:* golf, watching rugby and cricket. *Clubs:* Wimbledon Park Golf; Richmond Football.

MACDONALD, David Cameron; Chairman, Pittards, since 1985 (Director, 1984); Director: Coutts and Co., since 1980; Sears, since 1981; Merivale Moore, since 1985; Cogent Elliott Ltd, since 1986; Foster Yeoman Ltd, since 1993; *b* 5 July 1936; *s* of James Fraser Macdonald, OBE, FRCS and Anne Sylvia Macdonald (*née* Hutcheson); *m* 1st, 1968, Melody Jane Coles (marr. diss. 1980); two *d*; 2nd, 1983, Mrs Sally Robertson; one *s* one *d. Educ:* St George's Sch., Harpenden; Newport Grammar Sch. Admitted a solicitor with Slaughter and May, 1962; joined Philip Hill Higginson Erlangers, later Hill Samuel & Co. Ltd, 1964: Dir, 1968; Dep. Chm., 1979–80; Dir, Hill Samuel Gp Ltd, 1979–80; Chief Exec., Antony Gibbs Holdings Ltd and Chm., Antony Gibbs & Sons, 1980–83; Chairman: Bath and Portland Gp, 1982–85; Sound Diffusion, 1987–89. Sn. UK Advr, Credit Suisse First Boston, 1983–91. Dir Gen., Panel on Takeovers and Mergers, 1977–79. Adviser to Govt on Upper Clyde Shipbuilders crisis, 1971. Chm., Issuing Houses Assoc., 1975–77. Mem., BTA, 1971–82. Trustee, London City Ballet, 1983–87. *Recreations:* music, fishing. *Address:* Lovel House, Upton Noble, near Shepton Mallet, Somerset BA4 6BA. *T:* Upton Noble (01749) 850572.

McDONALD, David Wylie, CMG 1978; DA, RIBA, ARIAS, FHKIA; Secretary for Lands and Works, Hong Kong, 1981–83; MLC Hong Kong, 1974–83; *b* 9 Oct. 1927; *s* of William McDonald and Rebecca (*née* Wylie); *m* 1951, Eliza Roberts Steele; two *d. Educ:* Harris Acad., Dundee; School of Architecture, Dundee Coll. of Art (Lorimer Meml

Prize, RIAS, 1950; City Coronation Design Prize, Corporation of Dundee, 1953; DA 1953). Architect with Gauldie, Hardie, Wright and Needham, Chartered Architects, Dundee, 1953–55; Public Works Department, Hong Kong: Architect, 1955; Sen. Architect, 1964; Chief Architect, 1967; Govt Architect, 1970; Principal Govt Architect, 1972; Dir of Building Develt, 1973; Dir of Public Works, 1974. Member: Finance Cttee, Legislative Council, 1974–83; Commonwealth Parly Assoc., 1974–. Director: Mass Transit Railway Corp., Hong Kong, 1975–83; Ocean Park Ltd, Hong Kong, 1976–83; Hong Kong Industrial Estate Corp., 1981–83; Mem., Hong Kong Housing Auth., 1982–83. Mem. Exec. Cttee: Girl Guides Assoc. (Hong Kong Br.), 1977–83; Hong Kong Red Cross, 1981–83. Mem. Cttee of Management, Margaret Blackwood Hsg Assoc., 1984–; Trustee, Scottish Trust for Physically Disabled, 1984–. Mem., Mensa, 1968–. JP Hong Kong, 1972–83. Silver Jubilee Medal, 1977. *Recreations:* swimming (Coach and Manager, Hong Kong Swimming Team at Commonwealth Games, Christchurch, NZ, 1974), drawing, painting and calligraphy. *Address:* Northbank, Backmuir of Liff, by Dundee DD2 5QU. *T:* Dundee (01382) 580483. *Clubs:* Hong Kong (Hong Kong) (Chairman, 1977); Royal Hong Kong Jockey (Hong Kong).

MACDONALD, Hon. Donald (Stovel), PC (Canada) 1968; CC 1994; lawyer; Counsel, McCarthy Tétrault, Toronto, since 1991; *b* 1 March 1932; *s* of Donald Angus Macdonald and Marjorie Stovel Macdonald; *m* 1st, 1961, Ruth Hutchison (*d* 1987), Ottawa; four *d*; 2nd, 1988, Adrian Lang; three step *s* three step *d* (and one step *d* decd). *Educ:* Univ. of Toronto (BA 1951); Osgoode Hall Law Sch. 1955 (LLB *ex post facto* 1991); Harvard Law Sch. (LLM 1956); Cambridge Univ. (Dip. in Internat. Law, 1957). Called to Ont Bar, 1955; Prize in Insurance Law, Law Soc. of Upper Canada, 1955; Rowell Fellow, Canadian Inst. of Internat. Affairs, 1956; McCarthy & McCarthy, law firm, Toronto, 1957–62, Partner, 1978–88; High Comr for Canada in UK, 1988–91. Special Lectr, Univ. of Toronto Law Sch., 1978–83, 1986–88. MP Rosedale, 1962–78; Parly Sec. to Ministers of Justice, Finance, Ext. Affairs, Industry, 1963–68; Minister without Portfolio, 1968; Pres., Queen's Privy Council, and Govt House Leader, 1968–70; Minister of National Defence, 1970–72; Minister of Energy, Mines and Resources, 1972–75; Minister of Finance, 1975–77. Director: McDonnell Douglas Corp., 1978–88; Du Pont Canada Inc., 1978–88; Bank of Nova Scotia, 1980–88; Alberta Energy Co. Ltd, 1981–88; MacMillan-Bloedel Ltd, 1986–88; Celanese Canada, 1991–; Sun Life Assurance Co. of Canada, 1991–; TransCanada Pipelines, 1991–; Slough Estates Canada Ltd, 1991–; Siemens Electric Ltd, 1991– (Chm., 1991–); Alberta Energy Co. Ltd, 1992–; Hambros Canada Inc., 1994–; Banister Foundn Inc., 1994–; Rainy River Forest Products Inc., 1994–. Chairman: Internat. Develt Res. Centre, Canada, 1981–84; Inst. for Res. on Public Policy, Montreal, 1991–; Design Exchange, 1993–. Chm., Royal Commn on Econ. Union and Develt Prospects for Canada, 1982–85. Trustee, Clan Donald Lands Trust, Armadale, Skye, 1991–. Chm., Canadian Friends of Cambridge, 1993–. Freeman, City of London, 1990; Liveryman, Distillers' Co. Hon. Fellow, Trinity Hall, Cambridge, 1994. LLD (*hc*): St Lawrence Univ., 1974; Univ. of New Brunswick at Saint John, 1990; Hon. DEng Colorado Sch. of Mines, 1976. *Recreations:* cross-country skiing, tennis. *Address:* 27 Marlborough Avenue, Toronto, Ont M5R 1X5, Canada. *T:* (416) 9646757; McCarthy Tétrault, Toronto Dominion Tower, PO Box 48, Toronto-Dominion Centre, Toronto, Ont M5K 1E6. *T:* (416) 6017932. *Clubs:* Reform; York, Toronto (Toronto).

McDONALD, Sir Duncan, Kt 1983; CBE 1976; BSc, FH-WC, FRSE, FEng; CIMgt; SMIEE; Chairman, Northern Engineering Industries plc, 1980–86 (Group Managing Director, 1977–80; Chief Executive, 1980–83); *b* 20 Sept. 1921; *s* of Robert McDonald and Helen Orrick; *m* 1955, Jane Anne Guckian; three *s* one *d*. *Educ:* Inverkeithing Public Sch.; Dunfermline High Sch.; Edinburgh Univ. (BSc). Grad. App., BTH, Rugby, 1942–45; Transformer Design, Research and Develt, BTH, 1945–54. Bruce Peebles Industries Ltd: Chief Transformer Designer, 1954–59; Chief Engr, 1959; Dir and Chief Engr, 1960; Managing Dir, 1962; Chm. and Chief Exec. (and of A. Reyrolle & Co. Ltd), 1974; Reyrolle Parsons Ltd: Dir, 1973–77; Chief Exec., 1976–77. Director: Barclays Bank (Newcastle), 1980–86; Nat. Nuclear Corp., 1982–86; General Accident, 1983–92; Northern Rock (Scotland), 1986–; Adv. Dir, Barclays Bank (Scotland), 1986–91. Member: Scottish Council Develt and Industry, 1967– (Vice-Pres., 1984–90); Scottish Economic Council, 1975–87. Mem. Court, Heriot-Watt Univ., 1984–90. Pres. Watt Club, 1986–87. FH-WC 1962. Fellow, Scottish Council (Develt and Industry), 1987. FRSA 1965. Hon. FIEE 1984. Hon. DSc Heriot-Watt, 1982; Hon. DEng Newcastle, 1984. *Publications:* various papers to learned socs, nat. and internat. *Recreations:* fishing, golf. *Address:* Duncliffe, Kinellan Road, Edinburgh EH12 6ES. *T:* 0131–337 4814. *Club:* New (Edinburgh).

McDONALD, (Edward) Lawson, MA, MD Cantab; FRCP; FACC; Hon. Consultant Cardiologist: National Heart Hospital, since 1983 (Consultant Cardiologist, 1961–83); Canadian Red Cross Memorial Hospital, Taplow, 1960–83; Consultant Cardiologist: King Edward VII's Hospital for Officers, London, 1968–88; to King Edward VII Hospital, Midhurst, 1970–92, Emeritus, 1992; Senior Lecturer to the Institute of Cardiology, 1961–83; *b* 1918; *s* of late Charles Seaver McDonald and Mabel Deborah (*née* Osborne); *m* 1953, Ellen Greig Rattray (marr. diss. 1972); one *s*. *Educ:* Felsted Sch.; Clare Coll., Cambridge; Middlesex Hospital; Harvard Univ. House appointments Middlesex Hospital, 1942–43. Temp. Surgeon-Lt, RNVR, 1943–46; served War of 1939–45, in N Atlantic and Normandy Campaigns (HMS Glasgow). RMO, Nat. Heart Hosp., 1946–47; Asst Registrar, Inst. of Cardiology, 1947–48; Med. Registrar, Middlesex Hosp., 1948–49; studied in Stockholm, 1949; Asst to Prof. of Medicine, Middlesex Hosp., 1949–52; Rockefeller Travelling Fellow in Medicine, 1952–53; Asst in Medicine, Med. Dept, Peter Bent Brigham Hosp., Boston, Mass. and Research Fellow in Medicine, Harvard Univ., 1952–53; Clinical and Research Asst, Dept of Cardiology, Middlesex Hosp., 1953–55; Asst Dir, Inst. of Cardiology and Hon. Asst Physician, Nat. Heart Hosp., 1955–61; Physician, and Physician to Cardiac Dept, London Hosp., 1960–78. Member: Bd of Governors, National Heart and Chest Hosps, 1975–82; Council, British Heart Foundn, 1975–83. Visiting Lecturer: American Coll. of Cardiology; American Heart Assoc.; Univ. of Toronto, Queen's Univ., Kingston, Ont; Univ. of Bombay; University of Barcelona, Eliseo Migoya Inst. of Cardiology, Bilbao, Spain; Istanbul Univ., Turkey; Univs of Chicago, Cincinnati and Kansas; Harvard Univ.; Mayo Foundation, USA; Univs of Belgrade, Ljubljana and Zagreb, Yugoslavia; Nat. Univ. of Cordoba, Argentine; Univ. of Chile, and Catholic Univ., Santiago; Nat. Univ. of Colombia; Nat. Inst. of Cardiology, Mexico; Nat. Univ. of Mexico; University of San Marcos and University of Cayetano Heredia, Peru; Nat. Univ. of Venezuela; Vis. Prof., Univ. of Oregon Med. Sch., since 1961, has addressed numerous cardiac societies in Europe, Africa, Australia, Canada, NZ, USA, People's Republic of China, USSR, and South America; St Cyres Lecturer, 1966; First Charles A. Berns Meml Lectr, Albert Einstein Coll. of Medicine, NY, 1973; Vth World Congress of Cardiology Souvenir Orator and Lectr's Gold Medallist, 1977. Advisor to the Malaysian Govt on Cardiac Services. Editorial Bd, New Istanbul Contribution to Clinical Science. Member: British Cardiac Soc.; Assoc. of Physicians of Great Britain and Ireland, and other societies; FACC; Corresp. Mem. or Hon. Mem. of various socs of Cardiology or Angiology in S America. Hon. Fellow, Turkish Med. Soc.; Internat. Fellow, Council on Clinical Cardiol., Amer. Heart Assoc.; Mem., Italian Soc. of Cardiology; Hon. Member: Pakistan Cardiac Soc,; Scientific Council, Revista Portuguesa de Cardiologia. Member, Most Honourable Order of the Crown of Johore, 1980. *Publications:* (ed) Pathogenesis and Treatment of Occlusive Arterial Disease, 1960; Medical and Surgical Cardiology, 1969; (ed) Very Early Recognition of Coronary Heart Disease, 1978; numerous contribs to learned jls; also papers and addresses. *Recreations:* art, ski-ing, mountain walking, sailing. *Address:* 9 Bentinck Mansions, Bentinck Street, W1M 5RJ. *T:* 0171–935 7101.

McDONALD, Elaine Maria, OBE 1983; Associate Artistic Director, Northern Ballet Theatre, since 1990; *b* 2 May 1943; *d* of Wilfrid Samuel and Ellen McDonald. *Educ:* Convent of the Ladies of Mary Grammar Sch., Scarborough; Royal Ballet Sch., London. Walter Gore's London Ballet, 1962–64; Western Theatre Ballet, 1964–69; Principal Dancer, 1969–89, Artistic Controller, 1988–89, Scottish Ballet; has also danced with London Fest. Ballet, Portuguese Nat. Ballet, Galina Samsova and Andre Prokovsky's New London Ballet, Cuban Nat. Ballet. Mem., Scottish Arts Council, 1986– (Mem., Dance and Mime Cttee, 1982–). Hon. LittD Strathclyde, 1990. *Relevant publication:* Elaine McDonald, ed J. S. Dixon, 1983. *Recreations:* physical therapy, theatre, travel, reading.

MacDONALD, Hon. Flora Isabel, OC 1993; Presenter, North/South, weekly television programme, since 1990; Chairperson, International Development Research Centre, since 1992; *b* N Sydney, Nova Scotia, 3 June 1926. *Educ:* schools in North Sydney, Nova Scotia; Empire Business Coll., Sydney, NS; Canadian Nat. Defence Coll. With Nat. HQ, Progressive Cons. Party, 1957–66 (Exec. Dir, 1961–66); Nat. Sec., Progressive Cons. Assoc. of Canada, 1966–69; Administrative Officer and Tutor, Dept of Political Studies, Queen's Univ., Kingston, 1967–73; MP (Progressive C) Kingston, Ontario, 1972–88; Sec. of State for External Affairs, Canada, 1979–80; Minister of Employment and Immigration, 1984–86; Minister for Communications, 1986–88. Vis. Scholar, Centre for Canadian Studies, Univ. of Edinburgh, 1989. Special Advr, Commonwealth of Learning, 1990–91. Dir, C. T. Financial Services, 1989–; Director: Canada Trust Co.; Canadian Civil Liberties Assoc.; Care Canada; Refugee Policy Gp, Washington; Canadian Crafts Council; Friends of Nat. Library. Patron, Commonwealth Human Rights Initiative. FRSA. Hon. degrees from Univs in Canada, US and UK. *Publications:* papers on political subjects. *Recreations:* speedskating, mountain climbing. *Address:* #502, 350 Queen Elizabeth Driveway, Ottawa, Ont K1S 3N1, Canada.

McDONALD, F(rancis) James; Chairman, Beaumont Hospital Board of Trustees, since 1992 (Chairman, Beaumont Hospital Foundation, 1987–92); President and Chief Operating Officer, General Motors, 1981–87; *b* Saginaw, Mich, 3 Aug. 1922; *s* of Francis and Mary McDonald; *m* 1944, Betty Ann Dettenthaler; two *s* one *d*. *Educ:* General Motors Inst. Served USN, 1944–46 (Lieut). Joined Saginaw Malleable Iron Plant, 1946; Transmission Div., Detroit, 1956–65; Pontiac Motor Div., 1965–68; Dir, Manufacturing Operations, Chevrolet Motor Div., 1968–69; Vice-Pres., and Mem. Admin Cttee, Gen. Motors, 1969; General Manager: Pontiac Motor Div., 1969–72; Chevrolet Motor Div., 1972–74; Exec. Vice-Pres. and a Dir, 1974; Mem. Finance Cttee, 1979; Chm., Exec. and Admin Cttees, 1981. Holds hon. degrees from univs and colls in the US, incl. Michigan State Univ. and Notre Dame Univ. *Address:* 1051 Indian Mound Trail, Vero Beach, FL 32963, USA.

MACDONALD, His Honour George Grant; a Circuit Judge, 1972–87; *b* 5 March 1921; *s* of late Patrick Macdonald, MA, Aberdeen, MB, ChB, Edinburgh, and Charlotte Primrose (*née* Rintoul); *m* 1967, Mary Dolores (*née* Gerrish), *widow* of G. G. Taylor; no *c*. *Educ:* Kelly Coll., Tavistock; Bristol Univ. (LLB (Hons)). Served War of 1939–45: in Royal Navy, Aug. 1941–July 1946, in Western Approaches, and Mine Sweeping, RNVR. Called to Bar, Gray's Inn, 1947; practised on Western Circuit, from Albion Chambers, Bristol; Dep.-Chm., Dorset QS, apptd 1969; Temp. Recorder of Barnstaple, Dec. 1971. *Recreations:* sailing, bridge, chess. *Address:* 32 Watership Drive, Hightown, Ringwood, Hants BH24 1QY. *T:* Ringwood (01425) 480507. *Club:* Clifton (Bristol).

McDONALD, Graeme Patrick Daniel, OBE 1988; Head of Drama, Ardent Productions, since 1994; *b* 30 July 1930; *s* of Daniel McDonald and Eileen (*née* McLean); unmarried. *Educ:* St Paul's Sch.; Jesus Coll., Cambridge. Entered TV, 1960; Dir, Granada TV, 1960–65; BBC Television: Producer, 1966–76: prodns include Thirty Minute Theatre, 1966–67, Wednesday Play, 1967–70 and Play for Today, 1970–76; Head of Drama Series and Serials, 1977–81; Head of Drama Gp, 1981–83; Controller, BBC 2, 1983–87; Man. Dir, Anglia Films Ltd, 1988–94. *Address:* c/o Ardent Productions, 74A Charlotte Street, W1P 2DA.

MACDONALD, Gus; *see* Macdonald, A. J.

MACDONALD, Howard; *see* Macdonald, J. H.

MACDONALD, Prof. (Hugh) Ian, OC 1977; Professor, Department of Economics and Faculty of Administrative Studies, since 1974, Director, Degree Programme in Public Management, since 1992, York University, Toronto; President Emeritus, York University, since 1984; *b* Toronto, 27 June 1929; *s* of Hugh and Winnifred Macdonald; *m* 1960, Dorothy Marion Vernon; two *s* three *d*. *Educ:* public schs, Toronto; Univ. of Toronto; Oxford Univ. BCom (Toronto), MA (Oxon), BPhil (Oxon). Univ. of Toronto: Lectr in Economics, 1955; Dean of Men, 1956; Asst Prof., Economics, 1962. Govt of Ontario: Chief Economist, 1965; Dep. Provincial Treas., 1967; Dep. Treas. and Dep. Minister of Economics, 1968; Dep. Treas. and Dep. Minister of Economics and Intergovernmental Affairs, 1972. Pres., York Univ., 1974–84; Dir, York Internat., 1984–94. Director: the AGF Cos, 1982–; CIBA-GEIGY Canada Ltd, 1980–; Aetna Life Insce Co. of Canada, 1985–; McGraw-Hill Ryerson Ltd, 1984–; Member, Board of Directors: Council for Canadian Unity, 1978–; World Encyclopaedia of Contemp. Theatre, 1984–; Member, Bd of Governors, York-Finch Hosp., 1977–; Chairman: Friends of Internat. Assoc. of Univs, 1992; The Commonwealth of Learning, 1994; Hockey Canada, 1987; Member: Canadian Economics Assoc.; Amer. Economics Assoc.; Royal Economic Soc. (London); Canadian Assoc. for Club of Rome; Inst. of Public Admin of Canada; Lambda Alpha Fraternity (Land Economics); Amer. Soc. for Public Admin; Past President: Empire Club of Canada; Ticker Club; Couchiching Inst. Public Affairs; Canadian Rhodes Scholars Foundn; World Univ. Service of Canada; Past Chairman: Bd, Corp. to Promote Innovation Develt for Employment Advancement (Govt of Ontario); Commn on Financing of Elementary and Secondary Educn in Ontario; Ont. Municipal Trng and Educn Adv. Council; Inst. for Political Involvement; Toronto Men's Br. of CIIA; Past Member: Admin. Bd, Internat. Assoc. of Univs; Council and Exec. Cttee, Interamerican Orgn for Higher Educn (Vice-Pres., Canada); Attorney General's Cttee on Securities Legislation; Economic Council of Canada. Hon. Councillor, Internat. Orgn for Higher Educn, 1992. KLJ 1978; Citation of Merit, Court of Canadian Citizenship, 1980. Hon. LLD Toronto, 1974. Canada Centennial Medal, 1967; Silver Jubilee Medal, 1977; Commemorative Medal, 125th Anniversary of Confedn of Canada, 1992. *Recreations:* hockey, tennis; public service in various organizations. *Address:* 7 Whitney Avenue, Toronto, Ont M4W 2A7, Canada. *T:* (416) 9212908; York University, 4700 Keele Street, N York, Ont M3J 1P3, Canada. *T:* (416) 7365632.

MACDONALD, Prof. Hugh John; Avis Blewett Professor of Music, Washington University, St Louis, since 1987; *b* 31 Jan. 1940; *s* of Stuart and Margaret Macdonald; *m*

1st, 1963, Naomi Butterworth; one *s* three *d*; 2nd, 1979, Elizabeth Babb; one *s*. *Educ:* Winchester College; Pembroke College, Cambridge (MA; PhD). FRCM 1987. Cambridge University: Asst Lectr, 1966–69; Lectr, 1969–71; Fellow, Pembroke Coll., 1963–71; Lectr, Oxford Univ., 1971–80, and Fellow, St John's Coll; Gardiner Prof. of Music, Glasgow Univ., 1980–87. Vis. Prof., Indiana Univ., 1979. Gen. Editor, New Berlioz Edition, 1966–. Szymanowski Medal, Poland, 1983. *Publications:* Berlioz Orchestral Music, 1969; Skryabin, 1978; Berlioz, 1981; (ed) Berlioz Selected Letters, 1995; articles in New Grove Dict. of Music and Musicians, Musical Times, Music and Letters, Revue de Musicologie. *Recreations:* bridges, typewriters. *Address:* Department of Music, Washington University, One Brookings Drive, St Louis, MO 63130–4899, USA. *T:* (314) 9355519.

MACDONALD, Iain Smith, CB 1988; MD; FRCPE, FFPHM; Chief Medical Officer, Scottish Home and Health Department, 1985–88, retired; *b* 14 July 1927; *s* of Angus Macdonald, MA and Jabina Urie Smith; *m* 1958, Sheila Foster; one *s* one *d*. *Educ:* Univ. of Glasgow (MD, DPH). Lectr, Univ. of Glasgow, 1955; Deputy Medical Officer of Health: Bury, 1957; Bolton, 1959; joined Scottish Home and Health Dept, 1964, Dep. Chief Med. Officer, 1974–85. Mem., MRC, 1985–88. QHP 1984–87. *Address:* 36 Dumyat Drive, Falkirk FK1 5PA. *T:* Falkirk (01324) 625100.

MacDONALD, Ian; *see* Mayfield, Hon. Lord.

MACDONALD, Ian; *see* Macdonald, H. I.

MACDONALD, Ian Alexander; QC 1988; *b* 12 Jan. 1939; *s* of late Ian Wilson Macdonald and Helen Nicolson, MA; *m* 1st, 1968, Judith Roberts (marr. diss.); two *s*; 2nd, 1978, Jennifer Hall (marr. diss.); one *s*; 3rd, 1991, Yasmin Sharif. *Educ:* Glasgow Acad.; Cargilfield Sch., Edinburgh; Rugby Sch.; Clare Coll., Cambridge (MA, LLB). Called to the Bar, Middle Temple, 1963; Astbury Scholar, 1962–65; SE Circuit. Lectr in Law, Kingston Polytechnic, 1968–72; Senior Legal Writer and Research Consultant, Incomes Data Services Ltd, 1974–80 (monitoring develts in employment law). Mem., Cttee of Inquiry into disappearance of Gen. Humberto Delgado, 1965; Chm., Indep. Inquiry into Racial Violence in Manchester Schs, 1987–88. Pres., Immigration Law Practitioners' Assoc., 1984–. Mem. Editl Adv. Bd, Immigration and Nationality Law and Practice. Grand Cross, Order of Liberty (Portugal), 1995. *Publications:* Resale Price Maintenance, 1964; (with D. P. Kerrigan) The Land Commission Act 1967, 1967; Race Relations and Immigration Law, 1969; Immigration Appeals Act 1969, 1969; Race Relations: the new law, 1977; (with N. Blake) The New Nationality Law, 1982; Immigration Law and Practice, 1983, 4th edn 1994; (Consulting Editor) Encyclopaedia of Forms and Precedents: Nationality, 1985; Murder in the Playground: report of Macdonald Inquiry into Racial Violence in Manchester Schools, 1990; (contrib.) Family Guide to the Law, 1971, 1972; articles in professional jls. *Recreations:* swimming, squash, watching football, reading. *Address:* 2 Garden Court, Temple, EC4Y 9BL. *T:* 0171–353 1633. *Club:* Cumberland Lawn Tennis.

MACDONALD, Prof. Ian Grant, FRS 1979; Professor of Pure Mathematics, Queen Mary and Westfield College (formerly Queen Mary College), University of London, 1976–87, now Emeritus; *b* 11 Oct. 1928; *s* of Douglas Grant Macdonald and Irene Alice Macdonald; *m* 1954, Margaretha Maria Lodewijk Van Goethem; two *s* three *d*. *Educ:* Winchester Coll.; Trinity Coll., Cambridge (MA). Asst Principal and Principal, Min. of Supply, 1952–57; Asst Lectr, Univ. of Manchester, 1957–60; Lectr, Univ. of Exeter, 1960–63; Fellow, Magdalen Coll., Oxford, 1963–72; Fielden Prof. of Pure Maths, Univ. of Manchester, 1972–76. *Publications:* Introduction to Commutative Algebra (with M. F. Atiyah), 1969; Algebraic Geometry, 1969; articles in math. jls. *Address:* 8 Blandford Avenue, Oxford OX2 8DY. *T:* Oxford (01865) 515373.

MacDONALD, Isabel Lillias, (Mrs J. G. MacDonald); *see* Sinclair, I. L.

McDONALD, Iverach; Associate Editor, The Times, 1967–73; Director, The Times Ltd, 1968–73; *b* 23 Oct. 1908; *s* of Benjamin McDonald, Strathcool, Caithness, and Janet Seel; *m* 1935, Gwendoline (*d* 1993), *o d* of late Captain Thomas R. Brown; one *s* one *d*. *Educ:* Leeds Gram. Sch. Asst Editor, Yorkshire Post, 1933; sub-editor, The Times, 1935; correspondent in Berlin, 1937; diplomatic correspondent 1938; Asst Editor, 1948; Foreign Editor, 1952; Managing Editor, 1965. War of 1939–45: Capt., Gen. Staff, 1939–40; travelled extensively in Soviet Union, Far East and America; reported all allied conferences after the war, including San Francisco, 1945, Paris, 1946 and 1947, Moscow, 1947, Colombo, 1950, and Bermuda, 1953. Sen. Associate Mem., St Antony's Coll., Oxford, 1976–. *Publications:* A Man of the Times, 1976; The History of The Times, vol. V, 1939–1966, 1984; chapters in: Walter Lippmann and His Times, 1959; The Times History of our Times, 1971. *Address:* Flat 25, Emden House, Barton Lane, Headington, Oxford OX3 9JU. *T:* Oxford (01865) 744150.

McDONALD, James; *see* McDonald, F. J.

MACDONALD, Most Rev. James; *see* St John's (Newfoundland), Archbishop of, (RC).

MACDONALD, Prof. James Alexander, BSc (Agric.), PhD (Edinburgh), DSc (St Andrews); Professor of Botany, University of St Andrews, 1961–77, now Emeritus; *b* 17 June 1908; *s* of late James Alexander Macdonald and Jessie Mary Simpson; *m* 1935, Constance Mary Simmie; one *d*. *Educ:* Inverness Royal Academy; Edinburgh Univ.; Steven Scholarship in Agriculture, 1930; DSc with Sykes Gold Medal, 1947. Asst Lecturer in Botany, East of Scot. Coll. of Agriculture, 1932–35; St Andrews University: Lecturer in Botany, 1935–52; Senior Lecturer, 1952–60; Dean, Faculty of Science, 1967–69. Pres., Botanical Soc. of Edinburgh, 1955–57; FRSE 1940 (Council Mem., 1956–59); Vice-Pres. RSE, 1961–64. Fellow, Inst. Biology. Silver Jubilee Medal, 1977. *Publications:* Introduction to Mycology, 1951; scientific papers in Trans Brit. Mycol. Soc., Annals Applied Biol., Mycologia, Proc. and Trans Bot. Soc. Edinburgh, Proc. and Trans Royal Soc. Edinburgh. *Recreations:* golf, fishing, philately. *Address:* 17 Hepburn Gardens, St Andrews, Fife KY16 9DF. *Club:* Royal and Ancient (St Andrews).

MACDONALD, John B(arfoot), OC 1991; DDS, MS, PhD; Chairman, Addiction Research Foundation, 1981–87 (President and Chief Executive Officer, 1976–81); Executive Director, Council of Ontario Universities, 1968–76; Professor of Higher Education, University of Toronto, 1968–76; *b* 23 Feb. 1918; *s* of Arthur A. Macdonald and Gladys L. Barfoot; *m*; two *s* one *d*; *m* 1967, Liba Kucera; two *d*. *Educ:* Univ. of Toronto, University of Illinois, Columbia Univ. DDS (with hons) Toronto, 1942; MS (Bact) Ill, 1948; PhD (Bact) Columbia, 1953. Lectr, Prev. Dentistry, University of Toronto, and private practice, 1942–44. Canadian Dental Corps, 1944–46 (Capt.) Instr, Bacteriol, University of Toronto, and private practice, 1946–47; Res. Asst, Univ. of Illinois, 1947–48; Kellogg Fellow and Canadian Dental Assoc. Res. Student, Columbia Univ., 1948–49; University of Toronto: Asst Prof. of Bacteriol., 1949–53; Assoc. Prof. of Bacteriol., 1953–56; Chm., Div. of Dental Res., 1953–56; Prof. of Bacteriol., 1956; Cons. in Dental Educn, University of BC, 1955–56; Dir, Forsyth Dental Infirmary, 1956–62 (Cons. in Bacteriol., 1962); Prof. of Microbiol., Harvard Sch., of Dental Med., 1956–62 (Dir of Postdoctoral Studies, 1960–62); President, Univ. of British Columbia, 1962–67. Consultant: Dental Med. Section of Corporate Research Div. of Colgate-Palmolive Co., 1958–62; Donwood Foundn, Toronto, 1967 (Chm. of Bd, 1972–75); Science Council of Canada, 1967–69; Addiction Research Foundn of Ontario, 1968–74 (Mem., 1974–76); Nat. Inst. of Health, 1968– (Mem., Dental Study Sect., 1961–65). Chm., Commn on Pharmaceutical Services of the Canadian Pharmaceutical Assoc., 1967; Mem. and Vice-Chm., Ontario Council of Health, 1981–84; Councillor-at-Large, Internat. Assoc. for Dental Research, 1963, Pres. 1968–69. Fellow, Mem. or Chm. of numerous assocs. etc, both Canadian and international. FACD 1955; Hon. FICD 1965. Hon. AM, Harvard Univ., 1956; Hon. LLD: Univ. of Manitoba, 1962; Simon Fraser Univ., 1965; Hon DSc Univ. of British Columbia, 1967; Hon. LLD: Wilfred Laurier Univ., 1976; Brock Univ., 1976; Univ. of W Ontario, 1977; Hon. DSc Univ. of Windsor, 1977. *Publications:* Higher Education in British Columbia and a Plan for the Future, 1962, etc.; numerous contribs to learned jls. *Recreations:* golf, fishing. *Address:* 30 Metropolitan Crescent, Keswick, Ont L4P 1L5, Canada. *Clubs:* University of BC Faculty, Vancouver (Vancouver); Arts and Letters Faculty, University of Toronto (Toronto).

MACDONALD, Air Commodore John Charles, CB 1964; CBE 1957; DFC 1940 (Bar 1942); AFC 1941; President, Abbeyfield (Weymouth) Society; *b* 25 Dec. 1910; *s* of late Robert Macdonald; *m* 1952, Gladys Joan, *d* of John Hine, Beaminster, Dorset; two *s*. *Educ:* Berkhamsted Sch.; RAF Cadet Coll., Cranwell. Commissioned RAF, 1930. Served War of 1939–45 in Bomber Command; POW Stalag Luft III, 1942–45, escaped April 1945. Commanded RAF Akrotiri during Suez campaign; UK National Military Representative, SHAPE, 1959–61; Comdr RAF East Africa, 1961–64; Min. of Defence, 1964; retd, 1964. Chevalier, Légion d'Honneur, 1958; Croix de Guerre, 1958. *Recreations:* golf, sailing, shooting. *Address:* Woodbine Cottage, Osmington, Dorset DT3 6EX. *T:* Preston (01305) 833259.

McDONALD, Prof. John Corbett, MD; FRCP, FFCM, FFOM; Professor of Epidemiology, and Head of School of Occupational Health, McGill University, 1981–83, Professor Emeritus, since 1988; Professor of Occupational Health, London School of Hygiene and Tropical Medicine, London University, 1976–81, Professor Emeritus, since 1981; Head, Epidemiological Research Unit, National Heart and Lung Institute (London Chest Hospital), University of London, since 1990; *b* 20 April 1918; *s* of John Forbes McDonald and Sarah Mary McDonald; *m* 1942, Alison Dunstan Wells; one *s* three *d*. *Educ:* London Univ. (MD); Harvard Univ. (MS). DPH, DIH; FRCP (Canada) 1970; FRCP 1976; FFCM 1976; FFOM 1978. Served War, MO, RAMC, 1942–46. Epidemiologist, Public Health Lab. Service, 1951–64 (Dir, Epidemiol Res. Lab., 1960–64); Prof. and Head, Dept of Epidemiology and Health, McGill Univ., Montreal, 1964–76; Dir, TUC Centenary Inst. of Occupational Health, 1976–81; Chm., Dept of Clinical Epidemiology, Nat. Heart and Lung (formerly Cardiothoracic) Inst. (Brompton Hosp.), Univ. of London, 1986–90. *Publications:* (ed) Recent Advances in Occupational Health, 1981; papers on epidemiol subjects. *Recreations:* skiing, cycling. *Address:* 232 Peabody Road, Mansonville, Quebec J0E 1X0, Canada; 4 Temple West Mews, West Square, SE11 4TJ. *Club:* Athenæum.

MacDONALD, Maj.-Gen. John Donald, CB 1993; CBE 1986 (OBE 1981); General Secretary: The Royal British Legion, Scotland, and The Earl Haig Fund (Scotland), since 1994; Officers Association (Scotland), since 1994; *b* 5 April 1938; *s* of Lt-Col John MacDonald, OBE: *m* 1964, Mary, *d* of Dr Graeme M. Warrack, CBE, DSO, TD; one *s* two *d*. *Educ:* George Watson's Coll., Edinburgh; RMA Sandhurst. Commnd, 1958; saw service with KOSB, RASC, RCT and Airborne Forces Berlin, UK, BAOR, N Africa, India (Defence Services Staff Coll.), 1958–71; ndc, 1976; Turkey NATO HQ Izmir, CO 4 Armoured Div., Transport Regt RCT, 1978–80; Instr Australian Comd and Staff Coll., 1980–82; Chief Instr and Comdt, RCT Officers' Sch., 1983; DCS 3 Armoured Div., 1983–86; Col Personnel Br. 8 Mil. Sec., 1987–88; Comdr Transport, 1st BR Corps and Garrison Comdr Bielefeld, 1988–91; DG Transport and Movements, MoD, 1991–93. Chm., Sportsmatch, 1993–; Mem., Sports Council, Scotland, 1994–. Queen's Councillor, Queen Victoria Sch., Dunblane, 1994–. Chm., Combined Services Rugby, 1991–. Freeman, City of London, 1991; Hon. Mem. Ct of Assts, Carmens' Co., 1991. *Recreations:* Rugby (played for Scotland, Barbarians, Combined Services and Army), ski-ing, golf, travel, moving house, collecting. *Address:* c/o Bank of Scotland, 141 Princes Street, Edinburgh. *Clubs:* Army and Navy, British Sportsman; London Scottish, Royal & Ancient (St Andrews), Honourable Co. of Edinburgh Golfers (Muirfield), Rugby Internationalists Golfing Society.

MacDONALD, John Grant, CBE 1989 (MBE 1962); HM Diplomatic Service, retired; re-employed at Foreign and Commonwealth Office, since 1993; *b* 26 Jan. 1932; *er s* of late John Nicol MacDonald and Margaret MacDonald (*née* Vasey); *m* 1955, Jean, *o c* of late J. K. K. Harrison; one *s* two *d*. *Educ:* George Heriot's School. Entered HM Foreign (later Diplomatic) Service, 1949; FO, 1949; served HM Forces, 1950–52; FO, 1952; Berne, 1954–59; Third Sec. and Vice Consul, Havana, 1960–62; FO, 1962; DSAO, 1965; Second, later First Sec. (Comm.), Lima, 1966–71; Nat. Defence Coll., Latimer, 1971–72; Parly Clerk of FCO, 1972–75; First Sec. (Comm.), Hd of Trade Promotion Sect., Washington, 1975–79; Hd of Chancery, Dhaka, 1980–81; Hd of Chancery and HM Consul, Bogotá, 1981–84; Counsellor, FCO, 1985–86; Ambassador to: Paraguay, 1986–89; Panama, 1989–92; Head, and Dep. Head (Political), UK Delegn, EC Monitor Mission, 1992; temp. duty as Charter Mark Assessor, Cabinet Office, 1994, 1995. *Recreations:* travel, photography, swimming. *Address:* c/o Foreign and Commonwealth Office, SW1A 2AH. *Clubs:* Naval and Military, Royal Over-Seas League.

MACDONALD, (John) Howard, CA; FCT; Director: BOC Group plc, since 1991; Weir Group plc, since 1991; McDermott International Inc., since 1985; J. Ray McDermott Inc., since 1985; *b* 5 June 1928; *s* of John and Helen Macdonald; *m* 1961, Anne Hunter; three *d*. *Educ:* Hermitage, Helensburgh. CA 1954. Thomson McLintock & Co. (served articles), 1949–55; Walter Mitchell & Sons, 1955–58; Aircraft Marine Products, 1958; Finance Manager, Keir & Cawder Arrow Drilling, 1958–60; Royal Dutch Shell Group, 1960–83, Group Treasurer, 1978–83; Chairman and Chief Executive: Dome Petroleum, 1983–88; NatWest Investment Bank, 1989–91; Dir, National Westminster Bank, 1989–91. Mem., Assoc. of Corporate Treasurers, 1979. *Recreations:* golf, theatre. *Address:* 18 Fairbourne, Cobham, Surrey KT11 2BP. *T:* Chertsey (01932) 862281. *Club:* Caledonian.

MACDONALD, John Reginald, QC 1976; barrister-at-law; Commercial, Chancery and Administrative Lawyer; *b* 26 Sept. 1931; *s* of Ranald Macdonald and Marion Olive (*née* Kirkby); *m* 1958; one *s* one *d*. *Educ:* St Edward's Sch., Oxford; Queens' Coll., Cambridge. Called to Bar, Lincoln's Inn, 1955, Bencher, 1985; called to Bar of Eastern Caribbean, 1988. Represented: the people of Ocean Island, 1975; Yuri Orlov, the Soviet dissident, 1977–86; Canadian Indians, 1982; the Ilios, who were removed from Diego Garcia to make way for a US base, 1983; appeared for the people of Barbuda at the Antigua Indep. Conf. at Lancaster House in 1980; an observer in Namibia, pre-election period, 1989; Mem., Internat. Commn of Jurists missions to investigate violence in S Africa, 1990, 1992, 1993. Drafted written constitution for the UK (We the People), proposed by Liberal Democrats, 1990, revised 1993. Contested: Wimbledon (L) 1966 and 1970; Folkestone and Hythe (L) 1983, (L/Alliance) 1987; E Kent (Lib Dem), Eur. election 1994. Chm., Assoc. of Liberal Lawyers, 1973–78. *Recreation:* the theatre. *Address:* 12 New Square, Lincoln's Inn, WC2A 3SW. *T:* 0171–405 3808. *Clubs:* National Liberal; MCC.

MacDONALD, John William; HM Diplomatic Service, retired; *b* 13 June 1938; *s* of John MacDonald and Anne MacDonald (*née* Richards); *m* 1960, Margaret Millam Burns. *Educ:* Boteler Grammar Sch; NDC; Manchester Businesss Sch. Foreign Office, 1955, and 1959–94; Royal Navy, 1957–59; Dipl. Service appts include Cairo, Tokyo, Dhaka, Dar es Salaam; Consul-Gen., Shanghai, 1991–94. *Recreations:* walking, golf, listening to music. *Address:* Cherry Orchard, Garden Reach, Chalfont St Giles, Bucks HP8 4BE. *Club:* Little Chalfont Golf.

MACDONALD, Sir Kenneth (Carmichael), KCB 1990 (CB 1983); Chairman: Cossor Electronics Ltd, since 1991; International Military Services Ltd, since 1993; Council of Voluntary Welfare Work, since 1993; *b* 25 July 1930; *s* of William Thomas and Janet Millar Macdonald; *m* 1960, Ann Elisabeth (*née* Pauer); one *s* two *d*. *Educ:* Hutchesons' Grammar Sch.; Glasgow Univ. MA (Hons Classics). RAF, 1952–54. Asst Principal, Air Ministry, 1954; Asst Private Sec. to Sec. of State, 1956–57; Private Sec. to Permanent Sec., 1958–61; HM Treasury, 1962–65; MoD, 1965; Asst Sec., 1968; Counsellor (Defence), UK Delegn to NATO, 1973–75; Asst Under-Sec. of State, 1975, Dep. Under-Sec. of State, 1980, Second Perm. Under-Sec. of State, 1988–90, MoD. Chm., Raytheon (Europe) Ltd, 1991–94. *Recreation:* golf. *Address:* c/o Barclays Bank, 357–366 Strand, WC2R 0NX. *Club:* Royal Air Force.

McDONALD, Lawson; *see* McDonald, E. L.

McDONALD, Leneen, (Mrs Angus McDonald); *see* Forde, M. M. L.

MacDONALD, Margaret; *see* Casson, M. MacD, (Lady Casson).

MacDONALD, Margo, (Mrs James Sillars); television and radio presenter and reporter; *b* 19 April 1943; *d* of Robert and Jean Aitken; *m* 1st, 1965, Peter MacDonald (marr. diss. 1980); two *d*; 2nd, 1981, James Sillars, *qv*. *Educ:* Hamilton Academy; Dunfermline Coll. (Diploma of Physical Educn). Contested (SNP) Paisley, Gen. Elec., 1970; MP (SNP) Glasgow (Govan), Nov. 1973–Feb. 1974; contested (SNP): Glasgow (Govan), Gen. Elec., Feb. 1974 and Oct. 1974; Hamilton, by-election, May 1978. Vice-Chm., Scottish National Party, 1972–79 (Senior Vice-Chm., 1974–78); Mem., SNP Nat. Exec., 1980–81; Chm., SNP '79 Group, 1978–81. Director of Shelter (Scotland), 1978–81. *Address:* 97 Grange Loan, Edinburgh EH9 2ED.

McDONALD, Mavis; Principal Establishment Officer, Department of the Environment, since 1995; *b* 23 Oct. 1944; *d* of late Richard Henry and of Elizabeth Lowe; *m* 1971, David Arthur McDonald, *qv*; one *s*. *Educ:* Chadderton Grammar Sch. for Girls; London Sch. of Econs and Pol Science (BSc Econ). Min. of Housing and Local Govt, subseq. DoE, 1966–: Asst Private Sec. to Minister for Housing and Local Govt, 1969–70, to Sec. of State for the Environment, 1970–71; Private Sec. to Perm. Sec., 1973–75; Asst Sec., Central Policy Planning Unit, 1981–83; Head of Personnel Management (Envmt) Div., 1983–86; Finance, Local Authority Grants, 1986; Dep. Dir, Local Govt Finance, 1987; Under Secretary: Directorate of Admin. Resources, 1988–90; Directorate of Personnel Management, 1990–91; Directorate of Housing Resources and Management, 1990–93; Directorate of Local Govt, 1994–95. Non-exec. Dir, Tarmac Housing Div., 1988–91.

MACDONALD, Morag, (Mrs Walter Simpson), CBE 1993; Secretary of the Post Office, 1985–94; *b* 8 Feb. 1947; *d* of Murdoch Macdonald Macdonald and Isobel Macdonald (*née* Black); *m* 1st, 1970, Adam Somerville; 2nd, 1983, Walter Simpson; one *d*. *Educ:* Bellahouston Academy, Glasgow; Univ. of Glasgow (LLB Hons); College of Law, London. Called to the Bar, Inner Temple, 1974. Joined Post Office as graduate trainee, 1968; posts in Telecommunications and Corporate HQ, 1969–79, PA to Managing Dir, Girobank, 1980; Dep. Sec., Post Office, 1983–85. Mem. Management Cttee, Industry and Parlt Trust, 1986–94. Council Mem., St George's Hosp. Med. Sch., 1994–. FRSA 1990. *Recreations:* walking, embroidery, very indifferent piano playing. *Address:* Red Sails, Hiham Green, Winchelsea, E Sussex TN36 4HB.

MACDONALD, Nigel Colin Lock; Partner, Ernst & Young, since 1976; President, Institute of Chartered Accountants of Scotland, 1993–94; *b* 15 June 1945; *s* of Trevor William and Barbara Evelyn Macdonald; *m* 1st, 1972, Elizabeth Ruth Leaney (*d* 1981); 2nd, 1983, Jennifer Margaret Webster; one *d*. *Educ:* Cranleigh Sch.; Inst. of Chartered Accountants of Scotland. Thomson McLintock & Co., 1962–68; Whinney Murray & Co., 1968–70; Whinney Murray Ernst & Ernst, Netherlands, 1970–72; Whinney Murray, later Ernst & Whinney, then Ernst & Young, 1972–. Dir, James Lock & Co., 1976– (Chm., 1986–). Mem. Council, Inst. of Chartered Accountants of Scotland, 1989 (Pres., 1993–94). Member: Cadbury Cttee on corporate governance, 1991; Review Panel, Financial Reporting Council, 1991; Bd, BSI, 1992; Industrial Develt Adv. Bd, 1995. FRSA 1993. Elder, St Andrew's URC, Cheam. *Recreations:* old cars, swimming, topography. *Address:* 10 Lynwood Road, Epsom, Surrey KT17 4LD. *T:* Epsom (01372) 720853. *Clubs:* Royal Automobile, City of London.

McDONALD, Dr Oonagh; management consultant, financial services industry; *b* Stockton-on-Tees, Co. Durham; *d* of Dr H. D. McDonald. *Educ:* Roan Sch. for Girls, Greenwich; East Barnet Grammar Sch.; Univ. of London (BD Hons 1959; MTh 1962, PhD 1974, King's Coll.). Teacher, St Barnabas Sch., S Woodford, 1959–62; Lectr for Dip. in Sociology, Toynbee Hall, 1964–65; Teacher, Hornsey Grammar Sch. and Boreham Wood Sch., 1964–65; Lectr in Philosophy, Bristol Univ., 1965–76. Gwilym Gibbon Res. Fellow, Nuffield Coll., Oxford, 1988–89; Sen. Res. Fellow, Univ. of Warwick, 1990. Contested (Lab): S Glos, Feb. and Oct. 1974; Thurrock, 1987. MP (Lab) Thurrock, July 1976–87. PPS to Chief Sec. to Treasury, 1977–79; Opposition front bench spokesman on defence, 1981–83, on Treasury and economic affairs, 1983–87, on Civil Service, 1983–87. Member: Public Accounts Cttee, 1977–78; Select Cttee on Employment, 1981; Jobs and Industry Policy Cttee, 1985–87. Mem., USDAW, 1990–; Industrial Policy sub-cttee, Labour Party NEC, 1976–83 (Finance and Economic Affairs sub-cttee, 1978–83). Mem. Council, Consumers' Assoc., 1988–. Consultant, Unity Trust Bank plc, 1987–88. Non-exec. Dir, Investors' Compensation Scheme, 1992–. Dir, SIB, 1993– (Chm., Consumer Panel, 1994–). Trustee, Res. Inst. for Consumer Affairs, 1992–. Gov., Birkbeck Coll., 1987–. Devised TV documentary, A Woman's Life. *Publications:* (jtly) The Economics of Prosperity, 1980; Own Your Own: social ownership examined, 1989; Parliament at Work, 1989; The Future of Whitehall, 1992; articles on taxation, child benefit, industrial strategy, etc. *T:* 0181–940 5563.

MACDONALD OF CLANRANALD, Ranald Alexander; 24th Chief and Captain of Clanranald; Chairman and Managing Director, Tektura Ltd; *b* 27 March 1934; *s* of late Captain Kenneth Macdonald of Inchkenneth, DSO, and late Marjory Broad Smith, Basingstoke; *S* kinsman as Chief of Clanranald, 1944; *m* 1961, Jane Campbell-Davys, *d* of late I. E. Campbell-Davys, Llandovey, Carms; two *s* one *d*. *Educ:* Christ's Hospital. Founded: Fairfix Contracts Ltd, 1963; Tektura Wallcoverings, 1970. Chm., British Contract Furnishing Assoc., 1975–76. Lieut (TA) Cameron Highlanders, 1958–68. Mem., Standing Council of Scottish Chiefs, 1957–; Pres., Highland Soc. of London, 1988–91 (Dir, 1959–80); Chief Exec., Clan Donald Lands Trust, 1978–80; Chm., Museum of the Isles, 1981–90; Founding Trustee, Lord of the Isles Gallery Proj., 1989–. Vice Pres., Les Avants Bobsleigh and Toboggan Club, 1987–. Kt of Justice Constantinian Order of St George, 1982. *Recreations:* sailing, fishing. *Heir:* *s* Ranald Og Angus Macdonald, younger of Clanranald, *b* 17 Sept. 1963. *Address:* Boisdale House, Rodney Street, N1 9JH. *T:* (office) 0171–837 8000. *Clubs:* Turf, Beefsteak, Pratt's; New, (Edinburgh).

McDONALD, Robert Howat; *see* McDonald, Hon. Lord.

MACDONALD, Vice-Adm. Sir Roderick (Douglas), KBE 1978 (CBE 1966); retired; artist, since 1979; *b* Java, 25 Feb. 1921; *s* of Douglas and Marjorie Macdonald; *m* 1st, 1943, Joan Willis (marr. diss. 1980); two *s* (and one *s* decd); 2nd, 1980, Mrs Pamela Bartosik. *Educ:* Fettes. Entered Royal Navy, 1939. Served War: Fleet and Convoy ops throughout 1939–45 (Atlantic, Norway, Mediterranean, Eastern Fleet, East Coast and Normandy). Commanded HMS Leeds Castle, 1953, also HMS Essington; Sen. Officer, 104th Mine-Sweeping Sqdn and HMS Walkerton, 1957 (despatches, Cyprus); Comdr Sea Trng, 1959; Comd HMS Falmouth, 1961; Comdr, Naval Forces and Jt Force Comdr, Borneo, 1965 (CBE); Comd HMS Galatea; Captain (D): Londonderry Sqdn, 1968; First Frigate Sqdn, Far East, 1969; Captain of the Fleet, 1970; Comd HMS Bristol, 1972; COS to C-in-C, Naval Home Command, 1973–76; ADC to the Queen, 1975; COS to Comdr, Allied Naval Forces Southern Europe, 1976–79. One-man exhibitions: Naples, 1978; Edinburgh, 1980, 1989; London, 1981, 1983, 1985, 1987, 1991. Younger Brother of Trinity House; Vice-Pres. 1976–85, and Fellow, Nautical Inst. Chieftain, Isle of Skye Highland Games; President: Isle of Skye Piping Soc.; Inverness Sea Cadets. Trustee, Clan Donald Lands Trust. *Publication:* The Figurehead, 1993. *Recreation:* gardening. *Address:* Ollach, Braes, Isle of Skye IV51 9LJ. *Clubs:* Caledonian; Royal Scottish Pipers Society (Edinburgh); Royal Naval Sailing Assoc.

MACDONALD, Roderick Francis; QC (Scot.) 1988; *b* 1 Feb. 1951; *s* of late Finlay Macdonald and of Catherine Maclean. *Educ:* St Mungo's Acad., Glasgow; Glasgow Univ. (LLB Hons). Admitted advocate, 1975; Advocate-Depute (Crown Counsel), 1987–93; Home Advocate-Depute (Sen. Crown Counsel), 1990–93. Legal Chm., Pension Appeal Tribunals for Scotland, 1995–; Mem., Criminal Injuries Compensation Bd, 1995–. *Recreations:* hill walking, cycling. *Address:* 6A Lennox Street, Edinburgh EH4 1QA. *T:* 0131–332 7240.

MACDONALD, Maj.-Gen. Ronald Clarence, CB 1965; DSO 1944 and Bar, 1945; OBE 1953; Director, Griffin Farms Ltd, Norfolk; *b* 1 Aug. 1911; 2nd *s* of late Col C. R. Macdonald, CMG; *m* 1st, 1939, Jessie Ross Anderson (*d* 1986); one *s* one *d*; 2nd, 1986, Constance Margaret Davies. *Educ:* Rugby; RMC, Sandhurst. Royal Warwicks Regt: Commissioned, 1931; Comdr 2nd Bn, 1945–46; Comdr 1st Bn, 1953–55; Bn Comdr, France, Germany Campaign, 1944–45; Mil. Asst to CIGS, 1946–49; GSO1, HQ, West Africa Comd, 1950–53; Col Gen. Staff, SHAPE, 1955–56; Comdr 10th Inf. Bde Gp, 1956–59; DDI, War Office, 1959–60; Chief of Staff, HQ Middle East Comd, 1960–62; Dep. Chief of Staff, Headquarters, Allied Land Forces, Central Europe, 1962–65; retired, 1965. Col Royal Warwicks Fusiliers, 1963–68; Dep. Col (Warwicks), The Royal Regt of Fusiliers, 1968–74. *Recreation:* golf. *Address:* 6 The Beeches, Shaw, Melksham, Wilts SN12 8EW.

MACDONALD, Ronald John, CEng, MIMechE; Director-General, Royal Ordnance Factories/Production, 1974–79, retired; *b* 2 Nov. 1919; *s* of Ronald Macdonald and Sarah Jane Macdonald; *m* 1944, Joan Margaret Crew; two *s*. *Educ:* Enfield Grammar Sch.; Enfield Technical Coll. Engrg apprenticeship at Royal Small Arms Factory, Enfield, 1936–40. Army service, REME, in India, China and Hong Kong, 1943–47 (Major). Established Civil Servant, Royal Small Arms Factory, 1948; Royal Ordnance Factory, Radway Green, 1949; ROF Headquarters, Mottingham, 1953; ROF, Blackburn, 1960; Director: ROF, Birtley, Co. Durham, 1964; Ordnance Factories/Ammunition, 1972. *Address:* 72 Lincoln Park, Amersham, Bucks HP7 9HF. *T:* Amersham (01494) 727402. *Club:* Army and Navy.

MacDONALD, Prof. Simon Gavin George, FRSE; Professor of Physics, University of Dundee, 1973–88, now Emeritus; *b* 5 Sept. 1923; *s* of Simon MacDonald and Jean H. Thomson; *m* 1948, Eva Leonie Austerlitz; one *s* one *d*. *Educ:* George Heriot's Sch., Edinburgh; Edinburgh Univ. (MA (1st Cl. Hons) Maths and Nat. Phil); PhD (St Andrews). FIP 1958, FRSE 1972. Jun. Scientific Officer, RAE, Farnborough, 1943–46; Lectr, Univ. of St Andrews, 1948–57; Senior Lecturer: University Coll. of the West Indies, 1957–62; Univ. of St Andrews, 1962–67; Visiting Prof., Ohio Univ., 1963; University of Dundee: Sen. Lectr, then Prof., 1967–88; Dean of Science, 1970–73; Vice-Principal, 1974–79. Convener, Scottish Univs Council on Entrance, 1977–83 (Dep. Convener, 1973–77); Chm., Stats Cttee, UCCA, 1989–93 (Mem. Exec. Cttee, 1977–93; Chm., Technical Cttee, 1979–83; Dep. Chm., 1983–89). Chm., Bd of Dirs, Dundee Rep. Th., 1975–89; Chm., Fedn of Scottish Theatres, 1978–80. *Publications:* Problems and Solutions in General Physics, 1967; Physics for Biology and Premedical Students, 1970, 2nd edn 1975; Physics for the Life and Health Sciences, 1975; articles in physics jls. *Recreations:* bridge, golf, fiction writing. *Address:* 10 Westerton Avenue, Dundee DD5 3NJ. *T:* Dundee (01382) 778692. *Club:* Commonwealth Trust.

MACDONALD, Rt. Rev. Thomas Brian, OBE 1970; Coadjutor Bishop of Perth, Western Australia, 1964–79, retired; *b* 25 Jan. 1911; *s* of Thomas Joseph Macdonald, MD, and Alice Daisy Macdonald; *m* 1936, Audrey May Collins; three *d*. *Educ:* Mercers' Sch., Holborn, EC. Licentiate of Theology 1932, Aust. Coll. of Theol. Deacon 1934, priest 1935, Diocese of Ballarat, Vic.; Deacon in charge of All Saints, Ballarat, 1934; Priest in charge of Landsborough, 1935; Rector of Williams, Dio. of Bunbury, 1935–39; Rector of Manjimup, WA, 1939–40. Chaplain, Australian Imperial Forces, 1940–44 (despatches). Rector of Christ Church, Claremont, Dio. of Perth, 1944–50; Chaplain of Collegiate Sch. of St Peter, Adelaide, S Australia, 1950–58; Dean of Perth, Western Australia, 1959–61; Archdeacon of Perth, 1961–63. Administrator, Diocese of Perth during 1963 and 1969. *Address:* 33 Thomas Street, Nedlands, WA 6009, Australia. *Club:* Weld (Perth).

MACDONALD, Air Vice-Marshal Thomas Conchar, CB 1962; AFC 1942; MD (retired); *b* 6 Aug. 1909; *s* of John Macdonald, MA, BSc, and Mary Jane Conchar; *m* 1937, Katharine Cairns Frew. *Educ:* Hermitage Sch.; Glasgow High Sch.; University of Glasgow; MB, ChB 1932; MD 1940; DPH (London) 1949. Joined RAF Medical Br., 1933; served in Iraq, Egypt and England, before 1939. War service included RAF Inst. of Aviation Med., Farnborough, as Asst to Consultant in Applied Physiology, 1939–41; USA and Canada, 1941–42; DPMO (Flying) Fighter Command, 1942–45; Far East, 1945–46 (despatches, AFC). Post-war appts include: PMO 2nd TAF (Germany), 1951–53; Dir of Hygiene and Research, Air Min., 1953–56 (Chm. Aero-Medical Panel of Advisory Gp for Research and Develt (AGARD) of NATO); PMO, Bomber Command, 1956–58; PMO Middle East Air Force, 1958–61; PMO Technical Training Command, RAF, 1961–66. Air Vice-Marshal, 1961. QHP 1961–66; CStJ 1961. *Publications:* contributions to various med. jls. *Recreations:* sailing, fishing. *Address:* Wakeners Wood, Midhurst Road, Haslemere, Surrey GU27 2PT. *T:* Haslemere (01428) 643685. *Club:* Royal Air Force.

McDONALD, Sir Tom, Kt 1991; OBE 1983; Director, Opera North, since 1982; *b* 5 Aug. 1923; *s* of Robert and Edna McDonald; *m* 1951, Pamela Anne Glaisby; three *s* one *d*. *Educ:* Dewsbury Wheelwright Grammar Sch.; Leeds Univ. (BCom Hons). FCA.

Armitage & Norton: Audit Manager, 1953–62; Partner, 1962–86; Chm., 1982–86. Chairman: Old Swan Hotel (Harrogate) Ltd, 1973–82; Yorkshire Chemicals, 1977–83; Yorks and Humberside and E Midlands Indust. Develt Bd, 1982–91; Educn Assets Bd, 1988–93; W Yorks Residuary Body, 1986–91; W Midlands Residuary Body, 1990–91; Yorkshire Enterprise Ltd, 1990–94; Director: Dale Electric International, 1988–93; S. Jerome & Sons (Holdings), 1988–93; Consultant, KPMG Peat Marwick, 1987–93. Pres., W Yorks Soc. of Chartered Accountants, 1986–87. *Recreations:* history, travel, music. *Address:* 10 Lime Crescent, Sandal, Wakefield, W Yorks WF2 6RY. *T:* Wakefield (01924) 258871.

McDONALD, Trevor, OBE 1992; newscaster, since 1990, main presenter, since 1992, News at Ten, ITN; *b* Trinidad, 16 Aug. 1939; *m*; two *s* one *d*. Work on newspapers, radio and television, Trinidad, 1960–69; producer for Caribbean Service and World Service, BBC Radio, London, 1969–73; Independent Television News: reporter, 1973–78; sports corresp., 1978–80; diplomatic corresp., 1980–82; diplomatic corresp. and newscaster, 1982–87, Diplomatic Ed., 1987–89, Channel Four News; newscaster, News at 5.40, 1989–90. Newscaster of the Year, TRIC, 1993. *Publications:* Clive Lloyd: a biography, 1985; Vivian Richards: a biography, 1987; Queen and Commonwealth, 1989; Fortunate Circumstances (autobiog.), 1993. *Address:* c/o ITN, 200 Gray's Inn Road, WC1 8XZ.

McDONALD, William, CA; JP; Chamberlain, 1962–89, and Secretary, 1971–89, Company of Merchants of City of Edinburgh; Bursar, Carnegie Trust for the Universities of Scotland, since 1990; *b* 9 Nov. 1929; *yr s* of late Joseph McDonald and Margaret Pringle (*née* Gibb); *m* 1956, Anne Kidd Laird Donald; one *s* one *d*. *Educ:* Perth Acad. Served RAF, 1952–54. Sec., South Mills and Grampian Investment, Dundee, 1957–62. Clerk and Treasurer, Incorp. of Guildry in Edinburgh, 1975–89; Jt Sec., Scottish Council of Independent Schs, 1978–89. Chm., Lothian Region Valuation Appeal Cttee, 1995– (Mem., 1990–95). Dep. Chief Comr of Scotland, Scout Assoc., 1977–79 (Hon. Treas., Scotland, 1989–93); Chm., Finance Cttee, Scout Assoc., 1993–; Chm., Scottish Environmental and Outdoor Centres Assoc. (formerly Scottish Nat. Camps Assoc.), 1986–91; Mem., High Constables of Edinburgh (Colinton Ward), 1983–; Mem., Rotary Club of Edinburgh, 1989–94. *Recreations:* Scout Association, bridge, golf. *Address:* 1/3 Wyvern Park, The Grange, Edinburgh EH9 2JY. *Club:* New (Edinburgh).

McDONALD, Very Rev. William James Gilmour; Moderator of the General Assembly of the Church of Scotland, 1989–90; Parish Minister of Mayfield, Edinburgh, 1959–92; *b* 3 June 1924; *s* of Hugh Gilmour McDonald and Grace Kennedy Hunter; *m* 1952, Margaret Patricia Watson; one *s* two *d*. *Educ:* Daniel Stewart's College, Edinburgh; Univ. of Edinburgh (MA, BD); Univ. of Göttingen. Served Royal Artillery and Indian Artillery, 1943–46. Parish Minister, Limekilns, Fife, 1953–59. Convener, Cttee on Education for the Ministry, 1974–78; Convener, Assembly Council, 1984–87. Warrack Lectr, Edinburgh and Aberdeen Univs, 1992, Glasgow and St Andrews Univs, 1995; Turnbull Trust Preacher, Scots Ch, Melbourne, 1993. Hon. DD Edinburgh, 1987. *Address:* 7 Blacket Place, Edinburgh EH9 1RN. *T:* 0131–667 2100.

McDONALD, Hon. Sir William (John Farquhar), Kt 1958; *b* 3 Oct. 1911; *s* of John Nicholson McDonald and Sarah McDonald (*née* McInnes); *m* 1935, Evelyn Margaret Koch; two *d*. *Educ:* Scotch Coll., Adelaide, South Australia. Served AIF, 1939–45, Capt. Councillor, Shire of Kowree, 1946–61. MLA, electorate of Dundas, Victoria, 1947–52, 1955–70; Speaker, Legislative Assembly, Victoria, 1955–67; Minister of Lands, Soldier Settlement, and for Conservation, 1967–70. Mem., Exec. Council, Victoria. Trustee, Shrine of Remembrance, 1955–70. Victoria State Pres., Poll Shorthorn Soc. of Aust., 1962–72; Trustee, Royal Agricultural Soc. of Victoria, 1968–. Trustee, Victoria Amateur Turf Club, 1969. *Address:* Brippick, 102 St Georges Road, Toorak, Vic 3142, Australia. *T:* (3) 8275839. *Clubs:* Hamilton (Hamilton, Victoria); Australian, Naval and Military, Melbourne (Melbourne).

MACDONALD, Prof. William Weir, PhD, DSc; FIBiol; Selwyn Lloyd Professor of Medical Entomology, 1980–94, now Professor Emeritus, and Dean, 1983–88, Liverpool School of Tropical Medicine; *b* 5 Dec. 1927; *s* of William Sutherland Macdonald and Ina Weir; *m* 1950, Margaret Lawrie; two *d*. *Educ:* Univ. of Glasgow (BSc 1948). MSc 1964, PhD 1965, Univ. of Liverpool; DSc 1973, Univ. of Glasgow; FIBiol 1966. Strang-Steel Scholar, Glasgow Univ., 1948; Colonial Office Res. Scholar, 1949–50; Entomologist, E African Fisheries Res. Org., Uganda, 1950–52; Res. Fellow, Inst. for Med. Res., Kuala Lumpur, 1953–60; Lectr, Sen. Lectr, and Reader, Liverpool Sch. of Trop. Medicine, 1960–76; Prof. of Med. Entomology, London Sch. of Hygiene and Trop. Medicine, 1977–80. Consultant: WHO; various overseas govts. Chalmers Medal, Royal Soc. of Trop. Medicine and Hygiene, 1972. *Publications:* papers on med. entomology in scientific jls. *Recreations:* golf, gardening. *Address:* 10 Headland Close, West Kirby, Merseyside L48 3JP. *T:* 0151–625 7857.

MACDONALD-BUCHANAN, John, MC 1945; Vice-Lord Lieutenant of Northamptonshire, since 1991; *b* 15 March 1925; *s* of Major Sir Reginald Macdonald-Buchanan, KCVO, MBE, MC and Hon. Lady Macdonald-Buchanan, OStJ, *o c* of 1st Baron Woolavington, GCVO; *m* 1st, 1950, Lady Rose Fane (*d* 1984), *d* of 14th Earl of Westmorland; one *s* two *d*; 2nd, 1969, Mrs Jill Rosamonde Trelawnay, *d* of Maj.-Gen. Cecil Benfield Fairbanks, CB, CBE; two *d*. *Educ:* Eton; RMC, Sandhurst; RAC, Cirencester. 2nd Lt, Scots Guards, 1943; served War, 1944–45, NW Europe; Malaya, 1948–50; retired, 1952. Mem., Horserace Betting Levy Bd, 1973–76. Steward of Jockey Club, 1969–72, Sen. Steward 1979–82. High Sheriff 1963–64, DL 1978, Northants. *Address:* Cottesbrooke Hall, Northampton NN6 8PF. *T:* Creaton (01604) 505732; 22 Cadogan Place, SW1X 9SA. *T:* 0171–235 8615. *Clubs:* White's, Turf.

MacDONALD SCOTT, Mary, (Mrs Michael MacDonald Scott); *see* Lavin, Mary.

MACDONALD-SMITH, Maj.-Gen. Hugh, CB 1977; *b* 8 Jan. 1923; *s* of Alexander and Ada Macdonald-Smith; *m* 1947, Désirée Violet (*née* Williamson); one *s* one *d* (and one *d* decd). *Educ:* Llanelli Grammar Sch.; Llandovery Coll.; Birmingham Univ. BSc. CEng, FIMechE, FIEE. Commissioned REME, 1944; served: India, 1945–47; Singapore, 1956–58; BAOR, 1961–63; Technical Staff Course, 1949–51; Staff Coll., Camberley, 1953; Lt-Col, 1963; Asst Dir, Electrical and Mechanical Engineering, HQ Western Comd, 1963–65; Asst Mil. Sec., MoD, 1965–66; Comd REME, 1 (BR) Corps Troops, 1966–67; Technical Gp, REME, 1967–72; Col, 1967; Brig. 1970; Dep. Dir, Electrical and Mechanical Engineering (Eng. Pol.), (Army), 1972–75; Dir, later Dir Gen., Electrical and Mech. Engrg (Army), 1975–78; retired 1978. Col Comdt, REME, 1978–83; Rep. Col Comdt, REME, 1979–80. Dir, TEMA, 1981–87 (Sec. to Council, 1979–80). Mem., Cttee of Inquiry into Engrg Profession, 1977–79. Mem. Council, IMechE, 1975–76. *Recreations:* golf, gardening, photography. *Address:* c/o Lloyds Bank, Llanelli.

McDONAUGH, James, CBE 1970 (OBE 1965); retired 1973; reappointed 1973–75, Director North Europe Department, British Council; *b* 26 July 1912; *s* of late Edward McDonaugh and late Christina, *d* of William Bissell; *m* 1944, Mary-Eithné Mitchell, *d* of James Vyvyan Mitchell; three *s* two *d*. *Educ:* Royal Grammar Sch., Worcester; St Edmund Hall, Oxford (Exhibitioner, MA). Asst Master, Ampleforth Coll., 1935–40; War Service, 1940–45; Lecturer, Graz and Innsbruck Univs, 1947–50; Asst Rep., British Council, Austria, 1950–54; Representative, Malta, 1954–58; Dep. Counsellor (Cultural), Bonn, 1958–59; Dep. Rep., Germany, 1958–61; Dir Specialist Tours Dept, 1961–65; Asst Controller, Education Div., 1965; Rep., Germany, 1966–73. *Address:* Old Rectory Cottage, Whitestaunton, Chard, Somerset TA20 3DL.

MacDONELL OF GLENGARRY, Air Cdre Aeneas Ranald Donald, CB 1964; DFC 1940; Hereditary 22nd Chief of Glengarry; *b* 15 Nov. 1913; *e s* of late Ranald MacDonell of Glengarry, CBE; *m* 1st, Diana Dorothy (*d* 1980), *yr d* of late Henry Keane, CBE; two *s* one *d*; 2nd, Lois Eirene Frances, *d* of Rev. Gerald Champion Streatfeild; one *s* one *d*. *Educ:* Hurstpierpoint Coll.; Royal Air Force Coll., Cranwell. No 54 Fighter Sqdn, 1934; Fleet Air Arm, 1935–37; Flying Instructor, 1938–39; Air Ministry, 1939–40; No 64 Fighter Sqdn, 1940–41; POW, 1941–45; Ministry of Defence, 1946–47; HQ Flying Training Command, 1947–49; Chief Flying Instructor, RAF Coll., Cranwell, 1949–51; Ministry of Defence, 1952–54; Senior RAF Instructor, Joint Services Staff Coll., 1954–56; Air Attaché, Moscow, 1956–58; Dir of Management and Work Study, Ministry of Defence, Air Force Dept, 1960–64, retd. Ops Res. Manager, CJB, 1964–67; Personnel Manager, CITB, 1967–73; Dept Head, Industrial Soc., 1973–76; Partner, John Courtis and Partners, 1976–80. Hon. Vice-Pres., Ross and Cromarty Br., SSAFA, 1983–; Trustee: Clan Donald Lands Trust, 1973–; Finlaggan Trust, 1984–; Invergarry Castle Trust, 1960–. MIMgt. *Recreations:* ciné photography, art, travel. *Address:* Elonbank, 23 Castle Street, Fortrose, Ross-shire IV10 8TH. *T:* Fortrose (01381) 620121. *Club:* Royal Air Force.

McDONNELL, family name of **Earl of Antrim.**

McDONNELL, Christopher Thomas, CB 1991; Deputy Under-Secretary of State, Ministry of Defence, 1988–91; *b* 3 Sept. 1931; *s* of Christopher Patrick McDonnell and Jane McDonnell; *m* 1955, Patricia Anne (*née* Harvey) (*d* 1967); three *s* one *d*. *Educ:* St Francis Xavier's Coll., Liverpool; Corpus Christi Coll., Oxford (MA). WO, 1954; HM Treasury, 1966–68; RCDS, 1973; Asst Under-Sec. of State, MoD, 1976–88.

McDONNELL, David Croft; National Managing Partner, Grant Thornton, since 1989; *b* 9 July 1943; *s* of Leslie and Catherine McDonnell; *m* 1967, Marieke (*née* Bos); three *d*. *Educ:* Quarry Bank High School, Liverpool. FCA. Qualified Chartered Accountant, 1965; Partner, Thornton Baker, later Grant Thornton, 1972. Chm. Bd of Trustees, Nat. Museums and Galls on Merseyside, 1995–. *Recreations:* sailing, motor racing (spectating), mountain walking. *Address:* Grant Thornton, Grant Thornton House, Melton Street, Euston Square, NW1 2EP. *T:* 0171–383 5100.

McDONNELL, His Honour Denis Lane, OBE 1945; a Circuit Judge (formerly a County Court Judge), 1967–86; *b* 2 March 1914; *o c* of late David McDonnell, LLD and Mary Nora (*née* Lane), Riversdale, Sundays Well, Cork and Fairy Hill, Monkstown, Co. Cork and *g s* of Denny Lane, poet and Young Irelander; *m* 1940, Florence Nina (Micky), *d* of late Lt-Col Hugh T. Ryan, DSO and Clare Emily (*née* Conry), Castle View, Ballincollig, Co. Cork; three *d* (and one *s* one *d* decd). *Educ:* Christian Brothers' Coll., Cork; Ampleforth Coll.; Sidney Sussex Coll., Cambridge (MA). Served in RAFVR, Equipment and Admin. and Special Duties Branches, 1940–45 in UK and with No. 84 Gp in NW Europe (Wing Comdr). Called to Bar, Middle Temple, 1936; Bencher, 1965. Practised at Bar, 1938–40 and 1946–67. Hon. Sec., Council of HM Circuit Judges, 1979–83 (Pres., 1985). *Publications:* Kerr on Fraud and Mistake (7th edn, with J. G. Monroe), 1952; titles on carriage in Encyclopædias of Forms and Precedents and Court Forms and Precedents, and in Halsbury's Laws of England. *Recreations:* family life, listening to music, golf, gardening. *Clubs:* Piltdown Golf, Rye Golf, Woking Golf, Royal Cinque Ports Golf.

McDONNELL, John; Secretary, Association of London Goverment, since 1995; *b* 8 Sept. 1951; *s* of Robert and Elsie McDonnell; *m* 1971, Marilyn Jean Cooper (marr. diss. 1987); two *d*. *Educ:* Great Yarmouth Grammar Sch.; Burnley Technical Coll.; Brunel Univ. (BSc); Birkbeck Coll., Univ. of London (MSc Politics and Sociology). Prodn worker, 1968–72; Research Assistant: NUM, 1976–78; TUC, 1978–82; full-time GLC Councillor, Hillingdon, Hayes and Harlington, 1982–86; Dep. Leader, GLC, 1984–85; Chm., GLC F and GP Cttee, 1982–85; Prin. Policy Advr, Camden Bor. Council, 1985–87; Sec., Assoc. of London Authorities, 1987–95. Editor, Labour Herald, 1985–88. Member: Gtr London Lab. Party Regl Exec. Cttee, 1982–87; for Gtr London, Lab. Party Nat. Policy Forum, 1993–; Chm., Lab. Party Irish Soc. Advr, Guildford Four Relatives Campaign, 1984–; Chair, Britain and Ireland Human Rights Centre, 1992–. Contested (Lab) Hampstead and Highgate, 1983; contested (Lab) Hayes and Harlington, 1992. Housefather (pt-time) of family unit, children's home, 1972–87. *Publications:* articles and pamphlets incl. contribs to Labour Herald, Briefing and Tribune. *Recreations:* gardening, reading, cycling, music, theatre, cinema, Wayfarer dinghy sailing, supporting Liverpool, Hayes and Yeading Football Clubs; generally fermenting the overthrow of capitalism. *Address:* Association of London Government, 36 Old Queen Street, SW1H 9JF; 38 Clayton Road, Hayes, Middlesex UB3 1AZ. *Clubs:* London Irish, Blues West 14; Hillingdon Irish Society; St Claret's, Working Men's (Hayes).

McDONNELL, John Beresford William; QC 1984; *b* 26 Dec. 1940; *s* of Beresford Conrad McDonnell and Charlotte Mary McDonnell (*née* Caldwell); *m* 1968, Susan Virginia, *d* of late Wing Comdr H. M. Styles, DSO and of Audrey (*née* Jorgensen, who *m* 2nd, 1947, Gen. Sir Charles Richardson, GCB, CBE, DSO); two *s* one *d*. *Educ:* City of London School (Carpenter Scholar); Balliol College, Oxford (Domus Scholar; Hon. Mention, Craven Scholarship, 1958; 1st Cl. Hon. Mods 1960; 2nd LitHum 1962, 2nd Jurisp 1964; MA); Harvard Law Sch. (LLM 1965). Called to the Bar, Inner Temple, 1968; Bencher, Lincoln's Inn, 1993. Pres., Oxford Union Soc. and Amer. Debating Tour, 1962; Harkness Fellowship, 1964–66; Amer. Political Science Assoc. Congressional Fellowship, 1965–66 (attached Rep. Frank Thompson Jr, NJ and Senator George McGovern, SDak); Cons. Research Dept, 1966–69; HM Diplomatic Service, 1969–71, First Sec., Asst Private Sec. to Sec. of State for Foreign and Commonwealth Affairs, 1970–71; practising at Chancery Bar, 1972–. Cllr, Lambeth Borough Council, 1968–69. London Rowing Club Grand VIII, Henley, 1958. FRSA 1994. *Recreation:* sculling. *Address:* 20 Brompton Square, SW3 2AD. *T:* 0171–584 1498; 1 New Square, Lincoln's Inn, WC2A 3SA. *T:* 0171–405 0884. *Club:* Athenæum.

McDOUGALL, Hon. Barbara Jean; PC (Can.) 1984; Secretary of State for External Affairs, Canada, 1991–93; *b* Toronto, 12 Nov. 1937. *Educ:* Univ. of Toronto (BA Hons Econ. and Pol Sci. 1960). Chartered Financial Analyst, 1973. Worked in financial sector in Vancouver, Edmonton and Toronto; Exec. Dir, Canadian Council Financial Analysts, 1982–84; financial columnist, national magazines and on TV. MP for St Paul's, Toronto, 1984–93; Minister of State: Finance, 1984–86; Privatisation, 1986–88; Minister Responsible for Status of Women, 1986–90 and for Regulatory Affairs, 1986–88; Minister, Employment and Immigration, 1988–91; Chairperson, Cabinet Cttee on Foreign Affairs and Defence Policy, 1991–93; Member Cabinet Cttees: Planning and Priorities, 1991–93; Canadian Unity and Constitutional Negotiations, 1991–93. Active in community organisations, including Community Occupational Therapy Associates, Elizabeth Fry Soc.

MacDOUGALL, Sir (George) Donald (Alastair), Kt 1953; CBE 1945 (OBE 1942); FBA 1966; economist; *b* 26 Oct. 1912; *s* of late Daniel Douglas MacDougall, Glasgow, and late Beatrice Amy Miller; *m* 1st, 1937, Bridget Christabel Bartrum (marr. diss. 1977); one *s* one *d*; 2nd, 1977, Laura Margaret Hall (*née* Linfoot) (*d* 1995). *Educ:* Kelvinside Acad., Glasgow; Shrewsbury Sch.; Balliol Coll., Oxford (Hon. Fellow, 1992). George Webb Medley Junior (1934) and Senior (1935) Scholarships in Political Economy; Asst Lecturer (later Lecturer) in Economics, University of Leeds, 1936–39; First Lord of the Admiralty's Statistical Branch, 1939–40; Prime Minister's Statistical Branch, 1940–45 (Chief Asst, 1942–45). Work on Reparations and German Industry, Moscow and Berlin, 1945; Mem. of Heavy Clothing Industry Working Party, 1946; Official Fellow of Wadham Coll., Oxford, 1945–50, Domestic Bursar, 1946–48, Hon. Fellow, 1964–; Econ. Dir, OEEC, Paris, 1948–49; Faculty Fellow, Nuffield Coll., 1947–50, Professorial Fellow, 1950–52, Official Fellow, 1952–64, First Bursar, 1958–64, Hon. Fellow, 1967–; Nuffield Reader in Internat. Economics, Oxford Univ., 1950–52; Chief Adviser, Prime Minister's Statistical Branch, 1951–53; Visiting Prof., Australian Nat. Univ., 1959; MIT Center for Internat. Studies, New Delhi, 1961; Dir, Investing in Success Equities, Ltd, 1959–62; Economic Dir, NEDO, 1962–64; Mem. Turnover Tax Cttee, 1963–64; Dir-Gen., Dept of Economic Affairs, 1964–68; Head of Govt Economic Service, and Chief Economic Adviser to the Treasury, 1969–73; Chief Economic Advr, CBI, 1973–84. Mem. Council, Royal Econ. Soc., 1950– (Hon. Sec., 1958–70; Vice-Pres., 1970–72, 1974–; Pres., 1972–74); Pres., Soc. for Strategic and Long Range Planning, 1977–85, Vice-Pres., 1968–77; Vice-Pres., Soc. of Business Economists, 1978–; Chm., Exec. Cttee NIESR, 1974–87; Mem., EEC Study Gp on Economic and Monetary Union, 1974–75; Chm., EEC Study Gp on Role of Public Finance in European Integration, 1975–77. Hon. LLD Strathclyde, 1968; Hon. LittD Leeds, 1971; Hon. DSc Aston, 1979. *Publications:* (part author) Measures for International Economic Stability, UN, 1951; The World Dollar Problem, 1957; (part author) The Fiscal System of Venezuela, 1959; The Dollar Problem: A Reappraisal, 1960; Studies in Political Economy (2 vols), 1975; Don and Mandarin: memoirs of an economist, 1987; contrib. to various economic and statistical jls. *Address:* Flat K, 19 Warwick Square, SW1V 2AB. *T:* 0171–821 1998. *Club:* Reform.

MACDOUGALL, Neil; Hon. Mr Justice Macdougall; Justice of Appeal, since 1989, and Vice-President of the Court of Appeal, since 1993, Supreme Court of Hong Kong; *b* 13 March 1932; *s* of Norman Macdougall and Gladys Clare Kennerly; *m* 1987, Helen Lui. *Educ:* Aquinas Coll., Perth, WA; Univ. of Western Australia (LLB 1954). Admitted Barrister and Solicitor of Supreme Court, WA, 1957, and of High Court of Australia, 1958; Solicitor of Supreme Court of England, 1976, and of Supreme Court of Hong Kong, 1977. Crown Counsel, Hong Kong, 1965; Director of Public Prosecutions, Hong Kong, 1978; a Judge of the High Court, Hong Kong, 1980; Comr, Supreme Court of Brunei, 1987. Chairman: Insider Dealing Tribunal, Hong Kong, 1987–88; Air Transport Licensing Authy, Hong Kong, 1992–. *Recreations:* classical music, study of natural history, photography. *Address:* 8B Severn Road, The Peak, Hong Kong. *T:* 8497077. *Club:* Hong Kong (Hong Kong).

MACDOUGALL, Patrick Lorn, FCA; Chief Executive, since 1985, and Chairman, since 1989, West Merchant Bank Ltd (formerly Standard Chartered Merchant Bank, then Chartered WestLB); *b* 21 June 1939; *s* of late James Archibald Macdougall, WS, and of Valerie Jean Macdougall; *m* 1st, 1967, Alison Noel Offer (marr. diss. 1982); two *s*; 2nd, 1983, Bridget Margaret Young; three *d*. *Educ:* schools in Kenya; Millfield; University Coll., Oxford (MA Jurisprudence). FCA 1976. Called to the Bar, Inner Temple, 1962. Manager, N. M. Rothschild & Sons Ltd, 1967–70; Exec. Dir, Amex Bank (formerly Rothschild Intercontinental Bank Ltd), 1970–77, Chief Exec., 1977–78; Exec. Dir, Jardine Matheson Holdings Ltd, 1978–85; Gp Exec. Dir, Standard Chartered PLC, 1988–89. Mem., Internat. Adv. Bd, Creditanstalt–Bankverein, Vienna, 1982–85. Director: Global Natural Resources Inc., USA, 1994–; Nuclear Electric plc, 1994–. FRSA 1988. *Recreations:* ski-ing, golf, opera, bridge. *Address:* 10 Stevenage Road, SW6 6ET. *T:* 0171–736 3506. *Clubs:* Hurlingham; Hongkong, Shek O (Hong Kong); Wisley Golf.

MacDOWALL, Dr David William, MA, DPhil; FSA, FRAS; Chairman, Society for South Asian Studies (formerly Society for Afghan Studies), since 1982 (Hon. Secretary, 1972–82); Hon. Research Fellow, Centre for Research in East Roman Studies, University of Warwick, since 1993; *b* 2 April 1930; *o s* of late William MacDowall and late Lilian May MacDowall (*née* Clarkson); *m* 1962, Mione Beryl, *yr d* of late Ernest Harold Lashmar and Dora Lashmar; two *d*. *Educ:* Liverpool Inst.; Corpus Christi Coll., Oxford; British Sch. at Rome. Hugh Oldham Scholar 1947, Pelham Student in Roman History 1951; Barclay Head Prize for Ancient Numismatics, 1953 and 1956. 2nd Lieut Royal Signals, 1952. Asst Principal, Min. of Works, 1955; Asst Keeper, Dept of Coins and Medals, British Museum, 1956; Principal, Min. of Educn, 1960; Principal, Univ. Grants Cttee, 1965; Asst Sec. 1970; Master of Univ. Coll., Durham, 1973; Hon. Lectr in Classics and in Oriental Studies, Univ. of Durham, 1975; Dir, Polytechnic of N London, 1980–85. Hon. Treasurer, Royal Numismatic Soc., 1966–73; Vice-Pres., British Archaeol Assoc., 1993– (Hon. Treas., 1989–93); Pres., Royal Asiatic Soc., 1994– (Vice-Pres., 1993–94). Mem. Governing Body, SOAS, 1990–. Trustee, UK Trust, Indian Nat. Trust for Archl and Cultural Heritage, 1994–. Corresponding Member: Istituto Italiano per il Medio ed Estremo Oriente, 1987; Amer. Numismatic Soc., 1991. *Publications:* Coin Collections, their preservation, classification and presentation, 1978; The Western Coinages of Nero, 1979; (contrib.) Mithraic Studies, 1975; (contrib.) The Archaeology of Afghanistan, 1978; (ed jtly) Indian Numismatics: history, art and culture, 1992; (jtly) The Roman Coins, Republic and Empire up to Nerva, in the Provinciaal Museum G. M. Kam at Nijmegen, 1992; articles in Numismatic Chron., Jl Numismatic Soc. India, Schweizer Münzblätter, Acta Numismatica, S Asian Archaeology, Afghan Studies, S Asian Studies; etc. *Recreations:* travel, antiquities, photography, natural history, gardening, genealogy. *Address:* Admont, Dancers End, Tring, Herts HP23 6JY. *Club:* Athenæum.

McDOWALL, Keith Desmond, CBE 1988; independent consultant on public affairs and government relations, since 1988; *b* 3 Oct. 1929; *s* of William Charteris McDowall and Edna Florence McDowall; *m* 1st, 1957, Shirley Margaret Russell Astbury (marr. diss. 1985); two *d*; 2nd, 1988, Brenda Dean (*see* Baroness Dean of Thornton-le-Fylde). *Educ:* Heath Clark Sch., Croydon, Surrey. Served RAF, National Service, 1947–49. South London Press, 1947–55; Daily Mail, 1955–67: Indust. Corresp., 1958; Indust. Editor, 1961–67; Man. Dir, Inca Construction (UK) Co. Ltd, 1967–69; Govt Information Service: successively Chief Inf. Officer, DEA, BoT, Min. of Housing and Local Govt, DoE, and Home Office, 1969–72; Dir of Inf., NI Office, 1972–74; Dir of Inf., Dept of Employment, 1974–78; Man. Dir Public Affairs, British Shipbuilders, 1978–80. Dir, Govan Shipbuilders Ltd, 1978–80. Dir of Information, 1981–86, Dep. Dir Gen., 1986–88, CBI. Chm., Kiss FM Radio, 1990–92 (Chm., steering cttee, 1989–90). *Publications:* articles in newspapers and various pubns. *Recreations:* sailing, golf, mingling. *Address:* 2 Malvern Terrace, N1 1HR. *Clubs:* Reform; Medway Yacht (Rochester); South Herts Golf.

McDOWALL, Stuart, CBE 1984; Chairman, Fife Healthcare NHS Trust, since 1994; economic consultant; Senior Lecturer in Economics, University of St Andrews, 1967–91; *b* 19 April 1926; *s* of Robert McDowall and Gertrude Mary Collister; *m* 1951, Margaret Burnside Woods Gyle; three *s*. *Educ:* Liverpool Institute; St Andrews University (MA hons 1950). Personnel Manager, Michael Nairn & Co., 1955–61; Lectr in Econs, St Andrews Univ., 1961–67; Master, United Coll. of St Salvator and St Leonard, 1976–80. Dep. Chm., Central Arbitration Cttee, 1976–; Local Govt Boundary Comr for Scotland, 1983–; Member: Monopolies and Mergers Commn, 1985–89; Restrictive Practices Court, 1993–. Econ. Consultant to UN in Saudi Arabia, 1985–89. Sec., Scottish Economic Soc., 1970–76. *Publications:* (with P. R. Draper) Trade Adjustment and the British Jute Industry, 1978; (with H. M. Begg) Industrial Performance and Prospects in Areas Affected by Oil Developments, 1981; articles on industrial economics and regional economics. *Recreations:* golf, hill walking. *Address:* 10 Woodburn Terrace, St Andrews, Fife KY16 8BA. *T:* St Andrews (01334) 73247. *Clubs:* Commonwealth Trust; Royal and Ancient Golf (St Andrews).

MacDOWELL, Prof. Douglas Maurice, DLitt; FRSE; FBA 1993; Professor of Greek, University of Glasgow, since 1971; *b* 8 March 1931; *s* of Maurice Alfred MacDowell and Dorothy Jean MacDowell (*née* Allan). *Educ:* Highgate Sch.; Balliol Coll., Oxford (1st Cl. Classical Mods 1952, 1st Cl. Lit. Hum. 1954; MA, DLitt). FRSE 1991. Classics Master: Allhallows Sch., 1954–56; Merchant Taylors' Sch., 1956–58; University of Manchester: Asst Lectr, Lectr and Sen. Lectr, 1958–70; Reader in Greek and Latin, 1970–71. Vis. Fellow, Merton Coll., Oxford, 1969. *Publications:* Andokides: On the Mysteries, 1962; Athenian Homicide Law, 1963; Aristophanes: Wasps, 1971; The Law in Classical Athens, 1978; Spartan Law, 1986; Demosthenes: Against Meidias, 1990; Aristophanes and Athens, 1995. *Address:* Department of Classics, University of Glasgow, G12 8QQ. *T:* 0141–339 8855. *Club:* United Oxford & Cambridge University.

McDOWELL, Sir Eric (Wallace), Kt 1990; CBE 1982; FCA; Chairman, Capita Management Consultants Ltd, since 1992; *b* 7 June 1925; *s* of Martin Wallace McDowell and Edith Florence (*née* Hillock); *m* 1954, Helen Lilian (*née* Montgomery); one *s* two *d*. *Educ:* Royal Belfast Academical Instn. FCA 1957. Served War, 1943–46. Student Chartered Accountant, 1942, qualified 1948; Partner, Wilson Hennessey & Crawford, and (after merger in 1973) Deloitte, Haskins & Sells, 1952–85 (Sen. Partner, Belfast, 1980–85, retd). Director: NI Transport Holding Co., 1971–74; Spence Bryson Ltd, 1986–89; TSB Northern Ireland, 1986–92; AIB Group Northern Ireland, 1992–; Capita Northern Ireland. Member: Council, Inst. of Chartered Accountants in Ireland, 1968–77 (Pres., 1974–75); Industries Develt Adv. Cttee, 1971–82 (Chm., 1978–82); Adv. Cttee of NI Central Investment Fund for Charities, 1975– (Chm., 1980–); NI Econ. Council, 1977–83; Industrial Develt Bd for NI, 1982–91 (Chm., 1986–91); Exec. Cttee, Relate: Marriage Guidance, NI, 1981– (Chm., 1992–); Nat. Exec. Cttee, Relate, 1992–; Broadcasting Council for NI, 1983–86; Financial Reporting Review Panel, 1990–94; Senate, QUB, 1993–. Trustee, Presbyterian Church in Ireland, 1983–. Treas., Abbeyfield Belfast Soc., 1986–. Governor, Royal Belfast Academical Instn, 1959– (Chm. of Governors, 1977–86); President: Belfast Old Instonians Assoc., 1993–94; Confedn of Ulster Socs, 1989–. Hon. DSc(Econ) QUB, 1989. *Recreations:* music, drama, foreign travel. *Address:* Beechcroft, 19 Beechlands, Belfast BT9 5HU. *T:* Belfast (01232) 668771. *Clubs:* Royal Over-Seas League; Ulster Reform (Belfast).

McDOWELL, George Roy Colquhoun, CBE 1988; CEng, FIEE; Chairman, British Standards Institution, 1985–88; *b* 1 Sept. 1922; *s* of Robert Henry McDowell and Jean McDowell; *m* 1948, Joan Annie Bryan; two *s*. *Educ:* Coleraine Academical Instn; Queen's Univ., Belfast (BSc Eng). Signals Officer, RAF, 1942–46. Works Manager, Distribn Transformer Div., subseq. Works Manager, Power Transformer Div., Ferranti Ltd, 1950–69, Dir, 1969–87, Man. Dir Designate, 1969–72, Chm. and Man. Dir, 1972–87, George H. Scholes. Director: WSK (Electrical), 1980–; Clipsal (UK), 1983–; L. T. Switchgear, 1984–; Peter Peregrinus, 1985–; Capstead Controls Ltd, 1986; Pentland Electronics Ltd, 1987; PDL-Wylex Sdn Bhd, Malaysia, 1980–; Clipsal Switchgear Pty, Australia, 1982–; Menvier-Swain Group, 1985– (Chm.). Chairman: Electrical Installation Equipment Manufacturers' Assoc., 1977–80; British Electrotechnical Cttee, BSI; Electrotechnical Council, BSI, 1982–85; President: British Electrical and Allied Manufacturers' Assoc., 1981–82; Internat. Electrotechnical Commn, 1987–; IEEIE; Institution of Electrical Engineers: Chm., Power Bd; Chm., Finance Cttee; Mem. Council. Grand Decoration of Honour for Services to the Republic of Austria, 1978. *Recreations:* golf, Rugby, cricket. *Address:* 24 Oak Drive, Bramhall, Stockport, Cheshire SK7 2AD. *T:* 0161–439 4552. *Club:* Army and Navy.

McDOWELL, Sir Henry (McLorinan), KBE 1964 (CBE 1959); retired; *b* Johannesburg, S Africa, 10 Dec. 1910; *s* of John McDowell and Margaret Elizabeth Bingham; *m* 1939, Norah (*d* 1995), *d* of Walter Slade Douthwaite; one *s* one *d*. *Educ:* Witwatersrand Univ.; Queen's Coll., Oxford; Yale Univ. Served War of 1939–45, 1 Bn Northern Rhodesia Regt, East Africa and South-East Asia, 1940–44. Entered HM Colonial Service (Cadet, Northern Rhodesia), 1938; Clerk, Legislative and Executive Councils, 1945; Assistant Secretary, 1950; Deputy Financial Secretary, 1952. Imperial Defence Coll., 1948; seconded Colonial Office, 1949. Economic and Financial Working Party, in preparation for federation of Rhodesias and Nyasaland, 1953; Federal Treasury, 1954; Secretary, Ministry of Transport, 1955; Secretary, Federal Treasury, 1959–63. Chm., Zimbabwe Board, Barclays Bank Internat. Ltd, 1969–79; Chm. or Dir, other cos in Zimbabwe, 1964–79. Chancellor, Univ. of Rhodesia, 1971–81; Chm. or Mem., governing bodies, educational institutions, Zimbabwe, 1964–79. Hon. LLD Witwatersrand, 1971; Hon. DLitt Rhodesia, 1975. *Recreations:* walking, reading. *Address:* 2 Donne Court, Burbage Road, SE24 9HH. *Club:* Harare.

See also J. H. McDowell.

McDOWELL, Prof. John Henry, FBA 1983; FAAAS; University Professor of Philosophy, University of Pittsburgh, since 1988 (Professor of Philosophy, 1986–88); *b* 7 March 1942; *s* of Sir Henry McDowell, *qv*; *m* 1977, Andrea Lee Lehrke. *Educ:* St John's College, Johannesburg; University College of Rhodesia and Nyasaland; New College, Oxford. BA London; MA Oxon. FAAAS 1993. Fellow and Praelector in Philosophy, UC, Oxford, 1966–86, Emeritus Fellow, 1988; Univ. Lectr (CUF), Oxford Univ., 1967–86. James C. Loeb Fellow in Classical Philosophy, Harvard Univ., 1969; Visiting Professor: Univ. of Michigan, 1975; Univ. of California, Los Angeles, 1977; Univ. of Minnesota, 1982; Jadavpur Univ., Calcutta, 1983; John Locke Lectr, Oxford Univ., 1991. Sen. Fellow, Council of Humanities, Princeton Univ., 1984. *Publications:* Plato, Theaetetus (trans. with notes), 1973; (ed with Gareth Evans) Truth and Meaning, 1976; (ed) Gareth Evans, The Varieties of Reference, 1982; (ed with Philip Pettit) Subject, Thought, and Context, 1986; Mind and World, 1994; articles in jls and anthologies. *Recreations:* reading, music, gardening, lawn tennis. *Address:* c/o Department of Philosophy, University of Pittsburgh, Pittsburgh, PA 15260, USA. *T:* (412)6245792.

McDOWELL, Malcolm, (Malcolm Taylor); actor; *b* 13 June 1943; *m* 1992, Kelley Kuhr; one *s* one *d* by prev. marriage. *Educ:* Leeds. *Stage:* RSC Stratford, 1965–66; Entertaining Mr Sloane, Royal Court, 1975; Look Back in Anger, NY, 1980; In Celebration, NY, 1984; Holiday, Old Vic, 1987; Another Time, NY, 1993; *films:* If, 1969; Figures in a Landscape, 1970; The Raging Moon, 1971; A Clockwork Orange, 1971; O Lucky Man, 1973; Royal Flash, 1975; Aces High, 1976; Voyage of the Damned,

1977; Caligula, 1977; The Passage, 1978; Time After Time, 1979; Cat People, 1981; Blue Thunder, 1983; Get Crazy, 1983; Britannia Hospital, 1984; Gulag, 1985; Cross Creek, 1985; Sunset, 1988; Assassin of the Tsar, 1991; Milk Money, 1993; Star Trek Generations, 1994; Tank Girl, 1995. *Address:* c/o ICM, 76 Oxford Street, W1R 1RB.

McDOWELL, Stanley; Town Clerk and Chief Executive, Belfast City Council, 1989–92; *b* 14 June 1941; *s* of William McDowell and Annie Storey; *m* 1966, Charlotte Elizabeth Stockdale; three *d*. *Educ:* Royal Belfast Academical Instn; Queen's Univ. of Belfast (BSc Econ). FCIS. Belfast City and Dist Water Comrs, 1959–70; Asst Sec. (Actg), Antrim County Council, 1971–73; Roads Service Divl Finance Officer, DoE (NI), 1973–79; Belfast City Council, 1979–92; Asst Town Clerk (Admin), 1979–89. *Address:* 12 Slievedarragh Park, Belfast BT14 8JA. *T:* Belfast (01232) 716472.

MACDUFF, Earl of; *now see* Earl of Southesk.

MacDUFF, Alistair Geoffrey; QC 1993; a Recorder, since 1987; *b* 26 May 1945; *s* of late Alexander MacDonald MacDuff and of Irish Emma Jarvis (*née* Gardner); 1st, 1969, Susan Christine Kitchener (*d* 1991); two *d*; 2nd 1993, Katherine Anne Buckley. *Educ:* Ecclesfield Grammar Sch., Sheffield; LSE (LLB 1965); Sheffield Univ. (LLM 1967). Called to the Bar, Lincoln's Inn, 1969; Asst Recorder, 1983–87. *Recreations:* theatre, opera, travel, golf, Association football. *Address:* Devereux Chambers, Devereux Court, WC2R 3JJ. *T:* 0171–353 7534. *Clubs:* Hendon Golf; Economicals Association Football (New Malden).

McDUFF, Prof. (Margaret) Dusa, PhD; FRS 1994; Professor of Mathematics, State University of New York at Stony Brook, since 1984; *b* 18 Oct. 1945; *d* of Conrad Hal Waddington and Margaret Justin (*née* Blanco White); *m* 1st, 1968, David William McDuff (marr. diss. 1978); one *d*; 2nd, 1984, John Willard Milnor; one *s*. *Educ:* Univ. of Edinburgh (BSc Hons); Girton Coll., Cambridge (PhD 1971). Lecturer: Univ. of York, 1972–76; Univ. of Warwick, 1976–78; Asst Prof., 1978–80, Associate Prof., 1980–84, SUNY at Stony Brook. Asst Prof., MIT, 1974–75; Mem., Inst. for Advanced Study, Princeton, 1976 and 1977; Vis. Prof., Univ of Calif, Berkeley, 1993. *Publications:* (with D. Salamon): J-Holomorphic Curves and Quantum Cohomology, 1994; Introduction to Symplectic Topology, 1995. *Recreations:* chamber music, reading, walking. *Address:* Mathematics Department, State University of New York, Stony Brook, NY 11794, USA. *T:* (516) 6328290.

MACE, Brian Anthony; Director, Savings and Investment Division, Board of Inland Revenue, since 1990; *b* 9 Sept. 1948; *s* of late Edward Laurence Mace and of Olive (*née* Bennett); *m* 1973, Anne Margaret Cornford. *Educ:* Maidstone Grammar Sch.; Gonville and Caius Coll., Cambridge (MA Mathematics). Admin trainee, Bd of Inland Revenue, 1971–73; seconded to Secretariat, Inflation Accounting Cttee, 1974–75; Inland Revenue: Principal, 1975–82; Asst Sec., 1982–90; Under Sec., 1990–. *Recreations:* opera, chamber music and song, theatre, cricket, historic buildings. *Address:* Board of Inland Revenue, South West Wing, Bush House, Strand, WC2B 4RD. *T:* 0171–438 6614.

MACE, Lt-Gen. Sir John (Airth), KBE 1990 (OBE 1974; MBE 1967); CB 1986; New Zealand Chief of Defence Force, 1987–91; *b* 29 June 1932; *m* 1962, Margaret Theodocia (*née* McCallum); one *s* one *d*. *Educ:* Ashburton High Sch., NZ; Nelson Coll., NZ; RMC Duntroon, Australia. Commissioned NZ Army, 1953; NZ SAS, 1955–57; active service in Malayan Emergency (despatches, 1958); Comd SAS Sqdn, 1960–62 and 1965; Comd Co. of 1 RNZIR 1st Bn, Borneo, 1966; Vietnam, 1967; appts include: Dir of Infantry and NZ SAS; CO, 1st Bn RNZIR, Singapore; Dir, Officer Postings; Comdr, Army Logistics Support Gp; Comdr, 1st Inf. Bde Gp; Army Staff Coll., Camberley; JSSC, Canberra; Comdr, NZ Force SE Asia, 1979–80; RCDS 1981; Dep. Chief of Defence Staff, 1982–84; Chief of General Staff, 1984–87. *Recreations:* golf, walking, reading. *Clubs:* Wellesley, Wellington, Wellington Golf (Wellington).

MacEACHEN, Hon. Allan Joseph, PC (Canada); Leader of Opposition in the Senate, 1984–91; *b* Inverness, Nova Scotia, 6 July 1921; *s* of Angus and Annie MacEachen. *Educ:* St Francis Xavier Univ. (BA 1944); Univ. of Toronto (MA 1946); Univ. of Chicago; MIT. Prof. of Economics, St Francis Xavier Univ., 1946–48; Head of Dept of Economics and Social Sciences; MP (L) Cape Breton Highlands-Canso, Nova Scotia, 1953–84; Special Asst and Consultant on Econ. Affairs to Hon. Lester Pearson, 1958; Minister: of Labour, 1963–65; of Nat. Health and Welfare, 1965–68; of Manpower and Immigration, 1968–70; of External Affairs, 1974–76; of Finance, 1980–82; Sec. of State for External Affairs, 1982–84; Pres., Privy Council and Govt Leader in House of Commons, Canada, 1970–74 and 1976–79; Dep. Prime Minister, 1977–79 and 1980–84; Dep. Leader of the Opposition and Opposition House Leader, 1979–80; called to Senate, 1984, Leader of Govt in Senate, 1984. Hon. Degrees: St Francis Xavier Univ.; Acadia Univ.; Loyola Coll; St Mary's Univ.; Dalhousie Univ.; Wilfrid Laurier Univ. *Address:* The Senate, Ottawa K1A 0A4, Canada.

McEACHERN, Allan; Hon. Chief Justice McEachern; Chief Justice of British Columbia, since 1988; *b* 20 May 1926; *s* of John A. and L. B. McEachern; *m* 1953, Gloria L.; two *d*. *Educ:* Univ. of British Columbia (BA 1949; LLB 1950). Called to the Bar of British Columbia, 1951. Partner, Russell and DuMoulin, Barristers, 1950–79; Chief Justice, Supreme Court of BC, 1979–88. Hon. LLM Univ. of BC, 1990. *Recreations:* walking, sailing, gardening. *Address:* The Law Courts, 800 Smithe Street, Vancouver, BC V6Z 2E1, Canada. *T:* (604)6602710.

McEACHRAN, Colin Neil, JD; QC (Scot.) 1982; *b* 14 Jan. 1940; *s* of Eric Robins McEachran and Nora Helen Bushe; *m* 1967, Katherine Charlotte Henderson; two *d*. *Educ:* Trinity Coll., Glenalmond; Merton Coll., Oxford (BA 1961); Univ. of Glasgow (LLB 1963); Univ. of Chicago (Commonwealth Fellow; JD 1965). Admitted Solicitor, 1966; admitted to Faculty of Advocates, 1968. Solicitor, Glasgow, 1966–67; Advocate Depute, 1975–78. Mem., Scottish Legal Aid Bd, 1990–. Vice Chm., Commonwealth Games Council for Scotland, 1991–. *Recreations:* target rifle shooting (Silver Medal, Commonwealth Games, NZ, 1974), hill walking. *Address:* 1 Saxe-Coburg Place, Edinburgh EH3 5BR. *T:* 0131–332 6820.

MACEDO, Prof. Helder Malta, PhD; Camoens Professor of Portuguese, University of London at King's College, since 1982; *b* 30 Nov. 1935; *s* of Adelino José de Macedo and Aida Malta de Macedo; *m* 1960, Suzette Armanda (*née* de Aguiar). *Educ:* Faculty of Law, Univ. of Lisbon; King's Coll., Univ. of London (BA, PhD); FKC 1991. Lectr in Portuguese and Brazilian Studies, KCL, 1971–82; Sec. of State for Culture, Portuguese Govt, 1979. Visiting Professor: Harvard Univ., 1981; Ecole des Hautes Etudes et Sciences Sociales, Paris, 1992, 1995. Pres., Internat. Assoc. of Lusitanists, 1994–. Fellow, Academia das Ciências de Lisboa, 1987. Editor, Portuguese Studies Jl, 1985–. Comendador, Ordem de Santiago da Espada (Portugal), 1993. *Publications:* Nós, Uma Leitura de Cesário Verde, 1975, 3rd edn 1986; Do Significado Oculto da 'Menina a Moça', 1977; Poesia 1957–77, 1978; Camões e a Viagem Iniciática, 1980; The Purpose of Praise: Past and Future in The Lusiads of Luís de Camões, 1983; Cesário Verde: O Romântico e o Feroz, 1988; Partes de Africa, 1991; Viagem de Inverno, 1994. *Address:* Department of Portuguese and Brazilian Studies, King's College London, Strand, WC2R 2LS. *T:* 0171–873 2507.

McELHERAN, John; Principal Assistant Solicitor (Under Secretary), Ministry of Agriculture, Fisheries and Food, 1983–89; *b* 18 Aug. 1929; *s* of late Joseph Samuel McElheran and Hilda McElheran (*née* Veale); *m* 1956, Jean Patricia Durham; one *s* two *d*. *Educ:* Archbishop Holgate's Grammar Sch., York; St Edmund Hall, Oxford (BA English, DipEd). Solicitor. Short period of teaching; articled clerk, Thomson & Hetherton, York, 1954; Asst Solicitor 1959, Partner 1962, Leathes Prior & Son, Norwich; Senior Legal Asst, Land Commn, Newcastle upon Tyne, 1967; Sen. Legal Asst 1971, Asst Solicitor 1974, Dept of Trade and Industry and successor Depts. *Recreation:* photography. *Address:* 12 Bedern, York YO1 2LP. *T:* York (01904) 628987. *Club:* Civil Service.

McENERY, John Hartnett; author, consultant and conceptual analyst, since 1981; *b* 5 Sept. 1925; *y s* of late Maurice Joseph and Elizabeth Margaret McEnery (*née* Maccabe); *m* 1977, Lilian Wendy, *yr d* of late Reginald Gibbons and Lilian Gibbons (*née* Cox). *Educ:* St Augustine's Sch., Coatbridge; St Aloysius Coll., Glasgow; Glasgow Univ. (MA(Hons)). Served War of 1939–45: RA, 1943–47; Staff Captain, Burma Command, 1946–47. Glasgow Univ., 1947–49. Asst Principal, Scottish Educn Dept, 1949; Principal, 1954; Cabinet Office, 1957; HM Treasury, 1959; Min. of Aviation, 1962; UK Delegn to NATO, 1964; Counsellor (Defence Supply), British Embassy, Bonn, 1966; Asst Sec., Min. of Technology, 1970; Dept of Trade and Industry, 1970–72; Under-Sec. and Regional Dir for Yorks and Humberside, DTI, 1972, Dept of Industry, 1974–76; Under Sec., Concorde and Nationalisation Compensation Div., Dept of Industry, 1977–81. *Publications:* Manufacturing Two Nations—the sociological trap created by the bias of British regional policy against service industry, 1981; Towards a New Concept of Conflict Evaluation, 1985; Epilogue in Burma 1945–48: the military dimension of British withdrawal, 1990; articles in Jl of Economic Affairs. *Recreations:* various games and sports, chess, travel. *Address:* 37 Leinster Avenue, East Sheen, SW14 7JW. *Club:* Hurlingham.

McENERY, Peter; actor; Associate Artist, Royal Shakespeare Co.; *b* 21 Feb. 1940; *s* of Charles and Mary McEnery; *m* 1978; one *d*. *Educ:* various state and private schs. First stage appearance, Brighton, 1956; first London appearance in Flowering Cherry, Haymarket, 1957; *stage:* rôles with RSC include, 1961–: Laertes, Tybalt, Johnny Hobnails in Afore Night Come, Bassanio, Lorenzaccio, Orlando, Sachs in The Jail Diary of Albie Sachs, Pericles, Brutus, Antipholus of Ephesus, Godber in A Dream of People; other rôles include: Rudge in Next Time I'll Sing to You, Criterion, 1963; Konstantin in The Seagull, Queen's, 1964; Harry Winter in The Collaborators, Duchess, 1973; Trigorin in The Seagull, Lyric, 1975; Edward Gover in Made in Bangkok, Aldwych, 1986; Fredrik in A Little Night Music, Chichester, transf. Piccadilly, 1989; Torvald in The Doll's House, Robert in Dangerous Corner, Chichester, 1994; Menelaus in Women of Troy, NT, 1995; directed: Richard III, Nottingham, 1971; The Wound, Young Vic, 1972. *Films* include: Tunes of Glory, 1961; Victim, 1961; The Moonspinners, 1963; Entertaining Mr Sloane, 1970; *television:* Clayhanger, 1976; The Jail Diary of Albie Sachs, 1980; Pictures, 1983; The Collectors, 1986; The Mistress, 1986; Witchcraft, 1992. *Recreations:* steam railway preservation, ski-ing, American football. *Address:* c/o Dennis Selinger, ICM, 76 Oxford Street, W1R 1RB.

McENTEE, Peter Donovan, CMG 1978; OBE 1963; HM Diplomatic Service, retired; Governor and Commander-in-Chief of Belize, 1976–80; *b* 27 June 1920; *s* of Ewen Brooke McEntee and Caroline Laura Clare (*née* Bayley); *m* 1945, Mary Elisabeth Sherwood; two *d*. *Educ:* Haileybury Coll., Herts. Served War, HM Forces, 1939–45, KAR (Major). HM Overseas Civil Service, 1946–63: Dist Commissioner; retired as Principal of Kenya Inst. of Administration; First Secretary: Commonwealth Relations Office, 1963; Lagos, 1964–67; Commonwealth Office (later Foreign and Commonwealth Office), 1967–72; Consul-Gen., Karachi, 1972–75. Chm., Royal Over-Seas League, 1992–. *Recreations:* music, natural history. *Address:* Woodlands, Church Lane, Danehill, Sussex RH17 7EU.

MACER, Dr Richard Charles Franklin, MA, PhD; consultant, since 1985; *b* 21 Oct. 1928; *s* of Lionel William Macer and Adie Elizabeth Macer; *m* 1952, Vera Gwendoline Jeapes; three *d*. *Educ:* Worthing High Sch.; St John's Coll., Cambridge. Research, St John's Coll., Cambridge, 1949–55, Hutchinson Res. Student, 1952–53; Hd of Plant Pathology Section, Plant Breeding Inst., Cambridge, 1955–66; Dir and Dir of Res., Rothwell Plant Breeders Ltd, Lincs, 1966–72; Prof. of Crop Production, Univ. of Edinburgh, 1972–76; Dir, Scottish Plant Breeding Station, 1976–81; Gen. Manager, Plant Royalty Bureau Ltd, 1981–85. *Publications:* papers on fungal diseases of cereals. *Recreations:* hill walking, archaeology, reading. *Club:* Farmers'.

McEVOY, David Dand; QC 1983; barrister-at-law; a Recorder of the Crown Court, since 1979; *b* 25 June 1938; *s* of David Dand McEvoy and Ann Elizabeth McEvoy (*née* Breslin); *m* 1974, Belinda Anne Robertson; three *d*. *Educ:* Mount St Mary's Coll.; Lincoln Coll., Oxford. BA (PPE). 2nd Lieut The Black Watch, RHR, 1958–59. Called to the Bar, Inner Temple, 1964. *Recreations:* golf, fishing. *Address:* Chambers Court, Longdon, Tewkesbury, Glos GL20 6AS. *T:* Birtsmorton (0168481) 626. *Clubs:* Blackwell Golf; Midland Flyfishers.

McEWAN, Geraldine, (Mrs Hugh Cruttwell); actress; *b* 9 May 1932; *d* of Donald and Norah McKeown; *m* 1953, Hugh Cruttwell, *qv*; one *s* one *d*. *Educ:* Windsor County Girls' School. Acted with Theatre Royal, Windsor, 1949–51; Who Goes There, 1951; Sweet Madness, 1952; For Better For Worse, 1953; Summertime, 1955; Love's Labour's Lost, Stratford-on-Avon, 1956; The Member of the Wedding, Royal Court Theatre, 1957; The Entertainer, Palace, 1957–58; Stratford-on-Avon, 1958: Pericles; Twelfth Night; Much Ado About Nothing; 1961: Much Ado About Nothing; Hamlet; Everything in the Garden, Arts and Duke of York's, 1962; School for Scandal, Haymarket, and USA, 1962; The Private Ear, and The Public Eye, USA, 1963; Loot, 1965; National Theatre, 1965–71: Armstrong's Last Goodnight; Love For Love; A Flea in Her Ear; The Dance of Death; Edward II; Home and Beauty; Rites; The Way of the World; The White Devil; Amphitryon 38; Dear Love, Comedy, 1973; Chez Nous, Globe, 1974; The Little Hut, Duke of York's, 1974; Oh Coward!, Criterion, 1975; On Approval, Haymarket, 1975; Look After Lulu, Chichester, and Haymarket, 1978; A Lie of the Mind, Royal Court, 1987; Lettice and Lovage, Globe, 1988; Hamlet, Riverside Studio, 1992; The Bird Sanctuary, Abbey, Dublin, 1994; National Theatre: The Browning Version and Harlequinade, 1980; The Provok'd Wife, 1980; The Rivals, 1983; Two Inches of Ivory, 1983; You Can't Take It With You, 1983. Directed: As You Like It, Birmingham Rep., transf. Phoenix, 1988; Treats, Hampstead, 1989; Waiting for Sir Larry, Edinburgh, 1990; Four Door Saloon, Hampstead, 1991; Keyboard Skills, Bush, 1993. *Television series:* The Prime of Miss Jean Brodie, 1978; The Barchester Chronicles, 1982; Mapp and Lucia, 1985, 1986; Oranges are not the only Fruit, 1990; Mulberry, 1992, 1993. *Films:* The Adventures of Tom Jones, 1975; Escape from the Dark, 1978; Foreign Body, 1986; Henry V, 1989; Robin Hood, Prince of Thieves, 1991. *Address:* c/o Marmont Management Ltd, Langham House, 302–308 Regent Street, W1R 5AL.

McEWAN, Ian Russell, FRSL 1982; author; *b* 21 June 1948; *s* of Major (retd) David McEwan and Rose Lilian Violet Moore; *m* 1982, Penny Allen (marr. diss. 1985); two *s* two *d*. *Educ:* Woolverstone Hall Sch.; Univ. of Sussex (BA Hons Eng. Lit.); Univ. of East

Anglia (MA Eng. Lit.). Began writing, 1970. Hon. DLitt Sussex, 1989; Hon. LittD E Anglia, 1993. *Films:* The Ploughman's Lunch, 1983; Last Day of Summer, 1984; Soursweet, 1988; The Innocent, 1993. *Publications:* First Love, Last Rites, 1975; In Between the Sheets, 1978; The Cement Garden, 1978 (filmed, 1993); The Imitation Game, 1981; The Comfort of Strangers, 1981; Or Shall we Die? (oratorio; score by Michael Berkeley), 1982; The Ploughman's Lunch (film script), 1985; The Child in Time, 1987 (Whitbread Award; Prix Fémina, 1993); Soursweet (film script), 1989; The Innocent, 1990; Black Dogs, 1992; The Daydreamer, 1994; The Short Stories, 1995. *Recreations:* hiking, tennis. *Address:* c/o Jonathan Cape, Random Century House, 20 Vauxhall Bridge Road, SW1V 2SA.

McEWAN, Robin Gilmour, QC (Scot.) 1981; PhD; Sheriff of South Strathclyde, Dumfries and Galloway at Ayr, since 1988 (at Lanark, 1982–88); Temporary Judge, Court of Session and High Court of Justiciary, since 1991; *b* 12 Dec. 1943; *s* of late Ian G. McEwan and of Mary McEwan, Paisley, Renfrewshire; *m* 1973, Sheena, *d* of late Stewart F. McIntyre and of Lilian McIntyre, Aberdour; two *d*. *Educ:* Paisley Grammar Sch.; Glasgow Univ. (1st Cl. Hons LLB; PhD). Faulds Fellow in Law, Glasgow Univ., 1965–68; admitted to Faculty of Advocates, 1967. Standing Jun. Counsel to Dept of Energy, 1974–76; Advocate Depute, 1976–79. Chm., Industrial Tribunals, 1981–; Mem., Scottish Legal Aid Bd, 1989–. *Publications:* Pleading in Court, 1980, 2nd edn 1995; (with Ann Paton) A Casebook on Damages in Scotland, 1983; contrib. Stair Memorial Encyclopaedia of the Laws of Scotland, 1987. *Recreation:* golf. *Address:* Sheriff's Chambers, Sheriff Court House, Wellington Square, Ayr KA7 1DR. *T:* Ayr (01292) 268474. *Clubs:* New (Edinburgh); Honourable Company of Edinburgh Golfers, Prestwick Golf.

MacEWEN, Ann Maitland, RIBA (DisTP), MRTPI; Planning Consultant; *b* 15 Aug. 1918; *d* of Dr Maitland Radford, MD, DPH, MOH St Pancras, and Dr Muriel Radford; *m* 1st, 1940, John Wheeler, ARIBA, AADip (Hons), Flt-Lt, RAF (killed on active service, 1945); two *d*; 2nd, 1947, Malcolm MacEwen, *qv*; one *d*. *Educ:* Howell's Sch., Denbigh, N Wales; Architectural Assoc. Sch. of Architecture (AA Dip., RIBA); Assoc. for Planning and Regional Reconstruction Sch. of Planning (SP Dip., MRTPI). Architectural Asst, 1945–46; Planning Asst, Hemel Hempstead New Town Master Plan, 1946–47; Architect-Planner with LCC, 1949–61; Mem., Colin Buchanan's Gp, Min. of Transport, which produced official report, Traffic in Towns, 1961–63; res. work, Transport Section, Civil Engineering Dept, Imperial Coll., 1963–64; Partner, Colin Buchanan and Partners, 1964–73. Senior Lectr, Bristol Univ. Sch. of Advanced Urban Studies, 1974–77; Hon. Res. Fellow, UCL, 1977–84. Mem., Noise Adv. Council, 1971–73. RIBA Distinction in Town Planning, 1967. *Publications:* National Parks—Cosmetics or Conservation? (with M. MacEwen), 1982; (with Joan Davidson) The Livable City, 1983; (with M. MacEwen) Greenprints for the Countryside? the story of Britain's National Parks, 1987. *Address:* Manor House, Wootton Courtenay, Minehead, Somerset TA24 8RD. *T:* Timberscombe (01643) 841325.

McEWEN, Hilary Mary; *see* Mantel, H. M.

McEWEN, Sir John (Roderick Hugh), 5th Bt *cr* 1953; *b* 4 Nov. 1965; *s* of Sir Robert Lindley McEwen, 3rd Bt, of Marchmont and Bardrochat, and of Brigid Cecilia, *d* of late James Laver, CBE, and Veronica Turleigh; *S* brother, 1983. *Educ:* Ampleforth; University Coll. London. *Heir: cousin* Adam Hugo McEwen, *b* 9 Feb. 1965. *Address:* 10 Leven Street, Edinburgh EH3 9LG.

MacEWEN, Malcolm; journalist; *b* 24 Dec. 1911; *s* of late Sir Alexander MacEwen and of Lady (Mary Beatrice) MacEwen; *m* 1st, 1937, Barbara Mary Stebbing, BSc (*d* 1944); one *d*; 2nd, 1947, Mrs Ann Maitland Wheeler (*see* Ann Maitland MacEwen); one *d* (and two step *d*). *Educ:* Edinburgh Univ. (MA, LLB). Member (Lab) Ross and Cromarty CC, 1938–40; wrote for Daily Worker, mainly as Parliamentary Correspondent, 1943–56; Asst Editor, Architects' Jl, 1956–60; Editor, RIBA Jl, 1964–71; RIBA: Head of Information Services, 1960–66; Publishing Services, 1966–70; Dir, Public Affairs, 1971–72. Leverhulme Res. Fellow, 1972–73; Research Fellow: UCL, 1977–84; Birkbeck Coll., 1985–88. Mem., Exmoor Nat. Park Cttee, 1973–81. Hon. Fellow, RIBA, 1974. *Publications:* Crisis in Architecture, 1974; (ed) Future Landscapes, 1976; (with Mrs A. M. MacEwen) National Parks—Cosmetics or Conservation?, 1982; (with G. Sinclair) New Life for the Hills, 1983; (jtly) Countryside Conflicts, 1986; (with A. M. MacEwen) Greenprints for the Countryside? the story of Britain's National Parks, 1987; The Greening of a Red, 1991. *Address:* Manor House, Wootton Courtenay, Somerset TA24 8RD. *T:* Timberscombe (01643) 841325.

MACEY, Rear-Adm. David Edward, CB 1984; Registrar and Secretary, Order of the Bath, since 1990; Receiver-General, Canterbury Cathedral, since 1984; *b* 15 June 1929; *s* of Frederick William Charles Macey and Florence May Macey; *m* 1st, 1958, Lorna Therese Verner (decd), *o d* of His Honour Judge Oliver William Verner; one *s* one *d*, and one step *s* two step *d*; 2nd, 1982, Fiona (marr. diss. 1994), *o d* of Vice-Adm. Sir William Beloe, KBE, CB, DSC. *Educ:* Sir Joseph Williamson's Mathematical Sch., Rochester; Royal Naval Coll., Dartmouth. Midshipman, 1948; Cruisers, Carriers, Destroyers, 1950–63; Comdr, 1963; Amer. Staff Coll., 1964; Comdr, RNC Dartmouth, 1970; Captain, 1972; Directorate Naval Plans, 1972–74; RCDS, 1975; Dir, RN Staff Coll., 1976–78; Dir, Naval Manpower, 1979–81; Rear-Adm., 1981; Dep. Asst Chief of Staff (Ops), SACEUR, 1981–84. ADC to HM the Queen, 1981. Gentleman Usher of the Scarlet Rod, Order of the Bath, 1985–90. Mem., Archbps' Commn on Cathedrals, 1992–. *Recreations:* walking, cricket, cooking. *Address:* 10 Lees Court, Sheldwich, near Faversham, Kent ME13 0NQ. *Clubs:* Anglo-Belgian, MCC; Band of Brothers (Kent).

MACEY, Air Vice-Marshal Eric Harold, OBE, 1975; Director General of Training (Royal Air Force), 1989–91, retired; *b* 9 April 1936; *s* of Harold Fred and Katrina Emma Mary Macey; *m* 1957, Brenda Ann Bracher; one *s* one *d*. *Educ:* Shaftesbury Grammar School; Southampton Tech. Coll. Asst Sci. Officer, Min. of Supply, 1953–54; RAF, 1954; commissioned, 1955; Pilot's Wings, 1956; RAF Staff Coll., 1966; RCDS 1983; AOC and Comdt, RAF Coll., Cranwell, 1985–87; ACDS (Policy and Nuclear), 1987–89. *Recreations:* music, walking, DIY. *Address:* Ebblemead, Homington, Salisbury, Wilts SP5 4NL. *Club:* Royal Air Force.

McFADDEN, Jean Alexandra, CBE 1992; JP; DL; MA, LLB; Leader, Glasgow District Council, 1980–86 and since 1992; Lecturer in Law, University of Strathclyde, since 1992; Vice Lord Lieutenant of City of Glasgow, 1980–92; *b* 26 Nov. 1941; *d* of John and Elma Hogg; *m* 1966, John McFadden (*d* 1991). *Educ:* Univ. of Glasgow (MA 1st Cl. Hons Classics); Univ. of Strathclyde (LLB 1st Cl. Hons). Principal Teacher of Classics, Strathclyde Schools, 1967–86; part-time Lectr in Law, Univ. of Glasgow, 1991–92. Entered Local Govt as Mem. of Glasgow Corp. for Cowcaddens Ward, 1971; Mem. for Scotstoun Ward, 1984– (due to boundary changes); Chm., Manpower Cttee, 1974–77; Leader of Labour Group, 1977–86, 1992–; Treasurer, Glasgow DC, 1986–92. Convener, Scottish Local Govt Information Unit, 1984–; Pres., Convention of Scottish Local Auths, 1990–92; Member Board: SDA, 1989–91; Glasgow Develt Agency, 1992–. Chm., Mayfest (Glasgow Internat. Arts Fest.), 1983–92. JP Glasgow, 1972; DL 1980. *Recreations:* cycling, theatre, walking, gliding, canoeing, golf. *Address:* 16 Lansdowne Crescent, Glasgow G20 6NQ. *T:* 0141–334 3522. *Club:* Tron Theatre (Glasgow).

McFADYEAN, Colin William; teacher, Avon Education Authority, since 1991; Coach, Cleve Rugby Football Club, since 1992; *b* 11 March 1943; *s* of Captain Angus John McFadyean, MC, 1st Bn London Scottish Regt (killed in action, 1944) and Joan Mary McFadyean (*née* Irish); *m* 1970, Jeanette Carol Payne; one *s*. *Educ:* Plymouth Coll.; Bristol Grammar Sch.; Loughborough Coll. of Education; Keele Univ. (DLC hons, Adv. DipEd). Phys. Educn teacher, Birmingham, 1965–67; Phys. Educn Lectr, 1967–72, Sen. Lectr, 1972–74, Cheshire; Dep. Dir, Nat. Sports Centre, Lilleshall, 1974–78; Chief Coach, Jubilee Sports Centre, Hong Kong, 1979–82; Sports Master and House Master, Dulwich Coll., 1983–85; Dir Gen., NPFA, 1985–87; with Croydon Educn Authy, 1988–90; Dir Coaching, Bristol FC (Rugby Union), 1990–1991; Coach, Moseley FC, 1991–93. Internat. Rugby career includes: 11 England caps, 1966–68; 4 Tests British Lions *v* NZ, 1966; (captain) *v* Ireland, 1968; (captain) *v* Wales, 1968; scored 5 tries, 1 dropped goal (in 15 Tests); other sport: coach to Hong Kong disabled team to Olympics, Arnhem, 1980; Adviser, Hong Kong table tennis team to World Championships, Yugoslavia, 1981. Broadcaster with Hong Kong TV and commercial radio. *Recreations:* tennis, golf, music. *Address:* The Barn, Parkfield Road, Pucklechurch, Bristol BS17 3PN. *Clubs:* British Sportsman's; England Rugby International's; Rugby Internationals Golf, Saltford Golf; Moseley Football (Vice-Pres.); Penguins Rugby Football (Vice-Pres).

MACFADYEN, Hon. Lord; Donald James Dobbie Macfadyen; a Senator of the College of Justice in Scotland, since 1995; *b* 8 Sept. 1945; *er s* of late Donald James Thomson Macfadyen and of Christina Dick Macfadyen; *m* 1971, Christine Balfour Gourlay Hunter; one *s* one *d*. *Educ:* Hutchesons' Boys' Grammar Sch., Glasgow; Glasgow Univ. (LLB 1967). Admitted to Faculty of Advocates, 1969, Vice-Dean 1992–95. Advocate Depute, 1979–82; Standing Jun. Counsel to Dept of Agric. and Fisheries for Scotland, 1977–79, to SHHD, 1982–83; QC (Scot.) 1983. Part-time Chm., Med. Appeal Tribunals and Vaccine Damage Tribunals, 1989–95; Temp. Judge, Court of Session, 1994–95. FCIArb 1993. *Address:* 66 Northumberland Street, Edinburgh EH3 6JE. *T:* 0131–556 6043, *Fax:* 0131–556 9149. *Club:* New (Edinburgh).

MACFADYEN, Donald James Dobbie; *see* Macfadyen, Hon. Lord.

MACFADYEN, Air Marshal Ian David, CB 1991; OBE 1984; FRAeS; Director General, Saudi Arabia Armed Forces Project, since 1994; *b* 19 Feb. 1942; *s* of Air Marshal Sir Douglas Macfadyen, KCB, CBE and of Lady Macfadyen (*née* Dafforn, now Mrs P. A. Rowan); *m* 1967, Sally Harvey; one *s* one *d*. *Educ:* Marlborough; RAF Coll., Cranwell. Joined RAF, 1960; Cranwell cadet, 1960–63; 19 Sqdn, 1965–68; HQ, RAF Strike Command, 1969; Flying Instructor, RAF Coll., Cranwell, 1970–73; RAF Staff Coll., 1973; 111 Sqdn, 1974–75; Flt Comdr, 43 Sqdn, 1976; HQ 2 ATAF, RAF Germany, 1976–79; comd 29 Sqdn, 1980–84; comd 23 Sqdn, 1984; MoD, 1984–85; comd RAF Leuchars, Fife, 1985–87; RCDS, 1988; MoD, 1989–90; COS, then Comdr, HQ British Forces ME, Riyadh, 1990–91; ACDS, Op. Requirements (Air Systems), 1991–94. Chm., 29 Sqdn Assoc.; Pres., RAF Clay Pigeon Shooting Assoc. Upper Freeman, GAPAN, 1992. QCVSA 1974. *Recreations:* shooting, photography, gliding, golf, aviation history, windsurfing. *Address:* c/o Lloyds Bank, Cox's & King's, PO Box 1190, 7 Pall Mall, SW1. *Clubs:* Royal Air Force; Royal & Ancient (St Andrews).

McFADZEAN, family name of **Baron McFadzean.**

McFADZEAN, Baron, *cr* 1966 (Life Peer); **William Hunter McFadzean,** KT 1976; Kt 1960; Director, Midland Bank, 1959–81 (Deputy Chairman, 1968–77); Hon. President, BICC plc, 1973 (Managing Director, 1954–61; Chairman, 1954–73); *b* Stranraer, 17 Dec. 1903; *s* of late Henry and of Agnes McFadzean, Stranraer; *m* 1933, Eileen, *e d* of Arthur Gordon, Blundellsands, Lancs.; one *s* one *d* (and one adopted *d* decd). *Educ:* Stranraer Academy and High Sch.; Glasgow Univ. Served articles with McLay, McAllister & McGibbon, Chartered Accountants, Glasgow, 1922–27; qualified as Chartered Accountant, 1927; with Chalmers Wade & Co., 1927–32; joined British Insulated Cables Ltd, as Accountant, 1932 (Financial Secretary, 1937; Exec. Manager, 1942); on amalgamation of British Insulated Cables Ltd and Callender's Cable & Construction Co. Ltd, in 1945, appointed to Board of British Insulated Callender's Cables Ltd as Exec. Director (Dep. Chairman, 1947; Chief Exec. Director, 1950), retd 1973; Chairman: Standard Broadcasting Corp. (UK) Ltd, 1972–79 (Hon. Pres., 1979–83); Home Oil (UK) Ltd, 1972–78; Scurry-Rainbow (UK) Ltd, 1974–78; Deputy Chairman: RTZ/BICC Aluminium Holdings Ltd, 1967–73; National Nuclear Corp., 1973–80; Canada Life Unit Trust Managers Ltd (Chm., 1971–82); Director: Anglesey Aluminium Ltd, 1968–73; Midland Bank Executor and Trustee Co., 1959–67; English Electric Co., 1966–68; Steel Co. of Wales Ltd, 1966–67; Canadian Imperial Bank of Commerce, 1967–74; Canada Life Assurance Co., 1969–79; Canada Life Assurance Co. of GB, 1971–84 (Dep. Chm., 1971–84); Home Oil Co. Ltd, 1972–77; Standard Broadcasting Corp. Ltd, 1976–79. Pres. FBI, 1959–61. Chairman: Council of Industrial Fedns of EFTA, 1960–63; (Founder) Export Council for Europe, 1960–64 (Hon. Pres. 1964–71); Commonwealth Export Council, 1964–66; British Nat. Export Council, 1964–66 (Pres. 1966–68); President: Brit. Electrical Power Convention, 1961–62; Brit. Nuclear Forum, 1964–66; Coal Trade Benevolent Assoc., 1967–68; Electrical and Electronics Industries Benevolent Assoc., 1968–69. Vice-President: Middle East Assoc., 1965; City of London Soc., 1965–72; British/Swedish Chamber of Commerce, 1963–74. Member: Inst. of Directors, 1954–76 (Council, 1954–74); Min. of Labour Adv. Bd on Resettlement of Ex-Regulars, 1957–60; Bd of Trade Adv. Council on ME Trade, 1958–60; MoT Shipping Adv. Panel, 1962–64; Ct of British Shippers' Council, 1964–74 (Pres., 1968–71); Council, Foreign Bondholders, 1968–74; Anglo-Danish Soc., 1965–75 (Chm., 1969–75; Hon. Pres., 1975); Adv. Cttee, Queen's Award for Industry, 1965–67 (Chm., Review Cttee, 1970). CompIEE 1956. JDipMA 1965. Commander Order of Dannebrog (Denmark), 1964, Grand Commander, 1974; Grande Oficial da Ordem do Infante Dom Henrique, Portugal, 1972. *Address:* 16 Lansdown Crescent, Bath, Avon BA1 5EX. *T:* Bath (01225) 335487.

McFALL, John; MP (Lab) Dumbarton, since 1987; *b* 4 Oct. 1944; *s* of John and Jean McFall; *m* 1969, Joan Ward; three *s* one *d*. *Educ:* St Patrick's Primary and Secondary Schools, Dumbarton; Paisley College (BSc Hons); Strathclyde Univ. (MBA); Open Univ. (BA). Schoolteacher, to Assistant Head Teacher, 1974–87. An Opposition Whip, 1989–91; Opposition front bench spokesman: for education and home affairs, 1992; on Scottish Affairs, 1992–. Member, House of Commons Select Committee: on Defence, 1988; on Sittings of the House, 1991; on Information, 1990–; Mem. Exec. Cttee, Parly Gp for Energy Studies, 1988–. Vis. Prof., Strathclyde Business Sch., Univ. of Strathclyde. *Recreations:* running, golf, reading. *Address:* 14 Oxhill Road, Dumbarton G82 4DG. *T:* Dumbarton (01389) 31437.

McFALL, Richard Graham; Chairman, 1980–86, Director, 1976–86, Fleming Enterprise Investment Trust plc (formerly Crossfriars Trust plc); *b* 31 Jan. 1920; 3rd *s* of Henry Joseph Marshall and Sarah Gertrude McFall; *m* 1945, Clara Louise Debonnaire Mitford; one *s* one *d*. *Educ:* Holmwood Prep. Sch., Lancs; Clifton Coll., Bristol. Joined Pacol Ltd, 1938; Mil. Service, HAC, 1939–40; Colonial Office, 1941–45 (Asst Sec., then Sec., W African Produce Control Bd); Motor & Air Products Ltd, 1946–48; re-joined Pacol Ltd, 1949, Dir 1951; Chm., London Cocoa Terminal Market Assoc., 1954–55; Chm., Cocoa Assoc.

of London, 1958–59; Dir 1962–82, Man. Dir 1965–74, Chm., 1970–76, Vice-Chm., 1976–78, Gill & Duffus Group PLC. *Recreation:* golf. *Address:* Springfold Cottage, Green Dene, East Horsley, Surrey KT24 5RG. *T:* East Horsley (01483) 283282. *Clubs:* Farmers'; Effingham Golf.

McFARLAND, Dr David John; Fellow, and Tutor in Psychology, Balliol College, Oxford, since 1966; University Reader in Animal Behaviour, University of Oxford, since 1974; *b* 31 Dec. 1938; *s* of John Cyril and Joan Elizabeth McFarland; *m* 1962, Frances Jill Tomlin; one *s* one *d. Educ:* Leighton Park Sch., Reading; Liverpool Univ. (BSc 1st Cl. Hons Zoology, 1961); Oxford Univ. (DPhil Psychology, 1965). Lecturer in Psychology: Durham Univ., 1964; Oxford Univ., 1966. Hofmeyer Fellow, Univ. of the Witwatersrand, 1974; Visiting Professor: Dalhousie Univ., 1968; Rutgers Univ., 1971; Univ. of Penn, 1977; SUNY, Stonybrook, 1978; Univ. of Oregon, 1978; Univ. of Münster, Germany, 1989. Pres., Internat. Ethological Conf., 1981. Editor, Animal Behaviour, 1969–74. *Publications:* (with J. McFarland) An Introduction to the Study of Behaviour, 1969; Feedback Mechanisms in Animal Behaviour, 1971; (ed) Motivational Control Systems Analysis, 1974; (ed) The Oxford Companion to Animal Behaviour, 1981; (with A. Houston) Quantitative Ethology: the state space approach, 1981; (ed) Functional Ontogeny, 1982; Animal Behaviour, 1985 (also USA); Problems of Animal Behaviour, 1989; Biologie des Verhaltens, (Germany) 1989; (with T. Bosser) Intelligent Behavior in Animals and Robots, (USA) 1993; articles in scientific learned jls. *Recreations:* keeping animals, pottery. *Address:* Balliol College, Oxford OX1 3BJ. *T:* Oxford (01865) 277760.

McFARLAND, Sir John (Talbot), 3rd Bt *cr* 1914, of Aberfoyle, Londonderry; TD 1967; Chairman: Lanes (Business Equipment), since 1977; J. T. McFarland Holdings, since 1984; McFarland Farms Ltd, since 1980; Director: G. Kinnaird & Son Ltd, since 1981; Windy Hills Ltd, since 1994; Erinwind Ltd, since 1994; *b* 3 Oct. 1927; *s* of Sir Basil Alexander Talbot McFarland, 2nd Bt, CBE, ERD, and Anne Kathleen (*d* 1952), *d* of late Andrew Henderson; *S* father, 1986; *m* 1957, Mary Scott, *d* of late Dr W. Scott Watson, Londonderry; two *s* two *d. Educ:* Marlborough College; Trinity Coll., Oxford. Captain RA (TA), retired 1967. Chairman: R. C. Malseed & Co. Ltd, 1957–90; Lanes (Derry) Ltd, 1977–84; Lanes (Fuel) Oils Ltd; Lanes Patent Fuels Ltd; Holmes Coal Ltd; Alexander Thompson & Co. Ltd; Nicholl Ballintyne Ltd; J. W. Corbett Ltd; Wattersons Ltd. Chm., Londonderry Lough Swilly Railway Co., 1978–81; Director: Londonderry Gaslight Co., 1958–89; Donegal Holdings Ltd, 1963–85. Member: Londonderry County Borough Council, 1955–69; NW HMC, 1960–73; Londonderry Port and Harbour Commrs, 1965–73. Jt Chm., Londonderry and Foyle Coll., 1971–76. High Sheriff, Co. Londonderry 1958, City of County of Londonderry 1965–67; DL Londonderry 1962, resigned 1982. *Recreations:* golf, shooting. *Heir: er s* Anthony Basil Scott McFarland [*b* 29 Nov. 1959; *m* 1988, Anne Margaret, *d* of T. K. Laidlaw, Gernonstown, Slane, Co. Meath. *Educ:* Marlborough Coll.; Trinity College, Dublin (BA). ACA]. *Address:* Dunmore House, Carrigans, Lifford, Co. Donegal. *T:* Letterkenny 40120. *Clubs:* Kildare Street and University (Dublin); Northern Counties (Londonderry).

MACFARLANE, family name of **Baron Macfarlane of Bearsden.**

MACFARLANE OF BEARSDEN, Baron *cr* 1991 (Life Peer), of Bearsden in the district of Bearsden and Milngavie; **Norman Somerville Macfarlane,** Kt 1983; DL; FRSE; Chairman: Macfarlane Group (Clansman) PLC, since 1973 (Managing Director, 1973–90); United Distillers PLC, since 1987; Lord High Commissioner, General Assembly, Church of Scotland, 1992 and 1993; *b* 5 March 1926; *s* of Daniel Robertson Macfarlane and Jessie Lindsay Somerville; *m* 1953, Marguerite Mary Campbell; one *s* four *d. Educ:* High Sch. of Glasgow. FRSE 1991. Commnd RA, 1945; served Palestine, 1945–47. Founded N. S. Macfarlane & Co. Ltd, 1949; became Macfarlane Group (Clansman) PLC, 1973. Underwriting Mem. of Lloyd's, 1978–; Chairman: The Fine Art Society PLC, 1976–; American Trust PLC, 1984– (Dir, 1980–); Guinness PLC, 1987–89 (Jt Dep. Chm., 1989–92); Director: Clydesdale Bank PLC, 1980–; General Accident Fire & Life Assce Corp. plc, 1984–; Edinburgh Fund Managers plc, 1980–. Dir, Glasgow Chamber of Commerce, 1976–79; Member: Council, CBI Scotland, 1975–81; Bd, Scottish Develt Agency, 1979–87. Chm., Glasgow Develt Agency (formerly Glasgow Action), 1985–92. Vice Chm., Scottish Ballet, 1983–87 (Dir, 1975–); Dir, Scottish National Orch., 1977–82; Pres., Royal Glasgow Inst. of the Fine Arts, 1976–87; Mem., Royal Fine Art Commn for Scotland, 1980–82; Scottish Patron, National Art Collection Fund, 1978–; Governor, Glasgow Sch. of Art, 1976–87; Trustee: Nat. Heritage Meml Fund, 1984–; Nat. Galls of Scotland, 1986–. Dir, Third Eye Centre, 1978–81. Chm. Governors, High Sch. of Glasgow, 1979–92; Mem. Court, Univ. of Glasgow, 1979–87. President: Stationers' Assoc. of GB and Ireland, 1965; Co. of Stationers of Glasgow, 1968–70; Glasgow High Sch. Club, 1970–72. DL Dunbartonshire, 1993. HRSA 1987; HRGI 1987; Hon. FRIAS 1984; Hon. FScotvec 1991; Hon. FRCPSGlas 1992; Hon. Fellow, Glasgow Sch. of Art, 1993. Hon. LLD: Strathclyde, 1986; Glasgow, 1988; Glasgow Caledonian, 1993; Aberdeen, 1995; DUniv Stirling, 1992; Dr (*hc*) Edinburgh, 1992. *Recreations:* golf, cricket, theatre, art. *Address:* Macfarlane Group (Clansman) PLC, Clansman House, 21 Newton Place, Glasgow G3 7PY; 50 Manse Road, Bearsden, Glasgow G61 3PN. *Clubs:* Art, Royal Scottish Automobile (Glasgow); Glasgow Golf.

McFARLANE OF LLANDAFF, Baroness *cr* 1979 (Life Peer), of Llandaff in the County of South Glamorgan; **Jean Kennedy McFarlane;** Professor and Head of Department of Nursing, University of Manchester, 1974–88, now Professor Emeritus; *b* 1 April 1926; *d* of late James and Elvina Alice McFarlane. *Educ:* Howell's Sch., Llandaff; Bedford and Birkbeck Colls, Univ. of London. MA, BSc(Soc); SRN, SCM, HV Tutor's Cert.; FRCN 1976; FCNA 1984. Staff Nurse, St Bartholomew's Hosp., 1950–51; Health Visitor, Cardiff CC, 1953–59; Royal Coll. of Nursing: Organising Tutor, Integrated Course, Educn Div., London, 1960–62; Educn Officer, Birmingham, 1962–66; Res. Project Ldr (DHSS sponsored), London, 1967–69; Dir of Educn, Inst. of Advanced Nursing Educn, London, 1969–71; Univ. of Manchester: Sen. Lectr in Nursing, Dept of Social and Preventive Medicine, 1971–73; Sen. Lectr and Head of Dept of Nursing, 1973–74. Member: Royal Commn on NHS, 1976–79; Commonwealth War Graves Commn, 1983–88. Chm., English Bd for Nursing, Midwifery and Health Visiting, 1980–83. Mem., Gen. Synod of C of E, 1990–. Hon. FRCP 1990. Hon. MSc Manchester, 1979; Hon. DSc Ulster, 1981; Hon. DEd CNAA, 1983; Hon. MD Liverpool, 1990. *Publications:* The Problems of Developing Criteria of Quality for Nursing Care (thesis), 1969; The Proper Study of the Nurse, 1970; (with G. Castledine) The Practice of Nursing using the Nursing Process, 1982. *Recreations:* music, walking, travelling, photography. *Address:* 5 Dovercourt Avenue, Heaton Mersey, Stockport SK4 3QB. *T:* 0161–432 8367.

MACFARLANE, Prof. Alan Donald James, FRAI; FRHistS; FBA 1986; Professor of Anthropological Science, University of Cambridge, since 1991; *b* 20 Dec. 1941; *s* of Donald Kennedy Macfarlane and Iris Stirling Macfarlane; *m* 1st, 1966, Gillian Ions; one *d*; 2nd, 1981, Sarah Harrison. *Educ:* Sedbergh School; Worcester College, Oxford (MA, DPhil); LSE (MPhil); SOAS (PhD). University of Cambridge: Senior Research Fellow in History, King's College, 1971–74; Univ. Lectr in Social Anthropology, 1975–81; Reader in Historical Anthropology, 1981–91. Lectures: Frazer Meml, Liverpool Univ., 1974; Malinowski Meml, LSE, 1978; Radcliffe-Brown Meml, Univ. of Lancaster, 1992; Marett Meml, Univ. of Oxford, 1995 . Rivers Meml Medal, RAI, 1984; William J. Goode Award, Amer. Sociol Assoc., 1987. *Publications:* Witchcraft in Tudor and Stuart England, 1970; The Family Life of Ralph Josselin, 1970; Resources and Population, 1976; (ed) The Diary of Ralph Josselin, 1976; Reconstructing Historical Communities, 1977; Origins of English Individualism, 1978; The Justice and the Mare's Ale, 1981; A Guide to English Historical Records, 1983; Marriage and Love in England, 1986; The Culture of Capitalism, 1987; The Cambridge Database System User Manual, 1990; The Nagas: hill peoples of North-east India, 1990; (ed and trans. with S. Harrison) Bernard Pignède, The Gurungs of Nepal, 1993. *Recreations:* walking, gardening, second-hand book hunting. *Address:* 25 Lode Road, Lode, near Cambridge CB5 9ER. *T:* Cambridge (01223) 811976.

MacFARLANE, Prof. Alistair George James, CBE 1987; FRS 1984; FEng 1981; FRSE; Principal and Vice-Chancellor of Heriot-Watt University, since 1989; *b* 9 May 1931; *s* of George R. MacFarlane; *m* 1954, Nora Williams; one *s. Educ:* Hamilton Academy; Univ. of Glasgow. BSc 1953, DSc 1969, Glasgow; PhD London 1964; MSc Manchester 1973; MA 1974, ScD 1979, Cantab. FIEE; FIEEE; FRSE 1990; CBIM 1991. Metropolitan-Vickers, Manchester, 1953–58; Lectr, Queen Mary Coll., Univ. of London, 1959–65, Reader 1965–66; Reader in Control Engrg, Univ. of Manchester Inst. of Sci. and Technology, 1966–69, Prof. 1969–74; Prof. of Engrg and Hd of Information Engrg Div., Univ. of Cambridge, 1974–88; Fellow, 1974–88, Vice-Master, 1980–88, Hon. Fellow, 1989–, Selwyn Coll., Cambridge. Chm., Cambridge Control Ltd, 1985–90; Non-Executive Director: Lothian and Edinburgh Enterprise Ltd, 1990–; British Nuclear Fuels plc, 1995–. Member: Council, SERC, 1981–85; Computer Board, 1983–88; Adv. Cttee for Safety of Nuclear Installations, 1987–90; Engineering Tech. Adv. Cttee, DTI, 1991–93. Comr, Nat. Commn on Educn, 1991–93; Chairman: Scottish Univs Wkg Party on Teaching and Learning in an Expanding Higher Educn System, 1991–92 (MacFarlane Report, 1992); Scottish Council for Res.in Educn, 1992–; Scottish Library and Information Council, 1994–. Trustee, Scottish Internat. Educn Trust, 1994–. Hon. DEng: UMIST, 1995; Glasgow, 1995. Medals: Centennial, ASME, 1980; Sir Harold Hartley, Inst. of Measurement and Control, 1982; Achievement, IEE, 1992; Faraday, IEE, 1993. *Publications:* Engineering Systems Analysis, 1964; Dynamical System Models, 1970; (with I. Postlethwaite) A Complex Variable Approach to the Analysis of Linear Multivariable Feedback Systems, 1979; (ed) Frequency-Response Methods in Control Systems, 1979; (ed) Complex Variable Methods for Linear Multivariable Feedback Systems, 1980; (with S. Hung) Multivariable Feedback: a quasi-classical approach, 1982; (with G. K. H. Pang) An Expert Systems Approach to Computer-Aided Design of Multivariable Systems, 1987. *Address:* Hermiston House, Hermiston, Edinburgh EH14 4AQ. *Club:* Caledonian.

MACFARLANE, Rev. Alwyn James Cecil; Parish Minister of Newlands (South), Church of Scotland, 1968–85; Extra Chaplain to the Queen in Scotland, since 1992 (Chaplain, 1977–92); *b* 14 June 1922; *s* of James Waddell Macfarlane and Ada Cecilia Rankin; *m* 1953, Joan Cowell Harris; one *s* one *d. Educ:* Cargilfield Sch.; Rugby Sch.; Oxford Univ. (MA); Edinburgh Univ. Served War: N Africa, Italy, Greece; Liaison Officer in Black Watch with 12th Bde, 1942–46. Ordained, 1951; served in parishes in Ross-shire, Edinburgh, Glasgow, Australia. *Recreations:* photography, walking. *Address:* 4/9 Belhaven Place, Edinburgh EH10 5JN.

MACFARLANE, Anne Bridget; Master of the Court of Protection, since 1982; *b* 26 Jan. 1930; *d* of late Dr David Griffith and Dr Grace Griffith; *m* 1957, James Douglas Macfarlane; two *d. Educ:* nine schools; Bristol Univ. (LLB). Admitted Solicitor, 1954. HM Land Registry, 1966–75; Registrar, Bromley County Court, 1975–82. *Publication:* (contrib.) Atkin's Court Forms, 2nd edn 1983. *Recreation:* collecting Victorian tiles. *Address:* Stewart House, 24 Kingsway, WC2B 6JX. *T:* 0171–269 7177. *Club:* Law Society.

MACFARLANE, Sir (David) Neil, Kt 1988; Chairman: Associated Nursing Services, since 1994; Rushman Lloyd PLC, since 1994; Securicor Group PLC, since 1995 (Director, since 1992); *b* 7 May 1936; *yr s* of late Robert and of Dulcie Macfarlane; *m* 1961, June Osmond King, Somerset; two *s* one *d. Educ:* St Aubyn's Prep. Sch.; Bancroft's, Woodford Green. Short Service Commission, Essex Regt, 1955–58; served TA, 265 LAA, RA, 1961–66. Joined Shell Mex and BP, 1959; contested (C): East Ham (North), 1970; Sutton and Cheam, by-election, 1972. Parly Under-Sec. of State (Dep. Minister for the Arts), DES, 1979–81; Parly Under-Sec. of State, DoE, 1981–85 (with spec. responsibility for Sport, 1981–85, for Children's Play, 1983–85). Mem., All Party Select Cttee on Science and Technology, 1974–79; MP (C) Sutton and Cheam, Feb. 1974–1992. Director: RMC; Bradford and Bingley Bldg Soc.; Zetters Pools. Chairman: Sports Aid Foundn, 1986–87; Golf Fund PLC; Vice-Pres. PGA, 1985–. Mem., National Trust, 1976–. *Publication:* Sport and Politics: a world divided, 1986. *Recreations:* golf, cricket-watching. *Clubs:* MCC, Lord's Taverners; Essex County Cricket; Royal & Ancient Golf; Huntercombe Golf; Sunningdale Golf; Wentworth Golf; Harlequins Rugby Football.

MACFARLANE, Sir George (Gray), Kt 1971; CB 1965; BSc; Dr Ing (Dresden); FEng; retired; Member of the Board, British Telecommunications Corporation, 1981–84; Corporate Director, British Telecom plc, 1984–87; *b* 8 Jan. 1916; *s* of late John Macfarlane, Airdrie, Lanarks; *m* 1941, Barbara Grant, *d* of Thomas Thomson, Airdrie, Lanarks; one *s* one *d. Educ:* Airdrie Academy; Glasgow Univ.; Technische Hochschule, Dresden, Germany. FIMA; FPhysS. On scientific staff, Air Ministry Research Establishment, Dundee and Swanage, 1939–41; Telecommunications Research Establishment (TRE), Malvern, 1941–60; Deputy Chief Scientific Officer (Individual Merit Post), 1954–60; Deputy Director, National Physical Laboratory, 1960–62; Director, Royal Radar Establishment, 1962–67; Controller (Research), Min. of Technology and Min. of Aviation Supply, 1967–71; Controller, Research and Develt Establishments and Research, MoD, 1971–75. Member: PO Review Cttee, 1976–77; PO Bd, 1977–81; NEB, 1980–85 and NRDC, 1981–85 (subseq. British Technology Gp). Mem., Bd of Trustees, Imperial War Museum, 1978–86. Deputy-Pres., IEE, 1976–78 (Vice-Pres., 1972–74), Hon. FIEE, 1988; Hunter Meml Lecturer, IEE, 1966; Council Mem., Fellowship of Engrg, 1982–87 (Vice-Pres. 1983–86). Hon. LLD Glasgow. Glazebrook Medal and Prize, Inst. of Physics, 1978. *Publications:* papers in IEE, Proc. Phys. Society, Phys. Review. *Recreations:* walking, gardening. *Address:* Red Tiles, 17 Orchard Way, Esher, Surrey KT10 9DY. *T:* Esher (01372) 463778. *Club:* Athenæum.

McFARLANE, Sir Ian, Kt 1984; Chairman and Managing Director: Southern Pacific Petroleum NL, since 1968; Central Pacific Minerals NL, since 1968; Chairman, Trans Pacific Consolidated Ltd, since 1964; *b* 25 Dec. 1923; *s* of Stuart Gordon McFarlane, CMG, MBE and Mary Grace McFarlane; *m* 1956, Ann, *d* of M. A. Shaw, Salt Lake City, USA; one *s* two *d. Educ:* Melbourne Grammar School; Harrow; Sydney Univ. (BSc, BE); MIT (MS). Served War of 1939–45, RANVR. Morgan Stanley & Co., 1949–59; Mem., Sydney Stock Exchange, 1959–64; Partner, Ord, Minnett, T. J. Thompson & Partners, 1959–64; Dep. Chm., Magellan Petroleum, 1964–70; Director: Trans City Discount Ltd, 1960–64; Consolidated Rutile Ltd, 1964–68; International Pacific Corp., 1967–73; Aust. Gen. Insurance Co., 1968–74; Mercantile Mutual Insurance Co., 1969–74; Concrete Construction, 1972–74; International Pacific Aust. Investments, 1972–73; Morgan Stanley Internat., NYC, 1976–80. Mem. Council, Imperial Soc. of Knights Bachelor, 1985–. Founder, Sir Ian McFarlane Travelling Professorship in Urology, 1980. Chm., Royal

Brisbane Hosp. Res. (formerly Hosp.) Foundn, 1985–93. Life Governor, Royal Prince Alfred Hosp., Sydney, 1982; Founding Governor, St Luke's Hosp. Foundn, Sydney, 1982–. Fellow Commoner, Christ's Coll., Cambridge, 1987. Hon. Col Kentucky, 1984–. *Address:* 40 Wentworth Road, Vaucluse, NSW 2030, Australia. *Clubs:* Australian (Sydney); Queensland (Brisbane); Commonwealth (Canberra); University (NY); Royal Sydney Golf; Cruising Yacht of Australia (Sydney); Monaco Yacht.

McFARLANE, Prof. Ian Dalrymple, MBE 1946; FBA 1978; Professor of French Literature, University of Oxford, 1971–83, now Emeritus; Professorial Fellow, Wadham College, Oxford, 1971–83, now Emeritus Fellow; *b* 7 Nov. 1915; *s* of James Blair McFarlane and Valérie Edith Liston Dalrymple; *m* 1939, Marjory Nan Hamilton; one *s* one *d. Educ:* Lycée St-Charles, Marseilles; Tormore Sch., Upper Deal, Kent; Westminster Sch.; St Andrews Univ. MA 1st class Hons, 1938; Carnegie Research Scholar, 1938–39. Served 1st Bn Black Watch, RHR, 1940–45. Apptd Lectr in French, Cambridge Univ., 1945; Gonville and Caius College: elected Fellow, 1947 (Hon. Fellow, 1990); appointed Senior Tutor, 1956; Prof. of French Language and Literature, St Andrews, 1961–70. Zaharoff Lectr, Oxford, 1984; Hon. Faculty Prof., University Coll., Cardiff, 1984. Hon. Sen. Res. Fellow, Inst. of Romance Studies, Univ. of London, 1990. Member, Scottish Cert. of Educn Examination Board, 1964; Member Academic Planning Board, University of Stirling, 1964–67; Mem. Cttee on Research and Develt in Modern Languages, 1966. Pres., MHRA, 1986. Doctor of Univ. of Paris, 1950; Dr *hc*, Univ. of Tours, 1982; Hon. DLitt St Andrews, 1982. Officier des Palmes Académiques, 1971. *Publications:* critical edn of M. Scève's Délie, 1966; Renaissance France 1470–1589, 1974; Buchanan, 1981; The Entry of Henri II into Paris, 1549, 1982; various, in learned periodicals. *Recreations:* cricket, music. *Address:* Wadham College, Oxford OX1 3PN.

McFARLANE, James Sinclair, CBE 1986; CEng, FIM; CIMgt; Director General, Engineering Employers' Federation, 1982–89; *b* 8 Nov. 1925; *s* of John Mills McFarlane and Hannah McFarlane; *m* 1951, Ruth May Harden; three *d. Educ:* Manchester Grammar Sch.; Emmanuel Coll., Cambridge (MA, PhD). CEng, FIM 1961. ICI Ltd, 1949–53; Henry Wiggin & Co. Ltd, 1953–69; Chm. and Man. Dir, Smith-Clayton Forge Ltd (GKN Ltd), 1969–76; Man. Dir, Garringtons Ltd (GKN Ltd), 1976–77; Guest Keen & Nettlefolds Ltd: Gen. Man., Personnel, 1977–79; Exec. Dir, 1979–82. Mem., NEDC, 1982–89; a Civil Service Comr (pt-time), 1983–88. *Publications:* contrib. scientific and technical jls. *Recreation:* music. *Address:* 24 Broad Street, Ludlow, Shropshire SY8 1NJ. *T:* Ludlow (01584) 872495. *Clubs:* Caledonian, United Oxford & Cambridge University.

McFARLANE, Prof. James Walter; Professor of European Literature, University of East Anglia, 1964–82, now Emeritus; *b* 12 Dec. 1920; *s* of James and Florence McFarlane; *m* 1944, Lillie Kathleen Crouch; two *s* one *d. Educ:* Bede Grammar Sch., Sunderland; St Catherine's Society, Univ. of Oxford. MA, BLitt 1948. War service, Intell. Corps, 1941–46 (Major); Oxford Soccer blue, 1947; Lectr and Sen. Lectr, Dept of German and Scandinavian Studies, King's Coll., Univ. of Durham, later Univ. of Newcastle upon Tyne, 1947–63; University of East Anglia: Founding Dean of European Studies, 1964–68; Public Orator, 1964–68, 1974–75, 1978–79; Pro-Vice-Chancellor, 1968–71; Professorial Fellow, 1982–86. Vis. Prof., Univ. of Auckland, NZ, 1967; Herbert F. Johnson Vis. Res. Prof., Inst. for Res. in Humanities, Univ. of Wisconsin-Madison, 1983–84. Mem., BBC Gen. Adv. Council, 1970–75; Chm., East Anglia Regional Adv. Council, 1970–75; Chm., Hunworth Crafts Trust, 1973–77; Mem. Exec., Eastern Arts Assoc., 1977–82. Founder Trustee, Norwich Puppet Theatre, 1979; Chm., The Wells Centre, Norfolk, 1981–88. Editor-at-large, Scandinavica: an International Journal of Scandinavian Studies, 1991– (Editor, 1975–90); Man. Editor, Norvik Press, 1985–. Leverhulme Faculty Fellow in European Studies, 1971–72; Brit. Acad. Wolfson Fellow. Fellow, Det Norske Videnskaps-Akademie, Oslo, 1977; Corresp. Mem., Svenska Litteratursällskapet i Finland, Helsinki, 1977; Foreign Member: Royal Norwegian Soc. of Sciences and Letters, 1982; Royal Danish Acad. of Sciences and Letters, 1983. Hon. Mem., Phi Beta Kappa, 1984. Hon. DLitt: Loughborough, 1990; Sunderland. Commander's Cross, Royal Norwegian Order of St Olav, 1975. *Publications:* Ibsen and the Temper of Norwegian Literature, 1960; Discussions of Ibsen, 1962; Henrik Ibsen, 1970; (with Malcolm Bradbury) Modernism: European Literature 1890–1930, 1976; Ibsen and Meaning, 1989; (editor and translator) The Oxford Ibsen, 1960–77: vol. 1, Early Plays, 1970; vol. 2, The Vikings at Helgeland, Love's Comedy, The Pretenders, 1962; vol. 3, Brand, Peer Gynt, 1972; vol. 4, The League of Youth, Emperor and Galilean, 1963; vol. 5, Pillars of Society, A Doll's House, Ghosts, 1961; vol. 6, An Enemy of the People, The Wild Duck, Rosmersholm, 1960; vol. 7, The Lady from the Sea, Hedda Gabler, The Master Builder, 1966; vol. 8, Little Eyolf, John Gabriel Borkman, When We Dead Awaken, 1977; (editor and translator with Janet Garton) Slaves of Love and other Norwegian short stories, 1982; (ed with Harald Næss) Knut Hamsun's Letters, vol. 1, 1990; (ed and contrib.) The Cambridge Companion to Henrik Ibsen, 1994; *translations:* Hamsun's Pan, 1955; Hamsun's Wayfarers, 1980; Obstfelder's A Priest's Diary, 1988; *festschrift:* (ed J. Garton) Facets of European Modernism: essays in honour of James McFarlane, 1985. *Recreation:* cyber-adventuring. *Address:* The Croft, Stody, Melton Constable, Norfolk NR24 2EE. *T:* Melton Constable (01263) 860505.

MACFARLANE, Sir Neil; *see* Macfarlane, Sir D. N.

MacFARLANE, Maj.-Gen. Robert Goudie, MBE 1952; FRCP; FRCPE; Deputy Secretary, Scottish Council for Postgraduate Medical Education, 1975–84; *b* 1 March 1917; *s* of late Archibald Forsyth MacFarlane and Jessie Robertson Goudie; *m* 1945, Mary Campbell Martin; three *s. Educ:* Hillhead High Sch., Glasgow; Glasgow Univ. MB, ChB, 1940; MD 1955; FRCPE 1964; MRCP 1970; FRCP 1979. Served War: commissioned RAMC, 1941; in Madagascar, India, Burma, 1941–45. Specialist in Medicine and Consultant Physician, 1948–; CO, British Mil. Hosp., Iserlohn, 1968–70; Prof. of Mil. Med., Royal Army Medical Coll., 1970–71; Consulting Physician, BAOR, 1971–73. Dir. of Army Medicine and Consulting Physician to the Army, 1973–74. QHP 1973. *Address:* 6 Redholm, Greenheads Road, North Berwick, East Lothian EH39 4RA.

MACFARLANE, Maj.-Gen. William Thomson, CB 1981; Consultant/Administrator, Sion College, 1984–93; *b* Bath, 2 Dec. 1925; *s* of late James and Agnes Macfarlane; *m* 1955, Dr Helen D. Meredith; one *d.* Commissioned Royal Signals, 1947. Served Europe, Near East, ME, and Far East. Commanded 16th Parachute Bde Signal Squadron, 1961–63; Military Asst, Commander FARELF, 1964–66; Comd 1st Div. HQ and Signal Regt, BAOR, 1967–70; Services Mem., Cabinet Office Secretariat, 1970–72; Comd, Corps Royal Signals, 1972–73; Dir of Public Relations (Army), MoD, 1973–75; C of S, UKLF, 1976–78; Chief, Jt Services Liaison Organisation, Bonn, 1978–80. Exec. Dir, Hong Kong Resort Co. Ltd, 1981–84; Chm., ICHIGO Ltd, 1990–; Dir, Compton Manor Estates (formerly Farms) Ltd, 1990–. Col Comdt, 1980–85, Rep. Col Comdt, 1985, Royal Corps of Signals. *Club:* Naval and Military.

MacFARQUHAR, Prof. Roderick Lemonde; Professor of Government, since 1984, and Leroy B. Williams Professor of History and Political Science, since 1990, Harvard University; *b* 2 Dec. 1930; *s* of Sir Alexander MacFarquhar, KBE, CIE, and of Berenice Whitburn; *m* 1964, Emily Jane Cohen; one *s* one *d. Educ:* Fettes Coll.; Oxford Univ. (BA); Harvard Univ. (AM); LSE (PhD). Specialist on China, Daily Telegraph (and later Sunday Telegraph), 1955–61; Founding Editor, China Quarterly, 1959–68; Rockefeller Grantee, 1962; Reporter, BBC TV programme Panorama, 1963–64. Associate Fellow, St Antony's Coll., Oxford, 1965–68. Mem., Editorial Bd, New Statesman, 1965–69; Ford Foundation Grant, 1968; Senior Research Fellow, Columbia Univ., 1969; Senior Research Fellow, RIIA, 1971–74 (Mem. Council, 1978–83); Co-presenter, BBC Gen. Overseas Services 24 Hours prog., 1972–74, 1979–80. Governor, SOAS, 1978–83; Dir, Fairbank Center for E Asian Res., Harvard Univ., 1986–92. Contested: (Lab) Ealing South, 1966; (Lab) Meriden, March 1968; (SDP) Derbys S, 1983. MP (Lab) Belper, Feb. 1974–1979; PPS to Minister of State, FCO, March 1974; resignation accepted, April 1975; reappointed June 1975; PPS to Sec. of State, DHSS, 1976–78. Member: N Atlantic Assembly, 1974–79; Select Cttee for Sci. and Technology, 1976–79; Trilateral Commn, 1976–(Mem. Exec. Cttee, 1976–84); Exec. Cttee, Fabian Soc., 1976–80. Leverhulme Res. Fellow, 1980–83; Fellow: Woodrow Wilson Center, Smithsonian Instn, 1980–81; Amer. Acad. of Arts and Scis, 1986–. Vis. Prof. of Govt, Harvard, 1982; Vis. Fellow, St Antony's Coll., Oxford, 1983; inaugurated Inchon Meml Lectureship, Korea Univ., 1987. *Publications:* The Hundred Flowers, 1960; The Sino-Soviet Dispute, 1961; Chinese Ambitions and British Policy (Fabian Pamphlet), 1966; (ed) China under Mao, 1966; Sino-American Relations, 1949–71, 1972; The Forbidden City, 1972; The Origins of the Cultural Revolution: Vol. 1, Contradictions among the People 1956–1957, 1974; Vol. 2, The Great Leap Forward 1958–1960, 1983; (ed jtly) Cambridge History of China, Vol. 14, 1987, Vol. 15, 1991; (ed jtly) The Secret Speeches of Chairman Mao, 1989; (ed) The Politics of China 1949–1989, 1993; articles in Foreign Affairs, The World Today, Atlantic Monthly, Pacific Affairs, Commentary, Newsweek, NY Review of Books, etc. *Recreations:* reading, listening to music, travel. *Address:* Fairbank Center, 1737 Cambridge Street, Cambridge, MA 02138, USA.

McFEELY, Elizabeth Sarah Anne C.; *see* Craig McFeely.

McFETRICH, (Charles) Alan; Managing Partner, External Affairs, Coopers & Lybrand, since 1994 (Executive Partner, 1992–94); *b* 15 Dec. 1940; *s* of late Cecil McFetrich, OBE, FCA and of Kathleen M. McFetrich (*née* Proom); *m* 1990, Janet Elizabeth Henkel (*née* Munro); two *s* one *d* from previous *m. Educ:* Oundle Sch.; Magdalene Coll., Cambridge. FCA. Trainee Accountant, Graham Proom & Smith, 1959–61 and 1964–66; Deloitte Haskins & Sells: Accountant, 1966–68; Consultant, 1968–73; Consultancy Partner, 1973–80; seconded to Dept of Industry, 1981–82; Nat. Operations Partner, 1983–85; Nat. Managing Partner, 1985–90; Man. Partner, 1990–92. FRSA 1989. *Recreations:* gardening, theatre. *Address:* Coopers & Lybrand, 1 Embankment Place, WC2N 6NN. *T:* 0171–583 5000.

McGAHERN, John, FRSL; author; *b* 12 Nov. 1934; *s* of Francis McGahern and Susan McManus; *m* 1973, Madeline Green. Research Fellow, Univ. of Reading, 1968–71; O'Connor Prof., Colgate Univ., 1969, 1972, 1977, 1979 and 1983. Member: Aosdana Irish Acad of Letters. British Northern Arts Fellow, 1974–76. McCauley Fellowship, 1964; British Arts Council Award, 1967; Soc. of Authors Award, 1975; Amer. Irish Foundn Literary Award, 1985; Irish Times/Aer Lingus Award, 1990; GPA Award, 1992. Hon. LitD TCD, 1991. Chevalier de l'Ordre des Arts et des Lettres (France), 1989. *Publications:* The Barracks, 1962 (AE Meml Award, 1962); The Dark, 1965; Nightlines, 1970; The Leavetaking, 1975; Getting Through, 1978; The Pornographer, 1979; High Ground, 1985; The Rockingham Shoot, 1987; Amongst Women, 1990; The Power of Darkness, 1991; The Collected Stories, 1992. *Address:* c/o Faber & Faber, 3 Queen Square, WC1N 3AU.

McGANN, Prof. Jerome John, PhD; John Stewart Bryan Professor of English, University of Virginia, since 1987; Director, Commonwealth Center for Cultural Change, since 1995; *b* 22 July 1937; *s* of John J. McGann and Marie V. McGann (*née* Lecouffe); *m* 1960, Anne Lanni; two *s* one *d. Educ:* Le Moyne Coll. (BS); Syracuse Univ. (MA); Yale Univ. (PhD 1966). Asst Prof., then Prof., Univ. of Chicago, 1966–75; Professor: Johns Hopkins Univ., 1975–81; CIT, 1981–87. Fulbright Fellow, 1965–66; Guggenheim Fellow, 1970–71 and 1976–77; NEH Fellow, 1975–76 and 1987–89. Lectures: Clark, Trinity Coll., Cambridge, 1988; Carpenter, Univ. of Chicago, 1988; Alexander, Univ. of Toronto, 1986; Lansdowne, Univ. of Victoria, 1994. Fellow, Amer. Acad. of Arts and Scis, 1994. Melville Kane Award, Amer. Poetry Soc., 1973; Distinguished Schol. Award, Byron Soc., 1989; Wilbur Cross Medal, Yale Univ., 1994. *Publications:* Fiery Dust: Byron's poetic development, 1969; (ed) Pelham, or The Adventures of a Gentleman, by Edward Bulwer-Lytton, 1972; Swinburne: an experiment in criticism, 1972; Don Juan in Context, 1976; Air Heart Sermons (poems), 1976; (with J. Kauffman) Writing Home (poems), 1978; (with J. Kahn) Nerves in Patterns (poems), 1979; (ed) Byron: the complete poetical works, Vol. I 1980, Vols II and III 1981, Vols IV and V 1986, Vol. VI 1991, Vol. VII 1993; The Romantic Ideology: a critical investigation, 1983; A Critique of Modern Textual Criticism, 1983, 2nd edn 1992; The Beauty of Inflections: literary investigations in historical method and theory, 1985; (ed) Textual Studies and Literary Interpretation, 1985; (ed jtly) The Manuscripts of the Younger Romantics: Byron, Vol. I 1985, Vol. II 1986, Vols III and IV 1988; (ed) Historical Studies and Literary Criticism, 1985; (ed) The Oxford Authors Byron, 1986; Social Values and Poetic Acts, 1987; Towards a Literature of Knowledge, 1989; (ed) Victorian Connections, 1989; (ed) Postmodern Poetries, 1990; The Textual Condition, 1991; (ed) The New Oxford Book of Romantic Period Verse, 1993; Black Riders: the visible language of modernism, 1993; (ed) A Symposium on Russian Postmodernism, 1993; (ed) Byron: the Oxford poetry library, 1994; Poetics of Sensibility: a revolution in literary style, 1995. *Recreation:* squash. *Address:* 555 Spring Lane, Charlottesville, VA 22903, USA. *T:* (804) 9795127.

McGARRITY, J(ames) Forsyth, CB 1981; MA, MEd, BSc; HM Senior Chief Inspector of Schools (Scotland), 1973–81; *b* 16 April 1921; *s* of late James McGarrity and Margaret Davidson; *m* 1951, Violet S. G. Philp, MA; one *s* one *d. Educ:* Bathgate Academy; Glasgow Univ. Schoolmaster, 1949–57; HM Inspector of Schools, 1957–68; HM Chief Inspector of Schools, 1968–73. *Recreations:* golf, gardening. *Address:* 30 Oatlands Park, Linlithgow, Scotland EH49 6AS. *T:* Linlithgow (01506) 843258.

McGARRY, Ian; General Secretary, British Actors' Equity Association, since 1991; *b* 27 Feb. 1941; *s* of John and Jean McGarry; *m* 1964, Christine Smith (marr. diss. 1989); one *s. Educ:* Chichester High Sch.; Lewes County Grammar Sch. Labour Party Constituency Agent, Putney, 1964–76; Asst General Sec., Equity, 1976–91. *Recreations:* golf, football (spectator), horse racing. *Address:* Guild House, Upper St Martin's Lane, WC2H 9EG. *T:* 0171–379 6000.

McGARVEY, Alan; specialist, industrial development and investment, in Eastern Europe and elsewhere, since 1990; Senior Consultant, Warwick Research Institute, since 1989; *b* 22 June 1942; *s* of William Johnson McGarvey and Rosina McGarvey; *m* 1967, Eileen Cook (*d* 1992). *Educ:* Wallsend Grammar Sch.; Coll. of Further Educn; Newcastle Univ. (BSc); Cranfield Sch. of Management (MBA). C. A. Parsons, 1958–64 (apprentice); RTZ, 1968–71; Decca Gp, 1972–76; MK Electric, 1976–78; Director, Small Company Div., NEB, 1978–82; Chief Exec., Greater London Enterprise Bd, 1982–86; management consultant, 1986–88; Man. Dir, Greater Manchester Econ. Develt Ltd, 1987–90; regl develt specialist, 1990–93; consultant, CEC, 1993–. Labour Party, 1974–; Mem., Wandsworth Borough Council, 1981–86 (Dep. Opposition Leader, 1982–83); Chm., Battersea Constituency Labour Parties, 1978–82. Exec. Mem., Wandsworth CRC, 1973–82; Board Member: Battersea Arts Centre Trust, 1982–88; Northern Chamber Orch., 1988–93; Member: Jt Governing Board, Centre for Development of Industry (EEC–ACP Lomé), 1981–90; Adv. Council, Cttee for Industrial Co-operation (EEC–ACP), 1990–. Governor, Polytech. of South Bank, 1985–87; Chm. Govs, Medlock Sch., Manchester, 1989–91. *Recreations:* home and garden, science fiction; amateur sculptor. *Address:* 11 Old Hall Mews, Old Hall Lane, Bolton BL1 7PW. *T:* Bolton (01204) 840141, *Fax:* Bolton (01204) 840723; Rue Fulton 1, 1040 Brussels, Belgium. *T:* (2) 2959161, *Fax:* (2) 2964251.

McGARVIE, Hon. Richard Elgin, AC 1994; Governor of Victoria, since 1992; *b* 21 May 1926; *s* of Richard Fleming McGarvie and Mabel Catherine McGarvie; *m* 1953, Lesley, *d* of K. G. and G. D. Kerr; two *s* two *d. Educ:* Camperdown High Sch.; Univ. of Melbourne (LLB Hons, BCom). AB, RAustNR, 1944–46. Admitted Victorian Bar, 1952; QC 1963; Judge, Supreme Court of Victoria, 1976–92. Mem., Law Faculty, Melbourne Univ., 1957–88. Chm., Nat. Cttee on Discrimination in Employment and Occupation, 1973–76; Mem., Adv. Cttee on Aust. Judicial System, Constitutional Commn, 1985–87. Chm., Victorian Bar Council, 1973–75; Treas., Exec. Law Council of Aust., 1974–76; Dep. Chm., then Chm., Aust. Inst. of Judicial Admin, 1980–86 (Mem., 1976–). Mem. Council, Monash Univ., 1980; Chancellor, La Trobe Univ., 1981–92. Hon. LLD Melbourne, 1990. *Publications:* (jtly) Cases and Materials on Contract, 1962, 4 edns; papers on law. *Recreations:* reading, sailing, bush camping and walking, vegetable gardening. *Address:* Government House, Melbourne, Vic 3004, Australia. *T:* (3) 96514211. *Club:* Royal Automobile (Victoria).

McGEE, Prof. James O'Donnell; Professor of Morbid Anatomy, University of Oxford, Fellow of Linacre College, Oxford, since Oct. 1975; *b* 27 July 1939; *s* of Michael and Bridget McGee; *m* 1961, Anne Lee; one *s* two *d. Educ:* Univ. of Glasgow. MB, ChB, PhD, MD; MA (Oxon). FRCPath 1986; FRCPGlas 1989. Various appts in Univ. Dept of Pathology, Royal Infirmary, Glasgow, 1962–69; Roche Inst. of Molecular Biology, Nutley, NJ: MRC Fellow 1969–70; Vis. Scientist 1970–71; Distinguished Vis. Scientist, 1981 and 1989; Dept of Pathology, Royal Infirmary, Glasgow: Lectr 1971–74; Sen. Lectr, 1974–75. Member: Scientific Cttee, 1978–88, Grants Cttee, 1988–92, Cancer Res. Campaign; Cttee on Safety of Medicines, 1987–89 (Safety and Efficacy Sub Cttee, 1984–87); Kettle Meml Lectr, RCPath, 1980; Annual Guest Lecturer: Royal Coll. of Physicians, Ireland, 1986; Royal Acad. of Medicine (Ireland), 1985. Bellahouston Gold Medal, Glasgow Univ., 1973. *Publications:* Biopsy Pathology of Liver, 1980, 2nd edn 1988; In Situ Hybridisation: principles and practice, 1990; Oxford Textbook of Pathology, 1992: vol 1, Principles of Pathology, vols 2a, 2b, Pathology of Systems; The Natural Immune System: The Macrophage, 1992; The Natural Killer Cell, 1992; Diagnostic Molecular Pathology, vols 1 and 2, 1992; papers in scientific jls on liver disease, non-istopic methods of gene detection, breast and cervical cancers. *Recreations:* talking with my family, swimming. *Address:* Nuffield Department of Pathology and Bacteriology, Level 4, John Radcliffe Hospital, Headington, Oxford OX3 9DU.

McGEOCH, Vice-Adm. Sir Ian (Lachlan Mackay), KCB 1969 (CB 1966); DSO 1943; DSC 1943; Director, Midar Systems Ltd, since 1986; *b* 26 March 1914; 3rd *s* of L. A. McGeoch of Dalmuir; *m* 1937, Eleanor Somers, *d* of Rev. Canon Hugh Farrie; two *s* two *d. Educ:* Pangbourne Coll. Joined RN, 1932. Comd HM Submarine Splendid, 1942–43; Staff Officer (Ops) 4th Cruiser Sqdn, 1944–45; Comd: HMS Fernie, 1946–47; 4th Submarine Squadron, 1949–51; 3rd Submarine Squadron, 1956–57; Dir of Undersurface Warfare, Admiralty, 1959; IDC 1961; Comd HMS Lion 1962–64; Admiral Pres., RNC, Greenwich, 1964–65; Flag Officer Submarines, 1965–67; Flag Officer, Scotland and Northern Ireland, 1968–70. Trustee, Imperial War Mus., 1977–87. Mem., The Queen's Body Guard for Scotland, Royal Co. of Archers, 1969–. MPhil Edinburgh, 1975. FNI 1986. Editor, The Naval Review, 1972–80. *Publications:* (jtly) The Third World War: a future history, 1978; The Third World War: the untold story, 1982; An Affair of Chances, 1991. *Recreations:* sailing, walking. *Address:* c/o Coutts & Co., 440 Strand, WC2R 0QS. *Clubs:* Army and Navy, Special Forces; Royal Yacht Squadron, Royal Naval Sailing Association (Cdre 1968–70), Royal Cruising.

McGEOUGH, Prof. Joseph Anthony, CEng, FIMechE, FIEE; Regius Professor of Engineering, University of Edinburgh, since 1983 (Head, Department of Mechanical Engineering, 1983–91); *b* 29 May 1940; *s* of late Patrick Joseph McGeough and Gertrude (*née* Darroch); *m* 1972, Brenda Nicholson; two *s* one *d. Educ:* St Michael's Coll., Irvine; Glasgow Univ. (BSc, PhD); Aberdeen Univ. (DSc). Vacation-apprentice, Malcolm & Allan Ltd, 1957–61; Research Demonstrator, Leicester Univ., 1966; Sen. Res. Fellow, Queensland Univ., 1967; Res. Metallurgist, International Research & Development Co. Ltd, Newcastle upon Tyne, 1968–69; Sen. Res. Fellow, Strathclyde Univ., 1969–72; Lectr 1972–77, Sen. Lectr 1977–80, Reader 1980–83, Dept of Engineering, Aberdeen Univ. Royal Society/SERC Industrial Fellow, 1987–89; Hon. Prof., Nanjing Univ. of Aeronautics and Astronautics, 1992–; Vis. Prof., Univ. degli Studi di Napoli Federico II, 1994. Member: Technical Adv. Cttee, Scottish Centre of Agricultural Engineering, 1987–93; Engrg Res. Bd, AFRC, 1992–94; Chm., Scottish Br., IMechE, 1993–95 (Chm., Edinburgh and SE Scotland Panel, 1988–92); Pres., CIRP Tech. Cttee on Electrophysical and Chemical Processes, 1992–95. Chm., Dyce Academy College Council, 1980–83; Hon. Vice-Pres., Aberdeen Univ. Athletic Assoc., 1981–; Hon. Pres., Lichfield Sci. and Engrg Soc., 1988–89. Editor, Processing of Advanced Materials, 1991–94; CIRP Ed., Jl of Materials Processing Technol., 1995–. FRSE 1990. *Publications:* Principles of Electrochemical Machining, 1974; Advanced Methods of Machining, 1988; papers mainly in Journals of: Mech. Engrg Science, Applied Electrochemistry; contrib. Encyclopaedia Britannica, Encyclopaedia of Electrochemistry; various patents. *Recreations:* gardening, golf, walking. *Address:* 39 Dreghorn Loan, Colinton, Edinburgh EH13 0DF. *T:* 0131–441 1302.

McGEOWN, Prof. Mary Graham, (Mrs J. M. Freeland), CBE 1985; FRCP, FRCPE, FRCPI; Professorial Fellow, Queen's University of Belfast, since 1988; *b* 19 July 1923; *d* of James Edward McGeown and Sarah Graham Quinn; *m* 1949, Joseph Maxwell Freeland (*d* 1982); three *s. Educ:* Lurgan College; Queen's University of Belfast (MB, BCh, BAO, with hons, 1946; MD, PhD). House Physician and Surgeon, Royal Victoria Hosp., Belfast, 1947–48; Sen. House Physician, Royal Belfast Hosp. for Sick Children, 1948; Asst Lectr in Pathology, 1948–50, in Biochemistry, 1950–53, QUB; res. grant, MRC, 1953–56; Res. Fellow, Royal Victoria Hosp., 1956–58; Belfast City Hospital: Sen. Hosp. MO, 1958–62; Consultant Nephrologist, 1962–88; Physician in Admin. Charge, Renal Unit, 1968–88. Hon. Reader in Nephrology, QUB, 1972–87. Chm., UK Transplant Management Cttee, 1983–91; Hon. Treas., Renal Assoc., 1986–89 (Pres., 1983–86); Pres., Ulster Med. Soc., 1985–86. Chm., Corrigan Club, 1987. Mem., Unrelated Living Transplants Regulatory Authority, 1990–; Hon. Member: British Transplantation Soc.; Eur. Dialysis Transplant/Eur. Renal Assoc.; Graves Lectr, Royal Acad. of Medicine, Ireland, 1963. Hon. DSc New Univ. of Ulster, 1983; Hon. DMSc QUB, 1991. *Publications:* Clinical Management of Electrolyte Disorders, 1983; Clinical Management of Renal Transplantation, 1992; numerous papers and chapters in books on calcium metabolism, renal stones, phosphate metabolism, parathyroid function and disease, renal transplantation, kidney diseases. *Recreations:* gardening, antique collecting, genealogy. *Address:* 14 Osborne Gardens, Belfast BT9 6LE. *T:* Belfast (01232) 669918.

McGHEE, George Crews, Legion of Merit; businessman; former diplomat; Director: Mobil Oil Co., 1969–82; Procter and Gamble Co., 1969–82; American Security & Trust Co., 1969–82; Trans World Airlines, 1976–82; *b* Waco, Texas, 10 March 1912; *s* of George Summers McGhee and Magnolia (*née* Spruce); *m* 1938, Cecilia Jeanne DeGolyer; two *s* four *d. Educ:* Southern Methodist Univ., Dallas; Univ. of Oklahoma; Oxford Univ. (Rhodes Schol.); Univ. of London. BS (Oklahoma) 1933; DPhil (Oxon) 1937. Served with US Navy, 1943–45 (Asiatic ribbon with three battle stars). Geologist and geophysicist, 1930–40; Oil producer, sole owner, McGhee Production Co., 1940–. Special Asst to Under-Sec of State for Economic Affairs, 1946; Coordinator for Aid to Greece and Turkey, 1947; Asst Sec. of State for Near Eastern, South Asian and African Affairs, 1949; US Ambassador to Turkey, 1951–53; Consultant, Nat. Security Council, 1958; Mem. President's Cttee to Study Mil. Asst Program, 1958; Counselor of Dept of State and Chm. of State Dept Policy Planning Council, 1961; Under-Sec. of State for Political Affairs, 1961; Bd, Panama Canal Co., 1962; US Ambassador to the Federal Republic of Germany, 1963–68; Ambassador-at-Large, 1968–69. Chairman: English Speaking Union of US, 1969–74; Business Council for Internat. Understanding, 1969–73; Vice-Chm., Inst. for Study of Diplomacy, 1978–; Member Board: Geo. C. Marshall Res. Foundn, 1972–85; German–American Cultural Fund, 1992–; Amer. Council on Germany, 1969–86; Resources for Future, 1977–82; Asia Foundn, 1974–84; Atlantic Council, 1975–; Atlantic Inst. for Internat. Affairs, 1977–88; Smithsonian Nat. Associates, 1971– (Chm., 1975–76); Population Crisis Cttee, 1969–82; Council of Amer. Ambassadors, 1983–; Amer. Inst. for Contemp. German Studies, 1983–; Nat. Tree Trust, 1992–; President's Circle, Nat. Acad. of Scis, 1989–; Circle, Nat. Gall. of Art, 1991–; Carnegie Council, 1990–; Council for Econ. Develt Sub-cttee on Global Econ. Strategy for US, 1991–. Member: Inst. of Turkish Studies, 1983–86; Sackler Gall. Vis. Cttee, Smithsonian Instn. Trustee: Duke Univ.; Cttee for Economic Develt, 1957–72; Aspen Inst. for Humanistic Studies, 1958–; Salzburg Seminar, 1969–71; Nat. Civil Service League, 1969–71; Folger Library Council, 1983–85. Chm., Saturday Review World, 1974–77. Mem., Amer. Philos. Soc., 1993–. Hon. Fellow, Queen's Coll., Oxford, 1969. Distinguished Service Citation, Univ. of Oklahoma, 1952; Hon. DCL, Southern Methodist Univ., 1953; Hon. LLD: Tulane Univ., 1957; Univ. of Maryland, 1965; Hon. DSc, Univ. of Tampa, 1969. Ouissam Alaouite Cherifien, Govt Morocco, 1950; Hon. Citizen, Ankara, Turkey, 1954; Outstanding Citizen Award, Amer. Friends of Turkey, 1983. *Publications:* Envoy to the Middle World, 1983; (ed) Diplomacy for the Future, 1987; At the Creation of a New Germany, 1989; (ed) National Interest and Global Goals, 1989; The US-Turkish-NATO Middle East Connection, 1990; Dance of the Billions, 1990; International Community: a goal for a New World Order, 1992; Life in Alanya: Turkish delight, 1992; contribs to Foreign Affairs, Gewerkschaftliche Rundschau, Werk und Wir, Europa Archiv, Universitas, Ruperto-Carola Weltraumfahrt-Raketentechnik, Europa, Washington Post, New York Times, etc. *Recreations:* hunting, tennis, photography. *Address:* Farmer's Delight, 36276 Mountville Road, Middleburg, VA 22117, USA. *Clubs:* Bohemian (California); Metropolitan, Cosmos (Washington, DC); Century Association (New York); Colonnade (Univ. of Virginia).

McGHIE, James Marshall; QC (Scot.) 1983; *b* 15 Oct. 1944; *s* of James Drummond McGhie and Jessie Eadie Bennie; *m* 1968, Ann Manuel Cockburn; one *s* one *d. Educ:* Perth Acad.; Edinburgh Univ. (LLB Hons). Called to the Scottish Bar, 1969; Advocate-depute, 1983–86. Pt-time Chm., Medical Appeal Tribunal, 1987–92; Mem., Criminal Injuries Compensation Bd, 1992–. *Recreations:* dining and Dunning. *Address:* 3 Lauder Road, Edinburgh EH9 2EW. *T:* 0131–667 8325.

MacGIBBON, Dr Barbara Haig, (Mrs John Roberts), CB 1988; FRCPath; Assistant Director (Medical), National Radiological Protection Board, 1988–93; *b* 7 Feb. 1928; *d* of Ronald Ross MacGibbon and Margaret Fraser; *m* 1954, John Roberts; one *s* one *d. Educ:* Lady Margaret Hall, Oxford; University College Hosp. Registrar, then Res. Assistant, Dept of Haematology, Royal Postgraduate Med. Sch., 1957–64; Sen. Registrar, Sen. Lectr/Hon. Consultant, then Sen. Res. Fellow, Dept of Haematology, St Thomas' Hosp. Med. Sch., 1969–79; SMO, then PMO, Toxicology and Environmental Health, DHSS, 1979; SPMO, DHSS, 1983–88. Chm., Panel on Energy, WHO Commn on Health and Envmt, 1990–92. *Publications:* articles in various med. jls.

McGILL, Angus, MBE 1990; journalist; *b* 26 Nov. 1927; *s* of Kenneth and Janet McGill. *Educ:* Warehousemen, Clerks' and Drapers' Schools, Addington, Surrey. Reporter, Shields Gazette, 1944; Army service; feature writer, Evening Chronicle, Newcastle, 1948; Londoner's Diary, Evening Standard, 1957; columnist, Evening Standard, 1961–92. British Press Award, descriptive writer of the Year, 1968. *Publications:* Augusta, daily comic strip (drawn by Dominic Poelsma), 1968–; Yea Yea Yea (novel), 1969; (with Kenneth Thomson) Live Wires, 1982; London Pub Guide, 1995. *Address:* 83 Winchester Court, Vicarage Gate, W8 4AF. *T:* 0171–937 2166.

MacGILL, George Roy Buchanan, CBE 1965; General Manager, Cumbernauld Development Corporation, 1956–70; Deputy Chairman, Scottish Special Housing Association, 1971–76; *b* 20 Dec. 1905; *s* of George Buchanan MacGill; *m* 1934, Jean Ferguson Anderson; two *d. Educ:* Glasgow High Sch. Chartered Accountant, 1928. FIMTA 1938. Town Chamberlain, Airdrie, 1932; Burgh Chamberlain, Dunfermline, 1947. *Recreations:* golf, music. *Address:* 28 Roman Court, Bearsden, Glasgow G61 2HS.

McGILL, Maj.-Gen. Nigel Harry Duncan, CB 1966; Chief of Staff to Commandant-General, Royal Marines, 1967–68, retired, 1968; *b* 15 Oct. 1916; *s* of Lt-Col H. R. McGill; *m* 1944, Margaret Constance Killen; two *s* one *d. Educ:* Victoria Coll., Jersey. Commissioned 2nd Lt RM 1934; Maj.-Gen. 1964; Comdr, Portsmouth Group, RM, 1964–67. Representative Col Comdt RM, 1977–78. Exec., Rolls Royce Ltd, 1968–78. *Recreation:* golf. *Address:* Alderwood, Manor Farm Road, Fordingbridge, Hants SP6 1DY.

McGILL, Rt. Rev. Stephen; Bishop of Paisley, (RC), 1968–88, now Bishop Emeritus; *b* Glasgow, 4 Jan. 1912; *s* of Peter McGill and Charlotte Connolly. *Educ:* St Aloysius', Glasgow; Blairs College, Aberdeen; Coutances, France; Institut Catholique, Paris. Ordained Priest of St Sulpice, 1936. STL Paris. St Mary's College, Blairs, Aberdeen: Spiritual Director, 1940–51; Rector, 1951–60; Bishop of Argyll and the Isles, 1960–68. *Address:* 13 Newark Street, Greenock PA16 7UH.

MacGILLIVRAY, Barron Bruce, FRCP; Consultant in Clinical Neurophysiology and Neurology, Royal Free Hospital, 1964–93 (Dean, School of Medicine, 1975–89); Consultant in Clinical Neurophysiology, National Hospital for Nervous Diseases, 1971–93; *b* 21 Aug. 1927; *s* of late John MacGillivray and of Doreene (*née* Eastwood), S Africa; *m* 1955, Ruth Valentine; two *s* one *d. Educ:* King Edward VII Sch., Johannesburg; Univ. of Witwatersrand (BSc Hons 1949); Univ. of Manchester; Univ. of London (MB, BS 1962). FRCP 1973. House Surg., House Phys., Manchester Royal Infirm., 1955–56; RMO,

Stockport and Stepping Hill Hosp., 1957–59; Registrar, subseq. Sen. Registrar, Nat. Hosp. for Nervous Diseases, Queen Sq., London, 1959–64; Res. Fellow, UCLA, 1964–65. Pro-Vice Chancellor, Medicine, Univ. of London, 1985–87. Member: Camden and Islington AHA(T), 1975–78; NE Thames RHA, 1979–84; CVCP, 1983–87; Senate, Collegiate Council, Univ. of London; Univ. rep., Council, Sch. of Pharmacy, St George's Hosp. Med. Sch. and British Postgraduate Med. Fedn; Examr and Teacher, Univ. of London. Mem., Complaints Review Cttee, DHSS, 1993–94. Pres., Electrophys. Technicians Assoc., 1976–82. MRI 1975; FRSocMed; FRSA. *Publications:* papers in sci. jls on cerebral electrophysiol., epilepsy, computing and cerebral death. *Recreations:* flying, photography, D-I-Y. *Address:* Rosslyn Tower, 18 St John's Avenue, Putney, SW15 2AA. *T:* 0181–788 5213.

MacGILLIVRAY, Prof. Ian, MD, FRCP; FRCOG; Regius Professor of Obstetrics and Gynæcology, University of Aberdeen, 1965–84 (Dean of Medical Faculty, 1976–79), now Emeritus Professor; *b* 25 Oct. 1920; *yr s* of W. and A. MacGillivray; *m* 1950, Edith Mary Margaret Cook; one *s* twin *d. Educ:* Vale of Leven Academy, Alexandria; University of Glasgow (MB, ChB 1944; MD 1953); MRCOG 1949, FRCOG 1959; FRCPGlas 1973. Gardiner Research Schol., 1949–51, Lectr in Midwifery, 1951–53, Univ. of Glasgow; Senior Lecturer: in Obstetrics and Gynæcology, Univ. of Bristol, 1953–55; in Midwifery and Gynæcology, Univ. of Aberdeen, 1955–61; Prof. of Obstetrics and Gynæcology, University of London, at St Mary's Hospital Medical Sch., 1961–65. Mem., GMC, 1979–84. Founder Pres., Internat. Soc. for Study of Hypertension in Pregnancy, 1976–80; Pres., Internat. Soc. for Twin Studies, 1980–83; Mem. Council, RCOG, 1974–80. *Publications:* Outline of Human Reproduction, 1963; Combined Textbook of Obstetrics and Gynaecology, 1976; Human Multiple Reproduction, 1976; Pre-eclampsia: the hypertensive disease of pregnancy, 1983; contrib. to: British Medical Journal, Lancet, Journal of Obstetrics and Gynæcology of the British Empire; Clinical Science. *Address:* Errogie, 35A Coombe Lane, Stoke Bishop, Bristol BS9 2BL. *T:* Bristol (0117) 940 0478.

McGILLIVRAY, Robert, CEng, FICE, FIWEM; Chairman, Fisheries Committee for Hydro-Electric Schemes, Scotland, since 1992; Chief Engineer and Under Secretary, Scottish Development Department, 1987–91; *b* 11 May 1931; *o s* of late William Gilchrist McGillivray and of Janet Love Jamieson; *m* 1955, Pauline, *e d* of late Alexander Davie; one *s. Educ:* Boroughmuir Sch., Edinburgh; Univ. of Edinburgh (BSc CivEng.). National Service, 1949–51. Training with J. & A. Leslie & Reid, CE, 1955–57; Asst Engr, Midlothian CC, 1957–60; CE, Dept of Agric. & Fisheries for Scotland, 1960–72; Scottish Development Department: Prin. CE, 1972–75; Engrg Inspector, 1976–80; Asst Chief Engr, 1980–85; Dep. Chief Engr, 1985–87. *Publication:* A History of the Clan MacGillivray (with George B. Macgillivray), 1973. *Recreations:* music, genealogy, Highland history. *Address:* Fairview, 88/3 Barnton Park View, Edinburgh EH4 6HJ. *T:* 0131–339 1667.

McGILVRAY, Prof. James William; Professor of Economics, University of Strathclyde, since 1988; *b* 21 Feb. 1938; *m* 1966, Alison Ann Wingfield; one *s* one *d. Educ:* St Columba's Coll., Dublin; Univ. of Edinburgh (MA); Trinity Coll., Dublin (MLitt). Lectr in Econs, TCD, 1962–69; Res. Fellow, Harvard Univ., 1969–70; Sen. Lectr, Univ. of Stirling, 1970–75; Res. Prof., 1975–80, Dir, 1980–85, Fraser of Allander Inst., Univ. of Strathclyde; Dir of Econs, Dar Al-Handasah Consultants, 1985–88. *Publications:* Irish Economic Statistics, 1968, 2nd edn 1983; Use and Interpretation of Medical Statistics (with G. J. Bourke), 1969, 4th edn 1991; articles in Econometrica, Economic Jl, Rev. of Econs and Statistics, Jl of Reg. Sci., etc. *Recreations:* golf, gardening. *Address:* Gartinstarry Lodge, Buchlyvie, Stirling FK8 3PD. *Club:* Fitzwilliam (Dublin).

McGIRR, Prof. Edward McCombie, CBE 1978; BSc, MD Glasgow; FRCP, FRCPE, FRCPGlas; FACP (Hon.); FFCM; FRSE; Dean, 1974–81, Administrative Dean, 1978–81, and Professor of Administrative Medicine, 1978–81 now Professor Emeritus, Faculty of Medicine, University of Glasgow; Dean of Faculties, University of Glasgow, since 1992; Physician, Glasgow Royal Infirmary, 1952–81; Honorary Consultant Physician to the Army in Scotland, 1975–81; *b* 15 June 1916; *yr s* of William and Ann McGirr, Hamilton, Lanarkshire; *m* 1949, Diane Curzon, *y c* of Alexander Woods, MBE, TD, DL, and Edith E. C. Woods, Birmingham and London; one *s* three *d. Educ:* Hamilton Academy; Glasgow Univ. BSc 1937; MB, ChB (Hons) Glasgow, 1940; MD (Hons) and Bellahouston Medal, 1960. Served RAMC, 1941–46, in UK, India, Burma, Siam, Indo-China; Medical Specialist; demobilized with hon. rank of Major. Glasgow University: various appointments incl. Lectr and Sen. Lectr in Medicine, at Royal Infirmary, Glasgow, 1947–61; Muirhead Prof. of Medicine, 1961–78. Visitor, Royal Coll. of Physicians and Surgeons of Glasgow, 1968–70, President 1970–72. Member: Medical Appeals Tribunals, 1961–88; Nat. Radiological Protection Bd, 1976–83; Scottish Health Service Planning Council, 1977–84 (Chm., 1978–84); Nat. Med. Consultative Cttee, 1977–81; Med. Sub-Cttee, UGC, 1977–81; GNC for Scotland, 1978–83; Greater Glasgow Health Bd, 1979–85; Nat. Bd for Nursing, Midwifery and Health Visiting for Scotland, 1980–83; Cttee of ten, Tenovus-Scotland, 1981–89; BBC/IBA Scottish Appeals Adv. Cttee, 1982–86; Chairman: Scottish Council for Postgrad. Med. Educn, 1979–85; Scottish Council for Opportunities for Play Experience, 1985–87; Professional Adv. Panel, Prince and Princess of Wales Hospice, 1985–87; Working Party on Play in Scotland, 1986–87; Clyde Estuary Amenity Council, 1986–90. Member: Assoc. of Physicians of Gt Britain and Ireland, 1955– (mem. of editorial panel, Quarterly Journal of Medicine, 1968–76; Mem. Council, 1972–76; Hon. Mem., 1990–); Scottish Soc. of Physicians; Scottish Soc. for Experimental Med. (Treas., 1960–66); Pres., Harveian Soc. of Edin., 1979; Corresp. Member: Amer. Thyroid Assoc.; Medical Research Soc. (mem. of council, 1967–69); Royal Medico-Chirurgical Soc. of Glasgow (Pres., 1965–66). Hon. DSc Glasgow, 1994. *Publications:* chiefly in relation to thyroid gland dysfunction, nuclear medicine, medical education, policy planning in the NHS, and 18th century medical history. *Recreations:* family life, curling. *Address:* Anchorage House, Bothwell, by Glasgow G71 8NF. *T:* Bothwell (01698) 852194. *Club:* Royal Scottish Automobile.

McGIVERN, Eugene; Under Secretary, Board of Inland Revenue, since 1986; *b* 15 Sept. 1938; *s* of late James McGivern and of Eileen McGivern; *m* 1960, Teresa Doran; two *s* one *d. Educ:* St Mary's Grammar School, Belfast. Joined Inland Revenue, 1955; seconded to Welsh Office as Private Sec. to Minister of State, 1967–69; Inland Revenue, 1969–. *Address:* Board of Inland Revenue, Somerset House, Strand, WC2R 1LB. *T:* 0171–438 6622.

McGLASHAN, John Reid Curtis, CBE 1974; HM Diplomatic Service, retired 1979; *b* 12 Dec. 1921; *s* of late John Adamson McGlashan and Emma Rose May McGlashan; *m* 1947, Dilys Bagnall (*née* Buxton Knight); one *s* two *d. Educ:* Fettes; Christ Church, Oxford (Rugger Blue, 1945). RAF (Bomber Command), 1940–45 (POW, 1941–45). Entered Foreign Service, 1953; Baghdad, 1955; Tripoli, 1963; Madrid, 1968; Counsellor, FCO, 1970–79. *Recreations:* gardening, reading. *Address:* Allendale, Selsey Bill, West Sussex PO20 9DB. *Club:* Vincent's (Oxford).

MacGLASHAN, Maureen Elizabeth; HM Diplomatic Service; Ambassador to the Holy See, since 1995; *b* 7 Jan. 1938; *d* of Kenneth and Elizabeth MacGlashan. *Educ:* Luton High Sch.; Girton Coll., Cambridge (MA, LLM). Joined FO, 1961; 2nd Sec., Tel Aviv, 1964–67; FCO, 1967–72; Head of Chancery, East Berlin, 1973–75; UK Representation to EEC, 1975–77; seconded to Home Civil Service, 1977–82; Counsellor, Bucharest, 1982–86; Asst Dir, Res. Centre for Internat. Law, and bye-Fellow, Girton Coll., Cambridge Univ., 1986–90; Counsellor, Consul-Gen. and Dep. Head of Mission, Belgrade, 1990; Head, Western European Dept, FCO, 1991–92; on secondment to CSSB, 1992;95. Ed., Iran–US Claims Tribunal Reports, vols 8–22. *Publication:* (trans.) Weil, Maritime Delimitation, Consolidated Index to the International Law Reports, vols 36–80. *Address:* c/o Foreign and Commonwealth Office, SW1A 2AH. *Club:* University Women's.

McGLASHAN, Prof. Maxwell Len, FRSC; Professor of Chemistry and Head of the Department of Chemistry, University College London, 1974–89, now Professor Emeritus; Hon. Research Fellow, since 1989; *b* 1 April 1924; *s* of late Leonard Day McGlashan and late Margaret Cordelia McGlashan; *m* 1947, Susan Jane, *d* of late Col H. E. Crosse, MC, OBE, and late Mrs D. Crosse, Patoka Station, Hawkes Bay, NZ. *Educ:* Greymouth, NZ; Canterbury Univ. Coll., Christchurch, NZ; Univ. of Reading. MSc (NZ) 1946, PhD (Reading) 1951, DSc (Reading) 1962. Asst Lectr, 1946–48, Lectr, 1948–53, Sen. Lectr, 1953, in Chemistry, at Canterbury Univ. Coll., Christchurch, NZ. Sims Empire Scholar, 1949–52; Lectr in Chem., Univ. of Reading, 1954–61; Reader in Chem., Univ. of Reading, 1962–64; Prof. of Physical Chem., Univ. of Exeter, 1964–74 (Dean, Faculty of Science, 1973–74). Mem., 1963–65, Vice-Chm., 1965–67, Chm., 1967–71, Commn on Physicochemical Symbols, Terminology, and Units. Chm., Interdivl Cttee on Nomenclature and Symbols, Internat. Union of Pure and Applied Chem., 1971–76; Member: Royal Society Symbols Cttee, 1963–88; BSI's Tech. Cttee on physical quantities and units, 1963– (Chm., 1978–); Council, Faraday Soc., 1965–67; Metrication Bd, 1969–80; Comité Consultatif des Unités (Metre Convention), 1969–; Council, Chem. Soc., 1970–73; SRC Chem. Cttee, 1974–76; Data Compilation Cttee, 1974–77; Res. Cttee, British Gas Corp., 1979–90; Trustee, Ramsay Meml Fellowships Trust, 1982– (Chm. Adv. Council, 1975–89). Editor, Jl of Chemical Thermodynamics, 1969–. Hon. Fellow, UCL, 1991. *Publications:* Physicochemical Quantities and Units, 1968 (Royal Inst. of Chem.), 2nd edn, 1971; Chemical Thermodynamics, 1979; papers on chemical thermodynamics and statistical mechanics in Proc. Roy. Soc., Trans Faraday Soc., Jl Chem. Thermodynamics, etc. *Recreations:* climbing in the Alps, gardening, the theatre. *Address:* Patoka, Fairwarp, Uckfield, E Sussex TN22 3DT. *T:* Nutley (01825) 712172. *Club:* Athenæum.

McGONAGLE, Stephen; Senator, Seanad Éireann, Dublin, 1983–87; *b* 17 Nov. 1914; *m*; five *s* one *d. Educ:* Christian Brothers', Derry. Chairman, NI Cttee, Irish Congress of Trade Unions, 1959; Vice-Chm., Derry Develt Commn, 1969–71; Pres., Irish Congress of Trade Unions, 1972–73; Mem., NI Economic Council, Indust. Tribunal, Indust. Ct, until 1973; Dist Sec., Irish Transport and General Workers' Union, Dec. 1973; NI Parly Comr For Admin, and Comr for Complaints, 1974–79; Chm., NI Police Complaints Bd, 1977–83. *Recreations:* fishing, boating, reading. *Address:* 10 Kingsfort Park, Derry.

MACGOUGAN, John; Member, Central Arbitration Committee, 1977–83; *b* 21 Aug. 1913; *m* 1941, Lizzie Faulkner; three *s* one *d. Educ:* various Northern Ireland Schs; Technical Sch.; Correspondence courses. Accountancy profession, 1930–45. Irish Officer, NUTGW, in charge of all Irish affairs, 1945–69; Gen. Sec., NUTGW, 1969–79. Contested (Irish Labour) N Ireland Parly Elections, Oldpark 1938, Falls Div. 1951; Westminster Parly Election, South Down 1950; Member: Belfast Corporation, 1949–58; Executive, Irish TUC, 1950–69 (Pres. 1957–58 and 1963–64); TUC Gen. Council, 1970–79, MSC, 1977–79, Economic and Social Cttee, EEC, 1978–80. Irish and UK Rep., ILO, 1962–85. *Recreations:* proletarian pastimes. *Address:* 96 Whalley Drive, Bletchley, Milton Keynes, Bucks MK3 6HU. *T:* Milton Keynes (01908) 372174.

McGOUGH, Roger; poet; *b* 9 Nov. 1937; *s* of Roger Francis and Mary Agnes McGough; *m* 1st, 1970 (marr. diss. 1980); two *s*; 2nd, 1986, Hilary Clough; one *s* one *d. Educ:* St Mary's Coll., Crosby, Liverpool; Hull Univ. (BA, Grad. Cert. Ed.). Fellow of Poetry, Univ. of Loughborough, 1973–75. Mem. Exec. Council, Poetry Soc., 1989–. Hon. Prof., Thames Valley Univ., 1993. *Television:* Kurt, Mungo, BP and Me (BAFTA Award), 1984. Lyrics for Wind in the Willows, Broadway, 1985–86; The Elements (RTS Award), 1993. *Publications:* Watchwords, 1969; After The Merrymaking, 1971; Out of Sequence, 1972; Gig, 1972; Sporting Relations, 1974; In The Glassroom, 1976; Summer with Monika, 1978; Holiday on Death Row, 1979; Unlucky For Some, 1981; Waving at Trains, 1982; Melting into the Foreground, 1986; Selected Poems 1967–1987, 1989; You at the Back, 1991; Defying Gravity, 1992; *children's books:* Mr Noselighter, 1977; The Great Smile Robbery, 1982; Sky in the Pie, 1983; The Stowaways, 1986; Noah's Ark, 1986; Nailing the Shadow, 1987; An Imaginary Menagerie, 1988; Helen Highwater, 1989; Counting by Numbers, 1989; Pillow Talk, 1990; The Lighthouse That Ran Away, 1991; My Dad's a Fire-eater, 1992; Another Custard Pie, 1993; Lucky, 1993; Stinkers Ahoy!, 1995; The Magic Fountain, 1995; contributed to: Penguin Modern Poets, No 10, Mersey Sound, 1967, rev. edn 1983; Oxford Book of 20th Century Verse, 1973; The Norton Anthology of Modern Poetry, 1973; Penguin Modern Poets, No 4 (new series), 1995; edited: Strictly Private, 1981; Kingfisher Book of Comic Verse, 1986. *Address:* c/o Peters Fraser and Dunlop, 5th floor, The Chambers, Chelsea Harbour, Lots Road, SW10 0XF. *T:* 0171–376 7676. *Club:* Chelsea Arts (Chm., 1984–86; Trustee, 1992–).

McGOVERN, George Stanley; United States Senator, 1963–81; *b* Avon, S Dakota, 19 July 1922; *s* of Rev. Joseph C. McGovern and Francis (*née* McLean); *m* 1943, Eleanor Faye Stegeberg; one *s* three *d* (and one *d* decd). *Educ:* Dakota Wesleyan Univ. (BA); Northwestern Univ. (MA, PhD). Served World War II, USAAF (DFC). Prof. of History and Govt, Dakota Wesleyan Univ., 1950–53. Exec. Sec., S Dakota Democratic Party, 1953–56; Mem., 1st Dist, S Dakota, US House of Reps, 1957–61; Dir, Food for Peace Programme, 1961–62; Senator from South Dakota, 1963–81. Democratic nominee for US President, 1972. Visiting Professor: Columbia Univ., 1977; Univ. of Pa, 1978; Northwestern Univ., 1981; Univ. of New Orleans, 1982; University Coll., Dublin, 1982; Duke Univ., 1985; Univ. of Munich, 1987. Mem., Amer. Hist. Assoc. *Publications:* The Colorado Coal Strike, 1913–14, 1953; War Against Want, 1964; Agricultural Thought in the Twentieth Century, 1967; A Time of War, A Time of Peace, 1968; (with Leonard F. Guttridge) The Great Coalfield War, 1972; An American Journey, 1974; Grassroots, an Autobiography, 1978. *Address:* PO Box 5591, Friendship Station, Washington, DC 20016, USA.

McGOWAN, family name of **Baron McGowan.**

McGOWAN, 3rd Baron, *cr* 1937; **Harry Duncan Cory McGowan;** Partner, Panmure, Gordon & Co., since 1971; *b* 20 July 1938; *e s* of Harry Wilson McGowan, 2nd Baron McGowan, and Carmen, *d* of Sir (James) Herbert Cory, 1st Bt; *S* father, 1966; *m* 1962, Lady Gillian Angela Pepys, *d* of 7th Earl of Cottenham; one *s* two *d. Educ:* Eton. *Heir: s* Hon. Harry John Charles McGowan, *b* 23 June 1971. *Address:* House of Lords, Westminster, SW1A 0PW; Highway House, Lower Froyle, Alton, Hants GU34 4NB. *T:* Bentley (01420) 22104; 12 Stanhope Mews East, SW7 5QU. *T:* 0171–370 2346. *Club:* Boodle's.

McGOWAN, Alan Patrick, PhD; Archivist, Royal Naval College, Greenwich, since 1989; Callendar Curator, National Maritime Museum, since 1989 (Chief Curator, 1986–88); *b* 16 Nov. 1928; *s* of Hugh McGowan and Alice Chilton; *m* 1958, Betty Eileen, *e d* of Mr and Mrs F. L. MacDougall, Ontario; three *s*. *Educ:* Spring Grove Grammar Sch.; Borough Road Coll.; Univ. of Western Ontario (BA, MA); Univ. of London (PhD). Served RASC (Air Freight), 1947–49. Asst Master (History), 1953–63; Lectr, Univ. of Western Ont Summer Sch., 1964; Canada Council Fellow, 1964–66; Asst Keeper, 1967–71, Head, 1971–86, Dept of Ships, National Maritime Museum. Associate Prof. of History, Univ. of Western Ont Summer Sch., 1977. Member: Council, Navy Records Soc., 1968–; Adv. Council on Export of Works of Art, 1972–88; Victory Adv. Technical Cttee, 1974– (Chm., 1983–); Mary Rose Adv. Cttee, 1974–78; Ships Cttee, Maritime Trust, 1977–88; Council, Soc. for Nautical Res., 1981–; Cttee, Falkland Islands Foundn, 1981–83. Associate RINA, 1980–88. *Publications:* (ed) Jacobean Commissions of Enquiry, 1608 and 1618, vol. 113 of Navy Records Society, 1971; Royal Yachts, 1975; (with J. Fabb) The Victorian and Edwardian Navy in Photographs, 1976; (ed and prefaced) Steel's Naval Architecture, 1976; Sailor, 1977; (ed and prefaced) Steel's Rigging and Seamanship, 1978; The Century before Steam, 1980; Tiller and Whipstaff, 1981; articles in jls of history and in encyclopaedia. *Recreations:* golf, reading, music. *Address:* c/o National Maritime Museum, Greenwich, SE10 9NF.

McGOWAN, Bruce Henry, MA; FRSA; Headmaster, Haberdashers' Aske's School, Elstree, 1973–87; *b* 27 June 1924; *er s* of late Rt Rev. Henry McGowan, sometime Bishop of Wakefield, and Nora Heath McGowan (*née* Godwin); *m* 1947, Beryl McKenzie (*née* Liggitt); one *s* three *d*. *Educ:* King Edward's Sch., Birmingham; Jesus Coll., Cambridge. War service, Royal Artillery, 1943–46 (India and Burma). Asst Master, King's Sch., Rochester, 1949–53; Senior History Master, Wallasey Gram. Sch., 1953–57; Headmaster: De Aston Sch., Market Rasen, Lincs, 1957–64; Solihull Sch., 1964–73. Page Scholar of the English-Speaking Union, 1961. Member: Church Assembly, 1963–70; Public Schools Commn, 1968–70; Council, Church Schools Co., 1986–92 (Chm., 1987–92); Cttee, GBGSA, 1989–93; GBA, 1992–95; Chairman: Boarding Schools Assoc., 1967–69; Headmasters' Conference, 1985 (Chairman: London Div. 1977; Community Service Cttee, 1976–80; Political and Public Relations Cttee, 1981–84). Comr, Duke of York's Royal Mil. Sch., Dover, 1986–; Governor: Bristol Grammar Sch., 1983–95; St George's Sch., Harpenden, 1977–81, 1984–; Greycotes Sch., Oxford, 1987–; Ellesmere Coll., 1992–94; Adv. Gov., St Benedict's Sch., Ealing, 1989–. Church Warden, St Mary's, N Leigh, Oxford, 1993–. Fellow Woodard Corp., 1990–94. *Recreations:* foreign travel, walking, music, the theatre. *Address:* The Bell House, 29 Union Street, Woodstock, Oxon OX20 1JF. *Club:* East India.

McGOWAN, Ian Duncan; Librarian, National Library of Scotland, since 1990; *b* 19 Sept. 1945; *s* of Alexander McGowan and Dora (*née* Sharp); *m* 1971, Elizabeth Ann Weir; two *d*. *Educ:* Liverpool Inst.; Exeter Coll., Oxford (BA 1st Cl. Hons Russian Lang. and Lit., 1967); Sch. of Slavonic and E European Studies, Univ. of London. National Library of Scotland: Asst Keeper, 1971–78; Keeper (Catalogues and Automation), 1978–88; Sec. of the Library, 1988–90. Chm., Nat. Preservation Adv. Cttee, 1994–. *Recreations:* books, gardens. *Address:* 23 Blackford Road, Edinburgh EH9 2DT. *T:* 0131–667 2432. *Club:* New (Edinburgh).

McGOWAN, John; Sheriff in Glasgow, since 1993; *b* 15 Jan. 1944; *s* of Arthur McGowan and Bridget McCluskey; *m* 1966, Elise Smith; two *s*. *Educ:* St Joseph's Acad., Kilmarnock; Glasgow Univ. (LLB). Admitted Solicitor, 1967; Temp. Sheriff, 1986–93. Chm., DHSS Appeal Tribunal, 1980–86. Mem. Council, Law Soc. of Scotland, 1982–85. *Recreations:* golf, tennis, curling, singing in church choir. *Address:* 19 Auchentrae Crescent, Ayr KA7 4BD. *T:* Ayr (01292) 260139.

McGOWAN, Prof. Margaret Mary, (Mrs Sydney Anglo), PhD; FBA 1993; Professor of French, since 1974, Senior Pro-Vice-Chancellor, since 1992, University of Sussex; *b* 21 Dec. 1931; *d* of George McGowan and Elizabeth (*née* McGrail); *m* 1964, Prof. Sydney Anglo. *Educ:* Stamford High Sch.; Univ. of Reading (BA, PhD). Lecturer: Univ. of Strasbourg, 1955–57; Univ. of Glasgow, 1957–64; University of Sussex: Lectr, 1964–68; Reader, 1968–74; Dean, Sch. of European Studies, 1977–80; Pro-Vice-Chancellor (Arts and Social Studies), 1981–86. Vice-Chm. Bd, British Inst. in Paris, 1978–. Freeman, City of Tours, 1986. *Publications:* L'Art du Ballet de Cour, 1963; Montaigne's Deceits, 1974; Ideal Forms in the Age of Ronsard, 1985; Louis XIII's Court Ballets, 1989; Moy qui me voy: studies of the self, 1990. *Recreations:* music, cooking, tennis. *Address:* 59 Green Ridge, Withdean, Brighton BN1 5LU.

McGOWAN, Michael; Member (Lab) Leeds, European Parliament, since 1984; *b* 19 May 1940; *m*; two *s* one *d*. *Educ:* Leicester University. Formerly: lecturer; BBC journalist; cooperative employment development officer, Kirklees Council, to 1984. *Address:* 3 Grosvenor Terrace, Otley, West Yorks LS21 1HJ.

McGRADY, Edward Kevin; MP (SDLP) Down South, since 1987; Partner, M. B. McGrady & Co., chartered accountants and insurance brokers; *b* 3 June 1935; *y s* of late Michael McGrady and late Lilian Leatham; *m* 1959, Patricia, *d* of Wm Swail and Margaret Breen; two *s* one *d*. *Educ:* St Patrick's High Sch., Downpatrick. ACA 1957, FCA 1962. Councillor, Downpatrick UDC, 1961–89; Chm. of UDC, 1964–73; Vice-Chm., Down District Council, 1973, 1975–76, 1977, Chm. 1974, 1976, 1978, 1981, 1982. 1st Chm. of SDLP, 1971–73; 1st Chm. of SDLP Assembly Party. Mem. (SDLP) S Down: NI Assembly, 1973–75; NI Constitutional Convention, 1975–76; NI Assembly, 1982–86; Head of Office of Executive Planning and Co-ordination (Minister for Co-ordination, Jan.-May 1974); contested (SDLP) Down S, gen. elections, 1979, 1983 and 1986. *Recreations:* golf, badminton, choral work. *Address:* Cois Na Cille, Saul Brae, Downpatrick, Co. Down BT30 6NL. *T:* Downpatrick 612882; House of Commons, SW1A 0AA. *T:* 0171–219 4481.

McGRAIL, Prof. Sean Francis, FSA; Visiting Professor of Maritime Archaeology, University of Southampton, since 1991; Chief Archaeologist, National Maritime Museum, 1976–89; *b* 5 May 1928; *m* 1955, Ursula Anne Yates, BA; one *s* three *d*. *Educ:* Royal Navy (Master Mariner); Univ. of Bristol (BA); Univ. of London (PhD); MA 1988, DSc 1989, Oxon. FSA 1981. Served RN, 1946–68: Seaman Officer; awarded Wings (pilot), 1952; comd 849 Sqdn, FAA, 1962–63. Undergrad., Univ. of Bristol, 1968–71 (Harry Crook Scholar, 1969–71); Postgrad. Student, Inst. of Archaeology, London, 1972–73; Postgrad. Student (pt-time), UCL, 1973–78; National Maritime Museum, 1972–89, Hd of Archaeol Res. Centre, 1976–86. Leverhulme Res. Fellow, 1991–94; Vis. Prof. of Maritime Archæology, Oxford Univ., 1986–93. Mem., Adv. Cttee on Historic Wrecks, Dept. of Nat. Heritage (formerly DoE), 1975–. Vice-Chm., Trust for Preservation of Oxford Coll. Barges, 1987–. *Publications:* Building and Trials of a Replica of an Ancient Boat, 1974; Logboats of England and Wales, 1978; Rafts, Boats and Ships, 1981; Ancient Boats, 1983; Ancient Boats of North West Europe, 1987; Medieval Boat and Ship Timbers from Dublin, 1993; *edited:* Sources and Techniques in Boat Archaeology, 1977; Medieval Ships and Harbours, 1979; Paul Johnstone, Seacraft of Prehistory, 1980, 2nd edn 1988; Brigg 'raft' and her Prehistoric Environment, 1981; Woodworking Techniques before 1500, 1982; Aspects of Maritime Archaeology and Ethnography, 1984; (with J. Coates) Greek Trireme of 5th Century BC, 1984; (with E. Kentley) Sewn Plank Boats, 1985; Maritime Celts, Saxons and Frisians, 1990; articles in archaeological and maritime jls. *Recreations:* strategic gardening, real ale specialist. *Address:* Institute of Archaeology, 36 Beaumont Street, Oxford OX1 2PG. *T:* Oxford (01865) 278240.

McGRATH, Dr Alister Edgar; Principal, Wycliffe Hall, Oxford, since 1995; *b* 23 Jan. 1953; *s* of Edgar P. McGrath and Annie J. M. McGrath (*née* McBride); *m* 1980, Joanna Ruth Collicutt; one *s* one *d*. *Educ:* Wadham Coll., Oxford (BA 1975); Linacre Coll., Oxford; Merton Coll., Oxford (MA, DPhil 1978; BD 1983); St John's Coll., Cambridge. Ordained deacon, 1980, priest, 1981; Curate, St Leonard's Ch, Wollaton, Nottingham, 1980–83; Lectr, Wycliffe Hall, Oxford, 1983–95. *Publications:* Explaining Your Faith. . . Without Losing Your Friends, 1988; Justification by Faith, 1988; Justitia Dei: history of the Christian doctrine of justification, Vol. I 1989, Vol. II 1993; Doubt: handling it honestly, 1990; Luther's Theology of the Cross: Martin Luther's theological breakthrough, 1990; Cloud of Witnesses: ten great Christian thinkers, 1990; Genesis of Doctrine, 1990; Life of John Calvin: a study in the shaping of Western culture, 1990; Affirming Your Faith: exploring the Apostles' Creed, 1991; Bridge Building: creative Christian apologetics, 1992; Intellectual Origins of the European Reformation, 1992; Making Sense of the Cross, 1992; Reformation Thought: an introduction, 1992; Roots that Refresh, 1992; Suffering, 1992; (with J. McGrath) Dilemma of Self Esteem: the Cross and Christian confidence, 1992; (ed) Blackwell Encyclopedia of Modern Christian Thought, 1993; Christian Theology: an introduction, 1993; Making of Modern German Christology: from the Enlightenment to Pannenberg, 1993; Renewal of Anglicanism: is Anglicanism strong enough to survive?, 1993; Jesus: who He is and why He matters, 1994; Evangelicalism and the Future of Christianity, 1994; contrib. articles to learned jls. *Recreations:* walking, Australian wines. *Address:* Wycliffe Hall, Oxford OX2 6PW. *T:* Oxford (01865) 274200.

McGRATH, Sir Brian (Henry), KCVO 1993 (CVO 1988); Treasurer to the Duke of Edinburgh, 1984–95 (Assistant Private Secretary, 1982; Private Secretary, 1982–92); *b* 27 Oct. 1925; *s* of William Henry and Hermione Gioja McGrath; *m* 1959, Elizabeth Joan Bruce (*née* Gregson-Ellis) (*d* 1977); two *s*, and one step *d*. *Educ:* Eton College. Served War of 1939–45, Irish Guards, 1943–46, Lieut. Cannon Brewery Co., 1946–48; Victoria Wine Co.: joined, 1948; Dir, 1949; Chm., 1960–82; Dir, 1960, Chm., 1975–82, Grants of St James's Ltd; Dir, Allied Breweries Ltd (subseq. Allied-Lyons plc), 1970–82; Chm., Broad Street Securities, 1983–92. Younger Brother of Trinity House, 1993. Master of Wine. *Recreations:* golf, tennis, shooting. *Address:* Flat 3, 9 Cheyne Gardens, SW3 5QU. *Clubs:* Boodle's, White's.

McGRATH, James Aloysius; Hotspur, Racing Correspondent of the Daily Telegraph, since 1991; racing commentator; *b* 13 June 1952; *s* of Brian James McGrath and Kathleen May McGrath; *m* 1977, Anita Lee; two *s* two *d*. *Educ:* Xavier Coll., Melbourne. Cadet racing writer, The Australian, 1972–73; Racing Corresp., China Mail (Hong Kong), 1973–74; Chief Racing Writer, South China Morning Post (Hong Kong), 1975–86; writer, Racing Post, 1986–90. Racing Commentator: BBC, 1992–; Satellite Information Services, 1993–. *Recreations:* golf, ski-ing, watching cricket. *Address:* The Travers, Chobham, Woking, Surrey GU24 8SZ. *T:* Chobham (01276) 857155. *Clubs:* Royal Hong Kong Jockey, Royal Hong Kong Golf, Hong Kong Football (Hong Kong).

McGRATH, Prof. John Christie; Regius Professor of Physiology, University of Glasgow, since 1991; *b* 8 March 1949; *s* of John Christie McGrath and Margaret Gilmore Cochrane McGrath (*née* Murray); *m* 1970, Wilma Nicol; one *s* one *d*. *Educ:* Cross Arthurlie Primary Sch.; John Neilson Instn; Univ. of Glasgow (BSc 1st class Hons 1970; PhD 1974). Wellcome Interdisciplinary Research Fellowship, Dept of Pharmacology and Univ. Dept of Anaesthesia, Glasgow Royal Infirmary, Univ. of Glasgow, 1973–75; Institute of Physiology, University of Glasgow: Lectr, 1975; Wellcome Trust Research Leave Fellowship, 1982; Sen. Lectr, Reader, Titular Prof., 1983–91; Co-Dir, Clinical Res. Initiative, 1994–. Member: British Pharmacol Soc. 1975 (Sandoz Prize, 1980); Cttee, Physiolog. Soc., 1988– (Mem., 1978); Internat. Soc. for Heart Research, 1989; Amer. Soc. for Pharmacology and Experimental Therapeutics, 1991; Amer. Physiol Soc., 1994. Mem., Labour Party. Member Editorial Board: British Jl of Pharmacology, 1985–91; Jl of Cardiovascular Pharmacology, 1988–; Pharmacological Reviews, 1990–; Jl of Vascular Res., 1991–. 1st Pfizer Award for Biology, 1983. *Publications:* contribs to learned jls in fields of pharmacology and physiology. *Recreations:* running, politics. *Address:* Institute of Physiology, University of Glasgow, Glasgow G12 8QQ. *T:* 0141–330 4483, *Fax:* 0141–330 4100, 0141–337 1651.

McGRATH, John Peter; writer and director, theatre, film and television; Director: Freeway Films, since 1983; Channel Four Television, since 1989; *b* 1 June 1935; *s* of John Francis McGrath and Margaret McGrath; *m* 1962, Elizabeth Maclennan; two *s* one *d*. *Educ:* Alun Grammar Sch., Mold; St John's Coll., Oxford. Theatre (playwright), 1958–61; BBC Television, 1960–65; film (screenwriting) and theatre (writing and directing), 1965–70; theatre, with regular forays into television and film, as writer and director, 1970–; founded 7:84 Theatre Co., 1971, Artistic Dir, 1971–88. Has produced or directed over 75 plays in the theatre, and written over 40 plays, including: Why the Chicken, 1959; The Tent, 1960; Comrade Jacob, 1968; Soft or a Girl, 1971; Trees in the Wind, 1971; Sergeant Musgrave Dances On (adaptation), 1972; Boom, 1974; Lay Off, 1975; Out of Our Heads, 1976; Trembling Giant, 1977; Bitter Apples, 1979; Nightclass, 1981; Rejoice!, 1982; The Catch, 1982; Women in Power, 1983; Women of the Dunes, 1983; Six Men of Dorset (adaptation), 1984; The Albannach (adaptation), 1984; The Baby and the Bathwater, 1984; All the Fun of the Fair, 1985; There is a Happy Land, 1986; Mairi Mhor, 1987; Border Warfare, 1989; John Brown's Body, 1990; Watching for Dolphins, 1991; The Wicked Old Man, 1992; The Silver Darlings (adaptation), 1994; many TV plays performed on BBC and ITV; prod. film Carrington, 1995; screenplays: The Bofors Gun, 1967; Billion Dollar Brain, 1967; The Virgin Soldiers (adaptation), 1968; The Reckoning, 1968; Blood Red Roses, 1986 (dir); The Dressmaker, 1988 (exec. producer); wrote libretto for Alexander Goehr's opera, Behold the Sun; writes songs and poems. *Publications: plays:* Events While Guarding the Bofors Gun, 1966; Random Happenings in the Hebrides, 1972; Bakke's Night of Fame, 1973; The Cheviot, The Stag and The Black Black Oil, 1974, 2nd edn 1981; The Game's A Bogey, 1974; Fish in the Sea, 1977; Little Red Hen, 1977; Yobbo Nowt, 1978; Joe's Drum, 1979; Blood Red Roses (filmed for TV, 1986), and Swings and Roundabouts, 1981; *general:* A Good Night Out, 1981; The Bone Won't Break, 1990. *Address:* c/o Freeway Films, 67 George Street, Edinburgh EH2 2JG.

McGRATH, William Joseph; Chief Executive Officer, Pentos Group, since 1994; *b* 30 Sept. 1940; *s* of William George McGrath and Wallis (*née* Reinwold); *m* 1965, Mary Teresa Bridget Galvin; two *d*. *Educ:* St John's RC Sch., Tamworth, Staffs; Open Univ. (BA Hons). With Cunard Steamship Co. Ltd, 1956–68; G. J. Keddie & Sons Ltd, 1968–75; Director: Asda Stores Ltd, 1975–81; Comet PLC, 1981–84; Founder and Chief Exec. Officer, Builders Mate, 1984–87; Dir, Wickes PLC, 1990–93 (Dep. Chm., 1993). MInstD 1984; MCIM 1989. FRSA 1994. Wine and Spirit Educn Trust (Cert., Higher

Cert. Dist. and Dip.). KSC 1962. *Recreations:* chess, walking, gardening. *Address:* 4 Sovereign View, SE16 1XH. *T:* 0171–232 2804. *Club:* East India.

McGREGOR, family name of **Baron McGregor of Durris.**

McGREGOR OF DURRIS, Baron *cr* 1978 (Life Peer), of Hampstead; **Oliver Ross McGregor;** Chairman, Press Complaints Commission, 1991–94; Professor of Social Institutions in the University of London, 1964–85; Head of Department of Sociology, at Bedford College, 1964–77; Joint Director, Rowntree Legal Research Unit, 1966–84; *b* 25 Aug. 1921; *s* of late William McGregor and late Anne Olivia Ross; *m* 1944, Nellie Weate; three *s*. *Educ:* Worksop Coll.; University of Aberdeen; London School of Economics (Hon. Fellow 1977). Temp. civil servant, War Office and Ministry of Agriculture, 1940–44. Asst Lecturer and Lecturer in Economic History, University of Hull, 1945–47; Lecturer, Bedford Coll., 1947–60, Reader in University of London, 1960–64; Simon Senior Research Fellow, University of Manchester, 1959–60. Fellow of Wolfson Coll., Oxford, 1972–75; Dir, Centre for Socio-Legal Studies, Univ. of Oxford, 1972–75. Member: Cttee on Enforcement of Judgment Debts, 1965; Cttee on Statutory Maintenance Limits, 1966; Cttee on Land Use (Recreation and Leisure), 1967; National Parks Commission, 1966–68; Independent Television Authority's General Advisory Council, 1967–73; Countryside Commission, 1968–80; Legal Aid Adv. Cttee, 1969–78; Cttee on One-Parent Families, 1969–74; Chairman: Royal Commn on Press, 1975–77 (Mem., 1974); Advertising Standards Authy, 1980–90; Forest Philharmonic Soc., 1975–. President: Nat. Council for One Parent Families, 1975–91; Nat. Assoc. of Citizens' Advice Bureaux, 1981–86. Chm., Reuters Founders Share Co., 1987– (Independent Trustee, 1984–). Lectures: Fawcett Meml, Bedford Coll., 1966; James Seth Meml, Edinburgh Univ., 1968; Hobhouse Meml, LSE, 1971; Maccabaean in Jurisprudence, British Acad., 1973; Hamlyn, Univ. of Kent, 1979; Eleanor Rathbone Meml, Durham Univ., 1979; Ian Gulland, Goldsmiths' Coll., 1980; 150th Anniversary of Univ. of London, LSE, 1986; Tom Olsen, St Bride's Church, 1991. Hon. LLD Bristol, 1986. *Publications:* Divorce in England, 1957; (ed) Lord Ernle, English Farming Past and Present, 6th edn, 1960; (jtly) Separated Spouses, 1970; Social History and Law Reform, 1981; various papers in British Journal of Sociology and other journals. *Address:* Far End, Wyldes Close, NW11 7JB. *T:* 0181–458 2856. *Club:* Garrick.

MacGREGOR, Alastair Rankin; QC 1994; *b* 23 Dec. 1951; *s* of Alexander MacGregor and Anna MacGregor (*née* Neil); *m* 1982, Rosemary Kerslake; one *s* one *d*. *Educ:* Glasgow Acad.; Edinburgh Univ.; New Coll., Oxford Univ. (MA). Called to the Bar, Lincoln's Inn, 1974. *Address:* One Essex Court, Temple, EC4Y 9AR. *T:* 0171–583 2000.
See also R. N. MacGregor

McGREGOR, Rev. Alistair Gerald Crichton; QC (Scot.) 1982; WS; Minister, North Leith Parish Church, Edinburgh, since 1987; *b* 15 Oct. 1937; *s* of late James Reid McGregor, CB, CBE, MC, and Dorothy McGregor; *m* 1965, Margaret Lees or McGregor; two *s* one *d*. *Educ:* Charterhouse; Pembroke Coll., Oxford (BA (Hons) Jurisprudence); Edinburgh Univ. (LLB; BD). Intelligence Corps, 1956–58. Solicitor and WS, 1965–66; Advocate, 1967–82. Clerk to Court of Session Rules Council, 1972–75; Standing Junior Counsel to: SHHD, 1977–79; Scottish Develt Dept, 1979–82. Chm., Family Care (Scotland), 1983–88; Director: Apex (Scotland), 1988–; Kirk Care Housing Assoc., 1994–. Licensed, Church of Scotland, 1986. *Recreations:* squash, tennis. *Address:* 22 Primrose Bank Road, Edinburgh EH5 3JG. *T:* 0131–551 2802. *Clubs:* University Staff, Sports (Edinburgh).

McGREGOR, Dr Angus; Regional Medical Officer, West Midlands Regional Health Authority, 1979–88; Visiting Professor, University of Keele, 1988–94; *b* 26 Dec. 1926; *s* of Dr William Hector Scott McGregor and Dr Olwen May Richards; *m* 1951, May Burke, BA; one *d*. *Educ:* Solihull Sch.; St John's Coll., Cambridge. MA, MD; FRCP; FFCM; DPH. Junior hospital posts, 1950; Army service, RAMC, 1951–52; general practice, 1953; Asst MOH, Chester, 1954–56; Deputy Medical Officer of Health: Swindon, 1957–58; Hull, 1958–65; MOH and Port MO, Southampton, 1965–74; District Community Physician, East Dorset, 1974–79. Mem. Bd, FCM, RCP, 1982–88. FRSA 1986. *Publications:* (with T. Bunbury) Disciplining and Dismissing Doctors in the NHS, 1988; contrib. papers to medical journals. *Recreation:* piano. *Address:* (home) 4 Meon Close, Upper Quinton, Stratford-upon-Avon CV37 8SX. *T:* Stratford-upon-Avon (01789) 720149. *Club:* Royal Over-Seas League.

MACGREGOR, Sir Edwin (Robert), 7th Bt *cr* 1828; Deputy Minister, Ministry of Lands and Parks, Province of British Columbia, Victoria, BC, 1991–92, retired; *b* 4 Dec. 1931; *e s* of Sir Robert McConnell Macgregor, 6th Bt, and of Annie Mary Lane; *S* father, 1963; *m* 1st, 1952, (Margaret Alice) Jean Peake (marr. diss. 1981); one *s* two *d* (and one *s* decd); 2nd, 1982, Helen Linda Herriott; two step *d*. *Educ:* University of British Columbia. BASc 1955, MASc 1957, Metallurgical Engineering. Plant Manager, 1965–72, Marketing Manager, Metals, 1972–74, Union Carbide Canada Ltd. Dep. Minister, Min. of Crown Lands, BC, 1989–91. Member: Assoc. of Professional Engrs, Province of British Columbia; Canadian Inst. of Mining and Metallurgy. *Publications:* contribs to Trans Amer. Inst. of Mining, Metallurgical and Petroleum Engrg, Jl Amer. Chem. Soc. *Recreations:* reading; participation in several outdoor sports such as golf, swimming, fishing, etc.; music. *Heir: s* Ian Grant Macgregor, *b* 22 Feb. 1959. *Address:* 6136 Kirby Road, RR3, Sooke, BC V0S 1N0, Canada.

MacGREGOR, Geddes; *see* MacGregor, J. G.

McGREGOR, Prof. Gordon Peter, DPhil; Professor of Education, University of Leeds, 1991–95, now Emeritus; *b* Aldershot, Hants, 13 June 1932; 2nd *s* of William A. K. McGregor and Mary A. McGregor (*née* O'Brien); *m* 1957, Jean Olga Lewis; three *d*. *Educ:* Bishop Road Jun. Sch., Bristol; St Brendan's Coll., Bristol (Open Scholar); Univ. of Bristol (BA Hons); Univ. of East Africa (MEd); Univ. of Sussex (DPhil); Dip. Coll. of Teachers of the Blind. Educn Officer, RAF, 1953–56; Asst Master, Worcester Coll. for the Blind, 1956–59; Asst Master, King's Coll., Budo, Uganda, 1959–62; Lecturer in English Language, Makerere Univ. Coll., Uganda 1963–66; Univ. of Zambia: Sen Lecturer in Educn, 1966–68; Reader and Head of Dept of Education, 1968–70; Prof. of Educn, 1970; Principal, Bishop Otter Coll., Chichester, 1970–80; Principal, Coll., then UC, of Ripon and York St John, Leeds Univ., 1980–95. Danforth Fellow, Colorado Coll., USA, 1972; Commonwealth Educn Consultant, Sri Lanka, 1973; British Council ELT Consultant, Iraq, 1975. Chairman: York Diocesan Educn Council, 1980–; Council of Church and Associated Colls, 1990–; Member: York DHA, 1982–86; UK Commn for UNESCO, 1984–86; Voluntary Sector Consultative Council, 1985–89; Bd of Nat. Adv. Body for Higher Educn, 1987–88. Vice-Chm. Govs, York Theatre Royal, 1992–95. Hon. DLitt: Ripon Coll., Wisconsin, 1986; York Coll., Penn, 1993. *Publications:* King's College, Budo, The First Sixty Years, 1967; Educating the Handicapped, 1967; English for Education?, 1968; Teaching English as a Second Language (with J. A. Bright), 1970; English in Africa, (UNESCO), 1971; Bishop Otter College and Policy for Teacher Education 1839–1980, 1981; A Church College for the 21st Century?: the first 150 years of Ripon and York St John, 1991; Towards True Education, 1994; various articles. *Recreations:* music, literature, theatre, travel, swimming, walking, armchair Rugby and cricket, watching my wife bird-watching. *Address:* Hollyhocks, High Street, Selsey, W Sussex. *T:* Selsey (01243) 602680.

MACGREGOR, Rt. Rev. Gregor; *see* Moray, Ross and Caithness, Bishop of.

MacGREGOR OF MacGREGOR, Brig. Sir Gregor, 6th Bt, *cr* 1795; ADC 1979; 23rd Chief of Clan Gregor; *b* 22 Dec. 1925; *o s* of Capt. Sir Malcolm MacGregor of MacGregor, 5th Bt, CB, CMG, and Hon. Gylla Lady MacGregor of MacGregor, OBE (*d* 1980); *S* father 1958; *m* 1958, Fanny, *o d* of C. H. A. Butler, Shortgrove, Newport, Essex; two *s*. *Educ:* Eton. Commissioned Scots Guards, 1944; served War of 1939–45. Served in Palestine, 1947–48; Malaya, 1950–51; Borneo, 1965. Staff Coll. Course, 1960; Brigade Major, 16th Parachute Bde Gp, 1961–63; Joint Services Staff Coll., 1965; commanding 1st Bn Scots Guards, 1966–69; GSO1 (BLO) Fort Benning, USA, 1969–71; Col Recruiting, HQ Scotland, 1971; Lt-Col commanding Scots Guards, 1971–74; Defence and Mil. Attaché, British Embassy, Athens, 1975–78; Comdr, Lowlands, 1978–80. Grand Master Mason of Scotland, 1988–93. Mem. of the Royal Company of Archers (Queen's Body Guard for Scotland), 1949–. *Heir: s* Major Malcolm Gregor Charles MacGregor of MacGregor, Scots Guards [*b* 23 March 1959; *m* 1988, Cecilia, *er d* of Sir Ilay Campbell of Succoth, Bt, *qv*]. *Address:* Bannatyne, Newtyle, Blairgowrie, Perthshire PH12 8TR. *T:* Newtyle (018285) 314; R-5 Buttonwood Bay, 96000 Overseas Highway, Key Largo, FL 33037–2124, USA. *T:* (305) 8525740. *Clubs:* Pratt's; New (Edinburgh).

McGREGOR, Harvey, QC 1978; DCL; Fellow, 1972–Sept. 1996 (Hon. Fellow, 1996), and Warden, 1985–Sept 1996, New College, Oxford; *b* 25 Feb. 1926; *s* of late William Guthrie Robertson McGregor and Agnes (*née* Reid). *Educ:* Inverurie Acad.; Scarborough Boys' High Sch.; Queen's Coll., Oxford (Hastings Scholar; BA 1951, BCL 1952, MA 1955, DCL 1983). Dr of Juridical Science, Harvard, 1962. Called to the Bar, Inner Temple, 1955, Bencher, 1985. Flying Officer, RAF, 1946–48. Bigelow Teaching Fellow, Univ. of Chicago, 1950–51; Vis. Prof., New York Univ. and Rutgers Univ., 1963–69 (various times). Consultant to Law Commn 1966–73. Pres., Harvard Law Sch. Assoc. of UK, 1981–; Mem., Acad. of European Private Lawyers, 1994–. Ind. Chm., London and Provincial Theatre Councils, 1992– (Dep. Ind. Chm., 1971–92); Pres., Oxford Stage Co., 1992–; Trustee, Oxford Union Soc., 1977–. Fellow, Winchester Coll., 1985–. Mem. Editorial Cttee, 1967–86, Mem., Editorial Bd, 1986–, Modern Law Review. *Publications:* McGregor on Damages, 12th edn 1961– 15th edn 1988; Contract Code, 1993; (contrib.) International Encyclopedia of Comparative Law, 1972; articles in legal jls. *Recreations:* music, theatre, travel. *Address:* (until Sept. 1996) Warden's Lodgings, New College, Oxford OX1 3BN. *T:* Oxford (01865) 279501; (chambers) 4 Paper Buildings, Temple, EC4Y 7EX. *T:* 0171–353 3366; (residence) Gray's Inn Chambers, Gray's Inn, WC1R 5JA. *T:* 0171–242 4942. *Club:* Garrick.

McGREGOR, Sir Ian (Alexander), Kt 1982; CBE 1968 (OBE 1959); FRS 1981; FRSE; Visiting Professor (formerly Professorial Fellow), Department of Tropical Medicine, Liverpool School of Tropical Medicine, since 1981; *b* 26 Aug. 1922; *s* of John McGregor and Isabella (*née* Taylor), Cambuslang, Lanarks; *m* 1954, Nancy Joan, *d* of Frederick Small, Mapledurham, Oxon; one *s* one *d*. *Educ:* Rutherglen Academy; St Mungo Coll., Glasgow. LRCPE, LRCSE, LRFPS(G) 1945; DTM&H 1949; MRCP 1962; FRCP 1967; FFCM 1972; Hon. FRCPGlas 1984. Mil. Service, 1946–48 (despatches). Mem. Scientific Staff, Human Nutrition Research Unit, MRC, 1949–53; Dir, MRC Laboratories, The Gambia, 1954–74, 1978–80; Head of Laboratory of Trop. Community Studies, Nat. Inst. for Med. Research, Mill Hill, 1974–77; Mem., External Staff, MRC, 1981–84. Chm., WHO Expert Cttee on Malaria, 1985–89; Member: WHO Adv. Panel on Malaria, 1961–; Malaria Cttee, MRC, 1962–71; Cttee on Nutrition Surveys, Internat. Union of Nutrition Sciences, 1971–75; Tropical Medicine Res. Bd, MRC, 1974–77, 1981–83; Steering Cttee on Immunology of Malaria, WHO, 1978–89; Steering Cttee on Applied Field Res. in Malaria, WHO, 1984–90; Council, Royal Soc., 1985–87. Lectures: Heath Clark, London Sch. of Hygiene and Tropical Medicine, 1983–84; Fred Soper, Amer. Soc. of Trop. Medicine and Hygiene, 1983; Lord Cohen History of Medicine, Liverpool Univ., 1989; Albert Norman Meml, Inst. of Med. Lab. Scis, 1992; Manson Orator, RSTM&H, 1994. Pres., Royal Soc. of Trop. Medicine and Hygiene, 1983–85 (Vice-Pres., 1981–83; Hon. Fellow, 1995). FRSE 1987. Hon. Fellow Liverpool Sch. of Trop. Medicine, 1980; Hon. Member: Amer. Soc. of Trop. Medicine and Hygiene, 1983; British Soc. for Parasitology, 1988. Hon. LLD Univ. of Aberdeen, 1983; Hon. DSc Glasgow, 1984. Chalmers Medal, Royal Soc. Trop. Med. and Hygiene, 1963; Stewart Prize, BMA, 1970; Darling Foundn Medal, WHO, 1974; Laveran Medal, Société de Pathologie Exotique de Paris, 1983; Glaxo Prize for Medical Writing, 1989. *Publications:* (ed with W. Wernsdorfer) Malaria: the principles and practice of malariology, 1988; scientific papers on infections, nutrition, immunity, child health and community medicine in tropical environments. *Recreations:* ornithology, golf, fishing. *Address:* The Glebe House, Greenlooms, Hargrave, Chester CH3 7RX.

McGREGOR, Ian Alexander, FRCS, FRCSGlas; Director, West of Scotland Regional Plastic and Oral Surgery Unit, 1980–86; *b* 6 June 1921; *s* of late Walker McGregor and Mary Duncan (*née* Thompson); *m* 1st, 1950, Christeen Isabel Mackay (decd); three *s*; 2nd, 1970, Frances Mary Vint. *Educ:* North Kelvinside Secondary Sch.; Glasgow Univ. (MB, ChB 1944; ChM 1972). FRCS 1950, FRFPSG 1951, FRCSGlas 1962; Hon. FRACS 1977; Hon. FRCSI 1984; Hon. FRCSE 1985; Hon. FACS 1986. Served RAMC, 1945–48. Consultant Surgeon, Glasgow Royal Infirmary, 1957–59; Consultant Plastic Surgeon, Greater Glasgow Health Bd, 1959–80. Visitor, 1982–84, Pres., 1984–86, RCPSGlas. Hon. DSc Glasgow, 1986. *Publications:* Fundamental Techniques of Plastic Surgery, 1960, 9th edn (with A. D. McGregor) 1995; (with W. H. Reid) Plastic Surgery for Nurses, 1966; (with Frances M. McGregor) Cancer of the Face and Mouth, 1986; scientific papers to surgical jls on reconstructive aspects of plastic surgery. *Recreations:* music, literature, golf. *Address:* 7 Ledcameroch Road, Bearsden, Glasgow G61 4AB. *T:* 0141–942 3419.

MacGREGOR, Sir Ian (Kinloch), Kt 1986; Chairman: Holmes Protection Inc.; Goldcrest Films; Partner, McFarland, Dewey & Co., New York; *b* 21 Sept. 1912; *m* Sibyl Spencer; one *s* one *d*. *Educ:* George Watson's Coll., Edinburgh; Hillhead High Sch., Glasgow; Univ. of Glasgow. BSc (1st cl. Hons); Royal Coll. of Science and Technol. (now Univ. of Strathclyde) (Dip. with distinction). Pres. and Chief Exec., 1966, Chm., 1969–77, Amax Inc. (Hon. Chm., 1977–82); Deputy Chairman, BL Ltd, 1977–80; Chm. and Chief Exec., BSC, 1980–83; Chm., NCB, 1983–86. Non-exec. Dir, Lazard Brothers & Co., 1986–90. President of the International Chamber of Commerce, Paris, 1978. Hon. degrees from Univs. of Glasgow (LLD), Strathclyde (LLD), Denver (LLD), Montana State (DEng), Rochester (LLD), Colorado Sch. of Mines (DEng), Wyoming (LLD), and Tri-State Coll., Indiana (DSc). Jackling Medal, Amer. Inst. of Mining and Metallurgical Engrs; John Fritz Gold Medal, Amer. Inst. of Mining, Metallurgical and Petroleum Engrs, 1981; Bessemer Gold Medal, Metals Soc., London, 1983. Chevalier, Légion d'Honneur, 1972. *Publication:* The Enemies Within, 1986. *Address:* 79 North Main Street, Cohasset, Mass 02025, USA; 450 South Ocean Boulevard, Manalapan, FL 33462, USA.

McGREGOR, James Stalker; Chairman, Honeywell Ltd, 1981–89; *b* 30 Oct. 1927; *s* of John McGregor and Jean McCabe; *m* 1953, Iris Millar Clark; one *s*. *Educ:* Dumfries Acad.;

Royal Tech. Coll., Glasgow (ARTC); Glasgow Univ. BSc (Hons); CEng, MIMechE; CBIM. Production Engr, Rolls Royce Ltd, 1952–56; Sales Engr, Sandvik Swedish Steels, 1956–57; Honeywell Control Systems: Assembly Manager, later Production Control Manager and Admin Manager, 1957–65; Divl Dir, Temperature Controls Gp, 1965–71; Man. Dir, 1971–86. Hon. LLD Strathclyde, 1984. *Recreation:* golf. *Address:* 19 Burgess Wood Road, Beaconsfield, Bucks HP9 1EQ.

MacGREGOR, Prof. (John) Geddes, DèsL (Sorbonne), DPhil, DD Oxon, BD Edinburgh et Oxon, LLB Edinburgh; FRSL 1948; Distinguished Professor of Philosophy, University of Southern California, 1966–75, now Emeritus; Dean of Graduate School of Religion, 1960–66; first holder of Rufus Jones Chair of Philosophy and Religion, Bryn Mawr, USA, 1949–60; Canon Theologian of St Paul's Cathedral, Los Angeles, 1968–74; *b* 13 Nov. 1909; *o s* of late Thomas and Blanche Geddes MacGregor, Angus; *m* 1941, Elizabeth (*d* 1994), *e d* of late Archibald McAllister, Edinburgh; one *s* one *d*. *Educ:* Universities of Edinburgh, Paris, Heidelberg; The Queen's Coll., Oxford. Senior Assistant to Dean of Chapel Royal in Scotland, at St Giles' Cathedral, Edinburgh, 1939–41; served in Civil Defence, War of 1939–45; Minister, Trinity Church, Glasgow, S1, 1941–49; Assistant to Prof. of Logic and Metaphysics, Edinburgh Univ., 1947–49. Examiner: Swarthmore Coll., USA, 1950, 1953, 1955–57; Hebrew Union Coll., USA, 1959, 1961; Visiting Professor: Univ. of British Columbia, 1963, 1966, 1973; Hebrew Union Coll., 1964–65; Univ. of Santa Clara, 1968; World Campus Afloat (Orient, 1974; Mediterranean, 1975); McGill Univ., Montreal, 1976; Inst. for Shipboard Educn (round-the-world-voyage), 1977; Univ. of Iowa, 1979; Univ. of Saskatchewan, 1979; Visiting Fellow: Dept of Religious Studies, Yale Univ., 1967–68; Coll. of Preachers, Washington Nat. Cathedral, 1991; Occasional Lectr at many US and Canadian Univs (Birks, Montreal, 1976; Warren, Dubuque, 1979; Arnett, Kansas, 1982; Fairchild, Miss, 1982); Vis. Lectr, Rikkyo Univ., Tokyo, 1981; Guest Lectr, Univ. Complutense, Madrid, 1992. Program Speaker, Parliament of the World's Religions, 1993. Dir, Amer. Friends of the Univ. of Edinburgh, 1983–86; Hon. Fellow, Emporia State Univ., Kansas, 1982. Diplomate, Internat. Soc. for Philosophical Enquiry, 1986. Special Preacher: St Paul's Cathedral, London, 1969; Westminster Abbey, 1970. Regent, American-Scottish Foundation, Inc., NY; Hon. Chaplain and Historian, St Andrew's Soc. of LA, 1981– (Pres., 1987–88); Hon. Canon of San Diego, California, 1987. Hon. LHD Hebrew Union, 1978. Hon. Phi Kappa Phi, 1972 (Distinguished Award, 1982). Hon. Assoc., Order of Agape and Reconciliation, 1988. California Literature Award (Gold Medal, non-fiction), 1964; Medallist, Nat. Soc. of the Sons of the American Revolution, 1989; Distinguished Emeritus Award, Univ. of Southern California, 1993. *Publications:* Aesthetic Experience in Religion, 1947; Christian Doubt, 1951; Les Frontières de la Morale et de la Religion, 1952; From a Christian Ghetto, 1954; The Vatican Revolution, 1957; The Tichborne Impostor, 1957; The Thundering Scot, 1957; Corpus Christi, 1959; Introduction to Religious Philosophy, 1959; The Bible in the Making, 1959; The Coming Reformation, 1960; The Hemlock and the Cross, 1963; God Beyond Doubt, 1966; A Literary History of the Bible, 1968; The Sense of Absence, 1968; So Help Me God, 1970; Philosophical Issues in Religious Thought, 1973; The Rhythm of God, 1974; He Who Lets Us Be, 1975, rev. edn 1987; Reincarnation in Christianity, 1978 (trans. German as vol. I, Reinkarnation und Karma im Christentum, 1985); Gnosis, 1979; Scotland Forever Home, 1980, rev. edn 1984; The Nicene Creed, 1981; Reincarnation as a Christian Hope, 1982; The Gospels as a Mandala of Wisdom, 1982; The Christening of Karma, 1984 (trans. German as vol. II, Reinkarnation und Karma im Christentum, 1986); Apostles Extraordinary, 1986; (ed) Immortality and Human Destiny, 1986; Angels: ministers of grace, 1988; Dictionary of Religion and Philosophy, 1989; Scotland: an intimate portrait, 1990; Images of Afterlife: beliefs from antiquity to modern times, 1992 (trans. French as Enquête sur l'existence de la réincarnation, 1995). *Recreations:* manual labour; now oftener reading, music. *Address:* 876 Victoria Avenue, Los Angeles, CA 90005–3751, USA. *T:* (213)9384826. *Clubs:* Athenæum, English-Speaking Union, Commonwealth Trust; Union Society (Oxford); Automobile (Los Angeles).

MACGREGOR, John Malcolm, CVO 1992; HM Diplomatic Service; Director General for Trade Promotion in Germany and Consul-General, Düsseldorf, since 1995; *b* 3 Oct. 1946; *s* of late Dr D. F. Macgregor and of K. A. Macgregor (*née* Adams); *m* 1982, Judith Anne Brown; three *s* one *d*. *Educ:* Kibworth Beauchamp Grammar Sch., Leics; Balliol Coll., Oxford (BA 1967). ARCO 1965. Taught at Cranleigh Sch., Surrey, 1969–73; joined HM Diplomatic Service, 1973; 1st Sec. (political), New Delhi, 1975; FCO, 1979; Pvte Sec. to Minister of State, FCO, 1981; Assistant, Soviet Dept, FCO, 1983; Dep. Head of Mission, Prague, 1986; Head of Chancery, Paris, 1990–93; Head of EU Dept (Ext.), 1993–95. *Recreations:* music, languages, bricolage, travel. *Address:* c/o Foreign and Commonwealth Office, King Charles Street, SW1A 2AH. *T:* 0171–270 3000.

MacGREGOR, Rt. Hon. John (Roddick Russell), OBE 1971; PC 1985; MP (C) South Norfolk, since Feb. 1974; *b* 14 Feb. 1937; *s* of late Dr. N. S. R. MacGregor; *m* 1962, Jean Mary Elizabeth Dungey; one *s* two *d*. *Educ:* Merchiston Castle Sch., Edinburgh; St Andrews Univ. (MA, 1st cl. Hons); King's Coll., London (LLB; FKC 1988). Univ. Administrator, 1961–62; Editorial Staff, New Society, 1962–63; Special Asst to Prime Minister, Sir Alec Douglas-Home, 1963–64; Conservative Research Dept, 1964–65; Head of Private Office of Rt Hon. Edward Heath, Leader of Opposition, 1965–68; an Opposition Whip, 1977–79; a Lord Comr of HM Treasury, 1979–81; Parly Under-Sec. of State, DoI, 1981–83; Minister of State, MAFF, 1983–85; Chief Sec. to HM Treasury, 1985–87; Minister of Agriculture, Fisheries and Food, 1987–89; Sec. of State for Educn and Sci., 1989–90; Lord Pres. of the Council and Leader of H of C, 1990–92; Sec. of State for Transport, 1992–94. Hill Samuel & Co. Ltd, 1968–79 (Dir, 1973–79), Dep. Chm., 1994–; Director: Associated British Foods, 1994–; Slough Estates, 1995–. Chairman: Fedn of University Cons. and Unionist Assocs, 1959; Bow Group, 1963–64; 1st Pres., Conservative and Christian Democratic Youth Community, 1963–65; Vice-Pres., ACC, 1995–. Formerly Treasurer, Federal Trust for Educn and Research; formerly Trustee, European Educnl Research Trust. *Publications:* contrib. The Conservative Opportunity; also pamphlets. *Recreations:* music, reading, travelling, gardening, conjuring (Mem., Magic Circle, 1989). *Address:* House of Commons, SW1A 0AA.

MACGREGOR, His Honour John Roy; a Circuit Judge, 1974–87; Honorary Recorder of Margate, 1972–79; *b* Brooklyn, NY, 9 Sept. 1913; 4th *s* of Charles George McGregor, of Jamaica and New York. *Educ:* Bedford School. Called to the Bar, Gray's Inn, 1939; Inner Temple (*ad eundem*), 1968; Holker Sen. Scholar, Gray's Inn, 1947. Served in Royal Artillery, 1939–46; RA (TA) and Special Air Service (TA), 1950–61. Dep. Chm., Cambridgeshire and Isle of Ely QS, 1967–71; a Recorder, 1972–74. Legal Assessor to Gen. Optical Council, 1972–74. *Address:* Nether Gaulrig, Yardley Hastings, Northampton NN7 1HD. *T:* Yardley Hastings (01604) 696861. *Club:* Special Forces.

MacGREGOR, Neil; *see* MacGregor, R. N.

McGREGOR, Peter, CEng, FIEE; writer and consultant; Director General, Export Group for the Constructional Industries, 1984–91 (Consultant, 1991–94); *b* 20 May 1926; *s* of Peter McGregor and Margaret Thomson McGregor (*née* McAuslan); *m* 1954, Marion, *d* of H. T. Downer; one *s* one *d*. *Educ:* Cardiff High Sch.; Univ. of Birmingham; London Sch. of Economics (BSc (Econs)); CompIProdE; MCIM; FIMgt. National Service, RE, 1946–48. Various appointments, Ferranti Ltd, 1950–74, incl. Works Manager, Distribution Transformer Dept, Sales Manager, Transformer Div., Gen. Manager, Power Div.; Dir, Industrie Elettriche di Legnano (Italy), 1970–74; Associate Dir, Corporate Renewal Associates Ltd, 1988–93. Dir, Oxford Univ. Business Summer Sch., 1972; first Sec. Gen., Anglo-German Foundn for Study of Industrial Soc., 1974–81; Industrial Dir (Dep. Sec.), NEDO, 1981–84. Chm., Textile Machinery EDC, 1982–86; Dir, Templeton Technol. Seminar, 1985. Member: N American Adv. Gp, BOTB, 1968–74; Europ. Trade Cttee, BOTB, 1981–83; Adv. Bd, Public Policy Centre, 1984–88; Cttee on Exchange Rate, Public Policy Centre, 1984–87. Industrial Advr to Liberal Party, 1960–73; an Industrial Advr to Social and Liberal Democrats, 1988–90; Chm., Hazel Grove Liberal Assoc., 1971–74; contested (L) Ilford South, 1964. Mem., Königswinter Conf. steering cttee, 1976–90. Hon. Treasurer, Anglo-German Assoc., 1983–91. Elder and Hon. Treas., St Columba's Ch, Oxford. FRSA. *Publications:* various articles and pamphlets especially on industrial relations, company structure, market economy. *Recreations:* sailing, walking, reading, listening to music, writing, conversation, gardening, drawing attention to the Emperor's lack of clothes. *Clubs:* Athenæum, Caledonian.

MacGREGOR, (Robert) Neil; Director, National Gallery, since 1987; *b* 16 June 1946; *s* of Alexander Rankin MacGregor and Anna Fulton Scobie MacGregor (*née* Neil). *Educ:* Glasgow Acad.; New Coll., Oxford; Ecole Normale Supérieure, Paris; Univ. of Edinburgh; Courtauld Inst. of Art. Mem., Faculty of Advocates, Edinburgh, 1972. Lectr in History of Art and Architecture, Univ. of Reading, 1976; Editor, The Burlington Magazine, 1981–86. Trustee, Pilgrim Trust, 1990–. Kuratorium, Zentralinstitut für Kunstgeschichte, Munich, 1992–. DUniv York, 1992; Dr *hc* Edinburgh, 1994. *Publications:* A Victim of Anonymity: the master of the St Bartholomew Altarpiece, 1994; contribs to Apollo, The Burlington Magazine, etc. *Address:* National Gallery, Trafalgar Square, WC2.

See also A. R. MacGregor.

MacGREGOR, Susan Katriona, (Sue), OBE 1992; Presenter, Today, BBC Radio Four, since 1984; *b* 30 Aug. 1941; *d* of Dr James MacGregor and late Margaret MacGregor (*née* MacGregor). *Educ:* Herschel School, Cape, South Africa. Announcer/producer, South African Broadcasting Corp., 1962–67; BBC Radio reporter, World at One, World This Weekend, PM, 1967–72; Presenter: Woman's Hour, BBC Radio 4, 1972–87; Tuesday Call, 1973–86; Conversation Piece, 1978–; Around Westminster, BBC TV, 1990–92. Dir, Hemming Publishing (formerly Municipal Journal) Ltd, 1980–. Member: RCP Cttee on Ethical Issues in Medicine, 1985–; Marshall Aid Commemoration Commn, 1989–. FRSA; Hon. MRCP 1995. *Recreations:* theatre, cinema, ski-ing. *Address:* c/o BBC, Portland Place, W1A 1AA. *T:* 0171–765 5566.

McGRIGOR, Captain Sir Charles Edward, 5th Bt, *cr* 1831; DL; Rifle Brigade, retired; Member Royal Company of Archers (HM Body Guard for Scotland); *b* 5 Oct. 1922; *s* of Lieut-Colonel Sir Charles McGrigor, 4th Bt, OBE, and Lady McGrigor, *d* of Edward Lygon Somers Cocks, Bake, St Germans, Cornwall; *S* father, 1946; *m* 1948, Mary Bettine, *e d* of Sir Archibald Charles Edmonstone, 6th Bt; two *s* two *d*. *Educ:* Eton. War of 1939–45 (despatches); joined Army, 1941, from Eton; served with Rifle Bde, N. Africa, Italy, Austria. ADC to Duke of Gloucester, 1945–47, in Australia and England. Exon, Queen's Bodyguard, Yeoman of the Guard, 1970–85. Mem. Cttee of Management, and a Vice-Pres., RNLI. DL Argyll and Bute, 1987. *Recreations:* fishing, gardening. *Heir:* *s* James Angus Rhoderick Neil McGrigor [*b* 19 Oct. 1949; *m* 1987, Caroline, *d* of late Jacques Roboh, Paris; two *d*]. *Address:* Upper Sonachan, Dalmally, Argyll PA33 1BJ.

McGROUTHER, Prof. (Duncan) Angus, MD; FRCS, FRCSGlas, FRCSEd; Professor of Plastic and Reconstructive Surgery, University College London, since 1989 (first established British chair in this subject); *b* 3 March 1946; *s* of Dr John Ingram McGrouther and Margot Christina Cooke Gray; *m* 1967, Sandra Elizabeth Jackson; one *s* one *d*. *Educ:* Glasgow High Sch.; Univ. of Glasgow (MB ChB 1969; MD Hons 1988); Univ. of Strathclyde (MSc Bioengineering 1975). Glasgow Royal Infirmary, 1969–74; Cruden Med. Res. Fellow, Bioengrg Unit, Univ. of Strathclyde, 1972–73; Registrar and Sen. Registrar in Plastic Surgery, Canniesburn Hosp., Glasgow, 1975–78; Assistentarzt, Klinikum Rechts der Isar, Munich, 1978; Consultant Plastic Surgeon: Shotley Bridge Gen. Hosp. and Sunderland Dist Gen. Hosp., 1979–80; Canniesburn Hosp., 1981–89. Christine Kleinert Vis. Prof., Univ. of Louisville, 1988. Kay-Kilner Prize, British Assoc. of Plastic Surgeons, 1979; Pulvertaft Prize, British Soc. for Surgery of the Hand, 1981. *Publications:* papers on anatomy, biomechanics, plastic surgery, hand surgery, microsurgery, and wound healing. *Recreations:* mountains, sea, books, fundraising for Phoenix Appeal. *Address:* Department of Plastic and Reconstructive Surgery, University College London, Rayne Institute, University Street, WC1E 6JJ. *T:* 0171–209 6130.

McGUCKIAN, John Brendan; Chairman: Industrial Development Board for Northern Ireland, since 1991; Ulster Television, since 1990; *b* 13 Nov. 1939; *s* of late Brian McGuckian and of Pauline (*née* McKenna); *m* 1970, Carmel, *d* of Daniel McGowan; two *s* two *d*. *Educ:* St McNissis Coll., Garrontower; Queen's Univ. of Belfast (BSc). Chm., Cloughmills Mfg Co., 1967–; Director: Munster & Leinster Bank, 1972–; Allied Irish Bank plc, 1976–; Harbour Group Ltd, 1978–; Aer Lingus plc, 1979–84; Unidare plc, 1987–; Irish Ferries plc, 1988–; Derry Development Commn, 1968–71; Dep. Chm., Laganside Corp., 1988–; and other directorships. Chm., Internat. Fund for Ireland, 1990–93. Sen. Pro-Chancellor and Chm. of Senate, QUB. *Address:* Ardverna, Cloughmills, Ballymena, Co. Antrim, Northern Ireland. *T:* Cloughmills (0126563) 692; Lisgoole Abbey, Culkey, Enniskillen.

McGUFFIN, Prof. Peter, PhD; FRCP; FRCPsych; Professor of Psychological Medicine, University of Wales College of Medicine, since 1987; *b* 4 Feb. 1949; *s* of Captain W. B. McGuffin, RD, RNR and M. M. McGuffin; *m* 1972, Dr Anne E. Farmer; one *s* two *d*. *Educ:* Univ. of Leeds (MB ChB); Univ. of London (PhD). MRCP 1976, FRCP 1988; MRCPsych 1978, FRCPsych 1990. St James Univ. Hosp., Leeds, 1972–77; Registrar, Sen. Registrar, Maudsley Hosp., 1977–79; MRC Fellow, MRC Sen. Clinical Fellow, Inst. of Psychiatry, 1979–86; Hon. Consultant, Maudsley and King's Coll. Hosps, 1983–86. Vis. Fellow, Washington Univ., St Louis, 1981–82. *Publications:* Scientific Principles of Psychopathology, 1984; A Psychiatric Catechism, 1987; Schizophrenia, the Major Issues, 1988; The New Genetics of Mental Illness, 1991; Seminars in Psychiatric Genetics, 1994; articles, research papers on psychiatry and genetics. *Recreations:* classical guitar, music, tennis, running, horse riding. *Address:* 68 Heol-y-Delyn, Lisvane, Cardiff CF4 5SR.

MacGUIGAN, Hon. Mark Rudolph, PC (Can.) 1980; PhD, JSD; **Hon. Mr Justice MacGuigan;** Judge, Federal Court of Appeal, Canada, since 1984; *b* 17 Feb. 1931; *s* of Hon. Mark R. MacGuigan and Agnes V. Trainor; two *s* one *d*; *m* 1987, Judge Patricia Dougherty, Oklahoma Ct of Appeals. *Educ:* Queen Square Sch.; Prince of Wales (Jun.) Coll.; St Dunstan's Univ., Charlottetown (BA *summa cum laude*); Univ. of Toronto (MA, PhD); Osgoode Hall Law Sch. (LLB); Columbia Univ. (LLM, JSD). Admitted to Law Soc. of Upper Canada, 1958. Asst Prof. of Law, 1960–63, and Associate Prof. of Law, 1963–66, Univ. of Toronto; Prof. of Law, Osgoode Hall Law Sch., 1966–67; Dean, Faculty of Law, Univ. of Windsor, 1967–68. MP for Windsor–Walkerville, Ont, 1968–84; Parly Secretary: to Minister of Manpower and Immigration, 1972–74; to Minister of

Labour, 1974–75; Opposition Critic of Solicitor Gen., 1979–80; Sec. of State for External Affairs, 1980–82; Minister of Justice, 1982–84. Chairman: House of Commons Special Cttee on Statutory Instruments, 1968–69; Standing Cttee on Justice and Legal Affairs, 1975–79; Sub-Cttee on Penitentiary System in Canada, 1976–77; Co-Chairman, Special Jt Cttee on Constitution of Canada, 1970–72 and 1978. Hon. LLD: Univ. of PEI, 1971; St Thomas Univ., 1981; Law Soc. of Upper Canada, 1983; Univ. of Windsor, Ont, 1983. *Publications:* Cases and Materials on Creditors' Rights, 2nd edn 1967; Jurisprudence: readings and cases, 2nd edn 1966; Abortion, Conscience and Democracy, 1994. *Recreations:* running, tennis, skiing, swimming. *Address:* 23 Linden Terrace, Ottawa, Ont K1S 1Z1, Canada. *Club:* Cercle Universitaire (Ottawa).

McGUIGAN BURNS, Simon Hugh; *see* Burns.

McGUINNESS, Maj.-Gen. Brendan Peter, CB 1986; consultant in education and training; Adviser on Engineering to Schools and Colleges, University of Birmingham, since 1994; Director of Education and Training Liaison, Engineering Employers' Federation, West Midlands, 1988–94 (Head of Educational Liaison, 1987–88); *b* 26 June 1931; *s* of Bernard and May McGuinness; *m* 1968, Ethne Patricia (*née* Kelly); one *s* one *d*. *Educ:* Mount St Mary's College. psc, rcds. Commissioned Royal Artillery, 1950; regimental duty, 1950–60; Staff, 1960–62; sc 1963; Adjutant, 1964–65; Staff, 1965–68 (despatches,Borneo, 1966); Battery Comdr, 1968–70; Staff Coll. Directing Staff, 1970–72; CO 45 Medium Regt, 1972–75; CRA 1st Armd Div., 1975–77; RCDS 1978; MoD Staff, 1979–81; Dep. Comdr, NE District, 1981–83; GOC W Dist, 1983–86. Hon. Col, Birmingham Univ. OTC, 1987–; Hon. Regtl Col, 45 Field Regt, 1985–91. Mem. Cttee, Hereford and Worcester Br., STA, 1991–. Project Dir, 1987–88, Governor, 1988–, The City Technol. Coll., Kingshurst; Mem. Court, Birmingham Univ., 1992–. Dir, Acafess Community Trust, 1992–94 (Chm., 1992). *Recreations:* tennis, hill walking, beagling. *Address:* The Old Rectory, 14 Whittington Road, Worcester WR5 2JU. *T:* Worcester (01905) 360102. *Club:* Army and Navy.

McGUINNESS, Rt. Rev. James Joseph; *see* Nottingham, Bishop of, (RC).

McGUIRE, Gerald, OBE 1974; President, Council for National Parks, 1990–92 (Vice-President, 1983–90; Vice-Chairman, 1981–83); *b* 12 July 1918; *s* of John Charles McGuire and Adelaide Maud McGuire (*née* Davies); *m* 1942, Eveline Mary Jenkins; one *s* one *d*. *Educ:* Trinity County Sch., Wood Green. Youth Hostels Association: Reg. Sec., N Yorks, 1944–64; National Countryside and Educn Officer, 1964–74; Dep. Nat. Sec., 1974–82; Pres., N England Region, 1989–95. President: Ramblers Assoc., 1975–78 (Vice Pres., 1978–; Pres., Lake Dist Area, 1983–86; Pres., E Yorks and Derwent Area, 1987–90); Assoc. of National Park and Countryside Voluntary Wardens, 1978–80; Chm., Countryside Link Gp, 1982–86. Member: N York Moors Nat. Park Cttee, 1953–72, 1985–91; Exec. Cttee, CPRE, 1966–76, 1981–84; Gosling Cttee on Footpaths, 1967–68; Countryside Commn, 1976–79; Commn on Energy and the Environment, 1978–81; Recreation and Conservation Cttee, Yorks Water Authority, 1984–89; Yorks Regional Cttee, Nat. Trust, 1985–93; Jt Adv. Cttee, Howardian Hills Area of Outstanding Natural Beauty, 1992–. Vice Pres., Open Spaces Soc., 1982– (Vice Chm. 1971–76); Vice Chairman: Standing Cttee on Nat. Parks, 1970–76; Council for Environmental Conservation, 1981–82; Trustee, Gatliff Trust, 1983–94. Hon. Mem., Cyclists Touring Club, 1978–. Cert. of Merit, Internat. Youth Hostel Fedn, 1983; Richard Schirrmann (Founder's) Medal, German Youth Hostels Assoc., 1983; Nat. Blood Transfusion Service Award for 100 donations, 1983. *Recreations:* reading, music, walking in the countryside. *Address:* 24 Castle Howard Drive, Malton, North Yorks YO17 0BA. *T:* Malton (01653) 692521.

McGUIRE, Michael Thomas Francis; *b* 3 May 1926; *m* 1954, Marie T. Murphy; three *s* two *d*. *Educ:* Elementary Schools. Coal miner. Whole-time NUM Branch Secretary, 1957–64. Joined Lab. Party, 1951. MP (Lab): Ince, 1964–83; Makerfield, 1983–87. PPS to Minister of Sport, 1974–77. Member: Council of Europe, 1977–87; WEU, 1977–87. *Recreations:* most out-door sports, especially Rugby League football; traditional music, especially Irish traditional music. *Address:* 11A Daresbury Road, Eccleston, St Helens, Lancs WA10 5DR.

McGURK, Colin Thomas, OBE 1971 (MBE 1963); HM Diplomatic Service, retired; *b* 9 July 1922; *m* 1946, Ella Taylor; one *s*. *Educ:* St Mary's Coll., Middlesbrough. Served in Army, 1942–45. HM Foreign (subseq. Diplomatic) Service; served in British Embassies, Cairo, Addis Ababa, Ankara; 3rd Sec., HM Legation, Sofia, 1953–55; 2nd Sec. (Commercial), Athens, 1956–58; FO, 1958–62; HM Consul, Stanleyville, 1962; 1st Sec., Yaoundé, Brussels and Kuwait, 1962–70; Commercial Counsellor, Kuwait, 1971–72; Commercial Inspector, FCO, 1972–75; Counsellor (Economic and Commercial), New Delhi, 1975–77 and Canberra, 1977–81. Member: Burnham Art Club, 1993–; Nat. Acrylic Painters Assoc, 1993–. *Recreations:* computer programming, painting, sailing. *Address:* 113 High Street, Burnham-on-Crouch, Essex CM0 8AH. *T:* Maldon (01621) 782467. *Club:* Royal Burnham Yacht.

McGURK, Prof. Harry, PhD, FBPsS; Director, Australian Institute of Family Studies, since 1994; *b* 23 Feb. 1936; *s* of Harry McGurk and Katherine (*née* Gallagher); *m* 1961, Elizabeth Lockhart Hannah (separated 1985); one *d*. *Educ:* Univ. of Glasgow (Dip of Qualification in Social Work, 1961); Univ. of Strathclyde (BA 1968; PhD 1971). CPsychol 1987; FBPsS 1980. Probation Officer, Edinburgh, 1961–63; Relief Manager, Educn Authy of E Nigeria, 1963–64; Vis. Res. Fellow, Educnl Testing Service, Princeton, 1971–72; Lectr, New School for Social Research, NY, 1971–72; University of Surrey: Lectr in Psychology, 1972–76; Sen. Lectr, 1976–86; Prof. of Develtl Psychology, 1986–90; Dir, Thomas Coram Res. Univ., Inst. of Educn, London Univ., 1990–94. FRSocMed 1994. *Publications:* Growing and Changing: a primer of developmental psychology, 1975; Ecological Factors in Human Development, 1976; Issues in Childhood Social Development: contemporary perspectives, 1992; numerous papers and other pubns. *Recreations:* music, theatre, cycling, tennis, hill climbing. *Address:* 6/16 Huntingfield Road, Toorak, Melbourne, Vic 3142, Australia.

MACH, David Stefan; sculptor; *b* 18 March 1956; *s* of Joseph Mach and Martha (*née* Cassidy); *m* 1979, Lesley June White. *Educ:* Buckhaven High Sch.; Duncan of Jordanstone Coll. of Art (Dip. and Post Dip. in Art); Royal Coll. of Art (MA). Full-time sculptor and very occasional vis. lectr, 1982–; sculptures exhibited at galleries in England, Scotland, NY, São Paolo Biennale, Venice Biennale. City of Glasgow Lord Provost Prize, 1992. *Recreations:* gardening, tennis, travelling, driving, film, television. *Address:* 64 Canonbie Road, Forest Hill, SE23 3AG. *T:* 0181–699 1668. *Club:* Chelsea Arts.

McHALE, Keith Michael; His Honour Judge McHale; a Circuit Judge, since 1980; *b* 26 March 1928; *s* of late Cyril Michael McHale and Gladys McHale; *m* 1966, Rosemary Margaret Arthur; one *s* one *d*. Called to the Bar, Gray's Inn, 1951. *Address:* Oak Lodge, Albemarle Road, Beckenham, Kent BR3 2HS.

McHARDY, Prof. William Duff, CBE 1990; Regius Professor of Hebrew, Oxford University, and Student of Christ Church, 1960–78; *b* 26 May 1911; *o s* of late W. D. McHardy, Cullen, Banffshire; *m* 1941, Vera (*d* 1984), *y d* of late T. Kemp, York; one *d*. *Educ:* Fordyce Academy; Universities of Aberdeen, Edinburgh, and Oxford (St John's College). MA, BD (Aberdeen), MA (Edinburgh), DPhil (Oxford). Research Fellow in Syriac, Selly Oak Colleges, Birmingham, 1942; Lecturer in Aramaic and Syriac, University of Oxford, 1945; Samuel Davidson Professor of Old Testament Studies in the University of London, 1948–60. Examiner, Universities of Aberdeen, Cambridge, Durham, Edinburgh, Leeds, London, Oxford and University Colleges of the Gold Coast/Ghana and Ibadan. Hon. Curator of Mingana Collection of Oriental Manuscripts, 1947. Grinfield Lecturer on the Septuagint, Oxford, 1959–61. Dep. Dir, 1968, Jt Dir, 1971, New English Bible; Dir, Revised English Bible, 1973–90. Burgess, Royal Burgh of Cullen, 1975. Hon. DD Aberdeen, 1958. Hon. Fellow, Selly Oak Colleges, 1980. *Publications:* articles in journals. *Address:* 2 Ogilvie Park, Cullen, Banffshire AB56 2XZ. *T:* Cullen (01542) 841008.

McHENRY, Donald F.; University Research Professor of Diplomacy and International Affairs, Georgetown University, since 1981; *b* 13 Oct. 1936; *s* of Limas McHenry and Dora Lee Brooks; *m* Mary Williamson (marr. diss.); one *s* two *d*. *Educ:* Lincoln Senior High Sch., East St Louis, Ill; Illinois State Univ. (BS); Southern Illinois Univ. (MSc); Georgetown Univ. Taught at Howard Univ., Washington, 1959–62; joined Dept of State, 1963; Head of Dependent Areas Section, Office of UN Polit. Affairs, 1965–68; Asst to Sec. of State, US, 1969; Special Asst to Counsellor, Dept of State, 1969–71; Lectr, Sch. of Foreign Service, Georgetown Univ.; Guest Scholar, Brookings Inst., and Internat. Affairs Fellow, Council on Foreign Relations (on leave from State Dept), 1971–73; resigned from State Dept, 1973; Project Dir, Humanitarian Policy Studies, Carnegie Endowment for Internat. Peace, Washington, 1973–76; served in transition team of President Carter, 1976–77; Ambassador and Deputy Rep. of US to UN Security Council, 1977–79, Permanent Rep., 1979; US Ambassador to UN, 1979–81. Director: Internat. Paper Co., 1981–; First National Bank of Boston; Bank of Boston Corp., 1981–; SmithKline Beecham plc, 1982–; Coca-Cola, 1982–; American Telephone and Telegraph, 1987–; Inst. for Internat. Economics; American Ditchley Foundn. Chm., Bd of Dirs, Africare. Trustee: Mayo Foundn; Johnson Foundn; Brookings Instn; Member, Bd of Governors: UNA of USA; ME Inst. Mem., American Acad. of Arts and Scis, 1992. Hon. degrees: Dennison, Duke, Eastern Illinois, Georgetown, Harvard, Illinois State, Michigan, Princeton, Southern Illinois, Tufts, and Washington Univs; Amherst, Bates, Boston and Williams Colleges. Superior Honor Award, Dept of State, 1966. Mem. Council on Foreign Relations and Editorial Bd, Foreign Policy Magazine. *Publication:* Micronesia: Trust Betrayed, 1975. *Address:* Georgetown University, 37th and O Streets, NW, Washington, DC 20057, USA.

MACHIN, Arnold, OBE 1965; RA 1956 (ARA 1947); sculptor, FRBS 1955; Master of Sculpture, Royal Academy School, 1958–67; Tutor, Royal College of Art, 1951–58; *b* 1911; *s* of William James Machin, Stoke-on-Trent; *m* 1949, Patricia, *d* of late Lt-Col Henry Newton; one *s*. *Educ:* Stoke School of Art; Derby School of Art; Royal College of Art. Silver Medal and Travelling Scholarship for Sculpture, 1940; two works in terracotta: St John the Baptist and The Annunciation, purchased by Tate Gallery, 1943; Spring terracotta purchased by President and Council of Royal Academy under terms of Chantrey Bequest, 1947; designed: new coin effigy, 1964, 1967 (decimal coinage); definitive issue of postage stamp, 1967; Silver Wedding commemorative crown, 1972; commemorative Silver Jubilee crown, 1977. *Recreations:* music, garden design. *Address:* 4 Avenue Studios, Sydney Close, SW3 6HW; Garmelow Manor, near Eccleshall, Staffordshire ST21 6HL.

MACHIN, David; Under Treasurer, Gray's Inn, since 1989; *b* 25 April 1934; *s* of late Noel and Joan Machin; *m* 1963, Sarah Mary, *yr d* of late Col W. A. Chester-Master, DL; two *d*. *Educ:* Eton (Oppidan Scholar); Trinity Coll., Cambridge. National Service, 1952–54 (2nd Lieut Welsh Guards). Editor, William Heinemann Ltd, 1957–66; Literary Agent, Gregson & Wigan Ltd and London International, 1966–68; Partner, A. P. Watt & Son, 1968–70; Director: Jonathan Cape Ltd, 1970–78; Chatto, Bodley Head and Jonathan Cape Ltd, 1977–78, 1981–87; Jt Man. Dir, 1981, Man. Dir, 1982–87, The Bodley Head Ltd; Dir, Triad Paperbacks Ltd, 1983–86; Gen. Sec., The Society of Authors, 1978–81. Chm. of Trustees, Inns of Court Gainsford Trust, 1992–. Vice-Chm., Hammersmith Democrats, 1988–89. *Publications:* (contrib.) Outlook, 1963; articles in The Author, The Bookseller, Graya. *Address:* 5 Gray's Inn Square, WC1R 5AZ; 20 Lansdown Crescent, Bath BA1 5EX. *Club:* Garrick.

MACHIN, Edward Anthony, QC 1973; a Recorder of the Crown Court, 1976–90; a Judge of the Courts of Appeal of Jersey and Guernsey, 1988–95; *b* 28 June 1925; *s* of Edward Arthur Machin and Olive Muriel Smith; *m* 1953, Jean Margaret McKanna; two *s* one *d*. *Educ:* Christ's Coll., Finchley; New Coll., Oxford. MA 1950; BCL 1950; Vinerian Law Scholar, 1950; Tancred Student, 1950; Cassel Scholar, 1951. Called to Bar, Lincoln's Inn, 1951; Bencher, 1980. *Publications:* Redgrave's Factories Acts, 1962, 1966, 1972; Redgrave's Offices and Shops, 1965 and 1973; Redgrave's Health and Safety in Factories, 1976, 1982; Health and Safety at Work, 1980; Health and Safety, 1990; (contrib.) Medical Negligence, 1990. *Recreations:* music, sailing, languages. *Address:* Strand End, Strand, Topsham, Exeter EX3 0BB. *T:* Topsham (01392) 877992. *Club:* Bar Yacht.

MACHIN, Kenneth Arthur; QC 1977; **His Honour Judge Machin;** a Circuit Judge, since 1984 (Deputy Circuit Judge, 1976–79); Chief Social Security Commissioner, since 1990; Chief Child Support Commissioner, since 1993; *b* 13 July 1936; *o s* of Thomas Arthur Machin and Edith May Machin; *m* 1983, Amaryllis Francesca (Member of Court of Common Council, Cripplegate Ward, City of London), *o d* of Dr Donald and Lucille Bigley. *Educ:* St Albans School. Called to the Bar, Middle Temple, 1960; South Eastern Circuit and Central Criminal Court; a Recorder of the Crown Court, 1979–84. Freeman, City of London. *Recreations:* painting, martello towers, Scalextric. *Address:* New Court, Temple, EC4Y 9BE. *T:* 0171–353 7741; The Penthouse, 502 Ben Jonson House, Barbican, EC2Y 8DL.

McHUGH, James, CBE 1989; FEng 1986; Chairman, British Pipe Coaters Ltd, since 1991; *b* 4 May 1930; *s* of late Edward McHugh and Martha (*née* Smith); *m* 1953, Sheila (*née* Cape); two *d*. *Educ:* Carlisle Grammar Sch.; various colls. FIMechE, FIGasE, FInstPet; FIQA; CIMgt. FRSA. Served Army, National Service. Entered Gas Industry, 1947; technical and managerial appts in Northern and E Midlands Gas Bds; Prodn Engr 1967, Dir of Engrg 1971, W Midlands Gas Bd; British Gas Corporation, subseq. British Gas plc: Dir of Ops, 1975; Mem., 1979; Man. Dir, Prodn and Supply, 1982; Man. Dir, 1986; Gp Exec. Mem., 1986–91. Dir, Lloyd's Register Quality Assurance Ltd, 1985–. Member: Meteorological Cttee, MoD, 1981–85; Engrg Council, 1989–92; President: IGasE, 1986–87; Inst. of Quality Assurance, 1992–. Freeman, City of London, 1984; Liveryman, Engineers' Co., 1984–. *Recreations:* mountaineering, dinghy sailing. *Address:* British Pipe Coaters Ltd, 152 Grosvenor Road, SW1V 3JL. *T:* 0171–821 1444. *Clubs:* Royal Automobile, Anglo-Belgian.

McILVENNA, Maj.-Gen. John Antony, CB 1980; Director of Army Legal Services, 1978–80, retired; *b* 10 Dec. 1919; *s* of Joseph Henry McIlvenna and Dorothy (*née* Brown); *m* Dr Hildegard Paula Gertrud Overlack; one *s* one *d*. *Educ:* Royal Grammar School, Newcastle upon Tyne; Hymers Coll., Hull; Durham Univ. LLB 1940. Private, KOYLI; 2nd Lieut, DLI, 1941; despatches 1945; admitted Solicitor, 1947; Captain, Army Legal Services, 1950; served in Hong Kong, Aden, Egypt, Libya and BAOR; Maj.-Gen. and

Dir, newly formed Army Legal Corps, 1978. Chm. and Dir, United Services Catholic Assoc., 1979–81, Vice-Pres., 1981–. *Recreations:* swimming, music, history. *Address:* Westfield, Biddenden, Kent TN27 8BB. *Club:* Army and Navy.

McILWAIN, Alexander Edward, CBE 1985; WS; President, Law Society of Scotland, 1983–84; Senior Partner, Leonards, Solicitors, Hamilton, since 1984 (Partner, since 1963); *b* 4 July 1933; *s* of Edward Walker McIlwain and Gladys Edith Horne or McIlwain; *m* 1961, Moira Margaret Kinnaird; three *d.* *Educ:* Aberdeen Grammar Sch.; Aberdeen Univ. MA 1954; LLB 1956. Pres., Students Representative Council, Univ. of Aberdeen, 1956–57. Commnd RCS, 1957–59, Lieut. Admitted Solicitor in Scotland, 1957; SSC, 1966. Burgh Prosecutor, Hamilton, 1966–75; District Prosecutor, Hamilton, 1975–76; Dean, Soc. of Solicitors of Hamilton, 1981–83; Vice Pres., Law Soc. of Scotland, 1982–83; Hon. Sheriff, Sheriffdom of South Strathclyde, Dumfries and Galloway at Hamilton, 1982; Temp. Sheriff, 1984. WS 1985. Chairman: Legal Aid Central Cttee, 1985–87; Hamilton Sheriff Court Project, 1991–94; Member: Lanarkshire Health Bd, 1981–91; Central Adv. Cttee on Justices of the Peace, 1987–; Supreme Court (formerly Review) Cttee, Scottish Legal Aid Bd, 1987–93. Pres., Temporary Sheriffs' Assoc., 1995– (Vice Pres., 1993–95); Hon. Vice-Pres., Scottish Lawyers for Nuclear Disarmament, 1985–. Chm., Lanarkshire Scout Area, 1981–91; Mem. Council, Scout Assoc., 1987–. Hon. Mem., Amer. Bar Assoc., 1983. *Publications:* (jtly) Time Costing and Time Recording; Supporting Victims in the Criminal Justice System. *Recreations:* work, gardening, listening to music. *Address:* Craigievar, Bothwell Road, Uddingston, Glasgow G71 7EY. *T:* Uddingston (01698) 813368. *Club:* New (Edinburgh).

McINDOE, William Ian, CB 1978; Deputy Secretary, Department of the Environment, 1979–86; *b* 11 March 1929; *s* of John McIndoe, Leven, Fife and Agnes Scott; *m* 1st, 1954, Irene Armour Mudie (*d* 1966); one *s* two *d*; 2nd, 1971, Jamesanna Smart (*née* MacGregor). *Educ:* Sedbergh; Corpus Christi Coll., Oxford. 2nd Lieut 2 RHA, 1951–53; CRO, 1953–63, served in Canberra and Salisbury, 1956–62, Private Sec. to Sec. of State, 1962–63; Private Sec. to Sec. of Cabinet, later Asst Sec., Cabinet Office, 1963–66; Scottish Office, 1966–76, Under-Sec., 1971; Dep. Sec., Cabinet Office, 1976–79. Dep. Chm., Housing Corp., 1986–90. *Address:* Speedyburn House, Station Road, Gifford, E Lothian EH41 4QL. *T:* Gifford (01620) 810363. *Club:* New (Edinburgh).

McINERNEY, Prof. John Peter, OBE 1995; Glanely Professor of Agricultural Policy and Director of Agricultural Economics Unit, University of Exeter, since 1984; *b* 10 Jan. 1939; *s* of Peter McInerney and Eva McInerney; *m* 1961, Audrey M. Perry; one *s* one *d.* *Educ:* Colyton Grammar Sch., Colyford, Devon; Univ. of London (BScAgric Hons); Univ. of Oxford (DipAgricEcons); Iowa State Univ. (PhD). Lectr in Agricl Econs, Wye Coll., Univ. of London, 1964–66; Lectr and Sen. Lectr in Agricl Econs, Univ. of Manchester, 1967–78; Prof. of Agricl Econs and Management, Univ. of Reading, 1978–84. Research Economist and Cons., World Bank, Washington, DC, 1972–. Phi Kappa Phi 1964, Gamma Sigma Delta 1964. *Publications:* The Food Industry: economics and policy (jtly), 1983; Badgers and Bovine Tuberculosis (jtly), 1986; Disease in Farm Livestock: economics and policy (jtly), 1987; Diversification in the Use of Farm Resources, 1989; Economic Analysis of Milk Quotas, 1992; chapters in: Current Issues in Economic Policy, 1975, 2nd edn 1980; Resources Policy, 1982, etc; articles in Jl of Agricl Econs, Amer. Jl of Agricl Econs, Canadian Jl of Agricl Econs, Outlook on Agric. *Recreations:* doing it myself, tentative farming, introspection. *Address:* c/o Agricultural Economics Unit, University of Exeter, Exeter EX4 6TL. *T:* Exeter (01392) 263837. *Club:* Templeton Social.

MacINNES, Archibald, CVO 1977; Under Secretary, Property Services Agency, Department of the Environment, 1973–79; retired 1989; *b* 10 April 1919; *s* of Duncan and Catherine MacInnes; *m* 1950, Nancey Elisabeth Blyth (*d* 1976); one *s* two *d.* *Educ:* Kirkcudbright Academy; Royal Technical Coll., Glasgow. FIMechE. Scott's Shipbuilding and Engineering Co., Greenock, 1937–44; Colonial Service, Nigeria, 1945–59; War Office Works Organisation: Gibraltar, 1959–63; Southern Comd, Salisbury, Wilts, 1963–64; MPBW, Bristol, 1964–68; DoE, Germany, 1968–72; Dir, London Region, PSA, DoE, 1972–79; part-time Planning Inspector, DoE, 1980–89. FIMgt. Coronation Medal. *Recreations:* golf, shooting, fishing. *Address:* Lower Road, Homington, Salisbury, Wilts SP5 4NG. *T:* Coombe Bissett (01722) 718336.

MacINNES, Barbara Mary; *see* Stocking, B. M.

MacINNES, Hamish, OBE 1979; BEM; Founder and Leader, Glencoe Mountain Rescue Team, 1960–94; author and film consultant (safety and production), BBC and major movies; Director, Glencoe Productions Ltd, since 1989; Hon. Director, Leishman Memorial Research Centre, Glencoe, since 1975; *b* 7 July 1930. Dep. Leader, British Everest Expedition, 1975. Mountain Rescue Cttee for Scotland (Past Sec.). Founder and Hon. Pres., Search and Rescue Dog Assoc.; Past Pres., Alpine Climbing Group; Pres., Guide Dogs for the Blind Adventure Gp, 1986–. Designer of climbing equipment, incl. the first all metal ice axe, terrodactyl ice tools, the MacInnes stretchers, MacInnes Boxes for high altitude mountain camping. Hon. LLD Glasgow, 1983; Hon. DSc: Aberdeen, 1988; Heriot-Watt, 1992. *Publications:* Climbing, 1964; Scottish Climbs, 2 vols, 1971, 2nd edn (1 vol.) 1981; International Mountain Rescue Handbook, 1972, 2nd edn 1984 (also USA); Call-Out: mountain rescue, 1973, 4th edn 1986; Climb to the Lost World, 1974; Death Reel (novel), 1976; West Highland Walks, vols 1 and 2, 1979, Vol. 3, 1983, Vol. 4, 1988; Look Behind the Ranges, 1979; Scottish Winter Climbs, 1980; High Drama (stories), 1980; Beyond the Ranges, 1984; Sweep Search, 1985; The Price of Adventure, 1987; My Scotland, 1988; The Way Through the Glens, 1989; Land of Mountain and Mist, 1989; books have been translated into Russian, Japanese and German. *Address:* Tigh A'Voulin, Glencoe, Argyll PA39 4HX.

McINNES, John Colin; QC (Scot.) 1990; Sheriff of Tayside Central and Fife, since 1974 (at Cupar and Perth); *b* 21 Nov. 1938; *s* of late Mr I. W. McInnes, WS, and of Mrs Lucy McInnes, Cupar, Fife; *m* 1966, Elisabeth Mabel Neilson; one *s* one *d.* *Educ:* Cargilfield Sch., Edinburgh; Merchiston Castle Sch., Edinburgh; Brasenose Coll., Oxford (BA); Edinburgh Univ. (LLB). 2nd Lieut 8th Royal Tank Regt, 1957–58; Lieut Fife and Forfar Yeomanry/Scottish Horse (TA), 1958–64. Advocate, 1963. In practice at Scottish Bar, 1963–73; Tutor, Faculty of Law, Edinburgh Univ., 1965–73; Sheriff of the Lothians and Peebles, 1973–74. Member and Vice-President: Security Service Tribunal, 1989–; Intelligence Services Tribunal, 1994–. Director: R. Mackness & Co. Ltd, 1963–70; Fios Group Ltd, 1970–72 (Chm., 1970–72). Chm., Fife Family Conciliation Service, 1988–90. Mem. Court, St Andrews Univ., 1983–91. Hon. LLD St Andrews, 1994. Contested (C) Aberdeen North, 1964. *Publication:* Divorce Law and Practice in Scotland, 1990. *Recreations:* shooting, fishing, ski-ing, photography. *Address:* Perth Sheriff Court, Tay Street, Perth PH2 8NL. *T:* Perth (01738) 620546.

MacINNES, Keith Gordon, CMG 1984; HM Diplomatic Service, retired; Ambassador and UK Permanent Representative to OECD, Paris, 1992–95; *b* 17 July 1935; *s* of late Kenneth MacInnes and of Helen MacInnes (*née* Gordon); *m* 1st, 1966, Jennifer Anne Fennell (marr. diss. 1980); one *s* one *d*; 2nd, 1985, Hermione Pattinson. *Educ:* Rugby; Trinity Coll., Cambridge (MA); Pres., Cambridge Union Soc., 1957. HM Forces, 1953–55. FO, 1960; Third, later Second Secretary, Buenos Aires, 1961–64; FO, 1964 (First Sec., 1965); Private Sec. to Permanent Under-Sec., Commonwealth Office, 1965–68; First Sec. (Information), Madrid, 1968–70; FCO, 1970–74; Counsellor and Head of Chancery: Prague, 1974–77; Dep. Perm. Rep., UK Mission, Geneva, 1977–80; Head of Information Dept, FCO, 1980–83; Asst Under-Sec. of State and Principal Finance Officer, FCO, 1983–87; Ambassador to the Philippines, 1987–92. *Recreations:* golf, bridge. *Address:* Pound House, Shenley, Herts WD7 9BW.

McINTOSH, family name of **Baron McIntosh of Haringey.**

McINTOSH OF HARINGEY, Baron *cr* 1982 (Life Peer), of Haringey in Greater London; **Andrew Robert McIntosh;** Deputy Leader of the Opposition, House of Lords, since 1992; *b* 30 April 1933; *s* of late Prof. A. W. McIntosh and Jenny (*née* Britton); *m* 1962, Naomi Ellen Sargant; two *s.* *Educ:* Haberdashers' Aske's Hampstead Sch.; Royal Grammar Sch., High Wycombe; Jesus Coll., Oxford (MA); Ohio State Univ. (Fellow in Econs, 1956–57). Gallup Poll, 1957–61; Hoover Ltd, 1961–63; Market Res. Manager, Osram (GEC) Ltd, 1963–65; IFF Research Ltd: Man. Dir, 1965–81; Chm., 1981–88; Dep. Chm., 1988–. Chm., SVP United Kingdom Ltd, 1983–92. Member: Hornsey Bor. Council, 1963–65; Haringey Bor. Council, 1964–68 (Chm., Develt Control); Greater London Council: Member for Tottenham, 1973–83; Chm., NE Area Bd, 1973–74, W Area Bd, 1974–76, and Central Area Bd, 1976; Opposition Leader on Planning and Communications, 1977–80; Leader of the Opposition, 1980–81. Opposition spokesman on educn and science, 1985–87, on industry matters, 1983–87, on the environment, 1987–92, on home affairs, 1992–, House of Lords. Chairman: Market Res. Soc., 1972–73; Assoc. for Neighbourhood Councils, 1974–80; Computer Sub-Cttee, H of L Offices Cttee, 1984–; Mem., Metrop. Water Bd, 1967–68. Chm., Fabian Soc., 1985–86 (Mem., NEC, 1981–87). Principal, Working Men's Coll., NW1, 1988–; Governor, Drayton Sch., Tottenham, 1967–83. Editor, Jl of Market Res. Soc., 1963–67. *Publications:* Industry and Employment in the Inner City, 1979; (ed) Employment Policy in the UK and United States, 1980; Women and Work, 1981; jl articles on theory, practice and findings of survey research. *Recreations:* cooking, reading, music. *Address:* 27 Hurst Avenue, N6 5TX. *T:* 0181–340 1496.

See also N. E. Sargant.

McINTOSH, Prof. Angus, FRSE 1978; FBA 1989; consultant on linguistics problems; hon. consultant, Institute for Historical Dialectology (formerly Gayre Institute for Medieval English and Scottish Dialectology), University of Edinburgh, since 1986; *b* 10 Jan. 1914; *s* of late Kenneth and Mary McIntosh (*née* Thompson), Cleadon, Sunderland, Co. Durham; *m* 1st, 1939, Barbara (*d* 1988), *d* of late Dr William Seaman and Mrs Bainbridge (*née* June Wheeler), New York City; two *s* one *d*; 2nd, 1988, Karina Williamson (*née* Side), *widow* of Colin Williamson, Fellow of Jesus Coll., Oxford. *Educ:* Ryhope Grammar Sch., Co. Durham; Oriel Coll., Oxford (BA, 1st Class Hons, English Lang., and Lit., 1934); Merton Coll., Oxford (Harmsworth Scholar); (Dip. of Comparative Philology, University of Oxford, 1936); Harvard Univ. (Commonwealth Fund Fellow, AM, 1937). MA (Oxford) 1938. Lecturer, Dept of English, University College, Swansea, 1938–46. Served War of 1939–45, beginning as trooper in Tank Corps, finishing as Major in Intelligence Corps. University Lecturer in Mediæval English, Oxford, 1946–48; Lecturer in English, Christ Church, Oxford, 1946–47; Student of Christ Church, 1947–48; University of Edinburgh: Forbes Prof. of English Language and General Linguistics, 1948–64, later Forbes Prof. of Eng. Lang., 1964–79; Dir, Middle English Dialect Atlas Project, 1979–86; Hon. Sen. Res. Fellow, Dept of English Language, Glasgow Univ., 1993–. Co-Chm., Hon. Adv. Bd, Pergamon Encyclopedia of Lang. and Linguistics, 1988–94. Rockefeller Foundation Fellowship, US, June-Sept. 1949; Leverhulme Emeritus Res. Fellow, 1984–86. Hon. Pres., Scottish Text Soc., 1989– (Pres., 1977–89). For. Mem., Finnish Acad. of Science and Letters, 1976. Hon. DPhil Poznan Univ., 1972; Hon. DLitt: Durham, 1980; Glasgow, 1994. Sir Israel Gollancz Prize, British Acad., 1989. *Publications:* books, articles and reviews on English language and related topics. *Recreations:* gardening, painting, music. *Address:* 32 Blacket Place, Edinburgh EH9 1RL. *T:* 0131–667 5791.

McINTOSH, Anne Caroline Ballingall; Member (C) European Parliament, Essex North and Suffolk South, since 1994 (North-East Essex, 1989–94); *b* 20 Sept. 1954; *d* of Dr Alastair Ballingall McIntosh and Grethe-Lise McIntosh (*née* Thomsen); *m* 1992, John Harvey. *Educ:* Harrogate Coll., Harrogate, Yorks; Univ. of Edinburgh (LLB Hons); Univ. of Aarhus, Denmark. Admitted to Faculty of Advocates, 1982. Unqualified legal advr in private EEC practice, Brussels, 1979–80; Bar apprentice with Simpson and Marwick, WS, and devilling at Scottish Bar, 1980–82; private legal practice, Brussels, specialising in EEC law, 1982–83; Secretariat Mem., responsible for transport, youth, culture, educn and tourism, and relations with Scandinavia, Austria, Switzerland and Yugoslavia, EDG, Europ. Parlt, 1983–89. European Parliament: a Jun. Whip, EDG, 1989–92; Mem., Transport and Legal Affairs Cttees; EDG Spokesman on Rules Cttee, 1989–95, Transport and Tourism Cttee, 1992–; Mem., Norway Parly Delegn, 1989–95, Polish Parly Delegn, 1995–. *Recreations:* swimming, cinema, walking. *Address:* (constituency office) The Old Armoury, Museum Street, Saffron Walden, Essex CB10 1JN. *T:* Saffron Walden (01799) 523631; (European Parliament) 97 Rue Belliard, B-1040 Brussels. *T:* (22)2845239.

MACINTOSH, Dr Farquhar, CBE 1982; Rector (Headmaster), The Royal High School, Edinburgh, 1972–89; *b* 27 Oct. 1923; *s* of John Macintosh and Kate Ann Macintosh (*née* MacKinnon); *m* 1959, Margaret Mary Inglis, Peebles; two *s* two *d.* *Educ:* Portree High Sch., Skye; Edinburgh Univ. (MA); Glasgow Univ. (DipEd). Served RN, 1943–46; commnd RNVR, 1944. Headmaster, Portree High Sch., 1962–66; Rector, Oban High Sch., 1967–72. Member: Highlands and Islands Develt Consultative Council, 1965–82; Broadcasting Council for Scotland, 1975–79; Chairman: BBC Secondary Programme Cttee, 1972–80; School Broadcasting Council for Scotland, 1981–85; Scottish Examination Bd, 1977–90; Scottish Assoc. for Educnl Management and Admin, 1979–82; Highlands and Is Educn Trust, 1988–; Educn Cttee of European Movt (Scotland), 1993–. Chm. of Governors, Jordanhill Coll. of Educn, 1970–72; Mem. Court, Edinburgh Univ., 1975–91; Chm., Sabhal Mor Ostaig (Gaelic Coll.), Skye, 1991–. Governor: St Margaret's Sch., Edinburgh, 1989–; Royal Blind Sch., 1990–. Elder, Church of Scotland. FEIS 1970; FScotvec 1990. Hon. DLitt Heriot-Watt, 1980; Dr *hc* Edinburgh, 1992. *Publications:* regular contribs to TES Scotland; contrib. to European Jl of Educn. *Recreations:* hill-walking, occasional fishing, Gaelic, travel. *Address:* 12 Rothesay Place, Edinburgh EH3 7SQ. *T:* 0131–225 4404. *Clubs:* East India; Rotary of Murrayfield and Cramond (Edinburgh).

McINTOSH, Genista Mary; Executive Director, Royal National Theatre, since 1990; *b* 23 Sept. 1946; *d* of late Geoffrey Tandy and of Maire Tandy; *m* 1971, Neil Scott Wishart McIntosh, *qv* (marr. diss.); one *s* one *d.* *Educ:* Univ. of York (BA Philosophy and Sociology). Press Sec., York Festival of Arts, 1968–69; Royal Shakespeare Co.: Casting Dir, 1972–77; Planning Controller, 1977–84; Sen. Administrator, 1986–90; Associate Producer, 1990. Dir, Marmont Management Ltd, 1984–86. Chm., SE London Common Purpose, 1993–. *Address:* Royal National Theatre, Upper Ground, SE1 9PX. *T:* 0171–928 2033.

McINTOSH, Rev. Canon Hugh; Honorary Canon, St Mary's Cathedral, Glasgow, since 1983; *b* 5 June 1914; *s* of Hugh Burns McIntosh and Mary (*née* Winter); *m* 1951, Ruth

Georgina, *er d* of late Rev. William Skinner Wilson and Enid (*née* Sanders); two *s* one *d*. *Educ:* Hatfield Coll., Durham (Exhibr); Edinburgh Theological Coll. (Luscombe Schol.). LTh, 1941; BA (dist.), 1942; MA 1945. Deacon and Priest, 1942. Precentor and Senior Chaplain, St Paul's Cathedral, Dundee, 1942–46; Senior Chaplain, St Mary's Cathedral, Edinburgh, 1946–49; Curate, St Salvador's, Edinburgh, 1949–51; Rector, St Adrian's, Gullane, 1951–54; Rector, St John's, Dumfries, 1954–66; Canon of St Mary's Cathedral, Glasgow, and Synod Clerk of Glasgow and Galloway, 1959; Provost of St Mary's Cathedral, Glasgow, 1966–70; Rector, Christ Church, Lanark, 1970–83. *Recreations:* reading, writing, and (a little) arithmetic. *Address:* 2 Ridgepark Drive, Lanark ML11 7PG. *T:* Lanark (01555) 663458.

McINTOSH, Vice-Admiral Sir Ian (Stewart), KBE 1973 (MBE 1941); CB 1970; DSO 1944; DSC 1942; Management Selection Consultant, 1973–78; *b* 11 Oct. 1919; *s* of late A. J. McIntosh, Melbourne, Australia; *m* 1943, Elizabeth Rosemary Rasmussen; three *s* (one *d* decd). *Educ:* Geelong Grammar Sch. Entered RN, 1938; comd HM Submarine: H44, 1942; Sceptre, 1943–44; Alderney, 1946–48; Aeneas, 1950–51; Exec. Officer, HMS Ark Royal, 1956–58; comd 2nd Submarine Sqn, 1961–63; comd HMS Victorious, 1966–68; Dir-Gen., Weapons (Naval), 1968–70; Dep. Chief of Defence Staff (Op. Req.), 1971–73, retd 1973. Captain, 1959; Rear-Adm., 1968; Vice-Adm., 1971. Chairman: Sea Cadet Assoc., 1973–83; HMS Cavalier Trust, 1974–88. *Recreations:* friends, reading, music. *Address:* 19 The Crescent, Alverstoke, Hants PO12 2DH. *T:* Gosport (01705) 580510. *Club:* Royal Over-Seas League.

MACINTOSH, Joan, CBE 1978; Member, Scottish Constitutional Commn, 1994; *b* 23 Nov. 1919; *m* 1952, Ian Gillies Macintosh (*d* 1992); one *s* two *d* (and one *s* decd). *Educ:* Amer. and English schs; Oxford Univ. (MA Modern History). BBC, 1941–42; Amer. Div., Min. of Inf., 1942–45; HM Foreign Service, 1945–52; retd on marriage. Voluntary work in India, 1953–69; CAB Organiser, Glasgow, 1972–75. Chm. Council, Insurance Ombudsman Bureau, 1981–85; Lay Observer for Scotland (Solicitors (Scotland) Act), 1981–89; Chm., Scottish Child Law Centre, 1989–92; Mem., Royal Commn on Legal Services in Scotland, 1975–80. Chm., Scottish Consumer Council, 1975–80; Vice-Chm., National Consumer Council, 1976–84; Vice-Pres., Nat. Fedn of Consumer Gps, 1982–. Hon. Pres., Scottish Legal Action Group, 1990. Mem. Council, Victim Support Scotland, 1992–. Hon. LLD: Dundee, 1982; Strathclyde, 1991; DUniv Stirling, 1988. *Recreations:* tapestry, gardening. *Address:* Wynd End, Auchterarder, Perthshire PH3 1AD. *T:* Auchterarder (01764) 662499.

McINTOSH, John Charles; Headmaster, The London Oratory School, since 1977; *b* 6 Feb. 1946; *s* of Arthur and Betty McIntosh. *Educ:* Ebury Sch.; Shoreditch Coll.; Sussex Univ. (MA). The London Oratory School: Asst Master, 1967–71; Dep. Headmaster, 1971–77. Member: Nat. Curriculum Council, 1990–93; Centre for Policy Studies Educn Gp, 1982–; Inst. of Econ. Affairs Educn Adv. Council, 1988–91; Health Educn Council, 1985–88. Mem., Catholic Union of GB, 1978–. FRSA 1981. *Recreations:* playing the organ, opera, ballet, theatre. *Address:* The London Oratory School, Seagrave Road, SW6 1RX; 75 Alder Lodge, River Gardens, Stevenage Road, SW6 6NR. *T:* 0171–385 4576, *Fax:* 0171–610 0834. *Clubs:* Athenæum, East India.

McINTOSH, Dr Malcolm Kenneth; Chief of Defence Procurement, Ministry of Defence, since 1991; *b* Melbourne, 14 Dec. 1945; *s* of Kenneth Stuart McIntosh and Valerie McIntosh (*née* MacKenzie); *m* 1971, Margaret Beatrice (*née* Stevens); three *s* one *d*. *Educ:* Telopea Park; Australian National Univ. (BSc Hons, PhD Physics). Research Scientist, Aust. Weapons Res. Estabt, 1970–72; Aust. Army, 1972–74 (Major); Aust. Economic Ministries, 1974–82; Australian Department of Defence, 1982–90; Chief of Defence Production, 1987; Dep. Sec., Acquisition and Logistics, 1988; Sec., Aust. Dept of Industry, Technology and Commerce, 1990. *Address:* Procurement Executive, Ministry of Defence, Whitehall, SW1A 2HB.

McINTOSH, Melinda Jane Frances; *see* Letts, M. J. F.

McINTOSH, Prof. Naomi Ellen Sargant, (Lady McIntosh of Haringey); *see* Sargant, N. E.

McINTOSH, Neil Scott Wishart; Chief Executive, Centre for British Teachers, since 1990; *b* 24 July 1947; *s* of William Henderson McIntosh and Mary Catherine McIntosh; *m* 1st, 1971, Genista Mary Tandy (*see* G. M. McIntosh) (marr. diss. 1990); one *s* one *d*; 2nd, 1991, Melinda Jane Frances Letts, *qv*; one *s* one *d*. *Educ:* Merchiston Castle Sch., Edinburgh; Univ. of York (BA Politics); London Sch. of Econs (MSc Industrial Relations). Res. Associate, PEP, 1969–73; Res. Dir, Southwark Community Develt Proj., 1973–76; Dir, Shelter, 1976–84; Dir, VSO, 1985–90. Councillor, London Bor. of Camden, 1971–77; Chm., Housing Cttee, 1974–76. Dir, Stonham Housing Assoc., 1982–. Vice Pres., BSA, 1985–91. Founder and Chm., Homeless Internat., 1988–91; Treasurer, Campaign for Freedom of Information, 1984–; Mem., Independent Broadcasting Telethon Trust, 1987–94. *Publication:* The Right to Manage?, 1971 (2nd edn 1976). *Recreations:* golf, hill walking, theatre. *Clubs:* Reform; Highgate Golf.

McINTOSH, Neil William David, CBE 1990; Chief Executive, Strathclyde Regional Council, 1992–March 1996; *b* 30 Jan. 1940; *s* of Neil and Beatrice McIntosh; *m* 1965, Marie Elizabeth Lindsay; one *s* two *d*. *Educ:* King's Park Sen. Secondary Sch., Glasgow. FIPM; ACIS. J. & P. Coats, 1957; Honeywell Controls, 1959; Berks, Oxford and Reading Jt O&M Unit, 1962; Stewarts & Lloyds, 1964; Lanark CC, 1966; Inverness CC, 1969; Highland Regl Council, 1975; Chief Exec., Dumfries and Galloway Regl Council, 1985. Director: Training 2000 (Scotland) Ltd, 1993–; Quality Scotland Foundn, 1993–; Sportability Strathclyde, 1994–. Hon. DHL Syracuse Univ., USA, 1993. FRSA. *Recreations:* antique bottle collecting, bowling, local history, hill walking. *Address:* (until March 1996) Strathclyde Regional Council, India Street, Glasgow G2 4PF. *T:* 0141–227 3409; Birnock Lodge, Well Road, Moffat DG10 9JT.

McINTOSH, Sir Ronald (Robert Duncan), KCB 1975 (CB 1968); Chairman, APV plc, 1982–89; Director: S. G. Warburg & Co. Ltd, 1978–90; Foseco plc, 1978–90; London & Manchester Group plc, 1978–90; *b* 26 Sept. 1919; *s* of Thomas Steven McIntosh, MD, FRCP, MRCS, and Christina Jane McIntosh; *m* 1951, Doreen Frances, *o d* of Commander Andrew MacGinnity and Margaret MacGinnity, Frinton-on-Sea. *Educ:* Charterhouse (Scholar); Balliol Coll., Oxford. Served in Merchant Navy, 1939–45; Second Mate, 1943–45. Assistant Principal, Board of Trade, 1947; General Manager, Dollar Exports Board, 1949–51; Commercial Counsellor, UK High Commn, New Delhi, 1957–61; Under-Secretary: BoT, 1961–64; DEA, 1964–66; Dep. Under-Sec. of State, Dept of Economic Affairs, 1966–68; Dep. Secretary, Cabinet Office, 1968–70; Dep. Under-Sec. of State, Dept of Employment, 1970–72; Dep. Sec., HM Treasury, 1972–73; Dir-Gen. Nat. Economic Development Office, and Mem. NEDC, 1973–77. Dir, Fisons Ltd, 1978–81. Chairman: Danish–UK Chamber of Commerce, 1990–92; British Health Care Consortium (for the former Soviet Union), 1992–. Member: British Overseas Trade Adv. Cttee, 1975–77; Council, CBI, 1980–90; Co-Chm., British-Hungarian Round Table, 1980–84. Chm., Centre for Eur. Agricl Studies, Wye Coll., 1979–83. Patron, British-Hungarian Soc., 1990–. Patron, ReAction Trust, 1991. CIMgt; FRSA. Hon. DSc Aston, 1977. *Recreations:* sailing, travel. *Address:* 24 Ponsonby Terrace, SW1P 4QA. *Club:* Royal Thames Yacht.

MacINTYRE, Prof. Alasdair Chalmers; Arts and Sciences Professor of Philosophy, Duke University, since 1995; *b* 12 Jan. 1929; *o s* of Eneas John MacIntyre, MD (Glasgow), and Margaret Emily Chalmers, MB, ChB (Glasgow); *m* 1977, Lynn Sumida Joy; one *s* three *d* by previous marriages. *Educ:* Epsom Coll. and privately; Queen Mary Coll., Univ. of London (Fellow, 1984); Manchester Univ. BA (London); MA (Manchester); MA (Oxon). Lectr in Philosophy of Religion, Manchester Univ., 1951–57; Lectr in Philosophy, Leeds Univ., 1957–61; Research Fellow, Nuffield Coll., Oxford, 1961–62; Sen. Fellow, Council of Humanities, Princeton Univ., 1962–63; Fellow and Preceptor in Philosophy, University Coll., Oxford, 1963–66; Prof. of Sociology, Univ. of Essex, 1966–70; Prof. of History of Ideas, Brandeis Univ., 1970–72; Univ. Prof. in Philos. and Political Sci., Boston Univ., 1972–80; Luce Prof., Wellesley Coll., 1980–82; W. Alton Jones Prof. of Philosophy, Vanderbilt Univ., 1982–88; McMahon/Hank Prof. of Philosophy, Univ. of Notre Dame, Indiana, 1988–94. Pres., Eastern Div., Amer. Phil Assoc., 1984. Fellow, Amer. Acad. of Arts and Scis, 1985; Corresp. FBA, 1994. Hon. Mem., Phi Beta Kappa, 1973. Hon. DHL Swarthmore, 1983; Hon. DLit: QUB, 1988; Williams Coll., Mass, 1993; DU Essex, 1990. *Publications:* Marxism and Christianity, 1954 (revised, 1968); New Essays in Philosophical Theology (ed, with A. G. N. Flew), 1955; Metaphysical Beliefs (ed), 1956; The Unconscious: a conceptual analysis, 1958; A Short History of Ethics, 1965; Secularisation and Moral Change, 1967; Marcuse: an exposition and a polemic, 1970; Sociological Theory and Philosophical Analysis (ed with D. M. Emmet), 1971; Against the Self-Images of the Age, 1971; After Virtue, 1981; Whose Justice? Which Rationality?, 1988; Three Rival Versions of Moral Enquiry, 1990. *Address:* Department of Philosophy, Duke University, Durham, NC 27708, USA.

McINTYRE, Prof. Alasdair Duncan, CBE 1994; FRSE 1975; Emeritus Professor of Fisheries and Oceanography, Aberdeen University, since 1986; *b* 17 Nov. 1926; *s* of Alexander Walker McIntyre and Martha Jack McIntyre; *m* 1967, Catherine; one *d*. *Educ:* Hermitage Sch., Helensburgh; Glasgow Univ. BSc (1st class Hons Zoology) 1948; DSc 1973. Scottish Home Department (since 1960, DAFS) Marine Laboratory, Aberdeen: Develt Commn Grant-aided Student, 1948–49; Scientific Officer, 1950; Head, Lab. Environmental Gp, 1973; Dep. Dir, 1977; Dir, 1983. Dir of Fisheries Res. Services for Scotland, Dept of Agric. and Fisheries for Scotland, 1983–86. UK Co-ordinator, Fisheries Res. and Develt, 1986. President: Scottish Marine Biological Assoc., later Scottish Assoc. for Marine Sci., 1988–93; Estuarine and Coastal Scis Assoc., 1992–; Sir Alister Hardy Foundn for Ocean Sci., 1992–; Chairman: UN Gp of Experts on Scientific Aspects of Marine Pollution (GESAMP), 1981–84; Adv. Cttee on Marine Pollution, Internat. Council for the Exploration of the Sea, 1982–84; Marine Forum for Envmtl Issues, 1988–; Assessor, Donaldson Inquiry into protection of UK coastline from pollution by merchant shipping, 1993–94. Member: NCC for Scotland, 1991; Res. Bd, Scottish Natural Heritage, 1992–. Hon. Res. Prof., Aberdeen Univ., 1983–86. Chm., Trustees of Buckland Foundn, 1994– (Vice Chm., 1988–94). Ed., Fisheries Research, 1988–. *Publications:* some 70 articles in scientific jls on marine ecology and pollution. *Recreations:* cooking, wine, walking. *Address:* 63 Hamilton Place, Aberdeen AB2 4BW. *T:* Aberdeen (01224) 645633.

McINTYRE, Sir Alister; *see* McIntyre, Sir M. A.

McINTYRE, Sir Donald (Conroy), Kt 1992; CBE 1985 (OBE 1977); opera singer, free-lance; *b* 22 Oct. 1934; *s* of George Douglas McIntyre and Mrs Hermyn McIntyre; *m*; three *d*. *Educ:* Mount Albert Grammar Sch.; Auckland Teachers' Trng Coll.; Guildhall Sch. of Music. Debut in Britain, Welsh National Opera, 1959; Sadler's Wells Opera, many roles, 1960–67; Royal Opera, Covent Garden, from 1967; also Vienna, Bayreuth, La Scala, Milan and Metropolitan, NY. *Principal roles:* Barak, in Die Frau Ohne Schatten, Strauss; Wotan and Wanderer, in The Ring, Wagner; Hollander, Wagner; Hans Sachs, in Die Meistersinger von Nurnberg, Wagner; Heyst, in Victory, Richard Rodney Bennett; Macbeth, Verdi; Scarpia, in Tosca, Puccini; Count, in Figaro, Mozart; Dr Schön, in Wozzeck, Berg; title role in Cardillac, Hindemith; Siegfried, Metropolitan, NY; Rocco, in Fidelio; Prospero, in Un Re in Ascolto, Berio; Balstrode, in Peter Grimes, Britten; Bayreuth: Wotan, Wanderer, Hollander; Telramund, in Lohengrin; Klingsor, Amfortas and Gurnemanz in Parsifal; Bayreuth Centenary Ring, 1976–81. *Video and films include:* Der Fliegende Holländer, 1975; Electra, 1976; Die Meistersinger, 1984; Bayreuth Centenary Ring, 1976–81; recordings include Pelléas et Mélisande, Il Trovatore, The Messiah, Oedipus Rex, The Ring, Beethoven's 9th Symphony, Damnation of Faust, Bayreuth Centenary Ring. Fidelio Award, 1989. *Recreations:* gardening, swimming, tennis, farming. *Address:* Foxhill Farm, Jackass Lane, Keston, Bromley, Kent BR2 6AN. *T:* Farnborough (01689) 855368; c/o Ingpen & Williams, 14 Kensington Court, W8 5DN.

MacINTYRE, Rt. Hon. Duncan, CMG 1992; DSO 1945; OBE 1956; ED; PC (NZ) 1980; Deputy Prime Minister of New Zealand, 1981–84; *b* 1915; *s* of A. MacIntyre; *m* Diana, *d* of Percy Hunter; two *s* three *d*. Sheep farming, 1933–39 and 1946–. Served War, NZ Army, 1939–46; Territorial Force, 1949–60 (Brig. 1956); Col Comdt RNZAC, 1976. MP (National Party) Hastings, 1960–72, Bay of Plenty, 1975–78, East Cape, 1978–84; Minister: of Lands, of Forests, and i/c of Valuation Dept, 1966–72; of Maori Affairs and of Island Affairs, 1969–72; for the Environment, 1972; of Agriculture, of Fisheries, and i/c of Rural Banking and Finance Corp., 1975–84; of Maori Affairs, 1975–78. *Address:* Taikura, RD4, Waipukurau, New Zealand.

MacINTYRE, Prof. Iain; Professor and Associate Director, William Harvey Research Institute, St Bartholomew's Hospital Medical College, since 1991; Hon. Consultant Chemical Pathologist: Hammersmith Hospital, since 1960; Queen Charlotte's Hospital; *b* 30 Aug. 1924; *s* of John MacIntyre, Tobermory, and Margaret Fraser Shaw, Stratherick, Inverness-shire; *m* 1947, Mabel Wilson Jamieson, MA, *y d* of George Jamieson and J. C. K. K. Bell, Largs, Ayrshire; one *d*. *Educ:* Jordanhill Coll. Sch., Glasgow; Univ. of Glasgow. MB, ChB Glasgow 1947; PhD London 1960; MRCPath 1963 (Founder Mem.), FRCPath 1971; FRCP 1977 (MRCP 1969); DSc London 1970. Asst Clinical Pathologist, United Sheffield Hosps, and Hon. Demonstrator in Biochem., Sheffield Univ., 1948–52; Royal Postgraduate Medical School: Registrar in Chemical Pathology, 1952–54; Sir Jack Drummond Meml Fellow, 1954–56; Asst Lectr in Chem. Path., 1956–59; Reader in Chem. Path., 1963–67; Dir, Endocrine Unit, 1967–89; Chm., Academic Bd, 1986–89; Sen. Res. Fellow, Dept of Medicine, 1989–91; Prof., Chem. Path., London Univ., 1967–89, now Emeritus. Director: Dept of Chem. Path., Hammersmith Hosp., 1982–89; Chelsea Hosp. for Women, Queen Charlotte's Hosp. for Women, 1986–89. Vis. Scientist, Nat. Insts of Health, Bethesda, 1960–61; Visiting Professor: San Francisco Medical Center, 1964; Melbourne Univ., 1979–80; St George's Hosp. Med. Sch., 1989–; Vis. Lectr, Insts of Molecular Biol. and Cytol., USSR Acad. of Scis, 1978. Mem., Hammersmith and Queen Charlotte's SHA, 1982–89. Chm. Organizing Cttee, Hammersmith Internat. Symposium on Molecular Endocrinology, 1967–79; Member: Org Cttee, Hormone and Cell Regulation Symposia, 1976–79; Adv. Council, Workshop on Vitamin D, 1977–79. Pres., Bone and Tooth Soc., 1984–87; Member: Cttee, Soc. for Endocrinology, 1978–80; Biochem. Soc.; NIH Alumni Assoc; Amer. Endocrine Soc.; Amer. Soc. for Bone and Mineral Res.; European Calcified Tissue Soc.; Assoc. of Clin. Biochemists. Vice-Pres.,

English Chess Assoc., 1989–. Member Editorial Board: Clinical Endocrinology, 1975–79; Molecular and Cellular Endocrinology, 1975–80; Jl of Endocrinological Investigation; Jl of Mineral and Electrolyte Metabolism; Jl of Investigative and Cell Pathol.; Jl of Metabolic Bone Disease and Related Res. Hon. MD Turin, 1985. Gairdner Internat. Award, Toronto, 1967; Elsevier Award, Internat. Confs on Calcium Regulating Hormones, Inc., 1992. *Publications:* articles in endocrinology. *Recreations:* tennis, squash, chess, music. *Address:* Great Broadhurst Farm, Broad Oak, Heathfield, East Sussex TN21 8UX. *T:* Burwash (01435) 883515. *Clubs:* Athenæum; Queen's, Hurlingham.

McINTYRE, Ian James; writer and broadcaster; *b* Banchory, Kincardineshire, 9 Dec. 1931; *y s* of late Hector Harold McIntyre, Inverness, and late Annie Mary Michie, Ballater; *m* 1954, Leik Sommerfelt, 2nd *d* of late Benjamin Vogt, Kragerø, Norway; two *s* two *d. Educ:* Prescot Grammar Sch.; St John's Coll., Cambridge (Scholar; Med. and Mod. Langs Tripos, Pts I and II; BA 1953; MA); Coll. of Europe, Bruges. Pres., Cambridge Union, 1953. Commnd, Intelligence Corps, 1955–57. Current affairs talks producer, BBC, 1957; Editor, At Home and Abroad, 1959; Man. Trng Organiser, BBC Staff Trng Dept, 1960; Programme Services Officer, ITA, 1961; staff of Chm., Cons. Party in Scotland, 1962; Dir of Inf. and Res., Scottish Cons. Central Office, 1965; contested (C) Roxburgh, Selkirk and Peebles, 1966; long-term contract, writer and broadcaster, BBC, 1970–76; presenter and interviewer, Analysis, and other programmes on politics, for. affairs and the arts; travelled widely in Europe, N America, Africa, Asia and ME; Controller: BBC Radio 4, 1976–78; BBC Radio 3, 1978–87. Associate Ed., The Times, 1989–90. *Publications:* The Proud Doers: Israel after twenty years, 1968; (ed and contrib.) Words: reflections on the uses of language, 1975; Dogfight: the transatlantic battle over Airbus, 1992; The Expense of Glory: a life of John Reith, 1993; Dirt and Deity: a life of Robert Burns, 1995; articles and book reviews in The Listener, The Times, The Independent. *Recreation:* family life. *Address:* Spylaw House, Newlands Avenue, Radlett, Herts WD7 8EL. *T:* Radlett (01923) 853532. *Clubs:* Beefsteak; Union (Cambridge).

McINTYRE, Very Rev. Prof. John, CVO 1985; DD, DLitt; FRSE; Professor of Divinity, University of Edinburgh, 1956–86, now Emeritus; Dean of the Order of the Thistle, 1974–89; an Extra Chaplain to the Queen in Scotland, 1974–75 and since 1986 (Chaplain to the Queen in Scotland, 1975–86); Moderator of the General Assembly of the Church of Scotland, 1982; *b* 20 May 1916; *s* of late John C. McIntyre, Bathgate, Scotland, and Annie McIntyre; *m* 1945, Jessie B., *d* of late William Buick, Coupar Angus; two *s* one *d. Educ:* Bathgate Academy; University of Edinburgh; MA 1938; BD 1941; DLitt 1953. Ordained, 1941; Locum Tenens, Parish of Glenorchy and Inishail, 1941–43; Minister of Parish of Fenwick, Ayrshire, 1943–45; Hunter Baillie Prof. of Theology, St Andrew's Coll., University of Sydney, 1946–56; Principal of St Andrew's Coll., 1950–56 (Hon. Fellow, 1990); Principal Warden, Pollock Halls of Residence, Univ. of Edinburgh, 1960–71; actg Principal and Vice-Chancellor, Edinburgh Univ., 1973–74, 1979; Principal, New Coll., and Dean of Faculty of Divinity, 1968–74. FRSE 1977 (Vice-Pres., 1983–86). DD *hc* Glasgow, 1961; DHL *hc*, Coll. of Wooster, Ohio, 1983; Dr *hc* Edinburgh, 1987. *Publications:* St Anselm and His Critics, 1954; The Christian Doctrine of History, 1957; On the Love of God, 1962; The Shape of Christology, 1966; Faith, Theology and Imagination, 1987; The Shape of Soteriology, 1992; articles and reviews in various learned jls of Theology. *Address:* 22/4 Minto Street, Edinburgh EH9 1RQ. *T:* 0131–667 1203.

McINTYRE, Sir (Meredith) Alister, Kt 1992; Vice-Chancellor, University of the West Indies, since 1988; *b* Grenada, 29 March 1932; *s* of Meredith McIntyre and Cynthia Eileen McIntyre; *m* Marjorie Hope; three *s* one *d. Educ:* LSE (BSc (Econ) 1st Cl. Hons 1957); Nuffield Coll., Oxford (BLitt 1960). Fulbright-Hays Fellow, Columbia Univ., 1963–64; Asst Prof., Woodrow Wilson Sch. of Public Affairs, Princeton Univ., 1962; University of the West Indies: Lectr in Economics, 1960–64; Sen. Lectr and Chm. of Social Scis, 1964–67; Dir, Inst. of Social and Econ. Res., 1964–74; Sec.-Gen., Caribbean Community Secretariat, 1974–77; Dir, Commodities Div., UNCTAD, 1977–82; Dep. Sec.-Gen., UNCTAD, 1982–87; Asst Sec.-Gen., UN, 1987–88. Hon. LLD West Indies, 1978. Comdr, Order of Distinction (Jamaica), 1975; Cacique's Crown of Honour (Guyana), 1978; Order of Merit (Jamaica), 1992; Order of the Caribbean Community, 1994. *Recreations:* swimming, sailing, reading. *Address:* Office of the Vice-Chancellor, The University of the West Indies, Mona, Kingston 7, Jamaica. *T:* 9272406.

McINTYRE, Prof. Michael Edgeworth, PhD; FRS 1990; Professor of Atmospheric Dynamics, Cambridge University, since 1993; Co-director, Cambridge Centre for Atmospheric Science, since 1992; Science and Engineering Research Council Senior Research Fellow, Cambridge University, since 1992; *b* 28 July 1941; *s* of Archibald Keverall McIntyre and Anne Hartwell McIntyre; *m* 1968, Ruth Hecht; one step *d* two step *s. Educ:* King's High School, Dunedin, NZ; Univ. of Otago, NZ; Trinity Coll., Cambridge. PhD Cantab 1967 (geophysical fluid dynamics); postdoctoral Fellow, Woods Hole Oceanographic Inst., 1967. Research Associate, Dept of Meteorology, MIT, 1967; Cambridge University: Asst Dir of Research, 1969; Res. Fellow, St John's Coll., 1968–71; Univ. Lectr, 1972; Reader in Atmospheric Dynamics, 1987. Member: Atmospheric Sci. Cttee, NERC, 1989–94; Sci. Steering Gp, UK Univs Global Atmos. Modelling Programme, 1990–. Member: Academia Europaea, 1989; Euro. Geophys. Soc., Amer. Geophys. Union, Catgut Acoust. Soc.; FRMetS; Fellow, Amer. Met. Soc., 1991 (Carl-Gustaf Rossby Res. Medal, 1987). *Publications:* numerous papers in professional jls. *Recreations:* music, gliding. *Address:* 98 Windsor Road, Cambridge CB4 3JN.

McINTYRE, Prof. Neil, FRCP; Professor of Medicine, Royal Free Hospital School of Medicine, since 1978; Director of Medical Education, University College London Medical School and Royal Free Hospital School of Medicine, since 1993; Hon. Consultant Physician, Royal Free Hospital, since 1968; *b* 1 May 1934; *s* of John William McIntyre and Catherine (*née* Watkins); *m* 1966, Wendy Ann Kelsey; one *s* one *d. Educ:* Porth County School for Boys; King's Coll. London (BSc 1st Cl. Hons Physiol); King's Coll. Hosp. (MB BS (Hons), MD). House Officer: KCH, 1959; Hammersmith Hosp., 1960; RAF Med. Br. (Flt Lieut), 1960–63; MRC Res. Fellow, Registrar, Lectr in Medicine, Royal Free Hosp., 1963–66; MRC Travelling Fellowship, Harvard Med. Sch., 1966–68; Royal Free Hospital School of Medicine: Sen. Lectr 1968–73, Reader in Medicine 1973–78; Chm., Dept of Medicine, 1983–94; Vice Dean, 1993–. Non-Exec. Dir, N Middlesex Hosp. NHS Trust, 1991–. MRSM 1968. Liveryman, Soc. of Apothecaries, 1971–. Sam E. Roberts Medal, Univ. of Kansas Med. Sch., 1980. *Publications:* Therapeutic Agents and the Liver, 1965; The Problem Orientated Medical Record, 1979; Lipids and Lipoproteins, 1990; Clinical Hepatology, 1991; papers on liver disease, lipoprotein metabolism, med. educn. *Recreations:* reading, photographing medical statues, golf. *Address:* Royal Free Hospital School of Medicine, Pond Street, Hampstead, NW3 2QG. *T:* 0171–794 0500. *Clubs:* Athenæum; Highgate Golf.

McINTYRE, Robert Douglas, MB, ChB (Edinburgh), DPH (Glasgow); JP; Hon. Consultant, Stirling Royal Infirmary (Consultant Chest Physician, Stirlingshire and Clackmannan, 1951–79); Member, Stirling and Clackmannan Hospital Board, 1964–74; *b* Dec. 1913; 3rd *s* of Rev. John E. McIntyre and Catherine, *d* of Rev. William Morison, DD; *m* 1954, Letitia, *d* of Alexander Macleod; one *s. Educ:* Hamilton Acad.; Daniel Stewart's Coll.; University of Edinburgh. MP (Scottish Nationalist), Motherwell and Wishaw, April-July 1945. Contested (SNP): Motherwell, 1950; Perth and E Perthshire, 1951, 1955, 1959, 1964; W Stirlingshire, 1966, 1970; Stirling, Falkirk and Grangemouth, by-election 1971, Feb. and Oct. 1974. Chm., 1948–56, Pres., 1958–80, Scottish National Party; Mem., Stirling Town Council (Hon. Treas., 1958–64, Provost, 1967–75); Chancellor's Assessor, Stirling Univ. Court, 1979–. Fellow, Scottish Council, 1987. Freeman, Royal Burgh of Stirling, 1975. DUniv Stirling 1976. JP Co. Stirling. *Publications:* numerous articles on Scottish, political and medical subjects, including regular contribs to the Scots Independent. *Recreation:* yachting. *Address:* 8 Gladstone Place, Stirling FK8 2NN. *T:* Stirling (01786) 73456. *Clubs:* Scottish Arts (Edinburgh); Stirling and County.

MACINTYRE, William Ian, CB 1992; Head, Telecommunications Division, Department of Trade and Industry, since 1994; *b* 20 July 1943; *s* of late Robert Miller Macintyre, CBE and of Florence Mary Macintyre; *m* 1967, Jennifer Mary Pitblado; one *s* two *d. Educ:* Merchiston Castle School, Edinburgh; St Andrews University. MA. British Petroleum Co. Ltd, 1965–72; ECGD, 1972–73; DTI, later Dept of Energy, 1973–77; seconded to ICFC, 1977–79; Asst Sec., Dept of Energy, Gas Div., 1979–83; Under-Sec. 1983, Dir-Gen., Energy Efficiency Office, 1983–87; Under Sec., Electricity Div., 1987–88, Electricity Div. B, 1988–91, Dept of Energy; Under Sec., Coal Div., Dept of Energy, then DTI, 1991–94. *Address:* Department of Trade and Industry, 151 Buckingham Palace Road, SW1W 9SS.

McINTYRE, William Ian Mackay, CBE 1990; PhD; FRCVS; Professor Emeritus of Veterinary Medicine, University of Glasgow, since 1991 (Senior Lecturer, 1951–61, Professor, 1961–83); *b* 7 July 1919; *s* of George John and Jane McIntyre; *m* 1948, Ruth Dick Galbraith; three *s. Educ:* Altnaharra Primary and Golspie Secondary Sch., Sutherland; Royal (Dick) Veterinary Coll. (MRCVS); University of Edinburgh (PhD). FRCVS 1983. Clinical Asst, Royal (Dick) Veterinary Coll., 1944–48; Lectr, Vet. Med., Royal (Dick) Vet. Coll., 1948–51. Seconded to University of East Africa, University Coll., Nairobi, as Dean, Faculty of Veterinary Science, and Prof., Clinical Studies, 1963–67. Dir, International Trypanotolerance Centre, The Gambia, 1984–89. Hon. DVM Justus Liebig Univ., Giessen, 1987. *Publications:* various, on canine nephritis, parasitic diseases and vaccines, clinical communications, and African Trypanosomiasis. *Address:* Stuckenduff, Shandon, Helensburgh G84 8NW. *T:* Rhu (01436) 820571.

McIVOR, Rt. Hon. Basil; *see* McIvor, Rt Hon. W. B.

McIVOR, Donald Kenneth; Director and Senior Vice-President, Exxon Corporation, Irving, Texas (formerly New York), since 1985; *b* 12 April 1928; *s* of Kenneth MacIver McIvor and Nellie Beatrice McIvor (*née* Rutherford); *m* 1953, Avonia Isabel Forbes; four *s* one *d. Educ:* Univ. of Manitoba (BSc Hons in Geol.). Joined Imperial Oil, 1950; operational and res. assignments, Exploration Dept, 1950–58; gen. planning and res. management positions, 1958–68; Asst Manager and Manager, Corporate Planning, 1968–70; Exploration Manager, 1970–72; Nat. Defence Coll., 1972–73; Sen. Vice-Pres., 1973–75; Exec. Vice-Pres., 1975–77; Vice-Pres., oil and gas exploration and prodn, Exxon Corp., NY, 1977–81; Dep. Chm., Imperial Oil, 1981; Chm. and Chief Exec. Officer, Imperial Oil, 1982–85. *Address:* (office) 225 East John W. Carpenter Freeway, Irving, TX 75062, USA.

McIVOR, (Frances) Jill, CBE 1994; Northern Ireland Parliamentary Commissioner for Administration and for Complaints, since 1991; *b* 10 Aug. 1930; *d* of Cecil Reginald Johnston Anderson and Frances Ellen (*née* Henderson); *m* 1953, William Basil McIvor, *qv*; two *s* one *d. Educ:* Methodist Coll.; Lurgan Coll.; Queen's Univ. of Belfast (LLB Hons). Called to Bar of Northern Ireland, 1980. Asst Librarian (Law), QUB, 1954–55; Tutor in Legal Res., Law Faculty, QUB, 1965–74; editorial staff, NI Legal Qtly, 1966–76; Librarian, Dept of Dir of Public Prosecutions, 1977–79. NI Mem., IBA, 1980–86; Dep. Chm., Radio Authy, 1990–94. Chm., Lagan Valley Regional Park Cttee, 1984–89 (Mem., 1975); Member: Ulster Countryside Cttee, 1984–89; Fair Employment Agency, 1984–89; Fair Employment Commn, 1990–91; Lay Panel, Juvenile Court, 1976–77; GDC, 1979–91; Exec., Belfast Voluntary Welfare Soc., 1981–88; Adv. Council, 1985–90, Bd, 1987–90, Co-operation North; Adv. Panel on Community Radio, 1985–86; NI Adv. Cttee, British Council, 1986–. Chairman: Ulster–NZ Trust, 1987–; Educnl Guidance Service for Adults, 1988–90. Mem. Bd of Visitors, QUB, 1988–. FRSA 1988. QSM 1993. *Publications:* Irish Consultant (and contrib.), Manual of Law Librarianship, 1976; (ed) Elegantia Juris: selected writings of F. H. Newark, 1973; Chart of the English Reports (new edn), 1982. *Recreations:* New Zealand, gardening. *Address:* 98 Spa Road, Ballynahinch, Co. Down BT24 8PP. *T:* Ballynahinch (01238) 563534. *Club:* Royal Over-Seas League.

McIVOR, Rt. Hon. (William) Basil, OBE 1991; PC (NI) 1971; *b* 17 June 1928; 2nd *s* of Rev. Frederick McIvor, Methodist clergyman and Lilly McIvor; *m* 1953, Frances Jill Anderson (*see* F. J. McIvor); two *s* one *d. Educ:* Methodist Coll., Belfast; Queen's Univ., Belfast. LLB 1948. Called to NI Bar, 1950; Jun. Crown Counsel, Co. Down, Sept. 1974, Resident Magistrate, Dec. 1974. MP (UU) Larkfield, NI Parlt, 1969; Minister of Community Relations, NI, 1971–72; Member (UU) for S Belfast, NI Assembly, 1973–75; Minister of Education, NI, 1974. Founder Mem., 1976–, Chm., 1988–, Fold Housing Assoc. Chm., All Children Together (the pioneering movement for integrated educn by consent), 1990–92 (Mem., 1974–). Governor, Campbell Coll., 1975– (Chm., 1983–85); Chm. Bd of Governors, Lagan Coll., Belfast, 1981– (the first integrated RC and Protestant school in NI). *Recreations:* golf, music, gardening. *Address:* Larkhill, 98 Spa Road, Ballynahinch, Co. Down BT24 8PP. *T:* Ballynahinch (01238) 563534. *Club:* Commonwealth Trust.

MACK, Brian John, DPhil; FSA; Keeper of Ethnography, British Museum, since 1991; *b* 10 July 1949; *s* of Brian Mack and Joan Alexandra Mack (*née* Kelly); *m* 1975, Caroline Jenkins; one *s* one *d. Educ:* Campbell Coll., Belfast; Univ. of Sussex (MA); Merton Coll., Oxford (DPhil 1975). FSA 1994. Res. Asst, 1976, Asst Keeper, 1977, Dept of Ethnography, BM. Member: Council, British Inst. in Eastern Africa, 1981–; Council, RAI, 1983–86; Council, African Studies Assoc., 1986–88. Mem. Editl Bd, Art History, 1982–91. Nat. Art Collections Fund Award for Images of Africa, BM, 1991. *Publications:* (with J. Picton) African Textiles (Craft Adv. Council Book of the Year), 1979, 2nd edn 1989; Zulus, 1980; (with P. T. Robertshaw) Culture History in the Southern Sudan, 1982; (with M. D. McLeod) Ethnic Sculpture, 1984; Madagascar, Island of the Ancestors, 1986; Ethnic Jewellery, 1988; Malagasy Textiles, 1989; Emil Torday and the Art of the Congo 1900–1909, 1990; (with C. Spring) African Textile Design, 1991; Masks, the Art of Expression, 1994; articles and revs in learned jls. *Address:* 6 Burlington Gardens, W1X 2EX. *T:* 0171–636 1555.

MACK, Keith Robert; Director-General, European Organisation for the Safety of Air Navigation (Eurocontrol), 1989–93; *b* 2 March 1933; *s* of late David Stanley Mack and Dorothy Ivy Mack (*née* Bowes); *m* 1960, Eileen Mary Cuttell; two *s* four *d. Educ:* Edmonton County School. RAF Pilot, 1951–58; Civilian Air Traffic Control Officer, Scottish and Oceanic Air Traffic Control Centre, 1960–67; RAF Staff College, Bracknell, 1968; NATS HQ, 1969–71; ATC Watch Supervisor, Scottish ATCC, 1972–73; CAA Chief Officer, Cardiff Airport, 1974; NATS HQ, 1975–76; ATC Watch Supervisor, London ATCC, 1977; NATS Dep. Dir of Control (Airspace Policy), 1978–79; Supt,

London ATCC, 1980–82; Dep. Controller, NATS, 1983–84; Mem. (full-time) and Gp Dir, CAA, and Controller, NATS, 1985–88. *Recreations:* music, walking, photography. *Address:* 67 Forest House, Russell-Cotes Road, Bournemouth BH1 3UB.

MACK SMITH, Denis, CBE 1990; FBA 1976; FRSL; Extraordinary Fellow, Wolfson College, Oxford, since 1987; Emeritus Fellow, All Souls Coll., Oxford, 1987; *b* 3 March 1920; *s* of Wilfrid Mack Smith and Altiora Gauntlett; *m* 1963, Catharine Stevenson; two *d*. *Educ:* St Paul's Cathedral Choir Sch.; Haileybury Coll.; Peterhouse, Cambridge Univ. (organ and history schols). MA Cantab, MA Oxon. Asst Master, Clifton Coll., 1941–42; Cabinet Offices, 1942–46; Fellow of Peterhouse, Cambridge, 1947–62 (Hon. Fellow, 1986); Tutor of Peterhouse, 1948–58; Univ. Lectr, Cambridge, 1952–62; Sen. Res. Fellow, 1962–87, Sub-Warden, 1984–86, All Souls Coll., Oxford. Chm., Assoc. for Study of Modern Italy, 1987–. For. Hon. Mem., Amer. Acad. of Arts and Sciences. Commendatore dell'Ordine al Merito della Repubblica Italiana; Public Orator of the Repubblica di San Marino, 1982. Awards: Thirlwall, 1949; Serena, 1960; Elba, 1972; Villa di Chiesa, 1973; Mondello, 1975; Nove Muse, 1976; Duff Cooper Meml., 1977; Wolfson Literary, 1977; Rhegium Julii, 1983; Polifemo d'Argento, 1988; Fregene, 1990. *Publications:* Cavour and Garibaldi 1860, 1954, enlarged 2nd edn 1985; Garibaldi, 1957; (jtly) British Interests in the Mediterranean and Middle East, 1958; Italy, a Modern History, 1959 (enlarged edn 1969); Medieval Sicily, 1968; Modern Sicily, 1968; Da Cavour a Mussolini, 1968; (ed) The Making of Italy 1796–1870, 1968, 2nd edn 1988; (ed) Garibaldi, 1969; (ed) E. Quinet, Le Rivoluzioni d'Italia, 1970; Victor Emanuel, Cavour and the Risorgimento, 1971; (ed) G. La Farina, Scritti Politici, 1972; Vittorio Emanuele II, 1972, 2nd edn 1994; Mussolini's Roman Empire, 1976; (jtly) Un Monumento al Duce, 1976; Cento Anni di Vita Italiana attraverso il Corriere della Sera, 1978; L'Italia del Ventesimo Secolo, 1978; (ed) G. Bandi, I mille: da Genova a Capua, 1981; Mussolini, 1981; (ed) F. De Sanctis, Un Viaggio Elettorale, 1983; Cavour, 1985; (jtly) A History of Sicily, 1986; Italy and its Monarchy, 1989; Mazzini, 1993; Jt Editor, Nelson History of England, 1962–. *Address:* White Lodge, Osler Road, Headington, Oxford OX3 9BJ. *T:* Oxford (01865) 62878.

McKAIG, Adm. Sir (John) Rae, KCB 1973; CBE 1966; *b* 24 April 1922; *s* of late Sir John McKaig, KCB, DSO, and Lady (Annie Wright) McKaig (*née* Lee); *m* 1945, Barbara Dawn, *d* of Dr F. K. Marriott, MC, Yoxford, Suffolk; two *s* one *d*. *Educ:* Loretto Sch. Joined RN as Special Entry Cadet, 1939; served in cruisers and destroyers in Home and Mediterranean Waters, 1940–43; in Amphibious Force S at invasion of Normandy, 1944; in coastal forces until 1945; qual. in Communications, 1945; Commander, 1952; Captain, 1959; served as Dep. to Chief Polaris Exec., 1963–66; comd HM Signal Sch., 1966–68; Rear-Adm., 1968; Asst Chief of Naval Staff (Operational Requirements), 1968–70; Vice-Adm., 1970; Flag Officer, Plymouth, and Port Admiral, Devonport, 1970–73; Adm., 1973; UK Mil. Rep. to NATO, 1973–75. Chm. and Chief Exec., Gray Mackenzie & Co., 1983–86; Dir, Inchcape plc, 1981–86. Mem., Royal Patriotic Fund Corp., 1978–. Dir, ALVA, 1989–92. *Recreations:* offshore sailing, shooting, fishing. *Clubs:* Army and Navy, Royal Ocean Racing.

McKANE, Prof. William, FRSE 1984; FBA 1980; Professor of Hebrew and Oriental Languages, University of St Andrews, 1968–90, now Emeritus; Principal of St Mary's College, St Andrews, 1982–86; *b* 18 Feb. 1921; *s* of Thomas McKane and Jemima Smith McKane; *m* 1952, Agnes Mathie Howie; three *s* two *d*. *Educ:* Univ. of St Andrews (MA 1949); Univ. of Glasgow (MA 1952, PhD 1956, DLitt 1980). RAF, 1941–45. University of Glasgow: Asst in Hebrew, 1953–56; Lectr in Hebrew, 1956–65; Sen. Lectr, 1965–68; Dean, Faculty of Divinity, St Andrews, 1973–77. Fellow, Nat. Humanities Center, NC, USA, 1987–88. Foreign Sec., Soc. for Old Testament Study, 1981–86 (Pres., 1978); Chm., Peshitta project (Old Testament in Syriac), Internat. Org. for Study of Old Testament. DD (*hc*) Edinburgh, 1984. Burkitt Medal, British Acad., 1985. *Publications:* Prophets and Wise Men, 1965; Proverbs: a new approach, 1970; Studies in the Patriarchal Narratives, 1979; Jeremiah 1–25 (International Critical Commentary series), 1986; Selected Christian Hebraists, 1989; articles and reviews in British and European learned jls. *Recreations:* St Andrews association football blue (1949), walking. *Address:* 51 Irvine Crescent, St Andrews, Fife KY16 8LG. *T:* St Andrews (01334) 73797. *Club:* Royal and Ancient Golf (St Andrews).

MACKANESS, George Bellamy, MB, BS, DPhil; FRS 1976; President, Squibb Institute for Medical Research and Development, 1976–87, retired; *b* Sydney, Australia, 20 Aug. 1922; *s* of James V. Mackaness and Eleanor F. Mackaness; *m* 1945, Gwynneth Patterson; one *s*. *Educ:* Sydney Univ. (MB, BS Hons 1945); London Univ. (DCP 1948); Univ. of Oxford (Hon. MA 1949, DPhil 1953). Resident MO, Sydney Hosp., 1945–46; Resident Pathologist, Kanematsu Inst. of Pathology, Sydney Hosp., 1946–47; Dept of Path., Brit. Postgrad. Med. Sch., London Univ., 1947–48 (DCP); ANU Trav. Scholarship, Univ. of Oxford, 1948–51; Demonstrator and Tutor in Path., Sir William Dunn Sch. of Path., Oxford, 1949–53; Dept of Experimental Pathology, Australian National University: Sen. Fellow, 1954–58; Associate Prof. of Exp. Path., 1958–60; Professorial Fellow, 1960–63; Vis. Investigator, Rockefeller Univ., NY, 1959–60; Prof. of Microbiology, Univ. of Adelaide, 1963–65; Dir, Trudeau Inst. for Med. Res., NY, 1965–76; Adjunct Prof. of Path., NY Univ. Med. Center, 1969–. Director: Josiah Macy Jr Foundn, 1982–86; Squibb Corp., 1984–87. Member: Allergy and Immunol. Study Sect., Nat. Insts of Health, 1967–71; Bd of Sci. Counsellors, Nat. Inst. of Allergy and Infect. Diseases, 1971–75; Armed Forces Epidemicol Bd, 1967–73; Bd of Governors, W. Alton Jones Cell Science Center, 1970–72; Council, Tissue Culture Assoc., 1973–; Bd of Sci. Consultants, Sloan-Kettering Inst. Member: Amer. Assoc. of Immunologists; Amer. Assoc. for Advancement of Science; Reticuloendothelial Soc.; Lung Assoc.; Internat. Union Against Tuberculosis; Amer. Soc. of Microbiologists. Fellow, Amer. Acad. of Arts and Scis, 1978. Paul Ehrlich-Ludwig Darmstaedter Prize, 1975. *Address:* 2783 Little Creek, Johns Island, SC 29455, USA. *T:* (803) 7681620.

MACKAY, family name of **Earl of Inchcape, Lord Reay** and **Barons Mackay of Ardbrecknish, Mackay of Clashfern** and **Tanlaw.**

MACKAY OF ARDBRECKNISH, Baron *cr* 1991 (Life Peer), of Tayvallich in the District of Argyll and Bute; **John Jackson Mackay;** Minister of State, Department of Social Security, since 1994; *b* 15 Nov. 1938; *s* of Jackson and Jean Mackay; *m* 1961, Sheena Wagner; two *s* one *d*. *Educ:* Glasgow Univ. (BSc, DipEd). Formerly, Head of Maths Dept, Oban High Sch.; Chief Exec., Scottish Cons. Central Office, 1987–90; Chm., Sea Fish Industry Authy, 1990–93. MP (C): Argyll, 1979–83; Argyll and Bute, 1983–87; Parly Under-Sec. of State, Scottish Office, 1982–87; a Lord in Waiting (Govt Whip), 1993–94; Parly Under-Sec. of State, Dept of Transport, 1994. Member: H of L Select Cttee on EC, 1991–93; H of L Sub-Cttee on Energy, Industry and Transport, 1991–93; H of L Delegated Powers Scrutiny Cttee, 1992–93. Pres., Glasgow Bn, Boys' Brigade, 1993–. *Recreations:* fishing, sailing. *Address:* Innishail, 51 Springkell Drive, Pollokshields, Glasgow G41 4EZ.

MACKAY OF CLASHFERN, Baron *cr* 1979 (Life Peer), of Eddrachillis in the District of Sutherland; **James Peter Hymers Mackay;** PC 1979; FRSE 1984; Lord High Chancellor of Great Britain, since 1987; *b* 2 July 1927; *s* of James Mackay and Janet Hymers; *m* 1958, Elizabeth Gunn Hymers; one *s* two *d*. *Educ:* George Heriot's Sch., Edinburgh. MA Hons Maths and Nat. Philosophy, Edinburgh Univ., 1948; Lectr in Mathematics, Univ. of St Andrews, 1948–50; Major Schol., Trinity Coll., Cambridge, in Mathematics, 1947, taken up 1950; Senior Schol. 1951; BA (Cantab) 1952; LLB Edinburgh (with Distinction) 1955. Admitted to Faculty of Advocates, 1955; QC (Scot.) 1965; Standing Junior Counsel to: Queen's and Lord Treasurer's Remembrancer; Scottish Home and Health Dept; Commissioners of Inland Revenue in Scotland; Sheriff Principal, Renfrew and Argyll, 1972–74; Vice-Dean, Faculty of Advocates, 1973–76; Dean, 1976–79; Lord Advocate of Scotland, 1979–84; a Senator of Coll. of Justice in Scotland, 1984–85; a Lord of Appeal in Ordinary, 1985–87. Chancellor, Heriot-Watt Univ., 1991–. Part-time Mem., Scottish Law Commn, 1976–79. Hon. Master of the Bench, Inner Temple, 1979. Fellow: Internat. Acad. of Trial Lawyers, 1979; Inst. of Taxation, 1981; Amer. Coll. of Trial Lawyers, 1990. Dir, Stenhouse Holdings Ltd, 1976–77. Mem., Insurance Brokers' Registration Council, 1977–79. A Comr of Northern Lighthouses, 1975–84; Elder Brother of Trinity House, 1990. Hon. Mem., SPTL, 1986. Hon. Fellow: Trinity Coll., Cambridge, 1989; Girton Coll., Cambridge, 1990; Hon. FRCSE, 1989; Hon. FRCP 1990; Hon. FICE, 1988. Hon. LLD: Edinburgh, 1983; Dundee, 1983; Strathclyde, 1985; Aberdeen, 1987; St Andrews, 1989; Cambridge, 1989; Coll. of William and Mary, Va, 1989; Birmingham, 1990; Hon. DCL Newcastle, 1990. *Publication:* Armour on Valuation for Rating, 5th edn (Consultant Editor), 1985. *Recreation:* walking. *Address:* Lord Chancellor's Residence, House of Lords, SW1A 0PW. *Clubs:* Athenæum; New (Edinburgh).

MACKAY, Prof. Alan Lindsay, FRS 1988; Professor of Crystallography, Birkbeck College, University of London, 1986–91, now Emeritus; *b* 6 Sept. 1926; *s* of Robert Lindsay Mackay, OBE, MC, BSc, MD and Margaret Brown Mackay, OBE, MB ChB, JP; *m* 1951, Sheila Thorne Hague, MA; two *s* one *d*. *Educ:* Wolverhampton Grammar Sch.; Oundle Sch.; Trinity Coll., Cambridge (BA, MA); BSc, PhD, DSc London. Lectr, Reader, Prof., Dept of Crystallography, Birkbeck Coll., 1951–91. Visiting Professor: Univ. of Tokyo, 1969; Univ. of Tsukuba, 1980; Korean Advanced Inst. of Sci. and Tech., 1987; Hon. Professor: Central China Univ; Sichuan Inst. of Sci. Studies; China Inst. for Sci. Studies; Univ. de Paris-Sud, 1989. Zaheer Lectr, New Delhi, 1977. *Publications:* The Harvest of a Quiet Eye, 1977; (with A. N. Barrett) Spatial Structure and the Microcomputer, 1987; (ed) A Dictionary of Scientific Quotations, 1991; papers in learned jls. *Recreation:* Asian studies. *Address:* 22 Lanchester Road, N6 4TA. *T:* 0181–883 4810.

MACKAY, Alastair, CMG 1966; *b* 27 Sept. 1911; *s* of late Alexander Mackay; *m* 1st, 1939, Janetta Brown Ramsay (*d* 1973); one *s* one *d*; 2nd, 1975, Edith Whicher. *Educ:* George Heriot's Sch.; Edinburgh Univ.; Berlin Univ. Entered HM Treasury, 1940. Member UK Treasury and Supply Delegation, Washington, 1951–54; seconded to Foreign Service Inspectorate, 1957–59; Financial Adviser to the British High Commissioner in India, 1963–66; Under-Sec., HM Treasury, 1967–71; Financial and Development Sec., Gibraltar, 1971–75. *Recreation:* the garden. *Address:* Hazeldown Cottage, Church Lane, Osmington, Dorset DT3 6EJ.

McKAY, Prof. Alexander Gordon, OC 1988; FRSC 1965; Professor of Classics, McMaster University, 1957–90, now Emeritus; Adjunct Professor of Humanities, since 1990, and Fellow, Vanier College, since 1992, York University; President, Royal Society of Canada, 1984–87; *b* 24 Dec. 1924; *s* of Alexander Lynn McKay and Marjory Maude Redfern Nicoll McKay; *m* 1964, Helen Jean Zulauf; two step *d*. *Educ:* Trinity Coll., Toronto (Hons BA Classics 1946); Yale Univ. (MA 1947); Princeton Univ. (AM 1948; PhD 1950). Classics faculty: Wells Coll., NY, 1949–50; Univ. of Pennsylvania, 1950–51; Univ. of Manitoba, 1951–52; Mount Allison Univ., 1952–53; Waterloo Coll., Ont., 1953–55; Univ. of Manitoba, 1955–57; McMaster Univ., 1957–90: Chm. of Dept, 1962–68, 1976–79; Founding Dean of Humanities, 1968–73; Senator, 1968–73, 1985–87. Dist. Vis. Prof., Univ. of Colorado, 1973; Prof. i/c, Intercollegiate Center for Classical Studies in Rome (Stanford Univ.), 1975, Mem. Inst. for Advanced Study, Princeton, 1979, 1981; Vis. Schol., Univ. of Texas, Austin, 1987; Vis. Fellow Commoner, Trinity Coll., Cambridge, 1988; Distinguished Vis. Lectr, Concordia Univ., Montreal, 1992–93. Dir, Internat. Union of Academies, 1980–83, 1986–90 (Vice-Pres., 1983–86). Hon. LLD: Manitoba, 1986; Brock Univ., Ont, 1990; Queen's Univ., Kingston, 1991; Hon. DLitt: McMaster, 1992; Waterloo, 1993. KStJ 1986. Silver Jubilee Medal, 1977; 125th Anniversary of the Confederation of Canada Medal, 1992. *Publications:* Naples and Campania: texts and illustrations, 1962; Roman Lyric Poetry: Catullus and Horace, 1962; Vergil's Italy, 1970; Cumae and the Phlegraean Fields, 1972; Naples and Coastal Campania, 1972; Houses, Villas and Palaces in the Roman World, 1975, German edn 1980; Roman Satire, 1976; Vitruvius, Architect and Engineer, 1978; Roma Antiqua: Latium and Etruria, 1986; Selections from Vergil's Aeneid Books I, IV, VI: Dido and Aeneas, 1988; Tragedy, Love and Change, 1994. *Recreations:* pianoforte, travel. *Address:* 1 Turner Avenue, Hamilton, Ont L8P 3K4, Canada. *T:* (905) 5261331, *Fax:* (905) 5269245. *Clubs:* Yale (NY); University (Pittsburgh); Tamahaac (Ancaster, Hamilton); Arts and Letters, X, (Toronto); President's (McMaster Univ.).

McKAY, Maj.-Gen. Alexander Matthew, CB 1975; FEng 1984; Secretary, Institution of Mechanical Engineers, 1976–87; *b* 14 Feb. 1921; *s* of Colin and Anne McKay; *m* 1949, Betty Margaret Lee; one *s* one *d* (and one *d* decd). *Educ:* Esplanade House Sch.; RN Dockyard Sch.; Portsmouth Polytechnic. FIEE, FIMechE; psc, sm; MASME. Served War of 1939–45 (despatches); Palestine, 1945–48 (despatches); Malaya, 1954–56; with 16th Indep Para. Bde Gp and 6th Airborne Div.; Staff Coll., Quetta, 1954; staff appts include GS02, DAA&QMG, DAQMG, AQMG; Dir, Elect. and Mech. Engrg, Army, 1972–75; Col Comdt, REME, 1974–80. 2nd Lieut, 1943; Lieut 1944; Captain 1944; Major 1947; Lt-Col 1960; Col 1966; Brigadier 1968; Maj.-Gen. 1972. Gen. Sec., IChemE, 1975–76. Mem. Council, IEE, 1973–76. Chm., Stocklake Hldgs 1976–87; Vice-Chm., Mechanical Engrg Publications Ltd, 1976–87. Pres. and Chm., Winchester Div., SSAFA, 1988–; Vice-Pres., Itchen Valley Br., RBL, 1992–. FRSE, 1985. Freeman, City of London, 1984; Liveryman, Engineers' Co., 1984–88. *Publications:* papers in Proceedings IMechE and REME Institution. *Recreations:* fly fishing, gardening, restoring antique furniture. *Address:* Church Cottage, Martyr Worthy, near Winchester, Hants SO21 1DY.

McKAY, Allan George; Director of Information Services, British Gas, since 1994; *b* 5 Sept. 1935; *s* of George Allan McKay and Wilhelmina McKay; *m* 1962, Margaret Currie Baxter; one *s* two *d*. *Educ:* Royal High School, Edinburgh. FCCA, ACIS, CIGasE. Accountant, Scottish Gas Board, 1961; Dir of Finance, Scottish Gas, 1975; Deputy Chairman: British Gas East Midlands, 1982; British Gas North Thames, 1987; Chairman: British Gas North Eastern, 1989; British Gas North Western, 1993. *Recreation:* golf. *Address:* British Gas plc, 51 Homer Road, Solihull, West Midlands B91 3QJ. *T:* 0121–712 4401.

McKAY, Allen; JP; *b* 5 Feb. 1927; *s* of Fred and Martha Anne McKay; *m* 1949, June Simpson; one *s*. *Educ:* Hoyland Kirk Balk Secondary Modern School; extramural studies, Univ. of Sheffield. Clerical work, Steel Works, 1941–45; general mineworker, 1945–47; Mining Electrical Engineer, 1947–65; NCB Industrial Relations Trainee, 1965–66; Asst Manpower Officer, Barnsley Area, NCB, 1966–78. MP (Lab) Penistone, July 1978–1983;

Barnsley West and Penistone, 1983–92. Opposition Whip, 1981. JP Barnsley, 1971. *Recreation:* reading. *Address:* 24 Springwood Road, Hoyland, Barnsley, South Yorks S74 0AZ. *T:* Barnsley (01226) 743418.

MacKAY, Andrew James; MP (C) Berkshire East, since 1983; a Lord Commissioner of HM Treasury (Government Whip), since 1993; *b* 27 Aug. 1949; *s* of Robert James MacKay and Olive Margaret MacKay; *m* 1975, Diana Joy (*née* Kinchin) one *s* one *d*. *Educ:* Solihull. MP (C) Birmingham, Stechford, Mar. 1977–1979; PPS to Sec. of State for NI, 1986–89, to Sec. of State for Defence, 1989–92; an Asst Govt Whip, 1992–93. Mem., Environment Select Cttee, 1985–86; Sec., Cons. Parly For. Affairs Cttee, 1985–86. Mem., Conservative Party Nat. Exec., 1979–82. *Recreations:* golf, squash, good food. *Address:* House of Commons, SW1A 0AA. *T:* 0171–219 4109. *Clubs:* Berkshire Golf; Aberdovey Golf; Royal & Ancient Golf (St Andrews).

MACKAY, Prof. Angus Iain Kenneth, PhD; FRHistS; FBA 1991; Professor of History, University of Edinburgh, since 1985; *b* 1936; *m* 1962; one *s* one *d*. *Educ:* Edinburgh Univ. (MA 1962; PhD 1969). Lectr, Reading Univ., 1965–69; Lectr, then Sen. Lectr, 1969–82, Reader, 1982–85, Edinburgh Univ. *Publications:* Spain in the Middle Ages, 1977; Money, Prices and Politics in Fifteenth-century Castile, 1981; Society, Economy and Religion in late Mediaeval Castile, 1987; (with R. Bartlett) Mediaeval Frontier Societies, 1989; contribs to learned jls. *Address:* Department of History, University of Edinburgh, William Robertson Building, 50 George Square, Edinburgh EH8 9JY.

McKAY, Archibald Charles; Sheriff of Glasgow and Strathkelvin, 1979–95; *b* 18 Oct. 1929; *s* of Patrick McKay and Catherine (*née* McKinlay); *m* 1956, Ernestine Maria Tobia; one *s* three *d*. *Educ:* Knocknacarry, Co. Antrim; St Aloysius' Coll., Glasgow; Glasgow Univ. (MA, LLB 1954). National Service commn, 1955–56. Started practice in Glasgow as solicitor, 1957; estabd own firm of solicitors, 1961; apptd to the Bench, 1978. Pres., Glasgow Bar Assoc., 1967–68. *Recreations:* flying, motor cycling, amateur radio, tennis. *Address:* 96 Springkell Avenue, Pollokshields, Glasgow G41 4EL. *T:* 0141–427 1525.

MACKAY, A(rthur) Stewart, ROI 1949; Teacher, Hammersmith College of Art, 1960–68, retired; *b* 25 Feb. 1909; British. *Educ:* Wilson's Grammar Sch.; Regent Street Polytechnic School of Art. Art Master, Regent Street Polytechnic School of Art, 1936, Assistant Lecturer, 1936–60. Served War of 1939–45: enlisted Army, Jan. 1942; released with rank of Captain, 1946. Exhibitor: RA (44 pictures exhibited); Paris Salon; ROI; RBA; Leicester Galleries; Imperial War Museum; Royal Scottish Academy; New York. *Publications:* How to Make Lino Cuts, 1935; articles for Artist and Kent Life, 1953, 1963. *Recreations:* reading, writing, archaeology. *Address:* 4 Dog Kennel Hill, East Dulwich, SE22 8AA.

MACKAY, Charles, CB 1986; FIBiol; Chief Agricultural Officer, Department of Agriculture and Fisheries for Scotland, 1975–87; *b* 12 Jan. 1927; *s* of Hugh and Eliza Mackay; *m* 1956, Marie A. K. Mackay (*née* Mitchell); one *s* one *d*. *Educ:* Strathmore Sch., Sutherland; Lairg Higher Grade Sch., Sutherland; Univ. of Aberdeen (BScAgric); Univ. of Kentucky (MSc). Department of Agriculture and Fisheries for Scotland: Temporary Inspector, 1947–48; Asst Inspector, 1948–54; Inspector, 1954–64; Sen. Inspector, 1964–70; Technical Develt Officer, 1970–73; Dep. Chief Agricl Officer, 1973–75. Hon. Order of Kentucky Colonels, 1960. *Recreations:* fishing, golf. *Address:* 4/3 Craufurdland, Edinburgh EH4 6DL. *T:* 0131–339 8770.

MACKAY, Charles Dorsey; Deputy Chairman, Inchcape plc, since 1995 (Chief Executive, 1991–95); *b* 14 April 1940; *s* of late Brig. Kenneth Mackay, CBE, DSO and Evelyn Maud (*née* Ingram); *m* 1964, Annmarie Joder-Pfeiffer; one *s* one *d* (and one *s* decd). *Educ:* Cheltenham Coll.; Queens' Coll., Cambridge (MA); INSEAD (MBA). British Petroleum Co., 1957–69; commercial apprentice, 1957–59; univ. apprentice, Cambridge, 1959–62; marketing assistant, London, 1962–63; Regl Sales Manager, Algeria, 1963–65; Commercial Dir, Burundi/Rwanda/Zaire, 1965–68; sponsored at INSEAD, France, 1968–69; McKinsey & Co. Inc., 1969–76: Consultant; Sen. Engagement Manager, 1972–76; worked in London, Paris, Amsterdam, Dar es Salaam; Pakhoed Holding NV, Rotterdam, 1976–81: Dir, 1976–77, Chm., 1977–81, Paktrans Div.; Chloride Group plc, 1981–86: Dir, 1981–86; Chm., Overseas Div., 1981–85; Chm., Power Electronics Div., 1985–86; Inchcape plc, 1986–: Dir, 1986–; Chm., Inchcape (Hong Kong) Ltd and Dodwell and Co. Ltd, 1986–87; Chm. and Chief Exec., Inchcape Pacific Ltd, 1987–91. *Recreations:* travel, tennis, ski-ing, classical music, opera, chess. *Address:* Inchcape plc, St James's House, 23 King Street, SW1Y 6QY. *T:* 0171–321 0110. *Clubs:* Hong Kong (Hong Kong).

MACKAY, Colin Crichton; QC 1989; a Recorder, since 1992; *b* 26 Sept. 1943; *s* of Sir James Mackerron Mackay, KBE, CB, and Katherine Millar Crichton Mackay (*née* Hamilton); *m* 1969, Rosamond Diana Elizabeth Collins; one *d* two *s*. *Educ:* Radley Coll.; Corpus Christi Coll., Oxford (Open Classical Schol; MA). Harmsworth Entrance Exhibnr, 1965, and Astbury Schol., 1967; called to the Bar, Middle Temple, 1967, Bencher, 1995. *Recreations:* opera, sport, Scotland. *Address:* 39 Essex Street, WC2R 3AT. *T:* 0171–583 1111. *Club:* Vincent's (Oxford).

McKAY, Sheriff Colin Graham; Sheriff of North Strathclyde (Floater), since 1990; *b* 20 Jan. 1942; *s* of Patrick Joseph McKay and Mary Kieran; *m* 1966, Sandra Anne Coli; one *d* one *s*. *Educ:* St Aloysius' Coll., Glasgow; Clongowes Wood Coll., by Dublin; Univ. of Glasgow (MA, LLB). Admitted Solicitor, 1966; in private practice, 1966–90; Temporary Sheriff, 1985–90. *Recreations:* sailing, hillwalking, watching Rugby. *Address:* Sheriff Court House, St James Street, Paisley PA3 2HW.

MACKAY, David Ian; His Honour Judge Mackay; a Circuit Judge, since 1992; *b* 11 Nov. 1945; *s* of David and Jessie Mackay, Higher Tranmere, Birkenhead; *m* 1974, Mary Elizabeth Smith; one *s* two *d*. *Educ:* Birkenhead Sch.; Brasenose Coll., Oxford (Schol.; BA Jurisprudence 1968; MA 1992). Called to the Bar, Inner Temple, 1969; practised on Northern Circuit, 1970–92; Asst Recorder, 1986–89; Recorder, 1989–92. Legal Mem., Mental Health Rev. Tribunal, 1988–. Gov., Birkenhead Sch., 1979– (Chm., 1991–). *Recreations:* history, transport, France. *Address:* Queen Elizabeth II Law Courts, Derby Square, Liverpool L2 1XA. *Club:* Athenæum (Liverpool).

MACKAY, Donald George; Hon. Research Fellow, Aberdeen University, since 1990; *b* 25 Nov. 1929; *s* of William Morton Mackay and Annie Tainsh Higgs; *m* 1965, Elizabeth Ailsa Barr; two *s* one *d*. *Educ:* Morgan Academy, Dundee; St Andrews Univ. (MA); Aberdeen Univ. (PhD 1994). Assistant Principal, Scottish Home Dept, 1953; Asst Private Sec. to Sec. of State for Scotland, 1959–60; Asst Sec., Royal Commn on the Police, 1960–62; Principal, SHHD, 1962–66; Sec., Royal Commission on Local Govt in Scotland, 1966–69; Asst Sec., Scottish Develt Dept, 1969–79; Asst Sec., 1980–83, Under Sec., 1983–85, Dept of Agric. and Fisheries for Scotland; Under Sec., Scottish Develt Dept., 1985–88. Mem., Scottish Agricl Wages Bd, 1991–. *Publication:* Rural Land Use Agencies in Scotland, 1995. *Recreations:* hill walking, photography, music. *Address:* 38 Cluny Drive, Edinburgh EH10 6DX. *T:* 0131–447 1851.

MacKAY, Prof. Donald Iain, FRSE; Chairman: PIEDA plc, since 1974; Scottish Enterprise, since 1993; Consultant to Secretary of State for Scotland, since 1971; *b* 27 Feb. 1937; *s* of William and Rhona MacKay; *m* 1961, Diana Marjory (*née* Raffan); one *s* two *d*. *Educ:* Dollar Academy; Univ. of Aberdeen (MA). FRSE 1988. English Electric Co., 1959–62; Lectr in Political Economy, Univ. of Aberdeen, 1962–65; Lectr in Applied Economics, Univ. of Glasgow, 1965–68, Sen. Lectr, 1968–71; Prof. of Political Economy, Univ. of Aberdeen, 1971–76; Prof. of Economics, Heriot-Watt Univ., Edinburgh, 1976–82, Professorial Fellow 1982–90; Hon. Prof., 1990–. Dir, Grampian Holdings, 1987–. Mem., Scottish Econ. Council, 1985–. Gov., NIESR, 1981–. *Publications:* Geographical Mobility and the Brain Drain, 1969; Local Labour Markets and Wage Structures, 1970; Labour Markets under Different Employment Conditions, 1971; The Political Economy of North Sea Oil, 1975; (ed) Scotland 1980: the economics of self-government, 1977; articles in Econ. Jl, Oxford Econ. Papers, Manch. Sch., Scottish Jl Polit. Econ., Jl Royal Stat. Soc. *Recreations:* tennis, golf, bridge. *Address:* Newfield, 14 Gamekeeper's Road, Edinburgh EH4 6LU.

MACKAY, Donald Sage; QC (Scot.) 1987; Solicitor-General for Scotland, since 1995; *b* 30 Jan. 1946; *s* of Rev. Donald George Mackintosh Mackay and Jean Margaret Mackay; *m* 1979, Lesley Ann Waugh; one *s* two *d*. *Educ:* George Watson's Boys' Coll., Edinburgh; Univ. of Edinburgh (LLB 1966, LLM 1968); Univ. of Virginia (LLM 1969). Law apprentice, 1969–71; Solicitor with Allan McDougall & Co., SSC, Edinburgh, 1971–76; called to the Scottish Bar, 1976; Advocate Depute, 1982–85. Mem., Criminal Injuries Compensation Bd, 1989. *Recreations:* golf, gardening, Isle of Arran. *Address:* 39 Hermitage Gardens, Edinburgh EH10 6AZ. *T:* 0131–447 1412; Kinneil Cottage, Lamlash, Isle of Arran KA27 8JT. *T:* Lamlash (01770600) 646; Advocates' Library, Parliament House, Edinburgh EH1 1RF. *T:* 0131–226 5071. *Club:* Western (Glasgow).

MACKAY, Douglas Ian; QC (Scot) 1993; *b* 10 Aug. 1948; *s* of Walter Douglas Mackay and Karla Marie Anna Fröhlich; *m* 1970, Susan Anne Nicholson; two *s* one *d*. *Educ:* Inverness High Sch.; Aberdeen Univ. (LLB). Admitted advocate, 1980. *Recreations:* Scottish art, travel, searching for bargains. *Address:* St Ann's House, Lasswade, Midlothian EH18 1ND. *T:* 0131–660 2634.

MACKAY, Eileen Alison, (Mrs A. Muir Russell); Principal Finance Officer, Scottish Office, since 1992; *b* 7 July 1943; *d* of Alexander William Mackay and Alison Jack Ross; *m* 1983, A(lastair) Muir Russell, *qv*. *Educ:* Dingwall Acad.; Edinburgh Univ. (MA Hons Geography). Dept of Employment, Scottish HQ, 1965–72; Scottish Office, 1972–78; HM Treasury, 1978–80; CPRS, Cabinet Office, 1980–83; Scottish Office, 1983–: Under Sec., Housing, Envmt Dept, 1988–92. Chm., Castlemilk Partnership, 1988–92; Dir, Moray Firth Maltings, 1988–. *Address:* The Scottish Office, Victoria Street, Edinburgh.

MACKAY, Eric Beattie; Editor of The Scotsman, 1972–85; *b* 31 Dec. 1922; *s* of Lewis Mackay and Agnes Johnstone; *m* 1954, Moya Margaret Myles Connolly (*d* 1981); three *s* one *d*. *Educ:* Aberdeen Grammar Sch.; Aberdeen Univ. (MA). Aberdeen Bon-Accord, 1948; Elgin Courant, 1949; The Scotsman, 1950; Daily Telegraph, 1952; The Scotsman, 1953: London Editor, 1957; Dep. Editor, 1961. *Recreations:* travel, golf, theatre. *Address:* 5 Strathearn Place, Edinburgh EH9 2AL. *T:* 0131–447 7737.

MACKAY, Maj.-Gen. Eric MacLachlan, CBE 1971 (MBE 1944); *b* 26 Dec. 1921; *s* of Ian MacLachlan Mackay and Violet Aimée Scott-Smith; *m* 1954, Ruth Thérèse Roth (*d* 1985); one *s*. *Educ:* Fettes Coll., Edinburgh. Served War: enlisted Royal Scots Fusiliers, 1940; commissioned Oct. 1941, Royal Engineers; 2/Lieut-Major, 1st Parachute Sqdn, RE, 1941–45, N Africa, Sicily, Italy, Arnhem, PoW (escaped) Norway. OC, Field Company, 20 Indian Div., French Indo-China, 1945–46; 2 i/c 23 Indian Div. Engrs, Java, 1946; OC, 35 Indian Field Company, Malaya, 1947; Supplementary Engrg Course, SME, 1948; GSO 2 Intell., Jt Intell. Bureau, 1949–50; Staff Coll., 1951; GSO 2, Org. and Equipment, HQ, ALFCE, 1952–53; Sen. Instructor Tactics, SME, 1954–55; OC, 33 Field Sqdn, RE, Cyprus, Suez, 1956–58; GSO 2, Wpns, MoD, 1958–60; JSSC, 1960; 2 i/c 2 Div. Engrs, 1961–62; Chief Engr, Malaysian Army, Borneo/Malaya, 1963–65; GSO 1, Co-ord., Master-Gen. of the Ordnance, 1966–67; Col, GS, RSME, 1968–69; Chief Engr (Brig.): Army Strategic Command, 1970–71; UK Land Forces, 1972; Maj.-Gen. 1973; Chief Engr, BAOR, 1973–76, retired. Managing Director: Cementation Sico Oman Ltd, 1977; Galadari Cementation Pte Ltd, Dubai, 1978–83; Forum Develt Pte Ltd, Singapore, 1983–85; Regional Dir Iraq, Engineering Services Internat., 1981–82; Chm., Amorshield Security Products, 1986–90. CEng 1976; MICE 1976. DSC (USA), 1944; Pingat Peringatan Malaysia (PPM), 1965. *Recreations:* motoring, skiing, photography. *Address:* Marston Court, Marston Magna, Yeovil, Somerset BA22 8BZ.

McKAY, Frederick; *see* McKay, J. F.

MACKAY, Sir (George Patrick) Gordon, Kt 1966; CBE 1962; Director, World Bank, 1975–78; Member, Board of Crown Agents, 1980–82; *b* 12 Nov. 1914; *s* of Rev. Adam Mackay and Katie Forrest (*née* Lawrence); *m* 1954, Margaret Esmé Martin; one *s* two *d*. *Educ:* Gordon Sch., Huntly; Aberdeen Univ. Joined Kenya and Uganda Railways and Harbours (later East African Railways and Harbours), 1938; Chief Asst to Gen. Manager, 1948; Chief Operating Supt, 1954; Dep. General Manager, 1960, General Manager, 1961–64; with World Bank, 1965–78. FCIT (MInstT 1961). OStJ 1964. *Recreation:* golf. *Address:* Well Cottage, Sandhills, Brook, Surrey GU8 5UP. *T:* Wormley (01428) 682549. *Club:* Nairobi (Kenya).

MACKAY, Sir Gordon; *see* Mackay, Sir G. P. G.

McKAY, Rt. Hon. Ian Lloyd, PC 1992; **Rt. Hon. Justice McKay;** Judge of the Court of Appeal of New Zealand, since 1991; *b* 7 March 1929; *s* of Neville James McKay and Kathleen Mary (*née* McGrath); *m* 1958, Ruth Constance Younger; four *s* two *d*. *Educ:* Victoria Coll., Univ. of NZ (BA, LLB). FCIArb; FInstArb (NZ). FInstD. Barrister and Solicitor, High Court of NZ, 1952; in practice as barrister and solicitor with Swan Davies & McKay, Wellington, later Swan Davies McKay & Co., then Young Swan McKay & Co., subseq. Young Swan Morison McKay, and Kensington Swan, 1953–91; Sen. Partner, 1967–91. Chm., various govt law reform cttees, 1971–87. Dir, public and private cos, 1970–91. Fellow, Internat. Acad. Trial Lawyers, USA, 1982–. Hon. Mem., Amer. Bar Assoc., 1981. *Publications:* papers to nat. confs and jls of various professional bodies. *Recreations:* Highland bagpipe music, tennis. *Address:* Court of Appeal, PO Box 1606, Wellington, New Zealand. *T:* (4) 4713591. *Club:* Wellington (Wellington, NZ).

McKAY, Very Rev. (James) Frederick, CMG 1972; OBE 1964 (MBE 1953); retired; Associate Minister, St Stephen's Uniting (formerly Presbyterian) Church, Sydney, 1974–80; Chairman, Uniting Church Negotiators, NSW, 1976–80; recognised as a foundation minister of Uniting Church in Australia at time of Union, 1977; *b* 15 April 1907; father, Northern Ireland; mother, Australian; *m* 1938, Margaret Mary Robertson; one *s* three *d*. *Educ:* Thornburgh Coll., Charters Towers, Qld; Emmanuel Coll., Brisbane, Qld; University of Queensland. MA; BD. Ordained Minister, Presbyterian Church of Australia, 1935; Patrol Padre, Australian Inland Mission (working with Flynn of the Inland), 1935–41; Chaplain, RAAF, 1941–46; Command Chaplain, Middle East, 1943–45; Minister, Toowong Parish, Qld, 1946–50; Superintendent (succeeding Flynn of the Inland), Aust. Inland Mission, 1951–74, Archivist, 1974–85. Moderator, Presbyterian Church of NSW, 1965; Moderator-Gen., Presbyterian Church of Australia, 1970–73.

Editor, Frontier News, 1951–74. Hon. LLD Queensland, 1992. Vocational Award, Sydney Rotary, 1972. *Publication:* Traeger, the Pedal Radio Genius, 1995. *Address:* Hawkesbury Village, Chapel Street, Richmond, NSW 2753, Australia. *T:* (45) 784561. *Club:* Australian (Sydney).

MACKAY, John; Headmaster, Bristol Grammar School, 1960–75; *b* 23 June 1914; *s* of William Mackay, Nottingham, and Eliza Mackay; *m* 1952, Margaret Ogilvie; two *s* two *d*. *Educ:* Mundella Grammar Sch., Nottingham; University of Nottingham; Merton Coll., Oxford. BA London (External) 1st Class Hons (English), 1935; Cambridge Teacher's Certificate, 1936. On staff of SCM, 1936–38; English Lecturer, St John's Coll., York, 1938–40. Served War of 1939–45, in Royal Navy, 1940–46. Merton Coll., Oxford, 1946–48; DPhil (Oxon) 1953. English Master, Merchant Taylors' School, Crosby, Liverpool, 1948–54; Second Master, Cheltenham Coll., 1954–60. Chm., HMC, 1970, Treasurer, 1974–75. *Recreations:* literature, gardening, cricket, arguing, senile reminiscence. *Address:* The Old Post Office, Tormarton, Badminton, Avon GL9 1HU. *T:* Chipping Sodbury (01454) 218243. *Club:* East India, Devonshire, Sports and Public Schools.

McKAY, Sir John (Andrew), Kt 1972; CBE 1966; QPM 1968; HM Chief Inspector of Constabulary for England and Wales, 1970–72; *b* 28 Nov. 1912; *s* of late Denis McKay, Blantyre, Lanarkshire; *m* 1st, 1947, Gertrude Gillespie Deighan (*d* 1971); two *d*; 2nd, 1976, Mildred Grace Kilday, *d* of late Dr Emil Stern and Grace Mildred Pleasants, San Francisco. *Educ:* Glasgow Univ. MA Glasgow, 1934. Joined Metropolitan Police, 1935; seconded to Army for service with Military Govt in Italy and Austria, 1943–47 (Lt-Col); Asst Chief Constable, then Deputy Chief Constable, Birmingham, 1953–58; Chief Constable of Manchester, 1959–66; HM Inspector of Constabulary, 1966–70. Freeman of City of London, 1972. OStJ 1963. Hon. MA, Manchester, 1966; Hon. Fellow, Manchester Polytechnic, subseq. Manchester Metropolitan Univ., 1971. *Address:* 212 Mocking Bird Circle, Santa Rosa, CA 95409, USA. *T:* (707) 5388285.

McKAY, Dr John Henderson, CBE 1987; JP; DL; Vice President, Royal Caledonian Horticultural Society, since 1993; *b* 12 May 1929; *s* of Thomas Johnstone McKay and Patricia Madeleine Henderson; *m* 1964, Catherine Watson Taylor; one *s* one *d*. *Educ:* West Calder High School. BA Hons, PhD, Open University. Labourer, clerk, Pumpherston Oil Co. Ltd, 1948–50; National Service, Royal Artillery, 1950–52; Officer and Surveyor, Customs and Excise, 1952–85. Mem., 1974–77 and 1978–88, Lord Provost and Lord Lieutenant, 1984–88, City of Edinburgh DC; Chm., Edinburgh Internat. Fest. Soc., 1984–88; Jt Chm., Edinburgh Mil. Tattoo Policy Cttee, 1984–88; Councillor, Royal Caledonian Horticultural Soc., 1974–78, 1980–81, 1984–88 (Sec. and Treas., 1988–93). Convener, Business Cttee, Gen. Council of Edinburgh Univ., 1992–. Chm., Scottish Wkg People's History Trust, 1992–; Trustee: Inst. of Occupl Medicine Res. Trust, 1992–; Almond Valley Collections Trust, 1994–; Edinburgh Quartet Trust, 1994–; Hon. Pres., Scottish Craftsmanship Assoc., 1987–; Hon. Vice-Pres., St Andrew Soc., 1989–; Patron, Scotland Yard Adventure Centre, 1988–. JP 1984, DL 1988, Edinburgh. Dr *hc* Edinburgh, 1989. *Recreations:* gardening, listening to music. *Address:* 2 Buckstone Way, Edinburgh EH10 6PN. *T:* 0131–445 2865. *Club:* Lothianburn Golf (Edinburgh).

MACKAY, Maj.-Gen. Kenneth, CB 1969; MBE 1943; idc, psc; GOC, Field Force Command Australia, Nov. 1973–Feb. 1974, retired; *b* 17 Feb. 1917; *m* 1943, Judith, *d* of F. Littler; two *s* one *d*. *Educ:* University High Sch., Melbourne; RMC Duntroon. Served War of 1939–45: Artillery, and Liaison Officer HQ 9th Australian Division, Middle East, 1940–41; ME Staff Sch., 1942; Bde Maj. 26 Bde, 1942–44; MO 12, War Office, 1944–45; Joint Sec., JCOSA, 1945–48; CO, 67 Inf. Bn, 1948; CO, 3 Bn Royal Aust. Regt, 1949; AHQ, 1949–52; Chief Instructor, Sch. of Tactics and Admin. 1952–55; Asst Aust. Defence Rep. UK, 1955–57; successively Dir of Maintenance, Personnel Admin., Quartering and Military Training, 1957–61; IDC, 1962; Dir Military Operations and Plans, Army HQ, Canberra, 1962–66; Comdr Aust. Force Vietnam, 1966; Commander 1st Division Australian Army, 1967–68; QMG AHQ, 1968–71; GOC Eastern Comd, 1971–73. *Recreations:* fishing, golf. *Address:* Unit 31, 207 Forest Way, Belrose, NSW 2085, Australia. *Clubs:* Australian (Sydney); Gordon Golf, New South Wales Golf.

McKAY, Mrs Margaret; Public Relations Consultant; *b* Jan. 1911. *Educ:* Elementary. Joined Labour Party 1932. Chief woman officer, TUC, 1951–62; Member of Co-operative Society, 1928–. Held administrative posts with Civil Service Clerical Association and Transport and General Workers' Union. MP (Lab) Clapham, 1964–70. Commander, Order of the Cedar of Lebanon. World Culture Award, Accademia Italia, 1984. *Publications:* Generation in Revolt (pen name Margaret McCarthy), 1953; Women in Trade Union History (TUC), 1954; Arab Voices from the Past; Electronic Arabia, 1974; The Chainless Mind, 1974; Timeless Arabia, 1978; Strangers in Palestine, 1982; Gulf Saga, 1982; Eve's Daring Daughters, 1985; Boadicea's Daughters; Middle Eastern Legacy, 1992. *Address:* PO Box 668, Abu Dhabi, Union of Arab Emirates.

MacKAY, Prof. Norman, MD; FRCPGlas, FRCPE, FRCSE, FRCGP, FCPS(Pak); Dean of Postgraduate Medicine and Professor of Postgraduate Medical Education, University of Glasgow, since 1989; *b* 15 Sept. 1936; *s* of Donald MacKay and Catherine MacLeod; *m* 1961, Grace Violet McCaffer; two *s* two *d*. *Educ:* Glasgow Univ. (MB ChB, MD). FRCPGlas 1973; FRCPE 1975; FRCSE 1993; FRCGP 1993; FCPS(Pak) 1993. Junior posts, Glasgow hosps, 1959–66; Lectr in Medicine, Nairobi, 1966–67; Sen. Registrar, Victoria Infirmary, Glasgow, 1967–68; Acting Sen. Lectr, Materia Medica, Univ. of Glasgow, 1968–72; Acting Consultant Physician, Falkirk, 1972–73; Consultant Physician, Victoria Infirmary, 1973–89, Hon. Consultant, 1989–94. Visitor, RCPSG, 1992–94 (Pres., 1994–). Hon. Sec., (1973–83). Hon. FACP 1995. *Publications:* articles in med. jls. *Recreations:* gardening, golf, soccer. *Address:* 4 Erskine Avenue, Dumbreck, Glasgow G41 5AL. *T:* 0141–427 0900.

MACKAY, Peter, CB 1993; Secretary, Scottish Office Industry Department, 1990–95; *b* Arbroath, 6 July 1940; *s* of John S. Mackay, FRCS, and Patricia M. Atkinson; *m* 1964, Sarah Holdich; one *s* two *d*. *Educ:* Glasgow High Sch.; St Andrews Univ. (MA Political Economy). Teacher, Kyogle High Sch., NSW, 1962–63; joined Scottish Office as Asst Principal, 1963; various posts, incl. Private Sec. to successive Ministers of State, 1966–68 and Secs of State, 1973–75; Nuffield Travelling Fellow, Canada, Australia and NZ, 1978–79; seconded: as Dir for Scotland, MSC, 1983–85; as Under Sec., Manpower Policy, Dept of Employment, London, 1985–86; Under Sec., Further and Higher Educn, Scottish Educn Dept, 1987–89; Principal Establishment Officer, Scottish Office, 1989–90. *Recreations:* high altitudes and latitudes, dinghy sailing, sea canoeing. *Address:* 6 Henderland Road, Edinburgh EH12 6BB. *T:* 0131–337 2830. *Clubs:* Clyde Canoe, Scottish Arctic.

McKAY, William Robert; Clerk Assistant, House of Commons, since 1994; *b* 18 April 1939; *s* of late William Wallace McKay and of Margaret H. A. Foster; *m* 1962, Rev. Margaret M., *d* of E. M. Fillmore, OBE; twin *d*. *Educ:* Trinity Academy, Leith; Edinburgh Univ. (MA Hons). Clerk in the House of Commons, 1961; Clerk of Financial Cttees, H of C, 1985–87; Clerk of the Journals, H of C, 1987–91; Clerk of Public Bills, H of C, 1991–94. Secretary: to the House of Commons Commn, 1981–84; to the Public Accounts Commn, 1985–87. *Publications:* (ed) Erskine May's Private Journal 1883–86, 1984; Secretaries to Mr Speaker, 1986; Clerks in the House of Commons 1363–1989: a biographical list, 1989; (ed) Observations, Rules and Orders of the House of Commons: an early procedural collection, 1989; contrib. historical jls. *Recreation:* dry-stone walling. *Address:* 1 Howe Hall Cottages, Littlebury Green, Saffron Walden CB11 4XF; Lochan a'Bhaigh, Isle of Coll, Argyll.

MACKAY-DICK, Maj.-Gen. Iain Charles, MBE 1981; General Officer Commanding London District and Major-General Commanding Household Division, since 1994; *b* 24 Aug. 1945; *s* of John Mackay-Dick and Margaret Edith Mackay-Dick (*née* Forty); *m* 1971, Carolynn Hilary Holmes; three *d*. *Educ:* St Edmund's Sch., Hindhead; Sherborne Sch.; RMAS; Staff Coll., Camberley (psc, hcsc). Commnd, Scots Guards, 1965; served Malaysia, Borneo, Germany, Falkland Is, Cyprus and UK to 1986; Comdt, Jun. Div. Staff Coll., Warminster, 1986–88; Comdr, 11 Armoured Bde, 1989–91; Dep. Mil. Sec. (A), 1991–92; GOC 1st Armoured Div., Verden, 1992–93; GOC Lower Saxony Dist, Verden, 1993; Comdr British Forces Falkland Is, 1993–94. *Publication:* (contrib.) Central Region versus Out of Area (essays), 1990. *Recreations:* most sports (represented Army in lawn tennis and squash (Army Squash Champion, 1971)), walking, gardening, military history. *Address:* HQ Scots Guards, Wellington Barracks, Birdcage Walk, SW1E 6HQ. *Clubs:* Cavalry & Guards; Edinburgh Angus (Edinburgh); Jesters; Guards' Golfing Society, Army Golfing Society.

McKEAN, Prof. Charles Alexander, FSAScot; FRSA; Professor of Architecture, Dundee University, since 1995; *b* 16 July 1946; *s* of John Laurie McKean and Nancy Burns Lendrum; *m* 1975, Margaret Elizabeth Yeo; two *s*. *Educ:* Fettes Coll., Edinburgh; Univ. of Bristol (BA Hons). Regional Secretary, RIBA, 1968–79; Sec. and Treas., RIAS, 1979–94; Architectural Correspondent: The Times, 1977–83; Scotland on Sunday, 1988–89; Trustee, Thirlestane Castle Trust, 1983–; Director, Workshops and Artists Studios Scotland (WASPS), 1980–85; Member: Scottish Arts Council Exhibitions Panel, 1980–83; Adv. Council for the Arts in Scotland, 1984–87; Edinburgh Common Purpose Adv. Cttee, 1990–94. Lectures: Bossom, RSA, 1986; RCS Prestigious, 1992. Hon. Mem., Saltire Soc. Hon. FRIBA 1989; Hon. FRIAS 1994. General Editor, RIAS/Landmark Trust series to Scotland, 1982–. Architectural Journalist of the Year, 1979 and 1983; Building Journalist of the Year, 1983. *Publications:* (with David Atwell) Battle of Styles, 1974; Guide to Modern Buildings in London 1965–75, 1976; Fight Blight, 1977; Architectural Guide to Cambridge and East Anglia 1920–80, 1980; Edinburgh—an illustrated architectural guide, 1982, 3rd edn 1983; (with David Walker) Dundee—an illustrated introduction through its buildings, 1984, 2nd edn 1986; Stirling and the Trossachs, 1984; The Scottish Thirties, 1987; The District of Moray—an illustrated introduction, 1987; (jtly) Central Glasgow—an illustrated architectural guide, 1989; Banff and Buchan—an illustrated architectural guide, 1990; For a Wee Country, 1990; Edinburgh: portrait of a city, 1991; Edinburgh—an illustrated architectural guide, 1992; (with David Walker) Dundee—an illustrated architectural guide, 1993; Value or Cost, 1994. *Recreations:* gardening, topography, books and glass collecting. *Address:* 10 Hill Park Road, Edinburgh EH4 7AW. *T:* 0131–336 2753. *Club:* Scottish Arts.

McKEAN, Douglas, CB 1977; *b* 2 April 1917; *s* of late Alexander McKean, Enfield, Mddx; *m* 1942, Anne (*d* 1994), *d* of late Roger Clayton, Riding Mill, Northumberland; two *s*. *Educ:* Merchant Taylors' Sch.; St John's Coll., Oxford. War Office, 1940; transferred to HM Treasury, 1949; Asst Sec., 1956; Under-Sec., 1962; on loan to Dept of the Environment, 1970–72; retired as Under Sec., HM Treasury, 1977. Dir, Agric. Mortgage Corp., 1978–87. Dep. Sec., Central Bd of Finance, Church of England, 1978–83. Trustee, Irish Sailors and Soldiers Land Trust, 1980–; Governor, Whitelands Coll., 1984–89. *Publication:* Money Matters: a guide to the finances of the Church of England, 1987. *Recreation:* mountain walking. *Address:* The Dower House, Forty Hill, Enfield, Middlesex EN2 9EJ. *T:* 0181–363 2365. *Club:* United Oxford & Cambridge University.

MacKEAN, Thomas Neill; His Honour Judge MacKean; a Circuit Judge, since 1993; *b* 4 March 1934; *s* of late Andrew Neill MacKean and Mary Dale MacKean (*née* Nichol); *m* 1962, Muriel Hodder; four *d*. *Educ:* Sherborne; Trinity Hall, Cambridge (BA). 2nd Lt, Royal Hampshire Regt, 1952–54. Partner, Hepherd Winstanley & Pugh, solicitors, Southampton, 1960–93, Sen. Partner, 1990–93; HM Coroner, Southampton and New Forest, 1990–93; a Recorder, 1991–93. *Recreations:* sailing, walking, working. *Address:* St Margaret's Priory, Titchfield, Hants PO14 4BQ. *T:* Titchfield (01329) 842056. *Clubs:* Royal Cruising; Royal Southern Yacht (Hamble).

McKEARNEY, Philip, CMG 1983; HM Diplomatic Service, retired; *b* 15 Nov. 1926; *s* of Philip McKearney, OBE; *m* 1950, Jean Pamela Walker; two *s*. *Educ:* City of London Sch.; Hertford Coll., Oxford. 4/7th Dragoon Guards, 1946–53; joined HM Diplomatic Service, 1953; 3rd Sec., British Embassy, Damascus, 1955–56; 1st Sec., British Legation, Bucharest, 1959–62; British Political Agent, Qatar, 1962–65; Counsellor and Consul-Gen., Baghdad, 1968–70; Counsellor, Belgrade, 1970–74; Inspector, FCO, 1975–77; Consul-General: Zagreb, 1977–80; Boston, Mass, 1980–83; Amb. to Romania, 1983–86; Dir, Foreign Service Prog., Oxford Univ., 1987–88.

MACKECHNIE, Sir Alistair (John), Kt 1993; financial consultant, since 1992; *b* 15 Nov. 1934; *s* of Frank Harper McIvor Mackechnie and Ellen Annie (*née* Brophy); *m* 1961, Countess Alexandra Kinsky, *er d* of Count Frederick-Carl Kinsky; three *d*. *Educ:* St Patrick's Coll., Wellington, NZ; Victoria Univ. of Wellington, NZ. ACA 1957. Nat. Service: commnd NZ Scottish Regt, 1955. Director: Henderson Admin, 1976–88; BSI-Thornhill Investment Mgt, 1989–; Te Mata Estate Winery (UK), 1992–. Twickenham Conservative Association: Chm., 1985–88; Pres., 1989–; Greater London Area Conservatives: Dep. Chm., 1988–90; Chm., 1990–93; Mem., Exec. Cttee, Nat. Union of Cons. and Unionist Assocs, 1988–. Mem. Council, Nat. Back Pain Assoc., 1994–. *Recreations:* theatre, travel, bird-watching, hill-walking. *Address:* 15 Waldegrave Gardens, Twickenham, Middx TW1 4PQ. *T:* 0181–892 9871. *Clubs:* Carlton, City of London.

McKECHNIE, George; Editor, The Herald, Glasgow, since 1994; *b* 28 July 1946; *m* 1971, Janequin (*née* Morris); two *s*. *Educ:* Portobello Sen. Secondary Sch., Edinburgh. Reporter: Paisley and Renfrewshire Gazette, 1964–66; Edinburgh Evening News, 1966; Scottish Daily Mail, 1966–68; Daily Record, 1968–73; Dep. News Editor and News Editor, Sunday Mail, 1974–76; Asst Editor, 1976–81, Editor, 1981–94, Evening Times, Glasgow. Director: George Outram & Co., 1986–92; Caledonian Newspaper Publishing, 1992–. Member: Press Complaints Commn, 1992–94; Adv. Bd, Assoc. of British Editors; Chairman: Editor's Cttee, Scottish Daily News Soc., 1989–91; Scottish Foundn, 1985–. *Recreations:* reading, walking, cinema, Hearts FC. *Address:* The Herald, 195 Albion Street, Glasgow G1 1QP. *T:* 0141–552 6255; East Blackbyre Farm, Waterside, by Fenwick, Ayrshire KA3 6JH. *T:* Fenwick (01560) 600716.

McKECHNIE, Sheila Marshall, OBE 1995; Director, Consumers' Association, since 1995; *b* Falkirk, 3 May 1948. *Educ:* Falkirk High School; Edinburgh Univ. (MA Politics and History); Warwick Univ. (MA Industrial Relations). Research Asst, Oxford Univ., 1971–72; Asst Gen. Sec., Wall Paper Workers Union Staff Section, 1972–74; WEA Tutor, Manchester, 1974–76; Health and Safety Officer, ASTMS, 1976–85; Dir, Shelter, 1985–94. DUniv Open, 1994; Hon. DSc(SocSci) Edinburgh, 1994. *Address:* Consumers' Association, 2 Marylebone Road, NW1 4DF.

McKEE, Major Sir Cecil; *see* McKee, Major Sir William Cecil.

McKEE, (Charles Dean) Grant; Director of Programmes, Yorkshire Television, since 1993; *b* 18 Aug. 1951; *s* of Cdr Eric McKee, RN, OBE and Betty (*née* Dean); *m* 1991, Jill Turton; one *d*. *Educ:* Clifton Coll.; Exeter Coll., Oxford (LLB). Journalist: Goole Times, 1974–76; Yorkshire Post, 1976–78; Yorkshire Television, 1979–: journalist and documentary producer, 1979–88; Editor, First Tuesday, 1988–93; Controller, Documentaries and Current Affairs, 1988–93. *Publication:* (with R. Franey) Time Bomb: Irish bombers, English justice and the Guildford Four, 1988. *Recreations:* travel, cricket, countryside. *Address:* c/o Yorkshire Television, The Television Centre, Leeds LS3 1JS. *T:* Leeds (0113) 243 8283.

McKEE, Major Sir (William) Cecil, Kt 1959; ERD; JP; Estate Agent; *b* 13 April 1905; *s* of late W. B. McKee and M. G. B. Bulloch; *m* 1932, Florence Ethel Irene Gill; one *d*. *Educ:* Methodist Coll., Belfast; Queen's Univ., Belfast. Alderman, Belfast Corporation, 1934; High Sheriff, Belfast, 1946; Deputy Lord Mayor, 1947, Lord Mayor of Belfast, 1957–59. JP Belfast, 1957. Pres., NI Br., Inst. of Dirs, 1957–59. Served with Royal Artillery in War of 1939–45. KStJ. 1982. Hon. LLD Queen's Univ., Belfast, 1960. *Recreation:* golf. *Address:* 250 Malone Road, Belfast. *T:* Belfast (01232) 666979. *Clubs:* Ulster Reform (Belfast); Royal County Down Golf.

McKEE, Dr William James Ernest, MA, MD, FFCM; Regional Medical Officer and Advisor, Wessex Regional Health Authority, 1976–89; *b* 20 Feb. 1929; *s* of John Sloan McKee, MA, and Mrs Annie Emily McKee (*née* McKinley); *m* Josée Tucker; three *d*. *Educ:* Queen Elizabeth's, Wakefield; Trinity Coll., Cambridge; Queen's Coll., Oxford. MA, MD, BChir (Cantab); LRCP, MRCS, FFCM. Clinical trng and postgrad. clinical posts at Radcliffe Infirmary, Oxford, 1952–57; med. res., financed by Nuffield Provincial Hosps Trust, 1958–61; successive posts in community medicine with Metrop. Regional Hosp. Bds, 1961–69; Sen. Admin. Med. Officer, Liverpool Regional Hosp. Bd, 1970–74; Regional Med. Officer, Mersey RHA, 1974–76. Chairman: Regional Med. Officers' Gp, 1984–86; Wessex Regl Working Party to review policy for Mental Handicap Services, 1979; UK Head of Delegation, EEC Hosp. Cttee, 1986–89; Member: Council for Postgrad. Med. Educn in England and Wales, 1975–85; Hunter Working Party on Med. Admin, 1972–83; DHSS Adv. Cttee on Med. Manpower Planning, 1982–85; DHSS Jt Planning Adv. Cttee on Med. Manpower, 1985–89; Bd of Faculty of Medicine, Univ. of Southampton, 1976–89. QHP 1987–90. *Publications:* papers on tonsillectomy and adenoidectomy in learned jls. *Recreations:* fly-fishing, golf. *Address:* 22a Bereweeke Avenue, Winchester SO22 6BH. *T:* Winchester (01962) 861369.

MacKEIGAN, Hon. Ian Malcolm; Supernumerary Justice of Appeal Division of Supreme Court of Nova Scotia, 1985–90 (Chief Justice of Nova Scotia and Chief Justice of Appeal Division of Supreme Court of Nova Scotia, 1973–85); *b* 11 April 1915; *s* of Rev. Dr J. A. MacKeigan and Mabel (*née* McAvity); *m* 1942, Jean Catherine Geddes; two *s* one *d*. *Educ:* Univs of Saskatchewan, Dalhousie and Toronto. BA (Great Distinction) 1934, MA 1935, LLB 1938, Dalhousie; MA Toronto 1939. Member of Nova Scotia and Prince Edward Island Bars; QC (Nova Scotia) 1954. Dep. Enforcement Administrator, Wartime Prices and Trade Bd, Ottawa, 1942–46; Dep. Comr, Combines Investigation Commn, Ottawa, 1946–50; Partner, MacKeigan, Cox, Downie & Mitchell and predecessor firms, Halifax, NS, 1950–73; Chm., Atlantic Develt Bd, 1963–69; Dir, Gulf Oil (Canada) Ltd, 1968–73; Dir, John Labatt Ltd, 1971–73. Hon. LLD Dalhousie, 1975. Centennial Medal, 1967; Jubilee Medal, 1977. *Publications:* articles in Can. Bar Review and Can. Jl Polit. Sci. and Econs. *Recreations:* fishing, golf. *Address:* 833 Marlborough Avenue, Halifax, NS B3H 3G7, Canada. *T:* (902)4291043. *Clubs:* Halifax, Saraguay, Ashburn Golf (Halifax).

MacKEITH, Prof. Margaret Anne, PhD; FRTPI; FRGS; Dean, Faculty of Design and Technology, University of Central Lancashire (formerly Lancashire Polytechnic), since 1990; Royal Fine Art Commissioner, since 1993; *b* 26 June 1939; *d* of James and Gertrude Crane; *m* 1962, Charles Gordon MacKeith; two *s*. *Educ:* Shirebrook Grammar Sch., Derbyshire; Univ. of Manchester (DipTP, MA); Heriot Watt Univ. (PhD). FRTPI 1980; FRGS 1976; MIEnvSc 1977. Planning Officer, Lancs CC, 1961–63; Consultant to MacKeith Dickinson and Partners, 1963–74; Prin. Planning Officer, Blackpool BC, 1967–69 and 1974–75; Lancashire Polytechnic: Sen., then Prin. Lectr, 1975–87; Hd, Sch. of Construction and Surveying, 1987–90; Dean, Faculty of Technol., 1987–90. Member: BTEC Cttees, 1988–93; NW Cttee, OFFER, 1990–93; Landscape Adv. Cttee, Dept of Transport, 1991–93; NRA NW Cttee, 1994–. FRSA 1990. Dr *hc* Cluj, Romania, 1994. *Publications:* Shopping Arcades 1817–1939, 1985; History and Conservation of Shopping Arcades, 1986; articles and conf. papers on conservation, engrg educn and women in engrg and technol. *Recreations:* travel, architectural history, music, opera. *Address:* 104 Breck Road, Poulton-le-Fylde, Lancs FY6 7HT. *T:* Poulton-le-Fylde (01253) 884774; 4 Breton House, Barbican, EC2Y 8AB.

McKELLEN, Sir Ian (Murray), Kt 1991; CBE 1979; actor and director since 1961; *b* 25 May 1939; *s* of late Denis Murray McKellen and Margery (*née* Sutcliffe). *Educ:* Wigan Grammar Sch.; Bolton Sch.; St Catharine's Coll., Cambridge (BA; Hon. Fellow, 1982). Pres., Marlowe Soc., 1960–61. Elected to Council of Equity, 1971–72. 1st appearance (stage): Belgrade Theatre, Coventry, in a Man for all Seasons, Sept. 1961. Arts Theatre, Ipswich, 1962–63; Nottingham Playhouse, 1963–64; 1st London stage appearance, Duke of York's in A Scent of Flowers, 1964 (Clarence Derwent Award); Recruiting Officer, Chips with Everything, Cambridge Theatre Co., 1971; Founder Mem., Actors Company: Ruling the Roost, 'Tis Pity She's a Whore, Edin. Fest., 1972; Knots, Wood-Demon, Edin. Fest., 1973, and with King Lear, Brooklyn Acad. of Music, Wimbledon Theatre season, 1974; *London stage appearances:* A Lily in Little India, St Martin's; Man of Destiny/O'Flaherty VC, Mermaid Theatre; Their Very Own and Golden City, Royal Court, 1966; The Promise, Fortune, 1967 (also Broadway); White Lies/Black Comedy, Lyric; Richard II, Prospect Theatre Co., 1968 (revived with Edward II, Edin. Fest., British and European tours); Hamlet, Cambridge, 1971 (British and European tours); Ashes, Young Vic, 1975; Bent, Royal Court, Criterion, 1979 (SWET Award, 1979); Short List, Hampstead, 1983; Cowardice, Ambassadors, 1983; Henceforward, Vaudeville, 1988; *with Royal National Theatre:* Much Ado About Nothing, Old Vic, 1965; Armstrong's Last Goodnight, Trelawney of the Wells, Chichester Fest., 1965; Venice Preserv'd, Wild Honey (Laurence Olivier Award, Plays and Players Award; Los Angeles and NY, 1986–87), Coriolanus (London Standard Award), South Bank, 1984–85; As Assoc. Dir, produced and acted in The Duchess of Malfi, The Real Inspector Hound with The Critic, The Cherry Orchard (Paris and Chicago), 1984–85; Bent, 1990 (also Garrick); Kent in King Lear, and title role, Richard III, 1990 (Laurence Olivier Award; Assoc. Prod. for world tour, 1990–91); Napoli Milionaria, 1991; Uncle Vanya, 1992; Richard III, US tour, 1992; *with Royal Shakespeare Co.:* Dr Faustus, Edin. Fest. and Aldwych, 1974; Marquis of Keith, Aldwych, 1974–75; King John, Aldwych, 1975; Too Good to be True, Aldwych and Globe, 1975; Romeo and Juliet, The Winter's Tale, Macbeth (Plays and Players Award, 1976), Stratford, 1976–77; Every Good Boy Deserves Favour, RFH, 1977, Barbican, 1982; Romeo and Juliet, Macbeth, Pillars of the Community (SWET Award, 1977), Days of the Commune, The Alchemist (SWET Award, 1978), Aldwych and RSC Warehouse, 1977–78; Prod. RSC Tour, 1978: Three Sisters, Twelfth Night, Is There Honey Still for Tea; Iago in Othello, The Other Place, Stratford and Young Vic, 1989, BBC TV (Evening Standard and London Critics' Award); *Directed:* Liverpool Playhouse, 1969; Watford and Leicester, 1972; A Private Matter, Vaudeville, 1973; The Clandestine Marriage, Savoy, 1975; *other performances include:* Words, Words, Words (solo recital), Edin. Fest. and Belfast Fest., 1976 (with Acting Shakespeare, Edin. and Belfast, 1977); Amadeus, Broadhurst, NY, 1980–81 (Drama Desk, NY Drama League, Outer Critics' Circle and Tony Awards); *Acting Shakespeare tours:* Israel, Norway, Denmark, Sweden, 1980; Spain, France, Cyprus, Israel, Poland, Romania, 1982; Los Angeles and Ritz, NYC (Drama Desk Award), 1983; San Francisco, Washington DC, Los Angeles, Olney, Cleveland, San Diego, Boston (Elliot Norton Award), 1987 Playhouse, London, 1987–88; A Knight Out, NY, S Africa, UK, 1994–95. *Films,* 1968–: A Touch of Love, The Promise, Alfred the Great, Priest of Love, Scarlet Pimpernel, Plenty, Zina, Scandal, The Ballad of Little Jo, Six Degrees of Separation, The Shadow, Jack and Sarah, Restoration. Has appeared on television, 1966–, incl. Walter, 1982 (RTS Performance Award for 1982); Walter and June, 1983; Mister Shaw's Missing Millions, 1993; Tales of the City, 1993; Cold Comfort Farm, 1995. Cameron Mackintosh Prof. of Contemporary Theatre, Univ. of Oxford, 1991. Hon. DLitt Nottingham, 1989. *Address:* c/o ICM, Oxford House, 76 Oxford Street, W1N 0AX. *T:* 071–636 6565, *Fax:* 071–323 0101.

McKELVEY, Air Cdre John Wesley, CB 1969; MBE 1944; CEng, MRAeS; RAF, retired; *b* 25 June 1914; *s* of late Captain John Wesley McKelvey, Enfield, Mddx; *m* 1938, Eileen Amy Carter, *d* of John Charles Carter, Enfield; two *s*. *Educ:* George Spicer Sch., Enfield. RAF Aircraft Apprentice, 1929; commnd 1941 (Eng Branch); served 1939–45, Egypt, Syria, Iraq and Bomber Comd (despatches, 1943); Group Captain 1960; Dep. Dir Intelligence (Tech.), 1962–64; Dir of Aircraft and Asst Attaché, Defence Research and Development, British Embassy, Washington, 1964–66; Air Officer Wales and CO, RAF St Athan, 1966–69; retd Aug. 1969. RAF Benevolent Fund: Sec. (Appeals), 1971–77; Legacies and Trusts Officer, 1977–79. *Recreations:* bowls, gardening, photography. *Address:* 19 Greensome Drive, Ferndown, Dorset BH22 8BE. *T:* Ferndown (01202) 894464. *Club:* Royal Air Force.

McKELVEY, Rev. Dr Robert John; Principal, Northern College, Manchester, 1979–93; Moderator, General Assembly of the United Reformed Church, 1994–95; *b* 12 Oct. 1929; *s* of Robert John McKelvey and Eleanor McMaster McKelvey (*née* Earls); *m* 1957, Martha Esther Skelly; two *s* one *d*. *Educ:* Paton Congregational Coll.; Nottingham Univ. (BA 1955); Pittsburgh Theol Seminary (MTh 1956); Mansfield Coll., Oxford (DPhil 1959). Tutor, 1959–67, Principal, 1968–74, Adams United Coll., S Africa; Pres., Federal Theol Seminary of S Africa, 1970–71; Dir, Internship Trng, United Congregational Church of S Africa, 1975–78; Pres., Northern Fedn for Trng in Ministry, 1984–86. *Publications:* The New Temple: the Church in the New Testament, 1969; contributor to: New Bible Dictionary, 1962; The Illustrated Bible Dictionary, 1980; New 20th Century Encyclopedia of Religious Knowledge, 2nd edn 1991; learned jls incl. NT Studies, Jl of Theol Studies. *Recreations:* gardening, walking, travel, oddjobbery. *Address:* 64 Brooklawn Drive, Withington, Manchester M20 3GZ. *T:* 0161–434 4936.

McKELVEY, William; MP (Lab) Kilmarnock and Loudoun, since 1983 (Kilmarnock, 1979–83); *b* Dundee, July 1934; *m*; two *s*. *Educ:* Morgan Acad.; Dundee Coll. of Technology. Joined Labour Party, 1961; formerly Sec. Organiser, Lab. Party, and full-time union official. Mem., Dundee City Council. Chm., Select Cttee on Scottish Affairs, 1992–. *Address:* House of Commons, SW1A 0AA; 41 Main Street, Kilmaurs, Ayrshire KA3 2SY.

McKELVIE, Peter, FRCS, FRCSE; Consultant Ear, Nose and Throat Surgeon: London Hospital, since 1971; Royal National Throat, Nose and Ear Hospital, London, since 1972; *b* 21 Dec. 1932; *s* of William Bryce McKelvie, MD, ChM, FRCSE, DLO, and Agnes E. McKelvie (*née* Winstanley), Headmistress; *m* Myra Chadwick, FRCP, Cons. Dermatologist; one *d*. *Educ:* Manchester Grammar Sch.; Rugby Sch.; Univ. of Manchester (MB ChB, MD, ChM). FRCS 1962, FRCSE 1989. House Surgeon: Manchester Royal Inf., 1957; Royal Nat. Throat, Nose and Ear Hosp., London, 1958; Lectr in Anatomy, KCL, 1959; Casualty Surg., St Mary's Hosp., London, 1960; Reader in Laryngology, UCL, 1968–70; Dean, Inst. of Laryngology and Otology, London, 1984–89. Examiner: London Univ.; Royal Colls of Surgeons of England, Edinburgh and Glasgow. MRSM 1966 (Pres., Laryngology Sect., 1992–93). *Publications:* numerous, on head and neck cancer. *Recreations:* mirth, watching young surgeons develop, Mediterranean Basin. *Address:* Elmcroft, 9 Farm Way, Northwood, Mddx HA6 3EG. *T:* Northwood (01923) 823544.

McKENNA, David, CBE 1967 (OBE 1946; MBE 1943); FCIT; Member, British Railways Board, 1968–76 (part-time Member, 1976–78); *b* 16 Feb. 1911; *s* of late Rt Hon. Reginald McKenna and Pamela Margaret McKenna (*née* Jekyll); *m* 1934, Lady Cecilia Elizabeth Keppel, *d* of 9th Earl of Albemarle, MC; three *d*. *Educ:* Eton; Trinity Coll., Cambridge. London Passenger Transport Board, 1934–39, and 1946–55; Asst General Manager, Southern Region of BR, 1955–61; Chief Commercial Officer, HQ, BR, 1962; General Manager, Southern Region of BR, and Chairman Southern Railway Board, 1963–68; Chairman, British Transport Advertising, 1968–81. Mem., Dover Harbour Bd, 1969–80. Dir, Isles of Scilly Steamship Co., 1976–92. War Service with Transportation Service of Royal Engineers, 1939–45; Iraq, Turkey, India and Burma; Lieut-Colonel. Pres., Chartered Inst. of Transport, 1972. Chairman of Governors, Sadler's Wells, 1962–76. Vice-Pres., Royal College of Music; Chairman of Bach Choir, 1964–76. FRCM. Commandeur de l'Ordre National du Mérite, 1974. *Publications:* various papers on transport subjects. *Recreations:* music, sailing. *Address:* Rosteague, Portscatho, Truro, Cornwall TR2 5EF. *Clubs:* Brooks's; Royal Cornwall Yacht (Falmouth).

McKENNA, Hon. Francis Joseph, (Frank); PC (Can.) 1987; MLA (Liberal Party), Chatham, New Brunswick, since 1982; Premier of New Brunswick, since 1987; *b* 19 Jan. 1948; *s* of Durward and Olive McKenna; *m* Julie Friel; two *s* one *d*. *Educ:* Apohaqui Elementary Sch.; Sussex High Sch.; St Francis Xavier Univ. (BA); Queen's Univ.; Univ. of New Brunswick (LLB). Lawyer; Mem., NB and Canadian Bar Assocs; Founder and 1st Pres., Chatham Downtown Merchants' Assoc.; former Pres., Chatham Chamber of Commerce. Leader, NB Liberal Party, 1985–; Pres., Privy Council of Canada (Mem., Org. and Policy Cttees). Former Member: Standing Cttee, Law Amendments and Public Accounts; Select Cttee of Science and Technology. Hon. DSP Moncton, 1988; Hon. LLD New Brunswick, 1988. Vanier Award, 1988. *Address:* Office of the Premier, Fredericton, New Brunswick E3B 5H1, Canada.

MacKENNA, Robert Ogilvie, MA, ALA; University Librarian and Keeper of the Hunterian Books and MSS, Glasgow, 1951–78; *b* 21 March 1913; *s* of late Dr John G. MacKenna and Katherine Ogilvie; *m* 1942, Ray, *o d* of late Samuel Mullin, Glasgow. *Educ:* Paisley Grammar Sch.; Glasgow Univ. Assistant Librarian, Glasgow Univ., 1936; Sub-Librarian, Leeds Univ., 1946; Librarian, King's Coll., Newcastle upon Tyne (University of Durham), 1948–51. Served War as officer, RNVR, 1939–45. Trustee, National Library of Scotland, 1953–79. President, Scottish Library Association, 1966; Chairman, Standing Conference of National and University Libraries, 1967–69. President Scottish Cricket Union, 1968. Editor, The Philosophical Journal, 1976–77. *Publication:*

Glasgow University Athletic Club: the story of the first hundred years, 1981. *Recreations:* watching and talking cricket, hill-walking. *Address:* 40 Kelvin Court, Glasgow G12 0AE. *Club:* College (Glasgow).

MACKENZIE, family name of **Earl of Cromartie.**

MACKENZIE of Gairloch; *see under* Inglis of Glencorse.

MACKENZIE, Sir Alexander Alwyne H. C. B. M.; *see* Muir Mackenzie.

MACKENZIE, Archibald Robert Kerr, CBE 1967; HM Diplomatic Service, retired; *b* 22 Oct. 1915; *s* of James and Alexandrina Mackenzie; *m* 1963, Virginia Ruth Hutchison. *Educ:* Glasgow, Oxford, Chicago and Harvard Universities. Diplomatic Service, with duty at Washington, 1943–45; United Nations, 1946–49; Foreign Office, 1949–51; Bangkok, 1951–54; Cyprus, 1954; Foreign Office, 1955–57; OEEC, Paris, 1957–61; Commercial Counsellor, HM Embassy, Rangoon, 1961–65; Consul-General, Zagreb 1965–69; Ambassador, Tunisia, 1970–73; Minister (Econ. and Social Affairs), UK Mission to UN, 1973–75. Brandt Commission, 1978–80. *Recreation:* golf. *Address:* Strathcashel Cottage, Rowardennan, near Glasgow G63 0AW. *T:* Balmaha (01360) 870262. *Club:* Royal Scottish Automobile (Glasgow).

MACKENZIE, Major Colin Dalzell, MBE 1945; MC 1940; Vice Lord-Lieutenant of Inverness, 1986–94; *b* 23 March 1919; *s* of Lt-Col Douglas William Alexander Dalziel Mackenzie, CVO, DSO, DL; *m* 1947, Lady Anne FitzRoy, *d* of 10th Duke of Grafton; one *s* three *d* (and one *s* decd). *Educ:* Eton; RMC Sandhurst. Page of Honour to King George V, 1932–36; joined Seaforth Highlanders, 1939; ADC to Viceeroy of India, 1945–46, Dep. Mil. Sec. to Viceroy, 1946–47; retired Seaforth Highlanders, 1949. Mem., Queen's Body Guard for Scotland, Royal Company of Archers, 1959–. Mem., Inverness-shire County Council, 1949–51. *Recreation:* fishing. *Address:* Farr House, Inverness IV1 2XB. *T:* Farr (01808) 521202. *Clubs:* Turf, Pratt's; New (Edinburgh).

MACKENZIE, Colin Scott; DL; Sheriff of Grampian, Highland and Islands at Lerwick and Kirkwall, since 1992; Vice Lord-Lieutenant, Western Isles, 1984–92; *b* 7 July 1938; *s* of late Major Colin Scott Mackenzie, BL and Mrs Margaret S. Mackenzie, MA; *m* 1966, Christeen Elizabeth Drysdale McLauchlan. *Educ:* Nicolson Inst., Stornoway; Fettes Coll., Edinburgh; Edinburgh Univ. (BL 1959). Admitted Solicitor and Notary Public, 1960; Procurator Fiscal, Stornoway, 1969–92. Clerk to the Lieutenancy, Stornoway, 1975–92. Dir, Harris Tweed Assoc. Ltd, 1979–; Trustee, Western Isles Kidney Machine Trust, 1977–. Council Mem for Western Isles, Orkney, Shetland etc, Law Soc. of Scotland, 1985–92. General Assembly, Church of Scotland: Comr, Presbytery of Lewis, 1991–92; Mem., Bd of Social Responsibility, 1991–; Convenor, Study Gp into Young People and the Media, 1991–93. DL Islands Area of Western Isles, 1975. *Publication:* contrib. Stair Memorial Encyclopaedia of Laws of Scotland, 1987. *Recreations:* amateur radio, boating, fishing, local history, shooting, trying to grow trees. *Address:* Middlebank, 3 Bells Road, Lerwick, Shetland ZE1 0QB. *T:* Lerwick (01595) 5808; Park House, 8 Matheson Road, Stornoway, Western Isles PA87 2NQ. *T:* Stornoway (01851) 702008. *Clubs:* New (Edinburgh); Royal Scottish Automobile (Glasgow).

McKENZIE, Dan Peter, PhD; FRS 1976; Professor of Earth Sciences, Department of Earth Sciences, Cambridge University, since 1984; Fellow of King's College, Cambridge, 1965–73 and since 1977; *b* 21 Feb. 1942; *s* of William Stewart McKenzie and Nancy Mary McKenzie; *m* 1971, Indira Margaret Misra; one *s*. *Educ:* Westminster Sch.; King's Coll., Cambridge (BA 1963, PhD 1966). Cambridge University: Sen. Asst in Res., 1969–75; Asst Dir of Res., 1975–79; Reader in Tectonics, 1979–84. Hon. MA Cambridge, 1966. (Jtly) Geology and Geophysics Prize, Internat. Balzan Foundn of Italy and Switzerland, 1981; (jtly) Japan Prize, Science and Technology Foundn of Japan, 1990; Royal Medal, Royal Soc., 1991; Gold Medal, RAS, 1992. *Publications:* papers in learned jls. *Recreation:* gardening. *Address:* Bullard Laboratories, Madingley Road, Cambridge CB3 0EZ. *T:* Cambridge (01223) 337177.

MACKENZIE, Rear-Adm. David John, CB 1983; FNI; Royal Navy, retired 1983; Director, Atlantic Salmon Trust, since 1985; *b* 3 Oct. 1929; *s* of late David Mackenzie and of Alison Walker Lawrie; *m* 1965, Ursula Sybil Balfour; two *s* one *d*. *Educ:* Cargilfield Sch., Barnton, Edinburgh; Royal Naval Coll., Eaton Hall, Cheshire. Cadet to Comdr, 1943–72: served in East Indies, Germany, Far East, Home and Mediterranean Fleets, and commanded: HMML 6011, HM Ships: Brinkley, Barrington, Hardy, Lincoln, Hermione; Captain 1972; Senior Officers War Course, 1972; commanded HMS Phoenix (NBCD School), 1972–74; Captain F8 in HMS Ajax, 1974–76; Director of Naval Equipment, 1976–78; Captain: HMS Blake, 1979; HMS Hermes, 1980; Rear Admiral 1981; Flag Officer and Port Admiral, Gibraltar, Comdr Gibraltar Mediterranean, 1981–83. Younger Brother of Trinity House, 1971–. Member, Queen's Body Guard for Scotland (Royal Company of Archers), 1976–. Vice Pres., Nautical Inst., 1985–93. *Recreations:* shooting and fishing. *Address:* c/o Atlantic Salmon Trust, Moulin, Pitlochry, Perthshire PH16 5JQ. *Club:* New (Edinburgh).

McKENZIE, Prof. Donald Francis, FBA 1986; Professor of Bibliography and Textual Criticism, since 1989, and Professorial Fellow, Pembroke College, since 1986, University of Oxford; *b* 5 June 1931. *Educ:* Victoria UC, Wellington, NZ (BA 1954; DipJourn 1955; MA 1957); Corpus Christi Coll., Cambridge (PhD 1961); MA, DPhil Oxford, 1986. Public servant, NZ PO, 1949–56; various teaching positions, Victoria UC and Victoria Univ. of Wellington, 1956–69; Prof. of Eng. Lang. and Lit., Victoria Univ. of Wellington, 1969–87, now Emeritus; Reader in Textual Criticism, Oxford Univ., 1986–89. Fellow, Corpus Christi Coll., Cambridge, 1960–66; Sandars Reader in Bibliography, Cambridge, 1975–76; Lyell Reader in Bibliography, Oxford Univ., 1987–88. Panizzi Lectr, British Liby, 1985. Founder-manager, Wai-te-ata Press, 1961–86. Pres., Bibliographical Soc., 1982–83 (Gold Medal, 1990); Hon. Member: Bibliographical Soc. of America, 1986; Cambridge Bibliographical Soc., 1988. Corresp. FBA 1980; Hon. Fellow, Australian Acad. of Humanities, 1988. Mark Fitch Gold Medal for Bibliography, 1988; Walford Award, LA, 1994. *Publications:* (ed) Stationers' Company Apprentices 1605–1800, 3 vols, 1961–78; The Cambridge University Press 1696–1712: a bibliographical study, 1966; (ed with J. C. Ross) A Ledger of Charles Ackers, 1968; (ed) Robert Tailor, The Hogge hath lost his Pearl, 1972; Oral Culture, Literacy and Print in early New Zealand, 1985; Bibliography and the Sociology of Texts, 1986 (French trans. 1991); contribs to bibliographical jls. *Address:* 20 Bardwell Court, Bardwell Road, Oxford OX2 6SX. *T:* Oxford (01865) 58962.

MacKENZIE, Gillian Rachel, (Mrs N. I. MacKenzie); *see* Ford, G. R.

MACKENZIE, Sir Guy; *see* Mackenzie, Sir J. W. G.

MacKENZIE, Hector Uisdean; Associate General Secretary, UNISON, since 1993; *b* 25 Feb. 1940; *s* of George MacKenzie and Williamina Budge Sutherland; *m* 1961, Anna Morrison (marr. diss.); one *s* three *d*. *Educ:* Nicholson Inst., Stornaway, Isle of Lewis; Portree High Sch., Skye; Leverndale School of Nursing, Glasgow; West Cumberland School of Nursing, Whitehaven. RGN, RMN. Student Nurse, Leverndale Hosp., 1958–61; Asst Lighthouse Keeper, Clyde Lighthouses Trust, 1961–64; Student Nurse, 1964–66, Staff Nurse 1966–69, West Cumberland Hosp.; Confederation of Health Service Employees: Asst Regl Sec., 1969; Regl Sec., Yorks and E Midlands, 1970–74; Nat. Officer, 1974–83; Asst Gen. Sec., 1983–87; Gen. Sec., 1987–93. *Recreations:* work, reading, aviation. *Address:* UNISON Centre, 1 Mabledon Place, WC1H 9AJ. *T:* 0171–388 2366; Glen House, High Street, Banstead, Surrey SM7 2LH. *T:* Burgh Heath (01737) 353322.

MACKENZIE, Vice-Adm. Sir Hugh Stirling, KCB 1966 (CB 1963); DSO 1942 and Bar 1943; DSC 1945; *b* 3 July 1913; 3rd *s* of Dr and Mrs T. C. Mackenzie, Inverness; *m* 1946, Helen Maureen, *er d* of Major J. E. M. Bradish-Ellames; one *s* two *d*. *Educ:* Cargilfield Sch.; Royal Naval Coll., Dartmouth. Joined Royal Naval Coll., 1927; qualified in Submarines, 1935. Served throughout War of 1939–45 in Submarines, comdg HMS Thrasher, 1941–43; HMS Tantalus, 1943–45; Comdr 1946; Capt. 1951; Rear-Adm. 1961; Flag Officer, Submarines, 1961–63; Chief Polaris Executive, 1963–68; Vice-Adm. 1964; retired 1968. Chm., Navy League, 1969–74; Dir, Atlantic Salmon Research Trust Ltd, 1969–79 (renamed Atlantic Salmon Trust, 1979), Chm., 1979–83, Vice Pres., 1984–. Hon. Freeman, Borough of Shoreditch, 1942. CIMgt. *Recreation:* the country. *Address:* Sylvan Lodge, Puttenham, near Guildford, Surrey GU3 1BB. *Club:* Naval and Military.

MACKENZIE, Ian Clayton, CBE 1962; HM Diplomatic Service, retired; Ambassador to Korea, 1967–69; *b* 13 Jan. 1909; *m* 1948, Anne Helena Tylor; one *s* one *d*. *Educ:* Bedford Sch.; King's Coll., Cambridge. China Consular Service, 1932–41; Consul, Brazzaville, 1942–45, Foreign Office, 1945; 1st Sec., Commercial, Shanghai, 1946–49; Santiago, 1949–53; Commercial Counsellor: Oslo, 1953–58; Caracas, 1958–63; Stockholm, 1963–66. *Address:* Koryo, Armstrong Road, Brockenhurst, Hants SO42 7TA. *T:* Lymington (01590) 623453.

MACKENZIE, James, BSc; CEng, FIM; Chairman, Wade Building Services Ltd, since 1993; Director, Lloyds Register Quality Assurance Ltd, since 1985; *b* 2 Nov. 1924; *s* of James Mackenzie and Isobel Mary Chalmers; *m* 1950, Elizabeth Mary Ruttle; one *s* one *d*. *Educ:* Queen's Park Sch., Glasgow; Royal Technical Coll., Glasgow (BSc). The United Steel Companies Ltd, Research and Develt Dept, 1944–67; British Steel Corporation, 1967–85, a Man. Dir, 1976–85; former Dir, Geo. Cohen Sons & Co. Ltd. President: Inst. of Ceramics, 1965–67; Metals Soc., 1983–85. *Address:* Westhaven, Beech Waye, Gerrards Cross, Bucks SL9 8BL. *T:* Gerrards Cross (01753) 886461.

MacKENZIE, James Alexander Mackintosh, CB 1988; FEng 1982; Chief Road Engineer, Scottish Development Department, 1976–88, retired; *b* Inverness, 6 May 1928; *m* 1970, Pamela Dorothy Nixon; one *s* one *d*. *Educ:* Inverness Royal Acad. FICE, FIHT. Miscellaneous local govt appts, 1950–63; Chief Resident Engr, Durham County Council, 1963–67; Dep. Dir, 1967–71, Dir, 1971–76, North Eastern Road Construction Unit, MoT, later DoE. *Recreations:* golf, fishing. *Address:* Pendor, 2 Dean Park, Longniddry, East Lothian EH32 0QR. *T:* Longniddry (01875) 852643.

MacKENZIE, James Sargent Porteous, OBE 1963; *b* 18 June 1916; *s* of late Roderick and Daisy W. MacKenzie; *m* 1944, Flora Paterson; three *s*. *Educ:* Portree High Sch.; Edinburgh Univ. (MA Hons 1939); Glasgow Univ. (Dip. Social Studies 1947). War Service, 1939–45: Captain RA (Combined Ops, Burma and Normandy). Scottish HQ, Min. of Labour, 1947–56; Labour Advr, UK High Commn, New Delhi, 1956–62 (First Sec., 1956, Counsellor, 1959); Ministry of Labour: Asst Controller, Scottish HQ, 1962–65; Dep. Controller, Yorks and Humberside Regional Office, 1965–67; Principal Dep. Controller, Scottish HQ, Dept of Employment, 1967–72; Asst Sec., 1970; Counsellor (Labour) British Embassy, Bonn, 1972–77, retired 1977. Exec. Mem., Church of Scotland Cttee on Church and Nation, 1977–83. *Address:* 11 Baberton Park, Juniper Green, Edinburgh EH14 5DW.

MACKENZIE, Sir James William Guy, 5th Bt *cr* 1890, of Glen Muick, Aberdeenshire; Vice-Chairman, Kerrier Direct Services Board, since 1994; *b* 6 Oct. 1946; *s* of Lt-Col Eric Dighton Mackenzie, CMG, CVO, DSO (*d* 1972), 4th *s* of Sir Allan Russell Mackenzie, 2nd Bt, and Elizabeth Kathrine Mary, *d* of Captain James William Guy Innes, CBE; *S* cousin, 1993; *m* 1972, Paulene Patricia Simpson (marr. diss. 1980); two *d*. *Educ:* Stowe. Vice-Pres., Crown Royale Internat., USA, 1979–81. Vice-Chm., Portleven 2000 Charitable Trust, 1994–95. Mem. (Ind) Kerrier DC, 1993–. *Recreations:* watching cricket, music, unusual architecture. *Heir: b* Allan Walter Mackenzie, 6 Nov. 1952. *Address:* Tresowes Hill Farm, Ashton, near Helston, Cornwall TR13 9SY.

MACKENZIE, Gen. Sir Jeremy (John George), KCB 1992; OBE 1982; Deputy Supreme Allied Commander, Europe, since 1994; *b* 11 Feb. 1941; *s* of late Lt-Col John William Elliot Mackenzie, DSO, QPM and of Valerie (*née* Dawes); *m* 1969, Elizabeth Lyon (*née* Wertenbaker); one *s* one *d*. *Educ:* Duke of York Sch., Nairobi, Kenya. psc, HCSC. Commnd Queen's Own Highlanders, 1961; Canadian Forces Staff Coll., 1974; Bde Major, 24 Airportable Bde, 1975–76; CO 1 Queen's Own Highlanders, NI and Hong Kong, 1979–82; Instructor, Staff Coll., 1982–83; Col Army Staff Duties 2, 1983–84; Comdr 12th Armoured Bde, 1984–86; Service Fellowship, King's Coll., Univ. of London, 1987; Dep. Comdt, 1987–89, Comdt, 1989, Staff Coll; GOC 4th Armoured Div., BAOR, 1989–91; Comdr 1st (British) Corps, 1991–92; Comdr, Ace Rapid Reaction Corps, 1992–94. Colonel Commandant: WRAC, 1990–92; AGC, 1992–; Col, Highlanders Regt, 1994–. Mem., Queen's Body Guard for Scotland, Royal Company of Archers, 1986–. Pres., Services Br., British Deer Soc., 1993–. *Publication:* The British Army and the Operational Level of War, 1989. *Recreations:* shooting, fishing, painting. *Address:* c/o Lloyds Bank, Cox's & King's, PO Box 1190, SW1Y 5NA. *Club:* Army and Navy.

MACKENZIE, Brig. John Alexander, CBE 1955; DSO 1944 and Bar, 1944; MC 1940 and Bar, 1940; retired; *b* 9 March 1915; *s* of late Louis Robert Wilson Mackenzie; *m* 1952, Beryl Cathreen Culver; one *s*. *Educ:* Nautical Coll., Pangbourne; RMC, Sandhurst. 2nd Bn Gloucestershire Regt, 1935–43; Bn Comd, 2nd Bn Lancs Fusiliers, Tunisia, Sicily and Italy Campaigns, 1943–44 (despatches, 1944); Bde Comd: 11 Inf. Bde, Italy, 1944; 10 Inf. Bde, Greece, 1945–46; psc 1947; GSO1 HQ British Troops, Berlin, 1948–49; AAG (Organisation), HQ, BAOR, 1950; jssc 1951; GSO1 HQ Western Comd, 1951–54; Comd: Britcom Sub-area N, S Korea, 1955; Inf. Trng Team, HQ Jordan Arab Army, 1956; Jt Concealment Centre, 1957–58; Small Arms Sch., Hythe, 1958–59; idc 1960; Comd: 1 Bde, Nigeria, 1961–63; 3 Bde, Congo, 1962; Actg GOC, Royal Nigerian Army, 1963; BGS Army Trng, MoD, 1964–67; ADC to the Queen, 1967–70; Comdt and Inspector of Intelligence, 1967–70; retired 1970. *Recreation:* gardening. *Address:* Slaybrook Hall, Sandling Road, Saltwood, Hythe, Kent CT21 4HG.

McKENZIE, John Cormack, FEng 1984; FICE; Hon. Secretary, Overseas Affairs, Fellowship of Engineering, 1988–92; Vice-Chairman, Thomas Telford Ltd, 1982–90; Director, H. R. Wallingford plc; *b* 21 June 1927; *s* of William Joseph McKenzie and Elizabeth Frances Robinson; *m* 1954, Olga Caroline Cleland; three *s* one *d*. *Educ:* St Andrews Coll.; Trinity Coll., Dublin (MA, MAI); Queen's Univ., Belfast (MSc). FIPM, FIEI, FIE(Aust). McLaughlin & Harvey, and Sir Alexander Gibb & Partners, 1946–48; Asst Lectr, QUB, 1948–50; Edmund Nuttall Ltd, 1950–82, Dir, 1967–82; Chm., Nuttall

Geotechnical Services Ltd, 1967–82; Dir, British Wastewater Ltd, 1978–82. Secretary: ICE, 1982–90; Commonwealth Engineers' Council, 1983–; Sec. Gen., World Fedn of Engrg Orgs, 1987–; Vice-Pres., Register of Engrs for Disaster Relief. Pres., Beaconsfield Adv. Centre, 1978–. *Publications:* papers: Research into some Aspects of Soil Cement, 1952; Engineers: Administrators or Technologists?, 1971; (contrib.) Civil Engineering Procedure, 3rd edn 1979; Comparison of the Market and Command Economics, 1990; Wealth Creation, 1992. *Recreations:* philately, collecting ancient pottery, climbing. *Address:* 20 Ledborough Lane, Beaconsfield, Bucks HP9 2PZ. *Club:* Athenæum.

McKENZIE, Prof. John Crawford; Rector, 1986–Sept. 1996, and Governor and Director of International Development, The London Institute; *b* 12 Nov. 1937; *s* of late Donald Walter McKenzie and Emily Beatrice McKenzie; *m* 1960, Ann McKenzie (*née* Roberts); two *s*. *Educ:* London School of Economics and Political Science (BScEcon); Bedford Coll., London (MPhil). Lecturer, Queen Elizabeth Coll., Univ. of London, 1961; Dep. Director, Office of Health Econs, 1966; Market Inf. Manager, Allied Breweries Ltd, 1968; various posts, Kimpher Ltd, 1969, finally Chief Exec., Kimpher Marketing Services, 1973; Head of Dept, London Coll. of Printing, 1975; Principal: Ilkley Coll., 1978; Bolton Inst. of Higher Educn, 1982; Rector, Liverpool Poly., 1984. Visiting Professor: Queen Elizabeth Coll., 1976–80; Univ. of Newcastle, 1981–87. Director: Antiquarian Pastimes Ltd; Developments at The London Inst. Ltd; The Cochrane Theatre Co. Ltd; New Frontiers in Educn Ltd. Mem., Adv. Council, Univ. of Sarawak, Malaysia. Chevalier de l'Ordre des Arts et des Lettres (France), 1992. *Publications:* (ed jtly) Changing Food Habits, 1964; (ed jtly) Our Changing Fare, 1966; (ed jtly) The Food Consumer, 1987; many articles in Proc. Nutrition Soc., British Jl Nutrition, Nutrition Bull., etc. *Recreation:* collecting antiquarian books. *Address:* The London Institute, 65 Davies Street, W1Y 2AA. *T:* 0171–514 6000. *Clubs:* Athenæum, Chelsea Arts.

McKENZIE, Rear-Adm. John Foster, CB 1977; CBE 1974 (OBE 1962); *b* Waiuku, 24 June 1923; *s* of Dr J. C. McKenzie; *m* 1945, Doreen Elizabeth, *d* of Dr E. T. and Dr G. M. McElligott; one *s* one *d*. *Educ:* Timaru Boys' High Sch.; St Andrews Coll., Christchurch, NZ. Served War of 1939–45: Royal Navy; transferred to Royal New Zealand Navy, 1947; Head, Defence Liaison Staff, London, 1966–68; Imperial Defence Coll., 1969; Asst Chief of Defence Staff (Policy), Defence HQ, NZ, 1970–71; Deputy Chief of Naval Staff, 1972; Commodore, Auckland, 1973–75; Chief of Naval Staff, and Mem. Defence Council, 1975–77, retired 1977. ADC 1972–75. *Recreations:* gardening, fishing. *Address:* 64 Lohia Street, Khandallah, Wellington 4, New Zealand.

MACKENZIE of Mornish, John Hugh Munro; Chairman: SEET plc (formerly Scottish, English and European Textiles plc), since 1969; *b* 29 Aug. 1925; *s* of Lt-Col John Munro Mackenzie of Mornish, DSO, JP, Mil. Kt of Windsor, Henry VIII Gateway, Windsor Castle, and Mrs E. H. M. Mackenzie (*née* Taaffe); *m* 1951, Eileen Louise Agate, *d* of Alexander Shanks, OBE, MC, and Mrs Shanks; four *s* one *d* (and one *s* decd). *Educ:* Edinburgh Acad.; Loretto Sch.; Trinity Coll., Oxford (MA (Hons)); Hague Acad. of Internat. Law; Inns of Court Law Schs; McGill Univ., Montreal. Served Army, 1945–49: Captain, The Royal Scots (Royal Regt); war service, Europe; 1st KOSB, A Company, 9th Brigade, 3rd Inf. Div. (despatches, certs of gallantry) and Far East HQ Allied Land Forces SE Asia and HQ Ceylon Army Comd, Staff Captain, Mil. Sec's Branch; HM Guard of Honour, Balmoral, 1946; HQ 3rd Auto Aircraft Div., 1946–47, GSO III. Harmsworth Law Scholar, Middle Temple, 1950; called to the Bar, Middle Temple, 1950. United Dominions Trust Ltd, trainee, ICI Ltd, Legal Asst, Estates Dept, 1951; Hudson's Bay Scholar, 1952–53; ICI Ltd, Buyer Crop and misc. products, 1953–54; Trubenised (GB) Ltd and Associated Cos, Co. Sec. and Legal Advisor, 1955–56; Aspro-Nicholas Ltd, Gp Develt Officer, 1956–57; PA to Man. Dir, Knitmaster Holdings, 1957; formed: Grampian Holdings Ltd (Manager and Sec.), 1958, Man. Dir, 1960; London and Northern Gp Ltd (Dep. Chm. and Man. Dir), 1962, Chm., 1967–87; Tace plc (Chm., 1967–91); Scottish, English and European Textiles plc, 1969 (Chm.). Chairman: Pauling plc, 1976–87; Goring Kerr plc, 1983–91. Eight Queen's Awards for Export won by Group Cos. FRSA, CIMgt. *Recreations:* opera, bridge, shooting, fishing, all field sports. *Address:* Mortlake House, Vicarage Road, SW14 8RU; Scaliscro Lodge, Isle of Lewis, Outer Hebrides PA86 9EL; Shellwood Manor, Leigh, Surrey RH2 8NX. *Clubs:* Royal Automobile; New, Royal Scots (Edinburgh).

McKENZIE, Julia Kathleen, (Mrs Jerry Harte); actress, singer and director; *b* 17 Feb. 1941; *d* of Albion McKenzie and Kathleen Rowe; *m* 1972, Jerry Harte. *Educ:* Guildhall School of Music and Drama. Hon. FGSM, 1988. *Stage:* Maggie May, 1965; Mame, 1969; Promises, Promises, 1970; Company, 1972; Cowardy Custard, 1973; Cole, 1974; Side by Side by Sondheim, 1977 (London and Broadway); Norman Conquests, 1978; Ten Times Table, 1979; On the 20th Century, 1981; Guys and Dolls, NT, 1982; Schweyk in 2nd World War, NT, 1982; Woman in Mind, Vaudeville, 1986; Follies, Shaftesbury, 1987; Into the Woods, Phoenix, 1990; Sweeney Todd, NT, 1993; Communicating Doors, Gielgud, 1995; directed: Stepping Out, Duke of York's, 1984; Steel Magnolias, Lyric, 1989; Just So, Watermill, Bagnor, Berks, 1989; Putting it Together, Old Fire Station, Oxford, 1992, Manhattan Theatre Club, 1993; *films:* Shirley Valentine, 1989; The Old Curiosity Shop, 1994; *television films:* Those Glory Glory Days, 1980; Hotel Du Lac, 1986; Adam Bede, 1992; *series:* Fame is the Spur, 1982; Blott on the Landscape, 1985; Fresh Fields, 1984–86; French Fields, 1989–91; *television plays:* Dear Box No, 1983; Sharing Time, 1984; Absent Friends, 1985; Julia and Company (TV special), 1986; The Shadowy Third, 1995; numerous TV musicals. *Recreations:* cooking, gardening. *Address:* c/o April Young Ltd, 11 Woodlands Road, Barnes, SW13 0JZ. *T:* 0181–876 7030.

MacKENZIE, Kelvin Calder; Director, Mirror Group plc, since 1994; *b* 22 Oct. 1946; *m* 1969, Jacqueline Mary Holland; two *s* one *d*. Editor, The Sun, 1981–94; Man. Dir, British Sky Broadcasting, 1994. *Address:* Mirror Group, 1 Canada Square, Canary Wharf, E14 5AT.

MacKENZIE, Kenneth John; Deputy Secretary (Head of Economic and Domestic Affairs Secretariat), Cabinet Office, since 1995; *b* 1 May 1943; *s* of John Donald MacKenzie and Elizabeth Pennant Johnston Sutherland; *m* 1975, Irene Mary Hogarth; one *s* one *d*. *Educ:* Woodchurch Road Primary School, Birkenhead; Birkenhead School; Pembroke College, Oxford (Exbnr; MA Mod. Hist.); Stanford Univ., Calif (AM Hist.). Scottish Home and Health Dept, 1965; Private Sec. to Jt Parly Under Sec. of State, Scottish Office, 1969–70; Scottish Office Regional Develt Div., 1970–73; Scottish Educn Dept, 1973–76; Civil Service Fellow, Glasgow Univ., 1974–75; Principal Private Sec. to Sec. of State for Scotland, 1977–79; Asst Sec., Scottish Economic Planning Dept, 1979–83; Scottish Office: Finance Div., 1983–85; Principal Finance Officer, 1985–88; Under Sec., Home and Health Dept, 1988–91; Under Sec., 1991–92, Sec., 1992–95, Agric. and Fisheries Dept. Mem., BBSRC (formerly AFRC), 1992–95. Hon. Pres., Edinburgh CS Dramatic Soc. Convenor, Congregational Bd, St Cuthbert's Parish Church. *Address:* Cabinet Office, 70 Whitehall, SW1A 2AS.

MacKENZIE, Kenneth William Stewart, CMG 1958; CVO 1975; FRAI; Colonial Administrative Service, now retired; *b* 30 July 1915; *s* of late W. S. MacKenzie and E. MacKenzie (*née* Johnson); *m* 1939, Kathleen Joyce Ingram; one *s* one *d*. *Educ:* Whitcliffe Mount Gram. Sch., Cleckheaton; Downing Coll., Cambridge. 1st Cl. Hist. Tripos, Part I, 1935; Class II, Div. I, 1936; 1st Cl. Arch. and Anthrop. Tripos, Section A, 1937, BA 1936, MA 1962. Cadet, Colonial Administrative Service, Basutoland, 1938; Asst Sec., Mauritius, 1944; Administrative Officer, Kenya, 1948; Asst Financial Sec., Kenya, 1950; seconded to HM Treasury, 1951–53; Dep. Sec., 1954 and Permanent Sec., 1955, Treasury, Kenya; Minister for Finance and Development and Financial Sec., Kenya, 1959–62. MLC Kenya, 1955–62; MLA East Africa, 1959–62. Retired, 1963 to facilitate constitutional change. Re-employed as Principal, Colonial Office, 1963; Principal, HM Treasury, 1966–70; Asst Sec., DoE, 1970–75; Dir of Studies, RIPA (Overseas Unit), 1976–90. *Publication:* pamphlet, How Basutoland is Governed, 1944. *Recreations:* reading, gardening. *Address:* Beaumont, 28 Greenhurst Lane, Oxted, Surrey RH8 0LB. *T:* Oxted (01883) 713848. *Clubs:* Royal Over-Seas League; Achilles; Nairobi (Nairobi).

MACKENZIE, Lorimer David Maurice; Director, Budget and General Affairs, Directorate General of Fisheries, European Commission, since 1992; *b* 4 Aug. 1940; *s* of William David Beveridge Mackenzie and Elizabeth Reid (*née* Peters); *m* 1959, Penelope Marsh Happer; two *s* two *d*. *Educ:* Hermitage Park Sch., Leith; Royal High Sch., Edinburgh; Edinburgh Univ. (MA Hons Mental Philosophy). Department of Agriculture and Fisheries, Scottish Office: Asst Principal, 1964–68; Principal, 1968–73; Commission of the European Communities: Head of Division: Agricl Res., 1973–77; Food Aid, 1978–82; Develt of Trade, 1982–92. *Recreations:* Scottish history and literature. *Address:* Hoogvorstweg 4, 3080 Tervuren, Belgium; 41 Great King Street, Edinburgh EH3 6QR. *Clubs:* Commonwealth Trust, New (Edinburgh).

McKENZIE, Michael; QC 1991; Master of the Crown Office and Queen's Coroner and Attorney, Registrar of Criminal Appeals and of the Courts Martial Appeal Court, since 1988; *b* Hove, Sussex, 25 May 1943; *s* of Robert John McKenzie and Kitty Elizabeth McKenzie; *m* 1964, Peggy Dorothy, *d* of Thomas Edward William Russell and Dorothy Mabel Russell; three *s*. *Educ:* Varndean Grammar Sch., Brighton. Town Clerk's Dept, Brighton, 1961–63; Asst to Clerk of the Peace, Brighton Quarter Sessions, 1963–67; Sen. Clerk of the Court, 1967–70, Dep. Clerk of the Peace, 1970–71, Middlesex Quarter Sessions; called to the Bar, Middle Temple, 1970, Bencher, 1993; Deputy to Courts Administrator, Middlesex Crown Court, 1972–73; Courts Administrator (Newcastle), NE Circuit, 1974–79; Courts Administrator, Central Criminal Court, and Coordinator for Taxation of Crown Court Costs, S Eastern Circuit, 1979–84; Dep. Circuit Administrator, SE Circuit, 1984–86; Asst Registrar, Ct of Appeal Criminal Div., 1986–88. Freeman, City of London, 1979. FRSA 1990. Hon. Fellow, Kent Sch. of Law, Canterbury Univ., 1991. *Publication:* (ed) Rules of Court: criminal procedure, 1994. *Recreations:* Northumbrian stick dressing, fell walking. *Address:* Royal Courts of Justice, Strand, WC2A 2LL.

MACKENZIE, Michael Philip; Director-General, Food and Drink Federation, since 1986; *b* 26 June 1937; *s* of Brig. Maurice Mackenzie, DSO, and Mrs Vivienne Mackenzie; *m* 1966, Jill (*née* Beckley); one *s* one *d*. *Educ:* Downside Sch.; Lincoln Coll., Oxford (BA); Harvard Business Sch., USA. United Biscuits plc, 1966–86: Prodn Dir, various businesses within United Biscuits, 1974–83; Man. Dir, D. S. Crawford Bakeries, 1983–86. FRSA. *Recreations:* walking, gardening, opera, theatre. *Address:* Ebony Cottage, Reading Street, near Tenterden, Kent TN30 7HT. *Club:* Travellers'.

MACKENZIE, Sir Peter Douglas, 13th Bt *cr* 1673 (NS), of Coul, Ross-shire; *b* 23 April 1949; *s* of Henry Douglas Mackenzie (*d* 1965) and Irene Carter Freeman; *S* kinsman, 1990; *m* 1982, Jennifer, *d* of Ridley Boyce; two *d*. *Heir: kinsman* Miles Roderick Turing Mackenzie [*b* 18 April 1952; *m* 1983, Hiroko Sato].

MACKENZIE, Sir Roderick McQuhae, 12th Bt *cr* 1703, of Scatwell; FRCP(C); medical practitioner; *b* 17 April 1942; *s* of Captain Sir Roderick Edward François McQuhae Mackenzie, 11th Bt, CBE, DSC, RN and Marie Evelyn Campbell (*d* 1993), *o c* of late William Ernest Parkinson; *S* father, 1986; *m* 1970, Nadezhda, (Nadine), Baroness von Rorbas, *d* of Georges Frederic Schlatter, Baron von Rorbas; one *s* one *d*. *Educ:* Sedbergh; King's College London. MB, BS; MRCP; DCH. *Heir: s* Gregory Roderick McQuhae Mackenzie, *b* 8 May 1971. *Address:* 2431 Udell Road NW, Calgary, Alberta T2N 4H9, Canada.

McKENZIE, Sir Roy (Allan), ONZ 1995; KBE 1989; Director: Rangatira Ltd, 1946–93; James Cook Hotel Ltd, since 1970; *b* 7 Nov. 1922; *s* of John Robert McKenzie and Ann May McKenzie (*née* Wrigley); *m* 1949, Shirley Elizabeth Howard; two *s* one *d*. *Educ:* Timaru Boys' High Sch. ACA 1948. Executive, 1949–70, Exec. Dir, 1955, McKenzie NZ Ltd; Chairman: Rangatira Investment Co. Ltd, 1968–85; J. R. McKenzie Trust, 1970–87. Chairman and Founder: McKenzie Educn Foundation; Roy McKenzie Foundn; Chm., Te Omanga Hospice, 1979–. Patron, Outward Bound Trust NZ, 1977– (Chm., 1968). Hon. DLitt Massey, 1992. *Publication:* The Roydon Heritage, 1978. *Recrations:* tennis, ski-ing, tramping, breeding standardbreds (horses). *Address:* 21 Marine Drive, Lowry Bay, Eastbourne, New Zealand. *T:* (4)684492.

MACKENZIE, Wallace John, OBE 1974; Director, Slough Estates plc, 1972–91 (Group Managing Director, 1975–86); *b* 2 July 1921; *s* of Wallace D. Mackenzie and Ethel F. Williamson; *m* 1951, Barbara D. Hopson; two *s* one *d*. *Educ:* Harrow Weald County Grammar Sch. Gen. Manager, Slough Estates Canada Ltd, 1952–72; Dep. Man. Dir, Slough Estates Ltd, 1972–75. Dir, Investors in Industry plc, 1982–86; Chm., Trust Parts Ltd, 1986–94 (Dir, 1985). Member: Commn for New Towns, 1978–94; London Residuary Body, 1985–. *Recreations:* golf, bridge. *Address:* 1 Brampton Mews, Pound Lane, Marlow, Bucks SL7 2SY. *T:* Marlow (01628) 478310.

MACKENZIE, Prof. William James Millar, CBE 1963; FBA 1968; Professor of Politics, Glasgow University, 1966–74, now Emeritus; *b* 8 April 1909; *s* of Laurence Millar Mackenzie, WS, Edinburgh; *m* 1943, Pamela Muriel Malyon; one *s* four *d*. *Educ:* Edinburgh Academy; Balliol Coll., Oxford (MA) (Ireland Schol. 1929); Edinburgh Univ. (LLB); Fellow of Magdalen Coll., Oxford, 1933–48, Emeritus Fellow, 1990; Temp. Civil Servant, Air Ministry, 1939–44; Official War Historian, SOE, 1945–48. Faculty Fellow, Nuffield Coll., 1948; Lecturer in Politics, Oxford Univ., 1948; Prof. of Government, Manchester Univ., 1949–66, Glasgow Univ., 1966–74; Special Comr, for Constitutional Development, Tanganyika, 1952; Co-opted Mem., Manchester City Educn Cttee, 1953–64; apptd Mem., British Wool Marketing Board, 1954–66; Mem. Royal Commn on Local Govt in Greater London, 1957; Constitutional Adviser, Kenya, 1959; Vice-Chm., Bridges Cttee on Training in Public Administration for Overseas Countries, 1962; Member: Maud Cttee on Management in Local Govt, 1964–66; Cttee on Remuneration of Ministers and Members of Parliament, 1963–64; North-West Regional Economic Planning Council, 1965–66; SSRC, 1965–69; Parry Cttee on University Libraries, 1964–67; Chm., Children's Panel Adv. Cttee, Glasgow City, 1973–75. Hon. LLD: Dundee, 1968; Lancaster, 1970; Manchester, 1975; Hon. DLitt Warwick, 1972; Hon. DSc (Econ) Hull, 1981; DUniv Open Univ., 1984. *Publications:* (in part) British Government since 1918, 1950; (jtly) Central Administration in Great Britain, 1957; Free Elections, 1958; (ed with Prof. K. Robinson) Five Elections in Africa, 1959; Politics and Social Science, 1967; (jtly) Social Work in Scotland, 1969; Power, Violence, Decision, 1975; Explorations in Government, 1975; Political Identity, 1977; Biological Ideas in

Politics, 1978; Power and Responsibility in Health Care, 1979. *Address:* 12 Kirklee Circus, Glasgow G12 0TW.

McKENZIE JOHNSTON, Henry Butler, CB 1981; Vice-Chairman, Commission for Local Administration in England, 1982–84 (Commissioner, 1981–84); *b* 10 July 1921; *er s* of late Colin McKenzie Johnston and late Bernardine (*née* Fawcett Butler); *m* 1949, Marian Allardyce Middleton, *e d* of late Brig. A. A. Middleton and late Winifred (*née* Salvesen); one *s* two *d*. *Educ:* Rugby. Served with Black Watch (RHR), 1940–46; Adjt 6th Bn, 1944–45; Temp. Major 1945. Staff of HM Embassy, Athens, 1946–47; entered Foreign (subseq. Diplomatic) Service, 1947; Paris, 1948–51; British High Commn, Germany, 1951–54; FO, 1954–56; 1st Sec. (Commercial), Montevideo, 1956–60; FO, 1960–63; Counsellor (Information), Mexico City, 1963–66; Dep. High Comr, Port of Spain, 1966–67; seconded to Min. of Overseas Develt, 1968–70; Consul-Gen., Munich, 1971–73; seconded to Office of Parly Comr, 1973–79, transferred permanently, 1979–81; Dep. Parly Comr for Admin, 1974–81. Mem., Broadcasting Complaints Commn, 1986–90. Mem., Social Security Appeal Tribunal, Kensington, subseq. Central London, 1985–88. Chm., British-Mexican Soc., 1977–80. *Publication:* Missions to Mexico: a tale of British diplomacy in the 1820s, 1992. *Address:* 6 Pembroke Gardens, W8 6HS. *Clubs:* Athenæum, Hurlingham.

McKENZIE SMITH, Ian, OBE 1992; RSA 1987; PRSW (RSW 1981); FSAScot 1970; FMA 1987; City Arts and Recreation Officer, City of Aberdeen, since 1989; *b* 3 Aug. 1935; *s* of James McKenzie Smith and Mary Benzie; *m* 1963, Mary Rodger Fotheringham; two *s* one *d*. *Educ:* Robert Gordon's Coll., Aberdeen; Gray's Sch. of Art, Aberdeen; Hospitalfield Coll. of Art, Arbroath. Teacher of art, 1960–63; Educn Officer, Council of Industrial Design, Scottish Cttee, 1963–68; Dir, Aberdeen Art Gall. and Museums, 1968–89. Work in permanent collections: Scottish Nat. Gall. of Modern Art; Scottish Arts Council; Arts Council of NI; Contemp. Art Soc.; Aberdeen Art Gall. and Museums; Glasgow Art Gall. and Museums; City Art Centre, Edinburgh; Perth Art Gall.; Abbot Hall Art Gall., Kendal; Hunterian Mus., Glasgow; Nuffield Foundn; Carnegie Trust; Strathclyde Educn Authority; Lothian Educn Authority; RSA; DoE; Robert Fleming Holdings; IBM. Member: Scottish Arts Council, 1970–77; Cttee of Enquiry into Econ. Situation of Visual Artists, Gulbenkian Foundn, 1978. Pres., RSW, 1988–; Sec., RSA, 1991– (Dep. Pres. and Treas., 1990–91). Governor: Edinburgh Coll. of Art, 1976–88; The Robert Gordon Univ. (formerly Robert Gordon Inst. of Technology), 1989–. External Assessor: Glasgow Sch. of Art, 1982–86; Duncan of Jordanstone Coll. of Art, 1982–86. Board Member: Scottish Sculpture Workshop; Aberdeen Maritime Mus. Appeal; Friends of RSA; RSA Enterprises; Member: Nat. Heritage, Scottish Gp, 1977–; Curatorial Cttee, NT for Scotland, 1991–. FSS 1981; FRSA 1973. Hon. LLD Aberdeen, 1991. Inst. of Contemp. Prints Award, 1969; Guthrie Award, 1971, Gillies Award, 1980, RSA; ESU Thyne Scholarship, 1980. *Address:* 70 Hamilton Place, Aberdeen AB2 4BA. *T:* Aberdeen (01224) 644531. *Club:* Royal Northern (Aberdeen).

MACKENZIE SMITH, Peter; Director of Export Promotion, British Council, since 1994; *b* 12 Jan. 1946; *s* of Antony and Isobel Mackenzie Smith; *m* 1973, Sandra Gay-French; three *d*. *Educ:* Downside; Jesus Coll., Cambridge (BA Classical Tripos). Teacher: British Inst., Oporto, 1967–68; Internat. House, London, 1969; British Council, 1969–: Asst Rep., Lagos, 1969–72; Asst Cultural Attaché, Cairo, 1972–77; Regl Dir, Southampton, 1977–80; Educnl Contracts Dept, 1980–83; Dep. Rep., Cairo, 1983–87; Director: Educnl Contracts, 1987–89; Projects Div., 1989–92; Nigeria and W Africa, 1992–94. *Address:* 30 Prothero Road, SW6 7LZ.

MACKENZIE STUART, family name of **Baron Mackenzie-Stuart.**

MACKENZIE-STUART, Baron *cr* 1988 (Life Peer), of Dean in the District of the City of Edinburgh; **Alexander John Mackenzie Stuart;** President of the Court of Justice, European Communities at Luxembourg, 1984–88 (Judge of the Court of Justice, 1972–84); a Senator of the College of Justice in Scotland, 1972; *b* 18 Nov. 1924; *s* of late Prof. A. Mackenzie Stuart, KC, and Amy Margaret Dean, Aberdeen; *m* 1952, Anne Burtholme Millar, *d* of late J. S. L. Millar, WS, Edinburgh; four *d*. *Educ:* Fettes Coll., Edinburgh (open Schol.); Sidney Sussex Coll., Cambridge (schol. 1949, 1st cl. Pt II Law Tripos, BA 1949, Hon. Fellow, 1977); Edinburgh Univ. (LLB (dist.) 1951). Royal Engineers (Temp. Capt. 1946), 1942–47. Admitted Faculty of Advocates, 1951; QC (Scot.) 1963; Keeper of the Advocates Library, 1970–72. Standing Junior Counsel: to Scottish Home Dept, 1956–57; to Inland Revenue in Scotland, 1957–63. Sheriff-Principal of Aberdeen, Kincardine and Banff, 1971–72. President: British Acad. of Experts, 1989–92; European Movement (Scotland), 1991. Governor, Fettes College, 1962–72. Hon. Bencher: Middle Temple, 1978; King's Inn, Dublin, 1984; Hon. Mem., SPTL, 1982. FCIArb 1990; FRSE 1991. Hon. Prof., Collège d'Europe, Bruges, 1974–77. DUniv. Stirling, 1973; Hon. LLD: Exeter, 1978; Edinburgh, 1978; Glasgow, 1981; Aberdeen, 1983; Cambridge, 1987; Birmingham, 1988. Prix Bech for services to Europe, 1989. Grand Croix, Ordre Grand-Ducal de la Couronne de Chene de Luxembourg, 1988. *Publications:* Hamlyn Lectures: The European Communities and the Rule of Law, 1977; A French King at Holyrood, 1995; articles in legal publications. *Recreation:* collecting. *Address:* 7 Randolph Cliff, Edinburgh EH3 7TZ; Le Garidel, Gravières, 07140 Les Vans, Ardèche, France. *Clubs:* Athenæum; New (Edinburgh); Golf Club du Grand Guérin (Villefort).

McKEOWN, Prof. Patrick Arthur, OBE 1991; MSc; FEng 1986; FIEE; FIQA; FIMechE; Professor of Precision Engineering since 1974, Director of Cranfield Unit for Precision Engineering since 1969, Cranfield University (formerly Institute of Technology); Chairman, Cranfield Precision Engineering Ltd, since 1987 (Chief Executive, 1987–92); *b* 16 Aug. 1930; *s* of Robert Matthew McKeown and Augusta (*née* White); *m* 1954, Mary Patricia Heath; three *s*. *Educ:* Cambridge County High Sch. for Boys; Bristol Grammar Sch.; Cranfield Inst. of Technol. (MSc). CEng, MIMechE 1969; FIEE (FIProdE 1971); FIQA 1973. National Service, RE, 1949–51; Suez Campaign, 1956: Captain RE; port maintenance. Student apprentice, Bristol Aircraft Co. Ltd, Bristol, 1951–54 (HNC National State Scholarship); Cranfield Inst. of Technol., 1954–56; Société Genevoise, Newport Pagnell and Geneva, 1956–68 (Technical and Works Dir, 1965); Hd of Dept for Design of Machine Systems. Cranfield Inst. of Technol., 1975–85. Chairman: Cranfield Precision Systems Ltd, 1984–87; Cranfield Moulded Structures Ltd, 1984–91; non-executive Director: Control Techniques plc, 1990–95; AMTRI, 1990–92. Vice-Pres., Inst. of Qual. Assurance, 1976; Pres., CIRP (Internat. Instn for Prodn Engrg Research), 1988–89. Member: Evaluation Panel, National Bureau of Standards, Washington, USA; Metrology and Standards Requirements Bd, DTI, 1983–86; Advanced Manufg Technol. Cttee, DTI, 1983–87; Vis. Cttee, RCA, 1984–87; ACARD working gp, 1987–88. Internat. Advr, Gintic Inst. of Manufg Technology, Singapore, 1991–. Clayton Meml Lectr, IMechE, 1986. Charter Fellow, Soc. of Manufacturing Engineers, 1985. Fulbright Award (Vis. Prof. of Mechanical Engrg, Univ. of Wisconsin-Madison), 1982; F. W. Taylor Award, Soc. of Manufacturing Engrs, 1983; Thomas Hawksley Gold Medal, IMechE, 1987; Mensforth Gold Medal, IProdE, 1988. *Publications:* papers in CIRP Annals. *Recreations:* walking, travel, enjoyment of wine, good food, music, theatre. *Address:* 37 Church End, Biddenham, Bedford MK40 4AR. *T:* Bedford (01234) 267678.

MACKEOWN, Thomas Frederick William; Administrator and Secretary, University College Hospital, London, 1946–63; *b* 3 Jan. 1904; *s* of Rev. William Mackeown, Rushbrooke, Co. Cork; *m* 1936, Lorraine, *d* of Major R. Hayes, Sherburn-in-Elmet, Yorks; one *d*. *Educ:* Felsted; Worcester Coll., Oxford (MA). Qualified as Chartered Accountant, 1927. Hospital Administrator: Liverpool Stanley Hospital, 1934–37; Clayton Hospital, Wakefield, 1937–45; Royal Infirmary, Sunderland, 1945–46; Hill Homes, Highgate (actg), 1966; King Edward VII Memorial Hospital, Bermuda, 1967; Vice-Chm., Management Cttee, Harefield and Northwoods Hosps, 1960–74; undertook Hosp. Domestic Staff Survey under aegis of King Edward's Hosp. Fund for London, 1968. Lay FRSocMed, 1974. *Address:* Mary Feilding Guild, Kekewich House, 1 View Road, Highgate, N6 4DP. *T:* 0181–348 1952.

McKERN, Leo, (Reginald McKern), AO 1983; actor; *b* 16 March 1920; *s* of Norman Walton McKern and Vera (*née* Martin); *m* 1946, Joan Alice Southa (Jane Holland); two *d*. *Educ:* Sydney Techn. High Sch. Engrg apprentice, 1935–37; artist, 1937–40; AIF (Corp., Engrs), 1940–42; actor, 1944; arrived England, 1946; CSEU tour, Germany; Arts Council tours, 1947; Old Vic, 1949–52; Shakespeare Meml Theatre, 1952–54; Old Vic last season, 1962–63; New Nottingham Playhouse, 1963–64; *stage:* Toad of Toad Hall, Princes, 1954; Queen of the Rebels, Haymarket, 1955; Cat on a Hot Tin Roof, Aldwych, 1958; Brouhaha, Aldwych, 1958; Rollo, Strand, 1959; A Man for all Seasons, Globe, 1960; The Thwarting of Baron Bolligrew, RSC, Aldwych, 1965; Volpone, Garrick, 1967; The Wolf, Apollo, 1973; The Housekeeper, Apollo, 1982; Number One, Queen's, 1984; Boswell for the Defence, Australia, later Playhouse, 1989, tour 1991; Hobson's Choice, Chichester, 1995; *films:* The French Lieutenant's Woman, 1983; Ladyhawke, 1984; The Chain, 1985; Travelling North, 1986; On Our Selection, 1995; *television:* Rumpole of the Bailey (series), 1977–; Reilly—Ace of Spies, 1983; King Lear, 1983; Monsignor Quixote; Murder With Mirrors (film), 1985; The Master Builder, 1988; The Last Romantics (film), 1992; A Foreign Field, 1993. *Publication:* Just Resting (biographical memoir), 1983. *Recreations:* sailing, swimming, photography, painting, environment preservation. *Address:* c/o Richard Hatton Ltd, 29 Roehampton Gate, SW15 5JS.

MACKERRAS, Sir (Alan) Charles (MacLaurin), Kt 1979; CBE 1974; Hon. RAM 1969; FRCM 1987; Principal Guest Conductor: Scottish Chamber Orchestra, since 1992; San Francisco Opera, since 1993; Royal Philharmonic Orchestra, since 1993; Guest Conductor: Vienna State Opera; Paris Opera; Munich Opera; Royal Opera House Covent Garden; English National Opera; Metropolitan Opera; *b* Schenectady, USA, 17 Nov. 1925; *s* of late Alan Patrick and Catherine Mackerras, Sydney, Australia; *m* 1947, Helena Judith (*née* Wilkins); two *d*. *Educ:* Sydney Grammar Sch. Principal Oboist, Sydney Symphony Orchestra, 1943–46; Staff Conductor, Sadler's Wells Opera, 1949–53; Principal Conductor BBC Concert Orchestra, 1954–56; freelance conductor with most British and many continental orchestras; concert tours in USSR, S Africa, USA, 1957–66; First Conductor, Hamburg State Opera, 1966–69; Musical Dir, Sadler's Wells Opera, later ENO, 1970–77; Chief Guest Conductor, BBC SO, 1976–79; Chief Conductor, Sydney Symphony Orch., ABC, 1982–85; Principal Guest Conductor, Royal Liverpool Philharmonic Orch., 1986–88; Mus. Dir, WNO, 1987–92 (Conductor Emeritus, 1992–); frequent radio and TV broadcasts; many commercial recordings, notably Handel series for DGG and Janáček operas for Decca; appearances at many internat. festivals and opera houses. Hon. DMus: Hull, 1990; Nottingham, 1991; York, Brno, Brisbane, 1994. Evening Standard Award for Opera, 1977; Janáček Medal, 1978; Gramophone Record of the Year, 1977, 1980; Gramophone Operatic Record of the Year Award, 1983, 1984; Gramophone Best Choral Record, 1986; Grammy Award for best opera recording, 1981; Gramophone Best Opera Recording, 1994. *Publications:* ballet arrangements of Pineapple Poll and of Lady and the Fool; Arthur Sullivan's lost Cello Concerto, 1986; contrib. 4 appendices to Charles Mackerras: a musicians' musician, by Nancy Phelan 1987; articles in Opera Magazine, Music and Musicians and other musical jls. *Recreations:* languages, yachting. *Address:* 10 Hamilton Terrace, NW8 9UG. *T:* 0171–286 4047, *Fax:* 0171–289 5893.

McKERROW, June; Director, Mental Health Foundation, since 1992; *b* 17 June 1950; *d* of Alexander Donald and Lorna McKerrow. *Educ:* Brunel Univ. (MPhil 1977). Housing management in local govt and housing assocs, 1967–80; Dir, Stonham Housing Assoc., 1980–92. Trustee: Shelter, 1985–93; Homeless Internat., 1988–93; Cherwell Housing Trust, 1992–; Charity Projects, 1993–. *Address:* c/o Mental Health Foundation, 37 Mortimer Street, W1N 7RJ. *T:* 0171–580 0145.

MACKESON, Sir Rupert (Henry), 2nd Bt *cr* 1954; *b* 16 Nov. 1941; *s* of Brig. Sir Harry Ripley Mackeson, 1st Bt, and Alethea, Lady Mackeson (*d* 1979), *d* of late Comdr R. Talbot, RN; *S* father, 1964; *m* 1968, Hon. Camilla Keith (marr. diss. 1973), *d* of Baron Keith of Castleacre, *qv*. *Educ:* Harrow; Trinity Coll., Dublin (MA). Captain, Royal Horse Guards, 1967, retd 1968. *Publications:* (as Rupert Collens): (jtly) 'Snaffles' on Racing and Point-to-Pointing, 1988; (jtly) 'Snaffles' on Hunting, 1989; Look at Cecil Aldin's Dogs and Hounds, 1990; 25 Legal Luminaries from Vanity Fair, 1990; Cecil Aldin's Dog Models, 1994. *Recreations:* art, racing. *Heir:* none.

MACKESY, Dr Piers Gerald, FRHistS; FBA 1988; Fellow of Pembroke College, Oxford, 1954–87, now Emeritus; *b* 15 Sept. 1924; *s* of Maj.-Gen. Pierse Joseph Mackesy, CB, DSO, MC and Dorothy (*née* Cook), (Leonora Starr); *m* 1st, 1957, Sarah Davies; one *s* two *d*; 2nd, 1978, Patricia Timlin (*née* Gore). *Educ:* Wellington Coll.; Christ Church, Oxford (1st cl. Hons Modern Hist., 1950; DPhil 1953; DLitt 1978). FRHistS 1965. Lieut, The Royal Scots Greys (NW Europe, 1944–47); Captain, TA, 1950–57. Robinson Schol., Oriel Coll., Oxford, 1951–53; Harkness Fellow, Harvard Univ., 1953–54; Vis. Fellow, Inst. for Advanced Study, Princeton, 1962–63; Vis. Prof., CIT, 1966; Huntingdon Liby, San Marino, Calif, 1967. Lectures: Lees-Knowles, Cambridge, 1972; American Bicentennial, at Williamsburg, Va, Clark Univ., Naval War Coll., US Mil. Acad., Nat. War Coll., Peabody Mus., N Eastern Univ., Capitol Historical Soc. Member, Council: Inst. for Early Amer. Hist. and Culture, 1970–73; Nat. Army Mus., 1983–92; Soc. for Army Historical Res., 1985–94. *Publications:* The War in the Mediterranean 1803–10, 1957; The War for America 1775–83, 1964, 2nd edn 1993; Statesmen at War: the Strategy of Overthrow 1798–99, 1974; The Coward of Minden: the affair of Lord George Sackville, 1979; War without Victory: the downfall of Pitt 1799–1802, 1984; British Victory in Egypt, 1801: the end of Napoleon's conquest, 1995; contribs to various books and jls. *Recreations:* hunting, hill walking. *Address:* Leochel Cushnie House, Leochel Cushnie, Alford, Aberdeenshire AB33 8LJ. *T:* Muir of Fowlis (019755) 81379. *Club:* Army and Navy.

MACKEY, Prof. James Patrick; Thomas Chalmers Professor of Theology, since 1979, and Director of Graduate School and Associate Dean, since 1995, University of Edinburgh; *b* 9 Feb. 1934; *e s* of Peter Mackey and Esther Mackey (*née* Morrissey); *m* 1973, Hanorah Noelle Quinlan; one *s* one *d*. *Educ:* Mount St Joseph Coll., Roscrea; Nat. Univ. of Ireland (BA); Pontifical Univ., Maynooth (LPh, BD, STL, DD); Queen's Univ. Belfast (PhD); postgraduate study at Univs of Oxford, London, Strasbourg. Lectr in Philosophy, QUB, 1960–66; Lectr in Theology, St John's Coll., Waterford, 1966–69; Associate Prof. and Prof. of Systematic and Philosophical Theol., Univ. of San Francisco, 1969–79; Dean, Faculty of Divinity, Edinburgh Univ., 1984–88. Visiting Professor: Univ. of California,

Berkeley, 1974; Dartmouth Coll., NH, 1989; Mem., Centre for Hermeneutical Studies, Berkeley, 1974–79. Organiser, Internat. Conf. on the Cultures of Europe, Derry, 1992. *Television series:* The Hall of Mirrors, 1984; The Gods of War, 1986; Perspectives, 1986–87; radio programmes. Associate Editor: Herder Correspondence, 1966–69; Concilium (church history section), 1965–70; Horizons, 1973–79; Editor, Studies in World Christianity, 1995–. *Publications:* The Modern Theology of Tradition, 1962; Life and Grace, 1966; Tradition and Change in the Church, 1968; Contemporary Philosophy of Religion, 1968; (ed) Morals, Law and Authority, 1969; The Church: its credibility today, 1970; The Problems of Religious Faith, 1972; Jesus: the man and the myth, 1979; The Christian Experience of God as Trinity, 1983; (ed) Religious Imagination, 1986; Modern Theology: a sense of direction, 1987; (with Prof. J. D. G. Dunn) New Testament Theology in Dialogue, 1987; (ed) Introduction to Celtic Christianity, 1989; Power and Christian Ethics, 1993; (ed) The Cultures of Europe, 1994; contribs to theol. and philosoph. jls. *Recreations:* yachting; rediscovery of original Celtic culture of these islands. *Address:* 10 Randolph Crescent, Edinburgh EH3 7TT. *T:* 0131–225 9408. *Clubs:* Edinburgh University; Port Edgar Yacht (W Lothian).

MACKEY, Air Vice-Marshal Jefferson, QHDS; Director, RAF Dental Services, since 1990, and Defence Dental Services, since 1992; *b* 24 Oct. 1936; *s* of late James Mackey and of Cicely (*née* Hitchman); *m* 1959, Sheila Mary Taylor; one *s* two *d*. *Educ:* Latymer Upper Sch.; Guy's Hosp. (BDS, LDS RCS). Asst Dir, Defence Dental Services, 1982–86; Officer Comdg RAF Inst. of Dental Health and Trng, 1986–87; Principal Dental Officer, RAF Support Command, 1987–90. FISM; FIMgt; FRGS. *Address:* Takali, Oxford Road, Stone, Bucks HP17 8PB. *T:* Aylesbury (01296) 748823; 3 Shawfield Street, SW3 4BA. *Club:* Royal Air Force.

MACKEY, Most Rev. John, CBE 1983; Bishop of Auckland, NZ, (RC), 1974–83; *b* Bray, Co. Wicklow, 11 Jan. 1918; *s* of Malachy Mackey and Kathleen (*née* Byrne). *Educ:* Auckland Univ. (MA, DipEd); Notre Dame Univ., USA (PhD). Emigrated to NZ, 1924. Ordained priest, 1941; Adminr for Auckland Diocesan Schs, 1951–71; Lectr, Holy Cross Seminary, 1972–74; formerly Professor in Theological Faculty, National Seminary of Mosgiel, Dunedin. *Publications:* The Making of a State Education System, 1967; Reflections on Church History, 1975; Looking at Ourselves, 1994. *Address:* 3 Karaka Street, Takapuna, Auckland, New Zealand.

MACKEY, William Gawen; Partner, 1952, Managing Partner UK Operations, 1981–86, Ernst & Whinney; retired 1986; *b* 22 Sept. 1924; *s* of William Gawen Mackey and Jane Mackey; *m* 1948, Margaret Reeves Vinycomb; two *s*. *Educ:* Dame Allan's Sch., Newcastle upon Tyne. Qualified Chartered Accountant, 1949. Served RN, 1942–45 (Sub-Lt). Joined Ernst & Whinney, 1952, Newcastle; transf. London, 1973, with responsibility for corporate restructuring and insolvency services in UK. Receiver: Airfix; British Tanners; Laker; Stone-Platt. Chm., Insolvency Sub Cttee, CCAB, 1978–82; Dir, Inst. Corporate Insolvency Courses, 1974–80. *Publications:* articles and lectures on corporate management, restructuring and insolvency. *Recreations:* opera, gardening, France. *Address:* Eynesse, Ste Foy La Grande 33220, France. *T:* 57410042, *Fax:* 57410070.

MACKIE, family name of **Baron Mackie of Benshie.**

MACKIE OF BENSHIE, Baron *cr* 1974 (Life Peer), of Kirriemuir; **George Yull Mackie,** CBE 1971; DSO 1944; DFC 1944; Chairman: Caithness Glass Ltd, 1966–85; Caithness Pottery Co. Ltd, 1975–84; The Benshie Cattle Co. Ltd; Land and Timber Services Ltd, since 1986; *b* 10 July 1919; *s* of late Maitland Mackie, OBE, Hon. LLD; *m* 1st, 1944, Lindsay Lyall Sharp (*d* 1985), *y d* of late Alexander and Isabella Sharp, OBE, Aberdeen; three *d* (one *s* decd); 2nd, 1988, Jacqueline, *widow* of Andrew Lane, and *d* of late Col. Marcel Rauch. *Educ:* Aberdeen Grammar Sch.; Aberdeen Univ. Served War of 1939–45, RAF; Bomber Command, (DSO, DFC); Air Staff, 1944. Farming at Ballinshoe, Kirriemuir, 1945–89. Contested (L) South Angus, 1959; MP (L) Caithness and Sutherland, 1964–66; contested (L) Scotland NE, European Parliamentary election, 1979. Pres., Scottish Liberal Party, 1983–88 (Chm., 1965–70); Member: EEC Scrutiny Cttee (D), House of Lords; Liberal Shadow Admin; Exec., Inter-Parly Union; Governing Body, GB/East Europe Centre; Council of Europe, 1986–; WEU, 1986–; Liberal Spokesman, House of Lords: Devolution, Agriculture, Scotland, Industry. Chm., Cotswold Wine Co. (UK) Ltd, 1983–85. Dir, Scottish Ballet, 1986–88. Rector, Dundee Univ., 1980–83. Hon. LLD Dundee, 1982. *Publication:* Policy for Scottish Agriculture, 1963. *Address:* Cortachy House, by Kirriemuir, Angus DD8 4LY. *T:* Kirriemuir (01575) 4229. *Clubs:* Garrick, Farmers', Royal Air Force.

See also Sir Maitland Mackie, I. L. Aitken, A. G. Sharp, Sir R. L. Sharp.

MACKIE, Air Cdre (Retd) Alastair Cavendish Lindsay, CBE 1966; DFC 1943 and Bar 1944; Director General, Health Education Council, 1972–82; Director, Ansador Ltd, since 1983; *b* 3 Aug. 1922; *s* of George Mackie, DSO, OBE, MD, Malvern, Worcs and May (*née* Cavendish); *m* 1944, Rachel Goodson; two *s*. *Educ:* Charterhouse. Royal Air Force, 1940–68; Under Treas., Middle Temple, 1968; Registrar, Architects' Registration Council, 1970; Sec., British Dental Assoc., 1971; Pres., Internat. Union for Health Educn, 1979–82. Vice-Pres., CND, 1990–. *Recreation:* allotmenteering. *Address:* 4 Warwick Drive, SW15 6LB. *T:* 0181–789 4544. *Club:* Royal Air Force.

MACKIE, Prof. Andrew George; Professor of Applied Mathematics, 1968–88, Vice-Principal 1975–80, University of Edinburgh; *b* 7 March 1927; *s* of late Andrew Mackie and of Isobel Sigsworth Mackie (*née* Storey); *m* 1959, Elizabeth Maud Mackie (*née* Hebblethwaite); one *s* one *d*. *Educ:* Tain Royal Acad.; Univ. of Edinburgh (MA); Univ. of Cambridge (BA); Univ. of St Andrews (PhD). Lecturer, Univ. of Dundee, 1948–50; Bateman Res. Fellow and Instructor, CIT, 1953–55; Lecturer: Univ. of Strathclyde, 1955–56; Univ. of St Andrews, 1956–62; Prof. of Applied Maths, Victoria Univ. of Wellington, NZ, 1962–65; Res. Prof., Univ. of Maryland, 1966–68. Visiting Professor: CIT, 1984; Univ. of NSW, 1985. FRSE 1962. *Publications:* Boundary Value Problems, 1965, 2nd edn 1989; numerous contribs to mathematical and scientific jls. *Recreation:* golf. *Address:* 47 Cluny Drive, Edinburgh EH10 6DU. *T:* 0131–447 2164.

MACKIE, Clive David Andrew, FCA, FSS; Consultant, Institute of Actuaries, 1992–94; *b* 29 April 1929; *s* of David and Lilian Mackie; *m* 1953, Averil Ratcliff; one *s* three *d*. *Educ:* Tiffin Sch., Kingston-on-Thames. FCA 1956; FSS 1982. Director: cos in Grundy (Teddington) Group, 1959–67; D. Sebel & Co. Ltd, 1967–70; post in admin of higher educn, 1970–73; Institute of Actuaries: Dep. Sec., 1973–77; Sec., 1977–83; Sec.-Gen., 1983–92. Mem., Catenian Assoc., 1972–. *Recreations:* music (post 1800), cricket, carpentry, amateur dramatics, working with the Talking Newspapers Assoc. of UK. *Address:* Withermere, Burwash, East Sussex TN19 7HN. *T:* Burwash (01435) 882427. *Clubs:* Actuaries; Sussex CC.

MACKIE, Eric Dermott, OBE 1987; Chairman and Managing Director, Govan Kvaerner Ltd (formerly Govan Shipbuilders Ltd), 1979–90; *b* 4 Dec. 1924; *s* of James Girvan and Ellen Dorothy Mackie; *m* 1950, Mary Victoria Christie; one *s* one *d*. *Educ:* Coll. of Technology, Belfast. CEng; MIMechE, FIMarE, FRINA. 1st Class MoT Cert. (Steam and Diesel). Trained with James Mackie & Son (Textile Engrs), 1939–44; Design draughtsman, Harland & Wolff, Belfast, 1944–48; 2nd Engineer (sea-going) in both steam and diesel ships for Union Castle Mail Steamship Co., 1948–53; Harland & Wolff, Belfast, 1953–75: Test Engr; Manager, Shiprepair Dept; Gen. Manager i/c of Southampton branch; Gen. Manager i/c of ship prodn and shiprepair, Belfast; Man. Dir, James Brown Hamer, S Africa, 1975–79; Chief Exec. and Man. Dir of Shiprepair in UK, British Shipbuilders, 1979–81. Mem., Governing Bd, British Marine Technology. Denny Gold Medal, IMarE, 1987. *Publications:* articles for marine engrg instns on various subjects pertaining to marine engrg and gen. engrg. *Recreations:* golf, swimming, reading. *Address:* Middle Barton, Whittingham, near Alnwick, Northumberland NE66 4SU. *T:* Whittingham (0166574) 648. *Clubs:* Caledonian; Durban, Rand (Johannesburg, SA).

MACKIE, George, DFC 1944; RSW 1968; RDI 1973; freelance graphic artist and painter; Head of Design, Gray's School of Art, Aberdeen, 1958–80 (retd); *b* 17 July 1920; *s* of late David Mackie and late Kathleen Grantham; *m* 1952, Barbara Balmer, ARSA, RSW, RGI; two *d*. Served Royal Air Force, 1940–46. Consultant in book design to Edinburgh University Press, 1960–87. Paintings in various private and public collections incl. HRH the Duke of Edinburgh's and Scottish Nat. Gall. of Modern Art. Major retrospective exhibitions: Books, mostly scholarly, and some Ephemera, Nat. Library of Scotland, 1991; Dartmouth Coll., NH, USA, 1991. *Publication:* Lynton Lamb: Illustrator, 1979. *Address:* 32 Broad Street, Stamford, Lincs. PE9 1JP. *T:* Stamford (01780) 53296. *Club:* Double Crown.

MACKIE, Prof. George Owen, FRS 1991; DPhil; Professor of Biology, University of Victoria, 1968–94, Professor Emeritus since 1995; *b* 20 Oct. 1929; *s* of late Col (Frederick) Percival Mackie, CSI, OBE, IMS and Mary E. H. Mackie (*née* Owen); *m* 1956, Gillian V. Faulkner; three *s* two *d*. *Educ:* Oxford (BA 1954; MA 1956; DPhil 1956). FRSC 1982. Univ. of Alberta, 1957–68; Univ. of Victoria, 1968–; Chm., Biol. Dept, 1970–73. Editor, Canadian Jl of Zoology, 1980–89. Fry Medal, Canadian Soc. of Zoologists, 1989. *Publications:* (ed) Coelenterate Ecology and Behavior, 1976; numerous research articles in books and jls. *Recreations:* chamber music ('cello), earthenware pottery. *Address:* University of Victoria, Department of Biology, PO Box 1700, Victoria, BC V8W 2Y2, Canada. *T:* (604) 7217146.

MACKIE, Lily Edna Minerva, (Mrs John Betts), OBE 1986; Head Mistress, City of London School for Girls, 1972–86; *b* 14 April 1926; *d* of late Robert Wood Mackie and late Lilian Amelia Mackie (*née* Dennis); *m* 1985, John Betts (*d* 1992). *Educ:* Plaistow Grammar Sch.; University Coll., London (BA); Lycée de Jeunes Filles, Limoges; Université de Poitiers. Asst Mistress: Ilford County High Sch. for Girls, 1950–59; City of London Sch. for Girls, 1960–64; Head Mistress: Wimbledon County Sch., 1964–69; Ricards Lodge High Sch., Wimbledon, 1969–72. FRSA. *Recreations:* theatre, music, gardening, travel. *Address:* Cotswold, 59–61 Upper Tooting Park, SW17 7SU.

MACKIE, Sir Maitland, Kt 1982; CBE 1965; JP; farmer since 1932; *b* 16 Feb. 1912; *s* of late Dr Maitland Mackie, OBE and Mary (*née* Yull); *m* 1st, 1935, Isobel Ross (*d* 1960); two *s* four *d*; 2nd, 1963, Martha Pauline Turner (*d* 1993). *Educ:* Aberdeen Grammar Sch.; Aberdeen Univ. (BSCAgric). FEIS 1972; FRAgSS 1974; FInstM. County Councillor, Aberdeenshire, 1951–75 (Convener 1967–75); Chm., NE Devel Authority, 1969–75; Chairman: Jt Adv. Cttee, Scottish Farm Bldgs Investigation Unit, 1963–; Aberdeen Milk Marketing Bd, 1965–82; Peterhead Bay Management Co., 1975–86; Hanover (Scotland) Housing Assoc., 1981–86. Member: Agric. Sub-Cttee, UGC, 1965–75; Bd, Scottish Council for Development and Industry, 1975– (Chm., Oil Policy Cttee, 1975–); Clayson Cttee on Drink Laws in Scotland. Chm., Aberdeen Cable Services, 1983–87; Director: Scottish Telecommunications, 1969–85; Aberdeen Petroleum plc, 1980–. Governor: N of Scotland Coll. of Agriculture, 1968–82 (Vice-Chm., 1974–78); Rowett Inst., 1973–82. Fellow, Scottish Council Develt and Industry, 1986. Burgess of Guild, Aberdeen, 1978. JP 1956; Lord-Lieut, Aberdeenshire, 1975–87. KStJ 1977. Hon. LLD Aberdeen, 1977. *Publication:* A Lucky Chap, 1993. *Recreation:* travel. *Address:* The Stables, Westertown, Rothienorman, Aberdeenshire. *T:* Rothienorman (01651) 671392. *Clubs:* Farmers'; Royal Northern (Aberdeen).

See also I. L. Aitken, Baron Mackie of Benshie.

McKIE, Peter Halliday, CBE 1995; CChem, FRSC, FIQA; Chairman, Du Pont (UK) Ltd, since 1987; Manager, Du Pont Belle Plant, W Virginia, USA; *b* 20 March 1935; *s* of Harold and Winifred McKie; *m* 1959, Jennifer Anne Parkes; three *s* one *d*. *Educ:* Bangor Grammar Sch.; Queen's Univ., Belfast (BSc Chem.; Hon. DSc 1993). CChem, FRSC 1988; FIQA 1987. Shift Supervisor, Courtaulds Ltd, 1956–59; Supervisor, Du Pont Mfg, Londonderry, 1959–77; Manager, Du Pont Waynesbro Orlon Plant, USA, 1977–79; Asst Works Dir, Du Pont, Londonderry, 1979–81; Man. Dir, Du Pont Scandinavia and Du Pont Finland, 1981–84; Prodn Manager, Du Pont Europe, 1984–87. Vis. Prof., Dept of Engrg, QUB, 1991–. FInstD 1987. *Recreations:* photography, sport, classic cars and motor cycles. *Address:* Du Pont (UK) Ltd, PO Box 15, Londonderry, NI. *T:* Londonderry (0504) 864000.

McKIERNAN, Most Rev. Francis J.; *see* Kilmore, Bishop of, (RC).

MACKILLIGIN, David Patrick Robert, CMG 1994; HM Diplomatic Service; Governor, British Virgin Islands, since 1995; *b* 29 June 1939; *s* of R. S. Mackilligin, CMG, OBE, MC and Patricia (*née* Waldegrave); *m* 1976, Gillian Margaret Zuill Walker; two *d*. *Educ:* St Mary's Coll., Winchester; Pembroke Coll., Oxford (2nd Cl. Hons PPE). Asst Principal, CRO, 1961–62; Third, later Second Sec., Pakistan, 1962–66; Asst Private Sec. to Sec. of State for Commonwealth Relations, 1966–68; Private Sec. to Minister Without Portfolio, 1968–69; Dep. Comr, Anguilla, 1969–71 (Actg Comr, July–Aug. 1970); First Sec., Ghana, 1971–73; First Sec., Head of Chancery and Consul, Cambodia, 1973–75 (Chargé d'Affaires at various times); FCO, 1975–80 (Asst Head of W African Dept, 1978–80); Counsellor (Commercial and Aid), Indonesia, 1980–85; NATO Defence Coll., Rome, 1985–86; Counsellor (Economic and Commercial), and Dir of Trade Promotion, Canberra, 1986–90; High Comr, Belize, 1991–94. *Recreations:* walking and swimming in remote places, ruins, second-hand bookshops, theatre, literature. *Address:* c/o Foreign and Commonwealth Office, King Charles Street, SW1A 2AH. *Clubs:* United Oxford & Cambridge University, Commonwealth Trust.

MACKINLAY, Andrew Stuart; MP (Lab) Thurrock, since 1992; *b* 24 April 1949; *s* of Danny Mackinlay and Monica (*née* Beanes); *m* 1972, Ruth Segar; two *s* one *d*. *Educ:* Salesian Coll., Chertsey. ACIS; DMA. A clerk, Surrey CC, 1965–75; Nalgo official, 1975–92. An Opposition Whip, 1992–93; Mem., Transport Select Cttee. A Vice Pres., Assoc. of Dist Councils. *Recreations:* studying battlefields of World War I in France and Belgium, NON-league football. *Address:* House of Commons, SW1A 0AA. *T:* 0171–219 3000. *Club:* Chadwell Working Men's.

MacKINLAY, Sir Bruce, Kt 1978; CBE 1970; company director; *b* 4 Oct. 1912; *s* of Daniel Robertson MacKinlay and Alice Victoria Rice; *m* 1943, Erica Ruth Fleming; two *s*. *Educ:* Scotch Coll. Served War, AASC, 1940–45 (Lieut). Dir, J. Gadsden Australia Ltd, 1954–77. President: WA Chamber of Manufactures, 1958–61; Confedn of WA Industry, 1976–78; WA Employers' Fedn, 1974–75; Fremantle Rotary Club, 1956; Vice-Pres.,

Associated Chambers of Manufactures of Aust., 1960. Chairman: WA Inst. of Dirs, 1975–77; WA Div., National Packaging Assoc., 1967–69; WA Finance Cttee for the Duke of Edinburgh's Third Commonwealth Study Conf., 1967–68; Mem., Commonwealth Manufg Industries Adv. Council, 1962–70. Leader: Aust. Trade Mission, E Africa, 1968; WA Trade Mission, Italy, 1970; Employers' Rep., Internat. Labour Conf., 1977; Comr, State Electricity Commn, 1961–74. University of Western Australia: Mem. Senate, 1970–84; Chm., Master of Business Admin Appeal, 1973. Life Governor, Scotch Coll. Council (Chm., 1969–74); Chm. Nat. Council, Keep Australia Beautiful, 1984–86 (Mem. 1967–, Chm. 1981–86, WA Council); Councillor: Organising Council of Commonwealth and Empire Games, 1962; Aust. Council on Population and Ethnic Affairs, 1981–83. Pres., Most Excellent Order of the British Empire, WA Div., 1983–90. *Recreations:* swimming, gardening. *Address:* 9B Melville Street, Claremont, WA 6010, Australia. *T:* (9)3832220. *Clubs:* Weld, WACA, Claremont Football (WA).

McKINLAY, Peter; Chief Executive, Scottish Homes, since 1991; *b* 29 Dec. 1939; *s* of late Peter McKinlay and of Mary Clegg (*née* Hamill); *m* 1963, Anne Rogerson Aitken Thomson; two *s* one *d.* *Educ:* Univ. of Glasgow (MA Hons). GPO HQ, Edinburgh, 1963–67; Scottish Office, 1967–91: Private Sec. to Minister of State, 1974–75; Director, Scottish Prison Service, 1988–91. Nat. Exec., First Div. Assoc., 1977–80. Non-Exec. Dir, D. S. Crawford Ltd, 1984–86; Chairman: Campbeltown & Kintyre Enterprise Trust, 1992–; Bute Partnership, 1993–; Dir, Common Purpose, 1993–. *Recreations:* family, friends, garden, TV, reading, food, drink. *Address:* Thistle House, 91 Haymarket Terrace, Edinburgh EH12 5HE. *T:* 0131–479 5200. *Club:* Machrihanish Golf.

McKINLAY, Robert Murray, CBE 1993; FEng 1992; FRAeS; Chairman, United Bristol Healthcare NHS Trust, since 1994; President, Bristol Chamber of Commerce and Industry, since 1994; *b* 12 Jan. 1934; *s* of Robert Graham McKinlay and Mary Murray; *m* 1957, Ellen Aikman Stewart; two *s.* *Educ:* Vale of Leven Acad.; Royal Tech. Coll., Glasgow (BSc Hons, ARTC). Flight testing and project engineering, Bristol Helicopters and Westlands, 1956–66; British Aircraft Corporation, 1966–79: Systems Develt Manager; Designer in charge; Asst Chief Engr; Asst Dir, Flight Test; Concorde Design Dir; British Aerospace, 1979–94: Dir, Airbus; Gp Dir, Man. Dir, Airbus Div.; Man. Dir, Commercial Aircraft; Chm., Airbus, 1991–94. Vis. Prof., Dept Aerospace Engrg, Glasgow Univ., 1994–. Hon. DTech Bristol, 1991. *Recreations:* sailing, golf, piano, woodworking. *Address:* 43 Glenavon Park, Bristol BS9 1RW. *T:* Bristol (0117) 968 6253. *Clubs:* Society of Merchant Venturers (Bristol); Royal Western Yacht.

McKINLEY, Air Vice-Marshal David Cecil, CB 1966; CBE 1957; DFC 1940; AFC 1944, Bar 1945; RAF; *b* 18 Sept. 1913; *s* of David McKinley, Civil Engineer, and May McKinley (*née* Ward); *m* 1940, Brenda Alice (*née* Ridgway); three *s.* *Educ:* Bishop Foy Sch., Waterford; Trinity Coll., Dublin. Radio Engineering, Ferranti Ltd, 1935. Entered (regular) Royal Air Force, 1935; served continuously since that date; AOC Malta and Dep. C-in-C (Air), Allied Forces, Mediterranean, 1963–65; SASO, Transport Command, 1966, Air Support Command, 1967–68; retired 1968. Freeman, The Guild of Air Pilots and Air Navigators, 1959. FIN 1949. *Recreations:* sailing, fishing, water ski-ing, gardening. *Address:* 4 Courtil Lubin, Alderney, Channel Islands. *T:* Alderney (014812) 2497; Midland Bank, Alderney, CI. *Club:* Royal Air Force.

McKINLEY, John Key; Chairman and Chief Executive Officer, Texaco Inc., 1980–86 (President, 1971–83), retired; *b* Tuscaloosa, Ala, 24 March 1920; *s* of Virgil Parks McKinley and Mary Emma (*née* Key); *m* 1946, Helen Grace Heare; two *s* *Educ:* Univ. of Alabama (BS Chem. Engrg, 1940; MS Organic Chemistry, 1941); Harvard Univ. (Graduate, Advanced Management Program, 1962). Served War, AUS, Eur. Theatre of Ops, 1941–45 (Major, Bronze Star). Texaco Inc., 1941–86: Asst Dir of Res., Beacon, NY, 1957–59; Asst to the Vice-Pres., 1959–60; Manager of Commercial Develt Processes, 1960; Gen. Man., Worldwide Petrochemicals, NYC, 1960–67, Vice-Pres., Petrochem. Dept, 1967–71 (also Vice-Pres. i/c Supply and Distribution); Sen. Vice Pres., Worldwide Refining, Petrochems, Supply and Distbn, 1971, Pres. and Dir, 1971–83; Director: Texaco Inc., 1971–92; Merck & Co., Inc., 1982–90; Manufacturers Hanover Corp., 1980–90; Hanover Trust Co., 1980–90; Martin Marietta, 1985–90; Apollo Computer, 1987–89; Burlington Industries Inc., 1977–87; Federated Dept Stores, Inc., 1990–. Hon. Dir, Amer. Petroleum Inst. Man. Dir, Met. Opera Assoc., 1980–; National Chm., Met. Opera Centennial Fund, 1980. Dir, Americas Soc. Member: Bd of Overseers, Meml Sloan-Kettering Cancer Center, 1981–91; Brookings Council, 1986; Business Council. Fellow, Amer. Inst. of Chem. Engrs; Sesquicentennial Hon. Prof., Univ. of Alabama; Hon. LLD: Univ. of Alabama, 1972; Troy State Univ., 1974. *Address:* Tuscaloosa, AL, USA; Darien, CT 06820; Buffalo, Wyoming. *Clubs:* Links, Brook (NYC); Wee Burn Country (Darien); Augusta (Ga); National Golf, Blind Brook Country (Port Chester, NY); North River Yacht (Tuscaloosa).

McKINNEY, Judith, (Mrs J. P. McKinney); *see* Wright, Judith.

McKINNEY, (Sheila Mary) Deirdre; Her Honour Judge McKinney; a Circuit Judge, since 1981; *b* 20 Oct. 1928; *d* of Patrick Peter McKinney and Mary Edith (*née* Conoley). *Educ:* Convent of the Cross, Boscombe, Bournemouth. Called to the Bar, Lincoln's Inn, 1951; a Recorder of the Crown Court, 1978–81.

McKINNON, Rt. Hon. Donald Charles, PC 1992; MP (Nat. Party) Albany, New Zealand, since 1978; Deputy Prime Minister of New Zealand, and Minister of Foreign Affairs (formerly External Relations) and Trade, since 1990, and Minister of Pacific Island Affairs, since 1991; *b* 27 Feb. 1939; *s* of Maj.-Gen. Walter Sneddon McKinnon, *qv*; *m* 1964, Patricia Maude Moore (separated); three *s* one *d.* *Educ:* Lincoln Univ., New Zealand. AREINZ. Farm Manager, 1964–72; Farm Management Consultant, 1973–78; Real Estate Agent, 1974–78. Dep. Leader of the Opposition, 1987–90. *Recreations:* enthusiastic jogger and tennis player. *Address:* Parliament Building, Wellington, New Zealand. *T:* (4) 719997.

McKINNON, Sir James, Kt 1992; CA, FCMA; Chairman, Ionica, since 1993; Director General, Office of Gas Supply, 1986–93; *b* 1929. *Educ:* Camphill School. CA 1952, FCMA 1956. Company Secretary, Macfarlane Lang & Co. Ltd, Glasgow, 1955–65; Business Consultant, McLintock, Moores & Murray, Glasgow, 1965–67; Finance Director, Imperial Group plc, London, 1967–86. Pres., Inst. of Chartered Accountants of Scotland, 1985–86. *Publications:* papers to learned jls and articles in Accountants' magazine. *Recreation:* ski-ing.

McKINNON, Prof. Kenneth Richard, FACE; Vice-Chancellor, University of Wollongong, Australia, 1981–95, now Professor Emeritus; Chairman, McKinnon Walker Pty Ltd; Nuclear Research Reactor Review, since 1993; *b* 23 Feb. 1931; *s* of Charles and Grace McKinnon; *m* 1st, 1956 (marr. diss.); one *s*; 2nd, 1981, Suzanne H., *d* of W. Milligan. *Educ:* Univ. of Adelaide (BA); Univ. of Queensland (BEd); Harvard Univ. (EdD). FACE 1972. Teacher, headmaster and administrator, 1957–65; Dir of Educn, Papua New Guinea, 1966–73; Chairman: Australian Schs Commn, 1973–81; Bd of Educn, Vic, 1982–85; Australian Nat. Commn for UNESCO, 1984–88; Illawara Technology Corp., 1983–. Pres., AVCC, 1991–92. Member: Australia Council, 1974–77 (Dep. Chm., 1976–77); Primary Industries and Energy Res. Council, 1991–92; Prime Minister's Science Council, 1991–92. Consultant in the Arts, Aust. Govt, 1981. *Publications:* Realistic Educational Planning, 1973; articles in jls and papers. *Recreations:* swimming, theatre, music, reading. *Address:* 14 Norfolk House, 1 Sutherland Crescent, Darling Point, NSW 2027, Australia. *Club:* Commonwealth (Canberra, Australia).

MACKINNON, Dame Patricia; *see* Mackinnon, Dame U. P.

McKINNON, Hon. Sir Stuart (Neil), Kt 1988; **Hon. Mr Justice McKinnon;** a Judge of the High Court of Justice, Queen's Bench Division, since 1988; *b* 14 Aug. 1938; *s* of His Honour Neil Nairn McKinnon, QC; *m* 1966, Rev. Helena Jacoba Sara (*née* van Hoorn); two *d.* *Educ:* King's Coll. Sch., Wimbledon; Council of Legal Educn; Trinity Hall, Cambridge (BA, LLB 1963; MA 1967). Called to the Bar, Lincoln's Inn, 1960, Bencher, 1987; Junior at the Common Law Bar, 1964–80; QC 1980; a Recorder, 1985–88. Mem., Lord Chancellor's Mddx Adv. Cttee on JPs, 1990–. Pres., Cambridge Univ. Law Soc., 1962–63. *Recreation:* golf. *Address:* Royal Courts of Justice, Strand, WC2A 2LL. *Club:* Addington Golf.

MACKINNON, Dame (Una) Patricia, DBE 1977 (CBE 1972); *b* Brisbane, 24 July 1911; *d* of Ernest T. and Pauline Bell; *m* 1936, Alistair Scobie Mackinnon; one *s* one *d.* *Educ:* Glennie School and St Margaret's School, Queensland. Member Cttee of Management, Royal Children's Hospital, Melbourne, 1948–79; Vice-President, 1958; President, 1965–79; Chm., Research Bd, 1967–85. *Recreations:* gardening, reading history and biographies. *Address:* 5 Ross Street, Toorak, Vic 3142, Australia. *Club:* Alexandra (Melbourne).

McKINNON, Maj.-Gen. Walter Sneddon, CB 1966; CBE 1961 (OBE 1947); *b* 8 July 1910; *s* of Charles McKinnon and Janet Robertson McKinnon (*née* Sneddon); *m* 1937, Anna Bloomfield Plimmer; four *s* one *d.* *Educ:* Otago Boys High Sch., Dunedin, NZ; Otago Univ. (BSc); commissioned in NZ Army, 1935; various military courses, including Staff Coll., Camberley, England. Served War of 1939–45: Pacific, Italy (Lt-Col; despatches), Japan (occupation) (OBE); Brigadier, 1953; subsequent appointments: Comdr, Southern Mil. Dist (NZ), 1953; Head, NZ Joint Mil. Mission, Washington, DC, 1954–57; Comdr, Northern Military District, 1957–58; Adjutant-General, 1958–63; Quartermaster-General, 1963–65, Maj.-General, 1965; Chief of the General Staff, NZ Army, 1965–67; retired, 1967. Chairman: NZ Broadcasting Corp., 1969–74; Everton Trust Bd, Victoria Univ., 1969–73. Member: Taupo Borough Council, 1977–80; Tongariro United Council, 1979–80. Pres., Taupo Regional Museum and Art Centre, 1975–79; Mem., Social Develt Council, New Zealand, 1976–79. *Recreations:* golf, fishing and gardening. *Address:* 27/19 Liston Avenue, Taupo, New Zealand. *Clubs:* Wellesley (Wellington); Taupo Golf.

See also Rt Hon. D. C. McKinnon.

MACKINTOSH, family name of **Viscount Mackintosh of Halifax.**

MACKINTOSH OF HALIFAX, 3rd Viscount *cr* 1957; **John Clive Mackintosh;** Bt 1935; Baron 1948; FCA; *b* 9 Sept. 1958; *s* of 2nd Viscount Mackintosh of Halifax, OBE, BEM; *S* father, 1980; *m* 1982, Elizabeth (marr. diss. 1993), *o d* of late David G. Lakin; two *s*; *m* 1995, Claire Jane, *y d* of Stanislaw Nowak. *Educ:* The Leys School, Cambridge; Oriel College, Oxford (MA in PPE). President, Oxford Univ. Conservative Assoc., 1979. Chartered accountant; Partner, Price Waterhouse, 1992–. *Recreations:* cricket, bridge, golf. *Heir:* *s* Hon. Thomas Harold George Mackintosh, *b* 8 Feb. 1985. *Address:* House of Lords, SW1A 0PW. *Clubs:* MCC, Royal Automobile, Coningsby.

MACKINTOSH, Prof. Allan Roy, FRS 1991; Professor of Physics, University of Copenhagen, since 1970; *b* 22 Jan. 1936; *s* of Malcolm Roy Mackintosh and Alice Mackintosh (*née* Williams); *m* 1958, Jette Stannow; one *s* two *d.* *Educ:* Nottingham High Sch.; Peterhouse, Cambridge (scholar; BA, PhD). Associate Prof., Iowa State Univ., 1960–66; Res. Prof., Technical Univ. of Denmark, 1966–70; Dir, Risø Nat. Lab., Denmark, 1971–76; Dir, Nordic Inst. for Theoretical Physics, 1986–89. Alfred P. Sloan Res. Fellow, 1964–66; Lectures: D. K. C. MacDonald, Canada, 1975; F. H. Spedding, USA, 1983; Vis. Miller Prof., Univ. of California, Berkeley, 1989. Pres., European Phys. Soc., 1980–82. Member: Royal Danish Acad. of Scis and Letters, 1977; Norwegian Acad. of Sci. and Letters, 1993. Fil. Dr *hc* Uppsala, 1980. F. H. Spedding Award for Rare Earth Res., 1986. Kt of the Dannebrog (Denmark), 1975. *Publications:* Rare Earth Magnetism: structures and excitations (with Jens Jensen), 1991; articles on physics in learned jls. *Recreations:* sedate squash, listening to music, reading, walking. *Address:* Henrik Thomsenvej 4, 3460 Birkerød, Denmark. *T:* (45) 42815038; Physics Laboratory, H. C. Ørsted Institute, Universitetsparken 5, 2100 Copenhagen, Denmark. *T:* (45) 35320450.

MACKINTOSH, Cameron Anthony; producer of musicals; Chairman, Cameron Mackintosh, since 1981; Director, Delfont/Mackintosh, since 1991; *b* 17 Oct. 1946; *s* of Ian and Diana Mackintosh. *Educ:* Prior Park Coll., Bath. Hon. Fellow, St Catherine's Coll., Oxford, 1990. Decided to be producer of musical stage shows at age 8, after seeing Slade's Salad Days; spent brief period at Central Sch. of Speech and Drama; stage hand at Theatre Royal, Drury Lane; later Asst Stage Manager; worked with Emile Littler, 1966, with Robin Alexander, 1967; produced first musical, 1969. Co-owner, with First Leisure, of Prince Edward, Prince of Wales and Strand Theatres, 1991. *London productions:* Little Women, 1967; Anything Goes, 1969; Trelawney, 1972; The Card, 1973; Winnie the Pooh, 1974; Owl and Pussycat Went to See, 1975; Godspell, 1975; Side by Side by Sondheim, 1976; Oliver!, 1977, 1994; Diary of a Madam, 1977; After Shave, 1977; Gingerbread Man, 1978; Out on a Limb, 1978; My Fair Lady, 1979; Oklahoma!, 1980; Tomfoolery, 1980; Jeeves Takes Charge, 1981; Cats, 1981; Song and Dance, 1982; Blondel, 1983; Little Shop of Horrors, 1983; Abbacadabra, 1983; The Boyfriend, 1984; Les Misérables, 1985; Café Puccini, 1985; Phantom of the Opera, 1986; Follies, 1987; Miss Saigon, 1989; Just So, 1990; Five Guys Named Moe, 1991; Moby Dick, 1992; Putting It Together, 1992; Carousel, 1993. *Recreations:* taking holidays, cooking. *Address:* Cameron Mackintosh Ltd, 1 Bedford Square, WC1B 3RA. *T:* 0171–637 8866. *Club:* Groucho.

McKINTOSH, Ian; His Honour Judge McKintosh; a Circuit Judge, since 1988; *b* 23 April 1938; *s* of late Stanley and of Gertrude McKintosh; *m* 1967, Alison Rosemary, *e d* of Kenneth Blayney Large and Margaret Wharton Large; two *s* one *d.* *Educ:* Leeds Grammar Sch.; Exeter Coll., Oxford (MA). Admitted Solicitor of the Supreme Court, 1966. Served RAF, 1957–59. Articled to Town Clerk, Chester and to Laces & Co., Liverpool, 1962–66; Dept of Solicitor to Metropolitan Police, New Scotland Yard, 1966–69; Partner, Lemon & Co., Swindon, 1969–88; a Recorder, 1981–88. *Recreations:* cricket, sailing. *Address:* c/o Courts' Administrator, The Castle, Exeter EX4 3TH. *Clubs:* MCC, XL.

MACKINTOSH, (John) Malcolm, CMG 1975; HM Diplomatic Service, retired; *b* 25 Dec. 1921; *s* of late James Mackintosh, MD, LLD, FRCP, and Marjorie Mackintosh; *m* 1946, Elena Grafova; one *s* one *d* (and one *s* decd). *Educ:* Mill Hill; Edinburgh Academy; Glasgow Univ. MA (Hons) 1948. Served War, Middle East, Italy and Balkans, 1942–46; Allied Control Commn, Bulgaria, 1945–46. Glasgow Univ., 1946–48. Programme Organiser, BBC Overseas Service, 1948–60; Foreign Office, engaged on research, 1960–68; Asst Sec., Cabinet Office, 1968–87. Sen Fellow in Soviet Studies, IISS, 1989–91;

Hon. Sen. Res. Fellow, KCL, 1987–; Hon. Lectr in Internat. Affairs, St Andrews Univ., 1991–; Hon. Vis. Fellow, SSEES, 1994–. *Publications:* Strategy and Tactics of Soviet Foreign Policy, 1962, 2nd edn 1963; Juggernaut: a history of the Soviet armed forces, 1967. *Recreations:* walking, climbing. *Address:* 21 Ravensdale Avenue, N12 9HP. *T:* 0181–445 9714. *Club:* Garrick.

MACKINTOSH OF MACKINTOSH, Lt-Comdr Lachlan Ronald Duncan, OBE 1972; JP; 30th Chief of Clan Mackintosh; Lord-Lieutenant of Lochaber, Inverness, Badenoch and Strathspey, since 1985 (Vice-Lieutenant, 1971–85); Chairman, Highland Exhibitions Ltd, 1964–84; *b* 27 June 1928; *o s* of Vice-Adm. Lachlan Donald Mackintosh of Mackintosh, CB, DSO, DSC (*d* 1957); *m* 1962, Mabel Cecilia Helen (Celia), *yr d* of Captain Hon. John Bernard Bruce, RN; one *s* two *d* (and one *d* decd). *Educ:* Elstree; RNC Dartmouth. Flag Lieut to First Sea Lord, 1951; spec. communications, 1954; served in HM Yacht Britannia, 1957; retd 1963. Vice-Pres., Scottish Conservative and Unionist Assoc., 1969–71. DL 1965, CC 1970–75, Inverness-shire; Regional Cllr, Highland Region, 1974–; JP Inverness, 1982. *Heir:* *s* John Lachlan Mackintosh, younger of Mackintosh, *b* 2 Oct. 1969. *Address:* Moy Hall, Tomatin, Inverness IV13 7YQ. *T:* Tomatin (01808) 511211. *Club:* Naval and Military.

MACKINTOSH, Malcolm; *see* Mackintosh, J. M.

MACKINTOSH, Prof. Nicholas John, DPhil; FRS 1987; Professor of Experimental Psychology, and Professorial Fellow of King's College, University of Cambridge, since 1981; *b* 9 July 1935; *s* of Dr Ian and Daphne Mackintosh; *m* 1st, 1960, Janet Ann Scott (marr. diss. 1978); one *s* one *d*; 2nd, 1978, Bundy Wilson (marr. diss. 1989); two *s*; 3rd, 1992, Leonora Caroline Brosan, *d* of Dr G. S. Brosan, *qv*; one *s*. *Educ:* Winchester; Magdalen Coll., Oxford. BA 1960, MA, DPhil 1963. Univ. Lectr, Univ. of Oxford, 1964–67; Res. Fellow, Lincoln Coll., Oxford, 1966–67; Res. Prof., Dalhousie Univ., 1967–73; Prof., Univ. of Sussex, 1973–81. Visiting Professor: Univ. of Pennsylvania, 1965–66; Univ. of Hawaii, 1972–73; Bryn Mawr Coll., 1977. Editor, Qly Jl of Experimental Psychology, 1977–84. *Publications:* (ed with W. K. Honig) Fundamental Issues in Associative Learning, 1969; (with N. S. Sutherland) Mechanisms of Animal Discrimination Learning, 1971; The Psychology of Animal Learning, 1974; Conditioning and Associative Learning, 1983; Animal Learning and Cognition, 1994; Cyril Burt: fraud or framed, 1995; papers in psychological journals. *Address:* King's College, Cambridge CB2 1ST. *T:* Cambridge (01223) 351386.

McKITTERICK, Dr David John, FSA, FRHistS; FBA 1995; Fellow and Librarian, Trinity College, Cambridge, since 1986; *b* 9 Jan. 1948; *s* of Rev. Canon J. H. B. McKitterick and Marjory McKitterick (*née* Quarterman); *m* 1976, Rosamond Deborah Pierce (*see* R. D. McKitterick); one *d*. *Educ:* King's Coll. Sch., Wimbledon; St John's Coll., Cambridge (Scholar; BA 1969; MA 1973; LittD 1994); University College London (DipLib 1971). Staff, Cambridge Univ. Library, 1969–70, 1971–86; Fellow, Darwin Coll., Cambridge, 1978–86. Hon. Curator, Early Printed Books, Fitzwilliam Mus. Chm., Adv. Cttee on Books, Council for Care of Churches; Vice-Pres., Bibliog. Soc., 1990–; Pres., Cambridge Bibliog. Soc., 1991–. Trustee, Wordsworth Trust. *Publications:* The Library of Sir Thomas Knyvett of Ashwellthorpe 1539–1618, 1978; (ed) Stanley Morison and D. B. Updike: Selected Correspondence, 1979; (ed) Stanley Morison: selected essays on the history of letter forms in manuscript and print, 1981; (with John Dreyfus) A History of the Nonesuch Press, 1981; Four Hundred Years of University Printing and Publishing at Cambridge 1584–1984, 1984; Cambridge University Library: a history: the eighteenth and nineteenth centuries, 1986; A New Specimen Book of Curwen Pattern Papers, 1987; (ed jtly) T. F. Dibdin: *Horae Bibliographicae Cantabrigiensis*, 1988; Wallpapers by Edward Bawden, 1989; (ed) Andrew Perne: quartercentenary studies, 1991; Catalogue of the Pepys Library at Magdalene College, Cambridge, VII: facsimile of Pepys's catalogue, 1991; A History of Cambridge University Press, vol. 1: printing and the book trade in Cambridge 1534–1698, 1992; contribs to learned jls. *Address:* Trinity College, Cambridge CB2 1TQ. *T:* Cambridge (01223) 338513. *Club:* Double Crown (President, 1994–95).

McKITTERICK, Dr Rosamond Deborah, FRHistS; Reader in Early Mediaeval European History, University of Cambridge, since 1991; Fellow of Newnham College, Cambridge, since 1977; *b* Chesterfield, Derbys, 31 May 1949; *d* of Rev. Canon C. A. Pierce, OBE, MA, BD and Melissa (*née* Heaney); *m* 1976, David John McKitterick, *qv*; one *d*. *Educ:* Univ. of WA (BA 1st cl. Hons 1970); Univ. of Cambridge (MA 1977; PhD 1976; LittD 1991); Univ. of Munich (Graduate Student). FRHistS 1980; Fellow, European Medieval Acad., 1993. University of Cambridge: Asst Lectr, 1979–85; Lectr, 1985–91; Newnham College: Res. Fellow, 1974–77; Dir of Studies in Anglo-Saxon, Norse and Celtic, 1979–93. Guest Lectr in univs in Germany, Austria, USA, Australia, Denmark, France and Netherlands, 1978–; lecture tours: USA, 1982, 1990, 1994; Germany, 1987; UK; speaker, internat. confs on early medieval studies, Belgium, France, Netherlands, Germany, Italy, USA, UK and Eire, Austria. Vice-Pres., RHistS, 1994–. Editor: Cambridge Studies in Medieval Life and Thought; Cambridge Studies in Palaeography and Codicology, 1989–; Early Medieval Europe, 1992–. *Publications:* The Frankish Church and the Carolingian Reforms 789–895, 1977; The Frankish Kingdoms under the Carolingians 751–987, 1983; The Carolingians and the Written Word, 1989; The Uses of Literacy in early medieval Europe, 1990; (with Lida Lopes Cardozo) Lasting Letters, 1992; Carolingian Culture: emulation and innovation, 1993; Books, Scribes and Learning in the Frankish Kingdoms, Sixth to Ninth Centuries, 1994; (ed and contrib.) The New Cambridge Medieval History II, 700–900, 1995; Frankish Kings and Culture in the Early Middle Ages, 1995; articles in many collections of essays and conf. proc. and jls, incl. English Hist. Rev., Library, Studies in Church History, Francia, Scriptorium; reviews for TLS and English and continental learned jls. *Recreations:* music, fresh air. *Address:* Newnham College, Cambridge CB3 9DF. *T:* Cambridge (01223) 335700.

McKITTRICK, Neil Alastair; Stipendiary Magistrate, Middlesex, since 1989; *b* 1 Jan. 1948; *s* of late Ian James Arthur McKittrick and of Mary Patricia McKittrick (*née* Hobbs); *m* 1975, Jean Armstrong; one *s* one *d*. *Educ:* King's Sch., Ely; College of Law, Guildford. LLB London. Solicitor, 1972. Articled Clerk and Asst Solicitor, Cecil Godfrey & Son, Nottingham, 1967–73; Prosecuting Solicitor, Notts, 1973–77; Clerk to the Justices, 1977–89 (Darlington 1977, E Herts 1981, N Cambs 1986–89). Member: Council, Justices' Clerks' Soc., 1985–89 (Chm., Professional Purposes Cttee, 1987–89); President's Family Cttee, 1985–89; Justice Cttee on Witnesses, 1986; Domestic Courts Cttee, Magistrates' Assoc., 1988–91; Adv. Gp, Magistrates' Training Courses, 1989–; Middlesex Area Probation Cttee, 1990–. Editor, Justice of the Peace, 1985–89; Licensing Editor, Justice of the Peace Reports, 1983–; Editor, Jl of Criminal Law, 1990– (Mem., Editl Bd, 1985–). *Publications:* (ed jtly) Wilkinson's Road Traffic Offences, 14th edn to 17th edn, 1995; papers and articles in learned jls. *Recreations:* writing, walking, keeping the wolf from the door. *Address:* Magistrates' Courts Brent, Church End, 448 High Road, NW10 2DZ. *T:* 0181–451 7111. *Club:* Reform.

MACKLEY, Ian Warren, CMG 1989; HM Diplomatic Service; Head of Training, Foreign and Commonwealth Office, since 1993; *b* 31 March 1942; *s* of late Harold William Mackley and of Marjorie Rosa Sprawson (*née* Warren); *m* 1st, 1968, Jill Marion (*née* Saunders) (marr. diss. 1988); three *s*; 2nd, 1989, Sarah Anne Churchley; one *s* one *d*. *Educ:* Ardingly College. FO, 1960; Saigon, 1963; Asst Private Sec. to Ministers of State, FCO, 1967; Wellington, 1969; First Sec., 1972; FCO 1973; Head of Inf. Services, New Delhi, 1976; Asst Head, UN Dept, FCO, 1979; seconded to ICI, 1982; Counsellor, Dep. Hd of UK Delegn to Conf. on Confidence- and Security-Building Measures and Disarmament in Europe, Stockholm, 1984–86; Chargé d'Affaires, Kabul, 1987–89; Dep. High Comr, Canberra, 1989–93. Pres., Kabul Golf and Country Club, Afghanistan, 1987–89. *Recreations:* golf, armchair sport. *Address:* c/o Foreign and Commonwealth Office, SW1A 2AH.

MACKLIN, Sir Bruce (Roy), Kt 1981; OBE 1970; FCA; company director; Chairman: Standard Chartered Bank Australia Ltd, since 1987; Hyundai Automotive Distributors Australia Pty, since 1990; *b* 23 April 1917; *s* of Hubert Vivian Macklin and Lillian Mabel Macklin; *m* 1944, Dorothy Potts, Tynemouth, England; two *s* one *d*. *Educ:* St Peter's Coll., Adelaide; St Mark's Coll., Univ. of Adelaide (AUA Commerce). Served RAAF (Aircrew), 1941–45. Practising chartered accountant, 1947–69. Pres., Aust. Chamber of Commerce, 1967–69. Hon. Consul in S Aust. for Fed. Republic of Germany, 1968–74; Leader, Aust. Govt Mission to Papua New Guinea, 1971. Mem. Council of Governors, St Peter's Coll., 1962–69; Mem. Council, Univ. of Adelaide, 1965–71. A Founder, Adelaide Festival of Arts, 1958, Chm. Bd of Governors, 1972–78; Dep. Nat. Chm., Queen Elizabeth II Silver Jubilee Trust for Young Australians. Silver Jubilee Medal 1977; Commander's Cross, Order of Merit of Fed. Republic of Germany, 1986. *Recreations:* tennis, gardening, music. *Address:* Rothe Road, Echunga, SA 5153, Australia. *T:* (8) 3888180. *Clubs:* Adelaide, Naval, Military and Air Force (South Australia).

MACKLIN, David Drury, CBE 1989; DL; Member, Boundary Commission for England, since 1989; *b* 1 Sept. 1928; *s* of Laurence Hilary Macklin and Alice Dumergue (*née* Tait); *m* 1955, Janet Smallwood; four *s*. *Educ:* Felsted Sch., Essex; St John's Coll., Cambridge. MA. Articled to Baileys Shaw & Gillett, Solicitors, 1951–54; Assistant Solicitor: Coward Chance & Co., 1954–56; Warwickshire CC, 1956–61; Devon CC, 1961–69; Dep. Clerk, Derbyshire CC, 1969–73; Chief Executive: Lincolnshire CC, 1973–79; Devon CC, 1979–88. Chm., Community Council of Devon, 1992–; Mem., Devon and Cornwall Housing Assoc., 1989–. DL Devon, 1991. *Recreations:* sailing, music, golf, theatre, walking. *Address:* Randolls, Victoria Road, Topsham, Exeter EX3 0EU. *T:* Topsham (01392) 873160.

MACKNIGHT, Dame Ella (Annie Noble), DBE 1969; Consultant Emeritus (Obstetrician and Gynaecologist), Queen Victoria Hospital, Melbourne, since 1964; *b* 7 Aug. 1904; 4th *d* of Dr Conway Macknight. *Educ:* Toorak Coll., Melbourne; Univ. of Melbourne, resident student, Janet Clarke Hall. MB, BS 1928; MD Melbourne 1931; DGO Melbourne 1936; MRCOG 1951; FRCOG 1958; FRACS 1971; FAGO 1973; FRACOG (FAustCOG 1978); Fellow AMA, 1976. Hon. Obstetrician and Gynaecologist, Queen Victoria Hosp., Melbourne, 1935–64; Pres., Queen Victoria Hosp., Melbourne, 1971–77 (Vice-Pres., 1965–71); Hon. Sec., 1963–67, Vice-Pres., 1967–70, Pres., 1970–72, Australian Council, RCOG. Fellow, Asia and Oceania Fedn, 1993. Hon. MD Monash, 1972. *Recreation:* golf. *Address:* 8/16 Wooriguleen Road, Toorak, Vic 3142, Australia. *Clubs:* Lyceum (Melbourne); Royal Melbourne Golf.

MACKSEY, Kenneth John, MC 1944; freelance author, since 1968, and publisher, since 1982; *b* 1 July 1923; *s* of Henry George Macksey and Alice Lilian (*née* Nightingall); *m* 1946, Catherine Angela Joan Little; one *s* one *d*. *Educ:* Goudhurst Sch.; Sandhurst; Army Staff Coll., Camberley. Served War, RAC: trooper, 1941–44; commnd 141st Regt RAC (The Buffs), 1944; Western Europe, 1944–45; Royal Tank Regt, 1946; served: India, 1947; Korea, 1950; Germany, 1957 and 1960–62; Singapore, 1958–60; retd, 1968. Dep. Editor, Purnell's History of the Second World War, and History of the First World War, 1968–70. Consultant to Canadian Armed Forces, 1981–91; Mil. Consultant, Discovery Channel, 1993. Town Councillor, 1972–83. *Publications:* To the Green Fields Beyond, 1965 (2nd edn 1977); The Shadow of Vimy Ridge, 1965; Armoured Crusader: the biography of Major-General Sir Percy Hobart, 1967; Afrika Korps, 1968 (4th edn 1976); Panzer Division, 1968 (4th edn 1976); Crucible of Power, 1969; Tank, 1970 (3rd edn 1975); Tank Force, 1970; Beda Fomm, 1971; Tank Warfare, 1971; Vimy Ridge, 1972; Guinness Book of Tank Facts and Feats, 1972 (3rd edn 1980); The Guinness History of Land Warfare, 1973 (2nd edn 1976); Battle, 1974; The Partisans of Europe, 1975; (jtly) The Guinness History of Sea Warfare, 1975; Guderian, Panzer General, 1975 (3rd edn 1992); (with Joan Macksey) The Guinness Guide to Feminine Achievements, 1975; (jtly) The Guinness History of Air Warfare, 1976; The Guinness Book of 1952, 1977; The Guinness Book of 1953, 1978; The Guinness Book of 1954, 1978; Kesselring: the making of the Luftwaffe, 1978; Rommel: battles and campaigns, 1979; The Tanks, vol. 3, 1979; Invasion: the German invasion of England July 1940, 1980 (2nd edn 1990); The Tank Pioneers, 1981; A History of the Royal Armoured Corps, 1914–1975, 1983; Commando Strike, 1985; First Clash, 1985; Technology in War, 1986; Godwin's Saga, 1987; Military Errors of World War II, 1987; Tank versus Tank, 1988 (2nd edn 1991); For Want of a Nail, 1989; (jtly) The Penguin Encyclopedia of Modern Warfare, 1991, 2nd edn 1993; Penguin Encyclopedia of Weapons and Military Technology, 1994; (ed) The Hitler Options, 1995; contributor to DNB; articles and reviews in RUSI Jl, Army Qly, Brit. Army Rev., and The Tank. *Recreations:* umpiring ladies hockey, listening to music, living in Beaminster. *Address:* Whatley Mill, Beaminster, Dorset DT8 3EN. *T:* Beaminster (01308) 862321. *Club:* Social (Beaminster).

McKUEN, Rod; poet, composer, author, performer, columnist, classical composer; *b* Oakland, Calif, 29 April 1933. Has appeared in numerous films, TV, concerts, nightclubs, and with symphony orchestras. Composer: modern classical music; scores for motion pictures and TV. President: Stanyan Records; Discus Records; New Gramophone Soc.; Mr Kelly Prodns; Montcalm Prodns; Stanyan Books; Cheval Books; Biplane Books; Rod McKuen Enterprises; Vice-Pres., Tamarack Books; Dir, Animal Concern; Member, Advisory Board: Fund for Animals; Internat. Educn; Market Theatre, Johannesburg; Member, Board of Directors: National Ballet Theatre; Amer. Dance Ensemble; Amer. Guild of Authors and Composers; Exec. Pres., Amer. Guild of Variety Artists; Member: Amer. Soc. of Composers, Authors and Publishers; Writers' Guild; Amer. Fedn of TV and Radio Artists; Screen Actors' Guild; Equity; Modern Poetry Assoc.; Amer. Guild of Variety Artists; AGAC; Internat. Platform Assoc. Mem., Bd of Governors, National Acad. of Recording Arts and Sciences; Trustee: Univ. of Nebraska; Freedoms Foundn. Nat. spokesperson for Amer. Energy Awareness; Internat. spokesperson for Cttee for Prevention of Child Abuse (also Nat. Bd Mem.). Numerous awards, including: Grand Prix du Disc, Paris, 1966, 1974, 1975 and 1982; Golden Globe Award, 1969; Grammy for best spoken word album, Lonesome Cities, 1969; Entertainer of the Year, 1975; Man of the Year Award, Univ. of Detroit, 1978; awards from San Francisco, LA, Chattanooga, Topeka, Lincoln and Nebraska; Freedoms Foundn Patriot Medal, 1981; Salvation Army Man of the Year, 1982. Over 200 record albums; 41 Gold and Platinum records internationally; nominated Pulitzer Prize in classical music for The City, 1973. *Publications: poetry:* And Autumn Came, 1954; Stanyan Street and Other Sorrows, 1966; Listen to the Warm, 1967; Lonesome Cities, 1968; Twelve Years of Christmas, 1968; In Someone's Shadow, 1969;

A Man Alone, 1969; With Love, 1970; Caught in the Quiet, 1970; New Ballads, 1970; Fields of Wonder, 1971; The Carols of Christmas, 1971; And to Each Season, 1972; Pastorale, 1972; Grand Tour, 1972; Come to Me in Silence, 1973; America: an Affirmation, 1974; Seasons in the Sun, 1974; Moment to Moment, 1974; Beyond the Boardwalk, 1975; The Rod McKuen Omnibus, 1975; Alone, 1975; Celebrations of the Heart, 1975; Finding my Father: one man's search for identity (prose), 1976; The Sea Around Me, 1977; Hand in Hand, 1977; Coming Close to the Earth, 1978; We Touch the Sky, 1979; Love's Been Good to Me, 1979; Looking for a Friend, 1980; An Outstretched Hand (prose), 1980; The Power Bright and Shining, 1980; Too Many Midnights, 1981; Rod McKuen's Book of Days, 1981; The Beautiful Strangers, 1981; The Works of Rod McKuen: Vol. 1, Poetry, 1950–82, 1982; Watch for the Wind . . ., 1982; Rod McKuen—1984 Book of Days, 1983; The Sound of Solitude, 1983; Suspension Bridge, 1984; Another Beautiful Day, 1984, vol. 2, 1985; Valentines, 1986; Intervals, 1987; *major classical works:* Symphony No One; Concerto for Guitar and Orchestra; Concerto for Four Harpsichords; Concerto for Cello and Orch.; Concerto for Bassoon and Orch.; Seascapes; Concerto for Piano and Orchestra; Adagio for Harp and Strings; Piano Variations; The Black Eagle (opera); Birch Trees (Concerto for Orch.); various other classical commns; numerous lyrics; *film and television scores:* Joanna, 1968; Travels with Charley, 1968; The Prime of Miss Jean Brodie (Academy Award Nomination), 1969; Me, Natalie, 1969; The Loner, 1969; A Boy Named Charlie Brown (Academy Award Nomination), 1970; Come to your Senses, 1971; Scandalous John, 1971; Wildflowers, 1971; The Borrowers, 1973; Lisa Bright and Dark, 1973; Hello Again, 1974; Emily, 1975; The Unknown War, 1979; Man to Himself, 1980; Portrait of Rod McKuen, 1982; The Beach, 1984. *Address:* PO Box 2783, Los Angeles, CA 90078–2790, USA.

MACKWORTH, Commander Sir David Arthur Geoffrey, 9th Bt, *cr* 1776; RN retired; *b* 13 July 1912; *o s* of late Vice-Admiral Geoffrey Mackworth, CMG, DSO, and Noel Mabel, *d* of late William I. Langford; *S* uncle, 1952; *m* 1st, 1941, Mary Alice (marr. diss. 1972; she *d* 1993), *d* of Thomas Henry Grylls; one *s*; 2nd, 1973, Beryl Joan, formerly wife of late Ernest Henry Sparkes, and 3rd *d* of late Pembroke Henry Cockayn Cross and of Jeanie Cross. *Educ:* Farnborough Sch., Hants; RNC Dartmouth. Joined RN 1926; served HMS Eagle, HMS Suffolk, 1939–45; Commander, 1948; Naval Adviser to Director of Guided Weapon Research and Development, Ministry of Supply, 1945–49; retired, 1956. MRIN. *Recreations:* sailing, cruising. *Heir: s* Digby John Mackworth [*b* 2 Nov. 1945; *m* 1971, Antoinette Francesca, *d* of Henry James McKenna, Ilford, Essex; one *d*. *Educ:* Wellington Coll. Served Australian Army Aviation Corps, Malaysia and Vietnam (Lieut). With British Airways]. *Address:* 36 Wittering Road, Hayling Island, Hants. PO11 9SP. *Clubs:* Royal Ocean Racing; Royal Naval Sailing Association; Royal Yacht Squadron (Cowes).

MACKWORTH, Rosalind Jean, CBE 1994; Social Fund Commissioner for Great Britain, since 1987, and for Northern Ireland, since 1987; Senior Partner, Mackworth Rowland, Solicitors; *b* 10 Aug. 1928; *d* of Rev. Albert Walters, FRMetS and Alma Walters, sometime Comptroller to Archbishop of Canterbury; *m* Richard Charles Audley Mackworth, MA, MSc, DIC, CEng; two *d*. *Educ:* twelve small schools, following father's postings; Queen's Univ. Belfast (BA); Girton Coll., Cambridge (MA); Law Soc. professional exams. Joined Gregory Rowcliffe, Solicitors, 1956; set up own practice, 1967; amalgamated practice, Mackworth Rowland, 1982. Mem., VAT Tribunals, 1976–. Chm., Judicial Commn, Euro. Union of Women, 1984–87 (Vice-Chm., British Section, 1986–87). *Recreations:* everything except golf. *Address:* Mackworth Rowland, 3 Lenobia Mansions, Queen's Club Gardens, W14. *T:* 0171–385 4996; Independent Review Service for the Social Fund, Millbank Tower, 21–24 Millbank, SW1P 4QU.

MACKWORTH-YOUNG, Sir Robert Christopher, (Sir Robin Mackworth-Young), GCVO 1985 (KCVO 1975; CVO 1968; MVO 1961); Librarian Emeritus to HM the Queen; *b* 12 Feb. 1920; *s* of late Gerard Mackworth-Young, CIE; *m* 1953, Rosemarie, *d* of W. C. R. Aue, Menton, France; one *s*. *Educ:* Eton (King's Schol.); King's Coll., Cambridge. Pres., Cambridge Union Soc., 1948. Served in RAF, 1939–46. HM Foreign Service, 1948–55; Deputy Librarian, Windsor Castle, 1955–58; Librarian, Windsor Castle, and Asst Keeper of the Queen's Archives, 1958–85. Mem. Bd, British Library, 1984–90. FSA; Hon. FLA. *Recreations:* music, electronics, ski-ing. *Club:* Roxburghe.

McLACHLAN, Dr Andrew David, FRS 1989; Scientific Staff, Medical Research Council Laboratory of Molecular Biology, Cambridge, since 1967; Fellow of Trinity College, Cambridge, since 1959; *b* 25 Jan. 1935; *s* of Donald Harvey McLachlan and Katherine (*née* Harman); *m* 1959, Jennifer Margaret Lief Kerr; three *s*. *Educ:* Winchester Coll. (Schol.); Trinity Coll., Cambridge (BA, MA, PhD, ScD). Res. Fellow, Trinity Coll., 1958; Harkness Fellow, USA, 1959–61; Lectr in Physics, Trinity Coll., 1961–87; Lectr in Chemistry, Cambridge Univ., 1965–67. Visiting Professor: CIT, 1964; Brandeis Univ., 1975; UCLA, 1989. *Publications:* (with A. Carrington) Introduction to Magnetic Resonance, 1967; papers in various jls, including Jl of Molecular Biology, Nature, and Proceedings of the Royal Soc. *Recreations:* walking, music, camping. *Address:* Medical Research Laboratory of Molecular Biology, Hills Road, Cambridge CB2 2QH. *T:* Cambridge (01223) 248011; Trinity College, Cambridge CB2 1TQ. *T:* (home) Cambridge (01223) 361318.

McLACHLAN, Angus Henry; journalist; *b* 29 March 1908; *s* of James H. and Mabel McLachlan; unmarried. *Educ:* Scotch Coll., Melbourne; University of Melbourne. Melbourne Herald, 1928–36; joined Sydney Morning Herald, 1936; News Editor, 1937–49; General Manager, John Fairfax & Sons Ltd (publishers of Sydney Morning Herald, Australian Financial Review), 1949–64, Dir, 1965–80 (Man. Dir, 1965–70). Jt Man. Dir, Australian Associated Press Pty Ltd, 1965–82 (Chairman, 1958–59, 1964–65, 1975–77); Director: Reuters Ltd, London, 1966–71 (Trustee, 1979–84, Chm. 1980–84); Amalgamated Television Services Pty Ltd, 1955–85; Macquarie Broadcasting Holdings Ltd, 1966–80; David Syme & Co. Ltd, Publishers of The Age, 1970–79; Federal Capital Press Ltd, Publishers of Canberra Times, 1970–79; Mem. Council, Library of NSW, 1966–75 (Dep. Pres., 1974–75); Mem., Library Council of NSW, 1975–78; Member, Sydney University Extension Board, 1960–75. *Address:* Box 5303, GPO, Sydney, NSW 2001, Australia. *Clubs:* Australian, Union (Sydney); Royal Sydney Yacht Squadron.

McLACHLAN, Gordon, CBE 1967; BCom; FCA; Secretary, Nuffield Provincial Hospitals Trust, 1956–86; *b* 12 June 1918; *s* of late Gordon McLachlan and Mary McLachlan (*née* Baird); *m* 1951, Monica Mary Griffin; two *d*. *Educ:* Leith Academy; Edinburgh Univ. Served with RNVR, 1938–46; Gunnery Specialist, 1943–46. Accountant, Edinburgh Corp., 1946–48; Dep. Treas., NW Met. Regional Hosps Bd, 1948–53; Accountant Nuffield Foundn, Nuffield Provincial Hosps Trust, Nat. Corp. for Care of Old People, 1953–56. Asst Dir, Nuffield Foundn, 1955–56. Henry Cohen Lectr, Univ. of Jerusalem, 1969; Parker B. Francis Foundn Distinguished Lectr, Amer. Coll. of Hosp. Admin, 1976; Sir David Bruce Lectr, RAMC, 1982; Rock Carling Fellow, 1989–90. Consultant, American Hospitals Assoc. and American Hospitals Research and Educational Trust, 1964–65; Member Council, American Hospitals Research and Educational Trust, 1965–74 (citation for meritorious service, AHA, 1976); Mem., Inst. of Medicine, Nat. Acad. of Sciences, Washington DC, 1974–. General Editor, Nuffield Provincial Hospitals Trust publications, 1956–86; Consulting Editor, Health Services Research Journal (US), 1966–74. Hon. FRCGP 1978. Hon. LLD Birmingham, 1977. *Publications:* What Price Quality?, 1990; A History of the Nuffield Provincial Hospitals Trust 1940–90, 1992; editor of many publications on Nuffield Provincial Hospitals Trust list; contrib. to Lancet, Practitioner, Times, Twentieth Century, etc. *Recreations:* reading, watching ballet, theatre, Rugby football. *Address:* 95 Ravenscourt Road, W6 0UJ. *T:* 0181–748 8211. *Club:* Caledonian.

McLACHLAN, Peter John, OBE 1983; DL; Chief Executive (formerly Director), Bryson House, since 1980 (formerly General Secretary, Belfast Voluntary Welfare Society); Director: North City Training Ltd, since 1989; Lagan Watersports Ltd, since 1994; *b* 21 Aug. 1936; *s* of Rev. Dr Herbert John McLachlan and Joan Dorothy McLachlan (*née* Hall); *m* 1965, Gillian Mavis Lowe (marr. diss. 1992); two *d*. *Educ:* Magdalen College Sch., Oxford; Queen's Coll., Oxford (schol.; BA Lit. Hum.; MA). Administrative trainee, Min. of Finance, NICS, 1959–62; Administrator, NYO of GB, 1962–65 and 1966–69; Personal Asst to Chm., IPC, 1965–66; Cons. Res. Dept, 1970–72; Exec. Dir, Watney & Powell Ltd, 1972–73; Mem. (Unionist) S Antrim, NI Assembly, 1973–75; Gen. Manager, S. H. Watterson Engineering, 1975–77; Jt Man. Dir, Ulster Metalspinners Ltd, 1976–77; Projects Manager, Peace By Peace Ltd, 1977–79; Sec., Peace People Charitable Trust, 1977–79; Chm., Community of The Peace People, 1978–80. Founder Chairman: NI Fedn of Housing Assocs, 1976–78; Belfast Improved Houses Ltd, 1975–81 (Dir, 1975–); Lisnagarvey Housing Assoc., 1977–91; Dismas House, 1983–87 (Cttee Mem., 1983–89); Chm., NI Peace Forum, 1980–82; Vice-Chm., NI Hospice Ltd, 1981–90; Member: Minister's Adv. Cttee on Community Work, NI, 1982–84; Central Personal Social Services Adv. Cttee, 1984–88; Eastern Health and Social Services Bd, NI, 1991–94; Administrative Council: Royal Jubilee Trusts, 1975–81; NI Projects Trust, 1977–88; Advr, Children's Holiday Scheme NI, 1982–; Trustee: Buttle Trust, 1987–; Anchor Trust, 1987–90; Victoria Homes Trust, 1988–; Cecil King Meml Foundn, 1990–. Founder, NI Fedn Victims Support Schemes, (Hon. Sec., 1982–); Mem. Council, Victim Support UK, 1987–94 (Vice Chm., 1988–90). Mem., Bd of Visitors, HM Prison Maghaberry, 1986–91. Dir, Belfast Community Radio Ltd, 1989– (Chm., 1992–); Chairman: Belfast Br., Carers Nat. Assoc.; Forum for Community Work Educn, 1992–94; Belfast Hills Regl Park Cttee, 1994–; Mem., Adv. Council, Belfast Common Purpose, 1992–; Dir, Community Network Ltd; Cttee Mem., Belfast Civic Trust. Member: Corrymeela Community, 1975–; Cttee, Fellowship of Reconciliation, 1982– (Chm., 1992–). Mem., Internat. Advisory Cttee, Eisenhower Exchange Fellowships Foundn, Philadelphia, 1991–. DL Belfast, 1992. Salzburg Seminar Alumnus, 1979; UK Eisenhower Fellow, 1986. *Recreations:* piano playing, mountain walking, gardening, singing. *Address:* 9 Ashburne Mews, Belfast BT7 1SF. *T:* Belfast (01232) 325602. *Club:* New Cavendish.

MACLAGAN, Michael, CVO 1988; FSA; FRHistS; Richmond Herald of Arms, 1980–89; *b* 14 April 1914; *s* of Sir Eric Robert Dalrymple Maclagan, KCVO, CBE, and Helen Elizabeth (*née* Lascelles); *m* 1st, 1939, Brenda Alexander (marr. diss. 1946); one *s*; 2nd, 1949, Jean Elizabeth Brooksbank Garnett, *d* of late Lt-Col W. B. Garnett, DSO; two *d* (one *s* decd). *Educ:* Winchester Coll.; Christ Church, Oxford (BA 1st Cl. Hons Modern History, MA). FSA 1948; FRHistS 1961; FSG 1970; FHS 1972. Lectr, Christ Church, Oxford, 1937–39; Fellow of Trinity Coll., 1939–81, Emeritus Fellow 1981, Sen. Proctor, 1954–55. 2/Lieut TA, 1938; served war, 1939–46: 16/5 Lancers; sc; Major, GSOII War Office. Slains Pursuivant, 1948–70; Portcullis Pursuivant, 1970–80. Vis. Professor, Univ. of S Carolina, 1974; Fellow of Winchester Coll., 1975–89; Sen. Librarian, Oxford Union, 1960–70; Trustee, Oxford Union, 1970. Councillor, Oxford CBC, 1946–74; Sheriff, 1964–65; Lord Mayor of Oxford, 1970–71. Chm., Oxford Dio. Adv. Cttee, 1961–85. Master of Scriveners' Co., 1988–89. OStJ 1952. *Publications:* (ed) Bede: Ecclesiastical History I and II, 1949; Trinity College, 1955, rev. edn 1963; (jtly) The Colour of Heraldry, 1958; (ed) Richard de Bury: Philobiblon, 1960; 'Clemency' Canning, 1962 (Wheatley Gold Medal); City of Constantinople, 1968; (with J. Louda) Lines of Succession, 1981 (trans. French, 1984; 3rd edn 1992); articles in DNB, VCH, etc. *Recreations:* real tennis, wine, walking, travel. *Address:* 20 Northmoor Road, Oxford OX2 6UR. *T:* Oxford (01865) 58536; Trinity College, Oxford OX1 3BH. *Clubs:* Cavalry and Guards, Pratt's; Oxford Union (Oxford).

McLAGGAN, Murray Adams; JP; Lord Lieutenant of Mid Glamorgan, since 1990; *b* 29 Sept. 1929; *s* of Sir John Douglas McLaggan, KCVO, FRCS, FRCSE and Elsa Violet Lady McLaggan (*née* Adams), MD, DPH; *m* 1959, Jennifer Ann Nicholl; two *s* one *d*. *Educ:* Winchester College; New College, Oxford (MA 1st Cl. Hons). Called to the Bar, Lincoln's Inn, 1955; Student and Tutor in Law, Christ Church, Oxford, 1957–66. Member: Parly Boundary Commn for Wales, 1980–; Regl Adv. Bd, Wales, NRA (Chm., Regl Flood Defence Cttee, 1990–); former Chm., Forestry Commn Regional Adv. Cttee (Wales). Chm., Nat. Trust Cttee for Wales, 1991–94 (Dep. Chm., 1984–91). High Sheriff Mid Glamorgan, 1978–79, DL 1982; JP Glamorgan, 1968. *Recreations:* bibliophily, dendrology, amateur operatics. *Address:* Merthyr Mawr House, Bridgend, Mid Glamorgan CF32 0LR. *T:* Bridgend (01656) 652038.

McLAREN, family name of **Baron Aberconway.**

McLAREN, (Dame) Anne Laura, (Dr Anne McLaren), DBE 1993; DPhil; FRS 1975; FRCOG; Principal Research Associate, Wellcome/Cancer Research Campaign Institute, and Research Fellow, King's College, Cambridge, since 1992; *b* 26 April 1927; *d* of 2nd Baron Aberconway; *m* 1952, Donald Michie (marr. diss.); one *s* two *d*. *Educ:* Univ. of Oxford (MA, DPhil). FRCOG *ad eund* 1986. Post-doctoral research, UCL, 1952–55 and Royal Vet. Coll., London, 1955–59; joined staff of ARC Unit of Animal Genetics at Edinburgh Univ., 1959; Dir, MRC Mammalian Develt Unit, 1974–92. Mem., ARC, 1978–83. Vice-Pres., Royal Soc., 1992– (Mem. Council, 1985–87; Foreign Sec., 1991–); Pres., BAAS, 1993–94. Mem., Cttee of Managers, Royal Instn, 1976–81. Hon. Fellow, UCL, 1993. Scientific Medal, Zool Soc. London, 1967; Royal Medal, Royal Soc., 1990. *Publications:* Mammalian Chimaeras, 1976; Germ Cells and Soma, 1980; papers on reproductive biology, embryology, genetics and immunology in sci. jls. *Address:* Wellcome/CRC Institute, Tennis Court Road, Cambridge CB2 1QR; 40 Ainger Road, NW3 3AT.

McLAREN, Clare, (Mrs Andrew McLaren); *see* Tritton, E. C.

McLAREN, Prof. Digby Johns, OC 1987; PhD; FRS 1979; FRSC 1968; President, Royal Society of Canada, 1987–90; *b* 11 Dec. 1919; *s* of James McLaren and Louie Kinsey; *m* 1942, Phyllis Matkin; two *s* one *d*. *Educ:* Sedbergh Sch.; Queens' Coll., Cambridge (BA, MA); Univ. of Michigan (PhD). Served RA (Gunner to Captain), ME and Italy, 1940–46. Field Geologist, Geological Survey of Canada, in Alberta and British Columbia Rocky Mountains, District of Mackenzie, Yukon Territory, Arctic Islands, 1948–80; first Dir, Inst. of Sedimentary and Petroleum Geology, Calgary, Alberta, 1967–73; Dir Gen., Geological Survey of Canada, 1973–80; Prof., Dept of Geology, Univ. of Ottawa, 1981–89; Sen. Science Adviser, Dept of Energy, Mines and Resources, Ottawa, 1981–84. Pres., Commn on Stratigraphy, IUGS, 1972–76; Chm. of Bd, Internat. Geol Correlation Programme, UNESCO-IUGS, 1976–80; IUGS Deleg. to People's Republic of China to advise on participation in international science, 1977. President: Paleontol Soc., 1969;

Canadian Soc. Petroleum Geologists, 1971; Geol Soc. of America, 1981; Hon. Mem. and Leopold von Buch Medallist, Geol Soc. of Germany, 1982; Corresp. Mem., Geol Soc. of France, 1975; Foreign Associate, Nat. Acad. of Scis, USA, 1979. For. Mem., Amer. Philosophical Soc., 1994; For. Hon. Fellow, European Union of Geoscis, 1983; Hon. FGS 1989. Hon. DSc: Ottawa, 1980; Carleton, 1993; Waterloo, 1995. Gold Medal (for Pure and Applied Science), Professional Inst. of Public Service of Canada, 1979; Edward Coke Medal, Geol Soc. of London, 1985; Logan Medal, Geol Assoc. of Canada, 1987; Hollis D. Hedberg Award in Energy, Inst. for Study of Earth and Man, 1994. *Publications:* (ed) Resources and World Development (proceedings of 2 Dahlem Workshops), 1987; memoirs, bulletins, papers, geological maps, and scientific contribs to journals on regional geology, paleontology, geological time, correlation, extinctions and global change and resource depletion. *Recreations:* skiing, swimming, gardening, music. *Address:* 248 Marilyn Avenue, Ottawa, Ont K1V 7E5, Canada. *T:* (613) 7374360.

McLAREN, Ian Alban Bryant; QC 1993; Assistant Recorder, since 1992; *b* 3 July 1940; *yr s* of Alban McLaren and Doris (*née* Hurst); *m* 1964, Margaret Middleton, BA; two *s* one *d*. *Educ:* Sandbach Sch., Blackpool Grammar Sch.; Univ. of Nottingham (LLB 1961). Called to the Bar, Gray's Inn, 1962 (Macaskie Schol.); in practice at the Bar, 1962–; Law Tutor, Univ. of Nottingham, 1962–64. *Recreations:* gardening, photography. *Address:* 24 The Ropewalk, Nottingham NG1 5EF. *T:* Nottingham (0115) 947 2581.

McLAREN, Sir Robin (John Taylor), KCMG 1991 (CMG 1982); HM Diplomatic Service, retired; Director: Govett Oriental Investment Trust, since 1995; Invesco Asia Trust, since 1995; *b* 14 Aug. 1934; *s* of late Robert Taylor McLaren and of Marie Rose McLaren (*née* Simond); *m* 1964, Susan Ellen Hatherly; one *s* two *d*. *Educ:* Richmond and East Sheen County Grammar Sch. for Boys; Ardingly Coll.; St John's Coll., Cambridge (Schol.; MA). Royal Navy, 1953–55. Entered Foreign Service, 1958; language student, Hong Kong, 1959–60; Third Sec., Peking, 1960–61; FO, 1961–64; Asst Private Sec. to Lord Privy Seal (Mr Edward Heath), 1963–64; Second, later First Sec., Rome, 1964–68; seconded to Hong Kong Govt as Asst Political Adviser, 1968–69; First Sec., FCO, 1970–73; Dep. Head of Western Organisations Dept, 1974–75; Counsellor and Head of Chancery, Copenhagen, 1975–78; Head of Hong Kong and Gen. Dept, 1978–79, of Far Eastern Dept, 1979–81, FCO; Political Advr, Hong Kong, 1981–85; Ambassador to Philippines, 1985–87; Asst Under Sec. of State, FCO, 1987–90; Sen. British Rep., Sino-British Jt Liaison Gp, 1987–89; Dep. Under Sec. of State, FCO, 1990–91; Ambassador to People's Republic of China, 1991–94. *Recreations:* music, China, hill-walking. *Clubs:* United Oxford & Cambridge University; Hong Kong (Hong Kong).

McLAREN-THROCKMORTON, Clare; *see* Tritton, E. C.

McLAUCHLAN, Derek John, CEng, FIEE; FRAeS; Chief Executive, National Air Traffic Services, since 1991; Member of Board, Civil Aviation Authority, since 1991; *b* 5 May 1933; *s* of Frederick William McLauchlan and Nellie (*née* Summers); *m* 1960, Dr Sylvia June Smith (*see* S. J. McLauchlan); two *d*. *Educ:* Queen Elizabeth's Hospital, Bristol; Bristol Univ. (BSc). CEng, FIEE 1988; FRAeS 1993. BAC, 1954–66; European Space Technol. Centre, 1966–70; Marconi Space and Defence Systems, 1970–76; ICL, 1976–88; Renishaw Research, 1988–89; Dir Gen., Projects and Engrg, CAA, 1989–91. Non-exec. Chm., Architecture Projects Management Ltd, 1994–. Mem. Council, Air League, 1994–. *Recreations:* music, theatre, walking. *Address:* 7 Holmwood Close, East Horsley, Leatherhead, Surrey KT24 6SS. *T:* East Horsley (01483) 285144.

McLAUCHLAN, Dr Keith Alan, FRS 1992; Reader in Physical Chemistry, Oxford University, since 1994 (Lecturer, 1965–94); Fellow of Hertford College, Oxford, since 1965; *b* 8 Jan. 1936; *s* of Frederick William McLauchlan and Nellie (*née* Summers); *m* 1958, Joan Sheila Dickenson; one *s* one *d*. *Educ:* Queen Elizabeth's Hosp., Bristol; Univ. of Bristol (BSc, PhD); Univ. of Oxford (MA). Post-doctoral Fellow, NRCC, Ottawa, 1959–60; Post-doctoral Fellow, then Sen. Scientific Officer, NPL, Teddington, 1960–65. Oxford University: Chairman: Inter-deptl Cttee for Chemistry, 1990–93; Cttee of Heads of Sci. Depts, 1991–93; Mem. Gen. Bd, 1993–. Visiting Professor: Tata Inst., Bombay, 1986; Univ. of Konstanz, Germany, 1990. Chm., Electron Spin Resonance Discussion Gp, RSC, 1989–92. Pres., Internat. Soc. for Electron Paramagnetic Resonance, 1993–. Silver Award for Chemistry, IES, 1993. Radio and television appearances. *Publications:* Magnetic Resonance, 1972; contrib. chaps in books; papers and review articles in Molecular Physics, Chemical Physics Letters, etc. *Recreations:* gardening, walking, ski-ing, reading. *Address:* Physical Chemistry Laboratory, South Parks Road, Oxford OX1 3QZ. *T:* Oxford (01865) 275424; 29 Cumnor Hill, Oxford OX2 9EY. *T:* Oxford (01865) 862528.

McLAUCHLAN, Madeline Margaret Nicholls; Head Mistress, North London Collegiate School, 1965–85; *b* 4 June 1922; *o c* of late Robert and Gertrude McLauchlan, Birmingham. *Educ:* King Edward VI Grammar Sch. for Girls, Camp Hill, Birmingham; Royal Holloway College, University of London. Asst Mistress: Shrewsbury High Sch., GPDST, 1944; Manchester High Sch., 1952. Senior Walter Hines Page Scholar, E-SU, 1955. Head Mistress, Henrietta Barnett Sch., 1958. Chm., Schoolboy and Schoolgirl Exchange Cttee, E-SU (Mem., Educn Cttee, 1966); Member: Exec. Cttee, Assoc. of Head Mistresses, 1966–76, Chm., 1974–76; Exec. Cttee, UCCA, 1968–85; Direct Grant Cttee, GBGSA, 1972–; Assisted Places Cttee, ISJC, 1980–85; Council, Westfield Coll., Univ. of London, 1975–78; Council, The Francis Holland Schools Trust, 1985– (Chm., 1993–); Vice-Chm., Church Schs Co., 1988– (Mem. Council, 1985–). Governor: Imperial Coll., 1968–85; Bedford Coll., 1981–85; St Christopher's Sch., NW3, 1985–; Rougemont Sch., Newport, Gwent, 1988–92; Llanbedr Village Sch., 1989–; NYO, 1985–93 (Mem. Council, 1975, Vice-Chm. Council, 1981). Freeman, Goldsmiths' Co., 1986. *Recreations:* music, mountain walking, housekeeping. *Address:* The Coach House, Moor Park, Llanbedr, Crickhowell, Powys NP8 1SS. *Clubs:* English-Speaking Union, University Women's.

McLAUCHLAN, Dr Sylvia June, FFPHM; Director General, The Stroke Association, since 1993; *b* 8 June 1935; *d* of Sydney George Smith and Muriel May (*née* Treweek); *m* 1960, Derek John Alexander McLauchlan, *qv*; two *d*. *Educ:* High Sch. for Girls, Chichester; Univ. of Bristol (MB ChB 1959); Univ. of Manchester (MSc 1981). FFPHM 1989. GP, Bristol, 1960–66; MO, Dept of Public Health, Portsmouth, 1970–76; Clinical MO, Macclesfield, 1976–77; Community Medicine Dept, NW RHA, 1977–86; Public Health Dept, SW Thames RHA, 1986–91; Dir of Public Health, Ealing HA, 1991–93. *Recreations:* theatre, gardening, cooking. *Address:* The Stroke Association, CHSA House, Whitecross Street, EC1Y 8JJ. *T:* 0171–490 7999. *Club:* New Cavendish.

McLAUCHLAN, Thomas Joseph; Stipendiary Magistrate, 1966–82; *b* 15 May 1917; *s* of Alexander and Helen McLauchlan; *m* 1945, Rose Catherine Gray, MA. *Educ:* St Aloysius Coll., Glasgow; Univ. of Glasgow (BL). War service, Merchant Navy and RAF Y Section, Signals Intell., Wireless Officer, 1940–46. Legal Asst to Manager of large industrial insurance co., 1947–49; Clerk to Glasgow Police Courts, 1949–66. JP Scotland. *Address:* 1B Lennox Court, 14 Sutherland Avenue, Bearsden, Glasgow G61 3JW. *T:* 0141–942 9446.

McLAUGHLAN, Rear-Adm. Ian David, CB 1970; DSC 1941 and Bar, 1953; Admiral Commanding Reserves and Director General, Naval Recruiting, 1970–72, retired; *b* 2 May 1919; *s* of Richard John and Margaret McLaughlan; *m* 1942, Charity Pomeroy Simonds; two *d*. *Educ:* St Paul's Sch. Entered Navy, 1937; served in destroyers, 1940–45 (despatches three times); comd HMS: Flint Castle, 1948–50; Concord, 1950–52; jssc 1952; Armed Forces Staff Coll., Norfolk, Va, 1953; HMS Jupiter, 1953–55; comd HMS: Chieftain, 1955; Chevron, 1955–56 (despatches); Staff of C-in-C, Portsmouth, 1957–59; Asst Dir of Plans, Admty, 1959–61; Capt. (F), 2nd Frigate Sqdn, 1961–62; idc 1963; Dir, Naval Ops and Trade, 1964–66; comd HMS Hampshire, 1966–67; Chief of Staff to Comdr Far East Fleet, 1967–70. Comdr 1951; Capt. 1958; Rear-Adm. 1968. Commendador d'Aviz, 1956. *Recreations:* gardening. *Address:* The Five Gables, Mayfield, East Sussex TN20 6TZ. *T:* Mayfield (01435) 872218.

McLAUGHLIN, Eleanor Thomson, JP; DL; Lord Provost and Lord Lieutenant of Edinburgh, 1988–92; *b* 3 March 1938; *d* of Alexander Craig and Helen Thomson; *m* 1959, Hugh McLaughlin; one *s* two *d*. *Educ:* Broughton School. Mem. (Lab), Edinburgh District Council, 1974–. Chairman: Edinburgh Festival Soc., 1988–; Edinburgh Military Tattoo Ltd, 1988–. JP Edinburgh, 1975; DL Edinburgh, 1993. *Recreations:* Shetland lace knitting, gardening (Alpine plants). *Address:* 28 Oxgangs Green, Edinburgh EH13 9JS. *T:* 0131–445 4052.

McLAUGHLIN, Mrs (Florence) Patricia (Alice), OBE 1975; *b* 23 June 1916; *o d* of late Canon F. B. Aldwell; *m* 1937, Henry, *o s* of late Major W. McLaughlin, of McLaughlin & Harvey Ltd, London, Belfast and Dublin; one *s* two *d*. *Educ:* Ashleigh House, Belfast; Trinity Coll., Dublin. MP (UU) Belfast West, 1955–64; Hon. Sec., Parly Home Safety Cttee, 1956–64; Deleg. to Council of Europe and WEU, 1959–64. Past Chm., Unionist Soc.; Past Vice-Chm., Women's National Advisory Cttee of Cons. Party; Former Nat. Advisor on Women's Affairs to European Movement. Has been active in voluntary and consumer work for many years; Chairman: Steering Gp on Food Freshness, 1973–75; Housewife's Trust; Former Mem., Exec. Cttee, BSI. Vice-Pres., Royal Society for Prevention of Accidents, 1962–85. *Recreations:* talking and travelling. *Address:* 31 Headbourne Worthy House, Winchester, Hants SO23 7JG.

McLAUGHLIN, Mrs Patricia; *see* McLaughlin, Mrs F. P. A.

MacLAURIN, Sir Ian (Charter), Kt 1989; DL; Chairman, Tesco PLC, since 1985 (Managing Director, 1973–85; Deputy Chairman, 1983–85; Director, 1970); non-executive Director: Guinness PLC, since 1986; National Westminster Bank plc, since 1990; *b* Blackheath, 30 March 1937; *s* of Arthur George and Evelina Florence MacLaurin; *m* 1961, Ann Margaret (*née* Collar); one *s* two *d*. *Educ:* Malvern Coll., Worcs. Served in RAF, 1956–58. Joined Tesco, 1959. Director: Enterprise Oil, 1984–90; Gleneagles Hotels plc, 1992–. Chm., Food Policy Gp, Retail Consortium, 1980–84; Pres., Inst. of Grocery Distribution, 1989–92. Trustee, Royal Opera House Trust, 1992. Governor and Mem. Council, Malvern Coll. Mem. Cttee, MCC, 1986–. FRSA 1986; FIM 1987; Hon. FCGI 1992. Liveryman, Carmen's Co., 1982–. DL Herts, 1992. DUniv Stirling, 1987. *Recreation:* golf. *Address:* Tesco PLC, Tesco House, Delamare Road, Cheshunt, Herts EN8 9SL. *Clubs:* Royal Automobile; MCC, Lord's Taverners, XL, Band of Brothers.

MACLAY, family name of **Baron Maclay.**

MACLAY, 3rd Baron *cr* 1922, of Glasgow; **Joseph Paton Maclay,** DL; Bt 1914; Group Marketing Executive, Acomarit Group, since 1993; *b* 11 April 1942; *s* of 2nd Baron Maclay, KBE, and of Nancy Margaret, *d* of R. C. Greig, Hall of Caldwell, Uplawmoor, Renfrewshire; *S* father, 1969; *m* 1976, Elizabeth Anne, *o d* of G. M. Buchanan, Delamere, Pokataroo, NSW; two *s* one *d*. *Educ:* Winchester; Sorbonne Univ. Managing Director: Denholm Maclay Co. Ltd, 1970–83; Denholm Maclay (Offshore) Ltd, 1975–83; Triport Ferries (Management) Ltd, 1975–83; Dep. Man. Dir, Denholm Ship Management Ltd, 1982–83; Man. Dir, Milton Timber Services Ltd, 1984–90; Dir, Denholm Ship Management (Holdings) Ltd, 1991–93. Director: Milton Shipping Co. Ltd, 1970–83; Marine Shipping Mutual Insce Co., 1982–83; Altnamara Shipping PLC, 1994–; Pres., Hanover Shipping Inc., 1982–83. Director: British Steamship Short Trades Assoc, 1978–83; N of England Protection and Indemnity Assoc., 1976–83. Chm., Scottish Br., British Sailors Soc., 1979–81; Vice-Chm., Glasgow Shipowners & Shipbrokers Benevolent Assoc., 1982–83. DL Renfrewshire, 1986. *Heir: s* Hon. Joseph Paton Maclay, *b* 6 March 1977. *Address:* Duchal, Kilmacolm, Renfrewshire PA13 4RS.

McLAY, Hon. James Kenneth, (Jim); Managing Director and Principal, J. K. McLay Ltd (international business consultants), since 1987; *s* of late Robert McLay and of Joyce McLay; *m* 1983, Marcy Farden. *Educ:* St Helier's Sch.; King's Sch.; King's Coll.; Auckland Univ. (LLB 1967); Pennsylvania State Univ. (EMP 1987). Solicitor in practice on own account, 1971; barrister 1974. MP (National Party) for Birkenhead, NZ, 1975–87; Attorney-Gen. and Minister of Justice, 1978–84; Government Spokesperson for Women, 1979–84; Dep. Prime Minister, 1984; Leader, National Party and Leader of the Opposition, 1984–86. Mem., Ministerial Wkg Party on Accident Compensation and Incapacity, 1990–91; NZ Comr, Internat. Whaling Commn, 1993–. Chairman: Wholesale Electricity Market Study, 1991–92; Wholesale Electricity Market Develt Gp, 1993–94. *Recreation:* trout fishing. *Address:* PO Box 8885, Symonds Street Post Office, Auckland 1, New Zealand.

MacLEAN, Hon. Lord; Ranald Norman Munro MacLean; a Senator of the College of Justice in Scotland, since 1990; *b* 18 Dec. 1938; *s* of late John Alexander MacLean, CBE; *m* 1963, Pamela Ross (marr. diss. 1993); two *s* one *d* (and one *s* decd). *Educ:* Inverness Royal Acad.; Fettes Coll.; Clare Coll., Cambridge Univ. (BA); Edinburgh Univ. (LLB); Yale Univ., USA (LLM). Called to the Scottish Bar, 1964; QC (Scot.) 1977; Advocate Depute, 1972–75, Home Advocate Depute, 1979–82; Standing Jun. Counsel, Health and Safety Exec. (Scotland), 1975–77; Member Council on Tribunals, 1985–90 (Chm., Scottish Cttee, 1985–90); Scottish Legal Aid Bd, 1986–90. Mem., Stewart Cttee on Alternatives to Prosecution, 1977–82. Chm. of Council, Cockburn Assoc., 1988–. *Publication:* (ed jtly) Gloag and Henderson, Introduction to the Law of Scotland, 7th edn 1968, 8th edn 1980. *Recreations:* hill walking, Munro collecting, birdwatching. *Address:* 38 Royal Terrace, Edinburgh EH7 5AH. *Clubs:* Scottish Arts, New (Edinburgh).

MACLEAN of Dochgarroch, yr, Very Rev. Allan Murray; Provost of St John's Cathedral, Oban, since 1986; *b* 22 Oct. 1950; *o s* of Rev. Donald Maclean of Dochgarroch and Loraine Maclean of Dochgarroch (*née* Calvert); *m* 1990, Anne, *widow* of David Lindsay; one *s* one *d*. *Educ:* Dragon School, Oxford; Trinity College, Glenalmond; Univ. of Edinburgh (MA 1st cl. Hons Scottish History); Cuddesdon Coll. and Pusey House, Oxford. Deacon 1976, Priest 1977; Chaplain of St Mary's Cathedral, Edinburgh, 1976–81; Rector of Holy Trinity, Dunoon, 1981–86; Exam. Chaplain to Bishop of Argyll and the Isles, 1983–. Pres., Internat. Clan Maclean Assoc., 1994– (Vice-Pres., Clan Maclean Assoc., 1982–94). Editor: Clan Maclean, 1975–85; Argyll and the Isles, 1984–93. *Publication:* Telford's Highland Churches, 1989. *Recreations:* topography, history, genealogy, architecture. *Address:* The Rectory, Oban, Argyll PA34 5DJ. *T:* Oban (01631) 562323; 3 Rutland Square, Edinburgh EH1 2AS. *T:* 0131–228 6036. *Club:* New (Edinburgh).

McLEAN, Colin, CMG 1977; MBE 1964; HM Diplomatic Service, retired; UK Permanent Representative to the Council of Europe (with the personal rank of Ambassador), 1986–90; *b* 10 Aug. 1930; *s* of late Dr L. G. McLean and H. I. McLean; *m* 1953, Huguette Marie Suzette Leclerc; one *s* one *d*. *Educ:* Fettes; St Catharine's Coll., Cambridge (MA). 2RHA, 1953–54. District Officer, Kenya, 1955–63; Vice-Principal, Kenya Inst. of Administration, 1963–64; HM Diplomatic Service, 1964; served Wellington, Bogotá and FCO, 1964–77; Counsellor, Oslo, 1977–81; Head of Trade Relations and Export Dept, FCO, 1981–83; High Comr in Uganda, 1983–86. *Recreation:* sailing. *Address:* 28 The Heights, Foxgrove Road, Beckenham, Kent BR3 2BY. *T:* 0181–650 9565.

MACLEAN, Colin William, FRCVS; Director General, Meat and Livestock Commission, since 1992; *b* 19 June 1938; *s* of late Kenneth Percy Maclean and Elsie Violet (*née* Middleton); *m* 1959, Jacqueline Diana Brindley; two *d*. *Educ:* William Hulme's Grammar Sch., Manchester; Liverpool Univ. Sch. of Vet. Sci. (BVSc); MVSc 1971. MRCVS 1961, FRCVS 1969. Veterinary Surgeon and Partner, veterinary practice, Thornley, Glos, and Wickham, Hants, 1961–66; Unilever Ltd: Chief Vet. Advr, 1966–72; Manager, Pig Breeding, 1972–74; Man. Dir, Farm Mark Ltd and Masterbreeders Ltd, 1974–76; Area Gen. Manager (S), BOCM Silcock Ltd, 1980–83; Glaxo Group: Dep. Man. Dir, 1983–88; Product Develt Dir, Glaxo Animal Health Ltd, 1983–88; Technical Dir, MLC, 1988–92. *Publications:* contrib. to Veterinary Record, Res. Vet. Sci., Jl Comparative Pathology. *Recreations:* squash, Rugby, theatre, travel. *Address:* Meat and Livestock Commission, PO Box 44, Winterhill House, Snowdon Drive, Milton Keynes MK6 1AX. *T:* Milton Keynes (01908) 677577. *Club:* Farmers'.

MACLEAN, Rt Hon. David John; PC 1995; MP (C) Penrith and the Border, since July 1983; Minister of State, Home Office, since 1993; *b* 16 May 1953; *s* of John and Catherine Jane Maclean; *m* 1977, Jayalaluna Dawn Gallacher. Asst Govt Whip, 1987–88; a Lord Comr of HM Treasury (Govt Whip), 1988–89; Parly Sec., MAFF, 1989–92; Minister of State, DoE, 1992–93. *Address:* House of Commons, SW1A 0AA.

McLEAN, Denis Bazeley Gordon, CMG 1989; Jennings Randolph Distinguished Fellow, United States Institute of Peace, since 1994; *b* Napier, NZ, 18 Aug. 1930; *s* of John Gordon McLean and Renée Maitland Smith; *m* 1958, Anne Davidson, Venado Tuerto, Argentina; two *s* one *d*. *Educ:* Nelson Coll., NZ; Victoria Univ. Coll., NZ (MSc); Rhodes Schol. 1954; University Coll., Oxford (MA). Jun. Lectr in Geology, Victoria UC, 1953–54; joined Dept of External Affairs of NZ Govt, London, 1957; served in: Wellington, 1958–60; Washington, 1960–63; Paris, 1963–66; Kuala Lumpur, 1966–68; Asst Sec. (Policy), MoD, Wellington, 1969–72; RCDS, 1972; Dep. High Comr, London, 1973–77; Dep. Sec. of Defence, NZ, 1977, Sec. of Defence, 1979–88; Ambassador to US, 1991–94. Visiting Fellow: Strategic and Defence Studies Centre, ANU, Canberra, 1989; Guest Scholar, Woodrow Wilson Center, and Sen. Associate, Carnegie Endowment for Internat. Peace, Washington, 1990–91. *Publication:* The Long Pathway: Te Ara Roa, 1986. *Recreations:* walking, looking at art, writing, geology. *Address:* 11 Dekka Street, Wellington, New Zealand. *Clubs:* Travellers'; Wellington (NZ).

MACLEAN, Sir Donald (Og Grant), Kt 1985; optometrist, practising in Ayr, since 1965; *b* 13 Aug. 1930; *s* of Donald Og Maclean and Margaret Maclean (*née* Smith); *m* 1958, Muriel Giles (*d* 1984); one *s* one *d*. *Educ:* Morrison's Academy, Crieff; Heriot Watt Univ. FBOA; Fellow, British Coll. of Opticians. RAMC, 1952–54. Optical practice: Newcastle upon Tyne, 1954–57; Perth, 1957–65. Chm., Ayr Constituency Cons. Assoc., 1971–75; Scottish Conservative and Unionist Association: Vice-Pres., 1979–83; Pres., 1983–85; Chm., W of Scotland Area, 1977–79; Exec. Mem., Nat. Union, 1979–89; Scottish Conservative Party: Dep. Chm., 1985–89; Vice-Chm., 1989–91. Chm., Ayrshire and Arran Local Optical Cttee, 1986–88. Chm., Ayrshire Medical Support Ltd. Freeman: Spectacle Makers' Co., 1986 (Liveryman, 1989–); City of London, 1987. Dean of Guildry, Royal Burgh of Ayr, 1993–. *Recreations:* coastal shipping, reading, photography, philately. *Address:* Dun Beag II, 22 Woodend Road, Alloway, Ayr KA7 4QR.

MACLEAN, Rear-Adm. Euan, CB 1986; FRINA, FIMechE; Director General Fleet Support Policy and Services, 1983–86; *b* 7 July 1929; *s* of John Fraser Maclean and Dorothy Mary Maclean; *m* 1954, Renée Shaw; two *d*. *Educ:* BRNC Dartmouth; RNEC Keyham/Manadon. FRINA 1980; FIMechE 1980. Joined Exec. Br., RN, 1943; transf. to Engr Br., 1947; sea service in HMS Sirius, Illustrious, Gambia, Ocean, Indefatigable, Defender, Hermes, Eagle and Ark Royal, 1950–72; on loan to Royal Malaysian Navy, 1965–68; Prodn Dept, Portsmouth Dockyard, 1968–71; HMS Ark Royal, 1971–72; Exec. Officer, HMS Sultan, 1973; Dep. Prodn Man., Devonport Dockyard, 1974–77; Fleet Marine Engr Officer, 1977–79; student, RCDS, 1980; Prodn Man., Portsmouth Dockyard, 1981–83. ADC to the Queen, 1982. Comdr 1965, Captain 1974, Rear-Adm. 1983. *Recreation:* rough country.

MACLEAN of Dunconnel, Sir Fitzroy Hew, 1st Bt, *cr* 1957; KT 1993; CBE (mil.) 1944; 15th Hereditary Keeper and Captain of Dunconnel; *b* 11 March 1911; *s* of Major Charles Maclean, DSO; *m* 1946, Hon. Mrs Alan Phipps, 2nd *d* of 16th Baron Lovat, KT; two *s*. *Educ:* Eton; Cambridge. 3rd Sec., Foreign Office, 1933; transferred to Paris, 1934, and to Moscow, 1937; 2nd Sec., 1938; transferred to Foreign Office, 1939; resigned from Diplomatic Service, and enlisted as private in Cameron Highlanders; 2nd Lt Aug. 1941; joined 1st Special Air Service Regt Jan. 1942; Capt. Sept. 1942; Lt-Col 1943; Brig. Comdg British Military Mission to Jugoslav partisans, 1943–45. Lees Knowles Lecturer, Cambridge, 1953. MP (C) Lancaster, 1941–59, Bute and N Ayrshire, 1959–Feb. 1974; Parly Under-Sec. of State for War and Financial Sec. War Office, Oct. 1954–Jan. 1957. Member: UK Delegn to North Atlantic Assembly, 1962–74 (Chm., Mil. Cttee, 1964–74); Council of Europe and WEU, 1972–74. Hon. Col, 23rd SAS Regt, 1984–88. Hon. LLD: Glasgow 1969; Dalhousie 1971; Dundee, 1984; Hon. DLitt Acadia, 1970. French Croix de Guerre, 1943; Order of Kutusov, 1944; Partisan Star (First Class), 1945; Order of Merit, Yugoslavia, 1969; Order of the Yusoslav Star with Ribbon, 1981. *Publications:* Eastern Approaches, 1949; Disputed Barricade, 1957; A Person from England, 1958; Back to Bokhara, 1959; Jugoslavia, 1969; A Concise History of Scotland, 1970; The Battle of Neretva, 1970; To the Back of Beyond, 1974; To Caucasus, 1976; Take Nine Spies, 1978; Holy Russia, 1979; Tito, 1980; The Isles of the Sea, 1985; Portrait of the Soviet Union, 1988; Bonnie Prince Charlie, 1988; All The Russias, 1992; Highlanders, 1995. *Heir: s* Charles Maclean, yr of Dunconnel [*b* 31 Oct. 1946; *m* 1986, Deborah, *d* of Lawrence Young; three *d*]. *Address:* Strachur House, Argyll PA27 8BX. *T:* Strachur (0136986) 242. *Clubs:* White's, Pratt's; Puffin's, New (Edinburgh).

McLEAN, Sir Francis (Charles), Kt 1967; CBE 1953 (MBE 1945); *b* 6 Nov. 1904; *s* of Michael McLean; *m* 1930, Dorothy Mabel Blackstaffe; one *s* one *d*. *Educ:* University of Birmingham (BSc). Chief Engineer, Psychological Warfare Division, SHAEF, 1943–45. Dep. Chief Engineer, BBC, 1952–60; Dep. Dir of Engineering, BBC, 1960–63; Director, Engineering, BBC, 1963–68. Dir, Oxley Developments Ltd, 1961–. Chairman: BSI Telecommunications Industry Standards Cttee, 1960–77; Royal Commn on FM Broadcasting in Australia, 1974. Pres., Newbury Dist Field Club. FIEE. *Publications:* contrib. Journal of IEE. *Address:* Greenwood Copse, Tile Barn, Woolton Hill, Newbury, Berks. RG15 9XE. *T:* Newbury (01635) 253583.

McLEAN, Geoffrey Daniel, CBE 1988; QPM 1981; Assistant Commissioner (Territorial Operations), Metropolitan Police, 1984–91; *b* 4 March 1931; *s* of late William James McLean and Matilda Gladys (*née* Davies); *m* 1959, Patricia Edna Pope; two *s* two *d*. Following service in RA, joined Metropolitan Police, 1951; Chief Supt, 1969; Staff Officer to HMCIC, Home Office, 1970–72; Comdr, 1975; Graduate, RCDS, 1978; Dep. Asst Comr, 1979; Dep. Comdt, Police Staff Coll., 1981–83. *Recreations:* Met. Police Athletics Assoc. (Chm., 1984); Met. Police Football Club (Chm., 1984); Met. Police Race-Walking Club (Chm., 1978); riding. *Address:* c/o New Scotland Yard, Broadway, SW1H 0BG. *T:* 0171–230 1212.

MacLEAN, Vice-Adm. Sir Hector Charles Donald, KBE 1962; CB 1960; DSC 1941; JP; DL; *b* 7 Aug. 1908; *s* of late Captain D. C. H. Maclean, DSO, The Royal Scots; *m* 1933, Opre, *d* of late Captain Geoffrey Vyvyan, Royal Welch Fusiliers; one *s* two *d*. *Educ:* Wellington. Special Entry into Navy, 1926; Captain 1948; idc 1951; Comd HMS Saintes and 3rd Destroyer Sqdn, 1952–53; Dir of Plans, Admiralty, 1953–56; Comd HMS Eagle, 1956–57; Chief of Staff, Home Fleet, 1958–59; Chief of Allied Staff, Mediterranean, 1959–62; Vice-Adm. 1960; retired 1962. JP Norfolk, 1963; DL Norfolk, 1977. *Address:* Deepdale Old Rectory, Brancaster Staithe, King's Lynn, Norfolk PE31 8DD. *T:* Brancaster (01485) 210281. *Club:* Norfolk (Norwich).

McLEAN, Hector John Finlayson, CBE 1995; Secretary, Crown Appointments Commission, and Archbishops' Appointments Secretary, 1987–95; *b* 10 Feb. 1934; *s* of late Dr Murdoch McLean, MB ChB and Dr Edith Muriel Finlayson McLean (*née* McGill), MB ChB, DPH, DOMS; *m* 1959, Caroline Elizabeth Lithgow; one *s* two *d*. *Educ:* Dulwich Coll.; Pembroke Coll., Cambridge (BA Hons 1958); FIPD (FIPM 1965); Harvard Business Sch., Switzerland (SMP6 1976). 2nd Lieut, KOSB, 1954–55. Imperial Chemical Industries, 1958–87: Central Staff Dept, 1958; various personnel and admin. posts in Dyestuffs and Organics Divs, 1959–72; Personnel Manager, Organics Div., 1972–74; Polyurethanes Business Area Manager, 1974–75; Dir, Agricl Div., 1975–86. Non-exec. Chairman: People & Potential Ltd, 1987–; Positive People Develt (formerly Teesside Positive People), 1987–94. Mem. Exec. Cttee, N of England Develt Council, 1978–83; Teesside Industrial Mission: Mem., Management Cttee, 1978–85; Chm., 1982–85; Dir, Cleveland Enterprise Agency, 1982–87. Mem., Northern Regl Council, CBI, 1981–85; Trustee: NE Civic Trust, 1976–88; Northern Heritage Trust, 1984–87. Mem., Chemical and Allied Products ITB, 1979–82. Gov. Teesside Polytechnic, 1978–84; Mem. Council, Newcastle Univ., 1985–87. FRSA 1991. *Recreations:* music (especially choral music), travel, gardening, walking. *Address:* College Farm House, Purton, near Swindon, Wilts SN5 9AE. *T:* Swindon (01793) 770525. *Club:* United Oxford & Cambridge University.

MACLEAN, Hector Ronald; Sheriff of Lothian and Borders, at Linlithgow, since 1988; *b* 6 Dec. 1931; *s* of Donald Beaton Maclean and Lucy McAlister; *m* 1967, Hilary Elizabeth Jenkins; three *d*. *Educ:* High Sch. of Glasgow; Glasgow Univ. Admitted to Faculty of Advocates, 1959. Sheriff of N Strathclyde (formerly Renfrew and Argyll), 1968–88. *Recreation:* golf. *Address:* Barrfield, Houston, Renfrewshire. *T:* Bridge of Weir (01505) 612449.

McLEAN, Ian Graeme; His Honour Judge McLean; a Circuit Judge since 1980; *b* Edinburgh, 7 Sept. 1928; *s* of Lt-Gen. Sir Kenneth McLean, KCB, KBE; *m* 1957, Eleonore Maria Gmeiner, Bregenz, Austria; two *d*. *Educ:* Aldenham Sch.; Christ's Coll., Cambridge. BA Hons Law 1950; MA 1955. Intell. Corps, 1946–48. Called to English Bar, Middle Temple, Nov. 1951; admitted Faculty of Advocates, Edinburgh, 1985; practised London and on Western Circuit, 1951–55; Crown Counsel, Northern Nigeria, 1955–59; Sen. Lectr and Head of Legal Dept of Inst. of Administration, Northern Nigeria, 1959–62; Native Courts Adviser, 1959–62; returned to English Bar, 1962; practised London and South Eastern Circuit, 1962–70, occasional Dep. Chm., Inner, NE, SW and Middx Areas, London QS, 1968–70; occasional Dep. Recorder, Oxford, 1969–70, Adjudicator under Immigration Acts, 1969–70; Metropolitan Stipendiary Magistrate, 1970–80. *Publications:* Cumulative Index West African Court of Appeal Reports, 1958; (with Abubakar Sadiq) The Maliki Law of Homicide, 1959; (with Sir Lionel Brett) Criminal Law Procedure and Evidence of Lagos, Eastern and Western Nigeria, 1963; (with Cyprian Okonkwo) Cases on the Criminal Law, Procedure and Evidence of Nigeria, 1966; (with Peter Morrish) A Practical Guide to Appeals in Criminal Courts, 1970; (with Peter Morrish) The Crown Court, an index of common penalties, etc, 1972–92; (ed, with Peter Morrish) Harris's Criminal Law, 22nd edn, 1972; (with Peter Morrish) The Magistrates' Court, an index of common penalties, annually 1973–92; (with Peter Morrish) The Trial of Breathalyser Offences, 1975, 3rd edn 1990; A Practical Guide to Criminal Appeals, 1980; A Pattern of Sentencing, 1981; (with John Mulhern) The Industrial Tribunal: a practical guide to employment law and tribunal procedure, 1982; (with Sheriff Stone) Fact-Finding for Magistrates, 1990; contrib. Archbold's Criminal Pleadings, 38th edn, and Halsbury's Laws of England, 4th edn, title Criminal Law. *Recreations:* gardening, writing, languages.

MACLEAN, Dr Ian Walter Fitzroy, FRHistS; FBA 1994; Reader in French, University of Oxford, since 1994; Fellow, Queen's College, Oxford, since 1972; *b* 9 Feb. 1945; *s* of James Walter Maclean and Elsie May Maclean (*née* Davis); *m* 1971, Pauline Jennifer Henderson; one *s* two *d*. *Educ:* Christ's Hosp.; Wadham Coll., Oxford (BA 1st Cl. Hons Mod. Lang. 1966; MA, DPhil 1971). FRHistS 1989. Sen. Scholar, Wadham Coll., Oxford, 1967–69; Lectr in French, Univ. of Leeds, 1969–72; CUF Lectr in French, Univ. of Oxford, 1972–93. Dir, European Humanities Res. Centre, Oxford, 1994–. Vis. Fellow, Humanities Res. Centre, Canberra, 1983; Vis. Scholar, Herzog August Bibliothek, Wolfenbüttel, 1986, 1995; Vis. Prof., Catholic Univ. of Nijmegen, 1993; Dist. Vis. Schol., Centre for Renaissance and Reformation Studies, Victoria Univ., Univ. of Toronto, 1994. *Publications:* Woman Triumphant: feminism in French literature, 1977; The Renaissance Notion of Woman, 1980; (ed and contrib.) Montaigne, 1982; (ed and contrib.) The Political Responsibility of Intellectuals, 1990; Meaning and Interpretation in the Renaissance: the case of law, 1992; articles and essays in learned jls, collective vols, etc. *Recreations:* music, fishing, wine. *Address:* Queen's College, Oxford OX1 4AW. *T:* Oxford (01865) 279120.

McLEAN, John Alexander Lowry, QC 1974; Principal Secretary to Lord Chief Justice (formerly Permanent Secretary, Supreme Court of Northern Ireland) and Clerk of the Crown for Northern Ireland, 1966–93; *b* 21 Feb. 1921; *o s* of John McLean and Phoebe Jane (*née* Bowditch); *m* 1950, Diana Elisabeth Campbell (*d* 1986), *e d* of S. B. Boyd Campbell, MC, MD, FRCP, and Mary Isabel Ayre, St John's, Newfoundland; one *s* two *d*. *Educ:* Methodist Coll., Belfast; Queen's University Belfast. Served Intell. Corps, 1943–47. Called to Bar of Northern Ireland, 1949. Asst Sec., NI Supreme Court, and Private Sec. to Lord Chief Justice of NI 1956; Under Treas., Hon. Soc. of Inn of Court of NI, 1966; Clerk of Restrictive Practices Court in NI, 1957. Member: Jt Working Party on Enforcement of Judgments of NI Courts, 1963; Lord Chancellor's Cttee on NI Supreme Court, 1966; Lord Chancellor's Foreign Judgments Working Party, 1974. *Publications:* contrib. legal periodicals. *Recreations:* not golf. *Address:* 24 Marlborough Park

South, Belfast BT9 6HR. *T:* Belfast (01232) 667330; Lifeboat Cottage, Cloughey, Co. Down BT22 1HS. *T:* Portavogie (012477) 71313. *Club:* Commonwealth Trust.

MacLEAN, Hon. (John) Angus, OC 1992; PC 1957; DFC, CD; Premier of Prince Edward Island, 1979–81; *b* 15 May 1914; *s* of late George A. MacLean; *m* 1952, Gwendolyn Esther M. Burwash; two *s* two *d. Educ:* Mount Allison Academy; Summerside High Sch.; Univ. of British Columbia; Mount Allison Univ. BSc. Served War of 1939–45, RCAF: commanded Test and Development Estabt, 1943–45; Missing and Enquiry Unit, Europe, 1945–47, Wing Comdr (despatches). First elected to House of Commons by by-election, June 1951, re-elected 1953, 1957, 1958, 1962, 1963, 1965, 1968, 1972, 1974; Minister of Fisheries in the Diefenbaker Cabinet, 1957–63; elected Leader of PC Party of PEI, 1976; first elected to PEI Legislature at by-election, 1976, re-elected 1978 and 1979. PEI's Comr to EXPO '86. Member: PEI Energy Commn, 1984–87; Sen. Adv. Bd, Maritime Provinces Educn Foundn, 1983–86; Nat. Mus. of Natural Scis, Nat. Museums of Canada, 1985–88. Mem. Royal Air Forces Escaping Soc. (Canadian Br.). Hon. LLD: Mount Allison Univ., 1958; Univ. of PEI, 1985. OStJ 1982. *Recreations:* genealogical research, bird watching. *Address:* Lewes, RR3, Belle River, Prince Edward Island COA 1B0, Canada. *T:* Murray River, PEI (902) 9622235. *Clubs:* United Services, Charlottetown, RCAF Association, Masonic Lodge, AF and AM, Royal Canadian Legion, Charlottetown Chamber of Commerce, Canadian (PEI).

McLEAN, (John David) Ruari (McDowall Hardie), CBE 1973; DSC 1943; freelance typographer and author; *b* 10 June 1917; *s* of late John Thomson McLean and late Isabel Mary McLean (*née* Ireland); *m* 1945, Antonia Maxwell Carlisle; two *s* one *d. Educ:* Dragon Sch., Oxford; Eastbourne Coll. First studied printing under B. H. Newdigate at Shakespeare Head Press, Oxford, 1936. Industrial printing experience in Germany and England, 1936–38; with The Studio, 1938; Percy Lund Humphries, Bradford, 1939. Served Royal Navy, 1940–45. Penguin Books, 1945–46; Book Designer (freelance), 1946–53; Tutor in Typography, Royal College of Art, 1948–51; Typographic Adviser to Hulton Press, 1953; Founder Partner, Rainbird, McLean Ltd, 1951–58; Founder Editor, and Designer, Motif, 1958–67. Typographic Consultant to The Observer, 1960–64; Hon. Typographic Adviser to HM Stationery Office, 1966–80. Sandars Reader in Bibliography, Univ. of Cambridge, 1982–83; Alexander Stone Lectr in Bibliophily, Univ. of Glasgow, 1984. Member: Nat. Council for Diplomas in Art and Design, 1971; Vis. Cttee of RCA, 1977–83; Academic Adv. Cttee, Heriot-Watt Univ. for Edinburgh Coll. of Art, 1978–. Crown Trustee, Nat. Library of Scotland, 1981–. American Printing History Assoc. Individual Award, 1993. Croix de Guerre (French), 1942. *Publications:* George Cruikshank, 1948; Modern Book Design, 1958; Wood Engravings of Joan Hassall, 1960; Victorian Book Design, 1963, rev. edn 1972; Tschichold's Typographische Gestaltung (trans.), 1967; (ed) The Reminiscences of Edmund Evans, 1967; Magazine Design, 1969; Victorian Publishers' Book-bindings in Cloth and Leather, 1973; Jan Tschichold, Typographer, 1975; Joseph Cundall, 1976; (ed) Edward Bawden: A Book of Cuts, 1979; Thames and Hudson Manual of Typography, 1980; Victorian Publishers' Book-Bindings in Paper, 1983; The Last Cream Bun (drawings by Roger Pettiward), 1984; Benjamin Fawcett, Engraver and Colour Printer, 1988; (ed) Edward Bawden, War Artist, 1989; Nicolas Bentley drew the Pictures, 1990; Tschichold's Die neue Typographie (trans.), 1994; (ed) Typographers on Type, 1995. *Recreations:* reading, acquiring books. *Address:* Pier Cottage, Carsaig, Pennyghael, Isle of Mull PA70 6HD. *T:* and *Fax:* Pennyghael (01681) 704216. *Clubs:* Double Crown; New (Edinburgh).

McLEAN, Keith Richard, FCCA; Regional General Manager, Trent Regional Health Authority and Regional Director, NHS Executive, Trent, since 1994; *b* 27 Oct. 1947; *s* of Bertie and Elsie McLean; *m* 1973, Patricia Ann Morrell; one *d. Educ:* J. Rowntree Sch., York. FCCA 1975; IPFA 1989; MHSM 1992. Hospital Management Committees: Clerical Officer, York B, 1964–67; Higher Clerical Officer, Leicester No 4, 1967–68; Internal Auditor, Nottingham No 4, 1968–70; Sen. Accountant, Huddersfield, 1970–74; Dep. Area Treas., Calderdale HA, 1974–79; Dist Finance Officer, Derbys AHA, 1979–82; North Derbyshire Health Authority: Dist Treas., 1982–85; Dist Treas. and Dep. Dist Gen. Manager, 1985–87; Dir of Finance and Corporate Strategist, Leics HA, 1987–89; Yorkshire Regional Health Authority: Regl Dir of Finance, 1990–91; Regl Gen. Manager, 1991–94. Nat. Chm., Healthcare Financial Mgt Assoc., 1992–93. FRSA 1994. *Recreations:* golf, snooker. *Address:* Trent Regional Health Authority, Fulwood House, Fulwood, Sheffield S10 3TH. *T:* Sheffield (0114) 263 0300. *Clubs:* The Club, Oakdale Golf (Harrogate).

MacLEAN, Kenneth Smedley, MD, FRCP; Consultant Physician to Guy's Hospital, 1950–79, now Emeritus; *b* 22 Nov. 1914; *s* of Hugh MacLean and Ida Smedley; *m* 1939, Joan Hardaker; one *s* one *d* (and one *s* decd). *Educ:* Westminster; Clare Coll., Cambridge. MRCS, LRCP, 1939; House appts at Guy's, 1939; MB, BChir 1939. RNVR, 1939–46, Surg.-Lt and Surg.-Lt-Comdr. MRCP 1946; House Officer and Medical Registrar, Guy's Hosp., 1946–48; MD Cantab 1948; FRCP 1954; elected to Assoc. of Physicians of Great Britain and Ireland, 1956. Assistant Director, Dept of Medicine, Guy's Hospital Medical Sch., 1949, Director, 1961–63. Chm., University Hosps Assoc., 1975–78. Pres., Assurance Medical Soc., 1985–87. *Publication:* Medical Treatment, 1957. *Recreation:* golf. *Address:* 7 Icehouse Wood, Oxted, Surrey RH8 9DN. *T:* Oxted (01883) 716652.

MACLEAN, Hon. Sir Lachlan Hector Charles, 12th Bt *cr* 1631 (NS), of Duart and Morvern; DL; Major, Scots Guards, retired; 28th Chief of Clan Maclean; *b* 25 Aug. 1942; *s* of Baron Maclean, KT, GCVO, KBE, PC and of Elizabeth, *er d* of late Frank Mann; *S* to baronetcy of father, 1990; *m* 1966, Mary Helen, *e d* of W. G. Gordon; two *s* two *d* (and one *d* decd). *Educ:* Eton. DL Argyll and Bute, 1993. *Heir: s* Malcolm Lachlan Charles Maclean, *b* 20 Oct. 1972. *Address:* Arngask House, Glenfarg, Perthshire PH2 9QA.

McLEAN, Prof. Malcolm, PhD; CEng, FIM; Professor and Head of Department of Materials, Imperial College of Science, Technology and Medicine, University of London, since 1990; *b* 19 Dec. 1939; *s* of Andrew Bell McLean and Jane Pattison McLean (*née* Kilmartin); *m* 1967, Malinda Ruth Conner; two *s. Educ:* Ayr Acad.; Univ. of Glasgow (BSc Natural Phil. 1962; PhD 1965). CEng 1991; FIM 1984. Ohio State Univ., 1965–67; NPL, 1969–90 (Grade 6, Sect. Leader in mech. behaviour of materials at high temps). Fellow, Amer. Soc. Metals, 1992. Rosenhain Medallist, Inst. Metals, 1986. *Publications:* Directionally solidified materials for high temperature service, 1983; (Series Editor) Characterisation of high temperature materials, Vols 1–7, 1988–89; articles on materials sci. and engrg in learned jls. *Recreations:* travel, music, politics. *Address:* Department of Materials, Imperial College of Science, Technology and Medicine, Prince Consort Road, SW7 2BP; 20 Strawberry Hill Road, Twickenham, Middx TW1 4PT. *T:* 0181–892 0617.

MACLEAN, Murdo; Private Secretary to the Government Chief Whip, since 1979; *b* 21 Oct. 1943; *s* of Murdo Maclean and Johanna (*née* Martin). *Educ:* Glasgow. Temp. Clerk, Min. of Labour Employment Exchange, Govan, Glasgow, 1963–64; BoT, 1964–67; Prime Minister's Office, 1967–72; Dept of Industry, 1972–78. Freeman, City of London, 1994. FRSA 1990. *Address:* c/o 12 Downing Street, SW1A 2AD. *T:* 0171–219 3595/4400. *Club:* Garrick.

MACLEAN, Prof. Norman; JP; Professor of Genetics, since 1992, and Head of Department of Biology, since 1993; University of Southampton; *b* 23 Sept. 1932; *s* of late Alexander Maclean and Christine Walker; *m* 1962, Dr Jane Kay Smith; one *s* one *d. Educ:* George Heriot's Sch., Edinburgh; Edinburgh Sch. of Agriculture; Edinburgh Univ. (SDA, BSc 1st cl. Hons, PhD). FIBiol. Asst Lectr in Zoology, Edinburgh Univ., 1961–64; Sir Henry Wellcome Travelling Fellow, 1964–65; Res. Associate, Rockefeller Inst., NY, 1964; Lectr in Biology, Sen. Lectr and Reader, Southampton Univ., 1965–92. Edinburgh University: MacGillivray Prize in Zoology, 1956; Moira Lindsay Stuart Prize in Zoology, 1957; Gunning Victoria Jubilee Prize, 1960. JP Southampton, 1976. *Publications:* Control of Gene Expression, 1976; The Differentiation of Cells, 1977; Haemoglobin, 1978; Trout and Grayling: an angler's natural history, 1980; (jtly) DNA, Chromatin and Chromosomes, 1981; (ed jtly) Eukaryotic Genes: structure, activity and regulation, 1983; (ed) Oxford Surveys on Eurkaryotic Genes, vols 1–7, 1984–90; (jtly) Cell Commitment and Differentiation, 1987; Macmillan Dictionary of Genetic and Cell Biology, 1987; Genes and Gene Regulation, 1989, 3rd edn 1992; Animals with Novel Genes, 1994; articles in learned jls. *Recreations:* gardening, fly fishing, squash, reading. *Address:* 10 Russell Place, Southampton SO2 1NU. *T:* Southampton (01703) 557649. *Club:* Abbotts Barton Angling.

McLEAN, Peter Standley, CMG 1985; OBE 1965; Head of East Asia Department, Overseas Development Administration, 1985–87; *b* 18 Jan. 1927; *s* of late William and Alice McLean; *m* 1954, Margaret Ann Minns; two *s* two *d. Educ:* King Edward's Sch., Birmingham; Wadham Coll., Oxford (MA). Served Army, 1944–48; Lieut, 15/19th King's Royal Hussars. Colonial Service, Uganda, 1951–65, retired from HMOCS as Permanent Sec., Min. of Planning and Economic Develt; Ministry of Overseas Development: Principal, 1965; Private Sec. to Minister for Overseas Develt, 1973; Head of Eastern and Southern Africa Dept, 1975; Head of Bilateral Aid and Rural Develt Dept, 1979; Minister and UK Perm. Rep to FAO, 1980. Chm., Africa Grants Cttee, Comic Relief, 1989–92. *Recreations:* watching sport, DIY, painting. *Address:* 17 Woodfield Lane, Ashtead, Surrey KT21 2BQ. *T:* Ashtead (01372) 278146.

McLEAN, Philip Alexander, CMG 1994; HM Diplomatic Service; Ambassador to Cuba, since 1994; *b* 24 Oct. 1938; *s* of late Wm Alexander McLean and Doris McLean (*née* Campbell); *m* 1960, Dorothy Helen Kirkby; two *s* one *d. Educ:* King George V Sch., Southport; Keble Coll., Oxford (MA Hons). National Service, RAF, 1956–58. Industry, 1961–68; entered HM Diplomatic Service by Open Supplementary Competition, 1968; Second, later (1969) First, Secretary, FCO; La Paz, 1970–74: Head of Chancery, 1973; FCO, 1974–76; Dep. Director of British Trade Development Office and Head of Industrial Marketing, New York, 1976–80; Counsellor and Consul-Gen., Algiers, 1981–83; Diplomatic Service Inspector, 1983–85; Hd, S America Dept, FCO, 1985–87; Consul-Gen., Boston, 1988–91; Minister and Dep. Head of Mission, Peking, 1991–94. Hon. LLD American Internat. Coll., 1991. *Recreation:* free time. *Address:* c/o Foreign and Commonwealth Office, SW1A 2AH. *Club:* United Oxford & Cambridge University.

MacLEAN, Ranald Norman Munro; *see* MacLean, Hon. Lord.

MACLEAN, Sir Robert (Alexander), KBE 1973; Kt 1955; DL; Honorary President, Stoddard Holdings Ltd; *b* 11 April 1908; *s* of Andrew Johnston Maclean, JP, Cambuslang, Lanarkshire, and Mary Jane Cameron; *m* 1938, Vivienne Neville Bourke (*d* 1992), *d* of Captain Bertram Walter Bourke, JP, Heathfield, Co. Mayo; two *s* two *d. Educ:* High Sch. of Glasgow. JDipMA. President: Glasgow Chamber of Commerce, 1956–58; Association British Chambers of Commerce, 1966–68; Chairman: Council of Scottish Chambers of Commerce, 1960–62; Scottish Cttee, Council of Industrial Design, 1949–58 (Mem., CoID, 1948–58); Council of Management, Scottish Industries Exhibns, 1949, 1954 and 1959; Scottish Exports Cttee, 1966–70; Scottish Industrial Estates Corp., 1955–72 (Mem., 1946–72); Pres., British Industrial Exhibn, Moscow, 1966; Vice-Chm., Scottish Bd for Industry, 1952–60; Member: Pigs and Bacon Marketing Commn, 1955–56; BNEC, 1966–70; Scottish Aerodromes Bd, 1950–61; Export Council for Europe, 1960–64; BoT Trade Exhbns Adv. Cttee, 1961–65; Nat. Freight Corp., 1969–72; Regional Controller (Scotland): Board of Trade, 1944–46; Factory and Storage Premises, 1941–44. Director: Scottish Union & Nat. Insce Co., 1965–68; Scottish Adv. Bd, Norwich Union Insce Gp., 1965–81. Former Vice-Pres., Scottish Council (Develt and Industry), 1955–82. Trustee, Clyde Navigational Trust, 1956–58; Pres., Scottish Youth Clubs, 1959–68. DL Renfrewshire, 1970. CStJ 1975. FRSA; CIMgt. Hon. LLD Glasgow, 1970. *Recreations:* golf, fishing. *Address:* South Branchal Farm, Bridge of Weir, Renfrewshire PA11 3SJ. *Clubs:* Carlton; Western (Glasgow).

McLEAN, Ruari; *see* McLean, J. D. R. McD. H.

McLEAN, Dr Thomas Pearson, CB 1990; FRSE; CPhys, FInstP; CEng, FIEE; Professor of Electrical Engineering and Science, Royal Military College of Science, Shrivenham, since 1992; *b* Paisley, 21 Aug. 1930; *s* of Norman Stewart McLean and Margaret Pearson McLean (*née* Ferguson); *m* 1957, Grace Campbell Nokes; two *d. Educ:* John Neilson Instn, Paisley; Glasgow Univ. (BSc, PhD); Birmingham Univ. Royal Radar Estabt (becoming Royal Signals and Radar Estabt, 1976), 1955–80: Head of Physics Gp, 1973–77; Dep. Dir, 1977–80; Ministry of Defence: Under Sec., Dir Gen. Air Weapons and Electronic Systems, 1980–83; Dir, RARDE, 1984–86; Dep. Controller, Aircraft, 1987; Dir, Atomic Weapons Estabt, 1987–90. Member: Physics Cttee, SRC, 1968–73; Optoelectronics Cttee, Rank Prize Funds, 1972–81; Council, Inst. of Physics, 1980–84. Hon. Prof. of Physics, Birmingham Univ., 1977–80. Dep. Editor, Jl of Physics C, 1976–77. *Publications:* papers in Physical Rev., Jl of Physics, etc. *Recreations:* music, Scottish country dancing.

MacLEARY, Alistair Ronald; Member, Lands Tribunal for Scotland, since 1989; *b* 12 Jan. 1940; *s* of Donald Herbert MacLeary and Jean Spiers (*née* Leslie); *m* 1967, Mary-Claire Cecilia (*née* Leonard); one *s* one *d. Educ:* Inverness Royal Acad.; Coll. of Estate Management, London; Edinburgh Coll. of Art, Heriot-Watt Univ.; Strathclyde Univ. MSc, DipTP; FRICS, FRTPI. Gerald Eve & Co., 1963–65; Murrayfield Real Estate Co., 1965–67; Dept of Environment (on secondment), 1971–73; Wright, Partners, 1967–76; MacRobert Prof. of Land Economy, 1976–89, Dean, Faculty of Law, 1982–85, Aberdeen Univ. Univ. of Auckland Foundn Visitor and Fletcher Challenge Vis. Fellow, 1985; Memorialist, MacAuley Inst. for Soil Science, 1986–87. Mem., Cttee of Inquiry into Acquisition and Occupancy of Agricl Land, 1977–79; Chm., Watt Cttee, Energy Working Gp on Land Resources, 1977–79; Mem., Exec. Cttee, Commonwealth Assoc. of Surveying and Land Economy, 1980–85 (Chm., Bd of Surveying Educn, 1981–90); Member: Home Grown Timber Adv. Cttee, Forestry Commn, 1981–87; NERC, 1988–91 (Chm., Terrestrial and Freshwater Sci. Cttee, 1990–91). Mem., Gen. Council, RICS, 1983–87 (Pres., Planning and Develt Divl Council, 1984–85). Mem., MacTaggart Chair Adv. Bd, Glasgow Univ., 1992–. FRSA, FIMgt. Hon. Fellow, Commonwealth Assoc. of Surveying and Land Economy, 1992. Founder and Editor, Land Development Studies, 1983–90. *Publications:* (ed with N. Nanthakumeran) Property Investment Theory, 1988; National Taxation for Property Management and Valuation, 1990. *Recreations:* hill walking, field sports, ski-ing. *Address:* St Helen's, Ceres, Fife KY15 5NQ. *T:* Ceres (0133482) 8862. *Club:* Royal Northern and University (Aberdeen).

See also D. W. MacLeary.

MacLEARY, Donald Whyte; principal male dancer with the Royal Ballet since 1959; Senior Repetiteur to the Principal Artists, Royal Ballet, since 1994 (Repetiteur, 1981–94);

b Glasgow, 22 Aug. 1937; *s* of Donald Herbert MacLeary, MPS, and Jean Spiers (*née* Leslie). *Educ:* Inverness Royal Academy; The Royal Ballet School. Ballet Master, Royal Ballet, 1975–81. *Classical Ballets:* (full length) Swan Lake, Giselle, 1958; Sleeping Beauty, Cinderella, Sylvia, 1959; Ondine, La Fille Mal Gardée, 1960; (centre male rôle) in Ashton's Symphonic Variations, 1962; Sonnet Pas de Trois, 1964; Romeo and Juliet, 1965; Eugene Onegin, Stuttgart, 1966; Apollo, 1966; Nutcracker, 1968; Swan Lake with N. Makarova, 1972. *Creations:* (1954–74): Solitaire, The Burrow, Danse Concertante, Antigone, Diversions, Le Baiser de la Fée, Jabez and the Devil, Raymonda Pas de Deux (for Frederick Ashton), two episodes in Images of Love; Song of the Earth; Lilac Garden (revival); Jazz Calendar; Raymonda (for Nureyeff); The Man in Kenneth MacMillan's Checkpoint; leading role in Concerto no 2 (Balanchine's Ballet Imperial, renamed); Elite Syncopations, 1974; Kenneth MacMillan's Four Seasons Symphony; the Prince in Cinderella. Toured Brazil with Royal Ballet, Spring 1973. Guest dancer, Scottish Ballet, 1979. *Recreations:* reading, theatre, records (all types); riding, swimming. *Club:* Queen's.

See also A. R. MacLeary.

MACLEAY, Very Rev. John Henry James; Dean of Argyll and The Isles, since 1987; Rector of St Andrew's, Fort William, since 1978; *b* 7 Dec. 1931; *s* of James and Isabella Macleay; *m* 1970, Jane Speirs Cuthbert; one *s* one *d*. *Educ:* St Edmund Hall, Oxford (MA); College of the Resurrection, Mirfield. Deacon 1957, priest 1958, Southwark; Curate: St John's, East Dulwich, 1957–60; St Michael's, Inverness, 1960–62, Rector 1962–70; Priest-in-charge, St Columba's, Grantown-on-Spey with St John the Baptist's, Rothiemurchus, 1970–78; Canon of St Andrew's Cathedral, Inverness, 1977–78; Canon of St John's Cathedral, Oban and Synod Clerk, Diocese of Argyll and the Isles, 1980–87. *Recreations:* fishing, reading, visiting cathedrals and churches. *Address:* St Andrew's Rectory, Parade Road, Fort William PH33 6BA. *T:* Fort William (01397) 702979.

McLEAY, Hon. Leo Boyce; MP (Lab) Watson, New South Wales, since 1993 (Grayndler, 1979–93); Government Whip, House of Representatives, Australia, since 1993; *b* 5 Oct. 1945; *s* of Ron and Joan McLeay; *m* 1969, Janice Delaney; three *s*. *Educ:* De La Salle Sch., Marrickville; North Sydney Technical Coll. Telephone technician, 1962–76; Asst Gen. Sec., ALP (NSW), 1976–79; Dep. Speaker, 1986–89, Speaker, 1989–93, House of Representatives, Australia. *Recreations:* fishing, reading. *Address:* Parliament House, Canberra, ACT 2600, Australia. *T:* (62) 774083. *Clubs:* Olympic Soccer (Sydney); Canterbury Rugby League (NSW).

MACLEHOSE, family name of **Baron MacLehose of Beoch.**

MACLEHOSE OF BEOCH, Baron *cr* 1982 (Life Peer), of Maybole in the District of Kyle and Carrick, and of Victoria in Hong Kong; **Crawford Murray MacLehose,** KT 1983; GBE 1976 (MBE 1946); KCMG 1971 (CMG 1964); KCVO 1975; DL; HM Diplomatic Service, retired; *b* 16 Oct. 1917; *s* of Hamish A. MacLehose and Margaret Bruce Black; *m* 1947, Margaret Noël Dunlop; two *d*. *Educ:* Rugby; Balliol Coll., Oxford. Served War of 1939–45, Lieut, RNVR. Joined Colonial Service, Malaya, 1939; joined Foreign Service, 1947; Acting Consul, 1947, Acting Consul-General, 1948, Hankow; promoted First Secretary, 1949; transferred to Foreign Office, 1950; First Secretary (Commercial), and Consul, Prague, 1951; seconded to Commonwealth Relations Office, for service at Wellington, 1954; returned to Foreign Office and transferred to Paris, 1956; promoted Counsellor, 1959; seconded to Colonial Office and transferred to Hong Kong as Political Adviser; Counsellor, Foreign Office, 1963; Principal Private Secretary to Secretary of State, 1965–67; Ambassador: to Vietnam, 1967–69; to Denmark, 1969–71; Governor and C-in-C, Hong Kong, 1971–82. Dir, Nat. Westminster Bank, 1982–88. Chairman: Scottish Trust for the Physically Disabled, 1982–90; Margaret Blackwood Housing Assoc., 1982–90. Pres., GB-China Centre, 1982–93. Chm. Govs, SOAS, Univ. of London, 1985–90 (Hon. Fellow, 1983). DL Ayr and Arran, 1983. Hon. LLD: York, 1983; Strathclyde, 1984. KStJ 1972. *Recreations:* sailing, fishing. *Address:* Beoch, Maybole, Ayrshire KA19 8EN. *Clubs:* Athenæum, New (Edinburgh).

McLEISH, Henry Baird; MP (Lab) Central Fife, since 1987; *b* 15 June 1948; *s* of Harry McLeish and late Mary McLeish; *m* 1968, Margaret Thomson Drysdale (*d* 1995); one *s* one *d*. *Educ:* Heriot-Watt Univ. (BA Hons planning). Research Officer, Social Work Dept, Edinburgh, 1973–74; part time Lectr/Tutor, Heriot-Watt Univ., 1973–87. Planning Officer, Fife County Council, 1974–75; Planning Officer, Dunfermline DC, 1975–87. Part-time employment consultant, 1984–87. Member: Kirkcaldy DC (Chm., Planning Cttee, 1974–77); Fife Regl Council (Chm., Further Educn Cttee, 1978–82; Leader, Council, 1982–87). *Recreations:* reading, malt whisky (history and development of), history, life and works of Robert Burns, Highlands and Islands of Scotland. *Address:* 27 Braid Drive, Glenrothes, Fife KY7 4ES. *T:* Glenrothes (01592) 755330. *Clubs:* Denbeath Miners' Welfare; Glenrothes Football Recreation.

MacLELLAN, Maj.-Gen. (Andrew) Patrick (Withy), CB 1981; CVO 1989; MBE 1964; Resident Governor and Keeper of the Jewel House, HM Tower of London, 1984–89; *b* 29 Nov. 1925; *y s* of late Kenneth MacLellan and Rachel Madeline MacLellan (*née* Withy); *m* 1954, Kathleen Mary Bagnell; one *s* twin *d*. *Educ:* Uppingham. Commnd Coldstream Guards, 1944; served Palestine 1945–48, N Africa 1950–51, Egypt 1952–53, Germany 1955–56; psc 1957; DAA&QMG 4th Guards Brigade Group, 1958–59; Mil. Asst to Chief of Defence Staff, 1961–64; Instructor, Staff Coll., Camberley, 1964–66; GSO1 (Plans) Far East Comd, 1966–67; CO 1st Bn Coldstream Guards, 1968–70; Col GS Near East Land Forces, 1970–71; Comdr 8th Inf. Brigade, 1971–72; RCDS 1973; Dep. Comdr and COS, London District, 1974–77; Pres., Regular Commns Bd, 1978–80. Vice-Pres., Officers' Assoc. Mem. Cttee, Royal Humane Soc.; Adv. Council, Women's Transport Corps (FANY). FIMgt (FBIM 1970). Mem. (Walbrook Ward), Court of Common Council, City of London, 1989– (Chm., Police Cttee, 1995–). Freeman: City of London, 1984; Co. of Watermen and Lightermen; Liveryman, Fletchers' Co., 1986– (Mem., Ct of Assts, 1993–). Chevalier de la Légion d'Honneur, 1960. *Address:* c/o Bank of Scotland, London Chief Office, 38 Threadneedle Street, EC2P 2EH. *Clubs:* White's, Pratt's.

McLELLAN, Prof. David; DPhil; Professor of Political Theory, University of Kent, since 1975; *b* 10 Feb. 1940; *s* of Robert Douglas McLellan and Olive May Bush; *m* 1967, Annie Brassart; two *d*. *Educ:* Merchant Taylors' Sch.; St John's Coll., Oxford (MA, DPhil). Lectr in Politics, Univ. of Kent, 1966–71; Vis. Prof., State Univ. of New York, 1969; Guest Fellow in Politics, Indian Inst. of Advanced Studies, Simla, 1970; Sen. Lectr in Politics, Univ. of Kent, 1972, Reader in Political Theory, 1973. *Publications:* The Young Hegelians and Karl Marx, 1969 (French, German, Italian, Spanish and Japanese edns); Marx before Marxism, 1970, 2nd edn 1972; Karl Marx: The Early Texts, 1971; Marx's Grundrisse, 1971, 2nd edn 1973; The Thought of Karl Marx, 1971 (Portuguese and Italian edns); Karl Marx: His Life and Thought, 1973, 22nd edn 1976 (German, Italian, Spanish, Japanese, Swedish and Dutch edns); Marx (Fontana Modern Masters), 1975; Engels, 1977; Marxism after Marx, 1979; (ed) Marx: the first hundred years, 1983; Karl Marx: the legacy, 1983; Ideology, 1986; Marxism and Religion, 1987; Simone Weil: Utopian pessimist, 1989; Christianity and Politics, 1990; Religion and Public Life, 1992; Unto Caesar: the political relevance of Christianity, 1993. *Recreations:* chess, Raymond Chandler, hill walking. *Address:* Eliot College, University of Kent, Canterbury, Kent CT2 7NS. *T:* Canterbury (01227) 764000.

MacLELLAN, Prof. George Douglas Stephen, MA, PhD (Cantab); CEng; FIMechE, FIEE; Professor and Head of Department of Engineering, University of Leicester, 1965–88, now Emeritus Professor; *b* Glasgow, 1 Nov. 1922; *e s* of late Alexander Stephen MacLellan. *Educ:* Rugby Sch.; Pembroke Coll., Cambridge. Mech. Sci. Tripos, 1942. Dept of Colloid Science, Cambridge, and Callenders Cable and Construction Co. Ltd, 1942–44; Fellow, Pembroke Coll., 1944–59; Vickers-Armstrong Ltd, Newcastle upon Tyne, 1944–46; University Demonstrator and Lecturer in Engineering, Cambridge, 1947–59; Rankine Professor of Mechanical Engineering (Mechanics and Mechanism), University of Glasgow, 1959–65. Commonwealth Fund Fellow, MIT, 1948–49; Visiting Professor: Michigan State University, 1958; MIT, 1962; Nanyang Technological Inst., then Nanyang Technolog. Univ., Singapore, 1986, 1989–91, 1991–93; Nat. Univ. of Singapore, 1988–89. Member: CNAA, 1970–80; Engrg Bd, SRC, 1971–74; Vis. Cttee, RCA, 1973–82; Council, IMechE, 1974–76; Nominations Cttee, Engrg Council, 1984–; Council, Inst. of Measurement and Control, 1994– (Pres., Soc. of Instrument Technol., 1964–65). Mem. Council, Loughborough Univ. of Technology, 1979–91; Chm., Engrg Professors' Conference, 1983–85. Hon. DEd CNAA, 1992. *Publications:* contribs to mech. and elec. jls. *Address:* 6 Southmeads Close, Leicester LE2 2LT. *T:* Leicester (0116) 271 5402. *Clubs:* Athenæum, Leander.

MacLELLAN, Maj.-Gen. Patrick; *see* MacLellan, A. P. W.

McLELLAND, Charles James; Director General, Association of British Travel Agents, 1987; *b* 19 Nov. 1930; *s* of Charles John McLelland and Jessie Steele Barbour; *m* 1961, Philippa Mary Murphy; one *s* three *d*. *Educ:* Kilmarnock Acad.; Glasgow Acad.; Glasgow Univ. (MA). Commissioned Royal Artillery, 1952–54. Sub-Editor, Leader Writer, Glasgow Herald, 1954–58; Scriptwriter, European Productions, BBC, 1958–61; Head of Programmes, Radio Sarawak, 1962–64; Indian Programme Organiser, BBC, 1964–67; Asst Head, Arabic Service, BBC, 1967–71; Head of Arabic Service, 1971–75; Controller, BBC Radio 2, 1976–80 (also Radio 1, 1976–78); Dep. Man. Dir and Dir of Progs, BBC Radio, 1980–86. Chm., EBU Radio Prog. Cttee, 1985–86; Pres., Overseas Broadcasters' Club, 1985–89, Hon. Vice-Pres., 1990–. Mem. Council, Officers' Assoc., 1989–. Trustee, Bourke Trust, 1991–92. *Recreations:* gardening, reading, shooting. *Address:* Lamb Cottage, Hindon, Wilts SP3 6DR.

MacLENNAN, Maj.-Gen. Alastair, OBE 1945; Curator, Royal Army Medical Corps Historical Museum, Mytchett, Hants, 1969–Feb. 1977; *b* 16 Feb. 1912; *s* of Col. Farquhar MacLennan, DSO; *m* 1940, Constance Anne Cook; two *s* one *d*. *Educ:* Aberdeen Grammar Sch.; University of Aberdeen (MB, ChB). Commissioned Lieut, RAMC, 1934; Captain, 1935; Major, 1942; Lieut-Colonel, 1942; Colonel, 1952; Brigadier, 1964; Maj.-General, 1967; retired 1969. Appointments held include regimental, staff and Ministry of Defence in UK, Malta, NW Europe, India, Malaya, Korea, Egypt and Germany; ADGMS (Army), Min. of Defence, 1957–61; DDMS, HQ, BAOR, 1961–64; Inspector Army Medical Services, 1964–66; DDMS: 1 (Br) Corps, 1966–67; HQ Eastern Command, 1967–68; Dep. Dir-Gen., Army Med. Services, MoD, 1968–69; Col Comdt, RAMC, 1971–76. US Bronze Star Medal, 1952. OStJ, 1966. QHP, 1968–69. *Publications:* papers on history of military firearms and on Highland Regts in North America 1756–1783. *Recreations:* bird-watching, military history, collecting antique military firearms and swords, vintage motor-cars. *Address:* Gable House, Chequers Lane, North Crawley, Bucks MK16 9LJ. *T:* North Crawley (01234) 391700.

MacLENNAN, Dr David Herman, FRS 1994; FRSC 1985; University Professor, University of Toronto, since 1993; *b* 3 July 1937; *s* of Douglas Henry MacLennan and Sigridur MacLennan (*née* Sigurdson; *m* 1965, Linda Carol Vass; two *s* (one *d* decd). *Educ:* Swan River Collegiate Inst., Canada, Univ. of Manitoba (BSA 1959); Purdue Univ. (MS 1961; PhD 1963). Postdoctoral Fellow, 1963–64, Asst Prof., 1964–68, Inst. for Enzyme Res., Univ. of Wisconsin: Banting and Best Department of Medical Research, University of Toronto: Associate Prof., 1969–74; Prof., 1974–93; Acting Chm., 1978–80; Chm., 1980–90; J. W. Billes Prof. of Med. Res., 1987–. Consultant, Merck, Sharp & Dohme, PA, 1992–. Member: Med. Adv. Bd, Muscular Dystrophy Assoc., Canada, 1976–87; Scientists' Review Panel, MRC Canada, 1988–90; Univ. of Ottawa Heart Inst. Res. Review Panel, 1991–; Canadian Genetic Diseases Network, 1991–; Chm., Molecular Biol. and Pathol. Cttee, Heart and Stroke Foundn of Canada, 1995–. Awards include: Ayerst Award, Canadian Biochem. Soc., 1974; Internat. Lectr Award, Biophys. Soc., 1990; Gairdner Foundn Internat. Award, 1991. *Publications:* ed and contribs to numerous learned jls. *Recreations:* collecting and restoring Canadian antique furniture, reading fiction, listening to classical music, gardening. *Address:* Banting and Best Department of Medical Research, University of Toronto, C. H. Best Institute, 112 College Street, Toronto, Ontario M5G 1L6, Canada. *T:* (416) 9785008; 293 Lytton Boulevard, Toronto, Ontario M5N 1R7, Canada. *T:* (416) 4879729.

MacLENNAN, David Ross; HM Diplomatic Service; Counsellor, Head of Africa Department (Equatorial), Foreign and Commonwealth Office, and Commissioner, British Indian Ocean Territory, since 1994; *b* 12 Feb. 1945; *s* of David Ross MacLennan and Agnes McConnell; *m* 1964, Margaret Lytollis; two *d*. *Educ:* West Calder High Sch. FO, 1963; ME Centre for Arab Studies, 1966–69; Third, later Second Sec., Aden, 1969–71; Second, later First Sec., FCO, 1972–75; First Sec., UK Delegn to OECD, Paris, 1975–79; First Sec., Hd of Chancery, Abu Dhabi, 1979–82; Asst Hd, N America Dept, FCO, 1982–84; EEC, Brussels, 1984–85; Counsellor, Kuwait, 1985–88; Dep. High Comr, Nicosia, 1989–90; Consul Gen., Jerusalem, 1990–93. *Recreations:* gardening, natural history. *Address:* c/o Foreign and Commonwealth Office, SW1A 2AH.

MACLENNAN, Prof. Duncan; Director, Centre for Housing Research and Mactaggart Professor of Land Economics and Finance, University of Glasgow, since 1990; Member of Board, Scottish Homes, since 1989; *b* 12 March 1949; *s* of James Dempster Maclennan and Mary Mackechnie (*née* Campbell); *m* (separated); one *s* one *d*. *Educ:* Allan Glen's Sch., Glasgow; Univ. of Glasgow (MA, MPhil). Aberdeen University: Lectr in Pol Econ., 1976–79; Lectr in Applied Econs, 1979–81; Sen. Lectr, 1981–84; Titular Prof., 1984–88; Prof. of Urban Studies, 1988–90. Susman Prof. of Real Estate Finance, Wharton Bus. Sch., 1988. Chairman: Care and Repair (Scotland), 1987–; Shelter (Scotland) Adv. Council, 1989–; Dir, Joseph Rowntree Res. Programme, 1988–. FRSA 1993. *Publications:* Regional Policy in Britain, 1979; Housing Economics, 1982; Paying for Britain's Housing, 1990; The Housing Authority of the Future, 1991; contribs to Urban Studies, Housing Studies, Economic Jl, Applied Econs. *Recreations:* gardening, cooking, Rugby, watching Glasgow get better. *Address:* 3 Glenburn Road, Bearsden, Glasgow G61 4PT. *T:* 0141–942 1394.

McLENNAN, Gordon; General Secretary, Communist Party of Great Britain, 1975–89; *b* Glasgow, 12 May 1924; *s* of a shipyard worker; *m*; four *c*. *Educ:* Hamilton Crescent Sch., Partick, Glasgow. Engineering apprentice, Albion Motors Ltd, Scotstoun, 1939, later engineering draughtsman. Elected Glasgow Organiser, Communist Party, 1949; Sec., Communist Party in Scotland, 1957; Nat. Organiser, Communist Party of GB, 1966.

Recreations: golf and other sports; cultural interests. *Address:* c/o Democratic Left, 6 Cynthia Street, N1 9JF.

MacLENNAN, Graeme Andrew Yule, CA; non-executive Director: HTR Japanese Smaller Companies Trust, since 1993; Premium Trust, since 1993; *b* 24 Aug. 1942; *s* of Finlay and Helen MacLennan; *m* 1st, 1973, Diane Marion Gibbon (*née* Fyfe) (marr. diss. 1989); two *s* two *d*; 2nd, 1989, Diana Rosemary Steven (*née* Urie). *Educ:* Kelvinside Academy, Glasgow. Asst Investment Manager, Leopold Joseph & Sons Ltd, London, 1964–68; Investment Man., Murray Johnstone & Co., Glasgow, 1969–70; Edinburgh Fund Managers: Investment Man., 1970; Dir, 1980, Jt Man. Dir, 1983–88; Investment Dir, Ivory & Sime plc, 1988–90; Dir, Phillips & Drew Fund Management, subseq. PDFM, 1990–93. Mem. Cttee for Scotland, Malcolm Sargent Cancer Fund for Children, 1993–. *Recreations:* hill walking, fishing. *Address:* The Old School House, 5 Main Street, Killearn, Glasgow G63 9RJ. *T:* Killearn (01360) 550127.

McLENNAN, Sir Ian (Munro), KCMG 1979; KBE 1963 (CBE 1956); President, Australian Academy of Technological Sciences, 1976–83, The Foundation President, since 1983; *b* 30 Nov. 1909; *s* of R. B. and C. O. McLennan; *m* 1937, Dora H., *d* of J. H. Robertson; two *s* two *d*. *Educ:* Scotch Coll., Melbourne; Melbourne Univ. Broken Hill Pty Co. Ltd: Cadet engineer, 1933; Asst Manager, Newcastle Steelworks of BHP Co. Ltd, 1943; Asst Gen. Man., BHP Co. Ltd, 1947; Gen. Man., 1950; Sen. Gen. Man., 1956; Chief Gen. Man., 1959; Man. Dir, 1967–71; Chm., 1971–77; Chairman: BHP-GKN Hldgs Ltd, 1970–78; Tubemakers of Australia Ltd, 1973–79; Australia and New Zealand Banking Group Ltd, and Australia and New Zealand Group Hldgs Ltd, 1977–82; Interscan Australia Pty Ltd, 1978–84; Bank of Adelaide, 1979–80; Henry Jones IXL Ltd, 1981; Elders IXL Ltd, 1981–85; Dir, ICI Australia Ltd, 1976–79. Chairman: Defence (Industrial) Cttee, 1956–75; Ian Clunies Ross Meml Foundn; Australian Mineral Development Laboratories, 1959–67, Mem. Council, 1959–77; Dep. Chm., Immigration Planning Council, 1949–67. Former Dir, International Iron and Steel Inst.; Pres., Australia-Japan Business Co-operation Cttee, 1977–85; Member: Internat. Council, Morgan Guaranty Trust Co. of NY, 1973–79; Australian Mining Industry Council, 1967–77; Australasian Inst. of Mining and Metallurgy (Pres., 1951, 1957 and 1972); Australian Mineral Industries Research Assoc. Ltd, 1958–77; General Motors Australian Adv. Council, 1978–82; Adv. Council, CSIRO, 1979–82. Chm., Queen Elizabeth II Jubilee Trust for Young Australians, 1978–81. For. Associate, Nat. Acad. of Engrg (USA), 1978; For. Mem., Fellowship of Engrg, UK, 1986. FIAM 1978; FAA 1980. Hon. DEng: Melbourne, 1968; Newcastle, 1968; Hon. DSc Wollongong, 1978; Hon. LLD Melbourne, 1988. *Recreations:* golf, gardening. *Address:* Apt 3, 112–120 Walsh Street, South Yarra, Victoria 3141, Australia. *Clubs:* Melbourne, Athenæum, Australian (Melbourne); Royal Melbourne Golf; Melbourne Cricket.

MACLENNAN, Robert Adam Ross; MP Caithness and Sutherland, since 1966 (Lab 1966–81, SDP 1981–88, Lib Dem since 1988); President, Liberal Democrats, since 1994; Barrister-at-Law; *b* 26 June 1936; *e s* of late Sir Hector MacLennan and Isabel Margaret Adam; *m* 1968, Mrs Helen Noyes, *d* of late Judge Ammi Cutter, Cambridge, Mass, and *widow* of Paul H. Noyes; one *s* one *d*, and one step *s*. *Educ:* Glasgow Academy; Balliol Coll., Oxford; Trinity Coll., Cambridge; Columbia Univ., New York City. Called to the Bar, Gray's Inn, 1962. Parliamentary Private Secretary: to Secretary of State for Commonwealth Affairs, 1967–69; to Minister without Portfolio, 1969–70; an Opposition Spokesman: on Scottish Affairs, 1970–71; on Defence, 1971–72; Parly Under-Sec. of State, Dept of Prices and Consumer Protection, 1974–79; opposition spokesman on foreign affairs, 1980–81; SDP spokesman on agriculture, fisheries and food, 1981–87; Leader, SDP, 1987–88; Jt Leader, SLD, 1988; Lib Dem spokesman on home affairs and the arts, 1988–94, on constitutional affairs and nat. heritage, 1994–. Member: House of Commons Estimates Cttee, 1967–69; House of Commons Select Cttee on Scottish Affairs, 1969–70; Public Accounts Cttee, 1979–. Mem., Latey Cttee on Age of Majority, 1968. *Recreations:* theatre, music, art. *Address:* House of Commons, SW1A 0AA.

McLENNAN, William Patrick, AM 1992; Australian Statistician, Australian Bureau of Statistics, since 1995; *b* 26 Jan. 1942; *s* of William Freeman McLennan and Linda Maude Shannon; *m* 1968, Christine Elizabeth Alexander; one *s* one *d*. *Educ:* Australian National University (BEcon Hons). Statistician, Aust. Bureau of Statistics, 1960–92; Dep. Aust. Statistician, 1986–92; Dir, CSO, and Head of Govt Statistical Service, UK, 1992–95. Vis. Fellow, Nuffield Coll., Oxford, 1992–95. *Recreations:* sport, Rugby, squash, golf. *Address:* Australian Bureau of Statistics, PO Box 10, Belconnen, ACT 2616, Australia.

MACLEOD, family name of **Baroness Macleod of Borve.**

MACLEOD OF BORVE, Baroness *cr* 1971 (Life Peer), of Borve, Isle of Lewis; **Evelyn Hester Macleod,** JP; DL; *b* 19 Feb. 1915; *d* of Rev. Gervase Vanneck Blois (*d* 1961), and Hon. Hester Murray Pakington (*d* 1973), *y d* of 3rd Baron Hampton; *m* 1st, 1937, Mervyn Charles Mason (killed by enemy action, 1940); 2nd, 1941, Rt Hon. Iain Norman Macleod, MP (Minister of Health, 1952–55; Minister of Labour and Nat. Service, 1955–59; Secretary of State for the Colonies, 1959–61; Chancellor of the Duchy of Lancaster and Leader of the House of Commons, 1961–63; Chancellor of the Exchequer, June 1970) (*d* 1970), *e s* of late Norman A. Macleod, MD, Scaliscro, Isle of Lewis; one *s* one *d*. Chm., 1973–85, Pres., 1985–, Nat. Association of the Leagues of Hospital Friends; first Chm., Nat. Gas Consumers' Council, 1972–77; Member: IBA (formerly ITA), 1972–75; Energy Commn, 1977–78; Metrication Bd, 1978–80. Co-Founder, Crisis at Christmas, 1967; Pres., Nat. Assoc. of Widows, 1976–. Governor, Queenswood Sch., 1978–85. JP Middlesex, 1955; DL Greater London, 1977. *Recreation:* my family. *Address:* House of Lords, SW1A 0PW; Luckings Farm, Coleshill, Amersham, Bucks HP7 0LS.

MacLEOD, Aubrey Seymour H.; *see* Halford-MacLeod.

MacLEOD, Dr Calum Alexander, CBE 1991; Chairman: Britannia Building Society, since 1994 (Deputy Chairman, 1993–94); Grampian Television, since 1993 (Deputy Chairman, 1982–93); *b* 25 July 1935; *s* of Rev. Lachlan Macleod and Jessie Mary Morrison; *m* 1962, Elizabeth Margaret Davidson; two *s* one *d*. *Educ:* Nicolson Inst., Stornoway; Glenurquhart Sch.; Aberdeen Univ. Partner, Paull & Williamsons Advocates, Aberdeen, 1964–80; Chairman: Aberdeen Petroleum, 1982–92; Harris Tweed Assoc., 1984–93 (Vice-Chm., 1993–95); North of Scotland, subseq. Abtrust Scotland, Investment Co., 1986–; Deputy Chairman: Scottish Eastern Investment Trust, 1988–; Britannia Life, 1992–94 (Chm., 1990–92); Dir, Aberdeen Bd, Bank of Scotland, 1980–. Member: White Fish Authy, 1973–80; N of Scotland Hydro-Electric Bd, 1976–84; Highlands and Islands Develt Bd, 1984–91; Grampian Health Bd, 1991– (Chm., 1993–). Chairman: Chancellor's Assessor, Aberdeen Univ., 1979–90; Robert Gordon's Coll., 1981–94; SATRO North Scotland, 1986–90; Scottish Council of Indep. Schs, 1992–; Gov., Caledonian Res. Foundn, 1990–94. Hon LLD Aberdeen, 1986. *Recreations:* golf, motoring, hill-walking, reading, music. *Address:* 6 Westfield Terrace, Aberdeen AB2 4RU. *T:* Aberdeen (01224) 641614. *Clubs:* Royal Northern and University (Aberdeen); Royal Aberdeen Golf; Nairn Golf.

McLEOD, Sir Charles Henry, 3rd Bt, *cr* 1925; *b* 7 Nov. 1924; *o* surv. *s* of Sir Murdoch Campbell McLeod, 2nd Bt, and Annette Susan Mary (*d* 1964), *d* of Henry Whitehead, JP, 26 Pelham Crescent, SW7; *S* father 1950; *m* 1957, Gillian (*d* 1978), *d* of Henry Bowlby, London; one *s* two *d*. *Educ:* Winchester. Diploma Master Brewer, 1950. Member, London Stock Exchange, 1955–. Represented India, Squash Rackets Internat., 1956–58. *Heir: s* James Roderick Charles McLeod [*b* 26 Sept. 1960; *m* 1990, Helen M. Cooper, *d* of Captain George Cooper, OBE, RN].

MacLEOD, Donald Alexander; HM Diplomatic Service, retired; study course organiser, since 1990; *b* 23 Jan. 1938; *er s* of late Col Colin S. MacLeod of Glendale, OBE, TD, and of Margaret Drysdale Robertson MacLeod; *m* 1963, Rosemary Lilian Abel (*née* Randle); two *s* two *d*. *Educ:* Edinburgh Academy; Pembroke Coll., Cambridge, 1958–61 (BA). National Service, Queen's Own Cameron Highlanders, 1956–58. HM Foreign Service, 1961; School of Oriental and African Studies, London, 1961–62; British Embassy, Rangoon, 1962–66; Private Sec. to Minister of State, Commonwealth Office, 1966–69; First Secretary, Ottawa, 1969–73; FCO, 1973–78; First Sec./Head of Chancery, Bucharest, 1978–80; Counsellor (Econ. and Commercial), Singapore, 1981–84. Dep. High Comr, Bridgetown, 1984–87; Hd of Protocol Dept, FCO, 1987–89. *Address:* Kinlochfollart, by Dunvegan, Isle of Skye IV55 8WQ.

MACLEOD, Sir Hamish; *see* Macleod, Sir N. W. H.

MacLEOD, Prof. Iain Alasdair, PhD; CEng, FICE, FIStructE; Professor of Structural Engineering, University of Strathclyde, since 1981; *b* 4 May 1939; *s* of Donald MacLeod and Barbara (*née* MacKenzie); *m* 1967, Barbara Jean Booth; one *s* one *d*. *Educ:* Lenzie Acad.; Univ. of Glasgow (BSc 1960, PhD 1966). CEng 1968; FIStructE 1982; FICE 1984. Asst Engr, Crouch & Hogg, Glasgow, 1960–62; Asst Lectr in Civil Engrg, Univ. of Glasgow, 1962–66; Structural Engineer: H. A. Simons Internat., Vancouver, Canada, 1966–67; Portland Cement Assoc., Skokie, USA, 1968–69; Lectr in Civil Engrg, Univ. of Glasgow, 1969–73; Prof. and Head of Dept of Civil Engrg, Paisley Coll. of Technol., 1973–81. Vice-Pres., IStructE, 1989–90; Mem., Standing Cttee on Structural Safety, IStructE and ICE, 1990–. *Publications:* Analytical Modelling of Structural Systems, 1990; over 60 published papers. *Recreations:* sailing, hill walking, ski-ing. *Address:* Department of Civil Engineering, University of Strathclyde, Glasgow G4 0NG. *T:* 0141–552 4400, ext. 3275.

MACLEOD, Ian Buchanan, FRCSE; Hon. Secretary, Royal College of Surgeons of Edinburgh, since 1993; Consultant Surgeon, Royal Infirmary, Edinburgh, and Hon. Senior Lecturer, Department of Clinical Surgery, University of Edinburgh, 1969–93; Surgeon to the Queen in Scotland, 1987–93; *b* 20 May 1933; *s* of Donald Macleod, MB, ChB, and Katie Ann Buchanan; *m* 1961, Kathleen Gillean Large; one *s* one *d*. *Educ:* Wigan Grammar Sch.; Univ. of Edinburgh (BSc Hons; MB ChB Hons). FRCSE 1962. Resident appts, Royal Inf., Edinburgh, 1957–59. National Service, MO RAMC, 1959–61. Res. Fellow, Lectr and Sen. Lectr, Univ. of Edinburgh, 1962–93; Hon. and Cons. Surg., Royal Inf., Edinburgh, 1969–93. Editor, Journal of Royal College of Surgeons of Edinburgh, 1982–87. *Publications:* Principles and Practice of Surgery (with A. P. M. Forrest and D. C. Carter), 1985; (contrib.) A Companion to Medical Studies, 1968, 3rd edn 1985; (contrib.) Farquharson's Textbook of Operative Surgery, 1986; papers in surgical jls. *Recreations:* golf, photography. *Address:* Derwent House, 32 Cramond Road North, Edinburgh EH4 6JE. *T:* 0131–336 1541. *Clubs:* University Staff, Bruntsfield Links Golfing Society (Edinburgh).

See also N. R. B. Macleod.

McLEOD, Sir Ian (George), Kt 1984; JP; director of companies; *b* 17 Oct. 1926; *s* of George Gunn McLeod; *m* 1950, Audrey Davis; two *d*. *Educ:* Kearsney College, Natal; Natal University; ACIS. Played for Rosslyn Park Rugby Team, 1951. Chm., London Transport Passengers Cttee, 1979–83; Board Mem., SE Electricity Board, 1983–89; Dir, Seeboard plc, 1990–94. Chairman: Croydon Central Cons. Assoc., 1973–76; Greater London Area Conservatives, 1981–84; Cons. Policy Gp for London, 1984–87; Nat. Union of Cons. and Unionist Assocs, 1988–90 (Vice-Chm., 1985–87); Mem., Nat. Union Exec. Cttee, Cons. Party, 1974–91; Chm., Brighton Cons. Conf., 1988. Mem., Croydon Borough Council, 1974–78; Dep. Mayor, 1976–77. Governor, Old Palace Girls' Sch., Croydon, 1974–87. JP SE London, 1977. *Recreations:* politics, reading history. *Address:* Pine Ridge, Pine Coombe, Shirley Hills, Croydon, Surrey CR0 5HS. *T:* 0181–654 4869. *Clubs:* Carlton, MCC.

McLEOD, Rev. John; Minister of Resolis and Urquhart, 1986–94; Chaplain to the Queen in Scotland, 1978–Apr. 1996; *b* 8 April 1926; *s* of Angus McLeod and Catherine McDougall; *m* 1958, Sheila McLeod; three *s* two *d*. *Educ:* Inverness Royal Academy; Edinburgh Univ. (MA); New Coll., Edinburgh. Farming until 1952; at university, 1952–58; ordained, Inverness, 1958. Missionary in India: Jalna, 1959–68; Poona, 1969–74; involved in rural development with special emphasis on development and conservation of water resource; also responsible for pastoral work in Church of N India, St Mary's, Poona, 1970–74; Church of Scotland Minister, Livingston Ecumenical Team Ministry, 1974; Warden of Nether Dechmont Farm Community Centre, 1977–81. *Recreations:* hill walking, gardening. *Address:* Benview, 19 Balvaird, Muir of Ord, Ross-shire IV7 6RQ. *T:* Muir of Ord (01463) 871286.

MacLEOD, John; Director, National Institute of Agricultural Botany, Cambridge, since 1990; *b* 16 Aug. 1939; *s* of James Rae MacLeod and Mollie McKee MacLeod (*née* Shaw); *m* 1966, Janet Patricia Beavan, sculptor; one *s* (and one *s* decd). *Educ:* Nicolson Inst., Stornoway; Univ. of Glasgow (BSc Hons Agr. 1962); Michigan State Univ. (MS 1964). NAAS, later ADAS, MAFF, 1964–90. Director: Arthur Rickwood Exptl Farm, 1982–85; ADAS Exptl Farms, MAFF, 1985–90. Pres., Groupe Consultatif Internat. de Recherche sur le Colza, Paris, 1993–. *Recreations:* long term restoration of a 16th century farmhouse and garden, art, sculpture. *Address:* National Institute of Agricultural Botany, Huntingdon Road, Cambridge CB3 0LE. *T:* Cambridge (01223) 276381; Church Farm House, Over, Cambs CB4 5NX.

MacLEOD OF MacLEOD, John; 29th Chief of MacLeod; *b* 10 Aug. 1935; second *s* of late Captain Robert Wolrige-Gordon, MC, and Joan, *d* of Hubert Walter and Dame Flora MacLeod of MacLeod, DBE; officially recognised in name of MacLeod of MacLeod by decree of Lyon Court, 1951; *S* grandmother, 1976; *m* 1973, Melita Kolin; one *s* one *d*. *Educ:* Eton. *Heir: s* Hugh Magnus MacLeod, younger of MacLeod. *Address:* Dunvegan Castle, Isle of Skye. *T:* Dunvegan (0147022) 206.

See also P. Wolrige-Gordon.

McLEOD, Prof. John Bryce, DPhil; FRS 1992; Professor of Mathematics, University of Pittsburgh, since 1988; *b* 23 Dec. 1929; *s* of John McLeod and Adeline Annie (*née* Bryce); *m* 1956, Eunice Martin Third; three *s* one *d*. *Educ:* Aberdeen Grammar Sch.; Univ. of Aberdeen (MA 1950); Oxford Univ. (BA 1952, MA, DPhil 1958). Rotary Foundn Fellow, Univ. of BC, 1952–53; Educn Officer, RAF, 1953–55; Harmsworth Sen. Scholar, Merton Coll., Oxford, 1955–56; Jun. Lectr in Maths, Oxford Univ., 1956–58; Lectr, Univ. of Edinburgh, 1958–60; University of Oxford: Fellow, Wadham Coll., 1960–91;

Lectr in Maths, 1960–88; Jun. Proctor, 1963–64; Sen. Fellow, SERC, 1986–91. *Publications:* numerous papers in mathematical jls. *Recreations:* travel, music, gardening. *Address:* Department of Mathematics, University of Pittsburgh, Pittsburgh, PA 15260, USA. *T:* (412) 6241273.

MacLEOD, Hon. Sir (John) Maxwell (Norman), 5th Bt *cr* 1924, of Fuinary, Morven, Co. Argyll; *b* 23 Feb. 1952; *s* of Baron MacLeod of Fuinary (Life Peer), MC and Lorna Helen Janet (*d* 1984), *er d* of late Rev. Donald Macleod; *S* to baronetcy of father, 1991. *Educ:* Gordonstoun. *Heir: b* Hon. Neil David MacLeod, *b* 25 Dec. 1959. *Address:* Fuinary Manse, Loch Aline, Morven, Argyll PA34 5XU.

McLEOD, Keith Morrison, CBE 1975; Financial Controller, British Airports Authority, 1971–75; *b* 26 May 1920; *yr s* of John and Mary McLeod; *m* 1943, Patricia Carter; two *s* one *d*. *Educ:* Bancroft's School. Asst Auditor, Exchequer and Audit Dept, 1939; served RAF, 1941–46; Asst Principal, Min. of Supply, 1948; Principal, 1950; BJSM, Washington, 1955–57; Asst Sec., Min. of Supply, 1957; Cabinet Office, 1962; Finance Dir, British Airports Authority, 1966. *Address:* 161 Banstead Road, Banstead, Surrey SM7 1QH. *T:* 0181–393 9005.

McLEOD, Prof. Malcolm Donald, FRSE; Director, since 1990, and Professor, since 1993, Hunterian Museum and Art Gallery, Glasgow; *b* 19 May 1941; *s* of Donald McLeod and Ellen (*née* Fairclough); *m* 1st, 1965, Jacqueline Wynborne (marr. diss. 1980); two *s* one *d*; 2nd, 1980, Iris Barry. *Educ:* Birkenhead Sch.; Hertford and Exeter Colls, Oxford (MA, BLitt). FRSE 1995. Lectr, Dept of Sociology, Univ. of Ghana, 1967–69; Asst Curator, Museum of Archaeology and Ethnology, Cambridge, 1969–74; Lectr, Girton Coll., Cambridge, 1969–74; Fellow, Magdalene Coll., Cambridge, 1972–74; Keeper of Ethnography, British Museum, 1974–90. Member: Hist. and Current Affairs Selection Cttee, Nat. Film Archive, 1978–84; Council, Museums Assoc., 1983–86; UK Unesco Cultural Adv. Cttee, 1980–85. Hon. Lecturer: Anthropology Dept, UCL, 1976–81; Archæology Dept, Glasgow Univ., 1991–. Lectures: Marett, Exeter Coll., Oxford, 1982; Sydney Jones, Liverpool Univ., 1984; Arthur Batchelor, UEA, 1987; Rivers, Cambridge, 1993. Trustee: Sainsbury Unit, UEA, 1991–; Oriental Mus., Univ. of Durham, 1994–. *Publications:* The Asante, 1980; Treasures of African Art, 1980; (with J. Mack) Ethnic Art, 1984; (with E. Bassani) Jacob Epstein: collector, 1987; An English-Kriolu, Kriolu-English Dictionary, 1990; Collecting for the British Museum, 1994; articles and reviews in learned jls. *Address:* Mossfennan, Bowden, Roxburghshire TD6 0ST; 13 Kirklee Terrace, Glasgow G12 0TH. *Club:* Athenæum.

MacLEOD, Hon. Sir Maxwell; *see* MacLeod, Hon. Sir J. M. N.

MACLEOD, Sir (Nathaniel William) Hamish, KBE 1994 (CBE 1992); JP; Financial Secretary, Hong Kong, 1991–95; *b* 6 Jan. 1940; *s* of George Henry Torquil Macleod and Ruth Natalie Wade; *m* 1970, Fionna Mary Campbell; one *s* one *d*. *Educ:* Univ. of St Andrews (MA Soc. Sci. Hons); Univ. of Bristol (Dip. Soc. Sci. Sociology); Birmingham Coll. of Commerce. FCIS. Commercial trainee, Stewarts & Lloyds, Birmingham, 1958–62; Hong Kong Government: Admin. Officer, 1966; Dir of Trade and Chief Trade Negotiator, 1983–87; Secretary for Trade and Industry, 1987–89; Sec. for the Treasury, 1989–91. JP Hong Kong, 1979. *Recreations:* competitive sailing, ski-ing, tennis, walking. *Address:* 20 York Road, Trinity, Edinburgh. *Clubs:* Hong Kong, Royal Hong Kong Yacht.

MACLEOD, Nigel Ronald Buchanan, QC 1979; a Recorder of the Crown Court, since 1981; a Deputy High Court Judge, since 1992; *b* 7 Feb. 1936; *s* of Donald Macleod, MB, ChB, and Katherine Ann Macleod; *m* 1966, Susan Margaret (*née* Buckley); one *s* one *d*. *Educ:* Wigan Grammar Sch.; Christ Church, Oxford (MA, BCL). Served RAF, 1954–56. Called to the Bar, Gray's Inn, 1961 (Bencher, 1993), Inner Temple *ad eundem* 1984. Asst Comr, Boundary Commn for England, 1981–85. Vice Chm., Local Govt Planning and Envmtl Bar Assoc., 1994–. *Publications:* contribs to legal jls. *Recreations:* sailing, walking. *Address:* The Start, Start Lane, Whaley Bridge, Derbyshire SK12 7BP. *T:* Whaley Bridge (01663) 732732; 4 Verulam Buildings, Gray's Inn, WC1R 5LQ. *T:* 0171–404 7752.

See also I. B. Macleod.

MacLEOD, Norman Donald; QC (Scot) 1986; MA, LLB; Advocate; Sheriff Principal of Glasgow and Strathkelvin, since 1986; *b* 6 March 1932; *s* of late Rev. John MacLeod, Edinburgh and Catherine MacRitchie; *m* 1957, Ursula Jane, *y d* of late George H. Bromley, Inveresk; two *s* two *d*. *Educ:* Mill Hill Sch.; George Watson's Boys' Coll., Edinburgh; Edinburgh Univ.; Hertford Coll., Oxford. Passed Advocate, 1956. Colonial Administrative Service, Tanganyika: Dist. Officer, 1957–59; Crown Counsel, 1959–64; practised at Scots Bar, 1964–67; Sheriff of Glasgow and Strathkelvin (formerly Lanarkshire at Glasgow), 1967–86. Vis. Prof., Law Sch., Univ. of Strathclyde, 1988–. *Recreations:* sailing, gardening. *Address:* Sheriffs' Library, Sheriff Court, PO Box 23, 1 Carlton Place, Glasgow G5 9DA. *T:* 0141–429 8888.

MACLEOD-SMITH, Alastair Macleod, CMG 1956; retired; *b* 30 June 1916; *s* of late R. A. Smith, MIEE, and Mrs I. Macleod-Smith (*née* Kellner); *m* 1945, Ann (*née* Circuitt); one *s* one *d*. *Educ:* The Wells House, Malvern Wells, Worcs; Ellesmere Coll., Salop; The Queen's Coll., Oxford. BA Oxon 1938. Entered HM Oversea Service as administrative cadet, Nigeria, 1939; Asst Dist Officer, 1942, Dist Officer, Nigeria, 1949; seconded to Windward Islands as Financial and Economic Adviser, 1949–52; Financial Sec., Western Pacific High Commission, 1952–57; Financial Sec., Sierra Leone, 1957–61. Dir, Selection Trust Ltd, 1967–80; Consultant, National Westminster Bank, 1981–83. *Address:* Roughetts Lodge, Coldharbour Lane, Hildenborough, Kent TN11 9JX.

McLERNAN, Kieran Anthony; Sheriff of Grampian, Highlands and Islands at Banff and Peterhead, since 1991; *b* 29 April 1941; *s* of James John McLernan and Delia (*née* McEvaddy); *m* 1979, Joan Doherty Larkins; one *s* three *d*. *Educ:* St Aloysius' Coll., Glasgow; Glasgow Univ. (MA 1961; LLB 1965). Admitted solicitor, 1965; Tutor, Glasgow Univ., 1985–91. Temp. Sheriff, 1986–91. KHS 1990. *Recreations:* golf, hockey, etc. *Address:* Sheriff Courthouse, Low Street, Banff AB4 1AU; Peockstone Farm, Lochwinnoch, Strathclyde PA12 4LE. *T:* Lochwinnoch (01505) 842128.

McLINTOCK, (Charles) Alan, CA; Chairman: Woolwich Building Society, 1984–95 (Deputy Chairman, 1980–84; Director, 1970–95; President, since 1995); Govett Strategic Investment Trust (formerly Border and Southern Stockholders Investment Trust), 1975–94; Allchurches Trust, since 1986 (Director, since 1975); Central Board of Finance of the Church of England, since 1992; AJ's Family Restaurants, since 1987; *b* 28 May 1925; *s* of late Charles Henry McLintock, OBE, and Alison McLintock; *m* 1955, Sylvia Mary Foster Taylor; one *s* three *d*. *Educ:* Rugby School. Served Royal Artillery, 1943–47; commnd 1945; Captain RHA 1946. With Thomson McLintock & Co., Chartered Accountants, 1948–87; qualified, 1952; Partner, 1954; Sen. Partner, KMG Thomson McLintock, 1982–87; Partner, Klynveld Main Goerdeler (KMG), 1979–87. Chairman: Grange Trust, 1973–81 (Dir, 1958–81); Stockholders Investment Trust, subseq. Govett Atlantic Investment Trust, 1978–92; Ecclesiastical Insce Office, subseq. Ecclesiastical Insce Gp, 1981–93 (Dir, 1972–93); Director: Trust Houses Ltd, 1967–71; Lake View Investment Trust, later Govett Oriental Investment Trust, 1971–90 (Chm., 1975–90); National Westminster Bank, 1979–90 (Adv. Bd, 1990–91); M & G Gp, 1982–94; Acxiom UK (formerly Southwark Computer Services), 1988–90. Vice-Pres., Metropolitan Assoc. of Building Socs, 1985–90. Trustee, Church Urban Fund, 1990–. Chairman of Governors: Rugby Sch., 1988–95 (Gov., 1973–95); Westonbirt Sch., 1991– (Gov., 1977–); Vice-Pres., Clergy Orphan Corp. Cttee, 1984– (Mem., Cttee of Management, 1963–84); Member: Royal Alexandra and Albert Sch. Bd of Management, 1965–88; Court, London Univ., 1987–. Hon. DBA Greenwich, 1994. *Recreations:* music, family pursuits. *Address:* Manor House, Westhall Hill, Burford, Oxon OX18 4BJ. *T:* Burford (01993) 822276. *Club:* Army and Navy.

McLINTOCK, Sir Michael (William), 4th Bt *cr* 1934, of Sanquhar, Co. Dumfries; *b* 13 Aug. 1958; *s* of Sir William Traven McLintock, 3rd Bt and André, *d* of Richard Lonsdale-Hands; *S* father, 1987. *Heir: b* Andrew Thomson McLintock, *b* 2 Dec. 1960.

McLOUGHLIN, George Leeke, CB 1988; Deputy Director of Public Prosecutions for Northern Ireland, 1982–87; *b* 2 July 1921; *e s* of Charles M. and Rose W. McLoughlin; *m* 1953, Maureen Theresa McKaigney; two *s* six *d*. *Educ:* St Columb's College, Londonderry; Queen's Univ. Belfast (BA). Barrister, N Ireland, practised 1945–58; joined HMOCS 1958; Resident Magistrate, 1958, Crown Counsel, 1958–63, Northern Rhodesia; Parly Draftsman, Zambia, 1965; Solicitor General, Zambia, 1968–70, retired; Office of Law Reform, N Ireland, 1971–72; Sen. Asst Dir of Public Prosecutions, NI (Under Secretary, NI Civil Service), 1973–82. *Recreations:* gardening, photography, armchair sports following. *Address:* c/o Northern Bank, 12–13 Shaftesbury Square, Belfast, Northern Ireland.

McLOUGHLIN, Most Rev. James; *see* Galway and Kilmacduagh, Bishop of, (RC).

McLOUGHLIN, Patrick Allen; MP (C) W Derbyshire, since May 1986; an Assistant Government Whip, since 1995; *b* 30 Nov. 1957; *s* of Patrick and Gladys Victoria McLoughlin; *m* 1984, Lynne Newman; one *s* one *d*. *Educ:* Cardinal Griffin Roman Catholic Sch., Cannock. Mineworker, Littleton Colliery, 1979–85; Marketing Official, NCB, 1985–86. PPS to Sec. of State for Trade and Industry, 1988–89; Parly Under-Sec. of State, Dept of Transport, 1989–92, Dept of Employment, 1992–93, DTI, 1993–94. *Address:* House of Commons, SW1A 0AA.

MACLURE, Sir John (Robert Spencer), 4th Bt *cr* 1898; Headmaster, Croftinloan School, Pitlochry, Perthshire, 1978–92; *b* 25 March 1934; *s* of Sir John William Spencer Maclure, 3rd Bt, OBE, and Elspeth (*d* 1991), *er d* of late Alexander King Clark; *S* father, 1980; *m* 1964, Jane Monica, *d* of late Rt Rev. T. J. Savage, Bishop of Zululand and Swaziland; four *s*. *Educ:* Winchester College. IAPS Diploma. 2nd Lt, 2nd Bn KRRC, 1953–55, BAOR; Lt, Royal Hampshire Airborne Regt, TA. Assistant Master: Horris Hill, 1955–66 and 1974–78; St George's, Wanganui, NZ, 1967–68; Sacred Heart Coll., Auckland, NZ, 1969–70; St Edmund's, Hindhead, Surrey, 1971–74. *Heir: s* John Mark Maclure, *b* 27 Aug. 1965. *Address:* Wild Goose Cottage, Gooseham, Bude, N Cornwall EX23 9PG. *Clubs:* MCC; Royal Greenjackets; Royal and Ancient (St Andrews); Royal North Devon Golf.

MACLURE, (John) Stuart, CBE 1982; Editor, Times Educational Supplement, 1969–89; *b* 8 Aug. 1926; *s* of Hugh and Bertha Maclure, Highgate, N6; *m* 1951, Constance Mary Butler; one *s* two *d*. *Educ:* Highgate Sch.; Christ's Coll., Cambridge. MA. Joined The Times, 1950; The Times Educational Supplement, 1951; Editor, Education, 1954–69. Hon. Prof. of Educn, Keele Univ., 1981–84; Dist. Vis. Fellow, PSI, 1989–90; Associate Fellow, Centre for Educn and Industry, Warwick Univ., 1991–94. President: Br. Sect., Comparative Educn Soc. in Europe, 1979; Educnl Sect., BAAS, 1983; Member: Educnl Adv. Council, IBA, 1979–84; Consultative Cttee, Assessment of Performance Unit, 1974–82. Regents' Lecturer, Univ. of California, Berkeley, 1980. Gov., Commonwealth Inst., 1991–. Hon. Fellow, City of Sheffield Polytechnic, 1976; Hon. FCP 1985; Hon. Fellow, Westminster Coll., 1990. DUniv Open, 1991. *Publications:* Joint Editor (with T. E. Utley) Documents on Modern Political Thought, 1956; Editor, Educational Documents, 1816–1963, 1965; A Hundred Years of London Education, 1970; (with Tony Becher) The Politics of Curriculum Change, 1978; (ed with Tony Becher) Accountability in Education, 1979; Education and Youth Employment in Great Britain, 1979; Educational Development and School Building, 1945–1973, 1984; Education Re-formed, a guide to the Education Reform Act, 1988; A History of Education in London 1870–1990, 1990; Missing Links—The Challenge to Further Education, 1991; (ed with Peter Davies) Learning to Think—Thinking to Learn, 1992. *Address:* 109 College Road, Dulwich, SE21 7HN. *Club:* MCC.

McLUSKEY, Very Rev. J(ames) Fraser, MC; MA, BD, DD; Minister at St Columba's Church of Scotland, Pont Street, London, 1960–86; Moderator of the General Assembly of the Church of Scotland, 1983–84; *b* 1914; *s* of James Fraser McLuskey and Margaret Keltie; *m* 1st, 1939, Irene (*d* 1959), *d* of Pastor Calaminus, Wuppertal; two *s*; 2nd, 1966, Ruth Quartermaine (*née* Hunter), *widow* of Lt-Col Keith Briant. *Educ:* Aberdeen Grammar Sch.; Edinburgh Univ. Ordained Minister of Church of Scotland, 1938; Chaplain to Univ. of Glasgow, 1939–47. Service as Army Chaplain, 1943–46 (1st Special Air Service Regt, 1944–46); Sub Warden Royal Army Chaplains' Training Centre, 1947–50; Minister at Broughty Ferry East, 1950–55; Minister at New Kilpatrick, Bearsden, 1955–60. *Publications:* Parachute Padre, 1951; The Cloud and the Fire, 1994. *Recreations:* walking, music, reading. *Address:* 3 Grosvenor Crescent, Edinburgh EH12 5EP. *T:* 0131–225 6878. *Clubs:* Caledonian, Special Forces; New (Edinburgh).

McMAHON, Andrew, (Andy); *b* 18 March 1920; *s* of Andrew and Margaret McMahon; *m* 1944; one *s* one *d*. *Educ:* District School, Govan. Boilermaker, Govan shipyards, 1936; unemployed, 1971–79. MP (Lab) Glasgow, Govan, 1979–83; first and only Boilermaker to enter House of Commons. Member, Glasgow Dist. Council, 1973–79. Chm., Scottish Arab Friendship Assoc., 1972–85; Sec. Gen., British-Iraqi Friendship Assoc., 1989– (Pres., 1986–89). *Recreations:* youth work, care and comfort for elderly. *Address:* 21 Morefield Road, Govan, Glasgow G51 4NG.

McMAHON, Sir Brian (Patrick), 8th Bt *cr* 1817; engineer; *b* 9 June 1942; *s* of Sir (William) Patrick McMahon, 7th Bt, and Ruth Stella (*d* 1982), *yr d* of late Percy Robert Kenyon-Slaney; *S* father, 1977; *m* 1981, Kathleen Joan, *d* of late William Hopwood. *Educ:* Wellington. BSc, AIM. Assoc. Mem., Inst of Welding. *Heir: brother* Shaun Desmond McMahon [*b* 29 Oct. 1945; *m* 1971, Antonia Noel Adie; *m* 1985, Jill Rosamund, *yr d* of Dr Jack Cherry; two *s*].

McMAHON, Sir Christopher William, (Sir Kit), Kt 1986; Chairman, Coutts Consulting Group, since 1992; Director: Taylor Woodrow, since 1991; Angela Flowers, since 1992; Aegis, since 1993; FI Group, since 1994; *b* Melbourne, 10 July 1927; *s* of late Dr John Joseph McMahon and late Margaret Kate (*née* Brown); *m* 1st, 1956, Marion Kelso; two *s*; 2nd, 1982, Alison Barbara Braimbridge, *d* of late Dr J. G. Cormie and late Mrs B. E. Cormie. *Educ:* Melbourne Grammar Sch.; Univ. of Melbourne (BA Hons Hist. and English, 1949); Magdalen Coll., Oxford. 1st cl. hons PPE, 1953. Tutor in English Lit., Univ. of Melbourne, 1950; Econ. Asst, HM Treasury, 1953–57; Econ. Adviser, British Embassy, Washington, 1957–60; Fellow and Tutor in Econs, Magdalen Coll., Oxford, 1960–64 (Hon. Fellow, 1986); Tutor in Econs, Treasury Centre for Admin. Studies, 1963–64; Mem., Plowden Cttee on Aircraft Industry, 1964–65; entered Bank of England as Adviser, 1964; Adviser to the Governors, 1966–70; Exec. Dir, 1970–80; Dep. Governor, 1980–85; Chief Exec. and Dep. Chm., 1986–87, Chm., 1987–91, Midland Bank. Director: Eurotunnel, 1987–91; Hongkong and Shanghai Banking Corp., 1987–91; Royal Opera House, 1989–; Newspaper Publishing, 1993–94. Mem., Gp of Thirty, 1978–84; Chairman: Working Party 3, OECD, 1980–85; Young Enterprise, 1989–92; CSFI, 1993–95. Mem. Court, Univ. of London, 1984–86; Gov., Birkbeck Coll., 1991–. Trustee: Whitechapel Art Gall., 1984–92; Royal Opera House Trust, 1984–86. Hon. Fellow, UCNW, 1988. Chevalier, Légion d'Honneur (France), 1990. *Publications:* Sterling in the Sixties, 1964; (ed) Techniques of Economic Forecasting, 1965. *Recreations:* looking at pictures, buying books, going to the movies, gardening in good weather. *Address:* c/o Coutts Consulting Group, 25 Whitehall, SW1A 2BS. *Club:* Garrick.

MacMAHON, Gerald John, CB 1962; CMG 1955; *b* 26 Sept. 1909; 2nd *s* of late Jeremiah MacMahon and Kathleen MacMahon (*née* Dodd); unmarried. *Educ:* Clongowes Wood Coll., Co. Kildare, Ireland; Emmanuel Coll., Cambridge (BA). Entered Board of Trade, 1933; Asst Sec., 1942. Imperial Defence Coll., 1949. Senior UK Trade Commissioner in India, 1952–58; Under-Sec., Board of Trade 1958–62 and 1964–70; Admiralty, Nov. 1962–64. *Address:* 19 Lower Park, Putney Hill, SW15 6QY. *Club:* Reform.

McMAHON, Hugh Robertson; Member (Lab) Strathclyde West, European Parliament, since 1984; *b* 17 June 1938; *s* of Hugh McMahon and Margaret Fulton Robertson. *Educ:* Glasgow University (MA Hons); Jordanhill College. Assistant Teacher: Largs High School, 1962–63; Stevenston High School, 1963–64; Irvine Royal Academy, 1964–68; Principal Teacher of History, Mainholm Academy, Ayr, 1968–71; Principal Teacher of History and Modern Studies, 1971–72, Asst Head Teacher, 1972–84, Ravenspark Academy, Irvine. European Parliament: Vice-Chairman: Cttee on Social Affairs and Employment; Cttee on Disabled; Cttee on Ageing; Mem., Budgetary Control and Envmt Cttees; spokesman on social affairs and employment matters; Mem., Interparly Delegn with Sweden. Rep. of Scottish MEPs, Scottish Exec. Cttee, Labour Party. *Recreations:* golf, reading, walking, languages. *Address:* (office) 9 Low Road, Paisley PA2 6AQ. *T:* 0141–889 9990. *Clubs:* Saltcoats & Kilbirnie Labour; Ravenspark Golf; Irvine Bogside Golf.

McMAHON, Sir Kit; *see* McMahon, Sir C. W.

McMAHON, Rt. Rev. Thomas; *see* Brentwood, Bishop of, (RC).

McMANNERS, Rev. Prof. John, DLitt; FBA 1978; Fellow and Chaplain, All Souls College, Oxford, since 1984; *b* 25 Dec. 1916; *s* of Rev. Canon Joseph McManners and Mrs Ann McManners; *m* 1951, Sarah Carruthers Errington; two *s* two *d. Educ:* St Edmund Hall, Oxford (BA 1st cl. hons Mod. History, 1939; Hon. Fellow, 1983); Durham Univ. (DipTheol 1947; Hon. Fellow, St Chad's Coll., 1992). DLitt Oxon, 1980. Military Service, 1939–45 in Royal Northumberland Fusiliers (Major). Priest, 1948; St Edmund Hall, Oxford: Chaplain, 1948; Fellow, 1949; Dean, 1951; Prof., Univ. of Tasmania, 1956–59; Prof., Sydney Univ., 1959–66; Professorial Fellow, All Souls Coll., Oxford, 1965–66; Prof. of History, Univ. of Leicester, 1967–72; Canon of Christ Church and Regius Prof. of Ecclesiastical History, Oxford Univ., 1972–84. Lectures: Birkbeck, 1976, Trevelyan, 1989, Cambridge; John Coffin Meml, London Univ., 1982; Sir Owen Evans, Univ. of Wales, 1984; F. D. Maurice, King's Coll., London, 1985; Zaharoff, 1985, Hensley Henson, 1986, A.B. Emden Meml, 1992, Oxford. Dir d'études associé, Ecole Pratique des Hautes Etudes, sect. IV, Paris, 1980–81. Mem., Doctrinal Commn of C of E, 1978–82. Trustee, Nat. Portrait Gallery, 1970–78; Mem. Council, RHistS, 1971; Pres., Ecclesiastical Hist. Soc., 1977–78. FAHA 1970. Hon. DLitt Durham, 1984. Officer, Order of King George I of the Hellenes, 1945; Comdr, Ordre des Palmes académiques (France), 1991. *Publications:* French Ecclesiastical Society under the Ancien Régime: a study of Angers in the 18th Century, 1960; (ed) France, Government and Society, 1965, 2nd edn 1971; Lectures on European History 1789–1914: Men, Machines and Freedom, 1966; The French Revolution and the Church, 1969; Church and State in France 1870–1914, 1972; Death and the Enlightenment, 1981 (Wolfson Literary Award, 1982); (ed) The Oxford Illustrated History of Christianity, 1990; contrib.: New Cambridge Modern History vols VI and VIII; Studies in Church History, vols XII, XV and XXII. *Recreation:* tennis. *Address:* All Souls College, Oxford OX1 4AL. *T:* Oxford (01865) 279368.

MacMANUS, Dr Bernard Ronald; Vice-Chancellor, Bournemouth University, 1992–94; *b* 25 April 1936; *s* of Ronald MacManus and Doris Evelyn MacManus (*née* Sherriff); *m* 1959, Patricia Mary Greet; one *s* one *d. Educ:* St Boniface's Coll., Devon; Plymouth Poly.; Univ. of Birmingham (BScEng, PhD). Head, Dept of Mech. Production and Aeronautical Eng., Manchester Poly., 1972–73; Dean, Faculty of Eng., Sunderland Poly., 1973–78; Dep. Dir, Glasgow Coll. of Technology, 1978–83; Director: Dorset Inst. of Higher Educn, 1983–91; Bournemouth Poly., 1991–92. *Publications:* contribs to learned jls on manufacturing systems. *Recreations:* swimming, classic cars, music. *Address:* Thurlstone, Chapel Lane, Osmington, Dorset DT3 6ET.

McMANUS, Francis Joseph; solicitor; *b* 16 Aug. 1942; *s* of Patrick and Celia McManus; *m* 1971, Carmel V. Doherty, Lisnaskea, Co. Fermanagh; two *s* one *d. Educ:* St Michael's, Enniskillen; Queen's University, Belfast. BA 1965; Diploma in Education, 1966. Subsequently a Teacher. MP (Unity) Fermanagh and S Tyrone, 1970–Feb. 1974. Founder Mem. and Co-Chm., Irish Independence Party, 1977–. *Address:* Lissadell, Drumlin Heights, Enniskillen, Co. Fermanagh, N Ireland. *T:* Enniskillen (01365) 323401.

MacMANUS, His Honour John Leslie Edward, TD 1945; QC 1970; a Circuit Judge (formerly a Judge of County Courts), 1971–90, retired; *b* 7 April 1920; *o s* of E. H. MacManus and H. S. MacManus (*née* Colton); *m* 1942, Gertrude (Trudy) Mary Frances Koppenhagen; two *d. Educ:* Eastbourne College. Served 1939–45 with RA: Middle East, Italy, Crete, Yugoslavia; Captain 1942; Major 1945. Called to Bar, Middle Temple, 1947. Dep. Chm., East Sussex QS, 1964–71. *Recreations:* gardening, travel. *Address:* The Old Rectory, Twineham, Haywards Heath, West Sussex RH17 5NR. *T:* Bolney (01444) 881221.

McMASTER, Brian John, CBE 1987; Director, Edinburgh International Festival, since 1991; *b* 9 May 1943; *s* of Brian John McMaster and Mary Leila Hawkins. *Educ:* Wellington Coll.; Bristol Univ. LLB. International Artists' Dept, EMI Ltd, 1968–73; Controller of Opera Planning, ENO, 1973–76; Gen Administrator, subseq. Man. Dir, WNO, 1976–91; Artistic Dir, Vancouver Opera, 1984–89. *Address:* Edinburgh International Festival, 21 Market Street, Edinburgh EH1 1BW. *T:* 0131–226 4001.

McMASTER, Gordon James; MP (Lab) Paisley South since Nov. 1990; *b* 13 Feb. 1960; *s* of William McMaster, retired Parks Superintendent and Alison McMaster (*née* Maxwell), clerkess. *Educ:* Cochrane Castle Primary Sch.; Johnstone High Sch.; Woodburn House FE Centre (City and Guilds in Horticulture); West of Scotland Agr. Coll. (OND Hort.); Jordanhill Coll. of Education (Cert. in Further Educn.) Apprentice gardner, Renfrew DC, 1976–77; full time student, 1977–78 and 1979–80, trainee hort. technician, Renfrew DC, 1978–79; Craftsman Gardener, Renfrew DC, 1980; Lectr in Hort., Langside Coll., 1980–86, Sen. Lectr, 1986–88; Co-ordinator, Growing Concern Initiative, Strathclyde, 1988–90. Member: Johnstone Community Council 1980–84 (Chm., 1982–84); Renfrew DC, 1984–91 (Dep. Leader, 1987–88; Leader, 1988–90). Scottish opposition whip, 1992–94; Asst to Dep. Chief Opposition Whip, 1994–; Sec., All-Party Disablement Gp, 1992–. *Recreations:* reading, gardening, computers. *Address:* 47 Hagg Crescent, Johnstone PA5 8TB. *T:* Johnstone (01505) 336259; House of Commons, SW1A 0AA. *T.* 0171–219 5104. *Clubs:* United Services (Johnstone); Lilybank Bowling.

McMASTER, Hughan James Michael, RIBA; Chief Architect and Director of Works, Home Office, 1980–87, retired; *b* 27 July 1927; *s* of William James Michael and Emly McMaster; *m* 1950; one *s* two *d. Educ:* Christ's Coll., Finchley; Regent Street Polytechnic (DipArch). ARIBA 1951. Served RAF, India and Far East, 1946–48. Joined Civil Service, 1961; Navy Works, 1961–69; Whitehall Development Gp, Directorate of Home Estate Management and Directorate of Civil Accommodation, 1969–76; Defence Works (PE and Overseas), 1976–80. FRSA. *Recreations:* ski-ing, swimming, theatre, music.

McMASTER, Peter, CB 1991; FRICS; Member, Lord Chancellor's Panel of Independent Inspectors, since 1991; *b* 22 Nov. 1931; *s* of Peter McMaster and Ada Nellie (*née* Williams); *m* 1955, Catherine Ann Rosborough; one *s* one *d. Educ:* Kelvinside Academy, Glasgow; RMA Sandhurst; RMCS Shrivenham. BScEng London. Called to the Bar, Middle Temple, 1969. Commissioned into Royal Engineers, 1952; served Middle and Far East; retired (major), 1970; joined Civil Service, 1970; W Midland Region, Ordnance Survey, 1970–72; Caribbean Region, Directorate of Overseas Survey, 1972–74; Headquarters, 1974–91, Dir Gen., 1985–91, Ordnance Survey. Vis. Prof., Kingston Polytechnic, subseq. Kingston Univ., 1991–93. Member Council: BCS, 1983–92; RGS, 1990–93. FIIM 1990. *Recreations:* travel, walking, chess. *Address:* Hillhead, Stratton Road, Winchester, Hampshire SO23 0JQ. *T:* Winchester (01962) 862684.

McMICHAEL, Prof. Andrew James, FRS 1992; Medical Research Council Clinical Research Professor of Immunology, University of Oxford, since 1982; Fellow of Trinity College, Oxford, since 1983; *b* 8 Nov. 1943; *s* of Sir John McMichael, FRS and late Sybil McMichael; *m* 1968, Kathryn Elizabeth Cross; two *s* one *d. Educ:* St Paul's Sch., London; Gonville and Caius Coll., Cambridge (MA; BChir 1968; MB 1969); St Mary's Hosp. Med. Sch., London. PhD 1974; MRCP 1971; FRCP 1985. House Physician, St Mary's Hosp., Royal Northern Hosp., Hammersmith Hosp. and Brompton Hosp., 1968–71; MRC Jun. Res. Fellow, National Inst. for Med. Res., 1971–74; MRC Travelling Fellow, Stanford Univ. Med. Sch., 1974–76; Oxford University: Wellcome Sen. Clin. Fellow, Nuffield Depts of Medicine and Surgery, 1977–79; University Lectr in Medicine and Hon. Consultant Physician, 1979–82. Member: Adv. Bd. Beit Meml Trust, 1984–; MRC Systems Bd, 1987–91; MRC AIDS Steering Cttee, 1988–94; Res. Grants Council, Hong Kong, 1990–95. *Publications:* (ed with J. W. Fabre) Monoclonal Antibodies in Clinical Medicine, 1982; articles on genetic control of human immune response, antiviral immunity and AIDS. *Recreations:* working in the garden and getting wet.

MACMILLAN, family name of **Earl of Stockton.**

MACMILLAN OF OVENDEN, Viscount; Daniel Maurice Alan Macmillan; *b* 9 Oct. 1974; *s* and *heir* of Earl of Stockton, *qv. Address:* 8 The Little Boltons, SW10 9LP. *T:* 0171–373 6379.

McMILLAN, Alan Austen, CB 1986; Solicitor to the Secretary of State for Scotland, 1984–87; *b* 19 Jan. 1926; *s* of Allan McMillan and Mabel (*née* Austin); *m* 1949, Margaret Moncur; two *s* two *d. Educ:* Ayr Acad.; Glasgow Univ. Served in Army, 1944–47. Qualified Solicitor in Scotland, 1949; Legal Assistant, Ayr Town Council, 1949–55; Scottish Office: Legal Assistant, 1955–62; Sen. Legal Assistant, 1962–68; Asst Solicitor, 1968–82, seconded to Cabinet Office Constitution Unit, 1977–78; Dep. Solicitor, 1982–84. *Recreations:* reading, music, theatre.

MACMILLAN, Sir (Alexander McGregor) Graham, Kt 1983; Director, Scottish Conservative Party, 1975–84; *b* 14 Sept. 1920; *s* of James Orr Macmillan and Sarah Dunsmore (*née* Graham); *m* 1947, Christina Brash Beveridge; two *s* two *d. Educ:* Hillhead High Sch., Glasgow. Served War, RA, 1939–46. Conservative Agent: W Lothian, 1947–50; Haltemprice, 1950–53; Bury St Edmunds, 1953–60; Dep. Central Office Agent, NW Area, 1960–61; Central Office Agent, Yorks Area, 1961–75. Chairman: M & P Financial Services Ltd, 1986–87 (Dir, 1984–87); Mid-Anglian Enterprise Agency Ltd, 1988–92 (Gov., 1987–); Exec. Sec., YorCan Communications Ltd, 1989–94. Chairman: Bury St Edmunds Round Table, 1959–60; Bury St Edmunds Br., Multiple Sclerosis Soc., 1987–95. Mem., Transport Users' Consultative Cttee for E England, 1987–95. Hon. Sec., Suffolk Assoc. of Boys' Clubs, 1986–88. Governor, Leeds Grammar Sch., 1968–75. *Recreations:* fishing, watching cricket and rugby. *Address:* 46 Crown Street, Bury St Edmunds, Suffolk IP33 1QX. *T:* Bury St Edmunds (01284) 704443. *Club:* St Stephen's Constitutional.

MACMILLAN, Alexander Ross, FCIBS, CIMgt; Director, 1974–87, Chief General Manager, 1971–82, Clydesdale Bank PLC; *b* 25 March 1922; *s* of Donald and Johanna Macmillan; *m* 1961, Ursula Miriam Grayson; two *s* one *d. Educ:* Tain Royal Acad. FCIBS (FIBScot 1942); CIMgt (CBIM 1980). Served War, RAF, 1942–46 (despatches, King's Birthday Honours, 1945). Entered service of N of Scotland Bank Ltd, Tain, 1938; after War, returned to Tain, 1946; transf. to Supt's Dept, Aberdeen, and thereafter to Chief Accountant's Dept, Clydesdale Bank, Glasgow, 1950, on amalgamation with N of Scotland Bank; Chief London Office, 1952; Gen. Manager's Confidential Clerk, 1955; Manager, Piccadilly Circus Br., 1958; Supt of Branches, 1965; Gen. Manager's Asst, 1967; Asst Gen. Man., 1968. Director: The High Sch. of Glasgow Ltd, 1979–92; Caledonian Applied Technology Ltd, 1982–87; Highland-North Sea Ltd, 1982– (Chm., 1982–); John Laing plc, 1982–86; Martin-Black PLC, 1982–85; Radio Clyde Ltd, 1982–93; Scottish Develt Finance Ltd, 1982–92; Kelvin Technology Develts Ltd, 1982–; Compugraphics Internat. Ltd, 1982–87; Highland Deephaven Ltd, 1983–; TEG Products Ltd, 1986–87; New Generation Housing Soc. Ltd, 1986–; Castle Wynd Housing Soc. Ltd, 1987–89; Wilsons Garage (Argyll) Ltd, 1987–94; Wilsons Fuels Ltd, 1987–; EFT Gp (formerly Edinburgh Financial Trust) plc, 1987–93; Balmoral Gp Ltd, 1988–93; North of Scotland Radio Ltd, 1989–93; Radio Clyde Holdings plc, 1991–93; Chm., First Northern Corporate Finance Ltd, 1983–87. Chm., Nat. House Bldg Council (Scotland), 1982–88. Mem. Court, Univ. of Glasgow, 1981–. Freeman, Royal Burgh of Tain, 1975. DUniv Glasgow, 1989. *Recreation:* golf. *Address:* St Winnins, 16 Ledcameroch Road, Bearsden G61 4AB. *T:* 0141–942 6455. *Club:* Golf (Killermont).

MacMILLAN, Prof. Andrew, OBE 1992; RSA 1990; RIBA; FRIAS; Professor of Architecture, Glasgow University, and Head, Mackintosh School of Architecture, 1973–94; *b* 11 Dec. 1928; *s* of Andrew Harkness MacMillan of Murlaggan and Mary Jane McKelvie; *m* 1955, Angela Lillian McDowell; one *s* three *d. Educ:* Maryhill Public Sch.; North Kelvinside Sen. Secondary Sch., Glasgow; Glasgow Sch. of Architecture (MA 1973). FRIAS 1973. Apprenticeship, Glasgow Corp. Housing Dept, 1945–52; Architectural Asst, East Kilbride New Town Develt Corp., 1952–54; Asst Architect, 1954–63, Partner, 1966–88, Gillespie Kidd & Coia; consultant architect in private practice, 1988–. Davenport Vis. Prof., Yale Univ., 1986. Mem., Scottish Arts Council, 1978–82; Vice-Pres. for Educn, RIBA, 1981–85; Vice President: Prince and Princess of Wales

Hospice, 1981–; Charles Rennie Mackintosh Soc., 1984–; Patron, Arts Educn Trust, 1988–. Royal Scottish Acad. Gold Medal, 1975; RIBA Bronze Medal, 1985; RIBA Award for Arch., 1966, 1967, 1968 and 1982; Saltire awards and Civic Trust awards at various times. *Publications:* papers and articles mainly dealing with urban design, urban building, architectural educn, Glasgow arch. of 20th century, and Charles Rennie Mackintosh. *Recreations:* travel, sailing, watercolours. *Address:* 1 Falcon Terrace, Glasgow G20 0AG. *T:* 0141–946 4358.

McMILLAN, Col Donald, CB 1959; OBE 1945; Chairman, Cable & Wireless Ltd, and associated companies, 1967–72; *b* 22 Dec. 1906; *s* of Neil Munro McMillan and Isabella Jamieson; *m* 1946, Kathleen Ivy Bingham; one *s*. *Educ:* Sloane Sch., Chelsea; Battersea Polytechnic. Post Office Engineering Dept, 1925–54; Director External Telecommunications, Post Office External Telecommunications Executive, 1954–67. BSc Eng (London); FIEE. *Publications:* contribs to Institution Engineers Journal, Post Office Institution Engineers Journal. *Recreations:* golf and gardening. *Address:* 46 Gatehill Road, Northwood, Mddx HA6 3QP. *T:* Northwood (01923) 822682. *Club:* Grim's Dyke Golf.

McMILLAN, Rt. Rev. Monsignor Donald Neil; Parish Priest, St Nicholas' Church, Winchcombe, since 1986; *b* 21 May 1925; *s* of Daniel McMillan and Mary Cameron McMillan (*née* Farrell). *Educ:* St Brendan's Coll., Bristol; Prior Park Coll., Bath; Oscott Coll., Sutton Coldfield. Ordained Priest, Dio. Clifton, 1948; Curate: Bath, 1948–49; Gloucester, 1949–51; Taunton, 1951. Commissioned Army Chaplain, 1951; Served: BAOR, 1961–63, 1966–68, 1975–77; Middle East, 1956–59, 1968–70; Far East, 1952–55; Principal RC Chaplain and Vicar Gen. (Army), 1977–81; Parish Priest: St Augustine's Church, Matson Lane, Gloucester, 1981–85; St Teresa's Church, Filton, Bristol, 1985–86. Apptd Prelate of Honour by Pope Paul VI, 1977. *Recreations:* reading, walking. *Address:* St Nicholas Presbytery, Chandos Street, Winchcombe, Glos GL54 5HX. *T:* Cheltenham (01242) 602412. *Club:* Army and Navy.

MACMILLAN, Very Rev. Gilleasbuig Iain; Minister of St Giles', The High Kirk of Edinburgh, since 1973; Chaplain to the Queen in Scotland, since 1979; Dean of the Order of the Thistle, since 1989; *b* 21 Dec. 1942; *s* of Rev. Kenneth M. Macmillan and Mrs Mary Macmillan; *m* 1965, Maureen Stewart Thomson; one *d*. *Educ:* Oban High School; Univ. of Edinburgh. MA, BD. Asst Minister, St Michael's Parish, Linlithgow, 1967–69; Minister of Portree Parish, Isle of Skye, 1969–73. Extra Chaplain to the Queen in Scotland, 1978–79. Hon. Chaplain: Royal Scottish Academy; Royal Coll. of Surgeons of Edinburgh; Soc. of High Constables of City of Edinburgh. *Address:* St Giles' Cathedral, Edinburgh EH1 1RE. *T:* 0131–225 4363. *Club:* New (Edinburgh).

MACMILLAN, Sir Graham; *see* Macmillan, Sir A. M. G.

MACMILLAN, Iain Alexander, CBE 1978; LLD; Sheriff of South Strathclyde, Dumfries and Galloway at Hamilton, 1981–92; Temporary Sheriff, 1992–94; *b* 14 Nov. 1923; *s* of John and Eva Macmillan; *m* 1954, Edith Janet (*née* MacAulay); two *s* one *d*. *Educ:* Oban High Sch.; Glasgow Univ. (BL). Served war, RAF, France, Germany, India, 1944–47. Glasgow Univ., 1947–50. Subseq. law practice; Sen. Partner, J. & J. Sturrock & Co., Kilmarnock, 1952–81. Law Society of Scotland: Mem. Council, 1964–79; Pres., 1976–77. Pres., Temp. Sheriffs' Assoc., 1993–94. Chm. Lanarkshire Br., Scottish Assoc. for Study of Delinquency, 1986–92. Hon. LLD Aberdeen, 1975. *Recreation:* golf. *Address:* 2 Castle Drive, Kilmarnock KA3 1TN. *T:* Kilmarnock (01563) 25864.

MacMILLAN, Jake; *see* MacMillan, John.

MacMILLAN, Dr James Loy; composer, part-time teacher, Royal Scottish Academy of Music and Drama, since 1989; *b* 16 July 1959; *s* of James MacMillan and Ellen MacMillan (*née* Loy); *m* 1983, Lynne Frew; one *s* two *d*. *Educ:* Edinburgh Univ. (BMus); Durham Univ. (PhD 1987). Lectr, Univ. of Manchester, 1986–88; Composer in Residence, St Magnus Fest., Orkney, 1989; Featured Composer: Musica Nova, Glasgow, 1990; Huddersfield Contemp. Music Fest., 1991; Edinburgh Fest., 1993; Affiliate Composer, Scottish Chamber Orch., 1990–; Vis. Composer, Philharmonia, 1991–. DUniv Paisley, 1995. Gramophone Award, 1993; Classic CD Award, 1994; Royal Philharmonic Soc. Award, 1995. *Compositions* include: Busquéda, 1988; Tryst, 1989; Tuireadh, 1991; Confession of Isobel Gowdie, 1990; Veni, Veni Emmanuel, 1992; Visitatis Sepulchri, 1993; Seven Last Words, 1994. *Recreations:* fatherhood, Glasgow Celtic FC. *Address:* c/o Boosey & Hawkes Music Publishers Ltd, 295 Regent Street, W1R 8JH. *T:* 0171–580 2060.

MacMILLAN, Prof. John, (Jake), PhD Glasgow; DSc Bristol; FRS 1978; CChem, ARIC; Alfred Capper Pass Professor of Organic Chemistry, 1985–90, and Head of Department of Organic Chemistry, 1983–90, University of Bristol, now Professor Emeritus; *b* 13 Sept. 1924; *s* of John MacMillan and Barbara Lindsay; *m* 1952, Anne Levy; one *s* two *d*. *Educ:* Lanark Grammar Sch.; Glasgow Univ. Res. Chemist, Akers Res. Labs, ICI Ltd, 1949; Associate Res. Manager, Pharmaceuticals Div., ICI Ltd, 1962; Lectr in Org. Chemistry, Bristol Univ., 1963, Reader 1968, Prof. 1978. Pres., Internat. Plant Growth Substance Assoc., 1973–76. For. Associate, Nat. Acad. of Scis, USA, 1991. *Publications:* (ed) Encyclopedia of Plant Physiology, New Series vol. 9, 1980; (ed jtly) Gibberellins, 1991; (jtly) GC-MS of Gibberellins and Related Compounds: methodology and a library of reference spectra, 1991; research papers in learned jls on natural organic products, esp. plant growth hormones. *Recreations:* golf, gardening, theatre, music. *Address:* 1 Rylestone Grove, Bristol BS9 3UT. *T:* Bristol (0117) 962 0535.

MacMILLAN, Lt-Gen. Sir John Richard Alexander, KCB 1988; CBE 1978 (OBE 1973); fruit farmer; GOC Scotland and Governor of Edinburgh Castle, 1988–91; *b* 8 Feb. 1932; *m* 1964, Belinda Lumley Webb; one *s* two *d*. *Educ:* Trinity Coll., Cambridge (BA 1953; MA 1958); rcds, psc. Commnd Argyll and Sutherland Highlanders, 2nd Lieut, 1952; GSO2 (Ops Int. Trng), Trucial Oman Scouts, 1963–64; BM, HQ 24 Inf. Bde, 1967–69; Chief Recruiting and Liaison Staff, Scotland, 1970; CO, 1st Bn The Gordon Highlanders, 1971–73; GSO1 (DS), Staff Coll., 1973–75; Col GS, Mil. Ops 4, 1975–76; Brig., 1976; Bde Comd, 39 Inf. Bde, 1977–78; RCDS 1979; COS, 1 (Br.) Corps, 1980–82; Maj.-Gen., 1982; GOC Eastern Dist, 1982–84; ACGS, MoD, 1984–87; Lt-Gen., 1988. Col, The Gordon Highlanders, 1978–86; Col Comdt, Scottish Div., 1986–91; Hon. Col, Aberdeen Univ. OTC, 1987–. Chm. Exec Cttee, Scottish Conservation Projects Trust, 1992–; Chm., Princess Louise Scottish Hosp., 1995. *Address:* c/o Northern Bank, 9 Donegall Square North, Belfast BT1 5GJ.

MACMILLAN, Matthew, CBE 1983 (OBE 1977); educational consultant, since 1995; *b* 14 July 1926; *s* of late David Craig Macmillan and Barbara Cruikshank Macmillan (*née* Gow); *m* 1949, Winifred (*née* Sagar); one *s* two *d*. *Educ:* Robert Gordon's Coll., Aberdeen; Aberdeen Univ. (MA Hons); Manchester Univ. (Teacher's Dip.) Served Royal Air Force, 1944–47. Schoolmaster, Chatham House Grammar Sch., Ramsgate, 1951–57; Sen. Lectr, Univ. of Science and Technology, Kumasi, Ghana, 1958–62; Associate Prof., University Coll. of Cape Coast, Ghana, 1962–64; Prof. of English, Univ. of Khartoum, The Sudan, 1965–70; British Council, London: Director, English-Teaching Information Centre, 1970–72; Dep. Controller, English Teaching Div., 1972–74; Asst Educn Adviser (English Studies), British Council, India, 1974–78; Controller, English Lang. and Lit. Div., British Council, 1978–83; Prof. of English, 1983–89, Principal, 1986–89, University Coll., Univ. of E Asia, Macau; Prof., English Programmes, E Asia Open Inst., Hong Kong, 1989–90; educnl consultant, 1990–92; Chief Examr (Lang.), Trinity Coll. London, 1993–94. Mem., ESU. *Publications:* articles on the teaching of English as a second/foreign language. *Recreations:* gardening, walking. *Address:* Manor House Cottage, The Row, Elham, Canterbury, Kent CT4 6UL. *T:* Elham (01303) 840427. *Club:* Commonwealth Trust.

MACMILLAN, Dr Robert Hugh; Professor of Vehicle Design and Head of School of Automotive Studies, 1977–82, Dean of Engineering, 1980–82, Cranfield Institute of Technology; *b* Mussoorie, India, 27 June 1921; *s* of H. R. M. Macmillan and E. G. Macmillan (*née* Webb); *m* 1950, Anna Christina Roding, Amsterdam; one *s* two *d*. *Educ:* Felsted Sch.; Emmanuel Coll., Cambridge. Technical Branch, RAFVR, 1941; Dept of Engrg, Cambridge Univ., 1947; Asst Prof. MIT, 1950–51; Prof. of Mech. Engrg, Swansea, 1956; Dir, Motor Industry Res. Assoc., 1964–77; Associate Prof., Warwick Univ., 1965–77. 20th Leonardo Da Vinci Lectr, 1973. Mem. Council, Loughborough Univ., 1966–81, 1988–91; Chm. Council, Automobile Div., IMechE, 1976–77; Member: Noise Adv. Council, 1970–77; Internat. Technical Commn, FIA, 1975–88; FISITA: Mem. Council, 1970–80; Chm., London Congress, 1972. Approved Lectr for NADFAS, 1985–; official guide, Winslow Hall, 1985–, Ascott, 1988–93. Editor, The Netherlands Philatelist, 1984–88. FRSA; MIEE; FIMechE; FRPSL. Hon. DTech Loughborough, 1992. Gold Medal, FISITA, 1970. *Publications:* Theory of Control, 1951; Automation, 1956; Geometric Symmetry, 1978; Dynamics of Vehicle Collisions, 1983. *Recreations:* music, philately, national heritage. *Address:* 43 Church Road, Woburn Sands, Bucks MK17 8TG. *T:* Milton Keynes (01908) 584011. *Clubs:* Royal Air Force, Royal Over-Seas League.

MACMILLAN, Very Rev. William Boyd Robertson; Moderator of the General Assembly of the Church of Scotland, 1991–92; Chaplain to the Queen in Scotland, since 1988; *b* 3 July 1927; *s* of Robert and Annie Simpson Macmillan; *m* 1962, Mary Adams Bisset Murray. *Educ:* Royal High Sch., Edinburgh; Univ. of Aberdeen (MA, BD). Served RN, 1946–48. Minister: St Andrew's, Bo'ness, 1955–60; Fyvie, 1960–67; Bearsden, South, 1967–78; St Mary's, Dundee, 1978–93. Convener, General Assembly, Church of Scotland: Bd of Practice and Procedure, 1985–88; Business Cttee, 1985–88. Chm. Bd of Dirs, High Sch. of Dundee, 1993–. Chm., Murray Home, 1994–; Trustee, Scottish Nat. War Meml, 1994–. Freeman of Dundee, 1991. Hon. LLD Dundee, 1990; Hon. DD Aberdeen, 1991. ChStJ 1993 (Prelate, 1993). *Recreations:* reading, golf, stamp collecting. *Address:* 3/5 Craigend Park, Edinburgh EH16 5XY. *Club:* New (Edinburgh).

McMILLAN-SCOTT, Edward; Member (C) European Parliament, North Yorkshire, since 1994 (York, 1984–94); *b* 15 Aug. 1949; *s* of Walter Theodore Robin McMillan-Scott, ARIBA and Elizabeth Maud Derrington Hudson; *m* 1972, Henrietta Elizabeth Rumney Hudson, solicitor; two *d*. *Educ:* Blackfriars School, Llanarth; Blackfriars School, Laxton; Exeter Technical College. Tour director in Europe, Scandinavia, Africa and USSR, 1968–75; PR exec., then parly consultant, 1976–84; political adviser to Falkland Islands Govt, London office 1983–84. European Parliament: Member: For. Affairs and Security Cttee, 1989–; Transport Cttee, 1989–92; Chm., 1979 Cttee (Cons. back-bench cttee), 1994–. Vice-Pres., Yorks and Humberside Develt Assoc. Mem. Court, Univ. of York. *Recreations:* music, reading. *Address:* European Parliament, 2 Queen Anne's Gate, SW1H 9AA.

McMINN, Prof. Robert Matthew Hay; Emeritus Professor of Anatomy, Royal College of Surgeons and University of London; *b* 20 Sept. 1923; *o s* of late Robert Martin McMinn, MD, ChB, Auchinleck and Brighton, and Elsie Selene Kent; *m* 1948, Margaret Grieve Kirkwood, MB, ChB, DA; one *s* one *d*. *Educ:* Brighton Coll. (Schol.); Univ. of Glasgow. MB, ChB 1947, MD (commendation) 1958, Glasgow; PhD Sheffield 1956; FRCS 1978. Hosp. posts and RAF Med. Service, 1947–50; Demonstrator in Anatomy, Glasgow Univ., 1950–52; Lectr in Anatomy, Sheffield Univ., 1952–60; Reader 1960–66, Prof. of Anatomy 1966–70, King's Coll., London Univ.; Sir William Collins Prof. of Human and Comparative Anatomy, RCS, Conservator, Hunterian Museum, RCS, and Prof. of Anatomy, Inst. of Basic Med. Scis, London Univ., 1970–82, prematurely retd. Late Examnr to RCS, RCP&S Glasgow and Univs of London, Cambridge, Edinburgh, Belfast, Singapore, Malaya and Makerere. Arris and Gale Lectr, RCS, 1960; Arnott Demonstrator, RCS, 1970. Former Treas., Anatomical Soc. of Gt Britain and Ireland; Foundn Sec., British Assoc. of Clinical Anatomists; FRSocMed; Member: Amer. Assoc. of Anatomists; Amer. Assoc. of Clinical Anatomists; BMA; Trustee, Skin Res. Foundn. *Publications:* Tissue Repair, 1969; The Digestive System, 1974; The Human Gut, 1974; (jtly) Colour Atlas of Human Anatomy, 1977, 3rd edn 1993; (jtly) Colour Atlas of Head and Neck Anatomy, 1981, 2nd edn 1994; (jtly) Colour Atlas of Foot and Ankle Anatomy, 1982, 2nd edn 1995; (jtly) Colour Atlas of Applied Anatomy, 1984; (jtly) Picture Tests in Human Anatomy, 1986; (jtly) The Human Skeleton, 1987; (ed) Last's Anatomy, 8th edn 1990, 9th edn 1994; (jtly) McMinn's Functional and Clinical Anatomy, 1995; articles in various med. and sci. jls. *Recreations:* motoring, photography, archaeology, short-wave radio. *Address:* Tavistone Lodge, Commonside, Great Bookham, Leatherhead, Surrey KT23 3LA. *T:* Leatherhead (01372) 459271.

McMINNIES, John Gordon, OBE 1965; HM Diplomatic Service, retired 1977; *b* 1 Oct. 1919; *s* of late William Gordon McMinnies and Joyce Millicent McMinnies; *m* 1947, Mary (*née* Jackson) (*d* 1978), novelist. *Educ:* Bilton Grange; Rugby Sch.; Austria (language trng). Reporter: Western Mail, 1938; Reuters, 1939. Served War, Army, 1940–46: comd R Troop, RHA; retd, Major. HM Diplomatic Service (Athens, Warsaw, Bologna, Malaysia, Cyprus, Nairobi, Lusaka, New Delhi), 1946–77; retd, Counsellor. *Recreations:* crazy paving, crosswords, cricketology, the sea. *Address:* 2 rue de la République, 34300 Agde, France. *T:* 67214438.

McMULLAN, Rt. Rev. Gordon; *see* Down and Dromore, Bishop of.

McMULLAN, Michael Brian; His Honour Judge McMullan; a Circuit Judge, since 1980; *b* 15 Nov. 1926; *s* of late Joseph Patrick McMullan and Frances McMullan (*née* Burton); *m* 1960, Rosemary Jane Margaret, *d* of late Stanley Halse deL. de Ville; one *s* two *d*. *Educ:* Manor Farm Road Sch.; Tauntons Sch., Southampton; The Queen's College, Oxford (MA). Called to the Bar, Gray's Inn, 1960. National Service, Army, 1946–48. Colonial Administrative Service: Gold Coast and Ghana, Political Administration Ashanti, Min. of Finance, Accra, Agricl Development Corp., 1949–60. In practice as Barrister, SE Circuit, 1961–80; a Recorder of the Crown Court, 1979. *Club:* United Oxford & Cambridge University.

McMULLEN, Prof. David Lawrence, FBA 1994; Professor of Chinese, University of Cambridge, since 1989; Fellow of St John's College, Cambridge, since 1967; *b* 10 Aug. 1939; *m* 1983, Sarah Jane Clarice Croft; two *d*. *Educ:* Monkton Combe Sch., Bath; St John's Coll., Cambridge (BA, MA, PhD). National Service, RAF, 1957–59. Taiwan Min. of Educn Schol., 1963–64; Harkness Commonwealth Fellowship, 1965–67; Asst Lectr 1967, Lectr 1972, in Chinese Studies, Cambridge Univ. Pres., British Assoc. for Chinese Studies, 1985–87. *Publications:* Concordances and Indexes to Chinese Texts, 1975; State and Scholars in T'ang China, 1988; contribs to jls of E Asian studies. *Recreation:* gardening.

Address: Grove Cottage, 35 High Street, Grantchester, Cambridge CB3 9NF. *T:* Cambridge (01223) 840206.

McMULLEN, Jeremy John; QC 1994; *b* 14 Sept. 1948; *s* of John Ezra McMullen and Irene McMullen; *m* 1973, Deborah Cristman; one *s* one *d*. *Educ:* William Hulme's Grammar Sch., Manchester; Brasenose Coll., Oxford (MA); LSE (MSc). Called to the Bar, Middle Temple, 1971; Associate Attorney, New York, 1971–73; General, Municipal, Boilermakers' Union: Legal Officer, 1973–77; Regl Officer, London, 1977–84; in practice at the Bar, 1984–. Chm. (part-time), Industrial Tribunals. Chairman: Industrial Law Soc., 1989–93; Employment Law Bar Assoc., 1994–95. *Publications:* Rights at Work, 1978, 2nd edn 1983; (contrib.) Penguin Guide to Civil Liberties, 1989; Employment Tribunal Procedure, 1995. *Recreations:* squash, swimming. *Address:* Old Square Chambers, Verulam Buildings, Gray's Inn, WC1R 5LQ. *Club:* Reform.

McMULLIN, Rt. Hon. Sir Duncan (Wallace), Kt 1987; PC 1980; Judge of Court of Appeal, New Zealand, 1979–89; commercial arbitrator, since 1990; *b* 1 May 1927; *s* of Charles James McMullin and Kathleen Annie Shout; *m* 1955, Isobel Margaret, *d* of Robert Ronald Atkinson, ED; two *s* two *d*. *Educ:* Auckland Grammar Sch.; Univ. of Auckland (LLB). Judge of Supreme Court, 1970–79. Chm., Royal Commn on Contraception, Sterilisation and Abortion in NZ, 1975–77. Chairman: Wanganui Computer Centre Policy Cttee, 1989–93; Surveillance Panel, Electricity Marketing Corp., 1994. Chm., Bd of Trustees, Maruia Soc., 1992. FIArb of NZ, 1990. *Recreations:* forestry, farming. *Address:* 707 Remuera Road, Auckland, New Zealand. *T:* (9) 5246583.

McMURRAY, Dr Cecil Hugh, FRSC, FIFST; Chief Scientific Officer, Department of Agriculture for Northern Ireland, since 1988; *b* 19 Feb. 1942; *s* of late Edwin McMurray and of Margaret (*née* Smyth); *m* 1967, Ann Stuart; two *s* one *d*. *Educ:* Royal Belfast Academical Instn; Queen's University, Belfast (BSc 1965; BAgr 1966); PhD Bristol, 1970. FRSC 1981; FIFST 1987. Res. Fellow, Dept of Chem., Harvard Univ., 1970–72; Head of Biochem. Dept, Vet. Res. Lab., Dept of Agric. for NI, 1972–84; Prof. of Food and Agricl Chem., QUB, and concurrently DCSO, Dept of Agric. for NI, 1984–88. Expert Advr, WHO, 1983, 1986; Assessor to: AFRC, 1988–94; Priorities Bd for R&D in Agric. and Food, 1988–93; Technology Bd for NI, 1988–92; NERC, 1992–93; Adv. Cttee on microbiol safety of food, 1992–. Mem., Steering Gp on chem. aspects of food surveillance, 1992–. Pres., Agricl Gp, BAAS, 1986–87. Mem. Cttee, Coronary Prevention Gp, 1985–89. Trustee, Agricl Inst. for NI, 1985–; Mem. Governing Body, Rowett Res. Inst., Aberdeen, 1986–89, 1993–. Mem. Editl Bd, Fertiliser Res., 1985–92. *Publications:* over 100 scientific publications in various jls incl. Biochemical Jl, Jl of Amer. Chemical Soc., Clin. Chem., CIBA Foundn Symposia, Jl of Chromatography, British Vet. Jl, Vet. Record, Jl Assoc. of Anal Chem., Trace Metals in Man and Domestic Animals, Biology of Total Envmt. *Recreations:* reading, photography, walking, gardening. *Address:* Department of Agriculture for Northern Ireland, Dundonald House, Upper Newtownards Road, Belfast BT4 3SB. *T:* Belfast (01232) 524635.

McMURRAY, David Bruce, MA; Headmaster, Oundle School, since 1984; *b* 15 Dec. 1937; *s* of late James McMurray, CBE, and of Kathleen McMurray (*née* Goodwin); *m* 1962, Antonia Murray; three *d*. *Educ:* Loretto Sch.; Pembroke Coll., Cambridge (BA, MA). National service, Royal Scots, 1956–58, 2nd Lieut. Pembroke Coll., Cambridge, 1958–61; Asst Master, Stowe Sch., 1961–64; Fettes College: Asst Master, 1964–72; Head of English, 1967–72; Housemaster, 1972–76; Headmaster, Loretto Sch., 1976–84. HM Comr, Queen Victoria Sch., Dunblane, 1977–87; Mem., Edinburgh Fest. Council, 1980–84. FRSA 1989. CCF Medal, 1976, and Bar, 1984. *Recreations:* cricket, golf, sub-aqua diving, poetry. *Address:* Cobthorne, West Street, Oundle, Peterborough PE8 4EF. *T:* Oundle (01832) 272251. *Clubs:* East India, Devonshire, Sports and Public Schools, MCC, Free Foresters.

MacMURRAY, Mary Bell McMillan, (Mrs Ian Mills), QC 1979; **Her Honour Judge MacMurray;** a Circuit Judge, since 1988; *d* of Samuel Bell MacMurray and Constance Mary MacMurray (*née* Goodman); *m* 1971, Ian Donald Mills. *Educ:* Queen Margaret's School, Escrick, York. Called to the Bar, Lincoln's Inn, 1954, Bencher, 1986. Barrister-at-Law, 1954–88; a Recorder of the Crown Court, 1978–88. Coronation Medal, 1953. *Recreation:* golf. *Address:* c/o Courts Administrator, Westgate House, Westgate Road, Newcastle upon Tyne NE1 1RR. *Clubs:* Durham County; Whitburn Golf; Lady Taverners.

McMURTRY, Hon. (Roland) Roy; Chief Justice, Ontario Court of Justice (General Division), since 1994 (Associate Chief Justice, 1991–94); *b* 31 May 1932; *s* of Roland Roy McMurtry and Doris Elizabeth Belcher; *m* 1957, Ria Jean Macrae; three *s* three *d*. *Educ:* St Andrew's Coll., Aurora, Ont; Trinity Coll., Univ. of Toronto (BA Hons); Osgoode Hall Law Sch., Toronto (LLB). Called to the Bar of Ontario, 1958; QC 1970. Partner: Benson, McMurtry, Percival & Brown, Toronto, 1958–75; Blaney, McMurtry, Stapells, 1988–91. Elected to Ontario Legislature, 1975; re-elected, 1977 and 1981; Attorney General for Ontario, 1975–85; Solicitor General for Ontario, 1978–82. High Comr in UK, 1985–88. Freeman, City of London, 1986. Hon. LLD: Univ. of Ottawa, 1983; Law Soc. of Upper Canada, 1984; Univ. of Leeds, 1988; York Univ., 1991. *Recreations:* painting, skiing, tennis. *Address:* 130 Queen Street West, Toronto, Ont M5H 2N5, Canada. *T:* (416) 3275000. *Club:* Albany (Toronto).

MACNAB OF MACNAB, James Charles; The Macnab; 23rd Chief of Clan Macnab; *b* 14 April 1926; *e s* of late Lt-Col James Alexander Macnabb, OBE, TD (*de jure* 21st of Macnab), London, SW3, and Mrs Ursula Walford, Wokingham, Berks; *S* gt uncle Archibald Corrie Macnab of Macnab, (*de facto*) 22nd Chief, 1970; *m* 1959, Hon. Diana Mary, DL, *er d* of Baron Kilmany, PC, MC, and of Monica Helen, (Lady Kilmany), OBE, JP, *o c* of late Geoffrey Lambton, 2nd *s* of 4th Earl of Durham; two *s* two *d*. *Educ:* Cothill House; Radley Coll.; Ashbury Coll., Ottawa. Served in RAF and Scots Guards, 1944–45; Lieut, Seaforth Highldrs, 1945–48. Asst Supt, then Acting Dep. Supt, Fedn of Malaya Police Force, 1948; retd, 1957. Mem., Western DC of Perthshire, 1961–64; CC, Perth and Kinross Jt County Council, 1964–75; Mem., Central Regional Council, 1978–82. Exec., subseq. Sen., Consultant, Hill Samuel Investment Services, 1982–92. Member, Royal Company of Archers, Queen's Body Guard in Scotland. Capt., Seaforth Highldrs, TA, 1960–64. JP Perthshire, 1968–75, Stirling, 1975–86. *Recreations:* shooting, travel. *Heir:* *s* James William Archibald Macnab, younger of Macnab [*b* 22 March 1963; *m* 1994, Dr Jane Mackintosh, *d* of late Dr David Mackintosh]. *Address:* Leuchars Castle Farmhouse, Leuchars, St Andrews, Fife KY16 0EY. *T:* Leuchars (01334) 838777. *Club:* New (Edinburgh).

McNAB, John Stanley; Chief Executive, Port of Tilbury London Ltd (formerly Port of Tilbury (Port of London Authority)), since 1987; *b* 23 Sept. 1937; *s* of Robert Stanley McNab and Alice Mary McNab; *m* 1st, 1961, Carol Field (marr. diss. 1978); two *d*; 2nd, 1980, Jacqueline Scammell. *Educ:* Gravesend Grammar Sch. FCCA 1976; FCIT 1992. Nat. Service, Royal Engineers, Libya, 1956–58. Port of London Authority: joined 1954; Accountant, India and Millwall Docks, 1965, Upper Docks, 1970; Man. Dir, PLA (Thames) Stevedoring, 1973; Dir, Upper Docks, 1974; Exec. Dir (Manpower) and Group Board Mem., 1978; Dir, Tilbury, 1983. Dir, Internat. Transport Ltd, 1992–. FRSA 1991; MIMgt (MBIM 1970). Freeman: City of London, 1988; Co. of Watermen and Lightermen of River Thames, 1988. *Recreations:* walking the dogs, swimming, tennis, DIY, learning Spanish and Portuguese. *Address:* Port of Tilbury London Ltd, Leslie Ford House, Tilbury Docks, Essex RM18 7EH. *T:* Tilbury (01375) 852427.

McNAB JONES, Robin Francis, FRCS; Surgeon: ENT Department, St Bartholomew's Hospital, 1961–87; Royal National Throat, Nose and Ear Hospital, 1962–83; *b* 22 Oct. 1922; *s* of late E. C. H. Jones, CBE, and M. E. Jones, MBE; *m* 1950, Mary Garrett; one *s* three *d*. *Educ:* Manchester Grammar Sch.; Dulwich Coll.; Med. Coll., St Bartholomew's Hosp. (MB BS 1945); FRCS 1952. Ho. Surg., St Bart's, 1946–47; MO, RAF, 1947–50; Demonstrator of Anatomy, St Bart's, 1950–52; Registrar, Royal Nat. Throat, Nose and Ear Hosp., 1952–54; Sen. Registrar, ENT Dept, St Bart's, 1954–59; Lectr, Dept of Otolaryngology, Univ. of Manchester, 1959–61; Dean, Inst. of Laryngology and Otology, Univ. of London, 1971–76; Vice-Pres., St Bart's Hosp. Med. Coll., 1984–87. Mem., Court of Examiners, 1972–78, and Mem. Council (for Otolaryngology), 1982–87, RCS; External Examiner, RCSI, 1980–83, 1988–91. Hon. Sec., Sect. of Otology, 1965–68, Pres., Sect. of Laryngology, 1981–82, RSocMed. *Publications:* various chapters in standard med. textbooks; contribs to med. jls. *Recreations:* tennis, ski-ing, golf, fishing, gardening. *Address:* The Consulting Suite, Fitzroy Nuffield Hospital, 10–12 Bryanston Square, W1H 8BB. *T:* 0171–723 1288; 91 Barnfield Wood Road, Beckenham, Kent BR3 2ST. *T:* 0181–650 0217.

MACNAGHTEN, Sir Patrick (Alexander), 11th Bt *cr* 1836; farmer; *b* 24 Jan. 1927; *s* of Sir Antony Macnaghten, 10th Bt, and of Magdalene, *e d* of late Edmund Fisher; *S* father, 1972; *m* 1955, Marianne, *yr d* of Dr Erich Schaefer and Alice Schaefer, Cambridge; three *s*. *Educ:* Eton; Trinity Coll., Cambridge (BA Mechanical Sciences). Army (RE), 1945–48. Project Engineer, Cadbury Bros (later Cadbury Schweppes), 1950–69; in General Management, Cadbury-Schweppes Ltd, 1969–84. *Recreations:* fishing, shooting. *Heir:* *s* Malcolm Francis Macnaghten, *b* 21 Sept. 1956. *Address:* Dundarave, Bushmills, Co. Antrim, Northern Ireland. *T:* Bushmills (012657) 31215.

MACNAGHTEN, Robin Donnelly, MA; Headmaster of Sherborne, 1974–88; *b* 3 Aug. 1927; 2nd *s* of late Sir Henry P. W. Macnaghten and of Lady Macnaghten; *m* 1961, Petronella, *er d* of late Lt-Col A. T. Card and Mrs Card; two *s* one *d*. *Educ:* Eton (Schol.); King's Coll., Cambridge (Schol.). 1st cl. Class. Tripos Pt I, 1947; 1st cl. with dist. Pt II, 1948; Browne Medallist; MA 1954. Travelled in Italy and Turkey, 1949. Asst, Mackinnon Mackenzie & Co., Bombay, 1949–54. Asst Master, Eton Coll., 1954, and Housemaster, 1965. Hon. Sec. and Treas., 1970–74, Pres., 1991–92, OEA; Pres., Old Shirburnian Soc., 1984–85. Governor: Sandroyd Sch., 1986–; Dauntsey's Sch., 1988–; Chairman of Governors: Hall Sch., Wincanton, 1978–; Forres at Sandle Manor (formerly Forres) Sch., 1991– (Gov., 1974–88). *Publication:* trans. Vita Romana (by U. E. Paoli), 1963. *Recreations:* numismatics (FRNS), walking, gardening. *Address:* Prospect House, Tisbury, Wilts SP3 6QQ. *T:* Tisbury (01747) 870355. *Club:* Western India Turf (Bombay).

McNAIR, family name of **Baron McNair.**

McNAIR, 3rd Baron *cr* 1955, of Gleniffer; **Duncan James McNair;** *b* 26 June 1947; *s* of 2nd Baron McNair and Vera, *d* of Theodore James Faithfull; *S* father, 1989. *Educ:* Bryanston. *Heir:* *b* Hon. William Samuel Angus McNair, *b* 19 May 1958. *Address:* House of Lords, SW1A 0PW.

McNAIR, Archie, (Archibald Alister Jourdan); Co-founder, 1955, and Chairman, 1955–88, Mary Quant Group of Companies; Founder, 1971, and Chairman, 1971–88, Thomas Jourdan plc; *b* 16 Dec. 1919; *s* of late Donald McNair and Janie (*née* Jourdan); *m* 1954, Catherine Alice Jane, *d* of late John and Margaret Fleming; one *s* one *d*. *Educ:* Blundells. Articled to Ford Simey & Ford, Solicitors, Exeter, 1938. Served War, 1939–45: River Thames Formation. Photographer, 1950–57. Dir, City and Capital Hotels, 1986–92. *Recreations:* growing fruit, carving wood, tennis, chess. *Address:* c/o Coutts & Co., 440 Strand, WC2N 0QS.

See also D. J. E. Ingram, D. B. Vernon.

MACNAIR, His Honour Maurice John Peter; a Circuit Judge, 1972–91; *b* 27 Feb. 1919; *s* of late Brig. J. L. P. Macnair and Hon. Mrs Macnair (*née* Atkin); *m* 1952, Vickie Reynolds, *d* of Hugh Reynolds; one *s* two *d*. *Educ:* Bembridge Sch.; St Paul's Sch.; St Edmund Hall, Oxford. BA 1947. Served War of 1939–45, Western Desert, Sicily, Italy; wounded 1944; Captain, RA. Called to Bar, Gray's Inn, 1948. Dep. Chm., W Sussex QS, 1968–72. *Recreations:* walking, painting. *Address:* 28 Rawlings Street, SW3 2LS.

McNAIR-WILSON, Sir Patrick (Michael Ernest David), Kt 1989; MP (C) New Forest, since 1968 (Lewisham West, 1964–66); Consultant; *b* 28 May 1929; *s* of Dr Robert McNair-Wilson; *m* 1953, Diana Evelyn Kitty Campbell Methuen-Campbell, *d* of Hon. Laurence Methuen-Campbell; one *s* four *d*. *Educ:* Eton. Exec. in French Shipping Co., 1951–53; various appointments at Conservative Central Office, 1954–58; Staff of Conservative Political Centre, 1958–61; Director, London Municipal Society, 1961–63; Executive with The British Iron and Steel Federation, 1963–64. Opposition Front Bench Spokesman on fuel and power, 1965–66; Vice-Chm., Conservative Parly Power Cttee, 1969–70; PPS to Minister for Transport Industries, DoE, 1970–74; Opposition Front Bench Spokesman on Energy, 1974–76; Chm., Jt Lords and Commons Select Cttee on Private Bill Procedure, 1987–88; Mem., Select Cttee on Members Interests, 1985–86. Editor of The Londoner, 1961–63. *Recreations:* sailing, pottery. *Address:* House of Commons, SW1A 0AA.

McNALLY, Eryl Margaret; Member (Lab) for Bedfordshire and Milton Keynes, European Parliament, since 1994; *b* 11 April 1942; *d* of late Llywelyn Williams, MP and Elsie Williams; *m* 1964, James Frederick McNally; one *s* one *d*. *Educ:* Newbridge Grammar Sch.; Bristol Univ. (BA Langs); University Coll., Swansea (PGCE). Modern langs teacher, 1964–84; advisory work, Bucks CC, 1985–93; freelance schools inspector, OFSTED, 1993–94. Councillor: Abbots Langley Parish Council, 1970–73; Watford RDC, 1972–74; Three Rivers DC, 1973–77; Herts CC, 1986–95. *Publications:* articles on language teaching and teacher training in professional jls. *Recreations:* learning languages, reading, world music, films. *Address:* 146 Abbots Road, Abbots Langley, Herts WD5 0BL. *T:* Watford (01923) 264525.

McNALLY, Tom; Head of Public Affairs, Shandwick Consultants, since 1993; *b* 20 Feb. 1943; *s* of John P. McNally and Elizabeth May (*née* McCarthy); *m* 1st, 1970, Eileen Powell (marr. diss. 1990); 2nd, 1990, Juliet Lamy Hutchinson; two *s*. *Educ:* College of St Joseph, Blackpool; University Coll., London (BScEcon; Fellow 1995). President of Students' Union, UCL, 1965–66; Vice-Pres., Nat. Union of Students, 1966–67; Asst Gen. Sec. of Fabian Society, 1966–67; Labour Party researcher, 1967–68; Internat. Sec. of Labour Party, 1969–74; Political Adviser to: Foreign and Commonwealth Sec., 1974–76; Prime Minister, 1976–79. MP (Lab 1979–81, SDP 1981–83) Stockport S; SDP Parly spokesman on educn and sport, 1981–83. Mem., Select Cttee on Industry and Trade, 1979–83. Contested (SDP) Stockport, 1983. Public Affairs Adviser, GEC, 1983–84; Dir-Gen., Retail Consortium, and Dir, British Retailers Association, 1985–87; Head of Public Affairs, Hill & Knowlton, 1987–93. FRSA; MIPR. Pres., St Albans Lib Dems. *Recreations:*

playing and watching sport, reading political biographies. *Address:* 9 Barncroft Way, St Albans, Herts AL1 5QZ.

McNAMARA, (Joseph) Kevin; MP (Lab) Hull North, since 1983 (Kingston-upon-Hull North, Jan. 1966–1974; Kingston-upon-Hull Central, 1974–83); *b* 5 Sept. 1934; *s* of late Patrick and Agnes McNamara; *m* 1960, Nora (*née* Jones), Warrington; four *s* one *d*. *Educ:* various primary schools; St Mary's Coll., Crosby; Hull Univ. (LLB). Head of Dept of History, St Mary's Grammar Sch., Hull, 1958–64; Lecturer in Law, Hull Coll. of Commerce, 1964–66. Opposition spokesman on defence, 1982–83, on defence and disarmament, 1983–85, dep. opposition spokesman on defence, 1985–87, opposition spokesman on Northern Ireland, 1987–94, on Civil Service, 1994–95. Member: Select Cttee on For. Affairs, 1977–82 (former Chm., Overseas Develt Sub-Cttee); Parly Assembly, NATO, 1984–88; Vice-Chm., Economic Cttee, NATO, 1985–87; former Chairman: Select Cttee on Overseas Develt; PLP NI Gp; Sec., Parly Gp, TGWU. Former Mem., UK Delegn to Council of Europe. Commendatore, Order Al Merito della Repubblica Italiana, 1977. *Recreations:* family and outdoor activities. *Address:* House of Commons, SW1A 0AA; 145 Newland Park, Hull HU5 2DX.

McNAMARA, Air Chief Marshal Sir Neville (Patrick), KBE 1981 (CBE 1972); AO 1976; AFC 1961; Royal Australian Air Force, retired 1984; *b* Toogoolawah, Qld, 17 April 1923; *s* of late P. F. McNamara; *m* 1950, Dorothy Joan Miller; two *d*. *Educ:* Christian Brothers Coll., Nudgee, Qld. Enlisted RAAF, 1941; commnd 1944; Fighter Pilot WWII with No 75 Sqdn, Halmaheras and Borneo; served with No 77 Sqdn in Japan on cessation of hostilities; Air Traffic Control duties, HQ NE Area, 1948; Flying Instructor, Central Flying Sch., 1951–53; operational tour with No 77 Sqdn in Korean War; Pilot Trng Officer, HQ Trng Comd, 1954–55; Staff Officer, Fighter Operations Dept Air, 1955–57; CO No 25 Sqdn W Australia, 1957–59; CO No 2 Operational Conversion Unit, 1959–61; CO and Sen. Air Staff Officer, RAAF Staff, London, 1961–63; Director of Personnel (Officers), Dept Air, 1964–66; OC RAAF Contingent, Thailand, 1966–67; Air Staff Officer, RAAF Richmond, 1967–69; Dir-Gen., Organisation Dept Air, 1969–71; Comdr RAAF Forces Vietnam, 1971–72; Aust. Air Attaché, Washington, 1972–75; Dep. Chief of Air Staff, 1975–79; Chief of Air Staff, 1979–82; Chief of Defence Force Staff, 1982–84. RAAF psc, pfc, jssc. *Recreations:* golf, fishing. *Club:* Commonwealth (Canberra).

McNAMARA, Robert Strange; Medal of Freedom with Distinction; *b* San Francisco, 9 June 1916; *s* of Robert James McNamara and Clara Nell (*née* Strange); *m* 1940, Margaret McKinstry Craig (decd); one *s* two *d*. *Educ:* University of California (AB); Harvard Univ. (Master of Business Administration); Asst Professor of Business Administration, Harvard, 1940–43. Served in USAAF, England, India, China, Pacific, 1943–46 (Legion of Merit); released as Lieut-Colonel. Joined Ford Motor Co., 1946; Executive, 1946–61; Controller, 1949–53; Asst General Manager, Ford Div., 1953–55; Vice-President, and General Manager, Ford Div., 1955–57; Director, and Group Vice-President of Car Divisions, 1957–61, President, 1960–61; Secretary of Defense, United States of America, 1961–68; Pres., The World Bank, 1968–81; Director: Royal Dutch Petroleum, 1981–87; Bank of America, 1981–87; Corning, 1981–90; The Washington Post, 1981–89. Trustee: Urban Inst.; Trilateral Commn. Hon. degrees from: Harvard, Calif, Mich, Columbia, Ohio, Princeton, NY, Notre Dame, George Washington, Aberdeen, St Andrews, Fordham and Oxford Univs; Williams, Chatham and Amherst Colls. Phi Beta Kappa. Albert Pick Jr Award, Univ. of Chicago (first recipient), 1979; Albert Einstein Peace Prize, 1983; Franklin D. Roosevelt Freedom from Want Medal, 1983; Amer. Assembly Service to Democracy Award; Dag Hammarskjöld Hon. Medal; Extrepreneurial Excellence Medal, Yale Sch. of Organization and Management; Olive Branch Award for Outstanding Book on subject of World Peace, 1987; Sidney Hillman Foundn Award, 1987; Onassis Athinai Prize, 1988. *Publications:* The Essence of Security, 1968; One Hundred Countries, Two Billion People: the dimensions of development, 1975; The McNamara Years at the World Bank, 1981; Blundering into Disaster, 1987; Out of the Cold, 1990; In Retrospect: the tragedy and lessons of Vietnam, 1995. *Address:* 1455 Pennsylvania Avenue NW, Washington, DC 20004, USA.

McNAUGHT, John Graeme; His Honour Judge McNaught; a Circuit Judge, since 1987; *b* 21 Feb. 1941; *s* of Charles William McNaught and Isabella Mary McNaught; *m* 1966, Barbara Mary Smith; two *s* one *d*. *Educ:* King Edward VII Sch., Sheffield; The Queen's Coll., Oxford (BA Jurisprudence, 1962). Bacon Scholar, Gray's Inn, 1962; called to the Bar, Gray's Inn, 1963; a Recorder, 1981–87. *Address:* The Swindon Combined Court Centre, Islington Street, Swindon SN1 2HG.

McNAUGHTON, Lt-Col Ian Kenneth Arnold; Chief Inspecting Officer of Railways, Department of Transport, 1974–82; *b* 30 June 1920; *er s* of late Brig. F. L. McNaughton, CBE, DSO and Betty, *d* of late Rev. Arnold Pinchard, OBE; *m* 1946, Arthea, *d* of late Carel Begeer, Voorschoten, Holland; two *d*. *Educ:* Loretto Sch.; RMA Woolwich; RMCS Shrivenham. BScEng, CEng, FIMechE, FCIT, FIRSE. 2nd Lieut RE, 1939; served War of 1939–45, NW Europe (Captain) (despatches); GHQ MELF, 1949 (Major); Cyprus, 1955; OC 8 Rly Sqdn, 1958; Port Comdt Southampton, 1959 (Lt-Col); SOI Transportation HQ BAOR, 1960; retd 1963. Inspecting Officer of Rlys, Min. of Transport, 1963. Chm., Rlys Industry Adv. Cttee, Health and Safety Commn, 1978–82. *Recreations:* gardening, foreign travel. *Address:* Chawton Glebe, Alton, Hants GU34 1SH. *T:* Alton (01420) 83395.

MACNAUGHTON, Prof. Sir Malcolm (Campbell), Kt 1986; MD; FRCPG; FRCOG; FRSE; Muirhead Professor of Obstetrics and Gynaecology, University of Glasgow, 1970–90, now Emeritus; *b* 4 April 1925; *s* of James Hay and Mary Robieson Macnaughton; *m* 1955, Margaret-Ann Galt; two *s* three *d*. *Educ:* Glasgow Academy; Glasgow Univ. (MD). Lectr, Univ. of Aberdeen, 1957–61; Sen. Lectr, Univ. of St Andrews, 1961–66; Hon. Sen. Lectr, Univ. of Dundee, 1966–70. Pres., RCOG, 1984–87; Vice-Pres., Royal Coll. of Midwives, 1992–. Pres., British Fertility Soc., 1992–95. Hon. FACOG; Hon. FSLCOG; Hon. FRCAnaes; Hon. FRACOG. Hon. LLD Dundee, 1988. *Publications:* Combined Textbook of Obstetrics and Gynaecology (ed jtly), 9th edn 1976; (ed and contrib.) Handbook of Medical Gynaecology, 1985; numerous papers in obstetric, gynaecological, endocrine and general medical jls. *Recreations:* fishing, walking, curling. *Address:* Beechwood, 15 Boclair Road, Bearsden, Glasgow G61 2AF. *T:* 0141–942 1909. *Club:* Glasgow Academical (Glasgow).

McNEE, Sir David (Blackstock), Kt 1978; QPM 1975; Commissioner, Metropolitan Police, 1977–82; non-executive director and adviser to a number of public limited companies; *b* 23 March 1925; *s* of John McNee, Glasgow, Lanarkshire; *m* 1952, Isabella Clayton Hopkins; one *d*. *Educ:* Woodside Senior Secondary Sch., Glasgow. Joined City of Glasgow Police, 1946. Apptd Dep. Chief Constable, Dunbartonshire Constabulary, 1968; Chief Constable: City of Glasgow Police, 1971–75; Strathclyde Police, 1975–77. Lectures: Basil Henriques, Bristol Univ., 1978; London, in Contemporary Christianity, 1979; Dallas, Glasgow, 1980; Peter le Neve Foster Meml, RSA, 1981. President: Royal Life Saving Soc., 1982–90; National Bible Soc. of Scotland, 1983–; Glasgow City Cttee, Cancer Relief, 1987–93; Glasgow Battalion, Boys' Brigade, 1984–87; Hon. Vice-Pres., Boys' Bde, 1980–; Vice-Pres., London Fedn of Boys Clubs, 1982–. Patron, Scottish Motor Neurone Assoc., 1982–. Hon. Col, 32 (Scottish) Signal Regt (V), TA, 1988–92. Freeman of the City of London, 1977. FIMgt (FBIM 1977); FRSA 1981. KStJ 1991. *Publication:* McNee's Law, 1983. *Recreations:* fishing, golf, music. *Clubs:* Caledonian, Naval (Life Mem.).

McNEICE, Sir (Thomas) Percy (Fergus), Kt 1956; CMG 1953; OBE 1947; *b* 16 Aug. 1901; *s* of late Canon W. G. McNeice, MA, and Mary Masterson; *m* 1947, Yuen Peng Loke, *d* of late Dr Loke Yew, CMG, LLD; one *s* one *d*. *Educ:* Bradford Grammar Sch.; Keble Coll., Oxford (MA). Malayan Civil Service, 1925; Captain, Straits Settlements Volunteer Force (Prisoner of War, 1942–45). MLC, Singapore, 1949; MEC 1949; President of the City Council, Singapore, 1949–56, retired. FZS. *Recreations:* bird watching, walking and swimming. *Address:* 12 Jalan Sampurna, Singapore 1026. *Club:* Commonwealth Trust.

McNEIL, (David) John, CBE 1988; WS; NP; Partner, Morton Fraser Milligan, since 1968; President, Law Society of Scotland, 1986–87; *b* 24 March 1937; *s* of Donald S. McNeil and Elizabeth (*neé* Campbell); *m* 1962, Georgina Avril Sargent; one *s* two *d*. *Educ:* Daniel Stewart's Coll., Edinburgh; Edinburgh Univ. (MA Hons, LLB). Apprenticed to Davidson & Syme, WS, Edinburgh, 1959–62; admitted Solicitor in Scotland, 1962; WS 1964; Partner, Fraser, Stodart and Ballingall, 1964–68. Mem. Council, Law Soc. of Scotland, 1972–92. Mem., Warnock Inquiry into Aspects of Human Infertility and Embryology, 1982–84. *Recreations:* golf, snooker, music and opera, theatre. *Address:* St Catherine's Royal Terrace, Linlithgow, West Lothian EH49 6HQ. *T:* Linlithgow (01506) 843100. *Clubs:* New, Bruntsfield Golf (Edinburgh).

McNEIL, Ian Robert, JP; FCA; Partner, Moores Rowland, Chartered Accountants, since 1958; *b* 14 Dec. 1932; *s* of Robert and Doris Mary McNeil; *m* 1963, Ann Harries-Rees; two *d*. *Educ:* Brighton Coll. ACA 1955. Partner, Nevill Hovey Gardner (later amalgamated into Moores Rowland), 1958. Dep. Chm., Financial Reporting Council, 1991–92; Mem., Takeover Panel, 1991–92. Mem., Lord Chancellor's Adv. Cttee on Legal Educn and Conduct, 1994–. Institute of Chartered Accountants in England and Wales: Vice-Pres., 1989–90; Dep. Pres., 1990–91; Pres., 1991–92. Liveryman: Curriers' Co., 1959 (Master, 1994–95); Chartered Accountants' Co., 1989. JP Hove 1967 (Chm., Hove Bench, 1988–89); Mem. Council, Magistrates' Assoc., 1983–89. *Address:* Lancasters, West End Lane, Henfield, West Sussex BN5 9RB. *T:* Henfield (01273) 492606. *Club:* Athenæum.

MACNEIL OF BARRA, Prof. Ian Roderick; The Macneil of Barra; Chief of Clan Macneil and of that Ilk; Baron of Barra; Wigmore Professor of Law, Northwestern University, since 1980; *b* 20 June 1929; *s* of Robert Lister Macneil of Barra and Kathleen, *d* of Orlando Paul Metcalf, NYC, USA; *m* 1952, Nancy, *e d* of James Tilton Wilson, Ottawa, Canada; two *s* one *d* (and one *s* decd). *Educ:* Univ. of Vermont (BA 1950); Harvard Univ. (LLB 1955). Lieut, Infty, Army of US, 1951–53 (US Army Reserve, 1950–69, discharged honorably, rank of Major). Clerk, US Court of Appeals, 1955–56; law practice, Concord, NH, USA, 1956–59. Cornell Univ., USA: Asst Prof. of Law, 1959–62; Associate Prof., 1962–63; Prof. of Law, 1962–72 and 1974–76; Ingersoll Prof. of Law, 1976–80; Prof. of Law, Univ. of Virginia, 1972–74. Visiting Professor of Law: Univ. of East Africa, Dar es Salaam, Tanzania, 1965–67; Harvard Univ., 1988–89; Guggenheim Fellow, 1978–79; Vis. Fellow, Wolfson Coll., Oxford, 1979. Hon. Vis. Fellow, Faculty of Law, Edinburgh Univ., 1979 and 1987. Member: American Law Inst.; Standing Council of Scottish Chiefs. FSAScot. *Publications:* Bankruptcy Law in East Africa, 1966; (with R. B. Schlesinger, *et al*) Formation of Contracts: A Study of the Common Core of Legal Systems, 1968; Contracts: Instruments of Social Co-operation-East Africa, 1968; (with R. S. Morison) Students and Decision Making, 1970; Contracts: Exchange Transactions and Relations, 1971, 2nd edn 1978; The New Social Contract, 1980; American Arbitration Law, 1992; (jtly) Federal Arbitration Law, 1994. *Heir: s* Roderick Wilson Macneil, Younger of Barra [*b* 22 Oct. 1954; *m* 1988, Sau Ming, *d* of Chun Kwan, Hong Kong]. *Address:* 5/8 Fountainhall Road, Edinburgh EH9 2NL. *T:* 0131–667 6068; Kisimul Castle, Isle of Barra, Scotland. *T:* Castlebay (01871) 810300.

McNEIL, John; *see* McNeil, D. J.

MacNEIL, Most Rev. Joseph Neil; *see* Edmonton (Alberta), Archbishop of, (RC).

McNEILL, (Gordon) Keith; Editor, Woman's Own, since 1990; *b* 6 Aug. 1953; *s* of Gordon Francis McNeill and Vera McNeill; *m* 1983, Ruth Brotherhood. *Educ:* Slough Grammar School. Features Editor, Chat Magazine, 1985; London Evening News, 1988; Deputy Editor, Woman's Own, 1988. *Recreations:* walking, Bournemouth AFC, modern art, historical architecture. *Address:* Woman's Own, King's Reach Tower, Stamford Street, SE1 9LS. *T:* 0171–261 5500.

McNEILL, James Walker, QC (Scot) 1991; *b* 16 Feb. 1952; *s* of James McNeill and Edith Anna Howie Wardlaw; *m* 1986, Katherine Lawrence McDowall; two *s* one *d*. *Educ:* Dunoon Grammar Sch.; Cambridge Univ. (MA); Edinburgh Univ. (LLB). Advocate 1978; Standing Junior Counsel: to Dept of Transport in Scotland, 1984–88; to Inland Revenue in Scotland, 1988–91. *Recreations:* music, hill-walking, golf, sailing, travel. *Address:* 28 Kingsburgh Road, Edinburgh EH12 6DZ. *Clubs:* New (Edinburgh); Isle of Colonsay Golf.

McNEILL, Prof. John, PhD; Director, Royal Ontario Museum, and George R. Gardiner Museum of Ceramic Art, Toronto, since 1991; *b* 15 Sept. 1933; *s* of Thomas McNeill and Helen Lawrie Eagle; *m* 1st, 1961, Bridget Mariel Winterton (marr. diss. 1990); two *s*; 2nd, 1990, Marilyn Lois James. *Educ:* George Heriot's, Edinburgh; Univ. of Edinburgh (BSc Hons, PhD 1960). Asst Lectr and Lectr, Dept of Agricl Botany, Univ. of Reading, 1957–61; Lectr, Dept of Botany, Univ. of Liverpool, 1961–69; Plant (later Biosystematics) Research Institute, Agriculture Canada, Ottawa: Res. Scientist, 1969–77, Chief, Vascular Plant Taxonomy Sect., 1969–72; Sen. Res. Scientist, 1977–81; Prof. and Chm., Dept of Biology, Univ. of Ottawa, 1981–87; Regius Keeper, Royal Botanic Garden, Edinburgh, 1987–89; Associate Dir Curatorial, Royal Ontario Mus., Toronto, 1989–90, Acting Dir, 1990–91. Hon. Professor: Univ. of Edinburgh, 1989; Univ. of Toronto, 1990–; Adjunct Prof., Univ. of Ottawa, 1987–91. *Publications:* Phenetic and phylogenetic classification (jt ed), 1964; (jtly) Grasses of Ontario, 1977; (jt ed) International Code of Botanical Nomenclature, sexennially, 1983–; (jtly) Preliminary Inventory of Canadian Weeds, 1988; over 20 chapters or sections of sci. books and over 90 contribs to sci. res. jls. *Recreation:* botanical nomenclature. *Address:* Royal Ontario Museum, 100 Queen's Park, Toronto, Ont M5S 2C6, Canada.

McNEILL, Maj.-Gen. John Malcolm, CB 1963; CBE 1959 (MBE 1942); *b* 22 Feb. 1909; *s* of Brig.-General Angus McNeill, CB, CBE, DSO, TD, Seaforth Highlanders, and Lilian, *d* of Maj.-General Sir Harry Barron, KCVO; *m* 1939, Barbara, *d* of Colonel C. H. Marsh, DSO, Spilsby, Lincs; two *d*. *Educ:* Imperial Service Coll., Windsor; RMA, Woolwich. 2nd Lieut, RA, 1929. Served Western Desert, Sicily, Italy, N.W. Europe and Burma, 1939–45; Commanded 1st Regt RHA, 1948–51; Student Imperial Defence Coll., 1952; Dep. Secretary, Chiefs of Staff Cttee, Ministry of Defence, 1953–55; Comdr RA 2nd Div. 1955–58; Comdt School of Artillery, 1958–60; Commander, British Army Staff, and Military Attaché, Washington, DC, 1960–63; Col Comdt RA, 1964–74. Principal

Staff Officer to Sec. of State for Commonwealth Relations, 1964–69. ADC to the Queen, 1958–60. *Address:* Hole's Barn, Pilton, Shepton Mallet, Som BA4 4DF. *T:* Pilton (0174989) 0212. *Clubs:* Army and Navy, English-Speaking Union.

McNEILL, Keith; *see* McNeill, G. K.

McNEILL, Peter Grant Brass, PhD; QC (Scot) 1988; Sheriff of Lothian and Borders at Edinburgh, since 1982; *b* Glasgow, 3 March 1929; *s* of late William Arnot McNeill and late Lillias Philips Scrimgeour; *m* 1959, Matilda Farquhar Rose, *d* of Mrs Christina Rose; one *s* three *d*. *Educ:* Hillhead High Sch., Glasgow; Morrison's Academy, Crieff; Glasgow Univ. MA (Hons Hist.) 1951; LLB 1954; Law apprentice, Biggart Lumsden & Co., Glasgow, 1952–55; Carnegie Fellowship, 1955; Faulds Fellowship, 1956–59; Scottish Bar, 1956; PhD, 1961. Hon. Sheriff Substitute of Lanarkshire, and of Stirling, Clackmannan and Dumbarton, 1962; Standing Junior Counsel to Scottish Development Dept (Highways), 1964; Advocate Depute, 1964; Sheriff of Lanarks, subseq. redesignated Glasgow and Strathkelvin, at Glasgow, 1965–82. Pres., Sheriffs' Assoc., 1982–85. Chm., Review Bd, Chinook Helicopter Accident, 1988. Mem., Scottish Records Adv. Council, 1989–95. Chm. Council, Stair Soc., 1990. *Publications:* (ed) Balfour's Practicks (Stair Society), 1962–63; (ed jtly) An Historical Atlas of Scotland *c* 400–*c* 1600, 1975; Adoption of Children in Scotland, 1982, 2nd edn 1986; legal and historical articles in Encyclopaedia Britannica, Juridical Review, Scots Law Times, Glasgow Herald, etc. *Recreations:* legal history, gardening, bookbinding. *Address:* Sheriffs' Chambers, Sheriff Court House, 27 Chambers Street, Edinburgh EH1 1LA. *T:* 0131–225 2525.

McNEISH, Prof. Alexander Stewart, FRCP; Director, Medical Research Council Clinical Sciences Centre, Hammersmith Hospital, since 1995; *b* 13 April 1938; *s* of Angus Stewart McNeish and Minnie Howieson (*née* Dickson); *m* 1963, Joan Ralston (*née* Hamilton); two *s* one *d*. *Educ:* Glasgow Acad.; Univ. of Glasgow (MB); Univ. of Birmingham (MSc). FRCP 1977; FRCPGlas 1985. Sen. Lectr in Paediatrics and Child Health, Univ. of Birmingham, 1970–76; Foundn Prof. of Child Health, Univ. of Leicester, 1976–80; University of Birmingham: Leonard Parsons Prof. of Paediatrics and Child Health, 1980–95; Dir, Inst. of Child Health, 1980–93; Dean, Faculty of Medicine and Dentistry, 1987–92; Dir of R&D, W Midlands RHA, 1992–95. Mem., GMC, 1984–95. *Publications:* papers on paediatric gastroenterology in Lancet, BMJ and in Archives of Disease in Childhood. *Recreations:* golf, music. *Address:* MRC Clinical Sciences Centre, Royal Postgraduate Medical School, Hammersmith Hospital, Du Cane Road, W12 0NN; 128 Westfield Road, Edgbaston, Birmingham B15 3JQ. *T:* 0121–454 6081. *Clubs:* Athenæum; Blackwell Golf.

McNICOL, David Williamson, CBE 1966; Australian Diplomatic Service, retired; *b* 20 June 1913; *s* of late Donald McNicol, Adelaide; *m* 1947, Elsa Margaret, *d* of N. J. Hargrave, Adelaide; one *s*. *Educ:* Carey Grammar Sch., Melbourne; Kings Coll., Adelaide; Adelaide Univ. (BA). RAAF, 1940–45, Pilot, 201 and 230 Sqdns RAF, Atlantic, Madagascar, Italy and Dodecanese. Australian Minister to Cambodia, Laos and Vietnam, 1955–56; idc 1957; Australian Comr to Singapore, 1958–60; Asst Sec., Dept of External Affairs, Australia, 1960–62; Australian High Comr to Pakistan, 1962–65 and to New Zealand, 1965–68; Australian Ambassador to Thailand, 1968–69; Australian High Comr to Canada, 1969–73; Dep. High Comr for Australia in London, 1973–75; Ambassador to S Africa, and High Comr to Botswana, Lesotho and Swaziland, 1975–77. *Recreations:* golf, gardening. *Address:* 18 Fishburn Street, Red Hill, ACT 2603, Australia. *Clubs:* Naval and Military (Melbourne); Royal Canberra Golf.

McNICOL, Prof. Donald; Vice-Chancellor and Principal, University of Sydney, since 1990; *b* 18 April 1939; *s* of Ian Robertson McNicol and Sadie Isabelle Williams; *m* 1963, Kathleen Margaret Wells; one *s* two *d*. *Educ:* Unley High Sch.; Univ. of Adelaide (BA 1964); St John's Coll., Cambridge (PhD 1967). Fellow, Aust. Psych. Soc. Lectr in Psychology, Univ. of Adelaide, 1967–71; Research Fellow, St John's Coll., Cambridge, 1968–69; Sen. Lectr in Psych., Univ. of NSW, 1971–74; Associate Prof. in Psych., Univ. of NSW, 1975–81; Prof. of Psych., Univ. of Tasmania, 1981–86, now Emeritus Prof.; Comr for Univs and Chm., Univs Adv. Council, Commonwealth Tertiary Educn, 1986–88; Vice-Chancellor, Univ. of New England, NSW, 1988–90. Pres., AVCC, 1994–95. FRSA. *Publication:* A Primer of Signal Detection Theory, 1972. *Recreations:* walking, jazz, reading. *Address:* University of Sydney, NSW 2006, Australia. *T:* (2) 6923058.

McNICOL, Prof. George Paul, CBE 1992; FRSE 1984; Principal and Vice-Chancellor, University of Aberdeen, 1981–91; *b* 24 Sept. 1929; *s* of Martin and Elizabeth McNicol; *m* 1959, Susan Ritchie; one *s* two *d*. *Educ:* Hillhead High Sch., Glasgow; Univ. of Glasgow. MD, PhD, FRCP, FRCPG, FRCPE, FRCPath. House Surg., Western Infirmary, Glasgow, 1952; House Phys., Stobhill Gen. Hosp., Glasgow, 1953; Regimental MO, RAMC, 1953–55; Asst, Dept Materia Medica and Therapeutics, Registrar, Univ. Med. Unit, Stobhill Gen. Hosp., 1955–57; Univ. Dept of Medicine, Royal Infirmary, Glasgow: Registrar, 1957–59; Hon. Sen. Registrar, 1961–65; Lectr in Medicine, 1963–65; Hon. Cons. Phys., 1966–71; Sen. Lectr in Medicine, 1966–70; Reader in Medicine, 1970–71; Prof. of Medicine and Hon. Cons. Phys., Leeds Gen. Infirmary, 1971–81; Chm., Bd of Faculty of Medicine, Leeds Univ., 1978–81. Harkness Fellow, Commonwealth Fund, Dept of Internal Medicine, Washington Univ., 1959–61; Hon. Clinical Lectr and Hon. Cons. Phys., Makerere UC Med. Sch. Extension, Kenyatta Nat. Hosp., Nairobi (on secondment from Glasgow Univ.), 1965–66. Chm. Med. Adv. Cttee, Cttee of Vice-Chancellors and Principals, 1985–90; Member: British Council Cttee on Internat. Co-op. in Higher Educn, 1985–91; Council, ACU, 1988–91; Former Mem., Adv. Council on Misuse of Drugs. Chm., Part I Examining Bd, Royal Colls of Physicians (UK). Vice-Chm., Raigmore Hosp. NHS Trust, 1993–95. Chm., Bd of Governors, Rowett Res. Inst., 1981–89; Mem., Bd of Governors, N of Scotland Coll. of Agriculture, 1981–91. Mem., Exec. Cttee, Scottish Council (Develt and Industry), 1989–91. Mem. Aberdeen Local Bd, Bank of Scotland, 1983–92. FRSA 1985. Hon. FACP. Foreign Corresp. Mem., Belgian Royal Acad. of Medicine, 1985. Hon. DSc Wabash Coll., Indiana, 1989; Hon. LLD Aberdeen, 1992. *Publications:* papers in sci. and med. jls on thrombosis and bleeding disorders. *Recreations:* sailing, skiing. *Address:* Chanonry Green, Kincurdie Drive, Rosemarkie, Ross-shire IV10 8SJ. *T:* Fortrose (01381) 621211.

See also A. H. Smallwood.

McNISH, Althea Marjorie, (Althea McNish Weiss), CMT 1976; freelance textile designer, since 1957; *b* Trinidad; *d* of late J. Claude McNish, educnl reformer, and late Margaret (*née* Bourne); *m* 1969, John Weiss. *Educ:* Port-of-Spain, by her father and others; London Coll. of Printing; Central School of Art and Crafts; Royal Coll. of Art. NDD, DesRCA; FCSD (FSIA 1968, MSIA 1960). Painted throughout childhood; after design educn in London, freelance practice in textile and other design; commns from Ascher and Liberty's, 1957; new techniques for laminate murals, for SS Oriana and hosp. and coll. in Trinidad; Govt of Trinidad and Tobago travelling schol., 1962; interior design (for Govt of Trinidad and Tobago) in NY, Washington and London, 1962; Cotton Bd trav. schol. to report on export potential for British printed cotton goods in Europe, 1963; collection of dress fabric designs for ICI and Tootal Thomson for promotion of Terylene Toile, 1966; special features for Daily Mail Ideal Home Exhibn, 1966–78; (with John Weiss) etched silver dishes, 1973–; interior design for Sec.-Gen. of Commonwealth, 1975; bedlinen collection for Courtaulds, 1978; (with John Weiss) textile design develt for BRB, 1978–81; textile hangings for BRB Euston offices, 1979; banners for Design Centre, 1981; (with John Weiss) improvements to London office of High Comr for Trinidad and Tobago, 1981; advr on exhibn design for Govt of Trinidad and Tobago, Commonwealth Inst., 1982–84; fashion textile designs for Yugoslav textile printers, 1985–; furnishing textile designs for Fede Cheti, Milan, 1986–; murals and hangings for Royal Caribbean Cruise Line: MS Nordic Empress, 1990; MS Monarch of the Seas, 1991. Paintings and various work in exhibitions include: individual and gp exhibns, London, 1954–; paintings, Jamaica, 1975; hangings, Kilkenny, 1981; hangings, individual exhibn, Peoples Gall., 1982; hangings, Magazine Workspace, Leicester, 1983; textile designs in exhibitions: Inprint, Manchester and London, 1964–71; Design Council/BoT, USA and Sweden, 1969, London, 1970, London and USA, 1972; Design-In, Amsterdam, 1972–74; Design Council, 1975–80; The Way We Live Now, V&A Mus., 1978; Indigo, Lille, 1981–82; Commonwealth Fest. Art Exhibn, Brisbane, 1982; Designs for British Dress and Furnishing Fabrics, V&A Mus., 1986; Make or Break, Henry Moore Gall., 1986; Surtex, New York, 1987; Ascher, V&A Mus., 1987; work represented in permanent collection of V&A Mus. Research tours: Czechoslovakia, 1968; Yugoslavia, 1972; Tunisia, 1974; Caribbean and N America, 1976; Yugoslavia, 1985–. Vis. Lecturer: Central Sch. of Art and Crafts and other colls and polytechnics, 1960–; USA, 1972; Italy, W Germany and Yugoslavia, 1985–; Advisory Tutor in Furnishing and Surface Design, London Coll. of Furniture, 1972–90. External assessor for educnl and professional bodies, incl. CSD and NCDAD/CNAA, 1966–; Mem. jury for Leverhulme schols, 1968; Judge: Portuguese textile design comp., Lisbon, 1973; 'Living' Design Awards, 1974; Carnival selection panels, Arts Council, 1982 and 1983. Vice-Pres., SIAD, 1977–78; Design Council: Mem., selection panels for Design Awards and Design Index, 1968–80; Mem. Bd, 1974–81; Mem., Jubilee Souvenir Selection Panel, 1976; Mem., Royal Wedding Souvenir Selection Panel, 1981. Member: Fashion and Textiles Design Bd, CNAA, 1975–78; London Local Adv. Cttee, IBA, 1981–; Formation Cttee, London Inst., ILEA, 1985. Mem. Governing Body, Portsmouth Coll. of Art, 1972–81. *BBC-TV:* studio setting for Caribbean edn of Full House, 1973. Has appeared, with work, in films for COI and Gas Council. Chaconia Medal (Gold) (Trinidad and Tobago), 1976, for service to art and design. *Publications:* textile designs produced in many countries, 1957–; designs illustrated in: V. D. Mendes and F. M. Hinchcliffe, Ascher, 1987; Did Britain Make It?, ed P. Sparke, 1986; M. Schoeser, Fabrics and Wallpapers, 1986; published in Decorative Art, Designers in Britain and design jls. *Recreations:* ski-ing, travelling, music, gardening. *Address:* 142 West Green Road, N15 5AD. *T:* 0181–800 1686. *Club:* Soroptimist.

McNULTY, (Robert William) Roy, CBE 1992; Managing Director, and Chief Executive, Short Brothers PLC, since 1988; *b* 7 Nov. 1937; *s* of Jack and Nancy McNulty; *m* 1963, Ismay Ratcliffe Rome; one *s* two *d*. *Educ:* Portora Royal School, Enniskillen; Trinity College, Dublin (BA, BComm). Audit Manager, Peat Marwick Mitchell & Co., Glasgow, 1963–66; Accounting Methods Manager, Chrysler UK, Linwood, 1966–68; Harland & Wolff, Belfast: Management Accountant, 1968–72; Computer Services Manager, 1972–74; Management Services Manager, 1975–76; Sen. Management Consultant, Peat Marwick Mitchell & Co., Belfast, 1977–78; Short Brothers: Exec. Dir, Finance and Admin, 1978–85; Dep. Managing Dir, 1986–88. Mem., Council, SBAC, 1988. Mem., Regional Council, CBI, 1987; Council Mem., Co-operation North, 1989. Associate Fellow, Dept of Engineering, Univ. of Warwick. FRAeS 1993; CIMgt. *Recreations:* jogging, golf, reading. *Address:* Short Brothers PLC, Airport Road, Belfast BT3 9DZ.

MACOUN, Michael John, CMG 1964; OBE 1961; QPM 1954; Overseas Police Adviser, and Inspector-General of Police, Dependent Territories, Foreign and Commonwealth Office, 1967–79, retired; Police Training Adviser, Ministry of Overseas Development, 1967–79; *b* 27 Nov. 1914; *o s* of late John Horatio Macoun, Comr of Chinese Maritime Customs; *m* 1940, Geraldine Mabel, *o d* of late Brig.-Gen. G. C. Sladen, CB, CMG, DSO, MC; two *s*. *Educ:* Stowe Sch., Buckingham; Univ. of Oxford (MA); Munich Univ. (Diploma in German Language and Literature). At Metropolitan Police Coll., 1938; Tanganyika Police, 1939–42, 1945–58; War Service, 1943–44; Inspector-Gen. of Police, Uganda, 1959–64; Directing Staff, Police Coll., Bramshill, 1965; Commonwealth Office, 1966. Lecture tour: of USA, under auspices of British Information Services, 1964; of Eastern Canada, for Assoc. of Canadian Clubs, 1966; Vis. Lectr, Police Coll., Bramshill, 1980–86. Rep. of Sec. of State, Police Appointments Bd, Hong Kong Govt, 1980–86. Non-exec. Dir, Control Risks Gp, 1983–86. Colonial Police Medal, 1951; OStJ 1959. *Recreations:* travel, walking. *Address:* Furzedown, Rowledge, near Farnham, Surrey GU10 4EB. *T:* Frensham (0125125) 3196. *Clubs:* Commonwealth Trust; County (Guildford).

McPARTLIN, Noel; Advocate, since 1976; Sheriff of Grampian, Highland and Islands at Elgin, since 1985; *b* 25 Dec. 1939; *s* of Michael Joseph McPartlin and Ann Dunn or McPartlin; *m* 1965, June Anderson Whitehead; three *s* three *d*. *Educ:* Galashiels Acad.; Edinburgh Univ. (MA, LLB). Solicitor in Glasgow, Linlithgow and Stirling, 1964–76. Sheriff of Grampian, Highland and Islands at Peterhead and Banff, 1983–85. *Recreation:* country life. *Club:* Elgin.

MacPHAIL, Sir Bruce (Dugald), Kt 1992; FCA; Managing Director, Peninsular and Oriental Steam Navigation Co., since 1985; *b* 1 May 1939; *s* of late Dugald Ronald MacPhail and Winifred Marjorie MacPhail; *m* 1st, 1963, Susan Mary Gregory (*d* 1975); three *s*; 2nd, 1983, Caroline Ruth Grimston Curtis-Bennett (*née* Hubbard). *Educ:* Haileybury Coll.; Balliol Coll., Oxford (MA); Harvard Business Sch., Mass, USA (MBA 1967). FCA 1976. Articled, Price Waterhouse, 1961–65; Hill Samuel & Co. Ltd, 1967–69; Finance Director: Sterling Guarantee Trust Ltd, 1969–74; Town & City Properties Ltd, 1974–76; Man. Dir, Sterling Guarantee Trust, 1976–85. Gov., Royal Ballet Sch., 1982–; Life Gov. and Mem. Council, Haileybury Coll., 1992–; Chm. Council, Templeton Coll., Oxford, 1993– (Mem., 1987–). *Recreations:* reading, wine, scuba diving. *Address:* Thorpe Lubenham Hall, Lubenham, Market Harborough, Leics LE16 9TR.

MACPHAIL, Iain Duncan; QC (Scot.) 1989; Sheriff of Lothian and Borders, since 1995; *b* 24 Jan. 1938; *o s* of late Malcolm John Macphail and Mary Corbett Duncan; *m* 1970, Rosslyn Graham Lillias, *o d* of E. J. C. Hewitt, MD, TD, Edinburgh; one *s* one *d*. *Educ:* George Watson's Coll.; Edinburgh and Glasgow Univs. MA Hons History Edinburgh 1959, LLB Glasgow 1962. Admitted to Faculty of Advocates, 1963; in practice at Scottish Bar, 1963–73; Faulds Fellow in Law, Glasgow Univ., 1963–65; Lectr in Evidence and Procedure, Strathclyde Univ., 1968–69 and Edinburgh Univ., 1969–72; Standing Jun. Counsel to Scottish Home and Health Dept and to Dept of Health and Social Security, 1971–73; Extra Advocate-Depute, 1973; Sheriff: of Lanarks, later Glasgow and Strathkelvin, 1973–81; of Tayside, Central and Fife, 1981–82; of Lothian and Borders, 1982–89; Mem., Scottish Law Commn, 1990–94. Chm., Scottish Assoc. for Study of Delinquency, 1978–81. Hon. LLD Edinburgh, 1992. *Publications:* Law of Evidence in Scotland (Scottish Law Commn), 1979; Evidence, 1987; Sheriff Court Practice, 1988; articles and reviews in legal jls. *Address:* Sheriff Court House, 27 Chambers Street, Edinburgh EH1 1LB. *T:* 0131–225 2525. *Club:* New (Edinburgh).

MACPHERSON, family name of **Barons Macpherson of Drumochter** and **Strathcarron.**

MACPHERSON OF DRUMOCHTER, 2nd Baron, *cr* 1951; **(James) Gordon Macpherson;** Chairman and Managing Director of Macpherson, Train & Co. Ltd, and Subsidiary and Associated Companies, since 1964; Chairman, A. J. Macpherson & Co. Ltd (Bankers), since 1973; founder Chairman, Castle Dairies (Caerphilly) Ltd; *b* 22 Jan. 1924; *s* of 1st Baron (*d* 1965) and Lucy Lady Macpherson of Drumochter (*d* 1984); *S* father, 1965; *m* 1st, 1947, Dorothy Ruth Coulter (*d* 1974); two *d* (one *s* decd); 2nd, 1975, Catherine, *d* of Dr C. D. MacCarthy; one *s* two *d. Educ:* Loretto; Wells House, Malvern. Served War of 1939–45, with RAF; 1939–45 Campaign medal, Burma Star, Pacific Star, Defence Medal, Victory Medal. Founder Chm. and Patron, British Importers Confedn, 1968–72. Member: Council, London Chamber of Commerce, 1958–73; (Gen. Purposes Cttee, 1959–72); East European Trade Council, 1969–71; PLA, 1973–76; Exec. Cttee, W India Cttee, 1959–83 (Dep. Chm. and Treasurer, 1971, Chm. 1973–75). Freeman of City of London, 1969; Mem., Butchers' Co., 1969–. Governor, Brentwood Sch. JP Essex, 1961–76; Dep. Chm., Brentwood Bench, 1972–76; Mem. Essex Magistrates Court Cttee, 1974–76. Hon. Game Warden for Sudan, 1974; Chief of Scottish Clans Assoc. of London, 1972–74; Member: Macpherson Clan Assoc. (Chm., 1963–64); Sen. Golfers' Soc., 1981–91. Founder Mem., WWF, 1961. FRSA 1971; FRES 1940; FZS 1965. *Recreations:* shooting, fishing, golf. *Heir: s* Hon. James Anthony Macpherson, *b* 27 Feb. 1979. *Address:* Kyllachy, Tomatin, Inverness-shire IV13 7YA. *T:* Tomatin (01808) 511212. *Clubs:* Boodle's, East India, Devonshire, Sports and Public Schools, Shikar; House of Lords Yacht; Royal and Ancient (St Andrews); Thorndon Park Golf (capt. 1962–63); Hartswood Golf (Founder Pres., 1970–74).

MACPHERSON, Sheriff Alexander Calderwood; a Sheriff of South Strathclyde, Dumfries and Galloway, at Hamilton, since 1978; *b* 14 June 1939; *s* of Alexander and Jean Macpherson; *m* 1963, Christine Isobel Hutchison (marr. diss. 1985); two *s. Educ:* Glasgow Academy; Glasgow Univ. (MA 1959, LLB 1962). Qualified as solicitor, 1962; private practice, 1962–78; part-time Assistantship in Private Law at Glasgow Univ., 1962–69; Partner in West, Anderson & Co., Solicitors, Glasgow, 1968–78; Lectr in Evidence and Procedure at Strathclyde Univ., 1969–78. Chairman, Glasgow North and East Br., Multiple Sclerosis Soc., 1973–88. *Recreations:* piping (especially Piobaireachd), psychotherapy, reading. *Address:* Sheriff Court, Hamilton, Lanarks ML3 6AA. *Clubs:* Glasgow Highland, Glasgow Art, Royal Scottish Automobile (Glasgow); Royal Scottish Pipers' Society (Edinburgh).

McPHERSON, Prof. Andrew Francis, FBA 1993; Professor of Sociology, since 1989, and Co-Director, Centre for Educational Sociology, since 1972, University of Edinburgh; *b* 6 July 1942; *m* 1st, 1965, Eldwyth Mary Boyle; one *s* one *d*; 2nd, 1989, Alison Jean Elphinstone Edward or Arnott. *Educ:* Ripon Grammar Sch.; The Queen's Coll., Oxford (BA Hist.). DPSA; FEIS; FSCRE; FRSE. Lectr in Sociology, Univ. of Glasgow, 1965; University of Edinburgh: Res. Fellow in Education, 1968; Lectr in Sociology, 1973; Sen. Lectr, 1978; Reader, 1983. *Publications:* (with G. Neave) The Scottish Sixth, 1976; (with L. Gow) Tell Them from Me, 1980; (jtly) Reconstructions of Secondary Education, 1983; (with C. Raab) Governing Education, 1988; academic articles on history and sociology of education. *Recreations:* family, music, sport. *Address:* Centre for Educational Sociology, University of Edinburgh, 7 Buccleuch Place, Edinburgh EH8 9LW.

MACPHERSON, Ewen Cameron Stewart; Chief Executive, 3i Group plc, since 1992 (Director, since 1989); *b* 19 Jan. 1942; *s* of G. P. S. Macpherson and Elizabeth Margaret Cameron (*née* Small); *m* 1982, Hon. Laura Anne Baring, *d* of 5th Baron Northbrook; two *s. Educ:* Fettes Coll., Edinburgh; Queens' Coll., Cambridge (MA); London Business Sch. (MSc). Rep., Massey-Ferguson (Export) Ltd, 1964–68; various appointments, ICFC, 1970–82; 3i Group plc and subsidiaries: Dir, City Office, 1982–90; Mem., Exec. Cttee, 1985–; Man. Dir, Finance & Planning, 1990–92. Governor, NIESR, 1993–. *Recreations:* gardening, sailing. *Address:* (office) 91 Waterloo Road, SE1 8XP. *T:* 0171–928 3131. *Clubs:* Caledonian, City of London; Royal Lymington Yacht.

McPHERSON, James Alexander Strachan, CBE 1982; JP; FSA (Scot.); Lord-Lieutenant of Grampian Region (Banffshire), since 1987; Solicitor, since 1954; *b* 20 Nov. 1927; *s* of Peter John McPherson and Jean Geddie Strachan; *m* 1960, Helen Marjorie Perks, MA; one *s* one *d. Educ:* Banff Academy; Aberdeen Univ. MA, BL, LLB. National Service, 1952–54; commissioned RA. Solicitor; Partner, Alexander George & Co., Macduff, 1954–95 (Senior Partner, 1986–95; Consultant, 1995–). Macduff Town Council: Mem., 1958–75; Treasurer, 1965–72; (last) Provost, 1972–75; Banff County Council: Mem., 1958–75; Chm., Educn Cttee, 1967–70; Chm., Management and Finance Cttee, 1970–75; (last) Convener, County Council, 1970–75; Mem., Assoc. of County Councils for Scotland, 1965–75; Mem., Grampian Regional Council, 1974–90 (Chm., Public Protection Cttee, 1974–86). Mem., Scottish Solicitors Discipline Tribunal, 1990–; former mem., numerous Scottish Cttees and Boards. Mem. Court, Aberdeen Univ., 1993–. Chm., Banff and Buchan JP Adv. Cttee, 1987–; Hon. Sheriff of Banffshire, 1972–. JP Banff and Buchan, 1974. *Recreations:* sailing, swimming and reading. *Address:* Dun Alastair, Macduff, Banffshire AB44 1XD. *T:* (home) Macduff (01261) 832377; (office) Macduff (01261) 832201. *Clubs:* Banff Town and County; Duff House Royal Golf.

M'PHERSON, Prof. Philip Keith, CEng, FIEE; Managing Director, MacPherson Systems Ltd, since 1984; Visiting Professor: City University, since 1987; Royal College of Military Science, since 1990; *b* 10 March 1927; *s* of Ven. Kenneth M'Pherson and Dulce M'Pherson; *m* 1975, Rosalie Margaret, *d* of Richard and Mary Fowler. *Educ:* Marlborough Coll.; Royal Naval Engineering Coll.; Royal Naval Coll., Greenwich; Massachusetts Inst. of Technology (SM); MA Oxon. Engineer Officer, Royal Navy, 1948–59; research in Admiralty Gunnery Estabt, 1955–59, retired as Lt-Comdr, 1959. Head, Dynamics Gp, Atomic Energy Estabt, UKAEA, 1959–65, SPSO, 1963; Fellow of St John's Coll., Oxford, 1965–67; Prof. of Systems Sci., later Systems Engrg and Management, 1967–87, and Pro-Vice-Chancellor, 1982–87, City Univ. Vis. Scholar, Internat. Inst. of Applied Systems Analysis, Austria, 1976–77; Adjunct Prof., Xian Jiaotong Univ., China, 1980–84. Member: Executive Cttee, UK Automation Council, 1964–68; SRC Control Engrg Cttee, 1970–75; Chairman: IMechE Automatic Control Gp, 1967–69; IEE Systems Engrg Gp Cttee, 1966–69; IEE Control and Automation Div., 1967–69; IEE Systems Engrg Cttee, 1984–90; Soc. for General Systems Research (UK), 1973–76. Archbishops' Commn on Rural Areas, 1988–89. Freeman, City of London, 1985; Liveryman, Engineers' Co., 1986. *Publications:* many papers in the scientific literature. *Recreations:* walking, singing, making things. *Address:* The Wash, Dam Green, Kenninghall, Norfolk. *Club:* City Livery.

MACPHERSON, Roderick Ewen; Fellow, King's College, Cambridge, since 1942; Registrary, University of Cambridge, 1969–83; *b* 17 July 1916; *s* of Ewen Macpherson, Chief Charity Commissioner, and Dorothy Mildred Hensley; *m* 1941, Sheila Joan Hooper, *d* of H. P. Hooper; two *s* two *d. Educ:* Eton College; King's College, Cambridge. Math. Tripos, Part II, Wrangler; Math. Tripos, Part III, Distinction; Smith's Prizeman, 1940. Served RAFVR, 1940–46, Navigator (Radio). Fellow, King's Coll., Cambridge, 1942–; Third Bursar, King's College, 1947–50, Second Bursar, 1950–51, First Bursar, 1951–62; University Treasurer, Univ. of Cambridge, 1962–69; Member: Council of the Senate, 1957–62; Financial Board, 1955–62. Cambridge City Council, 1958–74, Hon. Councillor, 1974–. *Recreations:* gardening, hill-walking. *Address:* Orion, Coton Road, Grantchester, Cambridge CB3 9NX. *T:* Cambridge (01223) 840266.

MACPHERSON, Sir (Ronald) Thomas (Stewart), (Tommy), Kt 1992; CBE (mil.) 1968; MC 1943, Bars 1944 and 1945; TD 1960; DL; Chairman: Boustead plc, since 1986; Allstate Reinsurance Ltd, since 1983; Keller Group plc, since 1991; *b* 4 Oct. 1920; 5th *s* of late Sir Thomas Stewart Macpherson, CIE, LLD, and Lady (Helen) Macpherson, (*née* Cameron); *m* 1953, Jean Henrietta, *d* of late David Butler Wilson; two *s* one *d. Educ:* Edinburgh Acad.; Cargilfield; Fettes Coll. (scholar); Trinity Coll., Oxford (1st open classical scholar; MA 1st Cl. Hons PPE). Athletics Blue and Scottish International; British Team World Student Games, Paris, 1947; represented Oxford in Rugby football and hockey, 1946–47. Reader Middle Temple. 2nd Lieut. Queen's Own Cameron Highlanders TA, 1939; Scottish Commando, 1940; POW, 1941–43, escaped 1943; Major 1943; served Special Forces with French and Italian Resistance, 1944–45. Consultant, Italo-Yugoslav Border Commn, 1946. Comd 1st Bn London Scottish TA, 1961–64; Col TA London Dist, 1964–67. Mem., Queen's Body Guard for Scotland (Royal Co. of Archers). Chm., 1961–79, Pres., 1979–, Achilles Club; Vice-Pres., Newtonmore Camanachd Club. Chairman: Mallinson-Denny Gp, 1981–82 (Man. Dir, 1967–81); Allstate Insurance Co., 1983–87; Birmid Qualcast, 1984–88; Cosmopolitan Textile Co., 1984–91; Employment Conditions Abroad Ltd, 1984–93; Webb-Bowen Internat. Ltd, 1984–94; SNTC (France), 1985–; Owl Creek Investments plc, 1989–91; Exec. Dir, Brooke Bond Gp plc, 1981–82; Director: Transglobe Expedition Ltd, 1978–83; Scottish Mutual Assurance Soc., 1982–91; C. H. Industrials PLC, 1983–91; NCB, 1983–86; TSB Scotland, 1986–91; Independent Insurance plc, 1987–93; Fitzwilton (UK) plc, 1990–; Soc. Générale Merchant Bank, 1991–93; UK Consultant, Sears Roebuck & Co., Chicago, 1984–; Consultant: Bain & Co. (USA), 1987–; Candover Investment plc, 1989–. Founder Chairman: Nat. Employment Liaison Cttee for TA and Reserves, 1986–9294; ABCC, 1986–88; Pres., Eurochambres (Assoc. of European Chambers of Commerce), 1992–94; Vice-Pres., London Chamber of Commerce, 1985– (Chm., Council, 1980–82). Member: Council, CBI (Chm., London and SE Reg., CBI, 1975–77); Scottish Council, London; Prices and Incomes Bd, 1968–69; Council, GBA, 1979–83; Council, Strathclyde Univ. Business Sch., 1982–86. Governor, Fettes Coll., 1982–92. Prime Warden, Co. of Dyers, 1985–86. FRSA, FIMgt. DL 1977, High Sheriff, 1983–84, Greater London. Chevalier, Légion d'Honneur, and Croix de Guerre with 2 palms, France; Medaglia d'Argento and Resistance Medal, Italy; Kt of St Mary of Bethlehem. *Recreations:* shooting, outdoor sport, languages. *Address:* 27 Archery Close, W2 2BE. *T:* 0171–262 8487; Craig Dhu House, by Newtonmore, Inverness-shire PH20 1BS. *T:* Laggan (01528) 544200. *Clubs:* Hurlingham, MCC; New (Edinburgh).

MACPHERSON, Sir Thomas; *see* Macpherson, Sir R. T. S.

MACPHERSON OF CLUNY (and Blairgowrie), Hon. Sir William (Alan), Kt 1983; TD 1966; **Hon. Mr Justice Macpherson of Cluny;** Judge of the High Court of Justice, Queen's Bench Division, since 1983; Cluny Macpherson; 27th Chief of Clan Macpherson; *b* 1 April 1926; *s* of Brig. Alan David Macpherson, DSO, MC, RA (*d* 1969) and late Catharine Richardson Macpherson; *m* 1962, Sheila McDonald Brodie; two *s* one *d. Educ:* Wellington Coll., Berkshire; Trinity Coll., Oxford (MA; Hon. Fellow, 1991). Called to Bar, Inner Temple, 1952; Bencher, 1978; QC 1971; a Recorder of the Crown Court, 1972–83; Presiding Judge, Northern Circuit, 1985–88; Pres., Interception of Communications Tribunal, 1990–. Mem., Bar Council and Senate, 1981–83; Hon. Mem., Northern Circuit, 1987. Served, 1944–47, in Scots Guards (Capt.). Commanded (Lt-Col) 21st Special Air Service Regt (TA), 1962–65, Hon. Col, 1983–91; Mem., Queen's Body Guard for Scotland, Royal Co. of Archers, 1977–, Brigadier 1989. Gov., Royal Scottish Corporation, 1972– (Vice-Pres., 1989–). *Recreations:* golf, fishing; Past Pres., London Scottish FC. *Heir: s* Alan Thomas Macpherson yr of Cluny and Blairgowrie. *Address:* Newton Castle, Blairgowrie, Perthshire PH10 6SU; Royal Courts of Justice, Strand, WC2A 2LL. *Clubs:* Caledonian, Highland Society of London (Pres., 1991–94), Special Forces; Blairgowrie Golf; Denham Golf.

MACPHIE, Maj.-Gen. Duncan Love; Executive Director, St John Ambulance, since 1994 (Medical Director, 1993–94); *b* 15 Dec. 1930; *s* of Donald Macphie and Elizabeth Adam (*née* Gibson); *m* 1957, Isobel Mary Jenkins; one *s* two *d. Educ:* Hutchesons' Grammar Sch.; Glasgow Univ. MB ChB. Stonehouse and Hairmyres Hosps, 1957–58; commnd RAMC, 1958; RMO, 1st Bn The Royal Scots, 1958–61; GP, Glasgow, 1961–63; RMO, 3 RHA, 1963–67; CO, BMH Dharan, Nepal, 1970–72; CO, 24 Field Ambulance, 1972–75; CO, BMH Munster, 1976–78; ADMS, 4 Armd Div., 1978–80; Asst DGAMS, MoD, 1980–83; CO, Queen Elizabeth Mil. Hosp., Woolwich, 1983–85; Chief, Med. Plans Branch, SHAPE, 1985–87; Comdr Med., BAOR, 1987–90, retd. QHS 1985–90. OStJ. *Recreations:* gardening, Rugby, cricket, classical music, reading.

McQUAID, James, PhD; FEng, FIMinE; Director, Strategy and General Division, and Chief Scientist, Health and Safety Executive, since 1992; *b* 5 Nov. 1939; *s* of late James and Brigid McQuaid; *m* 1968, Catherine Anne, *d* of late Dr James John Hargan and of Dr Mary Helen Hargan; two *s* one *d. Educ:* Christian Brothers' Sch., Dundalk; University Coll., Dublin (BEng); Jesus Coll., Cambridge (PhD); DSc NUI 1978. MIMechE 1972; FIMinE 1986; FEng 1991. Graduate engrg apprentice, British Nylon Spinners, 1961–63; Sen. Res. Fellow 1966–68, Sen. Scientific Officer 1968–72, PSO 1972–78, Safety in Mines Res. Estabt; seconded as Safety Advr, Petrochemicals Div., ICI, 1976–77; Dep. Dir, Safety Engrg Lab., 1978–80, Dir, 1980–85; Res. Dir, HSE, 1985–92. Chm., Electrical Equipment Certification Management Bd, 1985–92; Member: Safety in Mines Res. Adv. Bd, 1985–92; Council, Midland Inst. of Mining Engrs, 1987– (Vice-Pres., 1991–93, Pres., 1993–94); Council, IMinE, 1991–; Adv. Bd for Mech. Engrg, Univ. of Liverpool, 1987–92; Court, 1985–, Council, 1993–, Univ. of Sheffield; Exec. Cttee, RoSPA, 1992–94. Pres., Sheffield Trades Hist. Soc., 1989–91. Mem., Council, S Yorks Trades Hist. Trust, 1989–. *Publications:* numerous papers in technical jls. *Recreations:* ornamental turning, model engineering, industrial archaeology. *Address:* 61 Pingle Road, Sheffield S7 2LL. *T:* Sheffield (0114) 236 5349. *Club:* Athenæum.

McQUAIL, Paul Christopher; Visiting Professor, Bartlett School of Architecture, University College London, since 1992; Consultant, Market Access International, since 1994; *b* 22 April 1934; *s* of Christopher McQuail and Anne (*née* Mullan); *m* 1964, Susan Adler; one *s* one *d. Educ:* St Anselm's, Birkenhead; Sidney Sussex Coll., Cambridge. Min. of Housing and Local Govt, 1957; Principal, 1962; Asst Sec., 1969; DoE, 1970; Special Asst to Permanent Sec. and Sec. of State, 1972–73; Sec., Royal Commn on the Press, 1974–77; Under Sec., DoE, 1977–88; Chief Exec., Hounslow Bor. Council, 1983–85 (on secondment); Dep. Sec., DoE, 1988–94. Member: Environment and Planning Cttee, ESRC, 1983–87; Policy Cttee, CPRE, 1995–; Chairman: Nat. Urban Forestry Unit, 1995–; Nat. Retail Planning Forum, 1995–. *Recreations:* alpinism, books and other harmless pleasures. *Address:* 158 Peckham Rye, SE22 9QH.

MACQUAKER, Donald Francis, CBE 1991; solicitor; Partner, T. C. Young & Son, Glasgow, 1957–93, Consultant, since 1993; *b* 21 Sept. 1932; *s* of Thomas Mason

Macquaker, MC, MA, BL and Caroline Bertha Floris Macquaker; *m* 1964, Susan Elizabeth, *d* of Mr and Mrs W. A. K. Finlayson, High Coodham, Symington, Ayrshire; one *s* one *d*. *Educ:* Winchester Coll.; Trinity Coll., Oxford (MA); Univ. of Glasgow (LLB). Admitted Solicitor, 1957. Mem. Bd of Management, Glasgow Royal Maternity Hosp. and associated hosps, 1965–74 (Vice-Chm., 1972–74); Greater Glasgow Health Board: Mem., 1973–87; Chm., 1983–87; Convener, F and GP Cttee, 1974–83; Chm., Common Services Agency for Scottish Health Service, 1987–91. Dir, Lithgows Ltd, 1987–. Dir, Prince and Princess of Wales Hospice, Glasgow, 1991–94. *Recreations:* shooting, fishing, travelling, gardening. *Address:* Blackbyres, by Ayr KA7 4TS. *T:* Alloway (01292) 441088. *Clubs:* The Western (Glasgow); Leander (Henley-on-Thames).

McQUARRIE, Sir Albert, Kt 1987; Chairman: A. McQuarrie & Son (Great Britain) Ltd, 1946–88; Sir Albert McQuarrie & Associates Ltd, since 1988; Haverstock Homes (formerly Haverstock) plc, since 1990; *b* 1 Jan. 1918; *s* of Algernon Stewart McQuarrie and Alice Maud Sharman; *m* 1st, 1945, Roseleen McCaffery (*d* 1986); one *s*; 2nd, 1989, Rhoda Annie Gall. *Educ:* Highlanders Acad., Greenock; Greenock High Sch.; Royal Coll. of Science and Technology, Univ. of Strathclyde. MSE, PEng 1945. Served in HM Forces, 1939–45 (Officer in RE). Director: Hunterston Develt Co., 1989–; British American Corp., 1991–; Prooftask Ltd, 1993–; Consultant: Bredero Projects Ltd, 1975–; Celtic PLC, 1994. Former Dean of Guild, Gourock Town Council; Chm., Fyvie/Rothienorman/Monquhitter Community Council, 1975–79. Contested (C): Kilmarnock, 1966; Caithness and Sutherland, Oct. 1974; Banff and Buchan, 1987; Highlands and Islands, European Parly elecn, 1989. MP (C): Aberdeenshire E, 1979–83; Banff and Buchan, 1983–87. Chm., British/Gibraltar All Party Gp, 1979–87; Vice Chm., Conservative Fisheries Sub Cttee, 1979–87; Secretary: Scotch Whisky All Party Gp, 1979–87; Scottish Cons. Backbench Cttee, 1985–87; Member: Select Cttees on Scottish Affairs, 1979–83, on Agriculture, 1983–85, on Private Bill Procedure, 1987; Speaker's Panel of Chairmen, 1986–87. Mem. Council, Soc. of Engineers, 1978–87. Dep. Chm., Ayr Cons. Assoc., 1992–; Hon. Pres., Banff and Buchan Cons. and Unionist Assoc., 1989–. Pres., Gourock Horticultural Soc., 1993– (Hon. Vice-Pres., 1954–93). FRSH 1952. Freeman, City of Gibraltar, 1982. KStJ 1991; KSJ 1995. Granted armorial bearings, 1991. *Recreations:* golf, bridge, music, soccer, swimming, horticulture. *Address:* Crimond, 11 Balcomie Crescent, Troon, Ayrshire KA10 7AR. *Clubs:* Lansdowne; Western (Ayr); Royal Scottish Automobile (Glasgow); Marine Highland (Troon).

MACQUARRIE, Rev. Prof. John, TD 1962; FBA 1984; Lady Margaret Professor of Divinity, University of Oxford, and Canon of Christ Church, 1970–86; *b* 27 June 1919; *s* of John Macquarrie and Robina Macquarrie (*née* McInnes); *m* 1949, Jenny Fallow (*née* Welsh); two *s* one *d*. *Educ:* Paisley Grammar Sch.; Univ. of Glasgow. MA 1940; BD 1943; PhD 1954; DLitt 1964; DD Oxon 1981. Royal Army Chaplains Dept, 1945–48; St Ninian's Church, Brechin, 1948–53; Lecturer, Univ. of Glasgow, 1953–62; Prof. of Systematic Theology, Union Theological Seminary, NY, 1962–70. Consultant, Lambeth Conf., 1968 and 1978. Hon. degrees: STD: Univ. of the South, USA, 1967; General Theological Seminary, NY, 1968; DD: Glasgow, 1969; Episcopal Seminary of SW, Austin, Texas, 1981; Virginia Theol Seminary, 1981; Dayton, 1994; DCnL, Nashotah House, Wisconsin, 1986. *Publications:* An Existentialist Theology, 1955; The Scope of Demythologising, 1960; Twentieth Century Religious Thought, 1963; Studies in Christian Existentialism, 1965; Principles of Christian Theology, 1966; God-Talk, 1967; God and Secularity, 1967; Martin Heidegger, 1968; Three Issues in Ethics, 1970; Existentialism, 1972; Paths in Spirituality, 1972; The Faith of the People of God, 1972; The Concept of Peace, 1973; Thinking about God, 1975; Christian Unity and Christian Diversity, 1975; The Humility of God, 1978; Christian Hope, 1978; In Search of Humanity, 1982; In Search of Deity (Gifford Lectures), 1984; Theology, Church and Ministry, 1986; Jesus Christ in Modern Thought, 1990 (HarperCollins Religious Book Prize, 1991); Mary for All Christians, 1991; Heidegger and Christianity, 1994; Invitation to Faith, 1995. *Address:* 206 Headley Way, Headington, Oxford OX3 7TA. *T:* Oxford (01865) 61889.

MacQUEEN, Prof. John; Professor of Scottish Literature and Oral Tradition, University of Edinburgh, 1972–88, now Professor Emeritus, and Hon. Fellow, Faculty of Arts, 1993; *b* 13 Feb. 1929; *s* of William L. and Grace P. MacQueen; *m* 1953, Winifred W. McWalter; three *s*. *Educ:* Hutchesons' Boys' Grammar Sch.; Glasgow Univ.; Cambridge Univ. MA English Lang. and Lit., Greek, Glasgow; BA, MA Archaeology and Anthropology, Section B, Cambridge. RAF, 1954–56 (Flying Officer). Asst Prof. of English, Washington Univ., Missouri, 1956–59; University of Edinburgh: Lectr in Medieval English and Scottish Literature, 1959–63; Masson Prof. of Medieval and Renaissance Literature, 1963–72; Dir, Sch. of Scottish Studies, 1969–88; Endowment Fellow, 1988–92. Barclay Acheson Vis. Prof. of Internat. Relations, Macalester Coll., Minnesota, 1967; Vis. Prof. in Medieval Studies, Australian Nat. Univ., 1971; Winegard Vis. Prof., Univ. of Guelph, Ont, 1981. Chairman: British Branch, Internat. Assoc. of Sound Archives, 1978–80; Exec. Cttee, Scottish Nat. Dictionary Assoc., 1978–87; Scottish Dictionary Jt Council, 1988–92; Pres., Scottish Text Soc., 1989–92; Mem., Scottish Film Council, 1981–92 (Chm., Archive Cttee, 1980–92). FRSE 1992. Hon. DLitt NUI, 1985. Fletcher of Saltoun Award, 1990. *Publications:* St Nynia, 1961, 2nd edn 1991; (with T. Scott) The Oxford Book of Scottish Verse, 1966; Robert Henryson, 1967; Ballattis of Luve, 1970; Allegory, 1970; (ed with Winifred MacQueen) A Choice of Scottish Verse, 1470–1570, 1972; Progress and Poetry, 1982; Numerology, 1985; The Rise of the Historical Novel, 1989; (ed with Winifred MacQueen) Scotichronicon, Bks III and IV, 1989, Bks I and II, 1993, Bk V, 1995; (ed) Humanism in Renaissance Scotland, 1990; articles and reviews in learned jls. *Recreations:* music, walking, archaeology. *Address:* Slewdonan, Damnaglaur, Drummore, Stranraer DG9 9QN. *T:* Drummore (01776) 840637. *Clubs:* University Staff, Scottish Arts (Edinburgh).

McQUIGGAN, John, MBE 1955; Executive Director, United Kingdom-South Africa Trade Association Ltd, 1978–86; retired at own request from HM Diplomatic Service, 1977; *b* 24 Nov. 1922; *s* of John and Sarah Elizabeth McQuiggan; *m* 1950, Doris Elsie Hadler; three *s* one *d*. *Educ:* St Edwards Coll., Liverpool. Served War, in RAF, 1942–47 (W Africa, Europe and Malta). Joined Dominions Office, 1940; Administration Officer, British High Commission, Canberra, Australia, 1950–54; Second Sec., Pakistan, Lahore and Dacca, 1954–57; First Sec. (Inf.), Lahore, 1957–58; Dep. Dir, UK Inf. Services, Australia (Canberra and Sydney), 1958–61; Dir, Brit. Inf. Services, Eastern Nigeria (Enugu), 1961–64; Dir, Brit. Inf. Services in Uganda, and concurrently First Sec., HM Embassy, Kigali, Rwanda, 1964–69; W African Dept, FCO, 1969–73; HM Consul, Chad, 1970–73 (London based); Dep. High Comr and Counsellor (Econ. and Commercial), Lusaka, Zambia, and sometime Actg High Comr, 1973–76. Dir-Gen., Brit. Industry Cttee on South Africa, 1986. Mem., Royal African Soc.; MIPR 1964; Mem., Internat. Public Relations Assoc., 1975. Fellow, Inst. of Dirs. *Publications:* pamphlets and contribs to trade and economic and technical woodworking jls. *Recreations:* tennis, carpentry, craftwork. *Address:* 7 Meadowcroft, Bickley, Kent BR1 2JD. *T:* 0181–467 0075. *Club:* Royal Over-Seas League.

McQUILLAN, William Rodger; HM Diplomatic Service, retired; *b* 18 March 1930; *s* of late Albert McQuillan and Isabella Glen McQuillan; *m* 1970, Sheriell May Fawcett; one *s* two *d*. *Educ:* Royal High Sch., Edinburgh; Edinburgh Univ.; Yale Univ. Served RAF, 1954–57. Asst Sec., Manchester Univ. Appointments Board, 1957–65; HM Diplomatic Service, 1965–83: First Sec., CRO, 1965; Lusaka, 1968, Head of Chancery, 1969; First Sec. (Commercial), Santiago, Chile, 1970; Counsellor and HM Consul, Guatemala City, 1974; Head of Inf. Policy Dept, FCO, 1978–81; Ambassador to Iceland, 1981–83. *Recreations:* walking the dog, writing verse, Scottish country dancing.

MacQUITTY, James Lloyd, OBE 1983; QC (NI) 1960; Chairman, Ulster Television Ltd, 1977–83; *b* 2 Nov. 1912; *s* of James MacQuitty and Henrietta Jane (*née* Little); *m* 1941, Irene Frances McDowell. *Educ:* Campbell Coll. and Methodist Coll., Belfast; St Catherine's Coll., Oxford (MA); Trinity Hall, Cambridge (MA, LLM). Vice-Pres., Cambridge Univ. Conservative Assoc., 1936. HG Instructor, 1940–43; HAA, 1943–44. Called to English Bar, 1938, to NI Bar, 1941. Chairman: Compensation Appeals Tribunal; Compensation Tribunal for Loss of Employment through Civil Unrest; Wages Councils in NI, 1951–89; Arbitrator under the Industrial Courts Act 1919, 1958–78; Mem., Industrial Injuries Adv. Council, 1960–86. Before reorganisation in 1973 of Local Govt in NI, was Chm. of former Jt Adv. Bds for Local Authorities' Services, Municipal Clerks, Rural Dist Clerks and County Chief Educn Officers and County Surveyors. Vice-Chm., Management Cttee, Glenlola Collegiate Sch., 1964–75; Chm., Trustees of Ulster Folk and Transport Museum, 1976–85 (Vice-Chm., 1969–76). Hon. LLD QUB, 1987. Freeman, City of London, 1967. Chevalier de l'Ordre de St Lazare, 1962. *Recreations:* swimming, sailing. *Address:* 10 Braemar Park, Bangor, Co. Down, Northern Ireland BT20 5HZ. *T:* Bangor (01247) 454420. *Clubs:* Carlton; Royal Ulster Yacht.

MacRAE, Sir (Alastair) Christopher (Donald Summerhayes), KCMG 1993 (CMG 1987); HM Diplomatic Service; High Commissioner to Pakistan, since 1994; *b* 3 May 1937; *s* of Dr Alexander Murray MacRae and Dr Grace Maria Lynton Summerhayes MacRae; *m* 1963, Mette Willert; two *d*. *Educ:* Rugby; Lincoln Coll., Oxford (BA Hons English); Harvard (Henry Fellow in Internat. Relations). RN, 1956–58. CRO, 1962; 3rd, later 2nd Sec., Dar es Salaam, 1963–65; ME Centre for Arab Studies, Lebanon, 1965–67; 2nd Sec., Beirut, 1967–68; FCO, 1968–70; 1st Sec. and Head of Chancery: Baghdad, 1970–71; Brussels, 1972–76; attached Directorate-Gen. VIII, European Commn, Brussels, on secondment from FCO, 1976–78; Ambassador to Gabon, 1978–80, and to Sao Tomé and Principé (non-resident), 1979–80; Head of W Africa Dept, FCO, 1980–83, and Ambassador (non-resident) to Chad, 1982–83; Political Counsellor and Head of Chancery, Paris, 1983–87; Minister and Head of British Interests Section, Tehran, 1987; Vis. Fellow, IISS, 1987–88; Support Services Scrutiny, FCO, 1988; Under Sec. (on secondment), Cabinet Office, 1988–91; High Comr to Nigeria, and concurrently Ambassador (non-resident) to Benin, 1991–94. *Address:* c/o Foreign and Commonwealth Office, King Charles Street, SW1A 2AH.

MacRAE, Prof. Donald Gunn; Martin White Professor of Sociology, University of London, 1978–87, now Emeritus; *b* 20 April 1921; *o s* of Donald MacRae and Elizabeth Maud Gunn; *m* 1st, 1948, Helen Grace McHardy; two *d*; 2nd, 1987, Mrs Jean Ridyard; one *s* one *d*. *Educ:* various schools in Scotland; Glasgow High Sch.; Glasgow Univ.; Balliol Coll., Oxford. MA Glasgow 1942; BA 1945, MA 1949, Oxon. Asst Lectr, LSE, 1945; Univ. Lectr in Sociology, Oxford, 1949; Reader in Sociology, London Univ., 1954; Prof. of Sociology: UC Gold Coast, 1956; Univ. of California, Berkeley, 1959; Univ. of London, 1961–87. Fellow, Center for Advanced Studies in Behavioral Sciences, Stanford, 1967. Vis. Prof., Univ. of the Witwatersrand, 1975; Senior Member, Keynes Coll., Darwin Coll., Univ. of Kent at Canterbury. Member: Council, CNAA (Chm. Cttee for Arts and Social Studies, to 1978); Archbp of Canterbury's Gp on Divorce Law, 1964–66; Gaitskell Commn of Inquiry into Advertising, 1962–66; Internat. Council on the Future of the University, 1973–82. Editor, British Jl of Sociology, from formation to 1965; Mem., Editl Adv. Cttees, Encyclopædia Britannica, 1968–. *Publications:* Ideology and Society, 1960; (ed) The World of J. B. Priestley, 1967; (ed with intro.) The Man Versus the State, by Herbert Spencer, 1969; Ages and Stages, 1973; Max Weber, 1974. *Recreations:* talking, music, walking. *Address:* Norfolk House, 44 High Street, Sandwich, Kent CT13 9EG. *Club:* Athenæum.

McRAE, Frances Anne, (Mrs Hamish McRae); *see* Cairncross, F. A.

McRAE, Hamish Malcolm Donald; Associate Editor, The Independent, since 1991; *b* 20 Oct. 1943; *s* of Donald and Barbara McRae (*née* Budd); *m* 1971, Frances Anne Cairncross, *qv*; two *d*. *Educ:* Fettes College; Trinity College, Dublin (BA Hons Economics and Political Science). Liverpool Post, 1966–67; The Banker, 1967–72 (Asst Editor, 1969, Dep. Editor, 1971); Editor, Euromoney, 1972–74; Financial Editor, The Guardian, 1975–89; Business and City Editor and an Asst Editor, The Independent, 1989–91. Wincott Foundn financial journalist of the year, 1979. *Publications:* (with Frances Cairncross) Capital City: London as a financial centre, 1973, 5th edn 1991; (with Frances Cairncross) The Second Great Crash, 1975; Japan's role in the emerging global securities market, 1985; The World in 2020, 1994. *Recreations:* walking, ski-ing, cooking. *Address:* 6 Canonbury Lane, N1 2AP.

MACRAE, John Esmond Campbell, CMG 1986; DPhil; HM Diplomatic Service, retired; *b* 8 Dec. 1932; *s* of Col Archibald Campbell Macrae, IMS, and Euretta Margaret Skelton; *m* 1962, Anne Catherine Sarah Strain; four *s*. *Educ:* Sheikh Bagh Sch., Kashmir; Fettes Coll., Edinburgh; Christ Church Oxford (Open Scholar); Princeton, USA. DPhil, MA. Atomic Energy and Disarmament Dept, Foreign Office, 1959–60; 2nd Sec., British Embassy, Tel Aviv, 1961–64; 1st Secretary: Djakarta, 1964; Vientiane, 1964–66; FO, NE African Dept, 1966; Central Dept, 1967–69; Southern African Dept, 1970–72; UK Mission to the UN, New York (dealing with social affairs, population and outer space), 1972–75; Counsellor, Science and Technology, Paris, 1975–80; Head of Cultural Relns Dept, FCO, 1980–85; RCDS, 1985; Ambassador: to Senegal, and (non-resident) to Mali, Cape Verde, Guinea and Guinea-Bissau, 1985–90; to Mauritania (non-resident), 1986–92 and to Morocco, 1990–92. *Recreations:* music, travel, picnics in unusual places. *Address:* Les Aires, 26110 Mirabel aux Baronnies, France.

MacRAE, Kenneth Charles; His Honour Judge MacRae; a Circuit Judge, since 1990; *b* 14 March 1944; *s* of William and Ann MacRae; *m* 1981, Hilary Vivien Williams; one *d*. *Educ:* Redruth County Grammar School; Cornwall Tech. Coll.; Fitzwilliam Coll., Cambridge (BA Hons). Called to the Bar, Lincoln's Inn, 1969; a Recorder of the Crown Court, 1985. *Recreations:* gardening, walking, music. *Address:* c/o Courts Administrator, 10 Sundial Court, Tolworth Rise South, Surbiton, Surrey KT5 9NN. *T:* 0181–335 3090.

MACRAE, Col Sir Robert (Andrew Alexander Scarth), KCVO 1990; MBE 1953; JP; Lord-Lieutenant of Orkney, 1972–90 (Vice-Lieutenant, 1967–72); Farmer; *b* 14 April 1915; *s* of late Robert Scarth Farquhar Macrae, CIE, CBE, Grindelay House, Orphir, Orkney; *m* 1945, Violet Maud, *d* of late Walter Scott MacLellan; two *s*. *Educ:* Lancing; RMC Sandhurst. 2nd Lt Seaforth Highlanders, 1935; Col 1963; retd 1968. Active Service: NW Europe, 1940–45 (despatches, 1945); Korea, 1952–53; E Africa, 1953–54. Member: Orkney CC, 1970–74; Orkney Islands Council, 1974–78; Vice Chairman: Orkney Hospital Bd, 1971–74; Orkney Health Bd, 1974–79. Hon. Sheriff, Grampian, Highlands and Islands, 1972. DL, Co. of Orkney, 1946; JP Orkney, 1975. Freedom of Orkney,

1990. *Recreations:* sailing, fishing. *Address:* Grindelay House, Orkney KW17 2RD. *T:* Orphir (0185681) 228. *Clubs:* Army and Navy; New, Puffin's (Edinburgh).

MACREADIE, John Lindsay; National Officer, since 1970 and Deputy General Secretary, since 1987, Civil and Public Services Association; *b* 19 Sept. 1946; *s* of John and Mary Macreadie; *m* 1967, Roisin Ann Boden; one *s* one *d*. *Educ:* Primary and Secondary State Schools, Glasgow. Civil Servant, 1964–70. Mem., TUC General Council, 1987–88. *Recreations:* politics, football, cinema. *Address:* 1 The Green, Morden, Surrey SM4 4HJ. *T:* 0181–542 5880. *Club:* William Morris Labour (Wimbledon).

MACREADY, Sir Nevil (John Wilfrid), 3rd Bt *cr* 1923; CBE 1983; Chairman, Mental Health Foundation, since 1993; *b* 7 Sept. 1921; *s* of Lt-Gen. Sir Gordon (Nevil) Macready, 2nd Bt, KBE, CB, CMG, DSO, MC, and Elisabeth (*d* 1969), *d* of Duc de Noailles; *S* father 1956; *m* 1949, Mary, *d* of late Sir Donald Fergusson, GCB; one *s* three *d*. *Educ:* Cheltenham; St John's Coll., Oxford. Served in RA (Field), 1942–47 (despatches); Staff Captain, 1945. BBC European Service, 1947–50. Vice-Pres. and Gen. Manager, Mobil Oil Française, 1972–75; Man. Dir, Mobil Oil Co. Ltd, 1975–85. Pres., Inst. of Petroleum, 1980–82. Chairman: Crafts Council, 1984–91; Horseracing Adv. Council, 1986–93; Dep. Chm., British Horseracing Bd, 1993–95. Pres., Royal Warrant Holders' Assoc., 1979–80; Trustee V&A Museum, 1985–. *Recreations:* racing, fishing, theatre, music. *Heir: s* Charles Nevil Macready [*b* 19 May 1955; *m* 1981, Lorraine, *d* of Brian McAdam (marr. diss. 1994); one *s* one *d*]. *Address:* The White House, Odiham, Hants RG29 1LG. *T:* Odiham (01256) 702976. *Clubs:* Boodle's; Jockey (Paris).

MacROBBIE, Prof. Enid Anne Campbell, FRS 1991; Professor of Plant Biophysics, University of Cambridge, since 1987; Fellow of Girton College, since 1958; *b* 5 Dec. 1931; *d* of late George MacRobbie and Agnes Kerr MacRobbie (*née* Campbell). *Educ:* Mary Erskine Sch., Edinburgh; Univ. of Edinburgh (BSc, PhD); MA, ScD Cantab. Res. Fellow, Univ. of Copenhagen, 1957–58; Cambridge University: Res. Fellow, Botany Sch., 1958–62; Demonstrator in Botany, 1962–66; Lectr in Botany, 1966–73; Reader in Plant Biophysics, 1973–87. *Publications:* papers in sci jls. *Address:* Girton College, Cambridge CB3 0JG. *T:* Cambridge (01223) 338999.

McROBERT, Rosemary Dawn Teresa, OBE 1985; Deputy Director, Consumers' Association, 1980–88; *b* Maymyo, Burma, 29 Aug. 1927; *e d* of late Lt-Col Ronald McRobert, MB, ChB, FRCOG, IMS, and Julie Rees. *Educ:* privately and at Gloucestershire College of Educn. Journalist and broadcaster on consumer subjects, 1957–63; Founder editor, Home Economics, 1954–63; Chief Information Officer, Consumer Council, 1965–70; Consumer Representation Officer, Consumers' Assoc., 1971–73; Adviser on consumer affairs in DTI and Dept of Prices and Consumer Protection, 1973–74; Dir, Retail Trading Standards Assoc., 1974–80. Member Council: Inst. of Consumer Ergonomics, 1974–81; Consumers' Assoc., 1974–79; Advertising Standards Authority, 1974–80; Member: Adv. Council on Energy Conservation, 1974–82; Design Council, 1975–84; Post Office Review Cttee, 1976; Policyholders' Protection Bd, 1976–92; Nuffield Enquiry into Pharmacy Services, 1984–86; Council for Licensed Conveyancers, 1989–94; British Hallmarking Council, 1989–. Chm., Management Cttee, Camden Consumer Aid Centres, 1977–80. Vice-Pres., Patients Assoc., 1988–. Dir, Investors Compensation Scheme, 1988–95. Liveryman, Glovers' Co., 1979. *Address:* 57 Lawford Road, NW5 2LG. *Club:* Reform.

MacRORY, Avril; Head of Music Programmes, BBC Television, since 1993; *b* 5 April 1956; *d* of Patrick Simon MacRory and Elizabeth (*née* Flynn); *m* 1983, Val Griffin; one *s*. *Educ:* University College, Dublin (BA Hons 1970). Producer and Director, RTE, 1979; Head of Variety, RTE, 1986; Commissioning Editor, Music, Channel 4, 1988. *Recreations:* sailing, music, reading. *Address:* BBC Music and Arts, East Tower, Television Centre, Wood Lane, W12 7RJ. *T:* 0181–895 6263.

MACRORY, Prof. Richard Brabazon; Professor of Environmental Law, IBM Director of the Environmental Change Unit, and Fellow of Linacre College, University of Oxford, since 1994; Barrister-at-law; *b* 30 March 1950; *s* of Sir Patrick Macrory and of Lady Marjorie Elizabeth Macrory; *m* 1979, Sarah Margaret Briant; two *s*. *Educ:* Westminster Sch.; Christ Church, Oxford (BA 1972; MA 1976). Called to the Bar, Gray's Inn, 1974; Legal Advr, Friends of the Earth Ltd, 1975–78; Imperial College, London: Lectr, 1980–89; Associate Dir, 1990–94, Centre for Envmtl Technol.; Reader in Envmtl Law, 1989–91; Denton Hall Prof. of Envmtl Law, 1991–94. Chairman: UK Envmtl Law Assoc., 1986–88; Hon. Standing Council, CPRE, 1981–92; Member: Envmtl Adv. Bd, Shanks and McKewan plc, 1989–91; UK Nat. Adv. Cttee on Eco-labelling, 1990–91; Royal Commn on Envmtl Pollution, 1991–. Specialist Adviser: H of L Select Cttee on EC, 1991–92; H of C Select Cttee on Envmt, 1989–92, 1993–. Mem. Bd, Durham Univ. European Law Inst., 1991–. Hon. Chm., Merchant Ivory Prodns Ltd, 1992–. Editor, Jl of Envmtl Law, 1988–; Legal Corresp., Ends Report, 1982–; Mem., Editl Bd, Rivista Giuridica dell' Ambiente, 1993–. *Publications:* Nuisance, 1982; Water Law: principles and practice, 1985; Water Act 1989, 1989; (with D. Gilbert) Pesticide Related Law, 1989; (with S. Hollins) Bibliography of Community Environmental Law, 1995; articles and reviews in legal and tech. jls. *Recreations:* cinema, board-games, reading. *Address:* Crossing Farmhouse, Tackley, Oxford OX5 3AT. *T:* Tackley (01869) 331566; Brick Court Chambers, 15–19 Devereux Court, WC2R 3JJ. *T:* 0171–583 0777, *Fax:* 0171–583 9401; Environmental Change Unit, 1a Mansfield Road, Oxford OX1 8TB. *T:* Oxford (01865) 281180, *Fax:* (01865) 281181.

MACROSSAN, Hon. John Murtagh, AC 1993; **Hon. Chief Justice Macrossan;** Chief Justice of the Supreme Court, Queensland, since 1989; *b* 12 Mar. 1930; *m* 1961, Margery Newton; one *s*. *Educ:* St Columban's Coll., Brisbane; Univ. of Queensland; Univ. of Oxford. Admitted Qld Bar, 1951; QC 1967; Judge of Supreme Court, Qld, 1980–89. Chancellor, Griffith Univ., 1988–. *Address:* Supreme Court of Queensland, Brisbane, Qld 4000, Australia.

MacSHANE, Denis, PhD; MP (Lab) Rotherham, since May 1994; *b* 21 May 1948; *e s* of late Jan Matyjaszek and of Isobel MacShane; *m* 1987, Nathalie Pham; one *s* four *d*. *Educ:* Merton Coll., Oxford (MA); Birkbeck Coll., London. (PhD). BBC reporter, 1969–77; Pres., NUJ, 1978–79; Policy Dir, Internat. Metalworkers Fedn, 1980–92; Dir, European Policy Inst., 1992–94. *Publications:* Solidarity: Poland's Independent Trade Union, 1981; François Mitterand: a political Odyssey, 1982; Black Workers, Unions and the Struggle for Democracy in South Africa, 1984; International Labour and the Origins of the Cold War, 1992. *Recreations:* walking, family, novels, poetry. *Address:* House of Commons, SW1A 0AA. *Club:* Rotherham Labour.

McSHARRY, Deirdre; *b* 4 April 1932; *d* of late Dr John McSharry and Mrs Mary McSharry. *Educ:* Dominican Convent, Wicklow; Trinity Coll., Dublin. Woman's Editor, Daily Express, 1962–66; Fashion Editor, The Sun, 1966–72; Editor, Cosmopolitan, 1973–85; Editor-in-Chief, Country Living, 1986–89; Consultant, Nat. Magazine Co., and Magazine Div., The Hearst Corp., 1990–95; Ed., Countryside mag., NY, 1991–92. Mem. Council, Amer. Mus. in Britain, Bath, 1995–. Magazine Editor of the Year, PPA, 1981, 1987; Mark Boxer Award, British Soc. of Magazine Editors, 1992. *Recreations:* architecture, design, travel. *Address:* 5 Widcombe Terrace, Bath BA2 6AJ.

MacSHARRY, Raymond; Director, Bank of Ireland, since 1993; Chairman, Ryanair, since 1993; Director, Jefferson Smurfit Group, since 1993; *b* Sligo, April 1938; *m* Elaine Neilan; three *s* three *d*. *Educ:* St Vincent's Nat. Sch., Sligo; Ballincutranta Nat. Sch., Beltra, Co. Sligo; Marist Brothers Nat. Sch., Sligo; Summerhill Coll., Sligo. TD (FF) for Sligo Leitrim, 1969–88; opposition front bench spokesman on Office of Public Works, 1973–75; Mem., Cttee of Public Accts, 1969–77; Minister of State, Dept of Finance and the Public Service, 1977–79; Minister of Agriculture, 1979–81; opposition spokesman on Agric., 1981–82; Tánaiste and Minister for Finance, 1982; Minister for Finance and the Public Service, 1987–88. Mem., Commn of EC, 1989–92. Formerly Member: New Ireland Forum; Nat. Exec., Fianna Fáil Party (later, also an Hon Treas.). Mem. for Connaught/Ulster, Europ. Parlt, 1984–87; Mem., Council of Ministers, 1984–87. Governor, Europ. Investment Bank, 1982. Director: Hannon's Poultry, Roscommon, 1993–; Galtee Deer Care, Cork, 1993–. Councillor, Sligo CC, 1967–78; Chairman: Bd of Management, Sligo Reg. Tech. Coll., 1974 (Mem., 1970–78); Sligo Hosp. Exec. Cttee, 1972–78; NW Health Bd, 1974–75 (Mem., 1971–78); Member: Sligo Corp., 1967–78 (Alderman, 1974–78); Town of Sligo Vocational Educn Cttee, 1967–78; Bd of Management, Sligo-Leitrim Reg. Develt Org., 1973–78; Sligo Jun. Chamber, 1965– (PP). Freeman, Borough of Sligo, 1993. Hon. Dr NUI, 1994; Hon. DEconSc Limerick, 1994. Grand Cross, Order of Leopold II (Belgium), 1993. *Address:* 46 Upper Mount Street, Dublin 2, Eire. *T:* (1) 6762459, *Fax:* 6762489; Alcantara, Pearse Road, Sligo, Eire.

MACTAGGART, Fiona; Chairman, Liberty (National Council for Civil Liberties), since 1994; *b* 12 Sept. 1953; *d* of Ian Auld Mactaggart and Rosemary Belhaven. *Educ:* Cheltenham Ladies' Coll.; King's Coll., London (BA Hons); Inst. of Educn, London (MA). Gen. Sec., London Students' Organisation, 1977–78; Vice-Pres., 1978–80, Nat. Sec., 1980–81, NUS; Gen. Sec., Jt Council for Welfare of Immigrants, 1982–86. Mem. (Lab) Wandsworth BC, 1986–90 (Leader of the Opposition, 1988–90). Teacher, Lyndhurst Sch., Camberwell, 1988–92; Lectr, Inst. of Educn, 1993–. *Address:* 61 Taybridge Road, SW11 5PX. *T:* 0171–228 4468.

MACTAGGART, Sir John (Auld), 4th Bt *cr* 1938, of King's Park, City of Glasgow; FRICS; *b* 21 Jan. 1951; *s* of Sir Ian Auld Mactaggart, 3rd Bt and of Rosemary, *d* of Sir Herbert Williams, 1st Bt, MP; *S* father, 1987; *m* 1st, 1977, Patricia (marr. diss. 1990), *y d* of late Major Harry Alastair Gordon, MC; 2nd, 1991, Caroline, *y d* of Eric Williams; one *s* one *d*. *Educ:* Shrewsbury; Trinity Coll., Cambridge (MA). Chairman: Central and City Holdings, 1981–; Western Heritable Investment Co. Ltd, 1987–. Dir, The Scottish Ballet, 1988–. *Heir: s* Jack Auld Mactaggart, *b* 11 Sept. 1993. *Address:* 22 Tregunter Road, SW10 9LH.

MACTAGGART, William Alexander, CBE 1964; JP; Chairman, 1960–70, and Managing Director, 1945–68, Pringle of Scotland Ltd, Knitwear Manufacturers, Hawick; *b* 17 Aug. 1906; *o s* of late William Alexander and Margaret Mactaggart, Woodgate, Hawick; *m* 1932, Marjorie Laing Innes; two *s* one *d*. *Educ:* Sedbergh Sch., Yorks. Joined Robert Pringle & Son Ltd (later Pringle of Scotland Ltd), 1925; Dir, 1932; Joint Managing Dir, 1933. Served War of 1939–45: Captain, RASC, Holland, Belgium, France, 1942–45. Elder of Lilliesleaf Parish Church. *Address:* Bewlie House, Lilliesleaf, Melrose, Roxburghshire TD6 9ER. *T:* Lilliesleaf (018357) 267.

MacTAGGART, Air Vice-Marshal William Keith, CBE 1976 (MBE 1956); CEng, FIMechE; FRAeS; Consultant: MPE Ltd, 1989–91 (Managing Director, 1981–89); Adwest plc, 1989–91; *b* 15 Jan. 1929; *s* of Duncan MacTaggart and Marion (*née* Keith); *m* 1st, 1949 Christina Carnegie Geddes (marr. diss. 1977); one *s* two *d*; 2nd, 1977, Barbara Smith Brown, *d* of Adm. Stirling P. Smith, late USN, and Mrs Smith; one step *d*. *Educ:* Aberdeen Grammar Sch.; Aberdeen Univ. (BScEng 1948). FIMechE 1973; FRAeS 1974; FIMgt (FBIM 1978). Commnd RAF, 1949; 1949–67: Engr Officer; Pilot; AWRE, Aldermaston (Montebello and Maralinga atomic trials); attended RAF Staff Coll., and Jt Services Staff Coll.; Def. Intell.; Systems Analyst, DOAE, West Byfleet, and MoD (Air); Head of Systems MDC, RAF Swanton Morley, 1968; OC RAF Newton, 1971 (Gp Captain); Dep. Comd Mech. Engr, HQ Strike Comd, 1973; Dir of Air Armament, MoD (PE), 1973 (Air Cdre); RCDS, 1977; Vice-Pres. (Air), Ordnance Bd, 1978 (Air Vice-Marshal), Pres., 1978–80. Dep. Chm., Tomash Holdings Ltd, 1980–84. *Recreations:* music, travel. *Address:* Croft Stones, Lothmore, Helmsdale, Sutherland KW8 6HP. *T:* Helmsdale (01431) 821439. *Club:* Royal Air Force.

MacTHOMAS OF FINEGAND, Andrew Patrick Clayhills; 19th Chief of Clan MacThomas (Mac Thomaidh Mhor); *b* 28 Aug. 1942; *o s* of late Captain Patrick Watt MacThomas of Finegand and of Elizabeth, *d* of late Becket Clayhills-Henderson, Invergowrie, Angus; *S* father 1970; *m* 1985, Anneke Cornelia Susanna, *o d* of A. and S. Kruyning-Van Hout, Netherlands; one *s* one *d*. *Educ:* St Edward's, Oxford. Head of Public Affairs, Barclays plc. FSA (Scot.) 1973. Pres., Clan MacThomas Soc., 1970–; Hon. Vice-Pres., Clan Chattan Assoc., 1970–. *Recreations:* steeplechasing, my young family. *Heir: s* Thomas David Alexander MacThomas, Yr of Finegand, *b* 1 Jan. 1987. *Address:* c/o Barclays Bank, Hide Hill, Berwick-upon-Tweed.

McVEIGH, (Robert) Desmond; Managing Director, Longdown Financial Services Ltd, since 1995; *b* 10 Jan. 1939; *s* of Rev. Robert Walker McVeigh and of late Evelyn Mary (*née* McCoubrey); *m* 1966, Gillian Ann Nash; two *s* one *d*. *Educ:* Methodist Coll., Belfast; QUB (LLB Hons); Univ. of Michigan (LLM). Citibank, London, 1967–71; GATX, London, 1971–72; Citibank, 1972–74; First Nat. Bank, Dallas, 1974–77; Saudi Internat. Bank, London, 1977–85; Lloyds Merchant Bank, 1985–87; independent consultant, 1987–92; Chief Exec., IDB for NI, 1993–95. Vis. Prof. of Finance and Industrial Relations, Warsaw Univ., 1994–. CIMgt 1994. *Recreations:* golf, tennis, music. *Address:* Tithebarns, Tithebarns Lane, Clandon Road, Send, Guildford, Surrey GU23 7LE. *T:* and *Fax:* Guildford (01483) 223391. *Club:* Royal Over-Seas League.

MacVICAR, Rev. Kenneth, MBE (mil.) 1968; DFC 1944; Extra Chaplain to the Queen in Scotland, since 1991 (Chaplain in Ordinary, 1974–91); Minister of Kenmore and Lawers, Perthshire, 1950–90; *b* 25 Aug. 1921; *s* of Rev. Angus John MacVicar, Southend, Kintyre; *m* 1946, Isobel Guild McKay; three *s* one *d*. *Educ:* Campbeltown Grammar Sch.; Edinburgh Univ.; St Andrews Univ. (MA); St Mary's Coll., St Andrews. Mem., Edinburgh Univ. Air Squadron, 1941; joined RAF, 1941: Pilot, 28 Sqdn, RAF, 1942–45, Flt Comdr, 1944–45 (despatches, 1945). Chaplain, Scottish Horse and Fife and Forfar Yeomanry/Scottish Horse, TA, 1953–65. Convener, Church of Scotland Cttee on Chaplains to HM Forces, 1968–73. Clerk to Presbytery of Dunkeld, 1955. District Councillor, 1951–74. *Recreation:* golf. *Address:* Illeray, Kenmore, Aberfeldy, Perthshire PH15 2HE. *T:* Kenmore (01887) 830514.

MACVICAR, Neil, QC (Scotland) 1960; MA, LLB; Sheriff of Lothian and Borders (formerly the Lothians and Peebles), at Edinburgh, 1968–85; *b* 16 May 1920; *s* of late Neil Macvicar, WS; *m* 1949, Maria, *d* of Count Spiridon Bulgari, Corfu; one *s* two *d*. *Educ:* Loretto Sch.; Oriel Coll., Oxford; Edinburgh Univ. Served RA, 1940–45. Called to

Scottish Bar, 1948. Chancellor, Dio. of Edinburgh, 1961–74. Chm. of Govs, Dean Orphanage and Cauvin's Trust, 1967–85. *Publications:* A Heart's Odyssey (memoirs), 1991; Grace Notes: variations on a Greek theme, 1995. *Address:* 25 Blackford Road, Edinburgh EH9 2DT. *T:* 0131–667 2362; Kapoutsi, Gastouri, Corfu, Greece. *Clubs:* New (Edinburgh); Anagnostiki Etairia (Corfu).

McVIE, Prof. (John) Gordon, MD; Scientific Director, Cancer Research Campaign, since 1989; *b* 13 Jan. 1945; *s* of John McVie and Lindsaye Woodburn McVie (*née* Mair); *m* 1966, Evelyn Mary Strang (separated); three *s*. *Educ:* Royal High Sch., Edinburgh; Univ. of Edinburgh (BSc Hons; MB, ChB; MD 1978) MRCP 1971. Edinburgh University: MRC Fellow, 1970–71; Lectr in Therapeutics, 1971–76; CRC Sen. Lectr in Oncology, Glasgow Univ., 1976–80; Netherlands Cancer Institute, Amsterdam: Hd, Clinical Res. Unit, 1980–84; Clinical Res. Dir, 1984–89. Vis. Prof., BPMF, London Univ., 1990–. Member: Council, Scottish Action for Smoking and Health, 1975–80; Royal College of Physicians: Collegiate Mems Cttee, 1975–80; Standing Cttee on Smoking, 1976–80; MRC Cancer Therapy Cttee UK, 1984–92; Bd of Dirs, Netherlands Cancer Inst., 1984–89; Permanent Cttee on Oncology, Min. of Health, Netherlands, 1986–89; European Organisation for Research and Treatment of Cancer: Chairman: Lung Cancer Co-operation Gp, 1981–88; Pharmacokinetics and Metabolism Gp, 1984–87 (Mem., 1981–87); Protocol Rev. Cttee, 1984–91; Pres., 1994. Examiner: RCPE, 1976–94; RCPSG, 1978–84. Chm., UICC Fellowships Prog., 1990–. Mem., editl bds of numerous jls related to cancer; Editor-in-Chief, European Cancer News, 1987–; European Ed., Jl Nat. Cancer Inst., 1994. Hon. FRCPE 1981; FRCPSGlas 1987. *Publications:* Cancer Assessment and Monitoring, 1979; Autologous Bone Marrow Transplantation and Solid Tumours, 1984; Microspheres and Drug Therapy, 1984; Clinical and Experimental Pathology and Biology of Lung Cancer, 1985; contrib. chapters in books and jls. *Recreations:* opera, theatre, cooking, Italian wine. *Address:* 10 Cambridge Terrace, NW1 4JL. *T:* 0171–224 1333. *Club:* New (Edinburgh).

McWATTERS, George Edward; Director of Corporate Affairs, HTV Group plc, 1989–91; Chairman: TVMM, 1988–91; HTV West, 1969–88; *b* India, 17 March 1922; *s* of Lt-Col George Alfred McWatters and Ellen Mary Christina McWatters (*née* Harvey); *m* 1st, 1946, Margery Robertson (*d* 1959); 2nd, 1960, Joy Anne Matthews; one *s*. *Educ:* Clifton Coll., Bristol. Vintners' Scholar, 1947. Served War of 1939–45: enlisted ranks Royal Scots, 1940; commissioned 14th Punjab Regt, Indian Army, 1941–46. John Harvey & Sons (family wine co.): joined, 1947; Dir, 1951; Chm., 1956–66; estab. a holding co. (Harveys of Bristol Ltd), 1962, but Showerings took over, 1966, and he remained Chm. until resignation, Aug. 1966; Chm., John White Footwear Holdings Ltd, later Ward White Gp Ltd, 1967–82; Actg Chm., HTV Group plc, 1985–86; Chm., HTV Ltd, 1986–88 (Vice-Chm., 1969–86). Chm., Bristol Avon Phoenix, 1987–90; Director: Bristol and West Bldg Soc., 1985–92 (Vice-Chm., 1988–92); Martins Bank, 1960–70; Local Adv. Dir (Peterborough), Barclays Bank, 1970–82; Local Dir (Northampton), Commercial Union Assce Co., 1969–82; Dir, Bain Clarkson Ltd, 1982–. Mem., CBI Grand Council, 1970–82. Mem. Cttee, Automobile Assoc., 1962–89. Chairman: Council, Order of St John, Avon, 1983–93; Bishop of Bristol's Urban Fund, 1989–; Vice-Pres., Avon Wildlife Trust, 1989– (Chm., Appeal Cttee, 1982). Pres., Avon and Bristol Fedn of Boys Clubs, 1985–94. Governor: Clifton Coll., 1958–; Kimbolton Sch., 1970–82. Master, Soc. of Merchant Venturers, 1986. City Councillor, Bristol, 1950–53. JP, Bristol, 1960–67; JP, Marylebone, 1969–71; High Sheriff, Cambridgeshire, 1979. *Recreations:* swimming, walking. *Address:* 4 Rivers Street, Bath, Avon BA1 2PZ. *T:* Bath (01225) 337725. *Club:* MCC.

McWATTERS, Stephen John; Headmaster, The Pilgrims' School, 1976–83, retired; *b* 24 April 1921; *er s* of late Sir Arthur Cecil McWatters, CIE; *m* 1957, Mary Gillian, *o d* of late D. C. Wilkinson and Mrs G. A. Wilkinson; one *s* two *d*. *Educ:* Eton (Scholar); Trinity Coll., Oxford (Scholar, MA). 1st Cl. Class. Mods, 1941. Served in The King's Royal Rifle Corps, 1941–45. Distinction in Philosophy section of Litterae Humaniores, Oxford, 1946. Asst Master, Eton Coll., 1947–63 (Master in Coll., 1949–57, Housemaster, 1961–63); Headmaster, Clifton Coll., 1963–75. *Recreations:* music, bird-watching. *Address:* 26 Edgar Road, Winchester SO23 9TN. *T:* Winchester (01962) 867523.

McWEENY, Prof. Roy; Professor of Theoretical Chemistry, University of Pisa, since 1982; *b* 19 May 1924; *o s* of late Maurice and Vera McWeeny; *m* 1947, Patricia M. Healey (marr. diss. 1979); one *s* one *d*; *m* 1982, Virginia Del Re. *Educ:* Univ. of Leeds; University Coll., Oxford. BSc (Physics) Leeds 1945; DPhil Oxon 1949. Lectr in Physical Chemistry, King's Coll., Univ. of Durham, 1948–57; Vis. Scientist, Physics Dept, MIT, USA, 1953–54; Lectr in Theoretical Chemistry, Univ. Coll. of N Staffs, 1957–62; Associate Dir, Quantum Chemistry Gp, Uppsala Univ., Sweden, 1960–61; Reader in Quantum Theory, 1962–64, Prof. of Theoretical Chemistry, 1964–66, Univ. of Keele; Prof. of Theoretical Chem., 1966–82, and Hd of Chemistry Dept, 1976–79, Sheffield Univ. Vis. Prof., America, Japan, Europe. Mem., Acad. Européenne des Scis, des Arts et des Lettres, 1988. *Publications:* Symmetry, an Introduction to Group Theory and its Applications, 1963; (with B. T. Sutcliffe) Methods of Molecular Quantum Mechanics, 1969, 2nd edn as sole author, 1989; Spins in Chemistry, 1970; Quantum Mechanics: principles and formalism, 1972; Quantum Mechanics: methods and basic applications, 1973; Coulson's Valence, 3rd rev. edn 1979; contrib. sections in other books and encyclopædias; many research papers on quantum theory of atomic and molecular structure in Proc. Royal Soc., Proc. Phys. Soc., Phys. Rev., Revs. Mod. Phys., Jl Chem. Phys., etc. *Recreations:* drawing, sculpture, travel. *Address:* Via Consoli del Mare 3, 56124 Pisa, Italy.

MACWHINNIE, Sir Gordon (Menzies), Kt 1992; CBE 1984 (OBE 1977); JP; FCA; Chairman, Leighton Asia Ltd, since 1990; Director, Allied Group Ltd, since 1993; *b* 13 Nov. 1922; *s* of Arthur William Philip Macwhinnie and Nellie Evelyn (*née* Rand); *m* 1948, Marjorie Grace Benwell; two *s*. *Educ:* Westminster Sch. FCA 1958 (ACA 1948). War Service, 1941–46: Capt., No 1 Commando, Burma and FE. Joined Peat Marwick Mitchell & Co., 1948, Sen. Partner, Hong Kong, 1968–78; chm. and dir of cos, 1978–; consultant in private practice, 1978–. Chm. and Mem., Govt cttees, 1978–. Council Mem., Hong Kong Univ. of Science and Technol., 1988–. Hon. DLitt Hong Kong Poly., 1991. *Recreations:* golf, horse-racing, watching cricket, football, athletics, etc. *Address:* Apt 3003, de Ricou, The Repulse Bay, 109 Repulse Bay Road, Hong Kong. *T:* 28031302, *Fax:* 28129874. *Clubs:* Oriental; Royal & Ancient Golf (St Andrews); Piltdown Golf; Royal Hong Kong Golf (Pres.), Hong Kong, Royal Hong Kong Jockey (Chm., 1989–91).

McWHIRTER, Norris Dewar, CBE 1980; author, publisher, broadcaster; Director, Guinness Publications Ltd (formerly Guinness Superlatives Ltd), since 1954 (Managing Director, 1954–76); *b* Winchmore Hall, N London, 12 Aug. 1925; *er (twin) s* of William Allan McWhirter, Managing Director of Associated Newspapers and Northcliffe Newspapers Group, and Margaret Williamson; *m* 1st, 1957, Carole (*d* 1987), *d* of George H. Eckert; one *s* one *d*; 2nd, 1991, Tessa Mary, *d* of late Joseph Dunsdon Pocock and Dorothy Pocock (*née* von Weichardt). *Educ:* Marlborough; Trinity Coll., Oxford. BA (Internat. Rel. and Econs), MA (Contract Law). Served RN, 1943–46: Sub-Lt RNVR, 2nd Escort Gp, Atlantic; minesweeping Pacific. Dir, McWhirter Twins Ltd, 1950–; Chm., Wm McWhirter & Sons, 1955–86; co-founder, Redwood Press (Chm., 1966–72); Dir, Gieves Group plc, 1972–. Founder Editor (with late Ross McWhirter till 1975) and compiler, Guinness Book of Records, 1954–86 (1st edn 1955), Adv. Editor, 1986–; by 1994, 345 edns in 37 languages; over 75 million sales. Athletics Correspondent: Observer, 1951–67; Star, 1951–60; BBC TV Commentator, Olympic Games, 1960–72; What's In the Picture, 1957; The Record Breakers, 1972–; Guinness Hall of Fame, 1986–. Mem., Sports Council, 1970–73. Chm., Freedom Assoc., 1983– (Dep. Chm., 1975–83). Pres., Marlburian Club, 1983–84. Contested (C) Orpington, 1964, 1966. Trustee: Ross McWhirter Foundn (Chm., 1994–); Police Convalescent and Rehabilitation Trust. *Publications:* Get To Your Marks, 1951; (ed) Athletics World, 1952–56; Dunlop Book of Facts, 5 edns, 1964–73; Guinness Book of Answers, 1976, 9th edn 1994; Ross: story of a shared life, 1976; Guinness Book of Essential Facts, 1979 (US); (jtly) Treason at Maastricht, 1994. *Recreations:* family tennis, watching athletics (Oxford 100 yds, Scotland 1950–52, GB in Norway 1951) and Rugby football (Mddx XV, 1950). *Address:* c/o 33 London Road, Enfield EN2 6DJ. *T:* 0181–367 4567. *Clubs:* Carlton; Vincent's (Oxford); Achilles.

McWIGGAN, Thomas Johnstone, CBE 1976; aviation electronics consultant; Secretary General, European Organisation for Civil Aviation Electronics, 1979–87; *b* 26 May 1918; *s* of late Thomas and Esther McWiggan; *m* 1947, Eileen Joyce Moughton; two *d*. *Educ:* UC Nottingham. Pharmaceutical Chemist. FIEE, FRAeS, SMIEEE. Signals Officer (Radar), RAFVR, 1941–46. Civil Air Attaché (Telecommunications) Washington, 1962–65; Dir of Telecommunications (Plans), Min. of Aviation, 1965; Dir of Telecommunications (Air Traffic Services), BoT, 1967; Dir Gen. Telecommunications, Nat. Air Traffic Services, 1969–79 (CAA, 1972–79). *Publications:* various technical papers. *Recreations:* photography, cabinet-making, gardening. *Address:* The Squirrels, Liberty Rise, Addlestone, Weybridge, Surrey KT15 1NU. *T:* Weybridge (01932) 843068.

MacWILLIAM, Very Rev. Alexander Gordon; Dean of St Davids Cathedral, 1984–90; *b* 22 Aug. 1923; *s* of Andrew George and Margaret MacWilliam; *m* 1951, Catherine Teresa (*née* Bogue); one *s*. *Educ:* Univ. of Wales (BA Hons Classics, 1943); Univ. of London (BD 2nd Cl. Hons, 1946, PhD 1952, DipEd 1962). Deacon 1946, priest 1947; Curate of Penygroes, Gwynedd, 1946–49; Minor Canon, Bangor Cathedral, 1949–55; Rector of Llanfaethlu, Gwynedd, 1955–58; Head of Dept of Theology, Trinity Coll., Carmarthen, Dyfed, 1958–74; Head of School of Society Studies, Trinity Coll. (Inst. of Higher Education, Univ. of Wales), 1974–84; Canon of St Davids Cathedral and Prebendary of Trefloden, 1978. Examining Chaplain to Bishop of St Davids, 1969. Vis. Prof. of Philosophy and Theology, Central Univ. of Iowa, USA, 1983. Prov. Grand Master, S Wales Western Div., United Grand Lodge of England, 1992–. *Publications:* contribs to Learning for Living (Brit. Jl of Religious Education), UCW Jl of Educn. *Recreations:* travel to archaeological sites and art centres, classical music, food and wine. *Address:* Pen Parc, Smyrna Road, Llangain, Carmarthen, Dyfed SA33 5AD.

McWILLIAM, John David; MP (Lab) Blaydon, since 1979; *b* 16 May 1941; *s* of Alexander and Josephine McWilliam; *m* 1st, 1965, Lesley Mary Catling; two *d*; 2nd, 1994, Mary McLoughlin. *Educ:* Leith Academy; Heriot Watt Coll.; Napier College of Science and Technology. Post Office Engineer, 1957–79. Councillor, Edinburgh CC, 1970–75 (last Treasurer of City of Edinburgh and only Labour one, 1974–75); Commissioner for Local Authority Accounts in Scotland, 1974–78. Member: Scottish Council for Technical Educn, 1973–85; Select Cttee on Educn, Science and the Arts, 1980–83; Select Cttee on Procedure, 1984–87; Services Cttee (Chm., Computer sub-cttee, 1983–87); Select Cttee on Defence, 1987–; Speaker's Panel of Chairmen, 1988–. Dep. to the Shadow Leader of the House of Commons, 1983; Opposition Whip, 1984–87. Mem., Gen. Adv. Council, BBC, 1984–89. *Recreations:* reading, listening to music, angling. *Clubs:* Bleach Green Labour (Blaydon); Chopwell Social, Chopwell RAOB (Chopwell); Dunston Social, Dunston Mechanics Institute (Dunston); Ryton Social (Ryton); Blackhall Mill Social (Blackhall Mill); Greenside and District Social (Greenside); Winlaton West End (Winlaton). *Address:* House of Commons, SW1A 0AA.

McWILLIAM, Michael Douglas; Director, School of Oriental and African Studies, University of London, since 1989; *b* 21 June 1933; *s* of Douglas and Margaret McWilliam; *m* 1960, Ruth Arnstein; two *s*. *Educ:* Cheltenham Coll.; Oriel Coll., Oxford (MA); Nuffield Coll., Oxford (BLitt). Kenya Treasury, 1958; Samuel Montagu & Co., 1962; joined Standard Bank, subseq. Standard Chartered Bank, 1966; Gen. Manager, 1973; Gp Man. Dir, 1983–88. Member: Bd, Commonwealth Development Corp., 1990–; Council, ODI, 1991–. Chm., Superannuation Fund, London Univ., 1990–; Dir, Shanghai Fund, Bangladesh Fund, Indo-Suez Gp, 1992–. Vice-Pres., Royal African Soc., 1991– (Mem. Council, 1979–91). Pres. Council, Cheltenham Coll., 1988–92 (Mem., 1977–92). *Address:* 82W Portland Place, W1N 3DH. *Club:* Commonwealth Trust (Mem. Bd, 1989–91).

McWILLIAMS, Sir Francis, GBE 1992; FEng 1991; conciliator and arbitrator, since 1978; Chairman, Centre for Economics and Business Research, since 1992; Lord Mayor of London, 1992–93; *b* 8 Feb. 1926; *s* of John J. and Mary Anne McWilliams; *m* 1950, Winifred (*née* Segger); two *s*. *Educ:* Holy Cross Acad., Edinburgh; Edinburgh Univ. (BSc Eng 1945); Inns of Court Sch. of Law. FICE; FCIArb. Engineer in local govt, 1945–54; Town Engineer, Petaling Jaya New Town, Malaysia, 1954–64; Consulting Civil and Struct. Engineer, Kuala Lumpur, 1964–76. Bar student, 1976–78; called to the Bar, Lincoln's Inn, 1978, Bencher, 1993. Dir, Hong Kong & Shanghai Bank (Malaysia), 1993–. Mem., Bar Assoc. for Commerce, Finance & Industry, 1989–; Pres., British–Southern Slav States Law Soc., 1993–. Mem., Common Council, City of London, 1978–80; Alderman, Ward of Aldersgate, 1980–; Sheriff, City of London, 1988–89. Master: Arbitrators' Co., 1985–86; Engineers' Co., 1990–91; Loriners' Co., 1995–; Pres., Aldersgate Ward Club, 1980–. Chm., St John's Ambulance City Br., 1992–. Pres., Instn of Incorp. Exec. Engrs, 1994–. Chm. Trustees, Foundn for Manufg and Industry, 1994–. FCGI. Hon. DCL City; Hon. DEng Kingston, 1994. KStJ 1992; KSG 1993. PJK, Selangor, Malaysia, 1963; Dato Seri Selera, Selangor, 1973. Order of Merit (Senegal), 1989; Order of Independence (Cl. III) (UAE), 1989. *Recreations:* golf, ski-ing. *Address:* Flat 1, 32 Shepherds Hill, Highgate, N6 5AH. *T:* 0181–340 5811. *Clubs:* City Livery; Hon. Company of Edinburgh Golfers, Muirfield, Verulam Golf; Royal Selangor Golf, Royal Alam Shah Golfing Society, Selangor, Lake (Kuala Lumpur).

MADARIAGA, Prof. Isabel Margaret de, FRHistS; FBA 1990; Professor of Russian Studies, University of London at School of Slavonic and East European Studies, 1981–85, now Professor Emerita; *b* 27 Aug. 1919; *d* of late Salvador de Madariaga and Constance Archibald, MA; *m* 1943, Leonard Bertram Schapiro, CBE, FBA (marr. diss 1976; he *d* 1983). *Educ:* Ecole Internationale, Geneva; Instituto Escuela, Madrid and fifteen other schools; Univ. of London (BA, PhD). FRHistS 1967. BBC Monitoring Service, 1940–43; Min. of Information (later COI), 1943–47; Economic Information Unit, HM Treasury, 1947–48; Editl Asst, Slavonic and East European Review, 1951–64; Asst Lectr and Lectr, LSE, intermittently, 1951–66; Lectr in Modern History, Univ. of Sussex, 1966–68; Sen. Lectr in Russian Hist., Univ. of Lancaster, 1968–71; Reader in Russian Studies, SSEES, Univ. of London, 1971–81. Corresp. Mem., Royal Spanish Acad. of History, 1991. Member, Editorial Boards: Government and Opposition, 1965–; Slavonic and E European Review, 1971–86; European History Qly, 1971–. *Publications:* Britain, Russia and the Armed Neutrality, 1963; (with G. Ionescu) Opposition, 1968; Russia in the Age of

Catherine the Great, 1981; Catherine the Great: a short history, 1990; articles in learned jls. *Recreation:* music. *Address:* 25 Southwood Lawn Road, Highgate, N6 5SD. *T:* 0181–341 0862. *Club:* United Oxford & Cambridge University.

MADDEN, (Albert) Frederick (McCulloch), DPhil; Reader in Commonwealth Government, Oxford, 1957–84; Professorial Fellow of Nuffield College, 1958–84, Emeritus Fellow since 1984, Pro-Proctor, 1988–89; *b* 27 Feb. 1917; *e s* of A. E. and G. McC. Madden; *m* 1941, Margaret, *d* of Dr R. D. Gifford; one *s* one *d. Educ:* privately, by mother; Bishop Vesey's Grammar Sch.; Christ Church, Oxford. Boulter and Gladstone exhibns; BA 1938, BLitt 1939, DPhil 1950. Dep. Sup., Rhodes House Library, 1946–48; Beit Lectr, 1947–57; Sen. Tutor to Overseas Service Courses, 1950–; Co-Dir, Foreign Service Course, 1959–72; Dir, Inst. of Commonwealth Studies, 1961–68; Vice-Chm., History Bd, 1968–73. Canadian Vis. Fellow, 1970; Vis. Prof., Cape Town, 1973; Vis. Fellow, Res. Sch., ANU, 1974. Dir, Hong Kong admin. course, 1975–86. Dir, Prospect Theatre, 1963–66. FRHistS 1952. *Publications:* (with V. Harlow) British Colonial Developments, 1774–1834, 1953; (with K. Robinson) Essays in Imperial Government, 1963; chapter in Cambridge History of British Empire III, 1959; Imperial Constitutional Documents, 1765–1965, 1966; (with W. Morris-Jones) Australia and Britain, 1980; (with D. K. Fieldhouse) Oxford and the Idea of Commonwealth, 1982; Perspectives on Imperialism and Decolonisation (Festschrift), 1984; Select Documents on the Constitutional History of the British Empire: Vol. I, The Empire of the Bretaignes 1165–1688, 1985; Vol. II, The Classical Period of the First British Empire 1689–1783, 1986; Vol. III, Imperial Reconstruction 1763–1840, 1987; Vol. IV, Settler Self-government 1840–1900, 1989; Vol. V, The Dependent Empire and Ireland 1840–1900, 1991; Vol. VI, The Dominions and India since 1900, 1993; Vol. VIII, The Dependent Empire 1900–48, 1994; reviews in English Historical Review, etc. *Recreations:* acting (Cranmer in Quatercentenary, St Mary's, Oxford, and 160 other parts); photographing islands and highlands, hill towns, country houses, churches; Renaissance art; writing music and listening. *Address:* Penstones Court, Marlborough Lane, Stanford-in-the-Vale, Oxfordshire SN7 8SW. *T:* Stanford-in-the-Vale (01367) 718068.

See also D. C. A. McC. Madden.

MADDEN, Admiral Sir Charles (Edward), 2nd Bt, *cr* 1919; GCB 1965 (KCB 1961; CB 1955); Vice Lord-Lieutenant of Greater London, 1969–81; *b* 15 June 1906; *s* of Admiral of the Fleet Sir Charles E. Madden, 1st Bart, GCB, OM, and Constance Winifred (*d* 1964), 3rd *d* of Sir Charles Cayzer, 1st Bart; *S* father, 1935; *m* 1942, Olive (*d* 1989), *d* of late G. W. Robins, Caldy, Cheshire; one *d. Educ:* Royal Naval Coll., Osborne. ADC to the Queen, 1955. Served War: Exec. Officer, HMS Warspite, 1940–42 (despatches); Captain, HMS Emperor, 1945 (despatches); Naval Asst to 1st Sea Lord, 1946–47. Captain, 1946; Rear-Admiral, 1955; Vice-Admiral, 1958; Admiral, 1961. Chief of Naval Staff, NZ, 1953–55; Dep. Chief of Naval Personnel, 1955–57; Flag Officer, Malta, 1957–59; Flag Officer, Flotillas, Home Fleet, 1959–60; C-in-C Plymouth, 1960–62; C-in-C Home Fleet and NATO C-in-C Eastern Atlantic Command, 1963–65; retired, 1965. Chairman, Royal National Mission to Deep Sea Fishermen, 1971–81 (Dep. Chm., 1966–71); Vice-Chairman, Sail Training Assoc., 1968–70. Trustee: National Maritime Museum, 1968– (Chm., 1972–77); Portsmouth Royal Naval Museum, 1973–77. Chm., Standing Council of the Baronetage, 1975–77. Dep. Warden, Christ Church, Victoria Rd, 1970–86. Grand Cross of Prince Henry the Navigator, Portugal, 1960. *Recreation:* painting. *Heir: nephew* Peter John Madden, *b* 10 Sept. 1942. *Address:* 21 Eldon Road, W8 5PT. *Club:* Arts.

MADDEN, Rear-Admiral Colin Duncan, CB 1966; CBE 1964; LVO 1954; DSC 1940 and Bar, 1944; Registrar and Secretary, Order of the Bath, 1979–85; *b* 19 Aug. 1915; *s* of late Archibald Maclean Madden, CMG, and Cecilia Catherine Moor; *m* 1943, Agnes Margaret, *d* of late H. K. Newcombe, OBE, Canada and London, and Eleanor Clare; two *d. Educ:* RN Coll., Dartmouth. During War of 1939–45, took part in blocking Ijmuiden harbour and Dutch evacuation; Navigating Officer of 7th Mine Sweeping Flotilla, HMS Arethusa; Assault Group J1 for invasion of Europe, and HMS Norfolk. Thence HMS Triumph. Commander, 1950; Comd HMS Crossbow, 1952; staff of Flag Officer Royal Yachts, SS Gothic and Comdr (N) HM Yacht Britannia, for Royal Commonwealth Tour, 1953–54; Captain, Naval Attaché, Rome; Captain D 7 in HMS Trafalgar; IDC. Comd HMS Albion, 1962; Rear-Admiral, 1965; Senior Naval Member Directing Staff, Imperial Defence Coll., 1965–67; retired, 1967. Dir, Nat. Trade Develt Assoc., 1967–69. Gentleman Usher of the Scarlet Rod to the Order of the Bath, 1968–79. Dir Gen., Brewers' Soc., 1969–80. *Recreations:* sailing, gardening, fishing, tapestry. *Clubs:* Army and Navy; Royal Naval Sailing Association.

MADDEN, David Christopher Andrew McCulloch; HM Diplomatic Service; High Commissioner, Republic of Cyprus, since 1994; *b* 25 July 1946; *s* of Dr A. F. McC. Madden, *qv*; *m* 1970, Penelope Anthea Johnston; one *s* two *d. Educ:* Magdalen Coll. Sch., Oxford; Merton Coll., Oxford (MA); Courtauld Inst. of Art, London Univ. (MA). FCO, 1970–72; British Mil. Govt, Berlin, 1972–75; Cabinet Office, 1975–77; Moscow, 1978–81; Athens, 1981–84; FCO, 1984–87; Counsellor, 1987; Dep. Hd of Mission, Belgrade, 1987–90; Head, Southern European Dept, FCO, 1990–94. *Recreations:* cricket, rowing, reading, pets, wildlife. *Address:* Foreign and Commonwealth Office, King Charles Street, SW1A 2AH.

MADDEN, Frederick; *see* Madden, A. F. McC.

MADDEN, Dr (John) Lionel; Librarian, National Library of Wales, since 1994; *b* 8 Aug. 1938; *s* of late Cyril Madden and of Edith (*née* Mottram); *m* 1965, Georgina Mary Hardwick; one *s* one *d. Educ:* King Edward VII Grammar Sch., Sheffield; Lincoln Coll., Oxford (MA 1964); University Coll. London (DipLib 1963); Univ. of Leicester (PhD 1970). ALA 1964. Asst Librarian, Univ. of Hull, 1963–67; Bibliographer, Univ. of Leicester Victorian Studies Centre, 1967–72, Sen. Lectr, Coll. of Librarianship, Wales, 1973–87; Keeper of Printed Books, Nat. Liby of Wales, 1987–94. Mem., Pubns Bd, Leicester Univ. Press, 1968–72; Chm., Pubns Bd, Tennyson Soc., 1973–77. Pres., Welsh Liby Assoc., 1994–; Mem., Liby and Inf. Services Council, Wales, 1994–; Vice-Chm., Welsh Books Council, 1994–. Trustee, St Deiniol's Liby, Hawarden, 1994–. Hon. Fellow, Dept of Inf. and Liby Studies, Univ. of Wales, Aberystwyth, 1989–93, Hon. Prof., 1993–. Hon. Mem., Gorsedd Beirdd Ynys Prydain, 1995–. *Publications:* Thomas Love Peacock, 1967; How to Find Out about the Victorian Period, 1970; Robert Southey: the critical heritage, 1972; Sir Charles Tennyson: an annotated bibliography, 1973; The Nineteenth Century Periodical Press in Britain, 1976; Primary Sources for Victorian Studies, 1977; (ed jtly) Investigating Victorian Journalism, 1990. *Recreation:* walking. *Address:* The National Library of Wales, Aberystwyth SY23 3BU. *T:* Aberystwyth (01970) 623816.

MADDEN, Max; MP (Lab) Bradford West, since 1983; *b* 29 Oct. 1941; *s* of late George Francis Leonard Madden and Rene Frances Madden; *m* 1972, Sheelagh Teresa Catherine Howard. *Educ:* Lascelles Secondary Modern Sch.; Pinner Grammar Sch. Journalist: East Essex Gazette; Tribune (political weekly); Sun, London; Scotsman, London; subseq. Press and Information Officer, British Gas Corp., London; Dir of Publicity, Labour Party, 1979–82. MP (Lab) Sowerby, Feb. 1974–1979. *Address:* House of Commons, SW1A 0AA.

MADDEN, Michael; Under Secretary, Ministry of Agriculture, Fisheries and Food, 1985–Feb. 1996; *b* 12 Feb. 1936; *s* of late Harold Madden and Alice Elizabeth (*née* Grenville); *m* 1960 (marr. diss. 1977); two *s* one *d*; *m* 1994, Angela Grace Abell. *Educ:* King Edward VII Sch., Sheffield. Exec. Officer, Min. of Transport and Civil Aviation, 1955; Ministry of Agriculture, Fisheries and Food: Asst Principal, 1963–67; Asst Private Sec. to Minister, 1966–67; Principal, 1967; Asst Sec. (as Head, Tropical Foods Div.), 1973; Under Sec., 1985; Head, Management Services Gp, 1985; Flood Defence, Plant Protection and Agricl Resources, 1990; Envmt Policy Gp, 1991. *Recreations:* walking, eating and drinking with friends, music, planning expeditions. *Address:* 2A Brampton Road, St Albans, Herts AL1 4PW.

MADDICOTT, Dr John Robert Lewendon, FSA; Fellow and Lecturer in Modern History, Exeter College, Oxford, since 1969; *b* Exeter, 22 July 1943; *e s* of late Robert Maddicott, Ipplepen, Devon, and Barbara (*née* Lewendon); *m* 1965, Hilary, *d* of late Thomas and Violet Owen; two *d. Educ:* Cheltenham Grammar Sch.; King Edward's Sch., Bath; Worcester Coll., Oxford (BA 1st cl. 1964; DPhil 1968). FSA 1980. Jun. Lectr, Magdalen Coll., Oxford, 1966–67; Asst Lectr, Univ. of Manchester, 1967–69; Sub-Rector, Exeter Coll., Oxford, 1988–90. Vis. Prof., Univ. of S Carolina, 1983. Jt Editor, English Hist. Review, 1990–. *Publications:* Thomas of Lancaster 1307–22, 1970; The English Peasantry and the Demands of the Crown, 1294–1341, 1975; Law and Lordship: Royal Justices as Retainers in Thirteenth- and Fourteenth-Century England, 1978; Simon de Montfort, 1994; contribs to learned jls. *Recreations:* hill walking, poetry, book collecting. *Address:* Exeter College, Oxford OX1 3DP. *T:* Oxford (01865) 279621.

MADDISON, Prof. Angus; Professor of Economics, University of Groningen, Netherlands, since 1978; *b* 6 Dec. 1926; *s* of Thomas Maddison and Jane (*née* Walker); *m* 1st, Carol Hopkins; two *s*; 2nd, Penelope Pearce; one *d. Educ:* Darlington Grammar Sch., Selwyn Coll., Cambridge (BA, MA); McGill Univ., Montreal; Johns Hopkins Univ.; Univ. Aix-en-Provence (docteur d'état). Pilot Officer, RAF, 1948–49. Lectr in Econ. Hist., Univ. of St Andrews, 1951–52; Head of Econs Div., later Dir, Develt Assistance, then Fellow, Develt Centre, OEEC and OECD, Paris, 1953–66; Dir, Res. Project on Econ. Growth, Twentieth Century Fund, NY, 1966–69; Res. Fellow and Econ. Advr, Harvard Univ. Centre for Internat. Affairs, 1969–71; Head, Central Analysis Div., OECD, Paris, 1971–78. Visiting Lecturer or Professor: Univ. of Calif, Berkeley, 1968; Nuffield Coll., Oxford, 1975; Université Paris Dauphine, 1981; ANU, 1982; St Antony's Coll., Oxford, 1988; Internat. Develt Centre, Japan, 1989; Universitá Ca' Foscari, Venice, 1990; Univ. of Turin, 1993; NY Univ., 1993. Consultant: EU, ECAFE, ECE, ECLAC, FAO, GATT, IADB, UNESCO, UN, UNIDO; World Bank; govts of Brazil, Ghana, Greece, Mexico and Pakistan. Corresp. FBA 1994. Foreign Hon. Mem., Amer. Econ. Assoc., 1989; Foreign Mem., Russian Acad. of Scis in Econs and Business, 1992. Medal, Univ. of Helsinki, 1986. *Publications:* Economic Growth in the West, 1964; Foreign Skills and Technical Assistance in Economic Development, 1965; Economic Growth in Japan and the USSR, 1969; Economic Progress and Policy in Developing Countries, 1970; Class Structure and Economic Growth: India and Pakistan since the Moghuls, 1971; Phases of Capitalist Development, 1982; Two Crises: Latin America and Asia 1929–38 and 1973–83, 1985; The World Economy in the Twentieth Century, 1989; Dynamic Forces in Capitalist Development, 1991; The Political Economy of Poverty, Equity and Growth: Brazil and Mexico, 1992; Explaining the Economic Performance of Nations: essays in time and space, 1995; Monitoring the World Economy, 1995; numerous articles in econ. and financial jls. *Recreations:* collecting furniture, books and hats. *Address:* Chevincourt, 60150, France. *T:* 44760532, *Fax:* 44766514.

MADDISON, David George; His Honour Judge Maddison; a Circuit Judge, since 1992; *b* 22 Jan. 1947; *s* of Claude and Clarice Maddison; *m* 1976, Indira Mary Antoinette Saverymuttu; three *s. Educ:* King's Sch., Chester; Grey Coll., Univ. of Durham (BA 1968). Called to the Bar, Inner Temple, 1970; practised on Northern Circuit, 1972–92; a Recorder, 1990–92. *Recreations:* classical music, playing the piano, singing, tennis, golf, watching football. *Address:* c/o Courts of Justice, Crown Square, Manchester M60 9DJ. *Clubs:* Athenæum (Liverpool); Liverpool Cricket.

MADDISON, Vincent Albert, CMG 1961; TD 1953; *b* 10 Aug. 1915; *s* of late Vincent Maddison; *m* 1954, Jennifer Christian Bernard; two *s* one *d. Educ:* Wellingborough Sch.; Downing Coll., Cambridge (MA). Colonial Administrative Service, 1939. Served War of 1939–45: Ethiopian and Burma Campaigns. District Officer, Kenya, 1947; seconded to Secretariat, 1948; Director, Trade and Supplies, 1953; Secretary, 1954, Perm. Secretary, 1957–63, Min. of Commerce and Industry; retired from Kenya Government, 1963; Chairman: East African Power and Lighting Co. Ltd, 1965–70; Tana River Development Co. Ltd, 1965–70; The Kenya Power Co. Ltd 1965–70; Director: Nyali Ltd, 1966–70; Kisauni Ltd, 1966–70; East African Trust and Investment Co. Ltd, 1966–70; East African Engineering Consultants, 1966–70. *Recreations:* ski-ing, gardening, sailing. *Address:* 1 Shobdon Court Mews, Shobdon, Leominster, Herefordshire HR6 9LZ. *T:* Kingsland (01568) 708688. *Club:* Muthaiga Country (Kenya).

MADDOCK, Diana Margaret; MP (Lib Dem) Christchurch, since July 1993; *b* 19 May 1945; *d* of Reginald Derbyshire and Margaret Evans; *m* 1966, Robert Frank Maddock; two *d. Educ:* Brockenhurst GS; Shenstone Training Coll.; Portsmouth Polytechnic. Teacher: Weston Park Girls' Sch., Southampton, 1966–69; Extra-Mural Dept, Stockholm Univ., 1969–72; Sholling Girls' Sch., Southampton, 1972–73; Anglo-Continental Sch. of English, Bournemouth, 1973–76; Greylands Sch. of English, Southampton, 1990–91. Councillor (L, subseq. Lib Dem), Southampton CC, 1984–93. Vice-Chm., All-Party Parly Gp on Homelessness and Housing Need. Contested (Lib Dem) Southampton Test, 1992. *Recreations:* theatre, music, reading, travel. *Address:* House of Commons, SW1A 0AA. *T:* 0171–219 3000.

MADDOCKS, Arthur Frederick, CMG 1974; HM Diplomatic Service, retired; Ambassador and UK Permanent Representative to OECD, Paris, 1977–82; *b* 20 May 1922; *s* of late Frederick William Maddocks and Celia Elizabeth Maddocks (*née* Beardwell); *m* 1945, Margaret Jean Crawford Holt; two *s* one *d. Educ:* Manchester Grammar Sch.; Corpus Christi Coll., Oxford. Army, 1942–46; Foreign (later Diplomatic) Service, 1946–82: Washington, 1946–48; FO, 1949–51; Bonn, 1951–55; Bangkok, 1955–58; UK Delegn to OEEC, 1958–60; FO, 1960–64; UK Delegn to European Communities, Brussels, 1964–68; Political Adviser, Hong Kong, 1968–72; Dep. High Comr and Minister (Commercial), Ottawa, 1972–76. Mem., OECD Appeals Tribunal, 1984–89. *Address:* Lynton House, 83 High Street, Wheatley, Oxford OX33 1XP. *Club:* Hong Kong (Hong Kong).

MADDOCKS, Bertram Catterall; His Honour Judge Maddocks; a Circuit Judge, since 1990; *b* 7 July 1932; *s* of His Honour George Maddocks and of Mary Maddocks (*née* Day); *m* 1964, Angela Vergette Forster; two *s* one *d. Educ:* Malsis Hall, near Keighley; Rugby; Trinity Hall, Cambridge (schol.; MA; Law Tripos Part 2 1st Cl. 1955). Nat. Service, 2nd Lieut, RA, 1951; Duke of Lancaster's Own Yeomanry (TA), 1958–67. Called to the Bar, Middle Temple, 1956; Harmsworth Schol.; Mem., Lincoln's Inn; a Recorder, 1983–90. Pt-time Chm., VAT Tribunals, 1977–92. *Recreations:* real tennis, lawn tennis, ski-ing, bridge. *Address:* Moor Hall Farm, Prescot Road, Aughton, Lancashire L39 6RT. *T:* Aughton Green (01695) 421601. *Clubs:* Queen's; Northern Counties (Newcastle); Manchester Tennis and Racquet.

MADDOCKS, Fiona Hamilton; Founding Editor, BBC Music Magazine, since 1992; Feature Writer, The Observer, The Independent, The Spectator and other publications, since 1991; *b* 1 June 1955; *d* of William Hunter Maddocks and Dorothy Christina Hill; *m* 1989, Robert James Cooper; two *d*. *Educ:* Blackheath High Sch. (GPDST), London; Royal Coll. of Music; Newnham Coll., Cambridge (English Tripos; MA; Associate, 1985). Taught English Literature, Istituto Orsoline, Cortina d'Ampezzo, Italy, 1977–78; Medici Soc., London, 1978–79; News trainee, Producer and Sen. Producer, LBC, 1979–82; Founder Producer/Editor, Comment, 1982–85, Asst Commng Editor, Music, 1985–86, Channel 4; The Independent: Dep. Arts Editor, 1986–88, and writer; Music Editor and Associate Arts Editor, 1988–91. Launched Garden Venture, project with Royal Opera House, 1988–89. Mem. Exec. Cttee, SPNM, 1990–91; Mem., Critics' Circle, 1995. BP Arts Journalism Press Award, 1991. *Recreations:* playing chamber music, Italy. *Address:* c/o BBC Worldwide, 80 Wood Land, W12 0TT.

MADDOCKS, Sir Kenneth (Phipson), KCMG 1958 (CMG 1956); KCVO 1963; *b* 8 Feb. 1907; *s* of Arthur P. Maddocks, Haywards Heath, Sussex; *m* 1st, 1951, Elnor Radcliffe, CStJ (*d* 1976), *d* of late Sir E. John Russell, OBE, FRS; no *c*; 2nd, 1980, Patricia Josephine, *d* of Algernon and Irma Hare Duke and *widow* of Sir George Mooring, KCMG. *Educ:* Bromsgrove Sch.; Wadham Coll., Oxford. Colonial Administrative Service, Nigeria, 1929; Civil Secretary, Northern Region, Nigeria, 1955–57; Dep. Governor, 1957–58. Acting Governor, Northern Region, Nigeria, 1956 and 1957. Governor and Commander-in-Chief of Fiji, 1958–63; Dir and Secretary, E Africa and Mauritius Assoc., 1964–69. KStJ (Mem. Chapter-Gen., Order of St John, 1969–75). *Recreation:* gardening. *Address:* 11 Lee Road, Aldeburgh, Suffolk IP15 5HG. *T:* Aldeburgh (01725) 453443.

MADDOCKS, Rt. Rev. Morris Henry St John; Adviser on the Ministry of Health and Healing to Archbishops of Canterbury and York, since 1983; Hon. Assistant Bishop, Diocese of Chichester, since 1987; Prebendary of Chichester Cathedral, since 1992; *b* 28 April 1928; *s* of late Rev. Canon Morris Arthur Maddocks and Gladys Mabel Sharpe; *m* 1955, Anne Miles; no *c*. *Educ:* St John's Sch., Leatherhead; Trinity Coll., Cambridge; Chichester Theological Coll. BA 1952, MA 1956, Cambridge. Ordained in St Paul's Cathedral, London, 1954. Curate: St Peter's, Ealing, 1954–55; St Andrews, Uxbridge, 1955–58; Vicar of: Weaverthorpe, Helperthorpe and Luttons Ambo, 1958–61; S Martin's on the Hill, Scarborough, 1961–71; Bishop Suffragan of Selby, 1972–83. Chm., Churches' Council for Health and Healing, 1982–85 (Co-Chm., 1975–82); Co-Founder, with wife, of Acorn Christian Healing Trust, 1983. *Publications:* The Christian Healing Ministry, 1981; The Christian Adventure, 1983; Journey to Wholeness, 1986; A Healing House of Prayer, 1987; Twenty Questions about Healing, 1988; The Vision of Dorothy Kerin, 1991. *Recreations:* music, walking, gardening. *Address:* 3 The Chantry, Cathedral Close, Chichester, W Sussex PO19 1PZ. *T:* Chichester (01243) 788888. *Club:* Army and Navy.

MADDOX, Sir John (Royden), Kt 1995; writer and broadcaster; Editor, Nature, 1966–73 and since 1980; *b* 27 Nov. 1925; *s* of A. J. and M. E. Maddox, Swansea; *m* 1st, 1949, Nancy Fanning (*d* 1960); one *s* one *d*; 2nd, 1960, Brenda Power Murphy; one *s* one *d*. *Educ:* Gowerton Boys' County Sch.; Christ Church, Oxford; King's Coll., London. Asst Lecturer, then Lecturer, Theoretical Physics, Manchester Univ., 1949–55; Science Correspondent, Guardian, 1955–64; Affiliate, Rockefeller Institute, New York, 1962–63; Asst Director, Nuffield Foundation, and Co-ordinator, Nuffield Foundation Science Teaching Project, 1964–66; Man. Dir, Macmillan Journals Ltd, 1970–72; Dir, Macmillan & Co. Ltd, 1968–73; Chm., Maddox Editorial Ltd, 1972–74; Dir, Nuffield Foundn, 1975–80. Member: Royal Commn on Environmental Pollution, 1976–81; Genetic Manipulation Adv. Gp, 1976–80; British Library Adv. Council, 1976–81; Council on Internat. Develt, 1977–79; Chm. Council, Queen Elizabeth Coll., 1980–85; Mem. Council, King's Coll. London, 1985–89. Mem., Crickadarn and Gwendwr Community Council, 1981–. Hon. DTech Surrey, 1982; Hon. DSc: UEA, 1992; Liverpool, 1994. *Publications:* (with Leonard Beaton) The Spread of Nuclear Weapons, 1962; Revolution in Biology, 1964; The Doomsday Syndrome, 1972; Beyond the Energy Crisis, 1975. *Address:* Porters South, 4–6 Crinan Street, N1 9SQ; 9 Pitt Street, W8 4NX. *T:* (office) 0171–836 6633; (home) 0171–937 9750. *Club:* Athenæum.

MADDOX, Ronald, PRI 1989 (RI 1959); artist, illustrator and designer; *b* 5 Oct. 1930; *s* of Harold George and Winifred Maddox; *m* 1958, Camilla Farrin; two *s*. *Educ:* Hertfordshire College of Art and Design, St Albans; London College of Printing and Graphic Art. FCSD, FSAI; Hon. RWS 1990. Nat. Service, RAF, 1949–51, Air Min. Design Unit. Designer, illustrator, art director, London advertising agencies, 1951–61; private practice, 1962–; commissioned by nat. and multinat. cos and corps, govt depts, public authorities, TV; designer British postage stamps and philatelic material, 1972– (winner Prix de l'art Philatelique, 1987); exhibns, RA, RI, London and provincial galls; paintings in royal, govt and public bodies' collections. Vice-Pres., RI, 1979; Hon. Member: Soc. of Architect Artists; Fedn of Canadian Artists; United Soc. of Artists; Campine Assoc. of Watercolours, Belgium; PS. FRSA. Winsor & Newton/RI Award, 1981, 1991. *Recreations:* compulsive drawing, walking, cycling, gardening. *Address:* Herons, 21 New Road, Digswell, Herts AL6 0AQ. *T:* Welwyn (01438) 714884.

MADDRELL, Geoffrey Keggen; Chairman: Macdonald Martin Distilleries plc, since 1994; Westbury plc, since 1992; Manx and Overseas plc, since 1991; ProShare, since 1994 (Chief Executive, 1991–94); *b* 18 July 1936; *s* of Captain Geoffrey Douglas Maddrell and Barbara Marie Kennaugh; *m* 1964, Winifred Mary Daniel Jones; two *s* one *d*. *Educ:* King William's Coll., Isle of Man; Corpus Christi Coll., Cambridge (MA Law and Econs); Columbia Univ., New York (MBA). Lieut, Parachute Regt, 1955–57. Shell Internat. Petroleum Co. Ltd, 1961–69; Boston Consulting Gp, Boston, USA, 1971–72; Bowater Corp., 1972–86, apptd to main bd, 1979; joined Tootal Gp as Man. Dir, 1986, Chief Exec., 1987–91. Dir, Transport Develt Gp, 1992–; Chm., Ivory and Sime ISIS Trust plc, 1993–. Chm., Manchester TEC, 1988–91; Civil Service Comr, 1992–. Gov., UMIST, 1987–. *Recreations:* club running, golf, travel. *Address:* 28 Sussex Street, SW1V 4RL. *T:* 0171–834 3874.

MADDRELL, Dr Simon Hugh Piper, FRS 1981; Fellow of Gonville and Caius College, Cambridge, since 1964; Hon. Reader, Cambridge University, since 1991; *b* 11 Dec. 1937; *s* of Hugh Edmund Fisher Maddrell and Barbara Agnes Mary Maddrell; *m* 1st, 1961, Anna Myers (marr. diss. 1985); three *s* one *d*; 2nd, 1990, Katherine Mona Mapes. *Educ:* Peter Symonds' Sch., Winchester; St Catharine's Coll., Cambridge. BA, MA, PhD 1964, ScD 1978. Res. Fellow, Dalhousie Univ., Canada, 1962–64; SPSO, AFRC Unit of Invertebrate Chem. and Physiology, subseq. Unit of Insect Neurophysiology and Pharmacology, Cambridge Univ., 1968–90; College Fellow and Lectr, Gonville and Caius Coll., Cambridge, 1968–. Financial Sec., Co. of Biologists Ltd, 1965–. Scientific Medal, Zool Soc. of London, 1976. *Publication:* Neurosecretion, 1979. *Recreations:* golf, gardening, wine-tasting, cinema. *Address:* Gonville and Caius College, Cambridge CB2 1TA; Ballamaddrell, Ballabeg, Arbory, Isle of Man. *T:* Castletown (IOM) (01624) 822787.

MADEL, Sir (William) David, Kt 1994; MP (C) Bedfordshire South West, since 1983 (South Bedfordshire, 1970–83); *b* 6 Aug. 1938; *s* of late William R. Madel and of Eileen Madel (*née* Nicholls); *m* 1971, Susan Catherine, *d* of late Lt-Comdr Hon. Peter Carew; one *s* one *d*. *Educ:* Uppingham Sch.; Keble Coll., Oxford. MA Oxon 1965. Graduate Management Trainee, 1963–64; Advertising Exec., Thomson Organisation, 1964–70. Contested (C) Erith and Crayford Nov. 1965, 1966. PPS to Parly Under-Sec. of State for Defence, 1973–74, to Minister of State for Defence, 1974. Chm., Cons. Backbench Educn Cttee, 1983–85; Vice-Chm., Cons. Backbench Employment Cttee, 1974–81; Member: Select Cttee on Educn, Sci. and Arts, 1979–83, on Transport, 1995–; H of C European Legislation Cttee, 1983–. *Recreations:* cricket, tennis, reading. *Address:* 120 Pickford Road, Markyate, Herts AL3 8RL. *Clubs:* Carlton, Coningsby; Mid-Cheshire Pitt (Chester).

MADELUNG, Prof. Wilferd Willy Ferdinand; Laudian Professor of Arabic, University of Oxford, since 1978; *b* 26 Dec. 1930; *s* of Georg Madelung and Elisabeth (*née* Messerschmitt); *m* 1963, A. Margaret (*née* Arent); one *s*. *Educ:* Eberhard Ludwig Gymnasium, Stuttgart; Univs of Georgetown, Cairo, Hamburg. PhD (Hamburg). Cultural Attaché, W German Embassy, Baghdad, 1958–60. Vis. Professor, Univ. of Texas, Austin, 1963; Privatdozent, Univ. of Hamburg, 1963–64; University of Chicago: Asst Prof., 1964; Associate Prof., 1966; Prof. of Islamic History, 1969. Guggenheim Fellowship, 1972–73. Decoration of Republic of Sudan (4th cl.), 1962. *Publications:* Der Imam al-Qāsim ibn Ibrāhīm und die Glaubenslehre der Zaiditen, 1965; Religious Schools and Sects in Medieval Islam, 1985; Religious Trends in Early Islamic Iran, 1988; Religious and Ethnic Movements in Medieval Islam, 1992; articles in learned jls and Encyc. of Islam. *Recreation:* travel. *Address:* The Oriental Institute, Pusey Lane, Oxford OX1 2LE. *T:* Oxford (01865) 59272.

MADEN, Margaret; County Education Officer, Warwickshire County Council, 1989–95; *b* 16 April 1940; *d* of Clifford and Frances Maden. *Educ:* Arnold High Sch. for Girls, Blackpool; Leeds Univ. (BA Hons); Univ. of London Inst of Educn (PGCE). Asst Teacher of Geography, Stockwell Manor Comprehensive Sch., SW9, 1962–66; Lectr, Sidney Webb Coll. of Educn, 1966–71; Dep. Head, Bicester Comprehensive Sch., Oxon, 1971–75; Headmistress, Islington Green Comprehensive Sch., 1975–82; Dir, Islington Sixth Form Centre, 1983–86; Principal Advr, Tertiary Develt, ILEA, 1986–87; Dep. County Educn Officer, Warwickshire CC, 1987–88. Mem., Nat. Commn on Educn, 1991–93. Mem. Council, PSI, 1994–. Hon. FCP 1994. *Publications:* contributions to: Dear Lord James, 1971; Teachers for Tomorrow (ed Calthrop and Owens), 1971; Education 2000 (ed Wilby and Pluckrose), 1979; The School and the University, an International Perspective (ed Burton R. Clark), 1984; School Co-operation: new forms of Governance (ed Ransom and Tomlinson), 1994; (ed jtly) Success Against the Odds, 1995. *Recreations:* European painting, writing and films; politics, opera. *Address:* Primrose Cottage, Shutford, Banbury, Oxon OX15 6PB.

MADGE, Charles Henry; *b* 10 Oct. 1912; *s* of Lieut-Colonel C. A. Madge and Barbara (*née* Hylton Foster); *m* 1st, Kathleen Raine (marr. diss.); one *s* one *d*; 2nd, Inez Pearn (*d* 1976); one *s* one *d*; 3rd, Evelyn Brown (*d* 1984). *Educ:* Winchester Coll. (Scholar); Magdalene Coll., Cambridge (Scholar). Reporter on Daily Mirror, 1935–36; founded Mass-Observation, 1937; directed survey of working-class saving and spending for National Institute of Economic and Social Research, 1940–42; Research staff of PEP, 1943; Director, Pilot Press, 1944; Social Development Officer, New Town of Stevenage, 1947; Prof. of Sociology, Univ. of Birmingham, 1950–70. Mission to Thailand on UN Technical Assistance, 1953–54. UNESCO Missions to India, 1957–58, to South-East Asia, 1959 and 1960 and Leader of Mission to Ghana for UN Economic Commission for Africa, 1963. *Publications:* The Disappearing Castle (poems), 1937; The Father Found (poems), 1941; part-author of Britain by Mass-Observation, 1938, and other books connected with this organisation; War-time Pattern of Saving and Spending, 1943; (ed) Pilot Papers: Social Essays and Documents, 1945–47; Society in the Mind, 1964; (with Barbara Weinberger) Art Students Observed, 1973; (with Peter Willmott) Inner City Poverty in Paris and London, 1981; (ed with Mary-Lou Jennings) Pandaemonium, by Humphrey Jennings, 1985; (with Tom Harrisson) Britain by Mass-Observation, 1986; (with Humphrey Jennings) May the Twelfth, 1987; Of Love, Time and Places (poems), 1994; contributions to Economic Journal, Town Planning Review, Human Relations, etc. *Address:* 28 Lynmouth Road, N2 9LS.

MADGE, James Richard, CB 1976; Deputy Secretary, Department of the Environment, on secondment as Chief Executive, Housing Corporation, 1973–84; *b* 18 June 1924; *s* of James Henry Madge and Elisabeth May Madge; *m* 1955, Alice June Annette (*d* 1975), *d* of late Major Horace Reid, Jamaica; two *d*. *Educ:* Bexhill Co. Sch.; New Coll., Oxford. Pilot in RAFVR, 1942–46. Joined Min. of Civil Aviation, 1947; Principal Private Secretary: to Paymaster-General, 1950–51; to Minister of Transport, 1960–61; Asst Secretary, Min. of Transport, 1961–66; Under-Sec., Road Safety Gp, 1966–69; Head of Policy Planning, 1969–70; Under-Sec., Housing Directorate, DoE, 1971–73. Churchwarden, St Mary Abbots, Kensington, 1987–. *Recreations:* lawn tennis, swimming, furniture-making. *Address:* 56 Gordon Place, Kensington, W8 4JF. *T:* 0171–937 1927.

MADIGAN, Sir Russel (Tullie), Kt 1981; OBE 1970; Chairman: Remproc Ltd, since 1991; Australian United Steel Industry Pty Ltd, since 1994; *b* 22 Nov. 1920; *s* of Dr Cecil T. Madigan and Wynnis K. Wollaston; *m* 1st, 1942, Margaret Symons (decd); four *s* one *d*; 2nd, 1981, Satsuko Tamura (decd). *Educ:* Univ. of Adelaide (BScEng 1941, BE 1946, ME 1954, LLB 1960). FSASM 1941; FTS. Joined Zinc Corp., 1946; Gowrie Schol. in Canada and USA, 1947–49; Underground Manager, Zinc Corp., NBHC Ltd, 1956–59; CRA, Conzinc Rio Tinto of Australia Ltd: Gen. Manager, Gen. Mining Div., 1960–64; Dir, 1968–87; Dep. Chm., 1978–87; Hamersley Iron: Man. Dir, 1965–71; Chm., 1971–81. Chairman: Blair Athol Coal Pty, 1971–80; Interstate Oil, 1972–81; Hamersley Hldgs, 1971–81; APV Asia Pacific, 1983–87; Muswellbrook Energy & Minerals, 1987–90; Director: Nat. Commercial Union, 1969–90; Rio Tinto Zinc Corp., 1971–85; APV Hldgs, 1983–87. Pres., Aust. Inst. of Internat. Affairs, 1984–89; Chairman: Aust.-Japan Foundn, 1977–81; Aust. Mineral Foundn, 1984–88; Aust. Pacific Econ. Co-operation Cttee, 1986–92; Member: Export Develt Council, 1970–86; Consultative Cttee on Relations with Japan, 1977–82; Life Mem., Pacific Basin Econ. Council, 1982; Councillor: Australasian Inst. of Mining and Metallurgy, 1958–87 (Pres., 1980); Aust. Acad. of Technological Scis and Engrg, 1978–89 (Treas., 1985–89). *Recreations:* flying, farming. *Address:* 99 Spring Street, Melbourne, Vic 3000, Australia. *Clubs:* Athenæum, Melbourne, Royal Melbourne Golf.

MAEHLER, Prof. Herwig Gustav Theodor, FBA 1986; Professor of Papyrology, University College London, since 1981; *b* 29 April 1935; *s* of Ludwig and Lisa Maehler; *m* 1963, Margaret Anderson; two *d*. *Educ:* Katharineum Lübeck (Grammar Sch.); Univs of Hamburg (PhD Classics and Classical Archaeol.), Tübingen and Basel. British Council Schol., Oxford, 1961–62; Res. Assistant, Hamburg Univ., 1962–63, Hamburg Univ. Liby, 1963–64; Keeper of Greek Papyri, Egyptian Mus., W Berlin, 1964–79; Habilitation for Classics, 1975, Lectr in Classics, 1975–79, Free Univ. of W Berlin; Reader in Papyrology, UCL, 1979–81. Corresp. Mem., German Archaeol Inst., 1979. *Publications:* Die Auffassung des Dichterberufs im frühen Griechentum bis zur Zeit Pindars, 1963; Die

Handschriften des S Jacobi-Kirche Hamburg, 1967; Urkunden römischer Zeit, (BGU XI), 1968; Papyri aus Hermupolis (BGU XII), 1974; Die Lieder des Bakchylides, 2 vols, 1982; (with G. Cavallo) Greek Bookhands of the Early Byzantine Period, 1987; editions of Bacchylides and Pindar, 1970, 1987, 1989, 1992; articles in learned jls. *Address:* Department of Greek and Latin, University College London, Gower Street, WC1E 6BT. *T:* 0171-380 7490.

MAFFEY, family name of **Baron Rugby.**

MAGEE, Bryan; writer; Visiting Professor, King's College, London, since 1994 (Hon. Senior Research Fellow in History of Ideas, 1984–94); *b* 12 April 1930; *s* of Frederick Magee and Sheila (*née* Lynch); *m* 1954, Ingrid Söderlund (marr. diss.); one *d.* *Educ:* Christ's Hospital; Lycée Hôche, Versailles; Keble Coll., Oxford (Open Scholar; Hon. Fellow, 1994). Pres., Oxford Union, 1953; MA 1956. Henry Fellow in Philosophy, Yale, 1955–56. Music criticism for many publications, 1959–; Theatre Critic, The Listener, 1966–67; regular columnist, The Times, 1974–76. Mem., Arts Council, 1993–94 (Chm., Music Panel, 1993–94). Current Affairs Reporter on TV; Critic of the Arts on BBC Radio 3; own broadcast series include: Conversations with Philosophers, BBC Radio 3, 1970–71; Men of Ideas, BBC TV 2, 1978; The Great Philosophers, BBC TV 2, 1987; What's the Big Idea?, BBC Radio 3, 1991–92. Silver Medal, RTS, 1978. Contested (Lab): Mid-Bedfordshire, Gen. Elec., 1959; By-Elec., 1960; MP (Lab 1974–82, SDP 1982–83) Leyton, Feb. 1974–1983; contested (SDP) Leyton, 1983. Elected to Critics' Circle, 1970, Pres., 1983–84. Judge: for Evening Standard annual Opera Award, 1973–84; for Laurence Olivier Annual Opera Awards, 1990–91, 1993–95; Chm. of Judges, Royal Philharmonic Soc. opera awards, 1991–96. Lectr in Philosophy, Balliol Coll., Oxford, 1970–71; Visiting Fellow: All Souls Coll., Oxford, 1973–74; New Coll., Oxford, 1995; Vis. Schol., 1991–93, Vis. Fellow, 1993–94, Wolfson Coll., Oxford; Vis. Schol. in Philos., Harvard, 1979, Sydney Univ., 1982, Univ. of California, Santa Barbara, 1989 (Girvetz Meml Lectr); German Marshall Fund Fellow to USA, 1989. Charles Carter Lectr, Univ. of Lancaster, 1985; Bithell Meml Lectr, Univ. of London, 1989. Lecturer: Seattle Opera, 1989, 1991, 1995; Royal Opera House, 1990; San Francisco Opera, 1990; Belgian Nat. Opera, 1991; Bayreuth Festspielhaus, 1994; Los Angeles Opera, 1995; Royal Inst. of Philosophy, 1992, 1994. Hon. Pres., Edinburgh Univ. Philosophy Soc., 1987–88. Governor, 1979–, Mem. Council, 1982–, Ditchley Foundn; Acad. Visitor, LSE, 1994–95. Hon. Fellow, QMC, 1988; Fellow: QMW, 1989; Royal Philharmonic Soc., 1990. *Publications:* Crucifixion and Other Poems, 1951; Go West Young Man, 1958; To Live in Danger, 1960; The New Radicalism, 1962; The Democratic Revolution, 1964; Towards 2000, 1965; One in Twenty, 1966; The Television Interviewer, 1966; Aspects of Wagner, 1968, rev. edn 1988; Modern British Philosophy, 1971; Popper, 1973; Facing Death, 1977; Men of Ideas, 1978; The Philosophy of Schopenhauer, 1983; The Great Philosophers, 1987; Misunderstanding Schopenhauer, 1990; (with M. Milligan) On Blindness, 1995. *Recreations:* music, theatre. *Address:* 12 Falkland House, Marloes Road, W8 5LF. *T:* 0171–937 1210. *Clubs:* Garrick, Savile.

MAGEE, Ian; Chief Executive, Information Technology Services Agency, Department of Social Security, since 1993; *b* 9 July 1946. *Educ:* Leeds Univ. (BA Hist.). Joined DHSS, 1969; Private Sec. to Minister for Social Security, 1976–78; Asst Controller, Management Services, London N, 1983–84; seconded to Cabinet Office Enterprise Unit, 1984–86; Department of Social Security, 1986–: Dep. to Dir of Personnel, 1986–89; Asst Sec., 1989–93; Territorial Dir, Benefits Agency, 1990–93. Non-exec. Dir, Laing Management Contracting, 1989–91. *Recreations:* sport, especially cricket, football, golf, National Hunt racing. *Address:* (office) 4th Floor, Verulam Point, Station Way, St Albans, Herts AL1 5HE. *T:* St Albans (01727) 815838. *Club:* MCC.

MAGGS, Air Vice-Marshal William Jack, CB 1967; OBE 1943; MA; Fellow and Domestic Bursar, Keble College, Oxford, 1969–77, Emeritus Fellow since 1981; *b* 2 Feb. 1914; *s* of late Frederick Wilfrid Maggs, Bristol; *m* 1940, Margaret Grace, *d* of late Thomas Liddell Hetherington, West Hartlepool; one *s* one *d.* *Educ:* Bristol Grammar Sch.; St John's Coll., Oxford (MA). Management Trainee, 1936–38. Joined RAF, 1939; Unit and Training duties, 1939–42; Student, Staff Coll., 1942; Planning Staffs, and participated in, Algerian, Sicilian and Italian landings, 1942–44; SESO Desert Air Force, 1944; Jt Admin. Plans Staff, Cabinet Offices, Whitehall, 1945–48; Instructor, RAF Coll., Cranwell, 1948–50; comd No 9 Maintenance Unit, 1950–52; exchange officer at HQ, USAF Washington, 1952–54; Student Jt Services Staff Coll., 1954–55; No 3 Maintenance Unit, 1955–57; Dep. Director of Equipment, Air Ministry, 1958–59; SESO, HQ, NEAF, Cyprus, 1959–61; Student, Imperial Defence Coll., 1962; Director of Mech. Transport and Marine Craft, Air Ministry, 1963–64; Director of Equipment, Ministry of Defence (Air), 1964–67; SASO, RAF Maintenance Comd, 1967–69. Group Captain, 1958; Air Commodore, 1963; Air Vice-Marshal, 1967. Governor, Bristol Grammar Sch., 1980–89. *Recreations:* golf, gardening. *Club:* Royal Air Force.

MAGILL, Air Vice-Marshal Graham Reese, CB 1966; CBE 1962 (OBE 1945); DFC 1941 and Bar, 1943; retired Jan. 1970; *b* 23 Jan. 1915; *s* of late Robert Wilson Magill and late Frances Elizabeth Magill, Te Aroha, NZ; *m* 1942, Blanche Marie Colson (*d* 1991); two *s.* *Educ:* Te Aroha High Sch.; Hamilton Technical Coll., NZ. Joined Royal Air Force, 1936. Served War of 1939–45, Sudan and Eritrea (despatches 1941), Egypt, UK, NW Europe; subsequently, UK, Egypt, France. Director of Operations (Bomber and Reconnaissance), Air Ministry, 1959–62; Commandant, RAF College of Air Warfare, Manby, Lincs, 1963–64; Director-General of Organisation (RAF), Ministry of Defence, 1964–67; AOC, 25 Group, RAF, 1967–68; AOC 22 Group, RAF, 1968–69. *Address:* c/o Holmhurst, The Southra, Dinas Powys, S Glamorgan CF64 4DL. *Club:* Royal Air Force.

MAGINNIS, John Edward, JP; *b* 7 March 1919; *s* of late Edward Maginnis and Mary E. Maginnis, Mandeville Hall, Mullahead, Tandragee; *m* 1944, Dorothy, *d* of late R. J. Rusk, JP, of Cavanaleck, Fivemiletown, Co. Tyrone; one *s* four *d.* *Educ:* Moyallon Sch., Co. Down; Portadown Technical Coll. Served War of 1939–45, Royal Ulster Constabulary. MP (UU) Armagh, Oct. 1959–Feb. 1974. JP, Co. Armagh, 1956. Group Secretary, North Armagh Group, Ulster Farmers' Union, 1956–59; Member, Co. Armagh Agricultural Society. Hon. LLD, 1990. *Recreations:* football, hunting, shooting. *Address:* Mandeville Hall, 68 Mullahead Road, Tandragee, Craigavon, Co. Armagh, N Ireland BT62 2LB. *T:* Tandragee (01762) 840260.

MAGINNIS, Ken; MP (UU) Fermanagh and South Tyrone, since 1983 (resigned seat Dec. 1985 in protest against Anglo-Irish Agreement; re-elected Jan. 1986); *b* 21 Jan. 1938; *m* 1961, Joy Stewart; two *s* two *d.* *Educ:* Royal Sch., Dungannon; Stranmillis Coll., Belfast. Served UDR, 1970–81, commissioned 1972, Major. Party spokesman on internal security and defence. Mem., Dungannon District Council, 1981–93; Mem. (UU) Fermanagh and S Tyrone, NI Assembly, 1982–86. Contested (UU) Fermanagh and S Tyrone, Aug. 1981. Mem., H of C Select Cttee on Defence, 1984–86, on NI, 1994–. Vice Pres., UU Council, 1990–. *Address:* House of Commons, SW1A 0AA; 1 Park Lane, Dungannon, Co. Tyrone.

MAGNUS, Sir Laurence (Henry Philip), 3rd Bt *cr* 1917, of Tangley Hill, Wonersh; Executive Director, since 1988, and Deputy Head, UK Corporate Finance Division, since 1994, Samuel Montagu & Co. Ltd, Merchant Bankers; *b* 24 Sept. 1955; *s* of Hilary Barrow Magnus, QC (*d* 1987), and of Rosemary Vera Anne Magnus (*née* Masefield); *S* uncle, Sir Philip Magnus-Allcroft, 2nd Bt, CBE, 1988; *m* 1983, Jocelyn Mary, *d* of R. H. F. Stanton; two *s* one *d.* *Educ:* Eton College; Christ Church, Oxford (MA). Corporate Finance Executive, Samuel Montagu & Co. Ltd, 1977–84; Head of Corporate Finance, Samuel Montagu & Co. Ltd (Singapore Branch), 1984–87; Group Country Manager, Singapore Region, Midland Bank plc (Singapore), 1987–88. *Recreations:* reading, fishing, walking. *Heir: s* Thomas Henry Philip Magnus, *b* 30 Sept. 1985. *Address:* c/o Samuel Montagu & Co. Ltd, 10 Lower Thames Street, EC3R 6AE. *T:* 0171–260 9440. *Club:* Millennium.

MAGNUS, Prof. Philip Douglas, FRS 1985; R. P. Doherty, Jr–Welch Regents Professor of Chemistry, University of Texas at Austin, since 1989; *b* 15 April 1943; *s* of Arthur Edwin and Lillian Edith Magnus; *m* 1963, Andrea Claire (*née* Parkinson); two *s.* *Educ:* Imperial College, Univ. of London (BSc, ARCS, PhD, DSc). Asst Lectr, 1967–70, Lectr, 1970–75, Imperial College; Associate Prof., Ohio State Univ., 1975–81; Prof. of Chemistry, 1981–87, Distinguished Prof., 1987–88, Indiana Univ. Corday Morgan Medal, RSC, 1978; Janssen Prize, Belgian Chemical Soc. and Janssen Foundn, 1992. *Publications:* papers in leading chemistry jls. *Recreations:* golf, chess. *Address:* 3111D Windsor Road, Austin, TX 78703, USA. *T:* (512) 4713966.

MAGNUSSON, Magnus, Hon. KBE 1989; MA (Oxon); FRSE 1980; FRSA; writer and broadcaster; *b* 12 Oct. 1929; *s* of late Sigursteinn Magnusson, Icelandic Consul-Gen. for Scotland, and Ingibjorg Sigurdardottir; *m* 1954, Mamie Baird; one *s* three *d* (and one *s* decd). *Educ:* Edinburgh Academy; Jesus Coll., Oxford (MA; Hon. Fellow, 1990). Subseq. Asst Editor, Scottish Daily Express and Asst Editor, The Scotsman. Presenter, various television and radio programmes including: Chronicle; Mastermind; Pebble Mill at One; BC, The Archaeology of the Bible Lands; Tonight; Cause for Concern; All Things Considered; Living Legends; Vikings!; Birds For All Seasons; Scottish Television Personality of the Year, 1974. Editor: The Bodley Head Archaeologies; Popular Archaeology, 1979–80. Chairman: Ancient Monuments Bd for Scotland, 1981–89; Cairngorms Working Party, 1991–93; NCC for Scotland, 1991–92; Scottish Natural Heritage, 1992–. Stewards, York Archaeol Trust; Scottish Churches Architectural Heritage Trust, 1978–85; Scottish Youth Theatre, 1976–78; Member: Bd of Trustees, Nat. Museums of Scotland, 1985–89; UK Cttee for European Year of the Environment, 1987; Pres., RSPB, 1985–90; Hon. Vice-President: Age Concern Scotland; RSSPCC. Rector, Edinburgh Univ., 1975–78. FSAScot 1974; FRSA 1983; Hon. FRIAS 1987; FSA 1991; FRSGS 1991. Dr *hc* Edinburgh, 1978; DUniv: York, 1981; Paisley, 1993; Hon. DLitt: Strathclyde, 1993; Napier Univ., 1994. Iceland Media Award, 1985; Medlicott Medal, HA, 1989. Knight of the Order of the Falcon (Iceland), 1975, Knight Commander, 1986; Silver Jubilee Medal, 1977. *Publications:* Introducing Archaeology, 1972; Viking Expansion Westwards, 1973; The Clacken and the Slate (Edinburgh Academy, 1824–1974), 1974; Hammer of the North (Norse mythology), 1976, 2nd edn, Viking Hammer of the North, 1980; BC, The Archaeology of the Bible Lands, 1977; Landlord or Tenant? a view of Irish history, 1978; Iceland, 1979; Vikings!, 1980; Magnus on the Move, 1980; Treasures of Scotland, 1981; Lindisfarne: The Cradle Island, 1984; Iceland Saga, 1987; *translations* (all with Hermann Pálsson): Njal's Saga, 1960; The Vinland Sagas, 1965; King Harald's Saga, 1966; Laxdaela Saga, 1969; (all by Halldor Laxness): The Atom Station, 1961; Paradise Reclaimed, 1962; The Fish Can Sing, 1966; World Light, 1969; Christianity Under Glacier, 1973; (by Samivel) Golden Iceland, 1967; *contributor:* The Glorious Privilege, 1967; The Future of the Highlands, 1968; Strange Stories, Amazing Facts, 1975; Pass the Port, 1976; Book of Bricks, 1978; Chronicle, 1978; Discovery of Lost Worlds, 1979; Pass the Port Again, 1981; Second Book of Bricks, 1981; *introduced:* Ancient China, 1974; The National Trust for Scotland Guide, 1976, Karluk, 1976; More Lives Than One?, 1976; Atlas of World Geography, 1977; Face to Face with the Turin Shroud, 1978; Modern Bible Atlas, 1979; Living Legends, 1980; The Hammer and the Cross, 1980; Household Ghosts, 1981; Great Books for Today, 1981; The Voyage of Odin's Raven, 1982; Robert Burns: Bawdy Verse & Folksongs, 1982; Mastermind 4, 1982; Northern Voices, 1984; The Village, 1985, Secrets of the Bible Seas, 1985; Beowulf, 1987; Complete Book of British Birds, 1988; Trustlands, 1989; The Wealth of a Nation, 1989; The Return of Cultural Treasures, 1990; *edited:* Echoes in Stone, 1983; Readers Digest Book of Facts, 1985; Chambers Biographical Dictionary, 5th edn 1990; The Nature of Scotland, 1991. *Recreations:* digging and delving. *Address:* Blairskaith House, Balmore-Torrance, Glasgow G64 4AX. *T:* Balmore (01360) 620226.

MAGONET, Rabbi Dr Jonathan David; Principal, Leo Baeck College, since 1985; *b* 2 Aug. 1942; *s* of Alexander Philip and Esther Magonet; *m* 1974, Dorothea (*née* Foth); one *s* one *d.* *Educ:* Westminster Sch.; Middlesex Hosp. Med. Sch. (MB BS). Leo Baeck Coll.; Univ. of Heidelberg (PhD). Junior hosp. doctor, 1966–67; Leo Baeck College: Rabbinic studies, 1967–71; Head of Dept of Bible Studies, 1974–85. Vis. Fellow, Tel Aviv Univ., 1990–91; Guest Prof., Kirchliche Hochschule, Wuppertal, Germany, 1992–93, 1995. Vice-Pres., World Union for Progressive Judaism, 1988–. Co-Editor, European Judaism, 1992– (Mem. Edtl Bd, 1978–); Member, Editorial Board: Christian-Jewish Relations, 1987–; Jl of Progressive Judaism, 1993–. *Publications:* Form and Meaning: studies in literary techniques in the Book of Jonah, 1976; (ed jtly) Forms of Prayer, vol. I, Daily and Sabbath Prayerbook, 1977, vol. III, Days of Awe Prayerbook, 1985, vol. II, Pilgrim Festival Prayerbook, 1995; (ed jtly) The Guide to the Here and Hereafter, 1988; A Rabbi's Bible, 1991; Bible Lives, 1992; (jtly) How to Get Up When Life Gets You Down, 1992; (ed jtly) The Little Blue Book of Prayer, 1993; A Rabbi Reads the Psalms, 1994; (jtly) Kindred Spirits, 1995; (ed) Jewish Explorations of Sexuality, 1995. *Address:* 18 Wellfield Avenue, N10 2EA. *T:* 0181–444 3025.

MAGRUTSCH, Dr Walter; Commander's Cross, Austria, 1988; Austrian Ambassador to the Court of St James's, 1987–93; *b* 16 July 1929; *s* of Hans and Magdalena Magrutsch; *m* 1955, Elisabeth Pihofsky; three *d.* *Educ:* Univ. of Vienna (Dr jur 1953), post-graduate studies in Paris. Practising law, Austrian courts, 1953–54; entered Austrian Diplomatic Service, 1954; Attaché, New Delhi, 1955–56; Secretary, Bonn, 1957–61; Counsellor, Prague, 1964–69; Envoy Extr. and Minister Plen., 1970; Head of Political Div. for Eastern Europe, China and Middle East, Min. of Foreign Affairs, 1970–74; Ambassador to Canada, 1974–78, to Brazil, 1978–81; Dir-Gen., Legal and Consular Affairs Section, MFA, 1982–87, concurrently Dep. Sec.-Gen. for Foreign Affairs, 1986–87. Decorations from FRG, Hungary, Indonesia, Brazil, France, Belgium. *Recreations:* mountaineering, tennis, piano playing. *Address:* Haizingergasse 52, 1180 Wien, Austria. *Clubs:* Travellers, Queen's.

MAGUIRE, (Albert) Michael, MC 1945; MM 1943; QC 1967; *b* 30 Dec. 1922; *s* of late Richard Maguire and Ruth Maguire. *Educ:* Hutton Grammar Sch.; Trinity Hall, Cambridge (BA 1948). Served War of 1939–45, North Irish Horse (Captain), in Africa (MM) and Italy (MC). Inns of Court Regt, 1946. War Crimes Investigation Unit, 1946. Called to the Bar, Middle Temple, 1949 (Harmsworth Scholar); Bencher, 1973; Leader, Northern Circuit, 1980–84. Last Recorder of Carlisle (1970–71). *Address:* Goldsmith Building, Temple, EC4Y 7BL; Chestnuts, 89 Lower Bank Road, Fulwood, Preston PR2 4NU. *T:* Preston (01772) 719291.

MAGUIRE, (Benjamin) Waldo, OBE 1973; *b* 31 May 1920; *s* of Benjamin Maguire and Elizabeth Ann Eldon; *m* 1944, Lilian Joan Martin; four *s.* *Educ:* Portadown Coll.; Trinity

Coll., Dublin. BA 1st cl. hons Philosophy. Intell. Service, WO and FO, 1942–45; BBC Latin American Service, 1945; BBC Radio News, 1946–55; BBC TV News, 1955; Editor, BBC TV News, 1962–64; Controller, News and Public Affairs, NZ Broadcasting Corp., 1965–66; BBC Controller, NI, 1966–72; Head of Information Programmes, NZ TV2, 1975–76. *Recreations:* gardening, conversation, angling. *Address:* 116 Park Avenue, Ruislip, Mddx HA4 7UP. *T:* Ruislip (01895) 635981.

MAGUIRE, Air Marshal Sir Harold John, KCB 1966 (CB 1958); DSO 1946; OBE 1949; Director, Commercial Union Assurance Co., 1975–82 (Political and Economic Adviser, 1972–79); *b* 12 April 1912; *s* of Michael Maguire, Maynooth, Ireland, and Harriett (*née* Warren), Kilkishen, Co. Clare, Ireland; *m* 1940, Mary Elisabeth Wild (*d* 1991), Dublin; one *s* one *d. Educ:* Wesley Coll., Dublin; Dublin Univ. Royal Air Force Commn, 1933; service in flying boats, 230 Sqdn, Egypt and Far East, 1935–38; commanded night fighter sqdn, UK, 1939–40 and day fighter sqdn, 1940; OC 266 (Fighter) Wing, Dutch E Indies, 1942; POW, Java, 1942; Staff Coll., 1947; Fighter Command Staff Duties, 1948–50; OC, RAF, Odiham, 1950–52; Senior Air Staff Officer, Malta, 1952–55; staff of CAS, Air Ministry, 1955–58; Senior Air Staff Officer, HQ No 11 Group, RAF, 1958–59; AOC No 13 Group, RAF, 1959–61; AOC No 11 Group, Fighter Command, 1961–62; SASO Far East Air Force, 1962–64; ACAS (Intelligence), 1964–65; Dep. Chief of Defence Staff (Intelligence), 1965–68; retired, 1968; Dir-Gen. of Intelligence, MoD, 1968–72. *Club:* Royal Air Force.

MAGUIRE, Hugh, FRAM; violinist and conductor; Director of Strings, Britten-Pears School for Advanced Music Studies, since 1978; Professor of Violin, Royal Academy of Music, since 1957; *b* 2 Aug. 1926; *m* 1st, 1953, Suzanne Lewis (marr. diss. 1987), of International Ballet; two *s* three *d*; 2nd, 1988, Tricia Catchpole. *Educ:* Belvedere Coll., SJ, Dublin; Royal Academy of Music, London (David Martin); Paris (Georges Enesco). Leader: Bournemouth Symphony Orchestra, 1952–56; London Symphony Orchestra, 1956–62; BBC Symphony Orchestra, 1962–67; Cremona String Quartet, 1966–68; Allegri String Quartet, 1968–76; Melos Ensemble, 1972–85; Orch. of Royal Opera House, Covent Garden, 1983–91. Artistic Dir, Irish Youth Orch. String coach, European Commn Youth Orch. Mem., Irish Arts Council. Hon. MMus Hull, 1975; Hon. DLitt Univ. of Ulster, 1986; Hon. DMus NUI, 1992. Harriet Cohen Internat. Award; Councils Gold Medal (Ireland), 1963; Cobbett Medal, Musicians' Co., 1982. *Address:* Manor Farm, Benhall, Suffolk IP17 1HN. *T:* Saxmundham (01728) 603245.

MAGUIRE, John Joseph; QC (Scot) 1990; Sheriff Principal of Tayside, Central and Fife, since 1990; *b* 30 Nov. 1934; *y s* of Robert Maguire, Solicitor, Glasgow, and Julia Maguire; *m* 1962, Eva O'Hara, Tralee, Co. Kerry; two *s* two *d. Educ:* St Mary's Coll., Blairs; Pontifical Gregorian Univ., Rome (PhL 1955); Edinburgh Univ. (LLB 1958). Mem., Faculty of Advocates, 1958; Standing Junior to MPBW, 1963–68; Sheriff Substitute: Airdrie, 1968; Glasgow, 1973. Mem., Deptl Cttee on Alternatives to Prosecution, 1977–82. Pres., Sheriffs' Assoc., 1989–90 (Sec., 1982–87). *Recreations:* reading, pottering in the garden. *Address:* Sheriff Principal's Chambers, Sheriff Court House, Tay Street, Perth PH2 8NL. *T:* (Court) Perth (01738) 620546; (home) Perth (01738) 636260. *Club:* New (Edinburgh).

MAGUIRE, Mairead C.; *see* Corrigan-Maguire.

MAGUIRE, Michael; *see* Maguire, A. M.

MAGUIRE, Rt. Rev. Robert Kenneth, MA, DD; Hon. Assisting Bishop: Diocese of Western New York, 1984–86; Diocese of Southeast Florida, 1984–89, retired; *b* 31 March 1923; *s* of late Robert Maguire and late Anne Crozier; unmarried. *Educ:* Trinity Coll., Dublin. BA 1945; Divinity Testimonium, 1947. Deacon, 1947; Priest, 1948. Curate of: St Mark, Armagh, 1947–49; St James the Apostle, Montreal, 1949–52; Dean of Residence, Trinity Coll., Dublin, 1952–60; Curate-in-charge of St Andrew's, Dublin, 1954–57; Minor Canon of St Patrick's Cathedral, Dublin, 1955–58; Dean and Rector of Christ Church Cathedral, Montreal, 1961–62; Bishop of Montreal, 1963–75. Co-ordinator: Canadian Conf., Theology '76, 1975–76; North American Consultation on the Future of Ministry, 1979–80. Assistant to the Primate, Anglican Church of Canada, 1980–84. DD (*jure dig.*): Dublin Univ., 1963; Montreal Diocesan Theolog. Coll., 1963; DCL (*hc*), Bishop's Univ., Lennoxville, Qué., 1963. *Address:* 4875 Dundas Street West, Apt 304, Islington, Ontario M9A 1B3, Canada.

MAGUIRE, Waldo; *see* Maguire, B. W.

MAHATHIR bin MOHAMAD, Dato Seri Dr; MHR for Kubang Pasu, since 1974; Prime Minister of Malaysia, since 1981, and Minister of Home Affairs, since 1986; *b* 20 Dec. 1925. *Educ:* Sultan Abdul Hamid Coll.; College of Medicine, Singapore (MB BS). Medical Officer, Kedah and Perlis, 1953–57; in private practice, 1957–64. MHR for Kota Star Selatan, 1964–69; Mem., Senate, 1972–74; Minister of: Education, 1974–77; Trade and Industry, 1977–81; Dep. Prime Minister, 1976–81. President, United Malays Nat. Organisation, 1981– (Mem., Supreme Council, 1972–). *Publication:* The Malay Dilemma, 1969. *Address:* Office of the Prime Minister, 5052 Kuala Lumpur, Malaysia.

MAHER, Terence; His Honour Judge Maher; a Circuit Judge, since 1995; *b* 20 Dec. 1941; *s* of late John Maher and of Bessie Maher; *m* 1965 (marr. diss. 1983); two *d. Educ:* Burnley Grammar Sch.; Univ. of Manchester. LLB (hons). Admitted Solicitor, 1966; articled to Town Clerk, Burnley; Asst Sol., City of Bradford, 1966–68; Prosecuting Sol., Birmingham Corp., 1968–70; Dep. Pros. Sol., Thames Valley Police, 1970–73; Asst Sol. and partner, Cole & Cole, Oxford, 1973–83; Metropolitan Stipendiary Magistrate, 1983–95; a Chm., Inner London Juvenile, subseq. Youth, Courts and Family Proceedings Court, 1985–95; a Recorder, 1989–95. Gen. Sec., Univ. of Manchester Students' Union, 1962–63; Chm., Chipping Norton Round Table, 1975–76; Treasurer/Vice-Chm. and Chm., Oxford and District Solicitors' Assoc., 1980–83; Mem., Law Society Standing Cttee on Criminal Law, 1980–85. Mem. Editl Bd, Jl of Criminal Law. *Recreations:* walking, reading, anything to do with France and the French. *Address:* c/o Wood Green Crown Court, Lordship Lane, N22. *Club:* Frewen (Oxford).

MAHER, Terence Anthony, FCCA; Chairman, Chalford Publishing Co. Ltd, since 1994; *b* 5 Dec. 1935; *s* of late Herbert and Lillian Maher; *m* 1960, Barbara (*née* Grunbaum); three *s. Educ:* Xaverian Coll., Manchester. ACCA 1960, FCCA 1970. Carborundum Co. Ltd, 1961–69; First National Finance Corp., 1969–72; Founder, Chm. and Chief Exec., Pentos plc, 1972–93; Chairman: Dillons Bookstores, 1977–93; Athena Internat., 1980–93; Ryman, 1987–93. Contested (L): Accrington, 1964; Runcorn, 1966. Founder Trustee, Lib Dem, 1988–. Trustee, Photographers' Gall., 1994–. FRSA 1988. *Publications:* (jtly) Counterblast, 1965; (jtly) Effective Politics, 1966; Against my better judgment, 1994. *Recreations:* reading, ski-ing, tennis, walking, music, bridge. *Address:* 33 Clarence Terrace, Regent's Park, NW1 4RD. *T:* 0171–723 4254; The Old House, Whichford, near Shipston-on-Stour, Warwickshire CV36 5PG. *T:* Long Compton (01608) 684614. *Club:* Savile.

MAHER, Very Rev. William Francis, SJ; Provincial Superior of the English Province of the Society of Jesus, 1976–81; *b* 20 June 1916. *Educ:* St Ignatius' College, Stamford Hill; Heythrop College, Oxon. STL. Entered the Society of Jesus, 1935; ordained priest, 1948; Principal, Heythrop College, 1974–76. *Address:* St Bernard's, 20A Southbourne Road, Holbury, Hants SO4 1NT.

MAHFOUZ, Naguib; Egyptian novelist; *b* 11 Dec. 1911; *m* Attiyah-Allah; *c. Educ:* King Fuad I Univ. (now Cairo Univ.). Sec., King Fuad I Univ.; Min. of Religious Affairs, 1939–54; screen writer (over 30 film scripts), 1945–; Dept of Arts, 1954; retired 1972. Nobel Prize for Literature, 1988. *Publications* include: trans. (into Arabic), James Baikie, Ancient Egypt, 1932; *novels:* 'Abath al-aqdar (Games of Fate), 1939; Radubis (Radobis), 1943; Kifah Tibah (The Struggle of Thebes), 1944; Al-Qahira al-jadida (New Cairo), 1946; Zuqaq al-middaq (Midaq Alley), 1947; Al-Sarab (The Mirage), 1949; Bidaya wa nihaya (The Beginning and the End), 1951; trilogy: Bayn al-qasrayn (Between the Two Palaces), vol. 1, 1956, Qasr al-shawq (The Palace of Desire), vol. 2, 1957, Al-Sukkariyya (The Sugar Bowl), vol. 3, 1957 (State Prize for Literature); trilogy, Awlad haritna (The Children of Our Lane), 1959; Al-Liss wa'l-kilab (The Thief and the Dogs), 1961; Al-Samman wa'l-kharif (Autumn Quail), 1962; Dunya'Illah (God's World), 1964; Al-Shahhat (The Beggar), 1965; Tharthara fawq al-nil (Small-talk on the Nile), 1966; Miramar, 1967; Hadrat al-muhtaram (Respected Sir), 1975; Afrah al-qubba (Wedding Songs), 1981; The Journey of Ibn Fattouma, 1993; Arabian Nights and Days, 1995; *short stories and plays for reading:* Taht al-mizalla (Under the Awning), 1969; Al-Mar'aya (Mirrors), 1972; Al'Hubb taht al-matar (Love in the Rain), 1973. *Address:* c/o Cinema Organisation, TV Building, Maspero Street, Cairo, Egypt.

MAHLER, Dr Halfdan Theodor; Director-General, World Health Organization, 1973–88, now Emeritus; Secretary-General, International Planned Parenthood Federation, since 1989; *b* 21 April 1923; *m* 1957, Dr Ebba Fischer-Simonsen; two *s. Educ:* Univ. of Copenhagen (MD, EOPH). Planning Officer, Internat. Tuberculosis Campaign, Ecuador, 1950–51; Sen. WHO Med. Officer, Nat. TB Programme, India, 1951–61; Chief MO, Tuberculosis Unit, WHO/HQ, Geneva, 1961–69; Dir, Project Systems Analysis, WHO/HQ, Geneva, 1969–70; Asst Dir-Gen., WHO, 1970–73. Hon. FFPHM 1975; Hon. FRSM 1976; Hon. FRCGP 1986; Hon. FRSTM&H, 1993; Hon. Fellow: Indian Soc. for Malaria and other Communicable Diseases, Delhi; Faculty of Community Med., RCP, 1975; Hon. Professor: Univ. Nacional Mayor de San Marcos, Lima, Peru, 1980; Fac. of Medicine, Univ. of Chile, 1982; Beijing Med. Coll., China, 1983; Shanghai Med. Univ., 1986; Bartel World Affairs Fellow, Cornell, 1988; Peking Univ., 1994; Hon. Advr, China FPA, 1994. Hon. Fellow: LSHTM, 1979; Coll. of Physicians and Surgeons, Dacca, Bangladesh, 1980; Hon. Member: Soc. médicale de Genève; Union internat. contre la Tuberculose; Société Française d'Hygiène, de Médecine Sociale et Génie Sanitaire, 1977; Med. Assoc. of Argentina, 1985; Latin American Med. Assoc., 1985; Italian Soc. of Tropical Medicine, 1986; APHA, 1988; Swedish Soc. of Medicine, 1988; Hon. Foreign Corresp. Mem., BMA, 1990; Hon. Life Mem., Uganda Medical Assoc., 1976; Assoc. Mem., Belgian Soc. of Trop. Medicine; List of Honour, Internat. Dental Fedn, 1984; Hon. Academician: Nat. Acad. of Medicine, Mexico, 1988; Nat. Acad. of Medicine, Buenos Aires, 1988. FRCP 1981. Hon. LLD: Nottingham, 1975; McMaster, 1989; Exeter, 1990; Toronto, 1990; Hon. MD: Karolinska Inst., 1977; Charles Univ., Prague, and Mahidol Univ., Bangkok, 1982; Aarhus, 1988; Copenhagen, 1988; Aga Khan, Pakistan, 1989; Newcastle upon Tyne, 1990; Hon. Dr de l'Univ. Toulouse (Sciences Sociales), 1977; Hon. Dr Public Health, Seoul Nat. Univ., 1979; Hon DSc: Lagos, 1979; Emory, Atlanta, 1989; SUNY, 1990; Hon. Dr Med. Warsaw Med. Acad., 1980; Hon. Dr Faculty of Medicine, Univ. of Ghent, Belgium, and Universidad Nacional Autonoma de Nicaragua, Managua, 1983; Hon. DHL CUNY, 1989; Dr *hc*: Universidad Nacional 'Federico Villarreal', Lima, Peru, 1980; Semmelweis Univ. of Medicine, Budapest, 1987. Jane Evangelisty Purkyne Medal, Prague, 1974; Comenius Univ. Gold Medal, Bratislava, 1974; Carlo Forlanini Gold Medal, 1975; Ernst Carlsens Foundn Prize, Copenhagen, 1980; Georg Barfred-Pedersen Prize, Copenhagen, 1982; Hagedorn Medal and Prize, Denmark, 1986; Freedom from Want Medal, Roosevelt Inst., 1988; Bourgeoisie d'Honneur, Geneva, 1989; UK–US Hewitt Award, RSM, 1992; Dr Ved Vias Puri Meml Award, 1994. Grand Officier: l'Ordre Nat. du Bénin, 1975; l'Ordre Nat. Voltaïque, 1978; l'Ordre du Mérite, République du Sénégal, 1982; Ordre National Malgache (Madagascar), 1987; Comdr (1st cl.), White Rose Order of Finland, 1983; Commandeur, l'Ordre National du Mali, 1982; Grand Cordon, Order of the Sacred Treasure (Japan), 1988; Storkors Af Dannebrogsordenen (Denmark), 1988; Grand Cross: Order of the Falcon (Iceland), 1988; Order of Merit (Luxembourg), 1990. *Publications:* papers etc on the epidemiology and control of tuberculosis, the political, social, economic and technological priority setting in the health sector, and the application of systems analysis to health care problems. *Recreations:* sailing, ski-ing. *Address:* 12 chemin du Pont-Ceard, 1290 Versoix, Switzerland.

MAHLER, Prof. Robert Frederick, FRCP, FRCPE; Editor, Journal of Royal College of Physicians, 1987–94, Editor Emeritus, since 1994; Consultant Physician, Clinical Research Centre, Northwick Park Hospital, Harrow, 1979–90, retired; *b* 31 Oct. 1924; *s* of Felix Mahler and Olga Lowy; *m* 1951, Maureen Calvert; two *s. Educ:* Edinburgh Academy; Edinburgh Univ. BSc; MB, ChB. Research fellowships and univ. posts in medicine, biochemistry and clinical pharmacology at various med. schs and univs: in Gt Britain: Royal Postgrad. Med. Sch., Guy's Hosp., Manchester, Dundee, Cardiff; in USA: Harvard Univ., Univ. of Indiana; in Sweden: Karolinska Inst., Stockholm; Prof. of Med., Univ. of Wales, 1970–79. Royal College of Physicians: Mem. Council, 1974–76; Censor, 1976–78; Bradshaw Lectr, 1977. Member: MRC, 1977–81; Commonwealth Scholarship Commn, 1980–93; Council, Imperial Cancer Res. Fund, 1984–94; Res. Cttee, British Diabetic Assoc., 1984–87; Scientific Co-ord. Cttee, Arthritis and Rheumatism Council, 1986–91. *Publications:* contribs to British and Amer. med. and scientific jls. *Recreations:* opera, music, theatre. *Address:* 14 Manley Street, NW1 8LT. *Club:* Royal Society of Medicine.

MAHON, Alice; MP (Lab) Halifax, since 1987; *b* 28 Sept. 1937; *m*; two *s*. Lectr, Bradford and Ilkeley Community Coll. Member: Calderdale Bor. Council, 1982–87; Calderdale DHA. *Address:* House of Commons, SW1A 0AA; 125 The Hough, Northowram, Halifax, W Yorks HX3 7DE.

MAHON, Charles Joseph; His Honour Judge Mahon; a Circuit Judge, since 1989; *b* 16 Aug. 1939; *s* of late Frank and Amy Agnes Mahon; *m* 1974, Lavinia Gough (*née* Breaks); one *d* and one step *s* two step *d. Educ:* Chetham's Hosp.; Gonville and Caius Coll., Cambridge (BA, LLB). Called to the Bar, Gray's Inn, 1962. Parachute Regt, TA, 1966–72. *Recreations:* music—playing and writing, books, walking.

MAHON, Sir Denis; *see* Mahon, Sir J. D.

MAHON, Sir (John) Denis, Kt 1986; CBE 1967; MA Oxon; FBA 1964; Art Historian; Trustee of the National Gallery, 1957–64 and 1966–73; Member, Advisory Panel, National Art-Collections Fund, since 1975; *b* 8 Nov. 1910; *s* of late John FitzGerald Mahon (4th *s* of Sir W. Mahon, 4th Bt) and Lady Alice Evelyn Browne (*d* 1970), *d* of 5th Marquess of Sligo. *Educ:* Eton; Christ Church, Oxford. Has specialised in the study of 17th-Century painting in Italy and has formed a collection of pictures of the period; is a member of the

Cttee of the Biennial Exhibitions at Bologna, Italy; was awarded, 1957, Medal for Benemeriti della Cultura by Pres. of Italy for services to criticism and history of Italian art; Archiginnasio d'Oro, City of Bologna, 1968; Serena Medal for Italian Studies, British Acad., 1972. Elected Accademico d'Onore, Clementine Acad., Bologna, 1964; Sen. Fellow, RCA, 1988; Corresp. Fellow: Accad. Raffaello, Urbino, 1968; Deputazione di Storia Patria per le provincie di Romagna, 1969. Ateneo Veneto, 1987. Hon. Citizen, Cento, 1982. Hon. DLitt: Newcastle, 1969; Oxford, 1994. *Publications:* Studies in Seicento Art and Theory, 1947; Mostra dei Carracci, Catalogo critico dei Disegni, 1956 (1963); Poussiniana, 1962; Catalogues of the Mostra del Guercino (Dipinti, 1968; Disegni, 1969); (with Nicholas Turner) The Drawings of Guercino in the Collection of Her Majesty the Queen at Windsor Castle, 1989; catalogues of exhibitions for 4th centenary of Guercino's birth, 1991–92; contributed to: Actes of Colloque Poussin, 1960; Friedlaender Festschrift, 1965; Problemi Guardeschi, 1967; (consultant) Luigi Salerno, I Dipinti del Guercino, 1988; articles, including a number on Caravaggio and Poussin, in art-historical periodicals, *eg,* The Burlington Magazine, Apollo, The Art Bulletin, Journal of the Warburg and Courtauld Institutes, Bulletin of the Metropolitan Museum of New York, Gazette des Beaux-Arts, Art de France, Paragone, Commentari, Zeitschrift für Kunstwissenschaft; has collaborated in the compilation of catalogues raisonnés of exhibitions, *eg,* Artists in 17th Century Rome (London, 1955), Italian Art and Britain (Royal Academy, 1960), L'Ideale Classico del Seicento in Italia (Bologna, 1962), Omaggio al Guercino (Cento, 1967). *Address:* 33 Cadogan Square, SW1X 0HU. *T:* 0171–235 7311, 0171–235 2530.

MAHON, Peter, JP; *b* 4 May 1909; *s* of late Alderman Simon Mahon, OBE, JP, Bootle, Liverpool; *m* 1935, Margaret Mahon (*née* Hannon). *Educ:* St James Elementary Sch.; St Edward's Coll. (Irish Christian Brothers). One of the longest serving Local Govt representatives in GB (42 years); Bootle Borough Council, 1933–70 (Mayor, 1954–55); Liverpool City Council, 1970–75; Liverpool DC, 1973–80 (Mem. (L) Old Swan Ward); Chm. or Dep. Chm. numerous cttees; Mem. Nat. Cttee of TGWU. Prospective Parly Candidate (Lab) Blackburn, 1952–54, contested (Lab) Preston, 1962–64; MP (Lab) Preston South, 1964–70; contested Liverpool Scotland, April 1971, as first Against Abortion candidate in UK; expelled from Labour Party. Talked out first Abortion Bill, House of Commons, 1966. *Recreations:* football and swimming enthusiast; fond of music. *Address:* Seahaven, Burbo Bank Road, Blundellsands, Liverpool L23 8TA.

MAHON, Colonel Sir William (Walter), 7th Bt *cr* 1819 (UK), of Castlegar, Co. Galway; *b* 4 Dec. 1940; *s* of Sir George Edward John Mahon, 6th Bt and Audrey Evelyn (*née* Jagger) (*d* 1957); *S* father, 1987; *m* 1968, Rosemary Jane, *yr d* of Lt-Col M. E. Melvill, OBE, Symington, Lanarks; one *s* two *d. Educ:* Eton. *Recreations:* shooting, watercolours, collecting, military history. *Heir: s* James William Mahon, *b* 29 Oct. 1976. *Club:* Army and Navy.

MAHONEY, Dennis Leonard; Deputy Chairman, Alexander Howden Group, since 1995; *b* 20 Sept. 1950; *s* of late Frederick Mahoney; *m* 1st, Julia McLaughlin (marr. diss.); one *s* one *d;* 2nd, 1988, Jacqueline Fox; one *s* one *d. Educ:* West Hatch Technical High School; Harvard Business Sch. (PMD 1983). Dir, Alexander & Alexander Services UK, 1969–; Managing Dir, Sedgwick Forbes N America, 1979; Dep. Chm., Sedgwick Forbes N America and Dir, Sedgwick Ltd, 1982; Chm., Alexander Howden Ltd, 1984. Dep. Chm., Lloyd's Insce Brokers Cttee, 1990. *Recreations:* ski-ing, shooting. *Address:* Alexander Howden Group, 8 Devonshire Square, EC2M 4PL.

MAHONEY, Rev. Prof. John Aloysius, (Jack), SJ; Dixons Professor of Business Ethics and Social Responsibility, London Business School, since 1993; *b* Coatbridge, 14 Jan. 1931; *s* of Patrick Mahoney and Margaret Cecilia Mahoney (*née* Doris). *Educ:* Our Lady's High Sch., Motherwell, St Aloysius' Coll., Glasgow; Univ. of Glasgow (MA 1951). LicPhil 1956; LicTheol 1963; DTheol *summa cum laude,* Pontifical Gregorian Univ., Rome, 1967. Entered Society of Jesus, 1951; ordained priest, 1962; Jesuit Tertianship, NY, 1963–64. Lectr in Moral and Pastoral Theology, Heythrop Coll., Oxon, 1967–70, and Heythrop Coll., London, 1970–86; Principal, Heythrop Coll., London, 1976–81; F. D. Maurice Prof. of Moral and Social Theology, KCL, 1986–93; Founding Dir, KCL Business Ethics Res. Centre, 1987–93; Dean, Faculty of Theol., London Univ., and Faculty of Theol. and Religious Studies, KCL, 1990–92. Mercers' Sch. Meml Prof. of Commerce, Gresham Coll., London, 1987–93; Martin D'Arcy Meml Lectr, Campion Hall, Oxford, 1981–82. Mem., Internat. Theol. Commn, Rome, 1974–80; Sector Pres., Nat. Pastoral Congress, 1980; Mem., Internat. Study Gp on Bioethics, Internat. Fedn of Catholic Univs. 1984–93. Pres., Catholic Theolog. Assoc., 1984–86. Chaplain to Tablet Table, 1983–; Domestic Chaplain to Lord Mayor of London, 1989–90. FRSA; CIMgt 1993. Founding Editor, Business Ethics, A European Review, 1992–. *Publications:* Seeking the Spirit, 1981; Bioethics and Belief, 1984; The Making of Moral Theology, 1987; The Ways of Wisdom, 1987; Teaching Business Ethics in the UK, Europe and USA, 1990; (ed) Business Ethics in a New Europe, 1992. *Recreations:* piano, sketching, unrequited golf. *Address:* Farm Street Church, 114 Mount Street, W1Y 6AH. *T:* 0171–493 7811.

MAHONY, Francis Joseph, CB 1980; OBE 1972; President, Repatriation Review Tribunal, Australia, 1979–84; *b* 15 March 1915; *s* of Cornelius J. Mahony and Angela M. Heagney; *m* 1939, Mary K. Sexton; seven *s* one *d. Educ:* De La Salle Coll., Armidale; Sydney Univ. (LLB 1940). Served War, CMF and AIF, 1942–44. Called to the Bar, Supreme Court of NSW, 1940; Commonwealth Crown Solicitor's Office, 1941; admitted Practitioner, High Ct of Australia, 1950; admitted Solicitor, Supreme Ct of NSW, 1952; Dep. Commonwealth Crown Solicitor, NSW, 1963–70; Dep. Sec., Attorney-Gen.'s Dept, Canberra, 1970–79. Leader, Aust. Delegn to Diplomatic Conf. on Humanitarian Law Applicable in Armed Conflicts, 1974–77. Chairman: Criminology Res. Council, 1972–79; Bd of Management, Aust. Inst. of Criminology, 1973–79; Mem. UN Cttee, Crime Prevention and Control, 1980–83. *Recreation:* golf. *Address:* 92 Cliff Avenue, Northbridge, NSW 2063, Australia. *T:* (2) 9587853. *Club:* Northbridge Golf.

MAHY, Brian Wilfred John, PhD, ScD; Director, Division of Viral and Rickettsial Diseases (formerly Division of Viral Diseases), Centers for Disease Control and Prevention, Atlanta, since 1989; Adjunct Professor, Emory University, since 1993; *b* 7 May 1937; *s* of Wilfred Mahy and Norah Dillingham; *m* 1st, 1959, Valerie Pouteaux (marr. diss. 1986); two *s* one *d;* 2nd, 1988, Penny Scott (*née* Cunningham). *Educ:* Elizabeth Coll., Guernsey; Univ. of Southampton (BSc, PhD); Univ. of Cambridge (MA, ScD). Res. Biologist, Dept of Cancer Res., London Hosp. Med. Coll., Univ. of London, 1962–65; Asst Dir, Res. Virology, Dept of Pathology, Cambridge Univ., 1965–79; Fellow and Tutor, University (Wolfson) Coll., 1967–84; Librarian, Wolfson Coll., 1975–80; Huddersfield Lectr in Special Path. (Virology), 1979–84; Head, Div. of Virology, Cambridge, 1979–84; Head, Pirbright Lab., AFRC Inst. for Animal Health (formerly Animal Virus Res. Inst. and AFRC Inst. for Animal Disease Res.), 1984–89. Vis. Prof., Univ. of Minnesota, 1968; Eleanor Roosevelt Internat. Cancer Fellow, Dept of Microbiol., Univ. of California, San Francisco, 1973–74; Vis. Prof., Inst. für Virologie, Univ. of Würzburg, 1980–81. Convener, Virus Group, 1980–84, Mem. Council, 1983–87, Soc. for General Microbiology; Vice-Chm., 1987–90, Chm., 1990–93, Past Chm., 1994–, Vice Pres., 1995–, Virology Div., Internat. Union of Microbiol Socs. FRSocMed 1985; Fellow, Infectious Diseases Soc. of America, 1992. Editor-in-Chief, Virus Research, 1983–; US Editor, Jl of Med. Virology, 1994–. *Publications:* (jtly) The Biology of Large RNA Viruses, 1970; Negative Strand Viruses, 1975; Negative Strand Virus and the Host Cell, 1978; Lactic Dehydrogenase Virus, 1975. A Dictionary of Virology, 1981; Virus Persistence, 1982; The Microbe 1984: pt 1, Viruses, 1984; Virology: a practical approach, 1985; The Biology of Negative Strand Viruses, 1987; Genetics and Pathogenicity of Negative Strand Viruses, 1989; Concepts in Virology: from Ivanovsky to the present, 1993; numerous articles on animal virology in learned jls. *Recreations:* playing the violin in chamber and orchestral groups, gardening. *Address:* Division of Viral and Rickettsial Diseases (A30), Centers for Disease Control and Prevention, 1600 Clifton Road, NE, Atlanta, GA 30333, USA.

MAHY, Margaret May, ONZ 1993; writer; *b* 21 March 1936; *d* of Francis George Mahy and Helen May Penlington; two *d. Educ:* Whakatane Primary and High Schs; Univ. of NZ (BA). Asst Librarian, Petone Public Library, 1959; Asst Children's Librarian, Christchurch Public Library, 1960; Librarian i/c of school requests, Sch. Library Service (Christchurch Br.), 1967; Children's Librarian, Christchurch Public Library, 1977; full time writer, 1980–. Hon. DLitt Canterbury, 1993. Carnegie Medal, 1982, 1984; Esther Glen Medal. *Publications: picture books:* The Dragon of an Ordinary Family, 1969; A Lion in the Meadow, 1969; Mrs Discombobulous, 1969; Pillycock's Shop, 1969; The Procession, 1969; The Little Witch, 1970; Sailor Jack and the Twenty Orphans, 1970; The Princes and the Clown, 1971; The Boy with Two Shadows, 1971; The Man whose Mother was a Pirate, 1972; The Railway Engine and the Hairy Brigands, 1973; Rooms for Rent/Rooms to Let, 1974; The Witch in the Cherry Tree, 1974; The Rare Spotted Birthday Party, 1974; Stepmother, 1974; The Ultra-Violet Catastrophe, 1975; The Great Millionaire Kidnap, 1975; The Wind Between the Stars, 1976; David's Witch Doctor, 1976; The Boy who was Followed Home, 1977; Leaf Magic, 1976; Jam, 1985; The Great White Maneating Shark, 1989; *collections of stories:* three Margaret Mahy Story Books, 1972, 1973, 1975; Nonstop Nonsense, 1977; The Great Piratical Rumbustification and The Librarian and the Robbers, 1978; The Chewing-Gum Rescue, 1982; The Birthday Burglar and a Very Wicked Headmistress, 1984; Ups and Downs, 1984; Wibble Wobble, 1984; The Dragon's Birthday, 1984; The Spider in the Shower, 1984; The Downhill Crocodile Whizz, 1986; Mahy Magic, 1986; The Three Wishes, 1986; The Door in the Air, 1988; Tick Tock Tales, 1994; *junior novels:* Clancy's Cabin, 1974; The Bus Under the Leaves, 1975; The Pirate Uncle, 1977; Raging Robots and Unruly Uncles, 1981; The Pirates' Mixed-Up Voyage, 1983; The Blood and Thunder Adventure on Hurricane Peak, 1989; The Cousins Quartet, books 1–4, 1994; *novels for older readers:* The Haunting, 1982; The Changeover, 1984; The Catalogue of the Universe, 1985; Aliens in the Family, 1986; The Tricksters, 1986; Memory, 1987; Dangerous Spuces, 1991; Underrunners, 1992; *for schools:* The Crocodile's Christmas Jandals, 1982; The Bubbling Crocodile, 1983; Mrs Bubble's Baby, 1983; Shopping with a Crocodile, 1983; Going to the Beach, 1984; The Great Grumbler and the Wonder Tree, 1984; Fantail Fantail, 1984; A Crocodile in the Garden, 1985; The Crocodile's Christmas Thongs, 1985; Horrakapotchin, 1985; *for emergent readers:* The Adventures of a Kite, 1985; Sophie's Singing Mother, 1985; The Earthquake, 1985; The Cake, 1985; The Catten, 1985; Out in the Big Wild World, 1985; A Vary Happy Bathday, 1985; Clever Hamburger, 1985; Muppy's Ball, 1986; Baby's Breakfast, 1986; The Tree Doctor, 1986; The Garden Party, 1986; The Man who Enjoyed Grumbling, 1986; The Trouble with Heathrow, 1986; The Pop Group, 1986; Feeling Funny, 1986; A Pet to the Vet, 1986; The New House Villain, 1986; Tai Taylor is Born, 1986; The Terrible Topsy-Turvy Tissy-Tossy Tangle, 1986; Trouble on the Bus, 1986; Mr Rumfitt, 1986; My Wonderful Aunt, 1986; *verse:* Seventeen Kings and Forty-Two Elephants, 1972; *non-fiction:* Look Under 'V', 1977. *Recreations:* reading, gardening. *Address:* No 1 RD, Lyttelton, New Zealand. *T:* (3) 299703

MAIDEN, Sir Colin (James), Kt 1992; ME, DPhil; Chairman: Fisher & Paykel Ltd, since 1978; National Insurance Company of New Zealand Ltd, since 1988; Independent Newspapers Ltd, since 1989; Vice Chancellor, University of Auckland, New Zealand, 1971–94; *b* 5 May 1933; *s* of Henry A. Maiden; *m* 1957, Jenefor Mary Rowe; one *s* three *d. Educ:* Auckland Grammar Sch.; Univ. of Auckland, NZ; Oxford Univ. ME(NZ), DPhil (Oxon). Post-doctorate research, Oxford Univ., Oxford, Eng. (supported by AERE, Harwell), 1957–58; Head of Hypersonic Physics Section, Canadian Armament Research and Develt Estabt, Quebec City, Canada, 1958–60; Sen. Lectr in Mechanical Engrg, Univ. of Auckland, 1960–61; Head of Material Sciences Laboratory, Gen. Motors Corp., Defense Research Laboratories, Santa Barbara, Calif, USA, 1961–66; Manager of Process Engineering, Gen. Motors Corp., Technl Centre, Warren, Michigan, USA, 1966–70. Chm., NZ Synthetic Fuels Corp. Ltd, 1980–90; Director: Mason Industries Ltd, 1971–78; Farmers Trading Co. Ltd, 1973–86; Wilkins & Davies Co. Ltd, 1986–89; Winstone Ltd, 1978–88; NZ Steel Ltd, 1988–92; ANZ Banking Gp (NZ) Ltd, 1990–93; NZ Refining Co. Ltd, 1991–; Progressive Enterprises Ltd, 1992–; Trans Power NZ Ltd, 1994–; DB Group Ltd, 1994–; Sedgwick Group (NZ) Ltd, 1994–; Tower Corp., 1995–. Chairman: NZ Energy R&D Cttee, 1974–81; Liquid Fuels Trust Bd, 1978–86; Chm., NZ Vice-Chancellors' Cttee, 1977–78, and 1991; Hon. Treasurer, ACU, 1988–. Member: Spirit of Adventure Trust Bd, 1972–80; NZ Metric Adv. Bd, 1973–77. NZ Agent for Joint NZ/US Sci. and Technol Agreement, 1974–81. Hon. LLD Auckland. Thomson Medal, Royal Soc. NZ, 1986; Medal, Univ. of Bonn, 1983. Silver Jubilee Medal, 1977. *Publications:* numerous scientific and technical papers. *Recreation:* tennis. *Address:* 7 Chatfield Place, Remuera, Auckland, New Zealand. *T:* (9) 5290380. *Clubs:* Vincent's (Oxford); Northern, Rotary (Auckland); Remuera Racquets, Eden Epsom Tennis, International Lawn Tennis of NZ, Auckland Golf.

MAIDEN, James Dennis, CEng; FFB; Director General, Federation of Master Builders, since 1991; *b* 28 June 1932; *s* of James William Maiden and Elsie (*née* Brotherton); *m* 1953, Irene Harris; one *s* one *d. Educ:* Wath-upon-Dearne Grammar Sch. CEng 1966; MIMechE 1966; FFB 1987. Engrg Consultant, Husband & Co., 1958–63; Chief Engr, British Shoe Corp., 1963–67; Construction Industry Training Board: Develt Manager, 1967–73; Gen. Manager, 1973–76; Dir of Trng, 1976–85; Chief Exec., 1985–90; Dir-Gen. designate, Fedn of Master Builders, 1990–91. Chief Exec., Construction Ind. Services Ltd, 1991–; Managing Director: Nat. Register of Warranted Builders Ltd, 1991–; Trade Debt Recovery Service Ltd, 1991–. Pres., Kings Lynn Inst. of Mgt, 1988. Trustee, Leonard Cheshire Foundn, 1987–92; Pres., Norfolk Outward Bound Assoc., 1988. Hon. Mem., C & G, 1981; CIMgt 1986; MIPM 1971. FRSA 1987. Freeman, City of London, 1988; Liveryman, Co of: Constructors, 1988; Plumbers, 1989. *Recreations:* golf, gardening, theatre. *Address:* 203 Gilbert House, The Barbican, EC2Y 8BD. *T:* 0171–588 6019; Micklebring, Church Lane, Bircham, Kings Lynn, Norfolk PE31 6QW. *T:* Kings Lynn (01485) 23336. *Clubs:* Royal Automobile; Hunstanton Golf.

MAIDEN, Robert Mitchell, FCIBS; Managing Director, Royal Bank of Scotland plc, and Executive Director, Royal Bank of Scotland Group plc, 1986–91; *b* 15 Sept. 1933; *s* of Harry and Georgina Maiden; *m* 1958, Margaret Mercer (*née* Nicolson). *Educ:* Montrose Acad., Tayside, Scotland. Royal Bank of Scotland: various appts, 1950–74; Supt of branches, 1974–76; Treasurer, 1976–77; Chief Accountant, 1977–81; Gen. Man. (Finance), 1981–82; Exec. Dir, 1982–86. Vice-Chm., CC-Bank AG, Germany, 1991–93; Chm., Lothian and Edinburgh Enterprise, 1994–. Mem., Commn for Local Authority Accounts in Scotland, 1992–. Gov., Napier Univ. (formerly Napier Poly.), 1988–. Trustee, C of S Pension Scheme, 1991–. FIMgt; FRSA. *Recreations:* music, golf, reading, hill walking. *Address:* Trinafour, 202 Braid Road, Edinburgh EH10 6HS. *Club:* New (Edinburgh).

MAIDMENT, Francis Edward, (Ted); Headmaster, Shrewsbury School, since 1988; *b* 23 Aug. 1942; *s* of Charles Edward and late Olive Mary Maidment. *Educ:* Pocklington Sch., York; Jesus Coll., Cambridge (Scholar). Asst Master, Lancing Coll., 1965–81 (Housemaster, 1975–81); Headmaster, Ellesmere Coll., Shropshire, 1982–88. *Recreations:* singing, medieval history, modest tennis. *Address:* Shrewsbury School, Shropshire SY3 7BA. *T:* Shrewsbury (01743) 344537.

MAIDMENT, Ted; *see* Maidment, F. E.

MAIDSTONE, Viscount; Daniel James Hatfield Finch Hatton; *b* 7 Oct. 1967; *s* and *heir* of 16th Earl of Winchilsea, *qv*; *m* Shelley Amanda Gillard. *Educ:* Ansford Comprehensive School, Castle Cary, Som. *Recreations:* swimming, cycling.

MAIDSTONE, Bishop Suffragan of, since 1992; **Rt. Rev. Gavin Hunter Reid;** *b* 24 May 1934; *s* of Arthur William Reid and Jean Smith Reid (*née* Guthrie); *m* 1959, Mary Eleanor Smith; two *s* one *d*. *Educ:* Roan Sch., Greenwich; Queen Mary Coll. and King's Coll., London Univ. (BA 1956); Oak Hill Theol Coll. Ordained, Chelmsford Cathedral: deacon, 1960; priest, 1961; Assistant Curate: St Paul's, East Ham, 1960–63; Rainham Parish Church, 1963–66; Publications Sec., CPAS, 1966–71; Editorial Sec., United Soc. for Christian Lit., 1971–74; Sec. for Evangelism, 1974–90, Consultant Missioner, 1990–92, CPAS; Advr, Gen. Synod Bd of Mission, 1990–92. Seconded: Nat. Dir, Mission England, 1982–85; Project Dir, Mission 89, 1988–89. *Publications:* The Gagging of God, 1969; The Elaborate Funeral, 1972; A New Happiness, 1974; To Be Confirmed, 1977; Good News to Share, 1979; Starting Out Together, 1981; To Reach a Nation, 1987; Beyond Aids, 1987; Lights that Shine, 1991; Brushing up on Believing, 1991; Our Place in his Story, 1994; various symposia. *Recreations:* golf, sailing, walking, birdwatching. *Address:* The Bishop's House, Pett Lane, Charing, Ashford, Kent TN27 0DL. *T:* Charing (01233) 712950.

MAIDSTONE, Archdeacon of; *see* Evans, Ven. P. A. S.

MAILER, Norman; *b* 31 Jan. 1923; *s* of Isaac Barnett Mailer and Fanny Schneider; *m* 1st, 1944, Beatrice Silverman (marr. diss., 1951); one *d*; 2nd, 1954, Adèle Morales (marr. diss., 1962); two *d*; 3rd, 1962, Lady Jeanne Campbell (marr. diss., 1963); one *d*; 4th, 1963, Beverly Bentley; two *s*; 5th, Carol Stevens; one *d*; 6th, Norris Church; one *s*. *Educ:* Harvard. Infantryman, US Army, 1944–46. Co-founder of Village Voice, 1955; an Editor of Dissent, 1953–63. Democratic Candidate, Mayoral Primaries, New York City, 1969. Directed films: Wild 90, 1967; Beyond the Law, 1967; Maidstone, 1968; Tough Guys Don't Dance, 1988. Pulitzer Prize for Fiction, 1980. *Publications:* The Naked and the Dead, 1948; Barbary Shore, 1951; The Deer Park, 1955 (dramatized, 1967); Advertisements for Myself, 1959; Deaths For The Ladies, 1962; The Presidential Papers, 1963; An American Dream, 1964; Cannibals and Christians, 1966; Why Are We In Vietnam?, 1967 (a novel); The Armies of the Night, 1968 (Pulitzer Prize, 1969); Miami and the Siege of Chicago, 1968 (National Book Award, 1969); Of a Fire on the Moon, 1970; The Prisoner of Sex, 1971; Existential Errands, 1972; St George and the Godfather, 1972; Marilyn, 1973; The Faith of Graffiti, 1974; The Fight, 1975; Some Honorable Men, 1975; Genius and Lust, 1976; A Transit to Narcissus, 1978; The Executioner's Song, 1979; Of a Small and Modest Malignancy, Wicked and Bristling with Dots, 1980; Of Women and Their Elegance, 1980; The Essential Mailer, 1982; Ancient Evenings, 1983; Tough Guys Don't Dance, 1984; Harlot's Ghost, 1991; Oswald's Tale: an American mystery, 1995. *Address:* c/o Rembar, 19 W 44th Street, New York, NY 10036, USA.

MAILLART, Ella (Kini); traveller; *b* 20 Feb. 1903; Swiss father and Danish mother; unmarried. *Educ:* Geneva; and also while teaching French at two schools in England. Took to the seas at 20, cruising with 3 ton Perlette, 10 ton Bonita, 45 ton Atalante-all these manned by girls; then 120 ton Volunteer, 125 ton Insoumise; in Mediterranean, Biscay, Channel; sailed for Switzerland, Olympic Games, Paris, 1924, single-handed competition; hockey for Switzerland as captain in 1931; skied for Switzerland in the FIS races in 1931–34; went to Russia for 6 months, 1930; travelled in Russian Turkestan for 6 months 1932; went to Manchoukuo for Petit Parisien, 1934; returned overland accompanied by Peter Fleming, via Koko Nor; travelled overland to Iran and Afghanistan in 1937 and 1939, in South India, 1940–45, Nepal, 1951, Everest Base Camp, 1965. Fellow RGS, London; Member: Royal Soc. for Asian Affairs; Club des Explorateurs, Paris; Hon. Mem., GB-China Centre. Sir Percy Sykes Medal. *Publications:* Parmi la Jeunesse Russe, 1932; Des Monts Célestes aux Sables Rouges, 1934 (in English as Turkestan Solo, 1934, repr. 1985); Oasis Interdites, 1937 (in English as Forbidden Journey, 1937, repr. 1983); Gipsy Afloat, 1942; Cruises and Caravans, 1942; The Cruel Way, 1947, repr. 1986; Ti-Puss, 1952; The Land of the Sherpas, 1955; La Vie Immédiate, 1991. *Recreations:* ski-ing, gardening. *Address:* 10 Avenue G. Vallette, 1206 Geneva, Switzerland. *T:* (22) 3464657; Atchala, Chandolin sur Sierre, Switzerland. *Clubs:* Kandahar, (hon.) Ski Club of Great Britain; (hon.) Alpine.

MAIN, Frank Fiddes, CB 1965; FRCPEd; Chief Medical Officer, Ministry of Health and Social Services, Northern Ireland, 1954–68, retired; *b* 9 June 1905; *s* of Frank and Mary Main, Edinburgh; *m* 1931, Minnie Roberta Paton; two *s* two *d*. *Educ:* Daniel Stewart's Coll., Edinburgh; Edinburgh Univ. MB, ChB 1927; DPH 1931; MRCPEd 1954; FRCPEd 1956. Medical Officer of Health, Perth, 1937–48; Senior Administrative Medical Officer, Eastern Regional Hosp. Bd (Scotland), 1948–54. Crown Mem., Gen. Med. Council, 1956–69. QHP 1956–59. *Recreation:* golf. *Address:* Balnacarron, 116 Hepburn Gardens, St Andrews, Fife KY16 9LT.

MAIN, Air Vice-Marshal John Bartram, OBE 1979 (MBE 1977); Air Officer Communications and Information Systems, and Air Officer Commanding Signals Unit, HQ Logistics Command, 1994–April 1996; Military Adviser, Matra Marconi Space UK Ltd, from April 1996; *b* 28 Jan. 1941; *s* of late Wing Comdr James Taylor Main, OBE and of Nellie Ethel Toleman; *m* 1965, Helen Joyce Lambert; two *d*. *Educ:* Portsmouth Grammar Sch.; Birmingham Univ. (BSc Elect. Eng.); RAF Tech. Coll., Henlow. CEng, FIEE, FIEIE, FRAeS. Commissioned Engr Branch, RAF, 1960; served Benson, Hiswa (Aden), Thorney Island; Dir of Sci. and Tech. Intell., MoD, 1970–74; OC No 33 Signals Unit, Cyprus, 1974–77; CO RAF Digby, 1977–79; RAF Staff Coll., 1979–80; RAF Signals Engrg Estabt, 1980–83; Head, Tech. Intell. (Air), 1983–87; RCDS 1986; Dep. Comd Aerosystems Engr, HQ Strike Comd, 1987–88; Comdt, RAF Sigs Engrg Estabt and Air Cdre Sigs, HQ RAF Support Comd, 1988–89; Dir, Command, Control, Communication and Inf. Systems (Policy and Op. Requirements), 1989–93; DG Support Services (RAF), 1993–94. *Recreations:* gardening, cycling, tennis, windsurfing, sailing, reading. *Address:* c/o Lloyds Bank, 38 London Road, North End, Portsmouth, Hants PO2 0LR. *Club:* Royal Air Force.

MAIN, His Honour John Roy, QC 1974; a Circuit Judge, 1976–95; *b* 21 June 1930; *yr s* of late A. C. Main, MIMechE; *m* 1955, Angela de la Condamine Davies, *er d* of late R. W. H. Davies, ICS; two *s* one *d*. *Educ:* Portsmouth Grammar Sch.; Hotchkiss Sch., USA; Brasenose Coll., Oxford (MA). Called to Bar, Inner Temple, 1954; a Recorder of Crown Court, 1972–76. Mem. Special Panel, Transport Tribunal, 1970–76; Dep. Chm., IoW QS, 1971. Gov., Portsmouth Grammar Sch., 1988–. *Recreations:* walking, gardening, music. *Address:* 4 Queen Anne Drive, Claygate, Surrey KT10 0PP. *T:* Esher (01372) 466380.

MAIN, Sir Peter (Tester), Kt 1985; ERD 1964; Chairman, The Boots Company PLC, 1982–85; *b* 21 March 1925; *s* of late Peter Tester Main and Esther Paterson (*née* Lawson); *m* 1st, 1952, Dr Margaret Fimister, MB, ChB (*née* Tweddle) (*d* 1984); two *s* one *d*; 2nd, 1986, May Hetherington Anderson (*née* McMillan). *Educ:* Robert Gordon's Coll., Aberdeen; Univ. of Aberdeen (MB, ChB 1948, MD 1963; Hon. LLD 1986). MRCPE 1981, FRCPE 1982. Captain, RAMC, 1949–51; MO with Field Ambulance attached to Commando Bde, Suez, 1956; Lt-Col RAMC (AER), retd 1964. House Surg., Aberdeen Royal Infirmary, 1948; House Physician, Woodend Hosp., Aberdeen, 1949; Demonstrator, Univ. of Durham, 1952; gen. practice, 1953–57; joined Res. Dept, Boots, 1957; Dir of Res., 1968; Man. Dir, Industrial Div., 1979–80; Dir, 1973–85, Vice-Chm., 1980–81, The Boots Company PLC. Chm., Inveresk Res. Internat., 1986–89; Dir, 1985–91, Vice-Chm., 1990–91, W. A. Baxter and Sons Ltd; Dir, John Fleming and Co., 1985–89. Chm., Cttee of Inquiry into Teachers' Pay and Conditions, Scotland, 1986; Member: NEDC, 1984–85; Scottish Health Service Policy Board, 1985–88; SDA, 1986–91. Governor, Henley Management Coll., 1983–86; Chm., Grantown Heritage Trust, 1987–91; Trustee, Univ. of Aberdeen Develt Trust, 1988–. CIMgt (FBIM 1978). *Recreations:* fly fishing, Scottish music. *Address:* Ninewells House, Chirnside, Duns, Berwickshire TD11 3XF.

MAINES, James Dennis, CEng, FIEE; Director General, Command Information Systems, Ministry of Defence, since 1995; *b* 26 July 1937; *s* of Arthur Burtonwood Maines and Lilian Maines (*née* Carter); *m* 1960, Janet Enid Kemp; three *s*. *Educ:* Leigh Grammar School; City University (BSc). Joined RSRE (then RRE), Malvern, 1956 (Sandwich course in applied physics, 1956–60); Head of Guided Weapons Optics and Electronics Group, 1981; Head, Microwave and Electro-optics Group, 1983; Head, Sensors, Electronic Warfare and Guided Weapons, ARE, Portsdown, 1984–86; Dep. Dir (Mission Systems), RAE, 1986–88; Dir Gen., Guided Weapons and Electronics Systems, MoD, 1988–95. Wolfe Award for outstanding MoD research (jtly), 1973. *Publications:* (jtly) Surface Wave Filters (ed Matthews), 1977; papers in learned jls. *Recreations:* sailing, cricket, squash, painting, non-labour intensive gardening. *Address:* Ministry of Defence, Room 316, Empress State Building, Lillie Road, SW6 1TR.

MAINGARD de la VILLE ès OFFRANS, Sir (Louis Pierre) René, (Sir René Maingard), Kt 1982; CBE 1961; company chairman and director, Mauritius; Chairman, Colonial Steamships Co. Ltd, since 1948; *b* 9 July 1917; *s* of Joseph René Maingard de la Ville ès Offrans and Véronique Hugnin; *m* 1946, Marie Hélène Françoise Raffray; three *d*. *Educ:* St Joseph's Coll.; Royal Coll. of Mauritius; Business Training Corp., London. Clerk, Rogers & Co. Ltd, 1936, Man. Dir, 1948. Chairman: Rogers & Co. Ltd, 1956–82; Mauritius Steam Navigation Co. Ltd, 1964–; Mauritius Portland Cement Co. Ltd, 1960–; De Chazal du Mée Associates Ltd, 1982–. Director: Mauritius Commercial Bank Ltd, 1956–; New Mauritius Dock Co. Ltd, 1948–. Formerly, Consul for Finland in Mauritius. Chevalier 1st Cl., Order of the White Rose, Finland, 1973. *Recreations:* golf, fishing, boating. *Address:* Rogers & Co. Ltd, PO Box 60, Port Louis, Mauritius. *T:* 086801. *Clubs:* Royal Air Force; Dodo, Mauritius Naval & Military Gymkhana (Mauritius).

MAINI, Sir Amar (Nath), Kt 1957; CBE 1953 (OBE 1948); *b* Nairobi, 31 July 1911; *e s* of late Nauhria Ram Maini, Nairobi, Kenya, and Ludhiana, Punjab, India; *m* 1935, Ram Saheli Mehra (*d* 1982), Ludhiana; two *s*. *Educ:* Govt Indian Sch., Nairobi; London Sch. of Economics (BCom, Hons 1932). Barrister-at-law, Middle Temple, London, 1933. Advocate of High Court of Kenya, and of High Court of Uganda. Sometime an actg MLC, Kenya, and Mem. Nairobi Municipal Council. From 1939 onwards, in Uganda; associated with family cotton business of Nauhria Ram & Sons (Uganda) Ltd. Formerly: Mem. Kampala Township Authority, Chm., Kampala Municipal Council, 1st Mayor of Kampala (1950–55); Dep. Chm., Uganda Electricity Board; Member: Uganda Development Corporation; Lint Marketing Board; Civil Defence Bd; Asian Manpower Cttee; Transport Bd; Supplies Bd; Immigration Advisory Bd; Advisory Bd of Health; Railway Advisory Council; Advisory Bd of Commerce; Rent Restriction Bd; Makerere Coll. Assembly, etc. Past Pres. Central Council of Indian Assocs in Uganda; Indian Assoc., Kampala; served on Cttees of Cotton Association. Formerly: Mem. Uganda Legislative and Exec. Councils; Development Council, Uganda; EA Legislative Assembly; EA Postal Advisory Bd; EA Transport Adv. Council; EA Air Adv Council, etc. Minister for Corporations and Regional Communications in the Government of Uganda, 1955–58; Minister of Commerce and Industry in Uganda, 1958–61; Speaker, E African Central Legislative Assembly, 1961–67; Mem., E African Common Market Tribunal, 1967–69. Dep. Chm. Kenya Broadcasting Corp., 1962–63. *Recreations:* walking, listening. *Address:* 55 Vicarage Road, East Sheen, SW14 8RY. *T:* 0181–878 1497. *Clubs:* Reform; Nairobi.
See also R. N. Maini.

MAINI, Prof. Ravinder Nath, FRCP; Professor of Rheumatology, Charing Cross and Westminster Medical School, University of London, since 1989; Director, Kennedy Institute of Rheumatology, since 1990 (Head, Clinical Immunology Division, since 1970); *b* 17 Nov. 1937; *s* of Sir Amar (Nath) Maini, *qv* and of late Saheli (*née* Mehra); *m* 1st, 1963, Marianne Gorm (marr. diss. 1986); one *s* one *d* (and one *s* decd); 2nd, 1987, Geraldine Room; two *s*. *Educ:* Cambridge Univ. (BA; MB, BChir 1962). MRCP 1966, FRCP 1977. Jun. med. appts, Guy's, Brompton and Charing Cross Hosps, 1962–70; Consultant Physician: St Stephen's Hosp., London, 1970–76; Rheumatology Dept, Charing Cross Hosp., 1970–; Prof. of Immunology of Rheumatic Diseases, Charing Cross and Westminster Med. Sch., 1981–89. President: Brit. Soc. Rheumatology, 1989–90 (Heberden Orator, 1988); Brit. League Against Rheumatism, 1985–89; Chm., Res. Subcttee, 1980–85, and Mem., Scientific Co-ordinating Cttee, 1980–, Arthritis and Rheumatism Council; Chm., Standing Cttee for Investigative Rheumatology, European League Against Rheumatism, 1990–; Mem., Exec. Cttee, Assoc. Physicians of GB and NI, 1989–91. Hon. Member: Australian Rheumatism Assoc., 1977; Norwegian Soc. for Rheumatology, 1988; Amer. Coll. of Rheumatology, 1988; Hellenic Rheumatology Soc., 1989; Hungarian Rheumatology Soc., 1990. *Publications:* Immunology of Rheumatic Diseases, 1977; (ed) Modulation of Autoimmune Disease, 1981; (contrib.) Textbook of the Rheumatic Diseases, 6th edn 1986; (ed) T cell activation in health and disease, 1989; (ed) Rheumatoid Arthritis, 1992; Immunopathogenisis of Rheumatoid Arthritis in Oxford Textbook of Rheumatology, 1993; articles in learned jls. *Recreations:* music appreciation, walking. *Address:* Kennedy Institute of Rheumatology, 6 Bute Gardens, W6 7DW. *T:* 0181–748 9966. *Club:* Reform.

MAINWARING, Captain Maurice K. C.; *see* Cavenagh-Mainwaring.

MAIR, Alexander, MBE 1967; Chief Executive and Director, Grampian Television Ltd, 1970–87, retired; *b* 5 Nov. 1922; *s* of Charles Mair and Helen Dickie; *m* 1953, Margaret Isobel Gowans Rennie. *Educ:* Skene, Aberdeenshire; Webster's Business Coll., Aberdeen; Sch. of Accountancy, Glasgow. Fellow, CIMA, 1992 (Associate, 1953). Chief Accountant,

Bydand Holdings Ltd, 1957–60; Company Sec., Grampian Television, 1961–70; apptd Dir, 1967; Director: ITN, 1980–87; Cablevision (Scotland) Ltd, 1983–88; TV Publication Ltd, 1970–87. Chairman: British Regional Television Assoc., 1973–75; ITCA Management Cttee, 1980–87; RGIT Ltd, 1989–. Pres., Aberdeen Junior Chamber of Commerce, 1960–61; Mem. Council, Aberdeen Chamber of Commerce, 1973– (Vice-Pres., 1987–89; Pres., 1989–91). Gov., Robert Gordon's Coll., Aberdeen, 1987–. FRSA 1973. FRTS 1987. *Recreations:* golf, ski-ing, gardening. *Address:* Ravenswood, 66 Rubislaw Den South, Aberdeen AB2 6AX. *T:* Aberdeen (01224) 317619. *Club:* Royal Northern (Aberdeen).

MAIR, Alexander Stirling Fraser, (Alistair), MBE 1987; DL; Chairman, since 1991, and Managing Director, since 1977, Caithness Glass Ltd; *b* 20 July 1935; *s* of Alexander W. R. Mair and Agnes W. (*née* Stirling); *m* 1st, 1961, Alice Anne Garrow (*d* 1975); four *s*; 2nd, 1977, Mary Crawford Bolton; one *d*. *Educ:* Robert Gordon's Coll., Aberdeen; Aberdeen Univ. (BSc Eng)). SSC, RAF, 1960–62. Rolls-Royce, Glasgow: grad. apprentice, 1957–59; various appts, until Product Centre Manager, 1963–71; Man. Dir, Caithness Glass, Wick, 1971–75; Marketing Dir, Worcester Royal Porcelain Co., 1975–77. Director: Grampian Television, 1986–; Crieff Hydro Ltd, 1994–. Vice Chm., Scottish Cons. and Unionist Party, 1992–93. Mem. Council, CBI, 1985– (Chm., Scotland, 1989–91). Dep. Pres., British Glass Manufacturers' Confedn, 1994–. Chm., Crieff Aux. Assoc. (Richmond House), 1993–. Mem. Court, Aberdeen Univ., 1993–; Gov., Morrison's Acad., Crieff, 1985–; Comr, Queen Victoria Sch., Dunblane, 1992–. FIMgt; FRSA 1986. DL Perth and Kinross 1993. *Recreations:* walking, gardening, swimming, current affairs. *Address:* Dungora, Crieff, Perthshire PH7 4AG. *T:* Crieff (01764) 652191. *Club:* Royal Scottish Automobile (Glasgow).

MAIR, John Magnus; Director of Social Work, Edinburgh, 1969–75; Lecturer in Social Medicine, University of Edinburgh, 1959–75; *b* 29 Dec. 1912; *s* of Joseph Alexander Mair and Jane Anderson; *m* 1940, Isobelle Margaret Williamson (*d* 1969); three *s*. *Educ:* Anderson Inst., Lerwick; Univs of Aberdeen (MB, ChB) and Edinburgh (DPH). MFCM. Asst GP, Highlands and Islands Medical Service, 1937–40; RAMC, 1940–45; Edinburgh Public Health Dept (latterly Sen. Depute Medical Officer of Health), 1945–69. *Recreation:* golf. *Address:* 46 Allington Road, Hendon, NW4 3DE. *T:* 0181–202 4186. *Clubs:* Edinburgh University Staff; Grampian (Corby).

MAIR, Prof. William Austyn, CBE 1969; MA; FEng 1984; Francis Mond Professor of Aeronautical Engineering, University of Cambridge, 1952–83; Head of Engineering Department, 1973–83; Fellow of Downing College, Cambridge, 1953–83, Hon. Fellow, 1983; *b* 24 Feb. 1917; *s* of William Mair, MD; *m* 1944, Mary Woodhouse Crofts; two *s*. *Educ:* Highgate Sch.; Clare Coll., Cambridge. Aerodynamics Dept, Royal Aircraft Establishment, Farnborough, 1940–46; Dir, Fluid Motion Laboratory, Univ. of Manchester, 1946–52. Mem. various cttees, Aeronautical Research Council, 1946–80. Dir, Hovercraft Development Ltd, 1962–81. John Orr Meml Lectr, S Africa, 1983. Chm., Editorial Bd, Aeronautical Qly, 1975–81. FRAeS (Silver Medal 1975). Hon. DSc Cranfield, 1990. *Publications:* (with D. L. Birdsall) Aircraft Performance, 1992; papers on aerodynamics. *Address:* 7 The Oast House, Pinehurst, Grange Road, Cambridge CB3 9AP. *T:* Cambridge (01223) 350137.

MAIS, Francis Thomas; Secretary, Royal Northern College of Music, 1982–90; *b* 27 June 1927; *s* of Charles Edward Mais and Emma (*née* McLoughlin); *m* 1st, Margaret Edythe Evans (*d* 1984); one *d*; 2nd, 1987, Joan Frost-Smith. *Educ:* Barnsley Grammar Sch.; Christ's Coll., Cambridge (MA). Northern Ireland Civil Service, 1951–82: Permanent Secretary: Dept of Commerce, 1979–81; Dept of Manpower Services, 1981–82. Governor, Associated Bd, Royal Schs of Music, 1985–92. Hon. RNCM 1987. *Address:* The Old Smithy, Rosgill, Penrith, Cumbria CA10 2QX. *T:* Shap (01931) 716113.

MAIS, Hon. Sir (Robert) Hugh, Kt 1971; Judge of the High Court of Justice, Queen's Bench Division, 1971–82; *b* 14 Sept. 1907; *s* of late Robert Stanley Oliver Mais, Chobham, Surrey; *m* 1938, Catherine (*d* 1987), *d* of J. P. Pattinson, *widow* of C. E. Kessler; one *s*, two step *s* (and one step *d* decd). *Educ:* Shrewsbury Sch.; Wadham Coll., Oxford (MA, 1948, Hon. Fellow, 1971). Called to the Bar, 1930, Bencher, Inner Temple, 1971; Mem. of Northern Circuit. Chancellor of the Diocese of: Manchester, 1948–71; Carlisle, 1950–71; Sheffield, 1950–71. Judge of County Courts: Circuit No 37 (West London), 1958–60; Circuit No 42 (Marylebone), 1960–71. Dep. Chm., Berkshire QS, 1964–71; Commissioner of Assize: SE Circuit, 1964, 1967; Oxford Circuit, 1968, 1969; NE Circuit, 1971. Mem., Winn Cttee on Personal Injuries Litigation. Served as Wing Comdr, RAF, 1940–44. *Recreations:* fishing, golf. *Address:* Ripton, Streatley-on-Thames, Berks RG8 9LE. *T:* Goring (01491) 872397.

MAISEY, Prof. Michael Norman, BSc, MD; FRCP; FRCR; Professor of Radiological Sciences, United Medical and Dental Schools of Guy's and St Thomas's Hospitals, since 1984; Medical Director and Chairman of the Management Board of Guy's Hospital, since 1991; Joint Medical Director, Guy's and St Thomas's NHS Trust, since 1993; *b* 10 June 1939; *s* of Harold Lionel Maisey and Kathleen Christine Maisey; *m* 1965, Irene Charlotte (*née* Askay); two *s*. *Educ:* Caterham Sch.; Guy's Hosp. Med. Sch. (BSc, MD). ABNM 1972; FRCP 1980. House appts, 1964–66; Registrar, Guy's Hosp., 1966–69; Fellow, Johns Hopkins Med. Instns, 1970–72; Sen. Registrar, Guy's Hosp., 1972–73; Consultant Physician, Endocrinology and Nuclear Medicine, Guy's Hosp., 1973–. Hon. Consultant to the Army in Nuclear Medicine, 1978–. *Publications:* Nuclear Medicine, 1980; Clinical Nuclear Medicine, 1982; books and papers on thyroid diseases and nuclear medicine. *Address:* Guy's Hospital, St Thomas Street, SE1 9RT. *T:* 0171–955 9000.

MAISNER, Air Vice-Marshal Aleksander, CB 1977; CBE 1969; AFC 1955; *b* 26 July 1921; *s* of Henryk Maisner and Helene Anne (*née* Brosin); *m* 1946, Mary (*née* Coverley); one *s* one *d*. *Educ:* High Sch. and Lyceum, Czestochowa, Poland; Warsaw Univ. Labour Camps, USSR, 1940–41; Polish Artillery, 1941–42; Polish Air Force, 1943–46; joined RAF, 1946; Flying Trng Comd, 1946–49, No 70 Sqdn Suez Canal Zone, 1950–52; No 50 Sqdn RAF Binbrook, 1953–55; No 230 (Vulcan) OCU, RAF Waddington, 1955–59; psa 1960; OC Flying Wing, RNZAF Ohakea, 1961–62; Dirg Staff, RAF Staff Coll., Andover, 1963–65; DD Air Plans, MoD, 1965–68; CO, RAF Seletar, Singapore, 1969–71; Asst Comdt, RAF Coll., Cranwell, 1971–73; Dir, Personnel (Policy and Plans), MoD, 1973–75; Asst Air Sec., 1975; Dir-Gen. of Personnel Management, RAF, 1976. Personnel Exec., Reed Internat. Ltd, 1977–82; Dir, Industry and Parlt Trust, 1984–87. Governor, Shiplake Coll., 1978–. Pres., Polish Air Force Assoc., 1982–. Comdr's Cross with Star, Order of Polonia Restituta (Poland), 1990; Comdr's Cross, OM (Poland), 1992. *Recreations:* gardening, reading. *Address:* c/o Lloyds Bank, 1 Reading Road, Henley-on-Thames, Oxon RG9 1AE. *Club:* Royal Air Force.

MAISONROUGE, Jacques Gaston; management consultant; *b* Cachan, Seine, 20 Sept. 1924; *s* of Paul Maisonrouge and Suzanne (*née* Cazas); *m* 1948, Françoise Andrée Féron; one *s* four *d*. *Educ:* Lycée Voltaire and Saint Louis, Paris. Studied engineering; gained dip. of Ecole Centrale des Arts et Manufactures. Engineer, 1948; various subseq. appts in IBM Corp., France; Chm. and Chief Exec. Officer, IBM World Trade Europe/ME/Africa Corp., 1974–81; Pres., IBM Europe, 1974–81; Sen. Vice-Pres., 1972–84, and Mem. Bd of Dirs, 1983–84, IBM Corp.; Chm., IBM World Trade Corp., 1976–84; Vice Chm., Liquid Air Corp., 1984–86; Dir-Gen. of Industry, France, 1986–87; Chm. of Bd, French Centre for Foreign Trade, 1987–89. Director: L'Air Liquide, 1964–94; IBM Europe/ME/Africa, 1987–. Chm., Bd of Trustees, Ecole Centrale des Arts et Manufactures, 1976–87; Chancellor, Internat. Acad. of Management, 1987–93. Commander: Ordre de la Légion d'Honneur; Ordre National du Mérite; des Palmes Académiques; Order of Merit of the Italian Republic; Order of Saint Sylvester; Order of Star of North (Sweden); Grand Officer, Order of Malta. *Publication:* Inside IBM: a European's story, 1985. *Recreations:* interested in sport (tennis). *Address:* 90 rue de la Faisanderie, 75116 Paris, France. *Club:* Automobile of France, Cercle Interallié.

MAITLAND, family name of **Earl of Lauderdale.**

MAITLAND, Viscount; Master of Lauderdale; **Ian Maitland;** Senior Regional Manager, Africa and Middle East, National Westminster Bank, since 1991; *b* 4 Nov. 1937; *s* and *heir* of Earl of Lauderdale, *qv*; *m* 1963, Ann Paule, *d* of Geoffrey Clark; one *s* one *d*. *Educ:* Radley Coll., Abingdon; Brasenose Coll., Oxford (MA Modern History). Various appointments since 1960; with Hedderwick Borthwick & Co., 1970–74; National Westminster Bank, 1974–: Regl Manager, Maghreb, 1986, ME and N Africa, 1989–91. Royal Naval Reserve (Lieutenant), 1963–73; Mem., Queen's Body Guard for Scotland, Royal Co. of Archers, 1986–. *Recreations:* photography, sailing. *Heir: s* Master of Maitland, *qv*. *Address:* 150 Tachbrook Street, SW1V 2NE. *Clubs:* Bankers, Royal Ocean Racing; New (Edinburgh).

MAITLAND, Master of; Hon. John Douglas Maitland; *b* 29 May 1965; *s* and *heir* of Viscount Maitland, *qv*. *Educ:* Emanuel School; Radley College; Van Mildert College, Durham (BSc). *Recreations:* cycling, camping, sailing. *Address:* 150 Tachbrook Street, SW1V 2NE.

MAITLAND, Alastair George, CBE 1966; Consul-General, Boston, 1971–75, retired; *b* 30 Jan. 1916; *s* of late Thomas Douglas Maitland, MBE, and Wilhelmina Sarah Dundas; *m* 1st, 1943, Betty Hamilton (*d* 1981); two *s* one *d*; 2nd, 1986, Hazel Margaret Porter. *Educ:* George Watson's Coll., Edinburgh; Universities of Edinburgh (MA First Class Hons), Grenoble and Paris, Ecole des Sciences Politiques. Vice-Consul: New York, 1938; Chicago, 1939; New York, 1939; Los Angeles, 1940; apptd to staff of UK High Commissioner at Ottawa, 1942; apptd to Foreign Office, 1945; Brit. Middle East Office, Cairo, 1948; Foreign Office, 1952; UK Delegation to OEEC, Paris, 1954; Consul-General: at New Orleans, 1958–62; at Jerusalem, 1962–64; at Cleveland, 1964–68; Dir-Gen., British Trade Develt Office, NY, 1968–71. Hon. LLD Lake Erie Coll., Ohio, 1971. CStJ. *Recreations:* music, golf, gardening, reading. *Address:* Box 31, Heath, MA 01346, USA.

MAITLAND, Charles Alexander, (10th Bt *cr* 1918, of Clifton, Midlothian); *b* 3 June 1986; *s* of Sir Richard John Maitland, 9th Bt (*d* 1994). Has not yet established his claim to the title.

MAITLAND, David Henry, CVO 1988; non-executive director of companies; *b* 9 May 1922; *s* of George and Mary Annie Maitland; *m* 1955, Judeth Mary Gold; three *d*. *Educ:* Eton; King's College, Cambridge. FCA. Army, 1941–46, Captain, Oxf. & Bucks Light Inf. Articled Whinney Smith & Whinney, 1946; qualified ACA 1950; Mobil Oil Co., 1952–60; Save & Prosper Group: Comptroller, 1960; Managing Dir and Chief Exec., 1966; Chm., 1979; non-exec. Dir, 1981; retired 1987. Dir, HFC Bank, 1989–. Chm., Unit Trust Assoc., 1973–75; Member: City Capital Markets Cttee, 1975–84; Inflation Accounting Steering Group, 1976–80; Council, Duchy of Lancaster, 1977–87; Bethlem Royal Hosp. and Maudsley Hosp. SHA, 1982–90; Royal Commn for 1851 Exhibn, 1984–; Lord Mayor Treloar Trust, 1984–. Vice-Chm., Crafts Council, 1989–90 (Mem., 1984–90). Chairman: Cttee of Management, Inst. of Psychiatry, 1987–90; Gabbitas Truman & Thring Educnl Trust, 1986–89. *Recreations:* gardening, golf. *Address:* St Paul's House, Upper Froyle, near Alton, Hants GU34 4LB. *T:* Bentley (01420) 22183. *Clubs:* City of London (Chm., 1986–88), Woking Golf.

MAITLAND, Sir Donald (James Dundas), GCMG 1977 (CMG 1967); Kt 1973; OBE 1960; Chairman, Health Education Authority, 1989–94; *b* 16 Aug. 1922; *s* of Thomas Douglas Maitland and Wilhelmina Sarah Dundas; *m* 1950, Jean Marie Young, *d* of Gordon Young; one *s* one *d*. *Educ:* George Watson's Coll.; Edinburgh Univ (MA). Served India, Middle East, and Burma, 1941–47 (Royal Scots; Rajputana Rifles). Joined Foreign Service, 1947; Consul, Amara, 1950; British Embassy, Baghdad, 1950–53; Private Sec. to Minister of State, Foreign Office, 1954–56; Director, Middle East Centre for Arab Studies, Lebanon, 1956–60; Foreign Office, 1960–63; Counsellor, British Embassy, Cairo, 1963–65; Head of News Dept, Foreign Office, 1965–67; Principal Private Sec. to Foreign and Commonwealth Secretary, 1967–69; Ambassador to Libya, 1969–70; Chief Press Sec., 10 Downing St, 1970–73; UK Permanent Rep. to UN, 1973–74; Dep. Under-Sec. of State, FCO, 1974–75; UK Mem., Commonwealth Group on Trade, Aid and Develt, 1975; Ambassador and UK Perm. Rep. to EEC, 1975–79; Dep. to Perm. Under-Sec. of State, FCO, Dec. 1979–June 1980; Perm. Under-Sec. of State, Dept of Energy, 1980–82. Chm., Independent Commn for World-Wide Telecommunications Develt, 1983–85. Govt Dir, Britoil, 1983–85; Director: Slough Estates, 1983–92; Northern Engrg Industries, 1986–89. Dep. Chm., IBA, 1986–89. Chairman: UK National Cttee for World Communications Year, 1983; Charlemagne Inst. (formerly Christians for Europe), 1984–. Mem., Commonwealth War Graves Commn, 1983–87. President: Bath Inst. for Rheumatic Diseases, 1986–95; Federal Trust for Educn and Res., 1987–; Vice-Pres., Centre Européen de Prospective et de Synthèse, Paris, 1990–95. Chm. of Govs, Westminster Coll., Oxford, 1994– (Gov., 1990–). *Recreations:* hill-walking, music. *Address:* Murhill Farm House, Limpley Stoke, Bath BA3 6HH. *T:* Limpley Stoke (01225) 723157.

MAITLAND, Lady (Helen) Olga, (Lady Olga Hay); MP (C) Sutton and Cheam, since 1992, journalist; *b* 23 May 1944; *er d* of Earl of Lauderdale, *qv*; *m* 1969, Robin Hay, *qv*; two *s* one *d*. *Educ:* Sch. of St Mary and St Anne, Abbots Bromley; Lycée Français de Londres. Reporter, Fleet St News Agency, Blackheath and Dist Reporter, 1965–67; journalist, Sunday Express, 1967–91. ILEA Candidate, Holborn and St Pancras, 1986; contested (C) Bethnal Green and Stepney, 1987. Member, Select Committee: on Educn; on Procedures. Secretary: Cons. Backbench Defence Cttee; Cons. Back bench NI Cttee. Founder and Chm., Families for Defence, 1983–; Pres., Defence and Security Forum, 1992–; Patron, St Raphael's Hospice Appeal, 1992–. *Publications:* Margaret Thatcher: the first ten years, 1989; (contrib.) Peace Studies in our Schools, 1984; (contrib.) Political Indoctrination in Schools, 1985. *Recreations:* family, gardening, the arts, travel. *Address:* House of Commons, SW1A 0AA. *T:* 0171–219 5239/6482; (constituency) 48 Benhill Avenue, Sutton, Surrey SM1 4DA. *T:* 0181–642 3791.

MAITLAND DAVIES, Keith Laurence; Metropolitan Stipendiary Magistrate, since 1984; *b* 3 Feb. 1938; *s* of Wyndham Matabele Davies, QC and Enid Maud Davies; *m* 1964, Angela Mary (*née* Fraser-Jenkins); two *d* one *s*. *Educ:* Winchester; Christ Church, Oxford (MA). Called to the Bar, Inner Temple, 1962; private practice, 1962–84. *Address:* c/o Marylebone Magistrates' Court, 181 Marylebone Road, NW1 5QJ.

MAITLAND-MAKGILL-CRICHTON; *see* Crichton.

MAITLAND SMITH, Geoffrey; Chairman, Sears plc (formerly Sears Holdings plc), 1985–95; chartered accountant; *b* 27 Feb. 1933; *s* of late Philip John Maitland Smith and of Kathleen (*née* Goff); *m* 1986, Lucinda Enid, *d* of late Lt-Col Gerald Owen Whyte. *Educ:* University Coll. Sch., London. Partner, Thornton Baker & Co., Chartered Accountants, 1960–70; Sears plc: Dir, 1971–95; Dep. Chm., 1978–84; Jt Chm., 1984; Chief Exec., 1978–88; Chairman: British Shoe Corp. Ltd, 1984–92; Selfridges Ltd, 1985–93 (Dep. Chm., 1978–85); Mallett plc, 1986–89 (Dir, 1986–89); Hammerson plc, 1993– (Dir, 1990–); Dep. Chm., Midland Bank plc, 1992– (Dir, 1986–); Director: Asprey plc, 1980–93; Central Independent Television plc, 1983–85; Courtaulds plc, 1983–90; Imperial Group plc, 1984–86; HSBC Holdings plc, 1992–. Mem. Bd, Financial Reporting Council, 1990–. Pres., Intercontinental Gp of Department Stores, 1990–95. Hon. Vice Pres., Inst. of Marketing, 1987–94. Chm. Council, University Coll. Sch. Liveryman, Worshipful Co. of Gardeners. *Recreations:* opera, music. *Address:* (office) 100 Park Lane, W1Y 4AR. *T:* 0171–887 1000.

MAITLIS, Prof. Peter Michael, FRS 1984; Professor of Chemistry, Sheffield University, since 1972; *b* 15 Jan. 1933; *s* of Jacob Maitlis and Judith Maitlis; *m* 1959, Marion (*née* Basco); three *d*. *Educ:* Univ. of Birmingham (BSc 1953); Univ. of London (PhD 1956, DSc 1971). Asst Lectr, London Univ., 1956–60; Fulbright Fellow and Res. Associate, Cornell Univ., 1960–61, Harvard Univ., 1961–62; Asst Prof, 1962–64, Associate Prof., 1964–67, Prof., 1967–72, McMaster Univ., Hamilton, Ont, Canada; Prof. of Inorganic Chemistry, Univ. of Sheffield, 1972–. Chm., Chemistry Cttee, SERC, 1985–88. Fellow, Alfred P. Sloan Foundn, USA, 1968–70; Tilden Lectr, RSC, London, 1979–80; Sir Edward Frankland Prize Lectr, RSC, 1985. Member: Royal Soc. of Chemistry (formerly Chem. Soc.), 1952– (Pres., Dalton Div., 1985–87); Amer. Chemical Soc., 1963–; Council, Royal Soc., 1991–93; BBC Sci. Consultative Gp, 1989–93. E. W. R. Steacie Prize (Canada), 1971; Medallist, RSC (Noble Metals and their Compounds), 1981. *Publications:* The Organic Chemistry of Palladium, vols 1 and 2, 1971; many research papers in learned jls. *Recreations:* travel, music, reading, swimming. *Address:* Department of Chemistry, The University, Sheffield S3 7HF. *T:* Sheffield (0114) 282 4480.

MAJOR; *see* Henniker-Major, family name of Baron Henniker.

MAJOR, Rt. Hon. John, PC 1987; MP (C) Huntingdon, since 1983 (Huntingdonshire, 1979–83); Prime Minister and First Lord of the Treasury, since 1990; *b* 29 March 1943; *s* of late Thomas Major and Gwendolyn Minny Coates; *m* 1970, Norma Christina Elizabeth (*née* Johnson); one *s* one *d*. *Educ:* Rutlish. AIB. Banker, Standard Chartered Bank: various executive posts in UK and overseas, 1965–79. Contested (C) St Pancras North (Camden), Feb. 1974 and Oct. 1974; PPS to Ministers of State at the Home Office, 1981–83; an Asst Govt Whip, 1983–84; a Lord Comr of HM Treasury (a Govt Whip), 1984–85; Parly Under-Sec. of State for Social Security, DHSS, 1985–86; Minister of State for Social ecurity, DHSS, 1986–87; Chief Sec. to HM Treasury, 1987–89; Sec. of State for Foreign Commonwealth Affairs, 1989; Chancellor of the Exchequer, 1989–90. Member, beth Borough Council, 1968–71 (Chm. Housing Cttee, 1970–71). Jt Sec., Cons. Party Environment Cttee, 1979–81; Parly Consultant, Guild of Glass Engravers, 1979–83. Mem. Bd, Warden Housing Assoc., 1975–83. Pres., Eastern Area Young Conservatives, 1983–85. *Recreations:* opera, cricket, football. *Address:* 10 Downing Street, SW1A 2AA. *Clubs:* Carlton, MCC.

MAJOR, John, FRICS; Land Agent to HM the Queen, Sandringham Estate, since 1991; *b* 16 June 1945; *s* of John Robert Major and Vera Major; *m* 1967, (Mary) Ruth Oddy; one *s* one *d*. *Educ:* Wellingborough Sch.; RAC, Cirencester. FRICS 1980. Partner, Osmond Tricks, Bristol, 1980–85; Land Agent, Castle Howard, N Yorks, 1986–91. *Recreation:* sailing. *Address:* Laycocks, Sandringham, King's Lynn, Norfolk PE35 6EB. *Club:* Farmers.

MAJOR, Kathleen, FBA 1977; Professor (part-time) of History, University of Nottingham, 1966–71; Principal of St Hilda's College, Oxford, 1955–65; Hon. Fellow, St Hilda's College, 1965; *b* 10 April 1906; *er d* of late George Major and Gertrude Blow. *Educ:* various private schools; St Hilda's College, Oxford. Honour School of Modern History, 1928; BLitt 1931. Librarian, St Hilda's College, 1931. Archivist to the Bishop of Lincoln, 1936; Lecturer, 1945, subsequently Reader in Diplomatic in the University of Oxford, until July 1955. Hon. Secretary, Lincoln Record Society, 1935–56 and 1965–74, Hon. Gen. Editor, 1935–75. Member Academic Planning Board for the University of Lancaster, 1962, and of Academic Advisory Cttee, 1964–70. Trustee of the Oxford Preservation Trust, 1961–65; a Vice-Pres., RHistS, 1967–71, Hon. Vice-Pres., 1981–; Pres., Lincoln Civic Trust, 1980–84. Hon. DLitt Nottingham, 1961. *Publications:* (joint editor with late Canon Foster) Registrum Antiquissimum of the Cathedral Church of Lincoln, vol. IV, 1938, (sole editor) vols V–X, 1940–73; *Acta Stephani Langton,* 1950; The D'Oyrys of South Lincolnshire, Norfolk and Holderness, 1984; (with S. R. Jones and J. Varley) A Survey of Ancient Houses in Lincoln, Fascicule I, Minster Yard I, 1984, Fascicule II, Minster Yard II, 1987, Fascicule III, Minster Yard III, 1990; articles in English Hist. Review, Journal of Ecclesiastical Hist., etc. *Recreation:* reading. *Address:* 21 Queensway, Lincoln LN2 4AJ.

MAJOR, Dame Malvina (Lorraine), DBE 1991 (OBE 1985); opera singer; *b* 28 Jan. 1943; *d* of Vincent William Major and Eva Gwendolen (*née* McCaw); *m* 1965, Winston William Richard Fleming (*d* 1990); one *s* two *d*. *Educ:* Hamilton Technical Coll.; London Opera Centre. Studied with Dame Sister Mary Leo, Auckland; winner: NZ Mobil Song Quest, 1963; Melbourne Sun Aria Contest, Australia, 1964; Kathleen Ferrier Award, London, 1966. Camden Fest., London; Salzburg Fest., 1968 (internat. début as Rosina in Barber of Seville), 1969, 1991; returned to NZ, 1970; La Finta Giardiniera, Th. de la Monnaie, Brussels, 1985; Vienna, Amsterdam, New York, Antwerp, Salt Lake City, 1986; Don Giovanni, Drottningholme, Brighton Fest., 1987; has also sung at Covent Garden (début as Rosalinde in Die Fledermaus, 1990), with Australian Opera, and in E Berlin. Performances include: La Bohème; Madame Butterfly; Faust; Il Seraglio; Rigoletto; Don Pasquale; Lucia di Lammermoor; Magic Flute; Tosca; Merry Widow; La Traviata; also concert perfs of works by Beethoven, Haydn, Mahler etc. TV and recordings. Established Dame Malvina Major Foundn for educn in performing arts, 1992. Entertainer and Internat. Performer of the Year, NZ, 1992; NZ Classical Disc Award, 1993 and 1994. *Recreations:* golf, sewing. *Address:* PO Box 11–175, Wellington, New Zealand.

MAJURY, Maj.-Gen. James Herbert Samuel, CB 1974; MBE 1961; Senior Steward, National Greyhound Racing Club, 1976–88; *b* 26 June 1921; *s* of Rev. Dr M. Majury, BA, DD, and Florence (*née* Stuart), Antrim, N Ireland; *m* 1948, Jeanetta Ann (*née* Le Fleming); two *s*. *Educ:* Royal Academical Institution, Belfast; Trinity College, Dublin. Royal Ulster Rifles, 1940; attached 15 Punjab Regt, 1942; seconded South Waziristan Scouts, 1943–47; Korean War, 1950 (Royal Ulster Rifles); Prisoner of War, Korea, 1950–53 (despatches 1954); Parachute Regiment, 1957–61; Comd Royal Irish Fusiliers, 1961–62; Comd 2nd Infantry Bde, 1965–67; GOC West Midland District, 1970–73. idc 1968. Col. Comdt, The King's Division, 1971–75, Col The Royal Irish Rangers, 1972–77; Hon. Col, 2nd Bn Mercian Volunteers, 1975–79. President: SSAFA for E Sussex, 1986–92; Indian Army Assoc., 1987–92. *Recreations:* golf, racing. *Address:* c/o Ulster Bank, 8 Market Square, Antrim BT41 4AT. *Club:* Naval and Military (Chm., 1983–88).

MAKAROVA, Natalia; dancer and choreographer; *b* Leningrad, 21 Nov. 1940; *m* 1976, Edward Karkar; one *s*. *Educ:* Vaganova Ballet Sch.; Leningrad Choreographic Sch. Mem., Kirov Ballet, 1959–70; London début, as Giselle, Covent Garden, 1961; joined American Ballet Theatre, 1970; formed dance co., Makarova & Co., 1980; Guest Artist: Royal Ballet, Covent Garden, 1972; London Festival Ballet, 1984. Has danced many classical and contemporary rôles in UK, Europe and USA, 1970–; appearances include: La Bayadère (which she also staged, and choreographed in part), NY Met, 1980, Manchester, 1985; On Your Toes, London and NY, 1984–86; choreographed new prodn of Swan Lake for London Fest. Ballet, London and tour, 1988. Honoured Artist of RSFSR, 1970. *Publications:* A Dance Autobiography, 1979; On Your Toes, 1984. *Address:* c/o Herbert Breslin Inc., 119 W 57th Street, New York, NY 10019, USA.

MAKEHAM, Peter Derek James; Head of Strategy and Employment Policy Division, Department for Education and Employment (formerly Department of Employment), since 1992; *b* 15 March 1948; *s* of Derrick James Stark Makeham and Margaret Helene Makeham; *m* 1972, Carolyne Rosemary Dawe; one *s* three *d*. *Educ:* Chichester High Sch. for Boys; Nottingham Univ. (BA); Leeds Univ. (MA Lab Econs). Economist, Dept of Employment, 1971–82; on secondment to Unilever, 1982–83; HM Treasury, 1983–84; Enterprise Unit, Cabinet Office, 1984–85; Dept of Employment, 1985–87; DTI, 1987–90; Dept of Employment, subseq. Dept for Educn and Employment, 1990–. *Recreation:* sailing. *Address:* Department for Education and Employment, Caxton House, Tothill Street, SW1H 9NF. *T:* 0171–273 5766.

MAKEPEACE, John, OBE 1988; FCSD; FIMgt, FRSA; designer and furniture maker, since 1961; Founder and Director: The Parnham Trust and Parnham College (formerly School for Craftsmen in Wood), 1977; Hooke Park College, 1989; *b* 6 July 1939; *m* 1st, 1964, Ann Sutton (marr. diss. 1979); 2nd, 1983, Jennie Moores (*née* Brinsden). *Educ:* Denstone Coll., Staffs. Study tours: Scandinavia 1957; N America, 1961; Italy, 1968; W Africa, 1972; USA, 1974; Australia, 1979; Japan, 1994. Furniture in private collections and Templeton Coll. and Keble Coll., Oxford, Nuffield Foundn, Portals plc, Reed International, Boots plc, Royal Soc. of Arts, Royal Museum of Scotland, Post Office, Lambeth Palace. *Public Collections:* Cardiff Museum; Fitzwilliam Museum, Cambridge; Leeds Museum; Art Inst., Chicago; Museum für Kunsthandwerk, Frankfurt; V & A Museum; Lewis Collection, Richmond, USA. *Exhibitions:* Herbert Art Gall., Coventry, 1963; New Art Centre, London, 1971; Fine Art Soc., London, 1977; Interior, Kortrijk, Belgium, 1978, 1992, 1994; Royal Show, Stoneleigh, 1981–87; Crafts Council Open, 1984; National Theatre, 1980, 1986; Parnham at Smiths Gall., 1988–91; Sotheby's, 1988, 1992, 1993; New Art Forms, Chicago, 1989–92; Tokyo, 1990; 1993: ARCO, Madrid; Chicago Contemporary Art Fair; Basel; Art '93, London; Conservation by Design, Providence, USA, 1993; Creation, Claridge's, 1994; Art Expo, Chicago, 1995; Banque de Luxembourg, 1995; British Embassy, Brussels, 1995. *Consultancies/Lectures:* Crafts Council, 1972–77; India Handicrafts Bd, 1975; Jammu and Kashmir Govt, 1977; Belgrade Univ., 1978; Artist in Context, V&A Mus., 1979; Chm., Wood Programme, World Crafts Conf., Kyoto, Japan, 1979; Australian Crafts Council, 1980; Loughborough Design Lecture, 1982; Oxford Farming Conf., 1990. Trustee, V & A Mus., 1987–91. *Television Films:* Made by Makepeace, 1975; History of English Furniture, 1978; Heritage in Danger, 1979; First Edition, 1980; Touch Wood, 1982; Tomorrow's World, 1986. Winner, Observer Kitchen Design, 1971; Hooke Park Coll. Winner, UK Conservation Award, 1987; British Construction Industry Award, 1990; Amer. Inst. of Archts Award, 1993. *Relevant publication:* John Makepeace: a spirit of adventure in craft and design, by Jeremy Myerson, 1995. *Recreations:* tree pruning, collecting works by young artists. *Address:* Parnham House, Beaminster, Dorset DT8 3NA. *T:* Beaminster (01308) 862204.

MAKEPEACE-WARNE, Maj.-Gen. Antony, CB 1992; MBE 1972; Commandant, Joint Service Defence College, 1990–92; *b* 3 Sept 1937; *e s* of late Keith Makepeace-Warne and Nora (*née* Kelstrup); *m* 1966, Jill Estelle Seath; two *d*. *Educ:* Taunton School; Open Univ. (BA Hons 1990). Commissioned KOYLI, 1960; served BAOR, Malaya, Aden, Berlin, MoD, to 1969; Staff College, 1970; 2nd Bn LI, 1971–72; 24 Airportable Bde, 1972–74; Instructor, Staff Coll., 1975–77; CO 1st Bn LI, 1977–80; Col ASD2, MoD, 1980–82; Comdr, Berlin Inf. Bde, 1982–84; RCDS 1985; ACOS HQ UKLF, 1986–88; GS Study of Indiv. Trg Orgn, 1988–89. Dep. Col, LI (Somerset and Cornwall), 1987–89; Colonel, The Light Infantry, 1990–92. *Publications:* Exceedingly Lucky: a history of the Light Infantry 1968–1993, 1993; The British Army Today and Tomorrow 1993/94, 1993; Brassey's Companion to the British Army, 1995. *Address:* c/o Lloyds Bank, Cox's & King's, 7 Pall Mall, SW1Y 5NA. *Club:* Army and Navy.

MAKGILL, family name of **Viscount of Oxfuird.**

MAKGILL CRICHTON MAITLAND, Major John David; Lord-Lieutenant of Renfrewshire, 1980–94; *b* 10 Sept. 1925; *e s* of late Col Mark Edward Makgill Crichton Maitland, CVO, DSO, DL, JP, The Island House, Wilton, Salisbury, Wilts, and late Patience Irene Fleetwood Makgill Crichton Maitland (*née* Fuller); *m* 1st, 1954, Jean Patricia (*d* 1985), *d* of late Maj.-Gen. Sir Michael Creagh, KBE, MC, Pigeon Hill, Homington, Salisbury; one *s* one *d*; 2nd, 1987, Mary Ann Vere, *o d* of late Major Charles Herbert Harberton Eales, MC, and *widow* of Capt. James Quintin Penn Curzon. *Educ:* Eton. Served War, 1944–45, Grenadier Guards. Continued serving until 1957 (temp. Major, 1952; retd 1957), rank Captain (Hon. Major). Renfrew CC, 1961–75. DL Renfrewshire 1962, Vice-Lieutenant 1972–80. *Address:* Daluaine, Rhynie, Huntly, Aberdeenshire AB54 4HL. *T:* Rhynie (01464) 861638.

MAKHULU, Most Rev. Walter Paul Khotso; *see* Central Africa, Archbishop of.

MAKIN, Claire Margaret, FRICS; Chief Executive, Royal Institution of Chartered Surveyors, since 1995; *b* 21 March 1951; *d* of James Ernest Makin and Mary Makin (*née* Morris); *m* 1978, David Anthony Bowman. *Educ:* City Univ. (MBA). FRICS 1988; ACIArb 1985. Partner, Richard Ellis, 1978–90; Consultant, Price Waterhouse, 1990–91; Partner Bernard Thorpe, 1991–93; Dir, DTZ Debenham Thorpe, 1993–95. FRSA 1991. *Recreations:* travelling, food and wine, restoring old houses. *Address:* Royal Institution of Chartered Surveyors, 12 Great George Street, Parliament Square, SW1P 3AD; 19 Queen Anne's Grove, Bedford Park, W4 1NW. *T:* 0181–994 2966.

MAKINS, family name of **Baron Sherfield.**

MAKINS, Nora; *see* Beloff, N.

MAKINS, Sir Paul (Vivian), 4th Bt *cr* 1903; Company Director, 1962–73; *b* 12 Nov. 1913; *yr s* of Sir Paul Makins, 2nd Bt, and Gladys Marie (*d* 1919), *d* of William Vivian, Queen's Gate, London; *S* brother, 1969; *m* 1945, Maisie (*d* 1986), *d* of Major Oswald Pedley and *widow* of Major C. L. J. Bowen, Irish Guards; no *c*. *Educ:* Eton Coll.; Trinity Coll. Cambridge (MA). Commissioned in Welsh Guards, 1935. Served War of 1939–45: France, 1940; Italy, 1944–45. Dir and Sec. Vitalba Co. Ltd (Gibraltar), 1962–73; Dir, Compañia Rentistica SA (Tangier), 1967–73. Kt of Magistral Grace, SMO Malta, 1955; JP Gibraltar, 1964–70. *Heir:* none. *Address:* Casas Cortijo 135, 11310 Sotogrande, Provincia de Cadiz, Spain. *Clubs:* Cavalry and Guards, Pratt's.
See also Archbishop of Southwark.

MAKINSON, William, CBE 1977; engineering management consultant; *b* 11 May 1915; *s* of Joshua Makinson and Martha (*née* Cunliffe); *m* 1952, Helen Elizabeth Parker; one *s* three *d*. *Educ:* Ashton-in-Makerfield Grammar Sch.; Manchester Univ. Asst Lecturer, Electronics, Manchester Univ., 1935–36; Education Officer, RAF Cranwell, 1936–39; RAE Farnborough, 1939–52; Hon. Squadron-Ldr, RAF, 1943–45; Superintendent, Blind Landing Experimental Unit, 1952–55; Defence Research Policy Staff, 1955–56; Managing Director, General Precision Systems Ltd, 1956–64; Group Jt Managing Director, Pullin, 1964–65; Mem., NRDC, 1967–80 (Man. Dir, 1974–80, Chief Exec., Engrg Dept, 1965–74). *Publications:* papers to Royal Aeronautical Society. *Recreation:* golf. *Address:* Ridings, Snows Paddock, Snows Ride, Windlesham, Surrey GU20 6LH. *T:* Ascot (01344) 22431.

MAKKAWI, Dr Khalil; Chevalier, Order of Cedar, Lebanon; Ambassador and Permanent Representative of Lebanon to the United Nations, New York, since 1990; *b* 15 Jan. 1930; *s* of Abdel Basset Makkawi and Rosa Makkawi; *m* 1958, Zahira Sibaei; one *s* one *d*. *Educ:* Amer. Univ. of Beirut (BA Polit. Science); Cairo Univ. (MA Polit. Science); Colombia Univ., NY, USA (PhD Internat. Relations). Joined Lebanese Min. of Foreign Affairs, 1957; UN Section at Min., 1957–59; Attaché to Perm. Mission of Lebanon to UN, New York, 1959, Dep. Perm. Rep., 1961–64; First Sec., Washington, 1964–66; Chief of Internat. Relations Dept, Min. of For. Affairs, Beirut, 1967–70; Counsellor, London, 1970–71; Minister Plenipotentiary, London, 1971–73; Ambassador to: German Democratic Republic, 1973–78; Court of St James's, and Republic of Ireland, 1979–83; Dir of Political Dept, Min. of Foreign Affairs, Beirut, 1983–85; Amb. to Italy, and Permanent Rep. to UNFAO, 1985–90. Mem., Lebanese Delegn to UN Gen. Assembly Meetings, 14th-39th Session; Chairman of Lebanese Delegations to: Confs and Councils, FAO, 1985–89; Governing Councils, IFAD, 1985–89; 16th Ministerial Meeting, Islamic conf. in Fès, 1986; 8th Summit Conf. of Non-Aligned Countries, Harare, 1986; Ministerial Meeting, Mediterranean Mems, Non-Aligned Countries, Brioni, Yugoslavia, 1987; IMO Conf., Rome, 1988; Vice-Pres., Lebanese delegn to ME peace negotiations, Washington, 1993–94. A Vice-Chm., Exec. Bd, UNICEF, 1993–. Grand Cross of Merit (Italian Republic). *Recreations:* sports, music. *Address:* Suite 531–33, 866 United Nations Plaza, New York, NY 10017, USA.

MAKLOUF, Raphael David; sculptor; painter; Chairman, Tower Mint, since 1975; *b* Jerusalem, 10 Dec. 1937; *m* 1968, Marillyn Christian Lewis, *d* of Gwilym Hugh Lewis, DFC; two *s* one *d*. *Educ:* studied art at Camberwell School of Art, under Karel Vogel, 1953–58. Official commissions: Tower of London, Carnegie Hall, NY, etc. New portrait effigy of the Queen on all UK and Commonwealth coinage from 1985, on Britannia gold coins, from 1989. Bronze portraits of the Queen, 1988, at Royal Nat. Theatre, Richmond Riverside Develt and Westminster Sch. Science Building, unveiled by the Queen. 15 Stations of Cross for new Brentwood Cathedral, 1992. Sitters have included: HM Queen; HRH Prince Philip; Rt Hon Margaret Thatcher; Joan Collins; Michael Parkinson; Bobby Moore; David Bailey; Sir Ian Mactaggart; Gen. Sir John Mogg; Lady Fall. FRSA 1985. *Address:* 3 St Helena Terrace, Richmond, Surrey TW9 1NR. *Clubs:* City Livery; St Helena Swimming (Richmond); Riverside Raquets.

MAKSYMIUK, Jerzy; conductor; Chief Conductor, 1984–93, Conductor Laureate, since 1993, BBC Scottish Symphony Orchestra; *b* Grodno, Poland, 9 April 1936. *Educ:* Warsaw Conservatory. First Prize, Paderewski Piano Comp., 1964; worked at Warsaw Grand Theatre, 1970–72; founded Polish Chamber Orchestra, 1972; UK début, 1977; toured all over world incl. European festivals of Aix-en-Provence and Vienna and BBC Promenade concerts; Principal Conductor, Polish Nat. Radio Orch., 1975–77; toured extensively in E Europe and USA; has conducted orchestras in Europe, USA and Japan including: Orch. Nat. de France, Tokyo Metropolitan Symphony, Ensemble Orchestral de Paris, Israel Chamber Orch. and Rotterdam Philharmonic; in UK has conducted BBC Welsh and BBC Philharmonic Orchs, CBSO, LSO, London Philharmonic, ENO, Bournemouth Sinfonietta and Royal Liverpool Phil. Orch.; début for ENO with Don Giovanni, London Coliseum, 1990. Has made numerous recordings. Hon. DLitt Strathclyde, 1990. *Address:* c/o IMG Artists (Europe), Media House, 3 Burlington Lane, Chiswick, W4 2TH.

MAKUTA, Hon. Friday Lewis; Chief Justice of Malaŵi, 1985–93; *b* 25 Oct. 1936; *s* of late Lewis and Anne Makuta; *m* 1962; four *s* one *d*. *Educ:* Malamulo Mission; Dedza Secondary Sch. Called to the Bar, Middle Temple, 1967. Joined Civil Service, Malaŵi, 1967; State Advocate, 1967; Chief Legal Aid Advocate, 1970; Dir of Public Prosecutions, 1972; Judge of the High Court, 1975; Attorney Gen. and Sec. for Justice, 1976; SC 1979; Dep. Sec. to the Pres. and Cabinet, 1984. *Club:* Civil Service (Lilongwe, Malaŵi).

MALAND, David; barrister; *b* 6 Oct. 1929; *s* of Rev. Gordon Albert Maland and Florence Maud Maland (*née* Bosence); *m* 1953, Edna Foulsham; two *s*. *Educ:* Kingswood Sch.; Wadham Coll., Oxford. BA Hons Mod. Hist., 1951; MA 1957; Robert Herbert Meml Prize Essay, 1959. Nat. service commn RAF, 1951–53. Asst Master, Brighton Grammar Sch., 1953–56; Senior History Master, Stamford Sch., 1957–66; Headmaster: Cardiff High Sch., 1966–68; Denstone Coll., 1969–78; High Master, Manchester Grammar Sch., 1978–85. Chm., Assisted Places Sub-Cttee of Headmasters' Conf., 1982–83. Called to the Bar, Gray's Inn, 1986. Gen. Gov., British Nutrition Foundn, 1987–. Governor: Stonyhurst Coll., 1973–80; Abingdon Sch., 1979–91; GPDST, 1984–88. *Publications:* Europe in the Seventeenth Century, 1966; Culture and Society in Seventeenth Century France, 1970; Europe in the Sixteenth Century, 1973; Europe at War, 1600–1650, 1980; (trans.) La Guerre de Trente Ans, by Pagès, 1971; articles and reviews in History. *Address:* Windrush, Underhill Lane, Westmeston, Hassocks, East Sussex BN6 8XG; 1 Garden Court, Temple, EC4Y 9BJ. *Club:* Athenæum.

MALCANGI, Evelyn Elizabeth Ann; *see* Glennie, E. E. A.

MALCOLM, Hon. David Kingsley, AC 1992; **Hon. Mr Justice Malcolm;** Chief Justice of Western Australia, since 1988, and Lieutenant-Governor, since 1990; *b* 6 May 1938; *s* of Colin Kingsley Malcolm and Jeanne (*née* Cowan); *m* 1965, Jennifer Birney; one *s*. *Educ:* Guildford Grammar Sch.; Univ. of Western Australia (LLB 1st Cl. Hons); Oxford Univ. (Rhodes Schol.; BCL 1st Cl. Hons). Partner, Muir Williams Nicholson, 1964–67; Counsel, Asst Gen. Counsel, Dep. Gen. Counsel, Asian Development Bank, Manila, 1967–70; Partner, Muir Williams Nicholson & Co., 1970–79; Independent Bar, 1980–88. QC: WA, 1980; NSW, 1983. Member: Law Reform Commn of WA, 1966–67 and 1975–82 (Chm., 1976, 1979–82); Copyright Tribunal, 1978–86; Chm., Town Planning Appeal Tribunal, 1979–86. Mem., Council of Law Soc. of WA, 1966–67, 1985–88 (Vice-Pres., 1986–88); Pres., WA Bar Assoc., 1982–84; Vice Pres., Aust. Bar Assoc., 1984; Dep. Chm., 1990–95, Chm., 1995–, Judicial Sect., LAWASIA. Chairman, Advisory Board: Neuromuscular Res. Inst. of Aust., 1989–; Crime Res. Centre, Univ. of WA, 1991–; Member: Senate, Univ. of WA, 1988–94; Constitutional Centenary Foundn Council, 1991–. *Publications:* articles in various learned jls, incl. Aust. Law Jl, Aust. Bar Rev., Aust. Business Law Rev., Univ. of WA Law Rev., LAWASIA Jl. *Recreations:* Rugby Union, equestrian sports, windsurfing. *Address:* Chief Justice's Chambers, Supreme Court, Perth, WA 6000, Australia. *T:* (chambers) (9) 4215337. *Clubs:* Weld (Perth, WA); Manila Polo (Manila).

MALCOLM, Sir David (Peter Michael), 11th Bt *cr* 1665; *b* 7 July 1919; *s* of Sir Michael Albert James Malcolm, 10th Bt, and Hon. Geraldine Margot (*d* 1965), *d* of 10th Baron Digby; *S* father, 1976; *m* 1959, Hermione, *d* of Sir David Home, 13th Bt; one *d*. *Educ:* Eton; Magdalene Coll., Cambridge (BA). Served with Scots Guards, 1939–46 (Major). Mem., Inst. of Chartered Accountants of Scotland, 1949. Member: Stock Exchange, 1956–80; Stock Exchange Council, 1971–80. Mem., Queen's Body Guard for Scotland, Royal Co. of Archers, 1952–. *Recreations:* shooting, golf. *Heir: cousin* James William Thomas Alexander Malcolm [*b* 15 May 1930; *m* 1955, Gillian Heather, *d* of Elton Humpherus; two *s* two *d*]. *Address:* Whiteholm, Gullane, East Lothian EH31 2BD. *Club:* New (Edinburgh).

MALCOLM, Derek Elliston Michael; Film Critic: The Guardian, since 1971; Cosmopolitan, since 1974; President: International Film Critics, since 1991 (Chairman, UK Section, since 1982); British Fedn of Film Societies, since 1993; *b* 12 May 1932; *s* of J. Douglas Malcolm and Dorothy Taylor; *m* 1962, Barbara Ibbott (marr. diss. 1966); one *d*. *Educ:* Eton; Merton College, Oxford (BA Hons Hist.). Actor, amateur rider (National Hunt), 1953–56; Drama Critic, Gloucestershire Echo, 1956–62; Sub-Editor, The Guardian, 1962–69; Racing correspondent, The Guardian, 1969–71. Dir, London Internat. Film Fest., 1984–86. Gov., BFI, 1989–92. Pres., Critics' Circle of UK, 1980 (Chm., Film Section, 1978–81). Internat. Publishing Cos Critic of the Year, 1972. *Publication:* Robert Mitchum, 1984. *Recreations:* cricket, tennis, squash, music. *Address:* 28 Avenue Road, Highgate, N6 5DW. *T:* 0181–348 2013.

MALCOLM, Dugald, CMG 1966; CVO 1964; TD 1945; HM Diplomatic Service, retired; Minister to the Holy See, 1975–77; *b* 22 Dec. 1917; 2nd *s* of late Maj.-Gen. Sir Neill Malcolm, KCB, DSO, and Lady (Angela) Malcolm; *m* 1st, 1957, Patricia Anne Gilbert-Lodge (*d* 1976), *widow* of Captain Peter Atkinson-Clark; one *d* one step *d*; 2nd, 1989, Margaret Roy Anderson, *d* of Rev. R. P. R. Anderson. *Educ:* Eton; New Coll., Oxford. Served Argyll and Sutherland Highlanders, 1939–45; discharged wounded. Appointed Foreign Office, Oct. 1945; Served Lima, Bonn, Seoul; HM Vice-Marshal of the Diplomatic Corps, 1957–65; Ambassador: to Luxembourg, 1966–70; to Panama, 1970–74. Member Queen's Body Guard for Scotland (Royal Company of Archers). *Address:* 3 South Cuil, Duror of Appin, Argyll PA38 4DA. *T:* Duror (0163174) 234. *Clubs:* Boodle's, Brooks's.

MALCOLM, Ellen, RSA 1976 (ARSA 1968); *b* 28 Sept. 1923; *d* of John and Ellen Malcolm; *m* 1962, Gordon Stewart Cameron, RSA (*d* 1994). *Educ:* Aberdeen Acad.; Gray's Sch. of Art, Aberdeen. DA (Aberdeen) 1944. Teacher of Art, Aberdeen Grammar Sch. and Aberdeen Acad., 1945–62. Paintings in public galleries in Southend, Aberdeen, Perth, Milngavie, Edinburgh, and in private collections in Scotland, England, Wales, America, Switzerland, Sweden and Australia. Chalmers-Jervise Prize, 1946; Guthrie Award, Royal Scottish Acad., 1952; David Cargill Award, Royal Glasgow Inst., 1973. *Recreation:* reading. *Address:* c/o Royal Scottish Academy, The Mound, Edinburgh EH2 2EL.

MALCOLM, George (John), CBE 1965; musician; *b* London, 28 Feb. 1917; *o s* of George Hope Malcolm, Edinburgh, and Johanna Malcolm (*née* Brosnahan). *Educ:* Wimbledon Coll.; Balliol Coll., Oxford (Scholar; MA, BMus; Hon. Fellow, 1966); Royal College of Music (Scholar). Served in RAFVR, 1940–46. Master of the Cathedral Music, Westminster Cathedral, 1947–59, training a famous boys' choir. Now mainly known as harpsichordist, pianist and conductor (making frequent concert tours). Hon. RAM, 1961; FRCM 1974; Hon. FRCO 1987. Hon. DMus Sheffield, 1978. Papal Knight of the Order of St Gregory the Great, 1970. *Address:* 99 Wimbledon Hill Road, SW19 7QT.

MALCOLM, Gerald; *see* Malcolm, W. G.

MALCOLM, Prof. John Laurence; Regius Professor of Physiology, University of Aberdeen, 1959–75, retired; *b* 28 Aug. 1913; *s* of late Professor J. Malcolm, Dunedin, New Zealand; *m* 1st, 1940, Sylvia Bramston (*d* 1958), *d* of late Basil B. Hooper, Auckland, New Zealand; one *s* one *d*; 2nd, 1961, Margaret Irvine Simpson (*d* 1967), *d* of late Colonel J. C. Simpson, Skene, Aberdeenshire. *Publications:* contributions to the Proceedings of Royal Society, Journal of Physiology, Journal of Neuro-physiology. *Address:* Heath Cottage, Crathie, Aberdeenshire AB3 5UP.

MALCOLM, Prof. Wilfred Gordon, CBE 1994; Vice-Chancellor, University of Waikato, New Zealand, 1985–94; *b* 29 Nov. 1933; *s* of Norman and Doris Malcolm; *m* 1959, Edmée Ruth Prebensen; two *s* four *d*. *Educ:* Victoria Univ. of Wellington (MA, PhD); Emmanuel Coll., Cambridge (BA). Victoria University of Wellington: Lectr in Mathematics, 1960–62; Gen. Sec., Inter Varsity Fellowship of Evangelical Unions, 1963–66; Lectr/Reader in Mathematics, 1967–74; Prof. of Pure Mathematics, 1975–84. *Address:* 76 Hamurana Road, Omokoroa, Bay of Plenty, New Zealand.

MALCOLM, (William) Gerald, CB 1976; MBE 1943; Member, Planning Appeals Commission (NI), 1978–83; Permanent Secretary, Department of the Environment for Northern Ireland, 1974–76; *b* Stirling, 19 Dec. 1916; *s* of late John and Jane M. Malcolm; *m* 1949, Margaret Cashel. *Educ:* High Sch. of Stirling; Glasgow Univ. (MA) (Hons French and German, 1945); London Univ. (BA 1945). Served War, Army, 1939–46: RASC and Intelligence Corps; Major, 1944; Africa and Italy Stars, 1939–45. Min. of Home Affairs for NI, Asst Principal, 1948; Min. of Agriculture for NI: Principal, 1956; Asst Sec., 1962; Sen. Asst Sec., 1966; Dep. Sec., 1970. *Recreations:* angling, swimming, ornithology, nature.

MALCOMSON, Thomas Herbert; HM Diplomatic Service, retired; Ambassador to Panama, 1992–96; *b* 9 Oct. 1937; *m* 1st, 1960, Barbara Hetherington (marr. diss. 1985); one *s* two *d*; 2nd, 1986, Blanca Ruiz de Castilla; twin *d*. Joined FO, subseq. FCO, 1961; Bangkok, 1963; São Paulo, 1967; FCO, 1971; Colombo, 1972; Consul, Chiang Mai, 1975; Second, later First, Sec., FCO, 1978; Dep. High Comr, Brunei, 1981; Acting High Comr, Solomon Is, 1984; First Secretary: Lima, 1985; FCO, 1989. *Address:* c/o Foreign and Commonwealth Office, SW1A 2AH.

MALDEN; *see* Scott-Malden.

MALDEN, Viscount; Frederick Paul de Vere Capell; Deputy Head Teacher, Skerton County Primary School, Lancaster, since 1990; *b* 29 May 1944; *s* and *heir* of 10th Earl of Essex, *qv*. *Educ:* Skerton Boys' School; Lancaster Royal Grammar School; Didsbury College of Education, Manchester; Northern School of Music. ACP, LLCM(TD). Assistant teacher, Marsh County Junior School, 1966–72; Deputy Head, 1972–75; Acting Head, 1975–77; Deputy Head Teacher, Marsh County Primary School, 1977–78; Head Teacher, Cockerham Parochial CE School, Cockerham, Lancaster, 1979–80; in charge of Pastoral Care, Curriculum Develt and Music, Skerton County Primary School, Lancaster, 1981–90. Patron, Morecambe Philharmonic Choir, 1990–. FRSA. *Recreations:* music, hi-fi. *Address:* 35 Pinewood Avenue, Brookhouse, Lancaster LA2 9NU.

MALE, David Ronald, CBE 1991; FRICS; Consultant, Gardiner & Theobald, Chartered Quantity Surveyors, since 1992 (Senior Partner, 1979–91); a Church Commissioner, 1989–93; *b* 12 Dec. 1929; *s* of Ronald Male and Gertrude Simpson; *m* 1959, Mary Louise

Evans; one *s* two *d*. *Educ:* Aldenham Sch., Herts. Served RA, 2nd Lieut, 1948–49. With Gardiner & Theobald, 1950–. Mem., Gen. Council, RICS, 1976–93 (Pres., 1989–90); Pres., Quantity Surveyors Divl Council, 1977–78. Member: Bd of Dirs, Building Centre, 1970–80; Govt Construction Panel, 1973–74; EDC for Building, 1982–86; Chm., NEDC Commercial Bldg Steering Gp, 1984–88; Dir, London and Bristol Developments, 1985–91. Member: Bd of Management, Cancer Relief Macmillan Fund, 1982–; Court of Benefactors, RSocMed, 1986–. Mem. Bd of Govs, Wilson Centre, Cambridge, 1993–; Gov., Aldenham Sch., 1974–93; Pres., Old Aldenhamian Soc., 1986–89. Master, Chartered Surveyors' Co., 1984–85; Liveryman, Painter-Stainers' Co., 1961–93. *Recreations:* opera and ballet, lawn tennis, Real tennis, golf. *Address:* 6 Bowland Yard, Kinnerton Street, SW1X 8EE. *Clubs:* Boodle's, Garrick, MCC (Mem. Cttee, 1984–95; Mem., Estates Sub-Cttee, 1984–).

MALE, Peter John Ellison, CMG 1967; MC 1945; HM Diplomatic Service, retired; Ambassador to Czechoslovakia, 1977–80; *b* 22 Aug. 1920; *s* of late H. J. G. Male and late Mrs E. A. Male; *m* 1947, Patricia Janet Payne; five *s* two *d*. *Educ:* Merchant Taylors' Sch.; Emmanuel Coll., Cambridge. HM Forces, 1940–45. HM Foreign Service (now HM Diplomatic Service), 1946; served in: Damascus, 1947–49; Wahnerheide, 1949–53; London, 1953–55; Guatemala City, 1955–57; Washington, 1957–60; London, 1960–62; Oslo, 1962–66; Bonn, 1966–70; New Delhi, 1970–74; Asst Under-Sec. of State, FCO, 1974–77. *Recreations:* gadgets, gardening. *Address:* Swinley Edge, Coronation Road, Ascot, Berks SL5 9LG. *Club:* United Oxford & Cambridge University.

MALECELA, Cigwiyemisi John Samwel; Prime Minister and First Vice President of the United Republic of Tanzania, since 1990; *b* 20 April 1934; *m*; four *c*. *Educ:* Alliance Secondary Sch., Dodoma; St Andrews Coll., Minaki, Dar es Salaam; Univ. of Bombay (BCom); post-grad. studies, Cambridge Univ. Dist Officer, Mbeya Region, 1960–61; appts for Tanganyikan Govt, 1962–64: Consul to USA and Sec. of Mission to UN, New York, 1962–63; Regl Comr, Lake Reg., 1963–64; for Tanzania: Ambassador to UN, 1964–68, to Ethiopia, 1968; Minister: for East African Community Affairs, 1969–71; for Foreign Affairs, 1972–75; for Agriculture, 1975–80; for Minerals, 1980–82; for Communications and Transport, 1982–85; Administrator, Tanzania's Public Debt, 1985; Regional Comr, Iringa, 1987; High Comr for Tanzania in UK, and non-resident Ambassador to Ireland, 1989–90. Member: Internat. Ind. Commn for Worldwide Telecommunication Develt, 1983; Commonwealth Eminent Persons Group on S Africa, 1985; Gp of 34 World Eminent Persons on Disarmament and Internat. Security, Stockholm, 1988.

MALEK, Redha; Prime Minister of Algeria, 1993–94; *b* 21 Dec. 1931; *m* 1963, Rafida Cheriet; two *s* one *d*. *Educ:* Algiers; Paris. BA. Mem. Governing Bd, Gen. Union of Moslem Algerian Students, 1956; Dir and Editor in Chief, El Moudjahid, party newspaper of Front de la Libération Nationale, 1957–62; Ambassador to: Yugoslavia, 1963–65; France, 1965–70; USSR, 1970–77; Minister of Information and Culture, Algeria, 1977–79; Ambassador to USA, 1979–82 (negotiated release of the 52 American hostages in Iran, 1980–81); Ambassador to UK, 1982–84. Mem. and spokesman, Algerian delegn to negotiations of Evian, 1961–62; Member, Drafting Committee: Programme of Tripoli, setting out FLN political programme, 1962; Nat. Charter, 1976. Mem., Central Cttee, FLN, 1979–. *Address:* 2 Rue Ahmed Bey, Algiers, Algeria.

MALET, Sir Harry (Douglas St Lo), 9th Bt *cr* 1791, of Wilbury, Wiltshire; JP; farmer, Australia and England; *b* 26 Oct. 1936; *o s* of Col Sir Edward William St Lo Malet, 8th Bt, OBE and Baroness Benedicta von Maasburg (*d* 1979); *S* father, 1990; *m* 1967, Julia Gresley, *d* of Charles Harper, Perth, WA; one *s*. *Educ:* Downside; Trinity Coll., Oxford (BA Eng. Lit.). Commnd QRIH, 1958–61. JP W Somerset, 1982. *Recreation:* equestrian sports. *Heir:* *s* Charles Edward St Lo Malet, *b* 30 Aug. 1970. *Address:* Wrestwood, RMB 184, Boyup Brook, WA 6244, Australia. *Club:* Weld (Perth).

MALIM, Rear-Adm. Nigel Hugh, CB 1971; LVO 1960; DL; FIMechE; *b* 5 April 1919; *s* of late John Malim, Pebmarsh, and Brenda Malim; *m* 1944, Moonyeen, *d* of late William and Winefride Maynard; two *s* one *d*. *Educ:* Weymouth Coll.; RNEC Keyham. Cadet, RN, 1936; HMS Manchester, 1940–41; HMS Norfolk, 1942; RNC Greenwich, 1943–45; HMS Jamaica, 1945–47; Staff of RNEC, 1948–50; Admty, 1951–54; HMS Triumph, 1954–56; Admty, 1956–58; HM Yacht Britannia, 1958–60; District Overseer, Scotland, 1960–62; Asst, and later Dep., Dir Marine Engrg, 1962–65; idc 1966; Captain, RNEC Manadon, 1967–69; Chief Staff Officer Technical to C-in-C, W Fleet, 1969–71, retd. Man. Dir, Humber Graving Dock & Engrg Co. Ltd, 1972–82. Chm., Fabric Council, Lincoln Cathedral, 1985–91. DL Lincoln, 1987. *Recreations:* offshore racing and cruising. *Address:* The Old Vicarage, Caistor, Lincoln LN7 6UG. *Clubs:* Royal Ocean Racing; Royal Naval Sailing Association.

MALIN, Prof. Stuart Robert Charles; Professor of Geophysics, Bosphorus University, Istanbul, since 1994; Visiting Professor, Department of Physics and Astronomy, University College London, since 1983; *b* 28 Sept. 1936; *s* of Cecil Henry Malin and Eleanor Mary Malin (*née* Howe); *m* 1963, Irene Saunders; two *d*. *Educ:* Royal Grammar Sch., High Wycombe; King's College, London. BSc 1958, PhD 1972, DSc 1981; FInstP 1971; CPhys 1985; FRAS 1961 (Mem. Council, 1975–78). Royal Greenwich Observatory, Herstmonceux: Asst Exptl Officer, 1958; Scientific Officer, 1961; Sen. Scientific Officer, 1965; Institute of Geological Sciences, Herstmonceux and Edinburgh: PSO, 1970; SPSO (individual merit), 1976, and Hd of Geomagnetism Unit, 1981; Hd of Astronomy and Navigation, Nat. Maritime Museum, 1982; Maths teacher: Dulwich Coll., 1988–91, 1992–94; Haberdashers' Aske's Hatcham Coll., 1991–92. Cape Observer, Radcliffe Observatory, Pretoria, 1963–65; Vis. Scientist, Nat. Center for Atmospheric Res., Boulder, Colorado, 1969; Green Schol., Scripps Instn of Oceanography, La Jolla, 1981. Pres., Jun. Astronomical Soc., 1989–91. Associate Editor, Qly Jl, RAS, 1987–92. *Publications:* (with Carole Stott) The Greenwich Meridian, 1984; Spaceworks, 1985; The Greenwich Guide to the Planets, 1987; The Greenwich Guide to Stars, Galaxies and Nebulae, 1989; The Story of the Earth, 1991; contribs to scientific jls. *Recreations:* croquet, clocks. *Address:* 30 Wemyss Road, Blackheath, SE3 0TG. *T:* 0181–318 3712; Boğaziçi University, PO Box 13, 81221 Çengelköy, Istanbul, Turkey.

MALINS, Humfrey Jonathan; lawyer and consultant; an Assistant Recorder, since 1991; Acting Metropolitan Stipendiary Magistrate, since 1992; *b* 31 July 1945; *s* of Rev. Peter Malins and late Lilian Joan Malins; *m* 1979, Lynda Ann; one *s* one *d*. *Educ:* St John's Sch., Leatherhead; Brasenose Coll., Oxford (MA Hons Law). College of Law, Guildford, 1967; joined Tuck and Mann, Solicitors, Dorking, 1967, qual. as solicitor, 1971; Partner, Tuck and Mann, 1973. Councillor, Mole Valley DC, Surrey, 1973–83 (Chm., Housing Cttee, 1980–81). Contested (C): Toxteth Division of Liverpool, Feb. and Oct. 1974; E Lewisham, 1979; Croydon NW, 1992; MP (C) Croydon NW, 1983–92. PPS to Minister of State, Home Office, 1987–89, to Minister of State, DoH, 1989–92. Chm. of Trustees, Immigration Adv. Service, 1993–. *Recreations:* Rugby football, golf, gardening. *Address:* Highbury, Westcott Street, Westcott, Dorking, Surrey RH4 3NU. *T:* Dorking (01306) 885554. *Clubs:* Coningsby; Vincent's (Oxford); Richmond Rugby Football; Walton Heath Golf.
See also J. H. Malins.

MALINS, Julian Henry; QC 1991; *b* 1 May 1950; *s* of Rev. Peter Malins and late (Lilian) Joan Malins (*née* Dingley); *m* 1972, Joanna Pearce; three *d*. *Educ:* St John's School, Leatherhead; Brasenose College, Oxford (MA). Called to the Bar, Middle Temple, 1972. Mem., General Council of the Bar, 1986–. Mem., Court of Common Council, City of London, 1981–. *Recreations:* fishing, chess, conversation. *Address:* Brick Court Chambers, 15/19 Devereux Court, WC2R 3JJ. *T:* 0171–583 0777.
See also H. J. Malins.

MALINS, Penelope, (Mrs John Malins); *see* Hobhouse, P.

MALJERS, Floris Anton, Hon. KBE 1992; Chairman, Unilever NV, and Vice Chairman, Unilever PLC, since 1984; *b* 12 Aug. 1933; *s* of A. C. J. Maljers and L. M. Maljers-Kole; *m* 1958, J. H. Maljers-de Jongh; two *s* (one *d* decd). *Educ:* Univ. of Amsterdam. Joined Unilever, 1959; various jobs in the Netherlands until 1965; Man. Dir, Unilever-Colombia, 1965–67; Man. Dir, Unilever-Turkey, 1967–70; Chairman, Van den Bergh & Jurgens, Netherlands, 1970–74; Co-ordinator of Man. Group, edible fats and dairy, and Dir of Unilever NV and Unilever PLC, 1974–. Member: Unilever's Special Committee, 1982–; Supervisory Bd, ABN Bank, Amsterdam, 1984–; Supervisory Bd, KLM Royal Dutch Airlines, 1991– (Vice Chm., 1994); Supervisory Bd, Philips Electronics NV, 1993– (Chm., 1994). Gov., Europ. Policy Forum, 1993–. Chm., Concertgebouw Foundn, 1987–. *Address:* Unilever PLC, Unilever House, Blackfriars, EC4P 4BQ. *T:* 0171–822 5531.

MALLABY, Sir Christopher (Leslie George), GCVO 1992; KCMG 1988 (CMG 1982); HM Diplomatic Service; Ambassador to France, since 1993; *b* 7 July 1936; *s* of late Brig. A. W. S. Mallaby, CIE, OBE, and Margaret Catherine Mallaby (*née* Jones); *m* 1961, Pascale Françoise Thierry-Mieg; one *s* three *d*. *Educ:* Eton; King's Coll., Cambridge. British Delegn to UN Gen. Assembly, 1960; 3rd Sec., British Embassy, Moscow, 1961–63; 2nd Sec., FO, 1963–66; 1st Sec., Berlin, 1966–69; 1st Sec., FCO, 1969–71; Harvard Business Sch., 1971; Dep. Dir, British Trade Develt Office, NY, 1971–74; Counsellor and Head of Chancery, Moscow, 1975–77; Head of Arms Control and Disarmament Dept, FCO, 1977–79, Head of East European and Soviet Dept, 1979–80, Head of Planning Staff, 1980–82, FCO; Minister, Bonn, 1982–85; Dep. Sec., Cabinet Office, 1985–88; Ambassador to Germany, 1988–92. *Recreations:* fishing, reading, travel. *Address:* c/o Foreign and Commonwealth Office, SW1A 2AH. *Clubs:* Brooks's, Beefsteak.

MALLALIEU, Baroness *cr* 1991 (Life Peer), of Studdridge in the County of Buckinghamshire; **Ann Mallalieu;** QC 1988; *b* 27 Nov. 1945; *d* of Sir (Joseph Percival) William Mallalieu and of Lady Mallalieu; *m* 1979, Timothy Felix Harold Cassel, *qv*; two *d*. *Educ:* Holton Park Girls' Grammar Sch., Wheatley, Oxon; Newnham Coll., Cambridge (MA, LLM; Hon. Fellow, 1992). (First woman) Pres., Cambridge Union Soc., 1967. Called to the Bar, Inner Temple, 1970, Bencher, 1992; a Recorder, 1985–93. Mem., Gen. Council of the Bar, 1973–75. *Recreations:* sheep, hunting, poetry, horseracing. *Address:* House of Lords, SW1A 0PW. *T:* 0171–219 3000.

MALLE, Louis; Film Director; *b* 30 Oct. 1932; *s* of Pierre Malle and Françoise Béghin; one *s*; *m* 1980, Candice Bergen; one *d*. *Educ:* Paris Univ.; Institut d'Etudes Politiques. Television, 1953; Asst to Comdt Cousteau on the Calypso, 1953–55. Films: Co-prod. Le Monde du Silence, 1955 (Palme d'Or, Cannes); Collab. techn of Robert Bresson for Un Condamné a mort s'est echappé, 1956; Author and Producer of: Ascenseur pour l'échafaud, 1957 (Prix Louis-Delluc, 1958); Les Amants, 1958 (Prix spécial du Jury du Festival de Venise, 1958); Zazie dans le métro, 1960; Vie privée, 1962; Le Feu Follet (again, Prix spécial, Venise, 1963); Viva Maria, 1965 (Grand Prix du Cinéma français); Le Voleur, 1966; Histoires extraordinaires (sketch), 1968; Calcutta, 1969 (prix de la Fraternité); Phantom India, 1969; Le Souffle au Coeur, 1971 (nominated Best Screenplay, US Acad. Awards, 1972); Humain, trop humain, 1972; Place de la République, 1973; Lacombe Lucien, 1974; Black Moon, 1975; Pretty Baby, 1977; films directed: Atlantic City, 1979 (Jt winner, Golden Lion, Venice Film Fest., 1980; Best Director, BAFTA awards, 1982; nominated Best Film and Best Director, US Acad. Awards, 1982); My Dinner With André, 1981; Crackers, 1984; Alamo Bay, 1985; (also cameraman) God's Country (for Public TV), 1985; And the Pursuit of Happiness, 1986; (also writer) Au Revoir Les Enfants, 1987 (Golden Lion, Venice Film Fest.; Best Film Director, BAFTA Award, 1988); Milou in May, 1990; Damage, 1993; Vanya on 42nd Street, 1994. *Publication:* Malle on Malle, 1993. *Address:* c/o NEF, 15 rue du Louvre, 75001 Paris, France.

MALLET, Sir Ivo; *see* Mallet, Sir W. I.

MALLET, John Valentine Granville, FSA; FRSA; Keeper, Department of Ceramics, Victoria and Albert Museum, 1976–89; *b* 15 Sept. 1930; *s* of late Sir Victor Mallet, GCMG, CVO, and Lady Mallet (*née* Andreae); *m* 1958, Felicity Ann Basset; one *s*. *Educ:* Winchester Coll.; Balliol Coll., Oxford (BA Modern History; Hon. Fellow, 1992). Mil. service in Army: commnd; held temp. rank of full Lieut in Intell. Corps, 1949–50. Messrs Sotheby & Co., London, 1955–62; Victoria and Albert Museum: Asst Keeper, Dept of Ceramics, 1962; Sec. to Adv. Council, 1967–73. Indep. Mem., Design Selection Cttee, Design Council, 1981–89; Member: Exec. Cttee, Nat. Art Collections Fund, 1989–; Art Adv. Cttee, Nat. Mus. of Wales, Cardiff, 1991–. Mem., Court of Assistants, Fishmongers' Co., 1970–, Prime Warden, 1983–84. *Publications:* articles on ceramics in Burlington Magazine, Apollo, Trans English Ceramic Circle, and Faenza. *Recreation:* tennis. *Address:* 11 Pembroke Square, W8 6PA.
See also P. L. V. Mallet.

MALLET, Philip Louis Victor, CMG 1980; HM Diplomatic Service, retired; *b* 3 Feb. 1926; *e s* of late Sir Victor Mallet, GCMG, CVO and Christiana Jean, *d* of Herman A. Andreae; *m* 1953, Mary Moyle Grenfell Borlase; three *s*. *Educ:* Winchester; Balliol Coll., Oxford. Army Service, 1944–47. Entered HM Foreign (subseq. Diplomatic) Service, 1949; served in: FO, 1949; Baghdad, 1950–53; FO, 1953–56; Cyprus, 1956–58; Aden, 1958; Bonn, 1958–62; FO, 1962–64; Tunis, 1964–66; FCO, 1967–69; Khartoum, 1969–73; Stockholm, 1973–76; Head of Republic of Ireland Dept, FCO, 1977–78; High Comr in Guyana and non-resident Ambassador to Suriname, 1978–82. *Address:* Wittersham House, Wittersham, Kent TN30 7ED. *Club:* Brooks's.
See also J. V. G. Mallet.

MALLET, Roger; Chairman, North Western Electricity Board, 1972–76, retired; *b* 7 June 1912; British; *m* 1942, Kathleen Els Walker; two *s* two *d*. *Educ:* Eastbourne Coll.; Trinity Hall, Cambridge. BA Mech. Sci. Tripos; CEng, FIEE. West Cambrian Power Co., S Wales, 1937–40; Buckrose Light & Power Co., Yorks, 1940–45; Shropshire, Worcestershire and Staffordshire Electric Power Co., 1945–47; Midlands Electricity Board, 1948–72. *Recreation:* golf.

MALLETT, Conrad Richard, FRICS; Member, Lands Tribunal, 1980–92; *b* 11 May 1919; *s* of Captain Raymond Mallett, OBE, MN and Joyce Mallett (*née* Humble); *m* 1942, Elisabeth (Paulina) Williams; one *s* two *d*. *Educ:* Wellingborough Sch. Ordinary Airman to Lieut Comdr (A), RNVR, 1939–46 (despatches 1941). Partner, Montagu Evans and Son, Chartered Surveyors, London and Edinburgh, 1950–80. *Recreation:* cruising under sail. *Address:* 2 Hadley Hurst Cottages, Hadley Common, Barnet, Herts EN5 5QF. *T:* 0181–449 5933.

MALLETT, Edmund Stansfield; Director of Applications Programmes, European Space Agency, Paris, 1981–85, retired; *b* 21 April 1923; *s* of Cecil Finer Mallett and Elsie Stansfield; *m* 1st, 1953, Nancy Campbell (*d* 1983); three *s*; 2nd, 1985, Jocelyn Maynard Ghent, BA, MA, PhD. *Educ:* Bradford Grammar Sch.; Leeds Univ. (BSc). CEng, MIEE; FBIS. Gramophone Co., 1944; Fairey Aviation Co., 1948; Royal Aircraft Establishment: joined 1950; Head, Data Transmission and Processing Div., 1961; Supt, Central Unit for Scientific Photography, 1966; Head, Instrumentation Div., 1968; Head of Instruments Br., Min. of Technol., 1969; Head of Instrumentation and Ranges Dept, RAE, 1971; Director Space, DoI, 1976; Under Sec., and Head of Res. and Technol. Requirements and Space Div., DoI, 1978; Dir, Nat. Maritime Inst., 1979. *Publications:* papers and articles on instrumentation and measurement. *Recreations:* music, art, genealogy, solving problems. *Address:* 580 Prospect Avenue, Rockcliffe Park, Ottawa, Ontario K1M 0X7, Canada. *T:* (613) 7487219.

MALLETT, Francis Anthony, CBE 1984; Chief Executive, South Yorkshire County Council, 1973–84; Clerk of the Lieutenancy, South Yorkshire, 1974–84; solicitor; *b* 13 March 1924; *s* of Francis Sidney and Marion Mallett; *m* 1956, Alison Shirley Melville, MA; two *s* one *d*. *Educ:* Mill Hill; London Univ. (LLB). Army, 1943–47: commissioned, Royal Hampshire Regt, 1944; served in Middle East, Italy and Germany. Second Dep. Clerk, Herts CC, 1966–69; Dep. Clerk, West Riding CC, 1969–74. Chairman: Assoc. of Local Authority Chief Execs, 1979–84; Crown Prosecution Service Staff Commn, 1985–87; Mem., W Yorks Residuary Body, 1985–91. *Recreations:* gardening, fishing, tennis. *Address:* Lurley Manor, Tiverton, Devon EX16 9QS. *T:* Tiverton (01884) 255363. *Club:* Lansdowne.

MALLETT, Ven. Peter, CB 1978; AKC; Chaplain-General to the Forces, 1974–80; Managing Director, Inter-Church Travel, 1981–86; *b* 1925; *s* of Edwin and Beatrice Mallett; *m* 1958, Joan Margaret Bremer; one *s* two *d*. *Educ:* King's Coll., London; St Boniface Coll., Warminster, Wilts. Deacon, 1951, priest, 1952. Curate, St Oswald's, Norbury, S London, 1951–54. Joined Royal Army Chaplains' Dept (CF), 1954, and has served overseas in Far East, Aden, Germany (despatches, Malaya, 1957). Has been Senior Chaplain of Aden Brigade, and at RMA, Sandhurst; Dep. Asst Chaplain-General, Berlin, 1968, in N Ireland, 1972; Asst Chaplain-General, BAOR, 1973. QHC 1973. Canon, dio. of Europe, 1982. Hon. Chaplain: RA Assoc., 1985–; RTR, 1987–; Queen's Regt/Princess of Wales Royal Regt, 1991–. OStJ 1976. FRGS 1987. Hon. DLitt Geneva Theol Coll., 1976. *Address:* Hawthorne Cottage, Hampstead Lane, Yalding, Kent ME18 6HJ. *T:* Maidstone (01622) 812607. *Clubs:* Army and Navy, Naval and Military (Hon.).

MALLIN, Rev. Canon Stewart Adam Thomson, CSG; Minister, St Paul's, Strathnairn, since 1991; *b* 12 Aug. 1924; *s* of George Garner Mallin and Elizabeth Thomson. *Educ:* Lasswade Secondary School; Coates Hall Theological Coll., Edinburgh. Deacon 1961, priest 1962; Curate, St Andrew's Cathedral, Inverness, 1961–64; Itinerant Priest, Diocese of Moray, Ross and Caithness, 1964–68; Priest-in-Charge of St Peter and the Holy Rood, Thurso, and St John's, Wick, 1968–77; Rector, St James, Dingwall and St Anne's, Strathpeffer, 1977–91; Dean of Moray, Ross and Caithness, 1983–91. Member of CSG, 1968–; Canon of St Andrew's Cathedral, Inverness, 1974. Hon. Chaplain, British Legion. Associate, Order of the Holy Cross (USA). OStJ 1995 (SBStJ 1992). *Recreations:* amateur drama, amateur opera. *Address:* St Paul's Parsonage, Croachy, Strathnairn, Inverness IV1 2UB. *Club:* Rotary (Thurso, then Dingwall; Pres., Dingwall, 1985–86).

MALLINCKRODT, Georg Wilhelm von; *see* von Mallinckrodt.

MALLINSON, Anthony William; Senior Partner, Slaughter and May, 1984–86; *b* 1 Dec. 1923; *s* of Stanley Tucker Mallinson and Dora Selina Mallinson (*née* Burridge); *m* 1955, Heather Mary Gardiner. *Educ:* Cheam School; Marlborough College; Gonville and Caius College, Cambridge (Exbnr 1948, Tapp Post-Graduate Scholar, 1949, BA, LLM). Served RA, 1943–47, Major. Admitted solicitor, England and Wales, 1952, Hong Kong, 1978; Partner, Slaughter and May, 1957–86; Solicitor to Fishmongers' Co., 1964–86. Mem. London Bd, Bank of Scotland, 1985–93; Director: Baring Stratton (formerly Stratton) Investment Trust, 1986–94; Morgan Grenfell Asset Management Ltd, 1986–91. Mem., BoT Cttee examining British Patent System (Banks Cttee), 1967–70; Chm., Cinematograph Films Council, 1973–76. Hon. Legal Adviser to Accounting Standards Cttee, 1982–86; Member: Council, Section on Business Law, Internat. Bar Assoc., 1984–90; (co-opted) Law Soc. Co. Law Cttee, 1986–92; Financial Services Tribunal, 1988–; Financial Reporting Review Panel, 1991–; Registration Cttee, TCCB, 1986–; Trustee, Essex CCC, 1990– (Mem. Exec. Cttee, 1986–92). *Recreations:* watching sport, particularly cricket, reading. *Address:* 15 Douro Place, W8 5PH. *T:* 0171–937 2739. *Club:* MCC.

MALLINSON, John Russell; Solicitor, Corporation of Lloyd's, since 1992; *b* 29 June 1943; *s* of Wilfred and Joyce Helen Mallinson; *m* 1968, Susan Rebecca Jane Godfree; one *s* one *d*. *Educ:* Giggleswick Sch.; Balliol Coll., Oxford (Keasbey Schol. 1963; BA). Solicitor (Hons.), 1972. Asst Solicitor, Coward Chance, 1972–74; Sen. Legal Assistant, DTI, 1974–79; Assistant Solicitor: Law Officers' Dept, AG's Chambers, 1979–81; DTI, 1982–84; Under Sec. (Legal), DTI, 1985–89; Gen. Manager, Corp. of Lloyd's, 1989–92; Mem., Lloyd's Regulatory Bd, 1993–. *Recreations:* reading, conversation, music, looking at paintings. *Address:* 4 Nunappleton Way, Hurst Green, Surrey RH8 9AW. *T:* Oxted (01883) 714775.

MALLINSON, William Arthur, CBE 1978; FEng 1985; Vice Chairman, Smiths Industries PLC, 1978–85; *b* 12 June 1922; *s* of Arthur Mallinson and Nellie Jane Mallinson; *m* 1948, Muriel Ella Parker; two *d*. *Educ:* William Hulme's Grammar Sch., Manchester; Faculty of Technol., Manchester Univ. (BScTech 1st Cl. Hons). MIEE, MIMechE, MRAeS; FIMgt (FBIM 1976). Electrical Officer, Tech. Br., RAFVR, 1943–47; Elec. Designer, Electro-Hydraulics Ltd, 1947–51; Ferranti Ltd: Proj. Engr, GW Dept, 1951–55; Chief Engr, Aircraft Equipment Dept, 1955–68; Smiths Industries Ltd, 1968–85: Technical Dir, then Gen. Man., Aviation Div.; Divl Man. Dir; Main Bd Dir; Corporate Man. Dir. Member: Airworthiness Requirements Bd, CAA, 1981–85; Electronics and Avionics Requirements Bd, DTI, 1983–85 (Chm., Aviation Cttee, 1984–85). *Recreations:* music, horticulture. *Address:* Chestnut Cottage, Dukes Covert, Bagshot, Surrey GU19 5HU. *T:* Bagshot (01276) 472479.

MALLINSON, Sir William (John), 4th Bt *cr* 1935, of Walthamstow; *b* 8 Oct. 1942; *s* of Sir William Paul Mallinson, 3rd Bt, FRCP, FRCPsych and Eila Mary (*d* 1985), *d* of Roland Graeme Guy; *S* father, 1989; *m* 1968, Rosalind Angela (marr. diss. 1978), *o d* of Rollo Hoare; one *s* one *d*. *Educ:* Charterhouse. *Recreations:* sailing, tennis, ski-ing. *Heir:* *s* William James Mallinson, *b* 22 April 1970. *Address:* 1 Hollywood Mews, Chelsea, SW10 9HU. *T:* 0171–352 3821; The Watch House, The Point, Bembridge, Isle of Wight PO35 5NQ. *T:* Isle of Wight (01983) 872019. *Club:* Bembridge Sailing.

MALLON, Rt. Rev. Mgr Joseph Laurence; Parish Priest, St Anne's, Ancoats, Manchester, since 1993; *b* 8 Aug. 1942; *s* of John Mallon and Mary (*née* O'Neill). *Educ:* St Nathy's Coll., Ballaghadereen; St Kiernan's Coll., Kilkenny. Ordained priest, Dio. of Salford, 1966; Curate: St Joseph's, Bury, 1966–67; St Anne's, Stretford, 1967–73; commnd into RAChD, 1973; service in England, NI, Germany and Cyprus; Sen. RC Chaplain, BAOR, 1988; Prin. RC Chaplain and VG (Army), 1989–93, retired. Prelate of Honour, 1989. *Recreations:* bridge, golf, recreational mathematics, The Times crossword. *Address:* St Anne's House, Carruthers Street, Ancoats, Manchester M4 7EQ.

MALLON, Seamus; MP (SDLP) Newry and Armagh, since Jan. 1986; *b* 17 Aug. 1936; *s* of Francis P. Mallon and Jane O'Flaherty; *m* 1966, Gertrude Cush; one *d*. *Educ:* St Joseph's Coll. of Educn. Member: NI Assembly, 1973–74 and 1982; NI Convention, 1975–76; Irish Senate, 1981–82; New Ireland Forum, 1983–84; Armagh Dist Council, 1973–. Dep. Leader, SDLP, 1978–. Member: Select Cttee on Agric., 1987–; Anglo-Irish Inter-Parly Body, 1990–. Author of play, Adam's Children, prod. radio, 1968, and stage, 1969. *Recreations:* angling, gardening. *Address:* 5 Castleview, Markethill, Armagh BT60 1QP. *T:* Markethill (01861) 551555; House of Commons, SW1A 0AA; (office) 2 Mill Street, Newry, Co. Down; (office) 6 Seven Houses, Armagh, Co. Armagh.

MALLORIE, Air Vice-Marshal Paul Richard, CB 1979; AFC 1947; retired RAF, 1980; Military Command and Control Systems Consultant; *b* 8 March 1923; *s* of late Rev. W. T. Mallorie and Margaret Mallorie; *m* 1951, Ursula Joyce Greig; three *s* one *d*. *Educ:* King's Sch., Canterbury. Flying Instructor, 1945; India and Middle East, 1946–49; Air Ministry, 1951–53; Staff Coll., 1954; No 139 Sqdn, 1955–57; JSSC, 1960; UK Mil. Advisers' Rep., SEATO, Bangkok, 1963–66; OC RAF Wittering, 1967–68; IDC, 1969; Min. of Defence, 1974–76; Asst Chief of Staff (Info. Systems), SHAPE, 1976–79. Res. Fellow, NATO, 1981–82. *Recreations:* gardening, computers. *Address:* c/o Barclays Bank, Framlingham, Woodbridge, Suffolk. *Club:* Royal Air Force.

MALLOWS, Surg. Rear-Adm. Harry Russell; Senior Medical Officer, Shell Centre, 1977–85; *b* 1 July 1920; *s* of Harry Mallows and Amy Mallows (*née* Law); *m* 1942, Rhona Frances Wyndham-Smith; one *s* two *d*. *Educ:* Wrekin Coll.; Christ's Coll., Cambridge (MA, MD); UCH, London. FFPHM, FFOM, DPH, DIH. SMO, HM Dockyards at Hong Kong, Sheerness, Gibraltar and Singapore, 1951–67; Naval MO of Health, Scotland and NI Comd, and Far East Stn, 1964–68; Dir of Environmental Medicine, Inst. of Naval Medicine, 1970–73; Comd MO, Naval Home Comd, 1973–75; QHP, 1974–77; Surgeon Rear-Adm. (Ships and Estabts), 1975–77; retd 1977. CStJ 1976. *Publications:* articles in BMJ, Royal Naval Med. Service Jl, Proc. RSM. *Recreations:* music, travel. *Address:* 1 Shear Hill, Petersfield, Hants GU31 4BB. *T:* Petersfield (01730) 263116.

MALMESBURY, 6th Earl of *cr* 1800; **William James Harris;** TD 1944 (2 Clasps); JP; DL; Baron Malmesbury, 1788; Viscount FitzHarris, 1800; Official Verderer of the New Forest, 1966–74; Lord-Lieutenant and Custos Rotulorum of Hampshire, 1973–82; served Royal Hampshire Regiment, TA; *b* 18 Nov. 1907; *o s* of 5th Earl and Hon. Dorothy Gough-Calthorpe (*d* 1973), CBE (Lady of Grace, Order of St John of Jerusalem, Order of Mercy, with bar), *y d* of 6th Lord Calthorpe; *S* father 1950; *m* 1st, 1932, Hon. Diana Carleton (*d* 1990), *e d* of 6th Baron Dorchester, OBE; one *s* two *d*; 2nd, 1991, Margaret Fleetwood (*née* Campbell-Preston), OBE (*d* 1994), *widow* of Raymond Baring; two step *s* one step *d*. *Educ:* Eton; Trinity Coll., Cambridge (MA). Vice-Pres. of the Cambridge Univ. Conservative Association, 1929; Professional Associate of Surveyors Institution, 1937. Personal Liaison Officer to Min. of Agric., SE Region, 1958–64; Mem., Agric. and Forestry Cttee, RICS, 1953–69; Chm., Hants Agric. Exec. Cttee, 1959–67; Cttee which produced White Paper on the Growing Demand for Water, 1961. Dir, Mid-Southern Water Co., 1961–78. Pres., New Forest 9th Centenary Trust, 1987– (Chm., 1977–87). Chairman: Hants Br., Country Landowners Assoc., 1954–56; T&AFA, Hants and IoW, 1960–68; first Chm., Eastern Wessex TA&VRA, 1968–70 (Vice-Pres., 1973–78; Pres., 1978–80); Hon. Col, 65th (M) Signal Regt, R Sigs (TA), 1959–66; Hon. Col, 2nd Bn The Wessex Regt (V), 1970–73. Mem. Basingstoke RDC, 1946–52; County Councillor, Hants CC, 1952; Vice-Lt, Co. Southampton, 1960–73; DL Hants, 1955 and 1983. Master, Worshipful Co. of Skinners, 1952–53. KStJ 1973. Coronation Medal, 1937, 1953; Silver Jubilee Medal, 1977. *Heir:* *s* Viscount FitzHarris, *qv*. *Address:* The Coach House, Greywell Hill, Basingstoke, Hants RG25 1DB. *T:* Odiham (01256) 702033. *Club:* Royal Yacht Squadron (Vice-Cdre, 1971–77).

See also Sir J. Baring, J. N. Maltby.

MALONE, Hon. Sir Denis (Eustace Gilbert), Kt 1977; Chief Justice of the Cayman Islands, 1990–93; *b* 24 Nov. 1922; *s* of Sir Clement Malone, OBE, QC, and Lady Malone; *m* 1963, Diana Malone (*née* Traynor). *Educ:* St Kitts-Nevis Grammar Sch.; Wycliffe Coll., Stonehouse, Glos; Lincoln Coll., Oxford (BA). Called to Bar, Middle Temple, 1950. Royal Air Force, Bomber Comd, 1942–46. Attorney General's Chambers, Barbados, WI, 1953–61, Solicitor-Gen., 1958–61; Puisne Judge: Belize, 1961–65; Trinidad and Tobago, 1966–74; Chief Justice of Belize, 1974–79; Puisne Judge, Bahamas, 1979–89. *Recreations:* tennis, swimming, walking, bridge, reading. *Address:* 21B Carefree Apartments, PO Box N-4811, Nassau, Bahamas, West Indies.

MALONE, (Peter) Gerald; MP (C) Winchester, since 1992; Minister of State, Department of Health, since 1994; Editor, The Sunday Times Scotland, 1989–90, Editorial Consultant, since 1990; *b* 21 July 1950; *s* of P. A. and J. Malone; *m* 1981, Dr Anne S. Blyth; two *s* one *d*. *Educ:* St Aloysius Coll., Glasgow; Glasgow Univ. (MA, LLB). Admitted solicitor, 1972. MP (C) Aberdeen S, 1983–87. PPS to Parly Under Secs of State, Dept of Energy, 1985, and to Sec. of State, DTI, 1985–86; an Asst Government Whip, 1986–87; Dep. Chm., Cons. Party, 1992–94. Dir of European Affairs, Energy and Envmtl Policy Center, Harvard Univ., 1987–90; Presenter, Talk In Sunday, Radio Clyde, 1988–90. Chm., CGA, 1991–. *Recreations:* opera, motoring. *Address:* c/o House of Commons, SW1A 0AA. *Club:* Conservative (Winchester).

MALONE, Rt. Rev. Vincent; an Auxiliary Bishop of Liverpool, (RC), and Titular Bishop of Abora, since 1989; *b* 11 Sept. 1931; *s* of Louis Malone and Elizabeth Malone (*née* McGrath). *Educ:* St Francis Xavier's Coll, Liverpool; St Joseph's Coll., Upholland; Liverpool Univ. (BSc 1959); Cambridge Univ. (CertEd 1960; DipEd 1964). FCP 1967. Chaplain to Notre Dame Training Coll., Liverpool, 1955–59; Curate, St Anne's, Liverpool, 1960–61; Asst Master, Cardinal Allen Grammar School, Liverpool, 1961–71; RC Chaplain to Liverpool Univ., 1971–79; Administrator, Liverpool Metropolitan Cathedral, 1979–89. *Address:* 17 West Oakhill Park, Liverpool L13 4BN. *T:* 0151–228 7637.

MALONE-LEE, Michael Charles, CB 1995; Vice Chancellor, Anglia Polytechnic University, since 1995; *b* 4 March 1941; *s* of Dr Gerard Brendan and Theresa Malone-Lee; *m* 1971, Claire Frances Cockin; two *s*. *Educ:* Stonyhurst College; Campion Hall, Oxford (MA). Ministry of Health, 1968; Principal Private Sec. to Sec. of State for Social Services, 1976–79; Asst Sec., 1977; Area Administrator, City and East London AHA, 1979–81; District Administrator, Bloomsbury Health Authy, 1982–84; Under Secretary, 1984, Dir, Personnel Management, 1984–87, DHSS; Prin. Fin. Officer, Home Office, 1987–90; Dep. Sec. (Dir of Corporate Affairs, NHS Management Exec.), DoH, 1990–93; Dep. Sec. (Head of Policy Gp), Lord Chancellor's Dept, 1993–95. Non-exec Dir, ICI (Agrochemicals), 1986–89. *Recreations:* natural history, marathon running. *Address:* Anglia Polytechnic University, Victoria Road South, Chelmsford, Essex CM1 1LL.

MALONEY, Michael John, JP; MA; Principal, Moreton Hall, 1990–92; *b* 26 July 1932; *s* of John William Maloney and Olive Lois Maloney; *m* 1960, Jancis Ann (*née* Ewing); one *s* one *d*. *Educ:* St Alban's Sch.; Trinity Coll., Oxford (MA). Nat. Service, 2nd Lieut RA, served with RWAFF, 1955–57. May & Baker Ltd, 1957–58; Asst Master, Shrewsbury Sch., 1958–66; Sen. Science Master, Housemaster, Dep. Headmaster, Eastbourne Coll., 1966–72; Headmaster: Welbeck Coll., 1972–85; Kamazu Acad., Malawi, 1986–89. JP Worksop, 1975–86, Shrewsbury, 1991. *Publication:* (with D. E. P. Hughes) Advanced Theoretical Chemistry, 1964. *Recreations:* ornithology, cryptography, very hard crosswords. *Address:* Lower Lane Cottage, Chirbury, Montgomery, Powys SY15 6UD. *T:* Chirbury (0193872) 303.

MALOTT, Deane Waldo; President Cornell University, Ithaca, NY, 1951–63, President Emeritus, 1963; Consultant, Association of American Colleges, 1963–70; *b* 10 July 1898; *s* of Michael Harvey Malott and Edith Gray Johnson; *m* 1925, Eleanor Sisson Thrum; one *s* two *d*. *Educ:* Univ. of Kansas (AB); Harvard Univ. (MBA). Asst Dean, Harvard Business Sch., 1923–29; Assoc. Prof. of Business, 1933–39; Vice-Pres., Hawaiian Pineapple Co., Honolulu, 1929–33; Chancellor, Univ. of Kansas, 1939–51. Educational Advisor, Ops Analysis Div., US Army Air Corps, 1943–45; Mem., Business Council, Washington, DC, 1944–; Trustee: Corning Museum of Glass, 1952–73; Teagle Foundation, 1952–85; William Allen White Foundation, 1952–; Kansas Univ. Endowment Assoc., 1962–; Nat. (formerly Pacific) Tropical Botanical Garden, 1964–; Mem. Bd, Univ. of Kansas Alumni Assoc., 1974–; Director: General Mills, Inc., 1948–70; Citizens Bank, Abilene, Kans, 1944–73; Pitney-Bowes, Inc., 1951–71; First Nat. Bank, Ithaca, NY, 1951–83; Owens-Corning Fiberglas Corp., 1951–72; Lane Bryant, Inc., 1963–77; Servomation Corp., 1963–74. Mem., Adv. Bd, Security Northstar Bank, 1983–. Hon. LLD: Washburn Univ., 1941; Bryant Coll., 1951; Hamilton Coll., 1951; Univ. of California 1954; Univ. of Liberia, 1962; Univ. of New Hampshire, 1963; Emory Univ., 1963; Juniata Coll., 1965; DCS, Univ. of Pittsburgh, 1957; Hon. DHL, Long Island Univ., 1967. Holds foreign Orders. *Publications:* Problems in Agricultural Marketing, 1938; (with Philip Cabot) Problems in Public Utility Management, 1927; (with J. C. Baker) Introduction to Corporate Finance, 1936; (with J. C. Baker and W. D. Kennedy) On Going into Business, 1936; (with B. F. Martin) The Agricultural Industries, 1939; Agriculture—the Great Dilemma (an essay in Business and Modern Society), 1951. *Address:* 322 Wait Avenue, Cornell University, Ithaca, NY 14850, USA. *Clubs:* University, Cornell (New York); Bohemian (San Francisco).

MALPAS, Prof. James Spencer, DPhil; FFPM; FRCR; FRCP; Consultant Physician, St Bartholomew's Hospital, since 1973; Professor of Medical Oncology, since 1979, and Director, Imperial Cancer Research Fund Medical Oncology Unit, since 1976, St Bartholomew's Hospital; *b* 15 Sept. 1931; *s* of Tom Spencer Malpas, BSc, MICE and Hilda Chalstrey; *m* 1957, Joyce May Cathcart; two *s*. *Educ:* Sutton County Grammar Sch.; St Bartholomew's Hosp., London Univ. Schol. in Sci., 1951; BSc Hons, 1952; MB BS, 1955; DPhil, 1965; FRCP 1971; FRCR 1983; FFPM 1989. Junior appts in medicine, St Bartholomew's Hosp. and Royal Post-Grad. Med. Sch.; Nat. Service in RAF, 1957–60; Aylwen Bursar, St Bartholomew's Hosp., 1961; Lectr in Medicine, Oxford Univ., 1962–65; St Bartholomew's Hospital: Sen. Registrar in Medicine, 1966–68; Sen. Lectr in Medicine, 1968–72; Dean, 1969–72, Gov., 1972–, Treasurer, 1986–87, and Vice Pres., 1987–93, of Med. Coll.; Dep. Dir (Clinical), ICRF, 1986–90. Cooper Res. Schol. in Med., 1966, 1967, 1968. Examiner in Medicine: Univ. of Oxford, 1974; Univ. of London, 1985, 1986. Asst Registrar, RCP, 1975–80; Treasurer, Postgrad. Med. Fellowship, 1984–87. Pres., Assoc. of Cancer Physicians, 1994–. Lockyer Lectr, RCP, 1978; Skinner Lectr, RCR, 1986; Subodh Mitra Meml Orator, New Delhi, 1991; Louise Buchanan Lectr, Assoc. of Cancer Physicians, 1993. Editor, British Jl of Cancer, 1992–. *Publications:* (ed jtly) Multiple Myeloma, 1994; contrib. many medical textbooks; papers in BMJ, Brit. Jl Haematology, Jl Clinical Oncology, etc. *Recreations:* travel, history, painting, sailing, wind surfing, avoiding gardening. *Address:* 213 Lauderdale Tower, Barbican, EC2Y 8BY. *T:* 0171–638 7177. *Club:* Little Ship.

MALPAS, Robert, CBE 1975; FEng 1978; FIMechE, FIChemE, FIMH; Chairman, Cookson Group, since 1991; Chairman, Natural Environment Research Council, since 1993; *b* 9 Aug. 1927; *s* of late Cheshyre Malpas and of Louise Marie Marcelle Malpas; *m* 1956, Josephine Dickenson. *Educ:* Taunton Sch.; St George's Coll., Buenos Aires; Durham Univ. BScMechEng (1st Cl. Hons). Joined ICI Ltd, 1948; moved to Alcudia SA (48.5 per cent ICI), Spain, 1963; ICI Europa Ltd, Brussels, 1965; Chm., ICI Europa Ltd, 1973; ICI Main Board Dir, 1975–78; Pres., Halcon International Inc., 1978–82; a Man. Dir, BP, 1983–89; Chm., PowerGen, 1990; Director: BOC Group, 1981–; Eurotunnel, 1987–; Repsol, SA, 1989–. Member: Engineering Council, 1983–88 (Vice-Chm., 1984–88); ACARD, 1983–86; Chm., LINK Steering Gp, 1987–93. Sen. Vice Pres., Fellowship of Engrg, 1988–92. Hon. DTech Loughborough, 1983; DUniv Surrey, 1984; Hon. DEng Newcastle, 1991; Hon. DSc Bath, 1991. Order of Civil Merit, Spain, 1967. *Recreations:* sport, music. *Address:* 2 Belgrave Mews West, SW1X 8HT. *Clubs:* Royal Automobile; River (NY); Mill Reef (Antigua).

MALPASS, Brian William, PhD; CChem; writer; Chief Executive, De La Rue Co. plc, 1987–89; *b* 12 Sept. 1937; *s* of William and Florence Malpass; *m* 1960, Hazel Anne; two *d*. *Educ:* Univ. of Birmingham (Open Schol.; Frankland Prize 1960; BScChem 1st Cl. Hons, PhD). MRSC. Passfield Res. Laboratories, 1963–68; De La Rue Co., 1968–89; Finance Dir, 1980–84; Man. Dir, Thomas De La Rue Currency Div., 1984–87. *Publications:* Bluff Your Way in Science, 1993; Bluff Your Way in Chess, 1993; numerous papers in scientific jls. *Recreations:* golf, cinema. *Address:* 13 Spinfield Mount, Marlow, Bucks SL7 2JU. *Club:* Maidenhead Golf.

MALTA, Archbishop of, (RC), since 1976; **Most Rev. Joseph Mercieca,** STD, JUD; *b* Victoria, Gozo, 11 Nov. 1928. *Educ:* Gozo Seminary; Univ. of London (BA); Gregorian Univ., Rome (STD); Lateran Univ., Rome (JUD). Priest, 1952; Rector of Gozo Seminary in late 1960s; Permanent Judge at Sacred Roman Rota and Commissioner to Congregation for the Sacraments and Congregation for the Doctrine of the Faith, 1969; Auxiliary Bishop of Malta, and Vicar-General, 1974–76. Consultor, Supreme Tribunal of Apostolic Segnatura suis, 1992. *Address:* Archbishop's Curia, PO Box 29, Valletta, Malta. *T:* 234317.

MALTBY, Antony John, JP; MA; Headmaster of Trent College, 1968–88; *b* 15 May 1928; *s* of late G. C. Maltby and Mrs Maltby (*née* Kingsnorth); *m* 1959, Jillian Winifred (*née* Burt); four *d*. *Educ:* Clayesmore Sch., Dorset; St John's Coll., Cambridge. BA Hons (History) 1950; MA. Schoolmaster: Dover Coll., 1951–58; Pocklington Sch., 1958–68. Mem. (C), Ashford BC, 1991. JP: Ilkeston, 1980; Ashford, 1992; DL Derbyshire, 1984–91. *Recreations:* squash, travel. *Address:* Little Singleton Farm, Great Chart, Ashford, Kent TN26 1JS. *T:* Ashford (01233) 629397. *Club:* Hawks (Cambridge).

MALTBY, Colin Charles; Chairman, Kleinwort Overseas Investment Trust plc, since 1992; *b* 8 Feb. 1951; *s* of George Frederick Maltby and Dorothy Maltby; *m* 1983, Victoria Angela Valerie Elton; one *s* two *d*. *Educ:* George Heriot's Sch., Edinburgh; King Edward's Sch., Birmingham; Christ Church, Oxford (MA, MSc); Stanford Business Sch. Pres., Oxford Union, 1973; Chm., Fedn of Cons. Students, 1974–75. With N. M. Rothschild & Sons, 1975–80; Director: Kleinwort Benson Investment Mgt Ltd, 1984–95 (Chief Exec., 1988–95); Banque Kleinwort Benson SA, Geneva, 1985–88; Kleinwort Benson Gp plc, 1989–95. *Recreations:* music, ski-ing. *Address:* 51 Addison Avenue, W11 4QU.

MALTBY, John Newcombe, CBE 1988; Chairman: Harrisons & Crosfield plc, 1991–94 (Director, 1987–94); Dover Harbour Board, since 1989; *b* 10 July 1928; *s* of Air Vice-Marshal Sir Paul Maltby, KCVO, KBE, CB, DSO, AFC, DL and Winifred Russell Paterson; *m* 1956, Lady Sylvia Veronica Anthea Harris, *d* of Earl of Malmesbury, *qv*; one *s* two *d*. *Educ:* Wellington Coll.; Clare Coll., Cambridge (MA Mech. Scis). Shell Internat. Petrolem, 1951–69; Founder and Man. Dir, Panocean Shipping & Terminals, 1969–75; Man. Dir, Panocean-Anco Ltd, 1975–79; The Burmah Oil plc: Dir, 1980–82; Dep. Chm., 1982–83; Gp Chief Exec., 1982–88; Chm., 1983–90. Director: J. Bibby and Sons plc, 1984–87; DRG plc, 1987–89. Mem., 1988–93, Chm., 1990–93, UKAEA. Chm., British Ports Fedn, 1992 (Dep. Chm., 1990–92). *Recreations:* history, gardening, sailing. *Address:* Broadford House, Stratfield Turgis, Hook, Hants RG27 0AS. *Club:* Brooks's.

MALTRAVERS, Lord; Henry Miles Fitzalan-Howard; *b* 3 Dec. 1987; *s* and *heir* of Earl of Arundel and Surrey, *qv*.

MALVERN, 3rd Viscount *cr* 1955, of Rhodesia and of Bexley, Kent; **Ashley Kevin Godfrey Huggins;** *b* 26 Oct. 1949; *s* of 2nd Viscount Malvern, and of Patricia Marjorie, *d* of Frank Renwick-Bower, Durban, S Africa; *S* father, 1978. *Heir: uncle* Hon. (Martin) James Huggins, *b* 13 Jan. 1928.

MAMALONI, Solomon; MP (People's Alliance Party), 1977; Prime Minister of Solomon Islands, 1981–85, 1989–93 and since 1994; *b* 1943. *Educ:* King George VI School; Te-Aute College, NZ. Exec. Officer, Civil Service, later Clerk to Legislative Council; MP Makira, 1970–76, West Makira, 1976–77 and 1980–; Chief Minister, British Solomon Islands, 1974–76; founder and leader, People's Progress Party (merged with Rural Alliance Party to form People's Alliance Party, 1979); Man. Dir, Patosha Co., 1977. *Address:* Office of the Prime Minister, Honiara, Guadalcanal, Solomon Islands.

MAMBA, George Mbikwakhe, Hon. GCVO 1987; Minister of Foreign Affairs, Swaziland, 1988–94; *b* 5 July 1932; *s* of Ndabazebelungu Mamba and Getrude Mthwalose Mamba, and *g s* of late Chief Bokweni Mamba; *m* 1960, Sophie Sidzandza Sibande; three *s* two *d*. *Educ:* Franson Christian High Sch.; Swazi National High Sch.; Morija Teacher Trng Coll.; Cambridge Inst. of Educn; Nairobi Univ. Head Teacher, Makhonza Mission Sch., 1956–60; Teacher, Kwaluseni Central Sch., 1961–65; Head Teacher, Enkamheni Central Sch., 1966–67; Inspector of Schs, Manzini Dist, 1969–70; Welfare/Aftercare Officer, Prison Dept, 1971–72; Counsellor, Swaziland High Commn, Nairobi, 1972–77; High Comr to UK and concurrently High Comr to Malta, Ambassador to Denmark, Sweden and Norway, and Perm. Deleg. to UNESCO, 1978–88, Sen. High Comr, 1984 and Doyen of Diplomatic Corps, 1985–88. Vice-Pres., Swaziland NUT, 1966–67. Field Comr, Swaziland Boy Scouts Assoc., 1967–68, Chief Comr, 1971–72. *Publication:* Children's Play, 1966. *Recreations:* scouting, reading. *Address:* c/o Ministry of Foreign Affairs, PO Box 518, Mbabane, Swaziland.

MAMET, David Alan; writer; stage and film director; *b* 30 Nov. 1947; *s* of Bernard Morris Mamet and Lenore June Mamet (*née* Silver); *m* 1st, 1977, Lindsay Crouse (marr. diss.); 2nd, 1991, Rebecca Pidgeon. *Educ:* Goddard College, Plainfield, Vt (BA Eng. Lit. 1969); Neighbourhood Playhouse Sch., NY. Founding Mem. and first Artistic Dir, St Nicholas Theater Co., Chicago, 1974. *Plays written and produced include:* American Buffalo, 1976; A Life in the Theatre, 1976; The Water Engine, 1976; The Woods, 1977; Glen Garry Glen Ross, 1984 (film, 1992); Speed the Plow, 1987; Bobby Gould in Hell, 1989; The Old Neighborhood, 1990; Oleanna, 1992; The Cryptogram, 1994; *written for films:* The Verdict, 1980; The Untouchables, 1986; House of Games, 1986; (with Shel Silverstein) Things Change, 1987; Hoffa, 1990; Homicide, 1991; Uncle Vanya on 42nd Street, 1994; *films directed:* House of Games, 1986; Things Change, 1988; Homicide, 1991. Pulitzer Prize for Drama, 1984. *Publications:* Writing in Restaurants, 1986; Some Freaks, 1989; The Hero Pony, 1990; On Directing Film, 1991; The Cabin, 1992; The Village, 1994. *Address:* c/o Howard Rosenstone, Rosenstone/Wender Agency, 3 East 48th Street, New York, NY 10017, USA.

MAMO, Sir Anthony (Joseph) Kt 1960; OBE 1955; Companion of Honour, National Order of Merit (Malta), 1990; *b* 9 Jan. 1909; *s* of late Joseph Mamo and late Carola (*née* Brincat); *m* 1939, Margaret Agius; one *s* two *d*. *Educ:* Royal Univ. of Malta. BA 1931; LLD 1934. Mem. Statute Law Revision Commn, 1936–42; Crown Counsel, 1942–51; Prof., Criminal Law, Malta Univ., 1943–57; Dep. Attorney-Gen., 1952–54, Attorney-Gen., 1955, Malta; Chief Justice and President, Court of Appeal, Malta, 1957–71; President, Constitutional Court, Malta, 1964–71; Governor-General, Malta, 1971–74; President, Republic of Malta, 1974–76. QC (Malta) 1957. Hon. DLitt Malta, 1969; Hon. LLD Libya, 1971. KStJ 1969. Gieh ir-Repubblika (Malta), 1992. *Publications:* Lectures on Criminal Law and Criminal Procedure delivered at the University of Malta. *Address:* 49 Stella Maris Street, Sliema, Malta. *T:* 330708. *Club:* Casino (1852).

MAN, Archdeacon of; *see* Willoughby, Ven. D. A.

MANASSEH, Leonard Sulla, OBE 1982; RA 1979 (ARA 1976); RWA; FRIBA; Partner, Leonard Manasseh Partnership (formerly Leonard Manasseh & Partners), since 1950; *b* 21 May 1916; *s* of late Alan Manasseh and Esther (*née* Elias); *m* 1st, 1947 (marr diss. 1956); two *s*; 2nd, 1957, Sarah Delaforce; two *s* (one *d* decd). *Educ:* Cheltenham College; The Architectural Assoc. Sch. of Architecture (AA Dip.). ARIBA 1941, FRIBA 1964; FCSD (FSIAD 1965); RWA 1972 (Pres., 1989–94, PPRWA 1995). Asst Architect, CRE N London and Guy Morgan & Partners; teaching staff, AA and Kingston Sch. of Art, 1941–43; Fleet Air Arm, 1943–46; Asst Architect, Herts CC, 1946–48; Senior Architect, Stevenage New Town Develt Corp., 1948–50; won Festival of Britain restaurant competition, 1950; started private practice, 1950; teaching staff, AA Sch. of Architecture, 1951–59; opened office in Singapore and Malaysia with James Cubitt & Partners (Cubitt Manasseh & Partners), 1953–54. Member: Council, Architectural Assoc., 1959–66 (Pres., 1964–65); Council of Industrial Design, 1965–68; Council, RIBA 1968–70, 1976–82 (Hon. Sec., 1979–81); Council, National Trust, 1977–91; Ancient Monuments Bd, 1978–84; Bd, Chatham Historic Dockyard Trust, 1984–. Pres., Franco-British Union of Architects, 1978–79. Governor: Alleyn's Sch., Dulwich, 1987–; Dulwich Coll., 1987–; Dulwich Picture Gallery, 1987–94. FRSA 1967. *Work includes:* houses, housing and schools; industrial work; power stations; conservation plan for Beaulieu Estate; Nat. Motor Museum, Beaulieu; Wellington Country Park, Stratfield Saye; Pumping Station, Weymouth; British Museum refurbishment; (jtly) New Research Centre, Loughborough, British Gas. *Publications:* Office Buildings (with 3rd Baron Cunliffe), 1962, Japanese edn 1964; Snowdon Summit Report (Countryside Commission), 1974; Eastbourne Harbour Study (Trustees, Chatsworth Settlement), 1976; (jtly) planning reports and studies. *Recreations:* photography, painting, being optimistic. *Address:* 6 Bacon's Lane, Highgate, N6 6BL. *T:* 0181–340 5528. *Clubs:* Athenæum, Arts, Royal Automobile.

MANCE, Hon. Sir Jonathan (Hugh), Kt 1993; **Hon. Mr Justice Mance;** a Judge of the High Court, Queen's Bench Division, Commercial List, since 1993; *b* 6 June 1943; *e s* of late Sir Henry Stenhouse Mance and of Lady (Joan Erica Robertson) Mance; *m* 1973, Mary Howarth Arden (*see* Hon. Dame M. H. Arden); *qv*; one *s* two *d*. *Educ:* Charterhouse; University Coll., Oxford (MA). Called to the Bar, Middle Temple, 1965, Bencher, 1990. QC 1982; a Recorder, 1990–93. Worked in Germany, 1965. Chm., Banking Appeal Tribunals, 1992–93. Dir, Bar Mutual Indemnity Fund Ltd, 1987–94. *Publications:* (asst editor) Chalmer's Sale of Goods, 1981; (ed jtly) Sale of Goods, Halsbury's Laws of England, 4th edn 1983; lectures and articles on insurance and other legal subjects. *Recreations:* tennis, languages, music. *Address:* Royal Courts of Justice, Strand, WC2A 2LL. *Club:* Cumberland Lawn Tennis.

MANCE, Dame Mary Howarth; *see* Arden, Hon. Dame M. H.

MANCHAM, Sir James Richard Marie, KBE 1976; international trade consultant, since 1981; Chairman, Airominor Ltd, since 1987; Founder and Chairman, Crusade for the Restoration of Democracy in Seychelles, since 1990; Leader of revived Seychelles Democratic Party, since 1992; President, Republic of the Seychelles, 1976–77; *b* 11 Aug. 1939; adopted British nationality, 1984; *e s* of late Richard Mancham and Evelyne Mancham, MBE (*née* Tirant); *m* 1963, Heather Jean Evans (marr. diss. 1974); one *s* one *d*; *m* 1985, Catherine Olsen; one *s*. *Educ:* Seychelles Coll.; Wilson Coll., London. Called to Bar, Middle Temple, 1961. Auditeur Libre à la Faculté de Droit ès Sciences Economiques, Univ. of Paris, 1962; Internat. Inst. of Labour Studies Study Course, Geneva, Spring 1968. Legal practice, Supreme Court of Seychelles. Seychelles Democratic Party (SDP), Pres. 1964; Mem. Seychelles Governing Council, 1967; Leader of Majority Party (SDP), 1967; Mem., Seychelles Legislative Assembly, 1970–76; Chief Minister, 1970–75; Prime Minister, 1975–76; led SDP to Seychelles Constitutional Conf., London, 1970 and 1976. Founder, Seychelles Weekly, 1962. Lecturer, 1981, on struggle for power in Indian Ocean, to US and Eur. univs and civic gps. Hon. Trustee, Cary Ann Lindblad Intrepid Foundn, 1986–. Hon. Citizen: Dade County, Florida, 1963; New Orleans, 1965. FRSA 1968. Cert. of Merit for Distinguished Contribn to Poetry, Internat. Who's Who in Poetry, 1974. Chevalier, Chaîne des Rôtisseurs, 1993. Officier de la Légion d'Honneur, 1976; Grande Médaille de la Francophonie, 1976; Grande médaille vermeille, Paris, 1976; Quaid-i-Azam Medallion (Pakistan), 1976; Gold Medal for Tourism, Mexico, 1977; Gold Medal of Chamber of Commerce and Industries of France, 1977; Gold Medal des Excellences Européennes, 1977; Plaque of Appreciation, Rotary Club of Manila, Philippines, 1987. *Publications:* Reflections and Echoes from Seychelles, 1972 (poetry); L'Air des Seychelles, 1974; Island Splendour, 1980; Paradise Raped, 1983; Galloo—The undiscovered paradise, 1984; New York's Robin Island, 1985; Peace of Mind, 1989; Adages of an Exile, 1991. *Recreations:* travel, water sports, tennis, writing. *Address:* c/o Lloyds Bank, 195 Edgware Road, W2 1EY. *Clubs:* Royal Automobile, Annabel's, Les Ambassadeurs, Wig and Pen; Intrepids (NY); Cercle Saint Germain des Prés (Paris).

MANCHESTER, 12th Duke of, *cr* 1719; **Angus Charles Drogo Montagu;** Baron Montagu, Viscount Mandeville, 1620; Earl of Manchester, 1626; *b* 9 Oct. 1938; *yr s* of 10th Duke of Manchester, OBE, and Nell Vere (*d* 1966); *S* brother, 1985; *m* 1st, 1961, Mary Eveleen McClure (marr. diss. 1970); two *s* one *d*; 2nd, 1971, Diane Pauline Plimsaul (marr. diss. 1985); 3rd, 1989, Mrs Ann-Louise Bird, *d* of Dr Alfred Butler Taylor, Cawthorne, S Yorks. *Educ:* Gordonstoun. *Address:* c/o House of Lords, SW1A 0PW.

MANCHESTER, Bishop of, since 1993; **Rt. Rev. Christopher John Mayfield;** *b* 18 Dec. 1935; *s* of Dr Roger Bolton Mayfield and Muriel Eileen Mayfield; *m* 1962, Caroline Ann Roberts; two *s* one *d*. *Educ:* Sedbergh School; Gonville and Caius Coll., Cambridge (MA 1961); Linacre House, Oxford (Dip. Theology). Deacon 1963, priest 1964, Birmingham; Curate of St Martin-in-the-Bull Ring, Birmingham, 1963–67; Lecturer at St Martin's, Birmingham, 1967–71; Chaplain at Children's Hospital, Birmingham, 1967–71; Vicar of Luton, 1971–80 (with East Hyde, 1971–76); RD of Luton, 1974–79; Archdeacon of Bedford, 1979–85; Bishop Suffragan of Wolverhampton, 1985–93. MSc Cranfield, 1984. *Recreations:* marriage, evangelism, walking. *Address:* Bishopscourt, Bury New Road, Manchester M7 0LE. *T:* 0161–792 2096.

MANCHESTER, Dean of; *see* Riley, Very Rev. K. J.

MANCHESTER, Archdeacon of; *see* Harris, Ven. R. B.

MANCHESTER, William; Purple Heart (US) 1945; author; Fellow, East College, 1968–86, writer in residence since 1974, and Adjunct Professor of History, 1979–92, now Professor Emeritus, Wesleyan University; Fellow, Pierson College, Yale University, since 1991; *b* 1 April 1922; *s* of William Raymond Manchester and Sallie E. R. (*née* Thompson); *m* 1948, Julia Brown Marshall; one *s* two *d*. *Educ:* Springfield Classical High School; Univ. of Massachusetts; Dartmouth Coll., NH; Univ. of Missouri. Served US Marine Corps, 1942–45. Reporter, Daily Oklahoman, 1945–46; Reporter, foreign corresp., war corresp., Baltimore Sun, 1947–55; Man. editor, Wesleyan Univ. Publications, 1955–64; Fellow, Center for Advanced Studies, 1959–60, Lectr in English, 1968–69, Wesleyan Univ. Trustee: Friends of Univ. of Massachusetts Library, 1970–76 (Pres., 1970–72); Winston Churchill Travelling Fellowships, 1992–; Mem., Soc. of Amer. Historians. Guggenheim Fellow, 1959; Hon. Dr of Humane Letters: Univ. of Mass, 1965; Univ. of New Haven, 1979; Hon. LittD: Skidmore Coll., 1987; Univ. of Richmond, 1988; Hon. LHD Russell Sage Coll., NY, 1990. Dag Hammarskjold Internat. Prize in Literature, 1967; Overseas Press Club (New York) Award for Best Book of the Year on Foreign Affairs, 1968; Univ. of Missouri Medal, 1969; Connecticut Book Award, 1974; President's Cabinet Award, Detroit Univ., 1981; Frederick S. Troy Medal, 1981; McConaughy Award, 1981; Lincoln Literary Award, 1983; Distinguished Public Service Award, Conn Bar Assoc., 1985; Sarah Josepha Hale Award, 1993. *Publications:* Disturber of the Peace, 1951 (publ. UK as The Sage of Baltimore, 1952); The City of Anger, 1953; Shadow of the Monsoon, 1956; Beard the Lion, 1958; A Rockefeller Family Portrait, 1959; The Long Gainer, 1961; Portrait of a President, 1962; The Death of a President, 1967; The Arms of Krupp, 1968; The Glory and the Dream, 1974; Controversy and other Essays in Journalism, 1976; American Caesar, 1978; Goodbye, Darkness, 1980; One Brief Shining Moment, 1983; The Last Lion: vol. 1, Visions of Glory, 1983; vol. 2, Alone, 1987 (publ. UK as The Caged Lion, Winston Spencer Churchill 1932–1940, 1988); This is Our Time, 1989; A World Lit Only By Fire, 1992; contrib. to Encyclopedia Britannica and to periodicals. *Recreation:* photography. *Address:* Wesleyan University, Middletown, CT 06459, USA. *T:* (203) 6853884. *Clubs:* Century, Williams (New York), University (Hartford).

MANCHESTER, Sir William (Maxwell), KBE 1987 (CBE 1973); FRCS, FRACS, FACS; retired; *b* 31 Oct. 1913; *s* of James Manchester and Martha Browne; *m* 1945, Lois Yardley Cameron (*d* 1990). *Educ:* Waimate Primary Sch.; Timaru Boys' High Sch.; Otago Univ. Med. Sch. MB ChB 1938. FRCS 1949; FRACS 1957; FACS 1973. NZ Medical Corps: joined as RMO, Feb. 1940; 2nd NZ Exped. Force, May 1940; seconded for training as plastic surgeon, Nov. 1940; served in UK, Egypt and NZ (mostly in plastic surgery) until 1947. Head of plastic surgical services, Auckland Hosp Bd, 1950–79; Prof. of Plastic and Reconstructive Surgery, Univ. of Auckland, 1977–79; private plastic surgery practice, 1979–89; Mem., Auckland Hosp. Bd, 1980–89. Mem., James IV Assoc. of Surgeons, 1969. *Publications:* chapters in: Operative Surgery, 1956, 3rd edn 1976; Long-term Results in Plastic and Reconstructive Surgery, 1980; The Artistry of Reconstructive Surgery, 1987; Management of Cleft Lip and Palate, ed J. Bardach and H. L. Morris, 1990; contribs to British and US med. jls. *Recreations:* classical music, gardening, cooking. *Address:* Watch Hill, Jeffs Road, RD1, Papatoetoe, Auckland, New Zealand. *T:* (9) 2746702. *Club:* Northern (Auckland).

MANCROFT, family name of **Baron Mancroft.**

MANCROFT, 3rd Baron *cr* 1937, of Mancroft in the City of Norwich; **Benjamin Lloyd Stormont Mancroft;** Bt 1932; *b* 16 May 1957; *s* of 2nd Baron Mancroft, KBE, TD and of Diana Elizabeth, *d* of late Lt-Col Horace Lloyd, DSO; *S* father, 1987; *m* 1990, Emma Louisa, *e d* of Thomas Peart; one *s* one *d*. *Educ:* Eton. MFH, Vale of White Horse Hunt, 1987–89. Chm., Inter Lotto (UK) Ltd. Chairman: Addiction Recovery Foundn, 1989–; Drug and Alcohol Foundn, 1993–; Deputy Chairman: British Field Sports Soc., 1993–; Phoenix House Housing Assoc., 1993–. Member Executive: Nat. Union of Cons. and Unionist Assocs, 1989–; Assoc. of Cons. Peers, 1990–. Patron: Sick Dentists' Trust, 1991–; Patsy Hardy Trust, 1991–. *Heir: s*, *b* 3 May 1995. *Address:* House of Lords, SW1A 0PW.

MANDELA, Nelson Rolihlahia, Hon. OM 1995; President of South Africa, since 1994; President, African National Congress, since 1991 (National Organizer and Vice-President, 1989–91); *b* 1918; *s* of Chief of Tembu tribe; *m* Winnie Mandela. *Educ:* Univ. Coll., Fort Hare; Univ. of Witwatersrand. Legal practice, Johannesburg, 1952. On trial for treason, 1956–61 (acquitted); sentenced to five years' imprisonment, 1962; tried for further charges, 1963–64, and sentenced to life imprisonment; released, 1990. Hon. DCL Oxford, 1994. Jawaharlal Nehru Award, India, 1979; Simon Bolivar Prize, UNESCO, 1983; Sakharov Prize, 1988; (with F. W. De Klerk) Nobel Peace Prize, 1993. *Publications:* No Easy Walk to Freedom, 1965; Long Walk to Freedom, 1994. *Address:* President's Office, Private Bag X 1000, Cape Town 8000, South Africa.

MANDELSON, Peter Benjamin; MP (Lab) Hartlepool, since 1992; *b* 21 Oct. 1953; *s* of George Mandelson and Mary (*née* Morrison). *Educ:* Hendon County Grammar Sch.; St Catherine's Coll., Oxford (Hons degree, PPE). Econ. Dept, TUC, 1977–78; Chm., British Youth Council, 1978–80; producer, LWT, 1982–85; Dir of Campaigns and Communications, Labour Party, 1985–90. An Opposition Whip, 1994–. Mem. Council, London Bor. of Lambeth, 1979–82. Industrial Consultant, SRU Gp, 1990–92. Mem., Internat. Adv. Cttee, Centre for Eur. Policy Studies, 1993–. Trustee, Whitechapel Art Gall., 1994–. *Publications:* Youth Unemployment: causes and cures, 1977; Broadcasting and Youth, 1980. *Recreations:* swimming, country walking. *Address:* 30 Hutton Avenue, Hartlepool, Cleveland TS26 9PN. *T:* Hartlepool (01429) 866173.

MANDELSTAM, Prof. Joel, FRS 1971; Emeritus Professor, University of Oxford, and Emeritus Fellow, Linacre College, since 1987; *b* S Africa, 13 Nov. 1919; *s* of Leo and Fanny Mandelstam; *m* 1954, Dorothy Hillier; one *s* one *d*; *m* 1975, Mary Maureen Dale. *Educ:* Jeppe High Sch., Johannesburg; University of Witwatersrand. Lecturer, Medical Sch., Johannesburg, 1942–47; Queen Elizabeth Coll., London, 1947–51; Scientific Staff, Nat. Institute for Med. Research, London, 1952–66; Iveagh Prof. of Microbiology, and Fellow of Linacre College, Univ. of Oxford, 1966–87; Deptl Demonstrator, Sir William Dunn Sch. of Pathology, Univ. of Oxford, 1987–90. Fulbright Fellow, US, 1958–59; Vis. Prof., Univ. of Adelaide, 1971. Mem., ARC, 1973–83. Leewenhoek Lectr, Royal Soc., 1975. Editorial Board, Biochemical Journal, 1960–66. *Publications:* Biochemistry of Bacterial Growth (with K. McQuillen and I. Dawes), 1968; articles in journals and books on microbial biochemistry. *Address:* 13 Cherwell Lodge, Water Eaton Road, Oxford OX2 7QH.

MANDELSTAM, Prof. Stanley, FRS 1962; Professor of Physics, University of California. *Educ:* University of the Witwatersrand, Johannesburg, Transvaal, South Africa (BSc); Trinity Coll., Cambridge (BA). PhD, Birmingham. Formerly Professor of Math. Physics, University of Birmingham; Prof. Associé, Univ. de Paris Sud, 1979–80 and 1984–85. Fellow, Amer. Acad. of Arts and Scis., 1992. Dirac Medal and Prize, Internat. Centre for Theoretical Physics, 1991; Dannie Heinemann Prize for Mathematical Physics, APS, 1992. *Publications:* (with W. Yourgrau) Variational Principles in Dynamics and Quantum Theory, 1955 (revised edn, 1956); papers in learned journals. *Address:* Department of Physics, University of California, Berkeley, CA 94720, USA.

MANDER, Sir Charles (Marcus), 3rd Bt, *cr* 1911; Underwriting Member of Lloyd's, 1957–92; Director: Manders (Holdings) Ltd, 1951–58; Mander Brothers Ltd, 1948–58; Headstaple Ltd, since 1977; *b* 22 Sept. 1921; *o s* of Sir Charles Arthur Mander, 2nd Bart, and late Monica Claire Cotterill, *d* of G. H. Neame; *S* father, 1951; *m* 1945, Maria Dolores Beatrice, *d* of late Alfred Brodermann, Hamburg; two *s* one *d*. *Educ:* Eton Coll., Windsor; Trinity Coll., Cambridge. Commissioned Coldstream Guards, 1942; served War of 1939–45, Canal Zone, 1943; Italy, 1943, Germany, 1944; War Office (ADC to Lieut-General R. G. Stone, CB), 1945. Chairman: Arlington Securities Ltd, 1977–83; London & Cambridge Investments Ltd, 1983–91. High Sheriff of Staffordshire, 1962–63. *Recreations:* shooting, music. *Heir: s* Charles Nicholas Mander [*b* 23 March 1950; *m* 1972, Karin Margareta, *d* of Arne Norin; four *s* one *d*]. *Address:* Little Barrow, Moreton-in-Marsh, Glos GL56 0XU. *T:* Cotswold (01451) 830265.

MANDER, Prof. Lewis Norman, FRS 1990; Professor of Chemistry, Australian National University, since 1980; *b* 8 Sept. 1939; *s* of John Eric and Anne Frances Mander; *m* 1965, Stephanie Vautin; one *s* two *d*. *Educ:* Mount Albert Grammar Sch.; Univ. of Sydney (PhD 1965). FRACI 1980; FAA 1983. Postdoctoral Fellow, Univ. of Michigan, 1964–65; Postdoctoral Associate, Caltech, 1965–66; Lectr and Sen. Lectr in Organic Chem., Univ. of Adelaide, 1966–75; Sen. Fellow, 1975–80, Dean, 1981–86 and 1992–95, Res. Sch. of Chem., ANU. Nuffield Commonwealth Fellow, Cambridge, 1972; Fulbright Sen. Schol., Caltech, 1977, Harvard, 1986. H. G. Smith Medal, RACI, 1981; Flintoff Medal and Prize, RSocChem, 1990. *Publications:* numerous articles in learned jls, mainly on synthesis of organic molecules. *Recreations:* bushwalking, speleology. *Address:* Research School of Chemistry, Australian National University, Canberra, ACT 0200, Australia. *T:* (6) 2493761, *Fax:* (6) 2495995.

MANDER, Michael Harold; His Honour Judge Mander; a Circuit Judge, since 1985 (Resident Judge, Shrewsbury Crown Court); *b* 27 Oct. 1936; *e s* of late Harold and Ann Mander; *m* 1960, Jancis Mary Dodd, *er d* of late Revd Charles and Edna Dodd. *Educ:* Workington Grammar School; Queen's College, Oxford (MA, 2nd cl. hons Jurisp.; Rigg Exbnr). Nat. Service, RA (2nd Lieut) to 1957. Articled clerk; solicitor, 2nd cl. hons, 1963; called to the Bar, Inner Temple, 1972. Asst Recorder, 1982–85. Dep. Chm., Agricultural Lands Tribunal, 1983–85. Freeman, Information Technologists' Co. *Recreation:* life under the Wrekin. *Address:* Garmston, Eaton Constantine, Shrewsbury SY5 6RL. *T:* Cressage (01952) 510288. *Club:* Wrekin Rotary (Hon. Mem.).

MANDER, Noel Percy, MBE 1979; FSA; Managing Director, N. P. Mander Ltd, since 1946; *b* 19 May 1912; *s* of late Percy Mander and Emily Pike, Hoxne, Suffolk; *m* 1948, Enid Watson; three *s* two *d*. *Educ:* Haberdashers Aske's Sch., Hatcham. Organ building from 1930, interrupted by war service with RA (Hampshire Bde) in N Africa, Italy and Syria, 1940–46. FSA 1974. Mem., Nat. Council of Christians and Jews (former Chm., N London Council). Former Governor, Sir John Cass Foundn. Liveryman, Musicians' Co.;

Past Master, Parish Clerks' Co. of City of London; Mem., Art Workers' Guild. Churchill Life Fellow, Westminster Coll., Fulton, 1982; Hon. Dr Arts Westminster Coll., 1984. Builder of Winston Churchill Meml Organ, Fulton, Missouri, and organs in many parts of world; organ builder to St Paul's Cathedral London and Canterbury Cathedral, and to HM Sultan of Oman. *Publications:* St Lawrence Jewry, A History of the Organs from the Earliest Times to the Present Day, 1956; St Vedast, Foster Lane, A History of the Organs from Earliest Times to the Present Day, 1961; St Vedast Foster Lane, in the City of London: a history of the 13 United Parishes, 1973; (with C. M. Houghton) St Botolph Aldgate: a history of the organs from the Restoration to the Twentieth Century, 1973. *Recreations:* archaeology, horology, reading. *Address:* The Street, Earl Soham, Woodbridge, Suffolk IP13 7SM. *T:* Earl Soham (01728) 685312; The Lodge, St Peter's Organ Works, St Peter's Close, E2 7AF. *T:* 0171–739 4746. *Club:* Savage.

MANDEVILLE, Viscount; Alexander Charles David Drogo Montagu; *b* 11 Dec. 1962; *s* and *heir* of 12th Duke of Manchester, *qv*. *Address:* 17138 Von Karman Avenue, Irvine, CA 92714, USA.

MANDUCA, John Alfred; High Commissioner for Malta in London, 1987–90; (concurrently) Ambassador to Norway, Sweden and Denmark, 1988–90, and to Ireland, 1990; *b* 14 Aug. 1927; *s* of Captain Philip dei Conti Manduca and Emma (*née* Pullicino); *m* 1954, Sylvia Parnis; two *s* two *d*. *Educ:* St Edward's Coll., Malta. Joined Allied Malta Newspapers Ltd, 1945, Dep. Editor, 1953–62; Malta Correspondent, The Daily Telegraph and The Sunday Telegraph, 1946–62; joined Broadcasting Authority, Malta, 1962; BBC attachment, 1963; Chief Exec., Broadcasting Authority, Malta, 1963–68; Dir and Manager, Malta Television Service Ltd, 1968–71; Man. Dir, Rediffusion Gp of Cos in Malta, 1971–76; Chm., Tourist Projects Ltd, 1976–83; Dir Gen., Confedn of Private Enterprises, 1983–87; Dir, RTK Radio, 1991–. Chairman: Malta Br., Inst. of Journalists, 1957, 1959 and 1961; Hotels and Catering Establishments Bd, 1970–71; Hon. Treas., Malta Br., Inst. of Dirs, 1975; Member: Tourist Bd, 1969–70; Broadcasting Authority, 1979–81. Chm. Bd of Governors, St Edward's Coll., 1995– (Mem., 1966–75, 1991–94). Served 11 HAA Regt, Royal Malta Artillery (T), 1952–55 (commnd 1953). Editor, Treasures of Malta, 1994–. *Publications:* Tourist Guide to Malta and Gozo, 1967, 7th edn 1980; Tourist Guide to Harbour Cruises, 1974, 3rd edn 1981; Connoisseur's Guide to City of Mdina, 1975, 3rd edn 1985; Gen. Ed., Malta Who's Who, 1987; (ed) Antique Maltese Clocks, 1992. *Recreations:* collecting Melitensia, current affairs, gardening. *Address:* Beaulieu, Bastion Square, Citta Vecchia (Mdina) RBT 12, Malta. *T:* 454009. *Club:* Casino Maltese (Malta).

MANDUCA, Paul Victor Sant; Chief Executive, Threadneedle Asset Management, since 1994; *b* 15 Nov. 1951; *s* of Victor Manduca and Elizabeth Manduca (*née* Johnson); *m* 1982, Ursula Vogt; two *s*. *Educ:* Harrow Sch.; Hertford Coll., Oxford (Hons Mod. Langs). Colegrave & Co., 1973–75; Rowe & Pitman, 1976–79; Hill Samuel Inv. Management, 1979–83; Touche Remnant, 1983–92: Dir 1986; Vice-Chm. 1987; Chm., 1989–92; Dir, TR Smaller Cos Investment Trust (formerly Trustees Group), 1986–; Man. Dir, TR Industrial & General, 1986–88; Chm., TR High Income, 1989–; Gp Dep. Man. Dir, Henderson Administration PLC, 1992–94. Director: Clydesdale IT, 1987–88; Eagle Star Hldgs, 1994–; Allied Dunbar Assurance, 1994–; Gresham Trust, 1994–. Chm., Assoc. of Investment Trust Cos, 1991–93 (Dep. Chm., 1989–91); Mem., Takeover Panel, 1991–93. *Recreations:* golf, squash, shooting. *Address:* 54 Brompton Square, SW3 2AG. *T:* 0171–584 3987. *Clubs:* Lansdowne; Wentworth Golf.

MANDUELL, Sir John, Kt 1989; CBE 1982; FRAM, FRCM, FRNCM, FRSAMD; composer; Principal, Royal Northern College of Music, 1971–April 1996; *b* 1928; *s* of Matthewman Donald Manduell, MC, MA, and Theodora (*née* Tharp); *m* 1955, Renna Kellaway; three *s* one *d*. *Educ:* Haileybury Coll.; Jesus Coll., Cambridge; Univ. of Strasbourg; Royal Acad. of Music. FRAM 1964; FRNCM 1974; FRCM 1980; FRSAMD 1982; FWCMD 1991; Hon. FTCL 1973; Hon. GSM 1986. BBC: music producer, 1956–61; Head of Music, Midlands and E Anglia, 1961–64; Chief Planner, The Music Programme, 1964–68; University of Lancaster: Dir of Music, 1968–71; Mem. Court and Council, 1972–77, 1979–83. University of Manchester: Hon. Lectr in Music, 1976–; Mem. Court, 1990–. Prog. Dir, Cheltenham Festival, 1969–94. Arts Council: Mem. Council, 1976–78, 1980–84; Mem. Music Panel, 1971–76, Dep. Chm., 1976–78, Chm., 1980–84; Mem. Touring Cttee, 1975–80, Chm., 1976–78; Mem. Trng Cttee, 1973–77. Mem. Music Adv. Cttee, British Council, 1963–72, Chm., 1973–80; Chm. Music Panel, North West Arts, 1973–79; Man., NW Arts Bd, 1991–. President: British Arts Fests Assoc., 1988– (Vice-Chm., 1977–81, Chm., 1981–88); European Assoc. of Music Academies (now Assoc. of European Conservatoires), 1988–; Manchester Olympic Fest., 1990; European Music Year (1985): Dep. Chm. UK Cttee, 1982–85; Member: Eur. Organising Cttee, 1982–86; Eur. Exec. Bureau, 1982–86; Internat. Prog. Cttee, 1982–84; Mem. Exec. Cttee, Composers' Guild of GB, 1984–87 (Vice Chm., 1987–89, Chm., 1989–92); Gulbenkian Foundn Enquiry into Trng Musicians, 1978; Mem. Opera Bd, 1988–95, Mem. Bd, 1989–95, Royal Opera House; Chairman: Cttee of Heads of Music Colls, 1986–90; Nat. Curriculum Music Working Gp, 1990–91; Governor: Chetham's Sch., 1971–; National Youth Orch., 1964–73, 1978–; President: Lakeland Sinfonia, 1972–89; Jubilate Choir, 1979–91; Pres., ISM, 1991–92; Director: London Opera Centre, 1971–79; Associated Bd of Royal Schools of Music, 1971–; Northern Ballet Theatre, 1973–86 (Chm., 1986–89); Manchester Palace Theatre Trust, 1978–84; London Orchestral Concert Bd, 1980–85; Young Concert Artists' Trust, 1983–93; Lake Dist Summer Music Fest., 1984–. Hon. Member: Roy. Soc. of Musicians, 1972; Chopin Soc. of Warsaw, 1973. Engagements and tours as composer and lectr in Canada, Europe, Hong Kong, S Africa and USA. Chairman: BBC TV Young Musicians of the Year, 1978, 1980, 1984; Munich Internat. Music Comp., 1979, 1982, 1984, 1985, 1995; Geneva Internat. Music Comp., 1986, 1990, 1991; Chm. or mem., national and internat. music competition juries. FRSA 1981; Fellow, Manchester Polytechnic, 1983. Hon. DMus: Lancaster, 1990; Manchester, 1992. First Leslie Boosey Award, Royal Phil. Soc. and PRS, 1980. Chevalier de l'Ordre des Arts et des Lettres (France), 1990. *Publications:* (contrib.) The Symphony, ed Simpson, 1966; *compositions:* Overture, Sunderland Point, 1969; Diversions for Orchestra, 1970; String Quartet, 1976; Prayers from the Ark, 1981; Double Concerto, 1985. *Recreations:* cricket; travel; French life, language and literature. *Address:* Royal Northern College of Music, Oxford Road, Manchester M13 9RD. *T:* 0161–273 6283. *Club:* MCC.

MANGHAM, Maj.-Gen. William Desmond, CB 1978; Director, The Brewers' Society, 1980–90; *b* 29 Aug. 1924; *s* of late Lt-Col William Patrick Mangham and Margaret Mary Mangham (*née* Donnachie); *m* 1960, Susan, *d* of late Col Henry Brabazon Humfrey; two *s* two *d*. *Educ:* Ampleforth College. 2nd Lieut RA, 1943; served India, Malaya, 1945–48; BMRA 1st Div. Egypt, 1955; Staff, HQ Middle East, Cyprus, 1956–58; Instructor, Staff Coll., Camberley and Canada, 1962–65; OC 3rd Regt Royal Horse Artillery, 1966–68; Comdr RA 2nd Div., 1969–70; Royal Coll. of Defence Studies, 1971; Chief of Staff, 1st British Corps, 1972–74; GOC 2nd Div., 1974–75; VQMG, MoD, 1976–79. Colonel Commandant: RA, 1979–88; RHA, 1983–88. Advisory Governor, Ampleforth Coll., 1990–. Mem., Gordon Foundn, 1980–. *Recreations:* shooting, golf. *Address:* Redwood House, Woolton Hill, Newbury, Berks RG15 9UZ. *Club:* Army and Navy.

MANGO, Prof. Cyril Alexander, FBA 1976; Bywater and Sotheby Professor of Byzantine and Modern Greek, 1973–95, and Fellow of Exeter College, Oxford University; *b* 14 April 1928; *s* of Alexander A. Mango and Adelaide Damonov; *m* 1st, 1953, Mabel Grover; one *d*; 2nd, 1964, Susan A. Gerstel; one *d*; 3rd, 1976, Maria C. Mundell. *Educ:* Univ. of St Andrews (MA); Univ. of Paris (Dr Univ Paris). From Jun. Fellow to Lectr in Byzantine Archaeology, Dumbarton Oaks Byzantine Center, Harvard Univ., 1951–63; Lectr in Fine Arts, Harvard Univ., 1957–58; Visiting Associate Prof. of Byzantine History, Univ. of California, Berkeley, 1960–61; Koraës Prof. of Modern Greek and of Byzantine History, Language and Literature, King's Coll., Univ. of London, 1963–68; Prof. of Byzantine Archaeology, Dumbarton Oaks Byzantine Center, 1968–73. FSA. *Publications:* The Homilies of Photius, 1958; The Brazen House, 1959; The Mosaics of St Sophia at Istanbul, 1962; The Art of the Byzantine Empire, Sources and Documents, 1972; Architettura bizantina, 1974; Byzantium, 1980; Byzantium and its Image, 1984; Le Développement Urbain de Constantinople, 1985. *Address:* Exeter College, Oxford OX1 3DP.

MANGOLD, Thomas Cornelius; Reporter, BBC TV Panorama, since 1976; *b* 20 Aug. 1934; *s* of Fritz Mangold and Dorothea Mangold; *m* 1972, Valerie Ann Hare (*née* Dean) (marr. diss. 1991); three *d*. *Educ:* Dorking Grammar Sch. Reporter, Croydon Advertiser, 1952. Served RA, 1952–54. Reporter: Croydon Advertiser, 1955–59; Sunday Pictorial, 1959–62; Daily Express, 1962–64; BBC TV News, 1964–70; BBC TV 24 Hours, later Midweek, 1970–76. *Publications:* (jtly) The File on the Tsar, 1976; (jtly) The Tunnels of Cu Chi, 1985; Cold Warrior, 1991. *Recreations:* writing, playing Blues harp. *Address:* c/o BBC TV, White City, W12 7TS. *T:* 0181–752 7100.

MANKOWITZ, (Cyril) Wolf; author; Honorary Consul to the Republic of Panama in Dublin, 1971; *b* 7 Nov. 1924; *s* of Solomon and Rebecca Mankowitz; *m* 1944, Ann Margaret Seligmann; three *s* (and one *s* decd). Educ: East Ham Grammar Sch.; Downing Coll., Cambridge (MA, English Tripos). Served World War II, as volunteer coal miner and in Army. Play and film producer: with Oscar Lewenstein, 1955–60; independently, 1960–70; with Laurence Harvey, 1970–72. Adjunct Prof. of English, Univ. of New Mexico, Albuquerque, 1982– (Adjunct Prof. of Theatre Arts, 1987–88). Exhibitions (Recent Collages): Davis Gall., Dublin, 1990; Grosvenor Gall., London, 1994. Soc. of Authors Award, for poetry, 1946; Cork Film Fest. Internat. Critics Prize, 1972, Grand Prize, 1973. *Plays include:* The Bespoke Overcoat, 1953 (filmed, 1955; Venice Film Fest. Prize, BAFTA Award, and Academy Award for best screenplay); The Boychick, 1954; The Mighty Hunter, 1956; The Last of the Cheesecake, 1956; (with Julian Moore) Expresso Bongo, 1958 (filmed, 1959); (with Beverley Cross) Belle, or The Ballad of Dr Crippen, 1961; Pickwick, 1963; Passion Flower Hotel (musical), 1965; Stand and Deliver, 1972; Samson and Delilah, 1978; The Irish Hebrew Lesson, 1978; *screenplays: include:* (some jtly): Make Me an Offer, 1954; A Kid for Two Farthings, 1955; The Millionairess, 1960; The Long and The Short and The Tall, 1961; The Day the Earth Caught Fire, 1961; The Waltz of the Toreadors, 1962; Where The Spies Are, 1965; Casino Royale, 1967; The Assassination Bureau, 1969; Bloomfield, 1970; Black Beauty, 1971; Treasure Island, 1972; The Hebrew Lesson (also dir.), 1972; The Hireling, 1973; (documentary) Almonds and Raisins (a treatment of Yiddish films, 1929–39), 1984; *television series:* Dickens of London, 1976. *Publications: novels:* Make Me An Offer, 1952 (televised, 1952); A Kid for Two Farthings, 1953; Laugh Till You Cry, 1955 (USA); My Old Man's a Dustman, 1956; Cockatrice, 1963; The Biggest Pig in Barbados, 1965; Raspberry Reich, 1979; ¡Abracadabra!, 1980; The Devil in Texas, 1984; Gioconda, 1987; The Magic Cabinet of Professor Smucker, 1988; Exquisite Cadaver, 1990; A Night with Casanova, 1991; *short stories:* The Mendelman Fire and Other Stories, 1957; Expresso Bongo: a Wolf Mankowitz Reader, 1961; The Blue Arabian Nights, 1973; The Day of the Women and The Night of the Men (fables), 1977; *biography:* Dickens of London, 1976; The Extraordinary Mr Poe, 1978; Mazeppa, 1982; *poetry:* XII Poems, 1971; *plays:* The Bespoke Overcoat and Other Plays, 1955; Five One-Act Plays, 1955; Expresso Bongo, 1960; The Samson Riddle, 1972; *miscellaneous:* The Portland Vase and the Wedgwood Copies, 1952; Wedgwood, 1953, rev. edn 1980; Majollika and Company (for childen), 1955; ABC of Show Business, 1956; (with R. G. Haggar) A Concise Encyclopedia of English Pottery and Porcelain, 1957; The Penguin Wolf Mankowitz, 1967. *Recreations:* sleeping or making collage. *Address:* The Bridge House, Ahakista, Durrus, near Bantry, Co. Cork, Ireland; 2322 Calle Halcon, Santa Fe, NM 87505, USA.

MANKTELOW, Rt. Rev. Michael Richard John; Hon. Assistant Bishop: of Chichester, since 1994; of Gibraltar in Europe, since 1994; *b* 23 Sept. 1927; *s* of late Sir Richard Manktelow, KBE, CB, and late Helen Manktelow; *m* 1966, Rosamund Mann; three *d*. *Educ:* Whitgift School, Croydon; Christ's Coll., Cambridge (MA 1952); Chichester Theological Coll. Deacon 1953, priest 1954, Lincoln; Asst Curate of Boston, Lincs, 1953–57; Chaplain of Christ's Coll., Cambridge, 1957–61; Chaplain of Lincoln Theological Coll., 1961–64, Sub-Warden, 1964–66; Vicar of Knaresborough, 1966–73; Rural Dean of Harrogate, 1972–77; Vicar of St Wilfrid's, Harrogate, 1973–77; Hon. Canon of Ripon Cathedral, 1975–77; Bishop Suffragan of Basingstoke, 1977–93; Canon Residentiary, 1977–91, Vice-Dean, 1987–91, Hon. Canon, 1991–93, Canon Emeritus, 1993, Winchester Cathedral. President: Anglican and Eastern Churches Assoc., 1980–; Assoc. for Promoting Retreats, 1982–87. *Publication:* Forbes Robinson: Disciple of Love, 1961. *Recreations:* music, walking. *Address:* 2 The Chantry, Canon Lane, Chichester, West Sussex PO19 1PZ. *T:* Chichester (01243) 531096.

MANLEY, Ivor Thomas, CB 1984; consultant in government/industry relations; Deputy Secretary, Department of Employment, 1987–91; *b* 4 March 1931; *s* of Frederick Stone and Louisa Manley; *m* 1952, Joan Waite; one *s* one *d*. *Educ:* Sutton High Sch., Plymouth. Entered Civil Service, 1951; Principal: Min. of Aviation, 1964–66; Min. of Technology, 1966–68; Private Secretary: to Rt Hon. Anthony Wedgwood Benn, 1968–70; to Rt Hon. Geoffrey Rippon, 1970; Principal Private Sec. to Rt Hon. John Davies, 1970–71; Asst Sec., DTI, 1971–74; Department of Energy: Under-Sec., Principal Estabt Officer, 1974–78, Under Sec., Atomic Energy Div., 1978–81; Dep. Sec., 1981–87. UK Governor, IAEA, 1978–81; Mem., UKAEA, 1981–86. Chm., Task Force on Tourism and the Envmt, 1990–91; Board Member: Business in the Community, 1988–89; BTA, 1991– (Chm., Marketing Cttee, 1991–); Volunteer Centre, UK, 1992;. *Recreations:* walking, reading. *Address:* 28 Highfield Avenue, Aldershot, Hants GU11 3BZ. *T:* Aldershot (01252) 22707.

MANLEY, Rt. Hon. Michael Norman, PC 1989; Prime Minister of Jamaica, 1972–80, and 1989–92; President, People's National Party, Jamaica, 1969–92 (Member, Executive, 1952–92); *b* St Andrew, Jamaica, 10 Dec. 1924; *s* of late Rt Excellent Norman W. Manley, QC, and Edna Manley (*née* Swithenbank); *m* 1972, Beverly Anderson (marr. diss. 1990); one *s* one *d*, and one *s* two *d* by previous marriages; *m* 1992, Glynne Ewart. *Educ:* Jamaica Coll.; London Sch. of Economics (BSc Econ Hons). Began as freelance journalist, working with BBC, 1950–51; returned to Jamaica, Dec. 1951, as Associate Editor of Public Opinion, 1952–53; Sugar Supervisor, Nat. Workers' Union, 1953–54; Island Supervisor and First Vice-Pres., 1955–72; Mem. Senate, 1962–67; MP for Central Kingston, Jamaica, 1967–92; Leader of the Opposition, 1969–72, and 1980–89. Has held various posts in Labour cttees and in Trade Union affairs; organised strike in sugar industry, 1959, which led to Goldenberg Commn of Inquiry; Pres., Nat. Workers Union, 1984–89. Vice-Pres., Socialist Internat., 1978. Hon. Doctor of Laws Morehouse Coll., Atlanta, 1973. UN Special Award for contrib. to struggle against apartheid, 1978; Joliot Curie Medal, World Peace Council, 1979. Order of the Liberator, Venezuela, 1973; Order of Mexican Eagle, 1975; Order of Jose Marti, Cuba, 1975. *Publications:* The Politics of Change, 1974; A Voice at the Workplace, 1976; The Search for Solutions, 1977; Jamaica: Struggle in the Periphery, 1982; A History of West Indies Cricket, 1988; The Poverty of Nations, 1991. *Recreations:* sports, music, gardening, reading. *Address:* 89 Old Hope Road, Kingston 6, Jamaica.

MANN; *see* Douglas-Mann.

MANN, Anthony; *see* Mann, G. A.

MANN, Prof. (Colin) Nicholas (Jocelyn), FBA 1992; Director, Warburg Institute, University of London, and Professor of the History of the Classical Tradition, since 1990; *b* 24 Oct. 1942; *s* of Colin Henry Mann and Marie Elise Mann (*née* Gosling); *m* 1964, Joëlle Bourcart; one *s* one *d*. *Educ:* Eton; King's Coll., Cambridge (MA, PhD). Res. Fellow, Clare Coll., Cambridge, 1965–67; Lectr, Univ. of Warwick, 1967–72; Vis. Fellow, All Souls Coll., Oxford, 1972; Fellow and Tutor, Pembroke Coll., Oxford, 1973–90, Emeritus Fellow, 1991–. Member Council: Mus. of Modern Art, Oxford, 1984–92 (Chm., 1988–90); Contemporary Applied Arts, 1994–. Fellow, European Medieval Acad., 1993. Romance Editor, Medium Ævum, 1982–90. *Publications:* Petrarch Manuscripts in the British Isles, 1975; Petrarch, 1984; A Concordance to Petrarch's Bucolicum Carmen, 1984; articles in learned jls. *Recreations:* yoga, sculpture. *Address:* Warburg Institute, Woburn Square, WC1H 0AB. *T:* 0171–580 9663.

MANN, David William; Deputy Chairman, Logica, 1993–94; Chairman, Cambridge Display Technology Ltd, since 1995; *b* 14 June 1944; *s* of William and Mary Mann; *m* 1968, Gillian Mary Edwards; two *s*. *Educ:* Felixstowe Grammar Sch.; Jesus Coll., Cambridge (MA). CEng; FBCS. CEIR, 1966–69; Logica: joined 1969; Dir, 1976; Man. Dir, UK Ops, 1979; Dep. Gp Man. Dir, 1982; Gp Man. Dir and Chief Exec., 1987. Dir, Industrial Control Services Gp, 1994–. Mem., Engineering Council, 1993–. Pres., British Computer Soc., 1994–95. Mem., Ct of Assts, Information Technologists' Co., 1992– (Jun. Warden, 1995–Oct. 1996). CIMgt. *Recreations:* gardening, walking, ski-ing, golf. *Address:* Theydon Copt, Forest Side, Epping, Essex CM16 4ED. *T:* Epping (01992) 575842.

MANN, Eric John; Controller, Capital Taxes Office, 1978–81; *b* 18 Dec. 1921; *s* of Percival John Mann and Marguerite Mann; *m* 1960, Gwendolen Margaret Salter; one *d* (one *s* decd). *Educ:* University Coll. Sch., Hampstead; Univ. of London (LLB). Entered Inland Revenue, 1946; Dep. Controller, Capital Taxes Office, 1974. *Publications:* (ed jtly) Green's Death Duties, 5th–7th edns, 1962–71. *Address:* Lawn Gate Cottage, Moccas, Herefordshire HR2 9LF.

MANN, Dr Felix Bernard; medical practitioner; *b* 10 April 1931; *s* of Leo and Caroline Mann; *m* 1986, Ruth Csorba von Borsai. *Educ:* Shrewsbury House; Malvern Coll.; Christ's Coll., Cambridge; Westminster Hosp. MB, BChir, LMCC. Practised medicine or studied acupuncture in England, Canada, Switzerland, France, Germany, Austria and China. Founder, Medical Acupuncture Soc., 1959. *Publications:* Acupuncture; the ancient Chinese art of healing, 1962, 2nd edn 1971; The Treatment of Disease by Acupuncture, 1963; The Meridians of Acupuncture, 1964; Atlas of Acupuncture, 1966; Acupuncture: cure of many diseases, 1971; Scientific Aspects of Acupuncture, 1977; Textbook of Acupuncture, 1987; Reinventing Acupuncture, 1992; also edns in Italian, Spanish, Dutch, Finnish, Portuguese, German, Japanese and Swedish; contrib. various jls on acupuncture. *Recreations:* walking in the country and mountains. *Address:* 15 Devonshire Place, W1N 1PB. *T:* 0171–935 7575. *Club:* Royal Society of Medicine.

MANN, (Francis) George, CBE 1983; DSO 1942; MC 1941; Director, 1977–87, and non-executive Deputy Chairman, 1980–86, Extel Group; *b* 6 Sept. 1917; *s* of Frank Mann and Enid Mann (*née* Tilney); *m* 1949, Margaret Hildegarde Marshall Clark (*d* 1995); three *s* one *d*. *Educ:* Eton; Cambridge Univ. BA. Served War of 1939–45, Scots Guards (DSO, MC). Director: Mann Crossman and Paulin, Watney Mann, Watney Mann and Truman Brewers, 1946–77. Middlesex County Cricket Club: first played, 1937; Captain, 1948–49; Pres., 1983–87; captained England in SA, 1948–49 and against NZ, 1949. Chairman: TCCB, 1978–83; Cricket Council, 1983. *Address:* West Woodhay, Newbury, Berks RG15 0BL. *T:* Inkpen (01488) 668243. *Club:* MCC (Pres., 1984–85; Hon. Life Vice-Pres., 1989).

MANN, George; *see* Mann, F. G.

MANN, George Anthony; QC 1992; *b* 21 May 1951; *s* of George Edgar and Ilse Beate Mann; *m* 1979, Margaret Ann Sherret; two *d*. *Educ:* Chesterfield Grammar Sch.; Perse Sch., Cambridge; St Peter's Coll., Oxford (BA 1973; MA 1977). Called to the Bar, Lincoln's Inn, 1974. *Recreations:* French horn playing, music, computers. *Address:* Enterprise Chambers, 9 Old Square, Lincoln's Inn, WC2A 3SR.

MANN, Prof. Jill, (Gillian Lesley Mann), FBA 1990; Professor of Medieval and Renaissance English, and Professorial Fellow of Girton College, University of Cambridge, since 1988; *b* 7 April 1943; *d* of late Edward William Ditchburn and Kathleen Ditchburn (*née* Bellamy); *m* 1964, Michael Mann (marr. diss. 1976). *Educ:* Bede Grammar Sch., Sunderland; St Anne's Coll., Oxford (BA 1964); Clare Hall, Cambridge (MA; PhD 1971). Research Fellow, Clare Hall, 1968–71; Lectr, Univ. of Kent at Canterbury, 1971–72; Official Fellow, Girton Coll., Cambridge, 1972–88; Asst Lectr, 1974–78, Lectr, 1978–88, Cambridge Univ. British Academy Research Reader, 1985–87. Hon. Fellow, St Anne's Coll., Oxford, 1990. *Publications:* Chaucer and Medieval Estates Satire, 1973; Ysengrimus, 1987; (ed with Piero Boitani) The Cambridge Chaucer Companion, 1986; Geoffrey Chaucer, 1991; articles on Middle English and Medieval Latin. *Recreations:* riding (badly), walking, travel. *Address:* Girton College, Cambridge CB3 0JG. *T:* Cambridge (01223) 338999.

MANN, John Frederick; educational consultant; Vice Chairman, Society of Education Consultants, since 1994 (Secretary, 1990–94); *b* 4 June 1930; *e s* of Frederick Mann and Hilda G. (*née* Johnson); *m* 1966, Margaret (*née* Moore); one *s* one *d*. *Educ:* Poole and Tavistock Grammar Schs; Trinity Coll., Oxford (MA). Asst Master, Colchester Royal Grammar Sch., 1954–61; Admin. Asst, Leeds County Bor., 1962–65; Asst Educn Officer, Essex CC, 1965–67; Dep. Educn Officer, Sheffield County Bor., 1967–78; Sec., Schools Council for the Curriculum and Exams, 1978–83; Dir of Educn, London Bor. of Harrow, 1983–88. Member: Iron and Steel Industry Trng Bd, 1975–78; Exec., Soc. of Educn Officers, 1976–78; Sch. Broadcasting Council, 1979–83; Council, British Educn Management and Admin Soc., 1979–84. Governor: Welbeck Coll., 1975–84; Hall Sch., 1985–88. Hon. Fellow, Sheffield Polytechnic, 1980; Hon. FCP, 1986. FRSA. JP Sheffield, 1976–79. *Publications:* Education, 1979; Highbury Fields School, 1994; contrib. to Victoria County History of Essex, Local Govt Studies, and Educn. *Recreations:* travel, books, theatre, gardening. *Address:* 109 Chatsworth Road, NW2 4BH. *T:* 0181–459 5419.

MANN, Martin Edward; QC 1983; a Recorder, since 1990; *b* 12 Sept. 1943; *s* of S. E. Mann and M. L. F. Mann; *m* 1966, Jacqueline Harriette (*née* Le Maître); two *d*. *Educ:* Cranleigh Sch. Called to the Bar, Gray's Inn, 1968 (Lord Justice Holker Sen. Exhibn), Lincoln's Inn, 1973 (*ad eund*); Bencher, Lincoln's Inn, 1991. Mem., Senate of the Inns of Court and the Bar, 1979–82; Chm., Bar Council Fees Collection Cttee, 1993–. *Publication:* (jtly) What Kind of Common Agricultural Policy for Europe, 1975. *Recreations:* ski-ing/mountaineering, farming, the arts. *Address:* 24 Old Buildings, Lincoln's Inn, WC2A 3UJ. *T:* 0171–404 0946; Kingston St Mary, Somerset. *Clubs:* Garrick, Royal Automobile.

MANN, Rt. Hon. Sir Michael, Kt 1982; PC 1988; a Lord Justice of Appeal, 1988–95; *b* 9 Dec. 1930; *s* of late Adrian Bernard Mann, CBE and of Mary Louise (*née* Keen); *m* 1st, 1957 (marr. diss. 1988); two *s*; 2nd, 1989, Audrey Edith Umpleby. *Educ:* Whitgift; King's Coll., London (LLB, PhD; FKC 1984). Called to Bar, Gray's Inn, 1953 (Bencher 1980; Master of the Estate, 1993; Chm., Management Cttee 1994); practised, 1955–82; Junior Counsel to the Land Commn (Common Law), 1967–71; QC 1972; a Recorder of the Crown Court, 1979–82; a Judge of the High Court of Justice, QBD, 1982–88. Asst Lectr 1954–57, Lectr 1957–64, in Law, LSE; part-time Legal Asst, FO, 1954–56. Inspector, Vale of Belvoir Coal Inquiry, 1979–80. Pres., Administrative Law Bar Assoc., 1993. *Publications:* (ed jtly) Dicey, Conflict of Laws, 7th edn, 1957; Dicey and Morris, Conflict of Laws, 8th edn 1967 to 10th edn, 1980.

MANN, Rt. Rev. Michael Ashley, KCVO 1989; Assistant Bishop, diocese of Gloucester, since 1989; Dean of Windsor, 1976–89; Chairman, St George's House, 1976–89; Register, Order of the Garter, 1976–89; Domestic Chaplain to the Queen, 1976–89; Prelate, Order of St John, since 1990; *b* 25 May 1924; *s* of late H. G. Mann and F. M. Mann, Harrow; *m* 1st, 1949, Jill Joan Jacques (*d* 1990); one *d* (one *s* decd); 2nd, 1991, Elizabeth Pepys. *Educ:* Harrow Sch.; RMC Sandhurst; Wells Theological Coll.; Graduate School of Business Admin., Harvard Univ. Served War of 1939–45: RMC, Sandhurst, 1942–43; 1st King's Dragoon Guards, 1943–46 (Middle East, Italy, Palestine). Colonial Admin. Service, Nigeria, 1946–55. Wells Theological Coll., 1955–57; Asst Curate, Wolborough, Newton Abbot, 1957–59; Vicar: Sparkwell, Plymouth, 1959–62; Christ Church, Port Harcourt, Nigeria, 1962–67; Dean, Port Harcourt Social and Industrial Mission; Home Secretary, The Missions to Seamen, 1967–69; Residentiary Canon, 1969–74, Vice-Dean, 1972–74, Norwich Cathedral; Adviser to Bp of Norwich on Industry, 1969–74; Bishop Suffragan of Dudley, 1974–76. Church Comr, 1977–85; Comr, Royal Hospital Chelsea, 1985–91. Trustee: Imperial War Museum, 1980– (Dep. Chm., 1990–); Army Museums Ogilby Trust, 1984–; British Library, 1990–93; Military Records Soc., 1992–. Chm., Soc. of Friends of Nat. Army Mus., 1989–. Governor: Harrow Sch., 1976–91 (Chm., 1980–88); Atlantic Coll., 1987–91. Nat. Chaplain, Royal British Legion, 1992–. CIMgt. KStJ 1990. *Publications:* A Windsor Correspondence, 1984; And They Rode On, 1984; A Particular Duty, 1986; China 1860, 1989; Some Windsor Sermons, 1989; Survival or Extinction, 1989; Regimental History of 1st Queen's Dragoon Guards, 1993; The Trucial Oman Scouts, 1994. *Recreations:* military history, philately, ornithology. *Address:* The Cottage, Lower End Farm, Eastington, Northleach, Glos GL54 3PN. *T:* Cotswold (01451) 860767. *Club:* Cavalry and Guards.

MANN, Murray G.; *see* Gell-Mann.

MANN, Nicholas; *see* Mann, C. N. J.

MANN, Patricia Kathleen Randall, (Mrs Pierre Walker); Director of External Affairs, J. Walter Thompson Group, and Vice President International, JWT, since 1981; Editor, Consumer Affairs, since 1978; *b* 26 Sept. 1937; *d* of late Charles Mann and of Marjorie Mann (*née* Heath); *m* 1962, Pierre George Armand Walker; one *d*. *Educ:* Clifton High School, Bristol. FCAM, FIPA; CIMgt. Joined J. Walter Thompson Co., 1959, Copywriter, 1959–77, Head of Public Affairs, 1978. Director: Yale and Valor plc, 1985–91; Woolwich (formerly Woolwich Equitable) Building Soc., 1983–. Mem., Monopolies and Mergers Commn, 1984–93. Member: Council, Inst. of Practitioners in Advertising, 1965– (Hon. Sec., 1979–83); Advertising Creative Circle, 1965–; Council, Nat. Advertising Benevolent Soc., 1973–77; Council, Advertising Standards Authy, 1973–86; Board, European Advertising Tripartite, 1981–; Board, European Assoc. of Advertising Agencies, 1984–; Gas Consumers Council, 1981–90; Board, UK CEED, 1984–; Food Adv. Cttee, MAFF, 1986–; Kingman Cttee on English, DES, 1987; EC Commerce and Distribution Commn, 1989–; Sen. Salaries Rev. Body, 1994–. Governor: CAM Educn Foundn, 1971–77; Admin. Staff Coll., Henley, 1976–92; Mem. Ct, Brunel Univ., 1976– (Council, 1976–86). Mem., Awards Nomination Panel, RTS, 1974–78. Mackintosh Medal, Advertising Assoc., 1977. FRSA. *Publications:* 150 Careers in Advertising, 1971; Advertising, 1979; (ed) Advertising and Marketing to Children, 1980; various articles. *Recreation:* word games. *Address:* c/o J. Walter Thompson, 40 Berkeley Square, W1X 6AD. *T:* 0171–499 4040. *Clubs:* Reform, Women's Advertising, London Cornish Association.

MANN, Pauline, (Mrs R. D. Mann); *see* Vogelpoel, P.

MANN, Rt. Rev. Peter Woodley, CBE 1994; Bishop of Dunedin, 1976–90; *b* 25 July 1924; *s* of Edgar Allen and Bessie May Mann; *m* 1955, Anne Victoria Norman; three *d*. *Educ:* Prince Alfred Coll., Adelaide; St John's Coll., Auckland (Fellow); Univ. of London (BD). Deacon, Dio. Waiapu, 1953; priest, 1954; Curate: Waiapu Cathedral, 1953–55; Rotorua, 1955–56; Vicar: Porangahau, 1956–61; Dannevirke, 1961–66; Vicar of Blenheim and Archdeacon of Marlborough, 1966–71; Vicar of St Mary's and Archdeacon of Timaru, 1971–75; Vicar of St James', Lower Hutt, 1975–76. *Recreations:* tennis, athletics. *Address:* 182 Maitland Street, Dunedin, New Zealand. *T:* (3) 4775245.

MANN, Sir Rupert (Edward), 3rd Bt *cr* 1905; *b* 11 Nov. 1946; *s* of Major Edward Charles Mann, DSO, MC (*g s* of 1st Bt) (*d* 1959), and of Pamela Margaret, *o d* of late Major Frank Haultain Hornsby; *S* great uncle, 1971; *m* 1974, Mary Rose, *d* of Geoffrey Butler, Stetchworth, Newmarket; two *s*. *Educ:* Malvern. *Heir:* *s* Alexander Rupert Mann, *b* 6 April 1978. *Address:* Billingford Hall, Diss, Norfolk IP21 4HN. *Clubs:* MCC; Norfolk.

MANN, William Neville, MD, FRCP; Consultant Physician Emeritus, Guy's Hospital, 1976; *b* 4 April 1911; *s* of William Frank Mann and Clara, *d* of John Chadwick; *m* Pamela, *yr d* of late H. E. Chasteney; two *s* four *d*. *Educ:* Alleyn's Sch.; Guy's Hospital. MB, BS (London), 1935; MRCP 1937; MD (London), 1937; FRCP, 1947. House Physician, Demonstrator of Pathology and Medical Registrar, Guy's Hospital, 1935–39. Served, 1940–45, in RAMC in Middle East and Indian Ocean (Temp. Lt-Col). Physician, Guy's Hosp., 1946–76. Hon. Visiting Physician to Johns Hopkins Hosp., Baltimore, USA. Physician: to HM Household, 1954–64; to HM the Queen, 1964–70; King Edward VII's Hosp. for Officers, 1965–76. Sen. Censor and Sen. Vice-Pres., RCP, 1969–70. Hon. DHL Johns Hopkins, 1986. *Publications:* Clinical Examination of Patients (jointly), 1950; The Medical Works of Hippocrates (jointly), 1950. Editor, Conybeare's Text-book of Medicine, 16th edn, 1975. *Address:* 90 Alleyn Road, SE21 8AH. T: 0181–670 2451. *Club:* Garrick.

MANNERS, family name of **Baron Manners,** and **Duke of Rutland.**

MANNERS, 5th Baron *cr* 1807; **John Robert Cecil Manners;** DL; Consultant, Osborne, Clarke & Co., Solicitors, Bristol (Partner, 1952–84); *b* 13 Feb. 1923; *s* of 4th Baron Manners, MC, and of Mary Edith, *d* of late Rt Rev. Lord William Cecil; *S* father, 1972; *m* 1949, Jennifer Selena, *d* of Ian Fairbairn; one *s* two *d*. *Educ:* Eton; Trinity College, Oxford. Served as Flt-Lieut, RAFVR, 1941–46. Solicitor to the Supreme Court, 1949. Official Verderer of the New Forest, 1983–. DL Hampshire, 1987. *Recreations:* hunting and shooting. *Heir: s* Hon. John Hugh Robert Manners [*b* 5 May 1956; *m* 1983, Lanya Mary Jackson, *d* of late Dr H. E. Heitz and of Mrs Ian Jackson; two *d*]. *Address:* Sabines, Avon, Christchurch, Dorset BH23 7BQ. *Club:* Brooks's.

MANNERS, Elizabeth Maude, TD 1962; MA; Headmistress of Felixstowe College, Suffolk, 1967–79; Member, East Anglia Regional Health Authority, 1982–85; *b* 20 July 1917; *d* of William George Manners and Anne Mary Manners (*née* Sced). *Educ:* Stockton-on-Tees Sec. Sch.; St Hild's Coll., Durham Univ. BA (Dunelm) 1938; MA 1941. Teacher of French at: Marton Grove Sch., Middlesbrough, 1939–40; Ramsey Gram. Sch., IOM, 1940–42; Consett Sec. Sch., Durham, 1942–44; Yarm Gram. Sch., Yorks, 1944–54; Deputy Head, Mexborough Gram. Sch., Yorks, 1954–59; Head Mistress, Central Gram. Sch. for Girls, Manchester, 1959–67. Vice-President: Girl Guides Assoc., Co. Manchester, 1959–67; Suffolk Agric. Assoc., 1967–82. Member: Educn Cttee, Brit. Fedn of Univ. Women, 1966–68; Council, Bible Reading Fellowship, 1973–81; Cttee, E Br., RSA, 1974–90; Cttee, ISIS East, 1974–79. Mem., Suffolk CC, 1977–85 (Member: Educn Cttee, 1977–85; Staff Joint and Personnel Cttees, 1981–85; Vice-Chm., Secondary Educn Cttee, 1981–85); Mem., Felixstowe Town Council, 1991–95; Mem., Suffolk War Pensions Cttee, 1980–90. Sponsor, the Responsible Society, 1982–90. Chm. Governors, Felixstowe Deben High Sch., 1985–88. Enlisted ATS (TA), 1947; commissioned, 1949. FRSA 1972. Coronation Medal, 1953. *Publications:* The Vulnerable Generation, 1971; The Story of Felixstowe College, 1980. *Recreations:* foreign travel, theatre, motoring, good food and wine. *Address:* 6 Graham Court, Hamilton Gardens, Felixstowe, Suffolk IP11 7ES.

MANNERS, Prof. Gerald; Professor of Geography, University College London, since 1980; Chairman, Sadler's Wells Foundation (formerly Sadler's Wells Foundation and Trust), since 1986 (Governor, since 1978); *b* 7 Aug. 1932; *s* of George William Manners and Louisa Hannah Manners; *m* 1st, 1959, Anne (*née* Sawyer) (marr. diss. 1982); one *s* two *d*; 2nd, 1982, Joy Edith Roberta (*née* Turner); one *s*. *Educ:* Wallington County Grammar School; St Catharine's College, Cambridge (MA). Lectr in Geography, University Coll. Swansea, 1957–67; Reader in Geography, UCL, 1967–80. Vis. Schol., Resources for the Future, Inc., Washington DC, 1964–65; Vis. Associate, Jt Center for Urban Studies, Harvard and MIT, 1972–73; Vis. Fellow, ANU, 1990. Dir, Economic Associates Ltd, 1964–74. Member: Council, Inst. of British Geographers, 1967–70; LOB 1970–80; SE Economic Planning Council, 1971–79; Council, TCPA, 1980–89; Subscriber, Centre for Environmental Studies Ltd, 1981–. Specialist Advisor to: H of C Select Cttee on Energy, 1980–92; H of L Select Cttee on Sustainable Develt, 1994–; Advr to Assoc. for Conservation of Energy, 1981–; Chairman: Regl Studies Assoc., 1981–84; RSA Panel of Inquiry into regl problem in UK, 1982–83. Mem., Central Governing Body, City Parochial Foundn, 1977– (Chm., Estate Cttee, 1987–). Trustee: Chelsea Physic Garden, 1980–83; EAGA Charitable Trust, 1993–. Vice-Chm., 1982–86, Chm. Theatre Bd, 1986–93, Sadler's Wells Foundn and Trust. Mem. Court, City Univ., 1985–. *Publications:* Geography of Energy, 1964, 2nd edn 1971; South Wales in the Sixties, 1964; Changing World Market for Iron Ore 1950–1980, 1971; (ed) Spatial Policy Problems of the British Economy, 1971; Minerals and Man, 1974; Regional Development in Britain, 1974, 2nd edn 1980; Coal in Britain, 1981; Office Policy in Britain, 1986; contribs to edited volumes and learned jls. *Recreations:* music, dance, theatre, walking, undergardening. *Address:* 338 Liverpool Road, Islington, N7 8PZ. *T:* 0171–607 7920, *Fax:* 0171–609 2306.

MANNERS, Hon. Thomas (Jasper); Director, Lazard Brothers, 1965–89 (Deputy Chairman, 1986–89); *b* 12 Dec. 1929; *y s* of 4th Baron Manners, MC, and of Mary Edith, *d* of late Rt Rev. Lord William Cecil; *m* 1955, Sarah, *d* of Brig. Roger Peake, DSO; three *s*. *Educ:* Eton. Lazard Brothers & Co. Ltd, 1955–89; Director: Legal & General Gp, 1972–93; Scapa Gp, 1970–; Davy Corp., 1985–91. *Recreations:* shooting, fishing. *Address:* The Old Malt House, Ashford Hill, Newbury, Berks RG15 8BN. *T:* Tadley (017356) 814865. *Clubs:* Pratt's, White's.

MANNING, Prof. Aubrey William George, DPhil, FRSE, FIBiol; Professor of Natural History, University of Edinburgh, since 1973; *b* 24 April 1930; *s* of William James Manning and Hilda Winifred (*née* Noble); *m* 1st, 1959, Margaret Bastock, DPhil (*d* 1982); two *s*; 2nd, 1985, Joan Herrmann, PhD; one *s*. *Educ:* Strode's School, Egham, Surrey; University Coll., London (BSc); Merton Coll., Oxford (DPhil). FRSE 1975; FIBiol 1980. Commnd RA, 1954–56. University of Edinburgh: Asst Lectr, 1956–59; Lectr, 1959–68; Reader, 1968–73. Sec. Gen., Internat. Ethological Cttee, 1971–79; Pres., Assoc. Study Animal Behaviour, 1983–86; Member: Scottish Cttee, NCC, 1982–88; NCC Adv. Cttee on Science, 1984–88; Pres., Biology Sect., BAAS, 1993; Chm. Council, Scottish Wildlife Trust, 1990–. Dr *hc* Univ. Paul Sabatier, Toulouse, 1981. Dobzhansky Meml Award, Behavior Genetics Assoc., 1994. *Publications:* An Introduction to Animal Behaviour, 1967, 4th edn (with Dr M. Dawkins) 1992; papers on animal behaviour in learned jls. *Recreations:* woodland regeneration, hill-walking, architecture, 19th century novels. *Address:* The Old Hall, Ormiston, East Lothian EH35 5NJ. *T:* Pencaitland (01875) 340536.

MANNING, David Geoffrey, CMG 1992; HM Diplomatic Service; Head of Policy Planning Staff, Foreign and Commonwealth Office, since 1994; *b* 5 Dec. 1949; *s* of John Robert Manning and Joan Barbara Manning; *m* 1973, Catherine Marjory Parkinson. *Educ:* Ardingly Coll.; Oriel Coll., Oxford. FCO, 1972; Warsaw, 1974–76; New Delhi, 1977–80; FCO, 1980–84; First Sec., Paris, 1984–88; Counsellor, seconded to Cabinet Office, 1988–90; Political Counsellor and Head of Political Sect., Moscow, 1990–93; Hd of Eastern Dept, FCO, 1993–94. British Mem., Contact Gp on Bosnia, Internat. Conf. on Former Yugoslavia, April–Nov. 1994. *Address:* c/o Foreign and Commonwealth Office, SW1A 2AH.

MANNING, Dr Geoffrey, CBE 1986; FInstP; independent consultant on parallel computing and networking; Visiting Professor, Department of Physics and Astronomy, University College London, since 1987; *b* 31 Aug. 1929; *s* of Jack Manning and Ruby Frances Lambe; *m* 1951, Anita Jacqueline Davis; two *s* one *d*. *Educ:* Tottenham Grammar Sch.; Imperial Coll., London Univ. BSc, PhD; ARCS. Asst Lectr in Physics, Imperial Coll., 1953–55; Research worker: English Electric Co., 1955–56; Canadian Atomic Energy Co., 1956–58; Calif Inst. of Technol., 1958–59; AERE, 1960–65; Rutherford Laboratory, Science Research Council: Gp Leader, 1965–69; Dep. Dir, 1969–79; Head of High Energy Physics Div., 1969–75; Head of Atlas Div., 1975–79; Dir, Rutherford (Rutherford & Appleton Labs), 1979–81; Dir, Rutherford Appleton Lab., SERC, 1981–86 (Hon. Scientist, 1994–); Chm., Active Memory Technology Ltd, 1986–92; non-exec. Dir, Recogniton Res., 1991–94; Consultant: to UFC on formation of UKERNA, 1991–93; Cambridge Parallel Processing, 1992–. Mem., Visiting Cttee, Physics Dept, Imperial Coll., 1988–92. Vis. Scientist, Fermi Nat. Accelerator Lab., 1994–95. Chairman: Parallel and Novel Architectures Sub Cttee, DTI, 1988–91; Systems Architecture Cttee, DTI/SERC, 1991–92 (Mem., 1988–91); Mem., IT Adv. Bd, DTI/SERC, 1991–92. Glazebrook Medal and Prize, Inst. of Physics, 1986. *Recreations:* golf, squash, ski-ing. *Address:* 38 Sunningwell Village, Abingdon, Oxon OX13 6RB. *T:* Oxford (01865) 736123.

MANNING, Dr Geoffrey Lewis, FRCSE; FDSRCS; Chairman, North Staffordshire Hospital NHS Trust, since 1993; *b* 21 Sept. 1931; *s* of late Isaac Harold Manning and Florence Hilda Manning (*née* Tomlin); *m* 1978, Patricia Margaret Wilson; one *d*. *Educ:* Rossall Sch., Fleetwood, Lancs; Univ. of Birmingham (LDS, BDS 1953; MB, ChB 1961). FDSRCS 1964; FRCSE 1986. Nat. service, Capt., RADC, 1954–56. Senior Registrar: Central Middx Hosp., 1964–66; Mt Vernon Hosp., 1966–68; Parkland Meml Hosp., Dallas, 1967; Consultant Oral Surgeon, N Staffs Hosp., 1968–93. Mem., N Staffs DHA, 1986–92. Leader, Health Task Force, Prince of Wales Business Leaders Forum, 1993–. British Fedn. of Pottery Manufacturers. *Recreations:* gardening, brick-laying, classic cars. *Address:* The Old Hall, Haughton, Stafford ST18 9HB. *T:* Stafford (01785) 780273. *Club:* Trentham Golf.

MANNING, Jane Marian, OBE 1990; freelance concert and opera singer (soprano), since 1965; *b* 20 Sept. 1938; *d* of Gerald Manville Manning and Lily Manning (*née* Thompson); *m* 1966, Anthony Edward Payne, composer. *Educ:* Norwich High Sch.; Royal Academy of Music (LRAM 1958); Scuola di Canto, Cureglia, Switzerland. GRSM 1960, ARCM 1962. London début (Park Lane Group), 1964; first BBC broadcast, 1965; début Henry Wood Promenade Concerts, 1972; founded own ensemble, Jane's Minstrels, 1988; regular appearances in leading concert halls and festivals in UK and Europe, with leading orchestras and conductors; many broadcasts and gramophone recordings, lectures and master classes. Specialist in contemporary music (over 300 world premières given); Warsaw Autumn Fest., 1975–78, 1987, 1992; Wexford Opera Fest., 1976; Scottish Opera, 1978; Brussels Opera, 1980. Canadian début, 1977; tours: of Australia and New Zealand, 1978, 1980, 1982, 1984, 1986; of Australia, 1990; of USA, 1981, 1983, 1985, 1986, 1987, 1988, 1989, 1991, 1993. Milhaud Vis. Prof., Mills Coll. Oakland, 1983; Lucie Stern Vis. Prof., Mills Coll., Oakland, 1981 and 1986; Vis. Artist, Univ. of Manitoba, Canada, 1992. Vice Pres., SPNM, 1984–. Member: Exec. Cttee, Musicians Benevolent Fund, 1989–; Arts Council Music Panel, 1990–95; Internat. Jury, Gaudeamus Young Interpreters Competition, Holland, 1976, 1979, 1987; Jury, Eur. Youth Competition for Composers, Eur. Cultural Foundn, 1985. Hon. ARAM 1972, Hon. FRAM 1984. Hon. DMus York, 1988. Special award, Composers Guild of Gt Britain, 1973. *Publications:* (chapter in) How Music Works, 1981; New Vocal Repertory, 1986, vol. II, 1995; (chapter in) A Messiaen Companion, 1995; articles in Composer, and Music and Musicians. *Recreations:* cooking, cinema, ornithology. *Address:* 2 Wilton Square, N1 3DL. *T:* 0171–359 1593, *Fax:* 0171–226 4369.

MANNING, Jeremy James C.; *see* Carter-Manning.

MANNING, Hon. Patrick Augustus Mervyn; MP (People's National Movement) San Fernando East, since 1971; Prime Minister, Trinidad and Tobago, since 1991; *b* 17 Aug. 1946; *s* of late Arnold and Elaine Manning; *m* 1972, Hazel Kinsale; two *s*. *Educ:* Rose Bank Private Sch.; San Fernando Govt Sch.; Presentation Coll.; Univ. of West Indies, Jamaica (BSc Special Hons Geology 1969). Texaco Trinidad Inc.: Refinery Operator, 1965–66; Geologist, 1969–71. Parliamentary Secretary: Min. of Petroleum and Mines, 1971–73; Office of the Prime Minister, 1973–74; Min. of Planning and Develt, 1974–75; Min. of Industry and Commerce, 1975–76; Min. of Works, Transport and Communications, 1976–78; Minister: Min. of Finance (Maintenance and Public Service), 1978–81; Prime Minister's Office (Information), 1979–81; Minister of: Inf. and of Industry and Commerce, 1981; Energy and Natural Resources, 1981–86; Leader of the Opposition, 1986–90; Leader, People's National Movement, 1987–. *Recreations:* table tennis, chess, reading. *Address:* Office of the Prime Minister, Central Bank Tower, Eric Williams Plaza, Independence Square, Port of Spain, Trinidad and Tobago. *T:* 6233656.

MANNING, Paul Andrew; Assistant Commissioner, Metropolitan Police, since 1994; *b* 29 May 1947; *s* of Owen Manning and Joyce Cynthia Manning (*née* Murgatroyd); *m* 1967, Margaret Anne Bucknall; two *s*. *Educ:* Forest of Needwood High Sch., Rolleston-on-Dove; Cranfield Inst. of Technology (MSc). Metropolitan Police Cadet, 1964; Constable, 1966, Chief Supt, 1985, Staffordshire Police; Asst Chief Constable, Avon and Somerset Constabulary, 1988; Dep. Chief Constable, Herts Constabulary, 1992. Mem., Amwell Rotary Club. *Recreations:* hill walking, Rotary. *Address:* Metropolitan Police, South West Area HQ, 3 Penrhyn Road, Kingston-upon-Thames, Surrey. *T:* 0181–247 5043.

MANNING, Thomas Henry, OC 1974; zoologist, now retired; *b* 22 Dec. 1911; *s* of Thomas E. and Dorothy (*née* Randall) Manning, Shrublands, Dallington, Northampton; *m* 1938, Ella Wallace Jackson. *Educ:* Harrow; Cambridge. Winter journey across Lapland, 1932–33; Survey and Zoological work on Southampton Island, 1933–35; Leader, Brit. Canadian-Arctic Exped., 1936–41; Royal Canadian Navy, 1941–45; Geodetic Service of Canada, 1945–47; Leader Geographical Bureau Expedition to Prince Charles I. (Foxe Basin), 1949; Zoological and Geographical work in James Bay, 1950; Leader Defence Research Board Expeditions: Beaufort Sea, 1951; Banks Island, 1952, 1953; Nat. Mus. Canada Expedition; King William Island, Adelaide Peninsula, 1957, Prince of Wales Island, 1958. Hon. LLD McMaster, 1979. Bruce Medal (Royal Society of Edinburgh, RPS, RSGS), 1944; Patron's Gold Medal, RGS, 1948; Massey Medal, Royal Canadian Geographical Soc., 1977. Guggenheim Fellow, 1959. *Publications:* The Birds of North Western Ungava, 1949; Birds of the West James Bay and Southern Hudson Bay Coasts, 1952; Birds of Banks Island, 1956; Mammals of Banks Island, 1958; A Biological Investigation of Prince of Wales Island, 1961; articles in The Auk, Journal Mamm. and Geog. Journal, Canadian Geog. Jl, Canadian Field-Naturalist, Arctic, Nat. Mus. Can. Bull., Canadian Jl of Zool., Syllogeus. *Recreations:* shooting, book-binding, cabinet-making, gardening. *Address:* RR4, Merrickville, Ont K0G IN0, Canada. *T:* (613)2694940.

MANNINGHAM-BULLER, family name of **Viscount Dilhorne.**

MANOR, Prof. James Gilmore, DPhil; Director, Institute of Commonwealth Studies and Professor of Commonwealth Politics, University of London, since 1994; *b* 21 April 1945; *s* of James Manor and Ann (*née* Jones); *m* 1974, Brenda Cohen; one *s*. *Educ:* Yale Univ. (BA 1967); Univ. of Sussex (DPhil 1975). Asst Lectr in History, Chinese Univ. of Hong Kong, 1967–69; Tutor, SOAS, 1973–75; Asst Prof. of History, Yale, 1975–76; Lectr in Politics, Univ. of Leicester, 1976–85; Prof. of Govt, Harvard, 1985–87; Professorial Fellow, Inst. of Develt Studies, 1987– (Head of Research, 1988–91). Sen. Res. Fellow, US Nat. Endowment for the Humanities, 1980–81; Vis Fellow, MIT, 1982. Consultant to: Dutch Govt, 1989–90; World Bank, 1994–95; Swedish Govt, 1995. Editor, Jl of Commonwealth and Comparative Politics, 1980–88. *Publications:* Political Change in an Indian State, 1977; (ed with P. Lyon) Transfer and Transformation, 1983; (ed) Sri Lanka in Change and Crisis, 1984; The Expedient Utopian, 1989; (ed) Rethinking Third World Politics, 1991; (ed with C. Colclough) States or Markets?, 1991; Power, Poverty and Poison, 1993; Nehru to the Nineties, 1994. *Recreations:* reading, theatre. *Address:* Institute for Commonwealth Studies, 27–28 Russell Square, WC1B 5DS. *T:* 0171–580 5876.

MANS, Keith Douglas Rowland; MP (C) Wyre, since 1987; *b* 10 Feb. 1946; *s* of Maj.-Gen. R. S. N. Mans, *qv; m* 1972, Rosalie Mary McCann; one *s* two *d*. *Educ:* Berkhamsted School; RAF College Cranwell; Open Univ. (BA). Pilot, RAF, 1964–77 (Flight Lieut); Pilot, RAF Reserve, 1977–. Retail Manager, John Lewis Partnership, 1978–87. PPS to Minister of State, Dept of Health, 1990–92, to Sec. of State for Health, 1992–95. Member: H of C Environment Select Cttee, 1987–91; Select Cttee on Defence, 1995–; Chairman: Parly Envmt Gp, 1993–; Parly Aviation Gp, 1994–; Vice-Chm., Backbench Fisheries Cttee, 1987–; Secretary: Backbench Aviation Cttee, 1987–90; Backbench Envmt Cttee, 1990–91; All Party Aviation Gp, 1991–94. *Recreation:* flying. *Address:* Underbank Cottage, Raikes Road, Thornton, Lancs FY5 5LS. *T:* Cleveleys (01253) 822502. *Clubs:* Army and Navy, Royal Air Force.

MANS, Maj.-Gen. Rowland Spencer Noel, CBE 1971 (OBE 1966, MBE 1956); Director, Military Assistance Office, 1973–76, retired; *b* 16 Jan. 1921; *s* of Thomas Frederick Mans and May Seigenberg; *m* 1945, Veeo Ellen Sutton; three *s*. *Educ:* Surbiton Grammar Sch.; RMC, Sandhurst; jssc, psc. Served War, Queen's Royal Regt and King's African Rifles, 1940–45. Regtl and Staff Duty, 1945–59; Instr, Staff Colleges, Camberley and Canada, 1959–63; Comd, 1st Tanganyika Rifles, 1963–64; Staff Duty, Far East and UK, 1964–68; Comd, Aldershot, 1969–72; DDPS (Army), 1972–73. Col, Queen's Regt, 1978–83 (Dep. Col (Surrey), 1973–77). Defence consultant and writer on defence and political affairs. Mem., Hampshire CC, 1984–89. *Publications:* Kenyatta's Middle Road in a Changing Africa, 1977; Canada's Constitutional Crisis, 1978. *Recreations:* writing, reading, gardening. *Address:* Ivy Bank Cottage, Vinegar Hill, Milford-on-Sea, Hants SO41 0RZ. *T:* Lymington (01590) 643982. *Clubs:* Army and Navy; Royal Lymington Yacht.
See also K. D. R. Mans.

MANSAGER, Felix Norman, Hon. KBE 1976 (Hon. CBE 1973); Honorary Director, Hoover Co. USA (President-Chairman, Hoover Co. and Hoover World-wide Corporation, 1966–75); Director, Hoover Ltd UK (Chairman, 1966–75); *b* 30 Jan. 1911; *s* of Hoff Mansager and Alice (*née* Qualseth); *m* Geraldine (*née* Larson); one *s* two *d*. *Educ:* South Dakota High Sch., Colton. Joined Hoover Co. as Salesman, 1929; Vice-Pres., Sales, 1959; Exec. Vice-Pres. and Dir, 1961. Dir, Belden and Blake Energy Co. Member: Council on Foreign Relations; Newcomen Soc. in N America; Trustee, Graduate Theological Union (Calif); The Pilgrims of the US; Assoc. of Ohio Commodores; Masonic Shrine (32nd degree Mason); Mem. and Governor, Ditchley Foundn; Member Board of Trustees: Ohio Foundn of Indep. Colls; Indep. Coll. Funds of America. Hon. Mem., World League of Norsemen. Marketing Award, British Inst. of Marketing, 1971. Executive Prof. of Business (Goodyear Chair), Univ. of Akron (Mem. Delta Sigma Pi; Hon. Mem., Beta Sigma Gamma). Hon. Fellow, UC Cardiff, 1973. Hon. Dr of Laws Capital Univ., 1967; Hon. LLD Strathclyde, 1970; Hon. DHL Malone Coll., Canton, Ohio, 1972; Hon. PhD Walsh Coll., Canton, 1974; Hon. Dr Humanities Wartburg Coll., Waverly, Iowa, 1976; Medal of Honor, Vassa Univ., Finland, 1973; Person of Year, Capital Univ. Chapter of Tau Pi Phi, 1981. Grand Officer, Dukes of Burgundy, 1968; Chevalier: Order of Leopold, 1969; Order of St Olav, Norway, 1971; Legion of Honour, France, 1973; Grande Officiale, Order Al Merito della Republica Italiana, 1975. *Recreation:* golf. *Address:* 3421 Lindel Court NW, Canton, OH 44718, USA. *Clubs:* Metropolitan (NYC); Congress Lake Country (Hartville, Ohio); Torske (Hon.) (Minneapolis).

MANSEL, Sir Philip, 15th Bt, *cr* 1621; FInstSM; Chairman and Managing Director of Eden-Vale Engineering Co. Ltd; *b* 3 March 1943; *s* of Sir John Mansel, 14th Bt and Hannah, *d* of Ben Rees; *S* father, 1947; *m* 1968, Margaret, *o d* of Arthur Docker; two *s* one *d*. *Heir: s* John Philip Mansel, *b* 19 April 1982. *Address:* 2 Deyncourt Close, Darras Hall, Ponteland, Northumberland NE20 9RP.

MANSEL, Prof. Robert Edward, FRCS; Professor of Surgery and Head of Department of Surgery, University of Wales College of Medicine, since 1992; *b* 1 Feb. 1948; *s* of Regnier Ranulf Dabridgecourt Mansel and Mary Germaine Mansel (*née* Littlewood); *m* 1987, Elizabeth Clare, *d* of John Francis Skone and Daphne Viola (*née* Rees); two *s* four *d*. *Educ:* Llandovery Coll.; Charing Cross Hosp. Med. Sch., Univ. of London (MB BS, MS). LRCP 1971; FRCS 1975. Res. Fellow, 1976–78, Lectr and Sen. Lectr, 1979–89, Univ. of Wales Coll. of Medicine; Prof. of Surgery, Univ. of Manchester, 1989–92. UICC Fellow, Univ. of Texas at San Antonio, 1982–83; Churchill Meml Fellowship, 1982; James IV Fellowship, James IV Assoc., 1989. Hunterian Prof., RCS, 1989. *Publications:* Fibrocystic Breast Disease, 1986; (with L. E. Hughes and D. J. T. Webster) Benign Breast Disease, 1989; Atlas of Breast Disease, 1994; contribs to surgical jls. *Recreations:* fishing, Rugby, travel, chess. *Address:* University Department of Surgery, University of Wales College of Medicine, Heath Park, Cardiff CF4 4XN. *T:* Cardiff (01222) 742749, *Fax:* (01222) 761623.

MANSEL-JONES, David; Chairman, Huntingdon Research Centre plc, 1978–86 (Vice-Chairman, 1974–78); *b* 8 Sept. 1926; *o s* of Rees Thomas Jones and Ceinwen Jones; *m* 1952, Mair Aeronwen Davies; one *s*. *Educ:* St Michael's Sch., Bryn; London Hospital. MB, BS 1950; MRCP 1973; FFPM 1992. Jun. Surgical Specialist, RAMC; Dep. Med. Dir, Wm R. Warner & Co. Ltd, 1957–59; Med. Dir, Richardson-Merrell Ltd, 1959–65; formerly PMO, SMO and MO, Cttee on Safety of Drugs; formerly Med. Assessor, Cttee on Safety of Medicines; Consultant to WHO, 1970–86; Senior PMO, Medicines Div., DHSS, 1971–74. Vis. Prof., Gulbenkian Science Inst., Portugal, 1981; Examiner, Dip. Pharm. Med., Royal Colls of Physicians, UK, 1980–87. *Publications:* papers related to safety of medicines. *Recreations:* music, painting. *Address:* 39 St John's Court, Princes Road, Felixstowe, Suffolk IP11 7SG. *T:* Felixstowe (01394) 275984.

MANSEL LEWIS, Sir David (Courtenay), KCVO 1995; Lord-Lieutenant of Dyfed, since 1979 (Lieutenant, 1974–79; HM Lieutenant for Carmarthenshire, 1973–74); JP; *b* 25 Oct. 1927; *s* of late Charlie Ronald Mansel Lewis and Lillian Georgina Warner, *d* of Col Sir Courtenay Warner, 1st Bt, CB; *m* 1953, Lady Mary Rosemary Marie-Gabrielle Montagu-Stuart-Wortley, OBE, JP, 4th *d* of 3rd Earl of Wharncliffe; one *s* two *d*. *Educ:* Eton; Keble Coll., Oxford (BA). Served in Welsh Guards, 1946–49; Lieut 1946, RARO. High Sheriff, Carmarthenshire, 1965; JP 1969; DL 1971. FRSA; KStJ. *Recreations:* music, sailing. *Address:* Stradey Castle, Llanelli, Dyfed SA15 4PL. *T:* Llanelli (01554) 774626. *Clubs:* Lansdowne; Royal Yacht Squadron (Cowes).

MANSELL, Gerard Evelyn Herbert, CBE 1977; Managing Director, External Broadcasting, BBC, 1972–81; Deputy Director-General, BBC, 1977–81; retired; *b* 16 Feb. 1921; 2nd *s* of late Herbert and Anne Mansell, Paris; *m* 1956, Diana Marion Sherar; two *s*. *Educ:* Lycée Hoche, Versailles; Lycée Buffon, Paris; Ecole des Sciences Politiques, Paris; Chelsea Sch. of Art. Joined HM Forces, 1940; served in Western Desert, Sicily and NW Europe, 1942–45 (despatches). Joined BBC European Service, 1951; Head, Overseas Talks and Features Dept, 1961; Controller, BBC Radio 4 (formerly Home Service), and Music Programme, 1965–69; Dir of Programmes, BBC, Radio, 1970. Chairman: British Cttee, Journalists in Europe, 1978–95; Jt Adv. Cttee on Radio Journalism Trng, 1981–87; Sony Radio Awards Organising Cttee, 1983–87; Communications Adv. Cttee, UK Nat. Commn for UNESCO, 1983–85; Friends of UNESCO, 1986–88; Member: Communication and Cultural Studies Bd, CNAA, 1982–87; Exec. Cttee, GB–China Centre, 1986– (Vice-Chm., 1988–); Franco-British Council, 1990–; Sandford St Martin Trust, 1991–. Governor, Falmouth Sch. of Art and Design, 1988–; Chairman: New Hampstead Garden Suburb Trust, 1984–90, 1992–93; Burgh House Trust, Hampstead, 1995–. Hon. Vis. Fellow, Grad. Centre for Journalism, City Univ., 1992–. FRSA 1979. Sony Gold Award for Services to Radio, 1988. French Croix de Guerre, 1945. *Publications:* Tragedy in Algeria, 1961; Let Truth be Told, 1982. *Address:* 15 Hampstead Hill Gardens, NW3 2PH.

MANSELL, Nigel Ernest James, OBE 1991; racing driver; *b* 8 Aug. 1953; *s* of Eric and Joyce Marshall; *m* Rosanne Elizabeth Perry; two *s* one *d*. *Educ:* Wellsbourne and Hall Green Bilateral Schools; Matthew Bolton Polytechnic; Solihull Tech. Coll.; N Birmingham Polytechnic (HND). Engineering apprenticeship with Lucas; lab. technician, Lucas Aerospace, later product manager; senior sales engineer, tractor div., Girling. Began racing in karts; won 11 regional championships, 1969–76; Formula Ford and Formula Three, 1976–79; Formula Two, later Formula One, 1980; Lotus team, 1981–84; Williams team, 1985–88 and 1991–92; Ferrari team, 1989–90; McLaren team, 1995; first competed in a Grand Prix, Austria, 1980; won 30 Grands Prix, 1980–92 (record); Formula One World Drivers Champion, 1992; American Newman-Haas IndyCar Team, 1993; IndyCar Champion, 1993. *Publications:* (with Derick Allsop) Driven to Win, 1988; (with Derick Allsop) Mansell and Williams, The Challenge for the Championship 1992; (with Jeremy Shaw) Nigel Mansell's IndyCar Racing, 1993. *Recreation:* golf. *Address:* c/o Sue Membery, The Old Smithy, Sealeys Farm, Church Road, West Huntspill, Somerset TA9 3SG. *T:* Burnham-on-Sea (01278) 789678.

MANSELL-JONES, Richard; Chairman: J. Bibby & Sons PLC, since 1988 (Director, since 1982); Brown, Shipley & Co., since 1992; *b* 4 April 1940; *s* of Arnaud Milward Jones and Winifred Mabel (*née* Foot); *m* 1971, Penelope Marion, *y d* of Major Sir David Henry Hawley, 7th Bt. *Educ:* Queen Elizabeth's, Carmarthen; Worcester College, Oxford (MA). FCA. Articled to Price, Waterhouse & Co., 1963–68; with N. M. Rothschild & Sons, 1968–72; Brown, Shipley & Co., 1972–88, Dir, 1974–88; Director: Brown, Shipley Holdings, 1985–92; Barr & Wallace Arnold Trust, 1984–93; Barlow Ltd (formerly Barlow Rand Ltd), 1988–; Rand Mines Ltd, 1988–93; Standard Bank London, 1992–. *Address:* 16 Stratford Place, W1N 9AF. *T:* 0171–629 6243. *Clubs:* Boodle's, Oriental, City of London.

MANSER, John; *see* Manser, P. J.

MANSER, Michael John, CBE 1993; RA 1995; architect in private practice, Manser Associates (formerly Michael Manser Associates), since 1961; President, Royal Institute of British Architects, 1983–85; *b* 23 March 1929; *s* of late Edmund George Manser and Augusta Madge Manser; *m* 1953, Dolores Josephine Bernini; one *s* one *d*. *Educ:* Sch. of Architecture, Polytechnic of Central London (DipArch). RIBA 1954; RWA 1994. Intermittent architectural journalism, including: News Editor, Architectural Design, 1961–64; Architectural Correspondent, The Observer and TV and radio, 1963–65. Councillor: RIBA, 1977–80 and 1982; RSA, 1987–93 (Chm., Art for Architecture Award Scheme, 1990–); Assessor, Art in the Workplace Awards, 1988–; RIBA Rep., Council, Nat. Trust, 1991–93; Mem., London Transport Design Policy Cttee, 1991–95. Hon. Fellow, Royal Architectural Inst. of Canada, 1985. Civic Trust Awards, 1967, 1973 and 1991; Award for Good Design in Housing, DoE, 1975; Heritage Year Award, 1975; Structural Steel Award, BSC, 1976; Commendation, RIBA Awards, 1977; RIBA Award and Regional Award, 1991. *Publications:* (with José Manser) Planning Your Kitchen, 1976; (contrib.) Psychiatry in the Elderly, 1991; (contrib.) Companion to Contemporary Architectural Thought, 1993. *Recreations:* going home, architecture, music, books, boats, sketching, gardening (under supervision). *Address:* Morton House, Chiswick Mall, W4 2PS. *Club:* Brooks's.

MANSER, (Peter) John, CBE 1992; FCA; Group Chief Executive, Robert Fleming Holdings Ltd, since 1990 (Director since 1972); Chairman, Robert Fleming & Co. Ltd, since 1990; Deputy Chairman, Robert Fleming Asset Management Ltd, since 1990; *b* 7 Dec. 1939; *s* of late Peter Robert Courtney Manser and Florence Delaplaine Manser; *m* 1969, Sarah Theresa Stuart (*née* Todd); two *d*. *Educ:* Marlborough Coll. Man. Dir, Jardine Fleming & Co. Ltd, 1975–79; Chief Exec., Save & Prosper Gp Ltd, 1983–88. Dir, Capital Shopping Centres, 1994–. Dep. Chm., FIMBRA, 1984–85; Dir, SIB, 1986–93; Chm., London Investment Banking Assoc., 1994–. Dir, Cancer Research Campaign, 1985–. *Recreations:* gardening, walking, shooting. *Address:* Chisenbury Priory, East Chisenbury, Pewsey, Wilts SN9 6AQ. *Clubs:* Boodle's, City of London, MCC.

MANSFIELD, family name of **Baron Sandhurst.**

MANSFIELD AND MANSFIELD, 8th Earl of, *cr* 1776 and 1792 (GB); **William David Mungo James Murray;** JP, DL; Baron Scone, 1605; Viscount Stormont, 1621; Baron Balvaird, 1641; (Earl of Dunbar, Viscount Drumcairn, and Baron Halldykes in the Jacobite Peerage); Hereditary Keeper of Bruce's Castle of Lochmaben; First Crown Estate Commissioner, since 1985; *b* 7 July 1930; *o s* of 7th Earl of Mansfield and Mansfield, and of Dorothea Helena (*d* 1985), *y d* of late Rt Hon. Sir Lancelot Carnegie, GCVO, KCMG; *S* father, 1971; *m* 1955, Pamela Joan, *o d* of W. N. Foster, CBE; two *s* one *d*. *Educ:* Eton; Christ Church, Oxford. Served as Lieut with Scots Guards, Malayan campaign, 1949–50. Called to Bar, Inner Temple, 1958; Barrister, 1958–71. Mem., British Delegn to European Parlt, 1973–75; an opposition spokesman in the House of Lords, 1975–79; Minister of State: Scottish Office, 1979–83; NI Office, 1983–84. Mem., Tay Salmon Fisheries Bd, 1971–79. Director: General Accident, Fire and Life Assurance Corp. Ltd, 1972–79, 1985–; American Trust, 1985–; Pinneys of Scotland, 1985–89; Ross Breeders Ltd, 1989–90. Ordinary Dir, Royal Highland and Agricl Soc., 1976–79. President: Fédn des Assocs de Chasse de l'Europe, 1977–79; Scottish Assoc. for Care and Resettlement of Offenders, 1974–79; Scottish Assoc. of Boys Clubs, 1976–79; Royal Scottish Country Dance Soc., 1977–; Chm., Scottish Branch, Historic Houses Assoc., 1976–79. Mem., Perth CC, 1971–75; Hon. Sheriff for Perthshire, 1974–; JP 1975, DL 1980, Perth and Kinross. Hon. Mem., RICS, 1994. *Publications:* articles on agriculture, land management and wine. *Heir: s* Viscount Stormont, *qv*. *Address:* Scone Palace, Perthshire PH2 6BE; 16 Thorburn House, Kinnerton Street, SW1X 8EX. *Clubs:* White's, Pratt's, Turf, Beefsteak.

MANSFIELD, Prof. Averil (Olive), (Mrs J. W. P. Bradley), FRCS; Professor of Vascular Surgery, and Director, Academic Surgical Unit, St Mary's Hospital and Medical School, since 1993; Consultant Surgeon, St Mary's Hospital, since 1982; *b* 21 June 1937; *m* 1987, John William Paulton Bradley. *Educ:* Liverpool Univ. (MB, ChM 1972). FRCS 1966. Consultant Surgeon: Royal Liverpool Hosp., 1972–80; Hillingdon Hosp., 1980–82; RPMS, 1980–. Royal College of Surgeons: Chm., Court of Examrs, 1990–92; Mem. Council, 1990–; Pres., Assoc. of Surgeons of GB and Ireland, 1992–93. Hon. MD Liverpool, 1994. *Publications:* Clinical Surgery in General, 1993; articles on vascular surgery. *Recreations:* playing the piano, walking in the Lake District, restoring old wrecks. *Address:* 31 Radnor Mews, W2 2SA.

MANSFIELD, Rear-Adm. David Parks, CB 1964; *b* 26 July 1912; *s* of Comdr D. Mansfield, RD, RNR; *m* 1939, Jean Craig Alexander (*d* 1984); one *s* one *d*. *Educ:* RN

Coll., Dartmouth; RN Engineering Coll., Keyham. Lt (E) 1934; HMS Nelson, 1934–36; Staff of C-in-C Med., 1936–39; HMS Mauritius, 1939–42; Lt-Comdr (E) 1942; HMS Kelvin, 1942–43; Chatham Dockyard, 1943–46; Comdr (E) 1945; Admty (Aircraft Maintenance Dept), 1946–49; Staff of FO Air (Home), 1949–51; HMS Kenya, 1951–53; RN Engrg Coll., 1953–55; Captain 1954; RNAS Anthorn (in command), 1955–57; RN Aircraft Yard, Fleetlands (Supt.), 1957–60; Admty Dir of Fleet Maintenance, 1960–62; Rear-Adm. 1963; Rear-Adm. Aircraft, on Staff of Flag Officer Naval Air Command, 1963–65. *Recreation:* family affairs. *Address:* The Outlook, Salisbury Road, St Margaret's Bay, Dover, Kent CT15 6DL. *T:* Dover (01304) 852237. *Club:* Army and Navy.

MANSFIELD, Vice-Adm. Sir (Edward) Gerard (Napier), KBE 1974; CVO 1981; retired 1975; *b* 13 July 1921; *s* of late Vice-Adm. Sir John Mansfield, KCB, DSO, DSC, and Alice Talbot Mansfield; *m* 1943, Joan Worship Byron, *d* of late Comdr John Byron, DSC and Bar, and late Frances Byron; two *d. Educ:* RNC, Dartmouth. Entered Royal Navy, 1935. Served War of 1939–45 in destroyers and Combined Ops (despatches), taking part in landings in N Africa and Sicily. Comdr, 1953; comd HMS Mounts Bay, 1956–58; Captain 1959; SHAPE, 1960–62; Captain (F) 20th Frigate Sqdn, 1963–64; Dir of Defence Plans (Navy), 1965–67; Cdre Amphibious Forces, 1967–68; Senior Naval Member, Directing Staff, IDC, 1969–70; Flag Officer Sea Training, 1971–72; Dep. Supreme Allied Comdr, Atlantic, 1973–75. Chm., Assoc. of RN Officers, 1975–86; Chm. Council, Operation Raleigh, 1984–89. Chm., Crondall Parish Council, 1977–81. Mem. Admin. Council, Royal Jubilee Trusts, 1978–81. *Recreations:* golf, gardening. *Address:* White Gate House, Heath Lane, Ewshot, Farnham, Surrey GU10 5AH. *T:* Aldershot (01252) 850325. *Club:* Army and Navy.

MANSFIELD, Dr Eric Harold, FRS 1971; FEng 1976; FRAeS, FIMA; Chief Scientific Officer (Individual Merit), Royal Aircraft Establishment, 1980–83; *b* 24 May 1923; *s* of Harold Goldsmith Mansfield and Grace Phundt; *m* 1947; two *s* one *d*; *m* 1974, Eunice Lily Kathleen Shuttleworth-Parker. *Educ:* St Lawrence Coll., Ramsgate; Trinity Hall, Cambridge. MA, ScD. Research in Structures Department, Royal Aircraft Establishment, Farnborough, Hants, 1943–83. Vis. Prof., Dept of Mechanical Engrg, Univ. of Surrey, 1984–90. Member: British Nat. Cttee for Theoretical and Applied Mechanics, 1973–79; Gen. Assembly of IUTAM, 1976–80; Council, Royal Soc., 1977–78. James Alfred Ewing Gold Medal for Engrg Res., ICE, 1991; Royal Medal, Royal Soc., 1994. UK winner (with I. T. Minhinnick), World Par Bridge Olympiad, 1951. Member, Editorial Advisory Boards: Internat. Jl of Non-linear Mechanics, 1965–95; Internat Jl of Mechanical Scis, 1977–84. *Publications:* The Bending and Stretching of Plates, 1964, 2nd edn 1989; Bridge: The Ultimate Limits, 1986; contribs to: Proc. Roy. Soc., Phil. Trans., Quarterly Jl Mech. Applied Math., Aero Quarterly, Aero Research Coun. reports and memos, and to technical press. *Recreations:* duplicate bridge, palaeontology, snorkling. *Address:* Manatoba, Dene Close, Lower Bourne, Farnham, Surrey GU10 3PP. *T:* Farnham (01252) 713558.

MANSFIELD, Sir Gerard; *see* Mansfield, Sir E. G. N.

MANSFIELD, Hon. Guy (Rhys John); QC 1994; a Recorder, since 1993; *b* 3 March 1949; *o s* and *heir* of 5th Baron Sandhurst, *qv*; *m* 1976, Philippa St Clair Verdon-Roe; one *s* one *d. Educ:* Harrow Sch.; Oriel Coll., Oxford (MA). Called to the Bar, Middle Temple, 1972. *Recreations:* cricket, opera. *Address:* 1 Crown Office Row, Temple, EC4Y 7HH. *T:* 0171–797 7500. *Clubs:* MCC; Leander (Henley-on-Thames); United (Jersey).

MANSFIELD, Michael; QC 1989; *b* 12 Oct. 1941; *s* of Frank Le Voir Mansfield and Marjorie Mansfield; *m* 1965, Melian Mansfield (*née* Bordes) (marr. diss. 1992); three *s* two *d*; 2nd, 1992, Yvette Vanson; one *s. Educ:* Highgate Sch.; Keele Univ. (BA Hons). Called to the Bar, Gray's Inn, 1967. Estabd set of chambers of which head, 1984. Hon. LLD South Bank Univ., 1995. *Recreations:* my children's interests. *Address:* 14 Tooks Court, Cursitor Street, EC4Y 1JY. *T:* 0171–405 8828.

MANSFIELD, Sir Peter, Kt 1993; FRS 1987; Professor of Physics, University of Nottingham, 1979–94, now Professor Emeritus; *b* 9 Oct. 1933; *s* of late Rose Lilian Mansfield (*née* Turner) and late Sidney George Mansfield; *m* 1962, Jean Margaret Kibble; two *d. Educ:* William Penn Sch., Peckham; Queen Mary Coll., London (BSc 1959, PhD 1962; Fellow, 1985). Research Associate, Dept of Physics, Univ. of Illinois, 1962–64; Lectr, Univ. of Nottingham, 1964, Sen. Lectr, 1968, Reader, 1970–79; Sen. Visitor, Max Planck Inst. für Medizinische Forschung, Heidelberg, 1972–73. Society of Magnetic Resonance in Medicine: Gold Medal, 1983; President, 1987–88. Hon. Member: Soc. of Magnetic Resonance Imaging, 1994; British Inst. of Radiology, 1993; Hon. FRCR 1992. Sylvanus Thompson Lectr and Medal, 1988, Barclay Medal, 1993, British Inst. of Radiology; Gold Medal, Royal Soc. Wellcome Foundn, 1984; Duddell Medal and Prize, Inst. of Physics, 1988; Antoine Béclère Medal, Internat. Radiol Soc. and Antoine Béclère Inst., 1989; Mullard Medal and Award, Royal Soc., 1990; ISMAR Prize, 1992; Gold Medal, Eur. Assoc. of Radiol., 1995; Garmisch-Partenkirchen Prize for Magnetic Resonance Imaging, 1995. *Publications:* NMR Imaging in Biomedicine (with P. G. Morris), 1982; (ed with E. L. Hahn) NMR Imaging, 1991; papers in learned jls on nuclear magnetic resonance. *Recreations:* languages, reading, travel, flying (Private Pilot's Licence, Private Pilot's Licence for Helicopters). *Address:* Magnetic Resonance Centre, Department of Physics, University of Nottingham, Nottingham NG7 2RD. *T:* (office) Nottingham (0115) 951 4740.

MANSFIELD, Sir Philip (Robert Aked), KCMG 1984 (CMG 1973); HM Diplomatic Service, retired; Ambassador to the Netherlands, 1981–84; *b* 9 May 1926; *s* of Philip Theodore Mansfield, CSI, CIE and Helen Rosamond Aked; *m* 1953, Elinor Russell MacHatton; two *s. Educ:* Winchester; Pembroke Coll., Cambridge. Grenadier Guards, 1944–47. Sudan Political Service, 1950–55. Entered HM Diplomatic Service, 1955; served in: Addis Ababa, Singapore, Paris, Buenos Aires; Counsellor and Head of Rhodesia Dept, FCO, 1969–72; RCDS, 1973; Counsellor and Head of Chancery, 1974–75, Dep. High Comr, 1976, Nairobi; Asst Under Sec. of State, FCO, 1976–79; Ambassador and Dep. Perm. Representative to UN, 1979–81. Consultant to: Rank Xerox, 1987–; BPB Industries, 1987–. *Recreations:* reading, walking, tree planting, cooking. *Address:* Gill Mill, Stanton Harcourt, Witney, Oxfordshire OX8 1AN. *T:* Witney (01993) 702554. *Clubs:* Commonwealth Trust; Aberdare Country (Kenya).

MANSFIELD, Prof. Terence Arthur, FRS 1987; FIBiol; Professor of Plant Physiology, since 1977, and Director, Institute of Environmental and Biological Sciences, since 1988, University of Lancaster; *b* 18 Jan. 1937; *s* of Sydney Walter Mansfield and Rose (*née* Sinfield); *m* 1963, Margaret Mary James; two *s. Educ:* Univ. of Nottingham (BSc); Univ. of Reading (PhD). FIBiol 1984. Lectr, then Reader, Univ. of Lancaster, 1965–77. Mem., AFRC, 1989–93. *Publications:* Physiology of Stomata, 1968; Effects of Air Pollutants on Plants, 1976; Stomatal Physiology, 1981; Plant Adaption to Environmental Stress, 1993; many contribs to books and jls in plant physiology. *Recreations:* cricket, hill walking, classical music. *Address:* 25 Wallace Lane, Forton, Lancs PR3 0BA. *T:* Forton (01524) 791338.

MANSFIELD, Terence Gordon; Managing Director, National Magazine Co., since 1982; Chairman, COMAG, since 1984; Director, Hearst Corporation USA, since 1993; *b* 3 Nov. 1938; *s* of Archer James Mansfield and Elizabeth Mansfield; *m* 1965, Helen Leonora Russell; two *d. Educ:* Maynard Road Jun. Sch., Essex; SW Essex Technical Sch. MInstM 1969; MInstD 1976. D. H. Brocklesby, Advertising Agents, 1954; S. H. Benson, Advertising Agents, 1956; served RAF, Christmas Island, 1957–59; Conde Nast Publications, 1960–66; Queen Magazine, 1966; National Magazine Co.: Advertisement Man., Harpers and Queen, 1969; Publisher, Harpers and Queen, 1975; Dep. Man. Dir, National Magazine Co., 1980. Member: Advertising Assoc.; Marketing Soc. 1975–; British Fashion Council, 1988–; Action Res. for Crippled Child, 1989–; Adv. Bd for Victim Support, 1990–. Friend of Epping Forest. *Recreations:* family, running, windsurfing, walking dogs. *Address:* 5 Grosvenor Gardens Mews North, SW1W 0JP. *T:* 0171–730 7740. *Clubs:* Mark's, Harry's Bar, Solus.

MANSON, Ian Stuart; Chief Crown Prosecutor, West Midlands Area, Crown Prosecution Service, 1986–89; *b* 15 March 1929; *s* of late David Alexander Manson and Elsie May (*née* Newton); *m* 1957, Pamela Horrocks-Taylor; three *s. Educ:* Heath Grammar Sch., Halifax; Clare Coll., Cambridge (Open Exhibnr; BA Hons). Admitted Solicitor, 1956. Asst Prosecuting Solicitor, Bradford, 1956–57; Prosecuting Solicitor: Southampton, 1957–58; Portsmouth, 1958–60; Asst Prosecuting Solicitor, Birmingham, 1960–66; Prosecuting Solicitor, W Midlands Police Authority, 1966–74; Chief Prosecuting Solicitor, W Midlands CC, 1974–86. *Recreations:* reading, music, gardening.

MANT, Prof. (Arthur) Keith, MD; FRCP; FRCPath; Emeritus Professor of Forensic Medicine, University of London, since 1984; *b* 11 Sept. 1919; *s* of George Arthur Mant and Elsie Muriel (*née* Slark); *m* 1947, Heather Smith, BA; two *s* one *d. Educ:* Denstone Coll., Staffs; St Mary's Hosp., Paddington. MB BS 1949, MD 1950; MRCS, LRCP 1943; FRCPath 1967; MRCP 1977; FRCP 1982. Dept Obst. and Gynæc., St Mary's Hosp., 1943; RAMC, i/c Path. Section, War Crimes Gp, 1945–48 (Major); Registrar (ex-service), Med. Unit, St Mary's Hosp., 1948–49; Dept of Forensic Medicine, Guy's Hospital, Univ. of London: Research Fellow, 1949–55; Lectr, 1955–66; Reader in Forensic Med., 1966–74; Prof. of Forensic Med., 1974–84; Head of Dept, 1972–84. Sen. Lectr in Forensic Med., 1965, Hon. Consultant in Forensic Med., 1967–84, KCH. WHO Consultant, Sri Lanka, 1982, 1984 and 1987. Visiting Lectr in Med. Jurisprudence and Toxicology, St Mary's Hosp., 1955–84; British Council Lectr, India, 1979; Visiting Professor: Univ. of Jordan, 1985; Nihon Univ., Japan, 1985. Lectures: Niels Dungal Meml, Reykjavic, 1979; J. B. Firth Meml, London, 1981; W. D. L. Fernando Meml, Sri Lanka, 1982; Douglas Kerr Meml, London, 1985. Examiner in Forensic Medicine: NUI, 1960; St Andrews Univ., 1967; Dundee Univ., 1968; RCPath, 1971; Soc. of Apothecaries, 1971; Univ. of Riyadh, Saudi Arabia, 1976; Univ. of Garyounis-Libya, 1976; Univ. of Tripoli, 1979. A. D. Williams Distinguished Scholar Fellowship, Univ. Med. Coll. of Virginia, 1963 and 1968. President: Internat. Assoc. in Accident and Traffic Med., 1972–83 (now Pres. Emeritus); British Acad. of Forensic Sci., 1975–76; President: Forensic Sci. Soc., 1963–65; British Assoc. in Forensic Med., 1970–71; Vice-Pres., Medico-Legal Soc. Nat. correspondent for GB, Internat. Acad. of Legal and Social Med.; Mem., Amer. Acad. of Forensic Sci.; Corresp. For. Mem., Soc. de Méd. Légale; Hon. Member: Brazilian Assoc. for Traffic Med.; Soc. de Méd. Légale, Belgium. Member, Editorial Board: Internat. Reference Org. in Forensic Med. (INFORM), 1971–; Amer. Jl of Forensic Medicine and Pathology, 1980–; Hon. Editor, Jl of Traffic Medicine, 1989–; formerly English Editor, Zeitschrift für Rechtsmedizin; Internat. Editorial Bd, Excerpta Medica (Forensic Sci. abstracts). Fellow: Indian Acad. of Forensic Sci.; Indian Assoc. in Forensic Medicine; Swedish Soc. of Med. Scis. Hon. DMJ(Path) Soc. of Apothecaries, 1979. *Publications:* Forensic Medicine: observation and interpretation, 1960; Modern Trends in Forensic Medicine, Series 3, 1973; (ed) Taylor's Principles and Practice of Medical Jurisprudence, 13th edn, 1984; contribs to med. and sci. literature. *Recreations:* fishing, orchid culture. *Address:* 29 Ashley Drive, Walton-on-Thames, Surrey KT12 1JT. *T:* Walton-on-Thames (01932) 225005.

MANT, Keith; *see* Mant, A. K.

MANTEL, Hilary Mary, (Mrs G. McEwen); author; *b* 6 July 1952; *d* of Henry Thompson and Margaret Mary Thompson (*née* Foster, later Mrs Jack Mantel); *m* 1973, Gerald McEwen. *Educ:* London Sch. of Econs; Sheffield Univ. (BJur). FRSL 1990. Shiva Naipaul Meml Prize, 1987; Winifred Holtby Award, RSL, 1990; Southern Arts Literature Prize, 1990; Cheltenham Fest. Prize, 1990; Book of Year Award, Sunday Express, 1992. *Publications:* Every Day is Mother's Day, 1985; Vacant Possession, 1986; Eight Months on Ghazzah Street, 1988; Fludd, 1990; A Place of Greater Safety, 1992; A Change of Climate, 1994; An Experiment in Love, 1995. *Recreation:* sleeping. *Address:* A. M. Heath & Co., 79 St Martin's Lane, WC2N 4AA.

MANTELL, Hon. Sir Charles (Barrie Knight), Kt 1990; **Hon. Mr Justice Mantell;** Judge of the High Court of Justice, Queen's Bench Division, since 1990; Presiding Judge, Western Circuit, since 1993; *b* 30 Jan. 1937; *s* of Francis Christopher Knight Mantell and Elsie Mantell; *m* 1960, Anne Shirley Mantell; two *d. Educ:* Manchester Grammar Sch.; Manchester Univ. (LLM). Called to the Bar, Gray's Inn, 1960, Bencher, 1990. Flying Officer, RAF, 1958–61. In practice at Bar, London and Manchester, 1961–82; a Recorder of the Crown Court, 1978–82; QC 1979; Judge of Supreme Court, Hong Kong, 1982–85; a Circuit Judge, 1985–90. *Recreations:* reading, watching cricket. *Address:* Royal Courts of Justice, Strand, WC2A 2LL. *Clubs:* Lansdowne; Hong Kong (Hong Kong).

MANTHORP, Brian Robert, MA; FCollP; Principal, Sandal Public School, Faisalabad, since 1994; *b* 28 July 1934; *s* of Alan Roy Manthorp and Stella Manthorp; *m* 1955, Jennifer Mary Caradine; three *s* one *d. Educ:* Framlingham Coll.; Pembroke Coll., Oxford (MA Hons English); Westcott House, Cambridge. Instructor Lieut, RN, 1955–58. Ordained priest, Guildford, 1961. Assistant Master, Charterhouse, 1958–65; Head of English: Lawrence Coll., Pakistan, 1965–67; Aitchison Coll., Pakistan, 1968–70; Oakbank Sch., Keighley, 1970–73; Headmaster, Holy Trinity Senior Sch., Halifax, 1973–80; Headmaster, Worcester Coll. for the Blind, 1980–87; Principal, RNIB New Coll., Worcester, 1987–94. *Publication:* Fifty Poems for Pakistan, 1971. *Recreations:* sport, sketching. *Address:* The Principal's House, Sandal Public School, Faisalabad, Pakistan. *Club:* East India.

MANTHORPE, John Jeremy, CB 1994; Chief Executive, since 1985, and Chief Land Registrar, since 1990, HM Land Registry; *b* 16 June 1936; *s* of Margaret Dora Manthorpe; *m* 1967, Kathleen Mary Ryan; three *s* one *d. Educ:* Beckenham and Penge Grammar School. HM Land Registry: Plans Branch, 1952; Principal Survey and Plans Officer, 1974; Controller (Registration), 1981–85. CIMgt 1994; Hon. ARICS 1992. *Recreations:* walking and watching the Ashdown Forest. *Address:* Beurles, Fairwarp, Uckfield, East Sussex TN22 3BG. *T:* Nutley (01825) 712795.

MANTLE, Richard John; General Director, Opera North, since 1994; *b* 21 Jan. 1947; *s* of George William Mantle, OBE and Doris Griffiths; *m* 1970, Carol June Mountain. *Educ:* Tiffin Sch.; Ealing Coll. of Advanced Technology. Personnel Officer, Beecham Group, 1969–72; Associate Dir, J. Walter Thompson Co., 1973–79; Personnel Dir, then Dep. Man. Dir, ENO, 1980–85; Man. Dir, Scottish Opera, 1985–91; Gen. Dir, Edmonton Opera, Canada, 1991–94. *Recreations:* music, reading, the country, English churches.

Address: Home Farm House, The Harewood House Estate, Leeds LS17 9LF. *T:* Leeds (0113) 2886179.

MANTON, 3rd Baron, *cr* 1922, of Compton Verney; **Joseph Rupert Eric Robert Watson;** DL; Landowner and Farmer; *b* 22 Jan. 1924; *s* of 2nd Baron Manton and Alethea (*d* 1979), 2nd *d* of late Colonel Philip Langdale, OBE; *S* father, 1968; *m* 1951, Mary Elizabeth, twin *d* of Major T. D. Hallinan, Ashbourne, Glounthaune, Co. Cork; two *s* three *d* (of whom two *s* one *d* are triplets). *Educ:* Eton. Joined Army, 1942; commissioned Life Guards, 1943; Captain, 1946; retired, 1947; rejoined 7th (QO) Hussars, 1951–56. DL Humberside, 1980. *Recreations:* hunting, shooting, racing. *Heir: s* Major the Hon. Miles Ronald Marcus Watson, Life Guards [*b* 7 May 1958; *m* 1984, Elizabeth, *e d* of J. R. Story; two *s*]. *Address:* Houghton Hall, Sancton, York YO4 3RE. *T:* Market Weighton (01430) 873234. *Clubs:* White's, Jockey.

See also Baron Hesketh.

MANTON, Sir Edwin (Alfred Grenville), Kt 1994; Senior Adviser, American International Group Inc., since 1982; *b* 22 Jan. 1909; *s* of John H. Manton and Emily C. Manton (*née* Denton); *m* 1936, Florence V. Brewer; one *d*. *Educ:* Shaftesbury GS; Coll. of Insurance, NY. AIIA. With B. W. Noble, Paris, 1927–33; American International Underwriters Corp.: Casualty Underwriter, 1933–37; Sec., 1937–38; Vice-Pres., 1938–42; Pres., 1942–69; Chm., 1969–75. Hon. DHL Coll. of Insurance, NY. *Publications:* various papers in insurance press. *Recreations:* walking, art, formerly cricket and hockey. *Address:* 40 Fifth Avenue, New York, NY 10011-8843, USA *T:* (212) 4776097; American International Group, 70 Pine Street, New York, NY 10270, USA.

MANWARING, Randle (Gilbert), MA; FSS, FPMI; poet and author; retired company director; *b* 3 May 1912; *s* of late George Ernest and Lilian Manwaring; *m* 1941, Betty Violet, *d* of H. P. Rout, Norwich; three *s* one *d*. *Educ:* private schools. MA Keele, 1982. Joined Clerical, Medical and Gen. Life Assce Soc., 1929. War service, RAF, 1940–46, W/Cdr; comd RAF Regt in Burma, 1945. Clerical, Medical & Gen. Pensions Rep., 1950; joined C. E. Heath & Co. Ltd, 1956: Asst Dir, 1960, Dir, 1964, Man. Dir. 1969; Founder Dir (Man.), C. E. Heath Urquhart (Life and Pensions), 1966–71, and a Founder Dir, Excess Life Assce Co., 1967–75; Dir, Excess Insurance Group, 1975–78; Insurance Adviser, Midland Bank, 1971; first Man. Dir, Midland Bank Ins. Services, 1972–74, Vice-Chm., 1974–77, Dir, 1977–78. Chm., Life Soc., Corp. of Insce Brokers, 1965–66; Dep. Chm., Corp. of Insce Brokers, 1970–71; Pres., Soc. of Pensions Consultants, 1968–70. Chairman of Governors: Luckley-Oakfield Sch., 1972–83; Northease Manor Sch., 1972–84. Diocesan Reader (Chichester), 1968–; Mem., Diocesan Synod, 1985–; Lay Chm., Uckfield Deanery Synod, 1993–; Churchwarden, St Peter-upon-Cornhill, London, 1985–90. Chm., Vine Books Ltd; Dir, Crusaders Union Ltd, 1960–91 (Vice-Pres., 1983–). Chm. of Trustees, Careforce, 1980–87. Chm., Probus Club, Uckfield, 1989–90. *Publications:* The Heart of this People, 1954; A Christian Guide to Daily Work, 1963; Thornhill Guide to Insurance, 1976; The Run of the Downs, 1984; From Controversy to Co-existence, 1985; The Good Fight, 1990; A Study of Hymnwriting and Hymnsinging in the Christian Church, 1991; *poems:* Posies Once Mine, 1951; Satires and Salvation, 1960; Under the Magnolia Tree, 1965; Slave to No Sect, 1966; Crossroads of the Year, 1975; From the Four Winds, 1976; In a Time of Unbelief, 1977; Poem Prayers for Growing People, 1980; The Swifts of Maggiore, 1981; In a Time of Change, 1983; Collected Poems, 1986; Some Late Lark Singing, 1992; Love So Amazing, 1995; contrib. poems and articles to learned jls in GB and Canada. *Recreations:* music, reading, following cricket. *Address:* Marbles Barn, Newick, Lewes, East Sussex BN8 4LG. *T:* Newick (01825) 723845. *Clubs:* Royal Air Force, MCC; Sussex County Cricket.

MANZIE, Sir (Andrew) Gordon, KCB 1987 (CB 1983); Director, Trafalgar House Corporation Development, since 1991; *b* 3 April 1930; *s* of late John Mair and Catherine Manzie; *m* 1955, Rosalind Clay; one *s* one *d*. *Educ:* Royal High Sch. of Edinburgh; London Sch. of Economics and Political Science (BScEcon). Joined Civil Service as Clerical Officer, Scottish Home Dept, 1947. National Service, RAF, 1949. Min. of Supply: Exec. Officer (Higher Exec. Officer, 1957). Private Sec. to Perm. Sec., Min. of Aviation, 1962; Sen. Exec. Officer, 1963; Principal, 1964; Sec. to Cttee of Inquiry into Civil Air Transport (Edwards Cttee), 1967; Asst Sec., Dept of Trade and Industry, on loan to Min. of Posts and Telecommunications, 1971; Dept of Industry, 1974; Under-Sec., Dir, Office for Scotland, Depts of Trade and Industry, 1975; Under Sec., Scottish Economic Planning Dept, 1975–79; Dir, Industrial Develt Unit, 1980–81, Dep. Sec., 1980–84, Dept of Industry (Dept of Trade and Industry, 1983–84); Second Perm. Sec. and Chief Exec., PSA, DoE, 1984–90, retd. Chairman: Anglo Japanese Construction Ltd, 1990–95; Forthspan Ltd, 1993–; Thistle Water, 1995–; Director: Altnacraig Shipping, 1990–; Motherwell Bridge Hldgs, 1990–; Altnamara Shipping, 1994–; Trafalgar House Construction Hldgs, 1991–; Mem., Adv. Bd, LEK Partnership, 1992–. Trustee, Stort Trust, 1990–. CIMgt (CBIM 1987); Hon. FCIOB 1990. *Recreations:* golf, reading. *Club:* Caledonian.

MANZINI, Raimondo; Italian Ambassador to the Court of St James's, 1968–75; *b* Bologna, 25 Nov. 1913. *Educ:* Univ. of California (Berkeley); Clark Univ., Mass. (MA); Dr of Law, Bologna Univ. Entered Diplomatic Service, 1940; served San Francisco, 1940–41; Lisbon, 1941–43; Min. of Foreign Affairs in Brindisi, Salerno, Rome, 1943–44; London, 1944–47; Consul General for Congo, Nigeria and Gold Coast, 1947–50; Consul General, Baden Baden, 1951–52; Head of Information Service, CED, Paris, 1952–53; Ministry of Foreign Affairs, 1953–55; Adviser to the Minister of Foreign Trade, 1955–58; Chef de Cabinet of Minister for Foreign Affairs, 1958; Diplomatic Adviser to the Prime Minister, 1958–59; Advr to Minister of Industry, 1960–64; Perm. Rep. to OECD, Paris, 1965–68; Sec.-Gen., Min. of Foreign Affairs, 1975–78. Gran Croce, Ordine Merito Repubblica, 1968; Hon. GCVO 1969; Commandeur, Légion d'Honneur (France), 1976. *Address:* Villa Bellochio, 83 Boulevard de Garavan, Menton, France.

MAPLE, Graham John; District Judge, Principal Registry of Family Division, High Court of Justice, since 1991; *b* 18 Dec. 1947; *s* of Sydney George and Thelma Olive Maple; *m* 1974, Heather Anderson; two *s*. *Educ:* Shirley Secondary Modern Sch.; John Ruskin Grammar Sch., Croydon; Bedford Coll., London (LLB 1973). Lord Chancellor's Dept, 1968; Sec., Principal Registry of Family Div., 1989. Mem., Outer London, Court Service Cttee, 1991–. Church Warden, St Mildred Parish Church, Tenterden, 1992–. *Publications:* (Co-Editor) Rayden and Jackson on Divorce, 12th edn 1974, to 16th edn 1991; (Co-Editor) The Practitioner's Probate Manual, 21st edn 1979; (ed) Holloway's Probate Handbook, 8th edn 1987. *Recreations:* archaeology, Roman Britain, steam and model railways. *Address:* Principal Registry, Family Division, High Court of Justice, Somerset House, WC2R 1LP.

MAPLES, Ven. Jeffrey Stanley; Archdeacon of Swindon and Hon. Canon Diocesan, Bristol Cathedral, 1974–82, Archdeacon Emeritus, 1982; *b* 8 Aug. 1916; *o s* of Arthur Stanley and Henrietta Georgina Maples; *m* 1945, Isobel Eileen Mabel Wren; four *s* (and one *s* decd). *Educ:* Downing Coll., Cambridge; Chichester Theological Coll. Asst Curate St James, Milton, Portsmouth, 1940–46; Asst Curate, Watlington, Diocese of Oxford, 1946–48. Vicar of Swinderby, Dio. Lincoln, and Diocesan Youth Chaplain, 1948–50; Vicar of St Michael-on-the-Mount, Lincoln, and Director of Religious Education: for Lincoln Dio., 1950–56; for Salisbury Dio., 1956–63; Canon of Lincoln, 1954–56; Chancellor of Salisbury Cathedral, 1960–67; Director of the Bible Reading Fellowship, 1963–67; Proctor in Convocation for Salisbury Diocese, 1957–70; Canon Emeritus of Salisbury Cathedral, 1967–; Vicar of St James, Milton, Portsmouth, 1967–74; Rural Dean of Portsmouth, 1968–73; Hon. Canon, Portsmouth Cathedral, 1972–74. *Address:* Flat 1, 95 Crane Street, Salisbury, Wilts SP1 2PU. *T:* Salisbury (01722) 323848.

MAPLES, John Cradock; Chairman and Chief Executive, Saatchi & Saatchi Government Communications Worldwide, since 1992; *b* 22 April 1943; *s* of late Thomas Cradock Maples and Hazel Mary Maples; *m* 1986, Jane Corbin. *Educ:* Marlborough Coll., Wiltshire; Downing Coll., Cambridge; Harvard Business Sch., USA. MP (C) W Lewisham, 1983–92; contested (C) W Lewisham, 1992. PPS to Financial Sec. to HM Treasury, 1987–90; Econ. Sec. to HM Treasury, 1990–92; Jt Dep. Chm., Cons. Party, 1994–95. *Recreations:* sailing, ski-ing. *Address:* (office) 67–69 Whitfield Street, W1P 5RL.

MAPLES EARLE, Ven. E. E.; *see* Earle.

MAR, Countess of (*suo jure*, 31st in line from Ruadri, 1st Earl of Mar, 1115); Premier Earldom of Scotland by descent; Lady Garioch, *c* 1320; **Margaret of Mar;** *b* 19 Sept. 1940; *er d* of 30th Earl of Mar, and Millicent Mary Salton; *S* father, 1975; recognised in surname "of Mar" by warrant of Court of Lord Lyon, 1967, when she abandoned her second forename; *m* 1st, 1959, Edwin Noel Artiss (marr. diss. 1976); one *d*; 2nd, 1976, (cousin) John Salton (marr. diss. 1981); 3rd, 1982, J. H. Jenkin, MA (Cantab), FRCO, LRAM, ARCM. Lay Mem., Immigration Appeal Tribunal, 1985–. Patron: Dispensing Doctors' Assoc., 1985–; Gulf Veterans Assoc., 1995–; Worcs Mobile Disabled Gp, 1991–; Pres., Elderly Accommodation Counsel, 1994–. Governor, King's Sch., Gloucester, 1984–87. *Heir: d* Mistress of Mar, *qv*. *Address:* St Michael's Farm, Great Witley, Worcester WR6 6JB. *T:* Great Witley (01299) 896608.

MAR, Mistress of; Lady Susan Helen of Mar; interior designer; *b* 31 May 1963; *d* and *heiress* of Countess of Mar, *qv*; *m* 1989, Bruce Alexander Wyllie; two *d*. *Educ:* King Charles I School, Kidderminster; Christie College, Cheltenham. *Address:* Firethorn Farm Cottage, Plough Lane, Ewhurst Green, Cranleigh, Surrey GU6 7SG.

MAR, 14th Earl of *cr* 1565, **and KELLIE,** 16th Earl of *cr* 1619; **James Thorne Erskine;** Baron Erskine 1429; Viscount Fentoun 1606; Baron Dirleton 1603; Premier Viscount of Scotland; Hereditary Keeper of Stirling Castle; DL; *b* 10 March 1949; *s* of 13th Earl of Mar and 15th Earl of Kellie, and of Pansy Constance Erskine (The Dowager Countess of Mar and Kellie, OBE); *S* father, 1993; *m* 1974, Mrs Mary Mooney, *yr d* of Dougal McD. Kirk. *Educ:* Eton; Moray Coll. of Education, 1968–71; Inverness Coll. (building course, 1987–88). Page of Honour to the Queen, 1962, 1963. Community Service Volunteer, York, 1967–68; Community Worker, Richmond-Craigmillar Parish Church, Edinburgh, 1971–73; Sen. Social Worker, Family and Community Services, Sheffield District Council, 1973–76; Social Worker: Grampian Regional Council, Elgin, 1976–77, Forres, 1977–78; Highland Regional Council, Aviemore, 1979; HM Prison, Inverness, 1979–81; Invernessd, Aug.–Dec. 1981; Community Worker, Merkinch Centre, Inverness, Jan.–July 1982; Community Service Supervisor, Inverness, 1983–87; building technician, 1989–91; project worker, SACRO Intensive Probation Project, Falkirk, 1991–93; boatbuilder, 1993. Pilot Officer, RAuxAF, 1979, attached to 2622 Highland Sqdn, RAuxAF Regt; Flying Officer, RAuxAF, 1982–86; RNXS, 1985–89. DL Clackmannan, 1991. *Heir: b* Hon. Alexander David Erskine [*b* 26 Oct. 1952; *m* 1977, Katherine Shawford, *e d* of Thomas Clark Capel; one *s* one *d*]. *Recreations:* canoeing, hill walking, railways, gardening, cycling, restoration of Alloa Tower. *Address:* Erskine House, Kirk Wynd, Clackmannan FK 10 4JF. *T:* Alloa (01259) 212438. *Clubs:* Farmers'; New (Edinburgh).

MARA, Rt. Hon. Ratu Sir Kamisese Kapaiwai Tuimacilai, GCMG 1983; KBE 1969 (OBE 1961), PC 1973; Tui Nayau; Tui Lau; President of the Republic of Fiji, since 1994; Hereditary High Chief of the Lau Islands; *b* 13 May 1920; *s* of late Ratu Tevita Uluilakeba, Tui Nayau; *m* 1951, Adi Lady Lala Mara (Roko Tui Dreketi); two *s* five *d* (and one *s* decd). *Educ:* Fiji; Sacred Heart Coll., NZ; Otago Univ., NZ; Wadham Coll., Oxford (MA), Hon. Fellow, 1971; London Sch. of Economics (Dip. Econ. & Social Admin.), Hon. Fellow, 1985. Administrative Officer, Colonial Service, Fiji, Oct. 1950; Fijian MLC, 1953–89, and MEC, 1959–61 (elected MLC and MEC, 1959). Member for Natural Resources and Leader of Govt Business; Alliance Party, 1964–66 (Founder of Party); Chief Minister and Mem., Council of Ministers, Fiji, 1967; Prime Minister, Fiji, 1970–87, Republic of Fiji, 1987–92; Minister for Foreign Affairs and Civil Aviation, 1986–87. Hon. Dr of Laws: Univ. of Guam, 1969; Univ. of Papua New Guinea, 1982; Hon. LLD: Univ. of Otago, 1973; New Delhi, 1975; Hon. DPolSc Korea, 1978; Hon. Dr Tokai Univ., 1980; DU Univ. of South Pacific, 1980. Man of the Pacific Award, 1984. Grand Cross, Order of Lion, Senegal, 1975; Order of Diplomatic Service Merit, Korea, 1978. *Recreations:* athletics, cricket, Rugby football, golf, fishing. *Address:* Government House, Suva, Fiji; Villa 1429, Pacific Harbour, Deuba. *Clubs:* United Oxford & Cambridge University, Achilles (London); Defence (Suva, Fiji).

See also Ratu E. Nailatikau.

MARA, Prof. Timothy Nicholas; professional artist; Professor of Printmaking, Royal College of Art, since 1990; *b* 27 Sept. 1948; *s* of Timothy Anthony Mara and Angela Mara; *m* 1970, Belinda Julie Reeves; two *d*. *Educ:* St Joseph's Coll., London; Epsom and Ewell Sch. of Art; Wolverhampton Polytechnic (DipAD 1st Class Hons); Royal Coll. of Art (MA). Lectr in Fine Art, Nat. Coll. of Art and Design, Dublin, 1977; Lectr in Printmaking, Brighton Polytechnic, 1978; Principal Lectr in Printmaking, Chelsea Sch. of Art, 1980–90. Gallery Artist with Flowers East and founder mem., Wildman Corner Studio, London, 1989–; one-man exhibitions, 1976–: ICA; Project Arts Centre, Dublin; Thumb Gallery; David Hendriks Gallery, Dublin, Angela Flowers Gallery; Flowers East; numerous group exhibns, UK and overseas; work in collections: Tate Gallery; V&A; BBC; Brooklyn Museum; NY Public Library; UCLA; Arts Council; British Council; commercial bodies. *Publication:* Thames and Hudson Technical Manual of Screenprinting, 1978. *Recreations:* tennis, reading. *Address:* Royal College of Art, Kensington Gore, SW7 2EU. *T:* 0171–584 5020. *Club:* Chelsea Arts.

MARAJ, Prof. James Ajodhya; Executive Director, Tertiary Education Commission, Mauritius, since 1995; *b* 28 Sept. 1930; *s* of Ramgoolam Maraj and Popo Maraj; *m* 1951, Etress (*née* Ouditt); two *s* two *d*. *Educ:* St Mary's Coll. and Govt Teachers' Coll., Trinidad; Univ. of Birmingham (BA, PhD). FRICS 1981. Teacher, Lectr, 1947–60; Sen. Lectr, Univ. of West Indies, 1965–70; Head, Inst. of Educn, UWI, 1968–70; Dir, Educn Div., Commonwealth Secretariat, 1970–72; Commonwealth Asst Sec.-Gen., 1973–75; Vice-Chancellor, Univ. of S Pacific, 1975–82 (Hon. Prof. of Educn, 1978–); Sen. Evaluation Officer, The World Bank, 1982–84; High Comr for Fiji in Australia, Malaysia and Singapore, 1985–86; Perm. Sec., Prime Minister's Office, Min. of Foreign Affairs, and Civil Aviation, Fiji, 1986–88; High Comr to India, 1986–87; Pres. and Chief Exec. Officer, Commonwealth of Learning, 1989–95. External Examr, Educn Adviser and Consultant to several countries; Chm. or Sec. nat. or internat. commns. Hon. Prof., Univ. of Mauritius, 1991; Adjunct Professor: Univ. of Vic, Canada, 1990; Simon Fraser Univ.,

1991. Hon. DLitt: Loughborough, 1980; Andhra Pradesh Univ., 1990; Indira Gandhi Nat. Open Univ., 1994; Hon. LLD Hull, 1993; Sri Lanka Open Univ., 1993; DU Univ. of South Pacific, 1983. Gold Medal of Merit, Trinidad and Tobago, 1974; Pacific Person of the Year, Fiji Times, 1978; Dist. Scholar's Award, British Council, 1979. Chevalier de la Légion d'Honneur, France, 1982. *Publications:* miscellaneous research papers. *Recreations:* sport: cricket, squash, horse-racing; poetry, music. *Address:* Tertiary Education Commission, 41 Mère Barthelemy Street, Port Louis, Mauritius. *Clubs:* Athenæum, Commonwealth Trust, Royal Over-Seas League.

MARAN, Prof. Arnold George Dominic, MD; FRCS, FRCSE, FRCPE, FACS; Professor of Otolaryngology, University of Edinburgh, since 1988; *b* 16 June 1936; *s* of John and Hilda Maran; *m* 1962, Anna De Marco; one *s* one *d. Educ:* Daniel Stewart's Coll., Edinburgh; Univ. of Edinburgh (MB, ChB 1959; MD 1963); Univ. of Iowa. FRCSE 1962; FACS 1974; FRCPE 1989; FRCS 1991. Basic trng in surgery, Edinburgh, followed by specialty head and neck trng, Univ. of Iowa; consultant otolaryngologist, Dundee Royal Infirmary, 1967–73; Prof. of otolaryngology, W Virginia Univ., 1974–75; consultant otolaryngologist, Royal Infirmary of Edinburgh, 1975–88. Chm., Intercollegiate Bd in Otolaryngology, 1988–91; Sec., Conf. of Royal Colls, Scotland, 1992. Royal College of Surgeons of Edinburgh: Hon. Treasurer, 1976–81; Mem. Council, 1981–86; Hon. Sec., 1988–92. President: Scottish Otolaryngol Soc., 1991–92; Laryngology Section, RSM, 1990. Sixteen visiting professorships; fifteen eponymous lectures. Hon. FDSRCS. Hon. Member: S African Otolaryngol Soc., 1986; S African Head and Neck Soc., 1986; Irish Otolaryngol Soc., 1990 (Wilde Medal, 1990); Assoc. of Surgeons of India, 1991. Yearsley Medal, 1985, Semon Medal, 1990, London Univ.; Jobson Horne Prize, BMA, 1985; W. J. Harrison Prize, 1989, Howells Prize, 1991, RSM; Leon Goldman Medal, Univ. of Cape Town, 1994. *Publications:* Head and Neck Surgery, 1972, 3rd edn 1993; Clinical Otolaryngology, 1979; Clinical Rhinology, 1990; Head and Neck Surgery for the General Surgeon, 1991; (ed) Logan Turner's Diseases of Nose, Throat and Ear, 11th edn, 1992; contribs to 14 textbooks; 150 articles. *Recreations:* golf, classical music, playing jazz piano. *Address:* 15 Cluny Drive, Edinburgh EH10 6DW. *T:* 0131–447 8519; 2 Double Dykes Road, St Andrews KY16 9DX. *T:* St Andrews (01334) 72939. *Clubs:* New (Edinburgh); Royal and Ancient Golf (St Andrews); Bruntsfield Golfing Society (Edinburgh).

MARCEAU, Marcel; Officier de la Légion d'Honneur; Commandeur de l'Ordre National du Mérite; Commandeur des Arts et Lettres de la République Française; mime; Founder and Director, Compagnie de Mime Marcel Marceau, since 1949; Director, International School of Mime of Paris Marcel Marceau; *b* Strasbourg, 22 March 1923; *s* of Charles and Anne Mangel; two *s* two *d. Educ:* Ecole des Beaux Arts; Arts Décoratifs, Limoges; Ecole Etienne Decroux; Ecole Charles Dullin. First stage appearance, in Paris, 1946; with Barrault/Renaud Co., 1946–49; founded his company, 1949; since then has toured constantly, playing in 65 countries. Created about 100 pantomimes (most famous are The Creation of the World, The Cage, The Maskmaker, The Tree, Bip Liontamer, Bip hunts Butterfly, Bip plays David and Goliath, Bip at a Society Party, Bip in the Modern and Future Life, Bip Soldier, etc), and 26 mimodrames, and in particular the character 'Bip' (1947); *Mimodrames:* Bip et la fille des rues, 1947; Bip et L'Oiseau, 1948; Death Before Dawn, 1948; The Fair, 1949; The Flute Player, 1949; The Overcoat, 1951; Moriana and Galvan, Pierrot of Montmartre, 1952; Les Trois Perruques, 1953; Un Soir aux Funambules, 1953; La Parade en bleu et noir, 1956; le 14 juillet, 1956; Le Mont de Piété, 1956; Le Loup de Tsu Ku Mi, 1956; Le Petit Cirque, 1958; Les Matadors, 1959; Paris qui rit, Paris qui pleure, 1959; Don Juan, 1964; Candide, 1970, with Ballet de l'Opéra de Hambourg; *films:* The Overcoat, 1951; Barbarella, 1967; Scrooge (BBC London), 1973; Shanks, US, 1973; Silent Movie, 1976. Has made frequent TV appearances and many short films for TV, incl. Pantomimes, 1954, A Public Garden, 1955, Le mime Marcel Marceau, 1965, The World of Marcel Marceau, 1966, 12 short films with Enc. Brit., NY, 1974. Member: Acad. of Arts and Letters (DDR); Akad. der schönen Künste, Munich; Acad. des Beaux Arts, Paris. Emmy Awards (US), 1955, 1968. Hon. Dr, Univ. of Oregon; Dr *hc* Univ. of Princeton, 1981. Gold Medal of Czechoslovak Republic (for contribution to cultural relations). *Publications:* Les 7 Péchés Capitaux (lithographs); Les Rêveries de Bip (lithographs); La Ballade de Paris et du Monde (text, lithographs, water-colours, drawings in ink and pencil); Alphabet Book; Counting Book; L'Histoire de Bip (text and lithographs); The Third Eye (lithoprint); Pimporello. *Recreations:* painting, poetry, fencing. *Address:* Compagnie de Mime Marcel Marceau, 32 rue de Londres, 75009 Paris, France. *T:* 42804832, *Fax:* 48749187.

MARCH AND KINRARA, Earl of; Charles Henry Gordon-Lennox; *b* 8 Jan. 1955; *s* and *heir* of Duke of Richmond and Gordon, *qv; m* 1st, 1976, Sally (marr. diss. 1989), *d* of late Maurice Clayton and of Mrs Denis Irwin; one *d;* 2nd, 1991, Hon. Janet Elizabeth, *d* of 3rd Viscount Astor and of Bronwen, *d* of His Honour Sir (John) Alan Pugh; one *s. Educ:* Eton. *Heir: s* Lord Settrington, *qv. Address:* Goodwood House, Chichester, West Sussex PO18 0PY.

MARCH, Lionel John, ScD; Professor, Department of Design and Computation, University of California, Los Angeles, since 1994; *b* 26 Jan. 1934; *o s* of Leonard James March and Rose (*née* Edwards); *m* 1st, 1960, Lindsey Miller (marr. diss. 1984); one *s* two *d;* 2nd, 1984, Maureen Vidler; one step *s* two step *d. Educ:* Hove Grammar Sch. for Boys; Magdalene Coll., Cambridge (MA, ScD). FIMA, FRSA. Nat. Service: Sub-Lt, RNVR, 1953–55. Harkness Fellow, Commonwealth Fund, Harvard Univ. and MIT, 1962–64; Asst to Sir Leslie Martin, 1964–66; Lectr in Architecture, Univ. of Cambridge, 1966–69; Dir, Centre for Land Use and Built Form Studies, Univ. of Cambridge, 1969–73; Prof., Dept of Systems Design, Univ. of Waterloo, Ontario, 1974–76; Prof. of Design, Faculty of Technology, Open Univ., 1976–81; Rector and Vice-Provost, RCA, 1981–84; Prof., Grad. Sch. of Architecture and Urban Planning, 1984–94, Hd of Architecture/Urban Design Prog. 1984–91, UCLA. Chm., Applied Res. of Cambridge Ltd, 1969–73. Mem., Governing Body, Imperial Coll. of Science and Technology, 1981–84. General Editor (with Leslie Martin), Cambridge Urban and Architectural Studies, 1970–; Founding Editor, Environment and Planning B, Planning and Design, 1974–. *Publications:* (with Philip Steadman) The Geometry of Environment, 1971; (ed with Leslie Martin) Urban Space and Structures, 1972; (ed) The Architecture of Form, 1976; (ed with Judith Sheine) R. M. Schindler: composition and construction, 1993. *Address:* The How House, 2422 Silver Ridge Avenue, Silver Lake, Los Angeles, CA 90039, USA. *T:* (213) 6617907.

MARCH, Prof. Norman Henry; Coulson Professor of Theoretical Chemistry, University of Oxford, 1977–94; Fellow of University College, Oxford, 1977–94, Emeritus since 1994; *b* 9 July 1927; *s* of William and Elsie March; *m* 1949, Margaret Joan Hoyle (*d* 1994); two *s. Educ:* King's Coll., London Univ. University of Sheffield: Lecturer in Physics, 1953–57; Reader in Theoretical Physics, 1957–61; Prof. of Physics, 1961–72; Prof. of Theoretical Solid State Physics, Imperial Coll., Univ. of London, 1973–77. Hon. DTech Chalmers, Gothenburg, 1980. *Publications:* The Many-Body Problem in Quantum Mechanics (with W. H. Young and S. Sampanthar), 1967; Liquid Metals, 1968; (with W. Jones) Theoretical Solid State Physics, 1973; Self-Consistent Fields in Atoms, 1974; Orbital Theories of Molecules and Solids, 1974; (with M. P. Tosi) Atomic Dynamics in Liquids, 1976; (with M. Parrinello) Collective Effects in Solids and Liquids, 1983; (with S. Lundqvist) The Theory of the Inhomogeneous Electron Gas, 1983; (with M. P. Tosi) Coulomb Liquids, 1984; (with M. P. Tosi) Polymers, Liquid Crystals and Low-Dimensional Solids, 1984; (with R. A. Street and M. P. Tosi) Amorphous Solids and the Liquid State, 1985; Chemical Bonds outside Metal Surfaces, 1986; (with P. N. Butcher and M. P. Tosi) Crystalline Semiconducting Materials and Devices, 1986; (with B. M. Deb) The Single Particle Density in Physics and Chemistry, 1987; (with S. Lundqvist and M. P. Tosi) Order and Chaos in Nonlinear Physical Systems, 1988; (with J. A. Alonso) Electrons in Metals and Alloys, 1989; Liquid Metals, 1990; Chemical Physics of Liquids, 1990; Electron Density Theory of Atoms and Molecules, 1992; (with J. F. Mucci) Chemical Physics of Free Molecules, 1993; Electron Correlaton in Molecules and Condensed Phases, 1995; many scientific papers on quantum mechanics and statistical mechanics in Proceedings Royal Society, Phil. Magazine, Phys. Rev., Jl of Chem. Phys, etc. *Recreations:* music, chess, cricket. *Address:* Elmstead, 6 Northcroft Road, Englefield Green, Egham, Surrey TW20 0DU. *T:* Egham (01784) 433078.

MARCH, Valerie, (Mrs Andrew March); *see* Masterson, V.

MARCHAMLEY, 4th Baron *cr* 1908; **William Francis Whiteley;** *b* 27 July 1968; *o s* of 3rd Baron Marchamley and of Sonia Kathleen Pedrick; *S* father, 1994. *Heir:* none. *Address:* House of Lords, SW1A 0PW.

MARCHANT, Catherine; *see* Cookson, Dame C.

MARCHANT, Edgar Vernon; retired; *b* 7 Dec. 1915; *s* of E. C. Marchant; *m* 1945, Joyce Allen Storey; one *s* two *d. Educ:* Marlborough Coll.; Lincoln Coll., Oxford. Engr, Bahrain Petroleum Co., 1938; various technical and scientific posts in Min. of Aircraft Production, Min. of Supply and RAE, 1940–51; Principal, Min. of Supply, 1951; Principal, BoT, 1955; Asst Sec., BoT, 1959; Asst Registrar of Restrictive Trading Agreements, 1964; Asst Sec., Dept of Economic Affairs, 1966; Nat. Board for Prices and Incomes: Asst Sec., 1967–68; Under-Sec., 1968–71; Under-Sec., DTI, 1971–75. Dir, Paddington Building Soc., 1977–87. Mem., CS Appeal Bd, 1976–84. *Recreations:* gardening, messing about in boats. *Address:* 87 New Forest Drive, Brockenhurst, Hants SO42 7QT. *Clubs:* Royal Southampton Yacht; Cruising Association.

MARCHANT, Ven. George John Charles; Archdeacon Emeritus and Canon Emeritus of Durham, since 1983; *b* 3 Jan. 1916; *s* of late T. Marchant, Little Stanmore, Mddx; *m* 1944, Eileen Lillian Kathleen, *d* of late F. J. Smith, FCIS; one *s* three *d. Educ:* St John's Coll., Durham (MA, BD); Tyndale Hall, Bristol. Deacon 1939, priest 1940, London; Curate of St Andrew's, Whitehall Park, N19, 1939–41; Licence to officiate, London dio., 1941–44 (in charge of Young Churchmen's Movement); Curate of St Andrew-the-Less, Cambridge (in charge of St Stephen's), 1944–48; Vicar of Holy Trinity, Skirbeck, Boston, 1948–54; Vicar of St Nicholas, Durham, 1954–74; Rural Dean of Durham, 1964–74; Hon. Canon of Durham Cathedral, 1972–74; Archdeacon of Auckland and Canon Residentiary, Durham Cathedral, 1974–83. Pre-Retirement Advr, Dio. Norwich Clergy, 1990–. Member of General Synod, 1970–80 (Proctor in Convocation for Dio. Durham). Chm. Editorial Bd, Anvil, 1983–91. *Publications:* contributed to: Baker's Dictionary of Theology, 1960; Bishops in the Church, 1966; articles in Evangelical Qly, Churchman, and Anvil; book reviews. *Recreations:* reading, music, bird watching, gardening. *Address:* 28 Greenways, Eaton, Norwich NR4 6PE. *T:* Norwich (01603) 458295.

MARCHANT, Graham Leslie; General Manager, Contemporary Dance Trust, since 1994; *b* 2 Feb. 1945; *s* of late Leslie and of Dorothy Marchant. *Educ:* King's School, Worcester; Selwyn College, Cambridge (MA). Administrator, Actors' Company, 1973–75; General Manager, English Music Theatre, 1975–78; Gen. Administrator, Opera North, 1978–82; Administrator, Tricycle Theatre, 1983–84; Chief Exec., Riverside Studios, 1984; Managing Dir, Playhouse Theatre Co., 1985–86; Dir, Arts Co-ordination, Arts Council, 1986–89; Head of Site Improvement, South Bank Centre, 1989–92. Director: Ballet Rambert Ltd, 1991–93; Lyric Theatre (Hammersmith) Trust, 1993–; Northern Ballet Theatre, 1993–94. *Recreations:* reading, gardening, walking. *Address:* 43 Canonbury Square, N1 2AW.

MARCHWOOD, 3rd Viscount *cr* 1945, of Penang and of Marchwood, Southampton; **David George Staveley Penny;** Bt 1933; Baron 1937; Managing Director, Moët & Chandon (London) Ltd, since 1987; *b* 22 May 1936; *s* of 2nd Viscount Marchwood, MBE and Pamela (*d* 1979), *o d* of John Staveley Colton-Fox; *S* father, 1979; *m* 1964, Tessa Jane, *d* of W. F. Norris; three *s. Educ:* Winchester College. 2nd Lt, Royal Horse Guards (The Blues), 1955–57. Joined Schweppes Ltd, 1958, and held various positions in the Cadbury Schweppes group before joining his present company. *Recreations:* cricket, shooting, racing. *Heir: s* Hon. Peter George Worsley Penny, *b* 8 Oct. 1965. *Address:* Filberts, Aston Tirrold, near Didcot, Oxon OX11 9DG. *T:* Blewbury (01235) 850386. *Clubs:* White's, MCC.

MARCKUS, Melvyn; City Editor, The Times, since 1993; *b* 1 Jan. 1944; *s* of late Norman Myer Marckus and of Violet Frances Mary Marckus (*née* Hughes); *m* 1st, 1970, Rosemary Virden (marr. diss. 1985); one *s* one *d;* 2nd, 1987, Rachel Mary Frances, *d* of Lord King of Wartnaby, *qv. Educ:* Worthing Grammar Sch. Journalist: Scotsman, 1962–66; Daily Mail, 1966–67; Guardian, 1967; Daily Mail, 1967–70; Daily Express, 1970–72; Sunday Telegraph, 1972–82 (Jt Dep. City Editor, 1979–82); Observer, 1982–93: City Editor, 1982–93; Editor, Observer Business, 1984–93; an Asst Editor, 1987; Exec. Dir, 1987. *Recreations:* fishing, films, literature. *Club:* Wig and Pen.

MARCUS, Frank Ulrich; playwright; Television Critic for Plays International Magazine, since 1984; *b* Breslau, Germany, 30 June 1928; *s* of late Frederick and Gertie Marcus; *m* 1951, Jacqueline (*née* Sylvester) (*d* 1993); one *s* two *d. Educ:* Bunce Court Sch., Kent (evac. to Shropshire during war); St Martin's Sch. of Art, London. Actor, Dir, Scenic Designer, Unity Theatre, Kensington (later Internat. Theatre Gp). Theatre Critic, Sunday Telegraph, 1968–78. *Stage plays:* Minuet for Stuffed Birds, 1950; The Man Who Bought a Battlefield, 1963; The Formation Dancers, 1964; The Killing of Sister George, 1965 (3 'Best Play of the Year' Awards: Evening Standard, Plays and Players, Variety); Cleo, 1965; Studies of the Nude, 1967; Mrs Mouse, Are You Within?, 1968; The Window, 1969; Notes on a Love Affair, 1972; Blank Pages, 1972; Carol's Christmas, 1973; Beauty and the Beast, 1975; Portrait of the Artist (mime scenario), 1977; Blind Date, 1977; The Ballad of Wilfred the Second, 1978; The Merman of Orford (mime scenario), 1978; *television plays:* A Temporary Typist, 1966; The Glove Puppet, 1968; *radio plays:* The Hospital Visitor, 1980; The Beverley Brooch, 1981; The Row over La Ronde, 1982; *translations:* Schnitzler's Reigen, 1952 (as La Ronde, TV, 1982); Liebelei (TV), 1954; Anatol, 1976; Molnar's The Guardsman, 1978 (first perf., 1969); Kaiser's From Morning Till Midnight, 1979; Hauptmann's The Weavers, 1980. *Publications:* The Formation Dancers, 1964; The Killing of Sister George, 1965; The Window, 1968; Mrs Mouse, Are You Within?, 1969; Notes on a Love Affair, 1972; Blank Pages, 1973; Beauty and the Beast, 1977; Blind Date, 1977; *translations:* Molnar, The Guardsman, 1978; Hauptmann, The Weavers, 1980; Schnitzler, La Ronde, and Anatol, 1982; contribs to: Behind the Scenes, 1972; Those Germans, 1973; On Theater, 1974 (US), etc, also to London Magazine, Plays and Players, Dramatists' Quarterly (US), New York Times, etc. *Recreation:* observing. *Address:* 79 Griffiths Road,

SW19 1ST. *T:* 0181-542 4728; c/o Casarotto Ramsay Ltd, 60–66 Wardour Street, W1V 3HP.

MARCUS, Prof. Rudolph Arthur; Arthur Amos Noyes Professor of Chemistry, California Institute of Technology, since 1978; *b* Montreal, 21 July 1923; *s* of Meyer Marcus and Esther Marcus (*née* Cohen); *m* 1949, Laura Hearne; three *s. Educ:* McGill Univ. (BSc Chemistry 1943; PhD 1946; Hon. DSc 1988). Postdoctoral research: NRCC, Ottawa, 1946–49; Univ. of N Carolina, 1949–51; Polytechnic Institute, Brooklyn: Asst Prof., 1951–54; Associate Prof., 1954–58; Prof., 1958–64; Acting Head, Div. of Phys. Chem., 1961–62; Prof., 1964–78, Head, Div. of Phys. Chem., 1967–68, Univ. of Illinois. Mem., Sci. Cttees and Nat. Adv. Cttees, incl. External Adv. Bd, Nat. Sci. Foundn Center for Photoinduced Charge Transfer, 1990–; Internat. Advr in Chem., World Scientific Publishing, 1987; mem., numerous editl bds; Lectr, USA, Asia, Australia, Canada, Europe, Israel, USSR. Mem., Nat. Acad. of Sciences and other learned bodies; Foreign Member: Royal Soc., 1987; RSCan, 1993. Hon. MRSC; Hon. Mem., Internat. Soc. of Electrochemistry. Prizes incl. Wolf Prize in Chem., 1985; Nat. Medal of Science, 1989; Nobel Prize in Chem., 1992. *Publications:* contribs to sci jls, incl. articles on electrochemistry, electron transfer, unimolecular reactions. *Recreations:* tennis, ski-ing, music. *Address:* Noyes Laboratory of Chemical Physics, Caltech 127–72, Pasadena, CA 91125, USA. *T:* (818) 3956566; 331 S Hill Avenue, Pasadena, CA 91106–3405, USA.

MARDELL, Peggy Joyce, CBE 1982; Regional Nursing Officer, North West Thames Regional Health Authority, 1974–82; *b* 8 July 1927; *d* of Alfred Edward and Edith Mary Mardell. *Educ:* George Spicer Sch., Enfield; Highlands Hosp., London (RFN); E Suffolk Hosp., Ipswich (Medallist, SRN); Queen Charlotte's Hosp. Battersea Coll. of Further Educn (Hons Dip., RNT). Queens Inst. of District Nursing, Guildford, 1951–52 (SCM); Ward Sister, Night Sister, Bethnal Green Hosp., 1953–55; Sister Tutor, Royal Surrey County Hosp., 1957–64; Asst Regional Nursing Officer, NE Metrop. Regional Hosp. Bd, 1964–70; Chief Regional Nursing Officer, NW Metrop. Regional Hosp. Bd, 1970–74. Lectr, British Red Cross, 1958–60; Examr, Gen. Nursing Council, 1962–70; Nurse Mem., Surrey AHA, 1977–82; Member: Royal Coll. of Nursing; Regional Nurse Trng Cttee, 1970–82; Assessor for Nat. Nursing Staff Cttee, 1970–82. *Recreations:* renovating old furniture, gardening, reading. *Address:* 3 Corvill Court, Shelley Road, Worthing, W Sussex BN11 4DF. *T:* Worthing (01903) 211876.

MARDEN, John Louis, CBE 1976; JP; Former Chairman, Wheelock, Marden and Co. Ltd; *b* Woodford, Essex, 12 Feb. 1919; *s* of late George Ernest Marden; *m* 1947, Anne Harris; one *s* three *d. Educ:* Gresham Sch., Norfolk; Trinity Hall, Cambridge (MA). Served War, as Captain 4th Regt RHA, in N Africa, France and Germany, 1940–46. Joined Wheelock, Marden & Co. Ltd, as trainee (secretarial and shipping, then insurance side of business), 1946; Dir of company, 1952, Chm., 1959. Chm., Hong Kong Shipowners' Assoc., 1978–79. JP Hong Kong, 1964. *Recreations:* solely sedentary and cerebral. *Address:* 14 Shek O, Hong Kong.

MARDER, Bernard Arthur; QC 1977; **His Honour Judge Marder;** a Circuit Judge, since 1983; President of the Lands Tribunal, since 1993 (Member, since 1989); *b* 25 Sept. 1928; *er s* of late Samuel and Marie Marder; *m* 1953, Sylvia Levy (MBE 1988); one *s* one *d. Educ:* Bury Grammar Sch.; Manchester Univ. (LLB 1951). Called to the Bar, Gray's Inn, 1952. A Recorder of the Crown Court, 1979–83. Formerly Asst Comr, Local Govt and Parly Boundary Commns; Chairman: Panel of Inquiry into W Yorks Structure Plan, 1979; Mental Health Review Tribunals, 1987–89. Mem. Bd, Orange Tree Theatre, 1986–; Chm. of Trustees, Richmond Parish Lands Charity, 1993– (Trustee, 1987–). Hon. FSVA 1994. *Recreations:* music, theatre, wine, walking. *Address:* Lands Tribunal, 48/49 Chancery Lane, WC2A 1JR.

MAREK, John, PhD; MP (Lab) Wrexham, since 1983; *b* 24 Dec. 1940; *m* 1964, Anne. *Educ:* Univ. of London (BSc (Hons), PhD). Lecturer in Applied Mathematics, University College of Wales, Aberystwyth, 1966–83. Opposition frontbench spokesman: on health, 1985–87; on treasury and economic affairs, and on the Civil Service, 1987–92. *Publications:* various research papers. *Address:* House of Commons, SW1A 0AA. *T:* 0171–219 4149.

MARGADALE, 1st Baron, *cr* 1964, of Islay, Co. Argyll; **John Granville Morrison,** TD; JP; DL; Lord-Lieutenant of Wiltshire, 1969–81; Member Royal Company of Archers (Queen's Body Guard for Scotland); *b* 16 Dec. 1906; *s* of late Hugh Morrison; *m* 1928, Hon. Margaret Esther Lucie Smith (*d* 1980), 2nd *d* of 2nd Viscount Hambleden; three *s* one *d. Educ:* Eton; Magdalene Coll., Cambridge. Served 1939–45 with Royal Wilts Yeomanry; in MEF, 1939–42. MP (C) Salisbury Division of Wilts, 1942–64; Chairman, Conservative Members' (1922) Cttee, 1955–64. Yeomanry Comdt and Chm., Yeomanry Assoc., 1965–71; Hon. Col, The Royal Wiltshire Yeomanry Sqdn, 1965–71; Hon. Col, The Royal Yeomanry, 1965–71; Dep. Hon. Col, The Wessex Yeomanry, 1971–. JP 1936, High Sheriff, 1938, DL 1950, Wilts. MFH S and W Wilts Foxhounds, 1932–65. KStJ 1972. *Heir: s* Hon. James Ian Morrison, *qv. Address:* Fonthill House, Tisbury, Salisbury, Wilts SP3 5SA. *T:* Tisbury (01747) 870202; Eallabus, Bridgend, Islay, Argyll PA44 7NZ. *T:* Bowmore (01496) 810223. *Clubs:* Turf, Jockey, White's.

See also Hon. Sir C. A. Morrison, Hon. M. A. Morrison.

MARGÁIN, Hugo B.; GCVO; Ambassador of Mexico to the United States, 1965–70 and 1977–82; *b* 13 Feb. 1913; *s* of Cesar R. Margáin and Maria Teresa Gleason de Margáin; *m* 1941, Margarita Charles de Margáin; two *s* three *d* (and one *s* decd). *Educ:* National Univ. of Mexico (UNAM); National Sch. of Jurisprudence (LLB). Prof. of Constitutional Law, 1947, of Constitutional Writs, 1951–56, and of Fiscal Law, 1952–56, Univ. of Mexico. Govt posts include: Dir-Gen., Mercantile Transactions Tax, 1951–52, and Dir-Gen., Income Tax, 1952–59, Min. for Finance. Official Mayor, Min. for Industry and Commerce, 1959–61; Dep. Minister of Finance, Sept. 1961–Dec. 1964; Sec. of Finance, Aug. 1970–May 1973; Ambassador to the UK, 1973–77. Chm., Nat. Commn on Corporate Profit-Sharing (ie labour participation), 1963–64; Govt Rep. on Bd of Nat. Inst. for Scientific Res., 1962–63 (Chm. of Bd, 1963–64). Holds hon. degrees from univs in USA. Hon. GCVO 1975. *Publications:* Avoidance of Double Taxation Based on the Theory of the Source of Taxable Income, 1956; Preliminary Study on Tax Codification, 1957; (with H. L. Gumpel) Taxation in Mexico, 1957; Civil Rights and the Writ of Amparo in Administrative Law, 1958; The Role of Fiscal Law in Economic Development, 1960; Profit Sharing Plan, 1964; Housing Projects for Workers (Infonavit), 1971. *Recreations:* riding, swimming. *Address:* Fujiyama No 745, Col. Las Aguilas, Del. Alvaro Obregón, México 01710 DF, México.

MARGASON, Geoffrey, CEng, FICE; Director, Transport and Road Research Laboratory, Crowthorne, 1984–88, retired (Deputy Director, 1980–84); *b* 19 Sept. 1933; *s* of Henry and Edna Margason; *m* 1958, Bernice Thompson; one *s* two *d. Educ:* Humberston Foundation Sch., Cleethorpes; Loughborough College of Advanced Technology (DLCEng). With British Transport Commission and Mouchel Associates, Consulting Engineers, until 1960; Transport and Road Research Laboratory: Researcher in Geotechnics, 1960–69; Research Manager in Construction Planning, Scottish Br. and Transport Planning, 1969–75; Sen. Research Manager in Transport Operations, 1975–78; Head of Research and Science Policy Unit, Depts of Environment and Transport, 1978–80. *Publications:* papers in jls of various professional instns and to nat. and internat. confs on range of topics in highway transportation; reports of TRRL. *Recreations:* pétanque, golf. *Address:* Franche Cottage, Pankridge Street, Crondall, Farnham, Surrey GU10 5QZ. *T:* Aldershot (01252) 850399. *Club:* Crondall Pétanque.

MARGERISON, Thomas Alan; author, journalist and broadcaster on scientific subjects; Consultant, British Nuclear Forum, since 1989; *b* 13 Nov. 1923; *s* of late Ernest Alan Margerison and Isabel McKenzie; *m* 1950, Pamela Alice Tilbrook; two *s. Educ:* Huntingdon Grammar Sch.; Hymers Coll., Hull; King's Sch., Macclesfield; Sheffield University. Research Physicist, 1949; film script writer, Film Producers Guild, 1950; Scientific Editor, Butterworths sci. pubns, Ed. Research, 1951–56; Man. Editor, Heywood Pubns and National Trade Press, 1956. First Scientific Editor, The New Scientist, 1956–61; Science Corresp., Sunday Times, 1961; Dep. Editor, Sunday Times Magazine, 1962; Man. Dir, Thomson Technical Developments Ltd, 1964; Dep. Man. Dir, 1967–69, Chief Exec., 1969–71, London Weekend Television; Dir, 1966, Chm., 1971–75, Computer Technology Ltd. Formerly Dir, Nuclear Electricity Information Gp. Chm., Communications Cttee, UK Nat. Commn for UNESCO. Worked for many years with Tonight team on BBC. Responsible for applying computers to evening newspapers in Reading and Hemel Hempstead. *Publications:* articles and television scripts, indifferent scientific papers; (ed) popular science books. *Recreation:* sailing. *Club:* Savile.

MARGESSON, family name of **Viscount Margesson.**

MARGESSON, 2nd Viscount *cr* 1942, of Rugby; **Francis Vere Hampden Margesson;** *b* 17 April 1922; *o s* of 1st Viscount Margesson, PC, MC, and Frances H. Leggett (*d* 1977), New York; *S* father, 1965; *m* 1958, Helena, *d* of late Heikki Backstrom, Finland; one *s* three *d. Educ:* Eton; Trinity Coll., Oxford. Served War of 1939–45, as Sub-Lt, RNVR. A Director of Thames & Hudson Publications, Inc., New York, 1949–53. ADC to Governor of the Bahamas, 1956; Information Officer, British Consulate-General, NY, 1964–70. *Heir: s* Major the Hon. Richard Francis David Margesson, Coldstream Guards [*b* 25 Dec. 1960; *m* 1990, Wendy Maree, *d* of James Hazelton]. *Address:* Ridgely Manor, Box 245, Stone Ridge, New York, NY 12484, USA.

MARGETSON, Sir John (William Denys), KCMG 1986 (CMG 1979); HM Diplomatic Service, retired; Special Representative of the Secretary of State for Foreign and Commonwealth Affairs, since 1994; Gentleman Usher of the Blue Rod, Order of St Michael and St George, since 1992; *b* 9 Oct. 1927; *yr s* of Very Rev. W. J. Margetson and Marion Jenoure; *m* 1963, Miranda, *d* of Sir William Menzies Coldstream, CBE and Mrs Nancy Spender; one *s* one *d. Educ:* Blundell's; St John's Coll., Cambridge (choral scholar; MA). Lieut, Life Guards, 1947–49. Colonial Service, District Officer, Tanganyika, 1951–60 (Private Sec. to Governor, Sir Edward Twining, subseq. Lord Twining, 1956–57); entered Foreign (subseq. Diplomatic) Service, 1960; The Hague, 1962–64; speech writer to Foreign Sec., Rt Hon. George Brown, MP, 1966–68; Head of Chancery, Saigon, 1968–70; Counsellor 1971, seconded to Cabinet Secretariat, 1971–74; Head of Chancery, UK Delegn to NATO, 1974–78; Ambassador to Vietnam, 1978–80; seconded to MoD as Senior Civilian Instructor, RCDS, 1981–82; Ambassador and Dep. Perm. Rep. to UN, NY, and Pres., UN Trusteeship Council, 1983–84; Ambassador to the Netherlands, 1984–87. Dir, John S. Cohen Foundn, 1988–93. Chm., Foster Parents Plan (UK), 1988–90. Patron, Suffolk Internat. Trade Gp, 1988–90; Jt Pres., Suffolk and SE Cambridgeshire 1992 Club, 1988–90. Chairman: RSCM, 1988–94; Jt Cttee, London Royal Schs of Music, 1991–94; Yehudi Menuhin Sch., 1990–94; Trustee: Fitzwilliam Museum Trust, 1990–; Ouseley Trust, 1991–; Music in Country Churches, 1993–. Hon. RCM 1992; FRSCM 1994. *Recreation:* music. *Club:* Brooks's.

MARGOLYES, Miriam; actress; *b* 18 May 1941; *d* of late Dr Joseph Margolyes and Ruth (*née* Walters). *Educ:* Oxford High Sch.; Newnham Coll., Cambridge; Guildhall Sch. of Music and Drama (LGSM 1959). *Films* include: Yentl, 1979; Little Shop of Horrors, 1985; The Good Father, 1985; Little Dorrit, 1986; I Love You to Death, 1989; The Age of Innocence, 1993; *theatre* includes: Dickens' Women (one-woman show), Players, 1991; She Stoops to Conquer, Queen's, 1993; *television* includes: Blackadder, 1983; Poor Little Rich Girl, 1984; Oliver Twist, 1985; The Life and Loves of a She Devil, 1986; *radio performances* include The Queen and I, 1993. Best Supporting Actress, LA Critics Circle, 1989; Best Supporting Actress, BAFTA, 1993. *Recreations:* reading, talking, eating, Italy. *Address:* c/o J. Altaras, 27 Floral Street, WC2E 9DP. *Fax:* 0171–627 2663.

MARGRIE, Victor Robert, CBE 1984; FCSD; studio potter; *b* 29 Dec. 1929; *s* of Robert and Emily Miriam Margrie; *m* 1955, Janet Smithers (separated); three *d. Educ:* Southgate County Grammar Sch.; Hornsey Sch. of Art (NDD, ATD 1952). FSIAD 1975. Part-time teaching at various London art colls, 1952–56; own workshop, making stoneware and latterly porcelain, 1954–71; Head of Ceramics Dept, Harrow Sch. of Art, 1956–71 (founded Studio Pottery Course, 1963); Sec., Crafts Adv. Cttee, 1971–77; Dir, Crafts Council, 1977–84; Professorial appt, RCA, 1984–85; own studio, Bristol, 1985. One-man exhibns, British Craft Centre (formerly Crafts Centre of GB), 1964, 1966 and 1968; represented in V&A Museum and other collections. Vice-Chm., Crafts Centre of GB, 1965; Member: Cttee for Art and Design, DATEC, 1979–84; Cttee for Art and Design, CNAA, 1981–84; Design Bursaries Bd, RSA, 1980–84; Working Party, Gulbenkian Craft Initiative, 1985–88; Fine Art Adv. Cttee, British Council, 1983–86; UK National Commn for UNESCO, 1984–85 (also Mem., Culture Adv. Cttee); Adv. Council, V&A Mus., 1979–84; Craftsmen Potters Assoc., 1960–89; Internat. Acad. of Ceramics, 1972–; Cttee, Nat. Video and Electronic Archive of the Crafts, 1993–. Ext. Examiner, Royal Coll. of Art: Dept of Ceramics and Glass, 1977; Dept of Silversmithing and Jewellery, 1978–80; Ext. Advisor, Dept of Ceramics, UWE (formerly Bristol Polytechnic), 1987–; Mem., Bd of Studies in Fine Art, Univ. of London, 1989–94; Advr, Faculty of Fine Art, Cardiff Inst. of Higher Educn, 1992–94, Vis. Prof., Univ. of Westminster (formerly Poly. of Central London), 1992–. Governor: Herts Coll. of Art and Design, 1977–79; Camberwell Sch. of Art and Crafts, 1975–84; W Surrey Coll. of Art and Design, 1978–87; Loughborough Coll. of Art and Design, 1984–89, 1990–93. Associate Editor, Studio Pottery, 1993–. *Publications:* contributed to: Oxford Dictionary of Decorative Arts, 1975; Europaischt Keramik Seit 1950, 1979; Lucie Rie, 1981; contrib. specialist pubns and museum catalogues. *Address:* Bowlders, Doccombe, Moretonhampstead, Devon TQ13 8SS. *T:* Moretonhampstead (01647) 40264.

MARÍN-GONZALEZ, Manuel; Grand Cross of Isabel la Católica; a Vice President, European Commission (formerly Commission of the European Communities), since 1986; *b* 21 Oct. 1949; *m*; *c. Educ:* Univ. of Madrid; Centre d'études européennes, Univ. of Nancy; Collège d'Europe, Bruges. MP for Ciudad Real, La Mancha, 1977–82; Sec. of State for relations with EEC, 1982–85. Mem., Spanish Socialist Party, 1974–. *Address:* c/o 200 rue de la Loi, 1049 Brussels, Belgium.

MARIO, Dr Ernest; Co-Chairman, and Chief Executive, Alza Corporation, Palo Alto, since 1993; *b* 12 June 1938; *s* of Jerry and Edith Mario; *m* 1961, Mildred Martha Daume; three *s. Educ:* Rutgers College of Pharmacy, New Brunswick, NJ (BSc Pharmacy); Univ. of Rhode Island (MS; PhD). Vice Pres., Manufacturing Operation, Smith Kline, 1974; E. R. Squibb & Sons: Vice Pres., Manufacturing for US Pharmaceutical Div., 1977; Vice

Pres. and Gen. Man., Chemical Div., 1979; Pres., Chemical Engrg Div. and Sen. Vice Pres. of company, 1981; Pres. and Chief Exec. Officer, Squibb Medical Product, 1983; elected to Bd, 1984; joined Glaxo Inc. as Pres. and Chief Exec. Officer, 1986; apptd to Bd of Glaxo Holdings, 1988; Chief Exec., 1989–93; Dep. Chm., 1991–93. Chairman: Nat. Foundn for Infectious Diseases, Washington, 1989; American Foundn for Pharmaceutical Educn, NY, 1991–. *Recreations:* golf, swimming. *Address:* Alza, 950 Page Mill Road, PO Box 10950, Palo Alto, CA 94303–0802, USA.

MARJORIBANKS, Sir James Alexander Milne, KCMG 1965 (CMG 1954); Chairman, Scotland in Europe, 1979–90; *b* 29 May 1911; *y s* of Rev. Thomas Marjoribanks of that Ilk, DD, and Mary Ord, *d* of William Logan, Madras CS; *m* 1936, Sonya Patricia (*d* 1981), *d* of David Stanley-Alder, Alderford Grange, Sible Hedingham, Essex, and Sylvia Marie Stanley; one *d*. *Educ:* Merchiston; Edinburgh Academy; Edinburgh Univ. (MA, 1st class hons). Entered Foreign Service, Nov. 1934; HM Embassy, Peking, 1935–38; Consulate-General, Hankow, 1938; Marseilles, 1939–40; Consul, Jacksonville, 1940–42; Vice-Consul, New York, 1942–44; Asst to UK Political Rep., Bucharest, 1944–45; Foreign Office, 1945–49; Dep. to Secretary of State for Foreign Affairs in Austrian Treaty negotiations, 1947–49; Official Secretary, UK High Commn, Canberra, 1950–52; Dep. Head of UK Delegation to High Authority of European Coal and Steel Community, 1952–55; Cabinet Office, 1955–57; HM Minister (Economic), Bonn, 1957–62; Asst Under-Secretary of State, Foreign Office, 1962–65; Ambassador and Head of UK Delegn to European Economic Community, European Atomic Energy Community and ECSC, 1965–71. Director: Scottish Council (Develt and Industry), 1971–81 (Vice-Pres., 1981–83); The Distillers Co. Ltd, 1971–76; Governing Mem., Inveresk Research International, 1978–90. Gen. Council Assessor, Edinburgh Univ. Ct, 1975–79. *Recreations:* hill walking, croquet. *Address:* 13 Regent Terrace, Edinburgh EH7 5BN; Lintonrig, Kirk Yetholm, Roxburghshire TD5 8PH. *Club:* New (Edinburgh).

MARJORIBANKS, Kevin McLeod, PhD; FSS; FASSA; FACE; Vice-Chancellor, University of Adelaide, 1987–93; *b* 25 July 1940; *s* of Hugh and Irene Marjoribanks; *m* 1962, Janice Humphreys; one *s* one *d*. *Educ:* Universities of: New South Wales (BSc); New England (BA); Harvard (MA); Toronto (PhD). FSS 1977; FASSA 1982; FACE 1983. Asst Prof., Univ. of Toronto, 1969; Lectr, Univ. of Oxford, 1970–74; University of Adelaide: Prof. of Educn, 1975–86; Pro Vice-Chancellor, 1986. Visiting Professor: Stanford Univ., 1979; Haifa Univ., 1983. *Publications:* Environments for Learning, 1974; Families and their Learning Environments, 1979; Ethnic Families and Children's Achievements, 1980; The Foundations of Children's Learning, 1989; Families, Schools and Learning: a study of children's learning environments, 1993. *Recreations:* writing, music listening, walking. *Address:* 81 Molesworth Street, North Adelaide, SA 5006, Australia. *Clubs:* Adelaide; Harvard of Australia.

MARK, James, MBE 1943; Under-Secretary, Ministry of Overseas Development, 1965–74, retired; *b* 12 June 1914; *s* of late John Mark and Louisa Mary (*née* Hobson); *m* 1941, Mary Trewent Rowland; three *s* two *d*. *Educ:* William Hulme's Grammar Sch., Manchester; Trinity Coll., Cambridge; Universities of Munich and Münster. MA 1939. PhD 1939, Cambridge. Intelligence Corps, 1940–46. Principal, Control Office for Germany and Austria, 1946–48; HM Treasury, 1948–64; Asst Secretary, 1950; Economic Counsellor, Washington, 1951–53. Jt Editor, Theology, 1976–83. *Publications:* The Question of Christian Stewardship, 1964; articles and reviews on theological and related subjects. *Recreations:* reading, music, theatre. *Address:* 16 South Row, SE3 0RY. *T:* 0181–852 9289.
See also Sir Robert Mark.

MARK, Sir Robert, GBE 1977; Kt 1973; QPM 1965; Commissioner, Metropolitan Police, 1972–77 (Deputy Commissioner, 1968–72); *b* Manchester, 13 March 1917; *y s* of late John Mark and Louisa Mark (*née* Hobson); *m* 1941, Kathleen Mary Leahy; one *s* one *d*. *Educ:* William Hulme's Grammar Sch., Manchester. Constable to Chief Superintendent, Manchester City Police, 1937–42, 1947–56; Chief Constable of Leicester, 1957–67; Assistant Commissioner, Metropolitan Police, 1967–68. Vis. Fellow, Nuffield Coll., Oxford, 1970–78 (MA Oxon 1971). Member: Standing Advisory Council of Penal System, 1966; Adv. Cttee on Police in Northern Ireland, 1969; Assessor to Lord Mountbatten during his Inquiry into Prison Security, 1966. Royal Armoured Corps, 1942–47: Lieut, Phantom (GHQ Liaison Regt), North-West Europe, 1944–45; Major, Control Commission for Germany, 1945–47. Lecture tour of N America for World Affairs Council and FCO, Oct. 1971; Edwin Stevens Lecture to the Laity, RCM, 1972; Dimbleby Meml Lecture (BBC TV), 1973. Director: Phoenix Assurance Co. Ltd, 1977–85; Control Risks Ltd, 1982–87. Mem. Cttee, AA, 1977–87; Governor and Mem. Admin. Bd, Corps of Commissionaires, 1977–86; Hon. Freeman, City of Westminster, 1977. Hon. LLM Leicester Univ., 1967; Hon. DLitt Loughborough, 1976; Hon. LLD: Manchester, 1978; Liverpool, 1978. KStJ 1977. *Publications:* Policing a Perplexed Society, 1977; In the Office of Constable, 1978. *Address:* Esher, Surrey KT10 8LU.
See also James Mark.

MARKESINIS, Prof. Basil Spyridonos, PhD, LLD, DCL; Professor of European Law, University of Oxford, and Founder Director, Centre for Advanced Study of European and Comparative Law, since 1995; Fellow, Lady Margaret Hall, Oxford, since 1995; Professor of Anglo-American Private Law, University of Leiden, since 1986; *b* 10 July 1944; *s* of Spyros B. Markesinis (former Prime Minister of Greece) and Ieta Markesinis; *m* 1970, Eugenie (*née* Trypanis); one *s* one *d*. *Educ:* Univ. of Athens (LLB, DIur); MA, PhD, LLD Cambridge; DCL Oxford. Asst Prof., Law Faculty, Univ. of Athens, 1965–68; Gulbenkian Res. Fellow, Churchill Coll., Cambridge, 1970–74; called to the Bar, Gray's Inn, 1973, Bencher, 1991; Fellow of Trinity Coll., Cambridge, and Univ. Lectr in Law, 1975–86; Denning Prof. of Comparative Law, Univ. of London, at QMC, subseq. QMW, 1986–93; Dep. Dir, Centre for Commercial Law Studies, Univ. of London, 1986–93; Prof. of Eur. Private Law, UCL, 1993–95. Founder and Dir, Leiden Inst. of Anglo-American Law, 1987–. Advocate to Greek Supreme Court, 1976–86. Visiting Professor: Univs of Paris I and II; Siena; Rome; Cornell; Michigan (Ann Arbor); Texas (Austin); Francqui Vis. Prof., Univ. of Gent, 1989–90. Lectures: Atkin, Reform Club, 1989; Shimizu, LSE, 1989; Lionel Cohen Meml, Hebrew Univ. of Jerusalem, 1993. Mem., Council of Management, British Inst. of Internat. and Comparative Law, 1993–. Associate Fellow, Internat. Acad. of Comp. Law, 1987; Mem., Amer. Law Inst., 1989; Corresponding Member: Royal Belgian Acad., 1990; Acad. of Athens, 1994; Foreign Mem., Royal Netherlands Acad. of Arts and Scis, 1995; Corresp. Collaborator, UNIDROIT, 1992. DIur (*hc*) Ghent, 1992. Humboldt Forschungspreise, 1995. Officer's Cross, Order of Merit (Germany), 1992; Officier, Ordre des Palmes Académiques (France), 1992; Cavaliere Ufficiale del Ordine al Merito (Italy), 1995; Chevalier, Légion d'Honneur (France), 1995. *Publications:* The Mother's right to Guardianship according to the Greek Civil Code, 1968; The Theory and Practice of Dissolution of Parliament, 1972 (Yorke Prize); The English Law of Torts, 1976; (jtly) An Outline of the Law of Agency, 1979, 3rd edn 1992; (jtly) Richterliche Rechtspolitik im Haftungsrecht, 1981; (jtly) Tortious Liability for unintentional harm in the Common Law and the Civil Law, 2 vols, 1982; (jtly) Tort Law, 1984, 3rd edn 1994; A Comparative Introduction to the German Law of Torts, 1986, 3rd edn 1994; (gen. ed. and contrib.) The Gradual Convergence: foreign ideas, foreign influences and English law on the eve of the 21st century, 1994; many articles in learned jls in Belgium, Canada, England, France, Germany, Greece, Israel, Italy and USA. *Recreations:* painting, music, archaeological digging, chess. *Address:* Faculty of Laws, St Cross Building, St Cross Road, Oxford OX1 3UR. *T:* Oxford (01865) 281610, *Fax:* (01865) 281611.

MARKEY, Air Vice-Marshal Peter Desmond, OBE 1986; Director General of Support Management, Royal Air Force, since 1995; *b* 28 March 1943; *s* of Althorpe Hazel Christopher Markey and Marjorie Joyce Markey (*née* Thomas); *m* 1966, Judith Mary Widdowson; one *s* one *d*. *Educ:* RAF Coll. Cranwell; Open Univ. (BA 1980); Cranfield Univ. (MSc 1994). RAF Supply Officer: commissioned 1964; served Singapore, France and UK to 1981; NDC, 1981–82; HQ Strike Comd, 1982–83; HQ AFCENT, Netherlands, 1983–85; MoD Carlisle, 1986–88; Station Comdr, Carlisle, 1988–89; RCDS 1990; MoD Central Staff, 1991; Dept of AMSO, 1991; HQ Logistics Comd, 1994. *Publications:* papers and contribs to learned jls. *Recreations:* running, mountain walking, caravanning. *Address:* HQ Logistics Command, RAF Brampton, Huntingdon, Cambs PE18 8QL. *T:* Huntingdon (01480) 52151. *Club:* Royal Air Force.

MARKHAM, Sir Charles (John), 3rd Bt, *cr* 1911; *b* 2 July 1924; *s* of Sir Charles Markham, 2nd Bt, and Gwladys, *e d* of late Hon. Rupert Beckett; *S* father 1952; *m* 1949, Valerie, *o d* of Lt-Col E. Barry-Johnston, Makuyu, Kenya; two *s* one *d*. *Educ:* Eton. Served War of 1939–45, Lieut in 11th Hussars (despatches). Vice-Chm., Nairobi Co. Council, 1953–55; MLC Kenya, 1955–60. Pres., Royal Agricultural Soc., Kenya, 1958. KStJ 1973. *Heir: s* Arthur David Markham [*b* 6 Dec. 1950; *m* 1977, Carolyn, *yr d* of Captain Mungo Park; two *d*]. *Address:* PO Box 42263, Nairobi, Kenya, East Africa. *Club:* Cavalry and Guards.

MARKING, Sir Henry (Ernest), KCVO 1978; CBE 1969; MC 1944; CompRAeS 1953; FCIT; Deputy Chairman and Managing Director, British Airways, 1972–77; *b* 11 March 1920; *s* of late Isaac and Hilda Jane Marking. *Educ:* Saffron Walden Gram. Sch.; University Coll., London. Served War of 1939–45: 2nd Bn The Sherwood Foresters, 1941–45; North Africa, Italy and Middle East; Adjutant, 1944–45. Middle East Centre of Arab Studies, Jerusalem, 1945–46. Admitted solicitor, 1948. Asst Solicitor, Cripps, Harries, Hall & Co., Tunbridge Wells, 1948–49; Asst Solicitor, 1949, Sec., 1950, Chief Exec., 1964–72, Chm., 1971–72, BEA; Mem. Bd, BOAC, 1971–72; Mem., British Airways Board, 1971–80. Chm., Rothmans UK, 1979–86; Director: Rothmans International, 1979–86; Barclays International, 1977–86. Mem., 1969–77, Chm., 1977–84, British Tourist Authority. Trustee, 1962–95, Chm. Internat. Cttee, 1970–91, Leonard Cheshire Foundn. FIMgt (FBIM 1971). *Club:* Reform.

MARKOVA, Dame Alicia, DBE 1963 (CBE 1958); **(Dame Lilian Alicia Marks);** Prima Ballerina Assoluta; Professor of Ballet and Performing Arts, College-Conservatory of Music, University of Cincinnati, since 1970; President, London Festival Ballet, since 1986; *b* London 1910; *d* of Arthur Tristman Marks and Eileen Barry. With Diaghilev's Russian Ballet Co., 1925–29; Rambert Ballet Club, 1931–33; Vic-Wells Ballet Co., 1933–35; Markova-Dolin Ballet Co., 1935–37; Ballet Russe de Monte Carlo, 1938–41; Ballet Theatre, USA, 1941–46. Appeared with Anton Dolin, guest and concert performances, 1948–50. Co-Founder and Prima Ballerina, Festival Ballet, 1950–51; Guest Prima Ballerina: Buenos Aires, 1952; Royal Ballet, 1953 and 1957; Royal Danish Ballet, 1955; Scala, Milan, 1956; Teatro Municipal, Rio de Janeiro, 1956; Festival Ballet, 1958 and 1959; Guest appearances at Metropolitan Opera House, New York, 1952, 1953–54, 1955, 1957, 1958; Dir, Metropolitan Opera Ballet, 1963–69; produced Les Sylphides for Festival Ballet and Aust. Ballet, 1976, for Royal Ballet School and Northern Ballet Theatre, 1978, for Royal Winnipeg Ballet, Canada, 1979. Guest Professor: Royal Ballet Sch., 1973–; Paris Opera Ballet, 1975; Australian Ballet Sch., 1976; Yorkshire Ballet Seminars, 1975–; Pres., All England Dance Competition, 1983–. Vice-Pres., Royal Acad. of Dancing, 1958–; Governor, Royal Ballet, 1973–; President: Pavlova Meml Mus., 1978; London Ballet Circle, 1981–; Trust of the Arts Educational Schs, 1984–;. Concert, television and guest appearances (general), 1952–61. BBC series, Markova's Ballet Call, 1960; Masterclass, BBC2, 1980. Queen Elizabeth II Coronation Award, Royal Acad. of Dancing, 1963; Special Ballet Award, Evening Standard, 1994. Hon. DMus: Leicester, 1966; East Anglia, 1982. *Publications:* Giselle and I, 1960; Markova Remembers, 1986. *Address:* c/o Barclays Bank, PO Box No 4599, SW3 1XE.

MARKOWITZ, Prof. Harry M., PhD; Professor of Finance and Economics, Baruch College, City University of New York, 1982–93; *b* 24 Aug. 1927; *s* of Morris Markowitz and Mildred (*née* Gruber); *m* Barbara Gay. *Educ:* Univ. of Chicago (PhB Liberal Arts 1947; MA 1950, PhD 1954 Econs). Res. Associate, Rand Corp., 1952–60 and 1961–63; Consultant, Gen. Electric Corp., 1960–61; Chm., Bd and Technical Dir, Consolidated Analysis Centres Inc., 1963–68; Prof. of Finance, UCLA, 1968–69; Pres., Arbitrage Management Co., 1969–72, Consultant, 1972–74; Vis. Prof. of Finance, Wharton Bus. Sch., 1972–74; Res. Staff Mem., T. J. Watson Res. Center, IBM, 1974–83; Adj. Prof. of Finance, Rutgers Univ., 1980–82; Consultant, Daiwa Securities, 1990–. Director: Amer. Finance Assoc.; TIMS. Fellow: Econometric Soc.; Amer. Acad. Arts and Sciences, 1987. Von Neumann Theory Prize, ORSA/TIMS, 1989; Nobel Prize for Economics, 1990. *Publications:* Portfolio Selection: efficient diversification of investments, 1959, 3rd edn 1991; Simscript: a simulation programming language, 1963; (jtly) Studies in Process Analysis: economy-wide production capabilities, 1963 (trans. Russian 1967); (jtly) The Simscript II Programming Language, 1969; (jtly) The EAS-E Programming Language, 1981; (jtly) Adverse Deviation, 1981; Mean-Variance Analysis in Portfolio Choice and Capital Markets, 1987; contrib. chapters to numerous books and papers in professional jls, incl. Jl of Finance, Management Science, Jl of Portfolio Management. *Recreations:* music, canoeing, snorkeling.

MARKS, family name of **Baron Marks of Broughton.**

MARKS OF BROUGHTON, 2nd Baron, *cr* 1961; **Michael Marks;** *b* 27 Aug. 1920; *o s* of 1st Baron and Miriam (*d* 1971), *d* of Ephraim Sieff; *S* father 1964; *m* (marr. diss.); one *s* two *d*. *Heir:* son.

MARKS, Bernard Montague, OBE 1984; Life President, Alfred Marks Bureau Group of Companies, 1985 (Managing Director, 1946–81 and Chairman, 1946–84); *b* 11 Oct. 1923; *s* of Alfred and Elizabeth Marks; *m* 1956, Norma Renton (*d* 1990); two *s*. *Educ:* Highgate Public Sch.; Royal Coll. of Science. Served Somerset LI, seconded to RWAFF (Staff Capt.), 1944–46. Chm. or Vice-Chm., Fedn of Personnel Services of GB, 1965–79, 1983–84. Mem., Equal Opportunities Commn, 1984–86. *Publication:* Once Upon A Typewriter, 1974. *Recreations:* bridge, golf, ski-ing. *Address:* Leyfield House, Onslow Road, Burwood Park, Walton-on-Thames, Surrey KT12 5AY. *Club:* St George's Hill Golf.

MARKS, Dennis Michael; General Director, English National Opera, since 1993; *b* 2 July 1948; *s* of Samuel Marks and Kitty Ostrovsky; *m*; one *s* one *d*. *Educ:* Haberdashers' Aske's Sch., Elstree; Trinity Coll., Cambridge (1st Cl. Hons English Tripos). British Broadcasting Corporation, 1969–81: TV researcher, 1969–71; Dir, TV music and arts, 1972–78;

Dir/Producer, Bristol Arts Unit, 1978–81; Dir/Producer, 3rd Eye Prodns, 1981–85; BBC TV: Editor, music progs, 1985–88; Asst Head of Music and Arts Dept, 1988–91; Hd of Music Progs, 1991–93. Pres., Internat. Music Centre, Vienna, 1989–92. *Publications:* Great Railway Journeys, 1981; Repercussions, 1985. *Recreations:* cooking, writing. *Address:* English National Opera, London Coliseum, St Martin's Lane, WC2N 4ES.

MARKS, Frederick Charles, OBE 1983; Commissioner for Local Administration in Scotland, since 1994; *b* 3 Dec. 1934; *s* of James Marks and Elizabeth (*née* McInnes); *m* 1959, Agnes Miller Bruce; two *s* one *d* (and one *s* decd). *Educ:* Wishaw High Sch.; Univ. of Glasgow (MA Hons; LLB). Admitted solicitor, 1960. Legal Asst, Burgh of Motherwell and Wishaw, 1957–61; Solicitor, Burgh of Kirkcaldy, 1961–63; Depute Town Clerk, City and Royal Burgh of Dunfermline, 1963–68; Town Clerk, Burgh of Hamilton, 1968–75; Chief Exec., Motherwell Dist, 1974–83; Gen. Manager, Scottish Special Housing Assoc., 1983–89; Dep. Chm., Local Govt Boundary Commn for Scotland, 1989–94. *Address:* 23 Walker Street, Edinburgh EH3 7HX. *T:* 0131–225 5300.

MARKS, John Emile, CBE 1970; Chairman, Peckerbond Ltd; *m* 1975, Averil May Hannah (*née* Davies); two *s* two *d* by former marriage. *Educ:* Eton College. Served War of 1939–45 (despatches 1944). *Recreations:* tennis, bowls. *Address:* Teignmouth, Devon.

MARKS, John Henry, MD; FRCGP; General Practitioner, Boreham Wood, 1954–90; Chairman of Council, British Medical Association, 1984–90; Medical Director, National Medical Examination Network (Definitech) Ltd, since 1992; *b* 30 May 1925; *s* of Lewis and Rose Marks; *m* 1954, Shirley Evelyn, *d* of Alic Nathan, OBE; one *s* two *d*. *Educ:* Tottenham County Sch.; Edinburgh Univ. MD; FRCGP; D(Obst)RCOG. Served RAMC, 1949–51. Chairman: Herts LMC, 1966–71; Herts Exec. Council, 1971–74; Member: NHS Management Study Steering Cttee, 1971–72; Standing Med. Adv. Cttee, 1984–90; Council for Postgrad. Med. Educn, 1984–90. British Medical Association: Fellow, 1976; Member: Gen. Med. Services Cttee, 1968–90 (Dep. Chm., 1974–79); Council, 1973–; GMC, 1979–84, 1990–94; Chairman: Representative Body, 1981–84; Foundn for AIDS, 1987–. Mem. Council, ASH, 1991–. *Publications:* The Conference of Local Medical Committees and its Executive: an historical view, 1979; papers on the NHS and general medical practice. *Recreations:* philately, walking, gardening. *Address:* Brown Gables, Barnet Lane, Elstree, Herts WD6 3RQ. *T:* 0181–953 7687.

MARKS, Jonathan Clive; QC 1995; *b* 19 Oct. 1952; *s* of Geoffrey Jack Marks, LDS RCS and Patricia Pauline Marks, LLB; *m* 1st, 1982, Sarah Ann Russell (marr. diss. 1991); one *s* one *d*; 2nd, 1993, Clementine Medina Cafopoulos. *Educ:* Harrow; University Coll., Oxford (BA Hons Jurisp.); Inns of Court Sch. of Law. Called to the Bar, Inner Temple, 1975; in practice, Common Law and Commercial Law, Western Circuit. Vis. Lecturer in Advocacy: Univs of Malaya and Mauritius; Sri Lanka Law Coll. Contested (SDP): Weston-Super-Mare, 1983; Falmouth and Camborne, 1987; EP elecn, Cornwall and Plymouth, 1984; Mem., Lib Dem Cttee for England, 1988–89. Freeman, City of London, 1975; Mem., Patternmakers' Co. *Recreations:* tennis, ski-ing, theatre, opera, food, wine, travel. *Address:* 4 Pump Court, Temple, EC4Y 7AN. *T:* 0171–353 2656. *CLub:* Royal Automobile.

MARKS, Dr Louis Frank; Producer, BBC Television Drama, since 1976; *b* 23 March 1928; *s* of Michael Marks and Sarah Abrahams; *m* 1957, Sonia Herbstman; two *d*. *Educ:* Christ's Coll., London; Balliol Coll., Oxford (MA, BLitt, DPhil 1957). Sen. History teacher, Beltane Sch., 1951–53; founder and editor, Books and Bookmen, 1956; freelance scriptwriter, TV series, 1958–69; joined BBC, 1970; Script Editor, Series Dept, 1970; Plays Dept, 1972; Drama Producer, 1974; productions include: The Lost Boys (RTS Award, 1979); Play of the Month, later Festival, 1979–86, incl. Lady Windermere's Fan and Ghosts (ACE Awards, 1988, 1992); films include: Silas Marner (Banff Film Fest. Award, 1986); Memento Mori (Writers' Guild Award, 1992); The Trial, 1993; TV adaptation: Middlemarch (serial), 1994 (Writers' Guild Award, BPG TV Award for best serial, Voice of the Listener and Viewer Award for excellence in broadcasting and best TV prog., 1994). *Publications:* (ed and trans.) Antonio Gramsci: the modern prince, 1957; articles in Archivio Storico Italiano and Italian Renaissance Studies. *Address:* Paddock Lodge, The Green, Hampton Court, East Molesey, Surrey KT8 9BW. *T:* 0181–979 5254.

MARKS, Michael John Paul; Chairman, Smith New Court, since 1995 (Chief Executive, 1987–94); *b* 28 Dec. 1941; *m* 1967, Rosemary Ann Brody; one *s* two *d*. *Educ:* St Paul's Sch. Joined Smith Brothers, subseq. Smith New Court, 1959; Partner, 1971–84; Man. Dir, Smith New Court International, 1984–87. Non-exec. Dir, Rothschilds Continuation, 1990–; Mem., Internat. Markets Adv. Bd, Nasdaq Stock Market, 1991–. Dir, London Stock Exchange, 1994–. *Address:* Smith New Court, Smith New Court House, 20 Farringdon Road, EC1M 3NH.

MARKS, Prof. Richard Charles, PhD; FSA; Professor in Medieval Stained Glass, University of York, since 1992; *b* 2 July 1945; *s* of William Henry Marks and Jeannie Eileen Marks (*née* Pigott); *m* 1970, Rita Spratley. *Educ:* Berkhamsted Sch.; Queen Mary Coll., Univ. of London (BA (Hons) History); Courtauld Inst. of Art, Univ. of London (MA, PhD, History of European Art). Research Asst for British Acad. *Corpus Vitrearum Medii Aevi* Cttee, 1970–73; Asst Keeper, Dept of Medieval and Later Antiquities, British Mus., 1973–79; Keeper of Burrell Collection and Asst Dir, Glasgow Museums and Art Galls, 1979–85; Dir, Royal Pavilion, Art Gall. and Museums in Brighton, 1985–92. Chm., Group of Directors of Museums, 1989–92; Mem. Cttee, 1985–, Pres. Internat. Bd, 1995, *Corpus Vitrearum Medii Aevi*, British Academy; Trustee, Stained Glass Museum Trust, 1990–. Liveryman, Glaziers' Co., 1990. FSA 1977 (Mem. Council, 1990–94; Vice-Pres., 1991–94). *Publications:* (jtly) British Heraldry from its origins to *c* 1800, 1978; (jtly) The Golden Age of English Manuscript Painting, 1980; Burrell Portrait of a Collector, 1983, 2nd edn 1988; The Glazing of the Collegiate Church of the Holy Trinity, Tattershall, Lincs, 1984; (jtly) Sussex Churches and Chapels, 1989; Stained Glass in England during the Middle Ages, 1993; articles and reviews in learned jls. *Recreations:* opera, cricket, rowing, parish churches, travelling in the Levant. *Address:* c/o Centre for Medieval Studies, University of York, The King's Manor, York Y01 2EP; 38 High Street, Wing, near Leighton Buzzard, Beds LU7 0NR. *Clubs:* MCC; Clydesdale Amateur Rowing (Glasgow); North British Rowing (the Borders).

MARKS, Prof. Shula Eta, PhD; FBA 1995; Professor of Southern African History, School of Oriental and African Studies, University of London, since 1993; *b* Cape Town, S Africa, 14 Oct. 1936; *d* of Chaim and Frieda Winokur; *m* 1957, Isaac M. Marks; one *s* one *d*. *Educ:* Univ. of Cape Town (Argus Scholar, 1958–59; BA 1959). PhD London, 1967. Came to London, 1960; Lectr in the History of Southern Africa, SOAS and Inst. of Commonwealth Studies, 1963–76, Reader, 1976–83; Dir, 1983–93, Prof. of Commonwealth Hist., 1984–93, Inst. of Commonwealth Studies, London Univ.; Vice-Chancellor's Visitor to NZ, 1978. Dir, Ford Foundn Grant to Univ. of London on S African History, 1975–78; Mem., Commonwealth Scholarships Commn, 1993–. Mem., Adv. Council on Public Records, 1989–94. Pres., African Studies Assoc. of UK, 1978; Chm., Soc. for Protection of Sci. and Learning, 1993–. Editor, Jl of African History, 1971–77; Mem. Council, Jl of Southern African Studies, 1974– (Founding Mem., 1974). Hon. DLitt Univ. of Cape Town, 1994. *Publications:* Reluctant Rebellion: an assessment of the 1906–8 disturbances in Natal, 1970; (ed with A. Atmore) Economy and Society in Pre-industrial South Africa, 1980; (ed with R. Rathbone) Industrialization and Social Change in South Africa, 1870–1930, 1982; (ed with P. Richardson) International Labour Migration: historical perspectives, 1983; The Ambiguities of Dependence in Southern Africa: class, nationalism and the state in twentieth-century Natal, 1986; (ed) Not either an experimental doll: the separate worlds of three South African women, 1987; (ed with Stanley Trapido) The Politics of Race, Class & Nationalism in Twentieth Century South Africa, 1987; Divided Sisterhood: race, class and gender in the South African nursing profession, 1994; chapters in Cambridge Hist. of Africa, vols 3, 4 and 6; contrib. Jl of African Hist. and Jl of Southern African Studies. *Address:* School of Oriental and African Studies, WC1H 0XG.

MARKUS, Prof. Robert Austin, FBA 1985; Professor of Medieval History, Nottingham University, 1974–82, now Emeritus; *b* 8 Oct. 1924; *s* of Victor Markus and Lily Markus (*née* Elek); *m* 1955, Margaret Catherine Bullen; two *s* one *d*. *Educ:* Univ. of Manchester (BSc 1944; MA 1948; PhD 1950). Mem., Dominican Order, 1950–54; Asst Librarian, Univ. of Birmingham, 1954–55; Liverpool University: Sub-Librarian, 1955–59; Lectr, Sen. Lectr, Reader in Medieval Hist., 1959–74. Mem., Inst. for Advanced Study, Princeton, 1986–87; Distinguished Prof. of Early Christian Studies, Catholic Univ. of America, Washington, 1988–89; Univ. of Notre Dame, 1993. Pres., Assoc. Internationale d'Etudes Patristiques, 1991–95. *Publications:* Christian Faith and Greek Philosophy (with A. H. Armstrong), 1964; Saeculum: history and society in the theology of St Augustine, 1970; Christianity in the Roman world, 1974; From Augustine to Gregory the Great, 1983; The End of Ancient Christianity, 1990; contribs to Jl of Ecclesiastical Hist., Jl of Theol Studies, Byzantion, Studies in Church Hist., etc. *Recreation:* music. *Address:* 100 Park Road, Chilwell, Beeston, Nottingham NG9 4DE. *T:* Nottingham (0115) 925 5965.

MARLAND, Michael, CBE 1977; Headmaster, North Westminster Community School, since 1980; *b* 28 Dec. 1934; *m* 1st, 1955, Eileen (*d* 1968); four *s* one *d*; 2nd, 1971, Rose (marr. diss. 1977); 3rd, 1989, Linda; one *s*. *Educ:* Christ's Hospital Sch.; Sidney Sussex Coll., Cambridge (MA). Head of English, Abbey Wood Sch., 1961–64; Head of English and subseq. Dir of Studies, Crown Woods Sch., 1964–71; Headmaster, Woodberry Down Sch., 1971–79. Hon. Prof., Dept of Educn, Univ. of Warwick, 1980–92. Member: many educn cttees, incl. Bullock Cttee, 1972–75; Commonwealth Inst. Educn Cttee, 1982–; Arts Council of GB Educn Cttee, 1988–92; Educn and Human Develt Cttee, ESRC (formerly SSRC), 1983–88; Nat. Assoc. for Educn in the Arts, 1986–; Nat. Book League Council, 1984; Finniston Cttee on Technol. in Educn, 1985–88; Video Adv. Cttee, British Bd of Film Censors, 1989–; Chairman: Schools Council English Cttee, 1978–81; Books in Curriculum Res. Project, 1982–; Royal Ballet Educn Adv. Council, 1983–; Nat. Assoc. for Pastoral Care in Educn, 1982–86; Royal Opera House Educnl Adv. Council, 1984–; Nat. Textbook Ref. Library Steering Cttee, 1984–. Mem., Paddington and N Kensington DHA, 1982–84. *Publications:* Towards The New Fifth, 1969; The Practice of English Teaching, 1970; Peter Grimes, 1971; Head of Department, 1971; Pastoral Care, 1974; The Craft of the Classroom, 1975; Language Across the Curriculum, 1977; Education for the Inner City, 1980; Departmental Management, 1981; Sex Differentiation and Schooling, 1983; Short Stories for Today, 1984; Meetings and Partings, 1984; School Management Skills, 1985; The Tutor and the Tutor Group, 1990; Marketing the School, 1991; General Editor of: The Student Drama Series; Longman Imprint Books; The Times Authors; Heinemann Organisation in Schools Series; Longman Tutorial Resources; contrib. Times Educnl Supplement. *Recreations:* music, literature. *Address:* 22 Compton Terrace, N1 2UN. *T:* 0171–226 0648; The Green Farmhouse, Cranmer Green, Walsham-le-Willows, Bury St Edmunds, Suffolk IP31 3BJ. *T:* Walsham-le-Willows (01359) 259483.

MARLAND, Paul; MP (C) Gloucestershire West, since 1979; *b* 19 March 1940; *s* of Alexander G. Marland and Elsa May Lindsey Marland; *m* 1st, 1965, Penelope Anne Barlow (marr. diss. 1982); one *s* two *d*; 2nd, 1984, Caroline Ann Rushton. *Educ:* Gordonstoun Sch., Elgin; Trinity Coll., Dublin (BA, BComm). Hopes Metal Windows, 1964; London Press Exchange, 1965–66; farmer, 1967–. Jt PPS to Financial Sec. to the Treasury and Economic Sec., 1981–83, to Minister of Agriculture, Fisheries and Food, 1983–86. Chm., back-bench Agric. Cttee, 1989–. *Recreations:* skiing, shooting, riding, fishing. *Address:* Ford Hill Farm, Temple Guiting, Cheltenham, Glos GL54 5XU. *Club:* Boodle's.

MARLAR, Robin Geoffrey; management consultant, since 1968; cricket correspondent, Sunday Times, 1970–96; *b* 2 Jan. 1931; *o s* of late E. A. G. Marlar and Winifred Marlar (*née* Stevens); *m* 1st, 1955, Wendy Ann Dumeresque; two *s* four *d*; 2nd, 1980, Hon. Gill Taylor, 2nd *d* of Baron Taylor of Hadfield. *Educ:* King Edward's Sch., Lichfield; Harrow; Magdalene Coll., Cambridge (BA). Asst Master, Eton Coll., 1953–54; Librarian, Arundel Castle, 1954–59; Captain, Sussex CCC, 1955–59; sportswriter, Daily Telegraph, 1954–60; De La Rue Co., 1960–68; Consultant and Partner, Spencer-Stuart and Associates, 1968–71; Founder, Marlar Group of Consultancies, 1971. Sunday Times, 1961–96. Contested (C): Bolsover, 1959; Leicester NE, July 1962; contested (Ind.) Newbury, May 1993. *Publications:* The Story of Cricket, 1978; (ed) The English Cricketers Trip to USA and Canada 1859, 1979; Decision Against England, 1983. *Recreations:* gardening, sport. *Clubs:* Garrick, MCC; Sussex CCC.

MARLBOROUGH, 11th Duke of, *cr* 1702; **John George Vanderbilt Henry Spencer-Churchill;** DL; Baron Spencer, 1603; Earl of Sunderland, 1643; Baron Churchill, 1685; Earl of Marlborough, 1689; Marquis of Blandford, 1702; Prince of the Holy Roman Empire; Prince of Mindelheim in Suabia; late Captain Life Guards; *b* 13 April 1926; *s* of 10th Duke of Marlborough and Hon. Alexandra Mary Hilda Cadogan, CBE (*d* 1961), *d* of late Henry Arthur, Viscount Chelsea; *S* father, 1972; *m* 1st, 1951, Susan Mary (marr diss., 1960, she *m* 1962, Alan Cyril Heber-Percy), *d* of Michael Hornby; one *s* one *d* (and one *s* decd); 2nd, 1961, Mrs Athina Livanos (marr. diss. 1971; she *d* 1974), *d* of late Stavros G. Livanos, Paris; 3rd, 1972, Rosita Douglas; one *s* one *d* (and one *s* decd). *Educ:* Eton. Lieut Life Guards, 1946; Captain, 1953; resigned commission, 1953. Chairman: Martini & Rossi, 1979–; London Paperweights Ltd, 1974–. Mem., Forte Council, 1994–. President: Thames and Chilterns Tourist Board, 1974–; Oxfordshire Branch, CLA, 1978–; Oxfordshire Assoc. for Young People, 1972–; Oxford Br., SSAFA, 1977–; Sports Aid Foundn (Southern), 1981–; Oxford United Football Club, 1964–; Dep. Pres., Nat. Assoc. of Boys' Clubs, 1987–; Mem. Council, Winston Churchill Meml Trust, 1966–; Patron, Oxfordshire Br., BRCS. CC 1961–64, Oxfordshire; JP 1962; DL 1974. *Heir:* *s* Marquis of Blandford, *qv*. *Address:* Blenheim Palace, Woodstock, Oxon OX20 1PX. *Clubs:* Portland, White's.

MARLER, David Steele, OBE 1984; Director, Turkey, British Council, since 1993; *b* 19 March 1941; *s* of Steele Edward and Dorothy Marler; *m* 1963, Belinda Mary Handisyde; two *s*. *Educ:* Brighton, Hove and Sussex Grammar Sch.; Merton Coll., Oxford (Postmaster; BA, MA). British Council, 1962–: seconded SOAS, 1962–63; Asst Rep., Bombay, 1963; Regional Officer, India, 1967; Dep. Rep., Ethiopia, 1970; Rep., Ibadan, Nigeria, 1974; Dir, Policy Res., 1977; Rep., Cyprus, 1980; seconded SOAS, 1984; National Univ., Singapore, 1985; Rep., China, 1987–90; Dir, Asia, Pacific and Americas Div., 1990–92.

Recreations: sailing, travel, reading, walking. *Address:* c/o British Council, 10 Spring Gardens, SW1A 2BN. *T:* 0171–930 8466. *Club:* Changi Sailing (Singapore).

MARLER, Dennis Ralph Greville, FRICS; Chairman, Falcon Property Trust, since 1988; *b* 15 June 1927; *s* of late Greville Sidney Marler, JP, FRICS and Ivy Victoria (*née* Boyle); *m* 1952, Angela (*née* Boundy); one *s* one *d*. *Educ:* Marlborough. Served Royal Lincolnshire Regt, Palestine, 1946–48; articled pupil, Knight, Frank & Rutley, 1948–50; Partner, Marler & Marler, 1950–83; Jt Man. Dir, 1966–76, Man. Dir, 1976–85, Chm., 1985–90, Capital & Counties plc; Chairman: Knightsbridge Green Hotel Ltd, 1966–; Pension Fund Property Unit Trust, 1987–89. Member: NEDO Working Party for Wood Report (Public Client and Construction Industry), 1974–75; Adv. Bd, Dept of Construction Management, Univ. of Reading, 1981–88; DHSS Nat. Property Adv. Gp, 1984–91; FCO *ad hoc* Adv. Panel on Diplomatic Estate, 1985–90; RSA Art for Architecture Panel, 1990–93. A Vice-Pres., TCPA, 1983–; Pres., British Property Fedn, 1983–84. A Vice-Pres., RNIB, 1994. Mem. Ct of Assistants, Merchant Taylors' Co., 1984–. CIMgt; FRSA. *Recreations:* reading, golf, gardening. *Address:* Stoptide, Rock, Cornwall PL27 6JZ. *T:* Trebetherick (01208) 862141; 16 Whaddon House, William Mews, SW1X 9HG. *T:* 0171–235 9215. *Clubs:* Royal Thames Yacht, Roehampton; St Enodoc Golf.

MARLESFORD, Baron *cr* 1991 (Life Peer), of Marlesford in the County of Suffolk; **Mark Shuldham Schreiber;** DL; political consultant, farmer and journalist; Chairman, Council for the Protection of Rural England, since 1993; *b* 11 Sept. 1931; *s* of late John Shuldham Schreiber, AE, DL, Marlesford Hall, Suffolk and Maureen Schreiber (*née* Dent); *m* 1969, Gabriella Federica, *d* of Conte Teodoro Veglio di Castelletto d'Uzzone; two *d*. *Educ:* Eton; Trinity Coll., Cambridge. Nat. Service in Coldstream Guards, 1950–51. Fisons Ltd, 1957–63; Conservative Research Dept, 1963–67; Dir, Conservative Party Public Sector Research Unit, 1967–70; Special Advr to the Govt, 1970–74; Special Adviser to Leader of the Opposition, 1974–75; Editorial Consultant, 1974–91, lobby correspondent, 1976–91, The Economist. Ind. Nat. Dir, Times Newspaper Holdings, 1991–; Director: Royal Ordnance Factories, 1972–74; British Railways (Anglia), 1988–92; Eastern Electricity plc, 1990–. Member: Govt Computer Agency Council, 1973–74; Countryside Commn, 1980–92; Rural Development Commn, 1985–93. Mem., East Suffolk CC, 1968–70. DL Suffolk, 1991. *Recreation:* fighting history. *Address:* Marlesford Hall, Woodbridge, Suffolk IP13 0AU; 5 Kersley Street, SW11 4PR. *Club:* Pratt's.

MARLING, Sir Charles (William Somerset), 5th Bt *cr* 1882; *b* 2 June 1951; *s* of Sir John Stanley Vincent Marling, 4th Bt, OBE, and Georgina Brenda (Betty) (*d* 1961), *o d* of late Henry Edward FitzRoy Somerset; *S* father, 1977; *m* 1979, Judi P. Futrille; three *d*. *Address:* The Barn, The Street, Eversley, Hants RG27 0PJ.

MARLOW, Antony Rivers; MP (C) Northampton North, since 1979; *b* 17 June 1940; *s* of late Major Thomas Keith Rivers Marlow, MBE, RE retd, and Beatrice Nora (*née* Hall); *m* 1962, Catherine Louise Howel (*née* Jones) (*d* 1994); three *s* two *d*. *Educ:* Wellington Coll.; RMA Sandhurst; St Catharine's Coll., Cambridge (2nd Cl. Hons (1) Mech. Sciences, MA). Served Army, 1958–69; retd, Captain RE; management consultant and industrial/commercial manager, 1969–79. *Recreations:* farming, Rugby spectator, opera, ballet. *Address:* House of Commons, SW1A 0AA.

MARLOW, David Ellis; Chief Executive, 3i Group, 1988–92; *b* 29 March 1935; *m* 1959, Margaret Anne Smith; one *d* (one *s* decd). Chartered Accountant. Investors in Industry, subseq. 3i, 1960–92. Director: Brixton Estate plc, 1993–; Trinity Internat. Hldgs, 1992–; Brunner Mond Hldgs, 1994–. Mem., South Bank Bd, 1992–. Trustee, Maxwell Pensioners' Trust, 1993–. *Recreations:* playing tennis, the piano, the organ and the 'cello; ski-ing and scrambling in the Alps. *Address:* The Platt, Elsted, Midhurst, Sussex GU29 0LA. *T:* Harting (01730) 825261. *Clubs:* Athenæum; Cercle de l'Union Interalliée (Paris).

MARLOWE, Hugh; *see* Patterson, Harry.

MARMION, Prof. Barrie P., AO 1994; Visiting Professor, Department of Pathology, University of Adelaide (Adelaide Medical School), since 1985; *b* 19 May 1920; *s* of J. P. and M. H. Marmion, Alverstoke, Hants; *m* 1953, Diana Ray Newling, *d* of Dr P. Ray Newling, Adelaide, SA; one *d*. *Educ:* University Coll. and University Coll. Hosp., London. MD London 1947, DSc London 1963; FRCPath 1962, FRCPA 1964, FRCPE 1970, FRACP 1984; FRSE 1976. House Surg., UCH, 1942; Bacteriologist, Public Health Laboratory Service, 1943–62; Rockefeller Trav. Fellow, at Walter and Eliza Hall Inst., Melbourne, 1951–52; Foundation Prof., Microbiology, Monash Univ., Melbourne, Australia, 1962–68; Prof. of Bacteriology, Univ. of Edinburgh, 1968–78; Dir, Div. of Virology, Inst. of Med. and Vet. Science, Adelaide, 1978–85, retd. DUniv Adelaide, 1990. Distinguished Fellow Award (Gold Medal), RCPath Australia, 1986. *Publications:* (ed) Mackie and McCartney's Medical Microbiology, 13th edn 1978, 14th edn 1995; numerous papers on bacteriology and virology. *Recreations:* swimming, music. *Address:* Department of Pathology, University of Adelaide, North Terrace, Adelaide, SA 5000, Australia.

MARMOT, Prof. Michael Gideon, PhD; FFPHM; Professor of Epidemiology and Public Health, University College London, since 1985, and London School of Hygiene and Tropical Medicine at University College London, since 1990; Director, International Centre for Health and Society, since 1994; *b* 26 Jan. 1945; *s* of Nathan Marmot and Alice Marmot (*née* Weiner); *m* 1971, Alexandra Naomi Ferster; two *s* one *d*. *Educ:* Univ. of Sydney (BSc Hons, MB BS Hons); Univ. of California, Berkeley (PhD Epidemiology). MFCM. RMO, Royal Prince Alfred Hosp., 1969–70, Fellowship in Thoracic Medicine, 1970–71, Univ. of Sydney; Res. Fellow and Lectr, Dept of Biomedical and Envmtl Health Scis, Univ. of California, Berkeley, 1971–76 (Fellowships from Berkeley and Amer. Heart Assoc., 1972–76); Lectr and Sen. Lectr in Epidemiology, LSH&TM, 1976–85; Hon. Consultant, Public Health Medicine, Camden (formerly Bloomsbury) and Islington DHA, 1990–. Vis. Prof., RSocMed, 1987. *Publications:* (ed jtly and contrib.) Coronary Heart Disease Epidemiology, 1992; contribs to OPCS Medical and Population Studies; numerous papers in learned jls. *Recreations:* tennis, viola. *Address:* Department of Epidemiology and Public Health, University College London, 1–19 Torrington Place, WC1E 6BT; Wildwood Cottage, 17 North End, NW3 7HR. *T:* 0181–458 2125.

MARNOCH, Hon. Lord; Michael Stewart Rae Bruce; Senator of the College of Justice in Scotland, since 1990; *b* 26 July 1938; *s* of late Alexander Eric Bruce, Advocate in Aberdeen, and late Mary Gordon Bruce (*née* Walker); *m* 1963, Alison Mary Monfries Stewart; two *d*. *Educ:*Loretto Sch.; Aberdeen Univ. (MA, LLB). Admitted Faculty of Advocates, 1963; QC Scot. 1975; Standing Counsel: to Dept of Agriculture and Fisheries for Scotland, 1973; to Highlands and Islands Develt Bd, 1973; Advocate Depute, 1983–86. Mem., Criminal Injuries Compensation Bd, 1986–90. Hon. Vice Pres., Salmon and Trout Assoc., 1994– (Chm., Scotland, 1989–94). *Recreations:* fishing, golf. *Clubs:* New (Edinburgh); Honourable Company of Edinburgh Golfers; Turriff Golf.

MAROWITZ, Charles; West Coast critic, Theatre Week magazine, since 1990; Artistic Director: Malibu Stage Company, since 1990; Texas Stage Company, since 1994; *b* 26 Jan. 1934; Austrian mother, Russian father; *m* 1982, Jane Elizabeth Allsop. *Educ:* Seward Park High Sch.; University Coll. London. Dir, In-Stage Experimental Theatre, 1958; Asst Dir, Royal Shakespeare Co., 1963–65; Artistic Director: Traverse Theatre, 1963–64; Open Space Theatre London, 1968–81; Open Space Theatre of Los Angeles, 1982; Associate Dir, LA Theater Center, 1984–89. Drama Critic: Encore Magazine, 1956–63; Plays and Players, 1958–74; The Village Voice, 1955–; The NY Times, 1966–. *West End* Director: Loot, Criterion, 1967; The Bellow Plays, Fortune, 1966; Fortune and Men's Eyes, Comedy, 1969; productions *abroad:* Woyzeck, 1965, The Shrew, 1979, Nat. Theatre, Bergen; Hedda, 1978, Enemy of the People, 1979, Nat. Theatre, Oslo; Measure for Measure, Oslo New Theatre, 1981; The Father, Trondheim, 1981; Ah Sweet Mystery of Life, Seattle, 1981; A Midsummer Night's Dream, Odense, Denmark, 1983; Tartuffe, Molde, Norway, 1985; Marat/Sade, Rutgers, 1993; Merry Wives of Windsor, Dallas Shakespeare Fest., 1993; productions in *Los Angeles:* Artaud at Rodez, 1982; Sherlock's Last Case, 1984; The Petrified Forest, 1985; The Fair Penitent, 1986; The Shrew, 1986; Importance of Being Earnest, 1987; What the Butler Saw, 1988; Wilde West, 1989; Variations on Measure for Measure, 1990; A MacBeth, 1991. Order of the Purple Sash, 1969. *Publications:* The Method as Means, 1960; The Marowitz Hamlet, 1967; A Macbeth, 1970; Confessions of a Counterfeit Critic, 1973; Open Space Plays, 1974; Measure for Measure, 1975; The Shrew, 1975; Artaud at Rodez, 1976; Variations on The Merchant of Venice; The Act of Being, 1977; The Marowitz Shakespeare, 1978; New Theatre Voices of the 50s and 60s, 1981; Sex Wars, 1982; Prospero's Staff, 1986; Potboilers (collection of plays), 1986; Recycling Shakespeare, 1991; Burnt Bridges, 1991; Directing The Action, 1992; (trans.) Cyrano de Bergerac, 1995. *Recreation:* balling. *Address:* 3058 Sequit Drive, Malibu, CA 90265, USA.

MARPLES, Brian John; Emeritus Professor of Zoology, University of Otago, NZ; *b* 31 March 1907; 2nd *s* of George and Anne Marples; *m* 1931, Mary Joyce Ransford; two *s*. *Educ:* St Bees Sch.; Exeter Coll., Oxford. Lecturer in Zoology, Univ. of Manchester, 1929–35; Lecturer in Zoology, Univ. of Bristol, 1935–37; Prof. of Zoology, Univ. of Otago, NZ, 1937–67. *Publications:* Freshwater Life in New Zealand, 1962; various technical zoological and archaeological papers. *Address:* 1 Vanbrugh Close, Old Woodstock, Oxon OX20 1YB.

MARQUAND, Prof. David (Ian), FRHistS; Professor of Politics, since 1991, and Director of Political Economy Research Centre, since 1993, University of Sheffield; Joint Editor, The Political Quarterly, since 1987; *b* 20 Sept. 1934; *s* of Rt Hon. Hilary Marquand, PC; *m* 1959, Judith Mary (*née* Reed); one *s* one *d*. *Educ:* Emanuel Sch.; Magdalen Coll., Oxford; St Antony's Coll., Oxford (Sen. Schol.). 1st cl. hons Mod. Hist., 1957. FRHistS 1986. Teaching Asst, Univ. of Calif., 1958–59; Leader Writer, The Guardian, 1959–62; Research Fellow, St Antony's Coll., Oxford, 1962–64; Lectr in Politics, Univ. of Sussex, 1964–66. Contested: (Lab) Barry, 1964; (SDP) High Peak, 1983; MP (Lab) Ashfield, 1966–77; PPS to Minister of Overseas Develt, 1967–69; Jun. Opposition Front-Bench Spokesman on econ. affairs, 1971–72; Member: Select Cttee on Estimates, 1966–68; Select Cttee on Procedure, 1968–73; Select Cttee on Corp. Tax, 1971; British Deleg. to Council of Europe, 1970–73. Chief Advr, Secretariat-Gen., European Commission, 1977–78; Prof. of Contemporary History and Politics, Salford Univ., 1978–91. Vis. Scholar, Hoover Instn, Stanford, USA, 1985–86. Member: Nat. Steering Cttee, SDP, 1981–88; Policy Cttee, Soc & Lib Dem, 1988–90. Member: Aspen Inst., Berlin, 1982–; Adv. Council, Inst. of Contemporary British History, 1987–; Bd of Trustees, IPPR, 1992–; Adv. Council, Demos, 1993–; Social Justice Commn, 1993–94; Commn on Wealth Creation and Social Cohesion, 1994–95. Thomas Jefferson Meml Lectr, Univ. of Calif at Berkeley, 1981. FRSA. George Orwell Meml Prize (jtly), 1980. *Publications:* Ramsay MacDonald, 1977; Parliament for Europe, 1979; (with David Butler) European Elections and British Politics, 1981; (ed) John Mackintosh on Politics, 1982; The Unprincipled Society, 1988; The Progressive Dilemma, 1991; contrib. to: The Age of Austerity, 1964; A Radical Future, 1967; Coalitions in British Politics, 1978; Britain in Europe, 1980; The Political Economy of Tolerable Survival, 1980; The Rebirth of Britain, 1982; European Monetary Union Progress and Prospects, 1982; Social Theory and Political Practice, 1982; The Changing Constitution, 1985; Thatcherism, 1987; The Radical Challenge, 1987; The Ruling Performance, 1987; The Alternative, 1990; Debating the Constitution, 1993; Re-inventing the Left, 1994; articles and reviews in The Guardian, The Times, The Sunday Times, New Statesman, Encounter, Commentary, and in academic jls. *Recreation:* walking. *Address:* Department of Politics, Sheffield University, Sheffield S10 2TN.

MÁRQUEZ, Gabriel García; Colombian novelist; *b* 1928; *m* Mercedes García Márquez; two *s*. *Educ:* Univ. of Bogotá; Univ. of Cartagena. Corresp., El Espectador, Rome and Paris; formed Cuban Press Agency, Bogotá; worked for Prensa Latina, Cuba, later as Dep. Head, NY office, 1961; lived in Venezuela, Cuba, USA, Spain, Mexico; returned to Colombia, 1982; divides time between Mexico and Columbia. Rómulo Gallegos Prize, 1972; Nobel Prize for Literature, 1982. *Publications:* La hojarasca, 1955 (Leaf Storm, 1973); El coronel no tiene quien la escriba, 1961 (No One Writes to the Colonel, 1971); La mala hora, 1962 (In Evil Hour, 1980); Los funerales de la Mamá Grande, 1962; Cien años de soledad, 1967 (One Hundred Years of Solitude, 1970); La increíble y triste historia de la cándida Eréndira, 1972 (Innocent Erendira and other stories, 1979); El otoño del patriarca, 1975 (The Autumn of the Patriarch, 1977); Crónica de una muerte anunciada, 1981 (Chronicle of a Death Foretold, 1982; filmed, 1987); (with P. Mendoza) El olor de la Guayaba, 1982 (Fragrance of Guava, ed T. Nairn, 1983); El amor en los tiempos del cólera, 1984 (Love in the Time of Cholera, 1988); Relato de un naufrago (The Story of a Shipwrecked Sailor, 1986); Clandestine in Chile: adventures of Miguel Littín, 1986; Amores Dificiles, 1989 (of Love and Other Demons, 1995); El General en su Laberinto, 1989 (The General in his Labyrinth, 1991); Collected Stories, 1991; Doce cuentos peregrinos, 1992 (Strange Pilgrims, 1993). *Address:* c/o Agencia Literaria Carmen Balcelos, Diagonal 580, Barcelona, Spain.

MARQUIS, family name of **Earl of Woolton.**

MARQUIS, James Douglas, DFC 1945; Managing Director, Irvine Development Corporation, 1972–81; *b* 16 Oct. 1921; *s* of James Charles Marquis and Jessica Amy (*née* Huggett); *m* 1945, Brenda Eleanor, *d* of Robert Reyner Davey; two *s*. *Educ:* Shooters Hill Sch., Woolwich. Local Govt, 1938–41. Served War: RAF: 1941–46 (RAF 1st cl. Air Navigation Warrant, 1945), Navigation Officer, 177 Sqdn, 224 Gp, and AHQ Malaya (Sqdn Ldr 1945). Local Govt, 1946–56; Harlow Develt Corp., 1957–68; Irvine Develt Corp.: Chief Finance Officer, 1968–72; Dir of Finance and Admin., 1972. Pres., Ayrshire Chamber of Industries, 1979–80. Mem., Scottish Bonsai Assoc. FRMetS 1945; IPFA 1950; FCIS 1953. *Publication:* An Ayrshire Sketchbook, 1979. *Recreations:* sketching and painting (five one-man exhibns, incl. one in Sweden; works in collections: Japan, Sweden, Norway, Denmark, Australia, USA, Canada); gardening, bonsai. *Address:* 3 Knoll Park, Ayr KA7 4RH. *T:* Alloway (01292) 442212.

MARR, (Sir) Leslie Lynn, (2nd Bt, *cr* 1919, but does not use the title); MA Cambridge; painter and draughtsman; late Flight Lieutenant RAF; *b* 14 Aug. 1922; *o s* of late Col John Lynn Marr, OBE, TD, (and *g s* of 1st Bt,) and Amelia Rachel, *d* of late Robert Thompson, Overdinsdale Hall, Darlington; *S* grandfather 1932; *m* 1st, 1948, Dinora Delores Mendelson (marr. diss. 1956); one *d*; 2nd, 1962, Lynn Heneage; two *d*. *Educ:* Shrewsbury; Pembroke Coll., Cambridge. Has exhibited at Ben Uri, Drian, Woodstock, Wildenstein, Whitechapel,

Campbell and Franks Galls, London; also in Norwich, Belfast, Birmingham, Newcastle upon Tyne, Bristol and Paris. *Publication:* From My Point of View, 1979. *Heir: cousin* James Allan Marr [*b* 17 May 1939; *m* 1965, Jennifer, *yr d* of late J. W. E. Gill; two *s* one *d*].

MARR-JOHNSON, Frederick James Maugham; His Honour Judge Marr-Johnson; a Circuit Judge, since 1991; *b* 17 Sept. 1936; *s* of late Kenneth Marr-Johnson and Hon. Diana Marr-Johnson; *m* 1966, Susan Eyre; one *s* one *d*. *Educ:* Winchester Coll.; Trinity Hall, Cambridge (MA). Called to the Bar, Lincoln's Inn, 1962; practised on SE Circuit, 1963–91. *Recreation:* sailing. *Address:* 33 Hestercombe Avenue, SW6 5LL. *T:* 0171–731 0412. *Club:* Royal Yacht Squadron (Cowes).

MARRACK, Rear-Adm. Philip Reginald, CB 1979; CEng, FIMechE, FIMarE; *b* 16 Nov. 1922; *s* of Captain Philip Marrack, RN and Annie Kathleen Marrack (*née* Proud); *m* 1954, Pauline Mary (*née* Haag); two *d*. *Educ:* Eltham Coll.; Plymouth Coll.; RNC Dartmouth; RN Engineering Coll., Manadon. War service at sea, HM Ships Orion and Argus, 1944–45; Advanced Engineering Course, RNC Greenwich, 1945–47; HM Submarines Templar and Token, 1947–50; served in Frigate Torquay, Aircraft Carriers Glory and Hermes, and MoD; Captain 1965; Commanded Admiralty Reactor Test Estab., Dounreay, 1967–70; CSO (Mat.) on Staff of Flag Officer Submarines, and Asst Dir (Nuclear), Dockyard Dept, 1970–74; Rear-Adm. 1974; Dir, Naval Ship Production, 1974–77; Dir, Dockyard Production and Support, 1977–81, retd. *Recreations:* fly fishing, gardening, viticulture, wine making.

MARRE, Romola Mary, (Lady Marre), CBE 1979; Vice Chairman, City Parochial Foundation, 1989–93 (Trustee, 1975–89); *b* 25 April 1920; *d* of late Aubrey John Gilling and Romola Marjorie Angier; *m* 1943, Sir Alan Samuel Marre, KCB (*d* 1990); one *s* one *d*. *Educ:* Chelmsford County High Sch. for Girls; Bedford Coll., Univ. of London. BA Hons Philosophy. Asst Principal (Temp.), Min. of Health, 1941–42; Sgt, subseq. Jun. Comdr, ATS Officer Selection Bd, 1942–45. Organiser, West Hampstead Citizen's Advice Bureau, 1962–65; Dep. Gen. Sec., Camden Council of Social Service, 1965–73; Adviser on Community Health Councils to DHSS, 1974–75; Chairman: London Voluntary Service Council (formerly London Council of Social Service), 1974–84; Cttee on the Future of the Legal Profession, 1986–88; Panel of Four Commn of Enquiry into Human Aids to Communication, 1990–92; Bloomsbury, Camden and Islington HA Dist Ethics Cttee, 1993–; Member: Lord Chancellor's Adv. Cttee on Legal Aid, 1975–80; Milk Marketing Bd, 1973–82; BBC and IBA Central Appeals Adv. Cttee, 1980–87 (Chm., 1984–87); Council of Management, Charity Projects, 1987–90; Dep. Chm., Royal Jubilee Trusts, 1981–88; Chairman: Volunteer Centre, 1973–78; Adv. Gp on Hospital Services for children with cancer in North Western Region, Jan.-June 1979; Prince of Wales' Adv. Gp on Disability, 1982–84; Founder Pres., Barnet Voluntary Service Council, 1979–. *Recreations:* cooking, gardening, walking, talking. *Address:* 27 Edmunds Walk, N2 0HU. *T:* 0181–883 4420.

MARRINER, Sir Neville, Kt 1985; CBE 1979; conductor; Founder and Director, Academy of St Martin in the Fields, since 1956; *b* 15 April 1924; *s* of Herbert Henry Marriner and Ethel May Roberts; *m* 1955, Elizabeth Mary Sims; one *s* one *d*. *Educ:* Lincoln Sch.; Royal College of Music (ARCM). Taught music at Eton Coll., 1948; Prof., Royal Coll. of Music, 1950. Martin String Quartet, 1949; Jacobean Ensemble, 1951; London Symphony Orchestra, 1954; Music Director: Los Angeles Chamber Orchestra, 1968–77; Minnesota Orchestra, 1979–86; Stuttgart Radio Symphony Orch., 1984–89. Artistic Director: South Bank Summer Music, 1975–77; Meadow Brook Festival, Detroit Symphony Orchestra, 1979–83; Barbican Summer Festival, 1985–87. Hon. ARAM; Hon. FRCM 1983. Kt, Order of the Star of the North (Sweden), 1984; Officer, Ordre des Arts et des Lettres (France), 1995. *Club:* Garrick.

MARRIOTT, Bryant Hayes; Director of Broadcasting, Seychelles Broadcasting Corporation (formerly Radio Television Seychelles), 1991–93; *b* 9 Sept. 1936; *s* of Rev. Horace Marriott and Barbara Marriott; *m* 1963, Alison Mary Eyles; one *s* two *d*. *Educ:* Tormore Sch., Upper Deal, Kent; Marlborough Coll., Wilts; New Coll., Oxford (MA). Joined BBC, 1961; Studio Manager, 1961; Producer, 1963; Staff Training Attachments Officer, 1973; Chief Asst to Controller Radio 1 and 2, 1976; Head of Recording Services, 1979; Controller, Radio Two, 1983; Controller, Special Duties, Radio BBC, 1990–91. *Recreations:* gardening, sailing, drumming. *Address:* 4 School Pasture, Burnham Deepdale, King's Lynn, Norfolk PE31 8DF. *Club:* Brancaster Staithe Sailing.

MARRIOTT, Sir Hugh Cavendish S.; *see* Smith-Marriott.

MARRIOTT, Sir John Brook, KCVO 1995 (CVO 1991; LVO 1978); Keeper of the Royal Philatelic Collection, 1969–95; *b* 27 July 1922; *er s* of late John Morley Marriott and Maud Marriott (*née* Brook); *m* 1952, Mary Eleanor Norcliffe Thompson; two *s*. *Educ:* Merchant Taylors' Sch., Northwood; St John's Coll., Cambridge (Wrangler Math. Tripos; MA). Army Op. Res. Gp., Min. of Supply, 1943; Foreign Office, Bletchley, 1944. Asst Master, Charterhouse, 1945–82, Housemaster 1960–75. Mem., Nat. Postal Mus. Bd, 1989; Royal Philatelic Society, London: Hon. Fellow, 1993; Council Mem., 1969; Vice-Pres., 1979–83; Pres., 1983–86; Tilleard Medal, 1968; Tapling Medal, 1976; London Medal, 1987. Corresp. Mem., l'Académie de Philatelie, Paris. Liveryman, Merchant Taylors' Co., 1950. Gov., St Edmund's Sch., Hindhead, 1979–87. Roll of Distinguished Philatelists, Philatelic Congress of GB, 1972; Alfred F. Lichtenstein Award, Collectors Club, NY, 1988; Lindenberg Medal, Berlin 1888 Philatelic Club, 1988. *Publications:* Philatelic History of Trinidad to 1862, 1963; contribs to London Philatelist. *Recreations:* cricket, football, philately. *Clubs:* Arts, Army and Navy, MCC: Hawks (Cambridge).

MARRIOTT, John Miles; Non-Executive Director, Phillips & Drew Fund Management Ltd, since 1986; *b* 11 Oct. 1935; *s* of Arthur James Marriott and May Lavinia (*née* Goodband); *m* 1967, Josephine Anne (*née* Shepherd). *Educ:* High Pavement Grammar Sch., Nottingham. CIPFA 1962; MBCS 1970. E Midlands Electricity Bd, Nottingham (incl. 2 yrs National Service in RAF), 1952–60; Morley Bor. Council, 1960–62; Wolverhampton County Bor. Council, 1962–67; Asst Bor. Treasurer, Torbay Co. Bor. Council, 1967–70; Dep. Bor. Treas., 1970–72, and Bor. Treas., 1972–73, Ipswich Co. Bor. Council; Dir of Finance, Bolton Metrop. Bor. Council, 1973–78; County Treasurer, Greater Manchester Council, 1978–86; Principal, Grant Thornton, Chartered Accountants, 1986–90. Non-Exec. Dir, Wigan and Bolton HA, 1992–. Gov., Bolton Inst. of Higher Educn, 1993–. *Publications:* papers in prof. jls. *Recreations:* golf, reading, bird watching, motoring. *Address:* 12 Martinsclough, Lostock, Bolton BL6 4PF. *T:* Bolton (01204) 847444.

MARRIOTT, Martin Marriott; Headmaster, Canford School, 1976–92; *b* 28 Feb. 1932; *s* of late Rt Rev. Philip Selwyn Abraham, Bishop of Newfoundland, and Elizabeth Dorothy Cicely, *d* of late Sir John Marriott; *m* 1956, Judith Caroline Guerney Lubbock; one *s* two *d*. *Educ:* Lancing College; New College, Oxford. MA, DipEd. RAF Educn Branch, 1956–59. Asst Master, Heversham Grammar Sch., 1959–66; Asst Master, Housemaster, Second Master, Acting Master, Haileybury College, 1966–76. Chm., HMC, 1989. *Recreations:* grandchildren, golf, sailing, gardening. *Address:* Morris' Farm House, Baverstock, near Dinton, Salisbury, Wilts SP3 5EL. *T:* Salisbury (01722) 716874. *Club:* East India.

MARRIS, James Hugh Spencer; Director, Newcastle Race Course, since 1994; Regional Chairman, British Gas, Northern, 1988–93; *b* 30 July 1937; *s* of Harry V. Marris and Agnes E. Hutchinson; *m* 1963, Susan Mary Husband; one *s* one *d*. *Educ:* King William's College, Isle of Man; Royal Technical College, Salford. ARTCS, CEng, FIGasE. Dir of Engineering, E Midlands Gas, 1978–82; Regional Dep. Chm., Eastern Gas, 1982–83; HQ Dir (Ops), British Gas, 1983–87. *Publications:* contribs to IGasE Jl. *Recreations:* golf, gardening. *Address:* 3 Apple Tree Rise, Corbridge, Northumberland NE45 5HD. *T:* Corbridge (01434) 633509.

MARRIS, Prof. Robin Lapthorn; Professor of Economics, 1981–86, and Head of Department of Economics, 1983–86, Birkbeck College, University of London, now Professor Emeritus; *b* 31 March 1924; *s* of Eric Denyer Marris, CB, and late Phyllis, *d* of T. H. F. Lapthorn, JP; *m* 1st, 1949, Marion Ellinger; 2nd, 1954, Jane Evelina Burney Ayres; one *s* two *d*; 3rd, 1972, Anne Fairclough Mansfield; one *d*. *Educ:* Bedales Sch.; King's Coll., Cambridge. BA 1946, ScD 1968, Cantab. Asst Principal, HM Treasury, 1947–50; UN, Geneva, 1950–52; Fellow of King's Coll., Cambridge, 1951–76; Lectr, 1951–72, Reader, 1972–76, in Econs, Univ. of Cambridge; Prof. 1976–81 and Chm., 1976–79, Dept of Economics, Univ. of Maryland. Visiting Professor: Univ. of California, Berkeley, 1961; Harvard, 1967; Trento Univ., Italy, 1989–91. Dir, World Economy Div., Min. of Overseas Develt, 1964–66. Mem., Vis. Cttee, Open Univ., 1982–. *Publications:* Economic Arithmetic, 1958; The Economic Theory of Managerial Capitalism, 1964; The Economics of Capital Utilisation, 1964; (with Adrian Wood) The Corporate Economy, 1971; The Corporate Society, 1974; The Theory and Future of the Corporate Economy and Society, 1979; The Higher Education Crisis, 1987; Reconstructing Keynsian Economics with Imperfect Competition, 1991; Economics, Bounded Rationality and the Cognitive Revolution, 1992; Managerial Capitalism in Retrospect, 1995; contrib. Econ. Jl, Rev. Econ. Studies, Economica, Jl Manchester Stat. Soc., Jl Royal Stat. Soc., Amer. Econ. Rev., Qly Jl of Econs, Jl of Economic Literature, etc. *Recreations:* cooking, ski-ing, sailing. *Address:* Lingard House, Chiswick Mall, W4 2PJ.

See also S. N. Marris.

MARRIS, Stephen Nicholson; economic consultant; *b* 7 Jan. 1930; *s* of Eric Denyer Marris, CB, and Phyllis May Marris (*née* Lapthorn); *m* 1955, Margaret Swindells; two *s* one *d*. *Educ:* Bryanston School; King's College, Cambridge. MA, PhD. Nat. Inst. of Economic and Social Research, 1953–54; economist and international civil servant; with Org. for European Economic Co-operation, later Org. for Economic Co-operation and Development (OECD), 1956–83: Dir, Economics Branch, 1970; Economic Advr to Sec.-Gen., 1975; Sen. Fellow, Inst. for Internat. Econs, Washington, 1983–88. Vis. Res. Prof. of Internat. Economics, Brookings Instn, Washington DC, 1969–70; Vis. Prof., Institut d'Etudes Politiques, Paris, 1986. Hon. Dr Stockholm Univ., 1978. *Publication:* Deficits and the Dollar: the World Economy at Risk, 1985. *Recreation:* sailing. *Address:* 8 Sentier des Pierres Blanches, 92190 Meudon, France. *T:* 46269812.

See also R. L. Marris.

MARRISON, Rev. Dr Geoffrey Edward; Hon. Fellow, South East Asian Studies, University of Hull, since 1992 (Associate, Centre for South-East Asian Studies, 1989–91); *b* 11 Jan. 1923; *s* of John and Rose Marrison; *m* 1958, Margaret Marian Millburn; one *s* three *d*. *Educ:* SOAS, Univ. of London; Bishops' Coll. Cheshunt; Kirchliche Hochschule, Berlin. BA Malay 1948, PhD Linguistics 1967, London. Indian Army, 1942–46. SOAS, 1941–42 and 1946–49; ordained Priest, Singapore, 1952; in Malaya with USPG, 1952–56; Vicar of St Timothy, Crookes, Sheffield, 1958–61; Linguistics Adviser British and Foreign Bible Soc., 1962–67, incl. service in Assam, 1962–64; Asst Keeper, British Museum, 1967–71, Dep. Keeper 1971–74; Dir and Keeper, Dept of Oriental Manuscripts and Printed Books, British Library, 1974–83, permission to officiate, dio. of Carlisle, 1983–; Tutor, Carlisle Diocesan Training Inst., 1984–90. Res. studies on Indonesian literatures, Leiden and Indonesia, 1990–91. Mem., Koninklijk Instituut voor Taal-, Land- en Volkenkunde, The Netherlands, 1983–. Hon. Canon of All Saints Pro-Cathedral, Shillong, 1963. FRAS. *Publications:* The Christian Approach to the Muslim, 1958; A Catalogue of the South-East Asian Collections of Professor M. A. Jaspan (1926–1975), 1989; A Catalogue of the South-East Asian History Collections of Dr D. K. Bassett (1931–1989), 1992; A Catalogue of the Collections of Rev. Dr Harry Parkin on Asian Religions and Batak Studies (1926–1990), 1993; A Catalogue of the Collections of Dr Roy Bruton on Sarawak, and on the Sociology of Education, 1994; articles in Jl Malayan Branch Royal Asiatic Soc., Bible Translator. *Recreations:* ethno-linguistics of South and South East Asia, Christian and oriental art. *Address:* 1 Ainsworth Street, Ulverston, Cumbria LA12 7EU. *T:* Ulverston (01229) 586874.

MARS-JONES, Adam; Film Critic, The Independent, since 1986; *b* 26 Oct. 1954; *s* of Hon. Sir William Mars-Jones, *qv*. *Educ:* Westminster School; Cambridge Univ. (BA 1976). *Publications:* Lantern Lecture, 1981 (Somerset Maugham Award 1982); (with Edmund White) The Darker Proof, 1987, 2nd edn 1988; Venus Envy, 1990; Monopolies of Loss, 1992; The Waters of Thirst, 1993. *Recreations:* organ-playing, baby-sitting. *Address:* 42B Calabria Road, Highbury, N5 1HU. *T:* 0171–226 2890. *Club:* London Apprentice.

MARS-JONES, Hon. Sir William (Lloyd), Kt 1969; MBE 1945; a Judge of the High Court of Justice, Queen's Bench Division, 1969–90; *b* 4 Sept. 1915; *s* of Henry and Jane Mars Jones, Llansannan, Denbighshire; *m* 1947, Sheila Mary Felicity Cobon; three *s*. *Educ:* Denbigh County Sch.; UCW, Aberystwyth (LLB Hons); St John's Coll., Cambridge (BA). Entrance Schol., Gray's Inn, 1936; Pres. Students' Rep. Counc. and Central Students' Rep. Counc., UCW, 1936–37; MacMahon Studentship, 1939; Barrister at Law, 1941, QC 1957. War of 1939–45, RNVR (MBE); Lt-Comdr RNVR 1945. Contested W Denbigh Parly Div., 1945. Joined Wales and Chester Circuit, 1947, Presiding Judge, 1971–75. Recorder of: Birkenhead, 1959–65; Swansea, 1965–68; Cardiff, 1968–69; Dep. Chm., Denbighshire Quarter Sessions, 1962–68. Bencher, Gray's Inn, 1964, Treasurer, 1982. Comr of Assize, Denbigh and Mold Summer Assize, 1965. Member: Bar Council, 1962; Home Office Inquiry into allegations against Metropolitan Police Officers, 1964; Home Secretary's Adv. Council on Penal System, 1966–68. President: N Wales Arts Assoc., 1976–; UCNW, Bangor, 1983–95; UCW Old Students' Assoc., 1987–88; London Welsh Trust, 1989–95. Hon. LLD UCW, Aberystwyth, 1973. *Recreations:* singing, acting, guitar. *Clubs:* Garrick, Royal Naval Reserve.

See also A. Mars-Jones.

MARSDEN, Arthur Whitcombe, MSc, DIC, ARCS; formerly Education Officer/Technical Editor, Animal Production and Health Division, FAO, Rome, 1964–73; *b* Buxton, Derbyshire, 14 June 1911; *o s* of late Hubert Marsden and Margaret Augusta Bidwell; *m* 1st, 1940, Ailsa Anderson (*d* 1992), *yr d* of late William Anderson McKellar, physician, and Jessie Reid Macfarlane, of Glasgow and Chester-le-Street, Co. Durham; one *s* two *d*; 2nd, 1994, Dr Peggy B. Houghton (*née* Taylor). *Educ:* St Paul's; Imperial Coll. (Royal College of Science), London. BSc Special and ARCS, 1933; research in agricultural chemistry at Imperial Coll., 1933–36; research asst, 1936; demonstrator,

1937; asst lecturer, 1939; MSc and DIC, 1940. Temp. Instr Lieut RN, 1942; HMS Diomede, 1943; HMS King Alfred, 1944; RN Coll., Greenwich, and HMS Superb, 1945. Lecturer, Imperial Coll., London, 1946; Dept Head, Seale-Hayne Agricultural Coll., Newton Abbot, 1946–48; dir of research to grain companies in Aberdeen, 1948–49. Dir of Commonwealth Bureau of Dairy Science and Technology, Shinfield, Reading, 1950–57; Organising Secretary: 15th International Dairy Congress, London, 1957–60; 2nd World Congress of Man-made Fibres, 1960–63. Hon. Sec., Agriculture Group, Soc. of Chem. Industry, 1947–52, Chm., 1954–56; Organising Cttee of 2nd International Congress of Crop Protection, London, 1949; delegate on OEEC Technical Assistance Mission in USA and Canada, 1951; toured research centres in Pakistan, India, Australia, NZ and USA, Oct. 1954–Feb. 1955. *Publications:* papers in scientific journals. *Recreations:* gardening, music, philately, making model ships. *Address:* 109 Willingdon Road, Eastbourne, East Sussex BN21 1TX. *T:* Eastbourne (01323) 733602.

MARSDEN, Prof. (Charles) David, DSc; FRCP; FRS 1983; Professor of Clinical Neurology, since 1987, Director, MRC Human Movement and Balance Unit, Institute of Neurology and National Hospitals for Neurology and Neurosurgery (formerly for Nervous Diseases), Queen Square, since 1988; *b* 15 April 1938; *s* of Charles Moustaka Marsden, CBE and Una Maud Marsden; *m* 1961, Jill Slaney Bullock; two *s* three *d*; *m* 1979, Jennifer Sandom; three *d*. *Educ:* Cheltenham Coll.; St Thomas's Hosp. Med. Sch. (MSc 1960; MB, BS 1963). FRCP 1975 (MRCP 1965); MRCPsych 1978. Sen. House Physician, National Hosp. for Nervous Diseases, 1968–70; Institute of Psychiatry and King's College Hospital, London: Sen. Lectr in Neurol., 1970–72; Prof. of Neurol., 1972–87. Mem., MRC, 1988–91. Mem. Council, Royal Soc., 1991–94. *Publications:* papers on human movement disorders, motor physiology, and basal ganglia pharmacology. *Recreation:* the human brain. *Address:* Institute of Neurology, National Hospital for Neurology and Neurosurgery, Queen Square, WC1N 3BG. *Club:* Athenæum.

MARSDEN, Edmund Murray; Assistant Director-General, British Council, since 1993; *b* 22 Sept. 1946; *s* of Christopher Marsden and Ruth Marsden (*née* Kershaw); *m* 1981, Megan McIntyre; one *s*. *Educ:* Winchester College; Trinity College, Cambridge. Partner, Compton Press, Salisbury, 1968–70; Nuffield Foundn Publications Unit, 1970–71; British Council: Ghana, 1971; Belgium, 1973; Algeria, 1975; Management Accountant, 1977; Syria, 1980; Dir, Educn Contracts, 1982; Turkey, 1987; Dir, Corporate Affairs, 1990. *Address:* British Council, 10 Spring Gardens, SW1A 2BN. *T:* 0171–389 4892.

MARSDEN, Frank; JP; *b* Everton, Liverpool, 15 Oct. 1923; *s* of Sidney Marsden and Harriet Marsden (*née* Needham); *m* 1943, Muriel Lightfoot; three *s*. *Educ:* Abbotsford Road Sec. Mod. Sch., Liverpool. Served War, with RAF Bomber Command, 115 Sqdn (Warrant Officer), 1941–46. Joined Lab. Party and Co-op. Movement, 1948. MP (Lab) Liverpool, Scotland, Apr. 1971–Feb. 1974. Local Councillor: Liverpool St Domingo Ward, May 1964–67; Liverpool Vauxhall Ward, 1969–71; Knowsley DC, 1976–. Chm. Liverpool Markets, 1965–67; Past Mem. Exec. Cttee: Liverpool Trades Council; Liverpool Lab. Party. JP (City of Liverpool), 1969. *Recreations:* jazz music, gardening. *Address:* 2 Thunderbolt Cottage, 6 Alder Lane, Knowsley, Prescot, Merseyside L34 9EQ. *T:* 0151–546 8666.

MARSDEN, Dr John Christopher; Executive Secretary, Linnean Society, since 1989; *b* 4 March 1937; *s* of Ewart and May Marsden; *m* 1962, Jessany Margaret Hazel Macdonald; two *s*. *Educ:* Bristol Grammar Sch.; Keble Coll., Oxford (MA, DPhil). FRSC; FIBiol. Lectr in Biology, Univ. of York, 1965–71; Sen. Res. Fellow, Inst. of Child Health, 1971–72; Reader in Cell Physiology, City of London Polytechnic, 1972–74; Polytechnic of Central London: Head of Life Scis, 1974–86; Dean, Faculty of Engrg and Sci., 1986–88, retired. *Publications:* Enzymes and Equilibria (with C. F. Stoneman), 1974; numerous contribs to biol. jls. *Recreations:* book collecting, cookery. *Address:* 7 Surrey Close, Tunbridge Wells, Kent TN2 5RF. *T:* Tunbridge Wells (01892) 533784.

MARSDEN, Sir Nigel (John Denton), 3rd Bt *cr* 1924, of Grimsby; gardener since 1983; *b* 26 May 1940; *s* of Sir John Denton Marsden, 2nd Bt and of Hope, *yr d* of late G. E. Llewelyn; *S* father, 1985; *m* 1961, Diana Jean, *d* of Air Marshal Sir Patrick Hunter Dunn, *qv*; three *d*. *Educ:* Ampleforth College, York. Vice-Chairman and Managing Director of family business, Consolidated Fisheries Ltd, of Grimsby, 1973 until 1982, when Company ceased trading and was sold. *Recreations:* walking, shooting, family. *Heir:* *b* Simon Neville Llewelyn Marsden [*b* 1 Dec. 1948; *m* 1970, Catherine Thérèse (marr. diss.), *d* of late Brig. James Charles Windsor-Lewis, DSO, MC; *m* 1984, Caroline, *y d* of John Stanton, Houghton St Giles, Norfolk; one *d*]. *Address:* The Homestead, 1 Grimsby Road, Waltham, Grimsby, South Humberside DN37 0PS. *T:* Grimsby (01472) 822166.

MARSDEN, Rear-Adm. Peter Nicholas; *b* 29 June 1932; *s* of Dr James Pickford Marsden and Evelyn (*née* Holman); *m* 1956, Jean Elizabeth Mather; two *s* one *d*. *Educ:* Felsted Sch., Essex. Joined RN, 1950; Commander, 1968; Captain, 1976; Commodore, Admiralty Interview Bd, 1983–84; Sen. Naval Mem., DS, RCDS, 1985–88. Exec. Dir, 21st Century Trust, 1989–92. *Recreations:* golf, beagling, gardening. *Address:* c/o National Westminster Bank, Standishgate, Wigan, Lancs WN1 1UJ.

MARSDEN, Dr Rosalind Mary; HM Diplomatic Service; Political Counsellor, Tokyo, since 1993; *b* 1950; *d* of late Major Walter Stancliffe Marsden and Winifred Howells. *Educ:* Woking County Grammar Sch. for Girls; Somerville Coll., Oxford (BA 1st Cl. Hons Mod. Hist.); St Antony's Coll., Oxford (DPhil). Joined FCO, 1974; Tokyo, 1976–80; Policy Planning Staff, 1980–82; EC Dept (Internal), 1983–84; Bonn, 1985–88; Hong Kong Dept, 1989–91; on secondment to National Westminster Bank Gp, 1991–93. *Recreations:* mountain walking, reading, travel. *Address:* c/o Foreign and Commonwealth Office, King Charles Street, SW1A 2AH.

MARSDEN, Susan; Part-time Chairman: Social Security Appeal Tribunals (Leeds), since 1987; Disability Appeal Tribunals, since 1992; *b* 6 Dec. 1931; *d* of late John Marsden-Smedley and Agatha (*née* Bethell). *Educ:* Downe House Sch.; Girton Coll., Cambridge (MA). Called to the Bar, Middle Temple, 1957. Worked in consumer organisations in Britain and US, 1957–65; Senior Research Officer, Consumer Council, 1966–70; Legal Officer, Nuffield Foundation Legal Advice Research Unit, 1970–72; Exec. Dir, 1972–78, and Course Dir, 1978–81, Legal Action Gp (Editor, LAG Bulletin, 1972–78); Sec., Public Sector Liaison, RIBA, 1981–84; Asst Dir, Nat. Assoc. of CAB, 1985–86. Chm., Greater London CAB Service, 1979–85; Member: Council, National Assoc. of CAB, 1980–84; Royal Commn on Legal Services, 1976–79; Yorks Regional Rivers Adv. Cttee, Nat. Rivers Authority, 1989–; Council, Leeds Civic Trust, 1989–92. Chair, EYE on the Aire, 1988–93. *Publication:* Justice Out of Reach, a case for Small Claims Courts, 1969. *Recreations:* conservation along the River Aire, tree planting and preservation, gardening, walking, looking at modern buildings. *Address:* Flat 5, 28 Newlay Lane, Horsforth, Leeds LS18 4LE. *T:* Leeds (0113) 258 0936.

MARSDEN, William, CMG 1991; HM Diplomatic Service; Assistant Under-Secretary of State (Americas), Foreign and Commonwealth Office, since 1994; *b* 15 Sept. 1940; *s* of Christopher Marsden and Ruth (*née* Kershaw); *m* 1964, Kaia Collingham; one *s* one *d*. *Educ:* Winchester Coll.; Lawrenceville Sch., USA; Trinity Coll., Cambridge (MA); London Univ. (BSc Econs). FO, 1962–64; UK Delegn to NATO, 1964–66; Rome, 1966–69; seconded as Asst to Gen. Manager, Joseph Lucas Ltd, 1970; First Sec., FCO, 1971–76; First Sec. and Cultural Attaché, Moscow, 1976–79; Asst Head, European Community Dept, FCO, 1979–81; Counsellor, UK Representation to EEC, 1981–85; Head, E Africa Dept, FCO, and Comr, British Indian Ocean Territory, 1985–88; Ambassador to Costa Rica, and concurrently Ambassador to Nicaragua, 1989–92; Minister (Trade), Washington, 1992–94. Chairman: Diplomatic Service Assoc., 1987–88; Twickenham Town Cttee, 1981–88. MIMgt. *Address:* c/o Foreign and Commonwealth Office, SW1A 2AH.

MARSH, family name of **Baron Marsh.**

MARSH, Baron *cr* 1981 (Life Peer), of Mannington in the County of Wiltshire; **Richard William Marsh;** PC 1966; Kt 1976; FZS; FCIT; Chairman: Mannington Management Services, since 1989; Laurentian Financial Group plc, since 1986; *b* 14 March 1928; *s* of William Marsh, Belvedere, Kent; *m* 1st, 1950, Evelyn Mary (marr. diss. 1973), *d* of Frederick Andrews, Southampton; two *s*; 2nd, 1973, Caroline Dutton (*d* 1975); 3rd, 1979, Felicity, *d* of Baron McFadzean of Kelvinside. *Educ:* Jennings Sch., Swindon; Woolwich Polytechnic; Ruskin Coll., Oxford. Health Services Officer, National Union of Public Employees, 1951–59; Mem., Clerical and Administrative Whitley Council for Health Service, 1953–59; MP (Lab) Greenwich, Oct. 1959–April 1971; promoted Offices Act 1961; Member: Select Cttee Estimates, 1961; Chm. Interdepartmental Cttee to Co-ordinate Govt Policy on Industrial Training, 1964; Parly Sec., Min. of Labour, 1964–65; Joint Parly Sec., Min. of Technology, 1965–66; Minister of Power, 1966–68; Minister of Transport, 1968–69. Chairman: British Railways Bd, 1971–76; Newspaper Publishers' Assoc., 1976–90; British Iron and Steel Consumers' Council, 1977–82; Allied Investments Ltd, 1977–81; Member: NEDC, 1971–; Freight Integration Council, 1971–; Council, CBI, 1970–. Chairman: Allied Medical Group, 1977–81; Vivat Hldgs PLC, 1982–88; TV-am, 1983–84 (Dep. Chm., 1980–83); China & Eastern Investments Trust, Hong Kong, 1990– (Dir, 1987–); Gartmore British Income & Growth Trust, 1994–; Deputy Chairman: United Medical Enterprises Ltd, 1978–81; Lopex PLC, 1986– (Dir, 1985–); Director: Imperial Life of Canada UK, 1983–; Imperial Life Assurance Co. of Canada, 1983–; Charles Church Developments, 1987–; Laurentian Group Corp. (Montreal), 1990–94; Advisor: Nissan Motor Co., 1981–; Fujitec, 1982–. Pres., Council ECSC, 1968. Governor: British Transport Staff Coll. (Chm.); London Business Sch. FIMgt; FInstD; FInstM. *Publication:* Off the Rails (autobiog.), 1978. *Address:* House of Lords, SW1A 0PW.

MARSH, Barrie; *see* Marsh, G. B.

MARSH, Ven. Bazil Roland, BA; Archdeacon of Northampton, Non-Residentiary Canon of Peterborough, and Rector of St Peter's, Northampton, 1964–91, now Archdeacon Emeritus; *b* Three Hills, Alta, Canada, 11 Aug. 1921; *s* of late Ven. Wilfred Carter Marsh and late Mary Jean (*née* Stott), Devil's Lake, North Dakota, USA; *m* 1946, Audrey Joan, *d* of late Owen George Oyler, farmer, of Brookmans Park, Hatfield, and Alma Lillian Oyler; three *s* one *d*. *Educ:* State schs in USA and Swindon, Wilts; Leeds Univ.; Coll. of the Resurrection, Mirfield, Yorks. Curate of: St Mary the Virgin, Cheshunt, Herts, 1944–46; St John Baptist, Coventry, 1946–47; St Giles-in-Reading, Berks, 1947–51; Rector of St Peter's, Townsville, Qld, Australia, 1951–56; Vicar of St Mary the Virgin, Far Cotton, Northampton, 1956–64. MLitt Lambeth, 1990. *Address:* 12 Parkway, Northampton NN3 3BS. *T:* Northampton (01604) 406644.

MARSH, Rt. Rev. Edward Frank; *see* Newfoundland, Central, Bishop of.

MARSH, Rear-Adm. Geoffrey Gordon Ward, CB 1985; OBE 1969; jssc; Project Manager, NATO Frigate 90, Hamburg, 1988–90, retired; *m*; one *s* one *d*. *Educ:* St Albans Sch.; Queens' Coll., Cambridge. Britannia Royal Naval Coll., 1947; served on HM Ships: Indefatigable; Victorious; Carron; Norfolk; Girdle Ness; Bristol; involved in develt of Sea Dart missile; Hd of Propulsion Machinery Control, Ship Dept; Asst Dir (Surface Warfare), Naval Op. Req.; Dir, Weapons Co-ordination and Acceptance (Naval), MoD, 1978–80; i/c HMS Thunderer, 1980–82; ACNS (Op. Req.), 1982–84; Dep. Controller, Warships Equipment, MoD (Navy), 1984–87; Chief Naval Engr Officer, 1985–87. *Address:* c/o The Naval Secretary, Ministry of Defence, Old Admiralty Building, Whitehall, SW1A 2BE.

MARSH, Gordon Victor, MA; FHSM; Member, Police Complaints Authority, 1989–94 and since 1995; *b* 14 May 1929; *s* of late Ven. Wilfred Carter Marsh, Devil's Lake, North Dakota, USA and Rosalie (*née* Holliday); *m* Millicent, *e d* of late Christopher Thomas and Edith Rowsell; one *s* one *d*. *Educ:* Grammar Schs, Swindon; Keble Coll., Oxford (MA); Inst. of Health Service Administrators (FHA 1964); Sloan Business Sch., Cornell Univ., USA. NHS admin. posts, England and Wales, 1952–72; Administrator and Sec., Bd of Governors, UCH, 1972–74; Area Administrator, Lambeth, Southwark and Lewisham AHA(T), 1974–82; Dep. Health Service Comr, 1982–89, retd. Vice-Chm., Assoc. of Chief Administrators of Health Authorities, 1980–82; Member: Council, National Assoc. of Health Authorities, 1979–82; Adv. Bd, Coll. of Occupational Therapists, 1974–95. Chm., Trelawn Cttee of Richmond Fellowship, 1970–83; Hon. Sec. to Congregational Meeting and Wandsman, St Paul's Cathedral, 1980–. *Publications:* articles in professional jls. *Recreations:* music, gardening. *Address:* Springwater, St Lucian's Lane, Wallingford, Oxon OX10 9ER. *T:* Wallingford (01491) 836660. *Club:* United Oxford & Cambridge University.

MARSH, (Graham) Barrie, FCIArb; solicitor; Senior Partner, Mace & Jones, Solicitors, Liverpool and Manchester, since 1980 (Partner, since 1959); *b* 18 July 1935; *s* of Ernest Heaps Marsh and Laura Greenhalgh Marsh; *m* 1961, Nancy Smith; one *s* two *d*. *Educ:* Bury Grammar Sch.; Loughborough Grammar Sch.; Liverpool Univ. (LLB Hons). FCIArb 1982. Admitted as Solicitor, 1957. Nat. Chm., Young Solicitors Gp, Law Soc., 1975; President: Liverpool Law Soc., 1978–79; Solicitors' Disciplinary Tribunal, 1988–; Liverpool Publicity Assoc., 1980. Chairman: Merseyside Chamber of Commerce and Industry, 1984–86; Radio City PLC, 1988–91. Hon. Belgian Consul, Liverpool, and for NW, 1987–. *Publications:* Employer and Employee: a complete and practical guide to the modern law of employment, 1977, 3rd edn 1990; contribs to legal and personnel jls on all aspects of employment law and industrial relations. *Recreations:* golf, Liverpool Football Club, bird-watching, hill-walking. *Address:* Calmer Hey, Benty Heath Lane, Willaston, South Wirral L64 1SA. *T:* 0151–327 4863; Mace & Jones, Drury House, 19 Water Street, Liverpool L2 0RP. *T:* 0151–236 8989. *Clubs:* Royal Anglo-Belgian; Racquet, Artists (Liverpool); Heswall Golf (Cheshire).

MARSH, Jean Lyndsey Torren; actress; Artistic Director, Adelphi University Theatre, Long Island, New York, 1981–83; *b* 1 July 1934; *d* of late Henry Charles and of Emmeline Susannah Marsh; *m* 1955, Jon Devon Roland Pertwee (marr. diss. 1960). Began as child actress and dancer; *films:* Return to Oz; Willow; danced in Tales of Hoffmann, Where's Charley?, etc; acted in repertory companies: Huddersfield, Nottingham, etc; Broadway debut in Much Ado About Nothing, 1959; West End debut, Bird of Time, 1961; *stage:* Habeas Corpus, The Importance of Being Earnest, Too True to be Good, Twelfth Night, Blithe Spirit, Whose Life is it Anyway?, Uncle Vanya, On the Rocks, Pygmalion, Hamlet,

The Chalk Garden; *television:* series, Nine to Five; co-created and co-starred (Rose) in series Upstairs Downstairs; co-created series, The House of Eliott. Hon. DH Maryland Coll., NY, 1980. *Publications:* The Illuminated Language of Flowers, 1978; The House of Eliott, 1993; articles for Sunday Times, Washington Post, New York Times, Los Angeles Times. *Recreations:* walking, cross-country skiing, reading, cooking, eating. *Address:* Hamstead Farm Cottage, Drift Lane, Chidham, W Sussex PO18 8PP.

MARSH, Prof. Leonard George, OBE 1992; MEd; DPhil; Principal, Bishop Grosseteste College, since 1974; *b* 23 Oct. 1930; third *c* of late Ernest Arthur Marsh and Anne Eliza (*née* Bean); *m* 1953, Ann Margaret Gilbert; one *s* one *d. Educ:* Ashford (Kent) Grammar Sch.; Borough Road Coll., London Inst. of Educn (London Univ. Teachers' Certif. and Academic Dip.); Leicester Univ. (MEd); DPhil York, 1988. Lectr in Educn and Mathematics, St Paul's Coll., Cheltenham, 1959–61; Lectr, 1961–63, Sen. Lectr, 1963–65, Principal Lectr and Head of Postgraduate Primary Educn Dept, 1965–74, Goldsmiths' Coll., London. Hon. Prof., Hull Univ., 1987–. Visiting Lectr, Bank Street Coll., New York, and Virginia Commonwealth Univ.; former Consultant, OECD, Portugal; Educnl Consultant, Teacher Trng Proj., Botswana, 1981; Dir, Sindh Pakistan Primary Educn Develt Prog., 1992–; Specialist tour to India for British Council; Mem., SCAA, 1993–. Dir (non-exec.), A & C Black plc, 1994–. Member: Gen. Adv. Council, IBA, 1977–82; N Lincolnshire AHA, 1984–90; Chm., Nat. Assoc. for Primary Educn, 1981–83. FRSA. Hon. FCP (FCP 1989). *Publications:* Let's Explore Mathematics, Books 1–4, 1964–67; Children Explore Mathematics, 1967, 3rd edn 1969; Exploring Shapes and Numbers, 1968, 2nd edn 1970; Exploring the Metric System, 1969, 2nd edn 1969; Exploring the Metric World, 1970; Approach to Mathematics, 1970; Alongside the Child in the Primary School, 1970; Let's Discover Mathematics, Books 1–5, 1971–72; Being A Teacher, 1973; Helping your Child with Maths—a parents' guide, 1980; The Guinness Mathematics Book, 1980; The Guinness Book for Young Scientists, 1982. *Recreations:* photography, theatre, walking, films. *Address:* The Principal's House, Bishop Grosseteste College, Lincoln LN1 3DY. *T:* Lincoln (01522) 528241. *Club:* Athenæum.

MARSH, Nevill Francis, CBE 1969; Director-General, St John Ambulance, 1972–76; *b* 13 Aug. 1907; *m* 1st, 1935, Betty Hide (decd); one *s* one *d*; 2nd, 1989, Gillian Hodnett. *Educ:* Oundle Sch., Northants; Clare Coll., Cambridge (MA). Traction Motor Design Staff, Metropolitan-Vickers Electrical Co. Ltd, 1930–32; Mid-Lincolnshire Electric Supply Co. Ltd: Dist Engineer, 1932–38; Engineer and Manager, 1938–48; Chief Commercial Officer, E Midlands Electricity Board, 1948–55; Dep.-Chm., N Eastern Electricity Board, 1955–57; Dep.-Chm., E Midlands Electricity Board, 1957–59; Chm., East Midlands Electricity Board, 1959–61; a Dep. Chm., Electricity Council, 1962–71; Chm., British Electrotechnical Cttee, 1970–72. Dir for Gtr London, St John Ambulance Assoc., 1971–72. Also formerly: Dir, Altrincham Electric Supply Ltd, and Public Utilities (Elec.) Ltd, and Supervising Engineer, Campbeltown & Mid-Argyll Elec. Supply Co. Ltd, and Thurso & District Elec. Supply Co. Ltd. FIEE; Pres. of Assoc. of Supervising Electrical Engineers, 1966–68. KStJ 1973. *Publications:* jt contrib. Jl Inst. Electrical Engineers, 1955. *Address:* Gill's Cottage, 23 High Street, Morton, near Bourne, Lincs PE10 0NR. *T:* Morton (01778) 570601. *Club:* Royal Air Force.

MARSH, Norman Stayner, CBE 1977; QC 1967; Law Commissioner, 1965–78; Member, Royal Commission on Civil Liability and Compensation for Personal Injury, 1973–78; *b* 26 July 1913; 2nd *s* of Horace Henry and Lucy Ann Marsh, Bath, Som; *m* 1939, Christiane Christinnecke, 2nd *d* of Professor Johannes and Käthe Christinnecke, Magdeburg, Germany; two *s* two *d. Educ:* Monkton Combe Sch.; Pembroke Coll., Oxford (2nd Class Hons, Final Honour Sch. of Jurisprudence, 1935; 1st Cl. Hons BCL; Hon. Fellow, 1978). Vinerian Scholar of Oxford Univ., Harmsworth Scholar of Middle Temple, called to Bar, 1937; practice in London and on Western Circuit, 1937–39; Lieut-Col Intelligence Corps and Control Commission for Germany, 1939–46. Stowell Civil Law Fellow, University Coll., Oxford, 1946–60; University Lecturer in Law, 1947–60; Estates Bursar, University Coll., 1948–56; Secretary-General, International Commission of Jurists, The Hague, Netherlands, 1956–58. Member: Bureau of Conference of Non-Governmental Organisations with Consultative Status with the United Nations, 1957–58; Internat. Cttee of Legal Science (Unesco), 1960–63. Dir of British Institute of International and Comparative Law, 1960–65. Mem., Younger Cttee on Privacy, 1970–72. Hon. Vis. Prof. in Law, KCL, 1972–77. Vice-Chm., Age Concern, England, 1979–86. General editor, International and Comparative Law Quarterly, 1961–65, Mem., Editorial Board, 1965–93. *Publications:* The Rule of Law as a supra-national concept, in Oxford Essays in Jurisprudence, 1960; The Rule of Law in a Free Society, 1960; Interpretation in a National and International Context, 1974; (editor and part-author) Public Access to Government-held Information, 1987; articles on common law and comparative law in English, American, French and German law jls. *Address:* Wren House, 13 North Side, Clapham Common, SW4 0RF. *T:* 0171–622 2865.

See also B. K. Cherry.

MARSH, Prof. Paul Rodney; Professor of Management and Finance, London Business School, since 1985; *b* 19 Aug. 1947; *s* of Harold Marsh and Constance (*née* Miller); *m* 1971, Stephanie Beatrice (*née* Simonow). *Educ:* Poole Grammar Sch.; London School of Economics (BScEcon, 1st Cl. Hons); London Business Sch. (PhD). Systems Analyst, Esso Petroleum, 1968–69; Scicon, 1970–71; London Business School, 1974–: Bank of England Res. Fellow, 1974–85; Dir, Sloan Fellowship Prog., 1980–83; Non-exec. Dir, Centre for Management Develt, 1984–; Mem. Gov. Body, 1986–90; Faculty Dean, 1987–90; Dep. Principal, 1989–90; Dir, Masters in Finance Prog., 1993–. Member: CBI Task Force on City-Industry Relationships, 1986–88. Exec. Cttee, British Acad. of Management, 1986–88. Non-exec. Dir, M&G Investment Management Ltd, 1989–; Dir, Hoare Govett Indices Ltd, 1991–. Gov. Examg Bd, Securities Inst., 1994–. *Publications:* Cases in Corporate Finance, 1988; Managing Strategic Investment Decisions, 1988, Accounting for Brands, 1989; Short-termism on Trial, 1990; The HGSC Smaller Companies Index, 1995; numerous articles in Jl of Financial Econs, Jl of Finance, Harvard Business Review, Jl of Inst. of Actuaries, Managerial Finance, Res. in Marketing, Mergers and Acquisitions, Investment Analyst, Long Range Planning, Investment Management Rev., etc. *Recreations:* gardening, investment. *Address:* London Business School, Sussex Place, Regent's Park, NW1 4SA. *T:* 0171–262 5050.

MARSHALL, family name of **Baron Marshall of Goring.**

MARSHALL OF GORING, Baron *cr* 1985 (Life Peer), of South Stoke in the County of Oxfordshire; **Walter Charles Marshall;** Kt 1982; CBE 1973; FRS 1971; Ambassador to World Association of Nuclear Operators, since 1993 (Chairman, 1989–93); *b* 5 March 1932; *s* of late Frank Marshall and Amy (*née* Pearson); *m* 1955, Ann Vivienne Sheppard; one *s* one *d. Educ:* Birmingham Univ. Scientific Officer, AERE, Harwell, 1954–57; Research Physicist: University of California, 1957–58; Harvard Univ., 1958–59; AERE, Harwell: Group Leader, Solid State Theory, 1959–60; Head of Theoretical Physics Div., 1960–66; Dep. Dir, 1966–68; Dir, 1966–75; Chief Scientist, Dept of Energy, 1974–77; United Kingdom Atomic Energy Authority: Dir, Research Gp, 1969–75; Mem., 1972–82; Dep. Chm., 1975–81; Chm., 1981–82; Chm., CEGB, 1982–89. Member: NRDC, 1969–75; NEDC, 1984–86; Chairman: Adv. Council on R&D for Fuel and Power, 1974–77; Offshore Energy Technology Bd, 1975–77. Adviser: Lloyd's nuclear insurance syndicate, 1991–; Inst. of Nuclear Safety System Inc., KANSAI Electric Power Co., Japan, 1992–. Pres., Assoc. of Science Educn, 1987. Editor, Oxford Internat. Series of Monographs on Physics, 1966–. Freeman, City of London, 1984. Fellow, Royal Swedish Acad. of Engrg Scis, 1977; For. Associate, Nat. Acad. of Engineering, USA. Hon. FWeldI, 1987; Hon. Fellow, St Hugh's Coll., Oxford, 1983; Hon. DSc Salford, 1977. Maxwell Medal, 1964; Glazebrook Medal, 1975. Henry DeWolf Smyth Nuclear Statesman Award, USA, 1985; Internat. Award, Canadian Nuclear Assoc., 1991. *Publications:* Thermal Neutron Scattering, 1971; Nuclear Power Technology, 1984; research papers on magnetism, neutron scattering and solid state theory. *Recreations:* gardening, origami, physics. *Address:* Bridleway House, Goring-on-Thames, Oxon RG8 0HS. *T:* Goring-on-Thames (01491) 875017, *Fax:* (01491) 875009.

MARSHALL, Mrs Alan R.; *see* Marshall, V. M.

MARSHALL, Alan Ralph; Managing Director, ARM Educational Consultants Ltd, since 1991; *s* of Ralph Marshall and Mabel Mills; *m* 1958, Caterina Gattico; one *s* one *d. Educ:* Shoreditch College (Teacher's Cert. 1953); London Univ. (Dip Ed 1959; MPhil 1965); Eastern Washington State Univ. (MEd 1964); Stanford Univ. (MA 1969). Teacher, schools in UK and USA, 1954–62; Lectr, Shoreditch Coll., 1962–68; Vis. Prof., Eastern Washington State Univ., 1964–65; Field Dir, Project Technology, Schools Council, 1970–72; Editor, Nat. Centre for School Technology, 1972–73; Course Team Chm., Open Univ., 1973–76; HM Inspector, DES, 1976–91, HM Chief Inspector of Schools, 1985–91. Hon. DEd CNAA, 1990. *Publications:* (ed) School Technology in Action, 1974; (with G. T. Page and J. B. Thomas) International Dictionary of Education, 1977; Giving Substance to a Vision, 1990; articles in jls. *Recreations:* travel, reading. *Address:* 98 Wheathampstead Road, Harpenden, Herts AL5 1JB.

MARSHALL, Alexander Badenoch, (Sandy); Director, Maersk Co. Ltd, since 1980 (Vice-Chairman, 1983–87; Chairman, 1987–93); *b* 31 Dec. 1924; *m* 1961, Mona Kurina Douglas Kirk, South Africa; two *s* one *d. Educ:* Trinity Coll., Glenalmond; Worcester Coll., Oxford (MA). Served War, Sub-Lieut RNVR, 1943–46. P&O Group of Companies: Mackinnon Mackenzie & Co., Calcutta, 1947–59; Gen. Manager, British India Steam Navigation Co., 1959–62; Man. Dir, Trident Tankers Ltd, 1962–68; Dir, 1968–72, Man. Dir, 1972–79, Peninsular and Oriental Steam Navigation Co.; Chairman: Bestobell Plc, 1979–85; Commercial Union Assurance Co. plc, 1983–90 (Dir, 1970–90); Royal Bank of Canada Hldgs UK Ltd, 1988–95; Vice-Chm., The Boots Co. Plc, 1985–91 (Dir, 1981–91); Dir, Royal Bank of Canada, 1985–95. Pres., Chamber of Shipping of UK, 1994–95. Co-Chm., British-N American Cttee, 1984–90. *Recreations:* travel, hill walking, golf. *Address:* Crest House, Woldingham, Surrey CR3 7DH. *T:* Woldingham (01883) 65229. *Clubs:* Oriental; Tollygunge (Calcutta).

MARSHALL, Sir Arthur Gregory George, Kt 1974; OBE 1948; DL; Life President, Marshall of Cambridge (Holdings), 1990; *b* 4 Dec. 1903; *s* of David Gregory Marshall, MBE, and Maude Edmunds Wing; *m* 1931, Rosemary Wynford Dimsdale (*d* 1988), *d* of Marcus Southwell Dimsdale; two *s* one *d. Educ:* Tonbridge Sch.; Jesus Coll., Cambridge (Hon. Fellow, 1990). Engrg, MA. Joined Garage Company of Marshall (Cambridge) Ltd, 1926, which resulted in estabt of Aircraft Company, now Marshall of Cambridge (Aerospace) Ltd, 1929, Chm. and Jt Man. Dir, 1942–89. Chm., Aerodrome Owners Assoc., 1964–65; Member: Air Cadet Council, 1951–59 and 1965–76; Adv. Council on Technology, 1967–70. Hon. Old Cranwellian, 1979; CRAeS 1980. JP, 1951–61; DL 1968, High Sheriff of Cambridgeshire and Isle of Ely, 1969–70. Hon. DSc Cranfield, 1992. Order of El Istiqlal, First Class (Jordan), 1990. *Publication:* The Marshall Story: a century of wheels and wings, 1994. *Recreations:* Cambridge Athletics Blue, Olympic Team Reserve, 1924; flying. *Address:* Horseheath Lodge, Linton, Cambridge CB1 6PT. *T:* Cambridge (01223) 891318. *Clubs:* Royal Air Force; Hawks (Cambridge).

See also M. J. Marshall.

MARSHALL, Arthur Stirling-Maxwell, CBE 1986 (OBE 1979); HM Diplomatic Service, retired; *b* 29 Jan. 1929; *s* of Victor Stirling-Maxwell Marshall and Jeannie Theodora Hunter; *m* 1st, 1955, Eleni Kapralou, Athens (*d* 1969); one *s* two *d*; 2nd, 1985, Cheryl Mary Hookens, Madras; one *d. Educ:* Daniel Stewart's Coll., Edinburgh. Served Royal Navy, 1947–59. Foreign Office, 1959; Middle East Centre for Arab Studies, Lebanon, 1959–61; Political Officer, British Political Agency, Bahrain and Registrar of HBM Court for Bahrain, 1961–64; Attaché, Athens, 1964–67; Information Officer, Rabat, Morocco, 1967–69; Commercial Secretary: Nicosia, Cyprus, 1970–75; Kuwait, 1975–79; Deputy High Commissioner, Madras, 1980–83; Counsellor, Kuwait, 1983–85; Ambassador to People's Democratic Republic of Yemen, 1986–89. *Recreations:* music, nature. *Address:* 147 Highbury Grove, N5 1HP.

MARSHALL, Hon. (Cedric) Russell; Chairman, New Zealand Commission for UNESCO, since 1990; *b* 15 Feb. 1936; *s* of Cedric Thomas Marshall and Gladys Margaret Marshall; *m* 1961, Barbara May Watson; two *s* one *d. Educ:* Nelson Coll.; Christchurch Teachers Coll.; Auckland Univ. (DipTeaching, 1966); BA Victoria Univ., 1992. Primary teacher, Nelson, 1955–56; Trinity Methodist Theol Coll., 1958–60; Methodist Minister: Christchurch, Spreydon, 1960–66; Masterton, 1967–71; teacher, Wanganui High Sch., 1972. MP (Lab) Wanganui, 1972–90; Opposition education spokesman, 1976–84; Chief Opposition Whip, 1978–79; Minister of Education, 1984–87, for the Environment, 1984–86, of Conservation, 1986–87, of Disarmament and Arms Control, 1987–89, of Foreign Affairs, 1987–90, for Pacific Island Affairs, 1988–90. Chairman: Commonwealth Observer Mission to Seychelles electon, 1993; Commonwealth Observer Mission to South Africa, 1994; Mem., Commonwealth Observer Mission to Lesotho elections, 1993. Chairman: Polytechnics Internat. New Zealand, 1994–; Cambodia Trust (Aotearoa–New Zealand), 1994–; Trustee: Africa Information Centre, 1978– (Chm., 1991–); Nelson Mandela Trust (NZ), 1995–. Patron, Genealogical Res. Inst. of NZ, 1987–. Hon. PhD Univ. of Khon Kaen, Thailand, 1989. *Recreations:* reading, listening to music, genealogy. *Address:* 26 Mana Esplanade, Paremata, Porirua, New Zealand. *T:* and *Fax:* (4) 2339178.

MARSHALL, Prof. Christopher John, DPhil; FRS 1995; Director, Cancer Research Campaign Centre for Cell and Molecular Biology, Institute of Cancer Research, since 1994; *b* 19 Jan. 1949; *s* of Lillian and James Marshall; *m* 1973, Vivien Roma Morrall (separated); two *s* one *d. Educ:* King Henry VIII Sch., Coventry; Churchill Coll., Cambridge (MA); Lincoln Coll., Oxford (DPhil). Postdoctoral Fellow: ICRF, 1973–78; Sidney Farber Cancer Inst., Boston, USA, 1978–80; Research Scientist, Inst. of Cancer Research, 1980–. Mem., EMBO, 1993. *Publications:* contribs to learned jls. *Recreation:* cycling. *Address:* Chester Beatty Laboratories, Institute of Cancer Research, 237 Fulham Road, SW3 6JB. *T:* 0171–352 9772. *Club:* Norwood Paragon Cycling.

MARSHALL, Sir Colin (Marsh), Kt 1987; Chief Executive, since 1983, and Chairman, since 1993, British Airways (Deputy Chairman, 1989–93); *b* 16 Nov. 1933; *s* of Marsh Edward Leslie and Florence Mary Marshall; *m* 1958, Janet Winifred (*née* Cracknell); one *d. Educ:* University College Sch., Hampstead. Progressively, cadet purser to Dep. Purser, OSNC, 1951–58; Hertz Corp., 1958–64: management trainee, Chicago and Toronto, 1958–59; Gen. Man., Mexico, Mexico City, 1959–60; Asst to Pres., New York, 1960;

Gen. Manager: UK London, 1961–62; UK Netherlands and Belgium, London, 1962–64; Avis Inc., 1964–79: Reg. Man./Vice-Pres., Europe, London, 1964–66; Vice-Pres. and Gen. Man., Europe and ME, London, 1966–69; Vice-Pres. and Gen. Man., International, London, 1969–71; Exec. Vice-Pres. and Chief Operating Officer, New York, 1971–75; Pres. and Chief Operating Officer, New York, 1975–76; Pres. and Chief Exec. Officer, New York, 1976–79; Norton Simon Inc., New York, 1979–81: Exec. Vice-Pres. and Sector Exec.; Mem., Office of the Chm.; co-Chm. of Avis Inc.; Dir and Dep. Chief Exec., Sears Holdings plc, 1981–83. Board Member: HSBC Holdings, 1992–; US Air, 1993–; Qantas, 1993–; British Telecommunications, 1995–. *Recreations:* tennis, skiing. *Address:* c/o British Airways Head Office, PO Box 10, Heathrow Airport London, Hounslow, Mddx TW6 2JA. *T:* 0181–562 5474. *Club:* Queen's.

MARSHALL, David; MP (Lab) Glasgow, Shettleston, since 1979 (sponsored by TGWU); former transport worker; *b* May 1941; *m*; two *s* one *d*. *Educ:* Larbert, Denny and Falkirk High Schs; Woodside Sen. Secondary Sch., Glasgow. Joined Labour Party, 1962; former Lab. Party Organiser for Glasgow; Member: TGWU, 1960–; Select Cttee, Scottish Affairs, 1981–83; Hon. Sec., Scottish Gp of Labour MPs, 1981–. Private Member's Bill, The Solvent Abuse (Scotland) Act, May 1983. Member: Glasgow Corp., 1972–75; Strathclyde Reg. Council, 1974–79 (Chm., Manpower Cttee); Chm., Manpower Cttee, Convention of Scottish Local Authorities; Mem., Local Authorities Conditions of Service Adv. Bd. *Address:* House of Commons, SW1A 0AA; 32 Enterkin Street, Glasgow G32 7BA.

MARSHALL, Sir Denis (Alfred), Kt 1982; solicitor; with Barlow Lyde & Gilbert, 1937–83, now a consultant; *b* 1 June 1916; *s* of Frederick Herbert Marshall and Winifred Mary Marshall; *m* 1st, 1949, Joan Edith Straker (*d* 1974); one *s*; 2nd, 1975, Jane Lygo. *Educ:* Dulwich Coll. Served War: HAC, 1939; XX Lancs Fusiliers (Temp. Major), 1940–46. Articled to Barlow Lyde & Gilbert, Solicitors, 1932–37; admitted Solicitor, 1937. Mem. Council, Law Soc., 1966–86, Vice-Pres., 1980–81, Pres., 1981–82. Member: Insurance Brokers Registration Council, 1979–91; Criminal Injuries Compensation Bd, 1982–90; Council, FIMBRA, 1986–90. *Recreations:* sailing, gardening. *Address:* Redways, Warfleet Road, Dartmouth, S Devon TQ6 9BZ. *Clubs:* Naval and Military; Royal Dart Yacht.

MARSHALL, Dr Edmund Ian; Lecturer in Management Science, University of Bradford, since 1984; *b* 31 May 1940; *s* of Harry and Koorali Marshall; *m* 1969, Margaret Pamela, *d* of John and Maud Antill, New Southgate, N11; one *d*. *Educ:* Magdalen Coll., Oxford (Mackinnon Schol.). Double 1st cl. hons Maths, and Junior Mathematical Prize, Oxon, 1961; PhD Liverpool, 1965. Various univ. appts in Pure Maths, 1962–66; mathematician in industry, 1967–71. Mem., Wallasey County Borough Council, 1963–65. Contested (L) Louth Div. of Lincs, 1964 and 1966; joined Labour Party, 1967. MP (Lab) Goole, May 1971–1983; PPS to Sec. of State for NI, 1974–76, to Home Sec., 1976–79; Chm., Trade and Industry sub-cttee of House of Commons Expenditure Cttee, 1976–79; Mem., Chairmen's Panel in House of Commons, 1981–82; Opposition Whip, 1982–83; joined SDP, 1985. Contested (SDP/Alliance) Bridlington, 1987. Non-Exec. Dir, Wakefield FHSA, 1990–; Dir, Wakefield Healthcare Commn, 1994–. Member: British Methodist Conf., 1969–72, 1980 and 1985 (Vice-Pres., 1992); World Methodist Conf., 1971; British Council of Churches, 1972–78; Sec., All-Party Parly Gp related to Council of Christian and Associated Colls, 1994–. Reader in C of E, 1994–. Governor: Woodhouse Grove Sch., Bradford, 1986–94; Wakefield Grammar Schools Foundn, 1989–. *Publications:* (jtly) Europe: What Next? (Fabian pamphlet), 1969; Parliament and the Public, 1982; Business and Society, 1993; various papers in mathematical and other jls. *Recreations:* word games, music. *Address:* 14 Belgravia Road, Wakefield, West Yorks WF1 3JP. *Club:* Yorks County Cricket.

MARSHALL, Dr Frank Graham, FIEE; Group Research and Development Director, Colt Group Ltd, since 1990; *b* 28 March 1942; *s* of Frank and Vera Marshall; *m* 1965, Patricia Anne (*née* Bestwick); two *s* one *d*. *Educ:* Birmingham Univ. (BSc Physics); Nottingham Univ. (PhD Physics). FIEE 1984. Joined Royal Signals and Radar Estabt (MoD) (Physics and Electronic Device Res.), 1966; Sen. Principal Scientific Officer, 1975–80; seconded to HM Diplomatic Service as Science and Technology Counsellor, Tokyo, 1980–82. Man. Dir, Plessey Electronic Systems Res., later Plessey Res. Roke Manor, 1983–87; Technical Dir, Plessey Naval Systems, 1987–90. (Jtly) IEEE Best Paper award, 1973; (jtly) Wolfe Award, 1973. *Publications:* numerous papers on electronic signal processing devices in various jls. *Recreations:* country life, electronics. *Address:* Colt Group Ltd, New Lane, Havant, Hants PO9 2LY.

MARSHALL, Fredda, (Mrs Herbert Marshall); *see* Brilliant, F.

MARSHALL, Geoffrey, MA, PhD; FBA 1971; Provost, The Queen's College, Oxford, since 1993 (Fellow and Tutor in Politics, 1957–93); *b* 22 April 1929; *s* of Leonard William and Kate Marshall; *m* 1957, Patricia Ann Christine Woodcock; two *s*. *Educ:* Arnold Sch., Blackpool, Lancs; Manchester Univ. MA Manchester, MA Oxon, PhD Glasgow. Research Fellow, Nuffield Coll., 1955–57. Andrew Dixon White Vis. Prof., Cornell Univ., Ithaca, NY, 1985–91. Mem. Oxford City Council, 1965–74; Sheriff of Oxford, 1970–71. *Publications:* Parliamentary Sovereignty and the Commonwealth, 1957; Some Problems of the Constitution (with G. C. Moodie), 1959; Police and Government, 1965; Constitutional Theory, 1971; Constitutional Conventions, 1984; Ministerial Responsibility, 1989. *Recreation:* middle-aged squash. *Address:* The Queen's College, Oxford OX1 4AW. *T:* Oxford (01865) 279123.

MARSHALL, Hazel Eleanor, (Mrs H. C. J. Marshall); *see* Williamson, H. E.

MARSHALL, Howard Wright; retired; Under Secretary, Department of Transport, 1978–82; *b* 11 June 1923; *s* of Philip Marshall, MBE, and Mary Marshall; *m* 1st (marr. diss.); two *s*; 2nd, 1963, Carol Yvonne (*née* Oddy); one *d*. *Educ:* Prudhoe West Elementary, Northumberland; Queen Elizabeth Grammar Sch., Hexham. Served War, RAF, 1941–46; POW, 1943–45. Min. of Health, Newcastle upon Tyne, 1940; Regional Offices, Ministries of Health, Local Govt and Planning, Housing and Local Govt, 1948–55; HQ, Min. of Housing and Local Govt, 1955–59; National Parks Commn, 1959–62; Min. of Housing and Local Govt, later DoE, 1962; Asst Sec., 1968; Under Sec., 1976; Regional Dir, Eastern Region, Depts of Environment and Transport, 1976–78; Chm., East Anglia Regional Economic Planning Bd, 1976–78. *Recreations:* gardening, sport. *Address:* Brackenwood, Farthing Green Lane, Stoke Poges, Bucks SL2 4JH. *T:* Fulmer (01753) 662974. *Clubs:* Caterpillar; Wexham Park Golf and Leisure.

MARSHALL, Rev. Canon Hugh Phillips; Chief Secretary, General Synod of Church of England's Advisory Board of Ministry, since 1990; *b* 13 July 1934; *s* of Dr Leslie Phillips Marshall and Dr (Catherine) Mary Marshall; *m* 1962, Diana Elizabeth Gosling; one *s* three *d*. *Educ:* Marlborough Coll.; Sidney Sussex Coll., Cambridge (BA, MA); Bishop's Hostel, Lincoln. RN, 1952–54. Ordained deacon 1959, priest 1960, Dio. London; Curate, St Stephen with St John, Westminster, 1959–65; Vicar of St Paul, Tupsley, Hereford, 1965–74; Vicar and Team Rector of Wimbledon, 1974–87; Rural Dean of Merton, 1979–85; Vicar of Mitcham, Surrey, 1987–90; Hon. Canon of Southwark Cathedral, 1989, Hon. Canon Emeritus, 1990. Commissary to Bishop of Matabeleland, 1989–. *Recreations:* DIY, cooking, gardening, travel. *Address:* 30 Woodville Road, Morden, Surrey SM4 5AF. *T:* 0181–542 3962; (office) Church House, Great Smith Street, SW1P 3NZ. *T:* 0171–222 9011.

MARSHALL, James; MP (Lab) Leicester South, Oct. 1974–1983, and since 1987; *b* 13 March 1941; *m* 1962, Shirley (marr. diss.), *d* of W. Ellis, Sheffield; one *s* one *d*; *m* 1986, Susan, *d* of G. Carter, Leicester. *Educ:* City Grammar Sch., Sheffield; Leeds Univ. BSc, PhD. Joined Lab Party, 1960. Mem., Leeds City Council, 1965–68; Leicester City Council: Mem., 1971–76; Chm., Finance Cttee, 1972–74; Leader, 1974. Contested (Lab): Harborough, 1970; Leicester South, Feb. 1974, 1983. An Asst Govt Whip, 1977–79. *Address:* Flat 15, The Woodlands, 31 Knighton Road, Leicester LE2 3HL. *T:* Leicester (0116) 270 8237.

MARSHALL, James; Assistant Auditor General, National Audit Office, since 1993; *b* 16 March 1944; *s* of James Marshall and Winifred (*née* Hopkins); *m* 1980, Patricia Anne Smallbone; one *s*. *Educ:* Sacred Heart Coll., Droitwich; King Charles I Grammar Sch., Kidderminster; Jesus Coll., Cambridge (MA). Joined Inland Revenue, 1966: Asst Principal, 1966–69; Private Sec. to Chm. of Bd, 1969–70; Principal, 1970–74; First Sec., Budget and Fiscal, UK Repn to EC, Brussels, 1974–77; First Asst, UK Mem. of Court, European Court of Auditors, 1977–80; Asst Sec., Inland Revenue, 1980–88; Consultant, CJA Mgt Recruitment, 1988–89; Dir, Nat. Audit Office, 1989–93. *Recreations:* reading, walking, opera. *Address:* National Audit Office, Buckingham Palace Road, SW1W 9SP; 56 Melody Road, SW18 2QF. *T:* 0181–870 3308.

MARSHALL, Jeremy; *see* Marshall, John J. S.

MARSHALL, John; *see* Sessions, J.

MARSHALL, John, MA; JP; Headmaster, Robert Gordon's College, Aberdeen, 1960–77; *b* 1 July 1915; *s* of Alexander Marshall and Margaret Nimmo Carmichael; *m* 1940, May Robinson Williamson; two *d*. *Educ:* Airdrie Acad.; Glasgow Univ. MA (1st cl. hons Classics), 1935; Medley Memorial Prizeman, History 1934; John Clark Schol., Classics, 1935. Asst Master: Bluevale Sch., 1937–39; Coatbridge Sec. Sch., 1939–41; Principal Teacher of Classics, North Berwick High Sch., 1941–50; Rector, North Berwick High Sch., 1950–60. Mem., Adv. Coun. on Educn for Scotland, 1955–57; Trustee, Scottish Sec. Schools Travel Trust, 1960–78 (Chm., 1971–78; Sec., 1978–80); Pres., Headmasters' Assoc. of Scotland, 1962–64; Member: HMC, 1960–77; Gen. Teaching Coun. for Scotland, 1966–70; Exec. Cttee, UCCA, 1970–78; Co-ordinator, Scottish Scheme of Oxford Colls' Admissions, 1978–84. Trustee, Gordon Cook Foundn, 1974– (Chm., 1992–93). JP City of Aberdeen, 1967. *Publications:* Off the Beaten Track in Switzerland, 1989; The Visitor's Guide to Switzerland, 1990, 2nd edn 1995; The Visitor's Guide to The Rhine and Mosel, 1992; numerous articles on educational and travel subjects. *Recreations:* photography, writing, language studies, travel. *Address:* 11 Hazledene Road, Aberdeen AB1 8LB. *T:* Aberdeen (01224) 318003. *Club:* Royal Northern and University (Aberdeen).

MARSHALL, Prof. John, CBE 1990; FRCP, FRCPE; Professor of Clinical Neurology in the University of London, 1971–87, now Emeritus; *b* 16 April 1922; *s* of James Herbert and Bertha Marshall; *m* 1946, Margaret Eileen Hughes; two *s* three *d*. *Educ:* Univ. of Manchester (MB ChB 1946, MD 1951, DSc 1981). FRCPE 1957, FRCP 1966; DPM 1952. Sen. Registrar, Manchester Royal Infirmary, 1947–49; Lt-Col RAMC, 1949–51; MRC research worker, 1951–53; Sen. Lectr in Neurology, Univ. of Edinburgh, 1954–56; Reader in Clinical Neurology, Univ. of London, 1956–71. Chm., Disability Living (formerly Attendance) Allowance Bd, 1982–93. Knight of the Order of St Sylvester (Holy See), 1962, KCSG 1986 (KSG 1964). Auenbrugger Medal, Univ. of Graz, 1983. *Publications:* The Management of Cerebrovascular Disease, 1965, 3rd edn 1976; The Infertile Period, Principles and Practice, 1963, 2nd rev. edn 1969. *Recreations:* gardening, walking. *Address:* 203 Robin Hood Way, SW20 0AA. *T:* 0181–942 5509.

MARSHALL, John Alexander, CB 1982; General Secretary, Distressed Gentlefolk's Aid Association, 1982–89; *b* 2 Sept. 1922; *s* of James Alexander Marshall and Mena Dorothy Marshall; *m* 1947, Pauline Mary (*née* Taylor); six *s*. *Educ:* LCC elem. sch.; Hackney Downs School. Paymaster General's Office, 1939; FO, 1943; HM Treasury, 1947: Principal, 1953; Asst Sec., 1963; Under-Sec., 1972; Cabinet Office, 1974–77; Northern Ireland Office, 1977–82, Dep. Sec., 1979–82. *Recreations:* literature, music. *Address:* 48 Long Lane, Ickenham, Mddx UB10 8TA. *T:* Ruislip (01895) 672020.

MARSHALL, (John) Jeremy (Seymour); Chief Executive, De La Rue Co. plc, since 1989; *b* 18 April 1938; *s* of late Edward Pope Marshall and of Nita Helen Marshall (*née* Seymour); *m* 1962, Juliette Butterley; one *s* two *d*. *Educ:* Sherborne Sch.; New Coll., Oxford (MA Chem.). Nat. Service, Royal Signals, 1956–58. Wiggins Teape, 1962–64; Riker Labs, 1964–67; CIBA Agrochemicals, 1967–71; Hanson Trust: Managing Director: Dufaylite Developments, 1971–76; SLD Olding, 1976–79; Chief Executive: Lindustries, 1979–86; Imperial Foods, 1986–87; BAA plc, 1987–89; Director: John Mowlem & Co., 1991–; Camelot Gp, 1993–. CIMgt (CBIM 1991); FCIT 1989. *Recreations:* squash, lawn tennis, shooting, music. *Address:* Willow House, Bourn, Cambridge CB3 7SQ. *T:* Caxton (01954) 719435. *Club:* Royal Automobile.

MARSHALL, John Leslie; MP (C) Hendon South, since 1987; *b* 19 Aug. 1940; *s* of late Prof. William Marshall and Margaret Marshall; *m* 1978, Susan Elizabeth, *d* of David Mount, Petham, Kent; two *s*. *Educ:* Glasgow Academy; St Andrews Univ. (MA). ACIS. Asst Lecturer in Economics, Glasgow Univ., 1962–66; Lectr in Economics, Aberdeen Univ., 1966–70; Mem., Internat. Stock Exchange; Carr Sebag & Co., 1979–82; Partner, 1983–86, Dir, 1986–90, Analyst, 1990–93, Kitcat & Aitken; Analyst, Mees Pierson Securities (UK) Ltd (formerly London Wall Equities), 1993–. Contested (C): Dundee East, 1964 and 1966; Lewisham East, Feb. 1974. MEP (C) London N, 1979–89; Asst Whip, EDG, Eur. Parlt, 1986–89. PPS to Minister for the Disabled, Dept of Social Security, 1989–90, to Sec. of State for Social Security, 1990–92, to Leader of H of C, 1992–95. Chairman: British Israel Parly Gp, 1991–; Anglo-Israel Assoc., 1994–. Member: Aberdeen Town Council, 1968–70; Ealing Borough Council, 1971–86 (Chm., Finance Bd, 1978–82; Chm., Local Services Cttee, 1982–84). Dir, Beta Global Emerging Markets Investment Trust plc, 1990–; Consultant, Bus and Coach Council, 1991–. Chm., Friends of the Northern Line, 1994–. *Publications:* articles on economics in several professional jls; pamphlets on economic questions for Aims. *Recreations:* watching cricket, football and Rugby; gardening, bridge, theatre. *Address:* c/o House of Commons, SW1A 0AA. *Clubs:* Carlton; Middlesex County Cricket.

MARSHALL, John Roger; Chief Executive, John Mowlem and Co. PLC, since 1994 (Managing Director, 1989–94); *b* 20 April 1944; *s* of John Henry Marshall and Betty Alaine Rosetta Marshall; *m* (marr. diss.); one *s* two *d*. *Educ:* Rendcomb College; Bristol Univ. (BSc Hons Civil Eng.). MICE, CEng, FIHT. Balfour Beatty Consultants, W. C. French and R. McGregor & Sons, 1966–70; Mears Construction, 1970–78; Henry Boot, 1978–83; Man. Dir, Mowlem Management, 1983–87; Dir, John Mowlem & Co., 1987–. *Recreations:* arts (visual, dramatic and operatic), exercise. *Address:* Teddington, Middlesex.

MARSHALL, Laurence Arthur; His Honour Judge Marshall; a Circuit Judge, since 1991; *b* 1 June 1931; *s* of Reginald Herbert Marshall and Nora Marshall; *m* 1st, 1959, Marian Charlotte Mowlem Burt (marr. diss. 1979); two *s* two *d*; 2nd, 1980, Gloria Elizabeth Kindersley. *Educ:* Ardingly Coll.; King's Coll., London (LLB). Called to the Bar, Gray's Inn, 1956. *Recreation:* building. *Address:* The Old Post Office, Stourton, Shipston on Stour, Warwicks CV36 5HG. *T:* Little Cherington (0160875) 363. *Club:* Royal London Yacht.

MARSHALL, Margaret Anne; concert and opera singer; soprano; *b* 4 Jan. 1949; *d* of Robert and Margaret Marshall; *m* 1970, Dr Graeme Griffiths King Davidson; two *d*. *Educ:* High School, Stirling; Royal Scottish Academy of Music and Drama (DRSAMD). Recital début, Wigmore Hall, 1975; performs regularly with all major British orchs, also with ENO and Scottish Opera; opera début as Euridice, in Orfeo, Florence; major rôles include: Countess Almaviva in The Marriage of Figaro; Fiordiligi in Così fan Tutte; Elvira and Donna Anna in Don Giovanni; Violetta in La Traviata; Marschallin in Der Rosenkavalier; Constanze in The Seraglio; many concert and opera performances in Europe and N America; numerous recordings. First Prize, Munich International Competition, 1974. *Recreations:* squash, golf. *Address:* Woodside, Main Street, Gargunnock, Stirling FK8 3BP. *Club:* Gleneagles Country.

MARSHALL, Mark Anthony, CMG 1991; HM Diplomatic Service, retired; Ambassador to the Republic of Yemen (formerly Yemen Arab Republic) and the Republic of Djibouti, 1987–93; *b* 8 Oct. 1937; *s* of late Thomas Humphrey Marshall, CMG and of Nadine, *d* of late Mark Hambourg; *m* 1970, Penelope Lesley Seymour; two *d*. *Educ:* Westminster Sch.; Trinity Coll., Cambridge (BA). MECAS, 1958; Third Sec., Amman, 1960; FO, 1962; Commercial Officer, Dubai, 1964; FO, 1965; Aden, 1967; First Sec., 1968; Asst Dir of Treasury Centre for Admin. Studies, 1968; UK Delegn to Brussels Conf., 1970; First Sec./Head of Chancery, Rabat, 1972; First Sec., FCO, 1976; Counsellor: Tripoli, 1979–80; Damascus, 1980–83; Head of Finance Dept, FCO, 1984–87. *Recreations:* swimming, golf, fell walking.

MARSHALL, Martin John, CMG 1967; HM Diplomatic Service, retired; *b* 21 March 1914; *s* of late Harry Edmund Marshall and late Kate Ann (*née* Bishop); *m* 1938, Olive Emily Alice, *d* of Thomas and Olive King; two *d*. *Educ:* Westminster City Sch.; London Sch. of Economics, University of London. Customs and Excise Officer, 1935–39; Technical Officer, Min. of Aircraft Prod., 1940–46; Principal, Min. of Supply, 1947–50. Called to Bar, Gray's Inn, 1947. Trade Commissioner: Montreal, 1950–52; Atlantic Provinces, 1953; Alberta, 1954–57; Principal Trade Commissioner: Montreal, 1957–60; Calcutta (for Eastern India), 1961–63; Dep. High Comr, Sydney, 1963–67; Consul-General, Cleveland, Ohio, 1968–71; Dep. High Comr, Bombay, 1971–74. Dir, Finance/Administration, Royal Assoc. for Disability and Rehabilitation, 1977–79. *Recreation:* golf. *Address:* 8 Sunnyside Place, SW19 4SJ. *T:* 0181–946 5570. *Club:* Royal Wimbledon Golf.

MARSHALL, Sir Michael; *see* Marshall, Sir R. M.

MARSHALL, Rt. Rev. Michael Eric, MA; Archbishops' Adviser on Evangelism, since 1992; an Assistant Bishop: Diocese of London, since 1984; Diocese of Chichester, since 1992; *b* Lincoln, 14 April 1936. *Educ:* Lincoln Sch.; Christ's Coll., Cambridge (Tancred Scholar, Upper II: Hist. Pt 1 and Theol Pt 1a, MA); Cuddesdon Theological Coll. Deacon, 1960; Curate, St Peter's, Spring Hill, Birmingham, 1960–62; Tutor, Ely Theological Coll. and Minor Canon of Ely Cath., 1962–64; Chaplain in London Univ., 1964–69; Vicar of All Saints', Margaret Street, W1, 1969–75; Bishop Suffragan of Woolwich, 1975–84. Preb. of Wightring in Chichester Cathedral and Wightring Theol Lectr, 1990–. Dir of Evangelism, Chichester Theol Coll., 1991–; Leader, Springboard, 1992–. Founder and Director: Inst. of Christian Studies, 1970; Internat. Inst. for Anglican Studies, 1982; Founding Episcopal Dir, Anglican Inst., St Louis, Missouri, 1984–92; Member: Gen. Synod, 1970, also Diocesan and Deanery Synods; Liturgical Commn; Anglican/Methodist Liaison Commn until 1974; SPCK Governing Body; USPG Governing Body; Exam. Chap. to Bp of London, 1974. Has frequently broadcast on BBC and commercial radio; also lectured, preached and broadcast in Canada and USA. *Publications:* A Pattern of Faith, 1966 (co-author); Glory under Your Feet, 1978; Pilgrimage and Promise, 1981; Renewal in Worship, 1982; The Anglican Church, Today and Tomorrow, 1984; Christian Orthodoxy Revisited, 1985; The Gospel Conspiracy in the Episcopal Church, 1986; The Restless Heart, 1987; The Gospel Connection, 1991; The Freedom of Holiness, 1992; Founder and co-editor, Christian Quarterly. *Recreations:* music, cooking. *Address:* 18 Andrewes House, The Barbican, EC2Y 8AX.

MARSHALL, Michael John, DL; Chairman and Chief Executive, Marshall of Cambridge (Holdings) Ltd, since 1990; Vice Lord-Lieutenant of Cambridgeshire, since 1992; *b* 27 Jan. 1932; *s* of Sir Arthur Gregory George Marshall, *qv*; *m* 1st, 1960, Bridget Wykham Pollock (marr. diss. 1977); two *s* two *d*; 2nd, 1979, Sibyl Mary Walkinshaw (*née* Hutton); two step *s*. *Educ:* Eton Coll.; Jesus Coll., Cambridge (MA Hist.; rowing Blue, 1954, rep. GB in Eur. championships, 1955). IEng; FRAeS; FIMI. Nat. Service, Flying Officer, RAF, 1950–52. Joined Marshall of Cambridge (Eng) Ltd, 1955: Dep. Chm. and Man. Dir, Marshall (Cambridge) Ltd, 1964–90. Dir, Eastern Electricity Bd, 1971–77; Chm., BL Cars Distributor Council, 1977, 1983 (Mem., 1975–84); Vice-President: Inst. Motor Ind., 1980–; EEF, 1993–; Chm., Cambs Manpower Cttee, 1980–83. Vice-Chm., Cambs Youth Involvement Cttee, Silver Jubilee Fund, 1977–78; Chm., Cambridge Olympic Appeal, 1984; Mem., Ely Cathedral Restoration Appeal Co. Cttee, 1987–; Pres., Cambridge Soc. for Blind, 1989–92; Chm., Prince's Trusts' Cambs Appeal Cttee, 1991–92. Chairman: Civilian Cttee, 104 (City of Cambridge) Sqdn, ATC, 1975–; Beds and Cambs Wing, ATC, 1987–93; Member: Air Cadet Council, 1994–; Air League, 1995–. FRSA. Freeman, City of London, 1988; Liveryman, GAPAN, 1989–. Cambridgeshire: High Sheriff, 1988–89; DL 1989. *Recreations:* flying, walking, rowing. *Address:* Swaffham Prior House, Swaffham Prior, Cambridge CB5 0LD. *T:* Newmarket (01638) 741327; (office) The Airport, Newmarket Road, Cambridge CB5 8RX. *T:* Cambridge (01223) 373231. *Clubs:* Royal Air Force; Hawks, University Pitt, Cambridge County (Cambridge); Leander (Henley-on-Thames); Eton Vikings.

MARSHALL, Noël Hedley, CMG 1986; HM Diplomatic Service, retired; *b* 26 Nov. 1934; *s* of late Arthur Hedley Marshall, CBE, and Margaret Louise Marshall (*née* Longhurst). *Educ:* Leighton Park Sch.; Lawrenceville Sch., NJ (E-SU Exchange Scholar, 1953–54); St John's Coll., Cambridge (BA 1957, MA 1992; Sir Joseph Larmor Award, 1957). Pres., Cambridge Union Soc., 1957. Entered Foreign (later Diplomatic) Service; FO, 1957–59; Third Sec., Prague, 1959–61; FO, 1961–63; Second (later First) Sec., Moscow, 1963–65; CRO, 1965–66; First Sec. (Economic): Karachi, 1966–67; Rawalpindi, 1967–70; Chargé d'affaires *ai*, Ulan Bator, 1967; FCO, 1970–74; First Sec. (later Counsellor) Press, Office of UK Permanent Rep. to European Communities, Brussels, 1974–77; NATO Defence Coll., Rome, 1977–78; Counsellor, UK Delegn to Cttee on Disarmament, Geneva, 1978–81; Head of N America Dept, FCO, 1982–85; Overseas Inspector, 1985–86; Minister, Moscow, 1986–89; Co-ordinator, British Days in the USSR, Kiev, 1990; UK Perm. Rep. to Council of Europe (with personal rank of Ambassador), 1990–93. *Recreations:* sailing, the theatre. *Clubs:* Royal Ocean Racing, Royal Cruising.

MARSHALL, Norman Bertram, MA, ScD; FRS 1970; Professor and Head of Department of Zoology and Comparative Physiology, Queen Mary College, University of London, 1972–77, now Professor Emeritus; *b* 5 Feb. 1915; *s* of Arthur Harold and Ruby Eva Marshall; *m* 1944, Olga Stonehouse; one *s* three *d*. *Educ:* Cambridgeshire High Sch.; Downing Coll., Cambridge. Plankton Biologist, Dept of Oceanography, UC Hull, 1937–41; Army (mostly involved in operational research), 1941–44; seconded from Army for Service in Operation Tabarin to Antarctic, 1944–46; British Museum (Natural History): Marine fishes, 1947–72; Sen. Principal Scientific Officer, 1962–72. In charge of Manihine Expedns to Red Sea, 1948–50; Senior Biologist, Te Vega Expedn, 1966–67. Polar Medal (Silver), 1948; Rosenstiel Gold Medal for distinguished services to marine science; Senior Queen's Fellow in Marine Science, Aust., 1982. *Publications:* Aspects of Deep Sea Biology, 1954; The Life of Fishes, 1965; Explorations in the Life of Fishes, 1970; Ocean Life, 1971; Developments in Deep Sea Biology, 1979; various papers in learned jls. *Recreations:* music, fishing, golf. *Address:* 5 St John's Close, Great Chesterford, Saffron Walden, Essex CB10 1PB. *T:* Saffron Walden (01799) 531347.

MARSHALL, Prof. Sir (Oshley) Roy, Kt 1974; CBE 1968; High Commissioner for Barbados in the United Kingdom, 1989–91; Vice-Chancellor, Hull University, 1979–85, Emeritus Professor since 1985; *b* 21 Oct. 1920; *s* of Fitz Roy and Corene Carmelita Marshall; *m* 1945, Eirwen Lloyd; one *s* three *d*. *Educ:* Harrison Coll., Barbados, WI; Pembroke Coll., Cambridge; University Coll., London (Fellow, 1985). Barbados Scholar, 1938; BA 1945, MA 1948 Cantab; PhD London 1948. Barrister-at-Law, Inner Temple, 1947. University Coll., London: Asst Lecturer, 1946–48; Lecturer, 1948–56; Sub-Dean, Faculty of Law, 1949–56; Prof. of Law and Head of Dept of Law, Univ. of Sheffield, 1956–69, Vis. Prof. in Faculty of Law, 1969–80; on secondment to University of Ife, Ibadan, Nigeria, as Prof. of Law and Dean of the Faculty of Law, 1963–65; Vice-Chancellor, Univ. of West Indies, 1969–74; Sec.-Gen., Cttee of Vice-Chancellors and Principals, 1974–79. Chairman: Commonwealth Educn Liaison Cttee, 1974–81; Cttee on Commonwealth Legal Co-operation, 1975; Commonwealth Standing Cttee on Student Mobility, 1982–94; Council for Educn in the Commonwealth, 1985–91; Review Cttee on Cave Hill Campus, Univ. of WI, 1986; Constitutional Commn on the Turks and Caicos Islands, 1986; Member: Police Complaints Bd, 1977–81; Council, RPMS, 1976–83; Council, ACU, 1979–85; Management Cttee, Universities Superannuation Scheme Ltd, 1980–85; UGC for Univ. of S Pacific, 1987; Chm., Bd of Governors, Hymers Coll., Hull, 1985–89; Vice-Chm., Governing Body of Commonwealth Inst., 1980–81; Mem., Bd of Governors, Commonwealth of Learning, 1988–91; Trustee, Commonwealth Foundn, 1981. Hon. LLD: Sheffield, 1972; West Indies, 1976; Hull, 1986; Hon. DLitt CNAA, 1992. *Publications:* The Assignment of Choses in Action, 1950; A Casebook on Trusts (with J. A. Nathan), 1967; Theobald on Wills, 12th edn, 1963. *Recreations:* racing and cricket. *Address:* Kirk House, Kirk Croft, Cottingham, North Humberside HU16 4AU. *Club:* Commonwealth Trust.

MARSHALL, Peter, QPM 1979; Commissioner of Police for the City of London, 1978–85; *b* 21 June 1930; *s* of late Christopher George Marshall and Sylvia Marshall; *m* 1954, Bridget Frances Humphreys; three *s* one *d*. *Educ:* St Clement Danes Holborn Estate Grammar Sch. Trooper, 8th Royal Tank Regt, 1948–50. Police Officer, Metropolitan Police, 1950–78. *Recreations:* reading, gardening. *Address:* The Cottage, Cock Lane, Elham, Canterbury, Kent CT4 6TL.

MARSHALL, Sir Peter (Harold Reginald), KCMG 1983 (CMG 1974); Chairman, Joint Commonwealth Societies Council, since 1993; *b* 30 July 1924; 3rd *s* of late R. H. Marshall; *m* 1st, 1957, Patricia Rendell Stoddart (*d* 1981); one *s* one *d*; 2nd, 1989, Judith, *widow* of E. W. F. Tomlin. *Educ:* Tonbridge; Corpus Christi Coll., Cambridge (Hon. Fellow 1989). RAFVR, 1943–46. HM Foreign (later Diplomatic) Service, 1949–83. FO, 1949–52; 2nd Sec. and Private Sec. to Ambassador, Washington, 1952–56; FO, 1956–60; on staff of Civil Service Selection Board, 1960; 1st Sec. and Head of Chancery, Baghdad, 1961, and Bangkok, 1962–64; Asst Dir of Treasury Centre for Administrative Studies, 1965–66; Counsellor, UK Mission, Geneva, 1966–69, Counsellor and Head of Chancery, Paris, 1969–71; Head of Financial Policy and Aid Dept, FCO, 1971–73; Asst Under-Sec. of State, FCO, 1973–75; UK Rep. on Econ. and Social Council of UN, 1975–79; Ambassador and UK Perm. Rep. to Office of UN and Other Internat. Organisations at Geneva, 1979–83; Commonwealth Dep. Sec. Gen. (Econ.), 1983–88. Chm., Commonwealth Trust and Royal Commonwealth Soc., 1988–92; Pres., Queen Elizabeth House, Oxford, 1990–94; Vice Pres., Council for Educn in World Citizenship, 1985–; Member: Exec. Cttee, Pilgrims, 1986–; Council, VSO, 1989–; ODI, 1989–; Governor, E-SU of the Commonwealth, 1984–90; Trustee: King George VI and Queen Elizabeth Foundn of St Catharine's, 1987–; Magna Carta Trust, 1993–. Vis. Lectr, Diplomatic Acad. of London, 1989–. Hon. Fellow, Univ. of Westminster, 1992. *Publications:* The Dynamics of Diplomacy, 1990; chapter in The United Kingdom—The United Nations (ed Jensen and Fisher), 1990. *Recreations:* music, golf. *Address:* 26 Queensdale Road, W11 4QB.

MARSHALL, Peter Izod; Chairman, Ocean Group (formerly Ocean Transport and Trading), since 1987; Deputy Chairman, Astec (BSR) plc, since 1989; *b* 16 April 1927; *s* of Charles and Gwendoline Marshall; *m* 1955, Davina Mary (*née* Hart); one *s* one *d*. *Educ:* Buxton College. FCA; LRAM. Commercial Dir, EMI Electronics, 1962–67; Dir of Finance, Norcros, 1967–77; Dep. Chief Exec., Plessey Co., 1977–87; Dir, Hogg Robinson plc, 1987–; Chm., Plessey Pension Trust Ltd, 1990–. *Recreations:* music, swimming, golf. *Address:* Moyns, Christchurch Road, Virginia Water, Surrey GU25 4PJ. *T:* Wentworth (01344) 842118. *Clubs:* Les Ambassadeurs; Wentworth.

MARSHALL, Prof. Peter James, FBA 1992; DPhil; Rhodes Professor of Imperial History, King's College, London, 1980–93, now Emeritus; *b* 28 Oct. 1933; *s* of Edward Hannaford Marshall and Madeleine (*née* Shuttleworth). *Educ:* Wellington College; Wadham Coll., Oxford (BA 1957, MA, DPhil 1962). Military service, King's African Rifles, Kenya, 1953–54. Assistant Lecturer, Lecturer, Reader, Professor, History Dept, King's Coll., London, 1959–80 (FKC 1991). Mem., History Wkg Gp, National Curriculum, 1989–90. Vice-Pres., RHistS, 1987–91. Editor, Journal of Imperial and Commonwealth History, 1975–81; Associate Editor, Writings and Speeches of Edmund Burke, 1976–. *Publications:* Impeachment of Warren Hastings, 1965; Problems of Empire: Britain and India 1757–1813, 1968; (ed, with J. A. Woods) Correspondence of Edmund Burke, vol. VII, 1968; The British Discovery of Hinduism, 1972; East India Fortunes, 1976; (ed) Writings and Speeches of Edmund Burke, vol. V, 1981, vol. VI, 1991; (with Glyndwr Williams) The Great Map of Mankind, 1982; Bengal: the British bridgehead (New Cambridge History of India, Vol. II, 2), 1988; Trade and Conquest: studies on the rise of British dominance in India, 1993; (ed) Cambridge Illustrated History of the British Empire, 1995; articles in Economic History Rev., History, Modern Asian Studies, etc. *Address:* 7 Malting Lane, Braughing, Ware, Herts SG11 2QZ. *T:* Ware (01920) 822232.

MARSHALL, Air Cdre Philippa Frances, CB 1971; OBE 1956; Director of the Women's Royal Air Force, 1969–73; *b* 4 Nov. 1920; *d* of late Horace Plant Marshall,

Stoke-on-Trent. *Educ:* St Dominic's High Sch., Stoke-on-Trent. Joined WAAF, 1941; Comd WRAF Admin. Officer, Strike Comd, 1968–69, Air Cdre 1969; ADC, 1969–73. *Recreations:* music, cookery. *Club:* Royal Air Force.

MARSHALL, Sir Robert (Braithwaite), KCB 1971 (CB 1968); MBE 1945; Chairman, National Water Council, 1978–82; *b* 10 Jan. 1920; *s* of Alexander Halford Marshall and Edith Mary Marshall (*née* Lockyer); *m* 1945, Diana Elizabeth Westlake; one *s* three *d. Educ:* Sherborne Sch.; Corpus Christi Coll., Cambridge. Mod. Langs, Pt I, 1938–39; Economics Pts I and II, 1945–47. BA Cambridge. Foreign Office temp. appointment, 1939–45. Entered Home Civil Service, 1947; Ministry of Works, 1947–50; Private Sec. to Sec., Cabinet Office, 1950–53; Min. of Works, 1953–62; Min. of Aviation, 1962–66; Min. of Power, 1966–69; Min. of Technology, 1969–70; Under-Sec., 1964; Dep. Sec. 1966; Second Perm. Sec., 1970; Secretary (Industry), DTI, 1970–73; Second Permanent Sec., DoE, 1973–78. Chm., Cair Ltd, 1985–86. Vice-Pres., Wateraid and mem. of other trusts. Mem. and Vice Chm. Council, Surrey Univ., 1975–87; Chm. Governors, W Surrey Coll. of Art, 1985–89. Coronation Medal, 1953. *Recreations:* travel, gardening, music and arts. *Address:* 1 Shatcombe, Uploders, Bridport, Dorset DT6 4NR. *T:* Powerstock (01308) 485348.

MARSHALL, Robert Leckie, OBE 1945; Principal, Co-operative College, and Chief Education Officer, Co-operative Union Ltd, 1946–77; *b* 27 Aug. 1913; *s* of Robert Marshall and Mary Marshall; *m* 1944, Beryl Broad; one *s. Educ:* Univ. of St Andrews (MA Mediaeval and Modern History; MA 1st Cl. Hons English Lit.); Commonwealth Fellow, Yale Univ. (MA Polit. Theory and Govt). Scottish Office, 1937–39. Served War, 1939–46: RASC and AEC; finally Comdt, Army Sch. of Educn. Pres., Co-op. Congress, 1976. Missions on Co-op. develt to Tanganyika, Nigeria, India, Kenya, S Yemen and Thailand. Member: Gen. Adv. Council and Complaints Rev. Bd, IBA, 1973–77; Monopolies and Mergers Commn, 1976–82; Distributive Studies Bd, Business Educn Council, 1976–79; Chm., Quest House, Loughborough, 1980–86; Vice-Chm., Charnwood Community Council, 1980–90. Mem. Court, Loughborough Univ. of Technol., 1981–91. Hon. MA Open Univ., 1977; Hon. DLitt Loughborough Univ. of Technol., 1977. Jt Editor, Jl of Soc. for Co-operative Studies, 1967–. *Publications:* Lippen on Angus—a celebration of North Angus Co-operative Society, 1983; contribs to educnl and co-op jls. *Recreations:* walking, reading, swimming, golf. *Address:* Holly Cottage, 15 Beacon Road, Woodhouse Eaves, Leics LE12 8RN. *T:* Woodhouse Eaves (01509) 890612.

MARSHALL, Sir (Robert) Michael, Kt 1990; MP (C) Arundel since Feb. 1974; *b* 21 June 1930; *s* of late Robert Ernest and Margaret Mary Marshall, Brookside Cottages, Hathersage; *m* 1972, Caroline Victoria Oliphant, *d* of late Alexander Hutchison of Strathairly; two step *d. Educ:* Bradfield Coll.; Harvard and Stanford Univs. MBA Harvard 1960. Joined United Steel Cos Ltd, 1951; Branch Man., Calcutta, 1954–58; Man. Dir, Bombay, 1960–64; Commercial Dir, Workington, 1964–66; Man. Dir, Head Wrightson Export Co. Ltd, 1967–69; Management Consultant, Urwick Orr & Partners Ltd, 1969–74. Parly Under-Sec. of State, DoI, 1979–81. Chairman: Parly Space Cttee, 1982–; IPU, 1987–90 (Vice Chm., 1985–87); Parly IT Cttee, 1986– (Vice-Chm., 1982–86); Vice-Chairman: Cons. Party Parly Industry Cttee, 1976–79; All Party Parly Cttee on Management, 1974–79; Member: Select Cttee on Defence, 1982–87; Procedure Cttee, 1994–; Parly Adviser: British Aerospace, 1982–; Cable and Wireless, 1982–; SWET, 1984–; Williams Hldgs, 1988–. Member: Equity; BAFTA. Hon. DL New England Coll., 1982. FRSA. *Publications:* Top Hat and Tails: the story of Jack Buchanan, 1978; (ed) The Stanley Holloway Monologues, 1979; More Monologues and Songs, 1980; The Book of Comic and Dramatic Monologues, 1981; The Timetable of Technology, 1982; No End of Jobs, 1984; Gentlemen and Players, 1987; (contrib.) A Celebration of Lords and Commons Cricket, 1989; My Lord's, 1990; Cricket at the Castle, 1995. *Recreations:* writing books and for radio and TV, cricket commentating, golf. *Address:* Old Inn House, Slindon, Arundel, W Sussex BN18 0RB. *Clubs:* Garrick, MCC, Lord's Taverners; Sussex; Royal & Ancient Golf (St Andrews), Goodwood Golf.

MARSHALL, Prof. Robin, PhD; FRS 1995; Professor of Experimental Physics, Manchester University, since 1992; *b* 5 Jan. 1940; *s* of Robert Marshall and Grace Eileen Marshall (*née* Ryder); *m* 1963, Ida Catherine Elias; two *s* one *d. Educ:* Ermysted's Grammar Sch., Skipton; Univ. of Manchester (BSc 1962; PhD 1965). DSIR Research Fellow, 1965–67; Vis. Scientist, Deutsches Elektronen Synchrotron, Hamburg, 1967–68; Res. Scientist, MIT, 1968–70; Scientist, Daresbury Lab., 1970–78; PSO, 1978–86, Sen. Principal (IM), 1986–92, Rutherford Appleton Lab. *Publications:* High Energy Electron-Positron Physics, 1988; Electron-Positron Annihilation Physics, 1990; numerous scientific papers. *Recreation:* nurturing ducks on Manchester's inner city canals. *Address:* Department of Physics and Astronomy, University of Manchester, Manchester M13 9PL. *T:* 0161–275 4170.

MARSHALL, Sir Roy; *see* Marshall, Sir O. R.

MARSHALL, Hon. Russell; *see* Marshall, Hon. C. R.

MARSHALL, Thomas Daniel; Member, Newcastle City Council, since 1986; *b* 6 Nov. 1929; *s* of James William and Leonora Mary Marshall; *m* 1953, Eileen James; one *s. Educ:* St George's RC Elementary Sch., Bell's Close, Newcastle upon Tyne; Ruskin Coll.; Open Univ. Post Office, then Nat. Assistance Board, 1960; DHSS, 1966. Councillor, Newburn UDC, 1967; Mem., Tyne and Wear CC, 1974–86 (Chm., 1978–79). Chairman: Northern Region IT Inst.; NE Region IT Enterprise Agency; Tyne and Wear Enterprise Trust; Throckley Community Hall Ltd; Newburn Riverside Recreation Assoc. Ltd; Grange Day Centre Ltd; Director: Tyne and Wear Innovation Centre and Development Co.; Bowes Railway Co.; Tyneside Stables Project Ltd; Newcastle Airport PLC; Owners Ltd; Tyne Theatre and Opera House; Newburn Sports Services Ltd; Tyne Leisure Ltd; Gateshead Enterprise Agency. Trustee: Industrial Monuments Trust; Building Preservation Trust Ltd; Grange Welfare Assoc. *Recreation:* reading. *Address:* 7 Hallow Drive, Throckley, Newcastle upon Tyne NE15 9AQ. *T:* 0191–267 0956. *Clubs:* Grange Welfare; Newburn Memorial (Newcastle).

MARSHALL, Valerie Margaret, (Mrs A. R. Marshall); Director, Greig, Middleton & Co. Ltd, since 1990; *b* 30 March 1945; *d* of Ernest Knagg and Marion Knagg; *m* 1972, Alan Roger Marshall; two *s* one *d. Educ:* Brighton and Hove High Sch.; Girton Coll., Cambridge (MA); London Graduate Sch. of Business Studies (MSc). LRAM. Financial Controller, ICFC, 1969–80; Scottish Development Agency: Investment Exec., 1980–84; Investment Man., 1984–88; Head of Business Enterprise, 1988–90. Director: Renfrew Development Co. Ltd, 1988–90; Scottish Food Fund, 1988–90. Member: Scottish Cttee, Design Council, 1975–77; Monopolies and Mergers Commn, 1976–81. Chm., Scottish Music Inf Centre, 1986–90. Governor: Glasgow Sch. of Art, 1989–90; Tonbridge GS for Girls, 1993–. *Recreations:* music, ballet, collecting antiquarian books, walking, entertaining. *Address:* 2 Farnaby Drive, Sevenoaks, Kent TN13 2LQ.

MARSHALL, William; Assistant Under-Secretary of State, Ministry of Defence (Navy), 1968–72, retired; *b* 30 Sept. 1912; *e s* of late Allan and Julia Marshall, Whitecraigs, Renfrewshire; *m* 1st, 1940, Jessie Gardner Miller (*d* 1962); one *s*; 2nd, 1963, Doreen Margaret Read. *Educ:* Allan Glen's Sch., Glasgow; Glasgow Univ. MA Glasgow 1932, LLB (*cum laude*) Glasgow 1935. War of 1939–45: Temp. Asst Principal, Air Ministry, 1940; Service with Royal Navy (Ord. Seaman), and Admin. Staff, Admty, 1941. Private Sec. to Permanent Sec. of Admty (Sir J. G. Lang), 1947–48; Principal Private Sec. to successive First Lords of Admty (Lord Hall, Lord Packenham and Rt Hon. J. P. L. Thomas, later Lord Cilcennin), 1951–54; Asst Sec. in Admty, 1954; on loan to HM Treasury, 1958–61; returned to Admiralty, 1961. Chm., cttee to review submarine escape trng, 1974. *Recreations:* golf, travel, gardening. *Address:* 37 West Drive, Cheam, Surrey SM2 7NB. *T:* 0181–642 3399.

MARSHALL-ANDREWS, Robert Graham; QC 1987; a Recorder of the Crown Court, since 1982; *b* 10 April 1944; *s* of Robin and Eileen Nora Marshall; *m* 1968, Gillian Diana Elliott; one *s* one *d. Educ:* Mill Hill Sch.; Univ. of Bristol (LLB; winner, Observer Mace Nat. Debating Competition, 1965). Called to the Bar, Gray's Inn, 1967; Recorder, Oxford and Midland Circuit, 1982–. Trustee: George Adamson Trust, 1988–; Geffrye Museum, 1990–. Chm. of Govs, Grey Court Sch., 1988–94. *Publication:* The Palace of Wisdom (novel), 1989. *Recreations:* theatre, reading, Rugby (watching), travelling about. *Address:* 4 Paper Buildings, Temple, EC4Y 7EX. *T:* 0171–353 3366. *Club:* Druidston (Broadhaven, Pembrokeshire).

MARSHALL EVANS, David; *see* Evans.

MARSHAM, family name of **Earl of Romney.**

MARSLAND, Prof. Edward Abson, BDS, PhD; FDSRCS, FRCPath; Vice-Chancellor and Principal, University of Birmingham, 1981–86; Professor of Oral Pathology, University of Birmingham, 1964–81, Emeritus since 1986; *b* Coventry, 18 May 1923; *s* of T. Marsland; *m* 1957, Jose, *d* of J. H. Evans; one *s* two *d. Educ:* King Edward's Sch. and Univ. of Birmingham. House Surgeon, Gen. and Dental Hosps, Birmingham, 1946; Birmingham University: Research Fellow, 1948–50; Lectr in Dental Pathology, 1950–58; Sen. Lectr, 1958–64; Pro-Vice-Chancellor, 1977–79; Vice-Principal, 1979–81; Dir, Birmingham Dental Sch., 1969–74. Chairman: Co-ord. Cttee for Welfare of Handicapped, Birmingham, 1972–81; W Midlands Council for Disabled People, 1977–83 (Pres., 1985–); Midlands Council for Preparatory Trng of Disabled, 1987–89 (Vice-Chm., 1976–87); Regional Council, Sense in the Midlands, 1990–; Member: W Midlands RHA, 1984–87 (Chm., Rehabilitation Cttee, 1987–93); Disablement Services Authority, 1987–91. Pres., Blue Coat Sch., Birmingham, 1984–; Hon. Vice-Pres., Ironbridge Museum Trust, 1986; Chairman: Council, Edgbaston C of E Coll. for Girls, 1988–91 (Mem. Council, 1984–88); Council of Management, St Mary's Hospice, 1990– (Mem. Council, 1987–90). Trustee: Selly Oak Colls, 1987– (Hon. Fellow, 1986); Sense in the Midlands Foundn, 1987–93; Royal Orthopaedic Hospital Trust, Birmingham, 1990–; Midland Assoc. for Spina Bifida and Hydrocephalus, 1990–. Hon. LLD Birmingham, 1987; DUniv Open, 1987. Gold Medal, Birmingham Civic Soc., 1988. *Publications:* An Atlas of Dental Histology, 1957; A Colour Atlas of Oral Histopathology, 1975; scientific papers in various jls; articles on disability. *Recreations:* work for disabled people, gardening, motoring, photography. *Address:* 9 Bryony Road, Selly Oak, Birmingham B29 4BY. *T:* 0121–608 1285.

MARSLEN-WILSON, Lorraine Komisarjevsky; *see* Tyler, L. K.

MARSON, Anthony; Group Finance Director, PSA Services, Department of the Environment, 1990–93; *b* 12 Jan. 1938; *m* 1963, Margaret Salmond; three *s. Educ:* Bristol Univ. (BA). Finance Dir, Pharmaceutical Div., Beecham Gp, 1968–90. *Address:* PSA Services, 2 Marsham Street, SW1P 3EB.

MARTELL, Vice-Adm. Sir Hugh (Colenso), KBE 1966 (CBE 1957); CB 1963; *b* 6 May 1912; *s* of late Engineer Capt. A. A. G. Martell, DSO, RN (Retd) and late Mrs S. Martell; *m* Margaret, *d* of late Major A. R. Glover. *Educ:* Edinburgh Academy; RNC Dartmouth. Royal Navy, 1926–67, retired; served War, 1940–45 (despatches): Gunnery Officer in HMS Berwick and HMS Illustrious. Naval Adviser to Dir Air Armament Research and Development, Min. of Supply, 1952–54; Capt. (F) 7 and in Comd HMS Bigbury Bay, 1954–55; Overall Operational Comdr, Nuclear Tests, in Monte Bello Is as Cdre, 1956; IDC, 1957; Capt., HMS Excellent, 1958; ADC, 1958; Dir of Tactical and Weapons Policy, Admiralty and Naval Mem. Defence Research Policy Staff, Min. of Defence, 1959–62; Admiral Commanding Reserves and Dir-Gen. of Naval Recruiting (as Rear-Adm.), 1962–65; Chief of Allied Staff, Mediterranean, Aegean and Black Sea (as Vice-Adm.), 1965–67. Life Mem., RNSA. *Recreation:* sailing. *Club:* Naval (Hon. Life Mem.).

MARTEN, Francis William, CMG 1967; MC 1943; formerly Counsellor, Foreign and Commonwealth Office; *b* 8 Nov. 1916; *er s* of late Vice-Adm. Sir Francis Arthur Marten and late Lady Marten (*née* Phyllis Raby Morgan); *m* 1940, Hon. Avice Irene Vernon (*d* 1964); one *s* one *d*; 2nd, 1967, Miss Anne Tan; one *s. Educ:* Winchester Coll.; Christ Church, Oxford. Served HM Forces, 1939–46. Entered HM Foreign Service, 1946; served FO, 1946–48; Washington, 1948–52; FO, 1952–54; Teheran, 1954–57; NATO Defence Coll., Paris, 1957–58; Bonn, 1958–62; Leopoldville, 1962–64; Imperial Defence Coll., 1964–65; Dep. High Comr, Eastern Malaysia, 1965–67; ODM, 1967–69. *Recreation:* gardening. *Address:* 113 Pepys Road, SE14 5SE. *T:* 0171–639 1060.

MARTIN; *see* Holland-Martin.

MARTIN, Archer John Porter, CBE 1960; FRS 1950; MA, PhD; *b* 1 March 1910; *s* of Dr W. A. P. and Mrs L. K. Martin; *m* 1943, Judith Bagenal; two *s* three *d. Educ:* Bedford Sch.; Peterhouse, Cambridge, Hon. Fellow, 1974. Nutritional Lab., Cambridge, 1933–38; Chemist, Wool Industries Research Assoc., Leeds, 1938–46; Research Dept, Boots Pure Drug Co., Nottingham, 1946–48; staff, Medical Research Council, 1948–52; Head of Phys. Chem. Div., National Inst. of Medical Research, 1952–56; Chemical Consultant, 1956–59; Director, Abbotsbury Laboratories Ltd, 1959–70; Consultant to Wellcome Research Laboratories, 1970–73. Extraordinary Prof., Technological Univ. of Eindhoven, 1965–73; Professorial Fellow, Univ. of Sussex, 1973–78; Robert A. Welch Prof. of Chemistry, Univ. of Houston, Texas, 1974–79; Invited Prof. of Chemistry, Ecole Polytechnique Fédérale de Lausanne, 1980–84. Berzelius Gold Medal, Swedish Medical Soc., 1951; (jointly with R. L. M. Synge) Nobel Prize for Chemistry, 1952; John Scott Award, 1958; John Price Wetherill Medal, 1959; Franklin Institute Medal, 1959; Leverhulme Medal, Royal Society, 1963; Koltoff Medal, Acad. of Pharmaceutical Science, 1969; Callendar Medal, Inst. of Measurement and Control, 1971; Fritz-Pregl Medal, Austrian Soc. of Microchem. and Analytical Chem., 1985. Hon. DSc Leeds, 1968; Hon. LLD Glasgow, 1973.

MARTIN, (Arthur) Bryan, CB 1987; Member of Health and Safety Executive, 1985–88, and Director, Resources and Planning Division, 1977–88; Head of UK Delegation, and Alternate Chairman, Channel Tunnel Safety Authority, 1989–92; *b* 16 July 1928; *s* of Frederick Arthur Martin and Edith Maud Martin; *m* 1953, Dyllis Naomi Eirne Johnstone-Hogg; two *s. Educ:* Bristol Grammar Sch.; Royal Mil. Coll. of Science (BSc). Joined Army, REME, 1948; commnd, 1948; Lt-Col, 1967–69; served in UK, Germany, Malaya, Cyprus and Aden; joined Civil Service (Dept of Employment), 1969, as direct entrant principal; Asst Sec., Factory Inspectorate, 1973; Under Sec., HSE, 1977. Dir, Docklands Light Railway, 1993–. *Address:* Ashford Old Farm, Ilton, near Ilminster, Som TA19 9ED.

MARTIN, Sir Bruce; *see* Martin, Sir R. B.

MARTIN, Bryan; See Martin, A. B.

MARTIN, Charles Edmund, MA; Headmaster, Bristol Grammar School, since 1986; *b* 19 Sept. 1939; *s* of late Flight Lieut Charles Stuart Martin and of Sheila Martin; *m* 1966, Emily Mary Bozman; one *s* one *d. Educ:* Lancing College; Selwyn College, Cambridge (Hons English; MA); Bristol University (PGCE). VSO, Sarawak, 1958–59; Asst Master, Leighton Park School, Reading, 1964–68; Day Housemaster and Sixth Form Master, Sevenoaks School, 1968–71; Head of English Dept and Dep. Headmaster, Pocklington School, 1971–80; Headmaster, King Edward VI Camp Hill Boys' School, Birmingham, 1980–86. Sec., 1992–93, Chm., 1993–94, HMC SW Div.; Divl Rep., HMC Cttee, 1992–93. *Recreations:* travel, hill walking, theatre, ornithology. *Address:* The Grammar School, University Road, Bristol BS8 1SR. *Club:* East India.

MARTIN, Charlie; *see* Martin, J. C.

MARTIN, Christopher George; management consultant; Director of Personnel, British Broadcasting Corporation, 1981–89, retired; *b* 29 May 1938; *s* of George and Lizbette Martin; *m* 1st, 1960, Moira Hughes (marr. diss. 1975); one *s* one *d*; 2nd, 1981, Elizabeth Buchanan Keith; one *s* decd. *Educ:* Beckenham Sch., Kent. Royal Marines, 1956–62. Group Personnel Manager: Viyella Internat., 1964–70; Great Universal Stores, 1970–74; Personnel Dir, Reed Paper & Board, 1974–76; UK Personnel Dir, Air Products Ltd, 1976–78; Gp Personnel Controller, Rank Organisation Ltd, 1978–81. CIMgt (CBIM 1984); FIPM 1984. *Publication:* contrib. Jl of Textile Inst. *Recreations:* music, sailing. *Address:* Cailhavel, 31540 St Felix-Lauragais, France.

MARTIN, Christopher Sanford; Headmaster, Millfield School, since 1990; *b* 23 Aug. 1938; *s* of Geoffrey Richard Rex Martin and Hazel Matthews; *m* 1968, Mary Julia Parry-Evans; one *s* one *d. Educ:* St Andrews Univ. (MA Mod. Langs; PGCE). Commissioned 2/10 Gurkha Rifles, 1957. Taught at Westminster Sch., 1963–78, at Philips, Exeter Acad., USA, 1966; Head Master, Bristol Cathedral Sch., 1979–90. Member: Privy Council Educnl Panel, 1986–; Engrg Council Educn Cttee, 1988–; Adv. Bd, Teacher Trng Agency, 1995–. Chairman: SW Div., HMC, 1987; Choir Schools' Assoc., 1987–89; HMC/SHA Working Party on teacher shortage, 1987–90; Nat. Rep., HMC Cttee, 1987–89. Founded Textbooks for Africa scheme (ODA), 1988. *Recreations:* walking, sailing, ski-ing, rebuilding a farmhouse in SW France. *Address:* Millfield School, Street, Somerset BA16 0YD. *T:* Street (01458) 442291.

MARTIN, Rev. Prof. David Alfred, PhD; Senior Professorial Fellow, Institute for the Study of Economic Culture, Boston University, 1990–95; Professor of Sociology, London School of Economics and Political Science, London University, 1971–89, now Emeritus; Hon. Professor, Lancaster University, since 1993; *b* 30 June 1929; *s* of late Frederick Martin and late Rhoda Miriam Martin; *m* 1st, 1953, Daphne Sylvia Treherne (*d* 1975); one *s*; 2nd, 1962, Bernice Thompson; two *s* one *d. Educ:* Richmond and East Sheen Grammar Sch.; Westminster Coll. (DipEd 1952); Westcott House, Cambridge. BSc (Ext.) 1st Cl. Hons, London Univ., 1959; PhD 1964. School teaching, 1952–59; postgrad. scholar, LSE, 1959–61; Asst Lectr, Sheffield Univ., 1961–62; Lectr, LSE, 1962–67, Reader, 1967–71. JSPS Scholar, Japan, 1978–79; Scurlock Prof. of Human Values, Southern Methodist Univ., Dallas, Texas, 1986–90. Lectures: Cadbury, Birmingham Univ., 1973; Ferguson, Manchester Univ., 1977; Gore, Westminster Abbey, 1977; Firth, Nottingham Univ., 1980; Forwood, Liverpool Univ., 1982; Prideaux, Exeter Univ., 1984; F. D. Maurice, KCL, 1991; Sarum, Oxford Univ., 1994–95; Select Preacher, Cambridge Univ., 1979. Pres., Internat. Conf. of Sociology of Religion, 1975–83. Ordained Deacon, 1983, Priest 1984; Hon. Asst Priest, Guildford Cathedral, 1983–. *Publications:* Pacifism, 1965; A Sociology of English Religion, 1967; The Religious and the Secular, 1969; Tracts against the Times, 1973; A General Theory of Secularisation, 1978; Dilemmas of Contemporary Religion, 1978; (ed) Crisis for Cranmer and King James, 1979; The Breaking of the Image, 1980; (ed jtly) Theology and Sociology, 1980; (ed jtly) No Alternative, 1981; (ed jtly) Unholy Warfare, 1983; Divinity in a Grain of Bread, 1989; Tongues of Fire, 1990; contrib. Encounter, TLS, THES, Daedalus, TES. *Recreation:* piano accompaniment. *Address:* Cripplegate Cottage, 174 St John's Road, Woking, Surrey GU21 1PQ. *T:* Woking (01483) 762134.

MARTIN, David John Pattison; MP (C) Portsmouth South, since 1987; *b* 5 Feb. 1945; *s* of late John Besley Martin, CBE and Muriel Martin; *m* 1977, Basia Dowmunt; one *s* three *d* (and one *d* decd). *Educ:* Norwood Sch., Exeter; Kelly College; Fitzwilliam College, Cambridge (BA Hons 1967). Governor, Dummer Academy, USA, 1963–64; called to the Bar, Inner Temple, 1969; practised until 1976; formerly Dir, family caravan and holiday business. Teignbridge District Councillor (C), 1979–83. Contested Yeovil, 1983. PPS to Minister of State, Defence Procurement, 1990, to Sec. of State, Foreign and Commonwealth Affairs, 1990–94. *Recreations:* music, golf, chief arbitrator of children's squabbles. *Address:* House of Commons, SW1A 0AA. *T:* 0171–219 6912. *Club:* Hawks (Cambridge).

MARTIN, David Weir; Member (Lab) Lothians, European Parliament, since 1984; a Vice President of the European Parliament, since 1989; *b* 26 Aug. 1954; *s* of William Martin and Marion Weir; *m* 1979, Margaret Mary Cook; one *s* one *d. Educ:* Liberton High School; Heriot-Watt University (BA Hons Econs). Stockbroker's clerk, 1970–74; animal rights campaigner, 1975–78. Lothian Regional Councillor, 1982–84. Leader, British Lab Gp, European Parliament, 1987–88. Mem. Council, RIIA, 1991–92. Vice-Pres., National Playbus Assoc., 1985–. Vice-Pres., Internat. Inst. for Democracy; Mem. Cttee, Advocates for Animals (formerly Scottish Soc. for Prevention of Vivisection), 1985–. Dir, St Andrew Animal Fund, 1986–. *Publications:* Europe: an ever closer union, 1991; Fabian pamphlets on the Common Market and on EC enlargement; Wheatley pamphlet on European Union. *Recreations:* soccer, reading. *Address:* (office) 4 Lothian Street, Dalkeith, Midlothian EH22 1DS. *T:* 0131–654 1606.

MARTIN, Prof. Derek H.; Professor of Physics, Queen Mary and Westfield College (formerly Queen Mary College), University of London, 1967–94, Emeritus Professor since 1995; *b* 18 May 1929; *s* of Alec Gooch Martin and Winifred Martin; *m* 1951, Joyce Sheila Leaper; one *s* one *d. Educ:* Hitchin Boys' Grammar Sch.; Eastbourne Grammar Sch.; Univ. of Nottingham. BSc; PhD. Queen Mary College, London: Lectr, 1954–58, 1962–63; Reader in Experimental Physics, 1963–67; Dean, Faculty of Science, 1968–70; Head of Dept of Physics, 1970–75. DSIR Res. Fellow, 1959–62; Visiting Professor: Univ. of Calif, Berkeley, 1965–66; Univ. of Essex, 1995–. Member: Astronomy, Space and Radio Bd, SRC, 1975–78; Bd, Athlone Press, 1973–79; Royal Greenwich Observatory Cttee, 1977–80; Senate, Univ. of London, 1981–86; Court, Univ. of Essex, 1986–94. Fellow, Inst. of Physics (Hon. Sec., 1984–94); Mem., Internat. Astronomical Union. NPL Metrology Award, 1983. Editor, Advances in Physics, 1974–84. *Publications:* Magnetism in Solids, 1967; Spectroscopic Techniques, 1967; numerous articles and papers in Proc. Royal Soc., Jl of Physics, etc. *Address:* Hermanus, Hillwood Grove, Brentwood, Essex CM13 2PD. *T:* Brentwood (01277) 210546. *Club:* Athenæum.

MARTIN, Evelyn Fairfax, OBE 1994; Company Secretary, National Council of Women of GB, since 1992 (National President, 1986–88); Co-Chair, Women's National Commission, 1991–93; *b* 12 Aug. 1926; *d* of late Kenneth Gordon Robinson and Beatrice Robinson (*née* Monro); *m* 1949, Dennis William Martin; three *d* (and one *d* decd). *Educ:* Belvedere Girls' Sch., Liverpool; Huyton Coll. for Girls, Liverpool; Mrs Hoster's Secretarial Coll. Foster parent, 1960–71. Chairman: Battered Wives Hostel, Calderdale, 1980–82; Calderdale Well Woman Centre, 1982–86; Calderdale CHC, 1982–84; Women's Health and Screening Delegn, 1985–91. FRSA 1991. *Recreations:* gardening, foreign travel, animals. *Address:* 32 Clifton Road, Halifax HX3 0BT. *T:* Halifax (01422) 360438. *Club:* University Women's.

MARTIN, (Francis) Troy K.; *see* Kennedy Martin.

MARTIN, Frank; Second Treasury Officer of Accounts, HM Treasury, since 1994; *b* 1 April 1946; *s* of Frank and Sylvia Martin; *m* 1975, Jean Richardson; one *s* one *d. Educ:* Alsop High Sch. for Boys, Liverpool; Sidney Sussex Coll., Cambridge (BA Hist.); LSE (MSc Internat. Relns). COI, 1969–73; DTI, 1973–76; HM Treasury, 1976–: Dep. Dir, Central Unit on Purchasing, 1987–89; Principal Establishment and Finance Officer, CSO, 1989–93, on secondment. *Recreations:* reading, gardening, holidays in France. *Address:* HM Treasury, Parliament Street, SW1P 3AQ. *T:* 0171–270 3000.

MARTIN, Frank Vernon, MA (Oxon); graphic artist; printmaker; engraver; illustrator; *b* Dulwich, 14 Jan. 1921; *er s* of late Thomas Martin; *m* 1942, Mary Irene Goodwin; three *d. Educ:* Uppingham Sch.; Hertford Coll., Oxford (History Schol.); St Martin's Sch. of Art. Army, 1941–46. Studied wood engraving with Gertrude Hermes and etching with John Buckland Wright. In free-lance professional practice as wood engraver and book illustrator, 1948–. Teacher of etching and engraving, Camberwell Sch. of Art, 1953–80 (Hd of Dept of Graphic Arts, 1976–80). Printmaker, 1966–; etchings, drypoints, woodcuts in colour. Nineteen one-man exhibitions in UK, Europe and USA, 1956–; works in various public and private collections in UK and abroad. RE 1955–74; MSIA 1955–71; Mem., Soc. of Wood Engravers; Hon. Academician, Accademia delle Arti del Disegno, Florence, 1962. *Address:* 55 St Mary's Grove, W4 3LW.

MARTIN, Frederick Royal, BSc, CEng, FICE, FIStructE; Under-Secretary, Department of the Environment and Director, Defence Services II, Property Services Agency, 1975–79, retired; *b* 10 Oct. 1919; *e s* of late Frederick Martin and Lois Martin (*née* Royal); *m* 1946, Elsie Winifred Parkes (*d* 1984); one *s* three *d. Educ:* Dudley Grammar Sch.; Univ. of Birmingham (BSc (Hons)). Asst Engr, Birmingham, Tame and Rea Dist Drainage Bd, 1940; entered Air Min. Directorate-Gen. of Works, as Engrg Asst, 1941; Asst Civil Engr: Heathrow, Cardington, London, 1944–48; Civil Engr: Cambridge, Iraq, Jordan, Persian Gulf, London, 1948–54; Sqdn Leader, RAF, 1949–52; Sen. CE, London, 1954–58; Suptg CE, London, also Chief Engr, Aden, Aden Protectorate, Persian Gulf and E Africa, 1958–62; Suptg CE, Exeter, 1962–64; Min. of Public Bdg and Works, Area Officer, Bournemouth, 1964–66; Suptg CE, Directorate of Civil Engrg Develt, 1966–70; Asst Dir, 1970–72; Dir of Directorate of Social and Research Services, Property Services Agency, 1972; Chief Engineer, Maplin Develt Authority, 1973–74. Crampton Prize, ICE, 1946. *Publications:* various papers and articles to Instn Civil Engrs, etc, on airfield pavements. *Recreations:* looking at medieval building, reading, gardening. *Address:* 25 East Avenue, Bournemouth, Dorset BH3 7BS. *T:* Bournemouth (01202) 555858.

MARTIN, Geoffrey; *see* Martin, T. G.

MARTIN, Prof. Geoffrey Haward, CBE 1986; DPhil; FSA, FRHistS; Research Professor of History, University of Essex, since 1990; *b* 27 Sept. 1928; *s* of late Ernest Leslie Martin and Mary H. Martin (*née* Haward), *m* 1953, Janet, *d* of late Douglas Hamer, MC and Enid Hamer; three *s* one *d. Educ:* Colchester Royal Grammar Sch.; Merton Coll., Oxford (MA, DPhil); Univ. of Manchester. FSA 1975; FRHistS 1958. University of Leicester (formerly University Coll. of Leicester): Lectr in Econ. History, 1952–65; Reader in History, 1966–73; Prof. of History, 1973–82; Public Orator, 1971–74; Dean, Faculty of Arts, 1972–75; Pro-Vice-Chancellor, 1979–82; Hon. Archivist, 1989–. Keeper of Public Records, 1982–88. Vis. Prof. of Medieval History, Carleton Univ., Ottawa, 1958–59 and 1967–68; Vis. Res. Fellow, 1971, Sen. Res. Fellow, 1990–93, Merton Coll., Oxford; Sen. Res. Fellow, Loughborough Univ. of Technol., 1987–; Hon. Res. Fellow, Dept of Library and Archive Studies, UCL, 1987–; Dist. Vis. Prof. of History, Univ. of Toronto, 1989; Emeritus Fellow, Leverhulme Trust, 1989–91. Evelyn Wrench Lectr, ESU, 1992. Chairman: Board of Leicester University Press, 1975–82; Selection Cttee, Miners' Welfare National Educn Fund, 1978–84; British Records Assoc., 1982–91 (Vice-Pres., 1992–); Commonwealth Archivists' Assoc., 1984–88; Arts and Humanities Res. Degrees Sub-Cttee, CNAA, 1986–92; Mem., RCHM, 1987–94. Vice-Pres., RHistS, 1984–88; Mem. Council, Soc. of Antiquaries, 1989–91. Gov., Museum of London, 1989–95. Hon. Gen. Editor, Suffolk Record Soc., 1956–94. Dist. Mem., Sistema Nacional de Archivos, Mexico, 1988. DUniv Essex, 1989. Besterman Medal, Library Assoc., 1972. *Publications:* The Town: a visual history, 1961; Royal Charters of Grantham, 1963; (with Sylvia McIntyre) Bibliography of British and Irish Municipal History, vol. 1, 1972; Ipswich Recognizance Rolls: a calendar, 1973; (with Philomena Connolly) The Dublin Guild Merchant Roll *c* 1190–1265, 1992; Portsmouth Royal Charters 1194–1994, 1995; Knighton's Chronicle 1337–96, 1995; contribs to various learned jls. *Recreations:* fell-walking, adjusting phrases, gardening. *Address:* 27 Woodside House, Woodside, Wimbledon, SW19 7QN. *T:* 0181–946 2570. *Clubs:* Commonwealth Trust, United Oxford & Cambridge University.

MARTIN, Prof. Geoffrey Thorndike, PhD, LittD; FSA; Edwards Professor of Egyptology and Head of Department of Egyptology, University College London, 1988–93, now Emeritus; *b* 28 May 1934; *s* of late Albert Thorndike Martin and Lily Martin (*née* Jackson). *Educ:* Palmer's Sch., Grays Thurrock; University Coll. London (BA 1963); Corpus Christi Coll., Cambridge; Christ's Coll., Cambridge (MA 1966; PhD 1969; LittD 1994). ALA; FSA 1975. Cataloguer, Brit. Nat. Bibliography, 1957–60; Lady Wallis Budge Res. Fellow in Egyptology, Christ's Coll., Cambridge, 1966–70; University College London: Lectr in Egyptology, 1970–78; Reader in Egyptian Archaeology, 1978–87; Prof. (*ad hominem*) of Egyptology, 1987–88. Vis. Prof., Collège de France, 1986. Assisted at excavations of Egypt Exploration Society at: Buhen, Sudan, 1963; Saqqara, Egypt, 1964–68, 1970–71 (Site Dir, 1971–74; Field Dir, 1975–); Field Dir, Epigraphic Mission, Amarna, Egypt, 1969, 1980. Mem. Cttee, Egypt Exploration Soc., 1969–; Rep. for GB, Council of Internat. Assoc. Egyptologists, 1976–82; Mem. Cttee, Bd of Management, Gerald Averay Wainwright Near Eastern Archaeol Fund, Oxford Univ., 1985–89. Wilbour Fellow, Brooklyn Museum, 1969. Corresp. Mem., German Archaeol Inst., 1982. *Publications:* Egyptian Administrative and Private-Name Seals, 1971; The Royal Tomb at El-Amarna, vol. 1, 1974, vol. 2, 1989; The Tomb of Hetepka, 1979; The Sacred Animal Necropolis at North Saqqara, 1981; (with V. Raisman) Canopic Equipment in the Petrie Collection, 1984; Scarabs, Cylinders and other Ancient Egyptian Seals, 1985; The Tomb Chapels of Paser and Raia, 1985; Corpus of Reliefs of the New Kingdom, vol. 1, 1987; (with A. El-

Khouly) Excavations in the Royal Necropolis at El-Amarna, 1987; The Memphite Tomb of Horemheb, 1989; The Hidden Tombs of Memphis, 1991 (German edn 1994); Bibliography of the Amarna Period and its aftermath, 1991; contribs to learned and other jls. *Recreations:* travel, English history, book collecting. *Address:* c/o Department of Egyptology, University College London, Gower Street, WC1E 6BT.

MARTIN, George Henry, CBE 1988; Chairman: AIR Group of companies, since 1965; Heart of London Radio, since 1994; Director, Chrysalis Group, since 1978; *b* 3 Jan. 1926; *s* of Henry and Bertha Beatrice Martin; *m* 1st, 1948, Sheena Rose Chisholm; one *s* one *d*; 2nd, 1966, Judy Lockhart Smith; one *s* one *d*. *Educ:* St Ignatius Coll., Stamford Hill, London; Bromley County Sch., Kent; Guildhall Sch. of Music and Drama. Sub-Lieut, FAA, RNVR, 1944–47. BBC, July 1950; EMI Records Ltd, Nov. 1950–1965; formed AIR Gp of cos (originally Associated Independent Recordings Ltd), 1965; built AIR Studios, 1969; built AIR Studios, Montserrat, 1979; completed new AIR Studios, Lyndhurst Hall, 1992; company merged with Chrysalis Gp, 1974; produced innumerable records, including all those featuring The Beatles; scored the music for fifteen films; nominated for Oscar for A Hard Day's Night, 1964; Grammy Awards, USA, 1964, 1967 (two), 1973, 1993; Ivor Novello Awards, 1963, 1979. Hon. DMus Berklee Coll. of Music, Boston, Mass, 1989; Hon. MA Salford, 1992. *Publications:* All You Need Is Ears, 1979; Making Music, 1983; Summer of Love, 1994. *Recreations:* boats, sculpture, tennis, snooker. *Address:* c/o AIR Studios, Lyndhurst Hall, Hampstead, NW3 5NG. *Clubs:* Oriental; Alderney Sailing.

MARTIN, Lt-Gen. Henry James, CBE 1943; DFC; Chief of Defence Staff, South African Defence Force, retired; *b* 10 June 1910; *s* of Stanley Charles Martin and Susan C. Fourie; *m* 1940, Renée Viljoen; one *s* two *d*. *Educ:* Grey Coll. Sch., Bloemfontein; Grey Univ. Coll., Bloemfontein. Joined S African Air Force, 1936, and played important rôle in British Empire Training Scheme in South Africa; commanded No 12 Sqdn in Western Desert (DFC, Croix Militaire de première classe Belgique); commanded No 3 Wing (a unit of Desert Air Force) and campaigned from El Alamein to Tunis; returned to Union, 1943. *Recreation:* rugger (represented Orange Free State, 1931–34, Transvaal, 1935–37, South Africa, 1937). *Address:* 169 Pennys Way, Lynnwood Glen, Pretoria 0081, S Africa.

MARTIN, Ian; Senior Associate, Carnegie Endowment for International Peace, since 1993; *b* 10 Aug. 1946; *s* of Collin and Betty Martin. *Educ:* Brentwood Sch.; Emmanuel Coll., Cambridge; Harvard Univ. Ford Foundn Representative's Staff, India, 1969–70, Pakistan, 1970–71, Bangladesh, 1972; Community Relations Officer, Redbridge Community Relations Council, 1973–75; Gen. Sec., Jt Council for the Welfare of Immigrants, 1977–82 (Dep. Gen. Sec., 1976–77; Exec. Cttee Mem., 1982–86); Gen. Sec., The Fabian Soc., 1982–85; Sec. Gen., Amnesty Internat., 1986–92 (Hd, Asia Res. Dept, 1985–86). Dir for Human Rights, UN/OAS Internat. Civilian Mission in Haiti, 1993. Member: Exec. Cttee, NCCL, 1983–85; Redbridge and Waltham Forest AHA, 1977–82; Redbridge HA, 1982–83. Councillor, London Borough of Redbridge, 1978–82. *Publications:* Immigration Law and Practice (with Larry Grant), 1982; *contributed to:* Labour and Equality, Fabian Essays, 1980; Civil Liberties, Cobden Trust Essays, 1984; Public Interest Law (ed J. Cooper and R. Dhavan), 1986. *Address:* Carnegie Endowment for International Peace, 2400 N Street NW, Washington, DC 20037, USA.

MARTIN, Ian Alexander; Chairman and Chief Executive, the Glenisla Group Ltd, since 1994; Chairman, Unigate plc, since 1995; *b* 28 Feb. 1935; *s* of Alexander Martin and Eva (*née* Gillman); *m* 1963, Phyllis Mitchell-Bey; one *s* two *d*. *Educ:* Univ. of St Andrews (MA). Mem., Inst. of Chartered Accountants, Scotland. Dir, Mine Safety Appliances Co. Ltd, 1969–72; Div. Dir, ITT Europe, 1977–79; Grand Metropolitan: Dir, 1985–94; Gp Man. Dir, 1991–93; Dep. Chm., 1993–94; Chairman: Intercontinental Hotels, 1986–88; Burger King Corp., 1989–93; Pillsbury Co., 1989–93; Internat. Distillers and Vintners, 1992–93; Director: St Paul Companies Inc., 1989–; Grocery Manufacturers of America, 1989–93; Granada Group, 1992–; House of Fraser, 1994–; Nat. Commn on Children, USA, 1990–93. Mem. Bd, World Industry Council for Envmt. Chm., Europe Cttee, CBI, 1993–94. Internat. Trustee, Duke of Edinburgh's Award Scheme, 1991–; Director: Friends of the Youth Award Inc., 1991–; Cities in Schools. Freeman, City of London, 1982. CIMgt (CBIM 1986). *Recreations:* angling, golf, music. *Address:* 3 St James's Square, SW1Y 4JU. *T:* 0171–839 2820. *Clubs:* Buck's; Frenchmans Creek Yacht and Country (Florida).

MARTIN, James Brown; General Secretary, Educational Institute of Scotland, since 1988; *b* 6 Dec. 1953; *s* of James and Annie Martin; *m* 1975, Anne McNaughton; one *s* one *d*. *Educ:* Larbert Village and High Schs; Heriot-Watt Univ. (BAEcon); Moray House College of Educn. Teacher, Falkirk High Sch., 1975–79; Field Officer 1979–83, Asst Sec. 1983–88, EIS. Member: Gen. Council, Scottish TUC, 1987; Exec., ETUCE, 1988; Exec., Education International, 1993–. Mem., Forth Valley Enterprise Bd, 1989. *Recreations:* Hibernian FC, watching football. *Address:* 46 Moray Place, Edinburgh EH3 6BH. *T:* 0131–225 6244.

MARTIN, Janet, (Mrs K. P. Martin); Relief Warden (Assisted Independence), Test Valley Housing, 1988–91; *b* Dorchester, Dorset, 8 Sept. 1927; *d* of James Wilkinson and Florence Steer; *m* 1951, Peter Martin (retired Southampton HA, Senior Consultant AT&T (ISTEL) Ltd); one *s* one *d*. *Educ:* Dorchester Grammar Sch., Dorset; Weymouth Tech. Coll.; occupational training courses. PA to Group Sec., Herrison HMC, 1949; admin./clerical work, NHS and other, 1956; social research fieldwork, mainly NHS (Wessex mental health care evaluation team), and Social Services (Hants CC and Nat. Inst. for Social Work), 1967–76; residential social worker (children with special needs), Southampton, 1976–78; Social Services Officer, Test Valley, 1978–86; Senior Residential Care Officer (Elderly), Test Valley Social Services, 1986–87. Interviewer, MRC 'National' Survey, 1970–85; Psychosexual Counsellor, Aldermoor Clinic, 1981–84. Mem., Press Council, 1973–78. *Recreations:* buildings, books. *Address:* Hunter's Lodge, Linden Avenue, Dorchester, Dorset DT1 1EJ. *T:* Dorchester (01305) 269839.

MARTIN, John; *see* Martin, L. J.

MARTIN, John Christopher, (Charlie), CBE 1989; Deputy Chief Scientific Officer (Special Merit), United Kingdom Atomic Energy Authority, 1974–86; *b* 21 Sept. 1926; *s* of late Percy Martin and Marjorie Etta Caselton. *Educ:* Edward Alleyn's Sch.; King's Coll., London (BSc (Hons Physics) 1946). MoS, Fort Halstead, Sept. 1947; Woolwich Arsenal, 1950; UKAEA/MoD, AWRE, Aldermaston, Nov. 1952–89. EMP Fellow, 1988. USA Defense Nuclear Agency Exceptional Public Service Gold Medal, 1977; (first) Erwin Marx Award in Pulse Power Technology, 3rd Internat. Meeting on Pulsed Power, 1981. *Publications:* contribs to learned jls. *Recreations:* friends, food, snorkling, science fiction and fact (not always distinguishable). *Address:* Boundary Hall, Tadley, Basingstoke, Hants RG26 6QD.

MARTIN, Vice-Adm. Sir John (Edward Ludgate), KCB 1972 (CB 1968); DSC 1943; FNI; retired; Lieutenant-Governor and Commander-in-Chief of Guernsey, 1974–80; *b* 10 May 1918; *s* of late Surgeon Rear-Admiral W. L. Martin, OBE, FRCS and Elsie Mary Martin (*née* Catford); *m* 1942, Rosemary Ann Deck; two *s* two *d*. *Educ:* RNC, Dartmouth. Sub Lt and Lt, HMS Pelican, 1938–41; 1st Lt, HMS Antelope, 1942; navigation course, 1942; Navigation Officer, 13th Minesweeping Flotilla, Mediterranean, 1943–44, including invasions N Africa, Sicily, Pantelleria, Salerno; RNAS Yeovilton, 1944; Navigation Officer: HMS Manxman and HMS Bermuda, 1944–46; HMS Nelson, 1947; HMS Victorious, 1948; Staff Coll., 1949; Navigation Officer, HMS Devonshire, 1950–51; Dirg Staff, Staff Coll., 1952–54; Jt Services Planning Staff, Far East, 1954–55; Exec. Off., HMS Superb, 1956–57; Jt Services Staff Coll., 1958; Dep. Dir Manpower Planning and Complementing Div., Admty, 1959–61; Sen. Naval Off., W Indies, 1961–62; Comdr Brit. Forces Caribbean Area, 1962–63; Capt. Britannia Royal Naval Coll., Dartmouth, 1963–66; Flag Officer, Middle East, 1966–67; Comdr, British Forces Gulf, 1967–68 (despatches); Dir-Gen., Naval Personal Services and Training, 1968–70; Dep. Supreme Allied Comdr, Atlantic, 1970–72. Comdr 1951; Captain 1957; Rear-Adm. 1966; Vice-Adm. 1970. Pres., Nautical Inst., 1975–78. *Recreations:* fishing, shooting, beagling (Jt Master Britannia Beagles, 1963–66), sailing. *Clubs:* Army and Navy; Royal Naval Sailing Association; Royal Yacht Squadron.

MARTIN, John Francis Ryde, CMG 1993; HM Diplomatic Service; High Commissioner to Republic of Malaŵi, since 1993; *b* 8 Feb. 1943; *s* of Frank George Martin and Phyllis Mary Wixcey; *m* 1st, 1966, Hélène Raymonde Henriette Pyronnet (marr. diss. 1984); two *s*; 2nd, 1985, Kathleen Marie White; one *s*. *Educ:* Bedford School; Brasenose College, Oxford (MA); Bologna Center, Johns Hopkins Univ. FCO, 1966; Buenos Aires, 1968–70; Athens, 1970–74; Private Sec. to Minister of State, FCO, 1976–78; Nicosia, 1978–81; Asst Sec., Internat. Telecommunications, DTI, 1983–84; Counsellor: Lagos, 1984–88; (Econ. and Social), UKMIS to UN, 1988–93. *Recreations:* travel, collecting, bibliomania. *Address:* c/o Foreign and Commonwealth Office, SW1A 2AH. *Club:* Travellers'.

MARTIN, Sir (John) Leslie, Kt 1957; RA 1986; MA, PhD Manchester; MA Cantab; MA Oxon; Hon. LittD Cantab; Hon. LLD Leicester, Hull, Manchester; DUniv Essex; Hon. FRSAMD; FRIBA; Professor of Architecture, University of Cambridge, 1956–72; Emeritus Professor, 1973; Fellow, Jesus College, Cambridge, 1956–73, Hon. Fellow 1973, Emeritus Fellow, 1976; *b* 17 Aug. 1908; *s* of late Robert Martin, FRIBA; *m* Sadie Speight, MA, ARIBA (*d* 1992); one *s* one *d*. *Educ:* Manchester Univ. Sch. of Architecture. Asst Lectr, Manchester Univ. Sch. of Architecture, 1930–34; Head of Sch. of Architecture, Hull, 1934–39; Principal Asst Architect, LMS Railway, 1939–48; Dep. Architect, LCC, 1948–53; Architect to the LCC, 1953–56. Slade Prof. of Fine Art, Oxford, 1965–66; Ferens Prof. of Fine Art, Hull, 1967–68; William Henry Bishop Vis. Prof. of Architecture, Univ. of Yale, 1973–74; Lethaby Prof., RCA, 1981. Lectures: Gropius, Harvard, 1966; Cordingley, Manchester, 1968; Kenneth Kassler, Princeton, 1974; annual, Soc. Arch. Historians, 1976; Townsend, UCL, 1976; Convocation, Leicester, 1978. Consultant to Gulbenkian Foundn, Lisbon, 1959–69. Buildings include: work in Cambridge and for Univs of Cambridge, Oxford, Leicester and Hull; RSAMD, Glasgow; Gall. of Modern Art, Gulbenkian Foundn, Lisbon; scheme design, Royal Concert Hall, Glasgow. Mem. Council, RIBA, 1952–58 (Vice-Pres., 1955–57); Mem. Royal Fine Art Commn, 1958–72. RIBA Recognised Schs Silver Medallist, 1929; Soane Medallist, 1930; London Architecture Bronze Medallist, 1954; RIBA Distinction in Town Planning, 1956; Civic Trust Award, Oxford, 1967; Commend. Cambridge, 1972; Concrete Soc. Award, Oxford, 1972; Royal Gold Medal for Architecture, RIBA, 1973; RIBA Trustees Medal, 1991; Architects' Jl Centenary Award, 1995. Hon. Mem. Assoc. of Finnish Architects, Accademico corrispondente National Acad. of S Luca, Rome. Comdr, Order of Santiago da Espada, Portugal. Hon. Fellow, Humberside Coll. of Educn. *Publications:* Jt Editor, Circle, 1937, repr. 1971; The Flat Book, 1939 (in collab. with wife); Whitehall: a Plan for a National and Government Centre, 1965; The Framework of Planning (Inaugural Lecture) Hull, 1967; Jt Editor, Cambridge Urban and Architectural Studies, Vol. I: Urban Space and Structure, 1972; Building and Ideas (1933–83) from the Studio of Leslie Martin, 1983; contrib. various jls; papers include: An Architect's Approach to Architecture; Education Without Walls; Education Around Architecture; Notes on a Developing Architecture. *Address:* The Barns, Church Street, Great Shelford, Cambridge CB2 5EL. *T:* Cambridge (01223) 842399.

MARTIN, John Neville, FEng; FICE; FIStructE; Chairman, Ove Arup Partnership, 1992–95; *b* 9 April 1932; *s* of Reginald Martin and Dorothy Sylvia Martin (*née* Bray); *m* 1964, Julia Mary Galpin; three *s* one *d*. *Educ:* Royal Grammar Sch., Guildford. FICE 1957; FIStructE 1957; FEng 1988. Articled pupil with Engr and Surveyor, Woking UDC, 1949–52; Nat. Service, RE, 1952–54; Asst Engr, Sir William Halcrow & Partners, Consulting Engrs, 1954–57; with Ove Arup Partnership, Consulting Engrs, 1957–. *Publications:* various papers for engrg jls (IStructE). *Recreations:* Scouting, mountain-walking, music, country dancing. *Address:* Broadheath, Nutcombe Lane, Hindhead, Surrey GU26 6BP. *T:* Hindhead (01428) 604616.

MARTIN, Prof. John Powell; Professor Emeritus, University of Southampton; Visiting Professor, Department of Social Policy and Social Work, Manchester University, since 1992; *b* 22 Dec. 1925; *s* of Bernard and Grace Martin; *m* 1st, 1951, Sheila Feather (marr. diss. 1981); three *s*; 2nd, 1983, Joan Higgins. *Educ:* Leighton Park Sch., Reading; Univ. of Reading (BA); London Sch. of Economics and Political Science (Certif. in Social Admin., PhD); Univ. of Cambridge (MA). Lectr, London Sch. of Economics, 1953–59; Asst Dir of Research, Inst. of Criminology, Univ. of Cambridge, 1960–66; Fellow, King's Coll., Cambridge, 1964–67; Prof. of Sociology and Social Admin, later of Social Policy, 1967–89, Res. Prof., 1989–92, Univ. of Southampton. Hill Foundn Vis. Prof., Univ. of Minnesota, 1973; Vis. Fellow, Yale Law Sch., 1974. Mem., Jellicoe Cttee on Boards of Visitors of Penal Instns, 1974–75. *Publications:* Social Aspects of Prescribing, 1957; Offenders as Employees, 1962; The Police: a study in manpower (with Gail Wilson), 1969; The Social Consequences of Conviction (with Douglas Webster), 1971; (ed) Violence and the Family, 1978; (jtly) The Future of the Prison System, 1980; Hospitals in Trouble, 1984; (with J. B. Coker) Licensed to Live, 1985; (with Douglas Webster) Probation Motor Projects in England and Wales, 1994; articles in: Lancet, British Jl of Criminology, British Jl of Sociology, International Review of Criminal Policy, etc. *Recreations:* sailing, photography, do-it-yourself. *Address:* 3 Gordon Place, Manchester M20 3LD. *Club:* Lymington Town Sailing.

MARTIN, John Sharp Buchanan; Under-Secretary, School Education and Sport, Scottish Office Education Department, since 1992; *b* 7 July 1946; *s* of David Buchanan Martin and Agnes Miller (*née* Craig) *m* 1971, Catriona Susan Stewart Meldrum; one *s* one *d*. *Educ:* Bell-Baxter High Sch., Cupar, Fife; Univ. of St Andrews (BSc). Asst Principal, Scottish Educn Dept, 1968–71; Private Sec. to Parly Under-Sec. of State for Scotland, 1971–73; Scottish Office: Principal, 1973–80, seconded to Rayner Scrutinies, 1979–80; Asst Sec., 1980–92. *Recreations:* tennis, cricket, philately. *Address:* c/o Scottish Office Education Department, New St Andrews House, Edinburgh EH1 3TG. *T:* 0131–244 4413. *Clubs:* Colinton Lawn Tennis, Woodcutters Cricket (Edinburgh).

MARTIN, John Sinclair, CBE 1977; farmer; Chairman, Anglian Flood Defence Committee, National Rivers Authority, since 1989; *b* 18 Sept. 1931; *s* of Joseph and Claire Martin, Littleport, Ely; *m* 1960, Katharine Elisabeth Barclay, MB, BS; three *s* one *d*. *Educ:* The Leys Sch., Cambridge; St John's Coll., Cambridge (MA, Dip. in Agriculture).

Chairman: Littleport and Downham IDB, 1971–88; JCO Arable Crops and Forage Bd, 1973–76; Eastern Regional Panel, MAFF, 1981–86 (Mem., 1972–78); Great Ouse Local Land Drainage Cttee, AWA, 1983–88; Anglian Drainage Cttee, 1988–89; Member: Eastern Counties Farmers' Management Cttee, 1960–70; ARC, 1968–78; Great Ouse River Authority, 1970–74; Lawes Agricl Trust Cttee, 1982–84; MAFF Priorities Bd, 1984–88; Anglian Water Authority, 1988–89; Vice-Pres., Assoc. of Drainage Authorities, 1986–. Chairman: Ely Br., NFU, 1963; Cambs NFU, 1979. High Sheriff, Cambs, 1985–86. *Address:* Denny Abbey, Waterbeach, Cambridge CB5 9PQ. *T:* Cambridge (01223) 860282. *Club:* Farmers'.

MARTIN, John Vandeleur; QC 1991; *b* 17 Jan. 1948; *s* of Col Graham Vandeleur Martin, MC and Margaret Helen (*née* Sherwood); *m* 1974, Stephanie Johnstone Smith; two *s* one *d.* *Educ:* Malvern Coll.; Pembroke Coll., Cambridge (MA). Called to the Bar, Lincoln's Inn, 1972. Dep. High Court Judge, Chancery Div., 1993. Liveryman, Drapers' Co., 1973. *Recreations:* almost any opera, swimming in warm water. *Address:* Wilberforce Chambers, 8 New Square, Lincoln's Inn, WC2A 3QP. *T:* 0171–306 0102.

MARTIN, John William Prior; HM Diplomatic Service, retired; Counsellor, Foreign and Commonwealth Office, 1985–89; *b* 23 July 1934; *er s* of Stanley Gordon Martin and Frances Heather (*née* Moore); *m* 1960, Jean Fleming; three *s* one *d.* *Educ:* CIM Sch., Chefoo and Kuling; Bristol Grammar Sch.; St John's Coll., Oxford (MA). National Service, 1953–55 (2nd Lieut Royal Signals). Joined FO, 1959; Beirut, 1960; Saigon, 1963; Language Student, Hong Kong, 1965–67; Dar es Salaam, 1968; FCO, 1971; Singapore, 1974; FCO, 1978; Kuala Lumpur, 1982. *Recreations:* conservation, travel, ornithology.

MARTIN, Jonathan Arthur, OBE 1995; Head of Sport and Events, BBC Television, since 1987 (Head of Sport, 1981–87); *b* 18 June 1942; *s* of Arthur Martin and Mabel Gladys Martin (*née* Bishop); *m* 1967, Joy Elizabeth Fulker; two *s.* *Educ:* Gravesend Grammar School; St Edmund Hall, Oxford (BA 1964, English; MA 1992). Joined BBC as general trainee, 1964; producer, Sportsnight 1969; producer, Match of the Day, 1970; editor, Sportsnight and Match of the Day, 1974; exec. producer, BBC TV Wimbledon tennis coverage, 1979–81; producer, Ski Sunday and Grand Prix, 1978–80; managing editor, Sport, 1980. Vice-Pres., EBU Sports Gp, 1984–. *Recreations:* skiing, golf, watching sport, watching television. *Address:* Arkle, Valentine Way, Chalfont St Giles, Bucks HP8 4JB; BBC, Kensington House, W14. *T:* 0181–743 1272. *Club:* Harewood Downs Golf.

MARTIN, Mrs Kenneth Peter; *see* Martin, Janet.

MARTIN, Sir Laurence (Woodward), Kt 1994; DL; Director, Royal Institute of International Affairs, since 1991; *b* 30 July 1928; *s* of Leonard and Florence Mary Martin; *m* 1951, Betty Parnall; one *s* one *d.* *Educ:* St Austell Grammar Sch.; Christ's Coll., Cambridge (MA); Yale Univ. (MA, PhD). Flying Officer, RAF, 1948–50; Instr, Yale Univ., 1955–56; Asst Prof., MIT, 1956–61; Rockefeller Fellow for Advanced Study, 1958–59; Associate Prof., Sch. of Advanced Internat. Studies, The Johns Hopkins Univ., 1961–64; Wilson Prof. of Internat. Politics, Univ. of Wales, 1964–68; Prof. of War Studies, King's Coll., Univ. of London, 1968–77, Fellow 1983–; Vice-Chancellor, Univ. of Newcastle upon Tyne, 1978–90, Emeritus Prof., 1991. Research Associate, Washington Center of Foreign Policy Research, 1964–76, 1979–; Vis. Prof., Univ. of Wales, 1985–. Lees-Knowles Lectr, Cambridge, 1981; BBC Reith Lectr, 1981. Member: SSRC, 1969–76 (Chm. Res. Grants Bd); Res. Council, Georgetown Center of Strategic Studies, 1969–77, 1979–; Council, IISS, 1975–83. Consultant, Sandia Labs. DL Tyne and Wear, 1986. Hon. DCL Newcastle, 1991. *Publications:* The Anglo-American Tradition in Foreign Affairs (with Arnold Wolfers), 1956; Peace without Victory, 1958; Neutralism and Non-Alignment, 1962; The Sea in Modern Strategy, 1967; (jtly) America in World Affairs, 1970; Arms and Strategy, 1973; (jtly) Retreat from Empire?, 1973; (jtly) Strategic Thought in the Nuclear Age, 1979; The Two-Edged Sword, 1982; Before the Day After, 1985; The Changing Face of Nuclear Warfare, 1987. *Address:* Royal Institute of International Affairs, Chatham House, 10 St James's Square, SW1Y 4LE.

MARTIN, (Leonard) John, CBE 1995; Consulting Actuary, R. Watson & Sons, since 1954; *b* 20 April 1929; *s* of Leonard A. Martin and Anne Elisabeth Martin (*née* Scudamore); *m* 1956, Elisabeth Veronica Hall Jones; one *s* one *d.* *Educ:* Ardingly Coll. FIA, FSS, FPMI. Joined R. Watson & Sons, 1952, Partner 1954, Sen. Partner 1984–94. Dir, NPI Insurance Co. Pres., Inst. of Actuaries, 1992–94; Chm., Consultative Group of Actuaries in Europe, 1988–91; Rapporteur, Cttee of Actuaries, UN, 1988–. Liveryman, GAPAN. *Recreations:* flying, sailing, singing. *Address:* Pitt House, Ducie Avenue, Bembridge, Isle of Wight. *Club:* Naval.

MARTIN, Sir Leslie; *see* Martin, Sir J. L.

MARTIN, Leslie Vaughan; Directing Actuary (Superannuation and Research), Government Actuary's Department, 1974–79; *b* 20 March 1919; *s* of late Hubert Charles Martin and late Rose Martin (*née* Skelton) *m* 1949, Winifred Dorothy Hopkins; one *s* one *d.* *Educ:* Price's Sch., Fareham. FIA 1947. Served with RAMC and REME, 1940–46. Deptl Clerical Officer, Customs and Excise, 1936–38; joined Govt Actuary's Dept, 1938; Asst Actuary, 1949; Actuary, 1954; Principal Actuary, 1962. Mem. Council, Inst. of Actuaries, 1971–76; Vice-Chm., CS Medical Aid Assoc., 1976–79. Churchwarden, St Barnabas, Dulwich, 1965–70, 1977–79, Vice-Chm. of PCC, 1970–79; Treasurer: Morchard Bishop Parochial Church Council, 1980–83; Cadbury Deanery Synod, 1981–88; Chulmleigh Deanery Synod, 1989–95; Lapford PCC, 1991–93. *Recreations:* crosswords, chess, scrabble. *Address:* Pickwick House, Down St Mary, Crediton, Devon EX17 6EQ. *T:* Copplestone (01363) 84581.

MARTIN, Michael John; MP (Lab) Springburn Division of Glasgow, since 1979; *b* 3 July 1945; *s* of Michael and Mary Martin; *m* 1965, Mary McLay; one *s* one *d.* *Educ:* St Patrick's Boys' Sch., Glasgow. Sheet metal worker; AUEW Shop Steward, Rolls Royce, Hillington, 1970–74; Trade Union Organiser, 1976–79; Mem., and sponsored by, Nat. Union of Sheet Metal Workers, Coppersmiths and Heating and Domestic Engineers; PPS to Rt Hon. Denis Healey, MP, 1981–83; Member: Select Cttee for Trade and Industry, 1983–; Speaker's Panel of Chairmen, 1987–; Chm., Scottish Grand Cttee. Councillor: for Fairfield Ward, Glasgow Corp., 1973–74; for Balornock Ward, Glasgow DC, 1974–79. Mem., Coll. of Piping, 1989–. *Recreations:* hill walking, local history. *Address:* 144 Broomfield Road, Balornock, Glasgow G21 3UE.

MARTIN, His Honour Oliver Samuel; QC 1970; a Circuit Judge, 1975–93; *b* 26 Nov. 1919; *s* of Sidney Edward Martin and Nita Martin; *m* 1st, 1954, Marion Eve (marr. diss. 1982); two *s*; 2nd, 1982, Gloria Audrey. *Educ:* King's College Sch., Wimbledon; London University. Served RNVR, 1939–46. Called to Bar, Gray's Inn, 1951. Dep. Chm. E Sussex QS, 1970–71; a Recorder of the Crown Court, 1972–75. *Recreations:* golf, music, reading, writing, holidays.

MARTIN, Patrick William, TD; JP; MA; Headmaster of Warwick School, 1962–77; *b* 20 June 1916; *e s* of Alan Pattinson Martin, Bowness-on-Windermere, Westmorland; *m* 1st, 1939, Gwendoline Elsie Helme (*d* 1987), MA, St Hilda's Coll., Oxford; two *d*; 2nd, 1989, Eileen Muriel Beattie, JP. *Educ:* Windermere Grammar Sch.; Balliol Coll., Oxford. 2nd cl. hons in Modern History, Balliol Coll., 1937. Asst Master, Abingdon Sch., Berks, 1938–40. Commissioned in TA, 1938; served War of 1939–45, on active service with Royal Artillery; Staff College, Quetta; GSO 2, and 1 HQRA 14th Army in Burma (despatches); British Mil. Mission to Belgium, 1946. Schoolmaster, 1946–49; Asst Dir of Educn, Brighton, 1950–52; Headmaster: Chipping Norton Grammar Sch., 1952–57; Lincoln Sch., 1958–62. Chm., Midland Div., Headmasters' Conf., 1972–; Pres., Headmasters' Assoc., 1976; Treasurer, Warwick Univ., 1983–89. CC Warwickshire, 1977–85 (Leader, 1981–83). JP Warwicks 1966, Dep. Chm., Warwick Petty Sessions. *Publications:* History of Heart of England Building Society, 1981; articles in educational and other periodicals. *Recreations:* books, music, foreign countries and people; being alone in the countryside. *Address:* 80 High Street, Kenilworth, Warwicks CV8 1LZ. *T:* Kenilworth (01926) 54140.

MARTIN, Hon. Paul; PC (Canada) 1993; MP (L) for Lasalle-Emard, Quebec, since 1988; Minister for Finance and Minister responsible for Federal Office of Regional Development, Canada, since 1993; *b* Windsor, Ont. 28 Aug. 1938; *s* of Paul Joseph James Martin and Eleanor Alice Martin; *m* 1965, Sheila Ann Cowan; three *s.* *Educ:* Univ. of Ottawa; Univ. of Toronto (BA Philos. and Hist. 1962); Univ. of Toronto Law Sch. (LLB 1965). Merchant seaman on salvage ops in Arctic; worked in Legal Dept, ECSC, Luxembourg; with Osler, Hoskin & Harcourt, Toronto; called to the Bar, Ontario, 1966; with Power Corp. of Canada; Chm. and Chief Exec. Officer, Canada Steamship Lines; Corporate Dir for several major cos. Critic for: Treasury Bd and Urban Develt, until 1991; Envmt and Associate Finance Critic, 1991–93. Co-Chm., Nat. Platform Cttee, Liberal Party of Canada, 1993. *Address:* House of Commons, Room 515 S, Center Block, Ottawa, Ont K1A 0A6, Canada. *T:* (613) 9924284, *Fax:* (614) 9924291.

MARTIN, Peter; *see* Martin, R. P.

MARTIN, Peter Anthony; Finance Director (formerly County Treasurer), Kent County Council, since 1986 (Deputy County Treasurer, 1981–86); *b* 8 Dec. 1946; *s* of Frank and Renie Martin; *m* 1970, Jennifer Margaret (*née* Shaw); one *s* four *d.* *Educ:* Nottingham High Sch.; St John's Coll., Oxford (BA Hons); Univ. of Kent at Canterbury (MA Management). CIPFA 1973. Accountant, Derbyshire CC, 1969–76; Asst County Treasurer, W Sussex CC, 1976–81. Local Authy Assocs' RSG Principal Negotiator, 1991–94. Vice Pres., Soc. of Co. Treasurers, 1995–96. *Recreations:* cricket, reading, family. *Address:* Woodside, Hadlow Park, Hadlow, Tonbridge, Kent TN11 0HZ.

MARTIN, Maj.-Gen. Peter Lawrence de Carteret, CBE 1968 (OBE 1964); President, Lady Grover's Hospital Fund for Officers' Families, since 1989 (Chairman, 1975–85; Vice President, 1985–89); Member, National Executive Committee, Forces Help Society, since 1975; President, Normandy Veterans' Association, since 1995 (Vice President, 1989–95); *b* 15 Feb. 1920; *s* of late Col Charles de Carteret Martin, MD, ChD, IMS and of Helen Margaret Hardinge Grover; *m* 1st, 1949, Elizabeth Felicia (marr. diss. 1967), *d* of late Col C. M. Keble; one *s* one *d*; 2nd, 1973, Mrs Valerie Singer. *Educ:* Wellington Coll.; RMC Sandhurst. FBIM 1979 (MBIM 1970). Commnd Cheshire Regt, 1939; BEF (Dunkirk), 1940; Middle East, 1941; N Africa 8th Army, 1942–43 (despatches); invasion of Sicily, 1943; Normandy landings and NW Europe, 1944 (despatches); Palestine, 1945–47; GSO2 (Int.), HQ British Troops Egypt, 1947; Instructor, RMA Sandhurst, 1948–50; psc 1951; Bde Major 126 Inf. Bde (TA), 1952–53; Chief Instructor MMG Div. Support Weapons Wing, Sch. of Infantry, 1954–56; Malayan Ops, 1957–58 (despatches); DAAG GHQ FARELF, 1958–60; CO 1 Cheshire, N Ireland and BAOR, 1961–63; AA&QMG Cyprus District, 1963–65; comd 48 Gurkha Inf. Bde, Hong Kong, 1966–68; Brig. AQ HQ Army Strategic Comd, 1968–71; Dir, Personal Services (Army), 1971–74. Col The 22nd (Cheshire) Regt, 1971–78; Col Comdt, Mil. Provost Staff Corps, 1972–74. Services Advr, Variety Club of GB, 1976–86. Mem., Ex-Services Mental Welfare Soc., 1977–91. *Recreations:* golf, ski-ing. *Address:* 17 Station Street, Lymington, Hants SO41 3BA. *T:* Lymington (01590) 672620. *Club:* Army and Navy.

MARTIN, Peter Lewis, CBE 1980; building services engineer, retired; *b* 22 Sept. 1918; *s* of George Lewis and Madeleine Mary Martin; *m* 1949, Elizabeth Grace, *d* of John David Melling; two *d.* *Educ:* Wyggeston Boys Sch., Leicester; Kibworth Beauchamp Grammar Sch.; Leicester Coll. of Art and Technology; Borough Polytechnic. CEng; MConsE. Apprenticed to engrg contractor, 1934–39. Served War, 1940–46, RAF Engrg Branch. Joined consulting engrg practice of Dr Oscar Faber, 1947; Partner, 1961–83; Consultant, 1983–85. Pres., IHVE, 1971–72; Chairman: Heating and Ventilating Res. Assoc., 1967–69; Assoc. of Consulting Engrs, 1983–84; Member: Cttee for Application of Computers to the Construction Industry, 1970–72; Technical Data on Fuel Cttee, World Energy Conf., 1971–77; Construction and Housing Res. Adv. Council, 1975–77; Building Services Bd, CNAA, 1975–80; Engrg Council, 1982–86. Vis. Prof., Univ. of Strathclyde, 1974–85; Hon. DSc Strathclyde, 1985. Governor, Herts Coll. of Building, 1970–74. Master, Plumbers' Co., 1979–80; Freeman: Fanmakers' Co.; Engineers' Co. Silver Medal, 1956, Bronze Medal, 1968, Gold Medal, 1976, IHVE. *Publications:* (jtly) Heating and Air Conditioning of Buildings, by Faber and Kell, 5th edn 1971 to 8th edn 1995; contribs to engrg jls and confs. *Recreation:* avoiding gardening. *Address:* Quietways, Lower Bodham, Holt, Norfolk NR25 6PS. *T:* Holt (01263) 712591. *Club:* Lansdowne.

MARTIN, Prof. Raymond Leslie, AO 1987; MSc, PhD, ScD, DSc; FRACI, FRSC, FTS, FAA; Professor of Chemistry, Monash University, Melbourne, 1987–92, now Emeritus (Vice-Chancellor, 1977–87); Chairman, Australian Science and Technology Council, 1988–92; *b* 3 Feb. 1926; *s* of Sir Leslie Harold Martin, CBE, FRS, FAA and late Gladys Maude Elaine, *d* of H. J. Bull; *m* 1954, Rena Lillian Laman; three *s* one *d.* *Educ:* Scotch Coll., Melbourne; Univ. of Melb. (BSc, MSc); Sidney Sussex Coll., Cambridge (PhD, ScD). FRACI 1956; FRSC (FRIC 1974); FTS 1989; FAA 1971. Resident Tutor in Chemistry, Queen's Coll., Melb., 1947–49 (Fellow, 1979–); Sidney Sussex Coll., Cambridge: 1851 Exhibn Overseas Scholar, 1949–51; Sen. Scholar, 1952–54; Res. Fellow, 1951–54; Sen. Lectr, Univ. of NSW, 1954–59; Section Leader, 1959–60, and Associate Res. Manager, 1960–62, ICIANZ; Prof. of Inorganic Chem., 1962–72, and Dean of Faculty of Science, 1971, Univ. of Melb.; Australian National University, Canberra: Prof. of Inorganic Chem., Inst. of Advanced Studies, 1972–77, Prof. Emeritus 1977; Dean, Res. Sch. of Chem., 1976–77; DSc. Vis. Scientist: Technische Hochschule, Stuttgart, 1953–54; Bell Telephone Labs, NJ, 1967; Vis. Prof., Columbia Univ., NY, 1972. Royal Aust. Chemical Institute: Smith Medal, 1968; Olle Prize, 1974; Inorganic Medal, 1978; Leighton Medal, 1989; Fed. Pres., 1968–69. Chm., Internat. Commn on Atomic Weights and Isotopic Abundances, 1983–87; Mem., Prime Minister's Science Council, 1989–92. Director: Circadian Technologies Ltd, 1986–; Heide Park and Art Gall., 1988–92; Winston Churchill Meml Trust (Dep. Nat. Chm., 1993–); Trustee, Selby Scientific Foundn, 1990–. Council Mem., Victorian Coll. of the Arts, 1984– (Dep. Pres., 1991; Pres., 1992–95). Hon. LLD Monash, 1992. *Publications:* papers and revs on physical and inorganic chem. mainly in jls of London, Amer. and Aust. Chem. Socs. *Recreations:* ski-ing, golf, lawn tennis (Cambridge Univ. team *v* Oxford, Full Blue; Cambs County Colours). *Address:* PO Box 98, Mount Eliza, Vic 3930, Australia. *Clubs:* Melbourne (Melbourne); Hawks (Cambridge); Frankston Golf (Victoria).

MARTIN, Richard Graham; Chairman, Allied-Domecq (formerly Allied-Lyons) Pensions and Trustee Services, since 1992; *b* 4 Oct. 1932; *s* of Horace Frederick Martin, MC and Phyllis Jeanette Martin; *m* 1958, Elizabeth Savage; two *s* one *d*. *Educ:* Sherborne School; St Thomas's Hosp. Med. Sch., 1953–54. 2nd Lt, RA, 1951–52. Joined Friary Holroyd & Healy's Brewery, 1955, Dir, 1959; Dir, Friary Meux, 1963–66; Managing Dir, Ind Coope (East Anglia), 1966–69; Director: Joshua Tetley & Son, 1969–72; Allied Breweries, 1972–92; Chief Exec., Joshua Tetley & Son, 1972–78; Vice-Chm., Joshua Tetley & Son and Tetley Walker, 1978–79; Chm., Ind Coope, 1979–85; Man. Dir, 1985–86, Chm. and Chief Exec., 1986–88, Allied Breweries; Allied-Lyons: Dir, 1981–92; Vice-Chm., 1988–92; Chief Exec., 1989–91; Chairman: J. Lyons & Co. Ltd, 1989–91; Hiram Walker, 1991 (Dir, 1989–91). Chm., Brewers' Soc., 1991–92 (Vice-Chm., 1989–91). Pres., Shire Horse Soc., 1981–82. *Recreations:* travel, music, food. *Address:* c/o Allied-Lyons PLC, 24 Portland Place, W1N 4BB. *T:* 0171–323 9000.

MARTIN, Sir (Robert) Bruce, Kt 1992; QC 1977; Chairman, North Western Regional Health Authority, 1988–94; *b* 2 Nov. 1938; *s* of late Robert Martin and Fay Martin; *m* 1967, Elizabeth Georgina (*née* Kiddie); one *s* one *d*. *Educ:* Shrewsbury Sch.; Liverpool Univ. (LLB Hons 1959). Called to the Bar, Middle Temple, 1960; a Recorder of the Crown Court, 1978–86. Chm., The Bob Martin Co., 1980–. Vice-Chm., Mersey RHA, 1986–88 (Mem., 1983–88). *Recreations:* music, golf, ski-ing. *Address:* 4 Montpelier Terrace, SW7 1JP. *T:* 0171–584 0649. *Club:* Royal Birkdale Golf.

MARTIN, Robert Logan, (Roy); QC (Scot.) 1988; *b* 31 July 1950; *s* of Robert Martin and Dr Janet Johnstone Logan or Martin; *m* 1984, Fiona Frances Neil; one *s* two *d*. *Educ:* Paisley Grammar Sch.; Univ. of Glasgow (LLB). Solicitor, 1973–76; admitted to Faculty of Advocates, 1976; Mem., Sheriff Court Rules Council, 1981–84; Standing Junior Counsel to Dept of Employment in Scotland, 1983–84; Advocate-Depute, 1984–87; called to the Bar, Lincoln's Inn, 1990. Admitted to Bar of NSW, 1987. Chairman: Industrial Tribunals, 1991–; Scottish Planning, Local Govt and Envmtl Bar Gp, 1991–. Hon. Sec., Wagering Club, 1982–91. *Recreations:* shooting, ski-ing, modern architecture, vintage motor cars. *Address:* Hardengreen House, by Eskbank, Midlothian EH22 3LF. *Club:* New (Edinburgh).

MARTIN, Robin Geoffrey; Director, Hewetson plc, since 1980 (Chairman, 1980–88); *b* 9 March 1921; *s* of Cecil Martin and Isabel Katherine Martin (*née* Hickman); *m* 1946, Margery Chester Yates; two *s* one *d*. *Educ:* Cheltenham Coll.; Jesus Coll., Cambridge (MA). FIQ. Tarmac Ltd: Dir 1955; Gp Man. Dir 1963; Dep. Chm. 1967; Chm. and Chief Exec., 1971–79; Dir, Serck Ltd, 1971, Dep. Chm., 1974, Chm., 1976–81; Director: Burmah Oil Co,. 1975–85; Ductile Steels Ltd, 1977–82. Mem., Midlands Adv. Bd, Legal and General Assurance Soc. Ltd, 1977–84. Chm., Ironbridge Gorge Develt Trust, 1976–78. Life Governor, Birmingham Univ., 1970–85. *Recreations:* gardening, bridge. *Club:* East India.

MARTIN, Robin Rupert; Principal Finance Officer, Board of Inland Revenue, since 1993; *b* 28 Feb. 1946; *s* of late Rupert Claude Martin and Ellen Martin (*née* Wood); *m* 1972, Jane Elizabeth Mackenzie Smith; three *s*. *Educ:* Harrow Sch.; Worcester Coll., Oxford (MA Hons). VSO, 1964–65 and 1969–70; joined Home Civil Service, 1970: Private Sec. to Chm., Bd of Inland Revenue, 1973–74; Office of Chancellor of Duchy of Lancaster, Cabinet Office, 1976–79; Asst Sec., 1981; Under Sec., 1993. *Recreations:* leisurely hill-walking, second hand books, cricket. *Address:* Board of Inland Revenue, Somerset House, WC2R 1LB. *Club:* MCC.

MARTIN, Roger John Adam; formerly HM Diplomatic Service; Director, Somerset Wildlife Trust (formerly Somerest Trust for Nature Conservation), since 1988; *b* 21 Jan. 1941; *s* of late Geoffrey (Richard Rex) Martin and of Hazel (*née* Matthews); *m* 1972, Ann Cornwell (*née* Sharp); one *s*. *Educ:* Westminster School; Brasenose College, Oxford (BA). VSO, Northern Rhodesia, 1959–60; Commonwealth Office, 1964–66; Second Sec., Djakarta, 1967, Saigon, 1968–70; First Sec., FCO, 1971–74, Geneva, 1975–79; seconded to Dept of Trade, as Head of Middle East/North Africa Br., 1981–83; Dep. High Comr, Harare, 1983–86; resigned. Vis. Fellow, Univ. of Bath. Mem., Nat. Exec., VSO, 1988–. *Publication:* Southern Africa: the price of apartheid, 1988. *Recreations:* environmental issues, walking, archaeology. *Address:* Coxley House, Coxley, near Wells, Somerset BA5 1QS. *T:* Wells (01749) 672180.

MARTIN, Ronald, MBE 1945; *b* 7 Nov. 1919; *o s* of late Albert and Clara Martin; *m* 1943, Bettina, *o d* of late H. E. M. Billing; one *d*. *Educ:* St Olave's Grammar Sch. Asst Traffic Superintendent, GPO, 1939. Served War of 1939–45, Royal Signals, NW Europe. GPO: Asst Princ., 1948; Princ., 1950; Treasury, 1954; Princ. Private Sec. to PMG, 1955; Staff Controller, GPO, London, 1956; Asst Sec., 1957; Dir Establishments and Organisation, GPO, 1966; Dir Telecommunications Personnel, 1967; Dir of Marketing, Telecommunications HQ, 1968–75; Sen. Dir, Customer Services, 1975–79. *Recreations:* music, motoring, horology. *Address:* 23 Birch Close, Send, Woking, Surrey GU23 7BZ.

MARTIN, Roy; *see* Martin, Robert L.

MARTIN, (Roy) Peter, MBE 1970; author and critic; *b* 5 Jan. 1931; *s* of Walter Martin and Annie Mabel Martin; *m* 1st, 1951, Marjorie Peacock (marr. diss. 1960); 2nd, Joan Drumwright (marr. diss. 1977); two *s*; 3rd, 1978, Catherine Sydee. *Educ:* Highbury Grammar Sch.; Univ. of London (BA 1953, MA 1956); Univ. of Tübingen. Nat. Service (RAF Educn Branch), 1949–51. Worked as local govt officer, schoolteacher and tutor in adult educn; then as British Council officer, 1960–83; service in Indonesia, Hungary (Cultural Attaché) and Japan (Cultural Counsellor). *Publications:* (with Joan Martin) Japanese Cooking, 1970; (as James Melville): The Wages of Zen, 1979; The Chrysanthemum Chain, 1980; A Sort of Samurai, 1981; The Ninth Netsuke, 1982; Sayonara, Sweet Amaryllis, 1983; Death of a Daimyo, 1984; The Death Ceremony, 1985; Go Gently Gaijin, 1986; The Imperial Way, 1986; Kimono For A Corpse, 1987; The Reluctant Ronin, 1988; A Haiku for Hanae, 1989; A Tarnished Phoenix, 1990; The Bogus Buddha, 1990; The Body Wore Brocade, 1992; Diplomatic Baggage, 1994; The Reluctant Spy, 1995; (as Hampton Charles): Miss Seeton At The Helm, 1990; Miss Seeton, By Appointment, 1990; Advantage Miss Seeton, 1990. *Recreations:* music, books. *Address:* c/o Curtis Brown, 28/29 Haymarket, SW1Y 4SP. *Clubs:* Travellers', Detection.

MARTIN, Samuel Frederick Radcliffe, CB 1979; First Legislative Draftsman, 1973–79; *b* 2 May 1918; 2nd *s* of late William and Margaret Martin; *m* 1947, Sarah, *y d* of late Rev. Joseph and Margaret McKane; three *s*. *Educ:* Royal Belfast Academical Instn; Queen's Univ., Belfast (LLB). Called to Bar, Gray's Inn, 1950. Examr, Estate Duty Office, NI, 1939; Professional Asst, Office of Parly Draftsmen, 1956. Legal Adviser to Examiner of Statutory Rules, NI, 1979–81; Asst Comr, Local Govt Boundaries' Commn, 1983–84. Northern Ireland Editor, Current Law, 1979–90. *Publications:* articles in NI Legal Qly and Gazette of Incorp. Law Soc. *Recreation:* golf. *Address:* Brynburn, 196 Upper Road, Greenisland, Carrickfergus, Co. Antrim BT38 8RW. *T:* Whiteabbey (01232) 862417.

MARTIN, Stanley William Frederick, CVO 1992 (LVO 1981); JP; HM Diplomatic Service, retired; Extra Gentleman Usher to the Queen, since 1993; Protocol Consultant, Foreign and Commonwealth Office, since 1993; Diplomatic Consultant, Hyde Park Hotel, since 1993; *b* 9 Dec. 1934; *s* of Stanley and Winifred Martin; *m* 1960, Hanni Aud Hansen, Copenhagen; one *s* one *d*. *Educ:* Bromley Grammar Sch.; University Coll., Oxford (MA Jurisprudence); Inner Temple (student Scholar). Nat. Service, 2nd Lieut RASC, 1953–55. Entered CRO, 1958; Asst Private Sec. to Sec. of State, 1959–62; First Secretary: Canberra, 1962–64; Kuala Lumpur, 1964–67; FCO (Planning Staff and Personnel Dept), 1967–70; seconded to CSD (CSSB), 1970–71; Asst Marshal of the Diplomatic Corps, 1972–81; First Asst Marshal, 1981–92; Associate Head of Protocol Dept, FCO, 1986–92. Vis. Prof., Diplomatic Acad., Poly. of Central London, subseq. Univ. of Westminster, 1987–. Member: Cttee, London Diplomatic Assoc., 1972–; Central Council, Royal Over-Seas League, 1982–; Council, Oxford Soc., 1993–. Trustee, Attlee Foundn, 1993–; Advr, Consular Corps of London, 1993–. FRSA 1985. JP Inner London, 1993. Freeman of the City of London, 1988. Companion, Order of Distinguished Service (Brunei), 1992. *Publications:* contribs to Jl of Orders and Medals Res. Soc. *Recreations:* collecting books and manuscripts, historical research and writing, walking. *Address:* 14 Great Spilmans, Dulwich, SE22 8SZ. *T:* 0181–693 8181. *Club:* Royal Over-Seas League.

MARTIN, Stephen Harcourt; Under Secretary, and Head of Education Department, Welsh Office, since 1992; *b* 4 Sept. 1952; *s* of Robert Harcourt Martin and Joan Winifred Martin (*née* Carpenter); *m* 1988, Amanda Suna Hodges; one *s* one *d*. *Educ:* Watford GS for Boys; Haywards Heath GS; Hull Univ. (Pol Studies). Nursing Assistant, De La Pole Psych. Hosp., Willerby, 1973–74; Welsh Office: Exec. Officer, Town and Country Planning Div., 1974–77; Admin Trainee, Health and Industry Depts, 1977–79; Pvte Sec. to successive Perm. Secs, 1979–81; Principal: Health Dept, 1981–85; Housing Div., 1985–87; Asst Sec., Health and Social Services Divs, 1987–92. *Recreations:* music, reading, Welsh. *Address:* Welsh Office, Crown Buildings, Cathays Park, Cardiff CF1 3NQ. *T:* Cardiff (01222) 823207.

MARTIN, Hon. Stephen Paul; MP (Lab) for Cunningham, NSW, since 1984; Speaker, House of Representatives, Australia, since 1993; *b* 24 June 1948; *s* of Harold and Vera Martin; *m* 1971, Carol O'Keeffe; one *s* three *d*. *Educ:* ANU (BA); Univ. of Alberta (MA); Sydney Univ. (MTCP); Univ. of NSW (Dip. Ed). High School teacher, 1970–74; Univ. Lectr, 1975–77; Town Planner, NSW Dept of Planning and Environment, 1977–84. Chm., Banking, Finance and Public Administration Cttee, 1987–91; Parly Sec. to Minister for Foreign Affairs and Trade, 1991–93. *Recreations:* swimming, Rugby League, movies. *Address:* House of Representatives, Parliament House, Canberra, ACT 2600, Australia. *T:* (6) 2774000. *Club:* Illawarra Steelers (Wollongong).

MARTIN, (Thomas) Geoffrey; Head of Representation of European Commission in the United Kingdom, since 1993; *b* 26 July 1940; *s* of Thomas Martin and Saidee Adelaide (*née* Day); *m* 1968, Gay (Madeleine Annesley) Brownrigg; one *s* three *d*. *Educ:* Queen's Univ., Belfast (BSc Hons). President, National Union of Students of England, Wales and Northern Ireland, 1966–68; City of London: Banking, Shipping, 1968–73; Director, Shelter, 1973–74; Diplomatic Staff, Commonwealth Secretariat, 1974–79; Head of EC Office, NI, 1979–85; Head of EC Press and Inf. Services, SE Asia, 1985–87; Hd of External Relations, EC Office, London, 1987–93. *Address:* European Commission, Jean Monnet House, 8 Storey's Gate, SW1P 3AT. *Club:* Travellers'.

MARTIN, Victor Cecil, OBE; HM Diplomatic Service, retired; *b* 12 Oct. 1915; *s* of late Cecil Martin and Isabel Katherine Martin (*née* Hickman). *Educ:* Cheltenham Coll.; Jesus Coll., Cambridge (Scholar; Classical Tripos Parts 1 and 2; MA). Asst Principal, Board of Education, 1939. Served Intelligence Corps, 1940–45; Major 1944, Persia and Iraq Force. Principal, Min. of Education, 1946; transferred to CRO, 1948; British High Commn, New Delhi, 1951–54, 1956–60; Asst Sec., CRO, 1962; Head of West Africa Dept, 1961–64; Head of S Asia Dept, 1964–66; Head of Cultural Relations Dept, 1966–68; Dep. High Comr, Madras, 1968–71; Special Adviser to High Comr, British High Commn, New Delhi, 1972–75. *Recreations:* ornithology, music. *Address:* 76 Swan Court, Flood Street, SW3 5UD. *Clubs:* United Oxford & Cambridge University, Commonwealth Trust, Royal Over-Seas League.

MARTIN, William McChesney, Jun.; Chairman, Board of Governors, Federal Reserve System, 1951–70; *b* St Louis, Mo, 17 Dec. 1906; *s* of William McChesney Martin and Rebecca (*née* Woods); *m* 1942, Cynthia Davis; one *s* two *d*. *Educ:* Yale Univ. (BA 1928); Benton Coll. of Law, St Louis, 1931. Graduate student (part time), Columbia Univ., 1931–37. Served in bank examination dept of Federal Reserve Bank of St Louis, 1928–29; Head of statistics dept, A. G. Edwards & Sons, St Louis, 1929–31; partner, May 1931–July 1938. Mem., New York Stock Exch., June 1931–July 1938; Gov., 1935–38; Chm. Cttee on Constitution, 1937–38; Sec. Conway Cttee to reorganize the Exchange, 1937–38; Chm. Bd and Pres. pro. tem. May-June 1938; Pres. July 1938–April 1941. Asst Exec. President's Soviet Protocol Cttee and Munitions Assignments Board, Wash., DC, 1942; appointed Mem. Export-Import Bank, Nov. 1945; Chm. and Pres., 1946–49 (as Chm. of Federal Reserve Board, served on National Advisory Council on Internat. Monetary and Financial Problems). Asst Sec. of the Treasury, Feb. 1949–April 1951; US Exec. Dir, IBRD, 1949–52. Dir of several corporations. Trustee: Berry Schs, Atlanta, Ga; Johns Hopkins Univ., Baltimore; Nat. Geographic Soc. Holds numerous Hon. Degrees from Univs in USA and Canada. Drafted, Selective Service Act, private, US Army, 1941, Sergeant, GHQ Army War Coll., 1941; Commnd 1st Lt, Inf., Feb. 1942; Captain Aug. 1942; Major, 1943; Lt-Col 1944; Col 1945. Legion of Merit, 1945. *Recreations:* tennis, squash. *Address:* 2861 Woodland Drive, NW, Washington, DC 20008, USA. *Clubs:* West Side Tennis, Yale; Metropolitan, Alibi (Washington); Chevy Chase (Md).

MARTIN-BATES, James Patrick, MA; JP; FCIS; CIMgt; Director: Atkins Holdings Ltd, 1986–90 (Chairman, 1987–89); W. S. Atkins Ltd, 1986–94; W. S. Atkins Group Ltd, 1970–86; *b* 17 April 1912; *er s* of late R. Martin-Bates, JP, Perth, Scotland; *m* 1939, Clare, *d* of late Prof. James Miller, MD, DSc; one *s* two *d*. *Educ:* Perth Academy; Glenalmond; Worcester Coll., Oxford. BA 1933; MA 1944. Lamson Industries, 1933–36; Dorman Long & Co. Ltd, 1936–38; PE Group, 1938–61: Man. Dir, Production Engineering Ltd, 1953–59; Vice-Chm., PE Holdings, 1959–61; Director: Hutchinson Ltd, 1958–78; Avery's Ltd, 1970–77; Charringtons Industrial Holdings Ltd, 1972–77. Principal, Administrative Staff Coll., Henley-on-Thames, 1961–72. Chm., Management Consultants Association, 1960; Member: Council, British Institute of Management, 1961–66; UK Advisory Council on Education for Management, 1961–66; Council, Glenalmond, 1963–82; Bd of Visitors, HM Borstal, Huntercombe, 1964–67; The Council for Technical Education and Training for Overseas Countries, 1962–73; Council, University Coll., Nairobi, 1965–68; Council, Chartered Institute of Secretaries, 1965–74; EDC for Rubber Industry, 1965–69; Council, Univ. of Buckingham (formerly University Coll. at Buckingham), 1977–87. Governor, Aylesbury Grammar Sch., 1983–89. UN Consultant in Iran, 1972–78. High Sheriff of Buckinghamshire, 1974; Chm., Marlow Bench, 1978–82. FCIS 1961; CIMgt (FBIM 1960); Fellow Internat. Acad. of Management, 1964. DUniv Buckingham, 1986. Burnham Medal, BIM, 1974. *Publications:* The History of the Maurice Lubbock Memorial Fund, 1993; various articles in Management Journals. *Recreations:* golf, fishing. *Address:* Ivy Cottage, Fingest, near Henley-on-Thames, Oxon RG9 6QD. *T:* Turville Heath (01491) 638202. *Clubs:* Caledonian; Royal and Ancient (St Andrews); Huntercombe.

MARTIN-JENKINS, Christopher Dennis Alexander; cricket correspondent, Daily Telegraph, since 1991; BBC cricket commentator, since 1973; *b* 20 Jan. 1945; *s* of late Dennis Frederick Martin-Jenkins, TD; *m* 1971, Judith Oswald Hayman; two *s* one *d*. *Educ:* Marlborough; Fitzwilliam Coll., Cambridge (BA (Modern Hist.); MA). Dep. Editor, The Cricketer, 1967–70; sports broadcaster, 1970–73, Cricket Correspondent, 1973–80, 1984–91, BBC; Editor, 1981–88, Editl Dir, 1988–91, The Cricketer International. Pres., Rugby Fives Assoc., 1993–95. *Publications:* Testing Time, 1974; Assault on the Ashes, 1975; MCC in India, 1977; The Jubilee Tests and the Packer Revolution, 1977; In Defence of the Ashes, 1979; Cricket Contest, 1980; The Complete Who's Who of Test Cricketers, 1980; The Wisden Book of County Cricket, 1981; Bedside Cricket, 1981; Twenty Years On: Cricket's years of change, 1984; Cricket: a way of life, 1984; (ed) Cricketer Book of Cricket Eccentrics, 1985; (ed) Seasons Past, 1986; (ed jtly) Quick Singles, 1986; Grand Slam, 1987; Cricket Characters, 1987; Sketches of a Season, 1989; Ball by Ball, 1990; (jtly) Summers Will Never Be the Same, 1994. *Recreations:* cricket, Rugby fives, tennis, golf, gardening, walking. *Address:* Daily Telegraph, 1 Canada Square, Canary Wharf, E14 9DT. *Clubs:* MCC; I Zingari, Free Foresters, Arabs, Marlborough Blues, Cranleigh Cricket, Albury Cricket, Rudgwick Cricket, Horsham Cricket.

MARTINDALE, Air Vice-Marshal Alan Rawes, CB 1984; Royal Air Force, retired; *b* 20 Jan. 1930; *s* of late Norman Martindale and Edith (*née* Rawes); *m* 1952, Eileen Alma Wrenn; three *d*. *Educ:* Kendal Grammar Sch.; University Coll., Leicester (BA History, London Univ., 1950). Commissioned RAF, 1951; served, 1951–71: RAF Driffield, Oakington, Eindhoven, Stafford, Wickenby, Faldingworth and Marham; Instructor, RAF Coll., Cranwell; Staff AHQ Malta; RAF Staff Coll., Bracknell, MoD, Jt Services Staff Coll. (student and Directing Staff), and HQ Maintenance Comd; Dep. Dir of Supply Management, MoD, Harrogate, 1971–72; Comd Supply Officer, RAF Germany, 1972–74; Dir of Supply Management, MoD, Harrogate, 1974–75; RCDS, 1976; Air Cdre Supply and Movements, RAF Support Comd, 1977; Dep. Gen. Man., NAMMA, 1978–81; Dir of Supply Policy (RAF), MoD, 1981–82; Dir Gen. of Supply (RAF), 1982–84; retd 1985. Dist Gen. Manager, Hastings HA, 1985–90; Census Area Manager, S Kent and Hastings, 1990–91. Chm., Battle Festival, 1991–. *Recreations:* golf, gardening. *Address:* Taylors Cottage, Mountfield, Robertsbridge, East Sussex TN32 5JZ. *Club:* Royal Air Force.

MARTINEAU, Charles Herman; Chairman, Electricity Consultative Council for South of Scotland, 1972–76; *b* 3 Sept. 1908; *s* of Prof. Charles E. Martineau, Birmingham; *m* 1939, Margaret Shirley Dolphin; two *s* one *d*. *Educ:* King Edward's Sch., Birmingham. Jas Williamson & Son Ltd, Lancaster and Nairn-Williamson Ltd, Kirkcaldy: Man. Dir, 1952–66. Part-time Mem., S of Scotland Electricity Bd, 1971–76. Mem., Fife CC, 1967 (Vice-Convener, 1970–73); Mem., Fife Regional Council, 1978–82. *Recreations:* chess, golf. *Address:* Gladsmuir, Hepburn Gardens, St Andrews, Fife. *T:* St Andrews (01334) 73069. *Club:* Royal and Ancient (St Andrews).

See also Rt Rev. R. A. S. Martineau.

MARTINEAU, David Nicholas Nettlefold; His Honour Judge Martineau; a Circuit Judge, since 1994; *b* 27 March 1941; *s* of Frederick Alan Martineau and Vera Ruth Martineau (*née* Naylor); *m* 1968, Elizabeth Mary Allom; one *s* one *d*. *Educ:* Eton; Trinity Coll., Cambridge (MA, LLM). Called to the Bar, Inner Temple, 1964; Asst Recorder, 1982–86; Recorder 1986–94. Mem., Exec. Cttee, Cystic Fibrosis Trust, 1990–. *Recreations:* ski-ing, water ski-ing, wind-surfing, music, wine and food. *Address:* 37 Bedford Gardens, W8 7EF. *T:* 0171–727 7825. *Clubs:* MCC; Hawks (Cambridge).

MARTINEAU, Rt. Rev. Robert Arnold Schürhoff, MA; *b* 22 Aug. 1913; *s* of late Prof. C. E. Martineau, MA, MCom, FCA, and Mrs Martineau, Birmingham; *m* 1941, Elinor Gertrude Ap-Thomas; one *s* two *d*. *Educ:* King Edward's Sch., Birmingham; Trinity Hall, Cambridge; Westcott House, Cambridge. Tyson Medal for Astronomy, 1935. Deacon 1938, priest 1939; Curate, Melksham, 1938–41. Chaplain: RAFVR, 1941–46; RAuxAF, 1947–52. Vicar: Ovenden, Halifax, 1946–52; Allerton, Liverpool, 1952–66, St Christopher, San Lorenzo, Calif, 1961–62. Hon. Canon of Liverpool, 1961–66; Rural Dean of Childwall, 1964–66. Proctor in Convocation, 1964–66. Bishop Suffragan of Huntingdon, 1966–72; Residentiary Canon of Ely, 1966–72; Bishop of Blackburn, 1972–81. First Jt Chm., C of E Bd of Educn and Nat. Soc. for Promoting Religious Educn, 1973–79. Chm., Central Readers Bd, C of E, 1971–76. *Publications:* The Church in Germany in Prayer (ed jtly), 1937; Rhodesian Wild Flowers, 1953; The Office and Work of a Reader, 1970; The Office and Work of a Priest, 1972; Moments that Matter, 1976; Preaching through the Christian Year; Truths that Endure, 1977; Travelling with Christ, 1981. *Recreations:* gardening, swimming. *Address:* Gwenallt, Park Street, Denbigh, Clwyd LL16 3DB.

See also C. H. Martineau.

MARTINEAU-WALKER, Roger Antony; *see* Walker.

MARTINI, His Eminence Cardinal Carlo Maria, SJ; Archbishop of Milan, since 1980; *b* 15 Feb. 1927; *s* of Leonardo and Olga Maggia. *Educ:* Pontifical Gregorian Univ. (DTheol); Pontifical Biblical Inst. (Doctorate in holy scripture). Ordained priest, 1952; Rector, Pontifical Biblical Inst., 1969–78; Rector, Gregorian Univ., 1978–79. Cardinal 1983. Pres., Consilium Conferentiarum Episcopalium Europae, 1987–93. *Address:* Piazza Fontana 2, 20122 Milano, Italy. *T:* (2) 85561.

MARTLEW, Eric Anthony; MP (Lab) Carlisle, since 1987; *b* 3 Jan. 1949; *m* 1970, Elsie Barbara Duggan. *Educ:* Harraby Secondary School, Carlisle; Carlisle Tech. Coll. Nestlé Co. Ltd, 1966–87: joined as lab. technician; later Personnel Manager, Dalston Factory, Carlisle. Member: Carlisle County Borough Council, 1972–74; Cumbria CC, 1973–88 (Chm., 1983–85). Mem., Cumbria Health Authy, later E Cumbria HA, 1977–87 (Chm., 1977–79). *Recreations:* photography, fell walking, horse racing, Rugby league. *Address:* 42 Beaumont Road, Carlisle CA2 4RQ. *T:* Carlisle (01228) 20077.

MARTONMERE, 2nd Baron *cr* 1964; **John Stephen Robinson;** *b* 10 July 1963; *s* of Hon. Richard Anthony Gasque Robinson (*d* 1979) and of Wendy Patricia (who *m* subseq. Ronald De Mara), *d* of late James Cecil Blagden; *S* grandfather, 1989. *Educ:* Lakefield College School; Senaca College. *Heir:* *b* David Alan Robinson, *b* 15 Sept. 1965. *Address:* 390 Russell Hill Road, Toronto, Ont M4V 2V2, Canada.

MARTYN, Charles Roger Nicholas; Master of the Supreme Court, 1973–95; Special Adjudicator, Immigration Appellate Authority, since 1995 (part-time Adjudicator, 1991–95); *b* 10 Dec. 1925; *s* of Rev. Charles Martyn; *m* 1960, Helen, *d* of Frank Everson; two *s* one *d*. *Educ:* Charterhouse, 1939–44; Merton Coll., Oxford, 1947–49. MA (Hons) Mod. Hist. Joined Regular Army, 1944; commissioned 60th Rifles (KRRC), 1945; CMF, 1946–47; special release, 1947. Articles, 1950–52, and admitted as solicitor, 1952. Sherwood & Co., Parly Agents (Partner), 1952–59; Lee, Bolton & Lee, Westminster (Partner), 1961–73; Notary Public, 1969. Mem. and Dep. Chm., No 14 Legal Aid Area Cttee, 1967–73; Hon. Legal Adviser to The Samaritans (Inc), 1955–73. Chm., Family Welfare Assoc., 1973–78 (Chief Trustee of 129 public charities and 6 almshouses); Member: Gtr London Citizens' Advice Bureaux Management Cttee, 1974–79; Council, St Gabriel's Coll. (Further Education), Camberwell, 1973–77 (Vice-Chm.); Council, Goldsmiths' Coll., Univ. of London, 1988– (Mem., Delegacy, 1977–88). *Recreations:* walking, sailing (Vice-Cdre, Thames Barge Sailing Club, 1962–65), observing people, do-it-yourself, nigrology. *Address:* 29 St Albans Road, NW5 1RG. *T:* 0171–267 1076.

MARTYN-HEMPHILL, family name of **Baron Hemphill.**

MARWICK, Prof. Arthur John Brereton, FRHistS; Professor of History, The Open University, since 1969; *b* 29 Feb. 1936; *s* of William Hutton Marwick and Maeve Cluna Brereton; unmarried; one *d*. *Educ:* George Heriot's School, Edinburgh; Edinburgh Univ. (MA, DLitt); Balliol Coll., Oxford (BLitt). Asst Lectr in History, Univ. of Aberdeen, 1959–60; Lectr in History, Univ. of Edinburgh, 1960–69; Dean and Dir of Studies in Arts, Open Univ., 1978–84. Vis. Prof. in History, State Univ. of NY at Buffalo, 1966–67; Vis. Scholar, Hoover Instn and Vis. Prof., Stanford Univ., 1984–85; Directeur d'études invité, l'Ecole des Hautes Etudes en Sciences Sociales, Paris, 1985; Visiting Professor: Rhodes Coll., Memphis, 1991; Univ. of Perugia, 1991. *Publications:* The Explosion of British Society, 1963; Clifford Allen, 1964; The Deluge, 1965, new edn 1991; Britain in the Century of Total War, 1968; The Nature of History, 1970, 3rd edn 1989; War and Social Change in the Twentieth Century, 1974; The Home Front, 1976; Women at War 1914–1918, 1977; Class: image and reality in Britain, France and USA since 1930, 1980, rev. edn 1990; (ed) Illustrated Dictionary of British History, 1980; British Society since 1945, 1982, 2nd edn 1990; Britain in Our Century, 1984; (ed) Class in the Twentieth Century, 1986; Beauty in History: society, politics and personal appearance c 1500 to the present, 1988; (ed) Total War and Social Change, 1988; (ed) The Arts, Literature and Society, 1990; Culture in Britain since 1945, 1991; contribs to English Hist. Review, Amer. Hist. Review, Jl of Contemporary Hist. *Recreations:* wine, women, football. *Address:* 67 Fitzjohns Avenue, Hampstead, NW3 6PE. *T:* 0171–794 4534. *Clubs:* Open University Football, Open University Tennis.

MARX, Enid Crystal Dorothy, RDI 1944; Painter and Designer; *b* London, 20 Oct. 1902; *y d* of Robert J. Marx. *Educ:* Roedean Sch.; Central Sch. of Arts and Crafts; Royal College of Art Painting Sch. Designing and printing handblock printed textiles, 1925–39. Exhibited in USA and Europe; various works purchased by Victoria and Albert Museum, Musée des Arts Décoratifs, Boston Museum, Scottish Arts Council, Sheffield Art Gall., etc. Mem. Society of Wood Engravers. Wood engraving and autolithography pattern papers, book jackets, book illustration and decorations, trademarks, etc; designed moquettes and posters for LPTB. Industrial designing for printed and woven furnishing fabrics, wallpapers, ceramics, plastics. Fellow, 1982, Senior Fellow, 1987, RCA; FRSA, FSIAD; original mem. National Register of Industrial Designers of Central Institute of Art and Design. Mem. of Bd of Trade design panel on utility furniture. Designed postage stamps: ½d–2d for first issue Elizabeth II; Christmas 1976 issue. Lectures on textiles and folk art. *Publications:* (jointly) English Popular and Traditional Art, 1947; (with Margaret Lambert) English Popular Art, 1951, 2nd edn 1988; articles and broadcasts on aspects of industrial design in various countries; author and illustrator of twelve books for children. *Recreations:* study of popular art in different countries; gardening. *Address:* The Studio, 39 Thornhill Road, Barnsbury Square, N1 1JS. *T:* 0171–607 2286.

MARYCHURCH, Sir Peter (Harvey), KCMG 1985; consultant; Chairman, Associated Board of the Royal Schools of Music, since 1994; Director, Government Communications Headquarters, 1983–89; *b* 13 June 1927; *s* of Eric William Alfred and Dorothy Margaret Marychurch; *m* 1965, June Daphne Ottaway (*née* Pareezer). *Educ:* Lower School of John Lyon, Harrow. Served RAF, 1945–48. Joined GCHQ, 1948; Asst Sec. 1975; Under Sec. 1979; Dep. Sec. 1983. Chairman: Cheltenham Arts Festivals Co., 1994–; Cheltenham Internat. Fest. of Music, 1993–; Cheltenham and Cotswold Relate, 1990–. *Recreations:* theatre, music (especially opera), gardening. *Address:* Midland Bank, 2 The Promenade, Cheltenham, Glos GL50 1LS. *Club:* Naval and Military.

MARYON DAVIS, Dr Alan Roger, FFPHM; Consultant in Public Health Medicine, Lambeth, Southwark and Lewisham Health Commission (formerly West Lambeth, then South East London, Health Authority), since 1988; Senior Lecturer in Public Health, United Medical and Dental Schools (St Thomas's Campus), since 1988; *b* 21 Jan. 1943; *s* of Cyril Edward Maryon Davis and Hilda May Maryon Davis; one *s*; *m* 1981, Glynis Anne Davies; two *d*. *Educ:* St Paul's Sch.; St John's Coll., Cambridge (MA 1968; MB BChir 1970); St Thomas's Hosp. Med. Sch.; London Sch. of Hygiene and Tropical Medicine. MSc (Social Med.) London 1978; MRCP 1972; FFPHM (FFCM 1986); FRIPHH 1989. Early med. career in gen. medicine and rheumatology, later in community medicine; MO, 1977–84, CMO, 1984–87, Health Educn Council; Sen. Med. Adviser, Health Educn Authority, 1987–88; Hon. Consultant, Paddington and N Kensington HA, 1985–88; Hon. Sen. Lectr in Community Medicine, St Mary's Hosp. Med. Sch., 1985–88. Member Council: RIPH&H, 1989–; RoSPA, 1990–. Trustee, Health Information Trust, 1987–; Patron, Healthcare Foundn, 1987–. Writer and broadcaster on health matters, 1975–; BBC radio series include Action Makes the Heart Grow Stronger (Med. Journalist's Assoc. Radio Award), 1983; BBC television series include: Body Matters, 1985–89; Health UK, 1990–91. Editor-in-Chief, Health Education Jl, 1984–88; Med. Advice Columnist, Woman magazine, 1988–. *Publications:* Family Health and Fitness, 1981; Body Facts, 1984; (with J. Thomas) Diet 2000, 1984; (with J. Rogers) How to Save a Life, 1987; PSSST—a Really Useful Guide to Alcohol, 1989; Cholesterol Check, 1991; The Good Health Guide, 1994; Ruby's Health Quest, 1995. *Recreations:* eating well, drinking well, singing (not so well) with the humorous group Instant Sunshine. *Address:* 4 Sibella Road, Clapham, SW4 6HX. *T:* 0171–720 5659.

MASCHLER, Fay; restaurant critic, Evening Standard, since 1972; *b* 15 July 1945; *d* of Mary and Arthur Frederick Coventry; *m* 1970, Thomas Michael Maschler, *qv* (marr. diss. 1987); one *s* two *d*. *Educ:* Convent of the Sacred Heart, Greenwich, Conn. Copywriter, J. Walter Thompson, 1964; journalist, Radio Times, 1969. *Publications:* Cooking is a Game You Can Eat, 1975; A Child's Book of Manners, 1979; Miserable Aunt Bertha, 1980; Fay Maschler's Guide to Eating Out in London, 1986; Eating In, 1987; Howard & Maschler on Food, 1987; Teach Your Child to Cook, 1988. *Address:* Epworth, Antrim Road, NW3 4XN. *T:* 0171–722 1376. *Clubs:* Groucho, Car Clamp.

MASCHLER, Thomas Michael; Publisher, Jonathan Cape Children's Books, since 1991; Director, Jonathan Cape Ltd, since 1960 (Chairman, 1970–91); *b* 16 Aug. 1933; *s* of Kurt Leo Maschler and of Rita Masseron (*née* Lechner); *m* 1970, Fay Coventry (*see* Fay Maschler) (marr. diss. 1987); one *s* two *d*; *m* 1988, Regina Kulinicz. *Educ:* Leighton Park School. Production Asst, Andre Deutsch, 1955; Editor, MacGibbon & Kee, 1956–58; Fiction Editor, Penguin Books, 1958–60; Jonathan Cape: Editorial Dir, 1960; Man. Dir, 1966. Associate Producer, The French Lieutenant's Woman (film), 1981. *Publications:* (ed) Declarations, 1957; (ed) New English Dramatists Series, 1959–63. *Address:* 20 Vauxhall Bridge Road, SW1V 2SA.

MASEFIELD, Charles Beech Gordon, CEng; FRAeS; FIMechE; Head, Defence Export Services Organisation, since 1994; *b* 7 Jan. 1940; *s* of Sir Peter (Gordon) Masefield, *qv*; *m* 1970, Fiona Anne Kessler; two *s*. *Educ:* Eastbourne Coll.; Jesus Coll., Cambridge (MA). CEng 1984; FRAeS 1980; FIMechE 1984. Sales Exec., Beagle Aircraft, 1964–70; Hawker

Siddeley Aviation: Test Pilot, 1970–76; Dep. Chief Test Pilot, Manchester, 1976–78; British Aerospace, Manchester: Chief Test Pilot, 1978–80; Project Dir, 1980–81; Prodn Dir, 1981–84; Gen. Manager, 1984–86; Man. Dir, BAe Hatfield, Manchester, Prestwick, 1986–92; President: BAe Commercial Aircraft, 1992–93; Avro Internat. Aerospace, 1993–94; Sen. Vice-Pres. and Commercial Dir, Airbus Industrie, Toulouse, 1994. Pres., RAeS, 1994–95. *Recreation:* occasional golf. *Address:* Ashlea, Kinsbourne Green, Harpenden, Herts AL5 3PW. *T:* Harpenden (01582) 763901.

MASEFIELD, (John) Thorold, CMG 1986; HM Diplomatic Service; High Commisssioner, Nigeria, also concurrently Ambassador (non-resident) to the Republics of Benin and of Chad, since 1994; *b* 1 Oct. 1939; *e s* of Dr Geoffrey Bussell Masefield, DSc and Mildred Joy Thorold Masefield (*née* Rogers); *m* 1962, Jennifer Mary, *d* of late Rev. Dr H. C. Trowell, OBE and late K. M. Trowell, MBE; two *s* one *d* (and one *d* decd). *Educ:* Dragon Sch., Oxford; Repton Sch.; St John's Coll., Cambridge (Scholar) (MA). Joined CRO, 1962; Private Sec. to Permanent Under Sec., 1963–64; Second Secretary: Kuala Lumpur, 1964–65; Warsaw, 1966–67; FCO, 1967–69; First Sec., UK Delegn to Disarmament Conf., 1970–74; Dep. Head, Planning Staff, FCO, 1974–77; Far Eastern Dept, FCO, 1977–79; Counsellor, Head of Chancery and Consul Gen., Islamabad, 1979–82; Head of Personnel Services Dept, FCO, 1982–85; Head, Far Eastern Dept, FCO, 1985–87; Fellow, Center for Internat. Affairs, Harvard Univ., 1987–88; seconded to CSSB, 1988–89; High Comr, Tanzania, 1989–92; Asst Under-Sec. of State, FCO, 1992–94. *Publication:* article in International Affairs. *Recreations:* fruit and vegetables. *Address:* c/o Foreign and Commonwealth Office, SW1A 2AH. *Clubs:* Commonwealth Trust; Metropolitan (Lagos).

MASEFIELD, Sir Peter (Gordon), Kt 1972; MA Cantab; CEng; Hon. FRAeS; FCIT; President: Brooklands Museum Trust, since 1993 (Chairman, 1987–93); British Association of Aviation Consultants, since 1972; Croydon Airport Society, since 1962; *b* Trentham, Staffs, 19 March 1914; *e s* of late Dr W. Gordon Masefield, CBE, MRCS, and Marian A. Masefield (*née* Lloyd-Owen); *m* 1936, Patricia Doreen, 3rd *d* of late Percy H. Rooney, Wallington, Surrey; three *s* one *d*. *Educ:* Westminster Sch.; Chillon Coll., Switzerland; Jesus Coll., Cambridge (BA (Eng) 1935). On Design Staff, The Fairey Aviation Co. Ltd, 1935–37; Pilot's licence, 1937–70; joined The Aeroplane newspaper, 1937, Technical Editor, 1939–43; Air Correspondent Sunday Times, 1940–43; War Corresp. with RAF and US Army Eighth Air Force on active service, 1939–43; Editor, The Aeroplane Spotter, 1941–43; Chm. Editorial Cttee, The Inter-Services Journal on Aircraft Recognition, MAP, 1942–45; Personal Adviser to the Lord Privy Seal (Lord Beaverbrook) and Sec. of War Cabinet Cttee on Post War Civil Air Transport, 1943–45; first British Civil Air Attaché, British Embassy, Washington, DC, 1945–46 (Signator to Anglo-American Bermuda Air Agreement, 1946); Dir-Gen. of Long Term Planning and Projects, Ministry of Civil Aviation, 1946–48; Chief Executive and Mem. of Board of BEA, 1949–55; Managing Dir, Bristol Aircraft Ltd, 1956–60; Man. Dir, Beagle Aircraft Ltd, 1960–67, Chm., 1968–70; Dir, Beagle Aviation Finance Ltd, 1962–71. Chm., British Airports Authority, 1965–71. Chm., Nat. Jt Council for Civil Air Transport, 1950–51; Member: Cairns Cttee on Aircraft Accident Investigation, 1960; Min. of Aviation Advisory Cttees on Civil Aircraft Control and on Private and Club Flying and Gliding; Aeronautical Research Council, 1958–61; Board, LTE, 1973–82 (Chm. and Chief Exec., London Transport, 1980–82); CAA Flight Time Limitations Bd, 1986–91. Mem., Cambridge Univ. Appointments Bd, 1956–69. Director: Pressed Steel Co. Ltd, 1960–68; Worldwide Estates Ltd, 1972–88; Nationwide Building Soc., 1973–86; British Caledonian Aviation Gp Plc, 1975–88 (Dep. Chm., 1978–87); LRT Internat., 1982–91; Chm., Project Management Ltd, 1972–88. RAeS: Mem. Council, 1945–65; Pres., 1959–60; President: Inst. of Travel Managers, 1967–70; Duxford Aviation Soc., 1970–; Internat. Fedn of Airworthiness, 1980–83 (Patron, 1983–88); Chm., Bd of Trustees, Imperial War Museum, 1977–78; Mem. Council, Royal Aero Club (Chm., Aviation Cttee, 1960–65; Chm., 1968–70). Chm., Bd of Governors, Reigate Grammar Sch., 1979–91; Governor, Ashridge Management Coll., 1981–91. Pres., IRTE, 1979–81. FRSA (Chm. Council, 1977–79; Vice-Pres., 1979, now Vice-Pres. Emeritus); CIMgt. Hon. FAIAA; Hon. FCASI; Hon. DSc Cranfield, 1977; Hon. DTech Loughborough, 1977. Liveryman, GAPAN; Freeman, City of London. *Publications:* To Ride the Storm, 1982; articles on aviation, transport, management, and First World War. *Recreations:* reading, writing, gardening. *Address:* Rosehill, Doods Way, Reigate, Surrey RH2 0JT. *T:* Reigate (01737) 242396. *Clubs:* Athenæum, Royal Aero; National Aviation (Washington).

See also C. B. G. Masefield.

MASEFIELD, Thorold; *see* Masefield, J. T.

MASERI, Attilio, MD; FRCP; FACC; Professor of Cardiology, and Director of Institute of Cardiology, Catholic University of Rome, Italy, since 1991; *b* 12 Nov. 1935; *s* of Adriano and Antonietta Albini, Italian nobles; *m* 1960, Countess Francesca Maseri Florio di Santo Stefano; one *s*. *Educ:* Classic Lycée Cividale, Italy; Padua Univ. Med. Sch. Special bds in Cardiology, 1963, in Nuclear Medicine, 1965, Italy. Research fellow: Univ. of Pisa, 1960–65; Columbia Univ., NY, 1965–66; Johns Hopkins Univ., Baltimore, 1966–67; University of Pisa: Asst Prof., 1967–70; Prof. of Internal Medicine, 1970; Prof. of Cardiovascular Pathophysiology, 1972–79; Prof. of Medicine (Locum), 1977–79; Sir John McMichael Prof. of Cardiovascular Medicine, RPMS, Univ. of London, 1979–91. King Faisal Prize for Medicine, 1992. Chevalier d'honneur et devotion, SMO Malta. *Publications:* Myocardial Blood Flow in Man, 1972; Primary and Secondary Angina, 1977; Perspectives on Coronary Care, 1979; Heart Disease: a rational basis for clinical practice and clinical research, 1995; articles in major internat. cardiological and med. jls. *Recreations:* skiing, tennis, sailing. *Address:* Via Zandonai 9–11, 00194 Rome, Italy. *Club:* Queen's.

MASHAM OF ILTON, Baroness *cr* 1970 (Life Peer); **Susan Lilian Primrose Cunliffe-Lister, (Countess of Swinton);** DL; *b* 14 April 1935; *d* of Sir Ronald Sinclair, 8th Bt and Reba Blair (who *m* 2nd, 1957, Lt-Col H. R. Hildreth, MBE; she *d* 1985), *d* of Anthony Inglis, MD; *m* 1959, Lord Masham (now Earl of Swinton, *qv*); one *s* one *d* (both adopted). *Educ:* Heathfield School, Ascot; London Polytechnic. Has made career in voluntary social work. Mem., Peterlee and Newton Aycliffe New Town Corp., 1973–85. Vice-Chairman: All-Party Parly Drug Misuse Cttee, 1984–; All-Party Parly AIDS Cttee; Member: Parly All-Party Disablement Cttee, 1970–; Parly All-Party Penal Affairs Cttee, 1975–; All-Party Children's Gp; All-Party Gps on Breast Cancer, 1993, on Skin, 1994, and on Epilepsy, 1994. President: N Yorks Red Cross, 1963–88 (Patron, 1989–); Yorks Assoc. for the Disabled, 1963–; Spinal Injuries Assoc., 1982–; Chartered Soc. of Physiotherapy, 1975–82; Papworth and Enham Village Settlements, 1973–85; Countrywide Workshops Charitable Trust, 1993–; Vice-President: British Sports Assoc. for the Disabled; Disabled Drivers Assoc.; Assoc. of Occupnl Therapists; Action for Dysphasic Adults; Hosp. Saving Assoc.; Chairman: Bd of Dirs, Phoenix House (Drug Rehabilitation), 1986–92 (Patron, 1992–); Home Office Working Gp on Young People and Alcohol, 1987; Member: Yorks RHA, 1982–90; N Yorks FHSA, 1990–; Bd of Visitors, Wetherby Young Offenders Instn (formerly Wetherby Youth Custody Centre), 1963–94; Winston Churchill Meml Trust, 1980–; Trustee, Spinal Res. Trust; Patron: Disablement Income Gp; Yorks Faculty of GPs; Mem. and Governor, Ditchley Foundn, 1980–; former Mem., Volunteer Centre. Freedom, Borough of Harrogate, 1989. DL North Yorks, 1991. Hon. FRCGP, 1981; Hon. Fellow, Bradford and Ilkley Community Coll., 1988. Hon. MA Open, 1981; DUniv York, 1985; Hon. LLD: Leeds, 1988; Teesside, 1993; Hon. DSc Ulster, 1990; Hon. DLitt Keele, 1993. *Publication:* The World Walks By, 1986. *Recreations:* breeding highland ponies, swimming, table tennis, fishing, flower decoration, gardening. *Address:* Dykes Hill House, Masham, near Ripon, N Yorks HG4 4NS. *T:* Ripon (01765) 689241; 46 Westminster Gardens, Marsham Street, SW1P 4JG. *T:* 0171–834 0700.

See also Sir J. R. N. B. Sinclair, Bt.

MASIRE, Quett Ketumile Joni, Hon. GCMG 1991; Naledi ya Botswana; MP; President of Botswana, since 1980; *b* 23 July 1925; *m* 1957, Gladys Olebile; three *s* three *d*. *Educ:* Kanye; Tiger Kloof. Founded Seepapitso Secondary School, 1950; reporter, later Dir, African Echo, 1958; Mem., Bangwaketse Tribal Council, Legislative Council (former Mem., Exec. Council); founder Mem., Botswana Democratic Party (Editor, Therisanyo, 1962–67); Member, Legislative Assembly (later National Assembly): Kanye S, 1966–69; Ngwaketse-Kgalagadi, 1974–79; Dep. Prime Minister, 1965–66; Vice-Pres. and Minister of Finance and Development Planning, 1966–80. *Address:* State House, Private Bag 001, Gaborone, Botswana. *T:* 350850; PO Box 70, Gaborone, Botswana. *T:* 353391.

MASLIN, David Michael E.; *see* Eckersley-Maslin.

MASON, family name of **Baron Mason of Barnsley.**

MASON OF BARNSLEY, Baron *cr* 1987 (Life Peer), of Barnsley in South Yorkshire; **Roy Mason,** PC 1968; DL; *b* 18 April 1924; *s* of Joseph and Mary Mason; *m* 1945, Marjorie, *d* of Ernest Sowden; two *d*. *Educ:* Carlton Junior Sch.; Royston Senior Sch.; London Sch. of Economics (TUC Scholarship). Went underground at 14 years of age, 1938–53; NUM branch official, 1947–53; mem. Yorks Miners' Council, 1949. MP (Lab): Barnsley, March 1953–1983; Barnsley Central, 1983–87. Labour party spokesman on Defence and Post Office affairs, 1960–64; Minister of State (Shipping), Bd of Trade, 1964–67; Minister of Defence (Equipment), 1967–April 1968; Postmaster-Gen., April-June 1968; Minister of Power, 1968–69; President, Bd of Trade, 1969–70; Labour party spokesman on Civil Aviation, Shipping, Tourism, Films and Trade matters, 1970–74; Secretary of State for: Defence, 1974–76; Northern Ireland, 1976–79; opposition spokesman on agriculture, fisheries and food, 1979–81. Mem., Council of Europe and WEU, 1973. Chm., Yorkshire Gp of Labour MPs, 1972–74; Chm., Miners Gp of MPs, 1974, Vice-Chm., 1980. DL South Yorks, 1992. Dr *hc* Sheffield Hallam, 1993. *Recreations:* work, provided one stays on top of it, fly-fishing, cravatology, tie-designing. *Address:* 12 Victoria Avenue, Barnsley, S Yorks S70 2BH.

MASON, Alastair Michael Stuart, FRCP; Partner, Partners in Care, since 1994; *b* 4 March 1944; *s* of Adair Stuart and Rosemary Mason; *m* 1967, Kay Marion; two *s* two *d*. *Educ:* Downside Sch.; London Hosp., London Univ. MB BS. MRCP, FRCP 1993; MRCS; FFPHM 1991. Hosp. junior appts, 1967–73; Sen. Medical Officer, Dept of Health, 1974–84; Sen. Manager, Arthur Andersen & Co., 1984–88; RMO, S Western RHA, 1988–94. *Publications:* (ed) Walk don't run, 1985; Information for Action, 1988. *Recreations:* walking, reading, theatre. *Address:* 29 Forester Road, Bathwick, Bath BA2 6QE.

MASON, Hon. Sir Anthony (Frank), AC 1988; KBE 1972 (CBE 1969); Chancellor, University of New South Wales, since 1995; Chief Justice, High Court of Australia, 1987–95; *b* Sydney, 21 April 1925; *s* of F. M. Mason; *m* 1950, Patricia Mary, *d* of Dr E. N. McQueen; two *s*. *Educ:* Sydney Grammar Sch.; Univ. of Sydney. BA, LLB. RAAF Flying Officer, 1944–45. Admitted to NSW Bar, 1951; QC 1964. Commonwealth Solicitor-General, 1964–69; Judge, Court of Appeal, Supreme Court of NSW, 1969–72; Justice, High Court of Australia, 1972–87. Vice-Chm., UN Commn on Internat. Trade Law, 1968. Member: Management Cttee, British Inst. of Internat. and Comparative Law, 1987–; Council, ANU, 1969–72; Pro-Chancellor, ANU, 1972–75; Hon. LLD: ANU, 1980; Sydney, 1988; Melbourne, 1992; Monash, 1995; Griffith, 1995. Hon. DCL Oxford, 1993. FASSA 1989. Hon. Bencher, Lincoln's Inn, 1987. *Recreations:* gardening, tennis, swimming. *Address:* Chancellor's Office, University of New South Wales, Kensington, NSW 2052, Australia.

MASON, Arthur Malcolm; Director, Reckitt & Colman Ltd, 1958–79 (Chairman, 1970–77); *b* 19 Dec. 1915; British parents; *m* 1938, Mary Hall (*d* 1981); one *s* (one *d* decd). *Educ:* Linton House, London; Blundells School. Trainee, Unilever Ltd, 1934–38; Chiswick Products Ltd: Asst Sales Man., 1938; Sales and Advertising Man., 1939; Dir, 1943; Chm., 1957; Reckitt & Colman Holdings Ltd: Assoc. Dir, 1957; Dir, 1958; Vice-Chm., 1965–70. FInstD. OStJ 1975. *Recreations:* sailing, sea fishing, gardening. *Clubs:* Seaview Yacht, Brading Haven Yacht.

MASON, Sir (Basil) John, Kt 1979; CB 1973; FRS 1965; DSc (London); Director-General of the Meteorological Office, 1965–83; Chancellor, University of Manchester Institute of Science and Technology, since 1994 (President, 1986–94); *b* 18 Aug. 1923; *s* of late John Robert and Olive Mason, Docking, Norfolk; *m* 1948, Doreen Sheila Jones; two *s*. *Educ:* Fakenham Grammar Sch.; University Coll., Nottingham. Commissioned, Radar Branch RAF, 1944–46. BSc 1st Cl. Hons Physics (London), 1947, MSc 1948; DSc (London) 1956. Shirley Res. Fellow, Univ. of Nottingham, 1947; Asst Lectr in Meteorology, 1948, Lectr, 1949, Imperial Coll.; Warren Res. Fellow, Royal Society, 1957; Vis. Prof. of Meteorology, Univ. of Calif, 1959–60; Prof. of Cloud Physics, Imperial Coll. of Science and Technology (Univ. of London), 1961–65. Dir, Royal Soc. prog. on Acidification of Surface Waters, 1983–90; Sen . Advr, Global Envt Res. Centre, Imperial Coll., 1990–; Chairman: WMO/ICSU Scientific Cttee, World Climate Res. Prog., 1984–88; Co-ordinating Cttee, Marine Science and Technol., 1988–91. Hon. Gen. Sec. British Assoc., 1965–70; President: Physics Section, British Assoc., 1965; Inst. of Physics, 1976–78; BAAS, 1982–83; Nat. Soc. for Clean Air, 1989–91; Assoc. for Science Educn, 1992; Pres., 1968–70, Hon. Mem., 1985, Royal Meteorol. Soc.; Sen. Vice-Pres., 1976–86, and Treasurer, 1976–86, Royal Soc. UK Perm. Rep., World Meteorological Orgn, 1965–83 (Mem. Exec. Cttee, 1966–75 and 1977–83). Member: ABRC, 1983–87; Astronomy, Space Radio Bd, SERC, 1981–85. Chm. Council, 1970–75, Pro-Chancellor, 1979–85, Surrey Univ. Lectures: James Forrest, ICE, 1967 and 1993; Kelvin, IEE, 1968; Dalton, RIC, 1968; Bakerian, Royal Soc., 1971; Hugh MacMillan, IES, 1975; Symons, Royal Meteorol. Soc., 1976; Halley, Oxford, 1977; Rutherford, Royal Soc., Larmor, Cambridge, Linacre, Oxford, and H. L. Welch, Toronto, 1990; Loretto, Edinburgh, 1993. Mem., Academia Europaea, 1989; Hon. Mem., Amer. Meteorol Soc., 1988; Foreign Mem., Norwegian Acad. of Sci. and Letters, 1993. Hon. Fellow: Imperial Coll. of Science and Technology, 1974; UMIST, 1979. Hon. DSc: Nottingham, 1966; Durham, 1970; Strathclyde, 1975; City, 1980; Sussex, 1983; Plymouth Polytechnic, 1990; Heriot-Watt Univ., 1991; UMIST, 1994; Hon. ScD East Anglia, 1988. Hugh Robert Mill Medal, Royal Meteorol. Soc., 1959; Charles Chree Medal and Prize, Inst. Physics and Phys. Soc., 1965; Rumford Medal, Royal Soc., 1972; Glazebrook Medal, Inst. Physics, 1974; Symons Meml Gold Medal, Royal Meteorol. Soc., 1975; Royal Medal, Royal Soc., 1991. *Publications:* The Physics of Clouds, 1957, 2nd edn 1971; Clouds, Rain and Rain-Making,

1962, 2nd edn 1975; The Surface Waters Acidification Programme, 1990; Acid Rain, 1992; papers in physics and meteorological journals. *Recreations:* foreign travel, music. *Address:* 64 Christchurch Road, East Sheen, SW14 7AW.

MASON, Catherine Emily, (Mrs R. K. Mason); *see* Lampert, C. E.

MASON, David Arthur; Director of Social Services, Warwickshire County Council, since 1991; *b* 13 May 1946; *s* of Arthur J. Mason and Vera M. Mason. *Educ:* Birmingham Polytechnic (Cert. Social Work, 1970); Univ. of Aston in Birmingham (MSc Public Sector Management, 1981). Social worker, 1966–70; Sen. Social worker, Hounslow, 1970–72; Unit Organiser, Birmingham Family Service Unit, 1972–75; Area Man., Birmingham, 1975–81; Divl Dir of Social Services, Warwickshire, 1981–84; Director of Social Services: Knowsley, 1985–87; Liverpool CC, 1987–91. *Address:* Warwickshire Social Services Department, PO Box 48, Shire Hall, Warwick CV34 4RD. *T:* Warwick (01926) 410410.

MASON, Sir David (Kean), Kt 1992; CBE 1987; BDS, MD; FRCSGlas, FDSRCPS Glas, FDSRCSE, FRCPath; Professor of Oral Medicine and Head of the Department of Oral Medicine and Pathology, University of Glasgow Dental School, 1967–92, now Professor Emeritus; Dean of Dental Education, University of Glasgow, 1980–90; *b* 5 Nov. 1928; *s* of George Hunter Mason and Margaret Kean; *m* 1967, Judith Anne Armstrong; two *s* one *d. Educ:* Paisley Grammar Sch.; Glasgow Acad.; St Andrews Univ. (LDS 1951, BDS 1952); Glasgow Univ. (MB, ChB 1962, MD (Commendation) 1967). FDSRCSE 1957; FDSRCPS Glas 1967; FRCSGlas 1973; FRCPath 1976 (MRCPath 1967); Hon. FFDRCSI 1988; Hon. FDSRCPS Glas 1990. Served RAF, Dental Br., 1952–54. Registrar in Oral Surgery, Dundee, 1954–56; gen. dental practice, 1956–62; Vis. Dental Surgeon, Glasgow Dental Hosp., 1956–62, Sen. Registrar 1962–64; Sen. Lectr in Dental Surgery and Pathology, Univ. of Glasgow, 1964–67; Hon. Consultant Dental Surgeon, Glasgow, 1964–67. Chm., National Dental Consultative Cttee, 1976–80 and 1983–; Member: Medicines Commn, 1976–80; Dental Cttee, MRC, 1973–; Physiol Systems Bd, MRC, 1976–80; Jt MRC/Health Depts/SERC Dental Cttee, 1984–87; GDC, 1976– (Mem., Disciplinary Cttee, 1980–85; Health Cttee, 1985–; Pres., 1989–); Dental Cttee, UGC, 1977–87 (Chm., 1983–87); Supervised Trng Gp, UGC, 1984–86; Dental Rev. Wkg Party, UGC, 1986–87; Jt Cttee for Higher Trng in Dentistry, 1977–84; Dental Strategy Rev. Gp, 1980–81; Scientific Prog. Cttee, FDI, 1980–; Consultant to Commn on Dental Res., FDI, 1973–80. President: W of Scotland Br., BDA, 1983–84; British Soc. for Dental Res., 1984–86; British Soc. for Oral Medicine, 1984–86; GDC, 1989–; Convener, Dental Council, RCPGlas, 1977–80. Lectures: Charles Tomes, RCS, 1975; Holme, UCH, London, 1977; Caldwell Meml, Univ. of Glasgow, 1983; Evelyn Sprawson, London Hosp. Med. Coll., 1984. Hon. DDS Wales, 1991; Hon. LLD Dundee, 1993. John Tomes Prize, RCS, 1979; Colyer Medal, RCS, 1992. *Publications:* (jtly) Salivary Glands in Health and Disease, 1975; (jtly) Introduction to Oral Medicine, 1978; (jtly) Self Assessment: Manual I, Oral Surgery, 1978; Manual II, Oral Medicine, 1978; (ed jtly) Oral Manifestations of Systemic Disease, 1980, 2nd edn 1990. *Recreations:* golf, tennis, gardening, enjoying the pleasures of the countryside. *Address:* Greystones, Houston Road, Kilmacolm, Renfrewshire PA13 4NY. *Clubs:* Royal Scottish Automobile (Glasgow); Royal & Ancient Golf, Elie Golf House, Kilmacolm Golf.

MASON, Vice-Adm. Dennis Howard, CB 1967; CVO 1978; *b* 7 Feb. 1916; *s* of Wilfred Howard Mason, Broadwater, Ipswich, and Gladys (Mouse) Mason (*née* Teague), Trevenson, Cornwall; *m* 1940, Patricia D. M. (*née* Hood); three *d. Educ:* Royal Naval Coll., Dartmouth. Served War of 1939–45, Coastal Forces, Frigates and Destroyers; Comdr 1951; Captain 1956; Senior Naval Officer, Northern Ireland, 1961–63; Dir RN Tactical Sch., 1964–65; Rear-Adm. 1965; Chief of Staff to Commander, Far East Fleet, 1965–67; Vice-Adm. 1968, Comdt, Jt Services Staff Coll., 1968–70, retired 1970. ADC 1964. With Paper and Paper Products Industry Training Bd, 1971–72; Warden, St George's House, Windsor Castle, 1972–77. Mem., East Hants DC, 1979–87. *Recreations:* fishing, gardening. *Address:* Church Cottage, East Meon, Hants GU32 1NJ. *T:* East Meon (01730) 823466.

See also Vice-Adm. Hon. Sir N. J. Hill-Norton.

MASON, Frances Jane, (Mrs A. S. Mason); *see* Gumley, F. J.

MASON, Sir Frederick (Cecil), KCVO 1968; CMG 1960; HM Diplomatic Service, retired; *b* 15 May 1913; *s* of late Ernest Mason and Sophia Charlotte Mason (*née* Dodson); *m* 1941, Karen Rørholm; two *s* one *d* (and two *d* decd). *Educ:* City of London Sch.; St Catharine's Coll., Cambridge. Vice-Consul: Antwerp, 1935–36; Paris, 1936–37; Leopoldville, 1937–39; Elisabethville, 1939–40; Consul at Thorshavn during British occupation of Faroes, 1940–42; Consul, Colon, Panama, 1943–45; First Sec., British Embassy, Santiago, Chile, 1946–48; First Sec. (Information), Oslo, 1948–50; Asst Labour Adviser, FO, 1950–53; First Sec. (Commercial), UK Control Commission, Bonn, 1954–55; Counsellor (Commercial), HM Embassy, Athens, 1955–56; Counsellor (Economic), HM Embassy, Tehran, 1957–60; Head of Economic Relations Dept, Foreign Office, 1960–64; Under-Sec., Ministry of Overseas Development, 1965, and CRO, 1966; Ambassador to Chile, 1966–70; Under-Sec. of State, FCO, Oct. 1970–Apr. 1971; Ambassador and Perm. UK Rep. to UN and other Internat. Orgns, Geneva, 1971–73. Dir, New Court Natural Resources, 1973–83. British Mem., Internat. Narcotics Control Bd, Geneva, 1974–77. Chm., Anglo-Chilean Soc., 1978–82. Grand Cross, Chilean Order of Merit, 1968. *Publication:* Ropley Past and Present, 1989. *Recreations:* ball games, walking, painting. *Address:* The Forge, Ropley, Hants SO24 0DS. *T:* Ropley (01962) 772285. *Club:* Canning.

MASON, His Honour (George Frederick) Peter; QC 1963; FCIArb 1986; a Circuit Judge, 1970–87; *b* 11 Dec. 1921; *s* of George Samuel and Florence May Mason, Keighley, Yorks; *m* 1st, 1950 (marr. diss. 1977); two *s* two *d* (and one *d* decd); 2nd, 1981, Sara, *er d* of Sir Robert Ricketts, Bt, *qv. Educ:* Lancaster Royal Grammar Sch.; St Catharine's Coll., Cambridge. Open Exhibnr St Catharine's Coll., 1940. Served with 78th Medium Regt RA (Duke of Lancaster's Own Yeo.) in Middle East and Italy, 1941–45, latterly as Staff Capt. RA, HQ 13 Corps. History Tripos Pt 1, 1st cl. hons with distinction, 1946; called to Bar, Lincoln's Inn, 1947; MA 1948; Cholmeley Schol., 1949. Asst Recorder of Huddersfield, 1961; Dep. Chairman: Agricultural Land Tribunal, W Yorks and Lancs, 1962; West Riding of Yorks Quarter Sessions, 1965–67; Recorder of York, 1965–67; Dep. Chm., Inner London QS, 1970; Dep. Chm., NE London QS, 1970–71; Senior Judge: Snaresbrook Crown Ct, 1974–81; Inner London Crown Court, 1983–87. Member: Council, Assoc. of Futures Brokers and Dealers, 1987–91; London Court of Internat. Arbitration, 1990–; Bd, Securities and Futures Authy, 1991–93; Amer. Arbitration Assoc., 1992–; Bd, Internat. Petroleum Exchange, 1993–. Freeman, City of London, 1977. Liveryman, Wax Chandlers' Co., 1980–. *Recreations:* music, golf, cycling, carpentry. *Address:* 11 King's Bench Walk, Temple, EC4Y 7EQ. *T:* 0171–353 3337/8; Lane Cottage, Amberley, Glos GL5 5AB. *T:* Amberley (01453) 872412. *Clubs:* Athenæum; Hawks.

MASON, Sir Gordon (Charles), Kt 1993; OBE 1982; JP; *b* 8 Nov. 1921; *s* of Joseph Henry Mason and May Louisa Mason; *m* 1944, Tui Audrey King; two *s* one *d. Educ:* Kaipara Flats. In local government, New Zealand, 1960–92: Dep. Chm., 1965–72, Co. Chm., 1972–89; Mayor, Rodney DC, 1989–92. Chm., Local Govt Trng Bd, 1981–89; Pres., NZ Counties Assoc., 1984–87. Past Master: Rodney Masonic Lodge; Rotary; Lions. JP NZ, 1968. *Recreations:* travel, gardening. *Address:* Kaipara Flats RD4, Warkworth, New Zealand. *T:* (9) 4225718. *Clubs:* Bowling (NZ); RSA (Warkworth, NZ).

MASON, James Stephen, CB 1988; Counsel to the Speaker, House of Commons, 1994; *b* 6 Feb. 1935; *s* of Albert Wesley Mason and Mabel (*née* Topham); *m* 1961, Tania Jane Moeran (*see* T. J. Mason); one *s* two *d. Educ:* Windsor County Grammar Sch.; Univ. of Oxford (MA, BCL). Called to the Bar, Middle Temple, 1958; in practice, 1961–67; Office of Parly Counsel, 1967–94: Parly Counsel, 1980–94. *Recreations:* being an indulgent father, reading, walking, playing the piano. *Address:* Cannon Cottage, Well Road, NW3 1LH.

MASON, Jane; *see* Mason, T. J.

MASON, Sir John; *see* Mason, Sir B. J.

MASON, Sir John (Charles Moir), KCMG 1980 (CMG 1976); Chairman: Pirelli Cables Australia Ltd, since 1993 (Director, since 1987); Board of Advice, Spencer Stuart and Associates, Sydney, since 1985; *b* 13 May 1927; *o s* of late Charles Moir Mason, CBE and late Madeline Mason; *m* 1954, Margaret Newton; one *s* one *d. Educ:* Manchester Grammar Sch.; Peterhouse, Cambridge. Lieut, XX Lancs Fusiliers, 1946–48; BA 1950, MA 1955, Cantab; Captain, Royal Ulster Rifles, 1950–51 (Korea); HM Foreign Service, 1952; 3rd Sec., FO, 1952–54; 2nd Sec. and Private Sec. to Ambassador, British Embassy, Rome, 1954–56; 2nd Sec., Warsaw, 1956–59; 1st Sec., FO, 1959–61; 1st Sec. (Commercial), Damascus, 1961–65; 1st Sec. and Asst Head of Dept, FO, 1965–68; Dir of Trade Develt and Dep. Consul-Gen., NY, 1968–71; Head of European Integration Dept, FCO, 1971–72; seconded as Under-Sec., ECGD, 1972–75; Asst Under-Sec. of State (Economic), FCO, 1975–76; Ambassador to Israel, 1976–80; High Commissioner to Australia, 1980–84. Chairman: Thorn-EMI (Australia), 1985–94; Lloyd's Bank (NZA), Sydney, 1985–90; Lloyds International Ltd, 1985–90; Vickers Shipbuilders (Australia), 1985–92; Multicon, 1987–92; Prudential (Australia and NZ), later Prudential Corp. Australia, 1987–92; Prudential Assets Management, 1987–92; Prudential Funds Management, 1987–92; Director: Nat. Bank of NZ, 1984–90; Wellcome (Australia) Ltd, 1985–90; Fluor Daniel (Australia) Ltd, 1985–93; Sen. Internat. Advr, Fluor Corp., USA, 1989–93. Public Mem., Australia Press Council, 1992–; Member: Professional Conduct Cttees, NSW Bar Assoc., 1992–; NSW Law Soc., 1994–. Chairman: North Shore Heart Foundn, Sydney, 1986–92; Bequests Cttee, RACP, 1992–95; Mem., Finance Cttee, State Cancer Council, NSW, 1993–. Nat. Dep. Chm., Churchill Meml Trust, Aust. *Address:* 147 Dover Road, Dover Heights, NSW 2030, Australia; c/o Lloyds Bank, 7 Pall Mall, SW1Y 5NA. *Clubs:* Melbourne (Melbourne); Union (Sydney).

MASON, Prof. John Kenyon French, CBE 1973; Regius Professor of Forensic Medicine, University of Edinburgh, 1973–85, now Emeritus; *b* 19 Dec. 1919; *s* of late Air Cdre J. M. Mason, CBE, DSC, DFC and late Alma French; *m* 1943, Elizabeth Latham (decd); two *s. Educ:* Downside Sch.; Cambridge Univ.; St Bartholomew's Hosp. MD, FRCPath, DMJ, DTM&H; LLD Edinburgh 1987. FRSE 1995. Joined RAF, 1943; Dir of RAF Dept of Aviation and Forensic Pathology, 1956; retd as Group Captain, Consultant in Pathology, 1973. Pres., British Assoc. in Forensic Medicine, 1981–83. L. G. Groves Prize for Aircraft Safety, 1957; R. F. Linton Meml Prize, 1958; James Martin Award for Flight Safety, 1972; Douglas Weightman Safety Award, 1973; Swiney Prize for Jurisprudence, 1978; Lederer Award for Aircraft Safety, 1985. *Publications:* Aviation Accident Pathology, 1962; (ed) Aerospace Pathology, 1973; Forensic Medicine for Lawyers, 1978, 2nd edn 1983; (ed) The Pathology of Violent Injury, 1978, 2nd edn as The Pathology of Trauma, 1993; Law and Medical Ethics, 1983, 4th edn 1994; Butterworth's Medico-Legal Encyclopaedia, 1987; Human Life and Medical Practice, 1989; Medico-legal Aspects of Reproduction, 1990; The Courts and the Doctor, 1990; (ed) Forensic Medicine: an illustrated text, 1993; papers in medical jls. *Address:* 66 Craiglea Drive, Edinburgh EH10 5PF. *Club:* Royal Air Force.

MASON, Sir John (Peter), Kt 1994; CBE 1989; solicitor; Chairman, Scunthorpe and Goole Hospitals NHS Trust, since 1993; Chairman, National Union of Conservative and Unionist Associations, 1992–93 (Vice Chairman, 1989–92); *b* 25 Dec. 1940; *m* Margaret; one *s* two *d. Educ:* Scunthorpe GS. Admitted solicitor, 1961; Sen. Partner, Mason Baggott & Garton, solicitors, Scunthorpe, 1976–. Chm., Scunthorpe HA, 1981–93. Conservative Party: Chm., E Midlands Area, 1985–89; Dep. Chm., Bd of Finance; Mem., Nat. Union Exec. Cttee, 1977– (Chm., European Cttee, 1989–92). *Address:* Mason, Baggott & Garton, 13/19 Wells Street, Scunthorpe, S Humberside DN15 6HN.

MASON, Rt. Rev. Kenneth Bruce, AM 1984; retired; Chairman, Australian Board of Missions, General Synod of the Anglican Church of Australia, 1983–93; *b* 4 Sept. 1928; *s* of Eric Leslie Mason and Gertrude Irene (*née* Pearce); unmarried. *Educ:* Bathurst High Sch.; Sydney Teachers' Coll.; St John's Theological Coll., Morpeth; Univ. of Queensland. Deacon, 1953; Priest, 1954. Primary Teacher, 1948–51; St John's Theological Coll., Morpeth, 1952–53 (ThL); Member, Brotherhood of the Good Shepherd, 1954; Parish of: Gilgandra, NSW, 1954–58; Darwin, NT, 1959–61; Alice Springs, NT, 1962; University of Queensland, 1963–64 (BA, Dip Div); resigned from Brotherhood, 1965; Trinity Coll., Melbourne Univ.: Asst Chaplain, 1965; Dean, 1966–67; Bishop of the Northern Territory, 1968–83. Member, Oratory of the Good Shepherd, 1962, Superior, 1981–87. *Recreations:* attending opera, listening to music, walking, railways. *Address:* PO Box 544, Glebe, NSW 2037, Australia.

MASON, Rev. Canon Kenneth Staveley; Canon Theologian, Scottish Episcopal Church, since 1995; Canon of St Mary's Cathedral, Edinburgh, since 1989; *b* 1 Nov. 1931; *s* of Rev. William Peter Mason and Anna Hester (*née* Pildrem); *m* 1958, Barbara Thomson; one *s* one *d. Educ:* Imperial College of Science, London (BSc, ARCS); BD (ext.) London; Wells Theological Coll. Assistant Curate: St Martin, Kingston upon Hull, 1958; Pocklington, 1961; Vicar of Thornton with Allerthorpe and Melbourne, 1963; Sub-Warden and Librarian, KCL, at St Augustine's Coll., Canterbury, 1969; Dir, Canterbury Sch. of Ministry, 1977, Principal, 1981. Examining Chaplain to Archbp of Canterbury, 1979–91; Six Preacher in Canterbury Cath., 1979–84; Hon. Canon of Canterbury, 1984–89; Principal, Edinburgh Theol Coll., later Dir, Theol Inst., Scottish Episcopal Church, 1989–95. *Publications:* George Herbert, Priest and Poet, 1980; Anglicanism, a Canterbury essay, 1987; Priesthood and Society, 1992; Catholic Tradition and the Ordination of Women, 1993. *Recreation:* bird-watching. *Address:* 9c Rosebery Crescent, Edinburgh EH12 5JP. *T:* 0131–337 0500.

MASON, Monica; Principal Répétiteur, since 1984, Assistant Director, since 1989, Royal Ballet; *b* 6 Sept. 1941; *d* of Richard Mason and Mrs E. Fabian; *m* 1968, Austin Bennett. *Educ:* Johannesburg, SA; Royal Ballet Sch., London. Joined Royal Ballet in Corps de Ballet, 1958; Sen. Principal until 1989; created role of Chosen Maiden in Rite of Spring, 1962; also created roles in: Diversions, Elite Syncopations, Electra, Manon, Romeo and Juliet, Rituals, Adieu, Isadora, The Four Seasons, The Ropes of Time. Assistant to the Principal Choreographer, Royal Ballet, 1980–84. *Address:* Royal Opera House, Covent Garden, WC2E 9DD.

MASON, Dr Pamela Georgina Walsh, FRCPsych; Vice-Chairman, Taunton and Somerset NHS Trust, since 1991; Senior Principal Medical Officer (Under Secretary), Department of Health and Social Security, 1979–86, retired; re-employed as Senior Medical Officer, Department of Health, 1986–90; *d* of late Captain George Mason and Marie Louise Walsh; god-daughter and ward of late Captain William Gregory, Hon. Co. of Master Mariners; *m* 1st, 1949, David Paltenghi (*d* 1961); two *s*; 2nd, 1965, Jan Darnley-Smith. *Educ:* Christ's Hosp. Sch.; Univ. of London, Royal Free Hosp. Sch. of Medicine (MRCS, LRCP, 1949; MB, BS 1950). DPM 1957; MRCPsych 1971. Various appointments at: Royal Free Hosp., 1951–53; Maudsley Hosp. and Bethlem Royal Hosp., 1954–58; Guy's Hosp., 1958–60; Home Office, 1961–71; DHSS, later DoH, 1971–90. Vis. Psychiatrist, Holloway Prison, 1962–67; Adviser: C of E Children's Soc., 1962–; Royal Philanthropic Soc., 1962–; WRAF Health Educn Scheme, 1962–67. Chairman: WHO Working Gp on Youth Advisory Services, 1976; WHO Meeting of Nat. Mental Health Advrs, 1979. Member: Council of Europe Select Cttee of Experts on Alcoholism, 1976–77; Cttee of Experts on Legal Problems in the Medical Field, 1979–80. FRSocMed. QHP 1984–87. *Publications:* contribs to various professional jls and Govt pubns. *Recreations:* antiquities, humanities, ballet, films, tennis, seafaring and expeditions. *Address:* Blindwell House, Nether Stowey, Bridgwater, Som TA5 1LT. *T:* Nether Stowey (01278) 732707.

MASON, Dr Paul James, FRS 1995; Chief Scientist and Director, Research and Development, Meteorological Office, since 1991; *b* 16 March 1946; *s* of Charles Ernest Edward Mason and Phyllis Mary Mason (*née* Swan); *m* 1968, Elizabeth Mary Slaney; one *s* one *d*. *Educ:* Univ. of Nottingham (BSc Physics 1967); Univ. of Reading (PhD Geophysics 1972). Meteorological Office: SO, 1967–71; SSO, 1971–74; PSO, 1974–79; Head, Meteorological Res. Unit, Cardington, 1979–85; Asst Dir, Boundary Layer Br., 1985–89; Dep. Dir, Physical Res., 1989–91. Member: Editing Cttee, Qly Jl Meteorology, 1983–88; Editl Bd, Boundary Layer Meteorology, 1988–. Royal Meteorological Society: Mem. Council, 1989–90; Vice Pres., 1990–92 and 1994–95; Pres., 1992–94. L. G. Groves Prize for Meteorology, MoD, 1980; Buchan Prize, RMetS, 1986. *Publications:* scientific papers in meteorology and fluid dynamics jls. *Recreations:* walking, exploring the countryside. *Address:* Meteorological Office, Room 321a, London Road, Bracknell, Berks RG12 2SZ. *T:* Bracknell (01344) 854604.

MASON, Peter; *see* Mason, G. F. P.

MASON, Peter Geoffrey, MBE 1946; High Master, Manchester Grammar School, 1962–78; *b* 22 Feb. 1914; *o s* of Harry Mason, Handsworth, Birmingham; *m* 1st, 1939, Mary Evelyn Davison (marr. diss.); three *d*; 2nd, 1978, Elizabeth June Bissell (*d* 1983); 3rd, 1985, Marjorie Payne. *Educ:* King Edward's Sch., Birmingham; Christ's Coll., Cambridge (Scholar). Goldsmith Exhibitioner, 1935; Porson Scholar, 1936; 1st Class, Classical Tripos, Pts 1 and 2, 1935, 1936. Sixth Form Classical Master, Cheltenham Coll., 1936–40, Rugby Sch., 1946–49; Headmaster, Aldenham Sch., 1949–61. War Service, 1940–46: commissioned into Intelligence Corps, 1940; various staff appointments including HQ 21 Army Group; later attached to a dept of the Foreign Office. Member: Advisory Cttee on Education in the Colonies, 1956; ITA Educnl Adv. Council, 1964–69; Council, University of Salford, 1969–87; Council, British Volunteer Programme (Chm., 1966–74); Chairman: Council of Educn for World Citizenship, 1966–83; Reg. Conf. on IVS, 1972–82; (first), Eur. Council of Nat. Assocs of Indep. Schs, 1988–94, Hon. Life Pres., 1994; Hon. Dir of Research, ISIS, 1981–. *Publications:* Private Education in the EEC, 1983; Private Education in the USA and Canada, 1985; Private Education in Australia and New Zealand, 1987; Independent Education in Southern Africa, 1990; Independent Education in Western Europe, 1992; articles and reviews in classical and educational journals. *Recreations:* travel, fly-fishing, walking. *Address:* Leeward, Longborough, Moreton-in-Marsh, Glos GL56 0QR. *T:* and *Fax:* Cotswold (01451) 830147. *Club:* Athenæum.

MASON, Rt. Rev. Peter Ralph; *see* Ontario, Bishop of.

MASON, Philip, CIE 1946; OBE 1942; writer; *b* 19 March 1906; *s* of Dr H. A. Mason, Duffield, Derbs; *m* 1935, Eileen Mary, *d* of Courtenay Hayes, Charmouth, Dorset; two *s* two *d*. *Educ:* Sedbergh; Balliol. 1st Cl. Hons Philosophy, Politics and Economics, Oxford, 1927; MA 1952; DLitt 1972. ICS: Asst Magistrate United Provinces, 1928–33; Under-Sec., Government of India, War Dept, 1933–36; Dep. Commissioner Garhwal, 1936–39; Dep. Sec. Govt of India, Defence Co-ordination and War Depts, 1939–42; Sec. Chiefs of Staff Cttee, India, and Head of Conf. Secretariat, SE Asia Command, 1942–44; represented War Dept in Central Assembly, 1946; Joint Sec. to Government of India, War Dept, 1944–47; Tutor and Governor to the Princes, Hyderabad, 1947; retd from ICS, 1947. Mem. Commn of Enquiry to examine problems of Minorities in Nigeria, 1957. Dir of Studies in Race Relations, Chatham House, 1952–58; Dir, Inst. of Race Relations, 1958–69. Chairman: National Cttee for Commonwealth Immigrants, 1964–65; Exec. Cttee, UK Council for Overseas Student Affairs, 1969–75; Trustees, S African Church Devlt Trust, 1976–83 (Pres., 1983–88). Hon. Fellow, Sch. of Oriental and African Studies, 1970; Hon. DSc Bristol, 1971. Received into Catholic Church, 1978. *Publications:* (as Philip Woodruff): Call the Next Witness, 1945; The Wild Sweet Witch, 1947; Whatever Dies, 1948; The Sword of Northumbria, 1948; The Island of Chamba, 1950; Hernshaw Castle, 1950; Colonel of Dragoons, 1951; The Founders, 1953; The Guardians, 1954; (as Philip Mason): Racial Tension, 1954; Christianity and Race, 1956; The Birth of a Dilemma, 1958; Year of Decision, 1960; (ed) Man, Race and Darwin, 1960; Common Sense about Race, 1961; Prospero's Magic, 1962; (ed) India and Ceylon: Unity and Diversity, 1967; Patterns of Dominance, 1970; Race Relations, 1970; How People Differ, 1971; A Matter of Honour, 1974; Kipling: The Glass The Shadow and The Fire, 1975; The Dove in Harness, 1976; A Shaft of Sunlight, 1978; Skinner of Skinner's Horse, 1979; The English Gentleman, 1982; A Thread of Silk, 1984; The Men who Ruled India (abridged from The Founders, and The Guardians), 1985. *Recreation:* living. *Address:* 97 Glebe Road, Cambridge CB1 4TE. *T:* Cambridge (01223) 213569.

MASON, Rachel Anne, (Mrs A. L. Mason); *see* Squire, R. A.

MASON, Richard; author; *b* 16 May 1919. *Educ:* Bryanston School. *Publications: novels:* The Wind Cannot Read, 1947; The Shadow and the Peak, 1949; The World of Suzie Wong, 1957; The Fever Tree, 1962. *Address:* c/o A. M. Heath & Co. Ltd, 79 St Martin's Lane, WC2N 4AA.

MASON, Air Vice-Marshal Richard Anthony, CB 1988; CBE 1981; Leverhulme Airpower Research Director, Foundation for International Security, since 1989; *b* 22 Oct. 1932; *s* of William and Maud Mason; *m* 1956, Margaret Stewart; one *d*. *Educ:* Bradford Grammar Sch.; St Andrews Univ. (MA); London Univ. (MA). Commissioned RAF, 1956; Director of Defence Studies, 1977; Director of Personnel (Ground), 1982; Deputy Air Secretary, 1984; Air Sec., 1985–89. Hon. Sen. Res. Fellow, Univ. of Birmingham, 1989–. *Publications:* Air Power in the Next Generation (ed), 1978; Readings in Air Power, 1979; (with M. J. Armitage) Air Power in the Nuclear Age, 1981; The RAF Today and Tomorrow, 1982; British Air Power in the 1980s, 1984; The Soviet Air Forces, 1986; War in the Third Dimension, 1986; Air Power and Technology, 1986; To Inherit the Skies, 1990; Air Power: a centennial appraisal, 1994; articles in internat. jls on defence policy and strategy. *Recreations:* Rugby, writing, gardening. *Address:* c/o Lloyds Bank, Montpelier Walk, Cheltenham GL50 1SH. *Club:* Royal Air Force.

MASON, Rev. Canon Richard John; Archdeacon of Tonbridge, 1977–95; Minister of St Luke's, Sevenoaks, 1983–95; *b* 26 April 1929; *s* of Vice-Adm. Sir Frank Mason, KCB and late Dora Margaret Mason. *Educ:* Shrewsbury School. Newspaper journalist, 1949–55; Lincoln Theological College, 1955–58; Asst Curate, Bishop's Hatfield, Herts, 1958–64; Domestic Chaplain to Bishop of London, 1964–69; Vicar of Riverhead with Dunton Green, Kent, 1969–73; Vicar of Edenbridge, 1973–83, also Priest in Charge of Crockham Hill, 1981–83. Canon Emeritus, Rochester Cathedral, 1995. *Address:* 61 Nelson Road, Ipswich, Suffolk IP4 4DU. *T:* Ipswich (01473) 726350.

MASON, Prof. Sir Ronald, KCB 1980; FRS 1975; Professor of Chemistry, University of Sussex, 1971–88 (Pro-Vice-Chancellor, 1977); Chairman: British Ceramic Research Ltd, since 1990; University College Hospitals NHS Trust, since 1993; *b* 22 July 1930; *o s* of David John Mason and Olwen Mason (*née* James); *m* 1952, E. Pauline Pattinson; three *d*; *m* 1979, Elizabeth Rosemary Grey-Edwards. *Educ:* Univs of Wales and London (Fellow, University College Cardiff, 1981). Research Assoc., British Empire Cancer Campaign, 1953–61; Lectr, Imperial Coll., 1961–63; Prof. of Inorganic Chemistry, Univ. of Sheffield, 1963–71; Chief Scientific Advr, MoD, 1977–83. Vis. Prof., Univs in Australia, Canada, France, Israel, NZ and US, inc. A. D. Little Prof., MIT, 1970; Univ. of California, Berkeley, 1975; Ohio State Univ., 1976; North Western Univ., 1977; Prof. associé, Univ. de Strasbourg, 1976; Erskine Vis. Prof., Christchurch, NZ, 1977; Prof., Texas, 1982; Vis. Prof. of Internat. Relns, UCW, 1985–. Schmidt Meml Lectr, Israel, 1977. SRC: Mem., 1971–75; Chm. Chemistry Cttee, 1969–72; Chm. Science Bd, 1972–75; Consultant and Council Mem., RUSI, 1984–88; UK Mem., UN Commn of Disarmament Studies, 1984–92; Chairman: Council for Arms Control, 1986–90; Engrg Technol. Cttee, DTI, 1991–93. Pres., BHRA, 1986–94 (Chm., BHR Gp, 1990–); Member: ABRC, 1977–83; BBC Adv. Group, 1975–79. Chairman: Hunting Engineering Ltd, 1987 (Dep. Chm., 1985–87); Science Applications Internat. Corp. (UK) Ltd, 1993–. Hon. DSc: Wales, 1986; Keele, 1992. Corday-Morgan Medallist, 1965, and Tilden Lectr, 1970, Chemical Society; Medal and Prize for Structural Chem., Chem. Soc., 1973. *Publications:* (ed) Advances in Radiation Biology, 1964 (3rd edn 1969); (ed) Advances in Structure Analysis by Diffraction Methods, 1968 (6th edn 1978); (ed) Physical Processes in Radiation Biology, 1964; many papers in Jl Chem. Soc., Proc. Royal Soc., etc, and on defence issues. *Address:* Chestnuts Farm, Weedon, Bucks HP22 4NH.

MASON, Prof. Stephen Finney, FRS 1982; FRSC; Emeritus Professor of Chemistry, University of London; *b* 6 July 1923; *s* of Leonard Stephen Mason and Christine Harriet Mason; *m* 1955, Joan Banus; three *s*. *Educ:* Wyggeston Sch., Leicester; Wadham Coll., Oxford. MA, DPhil, DSc. Demonstrator, Mus. of Hist. of Sci., Oxford Univ., 1947–53; Research Fellow in Med. Chemistry, ANU, 1953–56; Reader in Chemical Spectroscopy, Univ. of Exeter, 1956–64; Professor of Chemistry: Univ. of East Anglia, 1964–70; KCL, 1970–87. Fellow, Wolfson Coll., Cambridge, 1988–90. *Publications:* A History of the Sciences: main currents of scientific thought, 1953; Molecular Optical Activity and the Chiral Discriminations, 1982; Chemical Evolution: origin of the elements, molecules and living systems, 1991; articles in Jl Chem. Soc., 1945–. *Recreations:* history and philosophy of science. *Address:* Department of Chemistry, King's College, Strand, WC2R 2LS. *T:* 011–836 5454; 12 Hills Avenue, Cambridge CB1 4XA. *T:* Cambridge (01223) 247827.

MASON, (Tania) Jane; Regional Chairman of Industrial Tribunals, London South Region, since 1992; *b* 25 Sept. 1936; *d* of Edward Warner Moeran, *qv* and Pymonie (*née* Fincham); *m* 1961, James Stephen Mason, *qv*; one *s* two *d*. *Educ:* Frensham Heights Sch. Called to the Bar, Inner Temple, 1961. Law Reporter, Judicial Cttee of Privy Council, 1976–83; Asst Legal Advr, British Council, 1983–86; full-time Chm. of Industrial Tribunals, 1986–92. *Recreations:* country life, English novels, culinary arts. *Address:* Cannon Cottage, Well Road, Hampstead, NW3 1LH. *T:* 0171–435 2917. *Club:* Reform.

MASON, Timothy Ian Godson; Director, Museums and Galleries Commission, since 1995; *b* 11 March 1945; *s* of Ian Godson Mason and Muriel (*née* Vaile); *m* 1975, Marilyn Ailsa Williams; one *d* one *s*. *Educ:* St Alban's Sch., Washington, DC; Bradfield Coll., Berkshire; Christ Church, Oxford (MA). Assistant Manager, Oxford Playhouse, 1966–67; Assistant to Peter Daubeny, World Theatre Season, London, 1967–69; Administrator: Ballet Rambert, 1970–75; Royal Exchange Theatre, Manchester, 1975–77; Director: Western Australian Arts Council, 1977–80; Scottish Arts Council, 1980–90; Consultant on implementation of changes in structure of arts funding, Arts Council of GB, 1990–91; Chief Exec., London Arts Bd, 1991–95. Mem., Gen. Adv. Council, BBC, 1990–. *Recreations:* family, travelling, the arts. *Address:* 30 Chatsworth Way, SE27 9HN; Museums and Galleries Commission, 16 Queen Anne's Gate, SW1H 9AA. *T:* 0171–233 4200.

MASON, William Ernest, CB 1983; Deputy Secretary (Fisheries and Food), Ministry of Agriculture, Fisheries and Food, 1982–89, retired; Director, Allied-Domecq (formerly Allied-Lyons) PLC, since 1989; consultant on food and drink industry; *b* 12 Jan. 1929; *s* of Ernest George and Agnes Margaret Mason; *m* 1959, Jean (*née* Bossley); one *s* one *d*. *Educ:* Brockley Grammar Sch.; London Sch. of Economics (BScEcon). RAF, 1947–49; Min. of Food, 1949–54; MAFF, 1954; Principal 1963; Asst Sec. 1970; Under Sec., 1975; Fisheries Sec., 1980. Member: Econ. Devlt Cttee for Distrib. Trades, 1975–80; Econ. Devlt Cttee for Food and Drink Manufg Inds, 1976–80. FRSA 1989; FIGD 1989; Hon. FIFST 1989. Hon. Keeper of the Quaiche, 1989–. *Recreations:* music, reading, modern British painting. *Address:* 82 Beckenham Place Park, Beckenham, Kent BR3 2BT. *T:* 0181–650 8241. *Club:* Reform.

MASRI, Taher Nashat; Order of the Renaissance (Jewelled), Jordan, 1991; Order of Al-Kawkab, Jordan, 1974; Hon. GBE; MP Jordan, since 1989; *b* 5 March 1942; *s* of Nashat Masri and Hadiyah Solh; *m* 1968, Samar Bitar; one *s* one *d*. *Educ:* North Texas State Univ. (BBA 1965). Central Bank of Jordan, 1965–73; MP Nablus Dist, 1973–75 and 1984–88; Minister of State for Occupied Territories Affairs, 1973–74; Ambassador to: Spain, 1975–78; France, 1978–83; Belgium (non-resident), 1978–80; Britain, 1983–84; Perm. Delegate to UNESCO, 1978–83; Foreign Minister, 1984–89 and 1991; Dep. Prime Minister and Minister of State for Economic Affairs, April–Aug. 1989; Chm., Foreign Relations Cttee, 1989–91; Prime Minister of Jordan and Minister of Defence, June–Nov. 1991; Speaker of Lower House of Parlt, 1993–94. Rapporteur, Royal Commn for Drafting of Nat. Charter, 1989. Grand Cross, Order of Civil Merit, Spain, 1977; Order of Isabel the Catholic, Spain, 1978; Commander, Legion of Honour, France, 1981. *Address:* PO Box 5550, Amman, Jordan. *T:* (6) 810600, (office) 642227, *Fax:* (6) 642226.

MASSE, Hon. Marcel; MP (Progressive C) Frontenac, Québec, since 1984; *b* 27 May 1936; *s* of Rosaire Masse and Angeline Masse (*née* Clermont); *m* 1960, Cécile, *d* of René and Clementine Martin; one *s* one *d*. *Educ:* Ecole Normale Jacques-Cartier, Montréal; Univ. de Montréal; Inst. of Pol Sci., Paris; Sorbonne, Paris; City of London Coll.; Inst. Européen d'Admin. des Affaires, Fontainebleau. History teacher, Joliette, Québec, 1962–66; Mem., Québec Nat. Assembly, 1966–73 (Minister, 1966–70); Dir, Lavalin Inc., Montréal, 1974–84; Minister of Communications, Canada, 1984–86, 1989–91; Minister of Energy, Mines and Resources, 1986–89; Minister of National Defence, 1991–93.

Recreations: reading, music, fishing, ski-ing. *Address:* House of Commons, Ottawa, Ontario K1A 0E4, Canada. *Clubs:* Rideau (Ottawa); Albany.

MASSEREENE, 14th Viscount *cr* 1660, **AND FERRARD,** 7th Viscount *cr* 1797; **John David Clotworthy Whyte-Melville Foster Skeffington;** Baron Loughneugh (Ire.), 1660; Baron Oriel (Ire.), 1790; Baron Oriel (UK), 1821; stockbroker with Dunbar Boyle & Kingsley; *b* 3 June 1940; *s* of 13th Viscount and Annabelle Kathleen, *er d* of H. D. Lewis; *S* father, 1992; *m* 1970, Ann Denise, *er d* of late Norman Rowlandson; two *s* one *d*. *Educ:* St Peter's Court, Millfield; Institute Monte Rosa. Grenadier Guards, 1958–61. Stock Exchange, 1961–64; motor trade, 1964–70; Stock Exchange, 1970–; various dirships; landowner. *Recreations:* vintage cars, stalking, shooting. *Heir: s* Hon. Charles John Clotworthy Whyte-Melville Foster Skeffington, *b* 7 Feb. 1973. *Address:* Chilham Castle, near Canterbury, Kent CT4 8DB. *Clubs:* Turf, Pratt's.

MASSEVITCH, Prof. Alla Genrikhovna; Chief Scientist of the Astronomical Institute of the Russian Academy of Sciences, since 1988 (Vice-President, 1952–88); Professor of Astrophysics, Moscow University, since 1946; *b* Tbilisi, Georgia, USSR, 9 Oct. 1918; *d* of Genrick Massevitch and Natalie Zhgenti; *m* 1942, Joseph Friedlander; one *d*. *Educ:* Moscow Univ. Lectured at the Royal Festival Hall, London, and at the Free Trade Hall, Manchester, etc., on The Conquest of Space, 1960; she is in charge of network of stations for tracking Sputniks, in Russia. Pres. Working Group 1 (Tracking and Telemetring) of COSPAR (Internat. Cttee for Space Research) 1961–66. Pres., Commission 35 (Internal Structure of Stars) of the Internat. Astronom. Union, 1967–70; Dep. Sec. Gen., UNISPACE 82 (UN Conf. on Exploration and Peaceful Uses of Outer Space), Vienna, 1981–83. Chm., Space Science Studies Cttee, Internat. Acad. of Astronautics, 1983–86; Associate Editor, Astrophysics and Space Science, 1987–94; Mem. Editorial Bd, Astrophysics (Russian), 1985–. Foreign Member: Royal Astronomical Soc., 1963; Indian Nat. Acad. of Sciences, 1979; Austrian Acad. Scis, 1985; Internat. Acad. Astronautics, 1964. Vice-President: Inst. for Soviet-American Relations, 1967; USSR Peace Cttee, 1977–92 (Mem. Bd, 1965–92); Mem. Bd, Internat. Peace Cttee, 1965–92. Internat. Award for Astronautics (Prix Galabert), 1963; Govtl decorations, USSR, Sign of Honour, 1963, Red Banner, 1975; USSR State Prize, 1975. Hon. Scientist Emeritus, 1978. *Publications:* Use of Satellite Tracking Data for Geodesy (monograph), 1980; Physics and Evolution of Stars (monograph), 1989; 142 scientific papers on the internal structure of the stars, stellar evolution, and optical tracking of artificial satellites, in Russian and foreign astronomical and geophysical journals. *Address:* 48 Pjatnitskaja Street, Moscow 109017, Russia. *T:* 2313980; Khmeleva Street 6, Apt 4, Moscow 103045. *Club:* Club for Scientists (Moscow).

MASSEY, Anna (Raymond); actress; *b* 11 Aug. 1937; *d* of late Raymond Massey and Adrianne Allen; *m* 1st, 1958, Jeremy Huggins (marr. diss., 1963); one *s*; 2nd, 1988, Uri Andres. *Educ:* London; New York; Switzerland; Paris; Rome. *Plays:* The Reluctant Debutante, 1955; Dear Delinquent, 1957; The Elder Statesman, 1958; Double Yolk, 1959; The Last Joke, 1960; The Miracle Worker, 1961; The School for Scandal, 1962; The Doctor's Dilemma, 1963; The Right Honourable Gentleman, 1964; The Glass Menagerie, 1965; The Prime of Miss Jean Brodie, 1966; The Flip Side, 1967; First Day of a New Season, 1967; This Space is Mine, 1969; Hamlet, 1970; Spoiled, 1971; Slag, 1971; Jingo, 1975; Play, 1976; The Seagull, 1981; Broadway Bound, 1991; A Hard Heart, 1992; Grace, 1992; Moonlight, 1993; *at National Theatre:* Heartbreak House, 1975; Close of Play, 1979; Summer; The Importance of Being Earnest; A Kind of Alaska, and Family Voices, in Harold Pinter trio Other Places, 1982; King Lear, 1986. *Films:* Gideon's Day, 1957; Peeping Tom, 1960; Bunny Lake is Missing, 1965; The Looking Glass War, 1969; David Copperfield, 1969; De Sade, 1971; Frenzy, 1972; A Doll's House, 1973; Sweet William, 1979; The Corn is Green, 1979; Five Days One Summer, 1982; Another Country, 1984; The Chain, 1985; Le Couleur du Vent, 1988; The Tall Guy, 1989; Haunted, 1995; The Grotesque, 1995. *Films for television:* Journey into the Shadows, Sakharov, 1984; Sacred Hearts, 1985; Hotel du Lac, 1986; The Christmas Tree, 1987; Sunchild, 1988, A Tale of Two Cities, 1989; Man From the Pru, 1990; numerous appearances in TV plays, including Shalom, Joan Collins, 1990. *Address:* c/o Markham and Froggatt Ltd, 4 Windmill Street, W1P 1HF.

See also D. R. Massey.

MASSEY, Daniel (Raymond); actor; *b* London, 10 Oct. 1933; *s* of late Raymond Massey and Adrianne Allen; *m* 1st, Adrienne Corri (marr. diss.); 2nd, Penelope Alice Wilton (marr. diss.); one *d*. *Educ:* Eton; King's Coll., Cambridge. Connaught Theatre, Worthing, 1956–57. *Plays:* The Happiest Millionaire, Cambridge, 1957; Living for Pleasure, Garrick, 1958; Make Me an Offer (musical), New, 1959; The School for Scandal, Haymarket, 1962; The Three Musketeers, and A Subject of Scandal and Concern, Nottingham, 1962; She Loves Me (musical), NY, 1963; Julius Caesar, Royal Court, 1964; A Month in the Country, and Samson Agonistes, Guildford, 1965; Barefoot in the Park, Piccadilly, 1965; The Rivals, Haymarket, 1966; The Importance of Being Earnest, Haymarket, 1967; Spoiled, Glasgow, 1970; Abelard and Heloise, Wyndham's, 1970; Three Sisters, and Trelawny of The Wells, 1971; Becket, Guildford, 1972; Popkiss, Globe, 1972; Gigi, NY, 1973; Bloomsbury, Phoenix, 1974; The Gay Lord Quex, Albery, 1975; Othello, Nottingham, 1976; Rosmersholm, Haymarket, 1977; Don Juan comes back from the War, Betrayal, Nat. Theatre, 1978; The Philanderer, Nat. Theatre, 1979; Appearances, May Fair, 1980; Man and Superman, The Mayor of Zalamea, The Hypochondriac, Nat. Theatre, 1981; The Time of Your Life, Twelfth Night, Measure for Measure, RSC, 1983; Breaking the Silence, Waste, RSC, 1984; Follies, Shaftesbury, 1987; The Doll's House, Haymarket, Leicester, 1989; Heartbreak House, Haymarket, 1992; Love's Labour's Lost, RSC, 1993; The Devil's Disciple, NT, 1994; Taking Sides, Minerva, Chichester, transf. Criterion, 1995. *Films:* include: Girls at Sea, 1957; Upstairs and Downstairs; The Entertainer; The Queen's Guard, 1960; Go to Blazes, 1962; Moll Flanders, 1966; Star, 1968 (Best Supporting Actor, Hollywood Golden Globe Award, 1968); The Incredible Sarah, 1977; The Cat and the Canary, 1978; Escape to Victory, 1981; Stalin, 1992. *TV: serials:* Roads to Freedom, 1970; The Golden Bowl, 1972; Good Behaviour, 1982; Intimate Contact, 1987; GBH, 1991; numerous plays. Best Supporting Actor, Hollywood Golden Globe Award, 1968; Actor of the Year, SWET Award, 1981. *Recreations:* golf, classical music, reading. *Address:* c/o Julian Belfrage Associates, 68 St James's Street, SW1A 1PH.

MASSEY, Doreen Elizabeth; independent consultant in health education, sex education and sexual health; Director, Family Planning Association, 1989–94; *b* 5 Sept. 1938; *d* of Mary Ann Hall (*née* Sharrock) and Jack Hall; *m* 1966, Dr Leslie Massey; two *s* one *d*. *Educ:* Darwen Grammar Sch., Lancs; Birmingham Univ. (BA Hons French 1961); DipEd 1962; Inst. of Educn, London Univ. (MA 1985). Graduate service overseas, Gabon, 1962–63; teacher: S Hackney Sch., 1964–67; Springside Sch., Philadelphia, 1967–69; Pre-School Play Group Association, 1973–77; teacher, Walsingham Sch., London, 1977–83 (co-ordinator Health Educn, Head of Year, senior teacher); advisory teacher for personal, social and health educn, ILEA, 1983–85; Manager, Young People's Programme, Health Educn Council, 1985–87; Dir of Educn, FPA, 1987–89. Member: Nat. Council of Women; Bd, Women's Nationwide Cancer Control Campaign, 1991–; Pre-School Playgroup Assoc.; Nat. Trust; English Heritage; school governor. FRSA 1992. *Publications:* Sex Education: Why, What and How?, 1988; Sex Education Factpack, 1988; (jtly) Sex Education Training Manual, 1991; (ed) Sex Education Resource Book, 1994; articles on sex educn, family planning, health educn. *Recreations:* reading, cinema, theatre, opera, art and design, yoga, Chi-Gong, vegetarian cookery, travel. *Address:* 9 Kyrle Road, SW11 6BD. *T:* 0171–207 3723.

MASSEY, (Robert) Graham; independent television producer/consultant, since 1995; *b* 28 Sept. 1943; *s* of Robert Albert Massey and Violet Edith Massey (*née* Smith); *m* 1965, Allison Ruth Duerden; one *s* one *d*. *Educ:* Manchester Grammar Sch.; Balliol Coll., Oxford (BA 1st Cl. Hons History). Joined BBC 1965 as general trainee; Producer, Science and Features Dept, 1970; Producer, 1972; Editor, 1981–85, Horizon; Series Producer, Making of Mankind (with Richard Leakey), 1979–81; Head, Special Features Unit, BBC Drama, 1985–89; Head, Science and Features Dept, BBC, 1989–91; Dir, Co-productions, 1991–92, Dir, Internat., 1992–94, BBC Enterprises. *Recreations:* theatre, cinema, cooking. *Address:* 2 Gregory Place, Holland Street, W8 4NG.

MASSEY, Roy Cyril; Organist and Master of the Choristers, Hereford Cathedral, since 1974; *b* 9 May 1934; *s* of late Cyril Charles Massey and Beatrice May Massey; *m* 1975, Ruth Carol Craddock Grove. *Educ:* Univ. of Birmingham (BMus); privately with David Willcocks. FRCO (CHM); ADCM; ARCM; FRSCM (for distinguished services to church music) 1972. Organist: St Alban's, Conybere Street, Birmingham, 1953–60; St Augustine's, Edgbaston, 1960–65; Croydon Parish Church, 1965–68; Warden, RSCM, 1965–68; Conductor, Croydon Bach Soc., 1966–68; Special Comr of RSCM, 1964–; Organist to City of Birmingham Choir, 1954–; Organist and Master of Choristers, Birmingham Cath., 1968–74; Dir of Music, King Edward's Sch., Birmingham, 1968–74. Conductor, Hereford Choral Soc., 1974–; Conductor-in-Chief, alternate years Associate Conductor, Three Choirs Festival, 1975–; Advisor on organs to dioceses of Birmingham and Hereford, 1974–. Mem. Council and Examiner, RCO, 1970–94; Mem., Adv. Council, 1976–78, Council, 1984–, RSCM. President: Birmingham Organists' Assoc., 1970–75; Cathedral Organists' Assoc., 1982–84; IAO, 1991–93. Fellow, St Michael's Coll., Tenbury, 1976–85. DMus Lambeth, 1990. *Recreations:* motoring, old buildings, climbing the Malvern Hills. *Address:* 1 College Cloisters, Cathedral Close, Hereford HR1 2NG. *T:* Hereford (01432) 272011. *Club:* Conservative (Hereford).

MASSEY, Prof. Vincent, PhD; FRS 1977; J. Lawrence Oncley Distinguished University Professor of Biological Chemistry, Unversity of Michigan, since 1995; *b* 28 Nov. 1926; *s* of Walter Massey and Mary Ann Massey; *m* 1950, Margot Eva Ruth Grünewald; one *s* two *d*. *Educ:* Univ. of Sydney (BSc Hons 1947); Univ. of Cambridge (PhD 1952). Scientific Officer, CSIRO, Australia, 1947–50; Ian McMaster Scholar, Cambridge, 1950–53, ICI Fellow, 1953–55; Researcher, Henry Ford Hosp., Detroit, 1955–57; Lectr, then Sen. Lectr, Univ. of Sheffield, 1957–63; Prof. of Biol Chemistry, Univ. of Michigan, 1963–95. Visiting Professor: Univ. of Ill, 1960; Univ. of Konstanz, Germany, 1973–74 (Permanent Guest Prof., 1975–); Inst. of Applied Biochem., Mitake, Japan, 1985; Guest Prof., Yokohama City Univ., Japan, 1988. Mem., NAS, USA, 1995–. Hon. DSc Tokushima Univ. Med. Sch., 1994. *Publications:* Flavins and Flavoproteins (ed jtly), 1982; over 400 articles in scholarly jls and books. *Recreations:* walking, sailing, gardening. *Address:* Department of Biological Chemistry, University of Michigan, Ann Arbor, MI 48109, USA. *T:* (313) 7647196, *Fax:* (313) 7634581.

MASSIE, Allan Johnstone, FRSL 1982; author and journalist; *b* 19 Oct. 1938; *s* of Alexander Johnstone Massie and Evelyn Jane Wilson Massie (*née* Forbes); *m* 1973, Alison Agnes Graham Langlands; two *s* one *d*. *Educ:* Drumtochty Castle Sch.; Trinity College, Glenalmond; Trinity College, Cambridge (BA). Schoolmaster, Drumtochty Castle Sch., 1960–71; TEFL, Rome, 1972–75; fiction reviewer, The Scotsman, 1976–; Creative Writing Fellow: Edinburgh Univ., 1982–84; Glasgow and Strathclyde Univs, 1985–86; columnist: Glasgow Herald, 1985–88; Sunday Times Scotland, 1987–; Daily Telegraph, 1991–. Mem., Scottish Arts Council, 1989–91. *Publications: fiction:* Change and Decay In All Around I See, 1978; The Last Peacock, 1980; The Death of Men, 1981; One Night in Winter, 1984; Augustus, 1986; A Question of Loyalties, 1989; The Hanging Tree, 1990; Tiberius, 1991; The Sins of the Fathers, 1991; Caesar, 1993; These Enchanted Woods, 1993; The Ragged Lion, 1994; King David: a novel, 1995; *non-fiction:* Muriel Spark, 1979; Ill-Met by Gaslight, 1980; The Caesars, 1983; A Portrait of Scottish Rugby, 1984; Colette, 1986; 101 Great Scots, 1987; Byron's Travels, 1988; Glasgow, 1989; The Novel Today, 1990; Edinburgh, 1994; *plays:* Quintet in October; The Minstrel and the Shirra; contribs to Spectator, Sunday Telegraph. *Recreations:* reading, lunching; watching cricket, Rugby, horse-racing, and my daughter competing in Pony Club events; walking the dogs. *Address:* Thirladean House, Selkirk TD7 5LU. *T:* Selkirk (01750) 20393. *Clubs:* Academy; Selkirk RFC.

MASSIE, Herbert William, OBE 1984; Director, Royal Association for Disability and Rehabilitation, since 1990; *b* 31 March 1949; *s* of Herbert Douglas and Lucy Joan Massie. *Educ:* Portland Trng Coll. for Disabled, Mansfield; Hereward Coll., Coventry; Liverpool Poly. (BA Hons 1977); Manchester Poly. (CQSW). MIMgt (MBIM 1990). Wm Rainford Ltd, 1967–68; W Cheshire Newspapers Ltd, 1968–70; Liverpool Assoc. for Disabled, 1970–72; Disabled Living Foundn, 1977; RADAR, 1978–. Member: Management Cttee, Disabled Drivers Assoc., 1968–71; Exec. Cttee, Assoc. of Disabled Professionals, 1979– (Vice Chm., 1986–94); Careers Service Adv, Council for England, 1979–83; Voluntary Council for Handicapped Children (later Council for Disabled Children), 1980–93 (Vice-Chm., 1985–93); Exec. Cttee, OUTSET, 1983–91; MSC Wkg Party to Review Quota Scheme for Employment of Disabled People, 1984–85; Access Cttee for England, 1984–93; Disabled Persons Tspt Adv. Cttee, 1986–; BR Adv. Gp on Disabled People, 1986–94; Tripscope, 1986– (Vice-Chm., 1989); Nat. Adv. Council on Employment of People with Disabilities, 1991–; Independent Commn on Social Justice, 1993–94; DSS Panel of Experts on Incapacity Benefit, 1993–94; Cabinet Office Adv. Panel on Equal Opportunities in Sen. CS, 1994–95. 1990 BEAMA Foundation for Disabled People: Sec., 1986–90; Trustee, 1990–. UK Nat. Sec., Rehabilitation Internat., 1993–. Patron, Disabled Living Services (Manchester), 1990–; Trustee: Independent Living Fund, 1990–93; Habinteg Housing Assoc., 1991–. FRSA 1988. *Publications:* (with M. Greaves) Work and Disability, 1977, 1979; Aspects of the Employment of Disabled People in the Federal Republic of Germany, 1982; (jtly) Day Centres for Young Disabled People, 1984; Travelling with British Rail, 1985; (with J. Weyers) Wheelchairs and their Use, 1986; (with J. Male) Choosing a Wheelchair, 1990; (with J. Isaacs) Seat Belts and Disabled People, 1990; reports and numerous articles. *Recreations:* photography, trying to master water gardening. *Address:* RADAR, 12 City Forum, 250 City Road, EC1V 8AF. *T:* 0171–250 3222; 4 Moira Close, N17 6HZ. *T:* 0181–808 0185. *Club:* Rugby.

MASSINGHAM, John Dudley, CMG 1986; HM Diplomatic Service, retired; Consul General and Director of Trade Promotion, Johannesburg, 1987–90; *b* 1 Feb. 1930; *yr s* of Percy Massingham and Amy (*née* Sanders); *m* 1952, Jean Elizabeth Beech; two *s* two *d*. *Educ:* Dulwich Coll.; Magdalene Coll., Cambridge (MA); Magdalen Coll., Oxford. HM Overseas Civil Service, N Nigeria, 1954–59; BBC, 1959–64; HM Diplomatic Service, 1964–: First Secretary, CRO, 1964–66; Dep. High Comr and Head of Chancery,

Freetown, 1966–70; FCO, 1970–71; seconded to Pearce Commn, Jan.–May 1972; First Sec. (Information), later Aid (Kuala Lumpur), 1972–75; First Sec. and Head of Chancery, Kinshasa, 1976–77; Chief Sec., Falkland Islands Govt, 1977–79; Consul-General, Durban, June–Dec. 1979; Counsellor (Economic and Commercial), Nairobi, 1980–81; Governor and C-in-C, St Helena, 1981–84; High Comr to Guyana and non-resident Ambassador to Suriname, 1985–87. *Recreations:* bird watching, nature conservation work. *Address:* 24 Cherry Orchard, Pershore, Worcs WR10 1EL.

MASSY, family name of **Baron Massy.**

MASSY, 9th Baron *cr* 1776 (Ire.); **Hugh Hamon John Somerset Massy;** *b* 11 June 1921; *o s* of 8th Baron, and Margaret, 2nd *d* of late Richard Leonard, Meadsbrook, Ashbourne, Co. Limerick, and *widow* of Dr Moran, Tara, Co. Meath; *S* father 1958; *m* 1943, Margaret, *d* of late John Flower, Barry, Co. Meath; four *s* one *d*. *Educ:* Clongowes Wood Coll.; Clayesmore Sch. Served War, 1940–45, Private, RAOC. *Heir: s* Hon. David Hamon Somerset Massy, *b* 4 March 1947.

MASSY-GREENE, Sir (John) Brian, AC 1989; Kt 1972; Chairman, Hazelton Air Lines (formerly Hazelton Air Services Investments) Ltd, since 1984; *b* Tenterfield, NSW, 20 April 1916; *s* of late Sir Walter Massy-Greene, KCMG, and Lula May Lomax; *m* 1942, Margaret Elizabeth Ritchie Sharp, *d* of late Dr Walter Alexander Ramsay Sharp, OBE; two *s* two *d*. *Educ:* Sydney C of E Grammar Sch.; Geelong Grammar Sch.; Clare Coll., Cambridge (MA). Served War 1939–45: New Guinea, AIF, as Lieut, 1942–45. Joined Metal Manufacturers Ltd, as Staff Cadet, 1939; later transferred to their wholly-owned subsid. Austral Bronze Co. Pty Ltd; Gen. Manager, 1953–62. Managing Dir, 1962–76, and Chm., 1966–77, Consolidated Gold Fields Australia Ltd; Chairman: The Bellambi Coal Co. Ltd, 1964–72; Goldsworthy Mining Ltd, 1965–76; The Mount Lyell Mining & Railway Co. Ltd, 1964–76; Lawrenson Alumasc Holdings Ltd, 1964–73 (Dir, 1962–73); Pacific Dunlop (formerly Dunlop Olympic) Ltd, 1979–86 (Dir, 1968–86; Vice-Chm., 1977–79); Santos Ltd, 1984–88 (Dir, 1984); Commonwealth Banking Corp., 1985–88 (Dep. Chm., 1975–85; Dir, 1968–88); Director: Associated Minerals Consolidated Ltd, 1962–76; Commonwealth Mining Investments (Australia) Ltd, 1962–72 and 1978–85; Consolidated Gold Fields Ltd, London, 1963–76; Dalgety Australia Ltd, 1967–78 (Dep. Chm., 1975–78); Zip Holdings Ltd, 1964–73; Australian European Finance Corp., 1975–89 (Chm., 1987–88); Nat. Mutual Life Assoc. Ltd, 1977–85. Member: Exec. Cttee, Australian Mining Industry Council, 1967–78 (Pres. 1971); Manuf. Industries Adv. Council, 1968–77; NSW Adv. Cttee, CSIRO, 1968–75. Mem., Aust. Inst. Mining and Metallurgy. FAIM; FIEAust. *Recreations:* farming, fishing, flying. *Address:* Nandillyan Heights, Molong, NSW 2866, Australia. *T:* (63) 668028. *Club:* Australian.

MASTEL, Royston John, CVO 1977; CBE 1969; Assistant Commissioner (Administration and Operations), Metropolitan Police, 1972–76; *b* 30 May 1917; *s* of late John Mastel and late Rose Mastel (*née* Gorton); *m* 1940, Anne Kathleen Johnson; two *s*. *Educ:* Tottenham Grammar School. Joined Metropolitan Police as Constable, 1937; Pilot, RAF, 1941–45; Metro. Police: Sergeant 1946; Inspector 1951; Supt 1955; Comdr, No 2 District, 1966; subseq. Dep. Asst Comr, Head of Management Services Dept and D Dept (Personnel); Asst Comr (Personnel and Training), 1972. OStJ 1976. *Recreations:* Rugby football, golf. *Address:* The Retreat, Nottage, Porthcawl CF36 3RU.

MASTER, Simon Harcourt; Group Deputy Chairman, since 1989, and Chairman, General Books Division, since 1992, Random House (formerly Random Century) Group, (Group Managing Director, 1989–90); *b* 10 April 1944; *s* of Humphrey Ronald Master and Rachel Blanche Forshaw (*née* Plumbly); *m* 1969, Georgina Mary Cook Batsford, *d* of Sir Brian Batsford; two *s*. *Educ:* Ardingly Coll.; Univ. de La Rochelle. Hatchards Booksellers, 1963; Pan Books Ltd, 1964, Sen. Editor, 1967; Sen. Editor, B. T. Batsford Ltd, 1969; Pan Books Ltd: Editorial Dir, 1971; Publishing Dir, 1973; Man. Dir, 1980–87; Chief Exec., Random House UK Ltd, 1987–89; Vice Pres., Internat. Random House Inc., 1987–90; Chm. and Chief Exec., Arrow, 1990–92. Non-Exec. Dir, HMSO, 1990–95. Mem. Council, Publishers Assoc., 1989–95 (Vice Pres., 1995–Apr. 1996; Pres., Apr. 1996–). *Recreations:* gardening, scuba diving, golf, old cars. *Address:* 13 Patten Road, SW18 3RH. *T:* 0181–874 2204. *Clubs:* Groucho; Sherborne Golf.

MASTERMAN, Crispin Grant, FCIArb; **His Honour Judge Masterman;** a Circuit Judge, since 1995; *b* 1 June 1944; *s* of Osmond Janson Masterman and Anne Masterman (*née* Bouwens); *m* 1976, Clare Fletcher; one *s* two *d*. *Educ:* St Edward's Sch., Oxford; Univ. of Southampton (BA). FCIArb 1991. Called to the Bar, Middle Temple, 1971; a Recorder, 1988–95. *Recreations:* family and friends, running, ski-ing, golf. *Address:* 28 South Rise, Llanishen, Cardiff CF4 5RH. *T:* Cardiff (01222) 754072.

MASTERS, Brian Geoffrey John; author; *b* 25 May 1939; *s* of Geoffrey Howard Masters and Mabel Sophia Charlotte (*née* Ingledew). *Educ:* Wilson's Grammar Sch., London; University Coll., Cardiff (BA 1st cl. Hons 1961); Université de Montpellier. FRSA 1989. *Publications:* Molière, 1969; Sartre, 1969; Saint-Exupéry, 1970; Rabelais, 1971; Camus: a study, 1973; Wynyard Hall and the Londonderry Family, 1974; Dreams about HM The Queen, 1974; The Dukes, 1975; Now Barabbas Was A Rotter: the extraordinary life of Marie Corelli, 1978; The Mistresses of Charles II, 1980; Georgiana, Duchess of Devonshire, 1981; Great Hostesses, 1982; Killing for Company: the case of Dennis Nilsen, 1985 (Gold Dagger Award, CWA); The Swinging Sixties, 1985; The Passion of John Aspinall, 1988; Maharana: the Udaipur Dynasty, 1990; Gary, 1990; The Life of E. F. Benson, 1991; The Shrine of Jeffrey Dahmer, 1993; (ed and trans.) Voltaire on Tolerance, 1994; Masters on Murder, 1994; The Evil That Men Do, 1996. *Recreations:* etymology, stroking cats. *Address:* 47 Caithness Road, W14 0JD. *T:* 0171–603 6838. *Clubs:* Garrick, Beefsteak, Pratt's, Academy, Aspinall's.

MASTERS, Rt. Rev. Brian John; *see* Edmonton, Area Bishop of.

MASTERS, Dr Christopher; Chief Executive, Christian Salvesen, since 1989; *b* 2 May 1947; *s* of Wilfred and Mary Ann Masters; *m* 1971, Gillian Mary (*née* Hodson); two *d*. *Educ:* Richmond Sch.; King's Coll. London (BSc, AKC); Leeds Univ. (PhD). Research Chemist, Shell Research, Amsterdam, 1971–77; Corporate Planner, Shell Chemicals UK, 1977–79; Business Develt Manager, Christian Salvesen, 1979–81; Dir of Planning, Merchants Refrigerating Co., NY, 1981–82; Managing Director: Christian Salvesen Seafoods, 1983–86; Christian Salvesen Industrial Services, 1984–89. Director: British Assets Trust, 1990–; Scottish Widows' Fund or Life Assurance Soc, 1992–. Chairman: Young Enterprise Scotland; Quality Assessment Cttee, SHEFC, 1993–. Director: Scottish Opera, 1994–; Scottish Chamber Orch., 1995–. *Publications:* Homogeneous Transition—Metal Catalysis, 1981, Russian edn 1983; numerous research papers and patents. *Recreations:* music, wine. *Address:* Christian Salvesen, 50 East Fettes Avenue, Edinburgh EH4 1EQ. *T:* 0131–559 3600.

MASTERS, Sheila Valerie, (Mrs Barry Noakes); Partner, KPMG Peat Marwick (formerly Peat Marwick Mitchell & Co.), since 1983; a Director, Bank of England, since 1994; *d* of Albert Frederick Masters and Iris Sheila Masters (*née* Ratcliffe); *m* 1985, Colin Barry Noakes. *Educ:* Eltham Hill Grammar Sch.; Univ. of Bristol (LLB). FCA; Associate, Inst. of Taxation. Joined Peat Marwick Mitchell & Co., 1970; seconded to HM Treasury, 1979–81; seconded to Dept of Health as Dir of Finance, NHS Management Exec., 1988–91. Member: Council, ICAEW, 1987–; Inland Revenue Management Bd, 1992–; NHS Policy Bd, 1992–; Chancellor of Exchequer's Private Finance Panel, 1993–. *Recreations:* ski-ing, horse racing, opera, early classical music. *Address:* 1 Puddle Dock, Blackfriars, EC4V 3PD. *T:* 0171–236 8000. *Club:* Farmers'.

MASTERSON, Valerie, (Mrs Andrew March), CBE 1988; opera and concert singer; *d* of Edward Masterson and Rita McGrath; *m* 1965, Andrew March; one *s* one *d*. *Educ:* Holt Hill Convent; studied in London and Milan on scholarship, and with Edwardo Asquez. Début, Landestheater Salzburg; appearances with: D'Oyly Carte Opera, Glyndebourne Festival Opera, ENO, Royal Opera, Covent Garden, etc; appears in principal opera houses in Paris, Aix-en-Provence, Toulouse, Munich, Geneva, Barcelona, Milan, San Francisco, Chile, etc; leading roles in: La Traviata, Le Nozze di Figaro, Manon, Faust, Alcina, Die Entführung aus dem Serail, Così fan tutte, La Bohème, Semele (SWET award, 1983), Die Zauberflöte, Julius Caesar, Rigoletto, Romeo and Juliet, Carmen, Count Ory, Mireille, Louise, Idomeneo, Les Dialogues des Carmélites, The Merry Widow, Xerxes, Orlando, Lucia di Lammermoor. Recordings include: La Traviata; Elisabetta, Regina d'Inghilterra; Der Ring des Nibelungen; The Merry Widow; Julius Caesar; Scipione; several Gilbert and Sullivan operas. Broadcasts regularly on radio and TV. FRCM; Hon. RAM 1994. *Recreations:* tennis, swimming, ice skating. *Address:* c/o Music International, 13 Ardilaun Road, Highbury, N5 2QR.

MATACA, Most Rev. Petero; *see* Suva, Archbishop of, (RC).

MATANE, Sir Paulias (Nguna), Kt 1986; CMG 1980; OBE 1975; Director, Treid Pacific (PNG) Pty Ltd, since 1987 (Chairman, 1986–90); Chairman, Ocean Trading Co. Pty, since 1990 (Director, since 1987); *b* 21 Sept. 1931; *s* of Ilias Maila Matane and Elsa Toto; *m* 1957, Kaludia Peril Matane; two *s* two *d*. *Educ:* Teacher's College (Dip. Teaching and Education). Asst Teacher, Tauran Sch., PNG, 1957, Headmaster, 1958–61; School Inspector, 1962–66; Dist Sch. Inspector and Dist Educn Officer, 1967–68; Supt, Teacher Educn, 1969; Foundn Mem., Public Schs Bd, 1969–70; Sec., Dept of Business Develt, 1971–74; Ambassador to USA, Mexico and UN, and High Comr to Canada, 1975–80; Sec., Foreign Affairs, PNG, 1980–85. Chm., Newton Pacific (PNG) Pty Ltd, 1995–. Chairman: Review Cttee on Philosophy of Educn, 1986; Cocoa Industry Investigating Cttee, 1987; Foundn for Peoples of South Pacific, PNG, 1989–; PNG Censorship Bd, 1990–; Advance PNG, 1991–; Foundn for Peoples of South Pacific/International Mem. Council, Univ. of PNG, 1982–. Hon. DTech Univ. of Technol., Lae, 1985; Hon. PhD Univ. of PNG, 1986. UN 40th Anniv. Medal, 1985. *Publications:* Kum Tumun of Minj, 1966; A New Guinean Travels through Africa, 1971; My Childhood in New Guinea, 1972; What Good is Business?, 1972; Two New Guineans Travel through SE Asia, 1974; Aimbe the Challenger, 1974; Aimbe the School Dropout, 1974; Aimbe the Magician, 1976; Aimbe the Pastor, 1979; Two Papua New Guineans Discover the Bible Lands, 1987; To Serve with Love, 1989; Chit-Chat, 1991; East to West—the longest train trip in the world, 1991; Let's Do It PNG, 1994; Trekking Through the New Worlds, 1995. *Recreations:* reading, gardening, squash, fishing, writing. *Address:* PO Box 7184, Boroko, NCD, Papua New Guinea. *Clubs:* Tamukavar, Tauran Ex Student and Citizens', Cathay (Papua New Guinea).

MATE, Rt. Rev. Martin; Bishop of Eastern Newfoundland and Labrador, 1980–92; *b* 12 Nov. 1929; *s* of John Mate and Hilda Mate (*née* Toope); *m* 1962, Florence Hooper, Registered Nurse; two *s* three *d*. *Educ:* Meml Univ. of Newfoundland and Queen's Coll., St John's, Newfoundland (LTh); Bishop's Univ., Lennoxville, PQ. BA (1st Cl. Hons), MA. Deacon 1952, priest 1953; Curate, Cathedral of St John the Baptist, St John's, Newfoundland, 1952–53; Deacon-in-charge and Rector, Parish of Pushthrough, 1953–58; Incumbent, Mission of St Anthony, 1958–64; Rural Dean, St Barbe, 1958–64; Rector of Cookshire, Quebec, 1964–67; Rector of Catalina, Newfoundland, 1967–72; RD of Bonavista Bay, 1970–72; Rector of Pouch Cove/Torbay, 1972–76; Treasurer, Diocesan Synod of E Newfoundland and Labrador, 1976–80. *Publication:* Pentateuchal Criticism, 1967. *Recreations:* carpentry, hunting, fishing, camping. *Address:* 42 Dundas Street, St John's, Newfoundland A1B 1X2, Canada.

MATES, Lt-Col Michael John; MP (C) East Hampshire, since 1983 (Petersfield, Oct. 1974–1983); *b* 9 June 1934; *s* of Claude John Mates; *m* 1959, Mary Rosamund Paton (marr. diss. 1980); two *s* two *d*; *m* 1982, Rosellen, *d* of Mr and Mrs W. T. Bett; one *d*. *Educ:* Salisbury Cathedral Sch.; Blundell's Sch.; King's Coll., Cambridge (choral schol.). Joined Army, 1954; 2nd Lieut, RUR, 1955; Queen's Dragoon Guards, RAC, 1961; Major, 1967; Lt-Col, 1973; resigned commn 1974. Minister of State, NI Office, 1992–93. Vice-Chm., Cons. NI Cttee, 1979–81 (Sec., 1974–79); Chairman: Select Cttee on Defence, 1987–92 (Mem., 1979–92); Cons. Home Affairs Cttee, 1987–88 (Vice-Chm., 1979–87); All-Party Anglo-Irish Gp, 1979–92; Sec., 1922 Cttee, 1987–88; Mem., Intell. and Security Cttee, 1994–; introduced: Farriers Registration Act, 1975; Rent Amendment Act, 1985. Farriers' Co.: Liveryman, 1975–; Asst, 1981; Master, 1986–87. *Address:* House of Commons, SW1A 0AA.

MATHER, Lt-Col Anthony Charles McClure, OBE 1990 (MBE 1965); Secretary, Central Chancery of the Orders of Knighthood and Assistant Comptroller, Lord Chamberlain's Office, since 1991; *b* 21 April 1942; *s* of late Eric James Mather and Stella Mather (*née* McClure); *m* 1966, Gaye, *d* of late Dr Eric Lindsay Dickson and Mrs Louise Tillett; one *s* two *d*. *Educ:* Eton College. Commissioned, Grenadier Guards, 1962; served UK, British Guyana, Germany and Hong Kong; retired 1991. An Extra Equerry to the Queen, 1992–. *Recreations:* gardening, fishing, music. *Address:* The Horseshoes, Chirton, near Devizes, Wilts SN10 3QR. *T:* Devizes (01380) 840261. *Club:* Army and Navy.

MATHER, Sir Carol; *see* Mather, Sir D. C. MacD.

MATHER, Sir (David) Carol (Macdonell), Kt 1987; MC 1944; *b* 3 Jan. 1919; *s* of late Loris Emerson Mather, CBE; *m* 1951, Hon. Philippa Selina Bewicke-Copley, *o d* of 5th Baron Cromwell, DSO; one *s* three *d*. *Educ:* Harrow; Trinity Coll., Cambridge. War of 1939–45: commissioned Welsh Guards, 1940; served in Western Desert Campaigns, 1941–42; PoW, 1942; escaped, 1943; NW Europe, 1944–45 (despatches); wounded, 1945; Palestine Campaign, 1946–48. Asst Mil. Attaché, British Embassy, Athens, 1953–56; GSO 1, MI Directorate, War Office, 1957–61; Mil. Sec. to GOC-in-C, Eastern Command, 1961–62; retd as Lt-Col., 1962. Conservative Research Dept, 1962–70; contested (C) Leicester (NW), 1966. MP (C) Esher, 1970–87. An Opposition Whip, 1975–79; a Lord Comr of HM Treasury, 1979–81; Vice-Chamberlain of HM Household, 1981–83; Comptroller of HM Household, 1983–86. FRGS. *Publication:* Aftermath of War, 1992. *Club:* Brooks's.

See also Sir W. L. Mather.

MATHER, Graham Christopher Spencer; solicitor; Member (C) Hampshire North and Oxford, European Parliament, since 1994; President, European Policy Forum, since 1992; *b* 23 Oct. 1954; *er s* of Thomas and Doreen Mather; *m* 1981, Fiona Marion McMillan (marr. diss. 1995), *e d* of Sir Ronald McMillan Bell, QC, MP and of Lady Bell; two *s*. *Educ:* Hutton Grammar School; New College, Oxford (Burnet Law Scholar); MA Jurisp.

Institute of Directors: Asst to Dir Gen., 1980; Head of Policy Unit, 1983; Institute of Economic Affairs: Dep. Dir, 1987; Gen. Dir, 1987–92. Mem., HM Treasury Working Party on Freeports, 1982. Mem., Monopolies and Mergers Commission, 1989–94. Vis. Fellow, Nuffield Coll., Oxford, 1992–. Mem., Westminster City Council, 1982–86; contested (C) Blackburn, 1983. Radio and television broadcaster. Vice-President: Strategic Planning Soc., 1993–; Assoc. of Dist Councils, 1994–. *Publications:* lectures, papers and contribs to jls; contribs to The Times. *Address:* European Policy Forum, 20 Queen Anne's Gate, SW1H 9AA. *T:* 0171–222 0733, *Fax:* 0171–222 0554. *Club:* United Oxford & Cambridge University.

MATHER, John Douglas, FCIT, FILDM; CIMgt; Chief Executive, National Freight Consortium plc, 1984–93; *b* 27 Jan. 1936; *s* of John Dollandson and Emma May Mather; *m* 1958, Hilda Patricia (*née* Kirkwood); one *s* (one *d* decd). *Educ:* Manchester Univ. (BACom, MAEcon). MIPM. Personnel Management: Philips Electrical, 1959–66; Convoys Ltd, 1966–67; Personnel Management, Transport Management, National Freight Company, 1967–93. Non-Executive Director: Bletchley Motor Gp, 1993–; Computer Management Gp, 1993–; Miller Gp, 1993–. Chairman: Bedfordshire TEC, 1991–93; Camden Business Partnership, 1991–; London Regeneration Consortium plc, 1993–. Member: Adv. Bd, Cranfield Sch. of Management, 1992–; Council, Cranfield Univ., 1993–. Trustee, Help The Aged, 1993–. Mem., Worshipful Co. of Carmen. *Recreations:* golf, gardening, travel. *Address:* Roundhale, Love Lane, Kings Langley, Hertfordshire WD4 9HW. *T:* Kings Langley (019232) 63063. *Clubs:* Royal Automobile; Woburn Golf and Country; La Sella Golf and Country.

MATHER, Sir William (Loris), Kt 1968; CVO 1986; OBE 1957; MC 1945; TD and 2 clasps 1949; MA, CEng; Vice Lord-Lieutenant of Cheshire, 1975–90; *b* 17 Aug. 1913; *s* of Loris Emerson Mather, CBE; *m* 1937, Eleanor, *d* of Prof. R. H. George, Providence, RI, USA; two *s* two *d*. *Educ:* Oundle; Trinity Coll., Cambridge (MA Engrg and Law, 1939). Commissioned Cheshire Yeomanry, 1935; served War of 1939–45: Palestine, Syria, Iraq, Iran, Western Desert, Italy, Belgium, Holland, Germany (wounded twice, MC); Instructor, Staff Coll., Camberley, 2nd i/c 1st RTR, and GSO1, 1944–45. Chm., Mather & Platt Ltd, 1960–78; Divisional Dir, BSC, 1968–73; Chairman: CompAir Ltd, 1978–83 (Dir, 1973–83); Neolith Chemicals Ltd, 1983–88; Advanced Manufacturing Technology Group, 1985–88. Director: District Bank, 1960–84; National Westminster Bank, 1970–84 (Chm., Northern Bd, 1972–84); Manchester Ship Canal Co. Ltd, 1970–84; Wormold Internat. Ltd, 1975–78; Imperial Continental Gas Assoc. Ltd, 1980–84. Chairman: NW Regional Economic Planning Council, 1968–75; Inst. of Directors, 1979–82 (Manchester Inst. of Dirs, 1967–72); British Pump Manufrs Assoc., 1970–73; President: Manchester Chamber of Commerce, 1964–66 (Emeritus Dir, 1978–89); Manchester Guardian Soc. for Protection of Trade, 1971–85; British Mech. Engrg Confedn, 1975–78; Civic Trust for the NW, 1979–91 (Chm., 1961–78); Vice Pres., Assoc. of British Chambers of Commerce, 1979–85; Pres., Mech. Engrg Council, 1978–80; Member: Council of Industrial Design, 1960–71; Engineering Industries Council, 1976–80; Council, Duchy of Lancaster, 1977–85. Member Court: Manchester Univ., 1956–94; Salford Univ., 1968–86; Royal College of Art, 1967–85; Mem. Council, Manchester Business Sch., 1964–85; Governor: Manchester University Inst. of Science and Technology (Pres., 1976–85; Hon. Fellow, 1986); Manchester Grammar Sch., 1965–80; Feoffee, Chetham's Hosp. Sch., 1961–91; President: Manchester YMCA, 1982–91 (Chm., 1953–82); Greater Manchester East County Scout Council, 1978–94. Hon. Fellow, Manchester Coll. of Art and Design, 1967; Hon. DEng Liverpool, 1980; Hon. LLD Manchester, 1983. Comdr, Cheshire Yeomanry, 1954–57; Col and Dep. Comdr, 23 Armoured Bde, TA, 1957–60; ADC to the Queen, 1961–66. CIMgt; FRSA. DL City and County of Chester, 1963; High Sheriff of Cheshire, 1969–70. KLJ 1988. *Recreations:* field sports, golf, swimming. *Address:* Whirley Hall, Macclesfield, Cheshire SK10 4RN. *T:* Macclesfield (01625) 422077. *Club:* Leander (Henley-on-Thames).

See also Sir D. C. M. Mather.

MATHERS, Sir Robert (William), Kt 1981; Director: Finlayson Timber & Hardware Pty Ltd, since 1986; National Mutual Life Association of Australasia Ltd, since 1988; Kidston Gold Mines Ltd, since 1988; Buderim Ginger Ltd, since 1989; Coles Myer Ltd, since 1992; Leutenegger Ltd, since 1992; Touraust Funds Management Ltd, since 1994; Australian Tourism Co. Ltd, since 1994; *b* 2 Aug. 1928; *s* of William Mathers and Olive Ida (*née* Wohlsen); *m* 1957, Betty Estelle Greasley; three *d*. *Educ:* Church of England Grammar Sch., E Brisbane. FAIM; FRMIA 1982. Chm. and Man. Dir, Mathers Enterprises Ltd, 1973–88; Chm., Kinney Shoes (Australia) Ltd, 1988–90; Dep. Chm., Bligh Coal Ltd, 1981–88. Mem., Aust. Adv. Bd, Kmart Corp., USA, 1991–94. Life Mem., Retailers Assoc. of Qld, 1990 (Mem. Council, 1952–90); Pres., Footwear Retailers Assoc., 1960–63. Member: Council, Australian Bicentennial Authority, 1980–89; Finance Adv. Cttee for XII Commonwealth Games, 1979; Australiana Fund, 1980–94; Brisbane Adv. Bd, Salvation Army, 1990–; Adv. Bd, Bond Univ. Sch. of Business, 1991–; Councillor: Griffith Univ., 1978–88; Enterprise Australia, 1983–92; Deputy Chairman: Nat. Finance Cttee, Australian Stockman's Hall of Fame and Outback Heritage Centre, 1984–89; Organising Cttee, Brisbane Bid for 1992 Olympics, 1985–88. Trustee: WWF, Australia, 1981–87; Queensland Art Gall., 1983–87 (Founding Cttee Mem., Qld Art Gall. Foundn, 1979). Hon. FAMI 1984; FRSA 1989. DUniv Griffith, 1992. Cavaliere, Order of Merit (Italy), 1983. *Recreations:* golf, tennis, swimming. *Address:* 1 Wybelenna Street, Kenmore, Queensland 4069, Australia. *T:* (7) 3785503. *Clubs:* Brisbane, Rotary, Royal Queensland Yacht Squadron, Tattersalls, Brisbane Polo, Milton Tennis, Queensland Rugby Union, Indooroopilly Golf (Brisbane).

MATHESON, Alexander, OBE 1990; JP; FRPharmS; Vice Lord-Lieutenant of the Western Isles, since 1994; Chairman, Western Isles Health Board, since 1993; *b* 16 Nov. 1941; *s* of Alex Matheson, MB ChB and Catherine Agnes Matheson (*née* Smith), MA; *m* 1965, Irene Mary Davidson, BSc Hons, MSc; two *s* two *d*. *Educ:* Nicolson Inst., Stornoway; Robert Gordon Inst. of Technol., Aberdeen. MRPharmS 1965, FRPharmS 1993. Man. Dir, 1966–82 and Chm., 1967–, Roderick Smith Ltd. Member: Stornoway Town Council, 1967–75 (Provost, 1971–75); Ross and Cromarty CC, 1967–75. Member: Stornoway Trust Estate, 1967– (Chm., 1971–81); Stornoway Pier and Harbour Commn, 1968– (Chm., 1971–72 and 1993–); Western Isles Island Council, 1974–94 (Convener, 1982–90); Western Isles Health Bd, 1974–. Pres., Islands Commn of Peripheral Maritime Regions of Europe, 1988–93. JP Western Is, 1971; Hon. Sheriff, Stornoway, 1972. *Recreations:* genealogy, research and lecturing on local history. *Address:* 33 Newton Street, Stornoway, Isle of Lewis HS1 2RW. *T:* Stornoway (01851) 702082. *Club:* Royal Scottish Automobile (Glasgow).

MATHESON, Duncan, MA, LLM; QC 1989; a Recorder of the Crown Court, since 1985. Bencher, Inner Temple, 1994. *Address:* 1 Crown Office Row, Temple, EC4Y 7HH. *T:* 0171–797 7500.

MATHESON of Matheson, Major Sir Fergus (John), 7th Bt *cr* 1882, of Lochalsh, Co. Ross; Chief of Clan Matheson; one of HM Body Guard of the Honourable Corps of Gentlemen-at-Arms, since 1979 (Standard Bearer, since 1993); *b* 22 Feb. 1927; *yr s* of Gen. Sir Torquhil George Matheson, 5th Bt, KCB, CMG and Lady Elizabeth Matheson, ARRC (*d* 1986), *o d* of 8th Earl of Albemarle; *S* brother, 1993; *m* 1952, Hon. Jean Elizabeth Mary Willoughby, *yr d* of 11th Baron Middleton, KG, MC; one *s* two *d*. *Educ:* Eton. Major, Coldstream Guards, 1945–64, retd. Pres., St John Ambulance, Norfolk, 1993–. *Heir* (to baronetcy and chiefship): *s* Major Alexander Fergus Matheson, yr of Matheson, Coldstream Guards [*b* 26 Aug. 1954; *m* 1983, Katharine Davina Mary, *o d* of W. R. M. Oswald, *qv*; two *s* one *d*]. *Address:* The Old Rectory, Hedenham, Bungay, Norfolk NR35 2LD. *Clubs:* Army and Navy, Pratt's; Norfolk (Norwich).

MATHESON, Sir (James Adam) Louis, KBE 1976 (MBE 1944); CMG 1972; FTS; FEng; Vice-Chancellor, Monash University, Melbourne, 1959–76; Chancellor, Papua New Guinea University of Technology, 1973–75; Chairman, Australian Science and Technology Council, 1975–76; *b* 11 Feb. 1912; *s* of William and Lily Edith Matheson; *m* 1937, Audrey Elizabeth Wood; three *s*. *Educ:* Bootham Sch., York; Manchester Univ. (MSc 1933). Lectr, Birmingham Univ., 1938–46 (PhD 1946); Prof. of Civil Engineering, Univ. of Melbourne, Australia, 1946–50; Beyer Prof. of Engineering, Univ. of Manchester, 1951–59. Hon. FICE (Mem. Council, 1965); Hon. FIEAust (Mem. Council, 1961–81, Vice-Pres., 1970–74, Pres., 1975–76); Fellow, Aust. Acad. of Technological Scis and Engrg, 1976; Fellow, Fellowship of Engrg, 1980. Member: Mission on Technical Educn in W Indies, 1957; Royal Commn into failure of King's Bridge, 1963; Ramsay Cttee on Tertiary Educn in Victoria, 1961–63; CSIRO Adv. Council, 1962–67; Exec., Aust. Council for Educational Research, 1964–69; Interim Council, Univ. of Papua New Guinea, 1965–68; Enquiry into Post-Secondary Educn in Victoria, 1976–78; Chairman: Council, Papua New Guinea Inst. of Technology, 1966–73; Aust. Vice-Chancellors' Cttee, 1967–68; Assoc. of Commonwealth Univs, 1967–69; Newport Power Stn Review Panel, 1977; Schools Commn Buildings Cttee, 1977–81; Victorian Planning and Finance Cttee, Commonwealth Schools Commn, 1979–83; Sorrento Harbour Inquiries, 1984 and 1987; St Kilda Harbour Inquiry, 1986. Trustee, Inst. of Applied Science (later Science Mus. of Victoria), 1963–83 (Pres., 1969–73). Dir, Nauru Phosphate Corp., 1977–79. Hon. DSc Hong Kong, 1969; Hon. LLD: Manchester, 1972; Monash, 1975; Melbourne, 1975. Kernot Meml Medal, 1972; Peter Nicol Russell Medal, 1976. *Publications:* Hyperstatic Structures: Vol. 1, 1959; Vol. 2, 1960; Still Learning, 1980; various articles on engineering and education. *Recreations:* music, woodcraft. *Address:* 26/166 West Toorak Road, South Yarra, Victoria 3141, Australia.

MATHESON, Very Rev. James Gunn; Moderator of General Assembly of Church of Scotland, May 1975–76; *b* 1 March 1912; *s* of Norman Matheson and Henrietta Gunn; *m* 1937, Janet Elizabeth Clarkson; three *s* one *d* (and one *d* decd). *Educ:* Inverness Royal Academy; Edinburgh Univ. (MA, BD). Free Church of Olrig, Caithness, 1936–39; Chaplain to HM Forces, 1939–45 (POW Italy, 1941–43); St Columba's Church, Blackhall, Edinburgh, 1946–51; Knox Church, Dunedin, NZ, 1951–61; Sec. of Stewardship and Budget Cttee of Church of Scotland, 1961–73; Parish Minister, Portree, Isle of Skye, 1973–79; retired 1979. Hon. DD Edinburgh, 1975. *Publications:* Do You Believe This?, 1960; Saints and Sinners, 1975; contrib. theol jls. *Recreations:* gardening, fishing. *Address:* Husabost, Totaig, Dunvegan, Isle of Skye IV55 8ZU.

MATHESON, Maj.-Gen. John Mackenzie, OBE 1950; TD 1969; retired; *b* Gibraltar, 6 Aug. 1912; *s* of late John Matheson and late Nina Short, Cape Town; *m* 1942, Agnes, *d* of Henderson Purves, Dunfermline; one *d*. *Educ:* George Watson's Coll., Edinburgh; Edinburgh Univ. (Vans Dunlop Schol.). MB, ChB 1936; MRCP 1939; MD 1945; FRCSEd 1946; FRCS 1962; FRCP 1972. Royal Victoria Hosp. Tuberculosis Trust Research Fellow, 1936–37; Lieut, RAMC (TA), 1936. Served War of 1939–45: Middle East, N Africa and Italy; Regular RAMC Commn, 1944 (despatches). Clinical Tutor, Surgical Professorial Unit, Edinburgh Univ., 1947–48; Med. Liaison Officer to Surgeon-Gen. US Army, Washington, DC, 1948–50; Asst Chief, Section Gen. Surgery, Walter Reed Army Hosp., Washington, DC, 1950–51; Cons. Surgeon: MELF, 1963–64; BAOR, 1967; Far East, 1967–69; Jt Prof. Mil. Surg., RAM Coll. and RCS of Eng., 1964–67; Brig. 1967; Comdt and Dir of Studies, Royal Army Med. Coll., 1969–71; Postgrad. Dean, Faculty of Medicine, Univ. of Edinburgh, 1971–80. QHS 1969–71. Hon. Col, 205 (Scottish) Gen. Hosp., T&AVR, 1978–80. Alexander Medal, 1961; Simpson-Smith Memorial Lectr, 1967; Gordon-Watson Lectr, RCS of Eng., 1967; Mitchiner Meml Lectr, RAM Coll., Millbank, 1988. Senior Fellow, Assoc. of Surgeons of GB and Ireland; British Medical Association: Mem., Armed Forces Cttee, 1983–88; Mem., Bd of Educn and Science, 1985–88; Pres., Lothian Div., 1978–80. President: Scottish Br., Royal Soc. of Tropical Medicine and Hygiene, 1978–80; Military Surgical Soc., 1984–86; Edinburgh Univ. Graduates Assoc., 1987–89 (Vice-Pres., 1985–86); Chm. Council, Edinburgh Royal Infirmary Samaritan Soc., 1983–. *Publications:* (contrib.) Military Medicine, in Dictionary of Medical Ethics, 1977; papers (on gun-shot wounds, gas-gangrene and sterilisation) to medical jls. *Recreation:* travel. *Address:* 2 Orchard Brae, Edinburgh EH4 1NY.

MATHESON, Sir Louis; *see* Matheson, Sir J. A. L.

MATHESON, Stephen Charles Taylor, CB 1993; Deputy Secretary, since 1989, and Deputy Chairman, Inland Revenue, since 1993; *b* 27 June 1939; *s* of Robert Matheson and Olive Lovick; *m* 1960, Marna Rutherford Burnett; two *s*. *Educ:* Aberdeen Grammar Sch.; Aberdeen Univ. (MA hons English Lang. and Lit., 1961). HM Inspector of Taxes, 1961–70; Principal, Bd of Inland Revenue, 1970–75; Private Sec. to Paymaster General, 1975–76, to Chancellor of the Exchequer, 1976–77; Board of Inland Revenue, 1977–; Project Manager, Computerisation of Pay As You Earn Project; Under Sec., 1984; Dir of IT, 1984; Comr, 1989; Dir Gen. (Management), 1989. FBCS (Pres., 1991–92); Associate Mem., PITCOM. FRSA 1992. Hon. DBA De Montfort Univ., 1994. *Publication:* Maurice Walsh, Storyteller, 1985. *Recreations:* Scottish and Irish literature, book collecting, cooking, music. *Address:* Somerset House, WC2R 1LB. *T:* 0171–438 6789.

MATHEW, John Charles, QC 1977; *b* 3 May 1927; *s* of late Sir Theobald Mathew, KBE, MC, and Lady Mathew; *m* 1952, Jennifer Jane Mathew (*née* Lagden); two *d*. *Educ:* Beaumont Coll. Served, Royal Navy, 1945–47. Called to Bar, Lincoln's Inn, 1949; apptd Junior Prosecuting Counsel to the Crown, 1959; First Sen. Prosecuting Counsel to the Crown, 1974–77. Elected a Bencher of Lincoln's Inn, 1970. *Recreations:* golf, shooting, cinema. *Address:* 47 Abingdon Villas, W8 6XA. *T:* 0171–937 7535. *Club:* Garrick.

MATHEW, Robert Knox, (Robin); QC 1992; *b* 22 Jan. 1945; *s* of late Robert Mathew, TD, MP and Joan Leslie (*née* Bruce); *m* 1968, Anne Rosella Elliott; one *d*. *Educ:* Eton Coll.; Trinity Coll., Dublin (BA 1967). City and financial journalist, 1968–76. Called to the Bar, Lincoln's Inn, 1974. Asst Parly Boundary Comr, 1992–. *Recreations:* country pursuits, racing, ski-ing. *Address:* 5 Bell Yard, WC2A 2JR; Church Farm, Little Barrington, *via* Burford, Oxon OX18 5TE. *T:* Windrush (014518) 44311. *Club:* Boodle's.

MATHEW, Theobald David; Windsor Herald of Arms, since 1978; *b* 7 April 1942; *s* of Robert Mathew, Porchester Terrace, London, and West Mersea Hall, Essex, solicitor, and Joan Alison, *d* of Sir George Young, Bt, MVO, of Formosa. *Educ:* Downside; Balliol Coll., Oxford (MA). Green Staff Officer at Investiture of HRH the Prince of Wales, 1969; Rouge Dragon Pursuivant of Arms, 1970; Dep. Treasurer, Coll. of Arms, 1978–. OStJ 1986. *Recreations:* cricket and sailing. *Address:* 76 Clifton Hill, NW8 0JT. *T:* 0171–624

8448; College of Arms, EC4V 4BT. *T:* 0171–248 0893. *Clubs:* Athenæum, MCC, Middlesex CC.

MATHEWS, Hon. Jeremy Fell, CMG 1989; Attorney General of Hong Kong, since 1988; *b* 14 Dec. 1941; *s* of George James and Ivy Priscilla Mathews; *m* 1st, 1968, Sophie Lee (marr. diss. 1992); two *d*; 2nd, 1992, Halima Guterres. *Educ:* Palmer's Grammar Sch., England. Qualified as solicitor, London, 1963; private practice, London, 1963–65; Dep. Dist Registrar in the High Court of Australia, Sydney, 1966–67; Hong Kong Government: Crown Counsel, 1968; Dep. Law Draftsman, 1978; Dep. Crown Solicitor, 1981; Crown Solicitor, 1982. *Recreations:* reading, trekking, music. *Address:* Attorney General's Chambers, Queensway Government Offices, 66 Queensway, Hong Kong. *T:* 8672001. *Clubs:* Hong Kong; Hong Kong Football.

MATHEWS, Marina Sarah Dewe, (Mrs John Dewe Mathews); *see* Warner, M. S.

MATHEWS, Terence Francis, CBE 1995; Commissioner, Building Societies Commission, 1988–May 1996; *b* 1 May 1935; *s* of Frank Mathews and Alice Elizabeth (*née* Lever); *m* 1st, 1958, Anna Dawson (marr. diss. 1973); one *s* one *d*; 2nd, 1976, Barbara Scott. *Educ:* Balham Central Sch. Nat. Service, RAF, 1953–55. HM Treasury, 1952–86; Building Socs Commn, 1986–96, retd. *Recreation:* amateur theatre. *Address:* (until May 1996) Building Societies Commission, 15 Great Marlborough Street, W1V 2AX. *T:* 0171–494 6627; 24 Pyecombe Corner, N12 7AJ.

MATHEWSON, George Ross, CBE 1985; BSc, PhD, MBA; FRSE; CEng, MIEE; Group Chief Executive, Royal Bank of Scotland Group, since 1992 (Deputy Group Chief Executive, 1990–92); Director: Royal Bank of Scotland, since 1987; Royal Bank of Scotland Group, since 1987; *b* 14 May 1940; *s* of George Mathewson and Charlotte Gordon (*née* Ross); *m* 1966, Sheila Alexandra Graham (*née* Bennett); two *s*. *Educ:* Perth Academy; St Andrews Univ. (BSc, PhD); Canisius Coll., Buffalo, NY (MBA). Assistant Lecturer, St Andrews Univ., 1964–67; various posts in Research & Development, Avionics Engineering, Bell Aerospace, Buffalo, NY, 1967–72; joined Industrial & Commercial Finance Corp., Edinburgh, 1972; Area Manager, Aberdeen, 1974, and Asst General Manager and Director, 1979; Chief Exec. and Mem., Scottish Develt Agency, 1981–87; Dir of Strategic Planning and Develt, Royal Bank of Scotland Group, 1987–90; Director: Scottish Investment Trust Ltd, 1981–; Citizens Financial Gp, Inc., 1989–; Direct Line Insurance plc, 1990–. FCIBS 1994; CIMgt (CBIM 1985); FRSE 1988. Hon. LLD Dundee, 1983. *Publications:* various articles on engineering/finance. *Recreations:* geriatric Rugby, tennis, business. *Address:* 29 Saxe Coburg Place, Edinburgh EH3 5BP; Royal Bank of Scotland, 42 St Andrew Square, Edinburgh EH2 2YE. *Club:* New (Edinburgh).

MATHIAS, Prof. Christopher Joseph, DPhil; FRCP; Professor of Neurovascular Medicine, University of London at St Mary's Hospital Medical School, Imperial College of Science, Technology and Medicine, and Institute of Neurology, British Postgraduate Medical Federation, since 1991; Consultant Physician, since 1982: St Mary's Hospital; Western Eye Hospital; National Hospital for Neurology and Neurosurgery; *b* 16 March 1949; *s* of late Lt Elias Mathias, IN and Hilda Mathias (*née* Lobo); *m* 1977, Rosalind (Lindy) Margaret, *d* of late Ambrose Jolleys, Cons. Paediatric Surgeon and of Elizabeth, (Betty), Jolleys; two *s* one *d*. *Educ:* St Aloysius Sch., Visakhapatnam; St Joseph's E. H. Sch., Bangalore; St John's Med. Coll., Bangalore Univ. (MB BS 1972); Worcester Coll., Oxford; Wolfson Coll., Oxford (DPhil 1976). LRCSE, LRCPSGlas 1974; MRCP 1978, FRCP 1987. Rhodes Schol., 1972–75; Res. Officer and Hon. Registrar, Dept of Neurology, Churchill Hosp., Oxford, 1972–76; Clinical Asst and Res. Fellow, Nat. Spinal Injuries Centre, Stoke Mandeville Hosp., 1973–76; Sen. Hse Officer, Dept of Medicine, RPMS/Hammersmith Hosp., 1976–77; Registrar in Medicine, St Mary's Hosp., Portsmouth and Dept of Renal Medicine, Univ. of Southampton, 1977–79; Wellcome Trust Sen. Res. Fellow in Clinical Sci. at St Mary's Hosp. Med. Sch., 1979–84; Wellcome Trust Sen. Lectr in Med. Sci., St Mary's Hosp. Med. Sch. and Inst. of Neurol., 1984–92. Prof. Ruitinga Foundn Award and Vis. Prof., Acad. Med. Centre, Univ. of Amsterdam, 1988. Dr J. Thomas Meml Oration, St John's Med. Coll., Bangalore Univ., 1988; Lectures: Lord Florey Meml, and Dorothy Mortlock, Royal Adelaide Hosp., Univ. of Adelaide, 1991; BP Regl, RCP, 1992. Founder Editor-in-Chief, Clinical Autonomic Res., 1991–. Chairman: Clinical Autonomic Res. Soc., 1987–90 (first Sec., 1982–86) Res. Cttee, World Fedn of Neurol., 1993– (Mem., 1989–93); Scientific Panel, European Fedn of Neurol Socs, 1994–. *Publications:* (ed jtly) Mild Hypertension: current controversies and new approaches, 1984; (ed jtly) Concepts in Hypertension, 1989; (ed jtly) Autonomic Failure: a textbook of clinical disorders of the autonomic nervous system, 3rd edn 1992; chaps in neurol. and cardiovascular textbooks; papers on nervous system and hormonal control of circulation in neurological, cardiovascular and other medical disorders. *Recreations:* gardening, badminton, watching cricket and football, observing human (and recently, canine) behaviour. *Address:* Meadowcroft, West End Lane, Stoke Poges, Bucks SL2 4NE.

MATHIAS, Surg. Rear-Adm. (D) Frank Russell Bentley; retired 1985; Director, Naval Dental Services, 1983–85, and Deputy Director of Defence Dental Services (Organisation), Ministry of Defence, 1985; *b* 27 Dec. 1927; *s* of Thomas Bentley Mathias and Phebe Ann Mathias; *m* 1954, Margaret Joyce (*née* Daniels); one *s* one *d*. *Educ:* Narberth Grammar Sch.; Guy's Hosp., London. LDSRCS Eng. 1952. House Surgeon, Sussex County Hosp., Brighton, 1952–53; joined RN, 1953; principal appointments: Staff Dental Surgeon, Flag Officer Malta, 1972; Flotilla Dental Surgeon, Flag Officer Submarines, 1972–74; Comd Dental Surgeon, Flag Officer Naval Air Comd, 1974–76; Dep. Dir, Naval Dental Services, 1976–80; Comd Dental Surgeon to C-in-C Naval Home Comd, 1980–83. QHDS 1982–85. OStJ 1981.

MATHIAS, Pauline Mary; Headmistress, More House School, 1974–89; Member, Independent Television Commission, since 1991; *b* 4 Oct. 1928; *d* of Francis and Hilda Donovan; *m* 1954, Prof. Anthony Peter Mathias; two *s*. *Educ:* La Retraite High School; Bedford College, London (BA Hons; DipEd). Head of English Dept, London Oratory Sch., 1954–64; Sen. Lectr in English and Admissions Tutor, Coloma Coll. of Education, 1964–74. Pres., GSA, 1982–83; Vice-Pres., Women's Careers Foundn, 1985–89; Chairman: ISIS, 1984–86; GBGSA, 1994– (Dep. Chm., 1992–94). Governor: Westminster Cathedral Choir Sch., 1978–; ESU, 1986–92; St Felix Sch., Southwold, 1986– (Chm. Governors, 1990–). *Address:* 18 Lee Road, Aldeburgh, Suffolk IP15 5HG.

MATHIAS, Dr Peter, CBE 1984; MA, DLitt; FBA 1977; Master of Downing College, Cambridge, 1987–95 (Hon. Fellow, 1995); *b* 10 Jan. 1928; *o c* of John Samuel and Marion Helen Mathias; *m* 1958, Elizabeth Ann, *d* of Robert Blackmore, JP, Bath; two *s* one *d*. *Educ:* Colston's Sch., Bristol; Jesus Coll., Cambridge (Schol.; Hon. Fellow, 1987). 1st cl. (dist) Hist. Tripos, 1950, 1951; DLitt: Oxon, 1985; Cantab, 1987. Research Fellow, Jesus Coll., Cambridge, 1952–55; Asst Lectr and Lectr, Faculty of History, Cambridge, 1955–68; Dir of Studies in History and Fellow, Queens' Coll., Cambridge, 1955–68 (Hon. Fellow, 1987); Tutor, 1957–68; Senior Proctor, Cambridge Univ., 1965–66; Chichele Prof. of Economic History, Oxford Univ., and Fellow of All Souls Coll., Oxford, 1969–87. Mem., Council of the Senate, Cambridge Univ., 1991–94. Vis. Professor: Univ. of Toronto, 1961; School of Economics, Delhi, 1967; Univ. of California, Berkeley, 1967; Univ. of Pa, 1972; Virginia Gildersleeve, Barnard Coll., Columbia Univ., 1972; Johns Hopkins Univ., 1979; ANU, Canberra, 1981; Geneva, 1986; Leuven, 1990; San Marino, 1990. Chairman: Business Archives Council, 1968–72 (Vice-Pres., 1980–84; Pres., 1984–); Econ. and Social History Cttee, SSRC, 1975–77 (Mem., 1970–77); Acad. Adv. Council, University Coll., Buckingham, 1979–84 (Mem., 1984–); Wellcome Trust Adv. Panel for History of Medicine, 1981–88; Friends of Kettle's Yard, 1989–; Fitzwilliam Mus. Enterprises Ltd, 1990–; Syndic of Fitzwilliam Mus., 1987–; Bd of Continuing Educn, 1991–95; Nat. Adv. Council, British Library, 1994– (Mem., Adv. Cttee (Humanities and Social Scis), 1990–94); Member: ABRC, 1983–89; Round Table, Council of Industry and Higher Educn, 1989–; Beirat Wissenschaftskolleg, Berlin, 1992–. Treasurer, Econ. Hist. Soc., 1968–88 (Pres., 1989–92; Vice Pres., 1992–); Hon. Treasurer, British Acad., 1980–89; International Economic History Association: Sec., 1959–62; Pres., 1974–78; Hon. Pres., 1978–; Vice Pres., Internat. Inst. of Economic History Francesco Datini, Prato, 1987– (Mem. Exec. Cttee, 1972–); Jerusalem Cttee, 1978–93; Mem., Academia Europaea, 1989; Trustee and Mem. Council, GB Sasakawa Foundn, 1994–. Foreign Member: Royal Danish Acad., 1982; Royal Belgian Acad., 1988. Curator, Bodleian Library, 1972–87. FRHistS 1972 (Vice-Pres., 1976–80). Hon. DLitt: Buckingham, 1985; Birmingham, 1988; Hull, 1992; Warwick, 1995; De Montfort, 1995. Asst Editor, Econ. Hist. Rev., 1955–57; Gen. Editor, Debates in Economic History, 1967–86. *Publications:* The Brewing Industry in England 1700–1830, 1959, repr. 1993; English Trade Tokens, 1962; Retailing Revolution, 1967; The First Industrial Nation, 1969, rev. edn 1983; (ed) Science and Society 1600–1900, 1972; The Transformation of England, 1979; L'Economia Britannica dal 1815 al 1914, 1994; General Editor, Cambridge Economic History of Europe, 1968–. *Recreation:* travel. *Address:* Bassingbourn Mill, Mill Lane, Bassingbourn, near Royston, Herts SG8 5PP. *T:* Royston (01763) 248708.

MATHIES, Monika W.; *see* Wulf-Mathies.

MATHIESON, Hon. Dame Janet Hilary; *see* Smith, Hon. Dame J. H.

MATHIESON, William Allan Cunningham, CB 1970; CMG 1955; MBE 1945; consultant to international organisations; *b* 22 Feb. 1916; *e s* of Rev. William Miller Mathieson, BD, and Elizabeth Cunningham Mathieson (*née* Reid); *m* 1946, Elizabeth Frances, *y d* of late Henry Marvell Carr, RA; two *s*. *Educ:* High Sch. of Dundee; Edinburgh and Cambridge Univs. Joined Colonial Office, 1939; served War, 1940–45; Royal Artillery in UK, France and Germany (Major, despatches). Rejoined Colonial Office, 1945; Middle East Dept, 1945–48; Private Sec. to Minister of State, 1948–49; Asst Sec., Colonial Office, 1949; Counsellor (Colonial Affairs) UK Delegn to UN, New York, 1951–54; Head of East African Department, CO, 1955–58; Minister of Education, Labour and Lands, Kenya, 1958–60; Asst Sec., Dept of Technical Co-operation, 1961–64; Under-Sec., 1964–68, Dep. Sec., 1968–75, Min. of Overseas Development; Consultant, UN Develt Prog., 1976–81. Chm., Executive Council, Commonwealth Agricultural Bureaux, 1963; Member: Exec. Bd, Unesco, 1968–74; Bd of Trustees, Internat. Centre for Maize and Wheat Improvement (Mexico), 1976–86; Council, ODI, 1977–90; Council, Commonwealth Soc. for the Deaf, 1979–94; Bd of Management, LSHTM, 1981–84; Bd of Governors, Internat. Centre for Insect Physiol. and Ecol., Nairobi, 1985–90; Chm., Bd of Trustees, Internat. Service for Nat. Agr. Res., 1980–84. Hon. Fellow, Queen Elizabeth House, Oxford, 1973; Foreign Fellow, African Acad. of Scis, 1989. FRSA. *Recreations:* photography, travel. *Address:* 13 Sydney House, Woodstock Road, W4 1DP.

MATLHABAPHIRI, Hon. Gaotlhaetse Utlwang Sankoloba; MP, Botswana, 1979–80, and since 1989; *b* 6 Nov. 1949; *s* of late Sankoloba and Khumo Matlhabaphiri; four *d*. *Educ:* Diamond Corporation Training Sch.; London; Friederick Ebert Foundn, Gaborone (Labour Economics). Clerk, Standard Chartered Bank, 1971–72; teacher, also part-time Dep. Head Master, Capital Continuation Classes, Gaborone, 1971–72; diamond sorter valuator, 1973–79; Gen. Sec., Botswana Democratic Party Youth Wing, 1978–85 and 1992–96; Asst Minister of Agriculture, 1979–85; Mem., Central Cttee, Botswana Democratic Party, 1982–85 and 1991–95 (Chm., Labour Cttee, 1991); Ambassador of Botswana to Nordic countries, 1985–86; High Comr for Botswana in UK, 1986–88 (concurrently Ambassador (non-resident) to Romania and Yugoslavia). Asst Gen. Sec., Bank Employees Union, 1972; Gen. Sec., Botswana Diamond Sorters Valuators Union, 1976–79; Chairman: Botswana Fedn of Trade Unions, 1979; Parly Public Accounts Cttee, 1993–94; Law Reform Cttee, 1993–94. Member: CPA; Botswana Br., IPU Cttee, 1993; UEESA. Conductor/Dir, Botswana Democratic Party Internat. Choir. Governor, IFAD, 1980–84. *Recreations:* footballer, athlete; choral music. *Address:* c/o PO Box 28, Gaborone, Botswana. *Clubs:* Royal Over-Seas League, Commonwealth Trust; Gaborone Township Rollers.

MATLOCK, Jack Foust; American Career Diplomat; Kathryn and Shelby Cullom Davis Professor, Columbia University, since 1993; *b* 1 Oct. 1929; *s* of late Jack F. Matlock and of Nellie Matlock (*née* McSwain); *m* 1949, Rebecca Burrum; four *s* one *d*. *Educ:* Duke Univ. (BA 1950); Columbia Univ. (MA 1952). Editor and translator on Current Digest of the Soviet Press, 1952–53; Russian language and literature Instructor, Dartmouth Coll., 1953–56; joined US Foreign Service, 1956; served in Moscow, Austria, Ghana, Zanzibar, Tanzania; Vis. Prof. of Political Science, Vanderbilt Univ., 1978–79; Dep. Dir, Foreign Service Inst., 1979–80; Chargé d'Affaires, Moscow, 1981; Ambassador to Czechoslovakia, 1981; Special Asst to President for Nat. Security Affairs and Sen. Dir, European and Soviet Affairs on Nat. Security Council Staff, 1983–86; Ambassador to Soviet Union, 1987–91. Masaryk Award, 1983; Superior Honor Award, Dept of State, 1981; Presidential Meritorious Service Award, 1984, 1987. *Publications:* Handbook to Russian edn of Stalin's Works, 1972; Autopsy on an Empire: re-viewing the Soviet collapse, 1995; articles on US-Soviet relations. *Address:* (office) 420 West 118th Street, New York, NY 10027, USA; (home) 2913 P Street NW, Washington, DC 20007, USA; 448 Riverside Drive, New York, NY 10027, USA. *Club:* International (Washington DC).

MATOKA, Dr Peter Wilfred; Chairman and Managing Director, Filizam Project and Investment Centre Ltd, since 1992; Senior Lecturer, University of Zambia, since 1995; *b* 8 April 1930; *m* 1957, Grace Joyce; two *s* one *d*. *Educ:* Mwinilunga Sch.; Munali Secondary Sch.; University Coll. of Fort Hare (BA Rhodes); American Univ., Washington (Dipl. Internat. Relations); Univ. of Zambia (MA); Univ. of Warwick (PhD 1994). MP Mwinilunga, Parlt of Zambia, 1964–78; Minister: of Information and Postal Services, 1964–65; of Health, 1965–66; of Works, 1967; of Power, Transport and Works, 1968; of Luapula Province, 1969; High Comr for Zambia in UK and Ambassador to the Holy See, 1970–71; Minister of Health, 1971–72; Minister of Local Govt and Housing, 1972–77; Minister of Economic and Technical Co-operation, 1977–78; retd from active politics, 1992; Sen. Regl Advr, Econ. Commn for Africa, UN, Addis Ababa, 1979–83; High Comr in Zimbabwe, 1984–89. Mem. Central Cttee, United National Independence Party, 1971– (Chairman: Social and Cultural Cttee, 1989–90; Sci. and Technol. Cttee, 1990–91). Life Mem., CPA, 1974. Pres., AA of Zambia, 1969–70. Kt of St Gregory the Great, 1964; Mem., Knightly Assoc. of St George the Martyr, 1986–. *Recreations:* reading, walking, watching television. *Address:* (office) Ibex Hill Township, PO Box 50101, Lusaka, Zambia.

MATOLENGWE, Rt. Rev. Patrick Monwabisi; a Bishop Suffragan of Cape Town, 1976–88, retired; Dean and Bishop in Residence, All Saints' Cathedral, Diocese of Milwaukee, since 1990; *b* 12 May 1937; *s* of David and Emma Matolengwe; *m* 1967, Crecentia Nompumelelo (*née* Nxele); three *s* two *d*. *Educ:* Healdtown Institution, Fort Beaufort (matric.); Lovedale Teacher Training Coll., Alice; Bishop Gray Coll., Cape Town; Federal Theol Sem., Alice (Cert. Theol.). MTh and DD, Nashotah House Seminary, 1992. Teaching, 1959–60; Court Interpreter, 1960–61; theological studies, 1962–65; Curacy at Herschel, Dio. Grahamstown, 1965–68; Rector of Nyanga, Dio. Cape Town, 1968–76, of St Luke's Church, Whitewater, Dio. of Milwaukee, 1988–89. *Recreations:* scouting, singing, music, reading, tennis. *Address:* 818 E Juneau Avenue, Milwaukee, WI 53202, USA.

MATTHEW, Chessor Lillie, FRIBA, FRIAS; JP; Principal, Duncan of Jordanstone College of Art, Dundee, 1964–78, retired; *b* 22 Jan. 1913; *s* of William Matthew and Helen Chessor Matthew (*née* Milne); *m* 1939, Margarita Ellis; one *s*. *Educ:* Gray's School of Art; Robert Gordon's Coll., Aberdeen. Diploma in Architecture; AMRTPI. Lectr, Welsh Sch. of Architecture, Cardiff, 1936–40. Served RAF, 1940–46, Flt-Lt. Sen. Lectr, Welsh Sch. of Architecture, Cardiff, 1946–57; Head of Sch. of Architecture, Duncan of Jordanstone Coll. of Art, Dundee, 1958–64. *Recreations:* hill walking, foreign travel. *Address:* Craigmhor, 36 Albany Road, West Ferry, Dundee DD5 1NW. *T:* Dundee (01382) 778364.

MATTHEW, Prof. (Henry) Colin Gray, DPhil; FBA 1991; Editor, New Dictionary of National Biography, since 1992; Professor of Modern History, Oxford, since 1992; Fellow and Tutor in Modern History, St Hugh's College, Oxford, since 1978; Lecturer in Gladstone Studies, Christ Church, Oxford, since 1970; *b* 15 Jan. 1941; *s* of Henry Johnston Scott and Joyce Mary Matthew; *m* 1966, Sue Ann (*née* Curry); two *s* one *d*. *Educ:* Sedbergh Sch.; Christ Church, Oxford (MA, DPhil); Makerere Coll., Univ. of E Africa (DipEd). Education Officer, Grade IIA, Tanzanian Civil Service, 1963–66; Student of Christ Church, Oxford, 1976–78. Literary Dir, RHistS, 1985–89. Editor, The Gladstone Diaries, 1972–94. *Publications:* The Liberal Imperialists, 1973; (ed) The Gladstone Diaries: vols 3 and 4 (with M. R. D. Foot), 1974; vols 5 and 6, 1978; vols 7 and 8, 1982; vol. 9, 1986; vols 10 and 11, 1990; vols 12, 13 and 14, 1994; Gladstone 1809–1874, 1986; Gladstone 1875–1898, 1995; (ed with Jane Garnett) Religion and Revival since 1700, 1993; contributor to: Studies in Church History, vol. xv, Oxford Illustrated History of Britain, 1984, and learned jls. *Recreations:* fishing, bag-pipe playing, second-hand book buying. *Address:* 107 Southmoor Road, Oxford OX2 6RE. *T:* Oxford (01865) 274900 or 57959.

MATTHEWMAN, Keith; QC 1979; **His Honour Judge Matthewman;** a Circuit Judge, since 1983; *b* 8 Jan. 1936; *e s* of late Lieut Frank Matthewman and Elizabeth Matthewman; *m* 1962, Jane (*née* Maxwell); one *s*. *Educ:* Long Eaton Grammar Sch.; University College London (LLB). Called to the Bar, Middle Temple, 1960. School teacher, Barking, Essex and Heanor, Derbys, 1960–61; Commercial Assistant, Internat. Div., Rolls-Royce Ltd, 1961–62; practice at the Bar, 1962–83, Midland Circuit, later Midland and Oxford Circuit; a Recorder of the Crown Court, 1979–83. Mem. Cttee, Council of HM's Circuit Judges, 1984–89. Mem., Notts Probation Cttee, 1986–. A Pres., Mental Health Review Tribunals, 1993–. Mem., Heanor UDC, 1960–63. TV appearances include Crimestalker, Central TV, 1993. *Recreation:* gardening. *Address:* c/o Crown Court, Nottingham NG1 7EJ. *Club:* Beeston Fields Golf (Bramcote).

MATTHEWS, family name of **Baron Matthews**.

MATTHEWS, Baron *cr* 1980 (Life Peer), of Southgate in the London Borough of Enfield; **Victor Collin Matthews,** FRSA, CBIM; Trafalgar House plc: Deputy Chairman, 1973–85; Group Managing Director, 1968–77; Group Chief Executive, 1977–83; *b* 5 Dec. 1919; *s* of A. and J. Matthews; *m* 1942, Joyce Geraldine (*née* Pilbeam); one *s*. *Educ:* Highbury. Served RNVR, 1939–45. Chairman: Trafalgar House Develt Hldgs, 1970–83; Cunard Steam-Ship Co., 1971–83; Ritz Hotel (London), 1976–83; Trafalgar House Construction Hldgs, 1977–83; Express Newspapers plc, 1977–85 (Chief Exec., 1977–82); Cunard Cruise Ships, 1978–83; Cunard Line, 1978–83; Evening Standard Co. Ltd, 1980–85; Fleet Publishing Internat. Hldgs Ltd, 1978–82; Fleet Hldgs, 1982–85; (non-exec.) Ellerman Hldgs, 1983–86; Director: Associated Container Transportation (Australia) Ltd, 1972–83; Cunard Crusader World Travel Ltd, 1974–85; Racecourse Holdings Trust Ltd, 1977–85; Associated Communications Corp. plc, 1977–82; Goldquill Ltd, 1979–83; Darchart Ltd, 1980–83; Garmaine Ltd, 1980–83. *Recreations:* racehorse breeder/owner, cricket, golf. *Address:* Waverley Farm, Mont Arthur, St Brelades, Jersey, Channel Islands. *Clubs:* MCC, Royal Automobile; Royal & Ancient Golf.

MATTHEWS, Rt Rev. Anthony Francis Berners H.; *see* Hall-Matthews.

MATTHEWS, Colin, DPhil; composer; *b* 13 Feb. 1946; *s* of Herbert and Elsie Matthews; *m* 1977, Belinda Lloyd; one *s* two *d*. *Educ:* Univ. of Nottingham (BA Classics, MPhil Composition); Univ. of Sussex (DPhil). Studied composition with Arnold Whittall and Nicholas Maw, 1967–70; collaborated with Deryck Cooke on performing version of Mahler's Tenth Symphony, 1964–74; asst to Benjamin Britten, 1971–76; worked with Imogen Holst, 1972–84; taught at Univ. of Sussex, 1971–72, 1976–77. Associate Composer, LSO, 1990–. Dir, Holst Estate and Holst Foundn, 1973–; Trustee, Britten-Pears Foundn, and Dir, Britten Estate, 1983–; Mem. Council and Exec. Cttee, SPNM, 1981–93, 1994–; Exec. Mem. Council, Aldeburgh Foundn, 1984–93; Dir, PRS, 1992–. Founder, NMC Recordings Ltd, 1988. Patron, Musicians against Nuclear Arms, 1985–. *Principal works:* Fourth Sonata, 1974; Night Music, 1976; Sonata no 5 'Landscape', 1977–81; String Quartet no 1, 1979; Oboe Quartet, 1981; The Great Journey, 1981–88; Divertimento for Double String Quartet, 1982; Toccata Meccanica, 1984; Night's Mask, 1984; Cello Concerto, 1984; Suns Dance, 1985; Five Duos, 1985; Three Enigmas, 1985; String Quartet no 2, 1985; Pursuit (ballet), 1986; Monody, 1986–87; Eleven Studies in Velocity, 1987; Two Part Invention, 1987; Cortège, 1988; Hidden Variables, 1989; Quatrain, 1989; Second Oboe Quartet, 1990; Five Concertinos, 1990; Chiaroscuro, 1990; Machines and Dreams, 1990; Broken Symmetry, 1990–91; Contraflow, 1992; Memorial, 1992; String Quartet no 3, 1994; . . . through the glass, 1994. Scottish National Orch. Ian Whyte Award, 1975; Park Lane Group Composer Award, 1983. *Publications:* contribs to Musical Times, Tempo, TLS, etc. *Recreations:* wine, very amateur astrophysics. *Address:* c/o Faber Music Ltd, 3 Queen Square, WC1N 3AU. *T:* 0171–278 6881. *Club:* Leyton Orient Supporters'.

See also D. J. Matthews.

MATTHEWS, David; *see* Matthews, William D.

MATTHEWS, David John; composer; *b* 9 March 1943; *s* of Herbert and Elsie Matthews; *m* Jean Hasse. *Educ:* Bancroft's Sch., Woodford; Univ. of Nottingham (BA Classics). Studied composition with Anthony Milner, 1967–69; Asst to Benjamin Britten, 1966–70. Musical Dir, Deal Fest., 1989–. Collaborated with Deryck Cooke on performing version of Mahler's Tenth Symphony, 1964–74. *Compositions include:* 3 songs for soprano and orchestra, 1968; String Quartet No 1, 1970; Symphony No 1, 1975; String Quartet No 2, 1976; Symphony No 2, 1977; String Quartet No 3, 1977; September Music, for small orch., 1979; Ehmals und Jetzt, 6 songs for soprano and piano, 1979; The Company of Lovers, 5 choral songs, 1980; String Quartet No 4, 1981; Serenade, for chamber orch., 1982; Violin Concerto, 1982; The Golden Kingdom, 9 songs for high voice and piano, 1983; Piano Trio No. 1, 1983; Clarinet Quartet, 1984; Symphony No 3, 1985; In the Dark Time, for orch., 1985; Variations for strings, 1986; The Flaying of Marsyas, for oboe and string quartet, 1987; Chaconne, for orch., 1987; Cantiga, for soprano and chamber orch., 1988; The Ship of Death, for chorus, 1989; Piano Sonata, 1989; String Trio, 1989; Romanza, for 'cello and small orch., 1990; The Music of Dawn, for orch., 1990; Symphony No 4, 1990; Capriccio, for 2 horns and strings, 1991; String Quartet No 6, 1991; Oboe Concerto, 1992; The Sleeping Lord, for sop. and ensemble, 1992; A Vision and a Journey, for orch., 1993; Piano Trio No 2, 1993; A Congress of Passions, for voice, oboe and piano, 1994; Vespers, for soli, chorus and orch., 1994; Skies now are Skies, for tenor and string quartet, 1994; A Song and Dance Sketchbook, for piano quartet, 1995. *Publications:* Michael Tippett, 1980; Landscape into Sound, 1992; contribs to Tempo, TLS. *Recreations:* walking, sketching. *Address:* c/o Faber Music Ltd, 3 Queen Square, WC1N 3AU.

See also Colin Matthews.

MATTHEWS, David Napier, CBE 1976 (OBE 1945); MA, MD, MCh (Cambridge); FRCS; Hon. FDSRCS; retired; Consulting Plastic Surgeon, University College Hospital and Hospital for Sick Children; Civilian Consultant in Plastic Surgery to the Royal Navy since 1954; *b* 7 July 1911; *m* 1940, Betty Eileen Bailey Davies; two *s* one *d*. *Educ:* Leys Sch., Cambridge; Queens' Coll., Cambridge; Charing Cross Hosp. Qualified as doctor, 1935. Surgical Registrar, Westminster Hospital, until 1940; Surgeon Plastic Unit, East Grinstead, 1939–41; Surgical Specialist, RAFVR, 1941–46; Plastic Surgeon: UCH and Hosp. for Sick Children, 1946–76; Royal Nat. Orthopædic Hosp., 1947–54; King Edward's Hosp. for Officers, 1972–80. Adviser in Plastic Surgery, DHSS, 1962–77. Consulting Practice as Surgeon 1946–80; Hunterian Professor, RCS, 1941, 1944, 1976; President: British Assoc. of Plastic Surgeons, 1954 and 1971; Plastic Section, RSM, 1970–71; Sec., Harveian Soc. of London, 1951, Vice-Pres., 1954, Pres., 1962; Gen. Sec. Internat. Confederation for Plastic Surgery, 1959; Pres., Chelsea Clinical Soc., 1962. *Publications:* Surgery of Repair, 1943, 2nd edn, 1946; (Ed.) Recent Advances in the Surgery of Trauma, 1963; chapters in surgical books; contrib. to Lancet, BMJ and Post Graduate Jl etc. *Recreation:* fishing. *Address:* River Walk, Shooters Hill, Pangbourne, Reading RG8 7DU. *T:* Pangbourne (01734) 844476.

MATTHEWS, Douglas, BA; FLA; Librarian, The London Library, 1980–93; *b* 23 Aug. 1927; *s* of Benjamin Matthews and Mary (*née* Pearson); *m* 1968, Sarah Maria Williams (marr. diss. 1991); two *d*. *Educ:* Acklam Hall Sch., Middlesbrough; Durham Univ. Assistant: India Office Library, 1952–62; Kungl. Biblioteket, Stockholm, 1956–57; Librarian, Home Office, 1962–64; Dep. Librarian, London Library, 1965–80. Mem. Cttee, Royal Literary Fund, 1993–. Mem. Court, Univ. of Sussex, 1983–94. *Address:* 1 Priory Terrace, Mountfield Road, Lewes, Sussex BN7 2UT. *T:* Lewes (01273) 475635. *Club:* Garrick.

MATTHEWS, Dr Drummond Hoyle, VRD 1967; FRS 1974; Senior Research Associate, Scientific Director, British Institutions Reflection Profiling Syndicate, at the University of Cambridge, 1982–90; Fellow, Wolfson College, Cambridge, 1980–90; *b* 5 Feb. 1931; *s* of late Captain C. B. and late Mrs E. M. Matthews; *m* 1st, 1963, Elizabeth Rachel McMullen (marr. diss. 1980); one *s* one *d*; 2nd, 1987, Sandie Adam. *Educ:* Bryanston Sch.; King's Coll., Cambridge. BA 1954, MA 1959, PhD 1962. RNVR, 1949–51, retd 1967. Geologist, Falkland Islands Dependencies Survey, 1955–57; returned to Cambridge (BP student), 1958; Research Fellow, King's Coll., 1960; Sen. Asst in Research, Dept of Geophysics, 1960; Asst Dir of Research, 1966; Reader in Marine Geology, 1971. Balzan Prize (jtly), 1982. *Publications:* papers on marine geophysics in jls and books. *Recreations:* walking, sailing. *Address:* Orchard Cottage, Sparkhayes Lane, Porlock, Som TA24 8NE. *Clubs:* Antarctic, Cruising Association.

MATTHEWS, Edwin James Thomas, TD 1946; Chief Taxing Master of the Supreme Court, 1979–83 (Master, 1965–78); *b* 2 May 1915; *s* of Edwin Martin Matthews (killed in action, 1917); *m* 1939, Katherine Mary Hirst, BA (Oxon.), Dip. Soc. Sc. (Leeds); two *d*. *Educ:* Sedbergh Sch., Yorks. Admitted as Solicitor of Supreme Court, 1938; practice on own account in Middlesbrough, 1938–39. Served in Royal Artillery, 1939–46, UK, France and Belgium (Dunkirk 1940); released with rank of Major. Partner, Chadwick Son & Nicholson, Solicitors, Dewsbury, Yorks, 1946–50; Area Sec., No. 6 (W Midland) Legal Aid Area Cttee of Law Soc., 1950–56; Sec. of Law Soc. for Contentious Business (including responsibility for administration of Legal Aid and Advice Schemes), 1956–65. Toured Legal Aid Offices in USA for Ford Foundation and visited Toronto to advise Govt of Ontario, 1963. Mem., Council, British Academy of Forensic Sciences, 1965–68. Special Consultant to NBPI on Solicitors' Costs, 1967–68; General Consultant, Law Soc., 1983–84. Member: Lord Chancellor's Adv. Cttee on Legal Aid, 1972–77; Working Party on Legal Aid Legislation, 1974–76; Working Party on the Criminal Trial, 1980–83; Supreme Ct Procedure Cttee, 1982–83. Lectr, mainly on costs and remuneration for solicitors and counsel, for Coll. of Law, Legal Studies and Services Ltd and to various provincial Law Socs, 1983–89. *Publications:* contrib. Halsbury's Laws of England, 1961 and Atkins Encyclopaedia of Forms and Precedents, 1962; (with Master Graham-Green) Costs in Criminal Cases and Legal Aid, 1965; (jointly) Legal Aid and Advice Under the Legal Aid and Advice Acts, 1949 to 1964, 1971; (ed jtly) Supreme Court Practice; contribs to legal journals. *Recreations:* trout fishing, theatre, gardening, French wines. *Address:* 2 Downside Road, Winchester, Hants SO22 5LU. *T:* Winchester (01962) 862478. *Club:* Abbots Barton (Hants).

MATTHEWS, Prof. Ernest, DDS, PhD, MSc, ARCS, DIC, FDSRCS; Director of Prosthetics, University of Manchester, 1935–70, now Professor Emeritus; *b* 14 Dec. 1904; *s* of James Alfred Matthews, Portsmouth; *m* 1928, Doris Pipe (decd); one *d* (two *s* decd). *Educ:* Imperial Coll., London; Cambridge; Guy's Hospital, London. Demonstrator and Lecturer, Guy's Hospital Medical and Dental Schs, 1926–34; Prosthetic Dental Surgeon, Manchester Royal Infirmary, 1937; Dean and Dir, Turner Dental Sch., 1966–69; Cons. Dental Surgeon, Christie Hosp., 1945; Hon. Adviser in Dental Surgery to Manchester Regional Hospital Board, 1951. Silver Jubilee Medal, 1977. *Recreation:* gardening. *Address:* 16 The Spain, Petersfield, Hants GU32 3LA.

MATTHEWS, Prof. Geoffrey, MA, PhD; CMath, FIMA; Shell Professor of Mathematics Education, Centre for Science and Mathematics Education, Chelsea College, University of London, 1968–77, now Emeritus; *b* 1 Feb. 1917; *s* of Humphrey and Gladys Matthews; *m* 1st, 1941, Patricia Mary Jackson; one *s* one *d*; 2nd, 1972, Julia Comber. *Educ:* Marlborough; Jesus Coll., Cambridge (MA); PhD (London). CMath 1991; FIMA 1964. Wiltshire Regt, Intelligence Officer 43rd (Wessex) Div., 1939–45, Captain (dispatches, 1945; US Bronze Star, 1945). Teacher: Haberdashers' Aske's Sch., 1945–50; St Dunstan's Coll., 1950–64, Dep. Head and head of mathematics dept; Organiser, Nuffield Mathematics Teaching Project, 1964–72; Co-director (with Julia Matthews), Schools Council Early Mathematical Experiences project, 1974–79; Co-dir (with Prof. K. W. Keohane) SSRC funded prog. Concepts in Secondary Sch. Maths and Sci., 1974–79. Presenter of BBC TV programmes in series Tuesday Term, Middle School Mathematics, and Children and Mathematics; consultant to BBC series Maths in a Box and You and Me, and to ATV series Towards Mathematics. Consultant to maths teaching projects in Italy, Greece, Portugal, Sri Lanka and Thailand; has lectured extensively abroad. Pres., Mathematical Assoc., 1977–78 (Hon. Mem., 1990); Founder Mem., Commonwealth Assoc. of Sci. and Maths Educators, 1964; Member: Internat. Cttee, 3rd Congress, ICME, 1976; Council, Inst. of Maths and its Applications, 1978–81; Cttee, Soc. of Free Painters and Sculptors, 1978–89. One man shows, Loggia Gall., 1986, 1989; St Martin's-in-the-Fields Gall., 1993. *Publications:* Calculus, 1964; Matrices I & II, 1964; Mathematics through School, 1972; Mainly on the Bright Side, 1989; papers in Proc. Kon. Akad. Wetensch. (Amsterdam); numerous articles in Math. Gaz., etc. *Recreations:* painting, travel. *Address:* 50 Sydney Road, Bexleyheath, Kent DA6 8HG. *T:* 0181–303 4301.

MATTHEWS, Geoffrey Vernon Townsend, OBE 1986; Director of Research and Conservation, 1955–88, and Deputy Director, 1973–88, Wildfowl Trust, Slimbridge; *b* 16 June 1923; *s* of Geoffrey Tom Matthews and Muriel Ivy Townsend; *m* 1st, 1946, Josephine (marr. diss. 1961), *d* of Col Alured Charles Lowther O'Shea Bilderdeck; one *s* one *d*; 2nd, 1964, Janet Kear, *qv* (marr. diss. 1978); 3rd, 1980, Mary Elizabeth, *d* of William Evans; one *s* one *d*. *Educ:* Bedford Sch.; Christ's Coll., Cambridge (MA, PhD). RAF Operational Res., Bomber and SE Asia Comds (Sci. Officer/Flt Lieut), 1943–46. Post-doctoral res., Cambridge Univ., 1950–55; Special Lectr, Bristol Univ., 1965–88; Hon. Lectr 1966–69, Professorial Fellow 1970–90, UC, Cardiff. Dir, Internat. Waterfowl Res. Bureau, 1969–88, Counsellor of Honour, 1989–. Served on numerous non-govtl and govtl cttees; travelled widely. Pres., Assoc. for the Study of Animal Behaviour, 1971–74; Vice-Pres., British Ornithologists' Union, 1972–75, Union Medal, 1980. FIBiol, 1974; Corresp. Fellow, Amer. Ornithologists Union, 1969–. RSPB Medal, 1990. Officer, Dutch Order of Golden Ark, 1987. *Publications:* Bird Navigation, 1955, 2nd edn 1968; The Ramsar Convention on Wetlands, 1993 (trans. German and Japanese); chapters contributed to 43 multi-authored books; more than 100 papers in sci. and conservation jls. *Recreations:* fossil hunting, collecting zoological stamps, reading, household maintenance. *Address:* 32 Tetbury Street, Minchinhampton, Glos GL6 9JH. *T:* Stroud (01453) 884769. *Club:* Victory.

MATTHEWS, George Lloyd; Archivist, Democratic Left (formerly Communist Party of Great Britain); *b* 24 Jan. 1917; *s* of James and Ethel Matthews, Sandy, Beds; *m* 1940, Elisabeth Lynette Summers; no *c*. *Educ:* Bedford Modern Sch.; Reading Univ. Pres., Reading Univ. Students Union, 1938–39; Vice-Pres., Nat. Union of Students, 1939–40; Vice-Pres., University Labour Fedn, 1938–39. County Chm., Nat. Union of Agricultural Workers, 1945–49; Mem. Exec. Cttee, Communist Party, 1943–79; Asst Gen. Sec., Communist Party, 1949–57; Asst Editor, 1957–59, Editor, 1959–74, Daily Worker, later Morning Star; Head of Press and Publicity Dept, Communist Party of GB, 1974–79. *Publication:* (ed with F. King) About Turn, 1990. *Recreation:* music. *Address:* c/o Democratic Left, 6 Cynthia Street, N1 9JF. *T:* 0171–278 4443.

MATTHEWS, Gordon (Richards), CBE 1974; FCA; *b* 16 Dec. 1908; *m* 1st, 1934, Ruth Hillyard Brooks, *d* of Sir David Brooks, GBE (*d* 1980); one *s* one *d* (and one *d* decd); 2nd, 1982, Freda E. Evans (*née* Ledger). *Educ:* Repton Sch. Chartered Accountant, 1932. Contested (U) General Election, Deritend, Birmingham, 1945, and Yardley, Birmingham, 1950; MP (C) Meriden Division of Warwicks, 1959–64; PPS to the Postmaster-General, 1960–64. Hon. Treas., Deritend Unionist Assoc., 1937–45; Hon. Sec., Birmingham Unionist Association, 1948–53. Pres. City of Birmingham Friendly Soc., 1957–64; Mem. Board of Management, Linen and Woollen Drapers Institution and Cottage Homes, 1950–65 (Pres. of Appeal, 1954–55); Chm. of Exec. Cttee, Birmingham Area of YMCA, 1951–59; Mem., Nat. Council and Nat. Exec. Cttee, YMCA, 1968–71; Chm., Finance Cttee, YWCA, Birmingham Area, 1965–72. Chm., Oxfordshire Br., CPRE, 1978–81. Pres., West Midlands Cons. Council, 1983–85 (Dep. Chm., 1967–70; Chm., 1970–73). FRSA 1986. *Recreations:* fly-fishing and foreign travel. *Address:* 12 Cherry Orchard Close, Chipping Campden, Glos GL55 6DH. *T:* Evesham (01386) 840626.

MATTHEWS, Henry Melvin; Managing Director, Texaco Ltd, 1982–88; *b* 26 Feb. 1926; *s* of Phillip Lawrence and Agnes K. Matthews; *m* 1947, Margaret Goodridge; one *s* two *d*. *Educ:* Columbia University; Tufts Univ. (BSNS, BSME). Commnd Ensign, 1945, USNR; retired 1986. General Manager, Texaco Europe, USA, 1976; Vice Pres. Manufacture and Marketing, Texaco Europe, USA, 1980. Mem., US Navy League, London. *Recreations:* tennis, golf, swimming, gardening, music (choir), YMCA, Congregational Church. *Address:* (winter) 6280 Winged Foot Drive, Stuart, FL 34997, USA; (summer) Three Winds, 338 West Beach Road, Charlestown, RI 02813, USA. *Club:* Mariner Sands CC (Stuart, Fla).

MATTHEWS, Jeffery Edward, FCSD; freelance graphic designer and consultant, since 1952; *b* 3 April 1928; *s* of Henry Edward Matthews and Sybil Frances (*née* Cooke); *m* 1953, (Sylvia Lilian) Christine (*née* Hoar) (*d* 1994); one *s* one *d*. *Educ:* Alleyn's; Brixton Sch. of Building (Interior Design; NDD). AIBD 1951; FCSD (FSIAD 1978). Graphic designer with J. Edward Sander, 1949–52; part-time tutor, 1952–55. Lettering and calligraphy assessor for SIAD, 1970–. Designs for Post Office: decimal to pay labels, 1971; fount of numerals for definitive stamps, 1981; stamps: United Nations, 1965; British bridges, 1968; definitives for Scotland, Wales, NI and IOM, 1971; Royal Silver Wedding, 1972; 25th Anniversary of the Coronation, 1978; London, 1980; 80th birthday of the Queen Mother, 1980; Christmas, 1980; Wedding of Prince Charles and Lady Diana Spencer, 1981; Quincentenary of College of Arms, 1984; 60th birthday of the Queen, 1986; Wedding of Prince Andrew and Sarah Ferguson, 1986; Order of the Thistle Tercentenary of Revival, 1987; 150th Anniversary of the Penny Black, 1990; also first-day covers, postmarks, presentation packs, souvenir books and posters; one of three stamp designers featured in PO film, Picture to Post, 1969. Other design work includes: title banner lettering and coat of arms, Sunday Times, 1968; cover design and lettering for official prog., Royal Wedding, 1981; The Royal Mint, commemorative medal, Order of the Thistle, 1987; official heraldry and symbols, HMSO; hand-drawn lettering, COI; stamp designs, first-day covers, calligraphy, packaging, promotion and bookbinding designs, logotypes, brand images and hand-drawn lettering, for various firms including Unicover Corp., USA, Harrison & Sons Ltd, Metal Box Co., DRG, Reader's Digest Assoc. Ltd, Encyc. Britannica Internat. Ltd, ICI and H. R. Higgins (Coffee-man) Ltd. Work exhibited in A History of Bookplates in Britain, V&A Mus., 1979. Citizen and Goldsmith of London (Freedom by Patrimony), 1949. FRSA 1987. *Publications:* (contrib.) Designers in Britain, 1964, 1971; (contrib.) 45 Wood-engravers, 1982; (contrib.) Royal Mail Year Book, 1984, 1986, 1987. *Recreations:* furniture restoration, playing the guitar, gardening, DIY. *Address:* 46 Kings Hall Road, Beckenham, Kent BR3 1LS.

MATTHEWS, John, CBE 1990; FRAgS; Director, Institute of Engineering Research, Agricultural and Food Research Council (formerly National Institute of Agricultural Engineering), 1984–90; *b* 4 July 1930; *s* of John Frederick Matthews and Catherine Edith Matthews (*née* Terry); *m* 1982 (marr. diss. 1993); two *d*. *Educ:* Royal Latin School, Buckingham. BSc (Physics) London. CPhys, FInstP; CEng; FIAgrE 1970 (Hon. FIAgrE 1994). Scientist, GEC Res. Labs, 1951–59; National Institute of Agricultural Engineering: joined 1959; Head of Tractor Performance Dept, 1967–73; Head of Tractor and Cultivation Div., 1973–83; Asst Dir, 1983–84; Dir, 1984–90. Vis. Prof., Cranfield Inst. of Technology, 1987. Dir, Ceredigion and Mid-Wales NHS Trust, 1992–. Mem., Bd of Management, AFRC, 1986–90. Formerly Chm., Technical Cttees, Internat. Standards Orgn and OECD; Pres., Inst. of Agricl Engineers, 1986–88. Pro-Chancellor, Univ. of Luton, 1993– (Chm. of Govs, Luton Coll. of Higher Educn, 1989–93). Fellow: Ergonomics Soc.; Academie Georgofili, Italy, 1991. Research Medal, RASE, 1983. Max Eyth Medallion (Germany), 1990; Chevalier de Merite Agricole (France), 1992. *Publications:* (contrib.) Fream's Elements of Agriculture, 1984; (ed) Progress in Agricultural Physics and Engineering, 1991; contribs to other books and jls on agricultural engineering and ergonomics. *Recreations:* farming, gardening, Lions International club, travel. *Address:* Carron, Aberporth, Cardigan, Dyfed SA43 2DA.

MATTHEWS, Prof. John Burr Lumley, (Jack), FRSE; Director and Secretary, Scottish Association for Marine Science (formerly Scottish Marine Biological Association), since 1988; *b* 23 April 1935; *s* of Dr John Lumley Matthews and Susan Agnes Matthews; *m* 1962, Jane Rosemary Goldsmith; one *s* two *d*. *Educ:* Warwick Sch.; St John's Coll., Oxford (MA, DPhil). FRSE 1988. Res. Scientist, Oceanographic Lab., Edinburgh, 1961–67; University of Bergen: Lectr, Sen. Lectr, Marine Biology, 1967–78; Prof., Marine Biology, 1978–84; Dep. Dir, Scottish Marine Biol Assoc., 1984–88; Dir, Dunstaffnage Marine Lab., NERC, 1988–94. Vis. Prof., Oceanography, Univ. of British Columbia, 1977–78; Hon. Prof., Biology, Univ. of Stirling, 1984–. Member: Cttee for Scotland, Nature Conservancy Council, 1989–91; SW Regl Bd, Scottish Natural Heritage, 1992– (Dep. Chm., 1994–). Sec., Internat. Assoc. of Biol Oceanography. FRSA 1989. *Publications:* (ed jtly) Freshwater on the Sea, 1976; contribs to marine sci. jls. *Recreations:* country wines, pethau cymreig. *Address:* Grianaig, Rockfield Road, Oban, Argyll PA34 5DH. *T:* Oban (01631) 562734.

MATTHEWS, Dr John Duncan, CVO 1989; FRCPE; retired; Consultant Physician, Royal Infirmary, Edinburgh, 1955–86; Hon. Senior Lecturer, University of Edinburgh, 1976–86; *b* 19 Sept. 1921; *s* of Joseph Keith Matthews and Ethel Chambers; *m* 1945, Constance Margaret Moffat; two *s*. *Educ:* Shrewsbury; Univ. of Cambridge (BA); Univ. of Edinburgh (MB, ChB). FRCPE 1958. Surgeon, High Constables and Guard of Honour, Holyroodhouse, 1961–87, Moderator, 1987–89. Hon. Consultant in Medicine to the Army in Scotland, 1974–86; Examr in Medicine, Edinburgh and Cambridge Univs and Royal Colleges of Physicians. Vice-Pres., RCPE, 1982–85; Mem./Chm., various local and national NHS and coll. cttees. Sec., Edinburgh Medical Angling Club, 1963–86. *Publications:* occasional articles in med. jls on diabetes and heart disease. *Recreations:* cricket (Free Foresters, Grange, and Scotland), fishing, golf, gardening. *Address:* 3 Succoth Gardens, Edinburgh EH12 6BR.

MATTHEWS, Prof. John Frederick, DPhil; FRHistS; FSA; FBA 1990; Professor of Middle and Later Roman History, Oxford University, since 1992; Fellow, and Praelector in Ancient History, Queen's College, Oxford, since 1976; *b* 15 Feb. 1940; *s* of Jack and Mary Matthews; *m* 1965, Elaine Jackson (separated 1992); two *d*. *Educ:* Wyggeston Boys' Sch., Leicester; Queen's Coll., Oxford (MA 1965; DPhil 1970). FRHistS 1986; FSA 1993. Oxford University: Dyson Jun. Res. Fellow in Greek Culture, Balliol Coll., 1965–69; Conington Prize, 1971; Univ. Lectr in Middle and Late Roman Empire, 1969–90; Reader, 1990–92; Official Fellow, Corpus Christi Coll., 1969–76. Inst. for Advanced Study, Princeton, 1980–81; British Acad. Reader in Humanities, 1988–90; Chm. of Govs, Cheney Sch., Oxford, 1986–91. *Publications:* Western Aristocracies and Imperial Court AD 364–425, 1975; (with T. J. Cornell) Atlas of the Roman World, 1982; Political Life and Culture in late Roman Society, 1985; The Roman World of Ammianus, 1989; (with Peter Heather) The Goths in the Fourth Century, 1991. *Recreations:* playing the piano, listening to music, suburban gardening. *Address:* Queen's College, Oxford OX1 4AW. *T:* Oxford (01865) 279132.

MATTHEWS, Michael Gough; pianist, teacher, adjudicator and consultant; Director, Royal College of Music, 1985–93; *b* 12 July 1931; *s* of late Cecil Gough Matthews and Amelia Eleanor Mary Matthews. *Educ:* Chigwell School; Royal College of Music (Open Scholarship, 1947; Hopkinson Gold Medal, 1953; ARCM, FRCM 1972); ARCO; Diploma del Corso di Perfezionamento St Cecilia, Rome. Diploma of Honour and Prize, Chopin Internat. Piano Competition, 1955; Italian Govt Scholarship, 1956; Chopin Fellowship, Warsaw, 1959. Pianist; recitals, broadcasts, concerts, UK, Europe and Far East. Supervisor Junior Studies, RSAMD, 1964–71; Royal College of Music: Dir, Junior Dept, and Prof. of Piano, 1972–75; Registrar, 1975; Vice-Dir, 1978–84. Teacher and adjudicator of internat. competitions. Hon. Dir, Royal Music Foundn, Inc., USA, 1985–. Member: NYO GB; Royal Philharmonic Soc., 1985–; Music Study Gp, EEC, 1989–; Comité d'Honneur, Presence de l'Art, Paris, 1990–; Council, Purcell Tercentenary Trust, 1992. Vice-President: RCO, 1985–; Nat. Youth Choir, 1986–; Herbert Howells Soc., 1987–; Hon. Vice-Pres., Royal Choral Soc., 1992–. Consultant to HM the Sultan of Oman, 1993–, to Jaguar Cars, 1993–. Hon. FLCM 1976; Hon. RAM 1979; FRSAMD 1986; FRNCM 1991; FRSA; Hon. GSM 1987. Recordings of piano music of Fauré, Paris. *Publications:* various musical entertainments; arranger of educational music. *Recreation:* gardening. *Address:* Laurel Cottages, South Street, Mayfield, E Sussex TN20 6DD. *T* and *Fax:* Mayfield (01435) 873065. *Club:* Athenæum.

MATTHEWS, Mrs Pamela Winifred, (Mrs Peter Matthews), BSc (Econ.); Principal, Westfield College (University of London), 1962–65; *b* 4 Dec. 1914; *d* of Lt-Col C. C. Saunders-O'Mahony; *m* 1938, H. P. S. Matthews (*d* 1958); one *s* one *d*. *Educ:* St Paul's Girls' Sch.; London Sch. of Economics. Royal Institute of International Affairs, 1938–39; Foreign Office, 1939–40; The Economist Newspaper, 1940–43; Foreign Office, 1943–45; Reuters, 1945–61; Nat. Inst. for Social Work Trg, 1961–62. Independent Mem., Advertising Standards Authority, 1964–65; Industrial Tribunal rep. for CAB, 1974–89. Mem., RIIA, 1990. Governor: Northwood Coll., Middlesex, 1962–89; Cardinal Manning Boys' RC School, 1980–91. *Publications:* diplomatic correspondence for Reuters. *Recreations:* travel, theatre. *Address:* 1 Edwardes Place, Kensington High Street, W8 6LR. *T:* 0171–603 8458.

MATTHEWS, Percy; *b* 24 July 1921; *s* of Samuel and Minnie Matthews; *m* 1946, Audrey Rosenthal; one *s* two *d*. *Educ:* Parmiters Sch., London. Overseas Associate, J. O. Hambro & Co. Hon. Fellow, St Peter's Coll., Oxford. Freeman, City of London. *Recreations:* painting, golf.

MATTHEWS, Mrs Peter; *see* Matthews, Mrs Pamela W.

MATTHEWS, Sir Peter (Alec), Kt 1975; AO 1980; Chairman, Pegler-Hattersley plc, 1979–87 (Director, 1977–87); Director: Lloyds Bank, 1974–91 (Chairman, Central London Regional Board, 1978–91); Cookson Group (formerly Lead Industries Group), 1980–91; Hamilton Oil Great Britain, 1981–91; *b* 21 Sept. 1922; *s* of Major Alec Bryan Matthews and Elsie Lazarus Barlow; *m* 1946, Sheila Dorothy Bunting; four *s* one *d*. *Educ:* Shawnigan Lake Sch., Vancouver Island; Oundle Sch. Served Royal Engineers (retired as Major), 1940–46. Joined Stewarts and Lloyds Ltd, 1946; Director of Research and Technical Development, 1962; Member for R&D, BSC, 1968–70, Dep. Chm., 1973–76;

Vickers PLC: Man. Dir, 1970–79; Chm., 1980–84; Director: British Electric Traction Plc, 1976–87; Sun Alliance and London Insurance, 1979–89; Lloyds & Scottish, 1983–86. Chm., Armed Forces Pay Review Body, 1984–89; Mem., Top Salaries Review Body, 1984–89. Member: BOTB, 1973–77; Export Guarantees Adv. Council, 1973–78; Status Review Cttee, ECGD, 1983–84; Pres., Sino-British Trade Council, 1983–85. Member: NRDC, 1974–80; Engineering Industries Council, 1976–84 (Chm., 1980–84); Adv. Council for Applied R&D, 1976–80. Pres., Engineering Employers Fedn, 1982–84; Chm., Council, University Coll., London, 1980–89 (Hon. Fellow, 1982). CBIM, FRSA. *Recreations:* sailing, gardening. *Address:* Chalkwell, Nether Wallop, Stockbridge, Hants SO20 8HE. *T:* Andover (01264) 782136. *Club:* Royal Yacht Squadron (Cowes).

MATTHEWS, Prof. Peter Bryan Conrad, FRS 1973; MD, DSc; Professor of Sensorimotor Physiology, 1987–Oct. 1996, and Student of Christ Church since 1958, University of Oxford; *b* 23 Dec. 1928; *s* of Prof. Sir Bryan Matthews, CBE, FRS; *m* 1956, Margaret Rosemary Blears; one *s* one *d.* *Educ:* Marlborough Coll.; King's Coll., Cambridge; Oxford Univ. Clinical School. Oxford University: Univ. Lectr in Physiology, 1961–77; Reader, 1978–86; Tutor, Christ Church, 1958–86. Sir Lionel Whitby Medal, Cambridge Univ., 1959; Robert Bing Prize, Swiss Acad. of Med. Science, 1971. *Publications:* Mammalian Muscle Receptors and their Central Actions, 1972; papers on neurophysiology in various scientific jls. *Address:* University Laboratory of Physiology, Parks Road, Oxford OX1 3PT. *T:* Oxford (01865) 272500.

MATTHEWS, Prof. Peter Hugoe, LittD; FBA 1985; Professor and Head of Department of Linguistics, since 1980, and Fellow, since 1980, Praelector, since 1987, of St John's College, University of Cambridge; *b* 10 March 1934; *s* of John Hugo and Cecily Eileen Emsley Matthews; *m* 1984, Lucienne Marie Jeanne Schleich; one step *s* one step *d.* *Educ:* Montpellier Sch., Paignton; Clifton Coll.; St John's Coll., Cambridge (MA 1960; LittD 1988). Lectr in Linguistics, UCNW, 1961–65 (on leave Indiana Univ., Bloomington, 1963–64); University of Reading: Lectr in Linguistic Science, 1965–69; Reader, 1969–75; Prof., 1975–80 (on leave as Fellow, King's Coll., Cambridge, 1970–71, and as Fellow, Netherlands Inst. of Advanced Study, Wassenaar, 1977–78). Pres., Philological Soc., 1992–. An Editor, Jl of Linguistics, 1970–79. *Publications:* Inflectional Morphology, 1972; Morphology, 1974, 2nd edn 1991; Generative Grammar and Linguistic Competence, 1979; Syntax, 1981; Grammatical Theory in the United States from Bloomfield to Chomsky, 1993; articles and book chapters. *Recreations:* cycling, gardening. *Address:* 10 Fendon Close, Cambridge CB1 4RU. *T:* Cambridge (01223) 247553; 22 Rue Nina et Julien Lefevre, 1952 Luxembourg. *T:* 224146.

MATTHEWS, Sir Peter (Jack), Kt 1981; CVO 1978; OBE 1974; QPM 1970; DL; Chief Constable of Surrey, 1968–82; *b* 25 Dec. 1917; *s* of Thomas Francis Matthews and Agnes Jack; *m* 1944, Margaret, *er d* of Cecil Levett, London; one *s.* *Educ:* Blackridge Public Sch., West Lothian. Joined Metropolitan Police, 1937; Flt-Lt (pilot) RAF, 1942–46; Metropolitan Police, 1946–65; seconded Cyprus, 1955; Chief Supt P Div. 1963–65; Chief Constable: of East Suffolk, 1965–67; of Suffolk, 1967–68. President: British Section, Internat. Police Assoc., 1964–70 (Internat. Pres. 1966–70); Assoc. of Chief Police Officers of England, Wales and NI, 1976–77 (Chm., Sub-Cttee on Terrorism and Allied Matters, 1976–82; Rep. at Interpol, 1977–80); Chief Constables' Club, 1980–81; Vice-Chm., Home Office Standing Adv. Cttee on Police Dogs, 1982– (Chm., 1978–82; Chm., Training Sub-Cttee, 1972–82); led British Police Study Team to advise Singapore Police, 1982; specialist advr to Parly Select Cttee on Defence, 1984; Mem., MoD Police Review Cttee, 1985. Pres., Working Br., Aircrew Assoc., 1990–. Lecture tour of Canada and USA, 1979; Lecturer: Airline Training Associates Ltd, 1984–91; International Military Services Ltd, 1987–91. Final Reader, HM The Queen's Police Gold Medal Essay Competition, 1983–92. CIMgt (CBIM 1978). DL Surrey, 1981. *Club:* Royal Air Force.

MATTHEWS, Richard Bonnar, CBE 1971; QPM 1965; Chief Constable, Warwickshire, 1964–76 (Warwickshire and Coventry, 1969–74); *b* 18 Dec. 1915; *er s* of late Charles Richard Matthews, Worthing; *m* 1943, Joan, *d* of late Basil Worsley, Henstridge, Som; two *d.* *Educ:* Stowe School. Served War of 1939–45, Lieut, RNVR. Joined Metropolitan Police, 1936; Asst Chief Constable, E Sussex, 1954–56; Chief Constable of Cornwall and Isles of Scilly, 1956–64. Chm., Traffic Cttee, Assoc. of Chief Police Officers, 1973–76. Mem., Williams Cttee on Obscenity and Film Censorship, 1977–79; Chm., CS selection bds, 1979–85. Founder, Adv. Cttee on Beach Life Saving for Cornwall, 1959. Pres., Old Stoic Soc., 1986. *Recreations:* ski-ing, fishing, gardening. *Address:* Smoke Acre, Great Bedwyn, Marlborough, Wilts SN8 3LP. *T:* Marlborough (01672) 870584. *Club:* Naval.

MATTHEWS, Prof. Robert Charles Oliver, (Robin), CBE 1975; FBA 1968; Master, 1975–93, and Fellow, since 1993, Clare College, Cambridge; Professor of Political Economy, Cambridge University, 1980–91, now Emeritus; *b* 16 June 1927; *s* of Oliver Harwood Matthews, WS, and Ida Finlay; *m* 1948, Joyce Hilda Lloyds; one *d.* *Educ:* Edinburgh Academy; Corpus Christi Coll., Oxford (Hon. Fellow, 1976). Student, Nuffield Coll., Oxford, 1947–48; Lectr, Merton Coll., Oxford, 1948–49; University Asst Lectr in Economics, Cambridge, 1949–51, and Univ. Lectr, 1951–65; Fellow of St John's Coll., Cambridge, 1950–65; Drummond Prof. of Political Economy, Oxford, and Fellow of All Souls Coll., 1965–75. Vis. Prof., Univ. of California, Berkeley, 1961–62. Chm., SSRC, 1972–75. A Managing Trustee, Nuffield Foundn, 1975–; Trustee, Urwick Orr and Partners Ltd, 1978–86. Pres., Royal Econ. Soc., 1984–86; Mem., OECD Expert Group on Non-inflationary Growth, 1975–77. Chm., Bank of England Panel of Academic Consultants, 1977–93. FIDE Internat. Master of chess composition, 1965. For. Hon. Mem., Amer. Acad. of Arts and Scis, 1985; Hon. Mem., Amer. Econs Assoc., 1993. Hon. DLitt Warwick, 1980. *Publications:* A Study in Trade Cycle History, 1954; The Trade Cycle, 1958; (with M. Lipton and J. M. Rice) Chess Problems: introduction to an art, 1963; (with F. H. Hahn) Théorie de la Croissance Economique, 1972; (ed) Economic Growth: trends and factors, 1981; (with C. H. Feinstein and J. C. Odling-Smee) British Economic Growth 1856–1973, 1982; (ed with G. B. Stafford) The Grants Economy and Collective Consumption, 1982; (ed) Slower Growth in the Western World, 1982; (ed with J. R. Sargent) Contemporary Problems of Economic Policy: essays from the CLARE Group, 1983; (ed) Economy and Democracy, 1985; Mostly Three-Movers, 1995; articles in learned journals. *Address:* Clare College, Cambridge CB2 1TL. *Club:* Reform.

MATTHEWS, Sir Stanley, Kt 1965; CBE 1957; President, Stoke City Football Club, since 1990; *b* Hanley, Stoke-on-Trent, 1 Feb. 1915; *s* of late Jack Matthews, Seymour Street, Hanley; *m* 1st, 1935, Elizabeth Hall Vallance (marr. diss. 1975); one *s* one *d;* 2nd, 1975, Gertrud (Mila) Winterova. *Educ:* Wellington Sch., Hanley. Professional footballer: played in first Football League match, 1931; first played for England, 1934, and fifty-five times subsequently; Blackpool FC, 1947–61 (FA Cup, 1953); Stoke City FC, 1961–65. Freedom of Stoke-on-Trent, 1963. *Publication:* The Stanley Matthews Story, 1960. *Recreations:* golf, tennis. *Address:* Stoke City Football Club, Victoria Ground, Stoke-on-Trent. *Club:* National Sporting.

MATTHEWS, Suzan Patricia, (Mrs A. R. Matthews); QC 1993; a Recorder, since 1995; *b* 5 Dec. 1947; *y c* of late Sidney Herbert Clark and Susan Hadnett Clark (*née* Mathews); *m* 1970, Anthony Robert Matthews; one *s.* *Educ:* Univ. of Bradford (BSc Hons Business Admin 1972). Called to the Bar, Middle Temple, 1974. Asst Recorder, 1991–95. Asst Boundary Comr, 1992–. Councillor, SE Region, Gas Consumers' Council, 1987–. *Recreations:* historical research, music, cricket, gardening, boats. *Address:* Guildford Chambers, Stoke House, Leapale Lane, Guildford, Surrey GU1 4LY. *T:* Guildford (01483) 39131.

MATTHEWS, Timothy John; Chief Executive, Guy's and St Thomas' Hospital Trust, since 1993; *b* 24 June 1951; *s* of Kenneth James Matthews and Vera Joan Matthews (*née* Fittall); *m* 1984, Sally Vivien Davies; two *s.* *Educ:* Peterhouse, Cambridge (BA Hons History). Admin. Trainee, DHSS, 1974; Private Sec. to Perm. Sec., DHSS, 1978–79; Dist Gen. Administrator, Bloomsbury HA, 1984; Gen. Manager, Middlesex Hosp., 1985; Dist Gen. Manager, Maidstone HA, 1988; Chief Exec., St Thomas' Hosp., 1991. Trustee, Kent Community Housing Trust, 1991–94. *Recreations:* allotment gardening, opera. *Address:* 70 Rosendale Road, West Dulwich, SE21 8DP.

MATTHEWS, Rt Rev. Victoria; a Suffragan Bishop of Toronto (Bishop of the Credit Valley), since 1994; *b* 1954; *d* of Beverley Matthews and late Pauline Ritchie Matthews. *Educ:* Trinity Coll., Univ. of Toronto (BA (Hons) 1976; ThM 1987); Yale Univ. Divinity Sch. (MDiv 1979). Ordained deacon, 1979, priest, 1980; Asst Curate, St Andrew, Scarborough, 1979–83; Incumbent: Parish of Georgina, York-Simcoe, 1983–87; All Souls, Lansing, York-Scarborough, 1987–94. Regional Dean, Deanery of York Mills, 1989–94. N Amer. Theol Fellow, 1976–79. *Recreations:* reading, hiking, swimming, travel. *Address:* PO Box 74510, Mississauga, Ontario L5H 4J6, Canada. *T:* (905) 8234280, *Fax:* (905) 8234896.

MATTHEWS, Prof. Walter Bryan; Professor of Clinical Neurology, University of Oxford, 1970–87, now Emeritus; Fellow of St Edmund Hall, Oxford, 1970–87, now Emeritus; *b* 7 April 1920; *s* of Very Rev. Dr Walter Robert Matthews; *m* 1943, Margaret Forster; one *s* one *d.* *Educ:* Marlborough Coll.; University Coll., Oxford. MA, DM, FRCP. RAMC, 1943–46. Senior Registrar, Oxford, 1948; Chief Asst, Dept of Neurology, Manchester Royal Infirmary, 1949–52; Senior Registrar, King's College Hosp., 1952–54; Consultant Neurologist, Derbyshire Royal Infirmary, 1954–68; Consultant Neurologist, Manchester Royal Infirmary and Crumpsall Hosp., 1968–70. President: Section of Neurology, RSM, 1981; Assoc. of British Neurologists, 1982; Second Vice-Pres., RCP, 1986–87. Osler Orator, RCP, 1981. Editor-in-Chief, Jl of Neurological Scis, 1977–83. *Publications:* Practical Neurology, 1963, 3rd edn 1975; (with H. G. Miller) Diseases of the Nervous System, 1972, 3rd edn 1979; (ed) Recent Advances in Clinical Neurology I, 1975, II, 1978, IV, 1984; Multiple Sclerosis: the facts, 1978; (ed) McAlpine's Multiple Sclerosis, 1985, 2nd edn 1991; papers in Brain, Quarterly Jl of Medicine, etc. *Recreation:* walking. *Address:* Sandford House, Henley Road, Sandford-on-Thames, Oxford OX4 4YN.

MATTHEWS, (William) David; His Honour Judge Matthews; a Circuit Judge, since 1992; *b* 19 Nov. 1940; *s* of Edwin Kenneth William Matthews and Bessie Matthews; *m* 1965, Pauline Georgina May Lewis; two *s.* *Educ:* Wycliffe Coll. Admitted Solicitor, 1964; Partner, T. A. Matthews & Co., 1965–92; a Recorder, 1990–92. Pres., Herefordshire, Breconshire and Radnorshire Incorp. Law Soc., 1988–89. *Recreations:* cricket, boats, farming. *Address:* 6/7 King Street, Hereford HR4 9BS. *T:* Hereford (01432) 352121. *Club:* New Quay Yacht (New Quay, Dyfed).

MATTHÖFER, Hans; Member of the Bundestag (Social Democrat), 1961–87; *b* Bochum, 25 Sept. 1925; *m* Traute Matthöfer (*née* Mecklenburg). *Educ:* primary sch.; studied economics and social sciences in Frankfurt/Main and Madison, Wis, USA, 1948–53 (grad. Economics). Employed as manual and clerical worker, 1940–42; Reich Labour Service, 1942; conscripted into German Army, 1943 (Armoured Inf.), final rank NCO. Joined SPD (Social Democratic Party of Germany), 1950; employed in Economics Dept, Bd of Management, IG Metall (Metalworkers' Union) and specialized in problems arising in connection with automation and mechanization, 1953 (Head of Educn Dept, 1961). Member, OEEC Mission in Washington and Paris, 1957–61; Vice-Pres., Gp of Parliamentarians on Latin American Affairs (Editor of periodical Esprés Español until end of 1972); Mem., Patronage Cttee of German Section of Amnesty Internat.; Pres., Bd of Trustees, German Foundn for Developing Countries, 1971–73; Parly State Sec. in Federal Min. for Economic Co-operation, 1972; Federal Minister for Research and Technology, 1974, of Finance, 1978–82, for Posts and Telecommunications, 1982. Mem. of Presidency and Treasurer, SPD, 1985–87. Chm., Exec. Bd, Beteiligungsges. der Gewerkschaften (formerly für Gemeinwirtschaft) AG, trade union holding, 1987–. Publisher, Vorwärts, 1985–88. *Publications:* Der Unterschied zwischen den Tariflöhnen und den Effektivverdiensten in der Metallindustrie der Bundesrepublik, 1956; Technological Change in the Metal Industries (in two parts), 1961–62; Der Beitrag politischer Bildung zur Emanzipation der Arbeitnehmer—Materialien zur Frage des Bildungsurlaubs, 1970; Streiks und streikähnliche Formen des Kampfes der Arbeitnehmer im Kapitalismus, 1971; Für eine menschliche Zukunft—Sozialdemokratische Forschungs—und Technologiepolitik, 1976; Humanisierung der Arbeit und Produktivität in der Industriegesellschaft, 1977, 1978, 1980; Agenda 2000: Vorschläge zur Wirtschafts- und Gesellschaftspolitik, 1993; numerous articles on questions of trade union, development, research and finance policies. *Address:* Schreyerstrasse 38, 61476 Kronberg im Taunus, Germany.

MATTINGLY, Alan; Director (formerly Secretary), Ramblers' Association, since 1974; *b* 19 May 1949; *s* of Alexander and Patricia Mattingly; *m* 1980, Wendy Mallard. *Educ:* The Latymer Sch., Edmonton; St John's Coll., Cambridge (BA). Chm., Council for Nat. Parks, 1979–83, 1990–93; Vice-Pres., Countrywide Holidays Assoc., 1980–. Mem., (Lab) Newham Borough Council, 1980–86, Dep. Leader, 1983–85. *Publications:* Tackle Rambling, 1981; Walking in the National Parks, 1982. *Recreations:* walking, orienteering. *Address:* 45 Tonbridge Crescent, Kenton, Middlesex HA3 9LE.

MATTINGLY, Dr Stephen, TD 1964; FRCP; Consultant Physician, Middlesex Hospital, 1958–81, now Emeritus; Consultant Physician, 1956–82 and Medical Director, 1972–82, Garston Manor Rehabilitation Centre; Hon. Consultant in Rheumatology and Rehabilitation to the Army, 1976–81; *b* 1 March 1922; *s* of Harold Mattingly, CBE and Marion Grahame Meikleham; *m* 1945, Brenda Mary Pike; one *s.* *Educ:* Leighton Park Sch.; UCH (MB, BS); Dip. in Physical Med., 1953. FRCP 1970. House-surg., UCH, 1947; Regtl MO, 2/10 Gurkha Rifles, RAMC Far East, 1947–49; House-surg. and Registrar, UCH, 1950–55; Sen. Registrar, Mddx Hosp., 1955–56. Reg. Med. Consultant for London, S-Eastern, Eastern and Southern Regions, Dept of Employment, 1960–74. Mem., Attendance Allowance Bd, 1978–83. Lt-Col RAMC TA, 1952–67. *Publications:* (contrib.) Progress in Clinical Rheumatology, 1965; (contrib.) Textbook of Rheumatic Diseases, ed Copeman, 1969; (contrib.) Fractures and Joint Injuries, ed Watson Jones, 5th edn 1976, 6th edn 1982; (ed) Rehabilitation Today, 1977, 2nd edn 1981. *Recreation:* gardening. *Address:* Highfield House, Little Brington, Northants NN7 4HN. *T:* Northampton (01604) 770271.

MATUTES JUAN, Abel; Member (Partido Popular) for Spain, European Parliament, since 1994; *b* 31 Oct. 1941; *s* of Antonio Matutes and Carmen Juan; *m* Nieves Prats Prats;

one *s* three *d*. *Educ:* University of Barcelona (Law and Economic Sciences). Prof., Barcelona Univ., 1963; Vice-Pres., Employers Organization for Tourism, Ibiza-Formentera, 1964–79; Mayor of Ibiza, 1970–71; Senator, Ibiza and Formentera in Alianza Popular (opposition party), 1977–79; Vice-Pres., Partido Popular (formerly Alianza Popular), 1979– (Pres., Economy Cttee); Mem., EEC, 1986–94. Pres., Nat. Electoral Cttee; Spokesman for Economy and Finance, Grupo Popular in Congress (Parlt). *Recreation:* tennis. *Address:* POB 416, Ibiza. *Clubs:* Golf Rocalliza (Ibiza); de Campo Tennis (Ibiza).

MAUCERI, John Francis; Chief Conductor, Los Angeles Philharmonic Hollywood Bowl Orchestra, since 1991; *b* 12 Sept. 1945; *s* of Gene B. Mauceri and Mary Elizabeth (*née* Marino); *m* 1968, Betty Ann Weiss; one *s*. *Educ:* Yale Univ. (BA, MPhil). Music Dir, Yale Symphony Orch., 1968–74; Associate Prof., Yale Univ., 1974–84; Music Director: Washington Opera, 1979–82; Orchestras, Kennedy Center, 1979–; Amer. Symphony Orch., NYC, 1985–87; Scottish Opera, 1987–93; Leonard Bernstein Fest., LSO, 1986; Conductor, Amer. Nat. Tour, Boston Pops Orch., 1987; co-Producer, musical play, On Your Toes, 1983; Musical Supervisor, Song and Dance, Broadway, 1985. Dir, Charles Ives Soc., 1986– (Mem., 1986–); Mem., Adv. Bd, Amer. Inst. for Verdi Studies, 1986–; Consultant for Music Theater, Kennedy Center for Performing Arts, Washington, 1982–91; Trustee, Nat. Inst. for Music Theater, 1986–. Mem. Adv. Bd, Kurt Weill Edn, 1993–. Numerous recordings. Antoinette Perry Award, League of NY Theatres and Producers, 1983; Drama Desk Award, 1983; Outer Critics Circle Award, 1983; Arts award, Yale Univ., 1985; Grammy award for Candide recording, 1987; Olivier award for Best Musical for Candide, adaptation for Scottish Opera/Old Vic prodn, 1988; Wavenden All Music Award for Conductor of the Year, 1989. *Publications:* (contrib.) Sennets and Tuckets: a Bernstein celebration (ed Ledbetter), 1988; various articles for Scottish Opera programmes and newspapers. *Address:* c/o Jonathan Brill, CAMI, 165 West 57th Street, New York, NY 10019, USA.

MAUCHLINE, Lord; Michael Edward Abney-Hastings; ranger with New South Wales Pastures Protection Board; *b* 22 July 1942; *s* and *heir* of Countess of Loudoun (13th in line), *qv* and *s* of Captain Walter Strickland Lord (whose marriage to the Countess of Loudoun was dissolved, 1945; his son assumed, by deed poll, 1946, the surname of Abney-Hastings in lieu of his patronymic); *m* 1969, Noelene Margaret McCormick, 2nd *d* of Mr and Mrs W. J. McCormick, Barham, NSW; two *s* three *d* (of whom one *s* one *d* are twins). *Educ:* Ampleforth. *Address:* 74 Coreen Street, Jerilderie, NSW 2716, Australia.

MAUD, Hon. Sir Humphrey (John Hamilton), KCMG 1993 (CMG 1982); HM Diplomatic Service, retired; Deputy Secretary General (Economic and Social Affairs) of the Commonwealth, since 1993; *b* 17 April 1934; *s* of Baron Redcliffe-Maud, GCB, CBE and Jean, *yr d* of late J. B. Hamilton, Melrose; *m* 1963, Maria Eugenia Gazitua; three *s*. *Educ:* Eton (Oppidan Scholar); King's Coll., Cambridge (Scholar; Classics and History); MA. Mem., NYO, 1949–52. Instructor in Classics, Univ. of Minnesota, 1958–59; entered Foreign Service, 1959; FO, 1960–61; Madrid, 1961–63; Havana, 1963–65; FO, 1966–67; Cabinet Office, 1968–69; Paris, 1970–74; Nuffield Coll., Oxford (Econs), 1974–75; Head of Financial Relations Dept, FCO, 1975–79; Minister, Madrid, 1979–82; Ambassador, Luxembourg, 1982–85; Asst Under Sec. of State, FCO, 1985–88; High Comr, Cyprus, 1988–90; Ambassador to Argentina Rep., 1990–93. Member, Executive Committee: British Diabetic Assoc., 1986–90; RCM, 1987–. *Recreations:* golf, tennis, music ('cellist), bird-watching. *Address:* c/o Commonwealth Secretariat, Marlborough House, Pall Mall, SW1Y 5HX; 31 Queen Anne's Grove, W4 1HW. *Club:* United Oxford & Cambridge University.

MAUDE, family name of **Viscount Hawarden.**

MAUDE, Rt. Hon. Francis Anthony Aylmer; PC 1992; Board Member: Asda Group plc, since 1992; Morgan Stanley International Inc., since 1993; Chairman, Government's Deregulation Task Force, since 1994; *b* 4 July 1953; *s* of Baron Maude of Stratford-upon-Avon, TD, PC; *m* 1984, Christina Jane, *yr d* of late Peter Hadfield, Shrewsbury; two *s* two *d*. *Educ:* Abingdon Sch.; Corpus Christi Coll., Cambridge (MA (Hons) History; Avory Studentship; Halse Prize). Called to Bar, Inner Temple, 1977 (scholar; Forster Boulton Prize). Councillor, Westminster CC, 1978–84. MP (C) Warwicks N, 1983–92; contested (C) Warwicks N, 1992. PPS to Minister of State for Employment, 1984–85; an Asst Government Whip, 1985–87; Parly Under Sec. of State, DTI, 1987–89; Minister of State, FCO, 1989–90; Financial Sec. to HM Treasury, 1990–92. Dir, Salomon Brothers, 1992–93. *Recreations:* ski-ing, cricket, reading, music. *Address:* Morgan Stanley International, 25 Cabot Square, Canary Wharf, E14 4QA.

MAUGHAN, Air Vice-Marshal Charles Gilbert, CB 1976; CBE 1970; AFC; Independent Panel Inspector, Department of the Environment, 1983–94; *b* 3 March 1923. *Educ:* Sir George Monoux Grammar Sch.; Harrow County Sch. Served War, Fleet Air Arm (flying Swordfishes and Seafires), 1942–46. Joined RAF, 1949, serving with Meteor, Vampire and Venom sqdns in Britain and Germany; comd No 65 (Hunter) Sqdn, Duxford, Cambridgeshire (won Daily Mail Arch-to-Arc race, 1959). Subseq. comd: No 9 (Vulcan) Sqdn; flying bases of Honington (Suffolk) and Waddington (Lincs); held a staff post at former Bomber Comd, Air Staff (Ops), Strike Command, 1968–70; Air Attaché, Bonn, 1970–73; AOA Strike Command, 1974–75; SASO RAF Strike Command, 1975–77. Gen. Sec., Royal British Legion, 1978–83. *Address:* Whitestones, Tresham, Wotton-under-Edge, Glos GL12 7RW.

MAULEVERER, (Peter) Bruce; QC 1985; a Recorder, since 1985; *b* 22 Nov. 1946; *s* of late Algernon Arthur Mauleverer and Hazel Mary Mauleverer; *m* 1971, Sara (*née* Hudson-Evans); two *s* two *d*. *Educ:* Sherborne School; University College, Univ. of Durham (BA 1968). Called to the Bar, Inner Temple, 1969, Bencher 1993. Vice-Chm., Internat. Law Assoc., 1993– (Hon. Sec.-Gen., 1986–93). *Recreations:* sailing, ski-ing, travel. *Address:* Eliot Vale House, Eliot Vale, Blackheath, SE3 0UW. *T:* 0181–852 2070.

MAUND, Rt. Rev. John Arthur Arrowsmith, CBE 1975; MC 1946; Hon. Assistant Bishop, Worcester, 1983–93; *b* 1909; *s* of late Arthur Arrowsmith and Dorothy Jane Maund, Worcester, England; *m* 1948, Catherine Mary Maurice, Bromley, Kent; no *c*. *Educ:* Worcester Cathedral King's Sch.; Leeds Univ.; Mirfield Theological Coll. BA Leeds 1931; Asst Priest, All Saints and St Laurence, Evesham, Worcs, 1933–36; Asst Priest, All Saints, Blackheath, London, 1936–38; Asst Priest, Pretoria Native Mission, Pretoria, South Africa, 1938–40; CF 1940–46 (despatches, 1942); Asst Priest, Pretoria Native Mission, in charge Lady Selborne, Pretoria, 1946–50; Bishop of Lesotho, 1950–76 (diocese known as Basutoland, 1950–66). Chaplain to Hengrave Community and Hon. Asst Bishop, St Edmundsbury and Ipswich, 1977–83; Chaplain to Beauchamp Community, Malvern, 1983–89. Fellow Royal Commonwealth Society. *Recreations:* gardening, bridge, the daily newspaper. *Address:* Flat 1, Warden's Lodge, The Quadrangle, Newland, Malvern, Worcs WR13 5AX. *T:* Malvern (016845) 68072.

MAUNDER, Prof. Leonard, OBE 1977; BSc; PhD; ScD; FEng; FIMechE; Professor of Mechanical Engineering, 1967–92, now Emeritus (Professor of Applied Mechanics, 1961), Dean of the Faculty of Applied Science, 1973–78, University of Newcastle upon Tyne; *b* 10 May 1927; *s* of Thomas G. and Elizabeth A. Maunder; *m* 1958, Moira Anne Hudson; one *s* one *d*. *Educ:* Bishop Gore Grammar Sch., Swansea; University Coll. of Swansea (BSc; Hon. Fellow, 1989); Edinburgh Univ. (PhD); Massachusetts Institute of Technology (ScD). Instructor, 1950–53, and Asst Prof., 1953–54, in Dept of Mech. Engrg, MIT; Aeronautical Research Lab., Wright Air Development Center, US Air Force, 1954–56; Lecturer in Post-Graduate Sch. of Applied Dynamics, Edinburgh Univ., 1956–61. Christmas Lectr, Royal Instn, 1983. Member: NRDC, 1976–81; SRC Engrg Bd, 1976–80; Adv. Council on R&D for Fuel and Power, Dept of Energy, 1981–92; British Technology Gp, 1981–92; ACOST, 1987–93; Dep. Chm., Newcastle Hospitals Management Cttee, 1971–73. President: Internat. Fedn Theory of Machines and Mechanisms, 1976–79; Engrg, BAAS, 1980. Vice-Pres., IMechE, 1975–80. Hon. Foreign Mem., Polish Soc. Theoretical and Applied Mechanics, 1984. *Publications:* (with R. N. Arnold) Gyrodynamics and Its Engineering Applications, 1961; Machines in Motion, 1986; numerous papers in the field of applied mechanics. *Address:* The Old Forge Building, The University, Newcastle upon Tyne NE1 7RU.

MAUNDRELL, Rev. Canon Wolseley David; Priest-in-charge (NSM), Stonegate, 1989–94; Canon and Prebendary of Chichester Cathedral, 1981–89; *b* 2 Sept. 1920; *s* of late Rev. William Herbert Maundrell, RN, and Evelyn Helen Maundrell; *m* 1950, Barbara Katharine Simmons (*d* 1985); one *s* one *d*. *Educ:* Radley Coll.; New Coll., Oxford. Deacon, 1943; Priest, 1944; Curate of Haslemere, 1943; Resident Chaplain to Bishop of Chichester, 1949; Vicar of Sparsholt and Lainston, Winchester, 1950; Rector of Weeke, Winchester, 1956; Residentiary Canon of Winchester Cathedral, 1961–70 (Treasurer, 1961–70; Vice-Dean, 1966–70); Examining Chaplain to Bishop of Winchester, 1962–70; Asst Chaplain of Holy Trinity Church, Brussels, 1970–71; Vicar of Icklesham, E Sussex, 1972–82; Rural Dean of Rye, 1978–84; Rector of Rye, 1982–89. *Address:* 13 North Walls, Chichester, West Sussex PO19 1DA. *T:* Chichester (01243) 537359.

MAUNSELL, Susan Pamela; Director of Investigations, Office of the Parliamentary Commissioner for Administration, since 1993; *b* 30 Jan. 1942; *d* of George Cruickshank Smith and Alice Monica Smith (*née* Davies); *m* 1965, Michael Brooke Maunsell (marr. diss. 1986). *Educ:* Nottingham High Sch. for Girls (GPDST); Girton Coll., Cambridge (schol.; BA classics; MA). Ministry of Health: Asst Principal, 1964; Private Sec. to Perm. Sec., 1967, to Parly Sec., 1968; Department of Health and Social Security: Principal, 1969; Asst Sec., 1976; Regl Controller, London S Social Security Reg., 1981–85; various HQ policy posts, 1985–89; Under Sec., Policy Div. A, DSS, 1989–92. FRSA 1995. *Recreations:* travel, books, theatre, cinema, riding, food, wine, joint owner of French cottage. *Address:* 27 Longton Avenue, SE26 6RE. *T:* 0181–778 5605.

MAURICE, Dr Rita Joy; Director of Statistics, Home Office, 1977–89; *b* 10 May 1929; *d* of A. N. Maurice and F. A. Maurice (*née* Dean). *Educ:* East Grinstead County Sch.; University Coll., London. BSc (Econ) 1951; PhD 1958. Asst Lectr, subseq. Lectr in Economic Statistics, University Coll., London, 1951–58; Statistician, Min. of Health, 1959–62; Statistician, subseq. Chief Statistician, Central Statistical Office, 1962–72; Head of Economics and Statistics Div. 6, Depts of Industry, Trade and Prices and Consumer Protection, 1972–77. Member: Council, Royal Statistical Soc., 1978–82; Parole Bd, 1991–94; Retail Prices Index Adv. Cttee, 1992–94. *Publications:* (ed) National Accounts Statistics: sources and methods, 1968; articles in statistical jls. *Address:* 10 Fairfax Place, Swiss Cottage, NW6 4EH.

MAUROY, Pierre; Mayor of Lille, since 1973; Deputy, Nord, since 1986; *b* 5 July 1928; *s* of Henri Mauroy and Adrienne Mauroy (*née* Bronne) *m* 1951, Gilberte Deboudt; one *s*. *Educ:* Lycée de Cambrai; Ecole normale nationale d'apprentissage de Cachan. Joined Young Socialists at age of 16 (Nat. Sec., 1950–58); teacher of technical educn, Colombes, 1952; Sec.-Gen., Syndicat des collèges d'enseignement technique de la Fédération de l'Education nationale, 1955–59; Sec., Fedn of Socialist Parties of Nord, 1961; Mem., Political Bureau, 1963, Dep. Gen. Sec., 1966, Socialist Party; Mem. Exec. Cttee, Fédération de la gauche démocratique et socialiste, 1965–68; First Sec., Fedn of Socialist Parties of Nord and Nat. Co-ordination Sec., Socialist Party, 1971–79; First Sec., Socialist Party, 1988–92. Member, from Le Cateau, and Vice-Pres., Conseil Gen. du Nord, 1967–73; Town Councillor and Deputy Mayor of Lille, 1971, Vice-Pres., Town Corp., 1971–81; Deputy, Nord, 1973–81; Prime Minister of France, 1981–84. Pres., Regional Council, Nord-Pas-de-Calais, 1974–81; Socialist Rep. and Vice-Pres., Political Commn, EEC, 1979–81. Political Dir, Action Socialiste Hebdo, 1979–; President: Communauté Urbaine de Lille, 1989–; Fédération nationale Léo Lagrange; Fédération Nationale des Elus Socialistes et Républicains, 1987–90; Socialist International, 1992–. *Publications:* Héritiers de l'avenir, 1977; C'est ici le chemin, 1982; A gauche, 1985. *Address:* 17–19 rue Voltaire, 59800 Lille, France.

MAVOR, Prof. John, FEng; FRSE; Principal and Vice-Chancellor, Napier University, since 1994; *b* 18 July 1942; *s* of Gordon Hattersley Mavor and Wilhelmina Baillie McAllister; *m* 1968, Susan Christina Colton; two *d*. *Educ:* City Univ., London; London Univ. (BSc, PhD, DSc(Eng)). FRSE; FInstP; FIEEE; FIEE; FEng 1994. AEI Res. Labs, London, 1964–65; Texas Instruments Ltd, Bedford, 1968–70; Emihus Microcomponents, Glenrothes, 1970–71; University of Edinburgh: Lectr, 1971; Reader, 1979; Lothian Chair of Microelectronics, 1980; Head of Dept of Electrical Engrg, 1984–89; Prof. of Electrical Engrg, 1986–94; Dean, 1989–94, and Provost, 1992–94, Faculty of Sci. and Engrg. *Publications:* MOST Integrated Circuit Engineering, 1973; Introduction to MOS LSI Design, 1983; over 150 technical papers in professional electronics jls. *Recreations:* gardening, walking. *Address:* Napier University, 219 Colinton Road, Edinburgh EH14 1DJ.

MAVOR, Michael Barclay, CVO 1983; MA; Head Master, Rugby School, since 1990; *b* 29 Jan. 1947; *s* of William Ferrier Mavor and late Sheena Watson Mavor (*née* Barclay); *m* 1970, Jane Elizabeth Sucksmith; one *s* one *d*. *Educ:* Loretto School; St John's Coll., Cambridge (Exhibn and Trevelyan Schol.). MA (English); CertEd. Woodrow Wilson Teaching Fellow, Northwestern Univ., Evanston, Ill, 1969–72; Asst Master, Tonbridge Sch., 1972–78; Course Tutor (Drama), Open Univ., 1977–78; Headmaster, Gordonstoun Sch., 1979–90. *Recreations:* theatre, writing, golf, fishing, cricket. *Address:* Rugby School, Rugby, Warwicks CV22 5EH. *T:* Rugby (01788) 543465. *Club:* Hawks (Cambridge).

MAVOR, Ronald Henry Moray, CBE 1972; author; *b* 13 May 1925; *s* of late Dr O. H. Mavor, CBE (James Bridie) and Rona Bremner; *m* 1959, Sigrid Bruhn (marr. diss. 1989); one *s* one *d* (and one *d* decd). *Educ:* Merchiston Castle Sch.; Glasgow Univ. MB, ChB 1948; MRCPGlas 1955, FRCPGlas 1989. In medical practice until 1957, incl. periods in RAMC, at American Hosp., Paris, and Deeside Sanatoria. Drama Critic, The Scotsman, 1957–65; Dir, Scottish Arts Council, 1965–71. Prof., 1981–90, and Head, 1983–90, Dept of Drama, Univ. of Saskatchewan (Vis. Prof., 1977–78, 1979–81), Prof. Emeritus. Vice-Chm., Edinburgh Festival Council, 1975–81 (Mem., 1965–81); Mem. Gen. Adv. Council, BBC, 1971–76; Mem. Drama Panel, British Council, 1973–79. Vis. Lectr on Drama, Guelph, Ontario, and Minneapolis, 1976. FRSA 1991. *Plays:* The Keys of Paradise, 1959; Aurelie, 1960; Muir of Huntershill, 1962; The Partridge Dance, 1963; A Private Matter (originally A Life of the General), 1973; The Quartet, 1980; A House on Temperance, 1981; The Grand Inquisitor, 1990. *Publications:* Art the Hard Way, in, Scotland, 1972; A

Private Matter (play), 1974; Dr Mavor and Mr Bridie, 1988. *Address:* 19 Falkland Street, Glasgow G12 9PY. *T:* 0141–339 3149.

MAW, (John) Nicholas; composer; *b* 5 Nov. 1935; *s* of Clarence Frederick Maw and Hilda Ellen (*née* Chambers); *m* 1960, Karen Graham; one *s* one *d*. *Educ:* Wennington Sch., Wetherby, Yorks; Royal Academy of Music. Studied in Paris with Nadia Boulanger and Max Deutsch, 1958–59. Fellow Commoner in Creative Arts, Trinity Coll., Cambridge, 1966–70; Visiting Professor of Composition: Yale Music Sch., 1984–85, 1989; Boston Univ., 1986; Prof. of Music, Milton Avery Grad. Sch. of Arts, Bard Coll., NY, 1990–. Midsummer Prize, Corp. of London, 1980; Konssevitsky Foundn Award, 1990; Sudler Internat. Wind Band Prize, John Philip Sousa Soc., 1992; Stoeger Prize for Chamber Music, Chamber Music Soc., Lincoln Center, 1993. *Compositions include: operas:* One-Man Show, 1964; The Rising of The Moon, 1970; *for orchestra:* Sinfonia, 1966; Sonata for Strings and Two Horns, 1967; Serenade, for small orchestra, 1973, 1977; Life Studies, for 15 solo strings, 1973; Odyssey, 1974–86; Summer Dances, 1981; Spring Music, 1983; The World in the Evening, 1988; Shahnama, 1992; *for instrumental soloist and orchestra:* Sonata Notturna, for cello and string orchestra, 1985; Little Concert, for oboe and chamber orchestra, 1987; Violin Concerto, 1993; *for voice and orchestra:* Nocturne, 1958; Scenes and Arias, 1962; *for wind band:* American Games, 1991; *chamber music:* String Quartet, no 1, 1965, no 2, 1983, no 3, 1994; Chamber Music for wind and piano quintet, 1962; Flute Quartet, 1981; Ghost Dances, for chamber ensemble, 1988; Piano Trio, 1991; *instrumental music:* Sonatina for flute and piano, 1957; Essay for organ, 1961; Personae for piano, nos I–III, 1973, IV–VI, 1985; Music of Memory, for solo guitar, 1989; *vocal music:* The Voice of Love, for mezzo soprano and piano, 1966; Six Interiors, for high voice and guitar, 1966; La Vita Nuova, for soprano and chamber ensemble, 1979; Five American Folksongs, for high voice and piano, 1988; Roman Canticle, for mezzo soprano, flute, viola and harp, 1989; *choral music:* Five Epigrams, for chorus, 1960; Round, for chorus and piano, 1963; Five Irish Songs, for mixed chorus, 1973; Reverdie, five songs for male voices, 1975; Te Deum, for treble and tenor soli, chorus, congregation and organ, 1975; Nonsense Rhymes; songs and rounds for children, 1975–76; The Ruin, for double choir and solo horn, 1980; Three Hymns, for mixed choir and organ, 1989; One Foot in Eden Still, I Stand (motet for choir and soloists), 1990. *Address:* c/o Faber Music Ltd, 3 Queen Square, WC1N 3AU; c/o Faber Music Inc., 50 Cross Street, Winchester, MA 01890, USA.

MAWBY, Colin (John Beverley); Choral Director, Radio Telefis Eireann, since 1981; *b* 9 May 1936; *e s* of Bernard Mawby and Enid Mawby (*née* Vaux); *m* 1987, Beverley Courtney; two *s*. *Educ:* St Swithun's Primary Sch., Portsmouth; Westminster Cathedral Choir Sch.; Royal Coll. of Music. Organist and Choirmaster of Our Lady's Church, Warwick St, W1, 1953; Choirmaster of Plymouth Cath., 1955; Organist and Choirmaster of St Anne's, Vauxhall, 1957; Asst Master of Music, Westminster Cath., 1959; Master of Music, 1961–75; Dir of Music, Sacred Heart, Wimbledon, 1978–81. Conductor: Westminster Chamber Choir, 1971–78; Westminster Cathedral String Orchestra, 1971–78; New Westminster Chorus, 1972–80; Horniman Singers, 1979–80; Culwick Choral Soc., 1981–85. Prof. of Harmony, Trinity Coll. of Music, 1975–81. Director (Catholic) Publisher, L. J. Cary & Co., 1963; Vice-Pres., Brit. Fedn of *Pueri Cantores*, 1966; Member: Council, Latin Liturgical Assoc., 1969; Adv. Panel, Royal Sch. of Church Music, 1974; Music Sub-Cttee, Westminster Arts Council, 1974. Hon. FGCM 1988. Broadcaster and recording artist; free lance journalism. *Publications:* Church music including sixteen Masses, Anthems, Motets and Holy Week music. *Recreations:* gardening, wine drinking. *Address:* Gerrardstown, Garlow Cross, Navan, Co. Meath, Ireland. *T:* Navan (46) 29394.

MAWBY, Peter John; Headmaster, Lancaster Royal Grammar School, since 1983; *b* 17 Aug. 1941; *s* of Norman James Mawby and May Mawby (*née* Huse); *m* 1960, Gillian Fay Moore; one *s* one *d*. *Educ:* Sedburgh Sch.; Queen's Coll., Cambridge (MA 1966). Assistant Teacher: Shrewsbury Sch., 1964–65; St John's Sch., Leatherhead, 1965–68; Head of Biology, Edinburgh Acad., 1968–79; Head of Science, Cheltenham Coll., 1979–83. *Publications:* (with M. B. V. Roberts) Biology 11–13, 1983; Biology Questions, 1985; Longman Science 11–14: Biology, 1991. *Recreations:* sport, music, ornithology. *Address:* Headmaster's House, Wyresdale Road, Lancaster LA1 3DU; Lancaster Royal Grammar School, East Road, Lancaster LA1 3EF. *T:* Lancaster (01524) 381458. *Club:* East India.

MAWER, Philip John Courtney; Secretary-General, General Synod of the Church of England, since 1990; *b* 30 July 1947; *s* of Eric Douglas and Thora Constance Mawer; *m* 1972, Mary Ann Moxon; one *s* two *d*. *Educ:* Hull Grammar Sch.; Edinburgh Univ. (MA Hons Politics 1971); DPA (London Univ. External) 1973. Senior Pres., Student Representative Council, 1969–70. Home Office, 1971; Private Sec. to Minister of State, 1974–76; Nuffield and Leverhulme Travelling Fellowship, 1978–79; Sec., Lord Scarman's Inquiry into Brixton disturbances, 1981; Asst Sec., Head of Industrial Relations, Prison Dept, 1984–87; Principal Private Sec. to Home Sec. (Rt Hon. Douglas Hurd), 1987–89; Under-Secretary, Cabinet Office, 1989–90. Trustee, All Churches Trust, 1992–; Mem. Governing Body, SPCK, 1994–. FRSA 1991. *Recreations:* family and friends. *Address:* Church House, Great Smith Street, SW1P 3NZ. *T:* 0171–222 9011.

MAWER, Ronald K.; *see* Knox-Mawer.

MAWHINNEY, Rt Hon. Brian (Stanley), PC 1994; MP (C) Peterborough, since 1979; Chairman of the Conservative Party and Minister without Portfolio, since 1995; *b* 26 July 1940; *s* of Frederick Stanley Arnot Mawhinney and Coralie Jean Mawhinney; *m* 1965, Betty Louise Oja; two *s* one *d*. *Educ:* Royal Belfast Academical Instn; Queen's Univ., Belfast (BSc); Univ. of Michigan, USA (MSc); Univ. of London (PhD). Asst Prof. of Radiation Research, Univ. of Iowa, USA, 1968–70; Lectr, subsequently Sen. Lectr, Royal Free Hospital School of Medicine, 1970–84. Mem., MRC, 1980–83. Mem., Gen. Synod of C of E, 1985–90. PPS to Ministers in HM Treasury, Employment and NI, 1982–86; Under Sec. of State for NI, 1986–90; Minister of State: NI Office, 1990–92; DoH, 1992–94; Sec. of State for Transport, 1994–95. Pres., Cons. Trade Unionists, 1987–90 (Vice-Pres., 1984–87); Mem., AUT. Contested (C) Stockton on Tees, Oct. 1974. *Publication:* (jtly) Conflict and Christianity in Northern Ireland, 1976. *Recreations:* sport, reading. *Address:* House of Commons, SW1A 0AA.

MAWREY, Richard Brooks; QC 1986; a Recorder of the Crown Court, since 1986; *b* 20 Aug. 1942; *s* of Philip Stephen Mawrey and Alice Brooks Mawrey; *m* 1965, Gillian Margaret Butt, *d* of Francis Butt and Alice Margaret Butt; one *d*. *Educ:* Rossall School; Magdalen College, Oxford (BA, 1st class Hons Law, 1963; Eldon Law Scholar, 1964; MA 1967). Albion Richardson Scholar, Gray's Inn, 1964; called to the Bar, Gray's Inn, 1964; Lectr in Law, Magdalen College, Oxford, 1964–65, Trinity College, Oxford, 1965–69. Co-Founder and Trustee, Historic Gardens Foundn. *Publications:* Computers and the Law, 1988; specialist editor: Consumer Credit Legislation, 1983; Butterworth's County Court Precedents, 1985; Bullen & Leake & Jacob's Precedents of Pleadings, 1990. *Recreations:* history, opera, cooking. *Address:* 2 Harcourt Buildings, Temple, EC4Y 9DB. *T:* 0171–583 9020.

MAWSON, David, OBE 1990; JP; DL; FSA; Partner, Feilden and Mawson, Architects, Norwich, 1957–90, Consultant, since 1990; *b* 30 May 1924; *s* of John William Mawson and Evelyn Mary Mawson (*née* Bond); *m* 1951, Margaret Kathlyn Norton; one *s* one *d*. *Educ:* Merchant Taylors' Sch., Sandy Lodge; Wellington Coll., NZ; Auckland Univ., NZ; Kingston-upon-Thames Coll. of Art. MA. Royal Navy, 1945–47. Architect, 1952–. Architect, Norwich Cathedral, 1977–90. Chairman: Norfolk Soc. (CPRE), 1971–76 (Vice Pres. 1976–); 54 Gp, 1982–; Norfolk Professional Firms Gp, 1994–; Friends of Norwich Museums, 1985–; Founder and Chm., British Assoc. of Friends of Museums, 1973–89 (Vice-Pres., 1989–); Founder Pres., World Fedn of Friends of Museums, 1975–81, Past Pres., 1981–. Mem., Cttee of Nat. Heritage, 1973–89; Trustee: Norfolk Historic Bldgs Trust, 1975–90 (Dir, 1990–); Theatre Royal, Norwich, 1991–; Vice-Pres., Norfolk Gardens Trust, 1991– (Founder, and Chm., 1988–91). Mem., Norfolk Assoc. of Architects, 1952– (Pres., 1979–81); Hon. Treas., Heritage Co-ordination Gp, 1981–87. First Gov., Wymondham Coll., 1991–. JP Norwich, 1972; DL Norfolk, 1986. FRSA 1982; FSA 1983. *Publication:* paper on British Museum Friends Socs in Proc. of First Internat. Congress of Friends of Museums, Barcelona, 1972; contrib. Jl of Royal Soc. of Arts. *Recreations:* tennis, yachting. *Club:* Norfolk (Norwich) (Pres., 1986–87).

MAWSON, Stuart Radcliffe; Consultant Surgeon, Ear Nose and Throat Department, King's College Hospital, London, 1951–79, Head of Department, 1973–79, Hon. Consultant, 1979; *b* 4 March 1918; *s* of late Alec Robert Mawson, Chief Officer, Parks Dept, LCC, and Ena (*née* Grossmith), *d* of George Grossmith Jr, Actor Manager; *m* 1948, June Irene, *d* of George Percival; two *s* two *d*. *Educ:* Canford Sch.; Trinity Coll., Cambridge; St Thomas's Hosp., London. BA Cantab 1940, MA 1976; MRCS, LRCP 1943; MB, BChir Cantab 1946; FRCS 1947; DLO 1948. House Surg., St Thomas's Hosp., 1943; RMO XIth Para. Bn, 1st Airborne Div., Arnhem, POW, 1943–44; Chief Asst, ENT Dept, St Thomas's Hosp., 1950; Consultant ENT Surgeon: King's Coll. Hosp., 1951; Belgrave Hosp. for Children, 1951; Recog. Teacher of Oto-Rhino-Laryngology, Univ. of London, 1958. Chm., KCH Med. Cttee and Dist Management Team, 1977–79. FRSocMed (Pres. Section of Otology, 1974–75); Liveryman, Apothecaries' Soc.; former Mem. Council, Brit. Assoc. of Otolaryngologists. *Publications:* Diseases of the Ear, 1963, 5th edn 1988; (jtly) Essentials of Otolaryngology, 1967; (contrib.) Scott-Brown's Diseases of the Ear, Nose and Throat, 4th edn 1979; (contrib.) Modern Trends in Diseases of the Ear, Nose and Throat, 1972; Arnhem Doctor, 1981; numerous papers in sci. jls. *Address:* Whinbeck, Knodishall, Saxmundham, Suffolk IP17 1UF. *Clubs:* Aldeburgh Golf, Aldeburgh Yacht.

MAXEY, Peter Malcolm, CMG 1982; HM Diplomatic Service, retired 1986; *b* 26 Dec. 1930; *m* 1st, 1955, Joyce Diane Marshall; two *s* two *d*; 2nd, Christine Irene Spooner. *Educ:* Bedford Sch.; Corpus Christi Coll., Cambridge. Served HM Forces, 1949–50. Entered Foreign Office, 1953; Third Sec., Moscow, 1955; Second Sec., 1956; First Sec., Helsinki, 1962; Moscow, 1965; First Sec. and Head of Chancery, Colombo, 1968; seconded to Lazard Bros, 1971; Inspector, 1972; Deputy Head UK Delegation to CSCE, Geneva, 1973; Head of UN Dept, FCO, 1974; NATO Defence Coll., Rome, 1977; Dublin, 1977; on secondment as Under Sec., Cabinet Office, 1978–81; Ambassador, GDR, 1981–84; Ambassador and Dep. Perm. Rep. to UN, NY, 1984–86. Editorial Dir, Global Analysis Systems, 1986–88.

MAXTON, John Alston; MP (Lab) Glasgow, Cathcart, since 1979; *b* Oxford, 5 May 1936; *s* of John Maxton, agr. economist, and Jenny Maxton; *m* Christine Maxton; three *s*. *Educ:* Lord Williams' Grammar Sch., Thame; Oxford Univ. Lectr in Social Studies, Hamilton Coll. Chm., Assoc. of Lectrs in Colls of Educn, Scotland; Member: Educnl Inst. of Scotland; Socialist Educnl Assoc. Joined Lab. Party, 1970. Opposition spokesman on health, local govt, and housing in Scotland, 1985–87, on Scotland, 1987–92; Scottish and Treasury Whip, 1984–85. Member: Scottish Select Cttee, 1981–83; Public Accounts Cttee, 1983–84; Nat. Heritage Select Cttee, 1992–. Mem., ASTMS. *Recreations:* family, listening to jazz, running. *Address:* House of Commons, SW1A 0AA.

MAXWELL, family name of **Barons de Ros** and **Farnham.**

MAXWELL, David Campbell F.; *see* Finlay-Maxwell.

MAXWELL of Ardwell, Col Frederick Gordon, CBE 1967; TD; FCIT; *b* 2 May 1905; *s* of late Lt-Col Alexander Gordon Maxwell, OBE, Hon. Corps of Gentlemen-at-Arms; *m* 1st, 1935, Barbara Margaret (decd), *d* of late Edward Williams Hedley, MBE, MD, Thursley, Surrey; two *s* (one *d* decd); 2nd, 1965, True Hamilton Exley, *d* of Francis George Hamilton, Old Blundells Cottage, Tiverton, Devon. *Educ:* Eton. OC 2nd Bn The London Scottish, 1939–42; GSO1, 52nd (Lowland) Div., 1943–44, served in Holland and Germany (despatches); GSO1, Allied Land Forces SE Asia, 1945; OC 1st Bn The London Scottish, 1947–50. Joined London Transport, 1924; Operating Manager (Railways), London Transport, 1947–70, retired 1971; Protocol and Conference Dept, FCO, 1971–88. Mem., Co. of London T&AFA, 1947–68; Lt-Col RE (T&AVR, IV), 1956–70; Regimental Col, The London Scottish, 1969–73. DL, Co. of London, 1962; DL, Greater London, 1966–81. OStJ 1969. *Address:* 41 Cheyne Court, Cheyne Place, SW3 5TS. *T:* 0171–352 9801. *Clubs:* Naval and Military, Highland Brigade.

MAXWELL, Ian Robert Charles; Joint Managing Director, Maxwell Communication Corporation plc, 1988–91; Chairman and Publisher: Mirror Group Newspapers Ltd, 1991 (Director, 1987–91); The European Newspaper Ltd, 1991 (Director, 1990–91); *b* 15 June 1956; *s* of late (Ian) Robert Maxwell, MC; *m* 1991, Laura Plumb. *Educ:* Marlborough; Balliol Coll., Oxford (MA). Sen. management positions, France, Germany and USA, Pergamon Press, 1978–83; Prince's Charitable Trust, 1983–84; British Printing & Communication Corporation, later Maxwell Communication Corporation, 1985–91; Sales Develt Dir, 1985–86; Chief Exec., Maxwell Pergamon Publishing Corp., 1988–91; Chairman: Agence Centrale de Presse, 1986–89; Maxwell Media, Paris, 1986–92; Dir, Pergamon AGB, 1989–92. Mem., Nat. Theatre Develt Council, 1986–91; Pres., Club d'Investissement Media, 1988–91. Vice Chm., Derby County Football Club, 1987–91 (Chm., 1984–87). *Recreations:* music, ski-ing, water-skiing, football.

See also K. F. H. Maxwell.

MAXWELL, Kevin Francis Herbert; Chairman and Chief Executive, Maxwell Communication Corporation plc, 1991 (Director, 1986–91); Consultant, Westbourne Communications Ltd, since 1993; *b* 20 Feb. 1959; *s* of late (Ian) Robert Maxwell, MC; *m* 1984, Pandora Deborah Karen Warnford-Davis; one *s* four *d*. *Educ:* Marlborough Coll.; Balliol Coll., Oxford (MA Hons). Chm., Macmillan Inc., 1991 (Dir, 1988–91); Dir, Guinness Mahon Hldgs, 1989–92. Chm., Oxford United FC, 1987–92. Trustee, New Sch. for Social Research, NYC, 1989. *Recreations:* water colour painting, football. *Address:* Moulsford Manor, Moulsford, Oxon OX10 9HU.

See also I. R. C. Maxwell.

MAXWELL, Sir Michael (Eustace George), 9th Bt *cr* 1681 (NS), of Monreith, Wigtownshire; ARICS; *b* 28 Aug. 1943; *s* of Major Eustace Maxwell (*d* 1971) and of Dorothy Vivien, *d* of Captain George Bellville; *S* uncle, 1987. *Educ:* Eton; College of Estate Management. *Recreations:* microlights, curling, tennis, ski-ing. *Address:* Laundry House, Farming Woods, Brigstock, Northants NN14 3JA; 56 Queensmill Road, SW6 6JS. *Clubs:* Stranraer Rugby; Port William Tennis.

MAXWELL, Sir Nigel Mellor H.; *see* Heron-Maxwell.

MAXWELL, Peter; *see* Maxwell, Hon. Lord.

MAXWELL, Richard; QC 1988; a Recorder, since 1992; *b* 21 Dec. 1943; *s* of Thomas and Kathleen Marjorie Maxwell; *m* 1966, Judith Ann Maxwell; two *s* two *d*. *Educ:* Nottingham High Sch.; Hertford College, Oxford (MA). Lectr in Law, 1966–68; called to the Bar, Inner Temple, 1968. An Asst Recorder, 1989–92. *Recreations:* squash (daily), running (weekly), half marathon (annually), fly fishing (in season), ski-ing, mountain-biking, roller-blading, wine, single malt whisky. *Address:* 5 Castle Grove, The Park, Nottingham NG7 1DN. *T:* Nottingham (0115) 941 8063. *Clubs:* Nottingham and Notts United Services; Nottingham Squash Rackets; Darley Dale Flyfishers'.

MAXWELL, Robert James, CBE 1993; JP; Secretary and Chief Executive, The King's Fund, since 1980; *b* 26 June 1934; *s* of Dr George B. Maxwell, MC and Cathleen Maxwell; *m* 1960, Jane FitzGibbon; three *s* two *d*. *Educ:* Leighton Park Sch.; New Coll., Oxford (BA 1st Cl. Hons, MA; Newdigate Prize for Poetry); Univ. of Pennsylvania (MA); LSE (PhD); Univ. of Tromsø (Dip. in Health Econs). FCMA. 2nd Lieut, Cameronians (Scottish Rifles), 1952–54. Union Corp., 1958–66; McKinsey & Co., 1966–75; Administrator to Special Trustees, St Thomas' Hosp., 1975–80. Pres., European Healthcare Management Assoc., 1985–87; Pres., Open Section, RSocMed, 1986–88. Chm., Court, LSHTM, 1985–; Gov., UMDS, 1989–; Director: Guy's and Lewisham Trust, 1990–93; Lewisham NHS Trust, 1993–; Mem., Bd of Management, Med. Defence Union, 1990–. Chm., Leighton Park Sch., 1981–. Hon. FRCGP; Hon. MRCP; Hon. Mem., Assoc. of Anaesthetists. Trustee, Joseph Rowntree Foundn, 1994–. JP Inner London Youth and Family Courts (Chm.), 1971–. DUniv Brunel, 1993; Hon. DLitt West of England, 1993. *Publications:* Health Care: the growing dilemma, 1974; Health and Wealth, 1981; Reshaping the National Health Service, 1988; Spotlight on the Cities, 1989. *Recreations:* poetry, walking, stained glass, not quite catching up with correspondence. *Address:* Pitt Court Manor, North Nibley, Dursley, Glos GL11 6EL; 2 Palace Court, W2 4HS. *Clubs:* Brooks's, Royal Society of Medicine.

MAXWELL, Rear-Adm. Thomas Heron, CB 1967; DSC 1942; idc, jssc, psc; Director-General of Naval Training, Ministry of Defence, 1965–67; retired, 1967; *b* 10 April 1912; *s* of late H. G. Maxwell; *m* 1947, Maeve McKinley; two *s* two *d*. *Educ:* Campbell Coll., Belfast; Royal Naval Engineering Coll. Cadet, 1930; Commander, 1946; Captain, 1956; Rear-Adm., 1965. *Address:* Tokenbury, Shaft Road, Bath, Avon BA2 7HP.

MAXWELL-HYSLOP, Kathleen Rachel, FSA; FBA 1991; archaeologist, retired; *b* 27 March 1914; *d* of Sir Charles Clay, CB, FBA and Hon. Lady Clay; *m* 1938, Aymer Robert Maxwell-Hyslop (*d* 1993); one *s* two *d*. *Educ:* Downe House Sch.; Sorbonne; London Univ. (Acad. Postgrad. Dip. in Archaeology of Western Asia). FSA 1950. Institute of Archaeology, University of London: Asst Lectr, 1947–52; Lectr in W Asiatic Archaeology, 1952–66. Archaeol research and travel in Turkey, Cyprus, Iraq, Jordan, Israel, 1950–89; lectured in Philadelphia, MIT, Teheran, Amman; excavations in British Isles, Turkey, Cyprus, Iraq and Iran, 1936–90. *Publications:* Western Asiatic Jewellery *c.* 3000–612 BC, 1971; articles in Iraq, Levant, Jl of Archaeol Science, Anatolian Studies and jls in USA and Turkey. *Recreations:* gardening, painting, piano. *Address:* Water Lane House, Little Tew, Chipping Norton, Oxon OX7 4JG. *T:* Great Tew (01608) 683226.

MAXWELL-HYSLOP, Sir Robert John, (Sir Robin), Kt 1992; *b* 6 June 1931; 2nd *s* of late Capt. A. H. Maxwell-Hyslop, GC, RN, and late Mrs Maxwell-Hyslop; *m* 1968, Joanna Margaret, *er d* of Thomas McCosh; two *d*. *Educ:* Stowe; Christ Church, Oxford (MA). Hons Degree in PPE Oxon, 1954. Joined Rolls-Royce Ltd Aero Engine Div., as graduate apprentice, Sept. 1954; served 2 years as such, then joined Export Sales Dept; PA to Sir David Huddie, Dir and GM (Sales and Service), 1958; left Rolls-Royce, 1960. Contested (C) Derby (North), 1959; MP(C) Tiverton Div. of Devon, Nov. 1960–1992. Member: Trade and Industry Select Cttee, 1971–92; Standing Orders Cttee, 1977–92; Procedure Select Cttee, 1978–92. Former Chm., Anglo-Brazilian Parly Gp. Dir, Ugland Internat., 1993–. Hon. Associate, BVA, 1977. Politician of the Year Award (first recipient), Nat. Fedn of Self-employed and Small Businesses, 1989. *Recreations:* motoring, South American history. *Address:* 4 Tiverton Road, Silverton, Exeter, Devon EX5 4JQ.

MAXWELL SCOTT, Sir Dominic James, 14th Bt *cr* 1642, of Haggerston, Northumberland; *b* 22 July 1968; *s* of Sir Michael Fergus Maxwell Scott, 13th Bt and of Deirdre Moira, *d* of late Alexander McKechnie; *S* father, 1989. *Educ:* Eton; Sussex Univ. *Heir: b* Matthew Joseph Maxwell Scott, *b* 27 Aug. 1976. *Address:* c/o 130 Ritherdon Road, SW17 8QQ.

MAXWELL-SCOTT, Dame Jean (Mary Monica), DCVO 1984 (CVO 1969); Lady in Waiting to HRH Princess Alice, Duchess of Gloucester, since 1959; *b* 8 June 1923; *d* of Maj.-Gen. Sir Walter Maxwell-Scott of Abbotsford, Bt, CB, DSO, DL and Mairi MacDougall of Lunga. *Educ:* Couvent des Oiseaux, Westgate-on-Sea. VAD Red Cross Nurse, 1941–46. *Recreations:* gardening, reading, horses. *Address:* Abbotsford, Melrose, Roxburghshire TD6 9BQ. *T:* Galashiels (01896) 752043. *Club:* New Cavendish.

MAY, family name of **Baron May.**

MAY, 3rd Baron, *cr* 1935, of Weybridge; **Michael St John May;** 3rd Bt, *cr* 1931; late Lieut, Royal Corps of Signals; *b* 26 Sept. 1931; *o s* of 2nd Baron May and *d* of George Ricardo Thomas; *S* father 1950; *m* 1st, 1958, Dorothea Catherine Ann (marr. diss. 1963), *d* of Charles McCarthy, Boston, USA; 2nd, 1963, Jillian Mary, *d* of Albert Edward Shipton, Beggars Barn, Shutford, Oxon; one *s* one *d*. *Educ:* Wycliffe Coll., Stonehouse, Glos; Magdalene Coll., Cambridge. 2nd Lieut, Royal Signals, 1950. *Recreations:* sailing, travel. *Heir: s* Hon. Jasper Bertram St John May, *b* 24 Oct. 1965. *Address:* Gautherns Barn, Sibford Gower, Oxon OX15 5RY.

MAY, Hon. Sir Anthony (Tristram Kenneth), Kt 1991; **Hon. Mr Justice May;** a Judge of the High Court of Justice, Queen's Bench Division, since 1991; *b* 9 Sept. 1940; *s* of late Kenneth Sibley May and Joan Marguérite (*née* Oldaker); *m* 1968, Stella Gay Pattisson; one *s* two *d*. *Educ:* Bradfield Coll.; Worcester Coll., Oxford (Trevelyan Scholar 1960, Hon. Scholar 1962; MA). Inner Temple Scholar, 1965; called to the Bar, 1967, Bencher, 1985; QC 1979; a Recorder, 1985–91. Jun. Counsel to DoE for Land Commn Act Matters, 1972–75; Chm., Commn of Inquiry, Savings and Investment Bank Ltd, IoM, 1990. A Judge, Employment Appeal Tribunal, 1993–. Vice-Chm., Official Referees Bar Assoc., 1987–91. Vice-Pres., Guildford Choral Soc., 1991– (Chm., 1980–91). *Publication:* (ed) Keating on Building Contracts, 5th edn 1991, 6th edn 1995. *Recreations:* gardening, music, books, bonfires. *Address:* Royal Courts of Justice, Strand, WC2A 2LL.

MAY, Prof. Brian Albert, FEng 1990; independent development adviser; Professor of Agricultural Engineering, 1982–91, and Head, Cranfield Rural Institute, 1989–91, Cranfield Institute of Technology; Emeritus Professor, 1992; *b* 2 June 1936; *s* of Albert Robert and Eileen May; *m* 1961, Brenda Ann Smith; three *s*. *Educ:* Faversham Grammar Sch.; Aston Univ., Birmingham. FRAgS. Design Engineer, Massey Ferguson, 1958–63; National College of Agricultural Engineering: Lectr, 1963–68; Sen. Lectr, 1968–72; Principal Lectr, 1972–75; Head of Environmental Control and Processing Dept, 1972–75; Cranfield Institute of Technology: Prof. of Environmental Control and Processing, 1975–82; Head, Nat. Coll. of Agricl Engrg, later Silsoe Coll., 1976–89; Dean, Faculty of Agricl Engrg, Food Prodn and Rural Land Use, 1977–86. Dir, British Agricl Export Council, 1985–88. Member: Res. Requirements Bd on Plants and Soils, AFRC, 1980–86; Engrg Adv. Cttee, AFRC, 1984–88; Standing Cttee on University Entrance Requirements, 1984–91; Agric. and Vet. Cttee, 1985–91, Engrg and Technol. Adv. Cttee, 1991–95, British Council; Overseas Affairs Cttee, Fellowship of Engrg, 1991–95; Undergrad. Adv. Gp, Royal Acad. of Engrg. Pres., IAgrE, 1984–86; Mem. Council, Royal Agricl Soc. of England, 1984–91. Governor, British Soc. for Res. in Agricl Engrg, 1979–90. Chm., Ramsgate Soc. *Publications:* Power on the Land, 1974; papers in agricl and engrg jls. *Recreations:* cricket, gardening, reading. *Address:* 23 Spencer Square, Ramsgate, Kent CT11 9LA. *T:* Thanet (01843) 580746. *Club:* Farmers'.

MAY, Charles Alan Maynard, FEng, FIEE; lately Senior Director, Development and Technology, British Telecom; retired 1984; *b* 14 April 1924; *s* of late Cyril P. May and Katharine M. May; *m* 1947, Daphne, *o d* of late Bertram Carpenter; one *s* two *d*. *Educ:* The Grammar Sch., Ulverston, Cumbria; Christ's Coll., Cambridge (Mech. Sciences tripos 1944, MA). CEng, FIEE 1967. Served REME and Indian Army, 1944–47. Entered Post Office Engrg Dept, 1948; Head of Electronic Switching Gp, 1956; Staff Engr, Computer Engrg Br., 1966; Dep. Dir (Engrg), 1970; Dir of Research, Post Office, later British Telecom, 1975–83. Dir, SIRA Ltd, 1982–89. Chm., IEE Electronics Divl Bd, 1977–78; Member: Council, IEE, 1970–72 and 1976–80; BBC Engrg Adv. Cttee, 1978–84; Adv. Cttee on Calibration and Measurement, 1978–83; Adv. Cttee, Dept of Electronic and Electrical Engrg, Sheffield Univ., 1979–82; Communications Systems Adv. Panel, Council of Educnl Technology, 1980–83; Ind. Adv. Bd, Sch. of Eng. and Applied Scis, Sussex Univ., 1981–84; Council, ERA Technology, 1983–88. Graham Young Lectr, Glasgow Univ., 1979. Vis. Examr, Imperial Coll., Univ. of London, 1980–82; External Examnr, NE London Polytechnic, 1982–86. Governor, Suffolk Coll. of Higher and Further Educn, 1980–83. FRSA 1985. *Publications:* contribs on telecommunications to learned jls. *Recreations:* gardening, bridge. *Address:* Corner Cottage, High Park Avenue, East Horsley, Leatherhead, Surrey KT24 5DD. *T:* East Horsley (01483) 282521.

MAY, Douglas James; QC (Scot) 1989; a Social Security Commissioner and a Child Support Commissioner, since 1993; *b* 7 May 1946; *s* of Thomas May and Violet Mary Brough Boyd or May. *Educ:* George Heriot's Sch., Edinburgh; Edinburgh Univ. Advocate 1971. Temporary Sheriff, 1990–. Contested (C): Edinburgh E, Feb. 1974; Glasgow Cathcart, 1983. *Recreations:* golf, photography (LRPS), travel, concert going. *Address:* Office of the Social Security Commissioners, 23 Melville Street, Edinburgh EH3 7PW. *T:* 0131–225 2201. *Clubs:* Scottish Arts, University Staff (Edinburgh); Merchants of Edinburgh Golf, Bruntsfield Links Golfing Society.

MAY, Gordon Leslie, OBE 1982; retired solicitor; *b* 19 Nov. 1921; *s* of A. Carveth May and Isobella May; *m* 1945, Nina Cheek; one *s* two *d*. *Educ:* Worcester College for the Blind; Manchester Univ. War service, 1939–45. Admitted Solicitor, 1947; South Eastern Gas Board: Solicitor, 1956; Secretary, 1961; Executive Board Member, 1968; British Gas Corporation: Dep. Chairman, SW Region, 1974; Corp. Sec., 1977–84; Mem. Executive, 1982–84. Consultant, Keene Marsland, solicitors, 1984–87. Mem. Exec. Council, RNIB, 1975–89. Chm. Bd of Governors, Worcester Coll. for the Blind, 1980–87. Liveryman, Solicitors' Co., 1963. *Recreation:* sailing. *Address:* Walsall House, High Street, Upnor, Rochester, Kent ME2 4XG. *T:* Medway (01634) 297197. *Clubs:* Royal Automobile; Medway Yacht (Upnor); Alderney Sailing.

MAY, Graham; retired from Civil Service, 1981; *b* 15 Dec. 1923; *s* of Augustus May; *m* 1952, Marguerite Lucy Griffin; four *s*. *Educ:* Gravesend County Sch. for Boys; Balliol Coll., Oxford (BA). War Service, Royal Artillery, 1942–46. Asst Principal, Min. of Works, 1948, Principal 1952; seconded to Treasury, 1961–63; Asst Sec., MPBW, 1963; Under Sec., DoE, 1972–81. *Address:* 14 Wells Close, Tenterden, Kent TN30 6QJ.

MAY, James Nicholas Welby; Director-General, British Retail Consortium, since 1989; *b* 21 Feb. 1949; *s* of Richard Percy May and Caroline Rosemary Welby May (*née* Jack); *m* 1979, Diana Mary Tamplin; two *s*. *Educ:* Sherborne Sch., Dorset; Southampton Univ. (BSc 1970); College of Law. Called to the Bar, Lincoln's Inn, 1974. Programme Officer, UNEP, 1976–77; Project Officer, IUCN, 1977–78; Legal Officer, Friends of the Earth, 1978–79; Legal Adviser, NFU, 1980–89. Sec., Footwear Distributors' Fedn, 1989–; Member: Countryside Commn Common Land Forum, 1984–86; Nat. Retail Trng Council, 1989–; Distributive Occupational Standards Council, 1993–. Non-exec. Dir, Guild of Excellence plc, 1995–. FRSA; MInstD; AIMgt. *Recreations:* travel, ski-ing. *Address:* British Retail Consortium, Bedford House, 69–79 Fulham High Street, SW6 3JW.

MAY, Air Vice-Marshal John Anthony Gerard, CB 1995; CBE 1993; Air Officer Training and Air Officer Commanding Training Group, Headquarters Personnel and Training Command, since 1994; Chief Executive, Training Group Defence Agency; *b* 12 Nov. 1941; *s* of Anthony Frederick May and late Beatrice Mary (*née* Niblett); *m* 1964, Margaret Anne Chester; two *s*. *Educ:* City of London Sch. Joined RAF 1961; flying trng, then Qualified Flying Instr, Linton-on-Ouse; Lightning aircraft, 1966; served with Nos 56, 5 and 19 Sqns; Staff Coll., Camberley, 1977; Chief Flying Instr, RAF Cranwell, 1979; Stn Comdr, Binbrook, 1985; Dep. Dir of Air Defence, MoD, 1987; Air Cdre Policy and Plans, RAF Support Comd, 1989; AOC No 38 Gp, and SASO, HQ Strike Comd, 1993–94. QCVSA 1971. *Recreations:* alpine ski-ing, classic cars. *Address:* HQ Personnel and Training Command, RAF Innsworth, Glos GL3 1EZ. *Club:* Royal Air Force.

MAY, Rt. Hon. Sir John (Douglas), Kt 1972; PC 1982; a Lord Justice of Appeal, 1982–89; *b* 28 June 1923; *s* of late Mr and Mrs E. A. G. May, of Shanghai and Chelsea; *m* 1958, Mary, *er d* of Sir Owen Morshead, GCVO, KCB, DSO, MC, and Paquita, *d* of J. G. Hagemeyer; two *s* one *d*. *Educ:* Clifton Coll. (Scholar); Balliol Coll., Oxford (Schol.). Lieut (SpSc) RNVR, 1944–46. Barrister-at-Law, Inner Temple, 1947 (Schol.), Master of the Bench, 1972; QC 1965; Recorder of Maidstone, 1971; Leader, SE Circuit, 1971; Presiding Judge, Midland and Oxford Circuit, 1973–77; a Judge of the High Ct, Queen's Bench Division, 1972–82; a Judge of the Employment Appeal Tribunal, 1978–82. Member: Parole Bd, 1977–80 (Vice-Chm., 1980); Royal Commn on Criminal Justice, 1991–93; Chairman: Inquiry into UK Prison Services, 1978–79; University Comrs, 1989–; Guildford and Woolwich Inquiry, 1989–94. Treas., Inner Temple, 1993. Clifton College: Mem. Council, 1980–93; Pres., 1987–93. *Address:* Lindens, Sturminster Newton, Dorset DT10 1BU. *T:* Sturminster Newton (01258) 473321. *Club:* Vincent's (Oxford).

MAY, John Otto, CBE 1962 (OBE 1949); HM Diplomatic Service; retired; *b* 21 April 1913; *s* of late Otto May, FRCP, MD; *m* 1939, Maureen McNally; one *d*. *Educ:* Sherborne; St John's Coll., Cambridge. Apptd to Dept of Overseas Trade, 1937. Private Sec. to Comptroller-General, 1939; Asst Commercial Secretary: Copenhagen, 1939; Helsinki, 1940; Ministry of Economic Warfare (Representative in Caracas), 1942–44; First Sec. (Commercial): Rome, 1945, Bucharest, 1948; Foreign Office, 1950–53; First Sec., Helsinki, 1954. Acted as Chargé d'Affaires in 1954, 1955, and 1956; Counsellor (Commercial) and Consul-General, HM Embassy, Athens, 1957–60; Consul-General: Genoa, 1960–65; Rotterdam, 1965–68; Gothenburg, 1968–72. Coronation Medal, 1953.

Recreations: travel, photography, walking, philately. *Address:* 6 Millhedge Close, Cobham, Surrey KT11 3BE. *T:* Cobham (01932) 864645. *Club:* United Oxford & Cambridge University.

MAY, Sir Kenneth Spencer, Kt 1980; CBE 1976; Director: Advertiser Newspapers Ltd, Adelaide, since 1988; The News Corporation Ltd, 1979–89; *b* 10 Dec. 1914; *s* of late N. May; *m* 1943, Betty C. Scott; one *s* one *d. Educ:* Woodville High School. Editorial staff, News, 1930; political writer, 1946–59; Asst Manager, News, Adelaide, 1959–64, Manager, 1964–69; Dir, News Ltd, 1969–86; Man. Dir, News Ltd, Aust., 1977–80; Chm., Mirror Newspapers Ltd and Nationwide News Pty Ltd, 1969–80; Director: Independent Newspapers Ltd, Wellington, NZ, 1971–84; Santos Ltd, 1980–83. *Address:* 26 Waterfall Terrace, Burnside, SA 5066, Australia.

MAY, Paul, CBE 1970; retired 1970; *b* 12 July 1907; *s* of William Charles May and Katharine Edith May; *m* 1st, 1933, Dorothy Ida Makower (*d* 1961); two *s* one *d*; 2nd, 1969, Frances Maud Douglas (*née* Tarver); two step *s. Educ:* Westminster; Christ Church, Oxford (MA). United Africa Co. Ltd, 1930–32; John Lewis Partnership, 1932–40; Min. of Aircraft Production, 1940–45; John Lewis Partnership, 1945–70 (Dep. Chm., 1955–70). Mem. Exec. Cttee, Land Settlement Assoc. Ltd, 1962–71. *Recreations:* walking, reading, etc. *Address:* Chesterford, Whittingham, Northumberland NE66 4UP. *T:* Whittingham (01665) 574642.

MAY, Richard George; His Honour Judge May; a Circuit Judge, since 1987; *b* 12 Nov. 1938; *s* of George William May, MB, and late Phyllis May; *m* 1974, Radmila Monica, *er d* of late J. D. A. Barnicot, OBE, and Elizabeth Barnicot; one *s* two *d. Educ:* Haileybury; Selwyn Coll., Cambridge. National Service, 2nd Lieut, DLI, 1958–60. Called to the Bar, Inner Temple, 1965; Midland and Oxford Circuit; a Recorder, 1985–87. Contested (Lab): Dorset South, 1970; Finchley, 1979. Councillor, Westminster CC, 1971–78 (Leader of the Opposition, 1974–77). *Publications:* (ed jtly) Phipson on Evidence, 12th edn 1976, 13th edn 1982; Criminal Evidence, 1986, 3rd edn 1995. *Address:* Devereux Chambers, Devereux Court, WC2R 3JJ. *T:* 0171–353 7534. *Club:* Savile.

MAY, Prof. Robert McCredie, FRS 1979; Chief Scientific Adviser to the Government and Head of the Office of Science and Technology, since 1995; Royal Society Research Professor, Department of Zoology, Oxford University, and Imperial College, London, since 1988; Fellow of Merton College, Oxford, since 1988; *b* 8 Jan. 1936; *s* of Henry W. May and Kathleen M. May; *m* 1962, Judith (*née* Feiner); one *d. Educ:* Sydney Boys' High Sch.; Sydney Univ. BSc 1956, PhD (Theoretical Physics) 1959. Gordon Mackay Lectr in Applied Maths, Harvard Univ., 1959–61; Sydney Univ.: Sen. Lectr in Theoretical Physics, 1962–64; Reader, 1964–69; Personal Chair, 1969–73; Princeton University: Prof. of Biology, 1973–88; Class of 1877 Prof. of Zoology, 1975–88; Chm., Univ. Res. Bd, 1977–88. Vis. Prof., Imperial Coll., 1975–88; visiting appointments at: Harvard, 1966; California Inst. of Technology, 1967; UKAEA Culham Lab., 1971; Magdalen Coll., Oxford, 1971; Inst. for Advanced Study, Princeton, 1972; King's Coll., Cambridge, 1976. Pres., British Ecol Soc., 1992–93; Chm., Natural History Mus., 1994– (Trustee, 1991–93); Trustee: WWF (UK), 1990–94; Royal Botanic Gardens, Kew, 1991–; Nuffield Foundn, 1993–. Member: Smithsonian Council, USA, 1988–; Jt Nature Conservation Council, 1989–. Overseas Mem., Australian Acad. of Sci., 1991; For. Associate, US Nat. Acad. of Scis, 1992. Linnean Medal, 1991. *Publications:* Stability and Complexity in Model Ecosystems, 1973, 2nd edn 1974; Theoretical Ecology: Principles and Applications, 1976, 2nd edn 1981; Population Biology of Infectious Diseases, 1982; Exploitation of Marine Communities, 1984; Perspectives in Ecological Theory, 1989; Infectious Diseases of Humans: dynamics and control, 1991; Extinction Rates, 1994; articles in mathematical, biol and physics jls. *Recreations:* tennis, running, bridge. *Address:* Office of Science and Technology, Albany House, 84–86 Petty France, SW1H 9ST; Department of Zoology, South Parks Road, Oxford OX1 3PS. *Club:* Athenæum.

MAY, Stuart; *see* May, W. H. S.

MAY, Valentine Gilbert Delabere, CBE 1969; Director, Yvonne Arnaud Theatre, Guildford, since 1975; *b* 1 July 1927; *s* of Claude Jocelyn Delabere May and Olive Gilbert; *m* 1st, 1955, Penelope Sutton; one *d*; 2nd, 1980, Petra Schroeder; one *d. Educ:* Cranleigh Sch.; Peterhouse Coll., Cambridge. Trained at Old Vic Theatre Sch. Director: Ipswich Theatre, 1953–57; Nottingham Playhouse, 1957–61; Bristol Old Vic Company, 1961–75. Plays directed for Bristol Old Vic which subseq. transf. to London incl.: War and Peace, 1962; A Severed Head, 1963; Love's Labour's Lost, 1964 (which also went on a British Council European tour); Portrait of a Queen, 1965; The Killing of Sister George, 1965; The Italian Girl, 1968; Mrs Mouse, Are You Within, 1968; Conduct Unbecoming, 1969; It's a Two-Foot-Six Inches Above the Ground World, 1970; Poor Horace, 1970; Trelawny, 1972; The Card, 1973. Directed at Old Vic: Richard II, 1959; Mourning Becomes Electra, 1961; Tribute to the Lady, 1974–75. Plays directed for Arnaud Theatre transferred to London: Baggage, 1976; Banana Ridge, 1976; The Dark Horse, 1978; House Guest, 1981. Directed: Little Me, Prince of Wales, 1984; Royal Baccarat Scandal, Chichester Fest., 1988, London, 1989; Henry IV (by Pirandello), London, 1990. Overseas prodns include: Romeo and Juliet, and Hamlet (NY and USA tour); The Taming of the Shrew (Hong Kong Fest. and Latin America tour); Broadway prodns: A Severed Head; Portrait of a Queen; The Killing of Sister George; Conduct Unbecoming; Murder Among Friends; Pygmalion. Hon. MA Bristol, 1975. *Recreations:* reading, architecture, music, astronomy. *Address:* Yvonne Arnaud Theatre, Millbrook, Guildford, Surrey GU1 3UX. *T:* Guildford (01483) 64571.

MAY, (William Herbert) Stuart; Senior Partner, Theodore Goddard, Solicitors, since 1989; *b* 5 April 1937; *s* of Arthur Douglas May and Jean Reid; *m* 1966, Sarah Margaret (*née* Maples); four *s. Educ:* Taunton School; Wadham College, Oxford (MA). Qualified Solicitor, 1965, with Theodore Goddard, Partner 1970, Sen. Partner, 1989. *Recreations:* gardening, theatre, spectator sport. *Address:* (office) 150 Aldersgate Street, EC1A 4EJ; Lower Farm, Hadstock, Cambridge CB1 6PF.

MAYALL, Prof. James Bardsley Lawson; Professor of International Relations, London School of Economics, since 1991; *b* 14 April 1937; *s* of Robert Cecil Mayall and Rhoda Anne (*née* Stote); *m* 1st, 1964, Margaret Berry (marr. diss. 1990); one *d*; 2nd, 1991, Avril Doris Whalley. *Educ:* Shrewsbury Sch.; Sydney Sussex Coll., Cambridge (BA Hist. Tripos 1960). Sir John Dill Fellow, Princeton Univ., NJ, 1960–61; BoT, 1961–64; British High Commn, New Dehli, 1964–65; Dept of Internat. Relns, LSE, 1966–; Chm., Steering Cttee, Centre for Internat. Studies, LSE, 1991–. Mem. Council, RIIA, 1992– (Associate Editor, Survey and Documents of Internat. Affairs, 1967–71). *Publications:* Africa and the Cold War, 1971; (Associate Ed.) Survey of International Affairs 1963, 1977; (ed jtly) A New International Commodity Regime, 1979; (ed jtly) The End of the Post-War Era: documents on Great Power relns 1968–75, 1980; (ed) The Community of States: a study in international political theory, 1982; Nationalism and International Society, 1990; (ed jtly) The Fallacies of Hope: the post Colonial record of the Commonwealth Third World, 1991. *Recreations:* cooking, gardening, watching cricket, walking the dog. *Address:* Department of International Relations, London School of Economics, WC2A 2AE. *T:* 0171–955 7400. *Club:* MCC.

MAYER, Anthony; *see* Mayer, R. A. J.

MAYER, Prof. Colin Peter; Professor of Management Studies, Deputy Director (Academic), School of Management, and Fellow of Wadham College, University of Oxford, since 1994; *b* 12 May 1953; *s* of Harold Charles Mayer and late Anne Louise Mayer; *m* 1979, Annette Patricia Haynes; two *d. Educ:* St Paul's Sch.; Oriel College, Oxford; Wolfson College, Oxford (MA, MPhil, DPhil); Harvard Univ. HM Treasury, 1976–78; Harkness Fellow, Harvard, 1979–80; Fellow in Economics, St Anne's College, Oxford, 1980–86; Price Waterhouse Prof. of Corporate Finance, City Univ. Business Sch., 1987–92; Prof. of Econs and Finance, Univ. of Warwick, 1992–94. Chm., ESF Network in Financial Markets, 1989–94; Dir, Oxford Economic Research Associates Ltd, 1987–. Hon. Fellow, St Anne's Coll., Oxford, 1993; FRSA. Associate Editor: Jl of Internat. Financial Management; Jl of Corporate Finance; Jl of Industrial Econs; European Financial Management Jl; Review of Economic Policy; Review of Econs and Stats. *Publications:* (with J. Kay and J. Edwards) Economic Analysis of Accounting Profitability, 1986; (with J. Franks) Risk, Regulation and Investor Protection, 1989; (with A. Giovannini) European Financial Integration, 1991; (with X. Vives) Capital Markets and Financial Intermediation, 1993; (with T. Jenkinson) Hostile Takeovers, 1994; articles in economic jls. *Recreations:* piano, jogging, reading philosophy and science. *Address:* Wadham College, Oxford OX1 3PN. *T:* Oxford (01865) 228476.

MAYER, (Ralph) Anthony (Jeffrey); Chief Executive, Housing Corporation, since 1991; *b* 24 Feb. 1946; *s* of George Mayer and Margaret (*née* Jones); *m* 1971, Ann Gowen; one *s* one *d. Educ:* City of Bath Boys' Sch.; Lycée Michelet, Paris; St Edmund Hall, Oxford (BA Hons PPE). Ministry of Housing and Local Government, subseq. Department of the Environment, 1967–85: Asst Principal, 1967–72; seconded as Pvte Sec. to Parly Sec., CSD, 1971–72; Principal, 1972–81; seconded as Mem., CPRS, 1974–76, and as Prin. Pvte Sec. to Sec. of State for Transport, 1980–82; Asst Sec., 1981–85; Asst Dir, N. M. Rothschild and Sons, 1985–87; Man. Dir (Finance and Admin), Rothschild Asset Management, 1987–91. *Recreations:* hill walking, bridge, golf, yachting. *Address:* c/o Housing Corporation, 149 Tottenham Court Road, W1P 0BN. *T:* 0171–393 2000.

MAYER, Thomas, CBE 1985; FEng 1987; Chairman, Eldonray Ltd, since 1990; *b* 17 Dec. 1928; *s* of Hans and Jeanette Mayer; *m* 1st, 1956 (marr. diss. 1975); one *s* one *d*; 2nd, 1975, Jean Patricia Burrows. *Educ:* King's Sch., Harrow; Regent Street Polytechnic (BScEng). FIEE 1964; FRTS 1968; CRAeS 1990. Broadcasting Div., Marconi Co. Ltd, 1948–68; Man. Dir, Marconi Elliott Micro-Electronics Ltd, 1968–69; Man. Dir, Marconi Communication Systems Ltd, 1969–81; Man. Dir, 1981–86, Chm., 1981–90, THORN EMI Electronics Ltd; Chief Exec., THORN EMI Technology Gp, 1986–88; Exec. Dir, THORN EMI plc, 1987–90. Chairman: THORN EMI Varian Ltd, 1981–89; Holmes Protection Gp, 1990–91; ITT Defence Ltd, 1993–; Director: Thorn Ericsson, 1981–88; Systron Donner Corp., 1983–90; Inmos Corp., 1985–88; Babcock Thorn Ltd, 1985–90; THORN EMI Australia, 1987–88; non-executive Director: Devonport Management Ltd, 1990–; Electron House plc, 1991–. Member: Council, IEE, 1971–74; Council, Electronic Engrg Assoc., 1974–75, 1981–87 (Pres., 1982–83); Nat. Electronics Council, 1983–; SBAC, 1984–90 (Pres., 1987–88). Liveryman, Worshipful Co. of Engineers, 1984–. *Recreations:* golf, swimming, theatre. *Address:* 1590 A.D., Burton Lane, Monks Risborough, Bucks HP27 9JF. *T:* Princes Risborough (01844) 274549. *Club:* Whiteleaf Golf (Whiteleaf).

MAYES, Maj.-Gen. Frederick Brian, CB 1995; FRCS; QHS 1991; Director General, Army Medical Services, 1993–April 1996; *b* 24 Aug. 1934; *s* of late Harry Frederick and Constance Enid Mayes, *m* 1962, Mary Anna Georgina Roche; one *s* two *d* (and one *s* decd). *Educ:* Wyggeston Grammar Sch., Leicester; St Mary's Hosp. Med. Sch. (MB BS London 1958). Commissioned Lieut RAMC, 1960; served Aden, E Africa, BAOR, UK; Consultant in Surgery, 1972; CO, BMH Hannover, 1984–87; CO, Cambridge Mil. Hosp., Aldershot, 1987–88; Consultant Surgeon, HQ BAOR, 1988–90; Comdr Med., HQ BAOR, 1990–93. Pres., St John's Ambulance, Germany, 1990. CStJ 1993. *Recreations:* off-shore sailing, bridge, mountaineering. *Address:* Mornington, 9 Searle Road, Farnham, Surrey GU9 8LJ. *T:* Farnham (01252) 715453.

MAYES, Ian; QC 1993; *b* 11 Sept. 1951; *yr s* of Harold Mayes, journalist, and Beatrice Mayes; *m* 1986, Shirley A. Bothroyd, *qv*; two *s. Educ:* Highgate Sch. (Foundation Schol.); Trinity Coll., Cambridge. Called to the Bar, Middle Temple, 1974 (Harmsworth Schol.); Dept of Trade Inspection, London Capital Group Ltd, 1975–77; Standing Counsel to Inland Revenue, 1983–93. Chm., Disciplinary Cttee, Lloyd's of London. Mem., Justice Cttee on Fraud Trials. *Recreations:* ski-ing, scuba diving, paintings, pots. *Address:* Littleton Chambers, 3 King's Bench Walk North, Temple, EC4Y 7HR. *T:* 0171–797 8600.

MAYES, Rt. Rev. Michael Hugh Gunton; *see* Kilmore, Elphin and Ardagh, Bishop of.

MAYES, Shirley Ann, (Mrs Ian Mayes); *see* Bothroyd, S. A.

MAYFIELD, Hon. Lord; Ian MacDonald, MC 1945; a Senator of the College of Justice in Scotland, 1981–95; *b* 26 May 1921; *s* of H. J. and J. M. MacDonald; *m* 1946, Elizabeth de Vessey Lawson; one *s* one *d. Educ:* Colston's Sch., Bristol; Edinburgh Univ. (MA, LLB). Served 1939–46: Royal Tank Regt (Capt.). TA Lothians and Border Horse, later Queen's Own Lowland Yeomanry, 1948–62. Called to Bar, 1952; QC (Scot.) 1964. Mem., Criminal Injuries Compensation Board, 1972–74. Sheriff Principal of Dumfries and Galloway, Feb.-Dec. 1973; Pres., Industrial Tribunals for Scotland, 1973–81; Scottish Chm., Employment Appeal Tribunal, 1986–92. *Recreation:* sport. *Address:* 16 Mayfield Terrace, Edinburgh EH9 1SA. *T:* 0131–667 5542. *Clubs:* Royal Scottish Automobile (Glasgow); Hon. Company of Edinburgh Golfers.

MAYFIELD, Rt. Rev. Christopher John, *see* Manchester, Bishop of.

MAYFIELD, Lt-Col Richard, DSO 1972; Clerk of the Cheque and Adjutant, HM Body Guard of the Honourable Corps of Gentlemen-at-Arms, since 1994; *b* 2 Nov. 1930; *s* of Col Bryan Mayfield (formerly Scots Guards) and Rowena Lucy (*née* Hordern); *m* 1964, Rosemary Elisabeth Carlton, *d* of Col and Mrs Donald Matheson; one *s* two *d. Educ:* Radley Coll. Commnd Scots Guards, 1949; served FE, ME and Europe; Lt-Col 1971; in comd 1st Bn, Scots Guards, 1971–74; retd 1974. Mem., HM Body Guard of Hon. Corps of Gentlemen-at-Arms, 1981–. *Recreations:* shooting, ski-ing. *Address:* Ewhurst Park, Ramsdell, Basingstoke, Hants RG26 5RG. *T:* Basingstoke (01256) 850051. *Club:* Army and Navy.

MAYHEW, family name of **Baron Mayhew.**

MAYHEW, Baron *cr* 1981 (Life Peer), of Wimbledon in Greater London; **Christopher Paget Mayhew;** *b* 12 June 1915; *e s* of late Sir Basil Mayhew, KBE; *m* 1949, Cicely Elizabeth Ludlam; two *s* two *d. Educ:* Haileybury Coll. (Scholar); Christ Church, Oxford (Open Exhibitioner, MA). Junior George Webb-Medley Scholar (Economics), 1937; Pres., Union Soc., 1937. Gunner Surrey Yeomanry RA; BEF Sept. 1939–May 1940; served with BNAF and CMF; BLA 1944 (despatches); Major, 1944. MP (Lab) S Norfolk, 1945–50; MP (Lab) Woolwich East, later Greenwich, Woolwich East, June 1951–July

1974; PPS to Lord Pres. of the Council, 1945–46; Parly Under-Sec. of State for Foreign Affairs, 1946–50; Minister of Defence (RN), 1964, resigned 1966; left Lab. Party, joined Lib. Party, 1974; MP (L) Greenwich, Woolwich East, July-Sept. 1974; contested (L): Bath, Oct. 1974 and 1979; Surrey, for European Parlt, 1979; London SW, for European Parlt, Sept. 1979. Vice-Chm., Liberal Action Gp for Electoral Reform, 1974–80. Liberal Party Spokesman on Defence, 1980–. President: Parly Assoc. for Euro-Arab Co-operation, 1980– (former Chm.); ANAF Foundn, 1992 (former Chm.); Middle East International (Publishers) Ltd, 1992– (former Chm.); former Chm., MIND (Nat. Assoc. for Mental Health). Chm., Liverpool Victoria Staff Pensions Trustee Cos, 1976–95. *Publications:* Planned Investment—The Case for a National Investment Board, 1939; Socialist Economic Policy, 1946; "Those in Favour . . ." (television play), 1951; Dear Viewer . . ., 1953; Men Seeking God, 1955; Commercial Television: What is to be done?, 1959; Coexistence Plus, 1962; Britain's Role Tomorrow, 1967; Party Games, 1969; (jtly) Europe: the case for going in, 1971; (jtly) Publish It Not . . .: the Middle East cover-up, 1975; The Disillusioned Voter's Guide to Electoral Reform, 1976; Time To Explain: an autobiography, 1987. *Recreations:* music, golf. *Address:* 39 Wool Road, Wimbledon, SW20 0HN.

MAYHEW, Kenneth; Fellow and Tutor in Economics, Pembroke College, Oxford, since 1976; *b* 1 Sept. 1947; *s* of late Albert Chadwick Mayhew and of Alice Mayhew (*née* Leigh); *m* 1st, 1973, Margaret Humphreys (marr. diss. 1982); one *d*; 2nd, 1990, Gillian Alexandra McGrattan; one *s*. *Educ:* Manchester Grammar Sch.; Worcester Coll., Oxford (MA); London School of Economics (MScEcon). Economic Asst, HM Treasury, 1970–72; Res. Officer, Queen Elizabeth House, Oxford, 1972; Asst Res. Officer, then Res. Officer, Inst. of Economics and Statistics, Oxford, 1972–81; Economic Dir, NEDO, 1989–91. Vis. Associate Prof., Cornell Univ., 1981. Advr, CBI, 1983. Editor, Oxford Bull. of Econs and Stats, 1976–88; Associate Editor, Oxford Review of Economic Policy, 1984–. *Publications:* Trade Unions and the Labour Market, 1983; (ed with D. Robinson) Pay Policies for the Future, 1983; (ed with A. Bowen) Improving Incentives for the Low Paid, 1990; (ed with A. Bowen) Reducing Regional Inequalities, 1991; (ed jtly) Providing Health Care, 1991; reports and numerous articles on labour econs and industrial relns in learned jls. *Recreations:* travel, literature. *Address:* 49 Hamilton Road, Oxford OX2 7PY. *T:* Oxford (01865) 510977. *Club:* Reform.

MAYHEW, Rt. Hon. Sir Patrick (Barnabas Burke), Kt 1983; PC 1986; QC 1972; MP (C) Tunbridge Wells, since 1983 (Royal Tunbridge Wells, Feb. 1974–1983); Secretary of State for Northern Ireland, since 1992; *b* 11 Sept. 1929; *o* surv. *s* of late A. G. H. Mayhew, MC; *m* 1963, Jean Elizabeth Gurney, MA (Cantab), BD, AKC, *d* of John Gurney; four *s*. *Educ:* Tonbridge; Balliol Coll., Oxford (MA). President, Oxford Union Society, 1952. Commnd 4th/7th Royal Dragoon Guards, national service and AER, captain. Called to Bar, Middle Temple, 1955, Bencher 1980. Contested (C) Camberwell and Dulwich, in Gen. Election, 1970. Parly Under Sec. of State, Dept of Employment, 1979–81; Minister of State, Home Office, 1981–83; Solicitor General, 1983–87; Attorney General, 1987–92. Mem. Exec., 1922 Cttee, 1976–79; Vice Chm., Cons. Home Affairs Cttee, 1976–79. *Address:* House of Commons, SW1A 0AA. *Clubs:* Garrick, Pratt's, Beefsteak.

MAYHEW-SANDERS, Sir John (Reynolds), Kt 1982; MA; FCA; business and management consultant; *b* 25 Oct. 1931; *e s* of Jack Mayhew-Sanders, FCA; *m* 1958, Sylvia Mary (*d* 1995), *d* of George S. Colling; three *s* one *d*. *Educ:* Epsom Coll.; RNC, Dartmouth; Jesus Coll., Cambridge (MA Engrg). FCA 1958. RN, 1949–55. Mayhew-Sanders & Co., Chartered Accountants, 1955–58; P-E Consulting Gp Ltd, 1958–72 (Dir, 1968–72); Chief Exec., 1975–83, and Chm., 1978–83, John Brown PLC (Dir, 1972–83); Director: Dowty Gp, 1982–85; Rover Gp (formerly BL plc), 1980–89; Chm., Heidrick and Struggles UK, 1985–87; Chief Exec., Samuelson Gp, 1987. Member: Management Bd, Engineering Employers' Fedn, 1977–81; BOTB, 1980–83; BBC Consultative Gp on Industrial and Business Affairs, 1981–83; Chm., Overseas Projects Bd, 1980–83; Pres., British-Soviet Chamber of Commerce, 1982–88; Vice-Pres., Inst. of Export, 1982–. Governor, Sadler's Wells Foundn, 1983–89. CBIM 1980; FRSA 1983. *Recreations:* fishing, shooting, astronomy, gardening, music. *Address:* Earlstone House, Burghclere, Hants RG20 9HN. *T:* Burghclere (01635) 278288.

MAYLAND, Rev. Canon Ralph, VRD 1962 and bar 1972; non-stipendiary Priest-in-Charge, Brancepeth, since 1994; *b* 31 March 1927; *s* of James Henry and Lucy Mayland; *m* 1959, Jean Mary Goldstraw; one *d* and one adopted *d*. *Educ:* Cockburn High Sch., Leeds; Leeds City Training Coll.; Westminster Coll., London Univ.; Ripon Hall, Oxford. Schoolteacher, 1945–46; RN, 1946–51; perm. commn, RNR, 1952, Chaplain, 1961–82; 3rd yr student, 1951–52; schoolteacher, 1952–57; theol student, 1957–59. Curate of Lambeth, 1959–62; Priest-in-charge, St Paul's, Manton, Worksop, 1962–67; Vicar, St Margaret's, Brightside, 1968–72; Chaplain, Sheffield Industrial Mission, 1968–75; Vicar, St Mary's, Ecclesfield, 1972–82; Chaplain to Master Cutler, 1979–80; Canon and Treasurer, York Minster, 1982–94, Canon Emeritus, 1994–. Life Mem., Royal Naval Assoc. *Recreations:* collecting Victorian children's literature, goat-keeping and rearing. *Address:* The Rectory, Brancepeth, Durham DH7 8EL.

MAYNARD, Prof. Alan Keith; Professor of Economics and Director of Centre for Health Economics, University of York, since 1983; *b* 15 Dec. 1944; *s* of Edward Maynard and Hilda (*née* McCausland); *m* 1968, Elizabeth Shanahan; two *s* two *d*. *Educ:* Univ. of Newcastle upon Tyne (BA Hons 1st cl. 1967); Univ. of York (BPhil 1968). Asst Lectr and Lectr, Univ. of Exeter, 1968–71; University of York: Lectr in Econs, 1971–77; Sen. Lectr, then Reader in Econs and Dir, Grad. Programme in Health Econs, 1977–83. Mem., York HA, 1982–91; Non-Exec. Mem., York NHS Hosp. Trust, 1991–. Member: ESRC, 1986–88; Health Services Res. Cttee, MRC, 1986–92; Chm., Evaluation Panel, Fourth Health and Med. Res. Programme, EC, 1990–91. Hon. MFPHM. *Publications:* Health Care in the European Community, 1976; (ed jtly) The Public Private Mix for Health, 1982; (with A. B. Atkinson and C. Trinder) Parents and Children, 1983; (ed jtly) Preventing Alcohol and Tobacco Problems, 1989; (ed jtly) Controlling Legal Addictions, 1990; (ed jtly) Competition in Health Care, 1991; (ed jtly) Purchasing and Providing Cost Effective Health Care, 1993; contrib. numerous articles to various jls. *Recreations:* walking, reading, watching cricket, football. *Address:* Centre for Health Economics, University of York, York YO1 5DD. *T:* York (01904) 433645, *Fax:* (01904) 433644. *Clubs:* Royal Society of Medicine, Commonwealth Trust.

MAYNARD, Brian Alfred, CBE 1982; Partner, Coopers & Lybrand, Chartered Accountants, 1950–81; *b* 27 Sept. 1917; *s* of late Alfred A. Maynard and Clarissa L. (*née* Shawe); *m* 1946, Rosemary Graham, *y d* of late Col E. C. Boutflower; two *s*. *Educ:* Leighton Park Sch.; Cambridge Univ. (MA). RNVR Commission, 1939–46, served Middle East and Europe. Member: Oxford Univ. Appts Cttee, 1959–81; Cttee of Duke of Edinburgh's Award Scheme, 1961–67; Council, Industry for Management Educn, 1968–81; Cttee of Enquiry into the Financial Control of Catering in the Services, 1973; Cttee of Enquiry into Problems facing the Nat. Theatre, 1978; Council for the Securities Industry, 1978; Chm., Adv. Cttee on Local Govt Audit, 1979–82. Mem. Council, Inst. of Chartered Accountants in England and Wales, 1968–81 (Pres., 1977–78); Chm., Management Consultants Assoc., 1970; Pres., Inst. of Management Consultants, 1974; Vice-Pres., European Fedn of Management Consultants Assoc., 1972–75; Pres., OECD Mission to USA, on Computers, 1960. *Recreations:* racing, shooting, farming. *Address:* Cowick Farm, Hilmarton, Calne, Wilts SN11 8RZ. *T:* Hilmarton (01249) 760397.

MAYNARD, Edwin Francis George; Overseas Business Consultant; Member, Export Council Advisory Panel; HM Diplomatic Service, retired; Deputy High Commissioner, Calcutta, 1976–80; *b* 23 Feb. 1921; *s* of late Edwin Maynard, MD, FRCS, DPH, and late Nancy Frances Tully; *m* 1945, Patricia Baker; one *s* one *d*; *m* 1963, Anna McGettrick; two *s*. *Educ:* Westminster. Served with Indian Army (4/8th (PWO) Punjab Regt and General Staff) (Major, GSO II), Middle East and Burma, 1939–46. BBC French Service, 1947; Foreign Office, 1949; Consul and Oriental Sec., Jedda, 1950; Second, later First, Sec., Benghazi, 1952; FO 1954; Bogota, 1956; Khartoum, 1959; FO, 1960; Baghdad, 1962; Founder Dir, Diplomatic Service Language Centre, 1966; Counsellor, Aden, 1967; Counsellor, New Delhi, 1968–72; Minister (Commercial), 1972–76, Chargé d'Affaires, 1974–75, Buenos Aires. *Recreations:* shooting, fishing, languages, gardening. *Address:* Littlebourne Court, Littlebourne, Canterbury, Kent CT3 1TU. *Club:* Brooks's.

MAYNARD, Prof. Geoffrey Walter; Economic Consultant, Investcorp International Ltd, since 1986; Director of Economics, Europe and Middle East, Chase Manhattan Bank, 1977–86 (Economic consultant, 1974); Director, Chase Manhattan Ltd, 1977–86; *b* 27 Oct. 1921; *s* of Walter F. Maynard and Maisie Maynard (*née* Bristow); *m* 1949, Marie Lilian Wright; two *d*. *Educ:* London School of Economics. BSc(Econ); PhD. Lectr and Sen. Lectr, UC of S Wales, Cardiff, 1951–62; Economic Consultant, HM Treasury 1962–64; Economic Advr, Harvard Univ. Develt Adv. Gp in Argentina, 1964–65; University of Reading: Reader, 1966–68; Prof. of Economics, 1968–76; Vis. Prof. of Economics, 1976–. Editor, Bankers' Magazine, 1968–72; Under-Sec. (Econs), HM Treasury, 1972–74 (on leave of absence); Dep. Chief Economic Advr, HM Treasury, 1976–77; occasional consultant, IBRD, Overseas Develt Administration of FCO. Mem., Econ. Affairs Cttee, ESRC, 1982–85. Mem. Governing Body, Inst. of Develt Studies, Sussex, 1984–91; Mem. Council, Inst. of Fiscal Studies, 1988–. *Publications:* Economic Development and the Price Level, 1962; (jtly) International Monetary Reform and Latin America, 1966; (jtly) A World of Inflation, 1976; The Economy under Mrs Thatcher, 1988; chapters in: Development Policy: theory and practice, ed G. Papanek, 1968; Commonwealth Policy in a Global Context, ed Streeten and Corbet, 1971; Economic Analysis and the Multinational Enterprise, ed J. Dunning, 1974; Special Drawing Rights and Development Aid (paper), 1972; articles in Economic Jl, Oxford Economic Papers, Jl of Development Studies, World Development, etc. *Address:* 219 Queens Quay, 58 Upper Thames Street, EC4V 3EH. *Club:* Reform.

MAYNARD, Joan; *see* Maynard, V. J.

MAYNARD, Air Chief Marshal Sir Nigel (Martin), KCB 1973 (CB 1971); CBE 1963; DFC 1942; AFC 1946; *b* 28 Aug. 1921; *s* of late Air Vice-Marshal F. H. M. Maynard, CB, AFC, and of Irene (*née* Pim); *m* 1946, Daphne, *d* of late G R. P. Llewellyn, Baglan Hall, Abergavenny; one *s* one *d*. *Educ:* Aldenham; RAF Coll., Cranwell. Coastal Comd, UK, Mediterranean, W Africa, 1940–43; Flt-Lieut 1942; Sqdn-Ldr 1944; Mediterranean and Middle East, 1944; Transport Comd, 1945–49; comd 242 Sqdn on Berlin Air Lift; Air Staff, Air Min., 1949–51; Wing Comdr 1952; psa 1952; Staff Officer to Inspector Gen., 1953–54; Bomber Comd, 1954–57; jssc 1957; Gp Capt. 1957; SASO 25 Gp, 1958–59; CO, RAF Changi, 1960–62; Gp Capt. Ops, Transport Comd, 1963–64; Air Cdre 1965; Dir of Defence Plans (Air), 1965; Dir of Defence Plans and Chm. Defence Planning Staff, 1966; idc 1967; Air Vice-Marshal, 1968; Commandant, RAF Staff College, Bracknell, 1968–70; Commander, Far East Air Force, 1970–71; Air Marshal, 1972; Dep. C-in-C, Strike Command, 1972–73; C-in-C RAF Germany, and Comdr, 2nd Allied Tactical Air Force, 1973–76; Air Chief Marshal 1976; C-in-C, RAF Strike Command, and C-in-C, UK Air Forces, 1976–77. ADC to the Queen, 1961–65. *Address:* Manor House, Piddington, Bicester, Oxon OX6 0QB. *T:* Brill (01844) 238270. *Clubs:* Naval and Military, Royal Air Force; MCC.

MAYNARD, Roger Paul; Director of Corporate Strategy, British Airways, since 1991; Director: US Air, since 1993; Qantas, since 1993; *b* 10 Feb. 1943; *s* of Leonard John Maynard and May Gertrude Blake; *m* 1966, Ruth Elizabeth Wakeling; three *s* (including twin *s*). *Educ:* Purley Grammar Sch., Surrey; Queens' Coll., Cambridge (MA Hons Economics). Asst Principal, Bd of Trade, 1965; Second Secretary, UK Mission to UN and Internat. Organisations, Geneva, 1968; Principal: Dept of Industry, Shipbuilding Division, 1972; Dept of Trade, Airports Policy, 1975; Asst Sec., Dept of Industry, Air Division, 1978; Counsellor, Aviation and Shipping, British Embassy, Washington, 1982; British Airways: Vice Pres., Commercial Affairs, N America, 1987–89; Exec. Vice Pres., N America, 1989; Dir, Investor Relations and Marketplace Performance, 1989–91. *Recreations:* cricket, golf, music. *Address:* 43 Rosebank, Holyport Road, Fulham, SW6 6LO. *T:* (office) 0181–562 5596. *Club:* United Oxford & Cambridge University.

MAYNARD, (Vera) Joan; JP; *b* 1921. Mem. Labour Party Nat. Exec. Cttee, 1972–82, 1983–87; Sec., Yorks Area, Agricl and Allied Workers National Trade Group TGWU (formerly Nat. Union of Agricl and Allied Workers), 1956–78 (Nat. Vice Pres., 1966–72, sponsored as MP by the Union). MP (Lab) Sheffield, Brightside, Oct. 1974–1987. Mem., Parly Select Cttee on Agriculture, 1975–87; Vice-Chm., Labour Party, 1980–81. Chair, Campaign Gp of Lab. MPs, 1979–87. Former Parish Rural Dist and County Councillor, N Yorks. JP Thirsk, 1950. *Address:* Lansbury House, 76 Front Street, Sowerby, Thirsk, N Yorks YO7 1JF. *T:* Thirsk (01845) 522355.

MAYNARD SMITH, Prof. John, FRS 1977; Professor of Biology, University of Sussex, 1965–85, now Emeritus; *b* 6 Jan. 1920; *s* of Sidney Maynard Smith and Isobel Mary (*née* Pitman); *m* 1941; two *s* one *d*. *Educ:* Eton Coll.; Trinity Coll., Cambridge (BA Engrg, 1941); UCL (BSc Zool., 1951; Fellow, 1979). Aircraft stressman, 1942–47; Lectr in Zool., UCL, 1952–65; first Dean of Biol Sciences, Univ. of Sussex, 1965–72. For. Associate, US Nat. Acad. of Scis, 1982; Mem., Hungarian Acad. of Scis, 1993. Hon. DSc: Kent, 1983; Oxon, 1987; Sussex, 1988; Chicago, 1988. Balzan Prize, Fondazione Internazionale Premio E. Balzan, 1991; Darwin Medal, Royal Soc., 1986. *Publications:* The Theory of Evolution, 1958, 3rd edn 1975; Mathematical Ideas in Biology, 1968; On Evolution, 1972; Models in Ecology, 1974; The Evolution of Sex, 1978; Evolution and the Theory of Games, 1982; The Problems of Biology, 1985; Evolutionary Genetics, 1989; (with E. Szathmáry) The Major Transitions in Evolution, 1995. *Recreations:* gardening, fishing, talking. *Address:* The White House, Kingston Ridge, Lewes, East Sussex BN7 3JX. *T:* Lewes (01273) 474659.

MAYNE, Prof. David Quinn, FRS 1985; FEng 1987; Professor of Electrical and Computer Engineering, University of California, Davis, since 1989; *b* 23 April 1930; *s* of Leslie Harper Mayne and Jane Quin; *m* 1954, Josephine Mary Hess; three *d*. *Educ:* Univ. of the Witwatersrand, Johannesburg (BSc (Eng), MSc); DIC, PhD, DSc London. FIEE, FIEEE. Lectr, Univ. of Witwatersrand, 1950–54, 1956–59; R&D Engineer, British Thomson Houston Co., Rugby, 1955–56; Imperial College: Lectr, 1959–67, Reader, 1967–71; Prof. of Control Theory, 1971–89; Sen. Sci. Res. Fellow, 1979–80; Hd of Dept of Electrical Engrg, 1984–88. Research Consultant, at Univs of California (Berkeley),

Lund, Newcastle NSW, 1974–. Res. Fellow, Harvard Univ., 1970; Vis. Prof., Academia Sinica, Beijing, Shanghai and Guanzhou, 1981. Corresp. Mem., Nacional Acad. de Ingenieria, Mexico, 1983. Hon. DEng Lund Univ., 1995. *Publications:* Differential Dynamic Programming, vol. 24 in Modern Analytic and Computational Methods in Science and Mathematics (with D. H. Jacobson, ed R. Bellman), 1970; Geometric Methods in System Theory, proc. NATO Advanced Study Inst., (ed. with R. W. Brockett), 1973; contribs to learned jls. *Recreations:* walking, cross-country ski-ing. *Address:* 648 Lake Terrace Circle, Davis, CA 95616, USA.

MAYNE, Eric; Under Secretary, General Functions Group, Department of Economic Development, Northern Ireland, 1986–87, retired; *b* 2 Sept. 1928; *s* of Robert P. Mayne and Margaret Mayne; *m* 1954, Sarah Boyd (*née* Gray); three *s* two *d*. *Educ:* Bangor Grammar Sch. Univ. of Reading (BSc); Michigan State Univ. (MS). Horticultural Advisor, Min. of Agriculture, NI, 1949–56; Kellogg Foundation Fellow, 1956–57; Horticultural Advisor, HQ Min. of Agriculture, NI, 1957–64; Principal Officer, 1964–67; Gen. Manager, NI Agric. Trust, 1967–74; Sen. Asst Secretary, Dept of Agriculture, NI, 1974–79; Dep. Sec., Dept of Manpower Services, NI, 1979–82; Under Sec., Dept of Econ. Develt, NI, 1982–87. *Recreations:* gardening, winemaking.

MAYNE, John Fraser, CB 1986; management consultant; *b* 14 Sept. 1932; *s* of late John Leonard Mayne and Martha Laura (*née* Griffiths); *m* 1958, Gillian Mary (*née* Key); one *s* one *d*. *Educ:* Dulwich Coll.; Worcester Coll., Oxford. National Service, Royal Tank Regt, 1951–53. Air Min., 1956–64; HM Treasury, 1964–67; MoD, 1967–70; Asst Private Sec. to Sec. of State for Defence, 1968–70; Cabinet Office and Central Policy Rev. Staff, 1970–73; MoD, 1973–78; Private Sec. to Sec. of State for Def., 1975–76; Asst Under-Sec. of State (Air Staff), 1976–78; Principal Establishments and Finance Officer, NI Office, 1979–81; Dir Gen. of Management Audit, MoD, 1981–83; Dep. Sec., Cabinet Office (MPO), 1984–86; Principal Estab. and Finance Officer, DHSS, later Dept of Health, 1986–90. Non-exec. Mem., Hampstead HA, 1991–93. Associate, PA Consulting Group, 1990–. Member: Council, RUSI, 1986–89; Public Policy Unit, 1992–. Trustee, Nat. AIDS Trust, 1992–. Freeman, City of London, 1983. *Recreations:* music, fell-walking, cooking, work. *Address:* c/o Drummonds, 49 Charing Cross, SW1A 2DX.

MAYNE, Very Rev. Michael Clement Otway; Dean of Westminster, since 1986; Dean of the Order of the Bath, since 1986; *b* 10 Sept. 1929; *s* of Rev. Michael Ashton Otway Mayne and Sylvia Clementina Lumley Ellis; *m* 1965, Alison Geraldine McKie; one *s* one *d*. *Educ:* King's Sch., Canterbury; Corpus Christi Coll., Cambridge (MA); Cuddesdon Coll., Oxford. Curate, St John the Baptist, Harpenden, 1957–59; Domestic Chaplain to the Bishop of Southwark, 1959–65; Vicar of Norton, Letchworth, 1965–72; Head of Religious Progs, BBC Radio, 1972–79; Vicar of Great St Mary's, Cambridge (the University Church), 1979–86. Select Preacher: Univ. of Cambridge, 1988; Univ. of Oxford, 1989, 1993. Mem. Council, St Christopher's Hospice, 1988. Chairman: London Ecumenical AIDS Forum, 1992–; Sandford St Martin Trust, 1993–. Trustee: Royal Foundn of Grey Coat Hosp., 1986–; King George VI and Queen Elizabeth Foundn of St Catherine's, Cumberland Lodge, 1992–. Chm. Governors, Westminster Sch., 1986–. *Publications:* Prayers for Pastoral Occasions, 1982; (ed) Encounters, 1985; A Year Lost and Found, 1987; This Sunrise of Wonder, 1995. *Recreations:* theatre, bird-watching, books, silence. *Address:* The Deanery, Westminster, SW1P 3PA. *T:* 0171–222 2953.

MAYNE, Richard (John); writer; broadcaster; *b* 2 April 1926; *s* of John William Mayne and Kate Hilda (*née* Angus); *m* 1st, Margot Ellingworth Lyon; 2nd, Jocelyn Mudie Ferguson; two *d*. *Educ:* St Paul's Sch., London; Trinity Coll., Cambridge (1st Cl. Hons Pts I and II, Hist. Tripos; MA and PhD). War service, Royal Signals, 1944–47. Styring, Sen., and Res. Scholar, and Earl of Derby Student, Trinity Coll., Cambridge, 1947–53; Leverhulme European Scholar, Rome, and Rome Corresp., New Statesman, 1953–54; Asst Tutor, Cambridge Inst. of Educn, 1954–56; Official: ECSC, Luxembourg, 1956–58; EEC, Brussels, 1958–63; Dir of Documentation Centre, Action Cttee for United States of Europe, and Personal Asst to Jean Monnet, Paris, 1963–66; Paris Corresp., Encounter, 1966–71, Co-Editor, 1985–90, Contributing Editor, 1990–91. Vis. Prof., Univ. of Chicago, 1971; Dir of Federal Trust for Educn and Res., 1971–73; Head of UK Offices, 1973–79, Special Advr, 1979–80, EEC. Hon. Professorial Fellow, UCW, Aberystwyth, 1986–89. Film critic: Sunday Telegraph, 1987–89; The European, 1990–. *Publications:* The Community of Europe, 1962; The Institutions of the European Community, 1968; The Recovery of Europe, 1970 (rev. edn 1973); The Europeans, 1972; (ed) Europe Tomorrow, 1972; (ed) The New Atlantic Challenge, 1975; (trans.) The Memoirs of Jean Monnet, 1978 (Scott-Moncrieff Prize, 1979); Postwar: the dawn of today's Europe, 1983; (ed) Western Europe: a handbook, 1986; Federal Union: the pioneers, 1990; (trans.) Europe: a history of its peoples, 1990; (trans.) A History of Civilisations, 1993; (trans.) Illustrated History of Europe, 1993. *Recreations:* travel, sailing, fell-walking. *Address:* Albany Cottage, 24 Park Village East, Regent's Park, NW1 7PZ. *T:* 0171–387 6654. *Clubs:* Groucho; Les Misérables (Paris).

MAYNE, Mrs Roger; *see* Jellicoe, P. A.

MAYNE, William; writer; *b* 16 March 1928; *s* of William and Dorothy Mayne. *Educ:* Cathedral Choir Sch., Canterbury, 1937–42 (then irregularly). Has pursued a career as novelist and has had published a large number of stories for children and young people—about 90 altogether, beginning in 1953 and going on into the foreseeable future. Lectr in Creative Writing, Deakin Univ., Geelong, Vic, Aust., academic years, 1976 and 1977; Fellow in Creative Writing, Rolle Coll., Exmouth, 1979–80. Library Assoc's Carnegie Medal for best children's book of the year (1956), 1957. Guardian Award for Children's Fiction, 1993. *Address:* c/o David Higham Associates, 5–8 Lower John Street, Golden Square, W1R 4HA.

MAYO, 10th Earl of, *cr* 1785; **Terence Patrick Bourke,** Baron Naas, 1766, Viscount Mayo, 1781; Lieut RN (retired); Managing Director, Irish Marble Ltd, Merlin Park, Galway; *b* 26 Aug. 1929; *s* of Hon. Bryan Longley Bourke (*d* 1961) and Violet Wilmot Heathcote Bourke (*d* 1950); *S* uncle, 1962; *m* 1952, Margaret Jane Robinson Harrison (marr. diss. 1987; she *d* 1992); three *s*. *Educ:* St Aubyns, Rottingdean; RNC Dartmouth. Lieut, RN, 1952; Fleet Air Arm, 1952; Suez, 1956; Solo Aerobatic Displays, Farnborough, 1957; invalided, 1959. Mem., Gosport Borough Council, 1961–64; Pres., Gosport Chamber of Trade, 1962; Gov., Gosport Secondary Schs, 1963–64. Mem., Liberal Party, 1963–65; contested (L) Dorset South, 1964. *Recreations:* sailing, riding, shooting, fishing. *Heir:* *s* Lord Naas, *qv*. *Address:* Doon House, Maam, Co. Galway, Eire. *Club:* County Galway.

MAYO, Col (Edward) John, OBE 1976; Director General, Help the Aged, since 1983; *b* 24 May 1931; *s* of late Rev. Thomas Edward Mayo, JP, and Constance Muriel Mayo; *m* 1961, Jacqueline Margaret Anne Armstrong, MBE 1985, Lieut WRAC (*d* 1993), *d* of late Brig. C. D. Armstrong, CBE, DSO, MC; one *s*. *Educ:* King's Coll., Taunton. Commissioned into Royal Regt of Artillery, 1951; served Malta and N Africa 36 HAA Regt, 1951–55; ADC to Governor of Malta, 1953–54; 2nd Regt RHA, BAOR, 1955–58; ADC to C-in-C BAOR/Comdr Northern Army Gp, 1958–60; 20 Field Regt, RA UK, 1960–61; Adjt 20 Field Regt, RA Malaya, 1961–63; Adjt 254 (City of London) Regt RA(TA), 1963–64; Instr RMA, Sandhurst, 1964–66; GS03 Mil. Operations, MoD, 1966–68; Second in Comd 20 Heavy Regt, RA BAOR, 1968–70; GS02 Instr Staff Coll., 1970–72; commanded 17 Trng Regt and Depot RA, 1972–74, and The Depot Regt RA, 1974–75; GS01 Public Relations MoD, 1976–79; Col GS; Public Information BAOR, 1979–83; retired 1983. Member: Royal British Legion Benevolent Cttee; Welfare Cttee, SSAFA; Bd, HelpAge Sri Lanka; Trustee: HelpAge India; HelpAge Kenya; HelpAge Internat. *Publications:* miscellaneous articles on military matters. MIPR 1981. FRSA 1987. *Recreations:* fishing, gardening, sailing, riding, travelling, collecting and restoring antiques. *Address:* Help the Aged, St James's Walk, EC1R 0BE. *T:* 0171–253 0253; Sehore House, 24 Tekels Avenue, Camberley, Surrey GU15 2LB. *T:* Camberley (01276) 29653. *Clubs:* Army and Navy, Special Forces, MCC.

MAYO, Col John; *see* Mayo, Col E. J.

MAYO, Rear-Adm. Robert William, CB 1965; CBE 1962; *b* 9 Feb. 1909; *s* of late Frank Mayo, Charminster; *m* 1st, 1942, Sheila (*d* 1974), *d* of late John Colvill, JP, of Campbeltown; one *s*; 2nd, 1980, Mrs Betty Washbrook. *Educ:* Weymouth Coll.; HMS Conway. Royal Naval Reserve and officer with Royal Mail Steam Packet Co., 1926–37; Master's Certificate; transferred to Royal Navy, 1937. Served War, 1939–45; Korea, 1952; Capt., 1953; Rear-Adm., 1964; retired, 1966.

MAYO, Simon Herbert; Hon. Mr Justice Mayo; Justice of Appeal, Hong Kong, since 1995; *b* 15 Nov. 1937; *s* of late Herbert and Marjorie Mayo; *m* 1966, Catherine Yin Ying Young; one *s* one *d*. *Educ:* Harrow Sch. Admitted a solicitor, England and Wales, 1961, Hong Kong, 1963; called as barrister and solicitor, W Australia, 1967. Asst Legal Advr, GEC, 1961; Asst Solicitor, Deacons, Solicitors, Hong Kong, 1963; in private practice, WA, 1967; Asst Registrar, 1968, Registrar, 1976, Supreme Court of Hong Kong; a Judge of the High Court, Hong Kong, 1980–95. *Recreations:* golf, music, literature, walking. *Address:* Supreme Court, Hong Kong. *T:* 8254417. *Clubs:* Hong Kong, Sheko Country (Hong Kong).

MAYOH, Raymond Blanchflower; Under Secretary, Department of Health and Social Security, 1979–83, retired; *b* 11 Nov. 1925; *s* of Charles and Isabella Mayoh; *m* 1956, Daphne Yvonne Bayliss; one *s* one *d* (and one *s* decd). *Educ:* Colwyn Bay County Sch.; University College of North Wales. Assistant Principal, Ministry of Pensions, 1950; Principal, Ministry of Health, 1955; Assistant Secretary, 1965. *Recreations:* gardening, bird watching. *Address:* 20 Willingale Way, Thorpe Bay, Southend-on-Sea, Essex SS1 3SL. *T:* Southend (01702) 586650.

MAYOR, Hugh Robert; QC 1986; **His Honour Judge Mayor;** a Circuit Judge, since 1992; *b* 12 Oct. 1941; *s* of George and Grace Mayor; *m* 1970, Carolyn Ann Stubbs; one *s* one *d*. *Educ:* Kirkham Grammar Sch.; St John's Coll., Oxford (MA). Lectr, Univ. of Leicester, 1964 (MA). Called to the Bar, Gray's Inn, 1968; a Recorder, 1982–92. *Recreations:* history, sheep shearing. *Address:* The Grange, Slawston, Leics LE16 7UF. *T:* Hallaton (01858) 555200.

MAYOR ZARAGOZA, Federico; Director-General of UNESCO, since 1987; *b* Barcelona, 27 Jan. 1934; *s* of Federico Mayor and Juana Zaragoza; *m* 1956, Maria Angeles Menéndez; two *s* one *d*. *Educ:* Madrid Complutense Univ. Granada University: Prof. of Biochemistry, 1963–73; Rector, 1968–72; Prof. of Biochemistry, Univ. Autónoma, Madrid, 1973. Dir, 1974–78, Scientific Chm., 1983–87, Molecular Biology Centre, Higher Council for Scientific Research. Under-Sec., Min. for Educn and Science, 1974–75; Pres., Commn for Study of Special Set of Rules for the four Catalan Provinces, 1976; Mem., Cortes (Parliament) for Granada, 1977–78; Dep. Dir Gen., UNESCO, 1978–81; Minister for Educn and Science, Spain, 1981–82; Special Advr to Dir-Gen., UNESCO, 1982; Dir, Inst. of Sciences of Man, Madrid, 1983–87. Mem., European Parlt, 1987. *Address:* UNESCO, 7 place de Fontenoy, 75352 Paris 07 SP, France.

MAYR HARTING, Henry Maria Robert Egmont, DPhil; FBA 1992; Fellow, St Peter's College, since 1968, and Reader in Medieval History, since 1993, University of Oxford; *b* 6 April 1936; *s* of Herbert Mayr-Harting and Anna Mayr-Harting (*née* Münzer), Prague; *m* 1968, Caroline Henry; one *s* one *d*. *Educ:* Douai School; Merton Coll., Oxford (BA Mod. Hist. 1957; MA; DPhil 1961). Asst Lectr and Lectr in Medieval History, Univ. of Liverpool, 1960–68; Tutor in Medieval History, St Peter's Coll., Oxford, 1968–. Vis. Fellow, Peterhouse, Cambridge, 1983; Slade Prof. of Fine Art, Oxford Univ., 1987–88; Brown Foundn Fellow, Univ. of the South, Tennessee, 1992. *Publications:* The Acta of the Bishops of Chichester 1075–1207, 1965; The Coming of Christianity to Anglo-Saxon England, 1972, 3rd edn 1991; What to do in the Penwith Peninsula, Cornwall, in less than perfect weather, 1987, 2nd edn 1988; Ottonian Book Illumination: an historical study, 2 vols, 1991; articles in learned jls. *Recreations:* music, especially playing keyboard instruments; watching cricket. *Address:* St Peter's College, Oxford OX1 2DL. *T:* Oxford (01865) 278907.

MAYS, Colin Garth, CMG 1988; HM Diplomatic Service, retired; Bursar, Yehudi Menuhin School, since 1991; *b* 16 June 1931; *s* of William Albert Mays and Sophia May Mays (*née* Pattinson); *m* 1956, Margaret Patricia, *d* of Philemon Robert Lloyd and Gladys Irene (*née* Myers); one *s*. *Educ:* Acklam Hall Sch.; St John's Coll., Oxford (Heath Harrison Scholar). Served in Army, 1949–51; entered HM Foreign (subseq. Diplomatic) Service, 1955; FO, 1955–56; Sofia, 1956–58; Baghdad, 1958–60; FO, 1960; UK Delegn to Conf. of 18 Nation Cttee on Disarmament, Geneva, 1960; Bonn, 1960–65; FO, 1965–69; Prague, 1969–72; FCO, 1972–77; Head of Information Administration Dept, 1974–77; Counsellor (Commercial), Bucharest, 1977–80; seconded to PA Management Consultants, 1980–81; Diplomatic Service Overseas Inspector, 1981–83; High Commissioner: Seychelles, 1983–86; Bahamas, 1986–91. Liveryman, Painter-Stainers' Co., 1981. *Recreations:* sailing, swimming, travel. *Address:* Yehudi Menuhin School, Stoke d'Abernon, Cobham, Surrey KT11 3QQ. *Club:* Travellers'.

MAZANKOWSKI, Rt. Hon. Donald (Frank); PC (Can.) 1979; Deputy Prime Minister of Canada, 1986–93; Minister of Finance, 1991–93; *b* 27 July 1935; *s* of late Frank Mazankowski and Dora (*née* Lonowski); *m* 1958, Lorraine Poleschuk; three *s*. *Educ:* High Sch., Viking, Alberta. MP (Progressive Conservative), Vegreville, 1968–93; Minister for Transport and Minister responsible for Canadian Wheat Bd, 1979–80; Minister of Transport, 1984–86; Pres. of Queen's Privy Council for Canada, 1986–91; Minister of Agriculture, 1986–91; Minister responsible for Privatization, 1988. Govt House Leader, 1986–89. Hon. DEng Technical Univ. of Nova Scotia, 1987; Hon. LLD Alberta, 1993. *Address:* PO Box 1350, Vegreville, Alta T9C 1S5, Canada.

MAZRUI, Prof. Ali A., DPhil; Albert Schweitzer Professor in the Humanities, State University of New York, Binghamton, since 1989; *b* Kenya, 24 Feb. 1933; *s* of Al'Amin Ali Mazrui, Judge of Islamic Law, and Safia Suleiman Mazrui; marr. diss.; three *s*; two *s* by Pauline Uti. *Educ:* Univ. of Manchester (BA with distinction 1960); Columbia Univ. (MA 1961); Oxford Univ. (DPhil 1966). Makerere University, Kampala, Uganda: Lectr, 1963–65; Prof. and Head of Dept of Political Science, 1965–73; Dean, Faculty of Social Sciences, 1967–69; Res. Prof., Univ. of Jos, Nigeria, 1981–86; Prof. of Pol Science and of Afroamerican and African Studies, Univ. of Michigan, 1974–91; Sen. Scholar and Andrew

D. White Prof.-at-Large, Cornell Univ., 1986–92, now Emeritus. Vis. Prof., Univs of London, Manchester, Sussex, Leeds, Harvard, Calif (LA), Northwestern, Stanford, Colgate, Ohio State, Bridgewater State Coll., Mass, Denver, Pennsylvania State, McGill, Canada, Nairobi, Cairo, Baghdad, Singapore and Australian National, 1965–. Expert Adviser: World Bank, 1988–; UN Commn on Transnational Corps, 1987–. Member: Adv. Cttee, Trans-Africa Run for Wildlife Foundn, Inc., 1987–; Adv. Bd of Dirs, Detroit Chapter, AFRICARE, 1987–; Pan-African Adv. Council to UNICEF, 1988–. Pres., African Studies Assoc. of USA, 1978–79; Vice-President: Internat. Congress of African Studies, 1978–; Internat. African Inst., 1987–; World Congress of Black Intellectuals, 1988–. BBC Reith Lectr, 1979; Presenter, The Africans (BBC TV series), 1986. *Publications:* Towards a Pax Africana, 1967; The Anglo-African Commonwealth, 1967; On Heroes and Uhuru-Worship, 1967; Violence and Thought, 1969; (with R. I. Rotberg) Protest and Power in Black Africa, 1970; The Trial of Christopher Okigbo (novel), 1971; Cultural Engineering and Nation-Building in East Africa, 1972; (with Hasu Patel) Africa in World Affairs: the next thirty years, 1973; World Culture and the Black Experience, 1974; Soldiers and Kinsmen in Uganda, 1975; The Political Sociology of the English Language: an African perspective, 1975; A World Federation of Cultures: an African perspective, 1976; Africa's International Relations, 1977; The Warrior Tradition in Modern Africa, 1978; Political Values and the Educated Class in Africa, 1978; The African Condition (The Reith Lectures), 1980; (with Michael Tidy) Nationalism and New States of Africa, 1984; The Africans: a triple heritage, 1986; Cultural Forces in World Politics, 1990; Africa since 1935 (Vol. VIII, UNESCO General History of Africa), 1993. *Address:* Apartment 3E, 38–42 Front Street, Binghamton, NY 13905, USA. *T:* (607) 7774494.

MBEKEANI, Nyemba W.; Chief Executive, Mkulumadzi Farm Bakeries Ltd, since 1981; Chairman, Spearhead Holdings Ltd, since 1987; *b* 15 June 1929; Malawi parentage; *m* 1950, Lois Moses (*née* Chikankheni); two *s* three *d*. *Educ:* Henry Henderson Institute, Blantyre; London Sch. of Economics (Economic and Social Administration, 1963). Local Government Officer, 1945–58; political detention in Malawi and Southern Rhodesia, 1959–60; Business Executive, 1960–61; Local Govt Officer, 1963–64; Foreign Service, 1964; High Commissioner for Malawi in London, 1964–67; Ambassador to USA and Permanent Rep. at the UN, 1967–72; Ambassador to Ethiopia, 1972–73; Gen. Manager, Malaŵi Housing Corp., 1973–81. Farmer, company director, tea broker, baker, confectioner. Chm., Petroleum Control Commn, 1987–93; Board Member: Lingadzi Farming Co., 1987–; Sable Farming Co., 1987–. Trustee, Small Farmers Fertilizer Revolving Fund, 1988–93. Counsellor, Malaŵi Univ. Council, 1984–93; Chm., Malaŵi Polytechnic Bd of Govs, 1988–93. *Recreation:* flower gardening. *Address:* PO Box 2095, Blantyre, Malaŵi. *T:* 640633; *Telex:* 44847 Lumadzi MI.

M'BOW, Amadou-Mahtar; Director-General of Unesco, 1974–87; *b* 20 March 1921; *s* of Fara-N'Diaye M'Bow and N'Goné Casset, Senegal; *m* 1951, Raymonde Sylvain; one *s* two *d*. *Educ:* Univ. of Paris. Teacher, Rosso Coll., Mauritania, 1951–53; Dir, Service of Fundamental and Community Educn, Senegal, 1953–57; Min. of Education and Culture, 1957–58; Teacher at Lycée Faidherbe, St-Louis, Senegal, 1958–64; Prof., Ecole Normale Supérieure, Dakar, 1964–66; Minister of Educn, 1966–68; Mem. Nat. Assembly, Senegal, 1968–70; Minister of Culture, Youth and Sports 1968–70; Asst Dir-Gen. for Educn, UNESCO, 1970–74. Member: Acad. des Sciences d'Outre-Mer, 1977; Acad. of Kingdom of Morocco, 1981; Hon. Mem., Royal Acad. Fine Arts, San Temo, Spain, 1977; For. Mem., Acad. of Athens, 1983. Hon. Professor: Ecole normale supérieure, Dakar, 1979; Indep. Univ. of Santo Domingo, 1978; Nat. Indep. Univ. of Mexico, 1979. Hon. Dr: Buenos Aires, 1974; Granada (Lit. and Phil.), Sherbrooke (Educn), West Indies (Laws), 1975; Open, Kliment Okhridski, Sofia, Nairobi (Lit.), 1976; Malaya (Lit.), Philippines (Laws); Venice (Geog.), Uppsala (Soc. Scis), Moscow (Soc. Scis), Paris I, 1977; Andes (Philos.), Peru (Educn Scis), Haiti, Tribhunvan Univ., Nepal (Lit.), State Univ., Mongolia, Khartoum (Law), Sri Lanka, 1978; Charles Univ., Prague (Phil.), Tashkent, Québec, 1979; Nat. Univ. of Zaïre, Madras, Belgrade, Ivory Coast, Sierra Leone, 1980; Univ. Gama Filho, Brazil, 1981; Nat. Univ. of Lesotho, 1981; Univ. of Benin, 1981; Technical Univ. of Middle East, Ankara, 1981; Univ. of Ankara, 1981, Univ. of Gand, Belgium, 1982; Nat. Univ. of Seoul, 1982; State Univ. of Kiev, 1982; Laval Univ., Quebec, 1982; Quaid-i-Azam Univ., Islamabad, 1983; Jawaharlal Nehru Univ., New Delhi, 1983; Aix-Marseilles Univ., 1983; Beijing Univ., China, 1983; Kim Il Sung Univ., PDR of Korea (Pedagogy), 1983; Lucknow Univ., India (Lit.), 1983; Chulalongkorn Univ., Thailand (Pedagogy), 1983; Sokoto Univ., Nigeria (Lit.), 1984; Malta Univ., 1986; Polytechnic Univ. of Catalonia, Cauca Univ. Popayan (Colombia), Univ. of Mayor, Real y Pontificia de San Francisco Xavier de Chuquisara, Sucre (Bolivia), 1987; Grand Tribute, Univ. Candido Mendes, Brazil, 1981. Order of Merit, Senegal; Grand Cross: Order of the Liberator, Order of Andres Bello and Order of Francisco de Miranda, Venezuela; Order of Merit and Juan Montalvo National Order of Merit (Educn), Ecuador; Order of Miguel Antonio Caro y Rufino José Cuervo, Colombia; Order of Stara Planina, Bulgaria; Order of the Sun, Peru; Order of Merit of Duarte, Sanchez and Mella, Dominican Republic; National Order of the Lion, Senegal; Order of Alphonso X the Sabio, Spain; Order of the Southern Cross and Order of Merit of Guararapes, Brazil; Order of Distinguished Diplomatic Service Merit, Republic of Korea; Order of Sikatuna, Philippines; Order of Merit, Indonesia; Order of Merit, Syrian Arab Republic; Order of Merit, Jordan; Order of the Arab Republic of Egypt; Order of Felix Varela, Cuba; Grand Cross: Order of Nat. Flag (PDR of Korea); Order of Meritorious Action (Libya); Nat. Order of Andean Condor (Bolivia); Grand Order of Education (Bolivia); Grand Officer: National Order of Ivory Coast; National Order of Guinea; Order of Merit, Cameroon; National Order of Merit, Mauritania; Order of Independence, Tunisia; Commander: Order of Academic Palms; National Order of Upper Volta; Order of the Gabonese Merit; Order of Arts and Letters, France; Grand Medal, Order of the Inconfidência, State of Minas Gerais, Brazil; Medal: Order of Merit of Caetés, Olinda, Brazil; Order of Manual José Hurtado, Panama; Superior Decoration for Education, Jordan. Man and his World Peace Prize, Canada, 1978; Gold Medal of Olympic Order, 1981; Gold Medal of ALECSO (Arab Educnl, Cultural and Scientific Orgn), 1981; Internat. Dimitrov Prize, 1982; Gold Medal: Champion of Africa, 1986, of Andalucia, 1987. *Publications:* Le temps des peuples, ed R. Laffont, 1982; Where the Future Begins, 1982; Hope for the Future, 1984; Unesco: universality and international intellectual co-operation, 1985; numerous monographs, articles in educnl jls, textbooks, etc. *Address:* BP 5276, Dakar-Fann, Senegal; BP 434, R.P. Rabat, Morocco. *T:* Rabat 756871.

MEACHER, Michael Hugh; MP (Lab) Oldham (West) since 1970; *b* 4 Nov. 1939; *s* of George Hubert and Doris May Meacher; *m* 1st, 1962, Molly Christine (*née* Reid) (marr. diss. 1987); two *s* two *d*; 2nd, 1988, Mrs Lucianne Sawyer. *Educ:* Berkhamsted Sch., Herts; New College, Oxford. Greats, Class 1. Sec. to Danilo Dolci Trust, 1964; Research Fellow in Social Gerontology, Univ. of Essex, 1965–66; Lecturer in Social Administration: Univ. of York, 1967–69; London Sch. of Economics, 1970. Parly Under-Secretary of State: DoI, 1974–75; DHSS, 1975–76; Dept of Trade, 1976–79; Mem., Shadow Cabinet, 1983–; chief opposition spokesman on health and social security, 1983–87, on employment, 1987–89, on social security, 1989–92, on development and co-operation, 1992–93, on Citizen's Charter, 1993–94, on transport, 1994–. Mem., Treasury Select Cttee, 1980–83 (a Chm. of its sub-cttee). Chm., Labour Co-ordinating Cttee, 1978–83; Member: Nat. Exec.'s Campaign for Press Freedom; Labour Party NEC, 1983–88. Vis. Prof., Univ. of Surrey, Dept of Sociology, 1980–87. *Publications:* Taken for a Ride: Special Residential Homes for the Elderly Mentally Infirm, a study of separatism in social policy, 1972; Fabian pamphlets incl. The Care of the Old, 1969; Wealth: Labour's Achilles Heel, in Labour and Equality, ed P. Townsend and N. Bosanquet, 1972; Socialism with a Human Face, 1981; Diffusing Power: the key to Socialist revival, 1992; numerous articles. *Recreations:* music, sport, reading. *Address:* 34 Kingscliffe Gardens, SW19 6NR.

MEAD, Prof. William Richard, FBA 1994; Professor and Head of Department of Geography, University College, London, 1966–81, now Emeritus Professor; *b* 29 July 1915; *s* of William Mead and Catharine Sarah Stevens; unmarried. *Educ:* Aylesbury Gram. Sch. (Foundation Governor, 1981–); London Sch. of Economics (Hon. Fellow 1979). PhD 1946, DSc(Econ) 1968, London. Served RAF, 1940–46. Asst Lectr and Lectr, University of Liverpool, 1947–49; Rockefeller Fellowship, held in Finland, 1949–50; Lectr, 1950, Reader, 1953, University Coll., London. Chm. Council, Sch. of Slavonic and E European Studies, 1978–80. Chm., Anglo-Finnish Soc., 1966–; President: Inst. of British Geographers, 1971 (Hon. Mem., 1989); Geog. Assoc., 1981–82 (Hon. Mem., 1991); Hon. Sec., Royal Geographical Society, 1967–77 (Vice Pres., 1977–81, Hon. Vice-Pres., 1981–). Brown Meml Lectr, Univ. of Minnesota, 1983. Hon. Member: Finnish Geog. Soc.; Fenno-Ugrian Soc.; Porthan Soc.; Sydsvenska geografiska sällskapet; Det norske Videnskaps. Akademi, 1976; Det Norske Geografiske Selskab; Foreign Mem., Finnish Acad. of Science and Letters. Gill Memorial Award, 1951, Founder's Medal, 1980, RGS; Wahlberg Gold Medal, Swedish Geographical Soc., 1983; Fennia Medal, Finnish Geographical Soc., 1988; Res. Medal, RSGS, 1988. Dr *hc* University of Uppsala, 1966; DPhil *hc* Univ. of Helsinki, 1969; PhD *hc* Lund, 1987. Chevalier, Swedish Order of Vasa, 1962; Comdr, Orders of: Lion of Finland, 1963 (Chevalier, 1953); White Rose of Finland, 1976; Polar Star of Sweden, 1977. *Publications:* Farming in Finland, 1953; Economic Geography of Scandinavian States and Finland, 1958; (with Helmer Smeds) Winter in Finland, 1967; Finland (Modern Nations of the World Series), 1968; (with Wendy Hall) Scandinavia, 1972; The Scandinavian Northlands, 1973; (with Stig Jaatinen) The Åland Islands, 1974; An Historical Geography of Scandinavia, 1981; An Experience of Finland, 1993; other books on Norway, Sweden, Canada and USA. *Recreations:* riding, music. *Address:* 6 Lower Icknield Way, Aston Clinton, near Aylesbury, Bucks HP22 5JS.

MEADE, family name of **Earl of Clanwilliam.**

MEADE, Eric Cubitt, FCA; Senior Partner, Deloitte Haskins & Sells, Chartered Accountants, 1982–85; *b* 12 April 1923; *s* of William Charles Abbott Meade and Vera Alicia Maria Meade; *m* 1960, Margaret Arnott McCallum; two *s* one *d*. *Educ:* Ratcliffe College. FCA 1947. Served War, Hampshire Regt, 1942–46; N Africa, Italy, prisoner of war, 1944–45; Captain. Chartered Accountant, 1947. Mem. Council, Inst. of Chartered Accountants in England and Wales, 1969–79 (Chm., Parly and Law Cttee, 1974–76; Chm., Investigation Cttee, 1976–77); Chm., Consultative Cttee., Accountancy Bodies Ethics Cttee, 1977–83; Mem. Council, FIMBRA, 1986–87; Lay Mem., Solicitors Complaints Bureau, 1986–89; Mem., Audit Commn, 1986–89. *Recreations:* tennis, bowls. *Address:* 56 Hurlingham Court, Ranelagh Gardens, Fulham, SW6 3UP. *T:* 0171–736 5382. *Club:* Hurlingham.

MEADE, James Edward, CB 1947; FBA 1951; MA Oxon, MA Cantab; Hon. Dr, Universities of Basel, Bath, Essex, Glasgow, Hull, Oxford and Athens; Hon. Fellow: London School of Economics; Oriel College, Oxford; Hertford College, Oxford; Christ's College, Cambridge; Trinity College, Cambridge; *b* 23 June 1907; *s* of Charles Hippisley Meade and Kathleen Cotton-Stapleton; *m* 1933, Elizabeth Margaret, *d* of Alexander Cowan Wilson; one *s* three *d*. *Educ:* Malvern Coll.; Oriel Coll., Oxford; Trinity Coll., Cambridge. 1st Class Hon. Mods 1928; 1st Class Philosophy, Politics, and Economics, 1930. Fellow and Lecturer in Economics, 1930–37, and Bursar, 1934–37, Hertford Coll., Oxford; Mem. Economic Section of League of Nations, Geneva, 1938–40. Economic Asst (1940–45), and Dir (1946–47), Economic Section Cabinet Offices. Prof. of Commerce, with special reference to International Trade, London Sch. of Economics, 1947–57; Prof. of Political Economy, Cambridge, 1957–68; Nuffield Res. Fellow, 1969–74, and Fellow, Christ's Coll., Cambridge, 1957–74. Member: Coun. of Royal Economic Society, 1945–62 (Pres., 1964–66, Vice-Pres., 1966–); Council of Eugenics Soc., 1962–68 (Treasurer 1963–67). Visiting Prof., Australian National Univ., 1956. Pres. Section F, British Assoc. for the Advancement of Science, 1957; Chm. Economic Survey Mission, Mauritius, 1960. Trustee of Urwick, Orr and Partners Ltd, 1958–76. Governor: Nat. Inst. of Economic and Social Research, 1947–; LSE, 1960–74; Malvern Coll., 1972–. Chm., Cttee of Inst. for Fiscal Studies, 1975–77 (producing report on The Structure and Reform of Direct Taxation, 1978). Hon. Mem., Amer. Economic Assoc., 1962; For. Hon. Member: Soc. Royale d'Econ. Politique de Belgique, 1958; Amer. Acad. of Arts and Sciences, 1966; For. Associate, Nat. Acad. of Sciences, USA, 1981. (Jtly) Nobel Prize for Economics, 1977. *Publications:* Public Works in their International Aspect, 1933; The Rate of Interest in a Progressive State, 1933; Economic Analysis and Policy, 1936; Consumers' Credits and Unemployment, 1937; League of Nations' World Economic Surveys for 1937–38 and 1938–39; The Economic Basis of a Durable Peace, 1940; (with Richard Stone) National Income and Expenditure, 1944; Planning and the Price Mechanism, 1948; The Theory of International Economic Policy, Vol. I, 1951, Vol. II, 1955; A Geometry of International Trade, 1952; Problems of Economic Union, 1953; The Theory of Customs Unions, 1955; The Control of Inflation, 1958; A Neo-Classical Theory of Economic Growth, 1960; Three Case Studies in European Economic Union, 1962 (Joint Author); Efficiency, Equality, and the Ownership of Property, 1964; Principles of Political Economy, Vol. 1, The Stationary Economy, 1965, Vol. 2, The Growing Economy, 1968, Vol. 3, The Controlled Economy, 1972, Vol. 4, The Just Economy, 1976; The Theory of Indicative Planning, 1970; The Theory of Externalities, 1973; The Intelligent Radical's Guide to Economic Policy, 1975; Stagflation, vol. 1, Wage Fixing, 1982, vol. 2, (jtly) Demand Management, 1983; Alternative Systems of Business Organisation and of Workers' Remuneration, 1986; Collected Papers, vols 1, 2, 3, 1988, vol. 4, 1989; (jtly) Macroeconomic Policy: inflation, wealth and the exchange rate, 1989; Agathotopia: the economics of partnership, 1989; Liberty, Equality and Efficiency, 1993. *Address:* 40 High Street, Little Shelford, Cambridge CB2 5ES. *T:* Cambridge (01223) 842491.

See also P. S. Dasgupta, T. W. Meade, Sir Geoffrey Wilson.

MEADE, Patrick John, OBE 1944; consultant in meteorology to various international organisations; Director of Services, and Deputy Director-General, Meteorological Office, 1966–73; *b* 23 Feb. 1913; *s* of late John Meade, Caterham, Surrey; *m* 1937, Winifred Jessie, *d* of Bertram Kent, Fawley, Hants; one *s* one *d* (and one *s* decd). *Educ:* Sir Joseph Williamson's Math. Sch., Rochester; Imperial Coll. of Science and Technology (Royal College of Science). ARCSc, BSc; Lubbock Mem. Prize in Maths, London Univ., 1933. Entered Met. Office, 1936; Southampton, 1937; Flt Lt RAFVR, Fr., 1939–40; Sqdn Leader, Sen. Met. Off., GHQ Home Forces, 1940–42; Wing Comdr (Gp Capt. 1944), Chief Met. Off., MAAF, 1943–45; Chief Met. Off., ACSEA, 1945–46; Head of Met. Office Trng Sch., 1948–52; London Airport, 1952–55; Research, 1955–60; idc 1958;

Dep. Dir for Outstations Services, 1960–65. Hon. Sec., Royal Meteorological Society, 1956–61, Vice-Pres., 1961–63. *Publications:* papers in jls on aviation meteorology and on meteorological aspects of air pollution, atmospheric radioactivity and hydrology. *Recreations:* music, gardening. *Address:* Luccombe, Coronation Road, South Ascot, Berks SL5 9LP. *T:* Ascot (01344) 23206.

MEADE, Richard John Hannay, OBE 1974; Bureau Member, and Chairman of Northern European Group of Nations, International Equestrian Federation, since 1990; *b* 4 Dec. 1938; *s* of John Graham O'Mahony Meade and Phyllis Brenda Meade; *m* 1977, Angela Dorothy Farquhar; two *s* one *d* (and one *s* decd). *Educ:* Lancing College; Magdalene College, Cambridge (Engineering Degree). Competed for GB in 3-day equestrian events, 1963–82; won 3 Olympic gold medals: team gold, 1968; team and individual gold, Munich, 1972; World Championships team medals include: gold, Punchestown, 1970; gold, Luhmûhlen, 1982; European Championships team medals include: gold, Punchestown, 1967; gold, Burghley, 1971; gold, Horsens, 1981; won Burghley 1964 and Badminton 1970 and 1982. Mem., 3-day Event Cttee, Internat. Equestrian Fedn, 1977–80; Pres., British Equestrian Fedn, 1989–92; Chm., British Horse Foundn. *Publication:* Fit for Riding, 1984. *Address:* Church Farm, West Littleton, Chippenham, Wilts SN14 8JB. *T:* Bath (01225) 891226.

MEADE, Prof. Thomas Wilson, CBE 1994; DM; FRCP; Director, Medical Research Council Epidemiology and Medical Care Unit, Wolfson Institute of Preventive Medicine, Medical College of St Bartholomew's Hospital (formerly at Northwick Park Hospital, Harrow), since 1970; Professor of Epidemiology, Medical College of St Barthmolomew's Hospital; Hon. Director, Cardiovascular Epidemiology Research Group, British Heart Foundation, since 1982; *b* 21 Jan. 1936; *s* of James Edward Meade, *qv*; *m* 1962, Helen Elizabeth Perks; one *s* two *d*. *Educ:* Westminster Sch.; Christ Church, Oxford; St Bartholomew's Hosp. Sen. Lectr, Dept of Public Health, London Sch. of Hygiene and Tropical Medicine (on secondment to Schieffelin Leprosy Research Sanatorium, S India, 1969–70), 1968–70. Hon. Consultant in Epidemiology, Royal Hosps NHS Trust and Northwick Park and St Mark's NHS Trust. Member: MRC Physiological Systems and Disorders Bd, 1974–78; MRC Health Services Res. Panel and Cttee, 1981–90; Wellcome Trust Physiology and Pharmacology Panel, 1990–95. *Publications:* papers on thrombosis and arterial disease. *Recreation:* growing vegetables. *Address:* 28 Cholmeley Crescent, N6 5HA. *T:* 0181–340 6260. *Club:* Leander (Henley-on-Thames).

MEADE-KING, Charles Martin, MA; Headmaster, Plymouth College, 1955–73, retired; *b* 17 Aug. 1913; *s* of late G. C. Meade-King, solicitor, Bristol; *m* 1948, Mary (*née* Frazer); one *s* one *d*. *Educ:* Clifton Coll.; Exeter Coll., Oxford (Stapeldon Scholar). Asst Master, King's Sch., Worcester, 1935–38; Asst Master, Mill Hill Sch., 1938–40. Intelligence Corps, 1940–45. Housemaster, Mill Hill Sch., 1945–55. *Recreations:* history, arts, games. *Address:* Whistledown, Yelverton, near Plymouth PL20 6HX. *T:* Yelverton (01822) 852237.

MEADES, Jonathan Turner; journalist, writer and television performer; *b* 21 Jan. 1947; *s* of late John William Meades and Margery Agnes Meades (*née* Hogg); *m* 1st, Sally Dorothy Renée, *d* of Raymond Brown; twin *d*; 2nd, Frances Anne, *d* of Sir William Bentley, *qv*; two *d*. *Educ:* King's Coll., Taunton; RADA; Bordeaux Univ. Editor, Event, 1981–82; Features Editor, Tatler, 1982–85; Restaurant Critic, The Times, 1986–. Contributor to many magazines and newspapers, including: Books and Bookmen, Time Out, Observer, Architects Jl, Sunday Times, Harpers and Queen, Vogue, Literaty Review, Tatler, A La Carte, Independent, Sunday Correspondent, Mail on Sunday, Evening Standard. *TV series:* The Victorian House, 1987; Abroad in Britain, 1991; Further Abroad, 1994, Jerry-building, 1994; *film script:* L'Atlantide, 1991. *Publications:* This is Their Life, 1979; An Illustrated Atlas of the World's Great Buildings, 1980; Filthy English, 1984; Peter Knows what Dick Likes, 1989; Pompey, 1993. *Recreations:* buildings, mushrooms, sloth. *Address:* c/o Aitken, Stone & Wylie, 29 Fernshaw Road, SW10 0TG. *T:* 0171–351 7561. *Clubs:* Groucho, Academy.

MEADOW, Prof. (Samuel) Roy, FRCP; Head of Department of Paediatrics and Child Health, St James's University Hospital, Leeds, since 1980; President, British Paediatric Association, since 1994; *b* 9 June 1933; *m* 1st, 1962, Gillian Margaret Maclennan; one *s* one *d*; 2nd, 1978, Marianne Jane Harvey. *Educ:* Wigan Grammar Sch.; Bromsgrove Sch.; Worcester Coll., Oxford (BA Hons Physiol. 1957; MA, BM BCh 1960). DRCOG 1962; DCH 1963; MRCP 1964, FRCP 1974. Partner GP, Banbury, 1962–64; junior appts at Guy's Hosp., Evelina Children's Hosp., Hosp. for Sick Children, London and Royal Alexandra Hosp., Brighton, 1964–67; MRC Sen. Res. Fellow, Birmingham Univ., 1967–68; Sen. Lectr and Consultant Paediatrician, Leeds Univ., 1970–80. Blackwell Vis. Prof., NZ Paediatric Assoc., 1989; Kildorrory Lectr, Irish Paed. Assoc., 1987; Charles West Lectr, RCP, 1993. Chairman: Assoc. for Child Psychology and Psychiatry, 1983–84; Academic Bd, BPA, 1990–94. Editor, Archives of Diseases in Childhood, 1979–87. Dawson Williams Prize, BMA, 1994. *Publications:* Lecture Notes on Paediatrics, 1973, 6th edn 1991; Bladder Control and Enuresis, 1973; The Child and His Symptoms, 1978; ABC of Child Abuse, 1989, 2nd edn 1993; Paediatric Kidney Disease, 1992; reports and papers on teratogenicity of anticonvulsant drugs, Munchausen Syndrome by proxy child abuse, childhood urinary tract disorders and child abuse. *Recreation:* gardening. *Address:* Weeton Grange, Weeton, Leeds LS17 0AP. *T:* Harrogate (01423) 734234.

MEADOWCROFT, Michael James; writer and journalist; *b* 6 March 1942; marr. diss.; one *s* one *d*; *m* 2nd, 1987, Elizabeth Bee. *Educ:* King George V Sch., Southport; Bradford Univ. (MPhil 1978). Chm., Merseyside Regl Young Liberal Orgn, 1961; Liberal Party Local Govt Officer, 1962–67; Sec., Yorks Liberal Fedn, 1967–70; Asst Sec., Joseph Rowntree Social Service Trust, 1970–78; Gen. Sec., Bradford Metropolitan Council for Voluntary Service, 1978–83. Senior Vis. Fellow, PSI, 1989. Dir, Electoral Reform Consultancy Services, 1992–. Member: Leeds City Council, 1968–83; W Yorks MCC, 1973–76, 1981–83. Dir, Leeds Grand Theatre and Opera House, 1971–83. Chm., Liberal Party Assembly Cttee, 1977–81; Pres. Elect, Liberal Party, 1987–88. Contested (L) Leeds W, Feb. and Oct. 1974, 1987, 1992. MP (L) Leeds W, 1983–87. Chm., Electoral Reform Soc., 1989–. *Publications:* Liberal Party Local Government Handbook (with Pratap Chitnis), 1963; Success in Local Government, 1971; Liberals and a Popular Front, 1974; Local Government Finance, 1975; A Manifesto for Local Government, 1975; The Bluffer's Guide to Politics, 1976; Liberal Values for a New Decade, 1980; Social Democracy—Barrier or Bridge?, 1981; Liberalism and the Left, 1982; Liberalism and the Right, 1983; Liberalism Today and Tomorrow, 1989; The Politics of Electoral Reform, 1991; Diversity in Danger, 1992; The Case for the Liberal Party, 1992. *Recreations:* music (including jazz), cricket. *Address:* Waterloo Lodge, 72 Waterloo Lane, Bramley, Leeds LS13 2JF. *T:* Leeds (0113) 257 6232. *Clubs:* National Liberal; Armley Liberal, Bramley Liberal, Burley Liberal, Kirkstall Liberal, New Wortley Liberal, Upper and Lower Wortley Liberal (Leeds).

MEADOWS, Prof. Arthur Jack, FInstP; FLA; FIInfSc; Professor of Library and Information Studies, Loughborough University, since 1986; *b* 24 Jan. 1934; *s* of Arthur Harold Meadows and Alice Elson; *m* 1958, Isobel Jane Tanner Bryant; one *s* two *d*. *Educ:* New Coll., Oxford (MA Physics; DPhil Astronomy); University Coll. London (MSc History and Philosophy of Science). Fulbright Schol., Vis. Fellow, Mt Wilson and Palomar Observatories, Asst Prof., Univ. of Illinois, 1959–61; Lectr, Univ. of St Andrews, 1961–63; Asst Keeper, British Mus., 1963–65; University of Leicester: Hd of Dept and Prof., Astronomy and History of Science Depts, 1965–86; Hd of Primary Communications Res. Centre, 1975–86; Hd of Office for Humanities Communication, 1982–86. Hon. Life Vice-Pres., LA, 1995. *Publications:* Stellar Evolution, 1967; The High Firmament: a survey of astronomy in English literature, 1969; Early Solar Physics, 1970; Science and Controversy, 1972; Communication in Science, 1974; Greenwich Observatory: recent history (1836–1975), 1975; The Scientific Journal, 1979; (jtly) Dictionary of New Information Technology, 1982; (jtly) The Lamp of Learning: Taylor & Francis and the development of science publishing, 1984; (jtly) Maxwell's Equations and their Applications, 1985; Space Garbage, 1985; (jtly) Dictionary of Computing and Information Technology, 1987; The Origins of Information Science, 1987; (jtly) Principles and Practice of Journal Publishing, 1987; (jtly) The History of Scientific Discovery, 1987; Infotechnology, 1989; Innovation in Information, 1994; (jtly) Front Page Physics, 1994; (jtly) Project ELVYN, 1995; about 200 articles. *Recreation:* sleeping in meetings. *Address:* 47 Swan Street, Seagrave, Leics LE12 7NL. *T:* Sileby (0150981) 2557.

MEADOWS, Bernard William; sculptor; Professor of Sculpture, Royal College of Art, 1960–80; *b* Norwich, 19 Feb. 1915; *s* of W. A. F. and E. M. Meadows; *m* 1939, Marjorie Winifred Payne; two *d*. *Educ:* City of Norwich Sch. Studied at Norwich Sch. of Art, 1934–36; worked as Asst to Henry Moore, 1936–40; studied at Royal College of Art, 1938–40 and 1946–48. Served with RAF, 1941–46. Commissioned by Arts Council to produce a work for Festival of Britain, 1951. Rep. (Brit. Pavilion) in Exhib. of Recent Sculpture, Venice Biennale, 1952; in Exhib., Kassel, Germany, 1959, etc. Exhibited in International Exhibitions of Sculpture (Open Air): Battersea Park, 1951, 1960; Musée Rodin, Paris, 1956; Holland Park, 1957; in 4th International Biennial, São Paulo, Brazil, 1957; also in Exhibns (Open Air) in Belgium and Holland, 1953–. *One man exhibitions:* Gimpel Fils, London, 1957, 1959, 1963, 1965, 1967; Paul Rosenberg, New York, 1959, 1962, 1967; Taranman, London, 1979. *Works in Collections:* Tate Gallery; Victoria and Albert Museum; Arts Council; British Council; Museum of Modern Art, New York; also in public collections in N and S America, Israel, Australia, and in Europe. Mem., Royal Fine Art Commn, 1971–76. Awarded Italian State Scholarship, 1956. *Publication:* 34 etchings and box (for Molloy by Samuel Beckett), 1967. *Address:* 34 Belsize Grove, NW3 4TR. *T:* 0171–722 0772.

MEADOWS, Graham David; Director, Regional Policy, Commission of European Communities, since 1989; *b* 17 Dec. 1941; *s* of late Albert Edward Meadows and Jessica Maude Titmus; two *d*. *Educ:* Edinburgh Univ. MA Hons Political Economy. Journalist, 1958–69, specialising latterly in agric. affairs; European corresp., Farmers' Weekly (based in Brussels), 1973–75; EC 1975–; Mem., agric. policy unit; adviser on agricl, fisheries and envt policy, Office of Pres. of EEC (Gaston E. Thorn), 1981–84; Chef de Cabinet of Stanley Clinton Davis, Mem. of EEC responsible for transport, envmt and nuclear safety, 1985–89. *Recreations:* mountain walking, reading in the history of economic thought. *Address:* Commission of the European Communities, 200 rue de la Loi, 1049 Brussels, Belgium. *T:* (2) 235.61.81.

MEADOWS, Pamela Catherine, (Mrs P. A. Ormerod); Director, Policy Studies Institute, since 1993; *b* 9 Jan. 1949; *d* of Sidney James Meadows and Hilda Catherine (*née* Farley); *m* 1975, Paul Andrew Ormerod; one *s*. *Educ:* Kenya High Sch., Nairobi; Penrhos Coll., Colwyn Bay; Univ. of Durham (BA Econs 1970); Birkbeck Coll., Univ. of London (MSc Econs 1978). Research Officer, NIESR, 1970–74; Sen. Econ. Asst, then Econ. Advr, Home Office, 1974–78; Department of Employment: Econ. Advr, 1978–88; Grade 5, 1988–92; Chief Economic Advr, and Hd of Econs, Res. and Evaluation Div., 1992–93. Mem. Council, Public Finance Foundn, 1994–; Trustee, Employment Policy Inst., 1995–. *Address:* Policy Studies Institute, 100 Park Village East, NW1 3SR.

MEADOWS, Robert; company director, motor trade; Lord Mayor of Liverpool, 1972–73; *b* 28 June 1902; *m* 1st, 1926, Ivy L. Jenkinson (*d* 1963); three *s*; 2nd, 1967, Nora E. Bullen. *Educ:* locally and Bootle Technical Coll. Engineering, 1917–21. Liverpool: City Councillor, Fairfield Ward, 1945; City Alderman, Princes Park Ward, 1961–74. Pres., Exec. Cttee, Broadgreen Conservative Assoc. *Recreations:* motor vehicle development, property improvement, landscape gardening.

MEADWAY, (Richard) John, PhD; Head of Export Control and Non-Proliferation Division, Department of Trade and Industry, since 1994; *b* 30 Dec. 1944; *s* of late Norman Pardey Meadway and of Constance Meadway (now Kellaway); *m* 1968, Rev. Dr Jeanette Valerie (*née* Partis); two *d*. *Educ:* Collyer's Sch., Horsham; Peterhouse, Cambridge (MA NatScis); Edinburgh Univ. (PhD); Oxford Univ. (MA). Asst Principal, Min. of Technology, 1970; Private Secretary: to Minister for Trade and Consumer Affairs, 1973; to Sec. of State for Prices and Consumer Protection, 1974; to the Prime Minister, 1976–78; Asst Sec., 1979, Under Sec., 1989, Dept of Trade, later DTI; Hd of Overseas Trade Div. 2, DTI, 1989–94. UK Gov., IAEA, 1994–. FRSA 1995. *Publications:* papers on the amino-acid sequences of proteins. *Recreations:* reading, travel. *Address:* c/o Department of Trade and Industry, 66–74 Victoria Street, SW1E 6SW. *Club:* Reform.

MEAGER, Michael Anthony, ARIBA; Director of Estates, Department of Health, 1989–91; *b* 15 Feb. 1931; *s* of late Arthur Pattison Meager and Dora Edith Meager (*née* Greeves); *m* 1954, Val Cranmer Benson, *d* of late H. C. Benson; two *s* one *d*. *Educ:* Royal Naval Coll., Dartmouth; Clacton County High Sch.; Architectural Assoc. Sch. of Architecture. ARIBA 1955; AADip 1956. Architectural Asst, Moiret & Wood, 1954–55. National Service, RE, 1955–57: commnd 1956, served Cyprus, 1956–57. Architect, Hammett & Norton, 1957–58; HMOCS, Kenya, 1958–63: Dist Officer, Central Province, 1958–61; Asst Sec., Min. of Lands, Surveys and Town Planning, Nairobi, 1961–63; Architect: James Ralph, 1963–64; Tripe & Wakeham, 1964–66; Department of Health (formerly MoH and DHSS), 1966–91: Main Grade Architect, 1966–67; Prin. Arch., 1967–70; Suptg Arch., 1970–72; Asst Chief Arch., 1972–86; Chief Arch., 1986–88; Dir of Health Building, 1988–89. Dir, Isle of Jura Mill Co. Ltd, 1991–94. *Recreations:* boats, walking, listening to music. *Address:* 6 Garden Court, Greenacres, Eltham, SE9 5AZ.

MEAKIN, Wilfred, CB 1982; CEng, FIMechE; defence systems consultant (W. M. Associates); Executive Director, Royal Ordnance plc, 1986; Chairman, Royal Ordnance Inc., 1986; *b* 3 Oct. 1925. *Educ:* engineering apprenticeship in industry. Served War of 1939–45, RN. Technical Asst, ROF, Maltby, 1951; posts in ROF and former Inspectorate of Armaments; Asst Dir, ROF, Blackburn, 1966–72; Dir, ROF, Birtley, 1972–75; Dir, ROF Leeds, during 1975; Dir-Gen., Ordnance Factories (Weapons and Fighting Vehicles), 1975–79; Chief Exec. and Dep. Chm., Bd of ROF, later Royal Ordnance plc, 1979–86. Hon. FCGI.

MEALE, (Joseph) Alan; MP (Lab) Mansfield, since 1987; *b* 31 July 1949; *s* of Albert Henry and Elizabeth Meale; *m* 1983, Diana Gilhespy; one *s* one *d*. *Educ:* St Joseph's RC School; Ruskin College, Oxford. Seaman, British Merchant Navy, 1964–68; engineering worker, 1968–75; Nat. Employment Develt Officer, NACRO, 1977–80; Asst (Personal Research) to Gen. Sec., ASLEF, 1980–83; Parly and Political Advisor to Michael Meacher,

MP, 1983–87. An Opposition Whip, 1992–. Mem., Select Cttee on Home Affairs, 1989–; Treas., Parly All Party Football Gp, 1989; Chairman: PLP E Midland Gp; British Cyprus Cttee; Jt Vice-Chm., PLP Employment Cttee; Vice Chm., Parly Ukraine Cttee; Jt Sec., All Party Cults Cttee; Sec., All Party Animal Welfare Gp; Treas., British Section, CPA Cyprus Gp. Member: MSF Parly Cttee; Exec. Bd, SSAFA; Exec. Cttee on War Pensions. *Recreations:* reading, writing. *Address:* 5 Clumber Street, Mansfield, Notts NG18 1NT. *T:* Mansfield (01623) 660531; House of Commons, SW1A 0AA. *T:* 0171–219 4159. *Clubs:* Labour, Woodhouse Working Men's, Bellamy Road Working Men's (Mansfield).

MEANTI, Dr Luigi; Chairman, ENI SpA, Rome, since 1993; *b* Milan, 14 Aug. 1928; *m;* two *s*. *Educ:* Poly. of Milan (Dr Ing). Asst Prof., Poly. of Milan, 1954–57; SNAM SpA, Milan: mem. staff, R&D dept, 1958–65; with gas planning dept, 1966–69; Dep. Gen. Manager, 1970–72; Gen. Manager, 1973–80; Vice-Pres. and Man. Dir, 1981–91; Hon. Pres., 1991–. Pres., Internat. Gas Union, Zürich, 1991–94; Vice Pres., EUROGAS, 1991–93. Hon. Member: IGasE, 1992; Assoc. Tecnique de l'Industrie du Gaz, Paris, 1993. *Address:* c/o ENI SpA, Piazzale E. Mattei, 00144 Rome, Italy. *T:* (6) 5982326.

MEARS, Dr Adrian Leonard, CPhys, FInstP; Technical and Quality Director, Defence Research Agency, since 1991; *b* 27 May 1944; *s* of Leonard Mears and Marjorie (*née* Isaac); *m* 1969, Barbara Bayne; two *s*. *Educ:* Highgate Sch.; Christ Church, Oxford (DPhil, MA). Res. Associate, Univ. of Md, USA, 1969–71; joined RRE (later Royal Signals and Radar Establishment), 1971: worked on display technology, optoelectronics and lasers, 1971–81; Hd, Signal Processing, 1981–86; Dir of Science (Comd, Control, Communications and Inf. Systems), MoD, 1987–89; Dep. Dir and Commercial Dir, RSRE, 1990–91. *Recreations:* walking, DIY, music. *Address:* Defence Research Agency, Farnborough, Hants GU14 6TD. *T:* Farnborough (01252) 394555.

MEARS, Rt. Rev. John Cledan; Bishop of Bangor, 1983–92; *b* 8 Sept. 1922; *s* of Joseph and Anna Lloyd Mears; *m* 1949, Enid Margaret; one *s* one *d*. *Educ:* Univ. of Wales, Aberystwyth (BA Philosophy 1943); Wycliffe Hall, Oxford; St Deiniol's Library, Hawarden. MA Wales 1948 (research, Blaise Pascal). Deacon 1947, priest 1948, St Asaph; Curate: Mostyn, 1947–49; Rhosllannerchrugog, 1949–55; Vicar of Cwm, 1955–58; Lecturer, St Michael's Coll., Llandaff and Univ. of Wales, Cardiff, 1959–73; Chaplain, 1959–67; Sub-warden, 1967–73; Vicar of St Mark's, Gabalfa, Cardiff, 1973–82. Examining Chaplain, 1960–73; Hon. Canon of Llandaff Cathedral, 1981–82; Sec. of Governing Body, Church in Wales, 1977–82. *Publications:* reviews in Theology, articles in Efrydiau Athronyddol, Diwynyddiaeth, and Barn. *Recreations:* hiking, mountaineering. *Address:* 25 Avon Ridge, Thornhill, Cardiff CF4 9AU. *T:* Cardiff (01222) 615505.

MEARS, Martin John Patrick; President of the Law Society, since 1995; *b* 12 Feb. 1940; *s* of I. F. Mears and E. Mears; *m* 1st; seven *c;* 2nd, Susan. *Educ:* St Illtyd's College, Cardiff; Wadham Coll., Oxford (MA, BCL). Solicitor, 1966. *Publications:* numerous articles in national, regional and legal press. *Recreations:* Law Society, journalism. *Address:* Old Rectory, Haddiscoe, Great Yarmouth, Norwich. *Clubs:* United Oxford & Cambridge University; Norfolk (Norwich).

MEATH, 14th Earl of, *cr* 1627; **Anthony Windham Normand Brabazon;** Baron Ardee, Ireland, 1616; Baron Chaworth, of Eaton Hall, Co. Hereford, UK, 1831; late Major Grenadier Guards; *b* 3 Nov. 1910; *o s* of 13th Earl of Meath, CB, CBE and Lady Aileen Wyndham-Quin (*d* 1962), *d* of 4th Earl of Dunraven; *S* father 1949; *m* 1940, Elizabeth Mary, *d* of late Capt. Geoffrey Bowlby, Royal Horse Guards, and Hon. Mrs Geoffrey Bowlby, CVO; two *s* two *d*. *Educ:* Eton; RMC Sandhurst. Joined Grenadier Guards, 1930. ADC to Governor of Bengal, 1936; Capt., 1938; served War of 1939–45, Grenadier Guards (wounded, Italy, 1943); Major, 1941; retired, 1946. *Heir: s* Lord Ardee, *qv*. *Address:* Killruddery, Bray, Co. Wicklow, Ireland.

MEATH, Bishop of, (RC), since 1990; **Most Rev. Michael Smith;** *b* 6 June 1940; *s* of John Smith and Bridget Fagan. *Educ:* Gilson Endowed Sch., Oldcastle; St Finian's Coll., Mullingar; Lateran Univ., Rome (DCL 1966). Ordained priest, 1963; Curate, Clonmellon, 1967–68; Chaplain: St Loman's Hosp., 1968–74; Sacred Heart Hosp., 1975–84; Auxiliary Bp of Meath, 1984–88; Coadjutor Bp of Meath, 1988–90. Diocesan Sec., dio. of Meath, 1968–84; Sec., Irish Bishops' Conf., 1984– (Asst Sec., 1970–84). *Recreations:* golf, walking. *Address:* Bishop's House, Dublin Road, Mullingar, Co. Westmeath, Ireland. *T:* Mullingar (044) 48841, 42038, *Fax:* (044) 43020.

MEATH AND KILDARE, Bishop of, since 1985; **Most Rev. Walton Newcombe Francis Empey;** *b* 26 Oct. 1934; *m* 1960, Louise E. Hall; three *s* one *d*. *Educ:* Portora Royal School and Trinity College, Dublin. Curate Assistant, Glenageary, Dublin, 1958–60; Priest-in-charge, Grand Falls, NB, Canada, 1960–63; Parish Priest, Edmundston, NB, 1963–66; Incumbent, Stradbally, Co. Laois, Ireland, 1966–71; Dean of St Mary's Cathedral and Rector, Limerick City Parish, 1971–81; Bishop of Limerick and Killaloe, 1981–85. *Recreations:* reading, fishing and walking. *Address:* Moyglare, Maynooth, Co. Kildare, Ireland.

MEDAWAR, Nicholas Antoine Macbeth; QC 1984; **His Honour Judge Medawar;** a Circuit Judge, since 1987; *b* 25 April 1933; *e s* of Antoine Medawar and Innes (*née* Macbeth); *m* 1st, 1962, Joyce Catherine (*née* Crosland-Boyle) (marr. diss.); one *s* (one *d* decd); 2nd, 1977, Caroline Mary, *d* of Harry Samuel Collins, of Nottingham and Buckley. *Educ:* Keswick School; Trinity College, Dublin. BA Mod., LLB. Called to the Bar, Gray's Inn, 1957. Nat. Service, RASC, 1957–59, 2nd Lieut. A Recorder of the Crown Court, 1985–87. A Legal Assessor, Gen. Optical Council, 1984–87. Mem. Ethnic Minorities Adv. Cttee, Judicial Studies Bd, 1993–. *Recreations:* skittles, walking, mathematical diversions. *Address:* 4 Paper Buildings, Temple, EC4Y 7EX.

MEDD, David Leslie, OBE 1964; Consultant Architect, Department for Education (formerly Department of Education and Science), since 1978; *b* 5 Nov. 1917; *s* of Robert Tate Medd and Dorothy (*née* Rogers); *m* 1949, Mary Beaumont Crowley (*see* M. B. Medd). *Educ:* Oundle; Architectural Assoc. (AA Dip. Hons). ARIBA 1941. Architects' Dept, Herts CC, 1946–49. Develt Gp, Architects and Building Br., Min. of Educn, later DES, 1949–78; private architectural work, 1978–. Commonwealth Fund Fellowship, 1958–59. Hon. DSc: Edinburgh, 1974; Hull, 1993. SADG Medal (France), 1941; Distinguished Service Certificate, BSI, 1992. *Publications:* School Furniture, 1981; contrib. to numerous learned jls, incl. HMSO building bulletins. *Recreations:* art, music, furniture making, gardening. *Address:* 5 Pennyfathers Lane, Harmer Green, Welwyn, Herts AL6 0EN. *T:* Welwyn (01438) 714654. *Club:* Royal Over-Seas League.

MEDD, Mary Beaumont, (Mrs D. L. Medd), OBE 1964; retired; *b* 4 Aug. 1907; *d* of Ralph Henry Crowley and Muriel Crowley (*née* Priestman); *m* 1949, David Leslie Medd, *qv*. *Educ:* Bedales Sch.; Architectural Assoc. Pre-war work connected with housing and Building Centre, London; Hertfordshire County Council: Educn Dept, 1941–46; Architects' Dept, 1946–49; Develt Gp, Architects and Building Br., Min. of Educn, later DES, 1949–72; consultancy work, educnl and architectural, in England and abroad, 1972–93. Hon. DSc Hull, 1993. SADG Medal (France), 1932. *Publications:* contribs to jls and books, educnl and architectural, incl. HMSO building bulletins. *Recreations:* art, music, architecture, travel. *Address:* 5 Pennyfathers Lane, Harmer Green, Welwyn, Herts AL6 0EN. *T:* Welwyn (01438) 714654.

MEDD, His Honour Patrick William, OBE 1962; QC 1973; a Circuit Judge, 1981–92; *b* 26 May 1919; *s* of E. N. Medd; *m* 1st, 1945, Jeananne Spence Powell (marr. diss.); three *d;* 2nd, 1971, Elizabeth Spinks D'Albuquerque. *Educ:* Uppingham Sch.; Selwyn Coll., Cambridge. Served in Army, 1940–46, S Staffs Regt and E African Artillery, Major. Called to Bar, Middle Temple, 1947, Bencher 1969; Mem. Gen. Council of the Bar, 1965–67. Dep. Chm., Shropshire QS, 1967–71; Jun. Counsel to Comrs of Inland Revenue, 1968–73; Recorder of Abingdon, 1964–71 (Hon. Recorder, 1972–); a Recorder of the Crown Court, 1972–81. Chm., Bd of Referees, and Finance Act 1960 Tribunal, 1978–91; UK rep., panel of arbitrators, Internat. Centre for Settlement of Investment Disputes, 1979–87; Co-Pres., Nat. Reference Tribunal for Coalmining Ind., 1985–; Special Comr of Income Tax, 1986–92 (Presiding Special Comr, 1990–92); Pres., VAT Tribunals, 1988–92. *Publications:* (jtly) The Rule of Law, 1955; (jtly) Murder, 1956; (jtly) A Giant's Strength, 1958; Romilly, 1968. *Recreation:* gardening. *Address:* Little Place, Clifton Hampden, near Abingdon, Oxon OX14 3EQ.

MEDHURST, Brian; Managing Director (International Division), Prudential Corporation plc, 1985–94; *b* 18 March 1935; *s* of late Eric Gilbert Medhurst and Bertha May (*née* Kinggett); *m* 1960, Patricia Anne Beer; two *s* one *d*. *Educ:* Godalming Grammar Sch.; Trinity Coll., Cambridge (MA). FIA 1962 (Mem. Council, 1982–87). Joined Prudential Assurance Co. Ltd, 1958; Deputy Investment Manager, 1972; Investment Manager, 1975; Jt Chief Investment Manager, 1981; Gen. Manager, 1982. *Recreations:* squash, golf, piano duets, tree felling. *Address:* Longacre, Fitzroy Road, Fleet, Hants GU13 8JJ. *T:* Fleet (01252) 614159. *Clubs:* North Hants Golf; Royal Aldershot Officers'.

MEDINA, Earl of; Henry David Louis Mountbatten; *b* 19 Oct. 1991; *s* and *heir* of Marquess of Milford Haven, *qv*.

MEDLEY, George Julius, OBE 1989; Director, WWF-UK (World Wide Fund for Nature) (formerly World Wildlife Fund (UK)), 1978–93; *b* 2 Aug. 1930; *s* of late Brig. Edgar Julius Medley, DSO, OBE, MC and Norah Medley (*née* Templer); *m* 1952, Vera Frances Brand; one *s* one *d*. *Educ:* Winchester College; Wye College, Univ. of London. BSc (Hort.). Fruit farmer, 1952–56; Manager, Chemical Dept, Harrisons & Crosfield, Colombo, 1957–63; Dir, Fisons (Ceylon), 1960–63; Tech. Develt Manager, Tata Fison, Bangalore, 1963–64; Gen. Manager Pesticides Div., Tata Fison Industries, Bombay, 1964–68; Sales Manager, Western Hemisphere, Agrochemicals, Fisons Internat. Div., 1968–69; Overseas Manager, Fisons Agrochemical Div., 1970–71; Dep. Managing Dir, Glaxo Labs, India, 1972–73, Managing Dir, 1973–77. Chm., Alexis Productions Ltd, 1994–; Dir, Edward Jewson Services to Charities Ltd, 1993–. Mem., Radioactive Waste Management Adv. Cttee, 1991–. Vice-Pres., Organisation of Pharmaceutical Producers of India, 1974–77; Founder Mem. and Vice-Chm., Inst. of Charity Fundraising Managers, 1983 (Chm., 1984–85); Treasurer: Wilts WI Market Soc., 1993–; Wilts Wildlife Trust, 1994–; Trustee: Farming and Wildlife Adv. Gp, 1984–93; Internat. Inst. for Envmt and Develt, 1989–93; Falkland Islands Foundn, 1985–92. FIMgt; FICFM 1988; FRSA 1989. Officer, Order of Golden Ark (Netherlands), 1993. *Publications:* contrib. to Strategic Planning Soc. Jl. *Recreations:* gardening, DIY. *Address:* Hoddinotts House, Tisbury, Wilts SP3 6QQ. *T:* Tisbury (01747) 870677.

MEDLICOTT, Michael Geoffrey; Vice President, Europe, Delta Airlines Inc., since 1993; *b* 2 June 1943; *s* of Geoffrey Henry Medlicott and Beryl Ann Medlicott (*née* Burchell); *m* 1973, Diana Grace Fallaw; one *s* three *d*. *Educ:* Downside School; Lincoln College, Oxford (Scholar; MA). Management Trainee, P&O-Orient Lines, 1965–66; Shipping Asst, Mackinnon, Mackenzie & Co., Bombay, 1966–68, Tokyo, 1968–69; Asst to Management, P&O-Orient Lines, 1969–71; P&O Cruises: Develt Analyst, 1971–73; Asst Fleet Manager, 1973–75; Gen. Manager, Fleet, 1975–80; Gen. Manager, Europe, 1980–83; Dir, Europe, 1983–86; Man. Dir, Swan Hellenic, 1983–86; Man. Dir, P&O Air Holidays, 1980–86; Dir, P&O Travel, 1980–84; Chief Exec., BTA, 1986–93. Chm., European Travel Commn, 1992–93 (Chm., Planning Cttee, 1990–92). Member Council of Management: Passenger Shipping Assoc., 1983–86; Heritage of London Trust, 1987–; London Tourist Bd, 1992–93; Mem. Council, Tidy Britain Gp, 1988–. Member: Adv. Panel, Languages Lead Body, Dept of Employment, 1990–93; Adv. Council, Univ. of Surrey Tourism Dept, 1991–; Hon. Bd, Univ. Center of Hellenic and European Studies, Piraeus, 1994–. Trustee, British Travel & Educnl Trust, 1986–93. Mem., Royal Philatelic Soc. FRSA 1986. Queen Mother's Birthday Award for Envmtl Improvement, 1993. *Publications:* contribs to British West Indies Study Circle Bulletin, 1970–. *Recreations:* philately, theatre, gardening. *Address:* Delta Airlines Inc., 25 Buckingham Gate, SW1E 6LD.

MEDLYCOTT, Sir Mervyn (Tregonwell), 9th Bt *cr* 1808, of Ven House, Somerset; *b* 20 Feb. 1947; *s* of Thomas Anthony Hutchings Medlycott (*d* 1970) (2nd *s* of 7th Bt) and of Mrs Cecilia Mary Medlycott, Cowleaze, Edmondsham, Dorset, *d* of late Major Cecil Harold Eden; *S* uncle, 1986. Genealogist; FSG 1990; Mem., AGRA; Pres., Somerset and Dorset Family History Soc., 1986– (Founder and Hon. Sec., 1975–77; Chm., 1977–84; Vice-Pres., 1984–86). *Heir:* none. *Address:* The Manor House, Sandford Orcas, Sherborne, Dorset DT9 4SB. *T:* Corton Denham (01963) 220206.

MEDWAY, Lord; John Jason Gathorne-Hardy; *b* 26 Oct. 1968; *s* and *heir* of 5th Earl of Cranbrook, *qv*. *Educ:* Woodbridge Sch., Suffolk; Pembroke Coll., Oxford (BA). *Recreations:* natural history, drawing, photography. *Address:* 7 Woodfall Street, Chelsea, SW3 4DJ.

MEECHIE, Brig. Helen Guild, CBE 1986; Deputy Director General, Personal Services, Ministry of Defence, 1990–91, retired; *b* 19 Jan. 1938; *d* of John Strachan and Robina Guild Meechie. *Educ:* Morgan Academy, Dundee; St Andrew's University (MA). Commissioned 1960; served in UK, Cyprus and Hong Kong, 1961–76, in UK and Germany, 1977–82; Dir, WRAC, 1982–86; Mem., RCDS, 1987; Dir, Army Service Conditions, MoD, 1988–90. Hon. ADC to the Queen, 1982–86; ADC to the Queen, 1986. Hon. Col, Tayforth Univs OTC, 1986–91; Dep. Col Comdt, AGC, 1993–. Mem. Council, Union Jack Club, 1989–91. Gov., Royal Soldiers' Daughters' Sch., 1984–91. Freeman, City of London, 1983. CIMgt (CBIM 1986). Hon. LLD Dundee, 1986. *Recreations:* golf, gardening, travel. *Address:* 28 London Road, Amesbury, Salisbury, Wilts SP4 7DY.

MEEK, Brian Alexander, OBE 1982; JP; Deputy Chairman, Livingston Development Corporation, since 1986; Director, Capital Publicity Ltd, since 1987; Chairman, Ian McLauchlan Associates, since 1993; *b* 8 Feb. 1939; *s* of Walter Harold Meek and Elsbeth Dearden Meek; *m* 1st, 1962, Glenda (*née* Smith) (marr. diss. 1983); one *s* one *d;* 2nd, 1983, Frances (*née* Horsburgh). *Educ:* Royal High Sch. of Edinburgh; Edinburgh Commercial Coll. Sub-editor, The Scotsman and Edinburgh Evening Dispatch, 1958–63; Features and Leader Writer, Scottish Daily Express, 1963–74; Rugby Football Correspondent, Scottish Daily Express and Sunday Express, 1974–86; Political Columnist, Glasgow Herald, 1986–. Councillor: Edinburgh Corp., 1969–74; Edinburgh Dist Council, 1974–82 (Chm.,

Recreation Cttee, 1974–77); Lothian Regional Council, 1974–92 (Leader, Conservative Opposition, 1974–82, 1986–90; Convener and Leader of the Admin, 1982–86); Edinburgh DC, 1992–March 1996; City of Edinburgh Council, 1995–. Vice-Pres., Scottish Cons. and Unionist Assoc., 1989–92. Magistrate, Edinburgh, 1971, JP 1974. *Recreations:* golf, theatre, cinema, travel. *Address:* City Chambers, High Street, Edinburgh EH1 1PN. *T:* 0131–225 2424. *Club:* Caledonian (Edinburgh).

MEEK, Charles Innes, CMG 1961; Chief Executive, 1962–81, Chairman, 1973–81, White Fish Authority, retired; *b* 27 June 1920; *er s* of late Dr C. K. Meek; *m* 1947, Nona Corry Hurford; two *s* one *d*. *Educ:* King's Sch., Canterbury; Magdalen Coll., Oxford (MA). Demyship, Magdalen Coll., Oxford, 1939. Served in Army, 1940–41; District Officer, Tanganyika, 1941; Principal Asst Sec., Tanganyika, 1958; Permanent Sec., Chief Secretary's Office, 1959; Permanent Sec. to Prime Minister, Sec. to Cabinet, 1960; Government Dir, Williamson Diamonds; Head of the Civil Service, Tanganyika, 1961–62, retd. FRSA 1969. *Publications:* occasional articles in Journal of African Administration, etc. *Recreations:* travel, Spectator crossword, gardening. *Address:* Mariteau Cottage, German Street, Winchelsea, E Sussex TN36 4ES. *T:* Rye (01797) 226408. *Club:* Royal Over-Seas League.

MEEK, Prof. John Millar, CBE 1975; DEng; FEng 1976; FInstP; FIEE; David Jardine Professor of Electrical Engineering, University of Liverpool, 1946–78; Public Orator, 1973–76, and Pro-Vice-Chancellor, 1974–77, University of Liverpool; *b* Wallasey, 21 Dec. 1912; *s* of Alexander Meek and Edith Montgomery; *m* 1942, Marjorie, *d* of Bernard Ingleby; two *d*. *Educ:* Monkton Combe Sch.; University of Liverpool. College Apprentice, Metropolitan-Vickers Electrical Co. Ltd, 1934–36; Research Engineer, Metropolitan-Vickers Electrical Co. Ltd, 1936–38, 1940–46. Commonwealth Fund Research Fellow, Physics Dept, University of California, Berkeley, 1938–40. Mem. of Council, IEE, 1945–48, 1960–63 (Vice-Pres. 1964–68, Pres., 1968–69), Faraday Medal, 1975. Mem., IBA (formerly ITA), 1969–74. Hon. DSc Salford, 1971. *Publications:* The Mechanism of the Electric Spark (with L. B. Loeb), 1941; Electrical Breakdown of Gases (with J. D. Craggs), 1953, new edn 1978; High Voltage Laboratory Technique (with J. D. Craggs), 1954; papers in various scientific journals concerning research on electrical discharges in gases. *Recreations:* golf, gardening, theatre. *Address:* 4 The Kirklands, West Kirby, Merseyside L48 7HW. *T:* 0151–625 5850.

MEEK, Marshall, CBE 1989; RDI 1986; FEng 1990; FRINA; FIMarE; Chairman, Argonautics Maritime Technologies Ltd, since 1995; President, Royal Institution of Naval Architects, 1990–93 (Vice President, 1979–90); *b* 22 April 1925; *s* of Marshall Meek and Grace R. Smith; *m* 1957, Elfrida M. Cox; three *d*. *Educ:* Bell Baxter School, Cupar; Glasgow University (BSc). Caledon Shipbuilding Co., 1942–49; Asst Naval Architect, BSRA, 1949–53; Naval Architect, Ocean Fleets, 1953–79 (Dir, 1964–79); Head of Ship Technology, British Shipbuilders, 1979–84; Managing Dir, National Maritime Inst., 1984–85; Dep. Chm., 1985–86, Dir, 1986–88, Consultant, 1988–89, British Maritime Technology. Visiting Professor in Naval Architecture: Strathclyde Univ., 1972–83; UCL, 1983–86. Mem., Lloyds Register of Shipping Technical Cttee, 1979–. Chm., Marine Technology Bd, 1984–88; Member: Defence Scientific Adv. Council, 1989–94; Marine Safety Agency (formerly Surveyor General's) Res. Cttee, Dept of Transport, 1992–. Pres., NE Coast Inst. of Engrs and Shipbuilders, 1984–86. Chairman: NE Region, RSA, 1992; NE Coast Engrg Trust, 1994–March 1996. Mem., Northumberland Br., Gideons International in UK; Trustee, Northumberland and Newcastle upon Tyne Police Court Mission Fund, 1990–. JP City of Liverpool, 1977–79. FRSA. *Publications:* numerous papers to RINA and other marine jls. *Recreations:* gardening, reading. *Address:* Coppers, Hillside Road, Rothbury, Northumberland NE65 7PT. *T:* Rothbury (01669) 621403. *Club:* Caledonian.

MEERES, Norman Victor, CB 1963; Under-Secretary, Ministry of Defence, 1971–73, retired; *b* 1 Feb. 1913; *m* 1938, Elizabeth Powys Fowler; two *s* one *d*. *Educ:* Sloane Sch., Chelsea; Magdalene Coll., Cambridge. Asst Principal, Air Ministry, 1935, Principal, 1940, Asst Sec., 1944, Ministry of Aircraft Prod.; Asst Sec., Min. of Supply, 1946; Under Secretary: Min. of Supply, 1956; Min. of Aviation, 1959–67; seconded to Dipl. Service in Australia, with title Minister (Defence Research and Civil Aviation), 1965–68; Under-Sec., Min. of Technology, 1969–70. ARCM (piano teaching), 1974. *Recreations:* music, lawn tennis. *Address:* 89 Grove Way, Esher, Surrey KT10 8HF. *T:* 0181–398 1639.

MEESE, Edwin, III; lawyer; Distinguished Fellow, Heritage Foundation, Washington, since 1988; Distinguished Visiting Fellow, Hoover Institution, Stanford University, Calif, since 1988; *b* Oakland, Calif, 1931; *s* of Edwin Meese Jr and Leone Meese; *m* 1958, Ursula Herrick; one *s* one *d* (and one *s* decd). *Educ:* Oakland High Sch.; Yale Univ. (BA 1953); Univ. of Calif at Berkeley (JD 1958). Dep. Dist Attorney, Alameda County, 1959–67; Sec. of Legal Affairs to Gov. of Calif, Ronald Reagan, 1967–69; Exec. Assistant and C of S to Gov. of Calif, 1969–75; Vice-Pres., Rohr Industries, 1975–76; Attorney at Law, 1976–80; Dir, Center for Criminal Justice Policy and Management, Univ. of San Diego, 1977–81; Prof. of Law, Univ. of San Diego Law Sch., 1978–81; Counsellor to Pres. of USA, 1981–85; Attorney Gen. of USA, 1985–88. Hon. LLD: Delaware Law Sch.; Widener Univ.; Univ. of San Diego; Valparaiso Univ.; California Lutheran Coll.; Universidad Francisco Marroquin, Guatemala. *Publications:* contribs to professional jls. *Address:* The Heritage Foundation, 214 Massachusetts Avenue, NE, Washington, DC 20002, USA.

MEGAHEY, Leslie; writer and director, film and television; *b* 22 Dec. 1944; *s* of Rev. Thomas and Beatrice Megahey. *Educ:* King Edward VI Grammar Sch., Lichfield; Pembroke Coll., Oxford. BBC general trainee, 1965; radio drama, script editor, producer, 1967; director, producer, TV arts series, 1968–; Exec. Producer, Arena, 1978–79; Editor, Omnibus, 1979–81, Co-Editor, 1985–87; Head of Music and Arts, BBC TV, 1988–91; other *television:* The RKO Story; Artists and Models; The Orson Welles Story; numerous drama-documentaries; *films:* Schalcken the Painter, 1979; Cariani and the Courtesans, 1987; Duke Bluebeard's Castle (filmed opera), 1988; The Hour of the Pig, 1993; *theatre:* Jack—a night on the town, 1994. Mem., Arts Council Adv. Panel, Film and TV, 1985–89. Awards: BAFTA, 1980; Prague, 1975; Asolo, 1985; NY, 1987; Banff, 1987; Royal Philharmonic, 1989; Prix Italia, 1989. *Address:* c/o Peters Fraser & Dunlop, The Chambers, Chelsea Harbour, SW10 0XF.

MEGAHY, Thomas; Member (Lab) SW Yorkshire, European Parliament, since 1979; *b* 16 July 1929; *s* of Samuel and Mary Megahy; *m* 1954, Jean (*née* Renshaw); three *s*. *Educ:* Wishaw High Sch.; Ruskin Coll., Oxford, 1953–55; College of Educn (Technical), Huddersfield, 1955–56 and 1968–69; London Univ. (external student), 1959–63. BScEcon London; DipEcon and PolSci Oxon; DipFE Leeds. Left school at 14 to work on railway; National Service, RN, 1947–49; railway signalman, 1950–53. Lecturer: Rotherham Coll. of Technology, 1956–59; Huddersfield Technical Coll., 1960–65; Park Lane Coll., Leeds, 1965–79. European Parliament: Vice Pres., 1987–89; Dep. Leader, British Labour Group of MEPs, 1985–87; Member: Social Affairs Cttee, 1984–; Transport and Tourism Cttee; Hungarian Jt Cttee; Substitute Mem., Social Affairs Cttee. Active member of Labour Party, 1950–; Chm., Scottish Labour League of Youth; Executive Mem., Dewsbury CLP, 1962–. Councillor, Mirfield UDC, 1963–74; Leader, Kirklees Metropolitan Borough Council, 1973–76; Opposition Leader, 1976–78. Member, Yorks and Humberside REPC, 1974–77; Vice-President: AMA, 1979–; Yorks and Humberside Develt Assoc., 1981–. *Address:* 6 Lady Heton Grove, Mirfield, West Yorks WF14 9DY. *T:* Mirfield (01924) 492680.

MEGARRY, Rt. Hon. Sir Robert (Edgar), Kt 1967; PC 1978; FBA 1970; a Judge of the Chancery Division of the High Court of Justice, 1967–76; the Vice-Chancellor: of that Division, 1976–81; of the Supreme Court, 1982–85; *b* 1 June 1910; *e s* of late Robert Lindsay Megarry, OBE, MA, LLB, Belfast, and of late Irene, *d* of Maj.-Gen. E. G. Clark; *m* 1936, Iris, *e d* of late Elias Davies, Neath, Glam; three *d*. *Educ:* Lancing Coll.; Trinity Hall, Cambridge (Hon. Fellow, 1973). MA, LLD (Cantab); Music Critic, Varsity, 1930–32; Solicitor, 1935–41; taught for Bar and Solicitors' exams, 1935–39; Mem., Faculty of Law, Cambridge Univ., 1939–40; Certificate of Honour, and called to Bar, Lincoln's Inn, 1944, in practice, 1946–67; QC 1956–67; Bencher, Lincoln's Inn, 1962, Treasurer 1981. Principal, 1940–44, and Asst Sec., 1944–46, Min. of Supply; Book Review Editor and Asst Ed., Law Quarterly Review, 1944–67; Dir of Law Society's Refresher Courses, 1944–47; Sub-Lector, Trinity Coll., Cambridge, 1945–46; Asst Reader, 1946–51, Reader, 1951–67, Hon. Reader, 1967–71 in Equity in the Inns of Court (Council of Legal Educn); Member: Gen. Council of the Bar, 1948–52; Lord Chancellor's Law Reform Cttee, 1952–73; Senate of Inns of Court and Bar, 1966–70, 1980–82; Adv. Council on Public Records, 1980–85; Consultant to BBC for Law in Action series, 1953–66; Chairman: Notting Hill Housing Trust, 1967–68; Bd of Studies, and Vice-Chm., Council of Legal Educn, 1969–71; Friends of Lancing Chapel, 1969–93; Incorporated Council of Law Reporting, 1972–87; Comparative Law Sect., British Inst. of Internat. and Comp. Law, 1977–89; President: Soc. of Public Teachers of Law, 1965–66; Lancing Club, 1974–; Selden Soc., 1976–79. Visiting Professor: New York Univ. Sch. of Law, 1960–61; Osgoode Hall Law Sch., Toronto, 1964; Regents' Prof., UCLA, 1983; Lectures: John F. Sonnett, Fordham Univ., 1982; Tyrrell Williams, Washington Univ., St Louis, 1983; Leon Ladner, Univ. of British Columbia, 1984. Visitor: Essex Univ., 1983–90; Clare Hall, Cambridge, 1984–89. Hon. LLD: Hull, 1963; Nottingham, 1979; Law Soc. of Upper Canada (Osgoode Hall), 1982; London, 1988; DU Essex, 1991. Hon. Life Member: Canadian Bar Assoc., 1971; Amer. Law Inst., 1985. *Publications:* The Rent Acts, 1939, 11th edn, Vols 1 and 2, 1988, Vol. 3, 1989; A Manual of the Law of Real Property, 1946, 7th edn (ed with Prof. M. P. Thompson), 1993; Lectures on the Town and Country Planning Act, 1947, 1949; Miscellany-at-Law, 1955; (with Prof. Sir William Wade QC) The Law of Real Property, 1957, 6th edn 1996; Lawyer and Litigant in England (Hamlyn Lectures, 1962); Arabinesque-at-Law, 1969; Inns Ancient and Modern, 1972; A Second Miscellany-at-Law, 1973; Editor, Snell's Equity, 23rd edn 1947, 27th edn (with P. V. Baker, QC), 1973; contrib. to legal periodicals. *Recreations:* heterogeneous. *Address:* The Institute of Advanced Legal Studies, 17 Russell Square, WC1B 5DR. *T:* 0171–637 1731; 5 Stone Buildings, Lincoln's Inn, WC2A 3XT. *T:* 0171–242 8607.

MEGAW, Arthur Hubert Stanley, CBE 1951; MA Cantab; FSA; *b* Dublin, 1910; *s* of late Arthur Stanley Megaw; *m* 1937, Elene Elektra, *d* of late Helias Mangoletsi, Koritsa, Albania; no *c*. *Educ:* Campbell Coll., Belfast; Peterhouse, Cambridge. Walston Student (University of Cambridge), 1931. Macmillan Student, British School of Archæology at Athens, 1932–33, Asst Dir, 1935–36; Dir of Antiquities, Cyprus, 1936–60; Field Dir, Byzantine Institute, Istanbul, 1961–62; Dir, British Sch. of Archæology, Athens, 1962–68. CStJ 1967. *Publications:* (with A. J. B. Wace) Hermopolis Magna-Ashmunein, Alexandria, 1959; (with E. J. W. Hawkins) The Church of the Panagia Kanakariá in Cyprus, its Mosaics and Frescoes, 1977; various papers in archæological journals. *Recreation:* armchair travel. *Address:* 27 Perrin's Walk, NW3 6TH; PO Box 132, Paphos, Cyprus.

MEGAW, Rt. Hon. Sir John, PC 1969; Kt 1961, CBE 1956; TD 1951; a Lord Justice of Appeal, 1969–80; *b* 16 Sept. 1909; 2nd *s* of late Hon. Mr Justice Megaw, Belfast; *m* 1938, Eleanor Grace Chapman; one *s* two *d*. *Educ:* Royal Academical Institution, Belfast; St John's Coll., Cambridge Univ. (open schol. in classics; Hon. Fellow, 1967); Harvard Univ. Law Sch. (Choate Fellowship). Served War, 1939–45; Col, RA. Barrister-at-Law, Gray's Inn, 1934 (Certificate of Honour, Bar Final exam.); Bencher, 1958; Treasurer, 1976; QC 1953; QC (N Ire.) 1954; Recorder of Middlesbrough, 1957–61; Judge of the High Court of Justice, Queen's Bench Div., 1961–69; Pres., Restrictive Practices Court, 1962–68. Chm., Cttee of Inquiry into Civil Service Pay, 1981–82. Visitor: New Univ. of Ulster, 1976; Univ. of Ulster, 1984–89. Hon. LLD Queen's Univ., Belfast, 1968; Hon. DSc Ulster, 1990. Legion of Merit (US), 1946. Played Rugby football for Ireland, 1934, 1938.

MEGGESON, Michael; Solicitor and Notary Public; formerly Senior Partner, Warner, Goodman & Streat; a Recorder of the Crown Court, since 1981; *b* 6 Aug. 1930; *s* of Richard Ronald Hornsey Meggeson and Marjorie Meggeson; *m* 1975, Alison Margaret (*née* Wood). *Educ:* Sherborne; Gonville and Caius Coll., Cambridge. BA 1953; MA 1963. Nat. Service, RA, 1949–50; 5th Bn Royal Hampshire Regt, TA, 1950–63. Admitted a Solicitor, 1957; Asst Solicitor, 1957–59, Partner, 1959–95, Warner & Sons, subseq. Warner Goodman & Co., and Warner, Goodman & Streat; Dep. Circuit Judge, 1978–81. Mem. Cttee, Solicitors Staff Pension Fund, 1980– (Chm., Cttee of Management, 1988–92); Pres., Hampshire Incorp. Law Soc., 1981–82. *Recreations:* sailing, golf, gardening, music. *Address:* Church Farm, Langrish, near Petersfield, Hants GU32 1RQ. *T:* Petersfield (01730) 264470. *Clubs:* Royal Southern Yacht (Hamble); Hayling Island Golf, Liphook Golf.

MEHAFFEY, Rt. Rev. James; *see* Derry and Raphoe, Bishop of.

MEHEW, Peter; Assistant Under Secretary of State (Civilian Management) (C), Ministry of Defence, 1983–86, retired; *b* 22 Jan. 1931; *er s* of Oliver Mehew and Elsie (*née* Cox); *m* 1st, 1956, Gwyneth Sellors (*d* 1982); one *s* one *d*; 2nd, 1992, Margaret McComish; one step *s*. *Educ:* Bishop Wordsworth's Sch.; St Catharine's Coll., Cambridge (BA 1954). Asst Principal, Admiralty, 1954, Principal 1959; Assistant Secretary: CSD, 1970–73; MoD, 1973–80; Dep. Head, UK Delegn to Negotiations on Mutual and Balanced Force Reductions, 1975–77; Asst Under Sec. of State (Sales Admin), MoD, 1981–83. Fellow Commoner, CCC Cambridge, 1980. *Address:* 6 Anderson Road, Salisbury SP1 3DX. *T:* Salisbury (01722) 326364.

MEHROTRA, Prof. Ram Charan, MSc, DPhil, PhD, DSc; Vice-Chancellor, University of Allahabad, since 1991; Professor of Chemistry, University of Rajasthan, Jaipur, 1962–82, now Emeritus; *b* 16 Feb. 1922; *s* of late R. B. Mehrotra; *m* 1944, Suman; one *s* two *d*. *Educ:* Allahabad Univ. (MSc 1943, DPhil 1948); London Univ. (PhD 1952, DSc 1964). Research Chemist, Vigyan Kala Bhawan, Meerut, 1943–44; Lectr, Allahabad Univ., 1944–54; Reader, Lucknow Univ., 1954–58; Prof., 1958–62, Dean, Faculty of Science, 1959–62, Gorakhpur Univ.; Prof., 1962–74, Dean, Faculty of Science, 1962–65, Chief Rector, 1965–67, Vice-Chancellor, 1968–69 and 1972–73, Rajasthan Univ., Jaipur; Vice-Chancellor, Univ. of Delhi, 1974–79. Mem., UGC, 1982–. President: Chemistry Section, Indian Sci. Congress, 1967; Indian Chemical Soc., 1976–77; Indian Science Congress,

1978–79; Vice-Pres., Indian Nat. Science Acad., 1977–78; Member: Inorganic Chem. Div., IUPAC, 1977–81; Inorganic Nomenclature Commn, 1981–; Convener, Internat. Symposium, Nanjing, 1987. Fedn of Asian Chem. Socs Lecture, Seoul, 1987. Sir S. S. Bhatnagar award, 1965; Fedn of Indian Chambers of Commerce and Industry award, 1975; Prof. T. R. Seshadri's Birthday Commem. Medal, 1976; P. C. Ray Meml Medal, 1981; Golden Jubilee Medal, Inst. of Science, Bombay, 1983; Popularization of Science Award (by the Prime Minister), 1985; J. C. Ghosh Medal, Indian Chem. Soc., 1986; Achievement Award, Inst. of Oriental Phil., 1987; Platinum Jubilee Distinguished Service Award, Indian Science Congress, 1988; Atma Ram Award, for popularization of science, 1989; Dhar Meml Award, Diamond Jubilee Nat. Acad. of Science, 1991; Chatterjee Award, Indian Science Congress Assoc., 1991. Hon. DSc Meerut, 1976. *Publications:* (contrib.) Sol-Gel Science and Technology, 1989; Organometallic Chemistry, 1991; (contrib.) Chemistry, Spectroscopy and Applications of Sol-Gel Glasses, 1991; (contrib.) Chemistry of Silicon and Tin, 1991; treatises on: Metal Alkoxides and Metal β-Diketonates and Allied Derivatives, 1978; Metal Carboxylates, 1983; numerous research papers in nat. and internat. jls of chemistry; continuous references in the chemistry progress reports of Chem. Soc. London. *Recreation:* photography. *Address:* P4, University Campus, Jaipur 302004, India. *T:* (office) 510306; (home) 511476; Allahabad University, Allahabad–211002, India.

MEHTA, Ved (Parkash); writer; *b* Lahore, 21 March 1934; 2nd *s* of late Dr Amolak Ram Mehta (former Dep. Director General of Health Services, Govt of India), and Shanti Devi Mehta (*née* Mehra); naturalized citizen of USA, 1975; *m* 1983, Linn Fenimore Cooper, *d* of late William L. Cary; two *d. Educ:* Arkansas Sch. for the Blind; Pomona Coll.; Balliol Coll., Oxford; Harvard Univ. BA Pomona, 1956; BA Hons Mod. Hist. Oxon, 1959, MA 1962; MA Harvard, 1961. Phi Beta Kappa, 1955. Hazen Fellow, Oxford, 1956–59; Guggenheim Fellow, 1971–72, 1977–78; Ford Foundn Travel and Study Grantee, 1971–76, Public Policy Grantee, 1979–82; MacArthur Prize Fellow, 1982–87. Staff writer, The New Yorker, 1961–94. Yale University: Harvard Prize Fellow, 1959–60; Residential Fellow, Eliot House, 1959–61; Rosenkranz Chair in Writing, 1990–93; Lectr in History, 1990, 1991, 1992; Lectr in English, 1991–93; Associate Fellow, 1988–; Residential Fellow, 1990–93, Berkeley Coll. Vis. Schol., Case Western Reserve Univ., 1974; Beatty Lectr, McGill Univ., 1979; Vis. Prof. of Literature, Bard Coll., 1985, 1986; Noble Foundn Vis. Prof. of Art and Cultural History, Sarah Lawrence Coll., 1988; Vis. Fellow (Literature), Balliol Coll., 1988–89; Vis. Prof. of English, NY Univ., 1989–90; Arnold Bernhard Vis. Prof. of English and History, Williams Coll., 1994; Randolph Distinguished Vis. Prof. of English and History, Vassar Coll., 1994–Aug. 1996. Mem. Council on Foreign Relations, 1979–. Mem. Usage Panel, Amer. Heritage Dictionary, 1982. Fellow, NY Inst. for Humanities, 1988–92. Hon. DLitt: Pomona, 1972; Bard, 1982; Williams, 1986; Bowdoin Coll., 1995; DUniv Stirling, 1988. Assoc. of Indians in America Award, 1978; Silver Medal, Signet Soc., 1983; Distinguished Service Award, Asian/Pacific Americans Liby Assoc., 1986; NYC Mayor's Liberty Medal, 1986; Centenary Barrows Award, Pomona Coll., 1987; NY Public Liby Lion Medal, 1990; NY State Asian-American Heritage Month Award, 1991. *Publications:* Face to Face, 1957 (Secondary Educn Annual Book Award, 1958; serial reading on BBC Light prog., 1958, dramatization on Home prog., 1959; reissued 1967, 1978); Walking the Indian Streets, 1960 (rev. edn 1971); Fly and the Fly-Bottle, 1963, 2nd edn 1983 introd. Jasper Griffin; The New Theologian, 1966; Delinquent Chacha (fiction), 1967; Portrait of India, 1970, 2nd edn 1993; John Is Easy to Please, 1971; Mahatma Gandhi and His Apostles, 1977, reissued 1993; The New India, 1978; Photographs of Chachaji, 1980; A Family Affair: India under three Prime Ministers, 1982; Three Stories of the Raj (fiction), 1986; Rajiv Gandhi and Rama's Kingdom, 1995; Continents of Exile (autobiography): Daddyji, 1972; Mamaji, 1979; Vedi, 1982; The Ledge Between the Streams, 1984; Sound-Shadows of the New World, 1986; The Stolen Light, 1989; Up at Oxford, 1993; numerous translations; articles and stories in Amer., British and Indian newspapers and magazines, 1957–. Writer and commentator of TV documentary film Chachaji: My Poor Relation, PBS, 1978, BBC, 1980 (DuPont Columbia Award for Excellence in Broadcast Journalism, 1977–78). *Recreation:* listening to Indian and Western music. *Address:* 139 East 79th Street, New York, NY 10021, USA. *T:* (212) 5365662, *Fax:* (212) 8404035. *Club:* Century Association (NY) (Trustee, 1973–75).

MEHTA, Zubin; Music Director for life, Israel Philharmonic Orchestra (Musical Adviser, 1962–78); Artistic Director, Maggio Musicale Fiorentino, since 1986; *b* 29 April 1936; *s* of Mehli Mehta; *m* 1st, 1958, Carmen Lasky (marr. diss. 1964); one *s* one *d*; 2nd, 1969, Nancy Kovack. *Educ:* St Xavier's Coll., Bombay; Musikakademie, Vienna. First Concert, Vienna, 1958; first prize internat. comp., Liverpool, 1958; US debut, Philadelphia Orch., 1960; debut with Israel and Vienna Philharmonic Orchs, 1961; apptd Music Director, Montreal Symphony Orch., 1961; European tour with this orch., 1962; guest conducting, major European Orchs, 1962; Music Director: Los Angeles Philharmonic Orch., 1962–78; New York Philharmonic, 1978–91. Opera debut, Montreal, Tosca, 1964; debut Metropolitan Opera, Aida, 1965; operas at Metropolitan incl.: Tosca, Turandot, Otello, Carmen, Mourning becomes Elektra (world première), Trovatore, etc. Tours regularly with New York Philharmonic and Israel Philharmonic Orchs and occasionally with Vienna Phil. Orch.; regular guest conducting with Vienna Phil., Berlin Phil., Orch. de Paris. Hon. Doctorates: Colgate Univ.; Brooklyn Coll.; Westminster Coll.; Occidental Coll.; Sir George Williams Univ., Canada; Weizmann Inst. of Science, Israel; Tel-Aviv Univ. Holds numerous awards; Padma Bhushan (India), 1967; Commendatore of Italy; Médaille d'Or Verneil, City of Paris, 1984. *Address:* 27 Oakmont Drive, Los Angeles, CA 90049–1901, USA. *T:* (213) 4774444.

MEIER, Maj.-Gen. Anthony Leslie, CB 1995; OBE 1981; Director (non-executive), Eastbourne Hospitals NHS Trust, since 1994; Chairman, Management Board, Eastbourne Commercial Services, since 1995; *b* 3 Sept. 1937; *s* of late Eric Leslie Francis Meier and Vera Madge Meier (*née* Terry); *m* 1973, Susanne Jennifer Manley; two *s* one *d*. *Educ:* Latymer Upper Sch.; RMA Sandhurst. Commissioned RASC, 1957, later RCT; regtl appts, Germany and on secondment to Brigade of Gurkhas, Far East, 1958–68; Staff Coll., 1969; MoD, 31 Sqn GTR, NDC, BAOR, CO 8 Regt RCT, to 1981; Col GS Coord (COS), Staff Coll., 1981–84; NATO Defence Coll., Rome, 1984–85; HQ AFCENT, 1985–87; Dir of Intell. (Warsaw Pact), MoD, 1988–90; Dir-Gen., Management and Support of Intell., MoD, 1991–94. Dir, Macmillan Appeal for Brighton and Hove Hospice, 1994–. Chm., Bd of Govs, St Bede's Prep. Sch., Eastbourne, 1994–. *Publications:* Notes on the Warsaw Pact Ground Forces, 1972; articles in Internat. Defense Review. *Recreation:* sport. *Address:* c/o National Westminster Bank, 5 Meads Street, Eastbourne, E Sussex BN20 7QT.

MEIER, David Benjamin; His Honour Judge Meier; a Circuit Judge, since 1993; *b* 8 Oct. 1938; *s* of Arnold Meier, PhD and Irma Meier; *m* 1964, Kathleen Lesly Wilton; one *d. Educ:* Bury Grammar Sch.; King's College London (LLB). Admitted Law Society, 1964; Solicitor. Metropolitan Stipendiary Magistrate, 1985–93; a Recorder, 1991–93. Pres., Mental Health Tribunals, 1988–; Chairman: Juvenile Court, 1988–93; Family Panel, 1991–93. Pres., N Middx Law Soc., 1984–85. *Recreations:* riding, cricket, golf. *Address:* c/o Milton Keynes County Court, 351 Silbury Boulevard, Witan Gate East, Milton Keynes MK9 2DT.

MEINERTZHAGEN, Sir Peter, Kt 1980; CMG 1966; General Manager, Commonwealth Development Corporation, 1973–85; Director, Booker Tate Ltd, since 1989; *b* 24 March 1920; *y s* of late Louis Ernest Meinertzhagen, Theberton House, Leiston, Suffolk and Gwynnedd, *d* of Sir William Llewellyn, PRA; *m* 1949, Dido Pretty; one *s* one *d. Educ:* Eton. Served Royal Fusiliers, 1940–46 (Croix de Guerre, France, 1944). Alfred Booth & Co., 1946–57; Commonwealth Development Corporation, 1958–85. Member: Council, London Chamber of Commerce, 1968–69; Council, Overseas Develt Inst., 1979–85. *Address:* Mead House, Ramsbury, Wilts SN8 2QP. *T:* Marlborough (01672) 20715. *Club:* Muthaiga Country (Nairobi).

MEINERTZHAGEN, Peter Richard; Chairman, Hoare Govett, since 1991; *b* 16 April 1946; *s* of late Daniel Meinertzhagen and of Marguerite Meinertzhagen (*née* Leonard); *m* 1967, Nikki Phillips; five *d. Educ:* Eton College; Sorbonne. Hoare & Co.: joined 1965; Partner, 1973; Dir, Institutional Sales, 1973–90; Chm., Hoare Govett Corporate Finance, 1990–. *Recreations:* golf, tennis, horse-racing, music. *Address:* 20 Tite Street, SW3 4HZ. *T:* 0171–352 6806. *Club:* White's.

MEIRION-JONES, Prof. Gwyn Idris, FSA 1981; author and consultant on historic buildings; *b* 24 Dec. 1933; *e s* of late Maelgwyn Meirion-Jones and Enid Roberts, Manchester; *m* 1961, Monica, *e d* of late George and Marion Havard, Winchester. *Educ:* North Manchester Grammar School; King's College London (BSc, MPhil, PhD). National Service, RAF, 1954–56. Schoolmaster, 1959–68; Lectr in Geography, Kingston Coll. of Technology, 1968; Sir John Cass Coll., later City of London Polytechnic, now London Guildhall University: Sen. Lectr i/c Geography, 1969; Principal Lectr i/c, 1970; Head of Geography, 1970–89; Personal Chair, 1983–89, now Prof. Emeritus; Hon. Research Fellow, 1989–. Leverhulme Research Fellow, 1985–87; Vis. Prof. (Archaeol.), Univ. of Reading, 1995–. British Assoc. for the Advancement of Science: Sec., 1973–78, Recorder, 1978–83, Pres., 1992–93, Section H (Anthropology and Archaeology); Mem. Council, 1977–80; Mem. Gen. Cttee, 1977–83; Ancient Monuments Society: Mem. Council, 1974–79 and 1983–; Hon. Sec., 1976–79; Vice-Pres., 1979–; Editor, 1985–94. Member: Comité Scientifique des Musées du Finistère, 1984–; Royal Commn on Historical Monuments of England, 1985–; Adv. Cttee on Bldgs and Domestic Life, Welsh Folk Mus., 1991–. Hon. Pres., Domestic Buildings Res. Gp (Surrey), 1991– (Pres., 1986–91). Editor, Medieval Village Res. Gp, 1978–86. Hon. Corresp. Mem., Soc. Jersiaise, 1980–90 and 1990–; Corresp. Mem., Compagnie des Architectes en Chef des Monuments Historiques, 1989–. Exhibitions: vernacular architecture of Brittany, on tour 1982–89; Architecture vernaculaire en Bretagne (15e–20e siècles), Rennes and tour, 1984–89. *Publications:* La Maison traditionnelle (bibliog.), 1978; The Vernacular Architecture of Brittany, 1982; (with Michael Jones) Aimer les Châteaux de Bretagne, 1991 (trans. English and German); (with Michael Jones) Les Châteaux de Bretagne, 1992; (jtly) Manorial Domestic Buildings in England and Northern France, 1993; Historic Buildings and Dating by Dendrochronology, 1994; papers in sci., archaeol and ethnol jls. *Recreations:* food, wine, music, walking, swimming. *Address:* Department of Archaeology, University of Reading, Reading RG6 2AA. *T:* Reading (01734) 318132; 11 Avondale Road, Fleet, Hants GU13 9BH. *T:* and *Fax:* Fleet (01252) 614300. *Club:* Athenæum.

MEISEL, Prof. John, OC 1989; PhD; FRSC; President, Royal Society of Canada, 1992–95; Sir Edward Peacock Professor of Political Science, Queen's University, Canada, 1983–94, now Emeritus; Co-Editor (formerly Editor), International Political Science Review, since 1970; *b* 23 Oct. 1923; *s* of Fryda S. Meisel and Anne Meisel (*née* Heller); *m* 1949, Murie A. Kelly (decd). *Educ:* Pickering Coll.; Univ. of Toronto (BA, MA); LSE (PhD). FRSC 1974. Political scientist; Queen's University, Canada: Instructor to Prof., 1949–79; Hardy Prof. of Political Science, 1963–79. Vis. Prof., Yale, 1976–77; Commonwealth Dist. Vis. Prof., UK, 1978. Chm., Canadian Radio-TV and Telecommunications Commn, 1980–83. President: Canadian Pol. Sci. Assoc., 1973–74; Social Sci. Fedn of Canada, 1975–76. Canada Medals: Confedn Centennial, 1967; 125th Anniv. Confedn, 1992; Silver Jubilee Medal, 1977. *Publications:* The Canadian General Election of 1957, 1962; Papers on the 1962 Election, 1964; Working Papers on Canadian Politics, 1972; (with Vincent Lemieux) Ethnic Relations in Canadian Voluntary Associations, 1972; Cleavages, Parties and Values in Canada, 1974; (with Jean Laponce) Debating the Constitution, 1994; numerous articles in acad. jls. *Recreations:* visual and performing arts, swimming, cross-country ski-ing, hiking, bird watching, flower admiring, indoor gardening, printed word. *Address:* Colimaison, Tichborne, Ontario K0H 2V0, Canada. *T:* (613) 2792380, *Fax:* (613) 2793391; Queen's University, Kingston, Ontario K7L 3N6, Canada. *T:* (613) 5456227, *Fax:* (613) 5456848. *Club:* Cercle Universitaire (Ottawa).

MEIXNER, Helen Ann Elizabeth, (Mrs J. E. C. Thornton); JP; Deputy Director, Professional Services and Head, Consultancy Group, British Council, since 1994; *b* 26 May 1941; *d* of Henry Gerard and Valerie Meixner; *m* Jack Edward Clive Thornton, *qv*. *Educ:* Sydney C of E Grammar Sch. for Girls, Darlinghurst; Univ. of Queensland (BA 1961). Teacher, Abbotsleigh Girls' Sch., Wahroonga, 1962; Educn Asst, ABC, 1963–64; joined British Council, 1966; Recruitment Unit, Zagreb Office, Exchanges, Courses, Staff Recruitment, Dir-Gen's and Personnel Depts; Head, Design, Production and Publishing Dept, 1984–86; Dep. Dir, Personnel and Head, Personnel Dept, 1986–91; Dir of Libraries, Books and Information Div., 1991–94. Mem. Council, Ranfurly Liby Service, 1991–94. Dir, Cornerhouse, Manchester, 1993–. JP Inner London, 1988. *Recreations:* music, reading, walking, travel. *Address:* 131 Dalling Road, W6 0ET. *T:* 0181–748 7692; 15 Chepstow House, Chepstow Street, Manchester M1 5JF.

MELANESIA, Archbishop of, since 1994; **Most Rev. Ellison Leslie Pogo;** Bishop of Central Melanesia, since 1994; *b* 9 Dec. 1947; *s* of Stephen Zaku and Sarah Duri; *m* 1978, Roslyn (*née* Kairopo); one *s* two *d*. *Educ:* Bishop Patteson Theol Coll., Kohimarama, Solomon Is; St John's Theol Coll., Auckland, NZ (LTh). Asst Priest, Anderson's Bay, Dunedin, 1979–81; Bishop of Ysabel, Solomon Is, 1981–94. Mem., Exec. Cttee, Pacific Conf. of Churches, 1984–; Comr for Pacific Region, Unit IV (Sharing and Service), WCC, 1989–; Ex Officio Mem., Pacific Ecumenical Regl Gp, 1989–. Chm., Bd of Govs, Pacific Theol Coll., Suva, Fiji, 1994–. *Recreations:* reading, gardening. *Address:* Archbishop's House, PO Box 19, Honiara, Solomon Islands. *T:* (office) 21892, 21137, (home) 22339.

MELANESIA, CENTRAL, Bishop of; *see* Melanesia, Archbishop of.

MELBOURNE, Archbishop of, and Metropolitan of the Province of Victoria, since 1990; **Most Rev. Keith Rayner,** AO 1987; Primate of Australia, since 1991 (Acting Primate, 1989–91); *b* 22 Nov. 1929; *s* of Sidney and Gladys Rayner, Brisbane; *m* 1963, Audrey Fletcher; one *s* two *d*. *Educ:* C of E Grammar Sch., Brisbane; Univ. of Queensland (BA 1951; PhD 1964). Deacon, 1953; Priest, 1953. Chaplain, St Francis' Theol Coll., Brisbane, 1954; Mem., Brotherhood of St John, Dalby, 1955–58; Vice-Warden, St John's Coll., Brisbane, 1958; Rotary Foundn Fellow, Harvard Univ., 1958–59; Vicar, St Barnabas', Sunnybank, 1959–63; Rector, St Peter's, Wynnum, 1963–69; Bishop of Wangaratta, 1969–75; Archbishop of Adelaide and Metropolitan of South Australia, 1975–90. Pres., Christian Conference of Asia, 1977–81; Chm., International Anglican Theological and Doctrinal Commission, 1980–88. Hon. ThD Aust. Coll. of Theology,

1987. *Recreation:* tennis. *Address:* Bishopscourt, 120 Clarendon Street, East Melbourne, Vic 3002, Australia.

MELBOURNE, Archbishop of, (RC), since 1974; **Most Rev. Thomas Francis Little,** KBE 1977; DD, STD; *b* 30 Nov. 1925; *s* of Gerald Thompson Little and Kathleen McCormack. *Educ:* St Patrick's Coll., Ballarat; Corpus Christi Coll., Werribee; Pontifical Urban Coll., Rome. STD Rome, 1953. Priest 1950; Asst Priest, Carlton, 1953–55; Secretary, Apostolic Deleg. to Aust., NZ and Oceania, 1955–59; Asst Priest, St Patrick's Cathedral, Melbourne, 1959–65; Dean, 1965–70; Episcopal Vicar for Lay Apostolate, 1969; Pastor, St Ambrose, Brunswick, 1971–73; Auxiliary Bishop, Archdiocese of Melbourne, 1973. STD *hc,* Melbourne Coll. of Divinity, 1992. *Address:* St Patrick's Cathedral, Melbourne, Vic 3002, Australia. *T:* (3) 96670377.

MELBOURNE, Assistant Bishops of; *see* Curnow, Rt Rev. A. W.; Grant, Rt Rev. J. A.; Stewart, Rt Rev. J. C.; Wilson, Rt Rev. J. W.

MELCHETT, 4th Baron *cr* 1928; **Peter Robert Henry Mond;** Bt 1910; Executive Director, Greenpeace UK, since 1989 (Chairman, 1986–89); *b* 24 Feb. 1948; *s* of 3rd Baron Melchett and of Sonia Elizabeth Sinclair, *qv; S* father, 1973. *Educ:* Eton; Pembroke Coll., Cambridge (BA); Keele Univ. (MA). Res. Worker, LSE and Addiction Res. Unit, 1973–74. A Lord in Waiting (Govt Whip), 1974–75; Parly Under-Sec. of State, DoI, 1975–76; Minister of State, NI Office, 1976–79. Chm., working party on pop festivals, 1975–76; Chm., Community Industry, 1979–85. Chm., Wildlife Link, 1979–87; Vice-Pres., Ramblers' Assoc., 1984– (Pres., 1981–84). *Address:* House of Lords, SW1A 0PW.

MELCHIOR-BONNET, Christian; author; Director and founder, since 1946, Historia, Journal de la France; *b* Marseille, 10 April 1904; *s* of Daniel-Joseph Melchior-Bonnet and Geneviève (*née* de Luxer); *m* 1930, Bernardine Paul-Dubois-Taine (*g d* of the historian Taine, herself a historian, author of several historical works, recipient of Grand Prix Gobert of Académie Française); two *s* one *d. Educ:* St Jean de Béthune, Versailles; Ecole du Louvre, Faculté de droit de Paris. Secretary to Pierre de Nolhac, de l'Académie française, historian, at Jacquemart-André museum, 1927–36; formerly, Editor-in-Chief, Petit Journal, 1936–45 and Flambeau; Dir, historical and religious series of Editions Flammarion, 1932–46; Literary Dir, Fayard editions, 1946–67; Director of the reviews: Oeuvres Libres, 1946–64; Historia, 1946–; A la Page, 1964–69; Co-dir, Jardin des Arts; Literary Adviser to Nouvelles Littéraires, 1946–70. Privy Chamberlain to every Pope since 1946, incl. Pope John Paul II. Membre du jury: Prix Historia; Prix de la Fondation de France; Prix des Ambassadeurs. Officier de la Légion d'honneur; Commandeur de l'Ordre national du Mérite; Officier des Arts et des Lettres, et décorations étrangères. Prix du Rayonnement, Académie française, 1963. *Publications:* Scènes et portraits historiques de Chateaubriand, 1928; Les Mémoires du Comte Alexandre de Tilly, ancien page de la reine Marie-Antoinette, 1929; Les Mémoires du Cardinal de Retz, 1929; Principes d'action de Salazar, 1956; Le Napoléon de Chateaubriand, 1969; et nombreuses éditions de mémoires historiques. *Address:* 17 Boulevard de Beauséjour, 75016 Paris, France.

MELDRUM, Maj.-Gen. Bruce, CB 1991; OBE 1986; Chief of New Zealand General Staff, 1989–92; *b* 15 March 1938; *s* of late Ian Maitland Meldrum and of Vivienne Meldrum; *m* 1960, Janet Louise Boyling; one *s* one *d. Educ:* Feilding Agricl High Sch., NZ; RMC Duntroon. Lieut, RNZAC, 1959; Troop Comdr, Queen Alexandra's Regt, 1960–62; RAC Sch. of Tank Technol., UK, 1962–63; Sen. Instructor, then Chief Instructor, Sch. of Armour, Waiouru, 1963–66; OC 1 Armoured Sqdn, 1966–68; with US 11th Armoured Cavalry Regt, S Vietnam, Nov.–Dec. 1966; Staff Officer: Trng Directorate, Army HQ, 1968–69; HQ NZ Force Far East, Singapore, 1969–71; HQ NZ V Force, Saigon, 1971–72; Australian Comd and Staff Coll., 1972; Bde Maj., HQ 1 Inf. Bde, 1972–74; Lt-Col 1974; Staff Officer, HQ Field Force Comd, 1974–76; Dir, Ops and Plans, Army Gen. Staff, 1976–78; Australian JSSC, 1978; Special Projects Officer, 1978–80; Col 1980; Defence Advr, NZ High Commn, Kuala Lumpur, 1980–83; Comdr, Army Trng Gp, 1983–85; rcds, 1985–86; DCGS, 1986–89; Brig. 1987; Maj.-Gen. 1989. *Recreations:* golf, walking, reading. *Address:* 16/32 Hobson Street, Thorndon, Wellington, New Zealand. *T:* (4) 4991915. *Clubs:* Wellington, Wellesley (Wellington, NZ).

MELDRUM, Graham, CBE 1994; QFSM 1989; Chief Fire Officer, West Midlands Fire Service, since 1990; *b* 23 Oct. 1945; *s* of George Meldrum and Agnes (*née* Gordon); *m* 1964, Catherine Meier; one *s* one *d. Educ:* Inverurie Acad., Aberdeenshire. MIFireE. Fireman to Station Officer, London Fire Bde, 1963–73; Instructor, in the rank of Asst Divl Officer, Fire Service Coll., 1973–74; Divl Officer III, Hants Fire Service, 1974–76; Tyne and Wear: Divl Officer II, 1976–79; Divl Officer I, 1979–80; Sen. Divl Officer, 1980–83; West Midlands: Asst Chief Officer, 1983–84; Dep. Chief Fire Officer, 1984–90. Pres., Chief and Asst Chief Officers' Assoc., 1994–; Chm., Fire Services Nat. Benevolent Fund, 1994–. *Publications:* papers on fire engrg in jls. *Recreations:* computers, motor-cycling, railways, industrial archaeology, community work. *Address:* c/o West Midlands Fire Service, Lancaster Circus, Queensway, Birmingham B4 7DE. *T:* 0121–380 6001.

MELDRUM, Keith Cameron, CB 1995; Chief Veterinary Officer, Ministry of Agriculture, Fisheries and Food, since 1988; *b* 19 April 1937; *s* of Dr Walter James Meldrum and Mrs Eileen Lydia Meldrum; *m* 1st, 1962, Rosemary Ann (*née* Crawford) (marr. diss. 1980); two *s* one *d*; 2nd, 1982, Vivien Mary (*née* Fisher). *Educ:* Uppingham; Edinburgh Univ. Qualified as veterinary surgeon, 1961; general practice, Scunthorpe, 1961–63; joined MAFF, Oxford, 1963; Divl Vet. Officer, Tolworth, 1972, Leamington Spa, 1975; Dep. Regional Vet. Officer, Nottingham, 1978; Regional Vet. Officer, Tolworth, 1980; Asst Chief Vet. Officer, Tolworth, 1983; Dir of Vet. Field Service, 1986. *Recreations:* competitive target rifle shooting, outdoor activities. *Address:* Ministry of Agriculture, Fisheries and Food, Hook Rise South, Tolworth, Surbiton, Surrey KT6 7NF. *T:* 0181–330 8050. *Clubs:* Farmers'; North London Rifle (Bisley).

MELGUND, Viscount; Gilbert Timothy George Lariston Elliot-Murray-Kynynmound; *b* 1 Dec. 1953; *s* and *heir* of 6th Earl of Minto, *qv; m* 1983, Diana, *yr d* of Brian Trafford; two *s* one *d* (and one *s* decd). *Educ:* Eton; North East London Polytechnic (BSc Hons 1983). ARICS. Lieut, Scots Guards, 1972–76. Mem., Royal Co. of Archers, Queen's Body Guard for Scotland, 1983–. *Heir: s* Hon. Gilbert Francis Elliot-Murray-Kynynmound, *b* 15 Aug. 1984. *Club:* White's.

MELHUISH, Sir (Michael) Ramsay, KBE 1993; CMG 1982; HM Diplomatic Service, retired; *b* 17 March 1932; *s* of late Henry Whitfield Melhuish and Jeanette Ramsay Pender Melhuish; *m* 1961, Stella Phillips; two *s* two *d. Educ:* Royal Masonic Sch., Bushey; St John's Coll., Oxford (BA). FO, 1955; MECAS, 1956; Third Sec., Bahrain, 1957; FO, 1959; Second Sec., Singapore, 1961; First Sec. (Commercial) and Consul, Prague, 1963; First Sec. and Head of Chancery, Bahrain, 1966; DSAO (later FCO), 1968; First Sec., Washington, 1970; Counsellor, Amman, 1973; Head of N America Dept, FCO, 1976; Counsellor (Commercial), Warsaw, 1979–82; Ambassador, Kuwait, 1982–85; High Comr, Zimbabwe, 1985–89; Ambassador, Thailand, 1989–92. Head, EC Monitor Mission, Zagreb, July–Dec. 1992. *Recreations:* tennis, golf. *Address:* 9 Greycoat Gardens, Greycoat Place, SW1P 2QA. *Club:* United Oxford & Cambridge University.

MELIA, Dr Terence Patrick, CBE 1993; Chief Inspector, Further Education Funding Council, since 1993; *b* 17 Dec. 1934; *s* of John and Kathleen Melia (*née* Traynor); *m* 1976, Madeline (*née* Carney); one *d. Educ:* Sir John Deane's Grammar Sch., Northwich; Leeds Univ. (PhD). CChem, FRSC. Technical Officer, ICI, 1961–64; Lectr, then Sen. Lectr, Salford Univ., 1964–70; Principal, North Lindsey Coll. of Technology, 1970–74; HM Inspector of Schools, 1974–92: Regional Staff Inspector, 1982–84; Chief Inspector, Further and Higher Educn, 1985–86; Chief Inspector, Higher Educn, 1985–91; Sen. Chief Inspector, HM Inspectorate of Schs, 1991–92. Vis. Prof., Leeds Metropolitan Univ., 1993–. *Publications:* Masers and Lasers, 1967; papers on thermodynamics of polymerisation, thermal properties of polymers, effects of ionizing radiation, chemical thermodynamics, nucleation kinetics, thermal properties of transition metal compounds and gas kinetics. *Recreations:* golf, gardening.

MELINSKY, Rev. Canon (Michael Arthur) Hugh; Principal, Northern Ordination Course, 1978–88; *b* 25 Jan. 1924; *s* of late M. M. Melinsky and Mrs D. M. Melinsky; *m* 1949, Renate (*née* Ruhemann); three *d. Educ:* Whitgift Sch., Croydon; Christ's Coll., Cambridge (BA 1947, MA 1949); London Univ. Inst. of Education (TDip 1949); Ripon Hall, Oxford. Asst Master: Normanton Grammar Sch., 1949–52; Lancaster Royal Grammar Sch., 1952–57. Curate: Wimborne Minster, 1957–59; Wareham, 1959–61; Vicar of St Stephen's, Norwich, 1961–68; Chaplain of Norfolk and Norwich Hosp., 1961–68; Hon. Canon and Canon Missioner of Norwich, 1968–73; Chief Sec., ACCM, 1973–77. Chairman: C of E Commn on Euthanasia, 1972–75; Inst. of Religion and Medicine, 1973–77; Mem., Social Policy Cttee, C of E Bd for Social Responsibilty, 1982–; Mem. Cttee for Theological Educn, ACCM, 1985–88. Hon. Res. Fellow, Dept of Theol Studies, Manchester Univ., 1984. *Publications:* The Modern Reader's Guide to Matthew, 1963; the Modern Reader's Guide to Luke, 1963; Healing Miracles, 1967; (ed) Religion and Medicine, 1970; (ed) Religion and Medicine 2, 1973; Patterns of Ministry, 1974; (ed) On Dying Well, 1975; Foreword to Marriage, 1984; The Shape of the Ministry, 1992. *Address:* 15 Parson's Mead, Norwich, Norfolk NR4 6PG. *T:* Norwich (01603) 455042.

MELLAART, James, FSA; FBA 1980; Lecturer in Anatolian Archaeology, Institute of Archaeology, University of London, 1964–91; *b* 14 Nov. 1925; *s* of J. H. J. Mellaart and A. D. Van Der Beek; *m* 1954, Arlette Meryem Cenani; one *s. Educ:* University College, London. BA Hons (Ancient Hist. and Egyptology) 1951. Archaeol field surveys in Anatolia as Scholar and Fellow of British Inst. of Archaeol. at Ankara, 1951–56; excavations at Hacilar, 1957–60; Asst Dir, British Inst. of Archaeol. at Ankara, 1959–61; excavations at Çatal Hüyük, Turkey, 1961–63 and 1965; Foreign Specialist, Lectr at Istanbul Univ., 1961–63. Corresp. Mem., German Archaeol Inst., 1961. *Publications:* Earliest Civilisations of the Near East, 1965; The Chalcolithic and Early Bronze Ages in the Near East and Anatolia, 1966; Çatal Hüyük, a Neolithic Town in Anatolia, 1967; Excavations at Hacilar, 1970; The Neolithic of the Near East, 1975; The Archaeology of Ancient Turkey, 1978; Çatal Hüyük and Anatolian Kilims, 1989; (with Ann Murray) Beycesultan, vol. III 2, 1995; chapters in Cambridge Ancient History; numerous articles in Anatolian Studies, etc. *Recreations:* geology, Turkish ceramics, clan history, Gaelic and classical music, Seljuk art. *Address:* 13 Lichen Court, 79 Queen's Drive, N4 2BH. *T:* 0181–802 6984.

MELLARS, Paul Anthony, ScD; FBA 1990; Fellow, since 1981, President, since 1992, Corpus Christi College, Cambridge; University Reader in Archaeology, Cambridge University, since 1991 (University Lecturer, 1981–91); *b* 29 Oct. 1939; *s* of Herbert and Elaine Mellars; *m* 1969, Anny Chanut. *Educ:* Woodhouse Grammar Sch., Sheffield; Fitzwilliam Coll., Cambridge (Exhibnr; BA 1st Cl. Hons Archaeol. and Anthropol. 1962; MA 1965; PhD 1967; ScD 1988). FSA 1977. Sir James Knott Res. Fellow, Univ. of Newcastle upon Tyne, 1968–70; University of Sheffield: Lectr in Prehistory and Archaeol., 1970–75; Sen. Lectr, 1975–80; Reader, 1980–81. British Academy: Res. Reader, 1989–91; Reckitt Archaeol. Lectr, 1991; Vis. Prof., SUNY (Binghamton), 1974; Vis. Fellow, ANU, 1981; Danish Res. Council Vis. Lectr, Copenhagen and Aarhus Univs, 1985. Pres., Hunter Archaeol. Soc., 1975–80; Vice-Pres., Prehistoric Soc., 1992–; Chm., Archaeol. Sci. Cttee, Council for British Archaeol., 1980–87. *Publications:* (ed) The Early Postglacial Settlement of Northern Europe, 1976; Excavations of Oronsay, 1987; (ed) Research Priorities of Archaeological Science, 1987; (ed) The Human Revolution, 1989; (ed) The Emergence of Modern Humans, 1990; (ed) Middle Palaeolithic Adaptations in Eurasia, 1991; (ed) The Origin of Modern Humans and the Impact of Science-based Dating, 1992; articles in archaeol. jls. *Recreations:* music, foreign travel. *Address:* Long Gable, Elsworth, Cambs CB3 8HX. *T:* Elsworth (019547) 275; Department of Archaeology, Downing Street, Cambridge CB2 3DZ. *T:* Cambridge (01223) 333520.

MELLERS, Prof. Wilfrid Howard, OBE 1982; DMus; Composer; Professor of Music, University of York, 1964–81, now Emeritus; *b* 26 April 1914; *s* of Percy Wilfrid Mellers and Hilda Maria (*née* Lawrence); *m* 1st, 1940, Vera Muriel (*née* Hobbs) (marr. diss.); 2nd, 1950, Peggy Pauline (*née* Lewis) (marr. diss. 1975); two *d*; 3rd, 1987, Robin Hildyard. *Educ:* Leamington Coll.; Downing Coll., Cambridge. BA Cantab 1939; MA Cantab 1945; DMus Birmingham 1962. FGSM 1982. Supervisor in English and College Lecturer in Music, Downing Coll., Cambridge, 1945–48; Staff Tutor in Music, Extra Mural Dept, University of Birmingham, 1949–60; Visiting Mellon Prof. of Music, University of Pittsburgh, USA, 1960–62; Vis. Prof., City Univ., 1984–. Hon. DPhil City, 1981. *Publications:* Music and Society, 1946; Studies in Contemporary Music, 1948; François Couperin and the French Classical Tradition, 1950, 2nd edn 1987; Music in the Making, 1951; Man and his Music, 1957; Harmonious Meeting, 1964; Music in a New Found Land, 1964; Caliban Reborn: renewal in 20th-century music, 1967 (US), 1968 (GB); Twilight of the Gods: the Beatles in retrospect, 1973; Bach and the Dance of God, 1981; Beethoven and the Voice of God, 1983; A Darker Shade of Pale: a backdrop to Bob Dylan, 1984; Angels of the Night: popular female singers of our time, 1986; The Masks of Orpheus, 1987; Vaughan Williams and the Vision of Albion, 1989; Le Jardin Parfumé: homage to Federico Mompou, 1990; The Music of Percy Grainger, 1992; The Music of Francis Poulenc, 1993; *compositions* include: Canticum Incarnations, 1960; Alba in 9 Metamorphoses, 1962; Rose of May, 1964; Life-Cycle, 1967; Yeibichai, 1968; Canticum Resurrectionis, 1968; Natalis Invicti Solis, 1969; The Word Unborn, 1970; The Ancient Wound, 1970; De Vegetabilis et Animalibus, 1971; Venery for Six Plus, 1971; Sun-flower: the Quaternity of William Blake, 1972–73; The Key of the Kingdom, 1976; Rosae Hermeticae, 1977; Shaman Songs, 1980; The Wellspring of Loves, 1981; Hortus Rosarium, 1986. *Address:* Oliver Sheldon House, 17 Aldwark, York YO1 2BX. *T:* York (01904) 638686.

MELLERSH, Air Vice-Marshal Francis Richard Lee, CB 1977; DFC 1943 and Bar 1944; Air Officer Flying and Officer Training, HQ Training Command, 1974–77; *b* 30 July 1922; *s* of Air Vice-Marshal Sir Francis Mellersh, KBE, AFC; *m* 1967, Elisabeth Nathalie Komaroff; two *s* one *d. Educ:* Winchester House Sch.; Imperial Service College. Joined RAFVR, 1940; Nos 29, 600 and 96 Sqdns, 1941–45; various staff and flying appts, 1946–57; Dirg Staff, RAF Staff Coll., 1957–59; Staff of Chief of Defence Staff, 1959–61; Dep. Dir Ops (F), 1961–63; OC RAF West Raynham, 1965–67; Chief Current Plans, SHAPE, 1967–68; RCDS 1969; SASO, RAF Germany, 1970–72; ACDS (Ops), 1972–74.

Address: Rother Lea, Lossenham Lane, Newenden, Kent TN18 5QD. *Club:* Royal Air Force.

MELLING, Cecil Thomas, CBE 1955; MScTech, CEng, Hon. FIEE, FIMechE, Sen. FInstE, CIMgt; *b* Wigan, 12 Dec. 1899; *s* of William and Emma Melling; *m* 1929, Ursula Thorburn Thorburn; two *s* one *d* (and one *s* and one *d* decd). *Educ:* Manchester Central High Sch.; College of Technology, University of Manchester. 2nd Lieut RE 1918. Metropolitan Vickers Electrical Co. Ltd, 1920–34; Yorkshire Electric Power Co., 1934–35; Edmundson's Electricity Corporation Ltd, 1935–43. Borough Electrical Engineer, Luton, 1943–48. Chm., Eastern Electricity Board, 1948–57; Member: British Electricity Authority, 1952–53 and 1957; Electricity Council, 1957–61 (a Dep. Chm., 1961–65); Clean Air Council, 1961–64; Adv. Cttee on R&D, 1961–64. Chm. Utilization Sect., Institution of Electrical Engineers, 1949–50, Vice-Pres., IEE, 1957–62, Pres., 1962–63; Chm. of Council, British Electrical Development Association, 1951–52; Founder-Chm. 1945, and Pres. 1947, Luton Electrical Soc.; Pres. Ipswich & District Electrical Assoc., 1948–57; Chm. of Council, British Electrical and Allied Industries Research Assoc., 1953–55; Pres. Assoc. of Supervising Electrical Engineers, 1952–54; Chm., British Nat. Cttee for Electro-Heat, 1958–68; Mem. Council, BIM, 1961–78; Vice-Pres. Internat. Union for Electro-Heat, 1964–68, Pres., 1968–72; Pres., Manchester Technol. Assoc., 1967; Pres., British Electrotechnical Approvals Bd, 1974–84 (Chm., 1964–73); Chm., Electricity Supply Industry Trg Bd, 1965–68; Vice-Pres., Union of Internat. Engineering Organisations, 1969–75; Pres., Soc. of Retired Chartered Engrs in SE Kent, 1988– (Founder Chm., 1982–84). *Publications:* Light in the East, 1987; Memories of an Edwardian Childhood, 1993 (family circulation); contribs to Proc. Engineering Instns and Confs. *Address:* Durham Suite, The Grand, Folkestone CT20 2LR. *Club:* Athenæum.

MELLING, Dr Jack; Director, Centre for Applied Microbiology and Research, Porton Down, since 1993; *b* 8 Feb. 1940; *s* of John Melling and Mary (*née* Marsden); *m* 1967, Susan Ewart. *Educ:* Rivington and Blackrod Grammar Sch.; Manchester Univ. (BSc, MSc); Bath Univ. (PhD). FRPharmS 1977; FIBiol 1979. Res. Asst, Bath Univ., 1965–68; Lectr, Heriot-Watt Univ., 1968–69; SSO, then PSO, MoD, 1969–79; Dir, Vaccine Res. and Prodn Lab., PHLS, 1979–87; Dep. Dir, Centre for Applied Microbiology and Res., Porton Down, 1987–93. Visiting Professor: Rutgers Univ., 1979–84; Aston Univ., 1981–. Editor, Jl of Chem. Technol. and Biotechnol., 1985–. Lampitt Medal, SCI, 1993. *Publications:* Continuous Culture Applications and New Fields, 1977; Adhesion of Micro-organisms to Surfaces, 1979; The Microbial Cell Surface and Adhesion, 1981; Biosafety in Industrial Technology, 1994; papers in scientific jls. *Recreations:* ski-ing, shooting, walking. *Address:* Centre for Applied Microbiology and Research, Porton Down, Salisbury, Wilts SP4 0JG. *T:* Idmiston (01980) 612100. *Clubs:* Royal Society of Medicine; Parkstone Yacht (Poole).

MELLISH, family name of **Baron Mellish.**

MELLISH, Baron *cr* 1985 (Life Peer), of Bermondsey in Greater London; **Robert Joseph Mellish;** PC 1967; *b* 1913; *m* 1938, Anne Elizabeth, *d* of George Warner; five *s.* Served War of 1939–45, Captain RE, SEAC. Official, TGWU, 1938–46. MP (Lab 1946–82, Ind. 1982) Bermondsey, Rotherhithe 1946–50, Bermondsey 1950–74, Southwark, Bermondsey 1974–82. PPS to Minister of Pensions, 1951 (to Minister of Supply, 1950–51); Jt Parly Sec., Min. of Housing, 1964–67; Minister of Public Building and Works, 1967–69; Parly Sec. to Treasury and Govt Chief Whip, 1969–70 and 1974–76; Opposition Chief Whip, 1970–74. Chm., London Regional Lab. Party, 1956–77. Dep. Chm., LDDC, 1981–85. *Address:* House of Lords, SW1A 0PW.

MELLITT, Prof. Brian, FEng 1990; Director of Engineering and Production, Railtrack PLC, since 1995; *b* 29 May 1940; *s* of John and Nellie Mellitt; *m* 1961, Lyn Waring; one *s* one *d.* *Educ:* Loughborough Univ.; Imperial College, London Univ. (BTechEng, DIC). FIEE, FIMechE, FIRSE. Student apprentice, 1956, Junior Engineer, 1962, R&D Engineer, 1964, English Electric Co.; Lectr and Sen. Lectr, Huddersfield Polytechnic, 1966–67; Research Dept, British Rlys Bd, 1968–70; University of Birmingham: Lectr, 1971; Sen. Lectr, 1979; Prof., 1982; Head of Dept of Electronic and Electrical Engrg, 1986; Dean, Faculty of Engrng, 1987–88; Hon. Prof. of Electronic Engrg, 1989; Dir Engrg, London Underground Ltd, 1989–95; Dir, Metro Power, 1990–95. Consultant Engineer, railway related organisations, 1972–88. Editor, IEE Procs (B), 1978–. Hon. DTech Loughborough, 1991. Leonardo da Vinci Award, Italian Assoc. for Industrial Design, 1989. *Publications:* contribs on electric railway topics to learned jls. *Recreation:* bridge. *Address:* The Priory, 36 Church Street, Stilton, Cambs PE7 3RF. *T:* Peterborough (01733) 240573. *Club:* Athenæum.

MELLON, Sir James, KCMG 1988 (CMG 1979); HM Diplomatic Service, retired; Chairman: Scottish Homes, since 1989; Thamesmead Town, since 1993; *b* 25 Jan. 1929; *m* 1st, 1956, Frances Murray (*d* 1976); one *s* three *d*; 2nd, 1979, Mrs Philippa Shuttleworth (*née* Hartley). *Educ:* Glasgow Univ (MA). Dept of Agriculture for Scotland, 1953–60; Agricultural Attaché, Copenhagen and The Hague, 1960–63; FO, 1963–64; Head of Chancery, Dakar, 1964–66; UK Delegn to European Communities, 1967–72; Counsellor, 1970; Hd of Sci. and Technol. Dept, FCO, 1973–75; Commercial Counsellor, East Berlin, 1975–76; Head of Trade Relations and Export Dept, FCO, 1976–78; High Comr in Ghana and Ambassador to Togo, 1978–83; Ambassador to Denmark, 1983–86; Dir-Gen. for Trade and Investment, USA, and Consul-Gen., New York, 1986–88. *Publications:* A Danish Gospel, 1986; Og Gamle Danmark, 1992. *Address:* Scottish Homes, Thistle House, 91 Haymarket Terrace, Edinburgh EH12 5HE. *Club:* New (Edinburgh).

MELLON, Paul, Hon. KBE 1974; Hon. RA 1978; Hon. Trustee, National Gallery of Art, Washington, DC, since 1985 (Trustee, 1945–85; President, 1963–79; Chairman of Trustees, 1979–85); *b* 11 June 1907; *s* of late Andrew William Mellon and late Nora McMullen Mellon; *m* 1st, 1935, Mary Conover (decd); one *s* one *d*; 2nd, 1948, Rachel Lambert. *Educ:* Choate Sch., Wallingford, Conn; Yale Univ.; Univ. of Cambridge (BA 1931; MA 1938; Hon. LLD 1983). Trustee: Andrew W. Mellon Foundn (successor to merged Old Dominion and Avalon Foundns), 1969–; Virginia Mus. of Fine Arts, Richmond, Va, 1938–68, 1969–79. Fellow, Amer. Acad. of Arts and Scis, 1992; Member: Amer. Philosophical Soc., Philadelphia, 1971; Grolier Soc.; Soc. of Dilettanti; Roxburghe Club. Hon. Citizen, University of Vienna, 1965. Yale Medal, 1953; Horace Marden Albright Scenic Preservation Medal, 1957; Distinguished Service to Arts Award, Nat. Inst. Arts and Letters, 1962; Benjamin Franklin Medal, Royal Society of Arts, 1965, Benjamin Franklin Fellow, 1969; Alumni Seal Prize Award, Choate Sch., 1966; Skowhegan Gertrude Vanderbilt Whitney Award, 1972; Nat. Medal of Arts, USA, 1985; Medal in Architecture, Thomas Jefferson Meml Foundn, 1989; Hadrian Award, World Monuments Fund, 1989; Benjamin Franklin Award, Amer. Philosophical Soc., 1989; Medal for Distinguished Philanthropy, Amer. Assoc. of Museums, 1993. Hon. FRIBA 1978; Hon. FBA 1994. Hon. DLitt Oxford Univ., 1961; Hon. LLD Carnegie Inst. of Tech., 1967; Hon. DHL Yale, 1967; Hon. DVM London, 1991. *Publication:* (with John Baskett) Reflections in a Silver Spoon: a memoir, 1992. *Recreations:* fox-hunting, thoroughbred breeding and racing, sailing, swimming. *Address:* (office) 1729 H Street NW, Washington, DC 20006, USA; (home) Oak Spring, 8554 Oak Spring Road, Upperville, VA 22176. *Clubs:* Buck's; Travellers' (Paris); Jockey, Knickerbocker, Links, Racquet and Tennis, River, Yale (New York); Metropolitan, 1925 F Street (Washington).

MELLOR, David, OBE 1981; DesRCA; RDI 1962; FCSD; designer, manufacturer and retailer; Chairman, Crafts Council, 1982–84; *b* 5 Oct. 1930; *s* of Colin Mellor; *m* 1966, Fiona MacCarthy; one *s* one *d.* *Educ:* Sheffield College of Art; Royal College of Art (DesRCA and Silver Medal, 1953, Hon. Fellow 1966); British School at Rome. Set up silver-smithing workshop, Sheffield, 1954; designer and maker of silver for Worshipful Co. of Goldsmiths, Cutlers' Co., Southwell Minster, Essex Univ., Darwin Coll., Cambridge, among others, and range of silver tableware for use in British embassies; designer of fountain in bronze for Botanic Gdns, Cambridge, 1970; concurrently opened industrial design office. Consultancies, 1954–, include: Walker & Hall, Abacus Municipal, Glacier Metal, ITT, Post Office, British Rail, James Neill Tools; Cons. to DoE on design of traffic signals, 1965–70, and on design of automatic half-barrier crossing, as result of Gibbens report, 1969; Chm., Design Council Cttee of Inquiry into standards of design in consumer goods in Britain, 1982–84; Mem., Art and Design Working Gp, Nat. Adv. Body for Local Auth. Higher Educn, 1982–84. Trustee: V & A Museum, 1984–88; Peak Park Trust, 1992–. *Work in collections:* Goldsmiths' Co., V&A, Sheffield City Mus., Mus. of Modern Art, NY. *Awards:* Design Centre: 1957, 1959, 1962, 1965, 1966; Design Council: 1974, 1977; RSA Presidential Award for Design Management, 1981. Liveryman, Goldsmiths' Co., 1980; Freeman, Cutlers' Co. of Hallamshire, 1981. FCSD (FSIAD 1964; CSD Medal 1988). Hon. Fellow, Sheffield City Polytechnic, 1979; Hon. DLitt Sheffield Univ., 1986. *Address:* The Round Building, Hathersage, Sheffield S30 1BA. *T:* Hope Valley (01433) 650220.

MELLOR, Prof. David Hugh, FBA 1983; Professor of Philosophy, University of Cambridge, since 1986; Fellow, Darwin College, Cambridge, since 1971 (Vice-Master, 1983–87); *b* 10 July 1938; *s* of Sydney David Mellor and Ethel Naomi Mellor (*née* Hughes). *Educ:* Manchester Grammar School; Pembroke College, Cambridge (BA Nat. Scis and Chem. Eng, 1960; MA; PhD 1968; ScD 1990; MEng 1992); Univ. of Minnesota (Harkness Fellowship; MSc Chem. Eng, 1962). Technical Officer, ICI Central Instruments Lab., 1962–63; Cambridge University: Research Student in Philosophy, Pembroke Coll., 1963–68; Fellow, Pembroke Coll., 1965–70; Univ. Asst Lectr in Philosophy, 1965–70; Univ. Lectr in Philosophy, 1970–83; Univ. Reader in Metaphysics, 1983–85. Vis. Fellow in Philosophy, ANU, 1975; Radcliffe Trust Fellow in Philosophy, 1978–80. Hon. Prof. of Philosophy, Univ. of Keele, 1989–92. President: British Soc. for the Philos. of Science, 1985–87; Aristotelian Soc., 1992–93. Editor: British Journal for the Philosophy of Science, 1968–70; Cambridge Studies in Philosophy, 1978–82. *Publications:* The Matter of Chance, 1971; Real Time, 1981; Matters of Metaphysics, 1991; The Facts of Causation, 1995; articles in Mind, Analysis, Philosophy of Science, Philosophy, Philosophical Review, Ratio, Isis, British Jl for Philosophy of Science, Jl of Philosophy. *Recreation:* theatre. *Address:* 25 Orchard Street, Cambridge CB1 1JS. *T:* Cambridge (01223) 564724.

MELLOR, Rt. Hon. David John, PC 1990; QC 1987; MP (C) Putney, since 1979; *b* 12 March 1949; *s* of Mr and Mrs Douglas H. Mellor; *m* 1974, Judith Mary Hall (marr. diss. 1995); two *s.* *Educ:* Swanage Grammar Sch.; Christ's Coll., Cambridge (BA Hons 1970). FZS 1981. Called to the Bar, Inner Temple, 1972; in practice thereafter. Chm., Cambridge Univ. Conservative Assoc., 1970; contested West Bromwich E, Oct. 1974. PPS to Leader of Commons and Chancellor of the Duchy of Lancaster, 1981; Parly Under-Sec. of State, Dept of Energy, 1981–83, Home Office, 1983–86; Minister of State: Home Office, 1986–87; Foreign and Commonwealth Office, 1987–88; Dept of Health, 1988–89; Home Office, 1989–90; Privy Council Office (Minister for the Arts), 1990; Chief Sec. to the Treasury, 1990–92; Sec. of State for Nat. Heritage, 1992. Sec., Cons. Parly Legal Cttee, 1979–81; Vice-Chm., Greater London Cons. Members Cttee, 1980–81. Special Trustee, Westminster Hosp., 1980–87; Mem. Council, NYO, 1981–86; Mem. Bd, ENO, 1993–. BBC Radio Personality of the Year, Variety Club of GB, 1995. Hon. Associate, BVA, 1986. *Recreations:* classical music, reading, football. *Address:* House of Commons, SW1A 0AA. *T:* 0171–219 5481.

MELLOR, David John; His Honour Judge David Mellor; a Circuit Judge, since 1989; *b* 12 Oct. 1940; *s* of John Robert Mellor and Muriel Mary (*née* Field); *m* 1966, Carol Mary Clement, LLB, BA, AKC, Barrister, *o d* of David Morris Clement, *qv*; two *d.* *Educ:* Plumtree Sch., S Rhodesia; King's Coll., London (LLB). Called to the Bar, Inner Temple, 1964; a Recorder, 1986–89; Principal Judge in Civil Matters for counties of Cambridge, Norfolk and Suffolk, 1991–. *Address:* Norwich Combined Court, Bishopsgate, Norwich. *T:* Norwich (01603) 761776. *Club:* Norfolk (Norwich).

MELLOR, Derrick, CBE 1984; HM Diplomatic Service; retired; re-employed at Foreign and Commonwealth Office, since 1984; Occasional Lecturer, School of Oriental and African Studies, since 1987; *b* 11 Jan. 1926; *s* of William Mellor and Alice (*née* Hurst); *m* 1954, Kathleen (*née* Hodgson); two *s* one *d.* Served Army, 1945–49. Board of Trade, 1950–57; Trade Commission Service, 1958–64: served Kuala Lumpur and Sydney; HM Diplomatic Service, 1964–: served Copenhagen, Caracas, Asuncion (Ambassador, 1979–84) and London; Project Dir for S Amer., GAP Activity Projects (GAP) Ltd. *Recreations:* tennis, golf, skiing. *Address:* Summerford Farmhouse, Withyham, E Sussex TN7 4DA. *T:* Hartfield (01892) 770826. *Clubs:* Commonwealth Trust, Travellers'.

MELLOR, Hugh Wright; Secretary and Director, National Corporation for Care of Old People (now Centre for Policy on Ageing), 1973–80; *b* 11 Aug. 1920; *s* of late William Algernon and Katherine Mildred Mellor; *m* 1944, Winifred Joyce Yates. *Educ:* Leys Sch., Cambridge; London Univ. (BScEcon). Friends Relief Service, 1940–45; Sec., St Albans Council of Social Service, 1945–48; Community Develt Officer, Hemel Hempstead Develt Corp., 1948–50; Asst Sec., Nat. Corp. for Care of Old People, 1951–73. Pres., Hanover Housing Assoc., 1994– (Chm., 1980–85). *Publication:* The Role of Voluntary Organisations in Social Welfare, 1985. *Recreations:* walking, reading, music. *Address:* Lark Rise, Risborough Road, Great Kimble, Aylesbury, Bucks HP17 0XS. *Club:* Commonwealth Trust.

MELLOR, Brig. James Frederick McLean, CBE 1964 (OBE 1945); Norfolk County Commandant, Army Cadet Force, 1969–72; *b* 6 June 1912; *s* of late Col A. J. Mellor, RM, Kingsland, Hereford; *m* 1942, Margaret Ashley, *d* of Major F. A. Phillips, DSO, Holmer, Hereford; one *s* one *d.* *Educ:* Radley Coll.; Faraday House. C. A. Parsons, 1933; Yorkshire Electric Power, 1935. Commnd in Regular Army as Ordnance Mechanical Engr, 1936; France, Belgium, Dunkirk, 1940; Burma, Malaya, HQ, SEAC, 1944–47 (despatches, 1945); Brig. A/Q Northern Comd, 1961–64; Dir of Technical Trng and Inspector of Boys' Trng (Army), MoD, 1966–69; ADC to the Queen, 1963–69. Various appts in engineering and technical educn. Chm., IMechE Eastern Branch, 1971–72. DFH, FIMechE, FIEE. *Address:* Pinewood, Saxlingham Road, Blakeney, Holt, Norfolk NR25 7PB. *T:* Cley (01263) 740990. *Clubs:* Naval and Military, Royal Automobile; Norfolk (Norwich).

MELLOR, Kenneth Wilson, QC 1975; **His Honour Judge Mellor;** a Circuit Judge, since 1984; *b* 4 March 1927; *s* of Samuel Herbert Mellor; *m* 1957, Sheila Gale; one *s* three *d. Educ:* King's College Cambridge (BA 1949; LLB 1950; MA 1951). RNVR, 1944–47 (Sub Lieut). Called to the Bar, Lincoln's Inn, 1950. Dep. Chm., Hereford QS, 1969–71; a Recorder, 1972–84. Chm., Agricultural Land Tribunal (West Midlands). *Address:* 5 Fountain Court, Steelhouse Lane, Birmingham B4 6DR; 1 Paper Buildings, Temple, EC4.

MELLOR, Ronald William, CBE 1984; FEng; FIMechE; Secretary, Institution of Mechanical Engineers, 1987–93; *b* 8 Dec. 1930; *s* of William and Helen Edna Mellor; *m* 1956, Jean Sephton; one *s* one *d. Educ:* Highgate School; King's College London (BSc Eng). Ford Motor Co.: Manager Cortina Product Planning, 1964; Manager Truck Product Planning, 1965; Chief Research Engineer, 1969; Chief Engine Engineer, 1970; Chief Body Engineer, Ford Werke AG, W Germany, 1974; Vice Pres. Car Engineering, Ford of Europe Inc., 1975; Dir, Ford Motor Co. Ltd, 1983–87. Mem., Bd of Govs, Anglia Polytechnic Univ., 1993–. Liveryman, Co. of Carmen, 1990–. Thomas Hawksley Lectr, IMechE, 1983. *Recreation:* yachting.

MELLOWS, Prof. Anthony Roger, TD 1969; PhD, LLD; Solicitor of the Supreme Court, since 1960; Professor of the Law of Property in the University of London, 1974–90, now Emeritus; Chancellor, Order of St John, since 1991; *b* 30 July 1936; *s* of L. B. and M. P. Mellows; *m* 1973, Elizabeth, CStJ, *d* of Ven. B. G. B. Fox, MC, TD, and of Hon. Margaret Joan Fox, *d* of 1st Viscount Davidson, PC, GCVO, CH, CB. *Educ:* King's Coll., London. LLB 1957; LLM 1959; PhD 1962; BD 1968; LLD 1973; Fellow 1980. Commissioned Intelligence Corps (TA), 1959, Captain 1964; served Intell. Corps (TA) and (T&AVR) and on the Staff, 1959–71; RARO, 1971–91. Admitted a solicitor, 1960; private practice, 1960–; Sen. Partner, Messrs Alexanders Easton Kinch. Asst Lectr in Law, King's Coll., London, 1962, Lectr, 1964, Reader, 1971; Dir of Conveyancing Studies, 1969; Dean, Fac. of Laws, Univ. of London, 1981–84, and of Fac. of Laws, KCL, 1981–85; Hd of Dept of Laws, KCL, 1984–87; Mem. Council, KCL, 1972–80. Trustee: Kincardine Foundn, 1972–84; Nineveh Trust, 1985–90; London Law Trust, 1968– (Chm. Trustees); Order of St John and British Red Cross Soc. Jt Cttee, 1987–. AKC, London, 1957; FRSA 1959. GCStJ 1991 (KStJ 1988; CStJ 1985; OStJ 1981; Mem. Council, 1981–88; Registrar, 1988–91). Freeman of the City of London, 1963. *Publications:* Local Searches and Enquiries, 1964, 2nd edn 1967; Conveyancing Searches, 1964, 2nd edn 1975; Land Charges, 1966; The Preservation and Felling of Trees, 1964; The Trustee's Handbook, 1965, 3rd edn 1975; Taxation for Executors and Trustees, 1967, 6th edn 1984; (jtly) The Modern Law of Trusts, 1966, 5th edn 1983; The Law of Succession, 1970, 4th edn 1983; Taxation of Land Transactions, 1973, 3rd edn 1982. *Address:* 22 Devereux Court, Temple Bar, WC2R 3JJ. *Club:* Athenæum.

MELLY, (Alan) George (Heywood); professional jazz singer; with John Chilton's Feetwarmers, since 1974; *b* 17 Aug. 1926; *s* of Francis Heywood and Edith Maud Melly; *m* 1955, Victoria Vaughan (marr. diss. 1962); one *d*; *m* 1963, Diana Margaret Campion Dawson; one *s* and one step *d. Educ:* Stowe School. Able Seaman, RN, 1944–47. Art Gallery Asst, London Gallery, 1948–50; sang with Mick Mulligan's Jazz Band, 1949–61. Wrote Flook strip cartoon balloons (drawn by Trog (Wally Fawkes)), 1956–71. Critic, The Observer: pop music, 1965–67; TV, 1967–71; films, 1971–73. Film scriptwriter: Smashing Time, 1968; Take a Girl Like You, 1970. Pres., British Humanist Assoc., 1972–74. Critic of the Year, IPC Nat. Press Awards, 1970. *Publications:* I Flook, 1962; Owning Up, 1965; Revolt into Style, 1970; Flook by Trog, 1970; Rum Bum and Concertina, 1977; (with Barry Fantoni) The Media Mob, 1980; Tribe of One: Great Naive and Primitive Painters of the British Isles, 1981; (with Walter Dorin) Great Lovers, 1981; Mellymobile, 1982; (ed) Edward James, Swans Reflecting Elephants: my early years, 1982; Scouse Mouse, 1984; It's All Writ Out for You: the life and work of Scottie Wilson, 1986; (with Michael Woods) Paris and the Surrealists, 1991. *Recreations:* trout fishing, singing and listening to blues of 1920s, collecting modern paintings. *Address:* 33 St Lawrence Terrace, W10 5SR. *Clubs:* Colony Room, Chelsea Arts.

MELMOTH, Christopher George Frederick Frampton, CMG 1959; South Asia Department, International Bank for Reconstruction and Development, 1962–75, retired; *b* 25 Sept. 1912; *s* of late George Melmoth and Florence Melmoth; *m* 1946, Maureen Joan (*née* Brennan); three *d. Educ:* Sandringham Sch., Forest Gate. Accountant Officer, Co-ordination of Supplies Fund, Malta, 1942–45; Administrative Officer, Hong Kong, 1946–55; Minister of Finance, Uganda, 1956–62. *Recreations:* tennis, golf, walking. *Address:* Hoptons Cottage, Kemerton, Tewkesbury, Glos GL20 7JE.

MELROSE, Prof. Denis Graham; Professor of Surgical Science, Royal Postgraduate Medical School, 1968–83, Emeritus since 1983; *b* 20 June 1921; *s* of late Thomas Robert Gray Melrose, FRCS and Floray Collings; *m* 1945, Ann, *d* of late Kathleen Tatham Warter; two *s. Educ:* Sedbergh Sch.; University Coll., Oxford; UCH London. MA, BM, BCh, MRCP, FRCS. Junior appts at Hammersmith Hosp. and Redhill County Hosp., Edgware, 1945; RNVR, 1946–48; subseq. Lectr, later Reader, Royal Postgrad. Med. Sch.; Nuffield Travelling Fellow, USA, 1956; Fulbright Fellow, 1957; Associate in Surgery, Stanford Univ. Med. Sch., 1958. Fellow, RPMS, 1993. *Publications:* numerous papers in learned jls and chapters in books, particularly on heart surgery, heart lung machine and med. engrg. *Recreations:* sailing, ski-ing. *Address:* Can Serreta, Apartado 19, 07820 San Antonio Abad, Ibiza, Baleares, Spain. *T:* 71 343364. *Club:* Royal Naval Sailing Association.

MELVILL JONES, Prof. Geoffrey, FRS 1979; FRSC 1979; FCASI; FRAeS; Emeritus Professor, McGill University, since 1992; Adjunct Professor, University of Calgary, since 1992; *b* 14 Jan. 1923; *s* of Sir Bennett Melvill Jones, CBE, AFC, FRS and Dorothy Laxton Jotham; *m* 1953, Jenny Marigold Burnaby; two *s* two *d. Educ:* King's Choir Sch.; Dauntsey's Sch.; Cambridge Univ. (BA, MA, MB, BCh). Appointments in UK, 1950–61: House Surgeon, Middlesex Hosp., 1950; Sen. Ho. Surg., Otolaryngology, Addenbrooke's Hosp., Cambridge, 1950–51; MO, RAF, 1951; Scientific MO, RAF Inst. of Aviation Medicine, Farnborough, Hants, 1951–55; Scientific Officer (external staff), Medical Research Council of Gt Britain, 1955–61; McGill University: Dir, Aviation, later Aerospace Med. Res. Unit, 1961–88; Associate Prof., 1961–68; Full Prof., 1968–91; Hosmer Res. Prof. of Physiol., 1978–91. Fellow, Aerospace Medical Assoc., 1969; FCASI 1965; FRAeS 1981. First recipient, Dohlman Medal for research in the field of orientation and postural control, 1986; Robert Bárány Jubilee Gold Medal for most significant research on vestibular function during past 5 years; Ashton Graybiel Lectureship Award, US Navy, 1989; Stewart Meml Lectureship Award, RAeS, 1989; Buchanan-Barbour Award, RAeS, 1990; McLaughlan Medal, RSCan, 1991. *Publications:* Mammalian Vestibular Physiology, 1979 (NY); Adaptive Mechanisms in Gaze Control, 1985; research papers in physiological jls. *Recreations:* outdoor activities, music. *Address:* Department of Clinical Neurosciences, Faculty of Medicine, University of Calgary, 3330 Hospital Drive NW, Calgary, Alta T2N 4N1, Canada. *T:* (403) 220 8764/5911. *Fax:* (403) 283 8731.

MELVILLE; *see* Leslie Melville, family name of Earl of Leven and Melville.

MELVILLE, 9th Viscount *cr* 1802; **Robert David Ross Dundas;** Baron Duneira 1802; *b* 28 May 1937; *s* of Hon. Robert Maldred St John Melville Dundas (2nd *s* of 7th Viscount) (killed in action, 1940), and of Margaret Connell (who *m* 2nd, 1946, Gerald Bristowe Sanderson), *d* of late Percy Cruden Ross; *S* uncle, 1971; *m* 1982, Fiona Margaret Stilgoe, *d* of late Roger and of Mrs Stilgoe, Stogumber, Som; two *s. Educ:* Wellington College. District Councillor, Lasswade, Midlothian; Mem., Midlothian CC, 1964–67. Pres., Lasswade Civic Soc. Lieutenant, Ayrshire Yeomanry; Captain (Reserve), Scots Guards. *Recreations:* fishing, shooting, golf, chess. *Heir: s* Hon. Robert Henry Kirkpatrick Dundas, *b* 23 April 1984. *Address:* Solomon's Court, Chalford, near Stroud, Glos GL6 8LY. *T:* Brimscombe (01453) 883351; 3 Roland Way, Fulham, SW7. *T:* 0171–370 3553. *Clubs:* Cavalry and Guards; House of Lords Motor; Midlothian County; Bonnyrigg and Lasswade District Ex-Servicemen's.

MELVILLE, Anthony Edwin; Headmaster, The Perse School, Cambridge, 1969–87; *b* 28 April 1929; *yr s* of Sir Leslie Melville, *qv*; *m* 1964, Pauline Marianne Surtees Simpson, *d* of Major A. F. Simpson, Indian Army; two *d. Educ:* Sydney Church of England Grammar Sch.; Univ. of Sydney (BA); King's Coll., Cambridge (MA). Sydney Univ. Medal in English, 1950; Pt II History Tripos, 1st cl. with dist., 1952; Lightfoot Schol. in Eccles. History, 1954. Asst Master, Haileybury Coll., 1953. *Recreations:* reading, gardening, music. *Address:* 4 Field Way, Cambridge CBI 4RW. *Club:* East India.

MELVILLE, Prof. David, PhD; CPhys, FInstP; Vice-Chancellor, Middlesex University, since 1992 (Director, Middlesex Polytechnic, 1991–92); *b* 4 April 1944; *s* of late Frederick George Melville and Mary Melville; *m* 1968; one *s* two *d. Educ:* Clitheroe Royal Grammar Sch.; Sheffield Univ. (BSc 1st Cl. Hons 1965; PhD 1969); Columbia Univ. CPhys, FInstP 1978. Southampton University: Lectr in Physics, 1968–78; Sen. Lectr, 1978–84; Lancashire Polytechnic: Prof. of Physics and Head, Sch. of Physics and Astronomy, 1985–86; Asst Dir, 1986–89; Vice-Rector, 1989–91. ICI Res. Fellow, 1968; Visiting Professor: Univ. of Parma, Italy, 1974–80; Oporto Univ., Portugal, 1983; Visiting Scientist: ICI Corporate Lab., Runcorn, 1975; Consiglio Nazionale delle Ricerche, Italy, 1976–80. Vice-Pres., CVCP, 1995–. Member: Council, BNF Metals Technol. Centre, 1986–92; SERC Materials Commn, 1988–92; SERC Condensed Matter Sub-Cttee, 1986–88; SERC Physics Cttee, 1988–92; SERC Metals and Magnetic Materials Cttee, 1988–92; Council for Industry and Higher Educn, 1994–; Chairman: SERC Magnetism and Magnetic Materials Initiative, 1989–91; UK and Republic of Ireland Chapter, Magnetics Soc., IEEE, 1988–93; Internat. Congress on Magnetism, Edinburgh, 1991. Hon. Pres., Co. of Middx Trust, 1992–. *Publications:* articles on magnetism, magnetic materials and biophysics in scientific and engrg jls. *Recreations:* sailing, walking, ski-ing. *Address:* Principal's Lodge, Trent Park, Cockfosters Road, Barnet, Herts EN4 0PS. *T:* 0181–362 5606. *Club:* Grafham Water Sailing (Huntingdon).

MELVILLE, Sir Harry (Work), KCB 1958; FRS 1941; FRSC; PhD Edinburgh and Cantab; DSc Edinburgh; MSc Birmingham; Principal, Queen Mary College, University of London, 1967–76; *b* 27 April 1908; *s* of Thomas and Esther Burnett Melville; *m* 1942, Janet Marian, *d* of late Hugh Porteous and Sarah Cameron; two *d. Educ:* George Heriot's Sch., Edinburgh; Edinburgh Univ. (Carnegie Res. Scholar); Trinity Coll., Cambridge (1851 Exhibitioner). Fellow of Trinity College, Cambridge, 1933–44. Meldola Medal, Inst. of Chemistry, 1936; Davy Medal, Royal Society, 1955; Colwyn Medal, Instn of the Rubber Industry. Asst Dir, Colloid Science Laboratory, Cambridge, 1938–40; Prof. of Chemistry, Univ. of Aberdeen, 1940–48; Scientific Adviser to Chief Superintendent Chemical Defence, Min. of Supply, 1940–43; Superintendent, Radar Res. Station, 1943–45; Mason Prof. of Chemistry, Univ. of Birmingham, 1948–56. Chief Scientific Adviser for Civil Defence, Midlands Region, 1952–56; Bakerian Lecture, Royal Society, 1956. Member: Min. of Aviation Scientific Adv. Council, 1949–51; Adv. Council, Dept of Scientific and Industrial Res., 1946–51, Res. Council, British Electricity Authority, 1949–56; Royal Commn on Univ. Educn in Dundee, 1951–52; Res. Council, DSIR, 1961–65; Chm., Adv. Council on Research and Develt, DTI, 1970–74; Member: Nuclear Safety Adv. Cttee, DTI, 1972–; Cttee of Managers, Royal Institution, 1976–; Sec. to Cttee of the Privy Council for Scientific and Industrial Research, 1956–65; Chm., SRC, 1965–67. Mem., London Electricity Bd, 1968–75. Mem., Parly and Scientific Cttee, 1971–75; Pres., Plastics Inst., 1970–75. Hon. LLD Aberdeen; Hon. DCL Kent; Hon. DSc: Exeter; Birmingham; Liverpool; Leeds; Heriot-Watt; Essex; Hon. DTech Bradford. *Publications:* papers in Proceedings of Royal Society, etc. *Address:* Norwood, Dodds Lane, Chalfont St Giles, Bucks HP8 4EL. *T:* Chalfont St Giles (01494) 872222.

MELVILLE, James; *see* Martin, R. P.

MELVILLE, Sir Leslie Galfreid, KBE 1957 (CBE 1953); Member of the Board of the Reserve Bank, Australia, 1959–63, and 1965–74; Member, Commonwealth Grants Commission, 1979–82 (Chairman, 1966–74); *b* 26 March 1902; *s* of Richard Ernest Melville and Lilian Evelyn Thatcher; *m* 1925, Mary Maud Scales; two *s. Educ:* Sydney Church of England Grammar Sch. Bachelor of Economics, University of Sydney, 1925; Public Actuary of South Australia, 1924–28; Prof. of Economics, University of Adelaide, 1929–31; Economic Adviser to Commonwealth Bank of Australia, 1931–49; Asst Gov. (Central Banking) Commonwealth Bank of Australia, 1949–53; Mem. of Commonwealth Bank Bd, 1951–53; Exec. Dir of International Monetary Fund and International Bank for Reconstruction and Development, 1950–53. Mem. of Cttees on Australian Finances and Unemployment, 1931 and 1932; Financial Adviser to Australian Delegates at Imperial Economic Conference, 1932; Financial Adviser to Australian Delegate at World Economic Conference, 1933; Mem. of Financial and Economic Advisory Cttee, 1939; Chm. of Australian Delegation to United Nations Monetary Conf. at Bretton Woods, 1944; Mem. of Advisory Council of Commonwealth Bank, 1945–51; Chm. UN Sub-Commn on Employment and Economic Stability, 1947–50; Member: Immigration Planning Council, 1956–61; Develt Adv. Service of Internat. Bank, 1963–65; Chm. of Tariff Bd, Australia, 1960–62; Chm., Tariff Adv. Cttee of Papua and New Guinea, 1969–71. Vice-Chancellor Australian National Univ., Canberra, ACT, 1953–60. Hon. LLD: Toronto, 1958; ANU, 1978; Hon. DSc Econ Sydney, 1980. *Address:* UNit 61 The Grange, 67 MacGregor Street, Deakin, Canberra, ACT 2600, Australia. *Club:* Commonwealth.
See also A. E. Melville.

MELVILLE, Sir Ronald (Henry), KCB 1964 (CB 1952); *b* 9 March 1912; *e s* of Henry Edward Melville; *m* 1940, Enid Dorcas Margaret, *d* of late Harold G. Kenyon, Ware; two *s* one *d. Educ:* Charterhouse; Magdalene Coll., Cambridge. 1st Class Classical Tripos, Pts I and II, Charles Oldham Scholarship. Entered Air Ministry, 1934; Private Sec. to Chief of Air Staff, 1936, to Sec. of State, 1940; Asst Under-Sec., 1946; Dep. Under-Sec., 1958; Dep. Under-Sec., War Office, 1960–63; Second Permanent Under-Sec. of State, Ministry of Defence, 1963–66; Permanent Sec., Ministry of Aviation, 1966; Permanent Sec., attached Civil Service Dept, 1971–72; Director: Electronic Components Industry Fedn, 1972–81; Westland Aircraft, 1974–83. Chairman: Nat. Rifle Assoc., 1972–84 (Captain, GB Rifle Team, touring USA and Canada, 1976, and for Kolapore match in UK, 1977); Jt Shooting Cttee for GB, 1985–89; President: Council for Cadet Rifle Shooting, 1990–; Herts Rifle Assoc., 1960–; has represented Cambridge Univ., TA and Scotland (40 times) at rifle shooting. Member Council: Herts TAA, 1960–80; Herts Conservation Soc. (formerly Herts Soc.), 1963–; ACFA, 1972–84. *Recreations:* painting, gardening. *Address:* The Old Rose and Crown, Braughing, Ware, Herts SG11 2QA. *Club:* Brooks's.

MELVILLE-ROSS, Timothy David; Director General, Institute of Directors, since 1994; *b* 3 Oct. 1944; *s* of late Antony Stuart Melville-Ross and of Anne Barclay Fane; *m* 1967, Camilla Mary Harlackenden; two *s* one *d*. *Educ:* Uppingham School; Portsmouth College of Technology (Dip Business Studies, 2nd cl. hons). FCIS. British Petroleum, 1963–73; Rowe, Swann & Co., stockbrokers, 1973–74; joined Nationwide Building Soc., 1974: Dir and Chief Gen. Man., 1985–87; Dir and Chief Exec., 1987–94. Dir, Monument Oil and Gas plc, 1992–. Mem. Council, Industrial Soc., 1986–. Trustee, Uppingham Sch., 1988–. FRSA; CIMgt; FCIB. *Recreations:* music, reading, bridge, tennis, the countryside.

MELVIN, John Turcan, TD and star; MA Cantab; *b* 19 March 1916; *m* 1951, Elizabeth Ann Parry-Jones; one *s* three *d*. *Educ:* Stowe Sch.; Trinity Coll., Cambridge; Berlin Univ. (Schol.). Asst Master, Sherborne Sch., 1938. Served with Dorset Regt, 1939–46. Housemaster, Sherborne Sch., 1950; Headmaster, Kelly Coll., 1959–72; Hd of German Dept, Foster's Sch., 1972–75; Sixth Form Tutor, Sherborne Sch., 1975–82. Gov., Hall Sch. Trust, Wincanton. *Recreations:* walking, reading, tennis, dramatics. *Address:* Culverhayes Lodge, Sherborne, Dorset DT9 3BY. *Club:* English-Speaking Union.

MELVYN HOWE, Prof. George; *see* Howe, Prof. G. M.

MENCHÚ, Rigoberta; human rights activist; *b* 1959; *d* of late Vicente Menchú, Mayan resistance leader and founder, Cttee of Peasant Unity (CUC), Guatemala, and Juana Menchú. Works for indigenous peoples' rights; founded Vicente Menchú Foundn, Mexico City; Member: CUC; United Representation of Guatemalan Opposition; Five Hundred Years of Resistance Campaign; UN Working Group on Indigenous Populations; UN Internat. Indian Treaty Council. Nobel Peace Prize, 1992. *Publication:* I, Rigoberta Menchú (with Elisabeth Burgos-Debray), 1983 (trans. English 1984; in 12 other langs). *Address:* c/o Vicente Menchú Foundation, PO Box 5274, Berkeley, CA 94705, USA.

MENDE, Dr Erich; Member of the Bundestag, German Federal Republic, 1949–80; *b* 28 Oct. 1916; *m* 1948, Margot (*née* Hattje); three *s* one *d*. *Educ:* Humane Coll., Gross-Strehlitz; Universities of Cologne and Bonn (Dr jur). Military service in Infantry Regt 84, Gleiwitz. Served War of 1939–45, Comdr of a Regt (wounded twice, prisoner of war); Major, 1944. Co-founder of FDP (Free Democratic Party), 1945; Mem. Exec. Cttee, British Zone, FDP, 1947; Parliamentary Group of FDP: Whip, and Mem. Exec. Cttee, 1950–53; Dep. Chm., 1953; Chm., 1957; Chm. of FDP, 1960–68; joined CDU, 1970. Vice-Chancellor and Minister for All-German Affairs, Federal Republic of Germany, 1963–66. Mem., CDU Hessen, 1970. *Publications:* autobiography: Das verdammte Gewissen 1921–1945, 1982; Die neue Freiheit 1945–1961, 1984; Von Wende zu Wende 1962–1982, 1986. *Address:* Am Stadtwald 62, 53177 Bonn, Germany.

MENDEL, Paul David; Director, Council of Christians and Jews, since 1992; broadcaster and speaker; *b* 14 Oct. 1930; *s* of late Eric Lazarus Mendel and Esther (*née* Graber); *m* 1st, 1952, Marion Leigh (marr. diss. 1967); one *s* one *d*; 2nd, 1967, Ada Marianne Levinson (marr. diss. 1983); 3rd, 1989, Rosalind Alder. *Educ:* St Christopher's Sch., Letchworth. Nat. Service, 1949–51, Capt. RMP. Engaged in family automotive business, 1951–. Former Member: Middx CC; Barnet BC. Dep. Dir, Defence and Gp Relns, Bd of Deputies of British Jews, 1982–84; Council of Christians and Jews: Asst Dir, 1985–87; Dep. Dir, 1987–92. Member: Interfaith Network Exec., 1987–; Exec. Cttee, ICCJ. JP Juvenile and W Central PSD, 1955–83 (sometime Chm.). *Recreations:* travel, reading. *Address:* 100 Lyncroft Mansions, Lyncroft Gardens, NW6 1JY. *T:* 0171–794 6989. *Club:* New Cavendish.

MENDELSON, Prof. Maurice Harvey, QC 1992; DPhil; Professor of International Law, University of London at University College London, since 1987; *b* 27 Aug. 1943; *s* of William Maizel Mendelson and Anne (*née* Aaronson); *m* 1968, Katharine Julia Olga Kertesz; two *d*. *Educ:* St Marylebone Grammar Sch.; New Coll., Oxford (BA 1st Cl. Hons Jurisprudence 1964; MA; DPhil 1971). Called to the Bar, Lincoln's Inn, 1965; Internat. Law Fund Schol., 1966; Leverhulme European Res. Schol., 1966–67; Lectr in Laws, KCL, 1968–74; Kennedy Law Schol., Lincoln's Inn, 1970–73; Official Fellow and Tutor in Law, St John's Coll., Oxford, and Univ. Lectr in Law, Oxford, 1975–86. Fulbright Vis. Schol., Harvard Law Sch., 1977; Visiting Professor: Univ. of N Carolina, 1982; Univ. of Pennsylvania, 1986; Univ. of Paris II, 1993. Mem., Bd of Editors, British Yearbook of Internat. Law. *Publications:* articles in internat. law jls, etc; reports to Internat. Law Assoc. *Recreations:* the arts, painting, swimming, tennis, riding. *Address:* Faculty of Laws, University College London, Bentham House, 4 Endsleigh Gardens, WC1H 0EG. *T:* 0171–391 1446; 2 Hare Court, Temple, EC4Y 7BH. *T:* 0171–583 1770. *Club:* Athenæum.

MENDES, Samuel Alexander; Artistic Director, Donmar Warehouse Theatre, since 1992; *b* 1 Aug. 1965; *s* of Valerie Hélène Mendes (*née* Barnett) and James Peter Mendes. *Educ:* Magdalen Coll. Sch., Oxford; Peterhouse, Cambridge (BA English, 1st Cl. Hons). Asst Dir, Chichester Festival, 1987–88, Artistic Director, Minerva Studio Theatre, 1989: productions included: Heartlands; Summerfolk; Love's Labour's Lost; productions at *Donmar Warehouse*, 1992–, include: Assassins; Translations; Cabaret; Glengarry Glen Ross; productions as freelance director: *Royal Shakespeare Co.:* Troilus and Cressida; The Alchemist; Richard III; The Tempest; *Royal National Theatre:* The Sea; The Rise and Fall of Little Voice; The Birthday Party; Kean, Old Vic; The Plough and the Stars, Young Vic; Oliver, Palladium. Numerous awards. *Recreations:* cricket, football, theatre administration. *Address:* c/o Donmar Warehouse, 41 Earlham Street, WC2H 9LD. *T:* 0171–240 4882. *Clubs:* Peg's, Groucho.

MENDL, His Honour James Henry Embleton; a Circuit Judge at Knightsbridge Crown Court, 1974–93; *b* 23 Oct. 1927; *s* of late R. W. S. Mendl, barrister and author, and of Dorothy Williams Mendl (*née* Burnett), and *g s* of late Sir S. F. Mendl, KBE; *m* 1971, Helena Augusta Maria Schrama, *d* of late J. H. and H. H. Schrama-Jekat, The Netherlands. *Educ:* Harrow; University Coll., Oxford (MA). Called to Bar, Inner Temple, 1953; South Eastern Circuit. Commissioned, Worcestershire Regt, 1947; served: Egypt, with 2nd N Staffs, 1947–48; with Royal Signals (TA), 1952–54, and Queen's Royal Regt (TA) (Captain, 1955), 1954–56. Councillor, Royal Borough of Kensington and Chelsea, 1964–74 (Vice-Chm., Town Planning Cttee, 1969; Chm. (Vice-Chm. 1970), Libraries Cttee, 1971). Contested (C) Gateshead East, 1966. *Recreations:* music, reading, theatre.

MENDOZA, June Yvonne, AO 1989; RP; ROI; artist; *d* of John Morton and Dot (*née* Mendoza), musicians; *m* Keith Ashley V. Mackrell; one *s* three *d*. *Educ:* Lauriston Girls' Sch., Melbourne; St Martin's Sch. of Art. Member: RP 1970; ROI 1968. Portraits for govt, regts, industry and commerce, academia, medicine, theatre, sport (*eg* Chris Evert for Wimbledon Mus.), and in public and private collections internationally. These include: Queen Elizabeth II; Queen Elizabeth the Queen Mother; Prince and Princess of Wales; Margaret Thatcher; Prime Minister of Australia, Sir John Gorton; Prime Minister of Fiji, Ratu Sir Kamisese Mara; Pres. of Iceland, Vigdis Finnbogadottir; Pres. of Philippines, Corazón Aquino; Donald Coggan, Robert Runcie, and George Carey, severally, while Archbishop of Canterbury; large group paintings include: The House of Commons in Session, 1986; House of Representatives, for new Parliament building in Canberra; private series of musicians include: Sir Yehudi Menuhin; Sir Georg Solti; Dame Joan Sutherland; Paul Tortelier; Sir Michael Tippett. Lectures internationally; appearances on art programmes, TV and radio. Hon. DLitt: Bath, 1986; Loughborough. *Address:* 34 Inner Park Road, SW19 6DD.

MENDOZA, Maurice, CVO 1982; MSM 1946; heritage consultant; Secretary, Heritage Building Contractors Group (UK), since 1993; Under Secretary, Ancient Monuments and Historic Buildings, Department of the Environment, 1978–81; *b* 1 May 1921; *e s* of Daniel and Rachel Mendoza; *m* 1949, Phyllis Kriger. *Educ:* Sir Henry Raine's Foundation. Dip. Sociology London. Clerical Officer, HM Office of Works, 1938; served Royal Signals and Cheshire Yeo., 1941–46 (Sgt); Mil. Mission to Belgium, 1944–46; Organisation Officer, Treasury, 1956–61; Principal, MPBW, 1963; Asst Sec. 1968; DoE, 1970; Under-Sec., 1973; Dir of Manpower and Management Services, DoE and later, also Dept of Transport, 1974–78. Chairman: Friends of the Ridgeway, 1982–94; Common Land Forum, 1984–86; Sec., British Architectural Library Review Gp, 1987–88. Hon. Mem., 10th Battalion Transportation Corps, US Army, 1977. *Recreations:* theatre, walking, photography. *Address:* 45 Grange Grove, Canonbury, N1 2NP. *Clubs:* Athenæum, Civil Service.

MENDOZA, Vivian P.; *see* Pereira-Mendoza.

MENEVIA, Bishop of, (RC), since 1987; **Rt. Rev. Daniel Joseph Mullins;** *b* 10 July 1929; *s* of Timothy Mullins. *Educ:* Mount Melleray; St Mary's, Aberystwyth; Oscott Coll.; UC of S Wales and Mon, Cardiff (Fellow, University Coll., Cardiff). Hon. Fellow, St David's University Coll., Lampeter. Priest, 1953. Curate at: Barry, 1953–56; Newbridge, 1956; Bargoed, 1956–57; Maesteg, 1957–60; Asst Chaplain to UC Cardiff, 1960–64; Sec. to Archbp of Cardiff, 1964–68; Vicar General of Archdiocese of Cardiff, 1968; Titular Bishop of Stowe and Auxiliary Bishop in Swansea, 1970–87. Pres., Catholic Record Soc.; Chm., Cttee for Catechesis. Member of Court, UC, Swansea; Governor, Digby Stuart Coll. *Recreations:* golf, walking. *Address:* Bryn Rhos, 79 Walter Road, Swansea, West Glamorgan SA1 4PS.

MENHENNET, Dr David, CB 1991; Librarian of the House of Commons, 1976–91; Visiting Research Fellow, Goldsmiths' College, London University, since 1990; *b* 4 Dec. 1928; *s* of William and Everill Menhennet, Redruth, Cornwall; *m* 1954, Audrey, *o d* of William and Alice Holmes, Accrington, Lancs; two *s*. *Educ:* Truro Sch., Cornwall; Oriel Coll., Oxford (BA 1st Cl. Hons 1952); Queen's Coll., Oxford. Open Scholarship in Mod. Langs, Oriel Coll., Oxford, 1946; Heath Harrison Trav. Scholarship, 1951; Bishop Fraser Res. Scholar, Oriel Coll., 1952–53; Laming Fellow, Queen's Coll., Oxford, 1953–54; Zaharoff Trav. Scholarship, 1953–54. MA 1956, DPhil 1960, Oxon. Library Clerk, House of Commons Library, 1954; Asst Librarian i/c Res. Div., 1964–67; Dep. Librarian, 1967–76. Mem., Study of Parliament Gp, 1964–90; Chm. Adv. Cttee, Bibliographic Services, British Library, 1986–92 (Mem., 1975–86); Mem. Exec. Cttee, Friends of Nat. Libraries, 1991–95. FRSA 1966. Liveryman, Stationers' Co., 1990. Gen. Editor, House of Commons Library Documents series, 1972–90. *Publications:* (with J. Palmer) Parliament in Perspective, 1967; The Journal of the House of Commons: a bibliographical and historical guide, 1971; (ed with D. C. L. Holland) Erskine May's Private Journal, 1857–1882, 1972; (contrib.) The House of Commons in the Twentieth Century, ed S. A. Walkland, 1979; (contrib.) The House of Commons: Services and Facilities 1972–1982, ed M. Rush, 1983; The House of Commons Library: a history, 1991; articles in Lib. Assoc. Record, Parliamentarian, Parly Affairs, Polit. Qly, New Scientist, Contemp. Rev., Jl of Librarianship, Jl of Documentation, Book Collector. *Recreations:* walking, gardening, visiting old churches, French literature. *Address:* 50 Kelsey Lane, Beckenham, Kent BR3 3NE. *T:* 0181–650 7787. *Club:* Athenæum.

MENIN, Rt. Rev. Malcolm James; *see* Knaresborough, Bishop Suffragan of.

MENKES, Suzy Peta, (Mrs D. G. Spanier); Fashion Editor, International Herald Tribune, since 1988; *b* 24 Dec. 1943; *d* of Edouard Gerald Lionel Menkès and Betty Curtis Lightfoot; *m* 1969, David Graham Spanier; three *s* (one *d* decd). *Educ:* Univ. of Cambridge (MA). Editor, Varsity newspaper, Cambridge, 1966; Jun. Reporter, The Times, 1966–69; Fashion Editor, Evening Standard, 1969–77; Women's Editor, Daily Express, 1977–80; Fashion Editor: The Times, 1980–87; The Independent, 1987–88. Freeman: City of Milan, 1986; City of London, 1987. British Press Awards Commendations, 1983 and 1984. *Publications:* The Knitwear Revolution, 1983; The Royal Jewels, 1985, 3rd edn 1988; The Windsor Style, 1987; Queen and Country, 1992. *Recreations:* family life, reading, opera, Royal history. *Address:* c/o International Herald Tribune, 181 avenue Charles de Gaulle, 92521 Neuilly Cedex, Paris, France. *T:* 41439300.

MENNEER, Stephen Snow, CB 1967; retired, 1970, as Assistant Under-Secretary of State, Department of Health and Social Security; *b* 6 March 1910; *s* of Sydney Charles Menneer, LLD, and Minnie Elizabeth Menneer; *m* 1935, Margaret Longstaff Smith (*d* 1976); one *s* one *d*. *Educ:* Rugby Sch.; Oriel Coll., Oxford. Min. of Information, 1939; Min. of National Insurance, 1948; Under-Sec., Min. of Pensions and Nat. Insurance, then Min. of Social Security, 1961. *Address:* Wester Ground, Chittlehamholt, Umberleigh, N Devon EX37 9NU.

MENON, Prof. Mambillikalathil Govind Kumar, MSc, PhD; FRS 1970; MP (Janata Dal) Rajasthan, Rajya Sabha, since 1990; President, International Council of Scientific Unions, 1988–93; *b* 28 Aug. 1928; *s* of Kizhekepat Sankara Menon and Mambillikalathil Narayaniamma; *m* 1955, Indumati Patel; one *s* one *d*. *Educ:* Jaswant Coll., Jodhpur; Royal Inst. of Science, Bombay (MSc); Univ. of Bristol (PhD). Tata Inst. of Fundamental Research: Reader, 1955–58; Associate Prof., 1958–60; Prof. of Physics and Dean of Physics Faculty, 1960–64; Senior Prof. and Dep. Dir (Physics), 1964–66, Dir, 1966–75. Chm., Electronics Commn, and Sec., Dept of Electronics, Govt of India, 1971–78; Scientific Advr to Minister of Defence, Dir-Gen. of Defence Res. and Develt Orgn, and Sec. in the Ministry of Defence for Defence Res., 1974–78; Dir-Gen., Council of Scientific and Industrial Res., 1978–81; Sec. to Govt of India, Dept of Science and Technology, 1978–82, Dept of the Envmt, 1980–81; Chm., Commn for Addtnl Sources of Energy, 1981–82; Mem., Planning Commn, 1982–89; Chm., Science Adv. Cttee to the Cabinet, 1982–85; Scientific Advr to the Prime Minister, 1986–89; Minister of State for Sci. and Technology, India, 1989–90. Pres., India Internat. Centre, 1983–88; Member: UN Sec.-Gen.'s Adv. Cttee on Application of Sci. and Technol. to Develt, 1972–79 (Chm. for 2 yrs); Bd of Dirs, Internat. Fedn of Insts for Advanced Study, Stockholm, 1992–. President: Indian Sci. Congress Assoc., 1981–82; Indian Statistical Inst., 1990–. Fellow: Indian Acad. of Sciences (Pres., 1974–76); Indian Nat. Science Acad. (Pres., 1981–82); Founding Fellow, Third World Acad. of Sciences; Hon. Fellow: Nat. Acad. of Sciences, India (Pres., 1987–88); Indian Inst. of Sciences, Bangalore; For. Hon. Member: Amer. Acad. of Arts and Scis; Russian Acad. of Scis; Mem., Pontifical Acad. of Scis, Vatican; Hon. Pres., Asia Electronics Union; Hon. Mem., Instn of Electrical & Electronics Engrs Inc., USA. Mem. Governing Council, UN Univ., 1986–92. Hon. DSc: Jodhpur Univ., 1970; Delhi Univ., 1973; Sardar Patel Univ., 1973; Allahabad Univ., 1977; Roorkee Univ., 1979; Banaras Hindu Univ., 1981; Jadavpur Univ., 1981; Sri Venkateswara Univ., 1982; Indian Inst. of Tech. Madras, 1982; Andhra Univ., 1984; Utkal Univ., 1984; Aligarh Muslim Univ., 1986; Bristol Univ., 1990; N Bengal Univ., 1989; Indian Inst. of Technology, Kharagpur, 1990; Hon. Dr Engrg Stevens Inst. of Tech., USA, 1984. Royal

Commn for Exhibn of 1851 Senior Award, 1953–55; Shanti Swarup Bhatnagar Award for Physical Sciences, Council of Scientific and Industrial Research, 1960; Khaitan Medal, RAS, 1973; Pandit Jawaharlal Nehru Award for Sciences, Madhya Pradesh Govt, 1983; G. P. Chatterjee Award, 1984; Om Prakash Bhasin Award for Science and Technol., 1985; C. V. Raman Medal, INSA, 1985; J. C. Bose Triennial Gold Medal, Bose Inst., 1983; (first) Ashutosh Mukherjee Gold Medal, Indian Science Congress Assoc., 1988; National Awards: Padma Shri, 1961; Padma Bhushan, 1968; Padma Vibhushan, 1985. *Publications:* 135, on cosmic rays and elementary particle physics. *Recreations:* photography, bird-watching. *Address:* 77 Lodi Estate, New Delhi 110003, India. *T:* (11) 4620062. *Clubs:* National Liberal; India International Centre (New Delhi).

MENOTTI, Gian Carlo; composer; Founder and President, Spoleto Festivals, Italy and Charleston, USA; *b* Cadegliano, Italy, 7 July 1911. *Educ:* The Curtis Institute of Music, Philadelphia, Pa. Has been resident in the United States since 1928. Teacher of Composition at Curtis Inst. of Music, 1948–55. First performances of works include: Amelia Goes to the Ball (opera), 1936; The Old Maid and the Thief (radio opera), 1939 (later staged); The Island God, 1942; Sebastian (Ballet), 1943; Piano Concerto in F, 1945; The Medium (opera), 1946 (later filmed); The Telephone (opera), 1947; Errand into the Maze (ballet), 1947; The Consul (opera), 1950 (Pulitzer Prize); Apocalypse (orchestral), 1951; Amahl and the Night Visitors (television opera), 1951; Violin Concerto in A Minor, 1952; The Saint of Bleeker Street (opera), 1954 (Pulitzer Prize); The Unicorn, The Gorgon, and the Manticore, 1956; Maria Golovin (television opera), 1958; The Last Savage (opera), 1963; The Death of the Bishop of Brindisi (oratorio), 1963; Martin's Lie (opera), 1964; Canti della Lontananza (song cycle), 1967; Help, Help, the Globolinks (opera), 1968; The Leper (drama), 1970; Triplo Concerto a Tre (symphonic piece), 1970; The Most Important Man (opera), 1971; Fantasia for 'cello and orch., 1971; Tamu-Tamu (opera), 1973; The Egg (opera), 1976; The Trial of the Gypsy (opera), 1976; Landscapes & Remembrances, for chorus and orch., 1976; Symphony no 1, 1976; Chip & his Dog (opera), 1978; Juana la Loca (opera), 1979; Mass, O Pulchritudo, 1979; Song of Hope (cantata), 1980; A Bride from Pluto (opera), 1982; St Teresa (cantata), 1982; The Boy Who Grew Too Fast (opera), 1982; Goya (opera), 1986; Giorno di Nozze (opera), 1988; wrote libretto for Vanessa (opera, by Samuel Barber), 1958. Internationally recognised as a producer; has worked at the greatest opera houses, including La Scala, Metropolitan, Paris Opéra, Vienna Staatsoper. Guggenheim Award, 1946, 1947; Kennedy Centre Award, 1984; NYC Mayor's Liberty Award; Hon. Association, Nat. Inst. of Arts and Letters. *Publications:* his major works have been published, also some minor ones; he is the author of all his libretti, most of which have been written in English. *Address:* c/o Thea Dispeker, 59 East 54th Street, New York, NY 10022, USA; Yester House, Gifford, Haddington, East Lothian EH41 4JF.

MENSFORTH, Sir Eric, Kt 1962; CBE 1945; DL; MA Cantab; FEng; FIMechE; FRAeS; Hon. FIEE; Vice Lord-Lieutenant, South Yorkshire, 1974–81; President, Westland Aircraft Ltd, 1979–85; (Director, 1968–83; Managing Director 1938–45; Vice-Chairman, 1945–53, 1968–71; Chairman, 1953–68); Director, John Brown & Co. Ltd, 1948–83 (Deputy Chairman, 1959–78); *b* 17 May 1906; 2nd *s* of late Sir Holberry Mensforth, KCB, CBE; *m* 1934, Betty, *d* of late Rev. Picton W. Francis; three *d*. *Educ:* Altrincham County High Sch.; University Coll. Sch.; King's Coll., Cambridge (Price Exhibn) (1st class mechanical sciences tripos). Engineering work at Woolwich Arsenal, Mather & Platt Ltd, Bolckow Vaughan Ltd, Kloecknerwerke A. G., Dorman Long Ltd, English Electric Ltd (Founder, Domestic Appliance Div., 1931), Markham & Co. Ltd, T. Firth & John Brown Ltd, Firth Brown Tools Ltd, Wickman Ltd, Boddy Industries Ltd, Rhodesian Alloys Ltd (Founder, 1949), Normalair Ltd; Chief Production Adviser to: Chief Executive, Ministry of Aircraft Production, 1943–45; first Naval Dragonfly helicopter, 1950; 100 KW Orkney Windmill, 1951; Surform, 1956; London Battersea Heliport, 1959; SRN3 Hovercraft ascent of Lachine Rapids, 1963. Master Cutler, Sheffield, 1965–66. Chairman: EDC for Electronics Industry, 1968–70; Cttee on Quality Assurance, 1968–70; Council of Engineering Instns, 1969–72; Governing Body, Sheffield Polytechnic, 1969–75; Member: British Productivity Council, 1964–69; Royal Ordnance Factories Bd, 1968–72; Council, RGS, 1968–70; Smeatonian Soc. of Civil Engrs, 1966–77; Treasurer, BAAS, 1970–75; Pres., IProdE, 1967–69; a founder Vice-Pres., Fellowship of Engineering, 1977. President: Helicopter Assoc. of GB, 1953–55; S Yorks Scouts' Assoc., 1969–76; CPRE (Sheffield and Peak District Branch), 1975–86. Hon. Fellow, Sheffield City Polytech. Hon. DEng Sheffield, 1967; Hon. DSc Southampton, 1970. Freeman, Coachmakers' and Coach-Harness Makers' Co, 1950. DL S (formerly WR) Yorks, 1971. *Publications:* Air Frame Production, 1947 (Instn Prize, IMechE); Future of the Aeroplane (Cantor Lectures), 1959; Production of Helicopters and Hovercraft (Lord Sempill Lecture, IProdE), 1964; Future of Rotorcraft and Hovercraft (Cierva Meml Lecture, RAeS), 1967; Extracts from the Records of the Cutlers' Company, 1972; Family Engineers, 1981; Clogs to Clogs, 1991. *Address:* 42 Oakmead Green, Woodcote Side, Surrey KT18 7JS. *T:* Epsom (01372) 742313. *Clubs:* Alpine, Royal Automobile.

MENTER, Sir James (Woodham), Kt 1973; MA, PhD, ScD Cantab; FRS 1966; CPhys; FInstP; Principal, 1976–86, Fellow, 1986, Queen Mary College, London University; *b* 22 Aug. 1921; *s* of late Horace Menter and late Jane Anne Lackenby; *m* 1947, Marjorie Jean, *d* of late Thomas Stodart Whyte-Smith, WS; two *s* one *d*. *Educ:* Dover Grammar Sch.; Peterhouse, Cambridge. PhD 1949, ScD 1960. Experimental Officer, Admty, 1942–45; Research, Cambridge Univ., 1946–54 (ICI Fellow, 1951–54; Sir George Beilby Mem. Award, 1954); Tube Investments Research Laboratories, Hinxton Hall, 1954–68; Dir of Research and Develt, Tube Investments Ltd, 1965–76. Director: Tube Investments Res. Labs, 1961–68; Tube Investments Ltd, 1965–86; Round Oak Steelworks Ltd, 1967–76; British Petroleum Co., 1976–87; Steetley Co., 1981–85. Member: SRC, 1967–72; Cttee of Inquiry into Engrg Profession, 1977–79; a Vice-Pres., Royal Society, 1971–76, Treasurer, 1972–76; Royal Institution: a Manager, 1982–84; a Vice-Pres., 1983–85; Chm. Council, 1981–85. Fellow, Churchill Coll., Cambridge, 1966–88. President: Inst. of Physics, 1970–72; Metals Soc., 1976; Dep. Chm., Adv. Council Applied R&D, 1976–79. Mem. (part-time), BSC, 1976–79. Member: Bd of Govs, London Hosp. Med. Coll., 1976–86; Ct of Governors, City of London Polytechnic, 1982–85; Court, Stirling Univ., 1988–. Hon. FRSE 1992. Hon. DTech Brunel, 1974; DUniv Stirling, 1995. Bessemer Medal, Iron and Steel Inst., 1973; Glazebrook Medal and Prize, Inst. of Physics, 1977. *Publications:* scientific papers in Proc. Royal Society, Advances in Physics, Jl Iron and Steel Inst., etc. *Recreation:* fishing. *Address:* Carie, Kinloch Rannoch, by Pitlochry, Perthshire PH17 2QJ. *T:* Kinloch Rannoch (01882) 632341.

MENTETH, Sir James (Wallace) Stuart-, 6th Bt, *cr* 1838; *b* 13 Nov. 1922; *e s* of 5th Bt and Winifred Melville (*d* 1968), *d* of Daniel Francis and *widow* of Capt. Rupert G. Raw, DSO; *S* father, 1952; *m* 1949, Dorothy Patricia, *d* of late Frank Greaves Warburton; two *s*. *Educ:* Fettes; St Andrews Univ.; Trinity Coll., Oxford (MA). Served War of 1939–45, with Scots Guards, 1942–44; on active service in North Africa and Italy (Anzio) (severely wounded). *Recreations:* gardening, ornithology. *Heir: s* Charles Greaves Stuart-Menteth [*b* 25 Nov. 1950; *m* 1976, Nicola St Lawrence; three *d*].

MENTZ, Donald, AM 1994; Director General, CAB International (formerly Commonwealth Agricultural Bureaux), 1985–92, now retired; *b* 20 Oct. 1933; *s* of Stanley Mentz and Marie Agnes (*née* Bryant); *m* 1959, Mary Josephine (*née* Goldsworthy); one *s* two *d*. *Educ:* Hampton High School, Victoria; Dookie Agricultural College, Victoria (DDA); Melbourne Univ. (BAgSci); Australian Nat. Univ. (BEcon). Dept of External Territories, Australia, 1969–73; Aust. Develt Assistance Bureau, Dept of Foreign Affairs, 1973–77; Dept of Business and Consumer Affairs, 1977–78; Dir of Operations, Asian Develt Bank, Philippines, 1979–81; Dep. Sec., Dept of Business and Consumer Affairs, Aust., 1981–82; Dep. Sec., Dept of Territories and Local Govt., 1983–84. *Recreations:* skiing, gardening. *Address:* Flat 1, 25 Longridge Road, Earls Court, SW5 9SB. *T:* 0171–835 1208. *Clubs:* Athenæum; Commonwealth (Canberra).

MENUHIN, family name of **Baron Menuhin**.

MENUHIN, Baron *cr* 1993 (Life Peer), of Stoke d'Abernon in the County of Surrey; **Yehudi Menuhin,** OM 1987; KBE 1965; violinist, conductor; *b* New York, 22 April 1916; adopted British nationality, 1985; *s* of Moshe and Marutha Menuhin; *m* 1938, Nola Ruby, *d* of George Nicholas, Melbourne, Australia; one *s* one *d*; *m* 1947, Diana Rosamond, *d* of late G. L. E. Gould and late Lady Harcourt (Evelyn Suart); two *s*. *Educ:* private tutors; studied music under Sigmund Anker and Louis Persinger, in San Francisco; Georges Enesco, Rumania and Paris; Adolph Busch, Switzerland. Made début with orchestra, San Francisco, aged 7, Paris, aged 10, New York, 11, Berlin, 13; since then has played with most of world's orchestras and conductors; has introduced among contemp. works Sonata for Violin alone, by Béla Bartók (composed for Sir Yehudi Menuhin), as well as works by William Walton, Ben-Haim, Georges Enesco, Pizzetti, Ernest Bloch, etc. During War of 1939–45 devoted larger part of his time to concerts for US and Allied armed forces and benefit concerts for Red Cross, etc (500 concerts). Series of concerts in Moscow (by invitation), 1945; seven visits to Israel, 1950–; first tour of Japan, 1951; first tour of India (invitation of Prime Minister), 1952. Largely responsible for cultural exchange programme between US and Russia, 1955, and for bringing Indian music and musicians to West. Initiated his own annual music festival in Gstaad, Switzerland, 1957, and in Bath, 1959–68; Jt Artistic Dir, Windsor Festival, 1969–72. Founder, Live Music Now, 1977. Founded Yehudi Menuhin Sch. of Music, Stoke d'Abernon, Surrey, 1963; Founder/Pres., Internat. Menuhin Music Acad., Gstaad, 1976; President: Trinity Coll. of Music, 1971; Young Musicians' Symphony Orch., 1989–; Hallé Orch., 1992–; Associate Conductor and Pres., Royal Philharmonic Orch., 1982–; Principal Guest Conductor: English String Orch., 1988–; Warsaw Sinfonia, 1982–. Good Will Ambassador, UNESCO, 1992. Mem., Comité d'Honneur Service Européen d'Information Ministerielle et Parlementaire, 1987; Hon. Fellow: St Catharine's Coll., Cambridge, 1970; Fitzwilliam Coll., Cambridge, 1991; Hon. DMus: Oxford, 1962; Cambridge, 1970; Sorbonne, 1976; Toronto, 1984; Virginia Commonwealth Univ., 1987; Hartford, Conn, 1987; Santa Clara, Calif, 1988; Hon. Dr Gakushuin, Tokyo, 1988, and 10 other degrees from Brit. Univs. Freedom of the City of Edinburgh, 1965; City of Bath, 1966. He records for several companies, both as soloist and as Conductor of Menuhin Festival Orch., with which has toured USA, Australia, NZ and Europe; appears regularly on American and British Television. Gold Medal, Royal Philharmonic Soc., 1962; Jawaharlal Nehru Award for International Understanding, 1970; Sonning Music Prize, Denmark, 1972; Handel Medal, NY; City of Jerusalem Medal; Peace Prize, Börsenverein des Deutschen Buchhandels, 1979; Albert Medal, RSA, 1981; Una Vita Nella Musica, Omaggio a Venezia, 1983; Grande Plaque du Bimillenaire de Paris, 1984; Ernst von Siemens Prize, 1984; Moses-Mendelssohn-Preis des Landes Berlin; Internat. Soc. of Performing Arts Administrators Award, 1987; Brahms Medal, City of Hamburg, 1987; Preis der Stiftung für Freiheit und Menschenrechte, Bern, 1987; Golden Viotti Prize, Vercelli, Italy, 1987; Diploma Magistrale, Italy, 1987; Buber-Rosenzweig Medal, Ges. für Christlich-Jüdische Zusammenarbeit, 1989; Epée d'Academicien, Académie des Beaux Arts, 1988; Wolf Foundn Prize, 1991. Decorations include: Grand Officier de la Légion d'Honneur, 1986; Commander: Order of Arts and Letters (France); Order of Leopold (Belgium); Grand Officer, Order of Merit of the Republic (Italy), 1987; Officer, Ordre de la Couronne (Belgium); Kt Comdr Order of Merit (Fed. Rep. of Germany), Royal Order of the Phœnix (Greece); Comdr, Order of Orange-Nassau (Netherlands); Grand Cross, Order of Merit (FRG); Hon. Citizen of Switzerland, 1970. *Publications:* The Violin: six lessons by Yehudi Menuhin, 1971; Theme and Variations, 1972; Violin and Viola, 1976; Sir Edward Elgar: My Musical Grandfather (essay), 1976; (autobiography) Unfinished Journey, 1977; The Music of Man, 1980; (with Christopher Hope) The King, the Cat and the Fiddle, (children's book), 1983; Life Class, 1986; *Relevant Publication:* Yehudi Menuhin, The Story of the Man and the Musician, by Robert Magidoff, 1956 (USA); Conversations with Menuhin, by Robin Daniels, 1979. *Films:* Stage Door Canteen; Magic Bow; The Way of Light (biog.). *Television series:* The Music of Man. *Address:* SYM Music Company Ltd, PO Box 6160, SW1W 0XJ. *Clubs:* Athenæum, Garrick.

See also J. C. M. Benthall.

MENZIES, Duncan Adam Young; QC (Scot.) 1991; *b* 28 Aug. 1953; *s* of Douglas William Livingstone Menzies and Margaret Adam (*née* Young); *m* 1979, Hilary Elizabeth McLauchlan Weston; two *s*. *Educ:* Cargilfield; Glenalmond; Wadham Coll., Oxford (MA); Edinburgh Univ. (LLB). Admitted Advocate, 1978; Standing Junior Counsel to Admiralty, 1984–91. Contested (C): Midlothian, 1983; Edinburgh Leith, 1987. Founder, Scottish Wine Soc., 1976. *Recreations:* shooting, golf, wine. *Address:* Leaston House, Humbie, East Lothian EH36 5PD. *T:* Humbie (01875) 833219. *Clubs:* New (Edinburgh); Honourable Company of Edinburgh Golfers.

MENZIES, John Maxwell; Chairman, John Menzies, since 1952; *b* 13 Oct. 1926; *s* of late John Francis Menzies, and of Cynthia Mary Graham; *m* 1953, Patricia Eleanor, *d* of late Comdr Sir Hugh Dawson, Bt, CBE and Lady Dawson; four *d*. *Educ:* Eton. Lieut Grenadier Guards. Berwickshire CC, 1954–57. Director: Scottish American Mortgage Co., 1959–63; Standard Life Assurance Co., 1960–63; Vidal Sassoon Inc., 1969–80; Gordon & Gotch plc, 1970–85; Atlantic Assets Trust, 1973–88 (Chm., 1983–88); Ivory & Sime Enterprise Capital plc (formerly Independent Investment Co. plc), 1973– (Chm., 1983–); Fairhaven International (formerly Nimslo International), 1980–88; Rocky Mountains Oil & Gas, 1980–85; Ivory & Sime plc, 1980–83; Personal Assets Trust PLC, 1981–92; Bank of Scotland, 1984–94; Guardian Royal Exchange, 1985–; Malcolm Innes & Partners Ltd, 1989–. Trustee, Newsvendors' Benevolent Instn, 1974– (Pres., 1968–74). Mem. Bd of Trustees, Nat. Library of Scotland, 1991–. Mem., Royal Co. of Archers, HM's Body Guard for Scotland. *Recreations:* farming, shooting, reading, travel. *Address:* Kames, Duns, Berwickshire. *T:* Leitholm (01890) 840202. *Clubs:* Boodle's, Beefsteak; New (Edinburgh).

MENZIES, Sir Peter (Thomson), Kt 1972; Director: National Westminster Bank Ltd, 1968–82; Commercial Union Assurance Co. Ltd, 1962–82; *b* 15 April 1912; *s* of late John C. Menzies and late Helen S. Aikman; *m* 1st, 1938, Mary McPherson Alexander (*d* 1992), *d* of late John T. Menzies and late Agnes Anderson; one *s* one *d*; 2nd, 1994, Muriel, *d* of late Harold McKee Langton and Ethel Miles. *Educ:* Musselburgh Grammar Sch.; University of Edinburgh. MA, 1st Class Hons Math. and Natural Philosophy, 1934. Inland Revenue Dept, 1933–39; Treasurer's Dept, Imperial Chemical Industries Ltd, 1939–56 (Asst Treas. 1947, Dep. Treas. 1952); Director: Imperial Chemical Industries Ltd, 1956–72 (Dep. Chm., 1967–72); Imperial Metal Industries Ltd, 1962–72 (Chm., 1964–72). Part-time

Mem., CEGB, 1960–72; Mem., Review Body on Doctors' and Dentists' Remuneration, 1971–83; Chairman: Electricity Council, 1972–77; London Exec. Cttee, Scottish Council (Develt and Industry), 1977–82. A Vice-Pres., Siol na Meinnrich; Pres., UNIPEDE, 1973–76; Vice-Pres. and Gen. Treas., BAAS, 1982–86. FInstP; CompIEE. *Address:* 9 Fern Grove, Welwyn Garden City, Herts AL8 7ND. *T:* Welwyn Garden City (01707) 327234. *Club:* Caledonian.

MENZIES-WILSON, William Napier, CBE 1985; Chairman: Edinburgh Tankers plc, since 1986; Forth Tankers plc, since 1991; Celtic Tankers, since 1992; *b* 4 Dec. 1926; *s* of James Robert Menzies-Wilson and Jacobine Napier Williamson-Napier; *m* 1953, Mary Elizabeth Darnell Juckes; two *s* one *d. Educ:* Winchester; New Coll., Oxford (MA); North Western Univ., Chicago. Joined Stewarts & Lloyds Ltd, 1950; Managing Director, Stewarts & Lloyds of South Africa Ltd, 1954–61, Chairman, 1961; Director, Stewarts & Lloyds Ltd, 1964; Dir, Supplies & Transport, British Steel Corporation, 1967–73; Chairman: Wm Cory & Son Ltd, 1973–77; Ocean Transport & Trading plc, Liverpool, 1980–86 (Dir, 1973–88); Viking Resources Trust, 1986–89; Director: Overseas Containers Holdings, 1979–86; Dunlop Holdings, 1982–84; NFC, 1986–95. Pres., Gen. Council of British Shipping, 1984–85; Mem. Exec. Bd, Lloyd's Register of Shipping, 1984–87. Chm., Bd of Trustees, Help the Aged, 1988–. *Recreations:* shooting, golf, gardening. *Address:* Last House, Old, Northampton NN6 9RJ. *T:* Northampton (01604) 781346. *Clubs:* Brooks's; Hon. Co. of Edinburgh Golfers.

MERCER, Prof. Alan; Professor of Operational Research, University of Lancaster, since 1968; *b* 22 Aug. 1931; *s* of Harold Mercer and Alice Ellen (*née* Catterall); *m* 1954, Lillian Iris (*née* Pigott); two *s. Educ:* Penistone Grammar Sch.; Cambridge Univ. (MA; DipMathStat); London Univ. (PhD). NCB, 1954–56; UKAEA, 1956–62; Armour & Co. Ltd, 1962–64; Univ. of Lancaster, 1964–: Chm., Sch. of Management and Organisational Scis, 1982–85. Mem., Central Lancashire Develt Corp., 1971–85; Mem., 1985–89, Chm., 1986–89, Warrington and Runcorn Develt Corp. Chm., Employers' Side of Whitley Council for New Towns Staff, 1979–89 (Mem., 1971–89); Mem., Management and Industrial Relns Cttee, SSRC, 1972–76, 1980–82; Chm., Industry and Employment Cttee, ESRC, 1984–87 (Vice Chm., 1982–84); Mem., NW Econ. Planning Council, 1973–79. Jt Editor, European Journal of Operational Research, 1977–. *Publications:* Operational Distribution Research (jtly), 1978; Innovative Marketing Research, 1991; numerous papers in learned jls. *Recreations:* travel, bridge, sport. *Address:* South Cottage, Calton, Airton, Skipton, North Yorks BD23 4AD. *T:* Airton (01729) 830542.

MERCER, Rt. Rev. Eric Arthur John; *b* 6 Dec. 1917; *s* of Ambrose John Mercer, Kent; *m* 1951, Rosemary Wilma, *d* of John William Denby, Lincs; one *s* one *d. Educ:* Dover Gram. Sch.; Kelham Theol. Coll. Enlisted Sherwood Foresters, 1940; Capt. and Adjt, 14th Foresters, 1943; served Italy (despatches), 1944; Staff Coll., Haifa, 1944; DAA&QMG, 66 Inf. Bde, Palestine, 1945; GSO2 (SD), HQ, MEF, 1945. Returned Kelham Theol. Coll., 1946–47. Ordained, Chester; Curate, Coppenhall, Crewe, 1947–51; Priest in charge, Heald Green, 1951–53; Rector, St Thomas', Stockport, 1953–59; Chester Diocesan Missioner, 1959–65; Rector, Chester St Bridget, 1959–65; Hon. Canon of Chester Cathedral, 1964; Bishop Suffragan of Birkenhead, 1965–73; Bishop of Exeter, 1973–85. Church Commissioners: Dep. Chm., Pastoral Cttee, 1976–85; Mem., Bd of Governors, 1980–85. Nat. Chm., CEMS, 1974–78. *Publication:* (contrib.) Worship in a Changing Church, 1965. *Address:* Frickers House, Chilmark, Salisbury SP3 5AJ. *T:* Teffont (01722) 761400.

MERCER, Geoffrey Dallas; His Honour Judge Mercer; a Circuit Judge, South Eastern Circuit, since 1991; *b* 17 Dec. 1935; *s* of Leon Dallas Mercer, FRCS and Veronica Kathleen Mary Lillian Mercer (*née* Pitt-Lancaster). *Educ:* Clifton Coll., Bristol; St John's Coll., Cambridge (MA, LLM). Called to the Bar, Gray's Inn, 1960; practised at the Bar, 1961–91; Hd of Chambers, 1985–91. Former English Youth International and Cheshire County golfer. *Recreations:* golf, music.

MERCER, Prof. Ian Dews; Hon. Professor of Rural Conservation Practice, University of Wales, since 1991; Secretary General, Association of National Park Authorities, since 1995; *b* 25 Jan. 1933; *s* of Eric Baden Royds Mercer and Nellie Irene Mercer; *m* 1st, 1957, Valerie Jean Hodgson; four *s*; 2nd, 1976, Pamela Margaret Gillies (*née* Clarkson). *Educ:* King Edward VI Sch., Stourbridge; Univ. of Birmingham (BA Hons). Sub-Lieut RNR, 1954–56. Field Centre appts, Preston Montford, 1956–57, Juniper Hall, 1957–59, Slapton Ley, 1959–68; Lectr, St Luke's Coll., Exeter, 1968–70; Warden, Malham Tarn Field Centre, 1970–71; County Conservation Officer, Devon CC; 1971–73; National Park Officer, Dartmoor, 1973–90; Chief Exec., Countryside Council for Wales, 1990–95. Hon. LLD Exeter, 1994; Hon. DSc Plymouth, 1995. *Publications:* Nature Guide to the West Country, 1981; chapters in books on conservation matters. *Recreations:* painting, golf, France, teaching adults birds and landscape, watching sons play Rugby. *Address:* Ponsford House, Moretonhampstead, Newton Abbot, Devon TQ13 8NL. *T:* Moretonhampstead (01647) 440612.

MERCER, John Charles Kenneth; a Recorder of the Crown Court, 1975–82; *b* 17 Sept. 1917; *s* of late Charles Wilfred Mercer and Cecil Maud Mercer; *m* 1944, Barbara Joan, *d* of late Arnold Sydney Whitehead, CB, CBE, and Maud Ethel Whitehead; one *s* one *d. Educ:* Ellesmere Coll.; Law Sch., Swansea University Coll. (LLB). Solicitor. War Service, 1940–45, Captain RA. Partner, Douglas-Jones & Mercer, 1946–88, now Consultant. Mem., Royal Commn on Criminal Procedure, 1978–81; Mem., SW Wales River Authority, 1960–74. *Recreations:* fishing, shooting, golf, watching sport. *Address:* 334 Gower Road, Killay, Swansea, West Glamorgan SA2 7AE. *T:* Swansea (01792) 202931. *Club:* Clyne Golf (Swansea).

MERCER, Dr Robert Giles Graham; Headmaster, Stonyhurst College, since 1985; *b* 30 May 1949; *s* of late Leonard and Florence Elizabeth Mercer; *m* 1974, Caroline Mary Brougham; one *s. Educ:* Austin Friars School, Carlisle; Churchill College, Cambridge (Scholar; 1st cl. Hist. Tripos, Pts I and II; MA); St John's College, Oxford (Sen. Schol., DPhil). Head of History, Charterhouse, 1974–76; Asst Principal, MoD, 1976–78; Dir of Studies and Head of History, Sherborne School, 1979–85. Gov., Austin Friars Sch, 1987–. FRSA. *Publication:* The Teaching of Gasparino Barzizza, 1979. *Recreations:* art, music, travel, swimming. *Address:* St Philip's, Stonyhurst, Lancs BB6 9PT. *T:* Stonyhurst (01254) 826345. *Clubs:* Athenæum, East India.

MERCER, Rt. Rev. Robert William Stanley, CR; Diocesan Bishop, Anglican Catholic Church of Canada, since 1989 (Assistant Bishop, 1988–89); *b* 10 Jan. 1935; *s* of Harold Windrum Mercer and Kathleen Frampton. *Educ:* Grey School, Port Elizabeth, S Africa; St Paul's Theological Coll., Grahamstown, SA (LTh). Deacon 1959, priest 1960, Matabeleland; Asst Curate, Hillside, Bulawayo, 1959–63; Novice, CR, 1963; professed, 1965; at Mirfield, 1963–66; at St Teilo's Priory, Cardiff, 1966–68; Prior and Rector of Stellenbosch, S Africa, 1968–70; deported from SA, 1970; Chaplain, St Augustine's School, Penhalonga, Rhodesia, 1971–72; Rector of Borrowdale, Salisbury, Rhodesia, 1972–77; Bishop of Matabeleland, 1977–87. Sub-Prelate, Order of St John of Jerusalem, 1981. *Address:* 225 First Avenue, Ottawa, Ontario K1S 2G5, Canada.

MERCER, Roger James, FSA, FSAScot; FRSE; Secretary, Royal Commission on the Ancient and Historical Monuments of Scotland, since 1990; *b* 12 Sept. 1944; *o s* of Alan Mercer and Patricia (*née* Hicks); *m* 1970, Susan Jane Fowlie; one *s* one *d. Educ:* Harrow County Grammar Sch.; Edinburgh Univ. (MA). MIFA. Inspector of Ancient Monuments, DoE, 1969–74; Lectr and Reader, Dept of Archaeology, Univ. of Edinburgh, 1974–89. Mem., Ancient Monuments Bd for Scotland, 1988–; Vice President: Soc. of Antiquaries of Scotland, 1988–91; Council for British Archaeology, 1990–94; Prehistoric Soc., 1989–92. British Acad. Readership, 1989. *Publications:* Beaker Studies in Europe (ed), 1979; Hambledon Hill—a Neolithic Landscape, 1980; Grimes Graves—Excavations 1971–72, 1981; Carn Brea—a Neolithic Defensive Complex, 1981; (ed) Farming Practice in British Prehistory, 1981; Causewayed Enclosures, 1990; articles and reviews in learned jls. *Recreations:* music, books, good food. *Address:* Home House, 4 Old Church Lane, Duddingston, Edinburgh EH15 3PX. *T:* 0131–661 2931. *Club:* New (Edinburgh).

MERCER NAIRNE PETTY-FITZMAURICE, family name of **Marquess of Lansdowne.**

MERCHANT, Ismail; film producer, since 1960; Partner, Merchant Ivory Productions, since formation, 1961; *b* 25 Dec. 1936; *s* of Noormohamed Haji Abdul Rehman and Hazra Memon. *Educ:* St Xavier's Coll., Bombay (BA); New York Univ. (MBA). Collaborator with Ruth Prawer Jhabvala and James Ivory on most of the following: *feature films:* The Householder, 1963; Shakespeare Wallah, 1965 (won Best Actress award, Berlin Film Fest., 1965); The Guru, 1969; Bombay Talkie, 1970; Savages, 1972; The Wild Party, 1975; Roseland, 1977; The Europeans, 1979 (official Brit. entry, Cannes Film Fest.); Quartet, 1981; Heat and Dust, 1982 (Brit. entry, Cannes Film Fest.); The Bostonians, 1984 (feature, Cannes Film Fest.); A Room with a View, 1986; Maurice, 1987 (Silver Lions for Best Picture, Best Actor and Best Composer); Slaves of New York, 1989; Mr and Mrs Bridge, 1990; Howards End, 1992; The Remains of the Day, 1993; (directed) In Custody, 1994; Jefferson in Paris, 1995; *shorts:* The Creation of Woman, 1960 (Academy award nomination); Helen, Queen of the Nautch Girls, 1973; (directed) Mahatma and the Mad Boy, 1973; Sweet Sounds, 1976; *television:* Adventures of a Brown Man in Search of Civilization, 1971 (BBC); Autobiography of a Princess, 1975 (TV special, NY); Hullabaloo over Georgie and Bonnie's Pictures, 1978 (feature, LWT); Jane Austen in Manhattan, 1980 (feature, LWT and Polytel); (directed for Channel 4) The Courtesans of Bombay, 1983; The Curry Connection, 1990 (series, Channel 4). *Publications:* Ismail Merchant's Indian Cuisine, 1986; Hullabaloo In Old Jaypoore, 1988; Ismail Merchant's Florence, 1994; Ismail Merchant's Passionate Meals, 1994. *Recreations:* squash, bicycling, cooking. *Address:* 400 East 52nd Street, New York, NY 10022, USA. *T:* (212) 7593694; Garden View, Sutter Street, Bombay, India. *T:* 3094576.

MERCHANT, John Richard; Director of Resources, Voluntary Service Overseas, since 1995; *b* 4 June 1945; *s* of William Henry Merchant and Eileen Merchant; *m* 1966, Eileen McGill; two *s. Educ:* Gravesend Grammar Sch.; Sheffield Univ. (BSc); Cranfield Inst. of Technol. (MSc). FIS. Lyons Bakery Ltd, 1966–69; Lectr, Cranfield Inst. of Technol., 1969–75; Statistician, MoD, 1975–79; Chief Statistician, CS Coll., 1979–82; Asst Sec., Cabinet Office (MPO), 1982–84; Principal Finance and Estabt Officer, DPP, 1984–86, Crown Prosecution Service, 1986–88; Under Sec., 1985; Sec. and Dir, Council Policy and Admin, SERC, 1988–94; Grade 3, Office of Public Service and Science, 1994. *Recreations:* Nigerian postal history, fishing. *Address:* (office) 317 Putney Bridge Road, SW15 2PN. *T:* 0181–780 2266.

MERCHANT, Piers Rolf Garfield; MP (C) Beckenham, since 1992; *b* 2 Jan. 1951; *s* of Garfield Frederick Merchant and Audrey Mary Rolfe-Martin; *m* 1977, Helen Joan Burrluck; one *s* one *d. Educ:* Nottingham High School; Univ. of Durham. BA (Hons) Law and Politics, MA Political Philosophy. Reporter, Municipal Correspondent, Chief Reporter, Dep. News Editor, The Journal, 1973–80; News Editor, The Journal, 1980–82; Editor, Conservative Newsline, 1982–84. Dir of Corporate Publicity, NEI plc, 1987–90; Dir of Public Affairs, The Advertising Assoc., 1990–92. Contested (C) Newcastle upon Tyne Central, 1979. MP (C) Newcastle upon Tyne Central, 1983–87. PPS to Sec. of State for Social Security, 1992–. Co-Chm., Freeflow of Information Cttee, Internat. Parly Gp, 1986–91; Vice-Chm., All-Party Parly Cttee on AIDS, 1987. Mem., Senior Common Room, University Coll., Durham. *Publications:* newspaper articles and features. *Recreations:* swimming, walking, genealogy, electronics, computers. *Address:* c/o House of Commons, SW1A 0AA.

MERCHANT, Rev. Prof. William Moelwyn, FRSL; writer and sculptor; *b* 5 June 1913; *s* of late William Selwyn and Elizabeth Ann Merchant, Port Talbot, Glamorgan; *m* 1938, Maria Eluned Hughes, Llanelly; one *s* one *d. Educ:* Port Talbot Grammar Sch.; (Exhibnr) University Coll., Cardiff. BA, 1st Cl. English hons 1933; 2nd Cl. 1st div. Hist., 1934; MA 1950; DLitt 1960; Hon. Fellow, University Coll., Cardiff, 1981. Hist. Master, Carmarthen Grammar Sch., 1935; English Master, Newport High Sch., 1936; English Lectr, Caerleon Trg Coll., 1937; University Coll. Cardiff: Lectr in Eng. Lang. and Lit., 1939; Sen. Lectr, 1950; Reader, 1961; Prof. of English, Univ. of Exeter, 1961–74; Vicar of Llanddewi Brefi, dio. St Davids, 1974–78; Hon. Lectr, All Saints Church, Leamington Spa, 1979. Fellow, Folger Shakespeare Library, Washington, DC, and Fulbright Fellow, 1957; Woodward Lectr, Yale Univ., 1957; Dupont Lectr, Sewanee Univ., Tenn, 1963; Willett Prof. of English and Theology, Univ. of Chicago, 1971. Founded Rougemont Press, 1970 (with Ted Hughes, Eric Cleave and Paul Merchant). Welsh Cttee of Arts Council of Gt Brit., 1960 and 1975–; Council, Llandaff Festival, 1958–61. Consultant and script-writer on film, The Bible, Rome, 1960–64. Ordained to Anglican Orders, 1940; Examining Chaplain to the Bishop of Salisbury; Canon of Salisbury Cathedral, 1967–73, Canon Emeritus, 1973 (Chancellor, 1967–71); Mem., Archbishops' Commn on Faculty Jurisdiction, 1979–. Founded Llanddewi Brefi Arts Fest., 1975. Mem., Welsh Acad., 1991. FRSL 1976; Hon. Fellow, University Coll. of Wales, Aberystwyth, 1975. Hon. Prof. of Drama, UC Aberystwyth, 1985–87; Lyttelton Lectr, Eton Coll., 1983; Hon. Mem., Old Etonian Assoc., 1990. Hon HLD Wittenberg Univ., Ohio, 1973. *Publications:* Wordsworth's Guide to the Lakes (illus. John Piper), 1952 (US 1953); Reynard Library Wordsworth, 1955 (US 1955); Shakespeare and the Artist, 1959; Creed and Drama, 1965; (ed) Merchant of Venice, 1967; (ed) Marlowe's Edward the Second, 1967; Comedy, 1972; Tree of Life (libretto, music by Alun Hoddinott), 1972; Breaking the Code (poems), 1975; (ed) Essays and Studies, 1977; No Dark Glass (poems), 1979; R. S. Thomas, a critical evaluation, 1979 (US 1990); Confrontation of Angels (poems), 1986; Jeshua (novel), 1987 (US 1991); Fire from the Heights (novel), 1989 (US 1991); A Bundle of Papyrus (novel), 1989; Fragments of a Life (autobiog.), 1990 (Welsh Arts Council Literary Award, 1991); Inherit the Land (short stories), 1992; Triple Heritage (novel), 1994; Preaching the Word, 1994; The Boy Hasid and Other Tales, 1995; articles in Times Literary Supplement, Warburg Jl, Shakespeare Survey, Shakespeare Quarterly, Shakespeare Jahrbuch, Encyc. Britannica, etc. *Recreations:* theatre, typography, sculpting (thirty one-man exhibns at Exeter, Cardiff, Swansea, Plymouth, Southampton, Aberystwyth, Glasgow, Stirling, Birmingham, London, 1971–89). *Address:* 32A Willes Road, Leamington Spa, Warwicks CV31 1BN. *T:* Leamington (01926) 314253.

MERCIECA, Most Rev. Joseph; *see* Malta, Archbishop of, (RC).

MEREDITH, Most Rev. Bevan; *see* Papua New Guinea, Archbishop of.

MEREDITH, John Michael; barrister-at-law; Magistrate, Hong Kong, 1988–94, retired; *b* 23 Oct. 1934; *s* of late John Stanley Meredith and Lily Meredith; *m*; one *s* three *d*; *m* 1988, Linda (*née* Crossland). *Educ:* Crossley and Porter Schs, Halifax, Yorks; Leeds Univ. (LLB Hons 1956) Called to the Bar, Gray's Inn, 1958; Junior, NE Circuit, 1964; a Recorder, 1976–88. Dir, 1955–64, Chm. Dirs, 1964–88, J. T. Meredith (Carboniser) Ltd. *Recreations:* shooting, sailing. *Address:* China Rose, c/o Puerto Galera Yacht Club, Puerto Galera, Mindoro Island, Philippines. *Clubs:* Pwllheli Sailing (N Wales); Royal Hong Kong Yacht (Life Mem.); Puerto Galera Yacht.

MEREDITH, Richard Alban Creed, MA; Church Missionary Society Area Secretary, dioceses of Derby, Leicester and Southwell, since 1990; *b* 1 Feb. 1935; *s* of late Canon R. Creed Meredith; *m* 1968, Hazel Eveline Mercia Parry; one *s* one *d*. *Educ:* Stowe Sch.; Jesus Coll., Cambridge. Asst Master (Modern Langs), 1957–70, Housemaster, 1962–70, King's Sch., Canterbury; Headmaster, Giggleswick Sch., 1970–78; Head Master, Monkton Combe Sch., 1978–90. *Recreations:* walking, foreign travel, music, gardening. *Address:* Beacon Knoll, 334 Beacon Road, Loughborough LE11 2RD. *T:* Loughborough (01509) 212008.

MEREDITH DAVIES, (James) Brian; *see* Davies.

MERIFIELD, Anthony James, CB 1994; The Ceremonial Officer, Cabinet Office, since 1994; *b* 5 March 1934; *s* of late Francis Bertram Merifield and Richardina (*née* Parker); *m* 1980, Pamela Pratt. *Educ:* Chesterfield Sch.; Shrewsbury Sch.; Wadham Coll., Oxford (MA). National Service, 1952–54, Royal Tank Regt. HM Overseas Civil Service, Kenya, 1958–65; Department of Health and Social Security: Principal, 1965–71; Asst Sec., 1971–77; Under Secretary, 1978–82; Under Sec., NI Office, 1982–85; Dir of Regl Liaison, NHS Management Bd, DHSS, subseq. NHS Management Exec., DoH, 1986–91; Head of Sen. and Public Appts Gp, Cabinet Office, 1991–94. FRSA. *Address:* Cabinet Office, Ceremonial Branch, 53 Parliament Street, SW1A 2NG. *T:* 0171–210 5058, *Fax:* 0171–210 5046. *Club:* Commonwealth Trust.

MERLE, Robert; Croix du Combattant, 1945; Officier de l'Instruction publique, 1953; Professor of English Literature, University of Paris X, Nanterre, since 1965; Titular Professor: University of Rennes, Brittany, since 1944 (on leave, 1950–51); University of Toulouse, since 1957; University of Caen-Rouen, since 1960; University of Algiers, since 1963; *b* 29 Aug. 1908; father an officer; *m* 1st; one *d*; *m* 2nd, 1949; three *s* one *d*; 3rd, 1965; one *s*. *Educ:* Lycée Michelet, Paris; Sorbonne, Paris. Professor, 1944. Mobilised, 1939; Liaison agent with BEF (prisoner, 1940–43). *Publications:* Oscar Wilde, 1948; Week-end à Zuydcoote, 1949 (awarded Prix Goncourt); La Mort est mon métier, 1953; L'Ile, 1962 (awarded Prix de la Fraternité) (translated, as The Island, 1964); Un Animal doué de raison, 1967 (translated, as The Day of the Dolphin, 1969); Derrière la vitre, 1970; Malevil, 1972 (Campbell Award, USA); Les hommes protégés, 1974 (translated, as The Virility Factor, 1977); Madrapour, 1976; Fortune de France, 1978; En nos vertes années, 1979; Paris ma bonne ville, 1980; Le Prince que voilà, 1982; La violente amour, 1983; La Pique du jour, 1985; Le Jour ne se lève pas pour nous, 1986; L'Idole, 1987 (translated, as The Idol, 1989); Le Propre de l'Homme, 1989; La Volte des Vestugadins, 1991; L'Enfant-roi, 1993; *plays:* Flamineo (inspired by Webster's White Devil), 1953; Nouveau Sisyphe; *historical essays:* Moncada, 1965; Ben Bella, 1965; translations, articles. *Recreations:* swimming, tennis, yachting. *Address:* La Malmaison, Grosrouvre, 78490 Montfort L'Amaury, France.

MERLO, David, CEng; Director of Research, British Telecommunications plc, 1983–89; *b* 16 June 1931; *s* of Carlo G. Merlo and Catherine E. Merlo (*née* Stringer); *m* 1952, Patricia Victoria Jackson; two *s*. *Educ:* Kilburn Grammar Sch., London; London Univ. (BScEng 1st Cl. Hons 1954); W. B. Esson schol. of IEE, 1953, and IEE Electronics Premium, 1966. CEng 1967, FIEE 1973. Post Office Research Br., 1948; Executive Engineer, 1955; Sen. Scientific Officer, 1959; Principal Sci. Officer, 1967; Head of Division, 1974; Dep. Director of Research, 1977. Visiting Lecturer: Northampton Polytechnic, 1955–61; Regent Street Polytechnic, 1960–69; Governor, Suffolk College of Higher and Further Education, 1984–89. Served on numerous technical committees in telecommunications field. FRSA 1988. Patent award, 1970. *Publications:* miscellaneous contribs to learned jls. *Recreations:* reading, photography, wine. *Address:* Heather Lodge, Levington, Ipswich IP10 0NA. *T:* Nacton (01473) 659508.

MERLYN-REES, family name of **Baron Merlyn-Rees.**

MERLYN-REES, Baron *cr* 1992 (Life Peer), of Morley and South Leeds in the County of West Yorkshire and of Cilfynydd in the County of Mid Glamorgan; **Merlyn Merlyn-Rees,** PC 1974; *b* Cilfynydd, South Wales, 18 Dec. 1920; *s* of late L. D. and E. M. Rees; name changed to Merlyn-Rees by deed poll, 1992; *m* 1949, Colleen Faith (*née* Cleveley); three *s*. *Educ:* Elementary Schools, S Wales and Wembley, Middx; Harrow Weald Grammar School; London School of Economics; London Univ. Institute of Education. Nottingham Univ. Air Sqdn; Served RAF, 1941–46; demobilised as Sqdn Ldr. Teacher in Economics and History, Harrow Weald Grammar School, 1949–60. Organised Festival of Labour, 1960–62. Lecturer in Economics, Luton Coll. of Technology, 1962–63; contested (Lab) Harrow East, Gen. Elections 1955 and 1959 and by-election, 1959. MP (Lab) South Leeds, June 1963–83, Morley and Leeds South, 1983–92. PPS to Chancellor of the Exchequer, 1964; Parly Under-Sec. of State, MoD (Army), 1965–66; MoD (RAF), 1966–68; Home Office, 1968–70; Mem., Shadow Cabinet, 1972–74; Opposition spokesman on NI affairs, 1972–74; Sec. of State for NI, 1974–76; Home Sec., 1976–79; Shadow Home Sec., 1979–80; Opposition spokesman on Energy, 1980–83. Member: Cttee to examine operation of Section 2 of Official Secrets Act, 1971; Falklands Is Inquiry Cttee, 1982. Pres., Video Standards Council, 1990–. Chm., South Leeds Groundwork Trust, 1987– (Mem. Bd, Groundwork Foundn, 1990–). Chancellor, Univ. of Glamorgan, 1994–. Hon. Fellow, Goldsmiths' Coll., London Univ., 1984. Hon. LLD: Wales, 1987; Leeds, 1992. *Publications:* The Public Sector in the Mixed Economy, 1973; Northern Ireland: a personal perspective, 1985. *Recreation:* reading. *Address:* c/o House of Lords, SW1A 0PW.

MERMAGEN, Air Commodore Herbert Waldemar, CB 1960; CBE 1945 (OBE 1941); AFC 1940; retired, 1960; Director, Sharps, Pixley Ltd (Bullion Brokers), 1962–77; *b* 1 Feb. 1912; *s* of late L. W. R. Mermagen, Southsea; *m* 1937, Rosemary, *d* of late Maj. Mainwaring Williams, DSO and late Mrs Tristram Fox, Cheltenham; two *s*. *Educ:* Brighton Coll., Sussex. Joined RAF, 1930; 43(F) Sqdn, 1931–34; Instructor CFS, 1936–38; Squadron Leader, 1938; served War of 1939–45 in Fighter Command, UK, Middle East, France and Germany (SHAEF); AOC British Air Command, Berlin, 1945–46; Sen. RAF Liaison Officer, UK Services Liaison Staff, Australia, 1948–50; AOC, RAF Ceylon, 1955–57; Air Officer i/c Administration, Headquarters, RAF Transport Command, 1958–60. Air Commodore, 1955. Comdr Legion of Merit (USA), 1946; Medal for Distinguished Services (USSR), 1945; Chevalier, Légion d'Honneur (France) 1951. *Recreations:* rugby (RAF (colours), Sussex, Richmond), golf, gardening. *Address:* Allandale, Vicarage Street, Painswick, Glos GL6 6XS. *Club:* Royal Air Force.

MERRICKS, Walter Hugh; Assistant Secretary-General (Communications), Law Society, since 1987; *b* 4 June 1945; 2nd *s* of Dick and late Phoebe Merricks, Icklesham, Sussex; *m* 1982, Olivia Montuschi; one *s* one *d*, and one step *s*. *Educ:* Bradfield College, Berks; Trinity College, Oxford. MA Hons (Jurisp). Articled Clerk with Batt, Holden, 1968–70; admitted Solicitor, 1970; Hubbard Travelling Scholar, Montreal, 1971; Dir, Camden Community Law Centre, 1972–76; Lectr in Law, Brunel Univ., 1976–81; legal affairs writer, New Law Journal, 1982–85; Sec., Professional and Public Relations, Law Soc., 1985–87. Member: Royal Commn on Criminal Procedure, 1978–81; Fraud Trials (Roskill) Cttee, 1984–86. Mem., Victim Support Wkg Party on Financial Compensation, 1992–93. Mem. Council, King Alfred Sch., 1991–. Membership Sec., DI Network, 1993–. *Address:* 32 Cholmeley Crescent, N6 5HA. *T:* 0181–341 0406; c/o The Law Society, 113 Chancery Lane, WC2A 1PL. *T:* 0171–242 1222.

MERRIFIELD, Prof. Robert Bruce; Professor, since 1966, John D. Rockefeller Jr Professor, since 1984, Rockefeller University; *b* 15 July 1921; *s* of George and Lorene Merrifield; *m* 1949, Elizabeth L. Furlong; one *s* five *d*. *Educ:* Univ. of California, Los Angeles (BA 1943, Chemistry; PhD 1949, Biochemistry). Chemist, Philip R. Park Research Foundn, 1943–44; Research Asst, UCLA Med. Sch., 1948–49; Asst to Associate Prof., Rockefeller Inst. for Med. Research, 1949–66. Nobel Guest Prof., Uppsala, 1968. Member: Amer. Chem. Soc.; Amer. Soc. of Biological Chemists; Amer. Inst. of Chemists; Nat. Acad. of Sciences. Associate Editor, Internat. Jl of Peptide and Protein Research; Mem. Editl Bd of Analytical Biochemistry. Numerous hon. degrees from Amer. univs and colls. Lasker Award for Basic Med. Research, 1969; Gairdner Award, 1970; Intra-Science Award, 1970; Amer. Chem. Soc. Award for Creative Work in Synthetic Organic Chemistry, 1972; Nichols Medal, 1973; Instrument Specialties Co. Award, Univ. of Nebraska, 1977; Alan E. Pierce Award, 1979; Nobel Prize in Chemistry, 1984; Hirschmann Award in Peptide Chem., ACS, 1990; Josef Rudinger Award, Eur. Peptide Soc., 1990. Order of San Carlos (Columbia), 1984. *Publications:* numerous papers in sci. jls, esp. on peptide chemistry, solid phase peptide synthesis. *Address:* The Rockefeller University, 1230 York Avenue, New York, NY 10021, USA. *T:* (212) 3278244.

MERRILL, Fiona Claire, (Mrs R. W. T. Merrill); *see* Reynolds, F. C.

MERRIMAN, Air Vice-Marshal Alan; *see* Merriman, H. A.

MERRIMAN, Dr Basil Mandeville; FRAS, FRAI, FRGS; *b* 28 March 1911; *s* of Thomas Henry Merriman and Ida, *d* of Mandeville Blackwood Phillips; *m* 1938, Yvonne Flavelle (*d* 1974); one *s*. *Educ:* Colet Court Prep. Sch.; St Paul's School; St Bartholomew's Hospital Med. Coll.; MRCS, LRCP 1934. House Appointments, St Bartholomew's Hosp., 1934–36; post graduate studies, Berlin, Vienna, Prague, 1936–38; Medical Adviser, British Drug Houses, 1938; Med. Dir, Carter Foundn, 1956; Consultant, Home Office Prison Department, 1963. FRAS 1972; Fellow, Royal Soc. for Asian Affairs, 1973; FRAI 1974; FRGS 1976. *Publications:* contribs to medical and social jls on drug action and drug addiction and their relationship to crime, also various related aspects of social anthropology. *Recreation:* travel of all forms, particularly Asiatic (journeys mainly in Arab Asia, Central Asiatic region, and Japan). *Address:* 85 Holland Park, W11 3RZ. *T:* 0171–727 8228.

MERRIMAN, Air Vice-Marshal (Henry) Alan, CB 1985; CBE 1973; AFC 1957, and Bar 1961; DL; defence and aerospace consultant; *b* 17 May 1929; *s* of Henry Victor Merriman and Winifred Ellen Merriman; *m* 1965, Mary Brenda Stephenson; three *d*. *Educ:* Hertford Grammar Sch.; RAF Coll., Cranwell. Graduate, Empire Test Pilots Sch. FRAeS 1977. Commnd, 1951; Qual. Flying Instr, 263 F Sqdn, Empire Test Pilots Sch., Fighter Test Sqdn, A&AEE, Central Fighter Estabt, and RAF Staff Coll., 1952–63; Personal Air Sec. to Minister of Defence for RAF, 1964–66; Jt Services Staff Coll., 1966; OC Fighter Test Sqdn, A&AEE, 1966–69; HQ 38 Gp, 1969–70; Stn Comdr, RAF Wittering, 1970–72; RCDS, 1973; CO Empire Test Pilots Sch., 1974–75; Comdt, A&AEE, 1975–77; Dir, Operational Requirements (1), 1977–81; Mil. Dep. to Head of Defence Sales, 1981–84. Director: Falcon Equipment & Systems Ltd, 1991–; Ridgerunners Flying Centres Ltd, 1993–. Pres., NW Essex Aircrew Assoc., 1990–; Vice-Pres., N Herts Aircrew Assoc., 1992–; Herts County Rep., RAF Benevolent Fund, 1995. Queen's Commendation for Valuable Services in the Air, 1956. DL Herts, 1995. *Recreations:* microlight flying, gardening. *Address:* Kingswood, Millfield Lane, Hitchin, Herts SG4 7NH. *Club:* Royal Air Force.

MERRIMAN, James Henry Herbert, CB 1969; OBE 1961; MSc, MInstP, FEng, FIEE, FIEEIE; Chairman, National Computing Centre, 1977–83; Member for Technology, Post Office Corporation, 1969–76; *b* 1 Jan. 1915; *s* of Thomas P. Merriman, AMINA and A. Margaretta Jenkins; *m* 1942, Joan B. Frost; twin *s* one *d*. *Educ:* King's Coll. Sch., Wimbledon; King's Coll., University of London. BSc (Hons) 1935; MSc (Thesis) 1936. Entered GPO Engrg Dept (Research), 1936; Officer i/c Castleton Radio Stn, 1940; Asst Staff Engr, Radio Br., 1951; Imp. Def. Coll., 1954; Dep. Dir, Organisation and Methods, HM Treasury, 1956; GPO: Dep. Engr-in-Chief, 1965; Sen. Dir Engrg, 1967. Chairman: NEDO Sector Working Party on Office Machinery, 1979–83; NEDO Information Technology Cttee, 1980–83 (Mem. NEDO Electronics EDC, 1980–83); SERC/DoI/Industry Project Universe Steering Cttee, 1981–83; Home Office Radio Spectrum Review Cttee, 1982–83. Vis. Prof. of Electronic Science and Telecommunications, Strathclyde Univ., 1969–79. Governor, Imperial College, Univ. of London, 1971–83; Chm., Inspec, 1975–79; Dir, Infoline, 1976–80; Member: Nat. Electronics Council, 1969–76; Computer Bd for Univ. and Res. Councils, 1976–81; Exec. Bd, BSI, 1981–85 (Chm. Council for Inf. Systems); Science Museum Adv. Council, 1976–81; Council, Spurgeon's Coll., 1972–87. Mem. Council, IEE, 1965–80 (Chm. Electronics Div. Bd, 1968; Vice-Pres., 1969–72, Dep. Pres., 1972; Pres., 1974–75; Hon. FIEE 1981; Faraday Lectr, 1969–70); Royal Instn Discourse, 1971. FKC 1972. Mem., Hon. Soc. of Cymmrodorion, 1979–89. Hon. DSc Strathclyde, 1974. *Publications:* contribs to scientific and professional jls on tele-communications and inf. technology subjects. *Recreations:* walking, music, cactus growing.

MERRITT, Prof. John Edward; Emeritus Professor, The Open University, since 1987; educational research in association with Charlotte Mason College, Ambleside, since 1985; *b* 13 June 1926; *s* of Leonard Merritt and Janet (*née* Hartford); *m* 1948, Denise Edmondson; two *s*. *Educ:* Univ. of Durham (BA); Univ. of London (DipEdPsychol). ABPsS; FRSA. Sandhurst, 1945–46; Trng Officer, Border Regt, 1946–48. Educnl Psychologist, Lancs LEA, 1957–59; Sen. Educnl Psychologist, Hull LEA, 1959–63; Lectr, Inst. of Educn, Univ. of Durham, 1964–71; Prof. of Teacher Educn, Open Univ., 1971–85, retd. Emeritus Fellow, Leverhulme Trust, 1986–88. Pres., UK Reading Assoc., 1969–70; Chm., 5th World Congress on Reading, Vienna, 1974; Mem., Nat. Cttee of Inquiry into Reading and Use of English (Bullock Cttee), 1973–75. Hon. FCP 1994. *Publications:* Reading and the Curriculum (ed), 1971; A Framework for Curriculum Design, 1972; (ed jtly) Reading Today and Tomorrow, 1972; (ed jtly) The Reading Curriculum, 1972; Perspectives on Reading, 1973; What Shall We Teach, 1974; numerous papers in educnl jls. *Recreations:* fell walking, climbing, ski-ing, theatre. *Address:* Wetherlam, 20 Fisherbeck Park, Ambleside, Cumbria LA22 0AJ. *T:* Ambleside (015394) 32259.

MERRITT, Prof. Neil; Vice-Chancellor, University of Portsmouth, 1992–94 (President, Portsmouth Polytechnic, 1991–92); *b* 3 March 1939; *s* of the late Leslie Alfred Merritt and Gladys Irene (*née* Green); *m* 1961, Jean Fisher (Headmistress, Heathfield Sch., GPDST, Pinner); one *s* one *d*. *Educ:* Ilford County High Sch.; Univ. of Hull (LLB). Asst Lectr, City of London Coll., 1962–63; Lectr, Slough Coll., 1963–65; Staff Tutor, Further Educn Staff Coll., 1965–68; Head, Faculty of Management and Arts, Norfolk Coll. of Arts and Technology, 1968–73; Vice-Principal, Mid-Essex Technical Coll., 1973–74; Pro-Dir, Chelmer Inst. of Higher Educn, 1975–76; Vis. Prof. of Law, Indiana Univ., 1974 and 1976; Dir, Ealing Tech. Coll., later Ealing Coll. of Higher Educn, then Polytechnic of W London, 1977–91 (Prof. *ad hominem*, 1989). Secretary, then Chairman: Assoc. of Law Teachers, 1965–71; Standing Conf. of Principals, 1977–91; Member: Adv. Cttee on Legal Educn, 1972–76; CNAA Legal Studies Bd, 1978–84; Nat. Adv. Body for Public Sector Higher Educn Bd, 1982–88 (Mem., Chm.'s Study Gp, 1983–88); Trustee, then Vice-Chm., Central Bureau for Educnl Visits and Exchanges, 1980–88; Chairman: Cttee for Business and Finance, BTEC, 1982–85; Polytechnic and Colls Employers Forum, 1990–92; Pres., European Assoc. of Higher Educn, 1990–92; Co-Chm., Cttee for Higher Educn in EC, 1991–92. Chm., Hillingdon Hosp. Trust, 1991–94. FRSA. *Publications:* (with E. G. H. Clayton) Business Law, 1966; articles in professional jls on law, and higher educn policy. *Recreations:* reading, opera, travel, sailing, shortening meetings.

MERRIVALE, 3rd Baron, *cr* 1925, of Walkhampton, Co. Devon; **Jack Henry Edmond Duke;** *b* 27 Jan. 1917; *o s* of 2nd Baron Merrivale, OBE, and Odette, *d* of Edmond Roger, Paris; *S* father 1951; *m* 1st, 1939, Colette (marr. diss. 1974), *d* of John Douglas Wise, Bordeaux, France; one *s* one *d*; 2nd, 1975, Betty, *widow* of Paul Baron. *Educ:* Dulwich; Ecole des Sciences Politiques, Paris. Served War of 1939–45, RAF, 1940; Flight-Lieut, 1944 (despatches). Formerly Chm., Scotia Investments Plc; Chm., Grecian Investments (Gibraltar) Ltd (formerly Leisure Investments (Gibraltar) Ltd), 1990–; Pres., Inst. of Traffic Administration, 1953–70; Chairman: Anglo-Malagasy Soc., 1961; British Cttee for Furthering of Relations with French-speaking Africa, 1973; GB–Senegal Friendship Assoc., 1990. Founder Mem., Club de Dakar, 1974. Freeman, City of London, 1979. FRSA 1964. Chevalier, Nat. Order of Malagasy, 1968; Commander, Nat. Order of the Lion (Senegal), 1992. *Recreations:* sailing, riding, photography. *Heir: s* Hon. Derek John Philip Duke, *b* 16 March 1948. *Address:* 16 Brompton Lodge, SW7 2JA. *T:* 0171–581 5678.

MERSEY, 4th Viscount *cr* 1916, of Toxteth; **Richard Maurice Clive Bigham;** Baron 1910; Master of Nairne; film director; *b* 8 July 1934; *e s* of 3rd Viscount Mersey, and of 12th Lady Nairne, *qv*; *S* father, 1979; *m* 1961, Joanna, *d* of late John A. R. G. Murray, CBE; one *s*. *Educ:* Eton and Balliol. Irish Guards, 1952–54 (final rank Lt). Films incl. documentaries for Shell, LEPRA and Government (various awards, London and Venice). President: SIESO, 1987–91; Combined Heat and Power Assoc., 1989–92. FRGS. *Publication:* The Hills of Cork and Kerry, 1987. *Heir: s* Hon. Edward John Hallam Bigham [*b* 23 May 1966; *m* 1994, Claire, *d* of David Haigh]. *Address:* Bignor Park, Pulborough, West Sussex RH20 1HG. *T:* Sutton (01798) 869214.

MERTENS DE WILMARS, Baron Josse (Marie Honoré Charles); Grand Croix de l'Ordre de la Couronne; Chevalier de l'Ordre de Léopold; Judge, 1967–80, and President, 1980–84, Court of Justice of the European Communities; Emeritus Professor, Faculty of Law, Catholic University of Leuven, since 1971; Member of the University Curatorium, 1972–90; *b* 12 June 1912; *s* of (Marie Antoine Joseph) Albert Mertens de Wilmars and Jeanne Eugénie Marie Anne Meert; *m* 1939, Elisabeth Simonne M. Hubertine van Ormelingen; three *s* five *d*. *Educ:* Abdijschool, Zevenkerke, Bruges; Catholic Univ. of Leuven (Dr in Law, Dr in Pol. and Diplomatic Science). Hon. Assessor, Legislative Dept of Council of State (Conseil d'Etat) (Assessor, 1950–52). Mem., Chambre des Représentants de Belgique (Lower House of Parlt), 1952–62; former Mem., Bar Council. Hon. Mem., Bar of Antwerp. Chief Editor, Revue Internationale Droit Economique, 1989–93. CStJ. Groot kruis van de Orde van Orange Nassau (Neth.); Grand Croix de l'Ordre de la Couronne de Chêne (Lux.); Grosskreuz des Verdienstordens der Bundesrepublik Deutschland. *Publications:* several works on Belgian and European Law. *Address:* 192 Jan Van Rijswijcklaan, 2020 Antwerpen, Belgium. *T:* (3) 2380768.

MERTHYR, Barony of (*cr* 1911); title disclaimed by 4th Baron; *see under* Lewis, Trevor Oswin.

MERTON, Viscount; Simon John Horatio Nelson; *b* 21 Sept. 1971; *s* and *heir* of 9th Earl Nelson, *qv*.

MERTON, John Ralph, MBE 1942; painter; *b* 7 May 1913; *s* of late Sir Thomas Merton, KBE, FRS; *m* 1939, Viola Penelope von Bernd; two *d* (and one *d* decd). *Educ:* Eton; Balliol Coll., Oxford. Served War of 1939–45 (MBE); Air Photo reconnaissance research, Lieut-Col 1944. Works include: Mrs Daphne Wall, 1948; The Artist's daughter, Sarah, 1949; Altar piece, 1952; The Countess of Dalkeith, at Drumlanrig, 1958; A myth of Delos, 1959; Clarissa, 1960; Mrs Julian Sheffield, 1970; Sir Charles Evans, 1973; Iona Colquhoun Duchess of Argyll, 1982; Triple Portrait of Sir David Piper, 1984 (in Nat. Portrait Gall.); James Meade, 1987; Triple Portrait of HRH The Princess of Wales (for Cardiff City Hall), 1987; HM The Queen (at Windsor Castle), 1989; Paul H. Nitze (in Johns Hopkins Univ.), 1991; Triple Portrait of Duke of Grafton (for Nat. Portrait Gall.), 1992. Legion of Merit (USA), 1945. *Publication:* A Journey Through an Artist's Life, 1994. *Recreations:* music, making things, underwater photography. *Address:* Pound House, Oare, near Marlborough, Wilts SN8 4JA. *T:* Marlborough (01672) 563539.

See also Hon. Sir R. A. Morritt.

MERTON, Patrick Anthony, MD; FRCP; FRS 1979; Professor of Human Physiology, University of Cambridge, 1984–88; Fellow of Trinity College, Cambridge, since 1962; *b* 8 Oct. 1920; *s* of late Gerald Merton, MC, PhD, FRAS; *m* 1951, Anna Gabriel Howe; one *s* three *d*. *Educ:* The Leys; Beaumont; Trinity Coll., Cambridge (MB 1946; MD 1982); St Thomas's Hosp. FRCP 1991. On staff of MRC's Neurol. Res. Unit, National Hosp., Queen Sq., 1946–57; Nobel Inst. for Neurophysiology, Stockholm, 1952–54; Lectr, 1957–77, Reader, 1977–84, Univ. of Cambridge; Hon. Consultant in Clin. Neurophysiol., Nat. Hosp., Queen Sq., 1979–; Hon. Sen. Res. Fellow, Royal Postgrad. Med. Sch., 1981–82. *Publications:* scientific papers. *Address:* Trinity College, Cambridge CB2 1TQ.

MERVYN DAVIES, David Herbert; *see* Davies, D. H. M.

MESHER, John; Social Security Commissioner and Child Support Commissioner, since 1993; *b* 25 June 1947; *s* of Percy Charles Mesher and Dorothy Mesher; *m* 1973, Hilary Anne Wilkens; one *s* and *d* (and one *d* decd). *Educ:* Bancroft's Sch.; University Coll., Oxford (BA Jurisp, BCL); Yale Law Sch. (LLM). Called to the Bar, Gray's Inn, 1970; Lectr in Laws, QMC, 1969–76; University of Sheffield: Lectr in Law, Sen. Lectr and Reader, 1976–93; Simmons & Simmons Res. Fellow in Pensions Law, 1988–93; Prof. Associate, 1993–. Part-time Chm. of Social Security, Medical, and Disability Appeals Tribunals, 1981–93, Pensions Appeal Tribunals, 1995–; Dep. Social Security Comr, 1991–93. Editor, Occupational Pensions Law Reports, 1992–; Section Editor, Encyclopedia of Employment Law, 1991–. *Publications:* Compensation for Unemployment, 1976; (ed) CPAG's Supplementary Benefit Legislation Annotated, 1983, 10th edn, as Income-Related Benefits: the Legislation, 1993; contribs to learned jls. *Address:* Office of the Social Security and Child Support Commissioners, Harp House, 83 Farringdon Street, EC4A 4DH. *T:* 0171–353 5145.

MESSEL, Prof. Harry, CBE 1979; BA, BSc, BMilSci; PhD (NUI) 1951; Professor and Head of the School of Physics, and Director of Science Foundation for Physics, University of Sydney, Australia, 1952–87, now Emeritus Professor; Executive Chancellor, Bond University, since 1993 (Chancellor, 1992); *b* 3 March 1922. *Educ:* Rivers Public High Sch., Rivers, Manitoba. Entered RMC of Canada, 1940, grad. with Governor-General's Silver Medal, 1942. Served War of 1939–45: Canadian Armed Forces, Lieut, Canada and overseas, 1942–45. Queen's Univ., Kingston, Ont., 1945–48 (BA 1st Cl. Hons in Mathematics, 1948; BSc Hons in Engineering Physics, 1948); St Andrews Univ., Scotland, 1948–49; Institute for Advanced Studies, Dublin, Eire, 1949–51; Sen. Lectr in Mathematical Physics, University of Adelaide, Australia, 1951–52. Mem., Aust. Atomic Energy Commn, 1974–81; Sen. Vice-Chm., Species Survival Commn, IUCN, 1978– (Chm., Crocodile Specialist Gp, 1989–). Hon. DSc Sydney; Hon. DHL. *Publications:* Chap. 4, Progress in Cosmic Ray Physics, vol. 2, (North Holland Publishing Company), 1953; co-author and editor of: A Modern Introduction to Physics (Horwitz-Grahame, Vols I, II, III, 1959, 1960, 1962); Selected Lectures in Modern Physics, 1958; Space and the Atom, 1961; A Journey through Space and the Atom, 1962; The Universe of Time and Space, 1963; Light and Life in the Universe, 1964; Science for High School Students, 1964; Time, 1965; Senior Science for High School Students, 1966; (jt) Electron-Photon Shower Distribution Function, 1970; (jt) Multistrand Senior Science for High School Students, 1975; Australian Animals and their Environment, 1977; Time and Man, 1978; Tidal Rivers in Northern Australia and their Crocodile Populations (20 monographs), 1979–87; The Study of Populations, 1985; editor of: From Nucleus to Universe, 1960; Atoms to Andromeda, 1966; Apollo and the Universe, 1967; Man in Inner and Outer Space, 1968; Nuclear Energy Today and Tomorrow, 1969; Pioneering in Outer Space, 1970; Molecules to Man, 1971; Brain Mechanisms and the Control of Behaviour, 1972; Focus on the Stars, 1973; Solar Energy, 1974; Our Earth, 1975; Energy for Survival, 1979; The Biological Manipulation of Life, 1981; Science Update, 1983; The Study of Population, 1985; Highlights in Science, 1987; numerous papers published in: Proc. Physical Soc., London; Philosophical Magazine, London; Physical Review of America. *Recreations:* conservation, water ski-ing, hunting, fishing and photography. *Address:* Bond University, Gold Coast, Qld 4229, Australia. *T:* (75) 951044, *Fax:* (75) 951046.

MESSER, Cholmeley Joseph; Chairman, London Pension Funds Authority, since 1992 (Member, 1989–92); Director, HFC Bank plc, since 1993; *b* 20 March 1929; *s* of late Col Arthur Albert Messer, DSO. CBE, FRIBA, and Lilian Hope Messer (*née* Dowling); *m* 1956, Ann Mary Power; two *d*. *Educ:* Wellington Coll. Solicitor. Served KRRC, 2nd Lieut, 1948–49. Articled Lawrance Messer & Co., Solicitors, London 1949–54; Partner, 1957–66; Save & Prosper Group: Exec. Dir, 1967–72; Dep. Man. Dir, 1973–80; Man. Dir, 1980–84; Chm., 1981–89. Chm., Code of Advertising Practice Cttee, Advertising Standards Authority, 1977–78; Vice-Chm., Internat. Bar Assoc. Cttee on Investment Cos Funds and Trusts, 1978–81; Chm., Unit Trust Assoc., 1981–83; Chm., British Bobsleigh Assoc., 1989–92. *Recreations:* armchair sport, gardening, golf, railways. *Address:* The Manor House, Normandy, Guildford, Surrey GU3 2AP. *T:* Guildford (01483) 810910. *Club:* City of London.

MESSITER, Malcolm; oboist; Founder and Managing Director: Messiter Software, since 1985; Trans-Send International Ltd, since 1992; *b* 1 April 1949; *s* of Ian and Enid Messiter; *m* 1972, Christine (marr. diss. 1990); one *d*. *Educ:* Bryanston Sch.; Paris Conservatoire; Royal Coll. of Music (ARCM Hons 1971). First Oboe: BBC Concert Orchestra, 1971–77; London Mozart Players, 1977–83; London Festival Orchestra, 1985–; many solo concerts. Several recordings. *Publications:* personal computer software and manuals. *Recreations:* wine, music, opera, model aeroplanes. *Address:* 47 Sutton Crescent, Barnet, Herts EN5 2SW.

MESSMER, Pierre Auguste Joseph; Grand Croix de la Légion d'Honneur; Compagnon de la Libération; Croix de Guerre, 1939–45; Médaille de la Résistance; Député (RPR) from Moselle, 1968–88; *b* Vincennes (Seine), 20 March 1916; *s* of Joseph Messmer, industrialist, and of Marthe (*née* Farcy); *m* 1947, Gilberte Duprez. *Educ:* Lycées Charlemagne and Louis-le Grand; Faculty of Law, Paris; Ecole Nationale de la France d'Outre-Mer. Pupil Administrator of Colonies, 1938. Served War of 1939–45: Free French Forces, 1940; African Campaigns (Bir-Hakeim), France, Germany; parachuted Tonkin; PoW of Vietminh, 1945. Sec.-Gen., Interministerial Cttee of Indochina, 1946; Dir of Cabinet of E. Bollaert (High Commissioner, Indochina), 1947–48; Administrator-in-Chief of France Overseas, 1950; Governor: of Mauritania, 1952, of Ivory Coast, 1954–56; Dir of Cabinet of G. Defferre (Minister, France Overseas), Jan.–April 1956; High Commissioner: Republic of Cameroon, 1956–58; French Equatorial Africa, 1958; French West Africa, July 1958–Dec. 1959; Minister of Armed Forces: (Cabinets: M. Debré, 5 Feb. 1958–14 April 1962; G. Pompidou, April–Nov. 1962, 6 Dec. 1962–7 Jan. 1966, 8 Jan. 1966–1 April 1967, 7 April 1967–10 July 1968; M. Couve de Murville, 12 July 1968–20 June 1969); Minister of State in charge of Depts and Territories Overseas, Feb. 1971–72; Prime Minister, 1972–74; Mem. European Parliament, 1979–80. Pres., RPR Federal Cttee, Moselle, 1969–88. Mayor of Sarrebourg, 1971–89. Mem., l'Institut (Académie des Sciences Morales et Politiques), 1988. Officer, American Legion. *Publications:* (jtly) Les écrits militaires de Charles de Gaulle: essai d'analyse thématique, 1986; Après tant de batailles, 1992. *Recreations:* tennis, sailing. *Address:* 1 rue du Général Delanne, 92 Neuilly-sur-Seine, France.

MESTEL, Prof. Leon, PhD; FRS 1977; Professor of Astronomy, University of Sussex, 1973–92, now Emeritus; *b* 5 Aug. 1927; *s* of late Rabbi Solomon Mestel and Rachel (*née* Brodetsky); *m* 1951, Sylvia Louise Cole; two *s* two *d*. *Educ:* West Ham Secondary Sch., London; Trinity Coll., Cambridge (BA 1948, PhD 1952). ICI Res. Fellow, Dept of Maths, Univ. of Leeds, 1951–54; Commonwealth Fund Fellow, Princeton Univ. Observatory, 1954–55; University of Cambridge: Univ. Asst Lectr in Maths, 1955–58; Univ. Lectr in Maths, 1958–66; Fellow of St John's Coll., 1957–66; Vis. Mem., Inst. for Advanced Study, Princeton, 1961–62; J. F. Kennedy Fellow, Weizmann Inst. of Science, Israel, 1966–67; Prof. of Applied Maths, Manchester Univ., 1967–73. Eddington Medal, RAS, 1993. *Publications:* Magnetohydrodynamics (with N. O. Weiss), 1974 (Geneva Observatory); papers, revs and conf. reports on different branches of theoretical astrophysics. *Recreations:* reading, music. *Address:* 13 Prince Edward's Road, Lewes, E Sussex BN7 1BJ. *T:* Lewes (01273) 472731.

MESTON, family name of **Baron Meston.**

MESTON, 3rd Baron *cr* 1919, of Agra and Dunottar; **James Meston;** *b* 10 Feb. 1950; *s* of 2nd Baron Meston and of Diana Mary Came, *d* of Capt. O. S. Doll; *S* father, 1984; *m* 1974, Jean Rebecca Anne, *d* of John Carder; one *s* two *d*. *Educ:* Wellington College; St Catharine's Coll., Cambridge (MA); Leicester Univ. (LLM). Barrister, Middle Temple,

1973; Jun. Counsel to Queen's Proctor, 1992–. Legal Assessor, UKCC, 1991–. Appeal Steward, BBB of C, 1993–. Pres., British Soc. of Commerce, 1984–92. *Heir: s* Hon. Thomas James Dougall Meston, *b* 21 Oct. 1977. *Address:* Queen Elizabeth Building, Temple, EC4Y 9BS. *T:* 0171–797 7837. *Club:* Hawks (Cambridge).

METCALF, Prof. David Harry, PhD; Professor of Industrial Relations, London School of Economics, since 1985; *b* 15 May 1942; *s* of Geoffrey and Dorothy Metcalf; *m* 1968, Helen Pitt; one *s*. *Educ:* Manchester Univ. (BA Econ 1964; MA 1966); London Univ. (PhD 1971). Apprentice welder, English Electric, 1959–61; Lectr in Econs, LSE, 1967–75; Special Advr to Minister for Social Security, 1976–79; Prof. of Econs, Kent Univ., 1978–85. Editor, British Jl Industrial Relns, 1990–. *Publications:* Low Pay, Occupational Mobility and Minimum Wage Policy in Britain, 1983; New Perspectives on Industrial Disputes, 1993; articles in Econ. Jl, Industrial and Labor Relns Rev., etc. *Recreations:* horse-racing (owner and investor), watching Tottenham Hotspur FC. *Address:* 18 St Georges Avenue, N7 0HD. *T:* 0171–607 5902. *Club:* MCC.

METCALF, David Michael, DPhil, DLitt; Keeper of Heberden Coin Room, Ashmolean Museum, Oxford, since 1982; Fellow of Wolfson College, Oxford, since 1982; *b* 8 May 1933; *s* of Rev. Thomas Metcalf and Gladys Metcalf; *m* 1958, Dorothy Evelyn (*née* Uren); two *s* one *d*. *Educ:* St John's College, Cambridge. MA, DPhil, DLitt; FSA. Asst Keeper, Ashmolean Museum, 1963. Pres., Royal Numismatic Soc., 1994– (Sec., and Editor, Numismatic Chronicle, 1974–84). *Publications:* Coinage in South-eastern Europe 820–1396, 1979; Coinage of the Crusades and the Latin East, 1983; (ed with D. H. Hill) Sceattas in England and on the Continent, 1984; Coinage in Ninth-century Northumbria, 1987; Thrymsas and Sceattas in the Ashmolean Museum, Oxford: vol. 1, 1993, vol. 2, 1993, vol. 3, 1994; articles on numismatics in various jls. *Address:* 40 St Margaret's Road, Oxford OX2 6LD; Ashmolean Museum, Oxford OX1 2PH.

METCALF, Prof. Donald, AC 1993 (AO 1976); FRS 1983, FRACP, FRCPA, FAA; Head of Cancer Research Unit, Walter and Eliza Hall Institute of Medical Research, Melbourne, since 1965; Research Professor of Cancer Biology, University of Melbourne, since 1986; *b* 26 Feb. 1929; *s* of Donald Davidson Metcalf and Enid Victoria Metcalf (*née* Thomas); *m* 1954, Josephine Emily Lentaigne; four *d*. *Educ:* Sydney University. MD, BSc (med). Resident MO, Royal Prince Alfred Hosp., Sydney, 1953–54; Surgeon-Lieut, RANR, 1953–58; Carden Fellow in Cancer Res., 1954–65, Asst Director and Head of Cancer Res. Unit, 1965–, Walter and Eliza Hall Inst. Vis. Fellow, Harvard Med. Sch., 1956–58; Visiting Scientist: Roswell Park Meml Inst., Buffalo, 1966–67; Swiss Inst. for Experimental Cancer Res., Lausanne, 1974–75; Radiobiological Res. Inst., Rijswijk, 1980–81; Royal Soc. Guest Res. Fellow, Cambridge Univ., 1981. *Publications:* The Thymus, 1966; (with M. A. S. Moore) Haemopoietic Cells, 1971; Hemopoietic Colonies, 1977; Hemopoietic Colony Stimulating Factors, 1984; The Molecular Control of Blood Cells, 1988; (with N. A. Nicola) The Hemopoietic Colony Stimulating Factors, 1995; numerous scientific papers on cancer and leukaemia. *Recreations:* music, tennis. *Address:* 268 Union Road, Balwyn, Victoria 3103, Australia. *T:* (3) 98361343.

METCALF, Malcolm, MC 1944; DL; Chairman, Surrey County Council, 1978–81; *b* 1 Dec. 1917; *s* of Charles Almond Metcalf and Martha Fatherly Atkins Metcalf; *m* 1945, Charis Thomas; two *s*. *Educ:* Merchant Taylors' Sch., Crosby. ACIS. Army service, 1939–46. Contested (C) Barrow-in-Furness, 1959; Mem., Surrey CC, 1965–89 (Leader, 1973–77; Vice-Chm., 1977–78); Member: Metrop. Water Board, 1965–74 (Vice-Chm. 1971–72); Thames Conservancy, 1970–74; Thames Water Authority, 1973–78, 1981–87. Mem., Assoc. of County Councils, 1975–88. DL Surrey, 1979. *Address:* 1 The Lodge, Watts Road, Thames Ditton KT7 0DE. *T:* 0181–398 3057. *Clubs:* MCC, Burhill Golf (Walton-on-Thames).

METCALF, Ven. Robert Laurence; Archdeacon of Liverpool, since 1994; *b* 18 Nov. 1935; *s* of late Victor Noel Metcalf and Phyllis Maud Metcalf (*née* Dunwell); *m* 1964, Rachel Margaret Herring; two *s* three *d*. *Educ:* St John's Coll., Durham Univ. (BA 1960; rowing colours, 1960); Cranmer Hall, Durham (DipTheol 1962). Nat. Service, REME, 1955–57. Ordained deacon, 1962, priest, 1963; Curate: Christ Church, Bootle, 1962–65; i/c St John's, Widnes, 1965–67; Vicar, St Catharine, Wigan, 1967–75; Dir, Wigan Br., Samaritans, 1970–75; Rector, Holy Trinity, Wavertree, 1974–94; Chaplain: Liverpool Royal Sch. for the Blind, 1975–94; Blue Coat Sch., Liverpool, 1975–94; Diocesan Dir of Ordinands, Liverpool, 1982–94; Hon. Canon, Liverpool Cathedral, 1988. Occasional broadcaster, BBC Radio Merseyside. *Publications:* contrib.: Prayers for Today's Church, 1972; For All the Family, 1984; Prayers for Today's World, 1993; Reconciliation. *Recreations:* walking, rowing, reading novels (political intrigue!), holidaying. *Address:* 38 Menlove Avenue, Allerton, Liverpool L18 2EF. *T:* 0151–724 3956.

METCALFE, Adrian Peter; Director of Venue Production, Atlantic Olympic Games, since 1996; *b* 2 March 1942; *s* of Hylton and Cora Metcalfe; *m* 1966 (marr. diss. 1993); one *s* one *d*; *m* 1994, Baroness von Delviq. *Educ:* Roundhay Sch., Leeds; Magdalen Coll., Oxford. Reporter, Sunday Express, 1964; Dep. Editor, World of Sport, ABC TV, 1965; Producer, Sports Arena, LWT, 1968; Vice Pres., Marvin H. Sugarman, 1972; Presenter, CBS Sports Spectacular, 1972–76; Man. Dir, AMO Productions, 1976; Sen. Commissioning Editor, Sport and Features, Channel 4 TV, 1981; Commentator, ITV, 1966–87; Director of Programmes: Eurosport, Satellite TV, 1989–91; Tyne Tees Television Ltd, 1991–92; Dir, Tyne Tees Television Hldgs, 1991–92; Man. Dir, Lifetime Broadcast, 1992–94. GB Record, 400m, 45·7, ranked No 1 in the world at 400m, 1961; Silver Medal, 4×400m, European and Commonwealth Games, 1962; Gold Medal, 400m and 4×400m, World Student Games, 1963; Silver Medal, 4×400m, Tokyo Olympics, 1964; 9 victories, Oxford *v* Cambridge, 1961–64; 7 British Records, 4 European Records, 1961–64. Pres., OUAC, 1962–63. Hon. Vice-Pres. and Trustee, Sports Aid Foundn, 1990–. Governor, Bracknell Coll., 1990–. *Recreations:* choral music, theatre, horses. *Address:* 15 Tunis Road, W12 7EZ. *T.* 0181–749 9233.

METCALFE, Prof. David Henry Harold, OBE 1989; Senior Adviser on Curricular Development, University of Manchester School of Medicine, since 1993; Professor of General Practice, University of Manchester School of Medicine, 1978–92, now Professor Emeritus; *b* 3 Jan. 1930; *s* of Henry R. Metcalfe and Mary Metcalfe (*née* Evans); *m* 1957, Anne (*née* Page); three *s*. *Educ:* Leys School, Cambridge; Cambridge Univ. (clinical course at Liverpool) (MA, MB, BChir); MSc Manchester. FRCGP; FFPHM. United Liverpool Hosps, 1956–58; Principal in gen. practice, Hessle, E Yorks, 1960–70; Asst Prof. in Family Medicine, Univ. of Rochester, NY, 1970–72; Sen. Lectr (GP), Dept of Community Health, Nottingham Univ. Med. Sch., 1972–78. Dir, DHSS Urban Primary Care Res. Unit, 1978–92. Vice-Chm., RCGP, 1983–84. *Publications:* papers on medical information handling, doctor-patient communication, patterns of general practice, and medical educn. *Recreations:* photography, sailing, hill walking. *Address:* Westgate Barn, Milburn, Penrith, Cumbria CA10 1TW. *T:* Penrith (017683) 61947.

METCALFE, Hugh, OBE 1969; FEng; FRAeS; Director, Ricardo Group plc (formerly SAC International, then Ricardo International), since 1989; *b* 26 June 1928; *s* of late Clifford Metcalfe, CBE and Florence Ellen Metcalfe; *m* 1952, Pearl Allison Carter; three *s*. *Educ:* Harrow County Grammar School; Imperial College, Univ. of London. BSc, ARCS. RAF, 1946–48; joined Bristol Aeroplane Co., 1951; Divisional Dir, 1974; British Aerospace Dynamics Group: Group Dir, Naval Weapons, 1978; Man. Dir, Bristol Div., 1980; Man. Dir, Hatfield Div., 1981; Chief Exec., 1982; Dir, 1982–88, and Dep. Chief Exec. (Ops), 1986–88, BAe. Pres., RAeS, 1989–90. Hon. DSc Hatfield Polytechnic, 1988; Hon. DEng Bristol Univ., 1992. RAeS gold medal, 1984. *Recreation:* choral music. *Address:* Amberley, 28 Druid Stoke Avenue, Stoke Bishop, Bristol BS9 1DD. *Clubs:* Athenæum; Leander; Savage's (Bristol).

METCALFE, Air Commodore Joan, CB 1981; RRC 1976; Director of RAF Nursing Services, and Matron in Chief, Princess Mary's Royal Air Force Nursing Service, 1978–81; *b* 8 Jan. 1923; *d* of late W. and S. H. Metcalfe. *Educ:* West Leeds High Sch. for Girls; Leeds Coll. of Commerce. St James's Hosp., Leeds, 1943–47 (SRN); St James's Hosp. and Redcourt Hostel, Leeds, 1947–48 (SCM), PMRAFNS 1948. Served in RAF Hospitals in Egypt, Iraq, Libya, Cyprus, Germany, Singapore, and UK. Sen. Matron, 1970; Principal Matron, 1973. QHNS 1978–81. OStJ 1977. *Recreations:* classical music, theatre, needlework, gardening, non-fiction literature. *Address:* 10 Amport Close, Harestock, Winchester, Hants SO22 6LP. *T:* Winchester (01962) 880260. *Club:* Royal Air Force.

METCALFE, Stanley Gordon; Chairman: Queens Moat Houses plc, since 1993; Ranks Hovis McDougall PLC, 1989–93, retired (Managing Director, 1981–89, Chief Executive, 1984–89, and Deputy Chairman, 1987–89); *b* 20 June 1932; *s* of Stanley Hudson Metcalfe and Jane Metcalfe; *m* 1968, Sarah Harter; two *d*. *Educ:* Leeds Grammar Sch.; Pembroke Coll., Oxford (MA). Commnd Duke of Wellington's Regt, 1952. Trainee, Ranks, Hovis McDougall, 1956–59; Director, Stokes & Dalton, Leeds, 1963–66; Managing Director, McDougalls, 1966–69; Director, Cerebos Ltd, 1969–70; Managing Director: RHM Overseas Ltd, 1970–73; RHM Cereals Ltd, 1973–79; Director, Ranks Hovis McDougall Ltd, 1979. Member: Exec. Cttee, FDF, 1987–93 (Pres., 1990–92); Priorities Bd for R&D in Agriculture and Food, 1987–92; CBI President's Cttee, 1990–93; Council, Business in the Community, 1990–93. Chm., Adv. Bd, Inst. of Food Research, 1988–. President, Nat. Assoc. of British and Irish Millers, 1978. *Recreations:* cricket, golf, theatre. *Address:* The Oast House, Lower Froyle, Alton, Hants GU34 4LX. *T:* Bentley (01420) 22310. *Clubs:* Boodle's, MCC; IZ, Arabs.

METFORD, Prof. John Callan James; Professor of Spanish, 1960–81, now Emeritus Professor, Head of Department of Hispanic and Latin American Studies, 1973–81, University of Bristol; *b* 29 Jan. 1916; *s* of Oliver Metford and Florence Stowe Thomas; *m* 1944, Edith Donald; one *d*. *Educ:* Porth Grammar Sch.; Universities of Liverpool, Yale and California. Commonwealth Fund Fellow, 1939–41; British Council Lecturer in Brazil, 1942–44; Regional Officer, Latin American Department of the British Council, 1944–46; Lectr in Latin American Studies, Univ. of Glasgow, 1946–55; Bristol University: Head of Dept of Spanish and Portuguese, 1955–73; Prof., 1960–81; Dean of Faculty of Arts, 1973–76; Chm., Sch. of Modern Langs, 1976–79. Vis. Prof., Lehigh Univ., USA, 1968–69. Chm., Council of Westonbirt Sch., 1976–83; Mem., Central Cttee of Allied Schs, 1970–83; Governor, Coll. of St Matthias, Bristol, 1960–79; Mem., St Matthias Trust; Professorial Mem., Council of Univ. of Bristol, 1972–74; Founder Trustee, The Octagon, Univ. of West England (formerly Bristol Poly.), 1993–. Mem., Diocesan Adv. Cttee, Bristol, 1984–93. *Publications:* British Contributions to Spanish and Spanish American Studies, 1950; San Martín the Liberator, 1950, 2nd edn 1970; Modern Latin America, 1964; The Golden Age of Spanish Drama, 1969; Falklands or Malvinas?, rev. edn of J. Goebel: The Struggle for the Falkland Islands, 1982; Dictionary of Christian Lore and Legend, 1983; The Christian Year, 1991; articles in Bull. of Spanish Studies, Bull. of Hispanic Studies, Liverpool Studies in Spanish, International Affairs, Contemporary Review, etc. *Recreations:* opera, iconography. *Address:* 58 Westfield House, Cote Lane, Westbury-on-Trym, Bristol BS8 3UN. *T:* Bristol (0117) 949 4858.

METGE, Dame (Alice) Joan, DBE 1987; research anthropologist and writer; *b* 21 Feb. 1930; *d* of Cedric Leslie Metge and Alice Mary (*née* Rigg). *Educ:* Auckland Univ. (MA); London School of Economics (PhD). Jun. Lectr, Geography Dept, Auckland Univ., 1952; research and doctoral study, 1953–61; Lectr, Univ. Extension, Auckland Univ., 1961–64; University of Wellington: Sen. Lectr, Anthropology Dept, 1965–67, Associate Prof., 1968–88. Fifth Captain James Cook Res. Fellow, 1981–83. Hutchinson Medal, LSE, 1958, Elsdon Best Meml Medal, Polynesian Soc., 1987. *Publications:* A New Maori Migration, 1964; The Maoris of New Zealand, 1967, rev. edn 1976; (with Patricia Kinloch) Talking Past Each Other, 1978; In and Out of Touch, 1986; Te Kohao o Te Ngira, 1990. *Recreations:* theatre, music, reading, gardening. *Address:* 8 Paisley Terrace, Karori, Wellington 6005, New Zealand. *T:* (4)4766980.

METHUEN, family name of **Baron Methuen.**

METHUEN, 7th Baron *cr* 1838; **Robert Alexander Holt Methuen;** electrical engineer, retired from Roll-Royce plc, 1994; *b* 22 July 1931; *y s* of 5th Baron Methuen and Grace (*d* 1972), *d* of Sir Richard Durning Holt, 1st Bt; *S* brother, 1994; *m* 1st, 1958, Mary Catharine Jane (marr. diss. 1993), *o d* of late Ven. C. G. Hooper; two *d*; 2nd, 1994, Margrit Andrea, *o d* of Friedrich Hadwiger. *Educ:* Shrewsbury; Trinity Coll., Cambridge. *Heir: cousin* Christopher Paul Mansel Campbell Methuen-Campbell [*b* 23 March 1928; *m* 1st, 1950, Oona Cicily, *o d* of John Dalrymple Winn Treherne; one *s* three *d*; 2nd, 1975, Mrs Judith Anne Basset (*née* Crowther); one *s*]. *Address:* The Cascades, Nether Green, Bonsall, Derbyshire DE4 2AH.

METHUEN, Very Rev. John Alan Robert; Dean of Ripon, since 1995; *b* 14 Aug. 1947; *s* of late Rev. Alan Robert Methuen and Ruth Josephine Tyrrell Methuen; *m* 1970, Bridget Mary (*née* Andrews); two *d*. *Educ:* Upton Prep. Sch., Windsor; Eton Coll. Choir Sch.; St John's Sch., Leatherhead; Brasenose Coll., Oxford (Colquitt Exhibnr 1966; BA 1969; MA 1972); Cuddesdon Coll., Oxford. Asst Curate, Fenny Stratford and Water Eaton Team Ministry, Milton Keynes, 1971–74; Asst Chaplain, Eton Coll., 1974–77; Priest-in-Charge, St James, Dorney and Warden of Dorney Parish-Eton Coll. Conf. Centre, 1974–77; Vicar, St Mark, Reading, 1977–83; Rector, The Ascension, Hulme, Manchester, 1983–95. Mem., Egypt Exploration Soc. Gerald Avery Near Eastern Archaeolog. Prize, Oxford Univ., 1965. *Publications:* various lectures and papers. *Recreations:* drama and theatre, concerts and music-making; film-making, writing and broadcasting; history and archaeology; pilgrimage and travel (especially as leader and lecturer). *Address:* The Minster House, Ripon, North Yorkshire HG4 1PE. *T:* Ripon (01765) 603615.

METTERS, Dr Jeremy Stanley, CB 1994; FRCOG; Deputy Chief Medical Officer, Department of Health, since 1989; *b* 6 June 1939; *s* of late Thomas Lee Metters and Henrietta Currey; *m* 1962, Margaret Howell; two *s* one *d*. *Educ:* Eton; Magdalene College, Cambridge; St Thomas' Hosp. (MB BChir 1963, MA 1965). MRCOG 1970, FRCOG 1982. House officer posts, St Thomas' Hosp. and Reading, 1963–66; Lectr in Obst. and Gyn., St Thomas' Hosp., 1968–70; Registrar in Radiotherapy, 1970–72; DHSS 1972; SPMO (Under Sec.), 1984; Dep. Chief Scientist, DHSS, later Dept of Health, 1986–89. Member: Council of Europe Cttee on Bioethics (formerly Ethical and Legal Problems relating to Human Genetics), 1983–89; ESRC, 1986–88. *Publications:* papers in med. and sci. jls. *Recreations:* DIY, steam preservation.

METTYEAR, Michael King; His Honour Judge Mettyear; a Circuit Judge, since 1992; *b* 22 Sept. 1946; *s* of Charles Frank Henry King and Vera May (*née* Moore); *m* 1984, Gail Stafford; one *s* one *d*. *Educ:* LLB London (external). Called to the Bar, Middle Temple, 1973; a Recorder, 1990–92. *Recreations:* tennis, travel. *Address:* Hull Combined Court Centre, Lowgate, Hull HU1 2EZ. *T:* Hull (01482) 586161.

METZGER, Rev. Prof. Bruce Manning; George L. Collord Professor of New Testament Language and Literature, Princeton Theological Seminary, 1964–84, now Emeritus; *b* Middletown, Pa, 9 Feb. 1914; *o s* of late Maurice R. Metzger and Anna Manning Metzger; *m* 1944, Isobel Elizabeth, *e d* of late Rev. John Alexander Mackay, DD; two *s*. *Educ:* Lebanon Valley Coll. (BA 1935); Princeton Theol Seminary (ThB 1938, ThM 1939); Princeton Univ. (MA 1940, PhD 1942, Classics). Ordained, United Presbyterian Church, USA, 1939; Princeton Theological Seminary: Teaching Fellow in NT Greek, 1938–40; Instr. in NT, 1940–44; Asst Prof., 1944–48; Associate Prof., 1948–54; Prof., 1954–64. Dist. Vis. Prof., Fuller Theol Sem., 1970; Visiting Professor: Gordon-Conwell Theol Sem., 1978; Caribbean Grad. Sch. of Theol., Jamaica, 1990; Seminario Internacional Teológico Bautista, Buenos Aires, 1991; Schol. in Residence, Tyndale Hse, Cambridge, 1969; Visiting Fellow: Clare Hall, Cambridge, 1974; Wolfson Coll., Oxford, 1979; Vis. Lectr, Sem. Theol. Presbyt. do Sul, Campinas, Brazil, 1952; Lectr, New Coll. for Advanced Christian Studies, Berkeley, 1978; many lectures to some 100 other academic instns on 5 continents. Chairman, Amer. Cttee on Versions, Internat. Greek NT Project, 1950–; Secretary: Panel of Translators, Rev. Standard Version of Apocrypha, 1952–57; Amer. Textual Criticism Seminar, 1954–56; Member: Kurat. of Vetus Latina Inst., Beuron, 1959–; Adv. Cttee, Inst. of NT Textual Res., Münster, Germany, 1961–; Inst. for Advanced Study, Princeton, 1964 and 1974; Chairman: Cttee on Trans., Amer. Bible Soc., 1964–70; Amer. Exec. Cttee, Internat. Greek NT Project, 1970–88; Cttee of Translators, New RSV of the Bible, 1977–90. President: Soc. of Biblical Lit., 1971; Stud. Novi Test. Soc., 1971–72; N Amer. Patristic Soc., 1972; Soc. for Textual Scholarship, 1995; Corresp. Fellow Brit. Acad., 1978; Hon. Fellow and Corresp. Mem., Higher Inst. of Coptic Studies, Cairo, 1955; Mem., Amer. Philosophical Soc., 1986–. Hon. DD: Lebanon Valley Coll., 1951 (also Dist. Alumnus award of Alumni Assoc. 1961); St Andrews, 1964; Hon. DTheol Münster, 1971; Hon. LHD Findlay Coll., 1962; Hon. DLitt Potchefstroom, 1985. *Publications:* The Saturday and Sunday Lessons from Luke in the Greek Gospel Lectionary, 1944; Lexical Aids for Students of New Testament Greek, 1946, enlarged edn 1955 (trans. Malagasy, Korean); A Guide to the Preparation of a Thesis, 1950, 2nd edn 1961; Index of Articles on the New Testament and the Early Church Published in Festschriften, 1951, Supplement 1955; Annotated Bibliography of the Textual Criticism of the New Testament, 1955; (jtly) The Text, Canon, and Principal Versions of the Bible, 1956; An Introduction to the Apocrypha, 1957 (trans. Korean); Index to Periodical Literature on the Apostle Paul, 1960, 2nd edn 1970; Lists of Words Occurring Frequently in the Coptic New Testament (Sahidic Dialect), 1961; (jtly) The Oxford Concise Concordance to the Revised Standard Version of the Holy Bible, 1962; (jtly) The Oxford Annotated Bible, 1962; Chapters in the History of New Testament Textual Criticism, 1963; The Text of the New Testament, its Transmission, Corruption, and Restoration, 1964 (trans. German, Japanese, Korean, Chinese), 3rd enlarged edn 1992; The Oxford Annotated Apocrypha, 1965; The New Testament, its Background, Growth, and Content, 1965 (trans. Chinese, Korean); Index to Periodical Literature on Christ and the Gospels, 1966; Historical and Literary Studies, Pagan, Jewish, and Christian, 1968; A Textual Commentary on the Greek New Testament, 1971, 2nd edn 1994; The New Oxford Annotated Bible with the Apocrypha, expanded edn 1977; The Early Versions of the New Testament, their Origin, Transmission, and Limitations, 1977; New Testament Studies, Philological, Versional, and Patristic, 1980; Manuscripts of the Greek Bible, an Introduction to Greek Palaeography, 1981 (trans. Japanese); The Canon of the New Testament, its Origin, Development, and Significance, 1987 (trans. Korean, German); (jtly) The Making of the New Revised Standard Version of the Bible, 1991; Breaking the Code, Understanding the Book of Revelation, 1993; (ed) The Oxford Companion to the Bible, 1993; (general editor) Reader's Digest Condensed Bible, 1982 (trans. Italian, Korean); (ed) New Testament Tools and Studies, eighteen vols, 1960–93; (ed jtly) The Greek New Testament, 1966, 4th edn 1993; numerous articles in learned jls and encycs. *Recreations:* reading, woodworking. *Address:* 20 Cleveland Lane, Princeton, New Jersey 08540, USA. *T:* (609) 9244060. *Club:* Nassau (Princeton, New Jersey).

MEXBOROUGH, 8th Earl of, *cr* 1766; **John Christopher George Savile;** Baron Pollington, 1753; Viscount Pollington, 1766; *b* 16 May 1931; *s* of 7th Earl of Mexborough, and Josephine Bertha Emily (*d* 1992), *d* of late Captain Andrew Mansel Talbot Fletcher; *S* father, 1980; *m* 1st, 1958, Lady Elizabeth Hariot (marr. diss. 1972; she *d* 1987), *d* of 6th Earl of Verulam; one *s* (one *d* decd); 2nd, 1972, Mrs Catherine Joyce Vivian, *d* of late J. K. Hope, CBE; one *s* one *d*. MIMI. *Heir: s* Viscount Pollington, *qv*. *Address:* Arden Hall, Hawnby, York YO6 5LS. *T:* Bilsdale (01439) 798348; 14 Lennox Garden Mews, SW1X 0DP. *T:* 0171–589 3669. *Clubs:* All England Lawn Tennis and Croquet, Air Squadron; Mill Reef (Antigua).

MEYER, Sir Anthony John Charles, 3rd Bt, *cr* 1910; Policy Director, European Movement (UK), since 1992; *b* 27 Oct. 1920; *o s* of Sir Frank Meyer, MP, 2nd Bt, Ayot House, Ayot St Lawrence, Herts; *S* father, 1935; *m* 1941, Barbadee Violet, *o c* of late A. Charles Knight, JP, and of Mrs Charles Knight, Herne Place, Sunningdale; one *s* three *d*. *Educ:* Eton (Capt. of Oppidans); New Coll., Oxford. Served Scots Guards, 1941–45 (wounded); HM Treasury, 1945–46; entered HM Foreign Service, 1946; HM Embassy, Paris, 1951; 1st Sec., 1953; transferred to HM Embassy, Moscow, 1956; London, 1958. Cons. Research Dept, 1968. MP (C): Eton and Slough, 1964–66; W Flint, 1970–83, Clwyd NW, 1983–92. PPS to Chief Sec., Treasury, 1970–72; PPS to Sec. of State for Employment, 1972–74. Chm., Franco-British Parly Relations Cttee, 1979–92; Vice-Chm., Cons. European Affairs Cttee, 1979–89; Mem., Panel of Chairmen, House of Commons, 1985–92. Vice-Chm., Franco-British Council, 1986–; Mem. Bd, British Council of European Movement, 1990–. Trustee of Shakespeare National Memorial Theatre. Founder and Dir of political jl, Solon, 1969. Officier, Légion d'Honneur, France, 1983. *Publications:* A European Technological Community, 1966; Stand Up and Be Counted, 1990. *Recreations:* music, travel, skiing, cooking. *Heir: s* Anthony Ashley Frank Meyer [*b* 23 Aug. 1944; *m* 1966, Susan Mathilda (marr. diss. 1980), *d* of John Freestone; one *d*]. *Address:* Cottage Place, Brompton Square, SW3 2BE. *T:* 0171–589 7416. *Club:* Beefsteak.

MEYER, Christopher John Rome, CMG 1988; HM Diplomatic Service, on secondment to the Cabinet Office; Press Secretary to the Prime Minister, since 1994; *b* 22 Feb. 1944; *s* of Flight Lieut R. H. R. Meyer (killed in action 1944) and Mrs E. P. L. Meyer (now Mrs S. Landells); *m* 1976, Françoise Elizabeth Hedges, *d* of Air Cdre Sir Archibald Winskill, *qv*; two *s* one step *s*. *Educ:* Lancing College; Peterhouse, Cambridge (MA History); Johns Hopkins Sch. of Advanced Internat. Studies, Bologna. Third Sec., FO, 1966–67; Army Sch. of Education, 1967–68; Third, later Second, Sec., Moscow, 1968–70; Second Sec., Madrid, 1970–73; First Sec., FCO, 1973–78; First Sec., UK Perm. Rep. to European Communities, 1978–82; Counsellor and Hd of Chancery, Moscow, 1982–84; Head of News Dept, FCO, 1984–88; Fellow, Center for Internat. Affairs, Harvard, 1988–89; Minister (Commercial), 1989–92, Minister and Dep. Hd of Mission, 1992–93, Washington. *Address:* 10 Downing Street, SW1A 2AA.

MEYER, Rev. Conrad John Eustace; *b* 2 July 1922; *s* of William Eustace and Marcia Meyer; *m* 1960, Mary Wiltshire; no *c*. *Educ:* Clifton Coll.; Pembroke Coll., Cambridge; Westcott House. BA 1946, MA 1948. Served War of 1939–45: Royal Navy (commissioned from lower deck), 1942–46. Lieut (S) RNVR, post war, until apptd Chaplain, RNVR, 1950–54. Deacon, 1948; Priest, 1949; Asst Curate: St Francis, Ashton Gate, Bristol, 1948–51; Kenwyn, Truro, 1951; Falmouth Parish Church, 1954; Vicar of Devoran, Truro, 1956–65; Diocesan Youth Chaplain, 1956; Asst Dir of Religious Educn, 1958; Diocesan Sec. for Educn, 1960–69; Archdeacon of Bodmin, 1969–79; Hon. Canon of Truro, 1966–79; Examining Chaplain to Bishop of Truro, 1973–79; Bishop Suffragan of Dorchester, 1979–87 (Area Bishop, 1985–87); Hon. Asst Bishop, dio. of Truro, 1990–94. Received into RC Ch, 1994; ordained priest, 1995. Hon. Diocesan Sec., Nat. Soc., 1960–69. Society for Promoting Christian Knowledge: Mem. Governing Body, 1972–90; Chairman: Projects Cttee, 1973–87; Appeals Cttee, 1987–90; Vice Chm., 1988–90; Vice-Pres., 1990–. Chairman: Federation of Catholic Priests, 1976–79; Church Union Exec. Cttee, 1979–84; The Churches' Group on Funerals at Cemeteries and Crematoria, 1980–89. Fellow, Woodard Corp. of Schools, 1967–92; Provost, Western Div., Woodard Corp., 1970–92 (Hon. Fellow, 1993–94). Hon. FICD. *Recreations:* swimming, walking, military history, civil defence, archaeology. *Address:* Hawk's Cliff, 38 Praze Road, Newquay, Cornwall TR7 3AF. *Club:* Commonwealth Trust.

MEYER, Michael Leverson; free-lance writer since 1950; *b* London, 11 June 1921; 3rd and *y s* of Percy Barrington Meyer and Eleanor Rachel Meyer (*née* Benjamin); unmarried; one *d*. *Educ:* Wellington Coll.; Christ Church, Oxford (MA). Operational Res. Section, Bomber Comd HQ, 1942–45; Lectr in English Lit., Uppsala Univ., 1947–50. Visiting Professor of Drama: Dartmouth Coll., USA, 1978; Univ. of Colorado, 1986; Colorado Coll., 1988; Hofstra Univ., 1989; UCLA 1991. Mem. Editorial Adv. Bd, Good Food Guide, 1958–72. FRSL. Gold Medal, Swedish Academy, 1964. Knight Commander, Polar Star (1st class), Sweden, 1977; Order of Merit (Norway), 1995. *Publications:* (ed, with Sidney Keyes, and contrib.) Eight Oxford Poets, 1941; (ed) Collected Poems of Sidney Keyes, 1945, rev. edn 1989; (ed) The Minos of Crete, by Sidney Keyes, 1948; The End of the Corridor (novel), 1951; The Ortolan (play), 1967; Henrik Ibsen: The Making of a Dramatist, 1967; Henrik Ibsen: The Farewell to Poetry, 1971; Henrik Ibsen: The Top of a Cold Mountain, 1971 (Whitbread Biography Prize, 1971); Lunatic and Lover (play), 1981; (ed) Summer Days, 1981; Ibsen on File, 1985; Strindberg: a biography, 1985; File on Strindberg, 1986; Not Prince Hamlet (memoirs; US edn as Words through a Window Pane), 1989; The Odd Women (play, after the novel by George Gissing), 1993; *translated:* The Long Ships, by Frans G. Bengtsson, 1954; Ibsen: Brand, The Lady from the Sea, John Gabriel Borkman, When We Dead Awaken, 1960; The Master Builder, Little Eyolf, 1961; Ghosts, The Wild Duck, Hedda Gabler, 1962; Peer Gynt, An Enemy of the People, The Pillars of Society, 1963; The Pretenders, 1964; A Doll's House, 1965; Rosmersholm, 1966; Emperor and Galilean, 1986; Strindberg: The Father, Miss Julie, Creditors, The Stronger, Playing with Fire, Erik the Fourteenth, Storm, The Ghost Sonata, 1964; A Dream Play, 1973; To Damascus, Easter, The Dance of Death, The Virgin Bride, 1975; Master Olof, 1991; Fragments of a Life, by Hedi Fried, 1990. *Recreations:* real tennis, eating, sleeping. *Address:* 4 Montagu Square, W1H 1RA. *T:* 0171–486 2573. *Clubs:* Savile, Garrick, MCC.

MEYER, Michael Siegfried; Chairman and Chief Executive, EMESS plc, since 1983; *b* 2 May 1950; *s* of Ernest Meyer and Gretta Gillis; *m* 1st, 1984, Jill Benedict (marr. diss. 1990); one *d*; 2nd, 1994, Livia Hannah, *o d* of Maj.-Gen. Mark Green. *Educ:* South African College School, Cape Town. FCIS. Company Secretary, Heenan Beddow International, 1973–75; Director, 1976–79, Chief Exec., 1980–82, EMESS; Director: Royal Sovereign Group, 1986–90; TR Smaller Cos Investment Trust, 1990–; Walker Greenbank, 1991–. *Recreations:* cricket, Rugby, theatre. *Address:* EMESS, 20 St James's Street, SW1A 1HA. *T:* 0171–321 0127. *Clubs:* MCC, Lansdowne; Wanderers (Johannesburg).

MEYER, Roelof Petrus, (Roelf Meyer); MP (National Party) Johannesburg West, since 1979; Minister of Constitutional Development, since 1992, and of Provincial Affairs, since 1994, South Africa; *b* 16 July 1947; *m* 1971, Carenè Lubbe; two *s* two *d*. *Educ:* Ficksburg High Sch.; Univ. of OFS (BComm, LLB). Practised as attorney, Pretoria and Johannesburg, 1980; Deputy Minister of: Law and Order, 1986–88; Constitutional Development, 1988–91; Information Services, 1990–91; Minister of: Defence, 1991–92; Communication, 1992–94. *Recreations:* reading, jogging, cycling. *Address:* Ministry of Provincial Affairs and Constitutional Development, Private Bag X802, Pretoria 0001, South Africa. *T:* (12) 3411380.

MEYJES, Sir Richard (Anthony), Kt 1972; DL; Deputy Chairman, Foseco plc (formerly Foseco Minsep), 1986–89 (Director, 1976–89); Director, Coates Bros plc, 1976–83 (Chairman, 1978–83); *b* 30 June 1918; *s* of late Anthony Charles Dorian Meyjes and Norah Isobel Meyjes; *m* 1939, Margaret Doreen Morris; three *s*. *Educ:* University College School, Hampstead. War Service, RASC, Sept. 1939–Jan. 1946 (temp. Captain). Qualified as Solicitor, June 1946; Legal Dept, Anglo-Saxon Petroleum Co., 1946–56; Manager, Thailand and Vietnam Division, Shell International Petroleum Co., 1956–58; Marketing Manager, Shell Co. of Philippines, Ltd, Manila, 1958–61; President, 1961–64; Head of Regional Marketing Div., Shell International Petroleum Co., London, 1964–66; Marketing Coordinator, 1966–70. Seconded to HM Govt (Mr Heath's Admin) as Head of Business Team, 1970–72; Dir and Group Personnel Co-ordinator, Shell International Petroleum Co. Ltd, 1972–76; Dir, Portals Hldgs, 1976–88. Vice-Pres., Assoc. of Optometrists, 1988–. Chm. Council, Univ. of Surrey, 1980–85. DL, 1983, High Sheriff, 1984, Surrey. Master, Worshipful Co. of Spectacle Makers, 1985–87. CIMgt; FInstD; Hon. FBCO; FRSA. DUniv Surrey, 1988. Officer of Philippine Legion of Honour, 1964. *Recreations:* gardening, walking. *Address:* Long Hill House, The Sands, near Farnham, Surrey GU10 1NQ. *T:* Runfold (01252) 782601. *Clubs:* Royal Over-Seas League, City Livery, Institute of Directors.

MEYLER, John William F.; *see* Forbes-Meyler.

MEYNELL, Dame Alix (Hester Marie), (Lady Meynell), DBE 1949; *b* 2 Feb. 1903; *d* of late Surgeon Commander L. Kilroy, RN, and late Hester Kilroy; *m* 1946, Sir Francis Meynell, RDI (*d* 1975); no *c*. *Educ:* Malvern Girls' Coll.; Somerville Coll., Oxford. Joined civil service, Board of Trade, 1925. Seconded to the Monopolies and Restrictive Practices Commission as Sec., 1949–52; Under-Sec., Board of Trade, 1946–55; resigned from the Civil Service, 1955. Called to the Bar, 1956. Man. Dir, Nonesuch Press Ltd, 1976–86. Member: SE Gas Board, 1956–69 (Chm. Cons. Council, 1956–63); Harlow New Town Corpn, 1956–65; Performing Right Tribunal, 1956–65; Cttees of Investigation for England, Scotland and Great Britain under Agricultural Marketing Acts, 1956–65; Monopolies Commn, 1965–68; Cosford RDC, 1970–74. *Publication:* Public Servant, Private Woman (autobiog.), 1988. *Recreations:* family bridge, entertaining my friends and being entertained. *Address:* Lion House, Lavenham, Sudbury, Suffolk CO10 9PR. *T:* Lavenham (01787) 247526.

MEYNELL, Benedict William; Hon. Director-General, Commission of the European Communities, since 1981; *b* 17 Feb. 1930; *s* of late Sir Francis Meynell, RDI, and of Lady (Vera) Meynell, MA; *m* 1st, 1950, Hildamarie (*née* Hendricks); two *d*; 2nd, 1967, Diana (*née* Himbury). *Educ:* Beltane Sch.; Geneva Univ. (Licencié-ès-sciences politiques); Magdalen Coll., Oxford (Doncaster schol.; MA). Asst Principal, Bd of Inland Revenue, 1954–56; Asst Principal, BoT, 1957–59, Principal, 1959–68; Principal British Trade Commissioner, Kenya, 1962–64; Board of Trade: Principal Private Sec. to Pres., 1967–68; Asst Sec., 1968–70; Commercial Counsellor, Brit. Embassy, Washington, DC, 1970–73; a Dir, EEC, responsible for relations with Far East, and for commercial safeguards and textiles negotiations, 1973–77, for relations with N America, Japan and Australasia, 1977–81. *Publications:* (paper) International Regulation of Aircraft Noise, 1971; contribs: Japan and Western Europe, ed Tsoukalis and White, 1982; A Survey of External Relations, in Yearbook of European Law 1982; Servir l'Etat, 1987 (Cahiers de l'Homme series). *Address:* 49 rue Père Eudore Devroye, 1040 Bruxelles, Belgium. *T:* (2) 7364916.

MEYRIC HUGHES, Henry Andrew Carne; Director of Exhibitions, South Bank Centre (Hayward Gallery, National Touring Exhibitions, Arts Council Collection), since 1992; *b* 1 April 1942; *s* of late Reginald Richard Meyric Hughes and of Jean Mary Carne Meyric Hughes (*née* Pratt); *m* 1968, Alison Hamilton Faulds; one *s* one *d*. *Educ:* Shewsbury Sch.; Univs of Rennes and Munich; University Coll., Oxford (BA Hons); Univ. of Sussex (MA). British Council, 1968–92: Berlin, Lima, Paris, Milan, London; Dir, Fine Arts Dept, later Visual Arts Dept, 1986–92. British Comr, Venice Biennale and São Paulo Bienal, 1986–92. Dir, Riverside Trust, 1986–; Mem. Court, RCA, 1986; Mem., Faculty of Fine Arts, British Sch. at Rome, 1988–94. Board Member: Eur. Visual Arts Manifestation, Rotterdam; Internat. Assoc. of Curators of Contemp. Art Exhibs, Frankfurt; Inst. of Internat. Visual Arts, London. Silver Medal, Czech Soc. for Internat. Cultural Relations, 1986. *Publications:* contrib. catalogues for art exhibns, UK and overseas, 1966–. *Recreations:* music, reading. *Address:* Hayward Gallery, South Bank Centre, Royal Festival Hall, SE1 8XX. *T:* 0171–921 0856; 13 Ashchurch Grove, W12 9BT.

MEYRICK, Sir David (John Charlton), 4th Bt *cr* 1880; *b* 2 Dec. 1926; *s* of Colonel Sir Thomas Frederick Meyrick, 3rd Bt, TD, DL, JP, and Ivy Frances (*d* 1947), *d* of Lt-Col F. C. Pilkington, DSO; *S* father, 1983; *m* 1962, Penelope Anne, *d* of late Comdr John Bertram Aubrey Marsden-Smedley, RN; three *s*. *Educ:* Eton; Trinity Hall, Cambridge (MA). FRICS. *Heir: s* Timothy Thomas Charlton Meyrick, [*b* 5 Nov. 1963. *Educ:* Eton; Bristol Univ.]. *Address:* Bush House, Gumfreston, Tenby, Dyfed SA70 8RA.

MEYRICK, Sir George (Christopher Cadafael Tapps Gervis), 7th Bt *cr* 1791, of Hinton Admiral; *b* 10 March 1941; *s* of Sir George David Eliott Tapps Gervis Meyrick, 6th Bt, MC and of Ann, *d* of late Clive Miller; *S* father, 1988; *m* 1968, Jean Louise, *d* of late Lord William Montagu Douglas Scott and of Lady William Montagu Douglas Scott; two *s* one *d*. *Educ:* Eton; Trinity College, Cambridge (MA). FRICS. *Heir: s* George William Owen Tapps Gervis Meyrick, *b* 3 April 1970. *Address:* Hinton Admiral, Christchurch, Dorset; Bodorgan, Isle of Anglesey. *Club:* Boodle's.

MEYSEY-THOMPSON, Sir (Humphrey) Simon, 4th Bt *cr* 1874; *b* 31 March 1935; *s* of Guy Herbert Meysey-Thompson (*d* 1961), and Miriam Beryl Meysey-Thompson (*d* 1985); *S* kinsman, Sir Algar de Clifford Charles Meysey-Thompson, 1967. *Address:* 10 Church Street, Woodbridge, Suffolk IP12 1DH.

MIAKWE, Hon. Sir Akepa, KBE 1989 (OBE 1982); Chairman, Eastern Highlands Development Corporation, Papua New Guinea, since 1982; *b* 1934; *s* of Umakue Miakwe and Obio Opae; *m* Kora Maho; seven *s* five *d*. *Educ:* Grade 3, Kabiufa Primary Sch. Local Govt Councillor, 1960–77 (Pres., 1962–64, Sen. Vice-Pres., 1965–72); MP Goroka, 1972–76, Unggai/Bena, 1977–82; Minister for Correctional Services and Liquor Licensing under Nat. Party. Mem. Bd Dirs, Eastern Highlands Capital Authority, 1989–; Dir, New Guinea Highlands Coffee Exports Pty Ltd, 1992–. Mem. Council, Univ. of Papua New Guinea, 1991–94. *Address:* Eastern Highlands Development Corporation Pty Ltd, PO Box 354, Goroka, Papua New Guinea. *T:* 721653.

MIALL, (Rowland) Leonard, OBE 1961; research historian; *b* 6 Nov. 1914; *e s* of late Rowland Miall and S. Grace Miall; *m* 1st, 1941, Lorna (*d* 1974), *o d* of late G. John Rackham; three *s* one *d*; 2nd, 1975, Sally Bicknell, *e d* of late Gordon Leith. *Educ:* Bootham Sch., York (Scholar); Freiburg Univ.; St John's Coll., Cambridge (Sizar), MA. Pres. Cambridge Union, 1936; Ed. Cambridge Review, 1936. Lectured in US, 1937; Sec. British-American Associates, 1937–39; joined BBC; inaugurated talks broadcast to Europe, 1939; BBC German Talks and Features Editor, 1940–42. Mem. British Political Warfare Mission to US, 1942–44 (Dir of News, San Francisco, 1943; Head of New York Office, 1944); Personal Asst to Dep. Dir-Gen., Political Warfare Exec., London, 1944; attached to Psychological Warfare Division of SHAEF, Luxembourg, 1945. Rejoined BBC: Special Correspondent, Czechoslovakia, 1945; Actg Diplomatic Corresp., 1945; Chief Corresp. in US, 1945–53; Head of Television Talks, 1954; Asst Controller, Current Affairs and Talks, Television, 1961; Special Asst to Dir of Television, planning start of BBC-2, 1962; Asst Controller, Programme Services, Television, BBC, 1963–66; BBC Rep. in US, 1966–70; Controller, Overseas and Foreign Relations, BBC, 1971–74; Research Historian, BBC, 1975–84. Inaugurated BBC Lunchtime Lectures, 1962; Advisor, Cttee on Broadcasting, New Delhi, 1965; Delegate to Commonwealth Broadcasting Confs, Jamaica, 1970, Kenya, 1972, Malta, 1974. Dir, Visnews Ltd (Dep. Chm., 1984–85); Overseas Dir, BAFTA, 1974–; Mem. Council, RTS, 1984–91. FRTS 1986; FRSA. Cert. of Appreciation, NY City, 1970. *Publications:* Richard Dimbleby, Broadcaster, 1966; Inside the BBC, 1994; contribs to DNB and various jls. *Recreations:* writing, gardening. *Address:* Maryfield Cottage, Taplow, Maidenhead, Berks SL6 0EX. *T:* Burnham (01628) 604195. *Clubs:* Garrick; Union (Cambridge).

MICHAEL, Alun Edward; JP; MP (Lab) Cardiff South and Penarth, since 1987; *b* 22 Aug. 1943; *m*; five *c*. *Educ:* Colwyn Bay GS; Keele Univ. (BA Hons English and Phil.). Journalist, South Wales Echo, 1966–71; Youth and Community Worker, Cardiff, 1972–84; Area Community Education Officer, Grangetown and Butetown, 1984–87. Mem., Cardiff City Council, 1973– 89 (sometime Chm., Finance, Planning, Performance Review, and Econ. Develt, and Chief Whip, Labour Gp). Dir, Cardiff and Vale Enterprise. An Opposition Whip, 1987–88; Opposition frontbench spokesman: on Welsh Affairs, 1988–92; on Home Affairs, 1992–. Chairman: Co-operative Parly Gp, 1988–92; Parly Friends of Co-operative Ideal, 1988–92; Member: Nat. Exec., Co-op. Party, 1988–92; Parly Cttee, Co-op. Union, 1988–. Chairman: All-Party Gp on Alcohol Misuse, 1991–93; Parly Friends of WNO, 1991–; Jt Chm., All-Party Gp on Somalia, 1989–; Vice-Chm., All-Party Penal Affairs Gp, 1991–; Jt Sec., All-Party Gp for Further and Tertiary Educn, 1990–; Sec., All-Party Panel for Personal Social Services, 1990–93. Vice-Pres., YHA; formerly Mem. Exec., Nat. Youth Bureau. Formerly Vice-Pres., Bldg Socs Assoc. Plays leading role locally in community develt projects. JP Cardiff, 1972 (Chm., Cardiff Juvenile Bench, 1986–87; formerly Mem., S Glam Probation Cttee). *Recreations:* long-distance running, mountain walking, opera, listening to classical music, reading. *Address:* House of Commons, SW1A 0AA. *T:* 0171–219 3441; (office) Cardiff (01222) 223533. *Clubs:* Penarth Labour; Grange Stars; Earlswood.

MICHAEL, Dr Duncan, FEng 1984; Chairman, Ove Arup Partnership, since 1995 (Director, since 1977); *b* 26 May 1937; *s* of Donald Michael and Lydia Cameron MacKenzie; *m* 1960, Joan Clay; two *s* one *d*. *Educ:* Beauly Public School; Inverness Royal Academy. BSc Edinburgh; PhD Leeds. FICE; FIStructE; FHKIE. Lectr, Leeds Univ., 1961; Engineer, Ove Arup Partnership, 1962. Member: Council, IStructE, 1977–80, 1983–89; SE Asia Trade Adv. Group, BOTB, 1982–85; Civil Engineering Cttee, SERC, 1980–83; Council, Royal Acad. Engrg, 1994; Vice-Chm., Council of Tall Buildings & Urban Habitat, 1980–. Fellowship of Engrg Vis. Prof., Aberdeen Univ., 1989–94; Vis. Prof., Leeds Univ., 1990–. *Publications:* Skyscrapers, 1987; lectures and engineering papers in technical jls. *Recreations:* garden, Scottish archaeology, opera. *Address:* 21 Marryat Road, SW19 5BB. *Club:* Caledonian.

MICHAEL, Prof. Ian David Lewis; King Alfonso XIII Professor of Spanish Studies, University of Oxford, since 1982; Fellow, Exeter College, Oxford, since 1982; *b* 26 May 1936; *o s* of late Cyril George Michael and of Glenys Morwen (*née* Lewis). *Educ:* Neath Grammar Sch.; King's Coll., London (BA First Class Hons Spanish 1957); PhD Manchester 1967. University of Manchester: Asst Lectr in Spanish, 1957–60; Lectr in Spanish, 1960–69; Sen. Lectr in Spanish, 1969–70; University of Southampton: Prof. of Spanish and Hd of Spanish Dept, 1971–82; Dep. Dean, Faculty of Arts, 1975–77, 1980–82; Sen. Curator and Chm., Univ. Library Cttee, 1980–82. Leverhulme Faculty Fellow in European Studies (at Madrid), 1977–78; first British-Spanish Foundn Vis. Prof., Complutensian Univ., Madrid, 1993–94. Mem., Gp of Three for Spain (Humanities research review), Eur. Science Foundn, 1987. Pres., Assoc. of Hispanists of GB and Ire., 1990–92. Comdr, Order of Isabel la Católica (Spain), 1986. *Publications:* The Treatment of Classical Material in the Libro de Alexandre, 1970; Spanish Literature and Learning to 1474, in, Spain: a Companion to Spanish studies, 1973, 3rd edn 1977; The Poem of the Cid, 1975, new edn 1984; Poema de Mio Cid, 1976, 2nd edn 1979; Gwyn Thomas, 1977; chapter on Poem of My Cid in New Pelican Guide to English Literature. I ii, 1983; articles in various learned jls and Festschriften; *as David Serafín:* Saturday of Glory, 1979 (John Creasey Meml Award, CWA, 1980); Madrid Underground, 1982; Christmas Rising, 1982; The Body in Cadiz Bay, 1985; Port of Light, 1987; The Angel of Torremolinos, 1988. *Recreations:* horticulture; collecting Art Nouveau and Art Déco, particularly ceramics; writing pseudonymous fiction; opera. *Address:* Exeter College, Oxford OX1 3DP. *T:* Oxford (01865) 270484, *Fax:* (01865) 270757. *Clubs:* Reform, Organon.

MICHAEL, Ian (Lockie), CBE 1972; Deputy Director, Institute of Education, University of London, 1973–78; *b* 30 Nov. 1915; 4th *c* of late Reginald Warburton Michael and Margaret Campbell Kerr; *m* 1942, Mary Harborne Bayley, *e c* of late Rev. William Henry Bayley; one *s* one *d*. *Educ:* St Bees Sch.; private study. BA (London) 1938; PhD (Bristol) 1963. Schoolmaster: St Faith's Sch., Cambridge, 1935–40; Junior Sch., Leighton Park, 1941–45, Headmaster, 1946–49; Lectr in Educn, Bristol Univ., 1950–63; Prof. of Educn, Khartoum Univ., 1963–64; Vice-Chancellor, Univ. of Malaŵi, 1964–73. Leverhulme Emeritus Fellowship, 1978–79, 1979–80; Vis. Prof. of Educn, Univ. of Cape Town, 1981. Hon. DLitt Malaŵi, 1974. *Publications:* English Grammatical Categories and the Tradition to 1800, 1970; The Teaching of English from the Sixteenth Century to 1870, 1987; Early Textbooks of English, 1993. *Address:* 9 Cornwallis House, Cornwallis Grove, Bristol BS8 4PG. *T:* Bristol (0117) 973 5977.

MICHAEL, Sir Peter (Colin), Kt 1989; CBE 1983; CIMgt; Chairman: Classic FM, since 1993 (Director, since 1991); Pilot Investment Trust, since 1993; *b* 17 June 1938; *s* of Albert and Enid Michael; *m* 1962, Margaret Baldwin; two *s*. *Educ:* Whitgift Sch., Croydon; Queen Mary Coll., Univ. of London (BSc Elec. Engrg; Fellow, 1983). Chairman: Micro Consultants Group, 1969–85; Quantel Ltd, 1974–89; Databasix Ltd, 1986–88; UEI plc, 1986–89 (Dep. Chm., 1981–85); Cray Electronics, 1989–93. Member: Adv. Council for Applied R&D, 1982–85; NCB, 1983–86; ACARD Sub-Gp on Annual Review of Govt Funded R&D, 1985–86; Technol. Requirements Bd, DTI, 1986–88. Paper on City financing of electronics companies to PITCOM, 1988. Chairman: Royal Soc. of British Sculptors Appeal, 1992; Chelsea Harbour '93 Internat. Sculpture Exhibn Appeal; The Sculpture Company, 1994. Lectures: Humphrey Davies, QMC, 1984; IEE Electronics, 1984. Freeman, Goldsmiths' Co., 1984. Freeman, City of London, 1984; Liveryman, Goldsmiths' Co., 1988. CIMgt (CBIM 1982). FRSA 1984. Hon. FBKSTS 1981. The Guardian Young Businessman of the Year, 1982. *Recreations:* tennis, opera, classical music, wine, sculpture. *Address:* (office) 3 The Pentangle, Park Street, Newbury, Berks RG13 1EA. *T:* Newbury (01635) 552502.

MICHAELS, Prof. Leslie, MD; FRCPath, FRCP(C); Professor of Pathology, Institute of Laryngology and Otology, 1973–90 (Dean, 1976–81); Emeritus Professor, Department of Histopathology, University College London Medical School, since 1990; *b* 24 July 1925; *s* of Henry and Minnie Michaels; *m* Edith (*née* Waldstein); two *d*. *Educ:* Parmiter's Sch., London; King's Coll., London; Westminster Med. Sch., London (MB, BS; MD). FRCPath 1963, FRCP(C) 1962. Asst Lectr in Pathology, Univ. of Manchester, 1955–57; Lectr in Path., St Mary's Hosp. Med. Sch., London, 1957–59; Asst Prof. of Path., Albert Einstein Coll. of Medicine, New York, 1959–61; Hosp. Pathologist, Northern Ont, Canada, 1961–70; Sen. Lectr, Inst. of Laryn. and Otol., 1970–73. *Publications:* Pathology of the Larynx, 1984; Ear, Nose and Throat Histopathology, 1987; scientific articles in jls of medicine, pathology and otolaryngology. *Recreations:* reading, music, walking. *Address:* Romany Ridge, Hillbrow Road, Bromley, Kent BR1 4JL.

MICHEL, Prof. (Christopher) Charles, DPhil; Professor of Physiology and Head of Department of Physiology and Biophysics, St Mary's Hospital Medical School, since 1984; *b* 23 March 1938; *s* of late Maurice and May Michel; *m* 1965, Rosalind McCrink; one *s* one *d*. *Educ:* Leeds Grammar Sch.; Queen's Coll., Oxford (BA 1956, 1st cl. Physiol.; MA, DPhil 1962; BM BCh 1965). MRCP 1986. US Public Health Postdoctoral Res. Fellow, 1962; Oxford University: Deptl Demonstrator in Physiol., 1964–67; Univ. Lectr in Physiol., 1967–84; Fellow and Praelector in Physiol., Queen's Coll., 1966–84. Lectures: Oliver-Sharpey, RCP, 1985; Annual Prize Review, Physiol. Soc., 1987. Sec., Physiol Soc., 1980–83; Chm., RN Personnel Res. Cttee, 1991–, Army Personnel Res. Cttee, 1993–94, MRC. Hon. Mem., Amer. Physiol. Soc., 1993. Malpighi Prize, Eur. Soc. for Micro-circulation, 1984. *Publications:* (ed with E. M. Renkin) American Handbook of Physiology: the microcirculation, 1984; articles in learned jls. *Recreations:* running, walking, reading. *Address:* Department of Physiology and Biophysics, St Mary's Hospital Medical School, Imperial College of Science, Technology and Medicine, W2 1PG. *Club:* Garrick.

MICHEL, Prof. Dr Hartmut; Director, Max-Planck-Institut of Biophysics, Frankfurt am Main, since 1987; *b* Ludwigsburg, W Germany, 18 July 1948; *s* of Karl Michel and Frieda Michel; *m* 1979, Ilona Leger-Michel; one *s* one *d*. *Educ:* Universities of: Tübingen (Dip. in biochem.); Würzburg (PhD); Munich (habilitation for biochemistry, 1986). Res. associate with D. Oesterhelt, Univ. of Würzburg, 1977–79; group leader in D. Oesterhelt's dept, Max-Planck-Inst. of Biochemistry, Martinsried, until 1987. Various prizes, including: Biophysics Prize of Amer. Phys. Soc., 1986; Otto Klung Prize for Chemistry, 1986; (jtly) Otto Bayer Prize, 1988; (jtly) Nobel Prize for Chemistry, 1988. *Publication:* (ed) Crystallization of Membrane Proteins, 1990. *Recreations:* nature, wild life, physical exercise, readings on history and travel. *Address:* Max-Planck-Institut für Biophysik, Heinrich-Hoffmann-Strasse 7, 60528 Frankfurt am Main, Germany. *T:* (69) 96769401, *Fax:* (69) 96769423.

MICHELIN, Reginald Townend, CMG 1957; CVO 1953; OBE 1952; General Manager: Agualta Vale Estates, Jamaica, 1958–64; Jamaica Tourist Board, 1964–73; *b* 31 Dec. 1903; *s* of V. A. Michelin, Planter, Jamaica; *m* 1940, Nina Gladys Faulkner, Iffley, Oxford; one *s* one *d*. *Educ:* Exeter Sch., England. Sub-Inspector, Police, Jamaica, 1924; Inspector, Police, Leeward Islands, 1928; Asst Commissioner of Police, Nigeria, 1930; Comr of Police, Barbados, 1949; Commissioner of Police, Jamaica, 1953–58, retd. *Address:* Box 267, Montego Bay, Jamaica, West Indies.

MICHELL, Keith; actor since 1948; *b* Adelaide; *s* of Joseph Michell and Alice Maud (*née* Aslat); *m* 1957, Jeannette Sterke; one *s* one *d*. *Educ:* Port Pirie High Sch.; Adelaide Teachers' Coll.; Sch. of Arts and Crafts; Adelaide Univ.; Old Vic Theatre School. Formerly taught art. *Stage:* First appearance, Playbox, Adelaide, 1947; Young Vic Theatre Co., 1950–51; first London appearance, And So To Bed, 1951; Shakespeare Meml. Theatre Co., 1952–56, inc. Australian tour, 1952–53 (Henry IV Part 1, As You Like It, Midsummer Night's Dream, Troilus and Cressida, Romeo and Juliet, Taming of the Shrew, All's Well That Ends Well, Macbeth, Merry Wives of Windsor); Don Juan, Royal Court, 1956; Old Vic Co., 1956 (Antony and Cleopatra, Much Ado about Nothing, Two Gentlemen of Verona, Titus Andronicus); Irma La Douce, Lyric, 1958, Washington, DC, 1960 and Broadway, 1960–61; The Chances, Chichester Festival, 1962; The Rehearsal, NY, 1963; The First Four Hundred Years, Australia and NZ, 1964; Robert and Elizabeth, Lyric, 1964; The King's Mare, 1966; Man of La Mancha, 1968–69, NY, 1970; Abelard and Heloise, 1970, Los Angeles and NY, 1971; Hamlet, Globe, 1972; Dear Love, Comedy, 1973; The Crucifer of Blood, Haymarket, 1979; On the Twentieth Century (musical), Her Majesty's, 1980; Pete McGynty and the Dreamtime (own adap. of Peer Gynt), Melbourne Theatre Co., 1981; Captain Beaky Christmas Show, Lyric, Shaftesbury Ave., 1981–82; The Tempest, Brisbane, 1982; opened Keith Michell Theatre, Port Pirie, with one-man show, 1982; Amadeus (UK tour), 1983; La Cage Aux Folles, San Francisco and NY, 1984, Sydney and Melbourne, 1985; Portraits, Malvern Fest., 1987; Aspects of Love, Edmonton and Toronto, 1991–92, Chicago, 1992; Scrooge, Melbourne, 1993; Caesar and Cleopatra, Edmonton, 1994; *Chichester Festival Theatre:* Artistic Director, 1974–77; Tonight We Improvise, Oedipus Tyrannus, 1974; Cyrano de Bergerac, Othello, 1975; (dir and designed) Twelfth Night, 1976; Monsieur Perrichon's Travel, 1976; The Apple Cart, 1977; (dir and designed) In Order of Appearance, 1977; Murder in the Cathedral (Chichester Cathedral), 1977; Henry VIII, 1991; toured Australia with Chichester Co., 1978 (Othello, The Apple Cart); acted in: On the Rocks, 1982; Jane Eyre, 1986; The Royal Baccarat Scandal, 1988, transf. Theatre Royal Haymarket, 1989; Henry VIII, 1991. *Films include:* Dangerous Exile; The Hell Fire Club; Seven Seas to Calais; The Executioner; House of Cards; Prudence and the Pill; Henry VIII and his Six Wives; Moments, The Deceivers. *Television includes:* Henry VIII in the Six Wives of Henry VIII (series), 1972; Keith Michell at Chichester, 1974; My Brother Tom, 1986; Captain James Cook, 1987; Murder She Wrote (series), 1990. Many recordings. First exhibn of paintings, 1959; subseq. one-man exhibns at John Whibley Gall., London, Wright Hepburn and Webster Gall., NY, Century Gall., Henley-on-Thames, Wylma Wayne Gall., London, Vincent Gall., Adelaide. Many awards. *Publications:* (ed and illus.) Twelve Shakespeare Sonnets (series of lithographs produced 1974), 1981; illus. and recorded Captain Beaky series, 1975; (also illus.) Practically Macrobiotic, 1987. *Recreations:* painting, photography, swimming, cooking. *Address:* c/o London Management and Representation Ltd, 24 Noel Street, W1V 3RB.

MICHELL, Michael John; Head of Oil and Gas Division, Department of Trade and Industry, since 1993; *b* 12 Dec. 1942; *s* of John Martin Michell and Pamela Mary Michell; *m* 1st, 1965, Pamela Marianne Tombs (marr. diss. 1978); two *s* (one *d* decd); 2nd, 1978, Alison Mary Macfarlane; two *s*. *Educ:* Marlborough College; Corpus Christi College, Cambridge (BA 1964). Min. of Aviation, 1964; Private Sec. to Sir Ronald Melville, 1968–69; Concorde Div., 1969–73; Sec. to Sandilands Cttee on inflation accounting, 1973–75; Private Sec. to Sec. of State for Industry, 1975–77; HM Treasury, 1977–80; Industrial Policy Div., Dept. of Industry, 1980–82; RCDS 1983; Head, Air Div., DTI, 1984–88; Chief Exec., Radio Div., subseq. Radiocommunications Agency, DTI, 1988–93. *Address:* Department of Trade and Industry, Waterloo Bridge House, SE1 8UA. *T:* 0171–215 2000.

MICHELL, Prof. Robert Hall, FRS 1986; Royal Society Research Professor at the University of Birmingham, since 1987; *b* 16 April 1941; *s* of Rowland Charles Michell and Elsie Lorna Michell; two *s* one *d*. *Educ:* Crewkerne School, Somerset; Univ. of Birmingham (BSc Med. Biochem. and Pharmacol. 1962; PhD Med. Biochem. 1965; DSc 1978). Research Fellow, Birmingham, 1965–66, 1968–70, Harvard Med. Sch., 1966–68; Birmingham University: Lectr in Biochemistry, 1970–81; Sen. Lectr, 1981–84; Reader, 1984–86; Prof. of Biochemistry, 1986–87. Mem., Physiol. Systems and Disorders Bd, 1985–90, Chm., Grants Cttee B, 1988–90, MRC; Member: Fellowships Cttee, BHF, 1992–; Adv. Bd, Beit Meml Trust, 1993–; Pres., Med. Scis Sect., BAAS, 1993–94. Mem., EMBO, 1991. Member, Editorial Boards: Jl Neurochem., 1975–80; Cell Calcium, 1979–89; Biochem. Jl, 1983–88; Current Opinion in Cell Biology, 1988–; Procs Roy. Soc. B, 1989–; Jl of Molecular Endocrinology, 1992–; Molecular Membrane Biology, 1993–. CIBA Medal, Biochemical Soc., 1988. *Publications:* (with J. B. Finean and R. Coleman) Membranes and their Cellular Functions, 1974, 3rd edn 1984; (ed with J. B. Finean) Membrane Structure, vol. 1 of New Comprehensive Biochemistry, 1981; (ed with J. W. Putney, Jr) Inositol Lipids in Cellular Signalling, 1987; (ed with M. J. Berridge) Inositol Lipids and Transmembrane Signalling, 1988; (ed jtly) Inositol Lipids and Cellular Signalling, 1989; contribs to Nature, Biochem. Jl and sci. jls. *Recreations:* birdwatching, wilderness. *Address:* 59 Weoley Park Road, Birmingham B29 6QZ. *T:* 0121–472 1356.

MICHELMORE, Clifford Arthur, CBE 1969; Television Broadcaster and Producer; Managing Director: Michelmore Enterprises Ltd, since 1969; Communications Consultants Ltd, since 1969; Director, CP Video, since 1988; *b* 11 Dec. 1919; *s* of late Herbert Michelmore and Ellen Alford; *m* 1950, Jean Metcalfe (Broadcaster); one *s* one *d*. *Educ:* Cowes Senior Sch., Isle of Wight. Entered RAF, 1935; commnd 1940; left RAF 1947. Head, Outside Broadcasts and Variety, BFN, 1948; Dep. Station Dir, BFN, also returned to freelance as Commentator and Producer, 1949. Entered Television, 1950. Man. Dir, RM/EMI Visual Programmes, 1971–81. Has taken part in numerous radio and television programmes in Britain, Europe and the USA. Introduced: "Tonight" series, 1957–65; 24 Hours series, 1965–68; General Election Results programmes, 1964, 1966, 1970; So You Think . . . ., 1966–; Our World, 1967; With Michelmore (interviews); Talkback; Apollo Space Programmes, 1960–70; Holiday, 1969–86; Chance to Meet, 1970–73; Wheelbase, 1972; Getaway, 1975; Globetrotter, 1975; Opinions Unlimited, 1977–79; Presenter: Day by Day (Southern TV), 1980; Sudden Change (HTV), 1982; Cliff Michelmore Show (BBC Radio), 1982–83; Home on Sunday (BBC TV), 1983–90; Waterlines (BBC Radio Four), 1984–94; Lifeline (BBC TV), 1986–; Coastline (BBC Radio Four), 1991–94; Cliff's Country, 1992 (BBC Radio Four). Made films: Shaping of a Writer, 1977; Hong Kong: the challenge, 1978. FRSA, 1975. Television Society Silver Medal, 1957; Guild of TV Producers Award, Personality of the Year, 1958; TV Review Critics Award, 1959; Variety Club Award, 1961. *Publications:* (ed) The Businessman's Book of Golf, 1981; Cliff Michelmore's Holidays By Rail, 1986; (with Jean Metcalfe) Two-Way Story (autobiog.), 1986; Some of These Days, 1987; contribs to Highlife, Financial Weekly; various articles on television, broadcasting and travel. *Recreations:* golf, reading and doing nothing. *Address:* White House, Reigate, Surrey RH2 9BU; Brookfield, Bembridge, Isle of Wight PO35 5XW. *T:* Reigate (01737) 245014. *Clubs:* Garrick, Royal Air Force, MCC.

MICHELS, David Michael Charles; Chief Executive, Stakis, since 1991; *b* 8 Dec. 1946; *s* of Klaus Peter and Thelma Sadie Michels; *m* 1973, Michele Ann Arnold; one *s* one *d*. *Educ:* Clarks Coll. FHCIMA. Grand Metropolitan, 1966–81; Ladbrokes: Sales and Marketing Dir, Hotels, 1981–83; Man. Dir, Leisure Div., 1983–85; Man. Dir, Ladbroke Hotels, 1985–87; Hilton International: Sen. Vice-Pres., Sales and Marketing, 1987–89; Dep. Chm., Hilton UK and Exec. Vice-Pres., Hilton Worldwide, 1989–91. Hon. DLitt Glasgow Caledonian, 1993. *Recreations:* tennis, poker, reading. *Address:* Stakis, 3 Atlantic Quay, York Street, Glasgow G2 8JH. *T:* 0141–204 4321. *Club:* Vanderbilt.

MICHENER, James Albert; author; *b* New York City, 3 Feb. 1907; parents unknown; raised by Mabel Michener (*née* Haddock); *m* 1st, 1935, Patti Koon (marr. diss. 1948); 2nd, 1948, Vange Nord (marr. diss., 1955); 3rd, 1955, Mari Yoriko Sabusawa (*d* 1994); no *c*. *Educ:* Swarthmore Coll., Pennsylvania; St Andrews Univ., Scotland; Harvard Coll., Mass. Teacher, George Sch., Pa, 1933–36; Prof., Colorado State Coll. of Educn, 1936–41; Visiting Prof., Harvard, 1940–41; Associate Editor, Macmillan Co., 1941–49. Member: Adv. Cttee on the arts, US State Dept, 1957; Adv. Cttee, US Information Agency, 1970–76; Cttee to reorganise USIS, 1976; US Postal Service Adv. Cttee, 1978–87; NASA Adv. Council, 1979–83; US Internat. Broadcasting Bd, 1983–89. Served with USNR on active duty in South Pacific, 1942–45. Sec., Pennsylvania Constitutional Convention, 1968. Hon. DHL, LLD, LittD, DSci and DHum, from numerous univs. US Medal of Freedom, 1977. *Publications:* Unit in the Social Studies, 1940; (ed) Future of Social Studies, for NEA, 1940; Tales of the South Pacific (Pulitzer prize for fiction), 1947; The Fires of Spring, 1949; Return to Paradise, 1951; The Voice of Asia, 1951; The Bridges at Toko-ri, 1953; Sayonara, 1954; Floating World, 1955; The Bridge at Andau, 1957; (with A. Grove Day) Rascals in Paradise, 1957; Selected Writings, 1957; The Hokusai Sketchbook, 1958; Japanese Prints, 1959; Hawaii, 1959; Report of the County Chairman, 1961; Caravans, 1964; The Source, 1965; Iberia, 1968; Presidential Lottery, 1969; America *vs* America, 1969; The Quality of Life, 1970; Kent State, 1971; The Drifters, 1971; Centennial, 1974; Sports in America, 1976; Chesapeake, 1978; The Covenant, 1980; Space, 1982 (televised, 1987); Poland, 1983; Texas, 1985; Legacy, 1987; Alaska, 1988; Journey, 1988; Caribbean, 1989; (with John Kings) Six Days in Havana, 1989; The Novel, 1991; The Eagle and the Raven, 1990; Pilgrimage, 1990; The World is My Home, 1992; Mexico, 1992; My Lost Mexico, 1992; James A. Michener's Writer's Handbook, 1992; Creatures of the Kingdom, 1993; Literary Reflections, 1993; Recessional, 1994. *Address:* Texas Center for Writers, PCL 3.102, University of Texas, Austin, TX 78713, USA.

MICHIE, Prof. David Alan Redpath, RSA 1972 (ARSA 1964); RGI 1984; RWA 1991; Head, School of Drawing and Painting, Edinburgh College of Art, 1982–90; Professor Emeritus, Heriot-Watt University, 1991; *b* 30 Nov. 1928; *s* of late James Michie and late Anne Redpath, OBE, ARA, RSA; *m* 1951, Eileen Anderson Michie; two *d*. *Educ:* Edinburgh Coll. of Art (DA). National Service, 1947–49; Edinburgh Coll. of Art, 1949–53 (studied painting); travelling scholarship, Italy, 1953–54; Lectr in Painting, Gray's Sch. of Art, Aberdeen, 1958–62; Lectr in Painting, Edinburgh Coll. of Art, 1962–82, Vice-Principal, 1974–77. Visiting Professor of Painting: Acad. of Fine Art, Belgrade, 1979; Univ. of Calif, Santa Barbara, 1992. Member: Gen. Teaching Council for Scotland, 1976–80; Edinburgh Festival Soc., 1976–; Museums and Galls Commn, 1991–. Pres., Soc. of Scottish Artists, 1961–63. One Man Exhibitions: Mercury Gallery, London, 1967, 1969, 1971, 1974, 1980, 1983, 1992; Mercury Gall., Edinburgh, 1986; Lothian Region Chambers, 1977; Scottish Gall., Edinburgh, 1980, 1994; Kasteel de Hooge Vuursche, Baarn, Netherlands, 1991. FRSA 1990. *Recreation:* music. *Address:* 17 Gilmour Road, Edinburgh EH16 5NS. *T:* 0131–667 2684.

MICHIE, Prof. Donald, DPhil (Oxon), DSc (Oxon); Professor of Machine Intelligence, Edinburgh University, 1967–84, Professor Emeritus, since 1984; *b* 11 Nov. 1923; *s* of late James Kilgour Michie and late Marjorie Crain Michie; *m* 1st, 1949, Zena Margaret Davies (marr. diss.); one *s*; 2nd, 1952, Anne McLaren (marr. diss.); one *s* two *d*; 3rd, 1971, Jean Elizabeth Hayes (*née* Crouch). *Educ:* Rugby Sch.; Balliol Coll., Oxford (Schol., MA). Sci. Fellow Zool Soc. of London, 1953; Fellow Royal Soc. Edinburgh 1969; Fellow Brit. Computer Soc., 1971. War Service in FO, Bletchley, 1942–45; Res. Associate, Univ. of London, 1952–58; University of Edinburgh: Sen. Lectr, Surg. Science, 1958; Reader in Surg. Science, 1962; Dir of Expermtl Programming Unit, 1965; Chm. of Dept of Machine Intelligence and Perception, 1966; Dir, Machine Intelligence Res. Unit, 1974–84; Prof., Univ. of Strathclyde, 1984–92; Turing Institute, Glasgow: Dir of Res., 1984–86; Chief Scientist, 1986–92; Sen. Fellow, 1992–. Technical Dir, Intelligent Terminals Ltd (Knowledgelink), 1984–92. Royal Soc. Lectr in USSR, 1965; Wm Withering Lectr, Univ. of Birmingham, 1972; Vis. Lectr, USSR Acad. Sci., 1973, 1985; Geo. A. Miller Lectr, Univ. of Illinois, 1974, 1984; Herbert Spencer Lectr, Univ. of Oxford, 1976; Samuel Wilks Meml Lectr, Princeton Univ., 1978; S. L. A. Marshall Lectr, US Army Res. Inst. for the Behavioural and Soc. Scis, 1990; C. C. Garvin Lectr, Virginia Polytech. Inst. and State Univ., 1992; Vis. Fellow, St Cross Coll., Oxford, 1970; Vis. Scholar, Wolfson Coll., Oxford, 1994; Visiting Professor: Stanford Univ., 1962, 1978, 1991; Syracuse Univ., USA, 1970, 1971; Virginia Polytechnic Inst. and State Univ., 1974, 1992; Illinois Univ., 1976, 1979–81. Chief Editor, Machine Intelligence series, 1967–. Chm., A. M. Turing Trust, 1975–86. Treas., Human-Computer Learning Foundn, 1995–. Fellow, Amer. Assoc. Artificial Intell., 1990. Hon. DSc: CNAA, 1991; Salford, 1992. (With A. McLaren) Pioneer Award, Internat. Embryo Transfer Soc., 1988. *Publications:* (jtly) An Introduction to Molecular Biology, 1964; On Machine Intelligence, 1974, 2nd edn 1986; Machine Intelligence and Related Topics, 1982; (jtly) The Creative Computer, 1984; papers in tech. and sci. jls. *Recreations:* chess, travel. *Address:* 39 Lady Somerset Road, NW5 1TX. *Clubs:* Athenæum; New (Edinburgh).

MICHIE, (Janet) Ray; MP Argyll and Bute, since 1987 (L 1987–88, Lib Dem, since 1988); *b* 4 Feb. 1934; *d* of Baron Bannerman of Kildonan, OBE; *m* 1957, Dr Iain Michie, MB, FRCP; three *d*. *Educ:* Aberdeen High Sch. for Girls; Lansdowne House Sch., Edinburgh; Edinburgh Coll. of Speech Therapy. LCST, MCST. Area Speech Therapist, Argyll and Clyde Health Board, 1977–87. Chm., Argyll Lib. Assoc., 1973–76; Vice-Chm., Scottish Lib. Party, 1977–79; Chair, Scottish Lib. Democrats, 1992–93. Lib Dem spokesman on Scotland, 1988–. Member: Scottish NFU; Scottish Crofters' Union; An Comunn Gaidhealach. Vice-Pres., Coll. of Speech and Language Therapists, 1989–. Contested (L): Argyll, 1979; Argyll and Bute, 1983. *Recreations:* golf, swimming, gardening. *Club:* National Liberal.

MICHIE, William, (Bill); MP (Lab) Sheffield Heeley, since 1983; *b* 24 Nov. 1935; *m*; two *s*. *Educ:* Abbeydale Secondary Sch., Sheffield. Nat. Service, RAF, 1957–59. Formerly:

apprentice electrician; maintenance electrician; Lab. Technician, Computer Applications; unemployed, 1981–83. Joined Labour Party, 1965; Co-op. Party, 1966. Mem., AEEU (formerly AUEW, then AEU), 1952– (former Br. Trustee; former Standing Orders Cttee Deleg., Lab. Party Yorks Regl Conf.; AEU sponsored MP, 1983–). Member: Sheffield City Council, 1970–84 (Chairman: Planning, 1974–81; Employment, 1981–83; Gp Sec./Chief Whip, 1974–83); South Yorks CC, 1974–86 (Area Planning Chm., 1974–81). Member: Privileges Select Cttee, 1994; Members' Interests Select Cttee, 1993. *Recreations:* pub darts, gardening. *Address:* House of Commons, SW1A 0AA. *T:* 0171–219 4023; Barkers Pool House, Burgess Street, Sheffield S1 2HF. *T:* Sheffield (0114) 270 1881.

MIDDLEMAS, Prof. Robert Keith; Professor of History, University of Sussex, since 1986; *b* 26 May 1935; *s* of late Robert James Middlemas, Solicitor and of Eleanor Mary (*née* Crane), Howick, Northumberland; *m* 1958, Susan Mary, *d* of Laurence Edward Paul Tremlett and Marjorie Isobel Derrington Bell; one *s* three *d*. *Educ:* Stowe Sch.; Pembroke Coll., Cambridge (Exhibnr, scholar, BA 1st cl. History 1958); DPhil 1972, DLitt 1982, Sussex. 2nd Lieut, Northumberland Fusiliers, 1954–55 (served in Kenya); Clerk, House of Commons, 1958–66; Lectr in History, Univ. of Sussex, 1966–76, Reader, 1976–86. Visiting Professor: Stanford Univ. and Hoover Instn, Stanford, 1984; Univ. of Beijing, 1989. Member: UK Nat. Cttee, Unesco, 1980–86; Council, Inst. of Contemporary British History; Council and Res. Cttee, Foundn for Manufg and Industry, 1993–. FRSA. Co-Founder and Editor, Catalyst: a jl of public debate, 1985–87. *Publications:* The Master Builders, 1963; The Clydesiders, 1965; (with John Barnes) Baldwin, 1969; Diplomacy of Illusion, 1972; (ed) Thomas Jones: Whitehall Diary, vols I and II, 1969–70, vol. III, 1972; Politics in Industrial Society, 1979; Cabora Bassa, 1975; Power and the Party, 1980; Industry, Unions and Government, 1984; Power, Competition and the State, vol. I, Britain in Search of Balance 1940–61, 1986, vol. 2, Threats to the Post-War Settlement: Britain 1961–74, 1990; vol. 3, The End of the Post-War Era: Britain since 1974, 1991; Informal Politics of the European Community since 1973, 1995; articles and reviews in learned jls. *Recreations:* sports, sailing, fishing, landscape gardening; Member, UK Nat. Rifle Team, Canadian tour, 1958. *Address:* West Burton House, West Burton, Pulborough, West Sussex RH20 1HD. *T:* Bury (01798) 831516. *Clubs:* Flyfishers'; North London Rifle (Bisley).

MIDDLESBROUGH, Bishop of, (RC), since 1993; **Rt. Rev. John Crowley;** *b* Newbury, 23 June 1941. Ordained priest, 1965; Holy Trinity Parish, Brook Green, W6, 1965–68; Catholic Missionary Soc., 1968–74; Private Sec. to Cardinal Hume, 1974–82; Vicar Gen. for Westminster dio., 1982–86; Auxiliary Bishop of Westminster (Bishop in Central London), and Titular Bishop of Tala, 1986–92. Chairman, Catholic Fund for Overseas Development, 1988–. *Address:* Bishop's House, 16 Cambridge Road, Middlesbrough, Cleveland TS5 5NN. *T:* Middlesbrough (01642) 818253.

MIDDLESBROUGH, Auxiliary Bishop of, (RC); *see* O'Brien, Rt Rev. T. K.

MIDDLESEX, Archdeacon of; *see* Raphael, Ven. T. J.

MIDDLETON, 12th Baron *cr* 1711; **Digby Michael Godfrey John Willoughby,** MC 1945; DL; Bt 1677; *b* 1 May 1921; *er s* of 11th Baron Middleton, KG, MC, TD, and Angela Florence Alfreda (*d* 1978), *er d* of Charles Hall, Eddlethorpe Hall, Malton, Yorks; *S* father, 1970; *m* 1947, Janet, *o d* of General Sir James Marshall-Cornwall, KCB, CBE, DSO, MC; three *s*. *Educ:* Eton; Trinity Coll., Cambridge. BA 1950; MA 1958. Served War of 1939–45: Coldstream Guards, 1940–46; NW Europe, 1944–45 (despatches, MC, Croix de Guerre); Hon. Col, 2nd Bn Yorkshire Volunteers, TAVR, 1976–88. Mem., H of L Select Cttee on Europ. Communities, 1985–. Chm., Legal and Parly Cttee, CLA, 1973–79; Pres., CLA, 1981–83; Member: Yorks and Humberside Econ. Planning Council, 1968–79; Nature Conservancy Council, 1986–89. DL 1963, JP 1958, CC 1964–74, ER of Yorks; CC N Yorks, 1974–77. *Heir: s* Hon. Michael Charles James Willoughby [*b* 14 July 1948; *m* 1974, Hon. Lucy Sidney, *y d* of 1st Viscount De L'Isle, VC, KG, GCMG, GCVO, PC; two *s* three *d*]. *Address:* Birdsall House, Malton, N Yorks YO17 9NR. *Club:* Boodle's.

MIDDLETON, Bishop Suffragan of, since 1994; **Rt. Rev. Stephen Squires Venner;** *b* 19 June 1944; *s* of Thomas Edward Venner and Hilda Lester Venner; *m* 1972, Judith Sivewright Johnstone; two *s* one *d*. *Educ:* Hardyes Sch., Dorchester; Birmingham Univ. (BA); Linacre Coll., Oxford (MA); London Univ. (PGCE). Curate, St Peter, Streatham, 1968–71; Hon. Curate: St Margaret, Streatham Hill, 1971–72; Ascension, Balham, 1972–74; Head of RE, St Paul's Girls' Sch., Hammersmith, 1972–74; Vicar, St Peter, Clapham and Bishop's Chaplain to Overseas Students, 1974–76; Vicar: St John, Trowbridge, 1976–82; Holy Trinity, Weymouth, 1982–94; RD of Weymouth, 1988–94; Canon and Prebendary of Salisbury Cathedral, 1989–94. *Recreations:* playing organ and piano, watersports, computing, reading adventure novels. *Address:* The Hollies, Manchester Road, Rochdale OL11 3QY. *T:* Rochdale (01706) 358550, *Fax:* (01706) 354851.

MIDDLETON, Donald King, CBE 1981; HM Diplomatic Service, retired; Chairman, Leominster Abbeyfield Society, since 1993; Member Council, Voluntary Service Overseas, since 1983; *b* 24 Feb. 1922; *s* of late Harold Ernest Middleton and Ellen Middleton; *m* 1945, Marion Elizabeth Ryder (*d* 1988); one *d*. *Educ:* King Edward's Sch., Birmingham; Saltley College. Min. of Health, 1958–61; joined Commonwealth Relations Office, 1961; First Sec., British High Commn, Lagos, 1961–65; Head of Chancery, British Embassy, Saigon, 1970–72; British Dep. High Commissioner, Ibadan, 1973–75; HM Chargé d'Affaires, Phnom Penh, 1975; seconded to NI Office, Belfast, 1975–77; High Comr, Papua New Guinea, 1977–82. *Address:* Stone House, Ledgemoor, near Weobley, Herefordshire HR4 8RN. *Club:* Commonwealth Trust.

MIDDLETON, Edward Bernard; Partner, Pannell Kerr Forster, Chartered Accountants; *b* 5 July 1948; *s* of Bernard and Bettie Middleton; *m* 1971, Rosemary Spence Brown; three *s*. *Educ:* Aldenham Sch., Elstree; Chartered Accountant, 1970. Joined London office of Pannell Kerr Forster, 1971; Nairobi office, 1973; Audit Manager, London office, 1975; Partner, 1979; seconded to DTI as Dir, Industrial Develt Unit, 1984–86. Dir, Purchasing Systems Ltd, 1995–. Mem. sub-cttee, Consultative Cttee of Accountancy Bodies, 1980–84. Hon. Treas., Hotel and Catering Benevolent Assoc., 1992–. *Recreations:* sailing, photography. *Address:* Barrans, Bury Green, Little Hadham, Ware, Herts SG11 2ES. *T:* Bishops Stortford (01279) 658684. *Club:* Salcombe Yacht.

MIDDLETON, Francis; Advocate; Sheriff of Glasgow and Strathkelvin (formerly of Lanarkshire) at Glasgow, 1956–78, retired; Temporary Sheriff, 1979; *b* 21 Nov. 1913; Scottish; *m* 1942, Edith Muir; two *s* one *d*. *Educ:* Rutherglen Academy; Glasgow Univ. MA, LLB 1937. Practising as Solicitor, 1937–39; volunteered Sept. 1939; Cameronian Scottish Rifles; commissioned to 6th Battn 11th Sikh Regt, Indian Army, 1940; Captain 1940; Major 1942, injured; Interpreter 1st Class in Hindustani, 1943; posted to Judge Advocate's Branch, 1944; released Dec. 1945. Admitted Faculty of Advocates in Scotland, 1946. Sheriff Substitute of Inverness, Moray, Nairn and Ross and Cromarty, 1949–52, Fife and Kinross, 1952–56. Mem., Rotary Club. *Recreations:* reading, gardening. *Address:* 20 Queens Court, Helensburgh G84 7AH. *T:* Helensburgh (01436) 678965.

MIDDLETON, Sir George (Humphrey), KCMG 1958 (CMG 1950); HM Diplomatic Service, retired; *b* 21 Jan. 1910; *e s* of George Close Middleton and Susan Sophie (*née* Harley, subsequently Elphinstone); *m* Marie Elisabeth Camille Françoise Sarthou, Bordeaux; one *s*; one step *s* one step *d*. *Educ:* St Lawrence Coll., Ramsgate; Magdalen Coll., Oxford. Entered Consular Service, 1933, Vice-Consul, Buenos Aires; transferred to Asuncion, 1934, with local rank of 3rd Sec. in Diplomatic Service; in charge of Legation, 1935; transferred to New York, 1936; to Lemberg (Lwow), 1939; local rank of Consul; in charge of Vice-Consulate at Cluj, 1939–40; appointed to Genoa, 1940, to Madeira, 1940, to Foreign Office, 1943; 2nd Sec. at Washington, 1944; 1st Sec. 1945; transferred to FO, 1947; Counsellor, 1949; Counsellor, British Embassy, Tehran, Jan. 1951; acted as Chargé d'Affaires, 1951 and 1952 (when diplomatic relations severed); Dep. High Comr for UK, in Delhi, 1953–56; British Ambassador at Beirut, 1956–58; Political Resident in the Persian Gulf, 1958–61; British Ambassador to: Argentina, 1961–64; United Arab Republic, 1964–66. Mem. *Ad hoc* Cttee for UN Finances, 1966. Consultant, Industrial Reorganisation Corporation, 1967–68; Chm., Mondial Expatriate Services Ltd, 1988–91; Director: Overseas Medical Supplies Ltd; Britarge Ltd; Decor France Ltd; Chm., Exec. Cttee, British Road Fedn, 1972; Chief Executive, British Industry Roads Campaign, 1969–76. Past Chairman: Bahrain Soc.; Anglo-Peruvian Soc.; British Moroccan Soc. FRSA. Comdr, Order of Merit, Peru, 1974; Chevalier, National Order of the Cedar, Lebanon, 1988. *Recreations:* gardening, talking. *Address:* 1 Carlyle Square, SW3 6EX. *T:* 0171–352 2962. *Club:* Travellers'.

MIDDLETON, Rear-Adm. John Patrick Windsor, CB 1992; Secretary, Royal Commission for the Exhibition of 1851, since 1995; *b* 15 March 1938; *s* of late Comdr John Henry Dudley Middleton, RN and Norna Mary Tessimond (*née* Hitchings); *m* 1962, Jane Rodwell Gibbs; one *s* one *d*. *Educ:* Cheltenham College; BRNC Dartmouth; RNEC Manadon. CEng, MIMechE, MIMarE. Entered Royal Navy 1954; CSO(E) to Flag Officer Submarines, 1981; CSO(E) Falkland Islands, 1983; Captain Naval Drafting, 1984; Dir, In Service Submarines, 1987; CSO (Engrg), later (Support), to C-in-C Fleet, 1989–92, retd. Gov., CARE for People with a Mental Handicap, 1993–. Liveryman, Co. of Armourers and Brasiers. *Recreations:* sailing, walking. *Address:* Manora, Chilmark, Wilts SP3 5AH. *T:* Teffont (01722) 716231. *Clubs:* Naval; Royal Naval Sailing Association (Portsmouth).

MIDDLETON, Lawrence John, CMG 1985; PhD; HM Diplomatic Service; Ambassador to the Republic of Korea, 1986–90, retired; *b* 27 March 1930; *s* of John James Middleton and Mary (*née* Horgan); *m* 1963, Sheila Elizabeth Hoey; two *s* one *d*. *Educ:* Finchley Catholic Grammar Sch.; King's Coll., London (BSc 1951, PhD 1954). Scientific Officer, ARC, 1954–60 and 1962–63; Cons. to FAO and to UN Cttee on Effects of Atomic Radiation, 1960–62; CENTO Inst. of Nuclear Science, 1963–65; Principal, Min. of Agriculture, 1966–68; First Sec., FO, 1968; Washington, 1969–71; Kuala Lumpur, 1971–74; Counsellor (Commercial), Belgrade, 1974–78; Dir of Research, FCO, 1978–80; Cabinet Office, 1980–82; Counsellor, UK Delegn to Conf. on Disarmament, Geneva, 1982–84; Sen. DS, RCDS, 1984–86. Mem. Council, Royal Asiatic Soc., 1994–. *Publications:* articles on plant physiology and nuclear science in biology, 1954–63. *Address:* 12 Polstead Road, Oxford OX2 6TN.

MIDDLETON, Sir Lawrence (Monck), 10th Bt *cr* 1662, of Belsay Castle, Northumberland; *b* 23 Oct. 1912; *s* of Lt Hugh Jeffery Middleton, RN (*d* 1914), 3rd *s* of Sir Arthur Middleton, 7th Bt, and Mary Katharine Middleton, OBE (*d* 1949); *S* brother, 1993; *m* 1984, Primrose Westcombe. *Educ:* Eton Coll.; Edinburgh Univ. (BSc Forestry). Forestry Commn, 1939–45. *Recreations:* mountaineering, birdwatching, gardening. *Heir:* cousin Henry Lambert Middleton [*b* 26 Aug. 1923; *m* 1961, Susan Jenifer, *er d* of W. A. F. Whittingstall, TD, QC; one *d*]. *Address:* Estate Office, Belsay Castle, Newcastle upon Tyne NE20 0DY.

MIDDLETON, Rear Adm. Linley Eric, CB 1986; DSO, FRAeS; *m* 1965, Pamela Mannerings (*née* Lewis); three *s*. *Educ:* Dale Coll., Kingwilliamstown. Qualified as FAA pilot, 1952; served HMS Indefatigable, HMS Centaur, HMS Bulwark, HMS Eagle, HMS Mounts Bay, HMS Victorious and HMS Ark Royal, 1952–63; BRNC Dartmouth, 1964–65; CO, 809 Naval Air Squadron in HMS Hermes, 1966–67; Naval Staff, MoD, 1968–69; CO, HMS Whitby, 1970–71; Staff of Flag Officer, Naval Air Comd, 1971–73; Capt. 2nd Frigate Sqn and CO, HMS Undaunted, 1973–74, and CO, HMS Apollo, 1974–75; Chief Staff Officer to Flag Officer Carriers & Amphibious Ships, 1975–77; Dir, Naval Air Warfare, 1978–79; CO, HMS Hermes, 1980–82; Asst Chief of Naval Staff (Ops), 1983–84; Flag Officer, Naval Air Comd, 1984–87, retired. Man. Dir, British Internat. Helicopters, 1987–92. Liveryman: Coach Makers' and Coach Harness Makers' Co., 1983; GAPAN, 1993 (Upper Freeman, 1987).

MIDDLETON, Michael Humfrey, CBE 1975; Director, Civic Trust, 1969–86; *b* 1 Dec. 1917; *s* of Humfrey Middleton and Lilian Irene (*née* Tillard); *m* 1954, Julie Margaret Harrison; one *s* two *d*. *Educ:* King's Sch., Canterbury. Art Critic, The Spectator, 1946–56; Art Editor and Asst Editor, Picture Post, 1949–53; Exec. Editor, Lilliput, 1953–54; Editor, House and Garden, 1955–57; Sec. and Dep. Dir, Civic Trust, 1957–69; Mem. Council, Soc. of Industrial Artists and Designers, 1953–55, 1968–70; UK Sec.-Gen., European Architectural Heritage Year, 1972–75. Member: Adv. Cttee on Trunk Road Assessment, 1977–80; UK Commn for UNESCO, 1976–80. Hon. Fellow: RIBA, 1974; Landscape Inst., 1986. Film scripts include A Future for the Past, 1972. Council of Europe Pro Merito Medal, 1976. *Publications:* Soldiers of Lead, 1948; Group Practice in Design, 1967; Man Made the Town, 1987; Cities in Transition, 1991; contributor to many conferences and jls, at home and abroad, on art, design and environmental matters. *Recreation:* looking. *Address:* 84 Sirdar Road, W11 4EG. *T:* 0171–727 9136.

MIDDLETON, Ven. Michael John; Archdeacon of Swindon, since 1992; *b* 21 July 1940; *s* of Bernard and Gladys Middleton; *m* 1965, Anne Elisabeth Parker; two *s* one *d*. *Educ:* Weymouth Grammar Sch.; St Cuthbert's Soc., Durham (BSc); Fitzwilliam Coll., Cambridge (MA); Westcott House, Cambridge. Ordained: deacon, 1966; priest, 1967; Curate, St George's Jesmond, Newcastle, 1966–69; Chaplain: St George's Grammar Sch., Cape Town, 1969–72; King's School, Tynemouth, 1972–77; Vicar, St George's, Jesmond, Newcastle, 1977–85; Rector of Hexham, 1985–92; Hon. Canon of Newcastle, 1990. Proctor in Convocation, 1980–92. *Recreations:* walking, Westerns. *Address:* 2 Louviers Way, Swindon, Wilts SN1 4DU. *T:* Swindon (01793) 644556, *Fax:* (01793) 495352.

MIDDLETON, Sir Peter (Edward), GCB 1989 (KCB 1984); a Deputy Chairman and Director, and Chairman of BZW Banking Division, Barclays Bank, since 1991; *b* 2 April 1934; *m* 1st, 1964, Valerie Ann Lindup (*d* 1987); one *d* (one *s* decd); 2nd, 1990, Constance Owen. *Educ:* Sheffield City Grammar Sch.; Sheffield Univ. (BA; Hon. DLitt 1984); Bristol Univ. Served RAPC, 1958–60. HM Treasury: Senior Information Officer, 1962; Principal, 1964; Asst Director, Centre for Administrative Studies, 1967–69; Private Sec. to Chancellor of the Exchequer, 1969–72; Treasury Press Secretary, 1972–75; Head of Monetary Policy Div., 1975; Under Secretary, 1976; Dep. Sec., 1980–83; Permanent Sec., 1983–91. Director: Bass PLC, 1992–; General Accident Fire & Life Assurance Corp. plc, 1992–; NW Water Gp, 1993–. Member: Adv. Bd, Nat. Econ. Res. Associates 1991; Exec. Cttee,

Centre for Econ. Policy Res. Vis. Fellow, Nuffield Coll., Oxford, 1981–89. Chm., Inst. of Contemporary British History, 1992–. Member Council: Manchester Business Sch., 1985–92; Sheffield Univ., 1991–; Governor: London Business Sch., 1984–90; Ditchley Foundn, 1985–; NIESR, 1991–. Dir, English Chamber Orch. and Music Soc., 1992–. Cdre, Civil Service Sailing Assoc., 1984–92. *Address:* Barclays Bank plc, 54 Lombard Street, EC3P 3AH. *Club:* Reform.

MIDDLETON, Peter James; Chief Executive, Lloyd's of London, since 1992; *b* 10 Feb. 1940; *s* of Roy and Freda Middleton; *m* 1968, Yvonne Summerson; two *s* one *d*. *Educ:* Univ. of Paris; Univ. of Hull (BA Hons). HM Diplomatic Service, 1969–85: Second Sec., Jakarta, 1969–71; First Sec., Dar-es-Salaam, 1973–74; Paris, 1978–82; Midland Bank, 1985–87, Head of Banking Ops, 1986–87; Gp Chief Exec., Thomas Cook Gp, 1987–92. *Recreations:* motor-bikes, Middlesbrough Football Club, athletics, music. *Address:* 1 Lime Street, EC3M 7HA. *T:* 0171–327 6225.

MIDDLETON, Ronald George, DSC 1945; solicitor; *b* 31 July 1913; *o s* of late Sir George Middleton; *m* 1959, Sybil Summerscale (*d* 1976); no *c*. *Educ:* Whitgift Middle Sch.; University Coll., London. Solicitor, 1936. RNVR, 1939–47 (Lt-Comdr); Radar Officer HMS Queen Elizabeth, 1944–45; Fleet Radar Officer, Indian Ocean, 1945. Partner, Coward, Chance & Co., 1949, Senior Partner, 1972–80. Part-time Mem., NBPI, 1965–68. *Recreation:* sailing. *Address:* Flat 18, 76 Jermyn Street, SW1Y 6NP. *T:* 0171–839 7993. *Clubs:* Reform, Garrick, Royal Ocean Racing.

MIDDLETON, Stanley; novelist; *b* Bulwell, Nottingham, 1 Aug. 1919; *y s* of Thomas and Elizabeth Ann Middleton; *m* 1951, Margaret Shirley, *y d* of Herbert and Winifred Vera Welch; two *d*. *Educ:* High Pavement Sch.; University Coll., Nottingham (later Univ. of Nottingham); Hon. MA Nottingham, 1975. Served Army (RA and AEC), 1940–46. Head of English Dept, High Pavement Coll., Nottingham, 1958–81. Judith E. Wilson Vis. Fellow, Emmanuel Coll., Cambridge, 1982–83. MUniv Open, 1995. *Publications:* novels: A Short Answer, 1958; Harris's Requiem, 1960; A Serious Woman, 1961; The Just Exchange, 1962; Two's Company, 1963; Him They Compelled, 1964; Terms of Reference, 1966; The Golden Evening, 1968; Wages of Virtue, 1969; Apple of the Eye, 1970; Brazen Prison, 1971; Cold Gradations, 1972; A Man Made of Smoke, 1973; Holiday (jtly, Booker Prize), 1974; Distractions, 1975; Still Waters, 1976; Ends and Means, 1977; Two Brothers, 1978; In A Strange Land, 1979; The Other Side, 1980; Blind Understanding, 1982; Entry into Jerusalem, 1983; The Daysman, 1984; Valley of Decision, 1985; An After Dinner's Sleep, 1986; After a Fashion, 1987; Recovery, 1988; Vacant Places, 1989; Changes and Chances, 1990; Beginning to End, 1991; A Place to Stand, 1992; Married Past Redemption, 1993; Catalysts, 1994; Toward the Sea, 1995. *Recreations:* music, walking, listening, argument. *Address:* 42 Caledon Road, Sherwood, Nottingham NG5 2NG. *T:* Nottingham (0115) 962 3085. *Club:* PEN.

MIDGLEY, Eric Atkinson, CMG 1965; MBE 1945; HM Diplomatic Service, retired; *b* 25 March 1913; *s* of Charles Ewart Midgley, Keighley, Yorks; *m* 1937, Catherine Gaminara; two *d*. *Educ:* Christ's Hosp.; Merton Coll., Oxford. Indian Civil Service, 1937; Trade Commissioner at Delhi, 1947; Board of Trade, 1957; Commercial Counsellor at The Hague, 1960; Minister (Economic) in India, 1963–67; Minister (Commercial), Washington, 1967–70; Ambassador to Switzerland, 1970–73. *Recreation:* sailing. *Address:* 2 Wellington Place, Captains Row, Lymington, Hants SO41 9RS. *Club:* Royal Lymington Yacht.

MIDLETON, 12th Viscount *cr* 1717 (Ire.); **Alan Henry Brodrick;** Baron Brodrick of Midleton, Co. Cork 1715; Baron Brodrick of Peper Harow 1796; Keeper of Horology, John Gershom Parkington Collection of Time Measurement Instruments, Bury St Edmunds, since 1986; *b* 4 Aug. 1949; *s* of Alan Rupert Brodrick (*d* 1972) (*g g s* of 7th Viscount) and of Alice Elizabeth, *d* of G. R. Roberts; *S* uncle, 1989; *m* 1978, Julia Helen, *d* of Michael Pitt; two *s* one *d*. *Educ:* St Edmund's School, Canterbury. FBHI. Mem. Council, 1993, Chm. Museum and Liby Cttee, 1994, British Horological Inst. *Recreations:* conservation of turret clocks, bicycling, medieval and Renaissance music. *Heir: s* Hon. Ashley Rupert Brodrick, *b* 25 Nov. 1980. *Address:* 2 Burrells Orchard, Westley, Bury St Edmunds, Suffolk IP33 3TH. *Club:* Athenæum.

MIDWINTER, Eric Clare, OBE 1992; MA, DPhil; Chairman, London Regional Passengers' Committee, since 1984; *b* 11 Feb. 1932; *m*; two *s* one *d*. *Educ:* St Catharine's Coll., Cambridge (BA Hons History); Univs of Liverpool (MA Educn) and York (DPhil). Educational posts, incl. Dir of Liverpool Educn Priority Area Project, 1955–75; Head, Public Affairs Unit, Nat. Consumer Council, 1975–80; Dir, Centre for Policy on Ageing, 1980–91. Chairman: Council, Adv. Centre for Educn, 1976–84; London Transport Users Consultative Cttee, 1977–84; Community Educn Develt Centre, 1995–; Mem., POW Adv. Cttee on Disability, 1990–. Vis. Prof. of Educn, Univ. of Exeter, 1993–. DUniv Open, 1989. *Publications:* Victorian Social Reform, 1968; Law and Order in Victorian Lancashire, 1968; Social Administration in Lancashire, 1969; Nineteenth Century Education, 1970; Old Liverpool, 1971; Projections: an education priority project at work, 1972; Social Environment and the Urban School, 1972; Priority Education, 1972; Patterns of Community Education, 1973; ed, Teaching in the Urban Community School, 1973; ed, Pre-School Priorities, 1974; Education and the Community, 1975; Education for Sale, 1977; Make 'Em Laugh: famous comedians and their world, 1978; Schools and Society, 1980; W. G. Grace: his life and times, 1981; Age is Opportunity: education and older people, 1982; (ed) Mutual Aid Universities, 1984; The Wage of Retirement: the case for a new pensions policy, 1985; Fair Game: myth and reality in sport, 1986; Caring for Cash: the issue of private domiciliary care, 1986; Redefining Old Age, 1987; The Lost Seasons: wartime cricket 1939–1945, 1987; (ed) Retired Leisure, 1987; Polls Apart? Older Voters and the 1987 General Election, 1987; New Design for Old, Function, Style and Older People, 1988; Red Roses Crest the Caps: a history of Lancashire cricket, 1989; Creating Chances: arts by older people, 1990; Old Order: crime and older people, 1990; Out of Focus: old age, the press and broadcasting, 1991; Brylcreem summer: the 1947 cricket season, 1991; An Illustrated History of County Cricket, 1992; Lifelines, 1994; The Development of Social Welfare in Britain, 1994; First Knock: cricket's opening pairs, 1994; European Year '93, 1995; 150 Years: a celebration: Surrey CCC, 1995; Thriving People: the growth and prospects of the U3A in the UK, 1995; State Educator: the life and enduring influence of W. E. Forster, 1995; Darling Old Oval: history of Surrey County Cricket Club, 1995. *Recreations:* sport, comedy. *Address:* London Regional Passengers' Committee, Golden Cross House, 8 Duncannon Street, WC2N 4JF. *Clubs:* Savage, MCC; Lancashire CCC.

MIDWINTER, Prof. John Edwin, OBE 1984; PhD; FRS 1985; FEng 1984; Pender Professor of Electronic Engineering, since 1991, Head of Department of Electronic and Electrical Engineering (formerly of Electronic Engineering), since 1988, and Vice Provost, since 1994, University College London; *b* 8 March 1938; *s* of Henry C. and Vera J. Midwinter; *m* 1961, Maureen Anne Holt; two *s* two *d*. *Educ:* St Bartholomew's Grammar Sch., Newbury, Berks; King's Coll., Univ. of London (BSc Physics, 1961; AKC 1961). PhD Physics, London (ext.), 1968. MInstP 1973; FIEE 1980; FIEEE 1983. Joined RRE, Malvern, as Scientific Officer, 1961 (research on lasers and non-linear optics); Sen. Scientific Officer, 1964–68; Perkin Elmer Corp., Norwalk, Conn, USA, 1968–70; Res. Center, Materials Research Center, Allied Chemical Corp., Morristown, NJ, USA, 1970–71; Head of Optical Fibre Develt, PO Res. Centre, Martlesham, 1971–77; Head, Optical Communications Technol., British Telecom Res. Labs, 1977–84; BT Prof. of Optoelectronics, UCL, 1984–91. Visiting Professor: Queen Mary Coll., London, 1979–84; Southampton Univ., 1979–84. Chm., Project 208, Cttee of Science and Technology, EEC, 1977–85. Vice Pres., IEE, 1994 (Chm., Electronics Div., 1991–92). Lectures: Bruce Preller, RSE, 1983; Clifford Patterson, Royal Soc.,1983; Cantor, RSA, 1984. Electronics Div. Premium, 1976, J. J. Thompson Medal, 1987, IEE. Editor, Optical and Quantum Electronics, 1972–; Associate Editor, Jl of Lightwave Technology, IEEE, 1983–. *Publications:* Applied Non-Linear Optics, 1972; Optical Fibers for Transmission, 1979 (Best Book in Technol. Award, Amer. Publishers' Assoc., 1980); over 70 papers on lasers, non-linear optics and optical communications. *Recreations:* country and mountain walking, ski-ing, bird-watching, cycling. *Address:* Department of Electronic and Electrical Engineering, University College London, Torrington Place, WC1E 7JE. *T:* 0171–388 0427, 0171–387 7050.

MIDWINTER, Stanley Walter, CB 1982; RIBA, FRTPI; architect and planning consultant; Chief Planning Inspector (Director of Planning Inspectorate), Departments of the Environment and Transport, 1978–84; *b* 8 Dec. 1922; *s* of late Lewis Midwinter and Beatrice (*née* Webb); *m* 1954, Audrey Mary Pepper (*d* 1988); one *d*. *Educ:* Regent Street Polytechnic Sch.; Sch. of Architecture (DipArch, ARIBA 1948); Sch. of Planning and Res. for Regional Develt (AMTPI 1952, FRTPI 1965); Dip. in Sociol., Univ. of London, 1976. Served War, RE, 1942–46: N Africa, Italy, Greece. Planning Officer, LCC, 1949–54; Bor. Architect and Planning Officer, Larne, NI, 1955–60; joined Housing and Planning Inspectorate, 1960; Dep. Chief Inspector, 1976. Assessor at Belvoir Coalfield Inquiry, 1979. Town Planning Institute: Exam. Prize, 1952; Thomas Adams Prize, 1955; President's Prize, 1958. *Publications:* articles in TPI Jl. *Address:* 14 Collett Way, Frome, Somerset BA11 2XR.

MIERS, Sir (Henry) David (Alastair Capel), KBE 1985; CMG 1979; HM Diplomatic Service; Ambassador to the Netherlands, since 1993; *b* 10 Jan. 1937; *s* of late Col R. D. M. C. Miers, DSO, QO Cameron Highlanders, and Honor (*née* Bucknill); *m* 1966, Imelda Maria Emilia, *d* of Jean-Baptiste Wouters, Huizingen, Belgium; two *s* one *d*. *Educ:* Winchester; University Coll., Oxford. Tokyo, 1963; Vientiane, 1966; Private Sec. to Minister of State, FO, 1968; Paris, 1972; Counsellor, Tehran, 1977–79; Hd, Middle Eastern Dept, FCO, 1980–83; Ambassador to Lebanon, 1983–85; Asst Under-Sec. of State, FCO, 1986–89; Ambassador to Greece, 1989–93. *Address:* c/o Foreign and Commonwealth Office, SW1A 2AH.

MIFLIN, Dr Benjamin John, PhD; Director, Institute of Arable Crops Research and IACR-Rothamsted, since 1994; *b* 7 Jan. 1939; *s* of late Stanley Miflin and Kathleen (*née* Davies); *m* 1964, Hilary Newman; three *d*. *Educ:* Univ. of Nottingham (BSc); Univ. of Illinois (MS); QMC and Imperial Coll., London (PhD 1965). Lectr in Plant Scis (Plant Biochem.), Sch. of Agric., Univ. of Newcastle upon Tyne, 1965–73; Hd, Biochem. Dept, 1973–85, and Div. of Molecular Scis, 1983–85, Rothamsted Exptl Stn, Harpenden; Hd, Internat. R & D, Ciba-Geigy Seeds, Basle, 1986–93. Vis. Prof., Univ. of Nottingham, 1981–85 and 1994–. Member: BBSRC Technol. Interaction Bd, 1994–; Adv. Cttee on Novel Foods and Processes, 1995–. Corresp. Mem., Amer. Soc. of Plant Physiologists, 1986. *Publications:* (ed) The Biochemistry of Plants, Vol. 5, 1980, (ed with P. J. Lea) Vol. 16, 1990; (ed) Oxford Surveys of Plant Cell and Molecular Biology, Vols 1–7, 1984–91; numerous papers in field of plant biochem. and related subjects. *Recreations:* ski-ing, gardening, photography. *Address:* IACR-Rothamsted, Harpenden, Herts AL5 2JQ. *T:* Harpenden (01582) 763133.

MIFSUD BONNICI, Dr Carmelo, BA, LLD; MP First District, since 1987; Prime Minister of Malta, 1984–87; *b* 17 July 1933; *s* of Dr Lorenzo Mifsud Bonnici, and Catherine (*née* Buttigieg). *Educ:* Govt sch. and Lyceum, Malta; Univ. of Malta (BA, LLD); Univ. Coll. London. Lectr in Industrial and Fiscal Law, Univ. of Malta, 1969–. Legal Consultant, General Workers' Union, 1969–83; Dep. Leader, Labour Party, responsible for Party affairs, 1980–82; Designate Leader of the Labour Movement, 1982; co-opted to Parlt, 1983, Minister of Labour and Social Services, 1983; Sen. Dep. Prime Minister, 1983–84; Leader, Labour Party, 1984–92. *Recreation:* reading. *Address:* House of Representatives, Valletta, Malta.

MIFSUD BONNICI, Dr Ugo; President of Malta, since 1994; *b* 8 Nov. 1932; *m* 1959, Gemma Bianco; two *s* one *d*. *Educ:* Lyceum, Malta; Univ. of Malta (BA 1952; LLD 1955). Elected MP, 2nd Electoral Div., 1966–; Shadow Minister of Educn, 1971; President: General Council, 1976; Admin. Council, 1976; Minister of: Educn, 1987; Educn and the Interior, 1987–92; Educn and Human Resources, 1992. Campanion of Honour, Nat. Order of Merit (Malta). *Publications:* Biex il-Futur Jerga' Jibda, 1976; Il-Linja t-Tajba, 1980; Biex il-Futur Rega' Beda, 1992. *Recreations:* reading, writing, listening to music. *Address:* San Anton Palace, Balzan, Malta. *T:* 440354; 18 Triq Erin Serracino Inglott, Bormla, Malta. *Club:* Casino Maltese.

MILAN, Archbishop of; *see* Martini, His Eminence Cardinal C. M.

MILBANK, Sir Anthony (Frederick), 5th Bt *cr* 1882; farmer and landowner since 1977; Chairman, Moorland Association, since 1986; *b* 16 Aug. 1939; *s* of Sir Mark Vane Milbank, 4th Bt, KCVO, MC, and Hon. Verena Aileen, Lady Milbank (*d* 1995), *yr d* of 11th Baron Farnham, DSO; *S* father, 1984; *m* 1970, Belinda Beatrice, *yr d* of Brig. Adrian Gore, DSO; two *s* one *d*. *Educ:* Eton College. Brown, Shipley & Co. Ltd, 1961–66; M&G Securities Ltd, 1966–77. Member: NCC Cttee for England, 1989–91; CLA Exec. Cttee, 1989–94; Council, RSPB, 1993–. High Sheriff of Durham, 1991–92. *Recreations:* various. *Heir: s* Edward Mark Somerset Milbank, *b* 9 April 1973. *Address:* Barningham Park, Richmond, N Yorks DL11 7DW.

MILBORNE-SWINNERTON-PILKINGTON, Sir T. H.; *see* Pilkington.

MILBOURN, Dr Graham Maurice; Director, National Institute of Agricultural Botany, 1981–90, retired; *b* 4 Sept. 1930; *s* of late Frank McLaren Milbourn, BSc and Winifred May Milbourn; *m* 1956, Louise Lawson, BSc Hons; three *s*. *Educ:* Reading Univ. (BSc, MSc, PhD). Asst Lectr, Reading Univ., 1953–56; Radiobiological Lab., ARC, 1956–61; Sen. Lectr, Crop Production, Wye Coll., London Univ., 1961–77; Prof. of Crop Production, Sch. of Agric., Edinburgh Univ., 1977–81. Vis. Prof., Silsoe Coll., Cranfield Univ. (formerly Inst. of Technology), 1991–. Pres., Assoc. Applied Biologists, 1991. *Publications:* papers on physiology of cereals and vegetables, uptake of radio-nucleides by crops. *Recreation:* sailing. *Address:* Elmwood, Cuckoo Lane, Lolworth, Cambridge CB3 8HF. *T:* Crafts Hill (01954) 780815.

MILBURN, Alan; MP (Lab) Darlington, since 1992; *b* 27 Jan. 1958; partner, Dr Ruth Briel; one *s*. *Educ:* Stokesley Comprehensive Sch.; Lancaster Univ. (BA). Co-ordinator, Trade Union Studies Information Unit, Newcastle, 1984–90; Sen. Business Development Officer, N Tyneside MBC, 1990–92. Mem., Public Accounts Cttee, 1994–. Chair, PLP Treasury Cttee, 1992–. *Address:* House of Commons, SW1A 0AA.

MILBURN, Sir Anthony (Rupert), 5th Bt *cr* 1905; landowner; *b* 17 April 1947; *s* of Major Rupert Leonard Eversley Milburn (*yr s* of 3rd Bt) (*d* 1974) and of Anne Mary, *d* of late Major Austin Scott Murray, MC; *S* uncle, 1985; *m* 1977, Olivia Shirley, *y d* of Captain Thomas Noel Catlow, CBE, DL, RN; two *s* one *d. Educ:* Hawtreys, Savernake Forest; Eton College; Cirencester Agricultural Coll. ARICS. Company Director. *Recreations:* sporting and rural pursuits. *Heir: s* Patrick Thomas Milburn, *b* 4 Dec. 1980. *Address:* Guyzance Hall, Acklington, Morpeth, Northumberland NE65 9AG. *T:* Alnwick (01665) 513047. *Club:* New (Edinburgh).

MILBURN, Donald B.; *see* Booker-Milburn.

MILBURN, Very Rev. Robert Leslie Pollington, MA; FSA; *b* 28 July 1907; *er s* of late George Leslie and Elizabeth Esther Milburn; *m* 1944, Margery Kathleen Mary (*d* 1993), *d* of Rev. Francis Graham Harvie; one *d* (one *s* decd). *Educ:* Oundle; Sidney Sussex Coll., Cambridge; New Coll., Oxford. Asst Master, Eton Coll., 1930–32; Select Preacher, University of Oxford, 1942–44; Fellow and Chaplain of Worcester Coll., Oxford, 1934–57, Tutor, 1945–57, Estates Bursar, 1946–57 (Junior Bursar, 1936–46), Hon. Fellow, 1978. University Lectr in Church History, 1947–57; Bampton Lectr, 1952. Examining Chaplain to Bishop of St Edmundsbury and Ipswich, 1941–53, to Bishop of Southwark, 1950–57, to Bishop of Oxford, 1952–57; Dean of Worcester, 1957–68, now Emeritus; Master of the Temple, 1968–80. Mem. of Oxford City Council, 1941–47. A Trustee, Wallace Collection, 1970–76. Grand Chaplain, United Grand Lodge of England, 1969. *Publications:* Saints and their Emblems in English Churches, 1949; Early Christian Interpretations of History, 1954; Early Christian Art and Architecture, 1988; articles in Journal of Theological Studies and Church Quarterly Review. *Address:* 5 St Barnabas, Newland, Malvern, Worcs WR13 5AX.

MILDON, Arthur Leonard, QC 1971; **His Honour Judge Mildon;** a Circuit Judge, since 1986; *b* 3 June 1923; *er s* of late Rev. Dr W. H. Mildon, Barnstaple; *m* 1950, Iva, *er d* of late G. H. C. Wallis, Plymouth; one *s* one *d. Educ:* Kingswood Sch., Bath; Wadham Coll., Oxford (MA). Pres., Oxford Univ. Liberal Club, 1948. Army Service, 1942–46: Lieut, 138th (City of London) Field Regt, RA; Captain, 1st Army Group, RA. Called to Bar, Middle Temple, 1950, Bencher, 1979; Member of Western Circuit; Dep. Chm., Isle of Wight QS, 1967–71; a Recorder, 1972–85. Mem., Bar Council, 1973–74. Pres., Medico-Legal Soc., 1994–95. *Recreation:* sailing. *Address:* c/o 2 Crown Office Row, Temple, EC4Y 7HJ. *T:* 0171–797 8000. *Clubs:* Ski Club of Great Britain; Royal Solent Yacht.

MILDON, Russell; Director, International Affairs relating to Agriculture, European Commission, since 1993; *b* 22 Aug. 1949; *s* of R. F. Mildon and J. Mildon (*née* Kröpfl); *m* 1973, Micheline Williams; two *s* one *d. Educ:* Royal Holloway Coll., London Univ. (Open Schol.; BSc Hons); Brunel Univ. (MTech). With Commission of the European Communities, 1974–: Statistics, studies and reports (Agricl), 1974–81; Gen. Affairs Gp, 1981–83; Private Sec. to Dep. Dir Gen., Agricl Markets, 1983–86; Advr to Vice-Pres., 1986–89; Head: Unit for Analysis of Situation of Agricl Holdings, 1989; Unit for Oilseeds and Protein Crops, 1989–93. *Recreations:* squash, chess, travel. *Address:* European Commission, 200 Rue de la Loi, 1049 Brussels, Belgium. *T:* (2) 2953224.

MILEDI, Prof. Ricardo, MD; FRS 1970; Distinguished Professor, University of California, Irvine, since 1984; *b* Mexico City, 15 Sept. 1927; *m* 1955, Ana Carmen (Mela) Garces; one *s. Educ:* Univ. Nacional Autónoma, Mexico City. BSc 1945; MD 1955. Research at Nat. Inst. of Cardiology, Mexico, 1952–54; Rockefeller Travelling Fellowship at ANU, 1956–58; research at Dept of Biophysics, UCL, 1958–84. Fellow, Amer. Acad. of Arts and Scis, 1986; Hon. Mem., Hungarian Acad. of Scis, 1988; For. Mem., Nat. Acad. of Scis, 1989; Corresp. Mem., Mexican Acad. of Scis, 1991; Titular Mem., Eur. Acad. of Arts, Scis and Humanities, 1992. Dr *hc* Universidad del País Vasco, Spain, 1992. Luigi Galvani Award, 1987; Internat. Prize for Science, King Faisal Foundn, 1988. *Address:* Laboratory of Cellular and Molecular Neurobiology, Department of Psychobiology, University of California, Irvine, CA 92717–4550, USA. *T:* (714) 8565693; 9 Gibbs Court, Irvine, CA 92715, USA. *T:* (714) 8562677.

MILES, Prof. Albert Edward William, LRCP; MRCS; FDS; DSc; Professor of Dental Pathology at The London Hospital Medical College, 1950–76, retired; Hon. Curator, Odontological Collection, Royal College of Surgeons of England, 1955–89; *b* 15 July 1912; *m* 1st, 1939, Sylvia Stuart; one *s* decd; 2nd, 1979, Diana Cross. *Educ:* Stationers' Company Sch.; Charing Cross and Royal Dental Hosps. John Tomes Prize, RCS, 1954–56. Part-time Lectr, Anatomy Dept, London Hosp. Med. Coll., 1977–85; Hon. Researcher, Dept of Palaeontology, Nat. Hist. Museum, 1993–. Charles Tomes Lecturer, RCS, 1957; Evelyn Sprawson Lectr, London Hosp. Med. Coll., 1977. Hunterian Trustee, 1978–. Hon. FRSM 1988. Howard Mummery Meml Prize, BDA, 1976; Colyer Gold Medal, RCS, 1978; Sir Arthur Keith Medal, RCS, 1990; Wood Jones Medal, RCS, 1993. Exec. Editor, Archives of Oral Biology, 1969–88. *Publications:* Structural and Chemical Organization of Teeth, 1967; Teeth and Their Origins, 1972; An Early Christian Chapel and Burial Ground in Outer Hebrides, with a Study of the Skeletal Remains, 1989; Colyer's Variations and Diseases of the Teeth in Animals, 1990; contrib. to scientific literature, latterly on physical anthropology. *Address:* 1 Cleaver Square, Kennington, SE11 4DW. *T:* 0171–735 5350; Department of Palaeontology, Natural History Museum, Cromwell Road, SW7 5BD. *Clubs:* Tetrapods, Zoo.

MILES, Anthony John; President, International Publishing Partners Inc., USA, since 1993; Executive Publisher, Globe Communications Corporation, Florida, USA, 1985–90; *b* 18 July 1930; *s* of Paul and Mollie Miles; *m* 1975, Anne Hardman. *Educ:* High Wycombe Royal Grammar Sch. On staff of (successively): Middlesex Advertiser; Nottingham Guardian; Brighton Evening Argus. Daily Mirror: Feature writer, 1954–66; Asst Editor, 1967–68; Associate Editor, 1968–71; Editor, 1971–74; Mirror Group Newspapers: Editorial Dir, 1975–84; Dep. Chm., 1977–79 and 1984; Chm., 1980–83. Dir, Reuters Ltd, 1978–84. Member: Press Council, 1975–78; British Exec. Cttee, IPI, 1976–84; Council, CPU, 1983–84; Life Vice-Pres., Newspaper Press Fund (Appeal Chm., 1982–83). *Address:* 23331 Drayton Drive, Boca Raton, FL 33433, USA. *Club:* Reform.

MILES, Lieut-Comdr Brian, CBE 1994; RD 1970; FNI; RNR (retired); Director, Royal National Lifeboat Institution, since 1988; *b* 23 Feb. 1937; *s* of Terence Clifford Miles and Muriel Irene Terry; *m* 1964, Elizabeth Anne Scott; one *s* two *d. Educ:* Reed's School, Cobham; HMS Conway; Merchant Navy Cadet School. Master Mariner (Foreign Going) Cert. P&O Orient Lines: Cadet, 1954–57; Deck Officer, 1958–64; RNLI: Divl Inspector, 1964–73; Asst to Director, 1974–79; Ops Staff Officer, 1979–81; Dep. Dir, 1982–87. FNI 1989; CIMgt 1994. Freeman, City of London, 1993; Mem., Master Mariners' Co., 1994–. Younger Brother, Trinity House, 1994. *Address:* 8 Longfield Drive, West Parley, Ferndown, Dorset BH22 8TY. *T:* Bournemouth (01202) 571739.

MILES, Mrs Caroline Mary; Chairman, APT Design and Development Ltd, since 1994; *b* 30 April 1929; *d* of Brig. A. J. R. M. Leslie, OBE. *Educ:* numerous schools; Somerville Coll., Oxford. HM Treasury, 1953–54; NIESR, 1954–56 and 1964–67; attached to UN Secretariat, NY, 1956–63. Associate Mem., Nuffield Coll., Oxford, 1972–74; Ian Ramsey Fellow, St Cross Coll., Oxford, 1988–94. Market Develt Consultant, Harwell Res. Lab., 1981–86. Chm., Oxfordshire HA, 1984–92. Member: Textile Council, 1968–71; Inflation Accounting Cttee (Sandilands Cttee), 1974–75; Monopolies and Mergers Commn, 1975–84; NEB, 1976–79; Nuffield Council on Bioethics, 1991–. Trustee, The Tablet, 1982–; Radcliffe Med. Foundn, 1986–; Governor: Ditchley Foundn, 1983–; Oxford Polytechnic, 1988–92. *Publications:* Lancashire Textiles, A Case Study of Industrial Change, 1968; numerous papers and articles. *Recreations:* music, picnics, poohsticks. *Address:* Millbrook, Brookend, Chadlington, Oxford OX7 3NF. *T:* Chadlington (01608) 676309.

MILES, Prof. Charles William Noel, CBE 1980; Head of Department of Land Management and Development, 1968–81, Dean of Faculty of Urban and Regional Studies, 1972–75, and Professor Emeritus 1981, University of Reading; Chairman, Agricultural Wages Board for England and Wales, 1972–81; *b* 3 Nov. 1915; 2nd *s* of late Lt-Col Sir Charles W. Miles, 5th Bt; *m* 1940, Jacqueline (Dickie) Cross; one *d* (one *s* decd). *Educ:* Stowe Sch.; Jesus Coll., Cambridge (MA). FRICS. Army Service, 1939–46; Univ. Demonstrator and Univ. Lectr, Dept of Estate Management, Cambridge, 1946–54; Chief Agent to Meyrick Estates in Hants and Anglesey, 1954–68; Agent to Bisterne Estate, 1957–68. Pres., Chartered Land Agents Soc., 1965–66; Mem., Cambs AEC, 1953–54; Mem., SE Region Adv. Cttee of Land Commn, 1967–70. Mem., Yates Cttee on Recreation Management Trng, 1977–82. Leverhulme Trust Emeritus Fellowship, 1982–84. *Publications:* Estate Finance and Business Management, 1953, 4th edn 1981; Estate Accounts, 1960; Recreational Land Management, 1977, 2nd edn 1992; (co-ed) Walmesley's Rural Estate Management, 6th edn, 1978; Running an Open house, 1986; Going Public, 1991; (jtly) Aspects of Rural Estate Management, 1995. *Recreations:* walking, gardening, theatre. *Address:* Wheelers, Vicarage Lane, Mattingley, Basingstoke, Hants RG27 8LE. *T:* Heckfield (01734) 326357. *Club:* Farmers'.

See also Sir W. N. M. Miles, Bt.

MILES, Prof. Christopher John; Professor of Film and Television, Royal College of Art, since 1989; film director and producer; *b* 19 April 1939; *s* of late John Miles, MC and Clarice Baskerville (*née* Remnant); *m* 1967, Susan Helen Howard Armstrong; one *d. Educ:* Winchester Coll.; Institut des Hautes Etudes Cinématographiques, Paris. Dir, Milesian Film Productions, 1962–; *films* include: Six Sided Triangle, 1963; The Virgin and the Gypsy, 1970 (Best Film Award, US and UK Critics, 1970); Time for Loving, 1972; The Maids, 1974; Alternative Three, 1976; Priest of Love: life of D. H. Lawrence, 1981; Lord Elgin and some stones of no value, 1985; Cyclone Warning Class 4, 1994; *theatre:* Skin of our Teeth, Chicago, 1973. Lecture tours: India, for British Council, 1985; USA, 1986. FRCA 1989. *Publications:* Alternative Three, 1977 (trans. 5 langs); (contrib.) H of C Report on Film, 1982; contrib. Image et Son, D. H. Lawrence Soc. Jl. *Recreations:* film-making, long walks and sketching in Arcadia. *Address:* Calstone House, Calstone, Calne, Wilts SN11 8PY; Aghios Leos, Methoni, Greece. *Club:* Garrick.

MILES, Dillwyn, FRGS 1946; The Herald Bard, since 1967; Director, Dyfed Rural Council, 1975–81; Chairman, National Association of Local Councils, 1977–87, Vice-President, since 1987; *b* 25 May 1916; *s* of Joshua Miles and Anne Mariah (*née* Lewis), Newport, Pembrokeshire; *m* 1944, Joyce Eileen (*d* 1976), *d* of Lewis Craven Ord, Montreal and London; one *s* one *d. Educ:* Fishguard County Sch.; University College of Wales, Aberystwyth. Served War of 1939–45, Middle East, Army Captain. National Organiser Palestine House, London, 1945–48; Extra-mural Lectr, Univ. of Wales, 1948–51; Community Centres Officer, Wales, 1951–54; Gen. Sec., Pembrokeshire Community Council, 1954–75. Founder: Jerusalem Welsh Soc., 1940; W Wales Tourist Assoc., 1962; Assoc. of Trusts for Nature Conservation in Wales, 1973; Hon. Sec., W Wales Naturalists Trust, 1958–75 (Vice-Pres., 1975–). Grand Sword Bearer, Gorsedd of Bards of Isle of Britain, 1959–67 (Mem. Bd, 1945–). Member: Pembrokeshire CC, 1947–63; Cemaes RDC, 1947–52; Newport Parish Council, 1946–52; Haverfordwest Bor. Council, 1957–63; Pembrokeshire Coast Nat. Park Cttee, 1952–75; Exec. Cttee, Council for Protection of Rural Wales, 1946–64; Nature Conservancy's Cttee for Wales, 1966–73; Council, Soc. for Promotion of Nature Reserves, 1961–73; Countryside in 1970 Cttee for Wales, 1969–70; Sports Council for Wales, 1965–69; Mental Health Rev. Tribunal for Wales, 1959–71; Rent Trib. for Wales, 1966–87; Court of Govs, Nat. Libr. for Wales, 1963–64; Court of Govs, Univ. of Wales, 1957–66; Pembroke TA Assoc., 1956–59; Council for Small Industries in Wales, 1968–72; Age Concern Wales, 1972–77; Exec. Cttee, Nat. Council for Social Service, 1978–81; Exec. Cttee, NPFA, 1977–81; Council, Royal Nat. Eisteddfod of Wales, 1967–; Prince of Wales Cttee, 1971–80 (former Chm., Dyfed Projects Gp); Welsh Environment Foundn, 1971–80; Heraldry Soc., 1974–; Rural Voice, 1980–87. Former Chairman: Further Educn and Libraries and Museums Cttees, Pembs CC; Pembs Cttee, Arthritis and Rheumatism Council; Pembs Jun. Ch. of Commerce; Pembs Community Health Council; Policy and Welsh Cttees, Nat. Assoc. of Local Councils. Chairman: Wales Playing Fields Assoc., 1965–81; Pembs PO and Telecom Adv. Cttee, 1984–94 (Vice-Chm., 1971–84); Pembs Wildlife Appeal, 1988–. Pres., Pembs Histl Soc., 1994–. Editor: The Pembrokeshire Historian, 1955–81; Nature in Wales, 1970–80. Mayor of Newport, Pembs, 1950, 1966, 1967, 1979, and Sen. Alderman. Mayor and Adm. of the Port, Haverfordwest, 1961, Sheriff 1963, Burgess Warden 1974–. Broadcaster, TV and radio, 1936–. *Publications:* ed, Pembrokeshire Coast National Park, 1973; (jtly) Writers of the West, 1974; The Sheriffs of the County of Pembroke, 1975; The Royal National Eisteddfod of Wales, 1978; A Pembrokeshire Anthology, 1982; The Castles of Pembrokeshire, 1979, 3rd edn 1988; Portrait of Pembrokeshire, 1984; The Pembrokeshire Coast National Park, 1987; The Secret of the Bards, 1992; The Description of Pembrokeshire, 1994. *Recreations:* natural history, local history, books, food and wine. *Address:* 9 St Anthony's Way, Haverfordwest, Dyfed, Wales SA61 1EL. *T:* Haverfordwest (01437) 765275. *Clubs:* Savile, Wig and Pen.

MILES, (Frank) Stephen, CMG 1964; HM Diplomatic Service, retired; *b* 7 Jan. 1920; *s* of Harry and Mary Miles; *m* 1953, Margaret Joy (*née* Theaker); three *d. Educ:* John Watson's Sch., Edinburgh; Daniel Stewart's Coll., Edinburgh; St Andrews Univ. (MA); Harvard Univ. (Commonwealth Fellowship; MPA). Served with Fleet Air Arm, 1942–46 (Lt (A) RNVR). Scottish Home Dept, 1948; FCO (previously CRO), 1948–80; served in: New Zealand, 1949–52; E and W Pakistan, 1954–57; Ghana, 1959–62; Uganda, 1962–63; British Dep. High Commissioner, Tanzania, 1963–65 (Acting High Commissioner, 1963–64); Acting High Commissioner in Ghana, March-April 1966; Consul-Gen., St Louis, 1967–70; Dep. High Comr, Calcutta, 1970–74; High Comr, Zambia, 1974–78; High Comr, Bangladesh, 1978–79. A Dir of Studies, Overseas Services Unit, RIPA, 1980–83. Councillor: Tandridge DC, Surrey, 1982–90; Limpsfield Parish Council, 1983–95 (Chm., 1987–89). *Recreations:* cricket, tennis, golf. *Address:* Maytrees, 71 Park Road, Limpsfield, Oxted, Surrey RH8 0AN. *T:* Oxted (01883) 713132. *Clubs:* Commonwealth Trust, Royal Over-Seas League, MCC; Tandridge Golf.

MILES, Geoffrey, OBE 1970; HM Diplomatic Service, retired; Consul-General, Perth, Western Australia, 1980–82; *b* 25 Oct. 1922; *s* of late Donald Frank Miles and Honorine Miles (*née* Lambert); *m* 1946, Mary Rozel Cottle (*d* 1989); one *s* one *d. Educ:* Eltham College. Joined Home Civil Service (Min. of Shipping), 1939; War service as pilot in RAF, 1941–46 (commnd 1945); Min. of Transport, 1946–50; British Embassy, Washington

1951; Sec., Copper-Zinc-Lead Cttee, Internat. Materials Conf., Washington 1952–53; BoT, 1953–55; Asst Trade Comr, Perth, 1955–59; Second Sec., Ottawa, 1960–63; First Sec., Salisbury, 1963–66, Dublin, 1967–71; Trade Comr (later Consul) and Head of Post, Edmonton, 1971–75, Consul-Gen., 1976–78; Consul-Gen., Philadelphia, 1979–80. *Recreations:* music, golf, amateur radio. *Address:* Farthings, Appledram Lane, Chichester, W Sussex PO20 7PE. *Clubs:* Royal Air Force; British Officers (Philadelphia); Goodwood Golf.

MILES, Gwyn; Surveyor of Collections, Victoria and Albert Museum, since 1989; *b* 17 Nov. 1947; *d* of Sir Morien Morgan, CB, FRS and of Lady Morgan (*née* Axford); *m* 1969, David Miles; one *s* one *d*. *Educ:* Bristol Univ. (BSc Physiol.); Bath Univ. (DipEd); Museums Assoc. (Cert. in Conservation). Research Assistant: McGill Univ., Montreal, 1969; Bristol Univ., 1969–70; Science Teacher, St Mary Redcliffe and Temple Sch., Bristol, 1971; Department of Antiquities, Ashmolean Museum, Oxford: Conservator, 1972–82; Head of Conservation, 1982–85; Dep. Keeper of Conservation, V&A, 1985–89. *Publications:* Traditional Knitting in the British Isles, 1979; articles on conservation, collections management and gardening. *Recreation:* combining career and family. *Address:* 21 Iffley Road, Oxford OX4 1EA. *T:* Oxford (01865) 241972.

MILES, Prof. Hamish Alexander Drummond, OBE 1987; Barber Professor of Fine Arts and Director of the Barber Institute, University of Birmingham, 1970–90, Professor at Large and Emeritus Director, 1990–91, Emeritus Professor, since 1992; *b* 19 Nov. 1925; *s* of J. E. (Hamish) Miles and Sheila Barbara Robertson; *m* 1957, Jean Marie, *d* of T. R. Smits, New York; two *s* two *d*. *Educ:* Douai Sch.; Univ. of Edinburgh (MA); Balliol Coll., Oxford. Served War: Army, 1944–47. Asst Curator, Glasgow Art Gallery, 1953–54; Asst Lectr, then Lectr in the History of Art, Univ. of Glasgow, 1954–66; Vis. Lectr, Smith Coll., Mass, 1960–61; Prof. of the History of Art, Univ. of Leicester, 1966–70. Trustee, National Galleries of Scotland, 1967–87; Mem., Museums and Galleries Commn, 1983–87. *Publications:* (jtly) The Paintings of James McNeill Whistler, 2 vols, 1980; sundry articles and catalogues. *Recreations:* beekeeping and woodland management. *Address:* 31 Drummond Place, Edinburgh EH3 6PW; Burnside, Kirkmichael, Blairgowrie, Perthshire PH10 7NA.

MILES, (Henry) Michael (Pearson), OBE 1989; Executive Director, John Swire & Sons Ltd, since 1988; Director, Baring Holding Co., since 1995; *b* 19 April 1936; *s* of late Brig. H. G. P. Miles and Margaret Miles; *m* 1967, Carol Jane Berg; two *s* one *d*. *Educ:* Wellington Coll. National Service, Duke of Wellington's Regt, 1955–57. Joined John Swire & Sons, 1958; Managing Director: John Swire & Sons (Japan) Ltd, 1973–76; Cathay Pacific Airways Ltd, 1978–84 (Chm., 1984–88); Chairman: Swire Pacific, 1984–88; John Swire & Sons (HK), 1984–88; Director: Baring PLC, 1989–95 (Jt Dep. Chm., 1994–95); Johnson Matthey, 1990–; Portals Holdings, 1990–95; BP, 1994–. Chm., Hong Kong Tourist Assoc., 1984–88. Gov., Wellington Coll., 1988–. *Recreations:* golf, tennis. *Address:* Shalbourne House, Shalbourne, near Marlborough, Wilts SN8 3QH. *Clubs:* White's; Queen's; Royal and Ancient Golf; Berkshire Golf.

MILES, Jenefer Mary; *see* Blackwell, J. M.

MILES, John Edwin Alfred, CBE 1979 (OBE 1961; MBE 1952); HM Diplomatic Service, retired; *b* 14 Aug. 1919; *s* of late John Miles and late Rose Miles (*née* Newlyn); *m* 1952, Barbara Fergus Ferguson; two *s* one *d*. *Educ:* Hornsey County Sch. Apptd to Dominions Office, 1937. Served War: joined Queen's Royal West Surrey Regt, 1940; commissioned in N Staffordshire Regt, 1941; attached Royal Indian Army Service Corps, 1942 (Maj. 1943); released, Sept. 1946, and returned to Dominions Office. Served in: Wellington, NZ, 1948–51; Calcutta, 1953–56; CRO, 1957–61; Trinidad (on staff of Governor-Gen.), 1961; Jamaica (Adviser to Governor, and later First Sec. in British High Commission), 1961–64; Wellington, NZ, 1964–68; Counsellor, 1968; Accra, Ghana, 1968–71; Dep. High Comr, Madras, India, 1971–75; High Comr to Swaziland, 1975–79. *Address:* Cartref, Ladyegate Road, Dorking, Surrey RH5 4AR. *T:* Dorking (01306) 884346.

MILES, Prof. John Richard; Head, School of Fashion and Textiles, Royal College of Art, since 1993 (Course Director, Textiles and Fashion, 1989–93); Director, Miles Whiston and Wright; *b* 22 June 1944; *s* of Thomas William Miles and Hilda Mary Miles (*née* Davis); *m* 1963, Judith Bud (marr. diss.). *Educ:* Croydon Coll. of Art; Royal Coll. of Art (MDes). Set up design studio, Miles Calver and Pound (now Calver and Pound), 1973–78 (Director); Founder Dir, Peppermint Prints, 1978–82; Head, Textiles and Fashion, Brighton Polytechnic, 1979–85; Design Dir, Courtaulds, 1985–87; Gen. Manager, Next, 1987–89. Consultant, Studio Claire and Lyn. Chm., Textile and Fashion Panel, CNAA, 1983–88; Mem., Industrial Lead Body, 1991–. Governor, Winchester Sch. of Art. *Recreations:* gardening, films, cooking, reading. *Address:* Rose Cottage Farmhouse, 43 North Street, Biddenden, Ashford, Kent TN27 8BA. *T:* Biddenden (01580) 291867.

MILES, John Seeley, FCSD, FSTD; typographer and partner in design group, Banks and Miles; *b* 11 Feb. 1931; *s* of Thomas William Miles and Winifred (*née* Seeley); *m* 1955, Louise Wilson; one *s* two *d*. *Educ:* Beckenham and Penge Grammar Sch.; Beckenham School of Art. FCSD (FSIAD 1973); FSTD 1974. UN travelling schol. to Netherlands to practise typography and punch cutting under Jan van Krimpen and S. L. Hartz, 1954–55; Assistant to Hans Schmoller at Penguin Books, 1955–58; joined Colin Banks, *qv*, to form design partnership, Banks and Miles, 1958. Consultant to: Zoological Soc., Regent's Park and Whipsnade, 1958–82; Expanded Metal Co., 1960–83; Consumers' Assoc., 1964–93; British Council, 1968–83; The Post Office, 1972–83; E Midlands Arts Assoc., 1974–79; Curwen Press, 1970–72; Basilisk Press, 1976–79; Enschedé en Zn, Netherlands, 1980–94; British Telecom, 1980–89; British Airports Auth., 1983–87; typographic advisor, HMSO, 1985–; design advisor: Agricl Inf. Workshop, Udaipur, India, 1973; Monotype Corp., 1985–92; hon. design advr, UEA, 1990–. Designed banknote series Netherlands Antilles, 1987. Member: PO Design Adv. Cttee, 1972–76; Icograda Internat. Archive Cttee, 1993–. American Heritage Lectr, New York, 1960; held seminar, Graphic Inst., Stockholm, 1977 and 1986. Chairman: Wynkyn de Worde Soc., 1973–74; Arbitration Cttee, Assoc. Typographique Internationale, 1984–95; Mem., Soc. Roy. des Bibliophiles et Iconophiles de Belgique, 1991–94. Governor, Central School of Arts and Crafts, 1978–85; External examiner: London Coll. of Printing, 1984–88; Technische Hoogschool Delft, 1986–87; Reading Univ., 1990–93; de Montfort Univ., 1994–. Mem. CGLI, 1986. Exhibitions: London, 1971, 1978; Amsterdam and Brussels, 1977; Hamburg, 1991. FRSA 1988. (With Colin Banks) Green Product Award, 1989; BBC Envmtl Award, 1990. *Publications:* Design for Desktop Publishing, 1987; articles and reviews in professional jls. *Recreations:* gardening, painting, reading aloud. *Address:* 24 Collins Street, Blackheath, SE3 0GU. *T:* 0181–318 4739. *Club:* Double Crown.

MILES, Michael; *see* Miles, H. M. P.

MILES, Oliver; *see* Miles, R. O.

MILES, Peter Charles H.; *see* Hubbard-Miles.

MILES, Sir Peter (Tremayne), KCVO 1986; an Extra Equerry to HM the Queen, since 1988; *b* 26 June 1924; *er s* of late Lt-Col E. W. T. Miles, MC; *m* 1956, Philippa Helen Tremlett; two *s* one *d*. *Educ:* Eton Coll.; RMC, Sandhurst. First The Royal Dragoons, 1944–49; J. F. Thomasson & Co., 1949–59; Gerrard & National Discount Co. Ltd, 1959–80 (Managing Director, 1964–80). Director: P. Murray-Jones Ltd, 1966–75; Astley & Pearce Holdings Ltd, 1975–80 (Chm., 1978–80). Keeper of the Privy Purse and Treas. to the Queen, 1981–87; Receiver-Gen., Duchy of Lancaster, 1981–87; Mem., Prince of Wales' Council, 1981–87. *Address:* Mill House, Southrop, Lechlade, Gloucestershire GL7 3NU. *Clubs:* Cavalry and Guards, Pratt's, White's; Swinley Forest Golf.

MILES, (Richard) Oliver, CMG 1984; HM Diplomatic Service; Ambassador to Greece, since 1993; *b* 6 March 1936; *s* of George Miles and Olive (*née* Clapham); *m* 1968, Julia, *d* of late Prof. J. S. Weiner; three *s* one *d*. *Educ:* Ampleforth Coll.; Merton Coll., Oxford (Oriental Studies). Entered Diplomatic Service, 1960; served in Abu Dhabi, Amman, Aden, Mukalla, Nicosia, Jedda; Counsellor, Athens, 1977–80; Head of Near East and N Africa Dept, FCO, 1980–83; Ambassador to: Libya, 1984; Luxembourg, 1985–88; Under-Sec. on loan to Home CS, 1988–90; Asst Under Sec. of State (Economic), FCO, 1990–91; Dir Gen. of Jt Directorate, Overseas Trade Services, FCO/DTI, 1991–93. Non-exec. Dir, Vickers Defence Systems, 1990–93. *Recreations:* bird-watching, playing the flute. *Address:* c/o Foreign and Commonwealth Office, SW1A 2AH. *Club:* Travellers'.

MILES, Roger Steele, PhD, DSc; freelance museum consultant; Head, Department of Public Services, The Natural History Museum (formerly British Museum (Natural History)), 1975–94; *b* 31 Aug. 1937; *s* of John Edward Miles and Dorothy Mildred (*née* Steele); *m* 1960, Ann Blake; one *s* one *d*. *Educ:* Malet Lambert High Sch., Hull; King's Coll., Univ. of Durham (BSc, PhD, DSc). Sen. Res. Award, DSIR, 1962–64; Sen. Res. Fellow, Royal Scottish Museum, 1964–66, Sen. Scientific Officer, 1966–68; Sen. Sci. Officer, BM (Nat. Hist.), 1968–71, Principal Sci. Officer, 1971–74. Hon. Fellow, Columbia Pacific Univ., 1983. *Publications:* 2nd edn, Palaeozoic Fishes, 1971 (1st edn, J. A. Moy-Thomas, 1939); (ed, with P. H. Greenwood and C. Patterson) Interrelationships of Fishes, 1973; (ed, with S. M. Andrews and A. D. Walker) Problems in Vertebrate Evolution, 1977; (with others) The Design of Educational Exhibits, 1982, 2nd edn 1988; (ed with L. Zavala) Towards the Museum of the Future, 1994; papers and monographs on anatomy and palaeontology of fishes, articles on museums, in jls. *Recreations:* music, twentieth century art and architecture. *Address:* 3 Eagle Lane, Snaresbrook, E11 1PF. *T:* 0181–989 5684.

MILES, Stephen; *see* Miles, F. S.

MILES, Wendy Ann; *see* Henry, W. A.

MILES, William; Chief Executive, West Yorkshire County Council, and Clerk to the Lieutenancy, West Yorkshire, 1984–86; *b* 26 Sept. 1933; *s* of William and Gladys Miles; *m* 1961, Jillian Anne Wilson; three *s*. *Educ:* Wyggeston School, Leicester; Trinity Hall, Cambridge (MA, LLM). Solicitor. Asst Solicitor, Leicester, Doncaster and Exeter County Boroughs, 1960–66; Asst Town Clerk, Leicester Co. Borough, 1966–69; Dep. Town Clerk, Blackpool Co. Borough, 1969–73; City Legal Adviser, Newcastle upon Tyne, 1973–74; Chief Exec., Gateshead Borough Council, 1974–84. *Recreations:* bridge, hill walking, sport. *Address:* 23 Moor Crescent, Gosforth, Newcastle upon Tyne NE3 4AP. *T:* 0191–285 1996.

MILES, Sir William (Napier Maurice), 6th Bt *cr* 1859; retired architect; *b* 19 Oct. 1913; *s* of Sir Charles William Miles, 5th Bt, OBE; *S* father, 1966; *m* 1946, Pamela, *d* of late Capt. Michael Dillon; one *s* two *d*. *Educ:* Stowe; University of Cambridge (BA). Architectural Assoc. Diploma, 1939. Mem., Voluntary Euthanasia Soc. *Recreation:* surviving. *Heir:* *s* Philip John Miles, *b* 10 Aug. 1953. *Address:* Old Rectory House, Walton-in-Gordano, near Clevedon, Avon. *T:* Clevedon (01275) 873365.
See also Prof. C. W. N. Miles.

MILFORD, 3rd Baron *cr* 1939; **Hugo John Laurence Philipps;** Bt 1919; farmer and forester; *b* 27 Aug. 1929; *o s* of 2nd Baron Milford and his 1st wife, Rosamond Nina Lehmann, CBE (*d* 1990); *S* father, 1993; *m* 1st, 1951, Margaret Heathcote (marr. diss. 1958); one *d*; 2nd, 1959, Hon. Mary Makins (marr. diss. 1984), *e d* of Baron Sherfield, *qv*; three *s* one *d*; 3rd, 1989, Felicity Ballantyne. *Educ:* Eton, King's Coll., Cambridge. Lloyd's, 1951–86. High Sheriff, Powys, 1976–77. *Recreations:* fishing, reading, motoring in Europe, watching 1st class cricket. *Heir:* Hon. Guy Wogan Philipps [*b* 25 July 1961; *m* 1988, Rececca, *yr d* of Nigel Nicolson, *qv*]. *Address:* Llanstephan House, Llanstephan, Brecon, Powys LD3 0YR. *T:* Erwood (01982) 560693. *Clubs:* Boodle's, Pratt's, MCC.

MILFORD, John Tillman; QC 1989; a Recorder, since 1985; *b* 4 Feb. 1946; *s* of late Dr Roy Douglas Milford, Strathtay, Perthshire, and Jessie Milford (*née* Rhind); *m* 1975, Mary Alice, *d* of late Dr E. A. Spriggs of Wylam, Northumberland; three *d*. *Educ:* The Cathedral School, Salisbury; Hurstpierpoint; Exeter Univ. (LLB). Called to the Bar, Inner Temple, 1969; in practice on NE Circuit, 1970–. *Recreations:* fishing, shooting, gardening. *Address:* (chambers) 12 Trinity Chare, Newcastle upon Tyne NE1 3DF. *T:* 0191–232 1927; Hill House, Haydon Bridge, Hexham, Northumberland NE47 6HL. *T:* Hexham (01434) 684234. *Clubs:* Northern Counties (Newcastle upon Tyne); Durham County (Durham).

MILFORD HAVEN, 4th Marquess of, *cr* 1917; **George Ivar Louis Mountbatten;** Earl of Medina, 1917; Viscount Alderney, 1917; *b* 6 June 1961; *s* of 3rd Marquess of Milford Haven, OBE, DSC, and of Janet Mercedes, *d* of late Major Francis Bryce, OBE; *S* father, 1970; *m* 1989, Sarah Georgina, *d* of George A. Walker, *qv*; one *s* one *d*. *Heir:* *s* Earl of Medina, *qv*. *Address:* Moyns Park, Birdbrook, near Halstead, Essex CO9 4BP.

MILINGO, Most Rev. Emanuel; Former Archbishop of Lusaka (Archbishop, 1969–83); Special Delegate to the Pontifical Commission for Tourism and Immigration, since 1983; *b* 13 June 1930; *s* of Yakobe Milingo Chilumbu and Tomaide Lumbiwe Miti. *Educ:* Kachebere Seminary, Malawi; Pastoral Inst., Rome; University Coll., Dublin. Curate: Minga Parish, Chipata Dio., 1958–60; St Mary's Parish, 1960–61; Chipata Cathedral, 1963–64; Parish Priest, Chipata Cathedral, 1964–65; Sec. for Communications at Catholic Secretariat, Lusaka, 1966–69. Founder, The Daughters of the Redeemer, Congregation for young ladies, 1971. *Publications:* Amake-Joni, 1972; To Die to Give Life, 1975; Summer Lectures for the Daughters of the Redeemer, 1976; The Way to Daughterhood; My God is a Living God, 1981; Lord Jesus, My Lord and Saviour, 1982; Demarcations, 1982; The Flower Garden of Jesus the Redeemer; My Prayers Are Not Heard; Precautions in the Ministry of Deliverance. *Recreation:* music. *Address:* Pontificia Commissione per la Pastorale delle Migrazioni e del Turismo, Palazzo San Calisto, Vatican City.

MILKINA, Nina, (Mrs A. R. M. Sedgwick); Hon. RAM; concert pianist; *b* Moscow, 27 Jan. 1919; *d* of Jacques and Sophie Milkine; *m* 1943, Alastair Robert Masson Sedgwick; one *s* one *d*. *Educ:* privately. Musical studies with the late Leon Conus of the Moscow Conservatoire and at the Paris Conservatoire, also with Profs Harold Craxton and Tobias Matthay, London. First public appearance at age of 11 with Lamoureux Orchestra, Paris; has since been broadcasting, televising, and touring in Great Britain and abroad. Was commissioned by BBC to broadcast series of all Mozart's piano sonatas; invited to give Mozart recital for bicentenary celebration of Mozart's birth, Edinburgh Festival. Major works recorded: Mozart piano concertos K271 and K467; Mozart recitals; complete

Chopin Mazurkas; Scarlatti Sonatas; Mozart and Haydn Sonatas; works by Rachmaninov, Prokofiev, Scriabin. Widely noted for interpretation of Mozart's piano works. *Publications:* works for piano. *Recreations:* swimming, chess, fly fishing. *Address:* 17 Montagu Square, W1H 1RD; Casa delle Colonne, San Pietro, Sardinia.

MILKOMANE, G. A. M.; *see* Sava, George.

MILL, Robert Duguid Forrest P.; *see* Pring-Mill.

MILLAIS, Sir Geoffroy Richard Everett, 6th Bt *cr* 1885, of Palace Gate, Kensington and Saint Ouen, Jersey; *b* 27 Dec. 1941; *s* of Sir Ralph Regnault Millais, 5th Bt and his 1st wife, Felicity Caroline Mary Ward Robinson (*d* 1994), *d* of Brig.-Gen. W. W. Warner, CMG; *S* father, 1992. *Heir: uncle* Edward Gray St Helier Millais [*b* 15 March 1918; *m* 1947, Rosemary Barbara Lucas; four *s* one *d*].

MILLAN, Rt. Hon. Bruce, PC 1975; Member, Commission of the European Communities, 1989–95; *b* 5 Oct. 1927; *s* of David Millan; *m* 1953, Gwendoline May Fairey; one *s* one *d*. *Educ:* Harris Academy, Dundee. Chartered Accountant, 1950–59. Contested: West Renfrewshire, 1951, Craigton Div. of Glasgow, 1955. MP (Lab): Glasgow, Craigton, 1959–83; Glasgow, Govan, 1983–88; Parly Under-Sec. of State: for Defence, (RAF), 1964–66; for Scotland, 1966–70; Minister of State, Scottish Office, 1974–76; Sec. of State for Scotland, 1976–79; opposition spokesman on Scotland, 1979–83. *Address:* 1 Torridon Avenue, Glasgow G41 5LA.

MILLAR, family name of **Baron Inchyra.**

MILLAR, Anthony Bruce; Chairman, Frensham Properties Ltd, since 1993; Hon. President, The Albert Fisher Group PLC, since 1992 (Chairman, 1982–92); *b* 5 Oct. 1941; *s* of late James Desmond Millar and of Josephine Georgina Millar (*née* Brice); *m* 1964, Judith Anne (*née* Jester); two *d*. *Educ:* Haileybury Imperial Service College. FCA. Asst to Group Management Accountant and Group Treasurer, Viyella Internat. Fedn, 1964–67; United Transport Overseas Ltd, Nairobi, and London (Dep. Group Financial Controller), 1967–72; Finance Dir, Fairfield Property Co. Ltd, 1972–75; Consultant, 1975–77; Managing Dir, Provincial Laundries Ltd, 1977–81; Dep. Chm., Hawley Group, 1981–82. CIMgt. *Recreations:* swimming, scuba diving, walking, bridge, travel. *Address:* Frensham Vale House, Lower Bourne, near Farnham, Surrey GU10 3JB. *Club:* Mark's.

MILLAR, Betty Phyllis Joy; Regional Nursing Officer, South Western Regional Health Authority, 1973–84, retired; *b* 19 March 1929; *o d* of late Sidney Hildersly Millar and May Phyllis Halliday. *Educ:* Ursuline High Sch. for Girls; Dumbarton Academy; Glasgow Royal Infirm.; Glasgow Royal Maternity Hosp.; Royal Coll. of Nursing, London. RGN 1950; SCM 1953; NA (Hosp.) Cert. 1961. Theatre Sister, Glasgow Royal Infirm., 1953–54; Ward and Theatre Sister, Henry Brock Meml Hosp., 1954–55; Nursing Sister, Iraq Petroleum Co., 1955–57; Clinical Instructor, Exper. Scheme of Nurse Trng, Glasgow, 1957–60; Admin. Student, Royal Coll. of Nursing, 1960–61; 2nd Asst Matron, Glasgow Royal Infirm., 1961–62; Asst Nursing Officer, Wessex Regional Hosp. Bd, 1962–67; Matron, Glasgow Royal Infirm., 1967–69; Chief Regional Nursing Officer, SW Regional Hosp. Bd, 1969–73. WHO Fellowship to study nursing services in Scandinavia, 1967. Mem. Jt Bd of Clinical Nursing Studies, 1970–82. *Address:* Pinedrift, 45 Stoneyfields, Easton-in-Gordano, Bristol BS20 0LL. *T:* Pill (01275) 372709.

MILLAR, Douglas George; Clerk of Select Committees, House of Commons, since 1994; *b* 15 Feb. 1946; *s* of late George Millar and of Doris Mary Millar (*née* Morris); *m* 1st, 1967, Susan Mary Farrow (marr. diss. 1986); one *s* one *d*; 2nd, 1987, (Jane) Victoria Howard Smith; one *s* one *d*. *Educ:* City of Norwich Sch.; Bristol Univ. (BA Hons History 1967); Reading Univ. (MA Politics 1968). A Clerk, H of C, 1968–; Clerk of Defence Cttee, 1979–83; Clerk i/c Private Members' Bills and Divs, 1983–87; Clerk of Home Affairs Cttee, 1987–89; Principal Clerk and Clerk of Financial Cttees and Treasury and Civil Service Cttee, 1989–91; Sec. to Public Accounts Commn, 1989–91; Second Clerk, Select Cttees, 1991–94. Jt Sec., Assoc. of Secs Gen. of Parlts, 1971–77. *Publications:* articles and reviews in parly and political jls. *Recreations:* watching Norwich City, family, golf. *Address:* Committee Office, House of Commons, SW1A 0AA. *T:* 0171–219 6257. *Club:* Roehampton.

MILLAR, Prof. Fergus Graham Burtholme, DPhil; DLitt; FSA; FBA 1976; Camden Professor of Ancient History, and Fellow of Brasenose College, Oxford University, since 1984; *b* 5 July 1935; *s* of late J. S. L. Millar and of Jean Burtholme (*née* Taylor); *m* 1959, Susanna Friedmann; two *s* one *d*. *Educ:* Edinburgh Acad.; Loretto Sch.; Trinity Coll., Oxford (1st Cl. Lit. Hum.; Hon. Fellow, 1992); DPhil 1962, DLitt 1988, Oxon. Fellow: All Souls Coll., Oxford, 1958–64; Queen's Coll., Oxford, 1964–76; Prof. of Ancient History, UCL, 1976–84. Conington Prize, 1963. President: Soc. for the Promotion of Roman Studies, 1989–92 (Vice-Pres., 1977–89); Classical Assoc., 1992–93. FSA 1978. Corresp. Member: German Archaeolog. Inst., 1978; Bavarian Acad., 1987; Finnish Acad., 1989. Hon. DPhil Helsinki, 1994. Editor, Jl of Roman Studies, 1975–79. *Publications:* A Study of Cassius Dio, 1964; The Roman Empire and its Neighbours, 1967; (ed with G. Vermes) E. Schürer, history of the Jewish people in the age of Jesus Christ (175 BC-AD 135), Vol. I, 1973, Vol. II, 1979, Vol. III, parts 1 and 2 (ed with G. Vermes and M. D. Goodman), 1986–87; The Emperor in the Roman World (31 BC-AD 337), 1977, 2nd edn 1992; (ed with E. Segal) Caesar Augustus: seven aspects, 1984; The Roman Near East, 1993. *Address:* Brasenose College, Oxford OX1 4AJ; 80 Harpes Road, Oxford OX2 7QL. *T:* Oxford (01865) 515782.

MILLAR, George Reid, DSO 1944; MC; farmer and writer; *b* 19 Sept. 1910; 2nd *s* of Thomas Andrew Millar, architect, and Mary Reid Morton; *m* 1945, Isabel Beatriz (*d* 1990), *d* of Montague Paske Smith, CMG, CBE; no *c*. *Educ:* Loretto; St John's, Cambridge. Architect, 1930–32; journalist, with Daily Telegraph and Daily Express, 1934–39; Paris correspondent Daily Express, 1939; served War of 1939–45, The Rifle Bde; escaped from German POW camp to England, then served as agent in France; Chevalier de la Légion d'Honneur; Croix de Guerre avec Palmes. Farmer of 1,000 acres, 1962–82. *Publications:* Maquis, 1945; Horned Pigeon, 1946; My Past was an Evil River, 1946; Isabel and the Sea, 1948; Through the Unicorn Gates, 1950; A White Boat from England, 1951; Siesta, 1952; Orellana, 1954; Oyster River, 1963; Horseman, 1970; The Bruneval Raid, 1974; Road to Resistance, 1979. *Recreation:* sailing. *Address:* Uploders Place, Bridport, Dorset DT6 4PF. *T:* Powerstock (01308) 485653. *Clubs:* Special Forces, Royal Cruising; Royal Yacht Squadron (Cowes).

MILLAR, Ian Alastair D.; *see* Duncan Millar.

MILLAR, John Stanley, CBE 1979; County Planning Officer, Greater Manchester Council, 1973–83; *b* 1925; *s* of late Nicholas William Stanley Millar and late Elsie Baxter Millar (*née* Flinn); *m* 1st, 1961, Patricia Mary (*née* Land) (*d* 1992); one *d*; 2nd, 1993, Christine (*née* Riley). *Educ:* Liverpool Coll.; Univ. of Liverpool. BArch, DipCD, PPRTPI, RIBA. Planning Asst, then Sen. Asst Architect, City of Liverpool, 1948–51; Sectional Planning Officer, then Dep. Asst County Planning Officer, Lancs CC 1951–61; Chief Asst Planning Officer, then Asst City Planning Officer, City of Manchester, 1961–64; City Planning Officer, Manchester, 1964–73. *Publications:* papers in professional and technical jls. *Recreations:* walking, listening to music, travel, the sea. *Address:* 55 Stanneylands Drive, Wilmslow, Cheshire SK9 4EU. *T:* Wilmslow (01625) 523616.

MILLAR, Sir Oliver Nicholas, GCVO 1988 (KCVO 1973; CVO 1963; MVO 1953); FBA 1970; Director of the Royal Collection, 1987–88; Surveyor of the Queen's Pictures, 1972–88, Surveyor Emeritus, since 1988; *b* 26 April 1923; *er s* of late Gerald Millar, MC and late Ruth Millar; *m* 1954, Delia Mary, 2nd *d* of late Lt-Col Cuthbert Dawnay, MC; one *s* three *d*. *Educ:* Rugby; Courtauld Institute of Art, University of London (Academic Diploma in History of Art). Unable, for medical reasons, to serve in War of 1939–45. Asst Surveyor of the King's Pictures, 1947–49, Dep. Surveyor 1949–72. Trustee, Nat. Portrait Gallery, 1972–. Member: Reviewing Cttee on Export of Works of Art, 1975–87; Exec. Cttee, Nat. Art Collections Fund, 1986–. Visitor, Ashmolean Mus., 1987–93. Trustee, Nat. Heritage Meml Fund, 1988–92. A Dir, Friends of the Tate Gall., 1989–; Chm., Patrons of British Art, 1989–. FSA. Corresponding Fellow: Ateneo Veneto, Venice; Koninklijke Academie voor Wetenschappen, Letteren en Schone Kunsten, Belgium. *Publications:* Gainsborough, 1949; William Dobson, Tate Gallery Exhibition, 1951; English Art, 1625–1714 (with Dr M. D. Whinney), 1957; Rubens's Whitehall Ceiling, 1958; Abraham van der Doort's Catalogue, 1960; Tudor, Stuart and Early Georgian Pictures in the Collection of HM the Queen, 1963; Zoffany and his Tribuna, 1967; Later Georgian Pictures in the Collection of HM the Queen, 1969; Inventories and Valuations of the King's Goods, 1972; The Age of Charles I (Tate Gallery Exhibn), 1972; The Queen's Pictures, 1977; Sir Peter Lely (Nat. Portrait Gall. Exhibn), 1978; Van Dyck in England (Nat. Portrait Gall. Exhibn), 1982; Victorian Pictures in the Collection of HM the Queen, 1992; articles in the Burlington Magazine, etc; numerous catalogues, principally for The Queen's Gallery. *Recreations:* grandchildren, drawing, gardening, reading, listening to music. *Address:* The Cottage, Ray's Lane, Penn, Bucks HP10 8LH. *T:* Penn (01494) 812124. *Clubs:* Brooks's, MCC.

MILLAR, Air Vice-Marshal Peter; Administrator, Sovereign Base Areas and Commander, British Forces Cyprus, since 1995; *b* 20 June 1942; *s* of Air Cdre John Christopher Millar, RAF and Patricia Millar (*née* Allen); *m* 1966, Annette McMillan; one *s* two *d*. *Educ:* Malvern Coll.; RAF Coll., Cranwell. Served RAF: No 20 Sqn, Singapore, 1964–66; No 4 FTS, RAF Valley, 1967–69; Central Flying Sch., RAF Kemble, 1969–71; 560 Trng Sqn, Randolph AFB, Texas, 1971–74; RAF Staff Coll., 1974; Flight Commander: No 20 Sqn, Wildenrath, 1975–77; No 4 Sqn, Gutersloh, 1977–78; MoD, 1978–79; Sqn Comdr, No 233 OCU, RAF Wittering, 1979–82; USAF Air Warfare Coll., Maxwell AFB, Alabama, 1982–83; Brit. Defence Staff, Washington, 1983–84; Stn Comdr, RAF Wittering, 1985–86; RCDS 1987; on staff, UK Mil. Rep., NATO HQ, 1988–90; Dir NATO, MoD, 1990–93; HQ AAFCE, Ramstein AFB, Germany, 1993–95. Mem., RUSI, 1978–. *Recreations:* ski-ing, golf, off-shore sailing. *Address:* British Forces Cyprus, BFPO 53. *Club:* Royal Air Force.

MILLAR, Peter Carmichael, OBE 1978; Deputy Keeper of HM Signet, 1983–91; *b* 19 Feb. 1927; *s* of late Rev. Peter Carmichael Millar, OBE, DD and of Ailsa Ross Brown Campbell or Millar; *m* 1953, Kirsteen Lindsay Carnegie, *d* of late Col David Carnegie, CB, OBE, TD, DL, Dep. Gen. Manager, Clydesdale Bank; two *s* two *d*. *Educ:* Aberdeen Grammar Sch.; Glasgow Univ.; St Andrews Univ.; Edinburgh Univ. MA, LLB; WS. Served RN, 1944–47. Partner in law firms, Messrs W. & T. P. Manuel, WS, 1954–62; Aitken, Kinnear & Co., WS, 1963–87; Aitken Nairn, WS, 1987–92. Clerk to Soc. of Writers to HM Signet, 1964–83. Chairman: Church of Scotland Gen. Trustees, 1973–85; Mental Welfare Commn for Scotland, 1983–91; (part-time) Medical Appeal Tribunals, 1991–; Pension Appeal Tribunals, 1992–. Convener, Scottish Child and Family Alliance, 1992–95. *Recreations:* golf, hill-walking, music. *Address:* 25 Cramond Road North, Edinburgh EH4 6LY. *T:* 0131–336 2069. *Clubs:* New (Edinburgh); Hon. Co. of Edinburgh Golfers, Bruntsfield Links Golfing Society.

MILLAR, Sir Ronald (Graeme), Kt 1980; playwright, screenwriter and political writer; Deputy Chairman, Theatre Royal Haymarket, since 1977; *b* 12 Nov. 1919; *s* of late Ronald Hugh Millar and Dorothy Ethel Dacre Millar (*née* Hill). *Educ:* Charterhouse; King's Coll., Cambridge. Served as Sub-Lt, RNVR, 1940–43 (invalided out). Began in the Theatre as an actor. First stage appearance, London, Swinging the Gate, Ambassadors', 1940, subseq. in Mr Bolfry, The Sacred Flame, Murder on the Nile, Jenny Jones, (own play) Zero Hour, 1944. Ealing Studios, 1946–48, worked on Frieda, Train of Events, etc; screenwriter, Hollywood, 1948–54: So Evil My Love, The Miniver Story, Scaramouche, Rose-Marie, The Unknown Man, Never Let Me Go, Betrayed. Plays produced in London: Frieda, 1946; Champagne for Delilah, 1948, Waiting for Gillian, 1954; The Bride and the Bachelor, 1956; The More the Merrier, 1960; The Bride Comes Back, 1960; The Affair (from C. P. Snow novel), 1961, The New Men (from C. P. Snow), 1962; The Masters (from C. P. Snow), 1963; (book and lyrics) Robert and Elizabeth (musical), 1964; Number 10, 1967; Abelard and Heloise, 1970; The Case in Question (from C. P. Snow), 1975; A Coat of Varnish (from C. P. Snow), 1982. *Publication:* A View from the Wings (autobiog.), 1993. *Recreations:* all kinds of music, all kinds of people. *Address:* 7 Sheffield Terrace, W8 7NG. *T:* 0171–727 8361. *Clubs:* Brooks's, Dramatists'.

MILLAR, Prof. William Malcolm, CBE 1971; MD; Crombie-Ross Professor of Mental Health, University of Aberdeen, 1949–77; *b* 20 April 1913; *s* of Rev. Gavin Millar, BD, Logiealmond, Perthshire, and Margaret Malcolm, Stanley, Perthshire; *m* 1st, 1941, Catherine McAuslin Rankin; two *s* four *d*; 2nd, 1981, Maria Helen Ramsay. *Educ:* George Heriot's Sch., Edinburgh; Edinburgh Univ. MB, ChB (Edinburgh) 1936; MD (Edinburgh) 1939; Dip. Psych. (Edinburgh) 1939; MRCPE 1958; FRCPE 1962. Asst Physician, Royal Edinburgh Hospital for Mental Disorders, 1937–39. Served 1939–46 (Lieut, Captain, Major), Specialist in Psychiatry, RAMC. Senior Lecturer, Dept of Mental Health, Aberdeen Univ., 1946–49. Dean, Faculty of Medicine, 1965–68. Member: MRC, 1960–64; Mental Welfare Commn for Scotland, 1964–78. FBPsS 1946. *Publications:* contributions to various learned journals. *Recreations:* golf, chess, gardening. *Address:* 35 Beechgrove Avenue, Aberdeen AB2 4HE.

MILLARD, Anthony Paul; Headmaster, Giggleswick School, since 1993; *b* 21 Sept. 1948; *s* of Leonard William Millard and Marjorie Ethel Millard (*née* Manley); *m* 1971, Lesley Margaret Baker; one *s* three *d*. *Educ:* Solihull Sch.; LSE (BSc Econ); Balliol Coll., Oxford (PGCE). Teaching in Zambia, 1971–74; Stagiaire (specialist trainee) with EC, 1974–75; Wells Cathedral School: Asst Master, 1975–77; Housemaster, 1977–86; Dep. Headmaster, 1982–86; Headmaster, Wycliffe Coll., Glos, 1987–93. Chairman: ISIS (Central), 1990–92; Bloxham Project Cttee, 1991–; Services Cttee, HMC, 1995–. MInstD 1994. FRSA 1986. *Recreations:* Rugby, squash, travel, mountains. *Address:* Headmaster's House, Giggleswick School, Settle, N Yorks BD24 0DE. *T:* Settle (01729) 822547. *Clubs:* East India, Devonshire, Sports and Public Schools.

MILLARD, Sir Guy (Elwin), KCMG 1972 (CMG 1957); CVO 1961; HM Diplomatic Service, retired; *b* 22 Jan. 1917; *s* of Col Baldwin Salter Millard, and Phyllis Mary Tetley; *m* 1st, 1946, Anne, *d* of Gordon Mackenzie; one *s* one *d*; 2nd, 1964, Mary Judy, *d* of James Dugdale and Pamela, *widow* of 9th Earl Aylesford; two *s*. *Educ:* Charterhouse; Pembroke

Coll., Cambridge. Served RN, World War II. HM Diplomatic Service, 1939–76: Ambassador to Hungary, 1967–69; Minister, Washington, 1970–71; Ambassador to Sweden, 1971–74; Ambassador to Italy, 1974–76. Chm., British-Italian Soc., 1977–83. Grand Officer, Order of Merit, Italy, 1981. *Address:* Fyfield Manor, Southrop, Glos GL7 3NZ. *T:* Southrop (01367) 850234.

MILLARD, Raymond Spencer, CMG 1967; PhD; FICE; FIHT; retired; *b* 5 June 1920; *s* of Arthur and Ellen Millard, Ashbourne, Derbs; *m* 1st, 1945, Irene Guy (marr. diss.); one *s* one *d*; 2nd, 1977, Sheila Taylor (*née* Akerman). *Educ:* Queen Elizabeth Grammar Sch., Ashbourne; University Coll., London (BSc (Eng)). RE and civil engineering contracting, 1941–44. Road Research Laboratory, 1944–74: Hd of Tropical Section, 1955–65; Dep. Dir, 1965–74; Partner, Peter Fraenkel & Partners, Asia, 1974–76; Highway Engrg Advisor, World Bank, 1976–82; Dir of Technical Affairs, British Aggregate Construction Inds, 1983–87. *Publications:* Road Building in the Tropics, 1993; technical papers on highway engineering. *Recreations:* bonsai culture, painting. *Address:* Drapers Cottage, 93 High Street, Odiham, Hook, Hants RG29 1LB.

MILLEN, Brig. Anthony Tristram Patrick; Defence Advisor to British High Commissioner, Ottawa, Canada, 1980–83, retired; *b* 15 Dec. 1928; *s* of Charles Reginald Millen and Annie Mary Martin; *m* 1954, Mary Alice Featherston Johnston; three *s* two *d* (and two *s* decd). *Educ:* Mount St Mary's Coll. 5th Royal Inniskilling Dragoon Guards, 1948; served in Germany, Korea, Cyprus, N Ireland, Hong Kong, USA. *Publications:* articles in US military jls. *Recreation:* sailing. *Address:* The Manor House, Hutton Sessay, near Thirsk, N Yorks YO7 3BA. *T:* Thirsk (01845) 501444.

MILLER, family name of **Baroness Miller of Hendon.**

MILLER OF HENDON, Baroness *cr* 1993 (Life Peer), of Gore in the London Borough of Barnet; **Doreen Miller,** MBE 1989; JP; a Baroness in Waiting (Government Whip), since 1994; *b* 13 June 1933; *d* of Bernard Henry Feldman and Hetty Feldman; *m* 1955, Henry Miller; three *s*. *Educ:* Brondesbury and Kilburn High Sch.; LSE. Chairman and Managing Director, 1971–88: Universal Beauty Club Ltd (UK); Cosmetic Club International GmbH (Germany); Universal Beauty Club (Pty) Ltd (Australia). Nat. Chm. and Exec. Dir, The 300 Group, 1985–88; Chm., Women Into Public Life Campaign, 1987–; Human Rights Advr, Soroptimist International, 1987–90; Trustee, Menerva Educnl Trust, 1992–. Chm., Barnet FHSA, 1990–94. Crown Agent, 1990–94; Mem., Monopolies and Mergers Commn, 1992–93. Jt Treas., 1990–93, Chm., 1993–96, Greater London Area, Nat. Union of Conservative & Unionist Party. FRSA. JP Brent, 1971. *Publication:* Let's Make Up, 1975. *Recreations:* politics, reading, football, sitting by sunlit swimming pools given the opportunity. *Address:* House of Lords, SW1A 0PW. *Clubs:* Carlton, Reform, St Stephen's Constitutional.

MILLER, (Alan) Cameron; MA; LLB; FCIT; advocate; Tutor at Fettes College, 1974–94; Temporary Sheriff, 1979–82; *b* 10 Jan. 1913; *o s* of late Arthur Miller, Edinburgh; *m* 1945, Audrey Main; one *s* one *d*. *Educ:* Fettes Coll.; Edinburgh Univ. MA 1934; LLB 1936. Advocate, 1938; served War of 1939–45, RN. Interim Sheriff-Substitute at Dundee, 1946; Sheriff-Substitute of Inverness, Moray, Nairn, Ross and Cromarty, at Fort William, 1946–52; Legal Adviser (Scotland): British Transport Commn, 1952–62; BR Board, 1962–73. Chm., Inst. of Transport (Scotland), 1971–72. *Recreations:* golf and music. *Address:* 12A Quality Street, North Berwick, Scotland.

MILLER, Alan John McCulloch, DSC 1941, VRD 1950; Chairman, Miller Insulation Ltd, 1975–86; *b* 21 April 1914; *s* of late Louis M. Miller and Mary McCulloch; *m* 1940, Kirsteen Ross Orr; three *s* one *d*. *Educ:* Kelvinside Academy; Strathclyde Univ. CEng, MRINA, MIESS, FBIM, FRSA. Family engrg business, 1933–39. Commnd RNVR (Clyde Div.), 1938; served RN, 1939–45: Far East, Indian Ocean, S Atlantic, HMS Dorsetshire, then destroyers; in comd, HMS Fitzroy, Wolverine, Holderness, St Nazaire, Dieppe raids, Russian convoys, 1943–44; psc 1944. Rejoined family business, 1945, until sold to Bestobell Ltd, 1951; Dir, Bestobell Ltd, 1951–73, Chm. and Man. Dir, 1965–73; Chm. and Man. Dir, Wm Simons & Co. Ltd, Shipbuilders, 1956–60; Dir, Truckline Ferries Ltd, 1972–88; Chairman: Antigua Slipway Ltd, 1966–86; Dev West Ltd, 1973–76; Low & Bonar, 1977–82. Chm., BNEC Southern Africa Cttee, 1970, until abolished. Member: Sports Council, 1973–80; Central Council of Physical Recreation. *Recreations:* sailing, golf, ski-ing, shooting. *Address:* Dollerie Lodge, by Crieff, Perthshire PH7 3NX. *T:* Crieff (01764) 652299. *Clubs:* Royal Thames Yacht, Royal Ocean Racing, Royal Cruising; Western (Glasgow); Royal and Ancient (St Andrews).

MILLER, Alastair Cheape, MBE 1948; TD; Prison Governor, retired 1972; *b* 13 March 1912 (twin-brother); *s* of John Charles Miller, Banker, Glasgow, and Jessie Amelia Miller; *m* 1943, Elizabeth S. Hubbard (marr. diss. 1967); one *s* one *d*. *Educ:* Melville Coll., Edinburgh; Bedford Sch., Bedford. Territorial Army, 1930–51; War Service (Gibraltar and Italy); 5th Bedfs and Herts Regt, 1st Herts Regt and 4th KOYLI, 1948–51. Barclays Bank Ltd; Junior Clerk to Cashier, 1929–45. Housemaster, Approved Sch., April-Nov. 1946. Prison Service: Asst Governor, Wakefield, Dec. 1946–Jan. 1953; Governor: Dover, 1953–59; Winchester, 1959–62; Hindley Borstal, 1962–65; Parkhurst Prison, 1966–70; Pentonville, 1970–72. Associated with St Mungo Community Trust i/c Old Charing Cross Hosp. project for homeless people, 1974–75. Freeman, City of London, 1980. *Publication:* Inside Outside, 1976. *Recreations:* golf, sailing. *Address:* 5 Cardigan Street, SE11 5PE. *Clubs:* Hampstead Golf; Seaford Golf (Seaford); Newport Golf (Pembs); Cowes Corinthian Yacht (Cowes); Newport Boat (Pembroke).

MILLER, Alexander Ronald, CBE 1970; President, Motherwell Bridge Holdings Ltd, since 1989 (Managing Director, 1958–85; Chairman, 1958–88); *b* 7 Nov. 1915; *s* of Thomas Ronald Miller and Elise Hay. *Educ:* Craigflower; Malvern Coll.; Royal Coll. of Science and Technology. Royal Engineers (Major) and Royal Bombay Sappers and Miners, 1940–46. Member: Scottish Council, CBI (formerly FBI), 1955–82 (Chm., 1963–65); Council, CBI, 1982–; Design Council (formerly CoID), 1965–71 (Chm. Scottish Cttee, 1965–67); Scottish Economic Planning Council, 1965–71 (Chm., Industrial Cttee, 1967–71); British Railways (Scottish) Board, 1966–70; British Rail Design Panel, 1966–82; Gen. Convocation, Univ. of Strathclyde, 1967–; Steering Cttee, W Central Scotland Plan, 1970–75; Lanarkshire Area Health Bd, 1973–85 (Chm., 1973–77); Oil Develt Council for Scotland, 1973–78; Instn of Royal Engineers; BIM Adv. Bd for Scotland, 1974–89; Coll. Council, Bell Coll. of Technology, Hamilton, 1976–89; Lloyd's Register of Shipping Scottish Cttee, 1977–89, Gen. Cttee, 1982–; Lloyd's Register Quality Assce Ltd, 1984–89; Incorporation of Hammermen, Merchants' House of Glasgow. Chm., Management Cttee, Scottish Health Servs Common Servs Agency, 1977–83. Pres., Lanarkshire (formerly Hamilton and Other Districts) Br., Forces Help Soc. and Lord Roberts Workshops, 1979–90. A Burgess of the City of Glasgow. DUniv Stirling, 1986. FRSA; AIMechE; CIMgt. *Address:* Lairfad, Auldhouse, by East Kilbride, Lanarks. *T:* East Kilbride (013552) 63275. *Clubs:* Directors; Royal Scottish Automobile (Glasgow), Western (Glasgow).

MILLER, Amelia, (Mrs Michael Miller); *see* Freedman, A.

MILLER, Prof. Andrew, PhD; FRSE; Principal and Vice-Chancellor, University of Stirling, since 1994; *b* 15 Feb. 1936; *s* of William Hamilton Miller and Susan Anderson (*née* Auld); *m* 1962, Rosemary Singleton Hannah Fyvie; one *s* one *d*. *Educ:* Beath High Sch.; Edinburgh Univ. (BSc Hons 1958; PhD 1962); Wolfson Coll., Oxford (MA 1967). Postdoctoral Fellow, CSIRO, Melbourne, 1962–65; Tutor in Chemistry, Ormond Coll., Melbourne Univ., 1963–65; Staff Scientist, MRC Lab. of Molecular Biol., Cambridge, 1965–66; Lectr in Molecular Biophysics, Oxford Univ., 1966–83; Fellow, Wolfson Coll., Oxford, 1967–83; on secondment as Hd, EMBL, Grenoble, 1975–80; Edinburgh University: Prof. of Biochem., 1984–94; on secondment as Dir of Res., European Synchrotron Radiation Facility, Grenoble, 1986–91; Vice-Dean of Medicine, 1991–93; Vice-Provost of Medicine and Veterinary Medicine, 1992–93; Vice-Principal, 1993–94. FRSE 1986. *Publications:* (ed jtly) Minerals in Biology, 1984; numerous papers on collagen and muscle in scientific jls incl. Nature, Jl Molecular Biol. *Recreations:* music, walking, reading, wondering. *Address:* Principal's Office, University of Stirling, Stirling FK9 4LA. *T:* Stirling (01786) 467011.

MILLER, Andrew Peter; MP (Lab) Ellesmere Port and Neston, since 1992; *b* 23 March 1949; *s* of Ernest William Thomas Miller and Daphne Mary Miller; *m* Frances Ewan; two *s* one *d*. *Educ:* Hayling Island Secondary Sch.; LSE (Mature Student; Dip. Indust. Relations 1976). Lab. Technician, Dept of Geology, Portsmouth Poly., specialising in X-RF and X-RD analysis, 1967–76; Divl Officer, ASTMS, subseq. MSF, 1977–92. Mem., Science and Technol. Select Cttee, 1992–; Vice Chm., PLP Cttee on Science and Technol., 1993–. *Publication:* (jtly) North West Economic Strategy, 1987. *Recreations:* re-building a listed building, walking, photography. *Address:* Hollytree Cottage, Commonside, Alvanley, Cheshire WA6 9HB. *T:* Helsby (01928) 722642.

MILLER, Arjay; Dean, and Professor of Management, Graduate School of Business, Stanford University, 1969–79, now Dean Emeritus; Vice-Chairman, Ford Motor Company, 1968–69 (President, 1963–68); *b* 4 March 1916; *s* of Rawley John Miller and Mary Gertrude Schade; *m* 1940, Frances Marion Fearing; one *s* one *d*. *Educ:* University of California at Los Angeles (BS with highest hons, 1937). Graduate Student and Teaching Asst, University of California at Berkeley, 1938–40; Research Technician, Calif. State Planning Bd, 1941; Economist, Federal Reserve Bank of San Francisco, 1941–43. Captain, US Air Force, 1943–46. Asst Treas, Ford Motor Co., 1947–53; Controller, 1953–57; Vice-Pres. and Controller, 1957–61; Vice-Pres. of Finance, 1961–62; Vice-Pres., Staff Group, 1962–63. Trustee: Brookings Instn, Washington; Internat. Exec. Service Corps; Urban Inst. Member, Board of Directors: SRI International; William and Flora Hewlett Foundn. Councillor, The Conference Board. Fellow, Amer. Acad. of Arts and Scis, 1990. Hon. LLD: Univ. of California (LA), 1964; Whitman Coll., 1965; Univ. of Nebraska, 1965; Ripon Coll., 1980; Washington Univ., St Louis, 1982. *Address:* 225 Mountain Home Road, Woodside, CA 94062, USA. *Clubs:* Bohemian, Pacific Union (San Francisco).

MILLER, Arthur; playwright; *b* 17 Oct. 1915; *s* of Isadore Miller and Augusta Barnett; *m* 1940, Mary Grace Slattery (marr. diss.); one *s* one *d*; *m* 1956, Marilyn Monroe (marr. diss. 1961; she *d* 1962); *m* 1962, Ingeborg Morath; one *d*. *Educ:* University of Michigan, USA (AB). Pres. of PEN Club, 1965–69. Cameron Mackintosh Prof. of Contemporary Theatre, Oxford Univ., 1995. *Publications:* Honors at Dawn, 1936; No Villains (They Too Arise), 1937; The Pussycat and the Expert Plumber who was a Man, 1941; William Ireland's Confession, 1941; The Man who had all the Luck, 1944; That They May Win, 1944; Situation Normal (reportage), 1944; Focus (novel), 1945; Grandpa and the Statue, 1945; The Story of Gus, 1947; Jane's Blanket, 1963; I Don't Need You Anymore (collected stories), 1967; (jt author) In Russia, 1969; Fame, and the Reason Why, 1970; The Portable Arthur Miller, 1971; (with Inge Morath) In the Country, 1977; (ed Robert Martin) The Theater Essays of Arthur Miller, 1978; (with Inge Morath) Chinese Encounters, 1979; Salesman in Beijing, 1984; Timebends (autobiog.), 1987; *plays:* All My Sons, 1947 (NY Drama Critics Award, 1948); Death of a Salesman (NY Drama Critics Award, Pulitzer Prize), 1949 (filmed 1985); The Crucible, 1953; A View from the Bridge, 1955 (filmed 1962); A Memory of Two Mondays, 1955; Collected Plays, 1958; After the Fall, 1963; Incident at Vichy, 1964; The Price, 1968 and 1990; The Creation of the World and Other Business, 1972 (musical version, Up From Paradise, 1974); The American Clock, 1980 (TV version, 1993); Playing for Time (Peabody Award, CBS–TV), 1981; Two Way Mirror, 1985; Danger: Memory!, 1986; Ride Down Mount Morgan, 1990; The Last Yankee, 1992; Broken Glass, 1994; *screenplays:* The Misfits, 1960; Everybody Wins, 1990; contrib. stories and essays to Esquire, Colliers, Atlantic Monthly, etc. *Address:* c/o ICM, 40 W 57th Street, New York, NY 10019, USA.

MILLER, Barry; Director General, Finance, Ministry of Defence, since 1995; *b* 11 May 1942; *s* of Lt-Col Howard Alan Miller and Margaret Yvonne Richardson; *m* 1968, Katrina Elizabeth Chandler; one *s* one *d*. *Educ:* Lancaster Royal Grammar Sch. Ministry of Defence: Exec. Officer, RAE Farnborough, 1961; Asst Principal, MoD, London, 1965; Principal: Defence Policy Staff, 1969; Naval Personnel Div., 1969; Equipment Secretariat (Army), 1972; Defence Secretariat, 1973; CSD, 1975; Asst Secretary: Civilian Management, 1977; Defence Secretariat, 1980; RCDS 1984; Asst Sec., Management Services (Organisation), 1985; Director General: Defence Quality Assurance, 1986; Test and Evaluation, 1992; Asst Under Sec. (Finance), PE, 1994. *Address:* Ministry of Defence, Whitehall, SW1A 2HB.

MILLER, Sir Bernard; *see* Miller, Sir O. B.

MILLER, Bill; Member (Lab) Glasgow, European Parliament, since 1994; *b* 22 July 1954; *s* of George and Janet Miller; one *s* one *d*. *Educ:* Paisley Coll.; Kingston Poly. (BSc Land Econs). DipTP; ARICS. Surveyor, Glasgow DC, 1978–94. Councillor (Lab) Strathclyde, 1986–94. *Recreations:* record collecting, Kilmarnock Football Club, golf. *Address:* 131 Clarkston Road, Cathcart, Glasgow G44 3BN. *T:* 0141–637 3845. *Club:* Castlemill Labour (Glasgow).

MILLER, Bruce; *see* Miller, John D. B.

MILLER, Cameron; *see* Miller, A. C.

MILLER, Cheryl; *see* Miller, D. C.

MILLER, Colin Brown; Sheriff of South Strathclyde, Dumfries and Galloway, since 1991; *b* 4 Oct. 1946; *s* of late James Miller and of Isabella Brown or Miller; *m* 1972, Joan Elizabeth Blyth; three *s*. *Educ:* Paisley Grammar Sch.; Glasgow Univ. (LLB 1967). NP, SSC. Legal apprentice, Mitchells Johnston & Co., Glasgow, 1967–69; Asst Solicitor, D. S. & W. Semple, Paisley, 1969–70, Partner, 1971; Partner, McFadyen & Semple, Paisley, 1971–91 (Sen. Partner, 1987–91). Mem. Council, Law Soc. of Scotland, 1983–91. Convenor: Conveyancing Cttee, 1986–89; Judicial Procedure Cttee, 1989–91; Rights of Audience in Supreme Courts Working Party, 1990–91. Legal Advr, Waverley Steam Navigation Co. and associate cos, 1976–91. Dean, Faculty of Procurators in Paisley, 1991. Chm., Blythswood Housing Assoc., 1982–91. *Recreations:* sailing (Paddle Steamer Waverley), railways, ships, motor vehicles, video and still photography. *Address:* Sheriffs' Chambers, Wellington Square, Ayr KA7 1DR. *T:* Ayr (01292) 268474.

MILLER, David; journalist and author; Chief Sports Correspondent, The Times, since 1983; *b* 1 March 1935; *er s* of late Wilfred Miller and Everilda Miller (*née* Milne-Redhead); *m* 1957, Marita Marjorie Malyon; one *s* one *d*. *Educ:* Charterhouse; Peterhouse, Cambridge (Nat. Sci. Tripos). Sub-editor, The Times, 1956–59; Sports Correspondent: Daily Telegraph, 1960–73; Sunday Telegraph, 1961–73; Chief Sports Corresp., Daily Express, 1973–82. Has covered 12 Olympic Games and 10 Football World Cups. Mem., Press Commns of FIFA, IAAF and IOC, 1988–. Chm., Sports Writers' Assoc. of GB, 1981–84; Mem., Internat. Soc. of Olympic Historians, 1993–. Sports Writer of Year Award, What the Papers Say, 1986. *Publications:* Father of Football: biography of Sir Matt Busby, 1970; World Cup, 1970; World Cup, 1974; The Argentina Story, 1978; Cup Magic, 1981; (with Sebastian Coe) Running Free, 1981; The World to Play For, 1982; Coming Back, 1984; England's Last Glory, 1986; Sports Writers' Eye (anthology), 1989; Stanley Matthews, 1990; Born to Run, 1992; (jtly) History of IAAF, 1992; Olympic Revolution: biography of Juan Antonio Samaranch, 1992 (trans. 8 langs); Official IOC books: Seoul '88; Albertville '92; Lillehammer '94. *Recreations:* sailing, reading. *Address:* Hadleycote, Gloucester Road, Barnet, Herts EN5 1RZ. *Fax:* 0181–447 1461. *Clubs:* Lansdowne; Royal Thames Yacht; Hawks (Cambridge); Pegasus Football (Oxford).

MILLER, Dr David Andrew Barclay, FRS 1995; Head, Advanced Photonic Research Department, AT&T Bell Laboratories, since 1987; *b* 19 Feb. 1954; *s* of Matthew Barclay Miller and Martha Sanders Miller (*née* Dalling); *m* 1976, Patricia Elizabeth Gillies; one *s* one *d*. *Educ:* St Andrews Univ. (BSc Hons 1976); Heriot-Watt Univ. (PhD Phys 1979). FIEEE 1995. Res. Associate, 1979, Lectr, 1980–81, Heriot-Watt Univ.; Technical Staff, 1981–87, AT&T Bell Laboratories, Holmdel, NJ. Pres., IEEE Lasers and Electro-Optics Soc., 1995. Fellow: Amer. Phys. Soc.; Optical Soc. of America (Adolph Lomb Medal, 1986; R. W. Wood Prize, 1988); Internat. Prize in Optics, Internat. Commn for Optics, 1991. *Publications:* numerous papers in learned jls. *Recreation:* clarinet and saxophone playing. *Address:* AT&T Bell Laboratories, 101 Crawfords Corner Road, Holmdel, NJ 07723, USA. *T:* (908) 9495458; 64 Hance Road, Fair Haven, NJ 07704, USA.

MILLER, Maj.-Gen. David Edwin, CB 1986; CBE 1980 (OBE 1973); MC 1967; JP; Chief of Staff Live Oak, SHAPE, 1984–86, retired; *b* 17 Aug. 1931; *s* of late Leonard and Beatrice Miller; *m* 1958, Mary Lamley Fisher; two *s*. *Educ:* Loughton Sch., Essex; Royal Military Academy, Sandhurst. psc, jssc, ndc. Commissioned, Border Regt, 1951; Comd 1st Bn King's Own Royal Border Regt, 1971–73; Instructor, National Defence Coll., 1973–76; Colonel GS MoD, 1976–78; Comd Ulster Defence Regt, 1978–80; Dep. Chief of Staff Headquarters BAOR, 1980–83. Colonel, King's Own Royal Border Regt, 1981–88. JP Barnstaple, 1989. *Recreations:* wine, clocks, forestry. *Address:* c/o Barclays Bank PLC, PO Box 2403, N18 2BY. *Club:* Army and Navy.

MILLER, David Ivimey, OBE 1991; HM Diplomatic Service; Ambassador to Armenia, since 1995; *b* 26 March 1937; *m* 1966, Caroline Ethel Jackson; two *d*. Served FO, subseq. FCO, and Moscow, 1964–72; Berlin, 1972–74; CSCE, Geneva, 1974, Belgrade, 1977; First Sec. and Head of Chancery, Belgrade, 1978–82; seconded to Cabinet Office, 1982–85, to NATO Secretariat, Brussels, 1985–90; Principal Res. Officer, FCO, 1990–95. *Address:* c/o Foreign and Commonwealth Office, SW1A 2AH.

MILLER, Prof. David Louis, MD; FRCP, FFPHM; Professor of Public Health Medicine, St Mary's Hospital Medical School, University of London, 1983–95, now Emeritus Professor; *b* 16 Sept. 1930; *s* of John Henry Charles Miller and Muriel (*née* Rogers); *m* 1955, Wendy Joy Clark; three *s* one *d*. *Educ:* The Leys, Cambridge; Peddie Sch., Hightstown, NJ, USA; Clare Coll., Cambridge (BA 1952, MA 1955; MB, BChir 1955; MD 1965); St Thomas's Hosp. Med. Sch. (Scholar). DPH 1964; FRCP 1978 (MRCP 1973); FFCM 1972. House Officer, St Thomas' Hosp., 1956–57; MO, RAF, 1957–60; Research Asst, RPMS, 1960–62; Epidemiologist, PHLS, 1962–71; US Public Health Service Internat. Res. Fellow, Johns Hopkins Sch. of Hygiene and Public Health, Md, 1965–66; Prof. of Community Medicine, Middlesex Hosp. Med. Sch., 1972–82. Aneurin Bevan Meml Fellowship, Govt of India, 1981. Pres., Sect. Epidemiology, RSocMed, 1986–88; Acad. Registrar, FPHM, RCP, 1989–94. Life Mem., Soc. of Scholars, Johns Hopkins Univ., 1983. Chm., 1977–, Pres., 1986–, Central YMCA. *Publications:* (jtly) Lecture Notes on Epidemiology and Public Health Medicine, 1975, 3rd edn 1991; Epidemiology of Diseases, 1982; pubns on epidemiology, esp. respiratory infections, vaccines, HIV and health services. *Recreations:* walking, music, youth and community. *Club:* Royal Society of Medicine.

MILLER, David Quentin; His Honour Judge Miller; a Circuit Judge, since 1987; *b* 22 Oct. 1936; *s* of Alfred Bowen Badger and Mair Angharad Evans. *Educ:* Ellesmere Coll., Shropshire; London Sch. of Econs and Pol. Science, London Univ. (LLB Hons 1956). Called to the Bar, Middle Temple, 1958; admitted Barrister and Solicitor of the Supreme Court of NZ, 1959. In practice, SE Circuit, 1960–82; Metropolitan Stipendiary Magistrate, 1982–87; a Recorder, 1986–87. *Recreations:* history, walking, gardening, art, music, Trollope Society. *Address:* 31 Edinburgh Gardens, Windsor, Berks SL4 2AN. *T:* Windsor (01753) 866597.

MILLER, Donald C.; *see* Crichton-Miller.

MILLER, Sir Donald (John), Kt 1990; FEng 1981; FIMechE, FIEE; FRSE; Chairman, ScottishPower (formerly South of Scotland Electricity Board), 1982–92; *b* 1927; *s* of John Miller and Maud (*née* White); *m* 1973, Fay Glendinning Herriot; one *s* two *d*. *Educ:* Banchory Academy; Univ. of Aberdeen. BSc(Eng). Metropolitan Vickers, 1947–53; British Electricity Authority, 1953–55; Preece, Cardew and Rider (Consulting Engrs), 1955–66; Chief Engr, North of Scotland Hydro-Electric Bd, 1966–74; Dir of Engrg, then Dep. Chm., SSEB, 1974–82. Vis. Prof., Strathclyde Univ., 1991–. Chm., Power Div., IEE, 1979. Hon. Mem., British Nuclear Energy Soc., 1989. DUniv Strathclyde, 1992. *Publications:* papers to IEE. *Recreations:* gardening, hill walking, sailing.

MILLER, (Dorothy) Cheryl; Head of Paid Service, East Sussex County Council, since 1994; *b* 31 Aug. 1954; *d* of Sidney Radcliffe and Dorothy (*née* Ainsworth); *m* 1976, Graham Edwin Miller; one *s* one *d*. *Educ:* Preston Park Sch., Lancs; Preston Sixth Form Coll.; Manchester Univ. (BA Hons Class 1 Geography). Admin. Trainee, CSD, 1975–77; HEO and Asst Private Sec. to Lord Privy Seal and Leader of House of Lords, 1977–78; Personnel Policy Br., CSD, 1979–80; Mem., PM's Advr on Efficiency (Lord Rayner) Scrutiny Team, 1980; Cabinet Office: Head, CS Policy on Retirement and Redundancy Conduct and Discipline Br., 1980–84; Head, Constitutional Br., Machinery of Govt Div., 1984–85; Asst Dir, then Dep. Dir, CSSB, 1986–90; Head, Staff Develt, DTI, 1991; County Personnel Officer, 1991–93 and Head, Exec. Office, 1992–93, E Sussex CC. *Recreations:* theatre, music, literature, women's equality issues, family activities, cooking, entertaining. *Address:* East Sussex County Council, Pelham House, St Andrew's Lane, Lewes, East Sussex BN7 1UN. *T:* Lewes (01273) 481560. *Club:* Sussex Women's Management Network.

MILLER, Sir Douglas; *see* Miller, Sir I. D.

MILLER, Sir Douglas (Sinclair), KCVO 1972; CBE 1956 (OBE 1948); HM Overseas Colonial Service, retired; *b* 30 July 1906; British parentage; *m* 1933, Valerie Madeleine Carter (*d* 1995); one *d*. *Educ:* Westminster Sch.; Merton Coll., Oxford. HM Overseas Colonial Service, 1930–61: Supt of Native Educn, N Rhodesia, 1930–45; Director of Education: Basutoland, 1945–48; Nyasaland, 1948–52; Uganda, 1952–58; Kenya, 1958–59; Dir of Educn and Permanent Sec., Min. of Educn, Kenya, 1959–60; Temp. Minister of Educn, Kenya, 1960–61; Sec., King George's Jubilee Trust, 1961–71; Develt Adviser, Duke of Edinburgh's Award Scheme, 1971–85. *Address:* The Lodge, 70 Grand Avenue, Worthing, Sussex. *T:* Worthing (01903) 501195. *Clubs:* Commonwealth Trust; Kampala (Uganda).

MILLER, Edward, FBA 1981; Master, Fitzwilliam College, Cambridge, 1971–81, Hon. Fellow, 1981; *b* Acklington, Northumberland, 16 July 1915; *e s* of Edward and Mary Lee Miller; *m* 1941, Fanny Zara Salingar; one *s*. *Educ:* King Edward VI's Grammar Sch., Morpeth; St John's Coll., Cambridge (Exhibnr, Schol.). BA 1937; MA 1945; Strathcona Res. Student, 1937–39, Fellow, 1939–65, and Hon. Fellow, 1974, St John's Coll., Cambridge. Nat. Service, 1940–45 in Durham Light Inf., RAC and Control Commn for Germany; Major. Dir of Studies in History, 1946–55 and Tutor, 1951–57, St John's Coll., Cambridge; Asst Lectr in History, 1946–50 and Lectr, 1950–65, University of Cambridge; Warden of Madingley Hall, Cambridge, 1961–65; Prof. of Medieval Hist., Sheffield Univ., 1965–71. FRHistS; Chm., Victoria Co. Histories Cttee of Inst. Hist. Research, 1972–79; Dep. Chm., Cttee to review Local Hist., 1978–79; Mem., St Albans Res. Cttee. Chm., Editorial Bd, History of Parliament Trust, 1975–89. Hon. LittD Sheffield, 1972. *Publications:* The Abbey and Bishopric of Ely, 1951; Portrait of a College, 1961; (Jt Ed.) Cambridge Economic History of Europe, vol. iii, 1963, vol. ii, 2nd edn, 1987; Historical Studies of the English Parliament, 2 vols, 1970; (jtly) Medieval England: rural society and economic change, 1978; (ed) Agrarian History of England and Wales, vol. iii, 1991; (jtly) Medieval England: towns, commerce and crafts, 1995; articles in Victoria County Histories of Cambridgeshire and York, Agrarian History of England and Wales, vol. ii, English Hist. Rev., Econ. History Rev., Trans Royal Historical Society, Past and Present, etc. *Recreations:* with advancing years watching any form of sport, especially Rugby and cricket. *Address:* 36 Almoners Avenue, Cambridge CB1 4PA. *T:* Cambridge (01223) 246794.

MILLER, Edward, CBE 1988; Director of Education, Strathclyde, 1974–88; *b* 30 March 1930; *s* of Andrew and Elizabeth Miller; *m* 1955; two *s*. *Educ:* Eastbank Academy; Glasgow Univ. (MA, MEd). Taught at Wishaw High Sch., 1955–57 and Whitehill Secondary Sch., 1957–59; Depute Dir of Educn, West Lothian, 1959–63; Sen. Asst Dir of Educn, Stirlingshire, 1963–66; Depute, later Sen. Depute Dir of Educn, Glasgow, 1966–74. Hon. MLitt Glasgow Coll., 1985. *Recreations:* golf, reading, sailing.

MILLER, Air Chief Marshal Frank Robert, CC (Canada) 1972; CBE 1946; CD; retired from military service, 1966; Director, United Aircraft of Canada Ltd, 1967–76; *b* Kamloops, BC, April 1908; *m* Dorothy Virginia Minor, Galveston, Texas. *Educ:* Alberta Univ. (BSc, Civil Engrg). Joined RCAF, 1931. Served War of 1939–45: commanded Air Navigation Schs at Rivers, Man., and Penfield Ridge, NB, and Gen. Reconnaisance Sch., Summerside, PEI; subseq. Dir of Trng Plans and Requirements and Dir of Trng, Air Force HQ; service overseas with Can. Bomber Gp as Station Comdr, later Base Comdr, 1944; Tiger Force, 1945 (despatches); Chief SO (later AOC), Air Material Comd, 1945; US Nat. War Coll., 1948; Air Mem. Ops and Trng, Air Force HQ, 1949; Vice Chief of Air Staff, 1951; Vice Air Deputy, SHAPE HQ, Paris, 1954; Dep. Minister, Dept of Nat. Defence, 1955; Chm., Chiefs of Staff, 1960; first Pres., NATO Mil. Cttee, 1963–64; Chief of Defence Staff, Canada, 1964–66. Air Chief Marshal, 1961. Hon. LLD Alta, 1965; Hon. DScMil, RMC Canada, 1968. *Recreations:* golf, fishing. *Address:* 1654 Brandywine Drive, Charlottesville, VA 22901, USA.

MILLER, G(eorge) William; Chairman, G. William Miller & Co., Inc., Merchant Banking, since 1983; *b* Oklahoma, USA, 9 March 1925; *s* of James Dick Miller and Hazle Deane Miller (*née* Orrick); *m* 1946, Ariadna Rogojarsky. *Educ:* Borger High Sch.; Amarillo Junior Coll.; US Coast Guard Acad. (BS 1945); School of Law, Univ. of California, Berkeley (JD 1952). Served as US Coast Guard Officer, Pacific Area, 1945–49, stationed (one year) in China. Admitted to Bar of California, 1952, New York Bar 1953; law practice with Cravath, Swaine & Moore, NYC, 1952–56. Joined Textron Inc., Providence, RI, 1956; Vice-Pres. 1957; Treas. 1958; Pres. 1960; Chief Exec. 1968–78, also Chm., 1974–78; Dir, Federal Reserve Bank of Boston, 1970–78; Chm., Bd of Governors of Federal Reserve System of US, 1978–79; Sec. of the Treasury, USA, 1979–81. Regent Lectr, Univ. of Calif at Berkeley, 1983–84; Lloyd Bentsen Prof. of Govt-Business Relations, Lyndon B. Johnson Sch. of Public Affairs, Univ. of Texas at Austin, 1984; Fannie Wilson Smith Eminent Scholars Chair, Florida State Univ., 1989; Fellow, Univ. of Calif at Berkeley. Chm. and Chief Exec. Officer, Federated Stores, Inc., 1990–92; Director: Federated Department Stores, Inc.; Repligen Corp.; Georgetown Industries, Inc.; Kleinwort Benson Aust. Income Fund, Inc.; Ralphs Grocery Co.; Chm., Supervising Cttee, Schroder Venture Trust. Chairman: Indust. Adv. Council, President's Cttee on Equal Employment Opportunity, 1963–65; The Conference Board, 1977–78; National Alliance of Business, 1978; US Industrial Payroll Savings Cttee, 1977; President's Cttee on HIRE, 1977; Co-Chairman: US-USSR Trade and Econ. Council; Polish-US Econ. Council; President's Circle, Nat. Acad. of Scis, 1989–92. Member: Distbn Cttee, RI Foundn; Adv. Bd, Coalition of Northeastern Govs; Bd, Wolf Trap Foundn for Performing Arts; Bd, Washington Opera. Treasurer, Amer. Red Cross, 1983–87. Mem., State Bar, California. Phi Delta Phi. *Publication:* (ed) Regrowing the American Economy, 1983. *Recreations:* music, golf. *Address:* 1215 19th Street NW, Washington, DC 20036, USA. *T:* (202) 4291780. *Clubs:* Chevy Chase (Maryland); The Brook (NY); Burning Tree (Bethesda, Md); Lyford Cay (Bahamas).

MILLER, Sir Hilary Duppa, (Sir Hal Miller), Kt 1988; Chairman and Chief Executive, Cosmopolitan Holdings Ltd, since 1993; *b* 6 March 1929; *s* of late Lt-Comdr John Bryan Peter Duppa-Miller, GC, *m* 1st, 1956, Fiona Margaret McDermid; two *s* two *d*; 2nd, 1976, Jacqueline Roe, *d* of T. C. W. Roe and of Lady Londesborough; one *s* one *d*. *Educ:* Eton; Merton Coll., Oxford; London Univ. MA (Oxon) 1956; BSc (Estate Management) (London), 1962. With Colonial Service, Hong Kong, 1955–68. Company Director. Chief Exec., SMMT, 1991–93. Contested: (C), Barrow-in-Furness, 1970; Bromsgrove by-elec. May 1971; MP (C) Bromsgrove and Redditch, Feb. 1974–1983, Bromsgrove, 1983–92. PPS to Sec. of State for Defence, 1979–81, to Chancellor of the Duchy of Lancaster, 1981, resigned; Vice-Chm., Conservative Party Orgn, and PPS to the Chm., 1984–87; Mem., UK delegn to Council of Europe, 1974–76. Jt Chm., All Party Motor Industry Gp, 1978. Fellow, Econ. Develt Inst. of World Bank, Washington. *Recreations:* sailing, fell walking, cricket, Rugby refereeing. *Address:* Cosmopolitan Holdings Ltd, Road Five, Industrial Estate, Winsford, Cheshire CW7 3QU. *Clubs:* United Oxford & Cambridge University; Vincent's (Oxford); Aston Fields Royal British Legion (Bromsgrove); Eton Ramblers, Free Foresters, Blackheath Football.

See also Michael Miller.

MILLER, Sir (Ian) Douglas, Kt 1961; FRCS, FRACS; Hon. Consulting Neurosurgeon, since 1960 (Hon. Neurosurgeon, 1948), St Vincent's Hospital, Sydney, and Repatriation General Hospital; Chairman of Board, St Vincent's Hospital, 1966–76; Dean of Clinical School, St Vincent's Hospital, Sydney, 1931–64; *b* Melbourne, 20 July 1900; *m* 1939,

Phyllis Laidley Mort; three *s* two *d*. *Educ:* Xavier Coll., Melbourne; University of Sydney. MB, ChM Sydney 1924; FRCS 1928. Hon. Asst Surgeon, St Vincent's Hosp., Sydney, 1929; Lectr in Surgical Anat., Univ. Sydney, 1930; Hon. Surg., Mater. Hosp. Sydney, 1934; Hon. Surg., St Vincent's Hosp., 1939; Major AIF, Surgical Specialist, 1940; Lt-Col (Surgical CO), 102 AGH, 1942; o/c Neurosurgical Centre, AIF. Chairman: Community Systems Foundn of Aust., 1965–72; Foundn of Forensic Scis, Aust. President: RACS, 1957–59 (Mem. Ct of Examrs, 1946; Mem. Council, 1947); Asian Australasian Soc. of Neurological Surgeons, 1964–67. Chairman: Editorial Cttee, ANZ Jl of Surgery, 1958–73; Editorial Bd, Modern Medicine in Australia, 1970–. Hon. FRCSE 1980. Hon. AM 1964, Hon. LittD 1974, Singapore; Hon. MD Sydney, 1979. *Publications:* A Surgeon's Story, 1985; Earlier Days, 1970; contrib. Med. Jl of Aust., 1956, 1960. *Recreation:* agriculture. *Address:* 170 Kurraba Road, Sydney, NSW 2089, Australia. *T:* 9092415. *Club:* Australian (Sydney).

MILLER, Dr Jacques Francis Albert Pierre, AO 1981; FRS 1970; FAA 1970; Head of Experimental Pathology Unit, Walter and Eliza Hall Institute of Medical Research, since 1966; *b* 2 April 1931; French parents; *m* 1956, Margaret Denise Houen. *Educ:* St Aloysius' Coll., Sydney. BSc (Med.) 1953, MB, BS 1955, Sydney; PhD 1960, DSc 1965, London. Sen. Scientist, Chester Beatty Res. Inst., London, 1960–66; Reader, Exper. Pathology, Univ. of London, 1965–66. Croonian Lectr, Royal Soc., 1992. For. Mem., Académie Royale de Médicine de Belgique, 1969; For. Associate, US Nat. Acad. Scis, 1982. Hon. MD Sydney, 1986. Langer-Teplitz Cancer Research Award (USA), 1965; Gairdner Foundn Award (Canada), 1966; Encyclopaedia Britannica (Australia) Award, 1966; Scientific Medal of Zoological Soc. of London, 1966; Burnet Medal, Austr. Acad. of Scis, 1971; Paul Ehrlich Award, Germany, 1974; Rabbi Shai Shacknai Meml Prize, Hadassah Med. Sch., Jerusalem, 1978; Saint-Vincent Internat. Prize for Med. Res., Italy, 1983; first Sandoz Immunology Prize, 1990; first Medawar Prize, Transplantation Soc., 1990. *Publications:* over 360 papers in scientific jls and several chapters in books, mainly dealing with thymus and immunity. *Recreations:* music, photography, art, literature. *Address:* Walter and Eliza Hall Institute of Medical Research, Royal Melbourne Hospital PO, Parkville, Victoria 3050, Australia. *T:* (3) 93452555.

MILLER, James, CBE 1986; Chairman, Miller Group Ltd (formerly James Miller & Partners), since 1970; *b* 1 Sept. 1934; *s* of Sir James Miller, GBE, and Lady Ella Jane Miller; *m* 1st, 1959, Kathleen Dewar; one *s* two *d*; 2nd, 1969, Iris Lloyd-Webb; one *d*. *Educ:* Edinburgh Acad.; Harrow Sch.; Balliol Coll., Oxford (MA Engrg Sci.). Joined James Miller & Partners, 1958; Board Mem., 1960; Man. Dir, 1970–91. Director: Life Assoc. of Scotland, 1981–93; British Linen Bank, 1983–; Britoil, 1988–90; Bank of Scotland, 1993–; Mem., Scottish Adv. Bd, British Petroleum, 1990–. Pres., FCEC, 1990–93 (Chm., 1985–86). Chm,. Court, Heriot-Watt Univ., 1990–. *Recreation:* shooting. *Address:* Miller Group Ltd, Miller House, 18 South Groathill Avenue, Edinburgh EH4 2LW. *T:* 0131–332 2585. *Club:* City Livery.

MILLER, James Francis Xavier; Headmaster, Royal Grammar School, Newcastle upon Tyne, since 1994; *b* 3 March 1950; *yr s* of Lt-Col John Francis Miller and Barbara Mary Miller (*née* Cooke); *m* 1976, Ruth Ellen Rowland (*née* Macbeth); two *s*. *Educ:* Douai Sch.; Merton Coll., Oxford (BA Classical Mods and PPE; MA). Winchester College: Asst Master, 1972–89; Hd of Econs, 1978–82; Housemaster, 1982–89; Headmaster, Framlingham Coll., 1989–94. Councillor, Winchester CC, 1976–83 (Chm., Health and Works Cttee, 1979–82). FRSA 1994. *Recreations:* golf, cricket, opera, crosswords. *Address:* The Royal Grammar School, Eskdale Terrace, Newcastle upon Tyne NE2 4DX. *T:* 0191–281 5711. *Clubs:* East India; Free Foresters.

MILLER, Prof. J(ohn) D(onald) Bruce; Executive Director, Academy of the Social Sciences in Australia, 1989–91; Professor of International Relations, Research School of Pacific Studies, Australian National University, 1962–87, now Emeritus; *b* 30 Aug. 1922; *s* of Donald and Marion Miller, Sydney, Australia; *m* 1st, 1943, Enid Huthnance; one *s*; 2nd, 1957, Margaret Martin; one *s*; 3rd, 1990, Judith Bennet. *Educ:* Sydney High Sch.; University of Sydney. BEc, 1944; MEc 1951; MA Cantab 1978. Announcer and Talks Officer, Australian Broadcasting Commission, Sydney and Canberra, 1939–46; Staff Tutor, Department of Tutorial Classes, University of Sydney, 1946–52; Asst Lecturer in Political Science and International Relations, London Sch. of Economics, 1953–55; Lecturer in Politics, University Coll., Leicester, 1955–57; Prof. of Politics, University of Leicester, 1957–62; Dean of Social Sciences, 1960–62; Public Orator, 1961–62. Res. Associate, Chatham House, 1965, 1969, 1973. Visiting Professor: Indian Sch. of International Studies, 1959; Columbia Univ., New York, 1962, 1966, 1981; Yale, 1977; Princeton, 1984, 1986; Overseas Vis. Fellow, St John's Coll., and Smuts Vis. Fellow, Cambridge Univ., 1977–78; Macrossan Lectr, University of Queensland, 1966. Member: Aust. Population and Immigration Council, 1975–81; Aust. Res. Grants Cttee, 1975–81. Joint Editor, Journal of Commonwealth Political Studies, 1961–62; Editor, Australian Outlook, 1963–69; Chm., Editorial Adv. Bd for Austr. documents on foreign relations, 1971–77; Austr. Nat. Commn for UNESCO, 1982–84, 1990–93. Canberra correspondent, The Economist, 1962–87. FASSA 1967 (Treas., 1979–83). *Publications:* Australian Government and Politics, 1954, 4th edn with B. Jinks 1970; Richard Jebb and the Problem of Empire, 1956; Politicians (inaugural), 1958; The Commonwealth in the World, 1958; The Nature of Politics, 1962; The Shape of Diplomacy (inaugural), 1963; Australia and Foreign Policy (Boyer Lectures), 1963; (ed with T. H. Rigby) The Disintegrating Monolith, 1965; Britain and the Old Dominions, 1966; Australia, 1966; The Politics of the Third World, 1966; (ed) India, Japan, Australia: Partners in Asia?, 1968; Survey of Commonwealth Affairs: problems of expansion and attrition 1953–1969, 1974; (ed) Australia's Economic Relations, 1975; The EEC and Australia, 1976; The World of States, 1981; Ideology and Foreign Policy, 1982; Norman Angell and the Futility of War, 1986; (ed) Australians and British, 1987; (ed with L. J. Evans) Policy and Practice, 1987; (ed with R. J. Vincent) Order and Violence, 1990. *Recreation:* staying alive. *Address:* 1 Mountbatten Park, Yarralumla, ACT 2600, Australia. *T:* Canberra (6) 2825599. *Club:* National Press (Canberra).

MILLER, John Harmsworth; architect in private practice; *b* 18 Aug. 1930; *s* of Charles Miller and Brenda Borrett; *m* 1st, 1957, Patricia Rhodes (marr. diss. 1975); two *d*; 2nd, 1985, Su Rogers. *Educ:* Charterhouse; Architectural Assoc. Sch. of Architecture (AA Dip. Hons 1957). ARIBA 1959. Private practice, Colquhoun and Miller, 1961–90, John Miller and Partners, 1990–; works include: Forest Gate High Sch., West Ham (Newham), 1965; Chemistry Labs, Royal Holloway Coll., London Univ., 1970; Melrose Activity Centre, Milton Keynes Develt Corp. (Commendation, Steel Awards, 1975); Pillwood House, Feock, Cornwall (RIBA Regional Award, 1975); housing, Caversham Road/Gaisford Street, Camden, 1978; single person flats, Hornsey Lane, Haringey, 1980; Oldbrook, Milton Keynes (Silver Award, Architectural Design, 1987; Highly Commended, Housing Design and Civic Trust Awards); Whitechapel Art Gall. extension, 1985 (RIBA Regl Award, 1988; Civic Trust Award, 1988); Gulbenkian Gall. for RCA, 1989; Stevens Bldg for RCA, and Nomura Gall. and bookshop for Tate Gall., 1991; Queen's building, UEA (RIBA Nat. Award) and new 20th century galls for Nat. Portrait Gall., 1993; Elizabeth Fry building, UEA, 1995. Exhibition Designs for Arts Council: Dada and Surrealism Reviewed, 1978; Ten Modern Houses, 1980; Picasso's Picassos, 1981; Adolf Loos, 1985. Tutor: RCA and AA, 1961–73; Cambridge Sch. of Arch., 1969–70; Prof. of Environmental Design, RCA, 1975–85, Fellow 1976, Hon. Fellow, 1985. FRSA 1985. Vis. Prof., Sch. of Arch., UC Dublin, 1985. Visiting Critic: Cornell Univ. Sch. of Arch., Ithaca, 1966, 1968 and 1971; Princeton Univ. Sch. of Arch., NJ, 1970; Dublin Univ. Sch. of Arch., 1972–73; Univ. of Toronto, 1985. European Prize for Architecture, 1988. *Publications:* contribs to architect. jls. *Address:* 23 Regent's Park Road, NW1 7TL. *T:* 0171–267 5800.

MILLER, Sir John Holmes, 11th Bt *cr* 1705, of Chichester, Sussex; *b* 1925; *er s* of 10th Bt and of Netta Mahalah Bennett; *S* father 1960; *m* 1950, Jocelyn Robson Edwards, Wairoa, NZ; two *d*. *Heir: b* Harry Holmes Miller [*b* 1927; *m* 1954, Gwynedd Margaret Sheriff; one *s* two *d*].

MILLER, John Ireland; Vice-President, Methodist Conference of Great Britain, 1973–74; *b* 20 June 1912; *s* of John William Miller and Emma Miller (*née* Minkley); *m* 1943, Vida Bertha Bracher; one *s* one *d*. *Educ:* Hardye's School, Dorchester; Taunton School, Taunton. Admitted Solicitor and Member of Law Society, 1933. HM Coroner: Poole Borough, 1972–74 (Deputy Coroner, 1939–72); East Dorset, 1974–85. *Address:* Jacksons Farm, Maltings Lane, Witham, Essex CM8 1DZ. *T:* Witham (01376) 513388.

MILLER, Air Vice-Marshal John Joseph, CB 1981; Director of Studies, St George's House, Windsor Castle, 1989–94; *b* 27 April 1928; *s* of Frederick George Miller and Freda Ruth Miller; *m* 1950, Adele Mary Colleypriest; one *s* two *d*. *Educ:* Portsmouth Grammar School. Commissioned RAF, 1947; called to the Bar, Gray's Inn, 1958; CO RAF Support Unit Fontainbleau, 1965; Directing Staff, RAF Staff Coll., 1967; DGPS (RAF) Staff, MoD, 1970; Group Captain Admin., RAF Halton, 1971; Comd Accountant, HQ Strike Comd, 1973; RCDS 1975; Dir, Personnel Management (Policy and Plans) RAF, MoD, 1976; Asst Chief of Defence Staff (Personnel and Logistics), 1978–81; Head of Administrative Branch, RAF, 1979–83; Dir Gen., Personal Services, RAF, 1982–83. Dir, Inst. of Personnel Management, 1983–89. Pres., Eur. Assoc. for Personnel Management, 1987–89. *Recreations:* walking, swimming, theatre, music, collecting (especially antiquarian books). *Address:* 35 Huntsmans Meadow, Ascot, Berks SL5 7PF. *T:* Ascot (01344) 20413. *Club:* Royal Air Force.

MILLER, Lt-Col Sir John (Mansel), GCVO 1987 (KCVO 1974; CVO 1966); DSO 1944; MC 1944; Crown Equerry, 1961–87, an Extra Equerry since 1987; *b* 4 Feb. 1919; 3rd *s* of Brig.-Gen. Alfred Douglas Miller, CBE, DSO, DL, JP, Royal Scots Greys, and of Ella Geraldine Fletcher, Saltoun, E Lothian. *Educ:* Eton; RMA, Sandhurst. 2nd Lieut Welsh Guards, 1939; Adjt 1942–44; ADC to F-M Lord Wilson, Washington, DC, 1945–47; Regtl Adjt, 1953–56; Brigade Major 1st Guards Brigade, 1956–58; comd 1st Bn Welsh Guards, 1958–61. President: Royal Internat. Horse Show, 1993–; Coaching Club, 1975–82; Hackney Horse Soc., 1978–79, 1994–; Nat. Light Horse Breeding Soc. (HIS), 1982; British Driving Soc., 1982–; Royal Windsor Horse Show Club, 1985–90; Horse Rangers Assoc., 1985–; Cleveland Bay Horse Soc., 1986–88; BSJA, 1988–93; BHS, 1992–94; Vice-Pres., Irish Draught Horse Soc., GB, 1990–. Patron: Side Saddle Assoc., 1984–; Coloured Horse and Pony Soc., 1988. President: Wheatley Br, RNLI, 1982–; Wheatley Scouts, 1982–. *Recreations:* hunting, shooting, polo, driving. *Address:* Shotover House, Wheatley, Oxon OX9 1QS. *T:* Wheatley (018677) 2450. *Clubs:* Pratt's, White's; Constitutional (Windsor).

MILLER, Dr Jonathan Wolfe, CBE 1983; Research Fellow in Neuro-psychology, University of Sussex; *b* 21 July 1934; *s* of late Emanuel Miller, DPM, FRCP; *m* 1956, Helen Rachel Collet; two *s* one *d*. *Educ:* St Paul's Sch.; St John's Coll., Cambridge (MB, BCh 1959; Hon. Fellow 1982). Res. Fellow in Hist. of Med., UCL, 1970–73. Associate Director, Nat. Theatre, 1973–75; Artistic Dir, Old Vic, 1988–90. Mem., Arts Council, 1975–76. Vis. Prof. in Drama, Westfield Coll., London, 1977–; Fellow, UCL, 1981–. Co-author and appeared in Beyond the Fringe, 1961–64; stage directing in London and NY, 1965–67; *television:* Editor, BBC Monitor, 1965; directed films for BBC TV (incl. Alice in Wonderland), 1966; The Body in Question, BBC series, 1978; Exec. Producer, BBC Shakespeare series, 1979–81; Madness, BBC series, 1991; *stage:* School for Scandal, 1968, The Seagull, 1969, The Malcontent, 1973, Nottingham Playhouse; King Lear, The Merchant of Venice, Old Vic, 1970; The Tempest, Mermaid, 1970; Hamlet, Arts Theatre, Cambridge, 1970; Danton's Death, 1971, School for Scandal, 1972, Measure for Measure, 1974, Marriage of Figaro, 1974, The Freeway, 1974, Nat. Theatre; The Taming of the Shrew, 1972, The Seagull, 1973, Chichester; Family Romances, 1974, The Importance of Being Earnest, 1975, All's Well, 1975, Greenwich; Three Sisters, Cambridge, 1976; She Would If She Could, Greenwich, 1979; Long Day's Journey Into Night, Haymarket, 1986; The Taming of the Shrew, RSC, Stratford, 1987, Barbican, 1988; (jtly adapted and directed) The Emperor, Royal Court, 1987 (televised, 1988); Andromache, One Way Pendulum, Bussy D'Ambois, The Tempest, Candide, Old Vic, 1988; King Lear, The Liar, Old Vic, 1989; The Way of the World, Gate Theatre, Dublin, 1992; *film:* Take a Girl Like You, 1970; *operas:* Arden Must Die, Sadler's Wells Theatre, 1974; The Cunning Little Vixen, Glyndebourne, 1975 and 1977; English National Opera: The Marriage of Figaro, 1978; The Turn of the Screw, 1979, 1991; Arabella, 1980; Otello, 1981; Rigoletto, 1982, 1985, 1995; Don Giovanni, 1985; The Magic Flute, 1986; Tosca, 1986; The Mikado, 1986, 1988, 1993; The Barber of Seville, 1987; Der Rosenkavalier, 1994; Kent Opera: Così Fan Tutte, 1975; Rigoletto, 1975; Orfeo, 1976; Eugene Onegin, 1977; La Traviata, 1979; Falstaff, 1980, 1981; Fidelio, 1982, 1983, 1988; La Scala: La Fanciulla del West, 1991; Manon Lescaut, 1992; Maggio Musicale, Florence: Don Giovanni, 1990; Così fan Tutte, Tosca, 1991; Marriage of Figaro, 1992; Katya Kabanova, New York, 1991; Marriage of Figaro, Vienna State Opera, 1991; Roberto Deveureux, Monte Carlo, 1992; Die Gezeichnete, Zürich, 1992; Maria Stuarda, Monte Carlo, 1993; The Secret Marriage, Opera North, 1993; Falstaff, Zürich, 1993; L'Incoronazione di Poppea, Glimmerglass Opera, 1994; Pelléas et Mélisande, Metropolitan Opera, NY, 1995; Così fan tutti, Royal Opera House, and Rome, 1995. Hon. Fellow, RA, 1991; Hon. DLitt Leicester, 1981. Silver Medal, Royal TV Soc., 1981; Albert Medal, RSA, 1990. *Publications:* McLuhan, 1971; (ed) Freud: the man, his world, his influence, 1972; The Body in Question, 1978; Subsequent Performances, 1986; (ed) The Don Giovanni Book: myths of seduction and betrayal, 1990. *Recreation:* deep sleep. *Address:* c/o IMG Artists (Europe), Media House, 3 Burlington Lane, W4 2TH.

MILLER, Judith Henderson; author and publishing consultant; Editor, Miller's Guides; *b* 16 Sept. 1951; *d* of Andrew and Bertha Cairns; *m* 1978, Martin John Miller, *qv* (marr. diss. 1992); two *d*. *Educ:* Galashiels Acad.; Edinburgh Univ. (MA Hons English, 1973). Copywriter, WHT Advertising, Auckland, NZ, 1973–74; Editor, Lyle Publications, Galashiels, 1974–75; Occupational Guidance Officer, Dept of Employment, 1975–79; Man. Dir and Editor, Miller Publications, 1979–; with Martin Miller opened Chilston Park Hotel, 1985; Man. Dir, MJM Publishing Projects, 1985–92; Co-Founder, Miller's Magazine, 1991. *Publications:* Period Kitchens, 1995; Period Fireplaces, 1995; How to Make Money out of Antiques, 1995; with Martin Miller: Miller's Antiques Price Guide, annually 1979–; The Antiques Directory—Furniture, 1985; Period Details, 1987; Miller's Antique Pocket Fact File, 1988; Period Style, 1989; Understanding Antiques, 1989; Miller's Collectables Price Guide, annually 1989–; Country Style, 1990; Miller's Collectors Cars Price Guide, annually 1991–; Miller's Art Deco Checklist, 1991; Furniture Checklist,

1991; Period Finishes and Effects, 1992; Victorian Style, 1993. *Recreations:* antiques!, bridge. *Club:* Groucho.

MILLER, Prof. Karl Fergus Connor; Lord Northcliffe Professor of Modern English Literature, University College London, 1974–92; Editor, 1979–92, and Co-Editor, 1989–92, London Review of Books; *b* 2 Aug. 1931; *s* of William and Marion Miller; *m* 1956, Jane Elisabeth Collet; two *s* one *d*. *Educ:* Royal High School, Edinburgh; Downing Coll., Cambridge. Asst Prin., HM Treasury, 1956–57; BBC TV Producer, 1957–58; Literary Editor, Spectator, 1958–61; Literary Editor, New Statesman, 1961–67; Editor, Listener, 1967–73. FRSL 1992. *Publications:* (ed) Poetry from Cambridge, 1952–54, 1955; (ed, with introd.) Writing in England Today: The Last Fifteen Years, 1968; (ed) Memoirs of a Modern Scotland, 1970; (ed) A Listener Anthology, August 1967–June 1970, 1970; (ed) A Second Listener Anthology, 1973; (ed) Henry Cockburn, Memorials of his Time, 1974; Cockburn's Millennium, 1975; (ed, with introd.) Robert Burns, 1981; Doubles: studies in literary history, 1985; Authors, 1989; Rebecca's Vest (autobiog.), 1993; Boswell and Hyde, 1995. *Recreation:* football. *Address:* 26 Limerston Street, SW10 0HA.

MILLER, Dr Kenneth Allan Glen, CBE 1988; FEng; FIMechE; CIMgt; Chairman, PCME Ltd (formerly Pollution Control and Measurement (Europe) Ltd), since 1993; Deputy Chairman: ECCTIS 2000 Ltd, since 1990; Standing Conference on Schools' Science and Technology, since 1991; *b* 27 July 1926; *s* of Dr Allan Frederick Miller and Margaret Hutchison (*née* Glen); *m* 1954, Dorothy Elaine Brown; three *s*. *Educ:* Upper Canada Coll., Toronto; Trinity Hall, Cambridge (BA 1946; MA 1950; Hon. Fellow, 1992); PhD Wales, 1949. Res. Asst to Prof. of Physics, Aberystwyth, 1946; joined ICI, Billingham, 1949; various posts on production and design, 1949–59; seconded to BTC, 1959–60; Asst Tech. Manager, 1960, Engrg Manager, 1963, Engrg Dir, 1965, HOC Div., ICI; Engrg Advr, ICI, 1971; Managing Director: APV Co., 1974; APV Holdings, 1977–82; Dir-Gen., Engrg Council, 1982–88. Member: Cttee for Industrial Technol., 1972–76; UGC, 1981–83; Chm., Steering Cttee for Manufrg Adv. Service, 1977–82. Member Council: Fellowship of Engrg, 1982–85; CRAC, 1987–. *Recreations:* gardening, photography. *Address:* 4 Montrose Gardens, Oxshott, Surrey KT22 0UU. *T:* Oxshott (01372) 842093. *Club:* Leander.

MILLER, Kenneth William, FCA; Chief Executive, Hunting plc, since 1989; *b* 4 Feb. 1939; *s* of Albert William Miller and Winifred (*née* Ashworth); *m* 1st, 1964, Carol Susan Hislop (marr. diss. 1987); one *s* one *d*; 2nd, 1988, Jean Helen McPhail McInnes. *Educ:* Surbiton County Grammar Sch. FCA 1961. Company Sec., Hunting Associated Industries, 1965–73; Asst Finance Dir, Hunting Gp, 1969–73; Commercial Dir, E. A. Gibson & Co. Ltd, 1973–78; Hunting Petroleum Services plc: Dir, 1978–87; Man. Dir, 1987–89. *Recreations:* sailing, reading, sport, music. *Address:* Hunting plc, 3 Cockspur Street, SW1Y 5BQ. *T:* 0171–321 0123. *Club:* Royal Automobile.

MILLER, Prof. Marcus Hay, PhD; Professor of Economics, since 1978, Director, Parliamentary Policy Unit, since 1985, University of Warwick; *b* 9 Sept. 1941; *s* of J. Irvine Miller and Rose H. (*née* Moir); *m* 1967, Margaret Ellen Hummel (marr. diss.); two *d*. *Educ:* Price's Sch., Fareham, Hants; University Coll., Oxford (BA 1st Cl. PPE); Yale Univ. (Henry Fellowship, MA, PhD Econ). Lecturer, London School of Economics, 1967–76; Prof. of Economics, Univ. of Manchester, 1976–78. Economist, 1972–73, Houblon-Norman Fellow, 1981–82, Bank of England; Vis. Associate Prof. of Internat. Finance, Univ. of Chicago, 1976; Vis. Prof. of Public and Internat. Affairs, Princeton Univ., 1983. Member, Academic Panel, HM Treasury, 1976– (Chm., 1979–80); Adviser, House of Commons Select Cttee on the Treasury and Civil Service, 1980–81. Mem. Management Cttee, NIESR, 1980–. Mem., Economic Policy Gp, SDP, 1981. *Publications:* joint editor: Monetary Policy and Economic Activity in West Germany, 1977; Essays on Fiscal and Monetary Policy, 1981; papers on macro and monetary economics, incl. effects of UK entry into EEC, reform of UK monetary system, inflation, exchange rates and liquidity preference, in Amer. Economic Rev., Economica, Nat. Inst. Economic Rev., Oxford Economic Papers, Rev. of Economic Studies. *Recreations:* swimming, orienteering. *Address:* Department of Economics, University of Warwick, Coventry CV4 7AL. *T:* Coventry (01203) 24011, ext. 2484.

MILLER, Martin John; Co-Founder and Managing Director, Milroy Estates Ltd, since 1983; Co-Founder and Publisher, Miller's Magazine, since 1991; Joint Proprietor, Chilston Park Hotel; *b* 24 Nov. 1946; *s* of Marcus and Phyllis Miller; *m* 1st, 1966, Elaine (marr. diss. 1975); three *d*; 2nd, 1978, Judith Henderson Cairns (*see* J. H. Miller) (marr. diss. 1992); two *d*. *Educ:* West Tarring Secondary Modern Sch., Worthing. Freelance photographer, 1965–68; Co-Founder, Lyle Publications, 1968–74; semi-retirement, 1974–79; Co-Founder, MJM Publications, 1979; with Judith Miller opened Chilston Park Hotel, 1985. *Publications: with Judith Miller:* Miller's Antiques Price Guide, annually, 1979–; The Antiques Directory—Furniture, 1985; Period Details, 1987; Miller's Antique Pocket Fact File, 1988; Period Style, 1989; Understanding Antiques, 1989; Miller's Collectables Price Guide, annually 1989–; Country Style, 1990; Miller's Collectors Cars Price Guide, annually 1991–; Miller's Art Deco Checklist, 1991; Furniture Checklist, 1991; Period Finishes and Effects, 1992; Victorian Style, 1993. *Recreations:* shooting, indulging in fine wines and gourmet food. *Address:* (office) Eldon Lodge, 52 Victoria Road, Kensington, W8 5RQ. *Club:* Groucho.

MILLER, Dame Mary Elizabeth H.; *see* Hedley-Miller.

MILLER, Maurice Solomon, MB; *b* 16 Aug. 1920; *s* of David Miller; *m* 1944, Renée, *d* of Joseph Modlin, Glasgow; two *s* two *d*. *Educ:* Shawlands Academy, Glasgow; Glasgow University. MB, ChB 1944. Elected Mem. of Glasgow Corporation, 1950; Bailie of Glasgow, 1954–57; JP Glasgow, 1957. MP (Lab): Glasgow Kelvingrove, 1964–74; E Kilbride, 1974–87. Asst Govt Whip, 1968–69. Visited Russia as mem. of medical delegation, 1955. *Publication:* Window on Russia, 1956.

MILLER, Prof. Merton Howard, PhD; Professor of Banking and Finance, Graduate School of Business, University of Chicago, since 1961; *b* 16 May 1923; *s* of Joel L. Miller and Sylvia F. Miller (*née* Starr). *Educ:* Harvard Univ.; Johns Hopkins Univ. Asst Lectr, LSE, 1952; Asst Prof. and Associate Prof., Graduate Sch. of Indust. Admin, Carnegie Inst. of Technology, Pittsburgh, 1958–61. Nobel Prize for Economics (jtly), 1990. *Publications:* Theory of Finance, 1972; Macroeconomics, 1974; Financial Innovations and Market Volatility, 1991. *Address:* University of Chicago Graduate School of Business, 1101 East 58th Street, Chicago, IL 60637, USA.

MILLER, Michael, RD 1966; QC 1974; Barrister since 1958; *b* 28 June 1933; 2nd *s* of late John Bryan Peter Duppa-Miller, GC; *m* 1st, 1958, Mary Elizabeth (marr. diss. 1991), *e d* of late Donald Spiers Monteagle Barlow, FRCS; two *s* two *d*; 2nd, 1991, Dr Barbara Lepine Goodwin, *d* of late Thomas Goodwin. *Educ:* Dragon Sch., Oxford; Westminster Sch. (King's Scholar); Christ Church, Oxford (Westminster Scholar). BA Lit. Hum. 1955; MA 1958. Ord. Seaman, RNVR, 1950; Sub-Lt 1956; qual. submarines, 1956; Lt-Comdr RNR. Called to Bar, Lincoln's Inn, 1958, Bencher 1984; practice at Chancery Bar from 1958; Mem. Bar Council, 1972–74 and 1988–92; Mem. Senate of Inns of Court and Bar, 1974–76. Author and editor of computer programs incl. expert systems; founder of Clarendon Software. *Recreations:* sailing, music, chess, football. *Address:* 8 Stone Buildings, Lincoln's Inn, WC2A 3TA.

See also Sir H. D. Miller.

MILLER, Michael A.; *see* Ashley-Miller.

MILLER, Sir (Oswald) Bernard, Kt 1967; *b* 25 March 1904; *s* of late Arthur Miller and Margaret Jane Miller; *m* 1931, Jessica Rose Marie ffoulkes (*d* 1985); three *s*. *Educ:* Sloane Sch.; Jesus Coll., Oxford (Hon. Fellow, 1968); Stanhope Prize, 1925; BA 1927; MA 1930. Joined John Lewis Partnership, 1927; Dir, 1935; Chm., 1955–72. Chm., Retail Distributors Assoc., 1953; Member: Council of Industrial Design, 1957–66; Monopolies Commission, 1961–69; EDC for Distributive Trades, 1964–71. Chm. Southern Region, RSA, 1974–80; Mem. Council, RSA, 1977–82. Treasurer, Southampton Univ., 1974–82, Chm. Council, 1982–87, Pro-Chancellor, 1983–90. Hon. LLD Southampton, 1981. *Publication:* Biography of Robert Harley, Earl of Oxford, 1927. *Recreations:* fishing, gardening, opera and theatre. *Address:* 3 Sutton Manor Mews, Sutton Scotney, Hants SO21 3JX. *T:* Winchester (01962) 760997.

MILLER, Rev. Canon Paul William; Canon Residentiary of Derby Cathedral, 1966–83, Canon Emeritus since 1983; Chaplain to the Queen, 1981–88; *b* 8 Oct. 1918; *s* of F. W. Miller, Barnet. *Educ:* Haileybury; Birmingham Univ. (Dip. Theology). Served in ranks with Sherwood Foresters, 1939–45; POW of Japanese, 1942–45; despatches 1946. Deacon, 1949; Curate: of Staveley, Derbyshire, 1949–52; of Matlock, Derbyshire, 1952–55; Vicar of Codnor, Derbyshire, 1955–61; Novice, Community of the Resurrection, Mirfield, 1961–63; Priest-in-charge, Buxton, 1963–64; Chaplain, Derby Cathedral, 1964–66. *Recreations:* painting, travel. *Address:* 15 Forester Street, Derby DE1 1PP. *T:* Derby (01332) 44773.

MILLER, Peter Francis Nigel, RIBA, FCSD; Surveyor to the Fabric of Ely Cathedral, since 1974; *b* 8 May 1924; *s* of Francis Gerald Miller and Dorothy Emily (*née* Leftwich); *m* 1950, Sheila Gillian Branthwayt, ARCA FCSD, (*née* Stratton); one *s* two *d*. *Educ:* King's Sch., Canterbury; Sch. of Architecture, Coll. of Art, Canterbury. ARIBA 1952; FRIBA 1968; MSIA 1956; FSIA 1968. Served army, 1942–47, NW Europe, Austria, Italy and India; commnd Duke of Cornwall's LI, 1943. Private practice: Peter Miller and Sheila Stratton, 1954; Miller and Tritton, 1956; Purcell Miller and Tritton, 1965; Sen. Partner, Purcell Miller Tritton and Partners, Architects, Surveyors and Design Consultants, 1973–88, Consultant, 1988–. Vice-Pres., SIAD, 1976. *Recreations:* deer stalking, shooting, wildfowling, fishing. *Address:* The Old Foundry House, Letheringsett, Holt, Norfolk NR25 7JL. *T:* Holt (01263) 712329; The Chapter House, The College, Ely, Cambs. *T:* Ely (01353) 667735. *Club:* Norfolk (Norwich).

MILLER, Sir Peter (North), Kt 1988; Chairman, Lloyd's, 1984–87; Chairman, The Miller Insurance Group Ltd (formerly Thos R. Miller & Son (Holdings)), 1971–83 and since 1988; *b* 28 Sept. 1930; *s* of Cyril Thomas Gibson Risch Miller, CBE and Dorothy Alice North Miller, JP; *m* 1991, Jane Herbertson; one *s* and two *s* one *d* by previous marriage. *Educ:* Rugby; Lincoln Coll., Oxford (MA Hons; Hon. Fellow, 1992); City Univ (DSc). National Service, Intelligence Corps, 1949–50. Joined Lloyd's, 1953; qualified as barrister, 1954; Partner, Thos R. Miller & Son (Insurance), 1959, Sen. Partner, 1971–; Dir, Miller Underwriting Agents Ltd (formerly Thos R. Miller & Son (Underwriting Agents) Ltd), 1983–. Dep. Chm., Lloyd's Insurance Brokers' Asoc., 1974–75, Chm. 1976–77; Mem., Cttee of Lloyd's, 1977–80 and 1982–89 (Mem. Council of Lloyd's, 1983–89); in charge of team responsible for passage of Lloyd's Bill (Fisher), 1980–82. Member: Baltic Exchange, 1966–; Insurance Brokers' Registration Council, 1977–81; Vice-Pres., British Insce Brokers' Assoc., 1978–; Chm., British Cttee of Bureau Veritas, 1980–. One of HM's Lieutenants for the City of London, 1987–. FRSA 1986. Commendatore, Ordine al Merito della Repubblica Italiana, 1989. Hon. DSc City, 1987. *Recreations:* all sport (except cricket), including tennis, running, sailing; wine, music, old churches, gardening. *Address:* Dawson House, 5 Jewry Street, EC3N 2EX. *Clubs:* Brooks's, City of London; Vincent's (Oxford); Thames Hare and Hounds.

MILLER, Prof. Richard Albert, OBE 1976; FRAeS; Director of Strategic Management, School of Defence Management, Royal Military College of Science, Cranfield University, since 1995; *b* 12 July 1936; *s* of Albert and Emily Kate Miller; *m* 1959, Beryl Marjorie Thompson; one *s* one *d*. *Educ:* Northampton Grammar Sch.; Coll. of Art, Nottingham; Open Univ. (DipEd, BA Hons); Poly. of E London (MA, MSc). Royal Air Force, 1956–82, Pilot; Flying Duties, 1957–70; RAF Advanced Staff Course, 1970; MoD, 1971–72; OC 36 Sqn, RAF Lyneham, 1973–75; Station Comdr, RAF Benson and Dep. Captain of Queen's Flight, 1976–78; ADC to the Queen, 1976–78; RAF Diamond Jubilee Fellow, Univ. of S Calif and Fitzwilliam Coll., Cambridge, 1979; Dir, Dept of Air Warfare, RAF Coll., 1980; Dir, Air Staff Briefing, MoD, 1981–82; Dir, PR (RAF), MoD, 1982–84; retired (Air Cdre). Executive Air Weapons, BAe Inc, USA, 1985–86; Dir, Defence Procurement Management Gp, 1986–88, Dean, Continuing Educn, 1987–89, Dir, Sch. of Defence Management, 1988–95, RMCS. FIMgt; MAIAA. Freedom, City of London, 1982. QCVSA 1965, 1970. *Recreations:* reading, significant DIY, computing. *Address:* Barnet House, Faringdon Road, Shippon, Abingdon, Oxon OX13 6LW. *T:* Abingdon (01235) 522106. *Club:* Royal Air Force.

MILLER, Richard Hugh; QC 1995; *b* 1 Feb. 1953; *s* of Sir Stephen James Hamilton Miller, *qv*. *Educ:* Charterhouse; Univ. of Sussex (BSc Chem. Physics). Called to the Bar, Middle Temple, 1976; specialising in patent matters. *Publication:* (ed jtly) Terrell on the Law of Patents, 14th edn, 1994. *Recreations:* travel, films. *Address:* 3 New Square, Lincoln's Inn, WC2A 3RS. *T:* 0171–405 1111.

MILLER, Richard Morgan; Vice-Chairman, since 1995, and Director, since 1990, Willis Corroon Group plc (Chief Executive, 1990–94); *b* Nashville, Tenn, 1931; *m* 1953, Betty Ruth Randolph; one *s* two *d*. *Educ:* Montgomery Bell Acad., Nashville; Vanderbilt Univ., Nashville (BA 1953); Wharton Sch., Univ. of Pennsylvania. Served Korean War, 1953–55, Lt US Marine Corps; retired from US Marine Corps Reserve, 1960, Capt. Salesman, Dominion Insce Agency, 1955–58; established Richard M. Miller & Co., 1958, Pres., 1958–70; merger with Synercon Corp., 1970: Founder, Dir, Pres. and Chief Exec. Officer, 1970–76 (also Pres. and Chief Exec. Officer subsid. cos); Synercon Corp. merged into Corroon & Black Corp., 1976: Exec. Vice-Pres., Chief Operating Officer and Dir, 1976–78; Pres., Chief Operating Officer and Dir, 1978–88; Chief Exec. Officer, Pres. and Dir, 1988–89; Chm. Bd, Chief Exec. Officer and Dir, 1990–93; Corroon & Black Corp. merged into Willis Faber plc, 1990. Member, National Associations of: Casualty and Surety Agents; Insurance Brokers; Surety Bond Producers; Mem., Nat. Fedn of Independent Business; Director: Consumer Benefit Life Insce Co.; Meridian Insce Co. (Bermuda); Third Nat. Bank, 1983–; Third Nat. Corp. Trustee and Member Executive Committee: Insce Inst. of America; Amer. Inst. for Property and Liability Underwriters. *Recreation:* golf. *Address:* c/o Willis Corroon Group plc, 10 Trinity Square, EC3P 3AX; Willis Corroon Corporation, Willis Corroon Plaza, 26 Century Boulevard, Nashville, TN 37214, USA. *Clubs:* City Midday, New York Athletic (New York); Belle Meade Country, Cumberland, Nashville City, Tennessee (Nashville, Tennessee); John's Island (Florida); Mid Ocean (Bermuda).

MILLER, Robert Alexander Gavin D.; *see* Douglas Miller.

MILLER, Robin Anthony; a Recorder of the Crown Court, since 1978; *b* 15 Sept. 1937; *s* of William Alexander Miller, CBE, BEM, and Winifred Miller; *m* 1962, Irene Joanna Kennedy; two *s* one *d. Educ:* Devonport High Sch., Plymouth; Wadham Coll., Oxford (MA). Called to the Bar, Middle Temple, 1960. *Address:* St Michael's Lodge, 192 Devonport Road, Stoke, Plymouth, Devon PL1 5RD. *T:* Plymouth (01752) 564943.

MILLER, Sir Ronald (Andrew Baird), Kt 1993; CBE 1985; CA; Chairman, Dawson International PLC, since 1991 (Chairman and Chief Executive, 1982–91); *b* 13 May 1937; *m* 1965, Elizabeth Ann Gordon; one *s* one *d. Educ:* Daniel Stewart's Coll.; Univ. of Edinburgh (BSc). Joined Dawson International, 1968. Director: Securities Trust of Scotland, 1983–; Christian Salvesen, 1987–; Scottish Amicable Life Assce Soc., 1987– (Dep. Chm., 1994–); Chm., Scottish Textile Assoc., 1992–; Chm., British Knitting and Clothing Export Council, 1993–; Member: N Amer. Adv. Gp, DTI, 1986–; Scottish Exports Forum, 1992–; SHEFC, 1992–. Dir, Quality Scotland Foundn, 1991. Gov., Napier Univ. (formerly Polytechnic), 1991–. DSc *hc* Heriot-Watt Univ., 1992. Liveryman, Woolmen's Co., 1992. *Address:* 7 Doune Terrace, Edinburgh EH3 6DY.

MILLER, Ronald Kinsman, CB 1989; Solicitor of Inland Revenue, 1986–90, retired; part-time Chairman, VAT Tribunals, since 1991; *b* 12 Nov. 1929; *s* of William Miller and Elsie May Kinsman; *m* 1952, Doris Alice Dew; one *s* one *d. Educ:* Colchester Royal Grammar Sch. Served RN, 1948–50. Called to the Bar, Gray's Inn, 1953. Joined Inland Revenue, 1950; Asst Solicitor, 1971; Law Officers' Dept, 1977–79; Principal Asst Solicitor, 1981–86. *Recreations:* gardening, reading, music. *Address:* 4 Liskeard Close, Chislehurst, Kent BR7 6RT. *T:* 0181–467 8041. *Club:* Athenæum.

MILLER, Dr Roy Frank; Vice-Principal, Royal Holloway and Bedford New College, University of London, since 1985; *b* 20 Sept. 1935; *s* of Thomas R. Miller and Margaret Ann Tattum; *m* 1961, Ruth Naomi Kenchington; one *s. Educ:* Wembley County Grammar Sch.; University Coll. SW England, Exeter; Royal Holloway Coll. BSc, PhD; CPhys, FInstP. Teacher, Halbutt Secondary Modern Sch., 1957; Royal Holloway College: Demonstrator, 1957, Asst Lectr, 1960, Lectr, 1963, Sen. Lectr, 1973, Physics Dept; Vice-Principal, 1978–81; Acting Principal, 1981–82; Principal, 1982–85. Research Associate and Teaching Fellow, Case Western Reserve Univ., Ohio, USA, 1967–68. Mem. Senate, Univ. of London, 1981–85; Chm., Bd, Inst. of Classical Studies, Univ. of London, 1983–; Trustee and Governor, Strode's Foundn, Strode's Coll., Egham, 1982–. MRI; FRSA. *Publications:* articles in Jl Phys C, Phil. Mag., Vacuum. *Recreations:* mountaineering, squash, music. *Address:* Royal Holloway and Bedford New College, University of London, Egham Hill, Egham, Surrey TW20 0EX. *T:* Egham (01784) 434455. *Club:* Athenæum.

MILLER, Sidney James, MA; Higher Executive Officer, Department for Education (formerly Department of Education and Science), since 1989; *b* 25 Jan. 1943; *s* of Sidney Tomsett Miller and Mary Ada Miller (*née* Marshall); *m* 1971, Judith Branney (*née* Passingham); three *s* one *d. Educ:* Clifton Coll., Bristol; Jesus Coll., Cambridge (MA); Harvard Univ. VIth Form Classical Master and House Tutor, Clifton Coll., Bristol, 1965–68; Asst Master and Classical Tutor, Eton Coll., 1968–73, Head of Classical Dept, 1971–73; Dep. Headmaster (Organisation), Bridgewater Hall, Stantonbury Campus, Milton Keynes, 1974–77; Headmaster, Kingston Grammar Sch., Kingston upon Thames, 1977–86; Head Master, Bedford Sch., 1986–88; Professional Officer, Sch. Exams and Assessment Council, 1988–89. Mem., Gen. Synod of C of E, 1994–95. *Publications:* (ed jtly) Greek Unprepared Translation, 1968; (ed jtly) Inscriptions of the Roman Empire AD14–117, 1971; article in Didaskalos, 1972. *Recreations:* watching sports, learning languages, choral singing. *Address:* 43 Waterloo Road, Bedford MK40 3PG. *Clubs:* MCC; Achilles.

MILLER, Sir Stephen (James Hamilton), KCVO 1979; MD, FRCS; Consulting Ophthalmic Surgeon, retired 1986; Hospitaller, St John Ophthalmic Hospital, Jerusalem, 1980–90; Surgeon-Oculist: to the Queen, 1974–80; to HM Household, 1965–74; Ophthalmic Surgeon: St George's Hospital, 1951–80; National Hospital, Queen Square, 1955–78; King Edward VII Hospital for Officers, 1965–80; Surgeon, Moorfields Eye Hospital, 1954–80; Recognised Teacher in Ophthalmology, St George's Medical School and Institute of Ophthalmology, University of London, retired; *b* 19 July 1915; *e s* of late Stephen Charles Miller and Isobel Hamilton; *m* 1949, Heather P. Motion; three *s. Educ:* Arbroath High Sch.; Aberdeen Univ. House Physician and Surgeon, Royal Infirmary, Hull, 1937–39. Surgeon Lieut-Comdr RNVR, 1939–46 (Naval Ophthalmic Specialist, RN Aux. Hosp., Kilmacolm and RN Hosp., Malta). Resident Surgical Officer, Glasgow Eye Infirmary, 1946; Registrar and Chief Clinical Asst, Moorfields Eye Hosp., 1947–50; Registrar St George's Hosp., 1949–51; Research Associate, Institute of Ophthalmology, 1949–80. Ophthalmic Surgeon, Royal Scottish Corp.; Advr in Ophthalmol., BUPA; Civilian Consultant in Ophthalmol. to RN and MoD, 1971–80, Emeritus, 1980. Member: Med. Commn for Accident Prevention. FRSocMed (Hon. Mem., Sect. of Ophthalmol.); Fellow Faculty of Ophthalmology; Editor, British Journal of Ophthalmology, 1973–83; Mem. Editorial Bd, Ophthalmic Literature; Ophthalmological Soc. of UK; Oxford Ophthalmological Congress (Master, 1969–70); Examiner in Ophthalmology: for Royal Colls and Brit. Orthoptic Bd; RCS and RCSE. Mem. Exec. Cttee, London Clinic, 1975–85; Governor, Moorfields Eye Hosp., 1961–67 and 1974–77. Chm., TFC Frost Charitable Trust (formerly Frost Foundn Charity), 1966–; Vice-Pres., Iris Fund, 1987–; Trustee, Guide Dogs for the Blind, 1981–91. Hon. FRCOphth (Hon. FCOphth 1989). Hon. Mem., Amer. Acad. of Ophthalmology. Freeman, City of London; Liveryman, Soc. of Apothecaries. Doyne Medal, 1972; Montgomery Medal, 1974. GCStJ 1987 (KStJ 1978). *Publications:* Modern Trends in Ophthalmology, 1973; Operative Surgery, 1976; Parsons' Diseases of the Eye, 16th edn 1978, to 18th edn 1990; Clinical Ophthalmology for the Post-Graduate, 1987; articles in BMJ, Brit. Jl of Ophthalmology, Ophthalmic Literature. *Recreations:* golf, fishing. *Address:* Sherma Cottage, Pond Road, Woking GU22 0JT. *T:* Woking (01483) 762287. *Clubs:* Caledonian; Woking Golf.
See also R. H. Miller.

MILLER of Glenlee, Sir Stephen (William Macdonald), 8th Bt *cr* 1788, of Glenlee, Kirkcudbrightshire; FRCS; General Practitioner, since 1986; *b* 20 June 1953; *s* of Sir Macdonald Miller of Glenlee, 7th Bt and of Marion Jane Audrey Pettit, (Audrey, Lady Miller of Glenlee); *S* father, 1991; *m* 1st, 1978, Mary (*d* 1989), *d* of G. B. Owens; one *s* one *d*; 2nd, 1990, Caroline Clark (*née* Chasemore); one step *s* one step *d. Educ:* Rugby Sch.; St Bartholomew's Hosp. MB; FRCS 1981; MRCGP 1986. Surgical Registrar, Sheffield, 1979–81; Orthopaedic Registrar, Newcastle, 1982–84. *Publications:* various papers in med. jls. *Recreations:* gardening, fishing. *Heir: s* James Stephen Macdonald Miller, *b* 25 July 1981. *Address:* The Lawn, Shebbear, Beaworthy, Devon EX21 5RU.

MILLER, Stewart Crichton, CBE 1990; FEng, FIMechE, FRAeS; Director, since 1985, Director, Engineering & Technology, since 1993, Rolls-Royce plc; *b* 2 July 1934; *s* of William Young Crichton Miller and Grace Margaret Miller (*née* Finlay); *m* 1960, Catherine Proudfoot (*née* McCourtie); two *s* two *d. Educ:* Kirkcaldy High Sch.; Univ. of Edinburgh (BSc). FRAeS 1986. FEng 1987; FIMechE 1987. Rolls-Royce plc, 1954–: training, 1954–56; technol. appts, 1956–76; Chief Engr, RB211-535, 1977–84; Dir of Engrg, 1985–90; Man. Dir, Aerospace Gp, 1991–92. Mem., EPSRC, 1994–. Chm. Council, Loughborough Univ. of Technol., 1995–. Hon. DTech Loughborough, 1992. British Gold Medal, RAeS, 1988. *Publications:* many papers to professional bodies on engrg and technol. *Recreations:* family, music, walking. *Address:* Rolls-Royce plc, 65 Buckingham Gate, SW1E 6AT. *T:* 0171–222 9020.

MILLER, Terence George, TD 1960; MA Cantab; Director, Polytechnic of North London, 1971–80; *b* 16 Jan. 1918; *o s* of late George Frederick Miller, Cambridge, and late Marion Johnston, Port William, Wigtownshire; *m* 1944, Inga Catriona, 3rd *d* of Austin Priestman, MD, Folkestone, Kent; one *s* three *d. Educ:* Perse (foundn schol.); Jesus Coll., Cambridge (schol.; Nat. Sci. Tripos, pt 1 cl. 1, pt 2 cl. 1). Wiltshire Prizeman, 1939. Served War of 1939–45: RA, Glider Pilot Regt; TA, 1947–67 (Lt.-Col. 1964). Harkness Scholar, 1948; Research Fellow, Jesus Coll., 1949–54. University Demonstrator, 1948; Lectr in Geology, Univ. of Keele, 1953; Sen. Lectr, 1963, Prof. of Geography, Univ. of Reading, 1965–67; Principal, University Coll. of Rhodesia, 1967–69; Vis. Prof., Reading Univ., 1969–71. *Publications:* Geology, 1950; Geology and Scenery in Britain, 1953; scientific papers in various jls. *Recreations:* trying to understand war, beachcombing, listening. *Address:* Plough House, Docking Road, Sedgeford, Norfolk PE36 5LR. *T:* Heacham (01485) 570923.

MILLER, Walter George, IPFA; FCCA; Chief Executive, Bristol City Council, 1990–91 (Acting Chief Executive, 1987–90); *b* 2 March 1932; *s* of Bert and Rosina Miller; *m* 1956, Sheila Mary Daw; one *s* two *d. Educ:* Howardian High Sch., Cardiff. Clerk, City Treasurer's Dept, Cardiff, 1948–50. Served RA, Hong Kong and Korea, 1950–52. Audit Asst, City Treasurer's Dept, Cardiff, 1952–55; Accountant, Treasurer's Dept: Nairobi, 1955–58; Cardiff, 1958–60; Caerphilly, 1960–63; Ilford, 1963–65; Redbridge, 1965; Bromley, 1965–68; Asst Borough Treasurer, Bromley, 1968–72; Bristol: Asst City Treasurer, 1972–73; Dep. City Treasurer, 1973–80; City Treasurer, 1980–90. Governor, St Joseph's Sch., Portishead, 1986–. *Publications:* Morgan at Gatehaven (novel), 1994; contrib. local government and accountancy press. *Recreations:* writing, gardening, walking. *Address:* 4 Nore Road, Portishead, Bristol BS20 9HN. *T:* Bristol (0117) 984 8559.

MILLER, William; *see* Miller, George William.

MILLER, Prof. William Lockley, PhD; FBA 1994; Edward Caird Professor of Politics, Glasgow University, since 1985; *b* 12 Aug. 1943; *s* of William Lockley Miller and Florence Ratcliffe; *m* 1967, Fiona Thomson; two *s* one *d. Educ:* Edinburgh Univ. (MA 1st Cl. Maths and Nat. Phil. 1965); Newcastle Univ. (PhD Computing 1970). Lectr in Politics, Sen Lectr and Prof., Strathclyde Univ., 1968–85. Vis. Prof. in Politics, Virginia Tech., Blacksburg, 1983–84. *Publications:* Electoral Dynamics, 1977; The End of British Politics?, 1981; The Survey Method, 1983; (with Martin Harrop) Elections and Voters, 1987; Irrelevant Elections?, 1988; (jtly) How Voters Change, 1990; Media and Voters, 1991; (jtly) Alternatives to Freedom, 1995. *Recreation:* hill walking. *Address:* Department of Politics, Adam Smith Building, The University, Glasgow G12 8RT. *T:* 0141–339 8855.

MILLER PARKER, Agnes; *see* Parker, A. M.

MILLER SMITH, Charles; Director, since 1994, Chief Executive, since 1995, Imperial Chemical Industries; *b* 7 Nov. 1939; *s* of William Smith and Margaret Pettigrew Brownlie Wardrope; adopted grandfather's surname, Miller Smith, 1963; *m* 1964, Dorothy Agnes Wilson Adams; one *s* two *d. Educ:* Glasgow Acad.; St Andrews Univ. (MA). ACCA. Unilever: Financial Dir, Vinyl Products, 1970–73; Head of Planning, 1974; Finance Dir, Walls Meat Co., 1976; Vice-Chm., Hindustan Lever, 1979–81; Speciality Chemicals Group, 1981; Chief Exec., PPF Internat., 1983; Chief Exec., Quest Internat., 1986; Financial Dir, Unilever Board, 1989; Exec., Unilever Foods, 1993–94. Non-Exec. Dir, Midland Bank. Hon. LLD St Andrews. *Recreations:* reading, walking. *Address:* Imperial Chemical Industries, 9 Millbank, SW1P 3JF. *T:* 0171–834 4444. *Club:* National.

MILLES-LADE, family name of **Earl Sondes.**

MILLETT, Anthea Christine; Chief Executive, Teacher Training Agency, since 1995; *b* 2 Nov. 1941; *d* of Rupert Millett and Lucy Millett. *Educ:* Erdington Grammar School for Girls, Birmingham; Bedford Coll., Univ. of London (BA Hons). Teacher: Channing School, Highgate, 1963–65; Bournville Grammar Tech. Sch., Birmingham, 1965–67; Solihull High Sch., 1967–71 (Head of Dept); Dep. Head, Tile Hill Comprehensive Sch., Coventry, 1972–77; HM Inspectorate of Schools, subseq. OFSTED, 1978–; Chief Inspector, 1987–92; Dir of Inspection, 1993–95. Mem., Cttee of Enquiry, Management and Government of Schools, 1975–77. *Recreations:* travel, walking, gardening, DIY. *Address:* OFSTED, Elizabeth House, York Road, Waterloo, SE1 7PH. *T:* 0171–925 6800.

MILLETT, Rt. Hon. Sir Peter (Julian), Kt 1986; PC 1994; **Rt. Hon. Lord Justice Millett;** a Lord Justice of Appeal, since 1994; *b* 23 June 1932; *s* of late Denis Millett and Adele Millett; *m* 1959, Ann Mireille, *d* of late David Harris; two *s* (and one *s* decd). *Educ:* Harrow; Trinity Hall, Cambridge (Schol.; MA; Hon. Fellow, 1994). Nat. Service, RAF, 1955–57 (Flying Officer). Called to Bar, Middle Temple, 1955, *ad eundem* Lincoln's Inn, 1959 (Bencher, 1980), Singapore, 1976, Hong Kong, 1979; at Chancery Bar, 1958–86; QC 1973; a Judge of the High Court of Justice, Chancery Div. 1986–94. Examnr and Lectr in Practical Conveyancing, Council of Legal Educn, 1962–76. Junior Counsel to Dept of Trade and Industry in Chancery matters, 1967–73. Mem., General Council of the Bar, 1971–75. Outside Mem., Law Commn on working party on co-ownership of matrimonial home, 1972–73; Mem., Dept of Trade Insolvency Law Review Cttee, 1977–82. Pres., West London Synagogue of British Jews, 1991–95. *Publications:* contrib. to Halsbury's Laws of England, Encycl. of Forms and Precedents; articles in legal jls. *Recreations:* philately, bridge, The Times crossword. *Address:* Royal Courts of Justice, Strand, WC2A 2LL; 18 Portman Close, W1H 9HJ. *T:* 0171–935 1152; St Andrews, Kewhurst Avenue, Cooden, Sussex.

MILLGATE, Prof. Michael Henry, PhD; FRSC; FRSL; University Professor of English, Emeritus, Toronto University, since 1994; *b* 19 July 1929; *s* of Stanley Millgate and Marjorie Louisa (*née* Norris); *m* 1960, Jane, *d* of Maurice and Marie Barr. *Educ:* St Catharine's Coll., Cambridge (MA); Michigan Univ.; Leeds Univ. (PhD). FRSC 1982. Tutor-Organizer, WEA, E Lindsey, 1953–56; Lectr in English Lit., Leeds Univ., 1958–64; Prof. of English and Chm. of the Dept, York Univ., Ont, 1964–67; Prof. of English, Toronto Univ., 1967–94 (University Prof., 1987–94). Killam Sen. Res. Schol., 1974–75, Killam Res. Fellow, 1986–88; John Simon Guggenheim Meml Fellow, 1977–78. FRSL 1984. *Publications:* William Faulkner, 1961; (ed) Tennyson: Selected Poems, 1963; American Social Fiction, 1964; (ed jtly) Transatlantic Dialogue, 1966; The Achievement of William Faulkner, 1966; (ed jtly) Lion in the Garden, 1968; Thomas Hardy: his career as a novelist, 1971; (ed jtly) The Collected Letters of Thomas Hardy, vols I-VII, 1978–88; Thomas Hardy: a biography, 1982; (ed) The Life and Work of Thomas Hardy, 1985; (ed) William Faulkner Manuscripts 20, 21, 22 and 23, 1987; (ed) New Essays on Light in August, 1987; (ed) Thomas Hardy: selected letters, 1990; Testamentary Acts: Browning, Tennyson, James, Hardy, 1992; (ed jtly) Thomas Hardy's 'Studies, Specimens &c'

Notebook, 1994; (ed) Letters of Emma and Florence Hardy, 1996. *Address:* 75 Highland Avenue, Toronto, Ont M4W 2A4, Canada. *T:* (416) 920 3717.

MILLICHIP, Sir Frederick Albert, (Sir Bert), Kt 1991; Chairman, The Football Association, since 1981 (Member of Council, since 1970; Life Vice President, since 1990); *b* 5 Aug. 1914; *s* of late Hugh Bowater Millichip; *m* 1950, Joan Barbara Brown; one *s* one *d*. *Educ:* Solihull Sch., Warwicks. Qualified as Solicitor, 1950; Sen. Partner, 1959–88, Consultant, 1988–, Tyndelwood & Millichip (formerly Sharpe & Millichip). Served War, 1939–45, in England, N Africa, Sicily and Italy; joined S Staffs Regt as private, commnd RA (Captain). Union of European Football Associations: Chairman: Cttee for Five-a-Side Football, 1988–92; Juridical Cttee, 1992–93; Member: Exec. Cttee, 1988–; Organising Cttee for European Championship, 1981–; Referees' Cttee, 1992–93 (Chm., 1994–). Mem., FIFA Organising Cttee for World Cup, 1983–; Chm., FA Disciplinary Cttee, 1978–81. West Bromwich Albion Football Club: Dir, 1964–84; Chm., 1976–83; Pres., 1984–. *Recreation:* golf. *Address:* Fairlight, 52 Twatling Road, Barnt Green, Birmingham B45 8HU. *T:* 0121–445 4688. *Club:* Blackwell Golf (Blackwell, Worcs).

MILLIGAN, Hon. Lord; James George Milligan; a Senator of the College of Justice in Scotland, since 1988; *b* 10 May 1934; *s* of Rt Hon. Lord Milligan; *m* 1st, 1961, Elizabeth Carnegie Thomson (*d* 1982), *e d* of late Hon. Lord Migdale and Louise (*née* Carnegie; later Mrs Thomson); two *s* three *d*; 2nd, 1985, Elizabeth Cynthia Rae Ashworth, *widow* of Rupert S. H. Ashworth, and *y d* of late P. Rae Shepherd. *Educ:* St Mary's Sch., Melrose; Rugby Sch.; Oxford Univ. (BA); Edinburgh Univ. (LLB). Admitted to Faculty of Advocates, 1959; Standing Junior Counsel to the Scottish Home and Health Dept and Dept of Health and Social Security in Scotland; Advocate-Depute, 1971–78; QC (Scot.) 1972; Chm., Med. Appeal Tribunal (Scotland), 1979–88. Chm., RSSPCC Edinburgh, 1978–92. *Publication:* (contrib. small part of) Armour on Valuation for Rating, 3rd edn, 1961. *Recreations:* gardening, golf. *Address:* Parliament House, Edinburgh EH1 1RQ.

MILLIGAN, Iain Anstruther; QC 1991; *b* 21 April 1950; *s* of Wyndham Macbeth Moir Milligan, *qv*; *m* 1979, Zara Ann Louise Spearman; one *s* two *d*. *Educ:* Eton; Magdalene College, Cambridge (MA); College of Law. Called to the Bar, Inner Temple, 1973. *Recreations:* forestry, walking. *Address:* 20 Essex Street, WC2R 3AL. *T:* 0171–583 9294; Dunesslin, Dunscore, Dumfries DG2 0UR. *T:* Dunscore (01387) 820345.

MILLIGAN, James George; *see* Milligan, Hon. Lord.

MILLIGAN, Terence Alan, (Spike Milligan), Hon. CBE 1992; actor; author; *b* 16 April 1918; *s* of late Captain L. A. Milligan, MSM, RA retd, and Florence Winifred Milligan; *m* (wife *d* 1978); one *s* three *d*; *m* 1983, Shelagh Sinclair. *Educ:* Convent of Jesus and Mary, Poona; Brothers de La Salle, Rangoon; SE London Polytechnic, Lewisham. Lifetime Achievement Award, British Comedy Awards, 1994. Appearances (comedy) as Spike Milligan: *stage:* The Bed-Sitting Room; Son of Oblomov; Ben Gunn, in Treasure Island, Mermaid, 1973, 1974; One man shows, 1979, 1980; writer, Ubu Roi, 1980; Spike Milligan and Friends, Lyric, 1982; *radio:* Goon Show (inc. special performance, 1972, to mark 50th Anniversary of BBC); Best British Radio Features Script, 1972; The Milligan Papers, 1987; *TV:* Show called Fred, ITV; World of Beachcomber, BBC; Q5, BBC; Oh in Colour, BBC; A Milligan for All Seasons, BBC, 1972–73; Marty Feldman's Comedy Machine, ITV (writing and appearing; awarded Golden Rose and special comedy award, Montreux, 1972); The Melting Pot, BBC, 1975; Q7, BBC series, 1977; Q8, 1978; Q9, 1979; TV Writer of the Year Award, 1956; *films:* The Magic Christian, 1971; The Devils, 1971; The Cherry Picker, 1972; Digby the Biggest Dog in the World, 1972; Alice's Adventures in Wonderland, 1972; The Three Musketeers, 1973; The Great McGonagall, 1975; The Last Remake of Beau Geste, 1977; The Hound of the Baskervilles, 1978; Monty Python Life of Brian, 1978; History of the World, Part 1, 1980; Yellowbeard, 1983. *Publications:* Dustbin of Milligan, 1961; Silly Verse for Kids, 1963; Puckoon, 1963; The Little Pot Boiler, 1965; A Book of Bits, 1965; Milliganimals, 1968; The Bedside Milligan, 1968; The Bed-Sitting Room (play), 1969; The Bald Twit Lion, 1970; Adolf Hitler, My Part in his Downfall, 1971 (filmed 1973; on record, 1980); Milligan's Ark, 1971; Small Dreams of a Scorpion, 1972; The Goon Show Scripts, 1972; Rommel: Gunner Who?, 1973; (for children) Badjelly the Witch, 1973; (with J. Hobbs) The Great McGonagall Scrapbook, 1975; The Milligan Book of Records, Games, Cartoons and Commercials, 1975; Dip the Puppy, 1975; Transports of Delight, 1975; William McGonagal, the truth at last, 1976; Monty, His Part in my Victory, 1976; Goblins (with Heath Robinson illus), 1978; Mussolini, His Part in my Downfall, 1978; Open Heart University, 1978; Spike Milligan's Q Annual, 1979; Get in the Q Annual, 1980; Unspun Socks from a Chicken's Laundry, 1981; Indefinite Articles and Scunthorpe, 1981; The 101 Best and Only Limericks of Spike Milligan, 1982; (for children) Sir Nobonk and the Terrible, Awful, Dreadful, Naughty, Nasty Dragon (illus. by Carol Barker), 1982; The Goon Cartoons, 1982; More Goon Cartoons, 1983; There's A Lot Of It About, 1983; The Melting Pot, 1983; Spike Milligan's Further Transports of Delight, 1985; Where have all the Bullets Gone? (autobiog.), 1985; Floored Masterpieces with Worse Verse (illus. by Tracey Boyd), 1985; Goodbye Soldier, 1986; The Looney: an Irish fantasy, 1987; The Mirror Running (poetry), 1987; Startling Verse for all the Family (children's poetry), 1987; The Lost Goon Shows, 1987; Milligan's War, 1988; McGonagall Meets George Gershwin, 1988; It Ends With Magic, 1990; Dear Robert, Dear Spike, 1991; Peacework (autobiog.), 1991; Condensed Animals, 1991; Hidden Words (poetry), 1993; (with A. Clare) Depression and How To Survive It, 1993; The Bible According to Spike Milligan, 1993; Lady Chatterly's Lover According to Spike Milligan, 1994; Wuthering Heights According to Spike Milligan, 1995; Fleas, Knees and Hidden Elephants (poetry), 1995. *Recreations:* restoration of antiques, oil painting, water colours, gardening, eating, drinking, talking, wine, jazz. *Address:* 9 Orme Court, W2 4RL. *T:* 0171–727 1544.

MILLIGAN, Timothy James; His Honour Judge Milligan; a Circuit Judge, since 1991; *b* 16 March 1940; *s* of Dr Peter James Wyatt Milligan and Rosemary Elizabeth Ann (*née* Dutton); *m* 1976, Sally Marcella (*née* Priest); two step *s*. *Educ:* Frilsham House Prep. School; Winchester Coll.; Grenoble Univ. (1st and 2nd Foreigner's Degrees). Articled Clerk, Taylor Garrett, 1960–65; admitted Solicitor, 1967; Asst Solicitor, Leeds Smith, Beds, 1967–69; Asst Solicitor, then Partner, Triggs Turner, Guildford, 1969–73; Solicitor, then Partner, Warner & Richardson, Winchester, 1973–91; HM Coroner, Central Hants, 1982–91; a Recorder of the Crown Court, 1988–91. Hon. Mem., Coroners Soc. of GB, 1991; Mem. of various Old Wykehamist clubs and assocs. *Recreations:* rackets, cricket, football, reading, music, theatre, cinema. *Address:* Marsh Court Farm, Stockbridge, Hampshire SO20 6JB. *T:* Andover (01264) 810866. *Clubs:* MCC; Hampshire (Winchester); Hampshire CC (Mem. Cttee, 1993–); Jesters; Tennis and Rackets Association (Mem., Rackets Cttee, 1988–).

MILLIGAN, Wyndham Macbeth Moir, MBE 1945; TD 1947; Principal of Wolsey Hall, Oxford, 1968–80, retired; *b* 21 Dec. 1907; *s* of Dr W. Anstruther Milligan, MD, London, W1; *m* 1941, Helen Penelope Eirene Cassavetti, London, W1; three *s* two *d*. *Educ:* Sherborne; Caius Coll., Cambridge (Christopher James Student, 1931; 1st Cl. Classical Tripos, Parts 1 and 2). Asst Master, Eton Coll., 1932–, House Master, Eton Coll., 1946; Warden, Radley Coll., 1954–68. Served 1939–45, with Scots Guards, in NW Europe (Major). Former Chm., N Berks Area Youth Cttee. Governor: St Mary's, Wantage (Chm.); Reed's Sch., Cobham; Lay Chm., Vale of White Horse Deanery Synod; Mem., Administrative Council, King George's Jubilee Trust. FRSA 1968. *Recreations:* gardening, sketching. *Address:* Church Hill House, Stalbridge, Sturminster Newton, Dorset DT10 2LR. *T:* Stalbridge (01963) 362815.

See also I. A. Milligan.

MILLING; *see* Crowley-Milling.

MILLING, Peter Francis, MB, BChir, FRCS; formerly: Surgeon, Ear, Nose and Throat Department, University College Hospital; Surgeon in charge, Throat and Ear Department, Brompton Hospital; Consultant Ear, Nose and Throat Surgeon: Epsom District Hospital; Oxted and Limpsfield Cottage Hospital; Visiting Laryngologist Benenden Chest Hospital. *Educ:* Cambridge University. BA Hons, 1937; MRCS, LRCP, 1940; MA, MB, BChir, 1941; FRCS, 1946. Formerly Chief Assistant, Ear, Nose and Throat Department, St Thomas' Hospital; Chief Clinical Assistant and Registrar, Ear, Nose and Throat Department, Guy's Hosp.; Surgical Registrar, Ear, Nose and Throat Dept, Royal Cancer Hospital. Member British Association of Otolaryngologists. *Publications:* contributions to medical text-books and journals. *Address:* 3 Homefield Park, Ballasalla, Isle of Man IM9 2EL. *T:* Douglas (01624) 823072.

MILLINGTON, Anthony Nigel Raymond; Director General, Tokyo Office, European Automobile Manufacturers Association, since 1995; *b* 29 Jan. 1945; *s* of Raymond and Nancy Millington; *m* 1969, Susan Carolyn (*née* Steilberg); two *s*. *Educ:* Ipswich School; Univ. of Grenoble; Trinity College, Cambridge (BA); Univ. of Chicago. Joined FCO, 1968; Tokyo, 1969–76; FCO, 1976–80; Paris, 1980–84; Japanese National Defence College, 1984–85; Head of Chancery, Tokyo, 1985–88; Head of Far Eastern Dept, FCO, 1989–90; joined Rolls-Royce PLC, 1990; Pres., Rolls-Royce (Far East) Ltd, 1990–94; rejoined FCO, 1994. *Recreations:* golf, tennis, walking in the countryside. *Address:* c/o European Automobile Manufacturers Association, PO Box 564, Ark Mori Building, 1–12–32 Akasaka, Minato-ku, Tokyo 107, Japan. *T:* (3) 35054963, *Fax:* (3) 35054871. *Clubs:* Royal Automobile; Tokyo Lawn Tennis.

MILLINGTON, Wing Comdr Ernest Rogers, DFC 1945; advisor on training, Youth Training Scheme, 1980–90; Teacher in charge of Teachers' Centre, London Borough of Newham, 1967–80, retired; Founder, and Editor, Project, 1967–80; *b* 15 Feb. 1916; *s* of Edmund Rogers Millington and Emily Craggs; *m* 1st, 1937 (marr. diss. 1974); four *d*; 2nd, 1975, Ivy Mary Robinson. *Educ:* Chigwell Sch., Essex; College of S Mark and S John, Chelsea; Birkbeck Coll., London Univ. Clerk; Accountant; Company Sec.; served War of 1939–45, soldier, gunner officer, pilot RAF, instructor and heavy bomber, CO of a Lancaster Sqdn. MP (Commonwealth) for Chelmsford, 1945–50. Re-joined Royal Air Force, 1954–57. Head of Social Educn, Shoreditch Comprehensive Sch., London, 1965–67. *Publications:* (edited): A Study of Film, 1972; The Royal Group of Docks, 1977; A Geography of London, 1979; National Parks, 1980. *Recreations:* Francophilia, travel, writing. *Address:* Villa Martine, Couze St Front, 24150 Lalinde, France. *T:* 53249431.

MILLNER, Ralph; QC 1965; *b* 25 Jan. 1912; *o s* of Ralph Millner, Merchant, Manchester; *m* 1st, 1935, Bruna, *d* of Arturo Rosa, Este, Italy (marr. diss. 1949); one *d* decd; 2nd, 1949, Monica, *d* of Prof. P. W. Robertson, Wellington, NZ; one *s* two *d*. *Educ:* William Hulme's Grammar Sch., Manchester; Clare Coll., Cambridge (MA); Bedford Coll., London (BA, Italian). Called to English Bar, Inner Temple, 1934; Ghana Bar (Gold Coast), 1950; Sierra Leone Bar, 1957; Nigerian Bar and S Cameroons Bar, 1959; Guyana Bar (formerly British Guiana), 1961; has also appeared in courts of Aden and Kenya. Lectr in Italian, QUB, 1972–77. Vis. Lectr in Italian, Univ. of Leicester, 1980–92. Member: Soc. for Italian Studies; Haldane Soc. *Address:* 69 Anson Road, N7 0AS.

MILLON, Charles; Minister of Defence, France, since 1995; *b* Belley, Ain, 12 Nov. 1945; *s* of Gabriel Millon and Suzanne Millon (*née* Gunet); *m* Chantal Delsol; six *c*. *Educ:* Lamartine Instn, Belley; Saint-Marie Sch., Lyon. Asst Lectr, 1969; legal and fiscal consultant, 1969–. Mayor of Belley, 1977–. Deputy (UDF-PR) for Belley-Gex, elected 1978, 1981, 1986, 1988, 1993; Mem., Regl Council for Rhône-Alpes, elected 1981, 1986 (Pres., 1988–); Mem., Gen. Council of the Ain (Canton of Belley), 1985–88; National Assembly: Vice-Pres., 1986–88; Mem., Foreign Cttee, 1988–; Pres., Parly Gp of UDF, 1989–95. Pres., Departmental Fedn, PR and UDF, 1983–85; Mem., Pol Bd, PR, 1984–. *Publications:* L'extravagante histoire des nationalisations, 1984; L'alternate-Vérité, 1986; La tentation du conservatisme, 1995. *Address:* Ministry of Defence, 14 rue Saint-Dominique, 00450 Armées, France. *T:* 42193011.

MILLS; *see* Platts-Mills.

MILLS, family name of **Viscount Mills.**

MILLS, 3rd Viscount *cr* 1962; **Christopher Philip Roger Mills;** Bt 1953; Baron 1957; Area Fisheries, Recreation and Ecology Manager, North West Region, National Rivers Authority, since 1991; *b* 20 May 1956; *s* of 2nd Viscount Mills and of Joan Dorothy, *d* of James Shirreff; *S* father, 1988; *m* 1980, Lesley Alison, *er d* of Alan Bailey. *Educ:* Oundle School; Univ. of London (BSc Hons Biolog. Sciences; MSc Applied Fish Biology); Plymouth Polytechnic. Biologist at Salmon Research Trust of Ireland, 1980–89; Technical Asst, NRA, 1989–91. *Publications:* papers in Aquaculture, Aquaculture and Fisheries Management, Fish Biology. *Recreations:* flyfishing, fine wines. *Address:* House of Lords, SW1A 0PW.

MILLS, Barbara Jean Lyon; QC 1986; Director of Public Prosecutions, since 1992; *b* 10 Aug. 1940; *d* of John and Kitty Warnock; *m* 1962, John Angus Donald Mills; four *c*. *Educ:* St Helen's Sch., Northwood, Lady Margaret Hall, Oxford (Gibbs Scholar, 1961; MA; Hon. Fellow, 1991). Called to the Bar, Middle Temple, 1963, Bencher, 1990; QC (NI) 1991. Jun. Treasury Counsel, Central Criminal Court, 1981–86; a Recorder, 1982–92; Dir, Serious Fraud Office, 1990–92. Member: Criminal Injuries Compensation Bd, 1988–90; Parole Bd, 1990; Legal Assessor to GMC and GDC, 1988–90. Mem., Gen. Adv. Council, BBC, 1991–92. CIMgt 1993. Hon. LLD: Hull, 1993; Nottingham Trent, 1993; London Guildhall, 1994. *Recreation:* my family. *Address:* Crown Prosecution Service, 50 Ludgate Hill, EC4M 7EX.

MILLS, Prof. Bernard Yarnton, AC 1976; FRS 1963; FAA 1959; DSc Eng; Professor of Physics (Astrophysics), University of Sydney, 1965–85, Emeritus Professor 1986; *b* 8 Aug. 1920; *s* of Ellice Yarnton Mills and Sylphide Mills. *Educ:* King's Sch., New South Wales; University of Sydney. BSc 1940, DSc Eng 1959 (Sydney). Joined the then Council for Scientific and Industrial Research and worked on Devélt of mil. radar systems; after working for many years on radioastronomy he joined Sydney Univ. to form a radioastronomy group in Sch. of Physics, 1960; Reader in Physics, 1960–65; responsible for Mills Cross radio-telescope, near Hoskinstown, NSW. Lyle Medal of Australian Academy of Science, 1957. *Publications:* (jtly) A Textbook of Radar, 1946; many contribs to sci. jls in Australia, England and America, mainly on subjects of radioastronomy and astrophysics. *Address:* 52 Victoria Street, Roseville, NSW 2069, Australia.

MILLS, Vice-Adm. Sir Charles (Piercy), KCB 1968 (CB 1964); CBE 1957; DSC 1953; *b* 4 Oct. 1914; *s* of late Capt. Thomas Piercy Mills, Woking, Surrey; *m* 1944, Anne Cumberlege; two *d.* *Educ:* RN College, Dartmouth. Joined Navy, 1928; Comdr 1947; Capt. 1953; Rear-Adm. 1963; Vice-Adm. 1966. Served War of 1939–45, Home Waters, Mediterranean and Far East; Korea, 1951–52; Flag Officer, Second in Command, Far East Fleet, 1966–67; C-in-C Plymouth, 1967–69; Lieut-Governor and C-in-C Guernsey, 1969–74. US Legion of Merit, 1955. KStJ 1969. *Recreations:* golf, yachting. *Address:* Aldewaye, Aldeburgh, Suffolk IP15 5ER.

MILLS, Edward (David), CBE 1959; FRIBA; Architect and Design Consultant in private practice since 1937; Senior Partner, Edward D. Mills & Partners, Architects, London, since 1956; *b* 19 March 1915; *s* of Edward Ernest Mills; *m* 1939, Elsie May Bryant; one *s* one *d.* *Educ:* Ensham Sch.; Polytechnic Sch. of Architecture. ARIBA 1937, FRIBA 1946. Mem. of RIBA Council, 1954–62 and 1964–69; Chm. RIBA Bd of Architectural Education, 1960–62 (Vice-Chm., 1958–60). RIBA Alfred Bossom Research Fellow, 1953; Churchill Fellow, 1969. FCSD (FSIAD 1975); Mem., Uganda Soc. of Architects. Chm., Faculty Architecture, British School at Rome; Patron, Soc. of Architectural Illustrators. Architect for British Industries Pavilion, Brussels Internat. Exhibn, 1958; works include: St Andrews Cathedral, Mbale, Uganda; Nat. Exhibn Centre, Birmingham; Birmingham Internat. Arena; churches, schools, industrial buildings, research centres, flats and houses in Great Britain and overseas. Hon. DLitt, 1993. *Publications:* The Modern Factory, 1951; The New Architecture in Great Britain, 1953; The Modern Church, 1956; Architects Details, Vols 1–6, 1952–61; Factory Building, 1967; The Changing Workplace, 1971; Planning, 5 vols, 9th edn 1972, 10th edn (combined Golden Jubilee vol.), 1985; The National Exhibition Centre, 1976; Building Maintenance and Preservation, 1980, 2nd edn 1994; Design for Holidays and Tourism, 1983; contribs to RIBA journal, Architectural Review, etc. *Recreations:* photography, foreign travel. *Address:* The Studio, Gate House Farm, Newchapel, Lingfield, Surrey RH7 6LF. *T:* Lingfield (01342) 832241.

MILLS, Eric Robertson, CBE 1981; Registrar of the Privy Council, 1966–83; *b* 27 July 1918; *s* of late Thomas Piercy Mills, Woking, Surrey; *m* 1950, Shirley Manger; two *d.* *Educ:* Charterhouse; Trinity Coll., Cambridge (BA). Served Royal Artillery, 1939–46; Major 1944. Called to Bar, Inner Temple, 1947; Mem. of Western Circuit. Dep. Judge Advocate, 1955; Chief Clerk, Judicial Cttee of Privy Council, 1963. *Publications:* contribs to legal text books. *Address:* Lamber Green, St Catherines Drive, Guildford, Surrey GU2 5HE. *T:* Guildford (01483) 37218.

MILLS, Prof. Eric William, AM 1986; CChem, FRSC; FRACI; Director, South Australian Institute of Technology, 1978–85, retired; *b* 22 April 1920; *s* of William and Lucy Margaret Mills; *m* 1st, 1945, Inge Julia Königsberger (*d* 1986); three *d*; 2nd, 1993, Natalya Khudyakova; one *d.* *Educ:* Liverpool Institute; Univ. of Liverpool (BSc, PhD). Chemist, British Insulated Cables, 1941–45; Research Chemist, British Oxygen Co., 1948–49; Sen. Lectr, Birmingham College of Advanced Technology, 1949–52; Head of Dept, Rutherford Coll. of Technology, 1952–57; Principal: Carlisle Technical Coll., 1959–60; Chesterfield Coll. of Technology, 1960–63; Asst Dir, SA Inst. of Technology, 1964–77. *Address:* 3 Pam Street, Beaumont, SA 5066, Australia. *T:* (8) 3796674.

MILLS, Sir Frank, KCVO 1983; CMG 1971; HM Diplomatic Service, retired; Chairman of Council, Royal Commonwealth Society for the Blind (Sight Savers), 1985–91; *b* 3 Dec. 1923; *s* of Joseph Francis Mills and Louisa Mills; *m* 1953, Trilby Foster; one *s* two *d.* *Educ:* King Edward VI Sch., Nuneaton; Emmanuel Coll., Cambridge. RAFVR, 1942–45. CRO, 1948; served in: Pakistan, 1949–51; S Africa, 1955–58; Malaysia, 1962–63; Singapore, 1964–66; India, 1972–75; High Comr, Ghana, 1975–78; Private Sec. to Sec. of State, 1960–62; RCDS, 1971; Dir of Communications, FCO, 1978–81; High Comr, Bangladesh, 1981–83. Chairman: Camberwell HA, 1984–89; Chichester CHC, 1993–95. *Recreations:* golf, water colours. *Clubs:* Royal Over-Seas League; Goodwood Golf.

MILLS, Geoffrey Thomas; Headmaster, Latymer School, since 1983; *b* 13 Nov. 1935; *s* of Thomas Henry Mills and Margaret Jane (*née* Lewington); *m* 1970, Dorothy Anne Williams; one *s* three *d.* *Educ:* Enfield Grammar Sch.; Clare Coll., Cambridge (MA). Nat. Service, Corporal Clerk, RASC, 1954–56. Foreign lang. asst, Lyons, France, 1960–61; teacher of French and Spanish, Guthlaxton Grammar Sch., Leicester, 1961–62; Hd of Spanish, Sweyne Grammar Tech. Sch., Rayleigh, Essex, 1962–65; Head of Modern Languages: Coborn Sch. for Girls, Bow, 1965–69; Woodhouse Grammar Sch., Finchley, 1969–73; Dir of Studies, Longdean Sch., Hemel Hempstead, 1973–78; Headmaster, Manhood High Sch. and Community Centre, Selsey, W Sussex, 1978–83. *Recreations:* golf (Blue, 1958), bridge, crosswords, reading. *Address:* 59 Wades Hill, Winchmore Hill, N21 1BD. *T:* 0181–360 7335. *Club:* Mid Herts Golf (Wheathampstead).

MILLS, (George) Ian, FCA, FIMC; Chairman: South East London Health Authority, since 1993; Lambeth, Southwark and Lewisham Heath Commission, since 1993; *b* 19 Nov. 1935; *s* of George Haxton Mills and Evelyn Mary (*née* Owen); *m* 1968, Margaret Elizabeth Dunstan; one *s* one *d* (and one *s* decd). *Educ:* Taunton's Grammar Sch., Southampton. FCA 1960; FIMC 1964; LHSM 1985. Articled to Beal, Young & Booth, Southampton, 1954–60; Price Waterhouse, London, 1960–65; seconded to World Bank team assisting Govt of Pakistan Treasury, 1962; Chief Accountant, Univ. of Ibadan, Nigeria, 1965–68; rejoined Price Waterhouse, 1968; London Office, 1968–70; Newcastle upon Tyne Office, as Manager i/c Northern and Scottish Management Consultancy Ops, 1970–73; Partner, 1973; London Office, 1973–85: i/c Africa Management Consultancy Services, 1975–83; Nat. Dir, Central Govt Services, 1983–85; Nation Health Service Management Board, 1985–89: Dir of Financial Management, 1985–88; Dir of Resource Management, 1988–89; rejoined Price Waterhouse, 1989; Sen. Partner, Business Development Europe, 1989–91. Chairman: Lewisham and N Southwark HA, 1991–93; SE London Commissioning Agency, 1991–93. Member: Blackheath Preservation Trust Ltd, 1991–; Bd of Govs, UMDS of Guy's and St Thomas' Hosps, 1991–; Editorial Adv. Bd, Health Services Jl, 1992–; IHSM Consultants, 1992–; Bd of Govs, St Christopher's Hospice, 1993–; Delegacy, KCH Med. Sch., 1993–. *Publications:* articles in financial, educnl and med. jls. *Recreations:* classical music, photography, travel. *Address:* 60 Belmont Hill, SE13 5DN. *T:* 0181–852 2457. *Club:* Commonwealth Trust.

MILLS, Maj.-Gen. Giles Hallam, CB 1977; CVO 1984; OBE 1964; retired; *b* 1 April 1922; 2nd *s* of late Col Sir John Digby Mills, TD, Bisterne Manor, Ringwood, Hampshire, and Lady Mills; *m* 1947, Emily Snowden Hallam, 2nd *d* of late Captain W. H. Tuck, Perrywood, Maryland, USA, and Mrs Tuck; two *s* one *d.* *Educ:* Eton Coll. Served War: 2nd Lieut, KRRC, 1941; 1st Bn, KRRC, N Africa, Italy (Adjt, despatches), 1943–47. Staff Coll., 1951; Armed Forces Staff Coll. (US), 1959; Mil. Asst to CIGS, 1961–63; CO, 2 Green Jackets, KRRC, 1963–65; Admin. Staff Coll., Henley, 1965; Regtl Col, Royal Green Jackets, 1966–67; Comd, 8 Infty Bde, 1968–69; IDC 1970; Comd, British Army Staff and Mil. Attaché, Washington, 1971–73; Divl Brig., The Light Div., 1973–74; Dir of Manning (Army), 1974–77, retd. Major and Resident Governor, HM Tower of London, and Keeper of the Jewel House, 1979–84. *Publications:* Annals of The King's Royal Rifle Corps, vol. VI (with Roger Nixon), 1971, vol. VII, 1979. *Recreations:* gardening, bird-watching, fishing, shooting, history. *Address:* Leeland House, Twyford, Winchester, Hants SO21 1NP. *Club:* Army and Navy.

MILLS, Harold Hernshaw, CB 1995; Secretary, Scottish Office Environment Department, since 1992; *b* 2 March 1938; *s* of late Harold and of Margaret Mills; *m* 1973, Marion Elizabeth Beattie, MA. *Educ:* Greenock High Sch.; Univ. of Glasgow (BSc, PhD). Cancer Research Scientist, Roswell Park Memorial Inst., Buffalo, NY, 1962–64; Lectr, Glasgow Univ., 1964–69; Principal, Scottish Home and Health Dept, 1970–76; Asst Secretary: Scottish Office, 1976–81; Privy Council Office, 1981–83; Scottish Development Dept, 1983–84; Under Sec., Scottish Develt Dept, 1984–88; Prin. Finance Officer, Scottish Office, 1988–92. *Publications:* scientific papers in jls of learned socs on the crystal structure of chemical compounds. *Address:* Scottish Office, New St Andrew's House, Edinburgh EH1 3TG.

MILLS, Iain Campbell; MP (C) Meriden, since 1979; *b* 21 April 1940; *s* of John Steel Mills and Margaret Leitch; *m* 1971, Gaynor Lynne Jeffries. *Educ:* Prince Edward Sch., Salisbury, Rhodesia. Dunlop Rhodesia Ltd, 1961–64; Dunlop Ltd, UK, 1964–79 (latterly Marketing Planning Manager). Parly Private Secretary: to Minister of State for Industry, 1981–82; to Sec. of State for Employment, 1982–83; to Sec. of State for Trade and Industry, 1983–85; to Chancellor of Duchy of Lancaster, 1985–87. Mem., Select Cttee on Employment, 1989–; Jt Chm., All Party Motor Industry Gp, 1992–; Chm., Community Trade Mark Cttee, 1984–; Vice-Chm., Transport Safety Cttee, 1984–. *Address:* House of Commons, SW1A 0AA.

MILLS, Ian; *see* Mills, George I.

MILLS, Ivor; writer and broadcaster; corporate affairs and media consultant; *b* 7 Dec. 1929; *e s* of John Mills and Matilda (*née* Breen); *m* 1956, Muriel (marr. diss. 1987), *o d* of Wilson and Muriel Hay; one *s* one *d.* *Educ:* High sch.; Stranmillis Coll.; Queen's Univ., Belfast. Radio and television journalist, and freelance writer, Ulster TV, 1959, and Southern TV, 1963; freelance writer/editor/producer/presenter, contrib. to BBC World Service and Home Radio Networks, and ITV Regions, 1964; joined ITN as Reporter, 1963; newscaster, 1967–78; Head of Public Affairs, Post Office, 1978–81; Head of Public Affairs and Dep. Dir, Corporate Relns, British Telecommunications plc, 1981–88. Media consultant. *Recreations:* art, music, theatre, tennis, food, wine. *Address:* 46B Glenhurst Avenue, Parliament Hill NW5 1PS.

MILLS, Ivor Henry, FRCP; Professor of Medicine in the University of Cambridge, 1963–88, now Emeritus; Fellow, Churchill College, Cambridge, 1963–88; Hon. Consultant to United Cambridge Hospitals since 1963; *b* 13 June 1921; 3rd *s* of late J. H. W. Mills and late Priscilla Mills; *m* 1947, Sydney Elizabeth Puleston (*née* Roberts); one *s* one *d.* *Educ:* Selhurst Grammar Sch., Croydon; Queen Mary Coll., London; Trinity Coll., Cambridge. BSc (London) 1942; PhD (London) 1946; BA (Cantab) 1948; MB, BChir Cantab 1951; MRCP 1953; MD Cantab 1956; MA Cantab 1963; FRCP 1964. Pres. Cambridge Univ. Medical Soc., 1947–48; Sen. Schol., Trinity Coll., Cambridge, 1948; MRC (Eli Lilly) Trav. Fellow, 1956; Vis. Scientist, Nat. Inst. of Health, 1957; Lectr in Medicine and Chem. Path., St Thomas's Hosp. Medical Sch., 1954; Reader in Medicine, St Thomas's Hosp. Medical Sch., London, 1962. Vis. Prof. in Physiology and Medicine, N Carolina Med. Sch., USA, 1972. Mem., Hunter Working Party on Medical Administrators, 1970–72. Royal College of Physicians: Mem. Council, 1971–74; Pro-Censor, 1974–75, Censor, 1975–76; Croonian Lectr, 1977; Sec., Soc. for Endocrinology, 1963–71; Chm., Scientific Adv. Cttee, Mason Med. Res. Foundation, 1982–88. Hon. FACP. *Publications:* Clinical Aspects of Adrenal Function, 1964; contrib. Lancet, Science Jl of Endocr., Clin. Science, etc. *Recreations:* gardening, letters to The Times. *Address:* 6 Spinney Drive, Great Shelford, Cambridge CB2 5LY.

MILLS, John Frederick; Chief Executive, Cornwall County Council, since 1995; *b* 6 Sept. 1950; *s* of Henry Alfred Mills and Jean Margaret Aitchison; *m* 1974, Jean Marie Correia; one *s* three *d.* *Educ:* Highgate Sch.; The Queen's Coll., Oxford (MA, BLitt (Mod. Hist.)); Merton Coll., Oxford (Domus Sen. Schol.). Department of Trade and Industry, 1974–95: Private Sec. to Minister of State for Industry, 1976–78; seconded to Govt of Hong Kong as Principal Asst Sec. for CS, 1981–85; Asst Sec., 1986; Mem., Prime Minister's Policy Unit, 1989–92; Under Sec. and Dir of Consumer Affairs, OFT, 1992–95. Gov., Highgate Sch., 1993–. *Address:* County Hall, Truro, Cornwall TR1 3AY. *T:* Truro (01872) 322000.

MILLS, Sir John (Lewis Ernest Watts), Kt 1976; CBE 1960; Actor, Producer, Director; *b* 22 Feb. 1908; *m* 1941, Mary Hayley Bell, playwright; one *s* two *d.* *Educ:* Norwich. 1st appearance, stage, 1929. *Plays:* Cavalcade, London Wall, Words and Music, Five O'clock Girl, Give Me a Ring, Jill Darling, Floodlight, Red Night, We at the Cross Roads, Of Mice and Men, Men in Shadow, Duet for Two Hands, etc.; Old Vic Season, 1938; Top of the Ladder; Figure of Fun, Aldwych; Ross, New York, 1961; Power of Persuasion, Garrick, 1963; Veterans, Royal Court, 1972; At the End of the Day, Savoy, 1973; The Good Companions, Her Majesty's, 1974; Separate Tables, Apollo, 1977; Goodbye, Mr Chips, Chichester Fest., 1982; Little Lies, Wyndham's, 1983; The Petition, NT, (transf. Wyndham's) 1986; Pygmalion, Guildford and NY, 1987; When the Wind Blows (TV play), 1987. *Films:* The Midshipmaid, Britannia of Billingsgate, Brown on Resolution, OHMS, Cottage To Let, The Young Mr Pitt, We Dive at Dawn, In Which We Serve, The Way to the Stars, Great Expectations, So Well Remembered, The October Man, Scott of the Antarctic, The History of Mr Polly, The Rocking Horse Winner, Morning Departure, Mr Denning Drives North, Gentle Gunman, The Long Memory, Hobson's Choice, The Colditz Story, The End of the Affair, Above Us the Waves, Town on Trial, Escapade, Its Great to be Young, The Baby and the Battleship, War and Peace, Around the World in Eighty Days, Dunkirk, Ice Cold in Alex, I Was Monty's Double, Summer of the Seventeenth Doll, Tiger Bay, Swiss Family Robinson, The Singer not the Song, Tunes of Glory, Flame in the Streets, The Valiant, Tiara Tahiti, The Chalk Garden, The Truth about Spring, King Rat, Operation X Bow, Red Waggon, Sky West and Crooked (directed), The Wrong Box, The Family Way, Chuka, Showdown, Oh! What a Lovely War, The Return of the Boomerang, Ryan's Daughter (Best Supporting Actor Award, Oscar Award, 1971), Run Wild, Run Free, Emma Hamilton, Dulcima, Lamb, Young Winston, Oklahoma Crude, Trial by Combat, The Devil's Advocate, Great Expectations, The Big Sleep, Zulu Dawn, The 39 Steps, The Human Factor, Gandhi, Masks of Death, Murder with Mirrors, Who's That Girl?, Frankenstein, the Real Story, Deadly Advice. Tribute to Her Majesty (film documentary), 1986. *TV and TV series:* The Zoo Gang, 1974; Quatermass, 1979; Tales of the Unexpected, 1979, 1980, 1981; Young at Heart, 1980, 1981, 1982; The True Story of Spit MacPhee; A Tale of Two Cities; Ending Up; A Woman of Substance; Harnessing Peacocks, 1993; The Big Freeze; Martin Chuzzlewit, 1994. Member: SFTA (Vice-Pres.); RADA Council, 1965–; Chm., Stars Organization for Spastics, 1975–79. Pres., Mountview Theatre Sch., 1983–. Patron Life Mem., Variety Club. *Publications:* Up in the Clouds, Gentlemen Please (autobiog.), 1980; Book of Famous Firsts, 1984. *Recreations:* ski-ing, golf, painting. *Address:* c/o ICM, 76 Oxford Street, W1R 1RB. *Clubs:* Garrick, St James's.

MILLS, John Robert, BSc; CEng, FIEE; CPhys, MInstP; Under Secretary and Deputy Director (Systems) Royal Signals and Radar Establishment, Ministry of Defence, 1976–77, retired; *b* 12 Nov. 1916; *s* of Robert Edward Mills and Constance H. Mills; *m* 1950, Pauline Phelps; two *s*. *Educ:* Kingston Grammar Sch., Kingston-upon-Thames; King's Coll., London (BSc 1939); MInstP; FIEE, 1971. Air Ministry Research Estab., Dundee, 1939; RAE Farnborough, 1940–42; TRE, later RRE, Malvern, 1942–60; Supt (Offensive), Airborne Radar, RRE, 1954–60; Asst Dir, Electronics R and D (Civil Aviation), Min. of Aviation, 1960–61; Head of Radio Dept, RAE Farnborough, 1961–65; Electronics Div., Min. of Technology, 1965–67; Dir, Signals R&D Establishment, Christchurch, 1967–76. *Publications:* (jointly) Radar article in Encyclopædia Britannica; various papers in journals. *Address:* Meadowbank, Holly Green, Upton-upon-Severn, Worcester WR8 0PG.

MILLS, John William, OBE 1945; QC 1962; *b* 24 Oct. 1914; *s* of late John William Mills, OBE and Jessie Mills; *m* 1942, Phyllis Mary, *yr d* of late Arthur Gibson Pears; no *c*. *Educ:* Clifton; Corpus Christi Coll., Cambridge (MA). Called to Bar, Middle Temple, 1938; Bencher, 1968; Treas., 1985; retired 1987. Lt-Col, Royal Signals, 1944; Comdr, Royal Signals, 46 Div., 1944; Hon. Lt-Col 1946. Member: Bar Council, 1961–64; Clifton Coll. Council, 1967–80. *Publication:* (editor/author) Wurtzburg, Law Relating to Building Societies, subseq. Wurtzburg and Mills, Building Society Law, 10th edn 1952 to 14th edn 1988, Ed. Emeritus of 15th edn 1989. *Recreations:* sailing, golf. *Address:* 38 Adam and Eve Mews, W8 6UJ. *T:* 0171–937 1259; Greenleas, Highleigh, Chichester, Sussex PO20 7NP. *T:* Sidlesham (01243) 641396.

MILLS, Lawrence William Robert; Senior Advisor, United Nations Development Programme; Managing Partner, Oscar, Mills & Associates, since 1994; *b* London, 7 May 1934; *m* 1992, Amira Hamdy (*née* Elsayed); two *d* by previous marriage. *Educ:* Reigate Grammar Sch., Surrey. National Service: RN, 1953; Intell. Corps, 1954. Formerly, Jun. Exec., K. F. Mayer Ltd, London. Hong Kong Govt (Mem. of HMOCS): Exec. Officer, Cl. II, 1958; Asst Trade Officer, 1960; Trade Officer, 1964; Sen. Trade Officer, 1968; Principal Trade Officer, 1969; Asst Dir of Commerce and Industry, 1971; Chief Trade Negotiator, 1974–75, 1977–79, 1981–83; Counsellor (Hong Kong Affairs), UK Mission, Geneva, 1976–77; Director of Trade, Hong Kong, 1977–79, 1981–83; Comr of Industry, 1979–81; Regional Sec., Hong Kong and Kowloon, 1983; Official MLC, Hong Kong, 1983; retired from Hong Kong Govt Service, 1983. Chief Exec., Laws Fashion Knitters Ltd, Hong Kong and Sri Lanka, 1983–85. Dir Gen., Fedn of Hong Kong Industries, 1985–89. Chief Exec., Dubai Commerce and Tourism Promotion Board, 1989–93. *Recreation:* music (classical jazz). *Address:* c/o 19 Bancroft Court, Reigate RH2 7RW. *Clubs:* Naval and Military; Hong Kong, Hong Kong Country (Hong Kong).

MILLS, Leif Anthony, CBE 1995; General Secretary, Banking, Insurance and Finance Union (formerly National Union of Bank Employees), since 1972; *b* 25 March 1936; *s* of English father and Norwegian mother; *m* 1958, Gillian Margaret Smith; two *s* two *d*. *Educ:* Balliol Coll., Oxford. MA Hons PPE. Commnd in Royal Military Police, 1957–59. Trade Union Official, Nat. Union of Bank Employees, 1960–: Research Officer, 1960; Asst Gen. Sec., 1962; Dep. Gen. Sec., 1968. Mem. various arbitration tribunals; Member: TUC Non-Manual Workers Adv. Cttee, 1967–72; TUC Gen. Council, 1983– (Pres., 1994–95); Office of Manpower Economics Adv. Cttee on Equal Pay, 1971; Monopolies and Mergers Commn, 1982–91; Financial Reporting Council, 1990–; Chairman: TUC Financial Services Cttee, 1983–; TUC Educn and Training Cttee, 1989–94. Member: Cttee to Review the Functioning of Financial Institutions, 1977–80; CS Pay Res. Unit Bd, 1978–81; BBC Consultative Gp on Social Effects of Television, 1978–80; Armed Forces Pay Review Body, 1980–87; Council, NCVQ, 1992–; Bd, Investors in People, 1992–. Contested (Lab) Salisbury, 1964, 1965 (by-elecn). Mem. Governing Body, London Business Sch., 1988–92. Trustee, Civic Trust, 1988–. FRGS 1992. *Publications:* biography (unpublished), Cook: A History of the Life and Explorations of Dr Frederick Albert Cook, SPRI ms 883, Cambridge, 1970. *Recreations:* rowing, chess. *Address:* 31 Station Road, West Byfleet, Surrey KT14 6DR. *T:* Byfleet (019323) 42829. *Clubs:* United Oxford & Cambridge University; Oxford University Boat, Weybridge Rowing.

MILLS, Leonard Sidney, CB 1970; Deputy Director General (2), Highways, Department of the Environment, 1970–74; *b* 20 Aug. 1914; *s* of late Albert Edward Mills; *m* 1940, Kathleen Joyce Cannicott; two *s*. *Educ:* Devonport High Sch.; London Sch. of Economics; Birkbeck Coll., University of London. Entered Exchequer and Audit Dept, 1933; transferred to Min. of Civil Aviation, 1946; Asst Sec., 1950; Min. of Transport: Under-Sec., 1959; Chief of Highway Administration, 1968–70. Commonwealth Fund Fellow, 1953–54. *Recreations:* walking, croquet, photography, gardening. *Address:* Pine Rise, 7A Bedlands Lane, Budleigh Salterton, Devon EX9 6QH.

MILLS, Mary Bell McMillan, (Mrs Ian Mills); *see* MacMurray, M. B. McM.

MILLS, Rt. Rev. Murray John; *see* Waiapu, Bishop of.

MILLS, Neil McLay; Chairman, Sedgwick Group plc, 1979–84; *b* 29 July 1923; *yr s* of late L. H. Mills; *m* 1950, Rosamund Mary Kimpton, *d* of Col and Hon. Mrs A. C. W. Kimpton; two *s* two *d*. *Educ:* Epsom Coll.; University Coll. London. Served War, 1940–46: commnd RN; Lieut RNVR; Coastal Forces (mentioned in despatches, 1944). Joined Bland Welch & Co. Ltd, 1948; Exec. Dir, 1955; Chm., 1965–74; Chm., Bland Payne Holdings Ltd, 1974–79. Underwriting Mem. of Lloyd's, 1955–91. Director: Montagu Trust Ltd, 1966–74; Midland Bank Ltd, 1974–79; Wadlow Grosvenor International Ltd, 1984–88; Threadneedle Publishing Co. (formerly AVI Ltd), 1987–93. Vice-President: Insurance Inst. of London, 1971–84; British Insurance Brokers Assoc., 1978–84 (Mem., Internat. Insurance Brokers Cttee); Mem. Cttee, Lloyd's Insurance Brokers Assoc., 1974–77. Member: Church Army Board, 1957–64 (Vice-Chm., 1959–64); Council, Oak Hill Theol Coll., 1958–62. Trustee and Governor, Lord Mayor Treloar Trust, 1975–81. *Recreations:* farming, mowing, cooking. *Address:* 23 Bury Walk, SW3 6QD. *T:* 0171–823 9636; The Dower House, Upton Grey, near Basingstoke, Hants RG25 2RY. *T:* Basingstoke (01256) 862435. *Club:* Pilgrims.

MILLS, Sir Peter (Frederick Leighton), 3rd Bt, *cr* 1921; *b* 9 July 1924; *s* of Major Sir Frederick Leighton Victor Mills, 2nd Bt, MC, RA, MICE, and Doris (*née* Armitage); *S* father 1955; *m* 1954, Pauline Mary, *d* of L. R. Allen, Calverton, Notts; one *s* (one adopted *d* decd). *Educ:* Eastbourne Coll.; Cedara Coll. of Agriculture, University of Natal (BSc Agric.). Served HM Forces, 1943–47. CS, Fedn Rhodesia and Nyasaland, 1953; with Rhodesia Min. of Agric., 1964, Zimbabwe Min. of Agric., 1980–90. *Heir:* *s* Michael Victor Leighton Mills [*b* 30 Aug. 1957; *m* 1981, Susan, *d* of J. Doig, Harare, Zimbabwe]. *Address:* PO Box A474, Avondale, Harare, Zimbabwe.

MILLS, Peter William; QC (Can.) 1985; Senior Vice President since 1988, General Counsel since 1980 and Director since 1982, The Woodbridge Company Limited (Vice President, 1980–87); *b* 22 July 1942; *s* of Joseph Roger Mills and Jane Eveyln (*née* Roscoe); *m* 1967, Eveline Jane (*née* Black); two *s*. *Educ:* Dalhousie Univ. Law Sch. (LLB); Dalhousie Univ. (BComm). Barrister and solicitor, Ont, Canada; with McInnes, Cooper and Robertson, Halifax, 1967; Solicitor, Canadian Pacific Ltd, Montreal and Toronto, 1967–71; Dir, Cammell Laird Shipbuilders Ltd, 1971–76; Mem. Org. Cttee for British Shipbuilders, 1976–77; Manager, Currie, Coopers & Lybrand Ltd, Toronto, 1977–79; Director: Corporate Develt, FP Publications Ltd, 1979–80; Augusta Newsprint Co., 1981–; Hudson's Bay Co., 1985–; Markborough Properties Inc., 1986–. *Recreations:* golf, sailing, travel, reading. *Address:* The Woodbridge Company Limited, 65 Queen Street West, Toronto, Ont M5H 2M8, Canada. *Fax:* (416) 367–3549; 390 Glencairn Avenue, Toronto, Ont M5N 1V1. *Clubs:* Board of Trade, York Downs Golf and Country (Toronto); Royal Liverpool Golf (Hoylake).

MILLS, Richard Michael; Chairman and Chief Executive, Delfont Mackintosh Theatres Ltd, since 1991; *b* 26 June 1931; *s* of Richard Henry Mills and Catherine Keeley; *m* 1st, 1960, Lynda Taylor (marr. diss. 1967); one *d*; 2nd, 1983, Sheila White; two *s*. Commenced working in the theatre as an Assistant Stage Manager in 1948, and worked in every capacity, including acting and stage management. Joined Bernard Delfont Ltd, 1962; Dir, 1967; Dep. Chm., 1970–79; Chm., 1979–91; Chief Exec., 1970–91; Managing Director: Prince of Wales Theatre, 1970–; Prince Edward Theatre, 1978–. Member: Nat. Theatre Bd, 1976–91; Finance and Gen. Purposes Cttee, NT, 1976–91; Drama Panel, Arts Council of GB, 1976–77; English Tourist Bd, 1982–85. Shows worked on in the West End, 1948–62, include: I Remember Mama, Tuppence Coloured, Medea, Adventure Story, Anne Veronica, The Devil's General, I Capture the Castle, No Escape, Three Times a Day, The Sun of York, To my Love, Be my Guest, Hunter's Moon, The Iceman Cometh, Brouhaha, Detour after Dark, The Ginger Man, Sound of Murder, Will You Walk a Little Faster, Pool's Paradise, Belle, Come Blow your Horn. Whilst Gen. Manager and Dir with Bernard Delfont Ltd: Never Too Late, Pickwick, 1962; Caligula, Maggie May, Little Me, Our Man Crichton, 1963; The Roar of the Greasepaint (NY), Pickwick (NY), Twang, Barefoot in the Park, 1964; The Owl and the Pussycat, The Matchgirls, Funny Girl, Joey Joey, The Odd Couple, 1965; Queenie, Sweet Charity, The Four Musketeers, 1966; Golden Boy, Look Back in Anger (revival), 1967; Mame, Cat Among the Pigeons, 1968; Carol Channing, Danny La Rue at the Palace, 1969; Kean, Lulu, 1970; Applause, The Unknown Soldier and his Wife, 1971. With Lord Delfont has presented in the West End: The Good Old Bad Old Days, Mardi Gras, Brief Lives, Queen Daniella, Cinderella, Henry IV, Harvey, Sammy Cahn's Songbook, Streetcar Named Desire, Good Companions, It's All Right if I Do It, Charley's Aunt, An Evening with Tommy Steele, Gomes, The Wolf, Danny La Rue Show, Beyond the Rainbow, Dad's Army, Plumber's Progress, Paul Daniels Magic Show, Underneath the Arches, Little Me, and over 100 pantomimes and summer season shows. *Recreations:* golf, poker. *Address:* Prince of Wales Theatre, Coventry Street, W1V 8AS. *T:* 0171–930 9901. *Clubs:* Royal Automobile; Royal Mid-Surrey Golf, Coombe Hill Golf.

MILLS, Robert Ferris; Under Secretary, Department of Finance and Personnel, Northern Ireland, since 1990; *b* 21 Sept. 1939; *s* of Robert and Rachel Mills; *m* 1st, 1968, Irene Sandra Miskelly (marr. diss. 1978); one *s* one *d*; 2nd, 1984, Frances Elizabeth Gillies; two step *d*. *Educ:* Sullivan Upper School, Holywood, Co. Down; Queen's Univ., Belfast (BA Hons). Inland Revenue, 1961–64; Min. of Commerce, NI, 1964–68; Dept of Housing and Local Govt, 1968–71; Dept of the Environment, NI, 1971–75; Asst Sec., 1975–83, Under Sec., 1983–90, Dept of Health and Social Services, NI. *Recreations:* golf, tennis. *Address:* Parliament Buildings, Belfast. *Club:* Helen's Bay Golf.

MILLS, Air Cdre Stanley Edwin Druce, CB 1968; CBE 1959; Royal Air Force, retired; *b* 1913; *s* of Edwin J. Mills; *m* 1938, Joan Mary, *d* of Robert Ralph James; one *s* one *d*. *Educ:* Collegiate Sch., Bournemouth, RAF Staff Coll. Entered RAF 1939; served RAF Middle East and Italy, 1942–45; Station Comdr, RAF Innsworth, 1957–60; Comd Accountant, RAF Germany, 1960–63; Dir of Personnel (Policy) (Air), MoD, 1963–65; Dir of Personal Services (Air), MoD, 1966–68. Bursar, Roedean Sch., 1968–73. FCA. *Recreation:* travel. *Address:* Maryland, Lullington Close, Seaford, E Sussex BN25 4JH. *T:* Seaford (01323) 895468. *Club:* Royal Air Force.

See also C. E. D. Chilvers.

MILLS, Stratton; *see* Mills, W. S.

MILLS, Tessa Jane Helen Douglas, (Mrs David Mills); *see* Jowell, T. J. H. D.

MILLS, (William) Stratton; Partner in Mills, Selig, Solicitors, Belfast; Company Director; Chairman, Hampden Group PLC (formerly Hampden Homecare plc), since 1992; *b* 1 July 1932; *o s* of late Dr J. V. S. Mills, CBE, Resident Magistrate for City of Belfast, and Margaret Florence (*née* Byford); *m* 1959, Merriel E. R. Whitla, *o d* of late Mr and Mrs R. J. Whitla, Belfast; three *s*. *Educ:* Campbell Coll., Belfast; Queen's Univ., Belfast (LLB). Vice-Chm., Federation of University Conservative and Unionist Assocs, 1952–53 and 1954–55; admitted a Solicitor, 1958. MP (UU) Belfast N, Oct. 1959–Dec. 1972; MP (Alliance) Belfast N, Apr. 1973–Feb. 1974; PPS to Parly Sec., Ministry of Transport, 1961–64; Member: Estimates Cttee, 1964–70; Exec. Cttee, 1922 Cttee, 1967–70, 1973; Hon. Sec. Conservative Broadcasting Cttee, 1963–70, Chm., 1970–73; Mem., Mr Speaker's Conference on Electoral Law, 1967. Mem., One Nation Gp, 1972–73. Chm., Ulster Orchestra Soc. Ltd, 1980–90. Mem. Council, Winston Churchill Meml Trust, 1990–95. *Address:* (office) 20 Callender Street, Belfast BT1 5BQ. *T:* Belfast (01232) 243878; (home) 17 Malone Park, Belfast BT9 6NJ. *T:* Belfast (01232) 665210. *Clubs:* Carlton; Reform (Belfast).

MILLSON, John Albert; Assistant Under-Secretary of State, Ministry of Defence, 1972–78; *b* 4 Oct. 1918; *s* of late George Charles Millson and Annie Millson, London; *m* 1953, Megan Laura Woodiss; one *s* one *d*. *Educ:* St Olave's. Entered Air Min., 1936; Private Sec. to Parly Under-Sec. of State for Air, 1947–50; Principal, Air Min., 1955; Asst Sec., MoD, 1961; Asst Under-Sec. of State, 1972. Chm. of Governors, Homefield Prep. Sch., Sutton, 1975. *Recreations:* walking, listening to music. *Address:* 9 The Highway, Sutton, Surrey SM2 5QT. *T:* 0181–642 3967.

MILLSON, Tony; HM Diplomatic Service; Ambassador to Macedonia, since 1993; *b* 25 Nov. 1951; *s* of Donald Millson and Joan (*née* Whittle). *Educ:* Grimsby Wintringham Grammar Sch. Entered HM Diplomatic Service, 1970; MECAS, 1973; Third Sec. (Commercial), Tripoli, 1974–76; Third, later Second Sec. (Develt), Amman, 1976–80; FCO, 1980–83; Second Sec., BMG Berlin, 1983–86; First Sec., FCO, 1986–88; Hd of Chancery, Kuwait, 1988–90; FCO, 1991–93. *Recreations:* reading, listening to music, bridge. *Address:* c/o Foreign and Commonwealth Office, King Charles Street, SW1A 2AH.

MILMAN, Andrée, (Mrs David Milman); *see* Grenfell, A.

MILMAN, Lt-Col Sir Derek, 9th Bt *cr* 1800, of Levaton-in-Woodland, Devonshire; MC 1941; *b* 23 June 1918; *s* of Brig.-Gen. Sir Lionel Charles Patrick Milman, 7th Bt, CMG and Marjorie Aletta (*d* 1980), *d* of Col A. H. Clark-Kennedy; *S* brother, 1990; *m* 1942, Margaret Christine Whitehouse; two *s*. *Educ:* Bedford School; Sandhurst. Commnd Unattached List IA, 1938; joined 3/2nd Punjab Regt, 1939; served War of 1939–45, Eritrea (MC, despatches), N Africa, Burma; with Pakistan Army, 1947–50; joined 1st Bn Beds and Herts Regt, 1950; Instructor, RMA Sandhurst, 1957; comd 5th Beds TA, 1959–61; retired, 1963. Instructor, Civil Defence Staff Coll. , 1963–68; London Business

School, 1970–83. *Recreation:* bird watching. *Heir: s* David Patrick Milman [*b* 24 Aug. 1945; *m* 1969, Christina Hunt; one *s* one *d*].

MILMINE, Rt. Rev. Douglas, CBE 1983; an Assistant Bishop, diocese of Chichester, since 1992; *b* 3 May 1921; *s* of Alexander Douglas Milmine and Rose Gertrude Milmine (*née* Moore); *m* 1945, Margaret Rosalind, *d* of Edward and Gladys Whitley, Kilmorie, Meadfoot, Torquay; three *s* one *d*. *Educ:* Sutton Valence School; St Peter's Hall, Oxford (MA 1946); Clifton Theological Coll. RAFVR, 1941–45; POW, 1943–45. Deacon 1947, priest 1948; Curate: SS Philip and James, Ilfracombe, 1947–50; St Paul's, Slough, 1950–53; missionary with South American Missionary Society: Maquehue, Chile, 1954; Temuco, 1955–60; Santiago, 1961–68; Archdeacon of N Chile, Bolivia and Peru, 1964–68; Hon. Canon of Chile, 1969–72; Midland Area Sec. of SAMS, 1969–72; Bishop in Paraguay, 1973–85; retired 1986. *Publications:* Stiff Upper Smile (autobiog.), 1993; La Comunión Anglicana en América Latina, 1993. *Recreations:* study of current affairs, walking. *Address:* 1c Clive Court, 24 Grand Parade, Eastbourne, East Sussex BN21 3DD. *T:* Eastbourne (01323) 734159.

MILMO, John Boyle Martin; QC 1984; a Recorder of the Crown Court, since 1982; *b* 19 Jan. 1943; *s* of late Dermod Hubert Francis Milmo, MB BCh and of Eileen Clare Milmo (*née* White). *Educ:* Downside Sch.; Trinity Coll., Dublin. MA, LLB. Called to the Bar, Lincoln's Inn, 1966, Bencher, 1992. Mem., Bar Council, 1992–. *Recreations:* opera, discography. *Address:* 1 High Pavement, Nottingham NG1 1HF. *T:* Nottingham (0115) 941 8218. *Club:* United Services (Nottingham).

MILMO, Patrick Helenus; QC 1985; *b* 11 May 1938; *s* of Sir Helenus Milmo; *m* 1968, Marina, *d* of late Alexis Schiray and of Xenia Schiray, rue Jules Simon, Paris; one *s* one *d*. *Educ:* Downside; Trinity Coll., Cambridge (BA 1961). Harmsworth Scholar; called to the Bar, Middle Temple, 1962, Bencher, 1994. *Recreations:* wine, horse-racing, cinema. *Address:* 5 Raymond Buildings, Gray's Inn, WC1R 5BP; 7 Baalbec Road, N5. *Club:* Lansdowne.

MILNE, family name of **Baron Milne.**

MILNE, 2nd Baron, *cr* 1933, of Salonika and of Rubislaw, Co. Aberdeen; **George Douglass Milne,** TD; *b* 10 Feb. 1909; *s* of 1st Baron Milne, GCB, GCMG, DSO, Field Marshal from 1928, and Claire Marjoribanks, MBE, DGStJ (*d* 1970), *d* of Sir John N. Maitland, 5th Bt; *S* father, 1948; *m* 1940, Cicely, 3rd *d* of late Ronald Leslie; two *s* one *d*. *Educ:* Winchester; New Coll., Oxford. Mem., Inst. of Chartered Accountants of Scotland. Partner, Arthur Young McClelland Moores Co., 1954–73; Dir, London & Northern Group Ltd, 1973–87 (Dep. Chm., 1981). Master of the Grocers' Company, 1961–62, Sen. Court Mem., 1984–90. Served War of 1939–45, Royal Artillery (TA); prisoner of war, 1941; NWEF and MEF (wounded, despatches). *Recreation:* art: has exhibited RA, ROI, RP. *Heir: s* Hon. George Alexander Milne, *b* 1 April 1941. *Address:* 33 Lonsdale Road, Barnes, SW13 9JP. *T:* 0181–748 6421.

MILNE, Alasdair David Gordon; Director-General, BBC, 1982–87; *b* 8 Oct. 1930; *s* of late Charles Gordon Shaw Milne and of Edith Reid Clark; *m* 1954, Sheila Kirsten Graucob (*d* 1992); two *s* one *d*. *Educ:* Winchester Coll.; New Coll., Oxford (Hon. Fellow, 1985). Commnd into 1st Bn Gordon Highlanders, 1949. Hon. Mods Oxon 1952; BA Oxon Mod. Langs, 1954. Joined BBC, 1954; Dep. Editor, 1957–61, Editor, 1961–62, of Tonight Programme; Head of Tonight Productions, 1963–65; Partner, Jay, Baverstock, Milne & Co., 1965–67; rejoined BBC, Oct. 1967; Controller, BBC Scotland, 1968–72; Dir of Programmes, 1973–77, Man. Dir, 1977–82, BBC TV; Dep. Dir-Gen., BBC, 1980–82. Chm., Darrell Waters Ltd, 1988–90. Vis. Prof., Univ. of Miami, 1989. Vice-Pres., RTS, 1986–87. DUniv Stirling, 1983. Cyril Bennett Award, RTS, 1987. *Publication:* DG: the memoirs of a British broadcaster, 1988. *Recreations:* piping, salmon fishing, golf, tennis. *Address:* 30 Holland Park Avenue, W11 3QU. *Club:* Travellers'.

MILNE, (Alexander) Berkeley, OBE 1968; HM Diplomatic Service, retired; *b* 12 Feb. 1924; *s* of George and Mary Milne; *m* 1952, Patricia Mary (*née* Holderness); one *s* two *d*. *Educ:* Keith Grammar and Buckie High Schs, Banffshire, Scotland; Univ. of Aberdeen (MA (Hons Mental Phil.) 1943); University Coll., Oxford (BA (Hons Persian and Arabic) 1949). 3/2nd Punjab Regt, Indian Army: service in India and Java, 1943–46. Scarborough Schol., Tehran Univ., 1950–51; Lectr in Persian, Edinburgh Univ., 1951–52. Foreign Office, 1952–53; BMEO, Cyprus, 1953–54; Third, later Second Sec., Tehran, 1954–57; FO, 1958–61; Second, later First Sec., Brussels, 1961–64; FO (later FCO), 1964–65; First Sec., British Residual Mission, Salisbury, Rhodesia, 1966–67; First Sec., Jedda, Saudi Arabia, 1968–70; FCO, 1971–74; Counsellor, Tehran, 1974–77; GCHQ, 1978–83. Consultant, Oman Govt, 1983–86. *Recreations:* gardening, reading; playing chamber music, preferably second violin in string quartets. *Address:* 3 Paragon Terrace, Cheltenham, Glos GL53 7LA. *T:* Cheltenham (01242) 234849.

MILNE, Berkeley; *see* Milne, A. B.

MILNE, David Calder; QC 1987; FCA; a Recorder, since 1994; *b* 22 Sept. 1945; *s* of late Ernest and of Helena Milne; *m* 1978, Rosemary (*née* Bond); one *d*. *Educ:* Harrow Sch.; Oxford Univ. (MA). ACA 1969; FCA 1974. Articled to Whinney Murray & Co., chartered accountants, 1966–69; called to Bar, Lincoln's Inn, 1970. Treas., London Common Law and Commercial Bar Assoc., 1975–88; Mem., Taxation and Retirement Benefit Cttee, Bar Council, 1978–. *Recreations:* natural history, music, golf, Rugby. *Address:* (chambers) 16 Bedford Row, WC1R 4EB. *T:* 0171–414 8080. *Clubs:* Garrick, Hurlingham, Gnomes; Walton Heath Golf.

MILNE, Denys Gordon, (Tiny), CBE 1982; *b* 12 Jan. 1926; *s* of late Dr George Gordon Milne and of Margaret (*née* Campbell); *m* 1951, Pamela Mary Senior; two *s* one *d*. *Educ:* Epsom Coll.; Brasenose Coll., Oxford (MA Hons Mod. History). Pilot Officer, RAF Regt, RAFVR, 1944–47. Colonial Admin. Service, Northern Nigeria, 1951–55; British Petroleum Company, 1955–81, retired as Man. Dir and Chief Exec., BP Oil Ltd; Dir, Business in the Community, 1981–84. Director: Silkolene Lubricants Plc, 1981–91; Fluor Daniel Ltd (formerly Fluor (GB)), 1981–90; The Weir Group Plc, 1983–92. Member: Scottish Economic Council, 1978–81; Adv. Cttee on Energy Conservation, 1980–81. President: UK Petroleum Industry Assoc., 1980–81; Inst. of Petroleum, 1978–80. Chm., Horder Centre for Arthritis, 1983–. Trustee, Nat. Motor Mus., 1979–89. Chm. Council, Epsom Coll., 1990–. Trustee and Dep. Chm., Centre for Southern African Studies, York Univ., 1990–. Mem., Court of Assistants, Tallow Chandlers' Co., 1986– (Master, 1993–94). *Recreations:* gardening, cruising. *Address:* Westbury, Old Lane, St Johns, Crowborough, East Sussex TN6 1RX. *T:* Crowborough (01892) 652634. *Clubs:* Caledonian, Royal Air Force; Inanda (Johannesburg).

MILNE, Maj.-Gen. Douglas Graeme; retired; Civilian Medical Officer, Ministry of Defence, 1979–84; Deputy Director General Army Medical Services, 1975–78; *b* 19 May 1919; *s* of George Milne and Mary Panton; *m* 1944, Jean Millicent Gove; one *d*. *Educ:* Robert Gordon's Coll.; Aberdeen Univ. MB, ChB, FFCM, DPH. Commnd into RAMC, 1943; service in W Africa, Malta, Egypt, BAOR, Singapore; Dir of Army Health and Research, 1973–75. QHS 1974–78. Col Comdt, RAMC, 1979–84. OStJ 1976. *Recreations:* gardening, reading. *Address:* 17 Stonehill Road, SW14 8RR.

MILNE, Ian Innes, CMG 1965; OBE 1946; a Senior Clerk, House of Commons, 1969–76; *b* 16 June 1912; *e s* of Kenneth John Milne, CBE, and Maud Innes; *m* 1939, Marie Mange (*d* 1989); one *d*. *Educ:* Westminster Sch.; Christ Church, Oxford. Advertising, 1935–40; RE, 1940–46 (Lieut-Col). FO, 1946–68; 2nd Sec., Teheran, 1948–51; 1st Sec., Berne, 1955–56; 1st Sec., Tokyo, 1960–63; retired 1968. US Legion of Merit (Off.), 1946. *Recreations:* gardening, music. *Address:* Red Willows, Urgashay, Yeovil, Somerset BA22 8HH.

MILNE, James L.; *see* Lees-Milne.

MILNE, Sir John (Drummond), Kt 1986; Chairman, Alfred McAlpine plc, since 1992; *b* 13 Aug. 1924; *s* of Frederick John and Minnie Elizabeth Milne; *m* 1948, Joan Akroyd; two *s* two *d*. *Educ:* Stowe Sch.; Trinity Coll., Cambridge. Served Coldstream Guards, 1943–47. APCM (now Blue Circle Industries): management trainee, 1948; Asst to Director i/c Overseas Investments, 1953; President, Ocean Cement, Vancouver, 1957; Director, APCM, 1964, Man. Dir and Chief Exec., 1975; Blue Circle Industries: Chm. and Managing Director, 1983; Chm., 1983–90 (non-exec., 1987–90). DRG plc (formerly The Dickinson Robinson Group): Dir, 1973–89; Chm., 1987–89; Director: Royal Insurance, 1982–95; Witan Investment Co., 1988–; Avon Rubber, 1989–95; Solvay & Cie SA, 1990–. *Recreations:* golf, shooting. *Address:* Chilton House, Chilton Candover, Hants SO24 9TX. *Clubs:* Boodle's, MCC; Berkshire Golf.

MILNE, Kenneth Lancelot, CBE 1971; chartered accountant; *b* 16 Aug. 1915; *s* of F. K. Milne, Adelaide; *m* 1st, 1941, Mary (*d* 1980), *d* of E. B. Hughes; two *s* one *d*; 2nd, 1982, Joan Constance Lee, *d* of Claude W. J. Lee. *Educ:* St Peter's Coll., Adelaide. Entered Public Practice as a Chartered Acct, 1946; Elected to State Council, 1951, Chm. 1958–60, Mem. Gen. Council, 1956–60. Served with RAAF, 1940–45, attaining rank of Flt Lieut. Municipality of Walkerville: Councillor, 1960; Mayor, 1961–63; Municipal Assoc. 1961–65 (Pres. 1964–65); Pres. SA Br Aust. Inst. of Internat. Affairs, 1958–60; Mem. Faculty of Economics, University of Adelaide, 1963–65; Agent Gen. and Trade Comr for S Aust. in UK, 1966–71. MLC (Australian Democrat) SA, 1979–85 (Parlt Leader, 1983–85). President: SA Branch, Royal Overseas League, 1975–; Royal Life Saving Soc. of SA, 1977–. Chm., State Govt Insce Commn, 1971–79; Member: Commn on Advanced Educn, 1973–77; Universities Commn, 1977. Chm., Stirling Dist Bicentennary Cttee, SA, 1987–89. Freeman, City of London, 1970. *Publications:* Ostrich Heads, 1937; Forgotten Freedom, 1952; The Accountant in Public Practice, 1959. *Recreations:* rowing, tennis, conchology. *Address:* 50 Birch Road, Stirling, SA 5152, Australia. *T:* (8) 3393674. *Clubs:* Naval, Military and Air Force (Adelaide); Adelaide Rowing (Pres., 1986–) (SA).

MILNE, Maurice, CB 1976; FEng 1980; Deputy Director General of Highways, Department of the Environment, 1970–76; retired; *b* 22 July 1916; *s* of James Daniel Milne, stone mason, and Isabella Robertson Milne; *m* 1947, Margaret Elizabeth Stewart Monro; one *d* decd. *Educ:* Robert Gordon's Coll., Aberdeen; Aberdeen University. BScEng (1st cl. Hons). FICE, FIStructE, FIHT, FRTPI. Chief Asst, D. A. Donald & Wishart, Cons. Engrs, Glasgow, 1947–48; Sen. Engr and Chief Engr, Crawley Develt Corp., 1948–59; Engr, Weir Wood Water Board, 1953–57; County Engr and Surveyor, W Sussex CC, 1960–68; Dir, S Eastern Road Construction Unit, MoT, 1968–70. Chairman: Downland Housing Soc. Ltd, 1978–83; London and SE Region Anchor Housing Assoc., 1982–88. Trustee: Humane Research Trust, 1983– (Dep. Chm., 1992–94); Rees Jeffreys Road Fund, 1976–. (Chm., 1990–93). Hon. Sec., County Surveyors' Soc., 1963–67; Pres., Instn Highway Engineers, 1974–75; Mem. Council, ICE, 1967–71 and 1972–75; Pres., Perm. Internat. Assoc. of Road Congresses, 1977–84 (Hon. Pres., 1988–). *Publications:* contributions to Jl Instn of Civil, Municipal and Highway Engrs. *Recreations:* gardening, painting, photography. *Address:* Struan, Walton Lane, Bosham, Chichester, West Sussex PO18 8QB. *T:* Bosham (01243) 573304.

MILNE, Nanette Lilian Margaret, OBE 1994; JP; Councillor, City of Aberdeen District Council, since 1988; *b* 27 April 1942; *d* of Harold G. Gordon and Hannah L. C. Gordon (*née* Stephen); *m* 1965, Alan Ducat Milne; one *s* one *d*. *Educ:* Aberdeen High Sch. for Girls; Univ. of Aberdeen (MB ChB 1965). FFARCS 1969. Medical Officer, Grampian Health Board, later Aberdeen Royal Hospitals NHS Trust: anaesthetics, 1966–73; oncology research, 1980–92. Vice-Chm., Scottish Cons. and Unionist Party, 1989–93. JP Aberdeen, 1993. *Publications:* contrib. to BMJ on cardiovascular effects of laparoscopy and on colorectal cancer. *Recreations:* gardening, sports. *Address:* The Briars, Golfview Road, Bieldside, Aberdeen AB1 9AA. *T:* Aberdeen (01224) 867816.

MILNE, Norman; Sheriff of North Strathclyde at Campbeltown and Oban, 1975–81, retired; *b* 31 Dec. 1915; *s* of William Milne and Jessie Ferguson; *m* 1947, Phyllis Christina Philip Rollo; no *c*. *Educ:* Logie Central Sch., Dundee. Solicitor, 1939. Army, 1939–46: active service in Madagascar, Sicily, Italy, and Germany (despatches). Procurator Fiscal Depute: Perth, 1946–51; Edinburgh, 1951–55; Senior Depute Fiscal, Glasgow, 1955–58; Procurator Fiscal: Banff, 1959–64; Kirkcaldy, 1964–65; Paisley, 1965–71; Edinburgh, 1971–75. *Recreation:* music. *Address:* The Anchorage, Machrihanish, Argyll PA28 6PT.

MILNE, Peter Alexander, PhD; Eur Ing, CEng, FIMechE, FIMarE; Director, AMRIE, since 1994; *b* 23 April 1935; *s* of late Alexander Ogston Milne and of Lilian Winifred Milne (*née* Murray); *m* 1961, Beatrice Taylor Reid; two *d*. *Educ:* Tynemouth Sch.; Harwell Reactor Sch. BSc Marine Engrg Univ. of Durham 1957; PhD Applied Sci. Univ. of Newcastle 1960. Practical experience with apprenticeship at Wallsend Slipway & Engineering and at sea with Union Castle Mail Steamship; Trainee Manager, Swan Hunter Gp, 1961; Technical Dir, Swan Hunter Shipbuilders, 1970–74, Man. Dir, 1974–77; British Shipbuilders HQ at formation of Corp., 1977; Man. Dir, Shipbuilding Ops, 1978–80, Mem. Bd, 1981–90 (Bd Mem. for Engrg, 1981–83, for Merchant Ship and Enginebuilding, 1985–90), Man. Dir, Merchant and Composite Div., 1984, British Shipbuilders; Man. Dir, BMT Cortec, 1990–94. Dir, Vosper Thornycroft, 1978–80. Bd Mem., SMRTB, 1971–75; Chm., BSI Ind. Cttee, 1972–76; Dir, Lloyds Register of Shipping, 1984–91; Chm., Northern Engrg Centre, 1990–94. Vis. Lectr in Marine Engrg, Newcastle Univ., 1970–75. Pres., NECInst, 1986–88. Liveryman, Shipwrights' Co., 1984–. *Publications:* papers related to science and industry. *Recreations:* squash, cricket. *Address:* 14 Woodland Close, Earsdon Village, Whitley Bay, Tyne and Wear NE25 9LL. *T:* 0191–252 2708.

MILNE HOME, John Gavin, TD; FRICS; Lord-Lieutenant of Dumfries and Galloway, 1988–91 (Vice-Lord-Lieutenant, 1983–88); *b* 20 Oct. 1916; *s* of Sir John Hepburn Milne Home and Lady (Mary Adelaide) Milne Home; *m* 1942, Rosemary Elwes; two *s* one *d*. *Educ:* Wellington College; Trinity College, Cambridge. BA Estate Management. Served with King's Own Scottish Borderers (4th Bn), 1939–45 (TA 1938–49); Factor for Buccleuch Estates Ltd and Duke of Buccleuch on part of Scottish estates, 1949–74; Mem., Dumfries County Council, 1949–75; DL Dumfries 1970. *Recreations:* fishing and shooting. *Address:* Kirkside of Middlebie, Lockerbie, Dumfriesshire DG11 3JW. *T:* Ecclefechan (01576) 300204.

MILNE-WATSON, Sir Michael, 3rd Bt *cr* 1937; Kt 1969; CBE 1953; MA; *b* 16 Feb. 1910; *yr s* of Sir David Milne-Watson, 1st Bt, and Olga Cecily (*d* 1952), *d* of Rev. George Herbert; *S* brother, 1982; *m* 1940, Mary Lisette (*d* 1993), *d* of late H. C. Bagnall, Auckland, New Zealand; one *s*. *Educ:* Eton; Balliol Coll., Oxford. Served War of 1939–45. RNVR, 1943–45. Joined Gas Light & Coke Co., 1933; Managing Dir, 1945; Governor, 1946–49; Chairman: North Thames Gas Board, 1949–64; Richard Thomas & Baldwins Ltd, 1964–67; The William Press Group of Companies, 1969–74; a Dep. Chm., BSC, 1967–69 (Mem. Organizing Cttee, 1966–67); Mem., Iron and Steel Adv. Cttee, 1967–69. Director: Industrial and Commercial Finance Corp. Ltd, 1963–80; Commercial Union Assurance Co. Ltd, 1968–81; Finance for Industry Ltd, 1974–80; Finance Corp. for Industry Ltd, 1974–80; Rose Thomson Young (Underwriting) Ltd, 1982–87. President: Soc. of British Gas Industries Guild, 1970–71; Pipeline Industries Guild, 1971–72. Vice-Pres., BUPA, 1981– (Chm., 1976–81). Liveryman, Grocers' Co., 1947. Governor: Council, Reading Univ., 1971–82 (Pres., 1975–80); *Heir: s* Andrew Michael Milne-Watson [*b* 10 Nov. 1944; *m* 1st, 1970, Beverley Jane Gabrielle (marr. diss. 1981), *e d* of Philip Cotton, Majorca; one *s* one *d*; 2nd, 1983, Gisella Tisdall; one *s*]. *Address:* 39 Cadogan Place, SW1X 9RX; The Stables, Oakfield, Mortimer, Berks RG7 3AJ. *T:* Burghfield Common (01734) 832373. *Clubs:* Athenæum, MCC; Leander.

MILNER, family name of **Baron Milner of Leeds.**

MILNER OF LEEDS, 2nd Baron, *cr* 1951; **Arthur James Michael Milner,** AE 1952; Consultant, Gregory, Rowcliffe & Milners (formerly Milners, Curry & Gaskell), Solicitors, London, since 1988 (Partner, 1953–88); *b* 12 Sept. 1923; *o s* of 1st Baron Milner of Leeds, PC, MC, TD and Lois Tinsdale (*d* 1982), *d* of Thomas Brown, Leeds; *S* father, 1967; *m* 1951, Sheila Margaret, *d* of Gerald Hartley, Leeds; one *s* one *d* (and one *d* decd). *Educ:* Oundle; Trinity Hall, Cambridge (MA). Served: RAFVR, 1942–46, Flt Lt; 609 (W Riding) Sqn, RAuxAF, 1947–52, Flt Lt. Admitted Solicitor, 1951. Opposition Whip, House of Lords, 1971–74. Member: Jt Cttee on Consolidation Bills, 1982–92; Select Cttees on Private Bills, 1990–93. Member: Clothworkers' Co.; Pilgrims; Hon. Treas, Soc. of Yorkshiremen in London, 1967–70. *Heir: s* Hon. Richard James Milner [*b* 16 May 1959; *m* 1988, Margaret, *y d* of G. F. Voisin; two *d*]. *Address:* 2 The Inner Court, Old Church Street, SW3 5BY. *Club:* Royal Air Force.

MILNER, Prof. Arthur John Robin Gorell, FRS 1988; FRSE; Professor of Computer Science, and Fellow of King's College, Cambridge University, since 1995; *b* 13 Jan. 1934; *s* of John Theodore Milner and Muriel Emily (*née* Barnes-Gorell); *m* 1963, Lucy Petronella Moor; two *s* one *d*. *Educ:* Eton Coll.; King's Coll., Cambridge (BA Maths, 1957). FRSE 1993. Maths teacher, Marylebone Grammar Sch., 1959–60; Ferranti Ltd, London, 1960–63; Lectr in Maths and Computing, City Univ., London, 1963–68; Research Fellow: University Coll., Swansea, 1968–70; Artificial Intelligence Lab., Stanford Univ., Calif, 1970–72; Edinburgh University: Lectr, 1973–75; Sen. Lectr, 1975–78; Reader, 1978–84; Prof. of Computation Theory, 1984–94. Founder Mem., Academia Europaea, 1988. Hon. DSc(Eng) Chalmers Univ., Gothenburg, Sweden, 1988. A. M. Turing Award, ACM, 1991. *Publications:* Calculus for Communication and Concurrency, 1989; The Definition of Standard ML, 1990; Commentary on Standard ML, 1990; contribs to Computer Science on mechanised logic of computation and on calculus of communicating systems. *Recreations:* music, carpentry, walking. *Address:* 24 Lyndewode Road, Cambridge CB1 2HN.

MILNER, Prof. Brenda (Atkinson), OC 1984; OQ 1985; FRS 1979, FRSC 1976; Professor of Psychology, Department of Neurology and Neurosurgery, McGill University, since 1970; Head of Neuropsychology Research Unit, Montreal Neurological Institute, 1970–91; *b* 15 July 1918; *d* of Samuel Langford and Clarice Frances Leslie (*née* Doig). *Educ:* Univ. of Cambridge (BA, MA, ScD); McGill Univ. (PhD). Experimental Officer, Min. of Supply, 1941–44; Professeur Agrégé, Inst. de Psychologie, Univ. de Montréal, 1944–52; Res. Associate, Psychology Dept, McGill Univ., 1952–53; Lectr, 1953–60, Asst Prof., 1960–64, Associate Prof., 1964–70, Dept of Neurology and Neurosurgery, McGill Univ. Dorothy J. Killam Prof., Montreal Neurological Inst., 1993. Hon. LLD Queen's Univ., Kingston, Ont, 1980; Hon. DSc: Manitoba, 1982; Lethbridge, 1986; Mount Holyoke, 1986; Toronto, 1987; McGill, 1991; Wesleyan, 1991; Acadia, 1991; St Andrews, 1992; Hon. DScSoc Laval, 1987; Hon. Dr Montreal, 1988; Hon. DHumL Mount St Vincent, 1988. Izaak Walton Killam Prize, Canada Council, 1983; Hermann von Helmholtz Prize, Inst. for Cognitive Neuroscience, USA, 1984; Ralph W. Gerard Prize, Soc. for Neuroscience, 1987; Wilder Penfield Prize, PQ, 1993. Grand Dame of Merit, Order of Malta, 1985. *Publications:* mainly articles in neurological and psychological jls. *Address:* Montreal Neurological Institute, 3801 University Street, Montreal, Quebec H3A 2B4, Canada. *T:* (514) 3988503, *Fax:* (514) 3988540.

MILNER, Sir (George Edward) Mordaunt, 9th Bt *cr* 1716; *b* 7 Feb. 1911; *er s* of Brig.-Gen. G. F. Milner, CMG, DSO; *S* cousin (Sir William Frederick Victor Mordaunt Milner, 8th Bt) 1960; *m* 1st, 1935, Barbara Audrey (*d* 1951), *d* of Henry Noel Belsham, Hunstanton, Norfolk; two *s* one *d*; 2nd, 1953, Katherine Moodie Bisset, *d* of D. H. Hoey, Dunfermline. *Educ:* Oundle. Served War of 1939–45, Royal Artillery. Stipendiary Steward, Jockey Club of South Africa, 1954–59; Steward, Cape Turf Club, 1959–75; Steward, Jockey Club of SA, 1977–80. Mem. Council, Thoroughbred Breeders Assoc., 1975–82. *Publications:* Thoroughbred Breeding: notes and comments, 1987; Sons of the Desert, 1987; The Godolphin Arabian, 1989; *novels:* Inspired Information, 1959; Vaulting Ambition, 1962; The Last Furlong, 1965. *Heir: s* Timothy William Lycett Milner, *b* 11 Oct. 1936. *Address:* Natte Valleij, Klapmuts, Cape, S Africa. *T:* 02211–5171. *Clubs:* Rand (Johannesburg); Jockey Club of SA.

MILNER, Joseph, CBE 1975; QFSM 1962; Chief Officer of the London Fire Brigade, 1970–76; *b* 5 Oct. 1922; *e s* of Joseph and Ann Milner; *m* 1943, Bella Grice (*d* 1976), *e d* of Frederick George Flinton; one *s* one *d*; *m* 1976, Anne Cunningham, *e d* of J. Cunningham. *Educ:* Ladybarn Sch., Manchester. Served King's Regt (Liverpool), 1940–46: India/Burma, 1943–46 (Wingate's Chindits). Nat. Fire Service, 1946–48; North Riding Fire Bde, 1948–50; Manchester Fire Bde, 1950–51; Hong Kong Fire Bde, 1951–60; Dep. Dir, Hong Kong Fire Services, 1961–65; Dir, Hong Kong Fire Services, and Unit Controller, Auxiliary Fire Service, 1965–70. Mem., Hong Kong Council, Order of St John, 1965–70; JP Hong Kong, 1965–70. Regional Fire Commander (designate), London, 1970–76. Mem. Bd, Fire Service College, 1970–76; Mem., Central Fire Brigades Adv. Council, 1970–76; Adviser, Nat. Jt Council for Local Authority Fire Brigades, 1970–76; Chm., London Fire Liaison Panel, 1970–76; Mem., London Local Adv. Cttee, IBA, 1974–78; Fire Adviser, Assoc. of Metrop. Authorities, 1970–76. Vice-President: Fire Services Nat. Benevolent Fund (Chm., 1975–77); GLC Br., Royal British Legion, 1977–. Mem., Caston Parish Council, 1980–; Community Controller, Civil Defence, 1981–; Fellow, Instn of Fire Engineers, 1971; Associate Mem., Inst. of British Engineers, 1953; Associate, LCSP, 1987. OStJ 1971. *Recreations:* walking, poetry, hacking, horse management, remedial therapies, oil painting. *Address:* Lam Low, Caston, Attleborough, Norfolk NR17 1DD. *T:* Caston (01953) 483697. *Club:* Hong Kong (Hong Kong).

MILNER, Sir Mordaunt; *see* Milner, Sir G. E. M.

MILNER, Ralph; *see* Millner, Ralph.

MILNER, Rt. Rev. Ronald James; Bishop Suffragan of Burnley, 1988–93; Hon. Assistant Bishop, diocese of Southwell, since 1994; *b* 16 May 1927; *s* of Maurice and Muriel Milner; *m* 1950, Audrey Cynthia Howard; two *s* two *d* (and one *d* decd). *Educ:* Hull Grammar School; Pembroke Coll., Cambridge (MA); Wycliffe Hall, Oxford. Succentor, Sheffield Cathedral, 1953–58; Vicar: Westwood, Coventry, 1958–64; St James, Fletchamstead, Coventry, 1964–70; Rector of St Mary's, Southampton, 1970–73; Rector of the Southampton Team Ministry, 1973–83; Archdeacon of Lincoln, 1983–88. *Recreations:* ornithology, walking, music. *Address:* 7 Crafts Way, Southwell, Notts NG25 0BL.

MILNES, Rodney; *see* Blumer, Rodney Milnes.

MILNES COATES, Prof. Sir Anthony (Robert), 4th Bt *cr* 1911; BSc, MB BS, MD, MRCS, MRCP; Professor of Medical Microbiology, St George's Hospital Medical School, since 1990; *b* 8 Dec. 1948; *s* of Sir Robert Edward James Clive Milnes Coates, 3rd Bt, DSO, and of Lady Patricia Ethel, *d* of 4th Earl of Listowel; *S* father, 1982; *m* 1978, Harriet Ann Burton; one *s* two *d*. *Educ:* Eton; St Thomas's Hospital, London University. BSc; MRCS 1973; MB BS 1973; MRCP (UK) 1978; MD 1984. MRC Trng Res. Fellow, Dept of Bacteriology, RPMS, 1979–82; Sen. Registrar in Bacteriology, RPMS, 1982–84; Sen. Lectr (Hon. Consultant), Dept of Medical Microbiology, London Hosp. Medical Coll., 1984–90. *Heir: s* Thomas Anthony Milnes Coates, *b* 19 Nov. 1986. *Address:* Hereford Cottage, 135 Gloucester Road, SW7 4TH. *Club:* Brooks's.

MILNOR, (Margaret) Dusa; *see* McDuff, M. D.

MILOSLAVSKY, Dimitry T.; *see* Tolstoy, Dimitry.

MILOSZ, Czeslaw; poet, author; Professor of Slavic Languages and Literatures, University of California, Berkeley, 1961–78, now Emeritus; *b* Lithuania, 30 June 1911; naturalised US citizen, 1970; *s* of Aleksander and Weronika Milosz. *Educ:* High Sch., Wilno; Univ. of Wilno. MJuris 1934. Programmer, Polish Nat. Radio, 1935–39; Mem., Polish diplomatic service, Washington, Paris, 1945–50. Vis. Lectr, Univ. of Calif, Berkeley, 1960–61. Guggenheim Fellow, 1976. Member: Polish Inst. Letters and Scis in America; Amer. Acad. of Arts and Scis; PEN Club in Exile; Amer. Inst. of Arts and Letters. Hon. LittD Michigan, 1977; Hon. doctorates: Catholic Univ. of Lublin, 1981; Harvard Univ., 1989; Jagiellonian Univ., Krakow, 1989; Rome Univ., 1992. Prix Littéraire Européen, Les Guildes du Livre, Geneva, 1953; Neustadt Internat. Prize for Literature, Univ. of Oklahama, 1978; citation, Univ. of Calif, Berkeley, 1978; Nobel Prize for Literature, 1980. *Publications:* Poemat o czasie zastyglym (Poem on Time Frozen), 1933; Trzy zimy (Three Winters), 1936; Ocalenie (Rescue), 1945; Zniewolony umysl (The Captive Mind), 1953; Zdobycie wladzy, 1953, trans. as The Usurpers (in US as Seizure of Power), 1955; Dolina Issy, 1955, trans. as The Issa Valley, 1981; Swiatlo dzienne (Daylight), 1955; Traktat poetycki (Poetic Treatise), 1957; Rodzinna Europa, 1958, trans. as Native Realm, 1968; Postwar Polish Poetry, 1965; Widzenia nad Zatoka San Francisco (Views from San Francisco Bay), 1969; The History of Polish Literature, 1970; Prywatne obowiazki (Private Obligations), 1972; Selected Poems, 1973, rev. edn 1981; Ziemia Ulro (The Land of Ulro), 1977; Emperor of the Earth, 1977; Bells in Winter, 1978; Hymn o perle, 1982; Visions from San Francisco Bay, 1983; The Witness of Poetry, 1983; Separate Notebooks, 1984; The Land of Ulro, 1985; Unattainable Earth, 1986; Collected Poems, 1988; Provinces, 1991; Beginning With My Streets, 1992; A Year of the Hunter, 1994; Facing the River, 1995. *Address:* Department of Slavic Languages and Literatures, 5416 Dwinelle Hall, University of California, Berkeley, CA 94720, USA.

MILROY, Very Rev. Dominic Liston, OSB; MA; Headmaster, Ampleforth College, 1980–92; *b* 18 April 1932; *s* of Adam Liston Milroy and Clarita Burns. *Educ:* Ampleforth Coll.; St Benet's Hall, Oxford (1st Cl. Mod. Langs, MA). Entered Ampleforth Abbey, 1950; teaching staff, Ampleforth Coll., 1957–74; Head of Mod. Langs, 1963–74; Housemaster, 1964–74; Prior of Internat. Benedictine Coll. of S Anselmo, Rome, 1974–79. Chm., HMC, 1992. *Address:* c/o Ampleforth Abbey, York YO6 4EN. *T:* Ampleforth (01439) 788225.

MILSOM, Stroud Francis Charles; QC 1985; FBA 1967; Professor of Law, Cambridge University, 1976–90; Fellow of St John's College, Cambridge, since 1976; *b* 2 May 1923; *yr s* of late Harry Lincoln Milsom and Isobel Vida Collins; *m* 1955, Irène, *d* of late Witold Szereszewski, Wola Krysztoporska, Poland. *Educ:* Charterhouse; Trinity Coll., Cambridge. Admiralty, 1944–45. Called to the Bar, Lincoln's Inn, 1947, Hon. Bencher, 1970; Commonwealth Fund Fellow, Univ. of Pennsylvania, 1947–48; Yorke Prize, Univ. of Cambridge, 1948; Prize Fellow, Fellow and Lectr, Trinity Coll., Cambridge, 1948–55; Fellow, Tutor and Dean, New Coll., Oxford, 1956–64; Prof. of Legal History, London Univ., 1964–76. Selden Society: Literary Dir, 1964–80; Pres., 1985–88. Mem., Royal Commn on Historical Manuscripts, 1975–. Vis. Lectr, New York Univ. Law Sch., several times, 1958–70; Visiting Professor: Yale Law Sch., several times, 1968–; Harvard Law Sch. and Dept of History, 1973; Associate Fellow, Trumbull Coll., Yale Univ., 1974–; Charles Inglis Thomson Prof., Colorado Univ. Law Sch., 1977. Maitland Meml Lectr, Cambridge, 1972; Addison Harris Meml Lectr, Indiana Univ. Law Sch., 1974; Vis. Prof. and Wilfred Fullagar Lectr, Monash Univ., 1981; Ford's Lectr, Oxford, 1986; Carpentier Lectr, Columbia Univ., 1995. Foreign Mem., Amer. Phil Soc., 1984. Hon. LLD: Glasgow, 1981; Chicago, 1985. Ames Prize, Harvard, 1972; Swiney Prize, RSA/RCP, 1974. *Publications:* Novae Narrationes (introd., trans. and notes), 1963; introd. reissue Pollock and Maitland, History of English Law, 1968; Historical Foundations of the Common Law, 1969, 2nd edn 1981; The Legal Framework of English Feudalism, 1976; Studies in the History of the Common Law (collected papers), 1985. *Address:* St John's College, Cambridge CB2 1TP; 113 Grantchester Meadows, Cambridge CB3 9JN. *T:* Cambridge (01223) 354100. *Club:* Athenæum.

MILSTEIN, César, CH 1995; PhD; FRS 1975; Scientific Staff of Medical Research Council, since 1963; Fellow, Darwin College, University of Cambridge, 1981–95, now Emeritus; Head, Division of Protein and Nucleic Acid Chemistry, MRC Laboratory of Molecular Biology, 1983–94 (Joint Head of Department, 1981–83); *b* 8 Oct. 1927; *s* of Lázaro and Máxima Milstein; *m* 1953, Celia Prilleltensky. *Educ:* Colegio Nacional de Bahia Blanca; Univ. Nacional de Buenos Aires; Fitzwilliam Coll., Cambridge (Hon. Fellow 1982). Licenciado en Ciencias Quimicas 1952; Doctor en Quimica 1957; PhD Cantab 1960. British Council Fellow, 1958–60; Scientific Staff, MRC, Dept of Biochemistry, Cambridge Univ., 1960–61; Staff of Instituto Nacional de Microbiologia, Buenos Aires, 1957–63; Head of Div. de Biologia Molecular, 1961–63; Staff of MRC Laboratory of Molecular Biology, 1963–: Mem. Governing Bd, 1975–79; Head of Sub-div. of Protein Chemistry, 1969–80; Head Sub-div. of Molecular Immunobiology, 1980. For. Associate, Nat. Acad. of Scis, USA, 1981. Hon. FRCP, 1983; Hon. FRCPath, 1987; Hon. FRSocMed, 1992. Biochem. Soc. Ciba Medal, 1978; Rosenstiel Medal, 1979; Avery-Landsteiner Preis, 1979; Rosenberg Prize, 1979; Mattia Award, 1979; Gross Horwitz Prize, 1980; Koch Preis, 1980; Wolf Prize in Med., 1980; Wellcome Foundn Medal, 1980; Gimenez Diaz Medal, 1981; William Bate Hardy Prize, Camb. Philos. Soc., 1981; Sloan Prize, General Motors Cancer Res. Foundn, 1981; Gairdner Award, Gairdner

Foundn, 1981; Royal Medal, Royal Soc., 1982; Nobel Prize for Physiology or Medicine (with Prof. N. Jerne and Dr G. Koehler), 1984; Dale Medal, Soc. for Endicronology, 1984; Galen Medal, Apothecaries' Soc., 1985; Walker Prize, RCS, 1986; Copley Medal, Royal Soc., 1989; Nat. Biotechnology Ventures Award, USA, 1990. Silver Jubilee Medal, 1977. *Publications:* original papers and review articles on structure, evolution and genetics of immunoglobulins and phosphoenzimes. *Recreations:* open air activities, cooking. *Address:* Medical Research Council Laboratory of Molecular Biology, Hills Road, Cambridge CB2 2QH. *Club:* Sefe (Cambridge).

MILTON, Derek Francis, CMG 1990; HM Diplomatic Service, retired; *b* 11 Nov. 1935; *s* of Francis Henry Milton and Florence Elizabeth Maud Kirby; *m* 1st, 1960, Helge Kahle; two *s*; 2nd, 1977, Catherine Walmsley. *Educ:* Preston Manor County Grammar Sch., Wembley; Manchester Univ. (BA Hons Politics and Modern History, 1959). RAF, 1954–56. Colonial Office, 1959–63; Asst Private Sec. to Commonwealth and Colonial Sec., 1962–64; Commonwealth Prime Ministers' Meeting Secretariat, 1964; First Secretary: CRO (later FO), 1964–67; UK Mission to UN, New York, 1967–71; Rome, 1972–75; FCO, 1975–77; Counsellor: Civil Service Res. Fellow, Glasgow Univ., 1977–78; Caracas, 1978–79; Dept of Trade, 1980–82; Overseas Inspectorate, 1982–84; Minister-Counsellor, Mexico City, 1984–87; RCDS, 1988; High Comr, Kingston, Jamaica, and non-resident Ambassador to Haiti, 1989–95. *Recreations:* QPR Football Club, Poland, The Guardian, travel, languages. *Address:* 71 Cumberland Road, Bromley, Kent BR2 0PL.

MILTON-THOMPSON, Surg. Vice-Adm. Sir Godfrey (James), KBE 1988; FRCP; Warden, St Katharine's House, Wantage, since 1993; Medical Director General (Naval), 1985–90; Surgeon General, Ministry of Defence, 1988–90; *b* 25 April 1930; *s* of Rev. James Milton-Thompson and May LeMare (*née* Hoare); *m* 1952, Noreen Helena Frances, *d* of Lt-Col Sir Desmond Fitzmaurice, CIE; three *d*. *Educ:* Eastbourne Coll.; Queens' Coll., Cambridge (MA); St Thomas' Hosp. (MB BChir); FRCP 1974 (MRCP 1961); DCH 1963. Joined Royal Navy, 1955; after general service and hosp. appts at home and abroad, Cons. Phys., RN Hosp., Plymouth, 1967–70 and 1972–75; Hon. Research Fellow, St Mark's Hosp., London, 1969–71; Prof. of Naval Medicine, 1975–80; RCDS 1981; Dep. Medical Director General (Naval), 1982–84; Surg. Rear-Adm. (Operational Med. Services), 1984–85; Dep. Surg. Gen. (Research and Trng), MoD, 1985–87. QHP, 1982–90. Chm., Cornwall Community Healthcare Trust, 1991–93. Member: Medical Research Soc., 1971–; British Soc. of Gastroenterology, 1972–. Hon. Col, 211 (Wessex) Field Hosp., RAMC(V), 1990–95. Errol-Eldridge Prize, 1974; Gilbert Blane Medal, 1976. KStJ 1989 (Mem., Chapter Gen., 1988–; Hospitaller, 1991–95). *Publications:* on clinical pharmacology of the gastro-intestinal tract and therapy of peptic ulcer, etc, in med. jls. *Recreations:* fishing, paintings and painting, literature. *Address:* c/o Barclays Bank PLC, The Parade, Liskeard, Cornwall PL14 6AR. *Club:* Naval and Military.

MILVERTON, 2nd Baron *cr* 1947, of Lagos and of Clifton; **Rev. Fraser Arthur Richard Richards;** Rector of Christian Malford with Sutton Benger and Tytherton Kellaways, 1967–93; *b* 21 July 1930; *s* of 1st Baron Milverton, GCMG, and Noelle Benda, *d* of Charles Basil Whitehead; *S* father, 1978; *m* 1957, Mary Dorothy, BD, *d* of late Leslie Fly, ARCM, Corsham, Wilts; two *d*. *Educ:* De Carteret Prep. Sch., Jamaica; Ridley Coll., Ontario; Clifton Coll.; Egerton Agric. Coll., Kenya; Bishop's Coll., Cheshunt. Royal Signals, 1949–50; Kenya Police, 1952–53. Deacon 1957, priest 1958, dio. Rochester; Curate: Beckenham, 1957–59; St John Baptist, Sevenoaks, 1959–60; Great Bookham, 1960–63; Vicar of Okewood with Forest Green, 1963–67. *Recreations:* family, reading, current affairs and history; enjoys music and walking; interested in tennis, swimming, cricket and Rugby Union. *Heir:* *b* Hon. Michael Hugh Richards [*b* 1 Aug. 1936; *m* 1960, Edna Leonie, *y d* of Col Leo Steveni, OBE, MC; one *s*]. *Address:* House of Lords, Westminster, SW1A 0PW.

MILWARD, Prof. Alan Steele, FBA 1987; Professor of Economic History, University of London, since 1986; Official Historian, Cabinet Office, since 1993; *b* 19 Jan. 1935; *s* of Joseph Thomas Milward and Dorothy Milward (*née* Steele); *m* 1963, Claudine Jeanne Amélie Lemaître (marr. diss. 1994); two *d*. *Educ:* University College London (BA 1956); LSE (PhD 1960); MA Manchester 1981. Asst Lectr in Indian Archaeology, Univ. of London, 1959; Lectr in Economic History, Univ. of Edinburgh, 1960; Sen. Lectr in Social Studies, Univ. of East Anglia, 1965; Associate Prof. of Economics, Stanford Univ., 1969; Prof. of European Studies, UMIST, 1971; Prof. of Contemp. Hist., 1983, External Prof. of History, 1986, European Univ. Inst. Visiting Professor: Stanford Univ., 1966; Ecole Pratique des Hautes Etudes, 1977, 1990; Univ. of Illinois, 1978; Univ.-Gesamthochschule, Siegen, 1980; Oslo Univ., 1990; Aarhus Univ., 1992; Trondheim Univ., 1993. Fellow, Royal Norwegian Acad. of Scis and Letters, 1994. *Publications:* The German Economy at War, 1965; The Social and Economic Effects of the Two World Wars on Britain, 1971, 2nd edn 1984; The New Order and the French Economy, 1972; The Fascist Economy in Norway, 1972; (with S. B. Saul) The Economic Development of Continental Europe 1780–1870, 1973; (with S. B. Saul) The Development of the Economies of Continental Europe 1870–1914, 1977; War, Economy and Society, 1977; The Reconstruction of Western Europe 1945–1951, 1984, 2nd edn 1987; (with B. Martin) Landwirtschaft und Ernährung im Zweiten Weltkrieg, 1984; The European Rescue of the Nation-State, 1992; The Frontier of National Sovereignty, 1993. *Recreations:* theatre, cricket, reading timetables. *Address:* Department of Economic History, London School of Economics, Houghton Street, WC2A 2AE. *T:* 0171–955 7077; Cabinet Office, Hepburn House, Marsham Street, SW1P 4HW. *T:* 0171–217 6037.

MIMS, Prof. Cedric Arthur, MD, FRCPath; Professor of Microbiology, Guy's Hospital Medical School, London, 1972–90; *b* 9 Dec. 1924; *s* of A. H. and Irene Mims; *m* 1952, Valerie Vickery; two *s* two *d*. *Educ:* Mill Hill Sch.; University Coll. London (BSc (Zool)); Middlesex Hosp. Med. Sch. (MB, BS, BSc, MD). Medical Research Officer, East African Virus Research Inst., Entebbe, Uganda, 1953–56; Research Fellow and Professorial Fellow, John Curtin Sch. of Med. Research, Australian Nat. Univ., Canberra, 1957–72; Rockefeller Foundn Fellow, Children's Hosp. Med. Centre, Boston, USA, 1963–64; Visiting Fellow, Wistar Inst., Philadelphia, USA, 1969–70. *Publications:* (jtly) The Biology of Animal Viruses, 1974; The Pathogenesis of Infectious Disease, 1976, 4th edn 1995; (with D. O. White) Viral Pathogenesis and Immunology, 1984; (jtly) Medical Microbiology, 1993; numerous papers on the pathogenesis of virus infections. *Address:* Sheriff House, Hammingden Lane, Ardingly, Sussex RH17 6SR. *T:* Ardingly (01444) 892243.

MINCHINTON, Prof. Walter Edward; Professor of Economic History, University of Exeter, 1964–86 (Head of Department, 1964–84), now Emeritus; *b* 29 April 1921; *s* of late Walter Edward and Annie Border Minchinton; *m* 1945, Marjorie Sargood; two *s* two *d*. *Educ:* Queen Elizabeth's Hosp., Bristol; LSE, Univ. of London. 1st cl. hons BSc (Econ). FRHistS. War Service, RAOC, REME, Royal Signals (Lieut), 1942–45. UC Swansea: Asst Lectr, 1948–50; Lectr, 1950–59; Sen. Lectr, 1959–64. Rockefeller Research Fellow, 1959–60; Fellow, John Carter Brown Liby, Providence, RI, 1993. Visiting Professor: Fourah Bay Coll., Sierra Leone, 1965; La Trobe Univ., Australia, 1981–82. Chairman: Confedn for Advancement of State Educn, 1964–67; Devon History Soc., 1967–86; Exeter Industrial Arch. Gp, 1967–92; SW Maritime History Soc., 1984–87 (Pres., 1987–); British Agricultural History Soc., 1968–71 (Mem. Council, 1952–86); Export Research Group, 1971–72; Exeter Educn Cttee, 1972; Devon Historic Buildings Trust, 1980–86 (Mem. Council, 1967–). Vice-President: Assoc. for the History of the Northern Seas, 1989– (Pres., 1982–89); Internat. Commn for Maritime History, 1968–80 (Mem. Council, 1985–90; Mem. Council, British Cttee, 1974–); Council Member: Economic History Soc., 1955–66; Soc. for Nautical Research, 1969–72, 1978–81. Alexander Prize, RHistS, 1953. General Editor: Exeter Papers in Economic History, 1964–86; British Records Relating to America in Microform, 1962–89. *Publications:* The British Tinplate Industry: a history, 1957, repr. 1995; (ed) The Trade of Bristol in the Eighteenth Century, 1957; (ed) Politics and the Port of Bristol in the Eighteenth Century, 1963; Industrial Archaeology in Devon, 1968; (ed) Essays in Agrarian History, 1968; (ed) Industrial South Wales 1750–1914, essays in Welsh economic history, 1969; (ed) Mercantilism, System or Expediency?, 1969; The Growth of English Overseas Trade in the Seventeenth and Eighteenth Centuries, 1969; Wage Regulation in Pre-industrial England, 1972; Devon at Work, 1974; Windmills of Devon, 1977; (with Peter Harper) American Papers in the House of Lords Record Office: a guide, 1983; A Limekiln Miscellany: the South-West and South Wales, 1984; (with Celia King and Peter Waite) Virginia Slave-Trade Statistics 1698–1775, 1984; A Guide to Industrial Archaeological Sites in Britain, 1984; Devon's Industrial Past: a guide, 1986; Life to the City: an illustrated history of Exeter's water supply from the Romans to the present day, 1987; (ed) Britain and the Northern Seas: some essays, 1988; (ed) The Northern Seas: politics, economics and culture: eight essays, 1989; (ed) People of the Northern Seas, 1992; articles in Econ. History Review, Explorations in Entrepreneurial History, Mariner's Mirror, Trans RHistS, etc. *Recreations:* walking, music, industrial archaeology. *Address:* 53 Homefield Road, Exeter EX1 2QX. *T:* Exeter (01392) 77602.

MINDHAM, Prof. Richard Hugh Shiels, MD; FRCPE, FRCPsych; Nuffield Professor of Psychiatry, University of Leeds, since 1977; *b* 25 March 1935; *s* of Thomas Raper Mindham and Winifred Gertrude Mindham; *m* 1971, Barbara Harris Reid; one *s* one *d*. *Educ:* Guy's Hosp. Medical Sch.; Inst. of Psychiatry, Univ. of London. MD 1974; FRCPsych 1977; FRCPE 1978. Nottingham University Medical School: Sen. Lectr in Psychiatry, 1972–76; Reader, 1976–77. Vis. Prof., Johns Hopkins Univ., Md, 1982. *Publications:* papers on psychiatry, psychopharmacology and Parkinson's disease. *Recreations:* music, architecture, walking. *Address:* Division of Psychiatry and Behavioural Sciences, 15 Hyde Terrace, Leeds LS2 9LT. *T:* Leeds (0113) 233 2723. *Club:* Royal Society of Medicine.

MINFORD, Prof. (Anthony) Patrick (Leslie); Edward Gonner Professor of Applied Economics, University of Liverpool, since 1976; *b* 17 May 1943; *s* of Leslie Mackay Minford and Patricia Mary (*née* Sale); *m* 1970, Rosemary Irene Allcorn; two *s* one *d*. *Educ:* Horris Hill; Winchester Coll. (scholar); Balliol Coll., Oxford (schol.; BA); London Sch. of Economics (grad. studies; MScEcon, PhD). Economic Asst, Min. of Overseas Development, London, 1966; Economist, Min. of Finance, Malawi, 1967–69; Economic Adviser: Director's Staff, Courtaulds Ltd, 1970–71; HM Treasury, 1971–73, and HM Treasury Delegn in Washington DC, 1973–74. Visiting Hallsworth Fellow, Manchester Univ., 1974–75. Dir, Merseyside Develt Corp., 1988–89. Mem., Monopolies and Mergers Commn, 1990–. Mem., HM Treasury's Panel of Economic Forecasters, 1993–. Editor: NIESR Review, 1975–76; Liverpool Quarterly Economic Bulletin, 1980–. *Publications:* Substitution Effects, Speculation and Exchange Rate Stability, 1978; (jtly) Unemployment—Cause and Cure, 1983, 2nd edn 1985; (jtly) Rational Expectations and the New Macroeconomics, 1983; (jtly) The Housing Morass, 1987; The Supply Side Revolution in Britain, 1991; (jtly) The Cost of Europe, 1992; Rational Expectations Macroeconomics, 1993; articles in learned jls on monetary and international economics. *Address:* Department of Economics and Accounting, University of Liverpool, PO Box 147, Liverpool L69 3BX.

MINGAY, (Frederick) Ray, CMG 1992; Director-General, Export Promotion, Department of Trade and Industry, and Head of DTI/FCO Joint Export Promotions Directorate, since 1993; *b* 7 July 1938; *s* of Cecil Stanley and Madge Elizabeth Mingay; *m* 1963, Joan Heather Roberts; three *s* one *d*. *Educ:* Tottenham Grammar Sch.; St Catharine's Coll., Cambridge (BA); London Univ. (Postgrad. Pub. Admin.). Nat. Service (2nd Lt RAEC) 1959–61. Administration, St Thomas' Hosp., 1961; Min. of Transport, 1962–64; BoT, 1964; Chrysler (UK) Ltd, 1968–70; Consul (Commercial), Milan, 1970–73; Asst Sec., Dept of Trade, 1973–78; Counsellor (Commercial), Washington, 1978–83; Under Secretary: Mechanical and Electrical Engrg Div., DTI, 1983–86; Investment and Develt Div., DTI, 1986–88; Consul-Gen., Chicago, 1988–92; Head of Overseas Trade Div. 3, DTI, 1992–93. Churchill Fellow, Westminster Coll., Fulton, Mo. FIMgt; FRSA. *Address:* Department of Trade and Industry, Kingsgate House, 66–74 Victoria Street, SW1E 6SW.

MINGOS, Prof. David Michael Patrick, DPhil; FRS 1992; CChem; FRSC; Sir Edward Frankland BP Professor of Inorganic Chemistry, Imperial College, University of London, since 1992; *b* 6 Aug. 1944; *s* of Vasso Mingos and Rose Enid Billie Hayes (*née* Griffiths); *m* 1967, Stacey Mary Hosken; one *s* one *d*. *Educ:* Univ. of Manchester (BSc); Univ. of Sussex (DPhil). CChem 1983; FRSC 1983. Fulbright Fellow, Northwestern Univ., 1968–70; ICI Fellow, Sussex Univ., 1970–71; Lectr, QMC, 1971–76; University of Oxford: Lectr, 1976–90; Reader, 1990–92; Fellow, Keble Coll., 1976–92 and by special election, 1993; Univ. Assessor, 1991–92. Governor, Harrow Sch., 1994–. Dist. Prof., Xi'an Petroleum Inst., China, 1994–; Wilhelm Manchot Res. Prof. and prize, Munich, 1995. Corday Morgan Medal, 1980, Tilden Medal, 1988, Chemistry of Noble Metals Award, 1983, RSC. *Publications:* Introduction to Cluster Chemistry, 1990; Essentials of Inorganic Chemistry, 1995; contribs to jls of learned socs. *Recreations:* cricket, tennis, walking. *Address:* Department of Chemistry, Imperial College of Science, Technology and Medicine, S Kensington, SW7 2AY. *T:* 0171–594 5753; 6 Hurlingham Road, SW6 3QY. *T:* 0171–731 3391.

MINNITT, Robert John, CMG 1955; *b* 2 April 1913; *s* of Charles Frederick Minnitt and Winifred May Minnitt (*née* Buddle); *m* 1st, 1943, Peggy Christine Sharp (*d* 1973); one *s* two *d*; 2nd, 1975, Hon. Primrose Keighley Muncaster, *widow* of Claude Muncaster. *Educ:* Marlborough Coll.; Trinity Coll., Cambridge. Appointed to Colonial Administrative Service, Hong Kong, 1935; Chief Sec., Western Pacific High Commission, 1952–58, retired. Furniture designer and craftsman, 1960–66; temp. Civil Servant, CO, 1966; FCO, 1968–69. *Address:* Whitelocks, Sutton, Pulborough, W Sussex RH20 1PS. *T:* Sutton (01798) 869216.

MINOGUE, Prof. Kenneth Robert; Professor of Political Science, London School of Economics and Political Science, University of London, since 1984; *b* 11 Sept. 1930; *s* of Denis Francis Minogue and Eunice Pearl Minogue (*née* Porter); *m* 1954, Valerie Pearson Hallett; one *s* one *d*. *Educ:* Sydney Boys' High Sch.; Sydney Univ. (BA); London School of Economics (BScEcon). Asst Lectr, Univ. of Exeter, 1955–56; London School of Economics: Asst Lectr, 1956; Sen. Lectr, 1964; Reader, 1971. *Publications:* The Liberal Mind, 1961; Nationalism, 1967; The Concept of a University, 1974; Alien Powers: the pure theory of ideology, 1985; numerous contribs to learned jls. *Recreations:* opera, tennis, walking. *Address:* 43 Perrymead Street, SW6 3SN. *T:* 0171–731 0421. *Club:* Garrick.

MINOGUE, Maj.-Gen. Patrick John O'Brien; retired; *b* 28 July 1922; *s* of Col M. J. Minogue, DSO, MC, late East Surrey Regt, and Mrs M. V. E. Minogue; *m* 1950, June Elizabeth (*née* Morris); one *s* two *d*. *Educ:* Brighton Coll.; RMCS. CIMgt, FBCS, FIWSP, FIMH; jssc, psc, ato. Indian Army, 1942–46; East Surrey Regt, 1947; RAOC, 1951; served UK, BAOR, USA, Cyprus; Col, 1969; Brig., 1971; Insp. RAOC, 1971–73; Comdt, Central Ord. Depot, Bicester, 1973–75; Maj.-Gen. 1975; Comdr, Base Orgn, RAOC, 1975–78. Hon. Col, RAOC (TAVR), 1975–78; Col Comdt, RAOC, 1980–87. Group Systems Controller, Lansing Bagnall Ltd, 1978–81; Chm., LT Electronics, 1979–81. Mem., Spanish Golf Fedn, 1982–; Pres., Cabrera Lawn Bowling Club, 1987–92. *Recreations:* cricket, sailing (Cdre Wayfarer Class, UK, 1975), golf, shooting, gun-dogs, athletics, lawn bowling. *Address:* La Casa Rosada, Apartado 4, Cortijo Grande, Turre, Almeria, Spain. *Clubs:* MCC; Army Sailing Association; Royal Logistic Corps Yacht; Milocarian Athletic; Staff College (Camberley); Cortijo Grande Golf.

MINTO, 6th Earl of, *cr* 1813; **Gilbert Edward George Lariston Elliot-Murray-Kynynmound,** OBE 1986 (MBE (mil.) 1955); JP; Bt 1700; Baron Minto, 1797; Viscount Melgund, 1813; late Captain Scots Guards; Vice Lord-Lieutenant, Borders Region (Roxburgh, Ettrick and Lauderdale), since 1992; *b* 19 June 1928; *er s* of 5th Earl of Minto and Marion, OBE (*d* 1974), *d* of G. W. Cook, Montreal; *S* father, 1975; *m* 1st, 1952, Lady Caroline Child-Villiers (from whom he obtained a divorce, 1965), *d* of 9th Earl of Jersey; one *s* one *d*; 2nd, 1965, Mary Elizabeth (*b* 29 Dec. 1936; *d* 24 Jan. 1983), *d* of late Peter Ballantine and of Mrs Ballantine, Gladstone, New Jersey, USA; 3rd, 1991, Mrs Caroline Larlham. *Educ:* Eton; RMA, Sandhurst. Served Malaya, 1949–51; ADC to C-in-C FARELF, 1951, to CIGS, 1953–55, to HE Governor and C-in-C Cyprus, 1955; transferred to RARO, 1956. Brigadier, Queen's Body Guard for Scotland (Royal Company of Archers). Director, Noel Penny Turbines Ltd, 1971–92. Regional Councillor (Hermitage Div.), Borders Region, 1974–80, 1986–; Convenor, Borders Regional Council, 1990–; Mem. Exec., COSLA, 1990–. Pres., Scottish Council on Alcohol, 1987– (Chm., 1973–87); Dep. Traffic Comr for Scotland, 1975–81; Pres., S of Scotland Chamber of Commerce, 1980–82 (Exec. Vice-Pres., 1978–80). JP Roxburghshire, 1961–; DL Borders Region, Roxburgh, Ettrick and Lauderdale, 1983. *Heir: s* Viscount Melgund, *qv*. *Address:* Minto, Hawick, Scotland TD9 8SB. *T:* Denholm (01450) 87321.

MINTO, Dr Alfred, FRCPsych; Consultant Psychiatrist (Rehabilitation), Southern Derbyshire Health Authority, 1988–90, retired 1991; *b* 23 Sept. 1928; *s* of Alfred Minto and Marjorie Mavor Goudie Leask; *m* 1949, Frances Oliver Bradbrook; two *s* two *d*. *Educ:* Aberdeen Central Sch.; Aberdeen Univ. (MB ChB 1951); DPM RCS&P London 1961; MRCPsych 1972, FRCPsych 1974. House Physician, Huddersfield Royal Inf., 1952; Sen. House Officer/Jun. Hosp. Med. Officer, Fairmile Hosp., Wallingford, 1952–56; Sen. Registrar, St Luke's Hosp., Middlesbrough, 1956–59; Sen. Hosp. Med. Officer, 1959–63, Conslt Psychiatrist, 1963, Mapperley Hosp., Nottingham; Conslt Psychiatrist i/c, Alcoholism and Drug Addiction Service, Sheffield RHB, 1963–68; Conslt Psychiatrist, St Ann's and Mapperley Hosps, 1968–81; Med. Dir, Rampton Hosp., 1981–85; Associate Prof. of Psychiatry, Univ. of Calgary, and Clinical Dir of Forensic Psychiatry, Calgary Gen. Hosp., Alberta, 1986–87. Clinical Teacher, Nottingham Univ. Med. Sch., 1971–85; Special Lectr in Forensic Psych., Nottingham Univ., 1982–85. Conslt Psychiatrist, CS Comrs, 1964–85. *Publications:* Key Issues in Mental Health, 1982; papers on alcoholism, community care, toxoplasmosis. *Recreations:* books, people. *Address:* 76 Walsingham Road, Nottingham, NG5 4NR.

MINTOFF, Hon. Dominic, (Dom), BSc, BE&A, MA, A&CE; MP; MLA (Malta Labour Party), since 1947; Prime Minister of Malta, 1971–84; Leader of Labour Party, 1949–84; *b* Cospicua, 6 Aug. 1916; *s* of Lawrence Mintoff and late Concetta (*née* Farrugia); *m* 1947, Moyra de Vere Bentick; two *d*. *Educ:* Govt Elem. Sch., Seminary and Lyceum, Malta; Univ. of Malta (BSc 1937; BE&A, A&CE 1939); Hertford Coll., Oxford (Govt Travelling Scholar; Rhodes Scholar; MA Engrg Science). Practised as civil engineer in Britain, 1941–43, and as architect in Malta, 1943–. Gen. Sec. Malta Labour Party, 1936–37, Mem., Council of Govt and Exec. Council, 1945; Dep. Prime Minister and Minister for Works and Reconstruction, 1947–49 (resigned); Prime Minister and Minister of Finance, 1955–58; resigned office in 1958 to lead the Maltese Liberation Movement; Leader of Opposition, 1962–71; Minister of Foreign Affairs, 1971–81; Minister of the Interior, 1976–81 and 1983–84. Mem., Labour delegns to UK, 1945, 1947, 1948 and 1949. Negotiated removal of British Military base, 1971 and other foreign mil. bases by 1979. Dr *hc* Univ. of Pol. Studies, Ponterios, Greece, 1976. Order of the Republic, Libya, 1971; Grand Cordon: Order of the Republic, Tunisia, 1973; Order of Oissam Alaouite, 1978. *Publications:* scientific, literary and artistic works. *Recreations:* horse-riding, swimming, water skiing, bočči. *Address:* The Olives, Tarxien, Malta.

MINTON, Yvonne Fay, CBE 1980; mezzo-soprano; *er d* of R. T. Minton, Sydney; *m* 1965, William Barclay; one *s* one *d*. *Educ:* Sydney Conservatorium of Music. Elsa Stralia Scholar, Sydney, 1957–60; won Canberra Operatic Aria Competition, 1960; won Kathleen Ferrier Prize at s'Hertogenbosch Vocal Competition, 1961. Joined Royal Opera House as a Principal Mezzo-Soprano, 1965. Major roles include: Octavian in Der Rosenkavalier; Dorabella in Cosi Fan Tutte; Marina in Boris Godounov; Helen in King Priam; Cherubino in Marriage of Figaro; Orfeo in Gluck's Orfeo; Sextus in La clemenza di Tito; Dido in The Trojans at Carthage; Kundry in Parsifal; Charlotte in Werther; Countess Geschwitz in Lulu. Recordings include Octavian in Der Rosenkavalier, Mozart Requiem, Elgar's The Kingdom, etc. Guest Artist with Cologne Opera Company, Oct. 1969–. Hon. RAM 1975. *Recreations:* reading, gardening. *Address:* c/o Ingpen and Williams, 14 Kensington Court, W8 5DN. *T:* 0171–937 5158.

MIQUEL, Raymond Clive, CBE 1981; Chairman and Managing Director, Lees Group Ltd, since 1992; Chairman, Scottish Sports Council, 1987–91; Member, Sports Council, 1988–91; *b* 28 May 1931; *m* 1958; one *s* two *d*. *Educ:* Allan Glen's Sch., Glasgow; Glasgow Technical Coll. Joined Arthur Bell & Sons Ltd as Works Study Engineer, 1956; Production Controller, 1958; Production Director, 1962; Dep. Managing Director, 1965; Man. Dir, 1968–85; Dep. Chairman, 1972; Chm., 1973–85. Chairman: Towmaster Transport Co. Ltd, 1974–86; Canning Town Glass Ltd, 1974–86; Wellington Importers Ltd, 1984–86; Gleneagles Hotels PLC, 1984–86; Chm. and Chief Exec., Belhaven plc, 1986–88. Dir, Golf Fund Plc, 1989–94. Vis. Prof. in Business Develt, Glasgow Univ., 1985–. Member: British Internat. Sports Cttee, 1987–91; CCPR, 1984–. Governor, Sports Aid Foundn, 1979–. CIMgt (CBIM 1981). *Address:* Whitedene, Caledonian Crescent, Gleneagles, Perthshire, Scotland PH3 1NG. *T:* Auchterarder (01764) 62642.

MIRMAN, Sophie, (Mrs R. P. Ross); Joint Managing Director, Trotters Childrenswear and Accessories, since 1990; *b* 28 Oct. 1956; *d* of Simone and Serge Mirman; *m* 1984, Richard Philip Ross; one *s* two *d*. *Educ:* French Lycée, London. Marks & Spencer, 1974–81; Man. Dir, Tie Rack, 1981–83; Co-Founder, Sock Shop International, 1983; Chm. and Joint Man. Dir, Sock Shop International plc, 1983–90. *Recreations:* family, sport. *Address:* 34 King's Road, SW3 4UD. *T:* 0171–259 9622.

MIRON, Wilfrid Lyonel, CBE 1969 (OBE 1945; MBE 1944); TD 1950; JP; DL; Regional Chairman (Midlands), National Coal Board, 1967–76 and Regional Chairman (South Wales), 1969–76; National Coal Board Member (with Regional responsibilities), 1971–76; *b* 27 Jan. 1913; *s* of late Solman Miron and late Minnie Pearl Miron; *m* 1958, Doreen (*née* Hill) (*d* 1992); no *c*. *Educ:* Llanelli Gram. Sch. Admitted Solicitor, 1934; private practice and Legal Adviser to Shipley Collieries and associated companies. TA Commn, Sherwood Foresters, 1939; served War of 1939–45: Home Forces, 1939; France and Dunkirk, 1940; IO 139 Inf. Bde, 1940–41; GSO3 Aldershot Dist, 1941–42; Staff Coll., Quetta, 1942 (SC); DAAG 17 Ind. Div., 1943–44, and AA&QMG 17 Ind. Div., 1944–45, Chin Hills, Imphal, Burma (despatches, 1944). E Midlands Div. NCB: Sec. and Legal Adviser, 1946–51; Dep. Chm., 1951–60; Chm., 1960–67. Pres., Midland Dist Miners' Fatal Accident Relief Soc.; Chairman: E Mids Regional Planning Council, 1976–79 (Mem., 1965–76); (part-time), Industrial Tribunals, 1976–85. Freeman (by redemption) City of London; Master, Pattenmakers' Company, 1979–80. Hon. Lieut-Col. JP Notts, 1964 (Chairman: Nottingham PSD, 1982–83; Notts Magistrates' Cts Cttee, 1981–83); DL Notts, 1970. FRSA 1965–86. OStJ 1961. Hon. Fellow, Trent Polytechnic, 1980. *Publications:* Bitter Sweet Seventeen, 1946; articles and papers in mining and other jls. *Recreations:* cricket, music, reading, crosswords. *Address:* Briar Croft, School Lane, Halam, Newark, Notts NG22 8AD. *T:* Southwell (01636) 812446. *Clubs:* Army and Navy, MCC; XL; Nottingham and Notts United Services (Nottingham).

MIRREN, Helen; actress; *b* 26 July 1945. *Theatre includes: RSC:* Troilus and Cressida, Much Ado About Nothing, 1968; Richard III, Hamlet, The Two Gentlemen of Verona, 1970; Miss Julie, 1971; Macbeth, 1974; Henry VI parts I, II and III, 1977; Antony and Cleopatra, The Roaring Girl, 1983; *other:* Teeth 'n' Smiles, Royal Court, 1974; The Bed Before Yesterday, Lyric, 1976; Measure for Measure, Riverside, 1979; The Duchess of Malfi, Manchester Royal Exchange, 1980; Faith Healer, Royal Court, 1981; Extremities, Duchess, 1984; Two Way Mirror, Young Vic, 1988; Sex Please, We're Italian, Young Vic, 1991; A Month in the Country, Albery, and Roundabout, Broadway, 1994. *Films include:* Age of Consent, 1969; Savage Messiah, 1971; O Lucky Man, 1973; Caligula, 1977; The Long Good Friday, 1980; Excalibur, 1981; Cal, 1984; 2010, 1985; White Nights, 1986; Heavenly Pursuits, 1986; The Mosquito Coast, 1987; Pascali's Island, 1988; When the Whales Came, 1988; Bethune: The Making of a Hero, 1989; The Cook, The Thief, his Wife and her Lover, 1989; The Comfort of Strangers, 1989; Where Angels Fear to Tread, 1990; The Madness of King George, 1994. *TV includes:* Prime Suspect (series), 1991–95. *Address:* c/o Ken McReddie Ltd, 91 Regent Street, W1R 7TB.

MIRRLEES, Prof. James Alexander, FBA 1984; Professor of Political Economy, University of Cambridge and Fellow of Trinity College, since 1995; *b* 5 July 1936; *s* of late George B. M. Mirrlees; *m* 1961, Gillian Marjorie Hughes (*d* 1993); two *d*. *Educ:* Douglas-Ewart High Sch., Newton Stewart; Edinburgh Univ.; Trinity Coll., Cambridge. MA Edinburgh Maths, 1957; BA Cantab Maths, 1959; PhD Cantab Econs, 1963. Adviser, MIT Center for Internat. Studies, New Delhi, 1962–63; Cambridge Univ. Asst Lectr in Econs and Fellow of Trinity Coll., 1963, University Lectr, 1965; Adviser to Govt of Swaziland, 1963; Res. Assoc., Pakistan Inst. of Develt Econs, Karachi, 1966–67; Edgeworth Prof. of Econs, and Fellow, Nuffield Coll., Oxford Univ., 1968–95. Visiting Professor: MIT, 1968, 1970, 1976, 1987; Univ. of California, Berkeley, 1986; Yale Univ., 1989. Mem., Treasury Cttee on Policy Optimisation, 1976–78. Econometric Society: Fellow, 1970; Vice-Pres., 1980, Pres., 1982; Chm., Assoc. of Univ. Teachers of Econs, 1983–87; Pres., Royal Economic Soc., 1989–92. For. Hon. Mem., Amer. Acad. of Arts and Scis, 1981; Hon. Mem., Amer. Economic Assoc., 1982. Hon. DLitt Warwick, 1982. *Publications:* (joint author) Manual of Industrial Project Analysis in Developing Countries, 1969; (ed jtly) Models of Economic Growth, 1973; (jt author) Project Appraisal and Planning, 1974; articles in economic jls. *Recreations:* reading detective stories and other forms of mathematics, playing the piano, travelling, listening. *Address:* Trinity College, Cambridge CB2 1TQ.

MIRRLEES, Robin Ian Evelyn Stuart de la Lanne-; Richmond Herald of Arms, 1962–67; *b* Paris, 13 Jan. 1925; grandson of Ambassador La Lanne, godson of 11th Duke of Argyll; one *s*. *Educ:* Merton Coll., Oxford (MA). Several language diplomas. Served India, 1942–46; Captain RA, 1944; Gen. Staff, New Delhi, 1946; Embassy Attaché, Tokyo, 1947; Rouge Dragon Pursuivant of Arms, 1952–62 (and as such attended Coronation). Co-editor, Annuaire de France, 1966–. ADC to HM the King of Yugoslavia, 1963–70. Has raised substantial funds for humanitarian organisations; undertook restoration of Inchdrewer Castle, Scotland, and others; Laird of Island of Bernera, pop. 350. Freeman of City of London, 1960. Patrician of San Marino, 1964. Succeeded to the title of Comte de Lalanne (France), 1962 and titular Prince of Coronata. Various foreign orders of knighthood. *Recreations:* foxhunting, piloting, travelling, painting, sculpture, mystic philosophy. *Address:* Bernera Lodge, Great Bernera Island, by Stornoway, Outer Hebrides, Scotland; 115 Rue de la Pompe, Paris 16me; Inchdrewer Castle, Banff, Scotland; Villa Lambins-Lalanne, Le Touquet, France; Schloss Ratzenegg, Carinthia, Austria. *Clubs:* Buck's; Travellers' (Paris).

MIRVISH, Edwin, OC 1987; CBE 1989; *b* 24 July 1914; *s* of David and Anna Mirvish; *m* 1941, Anne Maklin; one *s*. *Educ:* Toronto. Proprietor: Ed Mirvish Enterprises and other cos; Honest Ed's World Famous Bargain Shopping Centre; several restaurants; Royal Alexandra Theatre, Toronto; Old Vic Theatre, 1982–; Princess of Wales Theatre, Toronto, 1993–. Hon. LLD: Trent Univ., 1967; Univ. of Waterloo, 1969; Fellow, Ryerson Technical Inst., 1981. Freeman, City of London, 1984. Award of Merit, City of Toronto. *Recreation:* ballroom dancing. *Address:* 581 Bloor Street West, Toronto, Ontario M6G 1K3, Canada. *T:* (416) 5372111. *Clubs:* Empire, Canadian, Arts and Letters, Variety (Toronto).

MIRZOEFF, Edward, CVO 1993; Executive Producer, Documentaries, BBC Television, since 1983; *b* 11 April 1936; *s* of late Eliachar Mirzoeff and of Penina (*née* Asherov); *m* 1961, Judith Topper; three *s*. *Educ:* Hasmonean Grammar Sch.; Queen's Coll., Oxford (Open Scholarship in Mod. History). MA Oxon. Market Researcher, Social Surveys (Gallup Poll) Ltd, 1958–59; Public Relns Exec., Duncan McLeish & Associates, 1960–61; Asst Editor, Shoppers' Guide, 1961–63; with BBC Television, 1963–: director and producer of film documentaries incl. (with Sir John Betjeman) Metro-land, 1973, A Passion for Churches, 1974, and The Queen's Realm, 1977; Police – Harrow Road, 1975; The Regiment, 1977; The Front Garden, 1979; The Ritz, 1981; The Englishwoman and The Horse, 1981; Elizabeth R, 1992; Torvill and Dean: facing the music, 1994; Treasures in Trust, 1995; Editor, 40 Minutes, 1985–89; Series Editor: Bird's-Eye View, 1969–71; Year of the French, 1982–83; In At The Deep End, 1983–84; Just Another Day, 1983–85; Real Lives, 1985; Fire in the Blood, 1992; Pandora's Box, 1992; The Ark, 1993; True Brits, 1994; Situation Vacant, 1995; The Living Dead, 1995; Redcaps, 1995; Jancis Robinson's Wine Course, 1995; The House, 1995; The Richard Dimbleby Lecture, 1972–82; A. J. P. Taylor Lectures (three series). Chm., BAFTA, 1995–96 (Vice-Chm., TV, 1991–95). BAFTA Awards: Best Documentary, 1981; Best Factual Series, 1985, 1989; Alan Clarke Award, 1995; Samuelson Award, Birmingham Fest. 1988; BFI TV Award, 1988; British Video Award, 1992. *Recreations:* exploring the London Library, walking in Wiltshire, visiting Italy. *Address:* 9 Westmoreland Road, SW13 9RZ. *T:* 0181–748 9247.

MISCAMPBELL, Norman Alexander, QC 1974; barrister; a Recorder of the Crown Court, since 1977; *b* 20 Feb. 1925; *s* of late Alexander and Eileen Miscampbell; *m* 1961, Margaret Kendall; two *s* two *d. Educ:* St Edward's Sch., Oxford; Trinity Coll., Oxford. Called to Bar, Inner Temple, 1952, Bencher 1983; N Circuit. Mem., Hoylake UDC, 1955–61. Contested (C) Newton, 1955, 1959; MP (C) Blackpool North, 1962–92. *Address:* 7 Abbey Road, West Kirby, Wirral, Merseyside L48 7EN.

MISCHLER, Norman Martin; Chairman: Hoechst UK Ltd, 1975–84; Hoechst Ireland Ltd, 1976–84; Berger Jenson & Nicholson Ltd, 1979–84; *b* 9 Oct. 1920; *s* of late Martin Mischler and Martha Sarah (*née* Lambert); *m* 1949, Helen Dora Sinclair; one *s* one *d. Educ:* St Paul's Sch., London; St Catharine's Coll., Cambridge (MA). Cricket Blue, 1946. Indian Army, 1940; served in Burma Campaign; released, rank of Major, 1946. Joined Burt, Boulton & Haywood, 1947, Vice-Chm. 1963; Dep. Man. Dir, Hoechst UK Ltd, 1966; Chairman: Harlow Chemical Co. Ltd, 1972–74; Kalle Infotec Ltd, 1972–74; Director: Berger, Jenson & Nicholson Ltd, 1975–84; Ringsdorff Carbon Co. Ltd, 1968–84; Vice-Chm., German Chamber of Industry and Commerce in London, 1974–84; Mem. Council, Chemical Industries Assoc. Ltd, 1975–84. Freeman, City of London. Officer's Cross, German Order of Merit, 1985. *Recreations:* cricket, opera, and theatre. *Address:* Scott House, Earsham Street, Bungay, Suffolk NR35 1AF. *Clubs:* Hawks (Cambridge); Norfolk (Norwich).

MISHCON, family name of **Baron Mishcon.**

MISHCON, Baron *cr* 1978 (Life Peer), of Lambeth in Greater London; **Victor Mishcon;** DL; Solicitor; Senior Partner, Mishcon de Reya (formerly Victor Mishcon & Co.), 1988–92, now Consultant; *b* 14 Aug. 1915; *s* of Rabbi Arnold and Mrs Queenie Mishcon; *m* 1976, Joan Estelle Conrad; two *s* one *d* by previous marr. *Educ:* City of London Sch. Mem. Lambeth Borough Coun., 1945–49 (Chm. Finance Cttee, 1947–49); Mem. London CC for Brixton, 1946–65 (Chairman: Public Control Cttee, 1947–52; Gen. Purposes Cttee, 1952–54; Council, April 1954–55; Supplies Cttee, 1956–57; Fire Brigade Cttee, 1958–65); Mem. GLC for Lambeth, 1964–67 (Chm., Gen. Purposes Cttee, 1964–67); Mem., ILEA, 1964–67. Member: Jt Cttee with House of Commons on Consolidation of Bills, 1983–85; Law Sub-Cttee, House of Lords European Communities Cttee, 1978–86; House of Lords Select Cttee on Procedure, 1981–83; House of Lords Select Cttee on Med. Ethics, 1993; Opposition spokesman on home affairs, 1983–90, on legal affairs, 1983–92, House of Lords. Vice Chm., Lords and Commons Solicitors Gp, 1983–. Chm. Governors, Cormont and Loughborough Secondary Schools, 1947–60; Governor: Stockwell Manor Sch., 1960–78 (Chm. of Governors, 1960–67, 1970–78); JFS Comprehensive Sch., 1970–85; Philippa Fawcett Coll. of Educn, 1970–80. Member: Standing Joint Cttee, Co. of London Sessions, 1950–65 (Vice-Chm. 1959–61); Nat. Theatre Board, 1965–67, 1968–90; South Bank Theatre Board, 1977–82; London Orchestra Bd, 1966–67; Exec. Cttee, London Tourist Board, 1965–67; Government Cttee of Enquiry into London Transport, 1953–54; Departmental Cttee on Homosexual Offences and Prostitution, 1954–57. Vice-Chm., Council of Christians and Jews, 1976–77; Vice-Pres., Bd of Deputies of British Jews, 1967–73; Hon. President, Brit. Technion Soc.; Vice-Pres. (Past Pres.) Assoc. of Jewish Youth; Pres., British Council of the Shaare Zedek Hosp., Jerusalem. Contested (Lab) NW Leeds, 1950, Bath, 1951, Gravesend, 1955, 1959. DL Greater London. Hon. QC 1992. Hon. Fellow, UCL, 1993. Hon. LLD Birmingham, 1991. Comdr Royal Swedish Order of North Star, 1954; Star of Ethiopia, 1954. *Address:* House of Lords, SW1A 0PW.

MISKIN, Raymond John, CEng, FIMechE, FIEE, MRAeS, FIQA; consulting engineer; Chief Executive, Certification Authority for Dental Laboratories and Suppliers, 1989–93; *b* 4 July 1928; *s* of late Sydney George Miskin and Hilda (*née* Holdsworth); *m* 1st, 1951 (marr. diss. 1981); one *d* (one *s* decd); 2nd, 1991. *Educ:* Woking Grammar Sch.; Southall Technical Coll. The Fairey Aviation Co. Ltd: apprentice, 1945–49; develt engr, 1949–59; Dep. Chief Inspector, 1959–63; Quality Control Manager and Chief Inspector, Graviner Ltd, 1963–69; Sec., Inst. of Qual. Assurance, 1969–73; Dep. Sec., 1973–76, Sec., 1976–87, IProdE; Dir, IPRODE Ltd, 1976–87. Mem. Council and Hon. Treasurer, Inst. of Qual. Assurance, 1963–69; Mem., Bd, Nat. Council for Qual. and Reliability, 1969–81 (Chm., 1975–77). Hon. Mem., Amer. Inst. of Industrial Engrs, 1985. FSME 1994. Hon. FIIPE 1979. Freeman, City of London, 1985. Internat. Industrial Management Award, San Fernando Valley Engineers Council, USA, 1978; Internat. Achievement Award, Los Angeles Council of Engrs, 1981; GTE (Hungary) Technical Achievement Medal, 1984. *Publications:* articles in technical pubns. *Recreation:* golf. *Address:* 36 Hayes Drive, Mosborough, Sheffield S19 5TR. *Club:* Renishaw Park Golf.

MISSELBROOK, (Bertram) Desmond, CBE 1972; FRSE 1978; Chairman, Livingston Development Corporation, 1972–78; *b* 28 May 1913; *s* of late C. J. and E. P. Misselbrook; *m* 1949, Anne, *er d* of late F. O. Goodman; two *s. Educ:* Chatham House, Ramsgate; Bristol Univ. Admiralty Psychologist, 1942–45. Lectr in Psychology and Dir, Unit of Applied Psychology, Edinburgh Univ., 1945–49; Senr Res. Fellow in Business Studies, 1970–71, Hon. Fellow, 1971. Personnel Adviser, 1949, Dir. 1955, Dep. Chm. 1963–70, British-American Tobacco Co. Ltd; Chm., Evershed and Vignoles Ltd, 1961–65; Chm., Mardon Packaging International Ltd, 1962–70; Dir, 1963, Dep. Chm. 1966–69, Wiggins Teape Ltd; Dir, Charterhouse Gp Ltd, 1969–72; Deputy Chairman: Standard Life Assurance Co., 1977–80 (Dir, 1970–84); Anderson Mavor Ltd, 1971–74; Chairman: Anderson Strathclyde Ltd, 1974–77; Seaforth Maritime Ltd, 1977–78. Mem. Council, British Inst. of Management, 1967–72 (a Vice-Chm., 1969); Chairman: Bd of Governors, Oversea Service, 1963–70; Construction Ind. Trng Bd, 1970–73; Council, Scottish Business Sch., 1972–77; Economic Development Cttees for Building and Civil Engineering Industries, 1969–72; Member: Adv. Council on Social Work (Scotland), 1970–74; Economic Consultant, Scottish Office, 1970–72. Hon. DSc Edinburgh, 1977. *Recreations:* fishing, gardening, walking. *Address:* Mains of Auchenfranco, Lochfoot, Dumfries DG2 8NZ. *T:* Dumfries (01387) 730208.

MISTRY, Dhruva, RA 1991; sculptor; *b* 1 Jan. 1957; *s* of Pramodray and Kantaben Mistry. *Educ:* Maharaja Sayajirao Univ. of Baroda (MA 1981); RCA (British Council schol.; MA 1983). Artist-in-residence, Kettle's Yard, and Fellow of Churchill Coll., Cambridge, 1984–85. Rep. Britain at 3rd Rodin Grand Prize Exhibn, Japan, 1990. Works of art for Victoria Square, Birmingham, commnd by Birmingham CC. *Recreations:* photography, reading, walking. *Address:* The Cottage, Dodds Farm, Ingatestone, Essex CM4 0NW.

MITCHELL, Adrian; writer; *b* 24 Oct. 1932; *s* of James Mitchell and Kathleen Fabian. *Educ:* Greenways Sch.; Dauntsey's Sch.; Christ Church, Oxford. Worked as reporter on Oxford Mail, Evening Standard, 1955–63; subseq. free-lance journalist for Daily Mail, Sun, Sunday Times, New Statesman; Granada Fellow, Univ. of Lancaster, 1968–69; Fellow, Center for Humanities, Wesleyan Univ., 1972; Resident Writer, Sherman Theatre, Cardiff, 1974–75; Vis. writer, Billericay Comp. Sch., 1978–80; Judith E. Wilson Fellow, Cambridge Univ., 1980–81; Resident writer, Unicorn Theatre for Children, 1982–83. Poetry Editor, New Statesman and Society, 1994–. FRSL 1987. *Plays:* Marat/Sade (stage adaptation), RSC, 1964; Tyger, NT Co. at New Theatre, 1971; Man Friday, 7:84 Theatre Co., 1973 (TV 1972, Screenplay 1975); Mind Your Head, Liverpool Everyman, 1973; Daft as a Brush (TV), 1975; A Seventh Man, Hampstead, 1976; White Suit Blues, Nottingham, Edinburgh and Old Vic, 1977; Houdini, Amsterdam, 1977; Glad Day (TV), 1978; Uppendown Mooney, Welfare State Theatre Co., 1978; The White Deer, Unicorn Theatre, 1978; Hoagy, Bix and Wolfgang Beethoven Bunkhaus, King's Head Theatre, 1979; In the Unlikely Event of an Emergency, Bath, 1979; Peer Gynt (adaptation), Oxford Playhouse, 1980; You Must Believe All This (TV), 1981; The Tragedy of King Real, Welfare State Theatre Co., 1982; Mowgli's Jungle, Contact Theatre, Manchester, 1982; A Child's Christmas in Wales (with Jeremy Brooks), Great Lakes Fest., 1983; The Wild Animal Song Contest, Unicorn Theatre, 1983; Life's a Dream (adaptation with John Barton), RSC Stratford, 1983, Barbican, 1984; C'Mon Everybody, Tricycle Theatre, 1984; The Great Theatre of the World (adaptation), Mediaeval Players, 1984; Satie Day/Night, Lyric Studio, Hammersmith, 1986; Mirandolina (adaptation), Bristol Old Vic, 1987; The Last Wild Wood in Sector 88, Rugby Music Centre, 1987; Anna on Anna, Th. Workshop, Edin., 1988; Woman Overboard, The Patchwork Girl of Oz, Palace Th., Watford, 1988; The Snow Queen, NY, 1990; Vasilisa The Fair (adaptation), NY, 1991; Pieces of Peace (TV), 1991; Unicorn Island, Dartington, 1992; The Blue, Walk the Plank, Fitzcarraldo Theatre Ship, Glasson Dock, Lancs and other UK ports, 1992; A New World and The Tears of the Indians (adaptation), Nuffield Theatre, Southampton, 1992; Meet the Baron, Dartington, 1993; Sir Fool's Quest, Dartington and nat. tour, 1994; National Theatre: The Mayor of Zalamea (adaptation), 1981; Animal Farm (lyrics), 1984; The Government Inspector, 1985; The Pied Piper, 1986; Love Songs of World War Three, 1987; Fuente Ovejuna (adaptation), 1989; Triple Threat, 1989. *Publications: novels:* If You See Me Comin', 1962; The Bodyguard, 1970; Wartime, 1973; *poetry:* Poems, 1964; Out Loud, 1968; Ride the Nightmare, 1971; The Apeman Cometh, 1975; For Beauty Douglas, (Collected Poems 1953–1979), 1982; On the Beach at Cambridge, 1984; Nothingmas Day, 1984; Love Songs of World War Three, 1988; All My Own Stuff, 1991; Adrian Mitchell's Greatest Hits—The Top Forty, 1991; *for children:* The Baron Rides Out, 1985; The Baron on the Island of Cheese, 1986; The Baron All At Sea, 1987; Leonardo the Lion from Nowhere, 1987; Our Mammoth, 1987; Our Mammoth Goes to School, 1987; Our Mammoth in the Snow, 1988; The Pied Piper, 1988; Strawberry Drums, 1989; The Thirteen Secrets of Poetry, 1993; (ed) The Orchard Book of Poems, 1993; also plays. *Address:* c/o Peters, Fraser and Dunlop, 5th Floor, The Chambers, Chelsea Harbour, Lots Road, SW10 0XF. *Club:* Chelsea Arts.

MITCHELL, Alec Burton, MA; CEng, MIMechE, FRINA; Director, Admiralty Marine Technology Establishment, 1977–84, retired; Scientific Adviser to Director General Ships, Ministry of Defence, 1981–84; *b* 27 Aug. 1924; *er s* of Ronald Johnson Mitchell and Millicent Annie Mitchell; *m* 1952, Barbara, *d* of Arthur Edward and Katie Florence Jane Archer; three *s. Educ:* Purley County Sch.; St. John's Coll., Cambridge (MA). Mechanical Sciences Tripos, Cambridge, 1944. Aeronautical Engineer with Rolls Royce Ltd, Hucknall, 1944–46; Grad. apprentice and gas turbine design engr with English Electric Co Ltd, Rugby, 1946–48. Joined RN Scientific Service, 1948; Dep. Head of Hydrodynamic Research Div., Admty Research Lab., 1961; promoted Dep. CSO, 1966; Dep. Dir, Admty Research Laboratory, 1973, Dir, 1974–77. *Publications:* numerous scientific papers on hydrodynamics and under-water propulsion systems. *Recreations:* golf, horology, wood-work. *Address:* 32 Ormond Crescent, Hampton, Mddx TW12 2TH.

MITCHELL, Alexander Graham, CBE 1973; DFM 1945; Governor, Turks and Caicos Islands, 1973–75 (Administrator, 1971–73); *b* 2 Nov. 1923; *s* of Alexander Mitchell and Evelyn Mitchell (*née* Green); *m* 1954, Pamela Ann Borman; three *d. Educ:* Dulwich College; Downing Coll., Cambridge (Exhibnr). Served RAF, 1942–45. Sudan Government Civil Service, 1951–55; HM Overseas Civil Service, 1955; Western Pacific High Commission: various posts in British Solomon Islands Protectorate and British Residency, New Hebrides, 1955–71; Sec., Financial Affairs, British Residency, 1968–71; retired June 1977. Clerk to Governors, Dame Allan's Schools, Newcastle, 1977–88. *Recreations:* ancient and military history. *Address:* The Dene, Stocksfield, Northumberland NE43 7PB. *Club:* Royal Over-Seas League.

MITCHELL, Andrew John Bower; MP (C) Gedling, since 1987; Parliamentary Under Secretary of State, Department of Social Security, since 1995; *b* 23 March 1956; *s* of Sir David Bower Mitchell, *qv; m* 1985, Sharon Denise (*née* Bennett); two *d. Educ:* Rugby; Jesus Coll., Cambridge (MA History). 1st RTR (Short Service (Limited) Commission), 1975; served with UNFICYP. Pres., Cambridge Union, 1978; Chm., Cambridge Univ. Conservatives, 1977; rep. GB in E-SU American debating tour, 1978. Internat. and Corp. business, Lazard Brothers & Co., 1979–87, Consultant, 1987–92. Mem., Islington Health Authy, 1985–87. Contested (C) Sunderland South, 1983. PPS to Minister of State, FCO, 1988–90, to Sec. of State for Energy, 1990–92; a Vice-Chm., Cons. Party, with special responsibility for candidates, 1992–93; an Asst Govt Whip, 1992–94; a Lord Comr of HM Treasury (Govt Whip), 1994–95. Mem., Finance Bill Cttee, 1988–92; Sec., One Nation Gp of Conservative MPs, 1989–92. Chairman: Coningsby Club, 1983; Islington North Conservatives, 1983–85; Conservative Collegiate Forum, 1991–92. *Recreations:* ski-ing, music, travel. *Address:* 30 Gibson Square, N1 0RD. *T:* 0171–226 5519; Dovecote Farmhouse, Tithby, Notts NG13 8GT. *T:* Bingham (01949) 839587. *Clubs:* Carlton; Cambridge Union Society; Carlton and District Constitutional.

MITCHELL, Angus; *see* Mitchell, J. A. M.

MITCHELL, Air Cdre Sir (Arthur) Dennis, KBE 1977; CVO 1961; DFC 1944, and Bar, 1945; AFC 1943; Founder and Managing Director, Aero Systems SA, since 1972; an Extra Equerry to the Queen since 1962; *b* 26 May 1918; 2nd *s* of Col A. Mitchell, DSO, Carrickfergus, Belfast, N Ireland; *m* 1949, Comtesse Mireille Caroline Cornet de Ways Ruart; one *s. Educ:* Nautical Coll., Pangbourne; RAF Coll., Cranwell; Army Staff Coll., Camberley; RAF Flying Coll., Manby. Joined RAF, 1936. Served 1938–45, India, Burma, UK and NW Europe; RAF Delegn, Belgium, 1948–49; US Air Force, 1951–53; HQ Allied Air Forces Central Europe, NATO, Fontainebleau, 1953–56; o/c RAF Cottesmore Bomber Comd, 1959–62; Dep. Captain and Captain of the Queen's Flight, 1956–59 and 1962–64; ADC to the Queen, 1958–62. Founder: Brussels Airways; Aero Distributors SA. French Croix de Guerre, 1945. *Recreation:* golf. *Address:* 10 chemin des Chasseurs, 1380 Ohain, Belgium. *T:* (2) 6531301; (office) (2) 6522222. *Clubs:* Royal Air Force, Naval and Military.

MITCHELL, Austin Vernon, DPhil; MP (Lab) Great Grimsby, since 1983 (Grimsby, Apr. 1977–1983); *b* 19 Sept. 1934; *s* of Richard Vernon Mitchell and Ethel Mary Mitchell; *m* 1st, Patricia Dorothea Jackson (marr. diss.); two *d;* 2nd, Linda Mary McDougall; one *s* one *d. Educ:* Woodbottom Council Sch.; Bingley Grammar Sch.; Manchester Univ. (BA, MA); Nuffield Coll., Oxford (DPhil). Lectr in History, Univ. of Otago, Dunedin, NZ, 1959–63; Sen. Lectr in Politics, Univ. of Canterbury, Christchurch, NZ, 1963–67; Official Fellow, Nuffield Coll., Oxford, 1967–69; Journalist, Yorkshire Television, 1969–71; Presenter, BBC Current Affairs Gp, 1972–73; Journalist, Yorkshire TV, 1973–77; Co-presenter, Target, Sky TV, 1989–. Opposition frontbench spokesman on trade and industry, 1987–89. *Publications:* New Zealand Politics In Action, 1962; Government By Party, 1966; The Whigs in Opposition 1815–1830, 1969; Politics and People in New Zealand, 1970; Yorkshire Jokes, 1971; The Half-Gallon Quarter-Acre Pavlova Paradise,

1974; Can Labour Win Again, 1979; Westminster Man, 1982; The Case for Labour, 1983; Four Years in the Death of the Labour Party, 1983; Yorkshire Jokes, 1988; Teach Thissen Tyke, 1988; Britain: beyond the blue horizon, 1989; Competitive Socialism, 1989; Accounting for Change, 1993. *Recreation:* worriting (*sic*). *Address:* 15 New Cartergate, Grimsby, South Humberside DN31 1RB. *T:* Grimsby (01472) 342145; House of Commons, SW1A 0AA. *T:* 0171–219 4559.

MITCHELL, Prof. Basil George, DD; FBA 1983; Nolloth Professor of the Philosophy of the Christian Religion, Oxford University, 1968–84; Fellow of Oriel College, 1968–84, now Emeritus; *b* 9 April 1917; *s* of George William Mitchell and Mary Mitchell (*née* Loxston); *m* 1950, Margaret Eleanor Collin; one *s* three *d*. *Educ:* King Edward VI Sch., Southampton; Queen's Coll., Oxford (Southampton Exhibitioner. 1st cl. Lit Hum 1939). Served Royal Navy, 1940–46; Lt RNVR 1942, Instructor Lt RN 1945. Lectr, Christ Church, Oxford, 1946–47; Fellow and Tutor in Philosophy, Keble Coll., Oxford, 1947–67, Emeritus Fellow, 1981; Sen. Proctor, 1956–57; Hebdomadal Council, 1959–65. Visiting Professor: Princeton Univ., 1963; Colgate Univ., 1976. Lectures: Stanton, in Philosophy of Religion, Cambridge Univ., 1959–62; Edward Cadbury, University of Birmingham, 1966–67; Gifford, Glasgow Univ., 1974–76; Nathaniel Taylor, Yale, 1986; Martin, Univ. of Hong Kong, 1987; Norton, Southern Baptist Theol Seminary, Louisville, 1989; Sarum, Oxford Univ., 1992. Member: C of E Working Parties on Ethical Questions, 1964–78; Doctrine Commn, 1978–84. Hon. DD Glasgow, 1977; Hon. DLitHum Union Coll., Schenectady, 1979. *Publications:* (ed) Faith and Logic, 1957; Law, Morality and Religion in a Secular Society, 1967; Neutrality and Commitment, 1968; (ed) The Philosophy of Religion, 1971; The Justification of Religious Belief, 1973; Morality: Religious and Secular, 1980; How to Play Theological Ping Pong, 1990; Faith and Criticism, 1994; articles in philosophical and theological periodicals. *Address:* Bartholomew House, 9 Market Street, Woodstock, Oxford OX20 1SU. *T:* Woodstock (01993) 811265.

MITCHELL, Bob; *see* Mitchell, R. C.

MITCHELL, Charles Julian Humphrey; *see* Mitchell, Julian.

MITCHELL, Lt-Col Colin Campbell; former soldier and politician; Chairman, The HALO Trust, since 1987; *b* 17 Nov. 1925; *o s* of Colin Mitchell, MC, and Janet Bowie Gilmour; *m* 1956, Jean Hamilton Susan Phillips; two *s* one *d*. *Educ:* Whitgift Sch. British Army, 1943; commissioned Argyll and Sutherland Highlanders, 1944, serving in Italy (wounded); Palestine, 1945–48 (wounded); Korea, 1950–51; Cyprus, 1958–59; Borneo, 1964 (brevet Lt-Col); Aden, 1967 (despatches). Staff appts as ADC to GOC-in-C Scottish Command; Directorate of Mil. Ops (MO4), WO; Qualified Camberley Staff Coll., 1955; subsequently: GSO2, 51st Highland Div. (TA); Bde Major, King's African Rifles, and GSO1 Staff of Chief of Defence Staff at MoD. Retired at own request, 1968; subseq. Special Correspondent, Vietnam. MP (C) W Aberdeenshire, 1970–Feb. 1974 (not seeking re-election); PPS to Sec. of State for Scotland, 1972–73. Mem., Select Cttee on Armed Services, 1970–71. Specialist Consultant: Rhodesia, 1975–79; Mexico, 1980; Afghanistan, 1983; Nicaragua, 1985; Pakistan NWFP, 1986; Eritrea, 1987; Cambodia, 1990. Mem., UNHCR Mission to Cambodia, 1991. Freedom of City of London, 1979. *Publication:* Having Been A Soldier, 1969. *Address:* c/o Coutts & Co., 440 Strand, WC2R 0QS.

MITCHELL, Sir David (Bower), Kt 1988; DL; MP (C) Hampshire North West, since 1983 (Basingstoke, 1964–83); *b* June 1928; *er s* of James Mitchell, Naval Architect; *m* 1954, Pamela Elaine Haward (separated); two *s* one *d*. *Educ:* Aldenham. Farming, 1945–50; businessman, wine merchant, 1951–79. An Opposition Whip, 1965–67; PPS to Sec. of State for Social Services, 1970–74; Parly Under Sec. of State, DoI, 1979–81, NI Office, 1981–83, Dept of Transport, 1983–85; Minister of State for Transport, 1986–88. Chm., Cons. Parly Smaller Business Cttee, 1974–79. Founder, 1976, Trustee Mem., 1989–, Small Business Bureau. DL Hants, 1994. *Recreations:* gardening, walking, wine-tasting, travel. *Address:* House of Commons, SW1A 0AA. *Club:* Carlton.
See also A. J. B. Mitchell.

MITCHELL, David William, CBE 1983; Chairman, Cumbernauld New Town Development Corporation, since 1987 (Member since 1985); *b* 4 Jan. 1933; *m* 1965, Lynda Katherine Marion Guy; one *d*. *Educ:* Merchiston Castle School, Edinburgh. Western RHB, 1968–75; Jt Man. Dir, M & N Norman (Timber) Ltd, 1992–; Director: Mallinson, Denny (Scotland), 1975–89; Hunter Timber (Scotland), 1989–92. Member: Exec. Cttee, Scottish Council Develt and Industry, 1979–; Scottish Council, CBI, 1980–85; Scottish Exec. Cttee, Inst. of Directors, 1984–91. President: Timber Trade Benevolent Soc., 1974; Scottish Timber Trade Assoc., 1984. Pres., Scottish Cons. and Unionist Assoc., 1980–82; Treasurer, Scottish Cons. Party, 1990–93. Gov., Craighalbert Centre for Children with Motor Neurone Disease, 1992–. *Recreations:* golf, shooting, fishing. *Address:* Dunmullen House, Blanefield, Stirlingshire G63 9AJ. *T:* Blanefield (01360) 770885. *Clubs:* Western (Glasgow); Royal and Ancient Golf, Prestwick Golf.

MITCHELL, Sir Dennis; *see* Mitchell, Sir A. D.

MITCHELL, Sir Derek (Jack), KCB 1974 (CB 1967); CVO 1966; Member, Royal National Theatre Board, since 1977; Chairman, Jocelyn Burton Silversmith & Goldsmith Ltd, since 1991; *b* 5 March 1922; *s* of late Sidney Mitchell, Schoolmaster, and Gladys Mitchell; *m* 1944, Miriam (*d* 1993), *d* of late F. E. Jackson; one *s* two *d*. *Educ:* St Paul's Sch.; Christ Church, Oxford. Served War of 1939–45: Royal Armoured Corps and HQ London District, 1942–45. Asst Principal HM Treasury, 1947; Private Sec. to Economic Sec., 1948–49; Private Sec. to Permanent Sec. and Official Head of Civil Service (Sir Edward Bridges), 1954–56; Principal Private Sec. to: Chancellor of Exchequer (Mr Reginald Maudling), 1962–63; The Prime Minister (Mr Harold Wilson, previously Sir Alec Douglas-Home), 1964–66; Under-Sec., 1964; Dep. Under-Sec. of State, Dept of Economic Affairs, 1966–67; Dep. Sec., Min. of Agriculture, Fisheries and Food, 1967–69; Economic Minister and Head of UK Treasury and Supply Delegn, Washington, (also UK Executive Director for IMF and IBRD), 1969–72; Second Permanent Sec. (Overseas Finance), HM Treasury, 1973–77. Director: Guinness Mahon & Co., 1977–78; Bowater Corp., 1979–84; Bowater Industries, 1984–89; Bowater Inc., 1984–93; Standard Chartered, 1979–89; Indep. Dir, The Observer Ltd, 1981–93; Sen. Advr, Shearson Lehman Brothers Internat., 1979–88. Mem., PLA, 1979–82. Dir, Peter Hall Production Co. Ltd, 1989–90; Chm., Royal Nat. Theatre Foundn, 1989– (Treas., 1982–89). Mem. Council, University Coll. London, 1978–82; Governing Trustee, Nuffield Provincial Hospitals Trust, 1978–; Trustee, Royal Nat. Theatre Endowment Fund, 1990–. *Recreations:* opera, theatre, music, travel, motoring on minor roads. *Address:* 9 Holmbush Road, Putney, SW15 3LE. *T:* 0181–788 6581. *Club:* Garrick.

MITCHELL, Douglas Svärd; Controller of Personnel and Administrative Services, Greater London Council, 1972–78; *b* 21 Aug. 1918; *er s* of late James Livingstone Mitchell and Hilma Josefine (*née* Svärd); *m* 1943, Winifred Thornton Paterson, *d* of late William and Ellen Paterson; one *s* two *d*. *Educ:* Morgan Academy, Dundee. Royal Ordnance Factories, 1937–51; Principal, Min. of Supply, 1951–55; Dir of Personnel and Admin., in Industrial, Production and Engineering Groups, UKAEA, 1955–63; Authority Personnel Officer for UKAEA, 1963–64; Dir of Establishments, GLC, 1964–72. *Address:* The Manor House, Horncastle, Lincolnshire LN9 5HF. *T:* Horncastle (01507) 523553.

MITCHELL, Sir (Edgar) William (John), Kt 1990; CBE 1976; FRS 1986; Fellow of Wadham College, Oxford, 1978–92, now Emeritus Fellow; *b* Kingsbridge, S Devon, 25 Sept. 1925; *s* of late Edgar and Caroline Mitchell; *m* 1985, Prof. Margaret Davies (*née* Brown); one *s* by previous *m*. *Educ:* Univs of Sheffield (BSc, MSc) and Bristol (PhD). FInstP. Metropolitan Vickers Research Dept, 1946–48, 1950–51; Univ. of Bristol, 1948–50; University of Reading, 1951–78: Prof. of Physics, 1961–78; Dean, Faculty of Science, 1966–69; Dep. Vice-Chancellor, 1976–78; University of Oxford: Dr Lee's Prof. of Experimental Philosophy, 1978–88; Prof of Physics, 1988–89. Science and Engineering Research Council (formerly Science Research Council): Mem., 1970–74, 1982–85; Chm., 1985–90; Mem., 1965–70, Chm., 1967–70, Physics Cttee; Chm., Neutron Beam Res. Cttee, 1966–74 (devised scheme for extensive University use of nuclear res. reactors for condensed matter res.); Mem., Sci. Planning Gp for Spallation Neutron Source, 1978–85; Mem., Sci. Bd (formerly Univ. Sci. and Tech. Bd), 1967–70; Mem., Nuclear Physics Bd, 1980–85. Mem., Management Bd, British National Space Centre, 1986–90. Acting Jt Dir, 1973, Mem., 1973–80, Sci. Council of Inst. Laue-Langevin, Grenoble; Member: Comité de Direction, Solid State Physics Lab., Ecole Normale and Univ. of Paris VI, 1975–79; Exec. Cttee, Univ. Council for Non-Academic Staff, 1979–82; UGC Phys. Sci. Cttee, 1982–85; Council, Inst. of Physics, 1982–86; ABRC, 1985–90; Council, Foundn of Sci. and Technol., 1985–90; Innovation Adv. Bd, DTI, 1988–90; Scientific Adv. Cttee for Nat. Gall., 1988–; Chm., SE Reg. Computing Cttee, 1974–76; Vice-Pres., European Sci. Foundn, 1989–92; Member: Council, CERN, 1985–93 (Vice-Pres., 1990; Pres., 1991–93); CODEST, EEC, 1991–94; ESTA, EU, 1994–. Mem., Academia Europaea, 1989. Hon. DSc: Reading, 1987; Kent, 1988; Budapest, 1988; Birmingham, 1990. Officer's Cross, Order of Merit (Germany), 1990. *Publications:* numerous papers on solid state physics. *Recreations:* good food, opera, motoring, physics. *Address:* Wadham College, Oxford OX1 3PN.

MITCHELL, Mrs Eric; *see* Shacklock, Constance.

MITCHELL, Ewan; *see* Janner, Hon. G. E.

MITCHELL, Frank; *see* Mitchell, G. F.

MITCHELL, Rear-Adm. Geoffrey Charles, CB 1973; retired 1975; Director, The Old Granary Art and Craft Centre, Bishop's Waltham, Hants, 1975–86; *b* 21 July 1921; *s* of William C. Mitchell; *m* 1st, 1955, Jocelyn Rainger (*d* 1987), Auckland, NZ; one *s* two *d*; 2nd, 1990, Dr Hilary Gardiner. *Educ:* Marlborough College. Joined RN 1940; Captain 1961; Director Officer Recruiting, 1961–63; Captain (F), 2nd Frigate Sqdn, 1963–65; Director Naval Ops and Trade, 1965–67; Comdr, NATO Standing Naval Force Atlantic, 1968–69; Director Strategic Policy, to Supreme Allied Comdr Atlantic, 1969–71; Rear Adm. 1971; Dep. Asst Chief of Staff (Ops), SHAPE, 1971–74; Chm., RNR and Naval Cadet Forces Review Bd, 1974–75. *Recreations:* golf, painting, music, languages, sailing. *Address:* 10 Nelson Close, Stockbridge, Hants SO20 6ES. *T:* Stockbridge (01264) 810365.

MITCHELL, George Francis (Frank), FRS 1973; MRIA; environmental historian; *b* 15 Oct. 1912; *s* of late David William Mitchell and late Frances Elizabeth Kirby; *m* 1940, Lucy Margaret Gwynn (*d* 1987); two *d*. *Educ:* High Sch., Dublin; Trinity Coll., Dublin (MA, MSc); FTCD 1945. Joined staff of Trinity Coll., Dublin, 1934; Professor of Quaternary Studies, 1965–79. Pro-Chancellor, Univ. of Dublin, 1985–88. Pres., Internat. Union for Quaternary Research, 1969–73. MRIA 1939, PRIA 1976–79. HRHA 1981; Pres., An Taisce, 1991–93; Hon. Life Mem., RDS, 1981; Hon. Member: Prehistoric Soc., 1983; Quaternary Res. Assoc., 1983; Hon. FRSE 1984. DSc (*hc*): Queen's Univ., Belfast, 1976; NUI, 1977; fil.D (*hc*) Uppsala, 1977. *Publications:* The Irish Landscape, 1976; Treasures of Early Irish Art, 1977; Shell Guide to Reading the Irish Landscape, 1986; Archaeology and Environment in Early Dublin, 1987; Man and Environment on Valencia Island, Co. Kerry, 1989; The Way that I Followed, 1990; Where has Ireland come from?, 1994; (jtly) The Bog of Ardee, 1995. *Address:* Gardener's Cottage, Townley Hall, Drogheda, Co. Louth, Republic of Ireland. *T:* Drogheda 34615.

MITCHELL, Harry; QC 1987; Company Secretary, The Wellcome Foundation Ltd, 1976–92, and Wellcome plc, 1985–92; *b* 27 Oct. 1930; *s* of Harry and Lily Mitchell; *m* 1960, Mrs Megan Knill (*née* Watkins); one step *s* one step *d*. *Educ:* Bolton School; Corpus Christi College, Cambridge (BA). FCIS. Called to the Bar, Gray's Inn, 1968. Asst District Comr, Colonial Service, Sierra Leone, 1954–59; Company Sec., Asbestos Cement, Bombay, 1960–64; Asst Company Sec., British Aluminium Co., 1964–66; Legal Manager/Exec. Dir Legal, Hawker Siddeley Aviation, 1966–76. Chm., Bar Assoc. for Commerce, Finance and Industry, 1984–85 (Vice-Pres., 1986–); Mem. Senate of Inns of Court and Bar and Bar Council, 1978–81, 1983–86; Part-time Immigration Adjudicator, 1992–. Mem., CBI London Regional Council, 1990–92. Mem. Management Cttee, 1994–, Chm., 1995–, Sarsen Housing Assoc., Devizes. Trustee, Migraine Trust, 1995–. *Publications:* articles in New Law Jl and Business Law Review. *Recreations:* playing piano, opera, reading, travel. *Address:* c/o Immigration Appeals, York House, Dukes Green Avenue, Feltham, Middx TW14 0LR. *T:* 0181–893 1000.

MITCHELL, Helen Josephine; *see* Watts, H. J.

MITCHELL, Iain Grant; QC (Scot) 1992; a Temporary Sheriff, since 1992; *b* 15 Nov. 1951; *s* of John Grant Mitchell and Isobel (*née* Gilhespie). *Educ:* Perth Acad.; Edinburgh Univ. (LLB Hons 1973). Called to the Scottish Bar, 1976. Cons. local govt cand. on various occasions, 1973–82; contested (C): Falkirk W, 1983; Kirkcaldy, 1987; Cumbernauld and Kilsyth, 1992; Hon. Sec., Scottish Cons. & Unionist Assoc., 1993–; Vice-Chm., Edinburgh Central Cons. Assoc., 1994–. Member: Scottish Cttee, RIIA, 1985–; Exec. Cttee, Scottish Council, European Movement, 1992–; Scottish Cttee, Soc. for Computers and Law, 1991–; Cttee, Scottish Lawyers' European Gp, 1993–. Chm., Trust for an Internat. Opera Theatre of Scotland, 1984–; Vice-Chm., Scottish Baroque Ensemble Ltd, 1988–; Dir, Sinfonia of Scotland, 1990–93. FSA (Scot) 1974; FRSA 1988. *Recreations:* music and the arts, photography, cinema, walking, travel, finding enough hours in the day. *Address:* Advocates' Library, Parliament House, High Street, Edinburgh EH1 1RF. *T:* 0131–226 5071. *Clubs:* Caledonian, Edinburgh University Staff (Edinburgh).

MITCHELL, James; writer these many years; *b* South Shields, 12 March 1926; *s* of James Mitchell and Wilhelmina Mitchell; *m* 1968, Delia, *d* of Major and Mrs K. J. McCoy; two *s*. *Educ:* South Shields Grammar Sch.; St Edmund Hall, Oxford (BA 1948, MA 1950); King's Coll., Newcastle upon Tyne, Univ. of Durham (DipEd 1950). Worked in rep. theatre, 1948, then in shipyard, travel agency and Civil Service; taught for some fifteen years in almost every kind of instn from secondary modern sch. to coll. of art. Free-lance writer: novels; more than a hundred television scripts; several screenplays and a theatre play. *Publications:* Here's a Villain, 1957; A Way Back, 1959; Steady Boys, Steady, 1960; Among Arabian Sands, 1963; The Man Who Sold Death, 1964; Die Rich, Die Happy, 1965; The Money that Money can't Buy, 1967; The Innocent Bystanders, 1969; Ilion like a Mist, 1969; A Magnum for Schneider, 1969; The Winners, 1970; Russian Roulette, 1973; Death and Bright Water, 1974; Smear Job, 1975; When the Boat Comes In, 1976;

The Hungry Years, 1976; Upwards and Onwards, 1977; The Evil Ones, 1982; Sometimes You Could Die, 1985; Dead Ernest, 1986; Dying Day, 1988; A Woman To Be Loved, 1990; An Impossible Woman, 1992; Leading Lady, 1993. *Recreations:* travel, military history, aristology. *Club:* Lansdowne.

MITCHELL, James; Social Security Commissioner, since 1980; a Child Support Commissioner, since 1993; *b* 11 June 1926; *s* of James Hill Mitchell and Marjorie Kate Mitchell (*née* Williams); *m* 1957, Diane Iris Mackintosh; two *d*. *Educ:* Merchiston Castle Sch., Edinburgh; Brasenose Coll., Oxford, 1944–45 and 1948–51 (Open Exhibnr, BCL, MA). Served RAFVR, 1945–48. Assistant Master, Edge Grove Preparatory Sch., Herts, 1952–55; called to the Bar, Middle Temple, 1954; private practice as barrister/solicitor, Gold Coast/Ghana, 1956–58; practice as barrister, London, 1958–80. Most Hon. Order of Crown of Brunei, 3rd Cl. 1959, 2nd Cl. 1972. *Recreations:* sailing, walking, railways, the Jacobites. *Address:* (office) Harp House, 83/86 Farringdon Street, EC4A 4BL. *T:* 0171–353 5145.

MITCHELL, Dr James Clyde, FBA 1990; Emeritus Fellow, Nuffield College, Oxford, 1985 (Official Fellow, 1973–85); *b* 21 June 1918; *s* of George Shellard Mitchell and Rosina Kate Jones; *m* 1st, 1942, Edna Masken (*d* 1962); three *s* one *d*; 2nd, 1964, Hilary Flegg (*d* 1976); one step *d*; 3rd, 1987, Jean Edwards. *Educ:* Univ. of Natal (BA(Soc. Sci)); Univ. of Oxford (MA; DPhil 1950); Univ. of Manchester (MA). Served War, Air Navigator, SAAF, 1942–45. Rhodes-Livingstone Institute, Northern Rhodesia: Asst Anthropologist, 1945–50; Sen. Sociologist, 1950–52; Dir, 1952–55; Prof. of African Studies and Sociology, UC of Rhodesia and Nyasaland, 1955–65; Prof. of Urban Studies, Univ. of Manchester, 1966–73. Rivers Meml Medal, for distinguished fieldwork, RAI, 1964. *Publications:* The Yao Village, 1956, 3rd edn 1971; The Kalela Dance, 1957; (ed) Social Networks in Urban Situations, 1969, 2nd edn 1971; (ed with J. Boissevain) Network Analysis: studies in interaction, 1973; (ed) Numerical Techniques in Social Anthropology, 1980; Cities, Society and Social Perception, 1987; contrib. sociol and anthropol jls. *Recreations:* bird-watching, gardening. *Address:* 25 Staunton Road, Headington, Oxford OX3 7TJ. *T:* Oxford (01865) 62539.

MITCHELL, Rt. Hon. Sir James (Fitz Allen), KCMG 1995; PC 1985; MP for the Grenadines, since 1966; Prime Minister of St Vincent and the Grenadines, and Minister of Finance, since 1984; *b* 15 May 1931; *s* of Reginald and Lois Mitchell; *m* (marr. diss.); four *d*. *Educ:* Imperial College of Tropical Agriculture (DICTA); University of British Columbia (BSA). MIBiol 1965. Agronomist, 1958–65; owner, Hotel Frangipani, Bequia, 1966–, and other cos; Minister of Trade, Agriculture and Tourism, 1967–72; Premier, 1972–74; Minister of Foreign Affairs, 1984–92. Founder and Pres., New Democratic Party, 1975–; Chm., Caribbean Democrat Union, 1991–; Vice-Chm., Internat. Democrat Union, 1992–. Alumni Award of Distinction, Univ. of BC, 1988. Chevalier d'honneur, Chaîne des Rôtisseurs, 1995. Order of the Liberator, Venezuela, 1972. *Publications:* World Fungicide Usage, 1967; Caribbean Crusade, 1989. *Recreations:* farming, yachting, windsurfing. *Address:* Bequia, St Vincent, West Indies. *T:* 83263. *Clubs:* St Vincent Nat. Trust; Bequia Sailing.

MITCHELL, (James Lachlan) Martin, RD 1969; Sheriff of Lothian and Borders (formerly Lothians and Peebles), since 1974 (as a floating Sheriff, 1974–78, and at Edinburgh, 1978); *b* 13 June 1929; *o s* of late Dr L. M. V. Mitchell, OBE, MB, ChB and Harriet Doris Riggall; *m* 1993, Jane Anne, *d* of late Patrick Clement Cox. *Educ:* Cargilfield; Sedbergh; Univ. of Edinburgh. MA 1951, LLB 1953. Admitted Mem. Faculty of Advocates, 1957; Standing Junior Counsel in Scotland to Admty Bd, 1963–74. Nat. Service, RN, 1954–55; Sub-Lt (S) RNVR 1954; Perm. Reserve, 1956; Comdr RNR 1966, retd 1974. *Recreations:* fishing, photography, gramophone. *Address:* 3 Great Stuart Street, Edinburgh EH3 6AP. *T:* 0131–225 3384. *Clubs:* New (Edinburgh); Highland (Inverness).

MITCHELL, Jeremy George Swale Hamilton; consumer policy adviser; *b* 25 May 1929; *s* of late George Oswald Mitchell and Agnes Josephine Mitchell; *m* 1st, 1956, Margaret Mary Ayres (marr. diss. 1988); three *s* one *d*; 2nd, 1989, Janet Rosemary Powney. *Educ:* Ampleforth; Brasenose and Nuffield Colls, Oxford (MA). Dep. Research Dir, then Dir of Information, Consumers' Assoc. (Which?), 1958–65; Asst Sec., Nat. Econ. Develt Office, 1965–66; Scientific Sec., then Sec., SSRC, 1966–74; Under Sec., and Dir of Consumer Affairs, Office of Fair Trading, 1974–77; Under Sec. and Dir, Nat. Consumer Council, 1977–86. Member: Economic Develt Cttee for the Distributive Trades, 1981–86; Independent Cttee for Supervision of Telephone Information Services, 1989–; Direct Mail Services Standards Bd, 1990–95; Bd, PIA, 1994–; Scottish Consumer Council, 1995; Vice-Chm., Nat. Council on Gambling, 1981–. *Publications:* (ed) SSRC Reviews of Research, series, 1968–73; (ed jtly) Social Science Research and Industry, 1971; Betting, 1972; (ed) Marketing and the Consumer Movement, 1978; (ed jtly) The Information Society, 1985; (ed) Money and the Consumer, 1988; Electronic Banking and the Consumer, 1988; The Consumer and Financial Services, 1990; Banker's Racket or Consumer Benefit?, 1991; (ed jtly) Television and the Viewer Interest, 1994. *Recreation:* Swinburne. *Address:* 19 Eglinton Crescent, Edinburgh EH12 5BY.

MITCHELL, Prof. Joan Eileen, (Mrs James Cattermole); Professor of Political Economy, University of Nottingham, 1978–85; *b* 15 March 1920; *d* of late Albert Henry Mitchell, Paper Merchant, and Eva Mitchell; *m* 1956, James Cattermole; one *s* one *d*. *Educ:* Southend-on-Sea High Sch.; St Hilda's Coll., Oxford. Economist, Min. of Fuel and Power, 1942; Tutor, St Anne's Coll., Oxford, 1945; Economist, BoT, 1947; Research Officer, Labour Party, 1950; Lectr in Econs, Nottingham Univ., 1952, Reader in Econs, 1962. Mem., NBPI, 1965–68; personal economic adviser to Sec. of State for Prices and Consumer Protection, 1974–76. Member: Cttee to Review the Functioning of Financial Institutions, 1977–80 (Chm. Res. Panel); Standing Commn on Pay Comparability, 1979–81. *Publications:* Britain in Crisis 1951, 1963; Groundwork to Economic Planning, 1966; The National Board for Prices and Incomes, 1972; Price Determination and Prices Policy, 1978. *Recreations:* gardening, cooking. *Address:* 15 Ranmoor Road, Gedling, Nottingham NG4 3FW.

MITCHELL, (John) Angus (Macbeth), CB 1979; CVO 1961; MC 1946; Secretary, Scottish Education Department, 1976–84; *b* 25 Aug. 1924; *s* of late John Fowler Mitchell, CIE and Sheila Macbeth, MBE; *m* 1948, Ann Katharine Williamson, MA, MPhil, author; two *s* two *d*. *Educ:* Marlborough Coll.; Brasenose Coll., Oxford (Junior Hulme Scholar); BA Modern Hist., 1948. Served Royal Armoured Corps, 1943–46: Lieut, Inns of Court Regt, NW Europe, 1944–45; Captain East African Military Records, 1946. Entered Scottish Education Dept, 1949; Private Sec. to Sec. of State for Scotland, 1958–59; Asst Sec., Scottish Educn Dept, 1959–65; Dept of Agriculture and Fisheries for Scotland, 1965–68; Scottish Development Dept, 1968; Asst Under-Secretary of State, Scottish Office, 1968–69; Under Sec., Social Work Services Gp, Scottish Educn Dept, 1969–75; Under Sec., SHHD, 1975–76. Chairman: Scottish Marriage Guidance Council, 1965–69; Working Party on Social Work Services in NHS, 1976; Working Party on Relationships between Health Bds and Local Authorities, 1976; Consultative Cttee on the Curriculum, 1976–80; Stirling Univ. Court, 1984–92; Scottish Action on Dementia, 1985–94; Vice-Convener, Scottish Council for Voluntary Orgs, 1986–91; Member: Commn for Local Authority Accounts in Scotland, 1985–89; Historic Buildings Council for Scotland, 1988–94; Co-ordinator, Recording Scottish Graveyards Project, 1992–; Sec., Greyfriars Kirkyard Trust, 1992–. Hon. Fellow, Edinburgh Univ. Dept of Politics, 1984–88. Hon. LLD Dundee, 1983; DUniv Stirling, 1992. Kt, Order of Oranje-Nassau (Netherlands), 1946. *Publications:* Procedures for the Reorganisation of Schools in England (report), 1987; Recording of Monumental Inscriptions, 1991. *Recreations:* old Penguins; gravestones. *Address:* 20 Regent Terrace, Edinburgh EH7 5BS. *T:* 0131–556 7671. *Club:* New (Edinburgh).

See also J. J. Mitchell.

MITCHELL, John Gall, QC (Scot.) 1970; a Social Security (formerly National Insurance) Commissioner, since 1979; a Child Support Commissioner, since 1993; *b* 5 May 1931; *s* of late Rev. William G. Mitchell, MA; *m* 1st, 1959, Anne Bertram Jardine (*d* 1986); three *s* one *d*; 2nd, 1988, Margaret, *d* of J. W. Galbraith. *Educ:* Royal High Sch., Edinburgh; Edinburgh Univ. (MA, LLB). Commn, HM Forces, 1954–56 (Nat. Service). Advocate 1957. Standing Junior Counsel, Customs and Excise, Scotland, 1964–70; Chairman: Industrial Tribunals, Scotland, 1966–80; Legal Aid Supreme Court Cttee, Scotland, 1974–79; Pensions Appeals Tribunal, Scotland, 1974–80. Hon. Sheriff of Lanarkshire, 1970–74. *Address:* c/o Office of the Social Security Commissioners, 23 Melville Street, Edinburgh EH3 7PW.

MITCHELL, John Logan; QC (Scot) 1987; *b* 23 June 1947; *s* of Robert Mitchell and Dorothy Mitchell; *m* 1973, Christine Brownlee Thomson; one *s* one *d*. *Educ:* Royal High School, Edinburgh(Past Pres., FP Club); Edinburgh Univ. (LLB Hons). Called to the Bar, 1974; Standing Junior Counsel: to Dept of Agriculture and Fisheries for Scotland, 1979; Forestry Commission for Scotland, 1979; Advocate Depute, 1981–85. *Recreation:* golf. *Address:* 17 Braid Farm Road, Edinburgh. *T:* 0131–447 8099. *Club:* Mortonhall Golf.

MITCHELL, John Matthew, CBE 1976; PhD; Assistant Director-General, 1981–84, Senior Research Fellow, 1984–85, British Council; retired; *b* 22 March 1925; *s* of Clifford George Arthur Mitchell and Grace Maud Jamson; *m* 1952, Eva Maria von Rupprecht; three *s* one *d*. *Educ:* Ilford County High Sch.; Worcester Coll., Oxford; Queens' Coll., Cambridge (MA). PhD Vienna. Served War, RN, 1944–46. British Council: Lectr, Austria, 1949–52 and Egypt, 1952–56; Scotland, 1957–60; Dep. Rep., Japan, 1960–63; Reg. Dir, Zagreb, 1963–66; Reg. Rep., Dacca, 1966–69; Dep. Controller, Home Div., 1969–72; Rep., Federal Republic of Germany, 1973–77; Controller, Educn, Medicine and Sci. Div., 1977–81. Vis. Fellow, Wolfson Coll., Cambridge, 1972–73; former Lectr, univs of Vienna, Cairo and Tokyo. Fellow, Inst. of Linguists (Chairman: Translating Div., 1990–; Members' Cttee, 1992–). *Publications:* International Cultural Relations, 1986; verse, short stories and trans. from German and French. *Recreations:* ski-ing, theatre, cinema, opera. *Address:* The Cottage, Pains Hill Corner, Pains Hill, Limpsfield, Surrey RH8 0RB. *T:* Oxted (01883) 723354. *Clubs:* National Liberal; Tandridge Golf.

MITCHELL, John Wesley, FRS 1956; PhD, DSc; Senior Research Fellow and Emeritus Professor, University of Virginia, since 1979; *b* 3 Dec. 1913; *s* of late John Wesley Mitchell and late Lucy Ruth Mitchell; *m* 1976, Virginia Hill; one step *d* of former marriage. *Educ:* Canterbury University Coll., Christchurch, NZ; Univ. of Oxford. BSc 1934. MSc 1935, NZ; PhD 1938, DSc 1960, Oxford. Reader in Experimental Physics in the Univ. of Bristol, 1945–59; Prof. of Physics, Univ. of Virginia, 1959–63; Dir of the National Chemical Laboratory, Oct. 1963–Aug. 1964; William Barton Rogers Prof. of Physics, Univ. of Virginia, 1964–79. Commonwealth of Virginia Lifetime Achievement Award in Science, 1993. *Publications:* various on photographic sensitivity and on plastic deformation of crystals in scientific journals. *Recreations:* mountaineering, colour photography. *Address:* Department of Physics, University of Virginia, Charlottesville, VA 22901, USA. *Clubs:* Athenæum; Cosmos (Washington, DC).

MITCHELL, Jonathan James; QC (Scot) 1992; *b* 4 Aug. 1951; *s* of (John) Angus (Macbeth) Mitchell, *qv* and Ann Katharine (*née* Williamson); *m* 1987, Melinda McGarry; one *s* one *d*. *Educ:* Marlborough Coll.; New Coll., Oxford (BA); Edinburgh Univ. (LLB). Advocate, 1979; Temp. Sheriff, 1988–. Dep. Social Security Comr, 1994–. Mem., Scotch Malt Whisky Soc. *Publication:* Eviction and Rent Arrears, 1994. *Address:* 30 Warriston Crescent, Edinburgh EH3 5LB. *T:* 0131–557 0854, *Fax:* 0131–557 3210.

MITCHELL, Joseph Rodney; Director General of Defence Accounts, Ministry of Defence, 1973, retired; *b* 11 March 1914; *s* of late Joseph William and Martha Mitchell, Sheffield; *m* 1936, Marian Richardson; two *s* three *d*. *Educ:* Sheffield Central Secondary School. FCCA, ACMA, ACIS. Works Recorder and Junior Costs Clerk, United Steel Cos Ltd, Sheffield, 1930–35; Senior Accounts Clerk, Cargo Fleet Iron Co. Ltd, Middlesbrough, 1936–39; Royal Ordnance Factories, 1940–55: Chief Exec. Officer, 1951–55; Min. of Supply/Aviation/Technology, 1956–71: Dir of Accounts, 1967–71; Dep. Dir Gen. of Defence Accounts, MoD, 1971–72. *Recreation:* hill-walking. *Address:* 4 Orchard Court, Hathersage Road, Grindleford, Sheffield S30 1JH.

MITCHELL, Julian; writer; *b* 1 May 1935; *s* of late William Moncur Mitchell and of Christine Mary (*née* Browne). *Educ:* Winchester; Wadham Coll. Oxford. Nat. Service in Submarines, 1953–55; Temp. Acting Sub-Lieut, RNVR. Member: Literature Panel, Arts Council, 1966–69; Welsh Arts Council, 1988–92 (Chm. Drama Cttee, 1989–92). John Llewellyn Rhys Prize, 1965; Somerset Maugham Award, 1966. Television plays include: Shadow in the Sun; A Question of Degree; Rust; Abide With Me (Internat. Critics Prize, Monte Carlo, 1977); Survival of the Fittest; adaptations of: Persuasion; The Alien Corn; Staying On; The Good Soldier; The Mysterious Stranger; The Weather in the Streets; Inspector Morse; series, Jennie, Lady Randolph Churchill, 1974; television documentary: All the Waters of Wye, 1990. Films: Arabesque, 1965; Vincent and Theo, 1990. Theatre: Adelina Patti, 1987. *Publications: novels:* Imaginary Toys, 1961; A Disturbing Influence, 1962; As Far As You Can Go, 1963; The White Father, 1964; A Circle of Friends, 1966; The Undiscovered Country, 1968; *biography:* (with Peregrine Churchill) Jennie: Lady Randolph Churchill, 1974; *translation:* Henry IV (Pirandello), 1979 (John Florio Prize, 1980); *plays:* Half-Life, 1977; The Enemy Within, 1980; Another Country, 1981 (SWET play of the year, 1982; filmed, 1984); Francis, 1983; After Aida (or Verdi's Messiah), 1986; Falling Over England, 1994; August, 1994 (adapted from Chekhov's Uncle Vanya; filmed, 1995); (adapted from Ivy Compton-Burnett): A Heritage and Its History, 1965; A Family and a Fortune, 1975; contribs to: Welsh History Review, The Monmouthshire Antiquary. *Recreations:* local history, fishing. *Address:* 47 Draycott Place, SW3 3DB. *Club:* Garrick.

MITCHELL, Keith Kirkman, OBE 1979; Lecturer in Physical Education, University of Leeds, 1955–90; *b* 25 May 1927; *s* of John Stanley Mitchell and Annie Mitchell; *m* 1950, Hannah Forrest; two *s*. *Educ:* Loughborough Coll. (Hons Dip. in Physical Educn). Phys. Educn Master, Wisbech Grammar Sch., 1950–52; Dir of Phys. Recreation, Manchester YMCA, 1952–55. Chm. Exec. Cttee, CCPR, 1981–87; Mem., Sports Council, 1976–87. Dir, 1953–84, Pres., 1985–, English Basketball Assoc. *Recreations:* basketball, photography, gardening, golf. *Address:* 7 Park Crescent, Guiseley, West Yorks LS20 8EL. *T:* Guiseley (01943) 875248.

MITCHELL, Martin; *see* Mitchell, J. L. M.

MITCHELL, Dame Mona (Ann), DCVO 1992 (CVO 1985; LVO 1976); Extra Lady-in-Waiting to HRH Princess Alexandra, the Hon. Lady Ogilvy, since 1968; *b* 20 Feb. 1938; *d* of Maj.-Gen. Francis Neville Mitchell, CB, CBE, DSO and late Ann Christian Mitchell (*née* Livingstone-Learmouth; she *m* 2nd, 1962, Brig. Richard Headlam Keenlyside, CBE, DSO). *Educ:* North Foreland Lodge. Secretary to: Fulke Walwyn, 1958–62; E. Hardy Amies, 1963–68; Sec., 1968–74, Private Sec., 1974–91, to HRH Princess Alexandra. *Recreations:* gardening, music, the arts in general. *Address:* Valley Farm, Blackford, Yeovil, Somerset BA22 7EF. *T:* North Cadbury (01963) 440304. *Club:* Army and Navy.

MITCHELL, Very Rev. Patrick Reynolds; Dean of Windsor, since 1989; Register, Order of the Garter, since 1989; Domestic Chaplain to the Queen, since 1989; *b* 17 March 1930; *s* of late Lt-Col Percy Reynolds Mitchell, DSO; *m* 1st, 1959, Mary Evelyn (*née* Phillips) (*d* 1986); three *s* one *d*; 2nd, 1988, Pamela, *d* of late A. G. Le Marchant and *widow* of Henry Douglas-Pennant; one step *s* one step *d* (and two step *s* decd). *Educ:* Eton Coll.; Merton Coll., Oxford (MA Theol); Wells Theol Coll. Officer in Welsh Guards (National Service), 1948–49. Deacon, 1954; priest, 1955; Curate at St Mark's, Mansfield, 1954–57; Priest-Vicar of Wells Cathedral and Chaplain of Wells Theological Coll., 1957–60; Vicar of St James', Milton, Portsmouth, 1961–67; Vicar of Frome Selwood, Somerset, 1967–73; Dean of Wells, 1973–89; Director of Ordination Candidates for Bath and Wells, 1971–74. Res. Fellow, Merton Coll., Oxford, 1984. Member: Adv. Bd for Redundant Churches, 1978–92; Cathedrals Adv. Commn for England, 1981–91. Governor, Wellington Coll., 1994–. Hon. Freeman, City of Wells, 1986. FSA 1981. *Address:* The Deanery, Windsor Castle, Berks SL4 1NJ. *T:* Windsor (01753) 865561.

MITCHELL, Richard Charles, (Bob); Lecturer in Business Studies, Eastleigh College of Further Education, 1984–93; *b* 22 Aug. 1927; *s* of Charles and Elizabeth Mitchell; *m* 1950, Doreen Lilian Gregory; one *s* one *d*. *Educ:* Taunton's Sch., Southampton; Godalming County Gram. Sch.; Southampton Univ. BSc(Econ) Hons 1951. Bartley County Sec. Sch.: Senior Master and Head of Maths and Science Dept, 1957–65; Dep. Headmaster, 1965–66. MP (Lab) Southampton Test, 1966–70; MP (Lab 1971–81, SDP 1981–83) Southampton, Itchen, May 1971–1983. Contested Southampton, Itchen (SDP) 1983, (SDP/Alliance) 1987. Mem., European Parlt, 1975–79. Member: Bureau of European Socialist Gp, 1976–79; Chairman's Panel, House of Commons, 1979–83. Vice-Chm. Govs, Sholing Girls' Secondary Sch., 1991–; Gov., Itchen Sixth Form Coll., 1984–. *Publication:* (jtly) Public Administration: a casebook approach, 1991. *Recreation:* postal chess (rep. Brit. Correspondence Chess Assoc. against other countries). *Address:* 49 Devonshire Road, Polygon, Southampton SO15 2GL. *T:* Southampton (01703) 221781.

MITCHELL, Robert, OBE 1984; Chairman and Managing Director, R. Mitchell & Co. (Eng) Ltd, 1959–81; Councillor, Greater London Council, 1964–86; *b* 14 Dec. 1913; *s* of Robert Mitchell and Lizzie Mitchell (*née* Snowdon); *m* 1946, Reinholda Thorretta L. C. Kettlitz; two *s* one step *s*. *Educ:* West Ham Secondary Sch.; St John's Coll., Cambridge (MA Hons NatSci). Councillor, Wanstead and Woodford Council, 1958–65, Dep. Mayor, 1960–61. Chairman: GLC, 1971–72; Fire Brigade and Ambulance Cttees, 1967–71; Nat. Jt Negotiating Cttee for Local Authority Fire Brigades, 1970–71; Covent Gdn Jt Develt Cttee, 1972–73; Professional and Gen. Services Cttee, 1977–79; Greater London Jt Supply Bd, 1977–79. Member: CBI Cttee on State Intervention in Private Industry, 1976–78; London and SE Reg. Council, 1969–79; Smaller Firms Council, 1977–79; Policy Cttee, AMA, 1978–79. Wanstead and Woodford Conservative Association: Vice-Chm., 1961–65; Chm., 1965–68; Vice-Pres., 1968–; contested (C) West Ham South, 1964 and 1966 gen. elecs. Represented: Cambridge Univ., swimming and water polo, 1932–35 (Captain, 1935); England and Gt Britain, water polo, 1934–48, incl. Olympic Games, 1936 and 1948; Gt Britain, swimming and water polo, World Univ. Games, 1933, 1935; Rest of World *v* Champions, water polo, Univ. Games, 1935; Captain, 1946–49, Pres., 1955–56, Plaistow United Swimming Club; London Rep., Cambridge Univ. Swimming Club, 1953–75. Mem. Cttee, Crystal Palace Nat. Sports Centre, 1965–88. Chm., London Ecology Centre Ltd, 1986–88; Gov., London Ecology Centre Trust, 1985–88; Verderer, Epping Forest, 1976–; Mem., Lea Valley Regl Park Auth., 1982–85. Liveryman, Worshipful Co. of Gardeners, 1975–. Governor, Chigwell Sch., 1966– (Vice-Chm., 1968–88). Grand Officer, Order of Orange Nassau (Holland), 1972; Order of Star (Afghanistan), 1971; Order of Rising Sun (Japan), 1971. *Publications:* Bob Mitchell's Epping Forest Companion, 1991; newspaper and magazine articles mainly on countryside and political subjects. *Recreation:* planting trees, then sitting watching them grow. *Address:* Hatchwood House, Nursery Road, Loughton, Essex IG10 4EF. *T:* 0181–508 9135; Little Brigg, Bessingham, Norfolk NR11 7JR. *Clubs:* Carlton; Hawks (Cambridge).

MITCHELL, Hon. Dame Roma (Flinders), AC 1991; DBE 1982 (CBE 1971); Governor of South Australia, since 1991; Senior Puisne Judge, Supreme Court of South Australia, 1979–83 (Judge of Supreme Court, 1965–83); *b* 2 Oct. 1913; *d* of Harold Flinders Mitchell and Maude Imelda Victoria (*née* Wickham). *Educ:* St Aloysius Coll., Adelaide; Univ. of Adelaide (LLB 1934). Admitted as Practitioner, Supreme Court of SA, 1934; QC 1962 (first woman QC in Australia). Sen. Dep. Chancellor, 1972–83, Chancellor, 1983–90, Univ. of Adelaide. Chairman: Parole Bd of SA, 1974–81; Criminal Law Reform Cttee of SA, 1971–81; Human Rights Commn of Australia, 1981–86; State Heritage Cttee of SA, 1978–81; SA Council on Child Protection, 1988–90; National President: Winston Churchill Meml Trust, 1988–91 (Dep. Chm., 1975–84; Nat. Chm., 1984–88); Australian Assoc. of Ryder-Cheshire Foundn, 1979–91. Member: Council for Order of Australia, 1980–90; Bd of Governors, Adelaide Festival of Arts, 1981–84. Boyer Lectr, ABC, 1975. Hon. FRACP 1992. DUniv Adelaide, 1985; Hon. LLD: Queensland, 1992; Flinders Univ. of S Australia, 1993; Univ. of S Australia, 1994. Medal, Instn of Engrs, 1994. *Recreations:* theatre, music, art, swimming, walking. *Address:* Government House, Adelaide, SA 5000, Australia. *Clubs:* Queen Adelaide, Lyceum (Adelaide).

MITCHELL, Prof. Ross Galbraith, MD, FRCPE, DCH; Professor of Child Health, University of Dundee and Pædiatrician, Ninewells Hospital, Dundee, 1973–85, now Emeritus; *b* 18 Nov. 1920; *s* of late Richard Galbraith Mitchell, OBE and Ishobel, *d* of late James Ross, Broadford, Skye; *m* 1950, June Phylis Butcher; one *s* three *d*. *Educ:* Kelvinside Acad.; University of Edinburgh. MB, ChB Edinburgh, 1944. Surg-Lt, RNVR, 1944–47; Jun. hosp. posts, Liverpool, London, Edinburgh, 1947–52; Rockefeller Res. Fellow, Mayo Clinic, USA, 1952–53; Lectr in Child Health, Univ. of St Andrews, 1952–55; Cons. Pædiatrician, Dundee Teaching Hosps, 1955–63; Prof. of Child Health, Univ. of Aberdeen, Pædiatrician, Royal Aberdeen Children's and Aberdeen Maternity Hosps, 1963–72; Univ. of Dundee: Dean, Faculty of Medicine and Dentistry, 1978–81; Mem. Court, 1982–85. Chairman: Scottish Adv. Council on Child Care, 1966–69; Specialist Adv. Cttee on Pædiatrics, 1975–79; Academic Bd, British Pædiatric Assoc., 1975–78; Spastics Internat. Med. Pubns, 1981–85; Mac Keith Press, London, 1986–95; Mem., GMC, 1983–86. President: Harveian Soc., Edinburgh, 1982–83; Scottish Paediatric Soc., 1982–84. For. Corresp. Mem., Amer. Acad. of Cerebral Palsy and Developmental Medicine, 1965–. Jt Editor, Developmental Medicine and Child Neurology, 1968–80. *Publications:* Disease in Infancy and Childhood, (7th edn) 1973; Child Life and Health (5th edn), 1970; Child Health in the Community (2nd edn), 1980; contribs to textbooks of paediatrics, medicine and obstetrics and articles in scientific and medical jls. *Recreations:* Celtic language and literature, fishing. *Address:* Craigard, Abertay Gardens, Barnhill, Dundee DD5 2SQ.

MITCHELL, Hon. Sir Stephen (George), Kt 1993; **Hon. Mr Justice Mitchell;** a Judge of the High Court of Justice, Queen's Bench Division, since 1993; *b* 19 Sept. 1941; *s* of Sydney Mitchell and Joan Mitchell (*née* Dick); *m* 1978, Alison Clare (*née* Roseveare); two *d*. *Educ:* Bedford Sch.; Hertford Coll., Oxford (MA). Called to the Bar, Middle Temple, 1964, Bencher, 1993; Second Prosecuting Counsel to the Crown, Inner London Crown Court, 1975; Central Criminal Court: a Junior Prosecuting Counsel to the Crown, 1977; a Senior Prosecuting Counsel to the Crown, 1981–86; QC 1986; a Recorder, 1985–89; a Circuit Judge, 1989–93. Mem., Judicial Studies Bd, 1991–93. *Publications:* (ed) Phipson on Evidence, 11th edn, 1970; (ed) Archbold's Criminal Pleading Evidence and Practice, 1971–88. *Address:* Royal Courts of Justice, Strand, WC2A 2LL.

MITCHELL, Terence Croft; Keeper of Western Asiatic Antiquities, British Museum, 1985–89; *b* 17 June 1929; *s* of late Arthur Croft Mitchell and Evelyn Violet Mitchell (*née* Ware). *Educ:* Holderness School, New Hampshire, USA; Bradfield Coll., Berks; St Catharine's Coll., Cambridge (MA 1956). REME Craftsman, 1947–49. Asst Master, St Catherine's Sch., Almondsbury, 1954–56; Resident Study, Tyndale House, Cambridge, 1956–58; European Rep., Aust. Inst. of Archaeology, 1958–59; Dept of Western Asiatic Antiquities, British Museum, 1959, Dep. Keeper, 1974, Acting Keeper, 1983–85. Chm., Victoria Inst., 1986–; Vice Chm., British Inst. at Amman for Archaeology and History, 1990–93. Editor, Palestine Exploration Fund Monograph Series, 1990–. *Publications:* Sumerian Art at Ur and Al-'Ubaid, 1969; (ed) Sir Leonard Woolley, Ur Excavations VIII, The Kassite Period and the Period of the Assyrian Kings, 1965; VII, The Old Babylonian Period, 1976; (ed) Music and Civilization, 1980; chapters on Israel and Judah in Cambridge Ancient History, vol. 3, part 1, 1982, part 2, 1991; The Bible in the British Museum: interpreting the evidence, 1988; articles and reviews. *Recreations:* music, reading, landscape gardening. *Address:* 32 Mallord Street, Chelsea, SW3 6DU. *T:* 0171–352 3962. *Club:* Athenæum.

MITCHELL, Warren; *b* 14 Jan. 1926; *s* of Montague and Annie Misell, later Mitchell; *m* 1952, Constance Wake; three *s*. *Educ:* Southgate Co. Sch.; University Coll., Oxford; RADA. Demobbed RAF, 1946. First professional appearance, Finsbury Park Open Air Theatre, 1950; Theophile in Can-Can, Coliseum, 1954; Crookfinger Jake in The Threepenny Opera, Royal Court and Aldwych, 1956; Mr Godboy in Dutch Uncle, Aldwych, 1969; Satan in Council of Love, Criterion, 1970; Herbert in Jump, Queen's, 1971; Ion Will in The Great Caper, Royal Court, 1974; The Thoughts of Chairman Alf, Stratford E, 1976; Willie Loman in Death of a Salesman, Nat. Theatre, 1979; Ducking Out, Duke of York's, 1983; Harpagon in The Miser, Birmingham Rep, 1986; Max in The Homecoming, 1991; *films include:* Diamonds Before Breakfast; Assassination Bureau; Best House in London; Till Death Us Do Part; Moon Zero Two; Whatever Happened to Charlie Farthing; Jabberwocky; Stand Up Virgin Soldiers; Meetings with Remarkable Men; Norman Loves Rose; The Chain; *television:* Alf Garnett in Till Death Us Do Part, BBC, 1966–78, and In Sickness and in Health, BBC, 1985, 1986; Shylock in Merchant of Venice, BBC, 1981; Till Death, ITV, 1981; The Caretaker, BBC, 1981; So You Think You've Got Troubles, BBC; Wall of Silence, BBC. TV Actor of the Year Award, Guild of Film and TV Producers, 1966; Actor of Year Award: Evening Standard, 1979; Soc. of West End Theatres, 1979; Plays and Players, 1979. *Recreations:* sailing, tennis, playing clarinet. *Address:* c/o ICM, Oxford House, 76 Oxford Street, W1R 1RB.

MITCHELL, Dame Wendy, DBE 1992 (OBE 1986); President, National Union of Conservative and Unionist Associations, 1993–94 (Vice-Chairman, 1990–93); *b* 14 Sept. 1932; *d* of Guy Francis Dell and Sophia Dell; *m* 1963, Anthony John Mitchell; one *s* one *d*. *Educ:* Heathfield House High Sch., Cardiff. Cardiff Royal Infirmary (SRN); St David's Hosp. and Queen's Inst., Cardiff (SCM). Mem., SE Thames RHA, 1986–94, S Thames RHA, 1994–; Dep. Chm., Women's Nationwide Cancer Control Campaign, 1986–94. Councillor, London Borough of Greenwich, 1974–94; Chairman: W Woolwich (Eltham) Cons. Assoc., 1974–77 (Pres., 1988–91); Greater London Area Cons. Women's Cttee, 1983–86; Cons. Women's Nat. Cttee, 1987–90; Dep. Chm., Greater London Area Cons. Exec., 1987. FRSA. *Recreation:* reading. *T:* 0181–850 3591. *Club:* Royal Society of Medicine.

MITCHELL, Sir William; *see* Mitchell, Sir E. W. J.

MITCHELL, Rt. Rev. Mgr. William Joseph; Vicar General, Diocese of Clifton, since 1987; *b* 4 Jan. 1936; *s* of William Ernest and Catherine Mitchell. *Educ:* St Brendan's Coll., Bristol; Corpus Christi Coll., Oxford (MA); Séminaire S Sulpice, Paris; Gregorian Univ., Rome (LCL). Ordained Priest, Pro-Cathedral, Bristol, 1961; Curate, Pro-Cathedral, Bristol, 1963–64; Secretary to Bishop of Clifton, 1964–75; Parish Priest, St Bernadette, Bristol, 1975–78; Rector, Pontifical Beda Coll., Rome, 1978–87; Parish Priest, St John's, Bath, 1988–90. Prelate of Honour, 1978. *Address:* St Anthony's Presbytery, Satchfield Crescent, Henbury, Bristol BS10 7BE. *T:* Bristol (0117) 983 3906, *Fax:* (0117) 983 3934.

MITCHELL COTTS, Sir R. C.; *see* Cotts.

MITCHELL-INNES, Alistair Campbell; Chairman, Sidney Banks, since 1994; *b* 1 March 1934; *s* of Peter Campbell Mitchell-Innes and Frances Jocelyn (*née* Ash); *m* 1957, Penelope Ann Hill; one *s* two *d*. *Educ:* Charterhouse; Stanford Business Sch. (Executive Program). Dir, Brooke Bond Gp plc, 1979–84; Chief Exec., Nabisco Gp Ltd, 1985–88; Chief Exec., Isosceles plc, 1991–93; Dep. Chm., H. P. Bulmer (Holdings) plc, 1990–. Non-Executive Director: Next plc, 1989–; Evans Halshaw plc, 1989–. *Recreations:* golf, cricket, gardening. *Address:* Langton Lodge, Station Road, Sunningdale, Berks SL5 0QR. *Clubs:* Caledonian, MCC; Berkshire Golf.

MITCHELL-THOMSON, family name of **Baron Selsdon.**

MITCHISON, Avrion; *see* Mitchison, N. A.

MITCHISON, Prof. Denis Anthony, CMG 1984; Professor of Bacteriology, Royal Postgraduate Medical School, 1971–84, Professor Emeritus, London University, since 1984; at St George's Hospital Medical School, since 1993; Director, Medical Research Council's Unit for Laboratory Studies of Tuberculosis, 1956–84; *b* 6 Sept. 1919; *e s* of Baron Mitchison, CBE, QC, and of Naomi Margaret Mitchison, *qv*; *m* 1st, 1940, Ruth Sylvia (*d* 1992), *d* of Hubert Gill; two *s* two *d*; 2nd, 1993, Honora, *d* of Christopher Carlin. *Educ:* Abbotsholme Sch.; Trinity Coll., Cambridge; University Coll. Hosp., London (MB, ChB). House Physician Addenbrooke's Hosp., Royal Berkshire Hosp.; Asst to Pathologist, Brompton Hosp.; Prof. of Bacteriology (Infectious Diseases), RPGMS, 1968–71. FRCP; FRCPath. *Publications:* numerous papers on bacteriology and chemotherapy of tuberculosis. *Address:* 14 Marlborough Road, Richmond, Surrey TW10 6JR. *T:* 0181–940 4751.

See also J. M. Mitchison, N. A. Mitchison.

MITCHISON, Prof. John Murdoch, ScD; FRS 1978; FRSE 1966; Professor of Zoology, University of Edinburgh, 1963–88, now Professor Emeritus and Hon. Fellow; *b* 11 June 1922; *s* of Lord Mitchison, CBE, QC, and of N. Haldane (*see* Naomi M. Mitchison); *m* 1947, Rosalind Mary Wrong; one *s* three *d*. *Educ:* Winchester Coll.; Trinity Coll., Cambridge. Army Operational Research, 1941–46; Sen. and Research Scholar, Trinity Coll., Cambridge, 1946–50; Fellow, Trinity Coll., Cambridge, 1950–54; Edinburgh University: Lectr in Zoology, 1953–59; Reader in Zoology, 1959–62; Dean, Faculty of Science, 1984–85; Mem. of Court, 1971–74, 1985–88. J. W. Jenkinson Memorial Lectr, Oxford, 1971–72. Member: Council, Scottish Marine Biol. Assoc., 1961–67; Exec. Cttee, Internat. Soc. for Cell Biology, 1964–72; Biol Cttee, SRC, 1972–75; Royal Commn on Environmental Pollution, 1974–79; Science Bd, SRC, 1976–79; Working Gp on Biol Manpower, DES, 1968–71; Adv. Cttee on Safety of Nuclear Installations, Health and Safety Exec., 1981–84. Pres., British Soc. for Cell Biology, 1974–77. Mem., Academia Europaea, 1989. FInstBiol 1963. *Publications:* The Biology of the Cell Cycle, 1971; papers in scientific jls. *Address:* Great Yew, Ormiston, East Lothian EH35 5NJ. *T:* Pencaitland (01875) 340530.

See also D. A. Mitchison, N. A. Mitchison.

MITCHISON, Naomi Margaret, CBE 1985; **(Lady Mitchison** since 1964, but she still wishes to be called Naomi Mitchison); *b* Edinburgh, 1 Nov. 1897; *d* of late John Scott Haldane, CH, FRS, and Kathleen Trotter; *m* 1916, G. R. Mitchison (*d* 1970), CBE, QC, created a Baron (Life Peer), 1964; three *s* two *d*. *Educ:* Dragon Sch., Oxford; home student, Oxford. Officier d'Académie Française, 1924; Argyll CC, 1945–65, on and off; Highland and Island Advisory Panel, 1947–65; Highlands and Islands Develt Consult. Council, 1966–76; Tribal Mother to Bakgatla, Botswana, 1963–. DUniv.: Stirling, 1976; Dundee, 1985; DLitt Strathclyde, 1983. Hon. Fellow: St Anne's Coll., Oxford, 1980; Wolfson Coll., Oxford, 1983. *Publications:* The Conquered, 1923; When the Bough Breaks, 1924; Cloud Cuckoo Land, 1925; The Laburnum Branch, 1926; Black Sparta, 1928; Anna Comnena, 1928; Nix-Nought-Nothing, 1928; Barbarian Stories, 1929; The Hostages, 1930; Comments on Birth Control, 1930; The Corn King and the Spring Queen, 1931; The Price of Freedom (with L. E. Gielgud), 1931; Boys and Girls and Gods, 1931; The Powers of Light, 1932; (ed) An Outline for Boys and Girls, 1932; The Delicate Fire, 1933; Vienna Diary, 1934; The Home, 1934; We Have Been Warned, 1935; Beyond this Limit, 1935; The Fourth Pig, 1936; Socrates (with R. H. S. Crossman), 1937; An End and a Beginning, 1937; The Moral Basis of Politics, 1938; The Kingdom of Heaven, 1939; As It was in the Beginning (with L. E. Gielgud), 1939; The Blood of the Martyrs, 1939; (ed) Re-educating Scotland, 1944; The Bull Calves, 1947; Men and Herring (with D. Macintosh), 1949; The Big House, 1950; Spindrift (*play:* with D. Macintosh), Citizens' Theatre, Glasgow, 1951; Lobsters on the Agenda, 1952; Travel Light, 1952; The Swan's Road, 1954; Graeme and the Dragon, 1954; The Land the Ravens Found, 1955; To the Chapel Perilous, 1955; Little Boxes, 1956; Behold your King, 1957; The Far Harbour, 1957; Five Men and a Swan, 1958; Other People's Worlds, 1958; Judy and Lakshmi, 1959; The Rib of the Green Umbrella, 1960; The Young Alexander, 1960; Karensgaard, 1961; The Young Alfred the Great, 1962; Memoirs of a Space Woman, 1962; (ed) What the Human Race is Up To, 1962; The Fairy who Couldn't Tell a Lie, 1963; When we Become Men, 1965; Ketse and the Chief, 1965; Return to the Fairy Hill, 1966; Friends and Enemies, 1966; The Big Surprise, 1967; African Heroes, 1968; Don't Look Back, 1969; The Family at Ditlabeng, 1969; The Africans: a history, 1970; Sun and Moon, 1970; Cleopatra's People, 1972; A Danish Teapot, 1973; Sunrise Tomorrow, 1973; Small Talk: memoirs of an Edwardian childhood (autobiog.), 1973; A Life for Africa, 1973; Oil for the Highlands?, 1974; All Change Here (autobiog.), 1975; Solution Three, 1975; Snake!, 1976; The Two Magicians, 1979; The Cleansing of the Knife, 1979; You May Well Ask (autobiog.), 1979; Images of Africa, 1980; The Vegetable War, 1980; Mucking Around, 1980; What Do You Think Yourself, Scottish Stories, 1982; Not By Bread Alone, 1983; Among You Taking Notes, 1985; Beyond this Limit (short stories), 1986; Early in Orcadia, 1987; A Girl Must Live, 1990; Sea-Green Ribbons, 1991; The Oathtakers, 1991. *Recreation:* surviving so far. *Address:* Carradale House, Carradale, Campbeltown, Scotland PA28 6QQ.

See also D. A. Mitchison, J. M. Mitchison, N. A. Mitchison.

MITCHISON, Prof. (Nicholas) Avrion, FRS 1967; Scientific Director, Deutsches Rheuma-Forschungszentrum Berlin, since 1990; *b* 5 May 1928; 3rd *s* of Baron Mitchison, CBE, QC, and of Naomi Margaret Mitchison, *qv*; *m* 1957, Lorna Margaret, *d* of Maj.-Gen. J. S. S. Martin, CSI; two *s* three *d*. *Educ:* Leighton Park Sch.; New Coll., Oxford (MA 1949). Fellow of Magdalen College, 1950–52; Commonwealth Fund Fellow, 1952–54; Lecturer, Edinburgh Univ., 1954–61; Reader, Edinburgh Univ., 1961–62; Head of Div. of Experimental Biology, Nat. Inst. for Med. Research, 1962–71; Jodrell Prof. of Zoology and Comparative Anatomy, UCL, 1970–89 (Hon. Fellow, 1993). Hon. MD Edinburgh, 1977. *Publications:* articles in scientific journals. *Address:* 14 Belitha Villas, N1 1PD; Deutsches Rheuma-Forschungszentrum Berlin, Nordufer 20, Haus 11, 13353 Berlin, Germany.

See also D. A. Mitchison, J. M. Mitchison.

MITFORD, family name of **Baron Redesdale.**

MITFORD, Jessica Lucy, (Mrs Jessica Treuhaft); author; *b* 11 Sept. 1917; *d* of 2nd Baron Redesdale; *m* 1st, Esmond Marcus David Romilly (*d* 1941); one *d*; 2nd, 1943, Robert Edward Treuhaft; one *s*. Distinguished Prof., San José State Univ., Calif, 1973–74. *Publications:* (as Jessica Mitford): Hons and Rebels, 1960; The American Way of Death, 1963; The Trial of Dr Spock, 1969; Kind and Usual Punishment, 1974; The American Prison Business, 1975; A Fine Old Conflict, 1977; The Making of a Muckraker, 1979; Faces of Philip: a memoir of Philip Toynbee, 1984; Grace had an English Heart: the story of Grace Darling, heroine and Victorian superstar, 1988; The American Way of Birth, 1992. *Address:* 6411 Regent Street, Oakland, CA 94618, USA.

MITFORD-SLADE, Patrick Buxton; Partner, Cazenove & Co., 1972–April 1996; Managing Director, Cazenove Money Brokers, 1986–April 1996; *b* 7 Sept. 1936; *s* of late Col Cecil Townley Mitford-Slade and Phyllis, *d* of E. G. Buxton; *m* 1964, Anne Catharine Stanton, *d* of Major Arthur Holbrow Stanton, MBE; one *s* two *d*. *Educ:* Eton Coll.; RMA Sandhurst. Commissioned 60th Rifles, 1955, Captain; served Libya, NI, Berlin and British Guyana; Adjt, 1st Bn The Royal Green Jackets, 1962–65; Instructor, RMA Sandhurst, 1965–67. Stockbroker, Cazenove & Co., 1968–96. Asst Sec., Panel on Takeovers and Mergers, 1970–72; Mem., Stock Exchange, 1972–86, Internat. Stock Exchange, 1986–92 (Mem. Council, 1976–91; Dep. Chm., 1982–85); Chairman: City Telecommunications Cttee, 1983–92; Securities Industry Steering Cttee on Taurus, 1988–90; Money Brokers Assoc., 1990–96; Dep. Chm., Stock Borrowing and Lending Cttee, 1990–96. Chm., Officers' Assoc., 1985–; Dir, Royal British Legion (Marketing) Ltd, 1992–; Hon. Treasurer: British Commonwealth Ex-Services League, 1993–; St Luke's Hosp. for the Clergy, 1994–. *Recreations:* shooting, fishing. *Address:* Damales House, Borough Court Road, Hartley Wintney, Hook, Hants RG27 8JA. *Club:* City of London.

MITHEN, Dallas Alfred, CB 1983; Chairman, Forestry Training Council, 1984–93; Commissioner for Harvesting and Marketing, Forestry Commission, 1977–83; *b* 5 Nov. 1923; *m* 1st, 1947, Peggy (*née* Clarke) (decd); one *s* one *d*; 2nd, 1969, Avril Teresa Dodd (*née* Stein). *Educ:* Maidstone Grammar Sch.; UC of N Wales, Bangor. BSc (Forestry). Fleet Air Arm, 1942–46. Joined Forestry Commission as District Officer, 1950; Dep. Surveyor, New Forest and Conservator SE (England), 1968–71; Senior Officer (Scotland), 1971–75; Head of Forest Management Div., Edinburgh, 1975–76. Pres., Inst. of Chartered Foresters, 1984–86; Pres., Forestry Section, BAAS, 1985. Trustee, Central Scotland Woodland Trust, 1985–. *Recreations:* gardening, swimming, walking. *Address:* Kings Knot, Bonnington Road, Peebles EH45 9HF. *T:* Peebles (01721) 20738.

MITRA, Dr Ashesh Prosad, FRS 1988; FNA; Bhatnagar Fellow, Council of Scientific and Industrial Research, since 1991; *b* 21 Feb. 1927; *s* of late A. C. Mitra and Subarna Prova Mitra; *m* 1956, Sunanda Mitra; two *d*. *Educ:* University of Calcutta (DPhil 1955). FNA 1963. Res. Assistant, Calcutta Univ., 1949–51; Colombo Plan Fellow, CSIRO, Sydney, 1951; Vis. Asst Prof. of Engrg Res., 1952–53, Vis. Prof., 1953–54, Penn. State Univ.; National Physical Laboratory, New Delhi: Sec., Radio Res. Cttee, 1954–56; Head, Radio Propagation Unit, later Radio Sci. Div., 1956–86; Director-level Scientist, 1974–82; Dir., 1982–86; Sec. to Govt of India, Dept of Industrial & Scientific Res., and Dir-Gen., Council of Scientific and Industrial Res., 1986–91. Mem., Indian Acad. of Astronautics, 1974–; Fellow, Third World Acad. of Scis, Trieste, 1988. Hon. DSc Manipur, 1988. *Publications:* (ed) Proceedings of the International Geophysical Year Symposium, vols 1 & 2, 1962; The Chemistry of the Ionosphere, 1970; Advances in Space Exploration, vol. 6, 1979; 50 Years of Radio Science in India, 1984; (ed jtly) Handbook on Radio Propagation for Tropical and Subtropical Countries, 1987; 165 papers. *Recreation:* music. *Address:* National Physical Laboratory, Hillside Road, New Delhi 110012, India. *T:* 5745298. *Clubs:* Delhi Gymkhana (New Delhi); Calcutta (Calcutta).

MITSAKIS, Prof. Kariofilis; Professor of Modern Greek Literature, University of Athens, since 1978; *b* 12 May 1932; *s* of Christos and Crystalli Mitsakis; *m* 1966, Anthoula Chalkia; two *s*. *Educ:* Univs of Thessaloniki (BA, PhD), Oxford (MA, DPhil) and Munich. Scientific Collaborator, National Research Foundn of Greece, 1959–62; Associate Prof. of Byzantine and Modern Greek Literature, Univ. of Maryland, 1966–68; Chm. of Dept of Comparative Literature, Univ. of Maryland, 1967–68; Sotheby and Bywater Prof. of Byzantine and Modern Greek Language and Literature, Univ. of Oxford, 1968–72; Prof. of Modern Greek Lit., Univ. of Thessaloniki, 1972–75; Dir, Inst. for Balkan Studies, Thessaloniki, 1972–80. *Publications:* Problems Concerning the Text, the Sources and the Dating of the Achilleid, 1962 (in Greek); The Greek Sonnet, 1962 (in Greek); The Language of Romanos the Melodist, 1967 (in English); The Byzantine Alexanderromance from the Cod. Vindob. theol. gr. 244, 1967 (in German); Byzantine Hymnography, 1971 (in Greek); Petrarchism in Greece, 1973 (in Greek); Introduction to Modern Greek Literature, 1973 (in Greek); Homer in Modern Greek Literature, 1976 (in Greek); George Viziynos, 1977 (in Greek); Modern Greek Prose: the Generation of the '30s, 1978 (in Greek); Modern Greek Music and Poetry, 1979 (in Greek and English); March Through the Time, 1982; The Living Water, 1983; Points of Reference, 1987 (in Greek); The Cycles with their trails that rise and fall, 1991 (in Greek); The Boston Essays, 1993 (in Greek); The Oxford Essays, 1995 (in Greek); contribs to Balkan Studies, Byzantinisch-Neugriechische Jahrbücher, Byzantinische Zeitschrift, Comparative Literature Studies, Diptycha, Etudes Byzantines-Byzantine Studies, Glotta, Hellenika, Jahrbuch der Oesterreichischen Byzantinischen Gesellschaft, Nea Hestia, etc. *Recreations:* music, travelling. *Address:* 25 Troados Street, 15342 Aghia Paraskevi, Athens, Greece.

MITTERRAND, François Maurice Marie; Grand Croix de l'Ordre National de la Légion d'Honneur; Grand Croix de l'Ordre National du Mérite; Croix de Guerre (1939–45); President of the French Republic, 1981–95; advocate; *b* Jarnac, Charente, 26 Oct. 1916; *s* of Joseph Mitterrand and Yvonne (*née* Lorrain); *m* 1944, Danielle Gouze; two *s*. *Educ:* Coll. Saint-Paul, Angoulême; Facultés de droit et des lettres, Univ. of Paris. Licencié en droit, Lic. ès lettres; Dip. d'études supérieures de droit public. Served War, 1939–40 (prisoner, escaped; Rosette de la Résistance). Missions to London and to Algiers, 1943; Sec.-Gen., Organisation for Prisoners of War, War Victims and Refugees, 1944–46. Deputy from Nièvre, 1946–58 and 1962–81; Minister for Ex-Servicemen, 1947–48; Sec. of State for Information, attached Prime Minister's Office, 1948–49; Minister for Overseas Territories, 1950–51; Chm., UDSR, 1951–52; Minister of State, Jan.-Feb. 1952 and March 1952–July 1953; Deleg. to Council of Europe, July-Sept. 1953; Minister of the Interior, June 1954–Feb. 1955; Minister of State, 1956–57; Senator, 1959–62; Candidate for Presidency of France, 1965, 1974; Pres., Fedn of Democratic and Socialist Left, 1965–68; First Sec., Socialist Party, 1971–81. Vice-Pres., Socialist International, 1972–81. Pres., Conseil général de la Nièvre, 1964–81. *Publications:* Aux frontières de l'Union française, 1953; Présence française et abandon, 1957; La Chine au défi, 1961; Le Coup d'Etat permanent, 1964; Ma part de vérité, 1969; Un socialisme du possible, 1970; La rose au poing, 1973; La paille et le grain, 1975; Politique 1, 1977; L'Abeille et l'architecte, 1978; Ici et maintenant, 1980; Politique 2, 1981; Reflexions sur la politique extérieure de la France, 1986; numerous contribs to the Press. *Recreation:* golf. *Address:* 22 rue de Bièvre, 75005 Paris, France.

MITTING, John Edward; QC 1987; a Recorder, since 1988; *b* 8 Oct. 1947; *s* of Alison Kennard Mitting and Eleanor Mary Mitting; *m* 1977, Judith Clare (*née* Hampson); three *s*. *Educ:* Downside Sch.; Trinity Hall, Cambridge (BA, LLB). Called to the Bar, Gray's Inn, 1970. *Recreations:* wine, food, bridge. *Address:* Hollow Dene, Coton, Gnosall, near Stafford ST20 0EQ. *T:* Stafford (01785) 822395.

MITTLER, Prof. Peter Joseph, CBE 1981; MA, PhD, MEd; CPsychol; FBPsS; Professor of Special Education, 1973–95, Professor Emeritus, since 1995, and Dean, Faculty of Education and Director, School of Education, 1991–94, University of Manchester; *b* 2 April 1930; *s* of Dr Gustav Mittler and Gertrude Mittler; *m* 1955, Helle Katscher; three *s*. *Educ:* Merchant Taylors' Sch., Crosby; Pembroke Coll., Cambridge (MA); PhD London; MEd Manchester. Clinical Psychologist, Warneford and Park Hosps, Oxford, 1954–58; Principal Psychologist, Reading Area Psychiatric Services, 1958–63; Lectr in Psychology, Birkbeck Coll., Univ. of London, 1963–68; Manchester University: Dir, Hester Adrian Res. Centre, 1968–82; Dir, Centre for Educnl Guidance and Special Needs, Dept of Educn, 1977–91; Dep. Dir, Sch. of Educn, 1989–91. Chm., Nat Develt Gp for Mentally Handicapped, 1975–80; Mem., Schs Exams and Assessment Council, 1988–90. Pres., Internat. League of Socs for Persons with Mental Handicap, 1982–86 (Vice-Pres., 1978–82); Mem., Prince of Wales Adv. Gp on Disability, 1984–90; Advr on disability to UN, UNESCO, WHO, ILO. *Publications:* ed, Psychological Assessment of Mental and Physical Handicaps, 1970; The Study of Twins, 1971; ed, Assessment for Learning in the Mentally Handicapped, 1973; ed, Research to Practice in Mental Retardation (3 vols), 1977; People not Patients, 1979; (jtly) Teaching Language and Communication to the Mentally Handicapped, (Schools Council), 1979; (ed jtly) Advances in Mental Handicap Research, 1980; (ed) Frontiers of Knowledge in Mental Retardation (2 vols), 1981; (ed jtly) Approaches to Partnership: professionals and parents of mentally handicapped people, 1983; (ed jtly) Aspects of Competence in Mentally Handicapped People, 1983; (ed jtly) Staff Training in Mental Handicap, 1987; (jtly) Inset and Special Educational Needs: running short, school-focused inservice courses, 1988; (ed jtly) Special Needs Education

(World Yearbook of Education), 1993; Teacher Education for Special Educational Needs, 1993; (ed jtly) Teacher Education for Special Needs in Europe, 1995; (ed) Changing Policy and Practice for People with Learning Disabilities, 1995; (jtly) Disability and the Family, 1995; papers in psychol and educnl jls. *Recreations:* music, travel. *Address:* 10 Park Road, Cheadle Hulme, Cheshire SK8 7DA. *T:* 0161–485 6491, *Fax:* 0161–486 1136.

MITTON, Rev. Dr Charles Leslie, BA; MTh; PhD; Principal of Handsworth College, Birmingham, 1955–70 (Tutor, 1951–55); *b* 13 Feb. 1907; *s* of Rev. Charles W. Mitton, Bradford, Yorks; *m* 1937, Margaret J. Ramage; one *s* one *d*. *Educ:* Kingswood Sch., Bath; Manchester Univ.; Didsbury Coll., Manchester. Asst Tutor at Wesley Coll., Headingley, 1930–33; Minister in Methodist Church at: Dunbar, 1933–36; Keighley, 1936–39; Scunthorpe, 1939–45; Nottingham, 1945–51; Tutor in New Testament Studies at Handsworth Coll., Birmingham, 1951–70. Editor of Expository Times, 1965–76. Hon. DD, Aberdeen Univ., 1964. *Publications:* The Epistle to the Ephesians: Authorship, Origin and Purpose, 1951; Pauline Corpus of Letters, 1954; Preachers' Commentary on St Mark's Gospel, 1956; The Good News, 1961; The Epistle of James, 1966; Jesus: the fact behind the faith, 1974; The Epistle to the Ephesians: a commentary, 1976; Your Kingdom Come, 1978. *Recreations:* Rugby football, Association football, cricket, tennis. *Address:* 14 Cranbrook Road, Handsworth, Birmingham B21 8PJ. *T:* 0121–554 7892.

MKONA, Callisto Matekenya, DSM (Malaŵi) 1966; Hon. GCVO 1985; High Commissioner for Malaŵi in Nairobi, since 1988, concurrently accredited to Egypt, Israel and Uganda, since 1988; *b* 4 June 1930; *s* of late Benedicto Mkona and of Martha Matekenya Mkona; *m* 1971, Helen Victoria (*née* Sazuze); two *s* two *d*. *Educ:* Zomba, Malaŵi; Urbanian Univ., Rome (DCL, Dip. Soc. Scis). Secondary School teacher, 1962–64; Mission Educn Liaison Officer, 1964–67; Educn Attaché (First Sec.), Washington and London, 1967–71; Ambassador to Ethiopia, 1971–72; Minister, Washington, 1972–73; High Comr in Zambia, 1973–75; Ambassador in Bonn, 1975–78; Dep. Principal Sec., Min. of External Affairs, 1978–79; Principal Sec., Office of the President and Cabinet, 1979–81; High Comr in London, also concurrently accredited to Denmark, France, Norway, Portugal, Sweden and Switzerland, 1981–87; Chm., Malaŵi Public Service Commn, 1987–88; CS retd, 1988. Permanent Representative to: UN Centre for Human Settlements (HABITAT), 1988–; UNEP, 1988–. Malaŵi Silver Jubilee of Independence Medal, 1990. *Recreations:* reading, walking, tennis, golf. *Address:* Malaŵi High Commission, Waiyaki Way, PO Box 30453, Nairobi, Kenya.

MLINARIC, David; interior decorator and designer, since 1964; founded David Mlinaric Ltd, 1964, became Mlinaric, Henry and Zervudachi Ltd, 1989; *b* 12 March 1939; *s* of Franjo and Mabel Mlinaric; *m* 1969, Martha Laycock; one *s* two *d*. *Educ:* Downside Sch.; Bartlett Sch. of Architecture; University Coll. London. Private and commercial interior designing and decorating, often in historic bldgs. Recent work includes: rooms in Nat. Gall., London, 1986–; Spencer House, London, 1990; Wellcome Building, London, 1992. Hon. Fellow, RCA, 1987. *Recreations:* gardening, sightseeing. *Address:* 38 Bourne Street, SW1W 8JA. *T:* 0171–730 9072.

MO, Timothy Peter; writer; *b* 30 Dec. 1950; *s* of Peter Mo Wan Lung and Barbara Helena Falkingham. *Educ:* Convent of the Precious Blood, Hong Kong; Mill Hill School; St John's Coll., Oxford (BA; Gibbs Prize 1971). *Publications:* The Monkey King, 1978 (Geoffrey Faber Meml Prize, 1979); Sour Sweet, 1982 (Hawthornden Prize, 1983; filmed, 1989); An Insular Possession, 1986; The Redundancy of Courage, 1991 (E. M. Forster Award, Amer. Acad. and Inst. of Arts and Letters, 1992); Brownout on Breadfruit Boulevard, 1995. *Recreations:* scuba diving, weight training, gourmandising.

MOATE, Sir Roger (Denis), Kt 1993; MP (C) Faversham since 1970; Insurance Broker; *b* 12 May 1938; *m* 1st; one *s* one *d*; 2nd, Auriol (*née* Cran); one *d*. *Educ:* Latymer Upper Sch., Hammersmith. Joined Young Conservative Movement, in Brentford and Chiswick, 1954: Vice-Chm., Greater London Area Young Conservatives, 1964; contested (C) Faversham, Gen. Elec., 1966. *Recreation:* skiing. *Address:* House of Commons, SW1A 0AA.

MOBBS, Sir (Gerald) Nigel, Kt 1986; DL; Chairman and Chief Executive, Slough Estates plc, since 1976 and Director of principal subsidiaries; Director, Barclays Bank PLC, since 1979; *b* 22 Sept. 1937; *s* of Gerald Aubrey Mobbs and Elizabeth (*née* Lanchester); *m* 1961, Hon. Pamela Jane Marguerite Berry, 2nd *d* of 2nd Viscount Kemsley, *qv*; one *s* twin *d*. *Educ:* Marlborough Coll.; Christ Church, Oxford. Joined Slough Estates plc, 1961; Director, 1963, Man. Dir, 1971. Director: Barclays Bank Trust Co. Ltd, 1973–86 (Chm., 1985–86); Charterhouse Gp, 1974–84 (Chm., 1977–83); Kingfisher plc (formerly Woolworth Holdings), 1982– (Dep. Chm., 1990–95; Chm., 1995–); Cookson Gp plc, 1985–93; Howard de Walden Estates Ltd, 1989–; Chm., Groundwork Foundn, 1990–94. Chairman: Corporate Health (formerly Slough Occupational Health Service), 1976–; Slough Social Fund, 1975–; Property Services Agency Adv. Bd, 1980–86; Aims of Industry, 1985–; Adv. Panel on Deregulation, DTI, 1988–94. Pres., Slough & Dist Chamber of Commerce, 1969–72; Vice-Pres., Assoc. of British Chambers of Commerce, 1976–90 (Chm. 1974–76); Pres., British Property Fedn, 1979–81. Mem., Commonwealth War Graves Commn, 1988–; Trustee, Nat. Army Mus., 1994–. President: Bucks Assoc. of Boys' Clubs, 1984–; British Council for Offices, 1990–91. Chm., Council, Univ. of Buckingham, 1987–. CIMgt. Master, Spectacle Makers' Co., 1989. Hon. Fellow, Coll. of Estate Management, 1978; Hon. Mem., RICS, 1990. Hon. DSc City, 1988; DUniv Buckingham, 1993. High Sheriff, 1982, DL, 1985, Bucks. OStJ. *Recreations:* riding, hunting, ski-ing, golf, travel. *Address:* c/o Slough Estates plc, 234 Bath Road, Slough SL1 4EE. *Clubs:* Brooks's; Toronto (Toronto).

MOBERLY, Sir John (Campbell), KBE 1984; CMG 1976; HM Diplomatic Service, retired; Consultant, Middle East Programme, Royal Institute of International Affairs, since 1986; *b* 27 May 1925; *s* of Sir Walter Moberly, GBE, KCB, DSO; *m* 1959, Patience, *d* of Major Sir Richard George Proby, 1st Bt, MC; two *s* one *d*. *Educ:* Winchester College; Magdalen College, Oxford. War Service in Royal Navy, 1943–47 (despatches). Entered HM Foreign (now Diplomatic) Service, 1950; Political Officer, Kuwait, 1954–56; Political Agent, Doha, 1959–62; First Secretary, Athens, 1962–66; Counsellor, Washington, 1969–73; Dir, Middle East Centre for Arab Studies, 1973–75; Ambassador, Jordan, 1975–79; Asst Under-Sec. of State, FCO, 1979–82; Ambassador, Iraq, 1982–85. CStJ 1979. *Recreations:* mountain walking and climbing, skiing, swimming. *Address:* 35 Pymers Mead, West Dulwich, SE21 8NH. *T:* 0181–670 2680; The Cedars, Temple Sowerby, Penrith, Cumbria CA10 1RZ. *T:* Kirkby Thore (017683) 61437. *Clubs:* Royal Automobile; Leander (Henley-on-Thames).

MOBERLY, Sir Patrick (Hamilton), KCMG 1986 (CMG 1978); HM Diplomatic Service, retired; Ambassador to South Africa, 1984–87; *b* 2 Sept. 1928; *yr s* of G. H. Moberly; *m* 1955, Mary Penfold; two *s* one *d*. *Educ:* Winchester; Trinity Coll., Oxford (MA). HM Diplomatic Service, 1951–88; diplomatic posts in: Baghdad, 1953; Prague, 1957; Foreign Office, 1959; Dakar, 1962; Min. of Defence, 1965; Commonwealth Office, 1967; Canada, 1969; Israel, 1970; FCO, 1974; Asst Under-Sec. of State, 1976–81; Ambassador to Israel, 1981–84. *Recreations:* tennis, opera, canal boating. *Address:* 38 Lingfield Road, SW19 4PZ. *Club:* United Oxford & Cambridge University.

MOBERLY, Maj.-Gen. Richard James, CB 1957; OBE 1944; retired, 1960, and became Director, Communications Electronic Equipment, War Office, until 1964; *b* 2 July 1906; *o s* of late J. E. Moberly; *m* 1st, 1935, Mary Joyce Shelmerdine (*d* 1964); three *d*; 2nd, 1971, Mrs Vivien Mary Cameron (*d* 1981), *d* of Victor Bayley, CIE, CBE. *Educ:* Haileybury; Royal Military Academy, Woolwich. Commissioned Royal Signals, 1926; India, 1928–35; comd 1st Airborne Div. Signal Regt, 1942–43; CSO 1st Airborne Corps, 1943–45; Comdt Indian Signal Trng Centre, 1946–47; Dep. Comdt, Sch. of Signals, 1949–52; Dep. Dir of Signals, WO, 1952–54; CSO, Northern Army Gp, 1954–57; Signal Officer-in-Chief, WO, 1957–60. Col Comdt, Royal Signals, 1960–66. Comr for Dorset, St John Ambulance, 1968–76. KStJ 1986. *Address:* Steeple Cottage, Westport Road, Wareham, Dorset BH20 4PR. *T:* Wareham (01929) 552697.

MODARRESSI, Anne, (Mrs T. M. Modarressi); *see* Tyler, A.

MODIGLIANI, Prof. Franco; Institute Professor Emeritus, Massachusetts Institute of Technology, since 1988 (Professor of Economics and Finance, 1962–70; Institute Professor, 1970–88); *b* Rome, 1918; *s* of Enrico Modigliani and Olga (*née* Flaschel); *m* 1939, Serena Calabi; two *s*. *Educ:* Univ. of Rome (DJur 1939); DSocSci New Sch. for Social Research, New York, 1944. Instr in Economics and Statistics, New Jersey Coll. for Women, 1942; Instr, Associate in Economics and Statistics, Bard Coll. of Columbia Univ., 1942–44; Lectr, 1943–44, Asst Prof. of Math. Econ. and Econometrics, 1946–48, New Sch. for Social Research; Res. Associate and Chief Statistician, Inst. of World Affairs, NY, 1945–48; Res. Consultant, Cowles Commn for Res. in Economics, Univ. of Chicago, 1949–54; Associate Prof., 1949, Prof. of Economics, 1950–52, Univ. of Illinois; Prof. of Econ. and Indust. Admin, Carnegie Inst. of Technology, 1952–60; Prof. of Economics, Northwestern Univ., 1960–62. Social Science Research Council: Mem., Bd of Dirs, 1963–68; Mem., Cttee on Econ. Stability and Growth, 1970–; Jt Chm., Adv. Sub-Cttee on MIT-Pennsylvania SSRC Model, 1970–81; Mem., Sub-Cttee on Monetary Res., 1970–77. Academic Consultant, Bd of Governors, Federal Reserve System, 1966–; Sen. Adviser, Brookings Panel on Econ. Activity, 1971–; Consultant, Bank of Italy, Rome; Mem., Consiglio Italiano per le Scienze Sociali, 1974–; Perm. Mem., Conf. on Income and Wealth, Nat. Bureau of Econ. Res. Mem., Adv. Bd, Jl of Money, Credit and Banking, 1969–. Mem., Nat. Acad. of Scis, 1973–; Fellow, Econometric Soc., 1949; Fellow, 1960–, Council Mem., 1978–80, Amer. Acad. of Arts and Scis. Numerous hon. degrees. Nobel Prize in Economic Science, 1985. Kt Grand Cross, Italy, 1985. *Publications:* National Incomes and International Trade (with Hans Neisser), 1953; (jtly) Planning Production, Inventories and Work Forces, 1960; (with Kalman J. Cohen) The Role of Anticipations and Plans in Economic Behavior and their Use in Economic Analysis and Forecasting, 1961; (with Ezio Tarantelli) Mercato del Lavoro, Distribuzione del Reddito e Consumi Privati, 1975; (ed with Donald Lessard) New Mortgage Designs for Stable Housing in an Inflationary Environment, 1975; The Collected Papers of Franco Modigliani, vols 1, 2, 3, 1980, vols 4, 5, 1989 (trans. Hungarian, 1988); The Debate Over Stabilization Policy, 1986; Il caso Italia, 1986; Reddito, Interesse, Inflazione, 1987; (with Frank Fabozzi) Capital Markets—Institutions and Instruments, 1991; Consumo, Risparmio, Finanza, 1992; (with Frank Fabozzi) Mortgage and Mortgage Backed Securities Markets, 1992; contribs to Corriere Della Sera, periodicals and learned jls. *Address:* Massachusetts Institute of Technology, Sloan School of Management, Cambridge, MA 02139, USA.

MODISE, Johannes, (Joe); Minister of Defence, Republic of South Africa, since 1994; *b* Doornfontein, 23 May 1929. *Educ:* Fred Clark Meml Sch., Nancefield. Commander, Umkhonto we Sizwe, 1963; worked for underground movement and went into exile, 1963; returned to SA, 1990. African National Congress: Mem., NEC, 1963–; Mem., Nat. Wkg Cttee, 1963–; mem., first gp of ANC negotiators to hold talks with Pretoria govt, March 1990; mem., negotiating team of TEC Sub-Council on Defence until elections, April 1994. *Address:* Ministry of Defence, Pretoria 0001, South Africa.

MOELWYN-HUGHES, Edmwnd Goronwy; Vice Judge Advocate General, since 1994; *b* 29 Aug. 1937; twin *s* of late Dr E. A. Moelwyn-Hughes and of Mair Elen Moelwyn-Hughes (*née* Evans); *m* 1964, Carolyn, *o d* of John Sanders; one *s* two *d*. *Educ:* The Leys Sch., Cambridge; Trinity Hall, Cambridge (MA). Nat. Service, 1956–58, 2nd Lieut Royal Welch Fusiliers. Called to the Bar, Inner Temple, 1968; practised Wales and Chester Circuit, 1968–73. Dep. Judge Advocate, 1973–78; Asst JAG, 1978–94; Standing Civilian Court Magistrate, 1982; DJAG, British Forces in Germany, 1989–91; Recorder of the Crown Court, 1990. *Recreations:* reading, music, walking, theatre. *Address:* Office of the Judge Advocate General, 22 Kingsway, WC2B 6LE. *T:* 0171–305 7913. *Clubs:* Army and Navy, Commonwealth Trust.

MOERAN, Edward Warner; *b* 27 Nov. 1903; *s* of E. J. Moeran. *Educ:* Christ's Coll., Finchley; University of London. Solicitor. MP (Lab) South Beds, 1950–51. Pres., W London Law Soc., 1971–72. Chm., Solicitors' Ecology Gp, 1972–74. *Publications:* Practical Conveyancing, 1949; Invitation to Conveyancing, 1962; Practical Legal Aid, 1970; (jtly) Social Welfare Law, 1977; Legal Aid Summary, 1978; Introduction to Conveyancing, 1979.

MOFFAT, Alistair Murray; Director of Programmes, Scottish Television, since 1990; Chief Executive, Scottish Television Enterprises, since 1993; *b* 16 June 1950; *s* of John and Ellen Moffat; *m* 1976; Lindsay Anne Reid Thomas; one *s* two *d*. *Educ:* Kelso High Sch.; St Andrews Univ. (MA Hons); Edinburgh Univ. (CertEd); London Univ. (MPhil). Administrator, Edinburgh Festival Fringe, 1976–81; Scottish Television: Arts Corresp., 1981–86; Controller of Features, 1987–90. Mem., Scotch Malt Whisky Assoc, 1989–. *Publications:* The Edinburgh Fringe, 1978; Kelsae: a history from earliest times, 1985; Remembering Charles Rennie Mackintosh, 1989. *Recreations:* badminton, golf. *Address:* c/o Scottish Television, Cowcaddens, Glasgow G2 3PR. *T:* 0141–332 9999.

MOFFAT, Brian Scott, OBE 1982; Chief Executive, since 1991, and Chairman, since 1993, British Steel; *b* 6 Jan. 1939; *s* of Festus and Agnes Moffat; *m* 1964, Jacqueline Mary Cunliffe; one *s* one *d* (and one *s* decd). *Educ:* Hulme Grammar School. FCA. Peat Marwick Mitchell & Co., 1961–68; British Steel plc (formerly British Steel Corp.), 1968–; Man. Dir, Finance, 1986–91. *Recreations:* farming, fishing, shooting.

MOFFAT, Lt-Gen. Sir (William) Cameron, KBE 1985 (OBE 1975); FRCS; *b* 8 Sept. 1929; *s* of William Weir Moffat and Margaret Garrett; *m* 1953, Audrey Watson; one *s*. *Educ:* King's Park Sch., Glasgow; Univ. of Glasgow, Western Infirmary (MB ChB). DTM&H. House Surgeon, Western Inf., Glasgow, 1952; Ship's Surg., Anchor Line, 1953; MO Seaforth Highlanders, 1954; SMO Edinburgh, 1956–57; Hammersmith Hosp., 1962; Birmingham Accident Hosp., 1964; Surg., RAAF Hosp. Malaya, 1965–67; Cons. Surg., BMH Rinteln, 1968–70; Prof. Military Surgery, RAM Coll. and RCS, 1970–75; CO BMH Rinteln, 1978–80; Comd MED HQ 1 (Br) Corps, 1980–83; PMO, UKLF, 1983–84; Surg. Gen./Dir Gen. Army Med. Servs, MoD, 1985–87, retired. QHS 1984–88. Chief Med. Advr, BRCS, 1988–94. Hon. DSc Glasgow, 1991. CStJ 1985. *Publications:* contribs to surgical text books and jls on missile wounds and their management. *Recreations:* golf, travel, bird-watching. *Address:* Kippax, Pound Green, Freshwater, Isle of Wight PO40 9HH.

MOFFATT, Prof. Henry Keith, ScD; FRS 1986; FRSE; Professor of Mathematical Physics, University of Cambridge, since 1980, (Head of Department of Applied Mathematics and Theoretical Physics, 1983–91); Fellow, Trinity College, Cambridge, 1961–76, and since 1980; *b* 12 April 1935; *s* of late Frederick Henry Moffatt and of Emmeline Marchant Fleming; *m* 1960, Katharine, (Linty), Stiven, *d* of late Rev. D. S. Stiven, MC, DD; one *s* two *d* (and one *s* decd). *Educ:* George Watson's Coll., Edinburgh; Edinburgh Univ. (BSc); Cambridge Univ. (BA, PhD, ScD). Lecturer in Mathematics, Cambridge Univ., and Director of Studies in Mathematics, Trinity Coll., 1961–76; Tutor, 1971–75; Sen. Tutor, 1975; Professor of Applied Mathematics, Bristol Univ., 1977–80. Visiting appts, Stanford Univ. and Johns Hopkins Univ., 1965, Univ. of Paris VI, 1975–76, Institut de Mécanique, Grenoble, 1986, Univ. of California, San Diego, 1987, Santa Barbara, 1991, Ecole Polytechnique Palaiseau, 1992–, Kyoto Univ., 1993. Co-editor, Journal of Fluid Mechanics, 1966–83. Foreign Mem., Royal Netherlands Acad. of Arts and Scis, 1991. MAE 1994. FRSE 1988. *Dhc* Inst. Nat Polytechnique de Grenoble, 1987; Hon. DSc SUNY, 1990. *Publications:* Magnetic Field Generation in Electrically Conducting Fluids, 1978; (jt ed) Topological Fluid Mechanics, 1990; Topological Aspects of the Dynamics of Fluids and Plasmas, 1992; papers in fluid mechanics and dynamo theory in Jl Fluid Mech. and other jls. *Address:* Trinity College, Cambridge CB2 1TQ.

MOFFATT, John, MA, DPhil; Provost, The Queen's College, Oxford, 1987–93, Hon. Fellow, 1993; *b* 12 Oct. 1922; *s* of Jacob and Ethel Moffatt; *m* 1949, Una Lamorna Morris (*d* 1992); one *d*. *Educ:* Keighley Boys' Grammar Sch.; Magdalen Coll., Oxford (MA, DPhil). Radar research with British Thomson-Houston Co. Ltd, Rugby, 1942–46; Oxford University: Sen. Res. Officer, Clarendon Lab., 1950; Lectr, Dept of Nuclear Physics, 1965; The Queen's College: Fellow and Praelector in Physics, 1950; Sen. Tutor, 1972–76. *Publications:* articles on physics in various scientific jls. *Address:* 2 Cumnor Rise Road, Cumnor Hill, Oxford OX2 9HD.

MOGER, Christopher Richard Derwent; QC 1992; a Recorder, since 1993 (an Assistant Recorder, 1990–93); *b* 28 July 1949; *s* of Richard Vernon Derwent Moger and Cecile Eva Rosales Moger (*née* Power); *m* 1st, 1974, Victoria Trollope (marr. diss. 1991); three *s*; 2nd, 1991, Prudence Da Cunha. *Educ:* Sherborne School; Bristol Univ. (LLB Hons). Called to the Bar, Inner Temple, 1972. Member: Western Circuit; London Common Law Bar Assoc.; Commercial Bar Assoc.; Official Referee's Bar Assoc.; Barristers' Overseas Advocacy Cttee. *Recreations:* fishing, chess, walking. *Address:* 4 Pump Court, Temple, EC4Y 7AN. *T:* 0171–353 2656. *Club:* Garrick.

MOGG; *see* Rees-Mogg, family name of Baron Rees-Mogg.

MOGG, Gen. Sir John, GCB 1972 (KCB 1966; CB 1964); CBE 1960; DSO 1944; Bar, 1944; Deputy Supreme Allied Commander, Europe, 1973–76; *b* 17 Feb. 1913; *s* of late Capt. H. B. Mogg, MC and late Alice Mary (*née* Ballard); *m* 1939, Cecilia Margaret Molesworth; three *s*. *Educ:* Malvern Coll.; RMC Sandhurst. Coldstream Guards, 1933–35; RMC Sandhurst (Sword of Honour) 1935–37; commissioned Oxfordshire and Buckinghamshire Light Infantry, 1937. Served War of 1939–45 (despatches twice, 1944); comd 9 DLI (NW Europe), 1944–45; Instructor, Staff Coll., 1948–50; Commander 10th Parachute Bn, 1950–52; Chief Instructor, School of Infantry, Warminster, 1952–54; Instructor (GSO1), Imperial Defence Coll., 1954–56; Comdr, Commonwealth Brigade Gp, Malaya, 1958–60; Meritorious Medal (Perak, Malaya); Dir of Combat Development, War Office, 1961–62; Comdt, Royal Military Academy, Sandhurst, 1963–66; Comdr 1st (British) Corps, 1966–68; GOC-in-C Southern Comd, 1968; GOC-in-C Army Strategic Comd, 1968–70; Adjutant-Gen., MoD (Army), 1970–73. ADC Gen. to the Queen, 1971–74. Col Comdt: Army Air Corps, 1963–74; The Royal Green Jackets, 1965–73; Hon. Col, 10th Parachute Bn, TA, 1973–78. Kermit Roosevelt Lectr, 1969. President: Army Cricket Assoc.; Army Saddle Club, 1969; Army Boxing Assoc., 1970; Army Parachute Assoc., 1971; BHS, 1972; Ex Services Mental Welfare Soc.; Army Benevolent Fund, 1980– (Chm., 1976); Normandy Veterans Assoc., 1982–; Chairman: Army Free Fall Parachute Assoc., 1970; Army Football Assoc., 1960–63; Royal Soldiers' Daughters Sch., 1976; Operation Drake for Young Explorers, 1978–; Operation Drake Fellowship, 1980–83; Royal Internat. Horse Show, 1979; Vice-Pres., Operation Raleigh. Pres., Council Services Kinema Corp., 1970. Dir, Lloyds Bank S Midland Regional Bd, 1976. Member Council: Wessex TA&VRA, 1976; British Atlantic Cttee, 1977; Fairbridge Drake Soc., 1987. Comr, Royal Hospital Chelsea, 1976. Governor: Malvern College, 1967; Bradfield College, 1977; Chm. of Governors, Icknield Sch., 1981–. Hon. Liveryman, Fruiterers' Co. DL Oxfordshire, 1979, Vice Lord-Lieut, 1979–89. *Recreations:* cricket, most field sports, helicopter pilot. *Address:* Church Close, Watlington, Oxon OX9 5QR. *Clubs:* Army and Navy, Flyfishers', MCC, Cavalry and Guards, Pitt.

MOGG, John Frederick; Director-General, Directorate-General XV, European Commission, since 1993; *b* 5 Oct. 1943; *s* of Thomas W. Mogg and Cora M. Mogg; *m* 1967, Anne Smith; one *d* one *s*. *Educ:* Bishop Vesey's Grammar Sch., Sutton Coldfield; Birmingham Univ. (BA Hons). Rediffusion Ltd, 1965–74; Principal: Office of Fair Trading, 1974–76; Dept of Trade (Insurance Div.), 1976–79; First Sec., UK Perm. Representation, Brussels, 1979–82; Department of Trade and Industry: Asst Sec., Minerals and Metals Div., 1982–85; PPS to Sec. of State for Trade and Industry, 1985–86; Under Secretary: European Policy Div., 1986–87; Industrial Materials Market Div., 1987–89; Dep. Hd, European Secretariat, Cabinet Office, 1989–90; Dep. Dir Gen., DGIII, EC, 1990–93. *Address:* Commission of the European Communities, DGXV, Rue de la loi 200, Bruxelles.

MOGGACH, Deborah; novelist, journalist and script-writer; *b* 28 June 1948; *d* of Richard Alexander Hough, *qv* and Helen Charlotte (*née* Woodyatt); *m* 1971, Anthony Austin Moggach (marr. diss. 1988); one *s* one *d*. *Educ:* Camden Sch. for Girls; Bristol Univ. (BA Hons English); Inst. of Educn, Univ. of London (BEd English). Mem., Exec. Cttee, English PEN, 1992–. Television includes: Crown Court, 1983; To Have and to Hold, 1986; Stolen, 1990; Goggle Eyes (adaptation), 1993; stage play, Double Take, Liverpool Playhouse, 1990. Young Journalist of the Year, Westminster Arts Council, 1975; Writer's Guild Award, 1993. *Publications:* You Must Be Sisters, 1978; Close to Home, 1979; A Quiet Drink, 1980; Hot Water Man, 1982; Porky, 1983; To Have and To Hold, 1986; Smile and other stories, 1987; Driving in the Park, 1988; Stolen, 1990; The Stand-In, 1991; The Ex-Wives, 1993; Changing Babies, 1995. *Recreation:* walking around London looking into people's windows. *Address:* 24 Ivor Street, NW1 9PJ. *T:* 0171–267 0989.

MOGGRIDGE, Harry Traherne, (Hal), OBE 1986; PPLI; RIBA; FIHort; Senior Partner, Colvin and Moggridge, Landscape Consultants (established 1922), since 1981 (Partner, since 1969); Member, Royal Fine Art Commission, since 1988; *b* London, 2 Feb. 1936; *s* of late Lt-Col Harry Weston Moggridge, CMG, and Helen Mary Ferrier Taylor; *m* 1963, Catherine Greville Herbert; two *s* one *d*. *Educ:* Tonbridge Sch.; Architectural Assoc.; evening lectures in landscape design under Prof. P. Youngman. Notts CC, 1960; Asst to Geoffrey Jellicoe, 1961–63; Site architect for Sir Wm Halcrow & Ptrs, Tema Harbour, Ghana, 1964–65; Landscape asst, GLC, 1966–67; own practice; entered into partnership with late Brenda Colvin, CBE, PPILA, 1969, continuing in partnership with Christopher Carter, ALI, and staff of nine. Prof. of Landscape Architecture, Univ. of Sheffield, 1984–86. Mem. Council, Landscape Inst., 1970–83 (Hon. Sec., Vice Pres., Pres. 1979–81) and 1987–93 (Deleg. to Internat. Fedn of Landscape Architects, 1980–; Chm., Internat. Cttee, 1986–92); Mem., Nat. Trust Architectural Panel, 1991–. Landscape works include: Brenig Reservoir, Clwyd; White Horse Hill, a new car park and restoration of grass downland; Gale Common Hill, Yorkshire, woods and fields over 100 million cubic metres of waste ash and shale built over 60 years; quarries; countryside studies; reclamation; public and private gardens; Aldermaston Ct, near Reading, grounds for a new co. headquarters; current projects incl. restoration of historic parks (eg Blenheim, Knole, Castle Hill), creation of new parks and consultancy for Inner Royal Parks of London. FRSA. *Publications:* numerous articles and chapters of books describing works or technical subjects. *Recreations:* looking at pictures, gardens, buildings, towns, landscapes and people in these places; walking, scene painting, dry stone walling, theatre. *Address:* Filkins, Lechlade, Glos GL7 3JQ. *T:* Filkins (01367) 860225. *Clubs:* Farmers.

MOHYEDDIN, Zia; actor; producer and director, Central TV, 1980–94; *b* 20 June 1931. *Educ:* Punjab University (BA Hons). Freelance directing for Aust. broadcasting, 1951–52; RADA, 1953–54; Pakistan stage appearances, 1956–59; UK stage, 1959–71; Dir Gen., Pakistan Nat. Performing Ensemble, to 1977; *stage:* appearances include: A Passage to India, 1960; The Alchemist, 1964; The Merchant of Venice, 1966; Volpone, 1967; The Guide, 1968; On The Rocks, 1969; Measure for Measure, 1981; Film, Film, Film, 1986; *films:* Lawrence of Arabia, 1961; Sammy Going South, 1963; The Sailor from Gibraltar; Khartoum, 1965; Ashanti, 1982; Assam Garden, 1985; Immaculate Conception, 1992; *television series:* The Hidden Truth, 1964; Gangsters, 1979; Jewel in the Crown, 1983; King of the Ghetto, 1986; Mountbatten, 1988; Shalom Salaam, 1989; creator, Family Pride, Channel Four, 1990. *Recreations:* reading, bridge, watching cricket. *Address:* c/o Plunkett Greene Ltd, 4 Ovington Gardens, SW3 1LS. *Club:* Savile.

MOI, Hon. Daniel arap, EGH, EBS; President of Kenya, since 1978; Minister of Defence, since 1979; *b* Rift Valley Province, 1924. *Educ:* African Inland Mission Sch., Kabartonjo; Govt African Sch., Kapsabet. Teacher, 1946–56. MLC, 1957; Mem. for Baringo, House of Representatives, 1963–78; Minister for Educn, 1961; Minister for Local Govt, 1962–64; Minister for Home Affairs, 1964–67; Vice-Pres. of Kenya, 1967–78. Chm., Kenya African Democratic Union (KADU), 1960; Pres., Kenya African Nat. Union (KANU) for Rift Valley Province, 1966; Pres. of KANU, 1978–. Chm., Rift Valley Provincial Council. Former Member: Rift Valley Educn Bd; Kalenjin Language Cttee; Commonwealth Higher Educn Cttee; Kenya Meat Commn; Bd of Governors, African Girls' High Sch., Kikuyu. *Address:* Office of the President, PO Box 30510, Nairobi, Kenya; State House, PO Box 40530, Nairobi, Kenya.

MOIR, Sir Ernest Ian Royds, 3rd Bt, *cr* 1916; *b* 9 June 1925; *o s* of Sir Arrol Moir, 2nd Bt, and Dorothy Blanche, *d* of Admiral Sir Percy Royds, CB, CMG; *S* father, 1957; *m* 1954, Margaret Hanham Carter; three *s*. *Educ:* Rugby; Cambridge Univ. (BA). Served War of 1939–45 in Royal Engineers. *Heir: s* Christopher Ernest Moir [*b* 22 May 1955; *m* 1983, Mrs Vanessa Kirtikar, *yr d* of V. A. Crosby; twin *s*, and one step *d*].

MOIR, James William Charles; Deputy Director, Corporate Affairs, BBC, 1993–96; Controller, BBC Radio 2, from Feb. 1996; *b* 5 Nov. 1941; *s* of William Charles Moir and Mary Margaret Moir (*née* Daly); *m* 1966, Julia (*née* Smalley); two *s* one *d*. *Educ:* Gunnersbury Catholic Grammar School; Univ. of Nottingham (BA). Joined BBC TV Light Entertainment Group, 1963; Producer, Light Entertainment, 1970, Exec. Producer, 1979; Head of Variety, 1982–87; Head of Gp, 1987–93. Chm., EBU Working Pty on Light Entertainment, 1992–94. Hon. Mem. Council, NSPCC, 1990–. Mem., Vice Chancellor's Adv. Bd, Univ. of Nottingham, 1990–. FRTS 1990. *Address:* The Lawn, Elm Park Road, Pinner, Middx HA5 3LE. *Club:* Reform.

MOIR CAREY, D. M.; *see* Carey.

MOISEIWITSCH, Prof. Benjamin Lawrence; Professor of Applied Mathematics, Queen's University of Belfast, 1968–93, now Emeritus; *b* London, 6 Dec. 1927; *s* of Jacob Moiseiwitsch and Chana Kotlerman; *m* 1953, Sheelagh M. McKeon; two *s* two *d*. *Educ:* Royal Liberty Sch., Romford; University Coll., London (BSc, 1949, PhD 1952). Sir George Jessel Studentship in Maths, UCL, 1949; Queen's University, Belfast: Lectr and Reader in Applied Maths, 1952–68; Dean, Faculty of Science, 1972–75; Hd, Dept of Applied Maths and Theoretical Physics, 1977–89. MRIA 1969. *Publications:* Variational Principles, 1966; Integral Equations, 1977; articles on theoretical atomic physics in scientific jls. *Address:* 21 Knocktern Gardens, Belfast, Northern Ireland BT4 3LZ. *T:* Belfast (01232) 658332.

MOISEIWITSCH, Tanya, (Mrs Felix Krish), CBE 1976; designer for the theatre; *b* 3 Dec. 1914; *d* of late Benno Moiseiwitsch, CBE, and 1st wife, Daisy Kennedy; *m* 1942, Felix Krish (decd). *Educ:* various private schs; Central School of Arts and Crafts, London; Scenic painting student at Old Vic, London. Abbey Theatre, Dublin, 1935–39; Q. Theatre, 1940; 1st West End prod. Golden Cuckoo, Duchess, 1940; Weekly Repertory, Oxford Playhouse, 1941–44. Stage designs include: Bless the Bride, Adelphi, 1947; Peter Grimes, Covent Garden, 1947; Beggar's Opera, English Opera Group, Aldeburgh Festival, 1948; Treasure Hunt, Apollo, 1949; Home at Seven, Wyndham's, 1950; The Holly and the Ivy, Lyric (Hammersmith) and Duchess, 1950; Captain Carvallo, St James's, 1950; Figure of Fun, Aldwych, 1951. Has designed for Old Vic Company since 1944; at Playhouse, Liverpool, 1944–45; at Theatre Royal, Bristol, 1945–46; productions for Old Vic Company include: (at New Theatre): Uncle Vanya, The Critic, Cyrano de Bergerac, 1945–46, The Cherry Orchard, 1948, A Month in the Country, 1949; (at Old Vic): Midsummer Night's Dream, 1951, Timon of Athens, 1952, Henry VIII, 1953; Two Gentlemen of Verona, 1957. Has designed for Royal Shakespeare Theatre, Stratford upon Avon: Henry VIII, 1950; The History Cycle (assisted by Alix Stone), 1951; Othello, 1954; Measure for Measure, 1956; Much Ado about Nothing (scenery), 1958; All's Well that Ends Well, 1959; also for 1st, and subsequent seasons, Shakespearean Festival, Stratford, Ont, incl. Cymbeline, 1970; The Imaginary Invalid, 1974 (Australian tour for Elizabethan Theatre Trust); All's Well that Ends Well, 1977; Mary Stuart (costumes), 1982; Tartuffe, 1983; (with Polly Scranton Bohdanetzky) The Government Inspector, Stratford, Ont, 1985; for The Matchmaker, Edinburgh Festival, 1954, and New York, 1955; for Cherry Orchard, Piccolo Teatro, Milan, 1955; for Merchant of Venice, Habimah Theatre, Israel, 1959; Tyrone Guthrie Theatre, Minneapolis, USA: 1963: Hamlet, The Miser, Three Sisters; 1964: St Joan, Volpone; 1965: The Way of the World; Cherry Orchard; 1966: As You Like It; Skin of our Teeth (with Carolyn Parker); 1967: The House of Atreus; 1973: (with J. Jensen) The Government Inspector (costumes); Metropolitan Opera, New York: Peter Grimes, 1967; Rigoletto, 1977; La Traviata, 1981; National Theatre: Volpone, 1968; The Misanthrope, 1973; Phaedra Britannica, 1975; The Double Dealer, 1978; Macook's Corner, Ulster Players, Belfast, 1969; Caucasian Chalk Circle, Sheffield Playhouse, 1969; Swift, Abbey Theatre, Dublin, 1969; Uncle Vanya, Minneapolis, 1969; The Barber of Seville, Brighton Festival, 1971; The Misanthrope, St James' Theater, NY, 1975; The Voyage of Edgar Allan Poe (world première), Minnesota Opera Co., USA, 1976; Œdipus the King and Œdipus at Colonus (costumes and masks), Adelaide Fest., 1978; Red Roses for Me, Abbey Theatre, Dublin, 1980; The Clandestine Marriage,

Compass Theatre Co. tour and Albery, 1984. Cons. designer, Crucible Theatre, Sheffield, 1971–73. For Granada TV, King Lear (costumes), 1983. Assoc. Dir Laureate, Stratford Festival, Canada. Diplôme d'Honneur, Canadian Conference of the Arts; Hon. Fellow, Ontario Coll. of Art, 1979. Hon. DLitt: Birmingham, 1964; Waterloo, Ont, 1977; Minnesota, 1994; Hon. LLD Toronto, 1988. *Address:* 17B St Alban's Studios, St Alban's Grove, W8 5BT.

MOKAMA, Hon. Moleleki Didwell, BA (Rhodes), LLM (Harvard), LLM (London); **Hon. Mr Justice Mokama;** Advocate of the Supreme Court of Botswana; Chief Justice of Botswana, since 1992; *b* 2 Feb. 1933; *e s* of Mokama Moleleki and Baipoledi Moleleki, Maunatlala, Botswana; *m* 1962, Kgopodiso Vivien Robi; one *s*. *Educ:* Moeng; Fort Hare; London Univ. Called to the Bar, Inner Temple, 1962; Crown Counsel to Botswana Govt, 1963–66; High Comr for Botswana in London, 1966–69; Botswana Ambassador Extraordinary and Plenipotentiary: to France, 1967–69; to Germany, 1967–69; to Sweden, 1968–69; to Denmark, 1968–69; Attorney-Gen. of Botswana, 1969–91. Comr (1 of 11), African Commn on Human and People's Rights. Hon. Mem., American Soc. of International Law, 1965. *Recreations:* swimming, shooting, hunting. *Address:* Chief Justice's Chambers, Private Bag 1, Lobatse, Botswana. *Fax:* 332317, *Telex:* 2758 Court BD.

MOLAPO, Mooki Motsarapane; High Commissioner for Lesotho in the United Kingdom, 1979–82; *b* 28 April 1928; *s* of Motsarapane and Mathebe Molapo; *m* 1958, Emily Mamanasse Thamae; three *s* one *d*. *Educ:* Lesotho (then Basutoland) High School. Government Service, 1950–83, retired. *Recreations:* football fan, walking, movies, theatre. *Address:* PO Box 42, Maputsoe 350, Lesotho.

MOLE, David Richard Penton; QC 1990; a Recorder, since 1995; *b* 1 April 1943; *s* of Rev. Arthur Penton Mole and Margaret Isobel Mole; *m* 1969, Anu-Reet (*née* Nigol); three *s* one *d*. *Educ:* St John's School, Leatherhead; Trinity College, Dublin (MA); LSE (LLM). City of London College, 1967–74 (Sen. Lectr, 1971); called to the Bar, Inner Temple, 1970; Standing Junior Counsel to Inland Revenue in rating valuation matters, 1984. Part-time cartoonist, 1979–83. *Publications:* contribs to Jl of Planning Law. *Recreations:* sailing, walking, ski-ing, drawing, painting. *Address:* 4–5 Gray's Inn Square, Gray's Inn, WC1R 5AY. *T:* 0171–404 5252.

MOLESWORTH, family name of **Viscount Molesworth.**

MOLESWORTH, 11th Viscount, *cr* 1716 (Ireland); **Richard Gosset Molesworth;** Baron Philipstown, 1716; *b* 31 Oct. 1907; *s* of 10th Viscount and Elizabeth Gladys Langworthy (*d* 1974); *S* father, 1961; *m* 1958, Anne Florence Womersley, MA (*d* 1983); two *s*. *Educ:* Lancing Coll.; private tutors. Farmed for many years. Freeman, City of London, 1978. Served War, in RAF, 1941–44 (Middle East, 1941–43). *Recreations:* foreign travel, music. *Heir: s* Hon. Robert Bysse Kelham Molesworth [*b* 4 June 1959. *Educ:* Sussex Univ. (BA Hons)].

MOLESWORTH, Allen Henry Neville; management consultant; *b* 20 Aug. 1931; *s* of late Roger Bevil Molesworth (Colonel RA), and of Iris Alice Molesworth (*née* Kennion); *m* 1970, Gail Cheng Kwai Chan. *Educ:* Wellington Coll., Berks; Trinity Coll., Cambridge (MA). FCA, FCMA, MIMC. 2nd Lt, 4th Queen's Own Hussars, Malaya, 1950. Project Accounts, John Laing & Sons (Canada) Ltd, 1954–58; Singleton Fabian & Co., Chartered Accountants, 1959–63; Consultant: Standard Telephones & Cables Ltd, 1963–67; Coopers & Lybrand Associates Ltd, 1967–76: India, 1970; Kuwait, 1971; France, 1972; New Hebrides, 1972; Laos, 1974; Tonga, 1975; Financial and Admin. Controller, Crown Agents, 1976–84; Chief Accountant, British Telecom Property, 1984–90. *Recreations:* shooting, skiing, music, restoring antiques. *Address:* c/o Lloyds Bank, 8–10 Waterloo Place, SW1Y 4BE. *Clubs:* 1900, Coningsby.

MOLESWORTH-ST AUBYN, Lt-Col Sir (John) Arscott, 15th Bt *cr* 1689, of Pencarrow; MBE 1963; DL; JP; *b* 15 Dec. 1926; *s* of Sir John Molesworth-St Aubyn, 14th Bt, CBE, and Celia Marjorie (*d* 1965), *d* of Lt-Col Valentine Vivian, CMG, DSO, MVO; *S* father, 1985; *m* 1957, Iona Audrey Armatrude, *d* of late Adm. Sir Francis Loftus Tottenham, KCB, CBE; two *s* one *d*. *Educ:* Eton. 2nd Lieut KRRC 1946; Captain 1954; psc 1959; Major 1961; jssc 1964; served Malaya and Borneo, 1961–63 and 1965; Royal Green Jackets, 1966; Lt-Col 1967; retd 1969. County Comr, Scouts, Cornwall, 1969–79. Mem., Cornwall River Authority, 1969–74; Chairman: West Local Land Drainage Cttee, SW Water Authority, 1974–89; West Local Flood Alleviation Cttee, Nat. Rivers Authority, SW Region, 1989–92; Devon Exec. Cttee, 1975–77, and Cornwall Exec. Cttee, 1987–89, CLA. Wessex Region, Historic Houses Assoc., 1981–83. Pres., Royal Cornwall Agricl Assoc., 1976; Mem. Council, Devon County Agricl Assoc., 1979–82; JP Devon, 1971–84, now supp. list; DL Cornwall, 1971; High Sheriff Cornwall, 1975. *Recreations:* shooting, ornithology. *Heir: s* William Molesworth-St Aubyn [*b* 23 Nov. 1958; *m* 1988, Carolyn, *er d* of William Tozier]. *Address:* Pencarrow, Bodmin, Cornwall PL30 3AG. *T:* St Mabyn (01208) 841449. *Clubs:* Army and Navy; Cornish 1768.

MOLITOR, Edouard, Hon. KCMG 1976; Grand Officier, Ordre du Mérite (Luxembourg), 1990; Commandeur, Ordre de la Couronne de Chêne, 1985; Officier, Ordre Civil et Militaire d'Adolphe de Nassau, 1977; Ambassador of Luxembourg to Italy, since 1993; Permanent Representative to UN Food and Agriculture Organisation, since 1993; *b* Luxembourg City, 14 Feb. 1931; *s* of Joseph Molitor and Lucie Michels; *m* 1960, Constance Scholtes; three *s*. *Educ:* Univs of Grenoble, Nancy and Paris. Dr en droit. Barrister, Luxembourg, 1955–60; joined Diplomatic Service, 1960 (Political Affairs); First Sec. and Rep. to UNESCO, Paris, 1964–69; Counsellor and Consul-Gen., Brussels, 1969–73; Dir of Protocol and Juridical Affairs, Min. of Foreign Affairs, 1973–78; Mem., Commn de Contrôle, EC, 1973–77; Ambassador to Austria, 1978–89; Perm. Rep. to UNIDO, IAEA, 1978–89; Head of Luxembourg Delegn, MBFR Conf., 1978–89 and at CSCE Conf., Vienna, 1986–89; Ambassador to UK, Ireland and Iceland, and Perm. Rep. to Council of WEU, 1989–92. Foreign Decorations from: Norway, 1964; Italy, W Germany, Belgium, 1973; Greece, 1975; Denmark, Tunisia, Senegal, Netherlands, France, 1978; Vatican, Austria, 1989; Iceland, 1990. *Recreations:* swimming, hiking, ski-ing, shooting, music, literature. *Address:* Via Ardeatina 134, 00179 Rome, Italy. *Clubs:* Travellers', Royal Anglo-Belgian.

MOLLISON, Prof. Patrick Loudon, CBE 1979; MD; FRCP; FRCPath; FRCOG; FRS 1968; Professor of Hæmatology, St Mary's Hospital Medical School, London University, 1962–79, now Emeritus Professor; Hon. Consultant Immunohaematologist, North London Blood Transfusion Centre, since 1983; *b* 17 March 1914; *s* of William Mayhew Mollison, Cons. Surgeon (ENT), Guy's Hospital; *m* 1st, 1940, Dr Margaret D. Peirce (marr. diss., 1964); three *s*; 2nd, 1973, Dr Jennifer Jones. *Educ:* Rugby Sch.; Clare Coll., Cambridge; St Thomas' Hosp., London. MD Cantab 1944; FRCP 1959; FRCPath 1963; FRCOG *ad eund*, 1980. House Phys., Medical Unit, St Thomas' Hosp., 1939; Medical Officer, S London Blood Supply Depot, 1939–43; RAMC, 1943–46; Dir, MRC Blood Transfusion Res. Unit, Hammersmith Hosp., 1946–60; part-time Dir, MRC Experimental Hæmatology Unit, 1960–79; Hon. Lectr, then Sen. Lectr, Dept of Medicine, Post-grad. Medical Sch., 1948; Consultant Hæmatologist: Hammersmith Hosp., 1947–60; St Mary's Hosp., 1960–79. Hon. FRSM 1979; Landsteiner Meml Award, USA, 1960; P. Levine Award, USA, 1973; Oehlecker Medal, Germany, 1974. *Publications:* Blood Transfusion in Clinical Medicine, 1951, 9th edn (jtly) 1993; papers on red cell survival and blood group antibodies. *Recreations:* music, gardening. *Address:* 60 King Henry's Road, NW3 3RR. *T:* 0171–722 1947.

MOLLO, Joseph Molelekoa Kaibe; Ambassador of Lesotho to Republic of South Africa, since 1992; *b* 7 May 1944; *s* of Kaibe and Cyrian Mollo; *m* 1972, Makaibe; two *s* two *d*. *Educ:* Univ. of Botswana, Lesotho and Swaziland (BA Admin); Univ. of Saskatchewan (MCEd); Carleton Univ. (working on a Master's degree in Political Science since 1978). Asst Sec., Min. of Finance, 1971; Comr of Co-operatives, 1973; Dep. Perm. Sec., Finance, 1975; High Comr, Canada, 1976; Perm. Sec., Finance, 1980; High Comr in London, 1982–83; Ambassador to Denmark (also accredited to Sweden, Norway, Finland, Iceland, GDR and Poland), 1983–86; Man. Dir, Trading Corp. of Lesotho, 1986–88. Unpublished thesis: Profit versus Co-operation: the struggle of the Western Co-operative College. *Recreations:* jogging, dancing, music, soccer. *Address:* Lesotho Embassy, PO Box 55817, Arcadia 0007, South Africa.

MOLLOY, family name of **Baron Molloy.**

MOLLOY, Baron *cr* 1981 (Life Peer), of Ealing in Greater London; **William John Molloy,** TD 1945; FRGS; *b* 26 Oct. 1918; *m* Eva Lewis; one *d*. *Educ:* elementary sch., Swansea; University Coll., Swansea (Political Economy, extra-mural). Served TA, 1938, Field Co., RE, 1939–46. Member: TGWU 1936–46; Civil Service Union, 1946–52; Co-op and USDAW, 1952; Parliamentary Adviser: COHSE, 1974–; Civil Service Union, 1974–79. Editor, Civil Service Review, 1947–52; Chm., Staff-Side Whitley Council, Germany and Austria Sections, FO, 1948–52, and Staff-Side Lectr, 1946–52. Member: Fulham Borough Council, 1954–62 (Leader, 1959–62); Fulham and Hammersmith Council, 1962–66. MP (Lab) Ealing N, 1964–79; former Vice-Chm., Parly Labour Party Gp for Common Market and European Affairs; Chm., PLP Social Services Gp, 1974; Parly Adviser, London Trades Council Transport Cttee, 1968–79; Mem., House of Commons Estimates Cttee, 1968–70; PPS to Minister of Posts and Telecom., 1969–70. Chm., British Tunisia Soc., 1987–; Vice-Chm., All Party British/Tunisian Parly Gp, 1987–. Member: CPA, 1964; IPU, 1964 (Mem. Exec., 1984–); Assemblies, Council of Europe and WEU, 1969–73; European Parlt, 1976–79. Mem., Parly and Scientific Cttee, 1982–; EC Mem., CAABU. Political Consultant: Confedn of Health Service Employees, 1979–; British Library Assoc., 1984–; Consultant and Adviser to Arab League, 1982–88. Vice-Pres., and a Trustee, Health Visitors Assoc., 1987–. Pres., Metropolitan Area, 1984–, and Nat. Vice Pres., 1993–, Royal British Legion. Hon. Life Pres., London Univ. Debating Soc., 1970; Hon. Pres., London Univ. Union, 1983–; Hon. Patron, Stirling Univ. Debating Soc., 1991–; Mem. Court, Reading Univ., 1968–. FRGS 1967 (former Mem. Exec. Council); Fellow, World Assoc. of Arts and Sciences, 1982. Hon. Fellow, UC of Swansea, Wales, 1987; Hon. Associate, BVA, 1988. *Recreations:* horse-riding, music, collecting dictionaries. *Address:* 2a Uneeda Drive, Greenford, Mddx UB6 8QB. *T:* (office) 0171–219 6710; (home) 0181–578 7736.

MOLLOY, Michael John; writer; *b* 22 Dec. 1940; *s* of John George and Margaret Ellen Molloy; *m* 1964, Sandra June Foley; three *d*. *Educ:* Ealing School of Art. Sunday Pictorial, 1956; Daily Sketch, 1960; Daily Mirror, 1962–85: Editor, Mirror Magazine, 1969; Asst Editor, 1970; Dep. Editor, 1975; Editor, Dec. 1975–1985; Editor, Sunday Mirror, 1986–88; Mirror Group Newspapers: Director, 1976–90; Editor in Chief, 1985–90. *Publications:* The Black Dwarf, 1985; The Kid from Riga, 1987; The Harlot of Jericho, 1989; The Century, 1990; The Gallery, 1991; Sweet Sixteen, 1992; Cat's Paw, 1993; Home Before Dark, 1994; Dogsbody, 1995. *Recreations:* reading, writing. *Address:* 62 Culmington Road, W13 9NH. *Club:* Savile.

MOLONY, Thomas Desmond, 3rd Bt. Does not use the title, and his name is not on the Official Roll of Baronets.

MOLYNEAUX, Rt. Hon. James Henry; PC 1983; MP (UU) Lagan Valley, since 1983 (Antrim South, 1970–83); Leader, Ulster Unionist Party, 1979–95; *b* 27 Aug. 1920; *s* of late William Molyneaux, Seacash, Killead, Co. Antrim; unmarried. *Educ:* Aldergrove Sch., Co. Antrim. RAF, 1941–46. Vice-Chm., Eastern Special Care Hosp. Man. Cttee, 1966–73; Chm. Antrim Br., NI Assoc. for Mental Health, 1967–70; Hon. Sec., S Antrim Unionist Assoc., 1964–70; Vice-Pres., Ulster Unionist Council, 1974. Mem. (UU) S Antrim, NI Assembly, 1982–86. Leader, UU Party, House of Commons, 1974–. Dep. Grand Master of Orange Order and Hon. PGM of Canada; Sovereign Grand Master, Commonwealth Royal Black Instn, 1971. JP Antrim, 1957–87; CC Antrim, 1964–73. *Recreations:* gardening, music. *Address:* Aldergrove, Crumlin, Co. Antrim, N Ireland BT29 4AR. *T:* Crumlin (018494) 22545.

MOLYNEUX, Prof. David Hurst, DSc; Director, Liverpool School of Tropical Medicine and Professor of Tropical Health Sciences, University of Liverpool, since 1991; *b* 9 April 1943; *s* of Reginald Frank Molyneux and Monica Foden Molyneux; *m* 1969, Anita Elisabeth Bateson; one *s* one *d*. *Educ:* Denstone Coll.; Emmanuel Coll., Cambridge (BA 1965; PhD 1969; MA 1969; DSc 1992). FIBiol 1984. Lectr, Dept of Parasitology, Liverpool Sch. of Tropical Medicine, 1968–77; seconded as Research Officer to Nigerian Inst. for Trypanosomiasis, Kaduna, 1970–72, as Project Manager to UNDP/WHO, Bobo Dioulasso, Burkino Faso, 1975–77; Prof. of Biology, Univ. of Salford, 1977–91. Pres., British Soc. of Parasitology, 1992. Chalmers Medal, RSTM&H, 1987; Wright Medal, British Soc. of Parasitology, 1989. *Publications:* The Biology of Trypanosoma and Leishmania: parasites of man and domestic animals (with R. W. Ashford), 1983; numerous contribs to professional jls. *Recreations:* golf, music, travel, primitive art. *Address:* Liverpool School of Tropical Medicine, Pembroke Place, Liverpool L3 5QA. *T:* 0151–708 9393; Kingsley Cottage, Town Well, Kingsley, Cheshire WA6 8EZ. *T:* Kingsley (01928) 788397. *Club:* Delamere Forest Golf.

MOLYNEUX, Helena; Director of Personnel, British Council, since 1993; *b* 17 Aug. 1948; *d* of Joseph and Mary Molyneux. *Educ:* Manchester Univ. (BSc); Cranfield Inst. of Technol. (MBA). FIPD. United Biscuits, 1969–73; Univ. of Sierra Leone, 1973–76; Bank of America: Personnel Manager, Bank of Amer. Internat., 1979–80; Divl Personnel Manager, NT & SA, San Francisco, 1980–82; Head, Employee Relns and Personnel Planning, Eur., ME and Africa Div., 1982–87; Bankers Trust Co.: Head, Employee Relns and Staffing, Eur., 1987–89; Head, Corporate Personnel, Eur., 1989–93. Dep. Chm., Traidcraft plc. FRSA. *Recreations:* music, reading, gardening, Dorset, ski-ing.

MOLYNEUX, James Robert M.; *see* More-Molyneux.

MONCADA, Dr Salvador Enrique, FRCP; FRS 1988; Director of Research, Wellcome Foundation Ltd, since 1986; *b* 3 Dec. 1944; *s* of Dr Salvador Eduardo Moncada and Jenny Seidner; *m* 1966, Dorys Lemus Valiente; one *d*. *Educ:* Univ. of El Salvador (DMS 1970); London Univ. (DPhil 1973; DSc 1983). FRCP 1994. GP, Social Service of El Salvador, 1969; Associate Prof. of Pharmacol. and Physiol., Univ. of Honduras, 1974–75; Wellcome Research Laboratories, 1971–73 and 1975–: Sen. Scientist, 1975–77; Hd of Dept of Prostaglandin Res., 1977–85; Dir, Therapeutic Res. Div., 1984–86. Visiting Professor: KCL, 1988; KCH Sch. of Medicine and Dentistry, 1992. Consultant, Pan Amer. Health Orgn, 1972–. Member, Editorial Board: British Jl of Pharmacol., 1980–85; Atherosclerosis

(Jl of Amer. Heart Assoc.), 1980–; European Jl of Clin. Investigation, 1986–; Thrombosis Research, 1989–. Mem., British Pharmacol Soc., 1974. Associate Fellow, Third World Acad. of Sciences, 1988. Amer. Nat. Acad. of Scis, 1994. Dr *hc*: Univ. of Complutense de Madrid, 1986; Univ. of Honduras, 1987; Univ. of Cantabria, 1988; Hon. DSc: Sussex, 1994; Mt Sinai Sch. of Medicine, NY, 1995; Nottingham, 1995. Peter Debeye Prize (jtly), Limburg Univ., 1980; Nat. Sci. Prize, Republic of Honduras, 1985; Prince of Asturias Prize for Science and Technology, 1990; Royal Medal, Royal Soc., 1994. *Publications:* (Scientific Ed.) British Medical Bulletin, 39 pt 3: Prostacyclin, Thromboxane and Leukotrienes, 1983; Nitric oxide from L-arginine: a bioregulatory system, 1990; (ed jtly) The Biology of Nitric Oxide, pts 3 and 4, 1994. *Recreations:* music, literature, theatre. *Address:* 25 Hitherwood Drive, SE19 1XA. *T:* 0181–670 0298.

MONCASTER, John Anthony; Master of the Supreme Court, Chancery Division, since 1992; *b* Louth, Lincs, 15 Oct. 1939; *o c* of Jack Moncaster and Muriel, 2nd *d* of Henry Butterick; *m* 1966, Gillian Ann, *o d* of Rev. Royston York; two *s* two *d*. Called to the Bar, Gray's Inn, 1961; practised at Chancery Bar. *Recreation:* books. *Address:* Dukes, Layer Marney, Essex. *T:* Colchester (01206) 330184.

MONCEL, Lt-Gen. Robert William, OC 1968; DSO 1944; OBE 1944; CD 1944; retired 1966; *b* 9 April 1917; *s* of René Moncel and Edith Brady; *m* 1939, Nancy Allison, *d* of Ralph P. Bell; one *d*. *Educ:* Selwyn House Sch.; Bishop's Coll. Sch. Royal Canadian Regt, 1939; Staff Coll., 1940; Bde Major 1st Armd Bde, 1941; comd 18th Manitoba Dragoons, 1942; GSO1, HQ 2 Cdn Corps, 1943; comd 4th Armd Bde, 1944; Dir Canadian Armd Corps, 1946; Nat. War Coll., 1949; Canadian Jt Staff, London, 1949–54; Comdr 3 Inf. Bde, 1957; QMG, 1960; GOC Eastern Comd, 1963; Comptroller Gen., 1964; Vice-Chief of the Defence Staff, Canada, 1965–66. Col, 8th Canadian Hussars. Chm., Fishermen's Memorial Hosp., 1980–84; Dir, Nova Scotia Rehabilitation Center, 1986–. Mem. Bd of Regents, Mount Allison Univ., 1983–. Croix de Guerre, France, 1944; Légion d'Honneur, France, 1944. Hon. LLD Mount Allison Univ., 1968. *Recreations:* fishing, sailing, golf. *Address:* High Head, Murder Point, Nova Scotia B0J 2E0, Canada; Summer Gardens, 1470 Summer Street, Halifax, NS B3H 3A3, Canada. *Clubs:* Royal Ottawa Golf; Royal St Lawrence Yacht; Royal Nova Scotia Yacht.

MONCK, family name of **Viscount Monck.**

MONCK, 7th Viscount *cr* 1801; **Charles Stanley Monck;** *S* father, 1982 but does not use the title. *Heir: b* Hon. George Stanley Monck.

MONCK, Sir Nicholas (Jeremy), KCB 1994 (CB 1988); Permanent Secretary, Employment Department Group, 1993–95; *b* 9 March 1935; *s* of Bosworth Monck and Stella Mary (*née* Cock); *m* 1960, Elizabeth Mary Kirwan; three *s*. *Educ:* Eton; King's Coll., Cambridge; Univ. of Pennsylvania. Asst Principal, Min. of Power, 1959–62; NEDO, 1962–65; NBPI, 1965–66; Senior Economist, Min. of Agriculture, Tanzania, 1966–69; HM Treasury, 1969–92: Asst Sec., 1971; Principal Private Sec. to Chancellor of the Exchequer, 1976–77; Under Sec., 1977–84; Dep. Sec. (Industry), 1984–90; Second Perm. Sec. (Public Expenditure), 1990–92. Mem., BSC, 1978–80. *Address:* 31 Lady Margaret Road, NW5 2NG.

MONCKTON, family name of **Viscount Galway** and **Viscount Monckton of Brenchley.**

MONCKTON OF BRENCHLEY, 2nd Viscount *cr* 1957; **Maj.-Gen. Gilbert Walter Riversdale Monckton,** CB 1966; OBE 1956; MC 1940; DL; FSA; retired, 1967; *b* 3 Nov. 1915; *o s* of 1st Viscount Monckton of Brenchley, PC, GCVO, KCMG, MC, QC, and Mary A. S. (*d* 1964), *d* of Sir Thomas Colyer-Fergusson, 3rd Bt; *S* father, 1965; *m* 1950, Marianna Laetitia (Dame of Honour and Devotion, SMO Malta (also Cross of Merit), OStJ, Pres., St John's Ambulance, Kent, 1975–80, High Sheriff of Kent, 1981–82), 3rd *d* of late Comdr Robert T. Bower; four *s* one *d*. *Educ:* Harrow; Trinity Coll., Cambridge. BA 1939, MA 1942. 2/Lt 5th Royal Inniskilling Dragoon Guards, SR 1938; Reg. 1939; France and Belgium, 1939–40; Staff Coll., 1941; Bde Major Armd Bde, 1942; Comd and Gen. Staff Sch., USA, 1943; Sqdn Ldr, 3rd King's Own Hussars, 1944, Italy and Syria; Sqdn Ldr, 5th Royal Inniskilling Dragoon Gds, 1945. RAF Staff Coll., 1949; GSO2, 7th Armd Div., 1949; Sqdn Ldr and 2 i/c 5th Royal Inniskilling Dragoon Gds, Korea and Egypt, 1951–52; GSO1, Mil. Ops, WO, 1954–56; Mil. Adv., Brit. Delegn, Geneva Confs on Indo-China and Korea, 1954; transf. 12th Royal Lancers and comd, 1956–58; Comdr Royal Armd Corps, 3rd Div., 1958–60; psc, idc 1961; Dep. Dir, Personnel Admin., WO, 1962; Dir of Public Relations, WO (subseq. MoD), 1963–65; Chief of Staff, HQ BAOR, 1965–67; Col 9th/12th Royal Lancers (Prince of Wales's), 1967–73; Hon. Col, Kent and Sharpshooters Yeomanry Sqdn, 1974–79. President: Kent Assoc. of Boys' Clubs, 1965–78; Inst. of Heraldic and Genealogical Studies, 1965; Kent Archæological Soc., 1968–75; Medway Productivity Assoc., 1968–72; Kent Co. Rifle Assoc., 1970–75; Anglo-Belgian Union, 1973–83; Chm., Thurnham Parish Council, 1968–70. FSA 1987. DL Kent, 1970. Liveryman Broderers' Co., Master 1978; KStJ; Chm., Council of Order of St John for Kent, 1969–75; SMO Malta: Bailiff, Grand Cross of Obedience (Chancellor of the British Assoc., 1963–68, Vice-Pres., 1968–74, Pres., 1974–83); Grand Cross of Merit, 1980; Comdr, Order of Crown (Belgium), 1965; Bailiff, Grand Cross of Justice, Constantinian Order of St George, 1975; Grand Officer, Order of Leopold II (Belgium), 1978. *Recreation:* archaeology. *Heir: s* Hon. Christopher Walter Monckton, *qv*. *Address:* Runhams Farm, Runham Lane, Harrietsham, Maidstone, Kent ME17 1NJ. *T:* Maidstone (01622) 850313. *Clubs:* Brooks's, MCC; Casino Maltese (Valetta).

See also Hon. D. R. C. Lawson.

MONCKTON, Hon. Christopher Walter; DL; Director, Christopher Monckton Ltd, consultants, since 1987; *b* 14 Feb. 1952; *s* and *heir* of Viscount Monckton of Brenchley, *qv*; *m* 1990, Juliet Mary Anne, *y d* of Jørgen Malherbe Jensen. *Educ:* Harrow; Churchill Coll., Cambridge; University Coll., Cardiff. BA 1973, MA 1977 (Cantab); Dip. Journalism Studies (Wales), 1974. Standing Cttee, Cambridge Union Soc., 1973; Treas., Cambridge Univ. Conservative Assoc., 1973. Reporter, Yorkshire Post, 1974–75, Leader-Writer, 1975–77; Press Officer, Conservative Central Office, 1977–78; Editor-designate, The Universe, 1978, Editor, 1979–81; Managing Editor, Telegraph Sunday Magazine, 1981–82; Leader-Writer, The Standard, 1982; Special Advr to Prime Minister's Policy Unit, 1982–86; Asst Editor, Today, 1986–87; Consulting Editor, 1987–92, Chief Leader-Writer, 1990–92, Evening Standard. Freeman, City of London, and Liveryman, Worshipful Co. of Broderers, 1973–. Member: Internat. MENSA Ltd, 1975–; St John Amb. Brigade (Wetherby Div.), 1976–77; Hon. Soc. of the Middle Temple, 1979–; RC Mass Media Commn, 1979–; Sec. to Econ., Forward Strategy, Health, and Employment Study Gps, Centre For Policy Studies, 1980–82. Vis. Lectr in Business Studies, Columbia Univ., NY, 1980. Editor, Not the Church Times, 1982. Kt SMO, Malta, 1973; OStJ 1973. DL Greater London, 1988. *Publications:* The Laker Story (with Ivan Fallon), 1982, Anglican Orders: null and void?, 1986; The Aids Report, 1987. *Recreation:* romance. *Address:* Finnart Lodge, Bridge of Gaur, Rannoch, by Pitlochry, Perthshire PH17 2QF. *T:* Bridge of Gaur (01882) 633317/633318, *Fax:* (01882) 633319. *Clubs:* Brooks's, Beefsteak, Pratt's.

MONCKTON-ARUNDELL, family name of **Viscount Galway.**

MONCREIFF, family name of **Baron Moncreiff.**

MONCREIFF, 5th Baron *cr* 1873; **Harry Robert Wellwood Moncreiff;** Bt, Nova Scotia 1626, UK 1871; Lt-Col (Hon.) RASC, retired; *b* 4 Feb. 1915; *s* of 4th Baron; *S* father, 1942; *m* 1952, Enid Marion Watson (*d* 1985), *o d* of Major H. W. Locke, Belmont, Dollar; one *s*. *Educ:* Fettes Coll., Edinburgh. Served War of 1939–45 (despatches). Retired, 1958. *Recreations:* Rugby football, tennis, shooting. *Heir: s* Hon. Rhoderick Harry Wellwood Moncreiff [*b* 22 March 1954; *m* 1982, Alison Elizabeth Anne, *d* of late James Duncan Alastair Ross; two *s*]. *Address:* Tulliebole Castle, Fossoway, Kinross-shire KY13 7QN. *T:* Fossoway (015774) 236.

MONCREIFFE of Moncreiffe, Hon. Peregrine David Euan Malcolm; Executive Director, Buchanan Partners Ltd, since 1990; *b* 16 Feb. 1951; *s* of Sir Iain Moncreiffe of that Ilk, CVO, DL, QC and Diana, Countess of Erroll; *m* 1988, Miranda Fox-Pitt; one *s* two *d*. *Educ:* Eton; Christ Church, Oxford (MA Modern Hist.). Lieut, Atholl Highlanders, 1978. Investment banker: with White Weld & Co. Ltd/Credit Suisse First Boston Ltd, 1972–82; Lehman Brothers Kuhn Loeb/Shearson Lehman, 1982–86; E. F. Hutton & Co., 1986–88. Mem., Royal Commn on Ancient and Historical Monuments of Scotland, 1989–94. Chm., Scottish Ballet, 1988–90. Trustee, Save the Rhino, 1991–. Mem., Royal Co. of Archers (Queen's Body Guard for Scotland), 1979–. Freeman, City of London; Liveryman, Co. of Fishmongers, 1987–. *Address:* Easter Moncreiffe, Bridge of Earn, Perth PH2 8QA. *T:* Perth (01738) 812338. *Clubs:* White's, Turf, Pratt's; New (Edinburgh); Leander (Henley); Brook (New York).

MONCRIEFF, William S.; *see* Scott-Moncrieff.

MONCTON, Archbishop of, (RC), since 1972; **Most Rev. Donat Chiasson;** *b* Paquetville, NB, 2 Jan. 1930; *s* of Louis Chiasson and Anna Chiasson (*née* Godin). *Educ:* St Joseph's Univ., NB; Holy Heart Seminary, Halifax, NS; Theological and Catechetical studies, Rome and Lumen Vitae, Belgium. *Address:* PO Box 248, Chartersville, Moncton, NB, Canada. *T:* (506) 3899531.

MOND, family name of **Baron Melchett.**

MONDALE, Walter Frederick; American Ambassador to Japan, since 1993; *b* Ceylon, Minnesota, 5 Jan. 1928; *s* of Rev. Theodore Sigvaard Mondale and Claribel Hope (*née* Cowan); *m* 1955, Joan Adams; two *s* one *d*. *Educ:* public schs, Minnesota; Macalester Coll., Univ. of Minnesota (BA *cum laude*); Univ. of Minnesota Law Sch. (LLB). Served with Army, 1951–53. Admitted to Minn. Bar, 1956; private law practice, Minneapolis, 1956–60; Attorney-Gen., Minnesota, 1960–65; Senator from Minnesota, 1965–76; Vice-Pres., USA, 1977–81; Counsel with Winston & Strawn, 1981–87; Partner with Dorsey & Whitney, 1987–93. Democratic Candidate for Vice-Pres., USA, 1976, 1980; Democratic Candidate for Pres., USA, 1984. Chm., Nat. Democratic Inst. for Internat. Affairs, 1987–93. Mem., Democratic Farm Labor Party. *Publication:* The Accountability of Power. *Address:* American Embassy, 10–1, Akasaka 1-chome, Minato-ku, Tokyo 107, Japan.

MONDAY, Horace Reginald, CBE 1967 (OBE 1958); JP; *b* 26 Nov. 1907; *s* of late James Thomas Monday, Gambia Civil Servant, and late Rachel Ruth Davis; *m* 1932, Wilhelmina Roberta Juanita, *d* of late William Robertson Job Roberts, a Gambian businessman; one *s*. *Educ:* Methodist Mission Schools, in Banjul, The Gambia; correspondence course with (the then) London Sch. of Accountancy. Clerk, 1925–48; Asst Acct, Treasury, 1948–52; Acct and Storekeeper, Marine Dept, 1953–54; Acct-Gen., The Gambia Govt, 1954–65; Chm., Gambia Public Service Commn, 1965–68; High Comr for The Gambia in the UK and NI, 1968–71. MP Banjul Central, 1977–82. Chairman: Management Cttee, Banjul City Council, 1971–79; Gambia Utilities Corp., 1972–76. Dir, Gambia Currency Bd, 1964–68; Governor, Gambia High Sch., 1964–68; Pres., Gambia Red Cross Soc., 1967–68. JP 1944. Comdr, National Order of Republic of Senegal, 1968. *Address:* Rachelville, 24 Clarkson Street, Banjul, The Gambia. *T:* 27511.

MONE, Rt. Rev. John Aloysius; *see* Paisley, Bishop of, (RC).

MONEY, Ernle (David Drummond); Barrister-at-Law; *b* 17 Feb. 1931; *s* of late Lt-Col E. F. D. Money, DSO, late 4th Gurkha Rifles, and Sidney, *o d* of D. E. Anderson, Forfar; *m* 1st, 1960, Susan Barbara (marr. diss. 1985), *d* of Lt-Col D. S. Lister, MC, The Buffs; two *s* two *d*; 2nd, Bella Maharaj (*d* 1993), barrister-at-law. *Educ:* Marlborough Coll.; Oriel Coll., Oxford (open scholar). Served in Suffolk Regt, 1949–51, and 4th Bn, Suffolk Regt (TA), 1951–56; MA Hons degree (2nd cl.) in mod. hist., 1954. Tutor and lecturer, Swinton Conservative Coll., 1956. Called to Bar, Lincoln's Inn (Cholmeley Scholar), 1958. Mem., Bar Council, 1962–66. MP (C) Ipswich, 1970–Sept. 1974; Opposition Front Bench Spokesman on the Arts, 1974; Sec., Parly Cons. Arts and Amenities Cttee, 1970–73, Vice-Chm., 1974; Vice-Pres., Ipswich Cons. Assoc., 1979–81. Regular columnist, East Anglian Daily Times, for some years. Governor, Woolverstone Hall Sch., 1967–70; co-opted Mem., GLC Arts Cttee, 1972–73; Mem., GLC Arts Bd, 1974–76; Mem., Cttee of Gainsborough's Birthplace, Sudbury. Fine Arts Correspondent, Contemporary Review, 1968–88. Pres., Ipswich Town Football Club Supporters, 1974–80; Vice-Pres., E Suffolk and Ipswich Branch, RSPCA, 1974–77. Mem., Primrose League. *Publications:* (with Peter Johnson) The Nasmyth Family of Painters, 1970; Margaret Thatcher, First Lady of the House, 1975; regular contrib. various periodicals and newspapers on antiques and the arts. *Recreations:* music, pictures and antiques, watching Association football. *Address:* Westgate Chambers, 144 The High Street, Lewes, E Sussex BN7 1XT. *T:* Lewes (01273) 480510; Flat 3, 4 Jevington Gardens, Eastbourne, E Sussex BN21 4HN. *T:* Eastbourne (01323) 737018; 10 St John's Villas, N19 3EG. *T:* 0171–272 6815. *Clubs:* Carlton, Dinosaurs; Norfolk (Norwich).

MONEY, Hon. George Gilbert, CHB 1986; FCIB; Director, Barclays Bank International Ltd, 1955–81 (Vice-Chairman, 1965–73); *b* 17 Nov. 1914; 2nd *s* of late Maj.-Gen. Sir A. W. Money, KCB, KBE, CSI and late Lady Money (*née* Drummond). *Educ:* Charterhouse Sch. Clerk, L. Behrens & Soehne, Bankers, Hamburg, 1931–32; Clerk, Barclays Bank Ltd, 1932–35, Dir 1972–73; joined Barclays Bank DCO (now Barclays Bank PLC), London, 1935; served in Egypt, Palestine, Cyprus, Ethiopia, Cyrenaica, E Africa, 1936–52; Local Dir, W Indies, 1952; Director: Barclays Bank of California, 1965–75; Bermuda Provident Bank Ltd, 1969–89; Barclays Bank of the Netherlands, Antilles NV, 1970–86; Republic Finance Corp. Ltd, 1972–88; Republic Bank Ltd, 1972–88; Barclays Bank of Jamaica Ltd, 1972–77; Barclays Australia Ltd, 1972–75; New Zealand United Corp., 1972–75; Chairman: Bahamas Internat. Trust Co. Ltd, 1970–72; Cayman Internat. Trust Co. Ltd, 1970–72; Mem., Caribbean Bd, Barclays Bank PLC, 1952–88. *Publication:* Nine Lives of a Bush Banker, 1990. *Recreations:* water ski-ing, fishing, bridge. *Address:* Saltram, St Joseph, Barbados.

MONEY-COUTTS, family name of **Baron Latymer.**

MONEY-COUTTS, Sir David (Burdett), KCVO 1991; Chairman, M & G Group, since 1990 (Director, since 1987); *b* 19 July 1931; *s* of late Hon. Alexander B. Money-Coutts (2nd *s* of 6th Baron Latymer, TD), and Mary E., *er d* of Sir Reginald Hobhouse,

5th Bt; *m* 1958, Penelope Utten Todd; one *s* two *d*. *Educ:* Eton; New Coll., Oxford (MA). National Service, 1st Royal Dragoons, 1950–51; Royal Glos Hussars, TA, 1951–67. Joined Coutts & Co., 1954; Dir, 1958–; Man. Dir, 1970–86; Chm., 1976–93. Director: National Discount Co., 1964–69; Gerrard & National, 1969– (Dep. Chm. 1969–89); United States & General Trust Corp., 1964–73; Charities Investment Managers (Charifund), 1964– (Chm., 1984–); Dun & Bradstreet, 1973–87; Phoenix Assurance, 1978–85 (Dep. Chm., 1984–85); Sun Alliance & London Insurance, 1984–90. Mem. UK Adv. Bd, National Westminster Bank, 1990–92 (Regl Dir, 1969–88, Chm., SE Reg., 1986–88; Dir, 1976–90; Chm., S Adv. Bd, 1988–92). Member: Kensington and Chelsea and Westminster AHA, 1974–82 (Vice-Chm., 1978–82); Bloomsbury HA, 1982–90 (Vice-Chm., 1982–88); Health Educn Council, 1973–77. Middlesex Hospital: Governor, 1962–74 (Dep. Chm. Governors, 1973–74); Chm., Finance Cttee, 1965–74; Mem., Med. Sch. Council, 1963–88 (Chm., 1974–88; Chm., Special Trustees, 1974–). Mem., Council, UCL, 1987–. Trustee, Multiple Sclerosis Soc., 1967–. Hon. Treas., Nat. Assoc. of Almshouses, 1960–92; Hon. Sec., Old Etonian Trust, 1969–76, Chm. Council, 1976–; Trustee, Mansfield Coll., Oxford, 1988–95. *Recreations:* odd jobs, living in the country. *Address:* Magpie House, Peppard Common, Henley-on-Thames, Oxon RG9 5JG. *T:* Rotherfield Greys (01491) 628497. *Club:* Leander (Henley-on-Thames).

MONIER-WILLIAMS, His Honour Evelyn Faithfull; a Circuit Judge, 1972–92; continued sitting in Crown and County Courts until 1995; *b* 29 April 1920; *o s* of late R. T. Monier-Williams, OBE, Barrister-at-Law, and Mrs G. M. Monier-Williams; *m* 1948, Maria-Angela Oswald (*d* 1983); one *s* one *d*. *Educ:* Charterhouse; University Coll., Oxford (MA). Admitted to Inner Temple, 1940; served Royal Artillery, 1940–46 in UK, Egypt, Libya, Tunisia, Sicily (8th Army), France, Low Countries and Germany; called to Bar, Inner Temple, 1948; South Eastern Circuit; Master of the Bench, Inner Temple, 1967, Reader, 1987, Treas., 1988; Mem. Senate of Four Inns of Court, 1969–73; Mem. Council, Selden Soc., 1970– (Vice Pres., 1990–); Mem., Council of Legal Educn, 1971–87, Vice Chm., 1974–87; Mem., Adv. Cttee on Legal Educn, 1979–87; Mem., Council of the Inns of Court, 1987–88. Livery, Glaziers' Company, 1974. *Recreation:* collecting old books. *Address:* Inner Temple, EC4Y 7HL.

MONK, Alec; *see* Monk, D. A. G.

MONK, Rear-Adm. Anthony John, CBE 1973; Appeals Organizer, The Royal Marsden Hospital Cancer Fund, 1984–87; *b* 14 Nov. 1923; *s* of Frank Leonard and Barbara Monk; *m* 1951, Elizabeth Ann Samson; four *s* (one *d* decd). *Educ:* Whitgift Sch.; RNC Dartmouth; RNEC Keyham. MSc, BScEng, FIMarE, FRAeS, FIMechE. Engr Cadet, 1941; served War of 1939–45, Pacific Fleet; flying trng, Long Air Engrg Course, Cranfield, 1946; RN Air Stn Ford; RNEC Manadon, 1950; Prodn Controller and Man., RN Aircraft Yard, Belfast, 1953–56; Mem. Dockyard Work Measurement Team, subseq. Engr Officer HMS Apollo, Techn. Asst to Dir-Gen. Aircraft, Sqdn Engr Officer to Flag Officer Aircraft Carriers, 1963–65; Asst Dir of Marine Engrg, 1965–68; Dir of Aircraft Engrg, 1968; Comd Engrg Officer to Flag Officer Naval Air Comd; Naval Liaison Officer for NI and Supt RN Aircraft Yard, Belfast, 1970; Port Admiral, Rosyth, 1974–76; Rear-Adm. Engineering to Flag Officer Naval Air Comd, 1976–78. Comdr 1956; Captain 1964; Rear-Adm. 1974. Dir Gen., Brick Develt Assoc., 1979–84. *Recreation:* swimming (ASA teacher). *Address:* Morning Glory, Kingsdown, Deal, Kent CT14 8AT.

MONK, Arthur James; Director, Components, Valves and Devices, Ministry of Defence, 1981–84, retired; *b* 15 Jan. 1924; *s* of late Rev. Arthur S. Monk, AKC, and late Lydia E. Monk; *m* 1953, Murial V. Peacock; one *s* two *d*. *Educ:* Latymer Upper School, Hammersmith; London Univ. BSc Hons Physics 1953; FIEE 1964. Served RAF, 1943–48. Services Electronic Research Labs, 1949–63, Asst Director (Co-ord. Valve Development), MoD, 1963–68; Student, Imperial Defence Coll., 1969; idc 1970; Admiralty Underwater Weapons Establishment, 1970–73; Dep. Director, Underwater Weapons Projects (S/M), MoD, 1973–76; Counsellor, Def. Equipment Staff, Washington, 1977–81. *Publications:* papers on electronics in jls of learned societies. *Recreations:* caravan touring, photography, family history and genealogy. *Address:* 65 Wyke Road, Weymouth, Dorset DT4 9QN. *T:* Weymouth (01305) 782338.

MONK, (David) Alec (George); Chief Executive Officer, Tri-Delta Corporation Ltd, 1990–93; *b* 13 Dec. 1942; *s* of Philip Aylmer and Elizabeth Jane Monk; *m* 1965, Jean Ann Searle; two *s* two *d*. *Educ:* Jesus College, Oxford. MA (PPE). Research Staff, Corporate Finance and Taxation, Sheffield Univ., 1966 and London Business Sch., 1967; Senior Financial Asst, Treasurer's Dept, Esso Petroleum Co., 1968; various positions with The Rio Tinto-Zinc Corp., 1968–77, Dir, 1974–77; Vice-Pres. and Dir, AEA Investors Inc., 1977–81; Chm. and Chief Exec., The Gateway Corp. (formerly Dee Corp.) PLC, 1981–89. Director: Scottish Eastern Investment Trust, 1985–; Charles Wells Ltd, 1989–. Mem., NEDC, 1986–90. Pres., Inst. of Grocery Distribution, 1987–89. Vis. Indust. Fellow, Manchester Business Sch., 1984. Hon. Fellow, St Hugh's Coll., Oxford, 1985. Hon. LLD Sheffield, 1988. *Publication:* (with A. J. Merrett) Inflation, Taxation and Executive Remuneration, 1967. *Recreations:* sports, reading.

MONK, Elizabeth Margaret, (Mrs M. J. Monk); *see* Reid, E. M.

MONK BRETTON, 3rd Baron *cr* 1884; **John Charles Dodson,** DL; *b* 17 July 1924; *o s* of 2nd Baron and Ruth (*d* 1967), 2nd *d* of late Hon. Charles Brand; *S* father, 1933; *m* 1958, Zoë Diana Scott; two *s*. *Educ:* Westminster Sch.; New Coll., Oxford (MA). DL E Sussex, 1983. *Recreations:* hunting, farming. *Heir: s* Hon. Christopher Mark Dodson [*b* 2 Aug. 1958; *m* 1988, Karen, *o d* of B. J. McKelvain, Fairfield, Conn; two *s* one *d*]. *Address:* Shelley's Folly, Cooksbridge, near Lewes, East Sussex BN8 4SU. *T:* Barcombe (01273) 400231. *Club:* Brooks's.

MONKS, John Stephen; General Secretary, Trades Union Congress, since 1993; *b* 5 Aug. 1945; *s* of Charles Edward Monks and Bessie Evelyn Monks; *m* 1970, Francine Jacqueline Schenk; two *s* one *d*. *Educ:* Ducie Technical High Sch., Manchester; Nottingham Univ. (BA Econ). Joined TUC, 1969; Hd of Orgn and Industrial Relns Dept, 1977–87; Dep. Gen. Sec., 1987–93. Member: Council, ACAS, 1979–95; ESRC, 1988–91. Trustee, Nat. Museum of Labour History, 1988–. Governor: Sedgehill Sch., 1987–94; LSE, 1989–; Goldsmiths' Coll., 1994–. *Recreations:* squash, music. *Address:* Congress House, Great Russell Street, WC1 3LS. *T:* 0171–636 4030.

MONKSWELL, 5th Baron *cr* 1885; **Gerard Collier;** Parliamentary consultant, since 1990; *b* 28 Jan. 1947; *s* of William Adrian Larry Collier and Helen (*née* Dunbar); *S* to disclaimed barony of father, 1984; *m* 1974, Ann Valerie Collins; two *s* one *d*. *Educ:* Portsmouth Polytechnic (BSc Mech. Eng, 1971); Slough Polytechnic (Cert. in Works Management 1972). Massey Ferguson Manfg Co. Ltd: Product Quality Engineer, 1972; Service Administration Manager, 1984. Mem. (Lab), Manchester City Council, 1989–94. *Recreations:* politics, swimming, movies. *Heir: s* Hon. James Adrian Collier, *b* 29 March 1977. *Address:* 513 Barlow Moor Road, Chorlton, Manchester M21 8AQ. *T:* 0161–881 3887.

MONMOUTH, Bishop of, since 1992; **Rt. Rev. Rowan Douglas Williams,** FBA 1990; *b* 14 June 1950; *s* of Aneurin Williams and Nancy Delphine Williams; *m* 1981, Hilary Jane Paul; one *d* *Educ:* Dynevor School, Swansea; Christ's College, Cambridge (BA 1971, MA 1975); Christ Church and Wadham College, Oxford (DPhil 1975; DD 1989). Lectr, College of the Resurrection, Mirfield, 1975–77; ordained deacon, 1977, priest, 1978; Chaplain, Tutor and Director of Studies, Westcott House, Cambridge, 1977–80; Cambridge University: Univ. Lectr in Divinity, 1980–86; Fellow and Dean of Clare Coll., 1984–86; Lady Margaret Prof. of Divinity, and Canon of Christ Church, Oxford, 1986–92. Hon. Asst Priest, St George's, Cambridge, 1980–83; Canon Theologian, Leicester Cathedral, 1981–92. Examining Chaplain to Bishop of Manchester, 1987–92. Chm., Church in Wales Div. for Social Responsibility, 1992–. Hon. Fellow: UC, Swansea, 1993; Clare Coll., Cambridge, 1994. *Publications:* The Wound of Knowledge, 1979; Resurrection, 1982; The Truce of God, 1983; (with Mark Collier) Beginning Now; peacemaking theology, 1984; Arius: heresy and tradition, 1987; (ed) The Making of Orthodoxy, 1989; Teresa of Avila, 1991; Open to Judgement, 1994; After Silent Centuries, 1994; contribs to Theologische Realencyklopädie, Jl of Theological Studies, Downside Review, Eastern Churches Review, Sobornost, New Blackfriars. *Recreations:* music, fiction, languages. *Address:* Bishopstow, Newport, Gwent NP9 4EA. *T:* Newport (Gwent) (01633) 263510.

MONMOUTH, Dean of; *see* Lewis, Very Rev. D. G.

MONOD, Prof. Théodore, DèsSc; Commandeur de la Légion d'Honneur, 1989 (Officier, 1958); Professor Emeritus at National Museum of Natural History, Paris (Assistant 1922, Professor, 1942–73); *b* 9 April 1902; *s* of Rev. Wilfred Monod and Dorina Monod; *m* 1930, Olga Pickova; two *s* one *d*. *Educ:* Sorbonne (Paris). Docteur èssciences, 1926. Sec.-Gen. (later Dir) of l'Institut Français d'Afrique Noire, 1938; Prof., Univ. of Dakar, 1957–59; Doyen, Science Faculty, Dakar, 1957–58. Mem., Academy of Sciences; Member: Acad. des Sciences d'Outre-Mer; Académie de Marine; Corresp. Mem., Académie des Sciences de Lisbonne and Académie Royale des Sciences d'Outre-Mer. Dr *hc* Köln, 1965, Neuchâtel, 1968. Gold Medallist, Royal Geographical Soc., 1960; Gold Medallist, Amer. Geographical Soc., 1961; Haile Sellassie Award for African Research, 1967; Grande Médaille d'Or, Société pour l'Encouragement au Progrès, 1991; Lauréat, Prix Marguerite Yourcenar, 1991. Comdr, Ordre du Christ, 1953; Commandeur, Mérite Saharien, 1962; Officier de l'Ordre des Palmes Académiques, 1966, etc. *Publications:* Méharées, Explorations au vrai Sahara, 1937, 3rd edn 1989; L'Hippopotame et le philosophe, 1942; Bathyfolages, 1954, 2nd edn 1991; (ed) Pastoralism in Tropical Africa, 1976; L'Emeraude des Garamantes, Souvenirs d'un Saharien, 1984; Sahara, désert magique, 1986; Déserts, 1988; Mémoires d'un Naturaliste Voyageur, 1990; (with Brigitte Zanda) Le Fer de Dieu: histoire de la météorite de Chinguetti, 1992; many scientific papers in learned jls. *Address:* 14 quai d'Orléans, 75004 Paris, France. *T:* 43267950; Muséum national d'Histoire naturelle, 43 rue Cuvier, 75005 Paris, France. *T:* 40793750.

MONRO, (Andrew) Hugh; Headmaster, Clifton College, since 1990; *b* 2 March 1950; *s* of Andrew Killey Monro, FRCS and Diana Louise Rhys; *m* 1974, Elizabeth Clare Rust; one *s* one *d*. *Educ:* Rugby School; Pembroke College, Cambridge (MA; PGCE). Graduate trainee, Metal Box, 1973; Haileybury College, 1974–79; Noble & Greenough School, Boston, Mass, 1977–78; Loretto School, 1979–86; Headmaster, Worksop College, 1986–90. *Recreations:* running, golf, American literature. *Address:* Clifton College, Clifton, Bristol BS8 3JH. *T:* Bristol (0117) 973 5945. *Club:* Hawks (Cambridge).

MONRO, Rt Hon. Sir Hector (Seymour Peter), Kt 1981; AE; PC 1995; JP; DL; MP (C) Dumfries, since 1964; *b* 4 Oct. 1922; *s* of late Capt. Alastair Monro, Cameron Highlanders, and Mrs Monro, Craigcleuch, Langholm, Scotland; *m* 1st, 1949, (Elizabeth) Anne Welch (*d* 1994), Longstone Hall, Derbs; two *s*; 2nd, 1994, Mrs Doris Kaestner, Baltimore. *Educ:* Canford Sch.; King's Coll., Cambridge. RAF, 1941–46, Flight Lt; RAuxAF, 1946–53 (AE 1953). Mem. of Queen's Body Guard for Scotland, Royal Company of Archers. Dumfries CC, 1952–67 (Chm. Planning Cttee, and Police Cttee). Chm. Dumfriesshire Unionist Assoc., 1958–63. Scottish Cons. Whip, 1967–70; a Lord Comr of HM Treasury, 1970–71, Parly Under-Sec. of State, Scottish Office, 1971–74; Opposition Spokesman on: Scottish Affairs, 1974–75; Sport, 1974–79; Parliamentary Under-Secretary of State: (with special responsibility for sport), DoE, 1979–81; Scottish Office, 1992–95. Member, Select Committee: on Scottish Affairs, 1983–86; on Defence, 1987. Chairman: Scottish Cons. Members Cttee, 1983–92; Cons. Parly Cttee on Sport, 1984–85. Vice Chm., Cons. Members Agricl Cttee, 1983–87. Mem. Dumfries T&AFA, 1959–67; Hon. Air Cdre, No 2622 RAuxAF Regt Sqdn, 1982–; Hon. Insp. Gen., RAuxAF, 1990–. Member: Area Executive Cttee, Nat. Farmers' Union of Scotland; Nature Conservancy Council, 1982–91; Council, Nat. Trust for Scotland 1983–92. President: Auto-cycle Union, 1983–90; NSRA, 1987–92. JP 1963, DL 1973, Dumfries. *Recreations:* Rugby football (Mem. Scottish Rugby Union, 1958–77, Vice-Pres., 1975, Pres., 1976–77); golf, flying, country sports, vintage sports cars. *Address:* Williamwood, Kirtlebridge, Dumfriesshire DG11 3LN. *T:* Kirtlebridge (01461) 500213. *Clubs:* Royal Air Force, MCC; Royal Scottish Automobile (Glasgow).

MONRO, Hugh; *see* Monro, A. H.

MONRO DAVIES, William Llewellyn, QC 1974; **His Honour Judge Monro Davies;** a Circuit Judge, since 1976; *b* 12 Feb. 1927; *s* of Thomas Llewellyn Davies and Emily Constance Davies; *m* 1956, Jean, *d* of late E. G. Innes; one *s* one *d*. *Educ:* Christ Coll., Brecon; Trinity Coll., Oxford (MA, LitHum). Served in RNVR, 1945–48 (Sub-Lt). Called to the Bar, Inner Temple, 1954. Mem., Gen. Council of the Bar, 1971–75. A Recorder of the Crown Court, 1972–76. *Recreations:* the theatre and cinema; watching Rugby football. *Address:* Farrar's Buildings, Temple, EC4Y 7BD. *T:* 0171–583 9241. *Club:* Garrick.

MONSON, family name of **Baron Monson.**

MONSON, 11th Baron *cr* 1728; **John Monson;** Bt *cr* 1611; *b* 3 May 1932; *e s* of 10th Baron and of Bettie Northrup (who *m* 1962, Capt. James Arnold Phillips), *d* of late E. Alexander Powell; *S* father, 1958; *m* 1955, Emma, *o d* of late Anthony Devas, ARA, RP; three *s*. *Educ:* Eton; Trinity Coll., Cambridge (BA). Pres., Soc. for Individual Freedom. *Heir: s* Hon. Nicholas John Monson [*b* 19 Oct. 1955; *m* 1981, Hilary, *o d* of Kenneth Martin, Nairobi and Diani Beach; one *s* one *d*]. *Address:* Manor House, South Carlton, Lincoln LN1 2RN. *T:* Lincoln (01522) 730263.

MONTACUTE, Mervyn Charles; Managing Director, Westminster City Council, 1991–94; *b* 5 Jan. 1946; *s* of Charles Montacute and Myra Annie Mabel (*née* Chinnock); *m* 1975, Susan Arleen Aardal; two *d* *Educ:* Cheltenham Grammar Sch.; West Seattle High Sch.; King's Coll., London (LLB); Plymouth Polytechnic (Dip. Management Studies); Harvard Univ. (MPA). Articled Clerk, Northants CC, 1968–70; Assistant Solicitor: Glamorgan CC, 1970–72; Cornwall CC, 1972–75; New Zealand: City Solicitor, Wellington CC, 1975–79; City Manager, Tauranga CC, 1981–86; Chief Exec., Dunedin CC, 1986–90. *Recreations:* music, literature. *Address:* c/o Westminster City Council, Westminster City Hall, 64 Victoria Street, SW1E 6QP. *T:* 0171–798 2030.

MONTAGNIER, Prof. Luc; Head of Viral Oncology Unit, since 1972, Professor, since 1985, and Head of Department of AIDS and Retroviruses, since 1990, Pasteur Institute,

Paris; Director of Research, Centre national de la recherche scientifique, since 1974; *b* 18 Aug. 1932; *s* of Antoine Montagnier and Marianne (*née* Rousselet); *m* 1961, Dorothea Ackermann; one *s* two *d*. *Educ:* Collège de Châtellerault; Univ. de Poitiers; Univ. de Paris. Asst, 1955–60, Attaché, 1960, Head, 1963, Head of Research, 1967, Faculty of Science, Paris; Head of Lab., Inst. of Radium, 1965–71. Commandeur: Légion d'honneur; Ordre national du Mérite. *Publications:* Vaincre le Sida, 1986; Des virus et des hommes, 1994; scientific papers on research into AIDS virus, molecular biology, virology, etc. *Address:* Pasteur Institute, 28 rue du Docteur-Roux, 75724 Paris Cedex 15, France.

MONTAGU; *see* Douglas-Scott-Montagu.

MONTAGU, family name of **Duke of Manchester, Earl of Sandwich,** and **Baron Swaythling.**

MONTAGU OF BEAULIEU, 3rd Baron *cr* 1885; **Edward John Barrington Douglas-Scott-Montagu;** Chairman, Historic Buildings and Monuments Commission, 1983–92; *b* 20 Oct. 1926; *o s* of 2nd Baron and Pearl (who *m* 2nd, 1936, Captain Hon. Edward Pleydell-Bouverie, RN, MVO, *s* of 6th Earl of Radnor), *d* of late Major E. B. Crake, Rifle Brigade, and Mrs Barrington Crake; *S* father, 1929; *m* 1st, 1959, Elizabeth Belinda (marr. diss. 1974), *o d* of late Capt. the Hon. John de Bathe Crossley, and late Hon. Mrs Crossley; one *s* one *d*; 2nd, 1974, Fiona Herbert; one *s*. *Educ:* St Peter's Court, Broadstairs; Ridley Coll., St Catharines, Ont; Eton Coll.; New Coll., Oxford. Late Lt Grenadier Guards; released Army, 1948. Founded Montagu Motor Car Museum, 1952 and World's first Motor Cycle Museum, 1956; created Nat. Motor Museum Trust, 1970, to administer new Nat. Motor Museum at Beaulieu, opened 1972. Mem., Develt Commn, 1980–84. President: Museums Assoc., 1982–84; Historic Houses Assoc., 1973–78; Union of European Historic Houses, 1978–81; Fédération Internationale des Voitures Anciennes, 1980–83; Southern Tourist Bd; Tourism Soc.; Assoc. of Brit. Transport Museums; English Vineyards Assoc.; Fedn of British Historic Vehicle Clubs, 1989–; Vice-Pres., Inst. of Motor Industry; Chancellor, Wine Guild of UK; Patron, Assoc. of Independent Museums. FRSA. Hon. FMA. Commodore: Nelson Boat Owners' Club; Beaulieu River Sailing Club; Vice Cdre, H of L Yacht Club. Founder and Editor, Veteran and Vintage Magazine, 1956–79. *Publications:* The Motoring Montagus, 1959; Lost Causes of Motoring, 1960; Jaguar, A Biography, 1961, rev. edn, 1986; The Gordon Bennett Races, 1963; Rolls of Rolls-Royce, 1966; The Gilt and the Gingerbread, 1967; Lost Causes of Motoring: Europe, vol. i, 1969, vol. ii, 1971; More Equal than Others, 1970; History of the Steam Car, 1971; The Horseless Carriage, 1975; Early Days on the Road, 1976; Behind the Wheel, 1977; Royalty on the Road, 1980; Home James, 1982; The British Motorist, 1987; English Heritage, 1987; The Daimler Century, 1995. *Heir:* *s* Hon. Ralph Douglas-Scott-Montagu, *b* 13 March 1961. *Address:* Palace House, Beaulieu, Hants SO42 7ZN. *T:* Beaulieu (01590) 612345, *Fax:* (01590) 612623; Flat 11, 24 Bryanston Square, W1H 7FJ. *T:* 0171–262 2603, *Fax:* 0171–724 3262. *Clubs:* Historical Commercial Vehicle (Pres.), Disabled Drivers Motor (Pres.), Steam Boat Assoc. of Gt Britain (Vice-Pres.), and mem. of many historic vehicle clubs.

See also Sir E. John Chichester, Bt, Earl of Lindsay.

MONTAGU, Prof. Ashley; *b* 28 June 1905; *o c* of Charles and Mary Ehrenberg; *m* 1931, Helen Marjorie Peakes; one *s* two *d*. *Educ:* Central Foundation Sch., London; Univ. of London; Univ. of Florence; Columbia Univ. (PhD 1937). Research Worker, Brit. Mus. (Natural Hist.), 1926; Curator, Physical Anthropology, Wellcome Hist. Mus., London, 1929; Asst-Prof. of Anatomy, NY Univ., 1931–38; Dir, Div. of Child Growth and Develt, NY Univ., 1931–34; Assoc.-Prof. of Anat., Hahnemann Med. Coll. and Hosp., Phila, 1938–49; Prof. and Head of Dept of Anthropology, Rutgers Univ., 1949–55; Dir of Research, NJ Cttee on Growth and Develt, 1951–55. Chm., Anisfield-Wolf Award Cttee on Race Relations, 1950– (drafted Statement on Race, for Unesco, 1950). Vis. Lectr, Harvard Univ., 1945; Regent's Prof., Univ. of Calif, Santa Barbara, 1961; Lectr, Princeton Univ., 1978–83, and Dir, Inst. Natural Philosophy, 1979–85. Fellow, Stevenson Hall, Princeton Univ., 1978. Produced, directed and financed film, One World or None, 1946. DSc Grinnell Coll., Iowa, 1967; DLitt Ursinus Coll., Pa, 1972; DSc Univ. N Carolina, 1987. Distinguished Service Award, Amer. Anthropological Assoc., 1984; Phi Beta Kappa Distinguished Service Award, 1985; Distinguished Service Award, Nat. Assoc. of Parents and Professionals for Safe Alternatives in Childbirth, 1986; Distinguished Service Award, Rollo May Center for Humanistic Studies, 1991; Distinguished Service Award, Pre and Perinatal Psychology Assoc. of America, 1993; Lifetime Achievement and Charles Darwin Award, Amer. Assoc. of Physical Anthropologists, 1994. Eponymous annual award by US Common Bond Inst. and Harmony Inst. of Russia, instituted 1995. *Publications:* Coming Into Being Among the Australian Aborigines, 1937, 2nd edn 1974; Man's Most Dangerous Myth: The Fallacy of Race, 1942, 6th edn 1995; Edward Tyson, MD, FRS (1650–1708): And the Rise of Human and Comparative Anatomy in England, 1943; Introduction to Physical Anthropology, 1945, 3rd edn 1960; Adolescent Sterility, 1946; On Being Human, 1950, 2nd edn 1970; Statement on Race, 1951, 3rd edn 1972; On Being Intelligent, 1951, 3rd edn 1972; Darwin, Competition, and Cooperation, 1952; The Natural Superiority of Women, 1953, 4th edn 1992; Immortality, 1955; The Direction of Human Development, 1955, 2nd edn 1970; The Biosocial Nature of Man, 1956; Education and Human Relations, 1958; Anthropology and Human Nature, 1957; Man: His First Million Years, 1957, 2nd edn 1969; The Reproductive Development of the Female, 1957, 3rd edn 1979; The Cultured Man, 1958; Human Heredity, 1959, 2nd edn 1963; Anatomy and Physiology (with E. B. Steen), 2 vols, 1959, 2nd edn 1984; A Handbook of Anthropometry, 1960; Man in Process, 1961; The Humanization of Man, 1962; Prenatal Influences, 1962; Race, Science and Humanity, 1963; The Dolphin in History (with John Lilly), 1963; The Science of Man, 1964; Life Before Birth, 1964, 2nd edn 1978; The Human Revolution, 1965; The Idea of Race, 1965; Man's Evolution (with C. Loring Brace), 1965; Up the Ivy, 1966; The American Way of Life, 1967; The Anatomy of Swearing, 1967; The Prevalence of Nonsense (with E. Darling), 1967; The Human Dialogue (with Floyd Matson), 1967; Man Observed, 1968; Man: His First Two Million Years, 1969; Sex, Man and Society, 1969; The Ignorance of Certainty (with E. Darling), 1970; Textbook of Human Genetics (with M. Levitan), 1971, 2nd edn 1977; Immortality, Religion and Morals, 1971; Touching: the human significance of the skin, 1971, 3rd edn 1986; The Elephant Man, 1971, 3rd edn 1995; Man and the Computer (with S. S. Snyder), 1972; (ed) The Endangered Environment, 1973; (ed) Frontiers of Anthropology, 1974; (ed) Culture and Human Development, 1974; (ed) The Practice of Love, 1974; (ed) Race and IQ, 1975, 2nd edn 1995; The Nature of Human Aggression, 1976; Human Evolution (with C. L. Brace), 1977; The Human Connection (with F. Matson), 1979; Growing Young, 1981, 2nd edn 1989; The Dehumanization of Man (with F. Matson), 1983; What We Know About Race, 1985; Humanity Speaking to Humankind, 1986; Living and Loving, 1986; The Peace of the World, 1986; The World of Humanity, 1988; Coming into Being, 1988; Editor: Studies and Essays in the History of Science and Learning; The Meaning of Love, 1953; Toynbee and History, 1956; Genetic Mechanisms in Human Disease, 1961, Atlas of Human Anatomy, 1961; Culture and the Evolution of Man, 1962; International Pictorial Treasury of Knowledge, 6 vols, 1962–63; The Concept of Race, 1964; The Concept of the Primitive, 1967; Culture: Man's Adaptive Dimension, 1968; Man and Aggression, 1968; The Origin and Evolution of Man, 1973; Learning Non-Aggression, 1978; Sociobiology Examined, 1980; Science and Creationism, 1983. *Recreations:* book collecting, gardening. *Address:* 321 Cherry Hill Road, Princeton, NJ 08540, USA. *T:* (609) 9243756.

MONTAGU, Jennifer Iris Rachel, PhD; FBA 1986; Curator of the Photograph Collection, Warburg Institute, 1971–91, now Hon. Fellow; *b* 20 March 1931; *d* of late Hon. Ewen Edward Samuel Montagu, CBE, QC. *Educ:* Brearley Sch., New York; Benenden Sch., Kent; Lady Margaret Hall, Oxford (BA; Hon. Fellow 1985); Warburg Inst., London (PhD). Assistant Regional Director, Arts Council of Gt Britain, North West Region, 1953–54; Lecturer in the History of Art, Reading Univ., 1958–64; Asst Curator of the Photograph Collection, Warburg Inst., 1964–71. Slade Prof., and Fellow of Jesus Coll., Cambridge, 1980–81; Andrew W. Mellon Lectr, Nat. Gall. of Art, Washington, 1991; Invited Prof., Collège de France, 1994. Member: Academic Awards Cttee, British Fedn of University Women, 1963–89; Executive Cttee, National Art-Collections Fund, 1973–; Consultative Cttee, Burlington Magazine, 1975–; Cttee, The Jewish Museum, 1983–; Reviewing Cttee on Export of Works of Art, 1987–. Trustee: Wallace Collection, 1989–; BM, 1994–. Hon. Academician, Accademia Clementina, Bologna, 1988. Serena Medal for Italian Studies, British Acad., 1992. Officier, Ordre des Arts et des Lettres (France), 1991. *Publications:* Bronzes, 1963; (with Jacques Thuillier) Catalogue of exhibn Charles Le Brun, 1963; Alessandro Algardi, 1985 (special Mitchell Prize); Roman Baroque Sculpture: the industry of art, 1989; The Expression of the Passions, 1994; articles in learned periodicals. *Address:* 10 Roland Way, SW7 3RE. *T:* 0171–373 6691; Warburg Institute, Woburn Square, WC1H 0AB.

MONTAGU, Montague Francis Ashley; *see* Montagu, A.

MONTAGU, Nicholas Lionel John, CB 1993; Deputy Secretary, Infrastructure (formerly Public Transport), Department of Transport, since 1992; *b* 12 March 1944; *s* of late John Eric Montagu and Barbara Joyce Montagu, OBE; *m* 1974, Jennian Ford Geddes, *o d* of Ford Irvine Geddes, *qv*; two *d*. *Educ:* Rugby Sch.; New Coll., Oxford (MA). Asst Lectr 1966–69, Lectr 1969–74, in Philosophy, Univ. of Reading; Department of Social Security (formerly Department of Health and Social Security): Principal, 1974–81 (seconded to Cabinet Office, 1978–80); Asst Sec., 1981–86; Under Sec., 1986–90; Dep. Sec., 1990– (seconded to Dept of Transport, 1992–). *Publication:* Brought to Account (report of Rayner Scrutiny on National Insurance Contributions), 1981. *Recreations:* cooking, wild flowers. *Address:* Department of Transport, Great Munster House, Horseferry Road, SW1P 4DR. *Club:* Norwegian.

MONTAGU DOUGLAS SCOTT, family name of **Duke of Buccleuch.**

MONTAGU-DOUGLAS-SCOTT, Douglas Andrew; *see* Scott.

MONTAGU-POLLOCK, Sir Giles Hampden; *see* Pollock.

MONTAGU-STUART-WORTLEY, family name of **Earl of Wharncliffe.**

MONTAGUE, family name of **Baron Amwell.**

MONTAGUE, Michael Jacob, CBE 1970; Chairman, Montague Multinational Ltd, since 1991; Superframe plc, since 1995; *b* 10 March 1932; *s* of David Elias Montague and Eleanor Stagg. *Educ:* High Wycombe Royal Grammar Sch.; Magdalen Coll. Sch., Oxford. Founded Gatehill Beco Ltd, 1958 (sold to Valor Co., 1962); Man. Dir, 1963, Chm., 1965–91, Yale and Valor plc. Chairman: English Tourist Bd, 1979–84; Nat. Consumer Council, 1984–87; Member: BTA, 1979–84; Ordnance Survey Advisory Bd, 1983–85; Millennium Commn, 1994–. Pres., BAIE, 1983–85; Chairman: Asia Cttee, BNEC, 1968–71; Henley Festival Ltd, 1992–94; Non-executive Director: Pleasurama PLC, 1985–88; Jarvis Hotels Ltd, 1990–; Williams Hldgs plc, 1991–92. Pres., Econ. and Industrial Res. Soc., 1990–; Vice-Pres., Royal Albert Hall, 1992–94 (Mem. Council, 1985–). *Address:* 5 Clareville Grove, SW7 5AU. *Club:* Oriental.

MONTAGUE, Robert Joel, CBE 1990; founder, Chairman and Chief Executive, Tiphook plc, 1978–94; *b* 22 June 1948; *s* of Robert and Freda Montague; *m* 1972 (marr. diss.); two *s* one *d*; *m* 1990, Silke Kruse; two *s* one *d*. *Educ:* Bedstone Sch., Shropshire; Caius Sch., Brighton. Esso Petroleum Co. Ltd, 1964–69; Cables Montague Ltd, 1969–80. *Recreations:* children, shooting, fishing, opera, ballet. *Address:* Pusey House, Pusey, near Farringdon, Oxon SN7 8QB.

MONTAGUE, Air Cdre Ruth Mary Bryceson; Director, Women's Royal Air Force, 1989–94; *b* 1 June 1939; *d* of late Griffith John Griffiths and Nancy Bryceson Griffiths (*née* Wrigley); *m* 1966, Roland Arthur Montague. *Educ:* Cavendish Grammar Sch. for Girls, Buxton; Bedford Coll., Univ. of London (BSc). Commissioned RAF, 1962; UK and Far East, 1962–66; UK, 1966–80; HQ Strike Command, 1980–83; RAF Staff Coll., 1983–86; Dep. Dir, WRAF, 1986–89. ADC to the Queen, 1989–94. Mem., Council and F and GP Cttee, RAF Benevolent Fund, 1994–. Mem. Council, Royal Holloway, London Univ., 1994–. FRSA 1993. *Recreations:* cookery, tapestry, gardening, swimming, clay pigeon shooting, world travel. *Address:* c/o National Westminster Bank, 7 High Street, Marlow, Bucks SL7 1AY. *Club:* Royal Air Force.

MONTAGUE BROWNE, Anthony Arthur Duncan, CBE 1965 (OBE 1955); DFC 1945; *b* 8 May 1923; *s* of late Lt-Col A. D. Montague Browne, DSO, OBE, Bivia House, Goodrich, Ross-on-Wye, and Violet Evelyn (*née* Downes); *m* 1st, 1950, Noel Evelyn Arnold-Wallinger (marr. diss. 1970); one *d*; 2nd, 1970, Shelagh Macklin (*née* Mulligan). *Educ:* Stowe; Magdalen Coll., Oxford; abroad. Pilot RAF, 1941–45. Entered Foreign (now Diplomatic) Service, 1946; Foreign Office, 1946–49; Second Sec., British Embassy, Paris, 1949–52; seconded as Private Sec. to Prime Minister, 1952–55; seconded as Private Sec. to Rt Hon. Sir Winston Churchill, 1955–65; Counsellor, Diplomatic Service, 1964; seconded to HM Household, 1965–67. Dir, 1967–74, a Man. Dir, 1974–83, Gerrard and National PLC; Dir, Columbia (British) Productions, 1967–77; Chm., LandLeisure PLC, 1987–88; Dep. Chm., Highland Participants PLC, 1987–89. Trustee and Chm. of Council, Winston Churchill Memorial Trust; Vice-Pres., Univs Fedn for Animal Welfare, 1987–93 (Mem., Council, 1985–91); Chm., Internat. Certificate of Deposit Market Assoc., 1980–82. Freeman, City of London, 1987. Hon. DL Westminster Coll., Fulton, Missouri, 1988. *Publication:* Long Sunset, 1995. *Address:* Hawkridge Cottages, Bucklebury, Reading RG7 6EG. *T:* Reading (01734) 712578. *Clubs:* Boodle's, Pratt's, Royal Automobile.

MONTAGUE-JONES, Brigadier (retd) Ronald, CBE 1944 (MBE 1941); jssc; psc; *b* 10 Dec. 1909; *yr s* of late Edgar Montague Jones, until 1931 Headmaster of St Albans Sch., Herts, and of late Emmeline Mary Yates; *m* 1937, Denise Marguerite (marr. diss.), *y d* of late General Sir Hubert Gough, GCB, GCMG, KCVO; one *s*; *m* 1955, Pamela, *d* of late Lieut-Col Hastings Roy Harington, 8th Gurkha Rifles, and late Hon. Mrs Harington; one *s*. *Educ:* St Albans; RMA, Woolwich; St John's Coll., Cambridge (BA 1933, MA 1937). 2nd Lieut RE 1930; Temp. Brig. 1943; Bt Lt-Col 1952; Brig. 1958. Egypt, 1935; Palestine, 1936–39 (despatches twice); War of 1939–45 (MBE, CBE, US Bronze Star, Africa Star, 1939–45 Star, Italy Star, Burma Star, General Service Medal with Clasps Palestine, SE Asia and Malaya). CC Dorset, for Swanage, 1964–85. Br. Pres., Royal British

Legion. *Address:* 10 Battlemead, Swanage, Dorset BH19 1PH. *T:* Swanage (01929) 423186.

MONTEAGLE OF BRANDON, 6th Baron *cr* 1839; **Gerald Spring Rice;** late Captain, Irish Guards; one of HM Body Guard, Hon. Corps of Gentlemen-at-Arms, since 1978; *b* 5 July 1926; *s* of 5th Baron and Emilie de Kosenko (*d* 1981), *d* of Mrs Edward Brooks, Philadelphia, USA; *S* father 1946; *m* 1949, Anne, *d* of late Col G. J. Brownlow, Ballywhite, Portaferry, Co. Down; one *s* three *d* (of whom two are twins). *Educ:* Harrow. Member: London Stock Exchange, 1958–76; Lloyd's, 1978–. *Heir: s* Hon. Charles James Spring Rice [*b* 24 Feb. 1953; *m* 1987, Mary Teresa Glover; four *d*]. *Address:* 242A Fulham Road, SW10 9NA. *Clubs:* Cavalry and Guards, Pratt's; Kildare Street and University (Dublin).

MONTEFIORE, Harold Henry S.; *see* Sebag-Montefiore.

MONTEFIORE, Rt. Rev. Hugh William, MA, BD; Hon. DD; Hon. Assistant Bishop, Diocese of Southwark, since 1987; *b* 12 May 1920; *s* of late Charles Sebag-Montefiore, OBE, and Muriel Alice Ruth Sebag-Montefiore; *m* 1945, Elisabeth Mary Macdonald Paton, *d* of late Rev. William Paton, DD, and Mrs Grace Paton; three *d*. *Educ:* Rugby Sch.; St John's Coll., Oxford (Hon. Fellow, 1981). Served during war, 1940–45; Capt. RA (Royal Bucks Yeo). Deacon 1949, priest 1950. Curate, St George's, Jesmond, Newcastle, 1949–51; Chaplain and Tutor, Westcott House, Cambridge, 1951–53; Vice-Principal, 1953–54; Examining Chaplain: to Bishop of Newcastle, 1953–70; to Bishop of Worcester, 1957–60; to Bishop of Coventry, 1957–70; to Bishop of Blackburn, 1966–70; Fellow and Dean of Gonville and Caius Coll., 1954–63; Lectr in New Testament, Univ. of Cambridge, 1959–63; Vicar of Great Saint Mary's, Cambridge, 1963–70; Canon Theologian of Coventry, 1959–70; Hon. Canon of Ely, 1969–70; Bishop Suffragen of Kingston-upon-Thames, 1970–78; Bishop of Birmingham, 1978–87. Mem., Archbishops' Commn on Christian Doctrine, 1967–76; Chm., General Synod Bd for Social Responsibility, 1983–87. Chairman: Indep. Commn on Transport, 1973; Transport 2000, 1987–92; Friends of the Earth Trust, 1992–; Nat. Trust for the Homeless, 1992–. Hon. DD: Aberdeen, 1976; Birmingham, 1985. *Publications:* (contrib.) The Historic Episcopate and the Fullness of the Church, 1954; To Help You To Pray, 1957; (contrib.) Soundings, 1962; Josephus and the New Testament, 1962; (with H. E. W. Turner) Thomas and the Evangelists, 1962; Beyond Reasonable Doubt, 1963; (contrib.) God, Sex and War, 1963; Awkward Questions on Christian Love, 1964; A Commentary on the Epistle to the Hebrews, 1964; Truth to Tell, 1966; (ed) We Must Love One Another Or Die, 1966; (contrib.) The Responsible Church, 1966; Remarriage and Mixed Marriage, 1967; (contrib.) Journeys in Belief, 1968; (ed) Sermons From Great St Mary's, 1968; My Confirmation Notebook, 1968; The Question Mark, 1969; Can Man Survive, 1970; (ed) More Sermons From Great St Mary's, 1971; Doom or Deliverance?, 1972; (ed) Changing Directions, 1974; (ed) Man and Nature, 1976; Apocalypse, 1976; (ed) Nuclear Crisis, 1977; (ed) Yes to Women Priests, 1978; Taking our Past into our Future, 1978; Paul the Apostle, 1981; Jesus Across the Centuries, 1983; The Probability of God, 1985; So Near And Yet So Far, 1986; Communicating the Gospel in a Scientific Age, 1988; God, Sex and Love, 1989; Christianity and Politics, 1990; Reclaiming the High Ground, 1990; (ed) The Gospel and Contemporary Culture, 1992; The Womb and The Tomb, 1992; Preaching for Our Planet, 1992; Credible Christianity, 1994; contribs to New Testament and Theological jls. *Address:* White Lodge, 23 Bellevue Road, Wandsworth Common, SW17 7EB. *Club:* Commonwealth Trust.

See also Ven. M. J. M. Paton.

MONTEITH, Rt. Rev. George Rae, BA; *b* 14 Feb. 1904; *s* of John Hodge Monteith and Ellen (*née* Hall); *m* 1st, 1931, Kathleen Methven Mules; two *s* one *d*; 2nd, 1982, Hilary Llewellyn Etherington. *Educ:* St John's Coll., Auckland, Univ. of New Zealand. BA 1927. Deacon, 1928; priest, 1929; Curate: St Matthew's, Auckland, 1928–30; Stoke-on-Trent, 1931–33; Vicar of: Dargaville, NZ, 1934–37; Mt Eden, Auckland, NZ, 1937–49; St Mary's Cathedral Parish, Auckland, 1949–69; Dean of Auckland, 1949–69; Vicar-General, 1963–76; Asst Bishop of Auckland, NZ, 1965–76. *Address:* 10A Mahoe Avenue, Remuera, Auckland 1005, NZ. *T:* (9) 5221188.

MONTEITH, Prof. John Lennox, FRS 1971; FRSE 1972; Emeritus Professor of Environmental Physics, University of Nottingham, 1989; *b* 3 Sept. 1929; *s* of Rev. John and Margaret Monteith; *m* 1955, Elsa Marion Wotherspoon; four *s* one *d*. *Educ:* George Heriot's Sch.; Univ. of Edinburgh (BSc 1951; Hon. DSc 1989); Imperial Coll., London. DIC, PhD; FInstP, FIBiol. Mem. Physics Dept Staff, Rothamsted Experimental Station, 1954–67; Prof. of Environmental Physics, 1967–86, Dean of Faculty of Agricl Sci., 1985–86, Nottingham Univ.; Dir, Resource Management Programme, Internat. Crops Res. Inst. for the Semi-Arid Tropics, 1987–91 (Vis. Scientist, 1984); Sen. Vis. Fellow, NERC, 1992–94. Adjunct Prof., Depts of Agricl Engrg and Agronomy, Univ. of Florida, 1991–; Vis. Prof., Reading Univ., 1992–; Hon. Prof., Edinburgh Univ., 1992–. Governor: Grassland Res. Inst., 1976–83; Silsoe Res. Inst., 1993–. Vice Pres., British Ecological Soc., 1977–79; Pres., Royal Meteorol Soc., 1978–80. Member: NERC, 1980–84; British Nat. Cttee for the World Climate Programme, 1980–86; Lawes Agricl Trust Cttee, 1983–86. Nat. Res. Council Senior Res. Associate, Goddard Space Flight Center, Md, USA, 1985; Clive Behrens Lectr, Leeds Univ., 1986; York Distinguished Lectr, Univ. of Florida, 1991. Buchan Prize, 1962, Symon's Gold Medal, 1995, RMetS; Solco Tromp Award, Internat. Soc. of Biometeorology, 1983; Rank Fund Nutrition Prize, 1989. *Publications:* Instruments for Micrometeorology (ed), 1972; Principles of Environmental Physics, 1973, 2nd edn (with M. H. Unsworth), 1990; (ed with L. E. Mount) Heat Loss from Animals and Man, 1974; (ed) Vegetation and the Atmosphere, 1975; (ed with C. Webb) Soil Water and Nitrogen, 1981; (ed with R. K. Scott and M. H. Unsworth) Resource Capture by Crops, 1994; papers on Micrometeorology and Crop Science in: Quarterly Jl of RMetSoc.; Jl Applied Ecology, etc. *Recreations:* music, photography. *Address:* 21 St Alban's Road, Edinburgh EH9 2LT.

MONTGOMERIE, family name of **Earl of Eglinton.**

MONTGOMERIE, Lord; Hugh Archibald William Montgomerie; Shipping Operations Manager, Cadogan Tate; *b* 24 July 1966; *s* and *heir* of 18th Earl of Eglinton and Winton, *qv*; *m* 1991, Sara Alexandra, *e d* of Niel Redpath. RN officer, 1988–92. *Address:* 17 Ormiston Grove, W12.

MONTGOMERY, family name of **Viscount Montgomery of Alamein.**

MONTGOMERY OF ALAMEIN, 2nd Viscount *cr* 1946, of Hindhead; **David Bernard Montgomery,** CBE 1975; Managing Director, Terimar Services (Overseas Trade Consultancy), since 1974; Chairman, Baring Puma Fund, since 1992; *b* 18 Aug. 1928; *s* of 1st Viscount Montgomery of Alamein, KG, GCB, DSO, and Elizabeth (*d* 1937), *d* of late Robert Thompson Hobart, ICS; *S* father, 1976; *m* 1st, 1953, Mary Connell (marr. diss. 1967); one *s* one *d*; 2nd, 1970, Tessa, *d* of late Gen. Sir Frederick Browning, GCVO, KBE, CB, DSO, and Lady Browning, DBE (Dame Daphne du Maurier). *Educ:* Winchester; Trinity Coll., Cambridge (MA). Shell International, 1951–62; Yardley International (Director), 1963–74; Dir, Korn/Ferry International, 1977–93; Chm., Antofagasta (Chile) and Bolivia Railway Co., 1980–82; Dir, NEI, 1981–87. Editorial Adviser, Vision Interamericana, 1974–94. Chm., Economic Affairs Cttee, Canning House, 1973–75; Pres., British Industrial Exhibition, Sao Paulo, 1974. Councillor, Royal Borough of Kensington and Chelsea, 1974–78. Hon. Consul, Republic of El Salvador, 1973–77. Pres., Anglo-Argentine Soc., 1977–87; Chairman: Hispanic and Luso Brazilian Council, 1978–80 (Pres., 1987–94); Brazilian Chamber of Commerce in GB, 1980–82; European Atlantic Gp, 1992–94 (Pres., 1994–); Pres., Anglo-Belgian Soc., 1994–. Patron: D-Day and Normandy Fellowship, 1980–; 8th Army Veterans Assoc., 1985–. President: Redgrave Theatre, Farnham, 1977–89; Restaurateurs Assoc. of GB, 1982–90 (Patron, 1991–); Centre for International Briefing, Farnham Castle, 1985–. Pres., Amesbury Sch., 1992– (Gov., 1976–92). Gran Oficial: Orden Bernardo O'Higgins (Chile), 1989; Orden Libertador San Martin (Argentina), 1992; Orden Nacional Cruzeiro do Sul (Brazil), 1993; Orden de Isabel la Católica (Spain), 1993; Commander's Cross, Order of Merit (Germany), 1993; Order of Aztec Eagle (Mexico), 1994. *Publication:* (with Alistair Horne) The Lonely Leader: Monty 1944–45, 1994. *Heir: s* Hon. Henry David Montgomery [*b* 2 April 1954; *m* 1980, Caroline, *e d* of Richard Odey, Hotham Hall, York; three *d*]. *Address:* 54 Cadogan Square, SW1X 0JW. *T:* 0171–589 8747. *Clubs:* Garrick, Canning; Royal Fowey Yacht.

MONTGOMERY, Alan Everard, CMG 1993; PhD; HM Diplomatic Service; High Commissioner to Tanzania, since 1995; *b* 11 March 1938; *s* of Philip Napier Montgomery and Honor Violet Coleman (*née* Price); *m* 1960, Janet Barton (*d* 1994); one *s* one *d*. *Educ:* Royal Grammar Sch., Guildford; County of Stafford Training Coll. (Cert. of Educn); Birkbeck Coll., London (BA Hons, PhD). Served Mddx Regt, 1957–59. Teacher, Staffs and ILEA, 1961–65; Lectr, Univ. of Birmingham, 1969–72; entered FCO, 1972; 1st Secretary: FCO, 1972–75; Dhaka, 1975–77; Ottawa, 1977–80; FCO, 1980–83; Counsellor GATT/UNCTAD, UKMIS Geneva, 1983–87; Counsellor, Consul-Gen. and Hd of Chancery, Jakarta, 1987–89; Head of Migration and Visa Dept, FCO, 1989–92; Ambassador to the Philippines, 1992–95. *Publications:* (contrib.) Lloyd George: 12 essays, ed A. J. P. Taylor, 1971; contrib. Cambridge Hist. Jl. *Recreations:* historic buildings, jazz, swimming, theatre, opera. *Address:* c/o Foreign and Commonwealth Office, King Charles Street, SW1A 2AH. *Clubs:* Royal Over-Seas League; Manila Polo.

MONTGOMERY, Sir (Basil Henry) David, 9th Bt, *cr* 1801, of Stanhope; JP; landowner; Lord-Lieutenant of Perth and Kinross, since 1995; Chairman, Forestry Commission, 1979–89; *b* 20 March 1931; *s* of late Lt-Col H. K. Purvis-Montgomery, OBE, and of Mrs C. L. W. Purvis-Russell-Montgomery (*née* Maconochie Welwood); *S* uncle, 1964; *m* 1956, Delia, *o d* of Adm. Sir (John) Peter (Lorne) Reid, GCB, CVO; one *s* four *d* (and one *s* decd). *Educ:* Eton. National Service, Black Watch, 1949–51. Member: Nature Conservancy Council, 1973–79; Tayside Regional Authority, 1974–79. Comr, Mental Welfare Commn for Scotland, 1990–91. Trustee, Municipal Mutual Insurance Ltd, 1980–. Hon. LLD Dundee, 1977. DL Kinross-shire, 1960, Vice-Lieutenant 1966–74; JP 1966; DL Perth and Kinross, 1975. *Heir: s* James David Keith Montgomery [*b* 13 June 1957; *m* 1983, Elizabeth, *e d* of late E. Lyndon Evans, Pentyrch, Mid-Glamorgan; one *s* one *d*. Served The Black Watch, RHR, 1976–86]. *Address:* Kinross House, Kinross KY13 7ET. *T:* Kinross (01577) 63416.

MONTGOMERY, (Charles) John, CBE 1977; Director: Lloyds Bank Plc, 1972–84 (a Vice-Chairman, 1978–84); Lloyds Bank International, 1978–84; Yorkshire Bank, 1980–84; *b* 18 Feb. 1917; *s* of late Rev. Charles James Montgomery; *m* 1950, Gwenneth Mary McKendrick; two *d*. *Educ:* Colwyn Bay Grammar School. Served with RN, 1940–46. Entered Lloyds Bank, 1935; Jt Gen. Man. 1968; Asst Chief Gen. Man. 1970; Dep. Chief Gen. Man. 1973; Chief Gen. Man., 1973–78. Pres., Inst. of Bankers, 1976–77, Vice Pres., 1977–. Chm., Chief Exec. Officers' Cttee, Cttee of London Clearing Bankers, 1976–78. *Recreations:* walking, photography, travel. *Address:* High Cedar, 6 Cedar Copse, Bickley, Kent BR1 2NY. *T:* 0181–467 2410. *Clubs:* Naval, Bankers.

MONTGOMERY, Sir David; *see* Montgomery, Sir B. H. D.

MONTGOMERY, David, CMG 1984; OBE 1972; Foreign and Commonwealth Office, 1987–91; *b* 29 July 1927; *s* of late David Montgomery and of Mary (*née* Walker Cunningham); *m* 1955, Margaret Newman; one *s* one *d*. Royal Navy, 1945–48. Foreign Office, 1949–52; Bucharest, 1952–53; FO, 1953–55; Bonn, 1955–58; Düsseldorf, 1958–61; Rangoon, 1961–63; Ottawa, 1963–64; Regina, Saskatchewan, 1964–65; FCO, 1966–68; Bangkok, 1968–72; Zagreb, 1973–76; FCO, 1976–79; Dep. High Comr to Barbados, 1980–84, also (non-resident) to Antigua and Barbuda, Dominica, Grenada, St Kitts and Nevis, St Lucia, St Vincent and the Grenadines, 1980–84; FCO, 1984–85. *Recreations:* golf, music (light and opera). *Address:* 8 Ross Court, Putney Hill, SW15 3NY. *Club:* Royal Over-Seas League.

MONTGOMERY, David John; Chief Executive, Mirror Group Newspapers, since 1992; *b* 6 Nov. 1948; *s* of William John and Margaret Jean Montgomery; *m* 1st, 1971, Susan Frances Buchanan Russell (marr. diss. 1987); 2nd, 1989, Heidi Kingstone, *d* of Prof. Edward Kingstone, McMaster Univ., Ont. *Educ:* Queen's University, Belfast (BA Politics/History). Sub-Editor, Daily Mirror, London/Manchester, 1973–78; Assistant Chief Sub-Editor, Daily Mirror, 1978–80; Chief Sub-Editor, The Sun, 1980; Asst Editor, Sunday People, 1982; Asst Editor, 1984, Editor, 1985–87, News of the World; Editor, Today, 1987–91 (Newspaper of the Year, 1988); Man. Dir, News UK, 1987–91; Chief Exec., 1991, Dir, 1991–, London Live Television. Director: Satellite Television PLC, 1986–91; News Group Newspapers, 1986–91; Caledonian Publishing Co. (Glasgow Herald & Times), 1991–92; Donohue Inc., 1992–; Newspaper Publishing (The Independent, Independent on Sunday), 1994–. *Address:* 13 Warrington Crescent, W9 1ED.

MONTGOMERY, Prof. Desmond Alan Dill, CBE 1981 (MBE 1943); MD; FRCP, FRCPI; Chairman, Northern Ireland Council for Postgraduate Medical Education, 1979–87; *b* 6 June 1916; 3rd *s* of late Dr and Mrs J. Howard Montgomery, China and Belfast; *m* 1941, Dr Susan Holland, 2nd *d* of late Mr and Mrs F. J. Holland, Belfast; one *s* one *d*. *Educ:* Inchmarlo Prep. Sch.; Campbell Coll.; Queen's Univ., Belfast (3rd, 4th and final yr scholarships; MB, BCh, BAO 1st Cl. Hons 1940; MD (Gold Medal) 1946). Sinclair Medal in Surgery, Butterworth Prize in Medicine, Prize in Mental Disease, QUB. MRCP 1948, FRCP 1964; FRCPI 1975; FRCOG (*ae*) 1981. Served War, RAMC, 1941–46: Temp. Major India Comd; DADMS GHQ India, 1943–45. House Physician and Surgeon, Royal Victoria Hosp., Belfast, 1940–41, Registrar, 1946; Registrar, Royal Postgrad. Med. Sch. and Hammersmith Hosp., and National Heart Hosp., London, 1946–48; Royal Victoria Hosp., Belfast: Sen. Registrar, 1948–51; Consultant Physician, 1951–79, Hon. Consultant 1980–; Physician i/c Sir George E. Clark Metabolic Unit, 1958–79; Endocrinologist, Royal Maternity Hosp., Belfast, 1958–79; Hon. Reader in Endocrinol., Dept of Medicine, QUB, 1969–75, Hon. Prof., 1975–. Hon. Secretary: Royal Victoria Med. Staff Cttee, 1964–66 (Chm., 1975–77); Ulster Med. Soc., 1954–58 (Pres., 1975–76). Member: NI Council for Health and Personal Social Services, 1974–83 (Chm., Central Med. Adv. Cttee, 1974–83, Mem. 1983–87); NI Med. Manpower Adv. Cttee, 1974–83; Distinction and Meritorious Awards Cttee, 1975–87 (Chm., 1982–87); Faculty of Medicine, QUB, 1969–87 (Chm., Ethical Cttee, 1975–81); Senate, QUB, 1979–; GMC, 1979–84; Pres., QUB Assoc., 1988–89. Member: BMA; Assoc. of Physicians of GB and NI; Eur. Thyroid Assoc.; Corrigan Club (Chm., 1969); Irish Endocrine Soc.

(1st Chm., Founder Mem.); Internat. Soc. for Internal Medicine; formerly Mem., Eur. Soc. for Study of Diabetes; Hon. Mem., British Dietetic Assoc. Lectured in USA, India, Greece, Australia and Nigeria; visited Russia on behalf of British Council, 1975. Pres., Belfast City Mission, 1973–92; Mem., Bd of Trustees, Presbyterian Church in Ireland. DSc (*hc*) NUI, 1980. Jt Editor, Ulster Med. Jl, 1974–84. *Publications:* (contrib.) Whitla's Dictionary of Treatment, 1957; (contrib.) Good Health and Diabetes, 1961, 3rd edn 1976; (contrib.) R. Smith, Progress in Clinical Surgery, 1961; (with R. B. Welbourn) Clinical Endocrinology for Surgeons, 1963; (contrib.) Progress in Neurosurgery, 1964; (with R. B. Welbourn) Medical and Surgical Endocrinology, 1975; (contrib.) M. D. Vickers, Medicine for Anaesthetists, 1977; articles in med. jls on endocrinology, diabetes mellitus and related subjects. *Recreations:* travel, photography, music, gardening, philately. *Address:* 59 Church Road, Newtownbreda, Belfast BT8 4AN. *T:* Belfast (01232) 648326; 15 Carrickmore Road, Ballycastle BT54 6QS. *T:* Ballycastle (012657) 62361.

MONTGOMERY, Sir Fergus; *see* Montgomery, Sir (William) Fergus.

MONTGOMERY, Group Captain George Rodgers, CBE 1946; DL; RAF (Retired); Secretary, Norfolk Naturalists' Trust, 1963–75; Hon. Appeal Secretary, and Member of the Court, University of East Anglia, since Nov. 1966; *b* 31 May 1910; *s* of late John Montgomery, Belfast; *m* 1st, 1932, Margaret McHarry Heslip (*d* 1981), *d* of late William J. Heslip, Belfast; two *s*; 2nd, 1982, Margaret Stephanie (*née* Reynolds), *widow* of Colin Vanner Hedworth Foulkes. *Educ:* Royal Academy, Belfast. Commnd in RAF, 1928; retd 1958. Served in UK and ME, 1928–38. War of 1939–45: Bomber Comd, NI, Air Min. and ME. Served UK, Japan and W Europe, 1946–58: Comdr RAF Wilmslow, 1946–47; Air Adviser to UK Polit. Rep. in Japan, and Civil Air Attaché, Tokyo, 1948–49; Chief Instr RAF Officers' Advanced Trg Sch., 1950; Comdt RAF Sch. of Admin, Bircham Newton, 1951–52; Comdr RAF Hednesford, 1953–54; DDO (Estabts) Air Min. and Chm. RAF Western European Estabts Cttee, Germany, 1955–57. On retirement, Organising Sec. Friends of Norwich Cathedral, 1959–62; Appeal Sec., Univ. of East Anglia, 1961–66; Hon. Vice-President: Norfolk Naturalists' Trust, 1979–; Broads Soc., 1983–; Mem., Great Bustard Trust Council, 1972–. DL Norfolk, 1979. *Recreations:* river cruising, gardening. *Address:* 24 Cathedral Close, Norwich, Norfolk NR1 4DZ. *T:* Norwich (01603) 628024. *Clubs:* Royal Air Force; Norfolk (Norwich).

MONTGOMERY, Hugh Bryan Greville; Chairman, Andry Montgomery group of companies (organisers, managers and consultants in exhibitions), since 1988 (Managing Director, 1952–88); *b* 26 March 1929; *s* of Hugh Roger Greville Montgomery, MC, and Molly Audrey Montgomery, OBE (*née* Neele). *Educ:* Repton; Lincoln Coll., Oxford (MA PPE). Founder member, Oxford Univ. Wine and Food Soc. Consultant and adviser on trade fairs and developing countries for UN; Consultant, Internat. Garden Festival, Liverpool, 1984. Chairman: Brit. Assoc. of Exhibn Organisers, 1970; Internat. Cttee, Amer. Nat. Assoc. of Exposition Managers, 1980–82 and 1990–93; British Exhibn Promotion Council, 1982–83; Pres., Union des Foires Internat., 1994– (Vice Pres., 1987–94). Member: Adv. Bd, Hotel Inst. for Management, Montreux, 1986–; London Regl Cttee, CBI, 1987–90; BOTB, 1991–94. Mem. Council, Design and Industries Assoc., 1983–85. Chm. of Trustees of ECHO (Supply of Equipment to Charity Hosps Overseas), 1978–89; Chairman: The Building Museum, 1988–; British Architectural Library Trust, 1989–; Interbuild Fund, 1972–; Vice-Pres., Bldg Conservation Trust, 1992–94 (Vice-Chm., 1979–92); Trustee: The Cubitt Trust, 1982–; Music for the World, 1990–92; Hon. Treas., Contemporary Art Soc., 1980–82; Councillor, Acad. of St Martin-in-the-Fields Concert Soc., 1988–. Member Executive Committee: CGLI, 1974–; Nat. Fund for Research into Crippling Diseases, 1970–92. Mem. Court, Co. of World Traders, 1992– (Master, 1995). Liveryman, 1952, Master, 1980–81, Co. of Tylers and Bricklayers (Trustee, Charitable and Pension Trusts, 1981–). Silver Jubilee Medal, 1977; Pro Cultura Hungaria Medal, 1991; Brooch, City of Utrecht, 1992; Gold Medal, Belgrade Fair, 1995. *Publications:* Industrial Fairs and Developing Countries (UNIDO), 1975; Going into Trade Fairs (UNCTAD/GATT), 1982; Exhibition Planning and Design, 1989 (Russian edn 1991); contrib. to Internat. Trade Forum (ITC, Geneva). *Recreations:* collecting contemporary art, sculpture, wine tasting, travelling in Siberia. *Address:* 11 Manchester Square, W1M 5AB. *T:* 0171–486 1951; Snells Farm, Amersham Common, Bucks HP7 9QN. *Clubs:* United Oxford & Cambridge University, City Livery.

MONTGOMERY, John; *see* Montgomery, C. J.

MONTGOMERY, John Duncan; JP; Member, Monopolies and Mergers Commission, since 1989; *b* 12 Nov. 1928; *s* of Lionel Eric Montgomery and Katherine Mary Montgomery (*née* Ambler); *m* 1956, Pauline Mary Sutherland; two *d*. *Educ:* King's College Sch., Wimbledon; LSE (LLB, LLM). Admitted Solicitor 1951; Treasury Solicitor's Dept, 1960–68; Legal Adviser, Beecham Products, 1974–75; Head, Legal Div., Shell UK, 1975–88 and Company Sec., Shell UK, 1979–88. Former Chm., Youth Orgns, Merton. Freeman, City of London, 1987; Mem., Loriners' Co., 1988. JP SW London, 1985. *Recreations:* dinghy sailing, photography. *Address:* Monopolies and Mergers Commission, New Court, 48 Carey Street, WC2A 2JT. *T:* 0171–324 1467. *Clubs:* MCC, City Livery.

MONTGOMERY, John Matthew; Clerk of the Salters' Company, 1975–90; *b* 22 May 1930; *s* of Prof. George Allison Montgomery, QC, and Isobel A. (*née* Morison); *m* 1956, Gertrude Gillian Richards; two *s* one *d*. *Educ:* Rugby Sch.; Trinity Hall, Cambridge (MA). Various commercial appointments with Mobil Oil Corporation and First National City Bank, 1953–74. Member: Council, Surrey Trust for Nature Conservation Ltd, 1965–89 (Chm., 1973–83; Vice-Pres., 1983–); Council, Royal Soc. for Nature Conservation, 1980–89; Exec. Cttee, Nat. Assoc. of Almshouses, 1980–91; Exec. Cttee, Age Concern Gtr London, 1985– (Chm., 1988–91); Council, Botanical Soc. of British Isles, 1991–95. Founder Mem., London Wildlife Trust, 1981–. Trustee, Relate: Marriage Guidance, 1992–. *Recreations:* various natural history interests. *Address:* 22 Red Lane, Claygate, Esher, Surrey KT10 0ES. *T:* Esher (01372) 64780.

MONTGOMERY, Col John Rupert Patrick, OBE 1979; MC 1943; *b* 25 July 1913; *s* of George Howard and Mabella Montgomery; *m* 1st, 1940, Alice Vyvyan Patricia Mitchell (*d* 1976); one *s* two *d*; 2nd, 1981, Marguerite Beatrice Chambers (*née* Montgomery). *Educ:* Wellington Coll.; RMC, Sandhurst. Commissioned, Oxfordshire and Buckinghamshire LI, 1933; Regimental Service in India, 1935–40 and 1946–47. Served War in Middle East, N Africa and Italy, 1942–45. Commanded 17 Bn Parachute Regt (9 DLI), 1953–56; SHAPE Mission to Portugal, 1956–59; retired, 1962. Sec., Anti-Slavery Soc., 1963–80. Silver Medal, RSA, 1973. *Address:* The Oast House, Buxted, Sussex TN22 4PP. *Club:* Army and Navy.

MONTGOMERY, Sir (William) Fergus, Kt 1985; MP (C) Altrincham and Sale, since Oct. 1974; *b* 25 Nov. 1927; *s* of late William Montgomery and Winifred Montgomery; *m* Joyce, *d* of George Riddle. *Educ:* Jarrow Grammar Sch.; Bede Coll., Durham. Served in Royal Navy, 1946–48; Schoolmaster, 1950–59. Nat. Vice-Chm. Young Conservative Organisation, 1954–57, National Chm., 1957–58; contested (C) Consett Division, 1955; MP (C): Newcastle upon Tyne East, 1959–64; Brierley Hill, Apr. 1967–Feb. 1974; contested Dudley W, Feb. 1974; PPS to Sec. of State for Educn and Science, 1973–74, to Leader of the Opposition, 1975–76. Chm., H of C Cttee of Selection, 1992–; Mem. Exec. Cttee, British American Parly Gp, 1991–. Mem. Executive, CPA, 1983–. Councillor, Hebburn UDC, 1950–58. Has lectured extensively in the USA. *Recreations:* bridge, reading, going to theatre. *Address:* 181 Ashley Gardens, Emery Hill Street, SW1P 1DP. *T:* 0171–834 7905; 6 Groby Place, Altrincham, Cheshire WA1 4AL. *T:* 0161–928 1983.

MONTGOMERY CUNINGHAME, Sir John Christopher Foggo, 12th Bt *cr* 1672, of Corsehill, Ayrshire and Kirktonholm, Lanarkshire; Chairman: Ronald A. Lee PLC, since 1986; Euromax Electronics Ltd, since 1985; Director: Artemis Energy Co., since 1981 (Partner); Purolite International Ltd, since 1984; Ryobi Lawn & Garden, since 1990, and other companies; *b* 24 July 1935; 2nd *s* of Col Sir Thomas Montgomery-Cuninghame, 10th Bt, DSO (*d* 1945), and of Nancy Macaulay (his 2nd wife), *d* of late W. Stewart Foggo, Aberdeen (she *m* 2nd, 1946, Johan Frederik Christian Killander); *b* of Sir Andrew Montgomery-Cuninghame, 11th Bt; *S* brother, 1959; *m* 1964, Laura Violet, *d* of Sir Godfrey Nicholson, 1st Bt; three *d*. *Educ:* Fettes; Worcester Coll., Oxford (MA). 2nd Lieut, Rifle Brigade (NS), 1955–56; Lieut, London Rifle Brigade, TA, 1956–59. *Recreation:* fishing. *Heir:* none. *Address:* The Old Rectory, Brightwalton, Newbury, Berks RG16 0BL.

MONTGOMERY WATT, Prof. William; *see* Watt.

MONTLAKE, Henry Joseph; solicitor; Senior Partner, H. Montlake & Co., since 1954; a Recorder of the Crown Court, since 1983; *b* 22 Aug. 1930; *s* of Alfred and Hetty Montlake; *m* 1952, Ruth Rochelle Allen; four *s*. *Educ:* Ludlow Grammar Sch., Ludlow; London Univ. (LLB 1951). Law Soc.'s final exam., 1951; admitted Solicitor, 1952. National Service, commnd RASC, 1953. Dep. Registrar of County Courts, 1970–78; Dep. Circuit Judge and Asst Recorder, 1978–83. Pres., West Essex Law Soc., 1977–78. Mem. Ethics Cttee, BUPA Roding Hosp. IVF Unit, 1991–. Chm., Ilford Round Table, 1962–63; Pres., Assoc. of Jewish Golf Clubs and Socs, 1984–94 (Sec., 1977–84). Gov., Redbridge Coll. of Further Educn, 1991–92. *Recreations:* golf, The Times crossword, people, travel. *Address:* Chelston, 5 St Mary's Avenue, Wanstead, E11 2NR. *T:* 0181–989 7228. *Clubs:* Wig and Pen; Dyrham Park Golf; Abridge Golf (Chm. 1964, Captain 1965).

MONTMORENCY, Sir Arnold Geoffroy de; *see* de Montmorency.

MONTREAL, Archbishop of, (RC), since 1990; **His Eminence Cardinal Jean-Claude Turcotte;** *b* 1936. Ordained priest, 1959; consecrated bishop, 1982; Cardinal, 1994. *Address:* Office of the Archbishop, 2000 rue Sherbrooke Ouest, Montreal, PQ H3H 1G4, Canada.

MONTREAL, Bishop of, since 1990; **Rt. Rev. Andrew S. Hutchison;** *b* 19 Sept. 1938; *s* of Ralph Burton Hutchison and Kathleen Marian (*née* Van Nostrand); *m* 1960, Lois Arlene Knight; one *s*. *Educ:* Lakefield Coll. Sch.; Upper Canada Coll.; Trinity Coll. Toronto (LTh). Ordained deacon, 1969, priest, 1970; served fifteen years in the dio. of Toronto; Dean of Montreal, 1984–90. Pres., Montreal Diocesan Theol Coll., 1990–; Visitor, Bishops Univ., Lennoxville, 1990–; Chaplain: Canadian Grenadier Guards, 1986–; 6087 and 22 CAR, 1986–; Order of St John of Jerusalem, Quebec, 1987–; Last Post Fund, Quebec, 1986–. OStJ. *Address:* Bishopscourt, 3630 de la Montagne, Montreal, Quebec H3G 2A8, Canada. *T:* (514) 849 4089. *Clubs:* United Services, Montreal Faculty, McGill University (Montreal).

MONTROSE, 8th Duke of, *cr* 1707; **James Graham;** Lord Graham 1445; Earl of Montrose 1505; Bt (NS) 1625; Marquis of Montrose 1644; Duke of Montrose, Marquis of Graham and Buchanan, Earl of Kincardine, Viscount Dundaff, Lord Aberuthven, Mugdock, and Fintrie 1707; Earl and Baron Graham (Eng.) 1722; *b* 6 April 1935; *e s* of 7th Duke of Montrose, and Isobel Veronica (*d* 1990), *yr d* of Lt-Col T. B. Sellar, CMG, DSO; *S* father, 1992; *m* 1970, Catherine Elizabeth MacDonell, *d* of late Captain N. A. T. Young, and of Mrs Young, Ottawa; two *s* one *d*. *Educ:* Loretto. Brig. Royal Company of Archers (Queen's Body Guard for Scotland), 1986 (Mem., 1965–). Area Pres., Scottish NFU, 1986 (Mem. Council, 1982–86 and 1987–90). OStJ 1978. *Heir:* *s* Marquis of Graham, *qv*. *Address:* Auchmar, Drymen, Glasgow. *T:* Drymen (01360) 307.

MOODY, Helen Wills; *see* Roark, H. W.

MOODY, Ian Charles Hugh, DL; Commissioner-in-Chief, St John Ambulance, 1991–95; *b* 25 April 1928; *s* of William Thomas Charles Moody and Roberta (*née* Baxter); *m* 1952, Angela de Lisle Carey; one *s* two *d*. *Educ:* Cheltenham Coll.; RMA, Sandhurst. Served RWF, 1947–50. Industrial relations and personnel appointments with: Compania Shell de Venezuela, 1951–54; Shell Trinidad Ltd, 1954–59; Shell BP Nigeria Ltd, 1959–60; PT Shell Indonesia, 1960–64; Pakistan Shell Oil Ltd, 1964–68; Personnel Manager, Shell Nigeria Ltd, 1968–72; Employee Relations, Shell Internat. Petroleum Co. Ltd, 1974–76; Personnel Manager, Shell Internat. Trading Co., 1976–83; retd 1983. St John Ambulance, Devon: Comr, 1983–88; Comdr, 1988–91; Chm., 1995–. FIPD. KStJ 1991. DL Devon, 1991. *Recreations:* cricket, sailing, gardening. *Address:* The Queen Anne House, The Strand, Lympstone, Devon EX8 5JW. *T:* Exmouth (01395) 263189. *Club:* MCC.

MOODY, Leslie Howard; General Secretary, Civil Service Union, 1977–82; *b* 18 Aug. 1922; *s* of George Henry and Edith Jessie Moody; *m* 1944, Betty Doreen Walton; two *s*. *Educ:* Eltham College. Telephone Engineer, General Post Office, 1940–53. Served Royal Signals, Far East, 1944–47. Asst Sec., Civil Service Union, 1953, Dep. Gen. Sec., 1963. A Dep. Chm., Civil Service Appeal Bd, 1990–92. *Recreations:* walking, music, theatre, educating management. *Address:* 9 Lock Chase, Blackheath, SE3 9HB. *T:* 0181–318 1040. *Club:* Civil Service.

MOODY, Peter Edward, CBE 1981; Director: Prudential Corporation, 1981–91 (Deputy Chairman, 1984–88); The Laird Group, 1981–92; *b* 26 Aug. 1918; *s* of late Edward Thomas Moody and Gladys (*née* Flint); *m* 1945, Peggy Elizabeth *d* of Edward Henry Causer and Elizabeth Theodora (*née* Finke); one *s* one *d*. *Educ:* Christ's Coll., Finchley. FIA. Prudential Assurance Co. Ltd: Dep. Investment Manager, 1960; Jt Sec. and Chief Investment Manager, 1973–80; Jt Sec. and Group Chief Investment Manager, Prudential Corp., 1979–80; Director: Triton Petroleum Ltd, 1971–89; United Dominions Trust, 1972–81; British American and General Trust, 1981–85; Inmos International, 1981–84; 3i Group plc (formerly FFI, then Investors in Industry), 1981–89; Equity Trustee Ltd, 1985–90. Mem., PO Bd, 1981–85. Trustee, Thalidomide Trust, 1984–93. Institute of Actuaries: Hon. Sec., 1968–70; Vice-Pres., 1972–75; Pres., 1978–80; Master, Worshipful Co. of Actuaries, 1988–89. *Publications:* contrib. Jl of Inst. of Actuaries. *Recreation:* golf. *Address:* 46 Brookmans Avenue, Brookmans Park, Herts AL9 7QJ.

MOODY-STUART, Mark, PhD; FGS; Group Managing Director, Royal Dutch/Shell Group, since 1991; *b* 15 Sept. 1940; *s* of Sir Alexander Moody-Stuart, OBE, MC and Judith (*née* Henzell); *m* 1964, Judith McLeavy; three *s* one *d*. *Educ:* Shrewsbury Sch.; St John's Coll., Cambridge (MA, PhD). Joined Shell, 1966; worked for various Shell companies in: Holland, 1966; Spain, 1967; Oman, 1968; Brunei, 1968–72; Australia, 1972–76; UK, 1977–78; Brunei, 1978–79; Nigeria, 1979–82; Turkey, 1982–86; Malaysia, 1986–89; Holland, 1990–91. *Publications:* papers in Geol Mag., Jl of Sedimentary Petrology,

Bull. Amer. Assoc. Petrology and Geol., Norsk Polarinstitut. *Recreations:* sailing, travel, reading. *Address:* Shell Centre, SE1 7NA. *T:* 0171–934 4212. *Clubs:* Travellers', Cruising Association.

MOOKERJEE, Sir Birendra Nath, Kt 1942; MA Cantab, MIE (India); Partner of Martin & Co. and Burn & Co., Managing Director, Martin Burn Ltd, Engineers, Contractors, Merchants, Shipbuilders, etc; Chairman Steel Corporation of Bengal Ltd; President Calcutta Local Board of Imperial Bank of India; Director Darjeeling Himalayan Railway Co. Ltd and many other companies; *b* 14 Feb. 1899; *s* of late Sir Rajendra Nath Mookerjee, KCIE, KCVO, MIE (India), FASB, DSc (Eng); *m* 1925, Ranu Priti Adhikari, *d* of Phani Bhusan Adhikari, late Professor Benares Hindu Univ.; one *s* two *d*. *Educ:* Bishop's Collegiate Sch., Hastings House, Calcutta; Bengal Engineering Coll.; Trinity Coll., Cambridge. Mem., Viceroy's Nat. Defence Council; Adviser, Roger Mission; Mem., Munitions Production Adv. Cttee. Fellow Calcutta Univ.; Sheriff of Calcutta 1941. *Address:* 7 Harrington Street, Calcutta 700071, India; Martin Burn Ltd, Martin Burn House, 12 Mission Row, Calcutta 1, India. *Clubs:* National Liberal; Calcutta, Calcutta Polo, Royal Calcutta Turf, Calcutta South, Cricket Club of India (Calcutta), etc.

MOOLLAN, Sir (Abdool) Hamid (Adam), Kt 1986; QC (Mauritius) 1976; sometime Chairman, Bar Council, Mauritius, 1970–93; *b* 10 April 1933; *s* of Adam Sulliman Moollan and Khatija Moollan; *m* 1966, Sara Sidiot; three *s*. *Educ:* Soonee Surtee Musalman Society Aided School; Royal College School; King's College London (LLB); Faculté de Droit, Univ. de Paris. Called to the Bar, Middle Temple, 1956; joined Mauritian Bar, 1960. *Recreations:* tennis, horse racing, hunting, fishing. *Address:* (home) Railway Road, Phoenix, Mauritius. *T:* 6864983; (chambers) 43 Sir William Newton Street, Port-Louis, Mauritius. *T:* 2083881. *Clubs:* Royal Over-Seas League; Mauritius Gymkhana, Mauritius Turf.

MOOLLAN, Sir Cassam (Ismael), Kt 1982; Chief Justice, Supreme Court of Mauritius, 1982–88, retired; Acting Governor-General, several occasions in 1984, 1985, 1986, 1987, 1988; Commander-in-Chief of Mauritius, 1984; *b* 26 Feb. 1927; *s* of Ismael Mahomed Moollan and Fatimah Nazroo; *m* 1954, Rassoulbibie Adam Moollan; one *s* two *d*. *Educ:* Royal Coll., Port Louis and Curepipe; London Sch. of Econs and Pol. Science (LLB 1950). Called to the Bar, Lincoln's Inn, 1951. Private practice, 1951–55; Dist Magistrate, 1955–58; Crown Counsel, 1958–64; Sen. Crown Counsel, 1964–66; Solicitor Gen., 1966–70; QC (Mauritius) 1969; Puisne Judge, Supreme Court, 1970; Sen. Puisne Judge, 1978. Editor, Mauritius Law Reports, 1982–84. Chevalier, Légion d'Honneur (France), 1986. *Recreations:* table tennis, tennis, bridge, Indian classical and semi-classical music. *Address:* Chambers, 43 Sir William Newton Street, Port Louis, Mauritius. *T:* 2120794, 2083881; 22 Hitchcock Avenue, Quatre Bornes, Mauritius. *T:* 4546949.

MOON, Brenda Elizabeth, FRSE; FLA; University Librarian, University of Edinburgh, since 1980; *b* 11 April 1931; *d* of Clement Alfred Moon and Mabel (*née* Berks). *Educ:* King Edward's Grammar Sch. for Girls, Camp Hill, Birmingham; St Hilda's Coll., Oxford (MA). MPhil Leeds; FLA 1958; FRSE 1992. Asst Librarian, Univ. of Sheffield, 1955–62; Sub-Librarian, 1962–67, Dep. Librarian, 1967–79, Univ. of Hull. *Publications:* Mycenaean Civilisation: publications since 1935, 1957; Mycenaean Civilisation: publications 1956–1960, 1961; Periodicals for South-East Asian Studies: a union catalogue of holdings in British and selected European libraries, 1979; articles in prof. jls. *Recreations:* walking, gardening, cruising on canals. *Address:* 4 Cobden Road, Edinburgh EH9 2BJ. *T:* 0131–667 0071.

See also M. M. Moon.

MOON, Mary Marjorie; Head Mistress, Manchester High School for Girls, 1983–94; *b* 28 Sept. 1932; *d* of Clement Alfred Moon and Mable Moon (*née* Berks). *Educ:* King Edward's Grammar Sch. for Girls, Birmingham; Univ. of Manchester (BA Hons, MEd); Univ. of London Inst. of Education (PGCE). Asst English Teacher, 1955–59, Head of English Dept, 1959–63, Orme Girls' Sch., Newcastle-under-Lyme; Head of English, Bolton Sch. (Girls' Div.), 1963–71; Head Mistress, Pate's Grammar Sch. for Girls, Cheltenham, 1971–83. *Recreations:* photography, sketching, travel. *Address:* 18 South Parade, Bramhall, Stockport, Cheshire SK7 3BH.

See also B. E. Moon.

MOON, Michael, RA 1994; artist; *b* 9 Nov. 1937; *s* of Donald and Marjorie Moon; *m* 1977, Anjum Khan; two *s*. *Educ:* Chelsea Sch. of Art; RCA. One-man shows include: Tate Gall., 1976; Waddington Galls, London, 1969, 1970, 1972, 1978, 1984, 1986, 1992; Macquarie Galls, Sydney, 1982; Christine Abrahams Gall., Melbourne, 1983; Pace Prints, NY, 1987; Kass/Meridien Gall., Chicago, 1988; Linda Goodman Gall., Johannesburg, 1994; work in public collections include: Tate Gall.; Australian Nat. Gall., Canberra; Mus. of WA, Perth; Art Gall. of NSW, Sydney; Power Inst., Sydney; Walker Art Gall., Liverpool; Birmingham City Art Gall.; V&A Mus. *Recreation:* watching schoolboy cricket. *Address:* 10 Bowood Road, SW11 6PE. *T:* 0171–228 7358.

MOON, Sir Peter Wilfred Giles Graham-, 5th Bt, *cr* 1855; Chairman, Trans Continental Corporation, since 1990; *b* 24 Oct. 1942; *s* of Sir (Arthur) Wilfred Graham-Moon, 4th Bt, and 2nd wife, Doris Patricia, *yr d* of Thomas Baron Jobson, Dublin; *S* father, 1954; *m* 1967, Sarah Gillian Chater (marr. diss.) (formerly *m* Major Antony Chater; marr. diss. 1966), *e d* of late Lt-Col Michael Lyndon Smith, MC, MB, BS, and Mrs Michael Smith; two *s*; *m* 1993; Mrs Terry de Vries. *Recreations:* shooting, golf. *Heir:* *s* Rupert Francis Wilfred Graham-Moon, *b* 29 April 1968. *Clubs:* Cricketers; Royal Cork Yacht.

MOON, Sir Roger, 6th Bt *cr* 1887, of Copsewood, Stoke, Co. Warwick; retired; *b* 17 Nov. 1914; *s* of Jasper Moon (*d* 1975) (*g g s* of 1st Bt) and Isabel (*née* Logan); *S* brother, 1988; *m* 1950, Meg, *d* of late Arthur Mainwaring Maxwell, DSO, MC; three *d*. *Educ:* Sedbergh. Coffee planter, Kenya, 1933–35; Rubber planter, Malaya, 1939–41 and 1946–63; Oil palms planter, Malaya, 1963–67. *Recreations:* shooting, golf, gardening. *Heir:* *b* Humphrey Moon [*b* 9 Oct. 1919; *m* 1st, 1955, Diana Hobson (marr. diss. 1964); two *d*; 2nd, 1964, Elizabeth Anne (*d* 1994), *d* of late George Archibald Drummond Angus and *widow* of H. J. Butler; one *d*]. *Address:* The Barn House, Wykey, Ruyton-XI-Towns, Shropshire SY4 1JA. *T:* Baschurch (01939) 260354.

MOONEY, Bel; writer and broadcaster; *b* 8 Oct. 1946; *d* of Edward and Gladys Mooney; *m* 1968, Jonathan Dimbleby, *qv*; one *s* one *d*. *Educ:* Trowbridge Girls' High School; University College London (1st cl. Hons, Eng. Lang. and Lit., 1969; Fellow 1994). Freelance journalist, 1970–79; columnist: Daily Mirror, 1979–80; Sunday Times, 1982–83; The Listener, 1984–86; *television:* interview series: Mothers By Daughters, 1983; The Light of Experience Revisited, 1984; Fathers By Sons, 1985; Grief, 1995; various series for BBC Radio 4 (Sandford St Martin Trust award for Devout Sceptics, 1994) and films for BBC TV and Channel 4. Board Member: Natural Theatre Co., 1994–; Friends of Gt Ormond St, 1994–. Governor, Bristol Polytechnic, 1989–91. *Publications: novels:* The Windsurf Boy, 1983; The Anderson Question, 1985; The Fourth of July, 1988; Lost Footsteps, 1993; *for children:* Liza's Yellow Boat, 1980; I Don't Want To!, 1985; The Stove Haunting, 1986; I Can't Find It!, 1988; It's Not Fair!, 1989; A Flower of Jet, 1990; But You Promised!, 1990; Why Not?, 1990; I Know!, 1991; The Voices of Silence, 1994; I'm Scared!, 1994; I Wish!, 1995; The Mouse with Many Rooms, 1995; Why Me?, 1996; *miscellaneous:* The Year of the Child, 1979; Differences of Opinion (collected journalism), 1984; (with Gerald Scarfe) Father Kismass and Mother Claws, 1985; Bel Mooney's Somerset, 1989; From This Day Forward (Penguin Book of Marriage), 1989; Perspectives for Living, 1992. *Recreations:* reading, music, art, churches, friends. *Address:* c/o David Higham Associates, 5 Lower John Street, W1R 3PE. *T:* 0171–437 7888. *Club:* Groucho.

MOONIE, Lewis George; MP (Lab) Kirkcaldy, since 1987; *b* 25 Feb. 1947; *m*; two *c*. *Educ:* Grove Acad., Dundee; St Andrews Univ. (MB ChB 1970); Edinburgh Univ. (MSc 1981). MRCPsych 1979; MFCM 1984. Psychiatrist, Ciba-Geigy, Switzerland, and Organon Internat., Netherlands; Sen. Registrar (Community Medicine), subseq. Community Medicine Specialist, Fife Health Bd. Mem., Fife Regl Council, 1982–86. Mem., Social Services Select Cttee, 1987–89; opposition front-bench spokesman on technology, 1990–92, on science and technol., 1992–, and on industry, 1994–. *Address:* House of Commons, SW1A 0AA; 85 Sauchenbush Road, Kirkcaldy, Fife KY2 5RN.

MOONMAN, Eric, OBE 1991; Chairman, Essex Radio, since 1991; Visiting Professor, Systems Science, City University, since 1992; *b* 29 April 1929; *s* of Borach and Leah Moonman; *m* 1962, Jane (marr. diss. 1991); two *s* one *d*. *Educ:* Rathbone Sch., Liverpool; Christ Church, Southport; Univs of Liverpool and Manchester. Dipl. in Social Science, Liverpool, 1955. Human Relations Adviser, British Inst. of Management, 1956–62; Sen. Lectr in Industrial Relations, SW Essex Technical Coll., 1962–64; Sen. Research Fellow in Management Sciences, Univ. of Manchester, 1964–66. MSc Manchester Univ., 1967. MP (Lab) Billericay, 1966–70, Basildon, Feb. 1974–1979; PPS to Minister without Portfolio and Sec. of State for Educn, 1967–68. Chairman: All-Party Parly Mental Health Cttee, 1967–70 and 1974–79; New Towns and Urban Affairs Cttee, Parly Labour Party, 1974–79. Dir, Centre for Contemporary Studies, 1979–90; Dir, Nat. Hist. Mus. Develt Trust, 1990–91. Chm., Zionist Fedn, 1975–80; Sen. Vice-Pres., Bd of Deputies, 1985–91, 1994–. Member: Stepney Council, 1961–65 (Leader, 1964–65); Tower Hamlets Council, 1964–67. Chm., Islington HA, 1981–90; Mem., Bloomsbury and Islington HA, 1990–92. Mem., Council, Toynbee Hall Univ. Settlement (Chm., Finance Cttee); Governor, BFI, 1974–80. Consultant, Internat. Red Cross (Africa), 1991–. Trustee: Balfour Diamond Jubilee Trust, 1985–; Winnicott Trust, 1990–94. FRSA. *Publications:* The Manager and the Organization, 1961; Employee Security, 1962; European Science and Technology, 1968; Communication in an Expanding Organization, 1970; Reluctant Partnership, 1970; Alternative Government, 1984; (ed) The Violent Society, 1987. *Recreations:* football, theatre, cinema. *Address:* 1 Beacon Hill, N7 9LY.

MOOR, Dr Robert Michael, FRS 1994; Deputy Director, Babraham Institute, since 1993; *b* 28 Sept. 1937; *s* of Donald C. Moor and Gwendolen (*née* Whitby); *m* 1962, Felicia Alison Elizabeth Stephens; four *d*. *Educ:* Estcourt, Natal, S Africa; Gonville and Caius Coll., Cambridge Univ. (PhD 1965; ScD). Senior Scientist, ARC Unit of Reproductive Physiology and Biochemistry, 1965–86; Head, Dept of Molecular Embryology, AFRC Inst. of Animal Physiology and Genetics Res., 1986–93. Hon. Fellow, Italian Vet. Assoc., 1990. Hon. Dr Univ. of Milan, 1990. *Publications:* numerous contribs to learned jls. *Recreations:* mountaineering, music. *Address:* 19 Thornton Close, Cambridge CB3 0NF. *T:* Cambridge (01223) 276669. *Club:* Alpino Italiano (Milan).

MOORBATH, Prof. Stephen Erwin, DPhil, DSc; FRS 1977; Professor of Isotope Geology, Oxford University, 1992–Oct. 1996; Professorial Fellow of Linacre College, 1990–Oct. 1996 (Fellow, 1970–90); *b* 9 May 1929; *s* of Heinz Moosbach and Else Moosbach; *m* 1962, Pauline Tessier-Varlêt; one *s* one *d*. *Educ:* Lincoln Coll., Oxford Univ. (MA 1957, DPhil 1959). DSc Oxon 1969. Asst Experimental Officer, AERE, Harwell, 1948–51; Undergrad., Oxford Univ., 1951–54; Scientific Officer, AERE, Harwell, 1954–56; Research Fellow: Oxford Univ., 1956–61; MIT, 1961–62; Sen. Res. Officer, 1962–78, Reader in Geology, 1978–92, Oxford Univ. Wollaston Fund, Geol Soc. of London, 1968; Liverpool Geol Soc. Medal, 1968; Murchison Medal, Geol Soc. of London, 1978; Steno Medal, Geol Soc. of Denmark, 1979. *Publications:* contribs to scientific jls and books. *Recreations:* music, philately, travel, linguistics. *Address:* 53 Bagley Wood Road, Kennington, Oxford OX1 5LY. *T:* Oxford (01865) 739507.

MOORCRAFT, Dennis Harry; Under-Secretary, Inland Revenue, 1975–81; *b* 14 Aug. 1921; *s* of late Harry Moorcraft and Dorothy Moorcraft (*née* Simmons); *m* 1945, Ingeborg Utne, Bergen, Norway; one *s* one *d*. *Educ:* Gillingham County Grammar Sch. Tax Officer, Inland Revenue, 1938. RNVR, 1940–46. Inspector of Taxes, 1948; Sen. Inspector of Taxes, 1956; Principal Inspector of Taxes, 1963. *Recreations:* gardening, garden construction, croquet.

MOORE, family name of **Earl of Drogheda** and **Barons Moore of Lower Marsh** and **Moore of Wolvercote.**

MOORE, Viscount; Benjamin Garrett Henderson Moore; *b* 21 March 1983; *s* and *heir* of Earl of Drogheda, *qv*.

MOORE OF LOWER MARSH, Baron *cr* 1992 (Life Peer), of Lower Marsh in the London Borough of Lambeth; **John Edward Michael Moore,** PC 1986; *b* 26 Nov. 1937; *s* of Edward O. Moore; *m* 1962, Sheila Sarah Tillotson; two *s* one *d*. *Educ:* London Sch. of Economics (BSc Econ). Nat. Service, Royal Sussex Regt, Korea, 1955–57 (commnd). Chm. Conservative Soc., LSE, 1958–59; Pres. Students' Union, LSE, 1959–60. Took part in expedn from N Greece to India overland tracing Alexander's route, 1960. In Banking and Stockbroking instns, Chicago, 1961–65; Democratic Precinct Captain, Evanston, Ill, USA, 1962; Democratic Ward Chm. Evanston, Illinois, 1964; Dir, 1968–79, Chm., 1975–79, Dean Witter Internat. Ltd. An Underwriting Mem. of Lloyds, 1978–92. Councillor (C), London Borough of Merton, 1971–74; Chm., Stepney Green Cons. Assoc., 1968. MP (C) Croydon Central, Feb. 1974–1992. A Vice-Chm., Conservative Party, 1975–79; Parly Under Sec. of State, Dept. of Energy, 1979–83; HM Treasury: Economic Sec., June–Oct. 1983; Financial Sec., 1983–86; Secretary of State: for Transport, 1986–87; for Social Services, 1987–88; for Social Security, 1988–89. Chairman: Credit Suisse Asset Management, 1992–; Energy Saving Trust Ltd, 1992–; Director: Monitor Inc., 1990– (Chm., Monitor European Exec. Cttee, 1990–); Gartmore Investment Management, 1990–92; GTECH Corp., 1992–; Swiss American Inc., 1992–; Blue Circle Industries, 1993–; Camelot PLC, 1994–; Rolls-Royce plc; Member: Internat. Adv. Bd, Marvin & Palmer Associates Inc., 1989–; Adv. Bd, Sir Alexander Gibb & Partners, 1990–. Mem. Council, Inst. of Dirs, 1991–. Mem. Ct of Governors, LSE, 1977–. *Address:* House of Lords, SW1A 0PW. *Clubs:* Carlton, Royal Automobile.

MOORE OF WOLVERCOTE, Baron *cr* 1986 (Life Peer), of Wolvercote in the City of Oxford; **Philip Brian Cecil Moore,** GCB 1985 (KCB 1980; CB 1973); GCVO 1983 (KCVO 1976); CMG 1966; QSO 1986; PC 1977; Private Secretary to the Queen and Keeper of the Queen's Archives, 1977–86; a Permanent Lord-in-Waiting to the Queen, since 1990; *b* 6 April 1921; *s* of late Cecil Moore, Indian Civil Service; *m* 1945, Joan Ursula Greenop; two *d*. *Educ:* Dragon Sch.; Cheltenham Coll. (Scholar); Oxford Univ. Classical Exhibitioner, Brasenose Coll., Oxford, 1940. RAF Bomber Command, 1940–42 (prisoner of war, 1942–45). Brasenose Coll., Oxford, 1945–46 (Hon. Fellow 1981). Asst Private Sec. to First Lord of Admiralty, 1950–51; Principal Private Sec. to First Lord of

Admiralty, 1957–58; Dep. UK Commissioner, Singapore, 1961–63; British Dep. High Comr in Singapore, 1963–65; Chief of Public Relations, MoD, 1965–66; Asst Private Secretary to the Queen, 1966–72, Dep. Private Secretary, 1972–77. Dir, General Accident, Fire and Life Assurance Corp., 1986–91. Chm., King George VI and Queen Elizabeth Foundn of St Catharine's, Cumberland Lodge, 1986–. Vice-Pres., SPCK. *Recreations:* golf, Rugby football (Oxford Blue, 1945–46; International, England, 1951), hockey (Oxford Blue, 1946), cricket (Oxfordshire). *Address:* Hampton Court Palace, East Molesey, Surrey KT8 9AU. *Clubs:* Athenæum, MCC.

MOORE, Alan Edward, CBE 1980; Deputy Chief Executive and Treasurer, Lloyds Bank, since 1994; Director, Lloyds Bank, since 1989; *b* 5 June 1936; *s* of late Charles Edward and Ethel Florence Moore; *m* 1961, Margaret Patricia Beckley; one *s* one *d. Educ:* Berkhamsted Sch. AIB, ACIS, FCT. Glyn Mills & Co., then Williams & Glyn's Bank, London, 1953–74; Dir Gen., Bahrain Monetary Agency, 1974–79; Dir and Treas., Lloyds Bank Internat., 1980–84; Dir of Treasury, Lloyds Bank, 1985–88; Dir of Corporate Banking and Treasury, Lloyds Bank, 1988–94. *Recreations:* industrial archaeology, photography, steam railways. *Address:* Lloyds Bank plc, 71 Lombard Street, EC3P 3BS. *T:* 0171–626 1500.

MOORE, Alexander Wyndham Hume S.; *see* Stewart-Moore.

MOORE, Antony Ross, CMG 1965; *b* 30 May 1918; *o s* of late Arthur Moore and late Eileen Maillet; *m* 1st, 1941, Philippa Weigall (marr. diss.); two *d*; 2nd, 1963, Georgina Mary Galbraith (*see* G. M. Moore); one *s. Educ:* Rugby; King's Coll., Cambridge. Served in Friends Ambulance Unit, 1939–40; HM Forces, 1940–46. Apptd Mem. Foreign (subseq. Diplomatic) Service, Nov. 1946; transf. to Rome, 1947; FO, Nov. 1949; 1st Sec., 1950; transf. to Tel Aviv, 1952; acted as Chargé d'Affaires, 1953, 1954; apptd Consul, Sept. 1953; FO, 1955; UK Perm. Delegn to UN, NY, 1957; Counsellor and transf. to IDC, 1961; FO, 1962–64; Internat. Fellow, Center for Internat. Affairs, Harvard Univ., 1964–65; Regional Information Officer, Middle East, British Embassy, Beirut, 1965–67; Head of Eastern Dept, FO, 1967; retd from HM Diplomatic Service, Dec. 1968. Dir, Iranian Selection Trust, 1969–72. *Address:* Touchbridge, Boarstall, Aylesbury, Bucks HP18 9UJ. *T:* Brill (01844) 238247.

MOORE, Brian; novelist; *b* 25 Aug. 1921; *s* of James Bernard Moore, FRCS, Northern Ireland, and Eileen McFadden; *m* Jean Denney. Guggenheim Fellowship (USA), 1959; Canada Council Senior Fellowship (Canada), 1960; Scottish Arts Council Internat. Fellowship, 1983. National Institute of Arts and Letters (USA) Fiction Award 1960. *Publications: novels:* The Lonely Passion of Judith Hearne, 1955 (filmed, 1989); The Feast of Lupercal, 1956; The Luck of Ginger Coffey (Governor-Gen. of Canada's Award for Fiction), 1960 (filmed, 1963); An Answer from Limbo, 1962; The Emperor of Ice-Cream, 1965; I am Mary Dunne, 1968; Fergus, 1970; Catholics, 1972 (W. H. Smith Literary Award, 1973); The Great Victorian Collection (James Tait Black Meml Award; Governor Gen. of Canada's Award for Fiction), 1975; The Doctor's Wife, 1976; The Mangan Inheritance, 1979; The Temptation of Eileen Hughes, 1981; Cold Heaven, 1983 (filmed, 1990); Black Robe, 1985 (Heinemann Award, RSL, 1986; filmed 1991); The Colour of Blood (Sunday Express Book of the Year Award), 1987; Lies of Silence, 1990; No Other Life, 1993; *non-fiction:* Canada (with Editors of Life), 1964; The Revolution Script, 1972. *Address:* c/o Curtis Brown Ltd, 10 Astor Place, New York, NY 10003, USA.

MOORE, Brian Baden; Football Commentator/Presenter: London Weekend Television, since 1968; The Match, Independent Television, since 1988; *b* 28 Feb. 1932; *m* 1955, Betty (*née* Cole); two *s. Educ:* Cranbrook Sch., Kent. Sports Sub-Editor, World Sports, 1954–56; journalist: Exchange Telegraph, 1956–58; The Times, 1958–61; Football Commentator/Presenter: BBC Radio, 1961–68; Mid-Week Sports Special, Thames TV, 1978–86; Presenter, Brian Moore Meets (TV documentary series), 1979–. *Publication:* The Big Matches 1970–1980, 1980. *Recreations:* being at home, animal care, golf. *Address:* c/o London Weekend Television, London Television Centre, Upper Ground, SE1 9LT. *T:* 0171–827 7704/7605.

MOORE, Charles Hilary; Editor, The Sunday Telegraph, since 1992; *b* 31 Oct. 1956; *s* of Richard and Ann Moore; *m* 1981, Caroline Mary Baxter; twin *s* and *d. Educ:* Eton Coll.; Trinity Coll., Cambridge (BA Hons History). Joined editorial staff of Daily Telegraph, 1979, leader writer, 1981–83; Assistant Editor and political columnist, 1983–84, Editor, 1984–90, The Spectator; weekly columnist, Daily Express, 1987–90; Dep. Editor, Daily Telegraph, 1990–92. Trustee: Prayer Book Soc., 1989–94; Friends of the Union. *Publications:* (ed with C. Hawtree) 1936, 1986; (with A. N. Wilson and G. Stamp) The Church in Crisis, 1986; (ed with Simon Heffer) A Tory Seer: the selected journalism of T. E. Utley, 1989. *Address:* 16 Thornhill Square, N1 1BQ. *T:* 0171–607 8872. *Club:* Beefsteak.

MOORE, Air Vice-Marshal Charles Stuart, CB 1962; OBE 1945; *b* London, 27 Feb. 1910; *s* of late E. A. Moore and E. B. Moore (*née* Druce); *m* 1st, 1937, Anne (*d* 1957), *d* of Alfred Rogers; 2nd, 1961, Jean Mary (marr. diss. 1993), *d* of John Cameron Wilson; one *d. Educ:* Sutton Valence Sch.; RAF Coll., Cranwell. Commissioned in General Duties Branch, Dec. 1930; served in Egypt, 1932–34 and 1936–41; Sqdn Ldr 1938; Sudan, 1941–42; Wing Comdr 1940; 11 Group, 1943–44; Gp Capt. 1943; OC, OTU, 1944–45; Gp Capt. Org., HQFC, 1945–46; Staff Coll., Bracknell, 1946–47; Dep. Dir Plans, Air Ministry, London, 1947–49; Student, US National War Coll., Washington, 1949–50; Staff of USAF Air War Coll., Alabama, 1950–53; Air Commodore, 1953; AOC 66 Group, 1953–55; Dir of Intelligence, Air Ministry, London, 1955–58; AOA, NEAF, 1958–62; Actg Air Vice-Marshal, 1960; retired, 1962. Joined HM Foreign Service, Oct. 1962; posted to British Embassy, Tehran, Iran; left HM Diplomatic Service, March 1969. *Recreations:* music, photography and travelling. *Address:* Ferndene, The Avenue, Crowthorne, Berks RG45 6PB. *T:* Crowthorne (01344) 772300. *Club:* Royal Air Force.

MOORE, Cicely Frances (Mrs H. D. Moore); *see* Berry, C. F.

MOORE, David James Ladd; Partnership Secretary, Freshfields, since 1993; *b* 6 June 1937; *s* of James and Eilonwy Moore; *m* 1968, Kay Harrison; two *s. Educ:* King Edward VI Sch., Nuneaton; Brasenose Coll., Oxford (BA). PO, 1961–67 (Asst Principal 1961, Principal 1966); Cabinet Office, 1967–69; HM Treasury, 1969–80 (Asst Sec. 1973); Under Secretary: Cabinet Office, 1980–82; HM Treasury, 1982–83; Inland Revenue (Principal Finance Officer), 1983–85; HM Treasury, 1985–93. *Recreations:* reading, theatre, cinema, tennis, art. *Address:* Freshfields, 65 Fleet Street, EC4Y 1HS.

MOORE, Prof. Derek William, FRS 1990; Professor of Applied Mathematics, Imperial College, London, since 1973; *b* 19 April 1931; *s* of William McPherson Moore and Elsie Marjorie Moore (*née* Patterson). *Educ:* Jesus Coll., Cambridge (MA, PhD). Asst Lectr and Lectr in Maths, Bristol, 1958–64; Sen. Postdoctoral Res. Fellow, Nat. Acad. of Scis, USA, 1964; Imperial College London: Sen. Lectr, Dept of Maths, 1967; Reader in Theoretical Fluid Mechanics, 1968. Sherman Fairchild Dist. Scholar, CIT, 1986. Foreign Hon. Mem., Amer. Acad. of Arts and Scis, 1985. *Recreation:* jazz tenor saxophone. *Address:* 71 Boileau Road, W5 3AP. *T:* 0181–998 8572.

MOORE, Derry; *see* Drogheda, Earl of.

MOORE, Dudley Stuart John; actor (stage, films, TV and radio); composer (film music and incidental music for plays, etc); *b* 19 April 1935; *s* of late Ada Francis and John Moore; *m* 1st, 1958, Suzy Kendall (marr. diss.); 2nd, 1975, Tuesday Weld (marr. diss.); one *s*; 3rd, 1988, Brogan Lane (marr. diss.); 4th, 1994, Nicole Rothschild; one *s. Educ:* County High Sch., Dagenham, Essex; Guildhall Sch.; Magdalen Coll., Oxford (BA, BMus). *Stage:* Beyond the Fringe, 1960–62 (London), 1962–64 (Broadway, New York); Behind the Fridge, 1971–72; Good Evening, NY, 1974; Mikardo (Los Angeles, UK/LA Fest.), 1988; Vic Lewis, John Dankworth Jazz Bands, 1959–60; composed incidental music, Royal Court Theatre (various plays), 1958–60; Play it again Sam, Woody Allen, Globe Theatre, 1970; Behind the Fridge, Cambridge Theatre, 1972–73; Good Evening, Broadway, New York, 1973–74; tour of USA, 1975. *BBC TV:* own series with Peter Cook: Not only . . . but also, 1964, 1966, 1970; *series:* It's Lulu, not to mention Dudley Moore, 1973; in the sixties, *ITV:* Goodbye again; Royal Command Performance; *series:* Orchestra! (co-presenter with Sir Georg Solti), 1991; Concerto!, 1993. Various TV and radio guest spots with Jazz piano trio. *Films:* The Wrong Box, 1966; 30 is a Dangerous Age Cynthia, 1967; Bedazzled, 1968; Monte Carlo or Bust, The Bed-sitting room, 1969; Alice in Wonderland, 1972; The Hound of the Baskervilles, 1977; Foul Play, "10", 1979; Wholly Moses, 1980; Arthur, 1981; Lovesick, Romantic Comedy, 1982; Unfaithfully Yours, Best Defense, 1983; Mickey & Maude, 1984; Santa Claus—The Movie, 1985; Like Father Like Son, 1987; Arthur 2—On The Rocks, 1988; Crazy People, 1990; Blame it on the Bellboy, 1992. *Film music* composed for: Bedazzled, 30 is a dangerous age Cynthia, The Staircase, Inadmissable Evidence, Six Weeks, and various TV films. *Publications:* Dud and Pete: The Dagenham Dialogues, 1971, new edn 1988; Musical Bumps, 1986; The Complete Beyond the Fringe, 1987. *Recreations:* films, theatre, music. *Address:* c/o Louis Pitt, ICM, 8942 Wilshire Boulevard, Beverley Hills, CA 90210, USA. *Club:* St James's.

MOORE, Rt. Rev. Edward Francis Butler, DD; *b* 1906; *s* of Rev. W. R. R. Moore; *m* 1932, Frances Olivia Scott; two *s* two *d. Educ:* Trinity Coll., Dublin (MA, PhD, DD). Deacon, 1930; Priest, 1931; Curate, Bray, 1930–32; Hon. Clerical Vicar, Christ Church Cathedral, Dublin, 1931–35; Curate, Clontarf, 1932–34; Incumbent, Castledermot with Kinneagh, 1934–40; Greystones, Diocese of Glendalough, 1940–49; Chaplain to Duke of Leinster, 1934–40; Rural Dean, Delgany 1950–59; Canon of Christ Church, Dublin, 1951–57; Archdeacon of Glendalough, 1957–59; Bishop of Kilmore and Elphin and Ardagh, 1959–81. *Recreations:* tennis, golf, fishing. *Address:* Drumlona, Sea Road, Kilcoole, Co. Wicklow, Ireland. *Club:* Royal Dublin Society (Dublin).

MOORE, Maj.-Gen. (retired) Frederick David, CB 1955; CBE 1954; *b* 27 Nov. 1902; *s* of Sir Frederick W. Moore; *m* 1932, Anna Morrell Hamilton (*d* 1974), *d* of Col T. H. M. Clarke, CMG, DSO; one *s. Educ:* Wellington Coll.; RMA Woolwich. Commnd in RFA, 1923. Served War of 1939–45: BEF 1940, 5th Regt RHA; BLA, 1944–45, CO 5th Regt RHA and CRA 53rd (W) Div.; GOC 5th AA Group, 1953–55; retd, 1956. DL Beds, 1958, Vice-Lieutenant, 1964–70. Officer Order of Crown (Belgian); Croix de Guerre (Belgian), 1940, with palm, 1945. *Recreations:* country pursuits. *Address:* Riverview, Bunclody, Co. Wexford, Ireland. *T:* (54) 77184. *Club:* Army and Navy.

MOORE, Geoffrey Herbert; Professor of American Literature and Head of the Department of American Studies, University of Hull, 1962–82, now Professor Emeritus; *b* 10 June 1920; *e s* of late Herbert Jonathan Moore, Norwich; *m* 1947, Pamela Marguerite (marr. diss. 1962), *d* of Bertram Munn, Twickenham; one *s* one *d. Educ:* Mitcham Grammar Sch.; Emmanuel Coll., Cambridge; Univ. of Paris. 1st Cl. English Tripos, Cambridge, 1946; MA 1951. War Service (Air Ministry and RAF), 1939–43. Instr in English, Univ. of Wisconsin, 1947–49; Vis. Prof. of English, Univs of Kansas City and New Mexico, 1948, 1949; Asst Prof. of English, Tulane Univ., 1949–51; Vis. Prof. of English, Univ. of Southern California and Claremont Coll., 1950; Extra Mural Lectr, London and Cambridge Univs, 1951–52; Editor and Producer, BBC Television Talks, 1952–54; Rose Morgan Prof., Univ. of Kansas, 1954–55; Lectr in Amer. Lit., Manchester Univ., 1955–59; Vis. Lectr, Univs of Mainz, Göttingen and Frankfurt, 1959; Rockefeller Fellow, Harvard Univ., 1959–60; Sen. Lectr in Amer. Lit., Manchester Univ., 1960–62; Dean, Faculty of Arts, Univ. of Hull, 1967–69. Visiting Professor: Univs of Montpellier, Aix-en-Provence and Nice, 1967, 1971; Univs of Frankfurt, Heidelberg, Mainz, Saarbrücken, Tübingen, 1967, 1968; Univs of Perpignan, Turin, Florence, Pisa, Rome, New Delhi, Hyderabad, Madras, Bombay, Calcutta, 1971; York Univ., Toronto, 1969–70; Univ. of Tunis, Spring 1970, 1971; Harvard, 1971; Univs of Düsseldorf, Heidelberg, Freiburg, Mainz, 1972; Univs of Teheran, Shiraz, Isfahan, Mashad, 1978; Univs of Berlin, Bremen, Osnabrück, 1981; Univs of Münster, Duisburg, Bonn, Düsseldorf, Aachen, 1982; Univ. of Göttingen, 1983; Tällberg, Sweden, 1984; Univs of Madrid, Bilbao, Barcelona, 1985; Univs of Warsaw, Lodz, Katowice, Cracow, 1992; Univs of Athens and Thessaloniki, 1993; Fellow, Sch. of Letters, Indiana Univ., Summer 1970; Research Fellow: Univ. of California at San Diego, 1974; Rockefeller Centre, Bellagio, 1979. Mem. Cttee, British Assoc. for Amer. Studies, 1957–60. Sen. Scholar Award, Amer. Coun. of Learned Socs, 1965. Editor and Founder, The Bridge (Cambridge lit. mag.), 1946; reviewer, Financial Times, 1976–; Gen. Editor of Henry James for Penguin Classics, 1981–. *Publications:* Voyage to Chivalry (under pseud.), 1947; Poetry from Cambridge in Wartime, 1947; The Penguin Book of Modern American Verse, 1954; (ed) 58 Short Stories by O. Henry, 1956; Poetry Today, 1958; American Literature and the American Imagination, 1964; American Literature, 1964; The Penguin Book of American Verse, 1977, 2nd edn 1983; *edited:* Portrait of a Lady, 1984; Roderick Hudson, 1986; Daisy Miller, 1986; Selected Poems of Emily Dickinson, 1986; Selected Poems of Robert Frost, 1986; Selected Poems of Walt Whitman, 1987; Selected Poems of Edgar Allan Poe, 1988; Selected Poems of Longfellow, 1989; Selected Poems of Thomas Hardy, 1990; Selected Poems of John Keats, 1991; Selected Poems of Rudyard Kipling, 1992; Selected Poems of William Wordsworth, 1992; Selected Poems of Gerard Manley Hopkins, 1993; Selected Poems of Tennyson, 1994; articles in TLS, Amer. Mercury, BBC Quarterly, Kenyon Review, Review of English Lit., The Year's Work in English Studies, Jl of American Studies, Studi Americani and other scholarly and literary jls. *Recreations:* swimming, driving. *Club:* Savile.

MOORE, George; Chairman, Grayne Marketing Co. Ltd, since 1978; *b* 7 Oct. 1923; *s* of George Moore and Agnes Bryce Moore; *m* 1946, Marjorie Pamela Davies (*d* 1986); three *s. Educ:* University Coll. and Royal Technical Coll., Cardiff (Jt Engineering Diploma); Hull Univ. (Post Graduate Diploma in Economics). Served War, RN, 1942–46. Graduate Engineer, Electricity Authority, 1948–50; Development Engineer, Anglo-Iranian Oil Co., Abadan, 1950–52; Chief Electrical Engineer, Distillers' Solvents Div., 1952–58; Management Consultant, Urwick, Orr & Partners, 1958–64; Executive Dir, Burton Group, 1964–66; Group Managing Dir, Spear & Jackson International Ltd and Chm., USA Subsidiary, 1966–75; Dir of cos in Sweden, France, India, Australia, Canada, S Africa, 1966–75; Under Sec. and Regional Industrial Dir, NW Regional Office, DoI, 1976–78; Dir, Cordel Corporate Develt Ltd, 1978–. FIMgt (FBIM 1980); FInstD 1978; MIMC 1990. *Recreations:* golf, sailing. *Address:* Leasgill House, Leasgill, near Milnthorpe, Cumbria LA7 7ET. *Club:* Reform.

MOORE, George, OBE 1994; Member, South Yorkshire County Council, 1974–86 (Chairman, 1978–79); *b* 29 Jan. 1913; *s* of Charles Edward Moore and Edith Alice Moore;

m 1943, Hannah Kenworthy; two *d*. *Educ:* Woodhouse, Sheffield. Started work in pit at 14 yrs of age, 1927; worked in hotel business, 1930; publican in own right for several yrs, after which went into fruit and vegetable business, first as retailer and eventually as wholesaler and partner in small co. Served in RAF for short period during war. Barnsley Bor. Council, then Barnsley MBC, 1961–94: served as Vice Chm., Health and Housing Cttee, and Vice Chm., Fire and Licensing Dept; Chairman: Barnsley and Dist Refuse Disposal Cttee, 1959–64; Sanitary Cttee, Barnsley, 1963–73; first Chm., Fire Service Cttee, S Yorks CC, 1974–78. Chm., Barnsley Community Health Council, 1974–92. Chm., Barnsley and Dist, Talking Newspaper for the Blind, 1978–94. *Recreation:* aviculture. *Address:* 34 Derwent Road, Athersley South, Barnsley, S Yorks S71 3QT. *T:* Barnsley (01226) 206644.

MOORE, His Honour George Edgar; HM First Deemster and Clerk of the Rolls, Isle of Man, 1969–74; *b* 13 July 1907; *er s* of Ramsey Bignall Moore, OBE, formerly HM Attorney-General for Isle of Man, and Agnes Cannell Moore; *m* 1937, Joan Mary Kissack; one *s* one *d*. *Educ:* Rydal School. Served in RAF, 1940–45 (Sqdn Ldr). Admitted to Manx Bar, 1930; Attorney-General for Isle of Man, 1957–63; HM Second Deemster, 1963–69; MLC; Chairman: IoM Criminal Injuries Compensation Tribunal, 1967–69; IoM Income Tax Appeal Comrs, 1969–74; Tynwald Common Market Select Cttee, 1970–74; Mem., Exec. Council Manx Museum and Nat. Trust, 1970–74; Chm. of Directors: Commercial Bank of Wales (IoM) Ltd, 1975–84; Securicor (IoM) Ltd, 1975–83; Trustee, Manx Blind Welfare Soc.; Pres., Isle of Man Badminton Assoc., 1953–72; Hon. County Representative of Royal Air Force Benevolent Assoc., 1948–72. *Address:* Brookdale, 8 Cronkbourne Road, Douglas, Isle of Man. *Club:* Ellan Vannin (IoM).

MOORE, (Georgina) Mary, (Mrs A. R. Moore); Principal, St Hilda's College, Oxford, 1980–90, Hon. Fellow, 1990; *b* 8 April 1930; *yr d* of late Prof. V. H. Galbraith, FBA, and late Georgina Rosalie Galbraith (*née* Cole-Baker); *m* 1963, Antony Ross Moore, *qv*; one *s*. *Educ:* The Mount Sch., York; Lady Margaret Hall, Oxford (BA Modern History 1951; MA; Hon. Fellow, 1981). Joined HM Foreign (later Diplomatic) Service, 1951; posted to Budapest, 1954; UK Permanent Delegn to United Nations, New York, 1956; FO, 1959; First Secretary, 1961; resigned on marriage. Mem., Council for Industry and Higher Educn, 1986–90. A Trustee: British Museum, 1982–92; Rhodes Trust, 1984–; Pilgrim Trust, 1991– (Chm., 1993–). JP Bucks 1977–82. Hon. LLD Mount Holyoke Coll., 1991. Under the name Helena Osborne has written plays for television and radio, including: The Trial of Madame Fahmy, Granada TV, 1980; for BBC Radio 4: An Early Lunch, 1980; An Arranged Marriage, 1982; Testimonies, 1990. *Publications:* (also as Helena Osborne): *novels:* The Arcadian Affair, 1969; Pay-Day, 1972; White Poppy, 1977; The Joker, 1979. *Address:* Touchbridge, Boarstall, Aylesbury, Bucks HP18 9UJ. *T:* Brill (01844) 238247. *Club:* University Women's.

See also J. H. Galbraith.

MOORE, Gordon Charles; Chief Executive, City of Bradford Metropolitan Council, 1974–86, retired; *b* 23 July 1928; *s* of John Edward and Jessie Hamilton Moore; *m* 1956, Ursula Rawle; one *s* two *d*. *Educ:* Uppingham; St Catharine's Coll., Cambridge (MA, LLM). Solicitor. CBIM. Legal Asst, Cambs CC, 1955–56; Asst Solicitor: Worcester CB, 1956–58; Bath CB, 1958–60; Sen. Asst Solicitor: Bath CB, 1960–63; Croydon CB, 1963–65; Asst Town Clerk, Croydon LB, 1965; Dep. Town Clerk, Bradford CB, 1965–68, Town Clerk, 1968–74. FRSA. Hon. DLitt Bradford, 1986. Silver Jubilee Medal, 1977. *Recreations:* music, railways, supporting Yorkshire County Cricket. *Address:* 22 Fern Hill Road, Shipley, W Yorks BD18 4SL. *T:* Bradford (01274) 585606.

MOORE, Sir Harry, (Henry Roderick), Kt 1978; CBE 1971; *b* 19 Aug. 1915; *er s* of late Roderick Edward Moore; *m* 1944, Beatrice Margaret, *d* of late Major J. W. Seigne; one *s* one *d*. *Educ:* Malvern Coll.; Pembroke Coll., Cambridge. Qualified as mem. of Institute of Chartered Accountants, 1939. Served War of 1939–45: North Africa, Italy, Europe; 2nd Lt Royal Fusiliers, 1939; Lt-Col, 1944. Director: Hill Samuel Group Ltd, 1949–80; Estates House Investment Trust Ltd, 1975–76; Chairman: Associated Engineering Ltd, 1955–75; Staveley Industries, 1970–79; Molins plc, 1978–86; Vice-Chm., Philip Hill Investment Trust plc, 1949–86. Chm., Bd of Governors, The London Hospital, 1960–74; Mem. Council, British Heart Foundn; Dep. Chm., Adv. Panel on Institutional Finance in New Towns, 1970–81; Chm., North East Thames RHA, 1974–84. Trustee, Countryside Foundn, 1986–. High Sheriff of Bucks, 1966. *Address:* 70 Chesterfield House, Chesterfield Gardens, W1Y 5TD. *T:* 0171–491 0666. *Clubs:* White's, Pratt's; Leander; Rand (Johannesburg).

MOORE, Sir Henry Roderick; *see* Moore, Sir Harry.

MOORE, Rt. Rev. Henry Wylie; General Secretary, Church Missionary Society, 1986–90; *b* 2 Nov. 1923; *m* 1951, Betty Rose Basnett; two *s* three *d*. *Educ:* Univ. of Liverpool (BCom 1950); Wycliffe Hall, Oxford. MA (Organization Studies) Leeds, 1972. LMS Railway Clerk, 1940–42. Served War with King's Regt (Liverpool), 1942–43; Rajputana Rifles, 1943–46. Curate: Farnworth, Widnes, 1952–54; Middleton, 1954–56; CMS, Khuzistan, 1956–59; Rector: St Margaret, Burnage, 1960–63; Middleton, 1963–74; Home Sec. and later Executive Sec., CMS, 1974–83; Bishop in Cyprus and the Gulf, 1983–86. *Recreation:* family life. *Address:* Fernhill Cottage, Craven Arms, Shropshire SY7 8HD.

MOORE, James Antony Axel Herring; Executive Director, US-UK Educational Commission (Fulbright Commission), since 1993; *b* 26 April 1940; *s* of late Lieut A. D. W. Moore, RN (killed HMS Audacity, 1941) and of Agneta Moore (*née* Wachtmeister); *m* 1964, Marianne Jerlström; two *s* one *d*. *Educ:* Wellington Coll.; Trinity Coll., Cambridge (MA); London Univ. Inst. of Educn (PGCE). Teacher: Norway, 1962–63; Thailand, 1964–67; British Council: Warsaw, 1967–70; Beirut, 1971–73; Ottawa, 1973–75; London, 1975–80; Chinese lang. trng, 1980–81; Director: Manila, 1981–85; Copenhagen, 1985–89; General Manager, Fellowships and Scholarships, 1990–93. *Recreations:* music, ski-ing, walking, sailing. *Address:* Fulbright House, 62 Doughty Street, WC1N 2LS. *T:* 0171–404 6880.

See also Vice-Adm. M. A. C. Moore.

MOORE, Rt Rev. James Edward; *see* Connor, Bishop of.

MOORE, Maj.-Gen. Sir Jeremy; *see* Moore, Maj.-Gen. Sir John J.

MOORE, Hon. Sir John (Cochrane), AC 1986; Kt 1976; President, Australian Conciliation and Arbitration Commission, 1973–85; *b* 5 Nov. 1915; *s* of E. W. Moore and L. G. Moore; *m* 1st, 1946, Julia Fay (*d* 1986), *d* of Brig. G. Drake-Brockman; two *s* two *d*; 2nd, 1988, Freda Beryl. *Educ:* N Sydney Boys' High Sch.; Univ. of Sydney (BA, LLB). Private, AIF, 1940; R of O Hon. Captain 1945. Admitted NSW Bar, 1940; Dept of External Affairs, 1945; 2nd Sec., Aust. Mission to UN, 1946; practice, NSW Bar, 1947–59; Dep. Pres., Commonwealth Conciliation and Arbitration Commn, 1959–72, Actg Pres. 1972–73. Chm. (Pres.), Aust. Council of Nat. Trusts, 1969–82; President: Nat. Trust of Aust. (NSW), 1966–69; Ind. Relations Soc. of NSW, 1972–73; Ind. Relations Soc. of Aust., 1973–74. Pres., NSW Br., Scout Assoc. of Aust., 1978–82. Hon. Vis. Prof., Univ. of NSW, 1987; Hon. Res. Associate, Univ. of Sydney, 1987. *Recreations:* swimming, reading. *Address:* 117 The Grange, McAuley Place, Waitara, NSW 2077, Australia. *T:* 4898961.

MOORE, John David; Headmaster, St Dunstan's College, Catford, since 1993; *b* 16 Feb. 1943; *s* of John and Hilda Moore; *m* 1966, Ann Medora; one *s* one *d*. *Educ:* St John's Coll., Cambridge (BA Classics 1965; MA 1969); CertEd Cambridge Univ., 1966. Classics Master, Judd Sch., Tonbridge, 1966–69; trainee commodity trader, Gill and Duffus Ltd, 1969–70; English Master, Skinners' Sch., Tunbridge Wells, 1970–74; Head of General Studies and English Master, King's Sch., Macclesfield, Ches., 1974–80; Dep. Headmaster, Carre's Grammar Sch., Sleaford, Lincs, 1981–86; Headmaster, Ilford County High Sch. for Boys, London Borough of Redbridge, 1986–93. *Recreations:* cricket, walking, theatre, music. *Address:* St Dunstan's College, Catford, SE6 4TY. *T:* 0181–690 1274.

MOORE, Captain John Evelyn, RN; Editor: Jane's Fighting Ships, 1972–87; Jane's Naval Review, 1982–87; *b* Sant Ilario, Italy, 1 Nov. 1921; *s* of William John Moore and Evelyn Elizabeth (*née* Hooper); *m* 1st, 1945, Joan Pardoe; one *s* two *d*; 2nd, Barbara (*née* Kerry). *Educ:* Sherborne Sch., Dorset. Served War: entered Royal Navy, 1939; specialised in hydrographic surveying, then submarines, in 1943. Commanded HM Submarines: Totem, Alaric, Tradewind, Tactician, Telemachus. RN Staff course, 1950–51; Comdr, 1957; attached to Turkish Naval Staff, 1958–60; subseq. Plans Div., Admty; 1st Submarine Sqdn, then 7th Submarine Sqdn in comd; Captain, 1967; served as: Chief of Staff, C-in-C Naval Home Command; Capt. DI3 (Navy), Defence Intell. Staff; retired list at own request, 1972. FRGS 1942. Hon. Professor: Aberdeen Univ., 1987–90; St Andrews Univ., 1990–92. *Publications:* Jane's Major Warships, 1973; The Soviet Navy Today, 1975; Submarine Development, 1976; (jtly) Soviet War Machine, 1976; (jtly) Encyclopaedia of World's Warships, 1978; (jtly) World War 3, 1978; Seapower and Politics, 1979; Warships of the Royal Navy, 1979; Warships of the Soviet Navy, 1981; (jtly) Submarine Warfare: today and tomorrow, 1986; Watchers on the Shore, 1994; (ed) The Impact of Polaris, 1995. *Recreations:* gardening, swimming, archaeology. *Address:* Elmhurst, Rickney, Hailsham, Sussex BN27 1SF. *T:* Eastbourne (01323) 763294, 765862. *Club:* Naval.

MOORE, Maj.-Gen. Sir (John) Jeremy, KCB 1982 (CB 1982); OBE (mil.) 1973; MC 1952, Bar 1962; defence consultant; *b* 5 July 1928; *s* of Lt-Col Charles Percival Moore, MC, and Alice Hylda Mary (*née* Bibby); *m* 1966, Veryan Julia Margaret Acworth; one *s* two *d*. *Educ:* Brambletye Sch.; Cheltenham Coll. Joined RM as Probationary 2/Lt, 1947; training until 1950 (HMS Sirius, 1948); Troop subaltern, 40 Commando RM, 1950–53 (MC Malayan Emergency 1952); Housemaster, RM School of Music, 1954; ADC to MGRM Plymouth Gp, 1954–55; Instructor, NCO's Sch., RM, 1955–57; Adjt, 45 Cdo RM, 1957–59; Instr, RMA Sandhurst, 1959–62; Adjt and Company Comdr, 42 Cdo RM, 1962–63 (Bar to MC Brunei Revolt 1962); Australian Staff Coll., 1963–64; GSO2 Operations, HQ 17 Gurkha Div., 1965; Asst Sec., Chiefs of Staff Secretariat, MoD, 1966–68; HMS Bulwark, 1968–69; Officer Comdg, Officers Wing Commando Trng Centre RM, 1969–71; CO 42 Cdo RM, 1972–73 (OBE operational, NI 1973); Comdt RM School of Music (Purveyor of Music to the Royal Navy), 1973–75; RCDS 1976; Comdr 3rd Cdo Bde RM, 1977–79; Maj. Gen. Commando Forces, RM, 1979–82; Comdr, Land Forces, Falkland Islands, May–July 1982; MoD, 1982–83, retired. Col Comdt, RM, 1990–. Hon. Col, Wilts ACF, 1991–. Director-General: Food Manufacturers' Fedn, 1984–85; Food and Drink Fedn, 1984–85. Mem. Council, Cheltenham Coll.; Governor, Knighton House Sch., Blandford. Trustee, Suzy Lamplugh Trust. *Recreations:* music (no performing ability except on a gramophone), painting, sailing, hill walking. *Club:* Edward Bear (RMA Sandhurst).

MOORE, Sir John (Michael), KCVO 1983; CB 1974; DSC 1944, Chairman, Lymington Harbour Commission, since 1993 (Deputy Chairman, 1990–93); Second Crown Estate Commissioner, 1978–83; *b* 2 April 1921; *m* 1986, Jacqueline Cingel, MBE. *Educ:* Whitgift Middle Sch.; Selwyn Coll., Cambridge. Royal Navy, 1940–46. Royal Humane Society Bronze Medal, 1942. Ministry of Transport, 1946; Joint Principal Private Sec. to Minister (Rt Hon. Harold (later Lord) Watkinson), 1956–59; Asst Sec., 1959; Under-Sec. (Principal Estabt Officer), 1966; Under-Sec., DoE, 1970–72; Dep. Sec., CSD, 1972–78. *Recreations:* sailing, walking hills and mountains. *Address:* 38 Daniells Walk, Lymington, Hants SO41 3PN. *T:* Lymington (01590) 679963. *Club:* Royal Lymington Yacht.

MOORE, Dr John Michael; JP; Headmaster, The King's School, Worcester, since 1983; *b* 12 Dec. 1935; *s* of late Roy Moore, CBE; *m* 1960, Jill Mary Maycock; one *s*. *Educ:* Rugby Sch.; Clare Coll., Cambridge (John Stewart of Rannoch Scholar, 1956; George Charles Winter Warr Scholar, 1957; 1st Cl. Hons Classical Tripos; MA; PhD 1960). Asst Master: Winchester Coll., 1960–64; Radley Coll., 1964–83; Jun. Fellow, Center for Hellenic Studies, Washington, DC, 1970–71. Hon. Fellow, Inst. for Advanced Res. in the Humanities, Birmingham Univ., 1986. FRSA 1994. JP Worcester City, 1986. Silver Jubilee Medal, 1977. *Publications:* The Manuscript Tradition of Polybius, 1965; (ed with P. A. Brunt) Res Gestae Divi Augusti, 1967, repr. with corrections 1973; (with J. J. Evans) Variorum, 1969; Timecharts, 1969; Aristotle and Xenophon on Democracy and Oligarchy, 1975, 2nd edn 1983; articles and reviews in Gnomon, Jl Soc. for Promotion of Hellenic Studies, Classical Qly, Greek, Roman and Byzantine Studies. *Recreations:* painting, gardening, travel. *Address:* 9 College Green, Worcester WR1 2LH.

MOORE, John Royston, CBE 1983; BSc, CChem, FRSC; Chairman, Bradford Health Authority, 1982–88; *b* 2 May 1921; *s* of late Henry Roland and Jane Elizabeth Moore; *m* 1947, Dorothy Mackay Hick, *d* of late Charles and Edith Mackay Hick; two *s*. *Educ:* Manchester Central Grammar Sch.; Univ. of Manchester (BSc Hons). War service, research and manufacture of explosives. Lecturer in schools and college, Manchester; Principal, Bradford Technical Coll., 1959–75; Sen. Vice Principal and Dir of Planning and Resources, Bradford Coll., 1975–80, retired. Chm., Wool, Jute and Flax ITB, 1981–83. Leader, Baildon Urban DC, 1965–68, Councillor, West Riding CC, until 1973; West Yorkshire MCC: Member, 1973–86; Leader, 1978–81; Leader of the Opposition, 1981–86. Dir, Yorkshire Enterprise Ltd, 1981–90. President, Yorks Conservative Adv. Cttee on Educn, 1975–89; past Chm., Conservative Nat. Adv. Cttee on Educn. Hon. Mem., and Councillor, City and Guilds of London Inst., 1977–92. Hon. MA Bradford, 1986. *Recreations:* music, history, bridge. *Address:* Bicknor, 33 Station Road, Baildon, Shipley, West Yorkshire BD17 6HS. *T:* Bradford (01274) 581777.

MOORE, Jonathan Guy J.; *see* James-Moore.

MOORE, Julian Keith; Head of Management Development Group, Office of Public Service and Science, Cabinet Office, 1992–93; *b* 18 Aug. 1945; *s* of late George H. D. Moore and Amy (*née* Ashwell); *m* 1970, Susan (*née* Dand); one *s* one *d*. *Educ:* St Paul's School; New College, Oxford (Open Scholar, MA). HM Treasury, 1968; Civil Service Dept, 1968–72; Private Sec. to Minister of State, N Ireland Office, 1972–73; Civil Service Dept, 1973–77; Private Sec. to Lord Privy Seal and Leader of House of Lords, 1977–79; Assistant Secretary: CSD, 1979–82; Home Office, 1982–85; Cabinet Office (MPO), 1985–87; Civil Service Comr, 1987–92; Dir, CSSB, 1987–91; Head, Office of Civil Service Comrs, 1991–92. Mem., Careers Adv. Bd, Univ. of London, 1988–92; UK Mem., Bd of Admin, Europ. Inst. of Public Admin, 1993–. *Publications:* articles and reviews, Times Literary Supplement. *Recreations:* historical cryptography, walking. *Address:* 6 Priory Crescent, Lewes, E Sussex BN7 1HP. *Club:* Athenæum.

MOORE, Prof. Leslie Rowsell, BSc, PhD, DSc, CEng, FIMinE, FGS; Consultant Geologist; Professor of Geology, University of Sheffield, 1949–77, now Emeritus Professor; *b* 23 June 1912; *m* 1946, Margaret Wilson MacRae (*d* 1985); one *s*. *Educ:* Midsomer Norton Grammar Sch.; Bristol Univ. Univ. of Bristol, 1930–37; Lecturer and Senior Lecturer, Cardiff, 1939–46; Research Dir, Univ. of Glasgow, 1946–48; Reader in Geology, Univ. of Bristol, 1948–49. *Publications:* contributions to: Quarterly Journal Geol. Soc., London; Geological Magazine; S Wales Inst. Engineers. *Recreations:* soccer, cricket, golf. *Address:* 39 Packenham Village, Packenham Road, Edgbaston, Birmingham B15 2NE. *T:* 0121–440 1692.

MOORE, Mary; *see* Moore, G. M.

MOORE, Vice Adm. Michael Antony Claës, LVO 1981; Chief of Staff to Commander Allied Naval Forces Southern Europe, since 1994; *b* 6 Jan. 1942; *s* of Lieut A. D. W. Moore, RN (killed HMS Audacity, 1941) and of Agneta Moore (*née* Wachtmeister); *m* 1969, Penelope Jane, JP, *d* of Rear-Adm. F. C. W. Lawson, *qv*; one *s* three *d*. *Educ:* Wellington Coll.; RNC Dartmouth. Swedish Naval Interpreter. Joined RN, 1960; served HM Ships Gurkha, Britannia and Ashton, 1963–67; Flag Lieut to Comdr FEF, Singapore, 1967–68; i/c HMS Beachampton, 1969; qualified as Navigator, 1970; HM Ships Tenby, Brighton, Plymouth and Tartar (i/c), 1970–77; Naval Ops, MoD, 1977–79; HMY Britannia, 1979–81; Captain, 1981; Naval Asst to Chief of Fleet Support, MoD, 1981–82; i/c HMS Andromeda, and Capt. 8th Frigate Sqn, 1983–84; i/c Ops, Northwood MHQ, 1985–87; Dir, Naval Warfare, MoD, 1988–90; Rear Adm., 1990; Maritime Advr to SACEUR, 1990–93; Vice Adm. 1994. Hon. Mem., Swedish Royal Soc. of Naval Scis, 1992. Younger Brother, Trinity House, 1988. *Recreations:* classical music, organ, piano. *Address:* c/o Naval Secretary, Victory Building, Hill Naval Base, Portsmouth PO1 3LS.
See also J. A. A. H. Moore.

MOORE, Prof. Michael Arthur, DPhil; FRS 1989; Professor of Theoretical Physics, University of Manchester, since 1976; *b* 8 Oct. 1943; *s* of John Moore and Barbara Atkinson; *m* 1967, Susan Eadington; three *s* one *d*. *Educ:* Huddersfield New Coll.; Oriel Coll., Oxford (BA 1964; DPhil 1967). Prize Fellow, Magdalen Coll., Oxford, 1967–71; Res. Associate, Univ. of Illinois, USA, 1967–69; Lectr in Physics, Univ. of Sussex, 1971–76. *Publications:* papers in scientific jls. *Recreation:* tennis. *Address:* The Schuster Laboratory, The University, Manchester M13 9PL.

MOORE, Rt. Hon. Michael Kenneth; PC 1990; MP (Lab) Christchurch North, New Zealand; Leader of the Opposition, 1990–93; *b* 28 Jan. 1949; *m* 1975, Yvonne (*née* Dereany). *Educ:* Dilworth Sch.; Bay of Islands College (only Minister in Labour Govt without a degree). Worked as social worker, builder's labourer, meat freezing worker and printer; MP (Lab) Eden 1972–75 (youngest NZ MP ever elected); MP (Lab) Papanui, later named Christchurch North, 1978–; spokesperson on housing, regional, small town and community development, the environment, tourism, recreation and sport, overseas trade and marketing, external relations and trade, finance; Minister of Foreign Affairs and Trade, 1990; trade missions led incl. Japan, Europe, Soviet Union, Pakistan, Turkey; Prime Minister of NZ, Sept.–Oct. 1990. *Publications:* On Balance, 1980; Beyond Today, 1981; A Pacific Parliament, 1982; The Added Value Economy, 1984; Hard Labour, 1987; Fighting for New Zealand, 1993. *Address:* Parliament Buildings, Wellington, New Zealand.

MOORE, Michael Rodney Newton; Chairman: Tomkins, 1984–95; Quicks Group, since 1993; Linx Printing Technologies, since 1993; London International Group, since 1994; *b* 15 March 1936; *s* of Gen. Sir Rodney Moore, GCVO, KCB, CBE, DSO, PMN and Olive Marion, *d* of Sir Thomas Bilbe Robinson, GBE, KCMG; *m* 1986, Jan, *d* of Paul and Lilian Adorian; one *s*. *Educ:* Eton; Magdalen College, Oxford (MA); Harvard Business Sch. (MBA). Nat. Service Commission, Grenadier Guards, 1957–59, serving in Cyprus, Lebanon (as ski instructor to Lebanese Army), UK. Called to the Bar, Gray's Inn, 1961; practised until 1964; joined Hill Samuel & Co., 1966 (Dir, 1970–71); subseq. Chm./Dir, various UK, USA & Swedish cos. Dir, Clerical, Medical & General Life Assce Soc., 1993–. A Dir, Which?, 1993–. Chm., NSPCC, 1988–95. *Recreations:* visiting ruins, opera, tennis, reading. *Address:* (office) 32 Lower Belgrave Street, SW1W 0LN. *Clubs:* Pratt's, Boodle's, Lansdowne.

MOORE, Michael S.; *see* Stuart-Moore

MOORE, Noel Ernest Ackroyd; Under-Secretary, Management and Personnel Office (formerly Civil Service Department), 1975–86, and Principal of Civil Service College, 1981–86, retired; Official Side Member, Civil Service Appeal Board, since 1987; *b* 25 Nov. 1928; *s* of late Rowland H. Moore and Hilda Moore (*née* Ackroyd); *m* 1954, Mary Elizabeth Thorpe; two *s*. *Educ:* Penistone Grammar Sch., Yorks; Gonville and Caius Coll., Cambridge (MA; Major Scholar; Half-Blue for chess). Asst Principal, Post Office, 1952; Asst Private Sec. to Postmaster General, 1955–56; Private Sec. to Asst PMG, 1956–57; Principal, 1957; Sec., Cttee of Inquiry on Decimal Currency, 1961–63; Treasury, 1966; Asst Sec., 1967; Sec., Decimal Currency Bd, 1966–72; Civil Service Dept, 1972. Mem., Barking and Havering FHSA, 1992–. FIPM 1985; FITD 1985. *Publication:* The Decimalisation of Britain's Currency (HMSO), 1973. *Recreations:* wide reading, crosswords, pricing donated books for the local Oxfam shop. *Address:* 30 Spurgate, Hutton, Brentwood, Essex CM13 2LA.

MOORE, (Sir) Norman Winfrid (3rd Bt *cr* 1919; has established his claim but does not use the title); Senior Principal Scientific Officer, Nature Conservancy Council, 1965–83 (Principal Scientific Officer, 1958–65); Visiting Professor of Environmental Studies, Wye College, University of London, 1979–83; *b* 24 Feb. 1923; *s* of Sir Alan Hilary Moore, 2nd Bt; *S* father 1959; *m* 1950, Janet, *o d* of late Mrs Phyllis Singer; one *s* two *d*. *Educ:* Eton; Trinity Coll., Cambridge (MA); Univ. of Bristol (PhD). Served War, 1942–45, Germany and Holland (wounded, POW). *Publication:* The Bird of Time, 1987. *Heir:* *s* Peter Alan Cutlack Moore [*b* 21 Sept. 1951; *m* 1989, Pamela Edwards. *Educ:* Eton; Trinity Coll., Cambridge (MA); DPhil Oxon]. *Address:* The Farm House, Swavesey, Cambridge CB4 5RA.

MOORE, Patrick Alfred Caldwell-, CBE 1988 (OBE 1968); free-lance author since 1968; *b* 4 March 1923; *s* of late Capt. Charles Caldwell-Moore, MC, and of Mrs Gertrude Lilian Moore. *Educ:* privately (due to illness). Served with RAF, 1940–45: Navigator, Bomber Command. Concerned in running of a school, 1945–52; free-lance author, 1952–65; Dir of Armagh Planetarium, 1965–68. TV Series, BBC, The Sky at Night, 1957–; radio broadcaster. Composed and performed in Perseus and Andromeda (opera), 1975, and Theseus, 1982. Pres., British Astronomical Assoc., 1982–84. Honorary Member: Astronomic-Geodetic Soc. of USSR, 1971; Royal Astronomical Soc. of New Zealand, 1983, Royal Astronomical Soc. of Canada, 1994. Editor, Year Book of Astronomy, 1962–. Lorimer Gold Medal, 1962; Goodacre Gold Medal, 1968; Arturo Gold Medal (Italian Astronomical Socs), 1969; Jackson-Gwilt Medal, RAS, 1977; Roberts-Klumpke Medal, Astronom. Soc. of Pacific, 1979. Fellow, QMW. Hon. DSc: Lancaster, 1974; Hatfield Polytechnic, 1989; Birmingham, 1990. *Publications:* More than 60 books, mainly astronomical, including The Amateur Astronomer, 1970, rev. edn 1990; Atlas of the Universe, 1970, rev. edn 1995; Guide to the Planets, 1976; Guide to the Moon, 1976; Can You Speak Venusian?, 1977; Guide to the Stars, 1977; Guide to Mars, 1977; (jtly) Out of the Darkness: the Planet Pluto, 1980; The Unfolding Universe, 1982; Travellers in Space and Time, 1983; (jtly) The Return of Halley's Comet, 1984; Stargazing, 1985; Exploring the Night Sky with Binoculars, 1986; The A–Z of Astronomy, 1986; TV Astronomer, 1987; Astronomy for the Under-Tens, 1987; Astronomers' Stars, 1987; (jtly) The Planet Uranus, 1988; The Planet Neptune, 1989; Space Travel for the Under Tens, 1989; Mission to the Planets, 1990; A Passion for Astronomy, 1991; The Earth for Under Tens, 1992; Fireside Astronomy, 1992; The Starry Sky, 1994; The Great Astronomical Revolution, 1994; Stars of the Southern Skies, 1994; Guinness Book of Astronomy, 1995; Teach Yourself Astronomy, 1995. *Recreations:* cricket, chess, tennis, music, xylophone playing (composer of music in records The Ever Ready Band Plays Music by Patrick Moore, 1979 and The Music of Patrick Moore, 1986). *Address:* Farthings, 39 West Street, Selsey, West Sussex PO19 1RP. *Clubs:* Athenæum, Lord's Taverners; Sussex County Cricket.

MOORE, Sir Patrick (William Eisdell), Kt 1992; OBE 1982; FRCS, FRACS; Consultant Surgeon, Honorary Staff, Auckland Hospital Board; *b* 17 March 1918; *m* 1942, Doris McBeth (Beth) Beedie; four *s*. *Educ:* Auckland Grammar Sch.; Otago Univ. (MB ChB). DLO. Medical Officer, 28 Bn, 2 NZEF. Consultant Surgeon, Green Lane Hosp., 1951; Reader in Otolaryngology, Auckland Med. Sch., 1975–84. President: Deafness Res. Foundn, 1963–90; NZ Otolaryngological Soc., 1968–70; NZ Hunts Assoc., 1984–89. *Publication:* A Great Run, 1972. *Recreations:* hunting, sketching, writing. *Address:* Binswood, 229 Remuera Road, Auckland 1105, New Zealand. *T:* (9) 5202679.

MOORE, Very Rev. Peter Clement, OBE 1993; Dean of St Albans, 1973–93, now Dean Emeritus; *b* 4 June 1924; *s* of Rev. G. G. Moore and Vera (*née* Mylrea); *m* 1965, Mary Claire (*d* 1993), *o d* of P. A. M. Malcolm and Celia (*née* Oldham); one *s* one *d*. *Educ:* Cheltenham Coll.; Christ Church, Oxford (MA, DPhil); Cuddesdon Coll., Oxford. FSA. Minor Canon of Canterbury Cathedral and Asst Master, Cathedral Choir School, 1947–49; Curate of Bladon with Woodstock, 1949–51; Chaplain, New Coll., Oxford, 1949–51; Vicar of Alfrick with Lulsley, 1952–59; Hurd Librarian to Bishop of Worcester, 1953–62; Vicar of Pershore with Pinvin and Wick, 1959–67; Rural Dean of Pershore, 1965–67; Canon Residentiary of Ely Cathedral, 1967–73; Vice-Dean, 1971–73. Select Preacher, Oxford Univ., 1986–87. Member: Archbishops' Liturgical Commission, 1968–76; General Synod, 1978–85; Governing Body, SPCK. Past Master, Worshipful Co. of Glaziers and Painters of Glass. Mem., Woodard Corp. Trustee, Historic Churches Preservation Trust. OStJ 1987. *Publications:* Tomorrow is Too Late, 1970; Man, Woman and Priesthood, 1978; Footholds in the Faith, 1980; Crown in Glory, 1982; Bishops: but what kind?, 1982; In Vitro Veritas, 1985; The Synod of Westminster, 1985; Sharing the Glory, 1990. *Recreations:* gardening, music, fishing, barrel organs. *Address:* Thruxton House, Thruxton, Hereford HR2 9AX. *T:* Wormbridge (01981) 570376. *Club:* United Oxford & Cambridge University.

MOORE, Prof. Peter Gerald, TD 1963; PhD; FIA; Professor of Statistics, 1965–93, now Professor Emeritus, and Principal, 1984–89, London Business School (Hon. Fellow, 1993); *b* Richmond, Surrey, 5 April 1928; *s* of Leonard Moore and late Ruby Moore; *m* 1958, Sonja Enevoldson Thomas, Dulwich; two *s* one *d*. *Educ:* King's College Sch., Wimbledon; University Coll. London (BSc (1st Cl. Hons Statistics), PhD; Rosa Morison Meml Medal 1949; Fellow, 1988). Served with 3rd Regt RHA, 1949–51, TA, 1951–65, Major 1963. Lectr, UCL, 1951–57; Commonwealth Fund (Harkness) Fellow, Princeton, NJ, 1953–54; Asst to Economic Adviser, NCB, 1957–59; Head of Statistical Services, Reed Paper Gp, 1959–65; Dep. Principal, London Business Sch., 1972–84. Director: Shell UK, 1969–72; Copeman Paterson Ltd, 1978–87; Martin Paterson Associates, 1984–88; Elf Petroleum UK plc, 1989–94; Partner, Duncan C. Fraser, 1974–77. Consultant, Pugh-Roberts Associates Inc., US, 1989–94. Gresham Prof. of Rhetoric, 1992–. Member: Review Body on Doctors' and Dentists' Pay, 1971–89; Cttee on 1971 Census Security, 1971–73; UGC, 1979–84 (Vice-Chm., 1980–83); Cons. to Wilson Cttee on Financial Instns, 1977–80. Pres., Royal Statistical Soc., 1989–91 (Mem. Council, 1966–78, 1988–; Hon. Sec., 1968–74; Guy Medal, 1970; Chambers Medal, 1995); Pres., Inst. of Actuaries, 1984–86 (Mem. Council, 1966–90; Vice-Pres., 1973–76); Member: Internat. Stat. Inst., 1972– (Council, 1985–91); Council, Internat. Actuarial Assoc, 1984–87; Industry and Employment Cttee, ESRC, 1983–88; Jarratt Cttee on Univ. Efficiency, 1984–85; Council, Hong Kong Univ. of Science and Technology, 1986–91; Acad. Council, China Europe Management Inst., Beijing, 1986–94; Univ. of London Senate, 1988–92; Council, UCL, 1989–; Court, Cranfield Inst. of Technology, 1989–; Court, City Univ., 1990–; Chm., Council of Univ. Management Schs, 1974–76; a Governor: London Business Sch., 1968–89; NIESR, 1985–; Sevenoaks Sch., 1984–90. Mem., Court of Assts, 1987–, Master, 1994–95, Tallow Chandlers' Co. CIMgt (CBIM 1986). Hon. DSc Heriot-Watt, 1985. J. D. Scaife Medal, Instn of Prodn Engrs, 1964. *Publications include:* Principles of Statistical Techniques, 1958, 2nd edn 1969; (with D. E. Edwards) Standard Statistical Calculations, 1965; Statistics and the Manager, 1966; Basic Operational Research, 1968, 3rd edn 1986; Risk and Business Decisions, 1972; (jtly) Case Studies in Decision Analysis, 1975; (with H. Thomas) Anatomy of Decisions, 1976, 2nd rev. edn 1988; Reason by Numbers, 1980; The Business of Risk, 1983; articles in professional jls. *Recreations:* golf, opera, walking, travel (particularly by train). *Address:* London Business School, Sussex Place, Regent's Park, NW1 4SA. *T:* 0171–262 5050; 3 Chartway, Sevenoaks, Kent TN13 3RU. *T:* Sevenoaks (01732) 451936. *Clubs:* Athenæum; Knole Park Golf.

MOORE, Philip John, BMus; FRCO; Organist and Master of the Music, York Minster, since 1983; *b* 30 Sept. 1943; *s* of Cecil and Marjorie Moore; one *s* two *d*. *Educ:* Maidstone Grammar Sch.; Royal Coll. of Music (ARCM, GRSM). BMus Dunelm; FRCO 1965. Asst Music Master, Eton Coll., 1965–68; Asst Organist, Canterbury Cathedral, 1968–74; Organist and Master of the Choristers, Guildford Cathedral, 1974–83. *Publications:* anthems, services, cantatas, organ music, song cycles, chamber music. *Recreations:* flying kites, collecting old fountain pens, collecting Imari, malt whisky. *Address:* 1 Minster Court, York YO1 2JJ.

MOORE, Richard Valentine, GC 1940; CBE 1963; BSc (Eng); FIMechE; FIEE; retired; Managing Director (Reactor Group), UK Atomic Energy Authority, 1961–76; Member, 1971–76; *b* 14 Feb. 1916; *s* of Randall and Ellen Moore; *m* 1944, Ruby Edith Fair; three *s*. *Educ:* Strand Sch., London; London Univ. County of London Electric Supply Co., 1936–39. RNVR, 1939–46; HMS Effingham, 1939–40; HMS President, 1940–41; HMS Dido, 1942–44; British Admiralty Delegn, Washington, DC, 1944–46; Lieut-Comdr 1944. AERE Harwell, 1946–53; Dept of Atomic Energy, Risley, 1953; Design and Construction of Calder Hall, 1953–57; Chief Design Engineer, 1955; UKAEA, 1955; Dir of Reactor Design, 1958–61. Faraday Lectr, 1966. Hon. DTech Bradford, 1970. *Publications:* various papers to technical institutions. *Recreations:* golf, gardening. *Address:* Culleen House, Cann Lane, Appleton, Ches WA4 5NQ. *T:* Warrington (01925) 61023. *Club:* Naval.

MOORE, Robert, CBE 1973; Commissioner for Local Administration in Scotland, 1975–78; *b* 2 Nov. 1915; *m* 1940, Jean Laird Dick; two *s*. *Educ:* Dalziel High Sch., Motherwell; Glasgow Univ. (BL). Admitted solicitor, 1939. Town Clerk, Port Glasgow, 1943–48; Secretary, Eastern Regional Hosp. Bd, 1948–60; Principal Officer: Scottish Hosp. Administrative Staffs Cttee, 1960–74; Manpower Div., Scottish Health Service, 1974–75. Lectr in Administrative Law, St Andrews Univ., 1960–65; External Examr in Administrative Law, Glasgow Univ., 1967–71. Mem., Scottish Cttee, Council on Tribunals, 1964–82. *Address:* 20/35 Craiglea Place, Edinburgh EH10 5QD. *T:* 0131–447 5493.

MOORE, Robert Jeffery; His Honour Judge Moore; a Circuit Judge, since 1995; *b* 1947; *s* of Jeffery Moore and Doreen Moore; *m* 1979, Susan Elaine Hatcliffe; two *s*. *Educ:* Loughborough Grammar Sch.; Univ. of Manchester (LLB Hons 1968). Called to the Bar, Gray's Inn, 1970; practised on North Eastern Circuit, 1971–95. *Recreations:* my wife, my sons' sporting skills, Leicester Tigers Rugby club, tennis, Italian food. *Address:* The Crown Court, 50 West Bar, Sheffield S3 9PH. *Club:* Sheffield.

MOORE, Roger; actor; *b* London, 14 Oct. 1927; *m* 1st, Doorn van Steyn (marr. diss. 1953); 2nd, 1953, Dorothy Squires (marr. diss. 1969); 3rd, Luisa Mattioli; two *s* one *d*. *Educ:* RADA. Special Ambassador for UNICEF, 1991–. Golden Globe World Film Favourite Award, 1980. Stage début, Androcles and the Lion. *TV series include:* Ivanhoe, 1958; The Alaskans, 1960–61; Maverick, 1961; The Saint, 1962–69 (dir some episodes); The Persuaders, 1972–73; The Man Who Woundn't Die, 1992; The Quest, 1995; *films include:* The Last Time I Saw Paris, 1954; The Interrupted Melody, 1955; The King's Thief, 1955; Diane, 1956; The Miracle, 1959; Rachel Cade, 1961; Gold of the Seven Saints, 1961; The Rape of the Sabine Women, 1961; No Man's Land, 1961; Crossplot, 1969; The Man Who Haunted Himself, 1970; Live and Let Die, 1973; The Man With The Golden Gun, 1974; Gold, 1974; That Lucky Touch, 1975; Street People, 1975; Shout at the Devil, 1975; Sherlock Holmes in New York, 1976; The Spy Who Loved Me, 1976; The Wild Geese, 1977; Escape to Athena, 1978; Moonraker, 1978; North Sea Hijack, 1979; The Sea Wolves, 1980; Sunday Lovers, 1980; For Your Eyes Only, 1980; The Cannonball Run, 1981; Octopussy, 1983; The Naked Face, 1983; A View to a Kill, 1985; Bed and Breakfast, 1989; Bullseye!, 1989; Fire, Ice and Dynamite, 1990. *Publication:* James Bond Diary, 1973. *Address:* c/o ICM Ltd, 76 Oxford Street, W1R 1RB.

MOORE, Prof. Stuart Alfred; Chairman, Central Manchester Healthcare NHS Trust, since 1992; Robert Ottley Professor of Quantitive Studies, University of Manchester, since 1992; *b* 9 Oct. 1939; *s* of Alfred Moore and Kathleen (*née* Dodd); *m* 1966, Diana Mary Connery; two *s* one *d*. *Educ:* Stockport Sch.; Manchester Univ. (MA Econs 1967). University of Manchester: Computer Asst, 1960–64; Lectr, then Sen. Lectr in Econ. Stats, 1964–92; Dean, Fac. of Econ. and Social Studies, 1980–83; Pro Vice-Chancellor, 1985–90; Dep. Vice-Chancellor, 1990–; Actg Vice-Chancellor, 1990–92. *Publications:* various papers in learned jls. *Recreations:* gardening, photography, travel, thrillers, films. *Address:* The University, Manchester M13 9PL. *T:* 0161–275 7400; Central Manchester Healthcare NHS Trust, Cobbett House, Oxford Road, Manchester M13 9WL. *T:* 0161–276 4841; 2 Carisbrooke Avenue, Hazel Grove, Stockport SK7 5PL.

MOORE, Terence, CBE 1993; Group Managing Director and Chief Executive Officer, Conoco Ltd, since 1987; *b* 24 Dec. 1931; *s* of Arthur Doncaster Moore and Dorothy Irene Gladys (*née* Godwin); *m* 1955, Tessa Catherine (*née* Wynne); two *s* one *d*. *Educ:* Strand Sch., London. BScEcon, Univ. of London; ACII 1958; AICS 1959. Shell Internat. Petroleum Co., 1948–64; Locana Corp. Ltd (investment bank), 1964–65; Conoco Ltd, 1965–: Dep. Man. Dir, Marketing and Operations, 1975; Man. Dir, Supply and Trading, Europe, 1979. Gov., Greenwich Theatre, 1991– (Vice Chm. Govs, 1992 93). FRSA. *Publications:* articles in industry jls. *Recreations:* music (Very catholic), reading (mainly biography, politics, poetry), jogging, badminton, family and friends. *Address:* 4 Oaklands Road, Groombridge, near Tunbridge Wells, Kent TN3 9SB. *T:* Langton Green (01892) 864568; 5 Gun Wharf, 130 Wapping High Street, E1 9NH. *T:* 0171–481 0853.

MOORE, Thomas William, JP; Chairman (since inception) of Trojan Metals Ltd, Carseview Holdings Ltd, Dundee Timber Market Ltd, Inverlaw Property Co. Ltd; *b* 9 Aug. 1925; Scottish; *m* 1945, Mary Kathleen Thompson; four *s* two *d*. *Educ:* Stobswell Secondary Sch.; Leicester Coll. of Art and Technology. MBIM. Contested (Lab), Perth and East Perthshire, 1959. Lord Provost of Dundee, and Lord Lieutenant of County of City of Dundee, 1973–75; Chairman: Tay Road Bridge Jt Cttee, 1973; Tayside Steering Cttee. FInstD. *Recreations:* golf, reading. *Address:* 85 Blackness Avenue, Dundee DD2 1JN. *Club:* Royal Automobile.

MOORE, Sir William (Roger Clotworthy), 3rd Bt *cr* 1932; TD 1962; DL; *b* 17 May 1927; *s* of Sir William Samson Moore, 2nd Bt, and Ethel Cockburn Gordon (*d* 1973); *S* father, 1978; *m* 1954, Gillian, *d* of John Brown, Co. Antrim; one *s* one *d*. *Educ:* Marlborough; RMC, Sandhurst. Lieut Royal Inniskilling Fusiliers, 1945; Major North Irish Horse, 1956. High Sheriff, Co. Antrim, 1964; DL Co. Antrim, 1990. *Heir:* *s* Richard William Moore [*b* 8 May 1955. *Educ:* Portora; RMA. Lieut Royal Scots, 1974]. *Address:* Moore Lodge, Ballymoney, Co. Antrim, Northern Ireland. *Club:* Army and Navy.

MOORE-BICK, Hon. Sir Martin James, Kt 1995; **Hon. Mr Justice Moore-Bick;** a Judge of the High Court of Justice, Queen's Bench Division, since 1995; *b* 6 Dec. 1946; *s* of John Ninian Moore-Bick and Kathleen Margaret Moore-Bick (*née* Beall); *m* 1974, Tessa Penelope Gee; two *s* two *d*. *Educ:* The Skinners' Sch., Tunbridge Wells; Christ's Coll., Cambridge (MA). Called to the Bar, Inner Temple, 1969, Bencher, 1992; QC 1986; a Recorder, 1990–95. *Recreations:* early music, gardening, reading. *Address:* Royal Courts of Justice, Strand, WC2A 2LL.

MOORE-BRABAZON, family name of **Baron Brabazon of Tara.**

MOORER, Admiral Thomas Hinman; Defense Distinguished Service Medals, 1973 and 1974; Navy DSM 1965, 1967, 1968, 1970; Army DSM 1974; Air Force DSM 1974; Silver Star 1942; Legion of Merit, 1945; DFC 1942; Purple Heart, 1942; Presidential Unit Citation, 1942; Board Member: Blount Inc.; Fairchild Industries; USLICO; CACI; *b* Mount Willing, Alabama, 9 Feb. 1912; *s* of Dr R. R. Moorer and Hulda Hill Hinson, Eufaula, Ala; *m* 1935, Carrie Ellen Foy Moorer; three *s* one *d*. *Educ:* Cloverdale High Sch., Montgomery, Ala; USN Acad.; Naval Aviation Trg Sch.; Naval War Coll. First ship, 1933; serving at Pearl Harbour in Fleet Air Wing, Dec. 1941; Pacific and East Indies areas, 1942; Mining Observer, C-in-C, US Fleet in UK, 1943; Strategic Bombing Survey in Japan, 1945; Naval Aide to Asst Sec. of Navy (Air), 1956; CO, USS Salisbury Sound, 1957; Special Asst to CNO, 1959; Comdr, Carrier Div. Six, 1960; Dir, Long Range Objectives Group, CNO, 1962; Comdr Seventh Fleet, 1964; C-in-C: US Pacific Fleet, 1965; Atlantic and Atlantic Fleet, and Supreme Allied Commander, Atlantic, 1965–67; Chief of Naval Operations, 1967–70; Chm., Jt Chiefs of Staff, USA, 1970–74, retired US Navy 1974. Captain 1952; Rear-Adm. 1958; Vice-Adm. 1962; Adm. 1964. Enshrined in Nat. Aviation Hall of Fame, 1987; introduced into Naval Aviation Hall of Honor, 1988. Gold Medal, Nat. Football Hall of Fame, 1990. Holds seventeen foreign decorations. Hon. LLD Auburn, 1968; Hon. DH Samford, 1970; Hon. Dr Mil. Science, The Citadel, 1983. *Recreations:* golfing, fishing, hunting. *Address:* 6901 Lupine Lane, McLean, VA 22101–1580, USA. *Clubs:* Brook (New York); International, Army-Navy Town (Washington, DC); US Naval Inst. (Annapolis, Md); Chevy Chase (Chevy Chase, Md).

MOORES, Mrs Brian; *see* Moores, Yvonne.

MOORES, Hon. Frank Duff; formerly Chairman, Executive Committee, Government Consultants International; Chairman and Chief Executive Officer, SSF (Holdings) Inc.; Premier of the Province of Newfoundland, 1972–79; *b* 18 Feb. 1933; *s* of Silas Wilmot Moores and Dorothy Duff Moores; *m* 1982, Beth Champion; two *s* six *d* by former marriages. *Educ:* United Church Academy, Carbonear; St Andrew's Coll., Aurora, Ont. MP, Canada, for Bonavista-Trinity-Conception, 1968–71; MHA for Humber W, Newfoundland, 1971; Pres., Progressive Conservative Party in Canada, 1969; Leader, Progressive Conservative Party, Newfoundland, 1970–79. Mem., Royal Commn on Economic Prospects of Newfoundland. Director: Council for Canadian Unity; Atlantic Salmon Fedn (Canada). Gov., Olympia Trust. Is a Freemason. Hon. LLD Meml Univ. of Newfoundland, 1975. *Recreations:* tennis, salmon fishing, golf. *Address:* Westmount, Quebec, Canada. *Clubs:* Rideau (Ottawa); Forest and Stream (Montreal); Mid Ocean (Bermuda); Hobe Sound Golf (Florida).

MOORES, John, CBE 1993; DL; Director, The Littlewoods Organisation, since 1950; *b* 22 Nov. 1928; *s* of Sir John Moores, CBE; *m* 1st, 1949, Helen Sheila Moore; three *s* one *d*; 2nd, 1963, Jane Stavely-Dick; four *s* one *d*. *Educ:* Eton Coll.; Syracuse Univ., USA. Joined The Littlewoods Organisation, 1946, Dep. Chm., 1968–71; Chm., Littlewoods Equal Opportunities, 1963–; Chm., Madaillon Mode GmbH, 1968–71. Chancellor, Liverpool John Moores Univ., 1994– (Sen. Pro-Chancellor, and Chm. Bd of Govs, 1992–94). DL Merseyside, 1993. Hon. Freeman, City of Liverpool, 1994. *Recreations:* languages, history, politics, animal breeding. *Address:* The Littlewoods Organisation, 100 Old Hall Street, Liverpool L70 1AB. *T:* 0151–235 2222. *Club:* Boodle's.

See also P. Moores.

MOORES, Peter, CBE 1991; DL; Director, The Littlewoods Organisation, 1965–93 (Chairman, 1977–80); *b* 9 April 1932; *s* of Sir John Moores, CBE; *m* 1960, Luciana Pinto (marr. diss. 1984); one *s* one *d*. *Educ:* Eton; Christ Church, Oxford; Wiener Akademie der Musik und darstellenden Kunst. Worked in opera at Glyndebourne and Vienna State Opera; sponsor of complete recordings: in English translation: Der Ring des Nibelungen, La Traviata, Otello, Rigoletto, Mary Stuart and Julius Caesar by ENO; Parsifal, Destiny (Osud), Eugene Onegin and The Barber of Seville by WNO; Troilus and Cressida, The Cunning Little Vixen and Peter Grimes, Royal Opera; in original language: Maria Padilla, Emilia di Liverpool, L'Assedio di Calais, Il Crociato in Egitto, Medea in Corinto and Orazi e Curiazi with Opera Rara. Founded Peter Moores Foundn, 1964; Director: Singer & Friedlander, 1978–92; Scottish Opera, 1988–92. Trustee, Tate Gall., 1978–85; Governor of the BBC, 1981–83. DL Lancs, 1992. Hon. RNCM, 1985. Hon. MA Christ Church, 1975. Gold Medal of the Italian Republic, 1974. *Recreations:* opera, shooting, fishing. *Address:* Parbold Hall, Parbold, near Wigan, Lancs WN8 7TG. *Club:* Boodle's.

See also John Moores.

MOORES, Yvonne, (Mrs Brian Moores); Chief Nursing Officer and Director of Nursing, Department of Health, since 1992; *b* 14 June 1941; *d* of Tom Abraham Quick and of late Phyllis Quick (*née* Jeremiah); *m* 1st, 1969, Bruce Holmes Ramsden; 2nd, 1975, Brian Moores. *Educ:* Itchen Grammar Sch., Southampton; Royal South Hampshire Hosp. (RGN); Southampton Gen. Hosp. (RM). Ward Sister, Whittington Hosp. and Royal Hampshire County Hosp., 1964–70; Principal Nursing Officer: N London HMC, 1971–72; W Manchester, 1973–74; Dist Nursing Officer, N Manchester, 1974–76; Area Nursing Officer, Manchester AHA, 1976–81; Chief Nursing Officer: Welsh Office, 1982–88; Scottish Office, Home and Health Dept, 1988–92. Vice-Chm., NHS Supply Council, 1979–82; Pres., Infection Control Nurses Assoc., 1987–90. FRSH. Hon. DSc Portsmouth, 1993. *Recreations:* golf, bridge. *Address:* Richmond House, 79 Whitehall, SW1A 2NS.

MOOREY, Adrian Edward; Director of Corporate and Government Affairs, Cable and Wireless plc, since 1995; *b* 4 May 1946; *s* of Edward Alfred Moorey and Lily Elizabeth Moorey; *m* 1st, 1969, Sandra Ann Jeffrey (marr. diss.); one *s*; 2nd, 1987, Lesley Nicola Hancock. *Educ:* Sir Joseph Williamson's Mathematical Sch., Rochester. Advertising and Marketing Asst, Lonsdale-Hands Orgn, 1964–67; Asst Information Officer, 1967–69, Inf. Officer, 1969–72, Home Office; Press Officer, PM's Office, 1973; Department of Employment: Sen. Press Officer, 1974–75; Chief Press Officer, 1976–81; Head of Inf., 1982–86; Director of Information: DTI, 1987–90; Home Office, 1990–94. *Recreations:* cricket, golf. *Address:* The Pines, 16 Kent Road, East Molesey, Surrey KT8 9JZ. *T:* 0181–979 0096.

MOOREY, (Peter) Roger (Stuart), DPhil; FBA 1977; FSA; Keeper, Department of Antiquities, Ashmolean Museum, Oxford, since 1983; Fellow of Wolfson College, since 1976; *b* 30 May 1937; *s* of late Stuart Moorey and Freda (*née* Harris). *Educ:* Mill Hill Sch.; Corpus Christi Coll., Oxford (MA, DPhil). FSA 1967. Nat. Service, 1956–58, Intelligence Corps. Asst Keeper, 1961–73, Sen. Asst Keeper, 1973–82, Ashmolean Museum, Oxford. Editor of Levant, 1968–86. Pres., British Sch. of Archaeology in Jerusalem, 1990–. *Publications:* Catalogue of the Ancient Persian Bronzes in the Ashmolean Museum, 1971; Ancient Persian Bronzes in the Adam Collection, 1974; Biblical Lands, 1975; Kish Excavations 1923–1933, 1978; Cemeteries of the First Millennium BC at Deve Hüyük, 1980; Excavation in Palestine, 1981; (ed) C. L. Woolley, Ur of the Chaldees, revd edn 1982; (with B. Buchanan) Catalogue of Ancient Near Eastern Seals in the Ashmolean Museum, II, 1984, III, 1988; Materials and Manufacture in Ancient Mesopotamia: the evidence of archaeology and art, 1985; A Century of Biblical Archaeology, 1991; Ancient Mesopotamian Materials and Industries, 1994; museum booklets and articles in learned jls. *Recreations:* travel, walking. *Address:* Ashmolean Museum, Oxford. *T:* Oxford (01865) 278019, 278020.

MOORHOUSE, (Cecil) James (Olaf); Member (C) London South and Surrey East, European Parliament, since 1984 (London South, 1979–84); co-ordinator on human rights for European People's Party and British Conservatives; spokesman on external economic relations, since 1994; *b* 1 Jan. 1924; *s* of late Captain Sidney James Humphrey Moorhouse and Anna Sophie Hedvig de Løvenskiold; *m* 1958, Elizabeth Clive Huxtable, Sydney, Aust.; one *s* one *d*. *Educ:* St Paul's School; King's Coll. and Imperial Coll., Univ. of London. BSc (Eng); DIC (Advanced Aeronautics); CEng. Designer with de Havilland Aircraft Co., 1946–48; Project Engr, BOAC, 1948–53; Technical Advr 1953–68, and Environmental Conservation Advr 1968–72, Shell International Petroleum; Environmental Advr, Shell Group of Companies in UK, 1972–73; Group Environmental Affairs Advr, Rio-Tinto Zinc Corp., 1973–80, Consultant, 1980–84. Dir, Project Development International, 1985–90. Contested (C) St Pancras North, 1966 and 1970. European Parliament: spokesman, 1979–84, co-ordinator, 1987–89, on transport for EDG; spokesman on external economic relations for EDG, 1984–87 and 1989–94; dep. co-ordinator on external economic relations for EPP, 1992–94; Chm., delegn to N Europe and Nordic Council, 1979–84; First Vice-Chm, delegn to EFTA Parliamentarians,

1984–86; Vice-Pres., External Econ. Relations Cttee, 1989–92. *Publications:* (with Anthony Teasdale) Righting the Balance: a new agenda for Euro-Japanese trade, 1987; numerous articles and papers on aviation. *Recreations:* walking, reading, travelling, watching cricket. *Address:* 1 Dean Farrar Street, SW1H 0DY. *Clubs:* Carlton, Royal Automobile.

MOORHOUSE, Geoffrey, FRSL; writer; *b* Bolton, Lancs, 29 Nov. 1931; *s* of William Heald and Gladys Heald (*née* Hoyle, subseq. Moorhouse) and step *s* of Richard Moorhouse; *m* 1st, 1956, Janet Marion Murray; two *s* one *d* (and one *d* decd); 2nd, 1974, Barbara Jane Woodward (marr. diss. 1978); 3rd, 1983, Marilyn Isobel Edwards. *Educ:* Bury Grammar School. Nat. Service, Royal Navy (Coder), 1950–52; editorial staff: Bolton Evening News, 1952–54; Grey River Argus (NZ), Auckland Star (NZ), Christchurch Star-Sun (NZ), 1954–56; News Chronicle, 1957; (Manchester) Guardian, 1958–70 (Chief Features Writer, 1963–70). FRGS 1972; FRSL 1982. *Publications:* in numerous editions and translations: The Other England, 1964; The Press, 1964; Against All Reason, 1969; Calcutta, 1971; The Missionaries, 1973; The Fearful Void, 1974; The Diplomats, 1977; The Boat and The Town, 1979; The Best-Loved Game, 1979 (Cricket Soc. Award); India Britannica, 1983; Lord's, 1983; To the Frontier, 1984 (Thomas Cook Award, 1984); Imperial City: the rise and rise of New York, 1988; At the George (essays), 1989; Apples in the Snow, 1990; Hell's Foundations: a town, its myths and Gallipoli, 1992; Om: an Indian pilgrimage, 1993; A People's Game: the centenary history of Rugby League football, 1995. *Recreations:* music, hill-walking, looking at buildings, watching cricket and both codes of Rugby football. *Address:* Park House, Gayle, near Hawes, North Yorkshire DL8 3RT. *T:* Wensleydale (01969) 667456. *Club:* Lancashire County Cricket.

MOORHOUSE, James; *see* Moorhouse, C. J. O.

MOORHOUSE, (Kathleen) Tessa; a District Judge (formerly Registrar), Family Division of the High Court of Justice, since 1982; *b* 14 Sept. 1938; *d* of late Charles Elijah Hall, MRCVS and of Helen Barbara Hall; *m* 1959, Rodney Moorhouse. *Educ:* Presentation Convent, Derbyshire; Leeds Univ.; King's Coll., London. Called to the Bar, Inner Temple, 1971. Asst, Jardine's Bookshop, Manchester, 1953–56; student, Leeds Univ., 1956–59; teacher of educationally subnormal, 1959–61; student, King's Coll., London, 1961–62; Classifier, Remand Home, 1962–64; Lectr in Law, 1964–71; barrister in practice, 1971–82. *Address:* Somerset House, Strand, WC2R 1LP. *T:* 0171–936 6000; 4 Brick Court, Temple, EC4Y 9AD. *T:* 0171–797 7766.

MOORHOUSE, Peter William; Deputy Chairman, Police Complaints Authority, since 1991; *b* 25 Dec. 1938; *s* of Francis and Dorothy Moorhouse; *m* 1962, Jane Catton; two *s* one *d*. *Educ:* Stonyhurst Coll. Joined Schweppes Group, 1961, Divl Dir, 1980–87; Police Complaints Authy, 1988–. Mem., Local Review Cttee, Parole Bd, 1973–88 (Chm., 1977–79, 1986–88). Gov., Stonyhurst Coll., 1991–94. FRSA. *Recreations:* opera, art, walking, inland boating. *Address:* c/o Midland Bank, 1 High Street, Harpenden, Herts AL5 2RS.

MOORTHY, Arambamoorthy Thedchana; Sri Lanka Foreign Service, retired; private academic research and writing, since 1984; *b* 10 Aug. 1928; *s* of late Mr Arambamoorthy and Mrs Nesamma Arambamoorthy; *m* 1959, Suseela T. Moorthy, *d* of Justice P. Sri Skanda Rajah; one *s* two *d*. *Educ:* BAEcon Hons (Sri Lanka). Called to Bar, Gray's Inn, 1965. Entered Foreign Service of Sri Lanka, 1953; Second Secretary: Indonesia, 1955–57; China, 1957–59; First Secretary: London, 1961–63; Federal Republic of Germany, 1964–66; Chargé d'Affaires, *ai*, Thailand, and Permanent Representative of Sri Lanka to Economic Commn for Asia and Far East, 1969; Chargé d'Affaires, *ai*, Iraq, 1970; Ambassador in Pakistan, 1978–Dec. 1980, and concurrently, Jan–Dec. 1980, Ambassador to Iran with residence in Islamabad; High Comr in London, 1981–84. *Address:* 19 Caverleigh Way, Worcester Park, Surrey KT4 8DH. *T:* 0181–337 2792.

MOOSONEE, Bishop of, since 1980; **Rt. Rev. Caleb James Lawrence;** *b* 26 May 1941; *s* of James Otis Lawrence and Mildred Viola Burton; *m* 1966, Maureen Patricia Cuddy; one *s* two *d*. *Educ:* Univ. of King's College. BA (Dalhousie Univ.) 1962; BST 1964. Deacon 1963, priest 1965; Missionary at Anglican Mission, Great Whale River, Quebec, 1965–75; Rector of St Edmund's Parish, Great Whale River, 1975–79; Canon of St Jude's Cathedral, Frobisher Bay, Diocese of The Arctic, 1974; Archdeacon of Arctic Quebec, 1975–79; Bishop Coadjutor, Diocese of Moosonee, Jan.–Nov. 1980. Hon. DD, Univ. of King's Coll., Halifax, NS, 1980. *Recreations:* reading, photography. *Address:* The Diocese of Moosonee, Synod Office, Box 841, Schumacher, Ontario P0N 1G0, Canada. *T:* (705)2671129.

MORAES, Dom; Indian poet and author; *b* 1938; *s* of Frank Moraes (Editor of the Indian Express and biographer of Nehru); *m* 1970, Leela Naidu. *Educ:* Jesus Coll., Oxford. Read English, 1956–59. Took up residence in England at age of 16, after world-wide travel and a 2-yr stay in Ceylon. *Publications:* A Beginning (poems), 1957 (Hawthornden Prize, 1958); Gone Away (Travel), 1960; Poems, 1960; John Nobody (poems), 1965; The Brass Serpent (trans. from Hebrew poetry), 1964; Poems 1955–65 (collected poems), 1966; My Son's Father (autobiography), 1968; The People Time Forgot, 1972; The Tempest Within, 1972; A Matter of People, 1974; (ed) Voices for Life (essays), 1975; Mrs Gandhi, 1980; Bombay, 1980; Collected Poems 1957–1987, 1988; Serendip (poems), 1990; Never At Home (autobiog.), 1994. *Address:* 12 Sargent House, Allana Marg, Bombay 39, India.

MORAHAN, Christopher Thomas; television, film and theatre director; *b* 9 July 1929; *s* of Thomas Hugo Morahan and Nancy Charlotte Morahan (*née* Barker); *m* 1st, 1954, Joan (*née* Murray) (decd); two *s* (one *d* decd); 2nd, 1973, Anna (*née* Wilkinson, acting name Anna Carteret); two *d*. *Educ:* Highgate; Old Vic Theatre School. Directing for ATV, 1957–61; freelance director in TV for BBC and ITV, 1961–71; Head of Plays, BBC TV, 1972–76; National Theatre, 1977–88 (Dep. to Director, 1979–80); Director, Greenpoint Films, 1983–. *Stage:* Little Murders, RSC, Aldwych, 1967; This Story of Yours, Royal Court, 1968; Flint, Criterion, 1970; The Caretaker, Mermaid, 1972; Melon, Th. Royal, Haymarket, 1987; Major Barbara, Chichester Fest., 1988; for National Theatre: State of Revolution, Brand, Strife, The Philanderer, Richard III, The Wild Duck, Sisterly Feelings, Man and Superman, Wild Honey (London Standard, Olivier, British Theatre Assoc. and Plays and Players Awards for Best Dir of the Year, 1984), The Devil's Disciple; *films:* Clockwise, 1986; Paper Mask, 1990; *television: films:* The Gorge, 1967; In the Secret State, 1985; After Pilkington, 1987 (Special Jury Prize, San Francisco Film Fest., 1987, Prix Italia, 1987); Troubles, 1988; The Heat of the Day, 1989; Old Flames, 1990; Can You Hear Me Thinking?, 1990; Common Pursuit, 1992; The Bullion Boys, 1993 (Internat. Emmy Award, 1994); Summer Day's Dream, 1994; *series:* Emergency Ward 10; The Orwell Trilogy; Talking to a Stranger; Fathers and Families; Jewel in the Crown (Internat. Emmy Award, BAFTA Best Series Dir Award, BAFTA Desmond Davis Award, 1984; Peabody Award, 1985; Golden Globe Award, Primetime Emmy Award, 1985); Ashenden, 1991; Unnatural Pursuits, 1992 (Internat. Emmy Award, 1993); Peacock Spring, 1996. Best Play direction award, SFTA, 1969. *Recreations:* photography, bird watching. *Address:* c/o Michael Whitehall Ltd, 125 Gloucester Road, SW7 4TE. *T:* 0171–244 8466. *Club:* Garrick.

MORAN, 2nd Baron *cr* 1943; **Richard John McMoran Wilson,** KCMG 1981 (CMG 1970); *b* 22 Sept. 1924; *er s* of 1st Baron Moran, MC, MD, FRCP, and Dorothy (*d* 1983), MBE, *d* of late Samuel Felix Dufton, DSc; *S* father, 1977; *m* 1948, Shirley Rowntree Harris; two *s* one *d*. *Educ:* Eton; King's Coll., Cambridge. Served War of 1939–45; Ord. Seaman in HMS Belfast, 1943; Sub-Lt RNVR in Motor Torpedo Boats and HM Destroyer Oribi, 1944–45. Foreign Office, 1945; Third Sec., Ankara, 1948; Tel-Aviv, 1950; Second Sec., Rio de Janeiro, 1953; First Sec., FO, 1956; Washington, 1959; FO 1961; Counsellor, British Embassy in S Africa, 1965; Head of W African Dept, FCO, 1968–73, concurrently Ambassador to Chad (non-resident), 1970–73; Ambassador to Hungary, 1973–76, to Portugal, 1976–81; High Comr in Canada, 1981–84. Cross Bencher, H of L, 1984–; Mem., Envmt sub cttee, 1986–91, Agric. sub cttee, 1991–, sub cttee on the 1996 IGC, 1995–, EC Cttee; Chm., All Party Parly Conservation Gp, 1992– (Vice-Chm., 1989–92). Vice-Chm., Atlantic Salmon Trust, 1988–95 (Mem. Management Cttee, 1984–); Chm., Fisheries Adv. Cttee for Welsh Region, Nat. Rivers Authy, 1989–94; Mem., Regl Fisheries Adv. Cttee, Welsh Water Authority, 1987–89; Pres., Welsh Salmon and Trout Angling Assoc., 1988–. Chm., Wildlife and Countryside Link, 1992–95; Pres., Radnorshire Wildlife Trust, 1994–; Mem., Council, RSPB, 1989–94. Grand Cross, Order of the Infante (Portugal), 1978. *Publications:* (as John Wilson): C. B.: a life of Sir Henry Campbell-Bannerman, 1973 (Whitbread Award, 1973); Fairfax, 1985. *Recreations:* fishing, fly-tying, bird-watching. *Heir:* *s* Hon. James McMoran Wilson [*b* 6 Aug. 1952; *m* 1980, Hon. Jane Hepburne-Scott, *y d* of Lord Polwarth, *qv*; two *s*]. *Address:* House of Lords, SW1A 0PW. *Club:* Flyfishers' (Pres., 1987–88).

See also Baron Mountevans, Hon. G. H. Wilson.

MORAN, Andrew Gerard; QC 1994; *b* 19 Oct. 1953; *s* of Francis Michael Moran and Winifrede Moran; *m* 1977, Carole Jane Sullivan; five *s* one *d*. *Educ:* West Park Grammar Sch., St Helens, Lancs; Britannia Royal Naval Coll., Dartmouth; Balliol Coll., Oxford (BA Law). Called to Bar, Gray's Inn, 1976. *Recreations:* Rugby (now as spectator), travel. *Address:* Byrom Chambers, 25 Byrom Street, Manchester M3 4PF. *T:* 0161–834 5238; 61 Fleet Street, EC4Y 1JU. *T:* 0171–353 4363.

MORAN, Rt. Rev. Monsignor John, CBE 1985; Principal RC Chaplain and Vicar General (Army), 1981–85; *b* 3 Dec. 1929; *s* of Thomas Moran and Gertrude May (*née* Sheer). *Educ:* De La Salle Coll., Sheffield; Ushaw Coll., Durham. Ordained Priest, Leeds Diocese, 1956; Curate, Dewsbury, 1956–60; Prison Chaplain, Armley, 1960–61; commissioned Army Chaplain, 1961; service in BAOR, Singapore, Malaya, Hong Kong, UK; Chaplain, RMA Sandhurst, 1968–70, Staff Chaplain, 1970–71; Senior Chaplain, HQ BAOR, 1977–79, and HQ UKLF, 1979–80. *Recreations:* music, rivers, clocks. *Address:* St Aidan's, Baildon Road, Baildon, West Yorks BD17 6AQ. *T:* Bradford (01274) 583032.

MORAN, Air Vice-Marshal Manus Francis; Royal Air Force, retired; *b* 18 April 1927; *s* of John Thomas Moran and Katherine Mary (*née* Coyle); *m* 1955, Maureen Elizabeth Martin, *o d* of Martin Dilks; one *s* three *d* (and one *s* decd). *Educ:* Mount St Joseph Abbey, Roscrea; University College Dublin (MB ChB, BAO 1952; MCh 1964); DLO, RCP and RCS, 1963. St Vincent's Hosp., Dublin, 1952; GP, Lutterworth, 1953–54; joined RAF 1954; Department of Otorhinolaryngology: served London, 1955–56; Wroughton, 1956–58; Weeton, 1958–59; Akrotiri, 1959–61; Halton, 1963–65; Consultant in ORL, RAF, 1965; served Changi, Singapore, 1965–68; Vis. Consultant, Johore Bahru Gen. Hosp., 1966–68; Nocton Hall, 1968–75; Wegberg, 1975–78; Wroughton, 1978–83; Consultant Adviser in ORL (RAF), 1983–88; Dean of Air Force Medicine, 1988–90; Sen. Consultant, RAF, 1990–91; Civilian Consultant in ORL, RAF Hosp., Wrighton, 1991–. QHP, 1988–91. Lectr in ORL, IAM Farnborough, for Dip. in Aviation medicine, RCP, 1983–88. Consultant: Nuffield Hosp., Leicester, 1992–; Met. Police, 1994–. Chm., Gen. Cttee, 8th British Acad. Conf. in ORL, 1987–91. Member: Irish Otological Soc.; Midland Inst. of Otology (Vice-Pres., 1971, 1975); Otology Section, RSM (Vice-Pres., Section of Laryngology, 1988–91, Pres., 1991–92); Council, British Assoc. of Otolaryngologists, 1983–88; Joseph Soc., BMA; BS Cttee on Auditory Alarms in med. monitoring equipment, 1983–88; Bd, Co-operation North, 1992–. Chm., Marston Meysey Charitable Trust, 1989– (Vice-Chm., 1987–89); Special Trustee, Royal Nat. Throat, Nose and Ear Hosp., 1993–. Hon. FRCSI 1991. Liveryman, Apothecaries' Soc. (Chm., Livery Cttee, 1994–); Freeman, City of London. CStJ 1990. Med. Soc. (UCD) Gold Medal, 1951; Lady Cade Medal, RCS, 1980. *Publications:* Upper Respiratory Problems in Yellow Nail Syndrome (jtly), 1976; contribs to learned jls on ORL applied to aviation medicine, ureamic rhinitis, vestibular dysfunction, acoustic trauma and hearing conservation. *Recreations:* preservation of rural amenities, walking, poetry, theology, power boating. *Address:* The Old Forge House, Marston Meysey, Cricklade, Wilts SN6 6LQ. *T:* Cirencester (01285) 810511. *Club:* Royal Air Force.

MORAUTA, Sir Mekere, Kt 1991; Chairman: National Airline Commission; Delta Seafoods, since 1993; *b* 12 June 1946; *s* of Morauta Hasu and Morikoai Elavo; *m* Roslyn; two *s*. *Educ:* Univ. of Papua New Guinea (BEcon); Flinders Univ., SA. Res. Officer (Manpower Planning), Dept of Labour, 1971; Economist, Office of the Economic Advr, 1972; Sec. for Finance, Govt of PNG, 1973–82; Man. Dir, PNG Banking Corp., 1983–92. Chm., Govt Adv. Cttee; Director: Highlands Gold (PNG); PNG Associated Industries; Thomas Nationwide Transport (PNG); James Barnes PNG; former Dir, numerous public and commercial bodies. Mem. Fund Raising Cttees, Salvation Army and Red Cross. Hon. DTech Univ. of Technology, PNG, 1987. *Publications:* numerous papers on economic and allied subjects. *Address:* PO Box 1267, Port Moresby NCD, Papua New Guinea. *T:* 217986.

MORAY, 20th Earl of, *cr* 1562; **Douglas John Moray Stuart;** Lord Abernethy and Strathearn, 1562; Lord Doune, 1581; Baron of St Colme, 1611; Baron Stuart (GB), 1796; *b* 13 Feb. 1928; *e s* of 19th Earl of Moray and Mabel Helen Maud Wilson (*d* 1968); *S* father, 1974; *m* 1964, Lady Malvina Murray, *er d* of 7th Earl of Mansfield and Mansfield; one *s* one *d*. *Educ:* Trinity Coll., Cambridge (BA), FLAS 1958. *Heir:* *s* Lord Doune, *qv*. *Address:* Doune Park, Doune, Perthshire FK16 6HA. *T:* Doune (01786) 841333; Darnaway Castle, Forres, Moray. *Club:* New (Edinburgh).

MORAY, ROSS AND CAITHNESS, Bishop of, since 1994; **Rt. Rev. Gregor Macgregor;** *b* 17 Nov. 1933; *m* 1956, Elizabeth Jean Harris; one *s* three *d*. *Educ:* St Andrews Univ. (MA 1964; BD 1967). Ordained deacon, 1976, priest, 1977; NSM, Elie and Earlsferry, and Pittenweem, 1977–81; Rector, Glenrothes, 1981–86; Vice-Provost, Cumbrae, 1986; Rector, Dollar, 1987–90; Mission Priest, St Luke, Wester Hailes, 1991–94. *Address:* Bishop's House, 34 Rangemore Road, Inverness IV3 5EA. *T:* Inverness (01463) 231059.

MORAY, ROSS AND CAITHNESS, Dean of; *see* Forrest, Very Rev. R. W.

MORAY, Edward Bruce D.; *see* Dawson-Moray.

MORCOM, Rev. Canon Anthony John; *b* 24 July 1916; *s* of late Dr Alfred Farr Morcom and Sylvia Millicent Morcom (*née* Birchenough); *m* 1st, 1955, Pamela Cappel Bain (*d* 1963); 2nd, 1965, Richenda, *widow* of Frederick Williams. *Educ:* Repton; Clare Coll., Cambridge; Cuddesdon Coll. Curate: St Mary Magdalene, Paddington, 1939–42; St Mary the Virgin, Pimlico, 1942–47; Domestic Chaplain to the Bishop of London, 1947–55; Archdeacon of Middx, 1953–66; Vicar of St Cyprian's, Clarence Gate, 1955–66; Vicar of St Mary the Less, Cambridge, 1966–73; Rural Dean of Cambridge, 1971–73; Residentiary Canon, Ely Cathedral, 1974–84; Vice-Dean, 1981–84. *Recreation:* travel. *Address:* 33 Porson Road, Cambridge CB2 2ET. *T:* Cambridge (01223) 62352. *Clubs:* United Oxford & Cambridge University, MCC.

MORCOM, Christopher, QC 1991; *b* 4 Feb. 1939; *s* of Dr Rupert Morcom and Mary Morcom (*née* Carslake); *m* 1966, Diane, *d* of late Jose Antonio Toledo and Winifred Anne (*née* Wardlaw); one *s* two *d*. *Educ:* Sherborne Sch.; Trinity Coll., Cambridge (BA Hons 1961; MA 1964). Called to the Bar, Middle Temple, 1963 (Cert. Honour, Astbury Scholar); Barrister, Mauritius, 1979–. Mem. Senate, Law Soc. Jt Wking Party on Intellectual Property Law, 1976–. Chm., Competition Law Assoc., 1985–. Vice Pres., Ligue Internationale du Droit de la Concurrence, 1994–. *Publications:* Service Marks: a guide to the new law, 1987; A Guide to the Trade Marks Act 1994, 1994; legal articles in Law Soc. Gazette, Counsel, European Intellectual Property Rev. *Recreations:* music, walking. *Address:* 1 Essex Court, Temple, EC4Y 9AR. *T:* 0171–936 3030. *Club:* Athenæum.

MORCOM, John Brian; a Social Security Commissioner, since 1981; a Child Support Commissioner, since 1993; *b* 31 May 1925; *s* of Albert John Morcom and Alice Maud Morcom (*née* Jones), Carmarthen; *m* 1st, 1958, Valerie Lostie de Kerhor Rivington (*d* 1960); one *s*; 2nd, 1965, Sheila Myfanwy Adams-Lewis (*d* 1986); one *d*. *Educ:* Queen Elizabeth Grammar Sch., Carmarthen; Balliol Coll., Oxford (State schol., 1943; MA). Bevin Ballottee, Oakdale Colliery, 1944; Medical Orderly, RAMC, Talgarth Mil. Mental Hosp. and BMH Suez, 1944–47. Called to the Bar, Inner Temple, 1952, Lincoln's Inn, 1955; Wales and Chester Circuit, 1954–81. *Publications:* Estate Duty Saving, 1959, 5th edn 1972; (jtly) Capital Transfer Tax, 1976, 2nd edn 1978. *Recreations:* Welsh genealogy, forestry. *Address:* Social Security Commission, Harp House, 83–86 Farringdon Street, EC4A 4DH. *Clubs:* Commonwealth Trust, London Welsh Association.

MORCOS-ASAAD, Prof. Fikry Naguib; Professor of Architecture, Department of Architecture and Building Science, University of Strathclyde, 1970–85, Professor Emeritus since 1986; *b* 27 Sept. 1930; *s* of Naguib and Marie A. Morcos-Asaad; *m* 1958, Sarah Ann (*née* Gribben); three *s*. *Educ:* Cairo Univ. (BArch); Georgia Inst. of Techn. (MArch); MIT (SM); IIT (PhD). FRIAS. Lectr in Architecture, Fac. of Engrg, Cairo Univ., 1952–54 and 1958–63; Dir of Structural Studies, Sch. of Arch., Univ. of Liverpool, 1963–70; Design Critic and Vis. Prof. in Arch. Engrg, Calif State Polytechnic Univ., 1969, 1970 and 1973; Vis. Prof. of Architecture, Assuit Univ., Egypt, 1980; Vis. Prof. of Architecture, 1985, of Architecture and Res., 1986–89, Univ. of Jordan, Amman. Research into: culture and arch.; housing design in hot, dry climates; prefabricated multi-storey housing in developing countries. Comr, Royal Fine Art Commn for Scotland, 1972–86; formerly Mem. Educn Cttee, Architects Registration Council of UK; former Member Council: Glasgow Inst. of Architects; Royal Incorp. of Architects in Scotland; Mem. Council, Glasgow Coll. of Building and Printing. Mem., Rotary International. *Publications:* Circular Forms in Architecture, 1955; High Density Concretes for Radiation Shielding, 1956; Structural Parameters in Multi-Storey Buildings under Dynamic Loading, 1956; The Egyptian Village, 1956; Architectural Construction, vol. 1 1960, vol. 2 1961; Plastic Design in Steel, 1975; Large-span Structures, 1976; Brickwork: some pertinent points, 1978; Design and Building for a Tropical Environment, 1978; Structural Systems in Architectural Configuration, 1987; Understanding Architectural Structure, 1988; various papers on structural form in architecture and on socio-cultural considerations in urban design. *Recreations:* renovation of antique clocks, gardening, reading, travelling. *Address:* Staneacre House, Townhead Street, Hamilton ML3 7BP. *T:* Hamilton (01698) 420644. *Clubs:* Rotary, Burns, Hamilton Civic Society (Hamilton).

MORDA EVANS, Raymond John; *see* Evans.

MORDAUNT, Sir Richard (Nigel Charles), 14th Bt *cr* 1611; (does not use the title at present); *b* 12 May 1940; *s* of Lt-Col Sir Nigel John Mordaunt, 13th Bt, MBE, and Anne (*d* 1980), *d* of late Arthur F. Tritton; *S* father, 1979; *m* 1964, Myriam Atchia; one *s* one *d*. *Educ:* Wellington. *Heir: s* Kim John Mordaunt, *b* 11 June 1966.

MORDUE, Richard Eric; Director of Economics and Statistics, Ministry of Agriculture, Fisheries and Food, since 1989; *b* 14 June 1941; *s* of Ralph Yielder Mordue and Helen Mary Mordue; *m* 1979, Christine Phillips; one *s* one *d*. *Educ:* Royal Grammar Sch., Newcastle upon Tyne; King's Coll., Univ. of Durham (BSc); Michigan State Univ. (MS). Joined MAFF as Asst Economist, 1964; Sen. Economic Advr, 1978; Head of Horticulture Div., 1982. *Recreations:* golf, bridge. *Address:* Ministry of Agriculture, Fisheries and Food, 3 Whitehall Place, SW1A 2HH. *T:* 0171–270 8539.

MORE, Norman, FRICS; Managing Director, Redditch Development Corporation, 1979–85; *b* 20 Dec. 1921; *s* of Herbert and Anna More; *m* 1952, Kathleen Mary Chrystal; two *s* one *d*. *Educ:* Royal High Sch., Edinburgh; Edinburgh Univ. FRICS 1970 (ARICS 1951). Served in Royal Engineers, Middle East, N Africa, Italy, Greece and Germany, Major, 1941–48. Surveyor, Directorate of Lands and Accommodation, Min. of Works, 1948–58; Sen. Valuer, City Assessor's Office, Glasgow Corporation, 1958–63; Valuation and Estates Officer, East Kilbride Development Corp., 1963–65; Chief Estates Officer, Redditch Development Corp., 1965–79. Consultant Chartered Surveyor, to Grimley J. R. Eve, London and Birmingham, 1985–90. Mem., W Midlands Regl Bd, TSB Gp, 1984–89. Chairman, West Midlands Br., Royal Instn of Chartered Surveyors, 1974–75. Chm., Stratford-on-Avon Friendship Project for Children, 1992–. *Publications:* press articles and contribs to jls. *Recreations:* music, sport. *Address:* Mead Cottage, 192 Loxley Road, Stratford-upon-Avon, Warwickshire CV37 7DU. *T:* Stratford-upon-Avon (01789) 293763. *Club:* East India, Devonshire, Sports and Public Schools.

MORE-MOLYNEUX, James Robert, OBE 1983; Vice Lord-Lieutenant of Surrey, since 1983; *b* 17 June 1920; *s* of Brig. Gen. Francis Cecil More-Molyneux-Longbourne, CMG, DSO and Gwendoline Carew More-Molyneux; *m* 1948, Susan Bellinger; one *s*. *Educ:* Eton; Trinity Hall, Cambridge. War service in 4/7th Royal Dragoon Guards and 14th PWO The Scinde Horse, 1941–46; Founder Chm., Guildway Ltd, 1947–85 (introduced first manufactured timber frame houses with brick cladding to UK, 1960); founded Loseley Co-Partnership, 1950; Chm., Loseley Park Farms, 1950–92; opened Loseley House to public, 1950–; founded Loseley Dairy Products, 1967; part-time Dir, Seeboard, 1975–84. Founder: Loseley & Guildway Charitable Trust, 1973; Loseley Christian Trust, 1983. Mem. Exec. Cttee, Industrial Participation Assoc., 1952–77; Patron, Surrey Assoc. of Youth Clubs. Lay Pastoral Asst, 1986–. High Sheriff of Surrey, 1974; DL Surrey 1976. Bledisloe Gold Medal for Landowners, RASE, 1984. *Publication:* The Loseley Challenge, 1995. *Recreations:* countryside, riding, Christian Healing Ministry. *Address:* Loseley Park, Guildford, Surrey GU3 1HS. *T:* Guildford (01483) 304440. *Club:* Farmers'.

MOREAU, Jeanne; Officier, Ordre National du Mérite, 1988 (Chevalier, 1970); Officier de la Légion d'Honneur, 1991 (Chevalier, 1975); actress; *b* 23 Jan. 1928; *d* of Anatole-Désiré Moreau and Kathleen Moreau (*née* Buckley); *m* 1949, Jean-Louis Richard (marr. diss.); one *s*; *m* 1977, William Friedkin (marr. diss.). *Educ:* Collège Edgar-Quinet; Conservatoire national d'art dramatique. *Theatre:* Comédie Française, 1948–52; Théâtre National Populaire, 1953; Le Récit de la Servante Zerline, 1986–89; La Celestine, 1989. Over 60 *films* including: Les amants, 1958; Les liaisons dangereuses, 1959; Le dialogue des Carmelites, 1959; Moderato cantabile, 1960; Jules et Jim, 1961; La Baie des Anges, 1962; Journal d'une femme de chambre, 1963; Viva Maria, 1965; Mademoiselle, 1965; The Sailor from Gibraltar, 1965; The Immortal Story, 1966; Great Catherine, 1967; The Bride wore Black, 1967; Monte Walsh, 1969; Chère Louise, 1971; Nathalie Granger, 1972; La Race des Seigneurs, 1974; Mr Klein, 1976; Lumière (also Dir), 1976; Le Petit Théâtre de Jean Renoir, 1976; Madame Rosa, 1978; L'Intoxe, 1980; Querelle, La Truite, 1982; L'Arbre, 1983; Sauve-toi Lola, Le Paltoquet, Le Miracule, 1986; La Nuit de l'Ocean, 1987; Ennemonde, 1988; Jour après Jour, 1988; Nikita, 1989; La Comédie d'un Jour, 1989; Anna Karamazoff, 1989; La Femme Fardée, Until the End of the World, 1990; La Vielle Qui Marchait Dans La Mer, Le Pas Suspendu de la Cigogne, The Map of the Human Heart, L'Amant, 1991; A Demain, L'Absence, 1992; Je m'appelle Victor, 1992; *television* plays and series: Huis Clos, BBC, 1984; The Last Seance, Granada, 1984; Le Tiroir Secret, 1985; We Shall Meet Again, BBC, 1992; The Clothes in the Wardrobe, BBC, 1993; A Foreign Field, BBC, 1993. Chm. Jury, Cannes Film Festival, 1995. Commandeur des Arts et des Lettres, 1985 (Chevalier, 1966). *Recreation:* reading. *Address:* SPICA, 103 boulevard Haussmann, 75008 Paris, France.

MORELAND, Robert John; management consultant; Member, Economic and Social Committee, European Community, since 1986 (Chairman, Regional Policy and Town and Country Planning Section, since 1990); *b* 21 Aug. 1941; *s* of Samuel John Moreland and late Norah Mary, (Molly) (*née* Haines). *Educ:* Glasgow Acad.; Dean Close Sch., Cheltenham; Univ. of Nottingham (BA Econs); Inst. of World Affairs, Conn, and Warwick Univ. (postgrad. work). Civil Servant, Govt of NS, Canada, 1966–67, Govt of NB, 1967–72; Sen. Economist, W Central Scotland Planning Study, 1972–74; Management Consultant, Touche Ross and Co., London, 1974–; Consultant: Westminster and City Conferences Ltd, 1985–; Strategy Network Internat., 1988–93; Prima Europe, 1993–. Mem. for Knightsbridge, Westminster City Council, 1990– (Chief Whip, 1993–94; Chm. of Envmt, 1994–). Contested (C) Pontypool, Oct. 1974; Mem. (C) Staffs, European Parlt, 1979–84, contested same seat, 1984; Chm., Eur. Cttee, Bow Gp, 1977–78; Vice-Chm., Conservative Gp for Europe, 1985–88. *Publications:* contrib. to Crossbow. *Recreations:* tennis, skiing, watching cricket and Rugby, golf. *Address:* 7 Vauxhall Walk, SE11 5JT. *T:* 0171–582 2613. *Clubs:* Carlton, Royal Automobile.

MORETON, family name of **Earl of Ducie.**

MORETON, Lord; James Berkeley Moreton; *b* 6 May 1981; *s* and *heir* of 7th Earl of Ducie, *qv*.

MORETON, Sir John (Oscar), KCMG 1978 (CMG 1966); KCVO 1976; MC 1944; HM Diplomatic Service, retired; *b* 28 Dec. 1917; *s* of Rev. C. O. Moreton; *m* 1945, Margaret Katherine, *d* of late Sir John Fryer, KBE, FRS; three *d*. *Educ:* St Edward's Sch., Oxford; Trinity Coll., Oxford (MA). War Service with 99th (Royal Bucks Yeomanry) Field Regt RA, 1939–46: France, Belgium, 1940; India, Burma, 1942–45. Colonial Office, 1946; Private Sec. to Perm. Under-Sec. of State, 1949–50; seconded to Govt of Kenya, 1953–55; Private Sec. to Sec. of State for Colonies (Rt Hon. Alan Lennox-Boyd), 1955–59; transf. to CRO, 1960; Counsellor, British High Commn, Lagos, 1961–64; IDC 1965; Asst Under-Sec. of State, CRO, 1965–66, CO 1966–68, FCO 1968–69; Ambassador to Vietnam, 1969–71; High Comr, Malta, 1972–74; Dep. Perm. Representative, with personal rank of Ambassador, UK Mission to UN, NY, 1974–75; Minister, British Embassy, Washington, 1975–77. Dir, Wates Foundn, 1978–87. Gentleman Usher of the Blue Rod, Order of St Michael and St George, 1979–92. Governor, St Edward's Sch., Oxford, 1980–92. Hon. DL Hanover Coll., Indiana, 1976. *Recreations:* most outdoor activities, formerly athletics (Oxford Blue and International, 880 yds, 1939). *Address:* Woodside House, Woodside Road, Cobham, Surrey KT11 2QR. *Club:* Army and Navy.

MOREY, Anthony Bernard Nicholas, CBE 1993; HM Diplomatic Service; Deputy High Commissioner, Calcutta, since 1993; *b* 6 Dec. 1936; *s* of late Bernard Rowland Morey and Madeleine Morey; *m* 1961, Agni Campbell Kerr; two *s* one *d*. *Educ:* Wimbledon Coll. Nat. service, 1955–57. FO, 1957–60; Kuwait, 1960–62; FO, 1962–65; Madras, 1965–66; FO, 1966; Tehran, 1967; Kabul, 1968–71; FCO, 1971–72; Washington, 1972–76; Zagreb, 1976–80; Lagos, 1980–83; seconded to Guinness Mahon, 1983–85; Counsellor and Consul General, Moscow, 1985–88; Dep. High Comr, Madras, 1989–91; Ambassador to Mongolia, 1991–93. *Recreations:* gardening, music, cats. *Address:* c/o Foreign and Commonwealth Office, SW1A 2AH; The Coach House, Nutcombe Lane, Hindhead, Surrey GU26 6BP. *Clubs:* Commonwealth Trust, Oriental; Royal Calcutta Turf.

MORGAN; *see* Elystan-Morgan.

MORGAN, Rt. Rev. Alan Wyndham; *see* Sherwood, Bishop Suffragan of.

MORGAN, Anthony Hugh, CMG 1990; HM Diplomatic Service, retired; Consul-General, Zürich, Director of British Export Promotion in Switzerland and Consul-General, Liechtenstein, 1988–91; *b* 27 March 1931; *s* of late Cyril Egbert Morgan and late Muriel Dorothea (*née* Nash); *m* 1957, Cicely Alice Voysey; two *s* one *d*. *Educ:* King's Norton Grammar Sch.; Birmingham Univ. (BA 1952). Served HM Forces (RAF Educn Br.), 1952–55. Joined HM Foreign (later Diplomatic) Service, 1956; Cairo, then Cyprus, 1956; Khartoum, 1957; FO, 1959; Saigon, 1962; Second Sec., 1963; UK Delegn to NATO, 1965; First Sec., 1968; FCO, 1969; First Sec. and Head of Chancery, Calcutta, 1973; FCO, 1976; Dep. Head of Inf. Policy Dept, 1977; Counsellor: (Information), Brussels, 1977–79; (Commercial), Copenhagen, 1979–82; Vienna, 1982–88. Comdr, Order of Dannebrog, Denmark, 1979. *Recreations:* listening to music, looking at pictures. *Club:* Royal Air Force.

MORGAN, Arthur William Crawford, (Tony Morgan); Chief Executive, Industrial Society, since 1994; Non-executive Director, Alexander Corporation, since 1990; *b* 24 Aug. 1931; *s* of Arthur James and Violet Morgan; *m* 1955, Valerie Anne Williams; three *s*. *Educ:* Hereford High Sch.; Westcliff High Sch. Chm. and Chief Exec. Officer, Purle Bros Holdings, 1964–71; Dep. Chm., Wimpey Waste Management, 1974–81; Dir, Redland plc, 1971–73; Founder and Dir, Morgan Hemingway Investment Bank, 1973–78; working in California for non-profit organisations, incl. Hunger Project and Breakthrough Foundn, 1981–84; Chm., Wistech, 1984–90. Governor, BBC, 1972–77. Sailed Olympic Games, Tokyo; Silver Medal, Flying Dutchman, 1964; Jt Yachtsman of the Year, 1965; Member: British Olympic Yachting Appeal, 1970; Royal Yachting Assoc. Council, 1968–72. Chm., Hunger Project Trust, 1984–89; Trustee, Youth at Risk, 1991–. FRSA. *Publications:* various technical papers. *Recreations:* squash, skiing, sailing. *Address:* Bovingdon, Marlow Common, Bucks SL7 2QR. *T:* Marlow (01628) 890654; 16 Upper Wimpole Street, W1. *T:* 0171–486 0674/2597; Haus Arbgrat, Zermatt, Switzerland. *T:* 672395. *Club:* Royal Thames Yacht.

MORGAN, Rt. Rev. Barry Cennydd; *see* Bangor, Bishop of.

MORGAN, Bill; *see* Morgan, J. W. H.

MORGAN, Brian David Gwynne, FRSC; Consultant Plastic Surgeon, University College Hospital, London and Mount Vernon Hospital, since 1972; *b* 2 March 1935; *s* of Brig. John Gwynne Morgan and Ethel Lilian (*née* Bloomer); *m* 1962, Sally Ann Lewis; one *s* two *d.* *Educ:* Wycliffe Coll., Glos; University College Hosp., London (MB BS). FRCS 1963. University College Hospital: pre-registration house appts, 1959–61; Casualty Officer, 1961; Registrar in Surgery, St Richard's Hosp., Chichester, 1962–64; Registrar in Surgery, 1964–66, Sen. Registrar, 1967, UCH; Plastic Surgery Registrar and Sen. Registrar, Mt Vernon Hosp., 1967–70; Consultant Plastic Surgeon, Shotley Bridge, Durham, 1970–72. Mem. Council, RCS. Fellow, UCL, 1992. *Publication:* Essentials of Plastic and Reconstructive Surgery, 1986. *Recreations:* water-colour painting, sailing, scuba-diving, hang-gliding (retired). *Address:* University College London Hospitals, Private Patients' Wing, Grafton Way, WC1E 6AU. *T:* 0171–383 7395. *Club:* Royal Society of Medicine.

MORGAN, Rear-Adm. Brinley John, CB 1972; *b* 3 April 1916; *s* of Thomas Edward Morgan and Mary Morgan (*née* Parkhouse); *m* 1945, Margaret Mary Whittles; three *s.* *Educ:* Abersychan Grammar Sch.; University Coll., Cardiff (BSc 1937). Entered Royal Navy as Instr Lt, 1939. Served War of 1939–45: Cruisers Emerald and Newcastle, 1939–41; Aircraft Carrier Formidable, 1941–43; Naval Weather Service (Admty Forecast Section), 1943–45. Staff of C-in-C Medit., 1945–48; HQ, Naval Weather Service, 1948–50; Staff of Flag Officer Trg Sqdn in HM Ships Vanguard, Indefatigable and Implacable, 1950–52; Instr Comdr, 1951; Lectr, RN Coll., Greenwich, 1952–54; Headmaster, RN Schools, Malta, 1954–59; Instr Captain, 1960; Staff of Dir, Naval Educn Service, 1959–61 and 1963–64; Sen. Officers' War Course, 1961; HMS Ganges, 1961–63; Dean, RN Engineering Coll., Manadon, 1964–69; Instr Rear-Adm., 1970; Dir, Naval Educn Service, 1970–75, retired.

MORGAN, Bruce; Stipendiary Magistrate for West Midlands, since 1989; *b* 30 March 1945; *s* of Francis William Morgan, DFC, and Phyllis Marie Morgan; *m* 1988, Sandra Joy Beresford; twin *d.* *Educ:* Oswestry School; Open Univ. (BA 1994). Solicitor of Supreme Court. Articled Clerk, Stourbridge, Worcs, 1964–69; Asst Solicitor, London, SE10, 1969–72; Partner with Lickfolds Wiley & Powles, 1973–86. Member: London Criminal Courts Solicitors Assoc. Cttee, 1971–73; Criminal Law Cttee, Westminster Law Soc., 1981–86; No 14 Area Regl Duty Solicitors Cttee, 1986–87; Metropolitan Stipendiary Magistrate, 1987–89. Member: British Acad. of Forensic Sci., 1970; Legal Medico Soc., 1970–. Mem., Greenwich, Chelsea and Ludlow Rotary Clubs, 1969–; Chm., Greenwich Round Table, 1983–84. *Publications:* various articles in legal journals. *Recreations:* tennis, cricket, gardening, attending auctions, study of British birds, breeding English butterflies. *Address:* c/o Birmingham Magistrates' Court, Steelhouse Lane, Birmingham B6 6QJ.

MORGAN, Vice-Adm. Charles Christopher; Flag Officer Scotland, Northern England and Northern Ireland, since 1992; *b* 11 March 1939; *s* of late Captain Horace Leslie Morgan, CMG, DSO, RN and Kathleen Hilda Morgan; *m* 1970, Susan Caroline Goodbody; three *d.* *Educ:* Clifton College; BRNC Dartmouth. MRIN 1989. Joined RN, 1957; served Brunei, 1962–66; HMS Greatford in Comd, 1966; Specialist Navigation Course, 1967; HMS Eskimo in Comd, 1976; NDC 1978; Comdr Sea Training, 1979; MoD, 1981–83; RCDS, 1984; Captain 5th Destroyer Sqdn (HMS Southampton), 1985–87; Staff, Jt Service Defence Coll., 1987–89; Naval Sec., 1990–92. Younger Brother of Trinity House, 1977. Gov., Clifton Coll., 1994–. FIMgt. *Recreations:* golf, tennis (Pres. RN LTA), Rugby (Vice-Pres., RN RU), wine, gardening. *Address:* c/o Lloyds Bank, 75 Cheap Street, Sherborne, Dorset. *Clubs:* Army and Navy; Royal North Devon Golf, Sherborne Golf.

MORGAN, Clifford Isaac, CVO 1986; OBE 1977; Head of Outside Broadcasts Group, BBC Television, 1975–87; *b* 7 April 1930; *m* 1955, Nuala Martin; one *s* one *d.* *Educ:* Tonyrefail Grammar School, South Wales. Played International Rugby Union for Wales, British Lions and Barbarians. Joined BBC, 1958, as Sports Organiser, Wales; Editor, Sportsview and Grandstand, 1961–64; Producer, This Week, 1964–66; freelance writer and broadcaster, 1966–72; Editor, Sport Radio, 1972–74; Head of Outside Broadcasts, Radio, 1974–75. President: London Glamorgan Soc., 1974–; Welsh Sports Assoc. for Mental Handicap, 1988–; Wales Council for the Disabled, 1990–; Welsh Pres., Cystic Fibrosis Res. Trust, 1987–; Vice-President: Sequal, 1976–; Nat. Children's Home, 1987–. Chm., Saints and Sinners Club, 1984–85. Hon. Fellow, Polytechnic of Wales, 1989. Hon. MA Wales, 1988; DUniv Keele, 1989. *Recreation:* music. *Address:* 34 Kensington Mansions, Trebovir Road, SW5 9TQ.

MORGAN, (David) Dudley; retired from Theodore Goddard & Co., Solicitors, 1983; *b* 23 Oct. 1914; *y s* of Thomas Dudley Morgan; *m* 1948, Margaret Helene, *o d* of late David MacNaughton Duncan, Loanhead, Midlothian; two *d.* *Educ:* Swansea Grammar Sch.; Jesus Coll., Cambridge (MA, LLM). War Service with RAF in Intell. Br., UK, 1940–42 and Legal Br., India, 1942–46; Wing Comdr 1945. Admitted Solicitor, 1939, with Theodore Goddard & Co.; Partner 1948; Senior Partner, 1974–80; Consultant, 1980–83. An Underwriting Member of Lloyd's. *Recreation:* gardening. *Address:* St Leonard's House, St Leonard's Road, Nazeing, Waltham Abbey, Essex EN9 2HG. *T:* Nazeing (01992) 892124. *Club:* Carlton.

MORGAN, David Gethin; County Treasurer, Avon County Council, 1973–94; *b* 30 June 1929; *s* of Edgar and Ethel Morgan; *m* 1955, Marion Brook. *Educ:* Jesus Coll., Oxford (MA Hons English). IPFA, FInstAM(Dip). Graduate Accountancy Asst, Staffordshire CC, 1952–58; Computer Systems Officer, Sen. O&M Officer, Cheshire CC, 1958–62; County Management Services Officer, Durham CC, 1962–65; Leicestershire CC: Asst County Treasurer, 1965–68; Dep. County Treasurer, 1968–73. Vice Chm. and Chm., Local Govt Finance Exec., CIPFA, 1987–92; Pres., Soc. of County Treasurers in England and Wales, 1988–89. Hon. Freeman, City of London, 1989. *Publication:* Vol. XV Financial Information Service (IPFA). *Recreations:* local history, church architecture, tai chi. *Address:* 6 Wyecliffe Road, Henleaze, Bristol, Avon BS9 4NH. *T:* Bristol (0117) 962 9640.

MORGAN, David Glyn; His Honour Judge Glyn Morgan; a Circuit Judge, since 1984; *b* 31 March 1933; *s* of late Dr Richard Glyn Morgan, MC, and Nancy Morgan; *m* 1959, Ailsa Murray Strang; three *d.* *Educ:* Mill Hill Sch.; Merton Coll., Oxford (MA). Called to Bar, Middle Temple, 1958; practised Oxford Circuit, 1958–70; Wales and Chester Circuit, 1970–84. A Recorder of the Crown Court, 1974–84. 2nd Lieut, The Queen's Bays, 1955; Dep. Col, 1st The Queen's Dragoon Guards, 1976. An Hon. Pres., Royal Nat. Eisteddfod of Wales, Casnewydd, 1988. *Recreations:* fishing, Rugby football, gardening. *Address:* 2 Harcourt Buildings, Temple, EC4Y 9DB. *T:* 0171–353 8549; 30 Park Place, Cardiff. *T:* Cardiff (01222) 398421. *Clubs:* Cavalry and Guards; Cardiff and County (Cardiff).

MORGAN, Sir David John H.; *see* Hughes-Morgan.

MORGAN, David Leslie; Deputy Chairman and Managing Director, M&G Group plc, since 1994; *b* 23 Dec. 1933; *s* of Captain Horace Leslie Morgan, CMG, DSO, RN and Kathleen Hilda Morgan (*née* Bellhouse); *m* 1965, Clare Jean Lacy; one *s* one *d.* *Educ:* Clifton Coll., Bristol; University Coll., Oxford (BA Hons PPE 1957). Worked in FE, for Shell, and later stockbroking in Malaysia, 1957–65; banking and investment management, Deltec Internat., London and NY, 1965–70; Dir, E. D. Sassoon, 1970–72; M&G Group, 1972–: Dir, 1973–91, Man. Dir, 1991–, M&G Investment Management; Dep. Gp Man. Dir, 1991–94. MSI 1993. FRSA 1993. *Recreations:* walking, wine, theatre. *Address:* c/o M&G Group plc, Three Quays, Tower Hill, EC3R 6BQ. *T:* 0171–626 4588. *Clubs:* Royal Automobile; Royal North Devon Golf.

MORGAN, David Thomas; Chief Executive, Black Country Development Corporation, since 1987; *b* 22 Jan. 1946; *s* of Janet Catherine and Noel David Morgan; *m* 1968, Quita Valentine; two *d.* *Educ:* Alleyne's Grammar School, Stevenage; Univ. of Newcastle upon Tyne (BA Hons Land Use Studies 1968). MRTPI 1971. Somerset CC, 1968–70; Worcs CC, 1970–71; Peterborough Develt Corp., 1971–81; Housing Develt Manager, 1981–85, Dir, Planning Services, 1985–87, LDDC. *Recreations:* Rugby football, drama. *Address:* 3 Riverside Court, Caunsall, near Kidderminster, Worcs DY11 5YW. *T:* Kidderminster (01562) 851688.

MORGAN, Douglas; IPFA; County Treasurer, Lancashire County Council, 1985–92; *b* 5 June 1936; *s* of late Douglas Morgan and Margaret Gardner Morgan; *m* 1960, Julia (*née* Bywater); two *s.* *Educ:* High Pavement Grammar Sch., Nottingham. IPFA 1963 (4th place in final exam. and G. A. Johnston (Dundee) Prize). Nat. Service, RAF, 1954–56. Nottingham CBC, 1952–61; Herefordshire CC, 1961–64; Berkshire CC, 1964–67; Asst Co. Treas., W Suffolk CC, 1967–70; Asst, later Dep., Co. Treas., Lindsey CC, 1970–73; Dep. Co. Treas., Lancashire CC, 1973–85. Chm., NW & N Wales Region, CIPFA, 1985–86; Pres., NW & N Wales Region, Students' Soc., CIPFA, 1989–90. Treas., Lancs Cttee, Royal Jubilee & Prince's Trust, 1985–92; Hon. Treasurer: Lancs Playing Fields Assoc., 1985–92; NW Region Library System and NW Sound Archive, 1986–92. FRSA. *Publications:* articles for Public Finance & Accountancy and other local govt jls. *Recreations:* golf and "collecting" golf courses, jazz, playing "gypsy" in a motor caravan. *Address:* 8 Croyde Road, St Annes-on-Sea, Lancs FY8 1EX. *T:* St Annes (01253) 725808. *Club:* Fairhaven Golf (Centenary Captain, 1995–96).

MORGAN, Dudley; *see* Morgan, David D.

MORGAN, Prof. Edwin (George), OBE 1982; Titular Professor of English, University of Glasgow, 1975–80, now Emeritus; *b* 27 April 1920; *s* of Stanley Lawrence Morgan and Margaret McKillop Arnott. *Educ:* Rutherglen Academy; High Sch. of Glasgow; Univ. of Glasgow. MA 1st Cl. Hons, Eng. Lang. and Lit., 1947. Served War, RAMC, 1940–46. University of Glasgow: Asst, 1947, Lectr, 1950, Sen. Lectr, 1965, Reader, 1971, in English. Vis. Prof., Strathclyde Univ., 1987–90; Hon. Prof., UCW, 1991–95. Cholmondeley Award for Poets, 1968; Hungarian PEN Meml Medal, 1972; Scottish Arts Council Book Awards, 1968, 1973, 1975, 1977, 1978, 1983, 1985, 1991 and 1992; Soros Translation Award, NY, 1985. Visual/concrete poems in many internat. exhibns, 1965–. Opera librettos (unpublished): The Charcoal-Burner, 1969; Valentine, 1976; Columba, 1976; Spell, 1979. Hon. DLitt: Loughborough, 1981; Glasgow, 1990; Edinburgh, 1991; DUniv: Stirling, 1989; Waikato, 1992; MUniv Open, 1992. *Publications: poetry:* The Vision of Cathkin Braes, 1952; The Cape of Good Hope, 1955; (ed) Collins Albatross Book of Longer Poems, 1963; Starryveldt, 1965; Emergent Poems, 1967; Gnomes, 1968; The Second Life, 1968; Proverbfolder, 1969; Penguin Modern Poets 15, 1969; Twelve Songs, 1970; The Horseman's Word, 1970; (co-ed) Scottish Poetry 1–6, 1966–72; Glasgow Sonnets, 1972; Instamatic Poems, 1972; The Whittrick, 1973; From Glasgow to Saturn, 1973; The New Divan, 1977; Colour Poems, 1978; Star Gate, 1979; (ed) Scottish Satirical Verse, 1980; Poems of Thirty Years, 1982; Grafts/Takes, 1983; Sonnets From Scotland, 1984; Selected Poems, 1985; From the Video Box, 1986; Newspoems, 1987; Themes on a Variation, 1988; Tales from Limerick Zoo, 1988; Collected Poems, 1990; Hold Hands Among the Atoms, 1991; (ed) James Thomson, The City of Dreadful Night, 1993; Sweeping out the Dark, 1994; *prose:* Essays, 1974; East European Poets, 1976; Hugh MacDiarmid, 1976; Twentieth Century Scottish Classics, 1987; Nothing Not Giving Messages (interviews), 1990; Crossing the Border: essays in Scottish Literature, 1990; Language, Poetry, and Language Poetry, 1990; Evening Will Come They Will Sew the Blue Sail, 1991; *translations:* Beowulf, 1952; Poems from Eugenio Montale, 1959; Sovpoems, 1961; Mayakovsky, Wi the Haill Voice, 1972; Fifty Renascence Love Poems, 1975; Rites of Passage (selected poetic translations), 1976; Platen: selected poems, 1978; Master Peter Pathelin, 1983; Rostand, Cyrano de Bergerac: a new verse translation, 1992. *Recreations:* photography, scrapbooks, walking in cities. *Address:* 19 Whittingehame Court, Glasgow G12 0BG. *T:* 0141–339 6260.

MORGAN, Edwin John; Director, Civil Service Selection Board, 1981–87, retired; *b* 10 Jan. 1927; *s* of Thomas Grosvenor Morgan and Florence (*née* Binmore); *m* 1954, Joyce Beryl, *o d* of Reginald and Gladys Ashurst, Bebington, Wirral; two *s* one *d.* *Educ:* Dauntsey's Sch.; St Edmund Hall, Oxford (Sen. Scholar, BA 1st Cl. Hons 1951). Served Army, Intell. Corps, Palestine and Cyprus, 1944–48. Lecteur d'anglais, Ecole normale supérieure, Paris, 1952; Asst, Dept of French Studies, Glasgow Univ., 1953; Asst Principal, Air Min., 1957, Principal, 1960; MoD, 1965; Registrar, RMCS, 1968; Asst Sec., 1970; CSD, 1971; CS Commn, 1975; Under Sec., 1980; CS Comr, 1980–87. Chm., CS Retirement Fellowship, 1987–92. FIPM 1985. *Recreations:* reading, walking, music, swimming, domesticity. *Address:* Ashurst, 6 Links Drive, Robin Lane, High Bentham, Lancaster LA2 7BJ. *T:* Bentham (015242) 61406. *Club:* Civil Service.

MORGAN, Ellis, CMG 1961; HM Diplomatic Service, retired; *b* 26 Dec. 1916; *s* of late Ben Morgan and of Mary Morgan, The Grove, Three Crosses, Gower, S Wales; *m* 1st, 1948, Molly Darby (marr. diss.); three *d*; 2nd, 1975, Mary, *d* of late Slade Baker Stallard-Penoyre; one *s* twin *d* (one decd). *Educ:* Swansea Grammar Sch. (Bishop Gore Sch.). Dep. Librarian, County Borough of Swansea, 1937–39. Commissioned Royal Artillery, 1941; served War of 1939–45, in India, Burma, Malaya, 1943–47. Entered Foreign (subseq. Diplomatic) Service, 1948; 3rd Sec., 1948–50, 2nd Sec., 1951–53, subseq. 1st Sec., British Embassy, Rangoon; 1st Sec., British Embassy, Bangkok, 1954–55; 1st Sec., Office of Commissioner-Gen., Singapore, 1957–60; Student at Imperial Defence Coll., 1961; Counsellor: UK High Commission, New Delhi, 1964; FO, later FCO, 1966–73; Political and Economic Adviser, Commercial Union Assurance, 1973–79. *Club:* Farmers'.

MORGAN, Eluned; *see* Morgan, M. E.

MORGAN, (Evan) Roger; Under Secretary for International Relations and Youth, Department for Education and Employment (formerly Department for Education), since 1994; *b* 18 April 1945; *s* of Evan and Stella Morgan; *m* 1967, Elizabeth, (Libby) (*née* Lewis); one *s* one *d.* *Educ:* Whitgift Sch., South Croydon; Battersea Coll. of Advanced Technol. Career spent within Dept for Educn (formerly DES), with various postings across the range of its responsibilities; Under Sec., Further Educn, 1991–94. *Recreations:* making music, cycling, gadgets. *Address:* Department for Education and Employment, Sanctuary Buildings, Great Smith Street, SW1P 3BT. *T:* 0171–925 6050.

MORGAN, (Frank) Leslie, CBE 1988 (MBE 1973); Chairman, Morgan Bros (Mid Wales) Ltd, since 1959; Chairman, Development Board for Rural Wales (Mid Wales

Development), 1981–89 (Member, 1977–81); *b* 7 Nov. 1926; *s* of Edward Arthur Morgan and Beatrice Morgan; *m* 1962, Victoria Stoker (*née* Jeffery); one *s* two *d*. *Educ:* Llanfair Primary Sch.; Llanfair Grammar Sch.; University College of Wales (BA Econ Hons). Post graduate trainee and parts executive in motor industry, 1950–56. Chairman and President, Montgomery Conservative Assoc., 1964–81; Member, Welsh Council, 1970–79; Dep. Chm., Mid Wales New Town Development Corp., 1973–77; Director: Develt Corp. for Wales, 1981–83; Wales Adv. Bd, Abbey National (formerly Abbey National Bldg Soc.), 1982–90; Member: Welsh Development Agency, 1981–89; Wales Tourist Bd, 1982–89; Infrastructure Cttee, BTA, 1982–89; Design Council Welsh Cttee, 1981–85. Pres., Montgomeryshire Agricl Soc., 1986. Pres., Montgomery Cons. Assoc., 1989–. Chm., Policy Cttee, Campaign for Montgomeryshire. *Recreations:* reading, travel, jogging, swimming, cycling. *Address:* Wentworth House, Llangyniew, Welshpool, Powys SY21 9EL. *T:* Llanfair-Caereinion (01938) 810462.

MORGAN, Gemmell; *see* Morgan, H. G.

MORGAN, Geoffrey Thomas, CB 1991; Adviser, Coopers & Lybrand, since 1991; Under Secretary, Cabinet Office (Office of the Minister for the Civil Service), Director of Public Appointments Unit, 1985–91; *b* 12 April 1931; *s* of late Thomas Evan Morgan and Nora (*née* Flynn); *m* 1960, Heather, *d* of late William Henry Trick and of Margery Murrell Wells; two *d*. *Educ:* Roundhay Sch. National Service, Royal Signals, 1950–52; joined Civil Service, 1952; served in Mins of Supply and Aviation, 1952–65; HM Treasury, 1965–68 and 1981–83; CSD, 1968–81; seconded to Arthur Guinness Son & Co., 1970–72; Adviser to World Bank in Washington, 1977–78; Cabinet Office, 1983–91; Adviser to: UN in NY, 1987–88; People's Republic of China in Beijing, 1988–91; Govt of Hungary in Budapest, 1990–; Govt of Jamaica in Kingston, 1991. Chm., Public Admin Cttee, WEU, 1990–91. Panel Chm., CSSB, 1991–95; Advr, Southern Africa Develt Unit, CS Coll., 1991–. Trustee, Whitehall and Industry Gp, 1991–94. *Recreation:* preserving the mulberry for posterity and the silkworm. *Address:* c/o Coopers & Lybrand, 1 Embankment Place, WC2N 6NN. *T:* 0171–213 2963.

MORGAN, George Lewis Bush; Chief Registrar, Bank of England, 1978–83; *b* 1 Sept. 1925; *s* of late William James Charles Morgan and Eva Averill Morgan (*née* Bush); *m* 1949, Mary Rose (*née* Vine); three *s*. *Educ:* Cranbr Sch., Kent. Captain, Royal Sussex Regt, 1943–47. Entered Bank of England, 1947; Asst Chief Accountant, 1966; Asst Sec., 1969; Dep. Sec., 1973. Mem. Bd of Govs, Holmewood House Prep. Sch., Tunbridge Wells, 1983– (Chm., 1986–). *Recreations:* golf, gardening. *Address:* Hill Top House, Five Ashes, Mayfield, East Sussex TN20 6HT. *Club:* Piltdown Golf.

MORGAN, Gwyn; *see* Morgan, J. G.

MORGAN, Prof. (Henry) Gemmell; Professor of Pathological Biochemistry, University of Glasgow, 1965–88, now Professor Emeritus, and Hon. Senior Research Fellow, since 1988; *b* 25 Dec. 1922; *s* of John McIntosh Morgan, MC, MD, FRCPE, and Florence Ballantyne; *m* 1949, Margaret Duncan, BSc, MB, ChB; one *d*. *Educ:* Dundee High Sch.; Merchiston Castle Sch., Edinburgh; Univ. of St Andrews at University Coll., Dundee. BSc 1943; MB, ChB (distinction), 1946; FRCPE 1962; FRCPGlas 1968; FRCPath 1970; FRSE 1971. Hon. Consultant, Royal Infirmary, Glasgow, 1966–88. Chm., Med. Cttee, Royal Infirmary, Glasgow, 1984–87. Hon. Life Mem., Assoc. of Clinical Biochemists (UK), 1990 (Chm., 1982–85; Pres., 1985–87). Academic Advr, Univ. of London, 1970–72; External Examiner: in Biochem., Univ. of Dundee, 1974–77; Final in Pathology, Charing Cross and Westminster Med. Sch., 1985–88; UMDS of Guy's and St Thomas' Hosps, London, 1987–89; MSc and PhD Clinical Chemistry, Newcastle, 1972–74, Leeds, 1977–80, Dublin, 1979–82, Examnr in FRCS, RCPGlas, 1970–. Chm., Scottish Br., Nutrition Soc., 1967–68. Adviser to Greater Glasgow Health Ed, SHHD. MInstD. *Publications:* chapters; papers in medical jls on calcium, and lipoproteins. *Recreations:* golf, foreign travel, history. *Address:* Firwood House, 8 Eaglesham Road, Newton Mearns, Glasgow G77 5BG. *T:* 0141–639 4404. *Club:* Athenæum.

MORGAN, Hugh Marsden; His Honour Judge Hugh Morgan; a Circuit Judge, since 1995; *b* 17 March 1940; *s* of Hugh Thomas Morgan, Cyncoed, Cardiff and Irene Morgan (*née* Rees); *m* 1967, Amanda Jane Tapley; two *s* one *d*. *Educ:* Cardiff High Sch.; Magdalen Coll., Oxford (Demy; BCL; MA Jurisp.). Called to the Bar, Gray's Inn, 1964; in practice: Midland Circuit, 1965–71; SE Circuit, 1971–95; Asst Recorder, 1983–87; Recorder, 1987–95. Member: Matrimonial Causes Rule Cttee, 1989–91; Family Proceedings Rule Cttee, 1991–93; Fees and Legal Aid Cttee, Senate and Bar Council, 1976–82. Mem., Wine Exec. Cttee, SE Circuit, 1986–88. Mem. Cttee, Family Law Bar Assoc., 1976–89. *Recreations:* gardening, reading, travel in France, Roman remains. *Address:* c/o Kingston County Court, St James Road, Kingston upon Thames KT1 2AD.

MORGAN, (Hywel) Rhodri; MP (Lab) Cardiff West, since 1987; *b* 29 Sept. 1939; *s* of Thomas John and Huana Morgan; *m* 1967, Julie Edwards; one *s* two *d*. *Educ:* St John's College, Univ. of Oxford (Hons cl. 2, PPE 1961); Harvard Univ. (Masters in Govt 1963). Tutor Organiser, WEA, S Wales Area, 1963–65; Research Officer, Cardiff City Council, Welsh Office and DoE, 1965–71; Economic Adviser, DTI, 1972–74; Indust. Develt Officer, S Glamorgan County Council, 1974–80; Head of Bureau for Press and Inf., European Commn Office for Wales, 1980–87. Opposition spokesman on: Energy, 1988–92; Welsh Affairs, 1992–. *Publication:* Cardiff: half and half a capital, 1994. *Recreations:* long-distance running, wood carving, marine wildlife. *Address:* Lower House, Michaelston-le-Pit, Dinas Powys, South Glamorgan CF6 4HE. *T:* (home) Cardiff (01222) 514262; (office) Cardiff (01222) 223207.

MORGAN, Janet; *see* Balfour of Burleigh, Lady.

MORGAN, Sir John (Albert Leigh), KCMG 1989 (CMG 1982); HM Diplomatic Service, retired; Chairman: Invesco (formerly Drayton) Korea Trust plc, since 1993 (Director, 1991); LSE Foundation, since 1994; East European Development Trust, since 1994; Director: Invesco Group Ltd, since 1994; Japan Discovery Trust, since 1994; *b* 21 June 1929; *s* of late John Edward Rowland Morgan, Bridge, Kent; *m* 1st, 1961, Hon. Fionn Frances Bride O'Neill (marr. diss. 1975), *d* of 3rd Baron O'Neill, Shane's Castle, Antrim; one *s* two *d*; 2nd, 1976, Angela Mary Eleanor, *e d* of Patrick Warre Rathbone, MBE, Woolton, Liverpool; one *s* one *d*. *Educ:* London School of Economics (BSc(Econ) Hons Econs and Law; Hon. Fellow, 1984). Served in Army, 1947–49: commnd 1948; interpreter with French Army, 1949. Entered Foreign Service, 1951; FO, 1951–53; 3rd Sec. and Private Sec. to HM Ambassador, Moscow, 1953–56; 2nd Sec., Peking, 1956–58; FO, 1958–63 (attended Geneva Conf. of Foreign Ministers on Berlin, 1959, and on Laos (interpreter in Russian and Chinese), 1961; interpreter for Mr Khrushchev's visit to UK, 1956, for Mr Macmillan's visit to Soviet Union, 1959, and for Summit Conf. in Paris, 1960); 1st Sec., 1960; Head of Chancery, Rio de Janeiro, 1963–64; FO, 1964–65; Chargé d'Affaires, Ulan Bator, 1965; Moscow, 1965–67; Dep. Hd, Econ. Relns Dept, subseq. Export Promotion Dept, FO, 1968; Head of Far Eastern Dept, FCO, 1970–72; Head of Cultural Relations Dept, FCO, 1972–80 (Member: Reviewing Cttee on Export of Works of Art; Fulbright Scholarship Commn; Selection Cttee, US Bicentennial Scholarships Prog.); Ambassador and Consul Gen. to Republic of Korea, 1980–83; Ambassador to Poland, 1983–86; Ambassador to Mexico, 1986–89. Man. Dir (Internat. Relations), Maxwell Communications Corp., 1989–90; Director: The European, 1990–91; Christies, 1993–95; Pres., IFPI, 1990–93. Served on Earl Marshal's Staff for State Funeral of Sir Winston Churchill, 1965, and for Investiture of Prince of Wales, 1969. Trustee, BM, 1991– (Mem., Develt Trust, 1991–). Governor, LSE, 1971–. Chairman: Anglo-Korean Soc., 1990–; UK-Korea Forum for the Future, 1991–; Pestalozzi Children's Village Appeal, 1993–; Member: Internat. Council, United World Colleges, 1990–; Internat. and Current Affairs Cttee, ESU, 1993–. Royal Philharmonic Orchestra: Dir, 1993–; Chm., Development Trust, 1993–. FRSA; Fellow, Royal Asiatic Soc.; Hon. Life Mem., GB-China Centre. Hon. DSc (Politics) Korea Univ., 1983; Hon. LLD Mexico Acad. of Internat. Law, 1987. Order of the Aztec Eagle, 1st cl. (Mexico), 1994. *Publications:* (under a pseudonym): various works of French and Chinese literary criticism. *Recreations:* ornithology, oriental art, tennis. *Address:* 41 Hugh Street, SW1V 1QJ. *T:* 0171–821 1037; Beaumont Cottage, South Brewham, near Bruton, Somerset BA10 0JZ. *T:* Upton Noble (01749) 850606. *Club:* Travellers'.

MORGAN, John Alfred; Investment Director, Caviapen Investments Ltd, since 1993; Director, Yamaichi Bank (UK) plc, since 1994; *b* 16 Sept. 1931; *s* of late Alfred Morgan and of Lydia Amelia Morgan; *m* 1959, Janet Mary Sclater-Jones; one *d*. *Educ:* Rugeley Grammar Sch.; Peterhouse, Cambridge (BA). Investment Research, Cambridge, 1953–59; Investment Manager, S. G. Warburg & Co. Ltd, 1959–67; Director: Glyn, Mills & Co., 1967–70; Finance and Investment, Williams & Glyn's Bank Ltd, 1970–76; Rothschild Asset Management, 1976–78; Central Trustee Savings Bank Ltd, 1982–86; Zurich Life Assce Co. Ltd, 1970–87; Sealink UK Ltd, 1983–85. Gen. Manager, British Railways Pension Funds, 1978–86; Chief Exec., IMRO, 1986–93. Chm., Post Office Users' Nat. Council, 1978–82. *Recreations:* music, contemporary art, fell walking. *Address:* 5 Grange Road, Highgate, N6 4AR. *Club:* Reform.

MORGAN, John Ambrose; His Honour Judge John Morgan; a Circuit Judge, since 1990; *b* 22 Sept. 1934; *s* of Joseph Michael Morgan and Monica Morgan; *m* 1970, Rosalie Mary Tyson; two *s*. *Educ:* St Edward's Coll., Liverpool; Univ. of Liverpool (Emmott Meml Scholar 1953; Alsopp Prizewinner 1953; LLB 1955). Law Soc. Finals 1957 (Local Govt Prize). Nat. Service, RAF, 1958–60. Admitted Solicitor, 1958; practised in local govt and private practice, 1960–70; called to the Bar, Gray's Inn, 1970; N Circuit, 1970–90; Dep. Stipendiary Magistrate, 1982; Asst Recorder, 1983; Recorder, 1988. Chm. of Govs, St Edward's Coll., Liverpool, 1987–. *Recreations:* Rugby Union football (writing and broadcasting; Pres., Liverpool RFU, 1980–82), golf, cricket, music, amateur operatics. *Address:* Queen Elizabeth II Law Courts, Derby Square, Liverpool L2 1XA. *T:* 0151–473 7373. *Clubs:* Athenæum (Liverpool); Liverpool St Helen's RFC, Woolton Golf, Sefton Cricket.

MORGAN, (John) Gwyn(fryn); Ambassador-Head of Delegation of the European Commission to Thailand, Vietnam, Laos, Cambodia, Myanmar and Malaysia, since 1993; *b* 16 Feb. 1934; *s* of Arthur G. Morgan, coal miner, and Mary Walters; *m* 1st, 1960, Joan Margaret Taylor (marr. diss. 1974); one *d*; 2nd, 1979, Colette Anne Rumball (marr. diss. 1989); two *s* one *d*; 3rd, 1990, Margery Sue Greenfeld. *Educ:* Aberdare Boys' Grammar Sch.; UCW Aberystwyth. MA Classics 1957; Dip. Educn 1958. Senior Classics Master, The Regis Sch., Tettenhall, Staffs, 1958–60; Pres., National Union of Students, 1960–62; Sec.-Gen., Internat. Student Conf. (ISC), 1962–65; Head of Overseas Dept, British Labour Party, 1965–69; Asst Gen. Secretary, British Labour Party, 1969–72; Chef de Cabinet to Mr George Thomson, 1973–75; Head of Welsh Inf. Office, EEC, 1975–79; a Dir, Development Corp. for Wales, 1976–81, Hon. Consultant in Canada 1981–83; Head of EEC Press and Inf. Office for Canada, 1979–83; EEC Rep. in Turkey, 1983–86; Hd, Delgn of EEC to Israel, 1987–92. Mem., Hansard Commn on Electoral Reform, 1975–76. Adjunct Prof., Univ. of Guelph, 1980–. *Publications:* contribs to numerous British and foreign political jls. *Recreations:* cricket, Rugby football, crosswords, wine-tasting. *Address:* Mayfair Garden (17th Floor), 59 Sukhumvit Soi 16, Bangkok 10110, Thailand. *Clubs:* Commonwealth Trust, Reform; Cardiff and County.

MORGAN, John Lewis, OBE 1981; Member (C) Test Valley Borough Council, since 1974; *b* 12 May 1919; *s* of Charles Lewis Morgan and Elsie Winifred (*née* Smith); *m* 1943, Grace Barnes; one *s* three *d*. *Educ:* St Paul's Sch. Member: Wherwell Parish Council, 1947– (Chm., 1962–); Andover RDC, 1950–74 (Vice-Chm., 1960–72; Chm., 1972–74; Chm. of Finance, 1956–74); Hampshire CC, 1956–66; Mayor of Test Valley, 1977–78 and 1978–79. Mem., Assoc. of Dist Councils, 1974– (Chm., 1984–87, Vice-Chm., 1983–84; Chm. of Housing and Environmental Health, 1979–83); President: IULA/CEMR (British Sections), 1984– (Chm., 1980–84); CLRAE, Strasbourg, 1987–90 (Mem., 1975–; Vice-Pres., 1984–87; Pres., 1987–90; 1st Vice-Pres., 1990–94; Chm., Environment and Town Planning Cttee, 1983–85); Chm., Eur. Affairs Cttee, IULA, The Hague, 1981–86; Vice-Chm., CEMR Paris, 1981–87; Chm., Consultative Cttee, CEMR/IULA, Brussels, 1986–94. Church lay reader. *Recreations:* keen supporter of Southampton Football Club; avid gardener. *Address:* Dancing Ledge, Wherwell, Andover, Hants SP11 7JS. *T:* Andover (01264) 860296.

MORGAN, John William Harold, (Bill), FEng 1978; Chairman, Trafford Park Urban Development Corporation, since 1990; Director: AMEC plc, 1983–91 (Chairman, 1984–88); Hill Samuel & Co., 1983–89; *b* 13 Dec. 1927; *s* of John Henry and Florence Morgan; *m* 1952, Barbara (*née* Harrison); two *d*. *Educ:* Wednesbury Boys' High Sch.; Univ. of Birmingham (BScEng, 1st Cl. Hons). FIMechE, MIEE. National Service commn with RAF, 1949–51. Joined English Electric Co., Stafford, as design engr, subseq. Chief Development Engr (Machines), 1953; Chief Develt Engr (Mechanical), 1957; Chief Engr (DC Machines), 1960; Product Div. Manager, 1962; Gen. Man., Electrical Machines Gp, 1965; Managing Director, English Electric-AEI Machines Gp (following merger with GEC/AEI), 1968; Asst Man. Dir and main board director, GEC plc, 1973–83. Chm., Staffordshire Cable, 1989–; Dep. Chm., Petbow Holdings, 1983–86; Director: Simon Engineering, 1983–88; Pitney Bowes, 1989–92; Tekdata, 1989–; UMIST Ventures, 1989–. Mem., Monopolies and Mergers Commn, 1992–. Mem. Council, Fellowship of Engrg, 1987–90. FRSA 1988. S. G. Brown award for an outstanding contrib. to promotion and development of mechanical inventions, Royal Society, 1968. *Recreations:* craft activities, particularly woodworking. *Address:* Mullion, Whitmore Heath, near Newcastle, Staffs ST5 5HF. *T:* Newcastle (Staffs) (01782) 680462.

MORGAN, Prof. Keith John, DPhil; FRACI, FRSC; FAIM; Visiting Professor, Hiroshima University, 1995–96; *b* 14 Dec. 1929; *s* of C. F. J. Morgan and Winifred Burman (formerly Morgan, *née* Allen); *m* 1957, Hilary Chapman; one *d*. *Educ:* Manchester Grammar Sch.; Brasenose Coll., Oxford (MA, BSc, DPhil). Senior Research Fellow, Min. of Supply, 1955–57; ICI Res. Fellow, 1957–58; Lectr, Univ. of Birmingham, 1958–64; AEC Fellow, Purdue Univ., 1960–61; Lectr, Sen. Lectr, Prof., Dept. of Chemistry, Univ. of Lancaster, 1964–86 (Pro-Vice-Chancellor, 1973–78; Sen. Pro-Vice-Chancellor, 1978–86); Vice-Chancellor, Univ. of Newcastle, NSW, 1987–93; Prof., Univ. of Electro-Communications, Tokyo, 1993–95. Chm., Hunter Foundn for Cancer Res., 1992–93; Dep. Chm., Hunter Technol. Develt Centre, 1987–93; Member: Hunter Econ. Develt Council, 1989–93; Hunter Federal Task Force, 1991–93; Hunter Area Health Service Bd,

1992–93; Dir, Hunter Orch., 1991–93. Chm., Regl Council, AIM, 1989–93. Chm. of Govs, Newcastle Grammar Sch., 1991–93; Member: UCNS, 1980–86; Council, Lancashire Polytechnic, 1985–86. Mem., NSW Envmtl Res. Trust, 1990–93. Hon. DSc Newcastle, NSW, 1993. *Publications:* scientific papers in Jl Chm. Soc. and other jls. *Recreations:* mountains, Mozart, cricket. *Address:* Hiroshima University, Kagamiyama 1-chome, Higashi-Hiroshima 724, Japan. *Club:* Newcastle (NSW).

MORGAN, Kenneth, OBE 1978; journalist; consultant on Press ethics; Director: Press Council, 1980–90; Press Complaints Commission, 1991; *b* 3 Nov. 1928; *s* of Albert E. and Lily M. Morgan; *m* 1950, Margaret Cynthia, *d* of Roland E. Wilson; three *d. Educ:* Stockport Grammar School. Reporter, Stockport Express, 1944; Army, 1946, commissioned, 1947 (served Palestine, Egypt, GHQ MELF); journalism, 1949; Central London Sec., NUJ, 1962; Nat. Organiser, NUJ, 1966; Gen. Sec., NUJ, 1970–77, Mem. of Honour, 1978. Press Council: Consultative Mem., 1970–77; Jt Sec., 1977–78; Dep. Dir and Conciliator, 1978–79; Consultant, Press Complaints Commn, 1992. Director: Journalists in Europe Ltd, 1982–; Reuters Founder's Share Co., 1984–. Mem. Exec. Cttee: Printing and Kindred Trades Fedn, 1970–73; Nat. Fedn of Professional Workers, 1970–77; Fedn of Broadcasting Unions, 1970–77; Confedn of Entertainment Unions, 1970–77; Bureau, Internat. Fedn of Journalists, 1970–78. Member: NEDC for Printing and Publishing Industry, 1970; Printing Industries Cttee, TUC, 1974–77; Printing and Publishing Industries Trng Bd, 1975–77; Jt Standing Cttee, Nat. Newspaper Industry, 1976–77; British Cttee, Journalists in Europe, 1977–; C of E General Synod Cttee for Communications Press Panel, 1981–90; CRE Media Gp, 1981–85; Judge, Samuel Storey Editl Awards, 1981–; Internat. Ombudsman Inst., 1983–; Trustee, Reuters, 1984–. Vice Pres. (former Chm.), Dulwich UNA, 1989–. Gov., 1992–, Hon. Sec., 1993–, ESU. Associate Mem. IPI, 1980; FRSA 1980. Methodist Recorder Lectr, 1989. *Publications:* Press Conduct in the Sutcliffe Case, 1983; (with David Christie) New Connexions: the power to inform, 1989; *contributed to:* El Poder Judicial en le Conjunto de los Poderes del Estado y de la Sociedad, 1989; Media Freedom and Accountability, 1989; The Independence of the Journalist, Is de Klant of de Krant Koning, 1990; Beyond the Courtroom: alternatives for resolving press disputes, 1991. *Recreations:* theatre, military history, inland waterways, travel. *Address:* 151 Overhill Road, Dulwich, SE22 0PT. *T:* 0181–693 6585.

MORGAN, Prof. Kenneth Owen, FBA 1983, FRHistS 1964; Principal, University College of Wales, Aberystwyth and Professor in the University of Wales, 1989–95; Vice-Chancellor, then Senior Vice-Chancellor, University of Wales, 1993–95; *b* 16 May 1934; *s* of David James Morgan and Margaret Morgan (*née* Owen); *m* 1973, Jane Keeler (*d* 1992); one *s* one *d. Educ:* University College School, London; Oriel College, Oxford. MA, DPhil 1958, DLitt 1985. University College, Swansea: Lectr in History Dept, 1958–66 (Sen. Lectr, 1965–66); Hon. Fellow, 1985; Fellow and Praelector, Modern Hist. and Politics, Queen's Coll., Oxford, 1966–89 (Hon. Fellow, 1992); Faculty Lectr, 1995–. Supernumerary Fellow, Jesus Coll., Oxford, 1991–92. Amer. Council of Learned Socs Fellow, Columbia Univ., 1962–63; Vis. Prof., Columbia Univ., 1965. BBC (Wales) Lectr, 1995. Member: Council, RHistS, 1983–86; Bd of Celtic Studies, 1972–; Council, Nat. Library of Wales, 1991–95. Editor, Welsh History Review, 1961–; Jt Editor, 20th Century British History, 1994–. *Publications:* Wales in British Politics, 1963, 3rd edn 1980; David Lloyd George: Welsh radical as world statesman, 1963, 2nd edn 1982; Freedom or Sacrilege?, 1966; Keir Hardie, 1967; The Age of Lloyd George, 1971, 3rd edn 1978; (ed) Lloyd George: Family Letters, 1973; Lloyd George, 1974; Keir Hardie: radical and socialist, 1975, 2nd edn 1984 (Arts Council prize, 1976); Consensus and Disunity, 1979, 2nd edn 1986; (with Jane Morgan) Portrait of a Progressive, 1980; Rebirth of a Nation: Wales 1880–1980, 1981, 2nd edn 1982 (Arts Council prize, 1982); David Lloyd George, 1981; Labour in Power 1945–1951, 1984, 2nd edn 1985; (ed jtly) Welsh Society and Nationhood, 1984; (ed) The Oxford Illustrated History of Britain, 1984, new edn 1992; (ed) The Sphere Illustrated History of Britain, 1985; Labour People, 1987, new edn 1992; (ed) The Oxford History of Britain, 1988; The Red Dragon and the Red Flag, 1989; The People's Peace: British History 1945–1990, 1991, new edn 1992; Academic Leadership, 1991; Modern Wales: politics, places and people, 1995; Britain and Europe, 1995; many articles, reviews etc. *Recreations:* music, architecture, sport, travel. *Address:* The Croft, 63 Millwood End, Long Hanborough, Witney, Oxon OX8 8BP. *T:* Witney (01993) 881341. *Club:* Athenæum.

MORGAN, Kenneth Smith; Editor of the Official Report (Hansard), House of Commons, 1979–89; *b* 6 Aug. 1925; *er s* of Edward and Florence Morgan; *m* 1952, Patricia Hunt; one *s* one *d. Educ:* Battersea and Dartford Grammar Schools. Commissioned Royal West Kent Regt, 1944; Burma, 1944–46. Weekly newspapers, 1947–51; Derby Evening Telegraph, 1951–52; Reuters Parliamentary Staff, 1952–54; joined Official Report, 1954; Dep. Asst Editor, 1972, Dep. Editor, 1978. Founded Commonwealth Hansard Editors Assoc., 1984. *Publication:* The Falklands Campaign: a digest of parliamentary debates on the Falklands, 1982. *Recreations:* Napoleonic warfare history, model soldiers, cricket, bridge. *Address:* 3 Highfield Road, Bexleyheath, Kent DA6 7HX.

MORGAN, Leslie; *see* Morgan, F. L.

MORGAN, Loraine; Metropolitan Stipendiary Magistrate, since 1995; *b* 2 Dec. 1953; *d* of Enrico Bellisario and late Elizabeth Bellisario (*née* Coyle); *m* 1976, Comdr Dai Morgan, RN. *Educ:* St Augustine's Priory, Ealing; Univ. of Exeter; Coll. of Law, Guildford. Admitted Solicitor, 1981; Partner, Reynolds & Hetherington, Fareham, 1982–86, Allsworth & Spears, Fareham, 1986–88; Solicitor Advocate, 1988–95; Co-founder and Dir, Just Advocates Ltd, 1991–95. Mem., Crown Court Rules Cttee, 1994. Vice-Pres., Bracton Law Soc., 1974–75; Cttee Mem., Hampshire Inc. Law Soc., 1990–94; Sec. and Chm., Southampton Criminal Courts Solicitors' Assoc., 1990–94; Vice-Chm., Criminal Law Solicitors' Assoc., 1991–94. *Recreations:* good wine, good food, the company of good friends. *Address:* c/o Inner London Magistrates' Courts Service, 65 Romney Street, SW1P 3RD. *T:* 0171–799 3332.

MORGAN, (Mair) Eluned; Member (Lab) Mid and West Wales, European Parliament, since 1994; *b* 16 Feb. 1967; *d* of Rev. Bob Morgan and Elaine Morgan. *Educ:* Atlantic Coll., Univ. of Hull (BA); Univs of Strasbourg, Complutense and Javeriana. Stagiaire with Socialist Gp, Europe. Parlt, 1990; with S4C, 1991; researcher and reporter, Agenda TV, 1992; documentary researcher, BBC TV, 1993. *Recreations:* walking, singing. *Address:* 2 Queen Street, Carmarthen, Dyfed SA31 1JR. *T:* Carmarthen (01267) 222205, *Fax:* (01267) 223343.

MORGAN, Marilynne Ann; Solicitor and Legal Adviser, Department of the Environment, since 1992; *b* 22 June 1946; *d* of late J. Emlyn Williams and Roma Elizabeth Williams (*née* Ellis); *m* 1970, Nicholas Alan, *e s* of Rear-Adm. Sir Patrick Morgan, KCVO, CB, DSC. *Educ:* Gads Hill Place, Higham-by-Rochester; Bedford Coll., Univ. of London (BA Hons History). Called to the Bar, Middle Temple, 1972. Res. Asst, Special Historical Sect., FCO, 1967–71; Department of Health and Social Security: Legal Asst, 1973; Sen. Legal Asst, 1978; Asst Solicitor, 1982; Under Sec. and Principal Asst Solicitor, 1985–91, DSS, 1988–91, DoE, 1991–92; Chm., Departmental Task Force, 1994–. Vice-Chm. 1983–84, Chm. 1984–86, Legal Sect. of Assoc. of First Div. Civil Servants. Mem., General Council of the Bar, 1987–92. *Publications:* contributor, Halsbury's Laws of England, 1982, 1986; articles in learned jls. *Recreations:* homely pursuits. *Address:* Department of the Environment, 2 Marsham Street, SW1P 3EB. *Club:* University Women's.

MORGAN, Michael David; Chief Executive and General Manager, Telford Development Corporation, 1986–92, retired; *b* 19 Jan. 1942; *s* of Edward Arthur and Winifred Maud Morgan; *m* 1980, Ljiljana Radojcic; three *d. Educ:* Royal Liberty Sch., Romford; Prince Rupert Sch., Wilhemshaven, FRG; Coll. of Estate Management, London Univ. (BSc Est. Man.). FRICS. Sheffield City Council, 1964–67; Derby Borough Council, 1967–70; Telford Develt Corp., 1970–92. *Recreations:* cricket, jogging, swimming, gardening. *Address:* 42 London Road, Shrewsbury SY2 6NX. *T:* Shrewsbury (01743) 352800.

MORGAN, Michael Hugh, CMG 1978; HM Diplomatic Service, retired; *b* 18 April 1925; *s* of late H. P. Morgan; *m* 1957, Julian Bamfield; two *s. Educ:* Shrewsbury Sch.; Downing College, Cambridge; School of Oriental and African Studies, London Univ. Army Service 1943–46. HMOCS Malaya, 1946–56. Foreign Office, 1956–57; First Secretary, Peking, 1957–60; Belgrade 1960–64; attached to Industry, 1964; First Secretary, FCO, 1964–68; Counsellor and Head of Chancery, Cape Town/Pretoria, 1968–72; Counsellor, Peking, 1972–75; Inspector, FCO, 1975–77; High Comr, Sierra Leone, 1977–81; Ambassador to the Philippines, 1981–85. Consultant, British Rail Engrg, 1986–88; Dir, Swansea Overseas Trust, 1988–91. *Address:* Strefford House, Strefford, Craven Arms, Shropshire SY7 8DE.

MORGAN, Patrick; HM Diplomatic Service; Counsellor and Deputy Head of Post, Abu Dhabi, since 1995; *b* 31 Jan. 1944; *s* of Matthew Morgan and Margaret (*née* Docherty); *m* 1966, Marlene Collins Beaton; two *s* two *d. Educ:* St Columba's High Sch., Greenock. BoT, 1963–64; CRO, 1964–65; FCO, 1965–67; British Embassy: Bonn, 1967–69; Kuwait, 1969–71; La Paz, 1972–75; FCO, 1975–79; British Embassy: Washington DC, 1979–83; Jakarta, 1983–86; FCO, 1987–92; Ambassador to Honduras, 1992–95. *Recreations:* swimming, jogging (horizontal), music. *Address:* c/o Foreign and Commonwealth Office, King Charles Street, SW1A 2AH; British Embassy, Abu Dhabi, United Arab Emirates.

MORGAN, Paul Hyacinth; QC 1992; *b* 17 Aug. 1952; *s* of Daniel Morgan and Veronica Mary (*née* Elder); *m* 1980, Sheila Ruth Harvey; three *s. Educ:* St Columb's Coll., Londonderry; Peterhouse, Cambridge (BA 1974; MA 1979). Called to the Bar, Lincoln's Inn, 1975. *Publications:* (ed jtly) Megarry on Rent Acts, 11th edn, 1988; (ed jtly) Woodfall on Landlord and Tenant, 28th edn, 1990. *Address:* Falcon Chambers, Falcon Court, EC4Y 1AA. *T:* 0171–353 2484.

MORGAN, His Honour Peter Trevor Hopkin; QC 1972; a Circuit Judge, 1972–87; Liaison Judge to Gwent Magistrates, and Justice of the Peace, 1973–87; a Judge of the Provincial Court of the Church in Wales, 1976–87; *b* 5 Feb. 1919; *o s* of Cyril Richard Morgan and Muriel Arceta (*née* Hole); *m* 1942, Josephine Mouncey, *d* of Ben Travers, CBE, AFC; one *s* three *d. Educ:* Mill Hill Sch.; Magdalen Coll., Oxford (BA). Called to Bar, Middle Temple, 1949; Wales and Chester Circuit; Lectr in Law, Univ. of Wales (Cardiff and Swansea), 1950–55. Liveryman, Fishmongers' Company. *Recreations:* inland waterways, viniculture, wine making. *Address:* 26 Westmead Lane, Chippenham, Wilts SN15 3HZ.

MORGAN, Peter William Lloyd; Director-General, Institute of Directors, 1989–94; Deputy Chairman, National Provident Institution, since 1995; *b* 9 May 1936; *s* of late Matthew Morgan and of Margaret Gwynneth (*née* Lloyd); *m* 1964, Elisabeth Susanne Davis; three *d. Educ:* Llandovery Coll.; Trinity Hall, Cambridge (MA). Royal Signals, 1954–56 (2nd Lieut). Joined IBM UK Ltd, 1959; Data Processing Sales Dir, 1971–74; Gp Dir of Marketing, IBM Europe, Paris, 1975–80; Director: IBM UK Ltd, 1983–87; IBM UK Holdings Ltd, 1987–89. Director: NCC, 1981–89; South Wales Electricity PLC, 1989–; Director Publications Ltd, 1989–94; G. M. Firth (Holdings), 1994–; Zergo plc, 1994–. Member: Governing Body, ICC UK, 1989–; Economic and Social Cttee, EC, 1994–. Freeman, Worshipful Co. of Inf. Technologists, 1992. Radical of the Year, Radical Soc., 1990. *Recreations:* music, history, gardening, ski-ing, exercising my dogs. *Address:* 40 Catherine Place, SW1E 6HL. *Club:* United Oxford & Cambridge University.

MORGAN, Rev. Philip; Minister, St Andrew's United Reformed Church, Frognal, London, since 1990; *b* 22 June 1930; *s* of David Lewis and Pamela Morgan; *m* 1954, Greta Mary Hanson; one *s* one *d. Educ:* Overdale Coll.; Selly Oaks Colls; Univ. of Birmingham (BA Hons Theology). Ordained 1952; Ministries: Aberfan, Godreaman, Griffithstown, Merthyr Tydfil and Treharris, 1952–58; Eltham, London, 1958–62; Leicester and South Wigston, 1962–67; General Secretary, Churches of Christ in GB and Ireland, 1967–80; Gen. Sec., BCC, 1980–90. Moderator, URC, 1984–85. Hon. DD Christian Theological Seminary, USA, 1980. *Recreations:* hill walking, Celtic history, steam railways. *Address:* St Andrew's Manse, 33 Crediton Hill, West Hampstead, NW6 1H5.

MORGAN, Piers Stefan; Editor, Daily Mirror, since 1995; *b* 30 March 1965; *s* of Glynne and Gabrielle Pughe-Morgan; *m* 1991, Marion Elizabeth Shalloe; one *s. Educ:* Chailey Comprehensive Sch.; Lewes Priory Sixth Form Coll.; Harlow Journalism Coll. With Lloyd's of London, 1985–87; Reporter, Surrey and S London Newspapers, 1987–89; Showbusiness Editor, The Sun, 1989–94; Editor, News of the World, 1994–95. Editor of the Year, Newspaper Focus Awards, 1994. *Publications:* Private Lives of the Stars, 1990; Secret Lives of the Stars, 1991; Phillip Schofield: to dream a dream, 1992; Take That: our story, 1993; Take That: on the road, 1994. *Recreations:* cricket, Arsenal FC. *Address:* Daily Mirror, 1 Canada Square, Canary Wharf, E14 5AP. *T:* 0171–293 3000.

MORGAN, Rhodri; *see* Morgan, H. R.

MORGAN, Richard Martin, MA; Warden, Radley College, since 1991; *b* 25 June 1940; *s* of His Honour Trevor Morgan, MC, QC, and late Leslie Morgan; *m* 1968, Margaret Kathryn, *d* of late Anthony Agutter and of Mrs Launcelot Fleming; three *d. Educ:* Sherborne Sch.; Caius Coll., Cambridge (MA, DipEd); York Univ. Assistant Master, Radley Coll., 1963; Housemaster, 1969; Headmaster, Cheltenham College, 1978–90. Member, Adv. Council, Understanding British Industry, 1977–79. JP Glos, 1978–90. *Recreations:* reading, music, games. *Address:* Radley College, Abingdon, Oxon OX14 2HR. *T:* Abingdon (01235) 520294. *Clubs:* Free Foresters', Jesters'.

MORGAN, Robin Milne; Principal: Daniel Stewart's and Melville College, Edinburgh, 1977–89; The Mary Erskine School, 1979–89; *b* 2 Oct. 1930; *o s* of Robert Milne Morgan and Aida Forsyth Morgan; *m* 1955, Fiona Bruce MacLeod Douglas; three *s* one *d. Educ:* Mackie Academy, Stonehaven; Aberdeen Univ. (MA); London Univ. (BA, External). Nat. Service, 2nd Lieut The Gordon Highlanders, 1952–54; Asst Master: Arden House Prep. Sch., 1955–60; George Watson's Coll., 1960–71; Headmaster, Campbell Coll., Belfast, 1971–76. *Recreations:* music, archaeology, fishing, climbing. *Address:* Rose House, Nawton, York YO6 5TT.

MORGAN, Robin Richard; Consultant editor, The Sunday Times, since 1995; *b* 16 Sept. 1953; *s* of Raymond Morgan and Jean Edith Bennett; *m* 1977, Ruth Winefride Mary O'Shea; two *s* one *d*. *Educ:* King Edward VI Grammar Sch., Stourbridge, W Midlands. County Express, Stourbridge, 1971–73; Evening Echo, Hemel Hempstead, 1973–79; Sunday Times, London, 1979–89: Reporter, 1979–83; Dep. News Editor, 1983–85; Insight Editor, 1985–87; Features Editor, 1987–89; Editor, Sunday Express, 1989–91; Associate Editor, Sunday Times, 1991–92; Editor, Sunday Times Magazine, 1992–93; Editorial Dir designate, Reader's Digest, 1993–94. Campaigning Journalist of the Year: (commended) 1982; (winner) 1983. *Publications:* (jtly) The Falklands War, 1982; (jtly) Rainbow Warrior, 1986; (jtly) Bullion, 1988; (ed) Manpower, 1988; (jtly) Ambush, 1989. *Recreations:* reading, travel. *Address:* 66–68 East Smithfield, Admiral House, EC1.

MORGAN, Roger; *see* Morgan, E. R.

MORGAN, Roger Hugh Vaughan Charles, CBE 1991; Librarian, House of Lords, 1977–91; *b* 8 July 1926; *s* of late Charles Langbridge Morgan, and Hilda Vaughan, both novelists and playwrights; *m* 1st, 1951, Harriet Waterfield (marr. diss. 1965), *d* of Gordon Waterfield; one *s* one *d* (and one *s* decd); 2nd, 1965, Susan Vogel Marrian, *d* of Hugo Vogel, Milwaukee, USA; one *s*. *Educ:* Downs Sch., Colwall; Phillips Acad., Andover, USA; Eton Coll.; Brasenose Coll., Oxford. MA. Grenadier Guards, 1944–47 (Captain, 1946). House of Commons Library, 1951–63; House of Lords Library, 1963–91. *Recreations:* painting, photography, cooking. *Address:* 30 St Peter's Square, W6 9UH. *T:* 0181–741 0267; Cliff Cottage, Laugharne, Dyfed. *T:* Laugharne (01994) 427398. *Clubs:* Garrick, Beefsteak, Saintsbury.
See also Marchioness of Anglesey.

MORGAN, Prof. Roger Pearce; Professor of Political Science, European University Institute, since 1988; *b* 3 March 1932; *s* of Donald Emlyn Morgan and Esther Mary Morgan (*née* Pearce); *m* 1st, 1957, Annie-Françoise, (Annette) Combes (marr. diss. 1988); three *s* one *d*; 2nd, 1988, Mrs Catherine Howell. *Educ:* Wolverton Grammar Sch.; Leighton Park Sch.; Downing Coll., Cambridge (MA 1957; PhD 1959); Univs of Paris and Hamburg. Staff Tutor, Dept of Extra-Mural Studies, London Univ., 1957–59; Asst Lectr and Lectr in Internat. Politics, UCW, Aberystwyth, 1959–63; Lectr in Hist. and Internat. Relations, Sussex Univ., 1963–67; Asst, then Dep. Dir of Studies, RIIA, 1968–74; Prof. of European Politics, 1974–78, and Dean, Sch. of Human and Environmental Studies, 1976–78, Loughborough Univ.; Head of European Centre for Political Studies, PSI, 1978–86; Vis. Fellow, Centre for Internat. Studies, LSE, 1987–88. Visiting Professor: Columbia Univ., 1965; Johns Hopkins Univ., 1969–70, 1988; Cornell Univ., 1972; Surrey Univ., 1980–84; UCLA, 1993; Res. Associate, Center for Internat. Affairs, Harvard, 1965–66; Visiting Lecturer: Cambridge Univ., 1967; LSE, 1974, 1980–88; Associate Mem., Nuffield Coll., Oxford, 1980–83; Hon. Professorial Fellow, UCW, Aberystwyth, 1980–84, Hon. Prof., 1985–. Lectr at RCDS, CS Coll., RNC, etc. Member: Council, RIIA, 1976–85, 1986–92; Academic Council, Wilton Park, 1982–83. Trustee, Gilbert Murray Trust, 1973–88. *Publications:* The German Social Democrats and the First International 1864–72, 1965; Modern Germany, 1966; (ed jtly) Britain and West Germany: changing societies and the future of foreign policy, 1971 (German edn, 1970); West European Politics since 1945, 1972; (ed) The Study of International Affairs, 1972; High Politics, Low Politics: toward a foreign policy for Western Europe, 1973; The United States and West Germany 1945–1973: a study in alliance politics, 1974 (German edn 1975); West Germany's Foreign Policy Agenda, 1978; (ed jtly) Moderates and Conservatives in Western Europe, 1982 (Italian edn 1983); (ed jtly) Partners and Rivals in Western Europe: Britain, France and Germany, 1986; (ed) Regionalism in European Politics, 1986; (ed jtly) New Diplomacy in the Post-Cold War World, 1993; (ed jtly) The Third Pillar of the European Union, 1994; (ed jtly) Parliaments and Parties: the European Parliament in the political life of Europe, 1995; contribs to symposia and jls. *Recreations:* music, travel, watching cricket. *Address:* European University Institute, Badia Fiesolana, 50016 San Domenico di Fiesole (FI), Italy. *T:* (55) 46851. *Clubs:* Reform, PEN; Middlesex County Cricket, Surrey County Cricket.

MORGAN, Sally; Head of Party Liaison for Leader of the Opposition, since 1995; *b* 28 June 1959; *d* of Albert Edward Morgan and Margaret Morgan; *m* 1984, John Lyons; two *s*. *Educ:* Belvedere Girls' Sch., Liverpool; Durham Univ. (BA Geog. Hons); Univ. of London (PGCE, MA Educ.). Secondary Sch. Teacher, 1981–85; Labour Party: Student Organiser, 1985–87; Sen. Targetting Officer, 1987–93; Dir, Campaigns and Elecns, 1993–95. *Recreations:* relaxing with family and friends, cooking, gardening.

MORGAN, Rt. Rev. Thomas Oliver; *see* Saskatchewan, Bishop of.

MORGAN, Tom, CBE 1982; DL; JP; Lord Provost of the City of Edinburgh and Lord Lieutenant of the City and County of Edinburgh, 1980–84; *b* 24 Feb. 1914; *s* of Thomas Morgan; *m* 1940, Mary Montgomery (*d* 1991), *d* of Stephen McLauchlan; two *s*. *Educ:* Longside Public Sch., Aberdeenshire; Aberdeen Univ.; W of Scotland Coll. of Agriculture. Unigate Ltd for 36 yrs (Regional Dir for Scotland). Member, Edinburgh Corp., 1954–71 and Edinburgh DC, 1977–84. Chairman: Edinburgh Festival Soc., 1980–84; Edinburgh Mil. Tattoo Policy Cttee, 1980–84. Formerly: Magistrate; City Treasurer; Curator of Patronage, Univ. of Edinburgh; Governor, George Heriot's Trust; Governor, Edinburgh and E of Scotland Coll. of Agric.; Dir, Edinburgh Chamber of Commerce and Manufactures; Pres., Edinburgh City Business Club; Gen. Comr of Income Tax; Chm., Edinburgh Abbeyfield Soc. DL Edinburgh, 1984. OStJ. *Recreations:* golf, gardening. *Address:* 400 Lanark Road, Edinburgh EH13 0LX. *T:* 0131–441 3245.

MORGAN, Tony; *see* Morgan, A. W. C.

MORGAN, Rt. Rev. Mgr. Vaughan Frederick John, CBE 1982; Chaplain, The Oratory School, since 1984; *b* Upper Hutt, New Zealand, 21 March 1931; *o s* of late Godfrey Frederick Vaughan Morgan and Violet (Doreen) Vaughan Morgan. *Educ:* The Oratory Sch., S Oxon; Innsbruck Univ. Ordained, 1957; Archdiocese of St Andrews and Edinburgh, 1959–62; entered Royal Navy as Chaplain, 1962; Prin. RC Chaplain (Naval), and Vicar Gen. for RN, 1979–84. Prelate of Honour to HH Pope John Paul II, 1979. *Publications:* contribs to journals. *Recreations:* music, swimming, painting, heraldry. *Address:* The Oratory School, Woodcote, Reading RG8 0PJ. *T:* Checkendon (01491) 681074. *Club:* Army and Navy.

MORGAN, Walter Thomas James, CBE 1959; FRS 1949; Director, Lister Institute of Preventive Medicine, London, 1972–75 (Deputy Director, 1952–68); *b* London, 5 Oct. 1900; *s* of Walter and Annie E. Morgan; *m* 1930, Dorothy Irene Price (*d* 1993); one *s* two *d*. *Educ:* Univ. of London. Grocers' Company Scholar, 1925–27; Beit Memorial Med. Res. Fellow, 1927–28; First Asst and Biochemist, Lister Institute Serum Dept (Elstree), 1928–37; Rockefeller Research Fellow (Eidgenössiche Tech. Hochschule, Zürich), 1937. Reader, 1938–51, Lister Inst.; Prof. of Biochemistry, Univ. of London, 1951–68, now Prof. Emeritus. PhD 1927, DSc 1937, London Univ.; DrSc (Tech.) Zürich, 1938. CChem, FRSC (FRIC 1929). Hon. Secretary: Biochemical Soc., 1940–45; Biological Council, 1944–47. Chm. Bd of Studies, Biochem., Univ. of London, 1954–57; Member: Scientific Advisory Council, 1956–60; MRC, 1966–70. Mem., Lawes Agricl Trust Cttee, 1964–76. Guest Lecturer, 100th meeting of Gesellschaft Deutscher Naturforscher und Ärzte, Germany, 1959; Royal Society: Croonian Lectr, 1959; Vice-Pres., 1961–64; Royal Medal, 1968. Vis. Prof., Japan Soc. for Promotion of Science, 1979. Hon. Member: Biochem. Soc., 1969; Internat. Soc. Blood Transfusion, 1980; British Soc. Blood Transfusion, 1984; Internat. Endotoxic Soc., 1987; Hon. FRCP 1982. MD *hc* Basel, 1964; DSc *hc* Michigan, 1969. Conway Evans Prize (Royal College of Physicians, London), 1964; (jointly) Landsteiner Memorial Award (USA), 1967; (jointly) Paul Ehrlich and Ludwig Darmstädter Prizes (Germany), 1968; Philip Levine Medal, Amer. Soc. of Clinical Pathologists, 1990. *Publications:* papers on biochemistry, immunology and pathology. *Address:* 57 Woodbury Drive, Sutton, Surrey SM2 5RA. *T:* 0181–642 2319. *Club:* Athenæum.

MORGAN, Prof. William Basil; Professor of Geography, 1971–92, Professor Emeritus, since 1988, and Head of Geography Department, 1982–87, King's College London; *b* 22 Jan. 1927; *s* of William George Morgan and Eunice Mary (*née* Heys); *m* 1954, Joy Gardner; one *s* one *d*. *Educ:* King Edward's Sch., Birmingham; Jesus Coll., Oxford (MA); PhD Glasgow. Assistant, Glasgow Univ., 1948; Lecturer: University Coll., Ibadan, Nigeria, 1953; Univ. of Birmingham, 1959; Reader in Geography, KCL, 1967. Participant in various UN university res. projects and conferences. *Publications:* (with J. C. Pugh) West Africa, 1969; (with R. J. C. Munton) Agricultural Geography, 1971; Agriculture in the Third World: a spatial analysis, 1978; (with R. P. Moss) Fuelwood and rural energy production and supply in the humid tropics, 1981; contribs to geographical and other learned jls and to various conf. collections. *Recreation:* development geography, walking. *Address:* 57 St Augustine's Avenue, South Croydon, Surrey CR2 6JQ. *T:* 0181–688 5687, *Fax:* 0181–667 0201.

MORGAN, Air Vice-Marshal William Gwyn, CB 1968; CBE 1960 (OBE 1945); RAF, retired 1969; *b* 13 Aug. 1914; *s* of T. S. Morgan; *m* 1962, Joan Russell. *Educ:* Pagefield Coll., Swansea. Joined Royal Air Force, 1939; Group Capt., 1958; Command Acct, HQ, FEAF, 1962; Air Commodore, 1965; DPS (2), RAF, 1965–66; AOA Technical Training Comd, 1966–68, Training Comd, 1968–69. Air Vice-Marshal, 1967; jssc; psc; FCCA; ACMA. *Recreation:* fell walking. *Address:* c/o Lloyds Bank, 7 Pall Mall, SW1Y 5NH. *Club:* Royal Air Force.

MORGAN, Rt. Hon. William James, PC (Northern Ireland) 1961; JP; Member (UUUC), for North Belfast, Northern Ireland Constitutional Convention, 1975–76; *b* 1914; *m* 1942; two *s* one *d*. Retired company director. MP, Oldpark Div. of Belfast, 1949–58, Clifton Div. of Belfast, 1959–69, NI Parlt; Minister: of Health and Local Government, Northern Ireland, 1961–64; of Labour and National Insurance, 1964; of Health and Social Services, 1965–69; Mem. (U), N Belfast, NI Assembly, 1973–75. *Address:* 6 Demesne Grove, Holywood, Co. Down, N Ireland BT18 9NQ. *T:* Holywood (01232) 423925.

MORGAN-GILES, Rear-Adm. Sir Morgan (Charles), Kt 1985; DSO 1944; OBE 1943 (MBE 1942); GM 1941; DL; *b* 19 June 1914; *e s* of late F. C. Morgan-Giles, OBE, MINA, Teignmouth, Devon; *m* 1946, Pamela (*d* 1966), *d* of late Philip Bushell, Sydney, New South Wales; two *s* four *d*; *m* 1968, Marigold, *d* of late Percy Lowe. *Educ:* Clifton Coll. Entered Royal Navy, 1932; served on China Station, and in destroyers. War Service: Atlantic convoys and Mediterranean; Tobruk garrison and Western Desert, 1941; with RAF, 1942; Sen. Naval Officer, Vis. (Dalmatia) and liaison with Commandos and Marshal Tito's Partisan Forces, 1943–44. Captain 1953; Chief of Naval Intelligence, Far East, 1955–56; Captain (D) Dartmouth Training Sqdn, 1957–58; HMS Belfast, in command, 1961–62; Rear-Adm. 1962; Adm. Pres., Royal Naval Coll., Greenwich, 1962–64; retd 1964. MP (C) Winchester, May 1964–79. Vice-Chm., Conservative Defence Cttee, 1965–75. Chm., HMS Belfast Trust, 1971–78; Life Vice-Pres., RNLI, 1989. Prime Warden, Shipwrights' Company, 1987–88. DL Hants, 1983. *Recreations:* sailing, country pursuits. *Address:* Frenchmoor Farm, West Tytherley, Salisbury SP5 1NU. *T:* Lockerley (01794) 341045. *Clubs:* Royal Yacht Squadron; Australian (Sydney).
See also Baron Killearn.

MORGAN HUGHES, David; *see* Hughes, David M.

MORGAN-OWEN, John Gethin, CB 1984, MBE 1945; QC 1981; Judge Advocate General, 1979–84; *b* 22 Aug. 1914; *o s* of late Maj.-Gen. L. I. G. Morgan-Owen, CB, CMG, CBE, DSO, West Dene, Beech, Alton; *m* 1950, Mary, *d* of late F. J. Rimington, MBE, Master Mariner; two *s* one *d*. *Educ:* Shrewsbury; Trinity Coll., Oxford (BA). Called to Bar, Inner Temple, 1938; Wales and Chester Circuit, 1939; practised at Cardiff, 1939–52. 2nd Lieut Suppl. Reserve, S Wales Borderers, 1939; served 2nd Bn SWB, 1939–44: N Norway, 1940; NW Europe, 1944–45; DAA&QMG, 146 Inf. Bde, 1944–45; Hon. Major. Dep. Judge Advocate, 1952: Germany, 1953–56; Hong Kong, 1958–60; Cyprus, 1963–66; AJAG, 1966; DJAG, Germany, 1970–72; Vice JAG, 1972–79. Jt Chm., Disciplinary Appeals Cttee, ICA, 1985–87. *Recreations:* bad tennis, inland waterways, beagling. *Address:* St Nicholas House, Kingsley, Bordon, Hants GU35 9NW. *T:* Bordon (01420) 472040. *Club:* Army and Navy.

MORIARTY, Gerald Evelyn, QC 1974; a Recorder of the Crown Court, since 1976; *b* 23 Aug. 1928; *er s* of late Lt-Col G. R. O'N. Moriarty and Eileen Moriarty (*née* Moloney); *m* 1961, Judith Mary, *er d* of Hon. William Robert Atkin; four *s*. *Educ:* Downside Sch.; St John's Coll., Oxford (MA). Called to the Bar, Lincoln's Inn, 1951, Bencher, 1983. *Address:* 3 Stone Buildings, Lincoln's Inn, WC2A 3XL. *T:* 0171–430 2318. *Club:* Reform.

MORIARTY, Brig. Joan Olivia Elsie, CB 1979; RRC 1977; Matron-in-Chief and Director of Army Nursing Services, 1976–80; *b* 11 May 1923; *d* of late Lt-Col Oliver Nash Moriarty, DSO, RA, and Mrs Georgina Elsie Moriarty (*née* Moore). *Educ:* Royal Sch., Bath; St Thomas' Hosp. (nursing); Queen Charlotte's Hosp. (midwifery). SRN. VAD, Somerset, 1941–42; joined QAIMNS (R), 1947; Reg. QAIMNS (later QARANC), 1948, retired Jan. 1981; appts incl.: Staff Captain, WO; Instr, Corps Trng Centre; Liaison Officer, MoD; served in UK, Gibraltar, BAOR, Singapore, Malaya, Cyprus; Matron, Mil. Hosp., Catterick, 1973–76; Comdt, QARANC Trng Centre, Aldershot, 1976. Major 1960; Lt-Col 1971; Col 1973; Brig. 1977. QHNS, 1977–80. OStJ 1977. *Recreation:* country pursuits. *Club:* Naval and Military.

MORIARTY, Michael John, CB 1988; Deputy Under-Secretary of State and Principal Establishment Officer, Home Office, 1984–90; *b* 3 July 1930; *er s* of late Edward William Patrick Moriarty, OBE, and May Lilian Moriarty; *m* 1960, Rachel Milward, *d* of late J. S. Thompson and Isobel F. Thompson; one *s* two *d*. *Educ:* Reading Sch., Reading; St John's Coll., Oxford (Sir Thomas White schol.; MA Lit. Hum.). Entered Home Office as Asst Principal, 1954; Private Sec. to Parliamentary Under-Secretaries of State, 1957–59; Principal, 1959; Civil Service Selection Bd, 1962–63; Cabinet Office, 1965–67; Asst Sec., 1967; Private Sec. to Home Sec., 1968; Head of Crime Policy Planning Unit, 1974–75; Asst Under-Sec. of State, 1975–84; seconded to NI Office, 1979–81; Broadcasting Dept, 1981–84. UK Representative, 1976–79, and Chm., 1978–79, Council of Europe Cttee on Crime Problems. Mem., Radio Authority, 1991– (Dep. Chm., 1994–). Member: Redundant Churches Cttee, Church Comrs, 1992–; Disasters Emergency Cttee, 1992–;

Sub-Treas. and Mem. Council, Chichester Cathedral, 1991–. *Recreations:* music, walking, local interests. *Address:* 22 Westgate, Chichester, West Sussex PO19 3EU. *T:* Chichester (01243) 789985.

MORICE, Prof. Peter Beaumont, DSc, PhD; FEng 1989; FICE, FIStructE; Professor of Civil Engineering, University of Southampton, 1958–91, now Emeritus; *b* 15 May 1926; *o s* of Charles and Stephanie Morice; *m* 1st, 1952, Margaret Ransom (marr. diss. 1986); one *s* two *d*; 2nd, 1986, Rita Corless (*née* Dunk). *Educ:* Barfield Sch.; Farnham Grammar Sch.; University of Bristol; University of London. Surrey County Council, 1947–48; Research Div., Cement and Concrete Assoc., 1948–57. Vis. Prof., Ecole Nat. des Ponts et Chaussées, Paris; Mem. Foundn Cttee, Sultan Qaboos Univ., Oman, 1980–86. Compagnon du Beaujolais, 1987. Order of Sultan Qaboos (Oman), 1986. *Publications:* Linear Structural Analysis, 1958; Prestressed Concrete, 1958; papers on structural theory in various learned journals. *Recreations:* sailing, reading, listening to music. *Address:* 12 Abbotts Way, Highfield, Southampton SO17 1QT. *T:* Southampton (01703) 557641. *Club:* Island Sailing (Cowes).

MORINI, Erica; concert violinist; *b* Vienna, 5 Jan. 1910; *m* 1938, Felice Siracusano; no *c*. *Educ:* at age of 4 years under father, Prof. Oscar Morini, and then under Prof. Ottocar Sevcik, masterclass of Viennese Conservatory, at age of 8. Debut under Arthur Nikisch, at age of 9, in Leipzig Gewandhaus (Beethoven Festival); from there on Concert-tours to: Australia, Asia, Africa, Europe; to USA, 1920. Hon. Mem., Sigma Alpha Beta. Hon. MusD: Smith Coll., Mass, 1955; New England Conservatory of Music, Mass, 1963. Gold Medal, City of NY, 1976. *Recreations:* mountain climbing and chamber music. *Address:* 1200 Fifth Avenue, New York, NY 10029, USA.

MORISHIMA, Prof. Michio, FBA 1981; Sir John Hicks Professor of Economics, London School of Economics and Political Science, 1984–88 (Professor of Economics, 1970–84); Emeritus Professor, University of London, 1988; *b* 18 July 1923; *s* of Kameji and Tatsuo Morishima; *m* 1953, Yoko; two *s* one *d*. Assistant Professor: Kyoto Univ., 1950–51; Osaka Univ., 1951–63; Prof., Osaka Univ., 1963–69. *Publications:* Equilibrium, Stability and Growth, 1964; Theory of Economic Growth, 1969; The Working of Econometric Models, 1972; Marx's Economics, 1973; Theory of Demand: real and monetary, 1973; The Economic Theory of Modern Society, 1976; Walras' Economics, 1977; Value, Exploitation and Growth, 1978; Why Has Japan 'Succeeded'?, 1982; The Economics of Industrial Society, 1985; Ricardo's Economics, 1989; Capital and Credit, 1992. *Address:* Ker, Greenway, Hutton Mount, Brentwood, Essex CM13 2NP. *T:* Brentwood (01277) 219595.

MORISON, Hon. Lord; Alastair Malcolm Morison; a Senator of the College of Justice, Scotland, since 1985; *b* 12 Feb. 1931; 2nd *s* of Sir Ronald Peter Morison, QC (Scotland); *m* 1st, 1957, Lindsay Balfour Oatts (marr. diss. 1977); one *s* one *d*; 2nd, 1980, Birgitte Hendil. *Educ:* Cargilfield; Winchester Coll.; Edinburgh Univ. Admitted to Faculty of Advocates, 1956; QC (Scotland) 1968. Chairman: Medical Appeals Tribunal, 1972–85; Performing Right Tribunal, 1984–85. *Recreations:* golf, fishing. *Address:* 6 Carlton Terrace, Edinburgh EH7 5DD. *T:* 0131–556 6766. *Club:* New (Edinburgh).

MORISON, Hugh; Director General, Scotch Whisky Association, since 1994; *b* 22 Nov. 1943; *s* of Archibald Ian Morison and Enid Rose Morison (*née* Mawer); *m* 1st, 1971, Marion Smithers (marr. diss. 1993); two *d*; 2nd, 1993, Ilona Bellos (*née* Roth). *Educ:* Chichester High School for Boys; St Catherine's Coll., Oxford (MA English Language and Literature; DipEd). Asst Principal, SHHD, 1966–69; Private Sec. to Minister of State, Scottish Office, 1969–70; Principal: Scottish Educn Dept, 1971–73; Scottish Economic Planning Dept, 1973–74; Offshore Supplies Office, Dept of Energy, 1974–75; Scottish Economic Planning Dept, 1975–82, Asst Sec., 1979; Gwilym Gibbon Res, Fellow, Nuffield Coll., Oxford, 1982–83; Scottish Development Dept, 1983–84; Under Secretary: SHHD, 1984–88; Industry Dept for Scotland, subseq. Scottish Office Industry Dept, 1988–93. Dir, The Weir Gp, 1989–93. FRSA 1990. *Publications:* The Regeneration of Local Economies, 1987; (with Ilona Bellos) Dauphiné, 1991. *Recreations:* hill walking, cycling, sailing, music, looking at ruins. *Address:* c/o Scotch Whisky Association, 20 Atholl Crescent, Edinburgh EH3 8HF. *T:* 0131–229 4383. *Clubs:* Commonwealth Trust; New (Edinburgh).

MORISON, Niall Maclaine; Chief Executive, General Council of the Bar, since 1994; *b* 3 May 1944; *s* of Dr Neil Morison and Dorothy Morison; *m* 1969, Alison Linda Hill; three *s* one *d*. *Educ:* Edinburgh Academy. Asst Sec., Bar Council, 1973–74; Senate of the Inns of Court and the Bar: Asst Sec., 1974–85; Dep. Sec., 1985–86; Dep. Chief Exec., Gen. Council of the Bar, 1987–94. *Recreations:* family, music, watching Rugby, fishing, ski-ing. *Address:* Bramdean Cottage, Stonegate, Wadhurst, E Sussex TN5 7EP. *T:* Ticehurst (01580) 200142.

MORISON, Air Vice-Marshal Richard Trevor, CBE 1969 (MBE 1944); RAF retired; President, Ordnance Board, 1971–72; *s* of late Oscar Colin Morison and Margaret Valerie (*née* Cleaver); *m* 1964, Rosemary June Brett; one *s* one *d*. *Educ:* Perse Sch., Cambridge; De Havilland Sch. of Aeronautical Engineering. Commnd in RAF, 1940; RAF Staff Coll., 1952; Sen. Techn. Officer, RAF Gaydon, 1955–57; HQ Bomber Comd, 1958–60; STSO HQ 224 Group, Singapore, 1960–61; Dir of Techn. Services, Royal NZ Air Force, 1961–63; Comd Engrg Officer, HQ Bomber Comd, 1963–65; Air Officer i/c Engrg, HQ Flying Training Comd, 1966–68; Air Officer i/c Engrg, HQ Training Comd RAF, 1968–69; Vice-Pres. (Air) Ordnance Bd, 1969–70. *Recreation:* cabinet making. *Address:* Meadow House, Chedgrave, Loddon, Norfolk NR14 6BS.

MORISON, Hon. Sir Thomas (Richard Atkin), Kt 1993; **Hon. Mr Justice Morison;** a Judge of the High Court of Justice, Queen's Bench Division, since 1993; *b* 15 Jan. 1939; *s* of Harold Thomas Brash Morison and Hon. Nancy Morison; *m* 1963, Judith Rachel Walton Morris (marr. diss. 1992); one *s* one *d*; *m* 1993, Caroline Yates. *Educ:* Winchester Coll.; Worcester Coll., Oxford, 1959–62 (MA). Passed final Bar examinations, 1959; called to the Bar, Gray's Inn, 1960, Bencher, 1987; pupil in Chambers, 1962–63; started practice, 1963; QC 1979; a Recorder, 1987–93. *Recreations:* reading, gardening, cooking. *Address:* Royal Courts of Justice, Strand, WC2A 2LL. *Club:* Oriental.

MORITA, Akio, Hon. KBE 1992; Hon. Chairman, Sony Corporation, since 1994 (Chairman, 1976–94); *b* Nagoya, Japan, 26 Jan. 1921; *m* 1950, Yoshiko Kamei; two *s* one *d*. *Educ:* Osaka Imperial Univ. (BSc Physics). Sony Corporation, Tokyo (formerly Tokyo Tsushin Kogyo K. K.): co-founder, 1946; Man. Dir, 1947–55; Sen. Man. Dir, 1955–56; Exec. Vice-Pres., 1959–71; Pres., 1971–76; Chief Executive Officer, 1976–93; Sony Corporation of America: Pres., 1960–66, Chm., 1966–72; Chm. Finance Cttee, 1972–74; Chm. Exec. Cttee, 1974–77; Chm. Finance Cttee, 1977–81; Chm., Exec. Cttee, 1981–94. Dir, IBM World Trade Americas/Far East Corp., 1972–77; Mem., Internat. Council, Morgan Guaranty Trust Co. Chm., Cttee on Internat. Industrial Co-operation, Keidanren (Japan Fedn of Economic Organizations), 1981–94; Vice Chm., Bd of Councillors, Keidanren, 1992–94 (Chm., Council for Better Corporate Citizenship). Albert Medal, RSA, 1982. Officier de la Légion d'Honneur, France, 1984; Commander's Cross, Order of Merit, FRG. *Publications:* Gakureki Muyooron (Never Mind Education Records), 1966; Shin Jitsuryoku Shugi (A New Merit System), 1969; Made in Japan: Akio Morita and the Sony Corporation (autobiog.), 1987; (jtly) A Japan That Can Say No, 1989. *Recreations:* music, golf, tennis. *Address:* Sony Corporation, 6–7–35 Kitashinagawa, Shinagawa-ku, Tokyo 141, Japan. *T:* (3) 54482111.

MORLAND, Martin Robert, CMG 1985; HM Diplomatic Service, retired; Director, Public Affairs, British Nuclear Fuels plc, since 1994; *b* 23 Sept. 1933; *e s* of Sir Oscar Morland, GBE, KCMG and of Alice, *d* of Rt Hon. Sir F. O. Lindley, PC, GCMG; *m* 1964, Jennifer Avril Mary Hanbury-Tracy; two *s* one *d*. *Educ:* Ampleforth; King's Coll., Cambridge (BA). Nat. Service, Grenadier Guards, 1954–56; British Embassy, Rangoon, 1957–60; News Dept, FO, 1961; UK Delegn to Common Market negotiations, Brussels, 1962–63; FO, 1963–65; UK Disarmament Delegn, Geneva, 1965–67; Private Sec. to Lord Chalfont, 1967–68; European Integration Dept, FCO, 1968–73; Counsellor, 1973–77, Rome (seconded temporarily to Cabinet Office to head EEC Referendum Information Unit, 1975); Hd of Maritime Aviation and Environment Dept, FCO, 1977–79; Counsellor and Head of Chancery, Washington, 1979–82; seconded to Hardcastle & Co. Ltd, 1982–84; Under-Sec., Cabinet Office, 1984–86; Ambassador to Burma, 1986–90; Ambassador and UK Perm. Rep. to Office of UN and other internat. orgns, Geneva, 1990–93. *Address:* 50 Britannia Road, SW6 2JP. *Club:* Garrick.

MORLAND, Hon. Sir Michael, Kt 1989; **Hon. Mr Justice Morland;** a Judge of the High Court of Justice, Queen's Bench Division, since 1989; *b* 16 July 1929; *e s* of Edward Morland, Liverpool, and Jane Morland (*née* Beckett); *m* 1961, Lillian Jensen, Copenhagen; one *s* one *d*. *Educ:* Stowe; Christ Church, Oxford (MA). 2nd Lieut, Grenadier Guards, 1948–49; served in Malaya. Called to Bar, Inner Temple, 1953, Bencher 1979; Northern Circuit; QC 1972; a Recorder, 1972–89; Presiding Judge, Northern Circuit, 1991–95. Mem., Criminal Injuries Compensation Bd, 1980–89. *Address:* Royal Courts of Justice, Strand, WC2A 2LL.

MORLAND, Sir Robert (Kenelm), Kt 1990; General Manager, Exports: Tate & Lyle Sugars, 1987–93; Tate & Lyle International, 1987–93; Director, Tate & Lyle Norway A/S, 1987–93; *b* 7 April 1935; *s* of late Kenelm and Sybil Morland; *m* 1st, 1960, Eve Charters (marr. diss. 1965); one *s*; 2nd, 1972, Angela Fraser; one *s*. *Educ:* Birkenhead Sch.; Rydal Sch., Colwyn Bay. Joined Tate & Lyle, 1953; held various managerial positions. Member: Cheshire Riverboard Authy, 1962–65; Birkenhead Nat. Assistance Bd, Adv. Cttee, 1962–65. Member: Birkenhead CBC, 1959–65; Richmond upon Thames BC, 1968–71. Contested (C) Birkenhead, 1964. Chairman: Birkenhead Young Conservatives, 1955–58; Kew Conservatives, 1971–74; Richmond and Barnes Cons. Assoc., 1975–79 (Dep. Pres., 1985–); Cons. Docklands Action Cttee, 1990–92; Greenwich and Lewisham Cons. Action Gp, 1993–94; Dep. Chm., Nat. Trade and Industry Forum, Cons. Party, 1991–; Vice-Pres., Gtr London Conservatives, 1990– (Dep. Chm., 1978–81; Jt Hon. Treas., 1981–87; Chm., 1987–90); Vice-Pres., Newham S Cons. Assoc., 1989–; Member: Cons. Nat. Union Exec. Cttee, 1978–93; Cons. Bd of Finance, 1981–87. *Recreations:* theatre, travel, horseriding. *Clubs:* Carlton, Royal Automobile.

MORLEY; *see* Hope-Morley, family name of Baron Hollenden.

MORLEY, 6th Earl of, *cr* 1815; **John St Aubyn Parker,** JP; Lt-Col, Royal Fusiliers; Lord-Lieutenant of Devon, since 1982; Chairman, Plymouth Sound Ltd, since 1974; *b* 29 May 1923; *e s* of Hon. John Holford Parker (*y s* of 3rd Earl), Pound House, Yelverton, Devon; *S* uncle, 1962; *m* 1955, Johanna Katherine, *d* of Sir John Molesworth-St Aubyn, 14th Bt, CBE; one *s* one *d*. *Educ:* Eton. 2nd Lt, KRRC, 1942; served NW Europe, 1944–45; Palestine and Egypt, 1945–48; transferred to Royal Fusiliers, 1947; served Korea, 1952–53; Middle East, 1953–55 and 1956; Staff Coll., Camberley, 1957; Comd, 1st Bn Royal Fusiliers, 1965–67. Director: Lloyds Bank Ltd, 1974–78; Lloyds Bank UK Management Ltd, 1979–86; Chm., SW Region, Lloyds Bank, 1989–91 (Chm., Devon and Cornwall Regl Bd, 1974–89). Mem., Devon and Co. Cttee, Nat. Trust, 1969–84; President: Plymouth Incorporated Chamber of Trade and Commerce, 1970–; Cornwall Fedn of Chambers of Commerce and Trader Assocs, 1972–79; West Country Tourist Bd, 1971–89. Governor: Seale-Hayne Agric. Coll., 1973–93; Plymouth Polytechnic, 1975–82 (Chm., 1977–82). Pres., Council of Order of St John for Devon, 1979. DL 1973, Vice Lord-Lieutenant, 1978–82, Devon. JP Plymouth, 1972. Hon. Colonel: Devon ACF, 1979–87; 4th Bn Devonshire and Dorset Regl, 1987–92. *Heir:* *s* Viscount Boringdon, *qv*. *Address:* Pound House, Yelverton, Devon PL20 7LJ. *T:* Yelverton (01822) 853162.

MORLEY, Cecil Denis, CBE 1967; Secretary General, The Stock Exchange, London, 1965–71; retired; *b* 20 May 1911; *s* of Cornelius Cecil Morley and Mildred Irene Hutchinson; *m* 1936, Lily Florence Younge (*d* 1992); one *s*. *Educ:* Clifton; Trinity Coll., Cambridge. Solicitor. Asst Sec., Share & Loan Dept, Stock Exchange, 1936; Sec. to Coun. of Stock Exchange, 1949. Served War of 1939–45, Major RA (TA). *Recreations:* travel, gardening. *Address:* Bearsward, Coastal Road, Kingston Gorse, West Sussex BN16 1SJ. *T:* Rustington (01903) 782837.

MORLEY, Elliot Anthony; MP (Lab) Glanford and Scunthorpe, since 1987; *b* 6 July 1952; *m* 1975; one *s* one *d*. *Educ:* St Margaret's C of E High Sch., Liverpool. Remedial teacher, comprehensive sch., Hull; head of individual learning centre, until 1987. Mem., Kingston upon Hull City Council, 1979–85; Chair, Hull City Transport Cttee, 1981–85. Contested (Lab) Beverley, 1983. Opposition front bench spokesman on food, agriculture and rural affairs, 1989–; Labour spokesperson on animal welfare, 1992–; Mem., Select Cttee for Agriculture, 1987–90; Dep. Chair, PLP Educn Cttee, 1987–90. Vice-Pres., Wildlife and Countryside Link, 1990–; Member of Council: RSPB, 1989–93; British Trust for Ornithology, 1992–95. *Recreations:* ornithology, the environment. *Address:* House of Commons, SW1A 0AA; 9 West Street, Winterton, Scunthorpe, S Humberside DN15 9QG.

MORLEY, Eric Douglas; Chairman, Miss World Ltd; joined Mecca Ltd, 1946, Chairman on leaving, 1978; Director, Grand Metropolitan Group, 1970–78; orphaned age 11; *m* Julia Evelyn; four *s* (one *d* decd). *Educ:* grammar sch.; Army. Training ship, Exmouth, 1930–34; Royal Fusiliers Band Boy, 1934; left Army, 1945 (Captain). Creator: Come Dancing, 1949 (world's longest-running TV series); Miss World, 1951 (world's greatest beauty pageant with 87 countries entering in 1994); introduced commercial bingo to UK, 1961. President: Outward Bound Trust; Variety Clubs Internat., 1977–79 (world's greatest children's charity); with wife, Julia, has raised over £100 million for charity worldwide. Freeman and Liveryman, City of London. Contested (C) Dulwich, Oct. 1974 and 1979 (reduced majority of the then Attorney-Gen. from 7,500 to 122). Liveryman, Marketors' Co. *Publication:* Miss World Story, 1967. *Recreations:* London Marathon for charity, French horn. *Club:* MCC.

MORLEY, Herbert, CBE 1974; Director and General Works Manager, Samuel Fox & Co. Ltd, 1959–65; Director, United Steel Cos, 1966–70; *b* 19 March 1919; *s* of George Edward and Beatrice Morley; *m* 1st, 1942, Gladys Hardy (*d* 1991); one *s* one *d*; 2nd, 1994, Mrs Frances H. Suagee, Cincinnatti, Ohio. *Educ:* Almondbury Grammar Sch., Huddersfield; Sheffield Univ. (Assoc. Metallurgy); Univ. of Cincinnati (Post-Grad. Studies in Business Admin). Dir and Gen. Man., Steel Peech Tozer, 1965–68; British Steel

Corporation: Dir, Northern Tubes Gp, 1968–70; Man. Dir, Gen. Steel Div., 1970–73; Man. Dir, Planning and Capital Develt, 1973–76. Chm., Templeborough Rolling Mills Ltd, 1977–82; Dep. Chm. and Dir, Ellison Circlips Gp Ltd, 1990–92; Director: Ellison-Morlock, 1985–92; Bridon Ltd, 1973–85. *Recreations:* music, cricket lover, weekend golfer. *Address:* 350 Wood Avenue, Cincinnati, OH 45220, USA. *T:* (513) 2216851.

MORLEY, John Harwood, FMA; writer and consultant (buildings and interiors); Keeper of Furniture and Interior Design, Victoria and Albert Museum, 1985–89; *b* 5 Dec. 1933; *s* of George Frederick Morley and Doris Simpson Morley; *m* 1960, Jacqueline Morgan; three *d*. *Educ:* Henry Mellish Grammar Sch.; Exeter Coll., Oxford (MA). FMA 1965. Archivist, Ipswich Corp., 1958–59; Art Asst, Herbert Art Gall., Coventry, 1959–61; Keeper of Art, Leicester Museums, 1961–65; Director: Bradford City Museums, 1965–68; Royal Pavilion, Art Gall. and Museums, Brighton, 1968–85; exhibitions, 1969–85, incl. The Jazz Age, and Death, Heaven and the Victorians. Mem. Council, Nat. Trust, 1985–89; Chairman (and Founder Member): Decorative Arts Soc. 1890–1940, 1975– (Pres., 1989–); The Brighton Soc., 1973–75; Sec. (and Founder Mem.), Friends of the Royal Pavilion, 1972–85; Trustee: Edward James Foundn, 1976–82; Geffrye Mus., 1990–95; Patron, Twentieth Century Soc.; Mem. Council, Attingham Summer Sch. Trust, 1983–87. *Publications:* Death, Heaven and the Victorians, 1971; Designs and Drawings: The Making of the Royal Pavilion, 1984; Regency Design 1790–1840: Gardens: Buildings: Interiors: Furniture, 1993. *Recreations:* music, gardening, reading, museums and houses. *Address:* 11 Vine Place, Brighton, East Sussex BN1 3HE.

MORLEY, Prof. Leslie Sydney Dennis, DSc; FRS 1992; FEng; FIMA; FRAeS; Professorial Research Fellow, Institute of Computational Mathematics, Brunel University, since 1985; *b* 23 May 1924; *s* of late Sydney Victor Morley, RN (Chief Petty Officer (Gunnery), HMS Hood, killed in action with the Bismarck, 1941) and of Doris May Huntley (*née* Evans); *m* 1951, Norma Baker; two *s* one *d*. *Educ:* Portsmouth Northern Secondary Sch.; Portsmouth Municipal Tech. Sch.; Southampton Univ. Coll. (HNC 1945); Coll. Aeronautics, Cranfield (DCAe 1948; DSc 1971); Univ. of Cambridge (Post-Grad. Dip. Structures and Materials 1959). FRAeS 1962; FIMA 1964; FEng 1982. Airspeed Ltd: apprentice toolroom fitter, Portsmouth, 1940–45; Stress Office, Christchurch, 1945–46; Res. Officer, Nat Luchtvartlab., Amsterdam, 1948–49; Tech. Asst, Bristol Aeroplane Co., Filton, 1949–50; Structures Dept, RAE, 1950–84, DCSO, 1976. *Publications:* Skew Plates and Structures, 1963; numerous articles on structural mechanics, esp. finite element method, plate and shell theory, in learned jls in Britain and abroad. *Recreations:* family, British heritage, engine repair and maintenance, building work, photography, gardening. *Address:* Institute of Computational Mathematics, Brunel University, Middx UB8 3PH. *T:* Uxbridge (01895) 274000.

MORLEY, Malcolm A.; artist; *b* 1931. *Educ:* Camberwell Sch. of Arts and Crafts; Royal Coll. of Art (ARCA 1957). *One man exhibitions:* Kornblee Gall., NY, 1957, 1964, 1967, 1969; Galerie Gerald Piltzer, Paris, 1973; Stefanotty Gall., NY, 1973, 1974; Clocktower Gall., Inst. for Art & Urban Resources, 1976; Galerie Jurka, Amsterdam, 1977; Galerie Jollenbeck, Cologne, 1977; Nancy Hoffman Gall., NY, 1979; Suzanne Hilberry Gall., Birmingham, Mich, 1979; Xavier Fourcade, NY, 1981, 1982, 1984, 1986; Galerie Nicholine Pon, Zurich, 1984; Fabian Carlsson Gall., London, 1985; Pace Gall., NY, 1988, 1991; Anthony d'Offay Gall., London, 1990; Tate Gall., 1991; Mary Boone Gall., NY, 1993, 1995; retrospective: Whitechapel Art Gall., also shown in Europe and USA, 1983–84; Centre Georges Pompidou, Paris, 1993; Fundacio La Caixa, Madrid, 1995; *major exhibitions:* Wadsworth Atheneum, Hartford, Conn, 1980; Akron Art Mus., 1982; *work in collections:* Met. Mus. of Art, NY; Detroit Inst. of Art; Hirshhorn Mus. and Sculpture Gdn, Washington; Lousiana Mus., Humlebaek, Denmark; Neue Galerie der Stadt Aachen; Mus. of Contemp. Art, Chicago, Munson-Williams-Proctor Inst., Utica, NY; Mus. of Modern Art, NY; Mus. Moderner Kunst, Vienna; Nat. Gall. of Art, Washington; Mus. of Contemp. Art, LA; Wadsworth Atheneum, Hartford; Centre Georges Pompidou, Paris; Nelson–Atkins Mus., Kansas City; Ludwig Forum for Internat. Art, Aachen, Vienna, Budapest; Mus. van Hedendaagse Kunst, Utrecht. First Turner Prize, Tate Gall., 1984; Painting Award, Skowhegan Sch. of Painting and Sculpture, 1992. *Address:* c/o Mary Boone Gallery, 417 West Broadway, New York, NY 10012, USA.

MORLEY, Sheridan Robert; author, journalist and broadcaster; Film Critic, Spectator, since 1990; London Drama Critic, International Herald Tribune, since 1979; *b* Ascot, Berks, 5 Dec. 1941; *s* of late Robert Morley, CBE and of Joan Buckmaster; *m* 1965, Margaret Gudejko (marr. diss. 1990); one *s* two *d*; *m* 1995, Ruth Leon. *Educ:* Sizewell Hall, Suffolk; Merton Coll., Oxford (MA (Hons) 1964). Newscaster, reporter and scriptwriter, ITN, 1964–67; interviewer, Late Night Line Up, BBC2, 1967–71; Presenter, Film Night, BBC2, 1972; Dep. Features Editor, The Times, 1973–75; Arts Editor, 1975–88, Drama Critic, 1975–89, Punch; Arts Diarist and TV Critic, The Times, 1989–90; Film Critic, Sunday Express, 1992–95; Regular presenter: Kaleidoscope, BBC Radio 4; Meridian, BBC World Service; frequent radio and TV broadcasts on the performing arts, incl. Broadway Babes, Song by Song by Sondheim, and the Arts Programme (Radio 2), Sheridan Morley Meets (BBC1) and Countdown (C4). Mem., Drama Panel, British Council, 1982–89. Narrator: Side by Side by Sondheim, Guildford and Norwich, 1981–82; (also devised): Noël and Gertie (Coward anthology), King's Head, London, 1983, Sonning, 1985, Warehouse, London, 1986, Sydney, 1988, Comedy, London, 1989; Spread a Little Happiness (Vivian Ellis anthology), King's Head and Whitehall, London, 1992; cabaret seasons, Pizza on the Park, 1992, 1994 and 1995. BP Arts Journalist of the Year, 1989. *Publications:* A Talent to Amuse: the life of Noël Coward, 1969; Review Copies, 1975; Oscar Wilde, 1976; Sybil Thorndike, 1977; Marlene Dietrich, 1977; Gladys Cooper, 1979; (with Cole Lesley and Graham Payn) Noël Coward and his Friends, 1979; The Stephen Sondheim Songbook, 1979; Gertrude Lawrence, 1981; (ed, with Graham Payn) The Noël Coward Diaries, 1982; Tales from the Hollywood Raj, 1983; Shooting Stars, 1983; The Theatregoers' Quiz Book, 1983; Katharine Hepburn, 1984; The Other Side of the Moon, 1985; (ed) Bull's Eyes, 1985; Ingrid Bergman, 1985; The Great Stage Stars, 1986; Spread a Little Happiness, 1986; Out in the Midday Sun, 1988; Elizabeth Taylor, 1988; Odd Man Out: the life of James Mason, 1989; Our Theatres in the Eighties, 1990; Robert My Father, 1993; Audrey Hepburn, 1993; ed, series of theatre annuals and film and theatre studies, incl. Punch at the Theatre, 1980, Methuen Book of Theatrical Short Stories, 1992 and Methuen Book of Movie Stories, 1993; contribs to The Times, Sunday Telegraph, Evening Standard, Radio Times, Mail on Sunday, Playbill (NY), High Life, Sunday Times, Variety, and The Australian. *Recreations:* talking, swimming, eating, narrating Spread a Little Happiness and Noël and Gertie. *Address:* 5 Admiral Square, Chelsea Harbour, SW10 0UU. *Club:* Garrick.

MORNINGTON, Earl of; Arthur Gerald Wellesley; *b* 31 Jan. 1978; *s* and *heir* of Marquess of Douro, *qv*. *Educ:* Eton Coll. A Page of Honour to HM Queen Elizabeth the Queen Mother, 1993–95.

MORO, Peter, CBE 1977; FRIBA, FCSD; architect; *b* 27 May 1911; *s* of Prof. Ernst Moro and Grete Hönigswald; *m* 1940, Anne Vanneck (marr. diss. 1984); three *d*. *Educ:* Stuttgart, Berlin and Zürich. Swiss Dip. Architecture, 1936; FRIBA 1948; FSIA 1957. Practice with Tecton, 1937–39; Mem. Exec. Cttee, Mars Gp, 1938; Lectr, Sch. of Arch., Regent Street Polytechnic, 1941–47; LCC Associated Architect, Royal Festival Hall (now listed), 1948–51; Peter Moro Partnership, 1952–86; Tutor, Architectural Assoc., 1954–55. External Examiner: Strathclyde Univ., 1973, 1975; Manchester Univ., 1977, 1981; Visiting Critic: Thames Polytechnic; Bath Univ.; Oxford Polytechnic; Sheffield Univ.; QUB. Architect: Fairlawn Sch., LCC, 1957; own house, 1957 (listed 1988); Nottingham Playhouse, 1964 (listed 1994); alterations, Royal Opera House, Covent Garden, 1964; Birstall Sch., Leics, 1964; housing schemes, GLC and Southwark, 1967–80; theatre, Hull Univ., the Gulbenkian Centre, 1970; additions and alterations, Bristol Old Vic, 1972; theatre, New Univ. of Ulster, 1976; Plymouth Theatre Royal, 1982; Taliesin Theatre, UC Swansea, 1984; theatre planning consultants, Hong Kong Acad. for Performing Arts, 1983–85. Sen. Pres., Assoc. of British Theatre Technicians (Founder Mem.); Member: Council, RIBA, 1967–73; Housing the Arts Cttee, Arts Council of GB, 1975–78. Governor, Ravensbourne Coll. of Art and Design, 1976–87. Lectures in UK, Finland, Norway, Germany and Holland. Bronze Medal, RIBA, 1964; 4 Civic Trust Awards and Commendations; Heritage Award, 1975; Concrete Award, 1983. *Publications:* contribs to technical jls in UK, Germany, France, Italy, Portugal and Japan. *Recreation:* tennis. *Address:* 20 Blackheath Park, SE3 9RP. *T:* 0181–852 0250.

MORPETH, Sir Douglas (Spottiswoode), Kt 1981; TD 1959; FCA; Chairman, Clerical Medical and General Life Assurance Society, later Clerical Medical Investment Group, 1978–94; *b* 6 June 1924; *s* of late Robert Spottiswoode Morpeth and Louise Rankine Morpeth (*née* Dobson); *m* 1951, Anne Rutherford, *yr d* of Ian C. Bell, OBE, MC, Edinburgh; two *s* two *d*. *Educ:* George Watson's Coll., Edinburgh; Edinburgh Univ. (BCom). Commissioned RA; served 1943–47, India, Burma, Malaya. Mem., Inst. of Chartered Accountants in England and Wales, 1952, Fellow, 1957, Pres., 1972. Partner, 1958–85, Sen. Partner, 1977–85, Touche Ross & Co. Chairman: (of Trustees), British Telecom Staff Superannuation Scheme, 1983–92; British Borneo Petroleum Syndicate, 1985–95; Deputy Chairman: Brixton Estate plc, 1983–94; Leslie Langton Hldgs, 1987–91; Dir, Allied-Irish Banks, 1986–91. Mem., Investment Grants Advisory Cttee, 1968–71; Chm., Inflation Accounting Steering Gp, 1976–80; Vice-Chm., Accounting Standards Cttee, 1970–82. Chm., Taxation Cttee, CBI, 1973–76. Honourable Artillery Company: Member, 1949–; Lt-Col, comdg 1st Regt HAC (RHA), 1964–66; Master Gunner within the Tower of London, 1966–69. Master, Co. of Chartered Accountants in England and Wales, 1977–78. FRCM (Hon. Treasurer, RCM, 1983–). *Recreations:* golf, tennis, gardening. *Address:* Winterden House, Shamley Green, near Guildford, Surrey GU5 0UD. *Clubs:* Athenæum, Caledonian, Royal Automobile.

MORPHET, David Ian; Director, Government Affairs, BICC plc, since 1992; *b* 24 Jan. 1940; *s* of late A. Morphet and of Sarah Elizabeth Morphet; *m* 1968, Sarah Gillian Sedgwick; two *s* one *d*. *Educ:* King James's Grammar Sch., Almondbury, Yorks; St John's Coll., Cambridge (History Schol.; English Tripos, class I, Pts I and II). Foreign Office, 1961; Vice Consul, Taiz, 1963; Doha, 1963–64; FO, 1964–66; Asst Private Sec. to Foreign Secretary, 1966–68; First Sec., Madrid, 1969–72; Diplomatic Service Observer, CS Selection Board, 1972–74; transf. to Dept of Energy, 1974; Asst Sec., 1975; Dep. Chm., Midlands Electricity Board (on secondment), 1978–79; Under-Secretary: Electricity Div., 1979–83; Energy Policy Div., 1983–85; Atomic Energy Div., 1985–89; UK Governor: IEA, 1983–85; IAEA, 1985–89. Dir, BICC Cables Ltd, 1981–89; Dir, Planning and Develt, Balfour Beatty Ltd, 1989–91. Chm., Export Finance Cttee, CBI, 1992–; Mem. Council, CBI, 1995–. Chm., Nat. Schizophrenia Fellowship, 1977–83. *Recreations:* music, theatre, walking. *Address:* 11 Daisy Lane, SW6 3DD. *Club:* Athenæum.

MORPHET, Richard Edward; Keeper, Modern Collection, Tate Gallery, since 1986; *b* 2 Oct. 1938; *s* of Horace Taylor Morphet and Eleanor Morphet (*née* Shaw); *m* 1965, Sally Richmond; two *d*. *Educ:* Bootham Sch., York; London Sch. of Economics (BA Hons History). Fine Arts Dept, British Council, 1963–66; Tate Gallery: Asst Keeper, 1966–73; Dep. Keeper, Modern Collection, 1973–86. *Publications:* numerous exhibition catalogues, magazine articles. *Address:* Tate Gallery, Millbank, SW1P 4RG. *T:* 0171–887 8848, *Fax:* 0171–887 8859.

MORPURGO, Jack Eric; Professor of American Literature, University of Leeds, 1969–83, now Emeritus; author; *b* 26 April 1918; *s* of late Mark Morpurgo, Islington; *m* 1946, Catherine Noel Kippe (*d* 1993), *d* of late Prof. Emile Cammaerts; three *s* one *d*. *Educ:* Christ's Hosp.; Univ. of New Brunswick; Coll. of William and Mary, USA (BA); Durham Univ. Enlisted RA, 1939; served as regimental and staff officer in India, Middle East, Greece and Italy; GSO 2, Public Relations Directorate, War Office. Editorial Staff, Penguin Books, 1946–49; Editor Penguin Parade; General Editor, Pelican Histories, 1949–67; Asst Dir, Nuffield Foundation, 1950–54; Dir-Gen., Nat. Book League, 1955–69, Dep. Chm., 1969–71, Vice-Pres., 1971–87; Prof. of American Studies, Univ. of Geneva, 1968–70; Visiting Professor: Michigan State Univ., 1950; Free Univ., Berlin, 1958; George Washington Univ., 1970; Vanderbilt Univ., 1981; Scholar-in-residence: Rockefeller Res. Center, Italy, 1974; Coll. of Idaho, 1986; Vis. Fellow, ANU, 1975, 1977; has lectured in USA, Canada, Germany, India, Burma, etc. Dir of Unesco Seminar on Production of Reading Materials, Rangoon, 1957, Madras, 1959. Almoner, Christ's Hospital (Dep. Chm., 1980–84); Chm. Working Pty on Medical Libraries; Dir, William and Mary Historical Project, 1970–76. Director: Sexton Press Ltd, 1984–; P. and M. Youngman Carter Ltd, 1985–. Phi Beta Kappa, 1948; Hon. Fellow, Coll. of William and Mary, 1949. Hon. LitD Maine, 1961; Hon. DLitt Elmira, 1966; Hon. DHL William and Mary, 1970; Hon. DHum Idaho, 1984. Yorkshire Post Special Literary Award, 1980. *Publications:* American Excursion, 1949; Charles Lamb and Elia, 1949, rev. edn 1993; The Road to Athens, 1963; Barnes Wallis, 1972; Treason at West Point, 1975; Their Majesties Royall Colledge, 1976; Allen Lane: King Penguin, 1979; Verses Humorous and Post-Humorous, 1981; Master of None: an autobiography, 1990; Christ's Hospital: an introductory history, 1991; contributor to: The Impact of America, 1951; joint author of: History of The United States (with Russel B. Nye), 1955; Venice (with Martin Hurlimann), 1964; (with G. A. T. Allar) Christ's Hospital, 1984; edited: Leigh Hunt: Autobiography, 1949; E. J. Trelawny: Last Days of Shelley and Byron, 1952; Poems of John Keats, 1953, rev. edn 1985; Rugby Football: An Anthology (with Kenneth Pelmear), 1958; Cobbett: a year's residence in USA, 1964; Cooper: The Spy, 1968; Cobbett's America, 1985; Margery Allingham: The Return of Mr Campion, 1989. *Recreations:* watching Rugby football, music. *Address:* 12 Laurence Mews, Askew Road, W12 9AT. *Clubs:* Army and Navy, Pilgrims.

MORPURGO DAVIES, Anna Elbina; *see* Davies, A. E.

MORRELL, Prof. David Cameron, OBE 1982; FRCP; FRCGP; Wolfson Professor of General Practice, United Medical and Dental Schools of Guy's and St Thomas' Hospitals, 1974–93, Emeritus Professor of General Practice, 1993; *b* 6 Nov. 1929; *s* of William and Violet Morrell; *m* 1953, Alison Joyce Morrell; three *s* two *d*. *Educ:* Wimbledon Coll.; St Mary's Hosp. Med. Sch. (MB BS). DObstRCOG; FFPHM. Phys., RAF Med. Br., 1954–57; Principal in Gen. Practice, Hoddesdon, Herts, 1957–63; Lectr in Gen. Practice, Univ. of Edinburgh, 1963–67; Sen. Lectr, then Reader, in Gen. Practice, St Thomas's Hosp. Med. Sch., 1967–74. KSG 1982. *Publications:* The Art of General Practice, 1966, 4th edn 1991; An Introduction to Primary Medical Care, 1976, 2nd edn 1981; (with J.

Cormack and M. Marinker) Practice: a handbook of general practice, 1976, 2nd edn 1987. *Recreations:* gardening, walking. *Address:* 14 Higher Green, Ewell KT17 3BA. *T:* 0181–224 5781.

MORRELL, David William James; Scottish Legal Services Ombudsman, 1991–94; *b* 26 July 1933; *s* of Rev. W. W. Morrell, MBE, TD and Grace Morrell; *m* 1960, Margaret Rosemary Lewis; two *s* one *d*. *Educ:* George Watson's Coll., Edinburgh; Univ. of Edinburgh (MA Hons, LLB). Law Apprentice, Edinburgh, 1954–57; Admin. Asst, Univ. of Durham, 1957–60; Asst Registrar and Graduate Appts Officer, Univ. of Exeter, 1960–64; Sen. Asst Registrar, Univ. of Essex, 1964–66; Academic Registrar, 1966–73, Registrar, 1973–89, Univ. of Strathclyde; Lay Observer for Scotland, 1989–91. OECD Consultant on management in higher educn, 1990. Dir, Lomond Healthcare NHS Trust, 1995. Governor: Univ. of Paisley (formerly Paisley Coll.), 1990– (Vice-Chm., 1992–); Scottish Centre for Children with Motor Impairments, 1994. FRSA 1992. *Publications:* papers on higher education and on provision of legal services. *Recreations:* hill-walking, fishing. *Address:* 29 Barclay Drive, Helensburgh, Dunbartonshire G84 9RA. *T:* Helensburgh (01436) 674875.

MORRELL, Frances Maine; Director of Studies, European Citizenship 1999 Project, since 1994; *b* 28 Dec. 1937; *d* of Frank and Beatrice Galleway; *m* 1964, Brian Morrell; one *d*. *Educ:* Queen Anne Grammar Sch., York; Hull Univ. BA (Hons) English Lang. and Lit. Secondary Sch. Teacher, 1960–69; Press Officer, Fabian Soc. and NUS, 1970–72; Research into MPs' constituency role, 1973; Special Adviser to Tony Benn, as Sec. of State for Industry, then as Sec. of State for Energy, 1974–79. Dep. Leader, 1981–83, Leader, 1983–87, ILEA; Mem. for Islington S and Finsbury, GLC, 1981–86; Sec., Speaker's Commn on Citizenship, 1988–91; Exec. Dir, Inst. for Citizenship Studies, 1992–93. Senior Research Fellow: QMW, 1991–93; Federal Trust for Educn and Res., 1993–. Member: Oakes Cttee, Enquiry into Payment and Collection Methods for Gas and Electricity Bills (report publ. 1976); Exec., Campaign for Labour Party Democracy, 1979–; Co Founder: Labour Co-ordinating Cttee, 1978; Women's Action Cttee, 1980–. Contested (Lab) Chelmsford, Feb. 1974. Chair: Arts Inform, 1993–; NCVQ Performing Arts Adv. Cttee, 1994–; London Schs Newspaper Project, 1994–; Mem. Bd of Dirs, Sadler's Wells Theatre, 1982–88. *Publications:* (with Tony Benn and Francis Cripps) A Ten Year Industrial Strategy for Britain, 1975; (with Francis Cripps) The Case for a Planned Energy Policy, 1976; From the Electors of Bristol: the record of a year's correspondence between constituents and their Member of Parliament, 1977; (jtly) Manifesto—a radical strategy for Britain's future, 1981; Children of the Future: the battle for Britain's schools, 1989. *Recreations:* reading, cooking, gardening. *Address:* 91 Hemingford Road, N1 1BY.

MORRELL, Col (Herbert) William (James), OBE 1954; MC 1944; TD; MA Oxon; DL; JP; *b* 1 Aug. 1915; *er s* of James Herbert Morrell, MA, Headington Hill, Oxford; *m* 1947, Pamela Vivien Eleanor, *d* of Richard Stubbs, Willaston, Cheshire; one *s* two *d*. *Educ:* Eton; Magdalen Coll., Oxford. 2nd Lt RA, 1936; served War of 1939–45 (France, Madagascar, Burma); retired 1948. DL 1961, JP 1959, High Sheriff 1960, Oxon. *Recreations:* hunting, sailing. *Address:* Caphill, Sandford St Martin, Oxon OX7 7AL. *T:* Great Tew (01608) 683291.

MORRELL, James George; Founder Director, Henley Centre for Forecasting, 1974–79; author and business forecaster; *b* 1923; *s* of late Frederick Morrell and Violet (*née* Smart); *m* 1st, 1944, Elizabeth Bristow (marr. diss. 1970); one *s* two *d*; 2nd, 1972, Margaret Helen Nickolls. *Educ:* Christ's Hospital; Ruskin and Wadham Colls, Oxford. MA Oxon 1953. Served RAF, 1941–46. Ford Motor Co., 1955; Phillips & Drew, 1957; Econ. Advr, Charterhouse Group, 1964–95; founded James Morrell & Associates, 1967. Consultant to OECD, 1985–87. Visiting Professor, Univ. of Bradford, 1970–73; Associate Fellow, Oxford Centre for Management Studies, 1981–84. *Publications:* Business Forecasting for Finance and Industry, 1969; Business Decisions and the Role of Forecasting, 1972; Inflation and Business Management, 1974; 2002: Britain plus 25, 1977; The Regeneration of British Industry, 1979; Britain through the 1980s, 1980; The Future of the Dollar and the World Reserve System, 1981; Employment in Tourism, 1982, 2nd edn 1985; Business Forecasts for the Housing Market, annually 1985–; The Impact of Tourism on London, 1985; Business Forecasts for the Motor Trades, annually 1986–; The Productivity Performance Index, 1989; Business Forecasts for the Commercial Property Market, 1994. *Recreations:* canals, Samuel Pepys, stock market. *Address:* 81 Speed House, Barbican, EC2Y 8AU. *Club:* Middlesex CC.

MORRELL, Rt. Rev. James Herbert Lloyd; Canon and Prebend of Heathfield in Chichester Cathedral, 1959–82, Canon Emeritus since 1982; Provost of Lancing (Southern Division Woodard Schools), 1961–82; *b* 12 Aug. 1907; *s* of George Henry and Helen Adela Morrell. *Educ:* Dulwich Coll.; King's Coll., London; Ely Theological Coll. Deacon, 1931; Priest, 1932; Curate of St Alphage, Hendon, 1931–35; Curate of St Michael and All Angels, Brighton, 1935–39; Bishop of Chichester's Chaplain for men, 1939–41; Lecturer for The Church of England Moral Welfare Council, 1941–44; Vicar of Roffey, 1944–46; Archdeacon of Lewes, 1946–59; Bishop Suffragan of Lewes, 1959–77; Asst Bishop, Diocese of Chichester, 1978–85. Fellow of King's Coll., London, 1960. *Publications:* Four Words (broadcast talks to the Forces), 1941; The Heart of a Priest, 1958; A Priest's Notebook of Prayer, 1961; The Catholic Faith Today, 1964. *Recreations:* walking, photography. *Address:* 83 Davigdor Road, Hove BN3 1RA. *T:* Brighton (01273) 733971.

MORRELL, Leslie James, OBE 1986; JP; Chairman, Northern Ireland Water Council, 1982–93; *b* 26 Dec. 1931; *s* of James Morrell; *m* 1958, Anne Wallace, BSc; two *s* one *d*. *Educ:* Portora Royal Sch., Enniskillen; Queen's Univ., Belfast. BAgric 1955. Member: Londonderry CC, 1969–73; Coleraine Bor. Council, 1973–77; Mem. (U) for Londonderry, NI Assembly, 1973–75; Minister of Agriculture, NI Exec., 1973–74; Dep. Leader, Unionist Party of NI, 1974–80. Mem., BBC Gen. Adv. Cttee, 1980–86; Chm., BBC NI Agricl Adv. Cttee, 1986–91. Chm., NI Fedn of Housing Assocs, 1978–80; Hon. Secretary: Oaklee Housing Assoc., 1992– (James Butcher Housing Assoc. (NI), 1981–92 (Chm., 1976–81)); James Butcher Retirement Homes Ltd, 1985–. Mem. Exec., Assoc. of Governing Bodies of Voluntary Grammar Schs, 1978–84; Chm., Virus Tested Stem Cutting Potato Growers Assoc., 1977–88. JP Londonderry, 1966. *Address:* Dunboe House, Castlerock, Coleraine BT51 4UB. *T:* Castlerock (01265) 848352.

MORRELL, Peter Richard; His Honour Judge Morrell; a Circuit Judge, since 1992; *b* 25 May 1944; *s* of Frank Richard Morrell and Florence Ethel Morrell; *m* 1970, Helen Mary Vint Collins; two *d*. *Educ:* Westminster Sch.; University, Coll., Oxford (MA). Admitted Solicitor, 1970; called to the Bar, Gray's Inn, 1974; a Recorder, 1990–92. *Recreations:* shooting, fishing, photography. *Address:* Peterborough Combined Court Centre, Crown Buildings, Rivergate, Peterborough PE1 1EJ. *T:* Peterborough (01733) 346342.

MORRELL, Col William; *see* Morrell, Col H. W. J.

MORRICE, Norman; choreographer; Director: the Royal Ballet, 1977–86; Choreographic Studies, Royal Ballet School, since 1987; Royal Ballet Choreographic Group, since 1987; *b* Mexico, of British parents. *Educ:* Rambert School of Ballet. Joined the Ballet Rambert in early 1950s as a dancer; notably danced Dr Coppélius, in Coppélia, and subseq. also choreographer; first considerable success with his ballet, Two Brothers, in America, and at first London perf., Sept. 1958; première of his 2nd ballet, Hazaña, Sadler's Wells Theatre, 1958; the New Ballet Rambert Company was formed in 1966 and he was Co-Director with Marie Rambert, to create new works by unknown and established choreographers; his ballet, Hazard, was danced at Bath Festival, 1967; he composed 10 new ballets by 1968 and had taken his place with leading choreographers; *ballets include:* 1–2–3, Them and Us and Pastorale Variée, which were staged at the Jeanetta Cochrane Theatre, 1968–69; Ladies, Ladies!, perf. by Ballet Rambert at Young Vic, 1972; Spindrift, at Round House, 1974, etc. Has danced frequently overseas.

MORRICE, Philip; HM Diplomatic Service; Consul-General, Sydney, since 1995; *b* 31 Dec. 1943; *s* of late William Hunter Morrice and Catherine Jane Cowie; *m* 1988, Margaret Clare Bower; one *s* one *d*. *Educ:* Robert Gordon's College, Aberdeen. Entered HM Diplomatic Service, 1963; served Kuala Lumpur, 1964–67; CO, later FCO, 1967–69; Caracas, 1969–72; First Sec., UK Delegn to OECD, Paris, 1973–75; First Sec. (Energy), UK Perm. Rep. to EC, Brussels, 1975–78; FCO, 1978–81; First Sec. (Commercial), later Counsellor (Comm.), Rome, 1981–85; Counsellor (Econ. and Comm.), Lagos, 1986–88; Minister-Counsellor, Consul-Gen. and Dir of Trade Promotion, Brasilia, 1988–92; Director, Anglo-Taiwan Trade Cttee, subseq. British Trade and Cultural Office, Taipei (on secondment), 1992–95. *Publications:* The Schweppes Guide to Scotch, 1983; The Whisky Distilleries of Scotland and Ireland, 1987; The Teacher's Book of Whisky, 1993; numerous articles. *Recreations:* travel, tennis, golf. *Address:* c/o Foreign and Commonwealth Office, SW1A 2AH. *Clubs:* Royal Over-Seas League, Royal Automobile.

MORRILL, Dr John Stephen, FRHistS; FBA 1995; Reader in Early Modern History, Cambridge, since 1992; Fellow, since 1975, and Vice Master, since 1994, Selwyn College, Cambridge; *b* 12 June 1946; *s* of William Henry Morrill and Marjorie (*née* Ashton); *m* 1968, Frances Mead; four *d*. *Educ:* Altrincham County Grammar Sch.; Trinity Coll., Oxford (BA 1967; MA, DPhil 1971). Keasbey Lectr in Hist., 1970–71, Jun. Res. Fellow, 1971–74, Trinity Coll., Oxford; Coll. Lectr in Hist., St Catherine's Coll., Oxford, 1973–74; Lectr in Mod. Hist., Univ. of Stirling, 1974–75; Faculty of History, Cambridge: Asst Lectr and Lectr, 1975–92; Selwyn College Cambridge: Dir of Studies in Hist., 1975–91; Tutor, 1979–91; Admissions Tutor, 1983–87; Sen. Tutor, 1987–91. Vice-Pres., RHistS, 1993–. *Publications:* Cheshire 1630–1660, 1974; The Revolt of the Provinces 1630–1650, 1976, rev. edn 1980; The Cheshire Grand Jury 1625–1659, 1976; (with G. E. Aylmer) The Civil Wars and Interregnum: sources for local historians, 1979; Seventeenth-Century Britain, 1980; Reactions to the English Civil War, 1982; Land Men and Beliefs, 1985; Charles I, 1989; Oliver Cromwell and the English Revolution, 1990; The National Covenant in its British Context, 1990; The Impact of the English Civil War, 1991; Revolution and Restoration, 1992; The Nature of the English Revolution, 1993; (with P. Slack and D. Woolf) Public Men and Private Conscience in Seventeenth-Century England, 1993; contribs to learned jls. *Recreations:* classical music, beer, cricket. *Address:* Selwyn College, Cambridge CB3 9DQ; 1 Bradford's Close, Bottisham, Cambs CB5 9DW. *T:* Cambridge (01223) 811822.

MORRIS, family name of **Barons Killanin, Morris, Morris of Castle Morris** and **Morris of Kenwood.**

MORRIS, 3rd Baron *cr* 1918; **Michael David Morris;** *b* 9 Dec. 1937; *s* of 2nd Baron Morris and of Jean Beatrice (now Lady Salmon), *d* of late Lt-Col D. Maitland-Makgill-Crichton; *S* father, 1975; *m* 1st, 1959, Denise Eleanor (marr. diss. 1962), *o d* of Morley Richards; 2nd, 1962, Jennifer (marr. diss. 1969), *o d* of Squadron Leader Tristram Gilbert; two *d*; *m* 1980, Juliet, twin *d* of Anthony Buckingham; two *s* one *d*. *Educ:* Downside. FCA. *Heir:* *s* Hon. Thomas Anthony Salmon Morris, *b* 2 July 1982. *Address:* House of Lords, SW1A 0PW.

MORRIS OF CASTLE MORRIS, Baron *cr* 1990 (Life Peer), of St Dogmaels in the County of Dyfed; **Brian Robert Morris,** MA, DPhil; Principal, St David's University College, Lampeter, 1980–91; *b* 4 Dec. 1930; *o s* of William Robert Morris and Ellen Elizabeth Morris (*née* Shelley); *m* 1955, Sandra Mary James, JP; one *s* one *d*. *Educ:* Cardiff High School; Worcester Coll., Oxford (MA, DPhil). National service with Welch Regt, 1949–51. Fellow of Shakespeare Inst., Univ. of Birmingham, 1956–58; Asst Lectr 1958–60, Lectr 1960–65, Univ. of Reading; Lectr 1965–67, Sen. Lectr 1967–71, Univ. of York; Prof. of English Literature, Univ. of Sheffield, 1971–80. Gen. Editor: New Mermaid Dramatists, 1964–86; New Arden Shakespeare, 1974–82. Opposition Dep. Chief Whip, H of L, 1992–. Member: Council, Yorkshire Arts Assoc., 1973–81 (Chm. Literature Panel, 1973–77); Welsh Arts Council, 1983–86 (Mem. Lit. Cttee, 1978–86); Archbishops' Council on Evangelism, 1971–75; Yr Academi Gymreig, 1979–; British Library Bd, 1980–91; Council, Poetry Soc., 1980–90 (Vice-Pres., 1990–); Council, Nat. Library of Wales, 1981–91; Chairman: Museums and Galls Commn, 1985–90 (Mem., 1975– (formerly Standing Commn on Museums and Galls)); Council, Prince of Wales's Inst. of Architecture, 1993–. Pres., Welsh Historic Gdns Trust, 1990–; Vice President: Council for Nat. Parks, 1985–; Museums Assoc., 1985–; Prayer Book Soc., 1990–. Trustee: Nat. Portrait Gall., 1977– (Vice-Chm., 1993–); Nat. Heritage Meml Fund, 1980–91; Welsh Adv. Cttee, British Council, 1983–91; Anthony Panizzi Foundn, 1987–91; Museum of Empire and Commonwealth, 1991–; Campaign for the Protection of Rural Wales, 1991–. Broadcaster, scriptwriter and presenter of television programmes. Hon. LittD Sheffield, 1991; Hon. LLD Wales, 1992. *Publications:* John Cleveland: a Bibliography of his Poems, 1967; (with Eleanor Withington) The Poems of John Cleveland, 1967; (ed) New Mermaid Critical Commentaries I-III, 1969–72; Mary Quant's London, 1973; (ed) Ritual Murder, 1980; Harri Webb, 1993; *edited plays:* Ford's The Broken Heart, 1965, and 'Tis Pity She's a Whore, 1968; (with Roma Gill) Tourneur's The Atheist's Tragedy, 1976; Shakespeare's The Taming of the Shrew, 1981; *poetry:* Tide Race, 1976; Stones in the Brook, 1978; Dear Tokens, 1987; contribs to journals. *Recreations:* music, mountains, and museums. *Address:* The Old Hall, Foolow, Eyam, Sheffield S30 1QR. *T:* Hope Valley (01433) 631186. *Clubs:* Athenæum, Beefsteak.

MORRIS OF KENWOOD, 2nd Baron *cr* 1950, of Kenwood; **Philip Geoffrey Morris,** JP; Company Director, retired 1990; *b* 18 June 1928; *s* of 1st Baron Morris of Kenwood, and Florence (*d* 1982), *d* of Henry Isaacs, Leeds; *S* father, 1954; *m* 1958, Hon. Ruth, *o d* of late Baron Janner and Lady Janner; one *s* three *d*. *Educ:* Loughborough Coll., Leics. Served RAF, Nov. 1946–Feb. 1949, July 1951–Oct. 1955. JP Inner London, 1967. *Recreations:* tennis, golf, ski-ing. *Heir:* *s* Hon. Jonathan David Morris, *b* 5 Aug. 1968. *Address:* Lawn Cottage, Orchard Rise, Kingston, Surrey KT2 7EY. *T:* 0181–942 6321.

MORRIS, Albert, FCIB; Director, 1989–94, and Deputy Group Chief Executive, 1992–94, National Westminster Bank; *b* 21 Oct. 1934; *m* 1987, Patricia Lane. *Educ:* Skerry's Coll., Liverpool; City of Liverpool Coll. of Commerce; Admin Staff Coll., Henley; MIT. National Westminster Bank: Head of Money Transmission, 1979–83; Dep. Gen. Manager, 1983–85, Gen. Manager, 1985–88, Management Services Div.; Chief Exec., Support Services, 1989–92. Director: NatWest Estate Management & Development Ltd, 1989–94; National Westminster Life Assce Ltd, 1992–94; Regent Associates, 1995–.

Chairman: BACS Ltd, 1985–94; Centre-file Ltd, 1988–94; Founding Mem., 1985–87 and Mem. Council, 1990–94, UK Banking Ombudsman Scheme; Chm., APACS, 1993–94 (Dep. Chm., 1991–93; Dir, APACS Admin Ltd, 1987–94); Mem. Adv. Council, Sema Group; Special Advr, Ibos Ltd; non-exec. Mem., DSS Departmental Bd, 1993–. FCIB 1984 (Mem. Council, 1989–); FRSA 1989. Court Liveryman, Co. of Information Technologists. *Recreations:* golf, work, politics. *Address:* Stonebridge, 74 West Common, Harpenden, Herts AL5 2LD.

MORRIS, Air Marshal Sir Alec, KBE 1982; CB 1979; FEng 1989; *b* 11 March 1926; *s* of late Harry Morris; *m* 1946, Moyna Patricia, *d* of late Norman Boyle; one *s* one *d* (twins). *Educ:* King Edward VI Sch., East Retford; King's Coll., Univ. of London; Univ. of Southampton. Commnd RAF, 1945; radar duties, No 90 (Signals) Gp, 1945–50; Guided Weapons Dept, RAE, 1953–56; exchange duty, HQ USAF, 1958–60; space res., Min. of Supply, 1960–63; DS, RAF Staff Coll., 1963–65; OC Eng, No 2 Flying Trng Sch., Syerston, 1966–68; Asst Dir, Guided Weapons R&D, Min. of Tech., 1968–70; OC RAF Central Servicing Develt Estabt, Swanton Morley, 1970–72; SASO, HQ No 90 (Signals) Gp, 1972–74; RCDS, 1974; Dir of Signals (Air), MoD, 1975–76; Dir Gen. Strategic Electronic Systems, MoD (PE), 1976–79; Air Officer Engineering, RAF Strike Command, 1979–81; Chief Engineer, RAF, 1981–83. Exec., BAe, 1983–91, retd. *Recreations:* tennis, gardening. *Address:* 12 Southcot Place, Bath BA2 4PE. *Clubs:* Royal Air Force; Bath and County (Bath).

MORRIS, Rt. Hon. Alfred; PC 1979; QSO 1989; MP (Lab and Co-op) Manchester (Wythenshawe) since 1964; *b* 23 March 1928; *s* of late George Henry Morris and Jessie Morris (*née* Murphy); *m* 1950, Irene (*née* Jones); two *s* two *d*. *Educ:* elem. and evening schs, Manchester; Ruskin Coll., Oxford; St Catherine's, Univ. of Oxford (MA); Univ. of Manchester (Postgrad. certif. in Educn). Employed in office of a Manchester brewing firm from age 14 (HM Forces, 1946–48); Teacher and Lectr, Manchester, 1954–56; Industrial Relations Officer, The Electricity Coun., London, 1956–64. Nat. Chm., Labour League of Youth, 1950–52; contested Liverpool (Garston), Gen. Elec. 1951; Observer, Coun. of Europe, 1952–53; PPS to Minister of Agric., Fisheries and Food, 1964–67, and to Lord President of the Council and Leader of House of Commons, 1968–70; Opposition front bench spokesman on social services, specialising in the problems of disabled people, 1970–74 and 1979–92; Parly Under-Sec. of State, DHSS, as Britain's first-ever Minister for the Disabled, 1974–79. Treasurer, British Gp, IPU, 1971–74; Mem., UK Parly Delegn to UN Gen. Assembly, 1966; Chm., Food and Agriculture Gp of Parly Lab. Party, 1971–74; Representative of Privy Council on Council of RCVS, 1969–74; promoted Chronically Sick and Disabled Persons Act, 1970, Food and Drugs (Milk) Act, 1970, Police Act, 1972, as a Private Member; Parly Adviser to the Police Fedn, 1971–74; Chm., Co-operative Parly Group, 1971–72 and 1983–85; Vice-Chm., All-Party Parly Retail Trade Gp, 1972–74; Vice-Pres., Parly and Scientific Cttee, 1991– (Chm., 1988–91); Chairman: Managing Trustees, Parly Pensions Fund, 1983– (Man. Trustee, 1980–83); Managing Trustees, H of C Members' Fund, 1983–; Anzac Gp of MPs and Peers, 1982–; Jt Treasurer, British-Amer. Parly Gp, 1983–. Mem., Gen. Adv. Council, BBC, 1968–74, 1983–; Patron: Disablement Income Group, 1970–; Motability, 1978–; Mem., Exec. Cttee, Nat. Fund for Research into Crippling Diseases, 1970–74. Chm., World Cttee apptd to draft "Charter for the 1980's" for disabled people worldwide, 1980–81; Pres., N of England Regional Assoc. for the Deaf, 1980–; Trustee, Crisis at Christmas, 1982–. Hon. Fellow, Manchester Metropolitan Univ. (formerly Poly.), 1990. Field Marshal Lord Harding Award, 1971, for services to the disabled; Grimshaw Meml Award of Nat. Fedn of the Blind, 1971; Paul Harris Fellowship, Rotary Internat., for services to the disabled internationally, 1992. Hon. AO 1991. *Publications:* Value Added Tax: a tax on the consumer, 1970; The Growth of Parliamentary Scrutiny by Committee, 1970; (with A. Butler) No Feet to Drag, 1972, Ed. lectures (Human Relations in Industry), 1958; Ed. Jl (Jt Consultation) publ. Nat. Jt Adv. Coun. Elec. Supply Ind., 1959–61. *Recreations:* gardening, tennis, snooker, chess. *Address:* House of Commons, SW1A 0AA.

MORRIS, Alfred Cosler; Vice Chancellor, University of the West of England, Bristol, since 1992 (Director, Bristol Polytechnic, 1986–92); *b* 12 Nov. 1941; *s* of late Stanley Bernard Morris, Anlaby, E Yorks, and Jennie Fletcher; *m* 1970, Annette, *er d* of Eamonn and May Donovan, Cork, Eire; one *d*. *Educ:* Hymers Coll., Hull (E Riding Scholar); Univ. of Lancaster (MA Financial Control 1970). FCA; FSS. Articled clerk to Oliver Mackrill & Co., 1958–63; Company Sec., Financial Controller and Dir, several cos, 1963–71; Sen. Leverhulme Res. Fellow in Univ. Planning and Orgn, Univ. of Sussex, 1971–74; Vis. Lectr in Financial Management, Univ. of Warwick, 1973; Group Management Accountant, Arthur Guinness Ltd, 1974–76; Management Consultant, Deloitte Haskins & Sells, 1976–77; Financial Adviser, subsids of Arthur Guinness, 1977–80; Dep. Dir, Polytechnic of the South Bank, 1980–85, Acting Dir, 1985–86. Adviser to H of C Select Cttee on Educn, Sci. and Arts, 1979–83. Chm., PCFC Cttee on Performance Indicators in Higher Educn, 1989–90; Member: CNAA, 1988–93; Higher Educn Funding Council for Wales, 1992–; Higher Educn Quality Council, 1992–94; South West Arts, 1994–; Bd, Westec, 1995–. Dir, Bristol and West Building Soc., 1992–. Chairman: Bristol Old Vic Trust, 1992–94; Patrons of Bristol Old Vic, 1993–; Trustee, Bristol Cathedral Trust, 1988–; Mem. Exec. Cttee, Bristol Soc., 1992–. Mem. Council, Clifton High Sch., 1995–. Hon. Fellow, Humberside Univ., 1990. Hon. LLD Bristol, 1993. *Publications:* (ed jtly and contrib.) Resources and Higher Education, 1982; articles and contribs to jls on higher educn. *Recreations:* sailing, wind-surfing. *Address:* Park Court, Sodbury Common, Old Sodbury, Avon BS17 6PX. *T:* Chipping Sodbury (01454) 319900.

MORRIS, Andrew James; HM Diplomatic Service; High Commissioner, Kingdom of Tonga, and Consul for Pacific Islands under American sovereignty South of the Equator, since 1994; *b* 22 March 1939; *s* of late Albert Morris and of Clara Morris; *m* 1961, Ann Christine Healy; two *s*. Served Army, 1960–64. Entered FO, 1964; served Kuwait, Salisbury, Sofia, Muscat, and San Francisco, 1965–78; Consul, Los Angeles, 1978–82; FCO, 1982–86; First Sec., Kaduna, 1986–89; Dep. High Comr, Port Moresby, 1989–93; First Sec., FCO, 1993–94. *Recreations:* golf, travel. *Address:* c/o Foreign and Commonwealth Office, SW1A 2AH.

MORRIS, Anthony Paul; QC 1991; a Recorder of the Crown Court, since 1988; *b* 6 March 1948; *s* of late Isaac Morris Morris and Margaret Miriam Morris; *m* 1975, Jennie Foley; two *s*. *Educ:* Manchester Grammar Sch.; Keble Coll., Oxford (MA). Called to the Bar, Gray's Inn, 1970; practising on Northern Circuit, 1970–. *Recreations:* standing on the touch-line, making stripes. *Address:* Peel Court Chambers, 45 Hardman Street, Manchester M3 3HA. *Clubs:* Little Ship; Dunham Forest Golf; Bowdon Lawn Tennis (Cheshire).

MORRIS, Air Marshal Sir (Arnold) Alec; *see* Morris, Air Marshal Sir Alec.

MORRIS, Rt. Hon. Charles Richard; PC 1978; DL; *b* 14 Dec. 1926; *s* of George Henry Morris, Newton Heath, Manchester; *m* 1950, Pauline, *d* of Albert Dunn, Manchester; two *d*. *Educ:* Brookdale Park Sch., Manchester. Served with Royal Engineers, 1945–48. Pres., Clayton Labour Party, 1950–52. Mem. of Manchester Corporation, 1954–64: Chm. of Transport Cttee, 1959–62; Dep. Chm. of Establishment Cttee, 1963–64. Mem., Post Office Workers Union (Mem. Nat. Exec. Council, 1959–63). Contested (Lab) Cheadle Div. of Cheshire, 1959. MP (Lab) Manchester, Openshaw, Dec. 1963–1983; PPS to the Postmaster-General, 1964; Govt Asst Whip, 1966–67; Vice-Chamberlain, HM Household, 1967–69; Treasurer, HM Household (Deputy Chief Whip), 1969–70; PPS to Rt Hon. H. Wilson, MP, 1970–74; Minister of State: DoE, March–Oct. 1974; CSD, 1974–79; Dep. Shadow Leader of the House, 1980–83. Sec., NW Gp of Labour MPs, 1979–83. Dep. Chm., Ponti Gp, 1987–. Chm., Oldham–Rochdale Groundwork Trust, 1984–; Chm., Covent Garden Tenants' Adv. Gp, 1990–; Gov., Disley Sch., 1992–. DL Greater Manchester, 1985. *Address:* 24 Buxton Road West, Disley, Stockport, Cheshire. *T:* Disley (01663) 2450.

MORRIS, Christopher; Chairman, since 1992, and National Director, Corporate Special Services, since 1975, Touche Ross & Co.; *b* 28 April 1942; *s* of Richard Archibald Sutton Morris and Josephine Fanny Mary Morris (*née* Galliano); *m* 1968, Isabel Claire Ramsden Knowles (marr. diss.); two *s*. *Educ:* privately. Chartered Accountant, 1967; Partner, Touche Ross & Co., 1970. Major insolvency assignments: Banco Ambrosiano; Laker Airways; Rush & Tomkins; Polly Peck, BCCI. *Recreations:* racing, music, travel, food and wine, countryside. *Address:* Cedric House, East Harding Street, EC4A 3AS. *T:* 0171–936 3000. *Club:* Turf.

MORRIS, Rev. Dr Colin; Director, Centre for Religious Communication, Westminster College, Oxford, since 1991; *b* 13 Jan. 1929; *o s* of Daniel Manley Morris and Mary Alice Morris, Bolton, Lancs. *Educ:* Bolton County Grammar Sch.; Lincoln Coll., Oxford; Univ. of Manchester. Served RM, 1947–49. Student, Nuffield Coll., Oxford, 1953–56; Missionary, Northern Rhodesia, 1956–60; President: United Church of Central Africa, 1960–64; United Church of Zambia, 1965–68; Minister of Wesley's Chapel, London, 1969–73; Gen. Sec., Overseas Div., Methodist Church, 1973–78; Pres. of the Methodist Conference, 1976–77; Hd of Religious Programmes, BBC TV, 1978–84; Dep. Hd, 1978–79, Hd, 1979–87, Religious Broadcasting, BBC; Special Adviser to Dir-Gen., BBC, 1986–87; Controller, BBC NI, 1987–90. Chairman: Community and Race Relations Unit, BCC, 1974–76; Bd of Trustees, Refugee Legal Centre, 1993–95; Mem., Lord Chancellor's Adv. Cttee on Legal Educn and Conduct, 1991–94. Presenter, Sunday, BBC Radio 4, 1994–. Lectures: Willson, Univ. of Nebraska, 1968; Cousland, Univ. of Toronto, 1972; Voigt, S Illinois Conf. United Methodist Church, 1973; Hickman, Duke University, North Carolina, 1974; Palmer, Pacific NW Univ., 1976; Heslington, Univ. of York, 1983; Hibbert, BBC Radio 4, 1986; William Barclay Meml, Glasgow, 1986; Univ. of Ulster Convocation, 1988; St Cuthbert's, Edinburgh, 1990; Studdert-Kennedy, Univ. of Leeds, 1994; Coll. of Preachers, 1995. Select Preacher, Univ. of Cambridge, 1975, Oxford, 1976. Holds several hon. degrees. Officer-Companion, Order of Freedom (Zambia), 1966. *Publications:* Black Government (with President K. D. Kaunda), 1960; Hour After Midnight, 1961; Out of Africa's Crucible, 1961; End of the Missionary, 1961; Church and Challenge in a New Africa, 1965; Humanist in Africa (with President K. D. Kaunda), 1966; Include Me Out, 1968; Unyoung, Uncoloured, Unpoor, 1969; What the Papers Didn't Say, 1971; Mankind My Church, 1971; The Hammer of the Lord, 1973; Epistles to the Apostle, 1974; The Word and the Words, 1975; Bugles in the Afternoon, 1977; Get Through Till Nightfall, 1979; (ed) Kaunda on Violence, 1980; God-in-a-Box: Christian strategy in the TV age, 1984; A Week in the Life of God, 1986; Raising the Dead: a preacher's notebook, 1987; Drawing the Line: taste and standards in BBC programmes, 1987; Starting from Scratch, 1990; Let God be God: TV sermons, 1990; Wrestling with an Angel, 1990; Start Your Own Religion, 1992; *relevant publication:* Spark in the Stubble, by T. L. Charlton, 1969. *Recreations:* writing, walking, music. *Address:* Tile Cottage, 8 Houndean Rise, Lewes, E Sussex BN7 1EG.

MORRIS, David; *see* Morris, W. D.

MORRIS, David Elwyn; a District Judge (formerly Registrar) of the Principal Registry of the Family Division of the High Court of Justice, 1976–91; *b* 22 May 1920; *s* of Rev. S. M. Morris and K. W. Morris; *m* 1st, 1947, Joyce Hellyer (*d* 1977); one *s* one *d*; 2nd, 1978, Gwendolen Pearce (*d* 1988), *widow* of Dr John Pearce, 3rd, 1990, Mrs C. M. Tudor. *Educ:* Mill Hill Sch.; Brasenose Coll., Oxford (Hulme Exhibnr; MA). With Friends' Ambulance Unit in China, 1942–44; served British Army in India, 1944–46. Called to Bar, Inner Temple, 1949; admitted Solicitor of the Supreme Court, 1955; Mem., Matrimonial Causes Rule Cttee, 1967–75. Partner, Jaques & Co. until 1975. Adv. Editor, Atkin's Encyclopaedia of Court Forms in Civil Proceedings, 1982–88. *Publications:* China Changed My Mind, 1948; The End of Marriage, 1971; contrib. Marriage For and Against, 1972; Pilgrim through this Barren Land, 1974. *Recreation:* reading. *Address:* 42 Frenchay Road, Oxford OX2 6TG. *T:* Oxford (01865) 58390. *Club:* United Oxford & Cambridge University.

MORRIS, David Griffiths; His Honour Judge Morris; a Circuit Judge, since 1994; *b* 10 March 1940; *s* of Thomas Griffiths Morris and Margaret Eileen Morris; *m* 1971, Carolyn Mary (*née* Miller); one *s* one *d*. *Educ:* Abingdon Sch.; King's Coll., Univ. of London (LLB Hons). Called to the Bar, Lincoln's Inn, 1965. Pupillage in London (Temple and Lincoln's Inn), 1965–67; Tenant in London Chambers (Temple), 1967–72; Tenant in Cardiff Chambers, 1972–94; Asst Recorder, 1979–84; Local Junior for Cardiff Bar, 1981–87; Head of Chambers, June 1984; a Recorder, 1984–94. Founder Member: Llantwit Major Round Table and 41 Clubs; Llantwit Major Rotary Club (Pres., 1984–85); Llanmaes Community Council, 1982–84. *Recreations:* Rugby Union football, cricket, swimming, theatre, reading, gardening, family. *Address:* Bryn Hafren, Newport Road, Castleton, Cardiff CF3 8UN. *T:* Cardiff (01222) 398421. *Clubs:* Cardiff and County, United Services Mess (Cardiff); Pontypool Rugby Football (Sen. Vice-Pres.).

MORRIS, Rev. David Richard; Member (Lab) European Parliament, South Wales West, since 1994 (Mid and West Wales, 1984–94); *b* Llanelli, 28 Jan. 1930. *Educ:* Stebonheath Central Sch., Llanelli; Ruskin Coll., Oxford; University Coll., Swansea; Theological Coll., Aberystwyth. Former foundry labourer; Minister, Mid-Wales and Newport, Presbyterian Church of Wales, 1958–62; former district and county councillor; Educnl Advisor, Gwent CC, 1974–84. Contested (Lab) Brecon and Radnor, 1983. Member, European Parliament Committees: Social Affairs; Transport and Tourism (substitute); Full Mem., ACP/EEC Assembly. Vice-Pres., Welsh Parlt Campaign. Contributor, Low Pay Unit. Member: TGWU; Socialist Educnl Assoc.; Tribune Gp; European PLP; CND (Chm., CND Wales); Socialist Health Assoc. *Address:* 39 St James Crescent, Swansea SA1 6DR.

MORRIS, David Richard, CEng, FIMechE; Chairman, Northern Electric plc, since 1989; *b* 25 July 1934; *s* of Frederick George Morris and Marjorie Amy (*née* Brown); *m* 1961, (Ann) Carole Birch; two *s* one *d*. *Educ:* Imperial College (BSc(Eng)). ACGI. Graduate Engrg apprenticeship, D. Napier & Son, Divl Chief Develt Engr and Gen. Manager, 1956–69, English Electric; Divl Gen. Manager and Divl Dir, General Electric Co., 1969–75; Subsid. Co. Man. Dir, Sears Holdings plc, 1975–80; Delta Group plc: Divl Man. Dir, 1980–84; Gp Exec. Dir, 1984–88. *Recreations:* sailing, golf. *Address:* Northern Electric plc, Carliol House, Market Street, Newcastle upon Tyne NE1 6NE. *Club:* Northern Counties (Newcastle upon Tyne).

MORRIS, Prof. David William, PhD; FRAgS; dairy and sheep farmer, since 1983; agricultural consultant, since 1986; *b* 7 Dec. 1937; *s* of late David William Morris and

Mary Olwen Ann Lewis; *m* 1966, Cynthia Cooper; one *s* one *d*. *Educ:* Ardwyn Grammar Sch.; UC of Wales (BSc Agric.); Univ. of Newcastle upon Tyne (PhD). FRAgS 1974. Develt Officer, Agric. Div., ICI, 1963–64; Asst Dir, Cockle Park Exptl Farm, Newcastle upon Tyne Univ., 1964–68; Farms Manager for Marquis of Lansdowne, Bowood, Wilts, 1968–70; Principal, Welsh Agric. Coll., Aberystwyth, 1970–83; Prof. of Agric., UC Wales, Aberystwyth, 1979–83. Churchill Fellowship, 1973. *Publications:* Practical Milk Production, 1976, 3rd edn 1977; (with M. M. Cooper) Grass Farming, 5th edn 1984. *Recreation:* farming. *Address:* Wern Berni Farm, Llanboidy, Whitland, Dyfed SA34 0EY. *T:* Whitland (01994) 448214. *Club:* Farmers'.

MORRIS, Denis Edward, OBE 1958; Head, and ultimately Controller of Light Programme, BBC, 1960–67; *b* 29 June 1907; *s* of Philip and Edith Morris; *m* 1st, 1931, Angela Moore (marr. diss., 1942); one *s*; 2nd, 1943, Catharine Garrett (*née* Anderton); one *s*. *Educ:* Tonbridge Sch. BBC Talks Producer, 1936; BBC Midland Public Relations Officer, 1938; BBC Empire Public Relations Officer, 1939; MOI Dir, Midland Region, 1940–42; BBC Midland Regional Programme Dir, 1943–48; Head of Midland Regional Programmes, 1948–60. Wine Correspondent, Daily Telegraph, 1967–87. Leicester City Council, 1933–36; Chm., Findon Parish Council, 1971–74; Chm., Lord Mayor of Birmingham's War Relief Fund Publicity and Appeals Cttee, 1942–48; Pres., Shoreham Cons. Assoc., 1976–79 and 1983–86 (Chm., 1971–75); Member: Hosp. Management Cttee, St Francis Hosp. and Lady Chichester Hosp., 1966–71; Exec. Cttee, Nat. Cricket Assoc., 1969–74 (Chm., Public Relations Standing Cttee, 1969–72); Dep. Chm., Lord's Taverners' Council, 1963–65 (Mem., 1962–67); Public Relations Advisor to MCC and the Counties, 1967–68; Mem., Public Relations and Promotion Sub-Cttee, TCCB, 1968–75. *Publications:* Poultry-Keeping for Profit, 1949; The French Vineyards, 1958; A Guide to the Pleasures of Wine-Drinking, 1972; ABC of Wine, 1977. *Recreations:* bridge, drinking wine. *Clubs:* MCC; Incogniti CC; Sussex Martlets CC; Gentlemen of Leicestershire CC; Blackheath Rugby; Sussex Rugby Football.

See also T. D. Morris.

MORRIS, Derek James, MA, DPhil; Fellow and Tutor, Oriel College, Oxford; *b* 23 Dec. 1945; *s* of Denis William and Olive Margaret Morris; *m* 1975, Susan Mary Whittles; two *s*. *Educ:* Harrow County Grammar Sch.; St Edmund Hall, Oxford; Nuffield Coll., Oxford. MA (Oxon); DPhil. Research Fellow, Centre for Business and Industrial Studies, Warwick Univ., 1969–70; Fellow and Tutor in Economics, Oriel Coll., Oxford, 1970–; Tutor and Sen. Tutor, Oxford University Business Summer Sch., 1970–78; Visiting Fellow, Oxford Centre for Management Studies, 1977–81; Economic Dir, Nat. Economic Develt Office, 1981–84; Sir John Hicks Res. Fellow, 1991–92, Chm., Social Studies Bd, 1993–94, Oxford Univ. Vis. Lectr, Univ. of Calif, Irvine, 1986–87. Mem., Monopolies and Mergers Commn, 1991– (a Dep. Chm., 1995–). Mem., Cttee of Inquiry into the Future of Cowley, 1990. Chm., Oxford Economic Forecasting, 1984–; Dir, Oxford China Economics Ltd, 1993–; Member Editorial Board: Oxford Economic Papers, 1984–; Annual Register of World Events, 1985–; Asst Editor, Jl of Industrial Economics, 1984–87; Associate Editor, Oxford Review of Economic Policy, 1985–. *Publications:* (ed) The Economic System in the UK, 1977, 3rd edn 1985; (with D. Hay) Industrial Economics, Theory and Evidence, 1979, 2nd edn 1991; (with D. Hay) Unquoted Companies, 1984; (ed jtly) Strategic Behaviour and Industrial Competition, 1987; (with D. Hay) The Behaviour and Performance of Chinese State-Owned Enterprises, 1993; articles on unemployment, trade policy and performance, productivity growth, industrial policy, macroeconomic policy, the Chinese economy, exchange rates, profitability, the stock market and corporate control. *Recreations:* skiing, badminton, Rugby, reading history. *Club:* Reform.

MORRIS, Desmond John, DPhil; writer on animal and human behaviour; *b* 24 Jan. 1928; *s* of Capt. Harry Howe Morris and Dorothy Marjorie Fuller Morris (*née* Hunt); *m* 1952, Ramona Baulch; one *s*. *Educ:* Dauntsey's Sch.; Birmingham Univ. (BSc); Magdalen Coll., Oxford (DPhil). Postdoctoral research in Animal Behaviour, Dept of Zoology, Oxford Univ., 1954–56; Head of Granada TV and Film Unit at Zool. Soc. of London, 1956–59; Curator of Mammals, Zool. Soc. of London, 1959–67; Dir, Inst. of Contemp. Arts, London, 1967–68; Research Fellow, Wolfson Coll., Oxford, 1973–81. Chm. of TV programmes: Zootime (weekly), 1956–67; Life (fortnightly), 1965–68; TV series: The Human Race, 1982; The Animals Roadshow, 1987–89; The Animal Contract, 1990; Animal Country, 1991–95; The Human Animal, 1994. *Publications:* (Jt Ed.) International Zoo Yearbook, 1959–62; The Biology of Art, 1962; The Mammals: A Guide to the Living Species, 1965; (with Ramona Morris) Men and Snakes, 1965; (with Ramona Morris) Men and Apes, 1966; (with Ramona Morris) Men and Pandas, 1966; The Naked Ape, 1967; (ed) Primate Ethology, 1967; The Human Zoo, 1969; Patterns of Reproductive Behaviour, 1970; Intimate Behaviour, 1971; Manwatching: a field guide to human behaviour, 1977; (jtly) Gestures: their origins and distribution, 1979; Animal Days (autobiog.), 1979; The Giant Panda, 1981; The Soccer Tribe, 1981; Inrock (novel), 1983; The Book of Ages, 1983; The Art of Ancient Cyprus, 1985; Bodywatching: a field guide to the human species, 1985; The Illustrated Naked Ape, 1986; Catwatching, 1986; Dogwatching, 1986; The Secret Surrealist, 1987; Catlore, 1987; The Human Nest-builders, 1988; The Animals Roadshow, 1988; Horsewatching, 1988; The Animal Contract, 1990; Animal-Watching, 1990; Babywatching, 1991; Christmas Watching, 1992; The World of Animals, 1993; The Human Animal, 1994; The Naked Ape Trilogy, 1994; Bodytalk: a world guide to gestures, 1994; The Illustrated Catwatching, 1994; numerous papers in zoological jls. *Recreations:* painting, archæology. *Address:* c/o Jonathan Cape, Random Century House, 20 Vauxhall Bridge Road, SW1V 2SA.

MORRIS, Desmond Victor; HM Diplomatic Service, retired; *b* 26 June 1926; *s* of late John Walter Morris and Bessie (*née* Mason); *m* 1st, 1951, Peggy Iris Mumford; two *d*; 2nd, 1961, Patricia Irene Ward, *d* of Charles Daniel and Emma Camwell; one *d*. *Educ:* Portsmouth Southern Secondary Sch. for Boys; Durham Univ. Served RAF, 1945–48. Joined HM Diplomatic Service, 1948; served at Seattle, Budapest, Saigon, Addis Ababa, Berne, Ankara and Pretoria; Dep. High Comr, Georgetown, 1973–78; Dep. Head of Accommodation and Services Dept, FCO, 1979–82; Consul-Gen. and Counsellor (Administration), Washington, 1982–86. *Recreations:* gardening, music, paintings, travel. *Address:* Grayshott, Green Lane, Axminster, Devon EX13 5TD.

MORRIS, Edward Allan, CMG 1967; OBE 1961; *b* 8 Sept. 1910; *s* of late John and Edith Morris, Twickenham; *m* 1937, Phyllis, *d* of late Francis and Mary Guise, Twickenham; one *d* (one *s* decd). *Educ:* Hampton Grammar Sch.; Univ. of London (BCom). Entered Crown Agents' Office, 1928. RAFVR, 1942–46; Sqdn Leader (King's Commendation, 1946). Crown Agents' Office: Asst Head of Dept, 1956; Head of Dept, 1958; Asst Crown Agent, 1964; Crown Agent for Oversea Governments and Administrations, 1968–71. *Recreations:* cricket, Rugby Union football, church bells and change-ringing, preserving the riverside area of Twickenham. *Address:* 56 Lebanon Park, Twickenham, Mddx TW1 3DQ. *T:* 0181–892 5856. *Clubs:* Royal Air Force, MCC, Corona (Hon. Treas.); Harlequin Football.

MORRIS, Air Commodore Edward James, CB 1966; CBE 1959; DSO 1942; DFC 1944; RAF, retired 1968; *b* 6 April 1915; *s* of late D. G. Morris, and late Mrs E. Morris, Bulawayo, Southern Rhodesia; *m* 1945, Alison Joan, *d* of Sir Charles Henderson, KBE; two *s*. *Educ:* Michaelhouse, Natal, S Africa. Commnd, 1937; Fighter Comd, 1938–41; Desert Air Force, 1941–45; Staff Coll., 1945–46; BAFO Germany, 1946–49; Old Sarum, 1949–52; Caledonian Sector, Fighter Command, 1952–53; RAF Flying Coll., 1953–54; Exchange Posting with USAF, Florida, 1954–56; SASO HQ 12 Group, 1956–58; OC Wattisham, 1958–59; HQ Fighter Command, 1959–60; Air Ministry, 1960–64; Chief of Staff, Headquarters Middle East Command, 1964–66; AOC Air Cadets, and Comdt Air Training Corps, 1966–68. American DFC 1945. *Recreations:* golf, fishing. *Address:* 300 Amberfield, Private Bag X010, Howick 3290, South Africa.

MORRIS, Estelle; MP (Lab) Birmingham, Yardley, since 1992; *b* 17 June 1952; *d* of Rt Hon. Charles Richard Morris, *qv* and Pauline Morris. *Educ:* Whalley Range High Sch., Manchester; Coventry Coll. of Educn (TCert); BEd Warwick Univ. Teacher, 1974–92. Councillor, Warwick DC, 1979–91 (Labour Gp Leader, 1981–89). An Opposition Whip, 1994–. *Address:* House of Commons, SW1A 0AA. *T:* 0171–219 3000.

MORRIS, Gareth; *see* Morris, J. G.

MORRIS, Gareth (Charles Walter); flautist; Professor of the Flute, Royal Academy of Music, 1945–85; *b* Clevedon, Som, 13 May 1920, *e s* of late Walter and Enid Morris; *m* 1954; one *d*; *m* 1975, Patricia Mary, *y d* of Neil and Sheila Murray, Romsey, Hampshire; one *s* two *d*. *Educ:* Bristol Cathedral Sch.; Royal Academy of Music, London. First studied the flute at age of twelve under Robert Murchie and later won a scholarship to RAM. Career since then has been as soloist, chamber music and symphonic player, teacher and lecturer; Principal Flautist, 1949–72, Chm., 1966–72, Philharmonia Orch. Gave first British performances of works by Alwyn, Bowen, Gerhard, Ghedini, Honegger, Ibert, Jacob, Koechlin, Martin, Martinu, Piston, Poulenc, Prokofiev, Rawsthorne, Reizenstein, Roussel, Seiber, Wellesz. Has been mem. Arts Council Music Panel, and Warden of Incorporated Soc. of Musicians Soloists Section; Adjudicator, International Flute playing Competitions, Geneva, 1973, 1978, Munich, 1974, Leeds, 1977, 1980, Ancona, 1978, 1979, 1984. Played at Her Majesty's Coronation in Westminster Abbey in 1953. Gov., RSM; Trustee, Loan Fund for Musical Instruments. ARAM 1945; FRAM 1950; FRSA 1967 (Mem. Council, 1977–83; Chm., Music Cttee, 1981–83). *Publication:* Flute Technique, 1991. *Recreations:* reading and collecting books, astronomy, antiquarian horology. *Address:* 4 West Mall, Clifton, Bristol BS8 4BH. *T:* Bristol (0117) 973 4966. *Club:* Royal Over-Seas League.

MORRIS, Prof. Howard Redfern, FRS 1988; Professor of Biological Chemistry, Imperial College, University of London, since 1980; *b* 4 Aug. 1946; *s* of Marion Elizabeth and Herbert Morris, Bolton, Lancs; *m* 1st, 1969, Lene Verny Jensen (marr. diss.); two *d*; 2nd, 1988, Maria Panico; one *s* one *d*. *Educ:* Univ. of Leeds (BSc 1967; PhD 1970). SRC Fellow, Cambridge, 1970–72; Scientific Staff, MRC Lab. of Molecular Biol., Cambridge, 1972–75; Imperial College: Lectr, Dept of Biochem, 1975–78; Reader in Protein Chem., 1978–80; Hd, Dept of Biochem., 1985–88; Chm., Div. of Life Sciences, 1985–88. Founder Chm., M-Scan Ltd, analytical chem. consultants, 1979–. Visiting Professor: Univ. of Virginia, 1978; Soviet Acad. of Scis, 1982; Univ. of Naples, 1983; Life Scis Div., E. I. Dupont, USA, 1984–85; Dow Lectr in Analytical Chem., Univ. of British Columbia, 1989–90. Mem., EMBO, 1979–. BDH Gold Medal and Prize for analytical biochem., Biochem. Soc., 1978; Medal and Prize for macromolecules and polymers, RSC, 1982; Gold Medal for contribs to biopolymer sequencing and mass spectroscopy, Univ. of Naples/CNR Italy, 1989. *Publications:* (ed) Soft Ionisation Biological Mass Spectrometry, 1981; numerous contribs to learned jls, on enkephalin, SRS-A leukotrienes, interleukin, calcitonin gene related peptide, mass spectrometry, protein and glycoprotein structure elucidation. *Recreations:* fell walking, gardening, guitar. *Address:* Department of Biochemistry, Imperial College, Exhibition Road, SW7 2AZ. *T:* 0171–589 5111.

MORRIS, Ian; *see* Morris, James I.

MORRIS, Ivor Gray, CMG 1974; former Chairman and Managing Director, Morris Woollen Mills (Ipswich) Pty Ltd; Chairman Queensland Export Advisory Committee; *b* 28 March 1911; *s* of John and Annie Morris, Talybont, Cards, and Ipswich, Qld; *m* 1944, Jessie Josephine Halley; two *d*. *Educ:* Scotch Coll., Melbourne; Scots Coll., Warwick, Qld; Ipswich Grammar Sch., Qld; Leeds Univ. Founded Morris Woollen Mills (Ipswich) Pty Ltd, 1934. Former Mem. Exec., Wool Textile Manufrs Assoc. of Australia; Life Mem., Nuclear Physics Foundn; Former Mem., Trade Develt Council, Canberra. Former Chm. of Trustees, Ipswich Grammar Sch.; Vice-Pres., Qld Museum Trust, 1970–; Patron, St David's Welsh Soc.; Foundn Mem. and District Governor, Ipswich Apex Club (1st Apex Club formed in Austr.), 1938. *Recreations:* music, reading. *Address:* River Road, Redbank, Queensland 4301, Australia. *T:* 882935. *Clubs:* Tattersall's (Brisbane); Ipswich, Ipswich North Rotary (Ipswich, Qld).

MORRIS, James; *see* Morris, Jan.

MORRIS, Air Vice-Marshal James, CBE 1984 (OBE 1977); Chief Executive, Scottish Society for the Prevention of Cruelty to Animals, since 1991; *b* 8 July 1936; *s* of late James and Davina Swann Morris; *m* 1959, Anna Wann Provan; three *s*. *Educ:* Kirkcaldy High Sch.; Edinburgh Univ. (BSc). Commnd RAF, 1957; Flying/Staff Duties, RAF, USN, RN, 1960–72; Sqn Comdr 201 Sqdn, 1975–77; sc, 1977–78, psc; Station Comdr RAF Kinloss, 1981–84; Dir Operational Requirements (Air), MoD, 1986–89; AO Scotland and NI, 1989–91. President: Scottish Area, RAFA, 1991–; Scottish Union Jack Assoc., 1995–. Regl Chm., Scottish and NI Air Cadets, 1995–. *Recreations:* sailing, golf, curling. *Address:* c/o Lloyds Bank, George Street, Edinburgh EH2 4TF. *Club:* Royal Air Force.

MORRIS, (James) Ian; His Honour Judge Morris; a Circuit Judge, since 1994; *b* 6 Feb. 1944; *s* of late Thomas Orlando Morris and of Pearl Morris; *m* 1st, 1966, Maureen Ann Burton (marr. diss. 1978); one *s* one *d*; 2nd, 1979, Christine Ann Dyson (*d* 1980); 3rd, 1982, Alison Margaret Turner (marr. diss. 1988). *Educ:* King Henry VIII Grammar Sch., Coventry; Corpus Christi Coll., Oxford (BA Jurisp. 1967; MA 1970). Called to the Bar, Inner Temple, 1968; Asst Recorder, 1984, Recorder, 1988–94, Midland and Oxford Circuit. Chairman: Sandwell AHA Enquiry, 1979; Bromsgrove Hosp. Enquiry, 1982; RHA Counsel, Cttee of Enquiry, Legionnaires' Disease, Stafford, 1985. Founder and first Chm., Birmingham Cancer Support Gp, 1984. *Recreations:* writing poetry and children's stories, music, walking, living. *Address:* c/o Worcester Crown Court, Foregate Street, Worcester.

MORRIS, (James) Peter; public affairs analyst; *b* 17 Sept. 1926; *s* of Frank Morris and Annie (*née* Collindridge); *m* 1st, Peggy Giles (marr. diss.); 2nd, Margaret Law. *Educ:* Barnsley Holgate Grammar Sch.; Manchester Univ. (BA, Teaching Dip.). CAM Dip, 1976. MIPR 1965, FIPR 1990; AMInstR 1980; Fellow, Soc. of Assoc. Execs, 1985 (Pres., 1992–93). Served RAF, 1945–48; Research Dept, Labour Party, 1952–59; Govt Information Services, 1960–73; Dir of Information, GLC, 1973–77; Sec. Gen., Nat. Cold Storage Fedn, later Cold Storage and Distribn Fedn, 1977–90. Sen. Treas. and Mem. Travel Bd, NUS, 1952–56; Borough Councillor, Hackney, 1956–59; Member: Nat. Exec., IPCS, 1964–73; Council for Social Democracy, 1984–90; Council, CBI, 1989–90. Vice-Pres., Techl Cttee, European Refrigerated Warehouses Assoc., 1985–90. Consultant,

Europ. Assoc. of Addiction Treatment Providers, 1992–. *Publication:* Road Safety: a Study of Cost Benefit in Public Service Advertising, 1972. *Recreations:* painting, writing, cricket. *Address:* 88 Ridgmount Gardens, WC1E 7AY. *T:* 0171–637 2141. *Clubs:* MCC, Reform.

MORRIS, Sir (James) Richard (Samuel), Kt 1992; CBE 1985; FEng; Chairman and Managing Director, 1980–90, Non-Executive Chairman, 1990–92, Brown and Root Ltd; *b* 20 Nov. 1925; *o s* of James John Morris and Kathleen Mary Morris (*née* McNaughton); *m* 1958, Marion Reid Sinclair; two *s* two *d*. *Educ:* Ardingly Coll.; Birmingham Univ. BSc, 1st cl. hons Chem. Engrg; Vice-Chancellor's Prize, 1955; FEng, FIChemE. Captain Welsh Guards, 1944–48. Courtaulds Ltd, 1950–78: Man. Dir, National Plastics Ltd, 1959–64; Dep. Chm., British Cellophane Ltd, 1967–70; Chm., British Celanese Ltd, 1970–72; Chm., Northgate Gp Ltd, 1971–76; Chm., Meridian Ltd, 1972–76; Dir, 1967–78, Gp Technical Dir, 1976–78, Courtaulds Ltd. Chairman: Devonport Management Ltd, 1987–91; Devonport Royal Dockyard plc, 1987–91; UK Nirex, 1989–; Dir, British Nuclear Fuels Ltd, 1971–85; non-exec. Dir, OGC International plc, 1994–. Vis. Prof. of Chem. Engrg, Univ. of Strathclyde, 1979–88; Pro-Chancellor, 1982–86, Sen. Pro-Chancellor and Chm. of Council, 1986–95, Loughborough Univ. Chm., Cttee of Chairmen of Univ. Councils and Boards, 1991–94. Member: Nuclear Power Adv. Bd, 1973; Adv. Council for Energy Conservation, 1974–80; Adv. Bd for Res. Councils, 1981–90, Dep. Chm., 1988–90; Dep. Chm., NEB, 1978–79; Industrial Adviser to Barclays Bank, 1980–85; Dep. Chm., Foundn for Science and Technology, 1994–. Mem. Council, 1974, Vice-Pres., 1976, Pres., 1977, IChemE; Vice-Pres., Soc. of Chem. Industry, 1978–81; Hon. Sec., 1979–82, Hon. Sec. for Educn and Training, 1984–91, Vice Pres., 1987–91, Fellowship of Engineering; President: Pipeline Industries Guild, 1983–85; Engrg Sect., BAAS, 1989; Soc. for Underwater Technology, 1989–91; Assoc. of Science Educn, 1990. Chm. British Cttee, Det Norske Veritas. Gov., Repton Sch., 1987–. FRSA 1986. Hon. DSc: Leeds, 1981; Bath, 1981; Birmingham, 1985; Loughborough, 1991. *Recreations:* sheep farming, gardening, music. *Address:* Breadsall Manor, Derby DE21 5LL. *T:* Derby (01332) 831368. *Club:* Athenæum.

MORRIS, James Shepherd, RSA 1989 (ARSA 1975); RIBA, FRIAS; ALI; Partner, Morris & Steedman, Architects and Landscape Architects; *b* 22 Aug. 1931; *s* of Thomas Shepherd Morris and Johanna Sime Malcolm; *m* 1959, Eleanor Kenner Smith; two *s* one *d*. *Educ:* Daniel Stewart's Coll.; Edinburgh Sch. of Architecture (DipArch); Univ. of Pennsylvania (MLA). *Architectural works:* Edinburgh Univ., Strathclyde Univ., Princess Margaret Rose Hosp., Countryside Commn for Scotland. Member, Arts Council of Gt Britain, 1973–80; Vice-Chm., Scottish Arts Council, 1976–80 (Chm., Art Cttee, 1976–80; Mem., Enquiry into Community Arts, 1974); Mem., Council, RSA, 1991– (Hon. Treas., 1992–); Past Member: Council, RIAS and Edinburgh AA, 1969–71; Council of Cockburn Assoc., Edinburgh; Cttee of Management, Traverse Theatre, Edinburgh. Convenor, Fellowship Cttee, RIAS, 1985–87. Trustee, Nat. Mus. of Antiquities, 1980–86. RIBA Award, 1974; 9 Civic Trust Awards, 1962–75; British Steel Award, 1971; European Architectural Heritage Award, 1975; European Heritage Business & Industry Award, 1975. *Publications:* contribs to RIBA Jl. *Recreations:* golf, tennis, skiing, painting. *Address:* (office) 38 Young Street North Lane, Edinburgh EH2 4JD. *T:* (office) 0131–226 6563. *Clubs:* New (Edinburgh); Philadelphia Cricket (Philadelphia); Valderrama (Sotogrande, Spain).

MORRIS, Jan, MA Oxon; FRSL; writer; *b* 2 Oct. 1926. Commonwealth Fellow, USA, 1953; Editorial Staff, The Times, 1951–56; Editorial Staff, The Guardian, 1957–62. Member: Yr Academi Gymreig; Gorsedd of Bards, Nat. Eisteddfod of Wales. Hon. Fellow, UCW, 1992. Hon. DLitt Wales, 1993. *Publications* (as James Morris until 1973, subseq. as Jan Morris): Coast to Coast, 1956, rev. edn 1962; Sultan in Oman, 1957, rev. edn 1983; The Market of Seleukia, 1957; Coronation Everest, 1958; South African Winter, 1958; The Hashemite Kings, 1959; Venice, 1960, 3rd rev. edn 1993; The Upstairs Donkey, 1962 (for children); The World Bank, 1963; Cities, 1963; The Presence of Spain, 1964, rev. edns (as Spain), 1979, 1982, 1988; Oxford, 1965, 2nd edn 1986; Pax Britannica, 1968; The Great Port, 1970, rev. edn 1985; Places, 1972; Heaven's Command, 1973; Conundrum, 1974, Travels, 1976; Farewell the Trumpets, 1978; The Oxford Book of Oxford, 1978; Destinations, 1980; My Favourite Stories of Wales, 1980; The Venetian Empire, 1980, 2nd edn 1988; The Small Oxford Book of Wales, 1982; A Venetian Bestiary, 1982; The Spectacle of Empire, 1982; (with Paul Wakefield) Wales, The First Place, 1982; (with Simon Winchester) Stones of Empire, 1983; The Matter of Wales, 1984; Journeys, 1984; Among the Cities, 1985; Last Letters from Hav, 1985; (with Paul Wakefield) Scotland, The Place of Visions, 1986; Manhattan '45, 1987; Hong Kong, 1988, 2nd rev. edn 1993; Pleasures of a Tangled Life, 1989; (with Paul Wakefield) Ireland, Your Only Place, 1990; Sydney, 1992; O Canada!, 1992; Locations, 1992; (ed) Travels with Virginia Woolf, 1993; (with Twm Morys) A Machynlleth Triad, 1994; Fisher's Face, 1995. *Address:* Trefan Morys, Llanystumdwy, Cricieth, Gwynedd, Wales LL52 0LP. *T:* Cricieth (01766) 522222, *Fax:* (01766) 522426.

MORRIS, Prof. Jeremy Noah, CBE 1972; FRCP; Professor of Public Health, University of London, at London School of Hygiene and Tropical Medicine, 1967–78, Hon. Research Officer, since 1978; *b* 6 May 1910; *s* of Nathan and Annie Morris; *m* 1939, Galina Schuchalter; one *s* one *d*. *Educ:* Hutcheson's Grammar Sch., Glasgow; Univ. of Glasgow; University Coll. Hosp., London; London School of Hygiene and Tropical Medicine (Hon. Fellow 1979). MA, DSc, DPH. Qual., 1934; hosp. residencies, 1934–37; general practice, 1937–38; Asst MOH, Hendon and Harrow, 1939–41; Med. Spec., RAMC, 1941–46 (Lt-Col 1944–46); Rockefeller Fellow, Prev. Med., 1946–47; Dir, MRC Social Med. Unit, 1948–75; Prof., Social Med., London Hosp., 1959–67. Visiting Professor: Yale, 1957; Berkeley, 1963; Jerusalem, 1968, 1980; Adelaide, 1983. Consultant, Cardiology, WHO, 1960–. Lectures: Ernestine Henry, RCP London; Chadwick Trust; Gibson, RCP Edinburgh; Fleming, RCPS Glasgow; Carey Coombs, Univ. of Bristol; Brontë Stewart, Univ. of Glasgow; St Cyres, Nat. Heart Hosp.; Alumnus, Yale; Delamar, Johns Hopkins Univ.; Wade Hampton Frost, APHA; George Clarke, Univ. of Nottingham. Member: Royal Commission on Penal Reform; Cttee, Personal Social Services, Working Party Med. Admin, 1964–72; Health Educn Council, 1978–80; Chairman: Nat. Adv. Cttee on Nutrition Educn, 1979–83; Fitness and Health Adv. Gp, Sports Council, and Health Educn Authority (formerly Health Educn Council), 1980–. Hon. Member: Amer. Epid. Soc., 1976; Soc. for Social Medicine, 1978; British Cardiac Soc., 1982; Swedish Soc. for Sports Medicine, 1984. JP Middx, 1956–66. Hon. Fellow, Amer. Coll. of Sports Medicine, 1985; Hon. FFCM 1977; Hon. FRSM 1991. Hon. MD Edinburgh, 1974; Hon. DSc Hull, 1982. Bisset Hawkins Medal, RCP, 1980; Honor Award, Amer. Coll. of Sports Medicine, 1985; Jenner Medal, RSM, 1987. *Publications:* Uses of Epidemiology, 1957, 3rd edn 1975 (trans. Japanese, Spanish); papers on coronary disease and exercise, and on health and prevention. *Recreations:* walking, swimming, piano music. *Address:* 3 Briardale Gardens, NW3 7PN. *T:* 0171–435 5024.

MORRIS, Rt. Hon. John, PC 1970; QC 1973; MP (Lab) Aberavon Division of Glamorgan since Oct. 1959; a Recorder of the Crown Court, since 1982; Opposition Spokesman on Legal Affairs and Shadow Attorney General, since 1983; *b* Nov. 1931; *s* of late D. W. Morris, Penywern, Talybont, Cardiganshire; *m* 1959, Margaret M. Morris, JP, *d* of late Edward Lewis, OBE, JP, of Llandysul; three *d*. *Educ:* Ardwyn, Aberystwyth; University Coll. of Wales, Aberystwyth; Gonville and Caius Coll., Cambridge (LLM); Academy of International Law, The Hague; Holker Senior Exhibitioner, Gray's Inn. Commissioned Royal Welch Fusiliers and Welch Regt. Called to the Bar, Gray's Inn, 1954, Bencher, 1985. Parly Sec., Min. of Power, 1964–66; Jt Parly Sec., Min. of Transport, 1966–68; Minister of Defence (Equipment), 1968–70; Sec. of State for Wales, 1974–79. Dep. Gen. Sec. and Legal Adviser, Farmers' Union of Wales, 1956–58. Member: UK Delegn Consultative Assembly Council of Europe and Western European Union, 1963–64, 1982–83; N Atlantic Assembly, 1970–74. Chairman: Nat. Pneumoconiosis Jt Cttee, 1964–66; Joint Review of Finances and Management, British Railways, 1966–67; Nat. Road Safety Advisory Council, 1967; Mem. Courts of University Colls, Aberystwyth, Swansea and Cardiff. Hon. LLD Wales, 1983. *Address:* House of Commons, SW1A 0AA.

MORRIS, John Evan A.; *see* Artro Morris.

MORRIS, Prof. (John) Gareth, CBE 1994; FRS 1988; FIBiol; Professor of Microbiology, University of Wales, Aberystwyth, since 1971; *b* 25 Nov. 1932; *s* of Edwin Morris and Evelyn Amanda Morris (*née* Griffiths); *m* 1962, Áine Mary Kehoe; one *s* one *d*. *Educ:* Bridgend Grammar Sch.; Univ. of Leeds; Trinity Coll., Oxford. DPhil; FIBiol 1971. Guinness Res. Fellow, Univ. of Oxford, 1957–61; Rockefeller Fellow, Univ. of Calif at Berkeley, 1959–60; Tutor in Biochem., Balliol Coll., Oxford, 1960–61; Lectr, subseq. Sen. Lectr, Univ. of Leicester, 1961–71. Vis. Associate Prof., Purdue Univ., USA, 1965. Member: UGC, 1981–86; Royal Commn on Environmental Pollution, 1991–. *Publications:* A Biologist's Physical Chemistry, 1968, 2nd edn 1974; contribs on microbial biochemistry and physiology. *Recreations:* gardening, walking. *Address:* Cilgwyn, 16 Lôn Tyllwyd, Llanfarian, Aberystwyth, Dyfed SY23 4UH. *T:* Aberystwyth (01970) 612502.

MORRIS, John Michael Douglas; General Secretary, since 1986 and Company Secretary, since 1990, British Boxing Board of Control; *b* 10 Aug. 1935; *s* of Charles Edward Douglas Morris and Mary Kathleen (*née* Murphy); *m* 1958, Jill Margaret Walker; two *s* two *d*. *Educ:* John Fisher Sch.; Dulwich Coll. Reporter, Northampton Chronicle & Echo, 1953–60; Sports sub-editor, Evening Standard, 1960–67; Gp Sports Editor, United Newspapers, 1967–77; freelance writer and publican, 1977–79; John Morris Sports Agency, Northampton, 1979–86. Co. Sec., European Boxing Union, 1991–; Mem., Bd of Govs, World Boxing Council, 1986–. Commissioner of the Year: World Boxing Council, 1987, 1989 and 1994; World Boxing Assoc., 1988. *Publications:* Play Better Tennis (instructional booklet), 1969; Come in No 3: biography of cricketer David Steele, 1977; Box On: biography of boxing referee Harry Gibbs, 1981. *Recreations:* amateur drama, reading, all sport. *Address:* 1 Parkside, Court Downs Road, Beckenham, Kent BR3 2TN. *T:* 0181–658 4875.

MORRIS, Sir Keith Elliot Hedley, KBE 1994; CMG 1988; HM Diplomatic Service, retired; Ambassador to Colombia, 1990–94; *b* 24 Oct. 1934; *m* Maria del Carmen Carratala; two *s* two *d*. Entered Foreign Office, 1959; served Dakar, Algiers, Paris, Bogota; First Sec., FCO, 1971–76; Counsellor (Commercial), Warsaw, 1976–79; Minister-Counsellor, Mexico City, 1979–84; Head of Personnel Policy Dept, FCO, 1984–85; rcds, 1986; Minister (Commercial) and Consul-Gen., Milan, 1987–90.

MORRIS, Kenneth; Managing Director, Northumberland County Council, since 1992; *b* 17 April 1947; *s* of Thomas and Phyllis Morris; *m* 1988, Veronica Ann Young; two *s*. *Educ:* George Stephenson Grammar Sch., West Moor, Newcastle upon Tyne. Group Accountant, Newcastle upon Tyne CBC, 1972; Management Accountant, Tyne and Wear CC, 1974; Chief Accountant, 1976, Dep. Dir of Finance, 1982, Gateshead MBC; County Treasurer, Northumberland CC, 1988. *Recreations:* sport, reading, music. *Address:* 38 Gerrard Road, Whitley Bay, Tyne and Wear NE26 4NL. *T:* 0191–253 4907.

MORRIS, Max; educational propagandist and reformer; pioneer of the Comprehensive School; Headmaster, Willesden High School, 1967–78, retired; *s* of Nathan and Annie Morris; *m* 1961, Margaret Saunders (*née* Howard), historian. *Educ:* Hutcheson's, Glasgow; Kilburn Grammar Sch., Mddx; University Coll., Univ. of London (BA 1st cl. Hons History); Inst. of Education, Univ. of London (DipEd); LSE. Began teaching, 1936, in Willesden. Served War, 1941–46, demobilised as Captain RASC. Sen. Lectr, Colls of Education, 1946–50; Dep. Head, Tottenham, 1960, after nine years of political discrimination in Middlesex; Headmaster, Chamberlayne Wood Secondary Sch., Willesden, 1962–67. NUT: Mem. Exec., 1966–79; Pres., 1973–74; Chm. Action Cttee, 1976–79. Chairman: Mddx Regional Examining Bd, 1975–79; London Regional Examining Bd, 1979–90; Vice-Chairman: Centre for Information and Advice on Educnl Disadvantage, 1975–80; London and E Anglian Gp, GCSE; Member: Schools Council Cttees, 1967–84; Burnham Cttee, 1970–79; Board of NFER, 1970–80; CLEA/School Teachers Cttee, 1972–79; Schools Broadcasting Council, 1972–80; Nat. Adv. Cttee on Supply and Trng of Teachers, 1973–78; Sub-Cttee on Educn, Labour Party NEC, 1978–83; Council, Inst. of Educn; Jt Council, GCE and CSE Boards; Univ. of London Exams and Assessment Council. Mem. (Lab) Haringey Borough Council, 1984–86. *Publications:* The People's Schools, 1939; From Cobbett to the Chartists, 1948; Your Children's Future, 1953; (with Jack Jones) An A to Z of Trade Unionism and Industrial Relations, 1982, 2nd edn 1986; (ed jtly) Education: the wasted years 1973–1986?, 1988; contribs on educnl and historical subjects in newspapers, weeklies and jls. *Recreations:* baiting the Dept of Education and Science; ridiculing Trotskyists and trendies; tasting malt whisky. *Address:* 44 Coolhurst Road, N8 8EU. *T:* 0181–348 3980.

MORRIS, Michael Sachs; Director-General, British Insurance Brokers' Association, 1980–85; *b* 12 June 1924; *s* of late Prof. Noah Morris, MD, DSc, and Hattie Michaelis; *m* 1952, Vera Leonie, *er d* of late Paul and Lona Heller; one *s* one *d*. *Educ:* Glasgow Acad.; St Catharine's Coll., Cambridge. Wrangler, 1948. Scientific Officer, Admty Signals Estabt, 1943–46; Asst Principal, BoT, 1948; idc 1970; Under Secretary: Insurance Div., DoT, 1973, Shipping Policy Div., DoT, 1978–80. Chm., Consultative Shipping Gp, 1979–80. Mem., Barnet Health Authy, 1985–90. *Recreation:* sitting in the sun. *Address:* 5 Sunrise View, The Rise, Mill Hill, NW7 2LL. *T:* 0181–959 0837. *Club:* United Oxford & Cambridge University.

MORRIS, Rt Hon. Michael (Wolfgang Laurence); PC 1994; MP (C) Northampton South, since Feb. 1974; Chairman of Ways and Means and Deputy Speaker, House of Commons, since 1992; *b* 25 Nov. 1936; *m* 1960, Dr Ann Appleby (Dr Ann Morris, MB, BS, MRCS, MRCP); two *s* one *d*. *Educ:* Bedford Sch.; St Catharine's Coll., Cambridge (MA). BA Hons Econs. Trainee to Marketing Manager, UK, India and Ceylon, Reckitt & Colman Gp, 1960–63; Service Advertising Ltd, 1964–68; Marketing Exec. to Account Supervisor, Horniblow Cox-Freeman Ltd, 1968–71, Dir 1969–71; Dir, Benton & Bowles Ltd, 1971–81; Proprietor, A. M. International, 1980–92. Contested (C) Islington North, 1966. Islington Council: Councillor, 1968–70; Alderman, 1970–74; Chm. of Housing, 1968; Leader, 1969–71. PPS to Minister of State, NI Office, 1979–81; Member: Public Accounts Cttee, 1979–92; Select Cttee on Energy, 1982–85; Chairman's Panel, 1984–92; Mem. Council, Europe and Western European Union, 1983–91; Chairman: British Sri Lanka Cttee, 1979–92; British Singapore Cttee, 1985–92; British Malaysia Cttee, 1987–92; British Burma Cttee, 1989–92; Vice-Chm., British Indonesia Cttee; Treas., British Asean and Thai Cttees; Secretary: British Venezuela Cttee; Cons. Housing and Local Govt Cttee, 1974–76; Cons Trade Cttee, 1974–76; Cons. Environment Cttee, 1977–79; Vice-Chm., Cons. Energy Cttee, 1981–92; Founder, Parly Food and Health Forum. Captain, Parly Golf Soc., 1988–91. Chm., Govs, Bedford Sch., 1989– (Governor, 1982–). *Publications:* (jtly) Helping the Exporter, 1967; (contrib.) Marketing below the Line: Studies in Management, 1972; The Disaster of Direct Labour, 1978. *Recreations:* restoration work, cricket, tennis, golf, budgerigars, forestry. *Address:* Caesar's Camp, Sandy, Beds SG19 2AD. *T:* Sandy (01767) 680388. *Clubs:* Carlton, MCC; All England Lawn Tennis and Croquet; George Row, Conservative, Whitworth, Billing Road, St George's (Northampton); John O'Gaunt Golf.

MORRIS, Nigel Godfrey, CMG 1955; LVO 1966; QPM 1954; *b* 11 Nov. 1908; 2nd *s* of late Lt-Col G. M. Morris, 2/8th Gurkha Rifles and late Mrs Morris; *m* 1st, 1941, Mrs G. E. Baughan, *widow* (*d* 1982), *e d* of late J. C. Sidebottom; one *d* and one step *d;* 2nd, 1984, Mrs M. C. Berkeley-Owen (*née* Mullally). *Educ:* Wellington Coll. Asst Superintendent SS Police, 1928; Chinese language course, Amoy, China, 1929; Asst Supt of Police, Singapore CID 1931; Special Branch, 1935; Asst Supt of Police, Town Penang, 1939; interned by Japanese, 1942; repatriated to UK, 1945; Asst Dir, Malayan Security Service, 1946; Dir, Special Branch, Singapore, 1948; Dep. Commissioner, CID, Singapore, 1950, Comr, 1952; Deputy Inspector-General of Colonial Police, Colonial Office, 1957–63; Commissioner of Police, Bahamas, 1963–68, retired. Colonial Police Medal, 1949. *Address:* 119 Cranmer Court, SW3 3HE. *T:* 0171–584 9875. *Club:* Phyllis Court (Henley).

MORRIS, Norma Frances; Administrative Secretary, Medical Research Council, since 1989; *b* 17 April 1935; *d* of Henry Albert Bevis and Lilian Eliza Bevis (*née* Flexon); *m* 1960, Samuel Francis Morris; one *s* two *d. Educ:* Ilford County High Sch. for Girls; University College London (BA, MA). Assistante Anglaise, Paris, 1956–57; Asst Lectr, Univ. of Hull, 1959–60; MRC, 1960–. Mem., Nat. Biol Standards Bd, 1990–. *Recreations:* opera, edible fungi. *Address:* Medical Research Council, 20 Park Crescent, W1N 4AL. *T:* 0171–637 6016.

MORRIS, Prof. Norman Frederick, MD, FRCOG; Medical Director, In Vitro Fertilisation Unit, Cromwell Hospital, since 1986; Professor of Obstetrics and Gynæcology, University of London, Charing Cross and Westminster Medical School (formerly Charing Cross Hospital Medical School), 1958–85, now Emeritus; Dean, Faculty of Medicine, University of London, 1971–76; Deputy Vice-Chancellor, University of London, 1976–80; *b* Luton, 26 Feb. 1920; *s* of F. W. Morris, Luton; *m* 1944, Lucia Xenia Rivlin; two *s* two *d. Educ:* Dunstable Sch., Dunstable; St Mary's Hospital Medical Sch. MRCS, LRCP 1943; MRCOG 1949; MB, BS (London) 1943; MD (London) 1949; FRCOG 1959. House appts St Mary's Hosp., Paddington and Amersham, 1943–44; Res. Obstetrician and Surg. Officer, East Ham Memorial Hosp., E6, 1944–46; Surg. Specialist RAF (Sqdn Ldr), 1946–48; Registrar, St Mary's Hosp., W2, and East End Maternity Hosp., E1, 1948–50; Sen. Registrar (Obst. and Gynæcol.), Hammersmith Hosp., 1950–52; First Asst, Obstetric Unit, Univ. Coll. Hosp., WC1, 1953–56; Reader, Univ. of London in Obst. and Gynæcol., Inst. of Obstetrics and Gynæcology, 1956–58. Dep. Chm., NW Thames RHA, 1974–80; Chm., NW Thames Reg. Res. Cttee, 1981–86. External Examiner, Univs of Sheffield, Leeds, Dundee and Liverpool. President: (founder) Internat. Soc. of Psychosomatic Obstetrics and Gynaecology, 1972–80; Section of Obstetrics and Gynaecology, RSocMed, 1978–79; W London Medico-Chirurgical Soc., 1982; Chairman: Assoc. of Profs of Obstets and Gynaecol. of UK, 1981–86; British Soc. of Psychosomatic Obstets, Gynaecol. and Andrology, 1988–; Treas., Internat. Soc. for Investigation of Stress, 1991–. Mem., Academic Forum, DHSS, 1981–84; Chm., Commonwealth Health Devélt Prog., Commonwealth Secretariat, 1990–; Sec. Gen., Commonwealth Health Foundn, 1994–. Mem., Hammersmith and Fulham HA, 1983–84. Mem. Ct and Senate, Univ. of London, 1972–80; Governor: Wye Coll., 1973–80; St Paul's Sch., 1976–91. Trustee, Little Foundn, 1992– (Chm., Scientific Cttee, 1993). Fellow, Soc. Gyn. et Obst., Italy, 1970–. Formerly Chm., Assoc. of University Clinical Academic Staff. Editor, Midwife and Health Visitor Jl. *Publications:* Sterilisation, 1976; Contemporary Attitudes to Care in Labour (The Psychosomatic Approach), 1986; Factors Influencing Population Control, 1986; articles in medical jls related to obstetric and gynaecological problems, 1952–. *Recreations:* travelling, collecting glass, music. *Address:* 16 Provost Road, NW3 4ST. *T:* 0171–722 4244. *Clubs:* Athenæum, 1942.

MORRIS, Owen Humphrey, CB 1977; CMG 1967; Deputy Under-Secretary of State, Welsh Office, 1974–81, retired; *b* 15 June 1921; *o c* of late David Humphreys Morris, Ton Pentre, Rhondda, Glam., and Mrs Amy Ann Morris (*née* Jones); *m* 1972, Mair Annetta Evans, *d* of late Capt. Daniel Evans, DSC, Tynllys, Morfa Nefyn. *Educ:* Public Elem. Schs; King's Coll. Sch., Wimbledon (Schol.); Balliol Coll., Oxford (Schol.; MA). Served War of 1939–45: The Welch Regt and King's African Rifles, 1941–45 (Capt.). Asst Princ., Colonial Office, 1946; seconded Sierra Leone Administration, 1952–53; Asst Sec., 1955; Dept of Techn. Cooperation, 1962; Min. of Overseas Development, 1964; Min. of Housing and Local Govt, 1966; Welsh Office, 1969; Asst Under-Sec., 1970; Dep. Sec., 1974. Chm., Gwynedd Archaeol Trust, 1984–87. *Address:* Taltreuddyn Fawr, Dyffryn Ardudwy, Gwynedd LL44 2RQ.

MORRIS, Peter; *see* Morris, J. P.

MORRIS, Peter Christopher West; solicitor; *b* 24 Dec. 1937; *s* of C. T. R. and L. B. Morris; *m* 1st, 1959, Joy (marr. diss.); two *s* one *d*; 2nd, 1987, Terese; one step *s* two step *d. Educ:* Seaford Coll.; Christ's Coll., Cambridge, 1958–61 (MA, LLB). Hockey Blue, 1959, 1960, 1961; Hockey for Wales, 1962–65. National Service, 1956–58. Admitted Solicitor, 1965; Partner with Wild Hewitson & Shaw, 1967; a Recorder of the Crown Court, 1980–84; voluntary removal from Roll of Solicitors, 1982; called to the Bar, Middle Temple, 1982–84; company dir, 1985–93; name restored to Roll of Solicitors, 1993. *Recreations:* golf, gardening, cycling. *Address:* 1 Hawthorn Close, Saltdean, Sussex BN2 8HX. *Clubs:* Hawks (Cambridge); Cambridge University Hockey (Pres.).

MORRIS, Prof. Peter John, FRS 1994; Nuffield Professor of Surgery, Chairman, Department of Surgery and Director, Oxford Transplant Centre, Oxford University, since 1974; Fellow of Balliol College, since 1974; *b* 17 April 1934; *s* of Stanley Henry and Mary Lois Morris; *m* 1960, Mary Jocelyn Gorman; three *s* two *d. Educ:* Xavier Coll., Melbourne; Univ. of Melbourne (MB, BS, PhD). FRCS, FRACS, FACS. Jun. surg. appts at St Vincent's Hosp., Melbourne, Postgrad. Med. Sch., London, Southampton Gen. Hosp. and MGH Boston, 1958–64; Research Fellow, Harvard Med. Sch., 1965–66; Asst Prof. in Surgery, Med. Coll. of Virginia, 1967; 2nd Asst in Surgery, Univ. of Melbourne, 1968–69, 1st Asst 1970–71; Reader in Surgery, Univ. of Melbourne, 1972–74. WHO Consultant, 1970–84; Cons. to Walter and Eliza Hall Inst. of Med. Res., 1969–74. Pres., Transplantation Soc., 1984–86; Chm., Nat. Kidney Res. Fund, 1986–90; Member: MRC, 1983–87; Oxford RHA, 1988–90; Council, RCS, 1991–. Hunterian Prof., RCS, 1972. USA Nat. Kidney Foundn Prof., 1986; Nimmo Vis. Prof., Univ. of Adelaide, 1993; Ho Tam Kit Hing Vis. Prof., Univ. of Hong Kong, 1994; Walkman Walters Vis. Prof., Mayo Clinic, 1994. Lectures: Champ Lyons, Univ. of Alabama, 1989; Fraser Meml, Univ. of Edinburgh, 1990; Bennett, TCD, 1991; Graham, Washington Univ., 1991; Murdoch Meml, Aberdeen Univ., 1991; Shaw, RCPE, 1991; Pybus Meml, N of Eng. Surg. Soc., 1992; Gallie, Royal Coll. of Physicians and Surgeons, Canada, 1992; Agnew, Univ. of Penn, 1993; Grey Turner, Internat. Surg. Soc., 1993. Hon. Fellow: Amer. Surgical Assoc., 1982; Asian Surg. Soc., 1989; Hon. FACS 1986; Hon. FRACS, 1995; Hon. FRCSE 1995; Hon. Mem., Amer. Soc. of Transplant Surgeons, 1993. Selwyn Smith Prize, Univ. of Melbourne, 1971; Cecil Joll Prize, RCS, 1988. Editor, Transplantation, 1979–. *Publications:* Kidney Transplantation: principles and practice, 1979, 4th edn 1994; Tissue Transplantation, 1982; Transient Ischaemic Attacks, 1982; Progress in Transplantation, Vol. 1 1984, Vol. 2 1985, Vol. 3 1986; (ed) Oxford Textbook of Surgery, 1994; (ed) Transplantation Reviews, annually, 1987–; numerous sci. articles and chapters in books concerned mainly with transplantation and surgery. *Recreations:* golf, tennis, cricket. *Address:* 19 Lucerne Road, Oxford OX2 7QB. *Clubs:* United Oxford & Cambridge University, MCC; Frilford Heath Golf (Oxford); Oxfordshire County Cricket; St Cyprien Golf (France); Melbourne Cricket (Melbourne).

MORRIS, Peter T.; *see* Temple-Morris.

MORRIS, Sir Richard; *see* Morris, Sir J. R. S.

MORRIS, Richard Francis Maxwell; Chief Executive, Associated Board of the Royal Schools of Music, since 1993; *b* 11 Sept. 1944; *s* of Maxwell Morris and late Frederica (*née* Abelson); *m* 1st, 1974, Sarah Quill (marr. diss. 1978); 2nd, 1983, Marian Sperling; two *d. Educ:* Eton Coll.; New Coll., Oxford (MA); Coll. of Law, London. Solicitor, Farrer & Co., 1967–71; Legal Advr and Banker, Grindlay Brandts, 1971–75; Corporate Finance Manager, S. G. Warburg & Co., 1975–79; Hodder and Stoughton: Group Finance Dir, 1979; Man. Dir, Educnl and Acad. Publishing, 1987; Jt Man. Dir, 1989–91; Dir, The Lancet, 1986–91; Man. Dir, Edward Arnold, 1987–91. Director: Invicta Sound, 1984–91; Southern Radio, 1991–92. Mem. Council, Kent Opera, 1985–90; Founder, Almaviva Opera, 1989–. Hon. RCM. *Recreations:* opera singing, 'cello playing, golf. *Address:* Holdfast House, Edenbridge, Kent TN8 6SJ. *T:* Edenbridge (01732) 862439. *Club:* Athenæum.

MORRIS, Richard Keith, FSA; Director, Council for British Archaeology, since 1991; *b* 8 Oct. 1947; *s* of John Richard Morris and Elsie Myra (*née* Wearne); *m* 1972, Jane Whiteley; two *s* one *d. Educ:* Denstone Coll., Staffs; Pembroke Coll., Oxford (MA); Univ. of York (BPhil). FSA 1982; MIFA 1986. Musician, 1971–72; Res. Assistant, York Minster Archaeol. Office, 1972–75; Churches Officer, 1975–77, Res. Officer, 1978–88, Council for British Archaeol.; Hon. Lectr, Sch. of History, Univ. of Leeds, 1986–88; Lectr, Dept of Archaeol., Univ. of York, 1988–91. Frend Medal, Soc. of Antiquaries of London, 1992. *Publications:* Cathedrals and Abbeys of England and Wales, 1979; The Church in British Archaeology, 1983; Churches in the Landscape, 1989; Guy Gibson, 1994. *Recreations:* music, aviation history, writing. *Address:* Council for British Archaeology, Bowes Morrell House, 111 Walmgate, York YO1 2UA. *T:* York (01904) 671417.

MORRIS, Sir Robert (Byng), 10th Bt *cr* 1806, of Clasemont, Glamorganshire; *b* 25 Feb. 1913; *s* of Percy Byng Morris (*d* 1957) (*g s* of 2nd Bt), and Ethel Maud (*d* 1923), *d* of William Morley Glascott, Melbourne; *S* cousin, 1982; *m* 1947, Christina Kathleen, *d* of Archibald Field, Toddington, Glos; one *s* three *d. Heir: s* Allan Lindsay Morris [*b* 27 Nov. 1961; *m* 1986, Cheronne, *e d* of Dale Whitford, Par, Cornwall; one *d*]. *Address:* Norton Creek Stables (RR5), St Chrysostome, Quebec, Canada.

MORRIS, Robert Matthew; Assistant Under Secretary of State, Criminal Justice and Constitutional Department, Home Office, since 1991; Registrar of the Baronetage, since 1991; *b* 11 Oct. 1937; *s* of late William Alexander Morris and of Mary Morris (*née* Bryant); *m* 1965, Janet Elizabeth Gillingham; two *s* one *d. Educ:* Handsworth Grammar Sch.; Christ's Coll., Cambridge. S Staffords Regt, 1956–58. Joined Home Office, 1961; Asst Private Sec. to Home Sec., 1964–66; CSD, 1969–71; Principal Private Sec. to Home Sec., 1976–78; Sec. to UK Prison Services Inquiry (May Cttee), 1978–79; Head of Crime Policy Planning Unit, 1979–81; Asst Under Sec. of State, Fire and Emergency Planning, 1983, Immigration Policy, Nationality and Passports, 1986. *Address:* c/o Home Office, 50 Queen Anne's Gate, SW1H 9AT.

MORRIS, Rear-Adm. Roger Oliver, CB 1990; FRGS; FRIN; Hydrographer of the Navy, 1985–90; *b* 1 Sept. 1932; *s* of Dr Oliver N. Morris and H. S. (Mollie) Morris (*née* Hudson). *Educ:* Mount House School, Tavistock; Royal Naval College, Dartmouth. Entered Royal Navy, 1946, commissioned 1952; specialized in Hydrographic Surveying, 1956; commanded HM Ships Medusa, Beagle, Hydra, Fawn, Hecla, Hydra, 1964–80; RCDS 1978; Director of Hydrographic Plans and Surveys, 1980–81; Asst Hydrographer, 1982–84. Chm. of Council, Soc. for Nautical Res., 1989–94; Vice-Pres., Royal Inst. of Navigation, 1991–92. *Publication:* Charts and Surveys in Peace and War, 1995. *Recreations:* heraldry, opera, bird watching. *Address:* Orchard House, Quantock View, Bishops Lydeard, Somerset TA4 3AW. *Club:* Commonwealth Trust.

MORRIS, Air Vice-Marshal Ronald James Arthur, CB 1974; retired; *b* 27 Nov. 1915; *s* of late Dr James Arthur Morris, Ladybank, Fife; *m* 1945, Mary Kerr Mitchell; one *s* two *d. Educ:* Madras Coll., St Andrews; St Andrews Univ. MB, ChB 1939; DPH Edinburgh, 1953; MFCM 1972. Commnd RAF, 1939; served on Fighter Comd Stns, 1940–41; India and Burma Campaign, 1941–45; HQ Techn. Trng Comd, 1946–48; SMO, HQ Air Forces Western Europe, 1948–50; Sen. Trng Officer and Comdt Med. Trng Estabt, 1950–52; Exchange Officer, Sch. of Aviation Medicine (USAF), 1955–56; Dept MA7, Air Min., 1956–60; OC RAF Chessington, 1960–61; OC RAF Hosp. Wroughton, 1961–63; PMO, Signals Comd, 1963–65; Dep. PMO, Far East Air Forces, 1965–69; PMO, Maintenance Comd, 1969–70; DDGMS (RAF), 1971–73; PMO, RAF Strike Comd, 1974–75. QHS, 1971–75. CStJ 1974. *Recreations:* golf, fishing. *Address:* 2 Cairnsden Gardens, St Andrews, Fife KY16 8SQ. *T:* St Andrews (01334) 75326.

MORRIS, Simon C.; *see* Conway Morris.

MORRIS, Prof. Terence Patrick, JP; Emeritus Professor of Criminology and Criminal Justice, University of London, since 1994 (Professor of Social Institutions, 1981–94); *b* 8 June 1931; *s* of Albert and Norah Avis Morris; *m* 1954, Pauline Jeannette Peake (*née* Morris) (marr. diss. 1973); one *d*; *m* 1973, Penelope Jane, *y d* of Stanley and Alexandra Tomlinson. *Educ:* John Ruskin Grammar Sch., Croydon; LSE, Univ. of London (Leverhulme Schol.). BSc (Soc) 1953, PhD (Econ) 1955. Lectr in Sociology, LSE, 1955–63; Reader, 1963–69, Prof., 1969–81, Sociology (with special ref. to Criminology), London Univ.; Founder Dir, Mannheim Centre for Criminology and Criminal Justice, LSE. Vis. Prof. of Criminology, Univ. of California, 1964–65. Mem., Adv. Mission on Treatment of Offenders (Western Pacific, British Honduras, Bahamas), 1966. Vice-Pres., Howard League for Penal Reform, 1986–; Mem., Magistrates' Assoc. Treatment of Offenders Cttee (co-opted), 1969–77; Founder Mem., Inst. for Study of Drug Dependence. Man. Editor, British Jl of Sociology, 1965–74. JP Inner London, 1967. *Publications:* The Criminal Area, 1957; (with Pauline Morris) Pentonville: a sociological study of an English prison, 1963; (with L. J. Blom-Cooper) A Calendar of Murder, 1964; Deviance and Control: the secular heresy, 1976; Crime and Criminal Justice since 1945, 1989; contribs to Brit. Jl Criminology, Brit. Jl Sociology, Encycl. Britannica. *Recreations:* cycling, photography. *Address:* c/o London School of Economics, Houghton Street, WC2A 2AE. *Club:* Cyclists' Touring.

MORRIS, Most Rev. Thomas, DD; Archbishop of Cashel and Emly, (RC), 1960–88, now Emeritus; *b* Killenaule, Co. Tipperary, 16 Oct. 1914; *s* of James Morris and Johanna (*née* Carrigan). *Educ:* Christian Brothers Schs, Thurles; Maynooth Coll. Ordained priest, Maynooth, 1939; studied, Dunboyne Institute, 1939–41. (DD). Professor of Theology, St Patrick's Coll., Thurles, 1942–Dec. 1959, Vice-Pres., 1957–60; appointed Archbishop, 1959; consecrated, 1960; retired, 1988. *Recreation:* reading. *Address:* The Green, Holy Cross, Thurles, Co. Tipperary, Ireland. *T:* (0504) 43209.

MORRIS, Very Rev. Timothy David; Dean of Diocese of Edinburgh, Episcopal Church in Scotland, since 1992; Rector of St Peter's, Galashiels, since 1985; *b* 17 Aug. 1948; *s* of Joseph Ernest and Mabel Elizabeth Morris; *m* 1st, 1972, Dorothy Helen Ferguson (marr. diss. 1987); one *d*; 2nd, 1988, Irene Elizabeth Lyness. *Educ:* King Edward's Grammar Sch., Bath; Coll. of Estate Management, London Univ. (BSc Econs); Trinity Coll., Bristol and Bristol Univ. (DipTh). Asst Estate Surveyor, Min. of Public Building and Works, Edinburgh, 1969–72; Curate, St Thomas's Church, Edinburgh, 1975–77; Rector: St James's Episcopal Church, Leith, Edinburgh, 1977–83; St Ninian's, Troon, Ayrshire, 1983–85. *Recreations:* music, Rugby Union, cricket, gardening. *Address:* The Rectory, 6 Parsonage Road, Galashiels, Selkirkshire TD1 3HS. *T:* Galashiels (01896) 3118.

MORRIS, Timothy Denis, CBE 1994; DL; Director, Yattendon Investment Trust PLC, since 1985; Chairman: Herts & Essex Newspapers Ltd, since 1989; Burton Daily Mail Ltd, since 1991 (Director, since 1983); Cambridge Newspapers Ltd, since 1993 (Director, 1970–77 and since 1985); Staffordshire Newsletter Ltd, since 1994; *b* 15 Feb. 1935; *s* of D. E. Morris, OBE, *qv*, and Mrs P. H. Skey; *m* 1959, Caroline Wynn; one *s* one *d*. *Educ:* Tonbridge Sch.; Pembroke Coll., Cambridge (MA). Dir, The Birmingham Post & Mail Ltd, 1967–90 (Chm., 1982–90); Man. Dir, Coventry Newspapers Ltd, 1970–77 (Dir, 1985–90; Chm., 1988–90); Chairman: Packet Newspapers (Cornwall) Ltd, 1986–94; West of England Newspapers Ltd, 1990–94; Director: Press Association Ltd, 1980–87 (Chm., 1985–86); South Hams Newspapers Ltd, 1985–94 (Chm., 1985–86); Reuters Founders Share Co. Ltd, 1987–; Midland Newspapers Ltd, 1988–90; Coventry Building Soc., 1991–; Heart of England Radio Ltd, 1993–. Dir, W Midlands RHA, 1990–93. Chairman: Birmingham Civic Soc., 1979–83; Birmingham Hippodrome Theatre Trust, 1990– (Dir, 1980–); Director: Royal Opera House Ballet Bd, 1990–; Birmingham Royal Ballet, 1993–; Gov., Royal Ballet, 1992–. President: W Midlands Newspaper Soc., 1975–76; Newspaper Soc., 1984–85; Coventry Chamber of Commerce, 1976–77. County Comr, Warwickshire Scouts, 1974–77. DL West Midlands, 1975. *Recreations:* golf, philately. *Address:* c/o Yattendon Investment Trust PLC, 1 Waterloo Street, Birmingham B2 5PG. *Club:* Naval.

MORRIS, Trefor Alfred, CBE 1992; QPM 1985; HM Chief Inspector of Constabulary, since 1993; *b* 22 Dec. 1934; *s* of late Kenneth Alfred Morris and Amy Ursula (*née* Burgess); *m* 1958, Martha Margaret (*née* Wroe); two *d*. *Educ:* Ducie Technical High School, Manchester; Manchester University (Dip. Criminology); Nat. Exec. Inst., USA. Constable to Chief Superintendent, Manchester City Police, Manchester and Salford Police, Greater Manchester Police, 1955–76; Asst Chief Constable, Greater Manchester Police, 1976–79; Dep. Chief Constable, 1979–84, Chief Constable, 1984–90, Herts; HM Inspector of Constabulary, 1990–93. Pres., Police Mutual Assurance Soc., 1994–. Mem., St Albans Diocesan Synod, 1989–. Vice President: Herts Scouts, 1989–; Police Athletics Assoc.; Pres., Luton, N Herts Inst. of Mgt. CIMgt (CBIM 1986). FRSA 1993. OStJ 1984. *Recreations:* music, golf, wine, walking, gardening. *Address:* Home Office, Queen Anne's Gate, SW1H 9AT. *Club:* Royal Over-Seas League.

MORRIS, Prof. Trevor Raymond, FIBiol; Professor of Animal Production, since 1984, and Head of Department of Agriculture, 1984–91, University of Reading; *b* 11 April 1930; *s* of Ivor Raymond Morris and Dorothy May Morris; *m* 1st, 1954, Elisabeth Jean (*née* Warren) (*d* 1992); three *s* two *d*; 2nd, 1994, Mary (*née* Gillett). *Educ:* Rendcomb Coll., Glos; Reading Univ. (BSc, PhD, DSc). University of Reading: Asst Lectr, 1952–54, 1956–57; Lectr in Agric., 1957–69; Reader in Agric., 1969–81; Prof. of Agriculture, 1981–84. *Publications:* over 100 articles in sci. jls. *Recreations:* music, gardening. *Address:* 36 Shinfield Road, Reading RG2 7BW. *T:* Reading (01734) 872529.

MORRIS, Walter Frederick; LLB London; ACII; FBIM; HM Diplomatic Service, retired; *b* 15 Oct. 1914; *s* of late Captain Frederick James Morris and Elsie Eleanor (*née* Williams); *m* 1945, Marjorie Vaughan, *o d* of late Thomas Vaughan Phillips and Eleanor Mirren (*née* Jones); one *s* one *d*. *Educ:* Cardiff High Sch.; University Coll., Cardiff (Law Prizeman). Admitted Solicitor, 1936; Legal practice, 1936–39. Served RA (TA), 1939–45: GHQ Home Forces (Intelligence); WO Sch. of Military Administration; Certificate of Merit, Western Comd; GSO1 (Lt-Col), HQ 21st Army Gp, BLA (later BAOR); commanded Legal Aid Organisation, which provided legal assistance to all British Army and RAF personnel in Europe; legal practice (and Hon. District Army Welfare Officer), 1945–47; entered Administrative Home Civil Service, 1947; Min. of Social Security, 1947–68 (Prin. Dep. Chief Insce Off., Asst Sec.); Admin. Staff Coll., Henley, 1953; on loan to Export Credits Guarantee Dept, 1955–57; Manchester Business Sch., 1968; trans. to HM Diplomatic Service, 1968; HM Consul-Gen., Cairo, 1968–70; ME Centre for Arab Studies, Shemlan, Lebanon, 1969; Head of Claims Dept, FCO, 1970–72; Dep. High Comr, later Consul-Gen., Lahore, 1972–73; retired from HM Diplomatic Service and re-entered legal practice, 1973; Founder, 1973, Senior Partner, 1973–82 and Consultant, 1982–92, Morris, Scott & Co., Solicitors, Highcliffe, Christchurch, Dorset. Mem., Law Soc. Liveryman, City of London Solicitor's Co. *Recreations:* golf, travel. *Address:* 19463 Ravines Court, Pine Lakes Country Club, North Fort Myers, FL 33903, USA. *T:* (941) 7312262. *Clubs:* Civil Service; Pine Lakes Golf (Florida); Punjab (Lahore).

MORRIS, William; General Secretary, Transport and General Workers Union, since 1992 (Deputy General Secretary, 1986–92); *b* 19 Oct. 1938; *s* of William and Una Morris; *m* 1957, Minetta (*d* 1990); two *s*. *Educ:* Jamaica. TGWU: Dist Officer, Nottingham, 1973; Dist Sec., Northampton, 1976; Nat. Sec., Passenger Services, 1979–85. Mem., TUC Gen. Council, 1988–. Member: Commn for Racial Equality, 1977–87; IBA Gen. Adv. Council, 1981–86; Road Transport ITB, 1986–92; Prince's Youth Business Trust, 1987–90; BBC General Adv. Council, 1987–88; Employment Appeals Tribunal, 1988–; Economic and Social Cttee, EC, 1990–; NEDC, 1992. *Recreations:* walking, gardening, watching sports. *Address:* 156 St Agnells Lane, Grove Hill, Hemel Hempstead, Herts HP2 6EG. *T:* Hemel Hempstead (01442) 63110.

MORRIS, Prof. (William) David, PhD; Vice Principal, since 1991, and Professor of Mechanical Engineering, since 1985, University College of Swansea (Head of Department of Mechanical Engineering, 1985–91); *b* 14 March 1936; *s* of late William Daniel and Elizabeth Jane Morris; *m* 1959, Pamela Eira Evans; two *s* one *d*. *Educ:* Queen Mary College, London (1st Cl. Hons BSc Eng); Univ. Coll. of Swansea, Wales (PhD). CEng, FIMechE, FIEE. Bristol Siddeley Engine Co., 1958–60; James Clayton Res. Fellow, Univ. of Wales, Swansea, 1960–63; Lectr, Dept of Mech. Engrg, Univ. of Liverpool, 1963–67; Lectr, 1967–72, Reader, 1972–79, Sch. of Engrg, Univ. of Sussex; J. H. Fenner Prof. of Mech. Engrg and Head, Dept of Engrg Design, Univ. of Hull, 1979–85. *Publications:* Differential Equations for Engineers and Applied Scientists, 1979; Heat Transfer and Fluid Flow in Rotating Coolant Channels, 1981. *Recreations:* oil painting, DIY, walking. *Address:* Department of Mechanical Engineering, University College of Swansea, Singleton Park, Swansea SA2 8PP. *T:* Swansea (01792) 295534.

MORRIS, Prof. William Ian Clinch; Professor of Obstetrics and Gynaecology, University of Manchester, 1949–72, Professor Emeritus since 1972; *b* 10 May 1907; *s* of Dr J. M. Morris, Neath; *m* 1938, Mary Farquharson (*d* 1976); one *d*. *Educ:* Royal High Sch., Edinburgh; Edinburgh Univ. Obstetrician to Ayr County Council, 1937–46; Sen. Lectr in Obstetrics and Gynaecology, Univ. of Edinburgh, 1946–49. RAMC (TA) 1935; war service, 1939–43. *Publications:* (jointly) A Combined Text-book of Obstetrics and Gynaecology, 1950; contribs to Jl of Obstetrics and Gynaecology of British Commonwealth, Lancet, Edinburgh Med. Jl, etc. *Address:* Edenfield House, Springfield, by Cupar, Fife KY15 5RT. *T:* Cupar (01334) 657517.

MORRIS, Very Rev. William James, KCVO 1995; JP; Minister of Glasgow Cathedral, since 1967; a Chaplain to the Queen in Scotland, 1969–June 1996; Dean of the Chapel Royal in Scotland, 1991–June 1996; *b* Cardiff, 22 Aug. 1925; *o s* of William John Morris and Eliza Cecilia Cameron Johnson; *m* 1952, Jean Daveena Ogilvy Howie, CBE, LLD, *o c* of Rev. David Porter Howie and Veena Christie, Kilmarnock; one *s*. *Educ:* Cardiff High Sch.; Univ. of Wales; Edinburgh Univ. BA 1946, BD 1949, Wales; PhD Edinburgh, 1954. Ordained, 1951. Asst, Canongate Kirk, Edinburgh, 1949–51; Minister, Presbyterian Church of Wales, Cadoxton and Barry Is, 1951–53; Buckhaven (Fife): St David's, 1953–57; Peterhead Old Parish, 1957–67; Chaplain to the Lord High Comr to the General Assembly of the Church of Scotland, 1975–76; Chaplain: Peterhead Prison, 1963–67; Glasgow DC, 1967–; Trades House of Glasgow, 1967–; W of Scotland Engrs Assoc., 1967–; The High Sch. of Glasgow, 1974–76, 1983–; Glasgow Acad., 1976–; Strathclyde Police, 1977–; Queen's Body Guard for Scotland, Royal Co. of Archers, 1994–; Hon. Chaplain, The Royal Scottish Automobile Club; Moderator, Presbytery of Deer, 1965–66; Convener Adv. Bd, Church of Scotland, 1977–80; Vice-Chm., Bd of Nomination to Church Chairs, Church of Scotland, 1978–81. Mem. IBA, 1979–84 (Chm. Scottish Adv. Cttee). President: Rotary Club of Peterhead, 1965–66; Peterhead and Dist Professional and Business Club, 1967; St Andrew's Soc., Glasgow, 1992– (Vice-Pres., 1967–82); Chairman: Iona Cath. Trust, 1976– (Trustee, 1967); Council, Soc. of Friends of Glasgow Cath., 1967; Club Service Cttee, Dist 101, RIBI, 1964–66; Prison Chaplaincies Bd (Church of Scotland Home Bd), 1969–83; Member: Scottish Cttee, British Sailors' Soc., 1967–83; Bd of Management, W of Scotland Convalescent Home, 1967–; Gen. Convocation, Strathclyde Univ., 1967–; Council of Management, Quarriers' Homes, 1968–88; Bd of Management, Glasgow YMCA, 1973–88; Scottish Council on Crime, 1974–76; Church of Scotland Bd of Practice and Procedure, 1981–85; Bd of Governors, Jordanhill Coll. of Educn, Glasgow, 1983–91; Hon. Pres., Glasgow Soc. of Social Services Inc., 1984–. Hon. Mem., Scottish Ambulance Assoc., 1981. JP: Co. of Aberdeen, 1963–71; Co. of City of Glasgow, 1971. ChStJ 1991. Hon. LLD Strathclyde, 1974; Hon. DD Glasgow, 1979; FRCPS(Hon.) 1983. *Publication:* A Walk Around Glasgow Cathedral, 1986. *Recreations:* fishing, gardening. *Address:* 94 St Andrews Drive, Glasgow G41 4RX. *T:* 0141–427 2757. *Clubs:* New (Edinburgh); RNVR (Scotland) (Hon.); University of Strathclyde Staff (Hon.); Rotary of Dennistoun (Hon.); Rotary of Glasgow (Hon.).

MORRIS, Wyn, FRAM; conductor; *b* 14 Feb. 1929; *s* of late Haydn Morris and Sarah Eluned Phillips; *m* 1962, Ruth Marie McDowell; one *s* one *d*. *Educ:* Llanelli Grammar Sch.; Royal Academy of Music; Mozarteum, Salzburg. August Mann's Prize, 1950; Apprentice Conductor, Yorkshire Symph. Orch., 1950–51; Musical Dir, 17th Trg Regt, RA Band, 1951–53; Founder and Conductor of Welsh Symph. Orch., 1954–57; Koussevitsky Memorial Prize, Boston Symph. Orch., 1957; (on invitation George Szell) Observer, Cleveland Symph. Orch., 1957–60; Conductor: Ohio Bell Chorus, Cleveland Orpheus Choir and Cleveland Chamber Orch., 1958–60; Choir of Royal National Eisteddfod of Wales, 1960–62; London debut, Royal Festival Hall, with Royal Philharmonic Orch., 1963; Conductor: Royal Choral Society, 1968–70; Huddersfield Choral Soc., 1969–74; Ceremony for Investiture of Prince Charles as Prince of Wales, 1969; Royal Choral Soc. tour of USA, 1969; former Chief Conductor and Musical Dir, Symphonica of London. FRAM 1964. Specialises in conducting of Mahler; has recorded Des Knaben Wunderhorn (with Dame Janet Baker and Sir Geraint Evans), Das Klagende Lied, Symphonies 1, 2, 5, 8 and 10 in Deryck Cooke's final performing version. Mahler Memorial Medal (of Bruckner and Mahler Soc. of Amer.), 1968. *Recreations:* chess, Rugby football, climbing, cynghanedd and telling Welsh stories.

MORRIS-JONES, His Honour Ifor Henry, QC 1969; a Circuit Judge, 1977–92; *b* 5 March 1922; *s* of late Rev. Prof. and Mrs D. Morris-Jones; *m* 1950, Anne Diana, *d* of late S. E. Ferris, OBE, Blundellsands; one *s* two *d*. *Educ:* Taunton Sch.; Sidney Sussex Coll., Cambridge. Called to the Bar, Lincoln's Inn, 1947. Joined Northern Circuit, 1947; Assistant Recorder, Carlisle, 1962; Dep. Chm., Cumberland Sessions, 1969–72; a Recorder, 1972–76. Mem., Bar Council, 1972. *Recreation:* golf. *Address:* 3 Paddock Close, Blundellsands, Liverpool L23 8UX. *T:* 0151–924 4848. *Club:* Artists' (Liverpool).

MORRIS-JONES, Prof. Wyndraeth Humphreys; Emeritus Professor of University of London; *b* 1 Aug. 1918; *s* of late William James Jones, Carmarthen, and Annie Mary Jones (*née* Morris); *m* 1953, Graziella Bianca Genre; one *s* two *d*. *Educ:* University Coll. Sch., Hampstead; London Sch. of Economics (BSc(Econ.) First Class, 1938; Leverhulme Research Grant, 1939; Hon. Fellow, 1980); Christ's Coll., Cambridge, Research Schol., 1940. Indian Army, 1941–46 (Lt-Col, Public Relations Directorate, 1944); Constitutional Adviser to Viceroy of India, 1947; Lecturer in Political Science, London Sch. of Economics, 1946–55; Prof. of Political Theory and Instns, Univ. of Durham, 1955–65; Prof. of Commonwealth Affairs and Dir, Inst. of Commonwealth Studies, Univ. of London, 1966–83. Leverhulme Emeritus Fellow, 1984–87. Rockefeller Travel Grants, 1954, 1960 and 1967. Vis. Prof. of Commonwealth Hist. and Instns, Indian Sch. of Internat. Studies, New Delhi, 1960; Visiting Professor: Univ. of Chicago, 1962; Univ. of California, Berkeley, 1964–65. Editor, Jl of Commonwealth and Comparative Politics (formerly Commonwealth Polit. Studies), 1964–80. *Publications:* Parliament in India, 1957; Government and Politics of India, 1964, 4th edn 1987; (with Biplab Dasgupta) Patterns and Trends in Indian Politics, 1976; Politics Mainly Indian, 1978; articles in Polit. Studies, Asian Survey, Modern Asian Studies, etc. *Address:* 95 Ridgway, SW19 4SX.

MORRIS WILLIAMS, Christine Margaret; *see* Puxon, C. M.

MORRISH, John Edwin, (Jack); school governor and education consultant; Hon. General Secretary, Northamptonshire Association of School Governing Bodies, since 1992; Vice-Chairman, National Governor's Council, since 1994; *b* 23 Sept. 1915; *s* of Henry Edwin Morrish and Ada Minnie (*née* Tapping); *m* 1st, 1937, Norah Lake (marr. diss.); one *d*; 2nd, 1944, Violet Saunders (marr. diss.); one *s* one *d*; 3rd, 1984, Betty Lupton (*née* Wear) (*d* 1990). *Educ:* Fleet Road, Hampstead, Elem. Sch.; University Coll. Sch.; Northampton Polytechnic, London; various work-faces; MA Leicester, 1991. Post Office Techn. Officer, 1932–54; coalminer, 1944–45. Trade Union Official: Civil Service Union, 1954–72; Soc.

of Civil and Public Servants, 1972–76 (Gen. Sec., Customs and Excise Gp). Administrator, Northants Rural Community Council, 1979. Census Officer, 1980–81, 1990–91. Mem. (Lab), Dep. Leader, and Chm., Educn Cttee, Northants CC, 1981–85; Mem. (Lab), Hounslow BC, 1986–90 (Vice-Chm., Educn Cttee). Vice-Chm., E Midlands Further Educn Council, 1982–85; Member: Adv. Cttee, Supply and Educn of Teachers; Assoc. of County Councils, 1981–85; Burnham Cttee on Teachers' Pay, 1983–84, 1986–87; AMA, 1986–90. Hon. Chm., Northants Child Poverty Action Gp, 1980–84. Hon. Treas., UK Reading Assoc. (World Congress Local Arrangements Cttee), 1985–86. Chm., Nene Coll. Governors, 1981–85. *Publications:* The Future of Forestry, 1971; contrib. trade union and educn jls. *Recreations:* thinking, pursuit of justice, music, talking. *Address:* The Old Bakehouse, 1 Church Street, Broughton, Kettering, Northants NN14 1LU. *T:* Kettering (01536) 790914. *Club:* Civil Service.

MORRISON, family name of **Viscount Dunrossil** and of **Barons Margadale** and **Morrison.**

MORRISON, 2nd Baron *cr* 1945, of Tottenham; **Dennis Morrison;** Manufacturing Executive with The Metal Box Co. Ltd, 1957–72, retired; *b* 21 June 1914; *e* and *o* surv. *s* of 1st Baron Morrison, PC, and Grace, *d* of late Thomas Glossop; *S* father 1953; *m* 1940, Florence Alice Helena (marr. diss. 1958), *d* of late Augustus Hennes, Tottenham; *m* 1959, Joan (marr. diss. 1975), *d* of late W. R. Meech. *Educ:* Tottenham County Sch. Employed by The Metal Box Co. Ltd on research work, 1937–51; Quality Controller, 1952–57. Lord Lieutenant's Representative for Tottenham, 1955–. FSS 1953–57. Vice-Pres., Acton Chamber of Commerce, 1972 (Mem., Exec. Cttee, 1962). Hon. President: Robert Browning Settlement, 1967–; 5th Acton Scout Group, 1969. *Recreation:* gardening. *Heir:* none. *Address:* 7 Ullswater Avenue, Felixstowe, Suffolk IP11 9SD. *T:* Felixstowe (01394) 77405.

MORRISON, (Alexander) Fraser, CBE 1993; Managing Director, since 1976, and Chairman, since 1984, Morrison Construction Group Ltd; Chairman, Highlands & Islands Enterprise, since 1992 (Director, since 1991); *b* 20 March 1948; *s* of Alexander Ferrier Sharp Morrison and Catherine Colina (*née* Fraser); *m* 1972, Patricia Janice Murphy; one *s* two *d*. *Educ:* Tain Royal Acad.; Univ. of Edinburgh (BSc Hons Civil Engrg). CEng, FICE 1993; Eur Ing 1993; MIHT 1982. Joined Morrison Construction Gp Ltd as Dir, 1970; Director: Shand Ltd, 1978–89; Alexander Shand Holdings Ltd, 1982–86. Federation of Civil Engineering Contractors: Chm., Scottish Sect., 1991–92; Chm., Nat. Fedn, 1993–94; Vice Pres., 1994–95. FRSA 1990. *Recreations:* golf, ski-ing, shooting, opera, art. *Address:* Morrison Construction Group Ltd, Morrison House, 12 Atholl Crescent, Edinburgh EH3 8HA. *T:* 0131–228 4188.

MORRISON, Alexander John Henderson; His Honour Judge Morrison; a Circuit Judge, since 1980; *b* 16 Nov. 1927; *yr s* of late Dr Alexander Morrison and Mrs A. Morrison; *m* 1978, Hon. Philippa, *y d* of 1st Baron Hives. *Educ:* Derby Sch.; Emmanuel Coll., Cambridge. MA, LLB. Called to the Bar, Gray's Inn, 1951. Mem. of Midland Circuit; Dep. Chm., Derbyshire QS, 1964–71; Regional Chm. of Industrial Tribunals, Sheffield, 1971–80; a Recorder of the Crown Court, 1971–80. A Pres., Mental Health Review Tribunals, 1983–. Pres., Derbys Union of Golf Clubs, 1977–79. *Recreations:* golf, schools football. *Address:* Derby Combined Court, Morledge, Derby. *T:* Derby (01332) 622600.

MORRISON, (Andrew) Neil, QFSM 1989; FIFireE; HM Chief Inspector of Fire Services for Scotland, since 1994; *b* 8 Sept. 1937; *e s* of late Andrew Steel Morrison and Margueritta Wilkin Caird; *m* 1963, Kathleen Rutherford; one *s*. *Educ:* Arbroath High Sch.; Dundee Coll. of Technol. FIFireE 1991. Angus Fire Brigade: Fireman, 1962–70; Leading Fireman, 1970–71; Sub-officer, 1971–74; Station Officer, 1974–75; Tayside Fire Brigade: Station Officer, 1975–76; Asst Divl Officer, 1976; Divl Officer, Grade III, 1976–79; Divl Officer, Grade I, 1979–80; Grampian Fire Brigade: Dep. Firemaster, 1980–85; Firemaster, 1985–93. *Recreations:* curling, golf, hill-walking, swimming. *Address:* Mill of Cranhill, Banchory-Devenick, Aberdeen AB1 5XR. *T:* Aberdeen (01224) 869800; The Scottish Office, Home and Health Department, St Andrew's House, Edinburgh EH1 3DG. *T:* 0131–244 2342.

MORRISON, Blake; *see* Morrison, P. B.

MORRISON, Hon. Sir Charles (Andrew), Kt 1988; *b* 25 June 1932; 2nd *s* of 1st Baron Margadale, *qv*; *m* 1st, 1954, Hon. Sara Long (*see* Hon. Sara Morrison) (marr. diss. 1984); one *s* one *d*; 2nd, 1984, Mrs Rosalind Ward. *Educ:* Eton. Nat. Service in The Life Guards, 1950–52; Royal Wilts Yeo. (TA), 1952–66. County Councillor, Wilts, 1958–65 (Chm., Educn Cttee, 1963–64). MP (C) Devizes, May 1964–1992. Chm., Nat. Cttee for Electoral Reform, 1985–91; Mem. Bd of Dirs, Global Cttee of Parliamentarians on Population and Develt, 1984–91. Chairman: South West Regional Sports Council, 1966–68; Young Volunteer Force Foundn, 1971–74; British Trust for Conservation Volunteers, 1973–78; Game Conservancy, 1987–94; Allerton Res. and Educn Trust, 1994–; Mem., Council, Salmon and Trout Assoc. A Vice-Chm., 1922 Cttee, 1974–83 (Mem. Exec., 1972). Prime Warden, Fishmongers' Co., 1986–87. *Recreations:* gardening, shooting, fishing. *Address:* Madresfield Court, Madresfield, Malvern, Worcs WR13 5AU. *T:* Malvern (01684) 573024. *Clubs:* White's, Pratt's.

See also Hon. J. I. Morrison, Hon. M. A. Morrison.

MORRISON, Chloe Anthony, (Toni); writer; *b* 18 Feb. 1931; *d* of George Wofford and Ella Ramah Wofford (*née* Willis); *m* 1958, Harold Morrison (marr. diss. 1964); two *s*. *Educ:* Howard Univ.; Cornell Univ. (MA 1955). Lectr in English and Humanities: Texas Southern Univ., 1955–57; Howard Univ., 1957–64; Associate Prof. of English, NY State Univ. Coll., Purchase, 1971–72; Professor of Humanities: SUNY, Albany, 1984–89; Princeton Univ., 1989–. An Editor, Random House, NY, 1965. Numerous literary awards, incl Pulitzer Prize for Fiction, 1988; Nobel Prize for Literature, 1993. *Publications:* The Bluest Eye, 1970; Sula, 1974; Song of Solomon, 1977; Tar Baby, 1983; Beloved, 1987; Jazz, 1992; Playing in the Dark: whiteness and the literary imagination, 1992; (ed) Race-ing Justice, En-gendering Power, 1993. *Address:* c/o Suzanne Gluck, International Creative Management, 40 W 57th Street, New York, NY 10019, USA.

MORRISON, Dennis John; Director, Environment and Transport, Government Office for the East Midlands, since 1994; *b* 20 May 1942; *s* of Leonard Tait Morrison and Alice Morrison; *m* 1967, Frances Joan Pollard; one *s* one *d*. *Educ:* Ashton-upon-Mersey Boys' School; Lymm Grammar School; Manchester Univ. (BA, DipT&CP). MRTPI. Planning appointments: Lancs CC, 1966–70; Welsh Office, Cardiff, 1970–75; NW Region, DoE, Manchester, 1975–81; Regional Controller, NW Enterprise Unit, DoE, 1981–84; Regional Controller (Urban and Economic Affairs), Merseyside Task Force, Liverpool, 1984–89; Regl Dir, Depts of Envmt and Transport, E Midlands Region, 1989–94. FRGS. *Recreations:* antiquarian horologist, antiquarian book collector, hill walking, gardening. *Address:* Cranbrook House, Cranbrook Street, Nottingham NG1 1EY. *T:* Nottingham (0115) 935 0602.

MORRISON, Donald Alexander Campbell; Assistant Under-Secretary of State, Home Office, 1972–76; *b* 30 Nov. 1916; *s* of late George Alexander Morrison, sometime MP for Scottish Univs, and late Rachel Brown Morrison (*née* Campbell); *m* 1st, 1951, Elma Margaret Craig (*d* 1970); one *s* one *d* (and one *s* decd); 2nd, 1973, Jane Margaret Montgomery; one step *s*. *Educ:* Fettes Coll.; Christ Church, Oxford (BA). Home Office, 1939; Asst Sec., 1955. A Senior Clerk (acting), House of Commons, 1976–81. War Service, 1940–45: 79th (Scottish Horse) Medium Regt, RA, 1942–45. *Publications:* Haps and Such (poems), 1986; *children's operas:* The Granite and the Heather, 1990 (perf. Aboyne, 1990); Little Jenny Nobody, 1991 (perf. Aboyne, 1990, Canterbury Fest., 1992); The Golden Slave, 1992 (perf. Aboyne, 1992); Afternoon in Jericho, 1993 (perf. Wingham Fest., 1993); Smugglers at Bay, 1993 (perf. Canterbury Fest., 1993); Remember David, 1995 (perf. Wingham Fest., 1995). *Recreation:* music. *Address:* 27 High Street, Wingham, near Canterbury, Kent CT3 1AW. *T:* Canterbury (01227) 720774.

MORRISON, Fraser; *see* Morrison, A. F.

MORRISON, Garth; *see* Morrison, W. G.

MORRISON, Sir Howard (Leslie), Kt 1990; OBE 1976; entertainer, self-employed, since 1957; Youth Development Director for Maori Affairs, since 1978; *b* 18 Aug. 1935; *s* of late Temuera Leslie Morrison and Gertrude Harete Morrison (*née* Davidson); *m* 1957, Rangiwhata Anne (*née* Manahi); two *s* one *d*. *Educ:* Huiarau Primary Sch.; Rotorua Primary Sch.; Rotorua High Sch.; Te Aute College. Surveyor's Asst, 1954–59; performer with Maori concert party groups since childhood; formed Howard Morrison Quartet, 1957 (part-time, later full-time); numerous recordings, TV, national tours; quartet disbanded 1965; solo entertainer, 1965–; tours in NZ, S Pacific, SE Asia; TV and films. *Recreations:* golf, swimming. *Address:* Korokai Street, Ohinemutu Village, Rotorua, New Zealand. *T:* (73) 485735, *Fax:* (73) 480910. *Club:* Carbine (Auckland, NZ).

MORRISON, Air Vice-Marshal Ian Gordon, CB 1965; CBE 1957 (OBE 1946); RNZAF (retired); *b* 16 March 1914; *s* of W. G. Morrison; *m* 1938, Dorothy, *d* of W. H. Franks; one *s* two *d*. *Educ:* Christchurch Boys' High Sch., NZ. RAF 1935; RNZAF 1939; No 75 Sqdn, UK, 1939; Comd RNZAF, Omaka, 1941; Comd RNZAF, Gisborne, 1942; SASO, Islands Gp, 1943; Comd No 3 BR Sqdn Pacific, 1944–45; jssc, UK, 1950; Comd RNZAF, Ohakea, 1952; Air Mem. for Supply, 1954; idc, 1958; AOC, RNZAF, HQ London, 1959–60; Air Mem. for Personnel, 1961–62; Chief of the Air Staff, Royal New Zealand Air Force, 1962–66. Develt Dir, A. S. Cornish Gp, 1970–80; Dep. Chm., Wm Scollay & Co., 1980–85. Nat. Pres., Scout Assoc. of NZ, 1967–79. *Recreations:* golf and angling. *Address:* 11 Mayfair Village, Oteha Valley Road, Browns Bay, Auckland, New Zealand. *T:* (9) 4789986. *Clubs:* Wellington (Pres., 1978–82), Wellington Golf (both in NZ).

MORRISON, James, RSA 1992 (ARSA 1973); RSW 1968; painter in oil and water colours; *b* 11 April 1932; *s* of John Morrison and Margaret Thomson; *m* 1955, Dorothy McCormack; one *s* one *d*. *Educ:* Hillhead High Sch., Glasgow; Glasgow Sch. of Art (DA). Vis. Artist, Hospitalfield House, 1962, 1963; Duncan of Jordanstone College of Art, Dundee: Member of Staff, 1965–87; Head of Dept, 1978–87; Mem. Board, 1988–. Council Mem., Soc. of Scottish Artists, 1964–67. Painting in Europe, USA and Canada, 1968–; one-man exhibns, Scotland, London, Italy, Germany, Canada, 1956–; numerous works in public and private collections, UK and overseas. Torrance Award, RGI, 1958; Arts Council Travelling Award, 1968. DUniv Stirling, 1986. *Publication:* Aff the Squerr, 1976, 2nd edn 1990. *Recreation:* playing recorder in a chamber music group. *Address:* Craigview House, Usan, Montrose, Angus DD10 9SD. *T:* Montrose (01674) 672639. *Clubs:* Rotary (Montrose); Edzell Golf.

MORRISON, Hon. James Ian, TD, DL; director of companies; farmer; *b* 17 July 1930; *e s* and *heir* of Baron Margadale, *qv*; *m* 1952, Clare Barclay; two *s* one *d*. *Educ:* Eton Coll.; Royal Agricultural Coll., Cirencester. 2nd Lieut, Life Guards, 1949–50; Major, Royal Wilts Yeo., 1960–68; Hon. Colonel: A (RWY) Sqn Royal Yeomanry RAC TA, and B (RWY) Sqn Royal Wessex Yeomanry, 1982–89; Royal Wessex Yeomanry RAC TA, 1984–89. Member, Queen's Body Guard for Scotland, 1960–. County Councillor, Wilts, 1955 and 1973–77, County Alderman, 1969; Chairman, W Wilts Conservative Assoc., 1967–71, Pres., 1972–84; Chm., Wilts CLA, 1978–81. Chm., Tattersalls Cttee, 1969–80. DL 1977–, High Sheriff 1971, Wiltshire. *Recreations:* racing, shooting, hunting. *Address:* Hawking Down, Hindon, Salisbury, Wilts SP3 6DN; Islay Estate Office, Bridgend, Islay, Argyll PA44 7PA. *Clubs:* White's, Jockey.

See also Hon. Sir C. A. Morrison, Hon. M. A. Morrison, Viscount Trenchard.

MORRISON, Ven. John Anthony; Archdeacon of Buckingham, since 1990; *b* 11 March 1938; *s* of Major Leslie Claude Morrison and Mary Sharland Morrison (*née* Newson-Smith); *m* 1968, Angela, *d* of late Major Jonathan Eric Bush; two *s* one *d*. *Educ:* Haileybury; Jesus Coll., Cambridge (BA 1960; MA 1964); Lincoln Coll., Oxford (MA 1968); Chichester Theol Coll. Deacon 1964, priest 1965; Curate: St Peter, Birmingham, 1964–68; St Michael-at-the-Northgate, Oxford, 1968–74; Chaplain, Lincoln Coll., Oxford, 1968–74; Vicar, Basildon, Berks, 1974–82; RD Bradfield, 1978–82; Vicar, Aylesbury, Bucks, 1982–89, Team Rector, 1989–90; RD Aylesbury, 1985–89. Mem., Gen. Synod, 1980–90. Mem. Ct of Assts, Spectacle Makers' Co., 1994–. *Address:* 60 Wendover Road, Aylesbury, Bucks HP21 9LW. *T:* Aylesbury (01296) 23269. *Clubs:* Leander (Henley-on-Thames); Vincent's (Oxford).

MORRISON, John Lamb Murray, CBE 1957; DSc; FEng; FIMechE; Formerly Professor of Mechanical Engineering, University of Bristol, Emeritus 1971; *b* 22 May 1906; *s* of late Latto A. Morrison, Biggar, Lanarkshire; *m* 1936, Olga, *d* of late M. Nierenstein, DSc; two *s*. *Educ:* Biggar High Sch.; Univ. of Glasgow (DSc 1939). Lecturer in Mechanical Engineering; Reader in Mechanical Engineering, Univ. of Bristol. Pres., IMechE, 1970–71. Hon. DSc Salford, 1972. *Publications:* An Introduction to the Mechanics of Machines, 1964; various papers on strength of materials and design of machines. *Recreations:* gardening, golf. *Address:* Dreva, Rayleigh Road, Bristol BS9 2AU. *T:* Bristol (0117) 968 1193.

MORRISON, John Sinclair, CBE 1991; President, Wolfson College (formerly University College), Cambridge, 1966–80; *b* 15 June 1913; *s* of Sinclair Morrison (and *g s* of William Morrison, NY and Stagbury, Chipstead, Surrey) and Maria Elsie, *d* of William Lamaison, Salmons, Kenley, Surrey; *m* 1942, Elizabeth Helen, *d* of S. W. Sulman, Bexhill, Sussex; three *s* two *d*. *Educ:* Charterhouse; Trinity Coll., Cambridge. Fellow Trinity College, Cambridge, 1937–45; Asst Lecturer Manchester University, 1937–39; Editor of Cambridge Review, 1939–40. Ordinary Seaman (Volunteer), 1940–41. In service of British Council, Cairo, Zagazig, Baghdad, 1941–42; British Council Rep. in Palestine and Transjordan, 1942–45; Pres. Jerusalem Rotary Club, 1945; Prof. of Greek and Head of Dept of Classics and Ancient History at the Durham Colls of Univ. of Durham, 1945–50; Fellow Tutor and Senior Tutor of Trinity Coll., Cambridge, 1950–60; Vice-Master and Sen. Tutor of Churchill Coll., Cambridge, 1960–65, now Hon. Fellow. Leverhulme Fellow, 1965. Mellon Prof., 1976–77, Kenan Prof., 1981–82, Reed Coll., Oregon, USA; Leverhulme Emeritus Fellow, 1984–85. Member: Sierra Leone Educn Commission, 1954; Annan Cttee on Teaching of Russian, 1961; Hale Cttee on University Teaching Methods, 1961; Schools Council, 1965–67; Jt Working Party on 6th Form Curriculum and Examinations,

1968–72; Governing Bodies Assoc., 1965; Governor: Bradfield Coll., 1963–83; Wellington Coll., 1963–83; Charterhouse Sch., 1970–93. Jt Editor, Classical Review, 1968–75. Trustee, National Maritime Museum, 1975–82; Chm., Trireme Trust, 1984–. Hon. FBA 1988. Hon. DLitt Davidson Coll., N Carolina, 1987. Caird Medal, Nat. Maritime Mus., 1991. *Publications:* (with R. T. Williams) Greek Oared Ships, 1968; Long Ships and Round Ships, 1980; (with J. F. Coates) The Athenian Trireme, 1986; (with J. Coates) Greek and Roman Oared Warships, 1995. *Address:* Granhams, Granhams Road, Great Shelford, Cambridge CB2 5JX. *T:* Cambridge (01223) 843158.

MORRISON, Margaret, OBE 1991; BEM 1972; Co-Chairman, Women's National Commission, 1989–91; *b* 20 March 1924; *d* of William and May Campbell; *m* 1943, Thomas Morrison; one *d. Educ:* Royal Jubilee Juniors, Newcastle; Sandyford Secondary Modern, Newcastle. Civil Service Union: Nat. Exec. Cttee, 1968–78; Vice-Pres., 1978–79; Pres., 1980–87; Dep. Pres., Nat. Union of Civil and Public Servants, 1987–89; Vice-Chm., Northern Regional TUC, 1980– (Chm., Women's Adv. Gp, 1980–); Mem., TUC Women's Cttee, 1979–89; Director: Northern Development Co., 1984–89; Entrust, 1984–; Mem., European Women's TUC and Steering Cttee, 1982–. Mem., Civil Service Appeal Bd, 1991–. TUC Gold Badge, Woman Trade Unionist of the Year, 1973. *Publication:* (jtly) Homelessness Amongst Women, report, 1983. *Recreations:* music, reading, swimming, conversation. *Address:* Women's National Commission, Goverment Offices, Horse Guards Road, SW1P 3AL. *T:* 0171–270 5903. *Club:* Victory.

MORRISON, Hon. Mary Anne, DCVO 1982 (CVO 1970); Woman of the Bedchamber to the Queen since 1960; *b* 17 May 1937; *o d* of Baron Margadale, *qv. Educ:* Heathfield School. *Address:* Fonthill House, Tisbury, Wilts. *T:* Tisbury (01747) 870366; Eallabus, Bridgend, Isle of Islay, Argyllshire. *T:* Bowmore (01496) 810223.
See also Hon. Sir C. A. Morrison, Hon. J. I. Morrison.

MORRISON, Neil; *see* Morrison, A. N.

MORRISON, Nigel Murray Paton; QC (Scot.) 1988; *b* 18 March 1948; *o s* of late David Paton Morrison, FRICS, FLAS and Dilys Trenholm Pritchard or Morrison. *Educ:* Rannoch School. Called to the Bar, Inner Temple, 1972; admitted Scottish Bar, 1975; Asst Editor, Session Cases, 1976–82; Asst Clerk, Rules Council, 1978–84; Clerk of Faculty, Faculty of Advocates, 1979–87; Standing Junior Counsel to Scottish Develt Dept (Planning), 1982–86; Temporary Sheriff, 1982–; Second (formerly Junior) Counsel to Lord President of Court of Session, 1984–89; First Counsel to Lord President, 1989–; Counsel to Sec. of State under Private Legislation Procedure (Scotland) Act 1936, 1986–. Chairman: Social Security Appeal Tribunals, 1982–91; Medical Appeal Tribunals, 1991–. Trustee, Nat. Library of Scotland, 1989–. *Publications:* (jtly) Greens Annotated Rules of the Court of Session, 1994; (ed) Greens Civil Practice Bulletin; contribs to Stair Memorial Encyclopaedia of the Laws of Scotland. *Recreations:* music, riding, being taken for walks by my black labrador dog. *Address:* 11 India Street, Edinburgh EH3 6HA. *T:* 0131–225 8030. *Club:* New (Edinburgh).

MORRISON, (Philip) Blake, FRSL; Staff writer, The Independent on Sunday, since 1994 (Literary Editor, 1990–94); *b* 8 Oct. 1950; *s* of Arthur Blakemore Morrison and Agnes O'Shea; *m* 1976, Katherine Ann Drake; two *s* one *d. Educ:* Ermysteds Grammar Sch., Skipton; Nottingham Univ. (BA); McMaster Univ. (MA); University College London (PhD). FRSL 1988. Poetry and fiction editor, TLS, 1978–81; Dep. Literary Editor, 1981–86, Literary Editor, 1987–89, Observer. Eric Gregory Award, 1980; Somerset Maugham Award, 1984; Dylan Thomas Meml Prize, 1985; E. M. Forster Award, 1988. *Publications:* The Movement: English poetry and fiction of the 1950s, 1980; (ed jtly) The Penguin Book of Contemporary British Poetry, 1982; Seamus Heaney, 1982; Dark Glasses, 1984; The Ballad of the Yorkshire Ripper, 1987; The Yellow House, 1987; And When Did You Last See Your Father, 1993 (Waterstone's/Volvo/Esquire Non-Fiction Award, 1993; J. R. Ackerley Award, 1994). *Recreations:* football, tennis. *Address:* The Independent on Sunday, One Canada Square, Canary Wharf, E14 5DL. *T:* 071–293 2471.

MORRISON, Maj.-Gen. Reginald Joseph Gordon, CB 1969; CBE 1959; MD, FRCP; retired; Physician, The Royal Hospital, Chelsea, 1969–79; Director of Medicine, Ministry of Defence (Army), and Consulting Physician to the Army, 1965–68; *b* 29 March 1909; *s* of R. Morrison; *m* 1947, Norma Jacqueline Nicholson; two *s. Educ:* Dulwich Coll.; St Joseph's Coll., SE19; St Bartholomew's Hosp. House Phys., St Bart's Hosp., 1934; Res. MO, Hove Gen. Hosp. Commnd RAMC, 1936; served as Med. Specialist, RAMC. Adviser in Medicine, EA Command, 1947–50; OC, Med. Div., QA Mil. Hosp., 1950–56; Cons. Phys., Far East, 1956–59; Prof. of Trop. Med., Royal Army Medical College, 1959–65. QHP 1963–68. *Publications:* (with W. H. Hargreaves) The Practice of Tropical Medicine, 1965; chapter in: Exploration Medicine, 1965; Medicine in the Tropics, 1974; various articles in Lancet, BMJ, Proc. RSM, etc. *Recreations:* rose growing, golf. *Address:* 1 Hollingdon Court, High Street, Chislehurst, Kent BR7 5AJ.

MORRISON, Richard Duncan; Arts Editor, The Times, since 1990; *b* 24 July 1954; *s* of Donald and Mary Morrison; *m* 1977, Marian Plant; two *s* one *d. Educ:* Univesity Coll. Sch.; Magdalene Coll., Cambridge (MA). Asst Editor, Classical Music magazine, 1977–83; Dep. Editor, Early Music magazine, 1984–88; The Times, Music Critic, 1984–89; Dep. Arts Editor, 1989–90. *Recreations:* walking, organ-playing. *Address:* 11 Sunningfields Crescent, NW4 4RD. *T:* 0181–202 8028.

MORRISON, Hon. Sara Antoinette Sibell Frances, (Hon. Mrs Sara Morrison); *b* 9 Aug. 1934; *d* of 2nd Viscount Long and of Laura, Duchess of Marlborough; *m* 1954, Hon. Charles Andrew Morrison (*see* Hon. Sir C. A. Morrison) (marr. diss. 1984); one *s* one *d. Educ:* in England and France. Gen. Electric Co., 1975– (Dir 1980–); Non-Executive Director: Abbey National plc (formerly Abbey Nat. Building Soc.), 1979–95; Carlton TV, 1992–; Kleinwort Charter Trust, 1993–. Chairman: Nat. Council for Voluntary Orgns (formerly Nat. Council of Social Service), 1977–81; Nat. Adv. Council on Employment of Disabled People, 1981–84. County Councillor, then Alderman, Wilts, 1961–71; Chairman: Wilts Assoc. of Youth Clubs, 1958–63; Wilts Community Council, 1965–70; Vice-Chairman: Nat. Assoc. Youth Clubs, 1969–71; Conservative Party Organisation, 1971–75; Member: Governing Bd, Volunteer Centre, 1972–77; Annan Cttee of Enquiry into Broadcasting, 1974–77; Nat. Consumer Council, 1975–77; Bd, Fourth Channel TV Co., 1980–85; Video Appeals Cttee (Video Recordings Act, 1984), 1985–; Governing Council, Family Policy Studies Centre, 1983–; Nat. Radiological Protection Bd, 1989–; Council, PSI, 1980–93; Governing Body, Imperial Coll., London, 1986– (Hon. Fellow 1993). CIMgt. FRSA. *Address:* Wyndham's Farm, Wedhampton, Devizes, Wilts SN10 3QE. *T:* Chirton (01380) 840221; 16 Groom Place, SW1X 7BA. *T:* 0171–245 6553.

MORRISON, Stephen Roger; Managing Director, London Weekend Television, since 1994; *b* 3 March 1947; *s* of Hyman Michael Morrison and Rebecca (*née* Zolkwer); *m* 1979, Gayle Valerie Broughall; three *d. Educ:* High Sch., Glasgow; Edinburgh Univ. (MA Hons); Nat. Film Sch., Beaconsfield (ANFS). BBC Scotland (Radio and TV), 1970; Granada Television: Producer/Dir, Northern Documentary Unit, 1974; Ed., Granada Regl Progs, 1977; Hd of Arts and Features, 1981; Dir of Programmes, 1987–92; Man. Dir, Broadcasting, 1992–94; Man. Dir, 1993–94; Feature Films Producer: The Magic Toyshop, 1986; The Fruit Machine, 1988; (Exec. Producer) My Left Foot, 1989; (Exec. Producer) The Field, 1990. *Recreations:* tennis, reading, films and theatre, talking and dining, touring delicatessens. *Address:* London Weekend Television, London Television Centre, Upper Ground, SE1 9LT. *T:* 0171–620 1620. *Club:* Garrick.

MORRISON, Dr Stuart Love; Professor of Community Medicine, University of Edinburgh, 1964–75, retired; *b* 25 Nov. 1922; *o s* of late William James Morrison, Ironfounder, Glasgow and late Isabella Murdoch, Edinburgh; *m* 1947, Dr Audrey Butler Lornie, *yr d* of late Lt-Col W. S. Lornie, MC, TD, MRCVS, Perth; one *d. Educ:* Glasgow Acad.; Dundee High Sch.; St Andrews and London Univs. MB, ChB (St Andrews) 1951; DPH (London) 1954; MRCP Edinburgh, 1966; FRCP Edinburgh, 1968; FFCM 1975. Served in RAF, 1939–46; Hosp. and gen. practice, 1951–53; Public Health appts, 1954–56; Mem., Scientific Staff, MRC Social Medicine Research Unit, 1956–62; Vis. Fellow, Epidemiology and Statistics, Univ. of N Carolina, 1961–62; Sen. Lectr in Social Med., Univ. of Edinburgh, 1962–64; Professorial Fellow in Community Medicine, 1976–82 and Dir of Centre for Med. Res., 1979–82, Univ. of Sussex; Vis. Prof. of Community Medicine, LSHTM, 1982–84; Prof. of Community Medicine, Univ. of Malta, 1984–86. *Publications:* (jtly) The Image and the Reality, 1978; contribs to med. jls on epidemiology and medical care, and to Book Collector on bibliography. *Recreation:* book collecting. *Address:* 4 Roselands, Sidmouth, Devon EX10 8PB.

MORRISON, Toni; *see* Morrison, C. A.

MORRISON, William Charles Carnegie, CBE 1993; CA; Director, Bank of Scotland, since 1993; Chairman, British Linen Bank Group Ltd, since 1994; Financial Adviser, ScotRail, since 1993; Visiting Professor in Accountancy, University of Strathclyde, since 1983; *b* 10 Feb. 1938; *s* of late William and Grace Morrison; *m* 1st; two *d*; 2nd, 1977, Joceline Mary (*née* Saint). *Educ:* Kelvinside Acad., Lathallan; Merchiston Castle Sch. Thomson McLintock & Co., subseq. KMG Thomson McLintock: qual. CA (with distinction), 1961; Partner, 1966; Jt Sen. Partner, Glasgow and Edinburgh, 1974–80; UK managing partner, 1980–87; Dep. Sen. Partner, Peat Marwick McLintock, subseq. KPMG Peat Marwick, 1987–93. Director: Thomas Cook & Son Ltd, 1971–72; Scottish Amicable Life Assurance Soc., 1973–87, 1993–; Securities Trust of Scotland, 1976–80; Brownlee & Co., 1978–80. Pres., Inst. of Chartered Accountants of Scotland, 1984–85 (Vice-Pres., 1982–84). Chairman: Auditing Practices Bd of UK and Ireland, 1991–94; Exec. Cttee, Jt Disciplinary Scheme of UK Accounting Profession, 1993–; Mem., Financial Reporting Council, 1991–95. Vice Pres., Scottish Council (Develt and Industry), 1982–93 (mem. various cttees; Fellow, 1993); Member: Scottish Telecommunications Bd, 1978–80; Scottish Cttee, Design Council, 1978–81. Governor, Kelvinside Acad., 1967–80 (Chm. of Governors, 1975–80); Hon. Treasurer, Transport Trust, 1982–88; Trustee, Indep. Living Funds, 1993–. FRSA 1990. *Publications:* occasional professional papers. *Recreations:* vintage transport, model railways. *Address:* 87 Campden Hill Court, Holland Street, W8 7HW. *T:* 0171–937 2972. *Clubs:* Caledonian; Royal Scottish Automobile (Glasgow).

MORRISON, (William) Garth, CBE 1994; DL; Chief Scout, since 1988; Chairman, East and Midlothian NHS Trust, since 1994; *b* 8 April 1943; *s* of Walter Courtenay Morrison and Audrey Elizabeth Morrison (*née* Gilbert); *m* 1970, Gillian Cheetham; two *s* one *d. Educ:* Pangbourne Coll.; Pembroke Coll., Cambridge (BA 1966). CEng, MIEE 1973. Service in RN, retiring as Lieut, 1961–73; farming in family partnership, 1973–. Scouting: Area Comr, E Lothian, 1973–81; Chief Comr of Scotland, 1981–88; Mem., World Scout Cttee, 1991–. Member: Lothian Region Children's Panel, 1976–83; Scottish Community Educn Council, 1988–95 (Fellow, 1995). DL E Lothian, 1984. Argentine Gold Medal, 1962. *Publication:* chapter in The Scottish Juvenile Justice System, 1982. *Recreations:* golf, sailing, scouting. *Address:* West Fenton, North Berwick, East Lothian EH39 5AL. *T:* North Berwick (01620) 842154. *Clubs:* Naval; Hawks (Cambridge).

MORRISON-BELL, Sir William (Hollin Dayrell), 4th Bt *cr* 1905; solicitor; *b* 21 June 1956; *s* of Sir Charles Reginald Francis Morrison-Bell, 3rd Bt and of Prudence Caroline, *d* of late Lt-Col W. D. Davies, 60th Rifles (she *m* 2nd, Peter Gillbanks); *S* father, 1967; *m* 1984, Cynthia Hélène Marie White; one *s. Educ:* Eton; St Edmund Hall, Oxford. *Heir: s* Thomas Charles Edward Morrison-Bell, *b* 13 Feb. 1985. *Address:* Highgreen, Tarset, Hexham, Northumberland NE48 1RP. *T:* Bellingham (01434) 240223; 106 Bishops Road, SW6 7AR. *T:* 0171–736 4940.

MORRISON-LOW, Sir James; *see* Low.

MORRITT, Rt. Hon. Sir (Robert) Andrew, Kt 1988; CVO 1989; PC 1994; **Rt. Hon. Lord Justice Morritt;** a Lord Justice of Appeal, since 1994; *b* 5 Feb. 1938; *s* of Robert Augustus Morritt and Margaret Mary Morritt (*née* Tyldesley Jones); *m* 1962, Sarah Simonetta Merton, *d* of John Ralph Merton, *qv*; two *s. Educ:* Eton Coll.; Magdalene Coll., Cambridge (BA 1961). 2nd Lieut Scots Guards, 1956–58. Called to the Bar, Lincoln's Inn, 1962, Bencher, 1984; QC 1977. Junior Counsel: to Sec. of State for Trade in Chancery Matters, 1970–77; to Attorney-Gen. in Charity Matters, 1972–77; Attorney General to HRH The Prince of Wales, 1978–88; a Judge of High Court of Justice, Chancery Div., 1988–94. Vice-Chancellor of Co. Palatine of Lancaster, 1991–94. Member: Gen. Council of the Bar, 1969–73; Adv. Cttee on Legal Educn, 1972–76; Top Salaries Review Body, 1982–87. *Recreations:* fishing, shooting. *Address:* Royal Courts of Justice, Strand, WC2A 2LL. *Club:* Garrick.

MORROCCO, Alberto, OBE 1993; RSA 1963 (ARSA 1952); RSW 1965; RP 1977; RGI; Head of School of Painting, Duncan of Jordanstone College of Art, Dundee, 1950–82; *b* 14 Dec. 1917; *m* 1941, Vera Cockburn Mercer; two *s* one *d. Educ:* Gray's Sch. of Art, Aberdeen. Carnegie Schol., 1937; Brough Schol., 1938. In the Army, 1940–46. Guthrie Award, 1943; San Vito Prize, Rome, 1959. Pictures in: Scottish Modern Arts Coll.; Contemporary Arts Soc.; Scottish Arts Council Coll.; Hull, Aberdeen, Glasgow, Perth, Dundee and Edinburgh City Art Galleries and Scottish Gall. of Modern Art. Mem., Royal Fine Art Commn for Scotland, 1978–88. Mem., Arts and Crafts in Architecture Panel, Saltire Soc., 1983–. Hon. LLD Dundee, 1980; DUniv Stirling, 1987. *Recreations:* travel, swimming, eating. *Address:* Binrock, 456 Perth Road, Dundee DD2 1NG. *T:* Dundee (01382) 69319. *Club:* Scottish Arts.

MORROGH, Henton, CBE 1969; FRS 1964; FEng 1979; Director, BCIRA (formerly British Cast Iron Research Association), 1959–85; *b* 29 Sept. 1917; *s* of Clifford and Amy Morrogh; *m* 1949, Olive Joyce Ramsay; one *d.* Distinguished for his work on the microstructure and solidification of cast iron and for the development of ductile cast iron. Visiting Prof., Dept of Industrial Engineering and Management Univ. of Technology, Loughborough, 1967–72. President: Instn of Metallurgists, 1967–68; Inst. of British Foundrymen, 1972–73; Internat. Cttee of Foundry Technical Assocs, 1978. Hon. Member: Japanese Foundrymen's Soc., 1984; Inst. of British Foundrymen, 1986. DSc (*hc*), Univ. of Birmingham, 1965; Iron and Steel Inst. Andrew Carnegie Gold Medal, 1946; E. J. Fox Medal Inst. of Brit. Foundrymen, 1951; McFadden Gold Medal, Amer. Foundrymen's Soc., 1952; Robert Hadfield Medal, Iron & Steel Inst., 1956; Gold Medal, Amer. Gray Iron Founders' Soc., 1961; Bessemer Gold Medal, Metals Soc., 1977. *Address:* Cedarwood,

Penn Lane, Tanworth-in-Arden, Warwicks B94 5HH. *T:* Tanworth-in-Arden (01564) 742414.

MORROW, Cdre Anthony John Clare, RN; Commodore, Royal Yachts, since 1995; *b* 30 March 1944; *s* of late Capt. John Geoffrey Basil Morrow, CVO, DSC, RN and Dorothy April Bettine (*née* Mather); *m* 1st, 1969, Jackie Rogers (marr. diss. 1979); two *d*; 2nd, 1982, Julie, *d* of R. M. Philips and late Mrs M. Philips; one *s* one *d*. *Educ:* Summerfields, Oxford; Nautical Coll., Pangbourne; BRNC, Dartmouth. Entered RN, 1962: qualified Signals Officer, HMS Mercury, 1971; Lt-Comdr 1972; on staff of C-in-C Fleet, Signals Officer, HM Yacht Britannia, 1972–78; commanded HMS Lindisfarne, 1972–79; Comdr 1979; on staff, UK Mil. Rep. to NATO, 1980–83; commanded HMS Active, 1983–85; RN Exchange to CNO, US Navy, Washington, 1985–87; MoD, 1987–88; Capt. 1988; Captain, HMS Mercury, 1988–91; commanded Fourth Frigate Sqdn, HMS Active, 1991–93; ACOS, Plans and Policy, CINCHAN, Eastern Atlantic, 1993–94. *Recreations:* outdoor activities, sports. *Address:* HM Yacht Britannia, BFPO 239.

MORROW, Sir Ian (Thomas), Kt 1973; CA; FCMA, JDipMA, FIMgt; CompIEE; Chairman: MAI (formerly Mills and Allen International) plc, 1974–93 (Director, 1974–94); Additional Underwriting Agencies (No 3) Ltd, since 1985; Scotia Pharmaceuticals Ltd, Scotia (formerly Efamol) Holdings plc, 1986–95; Beale Dobie & Co. Ltd, since 1989; Thurne Group Ltd, since 1993; *b* 8 June 1912; *er s* of late Thomas George Morrow and Jamesina Hunter, Pilmour Links, St Andrews; *m* 1940, Elizabeth Mary Thackray (marr. diss. 1967); one *s* one *d*; *m* 1967, Sylvia Jane Taylor; one *d*. *Educ:* Dollar Academy, Dollar. Chartered Accountant 1936; FCMA 1945; Asst Accountant, Brocklehurst-Whiston Amalgamated Ltd, 1937–40; Partner, Robson, Morrow & Co., 1942–51; Financial Dir, 1951–52, Dep. Man. Dir, 1952–56, Joint Man. Dir, 1956–57, Man. Dir, 1957–58, The Brush Electrical Engineering Co. Ltd (now The Brush Group Ltd); Jt Man. Dir, H. Clarkson & Co. Ltd, 1961–72; Chairman: UKO International plc (formerly UK Optical & Industrial Holdings Ltd), 1959–86 (former Man. Dir and Chm. of subsidiary cos); Associated Fire Alarms Ltd, 1965–70; Rowe Bros & Co. (Holdings) Ltd, 1960–70; Kenwood Manufacturing Co. Ltd, 1961–68; Crane Fruehauf Trailers Ltd, 1969–71; Collett, Dickenson, Pearce Internat. Ltd, 1979–83; Scotia DAF Trucks Ltd, 1979–83; Agricultural Holdings Co. Ltd, 1981–84; W. M. Still & Sons Ltd, 1964–86; Martin-Black PLC, 1977–86; Strong & Fisher (Hldgs), 1981–90 (Dir, 1981–90); Argunex Ltd, 1985–89; Walbrook Insce Co., 1990–92; Brightstone Estates, 1990–92; Insport Consultants, 1988–93; Deputy Chairman, Rolls Royce Ltd, 1970–71, Rolls Royce (1971) Ltd, 1971–73 (Man. Dir, 1971–72); Director: Hambros Industrial Management Ltd, 1965–91; Hambros PLC, 1972–90 (Dep. Chm., 1983–86); The Laird Gp, 1973–92 (Chm., 1975–87); DAF Trucks (GB), 1977–83; Zeus Management Ltd, 1985–93; Psion PLC, 1987–; C. E. Heath Public Ltd Co., 1988–. Led Anglo-American Council on Productivity Team on Management Accounting to US, 1950. Council Member: British Electrical & Allied Manufacturers' Assoc., 1957–58; British Internal Combustion Engine Manufacturers' Assoc., 1957–58; Member: Grand Council, FBI, 1953–58; Council, Production Engineering Research Assoc., 1955–58; Council, Inst. of Cost and Works Accountants (now Inst. of Management Accountants), 1952–70 (Pres. 1956–57, Gold Medallist 1961); Performing Right Tribunal, 1968–74; Council, Inst. of Chartered Accountants of Scotland, 1968–72, 1979–82 (Vice-Pres. 1970–72, 1979–80, 1980–81, Pres., 1981–82); Inflation Accounting Steering Gp, 1976–79; Lay Member, Press Council, 1974–80; Freeman, City of London; Liveryman, Worshipful Co. of Spectaclemakers. DUniv. Stirling, 1979; Hon. DLitt Heriot-Watt, 1982. *Publications:* papers and addresses on professional and management subjects. *Recreations:* reading, music, golf, ski-ing. *Address:* 2 Albert Terrace Mews, NW1 7TA. *T:* 0171–722 7110. *Clubs:* National Liberal, Royal Automobile; Royal and Ancient (St Andrews).

MORROW, Martin S.; Stipendiary Magistrate, Glasgow, since 1972; *b* 16 Nov. 1923; *s* of late Thomas Morrow and Mary Lavery; *m* 1952, Nancy May, BMus, LRAM; one *s* two *d*. *Educ:* St Aloysius' Coll., Glasgow; Glasgow Univ. Solicitor. Private practice, 1951–56; Asst Procurator Fiscal, 1956–72. *Recreations:* music, golf, reading. *Address:* 33 Leicester Avenue, Glasgow G12 0LU. *T:* 0141–334 1324. *Club:* St Mungo (Glasgow).

MORSE, Prof. Christopher George John, (Robin); Professor of Law, King's College London, since 1992; *b* 28 June 1947; *s* of John Morse and Margaret Gwenllian Morse (*née* Maliphant); *m* 1983, Louise Angela Stott; one *s*. *Educ:* Malvern Coll.; Wadham Coll., Oxford (MA, BCL). Called to the Bar, Middle Temple, 1971; King's College London: Lectr in Law, 1971–88; Reader, 1988–92; Hd and Dean, Sch. of Law, 1992–93. Visiting Professor: John Marshall Law Sch., Chicago, 1979–80; Univ. of Leuven, 1982; Dir of Studies, Hague Acad. of Internat. Law, 1990. *Publications:* Torts in Private International Law, 1978; (ed jtly) Dicey and Morris on the Conflict of Laws, 11th edn 1987, 12th edn 1993; (ed jtly) Benjamin's Sale of Goods, 3rd edn 1987, 4th edn 1992; Public Policy in Transnational Relationships, 1991; (ed jtly) Chitty on Contracts, 27th edn 1994; articles in learned jls and contribs to books. *Recreations:* Swansea City Association Football Club, travel. *Address:* School of Law, King's College London, Strand, WC2R 2LS. *T:* 0171–836 5454.

MORSE, Sir Christopher Jeremy, KCMG 1975; Non-Executive Director, Bank of England, since 1993; Warden, Winchester College, since 1987 (Fellow, 1966–82); Chancellor, Bristol University, since 1989; *b* 10 Dec. 1928; *s* of late Francis John Morse and Kinbarra (*née* Armfield-Marrow); *m* 1955, Belinda Marianne, *d* of Lt-Col R. B. Y. Mills; three *s* one *d* (and one *d* decd). *Educ:* Winchester; New Coll., Oxford (Hon. Fellow, 1979). 1st Class Lit. Hum. 1953. 2nd Lt KRRC, 1948–49. Fellow, All Souls Coll., Oxford, 1953–68, 1983–. Trained in banking at Glyn, Mills & Co., and made a director in 1964; Executive Dir, Bank of England, 1965–72; Lloyds Bank: Dep. Chm., 1975–77; Chm., 1977–93; Lloyds Bank International: Chm., 1979–80; Dep. Chm., 1975–77 and 1980–85; Chm., Lloyds Merchant Bank Hldgs, 1985–88. Alternate Governor for UK of IMF, 1966–72; Chm. of Deputies of Cttee of Twenty, IMF, 1972–74; Chm., Cttee of London Clearing Bankers, 1980–82 (Dep. Chm., 1978–80); Mem., Council of Lloyd's, 1987–; President: London Forex Assoc., 1978–91; Institut Internat. d'Etudes Bancaires, 1982–83; British Overseas Bankers' Club, 1983–84; BBA, 1984–91 (Vice-Pres., 1991–92); Internat. Monetary Conf., 1985–86; Banking Fedn of EC, 1988–90; CIB, 1992–93 (Vice-Pres., 1991–92); Vice-Pres., BITC, 1992–. Mem., NEDC, 1977–81. Chm., City Communications Centre, 1985–87; non-executive Director: Alexanders Discount Co. Ltd, 1975–84; Legal & General Assce Soc., 1964 and 1975–87; ICI, 1981–93; Zeneca, 1993–. Hon. Mem., Lombard Assoc., 1989. Governor, Henley Management Coll., 1966–85. Chairman: Per Jacobsson Foundn, 1987–; Trustees, Beit Meml Fellowships for Med. Res., 1976–; GBA, 1994–; Mem., British Selection Cttee, Harkness Fellowships, 1986–90. Freeman, City of London, 1978; Chm., City Arts Trust, 1976–79. FIDE Internat. Judge for chess compositions, 1975–; Pres., British Chess Problem Soc., 1977–79; Hon. Life Mem., British Chess Fedn, 1988. Pres., Classical Assoc., 1989–90. Hon. DLitt City, 1977; Hon. DSc Aston, 1984; Hon. LLD Bristol, 1989. *Recreations:* poetry, problems and puzzles, coarse gardening, golf. *Address:* 102a Drayton Gardens, SW10 9RJ. *T:* 0171–370 2265. *Club:* Athenæum.

MORSE, Sir Jeremy; *see* Morse, Sir C. J.

MORSE, Robin; *see* Morse, C. G. J.

MORSON, Basil Clifford, CBE 1987; VRD 1963; MA, DM Oxon; FRCS; FRCPath; FRCP; Civilian Consultant in Pathology to the Royal Navy, 1976–86, now Emeritus; Consulting Pathologist and Research Consultant to St Mark's Hospital, since 1986 (Consultant Pathologist, 1956–86); Director, WHO International Reference Centre for Gastrointestinal Cancer, 1969–86; *b* 13 Nov. 1921; *s* of late A. Clifford Morson, OBE, FRCS; *m* 1st, 1950, Pamela Elizabeth Gilbert (marr. diss. 1982); one *s* two *d*; 2nd, 1983, Sylvia Dutton, MBE. *Educ:* Beaumont Coll.; Wadham Coll., Oxford; Middlesex Hosp. Medical Sch. House Surg., Middlesex Hosp., 1949; House Surg., Central Middlesex Hosp., 1950; Asst Pathologist, Bland-Sutton Institute of Pathology, Middlesex Hosp., 1950. Sub-Lt RNVR, 1943–46; Surgeon-Comdr RNR (London Div.), retd 1972. President: Sect. of Proctology, RSocMed, 1973–74; British Soc. of Gastroenterology, 1979–80 (Hon. Mem., 1987); British Div., Internat. Acad. of Pathology, 1978–; Treas., RCPath, 1983– (Vice-Pres., 1978–81). Vis. Prof. of Pathology, Univ. of Chicago, 1959; Sir Henry Wade Vis. Prof., RCSE, 1970; Vis. Prof of Pathology, Univ. of Texas System Cancer Center, 1980 (Joanne Vandenberg Hill Award); Lectures: Lettsomian, Med. Soc., 1970; Sir Arthur Hurst Meml, British Soc. of Gastroenterology, 1970; Richardson, Massachusetts Gen. Hosp., Boston, 1970; Skinner, RCR, 1983; Shelley Meml, Johns Hopkins Univ., 1983; Kettle, RCPath, 1987. FRCS 1972; FRCP 1979 (MRCP 1973); Hon. Fellow: Amer. Soc. of Colon and Rectal Surgeons, 1974; Amer. Coll. of Gastroenterology, 1978; French Nat. Soc. of Gastroenterology, 1982; RSM, 1989; RAeS, 1990. John Hunter Medal, RCS, 1987; Frederick Salmon Medal, Sect. of Coloproctology, RSM, 1991. *Publications:* Pathology of Alimentary Tract, in Systemic Pathology, ed W. St C. Symmers, 1966, 3rd edn 1987; (ed) Diseases of the Colon, Rectum and Anus, 1969; Textbook of Gastrointestinal Pathology, 1972, 3rd edn 1989; Histological Typing of Intestinal Tumours, 1976; The Pathogenesis of Colorectal Cancer, 1978; Pathology in Surgical Practice, 1985; Colour Atlas of Gastrointestinal Pathology, 1988; numerous articles in medical journals. *Recreations:* gardening, ornithology, travel. *Address:* 14 Crossways Park, West Chiltington, W Sussex RH20 2QZ. *T:* West Chiltington (01798) 813528.

MORT, Rt. Rev. John Ernest Llewelyn, CBE 1965; Assistant Bishop, Diocese of Leicester, since 1972; *b* 13 April 1915; *s* of late Trevor Ll. Mort, JP, and Ethel Mary Mort; *m* 1953, Barbara Gifford. *Educ:* Malvern Coll.; St Catharine's Coll., Cambridge (BA Hist. Tripos 1938; MA 1942); Westcott House, Cambridge. Asst Curate, Dudley, 1940–44; Worcester Diocesan Youth Organiser, 1944–48; Private Chaplain to Bishop of Worcester, 1943–52; Vicar of St John in Bedwardine, Worcester, 1948–52; Bishop of N Nigeria, 1952–69; Canon Residentiary and Treasurer of Leicester Cathedral, 1970–88. Hon. LLD Ahmadu Bello Univ., 1970. *Address:* 271 Forest Road, Old Woodhouse, Loughborough, Leics LE12 8TZ.

MORT, (Margaret) Marion; ordination training, Southern Dioceses Ministerial Training Scheme, since 1994; *b* 10 May 1937; *d* of Rev. Ivan H. Whittaker and Margaret Whittaker; *m* 1959, Colin James Mort; one *s* two *d*. *Educ:* St Mary's Sch., Wantage; Queen's Coll., Harley St; Edinburgh Univ. Nat. Sec., World Development Movement, 1970–72; Licensed Lay Reader, 1983–; Mem. Gen. Synod, 1985–90 (rep. in Partners in Mission consultation for Church in Kenya, 1988). World Develt Educn Adviser, Dio. Portsmouth, 1984–91; Co-ordinator, then Officer, Decade of Evangelism (C of E), 1990–93; Mission and Evangelism Sec., Bd of Mission, Gen. Synod, 1993–94. Dir, Ocean Sound (ILR), 1985–92; Member: Bd of Christian Aid, 1987–90; Gen. Cttee, British and Foreign Bible Soc., 1993–. *Publications:* (jtly) Mission Audit, 1983; (jtly) Called to Order, 1988; (jtly) Building Bridges, 1995; church educnl papers; contribs to Church press. *Recreations:* good cars, good beer, good conversation. *Address:* Rivendell, High Street, Shirrell Heath, Southampton SO32 2JN. *T:* and *Fax:* Wickham (01329) 832178.

MORTIMER, Hon. Barry; *see* Mortimer, Hon. J. B.

MORTIMER, Clifford Hiley, DSc, DrPhil; FRS 1958; Distinguished Professor in Zoology, University of Wisconsin-Milwaukee, 1966–81, now Distinguished Professor Emeritus; *b* Whitchurch, Som, 27 Feb. 1911; *er s* of Walter Herbert and Bessie Russell; *m* 1936, Ingeborg Margarete Closs, Stuttgart, Germany; two *d*. *Educ:* Sibford and Sidcot Schs; Univ. of Manchester. BSc (Manchester) 1932, DSc (Manchester) 1946; Dr Phil (Berlin) 1935. Served on scientific staff of Freshwater Biological Assoc., 1935–41 and 1946–56. Seconded to Admiralty scientific service, 1941–46. Sec. and Dir, Scottish Marine Biological Assoc., 1956–66; Dir, Center for Great Lakes Studies, Univ. of Wisconsin-Milwaukee, 1966–79. Hon. DSc Wisconsin–Milwaukee, 1985; DèsSc *hc* Ecole Polytechnique Fédérale de Lausanne, 1987. *Publications:* scientific papers on lakes and the physical and chemical conditions which control life in them. *Recreations:* music, travel. *Address:* Milwaukee Catholic Home, 2462 N Prospect Avenue, Milwaukee, WI 53211, USA.

MORTIMER, Gerald James, CBE 1979 (MBE (mil.) 1944); DL; FEng; Councillor, Surrey County Council, 1973–93 (Chairman, Policy Committee, 1986–90); *b* 2 Sept. 1918; *s* of late Rev. Fernley Mortimer and Grace Mortimer (*née* Whiting); *m*1st, 1942, Connie (*née* Dodd) (*d* 1989); two *s* two *d*; 2nd, 1990, Theresa Ella Walker. *Educ:* Caterham Sch.; Royal School of Mines, London Univ. (BSc (mining engrg), ARSM). Served War, Major, RE, UK and NW Europe, 1939–46. Mining official on Witwatersrand gold mines, S Africa, and in E Africa, 1946–55; Consolidated Gold Fields Ltd: Management staff, London, 1955–63; Exec. Dir, 1963–78; Dep. Chm., 1969–78; Gp Chief Exec., 1976–78; non. exec. Dir, 1978–80; Consultant, 1978–83; Dir, other Gp cos, 1957–79; in charge Goldsworthy iron ore project, W Australia, 1964–65; Exec. Chm., Amey Roadstone Corp. Ltd, 1967–75. President: Overseas Mining Assoc., 1972–73; Instn of Mining and Metallurgy, 1977–78; Inst. of Quarrying, 1980–81; Board Mem., 1978–83, Vice-Chm., 1981–82, Chm., 1982–83, CEI. Hon. Treas., Fellowship of Engrg, 1981–84. President: Old Caterhamians Assoc., 1970–71; RSM Assoc., 1976–77. Chm., E Surrey Cons. Assoc., 1980–82, Treasurer, 1982–83. Governor: Caterham Sch., 1965– (Vice-Chm., 1978–); Marden Lodge County Primary Sch., Surrey (Vice-Chm., 1973–81; Chm., 1981–). DL Surrey, 1990. FRSA; Hon. FIMM; Hon. FIQ. *Publication:* Never a Shot in Anger (autobiog.), 1993. *Recreations:* history, politics. *Address:* 40 Harestone Valley Road, Caterham, Surrey CR3 6HD. *T:* Caterham (01883) 344853.

MORTIMER, James Edward; General Secretary of the Labour Party, 1982–85; *b* 12 Jan. 1921; *m*; two *s* one *d*. *Educ:* Junior Techn. Sch., Portsmouth; Ruskin Coll., Oxford; London Sch. of Economics. Worked in Shipbuilding and Engrg Industries as Ship Fitter Apprentice, Machinist and Planning Engr; TUC Schol., Oxford, 1945–46; TUC Economic Dept, 1946–48; full-time Trade Union Official, Draughtsmen's and Allied Technicians' Assoc., 1948–68. Dir, London Co-operative Soc., 1968–71. Mem., NBPI, 1968–71; Mem., Bd, LTE, 1971–74. Chm., ACAS (formerly Conciliation and Arbitration Service), 1974–81. Member: Wilberforce Ct of Inquiry into the power dispute, 1970; Armed Forces Pay Review Body, 1971–74; EDC for Chemical Industry, 1973–74; Chm. EDC for Mechanical and Electrical Engineering Construction, 1974–82. Vis. Fellow, Admin. Staff Coll., Henley, 1976–82; Sen. Vis. Fellow, Bradford Univ., 1977–82; Vis.

Prof., Imperial Coll. of Sci. and Technol., London Univ., 1981–83; Ward-Perkins Res. Fellow, Pembroke Coll., Oxford, 1981. Chm. Editl Cttee, Socialist Campaign Group News, 1987–; Mem. Exec. Cttee, Inst. of Employment Rights, 1989–. Hon. DLitt Bradford, 1982. *Publications:* A History of Association of Engineering and Shipbuilding Draughtsmen, 1960; (with Clive Jenkins) British Trade Unions Today, 1965; (with Clive Jenkins) The Kind of Laws the Unions Ought to Want, 1968; Industrial Relations, 1968; Trade Unions and Technological Change, 1971; History of the Boilermakers' Society, vol. 1, 1973, vol. 2, 1982, vol. 3, 1993; (with Valerie Ellis) A Professional Union: the evolution of the Institution of Professional Civil Servants, 1980. *Address:* 5 Silverdale Drive, SE9 4DH. *T:* 0181–851 7866.

See also J. E. Mortimer.

MORTIMER, James Edward; Deputy Director and Treasury Officer of Accounts, since 1995; *b* 9 Nov. 1947; *s* of James Edward Mortimer, *qv* and Renee Mabel Mortimer (*née* Horton); *m* 1969, Lesley Patricia Young. *Educ:* Latymer Upper Sch.; Wadham Coll., Oxford (MA, BPhil). HM Treasury, 1971–: Economic Advr, 1974–81; Principal, 1981–83; Grade 5, 1983–91; Under Sec., 1991–; Head of Aid and Export Finance Gp, 1991–95. *Recreations:* football, golf, cricket, birdwatching, cinema. *Address:* HM Treasury, Parliament Street, SW1P 3AG. *T:* 0171–270 4479. *Clubs:* Old Latymerians Association; Sunbury Golf.

MORTIMER, Hon. (John) Barry; Hon. Mr Justice Mortimer; a Justice of Appeal of the Supreme Court of Hong Kong, since 1993; *b* 7 Aug. 1931; *s* of John William Mortimer and Maud (*née* Snarr) Mortimer; *m* 1958, Judith Mary (*née* Page); two *s* two *d*. *Educ:* St Peter's School, York (Headmasters' Exhibitioner 1945); Emmanuel College, Cambridge; BA 1955, MA 1959. Commissioned into 4 RTR, 1951; served in Egypt, 1951–52; 45/51 RTR (TA), 1952–57. Called to the Bar, Middle Temple, 1956 (Bencher 1980); Harmsworth Law Scholar 1957; Prosecuting Counsel on NE Circuit: to Post Office, 1965–69; to Inland Revenue, 1969–71; QC 1971; a Recorder, 1972–87; Judge, Supreme Court of Hong Kong, 1985–93. Chancellor, Dio. of Ripon, 1971–85. Chairman: Mental Health Review Tribunal, 1983–85; Overseas Trust Bank (Compensation) Tribunal, 1986–87; Member: Bar Council, 1970–75; Senate, 1979–85; Law Reform Commn, Hong Kong, 1990– (Chm., Sub-cttee on Privacy and Data Protection). Hon. Diplomate, Amer. Bd of Trial Advocates, 1994. *Recreations:* reading, shooting, tennis. *Address:* Supreme Court, Queensway, Hong Kong; The Grange, Staveley, Knaresborough, N Yorks HG5 9LD. *Club:* Hong Kong.

MORTIMER, John (Clifford), CBE 1986; QC 1966; FRSL; barrister; playwright and author; *b* 21 April 1923; *s* of Clifford Mortimer and Kathleen May (*née* Smith); *m* 1st, 1949, Penelope Ruth Fletcher (*see* Penelope (Ruth) Mortimer) (marr. diss.); one *s* one *d*; 2nd, Penelope (*née* Gollop); two *d*. *Educ:* Harrow; Brasenose Coll., Oxford. Called to the Bar, 1948; Master of the Bench, Inner Temple, 1975. Mem. Nat. Theatre Bd, 1968–88. Chairman: Council, RSL, 1989–; Royal Court Theatre, 1990–. Pres., Howard League for Penal Reform, 1991–. Pres., Berks, Bucks and Oxon Naturalists' Trust, 1984–90. FRSL 1973. Hon. DLitt: Susquehanna Univ., 1985; St Andrews, 1987; Nottingham, 1989; Hon. LLD: Exeter, 1986; Brunel, 1990. Won the Italia Prize with short play, The Dock Brief, 1958; another short play What Shall We Tell Caroline, 1958. Full-length plays: The Wrong Side of the Park, 1960; Two Stars for Comfort, 1962; (trans.) A Flea in Her Ear, 1966; The Judge, 1967; (trans.) Cat Among the Pigeons, 1969; Come as You Are, 1970; A Voyage Round My Father, 1970 (filmed, 1982); (trans.) The Captain of Köpenick, 1971; I, Claudius (adapted from Robert Graves), 1972; Collaborators, 1973; Mr Luby's Fear of Heaven (radio), 1976; Heaven and Hell, 1976; The Bells of Hell, 1977; (trans.) The Lady from Maxim's, 1977; (trans.) A Little Hotel on the Side, 1984; opera (trans.) Die Fledermaus, 1988; A Christmas Carol (adapted from Dickens), 1994. Film Scripts: John and Mary, 1970; Brideshead Revisited (TV), 1981; Edwin (TV), 1984. British Acad. Writers Award, 1979. *Publications: novels:* Charade, 1947; Rumming Park, 1948; Answer Yes or No, 1950; Like Men Betrayed, 1953, reissued 1987; Three Winters, 1956; Will Shakespeare: an entertainment, 1977; Rumpole of the Bailey, 1978 (televised; BAFTA Writer of the Year Award, 1980); The Trials of Rumpole, 1979; Rumpole's Return, 1980 (televised); Regina v Rumpole, 1981; Rumpole for the Defence, 1982; Rumpole and the Golden Thread, 1983 (televised); Paradise Postponed, 1985 (televised 1986); Rumpole's Last Case, 1987 (televised); Rumpole and the Age of Miracles, 1988 (televised); Summer's Lease, 1988 (televised 1989); Titmuss Regained, 1990 (televised 1991); Rumpole à la Carte, 1990; Dunster, 1992; Rumpole on Trial, 1992; Under the Hammer, 1994 (televised); *travel:* (in collab. with P. R. Mortimer) With Love and Lizards, 1957; *plays:* The Dock Brief and Other Plays, 1959; The Wrong Side of the Park, 1960; Lunch Hour and Other Plays, 1960; Two Stars for Comfort, 1962; (trans.) A Flea in Her Ear, 1965; A Voyage Round My Father, 1970; (trans.) The Captain of Köpenick, 1971; Five Plays, 1971; Collaborators, 1973; Edwin and Other Plays, 1984; (trans.) Die Fledermaus, 1989; *interviews:* In Character, 1983; Character Parts, 1986; *autobiography:* Clinging to the Wreckage (Book of the Year Award, Yorkshire Post), 1982; Murderers and Other Friends, 1994; writes TV plays (incl. six Rumpole series); contribs to periodicals. *Recreations:* working, gardening, going to opera. *Address:* c/o A. D. Peters, 5th Floor, The Chambers, Chelsea Harbour, Lots Road, SW10 0XF. *Club:* Garrick.

MORTIMER, Katharine Mary Hope, (Mrs Robert Dean); Consultant/Financial Adviser, Know How Fund for Eastern Europe, since 1990; *b* 28 May 1946; *d* of late Rt Rev. Robert Cecil Mortimer and Mary Hope (*née* Walker); *m* 1st, 1973, John Noel Nicholson (marr. diss. 1986); one *s*; 2nd, 1990, Robert Michael Dean. *Educ:* School of SS Mary and Anne, Abbots Bromley; Somerville Coll., Oxford. MA, BPhil Oxon. World Bank, 1969–72; Central Policy Review Staff, 1972–78; N. M. Rothschild Asset Management Ltd, 1978–84; Dir, N. M. Rothschild & Sons (International Corporate Finance, subseq. Internat. Asset Management), 1984–88; seconded as Dir of Policy, SIB, 1985–87; Chief Exec., Walker Books, 1988–89. Mem. Bd, Crown Agents, 1990–; Non Executive Director: National Bus Company, 1979–91; Inst. of Development Studies, 1983–; Mast Develt Co., 1989–93; IQI Ltd, 1991–92; British Nuclear Fuels plc, 1993–. Member: ESRC, 1983–86; Authorised Conveyancing Practitioners Bd, 1991–. Mem., Royal Commn for Exhibn of 1851, 1988–. Member, Governing Body: Centre for Economic Policy Res., 1986–91; Imperial Coll., 1987–90. Trustee, Inst. for Public Policy Res., 1989–92. *Address:* Lower Corscombe, Okehampton, Devon EX20 1SD.

MORTIMER, Penelope (Ruth), FRSL; writer; *b* 19 Sept. 1918; *d* of Rev. A. F. G. and Amy Caroline Fletcher; *m* 1st, 1937, Charles Dimont (marr. diss. 1949); four *d*; 2nd, 1949, John Clifford Mortimer, *qv* (marr. diss. 1972); one *s* one *d*. *Educ:* Croydon High Sch.; New Sch., Streatham; Blencathra, Rhyl; Garden Sch., Lane End; St Elphin's Sch. for Daughters of Clergy; Central Educnl Bureau for Women; University Coll., London. *Screenplay:* Portrait of a Marriage, 1990. *Publications:* Johanna (as Penelope Dimont), 1947; A Villa in Summer, 1954; The Bright Prison, 1956; (with John Mortimer) With Love and Lizards, 1957; Daddy's Gone A-Hunting, 1958; Saturday Lunch with the Brownings, 1960; The Pumpkin Eater, 1962; My Friend Says It's Bulletproof, 1967; The Home, 1971; Long Distance, 1974; About Time (autobiog.), 1979 (Whitbread Prize); The Handyman, 1983; Queen Elizabeth: a life of the Queen Mother, 1986; About Time Too (autobiog.), 1993. *Address:* 19 St Gabriel's Road, NW2 4DS. *T:* 0181–452 8551, *Fax:* 0181–208 1946.

MORTIMORE, Prof. Peter John, OBE 1994; PhD; FBPsS; Director, Institute of Education, London University, since 1994 (Professor of Education, since 1990); *b* 17 Jan. 1942; *s* of late Claude Mortimore and of Rose Mortimore; *m* 1965, Jo Hargaden; three *d*. *Educ:* Chiswick County Grammar Sch.; St Mary's Coll., Strawberry Hill; Birkbeck Coll., London Univ. (BSc); Inst. of Education (MSc); Inst. of Psychiatry (PhD). CPsychol 1989; FBPsS 1989. Teacher, Sacred Heart Sch., SE5, 1964–66; Teacher and Head of Dept, Stockwell Manor Sch., SW9, 1966–73; Res. Officer, Inst. of Psychiatry, 1975–78; Mem., HM Inspectorate, 1978; Inner London Education Authority: Dir, Res. and Stats Br., 1979–85; Asst Educn Officer (Secondary Schs), 1985–87; Prof. of Educn, Lancaster Univ., 1988–90; Dep. Dir, London Univ. Inst. of Educn, 1990–94. Member: Educn Res. Bd, SSRC, 1981–82; Educn and Human Develt Cttee, ESRC, 1982–85; Univ. of London Exams and Assessment Council, 1991; Council, VSO, 1991. Gov., SOAS, 1993–. Hon. FCP 1994. FRSA 1990. *Publications:* (jtly) Fifteen Thousand Hours: secondary schools and their effects on children, 1979; (jtly) Behaviour Problems in Schools, 1984; (jtly) Secondary School Examinations, 1986; (jtly) School Matters: the junior years, 1988; (jtly) The Primary Head: roles, responsibilities and reflections, 1991; The Secondary Head: roles, responsibilities and reflections, 1991; (jtly) Managing Associate Staff, 1994; (jtly) Planning Matters, 1995. *Recreations:* theatre, art, music, walking. *Address:* Institute of Education, 20 Bedford Way, WC1H 0AL.

MORTIMORE, Simon Anthony; QC 1991; *b* 12 April 1950; *s* of Robert Anthony Mortimore and Katherine Elizabeth Mackenzie Mortimore (*née* Caine); *m* 1983, Fiona Elizabeth Jacobson; one *s* one *d*. *Educ:* Westminster School; Exeter Univ. (LLB). Called to the Bar, Inner Temple, 1972. *Publications:* contribs to Bullen and Leake and Jacobs Precedents of Pleading, 13th edn 1990. *Recreations:* opera, general cultural interests, travel, golf. *Address:* 3/4 South Square, Gray's Inn, WC1R 5HP. *T:* 0171–696 9900. *Clubs:* Hurlingham; Royal Mid Surrey Golf, Royal St George's Golf.

MORTON, 22nd Earl of, *cr* 1458 (*de facto* 21st Earl, 22nd but for the Attainder); **John Charles Sholto Douglas;** Lord Aberdour, 1458; Lord-Lieutenant of West Lothian, since 1985; *b* 19 March 1927; *s* of Hon. Charles William Sholto Douglas (*d* 1960) (2nd *s* of 19th Earl) and Florence (*d* 1985), *er d* of late Major Henry Thomas Timson; *S* cousin, 1976; *m* 1949, Sheila Mary, *d* of late Rev. Canon John Stanley Gibbs, MC, Didmarton House, Badminton, Glos; two *s* one *d*. DL West Lothian, 1982. *Recreation:* polo. *Heir: s* Lord Aberdour, *qv*. *Address:* Dalmahoy, Kirknewton, Midlothian. *Clubs:* Farmers'; Edinburgh Polo, Dalmahoy Country.

MORTON, Sir Alastair; *see* Morton, Sir R. A. N.

MORTON, Rev. Andrew Queen; Minister of Culross Abbey, 1959–87; *b* 4 June 1919; *s* of Alexander Morton and Janet Queen; *m* 1948, Jean, *e d* of George Singleton and late Jean Wands; one *s* two *d*. *Educ:* Glasgow Univ. MA 1942, BD 1947, BSc 1948. Minister of St Andrews, Fraserburgh, 1949–59. Dept of Computer Science, Univ. of Edinburgh, 1965–86. Hon. Res. Fellow, Glasgow Univ., 1990. FRSE 1973. *Publications:* The Structure of the Fourth Gospel, 1961; Authorship and Integrity in the New Testament, 1963; (with G. H. C. Macgregor) The Structure of Luke and Acts, 1965; Paul the Man and the Myth, 1965; (with S. Michaelson) The Computer in Literary Research, 1973; Literary Detection, 1979; (with S. Michaelson and N. Hamilton-Smith) Justice for Helander, 1979; (with James McLeman) The Genesis of John, 1980; (with S. Michaelson) The Cusum Plot, 1990; (with M. G. Farringdon) Fielding and the Federalist, 1990; Proper Words in Proper Places, 1992; The Authorship and Integrity of the New Testament Epistles, 1993; The Making of Mark, 1995; contrib. ALLC Jl; TLS. *Recreations:* thinking, talking. *Address:* 4 Upper Adelaide Street, Helensburgh G84 7HT. *T:* Helensburgh (01436) 75152.

MORTON, Admiral Sir Anthony (Storrs), GBE 1982; KCB 1978; DL; King of Arms, Order of the British Empire, since 1983; Vice Admiral of the United Kingdom, 1990–94; *b* 6 Nov. 1923; *s* of late Dr Harold Morton. *Educ:* Loretto School. Joined RN 1941; war service in Atlantic, Mediterranean and Far East (despatches, HMS Wrangler, 1945); Commander 1956; Comd HMS Appleton and 100th MSS 1957–58; HMS Undine 1960; HMS Rocket 1960–62; Captain 1964; Captain (F) 20th Frigate Squadron, 1964–66; Chief Staff Officer, Plans and Policy, to Commander Far East Fleet, 1966–68; Senior Naval Officer, Northern Ireland, 1968–70; Senior Naval Mem., RCDS, 1971–72; ACDS (Policy), 1973–75; Flag Officer, First Flotilla, 1975–77; Vice-Chief of Defence Staff, 1977–78; Vice-Chief of Naval Staff, 1978–80; UK Mil. Rep. to NATO, 1980–83. Rear Adm. of the UK, 1988–90. Chairman: Govs, Royal Star and Garter Home, 1986–91 (Vice-Pres., 1992–); Trustees, RN Museum, Portsmouth, 1985–94; Vice Pres., King George's Fund for Sailors, 1993– (Chm., 1986–93). DL Hants, 1989. OStJ 1990. *Recreations:* fishing, sailing, shooting, watching Association football. *Address:* c/o Barclays Bank, Winchester, Hants SO23 8RG. *Clubs:* Royal Cruising; Royal Yacht Squadron; Irish Cruising.

MORTON, Rev. Arthur, CVO 1979; OBE 1961; Director, National Society for the Prevention of Cruelty to Children, 1954–79; *b* 29 June 1915; *s* of Arthur Morton and Kate Floyd Morton; *m* 1940, Medora Gertrude Harrison; two *d*. *Educ:* Imperial Service Coll., Windsor; Jesus Coll., Cambridge (MA); Wycliffe Hall, Oxford (GOE). Curate, St Catherine's, Neasden, NW2, 1938–41; Chaplain, Missions to Seamen, Manchester, 1941–51. Asst Dir, NSPCC, 1951–54. Member, Adv. Council in Child Care and of Central Trng Council, 1956–71; frequent broadcasts on work of NSPCC. Mem., Glaziers Co., 1976–. *Publication:* (with Anne Allen) This is Your Child: the story of the NSPCC, 1961. *Recreations:* golf, fishing, reading, gardening. *Address:* 25 Cottes Way, Hill Head, Fareham, Hants PO14 3NF. *T:* Stubbington (01329) 663511.

MORTON, Christopher; *see* Morton, D. C.

MORTON, Air Commodore Crichton Charles, CBE 1945; Command Electronics Officer, HQ Bomber Command, 1962–66, retired; *b* 26 July 1912; *s* of late Charles Crichton Morton, Ramsey, IOM; *m* 1956, Diana Yvonne (*d* 1992), *d* of late Maj.-Gen. R. C. Priest, CB, RMS and *widow* of Group Captain N. D. Gilbart-Smith, RAF; no *c*. *Educ:* King William's Coll., IOM; RAF Coll., Cranwell. Various flying duties, 1932–36; RAF Officers Long Signals Course, Cranwell, 1936–37; signals duties, 1937–39; radar duties at HQ Fighter Comd, No 5 Signals Wing France, HQ 60 Signals Gp, Air HQ Iceland, HQ Air Comd SE Asia, 1939–45; Dir of Radar and Dep. Dir of Signals, Air Min., 1945–49; jssc Latimer, 1949–50; OC No 3 Radio Sch., RAF Compton Bassett, 1950–52; OC Communications Gp, Allied Air Forces Central Europe, 1952–55; Inspector of Radio Services, 1955–58; Dep. Chief Signals Office, HQ, SHAPE, 1958–60; Chm. of Brit. Jt Communications Electronics Board, Ministry of Defence, 1960–62. AMIEE 1955; AFRAeS 1965; MIERE 1965; CEng 1966. *Recreation:* researching Visigothic remains. *Address:* Apartamento 102, Torre Tramontana, Apartado 50, 17250 Playa de Aro, Gerona, Spain. *T:* (72) 817871.

MORTON, (David) Christopher; His Honour Judge Morton; a Circuit Judge, since 1992; *b* 1 Dec. 1943; *s* of Rev. Alexander Francis Morton and Esther Ann Morton; *m*

1970, Sandra Jo Kobes; three *s* one *d*. *Educ:* Worksop Coll., Notts; Fitzwilliam Coll., Cambridge (BA, LLB). Called to the Bar, Inner Temple, 1968; Wales and Chester Circuit; practised in Swansea, 1969–92. *Recreations:* Welsh affairs and Welsh language education, railways, family. *Address:* 80 Eaton Crescent, Swansea SA1 4QN. *T:* Swansea (01792) 473569. *Club:* Royal Over-Seas League.

MORTON, Prof. Frank, CBE 1976 (OBE 1968); DSc 1952, PhD 1936 (Manchester); MSc Tech; FIChemE; Professor of Chemical Engineering, University of Manchester, 1956–73, now Professor Emeritus; a Pro-Vice-Chancellor, 1968–72; *b* Sheffield, 11 Aug. 1906; *s* of late Joseph Morton, Manchester; *m* 1936, Hilda May, *d* of John W. Seaston, Withington, Manchester; one *s*. *Educ:* Manchester Univ. Demonstrator in Chemical Technology, 1931–36; Research Chemist, Trinidad Leaseholds Ltd, 1936–40; Superintendent of Research and Development, Trinidad Leaseholds, Trinidad, 1940–45; Chief Chemist, Trinidad Leaseholds Ltd, UK, 1945–49; Prof. of Chemical Engineering, Univ. of Birmingham, 1949–56. Actg Principal, Manchester Coll. of Science and Technology, 1964–65; Dep. Principal, Univ. of Manchester Inst. of Science and Technology, 1966–71. Member: Council, Manchester Business Sch., 1964–72; Chemical and Allied Products Training Board, 1968–71; European Fedn of Chemical Engineering, 1968–72. Pres., IChemE, 1963–64 (Hon. FIChemE 1983). Society of Chemical Industry: Vice-Pres., 1967–; Jubilee Memorial Lectr, 1967; Medal, 1969. Hon. Fellow, UMIST, 1978. *Publications:* Report of Inquiry into the Safety of Natural Gas as a Fuel (Ministry of Technology), 1970; various papers on petroleum, organic chemistry, chemical engineering and allied subjects. *Recreation:* golf. *Address:* 47 Penrhyn Beach East, Llandudno, Gwynedd LL30 3RG. *T:* Llandudno (01492) 548037.

MORTON, George Martin; Principal (formerly Senior) Planner, Trafford Borough Council, since 1986; *b* 11 Feb. 1940; *s* of Rev. Thomas Ralph Morton, DD, and Janet Maclay MacGregor Morton (*née* Baird). *Educ:* Fettes Coll Edinburgh; Edinburgh Coll. of Art; Glasgow Univ. RIBA. Member: Manchester City Council, 1971–74; Greater Manchester Council, 1973–77. Sec., Tameside and Glossop CHC, 1984–86. MP (Lab) Manchester, Moss Side, July 1978–1983; an Opposition Whip, 1979–83. *Address:* 4 St Annes Road, Manchester M21 8TD. *T:* 0161–881 8195.

MORTON, Kathryn Mary Stuart; Under Secretary (Legal), Department of Trade and Industry, since 1992; *b* 2 June 1946; *d* of Samuel Stuart Morton and Joan Alice Bessie Morton (*née* Tapscott). *Educ:* Ealing Grammar Sch. for Girls; Univ. of Sussex (BA). Solicitor. Leverhulme Res. Scholarship, India, 1967–68; Res. Asst, Lancaster Univ., 1969–71; Res. Officer, ODI, 1971–74; Res. Associate, ODI, and free-lance economist, 1974–80; with Bird & Bird: articled clerk, 1978–80; Asst Solicitor, 1980–82; OFT, 1982–85; DTI, 1985–. *Publications:* Aid and Dependence, 1975; (with Peter Tulloch) Trade and Developing Countries, 1977. *Address:* c/o Department of Trade and Industry, 1 Palace Street, SW1E 5HE. *T:* 0171–238 3470.

MORTON, Prof. Keith William; Professor of Numerical Analysis, and Professorial Fellow of Balliol College, Oxford University, since 1983; *b* 28 May 1930; *s* of Keith Harvey Morton and Muriel Violet (*née* Hubbard); *m* 1952, Patricia Mary Pearson; two *s* two *d*. *Educ:* Sudbury Grammar Sch.; Corpus Christi Coll., Oxford (BA 1952; MA 1954); New York Univ. (PhD 1964). Theoretical Physics Div., AERE, Harwell, 1952–59; Res. Scientist, Courant Inst. of Mathematical Sci., NY Univ., 1959–64; Head of Computing and Applied Maths, Culham Lab., UKAEA, 1964–72; Prof. of Applied Maths, Reading Univ., 1972–83. *Publications:* (with R. D. Richtmyer) Difference Methods for Initial-value Problems, 1967; (ed with M. J. Baines) Numerical Methods for Fluid Dynamics, Vol. I 1982, Vol. II 1986, Vol. III 1988, Vol. IV 1993; (with D. F. Mayers) Numerical Solution of Partial Differential Equations: an introduction, 1994; Mu numerous articles on numerical analysis and applied maths in learned jls. *Recreations:* reading, tennis, walking, gardening, listening to music. *Address:* Roscarrock, 48 Jack Straw's Lane, Headington, Oxford OX3 0DW. *T:* Oxford (01865) 68823; Oxford University Computing Laboratory, Wolfson Building, Parks Road, Oxford OX1 3QD. *T:* Oxford (01865) 273886.

MORTON, Kenneth Valentine Freeland, CIE 1947; OBE 1971; Secretary East Anglian Regional Hospital Board, 1947–72, retired; *b* 13 May 1907; *s* of Kenneth John Morton; *m* 1936, Mary Hadwin Hargreaves; four *s* one *d*. *Educ:* Edinburgh Academy; University Coll., Oxford. Joined ICS, 1930; Under-Sec. (Political) Punjab Govt, 1934–36; Deputy Commissioner, 1936–39; Colonisation Officer, 1939–43; Deputy Sec., Development Dept, 1943–46; Sec. Electricity and Industries Depts, 1946–47; retired, 1947. *Address:* Temple End House, 27 Temple End, Great Wilbraham, Cambridge CB1 5JF. *T:* Cambridge (01223) 880691. *Club:* East India, Devonshire, Sports and Public Schools.

MORTON, Patricia Ann; *see* Jacobs, P. A.

MORTON, Sir (Robert) Alastair (Newton), Kt 1991; Co-Chairman, Eurotunnel, since 1987 (Group Chief Executive, 1990–94); *b* 11 Jan. 1938; *s* of late Harry Newton Morton and Elizabeth Martino; *m* 1964, Sara Bridget Stephens; one *s* one *d*. *Educ:* St John's Coll. and Witwatersrand Univ., Johannesburg (BA); Worcester Coll., Oxford (MA; Hon. Fellow, 1994). Special grad. student, MIT, 1964. Anglo American Corp. of SA (mining finance), London and Central Africa, 1959–63; Internat. Finance Corp., Washington, 1964–67; Industrial Reorganisation Corp., 1967–70; Exec. Dir, 117 Group of investment trusts, 1970–72; Chm., Draymont Securities, 1972–76; Man. Dir, BNOC, 1976–80; Chief Exec., 1982–87, Chm., 1987, Guinness Peat Gp. Chairman: Kent TEC, 1990–95; Chancellor's Private Finance Panel, 1993–. Chm., CIT, 1992–94; Mem. Council, RIIA, 1990–. Chm., NYO of GB, 1994–. Hon. LLD: Bath, 1990; Kent, 1992; DUniv Brunel, 1992; Hon. DSc Warwick, 1994. Commandeur de la Légion d'Honneur (France), 1994. *Recreations:* sailing, walking, touring in 2CV. *Address:* The Adelphi, John Adam Street, WC2N 6JT. *Clubs:* University (New York); Itchenor Sailing.

MORTON BOYD, John; *see* Boyd, J. M.

MORTON JACK, David; His Honour Judge Morton Jack; a Circuit Judge, since 1986; *b* 5 Nov. 1935; *o s* of late Col W. A. Morton Jack, OBE, and late Mrs Morton Jack (*née* Happell); *m* 1972, Rosemary, *o d* of F. G. Rentoul; four *s*. *Educ:* Stowe (scholar); Trinity Coll., Oxford (Cholmeley Schol., MA). 2nd Lieut, RIrF, 1955–57. Called to the Bar, Lincoln's Inn, 1962; a Recorder of the Crown Court, 1979–86. *Recreations:* country pursuits, sheep-keeping, reading, music, gardens. *Address:* 1 Harcourt Buildings, Temple, EC4Y 9DA.

MORTON-SANER, Robert, CVO 1966; CBE 1962 (OBE 1946; MBE 1941); HM Diplomatic Service, retired; *b* 30 December 1911; *o s* of late Major A. E. Saner; *m* 1943, Katharine Mary Gordon (*d* 1981); two *d*. *Educ:* Westminster Sch.; Christ Church, Oxford. ICS, 1935; served in United Provinces; Under Sec., Defence Department, Government of India, 1940; Deputy Secretary and Chief Administrative Officer, General Headquarters, New Delhi, 1943–45; served with Resettlement Directorate, 1945–47. Retired from Indian Civil Service and entered Foreign (subseq. Diplomatic) Service, 1947. Served in Madras, 1947–50; Foreign Office, 1950–52; Budapest, 1953–55; NATO Defence College, 1955; Counsellor and Consul-General, Djakarta, 1955–59; Counsellor, Buenos Aires, 1960–64; Consul-General, Antwerp, 1964–70. Acted as Chargé d'Affaires, 1953, 1954, 1956, 1958, 1959, 1960. Member, Skinners' Company. Commander, Order of Leopold II (Belgium). *Recreations:* gardening, old churches. *Address:* Hethe Cottage, Hethe, Oxon OX6 9EU. *Club:* Royal Anglo-Belgian.

MOSAR, Nicolas; barrister; Ambassador from Luxembourg to Italy, 1989–92; *b* Luxembourg, 25 Nov. 1927; *m*; three *c*. *Educ:* Athénée Grand-Ducal; Faculté de Droit, Paris University. Called to Bar, 1955. Mem. Town Council, Luxembourg, 1959–70, 1975–85. Member of Luxembourg Parliament, 1964–74, 1976–85. Social Christian Party: Sec.-Gen., 1959–72; Chm., 1972–74; Chm., Party Parly Gp, 1979–85. Mem., EEC, 1985–88. *Publications:* political and legal papers. *Address:* (office) 8 rue Notre-Dame, 2240 Luxembourg. *T:* 228023, 474020, *Fax:* 462676.

MOSDELL, Lionel Patrick; Judge of the High Court of Kenya, 1966–72, Tanganyika, 1960–64; *b* 29 Aug. 1912; *s* of late William George Mosdell and late Sarah Ellen Mosdell (*née* Gardiner); *m* 1945, Muriel Jean Sillem; one *s* one *d*. *Educ:* Abingdon Sch.; St Edmund Hall, Oxford (MA). Solicitor, England, 1938. Served War of 1939–45, Gunner, Sussex Yeomanry RA, 1939–41; Commnd Rifle Bde, 1941; Libyan Arab Force; Force 133; No 1 Special Force; Egypt, Cyrenaica, Eritrea, Abyssinia, Italy (Capt.). Registrar of Lands and Deeds, N Rhodesia, 1946; Resident Magistrate, 1950; Senior Resident Magistrate, 1956; Barrister, Gray's Inn, 1952; Asst Solicitor, Law Soc., 1964–66. Part-time Chairman: Surrey and Sussex Rent Assessment Panel, 1972–82; Nat. Insce Local Tribunal, London S Region, 1974–84; Immigration Appeal Tribunal, 1975–84; Pensions Appeal Tribunals, 1976–86. Volunteer, SSAFA, 1988–. *Recreation:* reading. *Address:* 10 Orpen Road, Hove, East Sussex BN3 6NJ. *Clubs:* Special Forces, Commonwealth Trust.

MOSELEY, Elwyn Rhys; Commissioner for Local Administration in Wales (Ombudsman), since 1991; *b* 6 Aug. 1943; *s* of late Rev. Luther Moseley and Megan Eiluned Moseley (*née* Howells); *m* 1968, Annick Andrée Guyomard; two *s* one *d*. *Educ:* Caterham Sch.; Queens' Coll., Cambridge (MA). Solicitor. Asst Solicitor, Newport CBC, 1969–72; Sen. Asst Solicitor, Cardiff CBC, 1972–74; Cardiff City Council: City Solicitor, 1974–91; Dep. Chief Exec., 1979–91; Dir of Admin. and Legal Services, 1987–91. *Recreation:* Rugby football. *Address:* (office) Derwen House, Court Road, Bridgend, Mid Glamorgan CF31 1BN. *T:* Bridgend (01656) 661325.
See also T. H. Moseley.

MOSELEY, Sir George (Walker), KCB 1982 (CB 1978); Chairman, British Cement Association, since 1987; *b* 7 Feb. 1925; *o c* of late William Moseley, MBE, and Bella Moseley; *m* 1st, 1950, Anne Mercer (*d* 1989); one *s* one *d*; 2nd, 1990, Madge James. *Educ:* High Sch., Glasgow; St Bees Sch., Cumberland; Wadham Coll., Oxford (MA). Pilot Officer, RAF Levies, Iraq, 1943–48. Asst Principal, Min. of Town and Country Planning, 1950; Asst Private Sec. to Minister of Housing and Local Govt, 1951–52; Private Sec. to Parly Sec., 1952–54; Principal Private Sec. to Minister of Housing and Local Govt, 1963–65; Asst Sec. 1965; Under-Sec. 1970–76; Dep. Sec., DoE, 1976–78, CSD, 1978–80; Second Permanent Sec., DoE, 1980–81, Perm. Sec., 1981–85. Chm., Cement Makers' Fedn, 1987–88. Member: Adv. Council on Public Records, 1989–91; Ancient Monuments Adv. Cttee, 1986–91; Historic Buildings and Monuments Commn for England, 1986–91. Trustee, Civic Trust, 1987– (Chm. Trustees, 1990–). *Address:* Churchmead, Church Lane, Widdington, Saffron Walden, Essex CB11 3SF. *Club:* Royal Air Force.

MOSELEY, (Thomas) Hywel; QC 1985; **His Honour Judge Moseley;** a Circuit Judge, since 1989; *b* 27 Sept. 1936; *s* of late Rev. Luther Moseley and Megan Eiluned Moseley; *m* 1960, Monique Germaine Thérèse Drufin; three *d*. *Educ:* Caterham Sch.; Queens' Coll., Cambridge (MA, LLM). Called to the Bar, Gray's Inn, 1964; in private practice, Cardiff, 1965–89, and London, 1977–89; a Recorder, 1981–89. Lectr in Law, 1960–65, Prof. of Law, 1970–82, UCW, Aberystwyth. Mem., Insolvency Rules Cttee, 1993–. *Publication:* (with B. Rudden) Outline of the Law of Mortgages, 4th edn 1967. *Recreation:* bee-keeping. *Address:* Nantceiro, Llanbadarn Fawr, Aberystwyth, Dyfed SY23 3HW. *T:* Aberystwyth (01970) 623532; 6 Belgrave Court, 25 Cowbridge Road East, Cardiff CF1 9BJ. *T:* Cardiff (01222) 237769.
See also E. R. Moseley.

MOSER, Sir Claus (Adolf), KCB 1973; CBE 1965; FBA 1969; Chairman, British Museum Development Trust, since 1993; Chancellor: University of Keele, since 1986; Open University of Israel, since 1994; Chairman, Harold Holt Ltd, since 1990; *b* Berlin, 24 Nov. 1922; *s* of late Dr Ernest Moser and Lotte Moser; *m* 1949, Mary Oxlin; one *s* two *d*. *Educ:* Frensham Heights Sch.; LSE, Univ. of London. RAF, 1943–46. London Sch. of Economics: Asst Lectr in Statistics, 1946–49; Lectr, 1949–55; Reader in Social Statistics, 1955–61; Prof. of Social Statistics, 1961–70; Vis. Prof. of Social Statistics, 1970–75; Oxford University: Vis. Fellow, Nuffield Coll., 1972–80; Warden, Wadham Coll., 1984–93 (Hon. Fellow, 1993); Pro-Vice Chancellor, 1991–93. Dir, Central Statistical Office and Hd of Govt Statistical Service, 1967–78. Statistical Adviser, Cttee on Higher Educn, 1961–64. Chm., Economist Intelligence Unit, 1979–83; Director: N. M. Rothschild & Sons, 1978–90 (Vice-Chm., 1978–84); The Economist Newspaper, 1979–93; Equity & Law Life Assurance Soc., 1980–87; International Medical Statistics Inc., 1982–88; Octopus Books Ltd, 1982–87; Property & Reversionary Investments plc, 1983–86. Chairman: Royal Opera House, 1974–87; Adv. Bd, Music at Oxford, 1985–; Oxford Playhouse, 1992–; Member: Governing Body, Royal Academy of Music, 1967–79; BBC Music Adv. Cttee, 1971–83; Court of Governors, Royal Shakespeare Theatre, 1982–93; British Amer. Arts Assoc., 1982–; Pilgrim Trust, 1982–; Nat. Commission on Educn, 1991–95. Trustee: BM, 1988–94; LPO, 1988–94; Glyndebourne Opera Arts Trust, 1989–93; Soros Foundn, 1993–. Pres., Royal Statistical Soc., 1978–80; Pres., BAAS, 1989–90. Hon. FRAM, 1970. Hon. Fellow, LSE, 1976; Hon. DSocSci Southampton, 1975; Hon. DSc: Leeds, 1977; City, 1977; Sussex, 1980; Wales, 1990; Liverpool, 1991; South Bank, 1994; Hon. DSc(Econ) London, 1991; Hull, 1994; DUniv: Surrey, 1977; Keele, 1979; York, 1980; Open, 1992; Hon. DTech Brunel, 1981; Dr *hc* Edinburgh, 1991; Heriot-Watt, 1995; Hon. DLitt: W of England, 1993; Brighton, 1994; Hon. DCL Northumbria, 1995. Comdr de l'Ordre National du Mérite (France), 1976; Commander's Cross, Order of Merit (FRG), 1985. *Publications:* Measurement of Levels of Living, 1957; Survey Methods in Social Investigation, 1958; (jtly) Social Conditions in England and Wales, 1958; (jtly) British Towns, 1961; papers in statistical jls. *Recreation:* music. *Address:* 3 Regent's Park Terrace, NW1 7EE. *T:* 0171–485 1619; 7 Ethelred Court, Old Headington, Oxford OX3 9DA. *T:* Oxford (01865) 61028. *Club:* Garrick.

MOSES, Alan George; QC 1990; a Recorder, since 1986; *b* 29 Nov. 1945; *s* of Eric George Rufus Moses, *qv*; *m* 1992, Dinah, *d* of Sir Hugh Casson, *qv* and of Margaret MacDonald Casson, *qv*; two *s* one *d* by a previous marriage. *Educ:* Bryanston Sch.; University Coll., Oxford (Quondam Exhibnr; BA). Called to the Bar, Middle Temple, 1968, Bencher, 1994; Mem., Panel of Junior Counsel to the Crown, Common Law, 1981–90; Junior Counsel to Inland Revenue, Common Law, 1985–90. *Address:* 4–5 Gray's Inn Square, WC1R 5AY.

MOSES, Eric George Rufus, CB 1973; Solicitor of Inland Revenue, 1970–79; *b* 6 April 1914; *s* of Michael and Emily Moses; *m* 1940, Pearl Lipton; one *s*. *Educ:* University Coll. Sch., London; Oriel Coll., Oxford. Called to Bar, Middle Temple, 1938, Hon. Bencher,

1979. Served Royal Artillery, 1940–46 (Major). Asst Solicitor, Inland Revenue, 1953–65, Principal Asst Solicitor, 1965–70. *Recreations:* walking, music. *Address:* Broome Cottage, Castle Hill, Nether Stowey, Bridgwater, Somerset TA5 1NB.

See also A. G. Moses.

MOSES, Very Rev. Dr John Henry; Provost of Chelmsford, since 1982; *b* 12 Jan. 1938; *s* of late Henry William Moses and of Ada Elizabeth Moses; *m* 1964, Susan Elizabeth; one *s* two *d*. *Educ:* Ealing Grammar School; Nottingham Univ. (Gladstone Meml Prize 1958, BA History 1959, PhD 1965); Trinity Hall, Cambridge (Cert. in Education 1960); Lincoln Theological Coll. Deacon 1964, priest 1965; Asst Curate, St Andrew, Bedford, 1964–70; Rector of Coventry East Team Ministry, 1970–77; Examining Chaplain to Bishop of Coventry, 1972–77; Rural Dean of Coventry East, 1973–77; Archdeacon of Southend, 1977–82. Member, Gen. Synod, 1985–. Church Commissioner, 1988–. Chm. Council, Centre for Study of Theology, Univ. of Essex, 1987–. Vis. Fellow, Wolfson Coll., Cambridge, 1987. Rector, Anglia Polytechnic Univ., 1992. *Publications:* The Sacrifice of God, 1992; A Broad and Living Way, 1995. *Address:* The Provost's House, 3 Harlings Grove, Waterloo Lane, Chelmsford, Essex CM1 1YQ. *T:* Chelmsford (01245) 354318.

MOSES, Rev. Leslie Alan; Vicar of All Saints', Margaret Street, London, since 1995; *b* 3 Nov. 1949; *s* of Leslie Moses and Edna (*née* Watson); *m* 1971, Theresa Frances O'Connor; one *s* one *d*. *Educ:* Univ. of Hull (BA Hons History); Univ. of Edinburgh (BD Hons); Edinburgh Theol. Coll. Asst Curate, Old St Paul's, Edinburgh, 1976–79; Rector, St Margaret of Scotland, Leven, 1979–85; Priest-in-Charge, St Margaret of Scotland, Edinburgh, 1986–92; Rector, Old St Paul's, Edinburgh, 1985–95. *Recreations:* reading, visiting museums, galleries, churches and other buildings, exploring places. *Address:* The Vicarage, 7 Margaret Street, W1N 8JQ. *T:* 0171–636 1788.

MOSHINSKY, Elijah; Associate Producer, Royal Opera House, since 1979; *b* 8 Jan. 1946; *s* of Abraham and Eva Moshinsky; *m* 1970, Ruth Dyttman; two *s*. *Educ:* Melbourne Univ. (BA); St Antony's Coll., Oxford. Apptd to Royal Opera House, 1973: work includes original productions of: Peter Grimes, 1975; Lohengrin, 1978; The Rake's Progress, 1979; Macbeth, 1981; Samson et Dalila, 1981; Tannhäuser, 1984; Otello, 1987; Die Entführung aus dem Serail, 1987; Attila, 1990; Simon Boccanegra, 1991; Stiffelio, 1993; Aida, 1994; for ENO: Le Grand Macabre, 1982; The Mastersingers of Nuremberg, 1984; The Bartered Bride, 1985, 1986; for Australian Opera: A Midsummer Night's Dream, 1978; Boris Godunov, 1980; Il Trovatore, 1983; Werther, Rigoletto, 1990; Les Dialogues des Carmélites; for Metropolitan Opera, NY: Un Ballo in Maschera, 1980; Samson, 1987; Ariadne auf Naxos, 1993; Otello, 1994; other opera productions include: Wozzeck, 1976; Antony and Cleopatra, Chicago, 1990; I Vespri Siciliani, Grand Théâtre, Geneva; La Bohème, 1989, La Forza del Destino, 1990, Scottish Opera; Beatrice and Benedict, WNO, 1994; Die Meistersinger von Nürnberg, Holland Fest.; Benvenuto Cellini, 50th Maggio Musicale, Florence, 1987. Producer: Three Sisters, Albery, 1987; Light up the Sky, Globe, 1987; Ivanov, Strand, 1989; Much Ado About Nothing, Strand, 1989; Another Time, Wyndham's, 1989; Shadowlands, Queen's, 1989; Cyrano de Bergerac, Theatre Royal, Haymarket, 1992; Lord of the Flies, RSC, 1995; productions at National Theatre: Troilus and Cressida, 1976; The Force of Habit, 1976; productions for the BBC: All's Well That Ends Well, 1980; A Midsummer Night's Dream, 1981; Cymbeline, 1982; Coriolanus, 1984; Love's Labour's Lost, 1985; Ghosts, 1986; The Rivals, 1987; The Green Man, 1990; Genghis Cohn, 1993; Danton, 1994. Director: Matador, Queen's, 1991; Beckett, Haymarket, 1991; Reflected Glory, Vaudeville, 1992. *Recreations:* telephone conversation, writing film scripts. *Address:* 28 Kidbrooke Grove, SE3 0LG. *T:* 0181–858 4179. *Club:* Garrick.

MOSIMANN, Anton; Owner, Mosimann's (formerly Belfry Club), since 1988; *b* 23 Feb. 1947; *s* of Otto and Olga Mosimann; *m* 1973, Kathrin Roth; two *s*. *Educ:* private school in Switzerland; youngest Chef to be awarded Chef de Cuisine Diplome; 3 degrees. Served apprenticeship in Hotel Baeren, Twann; worked in Canada, France, Italy, Japan, Sweden, Belgium, Switzerland, 1962–; cuisinier at: Villa Lorraine, Brussels; Les Près d'Eugénie, Eugénie-les-Bains; Les Frères Troisgros, Roanne; Paul Bocuse, Collonges au Mont d'Or; Moulin de Mougins; joined Dorchester Hotel, 1975, Maître Chef des Cuisines, 1976–88. Channel Four TV series: Cooking with Mosimann, 1989; Anton Mosimann Naturally, 1991. World Pres., Les Toques Blanches Internationales, 1989–93; Hon. Mem., Chefs' Assoc., Canada, Japan, Switzerland, S Africa. Dr of Culinary Arts *hc* Johnson & Wales Univ., RI, 1990. Numerous Gold Medals in Internat. Cookery Competitions; Chef Award, Caterer and Hotelkeeper, 1985; Personnalité de l'année award, 1986; Glenfiddich Awards Trophy, 1986; Chevalier, Ordre des Coteaux de Champagne, 1990; Grand Cordon Culinaire, Conseil Culinaire Français de Grande Bretagne, 1994. Le Croix de Chevalier du Mérite Agricole (France), 1988. *Publications:* Cuisine à la Carte, 1981; A New Style of Cooking, 1983; Cuisine Naturelle, 1985; Anton Mosimann's Fish Cuisine, 1988; The Art of Anton Mosimann, 1989; Cooking with Mosimann, 1989; Anton Mosimann Naturally, 1991; The Essential Mosimann, 1993. *ecreations:* jogging, travelling, collecting art. *Address:* c/o Mosimann's, 11B West Halkin Street, SW1X 8JL. *T:* 0171–235 9625. *Clubs:* Garrick, Reform.

MOSLEY, family name of **Baron Ravensdale.**

MOSLEY, Max Rufus; President, Fédération Internationale de l'Automobile, since 1993; *b* 13 April 1940; *s* of Sir Oswald Mosley, 6th Bt and Hon. Diana, *d* of 2nd Baron Redesdale; *m* 1960, Jean Taylor; two *s*. *Educ:* abroad; Christ Church, Oxford (MA Natural Sciences). Sec., Oxford Union Society, 1961. Called to the Bar, Gray's Inn, 1964; Dir, March Cars, 1969; Legal Adviser, Formula One Constructors' Assoc., 1971; Pres., Fédn Internat. du Sport Automobile, 1991 (Pres., Manufacturers' Commn, FISA, 1986). Grande Ufficiale dell' Ordine al Merito (Italy), 1994. *Recreations:* ski-ing, snow-boarding, walking. *Address:* Fédération Internationale de l'Automobile, 8 place de la Concorde, 75008 Paris, France. *T:* 43124455. *Club:* Automobile Club de France.

MOSLEY, Nicholas; *see* Ravensdale, 3rd Baron.

MOSS, Very Rev. Basil Stanley; Provost of Birmingham Cathedral, 1973–85; Rector, Cathedral parish of St Philip, 1973–85; *b* 7 Oct. 1918; *e s* of Canon Harry George Moss and Daisy Violet (*née* Jolly); *m* 1950, Rachel Margaret, *d* of Dr Cyril Bailey and Gemma (*née* Creighton); three *d*. *Educ:* Canon Slade Grammar Sch., Bolton; The Queen's Coll., Oxford. Asst Curate, Leigh Parish Church, 1943–45; Sub-Warden, Lincoln Theological Coll., 1946–51; Sen. Tutor, St Catharine's Cumberland Lodge, Windsor Gt Pk, 1951–53; Vicar of St Nathanael with St Katharine, Bristol, 1953–60; Dir, Ordination Training, Bristol Dioc., 1956–66; Residentiary Canon of Bristol Cath., 1960–66, Hon. Canon, 1966–72; Chief Secretary, Advisory Council for the Church's Ministry, 1966–72; Chaplain to Church House, Westminster, 1966–72; Examining Chaplain to Bishop of Bristol, 1956–72, to Bishop of Birmingham, 1985–. Chm., Birmingham Community Relations Council, 1973–81. *Publications:* Clergy Training Today, 1964; (ed) Crisis for Baptism, 1966; (contrib.) Living the Faith, 1980. *Recreations:* walking, music. *Address:* 25 Castle Grove, Old Swinford, Stourbridge DY8 2HH. *T:* Stourbridge (01384) 378799. *Club:* Stourbridge Rotary.

MOSS, Charles James, CBE 1977; Director, National Institute of Agricultural Engineering, 1964–77; *b* 18 Nov. 1917; *s* of James and Elizabeth Moss; *m* 1939, Joan Bernice Smith; two *d*. *Educ:* Queen Mary Coll., London Univ. (BSc). Rotol Ltd, Gloucester, 1939–43; RAE Farnborough, 1943–45; CIBA Ltd, Cambridge, 1945–51; ICI Ltd, Billingham, 1951–58; Central Engineering Estabt, NCB, Stanhope Bretby, 1958–61; Process Devlt Dept, NCB, London, 1961–63; Vis. Prof., Dept of Agric. Engrg, Univ. of Newcastle upon Tyne, 1972–75; Head of Agr. Engineering Dept, Internat. Rice Res. Inst., Philippines, 1977–80; Liaison scientist and agr. engineer, Internat. Rice Res. Inst., Cairo, 1980–81. *Publications:* papers in learned jls, confs., etc. *Recreations:* gardening, walking. *Address:* 1 Laurel Court, Endcliffe Vale Road, Sheffield, South Yorks S10 3DU.

MOSS, Christopher John; QC 1994; a Recorder, since 1993; *b* 4 Aug. 1948; *s* of John (Jack) Gordon Moss and Joyce (Joy) Mirren Moss (*née* Stephany); *m* 1st, 1971, Gail Susan Pearson (marr. diss. 1987); one *s* two *d*; 2nd, 1988, Tracy Louise Levy; one *s* one *d*. *Educ:* Bryanston Sch.; University Coll. London (LLB). Called to the Bar, Gray's Inn, 1972. *Recreations:* television soap operas, playing the piano and accordion. *Address:* 5 Essex Court, Temple, EC4Y 9AH. *T:* 0171–583 2825.

MOSS, David Christopher; Commercial Director, Railtrack, since 1993; Board Member, Railtrack Group plc and Railtrack plc, since 1994; *b* 17 April 1946; *s* of Charles Clifford Moss and Marjorie Sylvia Moss (*née* Hutchings); *m* 1971, Angela Mary Wood; one *s*. *Educ:* King's Sch., Chester; Magdalene Coll., Cambridge (BA). Asst Principal, MPBW, 1968; Principal, 1972, DoE, and subseq. Dept of Transport and HM Treasury; Asst Sec., 1980, Dept of Transport and DoE; Under Sec., Internat. Aviation, Dept of Transport, 1988–93. Pres, European Civil Aviation Conf., 1990–93; Bd Chm., Jt Aviation Authorities, 1990–93. *Recreations:* opera, ecclesiastical architecture, wine. *Address:* Railtrack, 40 Bernard Street, WC1N 1BY. *T:* 0171–344 7100. *Club:* United Oxford & Cambridge University.

MOSS, David John; Chief Executive, Southampton University Hospitals Trust, since 1993; *b* 23 May 1947; *s* of John Henry Moss and Doris (*née* Fenna); *m* 1975, Susan Elizabeth Runnalls; three *s*. *Educ:* Sevenoaks Sch.; St John's Coll., Cambridge (MA); Poly. of Central London (Dip. Management Studies). IPFA; MHSM; FCMA; FIMgt. Management Trainee and Management Accounting, Philips Lamps, 1968–73; St Thomas' Hosp., 1973–74; Dist Finance Office, Enfield Health Dist, 1974–79; Dist. Treasurer, E Dorset HA, 1979–86; General Manager: Poole Gen. Hosp., 1986–88; Southampton Gen. Hosp., 1988–91; Southampton Univ. Hosps, 1991–93. *Publications:* (jtly) Managing Nursing, 1984; articles in professional jls. *Recreations:* cricket, golf, tennis, badminton, history, opera, walking. *Address:* Tuckswood, 41 Pinewood Road, Ferndown, Dorset BH22 9RP.

MOSS, (Sir) David John E.; *see* Edwards-Moss.

MOSS, David Joseph, CMG 1989; HM Diplomatic Service; High Commissioner in Kuala Lumpur, since 1994; *b* 6 Nov. 1938; *s* of Herbert Joseph and Irene Gertrude Moss; *m* 1961, Joan Lillian Moss; one *d* (one *s* decd). *Educ:* Hampton Grammar Sch. CS Commn, 1956; FO, 1957; RAF, 1957–59; FO, 1959–62; Third Sec., Bangkok, 1962–65; FO, 1966–69; First Sec., La Paz, 1969–70; FCO, 1970–73; First Sec. and Head of Chancery, The Hague, 1974–77; First Sec., FCO, 1978–79, Counsellor, 1979–83; Counsellor, Hd of Chancery and Dep. Perm. Rep., UK Mission, Geneva, 1983–87; Asst. Under-Sec. of State, FCO, 1987–90; High Comr, New Zealand, 1990–94. *Recreations:* reading, listening to music. *Address:* c/o Foreign and Commonwealth Office, SW1A 2AH.

MOSS, Elaine Dora; Children's Books Adviser to The Good Book Guide, 1980–86; *b* 8 March 1924; *d* of Percy Philip Levy and Maude Agnes Levy (*née* Simmons); *m* 1950, John Edward Moss, FRICS, FAI; two *d*. *Educ:* St Paul's Girls' Sch.; Bedford Coll. for Women (BA Hons); Univ. of London Inst. of Educn (DipEd); University College London Sch. of Librarianship (ALA). Teacher, Stoatley Rough Sch., Haslemere, 1945–47; Asst Librarian, Bedford Coll., 1947–50; freelance journalist and broadcaster (Woman's Hour, The Times, TES, TLS, The Spectator, Signal, etc.), 1956 ; Editor and Selector, NBL's Children's Books of the Year, 1970–79; Librarian, Fleet Primary Sch., ILEA, 1976–82. Eleanor Farjeon Award, 1976. *Publications:* texts for several picture books, incl. Polar, 1976; catalogues for Children's Books of the Year, 1970–79; Picture Books for Young People 9–13, 1981, 3rd edn 1992; Part of the Pattern: a personal journey through the world of children's books 1960–1985, 1986. *Recreations:* walking, art galleries, reading, ballet. *Address:* 7 St Anne's Close, N6 6AR.

MOSS, Gabriel Stephen; QC 1989; *b* 8 Sept. 1949; *m* 1979, Judith; one *d*. *Educ:* University of Oxford (Eldon Schol. 1975; BA Jurisprudence, BCL, MA). Lectr, Univ. of Connecticut Law Sch., 1972–73. Called to the Bar, Lincoln's Inn, 1974; Hardwicke Schol., 1971, Cassel Schol., 1975. Jt DTI Inspector, Bestwood plc, 1989. Formerly (part-time) Lectr/ Tutor, Oxford, LSE, Council of Legal Educn. Member: Bd, Insolvency Res. Unit, KCL, 1991; Insolvency Law Sub-Cttee, Consumer and Commercial Law Cttee, Law Soc., 1991–; Chm. Editl Bd, Insolvency Intelligence, 1994– (Mem., 1991–). *Publications:* (ed with David Marks) Rowlatt on Principal and Surety, 4th edn 1982; (with Gavin Lightman) The Law of Receivers of Companies, 1986, 2nd edn 1994; (with Martin Pascoe) Insolvency chapter, Ryde on Rating, 1990. *Recreations:* chess, gardening, foreign travel, tennis. *Address:* 3/4 South Square, Gray's Inn, WC1R 5HP. *T:* 0171–696 9900, *Fax:* 0171–696 9911.

MOSS, James Richard Frederick, OBE 1955; FRINA; RCNC; Founder, Chairman, 1978–94, and President, since 1994, Polynous, Cambridge; Chief Executive, Balaena Structures (North Sea), 1974–77, retired; *b* 26 March 1916; *s* of late Lt-Cdr J. G. Moss, RN, and late Kathleen Moss (*née* Steinberg); *m* 1941, Celia Florence Lucas; three *d*. *Educ:* Marlborough College; Trinity Coll., Cambridge (1st Cl. Hons Mech. Sci. Tripos and Maths Pt I, MA); RCNC, 1941. Constructor Comdr to C-in-C, Far East Fleet, 1949–52; Chief Constructor, HM Dockyard, Singapore, 1955–58; Supt, Naval Construction Research Estab., Dunfermline, 1965–68; Dir, Naval Ship Production, 1968–74. *Recreations:* yachting, music. *Address:* 13 Beaufort Place, Thompsons Lane, Cambridge CB5 8AG. *T:* Cambridge (01223) 328583. *Club:* Royal Naval Sailing Association.

MOSS, Jane Hope; *see* Bown, J. H.

MOSS, (John) Michael; Command Secretary to Second Sea Lord and Commander-in-Chief Naval Home Command, since 1994, and Assistant Under-Secretary of State (Naval Personnel), since 1989, Ministry of Defence; *b* 21 April 1936; *s* of late Ernest and of Mary Moss. *Educ:* Accrington Grammar Sch.; King's Coll., Cambridge (Foundn Scholar; MA Math. Tripos, Pt I Cl. I, Pt II Wrangler, Pt III Hons with Dist.). National Service, RAF Educn Branch: Pilot Officer 1958; Flying Officer 1959; Flt Lieut 1960; RAF Technical Coll., Henlow, 1959–60. Asst Principal, Air Min., 1960–63; Private Sec. to Air Member for Supply and Orgn, 1962–63; Principal, Air Min., 1963–64, and MoD, 1964–70; Private Sec. to Parly Under- Sec. of State for Defence for the RAF, 1969–70; Asst Sec., MoD, 1971–72; Estab. Officer, Cabinet Office, 1972–75; Sec., Radcliffe Cttee of Privy Counsellors on Ministerial Memoirs, 1975; returned to MoD as Asst Sec., 1976–83; RCDS, 1983; Asst Under-Sec. of State (Air), MoD (PE), 1984–88; Fellow, Center for Internat. Affairs, Harvard Univ., 1988–89. Cantoris Bass, St Bartholomew-the-Great,

Smithfield, 1968–. *Recreations:* travel, photography, choral singing. *Address:* c/o Royal Bank of Scotland, 119 Blackburn Road, Accrington, Lancs BB5 1JJ. *Clubs:* Royal Air Force, United Oxford & Cambridge University.

MOSS, John Ringer, CB 1972; adviser to companies in Associated British Foods Group, since 1980; *b* 15 Feb. 1920; 2nd *s* of late James Moss and Louisa Moss; *m* 1946, Edith Bland Wheeler; two *s* one *d. Educ:* Manchester Gram. Sch.; Brasenose Coll., Oxford (MA). War Service, mainly India and Burma, 1940–46; Capt., RE, attached Royal Bombay Sappers and Miners. Entered Civil Service (MAFF) as Asst Princ., 1947; Princ. Private Sec. to Minister of Agric., Fisheries and Food, 1959–61; Asst Sec., 1961; Under-Sec., Gen. Agricultural Policy Gp, 1967–70; Dep. Sec., 1970–80. Mem., Economic Develt Cttee for Agriculture, 1969–70. Specialist Adviser to House of Lords' Select Cttee on European Communities, 1982–90. Chm. Council, RVC, 1983–90. *Recreations:* music, travel. *Address:* 16 Upper Hollis, Great Missenden, Bucks HP16 9HP. *T:* Great Missenden (01494) 862676.

MOSS, Ven. Leonard Godfrey; Archdeacon of Hereford and Canon Residentiary of Hereford Cathedral, since 1991; *b* 11 July 1932; *s* of Clarence Walter Moss and Frances Lilian Vera Moss; *m* 1954, Everell Annette (*née* Reed); two *s* one *d. Educ:* Regent St Poly., London; King's Coll., London and Warminster (BD, AKC 1959). Quantity Surveyor's Asst, L. A. Francis and Sons, 1948–54; RE (National Service), 1954–56. Ordained: deacon, 1960; priest, 1961; Assistant curate: St Margaret, Putney, 1960–63; St Dunstan, Cheam, 1963–67; Vicar: Much Dewchurch with Llanwarne and Llandinabo, 1967–72; Marden with Amberley and Wisteston, 1972–84; Hereford Diocesan Ecumenical Officer, 1969–83; Prebendary of Hereford Cathedral, 1979–; Bishop of Hereford's Officer for Social Responsibility and Non-Residentiary Canon of Hereford Cathedral, 1984–91; Priest-in-charge, Marden with Amberley and Wisteston, 1992–94. Proctor in Convocation, 1970–. *Publications:* (contrib.) The People, the Land and the Church, 1987; articles and reviews in theol jls. *Recreations:* reading, listening to music, walking, folk-dancing. *Address:* The Archdeacon's House, The Close, Hereford HR1 2NG. *T:* Hereford (01432) 272873.

MOSS, Malcolm Douglas; MP (C) Cambridgeshire North East, since 1987; *b* 6 March 1943; *s* of Norman Moss and Annie Moss (*née* Gay); *m* 1965, Vivien Lorraine (*née* Peake); two *d. Educ:* Audenshaw Grammar Sch.; St John's Coll., Cambridge (BA 1965, MA 1968). Teaching Cert 1966. Asst Master, 1966–68, Head of Dept, 1968–70, Blundell's Sch.; Insurance Consultant, 1970–72, Gen. Manager, 1972–74, Barwick Associates; Chairman: Mandrake Gp plc, 1986–88; Mandrake Associates Ltd (formerly Mandrake (Insurance and Finance Brokers)), 1986–93 (Dir, 1974–); Fens Business Enterprise Trust, 1983–87 (Dir, 1983–). *Recreations:* tennis, ski-ing, amateur dramatics, gardening. *Address:* Boston House, South Brink, Wisbech, Cambs PE14 0RT; 88 St George's Square, SW1V 3QX. *T:* 0171–821 0269. *Club:* United Oxford & Cambridge University.

MOSS, Martin Grenville, CBE 1975; Director of National Trust Enterprises Ltd, 1985–89; Chairman, Whitchurch Silk Mill (Trading) Ltd, since 1992; *b* 17 July 1923; *s* of late Horace Grenville Moss and Gladys Ethel (*née* Wootton); *m* 1953, Jane Hope Bown, *qv*; two *s* one *d. Educ:* Lancing Coll. Served RAF, 1942–46 (Sqdn Ldr, pilot). Managing Director: Woollands Knightsbridge, 1953–66; Debenham & Freebody, 1964–66; Simpson (Piccadilly) Ltd, 1966–73, 1981–85; Chm. and Chief Exec. Officer, May Department Stores Internat., USA, 1974–80. Member: Export Council of Europe, 1960–64; Design Council, 1964–75 (Dep. Chm., 1971–75); Council, RCA, 1953–58; Royal Fine Art Commn, 1982–84; Council, RSA, 1977–94 (Chm., 1983–85). Formerly Governor: Sevenoaks Sch.; Ravensbourne Coll. of Art and Design; W Surrey Coll. of Art and Design. Order of the Finnish Lion, 1970. *Recreations:* gardening, painting, classic cars. *Address:* Parsonage Farm, Bentworth, Alton, Hants GU34 5RB. *T:* Alton (01420) 562175. *Club:* Royal Air Force.

MOSS, Michael; *see* Moss, J. M.

MOSS, Norman J.; *see* Jordan-Moss.

MOSS, Ronald Trevor; His Honour Judge Moss; a Circuit Judge, since 1993; *b* 1 Oct. 1942; *s* of Maurice and Sarah Moss; *m* 1971, Cindy (*née* Fiddleman); one *s* one *d. Educ:* Hendon County Grammar School; Nottingham University (Upper Second BA; Hons Law). Admitted Solicitor, 1968; Partner, Moss Beachley, solicitors, 1973–84; Metropolitan Stipendiary Magistrate, 1984–93; Asst Recorder, 1986–90; Recorder, 1990–93. Chm., Inner London Juvenile Courts, subseq. Inner London Youth and Family Panel, 1986–93. Mem. Cttee, London Criminal Courts Solicitors' Assoc., 1982–84. *Recreations:* golf, Watford Football Club. *Address:* c/o Luton Crown Court, 7 George Street, Luton LU1 2AA. *Club:* Moor Park Golf.

MOSS, Stirling, OBE 1959; FIE; Racing Motorist, 1947–62, retired; Managing Director, Stirling Moss Ltd; Director: Designs Unlimited Ltd; SM Design & Interior Decorating Co.; Hankoe Stove Enamelling Ltd; *b* 17 Sept. 1929; *m* 1st, 1957, Kathleen Stuart (marr. diss. 1960), *y d* of F. Stuart Moison, Montreal, Canada; 2nd, 1964, Elaine (marr. diss. 1968), 2nd *d* of A. Barbarino, New York; one *d*; 3rd, 1980, Susan, *y d* of Stuart Paine, London; one *s. Educ:* Haileybury and Imperial Service Coll. Brit. Nat. Champion, 1950, 1951, 1952, 1954, 1955, 1956, 1957, 1958, 1959, 1961; Tourist Trophy, 1950, 1951, 1955, 1958, 1959, 1960, 1961; Coupe des Alpes, 1952, 1953, 1954; Alpine Gold Cup (three consecutive wins), 1954. Only Englishman to win Italian Mille Miglia, 1955. Competed in 494 races, rallies, sprints, land speed records and endurance runs, and won 222 of these. Successes include Targa Florio, 1955; Brit. Grand Prix, 1955, 1957; Ital. GP, 1956, 1957, 1959; NZ GP, 1956, 1959; Monaco GP, 1956, 1960, 1961; Leguna Seca GP, 1960, 1961; US GP, 1959, 1960; Aust. GP, 1956; Bari GP, 1956; Pescara GP, 1957; Swedish GP, 1957; Dutch GP, 1958; Argentine GP, 1958; Morocco GP, 1958; Buenos Aires GP, 1958; Melbourne GP, 1958; Villareal GP, 1958; Caen GP, 1958; Portuguese GP, 1959; S African GP, 1960; Cuban GP, 1960; Austrian GP, 1960; Cape GP, 1960; Watkins Glen GP, 1960; German GP, 1961; Modena GP, 1961. Twice voted Driver of the Year, 1954 and 1961. *Publications:* Stirling Moss's Book of Motor Sport, 1955; In the Track of Speed, 1957; Stirling Moss's Second Book of Motor Sport, 1958; Le Mans, 1959; My Favourite Car Stories, 1960; A Turn at the Wheel, 1961; All But My Life, 1963; Design and Behaviour of the Racing Car, 1964; How to Watch Motor Racing, 1975; Motor Racing and All That, 1980; My Cars, My Career, 1987; Great Drives in the Lakes and Dales, 1993; *relevant publication:* Stirling Moss, by Robert Raymond, 1953. *Recreations:* snow-ski-ing, water ski-ing, subaqua, designing, model making, the theatre, and designing. *Address:* (business) Stirling Moss Ltd, 46 Shepherd Street, W1Y 8JN; (residence) 44 Shepherd Street, W1Y 8JN. *Clubs:* British Racing Drivers', British Automobile Racing, British Racing and Sports Car, Road Racing Drivers of America, 200 mph, Lord's Taverners, Royal Automobile; Internationale des Anciens Pilotes des Grand Prix; Chm. or Pres. of 36 motoring clubs.

MOSS, Trevor Simpson, PhD, ScD; FInstP; Editor, Journal of Infra Red Physics and Technology, since 1961; *b* 28 Jan. 1921; *s* of William Moss and Florence Elizabeth (*née* Simpson); *m* 1948, Audrey (*née* Nelson). *Educ:* Alleynes, Uttoxeter; Downing Coll., Cambridge. MA, PhD, ScD Cantab. Research on radar, Royal Aircraft Establishment, 1941–43; research on radar and semiconductors, Telecommunications Research Estabt, 1943–53; RAE, 1953–78; Dep. Dir, Royal Signals and Radar Estabt, 1978–81. Mem., Lloyd's, 1979–. Various hon. commissions in RAF, 1942–45. Max Born Medal, German and British Physical Societies, 1975; Dennis Gabor award, Internat. Soc. of Optical Engrs, 1988. *Publications:* Photoconductivity, 1952; Optical Properties of Semiconductors, 1959; Semiconductor Optoelectronics, 1973; Handbook of Semiconductors, vol. I, Basic Properties of Semiconductors, 1980, 2nd edn (ed P. T. Landsberg) 1992, vol. II, Optical Properties of Semiconductors, 1980, 2nd edn (ed Balkanski) 1994, vol. III, Materials and Preparation, 1980, 2nd edn (ed Mahajari) 1994, vol. IV, Device Physics, 1980, 2nd edn (ed C. Hilsum) 1993; approx. 100 res. papers in internat. physics jls. *Address:* 2 Shelsley Meadow, Colwall, Malvern, Worcs WR13 6PX. *T:* Colwall (01684) 40079.

MÖSSBAUER, Rudolf L., PhD; Professor of Experimental Physics, Technische Universität München, since 1977; *b* Munich, 31 Jan. 1929; *m*; one *s* two *d. Educ:* High Sch. and Technische Hochschule, München (equiv. Bachelor's and Master's degrees). PhD (München) 1958. Thesis work, Max Planck Inst., Heidelberg, 1955–57; Research Fellow: Technische Hochschule, München, 1958–59, and at Caltech, 1960–61; Prof. of Physics, CIT, 1962–64; Prof. of Experimental Physics, München, 1965–71; Dir, Institut Max von Laue-Paul Langevin, and French-German-British High-Flux-Reactor at Grenoble, 1972–77. Member: Bavarian Acad. of Sci.; Nat. Acad. of Scis, Washington; Amer. Acad. of Arts and Scis; Pontifical Acad.; Soviet Acad. of Sci.; Acad. Leopoldina, etc. Hon. degrees Oxford, Leuwen, Madrid, Grenoble, etc. Nobel Prize for Physics (jtly), 1961, and numerous other awards. Bavarian Order of Merit, 1962. *Publications:* on gamma resonance spectroscopy (Mössbauer effect) and on neutrino physics. *Recreations:* photography, music, mountaineering. *Address:* Technische Universität München, Physik-Department E 15, James-Franck-Strasse, 85748 Garching, Germany.

MOSSELMANS, Carel Maurits, TD 1961; Chairman: Rothschild International Asset Management, since 1989; Exco (formerly Exco International) plc, since 1991; Janson Green Holdings, since 1993; Janson Green Ltd, since 1993; *b* 9 March 1929; *s* of Adriaan Willem Mosselmans and Jonkvrouwe Nancy Henriette Mosselmans (*née* van der Wyck); *m* 1962, Hon. Prudence Fiona McCorquodale, *d* of 1st Baron McCorquodale of Newton, KCVO, PC; two *s. Educ:* Stowe; Trinity Coll., Cambridge (MA Modern Langs and Hist.). Queen's Bays 2nd Dragoon Guards, 1947–49; City of London Yeomanry (Rough Riders), TA, 1949; Inns of Court and City Yeomanry, 1961; Lt-Col comdg Regt, 1963. Joined Sedgwick Collins & Co., 1952 (Dir, 1963); Director: Sedgwick Forbes Hldgs, 1978; Sedgwick Forbes Bland Payne, 1979; Chm., Sedgwick Ltd, 1981–84; Dep. Chm., 1982–84, Chm., 1984–89, Sedgwick Group plc; Chairman: Sedgwick Lloyd's Underwriting Agents (formerly Sedgwick Forbes (Lloyd's Underwriting Agents)), 1974–89; The Sumitomo Marine & Fire Insurance Co. (Europe), 1981–90 (Dir, 1975–81); Rothschild Asset Management, 1990–93 (Dir, 1989–); Director: Coutts & Co., 1981–95; Rothschilds Continuation Ltd, 1990–. Vice-Pres., BIIBA, 1987–89. *Recreations:* shooting, fishing, golf, music. *Address:* 15 Chelsea Square, SW3 6LF. *T:* 0171–352 0621. *Clubs:* White's, Cavalry and Guards.

MOSTYN, 5th Baron, *cr* 1831; **Roger Edward Lloyd Lloyd-Mostyn,** Bt 1778; MC 1943; *b* 17 April 1920; *e s* of 4th Baron Mostyn; *S* father, 1965; *m* 1943, Yvonne Margaret Stuart (marr. diss., 1957), *y d* of A. Stuart Johnston, Henshall Hall, Congleton, Cheshire; one *s* one *d*; 2nd, 1957, Mrs Sheila Edmondson Shaw, OBE, DL, *o c* of Major Reginald Fairweather, Stockwell Manor, Silverton, Devon, and of Mrs Fairweather, Yew Tree Cottage, Fordcombe, Kent. *Educ:* Eton; Royal Military College, Sandhurst. 2nd Lt, 9th Queen's Royal Lancers, 1939. Served War 1939–45, France, North Africa, and Italy (wounded, despatches, MC). Temp. Major, 1946. *Heir: s* Hon. Llewellyn Roger Lloyd Lloyd-Mostyn [*b* 26 Sept. 1948; *m* 1974, Denise Suzanne, *d* of Roger Duvanel; one *s* one *d. Educ:* Eton. Called to the Bar, Middle Temple, 1973]. *Address:* Mostyn Hall, Mostyn, Clwyd, North Wales. *T:* Mostyn (01745) 560222.

MOSTYN, Gen. Sir David; *see* Mostyn, Gen. Sir J. D. F.

MOSTYN, Gen. Sir (Joseph) David (Frederick), KCB 1984; CBE 1974 (MBE 1962); Adjutant General, 1986–88; Aide de Camp General to the Queen, 1987–89; *b* 28 Nov. 1928; *s* of late J. P. Mostyn, Arundel, and of Mrs J. D. S. Keenan, Farnham; *m* 1952, Diana Patricia Sheridan; four *s* two *d. Educ:* Downside; RMA Sandhurst; psc, rcds. Commnd Oxf. and Bucks LI, 1948; served BAOR, Greece, Cyprus, UK, 1948–58; Canadian Army Staff Coll., 1958; WO, 1959–61; Coy Comdr 1st Green Jackets, Malaya, Brunei, Borneo, 1962–63 (despatches); Instructor, Staff Coll., Camberley, 1964–67; MoD, 1967–69; CO 2 RGJ, BAOR and NI, 1969–71; Comdt Officers' Wing, Sch. of Infantry, 1972; Comdr 8 Inf. Bde, NI, 1972–74; Dep. Dir Army Training, 1974–75; RCDS 1976; BGS, HQ BAOR, 1977; Dir Personal Services (Army), 1978–80; GOC Berlin and Comdt British Sector, 1980–83; Military Sec., 1983–86. Col Commandant: The Light Div., 1983–86; Army Legal Corps, 1983–88. Special Comr, Duke of York's Royal Mil. Sch., Dover, 1989–. Chairman: Lyme Regis Hosp. Trust, 1990–; Council, Dorset Respite and Hosp. Trust, 1990–. President: Uplyme and Lym Valley Soc., 1990–; Devon County Royal British Legion, 1992–. Kt SMO Malta, 1974. *Publications:* articles in mil. and RUSI jls. *Recreations:* maintaining a home for the family; all field sports. *Address:* c/o Lloyds Bank Plc, 54 Broad Street, Lyme Regis, Dorset DT7 3QR. *Club:* Army and Navy.

MOSTYN, Sir William Basil John, 15th Bt *cr* 1670, of Talacre, Flintshire; *b* 15 Oct. 1975; *s* of Sir Jeremy John Anthony Mostyn, 14th Bt and of Cristina, *o d* of Marchese Orengo, Turin; *S* father, 1988. *Heir: uncle* Trevor Alexander Richard Mostyn, *b* 23 May 1946. *Address:* The Coach House, Church Lane, Lower Heyford, Oxon.

MOTHERWELL, Bishop of, (RC), since 1983; **Rt. Rev. Joseph Devine;** *b* 7 Aug. 1937; *s* of Joseph Devine and Christina Murphy. *Educ:* Blairs Coll., Aberdeen; St Peter's Coll., Dumbarton; Scots Coll., Rome. Ordained priest in Glasgow, 1960; postgraduate work in Rome (PhD), 1960–64; Private Sec. to Archbishop of Glasgow, 1964–65; Assistant Priest in a Glasgow parish, 1965–67; Lecturer in Philosophy, St Peter's Coll., Dumbarton, 1967–74; a Chaplain to Catholic Students in Glasgow Univ., 1974–77; Titular Bishop of Voli and Auxiliary to Archbishop of Glasgow, 1977–83. Papal Bene Merenti Medal, 1962. *Recreations:* general reading, music, Association football. *Address:* 17 Viewpark Road, Motherwell ML1 3ER. *T:* Motherwell (01698) 63715.

MOTION, Andrew; writer; Professor of Creative Writing, University of East Anglia, since 1995; *b* 26 Oct. 1952; *s* of Andrew Richard Motion and Catherine Gillian Motion; *m* 1st, 1973, Joanna Jane Powell (marr. diss. 1983); 2nd, 1985, Janet Elisabeth Dalley; two *s* one *d. Educ:* Radley Coll.; University Coll., Oxford (BA 1st Cl. Hons, MLitt). Lectr in English, Univ. of Hull, 1977–81; Editor of Poetry Review, 1981–83; Poetry Editor, 1983–89, Editl Dir, 1985–87, Chatto & Windus. FRSL 1982. *Publications: poetry:* The Pleasure Steamers, 1978, 3rd edn 1983; Independence, 1981; The Penguin Book of Contemporary British Poetry (anthology), 1982; Secret Narratives, 1983; Dangerous Play, 1984 (Rhys Meml Prize); Natural Causes, 1987 (Dylan Thomas Award); Love in a Life, 1991; The Price of Everything, 1994; *criticism:* The Poetry of Edward Thomas, 1981; Philip Larkin, 1982; (ed) William Barnes: selected poems, 1994; *biography:* The Lamberts, 1986 (Somerset Maugham Award, 1987); Philip Larkin: a writer's life, 1993 (Whitbread

Award, 1993); *novels:* The Pale Companion, 1989; Famous for the Creatures, 1991. *Recreation:* cooking. *Address:* c/o Faber & Faber, 3 Queen Square, WC1N 3AU.

MOTSON, John Walker; BBC Sports Commentator, since 1971; *b* 10 July 1945; *s* of late William and Gwendoline Motson; *m* 1976, Anne Jobling; one *s*. *Educ:* Culford Sch., Bury St Edmunds. Barnet Press, 1963–67; Morning Telegraph, Sheffield, 1967–68; BBC Radio Sport, 1968–71; BBC TV Sport, 1971–. Commentator: 17 FA Cup Finals, 1977–; 6 World Cup Series, 1974–; 5 European Championships, 1976–92. *Publications:* Second to None: great teams of post-war soccer, 1972; (with J. Rowlinson) History of the European Cup, 1980; Match of the Day: the complete record, 1992, 1994. *Recreation:* running half-marathons. *Address:* c/o BBC Sport, Kensington House, W14 0PX. *T:* 0181–895 6972. *Clubs:* Scribes West International; Rugby.

MOTT, Gregory George Sidney, CBE 1979; Managing Director, Vickers Shipbuilding and Engineering Ltd, 1979–84, retired; *b* 11 Feb. 1925; *s* of Sidney Cyril George Mott and Elizabeth Rolinda Mott; *m* 1949, Jean Metcalfe. *Educ:* Univ. of Melbourne (BMechE Hons). Trainee Manager, Vickers Armstrong Ltd Naval Yard, 1948–49; Supervising Engr, A. E. Turner and John Coates, London, 1950–52; Sen. Draughtsman, Melbourne Harbour Trust Comrs, 1952–56; joined Vickers Armstrong Ltd, Barrow, trng on submarine construction, 1956; seconded to Naval Section Harwell, for shielding design DS/MP1 (specialised in computer technol.), 1957–59; returned to Barrow as Project Manager, Dreadnought, 1959–61; Technical Manager, Nuclear, 1961–64; Projects Controller, 1964–67; Local Dir, Vickers Ltd Shipbuilding Gp, 1966; responsible for Special Projects Div., incl. Oceanics Dept, 1968–72; Man. Dir, Vickers Oceanics Ltd, on formation of company, 1972–75; Dir, Vickers Ltd Shipbuilding Gp, and Gen. Manager, Barrow Shipbuilding Works (retained directorship, Vickers Oceanics Ltd, resigned later), 1975–77; Dir, Vickers Shipbuilding Gp Ltd, 1977; Gen. Manager and Dir, Barrow Engrg Works, Vickers Shipbuilding Gp Ltd, 1978.

MOTT, John Charles Spencer, FEng; Chairman, William Sindall plc, 1990–94 (Director, 1989–94); *b* Beckenham, Kent, 18 Dec. 1926; *m* 1953, Patricia Mary (*née* Fowler); two *s*. *Educ:* Balgowan Central Sch., Beckenham, Kent; Brixton Sch. of Building; Battersea Polytechnic; Rutherford Coll. of Technology, Newcastle upon Tyne. FICE, FIStructE. Served war, Lieut, Royal Marines, 1943–46. Indentured as Engr with L. G. Mouchel & Partners, 1949–52; joined Kier Ltd, 1952; Agent on heavy civil engrg contracts, 1952–63; Chairman: French Kier Holdings plc, 1974–86 (Dir, on merger, 1973, Chief Exec., 1974–84); May Gurney Hldgs Ltd, 1986–89. Director: Kier Ltd, 1963; J. L. Kier & Co. Ltd (Holding Co.), 1968; RMC plc, 1986–94. Mem. Council, Fellowship of Engrg, 1983–86; Mem. Council, 1973–75, 1986–87, and Vice Pres., 1986–87, ICE; Mem., Bragg Cttee on Falsework, 1972–74. CIMgt. *Address:* 91 Long Road, Cambridge CB2 2HE. *Club:* Danish.

MOTT, Sir John (Harmar), 3rd Bt, *cr* 1930; Regional Medical Officer, Department of Health and Social Security, 1969–84; *b* 21 July 1922; *s* of 2nd Bt and Mary Katherine (*d* 1972) *d* of late Rev. A. H. Stanton; *S* father, 1964; *m* 1950, Elizabeth (*née* Carson); one *s* two *d*. *Educ:* Radley Coll.; New Coll., Oxford. MA Oxford, 1948; BM, BCh, 1951. Served War of 1939–45: Pilot, Royal Air Force, 1943–46. Middlesex Hospital: House Physician, 1951; House Surgeon, 1952. Mem., RCGP. *Recreation:* photography. *Heir:* *s* David Hugh Mott [*b* 1 May 1952; *m* 1980, Amanda Jane, *d* of Lt-Comdr D. W. P. Fryer, RN; two *s*]. *Address:* Staniford, Brookside, Kingsley, Cheshire WA6 8BG. *T:* Kingsley (01928) 88123.

MOTT, Michael Duncan; His Honour Judge Mott; a Circuit Judge, since 1985; *b* 8 Dec. 1940; *s* of Francis J. Mott and Gwendolen Mott; *m* 1970, Phyllis Ann Gavin; two *s*. *Educ:* Rugby Sch.; Caius Coll., Cambridge (Exhibnr, MA). Called to Bar, Inner Temple, 1963; practised Midland and Oxford Circuit, 1964–69; Resident Magistrate, Kenya, 1969–71; resumed practice, Midland and Oxford Circuit, 1972; a Deputy Circuit Judge, 1976–80; a Recorder, 1980–85. *Recreations:* tennis, ski-ing, travel, music. *Address:* c/o Circuit Administrator, Midland and Oxford Circuit, Priory Courts, 33 Bull Street, Birmingham B4 6DW. *Clubs:* Cambridge Union Society; Union and County (Worcester).

MOTT, Sir Nevill (Francis), CH 1995; Kt 1962; FRS 1936; MA Cantab; Cavendish Professor of Physics, Cambridge University, 1954–71; Senior Research Fellow, Imperial College, London, 1971–73, Fellow, 1978; *b* 30 Sept. 1905; *s* of C. F. Mott, late Dir of Educn, Liverpool, and Lilian Mary Reynolds; *m* 1930, Ruth Horder; two *d*. *Educ:* Clifton Coll.; St John's Coll., Cambridge. Lecturer at Manchester Univ., 1929–30; Fellow and Lecturer, Gonville and Caius Coll., Cambridge, 1930–33; Melville Wills Prof. of Theoretical Physics in the Univ. of Bristol, 1933–48; Henry Overton Wills Prof. and Dir of the Henry Herbert Wills Physical Laboratories, Univ. of Bristol, 1948–54. Master of Gonville and Caius Coll., Univ. of Cambridge, 1959–66. Corr. mem., Amer. Acad. of Arts and Sciences, 1954; Pres., International Union of Physics, 1951–57; Pres., Mod. Languages Assoc., 1955; Pres., Physical Soc., 1956–58; Mem. Governing Board of Nat. Inst. for Research in Nuclear Science, 1957–60; Mem. Central Advisory Council for Education for England, 1956–59; Mem. Academic Planning Cttee and Council of University Coll. of Sussex; Chm. Ministry of Education's Standing Cttee on Supply of Teachers, 1959–62; Chairman: Nuffield Foundation's Cttee on Physics Education, 1961–73; Physics Education Cttee (Royal Society and Inst. of Physics), 1965–71. Chairman, Taylor & Francis, Scientific Publishers, 1970–75, Pres., 1976–86. Foreign Associate, Nat. Acad. of Sciences of USA, 1957; Hon. Member: Akademie der Naturforscher Leopoldina, 1964; Société Française de Physique, 1970; Inst. of Metals, Japan, 1975; Sociedad Real Española de Fisica y Quimica, 1980; European Physical Soc., 1985; Hon. Fellow: St John's Coll., Cambridge, 1971; UMIST, 1975; Darwin Coll., Cambridge, 1977; For. Fellow, Indian Nat. Science Acad., 1982. Hon. DSc: Louvain, Grenoble, Paris, Poitiers, Bristol, Ottawa, Liverpool, Reading, Sheffield, London, Warwick, Lancaster, Heriot-Watt, Oxon, East Anglia, Bordeaux, St Andrews, Essex, William and Mary, Stuttgart, Sussex, Marburg, Bar Ilan, Lille, Rome, Lisbon, Cambridge; Hon. Doctorate of Technology, Linköping, Sweden. Hon. FInstP 1972. Hughes Medal of Royal Society, 1941; Royal Medal, 1953; Grande Médaille de la Société Française de Métallurgie, 1970; Copley Medal, 1972; Faraday Medal, IEE, 1973; (jtly) Nobel Prize for Physics, 1977. Chevalier, Ordre Nat. du Mérite, France, 1977. *Publications:* An Outline of Wave Mechanics, 1930; The Theory of Atomic Collisions (with H. S. W. Massey), 1933; The Theory of the Properties of Metals and Alloys (with H. Jones), 1936; Electronic Processes in Ionic Crystals (with R. W. Gurney), 1940; Wave Mechanics and its Applications (with I. N. Snedden), 1948; Elements of Wave Mechanics, 1952; Atomic Structure and the Strength of Metals, 1956; Electronic Processes in Non-Crystalline Materials (with E. A. Davis), 1971, 2nd edn 1979; Elementary Quantum Mechanics, 1972; Metal-Insulator Transitions, 1974, 2nd edn 1990; Conduction in Non-crystalline Materials, 1986, 2nd edn 1993; A Life in Science (autobiog.), 1986; (ed) Can Scientists Believe? some examples of the attitude of scientists to religion, 1991; (with A. Alexandrov) High Temperature Superconductors and other Superfluids, 1994; various contribs to scientific periodicals about Atomic Physics, Metals, Semi-conductors, Superconductors and Photographic Emulsions and Glasses. *Recreation:* photography. *Address:* The Cavendish Laboratory, Madingley Road, Cambridge CB3 0HE; 63 Mount Pleasant, Aspley Guise, Milton Keynes MK17 8JX. *Club:* Athenæum.

MOTT, Philip Charles; QC 1991; a Recorder of the Crown Court, since 1987; *b* 20 April 1948; *s* of Charles Kynaston Mott and Elsie (*née* Smith); *m* 1977, Penelope Ann Caffery; two *d*. *Educ:* King's Coll., Taunton; Worcester Coll., Oxford (MA). Called to the Bar, Inner Temple, 1970; in practice on Western Circuit, 1970–. *Recreations:* the countryside, sailing. *Address:* 35 Essex Street, Temple, WC2R 3AR. *T:* 0171–353 6381. *Club:* Bar Yacht.

MOTTELSON, Prof. Ben R., PhD; Danish physicist; Professor, Nordic Institute for Theoretical Atomic Physics, Copenhagen, since 1957; *b* Chicago, Ill, USA, 9 July 1926; *s* of Goodman Mottelson and Georgia Mottelson (*née* Blum); *m* 1948, Nancy Jane Reno; three *c*; became a Danish citizen, 1971. *Educ:* High Sch., La Grange, Ill; Purdue Univ. (officers' trng, USN, V12 program; BSc 1947); Harvard Univ. (grad. studies, PhD 1950). Sheldon Trav. Fellowship from Harvard at Inst. of Theoretical Physics, Copenhagen (later, the Niels Bohr Inst.), 1950–51. His Fellowship from US Atomic Energy Commn permitted continuation of work in Copenhagen for two more years, after which he held research position in CERN (European Organization for Nuclear Research) theoretical study group, formed in Copenhagen. Visiting Prof., Univ. of Calif at Berkeley, Spring term, 1959. Nobel Prize for Physics (jtly), 1975; awarded for work on theory of Atomic Nucleus, with Dr Aage Bohr (3 papers publ. 1952–53). *Publications:* Nuclear Structure, vol. I, 1969; vol. II, 1975 (with A. Bohr); contrib. Rev. Mod. Phys (jt), etc. *Address:* Nordita, Copenhagen, Denmark.

MOTTERSHEAD, Frank William, CB 1957; Deputy Secretary, Department of Health and Social Security (formerly Ministry of Health), 1965–71; *b* 7 Sept. 1911; *o s* of late Thomas Hastings and Adeline Mottershead; unmarried. *Educ:* King Edward's Sch., Birmingham; St John's Coll., Cambridge. BA 1933, MA 1973. Entered Secretary's Dept of Admiralty, 1934; Principal Private Sec. to First Lord, 1944–46; idc 1949; Under Sec., 1950; Transferred to Ministry of Defence, 1956; Deputy Sec., 1958; Deputy Under-Sec. of State, 1964. *Address:* Old Warden, Grevel Lane, Chipping Campden, Glos GL55 6HS. *T:* Evesham (01386) 840548. *Club:* United Oxford & Cambridge University.

MOTTISTONE, 4th Baron, *cr* 1933, of Mottistone; **David Peter Seely,** CBE 1984; Lord Lieutenant for Isle of Wight, since 1986; Governor of the Isle of Wight, since 1992; *b* 16 Dec. 1920; 4th *s* of 1st Baron Mottistone; *S* half brother, 1966; *m* 1944, Anthea, *er d* of T. V. W. McMullan, Cultra, Co. Down, N Ireland; two *s* two *d* (and one *d* decd). *Educ:* RN Coll., Dartmouth. Convoy escorting, Atlantic and Mediterranean, 1941–44; qualified in Communications, 1944; Served in Pacific, 1945; in comd HMS Cossack, FE Flt, 1958–59; in comd HMS Ajax and 24th Escort Sqdn, FE Flt (offensive ops against Indonesian confrontation) (despatches), 1963–65; Naval Advr to UK High Comr, Ottawa, 1965–66; retired at own request as a Captain, 1967. Dir of Personnel and Training, Radio Rentals Gp, 1967–69; Director: Distributive Industry Trng Bd, 1969–75; Cake and Biscuit Alliance, 1975–81; Export Secretary: Biscuit, Cake, Chocolate and Confectionery Alliance, 1981–83. FIEE; FIPD; FIMgt. DL Isle of Wight, 1981–86. Hon. DLitt Bournemouth, 1993. KStJ 1989. *Recreation:* yachting. *Heir:* *s* Hon. Peter John Philip Seely [*b* 29 Oct. 1949; *m* 1st, 1972, Joyce Cairns (marr. diss. 1975); one *s*; 2nd, 1982, Linda, *d* of W. Swain, Bulphan Fen, Essex; one *s* three *d*]. *Address:* The Old Parsonage, Mottistone, Isle of Wight PO30 4EE. *Clubs:* Commonwealth Trust; Royal Yacht Squadron, Royal Cruising, Island Sailing, Royal Navy Sailing Association.

MOTTRAM, Maj.-Gen. John Frederick, CB 1983; LVO 1976; OBE 1969; Chief Executive, General Council of the Bar, 1987–94; *b* 9 June 1930; *s* of Frederick Mottram and Margaret Mottram (*née* Butcher); *m* 1956, Jennifer Thomas; one *s* one *d*. *Educ:* Enfield Central Sch.; Enfield Technical Coll. Joined RM, 1948; 42 Commando, Malaya, ME, 1951–54; Special Boat Squadron, 1955–56; HMS Loch Lomond, Persian Gulf, 1957–58; Adjutant, Commando Trng Centre, 1959–62; Student, Army Staff Coll., 1963; Staff of CGRM and RM Equerry to HRH The Duke of Edinburgh, 1964–65; Bde Major, 3 Commando Bde, Far East, 1966–68; Directing Staff, Army Staff Coll., 1969–71; CO, 40 Commando, NI and Plymouth, 1972–74 (mentioned in Despatches, 1973); Student, Naval War Coll., 1974; Jt Warfare Attaché, British Embassy, Washington DC, 1974–77; Col GS, DCGRM and RM ADC to HM The Queen, 1978–80; Maj.-Gen., 1980; Maj.-Gen. Training and Reserve Forces, RM, 1980–83, retd. Dir Gen., Fertiliser Manufacturers Assoc., 1983–86. *Recreations:* fishing, watercolour painting. *Club:* Army and Navy.

MOTTRAM, Richard Clive; Permanent Secretary, Ministry of Defence, since 1995; *b* 23 April 1946; *s* of John Mottram and Florence Yates; *m* 1971, Fiona Margaret Erskine; three *s* one *d*. *Educ:* King Edward VI Camp Hill Sch., Birmingham; Univ. of Keele (1st Cl. Hons Internat. Relns). Entered Home Civil Service, 1968, assigned to Ministry of Defence: Asst Private Sec. to Sec. of State for Defence, 1971–72; Principal, Naval Programme and Budget, 1973; Cabinet Office, 1975–77; Ministry of Defence: Private Sec. to Perm. Under Sec., 1979–81; Asst Sec., Manpower Control and Audit, Procurement Exec., 1981; Private Sec. to Sec. of State for Defence, 1982–86; Asst. Under Sec. of State, 1986–89; Dep. Under Sec. of State (Policy), 1989–92; Perm. Sec., Office of Public Service and Sci., 1992–95. *Recreations:* cinema, theatre, tennis. *Address:* Ministry of Defence, Main Building, Whitehall, SW1A 2HB.

MOTYER, Rev. John Alexander; Minister of Christ Church, Westbourne, Bournemouth, 1981–89, retired; *b* 30 Aug. 1924; *s* of Robert Shankey and Elizabeth Maud Motyer; *m* 1948, Beryl Grace Mays; two *s* one *d*. *Educ:* High Sch., Dublin; Dublin Univ. (MA, BD); Wycliffe Hall, Oxford. Curate: St Philip, Penn Fields, Wolverhampton, 1947–50; Holy Trinity, Old Market, Bristol, 1950–54; Tutor, Clifton Theol Coll., Bristol, 1950–54, Vice-Principal, 1954–65; Vicar, St Luke's, Hampstead, 1965–70; Dep. Principal, Tyndale Hall, Bristol, 1970–71; Principal and Dean of College, Trinity Coll., Bristol, 1971–81. *Publications:* The Revelation of the Divine Name, 1959; After Death, 1965; The Richness of Christ (Epistle to the Philippians), 1966; The Tests of Faith (Epistle of James), 1970, 2nd edn 1975; (Old Testament Editor) New Bible Commentary Revised, 1970, New Bible Commentary 21st Century Edition, 1994; The Day of the Lion (Amos), 1975; The Image of God: Law and Liberty in Biblical Ethics (Laing Lecture), 1976; The Message of Philippians, 1984; The Message of James, 1985; The Prophecy of Isaiah, 1993; A Scenic Route Through the Old Testament, 1994; contributor: New Bible Dictionary; Expositor's Bible Commentary; Law and Life (monograph); New International Dictionary of New Testament Theology; Evangelical Dictionary of Theology. *Recreations:* reading, odd-jobbing. *Address:* 10 Littlefield, Bishopsteignton, Teignmouth, Devon TQ14 9SG. *T:* Teignmouth (01626) 770986.

MOUATT, (Richard) Brian; Chief Dental Officer, Deparment of Health, since 1991; *b* 4 Sept. 1936; *m* 1962, Ursula Wälti; one *s* one *d*. *Educ:* Blundell's Sch.; Edinburgh Univ. (BDS 1960). MGDS RCS 1979. RAF Dental Branch, 1960–65 (to Sqn Leader); Dept of Public Health, Bournemouth, 1965–68; FCO, Chief Dental Officer to Republic of Zambia under Overseas Aid Scheme contract, 1968–72; gen. dental practice, Dorset, 1972–84; Dept of Health, 1984–. Hon. Sen. Res. Fellow, Eastman Inst. of Dental Surgery.

Recreations: travel, water colour painting. *Address:* Department of Health, Richmond House, 79 Whitehall, SW1A 2NS. *T:* 0171–210 5247. *Club:* Athenæum.

MOULE, Rev. Prof. Charles Francis Digby, CBE 1985; FBA 1966; Lady Margaret's Professor of Divinity in the University of Cambridge, 1951–76; Fellow of Clare College, Cambridge, since 1944; Canon Theologian (non-residentiary) of Leicester, 1955–76; Honorary Member of Staff, Ridley Hall, Cambridge, 1976–80; *b* 3 Dec. 1908; *s* of late Rev. Henry William Moule and Laura Clements Pope; unmarried. *Educ:* Weymouth Coll., Dorset; Emmanuel Coll., Cambridge (scholar) (Hon. Fellow 1972); Ridley Hall, Cambridge. 1st Cl. Classical Tripos Part I, 1929; BA (1st Cl. Classical Tripos Part II), 1931; Evans Prize, 1931; Jeremie Septuagint Prize, 1932; Crosse Scholarship, 1933; MA 1934. Deacon, 1933, priest, 1934; Curate, St Mark's, Cambridge, and Tutor of Ridley Hall, 1933–34; Curate, St Andrew's, Rugby, 1934–36; Vice-Principal, Ridley Hall, 1936–44, and Curate of St Mary the Great, Cambridge, 1936–40. Dean of Clare Coll., Cambridge, 1944–51; Faculty Asst Lecturer in Divinity in the Univ. of Cambridge, 1944–47; Univ. Lecturer, 1947–51. Burkitt Medal for Biblical Studies, British Acad., 1970. Hon. DD: St Andrews, 1958; Cambridge, 1988. *Publications:* An Idiom Book of New Testament Greek, 1953; The Meaning of Hope, 1953; The Sacrifice of Christ, 1956; Colossians and Philemon (Cambridge Greek Testament Commentary), 1957; Worship in the New Testament, 1961; The Birth of the New Testament, 1962, 3rd edn 1981; The Phenomenon of the New Testament, 1967; (co-editor) Christian History and Interpretation, 1968; The Origin of Christology, 1977 (Collins Theological Book Prize, 1977); The Holy Spirit, 1978; Essays in New Testament Interpretation, 1982; (co-editor) Jesus and the Politics of His Day, 1984; contrib., Encyclopædia Britannica, Interpreter's Dictionary of the Bible, Biblisch-Historisches Handwörterbuch. *Address:* 1 King's Houses, Pevensey, East Sussex BN24 5JR.

MOULSON, (Roger) Harry; Managing Director, British Gas TransCo, since 1993; *b* 25 Jan. 1944; *s* of Frank and Mary Moulson; *m* Elaine Ann Douthwaite; one *s* one *d.* British Gas: Engineer, then Manager, 1962–69; Service Management/Dir and Computer Dir, 1971–81; Marketing Dir and New Business Develt Dir, 1981–92. Regl Chm., Wales Reg., 1991–93. *Recreations:* music, antiques, DIY, sport. *Address:* British Gas, 31 Homer Road, Solihull, W Midlands BS1 3LT. *T:* 0121–626 4431.

MOULTON, Alexander Eric, CBE 1976; RDI; FEng; Managing Director, Moulton Developments Ltd, since 1956; *b* 9 April 1920; *s* of John Coney Moulton, DSc, The Hall, Bradford-on-Avon, and Beryl Latimer Moulton. *Educ:* Marlborough Coll.; King's Coll., Cambridge (MA). Bristol Aeroplane Co., 1939–44: Engine Research Dept; George Spencer, Moulton & Co. Ltd, 1945–56; became Techn. Dir; estab. Research Dept (originated work on rubber suspensions for vehicles, incl. own design Flexitor); formed Moulton Developments Ltd, 1956 to do develt work on own designs of rubber suspensions for BLMC incl. Hydrolastic and Hydragas (Queen's Award to Industry, 1967); formed Moulton Bicycles Ltd to produce own design Moulton Bicycle, 1962 (Design Centre Award, 1964); designer of Moulton Coach, 1968–70; Chm., Moulton report on engrg design educn, Design Council, 1975–76; launched Alex Moulton Bicycle, 1983. Dir, SW Regional Bd, National Westminster Bank, 1982–87. RDI 1968 (Master, 1982–83); FRSA 1968; FEng 1980. Hon. Dr, RCA, 1967; Hon. DSc Bath, 1971. SIAD Design Medal, 1976; (jointly): James Clayton Prize, Crompton-Lanchester Medal, and Thomas Hawksley Gold Medal, IMechE, 1979; MacRobert Award (mem., jt winning team), FEng, 1991. *Publications:* numerous articles and papers on engineering and education. *Recreations:* cycling, canoeing, shooting. *Address:* The Hall, Bradford-on-Avon, Wilts BA15 1AJ. *T:* Bradford-on-Avon (01225) 862991. *Club:* Brooks's.

MOULTON, Air Vice-Marshal Leslie Howard, CB 1971; DFC 1941; with The Plessey Co., 1971–82, retired; *b* 3 Dec. 1915; *s* of late Peter Moulton, Nantwich, Cheshire; *m* Lesley, *d* of late P. C. Clarke, Ilford; two *s* two *d.* *Educ:* Nantwich and Acton School. Joined RAF, 1932; served War of 1939–45, Pilot; Operations with 14 Sqdn in Africa, 1940–42; CFS, 1942–44; specialised in Signals, 1945; Staff Coll., 1950; USAF, Strategic Air Comd, 1954–56; Dep. Dir Radio, Air Min., 1958–61; Comdt RAF Cosford, 1961–63; CSO Fighter Comd, 1963–65; Min. of Technology, 1965–68. Wing Comdr 1955; Gp Captain 1959; Air Cdre 1964; Air Vice-Marshal 1969; AOC No 90 (Signals) Group, RAF, 1969–71; retired 1971. FIEE, CEng, 1959. *Recreations:* gardening, golf, hill walking. *Address:* No 14 The Paddock, Willaston House, Willaston, Nantwich, Cheshire CW5 7EP. *T:* Nantwich (01270) 665308. *Club:* Royal Air Force.

MOUND, Laurence Alfred, DSc; FRES; Research Associate, Natural History Museum (formerly British Museum (Natural History)), since 1992 (Keeper of Entomology, 1981–92); *b* 22 April 1934; *s* of John Henry Mound and Laura May Cape; *m* 1st, 1958, Agnes Jean Solari (marr. diss. 1985); one *s* two *d*; 2nd, 1987, Sheila Helen Halsey (marr. diss. 1994). *Educ:* Warwick Sch.; Sir John Cass Coll., London; Imperial Coll., London (DIC); DSc London; Imperial Coll. of Tropical Agriculture, Trinidad (DipTropAgric). Nigerian Federal Dept of Agricl Research, 1959–61; Rockefeller Studentship, Washington and Calif, 1961; Empire Cotton Growing Corp., Republic of Sudan, 1961–64; Sen. Scientific Officer, BM (NH), 1964–69; Australian CSIRO Research Award, 1967–68; PSO, 1969–75, Dep. Keeper, Dept of Entomology, BM (NH), 1975–81. Sec., 1976–88, Vice-Chm., 1988–92, Council for Internat. Congresses of Entomology; Consultant Dir, Commonwealth Inst. of Entomology, 1981–92. Hon. Prof., Sch. of Pure and Applied Biology, Univ. of Wales at Cardiff, 1990–; McMaster Res. Fellow, CSIRO, 1995–96. Editor, Jl of Royal Entomological Soc. of London, 1973–81 (Vice-Pres., RES, 1975–76). Numerous expedns studying thrips in tropical countries. *Publications:* over 130 technical books and papers on biology of thrips and whitefly, particularly in Bull. of BM (NH), incl. Whitefly of the World (with S. H. Halsey). *Recreations:* thrips with everything. *Address:* c/o Natural History Museum, Cromwell Road, SW7 5BD. *T:* 0171–938 9124.

MOUND, Trevor Ernest John, CVO 1986; OBE 1977; HM Diplomatic Service, retired; writer; Chairman, Ephew II Consultants, since 1991; *b* 27 July 1930; *e s* of late Harvey Mound and late Margaret Webb; *m* 1955, Patricia Kathleen de Burgh (marr. diss. 1972); two *s.* *Educ:* Royal Grammar Sch., Worcester; RMA Sandhurst; Univs of London and Hong Kong. Enlisted Coldstream Gds; 2nd Lt, Worcs Regt (Malayan Campaign), 1951–54; Parachute Regt (ME), 1954–56; Adjutant, Airborne Forces, 1956–58; GSO 3, 16 Parachute Bde (ME), 1958–60; MoD, 1965–67; retired 1967; joined HM Diplomatic Service, 1967; First Secretary and Head of Chancery: Luxembourg, 1969–71; Calcutta, 1971–73; FCO, 1973–76; Beirut, 1976–77; Counsellor (Commercial), Peking, 1978–81; Counsellor (Econ.), Oslo, 1981–83; Counsellor (Hong Kong negotiations), FCO, 1984; Consul General: Shanghai, 1985–87; Marseilles Principality of Monaco, 1987–90. *Recreation:* astericology. *Address:* 8 Beaufort East, Bath BA1 6QD.

MOUNSEY, John Patrick David, MA, MD, FRCP; Provost, Welsh National School of Medicine, 1969–79, retired; *b* 1 Feb. 1914; *s* of late John Edward Mounsey and late Christine Frances Trail Robertson; *m* 1947, Vera Madeline Sara King (*d* 1990); one *s* one *d.* *Educ:* Eton Coll.; King's Coll., Cambridge; King's Coll. Hosp., London. Sherbrook Res. Fellow, Cardiac Dept, London Hosp., 1951; Royal Postgraduate Medical School: Lectr, 1960; Sen. Lectr and Sub-Dean, 1962; Cons. Cardiologist, Hammersmith Hosp., 1960; Dep. Dir, British Postgrad. Med. Fedn, 1967; Member: GMC, 1970–79; GDC, 1973–79; Council, St David's University Coll., Lampeter, 1975–83; South Glamorgan AHA (T); British Cardiac Soc.; Assoc. of Physicians; Soc. of Physicians in Wales. Corresp. Mem., Australasian Cardiac Soc.; late Asst Ed., British Heart Jl. Hon. LLD Wales, 1980. *Publications:* articles on cardiology mainly in British Heart Jl. *Recreations:* painting, gardening, music. *Address:* Esk House, Coombe Terrace, Wotton-under-Edge, Glos GL12 7NA. *T:* Dursley (01453) 842792. *Club:* Athenæum.

MOUNT, Air Cdre Christopher John, CBE 1956; DSO 1943; DFC 1940; DL; retired; *b* 14 Dec. 1913; *s* of Capt. F. Mount; *m* 1947, Audrey Mabel Clarke; two *s.* *Educ:* Eton; Trinity Coll., Oxford. Royal Auxiliary Air Force, 1935; Royal Air Force, 1938. Consultant, Wrights (formerly C. R. Thomas & Son), Solicitors, Maidenhead (partner, 1970–79). DL Berks, 1984. *Address:* Garden House, Bagshot Road, Sunninghill, Ascot, Berks SL5 9JL. *T:* Ascot (01344) 22225.

MOUNT, Ferdinand; *see* Mount, W. R. F.

MOUNT, (William Robert) Ferdinand, (3rd Bt *cr* 1921, of Wasing Place, Reading, Berks, but does not use the title); journalist; Editor, Times Literary Supplement, since 1991; *b* 2 July 1939; *s* of Robert Francis Mount (*d* 1969), 2nd *s* of Sir William Arthur Mount, 1st Bt, CBE and his 1st wife, Lady Julia Pakenham (*d* 1956), *d* of 5th Earl of Longford; *S* uncle, 1993; *m* 1968, Julia Margaret, *d* of late Archibald Julian and Hon. Mrs Lucas; two *s* one *d* (and one *s* decd). *Educ:* Eton; Christ Church, Oxford. Has worked for Sunday Telegraph, Conservative Research Dept, Daily Sketch, National Review, Daily Mail, The Times; Political Columnist: The Spectator, 1977–82 and 1985–87; The Standard, 1980–82; Daily Telegraph, 1984–90; Head of Prime Minister's Policy Unit, 1982–83. *Publications:* Very Like a Whale, 1967; The Theatre of Politics, 1972; The Man Who Rode Ampersand, 1975; The Clique, 1978; The Subversive Family, 1982; The Selkirk Strip, 1987; Of Love and Asthma, 1991 (Hawthornden Prize, 1992); The British Constitution Now, 1992; Umbrella, 1994. *Heir: s* William Robert Horatio Mount, *b* 12 May 1969. *Address:* 17 Ripplevale Grove, N1 1HS. *T:* 0171–607 5398.

MOUNT CHARLES, Earl of; Henry Vivian Pierpoint Conyngham; *b* 23 May 1951; *s* and *heir* of 7th Marquess Conyngham, *qv*; *m* 1st, 1971, Juliet Ann, *yr d* of Robert Kitson (marr. diss. 1985); one *s* one *d*; 2nd, 1985, Lady Iona Grimston, *yr d* of 6th Earl of Verulam; one *d.* *Educ:* Harrow; Harvard Univ. Irish Rep., 1976–78, Consultant, 1978–84, Sotheby's; Chairman: Slane Castle Ltd; Slane Castle Productions. Dir, Grapevine Arts Centre, Dublin. Trustee, Irish Youth Foundn. *Heir: s* Viscount Slane, *qv.* *Address:* Slane Castle, Co. Meath, Eire; Beau Parc House, Navan, Co. Meath, Eire. *Club:* Kildare Street and University (Dublin).

MOUNT EDGCUMBE, 8th Earl of, *cr* 1789; **Robert Charles Edgcumbe;** Baron Edgcumbe, 1742; Viscount Mount Edgcumbe and Valletort, 1781; Farm Manager, for Lands and Survey, New Zealand, 1975–84; *b* 1 June 1939; *s* of George Aubrey Valletort Edgcumbe (*d* 1977) and of Meta Blucher, *d* of late Robert Charles Lhoyer; *S* uncle, 1982; *m* 1960, Joan Ivy Wall (marr. diss. 1988); five *d.* *Educ:* Nelson College. Career from farm worker to farm manager, managing first farm, 1960; taking up family seat in Cornwall, 1984. *Recreations:* hunting game, restoring classic cars. *Heir: half-b* Piers Valletort Edgcumbe, *b* 23 Oct. 1946. *Address:* Empacombe House, Cremyll, Cornwall PL10 1H2.

MOUNTAIN, Sir Denis Mortimer, 3rd Bt *cr* 1922; Chairman and Managing Director: Eagle Star Insurance Co. Ltd, 1974–85; Eagle Star Holdings plc, 1979–85; Chairman, Eagle Star Insurance Co. of America, 1978–85; *b* 2 June 1929; *er s* of Sir Brian Edward Stanley Mountain, 2nd Bt, and of Doris Elsie, *e d* of late E. C. E. Lamb; *S* father, 1977; *m* 1958, Hélène Fleur Mary Kirwan-Taylor; two *s* one *d.* *Educ:* Eton. Late Lieut, Royal Horse Guards. Chairman: Australian Eagle Insurance Co. Ltd, 1977–85; South African Eagle Insurance Co. Ltd, 1977–85, and other companies both in UK and overseas; Pres., Compagnie de Bruxelles Risques Divers SA d'Assurances (Belgium), 1977–85; Director: Rank Organisation PLC, 1968–94; Grovewood Securities Ltd, 1969–85 (Dep. Chm.); Philip Hill Investment Trust plc, 1967–86; Bank of Nova Scotia (Toronto), 1978–; BAT Industries plc, 1984–85; Allied London Properties, 1986–, and other UK and overseas companies. *Recreations:* fishing, shooting. *Heir: s* Edward Brian Stanford Mountain [*b* 19 March 1961; *m* 1987, Charlotte Sarah Jesson, *d* of Judge Henry Pownall, *qv*; two *s* one *d*]. *Address:* The Manor, Morestead, Winchester, Hants SO2 1LZ. *T:* Owslebury (01962) 777237; 12 Queens Elm Square, Old Church Street, Chelsea, SW3 6ED. *T:* 0171–352 4331.

MOUNTBATTEN, family name of **Marquess of Milford Haven.**

MOUNTBATTEN OF BURMA, Countess (2nd in line) *cr* 1947; **Patricia Edwina Victoria Knatchbull,** CBE 1991; CD; JP; DL; Viscountess Mountbatten of Burma, 1946; Baroness Romsey, 1947; Vice Lord-Lieutenant of Kent, since 1984; *b* 14 Feb. 1924; *er d* of Admiral of the Fleet 1st Earl Mountbatten of Burma, KG, GCB, OM, GCSI, GCIE, GCVO, DSO, PC, FRS, and Countess Mountbatten of Burma, CI, GBE, DCVO, LLD (*d* 1960) (Hon. Edwina Cynthia Annette Ashley, *e d* of 1st and last Baron Mount Temple, PC); *S* father, 1979; *m* 1946, Baron Brabourne, *qv*; four *s* two *d* (and one *s* decd). *Educ:* Malta, England and New York City. Served War in WRNS, 1943–46. Colonel-in-Chief, Princess Patricia's Canadian Light Infantry. Vice-President: BRCS; NSPCC; Chm., Sir Ernest Cassel Educational Trust. President: SOS Children's Villages (UK); Friends of Cassel Hosp.; Friends of William Harvey Hosp.; Shaftesbury Homes and Arethusa; Kent Branches of NSPCC, Save the Children Fund and Marriage Guidance Council. Vice-President: FPA; Nat. Childbirth Trust; SSAFA; RLSS; Shaftesbury Soc.; Nat. Soc. for Cancer Relief; Kent Voluntary Service Council; The Aidis Trust; RCN; Royal Nat. Coll. for Blind. Hon. President: Soc. for Nautical Research; British Maritime Charitable Foundn; Patron: Commando Assoc.; HMS Cavalier Trust; Legion of Frontiersmen of the Commonwealth; Foudroyant Trust; HMS Kelly Reunion Assoc.; Nuclear Weapons Freeze; VADs (RN); Compassionate Friends; Nurses' Welfare Trust; Vice-Patron, Burma Star Assoc. Gov., Ashford School, Kent. JP 1971 and DL 1973, Kent. DStJ 1981. *Heir: s* Lord Romsey, *qv.* *Address:* Newhouse, Mersham, Ashford, Kent TN25 6NQ. *T:* Ashford (01233) 503636; 39 Montpelier Walk, SW7 1JH. *T:* 0171–589 8829.

MOUNTEVANS, 3rd Baron *cr* 1945, of Chelsea; **Edward Patrick Broke Evans;** Assistant Marketing Manager, British Tourist Authority, 1982–89, Advisor, since 1989; *b* 1 Feb. 1943; *s* of 2nd Baron Mountevans and of Deirdre Grace, *d* of John O'Connell, Cork; *S* father, 1974; *m* 1973, Johanna Keyzer, *d* of late Antonius Franciscus Keyzer, The Hague. *Educ:* Rugby; Trinity Coll., Oxford. Reserve Army Service, 1961–66; 74 MC Regt RCT, AER; Lt 1964. Joined management of Consolidated Gold Fields Ltd, 1966; British Tourist Authority, 1972: Manager, Sweden and Finland, 1973; Head of Promotion Services, 1976. *Heir: b* Hon. Jeffrey de Corban Richard Evans [*b* 13 May 1948; *m* 1972, Hon. Juliet, *d* of Baron Moran, *qv*; two *s*]. *Address:* c/o House of Lords, SW1A 0PW.

MOUNTFIELD, Peter; Executive Secretary, Development Committee, World Bank, 1991–95; *b* 2 April 1935; *s* of late Alexander Stuart Mountfield and Agnes Elizabeth (*née* Gurney); *m* 1958, Evelyn Margaret Smithies; three *s.* *Educ:* Merchant Taylors' Sch., Crosby; Trinity Coll., Cambridge (BA); Graduate Sch. of Public Admin, Harvard. RN,

1953–55. Asst Principal, HM Treasury, 1958; Principal, 1963; Asst Sec., 1970; Under Secretary: Cabinet Office, 1977; HM Treasury, 1980–91. *Recreations:* reading, walking, looking at buildings. *Address:* 42 Lambardes, New Ash Green, Kent DA3 8HX. *T:* Gravesend (01474) 873677.

See also R. Mountfield.

MOUNTFIELD, Robin, CB 1988; Permanent Secretary, Office of Public Service and Science, Cabinet Office, since 1995; *b* 16 Oct. 1939; *s* of late Alexander Stuart Mountfield and Agnes Elizabeth (*née* Gurney); *m* 1963, Anne Newsham; three *c. Educ:* Merchant Taylors' Sch., Crosby; Magdalen Coll., Oxford (BA). Assistant Principal, Ministry of Power, 1961, Principal, 1965; Private Sec. to Minister for Industry, 1973–74; Asst Sec., Dept of Industry, 1974, seconded to Stock Exchange, 1977–78; Under Sec., DoI, later, DTI, 1980–84; Deputy Secretary: DTI, 1984–92; HM Treasury, 1992–95. *Address:* Office of Public Service and Science, 70 Whitehall, SW1A 2AS. *T:* 0171–270 0002.

See also P. Mountfield.

MOUNTFORT, Guy Reginald, OBE 1970; retired as Director, Ogilvy & Mather International Inc., New York (1964–66); and as Managing Director, Ogilvy and Mather Ltd, London (1964–66); *b* 4 Dec. 1905; *s* of late Arnold George Mountfort, artist, and late Alice Edith (*née* Hughes); *m* 1931, Joan Hartley (*née* Pink); two *d. Educ:* Grammar Sch. General Motors Corporation (France), 1928–38. War service, 1939–46, 12 Regt HAC and British Army Staff (Washington) Lt-Col; service in N Africa, Italy, Burma, Pacific, Germany. Procter & Gamble Inc., USA, 1946–47; Mather & Crowther Ltd, 1947, Dir, 1949; Vice-Chm., Dollar Exports Bd Advertising Cttee, 1948–49. Hon. Sec., Brit. Ornithologists' Union, 1952–62, Pres. 1970–75 (Union Medal, 1967); Leader of scientific expedns to Coto Doñana, 1952, 1955, 1956; Bulgaria, 1960; Hungary, 1961; Jordan, 1963, 1965; Pakistan, 1966, 1967. Vice Pres., World Wildlife Fund (Gold Medal, 1978); Scientific FZS (Stamford Raffles Award, 1969). Medal of Société d'Acclimatation, 1936. Commander, Order of the Golden Ark, Netherlands, 1980. *Publications:* A Field Guide to the Birds of Europe (co-author), 1954, 5th edn, Birds of Britain and Europe, 1994; The Hawfinch, 1957; Portrait of a Wilderness, 1958; Portrait of a River, 1962; Portrait of a Desert, 1965; The Vanishing Jungle, 1969; Tigers, 1973; So Small a World, 1974; Back from the Brink, 1977; Saving the Tiger, 1981; Wild India, 1985; Rare Birds of the World, 1988; Memories of Three Lives, 1991; contribs to ornithological and other scientific jls; television and radio broadcasts on ornithology and exploration. *Recreations:* ornithology, gardening, photography, travel. *Address:* 8 Park Manor, St Aldhelm's Road, Poole, Dorset BH13 6BS.

MOUNTGARRET, 17th Viscount (Ireland) *cr* 1550; Baron (UK) *cr* 1911; **Richard Henry Piers Butler;** *b* 8 Nov. 1936; *s* of 16th Viscount; *S* father, 1966; *heir-pres.* to earldoms of Marquess of Ormonde, *qv*; *m* 1st, 1960, Gillian Margaret (marr. diss. 1970), *o d* of Cyril Francis Stuart Buckley, London, SW3; two *s* one *d*; 2nd, 1970, Mrs Jennifer Susan Melville Fattorini (marr. diss. 1983), *yr d* of Captain D. M. Wills, Barley Wood, Wrington, near Bristol; 3rd 1983, Mrs Angela Ruth Waddington, *e d* of T. G. Porter, The Croft, Church Fenton, Tadcaster. *Educ:* Eton; RMA, Sandhurst. Commissioned, Irish Guards, 1957; retd rank Capt., 1964. Pres., Yorks CCC, 1984–90. *Recreations:* shooting, stalking, cricket, golf. *Heir: s* Hon Piers James Richard Butler [*b* 15 April 1961; *m* 1995, Laura Brown Gary, *d* of Albert Dickens Williams, Jr]. *Address:* Stainley House, South Stainley, Harrogate, Yorks HG3 3LX. *T:* Harrogate (01423) 770087; 15 Queensgate Place, SW7. *T:* 0171–584 6998. *Clubs:* White's, Pratt's.

MOVERLEY, Rt. Rev. Gerald; *see* Hallam, Bishop of, (RC).

MOWAT, David McIvor; JP; consultant, business columnist and commentator; Managing Director, Iatros Ltd, since 1994; Director, St Andrews Golf Club Manufacturing Ltd; Consultant Director, InterExec Edinburgh Ltd; *b* 12 March 1939; *s* of Ian M. Mowat and Mary I. S. Steel; *m* 1964, Elinor Anne Birtwistle; three *d. Educ:* Edinburgh Academy; University of Edinburgh (MA); BA Open Univ., 1984. Chief Executive: Edinburgh Chamber of Commerce and Manufactures, 1967–90; Chamber Developments Ltd, 1971; Edinburghs Capital Ltd, 1986; Who's Who in Business in Scotland Ltd, 1989–90. Dep. Chm., Edinburgh Tourist Gp, 1985–90. Principal, Applied International Marketing, 1990–. Pres., British Chambers of Commerce Execs, 1987–89. JP Edinburgh, 1969. FRSA. *Address:* 37 Orchard Road South, Edinburgh EH4 3JA. *T:* 0131–332 6865.

MOWAT, John Stuart; QC (Scot.) 1988; Sheriff Principal of South Strathclyde, Dumfries and Galloway, 1988–93; *b* 30 Jan. 1923; *s* of George Mowat and Annie Barlow; *m* 1956, Anne Cameron Renfrew; two *s* two *d. Educ:* Glasgow High Sch.; Belmont House; Merchiston Castle Sch.; Glasgow Univ. (MA, LLB). Served RAF Transport Comd, 1941–46; Flt-Lt 1944. Journalist, 1947–52; Advocate, 1952; Sheriff-Substitute, then Sheriff, of Fife and Kinross at Dunfermline, 1960–72; Sheriff of Fife and Kinross at Cupar and Kinross, 1972–74; Sheriff of Lanark and Glasgow, subseq. Glasgow and Strathkelvin, 1974–88. Chm., Sheriff Court Rules Council, 1989–92. Contested (L) Caithness and Sutherland, 1955; Office-bearer, Scottish Liberal Party, 1954–58; Life Trustee: Carnegie Dunfermline Trust, 1967–73; Carnegie UK Trust, 1971–73. *Recreations:* golf, curling, watching football. *Address:* 31 Westbourne Gardens, Glasgow G12 9PF. *T:* 0141–334 3743; Drummond View, Fortingall, Perthshire PH15 2LL. *T:* Kenmore (01887) 830639.

MOWBRAY (26th Baron *cr* 1283), **SEGRAVE** (27th Baron *cr* 1283), **AND STOURTON,** of Stourton, Co. Wilts (23rd Baron *cr* 1448); **Charles Edward Stourton,** CBE 1982; *b* 11 March 1923; *s* of William Marmaduke Stourton, 25th Baron Mowbray, 26th Baron Segrave and 22nd Baron Stourton, MC, and Sheila (*d* 1975), *er d* of Hon. Edward Gully, CB; *S* father, 1965; *m* 1952, Hon. Jane de Yarburgh Bateson, *o c* of 5th Baron Deramore, and of Nina Lady Deramore, OBE, *d* of Alastair Macpherson-Grant; two *s. Educ:* Ampleforth; Christ Church, Oxford. Joined Army, 1942; Commissioned Gren. Guards, 1943; served with 2nd Armd Bn Gren. Gds, as Lt, 1943–44 (wounded, France, 1944; loss of eye and invalided, 1945). Mem. of Lloyd's 1952; Mem. Securicor, 1961–64; Chairman: Ghadeco (UK) Ltd, 1986–; Thames Estuary Airport Co. Ltd, 1993–; Director: Securicor (Scotland) Ltd, 1964–70; General Development Co. Ltd (Ghana), 1980–; EIRC Ghana Ltd, 1982–; EIRC (Canada) Inc., 1983–; EIRC Hldgs Ltd (Jersey), 1986–. Mem., Nidderdale RDC, 1954–58. A Conservative Whip in House of Lords, 1967–70, 1974–78; a Lord in Waiting (Govt Whip), and spokesman for DoE, 1970–74; Dep. Chief Opposition Whip in House of Lords, 1978–79; a Lord in Waiting (Govt Whip), and spokesman for the arts, envt and transport, 1979–80. Chm., Govt Picture Buying Cttee, 1972–74; Mem., British Parly Delegn to Bicentennial Celebrations, Washington, 1976. Trustee: College of Arms Trust, 1975–; Church, Convent and Hosp., St John and St Elizabeth. Chancellor, Primrose League, 1974–80, 1981–83. Life Governor, Imperial Cancer Res. Fund, 1983–. Hon. Pres., Safety Glazing Assoc., 1975–78. Patron, Tayside and Mearns Normandy Veterans Assoc., 1992–. Bicentennial Year Award of Baronial Order of Magna Charta, USA, 1976. Kt of Hon. and Devotion, SMO Malta, 1947; Kt Gr. Cross, Mil. Order of St Lazarus, 1970; Bailiff, Grand Cross of Justice, Constantinian Order of St George (Italy), 1985. *Recreations:* reading, shooting, gardening. *Heir: s* Hon. Edward William Stephen Stourton [*b* 17 April 1953; *m* 1980, Penelope, *e d* of Dr Peter Brunet; one *s* four *d*]. *Address:* Marcus, by Forfar, Angus DD8 3QH. *T:* Finavon (0130785) 219; 23 Warwick Square, SW1V 2AB. *Clubs:* Turf, White's, Pratt's, Beefsteak, Pilgrims, Roxburghe.

See also F. P. Crowder.

MOWBRAY, Sir John, Kt 1983; Chairman, Wellington Diocesan Board of Trustees (Anglican), 1970–95; *b* 23 Sept. 1916; *s* of Harry Logan Campbell Mowbray and Therese Josephine Mowbray; *m* 1946, Audrey Burt Steel; two *s* one *d. Educ:* King's Coll., Auckland; Auckland University Coll. BCom, Dip. in Banking, Univ. of NZ; FCA NZ 1973. Served War, 2nd NZ Div. Field Artillery, ME, 1940–46 (Lieut). Joined staff of The National Bank of New Zealand, 1934; Gen. Man.'s Asst, 1957; Asst Gen. Man., 1961; Gen. Man. and Chief Exec., 1966–76. Chairman: Develt Finance Corp. of NZ, 1976–85; GEC New Zealand Ltd, 1976–86; Motor Hlldgs Ltd, 1980–84; DIC Ltd, 1982–86. Chairman: NZ Bankers' Assoc., 1966, 1972 and 1975; Higher Salaries Cttee in the State Services, 1972–78; Bd of Trustees, NZ Inst. of Econ. Res., 1978–; Asean NZ Business Council, 1984–88; NZ Technol. Advancement Trust, 1984–; Japan/NZ Business Council, 1974–78; NZ Cttee, Pacific Basin Econ. Council, 1972–74. Life Member: NZ Admin. Staff Coll. (formerly Chm.); Arthritis and Rheumatism Foundn of NZ; Barnados NZ. FNZIM 1974; Hon. Fellow, NZ Inst. of Bankers, 1975; FRSA 1970. A Lay Canon Emeritus, Wellington Cathedral. *Recreations:* golf, bridge, gardening. *Address:* 167 Karori Road, Karori, Wellington 5, New Zealand. *T:* 766334. *Clubs:* Wellington (Wellington); Northern (Auckland); Wellington Golf.

MOWBRAY, Sir John Robert, 6th Bt *cr* 1880; DL; *b* 1 March 1932; *s* of Sir George Robert Mowbray, 5th Bt, KBE, and of Diana Margaret, *d* of Sir Robert Heywood Hughes, 12th Bt; *S* father, 1969; *m* 1957, Lavinia Mary, *d* of late Lt-Col Francis Edgar Hugonin, OBE, Stainton House, Stainton in Cleveland, Yorks; three *d. Educ:* Eton; New College, Oxford. DL Suffolk, 1993. *Address:* The Hill House, Duffs Hill, Glemsford, Suffolk CO10 7PP. *T:* Glemsford (01787) 281930.

MOWBRAY, William John, QC 1974; *b* 3 Sept. 1928; *s* of James Nathan Mowbray, sugar manufr and E. Ethel Mowbray; *m* 1960, Shirley Mary Neilan; one *s* three *d. Educ:* Upper Canada Coll.; Mill Hill Sch.; New Coll., Oxford. BA 1952. Called to Bar, Lincoln's Inn, 1953 (Bencher, 1983); called to Bahamian Bar, 1971. Chairman: Chancery Bar Assoc., 1985–; Westminster Assoc. for Mental Health, 1981–; Westminster Christian Council, 1986–87 (Vice-Chm., 1984–85). *Publications:* Lewin on Trusts, 16th edn, 1964; Estate Duty on Settled Property, 1969; articles in jls. *Recreations:* music, observing nature in Sussex garden. *Address:* 12 New Square, Lincoln's Inn, WC2A 3SW. *T:* 0171–405 3808/9, 0171–405 0988/9. *Club:* Travellers'.

MOWL, Colin John; Deputy Director, Macroeconomic Policy and Prospects (formerly Grade 3, and Head, Economic Analysis and Forecasting Group), HM Treasury, since 1990; *b* 19 Oct. 1947; *s* of Arthur Sidney and Ada Mowl; *m* 1980, Kathleen Patricia Gallagher; one *s* one *d. Educ:* Lawrence Sheriff Sch., Rugby; LSE (BSc Econs, MSc). Econ. Asst, MoT, 1970–72; Sen. Econ. Asst, Econ. Advr, HM Treasury, 1972–83; Res. Manager, Forex Research Ltd, 1983; Sen. Econ. Advr, HM Treasury, 1983–90. *Publications:* various Treasury working papers. *Recreations:* family, home, sport. *Address:* HM Treasury, Parliament Street, SW1P 3AG. *T:* 0171–270 4459.

MOWLAM, Dr Marjorie; MP (Lab) Redcar, since 1987; *b* 18 Sept. 1949. *Educ:* Coundon Court Comprehensive Sch., Coventry; Durham Univ. (BA Social Anthrop. 1971); Iowa Univ. (MA; PhD 1978). Lecturer: Florida State Univ., 1977–78; Newcastle upon Tyne Univ., 1979–83; Administrator, Northern Coll., Barnsley, 1984–87. Opposition frontbench spokesman on NI, 1988–89, on city and corporate affairs, 1989–92, on Citizen's Charter and women, 1992–93, on nat. heritage, 1993–94, on NI, 1994–; Mem., Shadow Cabinet, 1992. Has held various Labour Party offices at constituency and dist levels. *Publications:* (ed jtly) Debate on Disarmament, 1982; (contrib.) Over Our Dead Bodies, ed D. Thompson, 1983. *Recreations:* travelling, swimming, jigsaws. *Address:* House of Commons, SW1A 0AA. *T:* 0171–219 5066; Redcar (01642) 490404.

MOWLL, Christopher Martyn; Clerk to The Clothworkers' Company of the City of London and Secretary to The Clothworkers' Foundation, 1978–92; *b* 14 Aug. 1932; *s* of late Christopher Kilvinton Mowll and Doris Ellen (*née* Hutchinson) *m* 1958, Margaret Frances (*née* Laird); four *s. Educ:* Epsom Coll.; Gonville and Caius Coll., Cambridge (MA). Admitted Solicitor, 1956. Member: Council, National Library for the Blind, 1964–79; Council, Metropolitan Society for the Blind, 1964– (Treas., 1965–79; Vice-Chm., 1971–79; Chm., 1979–); Exec. Council, RNIB, 1982–; Britain-Australia Bicentennial Cttee, 1984–88; Exec. Cttee, Assoc. of Charitable Foundns, 1989–92; Council, Shaftesbury Soc., 1993–. Hon. LLD Leeds, 1992. *Address:* 15 West Hill, Sanderstead, South Croydon, Surrey CR2 0SB. *T:* 0181–657 1207.

MOWSCHENSON, Terence Rennie; QC 1995; *b* 7 June 1953; *s* of Henry and Hanny Mowschenson; *m* 1992, Judith Angela Strang. *Educ:* Eagle Sch., Umtali, Rhodesia; Peterhouse, Marandellas, Rhodesia; Queen Mary Coll., London (LLB Hons); Exeter Coll., Oxford (BCL Hons). FCIArb. Called to the Bar, Middle Temple, 1977. *Recreations:* opera, reading, travel. *Address:* 1 Essex Court, Temple, EC4Y 9AR. *T:* 0171–583 2000. *Club:* Royal Automobile.

MOXON, Rt. Rev. David John; *see* Waikato, Bishop of.

MOXON, Prof. (Edward) Richard, FRCP; Action Research Professor of Paediatrics, University of Oxford, since 1984; Fellow, Jesus College, Oxford, since 1984; Head, Molecular Infectious Diseases Group, Institute of Molecular Medicine, John Radcliffe Hospital, Oxford, since 1988; *b* 16 July 1941; *s* of late Gerald Richard Moxon and of Margaret Forster Mohun; *m* 1973, Marianne Graham; two *s* one *d. Educ:* Shrewsbury Sch.; St John's Coll., Cambridge (Keasby Award, 1961; BA 1963), St Thomas' Hosp. (MB, BChir 1966); MA Oxon 1984. MRCP 1968, FRCP 1984. Surgical House Officer, Kent and Canterbury Hosp., 1966; Medical House Officer, Peace Meml Hosp., Watford, 1966; Pathologist, St Thomas' Hosp., 1967; Sen. House Officer in Paediatrics: Whittington Hosp., 1968; Hosp. for Sick Children, Gt Ormond St, 1969; Children's Hosp. Medical Center, Boston, Mass, USA: Asst Resident in Pediatrics, 1970; Res. Fellow in Infectious Diseases Div., 1971–74; Johns Hopkins Hosp., Baltimore, Md, USA: Asst Prof. in Pediatrics, 1974–80; Associate Prof. in Pediatrics, 1980–84; Chief, Eudowood Div. of Pediatric Infectious Diseases, 1982–84. Vis. Scientist, Washington Univ., St Louis, 1990–91. Mitchell Lectr, RCP, 1992. Convenor, BPA Immunology and Infectious Diseases Gp, 1984–89; Chm., MRC Sub-Cttee, Polysaccharide Vaccines, 1986–90; Member: Steering Gp, Encapsulated Bacteria, WHO, 1987–93. Amer. Soc. Clinical Investigation. Fellow: Infectious Diseases Soc. of America; Amer. Soc. Pediatric Res. *Publications:* (with D. Isaacs) Neonatal Infections, 1991; contribs to: Sande's Bacterial Meningitis, 1985; McKhann's Diseases of the Nervous System, part II, 1986; Jann's Bacterial Capsules and Adhesins, 1988; Lambert's Infections of the Central Nervous System, 1990; Forfar and Arneil's Textbook of Paediatrics, 4th edn 1991; (editl advr) Lancet's Modern Vaccines, 1991; Mandell's Principles and Practice of Infectious Diseases, 3rd edn 1994; Oxford Textbook of Medicine, 2nd edn 1995; many papers on meningitis and molecular basis of bacterial virulence, esp. *Haemophilus influenzae* and *Neisseria* *meningitidis. Recreations:* tennis, music. *Address:* 17 Moreton Road, Oxford OX2 7AX. *T:* Oxford (01865) 515344.

MOXON, Rev. Canon Michael Anthony; Canon, St George's Chapel, Windsor and Chaplain to Windsor Great Park, since 1990; Chaplain to the Queen, since 1986; *b* 23 Jan. 1942; *s* of Rev. Canon Charles Moxon and Phyllis Moxon; *m* 1969, Sarah-Jane Cresswell; twin *s* one *d. Educ:* Merchant Taylors' Sch., Northwood, Mddx; Durham Univ.; Salisbury Theol Coll. BD London. Deacon, 1970; Priest, 1971; Curate, Lowestoft gp of parishes, 1970–74; Minor Canon, St Paul's Cathedral, 1974–81; Sacrist of St Paul's, 1977–81; Warden of Coll. of Minor Canons, 1979–81; Vicar of Tewkesbury with Walton Cardiff, 1981–90. Member: Gen. Synod of C of E, 1985–90; Council for the Care of Churches, 1986–90. *Recreations:* music, reading, cricket. *Address:* The Chaplain's Lodge, The Great Park, Windsor, Berks SL4 2HP. *T:* Egham (01784) 432434.

MOXON BROWNE, Robert William; QC 1990; a Recorder, since 1991; *b* 26 June 1946; *s* of Kendall Edward Moxon Browne and Sheila Heron Moxon Browne; *m* 1968, Kerstin Elizabet Warne; one *s* one *d. Educ:* Gordonstoun School; University College, Oxford (BA). Called to the Bar, Gray's Inn, 1969. *Recretations:* ski-ing, archery, walking, gardening, wine. *Address:* 2 Temple Gardens, EC4Y 9AY. *T:* 0171–583 6041. *Club:* Hampstead Bowmen.

MOYERS, Bill D., BJ, BD; journalist; Executive Editor, Public Affairs Television Inc., since 1987; *b* 5 June 1934; *s* of John Henry Moyers and Ruby Moyers (*née* Johnson); *m* 1954, Judith Suzanne Davidson; two *s* one *d. Educ:* High Sch., Marshall, Texas; Univ. of Texas; Univ. of Edinburgh; Southwestern Theological Seminary. BJ 1956; BD 1959. Personal Asst to Senator Lyndon B. Johnson, 1959–60; Executive Asst, 1960; US Peace Corps: Associate Dir, 1961–63; Dep. Dir, 1963. Special Asst to President Johnson, 1963–66; Press Sec., 1965–67; Publisher of Newsday, Long Island, 1967–70; Exec. Ed., Bill Moyers' Jl, Public Broadcasting Service, 1971–76, 1978–81; editor and chief reporter, CBS Reports, 1976–79; Sen. News Analyst, CBS Evening News, 1981–86. Contributing Editor, Newsweek Magazine. Twenty-two Emmy Awards, incl. most outstanding broadcaster, 1974; Lowell Medal, 1975; ABA Gavel Award for distinguished service to American system of law, 1974; ABA Cert. of Merit, 1975; Awards for The Fire Next Door: Monte Carlo TV Festival Grand Prize, Jurors Prize and Nymph Award, 1977; Robert F. Kennedy Journalism Grand Prize, 1978, 1988; Christopher Award, 1978; Sidney Hillman Prize for Distinguished Service, 1978, 1981, 1987; Distinguished Urban Journalism Award, Nat. Urban Coalition, 1978; George Polk Award, 1981, 1987; Alfred I. du Pont—Columbia Univ. Award, 1981, 1987, 1988, 1991; Peabody Award, 1977, 1981, annually 1986–89; Overseas Press Award, 1986. *Publications:* Listening to America, 1971; Report from Philadelphia, 1987; The Secret Government, 1988; Joseph Campbell and the Power of Myth, 1988; A World of Ideas, 1989, 2nd edn 1990. *Address:* 356 West 58th Street, New York, NY 10019, USA.

MOYES, Lt-Comdr Kenneth Jack, MBE (mil.) 1960; RN retd; Under-Secretary, Department of Health and Social Security, 1975–78; *b* 13 June 1918; *s* of Charles Wilfrid and Daisy Hilda Moyes; *m* 1943, Norma Ellen Outred Hillier; one *s* two *d. Educ:* Portsmouth Northern Grammar Sch. FCIS. Royal Navy, 1939–63. Principal, Dept of Health and Social Security, 1963; Asst Secretary, 1970. *Recreations:* gardening, tennis, squash, bridge. *Address:* Garden House, Darwin Road, Birchington, Kent CT7 9JL. *T:* Thanet (01843) 42015.

MOYLAN, His Honour (John) David (FitzGerald); a Circuit Judge (formerly Judge of the County Courts), 1967–88; *b* 8 Oct. 1915; *s* of late Sir John FitzGerald Moylan, CB, CBE, and late Lady Moylan (*née* FitzGerald); *m* 1946, Jean, *d* of late F. C. Marno-Edwards, Lavenham, Suffolk; one *s* two *d. Educ:* Charterhouse; Christ Church, Oxford. Served War of 1939–45, with Royal Marines. Inner Temple, 1946; practised on the Western Circuit. *Recreations:* travel and music. *Address:* Ufford Hall, Fressingfield, Diss, Norfolk IP21 5TA.

MOYLAN-JONES, Rear-Adm. Roger Charles, CEng, FIMechE; Director General Aircraft (Navy), 1992–95; *b* 18 April 1940; *s* of Brian Percy Jameson Moylan-Jones and Louie-Mae (*née* Brown); *m* 1961, Mary Howells; two *s* one *d. Educ:* King Edward VI Grammar Sch., Totnes; BRNC, Dartmouth; RNEC, Manadon (BSc Eng 1964). CEng, FIMechE 1958. Joined BRNC Dartmouth, 1958; service in 766, 890, 360 Sqdns and HMS Ark Royal, 1965–69; HMS Ganges, 1969–71; Air Engineering Officer, 706 Sqdn and 819 Sqdn; Staff of Flag Officer Carriers and Amphibious Ships, 1971–77; ndc 1978; Staff of: Flag Officer, Naval Air Comd, 1979–80; Dep. Chief of Defence Staff (OR), 1981–82; CSO to FONAC, 1983–84; Capt., HMS Daedalus, 1984–86; RCDS 1987; Director: Aircraft Support Policy (Navy), 1988–89; Naval Manning and Trng (Engrg), 1989–91. Capt., RN and Combined Services CC, 1969–73, 1982, 1983; Pres., RNCC, 1993–95 (Chm., 1985–89; Life Vice Pres., 1995). *Recreations:* cricket, golf. *Clubs:* Army and Navy, MCC; I Zingari, Free Foresters, Forty.

MOYLE, Rt. Hon. Roland (Dunstan); PC 1978; barrister-at-law; Deputy Chairman, Police Complaints Authority, 1985–91; *b* 12 March 1928; *s* of late Baron Moyle, CBE; *m* 1956, Shelagh Patricia Hogan; one *s* one *d. Educ:* Infants' and Jun. Elem. Schs, Bexleyheath, Kent; County Sch., Llanidloes, Mont.; UCW Aberystwyth (LLB); Trinity Hall, Cambridge (MA, LLM). Called to the Bar, Gray's Inn, 1954. Commnd in Royal Welch Fusiliers, 1949–51. Legal Dept, Wales Gas Bd, 1953–56; Industrial Relations Executive with Gas Industry, 1956–62, and Electricity Supply Industry, 1962–66. MP (Lab) Lewisham N, 1966–74, Lewisham E, 1974–83; PPS to Chief Secretary to the Treasury, 1966–69, to Home Secretary, 1969–70; opposition spokesman on higher educn and science, 1972–74; Parly Sec., MAFF, 1974; Minister of State: NI Dept, 1974–76; for Health, 1976–79; opposition spokesman on health, 1979–80; deputy foreign affairs spokesman, 1980–83; opposition spokesman on defence and disarmament, 1983. Mem., Select Cttee on Race Relations and Immigration, 1968–72; Vice-Chm., PLP Defence Group, 1968–72; Sec., 1971–74, Mem. Exec. Cttee, 1968–83, British Amer. Parly Gp. *Recreation:* pottering. *Address:* 19 Montpelier Row, Blackheath, SE3 0RL.

MOYNE, 3rd Baron *cr* 1932, of Bury St Edmunds; **Jonathan Bryan Guinness;** *b* 16 March 1930; *s* of 2nd Baron Moyne and of Hon. Diana (*née* Mitford, now Hon. Lady Mosley); *S* father, 1992; *m* 1st, 1951, Ingrid Wyndham (marr. diss. 1962); two *s* one *d*; 2nd, 1964, Suzanne Phillips (*née* Lisney); one *s* one *d. Educ:* Eton; Oxford (MA, Mod. Langs). Journalist at Reuters, 1953–56. Merchant Banker: trainee at Erlangers Ltd, 1956–59, and at Philip Hill, 1959–62; Exec. Dir, 1962–64, non-exec. Dir, 1964–91, Leopold Joseph; Dir, Arthur Guinness Son & Co. Ltd, 1961–88. CC Leicestershire, 1970–74; Chairman, Monday Club, 1972–74. *Publications:* (with Catherine Guinness) The House of Mitford, 1984; Shoe: the odyssey of a sixties survivor, 1989. *Heir: s* Hon. Jasper Jonathan Richard Guinness [*b* 9 March 1954; *m* 1985, Camilla Alexandra, *d* of Robie David Corbett Uniacke]. *Address:* Bosalverne, Green Bank, Alverton, Penzance, Cornwall TR18 4ST. *Club:* Beefsteak.

See also Hon. D. W. Guinness, Lord Neidpath.

MOYNIHAN, Barony *cr* 1929; dormant since 1991.

MOYNIHAN, Hon. Colin Berkeley; *b* 13 Sept. 1955; *s* of 2nd Baron Moynihan, OBE, TD, and of June Elizabeth (who *m* 1965, N. B. Hayman), *d* of Arthur Stanley Hopkins; *m* 1992, Gaynor-Louise Metcalf; two *s. Educ:* Monmouth Sch. (Music Scholar); University Coll., Oxford (BA PPE 1977, MA 1982). Pres., Oxford Union Soc., 1976. Personal Asst to Chm., Tate & Lyle Ltd, 1978–80; Manager, Tate & Lyle Agribusiness, resp. for marketing strategy and develt finance, 1980–82; Chief Exec., 1982–83, Chm., 1983–87, Ridgways Tea and Coffee Merchants; external consultant, Tate & Lyle PLC, 1983–87. MP (C) Lewisham East, 1983–92; contested (C) Lewisham East, 1992. Political Asst to the Foreign Sec., 1983; PPS to Minister of Health, 1985, to Paymaster General, 1985–87; Parly Under Sec. of State (Minister for Sport), DoE, 1987–90; Parly Under-Sec. of State, Dept of Energy, 1990–92. Chm., All-Party Parly Gp on Afghanistan, 1986; Vice Chm., Cons. Food and Drinks Sub-Cttee, 1983–85; Sec. Cons. Foreign and Commonwealth Affairs Cttee, 1983–85. Member: Paddington Conservative Management Cttee, 1980–81; Bow Group, 1978–92 (Mem., Industry Cttee, 1978–79, 1985–87); Chm., Trade & Industry Standing Cttee, 1983–87. Hon. Sec., Friends of British Council. Patron, Land & City Families Trust. Gov., Feltonfleet Sch. Member: Sports Council, 1982–85; Major Spectator Sports Cttee, CCPR, 1979–82; CCPR Enquiry into Sponsorship of Sport, 1982–83; Steward, British Boxing Bd of Control, 1979–87; Trustee: Oxford Univ. Boat Club, 1980–84; Sports Aid Trust, 1983–87; Patron, Cambridge Univ. Women's Boat Club Assoc., 1989–; Governor, Sports Aid Foundn (London and SE), 1980–82. Oxford Double Blue, Rowing and Boxing, 1976 and 1977; World Gold Medal for Lightweight Rowing, Internat. Rowing Fedn, 1978; Olympic Silver Medal for Rowing, 1980; World Silver Medal for Rowing, 1981. Freeman, City of London, 1978; Liveryman, Worshipful Co. of Haberdashers, 1981. *Recreations:* collecting Nonesuch Books, music, sport. *Clubs:* Brooks's, Commonwealth Trust (Mem. Council, 1980–82); Vincent's (Oxford).

MOYNIHAN, Daniel Patrick; US Senator from New York State, since 1977; *b* Tulsa, Oklahoma, 16 March 1927; *s* of John Henry and Margaret Ann Phipps Moynihan; *m* 1955, Elizabeth Therese Brennan; two *s* one *d. Educ:* City Coll., NY; Tufts Univ.; Fletcher Sch. of Law and Diplomacy. MA, PhD. Gunnery Officer, US Navy, 1944–47. Dir of Public Relations, Internat. Rescue Commn, 1954; successively Asst to Sec., Asst Sec., Acting Sec., to Governor of NY State, 1955–58; Mem., NY Tenure Commn, 1959–60; Dir, NY State Govt Res. Project, Syracuse Univ., 1959–61; Special Asst to Sec. of Labor, 1961–62; Exec. Asst to Sec., 1962–63, Asst Sec. of Labor, 1963–65; Dir, Jt Center Urban Studies, MIT and Harvard Univ., 1966–69; Prof. of Govt, 1972–77 and Senior Mem., 1966–77, Harvard (Prof. of Education and Urban Politics, 1966–73). Asst to Pres. of USA for Urban Affairs, 1969–70; Counsellor to Pres. (with Cabinet rank), 1969–70; Consultant to Pres., 1971–73; US Ambassador to India, 1973–75; US Permanent Rep. to the UN and Mem. of Cabinet, 1975–76. Ranking Minority Mem., Senate Finance Cttee; Member, Senate Committees: For. Relations, Rules, Envmt, Public Works, (jt) Taxation and Library. Chm., Commn on Protecting and Reducing Govt Secrecy. Mem., US delegn 26th Gen. Assembly, UN, 1971. Fellow, Amer. Acad. Arts and Scis; Member: Amer. Philosophical Soc.; AAAS (formerly Vice-Pres.); Nat. Acad. Public Admin; President's Sci. Adv. Cttee, 1971–73. Hon. Fellow, London Sch. of Economics, 1970. Holds numerous hon. degrees. Meritorius Service Award, US Dept of Labor, 1965; Internat. League for Human Rights Award, 1975; John LaFarge Award for Interracial Justice, 1980; Hubert Humphrey Award, Amer. Pol Sci. Assoc., 1983; Medallion, State Univ. of NY at Albany, 1984; Henry Medal, Smithsonian Instn, 1985; Seal Medallion, CIA, 1986; Meml Sloan-Kettering Cancer Center Medal, 1986; Britannica Award, 1986; AIA Award, 1992; Laetare Medal, Notre Dame Univ., 1993; Thomas Jefferson Medal, Amer. Philosophical Soc., 1993. *Publications:* (co-author) Beyond the Melting Pot, 1963; (ed) The Defenses of Freedom, 1966; (ed) On Understanding Poverty, 1969; Maximum Feasible Misunderstanding, 1969; (ed) Toward a National Urban Policy, 1970; (jt ed) On Equality of Educational Opportunity, 1972; The Politics of a Guaranteed Income, 1973; Coping: On the Practice of Government, 1974; (jt ed) Ethnicity: Theory and Experience, 1975; A Dangerous Place, 1979; Counting Our Blessings, 1980; Loyalties, 1984; Family and Nation, 1986; Came the Revolution, 1988; On the Law of Nations, 1990; Pandaemonium: ethnicity in international politics, 1993. *Address:* United States Senate, Washington, DC 20510, USA. *Clubs:* Century, Harvard (NYC); Federal City (Washington).

MOYNIHAN, Martin John, CMG 1972; MC; HM Diplomatic Service, retired; *b* 17 Feb. 1916; *e s* of late William John Moynihan and Phebe Alexander; *m* 1946, Monica Hopwood; one *s* one *d. Educ:* Birkenhead Sch.; Magdalen Coll., Oxford (MA). India Office, 1939. War of 1939–45: Indian Army, 1940; QVO Corps of Guides; served with Punjab Frontier Force, N-W Frontier and Burma (MC); Commonwealth Service: Delhi, Madras, Bombay and London, 1946–54; Deputy High Commissioner: Peshawar, 1954–56; Lahore, 1956–58; Kuala Lumpur, 1961–63; Port of Spain, 1964–66; HM Consul-General, Philadelphia, 1966–70; Ambassador to Liberia, 1970–73; High Comr in Lesotho, 1973–76. Administering Officer, Kennedy Meml Trust, 1977–79. Mem., Council, Hakluyt Soc., 1976. Associate Mem. in S African Studies, Clare Hall, Cambridge, 1977–78. Hon. Knight Grand Band of Humane Order of African Redemption (Liberia), 1973. *Publications:* The Strangers, 1946; South of Fort Hertz, 1956; The Latin Letters of C. S. Lewis, 1987; Letters: C. S. Lewis and Don Giovanni Calabria, 1988. *Address:* 5 The Green, Wimbledon Common, SW19 5AZ. *T:* 0181–946 7964. *Clubs:* Athenæum, Travellers'.

MOYOLA, Baron *cr* 1971 (Life Peer), of Castledawson; **James Dawson Chichester-Clark,** PC (Northern Ireland) 1966; DL; *b* 12 Feb. 1923; *s* of late Capt. J. L. C. Chichester-Clark, DSO and bar, DL, MP, and Mrs C. E. Brackenbury; *m* 1959, Moyra Maud Haughton (*née* Morris); two *d* one step *s. Educ:* Eton. Entered Army, 1942; 2nd Lieut Irish Guards, Dec. 1942; wounded, Italy, 1944; ADC to Governor-General of Canada (Field-Marshal Earl Alexander of Tunis), 1947–49; attended Staff Coll., Camberley, 1956; retired as Major, 1960. MP (U), S Derry, NI Parlt, 1960–72; Asst Whip, March 1963; Chief Whip, 1963–67; Leader of the House, 1966–67; Min. of Agriculture, 1967–69; Prime Minister, 1969–71. County Derry: DL 1954; Vice Lieut, 1975–93. *Recreations:* shooting, fishing, ski-ing. *Address:* Moyola Park, Castledawson, Co. Derry, N Ireland BT45 8ED.

See also Sir R. Chichester-Clark, P. Hobhouse.

MPUCHANE, Samuel Akuna; in business in Botswana, since 1991; *b* 15 Dec. 1943; *s* of Chiminya Thompson Mpuchane and Motshidiemang Phologolo; *m* Sisai Felicity Mokgokong; two *s* one *d. Educ:* Univ. of Botswana, Lesotho and Swaziland (BA Govt and Hist.); Southampton Univ. (MSc Internat. Affairs). External Affairs Officer, 1969–70; First Secretary: Botswana Mission to UN, 1970–71; Botswana Embassy, Washington, 1971–74; Under Sec., External Affairs, 1974–76; on study leave, 1976–77; Dep. Perm. Sec., Min. of Mineral Resources and Water Affairs, 1977–79; Admin. Sec., Office of Pres., 1979–80; Perm. Sec., Min. of Local Govt and Lands, 1980–81; High Comr for Botswana in UK, 1982–85; Perm. Sec. for External Affairs, 1986–90. Director, 1991–: Standard Chartered Bank (Botswana); Builders World; Building Materials Supplies; Royal Wholesalers; Parts World; Trade World; Blue Chip Investments; Continental Star Caterers. *Recreations:* playing and watching tennis, watching soccer.

MTESA, Love; High Commissioner for Zambia in London, since 1992; *b* 9 July 1942; *s* of late William Mutesa and Olive Mutesa; *m* Marie Madeleine; two *s* two *d. Educ:* Mercy

Coll., NY (BSc Pol Sci 1985); Internat. Inst. of Public Relations, Paris (Dipl. Internat. Relations 1994); Univ. of Westminster (MA Diplomatic Studies). Teacher, Ndola, Zambia, 1962–64; 2nd Sec., Zambian Embassy, Kinshasa, 1966–70; 1st Sec., Addis Ababa, 1970–73; Counsellor, Kinshasa, 1974–75; Dir, Africa and Middle East, Foreign Affairs, Lusaka, 1975–79; Dep. High Comr, Harare, 1980–82; Dep. Perm. Rep., UN, NY, 1982–85; resigned from Govt, June 1986; Chm. of Opposition Party, Movement for Multi-Party Democracy for Lusaka Dist, 1990–92; Sec., Internat. Relations Cttee, MMD, 1991–92. *Recreations:* table tennis, watching soccer. *Address:* Zambia House, 2 Palace Gate, W8 5NG. *T:* 0171–589 6655; 17 Courtenay Avenue, Hampstead, N6 4LR.

MUCH, Ian Fraser Robert; Executive Director, T & N, since 1988 (Chief Executive Operations, since 1995); *b* 8 Sept. 1944; *s* of Alan Fraser Much and Helen Isabella Much (*née* Barker); *m* 1978, Perena Amanda Richards; one *d*. *Educ:* Haileybury and ISC; Lincoln Coll., Oxford (MA Jurisp.). The Metal Box Co., 1966–73; Selkirk Metalbestos, 1974–78; Household International Inc., 1978–84; Factory Manager, Nampa, Idaho, 1978–80; Vice-Pres., Gen. Manager, Greensboro, N Carolina, 1980–84; BTR: Man. Dir, Dunlop Aviation Div., 1985–87; Gp Chief Exec., 1987–88; Dir, BTR Industries; Managing Director: Engineering & Industrial, T & N, 1990–91; Bearings and Industrial, T & N, 1991–95. *Recreations:* ski-ing, tennis, squash, golf, swimming, bridge, theatre, opera. *Address:* T & N, Bowdon House, Ashburton Road West, Trafford Park, Manchester M17 1RA; The Woodlands, Knutsford Road, Chelford, Cheshire SK11 9AS. *Clubs:* Mere Golf and Country; Alderley Edge Cricket.

MUDD, (William) David; *b* 2 June 1933; *o s* of Capt. W. N. Mudd and Mrs T. E. Mudd; *m*; one *s* one *d* (and one step *d*). *Educ:* Truro Cathedral Sch. Journalist, Broadcaster, TV Commentator; work on BBC and ITV (Westward Television). Editor of The Cornish Echo, 1952; Staff Reporter: Western Morning News, 1952–53 and 1959–62; Tavistock Gazette, 1963. Mem., Tavistock UDC, 1963–65. MP (C) Falmouth and Camborne, 1970–92. PPS, Dept of Energy, 1979–81; Mem., Transport Select Cttee, 1982–92. Secretary: Conservative West Country Cttee, 1973–76; Conservative Party Fisheries Sub-Cttee, 1974–75, 1981–82. Patron, Court Interpreters' Assoc., Supreme Court of Hong Kong, 1979–. *Publications:* Cornishmen and True, 1971; Murder in the West Country, 1975; Facets of Crime, 1975; The Innovators, 1976; Down Along Camborne and Redruth, 1978; The Falmouth Packets, 1978; Cornish Sea Lights, 1978; Cornwall and Scilly Peculiar, 1979; About the City, 1979; Home Along Falmouth and Penryn, 1980; Around and About the Roseland, 1980; The Cruel Cornish Sea, 1981; The Cornish Edwardians, 1982; Cornwall in Uproar, 1983; Around and About the Fal, 1989; Around and About the Smugglers' Ways, 1991; Strange Stories of Cornwall, 1992; Dartmoor Reflections, 1993; The Magic of Dartmoor, 1994. *Recreations:* jig-saw puzzles, boating, photography, ice skating, walking, cycling.

MUDDIMER, Robert Michael; Director, Tomkins plc, since 1986; Chairman, Ranks Hovis McDougall, since 1992; *b* 30 Jan. 1933; *m* 1959, Marguerite Conroy; two *s* one *d*. *Educ:* Kibworth Grammar Sch.; Univ. of Nottingham (BSc Mech. Eng 1956). FIEE (FIMfgE 1966). Materials Mgt, Lansing Bagnall, 1965–68; Director: BTR Ind. Ltd, 1969–80; Molins Tobacco Ind. Ltd, 1981–86. CIMgt (CBIM 1973). *Recreations:* golf, sailing, wooden clockmaking. *Address:* Ranks Hovis McDougall, Chapel House, Liston Road, Marlow, Bucks SL7 1TJ. *Clubs:* Leicestershire Golf; Dayton Racquet (Ohio).

MUDIE, George Edward; MP (Lab) Leeds East, since 1992; *b* 6 Feb. 1945; *m*; two *c*. *Educ:* state schs. Former Mem. (Lab) Leeds CC, and Leader of Council. Former Chm., AMA. *Address:* House of Commons, SW1A 0AA.

MUELLER, Dame Anne Elisabeth, DCB 1988 (CB 1980); Second Permanent Secretary, HM Treasury, 1987–90; Chancellor, De Montfort University (formerly Leicester Polytechnic), since 1991; *b* 15 Oct. 1930; *d* of late Herbert Constantin Mueller and Phoebe Ann Beevers; *m* 1958, James Hugh Robertson (marr. diss. 1978). *Educ:* Wakefield Girls' High Sch.; Somerville Coll., Oxford (Hon. Fellow, 1984). Entered Min. of Labour and Nat. Service, 1953; served with Orgn for European Econ. Co-op., 1955–56; Treasury, 1962; Dept of Economic Affairs, 1964; Min. of Technology, 1969; DTI 1970; Under-Sec., DTI, later DoI, 1972–77; Dep. Sec., DoI, later DTI, 1977–84; Second Perm. Sec., Cabinet Office (MPO), 1984–87. Director: EIB, 1978–84; STC plc, 1990–91; CARE Britain, 1990–; Phonepoint Ltd, 1990–92; British Sky Broadcasting, 1991–; Sedgwick Lloyd's Underwriting Agents Ltd, 1992–; CARE International, 1992– (Vice-Pres., 1992–). Ind. Investigator, SIB, 1990–94; Member: Bd, Business in the Community, 1984–88; Rural Develt Commn, 1990–; Nurses and Allied Professions Review Body, 1991–94; Vice Pres., Industrial Participation Assoc., 1986–90. Member Council: Inst. of Manpower Studies, 1981–95 (Vice-Pres., 1989–95); Templeton Coll., Oxford, 1985–; Manchester Business Sch., 1985–92; Queen Mary and Westfield Coll., 1990–; Trustee: Whitechapel Art Gall., 1985–; Duke of Edinburgh's Study Confs, 1986–93; Res. Inst. for Consumer Affairs, 1991–; Chm., European Centre for Public Affairs, 1992–. Ind. Gov., De Montfort Univ. (formerly Leicester Polytechnic), 1988–. CIMgt (CBIM 1978); FRSA 1981; FIPM 1986. Hon. DLitt: Warwick, 1985; CNAA, 1991; Hon. LLD Nottingham, 1993. *Address:* 46 Kensington Heights, Campden Hill Road, W8 7BD. *T:* 0171–727 4780. *Club:* United Oxford & Cambridge University.

MUELLER, Rudolf Gottfried; Chairman, UBS (formerly UBS Phillips & Drew) Ltd, since 1989 (Chief Executive, 1989–93); Executive Vice President Europe, Union Bank of Switzerland Group, since 1991; *b* 28 May 1934; *m* Christiane Béroud; two *s*. *Educ:* primary and secondary schools, St Gallen, Switzerland; Internat. Management Inst., Geneva. Swiss Fed. Commercial Dip. 1953; grad. 1969 from Univ. of Geneva with dip. equivalent to MBA. Adolph Saurer AG, Arbon, 1954–56; United Trading Co., Basle, in Basle and Nigeria, 1956–68; Head of European office, James Capel & Co., Geneva and Chm. and Man. Dir, James Capel Far East, 1969–77; Union Bank of Switzerland: Rep. in Singapore, 1977, Br. Manager, 1978–81; First Vice-Pres., 1981–82; Head of Securities Sales and Trading Worldwide, Zürich, 1982–83; Sen. Vice-Pres., 1983–87; Exec. Vice-Pres. (UK), 1987–91. Chm., SOFFEX, Zürich, 1986–88. Chm., BMBA Securities Trading Cttee, 1991–; Mem., Chms' Cttee, LIBA, 1992–. Dir, London Stock Exchange, 1991– (Mem., 1988). Member of Board: Internat. Management Inst., Kiev, 1993–; London First, 1994–; Royal Opera House Trust, 1992–. *Recreations:* golf, ski-ing, hiking, oenology. *Address:* Union Bank of Switzerland, 100 Liverpool Street, EC2M 2RH. *T:* 0171–901 3333.

MUFF, family name of **Baron Calverley.**

MUGABE, Robert Gabriel; President of Zimbabwe, since 1988; President, Zimbabwe African National Union-Patriotic Front, since 1988; *b* Kutama, 1924; *m* 1961, Sarah Francesca Hayfron (*d* 1992); one *s* decd. *Educ:* Kutama and Empanden Mission School; Fort Hare Univ. (BA (Educ), BSc (Econ)); London Univ. (by correspondence: BSc(Econ); BEd; LLB; LLM; MSc(Econ)); Univ. of S Africa (by correspondence BAdm). Teacher, 1942–58: Kutama, Mapanzure, Shabani, Empandeni Mission, Hope Fountain Mission, Driefontein Mission, South Africa; Mbizi Govt Sch., Mambo Sch., Chalimbana Trng Coll., Zambia; St Mary's Teacher Trng Coll., Ghana. Publ. Sec. of Nat. Dem. Party, 1960–61; Publicity Sec. and acting Sec.-Gen., Zimbabwe African People's Union, 1961–62. Political detention, 1962, escaped to Tanzania, 1963; became Sec.-Gen. ZANU, Aug. 1963, but in detention in Rhodesia, 1964–74; resident in Mozambique, 1975–79. Prime Minister and Minister of Defence, 1980–87, Minister of Public Service, 1981–87, First Sec. of Politburo and Minister of Industry and Technology, 1984–87, Zimbabwe. Jt Leader (with Joshua Nkomo) of the Patriotic Front, Oct. 1976; Pres. (Co-Founder, 1963), ZANU, 1977–87. Attended Confs: Geneva Constitutional Conf. on Rhodesia, 1976; Malta Conf., 1978; London Conf., 1979. Hon. LLD Ahmadu Bello. *Address:* Office of the President, Harare, Zimbabwe.

MUGNOZZA, Carlo S.; *see* Scarascia-Mugnozza.

MUHEIM, Franz Emmanuel; Professorial Lecturer, The Bologna Centre, Johns Hopkins University, since 1995; Swiss Ambassador to the Court of St James's, 1989–94; *b* 27 Sept. 1931; *s* of Hans Muheim and Hélène (*née* Ody); *m* 1962, Radmila Jovanovic. *Educ:* Univs of Fribourg (LèsL), Geneva and Paris (arts degree). Joined Swiss Federal Dept of Foreign Affairs, 1960; served successively in Belgrade, Rabat and London, 1961–70; Council of Europe, UN and Internat. Orgns Sect., Dept of Foreign Affairs, Berne, 1971–77; Dep. Head of Mission, Minister Plenipotentiary, Washington, 1978–81; Dep. Dir of Political Affairs and Head of Political Div. Europe and N America, with rank of Ambassador, Berne, 1982–83; Dir, Internat. Orgns, Dept of Foreign Affairs, 1984–89. Head of Swiss delegns to internat. confs, *inter alia* UNESCO, ESA, Red Cross, Non-Aligned Movement. Fellow, Center for Internat. Affairs, Harvard Univ., 1981–82. *Publication:* (ed jtly) Einblick in die Schweizerische Aussenpolitik: festschrift für Staatssekretär Raymond Probst, 1984; Multilateralism Today: festchrift zum 70. Geburtstag von a. Ständerat Franz Muheim, 1993. *Recreations:* walking, mountaineering, ski-ing, photography, music. *Address:* Es Chesaux, 1646 Echarlens, Switzerland. *T:* (029) 52474.

MUIR, Alec Andrew, CBE 1968; QPM 1961; DL; Chief Constable of Durham Constabulary, 1967–70; *b* 21 Aug. 1909; *s* of Dr Robert Douglas Muir, MD, and Edith Muir, The Limes, New Cross, SE14; *m* 1948, Hon. Helen (who *m* 1st, 1935, Wm Farr; marr. diss., 1948; she *d* 1994), *er d* of Baron du Parcq (*d* 1949); one *s* one *d*, and one step *s* one step *d*. *Educ:* Christ's Hosp.; Wadham Coll., Oxford (MA). Receivers' Office, Metropolitan Police, 1933; Metropolitan Police Coll., 1934; Supt, 1948; Chief Constable, Durham Co. Constabulary, 1950. DL, Co. Durham, 1964. OStJ 1957. *Recreations:* cricket, bowls, squash, sailing. *Address:* Beanlands Nursing Home, Crosshills, Keighley, W Yorks BD20 8PL.

MUIR, Prof. Alexander Laird, MD; FRCPE, FRCR, FRCSE; Postgraduate Dean of Medicine, since 1990, and Professor of Postgraduate Medicine, since 1993, University of Edinburgh; Honorary Consultant Physician, Edinburgh Royal Infirmary, since 1974; Physician to the Queen in Scotland, since 1985; Honorary Physician to the Army in Scotland, since 1986; *b* 12 April 1937; *s* of Andrew Muir and Helena Bauld; *m* 1968, Berenice Barker Snelgrove, FRCR; one *s* one *d*. *Educ:* Morrisons Acad.; Fettes Coll.; Univ. of Edinburgh. MB ChB; MD 1970; FRCPE 1975 (MRCPE 1967); FRCR 1986; FRCSE 1994. MO, British Antarctic Survey, 1963–65; MRC Fellow, McGill Univ., 1970–71; Consultant Physician, Manchester Royal Infirmary, 1973–74; Sen. Lectr in Medicine, 1974, Reader in Medicine, 1981–89, Univ. of Edinburgh. Canadian MRC Vis. Scientist, Univ. of British Columbia, 1982. Mem., Admin of Radioactive Substances Adv. Cttee, 1986–. Vice-Pres., RCPE, 1994–. Member Editorial Board: Thorax, 1981–86; British Heart Jl, 1986–. *Publications:* contribs on physiology and diseases of heart and lungs to medical books, symposia and jls. *Recreations:* gardening, reading, ski-ing, sailboarding. *Address:* 45 Cluny Drive, Edinburgh EH10 6DU. *T:* 0131–447 2652. *Club:* Edinburgh University Staff (Edinburgh).

MUIR, Frank, CBE 1980, writer and broadcaster; *b* 5 Feb. 1920; *s* of Charles James Muir and Margaret Harding; *m* 1949, Polly McIrvine; one *s* one *d*. *Educ:* Chatham House, Ramsgate; Leyton County High Sch. Served RAF, 1940–46. Wrote radio comedy-series and compered TV progs, 1946. With Denis Norden, 1947–64; collaborated for 17 years writing comedy scripts, including: (for radio): Take it from Here, 1947–58; Bedtime with Braden, 1950–54; (for TV): And so to Bentley, 1956; Whack-O,! 1958–60; The Seven Faces of Jim, 1961, and other series with Jimmy Edwards; resident in TV and radio panel-games; collaborated in film scripts, television commercials, and revues (Prince of Wales, 1951; Adelphi, 1952); joint Advisors and Consultants to BBC Television Light Entertainment Dept, 1960–64; jointly received Screenwriters Guild Award for Best Contribution to Light Entertainment, 1961; together on panel-games My Word!, 1956–, and My Music, 1967–. Asst Head of BBC Light Entertainment Gp, 1964–67; Head of Entertainment, London Weekend Television, 1968–69, resigned 1969, and reverted to being self-unemployed; resumed TV series Call My Bluff, 1970; began radio series Frank Muir Goes Into . . ., 1971; The Frank Muir Version, 1976. Pres., Johnson Soc., Lichfield, 1975–76. Rector, Univ. of St Andrews, 1977–79. (With Simon Brett) Writers' Guild Award for Best Radio Feature Script, 1973; (with Denis Norden) Variety Club of GB Award for Best Radio Personality of 1977; Radio Personality of the Year, Radio Industries Club, 1977; Sony Gold Award, 1983. Hon. LLD St Andrews, 1978; Hon. DLitt Kent, 1982. *Publications:* (with Patrick Campbell) Call My Bluff, 1972; (with Denis Norden) You Can't Have Your Kayak and Heat It, 1973; (with Denis Norden) Upon My Word!, 1974; Christmas Customs and Traditions, 1975; The Frank Muir Book: an irreverant companion to social history, 1976; What-a-Mess, 1977; (with Denis Norden) Take My Word for It, 1978; (with Simon Brett) Frank Muir Goes Into . . ., 1978; What-a-Mess the Good, 1978; (with Denis Norden) The Glums, 1979; (with Simon Brett) The Second Frank Muir Goes Into . . ., 1979; Prince What-a-Mess, 1979; Super What-a-Mess, 1980; (with Simon Brett) The Third Frank Muir Goes Into . . ., 1980; (with Simon Brett) Frank Muir on Children, 1980; (with Denis Norden) Oh, My Word!, 1980; What-a-Mess and the Cat-Next-Door, 1981; (with Simon Brett) The Fourth Frank Muir Goes Into . . ., 1981; (with Polly Muir) The Big Dipper, 1981; A Book at Bathtime, 1982; What-a-Mess in Spring, What-a-Mess in Summer, What-a-Mess in Autumn, What-a-Mess in Winter, 1982; (with Simon Brett) The Book of Comedy Sketches, 1982; What-a-Mess at the Seaside, 1983; (with Denis Norden) The Complete and Utter "My Word!" Collection, 1983; What-a-Mess goes to School, 1984; What-a-Mess has Breakfast, 1986; What-a-Mess has Lunch, 1986; What-a-Mess has Tea, 1986; What-a-Mess has Supper, 1986; What-a-Mess goes on Television, 1989; (with Denis Norden) You Have "My Word", 1989; The Oxford Book of Humorous Prose: from William Caxton to P. G. Wodehouse, a conducted tour, 1990; What-a-Mess and the Hairy Monster, 1990; Frank Muir Retells: Three Little Pigs, Jack and the Beanstalk, Goldilocks and the Three Bears, 1991; The Walpole Orange, 1993. *Recreations:* book collecting, staring silently into space. *Address:* Anners, Thorpe, Egham, Surrey TW20 8UE. *T:* Chertsey (01932) 562759. *Club:* Garrick.

MUIR, (Isabella) Helen (Mary), CBE 1981; MA, DPhil, DSc; FRS 1977; Director, Kennedy Institute of Rheumatology, London, 1977–90 (Head of Division of Biochemistry, 1966–86); *b* 20 Aug. 1920; *d* of late G. B. F. Muir, ICS, and Gwladys Muir (*née* Stack). *Educ:* Downe House, Newbury; Somerville Coll., Oxford (Hon. Fellow, 1978). MA 1944, DPhil (Oxon) 1947, DSc (Oxon) 1973. Research Fellow, Dunn's Sch. of Pathology, Oxford, 1947–48; Scientific Staff, Nat. Inst. for Med. Research, 1948–54; Empire Rheumatism Council Fellow, St Mary's Hosp., London, 1954–58; Pearl Research Fellow, St Mary's Hosp., 1959–66; Visiting Professor: Queen Elizabeth Coll., Univ. of London,

1981–85; Newcastle Univ., 1995–. Hon. Prof., Charing Cross and Westminster Med. Sch., 1979–. Scientific Mem. Council, Med. Research Council (first woman to serve), Oct. 1973–Sept. 1977. Mem., Connective Tissue Res. Adv. Bd, 1971–85; Governor, Strangeways Res. Lab., 1980–90; Trustee, Wellcome Trust, 1982–90. Heberden Orator, London, 1976; Bunim Lectr, US Arthritis Assoc., New Orleans, 1978. Member, Editorial Board: Biochemical Jl, 1964–69; Annals of the Rheumatic Diseases, 1971–77; Connective Tissue Res., 1971–85; Jl of Orthopaedic Res., 1983–. For. Mem., Royal Swedish Acad. of Scis, 1989; Honorary Member: Amer. Soc. of Biological Chemists, 1982; European Soc. of Arthrology, 1988. Hon. DSc: Edinburgh, 1982; Strathclyde, 1983; Brunel, 1990. Feldberg Foundn Award, 1977; Neil Hamilton Fairley Medal, RCP, 1981; Ciba Medal, Biochem. Soc., 1981; Steindler Award, Orthop. Soc., USA, 1982; Ciba Internat. Award, 1993. *Publications:* many scientific papers, mainly on biochem. of connective tissues in reln to arthritis and inherited diseases in Biochem. Jl, Biochim. et Biophys. Acta, Nature, etc; contribs to several specialist books. *Recreations:* gardening, music, horses, natural history and science in general. *Address:* Department of Biochemistry, Charing Cross and Westminster Medical School, Fulham Palace Road, W6 8RF. *T:* 0181–846 7053.

MUIR, Prof. Kenneth, FBA 1970; King Alfred Professor of English Literature, University of Liverpool, 1951–74, now Professor Emeritus; *b* 5 May 1907; *s* of Dr R. D. Muir; *m* 1936, Mary Ewen; one *s* one *d*. *Educ:* Epsom Coll.; St Edmund Hall, Oxford (Hon. Fellow, 1987). Lectr in English, St John's Coll., York, 1930–37; Lectr in English Literature, Leeds Univ., 1937–51; Liverpool University: Public Orator, 1961–65; Dean of the Faculty of Arts, 1958–61. Visiting Professor: Univ. of Pittsburgh, 1962–63; Univ. of Connecticut, 1973; Univ. of Pennsylvania, 1977. Editor, Shakespeare Survey, 1965–80; Vice-Pres., Internat. Shakespeare Assoc., 1986– (Chm., 1974–85); Pres., English Assoc., 1987. Leeds City Councillor, 1945–47, 1950–51; Chm. of Leeds Fabian Soc., 1941–46; Pres., Leeds Labour Party, 1951; Birkenhead Borough Councillor, 1954–57. FRSL 1978. Docteur de l'Université: de Rouen, 1967; de Dijon, 1976. *Publications:* The Nettle and the Flower, 1933; Jonah in the Whale, 1935; (with Sean O'Loughlin) The Voyage to Illyria, 1937; English Poetry, 1938; Collected Poems of Sir Thomas Wyatt, 1949; Arden edn Macbeth, 1951; King Lear, 1952; Elizabethan Lyrics, 1953; (ed) Wilkins' Painful Adventures of Pericles, 1953; John Milton, 1955; The Pelican Book of English Prose I, 1956; Shakespeare's Sources, 1957; (ed with F. P. Wilson) The Life and Death of Jack Straw, 1957; (ed) John Keats, 1958; Shakespeare and the Tragic Pattern, 1959; trans. Five Plays of Jean Racine, 1960; Shakespeare as Collaborator, 1960; editor Unpublished Poems by Sir Thomas Wyatt, 1961; Last Periods, 1961; (ed) U. Ellis-Fermor's Shakespeare the Dramatist, 1961; (ed) Richard II, 1963; Life and Letters of Sir Thomas Wyatt, 1963; Shakespeare: Hamlet, 1963; (ed) Shakespeare: The Comedies, 1965; Introduction to Elizabethan Literature, 1967; (ed) Othello, 1968; (ed) The Winter's Tale, 1968; (ed with Patricia Thomson) Collected Poems of Sir Thomas Wyatt, 1969; The Comedy of Manners, 1970; (ed) The Rivals, 1970; (ed) Double Falsehood, 1970; (ed with S. Schoenbaum) A New Companion to Shakespeare Studies, 1971; Shakespeare's Tragic Sequence, 1972; Shakespeare the Professional, 1973; (ed) Essays and Studies, 1974; (ed) Three Plays of Thomas Middleton, 1975; The Singularity of Shakespeare, 1977; The Sources of Shakespeare's Plays, 1977; Shakespeare's Comic Sequence, 1979; Shakespeare's Sonnets, 1979; (trans.) Four Comedies of Calderón, 1980; (ed) U. Ellis-Fermor's Shakespeare's Drama, 1980; (ed with S. Wells) Aspects of the Problem Plays, 1982; (ed with M. Allen) Shakespeare's Plays in Quarto, 1982; (ed) Troilus and Cressida, 1982; (ed with S. Wells) Aspects of King Lear, 1982; (ed with J. Halio and D. Palmer) Shakespeare: man of the theater, 1983; Shakespeare's Didactic Art, 1984; (ed) King Lear: Critical Essays, 1984; (ed) Interpretations of Shakespeare, 1985; Shakespeare: contrasts and controversies, 1985; (trans. with A. L. Mackenzie) Three Comedies of Calderón, 1985; King Lear: a critical study, 1986; Antony and Cleopatra: a critical study, 1987; Negative Capability and the Art of the Dramatist, 1987; (trans. with A. L. Mackenzie) Calderón's La Cisma de Inglaterra, 1990; (trans. with A. L. Mackenzie) Calderón, Jealousy the Worst Monster, 1995. *Recreation:* theatre. *Address:* 6 Chetwynd Road, Oxton, Birkenhead, Merseyside L43 2JJ. *T:* 0151–652 3301.

MUIR, Sir Laurence (Macdonald), Kt 1981; VRD 1954; company director; Deputy Chairman, National Science and Technology Centre Advisory Committee, since 1986; Founding Chairman, Canberra Development Board, 1979–86; *b* 3 March 1925; *s* of Andrew Muir and Agnes Campbell Macdonald; two *s* two *d*. *Educ:* Yallourn State Sch.; Scotch Coll., Melbourne; Univ. of Melbourne (LLB). Served RAN, 1942–46 (Lieut); Lt-Comdr, RANR, 1949–65. Admitted Barrister and Solicitor, Supreme Court of Victoria, 1950. Sharebroker, 1949–80; Mem., Stock Exchange of Melbourne, 1960–80; Partner, 1962–80, Sen. Partner, 1976–80, Potter Partners. Director: ANZ Banking Gp, 1980–91; ACI Internat. Ltd (formerly ACI Ltd), 1980–88; Nat. Commercial Union Assce Co. of Aust. Ltd (formerly Commercial Union Assce Co. of Aust.), 1979–91; Wormald Internat. Ltd, 1980–88; Herald and Weekly Times Ltd, 1982–87; ANZ Pensions Ltd, 1982–91; Alcoa of Australia Ltd, 1982–; Hudson Conway Ltd (formerly Australian Asset Management Ltd), 1987–; Templeton Global Growth Fund, 1987–; Greening Australia, 1985–90; Focus Books Pty Ltd, 1990–; Australian Consolidated Press Group, subseq. Publishing and Broadcasting Ltd, 1992–; Southern Sun Energy Pty Ltd, 1992–; Chairman: Aust. Biomedical Corp. Ltd, 1983–87; Liquid Air Australia Ltd, 1982–; Elders Austral Chartering Pty Ltd, 1984–90; University Paton Ltd, 1986–90; Vic. Br., Greening Australia. Chm., John Curtin Sch. of Medical Res. Adv. Bd, 1982–88; Member: Parlt House Construction Authority (Chm., Artworks Adv. Cttee); Council, Gen. Motors, Aust.; L'Air Liquide World Adv. Cttee; Victoria Garden State Cttee; Vic. Appeals Cttee, Anti-Cancer Council; Commn for the Future, 1991–; Consultant, Alfred Hosp. Bd, 1983–88. Patron: Baker Med. Res. Inst.; Microsurgery Foundn; Trustee and Board Member: Sir Robert Menzies Meml Trust; Earthwatch Australia; Founder and Trustee, Delta Soc. Aust.; Trustee, Aust. Scout Educn & Trng Foundn; Life Trustee, Cttee for Economic Develt of Aust. Mem. Exec. Cttee, World Athletic Cup 1985; Council Mem., HRH Duke of Edinburgh's 6th Commonwealth Study Conf. (Chm., Aust. Finance Cttee). Fellow: Securities Inst. of Australia, 1962; Australian Inst. of Dirs, 1967; FAIM 1965. *Recreations:* gardening, fishing. *Address:* 1 Belle Avenue, Brighton, Vic 3186, Australia. *Clubs:* Melbourne, Melbourne Cricket, Lawn Tennis Association of Victoria (Melbourne); Peninsula Country Golf.

MUIR, (Sir) Richard James Kay, (4th Bt *cr* 1892, of Deanston, Perthshire); *S* father, 1994, but does not use the title; *b* 25 May 1939; *s* of Sir John Harling Muir, 3rd Bt, TD and of Elizabeth Mary, *e d* of Frederick James Dundas; *m* 1st, 1965, Susan Elizabeth (marr. diss. 1974), *d* of George A. Gardener; two *d*; 2nd, 1975, Lady Linda Mary Cole, *d* of 6th Earl of Enniskillen, MBE; two *d*. *Heir:* *b* Ian Charles Muir [*b* 16 Sept. 1940; *m* 1967, Fiona Barbara Elspeth, *d* of Major Stuart Mackenzie; three *d*].

MUIR, Richard John Sutherland, CMG 1994; HM Diplomatic Service; Ambassador to Oman, since 1994; *b* 25 Aug. 1942; *s* of John Muir and Edna (*née* Hodges); *m* 1966, Caroline Simpson; one *s* one *d*. *Educ:* The Stationers' Co.'s Sch.; Univ. of Reading (BA Hons). Entered HM Diplomatic Service, 1964, FO, 1964–65; MECAS, Lebanon, 1965–67; Third, then Second Sec. (Commercial), Jedda, 1967–70; Second Sec., Tunis, 1970–72; FCO, 1972–75; First Sec., Washington, 1975–79; seconded to Dept of Energy, 1979–81; First Sec., Jedda, 1981–82; Counsellor, Jedda and Dir-Gen., British Liaison Office, Riyadh, 1983–85; FCO 1985–94: Hd of Information Dept, 1987–90; Principal Finance Officer and Chief Inspector, 1991–94. *Address:* c/o Foreign and Commonwealth Office, SW1A 2AH.

MUIR, Tom; Director, British Retail Consortium, since 1995; Under Secretary, Textiles and Retailing Division, Department of Trade and Industry, 1992–94; *b* 15 Feb. 1936; *s* of late William and Maria Muir; *m* 1968, Brenda Dew; one *s* one *d*. *Educ:* King Edward VI Sch., Stafford; Leeds Univ. (BA Econs 1962). FCIS 1994. English Electric Co. Ltd, 1954–59; BoT, 1962–68; UK Perm. Delegn to OECD (on secondment to HM Diplomatic Service), 1968–71; DTI, 1972–75; UK Perm. Repn to EC, 1975–79 (on secondment); DoI, 1979–81; Dept of Trade, 1981–83; DTI, 1983–94: Under Sec., Insce Div., 1982–87, Overseas Trade Div. 4, 1987–89, Ext. European Policy, later Internat. Trade Policy Div., 1989–92. FRSA 1992. *Recreations:* walking, swimming, reading, looking at buildings and pictures. *Address:* Westhanger Tower, Westbrook Road, Godalming, Surrey GU7 2QH.

MUIR BEDDALL, Hugh Richard; *see* Beddall.

MUIR MACKENZIE, Sir Alexander (Alwyne Henry Charles Brinton), 7th Bt *cr* 1805; *b* 8 Dec. 1955; *s* of Sir Robert Henry Muir Mackenzie, 6th Bt and Charmian Cecil de Vere (*d* 1962), *o d* of Col Cecil Charles Brinton; *S* father, 1970; *m* 1984, Susan Carolyn, *d* of John David Henzel Hayter; one *s* one *d*. *Educ:* Eton; Trinity Coll., Cambridge. *Heir:* *s* Archie Robert David Muir Mackenzie, *b* 17 Feb. 1989. *Address:* Buckshaw House, Holwell, near Sherborne, Dorset DT9 5LD.

MUIR WOOD, Sir Alan (Marshall), Kt 1982; FRS 1980; FEng; FICE; Consultant, Sir William Halcrow & Partners (Partner, 1964–84, Senior Partner, 1979–84); *b* 8 Aug. 1921; *s* of Edward Stephen Wood and Dorothy (*née* Webb); *m* 1943, Winifred Leyton Lanagan, (Dr W. L. Wood, mathematician); three *s*. *Educ:* Abbotsholme Sch.; Peterhouse, Cambridge Univ. (MA; Hon. Fellow 1982). FICE 1957; Fellow, Fellowship of Engrg, 1977 (a Vice-Pres., 1984–87). Engr Officer, RN, 1942–46. Asst Engr, British Rail, Southern Reg., 1946–50; Res. Asst, Docks and Inland Waterways Exec., 1950–52; Asst Engr, then Sen. Engr, Sir William Halcrow & Partners, 1952–64. Principally concerned with studies and works in fields of tunnelling, geotechnics, coastal engrg, energy, roads and railways; major projects include: (Proj. Engr) Clyde Tunnel and Potters Bar railway tunnels; (Partner) Cargo Tunnel at Heathrow Airport, and Cuilfail Tunnel, Lewes; studies and works for Channel Tunnel (intermittently from 1958); Dir, Orange-Fish Consultants, resp. for 80 km irrigation tunnel. Member: ACARD, 1980–84; SERC, 1981–84; Governing Body, Inst. of Development Studies, 1981–87; Council, ITDG, 1981–84; Chairman: SERC/ESRC Jt Cttee, 1983–85; Res. Councils Individual Merit Promotion Panel, 1989–94. Mem. Council, Royal Soc., 1983–84, a Vice-Pres., 1983–84; President: Internat. Tunnelling Assoc., 1975–77 (Hon. Life Pres., 1977); ICE, 1977–78. Fellow, Imperial Coll., 1981; Foreign Member, Royal Swedish Acad. of Engrg Sci., 1980; Hon. Fellow, Portsmouth Polytech., 1984. Hon. DSc: City, 1978; Southampton, 1986; Hon. LLD Dundee, 1985; Hon. DEng Bristol, 1991. Telford Medal, ICE, 1976; James Alfred Ewing Medal, ICE and Royal Soc., 1984. *Publications:* Coastal Hydraulics, 1969, (with C. A. Fleming) 2nd edn 1981; papers, mainly on tunnelling, coastal engrg and wider aspects of engrg, in Proc. ICE and elsewhere. *Address:* Franklands, Bere Court Road, Pangbourne, Berks RG8 8JY. *T:* Pangbourne (01734) 842833. *Club:* Athenæum.

MUIRHEAD, Sir David (Francis), KCMG 1976 (CMG 1964); CVO 1957; HM Diplomatic Service, retired; *b* 30 Dec. 1918; *s* of late David Muirhead, Kippen, Stirlingshire; *m* 1942, Hon. Elspeth Hope-Morley (*d* 1989), *d* of 2nd Baron Hollenden, and of Hon. Mary Gardner, *d* of 1st Baron Burghclere; two *s* one *d*. *Educ:* Cranbrook Sch. Commissioned Artists Rifles (Rifle Brigade), 1937; passed Officers Exam., RMC Sandhurst; apptd to Bedfs and Herts Regt, 1939; served War of 1939–45 in France, Belgium and SE Asia. Hon. Attaché, Brit. Embassy, Madrid, 1941. Passed Foreign Service Exam., 1946; appointed to Foreign Office, 1947; La Paz, 1948; Buenos Aires, 1949; Brussels, 1950; Foreign Office, 1953; Washington, 1955; Foreign Office, 1959; Under-Sec., Foreign Office, 1966–67; HM Ambassador: Peru, 1967–70; Portugal, 1970–74; Belgium, 1974–78. Special Rep. of Sec. of State for Foreign and Commonwealth Affairs, 1979–94. Mem. Council, St Dunstan's, 1981–89; Comr, Commonwealth War Graves Commn, 1981–86. Grand Cross, Military Order of Christ (Portugal); Grand Cross, Order of Distinguished Service (Peru). *Address:* 16 Pitt Street, W8 4NY. *T:* 0171–937 2443. *Club:* Travellers'.

MUKHERJEE, Pranab Kumar; Minister of External Affairs, India, since 1995; Member, Rajya Sabha, 1969–87 (Leader, 1980–85); *b* 11 Dec. 1935; *s* of Kamda Kinkar Mukherjee, of an illustrious family which was involved actively in the Freedom Movement of India; *m* 1957, Suvra Mukherjee; two *s* one *d*. *Educ:* Vidyasagar Coll., Suri; Calcutta Univ. (MA (Hist. and Pol Sci.); LLB). Dep. Minister, Mins of Industrial Develt and of Shipping and Transport, 1973–74; Minister of State, Finance Min., 1974–77; Cabinet Minister i/c of Mins of Commerce, Steel and Mines, 1980–82; became youngest Minister to hold Finance Portfolio in Independent India, 1982–85; Commerce Minister, 1993–95. Spokesman, All India Congress Cttee, 1991; Chm., Central Election Campaign Cttee of Congress Party for Lok Sabha Election, 1991. Dep. Chm., Planning Cttee, Govt of India, 1991–93. *Publications:* Crisis in Democracy; An Aspect of Constitutional Problems in Bengal, 1967; Mid-Term Poll, 1969; Beyond Survival: an emerging dimension of Indian economy, 1984; Off the Track: an analysis of Indian economy, 1987. *Recreations:* music, gardening, reading. *Address:* S-22, Greater Kailash, Part II, New Delhi 110048, India. *T:* (home) 6435656, 6474025/6; (office) 3014070, 3011127.

MUKHERJEE, Tara Kumar, FLIA; Managing Director: Owl Financial Services Ltd, since 1988; Greater London Translation Unit, since 1993; President, Confederation of Indian Organisations (UK), since 1975; *b* 20 Dec. 1923; *s* of Sushil Chandra Mukherjee and Sova Moyee Mukherjee; *m* 1951, Betty Patricia Mukherjee; one *s* one *d*. *Educ:* Scottish Church Collegiate Sch., Calcutta, India; Calcutta Univ. (matriculated 1939). Shop Manager, Bata Shoe Co. Ltd, India, 1941–44; Buyer, Brevitt Shoes, Leicester, 1951–56; Sundries Buyer, British Shoe Corp., 1956–66; Prodn Administrator, Priestley Footwear Ltd, Great Harwood, 1966–68; Head Stores Manager, Brit. Shoe Corp., 1968–70; Save & Prosper Group: Dist Manager, 1970–78; Br. Manager, 1978–84; Senior Sales Manager, 1984–85; Br. Manager, Guardian Royal Exchange PFM Ltd, 1985–88. Pres., India Film Soc., Leicester. Chairman: Charter 90 for Asians; Leicester Community Centre Project; Member: Brit. Europ. Movement, London; Exec. Council, Leics Europ. Movement; Pres., EC Migrants Forum, Brussels. Dir, Coronary Prevention Gp, 1986–; Trustee, Haymarket Theatre, Leicester. Patron, London Community Cricket Assoc., 1987–. FRSA. *Recreation:* cricket (1st Cl. cricketer; played for Bihar, Ranji Trophy, 1941; 2nd XI, Leics CCC, 1949). *Address:* Tallah, 1 Park Avenue, Hutton, Brentwood, Essex CM13 2QL. *T:* Brentwood (01277) 263207. *Club:* (Gen. Sec.) Indian National (Leicester).

MULCAHY, Sir Geoffrey (John), Kt 1993; Chief Executive, Kingfisher (formerly Woolworth Holdings) plc, since 1995; Chairman, F. W. Woolworth plc, since 1984; *b* 7 Feb. 1942; *s* of Maurice Frederick Mulcahy and Kathleen Love Mulcahy; *m* 1965, Valerie Elizabeth; one *s* one *d*. *Educ:* King's Sch., Worcester; Manchester Univ. (BSc); Harvard Univ. (MBA). Esso Petroleum, 1964–74; Norton Co., 1974–77; British Sugar, 1977–83;

Woolworth Holdings, subseq. Kingfisher, 1983–: Gp Man. Dir, 1984–86; Chief Exec., 1986–93; Chm., 1990–95. Dir, Bass, 1989–. *Recreations:* sailing, squash. *Club:* Lansdowne.

MULDOON, Dame Thea (Dale), DBE 1993; QSO 1986; *b* 13 March 1927; *d* of Stanley Arthur and Annie Eveleen Flyger; *m* 1951, Rt Hon. Sir Robert David Muldoon, GCMG, CH, PC (*d* 1992); one *s* two *d*. *Educ:* Takapuna Grammar Sch. Associated with many charities; Patron: North Shore Hospice; Hibiscus Coast Br., NZ Red Cross Soc.; Vice Patron, NZ Foundn for Conductive Educn. *Recreations:* walking, aerobics. *Address:* 7 Homewood Place, Birkenhead, Auckland 10, New Zealand. *T:* (9) 4190343.

MULDOWNEY, Diane Ellen, (Mrs Dominic Muldowney); *see* Trevis, D. E.

MULDOWNEY, Dominic John; Music Director, National Theatre, since 1976; *b* 19 July 1952; *s* of William and Barbara Muldowney; *m* 1986, Diane Ellen Trevis, *qv*; one *d*. *Educ:* Taunton's Grammar School, Southampton; York University. BA, BPhil. Composer in residence, Southern Arts Association, 1974–76; composer of chamber, choral, orchestral works, including work for theatre and TV; *music published:* Piano Concerto, 1983; The Duration of Exile, 1984; Saxophone Concerto, 1985; Sinfonietta, 1986; Ars Subtilior, 1987; Lonely Hearts, 1988; Violin Concerto, 1989; Three Pieces for Orchestra, 1990; Percussion Concerto, 1991; Oboe Concerto, 1992; Trumpet Concerto, 1993; Concerto for 4 Violins, 1994. *Recreation:* France.

MULGRAVE, Earl of; John Samuel Constantine Phipps; *b* 26 Nov. 1994; *s* and *heir* of Marquis of Normanby, *qv*.

MULHOLLAND, family name of **Baron Dunleath.**

MULHOLLAND, Clare; Director of Programmes, Independent Television Commission, since 1991; *b* 17 June 1939; *d* of James Mulholland and Elizabeth (*née* Lochrin). *Educ:* Notre Dame High Sch., Glasgow; Univ. of Glasgow (MA Hons). Gen. trainee, then Press Officer, ICI, 1961–64; Press Officer: Granada Television, 1964–65; TWW, 1965–68; Press Officer, then Educn Officer, HTV, 1968–71; joined Independent Broadcasting Authority, later Independent Television Commission, 1971–: Reg. Exec., Bristol, 1971–77; Reg. Officer, Midlands, 1977–82; Chief Asst, Television, 1982–83; Dep. Dir of Television, 1983–91. Member: Arts Council of GB, 1986–94; Scottish Film Prodn Fund, 1984–90. FRTS 1988. *Recreations:* travel, food. *Address:* c/o ITC, 33 Foley Street, W1P 7LB. *T:* 0171–306 7895.

MULKEARNS, Most Rev. Ronald Austin; *see* Ballarat, Bishop of, (RC).

MULKERN, John, CBE 1987; JP; FCIT; international airport and aviation consultant, since 1987; *b* 15 Jan. 1931; *s* of late Thomas Mulkern and Annie Tennant; *m* 1954, May Egerton (*née* Peters); one *s* three *d*. *Educ:* Stretford Grammar Sch. Dip. in Govt Admin. Harvard Business Sch. AMP, 1977. FCIT 1973 (Mem. Council, 1979–82). Ministries of Supply and Aviation, Civil Service, 1949–65: Exec. Officer, finally Principal, Audit, Purchasing, Finance, Personnel and Legislation branches; British Airports Authority, 1965–87: Dep. Gen. Man., Heathrow Airport, 1970–73; Dir, Gatwick Airport, 1973–77; Man. Dir and Mem. of Bd, 1977–87. Chairman: British Airports International Ltd, 1978–82; Manchester Handling Ltd, 1988–94; Granik Ltd, 1990–91 (Pres., 1992–94); Director: London Luton Airport Ltd, 1991–; Reliance Aviation Security Ltd, 1992–94. President: Western European Airports' Assoc., 1981–83; Internat. Civil Airports Assoc. (Europe), 1986–; Chm., Co-ordinating Council, Airports Assocs, 1982; Mem. Bd, Airport Operators Council Internat., 1978–81. CIMgt (CBIM 1981); FInstD 1982. JP Surrey, 1988. *Recreations:* family pursuits, opera, classical recorded music.

MULL, Very Rev. Gerald S.; *see* Stranraer-Mull.

MULLALY, Terence Frederick Stanley; art historian and critic; *b* 14 Nov. 1927; *s* of late Col B. R. Mullaly (4th *s* of Maj.-Gen. Sir Herbert Mullaly, KCMG, CB, CSI) and Eileen Dorothy (*née* Stanley); *m* 1949, Elizabeth Helen (*née* Burkitt). *Educ:* in India, England, Japan and Canada; Downing Coll., Cambridge (MA). FSA 1977; FRNS 1981 (Mem. Council, 1993–). Archæological studies in Tripolitania, 1948, and Sicily, 1949; has specialised in study of Italian art, particularly Venetian and Veronese painting of 16th and 17th centuries; lecturer and broadcaster; Art Critic, Daily Telegraph, 1958–86. Vis. Prof., Finch Coll., NY, 1967–72. Pres. Brit. Section, Internat. Assoc. of Art Critics, 1967–73; Chm., British Art Medal Soc., 1986– (Vice Chm., 1982–86); Member: Adv. Cttee, Cracow Art Festival, 1974, Palermo Art Festival, 1976; UK Delgn, Budapest Cultural Forum, 1985; Cttee, FIDEM Congress, 1992; Council: Attingham Summer Sch. Trust, 1984–90; Derby Porcelain Internat. Soc., 1985–; Artistic Adviser, Grand Tours, 1974–90; Director: Grand Tours, 1980–90; Specialtours, 1986. Editor, Jl of British–Italian Soc., 1995–. FRSA 1969. Commendatore, Order Al Merito, Italy, 1974 (Cavaliere Ufficiale, 1964); l'Ordre du Mérite Culturel, Poland, 1974; Order of Merit of Poland (Silver Medal), 1978; Bulgarian 1300th Anniversary Medal, 1981; Sacro Militare Ordine Costantiniano di S Giorgio (Silver Medal), 1982; Premio Pietro Torta per il restauro di Venezia, 1983; Socio Straniero, Ateneo Veneto, 1986. *Publications:* Ruskin a Verona, 1966; catalogue of exhibition, Disegni veronesi del Cinquecento, 1971; contrib. to catalogue of exhibition Cinquant' anni di pittura veronese: 1580–1630, 1974; ed and contrib. to catalogue of exhibition, Modern Hungarian Medal, 1984; contrib. to Affreschi del Rinascimento a Verona: interventi di restauro, 1987; Caterina Cornaro, Queen of Cyprus, 1989; Anne Redpath, 1995; contribs on history of art, to Burlington Magazine, Master Drawings, Arte Illustrata, Arte Documento, Antologia di Belle Arti, The Minneapolis Inst. of Arts Bulletin, Bull. Univ. of New Mexico Art Mus., British Numismatic Jl, Numismatic Chronicle, Jl of British Art Medal Soc., Apollo, etc. *Recreations:* collecting and travel. *Address:* Waterside House, Pulborough, Sussex RH20 2BH. *T:* Pulborough (01798) 872104.

MULLAN, Charles Heron, CBE 1979; VRD 1950; DL; Resident Magistrate, 1960–82, retired; Lieutenant-Commander RNVR; retired, 1951; *b* 17 Feb. 1912; *s* of Frederick Heron Mullan, BA, DL, Solicitor, Newry, Co. Down, and Minnie Mullan, formerly of Stow Longa, Huntingdonshire; *m* 1940, Marcella Elizabeth Sharpe, *er d* of J. A. McCullagh, Ballycastle, Co. Antrim; one *s*. *Educ:* Castle Park, Dalkey, Co. Dublin; Rossall Sch., Fleetwood; Clare Coll., Cambridge. Hons Degree Law, Cambridge, 1934; MA 1939. Joined Ulster Div. RNVR, 1936; called up for active service with Royal Navy, Aug. 1939; served throughout the war, HMS Rodney 1939–40; destroyers and escort vessels, Channel, North Sea, North Atlantic, etc, 1940–44 (with Royal Norwegian Navy, 1941–43); King Haakon VII War Decoration 1944. MP (UU) Co. Down, 1946–50, Westminster Parlt; contested S Down, 1945, for NI Parlt. Mem. Ulster Unionist Council, 1946–60. Solicitor 1948; JP 1960; Chm., Belfast Juvenile Courts, 1964–79. Member: N Ireland Section of British Delegn to 3rd UN Congress on Prevention of Crime and Treatment of Offenders, Stockholm, 1965; initial N Ireland Legal Aid Adv. Cttee, 1967–75; Mem. Exec. Cttee, British Juvenile Courts Soc., 1973–79; Vice-Pres., NI Juvenile Courts Assoc., 1980–93; NI Rep. to 9th Congress of Internat. Assoc. of Youth Magistrates, Oxford, 1974; Adviser, Internat. Assoc. of Youth Magistrates, 1974–82. Hon. Governor, South Down Hospitals Gp, 1965–73; Vice-Pres., Rossallian Club, 1974. DL Co. Down, 1974. *Recreations:* ornithology, walking, boating. *Address:* Casanbarra, Carrickmore Road, Ballycastle, Co. Antrim, Northern Ireland BT54 6QS. *T:* Ballycastle (012657) 62323.

MULLENS, Lt-Gen. Sir Anthony (Richard Guy), KCB 1989; OBE 1979 (MBE 1973); Deputy Chief of Defence Staff (Systems), Ministry of Defence, 1989–92, retired; Consultant, British Rail, since 1992; Associate, Varley Walker & Partners, since 1994; *b* 10 May 1936; *s* of late Brig. Guy John de Wette Mullens, OBE, and of Gwendoline Joan Maclean; *m* 1964, Dawn Elizabeth Hermione Pease. *Educ:* Eton; RMA Sandhurst. Commnd 4th/7th Royal Dragoon Guards, 1956; regtl service, BAOR, 1956–58; ADC to Comdr 1st British Corps, 1958–60; Adjt 1962–65; sc 1967, psc; MA to VCGS, MoD, 1968–70; regtl service, 1970–72; Bde Major, 1972–73; Directing Staff, Staff Coll., 1973–76; CO 4/7 DG, BAOR, 1976–78; HQ BAOR, 1978–80; Comdr 7th Armd Bde, 1980–82; MoD (DMS(A)), 1982–85; Comdr 1st Armoured Div., 1985–87; ACDS (Operational Requirements), Land Systems, MoD, 1987–89. Col, Royal Dragoon Guards, 1994–. Liveryman: Armourers' and Braziers' Co., 1974 (Mem., Ct of Assts, 1993–); Coachmakers' and Coachharness Makers' Co., 1976. Niedersachsen Verdienstkreuz am Bande, 1982, Erste Klasse, 1987. *Recreations:* travel, riding, shooting, ski-ing. *Address:* c/o Lloyds Bank Private Banking, 50 Grosvenor Street, W1X 9FH. *Club:* Cavalry and Guards.

MÜLLER, Alex; *see* Müller, K. A.

MULLER, Franz Joseph; QC 1978; a Recorder of the Crown Court, since 1977; *b* England, 19 Nov. 1938; *yr s* of late Wilhelm Muller and Anne Maria (*née* Ravens); *m* 1985, Helena, *y d* of Mieczyslaw Bartosz; two *s*. *Educ:* Mount St Mary's Coll.; Univ. of Sheffield (LLB). Called to the Bar, Gray's Inn, 1961, Bencher, 1994; called to NI Bar, 1982. Graduate Apprentice, United Steel Cos, 1960–61; Commercial Asst, Workington Iron and Steel Co. Ltd, 1961–63. Commenced practice at the Bar, 1964. Non-Executive Director: Richards of Sheffield (Holdings) PLC, 1969–77; Satinsteel Ltd, 1970–77; Joseph Rodgers and Son Ltd and Rodgers Wostenholm Ltd, 1975–77. Mem., Sen. Common Room, UC Durham, 1981. Gov., Mount St Mary's Coll., 1984–86. *Recreations:* the Georgians, fell walking, being in Greece, listening to music. *Address:* Slade Hooton Hall, Laughton en le Morthen, Yorks S31 7YQ; 11 King's Bench Walk, Temple, EC4Y 7EQ. *T:* 0171–353 3337.

MÜLLER, (Karl) Alex, PhD; physicist at IBM Zurich Research Laboratory, since 1963; *b* 20 April 1927. *Educ:* Swiss Federal Institute of Technology, Zürich (PhD 1958). Battelle Inst., Geneva, 1958–63; Lectr, 1962, Titular Prof., 1970, Prof., 1987, Univ. of Zürich; joined IBM Res. Lab, Zurich, 1963; Manager, Physics Dept, 1973; IBM Fellow, 1982. Hon. degrees from eleven European and American univs. Prizes and awards include Nobel Prize for Physics (jtly), 1987. *Publications:* over 200 papers on ferroelectric and superconducting materials. *Address:* IBM Zurich Research Laboratory, Säumerstrasse 4, 8803 Rüschlikon, Switzerland.

MULLER, Dr Ralph Louis Junius, FIBiol; Director, International Institute of Parasitology, CAB International, 1981–93; *b* 30 June 1933; *s* of Carl and Sarah Muller; *m* 1st, 1959, Gretta Shearer; one *s* one *d*; 2nd, 1979, Annie Badilla Delgado; one *s* one *d*. *Educ:* Summerhill Sch., Suffolk; London Univ. (BSc, PhD, DSc). Res. Fellow, KCL, 1958–59; ODM, 1959–61; Lectr, Univ. of Ibadan, 1961–66; Sen. Lectr, LSHTM, 1966–80. Pres., European Fedn of Parasitologists, 1988–92; Hon. Sec., British Soc. for Parasitology, 1995–. Editor: Advances in Parasitology, 1978–; Jl of Helminthology, 1986–. *Publications:* Worms and Disease, 1975, 2nd edn 1994 Onchocerciasis, 1987; Medical Parasitology, 1989. *Recreations:* beekeeping, writing instruments, sport, photography. *Address:* 22 Cranbrook Drive, St Albans, Herts AL4 0SS. *T:* St Albans (01727) 852605, *Fax:* (01727) 856871.

MULLER, Mrs Robert; *see* Whitelaw, Billie.

MULLETT, Aidan Anthony, (Tony), CBE 1993; QPM 1982; Director-General, National Criminal Intelligence Service, 1992–93; *b* 24 May 1933; *s* of Bartholomew Joseph and Mary Kate Mullett; *m* 1957, Monica Elizabeth Coney; one *s* one *d*. *Educ:* Moat Boys' Sch., Leicester. Served Royal Air Force, 1950–56; joined Leicester City Police, 1957; Leicestershire and Rutland Constabulary, 1966, Chief Superintendent, 1973; Asst Chief Constable, W Mercia Constabulary, 1975–82; Dep. Chief Constable, Dyfed Powys Police, 1982–85; Chief Constable, W Mercia Constabulary, 1985–91. Chm., Crime Cttee, ACPO, 1990–91 (Hon. Sec., 1989). *Recreations:* golf, swimming.

MULLETT, Leslie Baden; consultant; *b* 22 Aug. 1920; *s* of Joseph and Edith Mullett; *m* 1st, 1945, Katharine Lear (marr. diss. 1968); no *c*; 2nd, 1971, Gillian Pettit. *Educ:* Gram. Sch., Hales Owen, Worcs; Birmingham Univ. BSc (Hons Physics) 1941. Telecommunications Research Estab., 1941–46; AEA, 1946–60 (Head of Accelerator Div., 1958); Asst Dir, Rutherford High Energy Lab., SRC, 1960–68; on secondment to Res. Gp, Min. of Technology, 1966–68; CSO, Min. of Transport, 1968; CSO, Res. Requirements, DoE, 1970–74; Dep. Dir, Transport and Road Res. Lab., DoE/Dept of Transport, 1974–80. Vis. Prof., Univ. of Reading, 1982–90. *Publications:* A Guide to Transport for Disabled People, 1982; papers in learned jls on particle accelerators and solar energy. *Recreation:* gardening. *Address:* 42 Grosvenor Avenue, Grosvenor Park, Bourne, Lincs PE10 9HU. *T:* Bourne (01778) 423054.

MULLETT, Tony; *see* Mullett, A. A.

MULLIGAN, Andrew Armstrong; President: Mulligan Communications Inc., since 1983; European Satellite Radio Ltd; EuroMedia Group, since 1989; *b* 4 Feb. 1936; *s* of Col Hugh Waddell Mulligan, CMG, MD, DSc and late Rita Aimee Armstrong; *m* 1964, Pia Ursula Schioler; two *s* two *d*. *Educ:* Magdalene Coll., Cambridge (Geog. and Anthropol Tripos (Hons). Personal Asst to Man. Dir, De La Rue Co., London, 1958–60; special assignment to Australia and NZ for Irish Export Bd, 1961–62; Foreign Correspondent: Daily Telegraph and London Observer in Paris, 1962–68; Independent Television News at Ten, 1968; Producer and reporter, BBC's Panorama, 1969–73; Head of General Reports Div., EEC, Brussels, 1973–74; Dir of Press and Information, Delegn of Commn of European Communities to the US, 1975–83. Dir, American Ireland Fund (formerly Ireland Fund of the US), 1976–. Publisher, Europe magazine, 1975–82. *Publications:* Ouvert l'Après Midi, 1963; The All Blacks, 1964. *Recreations:* rugby, tennis, skiing, sailing, landscape painting. *Address:* 1855 Shepherd Street, Washington, DC 20011, USA. *Clubs:* Annabel's; Hawks (Cambridge); Kildare Street and University (Dublin); Anglo-American Press Association (Paris); National Press (Washington, DC).

MULLIGAN, Christopher James; Director General, Passenger Transport Executive, Greater Manchester, since 1991; *b* 24 Feb. 1950; *s* of James Frederick Mulligan and Dorothy Mulligan (*née* Kneill); *m* 1989, Rowena May Burns. *Educ:* Hull Univ. (BA Hons 1971). Mem., CIPFA. Manchester CC, 1971–73; Gtr Manchester CC, 1973–77; Greater Manchester Passenger Transport Executive, 1977–: Dir of Finance, 1987–91. *Recreations:* reading, walking, good food. *Address:* 9 Portland Street, Piccadilly Gardens, Manchester M60 1HX. *T:* 0161–242 6060. *Club:* St James's (Manchester).

MULLIGAN, Prof. William, FRSE; Professor of Veterinary Physiology, 1963–86, and Vice-Principal, 1980–83, University of Glasgow, now Professor Emeritus; *b* 18 Nov. 1921; *s* of John Mulligan and Mary Mulligan (*née* Kelly); *m* 1948, Norah Mary Cooper one *s* two *d*. *Educ:* Banbridge Academy; Queen's Univ. of Belfast (BSc); PhD London. FIBiol 1988. Assistant, Dept of Chemistry, QUB, 1943–45; Demonstrator/Lectr, St Bartholomew's Med. Coll., London, 1945–51; Sen. Lectr, Veterinary Biochemistry, Univ. of Glasgow, 1951–63; McMaster Fellow, McMaster Animal Health Laboratory, Sydney, Aust., 1958–60; Dean of Faculty of Veterinary Medicine, Univ. of Glasgow, 1977–80. Dr. med. vet. *hc* Copenhagen, 1983. *Publications:* (jtly) Isotopic Tracers, 1954, 2nd edn 1959; numerous contribs to scientific jls on immunology and use of radiation and radioisotopes in animal science. *Recreations:* golf, tennis, gardening, pigeon racing, theatre. *Address:* 1 Daisy Green, Groton, Sudbury, Suffolk CO10 5EN. *T:* Boxford (01787) 210868.

MULLIN, Christopher John, (Chris); journalist and author; MP (Lab) Sunderland South, since 1987; *b* 12 Dec. 1947; *s* of Leslie and Teresa Mullin; *m* 1987, Nguyen Thi Ngoc, *d* of Nguyen Tang Minh, Kontum, Vietnam; one *d*. *Educ:* Univ. of Hull (LLB). Freelance journalist, travelled extensively in Indo-China and China; sub editor, BBC World Service, 1974–78; Editor, Tribune, 1982–84. Executive Member: Campaign for Labour Party Democracy, 1975–83; Labour Co-ordinating Cttee, 1978–82. Contested (Lab): Devon N, 1970; Kingston upon Thames, Feb. 1974. Mem., Home Affairs Select Cttee, 1992–; Chm., All Party Cambodia Gp, 1992–; Sec., All Party Vietnam Gp, 1988–; Chm., PLP Civil Liberties Gp, 1992–. Hon. LLD City, 1992. Editor: Arguments for Socialism, by Tony Benn, 1979; Arguments for Democracy, by Tony Benn, 1981. *Publications: novels:* A Very British Coup, 1982 (televised 1988); The Last Man Out of Saigon, 1986; The Year of the Fire Monkey, 1991; *non-fiction:* Error of Judgement—the truth about the Birmingham bombings, 1986, rev. edn 1990; pamphlets: How to Select or Reselect your MP, 1981; The Tibetans, 1981. *Address:* House of Commons, SW1A 0AA.

MULLIN, Rt. Rev. Mgr (John Raymond) Noel; VG 1993; Principal Roman Catholic Chaplain (Naval) and Director, Naval Chaplaincy Services (Training and Programmes), Ministry of Defence, since 1993; *b* 21 Dec. 1947. *Educ:* Underley Hall Sch., Kirkby Lonsdale; Upholland Coll., Lancs. Ordained priest, 1972; joined RN as Chaplain, 1978; served at home and abroad, afloat and ashore, at peace and in conflict. *Recreations:* Rugby, cricket, fell walking, performing arts, food. *Address:* 203 Victory Building, HM Naval Base, Portsmouth, Hants PO1 3LS.

MULLIN, Prof. John William, DSc, PhD, FRSC, FEng, FIChemE; Ramsay Memorial Professor of Chemical Engineering, University College London, 1985–90, now Emeritus Professor; Hon. Research Fellow, University College London, since 1990; *b* Rock Ferry, Cheshire, 22 Aug. 1925; *er s* of late Frederick Mullin and Kathleen Nellie Mullin (*née* Oppy); *m* 1952, Averil Margaret Davies, Carmarthen; one *s* one *d*. *Educ:* Hawarden County Sch.; UCW Cardiff (Fellow, 1981); University Coll. London (Fellow, 1981). 8 yrs in organic fine chemicals industry; University College London: Lectr, 1956; Reader, 1961; Prof., 1969; Dean, Faculty of Engrg, 1975–77; Vice-Provost, 1980–86; Crabtree Orator, 1993; Dean, Faculty of Engrg, London Univ., 1979–85. Vis. Prof., Univ. New Brunswick, 1967. Chm. Bd of Staff Examrs, Chem. Eng, Univ. London, 1965–70. Hon. Librarian, IChemE, 1965–77 (Mem. Council, 1973–76); Mem., Materials Sci. Working Gp, European Space Agency, 1977–81; Founder Mem., Brit. Assoc. for Crystal Growth. Parly Gp for Engrg Develt, 1994–. Member: Cttee of Management, Inst. of Child Health, 1970–83; Court of Governors, University Coll., Cardiff, 1982–; Council, Sch. of Pharmacy, Univ. of London, 1983– (Vice-Chm., 1988–). Chm., BS and ISO Cttees on industrial screens, sieves, particle sizing, etc. Liveryman, Engineers' Co. Moulton Medal, IChemE, 1970; Kurnakov Meml Medal, Inst. of Gen. and Inorganic Chem., USSR Acad. of Scis, 1991. Dr *hc* Inst Nat. Polytechnique de Toulouse, 1989. *Publications:* Crystallization, 1961, 3rd edn 1993; (ed) Industrial Crystallization, 1976; papers in Trans IChemE, Chem. Engrg Sci., Jl Crystal Growth, etc. *Address:* 4 Milton Road, Ickenham, Mddx UB10 8NQ. *T:* Uxbridge (01895) 634950. *Club:* Athenæum.

MULLIN, Rt. Rev. Mgr Noel; *see* Mullin, Rt Rev. Mgr J. R. N.

MULLINS, Rt. Rev. Daniel Joseph; *see* Menevia, Bishop of, (RC).

MULLINS, Edwin Brandt; author, journalist and film-maker; *b* 14 Sept. 1933; *s* of Claud and Gwendolen Mullins; *m* 1st, 1960, Gillian Brydone (*d* 1982); one *s* two *d*; 2nd, 1984, Anne Kelleher. *Educ:* Midhurst Grammar Sch.; Merton Coll., Oxford (BA Hons, MA). London Editor, Two Cities, 1957–58; Sub-editor and Art Correspondent, Illustrated London News, 1958–62; Art Critic: Sunday Telegraph, 1962–69; Telegraph Sunday Magazine, 1964–86; contributor, 1962–, to The Guardian, Financial Times, Sunday Times, Director, Apollo, Art and Artists, Studio, Radio Times, TV Times, Country Living. Regular broadcaster on radio and television; scriptwriter and presenter of numerous BBC and Channel 4 TV documentaries, incl. 100 Great Paintings, The Pilgrimage of Everyman, Gustave Courbet, Fake?, Prison, The Great Art Collection, A Love Affair with Nature, Masterworks, Paradise on Earth, Montparnasse Revisited. *Publications:* Souza, 1962; Wallis, 1967; Josef Herman, 1967; Braque, 1968; The Art of Elisabeth Frink, 1972; The Pilgrimage to Santiago, 1974; (ed) Great Paintings, 1981; (ed) The Arts of Britain, 1983; The Painted Witch, 1985; A Love Affair with Nature, 1985; The Royal Collection, 1992; Alfred Wallis: Cornish Primitive, 1994; *novels:* Angels on the Point of a Pin, 1979; Sirens, 1983; The Golden Bird, 1987; The Lands of the Sea, 1988, and others under a pseudonym, 1992, 1993, 1994, 1995. *Recreations:* everything except football. *Address:* c/o Curtis Brown, 28–29 Haymarket, SW1Y 4SP.

MULLINS, Leonard, CMG 1976; PhD, DSc; Director of Research, Malaysian Rubber Producers' Research Association, Brickendonbury, Hertford, 1962–83; *b* 21 May 1918; *s* of Robert and Eugenie Alice Mullins; *m* 1943, Freda Elaine Churchouse; two *d*. *Educ:* Eltham Coll.; University Coll., London; Inst. of Educn, London. BSc (Hons), PhD, DSc. CPhys; FInstP; FIM. Experimental Officer, Min. of Supply, 1940–44; Scientific Officer, finally Head of Physics Gp, Research Assoc. of British Rubber Manufrs, 1944–49; Malaysian (previously British) Rubber Producers' Research Assoc., 1950–83; Scientific Advr, UNIDO projects in China, Côte d'Ivoire, Malaysia, Vietnam, 1984–91; Foundn Lectr, Instn of Rubber Industry, 1968. Pres., Plastics and Rubber Inst., 1981–83 (Chm., 1976–77; Vice-Pres., 1977–81); Chm., Adv. Cttee, Nat. Coll. of Rubber Technology, 1976–87; Vice-Pres., Rubber and Plastics Research Assoc., 1983–. Member: Court, Cranfield Inst. of Technology; Adv. Bd, Inst. of Technol., Loughborough Univ.; Council, Rubber and Plastics Res. Assoc. Discovered Mullins Effect, relating to elastic behaviour of rubber. Moore Meml Lecture, Bradford Univ., 1982. Governor of local schools. Colwyn Medal, IRI, 1966; Médaille de la Ville de Paris, 1982; Outstanding Service Award, PRI, 1985; Charles Goodyear Medal Award, Rubber Div., American Chem. Soc., 1986; Carl Dietrich Harries Medal, Deutsche Kautschuk Ges., 1988; Eminent Citizen's Medal, Ho Chi Minh City, 1988. Comdr, Malaysian Order of Chivalry, JMN, 1975. *Publications:* numerous original scientific papers in field of rubber physics. *Address:* 32 Sherrardspark Road, Welwyn Garden City, Herts AL8 7JS. *T:* Welwyn Garden (01707) 323633. *Club:* Athenæum.

MULLIS, Marjorie; *see* Allthorpe-Guyton, M.

MULLOVA, Viktoria Yuriyevna; violinist; *b* 27 Nov. 1959; *d* of Juri Mullov and Raisa Mullova; one *s* one *d*. *Educ:* Central Music Sch., Moscow; Moscow Conservatory. First prize, Sibelius Competition, Helsinki, 1980; Gold Medal, Tchaikovsky Competition, Moscow, 1982; left USSR, 1983. Has performed with most major orchestras; many festival appearances. Recordings include: violin concertos: Brahms, Tchaikovsky, Sibelius, Mendelssohn, Shostakovich No 1, Prokoviev No 2, Paganini No 1; Bach partitas; Bach sonatas for violin and piano; Vivaldi, Four Seasons. *Address:* c/o Harold Holt, 31 Sinclair Road, W14 0NS.

MULRONEY, Rt. Hon. (Martin) Brian, PC 1984; Senior Partner, Ogilvy, Renault, since 1993; *b* 20 March 1939; *s* of Benedict Mulroney and Irene O'Shea; *m* 1973, Mila Pivnicki; three *s* one *d*. *Educ:* St Francis Xavier Univ. (BA); Université Laval (LLL). Partner, Ogilvy, Renault (Montreal law firm), 1965–76; Pres., Iron Ore Co. of Canada, 1976–83. MP (Progressive Conservative): Central Nova, 1983–84; Manicouagan, 1984–88; Charlevoix, 1988–93. Leader of the Opposition, 1983–84; Prime Minister of Canada, 1984–93. Royal Comr, Cliche Commn investigating violence in Quebec construction industry, 1974. Hon. LLD: St Francis Xavier Univ., 1979; Meml Univ., 1980. *Publication:* Where I Stand, 1983. *Recreations:* tennis, swimming.

MULVANEY, Prof. Derek John, AO 1991; CMG 1982; Professor of Prehistory, Australian National University, 1971–85, now Emeritus; *b* 26 Oct. 1925; *s* of Richard and Frances Mulvaney; *m* 1954, Jean Campbell; four *s* two *d*. *Educ:* Univ. of Melbourne (MA); Clare Coll., Univ. of Cambridge (BA, MA 1959, PhD 1970). FAHA 1970, FSA 1977, corr. FBA 1983. Navigator, RAAF, 1943–46 (Flying Officer); Lectr and Senior Lectr in History, Univ. of Melbourne, 1954–64; Senior Fellow, ANU, 1965–70; Vis. Prof., Cambridge, 1976–77; Chair of Australian Studies, Harvard, 1984–85; Mem. Council, Aust. Inst. of Aboriginal Studies, 1964–80 (Chm., 1982–84); Australian Heritage Commissioner, 1976–82; Mem., Cttee of Inquiry, Museums and National Collections, 1974–75; Sec., Australian Acad. of Humanities, 1989–. ANZAAS medal, 1988. *Publications:* Cricket Walkabout, 1967, 2nd edn 1987; The Prehistory of Australia, 1969, 2nd edn 1975; Australians to 1788, 1987; Encounters in Place, 1989; Commandant of Solitude, 1992; numerous excavation reports and historical articles. *Recreation:* gardening. *Address:* 128 Schlich Street, Yarralumla, ACT 2600, Australia. *T:* Canberra 2812352.

MUMFORD, Prof. Enid; Professor of Organizational Behaviour, Manchester Business School, 1979–88, now Emeritus; *b* 6 March 1924; *d* of Arthur McFarland and Dorothy Evans; *m* 1947, Jim Mumford; one *s* one *d*. *Educ:* Wallasey High Sch.; Liverpool Univ. (BA, MA); Manchester Univ. (PhD). CIPM; FBCS. Personnel Officer, Rotol Ltd, 1946–47; Production Supervisor, J. D. Francis Ltd, 1947–48; Research Associate: Dept of Social Science, Liverpool Univ., 1948–56; Bureau of Public Health Economics, Univ. of Michigan, USA, 1956–57; Res. Lectr, Dept of Social Science, Liverpool Univ., 1957–65; Lectr, then Sen. Lectr and Reader, Manchester Business Sch., 1966–79. *Publications:* Chester Royal Infirmary 1856–1956, 1956; Living with a Computer, 1964; Computers Planning and Personnel Management, 1969; Systems Design for People, 1971; Job Satisfaction: a study of computer specialists, 1972; (with others) Coal and Conflict, 1963; (with O. Banks) The Computer and the Clerk, 1967; (with T. B. Ward) Computers: planning for people, 1968; (with A. Pettigrew) Implementing Strategic Decisions, 1975; (ed, with H. Sackman) Human Choice and Computers, 1975; (ed, with K. Legge) Designing Organizations for Efficiency and Satisfaction, 1978; (with D. Henshall) A Participative Approach to Computer Systems Design, 1978; (with M. Weir) Computer Systems in Work Design, 1979; (ed. with C. Cooper) The Quality of Working Life, 1979; (with others) The Impact of Systems Change in Organizations, 1980; Values, Technology and Work, 1980; Designing Secretaries, 1983; Designing Human Systems for New Technology, 1983; Designing Human Systems for Health Care, 1993; Using Computers for Business Success, 1986; (with W. B. MacDonald) XSEL's Progress, 1989; Tools for Change, 1994; Effective Systems Design and Requirements Analysis, 1995; contribs to books and journals. *Address:* 4 Windmill Close, Appleton, Warrington, Cheshire WA4 5JS. *T:* Warrington (01925) 601039.

MUMFORD, Lady Mary (Katharine), DCVO 1995 (CVO 1982); Lady-in-Waiting to HRH Princess Alexandra, since 1964; *b* 14 Aug. 1940; 2nd *d* of 16th Duke of Norfolk, KG, GCVO, GBE, TD, PC and of Lavinia, Duchess of Norfolk, *qv*; *heir presumptive* to Lordship of Herries of Terregles; *m* 1986, Gp Captain Anthony Mumford, CVO, OBE. *Address:* North Stoke Cottage, North Stoke, Arundel, West Sussex BN18 9LS. *T:* Bury (01798) 831203; Lantonside, Glencaple, Dumfries DG1 4RQ. *T:* Glencaple (01387) 770260.

See also Lady Herries of Terregles.

MUMFORD, William Frederick, CB 1989; Deputy Under-Secretary of State for Research Establishments, Ministry of Defence, 1989, retired; Chairman's Panel, Civil Service Selection Board, since 1989; government departments recruitment consultant; *b* 23 Jan. 1930; *s* of late Frederick Charles Mumford and Hester Leonora Mumford; *m* 1958, Elizabeth Marion, *d* of Nowell Hall; three *s* one *d*. *Educ:* St Albans Sch.; Lincoln Coll., Oxford (MA PPE). Nat. Service commission, Royal Artillery, 1949–50. Appointed to Home Civil Service, 1953; Asst Principal, 1953–58, Principal, 1958–60, Air Ministry; First Secretary, UK Delegn to NATO, Paris, 1960–65; Principal, 1965–67, Asst Sec., 1967–73, Defence Secretariat, MoD; Dep. Head of UK Delegn to MBFR Exploratory Talks, Vienna, 1973; Principal Private Sec. to Secretaries of State for Defence: Rt Hon. Lord Carrington, 1973–74, Rt Hon. Ian Gilmour, MP and Rt Hon. Roy Mason, MP, 1974–75; Under-Sec., Machinery of Govt Div., CSD, 1975–76; Asst Sec.-Gen. for Defence Planning and Policy, NATO, Brussels, 1976–80; Asst Under-Sec. of State (Material-Naval), MoD, 1980–84; Asst Under-Sec. of State (Estabts and Res.), MoD, 1984–90. Advr to Coopers & Lybrand, management consultants, 1991–95. *Recreations:* antique book collecting, music.

MUMMERY, Christopher John L.; *see* Lockhart-Mummery.

MUMMERY, Hon. Sir John Frank, Kt 1989; **Hon. Mr Justice Mummery;** a Judge of the High Court of Justice, Chancery Division, since 1989; President, Employment Appeal Tribunal, since 1993; *b* 5 Sept. 1938; *s* of Frank Stanley Mummery and Ruth Mummery (*née* Coleman) Coldred, Kent; *m* 1967, Elizabeth Anne Lamond Lackie, *d* of Dr D. G. L. Lackie and Ellen Lackie (*née* Easterbrook), Edinburgh; one *s* one *d*. *Educ:* Oakleigh House, Dover; Dover County Grammar Sch.; Pembroke Coll., Oxford, 1959–63 (MA, BCL; Winter Williams Prize in Law; Hon. Fellow, 1989). National Service, The Border Regt and RAEC, 1957–59. Called to Bar, Gray's Inn (Atkin Schol.), 1964, Bencher, 1985. Treasury Junior Counsel: in Charity Matters, 1977–81; Chancery, 1981–89; a Recorder, 1989. Member, Senate of Inns of Court and Bar, 1978–81. Member: Justice Cttee on Privacy and the Law, 1967–70; Art Registration Cttee, 1969–; Legal Adv. Commn, Gen. Synod of C of E, 1988–; Council of Legal Educn, 1989–92; Ecclesiastical Rule Cttee, 1992–. *Publication:* (co-ed) Copinger and Skone James on Copyright, 12th edn 1980, 13th edn 1991. *Recreation:* long walks with family, friends and alone. *Address:* Employment Appeal Tribunal, Audit House, 58 Victoria Embankment, EC4Y 0DS.

MUNBY, Dr John Latimer, OBE 1984; Director, British Council, Greece, since 1990; *b* 14 July 1937; *s* of late Lawrence St John Munby and Jennie Munby; *m* 1961, Lilian Cynthia Hogg; two *s*. *Educ:* King's Sch., Bruton; Lincoln Coll., Oxford (BA Jurisp., MA); Inst. of Educn, London Univ. (PGCE); Univ. of Essex (MA Applied Linguistics, PhD). Nat. service, 2nd Lieut, 1955–57. Educn Officer, Govt of Tanzania, 1961–68; joined British Council, 1969; seconded to Advanced Teachers' Coll., Zaria, then Ahmadu Bello Univ., Nigeria, 1969–72; Director: English Teaching Inf. Centre, 1974–76; English Lang. Consultancies Dept, 1976–78; Representative: Kuwait, 1978–81; Singapore, 1981–85; Dep. Controller, Home Div., 1985–87; Controller, Libraries, Books and Information Div., 1987–90. FRSA 1982. *Publications:* Read and Think, 1968; Communicative Syllabus Design, 1978; contrib. various jls. *Recreations:* music, sport, wine. *Address:* c/o The British Council, 10 Spring Gardens, SW1A 2BN. *T:* 0171–930 8466.

MUNDAY, John, FSA; Keeper of Weapons and Antiquities, National Maritime Museum, Greenwich, 1976–84, now Keeper Emeritus; *b* 10 Aug. 1924; *s* of Rodney H. J. Munday and Ethel Emma Cutting; *m* 1953, Brenda Warden; two *s*. *Educ:* Portsmouth Northern Grammar Sch.; King's Coll., Newcastle; Durham Univ. (BA 1950; MA 1961). FSA 1972. Assistant, Portsmouth Public Libraries and Museums Dept, 1940–42. Served RN, 1942–46; Sub Lieut (Ex. Sp.), RNVR. National Maritime Museum, Greenwich: Asst Keeper, Librarian, 1951; Curator of Presentation, 1964; Dep. Keeper, 1969; Curator of Weapons and Antiquities, 1971. Hon. Vice Pres., Soc. for Nautical Res., 1985 (Hon. Sec., 1979–84); Member: Develt Cttee, SS Great Britain Project, 1980; HMS Victory Adv. Technical Cttee, 1985. *Publications:* For Those in Peril . . . lifesaving, then and now, 1963; Oar Maces of Admiralty, 1966; Dress of the British Sailor, rev. edn 1977; Heads & Tails—the Necessary Seating (with drawings), 1978; Naval Cannon, 1987. *Recreations:* painting, collecting, considering. *Address:* Fourteen The Beach, Walmer, Kent CT14 7HE. *T:* Deal (01304) 374493.

MUNFORD, William Arthur, MBE 1946; PhD; FLA; Librarian Emeritus, National Library for the Blind; *b* 27 April 1911; *s* of late Ernest Charles Munford and Florence Margaret Munford; *m* 1934, Hazel Despard Wilmer; two *s* one *d*. *Educ:* Hornsey County Sch.; LSE (BScEcon, PhD). Asst, Hornsey Public Libraries, 1927–31; Chief Asst, Ilford Public Libraries, 1931–34; Borough Librarian, Dover, 1934–45 (Food Exec. Officer, 1939–45); City Librarian, Cambridge, 1945–53; Dir-Gen., Nat. Library for the Blind, 1954–82. Hon. Sec., Library Assoc., 1952–55, Hon. Fellow 1977. Trustee Emeritus, Ulverscroft Foundn. *Publications:* Books for Basic Stock, 1939; Penny Rate: aspects of British public library history, 1951; William Ewart, MP, 1960; Edward Edwards, 1963; (with W. G. Fry) Louis Stanley Jast, 1966; James Duff Brown, 1968; A History of the Library Association, 1877–1977, 1976; (with S. Godbolt) The Incomparable Mac (biog. of Sir J. Y. W. MacAlister), 1983; Who was Who in British Librarianship 1800–1985, 1987; contribs to Librarianship jls, 1933–. *Recreations:* reading, rough gardening, wood sawing, cycling, serendipity. *Address:* 11 Manor Court, Pinehurst, Grange Road, Cambridge CB3 9BE. *T:* Cambridge (01223) 62962. *Club:* National Liberal.

MUNIR, Ashley Edward, PhD; Barrister; Under Secretary, Ministry of Agriculture, Fisheries and Food, 1982–92; *b* 14 Feb. 1934; *s* of late Hon. Sir Mehmed Munir Bey, Kt, CBE, and late Lady (Vessime) Munir; *m* 1960, Sureyya S. V. Dormen; one *s*. *Educ:* Brentwood Sch.; St John's Coll., Cambridge; King's Coll., London (PhD 1992). Called to the Bar, Gray's Inn, 1956. Practised as barrister, 1956–60, 1992–; Crown Counsel, 1960–64; entered Govt Legal Service, 1964; Asst Solicitor, MAFF, 1975–82. *Publications:* Perinatal Rights, 1983; Fisheries after Factortame, 1991; Mentally Disordered Offenders, 1993. *Recreations:* walking, playing the double-bass, listening to music. *Address:*(chambers) 1 Harcourt Buildings, Temple, EC4Y 9DA. *T:* 0171–353 0375; Grassdale, 31 Kingwell Road, Hadley Wood, Herts EN4 0HZ; L'Acapulco, Appt 506, Avenue du Casino, 34280 La Grande Motte, France. *Club:* United Oxford & Cambridge University.

MUNN, Sir James, Kt 1985; OBE 1976; MA; *b* 27 July 1920; *s* of Douglas H. Munn and Margaret G. Dunn; *m* 1946, Muriel Jean Millar Moles; one *d*. *Educ:* Stirling High Sch.; Glasgow Univ. (MA (Hons)). Entered Indian Civil Service, 1941; served in Bihar, 1942–47. Taught in various schools in Glasgow, 1949–57; Principal Teacher of Modern Languages, Falkirk High Sch., 1957–62, Depute Rector, 1962–66; Rector: Rutherglen Acad., 1966–70; Cathkin High Sch., Cambuslang, Glasgow, 1970–83. Univ. Comr, 1988–95; Chairman: Manpower Services Cttee for Scotland, 1984–88; MSC, subseq. Training Commn, 1987–88; Scottish Adv. Bd, Open Coll., 1989–91; Pres., Inst. of Trng and Develt, 1989–92 (Fellow, 1989). Member: Consultative Cttee on Curriculum, 1968–80 (Chm., 1980–87); University Grants Cttee, 1973–82; Chm., Cttee to review structure of curriculum at SIII and SIV, 1975–77. Mem. Court, Strathclyde Univ., 1983–91. Fellow: Paisley Coll. of Technology, 1988; SCOTVEC, 1989. Chevalier des Palmes Académiques, 1967. DUniv Stirling, 1978; Hon. LLD Strathclyde, 1988; Hon. DEd Napier Polytechnic, 1989. *Address:* 4 Kincath Avenue, High Burnside, Glasgow G73 4RP. *T:* 0141–634 4654.

MUNNS, Victor George; Counsellor (Labour), Washington, 1983–86; *b* 17 June 1926; *s* of Frederick William Munns and Lilian Munns; *m* 1952, Pamela Ruth Wyatt; two *s*. *Educ:* Haberdashers' Aske's, Hatcham; University Coll., London (BA). Served HM Forces (Army Intell.), 1945–48. Min. of Labour Employment Service, 1951–61; ILO, Trinidad and Belize, 1962–63; Sec., Shipbldg Industry Trng Bd, 1964–66; Res. Staff, Royal Commn on Trade Unions, 1966; Principal, Dept of Employment (Indust. Trng and Indust. Relations), 1967–72; Dep. Chief Officer, Race Relations Bd, 1973–74; Sec., Health and Safety Commn, 1974–77; Asst Sec., Health and Safety Exec., 1977–82. Dir, Nailsworth Festival, 1993–. *Club:* Royal Over-Seas League.

MUNRO, Sir Alan (Gordon), KCMG 1990 (CMG 1984); HM Diplomatic Service, retired; Director, Schroder Asseily & Co. Ltd, since 1993; *b* 17 Aug. 1935; *s* of late Sir Gordon Munro, KCMG, MC and Lilian Muriel Beit; *m* 1962, Rosemary Grania Bacon; twin *s* two *d*. *Educ:* Wellington Coll.; Clare Coll., Cambridge (MA). MIPM. Mil. Service, 4/7 Dragoon Guards, 1953–55; Middle East Centre for Arab Studies, 1958–60; British Embassy, Beirut, 1960–62; Kuwait, 1961; FO, 1963–65; Head of Chancery, Benghazi, 1965–66 and Tripoli, 1966–68; FO, 1968–73; Consul (Commercial), 1973–74, Consul-Gen., 1974–77, Rio de Janeiro; Head of E African Dept, FCO, 1977–78; Head of Middle East Dept, FCO, 1979; Head of Personnel Ops Dept, FCO, 1979–81; Regl Marketing Dir (ME), MoD, 1981–83; Ambassador to Algeria, 1984–87; Dep. Under-Sec. of State, ME/Africa, FCO, 1987–89; Ambassador to Saudi Arabia, 1989–93. Adviser: General Electric Co.; Tate and Lyle; Sir Alexander Gibb and Partners; Director: Arab-British Chamber of Commerce; Brazilian Chamber of Commerce. Gov., Imperial Coll. Pres., Soc. for Algerian Studies; Chm., Beit Trust for Central Africa; Vice Chm., BRCS, 1994–. *Recreations:* historic buildings, gardening, music, history. *Club:* Travellers'.

MUNRO of Lindertis, Sir Alasdair (Thomas Ian), 6th Bt *cr* 1825; Marketing Consultant; *b* 6 July 1927; *s* of Sir Thomas Torquil Alfonso Munro, 5th Bt and Beatrice Maude (*d* 1974), *d* of Robert Sanderson Whitaker; *S* father, 1985; *m* 1954, Marguerite Lillian, *d* of late Franklin R. Loy, Dayton, Ohio, USA; one *s* one *d*. *Educ:* Georgetown Univ., Washington, DC (BSS 1946); Univ. of Pennsylvania (MBA 1951); IMEDE, Lausanne. 2nd Lieut, USAF (previously US Army), 1946–53. Senior Vice-Pres., McCann-Erickson, New York, 1952–69; Pres., Jennings Real Estate, Waitsfield, Vermont, 1970–83. Founder, Dir (and Past Pres.), St Andrew's Soc. of Vermont, 1972–; Vice-Chm., Assoc. Bd of Directors, Howard Bank, Waitsfield, 1974–84; Founder, sometime Dir and Pres., Valley Area Assoc., Waitsfield, 1972–80. Chairman: Munro, Jennings & Doig, 1983–90; Highland Develt Gp, 1987–91. *Recreations:* gardening, travel, collector/dealer in Scottish antiques, Scottish heritage matters. *Heir:* *s* Keith Gordon Munro, *b* 3 May 1959. *Address:* River Ridge, Box 940, Waitsfield, VT 05673, USA.

MUNRO, Dame Alison, DBE 1985 (CBE 1964); Chairman, Chichester Health Authority, 1982–88; *b* 12 Feb. 1914; *d* of late John Donald, MD; *m* 1939, Alan Lamont Munro (killed on active service, 1941); one *s*. *Educ:* Queen's Coll., Harley Street; Wynberg Girls' High Sch., South Africa; St Paul's Girls' Sch.; St Hilda's Coll., Oxford (MA). Ministry of Aircraft Production, 1942–45; Principal, Ministry of Civil Aviation, 1945; Asst Sec., 1949; Under-Sec., Ministry of Transport and Civil Aviation, 1958; Under-Sec., Ministry of Aviation, 1960; High Mistress, St Paul's Girls' Sch. Hammersmith, 1964–74. Chm., Merton, Sutton and Wandsworth AHA(T), 1974–82. Chairman: Training Council for Teachers of the Mentally Handicapped, 1966–69; Cttee of Inquiry into Children's Footwear, 1972; Central Transport Consultative Cttee, 1980–85; Maternity Services Adv. Cttee, 1981–85; Code Monitoring Cttee on Infant Formulae, 1985–89; Member: Board, BEA, 1966–73; Board, British Library, 1973–79; British Tourist Authority, 1973–81. Pres., Chichester and Dist Caledonian Soc., 1992–94. Governor: Charing Cross Group of Hospitals, 1967–74; Chichester High Sch. for Girls, 1990–. Chm., St Richard's Hosp. Appeal. *Recreations:* gardening, sailing, bridge, Scottish country dancing. *Address:* Harbour Way, Ellanore Lane, West Wittering, West Sussex PO20 8AN. *T:* Birdham (01243) 513274. *Club:* Goodwood Country.

MUNRO, Charles Rowcliffe; *b* 6 Nov. 1902; *s* of Charles John Munro, CA, Edinburgh, Hon. Sheriff Substitute, County of Selkirk, and of Edith Rowcliffe; *m* 1942, Moira Rennie Ainslie, *d* of Dr Alexander Cruickshank Ainslie; two *s*. *Educ:* Merchiston Castle Sch., Edinburgh. Hon. Treasurer W Edinburgh Unionist Assoc., 1945–61, Hon. Treas. Scottish Nat. Cttee English-Speaking Union of the Commonwealth 1952–64; Pres. Edinburgh Union of Boys' Clubs, 1957–66. *Recreation:* fishing. *Address:* 66 Murrayfield Avenue, Edinburgh EH12 6AY. *T:* 0131–337 2139.

MUNRO, Colin Andrew; HM Diplomatic Service; Head of Organisation for Security and Co-operation in Europe Unit, Foreign and Commonwealth Office, since 1993; *b* 24 Oct. 1946; *s* of Capt. Frederick Bertram Munro and Jane Eliza (*née* Taylor); *m* 1967, Ehrengard Maria Heinrich; two *s*. *Educ:* George Watson's Coll., Edinburgh; Edinburgh Univ. (MA Hons Mod. Langs 1968). Asst Principal, Bd of Inland Revenue, 1968–69; FCO, 1969–71; Third, later Second, Sec., Bonn, 1971–73; Second, later First, Sec., Kuala Lumpur, 1973–77; FCO, 1977; Private Sec. to Minister of State, 1979–80; Hd of Chancery, Bucharest, 1981–82; FCO, 1983; Asst Head of W European Dept, 1985–87; Dep. Hd of Mission, E Berlin, 1987–90; Consul Gen., Frankfurt, 1990–93. *Publication:* contrib. Jl of Prince Albert Soc. *Recreations:* sports especially hockey, cricket, ski-ing, history, music. *Address:* c/o Foreign and Commonwealth Office, King Charles Street, SW1A 2AH. *Clubs:* Reform; Royal Selangor (Kuala Lumpur).

MUNRO, Colin William Gordon R.; *see* Ross-Munro.

MUNRO, Graeme Neil, FSAScot; Director and Chief Executive, Historic Scotland, since 1991; *b* 28 Aug. 1944; *s* of Daniel Munro and Nancy Kirkwood (*née* Smith); *m* 1972, Nicola Susan Wells; one *s* one *d*. *Educ:* Daniel Stewart's Coll., Edinburgh; Univ. of St Andrews (MA Hons 1967). FSAScot 1990. Joined Scottish Office as Asst Principal, 1968; Scottish Development Department: Housing, 1968; Planning, 1968–70; Private Sec. to Head of Dept, 1971; Principal, Roads, 1972–74; Scottish Home and Health Department: Hosp. Services, 1974–76; Criminal Justice, 1976–79; Asssistant Secrtetary: Dept of Agriculture and Fisheries for Scotland (Fisheries), 1979–83; NHS Funding, Scottish Home and Health Dept, 1983–87; Management and Orgn, Scottish Office Central Services, 1987–90; Dir, Historic Buildings and Monuments, Scotland, 1990–91. *Recreations:* gardening, walking, travel, reading. *Address:* (office) Longmore House, Salisbury Place, Edinburgh EH9 1SH. *T:* 0131–668 8696.

MUNRO, Ian Arthur Hoyle, MB, FRCP; Editor of The Lancet, 1976–88; *b* 5 Nov. 1923; *o s* of Gordon Alexander and Muriel Rebecca Munro; *m* 1948, Olive Isabel, MRCS, LRCP, *o d* of Ernest and Isabella Jackson; three *s* two *d*. *Educ:* Huddersfield Coll.; Paston Sch., North Walsham; Royal Liberty Sch., Romford; Guy's Hosp. (MB 1946). FRCP 1984 (MRCP 1980). Served with RAMC, 1947–50. Joined staff of The Lancet, 1951, Dep. Editor, 1965–76. Regents' Lectr, UCLA, 1982. Pres., Physicians for Human Rights (UK), 1991–. *Recreations:* cricket, crosswords. *Address:* Oakwood, Bayley's Hill, Sevenoaks, Kent TN14 6HS. *T:* Sevenoaks (01732) 454993. *Clubs:* Athenæum; Yorkshire CC.

MUNRO of Foulis-Obsdale, Sir Ian Talbot, 15th Bt *cr* 1634; *b* 28 Dec. 1929; *s* of Robert Hector Munro (*d* 1965) (*n* of 12th and 13th Bts) and Ethel Amy Edith, *d* of Harry Hudson; *S* cousin, Sir Arthur Herman Munro, 14th Bt, 1972. *Heir:* *cousin* Hector George Hamilton Munro [*b* 25 July 1912; *m* 1947, Clarice Amelia Emily (marr. diss. 1975), *d* of Herbert Pitcher; two *d*]. *Address:* 22 rue d'Occitanie, 11120 Ginestas, Aude, France.

MUNRO, Sir Sydney Douglas G.; *see* Gun-Munro, S. D.

MUNROW, Roger Davis, CB 1993; Chief Master of the Supreme Court of Judicature (Chancery Division), 1986–92, retired (Master, 1985–86); *b* 20 March 1929; *s* of late William Davis Munrow, CBE and Constance Caroline Munrow (*née* Moorcroft); *m* 1957, Marie Jane Beresford; three *d*. *Educ:* Bryanston School; Oriel College, Oxford. MA; Solicitor. Entered Treasury Solicitor's Dept as Legal Assistant, 1959; Senior Legal Assistant, 1965; Assistant Treasury Solicitor, 1973; Principal Asst Treasury Solicitor, 1981. *Recreations:* swimming, cycling. *Address:* 20 Monahan Avenue, Purley, Surrey CR8 3BA. *T:* 0181–660 1872.

MUNSTER, 7th Earl of, *cr* 1831; **Anthony Charles FitzClarence;** Viscount FitzClarence, Baron Tewkesbury, 1831; stained glass conservator for Chapel Studio, Hertfordshire, 1983–90; *b* 21 March 1926; *s* of 6th Earl of Munster, and Monica Shiela Harrington (*d* 1958), *d* of Lt-Col Sir Henry Mulleneux Grayson, 1st Bt, KBE; *S* father, 1983; *m* 1st, 1949 (marr. diss. 1966); two *d*; 2nd, 1966 (marr. diss. 1979); one *d*; 3rd, 1979, Alexa Maxwell (*d* 1995). *Educ:* St Edward's School, Oxford. Served RN, 1942–47. Graphic Designer: Daily Mirror Newspapers, 1957–66; IPC Newspapers Division (Sun), 1966–69; freelance 1971–79; stained glass conservator for Burrell collection, 1979–83. MSIA 1960–69. FRSA 1987. *Recreations:* field sports, photography. *Heir:* none. *Address:* House of Lords, SW1A 0PW.

MURCHIE, John Ivor; DL; **His Honour Judge Murchie;** a Circuit Judge, since 1974; *b* 4 June 1928; *s* of Captain Peter Archibald Murchie, OBE, RD, RNR; *m* 1953, Jenifer Rosalie Luard; one *s* two *d*. *Educ:* Edinburgh Academy; Rossall Sch.; Exeter Coll., Oxford (MA). Called to the Bar, Middle Temple, 1953; Harmsworth Scholarship, 1956. Dep. Chm., Berkshire QS, 1969–71; a Recorder of the Crown Court, 1972–74; Dep. Sen.

Judge, Sovereign Base Areas, Cyprus (non-res.), 1987–. Mem., Criminal Cttee, Judicial Studies Bd, 1988–91. Chm. Council, Rossall Sch., 1979–94, Life Gov., 1994; Governor, Queen Anne's Sch., Caversham, 1991–. DL Berks, 1994. *Recreations:* versifying and diversifying, taking photographs and awaiting developments.

MURDIN, Paul Geoffrey, OBE 1988; PhD; FInstP; Head of Astronomy, Particle Physics and Astronomy Research Council, and Director of Science, British National Space Centre, since 1994; *b* 5 Jan. 1942; *s* of Robert Murdin and Ethel Murdin (*née* Chubb); *m* 1964, Lesley Carol Milburn; two *s* one *d*. *Educ:* Trinity School of John Whitgift; Wadham Coll., Oxford (BA Physics); Univ. of Rochester, NY (PhD Physics and Astronomy). FRAS 1970; FInstP 1992. Res. Associate, Univ. of Rochester, 1970–71; Sen. Res. Associate, Royal Greenwich Observatory, 1971–74; Sen. Res. Scientist, Anglo-Australian Observatory, NSW, 1975–78; Royal Greenwich Observatory: Prin. Sci. Officer, 1979–81; Hd of La Palma Operations, 1981–87; Hd of Astronomy Div., 1987–90; Dir, Royal Observatory, Edinburgh, 1991–93; Sen. Mem., Wolfson Coll., Cambridge, 1990–. Mem. Bd of Trustees, Nat. Maritime Museum, 1990–. Mem., Royal Astronomical Soc., 1963–; Pres., European Astronomical Soc., 1993– (Vice-Pres., 1991–93). FRSA 1992. *Publications:* The Astronomer's Telescope (with Patrick Moore), 1963; Radio Waves from Space, 1969; (with L. Murdin) The New Astronomy, 1974; (with D. Allen and D. Malin) Catalogue of the Universe, 1980; (with D. Malin) Colours of the Stars, 1985; End in Fire, 1989; over 150 pubns in astronom. and other sci. jls, principally Monthly Notices of RAS. *Recreations:* writing, music, natural history, history of art. *Address:* Particle Physics and Astronomy Research Council, Polaris House, North Star Avenue, Swindon SN2 1ET. *T:* Swindon (01793) 412075.

MURDOCH, Dame Elisabeth (Joy), AC 1989; DBE 1963 (CBE 1961); *b* 1909; *d* of Rupert Greene and Marie (*née* de Lancey Forth); *m* 1928, Sir Keith (Arthur) Murdoch (*d* 1952); one *s* three *d*. *Educ:* Clyde Sch., Woodend, Victoria. Pres., Royal Children's Hospital, Melbourne, Victoria, Australia, 1953–65. Trustee, National Gallery, Victoria, 1968–76. Hon. LLD Melbourne, 1982. *Recreation:* gardening. *Address:* Cruden Farm, Langwarrin, Victoria 3910, Australia. *Clubs:* Alexandra, Lyceum (Melbourne).

See also K. R. Murdoch.

MURDOCH, Gordon Stuart; QC 1995; a Recorder, South Eastern Circuit, since 1995; *b* 7 June 1947; *s* of late Ian William Murdoch and Margaret Henderson McLaren Murdoch; *m* 1976, Sally Kay Cummings; two *s*. *Educ:* Falkirk High Sch.; Sidney Sussex Coll., Cambridge (MA, LLB). Called to the Bar, Inner Temple, 1970. *Recreations:* music, walking. *Address:* 4 Paper Buildings, Temple, EC4Y 7EX. *T:* 0171–583 0816.

MURDOCH, Dame Iris; *see* Murdoch, Dame J. I.

MURDOCH, Dame (Jean) Iris, (Dame Iris Bayley), DBE 1987 (CBE 1976); CLit 1987; novelist and philosopher; Fellow of St Anne's College, Oxford, since 1948, Hon. Fellow, 1963; *b* Dublin, 15 July 1919; *d* of Wills John Hughes Murdoch and Irene Alice Richardson; *m* 1956, John Oliver Bayley, *qv*. *Educ:* Froebel Educational Inst., London; Badminton Sch., Bristol; Somerville Coll., Oxford (Lit. Hum. 1st Class 1942), Hon. Fellow 1977. Asst Principal, Treasury, 1942–44; Administrative Officer with UNRRA, working in London, Belgium, Austria, 1944–46; Sarah Smithson studentship in philosophy, Newnham Coll., Cambridge, 1947–48; Lectr, RCA, 1963–67. Mem., Irish Academy, 1970; Hon. Member: Amer. Acad. of Arts and Letters, 1975; Amer. Acad. of Arts and Sciences, 1982. Hon. Fellow, Newnham Coll., Cambridge, 1986. Hon. DLitt Oxford, 1987; Hon. LittD Cambridge, 1993. Shakespeare Prize, FVS Foundn, Hamburg, 1988. *Publications:* Sartre, Romantic Rationalist, 1953; Under the Net, 1954; The Flight from the Enchanter, 1955; The Sandcastle, 1957; The Bell, 1958; A Severed Head, 1961 (play, Criterion, 1963); An Unofficial Rose, 1962; The Unicorn, 1963; The Italian Girl, 1964 (play, Criterion, 1967); The Red and the Green, 1965; The Time of The Angels, 1966; The Nice and The Good, 1968; Bruno's Dream, 1969; A Fairly Honourable Defeat, 1970; The Sovereignty of Good, 1970; An Accidental Man, 1971; The Black Prince, 1973 (James Tait Black Meml Prize; play, Aldwych, 1989); The Sacred and Profane Love Machine, 1974 (Whitbread Prize); A Word Child, 1975; Henry and Cato, 1976; The Fire and the Sun, 1977; The Sea, the Sea, 1978 (Booker Prize, 1978); Nuns and Soldiers, 1980; The Philosopher's Pupil, 1983; The Good Apprentice, 1985; Acastos, 1986; The Book and the Brotherhood, 1987; The Message to the Planet, 1989; Metaphysics as a Guide to Morals, 1992; The Green Knight, 1993; *plays:* The Servants and the Snow (Greenwich), 1970; The Three Arrows (Arts, Cambridge), 1972; Art and Eros (Nat. Theatre), 1980; *poems:* A Year of Birds, 1978; papers in Proc. Aristotelian Soc., etc. *Recreation:* learning languages.

MURDOCH, John Derek Walter; Director, Courtauld Institute Galleries, since 1993; *b* 1 April 1945; *s* of James Duncan and Elsie Elizabeth Murdoch; *m* 1st, 1967, Prue Smijth-Windham (marr. diss. 1986); one *s* two *d*; 2nd, 1990, Susan Lambert. *Educ:* Shrewsbury Sch.; Magdalen Coll., Oxford (BA); King's Coll., London (MPhil). Asst Keeper, Birmingham City Art Gall., 1969–73; Victoria & Albert Museum: Asst, then Dep. Keeper, Dept of Paintings, 1973–86; Keeper of Prints, Drawings, Photographs and Paintings, 1986–89; Asst Dir in charge of Collections, 1989–93. Vis. Fellow, British Art Center, Yale Univ., 1979. Trustee: William Morris Gall., Walthamstow, 1975–; Dove Cottage, Grasmere, 1982–. *Publications:* David Cox, 1970; Byron, 1974; English Watercolours, 1977; The English Miniature, 1981; Discovery of the Lake District, 1984; A Sort of National Property, 1985; Painters and the Derby China Works, 1986; contrib. to Rev. of English Studies, Jl of Warburg and Courtauld Insts, Burlington Magazine. *Address:* 14 South End Row, W8 5BZ. *T:* 0171–938 2003.

MURDOCH, (Keith) Rupert, AC 1984; publisher; Chairman, since 1991 and Group Chief Executive, since 1979, The News Corporation Ltd, Australia; Director, News International plc, UK, since 1969 (Chairman, 1969–87 and 1994–95; Chief Executive, 1969–81; Managing Director, 1982–83); *b* 11 March 1931; *s* of late Sir Keith Murdoch and of Dame Elisabeth (Joy) Murdoch, *qv*; *m* 1967, Anna Torv; two *s* two *d*. Chm., News America Publishing Inc.; Dir, Times Newspapers Hldgs Ltd, 1981– (Chm., 1982–90 and 1994–); Chm. and Chief Exec. Officer, Twentieth Century Fox, 1992–, Fox Inc., 1992–. *Address:* 1211 Avenue of the Americas, New York, NY 10036, USA; 1 Virginia Street, E1 9XY.

MURDOCH, Rupert; *see* Murdoch, K. R.

MURDOCH, William Ridley Morton, CBE 1963; DSC 1940 and Bar, 1942; VRD 1949; Sheriff of Grampian, Highland and Islands (formerly Ross and Cromarty), at Dingwall and Tain, 1971–78; *b* 17 May 1917; *s* of William Ridley Carr Murdoch and Margaret Pauline Mackinnon; *m* 1941, Sylvia Maud Pearson; one *s* one *d*. *Educ:* Kelvinside Academy, Glasgow; Glasgow Univ. (MA, LLB). War Service in Navy, 1939–45; Captain, RNR, 1959. Solicitor in private practice, 1947–71; Dir, Glasgow Chamber of Commerce, 1955–71; Dean, Royal Faculty of Procurators in Glasgow, 1968–71. DL, County of City of Glasgow, 1963–75. OStJ 1976. *Recreations:* sailing, gardening. *Address:* Seaview, Shore Street, Gairloch, Ross-shire IV21 2BZ. *T:* Gairloch (01445) 712481.

MURE, Kenneth Nisbet; QC (Scot.) 1989; *b* 11 April 1947; *o s* of Robert and Katherine Mure. *Educ:* Glasgow High Sch.; Glasgow Univ. (MA, LLB). FTII 1971. Admitted to Scots Bar, 1975; called to English Bar, Gray's Inn, 1990. Lectr, Faculty of Law, Glasgow Univ., 1971–83. *Address:* Advocates' Library, Edinburgh EH1 1RF.

MURERWA, Dr Herbert Muchemwa; Minister for the Environment and Tourism, Zimbabwe, since 1990; *b* 31 May 1941; *m* 1969, Ruth Chipo; one *s* four *d*. *Educ:* Harvard University. EdD (Educational Planning). Economic Affairs Officer, UN Economic Commission for Africa, Addis Ababa, 1978–80; Permanent Sec., Min. of Manpower Planning, 1980–81; Permanent Sec., Min. of Labour and Social Services, 1982–84; High Comr in UK, 1984–90. *Address:* c/o Ministry of Environment and Tourism, Karigamombe Centre, Private Bag 7753, Causeway, Harare, Zimbabwe.

MURFIN, Dr David Edward; Vice Chairman of Council, Royal College of General Practitioners, since 1994; *b* 15 June 1946; *s* of Leslie Walter Murfin and Elizabeth Ann Murfin; *m* 1972, Ann Margaret Lewis; one *s* one *d*. *Educ:* Gowerton Boys' Grammar Sch.; King's Coll. London; St George's Hosp., London. Principal in General Practice, Ammanford, Dyfed, 1974–. Mem. Council, RCGP, 1984–90 and 1993–. *Recreations:* reading, walking, cycling. *Address:* Brynteg Surgery, Brynmawr Avenue, Ammanford, Dyfed SA18 2DA. *T:* Ammanford (01269) 592058.

MURGATROYD, Prof. Walter, PhD; Professor of Thermal Power, Imperial College of Science and Technology, 1968–86, now Professor Emeritus; Rockefeller International Fellow, Princeton University, 1979; *b* 15 Aug. 1921; *s* of Harry G. Murgatroyd and Martha W. Strachan; *m* 1952, Denise Geneviève, *d* of late Robert Adolphe Schlumberger, Paris and Bénouville; one *s* one *d* (and one *s* decd). *Educ:* St Catharine's Coll., Cambridge. BA 1946, PhD 1952. Hawker Aircraft Ltd, 1942–44; Rolls Royce Ltd, 1944–46; Univ. of Cambridge (Liquid Metal and Reactor heat transfer research), 1947–54; UK Atomic Energy Authority, Harwell, 1954–56; Head of Dept of Nuclear Engineering, Queen Mary Coll., Univ. of London, 1956–67, and Dean of Engineering, 1966–67. Member: British-Greek Mixed Commn, 1963–78; British-Belgian Mixed Commn, 1964–78; British-Austrian Mixed Commn, 1965–78. Specialist Adviser to H of C Select Cttee on Energy, 1980–. *Publications:* contrib. to various scientific and technical journals. *Recreation:* music. *Address:* 7 Currie Hill Close, SW19 7DX. *T:* 0181–946 0415.

MURIA, Hon. Sir (Gilbert) John Baptist, Kt 1995; Chief Justice, Solomon Islands, since 1993; *b* 2 Feb. 1953; *s* of late John Baptist Manumate and of Adriana Gala; *m* 1982, Rosemary Kekealu; one *s* two *d*. *Educ:* Univ. of Papua New Guinea (LLB). Called to the Bar: PNG, 1980; Solomon Is, 1981. Sen. Crown Counsel, Solomon Is, 1980; Sen. Legal Officer, 1981–83; Chief Legal Officer, 1984–87; Dep. Public Solicitor, 1987–89; Public Solicitor, 1989–91; Actg Attorney Gen., 1989; Puisne Judge, High Court of Solomon Is, 1991–93. *Address:* High Court of Solomon Islands, PO Box G21, Honiara, Solomon Islands. *T:* 21632.

MURLEY, John Tregarthen, CB 1988; DPhil; *b* 22 Aug. 1928; *s* of John Murley and Dorothea Birch; *m* 1954, Jean Patricia Harris; one *d*. *Educ:* University College, London (BA 1st Cl. Hons History); St Antony's Coll., Oxford (DPhil). Entered FO, 1955; Counsellor, Washington, 1976–80. *Publication:* The Origin and Outbreak of the Anglo-French War of 1793, 1959. *Recreations:* tennis, golf, piano.

MURLEY, Sir Reginald (Sydney), KBE 1979; TD 1946; FRCS; President, Royal College of Surgeons, 1977–80; *b* 2 Aug. 1916; *s* of Sydney Herbert Murley and Beatrice Maud Baylis; *m* 1947, Daphne, 2nd *d* of Ralph E. and Rowena Garrod; three *s* two *d* and one step *d*. *Educ:* Dulwich Coll.; Univ. of London; St Bartholomew's Hosp. (MB, BS Hons 1939, MS 1948). MRCS, LRCP 1939; FRCS 1946. Served War, RAMC, 1939–45: ME, E Africa, N Africa, Sicily, Italy and NW Europe; regtl and fld ambulance MO; Surgical Specialist, No 1 and 2 Maxillo-Facial Units and Fld Surg. Units; Major. St Bartholomew's Hospital: Jun. Scholarship, 1935; Sen. Schol., and Sir William Dunn Exhibn in Anat., Univ. of London, 1936; House Surg., 1939; Anat. Demonstrator, 1946; Surg. Chief Asst, 1946–49; Cattlin Res. Fellow and Mackenzie Mackinnon Res. Fellow, RCP and RCS, 1950–51; Surgeon: St Albans Hosp., 1947; Royal Northern Hosp., London, 1953; Hon. Consultant Surgeon, St Bartholomew's Hosp., 1979. Chm., Med. Council on Alcoholism, 1980–92. Royal Coll. of Surgeons: formerly Tutor and Reg. Adviser; Examiner, primary FRCS, 1966–72; Mem. Council, 1970–82; Hunterian Orator, 1981; Bradshaw Lectr, 1981; Mem. Ct of Patrons, 1981–; Chm., Trustees of Hunterian Mus., 1988– (Trustee, 1981–). Vis. Prof., Cleveland Clinic, USA, 1979, 1982 and 1986. Mitchiner Lectr, RAMC, 1981 and 1993. FRSM, 1947–83; Fellow, Assoc. of Surgeons of GB and Ireland. Member: Hunterian Soc. (former Mem. Council; Pres., 1970–71; Orator, 1978); Med. Soc. of London (former Mem. Council; Pres., 1982); Harveian Soc. (former Mem. Council; Pres., 1983); BMA (former Councillor); Exec. Cttee, Soc. Internat. de Chirurgie, 1979–83 (Vice-Pres., 1985–86; Hon. Mem., 1991); European and internat. cardiovascular socs.; Adv. Council, The Social Affairs Unit, 1981–; Adv. Council, Health and Welfare Unit (formerly Health Unit), Inst. of Economic Affairs, 1986–. Hon. Vice-Pres., Nat. Stroke Campaign, 1985; Hon. Member: Brit. Assoc. of Plastic Surgs, 1983; Brit. Assoc. of Clinical Anatomists, 1983; Reading Pathological Soc., 1985; First Hon. Mem. and Medallist, Indep. Doctors' Forum, 1995. Sundry eponymous lectures and orations; Hon. FRACS and Syme Orator, 1979; Hon. FCSSA 1979; Hon. FRCSI 1980; Hon. FDSRCS 1981; Hon. Fellow: Italian Soc. Surg., 1979; Polish Assoc. of Surgeons, 1983. President: Sir John Charnley Trust, 1983–; Alleyn Club, 1983; Fellowship for Freedom in Medicine 1972–86; Mem. Council, Freedom Assoc., 1982–; Patron: Med. Aid to Poland, 1984–; Jagiellonian Trust, 1984–; Sponsor, 1984, Trustee, 1986, Family & Youth Concern (The Responsible Soc.). Freeman, City of London, 1955; Hon. Freeman, Barbers' Co., 1986; Liveryman, Apothecaries' Co., 1955–. *Publications:* (contrib.) Financing Medical Care, 1962; Surgical Roots and Branches (autobiog.), 1990; (ed jtly) The Case Books of John Hunter, FRS, 1993; contrib. surg. textbooks; articles in med. literature on breast, thyroid and vascular diseases; articles on med. politics and econs. *Recreations:* gardening, music, reading history and economics. *Address:* (home) Cobden Hill House, 63 Cobden Hill, Radlett, Herts WD7 7JN. *T:* Radlett (01923) 856532; (office) Consulting Suite, Wellington Hospital, Wellington Place, NW8 9LE. *T:* 0171–586 5959. *Clubs:* Royal Automobile; Fountain (St Bart's Hospital).

MURPHY, Andrew John; Sheriff of Tayside Central and Fife at Falkirk, since 1991; *b* 16 Jan. 1946; *s* of Robert James Murphy and Robina Murphy (*née* Scott); *m* 1980, Susan Margaret Thomson; two *s* two *d*. *Educ:* Allan Glen's School, Glasgow; Edinburgh Univ. (MA, LLB). 2nd Lieut RA (V), 1971–73; Flt Lieut RAF, 1973–75. Admitted to Faculty of Advocates, Scottish Bar, 1970; called to Bar, Middle Temple, 1990; Crown Counsel, Hong Kong, 1976–79; Standing Junior Counsel to Registrar General for Scotland, 1982–85; Temporary Sheriff, 1983–85; Sheriff of Grampian, Highland and Islands at Banff and Peterhead, 1985–91. *Address:* c/o Sheriff's Chambers, Court House, Main Street, Camelon, Falkirk FK1 4AR.

MURPHY, Rear-Adm. Anthony Albert, CBE 1976; Special Project Executive, Ministry of Defence, 1977–82; retired, 1983; *b* 19 May 1924; *s* of Albert Edward Murphy and Jennie (*née* Giles); *m* 1954, Antonia Theresa (*née* Rayner); four *s*. *Educ:* Sir George Monoux

Grammar Sch. National Provincial Bank, 1940–42; joined RN, 1942; commnd, 1944; Western Approaches, 1944–45; HMS Vanguard (Royal Tour of S Africa), 1945–49; HMS Bulwark (Suez); Comdr 1960; HMS Yarmouth/6th Frigate Sqdn, Kuwait, 1961–63; HMS Eagle, 1965–67; Captain 1967; Dir, Naval Guided Weapons, 1970–73; in comd HMS Collingwood, 1973–76; Rear-Adm. 1977; Vice-Pres., and Senior Naval Mem., Ordnance Board, 1977. *Recreations:* cricket, soccer (Chm. RNFA, 1973–76), country activities.

MURPHY, Brian Gordon; Building Societies' Ombudsman, since 1992; *b* 18 Oct. 1940; *s* of Albert and Doris Murphy; *m* 1973, Judith Ann Parkinson. *Educ:* Mill Hill Sch. Articled Smiles & Co.; admitted Solicitor, 1966; with Roythorne & Co. and Russell & Dumoulin, Canada; Partner: Knapp Fishers, 1968–87; Farrer & Co., 1987–92. Pt-time Chm., Industrial Tribunals, 1991–92. Vice-Chm., Incorp. Council of Law Reporting for Eng. and Wales, 1992–; Mem. Council, Law Soc., 1982–93 (Chm., Employment Law Cttee, 1987–90); Pres., Westminster Law Soc., 1983–84. *Recreations:* golf, theatre, photography, travel, private flying. *Address:* Building Societies' Ombudsman Co., 35–37 Grosvenor Gardens, SW1X 7AW. *T:* 0171–931 0044. *Club:* Phyllis Court (Henley).

MURPHY, Mrs Brian Taunton; *see* Hufton, Prof. Olwen.

MURPHY, Christopher Philip Yorke; *b* 20 April 1947; *s* of Philip John and Dorothy Betty Murphy; *m* 1969, Sandra Gillian Ashton. *Educ:* Devonport High Sch.; The Queen's Coll., Oxford (MA). Formerly Associate Dir, D'Arcy MacManus & Masius. President, Oxford Univ. Conservative Assoc., 1967; held number of Conservative Party offices, 1968–72. Parish Councillor, Windlesham, Surrey, 1972–76. Contested (C): Bethnal Green and Bow, Feb. 1974, Oct. 1974. MP (C) Welwyn Hatfield, 1979–87. Vice-Chairman: Parly Urban and New Town Affairs Cttee, 1980–87; Parly Arts and Heritage Cttee, 1981–86; Mem., Select Cttee on Statutory Instruments, 1980–87 (rep of cttee on Commonwealth Delegated Legislation Cttee, 1980–87); UK Delegate to Council of Europe/WEU, 1983–87 (Hon. Associate, 1988). Vice-President: C of E Artistic Heritage Commn, 1984–87; C of E Youth & Drugs Commn, 1986–87. Member: Nat. Cttee for 900th Anniversary of Domesday Book, 1986; Chief Pleas of Sark (Parlt), 1989–90 (Vice-Pres., Internat. Cttee of Chief Pleas, 1989–90); Arts Council of Bailiwick of Guernsey, 1988–90; Council, Société Guernésiaise, 1988–90. Life Mem., CPA, 1987. Hon. Sec., Société Sercquiaise, 1988–90. Sec., Sodor & Man Diocesan Synod, and Bishop's Advr, 1991–; Chapter Clerk, St German's Cathedral, 1992–; Diocesan Sec., 1993–; Secretary: Diocesan Bd of Finance, 1993–; Church Comrs for IOM, 1993–. FRSA. Freeman, City of London, 1984. Hon. Citizen, Cork, 1985. *Recreations:* arts, heritage, travel, conservation, walking, horticulture. *Address:* Cooil Voorath, The Cronk, Ballaugh, Isle of Man. *Club:* Oxford Union Society.

MURPHY, Cornelius McCaffrey, (Neil Murphy), MBE 1982; Chairman, New Life Venues Ltd, since 1992; *b* 31 May 1936; 2nd *s* of Edward and Annie Murphy, Glasgow; *m* 1992, Carmel Murphy; two *s*; two *d* by previous *m*, and two step *d*. *Educ:* Holyrood Sch.; Univ. of Glasgow (MA 1958). Joined The Builder Group, 1962, following spells of teaching and management trng: Editor, 1974–83, Editor-in-Chief, 1983–87, Building Magazine; Dir, 1979–92; Man. Dir, Building (Publishers) Ltd, 1981–90, Group Man. Dir, 1990–92. Mem., Worshipful Co. of Tylers and Bricklayers. *Recreations:* reading, golf. *Address:* 122 Sea Lane, Goring by Sea, W Sussex BN12 4PU. *Club:* Royal Automobile.

MURPHY, Dervla; *b* 28 Nov. 1931; *d* of Fergus Murphy and Kathleen Rochfort-Dowling; one *d*. *Educ:* Ursuline Convent, Waterford. American Irish Foundn Literary Award, 1975; Christopher Ewart-Biggs Meml Prize, 1978; Irish Amer. Cultural Inst. Literary Award, 1985. *Publications:* Full Tilt, 1965, 7th edn 1984; Tibetan Foothold, 1966, 3rd edn 1968; The Waiting Land, 1967, 3rd edn 1969; In Ethiopia with a Mule, 1968, 4th edn 1985; On a Shoe String to Coorg, 1976, 3rd edn 1985; Where the Indus is Young, 1977, 2nd edn 1984; A Place Apart, 1978, 5th edn 1984; Wheels Within Wheels, 1979, 5th edn 1984; Race to the Finish?, 1981; Eight Feet in the Andes, 1983, 2nd edn 1985; Muddling Through in Madagascar, 1985, 3rd edn 1987; Ireland, 1985; Tales from Two Cities, 1987; (ed) Embassy to Constantinople, the Travels of Lady Mary Wortley Montague, 1988; In Cameroon with Egbert, 1989; Transylvania and Beyond, 1992; The Ukimwi Road, 1993; South Africa, 1995. *Recreations:* reading, music, cycling, swimming, walking. *Address:* Lismore, Co. Waterford, Ireland.

MURPHY, Prof. Elaine, MD; FRCPsych; Professor of Psychiatry of Old Age, United Medical and Dental Schools of Guy's and St Thomas' Hospitals, since 1983; *b* Nottingham, 16 Jan. 1947; *d* of Roger Lawson and Nell Lawson (*née* Allitt); *m* 1969, John Matthew Murphy. *Educ:* Univ. of Manchester Med. Sch. (MB, ChB 1971; MD 1979). FRCPsych 1986. Consultant Psychiatrist, Newham and Redbridge HAs, 1980–83; Dist Gen. Manager, Lewisham and N Southwark HA, 1988–90. Vice-Chm., Mental Health Act Commn, 1988–94; Mem. Panel, Ashworth Hosp. Inquiry, 1992. *Publications:* Dementia and Mental Illness in Older People, 1986, 2nd edn 1993; Affective Disorders in the Elderly, 1986; After the Asylums, 1991; papers on mental disorder and social policy on community care. *Recreations:* Italy, opera. *Address:* 382 Lauderdale Tower, Barbican, EC2Y 8NA; The Grange, Brockdish, Norfolk IP21 4JE.

MURPHY, Rev. Canon Gervase; *see* Murphy, Rev. Canon J. G. M. W.

MURPHY, Ian Patrick; QC 1992; a Recorder, since 1990; *b* 1 July 1949; *s* of Patrick Murphy and Irene Grace (*née* Hooper); *m* 1974, Penelope Gay; two *d*. *Educ:* St Illtyd's Coll., Cardiff; LSE (LLB). Chartering Clerk, Baltic Exchange, 1970–71; called to the Bar, Middle Temple, 1972; Asst Recorder, 1986–90. *Recreations:* golf, ski-ing, cricket. *Address:* 9 Park Place, Cardiff CF1 3DP. *T:* Cardiff (01222) 382731; 3 Llandaff Chase, Llandaff, Cardiff CF5 2NA. *Clubs:* Cardiff County; Royal Porthcawl Golf.

MURPHY, Sheriff James Patrick; Sheriff of Glasgow and Strathkelvin, since 1989; *b* 24 Jan. 1932; *s* of Henry Francis Murphy and Alice (*née* Rooney); *m* 1956, Maureen Coyne; two *s* one *d*. *Educ:* Notre Dame Convent; St Aloysius' Coll., Glasgow; Univ. of Glasgow (BL 1953). Admitted Solicitor, 1953; assumed partner, R. Maguire Cook & Co., Glasgow, 1959; founded, with J. Ross Harper, firm of Ross Harper & Murphy, Glasgow, 1961; Sheriff of N Strathclyde, 1976–89. President: Glasgow Juridical Soc., 1962–63; Glasgow Bar Assoc., 1966–67; Sheriffs' Assoc., 1991–92; Mem. Council, Law Soc. of Scotland, 1974–76. Governor, St Aloysius' Coll., Glasgow, 1978–86. *Recreations:* bird watching, canoeing, cycling, books, the history of writing, footering. *Address:* 1 Kelvin Crescent, Bearsden G61 1BT.

MURPHY, Most Rev. John A., DD; Archbishop Emeritus of Cardiff, (RC) (Archbishop, 1961–83); *b* Birkenhead, 21 Dec. 1905; *s* of John and Elizabeth Murphy. *Educ:* The English Coll., Lisbon. Ordained 1931; consecrated as Bishop of Appia and Coadjutor Bishop of Shrewsbury, 1948; Bishop of Shrewsbury, 1949–61. ChStJ 1974. *Address:* Ty Mair, St Joseph's Nursing Home, Malpas, Newport, Gwent NP9 6ZE.

MURPHY, Rev. Canon (John) Gervase (Maurice Walker), LVO 1987; MA; a Chaplain to the Queen, since 1987; Chaplain of the Chapel Royal of St Peter ad Vincula, Tower of London, since 1991; *b* 20 Aug. 1926; *s* of William Stafford and Yvonne Iris Murphy; *m* 1957, Joy Hilda Miriam Livermore; five *d*. *Educ:* Methodist Coll., Belfast; Trinity Coll., Dublin (BA 1952, MA 1955; Rugby football team, 1947–52 (Capt., 1951–52); cricket colours). Guardsman, Irish Guards, 1944–45; commissioned Royal Ulster Rifles, 1945–47. TCD, 1947–52 and Divinity Sch., TCD, 1949–52. Ordained, 1952; Curate, Shankill Parish, Lurgan, 1952–55. Royal Army Chaplains' Dept, 1955; served: Korea, 1955–57; Woolwich, 1957–59; Aden, 1959–62; Infantry Junior Leaders, Oswestry, 1962–64; Bagshot, 1964–65; Worthy Down, 1965; Commonwealth Bde Sen. Chaplain, 1965–67; Sen. Chaplain, Guards Depot, Pirbright, 1967–69; DACG, Rhine Area, 1969–72; Sen. Chaplain, RMA Sandhurst, 1972–74; Asst Chaplain General: BAOR, 1974–75; South East, 1975–77; Vicar of Ranworth and RD of Blofield, 1977–79; Chaplain for Holidaymakers on Norfolk Broads, 1977–79; Domestic Chaplain to the Queen, Rector of Sandringham and Leader of Sandringham Group of Parishes, 1979–87; RD of Heacham and Rising, 1985–87; Hon Canon of Norwich Cathedral, 1986, Emeritus, 1987–; Rector, Christ Church Cathedral, Falkland Is, 1987–91; Chaplain, Lord Mayor of London, 1993–94. Vice-Pres., British Assoc. for Physical Trng, 1988– (Hon. Fellow, 1988). Played: Internat. Rugby football for Ireland, 1952, 1954 and 1958; Rugby football for British Army 1957, and for Barbarians, 1958. *Publication:* Christ Church Cathedral, Falkland Islands: its life and times 1892–1992, 1992. *Recreations:* sport, walking, gardening, interior decorating. *Address:* HM Tower of London, EC3N 4AB. *Clubs:* East India (Hon. Chaplain), British Sportsman's, London Irish RFC, Public School Wanderers RFC; Leprechauns Cricket (Ireland); Mid-Ulster Cricket.

MURPHY, Sir Leslie (Frederick), Kt 1978; Chairman, National Enterprise Board, 1977–79 (Deputy Chairman, 1975–77); *b* 17 Nov. 1915; *s* of Frederick Charles and Lillian Annie Murphy; *m* 1st, 1940, Marjorie Iris Cowell (*d* 1991); one *s* one *d*; 2nd, 1993, Dorothy Anne Murray. *Educ:* Southall Grammar Sch.; Birkbeck Coll., Univ. of London. Principal Private Sec. to Minister of Fuel and Power, 1947–49; Asst Sec., Min. of Fuel and Power, 1949–52; Chm., Mobil Supply Co. Ltd and Mobil Shipping Co. Ltd, 1955–59; Finance Dir, Iraq Petroleum Co. Ltd, 1959–64; Director: J. Henry Schroder Wagg & Co. Ltd, 1964–75 (Dep. Chm. 1972–73); Schroders plc, 1979–90 (Dep. Chm., 1973–75); Unigate Ltd, 1968–75; Simon Engrg Ltd, 1980–85; Folksam International Insurance (UK) Ltd, 1980–90; Petroleum Economics Ltd, 1980–94 (Chm., 1980–87). Mem., NEDC, 1977–79. Mem. Royal Commn on Distribution of Income and Wealth, 1974–76; Board Mem., Church Army, 1964–94; Chm., Church Army Housing Ltd, 1973–82, Pres., 1982–84. Trustee, SDP, 1981–90. *Recreations:* music, golf. *Address:* Hedgerley, Barton Common Road, Barton-on-Sea, Hants BH25 5PR.

MURPHY, Michael Joseph Adrian; QC 1993; a Recorder, since 1989; *b* 1 Oct. 1949. *Educ:* Aberdare Grammar Sch., Mid-Glam.; Sheffield Univ. (LLB, MA). Called to the Bar, Inner Temple, 1973. *Address:* 12 Paradise Square, Sheffield S1 2DE. *T:* Sheffield (0114) 273 8951.

MURPHY, Neil; *see* Murphy, C. McC.

MURPHY, Patrick James, CMG 1985; HM Diplomatic Service, retired; *b* 11 March 1931; *e s* of late Dr James Murphy and Cicely Mary (*née* Crowley); *m* 1st, 1959, Barbara May Healey-Purse (marr. diss. 1969); two *s*; 2nd, 1974, Jutta Ulrike Oehlmann; one *s*. *Educ:* Cranbrook School; Gonville and Caius College, Cambridge (BA; Geography Tripos). Served RAF, 1950–52. Oxford and Cambridge Far Eastern Expedition, 1955–56; BBC Gen. Overseas Service, 1956; Joined FO, 1957; Frankfurt, 1958; Berlin, 1959; FO, 1962; Second Sec. (Commercial), Warsaw, 1962; First Sec., FO, 1965; First Sec. (Commercial) and Consul, Phnom Penh, 1966; Consul, Düsseldorf, 1969; Consul, Hamburg, 1971; FCO, 1974; First Sec., Vienna, 1977; Counsellor, FCO, 1981–87. Advr, Sultanate of Oman, 1987–90; Consultant, HM Diplomatic Service, 1990–95. *Recreations:* history, travel, wine, boating, Irish life. *Address:* 260 Dacre Park, SE13 5DD. *T:* 0181–852 2483. *Club:* Royal Air Force.

MURPHY, Patrick Wallace; Under Secretary, Land Use, Conservation and Countryside Group, Ministry of Agriculture, Fisheries and Food, since 1994; *b* 16 Aug. 1944; *s* of Lawrence Vincent Murphy and Agnes Dunn; *m* 1972, Denise Lillieth Fullarton-Fullarton; two *s*. *Educ:* St Chad's College, Wolverhampton; Trinity Hall, Cambridge (BA Hons). Joined MAFF, 1966; Asst Private Sec. to Minister of Agriculture, Fisheries and Food, 1970; First Sec. (Agriculture and Commercial), British Embassy, Washington, 1974–78; Controller of Plant Variety Rights, 1978–82; Head, Land Use and Tenure Div., 1982–86; Under Sec., 1986; Head, Milk and Potatoes Gp, 1986–89; Hd of Pesticides, Vet. Medicines, Emergencies and Biotechnol. Gp, 1989–93; Hd of EC Gp, 1993–94. Non-Exec. Dir, IDV (UK), 1985–88. *Recreations:* cricket, tennis, gardening. *Address:* Elstead, Surrey.

MURPHY, Paul Peter; MP (Lab) Torfaen, since 1987; *b* 25 Nov. 1948; *s* of Ronald and Marjorie Murphy. *Educ:* St Francis RC Primary Sch., Abersychan; West Monmouth Sch., Pontypool; Oriel Coll., Oxford (MA). Management Trainee, CWS, 1970–71; Lectr in History and Govt, Ebbw Vale Coll. of Further Education, 1971–87. Mem., Torfaen Borough Council, 1973–87 (Chm., Finance Cttee, 1976–86); Sec., Torfaen Constituency Labour Party, 1974–87. Opposition front bench spokesman for Wales, 1988–94; on NI, 1994–. *Recreation:* music. *Address:* 42 Wiston Path, Fairwater, Cwmbran, Gwent NP44 4PY. *T:* Cwmbran (01633) 67145. *Clubs:* St Joseph's (St Dials); Fairwater Sports and Social.

MURPHY, Dr Simon Francis; Member (Lab) Midlands West, European Parliament, since 1994; *b* 24 Feb. 1962; *s* of Patrick Joseph Murphy and Mary Frances Murphy; *m* 1992, Bridget Lee Brickley. *Educ:* Sacred Heart Coll., Droitwich; N Worcs Coll., Bromsgrove; UCW, Aberystwyth (BSc Econ 1983; PhD 1986). Tutor, Dept of Political Sci., UCW, Aberystwyth, 1984–86; Asst to Leader of Labour Gp, Wolverhampton MBC, 1986–89; Head of Research, Office of John Bird, MEP, 1989–94. Contested (Lab) Wolverhampton SW, 1992. *Publication:* (contrib.) chapter in Contemporary Minority Nationalisms, ed M. Watson, 1990. *Recreations:* running, reading, cooking, watching sport. *Address:* Rooms 2/3 Gresham Chambers, 14 Lichfield Street, Wolverhampton WV1 1DP. *T:* Wolverhampton (01902) 712366.

MURPHY, Thomas, CBE 1991; Managing Director, Civil Aviation Authority, 1987–95; *b* 13 Nov. 1928; *s* of Thomas Murphy and Elizabeth Gray Murphy (*née* Leckie); *m* 1962, Sheila Jean Dorothy Young; one *s* three *d*. *Educ:* St Mirin's Acad., Paisley; Glasgow Univ. (MA Hons). Served Royal Artillery, 1951–53. Marks and Spencer, 1953–55; British Petroleum, 1955–86: appts in Territory of Papua New Guinea, Trinidad, Scotland, Algeria, USA, 1955–68; Asst Gen. Man., BP Tanker Co., 1968–76; Gen. Man., Gp Personnel, 1976–81; Advr, Organisation Planning, 1981–86; Non-Exec. Dir, CAA, 1986–87. Internat. Sen. Managers Programme, Harvard Business Sch., 1973. *Recreations:* walking, coarse golf, destructive gardening. *Address:* Woodruffe, Onslow Road, Sunningdale, Berks SL5 0HW. *T:* Ascot (01344) 23261. *Club:* Wentworth.

MURPHY, Thomas A(quinas); Chairman, General Motors Corporation, 1974–80; *b* Hornell, NY, 10 Dec. 1915; *s* of John Joseph Murphy and Alma (*née* O'Grady); *m* 1941, Catherine Rita Maguire; one *s* two *d*. *Educ:* Leo High Sch., Chicago; Univ. of Illinois. US

Naval Reserve, 1943–46. Joined General Motors Corporation, 1938; Asst Treas., 1959; Comptroller, 1967; Treas., 1968–70; Vice-Pres. and Gp Exec., Car and Truck Div., 1970–72; Vice-Chm., 1972–74. *Address:* c/o General Motors Corporation, General Motors Building, Detroit, MI 48202, USA.

MURPHY, Thomas James; journalist, The Times, since 1990; professional singer; *b* 26 June 1956; *s* of James Murphy and Beatrice Murphy (*née* Strand); *m* 1976, Janet Sallis; four *s. Educ:* Salesian Sch., Chertsey; Sussex Univ. (BA History); Warwick Univ. (MBA). Kitchen porter and factory labourer, 1977; trainee journalist, Slough Observer, 1978; Sports editor, Buckinghamshire Advertiser, 1981; Editor: Staines Informer, 1983; East Grinstead Courier, 1984; Sub-editor, The Independent, 1986; Dep. Chief sub-editor, London Evening News, 1987; Editor, The Universe, 1988–90. *Recreation:* swimming. *Address:* 17 Reynolds Road, Hove, Sussex BN3 5RT. *T:* Brighton (01273) 885806.

MURPHY-O'CONNOR, Rt. Rev. Cormac; *see* Arundel and Brighton, Bishop of, (RC).

MURRAY; *see* Beasley-Murray.

MURRAY; *see* Erskine-Murray.

MURRAY, family name of **Duke of Atholl,** of **Earl of Dunmore,** of **Earl of Mansfield and Mansfield** and of **Baron Murray of Epping Forest.**

MURRAY, Rt. Hon. Lord; Ronald King Murray, PC 1974; a Senator of the College of Justice in Scotland, 1979–95; *b* 15 June 1922; *s* of James King Murray, MIEE, and Muriel (*née* Aitken), Glasgow; *m* 1950, Sheila Winifred Gamlin; one *s* one *d. Educ:* George Watson's Coll., Edinburgh; Univ. of Edinburgh; Jesus Coll., Oxford. MA (1st cl. hons Phil) Edinburgh, 1948; LLB Edinburgh, 1952. Served HM Forces, 1941–46; commnd in REME, 1942; India and SEAC, 1943–46. Asst in Moral Philosophy, Edinburgh Univ., 1949; called to Scottish Bar, 1953; QC (Scotland) 1967; Advocate-Depute, 1964–67; Senior Advocate-Depute, 1967–70. MP (Lab) Leith, Edinburgh, 1970–79; Lord Advocate, 1974–79. Vice-Chm., Edinburgh Univ. Court, 1990–93. Mem., Scottish Records Adv. Council, 1987–93. Hon. Pres., Leith Boys' Brigade, 1984–. *Publications:* articles in various jls. *Recreation:* boating. *Address:* 1 Inverleith Grove, Edinburgh EH3 5PB. *T:* 0131–551 5330. *Clubs:* Royal Forth Yacht, Forth Corinthian Yacht.

MURRAY OF EPPING FOREST, Baron *cr* 1985 (Life Peer), of Telford in the County of Shropshire; **Lionel Murray,** OBE 1966; PC 1976; General Secretary of the Trades Union Congress, 1973–84; *b* 2 Aug. 1922; *m* 1945, Heather Woolf; two *s* two *d. Educ:* Wellington (Salop) Gram. Sch.; Univ. of London, 1940–41; NCLC; New Coll., Oxford, 1945–47 (Hon. Fellow, 1975). War Service, KSLI. Economic Dept, TUC, 1947, Head of Dept, 1954–69; Asst Gen. Sec., TUC, 1969–73. Mem., NEDC, 1973–84; Vice-President: ICFTU, 1973; European Trade Union Confedn, 1974. Vice-Chm., Nat. Children's Home; Vice-President: Hearing and Speech Trust; British Heart Foundn; Ironbridge Mus. Trust; Wesley's Chapel. Trustee: Carnegie UK Trust; NUMAST; Crisis at Christmas; Prison Service Trust. Gov., Nat. Youth Theatre. Fellow, QMW, 1988; Hon. Fellow, Sheffield City Polytechnic, 1979. Hon. DSc: Aston, 1977; Salford, 1978; Hon. LLD: St Andrews, 1979; Leeds, 1985. *Address:* 29 The Crescent, Loughton, Essex IG10 4PY. *T:* 0181–508 4425.

MURRAY, Bishop of The, since 1989; **Rt. Rev. Graham Howard Walden;** *b* 19 March 1931; *s* of Leonard Howard Walden and Mary Ellen Walden (*née* Cahalane); *m* 1964, Margaret Ann (*née* Brett); two *s* one *d. Educ:* Univ. of Queensland (BA 1952; MA 1954); Australian Coll. of Theol. (ThL 1954); Christ Church, Oxford (BLitt 1960; MLitt 1980). Ordained deacon 1954, priest 1955; Assistant Curate: West Hackney, 1954–56; St Saviour's, Poplar, 1957–58; permission to officiate, dio. of Oxford, 1955–59; Mem., Bush Brotherhood of the Good Shepherd, NSW, 1959–63; Vice Principal, Torres Strait Mission Theol Coll., 1963–65; Rector of Mudgee, NSW, 1965–70; Archdeacon of Barker, 1968–70; Archdeacon and Vicar-Gen. of Ballarat, 1970–89; Asst Bishop of Ballarat, 1981–89; Rector of Hamilton and Bishop in Hamilton, 1981–84. Nat. Chm., Anglican Men's Soc., 1983–93; Anglican Chm., Jt Anglican RC Diocesan Commn, 1977–89; Vice-Chm., Internat. Bishops' Conf., 1992–; Member: Gen. Bd of Religious Educn, 1970–81; Anglican Lutheran Conversations constituted by Gen. Synod of Anglican Church of Australia, 1989–; Gen. Synod Commn on Doctrine, 1989– (Chm., 1992–). *Publications:* contrib. to jls and church papers. *Address:* Bishop's Lodge, 23 Ellendale Avenue, Murray Bridge, SA 5253, Australia. *T:* (85) 322240; PO Box 269, Murray Bridge, SA 5253, Australia. *T:* (85) 322270, *Fax:* (85) 325760.

MURRAY, Alexander, FRHistS; FBA 1995; Fellow and Praelector in Modern History, University College, Oxford, since 1980; *b* 14 May 1934; second *s* of late Stephen Hubert Murray and Margaret (*née* Gillett). *Educ:* Bedales Sch., Petersfield; New Coll., Oxford (BA Mod. Hist.; BPhil European Hist.). FRHistS 1971. Served RA, 1953–55. Asst Lectr in Medieval Hist., Univ. of Leeds, 1961–63; University of Newcastle upon Tyne: Lectr, 1963–77; Sen. Lectr, 1977–80; Public Orator, 1973–76. Directeur des Etudes Associé, Ecole des Hautes Etudes en Sciences Sociales, Paris, 1986; Vis. Prof. of Medieval Hist., Harvard Univ., 1989–90. *Publications:* Reason and Society in the Middle Ages, 1978; articles in learned jls and collective vols. *Recreations:* music, walking. *Address:* University College, Oxford OX1 4BH. *T:* Oxford (01865) 276602.

MURRAY, Dame (Alice) Rosemary, DBE 1977; MA, DPhil; JP; DL; President, New Hall, Cambridge, 1964–81 (Tutor in Charge, 1954–64); Vice-Chancellor, Cambridge University, 1975–77; *b* 28 July 1913; *d* of late Adm. A. J. L. Murray and Ellen Maxwell Spooner. *Educ:* Downe House, Newbury; Lady Margaret Hall, Oxford (Hon. Fellow, 1968). MA (Oxon and Cantab); BSc, DPhil (Oxon). Lecturer in chemistry: Royal Holloway Coll., 1938–41; Sheffield Univ., 1941–42. Served War of 1939–45, Experimental Officer, Admiralty Signals Establishment, 1941; WRNS, 1942–46, Chief Officer. Lectr in Chemistry, Girton Coll., Cambridge, 1946–54, Fellow, 1949, Tutor, 1951, Hon. Fellow, 1976; Demonstrator in Chemistry, Univ. of Cambridge, 1947–52. Dir, Midland Bank Ltd, 1978–84; Independent Dir, The Observer, 1981–93. Member: Lockwood Cttee on Higher Educn in NI, 1963–65; Wages Councils, 1968–93; Council, GPDST, 1969–93; Armed Forces Pay Review Body, 1971–81; Pres., Nat. Assoc. of Adult Educn, 1977–80, Vice-Pres., 1980–83. Governor and Chm., Keswick Coll. of Education, 1953–83; Mem. Delegacy, Goldsmiths' Coll., London Univ., 1986–89; Visitor, Homerton Coll., Cambridge, 1990–. Mem. Council, Toynbee Hall, 1983–89. Liveryman, Goldsmiths' Co., 1978–. JP City of Cambridge, 1953–83; DL Cambs, 1982. Hon. Fellow: LMH, Oxford, 1970; Girton Coll., Cambridge, 1975; New Hall, Cambridge, 1981; Robinson Coll., Cambridge, 1985. Hon. DSc: New Univ. of Ulster, 1972; Leeds, 1975; Pennsylvania, 1975; Wellesley Coll., 1976; Hon. DCL Oxon, 1976; Hon. DL Univ. Southern California, 1976; Hon. LLD: Sheffield, 1977; Cantab, 1988. *Recreations:* gardening, book binding and restoring. *Address:* 3 Oxford Road, Old Marston, Oxford OX3 0PQ. *Club:* University Women's.

MURRAY, Andrew Robin; HM Diplomatic Service; Counsellor (Economic and Commercial), Stockholm, since 1993; *b* 21 Sept. 1941; *s* of Robert Alexander Murray and Jean Agnes Murray (*née* Burnett); *m* 1965, Irene Dorothy Foy; one *s* one *d. Educ:* Trinity Coll., Glenalmond; Edinburgh Univ. (MA Hons 1965). Economist with Govt of Ontario, Canada, 1966; investment analyst, ICFC, 1969; joined HM Diplomatic Service, 1973; First Sec., Islamabad, 1975–78; Head of Chancery, Buenos Aires, 1979–81; FCO, 1982–84; Counsellor, UKMIS to UN, 1984–88; Counsellor and Dep. Head of Mission, Caracas, 1988–91; FCO, 1991–93. *Recreation:* sporadic sport. *Address:* c/o Foreign and Commonwealth Office, SW1A 2AH.

MURRAY, Ann; mezzo-soprano; *b* Dublin, 27 Aug. 1949; *m* 1981, Philip Langridge, *qv*; one *s. Educ:* Royal Manchester Coll. of Music. Roles include: *for English National Opera:* Ariodante; Beatrice; Charlotte; Rosina; Xerxes; *for Royal Opera:* Cherubino; Composer; Donna Elvira; Dorabella; Idamante; Oktavian; *other roles:* Cecilio; Cenerentola; Nicklausse; Sextus. Many recitals and concerts (European recital tours, 1990, 1993, 1994); festival appearances incl. Aldeburgh, Edinburgh, Munich, Salzburg. *Address:* c/o Lies Askonas, 6 Henrietta Street, WC2E 8LA.

MURRAY, Sir Antony; *see* Murray, Sir J. A. J.

MURRAY, Athol Laverick, PhD; FRHistS; Keeper of the Records of Scotland, 1985–90; *b* Tynemouth, Northumberland, 8 Nov. 1930; *s* of late George Murray and Margery Laverick; *m* 1958, Irene Joyce Cairns; one *s* one *d. Educ:* Royal Grammar Sch., Lancaster; Jesus Coll., Cambridge (BA, MA); Univ. of Edinburgh (LLB, PhD). Research Assistant, Foreign Office, 1953; Assistant Keeper, Scottish Record Office, 1953–83; Deputy Keeper, 1983–84. Consultant Archivist, Jersey Archives Steering Gp, 1990–92. Vice-Pres., Soc. of Antiquaries of Scotland, 1989–92. FRHistS 1971. *Publications:* The Royal Grammar School, Lancaster, 1951; articles in Scottish Historical Review, etc. *Address:* 33 Inverleith Gardens, Edinburgh EH3 5PR. *T:* 0131–552 4465. *Club:* Civil Service.

MURRAY, Charles Henry; Chairman, National Irish Bank (formerly Northern Bank (Ireland)) Ltd, 1986–89; *b* 1917; *s* of Charles and Teresa Murray; *m* 1942, Margaret Ryan; one *s* four *d. Educ:* Christian Brothers Sch., Synge Street, Dublin; London Univ. (BCom). Asst Secretary, Dept of Finance (Ireland), 1961, Secretary, 1969–76; Dir, 1969–76, Governor, 1976–81, Central Bank of Ireland. Dir, Northern Bank, 1982–88. Hon. LLD, NUI, 1977. *Recreations:* reading, theatre, golf. *Address:* 6 Washington Park, Dublin 14. *T:* 947781.

MURRAY, David Edward; Chairman, Murray International Holdings Ltd, since 1981; director of companies; *b* 14 Oct. 1951; *s* of late David Ian Murray and of Roma Murray; *m* 1972, Louise V. Densley (*d* 1992); two *s. Educ:* Fettes Coll.; Broughton High Sch. Formed: Murray International Metals Ltd, 1976; Murray International Holdings Ltd, 1981. Young Scottish Businessman of the Year, 1984. Chairman: UK2000 (Scotland), 1987; Rangers FC, 1989–. Gov., Clifton Hall Sch., 1987. DUniv Heriot-Watt, 1986. *Recreations:* watching sport, wine enthusiast. *Address:* Murray House, 4 Redheughs Rigg, South Gyle, Edinburgh EH12 9DQ. *T:* 0131–317 7000.

MURRAY, David Edward, FRICS; Deputy Chief Executive (Property), Crown Estate, since 1993; *b* 22 Jan. 1944; *s* of late Thomas and Emily Murray; *m* 1968, Barbara Collins, *d* of late Sir Geoffrey and Lady Collins, Dorset; two *s. Educ:* Abbotsholme Sch., Derbys; Manor Park Sch., Hants; Hammersmith Sch. of Art & Building. AIQS 1970; Dip. Contsr. Econs 1975; FRICS 1983. Sir Robert McAlpine & Sons, 1962–67; Planning & Transportation Dept, GLC, 1968–72; Royal County of Berkshire: Gp Quantity Surveyor, 1972–77; Co. Quantity Surveyor, 1977–88; Dir of Property, 1988–93. External Examiner: Coll. of Estate Mgt, 1978–92; Univ. of Portsmouth, 1994–. Pres., Soc. of Chief Quantity Surveyors in Local Govt, 1979; Royal Institution of Chartered Surveyors: Chm., Quantity Surveyor's R&D Cttee, 1983–84; Mem., Divl Council, 1975–; Mem., several panels and wkg parties. *Publications:* Cost Effectiveness in Property Management, 1984; Artificial Intelligence in Property Portfolio Management, 1988; papers on property mgt and procurement to various UK confs. *Recreations:* sport (especially sailing), reading, music. *Address:* Applecroft, 16 Elsenwood Drive, Camberley, Surrey GU15 2AZ. *T:* Camberley (01276) 24345. *Club:* Parkstone Yacht (Dorset).

MURRAY, Rt. Rev. David Owen; an Assistant Bishop of Perth, Western Australia, since 1991; *b* 23 Dec. 1940; *s* of George Lawrence Murray and Winifred Eva (*née* Morgan); *m* 1971, Janet Mary Chittleborough; two *s. Educ:* Swanbourne State Sch.; Claremont High Sch.; St Michael's House, Crafers, SA (Kelham, Aust.) (ThL 1968). Jun. Postal Officer, 1955; Postal Clerk, 1957–65. Ordained deacon, 1968, priest, 1969; Asst Curate, Bunbury, 1968–70; Rector: Lake Grace, 1970–74; Jerramungup, 1974–79; Mt Barker, 1979–83; Chaplain to the Bishop of Bunbury, 1978–83; Rector: S Perth, 1983–88; Fremantle, 1988–94; Archdeacon of Fremantle, 1988–91. Mem., WA Chamber of Commerce, Fremantle, 1990–. *Recreations:* bagpipe playing, walking, swimming, camping, caravaning, theatre, concerts, reading, entertaining. *Address:* 6 Donavon Rise, Murdoch, WA 6150, Australia. *T:* (9) 3394696.

MURRAY, Rt. Hon. Sir Donald (Bruce), Kt 1988; PC 1989; a Lord Justice of Appeal, Supreme Court of Northern Ireland, 1989–93; a Judge of the Restrictive Practices Court, 1987–93; *b* 24 Jan. 1923; *y s* of late Charles Benjamin Murray and late Agnes Mary Murray, Belfast; *m* 1953, Rhoda Margaret, *o c* of late Thomas and Anna Parke, Londonderry; two *s* one *d. Educ:* Belfast Royal Acad.; Queen's Univ. Belfast (LLB Hons); Trinity Coll. Dublin (BA). 1st Cl., Certif. of Honour, Gray's Inn Prize, English Bar Final Exam., 1944; Called to Bar, Gray's Inn, 1945, Hon Bencher, 1987. Asst Parly Draftsman to Govt of NI, 1945–51; Asst Lectr, Faculty of Law, QUB, 1951–53. Called to NI Bar, 1953, and to Inner Bar, NI, 1964; Bencher, Inn of Court, NI, 1971; Chm., Gen. Council of Bar of NI, 1972–75; Judge of the High Court of Justice, NI, 1975–89. Dep. Chm., Boundary Commn for NI, 1976–84. Chairman: Incorporated Council of Law Reporting for NI, 1974–87 (Mem., 1971); Bd, SLS Legal Publications (NI), 1988–94. Member: UK Delegn to Commn Consultative des Barreaux des Pays des Communautés Européennes, 1972–75; Jt Standing Cttee of Bars of UK and Bar of Ireland, 1972–75; Deptl Cttee on Registration of Title to Land in N Ireland. Chm., Deptl Cttee on Reform of Company Law in NI; Inspector apptd to report on siting of new prison in NI. Mem., Legal Adv. Cttee of Standing Cttee of General Synod of Church of Ireland. Governor, Belfast Royal Academy. *Publications:* articles in various legal periodicals. *Recreations:* playing the piano, DXing.

MURRAY, Sir Donald (Frederick), KCVO 1983; CMG 1973; DL; HM Diplomatic Service, retired; Channel Tunnel Complaints Commissioner, 1987–95; *b* 14 June 1924; *s* of A. T. Murray and F. M. Murray (*née* Byfield); *m* 1949, Marjorie Culverwell; three *s* one *d. Educ:* Colfe's Grammar Sch.; King's Sch., Canterbury (King's and Entrance Schols); Worcester Coll., Oxford. Royal Marines, 1943–46 (41 (RM) Commando). Entered Foreign Office, 1948; Third Sec., Warsaw, 1948; FO 1951; Second Sec., Vienna, 1953; First Sec., Political Office, ME Forces, 1956; FO, 1957; First Sec. (Comm.), Stockholm, 1958; Head of Chancery, Saigon, 1962; FO 1964; Counsellor, 1965; Head of SE Asia Dept, 1966; Counsellor, Tehran, 1969–72; RCDS, 1973; Ambassador to Libya, 1974–76; Asst Under-Sec. of State, FCO, 1977–80; Ambassador to Sweden, 1980–84. Assessor Chm., CS Selection Bd, 1984–86. Director: Goodlass Wall and Co., 1985–90; Winsor and Newton, subseq. Col Art Fine Art and Graphics, 1991–. Kent County Chm., SSAFA, 1985–90, Vice-Pres., 1991–; Trustee, World Resource Foundn, 1986–. DL Kent, 1992. Grand Cross, Order of North Star (Sweden), 1983. *Recreations:* gentle sports (Oxford v Cambridge cross-country, 1942; athletics, 1943; small-bore shooting, 1947), gardening, music. *Address:* Oxney House, Wittersham, Kent TN30 7ED.

MURRAY, George Sargent; Forestry Commissioner, 1981–84; *b* 2 Oct. 1924; *s* of James and Helen Murray; *m* 1951, Anita Garden Fraser; two *s*. *Educ:* Buckie High School. Inland Revenue, 1941–43; Royal Navy, 1943–46; Inland Revenue, 1946–49; Dept of Agriculture and Fisheries for Scotland, 1949–67; Scottish Development Dept, 1967–71; Scottish Economic Planning Dept, Scottish Office, 1971–76; Dept of Agriculture and Fisheries for Scotland, 1976–81. *Recreation:* golf. *Address:* 30 Easter Currie Terrace, Currie, Midlothian EH14 5LE. *T:* 0131–449 2538.

MURRAY, Gordon, CB 1994; PhD; Director, Scottish Courts Administration, since 1986; *b* 25 Aug. 1935; *s* of late James Murray, Aberdeen, and Annie Hardie (*née* Center); *m* 1964, Janet (*née* Yerrington); two *s* one *d*. *Educ:* Kirkcaldy High Sch.; Edinburgh Univ. (BSc (Hons), PhD). Research Fellow: Atomic Energy of Canada, 1960–62; UKAEA, Harwell, 1962–65; Lectr, Univ. of Manchester, 1965–69; Principal, Scottish Home and Health Dept, 1970–77; Assistant Secretary: Scottish Educn Dept, 1977–79; Central Services, Scottish Office, 1979–86. *Recreations:* reading, hill walking, gardening. *Address:* 26–27 Royal Terrace, Edinburgh EH7 5AH. *T:* 0131–556 0755.

MURRAY, Sir James, KCMG 1978 (CMG 1966); HM Diplomatic Service, retired; Ambassador and Permanent UK Representative to UN and other International Organisations at Geneva, 1978–79; *b* 3 Aug. 1919; *er s* of late James Hamilton Murray, King's Cross, Isle of Arran, and Hester Macneill Buie; *m* 1982, Mrs Jill Charmian Chapuisat, *d* of Maj.-Gen. Frederick William Gordon-Hall, CB, CBE; two step *d*. *Educ:* Bellahouston Acad.; Glasgow Univ. Royal Regt of Artillery, 1939; served India and Burma, 1943–45; Staff Coll., Quetta, 1945; Bde Major (RA) 19 Ind. Div.; GSO II (RA) ALFSEA; GSO II War Office. HM Foreign (subseq. Diplomatic) Service, 1947; Foreign Office, 1947–49; First Sec. (Information), HM Embassy, Cairo, 1949–54; Foreign Office, 1954–56; attached National Defence Coll. of Can., 1956–57; First Sec., HM Embassy, Paris, 1957–61; HM Consul in Ruanda-Urundi, 1961–62; Special Ambassador for Independence celebrations in Ruanda, July 1962, and in Burundi, Sept. 1962; Ambassador to Rwanda and Burundi, 1962–63; Deputy Head of UK Delegation to European Communities, 1963–65; Counsellor, Djakarta, 1965–67; Head of Far Eastern Dept, FCO, 1967–70; Consul-Gen., San Francisco, 1970–73; Asst Under-Sec. of State, FCO, 1973–74; Dep. Perm. Representative to UN, 1974–78 (Ambassador, 1976). Special Envoy of 5 Western Govts for negotiations on Namibia, 1979–80. Withrow Prof. of Govt, Deep Springs Coll., Calif, 1990; Adviser: Trade Policy Res. Centre, London, 1981–89; to Chm., Hanson Industries, NY, 1983–92. *Recreations:* horses, lawn tennis. *Address:* 220 Columbia Heights, Brooklyn Heights, New York, NY 11201, USA. *T:* (718) 8523320. *Clubs:* Brooks's, Beefsteak, Pratt's; Brook (New York).

MURRAY, Prof. James Dickson, FRS 1985; FRSE 1979; Professor of Mathematical Biology, 1986–92, now Emeritus Professor, Director, Centre for Mathematical Biology, 1983–92, and Professorial Fellow, Corpus Christi College, 1986–92, now Emeritus Fellow, University of Oxford; *b* 2 Jan. 1931; *s* of Peter and Sarah Murray; *m* 1959, Sheila Todd Murray; one *s* one *d*. *Educ:* Dumfries Acad.; Univ. of St Andrews (BSc 1953; Carstairs Medal; Miller Prize; PhD 1956); Univ. of Oxford (MA 1961; DSc 1968). FIBiol 1988. Lectr, Applied Maths, Kings Coll., Durham Univ., 1955–56; Gordon MacKay Lectr and Res. Fellow, Tutor in Applied Maths, Leverett House, Harvard, 1956–59; Lectr, Applied Maths, UCL, 1959–61; Fellow and Tutor in Maths, Hertford College, Oxford, 1961–63; Res. Associate, Harvard, 1963–64; Prof. of Engineering Mechanics, Univ. of Michigan, 1964–67; Prof. of Maths, New York Univ., 1967–70; Fellow and Tutor in Maths, 1970–85, Sen. Res. Fellow, 1985–86, Corpus Christi Coll., Oxford; Reader in Maths, Univ. of Oxford, 1972–86. Vis. Fellow, St Catherine's Coll., Oxford, 1967; Guggenheim Fellow, Pasteur Inst., Paris, 1968; Visiting Professor: Nat. Tsing Hua Univ., 1975; Univ. of Florence, 1976; MIT, 1979; Winegard Prof., Univ. of Iowa, 1979; Univ. of Utah, 1979, 1985; Ida Beam Prof., Univ. of Guelph, 1980; Univ. of Heidelberg, 1980; CIT, 1983; Univ. of Angers, 1993; La Chaire Européenne, Univ. of Paris, 1994; Stan Ulam Vis. Schol., Univ. of Calif. Berkeley's Los Alamos Nat. Lab., 1985; Philip Prof., Univ. of Washington, 1988–94; Lectures: Scott Hawkins, Southern Methodist Univ., Dallas, 1984; Landsdowne, Univ. of Victoria, 1990; Pinkham, Swedish Hosp., Seattle, 1992; Curle, Univ. of St Andrews, 1994; Smith, St Catherine's Coll., Oxford, 1994. Math. Comr, SERC, 1985–88; Pres., European Soc. for Mathematical and Theoretical Biol., 1991–94; Member: Bd of Dirs, Soc. for Mathematical Biol., USA, 1986–89; ESF Network Cttee, 1991–94. Hon. DSc St Andrews, 1994. Naylor Prize in Applied Math., London Math. Soc., 1989. Member Editorial Boards: Jl Theor. Biol.; Jl Math. Biol.; Jl Maths Applied in Medicine and Biol.; Bull. Math. Biol.; Lecture Notes in Biomaths; Biomaths Series; Applied Math. Letters; Biotheoretica; Jl Nonlinear Sci.; Bifurcation and Chaos. *Publications:* Asymptotic Analysis, 1974, 2nd edn 1984; Nonlinear Differential Equation Models in Biology, 1977 (Russian trans. 1983); (ed with S. Brenner and L. Wolpert) Theories of Biological Pattern Formation, 1981; (ed with W. Jäger) Modelling of Patterns in Space and Time, 1984; Mathematical Biology, 1989, 2nd edn 1993; (ed with H. G. Othmer and P. K. Maini) Experimental and Theoretical Advances in Biological Pattern Formation, 1993; numerous articles in learned jls. *Address:* (until April 1996) Applied Mathematics FS–20, University of Washington, Seattle, WA 98195, USA; (from April 1996) La Combe, St Laurent des Bâtons, 24510 Ste Alvère, France.

MURRAY, Jennifer Susan, (Jenni); Presenter, Woman's Hour, BBC, Radio 4, since 1987; *b* 12 May 1950; *d* of Alvin Bailey and Win Bailey (*née* Jones); *m* 1971, Brian Murray (marr. diss. 1978); partner, David Forgham-Bailey; two *s*. *Educ:* Barnsley Girls' High Sch.; Hull Univ. (BA Hons French/Drama). BBC Radio Bristol, 1973–78; BBC TV South, 1978–82; BBC Newsnight, 1982–85; BBC Radio 4 Today, 1985–87. TV documentaries include: Everyman: Stand By Your Man, 1987, Breaking the Chain, 1988, As We Forgive Them, 1989; The Duchy of Cornwall, 1985, Women in Politics, 1989; Here's Looking At You, 1991; Presenter: Points of View, 1993; This Sunday, 1993, 1994; Dilemmas, 1994. Vice-Pres., FPA. Hon. DLitt Bradford, 1994. *Publications:* The Woman's Hour Book of Humour, 1993; contrib. to newspapers and periodicals. *Recreations:* reading, theatre, riding. *Address:* c/o Woman's Hour, BBC, Broadcasting House, Portland Place, W1A 1AA. *T:* 0171–765 4314.

MURRAY, John; *see* Dervaird, Hon. Lord.

MURRAY, Sir (John) Antony (Jerningham), Kt 1987; CBE 1980; Hon. Adviser to Government of Barbados in United Kingdom, since 1961; *b* 21 Jan. 1921; *s* of Captain John Challenger Murray and Cecilia Annette Murray (*née* Jerningham); *m* 1943, Hon. Winifred Mary, *e d* of 2nd Baron Hardinge of Penshurst, PC, GCB, GCVO, MC; one *s*. *Educ:* Eton College; New College, Oxford (2 terms). Grenadier Guards, 1940–46 (Major); Dir, Christmas Island Phosphate Co. Ltd, 1947–51; Mem. Exec. Cttee, West India Cttee, 1957– (Chm., 1963–65; Vice-Pres., 1966–). *Recreation:* fishing. *Address:* Woodmancote Manor Cottage, Cirencester, Glos GL7 7ED. *T:* Cirencester (01285) 831226. *Clubs:* Boodle's, Royal Automobile, MCC.

MURRAY, Prof. Joseph Edward, MD, DSc; plastic surgeon; Professor of Surgery, Harvard University, since 1970; *b* 1 April 1919; *s* of William Andrew Murray and Mary Murray (*née* DePasquale); *m* 1945, Virginia Link; three *s* three *d*. *Educ:* Holy Cross Coll. (AB 1940); Harvard Univ. (MD 1943). US Army, 1944–47. Chief Plastic Surgeon: Peter Bent Brigham Hosp., 1951–86, Surgeon Emeritus, 1986; Children's Hosp., Boston, 1972–85. Hon. FRCS; Hon. FRCSI; Hon. FRACS. Hon. DSc: Holy Cross Coll., 1965; Rockford Coll., 1966; Roger Williams Coll., 1986. Numerous honours and awards from US sci. instns; (jtly) Nobel Prize for Medicine, 1990. *Address:* 108 Abbott Road, Wellesley Hills, MA 02181, USA.

MURRAY, Katherine Maud Elisabeth, MA, BLitt, FSA; Principal, Bishop Otter College, Chichester, 1948–70; *b* 3 Dec. 1909; *d* of Harold J. R. Murray (former HMI of Schools) and Kate M. Crosthwaite. *Educ:* Colchester County High Sch.; Somerville Coll., Oxford. Tutor and Librarian, Ashburne Hall, Manchester, 1935–37; Mary Somerville Research Fellow, Somerville Coll., Oxford, 1937–38; Asst Tutor and Registrar, 1938–44, Domestic Bursar, 1942–44, and Junior Bursar, 1944–48, Girton Coll., Cambridge. Chairman of Council, Sussex Archæological Soc., 1964–77, Pres., 1977–80. Mem., Chichester District Council, 1973–87 (Chm. Planning Cttee, 1979–82, Vice-Chm., 1976–79). Hon. DLitt: Sussex, 1978; Coll. of Wooster, Ohio, 1979. Chichester Civic Award, 1993. *Publications:* The Constitutional History of the Cinque Ports, 1935; Register of Daniel Rough, Kent Record Soc., 1945; Caught in the Web of Words: James A. H. Murray and the Oxford English Dictionary, 1977 (Crashaw Prize, British Academy, 1979); articles in Sussex Notes and Queries, Transactions of the Royal Historical Society, Archæologia Cantiana, English Historical Review. *Recreations:* archæology, downland and nature conservation. *Address:* Upper Cranmore, Heyshott, Midhurst, West Sussex GU29 0DL. *T:* Midhurst (01730) 812325.

MURRAY, Sir Kenneth, Kt 1993; PhD; FRCPath; FRS 1979; FRSE; Biogen Professor of Molecular Biology, University of Edinburgh, since 1984; *b* 30 Dec. 1930; *yr s* of Allen and Elizabeth Ann Murray; *m* 1958, Noreen Elizabeth Parker (*see* N. E. Murray). *Educ:* Birmingham Univ. FRCPath 1991. Dept of Molecular Biology, Univ. of Edinburgh: Sen. Lecturer, 1967–73; Reader, 1973–76; Prof., 1976–. Member: Biochemical Soc.; European Molecular Biology Organisation; British Biophysical Soc.; Academia Europaea. Chm., Darwin Trust, Edinburgh, 1984– (Founder, 1983). FRSE 1989. *Publications:* papers on nucleic acid biochem., molecular genetics, genetic engineering and viral hepatitis. *Address:* Institute of Cell and Molecular Biology, University of Edinburgh, Edinburgh EH9 3JR. *Clubs:* Athenæum; New (Edinburgh).

MURRAY, Kenneth Alexander George, CB 1977; MA, EdB; Special Adviser to the Home Office on Police Service, Prison Service, and Fire Service selection, 1977–80; Director, Civil Service Selection Board, and Civil Service Commissioner, 1964–77; *b* 16 June 1916; *s* of late George Dickie Murray and Isabella Murray; *m* 1942, Elizabeth Ward Simpson; one *d*. *Educ:* Skene Street and Central Schools, Aberdeen; Aberdeen Univ. (MA English (1st Cl. Hons), EdB Psychol. (1st Cl. Hons)). RAMC and War Office Selection Bd, 1940–45, Captain. Psychological Adviser, Govt of India, 1945–47; Lectr in Psychology, Univ. of Hull, 1948–50; Principal Psychologist and Chief Psychologist, CS Selection Bd, 1951–63. Adviser to Police Service in high-grade selection, 1963–, also to Fire and Prison Services, to Church of Scotland and C of E; Adviser (earlier) to Govts of Pakistan and Western Nigeria through their Public Service Commns. FBPsS 1984. *Recreations:* reading, walking, bridge, watching cricket and Rugby League. *Address:* 15 Melvinshaw, Leatherhead, Surrey KT22 8SX. *T:* Leatherhead (01372) 372995. *Clubs:* MCC, Commonwealth Trust.

MURRAY, Prof. Leo Gerard; Director, Cranfield School of Management, since 1986; Pro Vice-Chancellor, Cranfield University (formerly Institute of Technology), since 1992; *b* 21 May 1943; *s* of Patrick and Teresa Murray; *m* 1970, Pauline Ball; one *s* one *d*. *Educ:* St Aloysius' Coll., Glasgow; Glasgow Univ. (MA Hons 1965). British Petroleum Co., 1965–67; Courtaulds Gp, 1968–75; A. T. Kearney Ltd, 1975–79; Rothmans International Ltd, 1979–86: Man. Dir, Murray Sons & Co. Ltd, 1979–82; Dir, Overseas Mfg and Licensing, 1982–85; Dir, ME Region, 1985–86. Mem., Textile Sector Gp, NEDO, 1987–88. Chairman: ICL Cranfield Business Games Ltd, 1987–92; Cranfield Conference Centre, 1993–; Man. Dir, Cranfield Management Develt Ltd, 1993–. Director and Treasurer: Council of Univ. Management Schs, 1987–92; Assoc. of Business Schs, 1992–93; Membre Conseil d'Orientation, Ecole Internat. d'Affaires, Marseilles, 1988–91. Vice-Pres., Strategic Planning Soc., 1992–. Trustee, Blind in Business, 1992–. FCIM 1988; FRSA 1989. *Recreations:* family, work, golf. *Address:* The Beeches, 2 Church Lane, Lathbury, Bucks MK16 8JY. *T:* Milton Keynes (01908) 615574. *Clubs:* Reform; Woburn Golf and Country.

MURRAY, Leo Joseph, CB 1986; QC (Aust.) 1980; legislation consultant, since 1989; Parliamentary Counsel, Queensland, Australia, 1975–89; *b* 7 April 1927; *s* of William Francis Murray and Theresa Agnes Murray (*née* Sheehy); *m* 1957, Janet Barbara Weir (marr. diss. 1987); two *d*. *Educ:* St Columban's Coll., Brisbane; Univ. of Queensland (BA, LLB). Admitted Barrister, Supreme Court, Queensland, 1951; Asst Crown Prosecutor, 1958; Asst Parly Counsel, 1963. *Publications:* contrib. to Australian Law Jl. *Recreations:* golf, ski-ing. *Address:* 99 Red Hill Road, Nudgee, Qld 4014, Australia. *T:* (7) 2675786. *Clubs:* Irish, Nudgee Golf (Brisbane); Southern Alps Ski (Sydney).

MURRAY, Nigel; Master of the Supreme Court, Queen's Bench Division, since 1991; a Recorder, since 1994; *b* 22 Jan. 1944; *s* of late Dr Ronald Ormiston Murray, MBE and Dr Catherine Joan Suzette Gauvain, FFCM; *m* 1970, Shirley Arbuthnot; one *s* one *d*. *Educ:* Stowe. Called to the Bar, Inner Temple, 1965; Mem. of Bar, Republic of Ireland and Sierra Leone; in practice, Western Circuit, specialising in Privy Council Appeals and Commonwealth Law, 1966–90, save when Judge of High Court of Botswana, 1984–87; Asst Recorder, 1982–94. An Editor, Supreme Court Practice, 1991–. *Recreation:* golf. *Address:* Royal Courts of Justice, Strand, WC2A 2LL. *T:* 0171–936 6000/6722. *Clubs:* Garrick; Berkshire Golf, Rye Golf.

MURRAY of Blackbarony, Sir Nigel Andrew Digby, 15th Bt *cr* 1628; farmer; *b* 15 Aug. 1944; *s* of Sir Alan John Digby Murray of Blackbarony, 14th Bt, and of Mabel Elisabeth, *d* of late Arthur Bernard Schiele, Arias, Argentina; *S* father, 1978; *m* 1980, Diana Margaret, *yr d* of Robert C. Bray, Arias, Argentina; one *s* two *d*. *Educ:* St Paul's School, Argentina; Salesian Agricl Sch., Argentina; Royal Agricultural Coll., Cirencester. Farms dairy cattle, store cattle, crops and bees. Holds a private pilot's licence. *Heir: s* Alexander Nigel Robert Murray, *b* 1 July 1981. *Address:* Establecimiento Tinamú, cc 115, 2624 Arias, Provincia de Córdoba, Argentina. *T:* 0462–60031. *Club:* Venado Tuerto Polo and Athletic.

MURRAY, Prof. Noreen Elizabeth, (Lady Murray), PhD; FRS 1982; FRSE; Professor of Molecular Genetics, Institute of Cell and Molecular Biology (formerly Department of Molecular Biology), University of Edinburgh, since 1988; *b* 26 Feb. 1935; *d* of John and

Lillian Grace Parker; *m* 1958, Sir Kenneth Murray, *qv*. *Educ:* King's College London (BSc); Univ. of Birmingham (PhD). Research Associate: Stanford Univ., California, 1960–64; Univ. of Cambridge, 1964–67; Mem., MRC Molecular Genetics Unit, Edinburgh, 1968–74; Lectr, 1974, later Sen. Lectr, Reader, 1978–88, Dept. of Molecular Biology, Univ. of Edinburgh; scientist in European Molecular Biol. Lab., Heidelberg, 1980–82. Member: BBSRC, 1994–; EMBO, 1981–; Pres., Genetical Soc., 1987–90. FRSE 1989. *Publications:* original research papers and reviews in field of genetics and molecular biology. *Recreation:* gardening. *Address:* Institute of Cell and Molecular Biology, University of Edinburgh, Mayfield Road, Edinburgh EH9 3JR. *T:* 0131–650 5374.

MURRAY, Sir Patrick (Ian Keith), 12th Bt *cr* 1673; *b* 22 March 1965; *s* of Sir William Patrick Keith Murray, 11th Bt, and of Susan Elizabeth (who *m* 1976, J. C. Hudson, PhD), *d* of Stacey Jones; *S* father, 1977. *Educ:* Christ College, Brecon, Powys; LAMDA. *Heir: kinsman* Major Peter Keith-Murray, Canadian Forces [*b* July 1935; *m* 1960, Judith Anne, *d* of late Andrew Tinsley; one *s* one *d*]. *Address:* Sheephouse, Hay-on-Wye, Powys.

MURRAY, Peter, CMG 1959; HM Diplomatic Service, retired; *b* 18 July 1915; *m* 1960, E. M. Batchelor. *Educ:* Portsmouth Gram. Sch.; Merton Coll., Oxford. Burma Commission, 1937–49, Foreign Service, 1947; HM Ambassador to Cambodia, 1961–64; Ambassador to Ivory Coast, Upper Volta and Niger, 1970–72.

MURRAY, Prof. Robin MacGregor, MD; Professor of Psychological Medicine, University of London, at King's College London and the Institute of Psychiatry, since 1989; *b* 31 Jan. 1944; *s* of James Alistair Campbell Murray and Helen Murray; *m* 1970, Shelagh Harris; one *s* one *d*. *Educ:* Royal High Sch., Edinburgh; Glasgow Univ. (MB, ChB 1968; MD 1974). MRCP 1971; MRCPsych 1976; MPhil London, 1976; DSc London, 1989. Registrar, Dept of Medicine, Univ. of Glasgow/Western Infirmary, 1971; Sen. House Officer, successively Registrar and Sen. Registrar, Maudsley Hosp., 1972–76; Vis. Fellow, National Inst. of Health, Washington, DC, 1977; Sen. Lectr, 1978–82, Dean, 1982–89, Inst. of Psych. Pres., Assoc. of European Psychiatrists, 1995–Dec. 1996. *Publications:* (jtly) Essentials of Postgraduate Psychiatry, 1979; (jtly) Misuse of Psychotropic Drugs, 1981; Lectures on the History of Psychiatry, 1990; articles on schizophrenia, depression, alcoholism, genetics, analgesic abuse and psychiatric illness in doctors.

MURRAY, Roger; President, Cargill Europe Ltd, since 1982; Chairman, Cargill plc, since 1982; *b* 8 June 1936; *s* of Donald Murray and Nancy (*née* Irons); *m* 1960, Anthea Mary (*née* Turnbull); one *s* three *d*. *Educ:* Uppingham Sch.; Brasenose Coll., Oxford (MA). RNVR (Sub-Lieut), 1954–56. Joined Cargill Inc., Minneapolis, 1959; various positions in Hull and Geneva, 1960–70; Pres., Cargill Canada, 1973. Mem., Management Cttee, Cargill Inc., 1986–. Canadian and British citizen. *Recreations:* sailing, ski-ing. *Address:* 11 Pembridge Place, W2 4XB. *T:* 0171–243 0026.

MURRAY, Rt. Hon. Ronald King; *see* Murray, Rt Hon. Lord.

MURRAY, Dame Rosemary; *see* Murray, Dame A. R.

MURRAY, Sir Rowland William Patrick, 14th Bt *cr* 1630; retired hotel general manager; *b* 26 Oct. 1910; *s* of late Rowland William Murray, 2nd *s* of 12th Bt, and Gertrude Frances McCabe; *S* uncle 1958; *m* 1944, Josephine Margaret Murphy; four *s* two *d*. Served in US Army during War of 1939–45. Captain. *Heir: s* Rowland William Murray [*b* 22 Sept. 1947; *m* 1970, Nancy Diane, *d* of George C. Newberry; one *s* one *d*].

MURRELL, Geoffrey David George, CMG 1993; OBE 1987; HM Diplomatic Service, retired; *b* 19 Dec. 1934; *s* of Stanley Hector Murrell and Kathleen Murrell (Martin); *m* 1962, Kathleen Ruth Berton; one *s* three *d*. *Educ:* Minchenden Grammar School, Southgate; Oxford Univ. BA French and Russian. FCO Research Dept, 1959–61; Moscow, 1961–64; FCO, 1964–68; Moscow, 1968–70; Head, Soviet Section, FCO Research Dept, 1970–75; First Sec., Belgrade, 1975–78; Regional Dir, Soviet and East European Region, Research Dept, 1978–83; Counsellor, Moscow, 1983–87; Counsellor, Res. Dept, FCO, 1987–91; Minister-Counsellor, Moscow, 1991–94. *Recreations:* tennis, guitar. *Club:* United Oxford & Cambridge University.

MURRELL, Prof. John Norman, PhD; FRS 1991; FRSC; Professor of Chemistry, University of Sussex, since 1965 (Pro-Vice-Chancellor (Science), 1985–88); *b* London, 1932; *m* 1954, Dr D. Shirley Read; two *s* two *d*. *Educ:* Univ. of London (BSc); Univ. of Cambridge (PhD). University of Sussex: Dean, Sch. of Molecular Scis, 1979–84; Acad. Dir of Univ. Computing, 1984–85. Chm., Science Bd Computing Cttee, SERC, 1981–84. *Publications:* Theory of Electronic Spectra of Organic Molecules, 1960; (jointly): Valence Theory, 1965; Semi-empirical Self-consistent-field-molecular Theory of Molecules, 1971; Chemical Bond, 1978; Properties of Liquids and Solutions, 1982; Molecular Potential Energy Surfaces, 1985; Introduction to the Theory of Atomic and Molecular Scattering, 1989. *Address:* School of Molecular Sciences, University of Sussex, Falmer, Brighton BN1 9QJ.

MURRIN, Orlando Richard Charles; Editor, Woman and Home, since 1994; *b* 1 April 1958; *s* of Patrick John Murrin and Patricia Mary, *d* of W. J. Skardon, OBE, MIS. *Educ:* Blundell's Sch., Devon; Magdalene Coll., Cambridge (Exhibnr; BA Hons English). Radio 3 Sub-Editor, Radio Times, 1980–83; Chief Sub Ed., Living mag., 1983–85; Asst Ed., Country Homes and Interiors, 1985–87; advertising copywriter, 1987–90; Dep. Ed., Living mag., 1990–93; with Woman and Home, 1993–. Pianist, Kettner's Restaurant, 1983–. *Recreations:* music (especially 19th and early 20th century), cookery (BBC Masterchef semi-finalist), gardening (especially poisonous plants), kite-flying. *Address:* Woman and Home, King's Reach Tower, SE1 9LS. *Clubs:* Groucho, Soho House.

MURSELL, Sir Peter, Kt 1969; MBE 1941; Vice Lord-Lieutenant, West Sussex, 1974–90; *b* 20 Jan. 1913; *m* 1938, Cicely, *d* of late Mr and Mrs M. F. North; two *s* two *d*. *Educ:* Bedales Sch.; Downing Coll. Cambridge. Fruit growing, 1934. War Service: Air Transport Auxiliary, 1940–44, Sen. Comdr. West Sussex County Council: Mem., 1947–74; Chm., 1962–67 and 1969–74. Member: Cttee on Management in Local Govt, 1965–66; Royal Commn on Local Govt in England, 1966–69; Water Space Amenity Commn, 1973–76; Inland Waterways Amenity Adv. Council, 1974–77. DL West Sussex, 1962. *Recreations:* sailing, mountain walking, skiing, squash, canal cruising. *Address:* Taints Orchard, The Street, Washington, West Sussex RH20 4AS. *T:* Ashington (01903) 893062. *Club:* Farmers'.

MURTA, Prof. Kenneth Hall, FRIBA; Professor of Architecture, University of Sheffield, since 1974; *b* 24 Sept. 1929; *s* of John Henry Murta and Florence (*née* Hall); *m* 1955, Joan Wilson; two *s* two *d*. *Educ:* Bede Collegiate GS, Sunderland; King's Coll., Univ. of Durham (BArch, DipArch). Architect in private practice and public service, 1954–59; Sen. Lectr, Nigerian Coll. of Arts, Science and Technology, then Ahmadu Bello Univ., 1959–62; University of Sheffield: Lectr, then Sen. Lectr, 1962–74; Dean, Faculty of Architectural Studies, 1974–77, 1984–88. Major designs: Anglican Cathedral, Kaduna, Nigeria; St John, Sheffield Park; All Saints, Denaby Main; St Laurence, Heanor; St Lawrence, Frodingham; Christ Church, Pitsmoor; St Mary the less, St John's Coll., Univ. of Durham; Christ Church, Stannington; St Luke, Lodge Moor, Sheffield; St Leonard, Thrybergh, Rotherham; All Saints, Totley, Sheffield; All Saints, Breadshall, Derbys; Pilgrims, Fordcombe, Kent. Chm., Sheffield Cathedral Fabric Adv. Cttee, 1992–. Mem., Bd of Architectural Educn, ARCUK, 1986– (Vice-Chm., 1990–91; Chm., 1991–); Chm., RIBA Yorks Reg., 1984–85. Hon. Sec., Ecclesiological Soc., 1991–. *Publications:* contribs to Architectural Rev., Ecclesiologist, Churchbuilding, Trans RIBA, Architects' Jl, RIBA Jl. *Recreations:* cricket, soccer, churchwatching, travel, walking in cities on Sundays. *Address:* Underedge, Back Lane, Hathersage, Derbyshire S30 1AR. *T:* Hope Valley (01433) 650833. *Club:* Royal Over-Seas League.

MURTAGH, Miss Marion; Managing Director: Stats (MR) Ltd, 1985–87; CSB Data Processing Ltd, 1985–87; Chairman of both companies, 1970–85. *Educ:* Waverley Gram. Sch., Birmingham. Qualified as: Certified Accountant, 1947; Chartered Secretary, 1948. Proprietor, The Calculating Bureau, 1938–51, Joint Owner, 1951–61. Member: Anglo-Thai Soc.; West Midlands Bridge Club (Pres.). Pres., Dorridge Village Hall Assoc. *Recreation:* bridge. *Address:* 116 Chessetts Wood Road, Lapworth, Solihull, West Midlands B94 6EL. *T:* Lapworth (01564) 782089.

MURTON, family name of **Baron Murton of Lindisfarne.**

MURTON OF LINDISFARNE, Baron *cr* 1979 (Life Peer), of Hexham in the County of Northumberland; **(Henry) Oscar Murton,** PC 1976; OBE 1946; TD 1947 (Clasp 1951); JP; a Deputy Chairman of Committees, since 1981 and a Deputy Speaker, since 1983, House of Lords; *b* 8 May 1914; *o s* of late H. E. C. Murton, and of E. M. Murton (*née* Renton), Hexham, Northumberland; *m* 1st, 1939, Constance Frances (*d* 1977), *e d* of late F. O'L. Connell; one *s* (one *d* decd); 2nd, 1979, Pauline Teresa (Freeman, City of London, 1980), *y d* of late Thomas Keenan. *Educ:* Uppingham Sch. Commissioned, TA, 1934; Staff Capt., 149 Inf. Bde, TA, 1937–39; Staff Coll., Camberley, 1939; tsc; active service, Royal Northumberland Fusiliers, 1939–46; Lt-Col, Gen. Staff, 1942–46 (C-in-C's commendation for good service, 1942, 1944). Managing Dir, Henry A. Murton Ltd, Departmental Stores, Newcastle-upon-Tyne and Sunderland, 1949–57. MP (C) Poole, 1964–79; Sec., Cons. Parly Cttee for Housing, Local Government and Land, 1964–67, Vice-Chm., 1967–70; Chm., Cons. Parly Cttee for Public Building and Works, 1970; PPS to Minister of Local Government and Development, 1970–71; an Asst Govt Whip, 1971–72; a Lord Comr, HM Treasury, 1972–73; Second Dep. Chm., 1973–74, First Dep. Chm., 1974–76, Dep. Speaker and Chm. of Ways and Means, House of Commons, 1976–79. Member: Exec. Cttee, Inter-Parliamentary Union British Group, 1970–71; Panel of Chairmen of Standing Cttees, 1970–71; Jt Select Cttee of Lords and Commons on Private Bill Procedure, 1987–88. Introduced: The Highways (Amendment) Act 1965; The Access to Neighbouring Land Act, 1992. Mem., Poole BC, 1961–63; Pres., Poole Cons. Assoc., 1983–95; a former Vice-Pres., Assoc. of Municipal Corporations; Mem. Herrison (Dorchester) Hosp. Group Management Cttee, 1963–74. Governor, Canford Sch., 1972–76. Chancellor, Primrose League, 1983–88. Freeman, City of London, 1977; Freeman, Wax Chandlers' Co.; Past Master, Clockmakers' Co. JP, Poole, 1963. *Recreations:* sailing, painting. *Address:* 49 Carlisle Mansions, Carlisle Place, SW1P 1HY. *T:* 0171–834 8226.

MUSCROFT, Harold Colin; barrister; *b* Leeds, 12 June 1924; *s* of Harold and Meta Catrina Muscroft; *m* 1958; three *d*. *Educ:* Dept of Navigation, Southampton Univ.; home; Exeter Coll., Oxford (MA). Volunteer, Royal Corps of Signals, 1942; commnd RA, 1943; served in India, Burma (wounded), Malay and Java; demobilised 1947 (Captain). Oxford, 1947–51. Called to Bar, Inner Temple, 1953; practised NE Circuit; a Recorder of the Crown Court, 1972–82. Called to Hong Kong Bar, 1982. Huddersfield Town Councillor, 1958–59. *Recreation:* writing. *Address:* 11 Chelmsford Road, Harrogate, North Yorks HG1 5NA. *T:* Harrogate (01423) 503344; Les Oliviers, 28 Boulevard Eugene-Tripet, 06400 Cannes, France.

MUSEVENI, Lt-Gen. Yoweri Kaguta; President of the Republic of Uganda, since 1986; *b* 1945; *s* of Amos and Esteri Kaguta; *m* 1973, Janet Kataaha; one *s* three *d*. *Educ:* primary and secondary schs in Uganda; Univ. of Dar-es-Salaam, Tanzania (BA). Asst Sec. for Research in President's Office, 1970–71; Hd of Front for National Salvation and anti-Idi Amin armed gp, 1971–79; Minister of Defence, 1979–80, and Vice Chm. of ruling Military Commn; Chm., Uganda Patriotic Movement; Chm., High Comd of Nat. Resistance Army, 1981–. *Publications:* The Path of Liberation; Consolidating the Revolution; What is Africa's Problem?; essays on Southern Africa; National Resistance Movement selected writings. *Recreations:* karate, football. *Address:* Office of the President, Parliamentary Buildings, PO Box 7168, Kampala, Uganda. *T:* 254881/241176/243926/243943.

MUSGRAVE, Sir Christopher (Patrick Charles), 15th Bt *cr* 1611; *b* 14 April 1949; *s* of Sir Charles Musgrave, 14th Bt and of Olive Louise Avril, *o d* of Patrick Cringle, Norfolk; *S* father, 1970; *m* 1st, 1978 (marr. diss. 1992); two *d*; 2nd, Carol, *d* of Geoffrey Lawson. *Recreations:* sailing, tennis, table-tennis, painting. *Heir: b* Julian Nigel Chardin Musgrave, *b* 8 Dec. 1951. *Address:* c/o National Westminster Bank, 52–54 West Street, Fareham, Hants PO16 9XA.

MUSGRAVE, Dennis Charles, FICE; Director, British Water Industries Group, 1981–85; *b* 10 Feb. 1921; *s* of Frederick Charles Musgrave and Jane Elizabeth (*née* Gulliver); *m* 1942, Marjorie Cynthia (*née* Chaston); one *s*. *Educ:* privately. MIStructE, FIWES. Engineering Assistant: Howard Humphreys and Sons, Consulting Engrs; Coode and Partners, Cons. Engrs, 1938–45; Asst Port Engr, Lagos, Nigeria, 1945–47; Engrg Asst, Borough of Willesden, 1947–49; Agent, Ruddock and Meighan, Civil Engrg Contractors, 1949–56; Associate Partner, Sandford, Fawcett and Partners, Cons. Engrs, in Canada, 1956–63, in Westminster, 1963–66. Engineering Inspector, Min. of Housing and Local Govt, 1966, Sen. Inspector, 1971; Asst Dir, DoE, 1974; Chief Water Engr, DoE, 1977–82. *Publications:* various technical papers. *Recreations:* music, literature. *Address:* Gaywoods, Ringshall Road, Little Gaddesden, near Berkhamstead, Herts HP4 1PE. *T:* Little Gaddesden (0144284) 3501.

MUSGRAVE, Sir Richard James, 7th Bt, *cr* 1782; *b* 10 Feb. 1922; *s* of Sir Christopher Norman Musgrave, 6th Bt, OBE, and Kathleen (*d* 1967), 3rd *d* of late Robert Chapman, Co. Tyrone; *S* father 1956; *m* 1958, Maria, *d* of late Col M. Cambanis, and Mrs Cambanis, Athens, Greece; two *s* four *d*. *Educ:* Stowe. Capt., The Poona Horse (17th Queen Victoria's Own Cavalry), 1940–45. *Recreation:* shooting. *Heir: s* Christopher John Shane Musgrave, *b* 23 Oct. 1959. *Address:* Knightsbrook House, Trim, Co. Meath. *T:* 046 31372; Komito, Syros, Greece. *Club:* Kildare Street and University (Dublin).

MUSGRAVE, Rosanne Kimble, MA; Headmistress, Blackheath High School (GPDST), since 1989; *b* 31 Jan. 1952; *d* of Gp Captain John Musgrave, DSO, and Joanne Musgrave. *Educ:* Cheltenham Ladies' Coll.; St Anne's Coll., Oxford (MA); MA Reading Univ.; PGCE London Univ. Assistant teacher of English: Latymer Grammar Sch., 1976–79; Camden School for Girls (ILEA), 1979–82; Head of English: Channing Sch., Highgate, 1982–84; Haberdashers' Aske's School for Girls, Elstree, 1984–89. Corporate Mem., Cheltenham Ladies' Coll., 1989; Gov., Dover Coll., 1994–. FRSA 1994. Freeman, City of London, 1993. *Recreations:* letterpress printing, DIY. *Address:* Vanbrugh Park, SE3 7AG.

MUSGRAVE, Thea; composer; *b* 1928; *d* of James P. Musgrave and Joan Musgrave (*née* Hacking); *m* 1971, Peter, *s* of Irving Mark, NY. *Educ:* Moreton Hall, Oswestry; Edinburgh Univ.; Paris Conservatoire; privately with Nadia Boulanger. *Works include:* Cantata for a summer's day, 1954; The Abbot of Drimock (Chamber opera), 1955; Triptych for Tenor and orch., 1959; Colloquy for violin and piano, 1960; The Phoenix and the Turtle for chorus and orch., 1962; The Five Ages of Man for chorus and orch., 1963; The Decision (opera), 1964–65; Nocturnes and arias for orch., 1966; Chamber Concerto No. 2, in homage to Charles Ives, 1966; Chamber Concerto No 3 (Octet), 1966; Concerto for orchestra, 1967; Music for Horn and Piano, 1967; Clarinet Concerto, 1968; Beauty and the Beast (ballet), 1968; Night Music, 1969; Memento Vitae, a concerto in homage to Beethoven, 1970; Horn concerto, 1971; From One to Another, 1972; Viola Concerto, 1973; The Voice of Ariadne (opera), 1972–73; Rorate Coeli, for chorus, 1974; Space Play, 1974; Orfeo I and Orfeo II, 1975; Mary, Queen of Scots (opera), 1976–77; Christmas Carol (opera), 1979; An Occurrence at Owl Creek Bridge (radio opera), 1981; Peripeteia (orchestral), 1981; Harriet, the Woman called Moses (opera), 1984; Black Tambourine for women's chorus and piano, 1985; Pierrot, 1985; For the Time Being for chorus, 1986; The Golden Echo, 1987; Narcissus, 1988; The Seasons (orchestral), 1988; Rainbow (orchestral), 1990; Simón Bolivar (opera), 1993; Autumn Sonata, 1993; Journey through a Japanese Landscape (marimba concerto), 1993; On the Underground (vocal), 1994; Helios (oboe concerto), 1995. Performances and broadcasts: UK, France, Germany, Switzerland, Scandinavia, USA, USSR, etc., Edinburgh, Cheltenham, Aldeburgh, Zagreb, Venice and Warsaw Festivals. Hon. MusDoc, CNAA. *Address:* c/o Novello & Co. Ltd, 8/9 Frith Street, W1V 5TZ.

MUSGRAVE, Prof. William Kenneth Rodgerson, PhD, DSc (Birmingham); Professor of Organic Chemistry, 1960–81, now Emeritus, and Head of Department of Chemistry, 1968–71, 1974–77, 1980–81, University of Durham; *b* 16 Sept. 1918; *s* of late Charles Musgrave and late Sarah Alice Musgrave; *m* 1944, Joyce Cadman; two *s*. *Educ:* Stanley Grammar Sch., Co. Durham; Univ. of Birmingham. British-Canadian Atomic Energy Project, 1944–45; Univ. of Durham: Lecturer in Chemistry, 1945–56; Senior Lecturer, 1956–60; Personal Readership in Organic Chem., 1960; Second Pro-Vice-Chancellor, 1970–73; Pro-Vice-Chancellor and Sub-Warden, 1973–78; Acting Vice-Chancellor, 1979. *Publications:* (joint) Advances in Fluorine Chemistry, Vol. I, edited by Stacey, Tatlow and Sharpe, 1960; Rodd's Chemistry of Carbon Compounds, vols Ia and IIIa, edited by Coffey; scientific papers in chemical journals. *Recreations:* gardening, rough shooting. *Address:* Apt 14, Pegasus Court, 61–63 Broad Road, Sale, Greater Manchester M33 2ES.

MUSGROVE, Prof. Frank, DLitt; Sarah Fielden Professor of Education, University of Manchester, 1970–82, now Emeritus; Dean of the Faculty of Education, 1976–78; *b* 16 Dec. 1922; *e s* of late Thomas and Fanny Musgrove; *m* Dorothy Ellen (*née* Nicholls); one *d*. *Educ:* Henry Mellish Grammar Sch., Nottingham; Magdalen Coll., Oxford; Univ. of Nottingham. MA Oxon, PhD Nottingham, MEd Manchester. Served War, RAFVR, 1941–45; Navigator, Bomber Command (commnd), Ops 149 Sqdn (tour of bombing missions completed 1944). Educational appts in England and in the Colonial Educn Service, E Africa, 1947–57; Lectureships in Univs of Leicester and Leeds, 1957–65; Foundn Chair of Research in Educn, Univ. of Bradford, 1965–70. Visiting Professor: of Educn, Univ. of BC, 1965; of Sociology, Univ. of California (Davis), 1969; Guest lectr, Inst. of Sociology, Univ. of Utrecht, 1968; The Chancellor's Lectr, Univ. of Wellington, NZ, 1970; British Council Lectr, Univs of Grenoble, Aix-en-Provence, Nice, Paris, 1972; Raymond Priestley Lectr, Univ. of Birmingham, 1975. Hon. Prof., Univ. of Hull, 1985–88. Co-editor, Research in Education, 1971–76. FRAI 1952; FRSA 1971. DLitt Open, 1982. *Publications:* The Migratory Elite, 1963; Youth and the Social Order, 1964; The Family, Education and Society, 1966; Society and the Teacher's Role (with P. H. Taylor), 1969; Patterns of Power and Authority in English Education, 1971; Ecstasy and Holiness, 1974, new edn 1994; Margins of the Mind, 1977; School and the Social Order, 1979; Education and Anthropology, 1982; The North of England: from Roman to present times, 1990; research papers in: Africa; Sociological Review; Brit. Jl of Sociology; Brit. Jl of Educational Psychology; Economic History Review; Brit. Jl of Social and Clinical Psychology, etc. *Recreations:* fell walking, classical music, fly fishing. *Address:* Dib Scar, The Cedar Grove, Beverley, E Yorks HU17 7EP. *T:* Hull (01482) 868799. *Club:* Derwent Anglers (Scarborough).

MUSGROVE, Harold John; Chairman, Birmingham Heartlands Hospital NHS Trust, since 1994; *b* 19 Nov. 1930; *s* of Harold Musgrove; *m* 1959, Jacquelin Mary Hobbs; two *s* two *d*. *Educ:* King Edward Grammar Sch., Birmingham; Birmingham Tech. Coll. Nat. Cert. of Mech. Eng. Apprentice, Austin Motor Co., 1945; held various positions, incl. Chief Material Controller (Commission as Navigator, RAF, during this period); Senior Management, Truck and Bus Group, Leyland Motor Corp., 1963–78; Austin Morris: Dir of Manufacturing, 1978–79; Man. Dir, 1979–80; Chm. and Man. Dir, 1980–81; Chm., Light Medium Cars Group, 1981–82; Chm. and Chief Exec., Austin Rover Gp, 1982–86; Chloride plc: Dir, 1989–92; Chm., Industrial Battery Sector, 1989–91; Chm., Power Supplies and Lighting Gp, 1991–92. Chm., W Midlands Ambulance Service, 1992–94. Pres., Birmingham Chamber of Industry and Commerce, 1987–88. Director: Metalrax Gp, 1987–. Pres., Aston Villa FC, 1986–. FIMI 1985. Midlander of the Year Award, 1980; IProdE Internat. Award, 1981; Soc. of Engineers Churchill Medal, 1982. *Recreations:* golf, soccer. *Address:* The Lodge, Laverton, Broadway, Worcs WR12 7NA.

MUSGROVE, Prof. John, RIBA; Professor Emeritus, University of London; Haden-Pilkington Professor of Environmental Design and Engineering, 1978–85 and Head of the Bartlett School of Architecture and Planning, 1980–85, University College London; *b* 20 June 1920; *s* of James Musgrove and Betsy (*née* Jones); *m* 1941, Gladys Mary Webb; three *s*. *Educ:* Univ. of Durham (King's Coll.) (BArch, 1st Cl. Hons). Asst to late Baron Holford, RA, 1952–53; Research Architect, Nuffield Foundn, 1953–60; Sen. Lectr and Reader in Architecture, University Coll. London, 1960–70, Prof., 1970–78. Hon. Fellow, Inst. of Architects, Sri Lanka, 1972. *Publications:* (jtly) The Function and Design of Hospitals, 1955; (jtly) The Design of Research Laboratories, 1960; (ed) Sir Banister Fletcher's History of Architecture, 19th edn, 1987; numerous articles and papers in Architects' Jl, RIBA Jl, and reviews. *Recreations:* painting in oils, gardening. *Address:* Netherby, 79 Green End Road, Boxmoor, Hemel Hempstead, Herts HP1 1QW.

MUSKERRY, 9th Baron *cr* 1781 (Ire.); **Robert Fitzmaurice Deane;** Bt 1710 (Ire.); *b* 26 March 1948; *s* of 8th Baron Muskerry and Betty Fairbridge, *e d* of George Wilfred Reckless Palmer; *S* father, 1988; *m* 1975, Rita Brink, Pietermaritzburg; one *s* two *d*. *Educ:* Sandford Park School, Dublin; Trinity Coll., Dublin (BA, BAI). *Heir:* *s* Hon. Jonathan Fitzmaurice Deane, *b* 7 June 1986. *Address:* 74 Bank Terrace, Manor Gardens, Durban, South Africa.

MUSKIE, Edmund Sixtus; Secretary of State, USA, 1980–81; lawyer and politician; *b* Rumford, Maine, 28 March 1914; *s* of Stephen Muskie and Josephine Czarnecki; *m* 1948, Jane Frances Gray; two *s* three *d*. *Educ:* Bates Coll., Maine (AB); Cornell Law Sch., Ithaca, New York (LLB). Served War, Lt USNR, 1942–45. Admitted to Bar: Massachusetts, 1939; Maine, 1940, and practised at Waterville, Maine, 1940 and 1945–55; Federal District Court, 1941. Mem., Maine House of Reps, 1947–51; Democratic Floor Leader, 1949–51; Dist. Dir for Maine, Office of Price Stabilisation, 1951–52; City Solicitor, Waterville, Maine, 1954–55; Governor of State of Maine, 1955–59; US Senator from Maine, 1959–80; Senate Assistant Majority Whip, 1966–80; Chm., Senate Budget Cttee, 1974–80. Cand. for Vice-Presidency of US, 1968. Mem., Senate Foreign Relations Cttee, 1970–74, 1979–80; Former Chm., and Mem. *ex officio*, Democratic Senatorial Campaign Cttee; Chairman, Senate Sub-Cttees on: Environmental Pollution, Senate Environment and Public Wks Cttee; Intergovtl Relations, Senate Governmental Affairs Cttee, 1959–78; Former Member: Special Cttee on Aging; Exec. Cttee, Nat. Governors' Conf.; Chm., Roosevelt Campobello Internat. Park Commn. Mem, Amer. Acad. of Arts and Sciences. Has numerous hon. doctorates. Phi Beta Kappa; Phi Alpha Delta. Presidential Medal of Freedom, 1981; Notre Dame Laetare Medal, 1981; Distinguished Service Award, Former Members of Congress Assoc., 1981. *Publication:* Journeys, 1972. *Address:* Chadbourne Parke, 1101 Vermont Avenue, NW, Washington, DC 20005, USA.

MUSSON, Gen. Sir Geoffrey (Randolph Dixon), GCB 1970 (KCB 1965; CB 1959); CBE 1945; DSO 1944; BA; *b* 9 June 1910; *s* of late Robert Dixon Musson, Yockleton, Shrewsbury; *m* 1939, Hon. Elspeth L. Bailey, *d* of late Hon. Herbert Crawshay Bailey; one *s* (one *d* decd). *Educ:* Shrewsbury; Trinity Hall, Cambridge. 2nd Lt KSLI, 1930. Served War of 1939–45, North Africa and Italy; Comdr 2nd Bn DCLI, 1943–44; Comdr 36th Infantry Bde, 1944–46. Comdr Commonwealth Forces in Korea, 1954–55; Comdt Sch. of Infantry, 1956–58, Comdr 7th Armoured Div., BAOR, 1958; Maj.-Gen. 1958; Comdr, 5th Div., 1958–59. Chief of Staff, GHQ, Near East Land Forces, 1959–62; Vice-Adjutant-Gen., War Office, subseq. Min. of Defence, 1963–64; GOC-in-C, N Command, 1964–67; Adjutant-General, 1967–70, retired. Colonel: King's Shropshire Light Infantry, 1963–68; The Light Infantry, 1968–72. A Vice-Chm., Nat. Savings Cttee, 1970–78; Chairman: HM Forces Savings Cttee, 1970–78; Regular Forces Employment Assoc., 1978–80; Vice-Pres., Royal Patriotic Fund Corporation, 1974–83; Pres., Victory Services Club, 1970–80. *Address:* Barn Cottage, Hurstbourne Tarrant, Andover, Hants SP11 0BD. *T:* Hurstbourne Tarrant (01264) 736354. *Club:* Army and Navy.

MUSSON, Rear Adm. John Geoffrey Robin, CB 1993; Senior Naval Directing Staff, Royal College of Defence Studies, 1990–93; Chief Naval Supply and Secretariat Officer, 1991–93; *b* 30 May 1939; *s* of Geoffrey William Musson and Winifred Elizabeth Musson (*née* Whyman); *m* 1965, Joanna Marjorie Ward; two *s* one *d*. *Educ:* Luton Grammar Sch.; BRNC, Dartmouth. Entered RN, 1957; served HM Ships: Bulwark, 1960–61; Decoy, 1961–62; Cavalier, 1966–67; Forth, 1967–69; Kent, 1975–76; NDC, 1979; MA, VCDS (Personnel and Logistics), 1980–81; Sec. to Chief of Fleet Support, 1982–83; CSO (Personnel and Admin), FONAC, 1984–86; Dir, Naval Officer Appts (Supply and WRNS), 1986–88; Captain, HMS Cochrane, 1988–90. *Recreations:* hill walking, mending things, history, hedge laying.

MUSSON, John Nicholas Whitaker; Warden of Glenalmond College (formerly Trinity College, Glenalmond), 1972–87; *b* 2 Oct. 1927; *s* of late Dr J. P. T. Musson, OBE and Gwendoline Musson (*née* Whitaker); *m* 1953, Ann Priest; one *s* three *d*. *Educ:* Clifton; Brasenose Coll., Oxford (MA). Served with Welsh Guards and Lancs Fusiliers, 1945–48 (commnd); BA Hons Mod. Hist., Oxford, 1951; HM Colonial Admin. Service, 1951–59; District and Provincial Administration, N Nigeria; Lectr, Inst. of Administration, N Nigeria; Staff Dept, British Petroleum, London, 1959–61; Asst Master and Housemaster, Canford Sch., 1961–72. Chm., Scottish Div. HMC, 1981–83; Scottish Dir (formerly Scottish Sec.), ISCO, 1987–93. Governor: SCIS, 1993–; Clifton Coll., 1989– (Mem. Council, 1989–95); George Watson's Coll., Edinburgh, 1989–. *Recreations:* hill walking, fly fishing, painting. *Address:* 47 Spylaw Road, Edinburgh EH10 5BP. *T:* 0131–337 0089. *Club:* New (Edinburgh).

MUSTILL, family name of **Baron Mustill.**

MUSTILL, Baron *cr* 1992 (Life Peer), of Pateley Bridge in the County of North Yorkshire; **Michael John Mustill;** Kt 1978; PC 1985; a Lord of Appeal in Ordinary, since 1992; *b* 10 May 1931; *o s* of Clement William and late Marion Mustill; *m* 1st, Beryl Reid Davies (marr. diss.); 2nd, Caroline Phillips; two *s* and one step *d*. *Educ:* Oundle Sch.; St John's Coll., Cambridge (Hon. Fellow, 1992). LLD Cantab 1992. Royal Artillery, 1949–51 (commissioned, 1950). Called to Bar, Gray's Inn, 1955, Bencher, 1976. QC 1968. Dep. Chm., Hants QS, 1971; a Recorder of the Crown Court, 1972–78; Judge of High Court, QBD, 1978–85; a Lord Justice of Appeal, 1985–92. Presiding Judge, NE Circuit, 1981–84. Chairman: Civil Service Appeal Tribunal, 1971–78; Judicial Studies Board, 1985–89; Deptl Cttee on Law of Arbitration, 1985–90. President: British Maritime Law Assoc.; CIArb. *Publications:* The Law and Practice of Commercial Arbitration in England (with S. C. Boyd, QC), 1982, 2nd edn 1989; Anticipatory Breach of Contract, 1990; Joint Editor: Scrutton on Charterparties and Bills of Lading; Arnould on Marine Insurance; articles in legal periodicals. *Recreations:* visiting France, reading, music, active sports. *Address:* House of Lords, SW1A 0PW.

MUSTOE, Mrs Anne, MA; traveller, and educational consultant; *b* 24 May 1933; *d* of H.W. Revill; *m* 1960, Nelson Edwin Mustoe, QC (*d* 1976). *Educ:* Girton Coll., Cambridge (BA Classical Tripos 1955, MA 1958). DipIPM 1959. Guest, Keen & Nettlefolds Ltd, 1956–60; Head of Classics, Francis Holland School, NW1, 1965–69; independent travel agent, 1969–73; Dep. Headmistress, Cobham Hall, Kent, 1975–78; Headmistress, St Felix School, Southwold, 1978–87. Chm., ISIS, 1986–87; President, Girls' Schools Assoc., 1984–85; Mem., Board of Managers of Girls' Common Entrance Examinations, 1983–86. Governor: Hethersett Old Hall Sch., 1981–86; Cobham Hall, 1986–; James Allen's Girls' Sch., 1991–; Thornton Coll., 1992–. JP Suffolk, 1981–85. *Publications:* A Bike Ride: 12,000 miles around the world, 1991; Escaping the Winter, 1993. *Recreations:* music, cycling (world cycling tours, 1987–88, 1994–95). *Address:* c/o PCA Finance, 90 Gloucester Mews West, W2 6DY. *T:* 0171–402 9082.

MUSTON, Rt. Rev. Gerald Bruce; Bishop of North-West Australia, 1981–92; *b* 19 Jan. 1927; 3rd *s* of Stanley John and Emily Ruth Muston; *m* 1951, Laurel Wright; one *s* one *d*. *Educ:* N Sydney Chatswood High School; Moore Theological College, Sydney. ThL (Aust. Coll. of Theology). Rector, Wallerawang, NSW, 1951–53; Editorial Secretary, Church Missionary Society (Aust.), 1953–58; Rector, Tweed Heads, NSW, 1958–61; Vicar, Essendon, Vic, 1961–67; Rural Dean of Essendon, 1963–67; Rector of Darwin, NT, and Archdeacon of Northern Territory, 1967–69; Federal Secretary, Bush Church Aid Society of Aust., 1969–71; Bishop Coadjutor, dio. Melbourne (Bishop of the Western Region), 1971–81. *Recreations:* golf, reading. *Address:* 14a Bellingham Place, Padbury, WA 6025, Australia. *Club:* Melbourne (Melbourne).

MUSTOW, Stuart Norman, CBE 1995; FEng 1982; FICE; consulting engineer, since 1986; Consultant, W. S. Atkins Consultants; *b* 26 Nov. 1928; *s* of Norman Eric Mustow and Mabel Florence Mustow (*née* Purcell); *m* 1964, Sigrid Hertha Young; two *s* one *d*. *Educ:* Aston Univ. (BSc). FIHT. Mil. service, RA; Local Govt Engineering, 1949–69; City Engineer and Surveyor, Stoke on Trent, 1969–74; County Surveyor, W Midlands, responsible for roads, transport planning and Birmingham Airport, 1974–86. Mem., Engineering Council, 1995–. President: Inst. Municipal Engrs, 1980–81; ICE, 1993–94. Hon. DSc Aston, 1994. *Publications:* papers in learned jls. *Recreations:* outdoor life, church, social work. *Address:* 9 Knighton Road, Sutton Coldfield, West Midlands B74 4NY. *T:* 0121–353 9839.

MUTCH, Dr William Edward Scott, OBE 1989; FRSE; forestry and land use consultant, since 1989; Member of Board and Chairman, South East Region, Scottish Natural Heritage, 1992–94; *b* 14 Aug. 1925; *s* of Wilfred Ernest Mutch and Helen Anderson Mutch (*née* Bannerman); *m* 1950, Margaret Isobel McKay; one *d. Educ:* Royal High Sch., Edinburgh; Edinburgh Univ. (BSc Forestry, PhD); St John's Coll., Oxford. FICFor. Colonial Service Forest Dept, Nigeria, 1946; University of Edinburgh: Lectr in Forestry, 1953; Sen. Lectr, 1963; Head of Dept of Forestry and Natural Resources, 1981–87. Dir, Central Scotland Woodlands Ltd, subseq. Central Scotland Countryside Trust, 1989–. Member: Countryside Commn for Scotland, 1988–92; Nat. Forestry Res. Adv. Cttee, 1982–; Nature Conservancy Council, 1989–91; Nature Conservancy Council for Scotland, 1991–92. Institute of Chartered Foresters: Pres., 1982–84; Inst. Medal, 1986. Editor, Scottish Forestry, 1957–62. *Publications:* Public Recreation in National Forests, 1967; The Interaction of Forestry and Farming, 1980; Farm Woodland Management, 1987; contribs to professional jls. *Recreations:* cabinet making, travel, painting. *Address:* 19 Barnton Grove, Edinburgh EH4 6EQ. *T:* 0131–339 1400.

MUTI, Riccardo; Conductor Laureate, Philadelphia Orchestra, since 1992 (Principal Guest Conductor, 1977–80; Principal Conductor and Music Director, 1980–92); Music Director, La Scala, Milan, since 1986; *b* 28 July 1941; *m* 1969, Cristina Mazzavillani; two *s* one *d. Educ:* Diploma in pianoforte, Conservatorio di Napoli; Diploma in conducting and composition, Milan. Principal Conductor, 1973–82, Music Dir, 1979–82, New Philharmonia, later Philharmonia Orchestra; Principal Conductor, Orchestra Maggio Musicale Fiorentino, 1969–81. Concert tours in USA: with Boston, Chicago, and Philadelphia orchestras; concerts at Salzburg, Edinburgh, Lucerne, Flanders and Vienna Festivals; concerts with Berlin Philharmonic, Vienna Philharmonic, Concertgebouw Amsterdam; opera in Florence, Salzburg, Vienna, Munich, Covent Garden, Milan. Hon. degrees from Bologna Univ. and univs in England and USA. Recording prizes from France, Germany, Italy, Japan and USA. Accademico: dell'Accademia di Santa Cecilia, Rome; dell'Accademia Luigi Cherubini, Florence. Grande Ufficiale, Repubblica Italiana; Cavaliere, Gran Croce (Italy), 1991; Verdienstkreuz, 1st class (Germany), 1976. *Address:* Teatro alla Scala, Via Filodrammtici 2, Milan 20121, Italy.

MUTTER, Anne-Sophie; violinist; *b* Rheinfelden, Baden, 29 June 1963. *Educ:* studied with Prof. Aida Stucki in Switzerland. Début with Herbert von Karajan, Salzburg, 1977; soloist with major orchestras of the world; also plays with string trio and quartet. Guest teacher, RAM, 1985. Hon. Pres., Univ. of Oxford Mozart Soc., 1983. Jugend Musiziert Prize (FRG) for: violin, 1970 and 1974; piano, 1970; Künstler des Jahres Deutscher Schallplattenpreis, 1979; Grand Prix Internat. du Disque, Record Acad. Prize, Tokyo, 1982; Internat. Schallplattenpreis, 1993; Grammy, 1994. Bundesverdienstkreuz (1st Cl.), 1987. *Recreations:* graphic arts, sport. *Address:* Effnerstrasse 48, 81925 Munich, Germany. *T:* (89) 984418, *Fax:* (89) 9827186.

MWINYI, Ndugu Ali Hassan; President, United Republic of Tanzania, since 1985; *b* 8 May 1925; *s* of late Hassan Mwinyi Chande and Asha Mwinyishehe; *m* 1960, Siti A. Mwinyi (*née* Abdulla); five *s* four *d. Educ:* Mangapwani Sch. and Dole Sch., Zanzibar; Teachers' Training Coll., Zanzibar; Durham Univ. Inst. of Education. Primary sch. teacher, head teacher, Tutor, Principal, Zanzibar, 1945–64; Acting Principal Sec., Min. of Educn, 1964–65; Dep. Gen. Manager, State Trading Corp., 1965–70; Minister of State, President's Office, Dar es Salaam, 1970–72; Minister for Health, 1972–75; Minister for Home Affairs, 1975–77; Ambassador to Egypt, 1977–81; Minister for Natural Resources and Tourism, 1982–83; Minister of State, Vice-President's Office, 1983; Vice-Pres., Union Govt, 1984. Chama Cha Mapinduzi (Revolutionary Party): Member, 1977; Nat. Exec. Cttee, 1982; Central Cttee, 1984; Vice-Chm., 1984–90; Chm., 1990–; Mem., Afro-Shirazi Party, 1964. Chairman: Zanzibar Film Censorship Bd, 1964–65; E African Currency Bd, Zanzibar, 1964–67; Nat. Kiswahili Council, 1964–77; Tanzania Food and Nutrition Council, 1974–76. Mem.,Univ. Council of Dar es Salaam, 1964–65. *Address:* State House, Dar es Salaam, United Republic of Tanzania.

MYER, Sidney Baillieu, AC 1990; MA Cantab; Chairman, Myer Emporium Ltd, since 1978 (Director, since 1955); Deputy Chairman, Coles Myer Ltd, 1985–94; President, Myer Foundation, since 1992 (Vice-President, 1959–92); Director, N. M. Rothschild & Son (Australia); *b* 11 Jan. 1926; *s* of late Sidney Myer and late Dame (Margery) Merlyn Baillieu Myer, DBE; *m* 1955, Sarah J., *d* of late S. Hordern; two *s* one *d. Educ:* Geelong Grammar Sch.; Pembroke Coll., Cambridge (MA). Sub-Lieut, RANVR, 1944–46. Joined Myer Emporium, 1953. Director: Elders IXL Ltd, 1972–82 and 1986–90; Cadbury Schweppes Aust. Ltd, 1976–82; Commonwealth Banking Corp., 1979–83; Network Ten Holdings Ltd and associated Cos, 1985–87; Chm., Nat. Mutual Life Assoc. of Australasia, 1988–92 (Dir, 1978–92). Dir, Howard Florey Inst. of Experimental Physiology and Medicine, 1971– (Pres., 1992–); Part-time Mem. Executive, CSIRO, 1981–85. Pres., French Chamber of Commerce (Vic), 1962–64; Rep. Chm., Aust.-Japan Foundn, 1976–81; Member: Consultative Cttee on Relations with Japan, 1978–81; Aust.-China Council, 1979–81; Nat. Bicentennial Sci. Centre Adv. Cttee, 1986–89. Councillor: Aust. Conservation Foundn, 1964–73; Vic. Coll. of Arts, 1973–78; Chm., Art Foundn of Vic., 1986–88; Vice-Pres., Nat. Gall. Soc. of Vic., 1964–68; Trustee, Nat. Gall. of Vic., 1973–83 (Vice-Pres., 1977–83); Chm., Commonwealth Research Centres of Excellence Cttee, 1981–82. Hon. LLD, 1993. Chevalier de la Légion d'Honneur, 1976. *Address:* Level 45, 55 Collins Street, Melbourne, Victoria 3000, Australia. *Clubs:* Australian (Sydney); Leander (Henley-on-Thames).

MYERS, Dr David Milton, CMG 1974; Vice-Chancellor, La Trobe University, Melbourne, 1965–76; *b* 5 June 1911; *s* of W. H. Myers, Sydney; *m* 1st, 1937, Beverley A. H. (*d* 1993), *d* of Dr T. D. Delprat; three *s*; 2nd, 1994, Moyna Lien, *d* of Dr T. D. Delprat. *Educ:* Univs of Sydney and Oxford. BSc, BE, DScEng; FIE Aust., FIEE, FInstP. 1st Chief of Div. of Electrotechnology, CSIR, 1939–49; P. N. Russell Prof. of Elec. Engrg, Univ. of Sydney, 1949–59; Dean, Faculty of Applied Science, and Prof. of Elec. Engrg, Univ. of British Columbia, 1960–65. Mem. Adv. Council, CSIRO, 1949–55; Mem. Nat. Res. Council of Canada, 1965; Chairman: Cttee on Overseas Professional Qualifications, 1969–84; Inquiry into Unemployment Benefits, for Aust. Govt, 1977; Cttee of Inquiry into fluoridation of Victorian water supplies, 1979–80; Consultative Council on Victorian Mental Health Act, 1981. Pres., Aust. Inst. of Engineers, 1958. Kernot Meml Medal, 1974; P. N. Russell Meml Medal, 1977. *Publications:* various research papers in sci. jls. *Recreations:* golf, tennis, music. *Address:* 23 Ethel Street, Balgowlah, NSW 2093, Australia. *T:* (2) 4485776. *Club:* Melbourne (Melbourne).

MYERS, Brig. (Retired) Edmund Charles Wolf, CBE 1944; DSO 1943; BA Cantab; CEng, MICE; *b* 12 Oct. 1906; *er s* of late Dr C. S. Myers, CBE, FRS; *m* 1943, Louisa (*d* 1995), *er d* of late Aldred Bickham Sweet-Escott; one *d. Educ:* Haileybury; Royal Military Academy, Woolwich; Caius Coll., Cambridge. Commissioned into Royal Engineers, 1926. Served Palestine, 1936 (despatches); War of 1939–45; Comdr, British Mil. Mission to Greek Resistance Forces, 1942–43; Middle East, including Balkans, until 1944 (African Star, Italy Star, DSO, CBE); North-West Europe, 1944–45 (France and Germany Star, Dutch Bronze Lion, Norwegian Liberty Medal); Far East, 1945; Korea, 1951–52 (despatches, American Legion of Merit). Chief Engineer, British Troops in Egypt, 1955–56; Dep. Dir, Personnel Administration in the War Office, 1956–59; retired 1959. Chief Civil Engineer Cleveland Bridge & Engineering Co. Ltd, 1959–64. Construction Manager, Power Gas Corp. Ltd, Davy-Ashmore Group, 1964–67. Regional Sec., British Field Sports Soc., 1968–71. *Publication:* Greek Entanglement, 1955. *Recreations:* horse training and riding, sailing, flying (1st Sec. RE Flying Club, 1934–35), fishing. *Address:* 10 University Farm, Moreton-in-Marsh, Glos GL56 0DN. *T:* Cotswold (01451) 830183. *Clubs:* Army and Navy, Special Forces.

MYERS, Geoffrey, CBE 1984; CEng; FCIT; Chairman, TRANSAID, since 1988; Vice-Chairman, British Railways Board, 1985–87 (Member, 1980–87); *b* 12 July 1930; *s* of Ernest and Annie Myers; *m* 1959, Patricia Mary (*née* Hall); two *s. Educ:* Belle Vue Grammar Sch.; Bradford Technical Coll. (BScEng London). CEng, MICE 1963; FCIT 1973. RE, 1955–57. British Rail: civil engrg positions, 1957–64; Planning Officer, N Eastern Reg., 1964–66; Divl Movements Manager, Leeds Div., 1966–68; Dir of Studies, British Transport Staff Coll., 1968–70; Divl Man., Sheffield, 1970–76; Dep. Gen. Man., Eastern Reg., 1976–77, Gen. Man., 1977–78; Dir of Strategic Develt, 1978–80; Dep. Chief Exec. (Railways), 1983; Jt Managing Dir (Railways), 1984–85. Hon. Lectr, Leeds Univ., 1991–. Pres. Council, CIT, 1986–87. Mem. Council, Save the Children (UK), 1993–. Mem., Carmen's Co., 1983. Hon. DEng Bradford, 1988. OStJ 1979. *Recreations:* golf, walking. *Address:* The Spinney, Lands Lane, Knaresborough, N Yorks HG5 9DE. *T:* Harrogate (01423) 863719.

MYERS, Geoffrey Morris Price; Under-Secretary, Agricultural and Food Research Council, 1973–87; *b* 8 May 1927. *Educ:* Reigate Grammar Sch.; King's Coll., London. Civil Service, 1950; UKAEA, 1959–67; Nat. Econ. Develt Office, 1967–69; Agric. Research Council, 1970. *Address:* 4 Stanhope Road, Croydon CR0 5NS. *T:* 0181–680 0827.

MYERS, Gordon Elliot, CMG 1979; Under-Secretary, Arable Crops, Pigs and Poultry Group, Ministry of Agriculture, Fisheries and Food, 1986–89, retired; *b* 4 July 1929; *s* of William Lionel Myers and Yvonne (*née* Arthur); *m* 1963, Wendy Jane Lambert; two *s* one *d Educ:* Kilburn Grammar Sch.; University Coll., Oxford (BA 1st Cl. Hons Modern History). Asst Principal, MAFF, 1951; Principal, 1958; Asst Sec., 1966; Head successively of Land Drainage Div., Sugar and Tropical Foods Div., and EEC Div., 1966–74; Under-Sec., MAFF, 1975; Minister (Agriculture), Office of UK Perm. Rep. to EEC, 1975–79; Under-Sec., Food Policy Gp, 1980–85, Cereals and Sugar Gp, 1985–86, MAFF. Mem., Cttee on Simplification of Common Agricl Policy, EEC, 1990–94. *Address:* Woodlands, Nugents Park, Hatch End, Pinner, Mddx HA5 4RA. *Club:* United Oxford & Cambridge University.

MYERS, Harry Eric, QC 1967; QC Gibraltar 1977; *b* 10 Jan. 1914; *s* of Harry Moss Myers and Alice Muriel Serjeant; *m* 1951, Lorna Babette Kitson (*née* Blackburn); no *c. Educ:* Bedford Sch. HAC, City of London, 1931. Admitted Solicitor of Supreme Court, 1936; called to Bar, Middle Temple, 1945. Prosecuting Counsel to Bd of Inland Revenue on SE Circuit, 1965. *Address:* 202 Beatty House, Dolphin Square, SW1V 3PH; 10 King's Bench Walk, Temple, EC4Y 7EB.

MYERS, John David; Chairman of Industrial Tribunals, since 1982 (Regional Chairman for Newcastle, since 1994); *b* 30 Oct. 1937; *s* of Frank and Monica Myers; *m* 1974, Anne McGeough (*née* Purcell), *widow* of J. T. McGeough; one *s. Educ:* Marist College, Hull; Hull University. LLB Hons. Called to the Bar, Gray's Inn, 1968. Schoolmaster, 1958–64; University, 1964–67; pupillage with J. D. Walker (later Judge Walker); practice at Hull, 1969–82 (Junior, NE Circuit, 1975–76). *Recreations:* cooking, oenology. *Clubs:* Pen and Palette (Newcastle); Foxton Hall Golf.

MYERS, Sir Kenneth (Ben), Kt 1977; MBE 1944; FCA; Director, South British Insurance Co. Ltd, 1934–82 (Chairman, 1945–78); retired; *b* 5 March 1907; *s* of Hon. Sir Arthur Myers and Lady (Vera) Myers (*née* Levy); *m* 1933, Margaret Blair Pirie one *s* two *d. Educ:* Marlborough Coll.; Gonville and Caius Coll., Cambridge (BA 1928). FCA 1933. Returned to NZ, 1933; served War with 2nd NZEF, ME and Italy, 1940–45. *Recreation:* looking after my family. *Address:* 228 Victoria Avenue, Remuera, Auckland 5, New Zealand. *T:* (9) 5245499. *Clubs:* Boodle's; Northern (Auckland).

MYERS, Martin Trevor, FRICS; Chief Executive and Managing Director, Imry Holdings Ltd, since 1989; *b* 24 Sept. 1941; *s* of Bernard Myers and Sylvia Marjorie Myers (*née* Pearman); *m* 1981, Nicole Josephine Yerna; one *s* one *d. Educ:* Arnold House, St John's Wood; Latymer Upper Sch.; Coll. of Estate Management, London Univ. (BSc). FRICS 1975. Jones Lang Wootton, 1965–83: Partner, 1969; Proprietory Partner, 1972; Chm. and Chief Exec., Arbuthnot Properties, 1983; merged with Imry Property Holdings, 1987, and with City Merchant Developers, 1988. *Recreations:* golf, shooting, riding, exercise. *Address:* 1 Durham Place, SW3 4ET; Kingsdown House, Upper Lambourn, Berks RG16 7QU. *Clubs:* Royal Automobile; Wisley Golf (Ripley).

MYERS, Sir Philip (Alan), Kt 1985; OBE 1977; QPM 1972; DL; one of Her Majesty's Inspectors of Constabulary, 1982–93; *b* 7 Feb. 1931; *s* of John and Catherine Myers; *m* 1951, Hazel Gittings; two *s. Educ:* Grove Park, Wrexham. RAF, 1949–50. Shropshire Constabulary, 1950–67; West Mercia Police, 1967–68; Dep. Chief Constable, Gwynedd Constabulary, 1968–70; Chief Constable, North Wales Police, 1970–81. OStJ 1972. DL Clwyd, 1983.

MYERS, Sir Rupert (Horace), KBE 1981 (CBE 1976); AO 1995; FTS 1979; Professor Emeritus; Vice-Chancellor and Principal, University of New South Wales, 1969–81; Director, Energy Resources of Australia Ltd, since 1982; *b* 21 Feb. 1921; *s* of Horace Alexander Myers and Dorothy (*née* Harris); *m* 1944, Io Edwina King; one *s* three *d. Educ:* Melbourne High Sch.; Univ. of Melbourne. BSc 1942; MSc 1943; PhD 1947; CPEng, FIMMA, FRACI; FAIM; FAusIMM; FAICD. Commonwealth Res. Fellow, Univ. of Melbourne, 1942–47; Principal Res. Officer, CSIRO, AERE Harwell, 1947–52; University of New South Wales: Foundn Prof. of Metallurgy, 1952–81; Dean, Faculty of Applied Science, 1956–61; Pro-Vice-Chancellor, 1961–69. Chairman: NSW State Pollution Control Commn, 1971–89; Aust. Vice-Chancellors' Cttee, 1977–79; Cttee of Inquiry into Technol Change in Australia, 1979–80; Commonwealth Cttee of Review of Nat. Capital Develt Commn, 1982–83; Consultative Cttee for Nat. Conservation Strategy for Australia, 1983–85; Coastal Council of NSW, 1982–85; Cttee of Review of NZ Univs, 1987–88; Cttee of Review of Aust. Sci. and Technology Council, 1993; Cttee of Review, Co-operative Res. Centres Prog., 1995. Pres., Aust. Acad. of Technol Scis and Engrg, 1989–94 (Vice-Pres., 1985–88). Director: CSR Ltd, 1982–93; IBM Australia Ltd, 1988–91. Member: Nat. Energy Adv. Cttee, 1980–82; Australian Manufacturing Council, 1980–82. Mem., Sydney Opera House Trust, 1976–83; Foundn Pres., Friends of Royal Botanic Gdns, Sydney, 1982–85. Hon. FIE(Aust.), 1992. Hon. LLD Strathclyde, 1973; Hon. DSc Wollongong, 1976; Hon. DEng Newcastle, 1981; Hon. DLitt NSW, 1981. *Publications:* Technological Change in Australia, 1980; numerous on metallurgy and atomic energy (also patents). *Recreations:* tennis, bowls, music, working with silver. *Address:* 135 Neerim Road, Castlecove, NSW 2069, Australia. *T:* and *Fax:* (2) 4176586. *Club:* Australian (Sydney).

MYERSON, Arthur Levey, QC 1974; **His Honour Judge Myerson;** a Circuit Judge, since 1978; *b* 25 July 1928; *o s* of Bernard and Eda Myerson; *m* 1960, Elaine Shirley Harris; two *s. Educ:* Blackpool Grammar Sch.; Queens' Coll., Cambridge. BA 1950, LLB 1951; BA (Open Univ.) 1985. Called to the Bar, 1952. A Recorder of the Crown Court, 1972–78. RAF, 1946–48. Pres., HM Council of Circuit Judges, 1991. *Recreations:* walking, reading, sailing. *Address:* Leeds Combined Court Centre, Oxford Row, Leeds LS1 3BE. *T:* Leeds (0532) 830040. *Clubs:* Commonwealth Trust; Moor Allerton Golf (Leeds).

MYLAND, Howard David, CB 1988; Deputy Comptroller and Auditor General, National Audit Office, 1984–89; *b* 23 June 1929; *s* of John Tarrant and Frances Grace Myland; *m* 1951, Barbara Pearl Mills; two *s* one *d. Educ:* Fairfields Schs; Queen Mary's Sch., Basingstoke. Served Intelligence Corps, 1948–50. Entered Exchequer and Audit Dept, 1948; Dep. Dir of Audit, 1972; Dir of Audit, 1977; Dep. Sec. of Dept, 1979; an Asst Auditor Gen., National Audit Office, 1984. Mem., Basingstoke Round Table, 1962–70. *Publication:* Public Audit Law—Key Development Considerations, 1992. *Recreations:* travel, contract bridge. *Club:* Sloane.

MYLES, David Fairlie, CBE 1988; tenant hill farmer; *b* 30 May 1925; *s* of Robert C. Myles and Mary Anne S. (*née* Fairlie); *m* 1951, Janet I. (*née* Gall); two *s* two *d. Educ:* Edzell Primary Sch.; Brechin High Sch. National Farmers Union of Scotland: Mem. Council, 1970–79; Convenor of Organisation and Publicity Cttee, 1976–79. MP (C) Banff, 1979–83; Sec., Cons. backbench Cttees on European Affairs and on Agriculture, Fisheries and Food (Jt Sec.); Mem., Select Cttees on Agriculture and on European Legislation. Contested (C) Orkney and Shetland, 1983. Councillor, Angus DC, 1984– (Leader, Cons. Gp, 1992–). Chm., Dairy Produce Quota Tribunal for Scotland, 1984–; Member: Exec., Angus Tourist Bd, 1984–92; North of Scotland Hydro-Electric Bd, 1985–88; Extra-Parly Panel (Scotland), 1986–; Potato Marketing Bd, 1988–. Dean, Guildry of Brechin, 1993–. *Recreations:* curling, Scottish fiddle music. *Address:* Dalbog, Edzell, Brechin, Angus DD9 7UU; (home) The Gorse, Dunlappie Road, Edzell, Brechin, Angus DD9 7UB. *Clubs:* Farmers'; Brechin Rotary.

MYLLENT, Peter; *see* Hamylton Jones, K.

MYLNE, Nigel James; QC 1984; a Recorder, since 1985; *b* 11 June 1939; *s* of late Harold James Mylne and Dorothy Evelyn Mylne (later D. E. Hogg); *m* 1st, 1967, Julie Phillpotts (marr. diss. 1977); two *s* one *d*; 2nd, 1979, Judith Hamilton; one *s. Educ:* Eton College. National Service, 10th Royal Hussars, 1957–59. Called to the Bar, Middle Temple, 1963. *Recreation:* beekeeping. *Address:* 67 Thurleigh Road, SW12 8TZ. *T:* 0181–673 2200. *Clubs:* White's, Pratt's, Garrick.

MYNERS, Paul; Chairman, Gartmore plc, since 1987; *b* 1 April 1948; *s* of late Thomas Russell Myners and of Carolyn Molly Myners; *m* 1972, Tessa Stanford-Smith (marr. diss. 1990); three *d. Educ:* Truro Sch., Cornwall; Univ. of London Inst. of Educn (BEd). Daily Telegraph, 1970–74; N. M. Rothschild & Sons Ltd, 1974–85 (Dir, 1979); Chief Exec., Gartmore plc, 1985–93. Non-executive Director: English & Scottish Investors plc, 1986–; PowerGen plc, 1990–. Mem., Financial Reporting Council, 1995–. Chm., Assoc. of Investment Trust Cos, 1993–. Member: Adv. Council, LSO; Adv. Bd, Royal Acad. Trust. FRSA 1994. *Recreations:* opera, the countryside. *Address:* 16 Walton Street, SW3 1RE. *Clubs:* City of London, Oriental; Hong Kong.

MYNORS, Sir Richard (Baskerville), 2nd Bt *cr* 1964, of Treago, Co. Hereford; Director of Music, Belmont Abbey School, Hereford, 1988–89; *b* 5 May 1947; *s* of Sir Humphrey Charles Baskerville Mynors, 1st Bt and Lydia Marian (*d* 1992), *d* of Sir Ellis Minns, LittD, FSA, FBA; *S* father, 1989; *m* 1970, Fiona Bridget, *d* of late Rt. Rev. G. E. Reindorp; three *d. Educ:* Marlborough; Royal College of Music (ARCM, ARCO); Corpus Christi Coll., Cambridge (MA). Asst Director of Music, King's School, Macclesfield, 1970–73; Director of Music: Wolverhampton Grammar School, 1973–81; Merchant Taylors' School, Crosby, 1981–88. *Heir:* none. *Address:* Treago, St Weonards, Hereford HR2 8QB. *T:* St Weonards (01981) 580208.

MYRES, Rear-Adm. John Antony Lovell, CB 1993; Hydrographer of the Navy, 1990–94; *b* 11 April 1936; *yr s* of late Dr John Nowell Linton Myres, CBE and Joan Mary Lovell Myres (*née* Stevens); *m* 1965, Alison Anne, *d* of late Lieut David Lawrence Carr, RN and of Mrs James Pertwee; three *s. Educ:* Winchester College. FRICS 1975; FRGS 1993; FRIN 1994. Entered RN 1954; specialised Hydrographic Surveying, 1959; CO HM Ships Woodlark, 1969–71, Fox, 1972–73, Hecla, 1974, 1978–79, 1981–82; Hydrographer, RAustN, 1982–85. Younger Brother of Trinity House, 1990. Freeman, City of London, 1990; Liveryman, Chartered Surveyors' Co., 1990. Guild Burgess of Preston, 1952. *Publications:* articles in professional jls. *Recreations:* naval and medallic history, gardening. *Clubs:* Naval, Royal Navy of 1765 and 1785, Geographical, Antartic.

MYRTLE, Brig. Andrew Dewe, CB 1988; CBE 1979 (MBE 1967); Chief Executive and Secretary, Tennis and Rackets Association, since 1989; *b* 17 Dec. 1932; *s* of Lt-Col John Young Elphinstone Myrtle, DSO, KOSB (killed in action in World War II) and Doreen May Lake; *m* 1973, Mary Rose Ford; two *d. Educ:* Horris Hill Prep. Sch.; Winchester Coll.; RMA, Sandhurst; Army Staff Coll. Co. Comdr, 1 KOSB, 1964–66; Bde Major, 24 Infantry Bde, 1966–68; Co. Comdr, 1 KOSB, 1968–69, CO, 1969–71; MA to Adjt Gen., 1971–74; Comdt, Jun. Div., Staff Coll., 1974–77; Comd 8 Infantry Bde, 1977–79; student, RCDS, 1979; DDMO, MoD, 1980–83; Asst Comdt, RMA, Sandhurst, 1983–85; Comdr Land Forces, Cyprus, 1986–88. ADC to the Queen, 1985–88. *Recreations:* golf, lawn tennis, (Real) tennis, fly-fishing. *Address:* Pen Guen, Stonor, Henley-on-Thames, Oxon RG9 6HB. *Clubs:* Army and Navy, MCC; Huntercombe Golf.

N

NAAS, Lord; Charles Diarmuidh John Bourke; *b* 11 June 1953; *e s* and *heir* of 10th Earl of Mayo, *qv*; *m* 1st, 1975, Marie Antoinette Cronnelly (marr. diss. 1979); one *d*; 2nd, 1985, Marie Veronica Mannion; two *s*. *Educ:* St Aubyn's, Rottingdean; Portora Royal Sch., Enniskillen; QUB; Bolton Street Coll. of Technology, Dublin. *Heir: s* Hon. Richard Thomas Bourke, *b* 7 Dec. 1985. *Address:* Derryinver, Beach Road, Clifden, Co. Galway, Eire.

NABARRO, Prof. Frank Reginald Nunes, MBE 1946; FRS 1971; Professor of Physics, University of the Witwatersrand, 1953–84, now Hon. Professorial Research Fellow; Fellow, South African Council for Scientific and Industrial Research, since 1994; *b* 7 March 1916; *s* of late Stanley Nunes Nabarro and Leah Nabarro; *m* 1948, Margaret Constance, *d* of late James Dalziel, ARAM; three *s* two *d*. *Educ:* Nottingham High Sch.; New Coll., Oxford (MA, BSc). DSc Birmingham. Sen. Exper. Officer, Min. of Supply, 1941–45; Royal Soc. Warren Research Fellow, Univ. of Bristol, 1945–49; Lectr in Metallurgy, Univ. of Birmingham, 1949–53; University of Witwatersrand: Prof. and Head of Dept of Physics, 1953–77, City of Johannesburg Prof. of Physics, 1970–77; Dean, Faculty of Science, 1968–70; Representative of Senate on Council, 1967–77; Deputy Vice-Chancellor, 1978–80. Vis. Prof., Nat. Research Council, Ottawa, 1956; Republic Steel Vis. Prof., Dept of Metallurgy, Case Inst. of Techn., Cleveland, Ohio, 1964–65; Overseas Fellow of Churchill Coll., Cambridge, 1966–67; Gauss Prof., Akademie der Wissenschaften, Göttingen, 1970; Professeur-associé, Univ. Paris-Sud, 1971, Montpellier II, 1973; Vis. Prof., Dept of Material Science, Univ. of Calif., Berkeley, 1977; Vis. Fellow, Robinson Coll., Cambridge, 1981; Vis. Prof., Dept of Materials Engrg, Technion, Haifa, 1983. Hon. Mem., S African Inst. of Physics, 1992 (Vice-Pres., 1956–57); Hon. FRSSAf 1973 (Pres., 1989–92). Hon. DSc: Witwatersrand, 1987; Natal, 1988; Cape Town, 1988. Beilby Memorial Award, 1950; South Africa Medal, 1972; De Beers Gold Medal, 1980; Claude Harris Leon Foundn Award of Merit, 1983; J. F. W. Herschel Medal, 1989; R. F. Mehl Award, 1995. *Publications:* Theory of Crystal Dislocations, 1967, repr. 1987; (jtly) Physics of Creep, 1995; scientific papers, mainly on solid state physics. *Recreation:* gardening. *Address:* 32 Cookham Road, Auckland Park, Johannesburg 2092, South Africa. *T:* (11) 7267745.

NABARRO, Sir John (David Nunes), Kt 1983; MD; FRCP; Consultant Physician, The Middlesex Hospital, London, 1954–81, now Emeritus Consultant Physician; Hon. Research Associate, Departments of Medicine and Biochemistry, University College and Middlesex School of Medicine (formerly Middlesex Hospital Medical School), since 1981; Director, Cobbold Laboratories, Middlesex Hospital Medical School, 1970–81; Hon. Consultant Physician, Royal Prince Alfred Hospital, Sidney, since 1959; *b* 21 Dec. 1915; *s* of David Nunes Nabarro and Florence Nora Nabarro (*née* Webster); *m* 1948, Joan Margaret Cockrell; two *s* two *d*. *Educ:* Oundle Sch.; University Coll., London (Howard Cluff Meml Prize 1935; Fellow, UCL, 1963); University Coll. Hosp. Med. Sch. (Magrath Schol., Atkinson Morley Schol., Atchison Schol., 1938). MD London. Medical Specialist, OC Med. Div., RAMC, 1939–45: served in Iraq; 8th Army, Italy (Salerno Anzio); Middle East (despatches). UCH: House Phys., 1939; Med. Registrar, 1945–47; Res. Asst Phys., 1948–49; First Asst, Med. Unit, UCH Med. Sch., 1950–54; WHO Travelling Fellowship, 1952. Hon. Cons. Endocrinologist to Army, 1965–81. Examiner in Medicine, Univs of Cambridge, London and Sheffield. Chm., Jt Consultants Cttee, 1979–84. Mem., Assoc. of Physicians of GB and Ire., 1952; Pres., Sect. of Endocrinology, RSM, 1968–70; Chm., Med. and Sci. Sects, 1975–77, Chm. Council, 1986–90, Brit. Diabetic Assoc. RCP: Mem. Council, 1954–55; Oliver Sharpey Lectr, 1960; Joseph Senior White Fellow, 1960; Examiner for MRCP, 1964–81; Procensor, 1973; Censor, 1974; Croonian Lectr, 1976; Sen. Censor and First Vice-Pres., 1977. William McIlwrath Guest Prof., Royal Prince Alfred Hosp., Sidney, 1959; John Mathison Shaw Lectr, RCPE, 1963; Guest Visitor, St Vincent's Hosp., Sidney, 1963; Guest Lectr, Postgrad. Cttee, Christchurch Hosps, NZ, 1973; Banting Meml Lectr, Brit. Diabetic Assoc., 1978; Best Meml Lectr, Toronto Diabetes Assoc., 1984. Hon. FRSM 1988. *Publications:* Biochemical Investigations in Diagnosis and Treatment, 1954, 3rd edn, 1962; papers on endocrinology and diabetes in med. jls. *Recreation:* gardening. *Address:* 33 Woodside Avenue, N12 8AT. *T:* 0181–445 7925.

NADER, Ralph; author, lecturer, lawyer; *b* Winsted, Conn, USA, 27 Feb. 1934; *s* of Nadra Nader and Rose (*née* Bouziane). *Educ:* Gilbert Sch., Winsted; Woodrow Wilson Sch. of Public and Internat. Affairs, Princeton Univ. (AB *magna cum laude*); Harvard Univ. Law Sch. (LLB). Admitted to: Bar of Conn, 1958; Bar of Mass, 1959; US Supreme Court Bar, 1963. Served US Army, 1959. Law practice in Hartford, Conn, 1959–; Lectr in History and Govt, Univ. of Hartford, 1961–63; Lectr, Princeton Univ., 1967–68. Member: Amer. Bar Assoc., 1959–; AAAS, 1964–; Phi Beta Kappa. Has pursued actively better consumer protection and improvement in the lot of the American Indian; lobbied in Washington for safer food, drugs, air, water and against nuclear reactors; played very important role in work for passing of: National Traffic and Motor Vehicle Safety Act, 1966; Wholesome Meat Act, 1967; Occupational Safety and Health Act, 1970; Safe Drinking Water Act, 1974; Freedom of Information Act, 1974; National Cooperative Bank Act, 1978. Niemen Fellows Award, 1965–66; named one of the Ten Outstanding Young Men of the Year by US Jun. Chamber of Commerce, 1967. *Publications:* Unsafe at Any Speed: the designed-in dangers of the American automobile, 1965, rev. edn 1991; (jtly) What to do with Your Bad Car, 1971; Working on the System: a manual for citizen's access to federal agencies, 1972; (jtly) Action for a Change, 1972; (jtly) Whistleblowing, 1972; (jtly) You and Your Pension, 1973; (ed) The Consumer and Corporate Accountability, 1973; (co-ed) Corporate Power in America, 1973; (jtly) Taming the Giant Corporation, 1976; (co-ed) Verdicts on Lawyers, 1976; (jtly) Menace of Atomic Energy, 1977; (co-ed) Who's Poisoning America?, 1981; (jtly) The Big Boys: power and position in American business, 1986; (jtly) Winning the Insurance Game, 1990; contrib. articles to many magazines; has weekly syndicated newspaper column. *Address:* PO Box 19367, Washington, DC 20036, USA.

NADESAN, Pararajasingam, CMG 1955; OBE 1954; Governor, Rotary International, District 321; Member, Legislative Council, Rotary International; Director: Cargills (Ceylon) Ltd; Associated Hotels Co. Ltd; Past Chairman: Low Country Products Association; Air Ceylon; *b* 20 Dec. 1917; *s* of Sir Sangarapillai Pararajasingam, and Padmavati, *d* of Sir Ponnambalam Arunachalam; *m* 1st, 1941, Gauri Nair (decd); one *s* one *d*; 2nd, 1953, Kamala Nair; three *d*. *Educ:* Royal College, and Ceylon Univ. Coll.; Univ. of London (BA Hons). Tutor, Ceylon Univ. Coll., 1940; entered Ceylon Civil Service, 1941; held various appts in sphere of provincial administration, 1941–47; Asst Permanent Sec., Min. of Transport and Works, 1948–53; Dir of Civil Aviation in addition to duties as Asst Sec. Min. of Transport and Works, 1954–56; Sec. to the Prime Minister and Information Officer, Ceylon, 1954–56; Member: Ceylon Delegation to the Bandung Conf.; Commonwealth Prime Minister's Conf.; ICAO Gen. Assembly; ILO Cttee on Plantations. Past Mem., Nat. Planning Council. Pres. Emeritus and Life Mem., Ceylon Hotels Assoc.; FHCIMA. FCIT. Past President: Orchid Circle of Ceylon; Sri Lanka Horticultural Soc. Officer Order of Merit (Italy), 1954; Knight Comdr Order of the Crown, Thailand, 1955; Comdr Order of Orange Nassau, Netherlands, 1955; Defence Medal, 1947; Coronation Medal, 1953; Ceylon Armed Services Inauguration Medal, 1956. *Recreations:* golf, tennis, gardening, collecting antiques, stamps and coins. *Address:* 52/1 Flower Road, Colombo 3, Sri Lanka. *T:* 573687. *Clubs:* Colombo, Orient, Rotary (Colombo); Gymkhana.

NAGANO, Kent George; Music Director: Opéra de Lyon, since 1989; Hallé Orchestra, since 1992; *b* 22 Nov. 1951; *s* of George Kimiyoshi Nagano and Ruth Okamoto; *m* Mari Kodama. *Educ:* Univ. of Calif. Has performed with: Boston Symphony Orch., 1984; Paris Opera (World Première, St François d'Assise, by Messiaen); Metropolitan Opera, 1994; Salzburg Fest., 1994; also World Première, Death of Klinghoffer by John Adams, Brussels, Lyon and Vienna. Gramophone Record of Year, 1990; Gramophone Opera Award, 1993; Grammy Award, 1995. *Address:* c/o Van Walsum Management Ltd, 26 Wadham Road, SW15 2LR. *T:* 0181–874 6344, *Fax:* 0181–877 0077.

NAGDA, Kanti; Manager, Sancroft Community Centre, Harrow, since 1982; *b* 1 May 1946; *s* of Vershi Bhoja Nagda and Zaviben Nagda; *m* 1972, Bhagwati Desai; two *s*. *Educ:* City High Sch., Kampala, Uganda; Coll. of Further Educn, Chippenham, Wilts; E African Univ., Uganda. Sec.-Gen., Confedn of Indian Organisations (UK), 1975–; Pres., Nat. Congress of Gujarati Orgns, 1992–. Exec. Cttee Member: Harrow Community Relations Council, 1974–76; Gujarati Literary Acad. (GB), 1976–82. Mem., European Movement. President: Uganda Art Circle, 1968–71; Anglo Indian Circle, 1973–82 and 1985–; Indian Cricket Club, Harrow, 1976–80; Greenford (Willow Tree) Lions Club, 1988–89. Representative: Harrow Youth Council; Brent Youth Council; Harrow Arts Council. Hon. Editorial Consultant, International Asian Guide & Who's Who, 1975–; Asst Editor, Oswal News, 1977–84. *Publications:* Muratiyo Ke Nokar (Gujarati novel), Kenya 1967; stories and articles in newspapers and jls. *Recreations:* cricket, photography. *Address:* 170 Tolcarne Drive, Pinner, Middx HA5 2DR. *T:* 0181–863 9089. *Club:* Indian National.

NAGLE, Terence John, FRICS; Managing Director, Brixton Estate plc, since 1993; *b* 10 Nov. 1942; *s* of Richard and Bridget Nagle; *m* 1974, Elizabeth Mary Millett; two *s* two *d*. *Educ:* Ottershaw Sch. FRICS 1964. Property Dir, Brixton Estate plc, 1984–93. *Recreations:* gardening, tennis, antique restoring. *Address:* Pitch Place House, Worplesdon, Guildford, Surrey GU3 3LQ. *T:* Guildford (01483) 232036.

NAGLER, Neville Anthony; Chief Executive, Board of Deputies of British Jews, since 1991; *b* 2 Jan. 1945; *s* of Gerald and Sylvia Nagler; *m* 1971, Judy Mordant; one *s* one *d*. *Educ:* Christ's Coll., Finchley; Jesus Coll., Cambridge (MA). Asst Principal, HM Treasury, 1967–70; Private Sec. to Chancellor of Exchequer, 1970–71; Principal, 1972; transferred to Home Office, 1975; Asst Sec., Race Relations and Equal Opportunities, 1980–83; Head, Drugs and Extradition Div., 1983–88; Asst Sec., Home Office Finance Div., 1988–91. UK Rep. to UN Commn on Narcotic Drugs, 1983–88; Chm., Council of Europe Pompidou Gp, 1984–88. Haldane Essay Prize, Haldane Soc., 1979; Cert. of Appreciation, US Drug Enforcement Admin, 1988. *Publications:* articles in Public Administration and UN Jl of Narcotic Drugs. *Recreations:* wine-making, listening to music, theatre, walking. *Address:* Woburn House, Tavistock Square, WC1H 0EZ. *T:* 0171–387 3952.

NAILATIKAU, Brig.-Gen. Ratu Epeli, LVO 1977; OBE 1979; MSD 1988; Ambassador of the Republic of Fiji to the Court of St James's, since 1988; concurrently Ambassador to Denmark, Germany, Israel, the Holy See and Egypt; *b* 5 July 1941; *s* of Ratu Sir Edward Cakobau, KBE, MC, ED and Adi Lady Vasamaca Tuiburelevn; *m* 1981, Adi Koila Nailatikau (*née* Mara), *d* of Ratu Sir Kamisese Mara, *qv*; one *s* one *d*. *Educ:* Levuka Public Sch.; Queen Victoria Sch., Fiji; Wadham Coll., Oxford. Enlisted in Royal Fiji Military Forces, 1962; commnd Fiji Infantry Regt, 1963; seconded to First Bn, Royal NZ Infantry Regt, Malaysia and Borneo, 1966; ADC to Governor of Fiji, 1968–69; Foreign Service Course, Oxford Univ., 1969–70; Second Secretary: Fiji High Commn, Canberra, 1970–72; Fiji Mission to UN, 1973–74; Australian Army Staff Coll., Queenscliffe, 1976 (psc); CO Fiji Bn, Fiji Infantry Regt serving with UNIFIL, 1978–79; Jt Services Staff Coll., Canberra, Australia, 1980 (jssc); Sen. Plans Officer, UNIFIL HQ, 1981; CS, 1981–82, Comdr, 1982–87, Royal Fiji Mil. Forces. Fiji Equerry: to the Prince of Wales during Fiji Independence visit, 1970; to the Queen during Jubilee visit, 1977. OStJ 1985. *Recreations:* golf, tennis. *Address:* Embassy of the Republic of Fiji, 34 Hyde Park Gate, SW7 5DN. *T:* 0171–584 3661.

NAILOR, Prof. Peter; Provost of Gresham College, since 1988; *b* 16 Dec. 1928; *o s* of Leslie Nailor and Lily Matilda (*née* Jones). *Educ:* Mercers' Sch.; Wadham Coll., Oxford (BA 1952, MA 1955). Home Civil Service, 1952; Asst Principal, Admiralty, 1952; First Lord's Representative on Admiralty Interview Bd, 1960–62; Polaris Executive, 1962–67; Asst Sec., MoD, 1967–69; Professor of Politics, Univ. of Lancaster, 1969–77; Prof. of Hist., 1977–88, Dean, 1982–84 and 1986–88, RNC, Greenwich. Visiting research appts and professorships in Canada, Australia and India; Member: Political Science Cttee, SSRC, 1975–81; FCO adv. panel on arms control and disarmament, 1975–88; MoD adv. panel on historical records, 1979–88; Chairman, British International Studies Assoc., 1983–86. *Publications:* (ed) The Soviet Union and the Third World, 1981; The Nassau Connection, 1988; Learning from Precedent in Whitehall, 1991; articles in learned jls, pamphlets. *Address:* Gresham College, Barnard's Inn Hall, Holborn EC1N 2HH.

NAIPAUL, Sir Vidiadhar Surajprasad, (Sir Vidia), Kt 1990; author; *b* 17 Aug. 1932; *m* 1955, Patricia Ann Hale. *Educ:* Queen's Royal Coll., Trinidad; University Coll., Oxford (Hon. Fellow, 1983). Hon. Dr Letters Columbia Univ., NY, 1981; Hon. LittD: Cambridge, 1983; London, 1988; Oxford, 1992. British Literature Prize, 1993. *Publications:* The Middle Passage, 1962; An Area of Darkness, 1964; The Loss of El Dorado, 1969; The Overcrowded Barracoon, and other articles, 1972; India: a wounded civilization, 1977; The Return of Eva Perón, 1980; Among the Believers, 1981; Finding the Centre, 1984; A Turn in the South, 1989; India: a million mutinies now, 1990; *novels:* The Mystic Masseur, 1957 (John Llewelyn Rhys Memorial Prize, 1958); The Suffrage of Elvira, 1958; Miguel Street, 1959 (Somerset Maugham Award, 1961); A House for Mr Biswas, 1961; Mr Stone and the Knights Companion, 1963 (Hawthornden Prize, 1964); The Mimic Men, 1967 (W. H. Smith Award, 1968); A Flag on the Island, 1967; In a Free State, 1971 (Booker Prize, 1971); Guerrillas, 1975; A Bend in the River, 1979; The Enigma of Arrival, 1987; A Way in the World, 1994. *Address:* c/o Aitken & Stone Ltd, 29 Fernshaw Road, SW10 0TG.

NAIR, Chengara Veetil Devan; President of Singapore, 1981–85; *b* Malacca, Malaysia, 5 Aug. 1923; *s* of Karunakaran Illath Vayalakkara and Devaki Chengara Veetil Nair; *m* 1953, Avadai Dhanam Lakshimi; three *s* one *d*. *Educ:* Victoria Sch., Singapore. Teacher, St Andrew's Sch., 1949–51; Gen. Sec., Singapore Teachers' Union, 1949–51; Convenor, and Mem. Central Exec. Cttee, People's Action Party, 1954–56; Political Sec., Min. of Education, 1959–60; Chm., Singapore Adult Educn Bd, 1961–64; National Trades Union Congress: Sec. Gen., 1962–65, 1969–79; Dir, Res. Unit, 1969–81; Pres., 1979–81; Pres., Asian Regl Orgn, ICFTU, 1976–81. MP Malaysia, 1964–69, Singapore, 1979–81; first Sec. Gen., Democratic Action Party, Malaysia, 1964–69. Member: Nat. Wages Council, 1972–81; Housing and Develt Bd, 1975–81; Presidential Council for Minority Rights, 1979–81; Chm., Singapore Labour Foundn, 1977–81. Mem. Council, Nat. Univ. of Singapore, 1980–81; Chm., Hindu Adv. Bd, 1981. Life Member: Singapore Cancer Soc.; Ramakrishna Mission; Sri Aurobindo Soc. Hon. DLitt Nat. Univ. of Singapore, 1976. *Publications:* (ed) Who Lives if Malaysia Dies?, 1969; (ed) Singapore: Socialism that Works, 1976; (ed) Tomorrow: the peril and the promise, 1976; (ed) Asian Labour and the Dynamics of Change, 1977; (ed) Not by Wages Alone, 1982. *Address:* 1107 Graywell Drive, Bloomington, Ind 47401, USA.

NAIRN, Margaret, RGN, SCM; Chief Area Nursing Officer, Greater Glasgow Health Board, 1974–84; *b* 20 July 1924; *d* of James R. Nairn and Anne G. Nairn. *Educ:* Aberdeen Academy. Nurse Training: general: Aberdeen Royal Infirmary, to 1945 (RGN); midwifery: Aberdeen Maternity Hosp., until 1948 (State Certified Midwife); Health Visitors: Aberdeen Coll. for Health Visitors, until 1952 (Health Visitors Cert.); administrative: Royal Coll. of Nursing, London, to 1959 (Nursing Admin. Cert.); 6 months study in USA as British Commonwealth and Empire Nurses Scholar, 1956. Ward Sister and Night Supt, Aberdeen Maternity Hosp., 1945–52; Director of Nursing Services in Aberdeen and Glasgow, 1952–74. *Publications:* articles in medical and nursing press: A Study of 283 Families with Rent Arrears; Liaison Services between Hospital and Community Nursing Services; Health Visitors in General Practice. *Recreations:* reading, gardening, swimming, travel. *Address:* 12 Countesswells Terrace, Aberdeen AB1 8LQ.

NAIRN, Martin John L.; *see* Lambie-Nairn.

NAIRN, Sir Michael, 4th Bt *cr* 1904; *b* 1 July 1938; *s* of Sir Michael George Nairn, 3rd Bt, TD, and of Helen Louise, *yr d* of Major E. J. W. Bruce, Melbourne, Aust.; *S* father, 1984; *m* 1st, 1972, Diana (*d* 1982), *er d* of Leonard Bligh, NSW; two *s* one *d*; 2nd, 1986, Sally Jane, *d* of Major W. P. S. Hastings. *Educ:* Eton; INSEAD. *Heir: s* Michael Andrew Nairn, *b* 2 Nov. 1973. *Club:* Caledonian.

NAIRN, Sir Robert Arnold S.; *see* Spencer-Nairn.

NAIRNE, Lady (12th in line, of the Lordship *cr* 1681); **Katherine Evelyn Constance Bigham;** *b* 22 June 1912; *d* of 6th Marquess of Lansdowne and Elizabeth (she *m* 2nd, Lord Colum Crichton-Stuart, who *d* 1957; she *d* 1964); *S* to brother's Lordship of Nairne, 1944; *m* 1933, Hon. Edward Bigham (later 3rd Viscount Mersey, who *d* 1979); three *s*. *Heir: s* Viscount Mersey, *qv*. *Address:* Bignor Park, Pulborough, W Sussex RH20 1HG. *T:* Sutton (Sussex) (017987) 214.

NAIRNE, Alexander Robert, (Sandy); Director, Public and Regional Services, Tate Gallery, since 1994; *b* 8 June 1953; *s* of Rt Hon. Sir Patrick Nairne, *qv*; partner since 1981, Sylvia Elizabeth (Lisa) Tickner; one *s* one *d*. *Educ:* Radley Coll.; University Coll., Oxford (BA Modern History and Economics 1974; MA). Asst Dir, Museum of Modern Art, Oxford, 1974–76; Research Asst and Asst Keeper, Tate Gallery, 1976–79; Dir of Exhibitions, Inst. of Contemporary Arts, 1980–83; writer and associate producer, State of the Art, TV series, Channel 4, 1985–87; Dir of Visual Arts, Arts Council, 1987–92; Sen. Res. Fellow, Getty Grant Prog., 1992–93. *Publication:* State of the Art, 1987. *Recreation:* punting. *Address:* 43 Lady Somerset Road, NW5 1TY. *T:* 0171–485 7992, *Fax:* 0171–267 2652. *Clubs:* Chelsea Arts; Leander (Henley).

NAIRNE, Rt. Hon. Sir Patrick (Dalmahoy), GCB 1981 (KCB 1975; CB 1971); MC 1943; PC 1982; Master, St Catherine's College, Oxford, 1981–88 (Hon. Fellow, 1988); Chancellor, Essex University, since 1983; *b* 15 Aug. 1921; *s* of late Lt-Col C. S. and Mrs E. D. Nairne; *m* 1948, Penelope Chauncy Bridges, *d* of Lt-Col R. F. and Mrs L. C. Bridges; three *s* three *d*. *Educ:* Radley Coll.; University Coll., Oxford (Exhibr; Hon. Fellow, 1981). Seaforth Highlanders, 1941–45 (Capt.). 1st cl. hons Mod. Hist. (Oxon), 1947. Entered Civil Service and joined Admty, Dec. 1947; Private Sec. to First Lord of Admty, 1958–60; Asst Sec., 1960; Private Sec. to Sec. of State for Defence, 1965–67; Assistant Under-Sec. of State (Logistics), MoD, 1967–70; Dep. Under-Sec. of State, MoD, 1970–73; Second Perm. Sec., Cabinet Office, 1973–75; Perm. Sec., DHSS, 1975–81. Mem., Falkland Isles Review Cttee, 1982; Govt Monitor, Hong Kong, 1984. Central Independent TV: Mem. Bd, 1990–92; Dep. Chm., 1986–90, Chm., 1990–92, W Regl Bd. Church Comr, 1993–; Chairman: Irene Wellington Educnl Trust, 1987–; Adv. Bd, Oxford Mus. of Modern Art, 1988–; Nuffield Council on Bioethics, 1991–; Pres., Oxfordshire Craft Guild, 1993–; Vice-President: Soc. for Italic Handwriting, 1987– (Chm., 1981–87); Oxford Art Soc., 1990–; Trustee: Nat. Maritime Museum, 1981–91; Joseph Rowntree Foundn; Nat. AIDS Trust; Member: Radley Coll. Council, 1975–; Council, Ditchley Foundn, 1988–; President: Assoc. of CS Art Clubs, 1976–89; Radleian Soc., 1980–83; Seamen's Hosp. Soc. FRSA 1978. Hon. LLD: Leicester, 1980; St Andrews, 1984; DU Essex, 1983. *Recreations:* watercolour painting, calligraphy. *Address:* Yew Tree, Chilson, near Charlbury, Chipping Norton, Oxon OX7 3HU. *Club:* United Oxford & Cambridge University (Trustee, 1989–95).

See also A. R. Nairne.

NAIRNE, Sandy; *see* Nairne, A. R.

NAIROBI, Archbishop of, (RC), since 1971; **HE Cardinal Maurice Otunga;** *b* Jan. 1923. Priest, 1950; Titular Bishop of Tacape, 1957; Bishop of Kisii, 1960; Titular Archbishop of Bomarzo, 1969; Cardinal 1973. *Address:* Archbishop's House, PO Box 14231, Nairobi, Kenya.

NAISH, Sir (Charles) David, Kt 1994; DL; FRAgS; President, National Farmers' Union, since 1991; *b* 28 July 1940; *s* of Charles Naish and Muriel (*née* Turner); *m* 1966, Victoria Cockburn Mattock; two *s* one *d*. *Educ:* Worksop Coll.; RAC, Cirencester (MRAC). Jt Man.-Dir, J. B. Eastwood Ltd, 1969–73; Chm., Thornhill Country Produce Ltd, 1982–85. Dep. Pres., NFU, 1985–91. Pres., COPA, 1995–. FRAgS 1986; FRSA 1992. DL Notts, 1991. *Recreations:* shooting, vintage motor cars, golf. *Address:* South Farm, Budby, Newark, Notts NG22 9EX. *T:* Mansfield (01623) 822436. *Club:* Farmers' (Chm., 1980).

NAISH, Peter; Chief Executive, Equal Opportunities Commission, since 1994; *b* 24 Jan. 1945; *s* of Frederick and Ida Naish; *m* 1970, Janet Kemp (separated 1983); one *s* two *d*. *Educ:* Hampton Grammar Sch.; King's Coll., London. Area Manager, Notting Hill Housing Trust, 1970–73; Chief Executive: Irwell Valley Housing Assoc., 1973–77; English Churches' Housing Gp, 1971–89; Research and Development for Psychiatry, 1989–91; CLS Care Services, 1991–94. *Recreations:* walking, music, poetry. *Address:* Equal Opportunities Commission, Overseas House, Quay Street, Manchester M3 3HN.

NAKAJIMA, Hiroshi, MD, PhD; Director-General of the World Health Organization, since 1988; *b* Japan, 16 May 1928; *m* Martha Ann (*née* De Witt); two *s*. *Educ:* Nat. Sen. High Sch., Urawa; Tokyo Med. Coll. (MD 1955; PhD 1960); Faculty of Medicine, Univ. of Paris. Research, Nat. Inst. of Health and Med. Res., Paris, 1958–67; Dir of Res. and Admin, Nippon Roche Res. Centre, Tokyo, 1967–73; Scientist, Evaluation and Control of Drugs, 1973–76, Chief, Drug Policies and Management, 1976–79, WHO HQ, Geneva; Regional Dir, Western Pacific Region, WHO, 1979–88. Vis. Prof. in Public Health, Tokyo Med. Coll., 1987; Vis. Prof., Univ. of Tokyo, 1991. Corresp. Mem., Acad. de Pharmacie, France, 1988; Assoc. Foreign Mem., Acad. Nat. de Médecine de France, 1989; Hon. Mem., Japanese Pharmacological Soc., 1990; FCPS(Pak) 1990; Hon. Foreign Mem., Acad. Royale de Médecine de Belgique, 1991. DM (*hc*) Med. Univ., Ulan Bator, Mongolia, 1991. Kojima Prize, Japan, 1984; Okamoto Award, Japan, 1989. Order of Merit (Poland), 1990; Chevalier de la Légion d'Honneur (France), 1991; Commandeur, Ordre Nat. du Lion (Senegal), 1991. *Publications:* articles and reviews in Japanese, French and English pubns. *Address:* World Health Organization, 20 avenue Appia, 1211 Geneva 27, Switzerland. *T:* 7912111.

NAKASONE, Yasuhiro; Prime Minister of Japan, 1982–87; Chairman and President, International Institute for Global Peace, since 1988; *b* 27 May 1918; 2nd *s* of Matsugoroh Nakasone; *m* 1945, Tsutako Kobayashi; one *s* two *d*. *Educ:* Faculty of Law, Imperial Univ. (graduate). Joined Min. of Home Affairs, 1941; commd as Lt-Comdr, 1945. Elected to House of Representatives (first of 15 consecutive times), 1947; Minister of State, Dir-Gen. of Science and Technology Agency, 1959–60; Minister of Transport, 1967–68; Minister of State, Dir-Gen. of Defence Agency, 1970–71; Minister of Internat. Trade and Industry, 1972–74; Minister of State for Admin. Management Agency, 1980–82. Chm. Exec. Council, 1971–72, Sec. Gen., 1974–76, Liberal Democratic Party. Hon. DHL, Johns Hopkins, 1984. Médaille de la Chancellerie, Univs of Paris. *Publications:* The Ideals of Youth, 1947; Japan Speaks, 1954, The New Conservatism, 1978; Human Cities—a proposal for the 21st century, 1980. *Address:* 3-22-7, Kamikifazawa, Setagaya-ku, Tokyo, Japan.

NALL, Sir Michael (Joseph), 2nd Bt *cr* 1954; Vice Lord-Lieutenant of Nottinghamshire, 1989–91; *b* 6 Oct. 1921, *er s* of Colonel Sir Joseph Nall, 1st Bt; *S* father, 1958; *m* 1951, Angela Loveday Hanbury, *e d* of Air Chief Marshal Sir Alec Coryton, KCB, KBE, MVO, DFC; two *s*. *Educ:* Wellington College, Berks. Joined Royal Navy, 1939. Served War of 1939–45 (at sea); psc(mil.) 1949; Lt-Comdr, 1950–61, retired. General Manager, Guide Dogs for the Blind Association, 1961–64. Pres., Nottingham Chamber of Commerce and Industry, 1972–74. DL Notts, 1970; High Sheriff, Notts, 1971. Chairman: Notts Scout Assoc., 1968–88 (Silver Acorn, 1979; Silver Wolf, 1989); Papplewick Pumping Station Trust, 1974–. *Recreations:* field sports, flying. *Heir: s* Edward William Joseph Nall, *b* 24 Oct. 1952. *Address:* Hoveringham Hall, Nottingham NG14 7JR.

NALL-CAIN, family name of **Baron Brocket.**

NAMALIU, Rt. Hon. Rabbie Langanai, CMG 1979; PC 1989; MP for Kokopo (Pangu Pati), Papua New Guinea, since 1982; Speaker of National Parliament, Papua New Guinea, since 1994; *b* 3 April 1947; *s* of Darius Namaliu and Utul Ioan; *m* 1978, Margaret Nakikus; two *s*, and one step *d*. *Educ:* Univ. of Papua New Guinea (BA); Univ. of Victoria, BC (MA). Senior Tutor, later Lectr in History, Univ. of Papua New Guinea, 1973; Principal Private Sec. to Chief Minister (Hon. Michael Somare), 1974–75; Vis. Pacific Fellow, Centre for Pacific Studies, Univ. of California, Santa Cruz, 1975; Provincial Comr, East New Britain Province, 1976; Chm., Public Services Commn, 1976–79; Exec. Officer to Leader of the Opposition (Rt Hon. Michael Somare), 1980–81; Minister for Foreign Affairs and Trade, 1982–84, for Primary Industry, 1985; Dep. Leader, 1985–88, Leader, 1988–92, Pangu Pati; Prime Minister, PNG, 1988–92. Hon. LLD Univ. of Victoria, BC, 1983. *Recreations:* swimming, walking, reading. *Address:* PO Box 6655, Boroko, National Capital District, Papua New Guinea.

NANDY, Dipak; Head of Equal Opportunities, Social Services Department, Nottinghamshire County Council, since 1992; *b* 21 May 1936; *s* of B. C. Nandy and Leela Nandy; *m* 1st, 1964, Margaret Gracie (decd); 2nd, 1972, Hon. Luise Byers (marr. diss. 1991); two *d*. *Educ:* St Xavier's Coll., Calcutta; Univ. of Leeds BA 1st Cl. Hons English Literature, 1960; C. E. Vaughan Research Fellowship, 1960–62. Lectr, English Literature, Univ. of Leicester, 1962–66; Lectr and Fellow of Rutherford College, Univ. of Kent at Canterbury, 1966–68; founder-Director, The Runnymede Trust, 1968–73; Vis. Fellow, Adlai Stevenson Inst. of International Affairs, Chicago, 1970–73; Research Fellow, Social and Community Planning Research, 1973–75; Dep. Chief Exec., Equal Opportunities Commn, 1976–86; Chief Exec., Intermediate Technology Develt Gp, 1986–88; Hon. Lectr in Social Policy, Univ. of Birmingham, 1989–; Financial and Admin. Dir, RSP, Queen Elizabeth House, Oxford, 1991. Member: Cttee of Inquiry into Future of Broadcasting, 1974–77; Council, Nat. Assoc. Citizens' Advice Bureaux, 1983–86; BBC: Chm., Asian Programmes Adv. Cttee, 1983–88; Mem., General Adv. Council. Member: Council, Northern Chamber Orch., 1980–84; Royal Nat. Theatre Bd, 1992–; Governor, BFI, 1984–87. Trustee, CSV, 1981–91. Hon. Liaison, Employment and Labour Law

Sect., Amer. Bar Assoc., 1980–. *Publications:* numerous essays in books, periodicals and newspapers on literature, political thought, race relations, urban problems, equality for women, broadcasting policy and development issues. *Recreations:* collecting records, opera, computing. *Club:* National Liberal.

NANKIVELL, Owen; JP; economic and business consultant; Executive Director, Hinksey Centre, since 1982; *b* 6 April 1927; *s* of John Hamilton Nankivell and Sarah Ann Mares; *m* 1956, Mary Burman Earnshaw; one *s* two *d*. *Educ:* Torquay Grammar Sch.; Univ. of Manchester. BA (Econ) 1951, MA (Econ) 1963. FRSS. Admty, 1951–52; Colonial Office, 1952–55; Central Statistical Office, 1955–65; DEA, 1965–69; HM Treasury, 1969–72; Asst Dir, Central Statistical Office, 1972–79; Gp Chief Economist, Lucas Industries, 1979–82. JP Worcester, 1983–89, Torbay, 1989. *Publications:* All Good Gifts, 1978; Economics, Society and Values, 1995. *Recreations:* Christian, tennis, choral music, singing. *Address:* 18 Ash Hill Road, Torquay TQ1 3HZ. *T:* Torquay (01803) 297719.

NAPIER, family name of **Lord Napier and Ettrick** and **Baron Napier of Magdala.**

NAPIER, 14th Lord, *cr* 1627 (Scotland), **AND ETTRICK,** 5th Baron, *cr* 1872 (UK); **Francis Nigel Napier,** KCVO 1992 (CVO 1985; LVO 1980); DL; a Bt of Nova Scotia, 1666, 11th Bt of Thirlestane; Major, Scots Guards (Reserve of Officers); Private Secretary, Comptroller and Equerry to HRH the Princess Margaret, Countess of Snowdon, since 1973; *b* 5 Dec. 1930; *e s* of 13th Baron Napier and 4th Ettrick, TD, and Muir (*d* 1992), *e d* of Sir Percy Newson, Bt; *S* father 1954; *m* 1958, Delia Mary, *yr d* of A. D. B. Pearson; two *s* two *d*. *Educ:* Eton; RMA, Sandhurst. Commissioned, 1950; served Malaya, 1950–51 (invalided); Adjt 1st Bn Scots Guards, 1955–57. Equerry to His late Royal Highness The Duke of Gloucester, 1958–60, retd, 1960. Deputy Ceremonial and Protocol Secretary, CRO, 1962–66; Purple Staff Officer at State Funeral of Sir Winston Churchill, 1966. A Cons. Whip, House of Lords, 1970–71. On behalf of HM The Queen, handed over Instruments of Independence to Tuvalu (formerly Ellice Is), 1978. Member: Royal Co. of Archers (Queen's Body Guard for Scotland), 1953–; Exec. Cttee, Standing Council of the Baronetage, 1985–; Standing Council of Scottish Chiefs. Pres., St John Ambulance Assoc. and Brigade for County of London, 1975–83. DL Selkirkshire, 1974, Ettrick and Lauderdale, 1975–. Freeman, City of London; Liveryman, Worshipful Company of Grocers. Hon. DLitt Napier Univ., 1993. KStJ 1991 (CStJ 1988). *Heir: s* Master of Napier, *qv*. *Address:* Nottingham Cottage, Kensington Palace, W8 4PU; (seat) Thirlestane, Ettrick, Selkirkshire. *Clubs:* White's, Pratt's; Royal Caledonian Hunt (Edinburgh).

NAPIER OF MAGDALA, 6th Baron *cr* 1868; **Robert Alan Napier;** *b* 6 Sept. 1940; *s* of 5th Baron Napier of Magdala, OBE, and of Elizabeth Marian, *y d* of E. H. Hunt, FRCS; *S* father, 1987; *m* 1964, Frances Clare, *d* of late Alan Frank Skinner; one *s* one *d*. *Educ:* Winchester College; St John's Coll., Cambridge (BA 1st cl. Hons 1962; MA 1966). *Heir: s* Hon. James Robert Napier, *b* 29 Jan. 1966. *Address:* The Coach House, Kingsbury Street, Marlborough, Wilts SN8 1HU. *T:* Marlborough (01672) 512333. *Club:* Leander (Henley-on-Thames).

NAPIER, Master of; Hon. Francis David Charles Napier; with Heath Bloodstock (formerly Heath Fielding (Bloodstock)) Ltd, since 1992; *b* 3 Nov. 1962; *s* and *heir* of 14th Lord Napier (and 5th Baron Ettrick), *qv*; *m* 1993, Zara Jane, *o d* of Hugh McCalmont, Newmarket, Suffolk. *Educ:* Stanbridge Earls School; South Thames Coll., Wandsworth, 1986–87 (City and Guilds Computer Diploma). With a Lloyd's agency, 1984–92. *Recreations:* travelling, horse-racing, motorcycling, squash. *Address:* 23 Poyntz Road, SW11 5PH. *Clubs:* Turf, Pratt's.

NAPIER, Sir Charles Joseph, 6th Bt *cr* 1867, of Merrion Square, Dublin; *b* 15 April 1973; *o s* of Sir Robin Surtees Napier, 5th Bt and of Jennifer Beryl, *d* of H. Warwick Daw; *S* father, 1994. *Heir: uncle* John Lennox Napier [*b* 25 Jan. 1934; *m* 1967, Cecily Mary, *d* of late Arthur Mortimer; one *s* one *d*].

NAPIER, John; stage designer; *b* 1 March 1944; *s* of James Edward Thomas Napier and Lorrie Napier (*née* Godbold); *m* 1st, Andreane Neofitou; one *s* one *d*; 2nd, Donna King, one *s* one *d*. *Educ:* Hornsey Coll. of Art; Central Sch. of Arts and Crafts. Designed 1st production, A Penny for a Song, Pheonix, Leicester, 1967; *London productions:* Fortune and Men's Eyes, 1968; The Ruling Class, The Fun War, Muzeeka, George Frederick (ballet), La Turista, 1969; Cancer, Isabel's a Jezebel, 1970; Mister, The Foursome, The Lovers of Viorne, Lear, 1971; Jump, Sam Sam, Big Wolf, 1972; The Devils (ENO), Equus, The Party, 1973; Knuckle, 1974; Kings and Clowns, The Travelling Music Show, 1978; The Devils of Loudon, Lohengrin (Covent Garden); King John, Richard II, Cymbeline, Macbeth, Richard III, 1974; Hedda Gabler, 1975; Much Ado About Nothing, The Comedy of Errors, King Lear, Macbeth, 1976; A Midsummer Night's Dream, As You Like It, 1977; The Merry Wives of Windsor, Twelfth Night, Three Sisters, Once in a Lifetime, 1979; The Greeks, Nicholas Nickleby (SWET award, Tony Award), 1980; Cats (Tony award), 1981; Henry IV Parts I and II, Peter Pan, 1982; Macbeth (Covent Garden), 1983; Starlight Express, 1984 (Tony Award, 1987); Les Misérables, 1985 (Tony Award, 1987); Time, 1986; Miss Saigon, 1989; Children of Eden, 1990; Trelawny of the 'Wells', 1993; Sunset Boulevard, 1993; Burning Blue, 1995; *Glyndebourne:* Idomeneo, 1983; *USA:* Siegfried & Roy Show (Las Vegas; also co-dir), 1990; film designs incl. Hook, 1991; numerous designs for stage productions in Europe, Japan, Australia, USA and for TV. *Recreation:* photography. *Address:* c/o MLR, 200 Fulham Road, SW10.

NAPIER, Sir John Archibald Lennox, 14th Bt *cr* 1627 (NS), of Merchistoun; *b* 6 Dec. 1946; *s* of Sir William Archibald Napier, 13th Bt and of Kathleen Mabel, *d* of late Reginald Greaves; *S* father, 1990; *m* 1969, Erica, *d* of late Kurt Kingsfield; one *s* one *d*. *Educ:* St Stithians; Witwatersrand Univ., Johannesburg. MSc(Eng); PhD. *Heir: s* Hugh Robert Lennox Napier, *b* 1 Aug. 1977. *Address:* Merchistoun, PO Box 65177, Benmore 2010, South Africa.

NAPIER, Maj.-Gen. Lennox Alexander Hawkins, CB 1983; OBE 1970; MC 1957; DL; General Officer Commanding Wales, 1980–83, retired; Inspector of Public Inquiries, since 1983; *b* 28 June 1928; *s* of Major Charles McNaughton Napier and D. C. Napier; *m* 1959, Jennifer Dawn Wilson; one *s* two *d*. *Educ:* Radley; RMA Sandhurst. Joined Army, 1946; commnd into South Wales Borderers, 1948; commanded 1st Bn S Wales Borderers and 1st Bn Royal Regt of Wales, 1967–70; Instructor, JSSC, 1970–72; served Min. of Defence, 1972–74; Brigade Commander, Berlin Infantry Bde, 1974–76; Prince of Wales's Division: Divisional Brigadier, 1976–80; Col Commandant, 1980–83; Col, The Royal Regt of Wales, 1983–89; Hon. Col, Cardiff Univ. OTC, 1985–92. Gwent: DL 1983; High Sheriff 1988. *Recreations:* shooting, riding. *Address:* c/o Barclays Bank, Monmouth, Gwent. *Club:* Lansdowne.

NAPIER, Rev. Michael Scott; Priest of the London Oratory, since 1959; *b* 15 Feb. 1929; *s* of Maj.-Gen. Charles Scott Napier, CB, CBE and Ada Kathleen Napier (*née* Douetil). *Educ:* Wellington Coll.; Trinity Hall, Cambridge (MA). Ordained priest, 1959; Superior of London Oratory, 1969–81, 1991–94; Visitor or Delegate of Holy See for Oratory of St Philip Neri, 1982–94. *Recreations:* art and architecture, history, travel. *Address:* The Oratory, SW7 2RP. *T:* 0171–589 4811. *Clubs:* Athenæum, Chelsea Arts.

NAPIER, Sir Oliver John, Kt 1985; Senior Partner, Napier & Sons, Solicitors; Chairman, Standing Advisory Commission on Human Rights, 1988–92; *b* 11 July 1935; *e s* of James J. and Sheila Napier; *m* 1961, Brigid (*née* Barnes); three *s* five *d* (and one *s* decd). *Educ:* Ballycruttle Public Elem. Sch., Downpatrick; St Malachy's Coll., Belfast; Queen's Univ., Belfast (LLB). Qual. Solicitor, NI, 1959; Lectr and Mem. Bd of Examrs, Incorp. Law Soc. of NI, 1965–71. Mem. Exec., Ulster Liberal Party, 1962–69; Founder Mem., New Ulster Movt, 1969; Founder Mem., Alliance Party, 1970, Leader 1973–84, Pres., 1989–92. Mem. (Alliance), E Belfast, NI Assembly, 1973–75; Minister of Legal Affairs, NI Executive, Jan.–May 1974; Mem. (Alliance), N Ireland Constitutional Convention for E Belfast, 1975–76; Mem. (Alliance) Belfast E, NI Assembly, 1982–86. Contested (Alliance), E Belfast, 1979, 1983. Councillor for E Belfast, Belfast CC, 1977–89. Member: Lawyers Insolvency Assoc., 1991–; Council, Soc. of Practitioners of Insolvency, 1993–. *Recreations:* many and varied. *Address:* 83 Victoria Road, Holywood, Co. Down BT18 9BG; Napier & Sons, 1–9 Castle Arcade, Belfast BT1 5DF.

NAPIER, Robert Stewart; Group Managing Director, since 1987, Chief Executive, since 1991, Redland; *b* 21 July 1947; *s* of Andrew Napier and Lilian V. Napier (*née* Ritchie); *m* 1977, Patricia Stewart; one *d*. *Educ:* Sedbergh School; Sidney Sussex College, Cambridge (BA 1969; MA 1971); Harvard Business School (AMP 1987). RTZ Corp., 1969–73; Brandts, 1973–75; Fisons, 1975–81; Redland: Finance Dir, 1981–87; Managing Dir, 1987–. Dir, United Biscuits (Hldgs), 1992–. *Recreations:* hill walking, shooting, escaping to Scotland, the works of John Buchan. *Address:* Redland House, Reigate, Surrey RH2 0SJ. *T:* Reigate (01737) 242488.

NAPOLITAN, Leonard, CB 1970; Director of Economics and Statistics, Ministry of Agriculture, Fisheries and Food, 1965–77; *b* 9 April 1919; *s* of Domenic and Rose G. Napolitan; *m* 1945, Dorothy Laycock; two *d*. *Educ:* Univ. of London (BSc Econ. 1944); LSE (MSc Econ. 1946). Asst Agric. Economist, Univ. of Bristol, 1947–48; joined Min. of Agric. and Fisheries as Agric. Economist, 1948. Pres., Agric. Econs Soc., 1974–75. FRSA 1984. *Address:* 4 Rectory Gardens, Burway Road, Church Stretton, Shropshire SY6 6DP.

NAPPER, John (Pelham); painter; *b* London, 17 Sept. 1916; *e s* of late John Mortimer Napper and late Dorothy Charlotte (*née* Hill); *m* 1st, 1935, Hedvig Sophie Armour; 2nd, 1945, Pauline Davidson. *Educ:* Frensham Heights, Surrey and privately; Dundee Sch. of Art; Royal Acad. Schs of Art. Served War of 1939–45: commnd RA, 1941; Ceylon, 1942, War Artist to Ceylon comd, 1943–44; seconded to RNVR, 1944, E Africa, 1944; demobilised, 1945. Taught life painting at St Martin's Sch. of Art, London, 1949–57. Lived in France, 1957–70. One-man exhibitions: Leicester Galleries, London, 1949, 1961, 1962; The Adams Gallery, London, 1957 and 1959; La Maison de la Pensée Française, Paris, 1960; Galerie Lahumière, Paris, 1963; Galleries Hervé and Lahumière, Paris, 1965; Larcada Gallery, New York, 1968, 1970, 1972, 1975, 1977; Browse and Darby Gall., 1978, 1980; Ludlow Fest., 1985, 1994; Thos Agnew and Sons, 1986; Albemarle Gall., 1988, 1990, 1991; Gillian Jason Gall., London, 1993; Ludlow Fest., 1994; retrospective exhibitions: Walker Art Gall., Liverpool, 1959; Oldham Art Gall., 1984; Machynlleth Art Centre, 1993. Paintings acquired by: BM; Contemp. Art Soc.; Courtauld Inst.; Fitzwilliam Mus.; Walker Art Gall., Liverpool; Musée d'Art Moderne, Paris; Mus. of Art, Tel Aviv; Musée Municipale, Dieppe; Nat. Gall., Kenya; Columbus Gall. of Fine Arts, Ohio, and other public and pvte collections. Vis. Prof. of Fine Arts, Southern Illinois Univ., USA, 1968–69. Médaille d'argent, Salon des Artistes françaises, Paris, 1947; Awarded prize at International Exhibition of Fine Arts, Moscow, 1957; Awarded International Assoc. of Art Critics Prize, 1961. *Publication:* The Rose and the Flame, 1994. *Address:* Steadvallets Farmhouse, Bromfield, Shropshire SY8 2LB.

NARAIN, Sase, OR 1976; CMG 1969; SC (Guyana) 1985; JP (Guyana); solicitor/attorney-at-law; Speaker of the National Assembly, Guyana, 1971–92; Chairman, National Bank of Industry and Commerce (Guyana), 1986–93; *b* 27 Jan. 1925; *s* of Oudit and Sookdai Naraine; *m* 1952, Shamshun Narain (*née* Rayman); four *s*. *Educ:* Modern Educational Inst.; Gibson and Weldon Law Tutors. Solicitor, admitted in England and Guyana, 1957. Town Councillor, City of Georgetown, 1962–70; Member: History and Arts Council, 1969–; Republic Cttee of Guyana, 1969; Pres., Guyana Sanatan Dharma Maha Sabha, 1963–. Comr for Oaths to Affidavits, 1961; Notary Public, 1968. Dep. Chm., Public Service Commn, Guyana, 1966–71; Mem., Police Service Commn, 1966–71. Chm., Berger Paints (Guyana), 1966–78; Dir, Pegasus Hotels of Guyana, 1987–90. Member: Nat. Awards Cttee of Guyana, 1970–92; Bd of Governors, President's Coll., Guyana, 1985–. JP 1962. *Recreations:* golf, cricket, swimming. *Address:* 217 South Street, Lacytown, Georgetown, Demerara, Guyana. *T:* (2) 66611. *Clubs:* Wig and Pen; Georgetown Cricket, Everest Cricket (Guyana).

NARASIMHA, Prof. Roddam, FRS 1992; Professor Ramanathan Distinguished Professor, since 1995, and Chairman, since 1990, Fluid Mechanics Unit, Jawaharlal Nehru Centre for Advanced Scientific Research (INSA Golden Jubilee Research Professor, 1991–94); Professor, Department of Aerospace Engineering and Centre for Atmospheric Sciences, Indian Institute of Science, since 1970; *b* 20 July 1933; *s* of Shri R. L. Narasimhaiya and Smt R. N. Leela Devi; *m* 1965, Dr Neelima S. Rao; two *d*. *Educ:* University Coll. of Engineering, Bangalore (BE 1953); Indian Inst. of Science (DIISc 1955; AIISc 1957); California Inst. of Technology (PhD 1961). Res. Fellow, CIT, 1961–62; Indian Institute of Science: Asst and Associate Prof., 1962–70; Dean of Engrg Faculty, 1980–82; Chm., Dept of Aerospace Engrg, 1982–84; Chm., 1982–89, Prof., 1982–, Centre for Atmospheric Scis; Dir, Nat. Aeronautical Lab., subseq. Nat. Aerospace Labs, Bangalore, 1984–93. Chief Project Co-ordinator, Hindustan Aeronautics Ltd, 1977–79. Clark B. Millikan Vis. Prof., CIT, 1985–; Jawaharlal Nehru Vis. Prof., Cambridge, 1989–90. Pres., Indian Acad. of Scis, 1992–94. Fellow: Indian Nat. Sci. Acad., 1979; Third World Acad. of Scis, Italy, 1989; Foreign Associate, US Nat. Acad. of Engrg, 1989; Hon. Fellow, Aer. Soc. of India, 1985; Distinguished Alumnus: CIT, 1986; Indian Inst. of Sci., 1988. Bhatnagar Prize in Engrg, CSIR, India, 1976. Kannada Rajyotsava Award, Karnataka, 1976; Padmabhushan, India, 1987. *Publications:* (ed) Computer Simulation, 1979; (ed) Turbulence Management and Relaminarisation, 1987; (ed) Developments in Fluid Mechanics and Space Technology, 1988; Surveys in Fluid Mechanics, vol. III; numerous sci. papers in learned jls. *Recreations:* history, walking, music. *Address:* Centre for Atmospheric Sciences, Indian Institute of Science, Bangalore 560012, India. *T:* (80) 3342943, 3340450, *Fax:* (80) 3341683.

NARASIMHAN, Chakravarthi Vijayaraghava; Senior Fellow, UN Institute for Training and Research, 1978–93; *b* 21 May 1915; *s* of Chakravarthi V. and Janaki Vijayaraghavachari; *m* 1938, Janaki, *d* of Dr M. T. Chari; two *d*. *Educ:* University of Madras (BA); Oxford (MA). Indian Civil Service, 1936; Dep. Sec., Development Dept, Government of Madras, 1945–48; Min. of Agriculture, Govt of India, 1950–53; Joint Sec., Economic Affairs Dept, Ministry of Finance, 1953–56; Executive Sec., UN Economic Commission for Asia and Far East, 1956–59; Under-Sec. for Special Political Affairs, UN, 1959–62; Chef de Cabinet of the Sec.-Gen., UN, 1961–73; Under-Sec., 1962–67, Under-Sec.-Gen. 1967–69, for Gen. Assembly Affairs, UN; Dep. Administrator, UN Develt Prog., 1969–72; Under-Sec.-Gen. for Inter-Agency Affairs and Co-ordination, UN, 1973–78; Organizing Exec. Sec., Cotton Develt Internat., UN Develt Programme, 1979–81. Hon. Doctor of Laws,

Williams Coll. Williamstown, Mass, 1960; Hon. Dr of Humane Letters, Colgate Univ., 1966. *Publications:* The United Nations: an inside view, 1988; History of United Nations University, 1994. *Recreations:* Sanskrit literature, South Indian classical music, tennis. *Address:* 5527 Uppingham Street, Chevy Chase, MD 20815, USA. *T:* (301) 6578571.

NARAYAN, R. K., (Rasipuram Krishnaswamy); author; *b* Madras, 10 Oct. 1906. *Educ:* Maharaja's College, Mysore, India. Padma Bushan award for distinguished services to literature. Hon. LittD Leeds, 1967. *Publications: novels:* Swami and Friends, 1935; The Bachelor of Arts, 1937; The Dark Room, 1939; The English Teacher, 1945; Mr Sampath, 1947; The Financial Expert, 1952; Waiting for the Mahatma, 1955; The Guide, 1958; The Man-Eater of Malgudi, 1961; Gods, Demons and Others, 1964; The Sweet Vendor, 1967; The Painter of Signs, 1977; A Tiger for Malgudi, 1983; (ed) The Ramayana, 1973; (ed) The Mahabharata, 1978; Talkative Man, 1986; The World of Nagaraj, 1990; The Grandmother's Tale, 1993; *autobiography:* My Days, 1975; *short stories:* An Astrologer's Day; The Lawley Road; A Horse and Two Goats, 1970; Under the Banyan Tree and Other Stories, 1985, etc; *essays:* Next Sunday, 1955 (India); My Dateless Diary, 1960 (India). *Address:* c/o Anthony Sheil Associates, 43 Doughty Street, WC1N 2LF; Yadavagiri, Mysore 2, India.

NARAYAN, Rudy; *b* Guyana, 11 May 1938; *s* of Sase Narayan and Taijbertie (*née* Sawh); *m* 1988, Saeeda Begum Asif; two *d* by previous marriage. *Educ:* Lincoln's Inn. Came to UK, 1953; served HM Forces, BAOR and HQ MELF, 1958–65. Lincoln's Inn: Founder/1st Pres., Students Union, 1966; Chm. of Debates, and Captain of Cricket, 1967; called to the Bar, 1968. Vice-Chm., Lambeth Council for Community Relations 1974; Founder Chm., Lambeth Law Centre; Councillor, Lambeth, 1974–76. Founder, Black Rights (UK); Chm. and Dir, Civil Rights (UK); Legal Adviser: Caribbean Times, Asian Times, African Times (London). Formerly: Mem., Race Relations Bd; Legal Officer, W Indian Standing Conf.; Founder, Soc. of Black Lawyers (Pres., 1987–89). Contested (Ind) Vauxhall, June 1989. *Publications:* Black Community on Trial, 1976; Black England, 1977; Barrister for the Defence, 1985; Black Silk, 1985; When Judges Conspire, 1989. *Recreations:* cricket, debating, theatre, ballet, opera. *Address:* Justice House, 402 Brixton Road, SW9 7AW. *T:* 0171–978 8545; 0181–769 0444. *Club:* Wig and Pen.

NARAYANAN, Kocheril Raman; Vice-President of India, since 1992; MP for Ottapalam, Kerala, Lok Sabha, since 1984; *b* 4 Feb. 1921; *s* of late Raman Vaidyan Narayan; *m* 1951, Usha; two *d. Educ:* Travancore Univ.; LSE (Hon. Fellow, 1972). Entered Foreign Service, 1949; served Rangoon, Tokyo, London and Min. of External Affairs, 1949–60; Actg High Comr, Australia, 1961–62; Consul-Gen., Hanoi, 1962–63; Dir, China Div., 1963–67; Ambassador to Thailand, 1967–69; Jt Sec. for Policy Planning, 1969–70; Prof., Jawaharlal Nehru Univ., 1970–72; Ambassador to Turkey, 1973–75; Addtl Sec. for Policy Planning Div., 1975–76; Ambassador to China, 1976–78; Mem., Indian Delegn to UN Gen. Assembly, 1979; Ambassador to USA, 1980–84. Minister of State for: Planning, 1984–85; External Affairs, 1985–86; Atomic Energy, Space, Electronics and Ocean Develt, 1986–87; Sci. and Technol., 1986–89. Hon. Fellow, Centre for Develt Studies, Trivandrum. *Publications:* (jtly) India and America: essays in understanding; Images and Insights; (jtly) Nonalignment in Contemporary International Relations; contribs on internat. relns, Indian politics, and literature. *Address:* Office of the Vice-President, 6 Maulana Azad Road, New Delhi 110011, India.

NARJES, Karl-Heinz; Member, Commission of the European Communities, 1981–89 (Vice-President, 1985–89); *b* 30 Jan. 1924; *s* of Heinrich Narjes; *m* 1951, Eva-Maria Rahe; one *s* one *d. Educ:* Hamburg Univ. Entered Foreign Service, 1953; Chef du Cabinet, Pres. of EEC, 1963; Dir-Gen., Press and Inf. Directorate, EEC, 1968–69; Minister of Econs and of Transport, Schleswig-Holstein, 1969–73. Mem., Bundestag, 1972–88; Mem., For. Affairs Cttee, 1976–80; Pres., Econ. Affairs Cttee, 1972–76, 1980–88.

NARUEPUT, Owart S.; *see* Suthiwart-Narueput.

NASH, (Denis Frederic) Ellison, OBE 1982; AE; FRCS; Consulting Surgeon, St Bartholomew's Hospital; *b* 10 Feb. 1913; *m* 1938, Joan Mary Andrew; two *s* two *d. Educ:* Dulwich College; St Bartholomew's Medical College. MRCS, LRCP, 1935; FRCS 1938. Served war of 1939–45, RAFVR, Wing-Comdr (Air Efficiency Award, 1943). Hunterian Professor, 1949 and 1956. Arris and Gale Lecturer, 1950. Consultant Surgeon: St Bartholomew's Hosp., 1947–78; Chailey Heritage Hosp., 1952–78; Dean, St Bartholomew's Hospital Medical College, 1957–62; Special Trustee, St Bartholomew's Hosp., 1974–78; Regional Postgraduate Dean, and Asst Dir, British Postgraduate Medical Fedn, Univ. of London, 1948–74. Special interest in the education and care of the physically handicapped; Hon. Med. Adviser: Shaftesbury Soc.; John Groom's Assoc. for Disabled. Senior Member, British Assoc. of Urological Surgeons. Senior Fellow, British Orthopædic Assoc.; Fellow, Assoc. of Surgeons of GB. Hon. Fellow, Med. Artists Assoc. *Publications:* The Principles and Practice of Surgery for Nurses and Allied Professions, 1955, 7th revised edn, 1980; scientific papers in medical journals particularly concerned with surgery of childhood. *Recreations:* photography, fuchsias. *Address:* 23 Heath Park Drive, Bickley, Bromley, Kent BR1 2WQ. *T:* 0181–467 1142. *Club:* City of London Guild of Freemen.

See also T. M. E. Nash.

NASH, Ellison; *see* Nash, D. F. E., Nash, T. M. E.

NASH, John Edward; Member, Advisory Board, Bank S. G. Warburg Soditic AG, 1987–94; Chairman, S. G. Warburg Bank AG, 1980–87 (Director, 1977–87; Deputy Chairman, 1977–80); *b* 25 June 1925; *s* of Joseph and Madeleine Nash; *m* 1947, Ralda Everard Herring; two *s* two *d. Educ:* Univ. of Sydney (BEc); Balliol Coll., Oxford (BPhil). Teaching Fellow in Economics, Sydney Univ., 1947. Exec. Dir, Samuel Montagu & Co. Ltd, 1956; also Director, 1960–73: British Australian Investment Trust; Montagu Trust Ltd; Midland Montagu Industrial Finance Ltd; Capel Court Corp. (in Melb.); resigned all directorships on appt to Brussels, 1973; Dir of Monetary Affairs, EEC, 1973–77; Director: Reckitt & Colman plc, 1966–73 and 1977–86; S. G. Warburg & Co. Ltd, 1977–86. Dir, Oxford Univ. Business Summer Sch., 1965; Research Fellow, Nuffield Coll., Oxford (part-time), 1966–69. Hon. Treasurer, PEP, 1964–73. Mem. Bd of Trustees, WWF Internat., 1979–92, 1993–94 (Hon. Treas., 1985–92). *Recreations:* golf, skiing, horse-racing, music. *Address:* Chalet Gstelli, 3785 Gsteig bei Gstaad, Switzerland. *T:* (030) 51162. *Clubs:* Turf, Buck's, MCC, University (Sydney).

NASH, Philip; Commissioner of Customs and Excise, 1986–90; *b* 14 March 1930; *s* of late John Hollett Nash and Edith Grace Nash (*née* Knee); *m* 1953, Barbara Elizabeth Bangs; one *s. Educ:* Watford Grammar School. National Service, RAF, 1949–50. HM Customs and Excise, 1950–90; on loan to Civil Service College, 1970–73; Asst Sec. and Head of Management Services, 1978–81; Asst Sec., Customs Directorate, 1981–86; Director, Customs, 1986–90. *Recreation:* collecting things. *Address:* Nutwood, 37 Lower Golf Links Road, Broadstone, Dorset BH18 8BQ. *T:* Broadstone (01202) 601898.

NASH, Ronald Peter, LVO 1983; HM Diplomatic Service; Deputy High Commissioner, Colombo and (non-resident) Malé, 1992–95; *b* 18 Sept. 1946; *s* of John Henry Nash and Jean Carmichael Nash (*née* McIlwraith); *m* 1976, Annie Olsen; three *s. Educ:* Harefield Secondary Modern Sch.; Southall Tech. Sch.; Southall Grammar Tech. Sch.; Manchester Univ. FCO, 1970; Moscow, 1974–76; UK Delegn to MBFR, Vienna, 1976–79; FCO, 1979–83; New Delhi, 1983–86; FCO, 1986–87; Dep. Hd of Mission, Vienna, 1988–92. Chm. Bd Dirs, Overseas Children's Sch., Colombo, Sri Lanka, 1994–95. *Address:* c/o Foreign and Commonwealth Office, SW1A 2AH.

NASH, (Timothy Michael) Ellison; His Honour Judge Nash; a Circuit Judge, since 1994; *b* 10 Dec. 1939; *s* of Denis Frederick Ellison Nash, *qv*; *m* 1965, Gael Nash; two *s* one *d* (and one *c* decd). *Educ:* Dulwich Coll.; St Bartholomew's Hosp. Called to the Bar, Gray's Inn, 1964; Standing Counsel: DHSS, 1974–79; DTI, 1976–91; Asst Recorder, 1987–89; Recorder, 1990–94. Legal Assessor, GMC and Royal Dental Council, 1989–94; Chm., Home Office Police Appeal Tribunals, 1988–94. Metropolitan Police Special Constabulary, 1961–83. Examr, Dio. of Canterbury, 1990–94. *Recreation:* walking round in ever-increasing circles. *Address:* Riding Gate House, 37 Old Dover Road, Canterbury, Kent CT1 3JB.

NASH, Ven. Trevor Gifford; Executive Co-ordinator, Advisers for Churches' Ministry of Healing in England, since 1990 (Adviser, since 1973); *b* 3 May 1930; *s* of Frederick Walter Gifford Nash and Elsie Violet Louise Nash; *m* 1957, Wanda Elizabeth (*née* Freeston); four *d. Educ:* Haileybury College, Hertford; Clare Coll., Cambridge (MA); Cuddesdon Coll., Oxford. Curate: Cheshunt, 1955–57; Kingston-upon-Thames, 1957–61; Priest-in-Charge, Stevenage, 1961–63; Vicar, Leagrave, Luton, 1963–67; Senior Chaplain, St George's Hosp. Gp, London, 1967–73; Rector, St Lawrence with St Swithun, Winchester, 1973–82; Priest-in-Charge, Holy Trinity, Winchester, 1977–82; RD of Winchester, 1978–82; Archdeacon of Basingstoke, 1982–90, Archdeacon Emeritus, 1990; Hon. Canon of Winchester, 1980–. RAChD (TA), 1956–61. *Recreations:* water-colour painting, music, walking. *Address:* The Corner Stone, 50B Hyde Street, Winchester, Hants SO23 7DY. *T:* Winchester (01962) 861759.

NASHA, Margaret Nnananyana, (Mrs Lawrence Nasha); High Commissioner for Botswana in the UK, 1989–93; *b* 6 Aug. 1947; *d* of Sadinyana and Motlatshiping Ramontshonyana; *m* 1975, Lawrence Nasha; four *s. Educ:* Univ. of Botswana (BA 1976). Several posts as broadcaster, 1968–84; Dir of Information and Broadcasting, Botswana, 1985–89. *Recreations:* leisure walks, tennis. *Address:* PO Box 917, Gabarone, Botswana.

NASMITH; *see* Dunbar-Nasmith.

NASMYTH, Dr Kim Ashley, FRS 1989; Senior Scientist, Institute of Molecular Pathology, Vienna, since 1987; *b* 18 Oct. 1952; *s* of James Nasmyth and Jenny Hughes; *m* 1982, Anna Dowson; two *d. Educ:* Eton Coll.; York Univ. (BA); Edinburgh Univ. (PhD). Jane Coffin Childs Postdoctoral Fellow, Dept of Genetics, Univ. of Washington, 1978–80; Robertson Fellow, Cold Spring Harbor Lab., NY, 1980–81; Staff Mem., MRC Lab. of Molecular Biol., Cambridge, 1982–87; Unofficial Fellow, King's Coll., Cambridge, 1984–87. Member: European Molecular Biol. Orgn, 1985–; Academia Europaea, 1993–. *Recreations:* climbing, ski-ing. *Address:* Linke Wienzeile 4/2/5, 1060 Vienna, Austria. *T:* (1) 5869498.

NASON, Justin Patrick Pearse, OBE 1980; HM Diplomatic Service, retired; *b* 29 March 1937; *s* of John Lawrence Nason and Catherine Agnes (*née* McFadden). *Educ:* Ampleforth; University Coll., Oxford. National Service, RAF, 1956–58. BICC, 1962–63; entered HM Foreign Service, 1963; FO, 1964–65; Prague, 1965–67; FCO, 1967–71; First Sec., Pretoria and Cape Town, 1971–74; Head of Chancery, Saigon, 1974–75; FCO, 1975–79; Head of Chancery, Kampala, 1979–81; Nat. Defence Coll. of Canada, 1981–82; Dep. High Comr, Colombo, 1982–85; Barclays Bank (on secondment), 1986–87; Minister Counsellor, Mexico City, 1988–90; temp. duty, Accra, 1990–91; Ambassador to Guatemala, 1991–95. *Recreation:* golf. *Club:* United Oxford & Cambridge University.

NATAL, Bishop of, since 1982; **Rt. Rev. Michael Nuttall;** *b* 3 April 1934; *s* of Neville and Lucy Nuttall; *m* 1959, Dorris Marion Meyer; two *s* one *d. Educ:* Maritzburg Coll. (matric. 1951); Univ. of Natal (BA 1955); Rhodes Univ. (BA Hons in History 1956). MA (Cantab), MA, DipEd (Oxon), BD Hons (London). Teacher at Westville High Sch., Natal, 1958; Lectr in History, Rhodes Univ., 1959–62; Theological Student, St Paul's Coll., Grahamstown, 1963–64; ordained deacon, 1964, priest 1965; Assistant Priest, Cathedral of St Michael and St George, Grahamstown, 1965–68; Lectr in Ecclesiastical History, Rhodes Univ., 1969–74; Dean of Grahamstown, 1975; Bishop of Pretoria, 1975–81. *Publications:* chapters in: Better Than They Knew, Volume 2 (ed R. M. de Villiers), 1974; Authority in the Anglican Communion (ed Stephen W. Sykes), 1987; articles in Dictionary of S African Biography. *Recreations:* walking, bird watching. *Address:* Bishop's House, 52 Roberts Road, Pietermaritzburg, 3201, South Africa.

NATH, (Dhurma) Gian; Permanent Representative of Mauritius to the United Nations, since 1992; *b* Triolet, Mauritius, 29 May 1934; *s* of Anmole Facknath, OBE and Mrs B. Facknath; *m* 1961, Chitralekha, *d* of Dr and Mrs Chiranji Lal Sud; two *s* one *d. Educ:* Delhi Univ. (BA Hons English 1960, MA 1962); Postgrad. Inst. of Internat. Affairs, New Delhi. Educn Officer, John Kennedy Coll., Mauritius, 1963–66 (Head of Dept of English, 1965–66); entered Diplomatic Service, Mauritius, as trainee, 1966; apptd to Mauritius High Commn, London, 1968; Head of Chancery, 1969; Counsellor, Mauritius Mission to EEC, 1972–76; Dep. High Comr, London, 1976–82; Ambassador in Cairo, 1982–83; High Comr in UK, 1983–87; Ambassador to Pakistan and (non-resident), to China, 1988–90; Ambassador to Australia, and concurrently to NZ, Brunei and Indonesia, 1990–92. Sec., OAU Gp, London, 1973–82. Mem., Television Bd, Mauritius Broadcasting Corp., 1965–66. Representative of Mauritius at various internat. meetings. Kt of Order of Pius IX (Vatican), 1987. *Recreations:* bridge, history of World War II, golf. *Address:* 10 Rue Le Corbusier, Geneva 1208, Switzerland. *T:* (22) 7891150.

NATHAN, family name of **Baron Nathan.**

NATHAN, 2nd Baron, *cr* 1940; **Roger Carol Michael Nathan;** *b* 5 Dec. 1922; *s* of 1st Baron Nathan, PC, TD, and Eleanor Joan Clara (*d* 1972), *d* of C. Stettauer; *S* father, 1963; *m* 1950, Philippa Gertrude, *d* of Major Joseph Bernard Solomon, MC, Pulborough, Sussex; one *s* two *d. Educ:* Stowe Sch.; New Coll., Oxford (MA). Served War of 1939–45: Capt., 17/21 Lancers (despatches, wounded twice). Admitted Solicitor (Hons), 1950; Senior Partner, Herbert Oppenheimer Nathan & Vandyk, 1978–86; Consultant, Denton Hall Burgin & Warrens, 1989–92. Chm., Arbitration Panel, The Securities Assoc., 1988–92. Hon. Associate Mem., Bar Assoc. of City of New York. FSA; FRSA; FRGS. Pres., Jewish Welfare Board, 1967–71; Chairman: Central British Fund for Jewish Relief and Rehabilitation, 1971–77 (Hon. Pres., 1977–); Exec. Cttee, Cancer Research Campaign (formerly British Empire Cancer Campaign), 1970–75 (Hon. Treasurer, 1979–87, Vice-Chm., 1987–); Working Party on Energy and the Envmt (reported 1974); Animal Procedures Cttee, 1990–93; Wkg Party on Efficiency and Effectiveness in Voluntary Sector, 1989–90; Court of Discipline, Cambridge Univ., 1990–92; Vice Chm., Cttee on Charity Law and Practice (reported 1976); Mem., Royal Commn on Envmtl Pollution, 1979–89. Mem., H of L Select Cttee on European Communities, 1983–88 and 1990–92 (Chm., *ad hoc* Sub-Cttee on European Co. Statute, 1989–90; Chm., Sub-Cttee F (Envmt), 1983–87 and 1990–92), on Science and Technology, 1994–; Chm., H of L

Select Cttee on Murder and Life Imprisonment, 1988–89. Chm., RSA, 1975–77, Vice-Pres., 1977–. Chairman: Inst. of Envmtl Assessment, 1990–91; South Downs Conservation Bd, 1992–; President: UK Envmtl Law Assoc., 1987–92; Nat. Soc. for Clean Air, 1987–89; Soc. of Sussex Downsmen, 1987–92. Chm., City Festival of Flowers, 1964; Master, Worshipful Company of Gardeners, 1963–64. Hon. LLD Sussex, 1988. *Heir: s* Hon. Rupert Harry Bernard Nathan [*b* 26 May 1957; *m* 1987, Ann, *d* of A. S. Hewitt]. *Address:* Collyers Farm, Lickfold, Petworth, West Sussex GU28 9DU. *T:* Lodsworth (01798) 861284. *Clubs:* Athenæum, Cavalry and Guards.

See also Hon. Lady Waley-Cohen.

NATHAN, Stephen Andrew; QC 1993; an Assistant Recorder, since 1989; *b* 30 April 1947; *s* of Frederick Emil Nathan and Margot Sophie Jeanette Nathan (*née* Welch); one *s* one *d*. *Educ:* Hall Sch., Hampstead; Cranleigh Sch., Surrey (Schol.); New Coll., Oxford (BA Law 1968; MA 1972). Called to the Bar, Middle Temple, 1969; in practice at the Bar, 1970–. Dep. Chm., Guild of Guide Lectrs, 1975–76; Sec., Ponsonby Residents' Assoc., 1980–. *Recreations:* tennis, swimming, fine cooking. *Address:* 2 Hare Court, Temple, EC4Y 7BH. *T:* 0171–583 1770. *Clubs:* Royal Automobile; Riverside Tennis.

NATHANS, Prof. Daniel; Professor of Molecular Biology and Genetics, The Johns Hopkins University School of Medicine, since 1980; Senior Investigator, Howard Hughes Medical Institute, since 1982; *b* 30 Oct. 1928; *s* of Samuel Nathans and Sarah Nathans (*née* Levitan); *m* 1956, Joanne Gomberg; three *s*. *Educ:* Univ. of Delaware, Newark, Del (BS Chemistry); Washington Univ., St Louis, Mo (MD). Intern, 1954–55, and resident, 1957–59, in Medicine, Columbia-Presbyterian Medical Center, NYC; Clinical Associate, Nat. Cancer Inst., Bethesda, Md, 1955–57; Guest Investigator, Rockefeller Inst., NYC, 1959–62; Prof. of Microbiology, 1962 and Faculty Mem., Johns Hopkins Univ. Sch. of Medicine, Baltimore, Md, 1962–. Mem., President's Council of Advrs on Science and Technol., 1990–93. US Nat. Acad. of Scis Award in Molecular Biology, 1976; Nobel Prize in Physiology or Medicine, 1978; US Nat. Medal of Sci., 1993. *Address:* 2227 Crest Road, Baltimore, MD 21209, USA.

NAUGHTIE, (Alexander) James; journalist and broadcaster; Presenter, Today, BBC Radio 4, since 1994; *b* 9 Aug. 1951; *s* of Alexander and Isabella Naughtie; *m* 1986, Eleanor Updale; one *s* two *d*. *Educ:* Keith Grammar Sch.; Aberdeen Univ. (MA Hons); Syracuse Univ., New York (MA). The Press and Journal, 1975–77; The Scotsman, 1977–84; The Guardian, 1984–88, Chief Political Corresp., 1985–88; Presenter: The World at One, BBC Radio 4, 1988–94; Opera News, BBC Radio 3, 1990–93. Columnist, Scotland on Sunday, 1990–. Laurence M. Stern Fellow, Washington Post, 1981; Mem. Bd, Anglo-Irish Encounter, 1984–87. Radio documentary series include: A Nearby Country, 1991; The Power and the Glory? America's Crisis of Leadership, 1992; The Thin Blue Line, 1993. Hon. LLD Aberdeen, 1990. Personality of the Year, Sony Radio Awards, 1991. *Publications:* (ed) Playing the Palace: a Westminster collection, 1984; contribs to newspapers, magazines, journals. *Recreations:* books, opera. *Address:* BBC, Broadcasting House, W1A 1AA. *Club:* Travellers'.

NAUGHTON, Philip Anthony; QC 1988; *b* 18 May 1943; *s* of Francis and Madeleine Naughton; *m* 1968, Barbara, *d* of Prof. F. E. Bruce; two *s* one *d*. *Educ:* Wimbledon Coll.; Univ. of Nottingham (LLB). Called to the Bar, Gray's Inn, 1970. Marketing and public relations posts with BP Chemicals Ltd and Air Products Ltd, 1964–71; commenced practice as barrister, 1971. *Recreations:* walking with friends, sailing without them. *Address:* 3 Serjeants' Inn, EC4Y 1BQ. *T:* 0171–353 5537.

NAVARRETE, Jorge Eduardo; Mexican Under-Secretary (Vice-Minister) for Energy, since 1995; Member of South Commission; *b* 29 April 1940; *s* of Gabriel Navarrete and late Lucrecia López; *m* 1st, 1962, María Antonieta Linares (marr. diss. 1973); one *s*; 2nd, 1976, María de Navarrete (*d* 1985); 3rd, 1987, Angeles Salceda. *Educ:* Nat. Sch. of Economics, Nat. Autonomous Univ. of Mexico (equivalent BA Econ.); post-graduate studies in internat. economy. Center for Latin American Monetary Studies, Mexico, 1963–65; Nat. Foreign Trade Bank, Mexico, 1966–72; joined Mexican Foreign Service, 1972; Ambassador to: Venezuela, 1972–75; Austria, 1976–77; Yugoslavia, 1977–79; Dep. Perm Rep. to UN, NY, 1979; Under Sec. (Economics), Min. of Foreign Affairs, Mexico, 1979–85; Ambassador: to UK and Republic of Ireland, 1986–89; to China, 1989–93; to Chile, 1993–95. Holds decorations from Argentina, Brazil, Ecuador, Federal Republic of Germany, Italy, Panama, Poland, Sweden, Venezuela. *Publications:* The International Transfer of Technology (with G. Bueno and M. S. Wionczeck), 1969; Mexico's Economic Policy, 2 vols, 1971, 1972; Cancun 1981: the international meeting on co-operation and development, 1982; The External Debt of Latin America: issues and policies, 1987; numerous essays on Mexican and Latin American economic issues, in Mexican and foreign jls. *Recreation:* chess. *Address:* Faralton 121-A, 01900 Mexico City, Mexico.

NAVRATILOVA, Martina; tennis player; *b* Prague, 18 Oct. 1956; *d* of Jana Navratilova. Left Czechoslovakia, 1975; adopted American nationality, 1981. Professional player, 1975–94. Has won 167 singles and 167 doubles titles, including 18 Grand Slam singles titles (a record 9 Wimbledon singles wins) and 37 Grand Slam doubles titles. Pres., Women's Tennis Assoc., 1979–80, 1994–95. *Publications:* Martina (autobiog.), 1985; The Total Zone (novel), 1994; Feat of Clay, 1996. *Address:* c/o International Management Group, 1 Erieview Plaza, Cleveland, OH 44114, USA.

NAYAR, Kuldip; syndicated columnist; President, Citizens for Democracy; *b* 14 Aug. 1924; *m* 1949, Bharti; two *s*. *Educ:* Northwestern Univ., USA (BA Hons, LLB, MSc in journalism). Press Officer to Home Minister, India, 1954–56, to Prime Minister, India, 1960–64; Editor and General Manager, United News of India, 1964–67; Delhi Editor, The Statesman, 1967–75; Editor, Indian Express News Service, 1975–81; syndicated columnist, 1981–; correspondent, The Times, London, 1968–89. High Comr in UK, 1990. Numerous journalism awards. *Publications:* Between the Lines, 1967; India: the critical years, 1968; The Supersession of Judges, 1971; Distant Neighbours, 1972; India After Nehru, 1974; The Judgement, 1977; In Jail, 1979; A report on Afghanistan, 1982; The Tragedy of Punjab, 1985; India House, 1992. *Recreations:* music (Indian and Western); cricket, hockey. *Address:* D7/2 Vasant Vihar, New Delhi 110057, India.

NAYLER, Georgina Ruth; Director, National Heritage Memorial Fund, 1989–95; *b* 16 March 1959; *d* of Dennis Nayler and Yvonne (*née* Loader). *Educ:* Brentwood County High Sch. for Girls; Univ. of Warwick (BA). Joined Nat. Heritage Meml Fund, 1982: Asst Dir, 1987–88; Dep. Dir, 1988–89. Mem., Historic Bldgs Council for Scotland, 1990–. *Recreations:* gardening, interior decorating, collecting china and watercolours.

NAYLOR, Bernard; University Librarian, Southampton University, since 1977 (Co-ordinator of Information Services, 1988–93); *b* 7 May 1938; *s* of William Edward Naylor and Lilian Naylor (*née* Oakes); *m* 1967, Frances Gemma Trenaman; four *s* one *d*. *Educ:* Balliol Coll., Oxford (BA 1963; MA 1965); Sch. of Librarianship and Archive Administration, University Coll. London (Dip. Lib. 1966). ALA 1969. Asst, Foreign Accessions Dept, Bodleian Liby, 1964–66; Librarian and Bibliographer, Univ. of London Inst. of Latin American Studies, 1966–74; Sec., Library Resources Co-ordinating Cttee, Univ. of London, 1974–77. Member: British Liby Adv. Cttee on Lending Services, 1978–86 (Chm., 1981–85); Council, Standing Conf. of Nat. and Univ. Libraries, 1979–82, 1984–90 (Vice-Chm., 1984–86; Chm., 1986–88); British Council Libraries Adv. Cttee, 1982–95 (Chm., 1986–95). Chm., Hants Area Tech. Res. Indust. Commercial Service Exec., 1981–. *Publications:* Accounts of Nineteenth Century South America, 1969; Directory of Libraries and Special Collections on Latin America and the West Indies, 1975; articles in liby jls. *Recreations:* playing the piano (in private), making wine, learning foreign languages. *Address:* 12 Blenheim Avenue, Highfield, Southampton SO17 1DU. *T:* Southampton (01703) 554697.

NAYLOR, (Charles) John, OBE 1993; Secretary and Treasurer, Carnegie United Kingdom Trust, since 1993; *b* 17 Aug. 1943; *s* of late Arthur Edgar Naylor, MBE and Elizabeth Mary Naylor; *m* 1968, Margery Thomson; two *s*. *Educ:* Royal Grammar Sch., Newcastle upon Tyne; Haberdashers' Aske's Sch., Elstree; Clare Coll., Cambridge (MA History). Jun. and sen. exec. posts in industry, 1965–75; Dir, YMCA National Centre, Lakeside, Cumbria, 1975–80; Dep. National Sec., 1980–82, Nat. Sec., 1982–93, National Council of YMCAs; mem. and chm. of YMCA European and world cttees, 1976–92. Vice-Chm., Nat. Council for Voluntary Youth Services, 1985–88; Mem., Nat. Adv. Council for Youth Service, 1985–88. Chair: Assoc. of Heads of Outdoor Educn Centres, 1979–80; MSC and DES Working Party on Residential Experience and Unemployment, 1980–81. CIMgt; FRSA. *Publications:* contribs on outdoor educn to DES and MSC pubns; articles in national and internat. YMCA pubns. *Recreations:* running, the outdoors (partic. the mountains), theatre, church, embryonic golf. *Address:* Carnegie UK Trust, Comely Park House, Dunfermline, Fife, KY12 7EJ. *T:* (office) Dunfermline (01383) 721445.

NAYLOR, Maj.-Gen. David Murray, CB 1992; MBE 1972; DL; Director-General, Territorial Army and Organisation, Ministry of Defence, 1989–92; *b* 5 March 1938; *s* of Thomas Humphrey Naylor and Dorothy Isobel Durning Naylor (*née* Holt); *m* 1965, Rosemary Gillian Hicks Beach; three *s*. *Educ:* Eton Coll. psc, rcds. Joined Scots Guards, 1956; commnd as National Service and later as Regular Officer; commanded: 2nd Bn Scots Guards, 1976–79; 22nd Armoured Bde, 1982–83; Dep. Mil. Sec. (A), 1985–87; GOC NE Dist and Comdr 2nd Inf. Div., 1987–89. Chm., N Yorks Ambulance Service NHS Trust, 1992–. Gov., St Peter's Sch., York, 1991–. DL N Yorks, 1994. *Recreations:* shooting, walking, tennis, travel. *Address:* Minster Hill, Huttons Ambo, York YO6 7HJ. *T:* Malton (01653) 695008. *Clubs:* Boodle's, Cavalry and Guards.

NAYLOR, Prof. Ernest, PhD, DSc; FIBiol; Lloyd Roberts Professor of Marine Zoology (formerly Lloyd Roberts Professor of Zoology), since 1982, and Head of School of Ocean Sciences, since 1992, University College of North Wales, Bangor; *b* 19 May 1931; *s* of Joseph and Evelyn Naylor; *m* 1956, Carol Gillian Bruce; two *d*. *Educ:* Univ. of Sheffield (BSc); Univ. of Liverpool (PhD, DSc). FIBiol 1972. Successively Asst Lectr, Lectr, Sen. Lectr and Reader in Zoology, University Coll. of Swansea, Wales, 1956–71; Prof. of Marine Biology, Univ. of Liverpool, 1971–82; Dean of Sci., UCNW, Bangor, 1989–91. Vis. Professor: Duke Univ., USA, 1969, 1970; Univ. of Otago, NZ, 1982. Member Council, NERC, 1976–82; Marine Sci. and Technol. Bd, NERC, 1994–; Specialist Adviser to H of L Select Sub-Cttee on Marine Sci. and Technology, 1985; Indep. Mem., Co-ordinating Cttee on Marine Sci. and Technology, 1988–91; Indep. Assessor, Inter-Agency Cttee on Marine Sci. and Technol., 1991–; UK Rep., EC Adv. Cttee for Marine Science and Technol., 1989–. President: Estuarine and Coastal Sciences Assoc., 1986–89; Soc. for Expmtl Biology, 1989–91. *Publications:* British Marine Isopods, 1972; (co-ed with R. G. Hartnoll) Cyclic Phenomena in Marine Plants and Animals, 1979; over 130 papers in learned jls. *Recreation:* gardening. *Address:* School of Ocean Sciences, University of Wales, Bangor, Gwynedd LL57 2DG. *T:* Bangor (01248) 351151, *Fax:* (01248) 382612.

NAYLOR, John; *see* Naylor, C. J.

NAYLOR, Prof. Malcolm Neville, RD 1967; DL; BSc, BDS, PhD; FDSRCS; Hon. Senior Research Fellow, Institute of Dental Surgery, since 1991; Professor of Preventive Dentistry, University of London, 1970–91, now Professor Emeritus; Head of Department of Periodontology and Preventive Dentistry, Guy's Hospital Dental School, 1980–91; *b* 30 Jan. 1926; *er s* of late Roland B. Naylor, MBE and Mabel L. (*née* Neville), Walsall, Staffs; *m* 1956, Doreen Mary, *d* of late H. E. Jackson, CBE; one *s*. *Educ:* Queen Mary's Sch., Walsall; Univ. of Glasgow; Univ. of Birmingham (BSc 1951, BDS 1955; Nuffield Scholar, 1949–51); Univ. of London (PhD 1963). FDSRCS 1958; Hon. FDSRCPSGlas 1992. Hosp. appts, Birmingham and Dundee, 1955–59; Guy's Hosp. Dental School: Res. Fellow, 1959–62; Sen. Lectr in Preventive Dentistry, 1962–66; Reader in Preventive Dentistry, 1966–70; Hon. Consultant Dental Surgeon, Guy's Hosp., 1966–91, Consultant Emeritus, 1991. William Waldorf Astor Fellow, USA, 1963. President: British Div., IADR, 1990–92 (Hon. Treas., 1975–90); Odontol Sect., RSocMed, 1984–85; Mem., FDI Commn, 1992–. Served RNVR and RNR, retiring as Surg. Captain (D), 1943–76; Hon. Dental Surgeon to the Queen, 1976; Hon. Col, Univ. of London OTC, 1979–94; Sec., 1978–82, Chm., 1982–89, COMEC; Chairman: Mil. Educn Cttee, Univ. of London, 1979–; Sea Cadet Assoc., Sports Council, 1975–. Governor: Roehampton Inst. for Higher Educn, 1978–; Whitelands Coll., 1975–; Bacons Sch., Bermondsey, 1979–90 (Vice Chm., 1981–90); St Saviour's and St Olave's Sch., 1980–90 (Chm., 1988–); Wye Coll., Univ. of London, 1992–. Mem., St Saviour's and St Olave's Foundn, 1991– (Sub Warden, 1995–). Lay Reader, C of E, 1974–. Mem., Southwark Diocesan Synod, 1983–92. Freeman, City of London, 1983; Liveryman, Bakers' Co., 1983–. DL Greater London, 1992 (Rep. DL Lambeth, 1994). Hon. FDSRCPSGlas. Colgate Prize, IADR, 1961; Tomes Medal, BDA, 1987. *Publications:* papers and articles in prof. and scientific jls. *Recreations:* sailing, music, family and home. *Address:* Carrick Lodge, Roehampton, SW15 5BN. *T:* 0181–788 5045. *Clubs:* Royal Society of Medicine; Royal Naval Sailing Assoc.

NAYLOR, Maurice; *see* Naylor, W. M.

NAYLOR, Peter Brian, CBE 1987; Representative, British Council, Greece, 1983–86; *b* 10 July 1933; *s* of Eric Sydney Naylor and Phyllis Marian Jolly; *m* 1958, Barbara Pearson (*d* 1995); two *s* one *d* (and one *s* decd). *Educ:* Grange High Sch., Bradford; Selwyn Coll., Cambridge (Open Exhibnr; BA 1957). Wool Top Salesman, Hirsch, Son & Rhodes, Bradford, 1957; British Council: Asst Rep., Bangkok, 1959; Courses Dept and E Europe Dept, London, 1962; Asst Rep., Warsaw, 1967; Reg. Rep., Dacca, E Pakistan, 1969; Actg Rep., Athens, 1971; Rep., Argentina, 1972, Brazil, 1975; Controller, European Div., 1978–83. *Publication:* contrib. Blood Sweat and Tears, 1992. *Recreations:* reading, writing, drawing, looking. *Address:* 3 Farmadine Court, Saffron Walden, Essex CB11 3HT. *T:* Saffron Walden (01799) 527708. *Club:* Saffron Walden Golf.

NAYLOR, (William) Maurice, CBE 1973; FHSM; JP; Director, National Association of Health Authorities, 1981–84; *b* 1920; *s* of late Thomas Naylor; *m* 1948, Maureen Ann, *d* of John Walsh; one *s* two *d*. *Educ:* St Joseph's Coll., Market Drayton; Manchester Univ. (BA Admin). FHSM 1956. Sec., Sheffield Regional Hosp. Bd, 1963–73; Regional Administrator, Trent RHA, 1973–81. Pres., Inst. of Health Services Management, 1975–76 (Chm., Educn Cttee, 1980–86); Hon. FHSM 1987. Hon. MBA Sheffield, 1982. *Address:* 8 Middlefield Croft, Dore, Sheffield S17 3AS. *T:* Sheffield (0114) 235 0778.

NAYLOR-LEYLAND, Sir Philip (Vyvian), 4th Bt *cr* 1895, of Hyde Park House; Director: Nantclwyd Farms Ltd; B. M. S. S. PLC; Fitzwilliam Peterborough Properties; Milton Gate Development Co.; Milton (Peterborough) Estates Co.; *b* 9 Aug. 1953; *s* of Sir Vivyan Edward Naylor-Leyland, 3rd Bt and of Hon. Elizabeth Anne Fitzalan-Howard (who *m* 2nd, Sir Stephen Hastings, *qv*), *yr d* of 2nd Viscount FitzAlan of Derwent, OBE; *S* father, 1987; *m* 1980, Lady Isabella Lambton, *d* of Viscount Lambton, *qv*; three *s* one *d*. *Educ:* Eton; RMA Sandhurst; NY Univ. Business Sch.; RAC Cirencester. 2nd Lieut, Life Guards, 1973, Lieut, 1975–76. Vice-Chm., Peterborough Royal Foxhound Show Soc., 1988–; Pres., Nat. Coursing Club, 1988–. Jt Master, Fitzwilliam Hunt, 1987–. *Heir: s* Thomas Philip Naylor-Leyland, *b* 22 Jan. 1982. *Address:* Nantclwyd Hall, Ruthin, Clwyd LL15 2PR; The Ferry House, Milton Park, Peterborough PE6 7AB. *Club:* White's.

NAZARETH, Gerald Paul, CBE 1985 (OBE 1976); **Hon. Mr Justice Nazareth;** Vice President, Court of Appeal, Hong Kong, since 1994; *b* 27 Jan. 1932; *s* of Vincent Lionel Nazareth and Lily Isabel Monteiro; *m* 1959, Elba Maria Fonseca; three *d*. *Educ:* Nairobi; St Xavier's College, Bombay; LLB Bombay Univ. Called to the Bar, Lincoln's Inn, 1962. Public Prosecutor, and Senior Crown Counsel, Kenya, 1954–63; Solicitor General, British Solomon Islands, 1963–73; Attorney General and Legal Advisor, Western Pacific High Commn, 1973–76; Hong Kong: Law Draftsman, 1976–84; MLC, 1979–84; QC, 1982; Judge of the High Court, 1985–91; Justice of Appeal, Supreme Ct, 1991–94; Comr, Supreme Court, Brunei, 1989–93. Member: Law Reform Commn, Hong Kong, 1982–84 (Chm., Sub-Cttee on Copyright Law, 1987–92); Wkg Gp on Sino-British Jt Declaration on Hong Kong, Beijing, 1984. Vis. Fellow, ANU, 1972. Vice-Pres., Commonwealth Assoc. of Legislative Counsel, 1983–90. *Recreations:* music, reading, walking. *Address:* The Supreme Court, Hong Kong. *T:* Hong Kong 8254405.

NAZIR-ALI, Rt. Rev. Dr Michael; *see* Rochester, Bishop of.

NEAL, Prof. Bernard George, MA, PhD, ScD; FEng 1980; Emeritus Professor, since 1982 and Fellow, since 1986, Imperial College, London University (Professor of Applied Science, 1961–72, of Engineering Structures, 1972–81, of Civil Engineering, 1981–82, and Head of Civil Engineering Department, 1976–82); *b* 29 March 1922; *s* of late Horace Bernard Neal, Wembley, and Hilda Annie Webb; *m* 1948, Elizabeth Ann, *d* of late William George Toller, Woodbridge, and Bertha Catharine Toller; one *s* one *d*. *Educ:* Merchant Taylors'; Trinity College, Cambridge (Schol.). MA Cantab, 1947; PhD Cantab 1948; ScD Cantab 1965; FInstCE 1960; FIStructE 1966. Temp. Experimental Officer, Admiralty, 1942–45; Research Student, Univ. of Cambridge, 1945–48; Research Associate, Brown University, USA, 1948–49; Demonstrator, 1949–51, Lecturer, 1951–54, Univ. of Cambridge; Research Fellow, 1947–50, Staff Fellow, 1950–54, Trinity Hall, Cambridge; Prof. of Civil Engineering, University Coll. of Swansea, 1954–61. Pro-Rector, Imperial Coll., London, 1972–74. Dean of City and Guilds Coll., 1964–67; Visiting Prof., Brown Univ., USA, 1959–60. Telford Premium, 1951, Manby Premium, 1952, Instn Civil Engineers. *Publications:* The Plastic Methods of Structural Analysis, 1956; Structural Theorems and their Applications, 1964; technical papers on theory of structures, strength of materials. *Recreations:* lawn tennis, croquet. *Address:* 32 Napier Court, Ranelagh Gardens, SW6 3UU. *T:* 0171–731 6188. *Clubs:* All England Lawn Tennis and Croquet (Mem. Cttee, 1982–), Hurlingham; Cheltenham Croquet (Pres., 1995–).

NEAL, Sir Eric (James), AC 1988; Kt 1982; CVO 1992; Chairman: Atlas Copco Australia Pty Ltd, since 1989; Metal Manufacturers Ltd, since 1990 (Director, since 1987); Director, 1972–92, Chief Executive, 1973–87, Managing Director, 1982–87, Boral Ltd; *b* 3 June 1924; *s* of James and May Neal; *m* 1950, Thelma Joan, *d* of R. E. Bowden; two *s*. *Educ:* South Australian Sch. of Mines. CEng; FIGasE, FAIE, FAIM. Director: Westpac Banking Corp., 1985–92 (Dep. Chm., 1987–88, Chm., 1989–92); John Fairfax Ltd, 1987–88; BHP Co. Ltd, 1988–94; Coca Cola Amatil Ltd, 1987–. Mem., Australian Adv. Council, Gen. Motors, 1987–94. Mem., Cttee apptd by Fed. Govt to advise on Higher Defence Orgn, 1982. Member: Amer. Bureau of Shipping, 1976–90; Aust. Gas Assoc. (former Mem. Bd); Inst. of Dirs; first Nat. Pres., Aust. Inst. of Co. Dirs, 1990–92. Chm. Exec. Cttee, Duke of Edinburgh's Sixth Commonwealth Study Conf. 1986; Nat. Chm., Duke of Edinburgh's Award Scheme in Australia, 1984–92; Internat. Trustee, Duke of Edinburgh's Award Internat. Assoc., 1986–. Chief Comr, City of Sydney, 1987–88. Hon. FIE (Aust). Hon. DEng Sydney, 1989. *Recreations:* naval history, travel, reading, shipping. *Address:* 286 Moore Park Road, Paddington, NSW 2021, Australia. *T:* (2) 3316404, *Fax:* (2) 3321804. *Clubs:* Melbourne (Melbourne); Union, Australian Jockey, Australasian Pioneers (Sydney).

NEAL, Frederick Albert, CMG 1990; FIL; aviation consultant; UK Representative on Council of International Civil Aviation Organization, Montreal, 1983–93; *b* 22 Dec. 1932; *s* of Frederick William George Neal and Frances Elizabeth (*née* Duke); *m* 1958, Gloria Maria Moirano. *Educ:* Royal Grammar Sch., High Wycombe; Sch. of Slavonic Studies, Cambridge; Birkbeck Coll., London (BA). FIL 1965. Min. of Supply, 1953; Asst Defence Supply Attaché, Bonn, 1958–64; Principal, Min. of Technology (subseq. DTI), 1967; Asst Sec., DTI, 1974; Counsellor (Economic and Commercial), Ottawa, 1975–80; Asst Sec., Dept of Trade, 1980–83. *Recreations:* golf, bridge, music. *Address:* 2 Hambledon Court, 19B Crescent East, Hadley Wood, Herts EN4 0EY. *Clubs:* Naval and Military, Royal Over-Seas League; South Herts Golf.

NEAL, Harry Morton, CBE 1991; FIC; Chairman, Harry Neal (City) Ltd, since 1987; *b* 21 Nov. 1931; *s* of late Godfrey French Neal and Janet Bryce Morton; *m* 1954, Cecilia Elizabeth Crawford, *d* of late Col M. Crawford, DSO; one *s* three *d*. *Educ:* Uppingham Sch.; London Univ. (BSc(Eng)); City and Guilds Coll. (ACGI). Flying Officer, RAF, 1953. Chm., Connaught Hotel Ltd, 1980–94 (Dir, 1966–); Dir, Savoy Hotel Ltd, 1982–93; Chm., Harry Neal Ltd, 1985–90. Member of Lloyd's. Chm., City and Guilds of London Inst., 1979–91; Member: TEC, then BTEC, 1982–94; Court of City Univ., 1982–91; Delegacy, St Mary's Hosp. Med. Sch., 1993–; Board of Governors: Imperial Coll., London, 1990–; Willesden Tech. Coll., 1983–86; Francis Holland Sch., 1988–; Management Cttee, Courtauld Inst. of Art, 1983–. Pres., Greater London Mddx W County Scout Council, 1983–. Liveryman, Carpenters' Co., 1955– (Jun. Warden, 1994–95; Middle Warden, 1995–96). FCIOB, FRSA; FCGI 1983. Chevalier de Tastevin, 1981. *Recreations:* gardening, shooting. *Address:* Great Sarratt Hall, Sarratt, Rickmansworth, Herts WD3 4PD.

NEAL, Sir Leonard (Francis), Kt 1974; CBE 1971; FCIT; CIPM; Industrial Relations Consultant to number of industrial and commercial companies; *b* 27 Aug. 1913; *s* of Arthur Henry Neal and Mary Neal; *m* 1939, Mary Lilian Puttock; one *s* one *d*. *Educ:* London School of Economics; Trinity College, Cambridge (MA). Labour Manager, Esso, 1956; Employee Relations Manager, Fawley Refinery, 1961; Labour Relations Adviser, Esso Europe Inc. Mem., British Railways Board, 1967–71; Chm., Commn on Industrial Relations, 1971–74. Prof. (part-time) of Industrial Relations, UMIST, 1970–76; Chairman: MAT International Gp Ltd, 1974–85; Employment Conditions Abroad Ltd, 1977–84; Dir (non-exec.), Pilkington Bros, 1976–83. *Publication:* (with A. Robertson) The Managers Guide to Industrial Relations. *Recreations:* reading, gardening, motoring. *Address:* Towcester, Northants.

NEAL, Michael David; Headmaster, Cranborne Chase School, 1969–83; *b* 27 Jan. 1927; *s* of David Neal, FCA; *m* 1952, Barbara Lisette, *d* of late Harold Carter, MA; two *s* two *d*. *Educ:* Winchester; University Coll., Oxford (BA). Rifle Bde, 1945–48 (Captain); Asst Master, RNC Dartmouth, 1952–54; Eton Coll., 1954–69 (Housemaster, 1963–69). Mem., Eton UDC, 1960–63. *Address:* Wegnall's Mill, Presteigne, Powys LD8 2LD. *T:* Presteigne (01544) 267012.

NEALE, Sir Gerrard Anthony, (Sir Gerry), Kt 1990; solicitor; Head of Public Affairs, Radcliffes & Co., Solicitors, Westminster, since 1991; Director, Commercial Law Affiliates, Minnesota; *b* 25 June 1941; *s* of Charles Woodhouse Neale and Phyllis Muriel Neale; *m* 1965, Deirdre Elizabeth McCann; one *s* two *d*. *Educ:* Bedford Sch. Articled to solicitors, Bedford, 1961; admitted 1966. Dir, Telephone Rentals, 1979–89. Councillor, Borough of Milton Keynes, 1973–79, Mayor, 1976–77. Chm., Buckingham Constituency Cons. Assoc., 1974–76. Contested (C) N Cornwall, Oct. 1974, 1992; MP (C) N Cornwall, 1979–92. PPS to Minister for Consumer Affairs, 1981–82, to Minister of State for Trade, 1981–83, to Sec. of State for Transport, 1985–86, to Sec. of State for the Environment, 1986–87, to Sec. of State for Defence, 1987–89. *Recreations:* sailing, golf. *Address:* Radcliffes & Co., 5 Great College Street, SW1P 3SJ. *T:* 0171–222 7040.

NEALE, Rt. Rev. John Robert Geoffrey, AKC; Hon. Assistant Bishop, Diocese of Bath and Wells, since 1991; *b* 21 Sept. 1926; *s* of late Geoffrey Brockman Neale and Stella Beatrice (*née* Wild). *Educ:* Felsted Sch.; King's Coll., London Univ. Served War of 1939–45: Lieut RA; Army, 1944–48. Business, G. B. Neale & Co Ltd, EC2, 1948–51. King's Coll. London, 1951–55 (Jelf Prize, 1954). Deacon, 1955, priest, 1956; Curate, St Peter, St Helier, Dio. Southwark, 1955–58. Chaplain, Ardingly Coll., Sx, 1958–63; Recruitment Sec., CACTM (ACCM), 1963–67; Archbishops' Rep. for ordination candidates, 1967–68; Canon Missioner, Dio. Guildford, Hon. Canon of Guildford Cath. and Rector of Hascombe, Surrey, 1968–74; Suffragan Bishop (later Area Bishop) of Ramsbury, 1974–88; Hon. Canon of Salisbury Cathedral, 1974–88; Archdeacon of Wilts, 1974–80; Sec., Partnership for World Mission, 1989–91. FIC 1991. *Publication:* Ember Prayer, 1965. *Recreation:* horticulture. *Address:* 26 Prospect, Corsham, Wilts SN13 9AF. *T:* Corsham (01249) 712557.

NEALE, Keith Douglas; County Treasurer, Essex, since 1987; Treasurer, Essex Police Authority, since 1995; *b* 27 March 1947; *s* of Douglas Jeffrey and Dorothy Neale; *m* 1969, Mary Williamson; one *s* one *d*. East Midlands Electricity Board, 1964; Trainee Accountant, Blackwell RDC, 1965; County Treasurer's Dept, Lindsey CC, Lincs, 1968; Asst Dir of Finance, Humberside CC, 1974; Dep. County Treasurer, Essex, 1982. Treas., E Anglia Tourist Bd, 1987–. Jt Hon. Sec., Soc. of County Treasurers, 1991–; Advr, Policy Cttee, ACC, 1993–. Member: CIPFA (Mem., Superannuation Panel, 1994–); UK Steering Cttee on Local Govt Superannuation, 1991, 1995–. *Address:* County Treasurer's Department, Essex County Council, County Hall, Chelmsford, Essex CM1 1LX. *T:* Chelmsford (01245) 492211.

NEALE, Kenneth James, OBE 1959; FSA; consultant; author and lecturer; Assistant Under Secretary of State, Home Office, 1976–82; *b* 9 June 1922; *s* of late James Edward and Elsie Neale; *m* 1943, Dorothy Willett; three *s* one *d*. *Educ:* Hackney Downs (Grocers') Sch., London. Entered Civil Service as Clerical Officer, Tithe Redemption Commn, 1939. Lieut, RNVR, 1941–46. Exec. Officer, Min. of Nat. Insce, 1947–51; Asst Princ., 1951–55, Principal, 1955–64, Colonial Office; Sec. for Interior and Local Govt, Cyprus, 1957; Dep. Admin Sec., Cyprus, 1958–59; Central African Office, 1962–64; Asst Sec., Commonwealth Office, and Counsellor, Diplomatic Service, 1964–67; Home Office: Asst Sec., 1967–70; Dir, Industries and Supply, 1970–75; Controller, Planning and Develt, 1976–80; Dir, Regimes and Services, 1980–82. Member: Prisons Bd, 1967–69, 1976–82; European Cttee on Crime Problems, 1976–84; Chairman: Council of Europe Select Cttee on Standard Minimum Rules for Treatment of Prisoners, 1978–80; Council of Europe Cttee for Co-operation in Prison Affairs, 1981–84; Consultant: Council of Europe, 1984–; Open Univ., 1990–93. Chairman: Essex Archaeol and Historical Congress, 1984–87 (Pres., 1987–90); Friends of Historic Essex, 1986–; Member: Council, Essex Soc. for Archaeol. and Hist. (formerly Essex Archaeol Soc.), 1984–87; Library, Museum and Records Cttee, Essex CC, 1986–. Mem. Editl Bd, Essex Jl, 1989–. *Publications:* Discovering Essex in London, 1970; Victorian Horsham, 1975; Work in Penal Institutions, 1976; Essex in History, 1977; Her Majesty's Commissioners, 1978; (ed) Strategies for Education within Prison Regimes, 1986; (ed) An Essex Tribute, 1987; (contrib.) Imprisonment: European perspectives, 1991; (ed) Essex Heritage, 1992; (ed) Prison Service People, 1993; various articles and papers on local history, natural history, penology. *Recreations:* reading, local history, natural history. *Address:* Honeysuckle Cottage, Great Sampford, Saffron Walden, Essex CB10 2RW. *T:* Great Sampford (01799) 586304.

NEALE, Michael Cooper, CB 1987; CEng, FIMechE, FRAeS; industrial consultant; *b* 2 Dec. 1929; *s* of late Frank and Edith Kathleen Neale; *m* 1956, Thelma Weare; one *s* two *d*. *Educ:* West Bridgford Grammar Sch., Nottingham; Queen Mary Coll., Univ. of London (BScEng, MScEng). Postgraduate research on fuel injection in diesel engines, 1951–53; Engr Officer, Royal Air Force, 1953–56; joined Civil Service, 1956; Aeroplane and Armament Experimental Estabt, Boscombe Down, 1956–58; joined Nat. Gas Turbine Estabt, Pyestock, 1958; Asst Director of Engine Develt, MoD Headquarters, 1971; Dep. Director (R&D), Nat. Gas Turbine Estabt, 1973–80; Dir Gen. Engines (PE), MoD, 1980–87; Sec., Royal Commn for Exhibn of 1851, 1987–94; non-exec. dir of cos, 1988–93. Silver medallist, RAeS, 1987. *Publications:* papers in Aeronautical Research Council reports and memoranda series and elsewhere in the technical press, mainly concerning engines. *Recreations:* old railways, cricket. *Address:* 108 Wargrave Road, Twyford, Reading, Berks RG10 9PJ. *T:* Twyford (01734) 341759. *Club:* Athenæum.

NEALON, Dr Catherina Theresa, (Rina), CBE 1979; JP; Chairman, Lothian Health Board, 1973–81; *d* of John and Margaret O'Reilly, Glasgow; *m* 1940, James Patrick Nealon (*d* 1989); one *s*. *Educ:* Convent of Mercy, Garnethill, Glasgow. Mem., Edinburgh Town Council for Pilton Ward, 1949–74; served as Magistrate, 1954–57; Licensing Court, 1954–57; Judge of Police, 1957–62; Chm., Health Cttee, 1972–73. Member: Educn Cttee, Civil Defence Commn, 1949–73; Royal Infirmary and Associated Hosp's Bd of Management, 1952–56; NHS Exec. Council for City of Edinburgh, 1953–74 (Vice-Chm., May 1966–74); Exec. Cttee of Scottish Assoc. of Exec. Councils, 1967–74 (Vice-Pres., 1971, Pres., 1972); SE Regional Hosp. Bd, Scotland, 1966–74 (Chm., 1969–74); Med. Educn Cttee, 1969–74 (Chm., 1972–74); Livingston New Town Jt Health Service Adv. Cttee, 1969–73; Scottish Health Service Planning Council, 1974–81; Common Services Agency, Management Cttee, and Convenor, Estabt and Accommodation Sub-Cttee, Scottish Health Service, 1974–77; Univ. Liaison Cttee, 1974– (Chm., 1978–81); Edinburgh and SE District Cttee, Scottish Gas Consultative Council, 1967–74 (Chm., 1970–74; Mem. Council, 1969–74); Clean Air Council for Scotland, 1966–75; Nat. Soc. for Clean Air, Scottish Div., 1963– (Vice-Pres., 1970–72, Pres., 1972–74); A&C Whitley Council, 1973–81 (Vice-Chm., 1975–81); Nat. Negotiating Cttee; Ambulance Officers' Negotiating Cttee (Management Side Chm., 1979–81); Gen. Whitley Council (Mem., Gen. Purposes Cttee and Jt Negotiating Cttee, 1980–81); Nat. Appeals Panel; SE Dist Cttee, Gas Consumers' Council, 1981–87; Chm., Scottish Hosp. Supplies Steering Cttee,

1972–74. Former Member: Edin. and Lothian Probation Cttee; Animal Disease Res. Assoc.; Edin. Coll. of Art; Royal Blind Asylum and Sch.; Scottish Accident Prevention Council; Marriage Guidance Council; Nat. Assoc. for Maternal and Child Welfare; Nat. Council on recruitment of Nurses and Midwives; Scottish Assoc. for Mental Health; Assoc. of Sea and Airport Authorities; Edin. and Lothians Tourist Assoc.; Youth Employment Cttee; Extra-Mural Cttee, Edin. Univ., 1960–65; Mem. Bd of Governors: Napier Coll. of Science and Technology, 1964–73 (Vice-Chm., 1971–73); Telford Coll. for Further Education, 1969–72; Moray House Coll. of Educn; Wellington Farm Approved Sch.; Dr Guthrie's Girls' Sch. JP Edinburgh, 1957; Mem. Justices Cttee, 1975; Justice on District Court, 1975–83; Mem. Extra-Parliamentary Panel, 1976–86; Mem., Crossroads Cttee, 1987–. Attended 25th Anniv. Meeting, President's Cttee on Employment of Handicapped, Washington, 1972. Travelled to many countries with Internat. Hosp. Fedn study tours. Member, Church of Scotland. Dr *hc* Edinburgh, 1977. *Recreations:* reading, dressmaking. *Address:* 34 Learmonth Crescent, Edinburgh EH4 1DE. *T:* 0131–332 6191.

NEAME, Robert Harry Beale; DL; Chairman, Shepherd Neame Brewers, since 1971; *b* 25 Feb. 1934; *s* of Jasper Beale Neame and Violet Evelyn Neame; *m* 1st, Sally Elizabeth Corben; one *s* two *d* (and one *s* decd); 2nd, 1974, Yvonne Mary Mackenzie; one *d*. *Educ:* Harrow (Head of School). Joined Shepherd Neame, 1956; Dir, 1957–. SE Regional Director: National Westminster Bank, 1982–92; Royal Insurance Co., 1988–; Director: Folkestone Racecourse, 1985– (Chm., 1988–); Marr Taverns PLC, 1992–. Chairman: SE England Tourist Bd, 1979–90; Gatwick Airport Consultative Cttee, 1990–; Member: Canterbury and Thanet RHA, 1990–94; Inland Waterways Amenities Adv. Council, 1992–. Chairman, British Section: IULA, 1986–89; CEMR, 1986–89; Vice Chm., Consultative Council of Regl and Local Authorities, 1989. Mem. (C) for Faversham, Kent CC, 1965–89 (Leader, 1982–84). DL Kent, 1992. *Recreations:* cricket, squash, rackets (Army Rackets Champion, 1954), golf, shooting, ski-ing. *Address:* Dane Court Farmhouse, Kits Hill, Selling, Faversham, Kent ME13 9QP. *T:* Canterbury (01227) 752284. *Clubs:* Press; MCC, Free Foresters, I Zingari, Band of Brothers, Butterflies; Kandahar Ski; Escorts, Jesters; Royal St George's Golf (Sandwich).

NEAME, Ronald; film producer and director; *b* 23 Apr. 1911; *s* of Elwin Neame and Ivy Close; *m* 1933, Beryl Yolanda Heanly; one *s*. *Educ:* University College School; Hurstpierpoint College. Entered film industry, 1928; became Chief Cameraman, 1934. In charge of production on: In Which We Serve, This Happy Breed, Blithe Spirit, Brief Encounter, 1942–45; produced: Great Expectations, Oliver Twist, The Magic Box; directed: Take My Life, The Card, 1945–51; The Million Pound Note, 1953; The Man Who Never Was, 1954; Windom's Way, 1957; The Horse's Mouth, 1958; Tunes of Glory, 1960; I Could Go On Singing, 1962; The Chalk Garden, 1963; Mr Moses, 1964; Gambit, 1966; The Prime of Miss Jean Brodie, 1968; Scrooge, 1970; The Poseidon Adventure, 1972; Odessa File, 1973; Meteor, 1978; Hopscotch, 1979; First Monday in October, 1980; Foreign Body, 1985; The Magic Balloon, 1989. *Address:* 2317 Kimridge, Beverly Hills, CA 90210, USA. *Club:* Savile.

NEARS, Colin Gray; television producer; Member of Council, and Chairman of Advisory Panel on Dance, Arts Council of Great Britain, 1982–90; *b* 19 March 1933; *s* of William Charles Nears and Winifred Mildred Nears (*née* Gray). *Educ:* Ipswich Sch.; King's Coll., Cambridge (MA). Admin. Asst, RIBA, 1956; BBC, 1958–87; Producer: Schools Television, 1960; Music and Arts, 1967. Author and director of programmes on literature, the visual arts, music and dance. Dir, Royal Opera House, 1995– (Mem., 1990–, Dep. Chm., 1991–, Ballet Bd); Chm., Birmingham Royal Ballet Bd, 1993–; Governor: Royal Ballet Sch., 1993–; Royal Ballet, 1994–; Trustee: Royal Ballet Benevolent Fund, 1992–; Dancers' Resettlement Fund, 1991–; Mem. Bd, Riverside Trust, 1991–93. Editor, Review, 1971–72. FRSA. BAFTA award for Best Specialised Programme, 1973; Prix Italia music prize, 1982. *Recreations:* reading, gardening, painting. *Address:* 16 Ashchurch Terrace, W12 9SL. *T:* 0181–749 3615.

NEARY, Martin Gerard James; conductor and organist; Organist and Master of the Choristers, Westminster Abbey, since 1988; *b* 28 March 1940; *s* of Leonard Walter Neary and Jeanne Marguerite (*née* Thébault); *m* 1967, Penelope Jane, *d* of Sir Brian Warren, *qv*, and Dame A. J. M. T. Barnes, *qv*; one *s* two *d*. *Educ:* HM Chapels Royal, St James's Palace; City of London Sch.; Gonville and Caius Coll., Cambridge (Organ Schol.; MA Theol. and Music). FRCO. Organist, St Mary's, Hornsey Rise, 1958; St Margaret's, Westminster: Asst Organist, 1963–65; Organist and Master of Music, 1965–71; Prof. of Organ, Trinity Coll., London, 1963–72; Organist and Master of Music, Winchester Cathedral, 1972–87. Organ Advr to dio. of Winchester, 1975–87. Conductor, Twickenham Musical Soc., 1966–72; Founder and Conductor, St Margaret's Westminster Singers, 1967–71; Conductor, Waynflete Singers, 1972–88; Dir, Southern Cathedrals Festival, 1972, 1975, 1978, 1981, 1984, 1987; Conductor, Aspen Music Festival, 1980. President: Cathedral Organists' Assoc., 1985–88; RCO, 1988–90 (Mem. Council, 1982–; a Vice-Pres., 1990–); Organists' Benevolent League, 1988–; Chairman: Church Services Cttee, Musicians Benevolent Fund, 1993–; Herbert Howells Soc., 1993–. Many organ recitals and broadcasts in UK, incl. Royal Festival Hall; has conducted many premières of music by British composers incl. John Tavener's Ultimos Ritos, 1979, and Akathist, 1988, Jonathan Harvey's Hymn, 1979, and Passion and Resurrection, 1981; with Martin Neary Singers perf. madrigals and graces at 10 Downing Street, 1970–74. Toured US and Canada, 1963, 1968, 1971, 1973, 1975, 1977, 1979, 1982, 1984, 1986, 1988, 1992, appearances incl. Carnegie Hall, Lincoln Center, Kennedy Center, Roy Thomson Hall; many European tours, including Russia, 1994; BBC Promenade Concerts; sometime Conductor with: ECO; LSO; BBCSO; Bournemouth SO and Sinfonietta; Acad. of Ancient Music; Winchester Baroque Ensemble; Arts Council Contemporary Music Network Tour, 1993; many recordings, incl. Purcell, Music for Queen Mary, and Taverner, Akathist. Compositions include: What is man?; responses, carol arrangements, etc. Hon. FTCL, 1969; Hon. RAM, 1988. Hon. Citizen of Texas, 1971. Prizewinner, St Alban's Internat. Organ Festival, 1963; Conducting Scholarship, Berkshire Music Center, USA, 1963; Diploma, J. S. Bach Competn, Leipzig, 1968; UK/USA Bicentennial Fellow, 1979–80; Artist-in-residence, Univ. of California at Davis, 1984. *Publications:* edns of early organ music; contribs to organ jls. *Recreation:* watching cricket. *Address:* 2 Little Cloister, Westminster Abbey, SW1P 3PL. *T:* 0171–222 6923, *Fax:* 0171–222 1025. *Club:* Athenæum.

NEAVE, Julius Arthur Sheffield, CBE 1978 (MBE (mil.) 1945); JP; DL; General Manager, since 1966, Director since 1977, Mercantile & General Reinsurance Co. Ltd (Managing Director, 1980–82); *b* 17 July 1919; *s* of Col Richard Neave and Helen Mary Elizabeth (*née* Miller); *m* 1951, Helen Margery, *d* of Col P. M. Acton-Adams, DSO, Clarence Reserve, Marlborough, NZ; three *d*. *Educ:* Sherborne School. Joined Mercantile & General Reinsurance Co. Ltd, 1938. Served War, 1939–46: called as Territorial, commnd 13th/18th Royal Hussars, Adjt 3 years, final rank Major (despatches 1945). Returned to Mercantile & General, 1946; Asst Gen. Manager, 1964. Dir, Prudential Corp., 1982–92. (First) Chairman, Reinsurance Offices Assoc., 1969–74, Hon. Pres., 1974–82; Chm., Reinsurance Panel, British Insce Assoc., 1971–82; representative, Gt Britain: Cttee, annual internat. meeting of reinsurers, Monte Carlo, 1969–82; Vice-Pres., Assoc. Internat. pour l'Etude de l'Assurance, Geneva, 1976–83, Pres., 1983. Dir and Governor, Internat. Insce Seminars, 1977–82 (Founder's Gold Medal, 1977); President: Insce Inst. of London, 1976–77, 1983–84; Chartered Insce Inst., 1983–84 (Mem. Council, 1975–); Mem. Court, Insurers' Co., 1979– (Master, 1984–85). Hon. Fellow, RSA, 1975. Essex: JP (Brentwood), 1975; DL, 1983; High Sheriff, 1987–88. OStJ 1988. *Publications:* Speaking of Reinsurance, 1980; Still Speaking of Reinsurance, 1983. *Recreations:* shooting, fishing, golf, needlework. *Address:* Mill Green Park, Ingatestone, Essex CM4 0JB. *T:* Ingatestone (01277) 353036. *Club:* Cavalry and Guards.

NEAVE, Sir Paul (Arundell), 7th Bt *cr* 1795, of Dagnam Park, Essex; *b* 13 Dec. 1948; *s* of Sir Arundell Thomas Clifton Neave, 6th Bt and Richenda Alice Ione (*d* 1994), *d* of Sir Robert Joshua Paul, 5th Bt; *S* father, 1992; *m* 1976, Coralie Jane Louise, *e d* of Sir Robert Kinahan, *qv*; two *s*. *Educ:* Eton. Mem., Stock Exchange, 1980; Dir, Henderson Crosthwaite Ltd. *Heir: s* Frederick Paul Kinahan Neave, *b* 25 Jan. 1981. *Address:* Queen's House, Monk Sherborne, Hants RG26 5HH.

NEDD, Sir (Robert) Archibald, Kt 1985; Chief Justice of Grenada, 1979–86; *b* 7 Aug. 1916; *s* of late Robert and Ruth Nedd; *m* 1941, Annis (*née* McDowall); two *s* one *d*. *Educ:* King's Coll. London (LLB). Called to the Bar, Inner Temple, 1938. Registrar of High Court, and Addtl Magistrate, St Vincent, 1940–41, Dominica, 1941–43; Magistrate, St Lucia, 1943–44 (acted Crown Attorney); Crown Attorney, Dominica, 1944–49 (Officer administering Govt of Dominica, March 1945–Nov. 1946); Magistrate, full powers, Nigeria, 1949–53; private practice, Nigeria, 1953–70; Principal State Counsel, Rivers State, Nigeria, 1970–71 (exercising functions of legal draftsman); Legal draftsman, Rivers State, Nigeria, 1971–74 (occasionally perf. functions of Solicitor-Gen.); Puisne Judge of Supreme Court of Associated States of W Indies and Grenada, at Antigua, 1974–75, at Grenada, 1975–79. *Recreation:* reading. *Address:* Old Fort, St George's, Grenada, West Indies. *T:* 1225.

NEEDHAM, family name of **Earl of Kilmorey.**

NEEDHAM, Karen Ida Boalth; *see* Spärck Jones, K. I. B.

NEEDHAM, Phillip; Director of Operations, ADAS, since 1992; *b* 21 April 1940; *s* of Ephraim and Mabel Jessie Needham; *m* 1962, Patricia Ann (*née* Farr); two *s* two *d*. *Educ:* Dunstable Grammar Sch.; Univ. of Birmingham (BSc); Imperial Coll., London Univ. (MSc, DIC). National Agricultural Advisory Service, subseq. Agricultural Development and Advisory Service, MAFF: Soil Scientist, 1961; Regional Soil Scientist, Reading, 1979; Hd of Soil Science, London, 1982; Sen. Agricl Scientist, 1985; Dep. Dir of R&D, 1987; Dir, Farm and Countryside Service and Commercial Dir, 1988–92. *Publications:* contribs to books and jls on various aspects of crop nutrition and soil science. *Address:* ADAS Headquarters, Oxford Spires Business Park, The Boulevard, Kidlington, Oxon OX5 1NZ. *T:* Oxford (01865) 842742, *Fax:* (01865) 845055.

NEEDHAM, Rt. Hon. Richard (Francis); (6th Earl of Kilmorey, but does not use the title); PC 1994; MP (C) Wiltshire North, since 1983 (Chippenham, 1979–83); *b* 29 Jan. 1942; *e s* of 5th Earl of Kilmorey (*d* 1977), and of Helen (who *m* 2nd, 1978, Harold William Elliott, CBE), *y d* of Sir Lionel Faudel-Phillips, 3rd Bt; *m* 1965, Sigrid Juliane Thiessen-Gairdner, *o d* of late Ernst Thiessen and of Mrs John Gairdner, Hamburg; two *s* one *d*. *Educ:* Eton College. Chm., R. G. M. Print Holdings Ltd, 1967–85. CC Somerset, 1967–74. Contested (C): Pontefract and Castleford, Feb. 1974; Gravesend, Oct. 1974; Personal Asst to Rt Hon. James Prior, MP, 1974–79. PPS to Sec. of State for NI, 1983–84, to Sec. of State for the Environment, 1984–85; Parly Under-Sec. of State, NI Office, 1985–92 (Minister for Health and Social Security, 1988–89, for Envmt, and for Economy, 1989–92); Minister of State, DTI, 1992–95. Cons. Vice-Chm., Employment Cttee, 1981–83; Mem., Public Accts Cttee, 1982–83. Founder Member: Anglo-Japanese 2000 Gp, 1984–; Anglo-Korean Forum for the Future, 1993–. Governor, British Inst. of Florence, 1983–85. *Publication:* Honourable Member, 1983. *Heir: s* Viscount Newry and Morne, *qv*. *Address:* House of Commons, SW1A 0AA. *Clubs:* Pratt's, Beefsteak.

NEEDHAM, Prof. Roger Michael, FRS 1985; FEng 1993; Professor of Computer Systems, since 1981, Head of Computer Laboratory, since 1980, and Fellow of Wolfson College, since 1967, University of Cambridge; *b* 9 Feb. 1935; *s* of Leonard William Needham and Phyllis Mary Needham; *m* 1958, Karen Ida Boalth Spärck-Jones, *qv*. *Educ:* Cambridge Univ. (MA, PhD). FBCS. Cambridge University: Sen. Asst in Research, Computer Lab., 1963–64; Asst Dir of Research, 1964–73; Reader in Computer Systems, 1973–81. Mem., UGC, 1985–89. Member: Chesterton RDC, 1971–74; South Cambs DC, 1974–86. Fellow, Assoc. for Computing Machinery, USA, 1994. Hon. DSc: Kent, 1983; Birmingham, 1995. *Publications:* (with M. V. Wilkes) The Cambridge CAP Computer and its operating system, 1979; (with A. J. Herbert) The Cambridge Distributed Computing System, 1982; contribs to publications on computer operating systems, communications, security and protection. *Recreations:* sailing, politics. *Address:* 7 Brook Lane, Coton, Cambridge CB3 7PY. *T:* Madingley (01954) 210366; (work) Cambridge (01223) 334607. *Clubs:* Naval; Royal Harwich Yacht.

NEEDLE, Clive; Member (Lab) Norfolk, European Parliament, since 1994. *Educ:* Southend High Sch.; Aston Univ. *Address:* European Parliament, 97 Rue Belliard, 1040 Brussels, Belgium; Norfolk Euro Office, Norwich Labour Centre, 59 Bethel Street, Norwich NR2 1NL.

NEEL, Janet; *see* Cohen, J.

NÉEL, Prof. Louis Eugène Félix, Grand Croix de la Légion d'Honneur; Croix de Guerre avec Palme; Président d'Honneur, Institut National Polytechnique de Grenoble; *b* Lyon, 22 Nov. 1904; *m* 1931, Hélène Hourticq; one *s* two *d*. *Educ:* Ecole Normale Supérieure. Agrégé de l'Université; Dr Sc. Prof., Univ. Strasbourg, 1937–45. Dir, Centre d'Etudes Nucléaires, Grenoble, 1956–71, and Delegate of High Comr for Atomic Energy at the centre, 1971–76; rep. France at Scientific Council, NATO, 1960–83; Prés., Conseil Sup. Sûreté Nucléaire, 1973–86. Mem., Acad. of Science, Paris, 1953; For. Member: Acad. of Science, Russia (formerly USSR), 1959, Rumania, 1965, Poland, 1975; Royal Netherlands Acad., 1959; Deutsche Akademie der Naturforscher Leopoldina, 1964; Royal Society, 1966; Amer. Acad. of Arts and Sciences, 1966; Pres., Internat. Union of Pure and Applied Physics, 1963–66. Gold Medal, CNRS, 1965; Nobel Prize for Physics, 1970. Hon. Dr: Graz, 1948; Nottingham, 1951; Oxford, 1958; Louvain, 1965; Newcastle, 1965; Coïmbra, 1966; Sherbrooke, 1967; Madrid, 1978. *Publications:* numerous on magnetism. *Address:* 15 rue Marcel-Allégot, 92190 Meudon-Bellevue, France. *T:* 45343651.

NEGARA BRUNEI DARUSSALAM, HM Sultan of; Hassanal Bolkiah Mu'izzaddin Waddaulah, DKMB, DK, PSSUB, DPKG, DPKT, PSPNB, PSNB, PSLJ, SPMB, PANB; Hon. GCMG; DMN, DK (Kelantan), DK (Johor), DK (Negeri Sembilan), DK (Pahang); Ruler of Negara Brunei Darussalam (formerly Brunei), since 1967; Prime Minister, Finance and Home Affairs Minister, Negara Brunei Darussalam, since its independence, Jan. 1984; *b* 15 July 1946; *s* of Sultan Sir Muda Omar 'Ali Saifuddien Sa'adul Khairi Waddien, DKMB, DK, GCVO, KCMG, PSSUB, PHBS, PBLI (*d* 1986).

Educ: Victoria Inst., Kuala Lumpur; RMA Sandhurst (Hon. Captain, Coldstream Guards, 1968; Hon. General 1984). Collar of the Supreme Order of the Chrysanthemum; Grand Order of Mugunghwa. *Address:* Istana Nurul Iman, Bandar Seri Begawan, Negara Brunei Darussalam.

NEGUS, Norma Florence, (Mrs D. J. Turner-Samuels); Her Honour Judge Negus; a Circuit Judge, since 1990; *b* 31 July 1932; *d* of late George David Shellabear and Kate (*née* Calvert); *m* 1st, 1956, Richard Negus (marr. diss. 1960); 2nd, 1976, David Jessel Turner-Samuels, *qv*. *Educ:* Malvern Girls' Coll., Malvern, Worcs. Fashion promotion and advertising in UK, Canada and USA, 1950–61; Merchandise Editor, Harper's Bazaar, 1962–63; Asst Promotion Manager, Vogue and House & Garden, 1963–65; Unit Manager, Trends Merchandising and Fashion Promotion Unit, 1965–67; Export Marketing Manager and Advertising Manager, Glenoit (UK) Ltd, 1967–68. Called to the Bar, Gray's Inn, 1970; Mem., Middle Temple, 1984. In practice on SE Circuit, 1971–84; a Metropolitan Stipendiary Magistrate, 1984–90; a Recorder, 1989–90. Mem., Parole Bd, 1991–94. Mem., Central Criminal Court Bar Mess, 1978–84. *Recreations:* reading, writing, theatre, music, travel, swimming. *Address:* c/o Southwark Crown Court, 1 English Grounds, Battle Bridge Lane, SE1 2HU.

NEGUS, Richard; consultant designer; Senior Partner, Negus & Negus, 1967–87; *b* 29 August 1927; *s* of Bertie and Kate Negus; *m* 1949, Pamela Wheatcroft-Hancock; two *s* one *d*. *Educ:* Battersea Grammar Sch.; Camberwell Sch. of Arts and Crafts. FSTD. Staff designer, Festival of Britain, 1948–51; Partner, Negus & Sharland, 1951–67; Lecturer, Central Sch. of Art, 1951–53. Consultant to: Cotton Board Design Centre, 1960–67; BNEC, 1969–75; British Airways, 1973–84, 1990–; Pakistan Airlines, 1975–79 and 1989–; Rank Organisation, 1979–86; City of Westminster, 1973–75; National Exhibition Centre, 1974–77; Lloyds Bank, 1972–75; Godfrey Davis, 1971–80; John Laing, 1970–73; Andry Montgomery, 1967–; Celltech, 1980–83; Vickers Ltd, 1980–83; SDP, 1981–88; Historic Buildings and Monuments Commn, 1984–; Nat. Maritime Mus., 1984–; Royal Armouries, 1984–; The Emirates (Airline), 1985–88; Tower of London, 1986–; Science Museum, 1987–; Northern Foods, 1986–; Waterford/Wedgwood, 1987; DoE Royal Parks, 1987–88; Nature Conservation Council, 1987–89; John Lewis Partnership, 1987–89; Nat. Theatre, 1989–91; Internat. Youth Hostels, 1989; Dubai Tourist Bd, 1990–; Blue Circle Properties, 1990–. Member: Design Council Poster Awards Cttee, 1970–72; PO Stamps Adv. Cttee, 1977–; CNAA, 1980–85; Design Council, 1981–86; Art and Design Cttee, Technician Educn Council, 1981–86. Advisor, Norwich Sch. of Art, 1969–71; External Assessor: Birmingham and Bradford Colls of Art, 1969–73; Medway Coll. of Design, 1989–; Governor: Camberwell Sch. of Art, 1964–78; Chelsea Sch. of Art, 1977–85; Mem. Court, RCA, 1979–82. PPCSD (Pres., SIAD, 1977–79, Vice Pres. 1966–68). *Publications:* Designing for Export Printing, 1972; Display of Text in Museums, 1989; contribs to: Design Mag., The Designer, Graphis, Gebrauchgraphick, Architectural Review, Rolls Royce Mag., Creative Review, Art and Artists. *Recreations:* the countryside, sailing. *Address:* 15 St Clement's Church, Davey Close, N7 8BT. *T:* 0171–607 8642; Little Gravenhurst, Bolney, Sussex RH17 5PA. *T:* Bolney (01444) 881841.

NEHER, Prof. Dr Erwin; Research Director, Max-Planck-Institut für biophysikalische Chemie, Göttingen, since 1983; *b* 20 March 1944; *s* of Franz Xaver Neher and Elisabeth Neher; *m* 1978, Dr Eva-Maria Ruhr; three *s* two *d*. *Educ:* Technical Univ., Munich (PhD); Univ. of Wisconsin. Research Associate: Max-Planck-Inst. für Psychiatrie, Munich, 1970–72; Max-Planck-Inst. für biophysikalische Chemie, 1972–75 and 1976–83; Yale Univ., 1975–76; Fairchild Scholar, CIT, 1988–89. For. Mem., Royal Soc., 1994. Nat. and internat. sci. awards: (jtly) Nobel Prize in Physiology or Medicine, 1991. *Publications:* Elektronische Messtechnik in der Physiologie, 1974; (ed) Single Channel Recording, 1983. *Address:* Max-Planck-Institut für biophysikalische Chemie, Am Fassberg, Postfach 2841, 37077 Göttingen, Germany. *T:* (551) 2011675.

NEHRU, Braj Kumar; Chairman: Indian Advisory Board, Grindlays Bank, 1988–94; Hindustan Oil Exploration Co. Ltd, since 1987; Director, East India Hotels Ltd, since 1988; *b* Allahabad, 4 Sept. 1909; *s* of Brijlal and Rameshawri Nehru; *m* 1935, Magdalena Friedmann; three *s*. *Educ:* Allahabad Univ.; LSE (Fellow); Balliol Coll., Oxford. BSc; BSc(Econ.). Called to Bar, Inner Temple. Joined ICS, 1934; Asst Comr, 1934–39; Under-Sec., Dept of Education, Health and Lands, 1939; Mem., Indian Legislative Assembly, 1939; Officer on special duty, Reserve Bank of India, and Under-Sec., Finance Dept, 1940; Jt Sec., 1947; Exec. Dir, IBRD (World Bank), and Minister, Indian Embassy, Washington, 1949–54 and 1958–62; Sec., Dept of Econ. Affairs, 1957–58; Comr-Gen. for Econ. Affairs, Min. of Finance, 1958–61; Ambassador to USA, 1961–68; Governor: Assam and Nagaland, 1968–73; Meghalaya, Manipur and Tripura, 1972–73; High Comr in London, 1973–77; Governor: Jammu and Kashmir, 1981–84; Gujarat, 1984–86. Rep. of India: Reparations Conf., 1945; Commonwealth Finance Ministers Confs, UN Gen. Assembly, 1949–52, and 1960; FAO Confs, 1949–50; Sterling Balance Confs, 1947–49; Bandung Conf., 1955; deputed to enquire into Australian Fed. Finance, 1946; Mem., UN Adv. Cttee on Admin and Budgetry Questions, 1951–53; Advr to Sudan Govt, 1955; Mem., UN Investments Cttee, 1962–92 (Chm., 1977–91; Mem. Emeritus, 1992). Pres., Dyal Singh Coll. Trust, 1990–; Trustee: Indira Gandhi Meml Trust, 1985–; Tribune Trust, 1988–; World Meml Fund for Disaster Relief, 1989–; Pres., Dyal Singh Library Trust, 1988– (Trustee, 1988–). Hon. LLD Mo Valley Coll.; Hon. LittD Jacksonville; Hon. DLitt Punjab. *Publications:* Australian Federal Finance, 1947; Speaking of India, 1966; Thoughts on the Present Discontents, 1986. *Recreations:* bridge, reading, conversation. *Address:* Fair View, Kasauli-173204, India. *T:* (01793) 2189. *Club:* Gymkhana (Delhi).

NEIDPATH, Lord; Hon. James Donald Charteris, Lord Douglas of Neidpath, Lyne and Munard; *b* 22 June 1948; *s* and *heir* of 12th Earl of Wemyss and March, *qv*; *m* 1983, Catherine Ingrid (marr. diss. 1988), *d* of Baron Moyne, *qv*, and of Mrs Paul Channon; one *s* one *d*. *Educ:* Eton; University College, Oxford (BA 1969, MA 1974); St Antony's Coll., Oxford (DPhil 1975), Royal Agricultural Coll., Cirencester (Diploma, 1978); ARICS 1983. Page of Honour to HM Queen Elizabeth the Queen Mother, 1962–64. Mem., Royal Co. of Archers (Queen's Body Guard for Scotland), 1978–. Mem. Council, Nat. Trust for Scotland, 1987–92; Chm., Heart of England Reg., Hist. Houses Assoc., 1991–. *Publication:* The Singapore Naval Base and the Defence of Britain's Eastern Empire 1919–42, 1981. *Heir:* *s* Hon. Francis Richard Percy Charteris, *b* 15 Sept. 1984. *Address:* Stanway, Cheltenham, Glos GL54 5PQ. *T:* Stanton (0138673) 469. *Clubs:* Brooks's, Pratt's, Ognisko Polskie; Puffin's, New (Edinburgh).

NEIGHBOUR, Oliver Wray, FBA 1982; Music Librarian, Reference Division of the British Library, 1976–85; *b* 1 April 1923; *s* of Sydney William Neighbour, OBE, TD, and Gwenydd Joyce (*née* Prentis). *Educ:* Eastbourne Coll.; Birkbeck Coll., London (BA 1950). Entered Dept of Printed Books, BM, 1946; Asst Keeper in Music Room, 1951; Dep. Keeper, 1976. *Publications:* (with Alan Tyson) English Music Publishers' Plate Numbers, 1965; The Consort and Keyboard Music of William Byrd, 1978; (ed) Music and Bibliography: essays in honour of Alec Hyatt King, 1980; article on Schoenberg in New Grove Dictionary of Music and Musicians, 1980; editor of first publications of works by Schumann, Schoenberg and Byrd. *Recreations:* walking, ornithology. *Address:* 12 Treborough House, 1 Nottingham Place, W1M 3FP. *T:* 0171–935 1772.

NEIL, Andrew Ferguson; writer and broadcaster; columnist for The Sunday Times and Daily Mail; *b* Paisley, 21 May 1949; *s* of James and Mary Neil. *Educ:* Paisley Grammar Sch.; Univ. of Glasgow (MA Hons Politics and Economics, 1971). Conservative Res. Dept, 1971–72; joined The Economist, 1973; Reporter, Ulster, 1973–74; Lobby Correspondent, 1974–75; Labour Corresp., 1975–78; Amer. Corresp., Washington and New York, 1979–82; UK Editor, London, 1982–83; Editor, The Sunday Times, 1983–94; Exec. Editor and Chief Correspondent, Fox Network News, 1994. Chm., Sky TV, 1988–90; Co-Proprietor and Dir, CGA and Country Magazine; Contributing Editor, Vanity Fair, New York, 1995–. Appears regularly on various current affairs television and radio programmes in Britain and America; programmes include The Midnight Hour, Westminster On-Line, Is This Your Life. *Publications:* The Cable Revolution, 1982; Britain's Free Press: Does It Have One?, 1988. *Recreations:* dining out in London, New York, Aspen and the Côte d'Azur. *Address:* Glenborn Enterprises Ltd, PO Box 584, SW7 3QY. *T:* 0171–244 9968. *Clubs:* Royal Automobile, Tramp.

NEIL, Matthew, CBE 1976; Secretary and Chief Executive, Glasgow Chamber of Commerce, 1954–83; *b* 19 Dec. 1917; *er s* of John Neil and Jean Wallace. *Educ:* John Neilson High Sch., Paisley; Glasgow Univ. (MA, LLB). Served War, 1939–46: Far East, ME, Mediterranean and Western Europe; RHA, RA and Air Observation Post; RAuxAF, 1950–57. Admitted solicitor, 1947; Hon. Sheriff, Renfrew and Argyll, now N Strathclyde, 1973–. Mem., British Overseas Trade Adv. Council, 1975–82. Hon. LLD Glasgow, 1983. *Recreations:* skiing, golf, music. *Address:* 39 Arkleston Road, Paisley PA1 3TH. *T:* 0141–889 4975. *Clubs:* East India, Devonshire, Sports and Public Schools; Lamlash Golf, Prestwick Golf.

NEIL, Ronald John Baille; Managing Director, Regional Broadcasting, BBC, since 1989; *b* 16 June 1942; *s* of John Clark Neil and Jean McMillan Taylor; *m* 1967, Isobel Anne Clark. *Educ:* High Sch. of Glasgow. Reporter, Daily Express, 1961; BBC, 1967–: Newsreader/Reporter, Reporting Scotland, 1967; Producer, Nationwide and 24 Hours, 1969; Output Editor, Nationwide, 1973; Dep. Editor, Newsnight, 1979; Editor: That's Life, 1981; Newsnight, 1981; Breakfast Time, 1983; Six O'Clock News, 1984; TV News, 1985; Dep. Dir, 1987–88, Dir, 1988–89, News and Current Affairs. *Recreations:* tennis, food, wine. *Address:* BBC, Henry Wood House, W1A 1AA. *Club:* Reform.

NEIL, Thomas, CMG 1962; TD 1951; Director, Thomson Foundation, 1963–79; *b* 23 December 1913; *s* of late W. R. Neil; *m* 1939, Phyllis Selina Gertrude Sargeant; one *d*. *Educ:* King's College, University of Durham (now University of Newcastle upon Tyne) (BSc, NDA). Lectr in Agriculture, Devon County Council, 1936–39; Chief Technical Officer, 1946. Colonial Service: District Officer, Kenya, 1947; Assistant Chief Secretary, 1957; Permanent Secretary, 1957; Permanent Secretary, Ministry of State, Kenya, 1959–63. Directed Africanisation of CS. Director, Kenya Famine Relief, 1961–63. Lay Mem., Immigration Appeal Tribunal, 1971–84. Served War of 1939–45 with Devonshire Regiment (TA), Lieutenant-Colonel, in UK, E Africa, Middle East. *Recreation:* country life. *Address:* Summerhill, Bourne End, Bucks SL8 5JL. *T:* Bourne End (016285) 20403.

NEILAND, Brendan Robert, RA 1992; RE 1988; Gallery Artist, Redfern Gallery, since 1992; *b* 23 Oct. 1941; *s* of Arthur Neiland and Joan Agnes Bessie Whiley; *m* 1970, Hilary Vivienne Salter; two *d*. *Educ:* Birmingham Sch. of Art (DipAD Hons); Royal Coll. of Art (MA). Exhibited: Angela Flowers Gall., 1970–78; Fischer Fine Art, 1978–92; Redfern Gall., 1993. Scholar, Crabtree Foundn, 1982. Silver Medal, RCA, 1969; John Moores XI Prize, 1978; Daler Rowney Award, RA Summer Exhibn, 1989. *Recreations:* listening to the cricket commentary on Radio 4, drinking fine wines. *Address:* 24 The Chase, Clapham, SW4 0NH. *T:* 0171–720 3393; Crepe, La Grévé sur le Mignon, 17170 Courcon, France. *T:* 46016297. *Club:* Chelsea Arts.

NEILD, Prof. Robert Ralph; Professor of Economics, University of Cambridge, 1971–84, now Emeritus; Fellow of Trinity College, Cambridge, since 1971; *b* 10 Sept. 1924; *o s* of Ralph and Josephine Neild, Letchmore Heath, Hertfordshire; *m* 1st, 1957, Nora Clemens Sayre (marr. diss. 1961); 2nd, 1962, Elizabeth Walton Griffiths (marr. diss. 1986); one *s* four *d* (incl. twin *d*). *Educ:* Charterhouse; Trinity Coll., Cambridge. Royal Air Force, 1943–44; Operational Research, 1944–45. Secretariat of United Nations Economic Commission for Europe, Geneva, 1947–51; Economic Section, Cabinet Office and Treasury, 1951–56; Lecturer in Economics, and Fellow, Trinity College, Cambridge, 1956–58; National Institute of Economic and Social Research: at first as Editor of its Quarterly Economic Review; then as Deputy Director of the Institute, 1958–64; MIT Center for International Studies, India Project, New Delhi, 1962–63; Economic Adviser to HM Treasury, 1964–67; Dir, Stockholm Internat. Peace Research Inst., 1967–71. Vis. Fulbright Prof., Hampshire Coll. and Five Colls, Amherst, Mass, USA, 1985. Mem., Fulton Cttee on Reform of CS, 1966–68; Vice-Chm., Armstrong Cttee on Budgetary Reform in UK, Inst. for Fiscal Studies, 1979–80. Director: Nat. Mutual Life Assce Soc., 1959–64; Investing in Success Equities Ltd, 1961–64, 1972–87. *Publications:* Pricing and Employment in the Trade Cycle, 1964; (with T. S. Ward) The Measurement and Reform of Budgetary Policy, 1978; How to Make Up Your Mind about the Bomb, 1981; An Essay on Strategy, 1990; (ed with A. Boserup) The Foundations of Defensive Defence, 1990; various articles. *Address:* Trinity College, Cambridge CB2 1TQ.

NEILL, Alistair, FFA, FIA; General Manager, Scottish Widows' Fund & Life Assurance Society, 1988–92; President, Faculty of Actuaries in Scotland, 1990–92; *b* 18 Nov. 1932; *s* of Alexander Neill and Marion Wilson; *m* 1958, Mary Margaret Hunter; one *s* two *d*. *Educ:* George Watson's Coll., Edinburgh; Univ. of Edinburgh (John Welsh Math. Bursar; MA); Univ. of Wisconsin (Fulbright Grantee; MS). Instructor Lieut, RN, 1958–60. Actuarial management posts in Scottish Widows' Fund, 1961–92. *Publication:* Life Contingencies, 1977, 5th edn 1989. *Recreations:* golf, curling. *Address:* 24 Bonaly Crescent, Edinburgh EH13 0EW. *T:* 0131–441 2038.

NEILL, Rt. Hon. Sir Brian (Thomas), Kt 1978; PC 1985; **Rt. Hon. Lord Justice Neill;** a Lord Justice of Appeal, since 1985; *b* 2 Aug. 1923; *s* of late Sir Thomas Neill and Lady (Annie Strachan) Neill (*née* Bishop); *m* 1956, Sally Margaret, *d* of late Sydney Eric and Marguerite Backus; three *s*. *Educ:* Highgate Sch.; Corpus Christi Coll., Oxford (Hon. Fellow 1986). Rifle Brigade, 1942–46 (Capt.). MA Oxford. Called to the Bar, Inner Temple, 1949, Bencher, 1976. QC 1968; a Recorder of the Crown Court, 1972–78; a Judge of the High Court, Queen's Bench Div., 1978–84. A Judge of the Commercial and Admiralty Courts, 1980–84; a Judge of Employment Appeal Tribunal, 1981–84. Mem., Departmental Cttee to examine operation of Section 2 of Official Secrets Act, 1971; Chairman: Adv. Cttee on Rhodesia Travel Restrictions, 1973–78; IT and the Courts Cttee, 1985–; Supreme Court Procedure Cttee, 1986–90. Mem., Ct of Assts, 1972–, Master, 1980–81, Turners' Co. Governor, Highgate Sch., 1969–90. *Publication:* (with Colin Duncan) Defamation, 1978, 2nd edn (ed with R. Rampton), 1984. *Address:* c/o Royal Courts of Justice, Strand, WC2A 2LL. *Clubs:* MCC, Hurlingham.
See also Sir F. P. Neill.

NEILL, Rev. Bruce Ferguson; QHC 1991; Principal Chaplain, Naval, Church of Scotland and Free Churches, 1991–Feb. 1996; *b* 9 Jan. 1941; *s* of Thomas Ferguson Neill and Jane (*née* Bruce); *m* 1966, Ishbel Macdonald; two *s* one *d*. *Educ:* Lesmahagow Primary; Hamilton

Academy; Glasgow Univ. and Trinity Coll., Glasgow (MA, BD). Probationer Asst, Drumchapel Old Parish Church, 1964–66; Minister, Dunfermline Townhill Parish Church, 1966–71; commnd as Chaplain, RN, 1971; Naval appts include: HMS Drake, 1972; RM, 1972; HMS Seahawk, 1974; HMS Cochrane, 1976; ships of 1st and 2nd Flotillas, 1979; HMS Dryad, 1981; Britannia RNC, 1983; HMS Cochrane, 1986; ships of Minor War Vessels Flotilla, 1989–91. *Recreations:* gardening, hill walking, off-shore sailing, woodwork, music, model making. *Address:* (until Feb. 1996) Naval Chaplaincy Services, Victory Building, HM Naval Base, Portsmouth, Hants PO1 3LR.

NEILL, Prof. Derrick James, DFC 1943; Emeritus Professor of Prosthetic Dentistry, University of London; Sub-Dean of Dental Studies, Guy's Hospital Dental School, 1969–76; Consultant Dental Surgeon, Guy's Hospital, since 1960; *b* 14 March 1922; *s* of Jameson Leonard Neill, MBE, and Lynn Moyle; *m* 1st, 1952, Iris Jordan (*d* 1970); one *s* one *d*; 2nd, 1971, Catherine Mary Daughtry. *Educ:* East Sheen County Grammar Sch.; Guy's Hosp. Dental Sch., Univ. of London. LDSRCS 1952; FDSRCS 1955; MDS London, 1966. Served RAFVR, 1941–46, 150 Sqdn, Bomber Comd (Sqdn Ldr). Dept of Dental Prosthetics, Guy's Hosp. Dental School: Lectr, 1954; Sen. Lectr, 1959; Univ. Reader in Dental Prosthetics, 1967; Prof. of Prosthetic Dentistry, 1969. Council Member, Odontological Section, Royal Soc. of Medicine, 1966–73; Past Pres., British Soc. for Study of Prosthetic Dentistry. Mem. Council of Governors: Guy's Hosp. Med. Sch., 1980–82; United Med. Schs of Guy's and St Thomas's Hosps, 1982–87. Fellow, Internat. Coll. of Cranio-Mandibular Orthopedics, 1986. Mem. Editorial Bd, Internat. Jl of Prosthodontics. *Publications:* (jtly) Complete Dentures, 1968; Partial Denture Construction, 1976; Restoration of the Partially Dentate Mouth, 1984; numerous papers in dental jls. *Recreations:* golf, music. *Address:* Hurst, Clenches Farm Road, Kippington, Sevenoaks, Kent TN13 2LU. *T:* Sevenoaks (01732) 452374. *Club:* Royal Automobile.

NEILL, Sir (Francis) Patrick, Kt 1983; QC 1966; Warden of All Souls College, Oxford, 1977–95; a Judge of the Courts of Appeal of Jersey and Guernsey, 1977–94; *b* 8 Aug. 1926; *s* of late Sir Thomas Neill, JP, and Lady (Annie Strachan) Neill (*née* Bishop); *m* 1954, Caroline Susan, *d* of late Sir Piers Debenham, 2nd Bt, and Lady (Angela) Debenham; four *s* two *d*. *Educ:* Highgate Sch.; Magdalen College, Oxford (Hon. Fellow, 1988). Gibbs Law Scholar, 1949; Eldon Law Scholar, 1950. BA 1950; BCL 1951; MA 1972. Served Rifle Brigade, 1944–47 (Captain); GSO III (Training), British Troops Egypt, 1947. Fellow of All Souls, 1950–77, Sub-Warden 1972–74; Lectr in Air Law, LSE, 1955–58; Vice-Chancellor, Oxford Univ., 1985–89. Called to the Bar, Gray's Inn, 1951; Bencher, 1971; Vice-Treas., 1989; Treas., 1990; Member, Bar Council, 1967–71, Vice-Chm., 1973–74, Chm., 1974–75; Chm., Senate of the Inns of Court and the Bar, 1974–75; a Recorder of the Crown Court, 1975–78. Chm., Justice—All Souls Cttee for Rev. of Admin. Law, 1978–87. Chairman: Press Council, 1978–83; DTI Cttee of Inquiry into Regulatory Arrangements at Lloyd's, 1986–87; Feltrum Loss Review Cttee at Lloyd's, 1991–92; first Chm., Council for the Securities Industry, 1978–85; Vice-Chm., CVCP, 1987–89. Independent Nat. Dir, Times Newspaper Hldgs, 1988–. Hon. Prof. of Legal Ethics, Birmingham Univ., 1983–84. Hon. LLD: Hull, 1978; Buckingham, 1994; Hon. DCL Oxon, 1987. *Publication:* Administrative Justice: some necessary reforms, 1988. *Recreations:* music and forestry. *Address:* 1 Hare Court, Temple, EC4Y 7BE. *Clubs:* Athenæum, Garrick, Beefsteak.
See also Rt Hon. Sir Brian Neill.

NEILL, Hugh; *see* Neill, J. H.

NEILL, Major Rt. Hon. Sir Ivan, Kt 1973; PC (N Ireland) 1950; *b* Belfast 1 July 1906; *m* 1928, Margaret Helena Allen. *Educ:* Ravenscroft Nat. Sch., Belfast; Shaftesbury House Tutorial Coll., Belfast; Queen's Univ., Belfast (BSc Econ). FRGS. Served War of 1939–45: RE in UK and FE, 1939–46; Major. MP Ballynafeigh Div. of Belfast, Parlt of Northern Ireland, 1949–73; Government of Northern Ireland: Minister of Labour and National Insurance, 1950–62; Minister of Home Affairs, Aug.-Oct. 1952; Minister of Education, 1962–64; Minister of Finance, 1964–65; Leader of House of Commons, Oct. 1964; resigned from Govt, April 1965; Minister of Develt, Dec. 1968–March 1969; Speaker of House of Commons, 1969–73. Represented N Ireland at Internat. Labour Confs, 1950–61. Councillor and Alderman in Belfast Corp., 1946–50 (specialised in educn, housing and youth welfare). DL Belfast, 1966–86. *Publications:* Travel Experiences; A Story in Verse; Church and State. *Address:* Cranagh Cottage, Warren Road, Donaghadee, Co. Down, Northern Ireland BT21 0PQ.

NEILL, Very Rev. Ivan Delacherois, CB 1963; OBE 1958; Provost of Sheffield and Vicar of the Cathedral Church of St Peter and St Paul, 1966–74, now Emeritus; Chaplain to the Queen, 1962–66; *b* 10 July 1912; *s* of Rev. Robert Richard Neill and Bessie Montrose (*née* Purdon); *m* 1938, Enid Eyre Godson (*née* Bartholomew); one *s* one *d*. *Educ:* St Dunstan's College; Jesus College, Cambridge (MA); London College of Divinity. Curate: St Mary, West Kensington, 1936–38; Christ Church, Crouch End, 1938–39. CF 4th Cl., Chatham; served BEF and UK with 3rd Div., Orkneys, Sandhurst, 1941–43; Sen. Chaplain, N Aldershot, 1943; 43rd (Wessex) Div., 1943–45 (despatches); DACG, 1st British Corps, 1945–46; Sen. Chaplain, Guards Depot, Caterham, 1947–50; DACG, N Canal, Egypt, 1950–53; Catterick, 1953; Warden, Royal Army Chaplains Dept Trg Centre, 1954–57; Sen. Chaplain, SHAPE 1957–58; Asst Chaplain-Gen., Middle East Land Forces, 1958–60; QHC 1960; Chaplain General to HM Forces, 1960–66. Chairman of Governors, Monkton Combe Sch., Bath, 1969–81; Pres. of Foundn, St Paul's and St Mary's C of E Coll. of Educn, Cheltenham, 1978–88. Knight Officer, Order of Orange Nassau (with Swords) 1946. *Address:* Fair Oak, Aviemore Road, Crowborough, E Sussex TN6 1QU. *T:* Crowborough (01892) 662928. *Club:* National.

NEILL, (James) Hugh, CBE 1969; TD 1950; JP; Lord-Lieutenant for South Yorkshire, since 1985; President, James Neill Holdings, since 1989 (Chairman, 1963–89); *b* 29 March 1921; *o s* of Col Sir Frederick Neill, CBE, DSO, TD, DL, JP, and Lady (Winifred Margaret) Neill (*née* Colver); *m* 1st, 1943, Jane Margaret Shuttleworth (*d* 1980); two *d*; 2nd, 1982, Anne O'Leary; one *s*. *Educ:* Rugby School. War service with RE and Royal Bombay Sappers and Miners, UK, Norway, India, Burma and Germany, 1939–46 (despatches, Burma, 1945). Mem., British Overseas Trade Bd, 1973–78; Pres., European Tool Cttee, 1972–76; Mem., Trent Regional Health Authority, 1974–80; Chm. Exec. Cttee, Sheffield Council for Voluntary Service, 1953–87; Mem. Council, CBI, 1965–83; Chm., E and W Ridings Regional Council, FBI, 1962–64; Pres., Nat. Fedn of Engrs Tool Manufrs, 1963–65; Pres., Fedn of British Hand Tool Manufrs, 1960–61. Pres., Sheffield Chamber of Commerce, 1984–85. FIMgt. Hon. Col, 3rd Bn Yorks Vol., subseq. 3rd/4th Bn Yorks Vol., later 3rd Bn Duke of Wellington's, 1988–93. Chm., Yorks & Humberside TAVRA, 1991–94. Hon. Fellow, Sheffield City Polytechnic, 1978; Hon. LLD Sheffield, 1982. Master Cutler of Hallamshire, 1958; High Sheriff of Hallamshire, 1971; DL South Yorkshire, 1974, JP 1985. KStJ 1986. *Recreations:* golf, horse trials, racing, shooting. *Address:* Barn Cottage, Lindrick Common, near Worksop S81 8BA. *T:* Dinnington (01909) 562806. *Clubs:* East India; Sheffield (Sheffield); Lindrick (Worksop); Royal and Ancient (St Andrews); Hon. Co. of Edinburgh Golfers (Muirfield).

NEILL, Rt. Rev. John Robert Winder; *see* Tuam, Killala and Achonry, Bishop of.

NEILL, Sir Patrick; *see* Neill, Sir F. P.

NEILSON, Ian (Godfrey), DFC 1944; TD 1951; *b* 4 Dec. 1918; *er s* of James Wilson Neilson, solicitor, Glasgow; *m* 1945, D. Alison St Clair Aytoun, Ashintully; one *s* one *d*. *Educ:* Glasgow Acad.; Glasgow Univ. (BL). Legal Trng, Glasgow, 1935–39; Territorial Army, 1938; War Service, 1939–45: Field Artillery; Air Observation Post, 1941; RA Staff, 1944; Lt-Col comdg War Crimes Investigation Unit, Germany, 1945–46; formed and commanded No 666 (Scottish) Sqdn, RAuxAF, 1948–53. Enrolled Solicitor, 1946. Royal Institution of Chartered Surveyors: Scottish Sec., Edinburgh, 1946–53; Asst Sec., London, 1953–61; Under-Sec., 1961–65; The Boys' Brigade: Brigade Sec., 1966–74; Officer, 5th Mid-Surrey Co., 1972–78; Nat. Hon. Vice-Pres., 1982–; Hon. Vice-Pres., W of England Dist, 1983–; Hon. Vice-Pres., Wilts Bn, 1985–. Clerk to Governors of the Cripplegate Foundn, Cripplegate Educnl Foundn, Trustees of St Giles and St Luke's Jt Parochial Charities, and Governors of the Cripplegate Schs Foundn, 1974–81. Hon. Treasurer, Thames Youth Venture Adv. Council (City Parochial Foundn), 1968–76. Vice-Chm., British Council of Churches Youth Dept, 1971–74; Trustee: St George's Chapel, London Airport, 1978– (Chm., 1983–); Douglas Haig Meml Homes, 1979–; Mem., Nat. Council for Voluntary Youth Services, 1966–74; Pres., London Br., Glasgow Academical Club, 1977–79; Chm. of Governors, Lucas-Tooth Leadership Training Fund for Boys, 1976–83; Governor, Kingsway-Princeton Coll. of Further Educn, 1977–83. Elder, United Reformed Church, St Andrew's, Cheam, 1972–83; Lay Mem., Provincial Ministerial Cttee, URC, 1974–83; Dir and Jt Sec., URC Trust, 1982–95; Mem. Council: Christchurch, Marlborough, 1984–90, 1992–; St Peter's and St Paul's Trust, Marlborough, 1985–. BIM: Hon. Sec., City of London Branch, 1976–79, Chm., 1979–81, Vice Pres., 1981–87; Chm., Inner London Branches Area Cttee, 1981–83; FIMgt (FBIM 1980). Sen. Instr, Royal Yachting Assoc., 1977–87; Vice-Pres., Air Observation Post Officers Assoc., 1978–; Chm., Epsom Choral Soc., 1977–81. Freeman, GAPAN, 1976–78, Liveryman, 1978–; Freeman, City of London, 1975; Chm., Queenhithe Ward Club, 1977–78. Hon. Editor, Tower and Town, Marlborough, 1984–. *Recreations:* golf, music, gardening, sailing. *Address:* The Paddock, Kingsbury Street, Marlborough, Wilts SN8 1HZ. *T:* Marlborough (01672) 515114. *Clubs:* Athenæum; Marlborough Golf; Chartered Surveyors' Golfing Society (Hon. Mem.); GAPAN Golf Soc.

NEILSON, Nigel Fraser, MC 1943; Chairman, Nigel F. Neilson, Public Relations (formerly Neilson McCarthy, then Neilson Associates), since 1962; *b* 12 Dec. 1919; *s* of Lt-Col W. Neilson, DSO, 4th Hussars and Maud Alice Francis Anson; *m* 1949, Pamela Catherine Georgina Sheppard (*d* 1989); one *s* one *d*. *Educ:* Hereworth Sch.; Christ's Coll., New Zealand; RADA. Inns of Court Regt; commnd Staffs Yeomanry, 1939; seconded Cavalry Regt, Transjordanian Frontier Force; served Syrian Campaign; returned Staffs Yeo., Seventh Armoured Div., GSO 111 Ops; served desert and Italy; Staff Coll., 1944; served in Germany, Holland and France; C of S, Bergen area, Norway; served with SAS and French SAS. On demobilisation worked in theatre, cabaret, films, London, USA and NZ; joined J. Walter Thompson, 1951; became personal rep. to Aristotle Onassis, 1955, later consultant to his daughter, Christina; founded Neilson McCarthy Internat. Public Relations Consultants in UK, USA, Australia, NZ and SE Asia, 1962. Past Pres., NZ Soc., 1978–79. Chevalier de la Légion d'Honneur 1946, Croix de Guerre avec Palme 1946. *Recreations:* riding, shooting, music, theatre. *Address:* c/o Coutts & Co., 1 Old Park Lane, W1Y 4BS.

NEILSON, Richard Alvin, CMG 1987; LVO 1968; HM Diplomatic Service; High Commissioner to Trinidad and Tobago, since 1994; *b* 9 July 1937; *s* of Robert and Ethel Neilson; *m* 1961, Olive Tyler; one *s*. *Educ:* Burnley Grammar Sch.; Leeds Univ. (BA Hons 1958, MA 1960). Fulbright Fellow, Univ. of Wisconsin, 1959–60; Asst Lectr, Univ. of Edinburgh, 1960–61; joined FO, 1961; Third (later Second) Sec., Kinshasa, 1963–65; Treasury Centre for Admin. Studies, 1965; Second (later First) Sec. (Information), Santiago, 1966–69; First Sec., Canberra, 1969–73; FCO, 1973–77; Counsellor, seconded to NI Office as Head of Political Affairs Div., 1977–79; Dep. High Comr, Lusaka, 1979–80, Acting High Comr, Nov. 1979–June 1980; Dep. Governor and Political Advr, Gibraltar, 1981–84; Head of Southern European Dept, FCO, 1984–86; Ambassador to Colombia, 1987–90; Ambassador to Chile, 1990–93. *Publications:* contribs to geomorphological literature. *Address:* c/o Foreign and Commonwealth Office, SW1A 2AH; Maynes Hill Farm, Hoggeston, Buckingham, Bucks. *T:* Winslow (01296) 712308. *Club:* Commonwealth Trust.

NELDER, John Ashworth, DSc; FRS 1981; Visiting Professor, Imperial College of Science, Technology and Medicine (formerly Imperial College of Science and Technology), since 1971; Head of Statistics Department, 1968–84, and of Division of Biomathematics, Jan.-Oct. 1984, Rothamsted Experimental Station; *b* 8 Oct. 1924; *s* of Reginald Charles and Edith May Ashworth Nelder; *m* 1955, Mary Hawkes; one *s* one *d*. *Educ:* Blundell's Sch., Tiverton; Cambridge Univ. (MA); DSc Birmingham. Head, Statistics Section, National Vegetable Research Station, 1950–68. Pres., Royal Statistical Soc., 1985–86. Hon. DSc Paul Sabatier, Toulouse, 1981. *Publications:* Computers in Biology, 1974; (with P. McCullagh) Generalized Linear Models, 1983, 2nd edn 1989; responsible for statistical programs (computer), Genstat and GLIM; numerous papers in statistical and biological jls. *Recreations:* piano-playing, music, natural history. *Address:* Cumberland Cottage, 33 Crown Street, Redbourn, St Albans, Herts AL3 7JX. *T:* Redbourn (01582) 792907.

NELIGAN, Michael Hugh Desmond; His Honour Judge Neligan; a Circuit Judge, since 1990; *b* 2 Dec. 1936; *s* of late Desmond West Edmund Neligan, OBE and of Penelope Ann, *d* of Henry Mason; *m* 1965, Lynn (*née* Maidment); three *d*. *Educ:* Bradfield College; Jesus College, Cambridge. Commissioned Royal Sussex Regt, 1960–62; served East Africa with 23rd and 4th Bns, King's African Rifles. Called to the Bar, Middle Temple, 1965; Prosecuting Counsel to the Crown, 1972; Metropolitan Stipendiary Magistrate, 1987–90. *Recreations:* cabinet making, gardening, dog-walking. *Address:* The Law Courts, Barker Road, Maidstone, Kent ME16 8EQ.

NELLIST, David; Welfare Rights Adviser, Robert Zara & Co., since 1992; *b* 16 July 1952; *m* 1984, Jane Warner; one *s* three *d*. Mem., MSF. Mem., W Midlands CC, 1982–86. MP (Lab, 1983–91, Ind. Lab, 1991–92) Coventry SE; contested (Ind. Lab) Coventry SE, 1992. *Address:* 33 Coundon Road, Coventry CV1 4AR. *T:* (home) Coventry (01203) 552059, (office) Coventry (01203) 257487.

NELSON, family name of **Earl Nelson** and **Baron Nelson of Stafford.**

NELSON, 9th Earl *cr* 1805, of Trafalgar and of Merton; **Peter John Horatio Nelson;** Baron Nelson of the Nile and of Hilborough, Norfolk, 1801; Viscount Merton, 1805; *b* 9 Oct. 1941; *s* of Captain Hon. John Marie Joseph Horatio Nelson (*d* 1970) (*y s* of 5th Earl) and of Kathleen Mary, *d* of William Burr, Torquay; *S* uncle, 1981; *m* 1969, Maureen Diana, *d* of Edward Patrick Quinn, Kilkenny; one *s* one *d*; *m* 1992, Tracy Cowie. Chm., Retainacar Ltd, 1988–; Dir, British Navy Pusser's Rum, 1988–. President: Royal Naval Commando Assoc.; Nelson Soc.; Vice-Pres., Jubilee Sailing Trust; Mem. Council, Friends of Nat. Maritime Mus.; Hon. Life Member: Royal Naval Assoc.; Royal Naval Museum. *Heir: s* Viscount Merton, *qv*. *Address:* House of Lords, SW1A 0PW. *Club:* St James's.

NELSON OF STAFFORD, 3rd Baron, *cr* 1960; **Henry Roy George Nelson;** Bt 1955; Operations Director, TIB plc, since 1993; *b* 26 Oct. 1943; *er s* of 2nd Baron Nelson of Stafford and of Pamela Roy, *yr d* of Ernest Roy Bird, MP; *S* father, 1995; *m* 1968, Dorothy, *yr d* of Leslie Caley; one *s* one *d*. *Educ:* Ampleforth; King's Coll., Cambridge (MA). CEng, FIMechE, MIEE. Joined RHP Bearings, 1970: Gen. Manager, transmission bearings, 1973–78, automotive bearings, 1978–81; Manufacturing Dir, industrial bearings, 1981–83; Man. Dir, Hopkinsons Ltd, 1983–85; Man. Dir, industrial and distribution divs, Pegler-Hattersley plc, 1985–86; Gp Man. Dir, GSPK Ltd, 1986–90; Man. Dir, power transmission div., Fenner plc, 1991–92. Mem., Govt Cttee of Enquiry into Engrng Profession, 1978–80. *Heir: s* Hon. Alistair William Henry Nelson, *b* 3 June 1973. *Address:* Eastlands, Tibthorpe, Driffield, E Yorks YO25 9LD. *Club:* Farmers'.

NELSON, NZ, Bishop of, since 1990; **Rt. Rev. Derek Lionel Eaton,** QSM 1985; *b* 10 Sept. 1941; *s* of Henry Jackson Eaton and Ella Barbara (*née* McDouall); *m* 1964, Alice Janice Maslin; two *s* one *d*. *Educ:* Christchurch Boys' High Sch. (NZ); Univ. of Missouri (MA *cum laude*); Switzerland (Cert. Française); Univ. of Tunis (Cert. Arabic and Islamics); Missionary Training Coll., Australia (DipTheol): Trinity Theol Coll., Bristol. School teacher, 1964. Missionary with Worldwide Evangelisation Crusade, Tunisia, 1968–78; ordained deacon and priest, 1971; Curate, St Luke's, Bristol, 1971–72; Vicar of Tunis, 1972–78; Hon. Chaplain, British Embassy, Tunis, 1972–78; Provost, Cairo Cathedral, Egypt, 1978–83 (Emeritus, 1984); Hon. Chaplain, British Embassy, Egypt, 1978–83; with Church Missionary Society, 1980–84; Assoc. Vicar, Papanui, Bishopdale, NZ, 1984–85; Vicar, Sumner, Redcliffs, NZ, 1985–90. Hon. Canon, Cairo Cathedral, 1985. *Publications:* contrib. theol and missiological jls. *Recreations:* swimming, golf, reading, tennis. *Address:* Bishopdale, PO Box 100, Nelson, New Zealand. *T:* Nelson (3) 5488991.

NELSON, Anthony; *see* Nelson, R. A.

NELSON, Bertram James, OBE 1984; HM Diplomatic Service, retired; Consul-General, Antwerp, 1983–85; *b* 7 Dec. 1925; *s* of Herbert James Nelson and Adelaide Mabel Nelson (*née* Newton); *m* 1958, Constance Dangerfield; one *s* one *d*. *Educ:* North Kensington Central School. Grenadier Guards, 1944–47; Post Office and Cable and Wireless, 1947–54; Foreign Office, 1954; served Cairo, Budapest, Athens, Asunción, Zagreb, DSAO, 1966–69; Vice-Consul, Tokyo, 1969–71; Vice-Consul, Tehran, 1972–75; FCO, 1975–79; First Sec. and Consul, Brussels, 1979–83. *Recreation:* enjoying retirement. *Address:* 2 Hornbeam Close, Aldwick, Bognor Regis, West Sussex PO21 4AH.

NELSON, Air Cdre Eric Douglas Mackinlay, CB 1952; retired, Sept. 1963; *b* 2 Jan. 1912; *e s* of late Rear-Adm. R. D. Nelson, CBE, and the late Ethel Nelson (*née* MacKinlay); *m* 1939, Margaret Yvonne Taylor (*d* 1988); one *s* one *d*. *Educ:* Dover Coll.; RAF Coll., Cranwell. Commissioned RAF, 1932; served War of 1939–45 (despatches); CO 103 (HB) Sqdn Elsham Wolds, 1943–44; Group Capt., 1944; ADC to the Queen, 1953–57; Air Commodore, 1956; Commandant, RAF, Halton, 1956–58; Commandant, Royal Air Force Staff College, Andover, 1958–60; AOA Transport Command, 1960–61; Air Officer Commanding and Commandant, Royal Air Force College, Cranwell, 1961–63. DL Lincs, 1966. *Recreations:* sailing, beagling. *Address:* 23 The Link, Wellingore, Lincoln LN5 0BJ. *T:* Lincoln (01522) 810604. *Club:* Royal Air Force.

NELSON, Eric Victor, LVO 1975; HM Diplomatic Service, retired; *b* 11 Jan. 1927; *s* of Victor H. H. and E. Vera B. Nelson (*née* Collingwood); *m* 1960, Maria Teresa (Marité) Paul; one *d* (and one *d* decd). *Educ:* Western High School; George Washington University, Washington DC. Royal Air Force, 1945–48. Board of Trade, 1949; served FO, later FCO: Athens, Belgrade, Haiphong, Caracas; First Sec., Saigon, 1962; First Sec. and Consul, Bujumbura, 1964 (Chargé d'Affaires *ai.* 1966–67); FO 1968; First Sec. and Consul, Asunçión, 1971; First Sec., Mexico City, 1974; FCO, 1978; seconded to Brunei Govt Service as Special Adviser to HM Sultan of Brunei, for Establishment of Brunei Diplomatic Service, 1981–84; Consul-Gen., Bordeaux, 1984–87. Order of the Aztec Eagle, Mexico, 1975. *Recreations:* photography, giving illustrated talks, tourism, cartooning, sculpture. *Address:* 8 Purberry Grove, Ewell, Surrey KT17 1LU.

NELSON, Sir Jamie (Charles Vernon Hope), 4th Bt *cr* 1912, of Acton Park, Acton, Denbigh; *b* 23 Oct. 1949; *s* of Sir William Vernon Hope Nelson, OBE and Hon. Elizabeth Ann Bevil Cary, *er d* of 14th Viscount Falkland; *S* father, 1991; *m* 1983, Maralyn Hedge (*née* Pyatt); one *s*. *Heir. b* Dominic William Michael Nelson [*b* 13 March 1957; *m* 1981, Sarah, *e d* of late John Neil Hylton Jolliffe; three *s*]. *Address:* 39 Montacute Road, Tintinhull, Yeovil, Somerset BA22 8QD. *T:* Martock (01935) 822496.

NELSON, John Graeme; Group Managing Director, South and East, British Rail, since 1994; *b* 19 June 1947; *s* of Charles and Jean Nelson; *m* 1971, Pauline Dickinson; two *s* one *d*. *Educ:* Aylesbury and Slough Grammar Schs; Univ. of Manchester (BA Econ Hons). Management trainee, BR Western Reg., 1968; Asst Station Man., Liverpool Street, 1971; Area Passenger Man., Shenfield, 1973; Passenger Sales Officer, Leeds, 1977; Passenger Man., Sheffield Div., 1979; Personal Asst, Chief Exec. BRB, 1981; Parcels Man., Southern Reg., 1982; Nat. Business Man., Red Star Parcels, 1984; Gen. Man., BR Eastern Reg., 1987; Man. Dir, Network SouthEast, 1991. *Recreations:* piano, football, badminton. *Address:* Euston House, 24 Eversholt Street, NW1 1DZ. *T:* 0171–320 0254.

NELSON, Michael Edward; Chairman, Reuter Foundation, 1982–90; General Manager, 1976–89, and Deputy Managing Director, 1981–89, Reuters Ltd; *b* 30 April 1929; *s* of Thomas Alfred Nelson and Dorothy Pretoria Nelson; *m* 1960, Helga Johanna (*née* den Ouden); two *s* one *d*. *Educ:* Latymer Upper School; Magdalen College, Oxford (MA). Joined Reuters, London, as trainee financial journalist, 1952; assignments Asia, 1954–57; returned to London; Manager, Reuters Economic Services, 1962; Chairman, 1987–88: Reuters Asia; Reuters Europe; Reuters Overseas. Trustee: Visnews, 1990–92 (Chm., 1985–89); Internat. Inst. of Communications, 1989– (Chm., UK Chapter, 1989–92); Chm. Adv. Council, World Link, 1990–92. Mem., Newspaper Panel, MMC, 1989–95. Trustee, St Bride's Church, 1989–. *Recreations:* walking, music, photography. *Address:* 21 Lansdowne Road, W11 3AG. *T:* 0171–727 8533; Domaine de la Rose, 2 Chemin des Restanques, 06650 Opio, France. *T:* 93773232. *Club:* Garrick.

NELSON, Nicholas; Head Teacher, Queens' School, Bushey, since 1995 (teacher, 1992–95); *b* 20 Jan. 1947; *s* of late Peter Nelson and of Margaret Nelson; *m* 1972, Charmian Alice (*née* Bell); one *s* two *d*. *Educ:* Pudsey Grammar Sch., Yorkshire; Reading Univ. (BA (Hons) History; CertEd 1992). BOAC: Management Trainee, 1969; Air Cargo Sales Rep., 1971; Cargo Sales Man., Japan/Dep. Marketing Man., Japan, 1973; British Airways: Cargo Manager: Eastern Scotland, 1978; Midlands, 1979; DHL International (UK) Ltd: Gen. Man., 1981; Man. Dir, 1982; Regional Dir (Europe), 1987; Man. Dir, Parcels, PO, then Royal Mail Parcelforce, 1987–91. *Recreations:* cricket, motorcycling. *Address:* Queens' School, Aldenham Road, Bushey, Watford, Herts WD2 3TY.

NELSON, Air Marshal Sir Richard; *see* Nelson, Air Marshal Sir S. R. C.

NELSON, (Richard) Anthony; MP (C) Chichester, since Oct. 1974; Minister of State, Department of Trade and Industry, since 1995; *b* 11 June 1948; *o s* of late Gp Captain R. G. Nelson, BSc, CEng, FRAeS, MICE, and of Mrs J. M. Nelson; *m* 1974, Caroline Victoria Butler; one *s* one *d*. *Educ:* Harrow Sch.; Christ's Coll., Cambridge (MA (Hons) Economics and Law). State Scholarship to Harrow, 1961; Head of School, 1966; Rothschild Scholar, 1966. N. M. Rothschild & Sons Ltd, 1969–73. Mem., Bow Gp Council, 1973. Dir, Chichester Fest. Th., 1983–92. Contested (C) E Leeds, Feb. 1974. PPS to Minister for Housing and Construction, 1979–83, to Minister of State for the Armed Forces, 1983–85; Economic Sec., 1992–94, Minister of State, 1994–95, HM Treasury. Member: Select Cttee on Science and Technology, 1975–79; Select Cttee on Televising of Proceedings of the House, 1988–92. FRSA 1979. *Recreations:* music, Rugby. *Address:* House of Commons, SW1A 0AA.

NELSON, Dr (Richard) Stuart, FInstP; Member Board, United Kingdom Atomic Energy Authority, since 1991, and Executive Director, Operations, AEA Technology, since 1994; *b* 1 May 1937; *s* of Richard and Winifred Emily Nelson; *m* 1965, Veronica Mary Beck; one *s* two *d*. *Educ:* Univ. of Reading (BSc 1st Cl. Hons Physics, 1958; DSc 1969). FInstP 1968. Joined UKAEA, Harwell, 1958; Div. Head, Materials Develt Div., 1981; Dir, Nuclear Power Res., 1984; Dir, Northern Res. Labs, 1987–90 (including Risley, Springfield and Windscale Labs); Man. Dir, Industrial Business Gp, AEA Technology, 1991. Vis. Prof., Univ. of Sussex, 1970–. *Publications:* The Observation of Atomic Collisions in Crystalline Solids, 1968; Ion Implantation, 1973; 200 papers in scientific jls. *Recreations:* hockey (played for Berkshire), golf, tennis. *Address:* Harwell, Didcot, Oxfordshire OX11 0RA. *T:* Didcot (01235) 432814.

NELSON, Robert Franklyn; QC 1985; a Recorder, since 1986; *b* 19 Sept. 1942; *s* of Clarence William and Lucie Margaret Nelson; *m* 1968, Anne-Marie Sabina Hall; two *s*. *Educ:* Repton; St John's Coll., Cambridge (MA). Called to the Bar, Middle Temple, 1965 (Harmsworth Entrance Exhibn, 1963), Bencher, 1993. *Recreations:* cricket, opera, golf. *Address:* 1 Paper Buildings, Temple, EC4Y 7EP. *T:* 0171–583 7355.

NELSON, St Elmo Dudley, CMG 1964; Permanent Secretary, Military Governor's Office, Kano, 1968–76; Acting Secretary to Military Government, and Head of Kano State Civil Service, 1970, 1973 and 1975; *b* 18 March 1919; *s* of late Dudley Nelson and Dorothy Maida (*née* Browne), Highton, Victoria, Australia; *m* 1958, Lynette Margaret, *o d* of late Phillip Anthony Browne, Yarram and Frankston, Victoria, Australia. *Educ:* privately; Geelong School; Oxford University; Sorbonne. Served War of 1939–45 (despatches): 2/7 Australian Infantry Bn (Major); campaigns N Africa, Greece, Crete, New Guinea; Instructor Staff Coll., Cabalah, 1944. Joined HM Colonial Administrative Service. Nigeria: Cadet 1947; Administrative Officer (Class II), 1957; Resident, Plateau Province, 1961; Resident and Provincial Sec., Kabba Province, 1962; Provincial Sec., Kano Province, 1963–67, Sokoto, 1967–68. Chm., Cttee which divided assets of Northern Region between the six Northern States, 1967. Election supervisor, Rhodesian independence elecns, 1980. Gen. Tax Comr, S Wilts, 1980–. *Recreations:* fishing, polo, squash. *Address:* Home Farm House, Teffont Evias, Salisbury, Wilts SP3 5RG. *Club:* MCC.

NELSON, Air Marshal Sir (Sidney) Richard (Carlyle), KCB 1963 (CB 1962); OBE 1949; Director-General, Royal Air Force Medical Services, 1962–67; Director of Research and Medical Services, Aspro-Nicholas Ltd, 1967–72; *b* Ponoka, Alberta, Canada, 14 Nov. 1907; *s* of M. O. Nelson, BA; *m* 1939, Christina Elizabeth Powell; two *s*. *Educ:* University of Alberta (MD). Commissioned in RAF, 1935; served: England 1935–36; Egypt and Western Desert, 1936–42; Fighter Command, 1943; UK Delegation (Canada), 1943–44; British Jt Services Mission (Washington), 1945–48; RAF Staff Coll., 1949; Air Ministry, 1949–52; Comd RAF Hosp., Nocton Hall, 1953–55; SMO British Forces, Arabian Peninsula, 1956–57; PMO Technical Training Comd, 1957–59; Bomber Comd, 1959–62, QHP 1961–67. *Recreations:* fishing, golf. *Address:* Caffyn's Copse, Shappen Hill Lane, Burley, Hants BH24 4EP. *T:* Burley (01425) 403308. *Clubs:* Royal Air Force; Royal Lymington Yacht.

NELSON, Stuart; *see* Nelson, R. S.

NEMETZ, Hon. Nathaniel Theodore, CC 1989; Canada Medal 1967; Chief Justice of British Columbia and Administrator of the Province of British Columbia, 1979–88; *b* 8 Sept. 1913; *s* of Samuel and Rebecca (*née* Birch); *m* 1935, Bel Newman (*d* 1991); one *s*. *Educ:* Univ. of British Columbia (BA 1st Cl. Hons History). Called to the Bar, BC, 1937; KC (Canada) 1950. Justice, Supreme Court of BC, 1963–68; Justice, Court of Appeal of BC, 1968–73; Chief Justice, Supreme Court of BC, 1973–78. Exec. Mem., Canadian Judicial Council, 1973–88 (Vice-Chm., 1985–88). Special counsel to: City of Vancouver, City of New Westminster and Municipality of Burnaby; Electrical Assoc.; BC Hosp. Assoc.; Public Utilities Commn of BC; Royal Commission on: Expropriation, 1961; Fishing, 1964; Election Regulations, 1965; Forest Industry, 1966. Chm., Educational Delegn to People's Republic of China, 1974; Advisor to Canadian Govt Delegn, ILO, Geneva, 1973. University of British Columbia: Mem. Senate and Bd of Govs, 1957–68 (Chm. Bd of Govs, 1965–68); Chancellor, 1972–75, now Chancellor Emeritus; Pres., Alumni Assoc., 1957; Hon. Mem., Faculty Assoc., 1972; Chancellor's Medal, 1988. Mem., Bd of Governors, Canadian Inst. for Advanced Legal Studies, Cambridge, England. Hon. Fellow, Hebrew Univ., Jerusalem, 1976. Hon. LLD: Notre Dame (Nelson), 1972; Simon Fraser, 1975; British Columbia, 1975; Victoria, 1976. Freeman, City of Vancouver, 1988. Hon. Consul, Singapore, 1989–. Silver Jubilee Medal, 1977; Medal of Yugoslav Flag with Ribbon, 1989. *Publications:* articles on: Swedish Labour Law and Practice, 1967; Judicial Administration and Judicial Independence, 1976; The Jury and the Citizen, 1985; The Concept of the Independence of the Judiciary, 1985. *Recreations:* reading, travelling. *Address:* 5688 Newton Wynd, Vancouver, BC V6T 1H5, Canada. *T:* (604) 2245383. *Clubs:* Vancouver (Life Mem.), University (Life Mem.; Pres., 1961–62), Faculty of University of British Columbia (Hon. Life Mem.) (Vancouver).

NENDICK, David Alan Challoner, CBE 1990; Secretary for Monetary Affairs, Hong Kong Government, 1985–93; *b* 31 July 1932; *s* of late Cyril Arthur and Kathleen Nendick; *m* 1964, Miriam Louise Gibbons; one *s* two *d*. *Educ:* Haileybury College. National Service, commissioned RA, 1950–52. Bank of England, 1953–89 (seconded Bank of Mauritius, 1970–72 and Hong Kong Govt, 1985–89); Hong Kong Govt, 1989–93. Gov., Dean Close Sch., Cheltenham. *Recreations:* tennis, walking, watching cricket. *Address:* Hideaway House, 83 Cheap Street, Sherborne, Dorset DT9 3BA. *T:* Sherborne (01935) 814023; 26 St Stephens Gardens, W2 5QX. *T:* 0171–792 2940. *Clubs:* East India, Bankers'; Hong Kong Country, Hong Kong Overseas Bankers.

NEPEAN, Lt-Col Sir Evan Yorke, 6th Bt, *cr* 1802; late Royal Signals; *b* 23 Nov. 1909; *s* of Sir Charles Evan Molyneux Yorke Nepean, 5th Bt, and Mary Winifred, *o d* of Rev. William John Swayne, formerly Vicar of Heytesbury, Wilts, and Custos of St John's Hospital, Heytesbury; *S* father 1953; *m* 1940, (Georgiana) Cicely, *o d* of late Major Noel Edward Grey Willoughby, Middlesex Regiment, of Chancel End House, Heytesbury, Wilts; three *d*. *Educ:* Winchester; Downing College, Cambridge (BA 1931; MA 1946). CEng; MIEE. North West Frontier of India (Mohmand), 1935. Served War of 1939–45: GSO3, War Office, 1939–40; with Royal Signals (Lt-Col 1943), UK, and Middle East, Major 1946; on Staff Southern Command, 1947; GSO1 Royal Signals, Ministry of Defence, 1950–53; Lt-Col 1952; Cmdg 11 Air Formation Signal Regt, BAOR, 1955–56, retired. Civil Servant, 1957–59; CSO's branch at HQ Southern Command (Retired

Officers' Staff appt), 1959–73. Mem., Salisbury Diocesan Guild of Ringers. *Recreations:* bell-ringing, amateur radio. *Heir:* none. *Address:* Goldens, Teffont, Salisbury, Wilts SP3 5RP. *T:* Teffont (01722) 716275.

NERINA, Nadia; (*née* Nadine Judd); Prima Ballerina; Ballerina with Royal Ballet, 1951–69; *b* Cape Town, Oct. 1927; *m* 1955, Charles Gordon. Joined Sadler's Wells Sch., 1946; after two months joined Sadler's Wells Theatre Ballet; transferred Sadler's Wells Ballet, Royal Opera House (now Royal Ballet), as soloist, 1967. *Rôles:* Princess Aurora in The Sleeping Beauty; Ondine; Odette-Odile in Swan Lake; Swanhilda in Coppelia; Sylvia; Giselle; Cinderella; Firebird; Can Can Dancer in La Boutique Fantasque; Ballerina in Petrushka; Colombine in Carnaval; Mazurka, Little Waltz, Prelude, in Les Sylphides; Mam'zelle Angot; Ballet Imperial; Scènes de Ballet; Flower Festival of Genzano; Les Rendezvous; Polka in Façade; The Girl in Spectre de la Rose; Casse Noisette; Laurentia; Khadra; Vagabonds; The Bride in A Wedding Bouquet; *creations:* Circus Dancer in Mardi Gras; Fairy Spring in Cinderella; Queen of the Earth in Homage to the Queen; Faded Beauty in Noctambules; Variation on a Theme; Birthday Offering; Lise in La Fille Mal Gardée; Electra; The Girl in Home; Clorinda in Tancredi. Appeared with Royal Ballet: Europe; South Africa; USA; Canada; USSR; Bulgaria; Romania. Recital Tours with Alexis Rassine: South Africa, 1952–55; England, 1956–57; concert performances, Royal Albert Hall and Royal Festival Hall, 1958–60. *Guest appearances include:* Turkish Nat. Ballet, 1957; Bolshoi Ballet, Kirov Ballet, 1960; Munich Ballet, 1963; Nat. Finnish Ballet, Royal Danish Ballet, 1964; Stuttgart Ballet, 1965; Ballet Theatre, Opera House Chicago, 1967; Royal Command Variety Performances, 1963–66. Mounted, dir. and prod three Charity Gala performances, London Palladium, 1969, 1971, 1972. Many TV appearances, UK and USA. Hon. Consultant on Ballet, Ohio Univ., 1967–69. British Jury Member, 3rd Internat. Ballet Competition, Moscow, 1977. Fellow, 1959, Patron, 1964, Cecchetti Soc. Mem. Council, RSPCA, 1969–74. *Publications:* contrib.: La Fille Mal Gardée, 1960; Ballet and Modern Dance, 1974; *relevant publication:* Ballerina, ed Clement Crisp, 1975. *Address:* c/o Royal Opera House, Covent Garden, WC2.

NETHERTHORPE, 3rd Baron *cr* 1959, of Anston, W Riding; **James Frederick Turner;** *b* 7 Jan. 1964; *s* of 2nd Baron Netherthorpe, and of Belinda, *d* of F. Hedley Nicholson; *S* father, 1982; *m* 1989, Elizabeth Curran Fahan, *d* of Edward Fahan, Connecticut; one *s* one *d*. *Educ:* Heatherdown Prep. School; Harrow School. *Heir: s* Hon. Andrew James Edward Turner, *b* 24 March 1993. *Address:* Boothby Hall, Boothby Pagnell, Grantham, Lincs NG33 4PQ. *T:* Ingoldsby (0147685) 374.

NEUBERGER, Albert, CBE 1964; PhD (London), MD (Würzburg); FRCP; FRS 1951; FRSC; Professor of Chemical Pathology, St Mary's Hospital, University of London, 1955–73, now Emeritus Professor; *b* 15 April 1908; *s* of late Max Neuberger and Bertha Neuberger; *m* 1943, Lilian Ida, *d* of late Edmond Dreyfus and Marguerite Dreyfus, London; four *s* (one *d* decd). *Educ:* Gymnasium, Würzburg; Univs of Würzburg and London. Beit Memorial Research Fellow, 1936–40; Research at the Biochemistry Department, Cambridge, 1939–42; Mem. of Scientific Staff, Medical Research Council, 1943; Adviser to GHQ, Delhi (Medical Directorate), 1945; Head of Biochemistry Dept, Nat. Inst. for Medical Research, 1950–55; Principal of the Wright Fleming Institute of Microbiology, 1958–62. Visiting Lectr on Medicine, 1960, on Biol Chemistry, 1964, Harvard Univ., and Physician-in-Chief (*pro tem.*), Peter Bent Brigham Hosp., Boston; Merck, Sharp and Dohme Vis. Prof., Sch. of Medicine, Univ. of Washington, 1965; Royal Soc./Israel Acad. Vis. Res. Prof., 1969; Julius Schultz Vis. Prof., Univ. of Miami Sch. of Medicine, 1988. Mem. of Editorial Bd, Biochemical Jl, 1947–55, Chm., 1952–55; Associate Man. Editor, Biochimica et Biophysica Acta, 1968–81. Member: MRC, 1962–66; Council of Scientific Policy, 1968–69; ARC, 1969–79; Indep. Cttee on Smoking and Health, 1973–82; Sci. Adv. Cttee, Rank Prize Funds, 1974–86; Chm., Jt ARC/MRC Cttee on Food and Nutrition Res., 1971–73; Chairman: Governing Body, Lister Inst., 1971–88 (Mem., 1968–); Advisory Board, Beit Memorial Fellowships, 1967–73; Biochemical Soc., 1967–69 (Hon. Mem., Biochemical Soc., 1973); Dep. Chm., Bd of Governors, Hebrew Univ., Jerusalem. Pres., Assoc. of Clinical Biochemists, 1972–73; Hon. Pres., British Nutrition Foundn, 1982–86. For. Hon. Mem., Amer. Acad. Arts and Sciences, 1972. FRCPath 1964; FRCP 1966. William Julius Mickle Fellowship of Univ. of London, 1946–47; Heberden Medal, 1959; Frederick Gowland Hopkins Medal, 1960; Kaplun Prize, 1973. Hon. LLD, Aberdeen, 1967; Hon. PhD, Jerusalem, 1968; Hon. DSc Hull, 1981. *Publications:* papers in Biochemical Jl, Proceedings of Royal Society and other learned journals. *Address:* 37 Eton Court, Eton Avenue, NW3 3HJ. *T:* 0171–586 5470. *Club:* Athenæum.

See also D. E. Neuberger, M. S. Neuberger.

NEUBERGER, David Edmond; QC 1987; a Recorder, since 1990; *b* 10 Jan. 1948; *s* of Prof. Albert Neuberger, *qv; m* 1976, Angela, *d* of Brig. Peter Holdsworth; two *s* one *d*. *Educ:* Westminster; Christ Church, Oxford (MA). N. M. Rothschild & Sons, 1970–73; called to the Bar, Lincoln's Inn, 1974, Bencher, 1993. *Address:* Falcon Chambers, Falcon Court, EC4Y 1AA. *T:* 0171–353 2484.

See also M. S. Neuberger.

NEUBERGER, Rabbi Julia Babette Sarah; Chairman, Camden and Islington Community Health Services NHS Trust, since 1993; *b* 27 Feb. 1950; *d* of Walter and Alice Schwab; *m* 1973, Anthony John Neuberger; one *s* one *d*. *Educ:* South Hampstead High Sch.; Newnham Coll., Cambridge (BA, MA); Leo Baeck Coll., London (Rabbinic Dip.). Lectr and Associate Fellow, Leo Baeck Coll., 1979–; Associate, Newnham Coll., Cambridge, 1983–; Harkness Fellow, Harvard Univ., 1991–92; Associate Fellow, King's Fund Coll., 1993–. Rabbi, South London Liberal Synagogue, 1977–89; Chm., Rabbinic Conf., Union of Liberal and Progressive Synagogues, 1983–85. Member: Council, N London Hospice Gp, 1984–91; Ethics Adv. Gp, RCN, 1986–93; BMA Ethics Cttee, 1992–94; NHS Health Adv. Service, 1993–; Council, St George's Hosp. Med. Sch., 1987–93; Chairman: Patients' Assoc., 1988–91; RCN Commn on the Health Service, 1988; Adv. Cttee, UK Clearing House on Health Outcomes, Nuffield Inst., 1992–95. Member: Nat. Cttee, SDP, 1982–88; Policy Cttee, SDP, 1983–85; Convenor, SDP/Liberal Lawyers' Working Party on Legal Services, 1985–87; Mem., Editorial Bd, Political Qly, 1987–93. Presenter, Choices, BBC TV, 1986 and 1987; Member: Interim (formerly Voluntary) Licensing Authority for IVF, 1987–91; Human Fertilization and Embryology Authority, 1990–; GMC, 1993–; Exec., Anchor Housing Assoc. and Trust, 1985–87; Exec., NCVO, 1988–89; Exec., Unicef UK, 1989–91; Council, SCF, 1994–; Bd, Citizenship Foundn, 1989–92; Council, St George's House, Windsor, 1989–94; Council, Runnymede Trust, 1989–; Governor, British Inst. of Human Rights, 1989–93. Chancellor, Univ. of Ulster, 1993–. Member Council: RHBNC, 1991–93; UCL, 1993–; Mem. Visiting Cttee, Meml Church, Harvard Univ., 1994–; Governor: James Allen's Girls' Sch., 1994–; Dulwich Coll. Prep. Sch., 1995–. Booker Prize Judge, 1994. DUniv Humberside, 1992; Hon. DSc Ulster, 1994; Hon. DLitt City, 1994. *Publications:* The Story of Judaism (for children), 1986, 2nd edn 1988; (ed) Days of Decision (4 in series), 1987; Caring for Dying Patients of Different Faiths, 1987, 2nd edn 1994; (ed with John A. White) A Necessary End, 1991; Whatever's Happening to Women?, 1991; Ethics and Healthcare: the role of Research Ethics Committees in the UK, 1992; (ed) The Things That Matter (anthology of women's spiritual poetry), 1993; contribs to various books on cultural, religious and ethical factors in nursing, reviews for variety of jls and newspapers. *Recreations:* riding, sailing, Irish life, opera, setting up the old girls' network, children. *Address:* 36 Orlando Road, SW4 0LF. *T:* 0171–622 2995. *Club:* Groucho.

NEUBERGER, Dr Michael Samuel, FRS 1993; Member, Scientific Staff, Medical Research Council Laboratory of Molecular Biology, Cambridge, since 1980; Fellow, Trinity College, Cambridge, since 1985; *b* 2 Nov. 1953; *s* of Prof. Albert Neuberger, *qv* and Lilian Ida (*née* Dreyfus); *m* 1991, Gillian Anne, *d* of late James and Anne Pyman; two *d*. *Educ:* Westminster Sch.; Trinity Coll., Cambridge (BA 1974; MA); Imperial Coll., University of London (PhD 1978). Res. Fellow, Trinity Coll., Cambridge, 1977–81; SRC Postdoctoral Fellow, Imperial Coll., London, 1977–79; EMBO Postdoctoral Fellow, Inst. of Genetics, Cologne, 1979–80. Internat. Res. Scholar, Howard Hughes Med. Inst., 1992–. Mem., EMBO, 1989–. *Publications:* articles in learned jls on molecular biol. and immunology. *Address:* Medical Research Council Laboratory of Molecular Biology, Hills Road, Cambridge CB2 2QH. *T:* Cambridge (01223) 248011; Trinity College, Cambridge CB2 1TQ. *T:* Cambridge (01223) 338400.

See also D. E. Neuberger.

NEUBERT, Sir Michael (Jon), Kt 1990; MP (C) Romford, since Feb. 1974; *b* 3 Sept. 1933; *s* of Frederick Henry and Mathilda Marie Louise Neubert; *m* 1959, Sally Felicity Bilger; one *s*. *Educ:* Queen Elizabeth's Sch., Barnet; Bromley Grammar Sch.; Royal Coll. of Music; Downing Coll., Cambridge. MA (Cantab) Modern and Medieval Langs. Travel and industrial consultant. Councillor, Borough of Bromley, 1960–63; London Borough of Bromley: Councillor, 1964–68; Alderman, 1968–74; Leader of the Council, 1967–70; Mayor, 1972–73. Contested (C): N Hammersmith, 1966; Romford, 1970. PPS to: Minister for Social Security and for the Disabled, 1980; Ministers of State, NI Office, 1981; Minister of State for Employment, 1981–82; Sec. of State for Trade, 1982–83; Asst Govt Whip, 1983–86; a Lord Comr of HM Treasury, 1986–88; Vice-Chamberlain of HM Household, 1988; Parly Under-Sec. of State for the Armed Forces, 1988–89, for Defence Procurement, 1989–90, MoD. Chm., Cons. Backbench Employment Cttee, 1992–; Mem., 1922 Exec. Cttee, 1992–. Chm., Bromley Conservative Assoc., 1968–69. *Publication:* Running Your Own Society, 1967. *Recreations:* music, literature, cinema, theatre, the countryside. *Address:* House of Commons, SW1A 0AA. *Club:* Romford Conservative and Constitutional.

NEUMANN, Prof. Bernhard Hermann, AC 1994; FACE 1970; FAA 1964; FRS 1959; Honorary Research Fellow, CSIRO Division of Mathematics and Statistics, since 1978; *b* Berlin-Charlottenburg, 15 Oct. 1909; *s* of late Richard Neumann and late Else (*née* Aronstein); *m* 1st, 1938, Hanna Neumann (*née* von Caemmerer) (*d* 1971), DPhil, DSc, FAA, formerly Prof. and Head of Dept of Pure Mathematics, Sch. of Gen. Studies, ANU; three *s* two *d*; 2nd, 1973, Dorothea Neumann (*née* Zeim), MA, PhD. *Educ:* Herderschule, Berlin; Univs of Freiburg, Berlin, Cambridge. Dr phil Berlin, 1932; PhD Cambridge 1935; DSc Manchester 1954. Asst Lectr, University Coll, Cardiff, 1937–40. Army Service, 1940–45. Lectr, University Coll., Hull, 1946–48; Lectr, Senior Lectr, Reader, Univ. of Manchester, 1948–61; Prof. and Hd of Dept of Maths, Inst. of Advanced Studies, ANU, Canberra, 1962–74, Emeritus Prof., 1975–; Sen. Res. Fellow, CSIRO Div. of Maths and Stats, 1975–77. Visiting Lecturer: Australian Univs, 1959; Univ. of Cambridge, 1970; Monash Univ., 1980; Visiting Professor: Tata Inst. of Fundamental Research, Bombay, 1959; New York Univ., 1961–62; Univ. of Wisconsin, 1966–67; Vanderbilt Univ., 1969–70; G. A. Miller Vis. Prof., Univ. of Illinois at Urbana-Champaign, 1975; Univ. of Manitoba, 1979; Vis. Fellow, Fitzwilliam Coll., Cambridge, 1970; SERC Visiting Fellow: Univ. of Glasgow, 1985; Univ. of Wales Coll. of Cardiff, 1991; Deutscher Akademischer Austauschs-Dienst Visitor, Univ. of Bielefeld, 1987. Wiskundig Genootschap te Amsterdam Prize, 1949; Adams Prize, Univ. of Cambridge, 1952–53. Mem., Aust. Subcommn, Internat. Commn Math. Instruct., 1967–75 (Chm.), and 1979–83; Mem.-at-large, Internat. Commn Math. Instruct., 1975–82, Mem. Exec. Cttee, 1979–82; Mem., Programme Adv. Cttee, Congress Math. Educn, Karlsruhe, 1976, Berkeley, Calif., 1980, Adelaide, Australia, 1984. Member Council: London Math. Society, 1954–61 (Vice-Pres., 1957–59); Aust. Math. Society, 1963–79 (Vice-Pres., 1963–64, 1966–68, 1971–73, Pres., 1964–66; Hon. Mem. 1981–; Fellow, 1994); Aust. Acad. of Science, 1968–71 (a Vice-Pres., 1969–71). Mem. Aust. Nat. Cttee for Mathematics, 1963–75 (Chm., 1966–75); (Foundation) Pres., Aust. Assoc. Math. Teachers, 1966–68, Vice-Pres., 1968–69, Hon. Mem., 1975–; (Foundn) Pres., Canberra Math. Assoc., 1963–65, Vice-Pres., 1965–66, Hon. Mem., 1975–; Hon. Mem., NZ Math. Soc., 1975–; Member: Acad. Adv. Council, RAN Coll., 1978–87; Sci. and Industry Forum, 1989–93. Chairman: Internat. Math. Olympiad Site Cttee, 1981–83; Aust. Math. Olympiad Cttee, 1980–86. Hon. DSc: Univ. of Newcastle, NSW, 1974; Monash Univ., 1982; Univ. of WA, 1995; Univ. of Hull, 1995; Hon. DMath Univ. of Waterloo, 1986; Hon. Dr rer. nat. Humboldt Univ., 1992. Non-res. Fellow (Tutor), Bruce Hall, ANU, 1963–; Hon. Fellow: Dept of Maths, Inst. of Advanced Studies, Sch. of Mathematical Scis, ANU, 1975–; Inst. of Combinatories and its Applications, 1990–. Pres., Amateur Sinfonia of Canberra Inc., 1978–80, Vice-Pres., 1980–81, 1983–84, Hon. Mem., 1984–85; Vice-Pres., Friends of the Canberra Sch. of Music, 1983–; Pres., Woden Valley Chess Club, 1994–. Hon. Editor, Proc. London Math. Soc., 1959–61; Assoc. Editor, Pacific Jl Math., 1964–92; (Foundation) Editor, Bulletin of Aust. Math. Soc., 1969–79, Hon. Editor, 1979–; Member Editorial Board: Communications in Algebra, 1973–84; Houston Jl Math., 1974–; Mem., Adv. Bd, Zentralblatt Didaktik Math. 1970–84; Editorial Advr, SE Asian Math. Bull., 1987–; Founder Editor and Publisher, IMU Canberra Circular, 1972–; Hon. Editor, Algebra Colloquium, Beijing, 1994–Dec. 1996; Mem. and Regional Chm., IMU Exchange Commn, 1975–78. *Publications:* Appendix to German and Hungarian translations of A. G. Kuroš: Teoriya Grupp, 1953, 1955: Topics in the Theory of Infinite Groups, Bombay, 1961; Special Topics in Algebra, Vol. I: Universal Algebra, Vol. II: Order Techniques, New York, 1962; Selected Works of B. H. Neumann and Hanna Neumann, 6 vols, 1988; papers, mainly on theory of groups, in various mathematical journals. *Recreations:* chess, cycling, music. *Address:* 20 Talbot Street, Forrest, ACT 2603, Australia. *T:* (6) 2733447, *Fax:* (6) 2495549.

NEVILE, Sir Henry (Nicholas), KCVO 1992; Lord-Lieutenant of Lincolnshire, 1975–95; High Steward, Lincoln Cathedral, since 1985; *b* 13 March 1920; *e s* of late Charles Joseph Nevile, Wellingore, Lincoln and Muriel (*née* O'Conor), *m* 1944, Jean Rosita Mary, MBE 1984, *d* of Cyril James Winceslas Torr and Maude (*née* Walpole); two *s* three *d*. *Educ:* Ampleforth; Trinity Coll., Cambridge. Served war, Scots Guards, in NW Europe, 1940–46 (despatches). Member: Upper Witham IDB, 1952–83 (Chm., 1964–76); Lincs River Bd and Authy, 1962–82; Kesteven CC, 1964–72. Liveryman, Farmers' Co., 1975– (Master, 1991–92). JP 1950, DL 1962, High Sheriff, 1963, Lincolnshire. Hon. Col, Lincs ACF. Hon. LLD Hull, 1994. KStJ. *Address:* Aubourn Hall, Lincoln LN5 9DZ. *T:* Lincoln (01522) 788270. *Club:* Brooks's.

NEVILL, family name of **Marquess of Abergavenny.**

NEVILL, Prof. Bernard Richard, FCSD; designer; Professor of Textile Design, Royal College of Art, 1984–89 (Fellow, since 1984); Director, Bernard Nevill Ltd (own furnishing collections), since 1990; *b* 24 Sept. 1934; *s* of R. G. Nevill. *Educ:* privately; St Martin's Sch. of Art; Royal Coll. of Art. FSIA 1970. Designed exhibn, Opera and Ballet, for Cotton Bd, Manchester, 1950; lectured in art, fashion, history of costume, textile design and fashion drawing, Shoreditch Coll., 1954–56 (resp. for first dress show staged at GLC Chm's annual reception, County Hall); Lectr, St Martin's Sch. of Art and RCA, 1959–74 (liaised between Fashion and Textile Schs, devising projs and themes for finale to RCA annual diploma show); lectured in theatre design and book illustration, Central Sch. of Art and Design, 1957–60; freelance illustrator, Good Housekeeping, Woman's Jl, Vogue, Harper's Bazaar, incl. covers for Queen and Sketch, 1956–60; freelance journalist, Vogue, Sketch and textile and fashion periodicals, 1956–66; Art Critic, Vogue, 1965–66; Designer (later Design Dir), Liberty Prints, 1961: for next decade, produced collections which became fashion landmarks and re-estabd Liberty's as major source of fashion textiles worldwide; collections designed: Islamic, 1963 (anticipated Eastern revival in fashion); Jazz, 1964 (first re-appraisal of Art Deco); Tango, 1966; Renaissance, 1967; Chameleon, 1969 (co-ordinated prints); Designer and Design Dir, Ten Cate, Holland, 1969–71; Design Consultant in dress fabrics to Cantoni (founders of cotton industry in Italy), 1971–84: printed velvets and cottons have placed Cantoni in forefront of internat. ready-to-wear; designed printed sheet collection for Cantoni Casa, 1977; textile consultant and designer of dress fabrics, Unitika Ltd, Japan, 1990–; dress fabric collections for KBC, Germany, 1993–; furnishing textile designs commnd by Pierre Frey, France, 1991–; furnishing collections produced by DMC Texunion, France, 1992–; redesign and supervision of restoration of interiors: Lennoxlove Castle, 1988–89; Eastnor Castle, 1989–. Designed: two collections for Internat. Wool Secretariat, 1975–77; English Country House Collection for Sekers Internat., 1981–82 (used this collection when redesigning Long Gall., Lutyen's British Embassy, Washington); Collections for Romanex de Boussac, France, 1982–87, including English Gardens, Botanic, Figurative Porcelain Prints and Printed Damasks; furnishing collection for restored Château de Bagnole, France. Designed costumes: films: Genevieve, 1953; Next To No Time, 1955; The Admirable Crichton, 1957; musical: Marigold, 1958; opera: Così fan tutte (Glyndebourne), 1962. Engaged in restoration of Fonthill Abbey and woodlands, 1976–. Mem., Adv. Panel, National Dip. of Design, 1964–66; Governor, Croydon Coll. of Art, 1966–67. FRSA 1966, resigned 1977. Book reviewer, TLS, 1987–. Illustrated articles on his work have appeared in the Press. *Recreations:* looking at large well-built walls and buildings; passionate conservationist and environmentalist, collector, bibliophil; tree-worship, chamber music. *Address:* West House, 35 Glebe Place, SW3 5JP; Fonthill Abbey, Fonthill Gifford, near Salisbury, Wilts SP3 6PX.

NEVILL, Maj.-Gen. Cosmo Alexander Richard, CB 1958; CBE 1954; DSO 1944; War Office, 1958–60; Colonel, Royal Fusiliers, 1959–63, retired; *b* 14 July 1907; *s* of late Maj. Cosmo Charles Richard Nevill, DSO, OBE, Eccleston, Leamington Spa; *m* 1934, Grania, *d* of late Maj. G. V. Goodliffe, MC, Birdstown, co. Donegal; one *s* one *d*. *Educ:* Harrow; Royal Military College. Commissioned as Second Lieutenant, Royal Fusiliers, 1927; served War of 1939–45 (DSO, OBE): on staff, India; commanded 2nd battalion Devonshire Regiment, Normandy; Lieutenant-Colonel, 1944. A General Staff Officer, Military Staff Committee, United Nations, New York, 1946–48; Chief Instr, Sch. of Infantry, 1948–50; commanded 1st battalion Royal Fusiliers, 1950–51; a Brigade Commander, 1951–54; Commandant School of Infantry, 1954–56; Major-General 1957; GOC 2nd Infantry Division, 1956–58. CC West Suffolk, 1962–67. Lay Canon, St Edmundsbury Cathedral, 1979–85. Freeman, City of London, 1962. *Address:* Holt, Edwardstone, Sudbury, Suffolk CO10 5PJ. *T:* Boxford (01787) 210428. *Clubs:* Army and Navy; I Zingari.

NEVILLE, family name of **Baron Braybrooke.**

NEVILLE, Prof. Adam Matthew, CBE 1994; TD 1963; FEng 1986; FRSE 1979; arbitrator and consultant on concrete and structural design and failures; Partner (formerly Director), A & M Neville Engineering, since 1975; Principal and Vice-Chancellor, University of Dundee, 1978–87; *b* 5 Feb. 1923; *m* 1952, Mary Hallam Cousins; one *s* one *d*. BSc 1st cl. Hons, MSc, PhD, DSc (Eng) London; DSc Leeds; FICE, FIStructE. Served War, Polish Forces under British comd, MC; Major RE (TA), 1950–63. Lectr, Southampton Univ., 1950–51; Engr, Min. of Works, NZ, 1951–54; Lectr, Manchester Univ., 1955–60; Prof. of Civil Engrg, Nigerian Coll. of Technology, 1960–62; Dean of Engrg, Calgary Univ., 1963–67, also Dean of Graduate Studies, 1965–66; Vis. Prof., Swiss Federal Inst. of Technology, 1967–68; Prof. and Head of Dept of Civil Engineering, Univ. of Leeds, 1968–78. Chm., Cttee of Principals of Scottish Univs, 1984–86. Former Chm., Permanent Concrete Commn, RILEM (Internat. Union of Testing and Res. Labs for Materials and Structures); Dir, Petroleum Recovery Res. Inst.; Advr to Canadian Govt on management of concrete research. Member Council: Concrete Soc., 1968–77, (Pres., 1974–75); IStructE, 1976–79; Faculty of Building, 1976–80; Royal Acad. (formerly Fellowship) of Engrg, 1989–95 (Vice-Pres., 1991–95); Open University, 1979–87; Council of Europe Standing Conference on Univ. Problems, 1980–87 (Pres., 1984–86); Member: Bd, Architectural Educn, ARC, 1980–87; Exec. Cttee, IUPC, 1979–90 (Vice-Chm., 1983–85); British Library Adv. Council, 1989–94; SERC Envmt Cttee, 1988–91; Athlone-Vanier Fellowships Bd, 1990–. Mem. Editorial Boards of various technical jls. Fellow, Amer. Concrete Inst., 1973, Hon. Mem., 1986; Hon. Fellow: Inst. of Concrete Technology, 1976; Singapore Concrete Inst., 1987; Hon. For. Mem., Académie Royale des Sciences d'Outre-Mer, Belgium, 1974. Hon. LLD St Andrews, 1987. IStructE Research Award, 1960; Reinforced Concrete Assoc. Medal, 1961; Senior Research Fellowship, Nat. Research Council of Canada, 1967; Stanton Walker Award (US) 1968; Medal of Univ. of Liège (Belgium), 1970; Arthur R. Anderson Award, Amer. Concrete Inst., 1972; President's Medal, Soc. of Engrs, 1985; Silver Medal, Inst. of Concrete Technology, 1993. OStJ 1983. *Publications:* Properties of Concrete, 1963, 4 edns, trans. into 12 languages; (with J. B. Kennedy) Basic Statistical Methods, 1964, 3 edns; Creep of Concrete: plain, reinforced and prestressed, 1970; (with A. Ghali) Structural Analysis: a unified classical and matrix approach, 1971, 3rd edn 1989, trans. into Chinese; Hardened Concrete: physical and mechanical aspects, 1971; High Alumina Cement Concrete, 1975; (with W. H. Dilger and J. J. Brooks) Creep of Plain and Structural Concrete, 1983; (with J. J. Brooks) Concrete Technology, 1987; numerous research papers on concrete and concrete structures. *Recreations:* ski-ing, travel (Travelers' Century Club Plaque, 1990). *Address:* 24 Gun Wharf, 130 Wapping High Street, E1 9NH. *T:* 0171–265 1087. *Clubs:* Athenæum; New (Edinburgh).

NEVILLE, Prof. (Alexander) Munro, MD; FRCPath; Research Secretary and Administrator, Ludwig Institute for Cancer Research, since 1985; *b* 24 March 1935; *s* of Alexander Munro and Georgina Neville; *m* 1961, Anne Margaret Stroyan Black; one *s* one *d*. *Educ:* Hillhead High Sch.; Univ. of Glasgow (MB ChB 1959; PhD 1965; MD 1969); Harvard Med. Sch.; DSc London, 1985. MRCPath 1969, FRCPath 1981. Med. appts, Glasgow Royal and Victoria Infirmaries, 1960–65; Res. Fellow, Harvard Med. Sch., 1965–67; Sen. Lectr in Pathology, Univ. of Glasgow, 1967–70; Hon. Consultant Pathologist, Royal Marsden Hosp., 1970–85; Prof. of Experimental Pathology, Univ. of London, 1972–85; Dean, Inst. of Cancer Research, 1982–84; Dir, Ludwig Inst. for Cancer Research, London Branch, 1975–85. Vis. Prof. of Pathol., RPMS, 1992–. Hon. Treas., RCPath, 1993–. *Publications:* The Human Adrenal Cortex, 1982; numerous papers on oncology and pathology in primary jls. *Recreations:* golf, gardening. *Address:* (office) Glen House, Stag Place, SW1E 5AG. *T:* 0171–828 0202, *Fax:* 0171–828 5427; 6 Woodlands Park, Tadworth, Surrey KT20 7TL. *T:* Tadworth (01737) 844113, *Fax:* (01737) 844287. *Clubs:* Athenæum; Banstead Downs.

NEVILLE, (Eric) Graham; His Honour Judge Neville; a Circuit Judge, since 1980; *b* 12 Nov. 1933; *m* 1966, Jacqueline Catherine. *Educ:* Kelly Coll.; Sidney Sussex Coll., Cambridge. Served Royal Air Force, General Duties. Called to Bar, Middle Temple, 1958. A Recorder of the Crown Court, 1975–80. *Recreations:* sailing, fishing. *Address:* Exeter Crown Court, The Castle, Exeter EX4 3PS. *Club:* Royal Western Yacht (Plymouth).

NEVILLE, John, OBE 1965; actor, stage and film; Hon. Professor in Drama, Nottingham University, since 1967; Artistic Director, Festival Theatre, Stratford, Ontario, 1985–89; *b* Willesden, 2 May 1925; *s* of Reginald Daniel Neville and Mabel Lillian (*née* Fry); *m* 1949, Caroline Hooper; three *s* three *d*. *Educ:* Willesden and Chiswick County Schools; Royal Academy of Dramatic Art. Worked as a stores clerk before studying at RADA. First appearance on stage, walking-on part in Richard II; subseq. parts at Open Air Theatre, in repertory at Lowestoft, and with Birmingham Repertory Co.; Bristol Old Vic Co., 1950–53; Old Vic Co., London, 1953–61; Nottingham Playhouse, 1961–63; Theatre Director, Nottingham Playhouse, 1963–68; Dir, Park Theatre Co., Fortune, 1969; Theatre Director: Citadel Theatre, Edmonton, Canada, 1973–78; Neptune Theatre, Halifax, NS, 1978–83. Parts with Old Vic include: Ferdinand in The Tempest, Macduff, Richard II, Orlando in As You Like It, Henry Percy in Henry IV, Part I, Mark Antony; during Old Vic tour of Europe, 1958, Hamlet, Sir Andrew Aguecheek. Played lead in Irma La Douce, Lyric, 1959–60; produced Henry V, Old Vic, 1960; The Lady From the Sea, Queen's, 1961; The School for Scandal, Haymarket, 1962; Alfie, Mermaid and Duchess, 1963. Acted in: The Chichester Festival Theatre, 1962; Beware of the Dog, St Martin's, 1967; Iago in Othello, Nottingham Playhouse, 1967; Mr and Mrs, Palace, 1968; The Apple Cart, Mermaid, 1970; The Beggar's Opera, The Doctor's Dilemma, Chichester, 1972; Sherlock Holmes, NY, 1975; Happy Days, Nat. Theatre, 1977; Grand Theatre, London, Ontario: acted in Dear Antoine and Arsenic and Old Lace, directed Hamlet, 1983; Stratford, Ontario: acted in Loves Labours' Lost, 1983, Merchant of Venice, 1984, Intimate Admiration, 1987, My Fair Lady, 1988; directed Mother Courage, and Othello, 1987, Three Sisters, 1989; acted in: The School for Scandal, NT, 1990; The Dance of Death, Almeida, 1995. Tour W Africa (Jt Dir and acting), 1963. *Films:* Oscar Wilde; Topaze; Billy Budd; A Study in Terror; Adventures of Baron of Munchausen. Has appeared on television, incl. The First Churchills, series for BBC 2. Hon. Dr Dramatic Arts Lethbridge Univ., 1979; Hon. DFA Nova Scotia Coll. of Art and Design, 1981. *Address:* 99 Norman Street, Stratford, Ont N5A 5R8, Canada. *Club:* Savage.

NEVILLE, (John) Oliver, MA, PhD; Consultant to Royal Academy of Dramatic Art, since 1993 (Principal, 1984–93); *b* 14 Aug. 1929; *s* of Frederick and Ethel Neville; *m* 1st, 1952, Shirley Hall; one *s* one *d*; 2nd, 1964, Pat Heywood. *Educ:* Price's Sch., Fareham; King's Coll., Cambridge (Le Bas Student; BA Eng. Lit., MA, PhD). After National Service, engaged in following with ultimate aim of becoming a theatre director: studied theatre design under Reginald Leefe, 1949–51; joined Old Vic Co., walking on in Tyrone Guthrie's Tamburlaine, with Donald Wolfit, 1951; studied singing with Clive Carey and Frank Titterton; seasons of rep. at York, Scarborough, Worthing, Bristol, Birmingham and Manchester, 1952–58; re-joined Old Vic Co., 1958 (roles included Warwick in Henry VI Trilogy and Claudius in Hamlet); toured America, Poland, Russia, India, Pakistan, Ceylon, with Old Vic and Bristol Old Vic, as stage dir, actor and dir; Associate Dir, Old Vic Co., 1960–62 (directed Macbeth and The Tempest); Director: Library Theatre, Manchester, 1963–66; Arts Theatre, Ipswich, 1966–69; Mature Student, Cambridge, 1969–76 (PhD on Ben Jonson's Masques and Poetry); Caroline Spurgeon Res. Fellow, Bedford Coll., London, 1977–79; Sen. Lectr in Drama, Univ. of Bristol, 1979–84. *Recreations:* mediaeval church architecture and stained-glass, gardening. *Address:* c/o Peters, Fraser & Dunlop, 503 The Chambers, Chelsea Harbour, SW10 0XF.

NEVILLE, Munro; *see* Neville, A. M.

NEVILLE, Air Vice-Marshal Patrick, CB 1988; OBE 1976; AFC 1960; Chief of Air Staff, Royal New Zealand Air Force, 1986–89, retired; *b* 23 Sept. 1932; *s* of Patrick Joseph Neville and Helena Neville; *m* 1954, Barbara Howell; one *s* one *d*. *Educ:* Purbrook Park County High Sch. (SchCert). Commnd 1951; Navigator: RAF, 1951–55; RNZAF, 1955; CO No 14 Sqdn RNZAF, 1966–69; Base Comdr, RNZAF Base Ohakea, NZ, 1969–70; Hon. ADC to Gov. Gen., 1972; Sen. ASO, Air HQ, ANZUK Force Singapore; later, Dep. Comdr NZ Force SE Asia in Singapore, 1973–75; RNZAF Air Staff, 1975–77; Base Comdr, RNZAF Base Auckland, 1978–79; AOC RNZAF Support Gp, 1980–82; Asst CDS for Operations and Plans, Defence HQ, Wellington, 1982–83; Hd of NZ Defence Liaison Staff, London, 1984–86. Gp Captain 1973, Air Cdre 1980, Air Vice-Marshal 1986. FNZIM; FRAeS. *Recreations:* golf, fishing. *Address:* 12 Mark Place, Lynmore, Rotorua, New Zealand. *T:* (7) 3459650. *Club:* Rotorua Golf.

NEVILLE, Sir Roger (Albert Gartside), Kt 1994; VRD 1965; FCA; Group Chief Executive, Sun Alliance Group, 1987–94; *b* 23 Dec. 1931; *s* of Geoffrey Graham Gartside Neville and Veronica Lily Neville; *m* 1957, Brenda Mary Parke Hamilton; one *s* three *d*. Royal Navy, 1950–52; joined Sun Alliance Insurance, 1962; General Manager, 1977; Dep. Chief General Manager, 1984. *Recreations:* sailing, fly fishing, cabinet making. *Address:* Possingworth Manor, Blackboys, near Uckfield, East Sussex TN22 5HE. *Clubs:* Royal Automobile, Royal Ocean Racing.

NEVILLE, Royce Robert; Agent-General for Tasmania, in London, 1971–78; Governing Director, Neville Constructions Pty Ltd, Burnie; *b* 5 Oct. 1914; *s* of R. P. Neville, Launceston, Tasmania; *m* 1941, Joan, *d* of G. A. Scott; two *s* two *d*. *Educ:* Launceston Technical Coll. Served War, Sqdn Ldr (OC Flying, Chief Flying Instr, Gen Reconnaissance Sqdn), RAAF, 1941–45. OC Air Trg Corps, Burnie, 1947. Past President: Air Force Assoc., 1947; Tas. Apex, 1948; Tas. Master Builders' Assoc., 1965–67; Master Builders' Fedn of Aust., 1965–66; Comr of Oaths for Tasmania, 1971; Mem., Australia Soc., London; Life Mem., Tasmanian Master Builders' Assoc. FInstD, FRAIB, AFAIM, Fellow, Inst. of Dirs, Aust., 1971; MIEx 1973; FFB 1976; FIArb 1977. Freeman, City of London, 1975; Freeman, Guild of Air Pilots and Air Navigators, 1976. JP 1974. *Recreations:* boating, fishing, painting. *Address:* 57 Illabunda Drive, Malua Bay, NSW 2536, Australia. *Clubs:* Wig and Pen; Naval, Military and Air Force (Hobart).

NEVILLE-JONES, (Lilian) Pauline, CMG 1987; HM Diplomatic Service; Political Director and Deputy Under-Secretary of State, Foreign and Commonwealth Office, since 1994; *b* 2 Nov. 1939; *d* of Roland Neville-Jones and Cecilia Emily Millicent Rath. *Educ:* Leeds Girls' High Sch.; Lady Margaret Hall, Oxford (BA Hons Mod. History). Harkness Fellow of Commonwealth Fund, USA, 1961–63; joined FO, 1963; Third Sec., Salisbury, Rhodesia, 1964–65; Third, later Second Sec., Singapore, 1965–68; FCO, 1968–71; First Sec., Washington, 1971–75; FCO, 1975–77; Mem. Cabinet, later Chef de Cabinet to Christopher Tugendhat, European Comr for Budget, Financial Control, Financial Instns and Taxation, 1977–82; Vis. Fellow, RIIA, and Inst. français des relations internationales, 1982–83; Head of Planning Staff, FCO, 1983–87; Minister (Econ.), 1987–88, Minister, 1988–91, Bonn; Dep. Sec., Cabinet Office (on secondment), 1991–94; Chm., Jt Intelligence Cttee, Cabinet Office, 1993–94. FRSA 1986. *Recreations:* antiques, cooking, gardening. *Address:* Foreign and Commonwealth Office, SW1A 2AH.

NEVILLE-ROLFE, Lucy Jeanne; Director, Deregulation Unit, Cabinet Office (formerly Department of Trade and Industry), since 1995; *b* 2 Jan. 1953; *d* of Edmund and Margaret Neville-Rolfe; *m* Richard John Packer, *qv*; four *s*. *Educ:* Somerville Coll., Oxford (BA PPE; MA). Joined MAFF, 1973; Pvte Sec. to Minister of Agric., Fisheries and Food, 1977–79; EC Sheepmeat and Milk, 1979–86; Land Use, 1986–88; Food Safety Act, 1988–90; Head of Personnel, 1990–92; Mem., Prime Minister's Policy Unit, 1992–94; Under Sec., 1994. *Recreations:* cricket, racing, gardening, art, architecture, theatre. *Address:* Deregulation Unit, Ashdown House, 123 Victoria Street, SW1E 6RB. *T:* 0171–215 6637.
See also M. T. Neville-Rolfe.

NEVILLE-ROLFE, Marianne Teresa; Regional Director, Government Office for the North West, Department of Trade and Industry, since 1994; *b* 9 Oct 1944; *d* of Edmund Neville-Rolfe and Margaret (*née* Evans); *m* 1972, David William John Blake (marr. diss. 1992). *Educ:* St Mary's Convent, Shaftesbury; Lady Margaret Hall, Oxford (BA). CBI, 1965–73 (Head, Brussels Office, 1971–72); Principal, DTI, 1973, Asst Sec., 1982, Under Sec., Internal European Policy Div., 1987; Chief Exec., CS Coll., and Dir, Top Management Prog., OMCS, then OPSS, Cabinet Office, 1990. *Recreations:* travel, opera. *Address:* (office) Sunley Tower, Piccadilly Plaza, Manchester M1 4BA. *T:* 0161–952 4002.

NEVIN, His Honour (Thomas) Richard, TD 1949 (and Bar); JP; LLB; retired 1984, as senior Circuit Judge on NE Circuit; a Judge of County Courts, later a Circuit Judge, 1967–84; a Deputy High Court Judge, 1974–84; Hon. Life Member, Council of HM Circuit Judges; *b* 9 Dec. 1916; *e s* of late Thomas Nevin, JP, and Phyllis (*née* Strickland), Ebchester Hall and Mirfield; *m* 1955, Brenda Micaela (marr. diss. 1979), *e d* of Dr B. C. Andrade-Thompson, MC, Scarborough; one *s* (and one *s* decd). *Educ:* Bilton Grange; Shrewsbury School; Leeds University. LLB 1939. 2nd Lt, W Yorks Regt (Leeds Rifles) TA, 1935. Served London Bombardment, India and Burma, 1939–46; Indian Artillery, Lt-Col 1944 (despatches), SEAC; DJAG, XII Army, 1945. Major, TARO, 1951. WR Special Constab., 1938–66. Articled Clerk to Sir A. M. Ramsden, CB, Solicitor, 1935. Called to Bar, Inner Temple, 1948; practised 19 years on NE Circuit (Junior, 1951); Law Lectr, Leeds Coll. of Commerce, 1949–51; Asst Recorder of Leeds, 1961–64; Recorder of Doncaster, 1964–67; Dep. Chm., Quarter Sessions: W Riding, 1965–71; E Riding, 1968–71, Yorkshire; Chm., Northern Agricultural Land Tribunal, 1963–67 (Dep. Chm. 1961–63); a special Divorce Comr, 1967–72; Mem., County Court Rule Cttee, 1974–80; Chm., Lord Chancellor's Adv. Cttee on JP's, Hull, 1968–74; apptd by Minister of Transport to conduct enquiries under Merchant Shipping Acts, 1986–89. Founder Chm., Leeds Family Mediation Service, 1979–84. Director, Bowishott Estates Ltd; Member: Leeds Gp Hospital Management Cttee, 1965–67; Thoresby Soc.; Yorks Archæological Soc.; President, Yorks Numismatic Soc., 1968; Life Mem., Guild of Freemen of London; Vice-Pres. Leeds Univ. Law Graduates; Mem., Leeds Univ. Adv. Cttee on Law. FRNS; FRSA; FCIArb. Freeman of City of London. JP West Yorks 1965–. *Publications:* Hon. Editor, Yorkshire Numismatic Soc.; and various articles. *Recreations:* coinage, our past, retirement, and rest. *Address:* The Court House, 1 Oxford Row, Leeds LS2 7DG; 11 King's Bench Walk, Temple, EC4Y 7EQ.

NEW, Maj.-Gen. Sir Laurence (Anthony Wallis), Kt 1990; CB 1986; CBE 1980; Lieutenant Governor of the Isle of Man, and President of the Tynwald Court, 1985–90; International President, Association of Military Christian Fellowships, since 1991; *b* 25 Feb. 1932; *s* of Lt-Col S. W. New, MBE and Mrs C. M. New; *m* 1956, Anna Doreen Verity; two *s* two *d*. *Educ:* King William's College, Isle of Man; RMA Sandhurst, 1950–52; commissioned, RTR, 1952; service in Hong Kong, Germany, Malaya, Borneo; CO 4 RTR, 1971–73; Bde Major, 20th Armd Bde, 1969–70; Sec., Defence Policy Staff, 1970–71; Defence and Military Attaché, Tel Aviv, 1974–77; Col GS, MoD, 1977–79; Brig. GS, MoD, 1981–82; ACGS (Op. Reqs), 1983–84; ACDS (Land Systems), MoD, 1984–85; graduate Staff Coll., JSSC, RCDS. Col Comdt, RTR, 1986–93; Vice Pres., TA&VRA, 1985–90. Gen. Sec., Officers' Pensions Soc., 1990–95; Campaign Dir, War and Service Widows Pensions Campaign, 1995. Licenced Reader, C of E; Church Warden, St Peter upon Cornhill, 1986–95; Pres., Soldiers' and Airmen's Scripture Readers Assoc., 1985–; Vice Pres., Officers' Christian Union, 1988–93. County Pres., St John Ambulance Brigade and Assoc., 1985–90; Patron, I of M Red Cross, 1985–90; President: Manx Music Fest., 1985–90; Mananan Internat. Fest. of Music and the Arts, 1987–; Sunninghill Comrades Club, 1991–95; Chairman: Bishop Barrow's Trustees, 1985–90; Royal Jubilee and Prince's Trust (I of M), 1986–90; Pres., White House School, Wokingham, 1985–. Freeman, City of London, 1985. CIMgt (FBIM 1979; CBIM 1986). KStJ 1986. *Recreations:* family, music, water colour painting. *Address:* Ballaquark, Laxey, Isle of Man IM4 7PH. *Club:* Army and Navy.

NEW WESTMINSTER, Bishop of, since 1994; **Rt Rev. Michael Ingham;** *b* 25 Aug. 1949; *s* of Herbert Ingham and Dorothy (*née* Crerar); *m* 1982, Gwen Robbins; two *d*. *Educ:* Univ. of Edinburgh (MA 1970; BD 1973 (First Class Hons)). Ordained deacon and priest, 1974; Asst Curate, St John the Evangelist, Ottawa, Ontario, 1974–76; Rector: Christ the King, Burnaby, BC, 1976–80; St Francis-in-the-Wood, W Vancouver, 1980–89; Principal Sec. to the Primate, Toronto, 1989–92; Dean of Christ Church Cathedral, Vancouver, 1992–94. *Publication:* Rites for a New Age, 1985, 2nd edn 1990. *Recreations:* sailing, squash. *Address:* #302–814 Richards Street, Vancouver, BC V6B 3A7, Canada. *T:* (604) 6846306.

NEW ZEALAND, Primate and Archbishop of, since 1986; **Most Rev. Brian Newton Davis;** Bishop of Wellington, since 1986; *b* 28 Oct. 1934; *s* of Leonard Lancelot and Ethel May Davis; *m* 1961, Marie Lynette Waters: four *d*. *Educ:* Stratford Primary and Technical High School; Ardmore Teachers' Training Coll., Auckland; Victoria Univ. of Wellington (MA 1st class Hons Geog.); Christchurch Theol Coll. (LTh). Teacher, Stratford Primary School, 1954; Laboratory Asst, Victoria Univ., 1958. Deacon 1960, priest 1961; Assistant Curate: St Mark's, Wellington, 1960–62; Parish of Karori West and Makara, 1962–64; Vicar: Karon West and Makara, 1964–67; Dannevirke, 1967–73; Cathedral Parish of St John the Evangelist and Dean of Waiapu, 1973; Vicar General of Waiapu, 1979–80; Bishop of Waikato, 1980–86. *Publication:* (contrib.) An Encyclopaedia of New Zealand, 1966. *Recreations:* tennis, wood carving and turning, water colour painting. *Address:* Bishopscourt, PO Box 12–046, Wellington, New Zealand.

NEWALL, family name of **Baron Newall.**

NEWALL, 2nd Baron, *cr* 1946; **Francis Storer Eaton Newall;** DL; company director and Chairman of several companies; Chairman, British Greyhound Racing Board, since 1985; *b* 23 June 1930; *o s* of 1st Baron (Marshal of the RAF Lord) Newall, GCB, OM, GCMG, CBE, AM; *S* father, 1963; *m* 1956, Pamela Elizabeth, *e d* of E. H. L. Rowcliffe, Pinkney Park, Malmesbury, Wilts; two *s* one *d*. *Educ:* Eton College; RMA Sandhurst. Commissioned into 11th Hussars (Prince Albert's Own), 1950; served in: Germany, 1950–53; Malaya, 1953–55; on staff of GHQ FarELF, Singapore, 1955–56; Adjt Royal Gloucestershire Hussars, 1956–58; retired 1961. Introduced Farriers Registration Acts and Betting Gaming and Lotteries Amendment Acts (Greyhound Racing) in House of Lords. Cons. Whip and front bench spokesman, 1976–79; Founder Mem., House of Lords all party Defence Study Group; official visits to NATO, SHAPE, Norway, Morocco, Bonn, Cyprus, BAOR, Qatar, Oman, Bahrain and Romania; Deleg. to Council of Europe and WEU, 1983. Mem., Select Cttee on Laboratory Animals Protection Bill. Pres., Soc. for Protection of Animals Abroad. Mem., Merchant Taylors' Co (Master, 1985–86). DL Greater London, 1988. *Recreations:* sport, travel, meeting people. *Heir: s* Hon. Richard Hugh Eaton Newall, *b* 19 Feb. 1961. *Address:* 18 Lennox Gardens, SW1X 0DG; Wotton Underwood, near Aylesbury, Bucks HP18 0RZ. *Club:* Cavalry and Guards.

NEWALL, Sir Paul (Henry), Kt 1994; TD 1967; DL; Consultant, Lehman Brothers; Director (non-executive), Guardian Royal Exchange plc; Lord Mayor of London, 1993–94; *b* 17 Sept. 1934; *s* of late Leopold Newall and Frances Evelyn Newall (*née* Bean); *m* 1969, Penelope Moyra, *o d* of Sir Julian Ridsdale, *qv* and Lady Ridsdale (*see* V. E. P. Ridsdale); two *s*. *Educ:* Harrow; Magdalene Coll., Cambridge (MA Econs). Nat. Service, commnd Royal Fusiliers, 1953–55; TA 1955–70, Major. Partner, Loeb Rhoades & Co. (mem., NY Stock Exchange), 1971; Overseas Director: Shearson Loeb Rhoades Inc., 1978; Shearson Lehman American Express (UK) Hldgs, 1981; Exec. Dir, Lehman Brothers Securities, 1990; Dir, Lehman Brothers Ltd (formerly Shearson Lehman International Ltd), 1985–94 (Sen. Advr, 1993–94). Mem., Adv. Cttee, Energy Internat. NV, 1978–. City of London: Mem., Court of Common Council (Ward of Cripplegate), 1980–81; Alderman, Ward of Walbrook, 1981–; Sheriff, 1989–90; Chm., City of London TAVRA, 1986–89; Vice-Chm., TA&VRA for Gtr London, 1989; Hon. Col, The London Regt, 1995–; Master, Bakers' Co., 1990–91; Member: Guild of Freemen, 1988– (Court, 1988–91); Court, HAC, 1980–; Liveryman, Gold and Silver Wyre Drawers' Co., 1980–. Vice-Pres., City of London Sector, British Red Cross, 1986–; Member: Friends of St Paul's Cathedral; City Heritage Soc.; Samuel Pepys Club; Governor: MENCAP City Foundn, 1982–; City of London Boys' Sch., 1985–86; City of London Freemen's Sch., 1987–88; Trustee: Morden Coll., 1991–; Lord Mayor's 800th Anniversary Awards Trust, 1992–. Patron: Samaritans Nat. Appeal, 1989–; Internat. Centre for Child Studies, 1989–. One of HM Lieutenants of City of London, 1975–; DL Gtr London, 1977; JP City of London, 1981; Hon. Vis. Magistrate, HM Tower of London, 1988–. Hon. DLitt City, 1993. KStJ 1993. Churchwarden, St Stephen's, Walbrook. *Recreations:* fencing, fly fishing, shooting, water-skiing, tennis, trees. *Address:* PO Box 270, Guildhall, EC2V 2EJ. *Clubs:* East India, City Livery, United Wards, Walbrook Ward (Pres.), MCC, Pilgrims.

NEWARK, Archdeacon of; *see* Hawtin, Ven. D. C.

NEWBERRY, Raymond Scudamore, OBE 1989; Director, British Council in Brazil, 1990–93, retired 1994; *b* 8 Feb. 1935; *s* of James Henry Newberry and late Doris Ada Newberry; *m* 1967, Angelina Nance; one *s* one *d*. *Educ:* Bristol Grammar Sch.; Selwyn Coll., Cambridge (BA); Univ. of Leeds (DipESL); Univ. of Bristol (DipEd). National Service, 1953–55. Lectr, Coll. of Arts, Baghdad Univ., 1959–62; joined British Council, 1962; Lectr, Teheran, 1963–64; Educn Officer, Calcutta, 1964–66; Head of English Dept, Advanced Teacher Trng Coll., Winneba, Ghana, 1966–70; Advr on English Lang., Min. of Educn, Singapore, 1970–74; Rep., Colombia, 1975–80; Director: North and Latin American Dept, 1980–82; America and Pacific Dept, 1982–84; Rep., Australia, 1984–89. *Publication:* (with A. Maley) Between You and Me, 1974. *Recreations:* bookbinding, golf. *Address:* Silverwood, Wildwood Close, Woking, Surrey GU22 8PL. *T:* Byfleet (01932) 341826.

NEWBERY, Prof. David Michael Garrood, FBA 1991; Professor of Economics and Director of Department of Applied Economics, Cambridge, since 1988; Fellow, Churchill College, Cambridge, since 1966; *b* 1 June 1943; *s* of Alan James Garrood Newbery and Betty Amelia Newbery; *m* 1975, Dr Terri Eve Apter; two *d*. *Educ:* Portsmouth Grammar Sch.; Trinity Coll., Cambridge (BA, MA, PhD). Economist, Treasury, Tanzania, 1965–66; Cambridge University: Asst Lectr, 1966–71; Lectr, 1971–86; Reader, 1986–88. Associate Prof., Stanford Univ., 1976–77; Div. Chief, World Bank, Washington, 1981–83; Fellow, Centre for Economic Policy Res., 1984–; Vis. Prof., Princeton, 1985; Vis. Scholar, IMF, 1987; Ford Vis. Prof., Univ. of California, Berkeley, 1987–88; Sen. Res. Fellow, Inst. for Policy Reform, Washington, DC, 1990–. Pres., European Economic Assoc., 1996 (Vice-Pres., 1994); Mem. Council, REconS, 1984–89; Fellow, Econometric Soc., 1989 (Frisch Medal, 1990). Bd Mem, Review of Economic Studies, 1968–79; Associate Editor: Economic Jl, 1977–; European Economic Review, 1988–93. *Publications:* Project Appraisal in Practice, 1976; (with J. E. Stiglitz) The Theory of Commodity Price Stabilization, 1981; (with N. H. Stern) The Theory of Taxation for Developing Countries, 1987; articles in learned jls. *Address:* 9 Huntingdon Road, Cambridge CB3 0HH. *T:* Cambridge (01223) 360216.

NEWBIGGING, David Kennedy, OBE 1982; DL; Chairman: Faupel Trading Group plc, since 1994 (Director, since 1989); Maritime Transport Services Ltd, since 1993; *b* 19 Jan. 1934; *s* of late David Locke Newbigging, CBE, MC, and Lucy Margaret; *m* 1968, Carolyn Susan (*née* Band); one *s* two *d*. *Educ:* in Canada; Oundle Sch., Northants. Joined Jardine, Matheson & Co. Ltd, Hong Kong, 1954; Dir, 1967; Man. Dir, 1970; Chm. and Sen. Man. Dir, 1975–83; Chairman: Hongkong & Kowloon Wharf & Godown Co. Ltd, 1970–80; Jardine Matheson & Co. Ltd, 1975–83; Jardine Fleming Holdings Ltd, 1975–83; Hongkong Land Co. Ltd, 1975–83; Hongkong Electric Holdings Ltd, 1982–83 (Dir, 1975–83); Rentokil Gp, 1987–94 (Dir, 1986–94); Redfearn PLC, 1988; NM UK Ltd 1990–93; Ivory & Sime, 1992–95 (Dir, 1987–95); Dep. Chm., Provincial Gp plc, 1985–91 (Dir, 1984–91); Director: Hongkong & Shanghai Banking Corp., 1975–83; Hong Kong Telephone Co., 1975–83; Safmarine and Rennies Holdings Ltd (formerly Rennies Consolidated Holdings), 1975–85; PACCAR (UK) Ltd, 1986–; Internat. Financial Markets Trading Ltd, 1986–93; United Meridian Corp., USA, 1987–; Wah Kwong Shipping Hldgs Ltd (Hong Kong), 1992–; Provincial Insurance, 1984–86; Provincial Life Insurance Co., 1984–86; CIN Management, 1985–87; Market Bd, Corp. of Lloyd's, 1993–; Friends' Provident Life Office, 1993–. Dir, British Coal Corp. (formerly NCB), 1984–87. Mem., Internat. Council, Morgan Guaranty Trust Co. of NY, 1977–85. Chm. of Council, Missions to Seamen, 1993–. Chm. of Trustees, Wilts Community Foundn, 1991–; Trustee, King Mahendra UK Trust for Nature Conservation, 1988–. Member: Hong Kong Exec. Council, 1980–84; Hong Kong Legislative Council, 1978–82. Chairman: Hong Kong Tourist Assoc., 1977–82; Hong Kong Gen. Chamber of Commerce, 1980–82; Steward, Royal Hong Kong Jockey Club, 1975–84. JP (unofficial) Hong Kong, 1971; DL Wilts, 1993. *Recreations:* most outdoor sports; Chinese art. *Address:* Wah Kwong House, 9th Floor, 10 Albert Embankment, SE1 7SP. *T:* 0171–582 1234. *Clubs:* Boodle's; Hongkong (Hong Kong).

NEWBIGIN, Rt. Rev. (James Edward) Lesslie, CBE 1974; DD; Minister, United Reformed Church, Winson Green, 1980–88, retired; *b* 8 Dec. 1909; *s* of Edward Richmond Newbigin, Shipowner, Newcastle, and Annie Ellen Newbigin (*née* Affleck); *m* 1936, Helen Stewart, *d* of Rev. Robert Henderson; one *s* three *d*. *Educ:* Leighton Park Sch.; Queens' Coll., Cambridge; Westminster Coll., Cambridge. Intercollegiate Secretary,

Student Christian Movement, Glasgow, 1931–33. Ordained by Presbytery of Edinburgh and appointed to Madras Mission of Church of Scotland, 1936; served as missionary in Chingleput and Kancheepuram, 1936–46; Bishop in Madura and Ramnad, Church of South India, 1947. Chairman, Advisory Cttee on Main Theme for Second Assembly, World Council of Churches, 1954; Vice-Chairman, Commission on Faith and Order, 1956; Chairman, International Missionary Council, 1958. Resigned from See of Madura, 1959. General Secretary, International Missionary Council, 1959; Associate General Secretary, World Council of Churches, 1961–65; Bishop in Madras, 1965–74; Lectr in Theology, Selly Oak Colls, Birmingham, 1974–79. Moderator, Gen. Assembly of URC, 1978. Hon. DD: Chicago Theological Seminary, 1954; St Andrews Univ., 1958; Hamburg, 1960; Basel, 1965; Hull, 1975; Newcastle, 1981. *Publications:* Christian Freedom in the Modern World, 1937; The Reunion of the Church, 1948; South India Diary, 1951; The Household of God, 1953; Sin and Salvation, 1956; A Faith for This One World?, 1962; Honest Religion for Secular Man, 1966; The Finality of Christ, 1969; The Good Shepherd, 1977; The Open Secret, 1978; The Light has come, 1982; The Other Side of 1984, 1983; Unfinished Agenda, 1985; Foolishness to the Greeks, 1986; The Gospel in a Pluralist Society, 1989; Truth to Tell, 1991. *Recreations:* music, walking. *Address:* 91 Stradella Road, SE24 9HL.

NEWBOLD, Yvette Monica, (Yve); Chief Executive, Pro-Ned, since 1995; *b* 6 July 1940; *d* of late Thomas Peter Radcliffe and of Anne Gertrude Radcliffe (*née* Flynn); *m* 1958, Anthony Patrick Newbold; three *s* one *d*. *Educ:* Blessed Sacrament Convent, Brighton; LLB London; Solicitor, 1970. Staff Counsel: IBM, 1968–71; Rank Xerox, 1972–79; Internat. Counsel, Xerox (USA), 1979–82; European Counsel, Walt Disney Productions, 1983–85; Co. Sec., Hanson, 1986–95. Non-executive Director: BT, 1991–; Coults & Co., 1994–. Member: Royal Commn on Criminal Justice, 1991–93; Sen. Salaries Rev. Body, 1994–. Governor, London Business Sch., 1990–. *Recreations:* fell-walking, jogging. *Address:* Devonshire House, Mayfair Place, W1X 5FH.

NEWBOROUGH, 7th Baron, *cr* 1776; **Robert Charles Michael Vaughan Wynn,** Bt 1742; DSC 1942; *b* 24 April 1917; *er s* of 6th Baron Newborough, OBE, JP, DL, and Ruby Irene (*d* 1960), 3rd *d* of Edmund Wigley Severne, of Thenford, Northamptonshire and Wallop, Shropshire; *S* father, 1965; *m* 1st, 1945, Rosamund Lavington Barbour (marr. diss. 1971); one *s* two *d*; 2nd, 1971, Jennifer, *y d* of late Captain C. C. A. Allen, RN, and Lady Morgan. *Educ:* Oundle. Served as 2nd Lt, SR, 1935–39, with 9th Lancers, 5th Inniskilling Dragoon Guards, then as Lt with 16th/5th Lancers after 6 months attachment with Royal Dragoon Guards; invalided out of Army, 1940. Took command of vessel attached to Fleet Air Arm, 1940, as civilian, and took part in Dunkirk evacuation; then joined RNVR as Sub Lieut; later had command of MTB 74 and took part in St Nazaire raid, 1942 (wounded, despatches, DSC, POW, escaped from Colditz 1944). High Sheriff of Merionethshire, 1963. *Recreation:* yachting. *Heir: s* Hon. Robert Vaughan Wynn [*b* 11 Aug. 1949; *m* 1st, 1981, Sheila Christine (marr. diss. 1988), *d* of William A. Massey; one *d*; 2nd, 1988, Mrs Susan Elizabeth Hall, *d* of late Andrew Francis Lloyd]. *Address:* Rhug, Corwen, Clwyd, North Wales LL21 0EH. *T:* Corwen (01490) 2510. *Clubs:* Goat, Naval and Military.

NEWBURGH, 12th Earl of, *cr* 1660 (Scot.); **Don Filippo Giambattista Francesco Aldo Maria Rospigliosi;** Viscount Kynnaird, Baron Levingston, 1660; 11th Prince Rospigliosi (Holy Roman Empire), 11th Duke of Zagarolo, 14th Prince of Castiglione, Marquis of Giuliana, Count of Chiusa, Baron of La Miraglia and Valcorrente, Lord of Aidone, Burgio, Contessa and Trappeto, and Conscript Roman Noble, Patrician of Venice, Genoa and Pistoia; *b* 4 July 1942; *s* of 11th Earl of Newburgh and of Donna Giulia, *d* of Don Guido Carlo dei Duchi Visconti di Mondrone, Count of Lonate Pozzolo; *S* father, 1986; *m* 1972, Baronessa Donna Luisa, *d* of Count Annibale Caccia Dominioni; one *d*. *Heir: d* Princess Donna Benedetta Francesca Maria Rospigliosi, *b* 4 June 1974. *Address:* Piazza Sant'Ambrogio 16, 20123 Milan, Italy.

NEWBY, (George) Eric, CBE 1994; MC 1945; FRSL 1972; FRGS 1975; writer; *b* 6 Dec. 1919; *o s* of George Arthur Newby and Hilda Pomroy, London; *m* 1946, Wanda, *d* of Viktor Skof and Gisella Urdih, Trieste; one *s* one *d*. *Educ:* St Paul's School. With Dorland Advertising, London, 1936–38; apprentice and ord. seaman, 4-masted Finnish barque, Moshulu, 1938–39; served War of 1939–45, The Black Watch and Special Boat Section, POW 1942–45; Women's Fashion Business, 1946–56 (with Worth Paquin, 1955–56); explored in Nuristan and made unsuccessful attempt to climb Mir Samir, Afghan Hindu Kush, 1956; with Secker & Warburg, 1956–59; with John Lewis Partnership (Central Buyer, Model Dresses), 1959–63; descended Ganges with wife, 1963. Travel Editor, The Observer, and Gen. Editor, Time Off Books, 1964–73. Mem., Assoc. of Cape Horners. *Publications:* The Last Grain Race, 1956; A Short Walk in the Hindu Kush, 1958; Something Wholesale, 1962; Slowly Down the Ganges, 1966; Time Off in Southern Italy, 1966; Grain Race: Pictures of Life Before the Mast in a Windjammer, 1968; (jointly) The Wonders of Britain, 1968; (jointly) The Wonders of Ireland, 1969; Love and War in the Apennines, 1971; (jointly) The World of Evelyn Waugh, 1973; Ganga (with photographs by Raghubir Singh), 1973; World Atlas of Exploration, 1975; Great Ascents, 1977; The Big Red Train Ride, 1978; A Traveller's Life, 1982; On the Shores of the Mediterranean, 1984; A Book of Travellers' Tales, 1985; Round Ireland in Low Gear, 1987; What the Traveller Saw, 1989; A Small Place in Italy, 1994. *Recreations:* walking, cycling, gardening. *Address:* West Bucknowle House, Bucknowle, Wareham, Dorset BH20 5PQ. *T:* Corfe Castle (01929) 480374. *Club:* Garrick.

NEWBY, Prof. Howard Joseph, CBE 1995; Vice-Chancellor, Southampton University, since 1994; *b* 10 Dec. 1947; *s* of Alfred Joseph Newby and Constance Annie (*née* Potts); *m* 1970, Janet Elizabeth (*née* Craddock); two *s*. *Educ:* John Port Grammar Sch., Etwall, Derbyshire; Atlantic Coll., St Donat's, Glamorgan; Univ. of Essex (BA, PhD). University of Essex: Lectr in Sociology, 1972–75; Sen. Lectr, 1975–79; Reader, 1979–83; Prof. of Sociology, 1983–88; Dir, Data Archive, 1983–88, Chm. and Chief Exec., 1988–94, ESRC. Prof. of Sociology and Rural Sociology, Univ. of Wisconsin-Madison, 1980–83; visiting appointments: Univ. of NSW, 1976; Sydney, 1976; Newcastle upon Tyne, 1983–84. Member: UFC, 1991–93; Rural Develt Commn, 1991–; South and West RHA, 1994–. Hon. DLitt: City of London Poly., 1991; South Bank Univ., 1992; Surrey, 1992; Portsmouth, 1992 (Hon. Fellow, Portsmouth Poly., 1991); Ulster, 1994. *Publications:* (jtly) Community Studies, 1971; The Deferential Worker, 1977; (jtly) Property, Paternalism and Power, 1978; Green and Pleasant Land?, 1979, 2nd edn 1985; (jtly) The Problem of Sociology, 1983; (jtly) Approximación Teoretica a la Sociologia Rural, 1983; Country Life, 1987; The Countryside in Question, 1988; (jtly) Social Class in Modern Britain, 1988; *edited jointly:* The Sociology of Community, 1974; Doing Sociological Research, 1977; International Perspectives in Rural Sociology, 1978; The Rural Sociology of the Advanced Societies, 1980; Political Action and Social Identity, 1985; Restructuring Capital, 1985; over 50 papers in learned jls. *Recreations:* family life, gardening, Derby County and railway enthusiasms. *Address:* The Old Mill, Mill Lane, Corston, Malmesbury, Wilts SN16 0HH. *Club:* Athenæum.

NEWBY, Percy Howard, CBE 1972; novelist; *b* 25 June 1918; *o s* of Percy Newby and Isabel Clutsam Newby (*née* Bryant); *m* 1945, Joan Thompson; two *d*. *Educ:* Hanley Castle Grammar Sch., Worcester; St Paul's Coll., Cheltenham. Served War of 1939–45, RAMC, 1939–42; BEF, France, 1939–40; MEF, 1941–42; seconded as Lecturer in English Literature, Fouad 1st University, Cairo, 1942–46. Joined BBC, 1949; Controller: Third Programme, 1958–69; Radio Three, 1969–71; Dir of Programmes, Radio, 1971–75; Man. Dir, BBC Radio, 1975–78. Chm., English Stage Co., 1978–84. Atlantic Award, 1946; Somerset Maugham Prize, 1948; Yorkshire Post Fiction Award, 1968; Booker Prize, 1969 (first recipient). *Publications:* A Journey to the Interior, 1945; Agents and Witnesses, 1947; The Spirit of Jem, 1947; Mariner Dances, 1948; The Snow Pasture, 1949; The Loot Runners, 1949; Maria Edgeworth, 1950; The Young May Moon, 1950; The Novel, 1945–50, 1951; A Season in England, 1951; A Step to Silence, 1952; The Retreat, 1953; The Picnic at Sakkara, 1955; Revolution and Roses, 1957; Ten Miles from Anywhere, 1958; A Guest and his Going, 1959; The Barbary Light, 1962; One of the Founders, 1965; Something to Answer For, 1968; A Lot to Ask, 1973; Kith, 1977; (with F. Maroon) The Egypt Story, 1979; Warrior Pharaohs, 1980; Feelings Have Changed, 1981; Saladin in his Time, 1984; Leaning in the Wind, 1986; Coming in with the Tide, 1991; Something About Women, 1995. *Address:* Garsington House, Garsington, Oxford OX44 9AB. *T:* Garsington (01865) 361420.

NEWBY, Richard Mark, OBE 1990; Director, Matrix Communications Consultancy Ltd (formerly Matrix Public Affairs Consultants), since 1992; Chairman, Reform Publications Ltd, since 1993; *b* 14 Feb. 1953; *s* of Frank and Kathleen Newby; *m* 1978, Ailsa Ballantyne Thomson; two *s*. *Educ:* Rothwell Grammar Sch.; St Catherine's Coll., Oxford (MA). HM Customs and Excise: Administration trainee, 1974; Private Sec. to Permanent Sec., 1977–79; Principal, Planning Unit, 1979–81; Sec. to SDP Parly Cttee, 1981; joined SDP HQ Staff, 1981; Nat. Sec., SDP, 1983–88; Exec., 1988–90, Dir of Corporate Affairs, 1991, Rosehaugh plc. *Recreations:* family, politics. *Address:* 4 Rockwells Gardens, Dulwich Wood Park, SE19 1HW. *T:* 0181–244 5675. *Clubs:* Reform, MCC.

NEWCASTLE, Bishop of, since 1981; **Rt. Rev. Andrew Alexander Kenny Graham;** *b* 7 Aug. 1929; *o s* of late Andrew Harrison and Magdalene Graham; unmarried. *Educ:* Tonbridge Sch.; St John's Coll., Oxford (Hon. Fellow, 1986); Ely Theological College. Curate of Hove Parish Church, 1955–58; Chaplain and Lectr in Theology, Worcester Coll., Oxford, 1958–70; Fellow and Tutor, 1960–70, Hon. Fellow, 1981; Warden of Lincoln Theological Coll., 1970–77; Canon and Prebendary of Lincoln Cathedral, 1970–77. Examining Chaplain to: Bishop of Carlisle, 1967–77; Bishop of Bradford, 1972–77; Bishop of Lincoln, 1973–77; Bishop Suffragan of Bedford, 1977–81. Chairman: ACCM, 1984–87; Doctrine Commn, 1987–95. DD Lambeth, 1995. *Recreation:* hill walking. *Address:* Bishop's House, 29 Moor Road South, Newcastle upon Tyne NE3 1PA. *T:* 0191–285 2220. *Club:* United Oxford & Cambridge University.

NEWCASTLE, NSW, Bishop of, since 1993; **Rt. Rev. Roger Adrian Herft;** *b* 11 July 1948; *s* of Richard Clarence and Esmie Marie Herft; *m* 1976, Cheryl Oranee Jayasekera; two *s*. *Educ:* Royal College, Colombo; Theological Coll. of Lanka. BTh, BD (Serampore). Employed at Carson Cumberbatch & Co. Ltd, 1966–69; theol coll., 1969–73; deacon 1972, priest 1973; Assistant Curate: Holy Emmanuel Church, Moratuwa, 1972; St Luke's Church, Borella, with chaplaincy to Colombo Prison, 1973; Vicar: Holy Emmanuel, Moratuwa, 1976; SS Mary and John Nugegoda, 1979; Parish Consultant, Diocese of Waikato, 1983; Bishop of Waikato, 1986–93. *Publication:* (co-ed) Encounter with Reality, 1971. *Recreations:* reading, avid follower of cricket. *Address:* Bishopscourt, Newcastle, NSW 2300, Australia. *T:* (49) 262767; Bishop's Registry, 250 Darby Street, Newcastle, NSW 2300, Australia. *T:* (49) 263733, *Fax:* (49) 261968.

NEWCASTLE, Provost of; *see* Coulton, Very Rev. N. G.

NEWDEGATE; *see* FitzRoy Newdegate, family name of Viscount Daventry.

NEWELL, Christopher William Paul; Director (Casework), Crown Prosecution Service, since 1993; *b* 30 Nov. 1950; *s* of Nicolas Gambier Newell and Edith Alice Newell (*née* Edgill). *Educ:* Wellington College; Southampton Univ. (LLB Hons). Called to the Bar, Middle Temple, 1973; Department of Director of Public Prosecutions: Legal Asst, 1975–78; Sen. Legal Asst, 1978–79; Law Officers' Dept, 1979–83; Sen. Legal Asst, DPP, 1983–86; Asst DPP, 1986; Branch Crown Prosecutor, Crown Prosecution Service, 1986–87; Asst Legal Sec., Law Officers' Dept, 1987–89; Dir of HQ Casework, CPS, 1989–93. *Recreations:* sport, travel. *Address:* Crown Prosecution Service, 50 Ludgate Hill, EC4M 7EX. *T:* 0171–273 1208. *Club:* Royal Automobile.

NEWELL, Donald, FRICS; Senior Partner, Hillier Parker May & Rowden, since 1990; *b* 31 Aug. 1942; *s* of Stephen Newell and Ida Laura Newell (*née* Hatch); *m* 1968, Rosemary Litler-Jones; one *s* two *d*. *Educ:* Cheshunt Grammar Sch. FRICS 1968. Lander Bedells & Crompton, 1961–68; Hillier Parker May & Rowden, Chartered Surveyors, 1968–: Partner, 1973–; Man. Partner, 1986–90. Pres., Brit. Council for Offices, 1991–92. Liveryman, Company of: Pattenmakers, 1979; Chartered Surveyors, 1993–. *Recreations:* sport, farming. *Address:* 73 Sussex Square, W2 2SS. *T:* 0171–262 6440. *Clubs:* Buck's, MCC.

NEWELL, Rt. Rev. Phillip Keith; *see* Tasmania, Bishop of.

NEWELL, Robert Fraser; Director-General, Royal Over-Seas League, since 1991; *b* 3 May 1943; *m* 1969, Shahnaz Bakhtiar; two *d*. *Educ:* University Coll. Sch. MHCIMA 1986. Hotel mgt positions in London, Iran and Kenya, 1965–75; Dir of Admin, Kenya Utalii Coll., Nairobi, 1975–79; Gen. Manager, Royal Over-Seas League, 1979–91. Vis. Lectr in Hotel Financial Mgt, Ecole Hotelière de Lausanne, 1983–. Chm., Assoc. of London Clubs, 1992–95; Member: Club Secs and Managers Assoc., 1982–; Jt Commonwealth Socs Council, 1991–. Associate, Brit. Assoc. Hotel Accountants, 1988; FIMgt 1983. *Recreations:* tennis, wine, teaching, watching Spurs. *Address:* Royal Over-Seas League, Over-Seas House, Park Place, St James's Street, SW1A 1LR. *T:* 0171–408 0214. *Club:* Grafton Tennis.

NEWENS, (Arthur) Stanley; Member (Lab) London Central, European Parliament, since 1984; *b* 4 Feb. 1930; *s* of Arthur Ernest and Celia Jenny Newens, Bethnal Green; *m* 1st, 1954, Ann (*d* 1962), *d* of J. B. Sherratt, Stoke-on-Trent; two *d*; 2nd, 1966, Sandra Christina, *d* of J. A. Frith, Chingford; one *s* two *d*. *Educ:* Buckhurst Hill County High Sch.; University Coll., London (BA Hons History); Westminster Training Coll. (Post-Graduate Certificate of Education). Coal face worker in N Staffs mines, 1952–55. Secondary Sch. Teacher, 1956–65, 1970–74. MP (Lab) Epping, 1964–70 (NUT sponsored); MP (Lab and Co-op) Harlow, Feb. 1974–1983. Contested (Lab) Harlow, 1983 and 1987. Chairman: Eastern Area Gp of Lab. MPs, 1974–83; Tribune Gp of MPs, 1982–83 (Vice-Chm., 1981–82); PLP Foreign Affairs Gp, 1982–83 (Vice-Chm., 1976–77); Dep. Leader, British Lab. Gp of MEPs, 1988–89 (Chm., 1985–87); Chair, EP Central Amer. Delegn, 1994–; Vice-Chm., Labour Action for Peace. Active Member: Labour Party, holding numerous offices, 1949–; NUM, 1952–55; NUT, 1956–. Pres., Liberation (Movement for Colonial Freedom), 1992– (Chm., 1967–92). Dir, London Co-operative Soc., 1971–77 (Pres., 1977–81); Mem., Central Exec., Co-op. Union, 1974–80. Sec., Harlow Council for Voluntary Service, 1983–84. *Publications:* The Case Against NATO (pamphlet), 1972; Nicolae Ceausescu, 1972; Third World: change or chaos, 1977; A

History of North Weald Bassett and its People, 1985; A Short History of the London Co-op Society Political Committee, 1988; (with Ron Bill) Leah Manning, 1991; pamphlets and articles. *Recreations:* local historical research, family, reading. *Address:* The Leys, 18 Park Hill, Harlow, Essex CM17 0AE. *T:* Harlow (01279) 420108.

NEWEY, Sidney Brian; consultant in transport; Assistant to Chief Executive, Railways, British Rail, 1990–93, retired; *b* 8 Jan. 1937; *s* of Sidney Frank Newey and Edith Mary Newey; *m* 1967, Margaret Mary Stevens; one *s*. *Educ:* Burton upon Trent Grammar Sch.; Worcester Coll., Oxford (MA Mod. History). MCIT. British Rail: Traffic apprentice, Western Region, 1960; Stationmaster, Southall, Mddx, 1964; Freight Marketing Manager, Western Region, 1971; Divl Manager, Birmingham, 1978; Dep. General Manager, London Midland Region, 1980; Gen. Manager, Western Region, 1985–87; Director, Provincial, 1987–90. *Recreations:* fell walking, history, reading, village and church affairs. *Address:* Chestnut Cottage, The Green South, Warborough, Oxon OX10 7DN. *T:* Warborough (01865) 858322.

NEWFOUNDLAND, CENTRAL, Bishop of, since 1990; **Rt. Rev. Edward Frank Marsh;** *b* 25 Oct. 1935; *m* 1962, Emma Marsh; one *s* two *d*. *Educ:* Dalhousie Univ., NS (BCom 1956); Univ. of Newfoundland (BA 1960); Queen's Coll., Newfoundland (LTh 1961; BD 1969). Deacon 1959, priest 1960; Curate, Corner Brook, 1959–63; Incumbent, Harbour Breton, 1963–69; Curate, Wickford, 1969–71; Incumbent, Indian Bay, 1971–73; Curate, St John the Baptist Cathedral, St John's, 1973–77; Rector of Cartwright, dio. East Newfoundland, 1977–81; Rector, Holy Trinity, Grand Falls, 1981–90. *Address:* 34 Fraser Road, Gander, Newfoundland A1V 2E8, Canada.

NEWFOUNDLAND, EASTERN, AND LABRADOR, Bishop of, since 1993; **Rt Rev. Donald Frederick Harvey;** *b* St John's, Newfoundland, 13 Sept. 1939; *s* of Robert Joseph and Elsie May Harvey (*née* Vaters); *m* 1964, Gertrude, *d* of George and Jessie Hiscock. *Educ:* St Michael's Sch., 1956; Memorial Univ. (BA 1985; MA 1987); Queen's Theol Coll. (MDiv 1986). Sch. teacher, 1956–57; ordained deacon, 1963, priest, 1974; served in parishes: Portugal Cove, 1963–64, 1973–76; Twillingate, 1965; King's Cove, 1965–68; Happy Valley, Labrador, 1968–73; St Michael & All Angels, St John's, 1976–83; Anglican Chaplain, Meml Univ. of Newfoundland, 1984–87; Rector, and Dean, Cathedral of St John the Baptist, St John's, 1989–92. Rural Dean of Labrador, 1968–73. Lectr in Pastoral Theol., Queen's Coll., 1984–; Sessional Lectr, English, Meml Univ. of Newfoundland, 1985–89. Mem., Rotary Club, St John's NW. *Address:* (office) 19 King's Bridge Road, St John's, Newfoundland A1C 3K4, Canada; (home) 22 Church Hill, St John's, Newfoundland A1C 3Z9, Canada.

NEWFOUNDLAND, WESTERN, Archbishop of, since 1990; **Most Rev. S(idney) Stewart Payne;** Metropolitan of the Ecclesiastical Province of Canada; *b* 6 June 1932; *s* of Albert and Hilda Payne; *m* 1962, Selma Carlson Penney, St Anthony, Newfoundland; two *s* two *d*. *Educ:* Elementary and High School, Fogo, Newfoundland; Memorial Univ. of Newfoundland (BA); Queen's Coll., Newfoundland (LTh); BD(General Synod). Incumbent of Mission of Happy Valley, 1957–65; Rector, Parish of Bay Roberts, 1965–70; Rector, Parish of St Anthony, 1970–78; Bishop of Western Newfoundland, 1978–. DD *hc* Univ. of King's Coll., Halifax, NS, 1981. *Address:* 13 Cobb Lane, Corner Brook, Newfoundland A2H 2V3, Canada. *T:* (709) 6399987.

NEWHOUSE, Ven. Robert John Darrell; Archdeacon of Totnes and Canon Residentiary of Exeter Cathedral, 1966–76, now Archdeacon Emeritus and Canon Emeritus; Treasurer of Exeter Cathedral, 1970–76; *b* 11 May 1911; *s* of Rev. R. L. C. Newhouse; *m* 1938, Winifred (*née* Elton); two *s*. *Educ:* St Edward's Sch.; Worcester Coll., Oxford; Cuddesdon College. Ordained, 1936. Curate of: St John's, Peterborough, 1936–40; St Giles, Cambridge, 1940–46; Chaplain, RNVR, 1941–46; Rector of Ashwater, Devon, 1946–56; Rural Dean of Holsworthy, 1954–56; Vicar of Littleham-cum-Exmouth, 1956–66; Rural Dean of Aylesbeare, 1965–66. *Address:* Pound Cottage, Northlew, Okehampton, Devon EX20 3NN. *T:* Beaworthy (01409) 221532.

NEWING, John Frederick; QPM 1988; Chief Constable, Derbyshire Constabulary, since 1990; *b* 1 March 1940; *s* of Frederick George Newing and Emily Beatrice Newing (*née* Bettles); *m* 1963, Margaret May Kilborn; two *s* one *d*. *Educ:* Kettering Grammar Sch.; Leeds Univ. (BA Hons Social and Public Administration). Joined Metropolitan Police, 1963; Police Staff Coll., 1967–68; Bramshill Scholarship, Leeds Univ., 1969–72; Community Relations Bd, 1974; Staff Officer to Commissioner, 1977; Chief Supt i/c Marylebone Div., 1980; Senior Command Course, Police Staff Coll., 1981; Comdr, Community Relations, 1982, Public Order Branch, 1984; Dep. Asst Comr i/c W London Area, 1985–87; seconded to Home Office Science and Technology Gp, 1987–90. *Publications:* articles in Policing and other professional jls. *Recreations:* reading, walking the dog, voluntary youth work, such sports as age allows. *Address:* Derbyshire Constabulary HQ, Butterley Hall, Ripley, Derbyshire DE5 3RS. *T:* Ripley (01773) 570100.

NEWING, Rt. Rev. Dom Kenneth Albert, OSB; *b* 29 Aug. 1923; *s* of Albert James Pittock Newing and Nellie Louise Maude Newing; unmarried. *Educ:* Dover Grammar School; Selwyn College, Cambridge (MA); Theological College, Mirfield, Yorks. Deacon, 1955; priest, 1956; Assistant Curate, Plymstock, 1955–63; Rector of Plympton S Maurice, Plymouth, 1963–82; Archdeacon of Plymouth, 1978–82; Bishop Suffragan of Plymouth, 1982–88; joined Order of St Benedict, 1988; solemn (life) profession, 1989. *Address:* Elmore Abbey, Church Lane, Speen, Newbury, Berks RG13 1SA.

NEWINGTON, Sir Michael (John), KCMG 1993 (CMG 1982); HM Diplomatic Service, retired; Ambassador to Brazil, 1987–92; *b* 10 July 1932; *er s* of J. T. Newington, Spalding, Lincs; *m* 1956, Nina Gordon-Jones; one *s* one *d*. *Educ:* Stamford Sch.; St John's Coll., Oxford. MA. RAF, 1951–52, Pilot Officer. Joined Foreign Office, 1955; Economic Survey Section, Hong Kong, 1957–58; resigned 1958. ICI, 1959–60. Rejoined FO, 1960; Second, later First Sec. (Economic), Bonn, 1961–65; First Sec., Lagos, 1965–68; Asst Head of Science and Technology Dept, FCO, 1968–72; Counsellor (Scientific), Bonn, 1972–75; Counsellor and Consul-Gen., Tel Aviv, 1975–78; Head of Republic of Ireland Dept, FCO, 1978–81; Consul-Gen., Düsseldorf, 1981–85; Ambassador to Venezuela and concurrently (non-resident) to Dominican Republic, 1985–87. *Recreations:* ski-ing, golf, gardening. *Address:* Inces, Scaynes Hill, W Sussex RH17 7NG.

NEWIS, Kenneth, CB 1967; CVO 1970 (MVO 1958); *b* 9 Nov. 1916; *o s* of late H. T. and G. Newis, Manchester; *m* 1943, Kathleen, *o d* of late John Barrow, Davenport, Cheshire; two *d*. *Educ:* Manchester Grammar Sch.; St John's Coll., Cambridge (Scholar). BA 1938, MA 1942. Entered HM Office of Works, 1938; Private Sec. to Minister of Works (Rt Hon. C. W. Key), 1948–49; Asst Sec., 1949; Under-Sec., 1959; Dir of Management Services, MPBW, 1969–70; Under-Sec., Scottish Devolt Dept, 1970–73, Sec., 1973–76. Hon. Pres., Queen's Hall (Edinburgh) Ltd. Vice-Chm., Cockburn Assoc., 1986–94; Member: Historic Buildings Council for Scotland, 1978–88; Bd, Methodist Homes for the Aged (Vice-Chm., MHA Housing Assoc.), 1977–91; Bd, RSAMD, 1977–88 (FRSAMD 1995); Scottish Churches' Council, 1984–87 (Chm., Friends of Scottish Churches' Council, 1984–87). Conservator of Wimbledon and Putney Commons, 1963–70. Governor: Farrington's School, 1964–70; Richmond College, 1964–70. *Recreation:* music. *Address:* 11 Abbotsford Park, Edinburgh EH10 5DZ. *Club:* New (Edinburgh).

NEWLAND, Prof. David Edward, MA; ScD; FEng 1982; FIMechE, FIEE; Professor of Engineering (1875), since 1976, and Deputy Head, Engineering Department, since 1993, University of Cambridge; Fellow, Selwyn College, Cambridge, since 1976; consulting engineer (part-time), since 1963; *b* 8 May 1936; *s* of late Robert W. Newland and Marion A. Newland (*née* Dearman); *m* 1959, Patricia Frances Mayne; two *s*. *Educ:* Alleyne's Sch., Stevenage; Selwyn Coll., Cambridge (Lyttleton Scholar, 1956; Mech. Sciences Tripos: Rex Moir Prize, 1956, Ricardo Prize, 1957; MA 1961; ScD 1990); Massachusetts Inst. of Technol. (ScD thesis on nonlinear vibrations, 1963). English Electric Co., 1957–61; Instr and Asst Prof. of Mech. Engrg, MIT, 1961–64; Lectr and Sen. Lectr, Imperial Coll. of Science and Technol., 1964–67; Prof. of Mech. Engrg, Sheffield Univ., 1967–76. Mem., Royal Commn on Envmtl Pollution, 1984–89. Visitor, Transport and Road Res. Lab., 1990–92. Past or present mem., cttees of IMechE, DTI, BSI, SERC, Design Council, Engrg Council and Royal Academy (formerly Fellowship) of Engineering, including: Mem., Editorial Panel, 1968–82 and Consultant Editor, 1983–87, Jl Mech. Engrg Sci., Proc. IMechE, Part C; Engrg Awards Panel, Design Council, 1977–79; Council, Fellowship of Engrg, 1985–88; Working Party on Engineers and Risk Issues, Engrg Council, 1990–94; Member: SRC Transport Cttee, 1969–72; Mech. Engrg and Machine Tools Requirements Bd, 1977, 1978; Chm., BSI Tech. Cttee on bellows expansion jts, 1976–85. Technical witness, Flixborough Inquiry, 1974–75, and other legal cases. Governor, St Paul's Schs, 1978–93. Churchwarden, Ickleton, 1979–87. Charles S. Lake award, 1975, and T. Bernard Hall prize, IMechE, 1991, for papers in IMechE Procs. *Publications:* An Introduction to Random Vibrations and Spectral Analysis, 1975, 3rd edn, as Random Vibrations, Spectral and Wavelet Analysis, 1993; Mechanical Vibration Analysis and Computation, 1989; technical papers, mostly in British and Amer. engrg jls. *Recreations:* music, jogging (London Marathon, etc). *Address:* c/o University Engineering Department, Trumpington Street, Cambridge CB2 1PZ. *T:* Cambridge (01223) 332670. *Club:* Athenæum.

NEWLEY, (George) Anthony; actor since 1946; author, composer; *b* 24 Sept. 1931; *m* 1956, Ann Lynn; *m* 1963, Joan Henrietta Collins, *qv* (marr. diss. 1970); one *s* one *d*; *m* Dareth Rich; one *s* one *d*. *Educ:* Mandeville Street Sch., Clapton, E5. Appeared on West End stage in: Cranks, 1955; Stop the World, I Want to Get Off (co-author and co-composer, with Leslie Bricusse), 1961–62; subseq. starred in New York production, 1962–63, new production, Lyric, 1989 (also co-dir); The Good Old Bad Old Days (co-author and co-composer with Leslie Bricusse), 1972; The Roar of the Greasepaint–the Smell of the Crowd (co-author and composer, with Leslie Bricusse, star and director), New York, 1965; Chaplin, Los Angeles, 1983. Has acted in over 40 films in last 17 years. *Films include:* Adventures of Dusty Bates; Oliver Twist; Up To His Neck; Cockleshell Heroes; High Flight; Idle on Parade; Jazz Boat; The Small World of Sammy Lee; Dr Doolittle; Sweet November; (wrote, produced and acted) Can Heironymus Merkin ever forget Mercy Humppe and find True Happiness?; (directed) Summertree, 1970; (score) Willy Wonka and the Chocolate Factory (Academy Award nomination, 1972); Quilp, 1974; It Seemed Like a Good Idea at the Time, 1974. *TV appearances include:* Anthony Newley Shows; The Strange World of Gurney Slade, 1960–61; Johnny Darling Show, 1962; Lucy in London, 1966; appears on TV and stars in leading night clubs and theatres in US. He is also a successful recording star. *Recreations:* photography, painting, fishing. *Address:* c/o Peter Charlesworth, 2nd Floor, 68 Old Brompton Road, SW7 3LQ.

NEWMAN, Dr Barry Hilton; consultant; Director, Propellants, Explosives and Rocket Motor Establishment, and Head of Rocket Motor Executive, Ministry of Defence, 1980–84, retired; *b* 16 Sept. 1926; *s* of Charles Ernest Newman and Kathleen (*née* Hilton); *m* 1950, Dorothy Ashworth Truesdale; one *s* one *d*. *Educ:* Bishop Vesey's Grammar Sch., Sutton Coldfield; Univ. of Birmingham (BSc (Hons) 1947, PhD 1950). Joined Scientific Civil Service, 1950; Explosives R&D Estabt, 1950–63; Defence Research Staff, Washington, 1963–66; Supt Explosives Br., Royal Armament R&D Estabt, 1966–71; Asst Dir, Directorate General Weapons (Army), 1971–72; Dir, Research Armaments, 1972–74; RCDS 1975; Head of Terminal Effects Dept, RARDE, 1976–77; Dep. Dir, RARDE, 1977–80. FRSA. *Publications:* official reports. *Recreations:* cricket, bridge, reading, music. *Address:* c/o Barclays Bank, 80 High Street, Sevenoaks, Kent. *Club:* MCC.

NEWMAN, Catherine Mary; QC 1995; *b* 7 Feb. 1954; *d* of Dr Ernest Newman and Josephine (*née* McLaughlin); *m* 1982, Ian James Gouldsbrough; one *s* one *d*. *Educ:* University Coll. London (LLB 1st Cl. Hons 1978). Called to the Bar, Middle Temple, 1979 (Harmsworth Schol.); in practice in business and commercial fields, Chancery Div., 1980–; Dep. Registrar in Bankruptcy, 1991–. Mem., Bar Council, 1987–90. *Publication:* Bar Finals Guide, 1980, 3rd edn 1987. *Recreation:* family life. *Address:* 13 Old Square, Lincoln's Inn, WC2A 3UA. *T:* 0171–404 4800.

NEWMAN, Cyril Wilfred Francis; QC 1982; **His Honour Judge Newman;** a Circuit Judge, since 1986; an Official Referee, since 1994; *b* 2 July 1937; *s* of late Wilfred James Newman and Cecilia Beatrice Lily Newman; *m* 1966, Winifred de Kok; two *s* one *d*. *Educ:* Sacred Heart Coll., Droitwich; Lewes County Grammar Sch. for Boys; Merton Coll., Oxford (BA 1959, MA 1964). President: OU Law Soc., 1959; OU Middle Temple Soc., 1959. Blackstone Entrance Scholar, Blackstone Pupillage Prize, and Harmsworth Major Scholar, Middle Temple, 1958–60; called to the Bar, Middle Temple, 1960; a Recorder, 1982–86. Asst Comr, Boundary Commn for England, 1976; Mem., Criminal Injuries Compensation Bd, 1985–86. Hon. Treasurer, Bar Yacht Club, 1973–88 (Rear-Cdre, 1985–86). Mem., Ashford Choral Soc., 1992–. *Recreations:* sailing, shooting, swimming, opera, church music. *Address:* Orlestone Grange, near Ashford, Kent TN26 2EB. *Club:* Bar Yacht.

See also Hon. Sir G. M. Newman.

NEWMAN, Edward; Member (Lab) Greater Manchester Central, European Parliament, since 1984; *b* 14 May 1953; *m*; three *c*. Formerly in light engineering, cable making; postal worker, Manchester. Mem., Manchester CC, 1979–85. *Address:* 7th Floor, Graeme House, Wilbraham Road, Chorlton cum Hardy, Manchester M21 1AQ; 234 Ryebank Road, Chorlton cum Hardy, Manchester M21 1LU.

NEWMAN, Sir Francis (Hugh Cecil), 4th Bt *cr* 1912, of Cecil Lodge, Newmarket; *b* 12 June 1963; *s* of Sir Gerard Robert Henry Sigismund Newman, 3rd Bt and of Caroline Philippa, *d* of late Brig. Alfred Geoffrey Neville, CBE, MC; *S* father, 1987; *m* 1990, Katharine, *d* of Timothy Edwards; one *s* one *d*. *Educ:* Eton; Univ. of Pennsylvania (BA Econs). *Recreations:* stalking, fishing, rowing. *Heir:* *s* Thomas Ralph Gerard Newman, *b* 7 Jan. 1993. *Address:* Burloes Hall, Royston, Herts SG8 9NE. *Club:* Eton Vikings.

NEWMAN, Frederick Edward Fry, CBE 1986; MC 1945; Chairman: Dan-Air Services, 1953–89; Davies & Newman Holdings, 1971–90; *b* 14 July 1916; *s* of Frank Newman and Katharine Newman; *m* 1947, Margaret Helen (*née* Blackstone); two *s* one *d*. *Educ:* The Leys School, Cambridge. Joined Davies & Newman, 1937; served HAC and 9th Field Regt, RA, 1939–46; formed Dan-Air Services, 1953. *Address:* Cranstone, Hook Heath Road, Woking, Surrey GU22 0DT. *T:* Woking (01483) 772605.

NEWMAN, Sir Geoffrey (Robert), 6th Bt, *cr* 1836; *b* 2 June 1947; *s* of Sir Ralph Alured Newman, 5th Bt, and of Hon. Ann Rosemary Hope, *d* of late Hon. Claude Hope-Morley; *S* father, 1968; *m* 1980, Mary, *y d* of Colonel Sir Martin St John Valentine Gibbs, KCVO, CB, DSO, TD; one *s* three *d*. *Educ:* Heatherdown, Ascot; Kelly Coll., Tavistock. 1st Bn, Grenadier Guards, 1967–70. Dir, Blackpool Sands (Devon) Utilities Co. Ltd. FRGS. *Recreations:* sub-aqua, sailing, all sports. *Heir: s* Robert Melvil Newman, *b* 4 Oct. 1985. *Address:* Blackpool House, Dartmouth, Devon TQ6 0RG.

NEWMAN, Hon. Sir George Michael, Kt 1995; **Hon. Mr Justice Newman;** a Judge of the High Court of Justice, Queen's Bench Division, since 1995; *b* 4 July 1941; *s* of late Wilfred James Newman and Cecilia Beatrice Lily Newman; *m* 1966, Hilary Alice Gibbs (*née* Chandler); two *s* one *d*. *Educ:* Lewes County Grammar Sch.; St Catharine's Coll., Cambridge (BA Law). Called to the Bar, Middle Temple, 1965, Bencher, 1989; QC 1981; a Recorder, 1985–95. FRSA 1991. *Recreations:* tennis, skiing, the countryside. *Address:* Royal Courts of Justice, Strand, WC2A 2LL.

See also C. W. F. Newman.

NEWMAN, Sir Jack, Kt 1977; CBE 1963; FCIT 1955; JP; Founder, 1938, President, 1981, Newman Group Ltd (formerly TNL), Nelson, New Zealand; *b* 3 July, 1902; *s* of Thomas Newman and Christina Thomson; *m* 1926, Myrtle O. A. Thomas; four *d*. *Educ:* Nelson Coll. for Boys, NZ. Joined Newman Bros Ltd (family business), 1922; Manager, 1927; Managing Director, 1935. Past President and Life Member: NZ Cricket Council; NZ Travel Assoc.; NZ Passenger Transport Fedn; former Dir, Pacific Area Travel Assoc. Represented: NZ, at cricket, 1931–33; Nelson, Canterbury and Wellington, at cricket; Nelson, at Rugby football, golf, and lawn bowls. JP Nelson, 1950. *Recreation:* lawn bowls. *Clubs:* MCC; Wellesley (Wellington); Nelson (Nelson).

NEWMAN, Karl Max, CB 1979; Second Counsel to the Chairman of Committees and Legal Adviser to the European Communities Committee, House of Lords, 1982–87; *b* 26 March 1919; *s* of Karl Neumann, DrJur, and Licie Neumann; *m* 1952, Annette, *d* of late Ronald Cross Sheen; one *s* one *d*. *Educ:* Ottershaw Coll., Surrey; Christ Church, Oxford (MA). Bacon Scholar of Gray's Inn, 1939. Served War in Army, 1940–42. Called to Bar, Gray's Inn, 1946, Bencher 1987; joined Lord Chancellor's Office, 1949; Asst Solicitor, 1962; Under-Sec., 1972–82; part-time Legal Adviser to European Unit of Cabinet Office, 1972–82; Head of Delegn negotiating UK accession to EEC Convention on Jurisdiction and Judgments, 1972–78. Member: UK delegns to Internat. Diplomatic Confs on Nuclear Liability, 1962–63; expert Cttees of Council of Europe, 1961–68; 10th and 11th Session of Hague Conf. on Private Internat. Law, 1964–68. Mem., EEC expert cttees, 1972–82. Hon. Fellow, British Inst. of Internat. and Comparative Law, 1991. *Publications:* Das Englisch-Amerikanische Beweisrecht, 1949 (Heidelberg); contribs to legal publications on EEC law, internat. jurisdiction and recognition of judgments. *Recreations:* philately, looking at paintings. *Address:* 17 Marryat Road, Wimbledon, SW19 5BB. *T:* 0181–946 3430. *Club:* United Oxford & Cambridge University.

NEWMAN, Sir Kenneth (Leslie), GBE 1987; Kt 1978; QPM 1982; Commissioner of the Metropolitan Police, 1982–87; non-executive director of various companies; *b* 15 Aug. 1926; *s* of John William Newman and Florence Newman; *m* 1949, Eileen Lilian. *Educ:* London Univ. (LLB Hons). Served War, RAF, 1942–46. Palestine Police, 1946–48; Metropolitan Police, 1948–73; Comdr, New Scotland Yard, 1972; Royal Ulster Constab., 1973–79; Sen. Dep. Chief Constable, 1973; Chief Constable, 1976–79; Comdt, Police Staff Coll., and HM Inspector of Constabulary, 1980–82. Vis. Prof. of Law, Bristol University, 1987–88. Registrar, Imperial Soc. of Knights Bachelor, 1991–. Chairman: Disciplinary Cttee, Security Systems Inspectorate, British Security Industry Assoc., 1987–; Assoc. for Prevention of Theft in Shops, 1987–91; Pres., Assoc. of Police and Public Security Suppliers, 1993–; Vice Pres., Defence Manufacturers Assoc., 1987–. Trustee: Police Foundn, 1982– (Chm., Res. Cttee, 1991–); Community Action Trust (Crime Stoppers), 1987–; World Humanity Action Trust, 1993–. CIMgt (FBIM 1977). Freeman of the City of London, 1983. KStJ 1987 (CStJ 1984). Communicator of the Year, BAIE, 1984. Order of: Bahrain, Class 2, 1984; the Aztec Eagle, Cl. 2, Mexico, 1985. King Abdul Aziz, Cl. 1, Saudi Arabia, 1987; Grand Officer: Order of Orange-Nassau, Netherlands, 1982; Grand Order of the Lion, Malaŵi, 1985; Order of Ouissam Alouite, Morocco, 1987; Commander: National Order of Legion of Honour, France, 1984; Order of Military Merit, Spain, 1986; Kt Comdr, Order of Merit, West Germany, 1986; Medal of Merit, Cl. 1, Qatar, 1985. *Recreations:* walking, reading, bridge.

NEWMAN, Kevin; Chief Executive, First Direct, Leeds, since 1991; *b* 28 June 1957; *s* of John and Valerie Newman; *m* 1983, Catherine Stewart-Murray; two *s*. *Educ:* Keele Univ. (BA Amer. Studies and Politics); Essex Univ. (US Govt and Politics). Mars Gp Services, 1981–85; Inf. Centre Manager, Business Systems Manager and Management Inf. Systems Dir, Woolworth, 1985–89; First Direct: joined 1989; Ops Dir, 1990. *Recreations:* squash, tennis, ski-ing, golf, gym workout, watching American football, parenthood. *Address:* First Direct, Millshaw Park Lane, Leeds LS98 1FD. *T:* Leeds (0113) 276 6100.

NEWMAN, Dr Lotte Therese, (Mrs N. E. Aronsohn), OBE 1991; general practitioner since 1958; President, Royal College of General Practitioners, since 1994; Member, General Medical Council, since 1984; *b* 22 Jan. 1929; *d* of Dr George Newman and Dr Tilly Newman; *m* 1959, Norman Edward Aronsohn; three *s* one *d*. *Educ:* North London Collegiate Sch.; Univ. of Birmingham; King's College London and Westminster Hosp. Med. Schs. BSc 1951, MB BS 1957; LRCP, MRCS 1957; FRCGP 1977; FRSM 1977. Casualty Officer, Westminster Hosp.; Paediatric House Officer, Westminster Children's Hosp.; gen. medicine, St Stephen's Hosp. Director: Private Patients Plan, 1983–; Private Patients Plan (Lifetime) plc, 1991–. Mem. Council, 1980–94, Vice-Chm., 1987–89, former Provost, NE London Faculty and former Examr, RCGP; Hon. Sec., 1981–86, Pres. elect, 1986–87, Pres., 1987–88, Medical Women's Fedn, Pres., Internat. Soc. of Gen. Practice, 1988–; Europ. Regl Vice-Pres., World Orgn of Nat. Colls, Acads and Academic Assocs of GPs/Family Physicians, 1992–; Member: Council, BMA, 1985–89 (Member: Med. Ethics Cttee; General Med. Services Cttee, 1983–86 and 1988–91; Private Practice and Prof. Fees Cttee, 1985–89; Forensic Medicine Sub-Cttee, 1985–89); Home Office Misuse of Drugs Tribunal, 1993–; Chm., Camden and Islington Local Med. Cttee, 1986–89 (Vice-Chm., 1983–86); Chm., Regional Co-ordinating Cttee of Area Local Med. Cttees, 1985–87; Lectr, Royal Army Med. Coll., 1976–89 (first woman to give Sir David Bruce Lecture in Gen. Practice, 1989); temp. Adviser, WHO; formerly UK rep., OECD and Mem., Expert Cttees studying Primary Health Care in Germany, Switzerland, Sweden. Mem., Parole Bd, 1992–94. Mackenzie Lectr, RCGP, 1991; Dame Hilda Rose Lectr, Med. Women's Fedn, 1994. Member: Hunterian Soc.; Hampstead Medical Soc.; Assurance Med. Soc., 1987–. Freeman, City of London; Liveryman, Apothecaries' Soc. of London. Sir David Bruce Medal, RAMC, 1990; Purkinje Medal for Services to Medicine, Czech Soc. of Gen. Practice, 1985. *Publications:* papers on: women doctors; multidisciplinary training and courses of Primary Health Care Team; breast feeding; ENT conditions and management of mental health handicap in gen. practice. *Recreations:* listening, music, boating. *Address:* The White House, One Ardwick Road, NW2 2BX. *T:* 0171–435 6630. *Clubs:* Royal Automobile, City Livery, Little Ship.

NEWMAN, Malcolm, CIPFA; City Treasurer, since 1987, and Deputy Chief Executive, since 1990, Sheffield City Council; *b* 2 April 1946; *s* of John George and Elizabeth Newman; *m* 1980, Marilyn Wilson; one *s* one *d*. *Educ:* Jarrow Grammar Sch. Clerk, Hebburn UDC, 1962–66; Newcastle upon Tyne City Council: various positions, 1966–71; Sen. Audit Asst, 1971–72; Sen. Management Accountant, 1972–73; Chief Accountant, 1973–77; Asst City Treas. (Accounting), 1977–79; Man. (Cons.) and Gen. Man., Wilson Johnson, 1979–80; Asst Finance Officer (Audit and Tech.), Sefton MDC, 1980–82; Hd of Financial Services 1982–85, Bor. Treas. 1985–87, London Borough of Southwark. Dir, Hallamshire Investments plc, 1988–; Chm., START Fedn, 1994–. Governor: Sheffield Hallam Univ. (formerly Sheffield Poly.), 1989–94; Silverdale Sch., 1993–. *Recreations:* old house, young family, squash, jogging, reading. *Address:* 113 Knowle Lane, Sheffield S11 9SN.

NEWMAN, Nanette, (Mrs Bryan Forbes); actress and writer; *b* 29 May 1939; *d* of Sidney and Ruby Newman; *m* 1958, Bryan Forbes, *qv*; two *d*. *Educ:* Sternhold Coll., London; Italia Conti Stage Sch.; RADA. Appeared as a child in various films for Children's Film Foundn; other film appearances include: The L-Shaped Room, 1962; The Wrong Arm of the Law, 1962; Seance on a Wet Afternoon, 1963; The Wrong Box, 1965; The Whisperers, 1966; Deadfall, 1967; The Madwoman of Chaillot, 1968; The Raging Moon, 1971 (Variety Club Best Film Actress Award); The Stepford Wives, 1974; International Velvet, 1978 (Evening News Best Film Actress Award); The Mystery of Edwin Drood, 1992; *television:* Call My Bluff, What's My Line, The Fun Food Factory (own series), London Scene, Stay with me till Morning, Jessie (title role), Let There Be Love, A Breath of Fresh Air, Late Expectations, The Endless Game, The Mixer. *Publications:* God Bless Love, 1972 (repr. 16 times); Lots of Love, 1973 (repr. 7 times); Vote for Love, 1976 (repr. 4 times); All Our Love, 1978; Fun Food Factory, 1976 (repr. twice); Fun Food Feasts, 1978; The Root Children, 1978; The Pig Who Never Was, 1979; Amy Rainbow, 1980; The Facts of Love, 1980; That Dog, 1980; Reflections, 1981; The Dog Lovers Coffee Table Book, 1982; The Cat Lovers Coffee Table Book, 1983; My Granny was a Frightful Bore, 1983; A Cat and Mouse Love Story, 1984; Nanette Newman's Christmas Cook Book, 1984; Pigalev, 1985; The Best of Love, 1985; The Summer Cookbook, 1986; Archie, 1986; Small Beginnings, 1987; Bad Baby, 1988; Entertaining with Nanette Newman and her Daughters Sarah and Emma, 1988; Sharing, 1989; Charlie the Noisy Caterpillar, 1989; ABC, 1990; 123, 1991; Cooking for Friends, 1991; Spider the Horrible Cat, 1992; There's a Bear in the Bath, 1993; There's a Bear in the Classroom, 1995; The Importance of Being Ernest the Earwig, 1996. *Recreation:* needlepoint. *Address:* c/o The Bookshop, Virginia Water, Surrey GU25 4DP. *T:* Wentworth (01344) 842463.

NEWMAN, Paul; American actor and director; *b* 26 Jan. 1925; *s* of Arthur Newman and Theresa (*née* Fetzer); *m* 1st, 1949, Jacqueline Witte; two *d* (one *s* decd); 2nd, 1958, Joanne Woodward; three *d*. *Educ:* Kenyon Coll. (BA); Yale Drama Sch. Mil. Service, USNR, 1943–46. Chairman: Newman's Own; Salad King. Team owner, and formerly driver, IndyCar racing. *Stage appearances include:* Picnic, 1953–54; Sweet Bird of Youth, 1959; *films include:* Somebody Up There Likes Me, 1956; Cat on a Hot Tin Roof, 1958; The Hustler, 1961; Sweet Bird of Youth, 1962; Hud, 1963; Torn Curtain, 1966; Cool Hand Luke, 1967; Butch Cassidy and the Sundance Kid, 1969; The Sting, 1973; Drowning Pool, 1975; Quintet, 1979; Fort Apache, the Bronx (also dir), 1980; Absence of Malice, 1981; The Verdict, 1982; Harry and Son (also wrote and directed), 1984; The Color of Money, 1986 (Academy Award, 1987); Blaze, 1990; Shadow Makers, 1990; Mr and Mrs Bridge, 1991; The Hudsucker Proxy, 1994; Nobody's Fool, 1995; *films directed include:* Rachel, Rachel, 1968; When Time Ran Out, 1980; The Glass Menagerie, 1987. Hon Academy Award for career achievement, 1986. *Address:* Newman Haas Racing, 500 Tower Parkway, Lincolnshire, IL 60069, USA.

NEWMAN, Vice Adm. Sir Roy (Thomas), KCB 1992 (CB 1991); Flag Officer Plymouth, and Commander Central Sub Area Eastern Atlantic, since 1992; *b* 8 Sept. 1936; *s* of Mr and Mrs T. U. Newman; *m* 1960, Heather (*née* Macleod); four *s*. *Educ:* Queen Elizabeth's Grammar Sch., Barnet, Herts. Joined RN, 1954; specialised in anti-submarine warfare, 1963; joined Submarine Service, 1966; Comdr 1971, Captain 1979; commanded: HMS Onyx, 1970–71; HMS Naiad, 1978–79; First Submarine Sqn and HMS Dolphin, 1981–83; Seventh Frigate Sqn and HMS Cleopatra, 1984–85; Dir of Naval Warfare, 1986–88; Flag Officer Sea Trng, 1988–89; COS to C-in-C Fleet and Dep. Comdr Fleet, 1990–92. Freeman, City of London, 1989. *Recreations:* cricket, golf, music, reading. *Clubs:* Army and Navy, Institute of Directors.

NEWMAN, Col Sir Stuart (Richard), Kt 1993; CBE 1984; TD 1952; *b* 13 June 1919; *e s* of late Capt. Thomas Pacey Newman, MC, DCM, and Dorothy, *y d* of Richard Booth Beverley. *Address:* 47 Gilkes Crescent, Dulwich Village, SE21 7BP.

NEWMAN, Sydney Cecil, OC 1981; film and television producer and executive; President, Sydney Newman Enterprises; *b* Toronto, 1 April 1917; *m* 1944, Margaret Elizabeth (*d* 1981), *d* of Rev. Duncan McRae, DD; three *d*. *Educ:* Ogden Public School and Central Technical School, Toronto. Painter, stage, industrial and interior designer; still and cinema photographer, 1935–41. National Film Board of Canada: joined under John Grierson as splicer-boy, 1941. Editor and Dir of Armed Forces training films and war information shorts, 1942; Exec. Producer in charge of all films for cinemas, including short films, newsreels, films for children and travel, 1947–52 (assigned to NBC in New York by Canadian govt, to report on American television techniques, 1949–50); TV Dir of Features and Outside Broadcasts, Canadian Broadcasting Corp., 1953; Superviser of Drama and Producer of General Motors Theatre, On Camera, Ford Theatre, Graphic, 1954; Superviser of Drama and Producer, Armchair Theatre, ABC Television, England, 1958–62 (devised, The Avengers, 1961); Head of Drama Group, TV, BBC, 1963–67 (devised Dr Who, 1963, and Adam Adamant Lives!, 1966), Producer, Associated British Productions Ltd, Elstree, 1968–69; Special Advr to Chm. and Dir, Broadcast Programmes Branch, Canadian Radio and Television Commn, 1970; Canadian Govt Film Comr and Chm., Nat. Film Bd of Canada, 1970–75; Special Advr on Film to Sec. of State for Canada, 1975–77; Chief Creative Consultant, Canadian Film Develt Corp., 1978–84 (Dir, Montreal, 1970–75). Dir, Canadian Broadcasting Corp., 1972–75. Producer: Canada Carries On, 1945; over 300 documentaries, including: Suffer Little Children (UN), It's Fun to Sing (Venice Award), Ski Skill, After Prison What? (Canada Award); Stephen D, BBC TV, 1963; The Rise and Fall of the City of Mahagonny, BBC TV, 1965; The Tea Party, BBC TV, 1965; Britten's The Little Sweep, Channel 4, 1989; produced first plays by Arthur Hailey, inc. Flight into Danger, Course for Collision; commissioned and prod. first on-air plays of Alun Owen, Harold Pinter, Angus Wilson, Robert Muller, Peter Luke, and plays by Clive Exton, David Perry and Hugh Leonard. Trustee, Nat. Arts Center, Ottawa, 1970–75; Gov., Canadian Conf. of the Arts; Member: New Western Film and TV Foundn; BAFTA; FRTS 1991; FRSA 1967; Fellow Soc. of Film and Television Arts, 1958. Ohio State Award for Religious Drama, 1956; Liberty Award, Best Drama Series, 1957; Desmond Davis Award, 1967, Soc. of Film and Television Arts; President's Award, 1969, and Zeta Award, 1970, Writers Guild of GB; Canadian Picture Pioneers Special Award, 1973; Special Recognition Award, SMPTE, 1975. Kt of Mark Twain, USA. *Address:* (office) 3 Nesbitt Drive, Toronto, Ont M4W 2G2, Canada.

NEWMARCH, Michael George, (Mick); Chief Executive, Prudential Corporation plc, 1990–95; *b* 19 May 1938; *s* of late George Langdon Newmarch and Phyllis Georgina Newmarch; *m* 1959, Audrey Clarke; one *s* two *d*. *Educ:* Univ. of London (BSc (Econs) external). Joined Prudential, 1955, Econ. Intelligence Dept; Exec. Dir, Prudential Corp., 1985–95; Chairman: Prudential Money Funds, 1983–95; Prudential Holborn, 1986–89; Prudential Financial Services, 1987–95 (Chief Exec., 1987–89); Prudential Currency Fund, 1987–95; Prudential Assce Co., 1990–95; Prudential Portfolio Managers, 1990–95 (Chief Exec., 1982–89); Prudential Nominees, 1990–95; Prudential Services, 1990–95; Mercantile and Gen. Gp., 1990–95. Mem. Adv. Bd, J. P. Morgan. Dir, ABI. Dir, Princess Royal Trust for Carers; Mem. President's Adv. Council, Spastics Soc. *Recreations:* salmon and trout fishing, flytying, bridge, theatre, concerts. *Club:* Flyfishers'.

NEWNS, Sir (Alfred) Foley (Francis Polden), KCMG 1963 (CMG 1957); CVO 1961; MA Cantab; *b* 30 Jan. 1909; *s* of late Rev. Alfred Newns, AKC; *m* 1st, 1936, Jean (*d* 1984), *d* of late A. H. Bateman, MB, BS; one *s* one *d*; 2nd, 1988, Beryl Wattles, BEd Cantab, MSc London, AMBDA. *Educ:* Christ's Hospital; St Catharine's College, Cambridge. Colonial Administrative Service, Nigeria, 1932; served E Reg. and Colony; Enugu Secretariat, 1947; Lagos Secretariat, 1949; attached Cabinet Office, London, 1951; Resident, 1951; Secretary to Council of Ministers, 1951; Secretary to Governor-General and the Council of Ministers, Federation of Nigeria, 1955–59; Dep. Governor, Sierra Leone, 1960–61; Acting Gov. during 1960; Adviser to the Government of Sierra Leone after Independence, 1961–63; Sec. to Cabinet, Govt of the Bahamas, 1963–71. Consultant to several governments on internal political procedure. President: St Catharine's Coll. Soc., 1986–87 (Sec., 1976–85); Foxton Gardens Assoc., 1989–91 (Chm., 1973–89); Member: Cambridgeshire Wild Life Fundraising Cttee (formerly Trust Appeal), 1986–90; Cttee, UK Br., Nigerian Field Soc., 1983–90 (Life Mem., 1934); Life Member: Britain–Nigeria Assoc.; Sierra Leone Soc., and other societies. Hon. Treasurer, Cambridge Specific Learning Disabilities Gp, 1986–; Hon. Auditor, Cambridge Decorative and Fine Arts Soc., 1984–. FRSA 1969. *Publications:* various papers on Cabinet procedure and government machinery, circulated in Commonwealth. *Address:* 47 Barrow Road, Cambridge CB2 2AR. *T:* Cambridge (01223) 356903.

See also J. Ounsted.

NEWPORT, Viscount; Alexander Michael Orlando Bridgeman; *b* 6 Sept. 1980; *s* and *heir* of 7th Earl of Bradford, *qv*.

NEWRY AND MORNE, Viscount; Robert Francis John Needham; Business Development Manager, Inchcape NRG, since 1995; *b* 30 May 1966; *s* and *heir* to Earl of Kilmorey (*see* Rt Hon. R. F. Needham); *m* 1991, Laura Mary, *o d* of Michael Tregaskis. *Educ:* Sherborne Prep. School; Eton College; Lady Margaret Hall, Oxford (BA); Imperial Coll., London (MBA 1993). Management trainee, Benjamin Priest, 1988–90; Sales Man., Lewmar Marine Ltd, 1991–92; Asst Man., Business Develt, Inchcape Pacific Ltd, 1994–95. Mem., Chichester Fest. Theatre Soc. *Recreations:* squash, theatre, travelling. *Clubs:* Pratt's; Hong Kong Football.

NEWSAM, Sir Peter (Anthony), Kt 1987; Director, University of London Institute of Education, 1989–94; Deputy Vice-Chancellor, University of London, 1992–94; *b* 2 Nov. 1928; *s* of late W. O. Newsam and of Mrs D. E. Newsam; *m* 1st, 1953, Elizabeth Joy Greg (marr. diss. 1987); four *s* one *d*; 2nd, 1988, Sue Addinell; one *d*. *Educ:* Clifton Coll.; Queen's Coll., Oxford (MA, DipEd). Asst Principal, BoT, 1952–55; teacher, 1956–63; Asst Educn Officer, N Riding of Yorks, 1963–66; Asst Dir of Educn, Cumberland, 1966–70; Dep. Educn Officer: W Riding of Yorks, 1970–72; ILEA, 1972–76; Educn Officer, ILEA, 1977–82; Chm., CRE, 1982–87; Sec., ACC, 1987–89. *Address:* 44 Lady Somerset Road, NW5 1TU.

NEWSOM-DAVIS, Prof. John Michael, MD; FRCP; FRS 1991; Professor of Clinical Neurology, University of Oxford, since 1987; *b* 18 Oct. 1932; *s* of John Kenneth and Dorothy Eileen Newsom-Davis; *m* 1963, Rosemary Elisabeth (*née* Schmid); one *s* two *d*. *Educ:* Sherborne Sch.; Pembroke Coll., Cambridge (BA 1957 Nat. Scis); Middlesex Hosp. Med. Sch. (MB BChir 1960, MD 1966); FRCP 1973. RAF, 1951–53 (Pilot). Lectr, Univ. Dept of Clinical Neurology, Nat. Hosp. for Nervous Diseases, 1967–69; Neurological Research Fellow, Cornell Med. Center, New York Hosp., 1969–70; Consultant Neurologist, Royal Free Hosp. and Nat. Hosp. for Nervous Diseases, 1970–80; MRC Clinical Res. Prof. of Neurology, Royal Free Hosp. Med. Sch. and Inst. of Neurology, 1980–87; Hon. Consultant, Nat. Hosp. for Nervous Diseases, 1987–. Department of Health: consultant advr in neurology, 1985–94; Mem., Central R & D Cttee, 1991–. Mem., MRC, 1983–87 (Mem., Neurosciences Grants Cttee, 1978–80; Mem., 1980–83, 1992–, Chm., 1983–85, Neuroscis Bd); Pres., Biomedical Section, BAAS, 1982–83, 1994; Hon. Sec., Assoc. of British Neurologists, 1981–84; Vice-Pres., Internat. Soc. for Neuroimmunology, 1987–; Chm., Med. Adv. Cttee, British Council, 1995–. Corr. Mem., Amer. Acad. of Neurology. Mem., Governing Body, BPMF, 1987–91. Mem. Editorial Bds of Brain, Jl of Neurological Sci., Jl of Neuroimmunology. *Publications:* (with E. J. M. Campbell and E. Agostoni) Respiratory Muscles: mechanics and neural control, 1970; numerous papers in Neurol. and Immunol. jls. *Recreations:* music and France. *Address:* Department of Clinical Neurology, University of Oxford, Radcliffe Infirmary, Oxford OX2 6HE.

NEWSOME, David Hay, MA; LittD Cantab 1976; FRSL 1981; Master of Wellington College, 1980–89; *b* 15 June 1929; *s* of Captain C. T. Newsome, OBE; *m* 1955, Joan Florence, *d* of Lt-Col L. H. Trist, DSO, MC; four *d*. *Educ:* Rossall Sch., Fleetwood; Emmanuel Coll., Cambridge (Scholar). First Cl. in Hist. Tripos Parts I and II, 1952, 1953. Asst Master, Wellington Coll., 1954–59 (Head of History Dept, 1956–59); Fellow of Emmanuel Coll., Cambridge, 1959–70; Asst Lectr in Ecclesiastical History, Univ. of Cambridge, 1961–66; Univ. Lectr, 1966–70; Sen. Tutor, Emmanuel Coll., Cambridge, 1965–70; Headmaster of Christ's Hospital, 1970–79. Lectures: Gore Memorial, Westminster Abbey, 1965; Bishop Westcott Memorial, Cambridge, 1968; Birkbeck, Univ. of Cambridge, 1972. Council of: Ardingly Coll., 1965–69; Eastbourne Coll., 1966–70; Epsom Coll., 1966–70. FRHistS, 1970. *Publications:* A History of Wellington College, 1859–1959, 1959; Godliness and Good Learning, Four Studies in a Victorian Ideal, 1961; The Parting of Friends, a study of the Wilberforces and Henry Manning, 1966; Bishop Westcott and the Platonic Tradition, 1969; Two Classes of Men: Platonism and English Romantic Thought, 1974; On the Edge of Paradise: A. C. Benson the Diarist, 1980 (Whitbread Book of the Year Award); (ed) Edwardian Excursions, 1981; The Convert Cardinals: Newman and Manning, 1993; articles in Jl of Theological Studies, Jl of Ecclesiastical History, Theology, History Today, Historical Jl, Recusant History. *Recreations:* music, fell-walking. *Address:* The Retreat, Thornthwaite, Keswick, Cumbria CA12 5SA. *T:* Braithwaite (017687) 78372. *Club:* East India.

NEWSOME, William Antony; Director-General, Association of British Chambers of Commerce, 1974–84; *b* 8 Nov. 1919; *s* of William F. Newsome and Elizabeth (*née* Thompson); *m* 1951, Estella Ann (*née* Cope); one *s*. *Educ:* King Henry VIII Sch., Coventry; Bedford Modern Sch. Student Engineer, W. H. Allen, Sons & Co. Ltd, Bedford, 1937–40. Served War, Royal Engineers: N Africa, Sicily, Italy campaigns, 1940–47. Engrg Dept, Crown Agents for Oversea Governments and Administrations, 1949–61; Principal: Home Office, 1961–64; Min. of Technology, 1964–70; Dept of Trade and Industry, 1970–71; Asst Sec., Dept of Trade, 1971–74. Member: SITPRO, 1972–84; Production Statistics Adv. Cttee, 1975–84; Home Office Standing Cttee on Crime Prevention, 1978–84. *Recreations:* photography, swimming, golf. *Address:* Bourdon Lacey, Old Woking Road, Woking, Surrey GU22 8HR. *T:* Woking (01483) 762237.

NEWSON-SMITH, Sir John (Kenneth), 2nd Bt *cr* 1944; DL; *b* 9 Jan. 1911; *s* of Sir Frank Newson-Smith, 1st Bt and Dorothy (*d* 1955), *d* of late Sir Henry Tozer; *S* father, 1971; *m* 1st, 1945, Vera Margaret Allt (marr. diss. 1971); one *s* two *d*; 2nd, 1972, Anne (*d* 1987), *d* of late Harold Burns; 3rd, 1988, Sarah Ramsay, *d* of late Robert Bicknell. *Educ:* Dover Coll.; Jesus Coll., Cambridge (MA). Joined Newson-Smith & Co, 1933, Partner 1938. Served War, Royal Navy, 1939–40; RNVR 1940. Rejoined Newson-Smith & Co, 1946 (which subseq. became Fielding Newson-Smith & Co.). Master of Turners Co., 1969–70; Liveryman: Merchant Taylors' Co.; Spectaclemakers' Co. Court of Common Council, 1945–78; Deputy, Ward of Bassishaw, 1961–76. DL City of London, 1947. *Recreations:* travelling, gardening. *Heir: s* Peter Frank Graham Newson-Smith [*b* 8 May 1947; *m* 1974, Mrs Mary-Ann Owens, *o d* of Cyril C. Collins; one *s* one *d*]. *Address:* East End, 67 East Street, Warminster BA12 9BZ. *Club:* City Livery.

NEWSTROM, Prof. David Graham L.; *see* Lloyd-Newstrom.

NEWTON, 5th Baron *cr* 1892, of Newton-in-Makerfield, Co. Lancaster; **Richard Thomas Legh;** *b* 11 Jan. 1950; *er s* of 4th Baron Newton and of Priscilla Egerton-Warburton; *S* father, 1992; *m* 1978, Rosemary Whitfoot, *yr d* of Herbert Clarke; one *s* one *d*. *Educ:* Eton; Christ Church, Oxford (MA). Solicitor, May May & Merrimans, 1976–79. General Comr for Income Tax, 1983–. Mem., Wealden DC, 1987–. Mem., Sussex Downs Conservation Bd, 1992–. *Recreation:* bridge. *Heir: s* Hon. Piers Richard Legh, *b* 25 Oct. 1979. *Address:* Laughton Park Farm, Laughton, Lewes, East Sussex BN8 6BU. *T:* Halland (01825) 840627. *Clubs:* Pratt's, MCC.

NEWTON, Rt. Hon. Antony Harold, (Rt. Hon. Tony Newton), OBE 1972; PC 1988; MP (C) Braintree since Feb. 1974; Lord President of the Council and Leader of the House of Commons, since 1992; economist; *b* Aug. 1937; *m* 1st, 1962, Janet Huxley (marr. diss. 1986); two *d*; 2nd, 1986, Mrs Patricia Gilthorpe. *Educ:* Friends' Sch., Saffron Walden; Trinity Coll., Oxford. Hons PPE. President: OU Conservative Assoc., 1958; Oxford Union, 1959. Formerly Sec. and Research Sec., Bow Group. Head of Conservative Research Dept's Economic Section, 1965–70; Asst Dir, Conservative Research Dept, 1970–74. Chm. Coningsby Club, 1965–66. Contested (C) Sheffield, Brightside, 1970. An Asst Govt Whip, 1979–81; a Lord Comr of HM Treasury, 1981–82; Parly Under-Sec. of State for Social Security, 1982–84, and Minister for the Disabled, 1983–84, Minister of State (Minister for Social Security and the Disabled), 1984–86, Minister of State (Minister for Health) and Chm., NHS Management Bd, 1986–88, DHSS; Chancellor of Duchy of Lancaster and Minister of Trade and Industry, 1988–89; Sec. of State for Social Security, 1989–92. Vice-Chm., Fedn of Univ. Conservative and Unionist Assocs, 1959. Gov., Felsted Sch. Interested in taxation and social services. *Address:* House of Commons, SW1A 0AA.

NEWTON, Air Vice-Marshal Barry Hamilton, CB 1988; OBE 1975; a Gentleman Usher to The Queen, since 1989; *b* 1 April 1932; *s* of late Bernard Hamilton Newton, FCA and Dorothy Mary Newton; *m* 1959, Constance Lavinia, *d* of late Col J. J. Aitken, CMG, DSO, OBE; one *s* one *d*. *Educ:* Highgate; RAF College Cranwell. Commissioned 1953; 109 Sqn, 1954; 76 Sqn, Australia and Christmas Island, 1956; Flying Instr, RAF Coll. and No 6 Flying Trng Sch., 1959–63; HQ Flying Trng Comd, 1964; Staff Coll., Bracknell, 1966; Personal Staff Officer to Comdr, Second Allied Tactical Air Force, 1967; OC Ops Wing, RAF Cottesmore, 1969; Air Warfare Course, 1971; Defence Policy Staff, 1972; Cabinet Office, 1975; Asst Dir, Defence Policy, 1978; Cabinet Office, 1979; Air Cdre Flying Trng, HQ RAF Support Comd, 1982; Sen. Directing Staff (Air), RCDS, 1984; Comdt, JSDC, 1986–88; Special Project Officer, RCDS, 1988—89. Mem. Council, TA&VRA, 1989–. *Recreations:* shooting, walking, philately. *Address:* c/o National Westminster Bank, Blue Boar Row, Salisbury, Wilts SP1 1DF. *Club:* Royal Air Force.

NEWTON, Sir (Charles) Wilfrid, Kt 1993; CBE 1988; FCIT; Chairman: London Regional Transport, 1989–94 (Chief Executive, 1989–94); London Underground Ltd, 1989–94; *b* 11 Dec. 1928; *s* of late Gore Mansfield Newton and Catherine Knox Newton; *m* 1954, Felicity Mary Lynn Thomas; two *s* two *d*. *Educ:* Orange Grove Prep. Sch.; Highlands North High Sch.; Univ. of Witwatersrand, Johannesburg. FCIT 1989. Chartered Accountant (South Africa). Chartered Accountant, Saml Thomson & Young, 1947–55; Territory Accounting and Finance Manager, Mobil Oil Corp., S Africa, 1955–62; Controller, Mobil Sekiyu KK, Tokyo, 1962–63; Financial Manager/Dep. Gen. Manager, Mobil Oil, E Africa, Nairobi, 1963–65; Finance Dir, Mobil Sekiyu KK, Tokyo,, 1965–68; Turner & Newall: Finance Dir, 1968; Man. Dir of Finance and Planning, 1974, of Plastics, Chemicals and Mining, 1976; Gp Man. Dir, 1979; Gp Man. Dir and Chief Exec., 1982; Chairman: Mass Transit Railway Corp., Hong Kong, 1983–89; Hong Kong Futures Exchange Ltd, 1987–89; non-executive Chairman: Raglan Properties plc, 1994–; John I. Jacobs PLC, 1994–; non-executive Director: Hongkong & Shanghai Banking Corp., 1986–90; Sketchley PLC, 1990–; MetroPower Ltd, 1990–94; HSBC Hldgs plc, 1990–; Midland Bank, 1992–; Mountcity Investments Ltd, 1994–. CIMgt (CBIM 1974); FRSA 1990. Hon. FEng 1993; Hon. FHKIE 1994. JP Hong Kong, 1986–89. *Recreations:* sailing, reading. *Address:* Newtons Gate, 12 Ramley Road, Pennington, Lymington, Hants SO41 8GQ. *T:* Lymington (01590) 679750; 7A Balmoral House, Windsor Way, Brook Green, W14 0UF. *T:* 0171–602 4996. *Clubs:* Carlton, Little Ship; Wanderers (Johannesburg); Hong Kong, Aberdeen Boat, Royal Hong Kong Yacht (Hong Kong); Royal Lymington Yacht.

NEWTON, Clive Trevor, CB 1991; consumer affairs consultant; Chairman: Appeals Committee, Association of Authorised Public Accountants, since 1993; Authorisation Appeals Committee, Chartered Association of Certified Accountants, since 1994; *b* 26 Aug. 1931; *s* of late Frederick Norman and of Phyllis Laura Newton; *m* 1961, Elizabeth Waugh Plowman; one *s* one *d*. *Educ:* Hove Grammar School for Boys. LLB London; called to Bar, Middle Temple, 1969; certified accountant, 1962. Examiner, Insolvency Service, Board of Trade, 1952, Sen. Examiner, 1963, Asst Official Receiver, 1967; Principal, Marine Div., BoT, 1969; Sen. Principal, Marine Div., Dept of Trade, 1973; Asst Director of Consumer Credit, Office of Fair Trading, 1974; Asst Sec., Regional Development Grants Div., Dept of Industry, 1978; Dir of Consumer Affairs, OFT, 1980; Under Sec., Head of Consumer Affairs Div., DTI, 1986–91. Vice-Chm., Legislation Cttee, Nat. Fedn of Consumer Gps, 1993–; Independent Chairman, Disciplinary Committee: Nat. Assoc. of Funeral Dirs, 1995–; Nat. Assoc. for Pre-Paid Funeral Plans, 1995–. Dir, Concordia (YSV) Ltd, 1994–. *Recreations:* golf, watching cricket and football. *Address:* 115 Hangleton Way, Hove, E Sussex BN3 8AF. *Clubs:* Royal Automobile; Sussex County Cricket, East Brighton Golf.

NEWTON, David Alexander; Chief Executive Officer, Hillsdown Holdings plc, since 1993 (Director, since 1985); *b* 6 Oct. 1942; *s* of Alexander and Hazel Newton; *m* 1965,

Kathleen Mary Moore; one *s* one *d*. *Educ:* Morecambe Grammar Sch.; Wyvern Coll. Mgt trainee, J. Bibby & Sons Ltd, UK, 1964–67; Area Manager, Cobb Breeding Co., 1967–69; Gen. Manager and Dir, Anglian Food Gp, 1969–72; Agricl Dir, Sovereign Chicken Ltd, 1972–82; Ops Dir, Ross Poultry Ltd, 1982–84; Chief Exec. Officer and Dir, Buxted Poultry Ltd, 1984–85; Chm., Maple Leaf Mills Ltd, Toronto, 1987–90; Pres. and Chief Exec. Officer, Canada Packers Inc., 1990–92; Chief Operating Officer, Hillsdown Holdings plc, 1992–93. FIMgt (FBIM 1984); FInstD 1984. *Recreations:* golf, music, watching sports. *Address:* Hillsdown Holdings plc, 32 Hampstead High Street, NW3 1QD. *T:* 0171–794 0677. *Club:* Diss Golf (Norfolk).

NEWTON, Derek Henry; Chairman, C. E. Heath plc, 1984–87; *b* 14 March 1933; *s* of Sidney Wellington Newton and Sylvia May Newton (*née* Peacock); *m* 1957, Judith Ann (*d* 1995), *d* of Roland Hart, Kingston, Surrey; two *d*. *Educ:* Emanuel School. FCII. Commissioned Royal Artillery, 1952–54 (Lieut). Clerical, Medical & General Life Assurance Society, 1954–58; C. E. Heath Urquhart (Life & Pensions), 1958–83, Chm., 1971–84; Dir, C. E. Heath, 1975, Dep. Chm., 1983–84; Director: Glaxo Insurance (Bermuda), 1980–93; Glaxo Trustees, 1980–92; Clarges Pharmaceutical Trustees, 1985–92. Governor, BUPA Med. R&D, 1981–94. *Recreations:* cricket, golf. *Address:* Pantiles, Meadway, Oxshott, Surrey KT22 0LZ. *T:* Oxshott (01372) 842273. *Clubs:* MCC; Surrey County Cricket (Chm. 1979–94).

NEWTON, Sir Gordon; *see* Newton, Sir L. G.

NEWTON, Sir (Harry) Michael (Rex), 3rd Bt, *cr* 1900; *b* 7 Feb. 1923; 2nd and *e* surv. *s* of Sir Harry K. Newton, 2nd Bt, OBE, DL, and Myrtle Irene (*d* 1977), *e d* of W. W. Grantham, Balneath Manor, Lewes; *S* father, 1951; *m* 1958, Pauline Jane, *o d* of late R. J. F. Howgill, CBE; one *s*; three adopted *d*. *Educ:* Eastbourne College. Served War of 1939–45, with KRRC, in 8th Army and Middle East, 1941–46 (wounded). Master, Girdlers' Company, 1975–76; Freeman of City of London. *Recreation:* sailing (winner of 1953 Fastnet Race). *Heir: s* Rev. George Peter Howgill Newton [*b* 26 March 1962; *m* 1988, Jane, twin *d* of John Rymer; two *d*]. *Address:* Cliff House, Old Lyme Road, Charmouth, Dorset DT6 6BW. *T:* Charmouth (01297) 60704. *Club:* Royal Ocean Racing.

NEWTON, Ian; *see* Newton, R. E. I.

NEWTON, Prof. Ian, FRS 1993; FRSE; Head, Vertebrate Ecology Section, NERC Institute of Terrestrial Ecology, since 1989; *b* 17 Jan. 1940; *s* of Haydn Edwin Newton and Nellie Newton (*née* Stubbs); *m* 1962, Halina Teresa Bialkowska; two *s* one *d*. *Educ:* Bristol Univ. (BSc Zoology 1961); Worcester Coll., Oxford (DPhil Ornithology 1964; DSc 1982). FRSE 1994. Dept of Zoology, Oxford, 1964–67; Nature Conservancy, Edinburgh, 1967–73; Institute of Terrestrial Ecology, Natural Environment Research Council: Edinburgh, 1973–79; Huntingdon, 1979–; research on avian population ecology, incl. finches, waterfowl, birds of prey, impact of pesticides. Vice-Pres., BOU, 1989–93; Pres., British Ecological Soc., 1994–95. Hon. Mem., Amer. Ornith. Union. Union Medal, BOU, 1988; President's Medal, British Ecological Soc., 1989; Gold Medal, RSPB, 1991. *Publications:* Finches, 1972; Population Ecology of Raptors, 1979; The Sparrowhawk, 1986; (ed) Lifetime Reproduction in Birds, 1989; papers in sci. jls. *Recreations:* apple growing, walking. *Address:* NERC Institute of Terrestrial Ecology, Monks Wood, Abbots Ripton, Huntingdon, Cambs PE17 2LS. *T:* Abbots Ripton (01487) 773381.

NEWTON, Rev. Dr John Anthony; Warden, John Wesley's Chapel, Bristol, since 1995; *b* 28 Sept. 1930; *s* of late Charles Victor Newton and of Kathleen Marchant; *m* 1963, Rachel, *d* of late Rev. Maurice H. Giddings and of Hilda Giddings, Louth, Lincs; four *s*. *Educ:* Grammar School, Boston, Lincs; University Coll., Hull; London Univ.; Wesley House, Cambridge. BA, PhD (Lond), MA (Cantab). Jun. Research Fellow, Inst. of Historical Research, London Univ., 1953–55; Housemaster and actg Chaplain, Kent Coll., Canterbury, 1955–56; trained for Methodist Ministry, Wesley House, 1956–58, Asst Tutor, Richmond Coll., Surrey, 1958–61, having been ordained, 1960; Circuit Minister at Louth, Lincs, 1961–64, and Stockton-on-Tees, 1964–65; Tutor at Didsbury Coll. (from 1967, Wesley Coll.), Bristol, 1965–72; taught Church History, St Paul's United Theolog. Coll., Limuru, Kenya, and Univ. of Nairobi, 1972–73; Principal of Wesley Coll., Bristol, 1973–78; Superintendent Minister, London Mission (W London) Circuit, 1978–86; Chm., Liverpool Dist of Methodist Church, 1986–95. President of the Methodist Conference, 1981–82; Jt Pres., Merseyside and Region Churches' Ecumenical Assembly, 1987–95; Moderator, Free Church Federal Council, 1989–90 and 1993–94; a Pres., Churches Together in England, 1990–94. Hon. Canon, Lincoln Cathedral, 1988. Chm. of Governors, Westminster Coll., Oxford, 1979–88; Trustee, Wesley House, Cambridge, 1979–88. Governor, Rydal School, Colwyn Bay, 1986–95. Hon. Fellow, Liverpool John Moores Univ., 1993. Hon. DLitt Hull, 1982; DD Lambeth, 1995. *Publications:* Methodism and the Puritans, 1964; Susanna Wesley and the Puritan Tradition in Methodism, 1968; The Palestine Problem, 1972; Search for a Saint: Edward King, 1977; The Fruit of the Spirit in the Lives of Great Christians, 1979; A Man for All Churches: Marcus Ward, 1984; The Wesleys for Today, 1989; Heart Speaks to Heart: ecumenical studies in spirituality, 1994. *Recreations:* music, gardening, walking, book-collecting. *Address:* 3 College Road, Westbury-on-Trym, Bristol BS9 3EJ. *T:* Bristol (0117) 959 3225. *Clubs:* Penn; Athenæum (Liverpool).

NEWTON, John David; a Recorder of the Crown Court, 1983–92; *b* 4 April 1921; *s* of late Giffard and Mary Newton; *m* 1942, Mary Bevan; one *s* one *d*. *Educ:* Berkhamsted School; University College London. LLB 1947. Served war of 1939–45 in Royal Artillery and Indian Army (Major); called to the Bar, Middle Temple, 1948; Lectr in Law, University College, Hull, 1948–51; Lectr then Senior Lectr in Law, Liverpool University, 1951–82. Dir, Liverpool Philharmonic Hall Trust, 1986–88. *Publications:* (ed) Halsbury's Laws of England, 4th edn, 1982, Vol. 39, Rent Charges and Annuities; (ed jtly) Encyclopaedia of Forms and Precedents, 5th edn, 1988, Vol. 33, Rent Charges and Annuities. *Recreations:* fishing, golf. *Address:* 10 Rose Mount, Oxton, Birkenhead, Merseyside L43 5SW. *T:* 0151–652 4675. *Clubs:* Athenæum (Liverpool); Royal Liverpool Golf.

NEWTON, Prof. John Michael, DSc; Professor of Pharmaceutics, School of Pharmacy, University of London, since 1984; *b* 26 Dec. 1935; *s* of Richard and Dora Newton; *m* 1959, Janet Hinninghan (marr. diss. 1986); one *s* two *d*. *Educ:* Leigh Grammar Sch., Lancs; Sch. of Pharmacy, Univ. of London (BPharm; DSc 1990); Univ. of Nottingham (PhD). FRPharmS. Apprentice pharmacist, Royal Albert Edward Infirmary, Wigan, 1953–55; Demonstrator, Univ. of Nottingham, 1958–62; Sen. Lectr, Sunderland Polytechnic, 1962–64; Lectr, Univ. of Manchester, 1964–67; Sen. Scientist, Lilly Research Centre Ltd, 1968–71; Lectr, Univ. of Nottingham, 1972–78; Prof. of Pharmaceutics, Univ. of London, at Chelsea College, 1978–83. *Publications:* numerous articles in sci. jls associated with pharmaceutical technology. *Recreations:* fell walking, long distance running (Belgrave Harriers), gardening. *Address:* School of Pharmacy, 29–39 Brunswick Square, WC1N 1AX.

NEWTON, Sir Kenneth (Garnar), 3rd Bt *cr* 1924; OBE 1970 (MBE 1944); TD; Chairman, Garnar Booth plc, 1972–87 (Managing Director, 1961–83); *b* 4 June 1918; *s* of Sir Edgar Henry Newton, 2nd Bt, and Gladys Maud (*d* 1966), *d* of late Sir James Garnar; *S* father, 1971; *m* 1944, Margaret Isabel (*d* 1979), *d* of Rev. Dr George Blair, Dundee; two *s*. *Educ:* Wellington College, Berks. Served War of 1939–45 (MBE); Lt-Col, RASC (TA). Chm. Governors, Colfe's Sch., 1982–93. Pres., Internat. Council of Tanners, 1972–78; Past President, British Leather Federation (1968–69); Liveryman and Member of Court of Assistants, Leathersellers' Company (Master, 1977–78) and Feltmakers' Company (Master, 1983–84). *Heir: s* John Garnar Newton [*b* 10 July 1945; *m* 1972, Jacynth A. K. Miller; three *s* (incl. twins)]. *Address:* Wildways, High Broom Lane, Crowborough, Sussex TN6 3SP.

NEWTON, Sir (Leslie) Gordon, Kt 1966; Editor of The Financial Times, 1950–72, Director 1967–72; *b* 1907; *s* of John and Edith Newton; *m* 1935, Peggy Ellen Warren (*d* 1995); (one *s* decd). *Educ:* Blundell's School; Sidney Sussex College, Cambridge. Chm., LBC, 1974–77; Director: Trust Houses Forte Ltd, 1973–80; Mills & Allen (Internat.) Ltd, 1974–81. Hannen Swaffer Award for Journalist of the Year, 1966; Granada Television special award, 1970. *Address:* 51 Thames House, Phyllis Court Drive, Henley-on-Thames, Oxon RG9 2NA.

NEWTON, Margaret; Schools Officer, Diocese of Oxford, 1984–88, retired; *b* 20 Dec. 1927; 2nd *d* of F. L. Newton, KStJ, MB, ChB, and Mrs A. C. Newton, MBE, BA. *Educ:* Sherborne School for Girls; St Andrews Univ.; Oxford University. MA Hons St Andrews, 1950; Educn Dip. Oxon 1951. Asst Mistress, King Edward VI Grammar School, Handsworth, Birmingham, 1951–54; Classics Mistress, Queen Margaret's Sch., York, 1954–60 (House Mistress, 1957); House Mistress, Malvern Girls' College, 1960–64 (Head of Classics Dept, 1962); Headmistress, Westonbirt Sch., 1965–80; Gen. Sec., Friends of the Elderly, 1981–83. *Address:* The Comedy, Sherborne Street, Lechlade, Glos GL7 3AN.

NEWTON, Sir Michael; *see* Newton, Sir H. M. R.

NEWTON, Peter Marcus; HM Diplomatic Service; Ambassador to Guatemala, since 1995; *b* 16 Sept. 1942; *s* of Leslie Marcus Newton and Edith Mary Newton; *m* 1972, Sonia Maria Freire de Castilho; two *s* one *d*. *Educ:* Hamilton Academy; Glasgow Univ. (MA Hons); McGill Univ. (postgrad. studies). Third Sec., CRO, later CO, 1965; Kinshasa, 1967; Lima, 1968; First Sec., FCO, 1972; First Sec. (Econ.), Tokyo, 1975; First Sec. and Head of Chancery, Caracas, 1979; FCO, 1981; Counsellor, FCO, 1985–87; Consul-Gen., Montreal, 1987–89; Dep. High Comr, Ottawa, 1989–92; Head of S Atlantic and Antarctic Dept, FCO, 1992–95. *Address:* c/o Foreign and Commonwealth Office, SW1A 2AH.

NEWTON, Richard James; Chairman, National and Provincial Building Society, 1988–93; *b* 17 Nov. 1927; *s* of Alfred Richard Newton and Rosamond Newton (*née* Tunstill); *m* 1961, Elizabeth Seraphine Meuwissen (*d* 1986); four *s*. *Educ:* Clifton; St John's College, Cambridge (MA). Managerial positions at: Courtaulds, 1951–58; Midland Silicones, 1959–62; Chemstrand, 1963–66; Keith Shipton & Co., 1967–69; Man. Dir, Bury & Masco (Holdings), 1970–77; non-exec. Dir, Sketchley, 1978–87 (Chm., 1983–87); Dir, National & Provincial Building Soc., 1985–93. Fellow and Bursar, Trinity Hall, Cambridge, 1977–89. Gov., 1990–, Mem. Council, 1993–, Clifton Coll. *Recreations:* music, fell-walking, playing the piano. *Address:* The White House, Beeston, Norfolk PE32 2NF. *T:* Fakenham (01328) 701215.

NEWTON, (Robert Edward) Ian; educational consultant, since 1995; *b* 4 Aug. 1946; *o s* of John Newton and Ethel Alhiston; *m* 1969, Fiona Olive Pallant; one *s* one *d*. *Educ:* Dulwich Coll.; Oriel Coll., Oxford (BA Hons Nat. Sci. (Physics) 1967; MA 1973); Inst. of Education, London Univ. (Postgrad. CertEd 1968). Rugby School: Physics Teacher, 1968; Sixth Form girls' housemaster, 1976; Head of Physics, 1991; Headmaster, Bedales Sch., 1992–94. CFM 1983. *Publication:* Wave Physics, 1990. *Recreations:* sailing, playing the bassoon, walking. *Address:* 22 Hillmorton Road, Rugby, Warwicks CV22 5AA. *T:* Rugby (01788) 561393. *Club:* Royal Naval Sailing Association.

NEWTON, Trevor, OBE 1991; Deputy Chairman since 1990, Group Managing Director since 1991, Yorkshire Water plc; *b* 22 Sept. 1943; *m* 1968, Christine Diane Bingham. *Educ:* Acklam Hall Grammar Sch., Middlesbrough; Manchester Univ. (BA Hons Econs). CIPFA 1970. Local Government Finance: Middlesbrough, 1966–71; Coventry, 1971–73; Bradford, 1973–76; Yorkshire Water Authority: Asst Finance Dir, 1976–83; Finance Dir, 1983–89; Finance Dir, Yorks Water plc, 1989–90. *Publication:* Cost-Benefit Analysis in Administration, 1971. *Recreation:* gardening. *Address:* Upper Park House, 5 Park House Road, Low Moor, Bradford, W Yorks BD12 0QD. *T:* Bradford (01274) 677189. *Club:* Naval and Military.

NEWTON, Sir Wilfrid; *see* Newton, Sir C. W.

NEWTON-CLARE, Herbert Mitchell, (Bill), CBE 1976; MC 1943; Executive Chairman, Albemarle Group; *b* 5 May 1922; *s* of Herbert John and Eileen Margaret Newton-Clare; *m*; three *d*; *m* 1992, Harriet Mary Sheila Stormonth-Darling. *Educ:* Cheltenham Coll. TA, Middlesex Regt, 1938; served War of 1939–45: mobilised, 1939; commnd, Wiltshire Regt, 1941; wounded, Normandy, 1944; demobilised, 1945 (Major). Joined Bowyers (Wiltshire) Ltd, as trainee, 1945; Factory Manager, 1955, Gen. Manager, 1957, Man. Dir, 1960, Chm., 1966; following take-over by Unigate of Scot Bowyers (formerly Bowyers (Wiltshire) Ltd), became Director of Unigate, 1973, Vice-Chm., 1974–76; Dir, FMC Ltd, and ancillary cos, 1976–77. Chm., Meat Manufrs Assoc., 1970–82; Member: Exec. and Council, Food Manufrs Fedn, 1970–82; Food and Drink Industries Fedn, 1970–82; Exec. Centre de Liaison des Industries Transformatrice de Viandes de la Commune Européenne, 1970–82. *Recreations:* golf, tennis, swimming, fishing. *Address:* 4A Walham Grove, Fulham, SW6 1QP. *T:* 0171–381 0131. *Club:* Sunningdale Golf.

NEWTON DUNN, William Francis; *b* 3 Oct. 1941; *s* of late Lt-Col Owen Newton Dunn, OBE, and Barbara (*née* Brooke); *m* 1970, Anna Terez Arki; one *s* one *d*. *Educ:* Marlborough Coll. (scholar); Gonville and Caius Coll., Cambridge (MA); INSEAD Business Sch., Fontainebleau (MBA). With Fisons Ltd (Fertilizer Division), 1974–79. MEP (C) Lincolnshire, 1979–94; contested (C) Lincolnshire and Humberside S, 1994. European Parliament: Cons. Spokesman: on Transport, 1984–87; on Rules of Procedure, 1987–89; on Political Affairs, 1989–91; Chm., 1979 Cttee (Cons. backbench MEPs), 1983–88; Mem. Bureau, Cons. MEP Gp, 1988–94; Dep. Leader, EDG, 1991–93; Chm., British Cons. MEP Section, Eur. People's Party, 1993–94. Contested (C): general elections: Carmarthen, Feb. 1974; Cardiff West, Oct. 1974. *Publications:* Greater in Europe, 1986; Big Wing: biography of Air Chief Marshal Sir Trafford Leigh-Mallory, 1992; pamphlet on the EEC's democratic deficit. *Recreation:* spending time with his children. *Address:* 27 Sterndale Road, W14 0HT. *T:* 0171–602 6187.

NGAIZA, Christopher Pastor; Chairman and Managing Director, PES Consultants Ltd, Tanzania, since 1986; *b* 29 March 1930; parents decd; *m* 1952, Thereza; three *s* two *d* (and one *s* decd). *Educ:* Makerere University Coll.; Loughborough Co-operative College.

Local Courts Magistrate, 1952–53; Secretary/Manager, Bahaya Co-operative Consumer Stores, 1955–57; Loughborough Co-operative Coll., 1957–59; Auctioneer and Representative of Bukoba Native Co-operative Union, Mombasa, 1959–61; Foreign Service, 1961–; Counsellor, Mission to UN, 1961–62; Counsellor, Tanganyika High Commn, London, 1962–63; High Commissioner for United Republic of Tanganyika and Zanzibar in London, 1964–65; Tanzanian Ambassador: to Netherlands, 1965–67, to Arab Republic of Egypt, 1972–77; Mem., E African Common Market Tribunal, 1968–69; Tanzania's first High Comr to Zambia, 1969–72; Special Personal Assistant to Pres. of Tanzania, 1977–83; Comr for Kagera River Basin Orgn, 1978–83. *Recreations:* music, tennis. *Address:* PES Consultants Ltd, PO Box 4647, Dar-es-Salaam, Tanzania.

NGATA, Sir Henare Kohere, KBE 1982 (OBE); chartered accountant, retired; *b* Waiomatatini, 19 Dec. 1917; *s* of Sir Apirana Ngata and Arihia, *d* of Tuta Tamati; *m* 1940, Rora Lorna, *d* of Maihi Rangipo Mete Kingi; one *s*. *Educ:* Waiomatatini Sch.; Te Aute Coll., Victoria Univ. of Wellington, BA; BCom; FCA (NZ Soc. of Accountants). Served 28th Maori Bn, 1939–45: POW, Greece; Germany, 1941–45. Chm., Mangatu 1, 3 & 4 Blocks Incorp., 1959–87; Director: Fieldair Ltd, 1960–79; Gisborne Sheepfarmers Mercantile Co. Ltd; Gisborne Sheepfarmers Freezing Co. Ltd. Member: Gisborne Reg. Commn, NZ Historic Places Trust, 1962–70; NZ Maori Council, 1962–85; C of E Provincial Commn on Maori Schs, 1964–; Gisborne/East Coast Regional Develt Council, 1973–78; Finance Cttee, Bishopric of Aotearoa. Nat. Pres., 28th Maori Bn Assoc., 1964–66. Vice-Pres., NZ Nat. Party, 1967–69. Hon. LLD, Victoria Univ. of Wellington, 1979. *Address:* Grant Road, Gisborne, New Zealand.

NIAGARA, Bishop of, since 1991; **Rt. Rev. Walter Gordon Asbil;** *b* 3 Oct. 1932; *m* 1957, Mavis Asbil; three *s* one *d*. *Educ:* Concordia Univ., Montreal (BA); McGill Univ. (BD, STM). Ordained deacon, 1957, priest, 1957; Rector: Aylwin River Desert, 1957–60; Montreal South Shore, 1960–65; St Stephen's, Montreal, 1965–67; St George, St Anne de Bellevue, 1967–70; St George and St Catharine's, 1970–86; Rector and Dean, Christ Church Cathedral, Ottawa, 1986–90; Co-adjutor Bishop of Niagara, 1990–91. Hon. DD Montreal Dio. Theol Coll., 1991. *Address:* 67 Victoria Avenue South, Hamilton, Ontario L8N 2S8, Canada. *T:* (905) 5271278.

NIARCHOS, Stavros Spyros; Grand Cross of Order of the Phœnix (Greece), 1957; Commander of Order of George I of Greece, 1954; Commander of Order of St George and St Constantine (Greece), 1964; Head of Niarchos Group of Shipping Companies which controls over 5.75 million tons of shipping (operational and building); *b* 3 July 1909; *s* of late Spyros Niarchos and of Eugenie Niarchos; *m* 1st, 1939, Melpomene Capparis (marr. diss., 1947); no *c*; 2nd, 1947, Eugenie Livanos (*d* 1970); three *s* one *d*; 3rd, 1965, Charlotte Ford (marr. diss., 1967); one *d*; 4th, 1971, Mrs Athina Livanos (*d* 1974). *Educ:* Univ. of Athens (Dr of Laws). On leaving Univ. joined family grain and shipping business; started independent shipping concern, 1939. Joined Royal Hellenic Navy Volunteer Reserve, 1941; served on destroyer engaged in North Atlantic convoy work (despatches). Demobilised, 1945, with rank of Lieut-Comdr. Returned to Shipping business. Pioneered super-tankers. *Recreations:* yachting, ski-ing. *Address:* c/o Niarchos (London) Ltd, 41/43 Park Street, W1A 2JR. *T:* 0171–629 8400. *Clubs:* Athenian, Royal Yacht Club of Greece (both in Athens).

NIBLETT, Prof. William Roy, CBE 1970; BA, MLitt; Professor of Higher Education, University of London, 1967–73, now Professor Emeritus; *b* 25 July 1906; *m* 1938, Sheila Margaret, OBE 1975, *d* of A. C. Taylor, Peterborough; one *s* one *d*. *Educ:* Cotham Sch., Bristol; University of Bristol (1st cl. hons English; DipEd 1st cl.; John Stewart Schol.); St Edmund Hall, Oxford. Sen. English Master, Doncaster GS, 1930–34; Lectr in Educn, King's Coll., Newcastle, 1934–45 (Registrar, Durham Univ., 1940–44); Prof. of Educn, University Coll., Hull, 1945–47; Prof. of Education, and Dir, Inst. of Education, Univ. of Leeds, 1947–59; Dean, Univ. of London Inst. of Education, 1960–68. Hibbert Lectr, 1965; Fulbright Schol. (Harvard) and Kellogg International Fellow, 1954; sometime Visiting Professor, Universities of California, Melbourne, Otago and Japanese Govt Vis. Prof., Univs of Japan. Mem., UGC, 1949–59; Chairman: UGC Sub-Cttee on Halls of Residence, 1956 (Report 1957); Educn Dept, BCC, 1965–71; Higher Educn Policy Gp, 1969–72; President: European Assoc. for Res. in Higher Educn, 1972; Higher Educn Foundn, 1984– (Chm. Trustees, 1980–81). Vice-President: World Univ. Service (UK), 1963–90; Soc. for Res. in Higher Educn, 1978–. Member: Nat. Advisory Coun. on Trng and Supply of Teachers, 1950–61; Council on Army Educn, 1961–70; Council, Royal Holloway College, 1963–76; Council, Cheltenham Ladies' College, 1967–79; Trustee, Westhill Coll., Birmingham, 1979–91. Hon. FSRHE 1992. Chm., Editorial Bd, Studies in Higher Education, 1975–82. *Publications:* Education and the Modern Mind, 1954; Christian Education in a Secular Society, 1960; (ed) Moral Education in a Changing Society, 1963; (ed) Higher Education: Demand and Response, 1969; (ed with R. F. Butts) World Year Book of Education, 1972–73; Universities Between Two Worlds, 1974; (with D. Humphreys and J. Fairhurst) The University Connection, 1975; (ed) The Sciences, The Humanities and the Technological Threat, 1975; (contrib.) International Encyclopedia of Higher Education, 1977; (contrib.) The Study of Education, 1980; (contrib.) Validation in Higher Education, 1983; (contrib.) Academic Community: discourse or discord?, 1994. *Address:* 7 Blenheim Road, Bristol BS6 7JL. *T:* Bristol (0117) 973 5891.

NIBLOCK, Henry, (Pat), OBE 1972; HM Diplomatic Service, retired; HM Consul-General, Strasbourg, 1968–72; *b* 25 Nov. 1911; *s* of Joseph and Isabella Niblock, Belfast; *m* 1940, Barbara Mary Davies, *d* of late Captain R. W. Davies, Air Ministry; two *s*. Vice-Consul: Bremen, 1947–50; Bordeaux, 1951; Second Sec. (Commercial), Copenhagen, 1951–53; Consul, Frankfurt-on-Main, 1954–57; First Sec. and Consul, Monrovia, 1957–58; Consul, Houston, 1959–62; Chargé d'Affaires, Port-au-Prince, 1962–63; First Sec. and Consul, Brussels, 1964; Consul (Commercial), Cape Town, 1964–67. *Recreations:* walking, photography. *Address:* 10 Clifton House, 2 Park Avenue, Eastbourne, East Sussex BN22 9QN. *T:* Eastbourne (01323) 505695. *Club:* Civil Service.

NICE, Geoffrey; QC 1990; a Recorder, since 1987; *b* 21 Oct. 1945; *s* of William Charles Nice and Mahala Anne Nice (*née* Tarryer); *m* 1974, Philippa Mary Gross; three *d*. *Educ:* St Dunstan's College, Catford; Keble College, Oxford. Called to the Bar, Inner Temple, 1971; Contested (SDP/Liberal Alliance) Dover, 1983, 1987. *Address:* Farrar's Building, Temple, EC4Y 7BD. *T:* 0171–583 9241.

NICHOL, Comdt (Daphne) Patricia, CBE 1986; Director, Women's Royal Naval Service, 1982–86; *b* 25 Sept. 1932; *d* of Captain Ralph Geoffrey Swallow, RN and Daphne Lucy Regina Swallow (*née* Parry); *m* 1991, Capt. Peter Dale Nichol, RN. *Educ:* St George's Sch., Ascot; Portsmouth Polytechnic (Hon. Fellow, 1983). Joined WRNS as Signal Wren, 1950; qualified as WRNS Communications Officer, 1955; served in HMS Drake and Malta, 1956–58; Oslo, Portsmouth, HMS Mercury, Northwood and Gibraltar, 1958–67; HMS Pembroke and HMS Heron, 1968–71; passed Naval Staff Course, 1972; HMS Dauntless, 1973–74; Staff of C-in-C Naval Home Comd and MoD, 1974–76; National Defence College Latimer Course, 1976–77; Staff of Naval Secretary, 1977; Command Personnel Officer to C-in-C Naval Home Comd, 1977–79; Dep. Dir, WRNS, 1979–81; Staff Officer Training Co-ordination and Comd WRNS Officer to C-in-C Naval Home Comd, 1981–82; Hon. ADC to the Queen, 1982–86. Asst Sec., Benevolent Dept, Officers' Assoc., 1987–89; Case Sec., DGAA, 1989–90. Member: Nat. Exec. Cttee, Forces Help Soc. and Lord Roberts Workshops, 1986–95; Council and Exec. Cttee, Shipwrecked Fishermen and Mariners Royal Benevolent Soc., 1991–; Council, Soc. of Friends of RN Mus. and HMS Victory, Portsmouth, 1994–. Hon. Fellow, Univ. of Portsmouth, 1993. *Recreations:* tennis, dressmaking and needlework, reading, theatre, opera, music. *Address:* c/o Lloyds Bank, 23 Elm Grove, Hayling Island, Hants PO11 9EA.

NICHOL, Sir Duncan (Kirkbride), Kt 1993; CBE 1989; Professor of International Health Care Management, and Director, Health Services Management Unit, University of Manchester, since 1994; *b* 30 May 1941; *s* of James and Mabel Nichol; *m* 1972, Elizabeth Wilkinson; one *s* one *d*. *Educ:* Bradford Grammar Sch.; St Andrews Univ. (MA Hons). AHSM (AHA 1967); FFPHM 1991. Asst Gp Sec. and Hosp. Sec. to Manchester Royal Infirmary, 1969–73; Dep. Gp Sec. and Actg Gp Sec., Univ. Hosp. Management Cttee of S Manchester, 1973–74; Dist Administrator, Manchester S Dist, 1974–77; Area Administrator, Salford AHA(T), 1977–81; Regional Administrator, 1981–84, Regional Gen. Manager, 1984–89, Mersey RHA; Chief Exec., NHS Management Executive, 1989–94. A Director: HM Prison Service, 1994–; BUPA, 1994–. Member: Central Health Services Council, 1980–81; NHS Training Authy, 1983–85. Pres., Inst. of Health Services Management, 1984–85; Chm., Educn Cttee, King Edward's Hosp. Fund for London, 1987–94. *Publications:* contributed: Health Care in the United Kingdom, 1982; Management for Clinicians, 1982; Working with People, 1983; Managers as Strategists, 1987. *Recreations:* walking, golf, squash. *Address:* Health Services Management Unit, University of Manchester, Devonshire House, Precinct Centre, Oxford Road, Manchester M13 9PL. *Club:* Athenæum.

NICHOL, Prof. Lawrence Walter, DSc; FRACI; FAA; Vice-Chancellor, Australian National University, 1988–93; *b* 7 April 1935; *s* of Lawrence Gordon Nichol and Mavis Lillian Nichol (*née* Burgess); *m* 1963, Rosemary Esther (*née* White); three *s*. *Educ:* Univ. of Adelaide (BSc 1956, Hons 1957; PhD 1962; DSc 1974). Postdoctoral Fellow, Clark Univ., Mass, 1961–62; Res. Fellow, ANU, 1963–65; Sen. Lectr, then Reader, Univ. of Melbourne, 1966–70; Prof. of Phys. Biochem., ANU, 1971–85; Vice-Chancellor, Univ. of New England, 1985–88. FRACI 1971; FAA 1981; Fellow, Royal Soc. of NSW, 1986. David Syme Res. Prize, 1966; Lemberg Medal, Aust. Biochem. Soc., 1977. *Publications:* Migration of Interacting Systems, 1972; Protein-Protein Interactions, 1981; over 100 papers in internat. sci. jls. *Recreations:* philately, cinema, art, Spanish language. *Address:* Unit 36, 171 Walker Street, North Sydney, NSW 2060, Australia.

NICHOL, Comdt Patricia; *see* Nichol, Comdt D. P.

NICHOLAS, (Angela) Jane (Udale), OBE 1990; Dance Director, Arts Council of Great Britain, 1979–89, retired; *b* 14 June 1929; *d* of late Bernard Alexander Royle Shore, CBE; *m* 1964, William Alan Nicholas. *Educ:* Norland Place Sch.; Rambert Sch. of Ballet; Arts Educnl Trust; Sadler's Wells Ballet Sch. Founder Mem., Sadler's Wells Theatre Ballet, 1946–50; Mem., Sadler's Wells Ballet at Royal Opera House, 1950–52; freelance dancer, singer, actress, 1952–60; British Council Drama Officer, 1961–70; Arts Council of Great Britain: Dance Officer, 1970–75; Asst Dance Dir, 1975–79. Member: Exec. Cttee, Dance UK, 1989–; Creative Dance Artists Trust, 1990–93; Riverside Arts Trust, 1991–; Benesh Inst. Endowment Fund, 1992–; Bd, Birmingham Royal Ballet, 1993–. FRSA 1990. *Recreations:* pruning, weeding, collecting cracked porcelain. *Address:* 21 Stamford Brook Road, W6 0XJ. *T:* 0181–741 3035.

NICHOLAS, Barry; *see* Nicholas, J. K. B. M.

NICHOLAS, Sir David, Kt 1989; CBE 1982; Chief Executive, 1977–91, Chairman, 1989–91, Independent Television News; Director, Channel Four Television, since 1992; *b* 25 Jan. 1930; *m* 1952, Juliet Davies; one *s* one *d*. *Educ:* Neath Grammar School; University Coll. of Wales, Aberystwyth. BA (Hons) English. National Service, 1951–53. Journalist with Yorkshire Post, Daily Telegraph, Observer; joined ITN, 1960; Deputy Editor, 1963–77; Editor, 1977–89. Produced ITN General Election Results, Apollo coverage, and ITN special programmes. Chm., Talk Radio UK, 1994–; Dir, Channel One TV, 1994–. Visiting Editor: Graduate Sch. of Journalism, Berkeley, Calif, 1993; Sch. of Journalism, Univ. of Colorado, 1994. FRTS 1980. Fellow, UC Aberystwyth, 1990. Hon. LLD Wales, 1990. Producers' Guild Award 1967, on return of Sir Francis Chichester; Cyril Bennett Award, RTS, 1985; Judges' Award, RTS, 1991. *Recreations:* walking, sailing, riding. *Club:* Reform.

NICHOLAS, Sir Harry; *see* Nicholas, Sir Herbert Richard.

NICHOLAS, Prof. Herbert George, FBA 1969; Rhodes Professor of American History and Institutions, Oxford University, 1969–78; Fellow of New College, Oxford, 1951–78, Emeritus 1978–80, Honorary Fellow since 1980; Director, New College Development Fund, 1989–94; *b* 8 June 1911; *s* of late Rev. W. D. Nicholas. *Educ:* Mill Hill Sch.; New Coll., Oxford. Commonwealth Fund Fellow in Modern History, Yale, 1935–37; MA Oxon, 1938; Exeter College, Oxford: Lectr, 1938, Fellow, 1946–51; Amer. Div., Min. of Information, and HM Embassy, Washington, 1941–46; Faculty Fellow, Nuffield Coll., Oxford, 1948–57; Nuffield Reader in the Comparative Study of Institutions, Oxford Univ., 1956–69. Chm., British Assoc. for American Studies, 1960–62; Vice-Pres., British Academy, 1975–76. Vis. Prof., Brookings Instn, Washington, 1960; Albert Shaw Lectr in Diplomatic History, Johns Hopkins, 1961; Vis. Fellow, Inst. of Advanced Studies, Princeton, 1964; Vis. Faculty Fellow, Inst. of Politics, Harvard, 1968. Hon. DCL Pittsburgh, 1968. *Publications:* The American Union, 1948; The British General Election of 1950, 1951; To the Hustings, 1956; The United Nations as a Political Institution, 1959, 5th edn 1975; (ed) Tocqueville's De la Démocratie en Amérique, 1961; Britain and the United States, 1963; The American Past and The American Present, 1971; The United States and Britain, 1975; The Nature of American Politics, 1980, 2nd edn 1986; (ed) Washington Despatches, 1941–45, 1981; La Naturaleza de la Política Norteamericana, 1985; articles. *Recreations:* gardening, listening to music. *Address:* 2 Quarry Hollow, Headington, Oxford OX3 8JR. *T:* Oxford (01865) 63135. *Club:* Athenæum.

NICHOLAS, Sir Herbert Richard, (Sir Harry Nicholas), Kt 1970; OBE 1949; General Secretary of the Labour Party, 1968–72; *b* 13 March 1905; *s* of Richard Henry and Rosina Nicholas; *m* 1932, Rosina Grace Brown. *Educ:* Elementary sch., Avonmouth, Bristol; Evening Classes; Correspondence Courses. Clerk, Port of Bristol Authority, 1919–36. Transport and Gen. Workers Union: District Officer, Gloucester, 1936–38; Regional Officer, Bristol, 1938–40; National Officer, London: Commercial Road Transport Group, 1940–42; Chemical Section, 1942–44; Metal and Engineering Group, 1944–56; Asst Gen. Sec., 1956–68 (Acting Gen. Sec., Oct. 1964–July 66). Mem., TUC General Council, 1964–67. Mem., Labour Party Nat. Exec. Cttee, 1956–64, 1967–; Treasurer, Labour Party, 1960–64. *Publications:* occasional articles in press on Industrial Relations subjects. *Recreations:* Rugby football, fishing, reading, gardening. *Address:* 33 Madeira Road, Streatham, SW16 2DG. *T:* 0181–769 7989.

NICHOLAS, Jane; *see* Nicholas, A. J. U.

NICHOLAS, (John Keiran) Barry (Moylan), FBA 1990; Principal of Brasenose College, Oxford, 1978–89 (Fellow, 1947–78; Hon. Fellow, 1989); *b* 6 July 1919; *s* of Archibald John Nicholas and Rose (*née* Moylan); *m* 1948, Hildegart, *d* of Prof. Hans Cloos, Bonn; one *s* one *d*. *Educ:* Downside; Brasenose Coll., Oxford (Scholar). 1st cl. Class. Mods, 1939 and Jurisprudence, 1946. Royal Signals, 1939–45: Middle East, 1941–45; Major, 1943. Called to Bar, Inner Temple, 1950, Hon. Bencher, 1984. Tutor, 1947–71 and Vice-Principal, 1960–63, Brasenose Coll.; All Souls Reader in Roman Law, Oxford Univ., 1949–71; Prof. of Comparative Law, Oxford, 1971–78; Mem., Hebdomadal Council, 1975–83. Visiting Professor: Tulane Univ., 1960; Univ. of Rome, 1964, 1993; Fordham Univ., 1968; Georgetown Univ., 1990; Bacon-Kilkenny Dist. Vis. Prof., Fordham Univ., 1985. UK Deleg. to UN Conf. on Internat. Sales Law, 1980. Mem., Louisiana State Law Inst., 1960. Dr *hc* Paris V, 1987. *Publications:* Introduction to Roman Law, 1962; (trans. Spanish, 1987); Jolowicz's Historical Introduction to Roman Law, 3rd edn 1972; French Law of Contract, 1982, 2nd edn 1992. *Address:* 18A Charlbury Road, Oxford OX2 6UU. *T:* Oxford (01865) 58512.

NICHOLAS, Sir John (William), KCVO 1981; CMG 1979; HM Diplomatic Service, retired; *b* 13 Dec. 1924; *m* 1944, Rita (*née* Jones); two *s*. *Educ:* Birmingham Univ. Served 7th Rajput Regt, Indian Army, 1944–47; joined Home Civil Service, 1949; War Office, 1949–57; transf. to CRO 1957; First Sec., Brit. High Commn, Kuala Lumpur, 1957–61; Economic Div., CRO, 1961–63; Dep. High Comr in Malawi, 1964–66; Diplomatic Service Inspector, 1967–69; Dep. High Comr and Counsellor (Commercial), Ceylon, 1970–71; Dir, Establishments and Finance Div., Commonwealth Secretariat, 1971–73; Hd of Pacific Dependent Territories Dept, FCO, 1973–74; Dep. High Comr, Calcutta, 1974–76; Consul Gen., Melbourne, 1976–79; High Comr to Sri Lanka and (non-resident) to Republic of the Maldives, 1979–84.

NICHOLAS, Michael Bernard, FRCO; Chief Executive, Royal College of Organists, since 1994; *b* 31 Aug. 1938; *s* of Bernard Victor Herbert Nicholas and Dorothy (*née* Gilfillan); *m* 1975, Heather Grant Rowdon; two *s*. *Educ:* City of London Sch.; Jesus Coll., Oxford (MA). FRCO 1958. Organist and Choirmaster: Louth Parish Church, Lincs, 1960–64; St Matthew's Ch., Northampton, 1965–71; Organist and Master of Choristers, Norwich Cathedral, 1971–94; (part-time) Lectr in Music, UEA, 1971–94. Conductor, Norwich Philharmonic Chorus, 1972–94; Musical Dir, Allegri Singers, 1994–. Hon. DMus UEA, 1995. *Publications:* Sightsinging, 1966; Muse at St Matthew's, 1968; various choral and organ compositions. *Recreations:* bridge, sailing, real ale. *Address:* Royal College of Organists, 7 St Andrew Street, Holborn, EC4A 3LQ.

NICHOLAS, William Ford, OBE 1954; Director, London Chamber of Commerce and Industry, 1974–84; *b* 17 March 1923; *s* of William and Emma Nicholas; *m* 1954, Isobel Sybil Kennedy; two *s*. *Educ:* Stockport Grammar School. Called to Bar, Middle Temple, 1965. Joined S Rhodesia Civil Service, 1947; Private Sec. to Prime Minister, S Rhodesia, 1950; Private Sec. to Prime Minister, Fedn of Rhodesia and Nyasaland, 1953; Counsellor, High Comr's Office, London, 1960; retd 1963. Dir, UK Cttee, Fedn of Commonwealth Chambers of Commerce, 1964; Dep. Dir, London Chamber of Commerce, 1966. *Address:* 2 Lime Close, Frant, Tunbridge Wells, Kent. *T:* Frant (01892) 750428; Les Collines de Capitou, Bâtiment A, Appt 06, 06210 Mandelieu, France.

NICHOLL, Anthony John David; His Honour Judge Nicholl; a Circuit Judge, since 1988; *b* 3 May 1935; *s* of late Brig. and Mrs D. W. D. Nicholl; *m* 1961, Hermione Mary (*née* Landon); one *s* two *d*. *Educ:* Eton; Pembroke Coll., Oxford. Called to Bar, Lincoln's Inn, 1958. Practised in London, 1958–61, in Birmingham, 1961–88; Head of Chambers, 1976–87; Chm., Fountain Court Chambers (Birmingham) Ltd, 1984–88. A Recorder, 1978–88. *Recreations:* history, gardening and other rural pursuits. *Address:* c/o Birmingham Crown Court, Newton Street, Birmingham B4 6NE.

NICHOLLS; *see* Harmar-Nicholls.

NICHOLLS, family name of **Baron Nicholls of Birkenhead.**

NICHOLLS OF BIRKENHEAD, Baron *cr* 1994 (Life Peer), of Stoke D'Abernon in the County of Surrey; **Donald James Nicholls;** Kt 1983; PC 1986; a Lord of Appeal in Ordinary, since 1994; *b* 25 Jan. 1933; *yr s* of William Greenhow Nicholls and late Eleanor Jane; *m* 1960, Jennifer Mary, *yr d* of late W. E. C. Thomas, MB, BCh, MRCOG, JP; two *s* one *d*. *Educ:* Birkenhead Sch.; Liverpool Univ.; Trinity Hall, Cambridge (Foundn Schol.; Hon. Fellow, 1986). LLB 1st cl. hons Liverpool, BA 1st cl. hons with dist., Pt II Law Tripos Cantab, LLB 1st cl. hons with dist. Cantab. Certif. of Honour, Bar Final, 1958; called to Bar, Middle Temple, 1958, Bencher, 1981; in practice, Chancery Bar, 1958–83; QC 1974; Judge of High Court of Justice, Chancery Div., 1983–86; a Lord Justice of Appeal, 1986–91; Vice-Chancellor, Supreme Court, 1991–94. Mem., Senate of Inns of Court and the Bar, 1974–76. Pres., Birkenhead Sch., 1986–. Hon. LLD Liverpool, 1987. *Recreations:* walking, history, music. *Address:* House of Lords, SW1A 0PW. *Club:* Athenæum.

NICHOLLS, Brian; consultant, Scottish Enterprise, since 1991; *b* 21 Sept. 1928; *s* of late Ralph and Kathleen Nicholls; *m* 1961, Mary Elizabeth Harley; one *s* two *d*. *Educ:* Haberdashers' Aske's Sch., Hampstead; London Univ. (BSc Econ); Harvard Business Sch. George Wimpey & Co., 1951–55; Constructors John Brown Ltd, 1955–75; Director: CJB Projects Ltd, 1972–75; CJB Pipelines Ltd, 1974–75; Dep. Chm., CJB Mohandessi Iran Ltd, 1974–75; Industrial Adviser, Dept of Trade, 1975–78; Director: John Brown Engrg, 1979–91; John Brown Engrg Gas Turbines, 1979–91; Rugby Power Co., 1990–91; Vice Pres., John Brown Power Ltd, 1987–90. Member: Council, British Rly Industry Export Gp, 1976–78; Overseas Projects Bd, 1976–78; BOTB, 1978. Member: Council, British Chemical Engineering Contractors Assoc., 1973–75; Trade and Industry Cttee, British Algerian Soc., 1974–75; Scottish Council (Develt and Industry), 1983– (Vice Pres., 1991–). Dir, Scottish Opera, 1993–. Freeman Mem., Incorp. of Coopers of Glasgow, 1991; Mem., Trades House of Glasgow, 1990. *Recreations:* writing, walking, music. *Address:* Croy, Shandon, by Helensburgh, Dunbartonshire G84 8NN. *T:* Rhu (01436) 820388. *Clubs:* Western (Glasgow); Royal Northern and Clyde Yacht (Rhu).

NICHOLLS, Christine Stephanie, DPhil; writer; *b* 23 Jan. 1943; *d* of Christopher James Metcalfe, Mombasa, Kenya, and Olive Metcalfe (*née* Kennedy); *m* 1966, Anthony James Nicholls, *s* of Ernest Alfred Nicholls, Carshalton; one *s* two *d*. *Educ:* Kenya High School; Lady Margaret Hall, Oxford (BA); St Antony's Coll., Oxford (MA, DPhil). Henry Charles Chapman Res. Fellow, Inst. of Commonwealth Studies, London Univ., 1968–69; freelance writer for BBC, 1970–74; res. asst, 1975–76; Jt Editor, 1977–89, Editor, 1989–95, DNB. *Publications:* The Swahili Coast, 1971; (with Philip Awdry) Cataract, 1985; Power: a political history of the 20th Century, 1990; The Dictionary of National Biography: 1961–70, 1981; 1971–80, 1986; 1981–85, 1990; Missing Persons, 1993; 1986–90, 1996. *Recreations:* reading novels, playing the flute. *Address:* 27 Davenant Road, Oxford OX2 8BU. *T:* Oxford (01865) 511320.

NICHOLLS, Clive Victor, QC 1982; a Recorder, since 1984; *b* 29 Aug. 1932; twin *s* of late Alfred Charles Victor Nicholls and of Lilian Mary (*née* May); *m* 1960, Alison Virginia, *d* of late Arthur and Dorothy Oliver; three *s* three *d*. *Educ:* Brighton Coll.; Trinity Coll., Dublin (MA, LLB); Sidney Sussex Coll., Cambridge (BA *ad eund*; LLM). Called to the Bar: Gray's Inn, 1957 (Bencher, 1990); Australian Capital Territories, 1991. British Deleg. to Cttee on Extradition and Human Rights, Internat. Law Assoc. Trustee, Bob Champion Cancer Trust, 1994– (Chm. Trustees, 1982–94). *Recreations:* sailing, fishing. *Address:* 3 Raymond Buildings, Gray's Inn, WC1R 5BH. *T:* 0171–831 3833. *Clubs:* Garrick; Royal Western Yacht (Plymouth).

See also C. A. A. Nicholls.

NICHOLLS, Colin Alfred Arthur, QC 1981; a Recorder, since 1984; *b* 29 Aug. 1932; twin *s* of late Alfred Charles Victor Nicholls and of Lilian Mary (*née* May); *m* 1976, Clarissa Allison Spenlove, *d* of late Clive and of Theo Dixon; two *s*. *Educ:* Brighton Coll.; Trinity Coll., Dublin. MA, LLB. Called to the Bar, Gray's Inn, 1957 (Albion Richardson Schol.), Bencher, 1989. Auditor, 1956, and Hon. Mem., 1958–, TCD Historical Soc.; Mem. Council, 1987–, a Vice Pres., 1990–, Commonwealth Lawyers Assoc. *Recreations:* painting (exhib. RHA), sailing. *Address:* 3 Raymond Buildings, Gray's Inn, WC1R 5BH. *T:* 0171–831 3833. *Club:* Garrick.

See also C. V. Nicholls.

NICHOLLS, David Alan, CB 1989; CMG 1984; defence consultant; Senior Political-Military Associate, Institute for Foreign Policy Analysis, Cambridge, Mass, USA, since 1991; Associate, Align Consultants, The Netherlands, since 1994; *s* of Thomas Edward and Beatrice Winifred Nicholls; *m* 1955, Margaret (*née* Lewis); two *d*. *Educ:* Cheshunt Grammar School; St John's Coll., Cambridge (Schol., Wright's Prizeman 1952, 1953; BA Hons 1954; MA 1989). Served RAF (Flying Officer), 1950–51. Admiralty, 1954–64; Asst Principal, 1954; Private Sec. to Parliamentary Sec., 1958–59; Principal, 1959; MoD, 1964–75; Private Sec. to Minister of Defence for Admin, 1968–69; Asst Sec., 1969; Cabinet Office, 1975–77; Asst Under-Sec. of State, MoD, 1977–80; Asst Sec., Gen. for Defence Planning and Policy, NATO, 1980–84; Dep. Under Sec. of State (Policy), MoD, 1984–89. Vis. Fellow (Fellow Commoner), Magdalene Coll., Cambridge, 1989–90; Associate Fellow, RIIA, 1990–93; Hon. Fellow, Graduate Sch. of Internat. Studies, Univ. of Birmingham, 1992–. Mem., Defence and Security Cttee, London Chamber of Commerce and Industry, 1991–. Chm., Soc. for Italic Handwriting, 1987–. Mem., Visiting Cttee, RCA, 1991–92. *Recreations:* sketching, printmaking. *Address:* c/o Midland Bank, Church Stretton, Shropshire. *Club:* National Liberal.

NICHOLLS, Rear-Adm. (Francis) Brian (Price) B.; *see* Brayne-Nicholls.

NICHOLLS, Rt. Rev. John; *see* Lancaster, Bishop Suffragan of.

NICHOLLS, Prof. John Graham, FRS 1988; Professor of Pharmacology, Biocenter, University of Basel, since 1983; *b* 19 Dec. 1929; *s* of late Dr Nicolai and of Charlotte Nicholls; *m* (marr. diss.); two *s*. *Educ:* Berkhamsted Sch.; Charing Cross Hosp.; King's Coll. and University Coll., London. BSc (1st cl. Hons); PhD; MB, BS. Research and teaching in Neurobiology at: Oxford, 1962; Harvard, 1962–65; Yale, 1965–68; Harvard, 1968–73; Stanford, 1973–83. *Publications:* From Neuron to Brain (with S. Kuffler), 1976, 3rd edn 1992; The Search for Connections, 1987. *Recreations:* Latin American history, music. *Address:* Biocenter, Klingelbergstrasse 70, 4056 Basel, Switzerland. *T:* (61) 2672230. *Club:* Athenæum.

NICHOLLS, Air Marshal Sir John (Moreton), KCB 1978; CBE 1970; DFC 1953; AFC 1965; non-executive Director, James Paget Hospital NHS Trust, 1993–95; *b* 5 July 1926; *s* of Alfred Nicholls and Elsie (*née* French); *m* 1st, Enid Jean Marjorie Rose (*d* 1975); two *d*; 2nd, Shelagh Joyce Hall (*née* Strong). *Educ:* Liverpool Collegiate; St Edmund Hall, Oxford. RAF Coll., 1945–46; No 28 Sqdn and No 257 Sqdn; 335th Ftr Sqdn USAF, Korea, 1952; Fighter Leader Sch.; 435th and 83rd Ftr Sqdns USAF, 1956–58; attached British Aircraft Co., Lightning Project, 1959–61; psa 1961; Comd, Air Fighting Develt Sqdn; jssc 1964; MoD; comd RAF Leuchars, 1967–70; idc 1970; SASO 11 Gp, 1971; Principal Staff Officer to CDS, 1971–73; SASO, Strike Comd, 1973–75; ACAS (Op. Requirements), 1976–77; Air Mem. for Supply and Orgn, 1977–79; Vice-Chief of the Air Staff, 1979–80. Dir i/c, British Aircraft Co. (British Aerospace), Saudi Arabia, 1980–82. CIMgt. DFC (USA) and Air Medal (USA), 1953. *Club:* Royal Air Force.

NICHOLLS, Michael William Newbery, FRCPath; Hon. Senior Lecturer in Medical Microbiology, United Medical and Dental Schools, St Thomas' Hospital, since 1991; President, Fellowship of Postgraduate Medicine, since 1993; *b* 22 May 1931; *s* of William Stanley Nicholls, MBE and Florence May (*née* King); *m* 1957, Pamela Winifred Hemer; two *s*. *Educ:* Xaverian Coll., London; UCL; UCH Med. Sch. (MB, BS). MRCS, LRCP; FRCPath 1980. Resident hosp. posts and general practice, 1955–61; Asst Microbiologist and Registrar, UCH, 1961–70; Consultant Microbiologist, Chichester and Worthing HAs, 1972–90; Dean of Postgrad. Medicine, SE Thames Reg., Univ. of London, 1990–95; Chief Exec., Centre for Educn R and D, 1990–94. Mem., Worthing HA, 1982–90. Freeman, City of London, 1984; Liveryman, Soc. of Apothecaries, 1984. *Publications:* various contribs, usually of new or creatively provocative material on med. microbiol., med. educn and the needed reforms in postgrad. and continuing med. educn. *Recreations:* sailing, singing, chamber music, 19th and 20th Century Arabic history. *Address:* Creekside, Greenacres, Birdham, Chichester, W Sussex PO20 7HL. *T:* Birdham (01243) 512937, *Fax:* (01243) 511087. *Clubs:* Athenæum; Offshore Cruising (Southampton).

NICHOLLS, Nigel Hamilton, CBE 1982; Clerk of the Privy Council, since 1992; *b* 19 Feb. 1938; *s* of late Bernard Cecil Hamilton Nicholls and Enid Kathleen Nicholls (*née* Gwynne); *m* 1967, Isobel Judith, *d* of Rev. Canon Maurice Dean; two *s*. *Educ:* King's School, Canterbury; St John's College, Oxford (BA 1962; MA 1966). Asst Principal, Admiralty, 1962, MoD, 1964; Asst Private Sec. to Minister of Defence for RN, 1965–66; Principal, 1966; Directing Staff, RCDS, 1971–73; Asst Private Sec. to Sec. of State for Defence, 1973–74; Asst Sec., 1974; Defence Counsellor, UK Delegation to MBFR Talks, Vienna, 1977–80; Asst Under-Sec. of State, MoD, 1984; Under Sec., Cabinet Office, 1986–89; Asst Under-Sec. of State (Systems), MoD, 1989–92. *Recreations:* choral singing, genealogy, mountain walking. *Address:* Privy Council Office, Whitehall, SW1A 2AT. *Club:* United Oxford & Cambridge University.

NICHOLLS, Patrick Charles Martyn; MP (C) Teignbridge, since 1983; *b* 14 Nov. 1948; *s* of late Douglas Charles Martyn Nicholls and Margaret Josephine Nicholls; *m* 1976, Bridget Elizabeth Fergus Owens; one *s* two *d*. *Educ:* Redrice College, Andover. Qualified solicitor, 1974. Partner, Dunn & Baker, 1976–. Mem., E Devon District Council, 1980–84. PPS to Ministers of State: Home Office, 1984–86; MAFF, 1986–87; Parliamentary Under-Secretary of State: Dept of Employment, 1987–90; DoE, 1990; Vice-Chm., Cons. Party, 1993–94. Vice Chm., Social Security Select Cttee, 1990–93. Vice Chm., Soc. of Cons. Lawyers, 1986–87. Steward, British Boxing Bd of Control, 1985–87. *Recreations:* theatre, opera, historical research, ski-ing. *Address:* c/o House of Commons, SW1A 0AA. *T:* 0171–219 4077. *Club:* Carlton.

NICHOLLS, Philip, CB 1976; *b* 30 Aug. 1914; *yr s* of late W. H. Nicholls, Radlett; *m* 1955, Sue, *yr d* of late W. E. Shipton; two *s*. *Educ:* Malvern; Pembroke Coll., Cambridge. Asst Master, Malvern, 1936; Sen. Classical Master, 1939; resigned, 1947. Served in Army, 1940–46: 8th Bn, The Worcestershire Regt; HQ, East Africa Command; Allied Commn for Austria. Foreign Office (German Section), 1947; HM Treasury, 1949; a Forestry Commissioner (Finance and Administration), 1970–75, retired. Mem. Council, Malvern Coll., 1960–90 (Vice-Chm., 1963–88). *Address:* Barnards Green House, Barnards Green, Malvern, Worcs WR14 3NQ. *T:* Malvern (01684) 574446.

NICHOLLS, Robert Michael, CBE 1995; Executive Director, London Implementation Group, NHS Management Executive, since 1993; *b* 28 July 1939; *s* of late Herbert Edgar Nicholls and of Bennetta L'Estrange (*née* Burges); *m* 1961, Dr Deirín Deirdre (*née* O'Sullivan); four *s*. *Educ:* Hampton Sch.; University Coll. of Wales (BA 1961); Univ. of Manchester (DSA 1962). FHSM (AHA 1963; FHA 1993). Asst Sec., Torbay Hosp., 1964; House Governor, St Stephen's Hosp., Chelsea, 1966; Asst Clerk to the Governors, St Thomas' Hosp., 1968; Dep. Gp Sec., Southampton Univ. Hosp. Management Cttee, 1972; Dist Administrator, Southampton and SW Hampshire Health Dist, 1974; Area Administrator, Newcastle upon Tyne AHA(T), 1977; Regl Administrator, SW RHA, 1981; Dist Gen. Man., Southmead DHA, 1985; Regl Gen. Man., later Chief Exec., Oxford RHA, 1988–93. Member: Health Educn Council, 1984–87; CMO's EEC Med. Trng Wkg Pty, 1992–93. National Council, Inst. of Health Service Management (formerly IHA): Mem., 1976–86; Pres., 1983–84. Mem., Education Cttee, King Edward's Hosp. Fund for London, 1975–81. *Publications:* (contrib.) Resources in Medicine, 1970; (contrib.) Working with People, 1983; (contrib.) Rationing of Healthcare in Medicine, 1993. *Recreations:* bird-watching, jazz, opera, sport. *Address:* Charlton on Otmoor, Oxon.

NICHOLLS, Rt. Rev. Vernon Sampson; Hon. Assistant Bishop of Coventry, since 1983; *b* 3 Sept. 1917; *s* of Ernest C. Nicholls, Truro, Cornwall; *m* 1943, Phyllis, *d* of Edwin Potter, Stratford-on-Avon; one *s* one *d*. *Educ:* Truro Sch.; Univ. of Durham and Clifton Theological Coll., Bristol. Curate: St Oswald Bedminster Down, Bristol, 1941–42; Liskeard, Cornwall, 1942–43. CF, 1944–46 (Hon. CF 1946). Vicar of Meopham, 1946–56; Rural Dean of Cobham, 1953–56; Mem., Strood RDC, 1948–56; Vicar and Rural Dean of Walsall, and Chaplain to Walsall Gen. Hosp., 1956–67; Preb. of Curborough, Lichfield Cath., 1964–67; Archdeacon of Birmingham, 1967–74; Diocesan Planning Officer and Co-ordinating Officer for Christian Stewardship, 1967–74; Bishop of Sodor and Man, 1974–83; Dean of St German's Cathedral, Peel, 1974–83. MLC, Tynwald, IoM, 1974–83; Member: IoM Bd of Educn, 1974–83; Bd of Social Security, 1974–81; IoM Health Services Bd, 1981–83; Founder Chm., IoM Council on Alcoholism, 1979. Mem., S Warwicks Drug Adv. Cttee, 1984–90. JP, IoM, 1974–83. Provincial Grand Master, Warwicks Province of Freemasons, 1985–92. *Recreations:* meeting people, motoring. *Address:* Apartment 18, Lucy's Mill, Mill Lane, Stratford-upon-Avon, Warwickshire CV37 6DE. *T:* Stratford-upon-Avon (01789) 294478.

NICHOLS, Rt. Rev. Anthony Howard; *see* Australia, North-West, Bishop of.

NICHOLS, Clement Roy, CMG 1970; OBE 1956; Chairman, Alpha Spinning Mills Pty Ltd; *b* 4 Jan. 1909; *s* of C. J. Nichols, Melbourne; *m* 1933, Margareta, *d* of A. C. Pearse, Melbourne; one *s* one *d*. *Educ:* Scotch Coll., Melbourne. CText; ATI. Lifetime in wool worsted manufacturing. Past Pres., Wool Textile Mfrs of Australia; Vice-Pres., Internat. Wool Textile Organisation, 1970–75; President: Victorian Chamber of Mfrs, 1970–72, 1977–78; Associated Chambers of Mfrs of Australia, 1971–74. Mem., World Scouts' Cttee, 1959–65, 1967–73; Chm., Asia Pacific Region, 1962–64; Chief Comr, Scout Assoc., 1963–66; Chief Comr, Victorian Br., 1952–58; Nat. Chm., 1973–79; Vice-Pres., Scout Assoc. of Australia, 1979–88. *Address:* 82 Studley Park Road, Kew, Victoria 3101, Australia. *Clubs:* Australian (Melbourne); Rotary (Heidelberg).

NICHOLS, Dinah Alison, CB 1995; Deputy Secretary, Housing and Construction, Department of the Environment, since 1994; *b* 28 Sept. 1943; *d* of late Sydney Hirst Nichols and of Freda Nichols. *Educ:* Wyggeston Girls' Grammar Sch., Leicester; Bedford Coll., Univ. of London (Reid Arts Schol.; BA Hons History, 1965). Ministry of Transport: Asst Principal, 1965–69; Asst Private Sec. to Minister, 1969–70; Principal, 1970–74; Cabinet Office, 1974–77; Asst Sec., DoE, 1978–83; Principal Private Sec. to Sec. of State for Transport, 1983–85; Under Sec., 1985–91, Dep. Sec., 1991–, DoE. Director: John Laing ETE, 1987–90; Anglian Water plc, 1992–. Sec. of State for the Envmt's Rep., Commonwealth War Graves Commn, 1993–. Winston Churchill Meml Fellow, 1969. *Recreations:* mountaineering and walking, choral singing, music, theatre. *Address:* Department of the Environment, 2 Marsham Street, SW1P 3EB. *T:* 0171–276 3623. *Clubs:* Swiss Alpine; Hampstead Cricket.

NICHOLS, Jeremy Gareth Lane, MA; Headmaster, Stowe School, since 1989; *b* 20 May 1943; *yr s* of late Derek Aplin Douglas Lane Nichols and of Ruth Anne Baiss (formerly Nichols); *m* 1972, Patricia Anne, *d* of Cdre Alan Swanton, DSO, DFC and bar, RN; one *s* three *d*. *Educ:* Lancing Coll., Sussex; Fitzwilliam Coll., Cambridge (BA English Lit. 1966; MA); Perugia Univ. Assistant Master: Livorno Naval Acad., 1965; Rugby Sch., 1966–67; Eton Coll., 1967–89, House Master, 1981–89; Gilman Sch., Baltimore, USA, 1979–80. *Recreations:* outdoor pursuits, sport, music, old cars. *Address:* Kinloss, Stowe, Buckingham MK18 5EH. *Clubs:* Hawks (Cambridge); Free Foresters, Corinthian Casuals.

NICHOLS, John; *see* Nichols, K. J. H.

NICHOLS, John Winfrith de Lisle, BSc (Eng); CEng; FIEE; retired; Director: National Maritime Institute, 1976–79; Computer Aided Design Centre, Cambridge, 1977–79; *b* 7 June 1919; *er s* of late John F. Nichols, MC, PhD, FRHistS, FSA, Godalming; *m* 1942, Catherine Lilian (*d* 1984), *er d* of Capt. A. V. Grantham, RNR, Essex; two *s* two *d*. *Educ:* Sir Walter St John's Sch., Battersea; London Univ. Royal Navy, 1940–46; GPO, Dollis Hill, 1946–47; RN Scientific Service, 1947–55; Chief Research Officer, Corp. of Trinity House, 1955–59; UKAEA, 1959–65; Min. of Technology, later DTI and Dept of Industry, 1965–; Under-Sec., and Chm., Requirement Bd for Computers, Systems and Electronics, 1972–74; Under Sec., Research Contractors Div., DoI, 1974–76. *Recreations:* gardening, sailing, caravanning. *Address:* Leybourne End, Wormley, Godalming, Surrey GU8 5TP. *T:* Wormley (01428) 683252.

NICHOLS, (Kenneth) John (Heastey); Metropolitan Stipendiary Magistrate, 1972–92; *b* 6 Sept. 1923; *s* of Sidney Kenneth Nichols, MC and Dorothy Jennie Heastey Richardson; *m* 1st, 1946, Audrey Heather Powell; one *d*; 2nd, 1966, Pamela Marjorie Long, *qv*. *Educ:* Westminster School. Served War of 1939–45: 60th Rifles, 1941–43; Parachute Regt, NW Europe, SE Asia Comd, 1943–46 (Captain). Admitted Solicitor, 1949; Partner, Speechly, Mumford & Soames (Craig), 1949–69. Mem., Inner London Probation Service Cttee, 1975–91. Mem. Council of Law Soc., 1959–68. Pres., Newheels, 1980–86; Vice-Pres., David Isaacs Fund, 1982–86. *Recreations:* cricket, music. *Address:* Dolphin House, Porthgwarra, St Levan, Cornwall TR19 6JP; Flat 1, 36 Buckingham Gate, SW1E 6PB. *Club:* MCC.

NICHOLS, Pamela Marjorie, (Mrs John Nichols); *see* Long, P. M.

NICHOLS, Peter Richard, FRSL 1983; playwright since 1959; *b* 31 July 1927; *s* of late Richard George Nichols and Violet Annie Poole; *m* 1960, Thelma Reed; one *s* two *d* (and one *d* decd). *Educ:* Bristol Grammar Sch.; Bristol Old Vic Sch.; Trent Park Trng College. Actor, mostly in repertory, 1950–55; worked as teacher in primary and secondary schs, 1958–60. Mem., Arts Council Drama Panel, 1973–75. Playwright in residence, Guthrie Theatre, Minneapolis, 1976. *TV plays:* Walk on the Grass, 1959; Promenade, 1960; Ben Spray, 1961; The Reception, 1961; The Big Boys, 1961; Continuity Man, 1963; Ben Again, 1963; The Heart of the Country, 1963; The Hooded Terror, 1963; The Brick Umbrella, 1964; When the Wind Blows, 1964 (later adapted for radio); Daddy Kiss It Better, 1968; The Gorge, 1968; Hearts and Flowers, 1971; The Common, 1973; Greeks Bearing Gifts (Inspector Morse series), 1991; *films:* Catch Us If You Can, 1965; Georgy Girl, 1967; Joe Egg, 1971; The National Health, 1973; Privates on Parade, 1983; *stage plays:* A Day in The Death of Joe Egg, 1967 (Evening Standard Award, Best Play; Tony Award, Best Revival, 1985); The National Health, 1969 (Evening Standard Award, Best Play); Forget-me-not Lane, 1971; Chez Nous, 1973; The Freeway, 1974 (radio broadcast, 1991); Privates on Parade, 1977 (Evening Standard Best Comedy, Soc. of West End Theatres Best Comedy and Ivor Novello Best Musical Awards); Born in the Gardens, 1979 (televised 1986); Passion Play, 1980 (Standard Best Play award, 1981); A Piece of My Mind, 1986; *musical:* Poppy, 1982 (SWET Best Musical Award). *Publications:* Feeling You're Behind (autobiog.), 1984; some TV plays in anthologies; all above stage plays published separately and in 2 vols, Nichols: Plays One and Two, 1991. *Recreations:* listening to jazz, looking at cities. *Address:* c/o Rochelle Stevens & Co., 2 Terretts Place, Upper Street, N1 1QZ.

NICHOLS, Richard Everard; Senior Partner, Kelly Nichols & Blayney, Solicitors, since 1976 (Partner, since 1965); *b* 26 April 1938; *s* of late Guy Everard Nichols and of Patricia Mary (*née* Hurst); *m* 1966, Shelagh Mary Loveband; two *s* one *d*. *Educ:* Christ's Hosp., Horsham. Nat. Service, commnd RE, 1956–58. Admitted solicitor, 1963; Asst Solicitor, Gunston & Smart, Hong Kong, 1963–64. Almoner, Christ's Hosp., 1984–; Gov., City Literary Inst., 1990–. Alderman, Ward of Candlewick, 1984–; Sheriff, City of London, 1994–95. Master, Salters' Co., 1988. OStJ 1992. *Recreations:* wine, travel, coarse gardening. *Address:* Newhall Farm, Bucks Hill, Kings Langley, Herts WD4 9AH. *T:* Watford (01923) 269882. *Club:* City Livery.

NICHOLS, Rt. Rev. Vincent Gerard; Auxiliary Bishop of Westminster (Bishop in North London), (RC), since 1992; Titular Bishop of Othona; *b* 8 Nov. 1945; *s* of Henry Joseph Nichols and Mary Nichols (*née* Russell). *Educ:* St Mary's College, Crosby; Gregorian Univ., Rome (STL PhL); Manchester Univ. (MA Theol); Loyola Univ., Chicago (MEd). Chaplain, St John Rigby VI Form College, Wigan, 1972–77; Priest, inner city of Liverpool, 1978–81; Director, Upholland Northern Inst., with responsibility for in service training of clergy and for adult Christian educn, 1981–84; Gen. Sec. RC Bishops' Conf. of England and Wales, 1984–91. Advr to Cardinal Hume and Archbishop Worlock, Internat. Synods of Bishops, 1980, 1983, 1985, 1987. Deleg. of Bishops' Conf. to Synod of Bishops, 1994. *Publications:* articles in The Clergy Review. *Address:* Westminster House, Watford Way, Hendon, NW4 4TY. *T:* 0181–202 2371.

NICHOLS, William Henry, CB 1974; *b* 25 March 1913; *s* of William and Clara Nichols. *Educ:* Owens School. Entered Inland Revenue, 1930; Exchequer and Audit Dept, 1935, Secretary, 1973–75, retired. *Address:* 23 Church View, Haughley, Stowmarket, Suffolk IP14 3PS.

NICHOLS, William Reginald, CBE 1975; TD; MA; Clerk of the Worshipful Company of Salters, 1946–75, Master, 1978–79; *b* 23 July 1912; *s* of late Reginald H. Nichols, JP, FSA, Barrister-at-Law; *m* 1946, Imogen, *d* of late Rev. Percy Dearmer, DD, Canon of Westminster, and late Nancy (who *m* 1946, Sir John Sykes, KCB; he died, 1952); one *s* one *d*. *Educ:* Harrow; Gonville and Caius Coll., Cambridge (Sayer Classical Scholar). MA 1938. Called to the Bar, Gray's Inn, 1937. Served War of 1939–45 with Hertfordshire Regt (despatches) and on staff 21st Army Group. Former Jt Hon. Sec., CGLI; Governor of Christ's Hospital; former Governor of Grey Coat Hospital Foundation. *Address:* The Farriers Cottage, St Nicholas-at-Wade, Birchington, Kent CT7 0NR.

NICHOLSON, Air Commodore Angus Archibald Norman, CBE 1961; AE 1945; Deputy Secretary-General, International Shipping Secretariat, 1971–80; *b* 8 March 1919; *s* of Major Norman Nicholson and Alice Frances Nicholson (*née* Salvidge), Hoylake, Cheshire; *m* 1943, Joan Mary, *d* of Ernest Beaumont, MRCVS, DVSM; one *s* one *d*. *Educ:* Eton; King's Coll., Cambridge. Cambridge Univ. Air Sqn, 1938–39; commissioned, 1939. Served War 1939–45: flying duties in Bomber Command and Middle East. Air Cdre, 1966; Dir of Defence Plans (Air), Min. of Defence, 1966–67; Defence Adviser to British High Comr in Canada and Head of British Defence Liaison Staff, 1968–70; retired from RAF, 1970. FIMgt (MBIM 1967, FBIM 1980). *Recreations:* sailing, golf, music. *Address:* 8 Courtenay Place, Lymington, Hants. *Clubs:* Army and Navy; Leander (Henley); Royal Lymington Yacht.

NICHOLSON, Anthony Thomas Cuthbertson; a Recorder of the Crown Court, 1980–84; *b* 17 May 1929; *s* of Thomas and Emma Cuthbertson Nicholson, Stratford, E; *m* 1955, Sheila Rose, *er d* of Albert and Rose Pigram, Laindon, Essex; two *s* one *d*. *Educ:* St Bonaventure's Grammar Sch., Forest Gate, E7. Journalist, 1944–62. Served Army, 1947–49, RAF, 1950–53. Called to the Bar, Gray's Inn, 1962. *Publications:* (play) Van Call, 1954; Esprit de Law, 1973. *Recreation:* wildfowling. *Address:* The Old Vicarage, Burnham Road, Southminster, Essex CM0 7ES.

NICHOLSON, Brian Thomas Graves; Chairman, Advertising Standards Board of Finance, since 1989; *b* 27 June 1930; *s* of late Ivor Nicholson, CBE, and of Mrs Alan McGaw; *m* Henrietta, *d* of late Nevill Vintcent, OBE, DFC, and Mrs Ralph Dennis; two *s* (and one *s* decd). *Educ:* Charterhouse. Reporter, Newcastle Evening Chronicle, 1949–53; Montreal Star, Toronto Telegram, and Victoria Times, 1953–54; Manchester Evening Chronicle, 1954–56; Sunday Graphic, 1956–57; Advertisement Manager, Sunday Times, 1957–65; Director: Sunday Times, 1963–65; Beaverbrook Newspapers, 1967–77; Man. Dir, Evening Standard, 1972–77; Jt Man. Dir, Observer, 1977–84; Hd of Public Affairs, Lloyd's of London, 1990–92; Director: CompAir, 1977–85; Center for Communication (USA), 1981–95; Lloyd's of London Press, 1982–93; London Broadcasting Co., 1983–90; Royal Opera House Covent Garden, 1984–89; Royal Ballet, 1984–92; News (UK), 1985–87; CCA Galleries, 1986–89; Logie Bradshaw Media, 1986–; Messenger Newspapers Gp, 1986–89; Aurora Productions, 1987–91; Messenger Television Ltd, 1989–; Whitespace Software Ltd, 1990–; Home Counties Newspaper Holdings plc, 1991–; Messenger Leisure Ltd, 1994–; Chairman: Audit Bureau of Circulation, 1975–77; Marlar Internat. Ltd, 1985–90; Carthusian Trust, 1987–; SE Arts Bd (formerly Assoc.), 1989–95; Publicitas Hldg (UK) Ltd, 1989–; Adv. Cttee on Advertising, COI, 1993–. Vice President: CAM Foundn, 1975–; Royal Gen. Theatrical Fund Assoc., 1986–; Member: Council of Commonwealth Press Union, 1975–; Adv. Bd, New Perspective Fund (USA), 1984–; Trustee, Glyndebourne Opera Co., 1977–; Gov., British Liver Foundn, 1989–. Mem., Editorial Adv. Bd, Focus in Education Ltd, 1986–90. Churchwarden, St Bride's Church, Fleet Street, 1978–. *Recreations:* travelling, listening, playing games. *Address:* Bloomsbury House, 74–77 Great Russell Street, WC1B 3DA. *Clubs:* Beefsteak, Brooks's, Pratt's, MCC; Piltdown Golf; Wentworth Golf.

NICHOLSON, Sir Bryan Hubert, Kt 1987; Chairman: British United Provident Association, since 1992; Varity Europe (formerly Varity Holdings) Ltd, since 1993; *b* 6

June 1932; *s* of late Reginald Hubert and Clara Nicholson; *m* 1956, Mary Elizabeth, *er d* of A. C. Harrison of Oxford; one *s* one *d* (and one *s* decd). *Educ:* Palmers School, Grays, Essex; Oriel College, Oxford (MA PPE; Hon. Fellow, 1989). 2nd Lieut, RASC, 1950–52; Unilever Management Trainee, 1955–58; Dist. Manager, Van den Berghs, 1958–59; Sales Manager, Three Hands/Jeyes Group, 1960–64; Sperry Rand: Sales Dir, UK, Remington Div., 1964–66; Gen. Manager, Australia, Remington Div., 1966–69; Managing Dir, UK and France, Remington Div., 1969–72; Dir, Ops, Rank Xerox (UK), 1972–76; Dir, Overseas Subsidiaries, Rank Xerox, 1976; Exec. Main Bd Dir, Rank Xerox, 1976–84; Chm., Rank Xerox (UK) and Chm., Rank Xerox GmbH, 1979–84; Chm., MSC, 1984–87; Chm. and Chief Exec., PO, 1987–92. Dir and Dep. Chm., Financial Reporting Council Ltd, 1993–. Non-executive Director: Rank Xerox, 1984–87; Baker Perkins Holdings, 1982–84; Evode, 1981–84; Internat. Post Corp. SA, 1988–92; GKN, 1991–; Varity Corp., USA, 1993–. Confederation of British Industry: Mem. Council, 1987–; Mem., President's Cttee, 1990–; Dep. Pres., 1993–94, May 1996–; Pres., 1994–May 1996; Chairman: Task Force on Vocational Educn and Training, 1988–89; Educn and Training Affairs Cttee, 1990–93; Chairman: CNAA, 1988–91; NICG, 1988–90; NCVQ, 1990–93. Department of Employment: Member: Adv. Cttee on Women's Employment, 1985–87; Women's Issues Wkg Gp, 1992–93; Race Relns Adv. Gp, 1985–87; Member: NEDC, 1985–92; Council, Inst. of Manpower Studies, 1985–93; Governing Council, Business in the Community, 1985–93; Council, Prince's Youth Business Trust, 1986–; Council, Industrial Soc., 1988– (Chm., 1990–93); Editl Bd, European Business Jl, 1988–. President: Involvement and Participation Assoc., 1990–94; ACFHE, 1992–93; AFC, 1993–94; Vice President: SRHE, 1992–; Re-Solv (Soc. for Prevention of Solvent Abuse), 1985–; NCH Action for Children (formerly Nat. Children's Home), 1989–. Chancellor, Sheffield Hallam Univ., 1992–; Pro Chancellor and Chm. Council, Open Univ., June 1996–. Pres., Oriel Soc., 1988–92; Patron, Rathbone Soc., 1987–; Trustee, Babson Coll., Mass, USA, 1990–. CIMgt (CBIM 1985); FRSA 1985. FCGI (CGIA 1988); FCIM 1990. Hon. Fellow: Manchester Metropolitan Univ. (formerly Polytechnic), 1990; SCOTVEC, 1994. Hon. DEd CNAA, 1992; DUniv Open, 1994. UK Hon. Rep. for W Berlin, 1983–84. *Recreations:* tennis, bridge, political history. *Address:* c/o British United Provident Association, Provident House, Essex Street, WC2R 3AX. *Club:* United Oxford & Cambridge University.

NICHOLSON, Sir Charles (Christian), 3rd Bt *cr* 1912, of Harrington Gardens, Royal Borough of Kensington; *b* 15 Dec. 1941; *s* of Sir John Norris Nicholson, 2nd Bt, KBE, CIE and Vittoria Vivien (*d* 1991), *y d* of Percy Trewhella; *S* father, 1993; *m* 1975, Martha Don, *d* of Stuart Warren Don and *widow* of Niall Anstruther-Gough-Calthorpe. *Educ:* Ampleforth; Magdalen Coll., Oxford. *Heir: b* James Richard Nicholson [*b* 24 Oct. 1947; *m* 1980, Sarah Hazel, *d* of Richard Alan Budgett; one *s* one *d*]. *Address:* Turners Green Farm, Elvetham, Hartley Wintney, Hants RG27 8BE. *Clubs:* Brooks's, Pratt's; Royal Yacht Squadron.

See also Sir E. H. Anstruther-Gough-Calthorpe.

NICHOLSON, (Charles) Gordon (Brown); QC (Scot.) 1982; Sheriff Principal of Lothian and Borders and Sheriff of Chancery, since 1990; *b* 11 Sept. 1935; *s* of late William Addison Nicholson, former Director, Scottish Tourist Board, and Jean Brown; *m* 1963, Hazel Mary Nixon; two *s*. *Educ:* George Watson's Coll., Edinburgh; Edinburgh Univ. (Hon. Fellow, Faculty of Law, 1988). MA Hons (English Lit.) 1956, LLB 1958. 2nd Lieut Queen's Own Cameron Highlanders, 1958–60. Admitted Faculty of Advocates, Edinburgh, 1961; in practice at Bar; Standing Junior Counsel, Registrar of Restrictive Trading Agreements, 1968; Advocate-Depute, 1968–70; Sheriff of: South Strathclyde, Dumfries and Galloway, 1970–76; Lothian and Borders, 1976–82; Mem., Scottish Law Commn, 1982–90. Vice Pres., Sheriffs' Assoc., 1979–82 (Sec., 1975–79). Member: Scottish Council on Crime, 1972–75; Dunpark Cttee on Reparation by Offenders, 1974–77; May Cttee of Inquiry into UK Prison Service, 1978–79; Kincraig Review of Parole in Scotland, 1988–89; Hon. President; Scottish Assoc. of Victim Support Schemes, 1989– (Chm., 1987–89); Scottish Assoc. for Study of Delinquency, 1988– (Chm., 1974–79; Hon. Vice-Pres., 1982–88); Chm., Edinburgh CAB, 1979–82. Comr, Northern Lighthouse Bd, 1990– (Vice Chm., 1993–94; Chm., 1994–95). *Publications:* The Law and Practice of Sentencing in Scotland, 1981, 2nd edn 1992; contrib. to legal periodicals. *Recreations:* music, golf. *Address:* Back o'Redfern, 24C Colinton Road, Edinburgh EH10 5EQ. *T:* and *Fax:* 0131–447 4300. *Clubs:* New (Edinburgh); Hon. Company of Edinburgh Golfers.

NICHOLSON, David; racehorse trainer, National Hunt; *b* 19 March 1939; *s* of Herbert Charles Denton Nicholson (Frenchie) and Diana Nicholson; *m* 1962, Dinah Caroline Pugh; two *s*. *Educ:* Oakley Hall Prep. Sch.; Haileybury Coll. Professional National Hunt jockey, 1951–74 (won Whitbread Gold Cup, 1967, with Mill House); racehorse trainer, 1968– (won Gold Cup, 1988, with Charter Party). *Recreation:* watching sport. *Address:* Jackdaws Castle, Temple Guiting, Glos GL54 5XU. *T:* Stanton (01386) 584209. *Clubs:* MCC; Gloucester County Cricket.

NICHOLSON, Hon. Sir David (Eric), Kt 1972; Speaker of the Legislative Assembly of Queensland, 1960–72 (record term); MLA (CP) for Murrumba, 1950–72; *b* 26 May 1904; *s* of J. A. Nicholson; *m* 1934, Cecile F., *d* of M. E. Smith; two *s* two *d*. *Recreations:* bowls, swimming, gardening. *Address:* Villa 37, Peninsular Gardens, 56 Miller Street, Kippa Ring, Qld 4021, Australia. *Clubs:* Redcliffe Trotting (Life Mem.), Redcliffe Agricl, Horticultural and Industrial Soc. (Life Mem.); Caboolture, Returned Servicemen's (Life Mem.), Caboolture Bowls (Caboolture).

NICHOLSON, David John; MP (C) Taunton, since 1987; *b* 17 Aug. 1944; *s* of late John Francis Nicholson and of Lucy Warburton Nicholson (*née* Battrum); *m* 1981, Frances Mary, *d* of late Brig. T. E. H. Helby, MC; two *s* one *d*. *Educ:* Queen Elizabeth's Grammar School, Blackburn; Christ Church, Oxford (MA Hons Mod. Hist.). Dept of Employment, 1966; Research Fellow, Inst. of Historical Res., 1970; Cons. Res. Dept, 1972 (Head, Political Section, 1974–82); Assoc. of British Chambers of Commerce, 1982–87 (Dep. Dir-Gen., 1986–87). PPS to Minister for Overseas Develt, 1990–92. Member: Select Cttee on Parly Comr for Admin, 1992–; Public Accounts Cttee, 1992–94; Select Cttee on Employment, 1994–; Jt Sec., All-Party Parly Gp for Population and Develt, 1990–94; Treas., All-Party Parly Gp on Water, 1993–; Sec., Cons. Backbench Social Services Cttee, 1988–90; Chm., Cons. W Country Mems Cttee, 1994–95 (Vice-Chm., 1992–93). *Publication:* (ed with John Barnes) The Diaries of L. S. Amery: vol. I, 1896–1929, 1980; vol. II, The Empire at Bay, 1929–45, 1988. *Recreations:* travel, gardening, music, the country. *Address:* Allshire, near Brushford, Somerset EX16 9JG. *Clubs:* Taunton Conservative; Wellington Conservative.

NICHOLSON, (Edward) Max, CB 1948; CVO 1971; Chairman, Land Use Consultants, 1966–89; *b* 12 July 1904; *m* 1st, 1932, Eleanor Mary Crawford (marr. diss., 1964); two *s*; 2nd, Marie Antoinette Mauerhofer; one *s*. *Educ:* Sedbergh; Hertford Coll., Oxford (Hon. Fellow, 1993). Head of Allocation of Tonnage Division, Ministry of War Transport, 1942–45; Secretary of Office of The Lord President of the Council, 1945–52. Member Advisory Council on Scientific Policy, 1948–64; Dir-Gen., Nature Conservancy, 1952–66; Convener, Conservation Section, Internat. Biological Programme, 1963–74; Secretary, Duke of Edinburgh's Study Conference on the Countryside in 1970, 1963; Albright Lecturer, Univ. of California, 1964; a Dir and Managing Editor, Environmental Data Services Ltd, 1978–80. President: RSPB, 1980–85; Simon Population Trust, 1985–; Trust for Urban Ecology (formerly Ecological Parks Trust), 1987–88 (Chm., 1977–87); Vice-President: RSA, 1978–82; Wildfowl and Wetlands Trust; WWF, UK; Trustee, Earthwatch Europe, 1985–93; Member: Council, Internat. Inst. of Environment and Develt, 1972–88; Internat. Council, WWF, 1983–86. Chairman: Environmental Cttee, London Celebrations for the Queen's Silver Jubilee, 1976–77; London Looks Forward Conf., 1977; UK Standing Cttee for World Conservation Strategy Prog., 1981–83; Common Ground Internat., 1981–. Hon. Member: IUCN; British Ecol Soc.; WWF; RTPI. Hon. Fellow, American Ornithologists' Union. Hon. Fellow RIBA; Hon. LLD Aberdeen, 1964; Hon. Dr, RCA, 1970; Hon. DL Birmingham, 1983. John C. Phillips Medallist International Union for Conservation of Nature and Natural Resources, 1963; Europa Preis für Landespflege, 1972. Comdr, Order of Golden Ark, Netherlands, 1973. *Publications:* Birds in England, 1926; How Birds Live, 1927; Birds and Men, 1951; Britain's Nature Reserves, 1958; The System, 1967; The Environmental Revolution, 1970 (Premio Europeo Cortina-Ulisse, 1971); The Big Change, 1973; The New Environmental Age, 1987; (ed jtly) The Birds of the Western Palearctic, Vol. I, 1977, Vol. II, 1980, Vol. III, 1983, Vol. IV, 1985, Vol. V, 1988, Vol. VI, 1992, Vol. VII, 1993, Vol. VIII and Vol. IX, 1994, and other books, scientific papers and articles. *Address:* 13 Upper Cheyne Row, SW3 5JW. *Club:* Athenæum.

NICHOLSON, (Edward) Rupert, FCA; Partner, Peat Marwick Mitchell & Co. (UK), 1949–77; *b* 17 Sept. 1909; *s* of late Alfred Edward Nicholson and late Elise (*née* Dobson); *m* 1935, Mary Elley (*d* 1983); one *s* one *d*. *Educ:* Whitgift Sch., Croydon. Articled to father, 1928–33; joined Peat Marwick Mitchell & Co., 1933. Apptd Receiver, Rolls-Royce Ltd, 1971. Chm., Techn. Adv. Cttee, Inst. Chartered Accountants, 1969–70; Liquidator, Court Line Ltd, 1974; Mem., Post Office Review Cttee, 1976. Dep. Chm., Croydon Business Venture, 1990– (Chm., 1983–90). Governor, Whitgift Foundn, 1976–94 (Chm., 1978–91; Gov. Emeritus, 1994–). Master, Horners' Co., 1984–85. *Publications:* articles in learned jls. *Address:* Grey Wings, The Warren, Ashtead, Surrey KT21 2SL. *T:* Ashtead (01372) 272655. *Club:* Caledonian.

NICHOLSON, Emma Harriet; MP (C) Devon West and Torridge, since 1987; *b* 16 Oct. 1941; *d* of Sir Godfrey Nicholson, 1st Bt and late Lady Katharine Constance Lindsay, 5th *d* of 27th Earl of Crawford; *m* 1987, Sir Michael Harris Caine, *qv*; one adopted *s* two step *c*. *Educ:* St Mary's School, Wantage; Royal Academy of Music. LRAM, ARCM. Computer Programmer, Programming Instructor, Systems Analyst, ICL, 1962–66; Computer Consultant, John Tyzack & Partners, 1967–69; Gen. Management Consultant and Computer Consultant, McLintock Mann and Whinney Murray, 1969–74; joined Save the Children Fund, 1974, Dir of Fund Raising, 1977–85, Pres., Hatherleigh Dist Br. PPS to Minister of State, Home Office, 1992–93, MAFF, 1993–95, to Financial Sec. to HM Treasury, 1995–. Founder and Jt Chm., All Party Parly Gp for Romanian Children; formerly Chm., All Party Parly Gp for Iraqi-Shias; Vice Chm., All Party Gp on Penal Affairs, 1992; Member: Select Cttee on Employment, 1990–91; British-Turkish, Franco-British, British-Japanese, and Anglo-Botswana Parly Gps; All Party Parly Gp on AIDS; All Party Gp on Child Abduction; All Party Conservation Gp; All Party Jazz Gp; Parly Panel, RCN, 1990–92. Formerly Alternate Mem., UK Delegn to WEU and Council of Europe. Chm., Cons. Backbench Envmt Cttee, 1991 (Sec., 1990–91); Vice-Chm., Cons. Party, 1983–87; Vice-President: Cons. Technol. Forum; Cons. Disability Gp; Western Area Young Conservatives; Mem., Tony Green Initiative. Contested (C) Blyth Valley, 1979. Vis. Parly Fellow, St Antony's Coll., Oxford, 1995. Vice-Moderator, Movement for Ordination of Women, 1991–. Dir, Shelter; Member: Exec. Bd, UNICEF UK; MRC; Council, European Movement; Eur. Union of Women; POW Adv. Trust on Disability; Council, PITCOM; Centre for Policy Studies; RIIA; Adv. Bd, Women of Tomorrow Awards; RAM Appeal Cttee; Editl Panel, 300 Gp Newsletter. Fellow, Industry and Parliament Trust. Vice President: Small Farmers' Assoc.; Assoc. of Dist Councils. Deputy Chairman: Duke of Edinburgh's Award 30th Anniv. Tribute Project, 1986-88; Duke of Edinburgh's Internat. Project '87, 1987–88. President: Plymouth and W Devon Cassette, Talking Newspaper; W Regl Assoc. for the Deaf; Patron: Hospice Care Trust, N Devon; CRUSAID; Devon Care Trust; Trustee, Ross McWhirter Foundn; Chm. Adv. Cttee, Carnegie UK Trust Venues Improvement Programmes. *Publications:* Why does the West forget?, 1993; contrib. various periodicals. *Recreations:* music, chess, reading, walking. *Address:* c/o House of Commons, SW1A 0AA. *T:* 0171–219 3000. *Clubs:* Reform, St Stephen's Constitutional; Blyth Conservative (Life Mem.), Tavistock Conservative, Okehampton Conservative, Torrington and Bideford Conservative; House of Commons Yacht.

NICHOLSON, Rev. Prof. Ernest Wilson, DD; FBA 1987; Provost of Oriel College, Oxford, since 1990; Pro-Vice-Chancellor, University of Oxford, since 1993; *b* 26 Sept. 1938; *s* of Ernest Tedford Nicholson and Veronica Muriel Nicholson; *m* 1962, Hazel (*née* Jackson); one *s* three *d*. *Educ:* Portadown Coll.; Trinity Coll., Dublin (Scholar; BA 1960; MA 1964; Hon. Fellow, 1992); Glasgow Univ. (PhD 1964). MA (by incorporation) 1967, BD 1971, DD 1978, Cambridge; DD Oxford (by incorporation) 1979. Lectr in Hebrew and Semitic Languages, TCD, 1962–67; Univ. Lectr in Divinity, Cambridge Univ., 1967–79; Fellow: University Coll. (now Wolfson Coll.), Cambridge, 1967–69 (Hon. Fellow, 1992); Pembroke Coll., Cambridge, 1969–79; Chaplain, Pembroke Coll., Cambridge, 1969–73, Dean, 1973–79; Oriel Prof. of the Interpretation of Holy Scripture, and Fellow of Oriel Coll., Oxford Univ., 1979–90. At various times vis. prof. at univs and seminars in Europe, USA, Canada and Australia. Pres., SOTS, 1988. Chm., Jardine Foundn, 1993–. Hon. Fellow, St Peter's Coll., Oxford, 1994. Comdr, Order of Merit (Italian Republic), 1990. *Publications:* Deuteronomy and Tradition, 1967; Preaching to the Exiles, 1971; Exodus and Sinai in History and Tradition, 1973; (with J. Baker) The Commentary of Rabbi David Kimḥi on Psalms 120–150, 1973; Commentary on Jeremiah 1–25, 1973; Commentary on Jeremiah 26–52, 1975; God and His People: covenant and theology in the Old Testament, 1986; articles in biblical and Semitic jls. *Recreations:* music, the English countryside. *Address:* Oriel College, Oxford OX1 4EW.

NICHOLSON, Gordon; *see* Nicholson, C. G. B.

NICHOLSON, Dr Howard, FRCP; Physician, University College Hospital, since 1948; Physician, Brompton Hospital, 1952–77, retired; Fellow of University College, London, since 1959; *b* 1 Feb. 1912; *s* of Frederick and Sara Nicholson; *m* 1941, Winifrid Madeline Piercy. *Educ:* University Coll., London, and University Coll. Hospital. MB, BS, London, 1935; MD London 1938; MRCP 1938, FRCP 1949. House appointments and Registrarship, UCH, 1935–38; House Physician at Brompton Hosp., 1938. Served War, 1940–45, RAMC; Physician to Chest Surgical Team and Officer i/c Medical Div. (Lt-Col). Registrar, Brompton Hosp., and Chief Asst, Inst. of Diseases of Chest, 1945–48. Goulstonian Lecturer, RCP, 1950. *Publications:* sections on Diseases of Chest in The Practice of Medicine (ed J. S. Richardson), 1961, and in Progress in Clinical Medicine, 1961; articles in Thorax, Lancet, etc. *Recreations:* reading, going to the opera. *Address:* Chelwood, Laughton, Lewes, E Sussex BN8 6BE.

NICHOLSON, Jack; American film actor, director and producer; *b* 22 April 1937; *s* of John and Ethel May Nicholson; *m* 1961, Sandra Knight (marr. diss. 1966); one *d*. *Films include:* Cry-Baby Killer, 1958; Studs Lonigan, 1960; The Shooting (also produced); Easy Rider, 1969; Five Easy Pieces, 1970; The Last Detail, 1973; Chinatown, 1974; One Flew Over the Cuckoo's Nest, 1975 (Acad. Award for Best Actor, 1976); The Passenger, 1975; The Shining, 1980; The Postman Always Rings Twice, 1981; Reds, 1981; Terms of Endearment (Acad. Award for Best Supporting Actor), 1984; Prizzi's Honor, 1985; Heartburn, 1986; The Witches of Eastwick, 1986; Ironweed, 1987; Batman, 1988; The Two Jakes, 1991 (also dir.); A Few Good Men, 1992; Man Trouble, 1993; Hoffa, 1993; Wolf, 1994. *Address:* c/o Bresler Kelly & Associates, 15760 Ventura Boulevard, Suite 1730, Encino, CA 91436, USA.

NICHOLSON, James Frederick; farmer; Member (UUUP), Northern Ireland, European Parliament, since 1994 (OUP, 1989–94); *b* 29 Jan. 1945; *s* of Thomas and Matilda Nicholson; *m* 1968, Elizabeth Gibson; six *s*. *Educ:* Aghavilly Primary Sch. Member: Armagh Dist Council, 1975– (Chm., 1995–); Southern Health and Social Services Bd, 1977–. Mem. (OU) Newry and Armagh, NI Assembly, 1982–86. Contested (OUP) Newry and Armagh, 1987. MP (OU) Newry and Armagh, 1983–85.

NICHOLSON, Rt Hon. Sir (James) Michael (Anthony), Kt 1988; PC 1995; **Rt Hon. Lord Justice Nicholson;** a Lord Justice of Appeal, Supreme Court of Judicature, Northern Ireland, since 1995; *b* 4 Feb. 1933; *s* of late Cyril Nicholson, QC, DL and late Eleanor Nicholson (*née* Caffrey); *m* 1973, Augusta Mary Ada, *d* of late Thomas F. Doyle and of Mrs Elizabeth Doyle, Co. Cork; one *s* two *d*. *Educ:* Downside; Trinity College, Cambridge (MA). Called to the Bar of N Ireland, 1956; to English Bar, Gray's Inn, 1963 (Hon. Bencher, 1995); to Bar of Ireland, 1975; QC (NI), 1971; Bencher, Inn of Court of NI, 1978; Chm., Exec. Council of Inn of Court of NI and of Bar Council, 1983–85; Senior Crown Counsel: Co. Fermanagh, 1971–73; Co. Tyrone, 1973–77; Co. Londonderry, 1977–86; High Court Judge, NI, 1986–95. Chm., Mental Health Review Tribunal (NI), 1973–76; Mem., Standing Adv. Commn for Human Rights (NI), 1976–78. High Sheriff, Co. Londonderry, 1972. President: Irish Cricket Union, 1978; NW ICU, 1986–93. *Recreations:* cricket, chess. *Address:* Royal Courts of Justice, Chichester Street, Belfast, Northern Ireland. *Club:* MCC.

NICHOLSON, Lewis Frederick, CB 1963; *b* 1 May 1918; *s* of Harold and May Nicholson; *m* 1947, Diana Rosalind Fear; one *s* two *d*. *Educ:* Taunton Sch.; King's Coll., Cambridge. Research Laboratories of GEC, 1939; Royal Aircraft Establishment, 1939–59; Head of Aerodynamics Dept, RAE, 1953–59; Imperial Defence Coll., 1956; Director-General of Scientific Research (Air), Ministry of Aviation, 1959–63; Dep. Director (Air) Royal Aircraft Establishment, 1963–66; Chief Scientist, RAF, 1966–69; Vice Controller Aircraft, MoD (PE), 1969–78, retired. *Publications:* (Joint) Compressible Airflow-Tables; Compressible Airflow-Graphs; papers on aerodynamic subjects. *Address:* 15 Silver Birches Way, Elstead, Godalming, Surrey GU8 6JA. *T:* Elstead (01252) 702362.

NICHOLSON, Margaret Beda; *see* Yorke, M.

NICHOLSON, Max; *see* Nicholson, E. M.

NICHOLSON, Hon. Sir Michael; *see* Nicholson, Hon. Sir J. M. A.

NICHOLSON, Michael Constantine; a Recorder of the Crown Court, since 1980; *b* 3 Feb. 1932; *m* 1960, Kathleen Mary Strong; two *d*. *Educ:* Wycliffe Coll., Stonehouse; University Coll. of Wales, Aberystwyth (LLB). Called to the Bar, Gray's Inn, 1957; Crown Counsel, Nyasaland, 1960–63; Wales and Chester circuit, 1963–. *Recreations:* opera, cinema, theatre. *Address:* (chambers) 33 Park Place, Cardiff CF1 3BA. *T:* Cardiff (01222) 233313. *Club:* Cardiff Golf.

NICHOLSON, Michael Thomas, OBE 1992; Senior Foreign Correspondent, ITN, since 1991; *b* 9 Jan. 1937; *s* of Major Allan Nicholson and Doris Alice Nicholson; *m* 1968, Diana Margaret Slater; two *s*, and one adopted *d*. *Educ:* Leicester Univ. (BA). Joined ITN, 1963: News Editor, 1965–66; War Correspondent, 1968–94: Nigeria, Biafra, Beirut, Jordan, Cyprus, Congo, Israel, Indo-Pakistan, Rhodesia, Angola, Falklands, Gulf, Bosnia, Croatia; Southern Africa Corresp., 1977–81; Newscaster, 1982–86; Washington Corresp., Channel 4, 1989–90. Campaign Medal: Falklands War, 1982; Gulf War, 1991. *Publications:* Partridge Kite, 1976; Red Joker, 1978; December Ultimatum, 1981; Pilgrims Rest, 1983; Across the Limpopo, 1986; A Measure of Danger, 1991; Natasha's Story, 1993. *Recreations:* sailing, walking. *Address:* Grayswood House, Grayswood, Surrey GU27 2DR. *Clubs:* Reform, Groucho.

NICHOLSON, Sir Paul (Douglas), Kt 1993; DL; Chairman, Vaux Group, since 1976 (Managing Director, 1971–92); *b* 7 March 1938; *s* of late Douglas Nicholson, TD and Pauline Nicholson; *m* 1970, Sarah, *y d* of Sir Edmund Bacon, Bt, KG, KBE, TD; one *d*. *Educ:* Harrow; Clare College, Cambridge (MA). FCA. Lieut, Coldstream Guards, 1956–58; joined Vaux Breweries, 1965. Chm., Northern Investors Co., 1984–89; Director: Tyne Tees Television, then Yorkshire-Tyne Tees Television Hldgs, 1981–; Northern Development Co., 1986–; Northern Electric, 1990–. Chm., Urban Develt Corp. for Tyne and Wear, 1987–; Chm., N Region, CBI, 1977–79; Chm., N Regional Bd, British Technology Group, 1979–84. Vice-Chm., Brewers' Soc., 1992–. High Sheriff, Co. Durham, 1980–81; DL Co. Durham, 1980. *Recreations:* deerstalking, driving horses (Pres., Coaching Club, 1990–). *Address:* Quarry Hill, Brancepeth, Durham DH7 8DW. *T:* Durham (0191) 3780275. *Clubs:* Boodle's; Northern Counties (Newcastle upon Tyne).

NICHOLSON, Ralph Lambton Robb; Secretary, United Kingdom Atomic Energy Authority, 1984–86; *b* 26 Sept. 1924; *s* of Ralph Adam Nicholson and Kathleen Mary Nicholson (*née* Robb); *m* 1951, Mary Kennard; one *s* two *d*. *Educ:* Sherborne School; Cambridge Univ.; Imperial College, London (BSc; ACGI). FIChemE. Royal Engineers, 1943–47. Chemical engineer, Distillers Co., 1950–51; Wellcome Foundation, 1951–54; Fisons, 1954–58; planning and commercial manager, UKAEA, 1958–67; Dir, Min. of Technology Programmes Analysis Unit, 1967–71; Principal Programmes and Finance Officer, UKAEA, 1971–84. *Publications:* contribs to energy and management jls. *Recreations:* gardening, music, canals. *Address:* The Garth, Midgham, Reading, Berks RG7 5UJ. *T:* Woolhampton (01734) 712211.

NICHOLSON, Robert; publisher, designer, artist, writer; *b* Sydney, Australia, 8 April 1920; *m* 1951 (marr. diss. 1976); one *s* one *d*; *m* 1989. *Educ:* Troy Town Elementary Sch., Rochester; Rochester Tech. Sch.; Medway Sch. of Art. Served 1939–45, RAMC (mainly pathology in Middle East). Responsible with brother for major design projects during post-war design boom, 1945–55, including Festival of Britain Exhibition in Edinburgh, 1951 and Design Centre, London, 1956. Writer and publisher of guide books including: Nicholson's London Guide; Street Finder; Guide to Great Britain, guides to the Thames, the canals, etc. Benjamin Franklin medal, 1960. Exhibns of landscape painting in London, Spain, France, and annually in Kent and Sussex. Lives in Kent.

NICHOLSON, Sir Robin (Buchanan), Kt 1985; PhD; FRS 1978; FEng 1980; Director, Pilkington plc (formerly Pilkington Brothers plc), since 1986; *b* 12 Aug. 1934; *s* of late Carroll and Nancy Nicholson; *m* 1st, 1958, Elizabeth Mary Caffyn (*d* 1988); one *s* two *d*; 2nd, 1991, Yvonne, *d* of late Arthur Appleby and of Gwendoline Appleby. *Educ:* Oundle Sch.; St Catharine's Coll., Cambridge. BA 1956, PhD 1959, MA 1960. FIM; MInstP; CIMgt. University of Cambridge: Demonstrator in Metallurgy, 1960; Lectr in Metallurgy, 1964; Fellow of Christ's Coll., 1962–66, Hon. Fellow 1984; Prof. of Metallurgy, Univ. of Manchester, 1966. Inco Europe Ltd: Dir of Research Lab., 1972; Dir, 1975; Man. Dir, 1976–81; Co-Chm., Biogen NV, 1979–81. Chief Scientific Advr to Cabinet Office, 1983–85 (Central Policy Review Staff, 1981–83). Director: Rolls-Royce plc, 1986–; BP plc, 1987–. Chairman: CEST, 1987–90; ACOST, 1990–93. Member: SERC (formerly SRC), 1978–81; Council for Sci. and Technol., 1993–. Mem. Council: Royal Soc., 1983–85; Fellowship of Engrg, 1986–89; Foreign Associate, Nat. Acad. of Engrg, USA, 1983. Hon. FIChemE; Hon. Fellow UMIST, 1988. Hon. DSc: Cranfield, 1983; Aston, 1983; Manchester, 1985; Hon. DMet Sheffield, 1984; Hon. DEng Birmingham, 1986; DUniv. Open, 1987. Rosenhain Medallist, Inst. of Metals, 1971; Platinum Medal, Metals Soc., 1982. *Publications:* Precipitation Hardening (with A. Kelly), 1962; (jtly) Electron Microscopy of Thin Crystals, 1965; (ed and contrib. with A. Kelly) Strengthening Methods in Crystals, 1971; numerous papers to learned jls. *Recreations:* family life, gardening, music. *Address:* Whittington House, 8 Fisherwick Road, Whittington, near Lichfield, Staffs WS14 9LH. *T:* Whittington (01543) 432081. *Club:* MCC.

NICHOLSON, Rupert; *see* Nicholson, E. R.

NICKELL, Prof. Stephen John, FBA 1993; Professor of Economics, Director of the Institute of Economics and Statistics and Fellow of Nuffield College, University of Oxford, since 1984; *b* 25 April 1944; *s* of John Edward Hilary Nickell and Phyllis Nickell; *m* 1976, Susan Elizabeth (*née* Pegden); one *s* one *d*. *Educ:* Merchant Taylors' Sch.; Pembroke Coll., Cambridge (BA); LSE (MSc). Maths teacher, Hendon County Sch., 1965–68; London School of Economics: Lectr, 1970–77; Reader, 1977–79; Prof. of Economics, 1979–84. Member: Academic Panel, HM Treasury, 1981–89; Council, REconS, 1984–94; ESRC, 1990–94. Fellow, Econometric Soc., 1980. *Publications:* The Investment Decisions of Firms, 1978; (with R. Layard and R. Dornbusch) The Performance of the British Economy, 1988; (with R. Jackman and R. Layard) Unemployment, 1991; (with R. Jackman and R. Layard) The Unemployment Crisis, 1994; The Performance of Companies, 1995; articles in learned jls. *Recreations:* reading, riding, cooking. *Address:* The Old Bakehouse, Horn Hill, Barford St Michael, Banbury, Oxon OX15 0RQ.

NICKLAUS, Jack William; golfer; *b* 21 Jan. 1940; *s* of Louis Charles Nicklaus and Helen (*née* Schoener); *m* 1960, Barbara Jean Bash; four *s* one *d*. *Educ:* Upper Arlington High Sch.; Ohio State Univ. Won US Amateur golf championship, 1959, 1961; became professional golfer, 1961; designs golf courses in USA, Europe, and Far East; Chm., Golden Bear Internat. Inc. Captained US team which won 25th Ryder Cup, 1983. *Major wins include:* US Open, 1962, 1967, 1972, 1980; US Masters, 1963, 1965, 1966, 1972, 1975, 1986; US Professional Golfers' Assoc., 1963, 1971, 1973, 1975, 1980; British Open, 1966, 1970, 1978, and many other championships in USA, Europe, Australia and Far East. Hon. Dr Athletic Arts Ohio State, 1972; Hon. LLD St Andrews, 1984. *Publications:* My 55 Ways to Lower Your Golf Score, 1962; Take a Tip from Me, 1964; The Greatest Game of All, 1969 (autobiog.); Lesson Tee, 1972; Golf My Way, 1974; The Best Way to Better Your Golf, vols 1–3, 1974; Jack Nicklaus' Playing Lessons, 1976; Total Golf Techniques, 1977; On and Off the Fairway, 1979 (autobiog.); The Full Swing, 1982; My Most Memorable Shots in the Majors, 1988. *Address:* (office) 11780 US Highway #1, North Palm Beach, FL 33408, USA.

NICKOLS, Herbert Arthur; Headmaster, Westonbirt School, Tetbury, Gloucestershire, 1981–86; *b* 17 Jan. 1926; *s* of Herbert and Henrietta Elizabeth Nickols; *m* 1953, Joyce Peake; two *s* one *d*. *Educ:* Imperial Coll., Univ. of London (BSc). ACGI. Res. Demonstrator, Imperial Coll., 1947–49; Housemaster, Sen. Science Master and later Dep. Headmaster, St Edmund's Sch., Canterbury, Kent, 1949–81. *Recreations:* music, travel, cricket. *Address:* 146 New Dover Road, Canterbury, Kent CT1 3EJ. *T:* Canterbury (01227) 452605.

NICKSON, family mane of **Baron Nickson.**

NICKSON, Baron *cr* 1994 (Life Peer), of Renagour in the District of Stirling; **David Wigley Nickson,** KBE 1987 (CBE 1981); DL; CIMgt; FRSE; Chairman, Clydesdale Bank, since 1991 (Director, 1981–89; Deputy Chairman, 1990–91); *b* 27 Nov. 1929; *s* of late Geoffrey Wigley Nickson and Janet Mary Nickson; *m* 1952, Helen Louise Cockcraft; three *d*. *Educ:* Eton; RMA, Sandhurst. Commnd Coldstream Guards, 1949–54. Joined Wm Collins, 1954; Dir, 1961–85; Jt Man. Dir, 1967; Vice Chm., 1976–83; Gp Man. Dir, 1979–82; Chm., Pan Books, 1982. Director: Scottish United Investors plc, 1970–83; General Accident plc, 1971– (Dep. Chm., 1993–); Scottish & Newcastle (formerly Scottish & Newcastle Breweries) plc, 1981– (Dep. Chm., 1982–83; Chm., 1983–89); Radio Clyde PLC, 1982–85; Edinburgh Investment Trust plc, 1983–94; Hambro's PLC, 1989–; National Australia Bank Ltd, 1991–. Chm., Top Salaries, then Sen. Salaries, Rev. Body, 1989–95; Chairman: SDA, 1989–90, Scottish Enterprise, 1990–93; CBI in Scotland, 1979–81; Pres., CBI, 1986–88 (Dep. Pres., 1985–86). Member: Scottish Indust. Develt Adv. Bd, 1975–80; Scottish Econ. Council, 1980–; NEDC, 1985–88; Scottish Cttee, Design Council, 1978–81; Nat. Trng Task Force, 1989–91. Chairman: Countryside Commn for Scotland, 1983–85; Atlantic Salmon Trust, 1989– (Mem., Council of Management, 1982–); Vice Chm., Assoc. of Scottish Dist Salmon Fishery Bds, 1989–92; Trustee: Game Conservancy, 1988–91; Prince's Youth Business Trust, 1987–90; Princess Royal's Trust for Carers, 1990–94. Chancellor, Glasgow Caledonian Univ., 1993–. Brig., Queen's Body Guard for Scotland, Royal Co. of Archers. DL Stirling and Falkirk, 1982. CIMgt (CBIM 1980); FRSE 1987. Hon. Fellow, Paisley Coll., subseq. Univ. of Paisley, 1992. DUniv Stirling, 1986; Hon. DBA Napier Polytechnic, 1990; DUniv Glasgow Caledonian, 1993. *Recreations:* fishing, shooting, bird watching, the countryside. *Clubs:* Boodle's, Flyfishers', MCC; Western (Glasgow).

NICKSON, Francis; Chief Executive and Town Clerk, London Borough of Camden, 1977–90; *b* 9 Sept. 1929; *s* of Francis and Kathleen Nickson; *m* 1957, Helena (*née* Towers). *Educ:* Preston Catholic College; Liverpool Univ. (LLB). LMRTPI. Admitted Solicitor (Hons), 1953; Asst Solicitor, Newcastle-under-Lyme, 1953–56; Senior Asst Solicitor, Wood Green, 1956–60; Assistant Town Clerk, Enfield, 1960–71; Deputy Town Clerk, Camden, 1971–77. Hon. Clerk, Housing and Works Cttee, London Boroughs Assoc., 1979–84; Hon. Sec., London Boroughs Children's Regional Planning Cttee, 1977–90. Freeman, City of London, 1990. FRSA. *Recreations:* listening to music, country walking, discovering French wines. *Address:* 14 Waggon Road, Hadley Wood, Barnet, Herts EN4 0HL. *T:* 0181–449 9390.

NICOL, family name of **Baroness Nicol.**

NICOL, Baroness *cr* 1982 (Life Peer), of Newnham in the County of Cambridgeshire; **Olive Mary Wendy Nicol;** FRGS; *b* 21 March 1923; *d* of James and Harriet Rowe-Hunter; *m* 1947, Alexander Douglas Ian Nicol (CBE 1985); two *s* one *d*. Civil Service, 1943–48. Opposition Whip, 1983–87, Opposition Dep. Chief Whip, 1987–89, H of L;

Member: H of L Science and Technol. Select Cttee, 1990–93; Envmt and Social Affairs sub-cttee, European Communities Cttee, 1993–; Sustainable Develt Select Cttee, 1994–; Ecclesiastical Cttee, 1989–. Trustee, Cambridge United Charities, 1967–86; Director, Cambridge and District Co-operative Soc., 1975–81, Pres. 1981–85; Member: Supplementary Benefits Tribunal, 1976–78; Cambridge City Council, 1972–82; Assoc. of District Councils, Cambridge Branch, 1974–76 and 1980–82; various school Governing Bodies, 1974–80; Council, Granta Housing Soc., 1975–; Careers Service Consultative Group, 1978–81. JP Cambridge City, 1972–86. FRGS 1990. *Recreations:* reading, walking. *Address:* c/o House of Lords, SW1A 0PW.

NICOL, Andrew George Lindsay; QC 1995; *b* 9 May 1951; *s* of D. R. Nicol and Margaret (*née* Mason); two *s*. *Educ:* Selwyn Coll., Cambridge (BA, LLB); Harvard Law Sch. (LLM). Harkness Fellow, 1973–75; Special Assistant: to Dir of Housing and Community Develt, California, 1975–76; Allen Allen and Hemsley, solicitors, Sydney, NSW, 1976–77; Lectr in Law, LSE, 1977–87; called to the Bar, Middle Temple, 1978; barrister, 1979–. *Publications:* (with G. Robertson) Media Law, 1984, revd edn 1992; (with A. Dummett) Subjects, Citizens, Aliens and Others, 1990. *Recreations:* family, walking. *Address:* Doughty Street Chambers, 11 Doughty Street, WC1N 2PG. *T:* 0171–404 1313, *Fax:* 0171–404 2283.

NICOL, (Andrew) William, JP; BSc; FICE, FIMechE, FIEE; Chairman, 1987–93, and Chief Executive, 1990–93, South Western Electricity plc; *b* 29 April 1933; *s* of Arthur Edward Nicol and Ethel Isabel Gladstone Nicol (*née* Fairley); *m* 1960, Jane Gillian Margaret Mann; one *s*. *Educ:* King's College School, Wimbledon; Durham Univ. (BSc). W. S. Atkins & Partners, 1960–67; Electricity Council, 1967–69; London Electricity Board, 1969–81; Dep. Chm., SE Electricity Board, 1981–87. Chairman: Trustees, NICEIC Pension Fund, 1986; South Western Enterprises, 1992–93. JP Surrey 1976. *Recreation:* Honourable Artillery Company. *Address:* 23 Ruxley Ridge, Claygate, Esher, Surrey KT10 0HZ. *Club:* Caledonian.

NICOL, Angus Sebastian Torquil Eyers; barrister; a Recorder of the Crown Court, since 1982; *b* 11 April 1933; *s* of Henry James Nicol and Phyllis Mary Eyers; *m* 1968, Eleanor Denise Brodrick; two *d*. *Educ:* RNC, Dartmouth. Served RN, 1947–56. Called to the Bar, Middle Temple, 1963. A Chairman: Disciplinary Cttee, Potato Marketing Bd, 1988–; VAT Tribunal, 1988–. Founder Vice-Chm. and Mem. Council, Monday Club, 1961–68. Lectr in Gaelic, Central London Adult Educn Inst., 1983–; Sen. Steward, Argyllshire Gathering, 1983; Dir, 1981–, and Jt Sec., 1984–, Highland Soc. of London; Conductor, London Gaelic Choir, 1985–91; Comr of Clan MacNicol for all Territories of GB south of River Tweed, 1988–. FSA (Scot.). *Publications:* Gaelic poems and short stories in Gairm, etc. *Recreations:* music, Gaelic language and literature, shooting, fishing, sailing, gastronomy. *Address:* 5 Paper Buildings, Temple, EC4Y 7HB. *T:* 0171–353 8494. *Clubs:* Flyfishers'; Royal Highland Yacht.

NICOL, Prof. Donald MacGillivray, FBA 1981; FKC 1980; Koraës Professor of Modern Greek and Byzantine History, Language and Literature, University of London, King's College, 1970–88, now Emeritus; Vice Principal, King's College, 1980–81 (Assistant Principal, 1977–80); *b* 4 Feb. 1923; *s* of late Rev. George Manson Nicol and Mary Patterson (*née* MacGillivray); *m* 1950, Joan Mary Campbell, *d* of Sir Walter Campbell, KCIE; three *s*. *Educ:* King Edward VII Sch., Sheffield; St Paul's Sch., London; Pembroke Coll., Cambridge (MA, PhD). Friends' Ambulance Unit, 1942–46; Scholar at British Sch. of Archæology, Athens, 1949–50; Lectr in Classics, University Coll., Dublin, 1952–64; Vis. Fellow, Dumbarton Oaks, Washington, DC, 1964–65; Vis. Prof. of Byzantine History, Indiana Univ., 1965–66; Sen. Lectr and Reader in Byzantine History, Univ. of Edinburgh, 1966–70. Dir, Gennadius Library, Athens, 1989–92. Birkbeck Lectr, Cambridge, 1976–77. Pres., Ecclesiastical Hist. Soc., 1975–76. MRIA 1960; FRHistS 1971. Hon. Citizen of Arta, Greece, 1990. Editor, Byzantine and Modern Greek Studies, 1973–83. *Publications:* The Despotate of Epiros, 1957; Meteora, the Rock Monasteries of Thessaly, 1963, rev. edn, 1975; The Byzantine Family of Kantakouzenos (Cantacuzenus) ca 1100–1460: a genealogical and prosopographical study, 1968; The Last Centuries of Byzantium, 1261–1453, 1972, 2nd edn 1993; Byzantium: Its Ecclesiastical History and Relations with the Western World, 1972; Church and Society in the Last Centuries of Byzantium, 1979; The End of the Byzantine Empire, 1979; The Despotate of Epiros 1267–1479: a contribution to the history of Greece in the middle ages, 1984; Studies in Late Byzantine History and Prosopography, 1986; Byzantium and Venice: a study in diplomatic and cultural relations, 1988; Joannes Gennadios—The Man: a biographical sketch, 1990; A Biographical Dictionary of the Byzantine Empire, 1991; The Immortal Emporer: the life and legend of Constantine Palaiologos, last Emperor of the Romans, 1992; The Byzantine Lady: ten portraits 1250–1500, 1994; articles in Byzantine, classical and historical jls. *Recreation:* bookbinding. *Address:* 16 Courtyards, Little Shelford, Cambridge CB2 5ER. *T:* Cambridge (01223) 843406. *Club:* Athenæum.

NICOL, Dr Joseph Arthur Colin, FRS 1967; Professor of Zoology, University of Texas Institute of Marine Science, 1967–80, now Professor Emeritus; *b* 5 Dec. 1915; *s* of George Nicol and Noele Petrie; *m* 1941, Helen Wilhelmina Cameron; one *d*. *Educ:* Universities of McGill, Western Ontario and Oxford. BSc (hons Zool.) 1938, McGill; MA 1940, Western Ontario; DPhil 1947, DSc 1961, Oxford. Canadian Army, RCCS, 1941–45. Asst Professor in Zoology, University of British Columbia, 1947–49; Experimental Zoologist, Marine Biological Assoc., UK, 1949 (research on marine animals, comparative physiology, luminescence, vision, at Plymouth Laboratory, 1949–66). Guggenheim Fellow, Scripps Inst. Oceanography, 1953–54. Vis. Prof., Univ. of Texas, 1966–67. *Publications:* Biology of Marine Animals, 1960; Eyes of Fishes, 1989; papers on comparative physiology and anatomy in Jl Marine Biol. Assoc. UK, Proc. Royal Soc, Jl Exp. Biol., Biol. Review, etc. *Recreation:* English literature. *Address:* Ribby, Lerryn, Lostwithiel, Cornwall PL22 0PG. *T:* Bodmin (01208) 872319.

NICOL, William; *see* Nicol, A. W.

NICOLI, Eric Luciano; Group Chief Executive, United Biscuits (Holdings) Plc, since 1991; *b* 5 Aug. 1950; *s* of Virgilio and Ida Nicoli; *m* 1977, Rosalind West; one *s* one *d*. *Educ:* Diss Grammar Sch.; King's College London (BSc Hons 1st class Physics). Marketing, Rowntree Mackintosh, 1972–80; United Biscuits: Sen. Marketing Controller, 1980; Marketing Dir, Biscuits Div., 1981; UK Group Business Planning Dir, 1984; Managing Dir, Frozen Food Div., 1985, Biscuit and Confectionery Div., 1986; Chief Exec., Eur. Ops and Group Chief Exec. designate, 1989–91. Dir, Thorn EMI plc, 1993–. Dep. Chm., BITC, 1991–; Member: Exec. Cttee, FDF, 1990–; Adv. Council on Advertising, COI, 1990–; Policy Issues Council, Inst. of Grocery Distbn, 1991–; Council, ISBA, 1987–92. Dep. Chm., Per Cent Club, 1993–. CIMgt. *Recreations:* sport, food, music. *Address:* United Biscuits (Holdings) plc, Church Road, West Drayton, Middlesex UB7 7PR. *T:* West Drayton (01895) 432100.

NICOLL, Douglas Robertson, CB 1980; retired; *b* 12 May 1920; *s* of James George Nicoll and Mabel Nicoll (*née* Styles); *m* 1st, 1949, Winifred Campion (*d* 1987); two *s*; 2nd, 1992, Mrs Cathryn Sansom. *Educ:* Merchant Taylors' School; St John's College, Oxford (MA 1946). FCO (GCHQ), 1946–80; Joint Services' Staff College, 1953; Under Secretary, 1977–80. *Address:* c/o National Westminster Bank, 31 The Promenade, Cheltenham, Glos GL50 1LH. *Club:* Travellers'.

NICOLL, Sir William, KCMG 1992 (CMG 1974); a Director General, Council of European Communities, 1982–91; *b* 28 June 1927; *s* of Ralph Nicoll and Christina Mowbray Nicoll (*née* Melville); *m* 1954, Helen Morison Martin; two *d*. *Educ:* Morgan Acad., Dundee; St Andrews Univ. Entered BoT, 1949; British Trade Comr, India, 1955–59; Private Sec. to Pres. of BoT, 1964–67; Commercial Inspector, FCO, 1967–69; DTI, 1969–72; Office of UK Perm. Rep. to European Communities, 1972–75; Under Sec., Dept of Prices and Consumer Protection, 1975–77; Dep. UK Rep. to EEC, 1977–82. Fulbright Fellow, George Mason Univ., Va, USA, 1991–92. Editor, European Business Jl, 1993–. Hon. LLD Dundee, 1983. *Publications:* (ed and contrib.) Competition Policy Enquiry, 1988; (with T. C. Salmon) Understanding the European Communities, 1990; (with T. C. Salmon) Understanding the New European Community, 1993; (ed jtly) Perspectives on European Business, 1995; contributed to: Government and Industry, ed W. Rodgers, 1986; The State of the EC, ed G. Rosendahl, 1993; Margaret Thatcher, Prime Minister Indomitable, ed W. Thompson, 1994; Maastricht and Beyond, ed A. N. Duff, 1994; contribs to various jls on European subjects. *Address:* Outback, Nackington Road, Canterbury, Kent CT4 7AX. *T:* Canterbury (01227) 456495.

NICOLLE, Anthony William, OBE 1991; Adviser, Palestine Monetary Authority; General Manager for Hong Kong and China, Standard Chartered Bank, 1991–94; *b* 13 April 1935; *s* of late Roland Nicolle and Dorothy May Pearce; *m* 1960, Josephine Anne (*née* Read); one *s* one *d*. *Educ:* Tiffin Sch.; King's Coll., London (LLB). Served RA, 1956–58. Joined Bank of England, 1958; seconded to NEDO, 1968–70; Econ. Intelligence Dept, 1970–77; seconded to Royal Commn on Distribn of Income and Wealth, 1974–75; banking supervision, 1977–80; Banking Dept, 1980–83; banking supervision, 1983–87; Comr of Banking, Hong Kong, 1987–91. *Recreations:* walking (a little), gardening (occasionally). *Address:* Upper Fields, Little Bognor, Fittleworth, Pulborough, W Sussex RH20 1JT. *Club:* Oriental.

NICOLLE, Dr Hilary Ann; Director of Education, London Borough of Islington, since 1993; *b* 12 April 1945; *d* of A. H. and E. V. Upton; *m* 1st, 1970, Noël Leo Nicolle; two *s*; 2nd, 1985, Paul Newman Hudson Clokie; one step *s* one step *d*. *Educ:* St Hilda's Coll., Oxford (BA 1st Class Hons; MA); LSE (PhD); London Univ. (PGCE 1977). HM Diplomatic Service, 1967–70; PhD research and univ. lecturing, 1970–76; school teacher, 1977–82; Headmistress, Tiffin Girls' Sch., Kingston upon Thames, 1982–88; Dep. Dir of Educn, London Borough of Wandsworth, 1988–92; Chief Exec., Sch. Examinations and Assessment Council, 1992–93. *Recreations:* family, foreign travel, history, choral music, National Trust. *Address:* Education Department, Laycock Street, N1 1TH. *Club:* Reform.

NICOLLE, Stéphanie Claire; QC (Jersey) 1995; HM Solicitor General for Jersey, since 1994; *b* 11 March 1948; *d* of Walter Arthur Nicolle and Madeleine Claire Nicolle (*née* Vitel). *Educ:* Convent of the Faithful Companions of Jesus, Jersey; St Aidan's Coll., Univ. of Durham. Called to the Bar, Gray's Inn, 1976; called to the Jersey Bar, 1978; Crown Advocate, 1986–94. *Publication:* (with P. Matthews) The Jersey Law of Property, 1991. *Address:* Solicitor General's Chambers, Royal Court House, Royal Square, St Helier, Jersey, Channel Islands.

NICOLSON, family name of **Baron Carnock.**

NICOLSON, Sir David (Lancaster), Kt 1975; FEng 1977; company chairman and business consultant, retired; *b* 20 Sept. 1922; *s* of Charles Tupper Nicolson, consulting engineer, and Margaret Lancaster Nicolson; *m* 1st, 1945, Joan Eileen (*d* 1991), *d* of Major W. H. Griffiths, RA; one *s* two *d*; 2nd, 1992, Beryl, *widow* of Sir Gerald Thorley, TD, FRICS. *Educ:* Haileybury; Imperial Coll., London Univ. (BSc; Hon. Fellow 1971). FCGI, FIMechE, FIProdE; FIMgt; FRSA. Constructor Lt, Royal Corps Naval Constructors, 1942–45; served N Atlantic and Normandy, 1944 (despatches). Production Manager, Bucyrus-Erie Co., Milwaukee, 1950–52; Manager, later Dir, Production-Engineering Ltd, 1953–62; Chairman: P-E Consulting Gp, 1963–68; British Airways Board, 1971–75; BTR plc, 1969–84 (Dep. Chm., 1965–69, Dir, 1984–); Rothmans International plc, 1975–84; Bulk Transport Ltd, 1984–89; German Securities Investment Trust, 1985–89; Lazard Leisure Fund, 1985–91; VSEL (Vickers Shipbuilding and Engineering), 1986–87; British Rail Engineering, 1987–89; Union Group, 1988–; DRG Ltd, 1989–; TACE PLC, 1991–93; Director: Delta Metal Co., 1967–79; Bank of Montreal, 1970–85; Richard Costain, 1970–78; MEPC, 1976–80; Todd Shipyards Corp., 1976–91; CIBA-Geigy (UK), 1978–90; GKN Plc, 1984–89; London & Scottish Marine Oil, 1983–92; Northern Telecom Ltd, 1987–92; Britannia Arrow Holdings plc, later Invesco MIM PLC, 1987–93; STC PLC, 1987–91; Dawnay Day & Co., 1988–; Brel Group Ltd, 1989–; Southern Water plc, 1989–93; Churchill Leisure Internat., 1989–90; Strategic Hldgs SA, 1991–93. European Adviser, NY Stock Exchange, 1985–. Mem. (C) London Central, European Parlt, 1979–84. Mem. Council: CBI, 1972– (Chm., Environment Cttee, 1976–79); Inst. of Directors, 1971–76; Brit. Inst. of Management, 1964–69; Inst. of Production Engrs, 1966–68; City and Guilds of London Inst., 1968–76; Mem., SRC Engineering Bd, 1969–71; Chm. Management Consultants Assoc., 1964; Mem. Brit. Shipbuilding Mission to India, 1957; Chairman: Cttee for Hosiery and Knitwear, NEDC, 1966–68; BNEC Cttee for Canada, 1967–71. Pres., ABCC, 1983–86. Chm., Amer. European Community Assoc., 1981–; Chm., European Movement, 1985–. Mem. Council, Templeton Coll. (formerly Oxford Centre for Management Studies), 1982–; Governor: Imperial Coll., London Univ., 1966–77; Cranleigh Sch., 1979–90; Pro-Chancellor, Surrey Univ., 1987–93. *Publications:* contribs to technical jls; lectures and broadcasts on management subjects in UK, USA, Australia, etc. *Recreation:* sailing. *Address:* Church House, Bale, near Fakenham, Norfolk NR21 0QR. *T:* Fakenham (01328) 878314. *Clubs:* Brooks's; Royal Thames Yacht.

NICOLSON, Malise Allen, MC 1945; Chairman: Bangor-on-Dee Races Ltd, 1984–94 (Director, since 1972); *b* 31 Oct. 1921; *e s* of late Sir Kenneth Nicolson, MC; *m* 1946, Vivien Bridget, *y d* of late Arthur Hilton Ridley, CBE; one *s* two *d*. *Educ:* Eton. Served War, Probyn's Horse, 1940–45 (MC; Burma); served 1st Royal Dragoons, 1946–47. Gladstone, Lyall Ltd, Calcutta, 1948–55; joined Booker McConnell, 1956; Dir, 1968–83; Chairman: Booker Line, 1968–83 (Dir, 1957–83); Coe Metcalf Shipping, 1977–83; McConnell Salmon Ltd, 1980–90 (Dir, 1973–90); Govt 'A' Dir, Mersey Docks and Harbour Co., 1974–80. Chairman: Liverpool Steam Ship Owners, 1971–72; Employers Assoc., Port of Liverpool, 1972–74; Vice-Chm., British Shipping Fedn, 1968–71; Pres., Gen. Council of British Shipping, 1982–83; Mem., Nat. Dock Labour Bd, 1986–90. Dir, The Racecourse Assoc. Ltd, 1984–90. *Recreation:* country sports. *Address:* Frog Hall, Tilston, Malpas, Cheshire SY14 7HB. *T:* Tilston (01829) 250320. *Club:* Army and Navy.

NICOLSON, Nigel, MBE 1945; FSA; FRSL; author; Director of Weidenfeld and Nicolson Ltd, 1948–92; *b* 19 Jan. 1917; 2nd *s* of late Hon. Sir Harold Nicolson, KCVO, CMG and Hon. V. Sackville-West, CH; *heir-pres.* to 4th Baron Carnock, *qv*; *m* 1953, Philippa Janet (marr. diss. 1970; she *d* 1987), *d* of Sir Gervais Tennyson d'Eyncourt, 2nd Bt; one *s* two *d*. *Educ:* Eton Coll.; Balliol Coll., Oxford. Capt. Grenadier Guards. Served War of 1939–45 in Tunisian and Italian Campaigns (MBE). Contested (C) NW Leicester, 1950, and

Falmouth and Camborne, 1951; MP (C) Bournemouth East and Christchurch, Feb. 1952–Sept. 1959. Chm. Exec. Cttee, UNA, 1961–66. Long Life Columnist, The Spectator, 1992–. *Publications:* The Grenadier Guards, 1939–45, 1949 (official history); People and Parliament, 1958; Lord of the Isles, 1960; Great Houses of Britain, 1965, revd edn 1978; (editor) Harold Nicolson: Diaries and Letters, 3 vols, 1966–68; Great Houses, 1968; Alex (FM Alexander of Tunis), 1973; Portrait of a Marriage, 1973; (ed) Letters of Virginia Woolf, 1975–80 (6 vols); The Himalayas, 1975; Mary Curzon, 1977 (Whitbread Award); Napoleon: 1812, 1985; (with Adam Nicolson) Two Roads to Dodge City, 1986; Kent, 1988; The World of Jane Austen, 1991; Vita and Harold: the letters of Vita Sackville-West and Harold Nicolson 1910–1962, 1992. *Recreation:* archæology. *Address:* Sissinghurst Castle, Cranbrook, Kent TN17 2AB. *T:* Cranbrook (01580) 714239. *Club:* Beefsteak.

NICOLSON, Roy Macdonald; Managing Director, Scottish Amicable Life Assurance Society, since 1990; *b* 12 June 1944; *s* of Alan Neil Nicolson and Mary Nicolson; *m* 1972, Jennifer Margaret Miller; one *s* one *d. Educ:* Paisley Grammar School. FFA, FPMI. Joined Scottish Amicable, 1960; Asst London Secretary, 1971; Asst Actuary, 1973; Pensions Manager (Operations), 1976; Asst Gen. Manager (Pensions), 1982; Gen. Manager (Systems), 1985; Dep. Chief Gen. Manager, 1990. *Recreations:* golf, bridge. *Address:* Scottish Amicable, Amicable House, 150 St Vincent Street, Glasgow G2 5NQ; Ardgarten, Doune Road, Dunblane, Perthshire FK15 9HR. *T:* Dunblane (01786) 823849. *Clubs:* Dunblane New Golf; Dun Whinny (Gleneagles).

NIEDUSZYŃSKI, Anthony John; Secretary to Monopolies and Mergers Commission, since 1993; *b* 7 Jan. 1939; *er s* of Tadeusz Adolf Antoni Nieduszyński, LLD and Madaleine Gladys Lilian (*née* Huggler); *m* 1980, Frances, *yr d* of Wing Comdr Max Oxford, OBE; one *d. Educ:* St Paul's School (Foundation Scholar); Merton College, Oxford (Postmaster; 1st cl. Hon. Mods 1959; 1st cl. Lit Hum 1961; MA). Board of Trade, 1964; Private Sec. to Pres. of BoT, 1967–68; Principal Private Sec. to Minister for Trade and Consumer Affairs, 1972–74 and to Sec. of State for Trade, 1974; Asst Sec., Dept of Prices and Consumer Protection, 1974, Dept of Industry, 1977, Home Office, 1982; Under Sec., DTI, 1985–93; Head: of Radiocommunications Div., 1985; of Air Div., 1988; of Business Task Forces Div. 2, 1990; of Aerospace Div., 1992. *Recreations:* gardening, fell walking, skating, linguistics, opera. *Address:* c/o Monopolies and Mergers Commission, New Court, 48 Carey Street, WC2A 2JT.

NIELD, Sir Basil Edward, Kt 1957; CBE 1956 (MBE 1943); DL; Judge of High Court of Justice, Queen's Bench Division, 1960–78; *b* 7 May 1903; *yr s* of late Charles Edwin Nield, JP, and Mrs F. E. L. Nield, MBE, Upton-by-Chester. *Educ:* Harrow Sch.; Magdalen Coll., Oxford (MA). Officers Emergency Reserve, 1938; served War of 1939–45: commnd Captain, 1940; GHQ MEF (Major), HQs E Africa Force, Palestine; Pres., Palestine Military Courts in Jerusalem; 9th Army, Beirut; HQs Eritrea and 8th Army; 1943: HQ Persia and Iraq; Asst Dep. Judge Advocate-Gen., ME (Lt-Col; despatches; MBE (mil.)); 21 Army Gp; HQ Lines of Communication, BLA, Normandy; HQ 2nd Army, Low Countries, Rhine; RARO until 1948. Called to Bar, Inner Temple, 1925, Master of the Bench, 1952, Reader, 1976, Treasurer, 1977; Northern Circuit, Chambers in Liverpool; KC 1945; Recorder of Salford, 1948–56; Recorder and first permanent Judge of Crown Court at Manchester, 1956–60; the only Judge to have presided at all sixty-one Assize towns in England and Wales before abolition of Assize system, 1972. Mem., Gen. Council of Bar, 1951. MP (C) City of Chester, 1940–56; sponsored as Private Member's Bill the Adoption of Children Act, 1949; Hon. Parly Chm., Dock and Harbour Authorities Assoc., 1944–50; Mem. Exec., 1922 Cttee; Mem., Special Cttee under Reorganisation Areas Measure for Province of York, 1944. Member: Magistrates' Rules Cttee, 1952–56; Legal Bd, Church Assembly, 1952–56; Home Secretary's Adv. Cttee on Treatment of Offenders, 1957. Chancellor, Diocese of Liverpool, 1948–56. Vice-President: Nat. Chamber of Trade, 1948–56; Graduate Teachers Assoc., 1950–56; Corp. of Secretaries, 1950; Assoc. of Managers of Approved Schools, 1956; Cheshire Soc. in London; Spastics Soc., Manchester. Chm., Chester Conservative Assoc., 1930–40. Member: Court, Liverpool Univ., 1948–56; Adv. Council, E-SU, 1951; Oxford Soc.; Imperial Soc. of Knights Bachelor; Life Mem., Royal Soc. of St George. Governor, Harrow Sch., 1961–71. FAMS. DL County Palatine of Chester, 1962–. Freeman, City of London, 1963. *Publication:* Farewell to the Assizes, 1972. *Address:* Osborne House, Isle of Wight PO32 6JY. *T:* Isle of Wight (01983) 200056. *Clubs:* Carlton; City, Grosvenor (Chester).

NIELSEN, Aksel Christopher W.; *see* Wiin-Nielsen.

NIELSEN, Hon. Erik H., DFC; PC (Can.) 1984; QC (Can.) 1962; Principal, Solar Electric Engineering Distributors, Canada, since 1992; President: Solar Electric Engineering Hawaii Inc., since 1993; Electricycle Inc., since 1994; *b* 24 Feb. 1924; *m* 1st, Pamela Hall (*d* 1969); three *c*; 2nd, 1983, Shelley Coxford. *Educ:* Dalhousie Univ. (LLB). Royal Canadian Air Force, 1942–51; flew Lancaster bombers, War of 1939–45. Called to the Bar of Nova Scotia, 1951; legal practice in Whitehorse, Yukon, 1952–. MP (PC) Yukon, 1957–87; Minister of Public Works, 1979–80; Dep. Opposition House Leader, Opposition House Leader, Leader of the Opposition, and Dep. Leader of the Opposition, 1980–84; Dep. Leader, Progressive Cons. Party, 1983; Dep. Prime Minister and Pres. of the Queen's Privy Council for Canada, 1984–85; Minister of Nat. Defence, 1985–86. Pres., Canadian Transport Commn, 1987; Chm., Nat. Transportation Agency of Canada, 1987–92. Dep. House Leader, 1980–81; Opposition appts, 1981–83. Chm., Ministerial Task Force on Program Review (report published, 1985). Member: Canadian Bar Assoc; Yukon Law Soc.; NS Barristers' Soc.; Hon. Mem., Whitehorse Chamber of Commerce; Hon. Life Mem., Yukon Chamber of Mines. *Publications:* Water Boy, 1987; The House is Not a Home, 1989. *Address:* MSPO PO Box 31024, Whitehorse, Yukon Y1A 5P7, Canada.

NIEMEYER, Oscar; architect; *b* Rio de Janeiro, 15 Dec. 1907; *s* of Oscar Niemeyer Soares; *m* Anita Niemeyer; one *d. Educ:* Escola Nacional de Beles Artes, Univ. of Brazil. Joined office of Lúcio Costa, 1935; worked on Min. of Education and Health Building, Rio de Janeiro, Brazilian Pavilion, NY World Fair, etc., 1936–41. Major projects include: Pamphulha, Belo Horizonte, 1941–43; also Quintandinha, Petrópolis; Exhibition Hall, São Paulo, 1953; Brasilia (Dir of Architecture), 1957–. Brazilian Rep., UN Bd of Design Consultants, 1947. Lenin Peace Prize, 1963; Prix Internat. de l'Architecture Aujourd'hui, 1966. *Address:* 3940 avenida Atlântica, Rio de Janeiro, Brazil.

NIENOW, Prof. Alvin William, FEng 1985; Professor and Director of Biochemical Engineering, BBSRC (formerly SERC) Centre for Biochemical Engineering, University of Birmingham, since 1989; *b* 19 June 1937; *o s* of late Alvin William Nienow and Mary May Nienow (*née* Hawthorn); *m* 1959, Helen Mary Sparkes; two *s* one *d. Educ:* St Clement Danes Grammar Sch.; University Coll. London (BSc Eng, 1st Cl. Hons; PhD; DSc Eng). FIChemE, CEng. Industry, 1958–61; Lectr and Sen. Lectr, 1963–80, Hon. Res. Fellow, 1980–, Dept of Chem. and Biochem. Engineering, UCL; University of Birmingham: Prof. of Chem. Engineering, 1980–89. Vis. Prof., Fellow and Lectr, China and Japan. Member: AFRC, 1987–90; Biotechnol. Directorate, SERC, 1990–93; Engrg Bd, SERC, then EPSRC, 1991–94; Planning and Resources Bd, BBSRC, 1994–; Council, IChemE, 1984–89; Scientific Adv. Cttee, EFCE, 1987–94; numerous other scientific and engrg bodies. Consultant: BHR Gp Fluid Mixing Processes, 1985–; Rhône-Poulenc Conseil Technologique, 1988–. Moulton Medal, IChemE, 1984; Jan E. Purkyne Medal, Czech Acad. of Science, 1993. *Publications:* (jtly) Mixing in the Process Industries, 1985, 2nd edn 1992; (ed) Bioreactor and Bioprocess Fluid Dynamics, 1993; numerous papers on mixing, fluidisation and biochem. engrg in learned jls. *Recreations:* sport, travel, dancing, music, real ale. *Address:* BBSRC Centre for Biochemical Engineering, School of Chemical Engineering, The University, Edgbaston, Birmingham B15 2TT. *T:* 0121–414 5325. *Clubs:* Athenæum, MCC; Edgbaston Priory, Reading Cricket.

NIGERIA, Metropolitan Archbishop and Primate of, since 1988; **Most Rev. Joseph Abiodun Adetiloye;** Bishop of Lagos, since 1985. *Educ:* Melville Hall, Ibadan; King's Coll., London (BD); Wycliffe Hall, Oxford. Ordained, dio. of Lagos, 1954; Lect, 1962, Vice Principal, 1963–66, Immanuel Coll., Ibadan; Provost, Ibadan Cathedral, 1966–70; Bishop of Ekiti, 1970–85. Mem., Eames Commn. *Address:* PO Box 13 (Bishopscourt, 29 Marina), Lagos, Nigeria. *Fax:* (1) 631264.

NIGHTINGALE, Benedict; *see* Nightingale, W. B. H.

NIGHTINGALE, Sir Charles (Manners Gamaliel), 17th Bt *cr* 1628; Senior Executive Officer, Department of Health, since 1989; *b* 21 Feb. 1947; *s* of Sir Charles Athelstan Nightingale, 16th Bt, and Evelyn Nadine Frances (*d* 1995), *d* of late Charles Arthur Diggens; *S* father, 1977. *Educ:* St Paul's School. BA Hons Open Univ., 1990. Entered DHSS as Executive Officer, 1969; Higher Executive Officer, 1977. *Heir: cousin* Edward Lacy George Nightingale, *b* 11 May 1938. *Address:* 16 Unity Grove, Harrogate HG1 2AQ.

NIGHTINGALE, Edward Humphrey, CMG 1955; farmer in Kenya since 1954; *b* 19 Aug. 1904; *s* of Rev. Edward Charles Nightingale and Ada Mary Nightingale; *m* 1944, Evelyn Mary Ray; three *s* one *d. Educ:* Rugby Sch.; Emmanuel Coll., Cambridge. Joined Sudan Political Service, 1926; Dep. Civil Sec., Sudan Government, 1951–52; Gov., Equatoria Province, Sudan, 1952–54. Order of the Nile, 4th Class, 1940. *Recreations:* carpentry, ornithology, photography. *Address:* Nunjoro Farm, PO Box 100, Naivasha, Kenya. *T:* (311) 21100. *Clubs:* Muthaiga Country (Nairobi); Naivasha Sports (Naivasha).

NIGHTINGALE, Sir John (Cyprian), Kt 1975; CBE 1970; BEM 1941; QPM 1965; DL; Chief Constable, Essex, 1962–69 and 1974–78, retired (Essex and Southend-on-Sea Joint Constabulary, 1969–74); *b* 16 Sept. 1913; *s* of Herbert Paul Nightingale, Sydenham, London; *m* 1947, Patricia Mary, *d* of Norman Maclaren, Glasgow University. *Educ:* Cardinal Vaughan Sch., Kensington; University Coll., London. Joined Metropolitan Police, 1935; Asst Chief Constable, Essex, 1958. Chm., Police Council, 1976–78; Mem., Parole Bd, 1978–82. Served with RNVR, 1943–45. DL Essex 1975. *Publications:* various police pubns. *Address:* Great Whitman's Farm, Purleigh, Essex CM3 6RW.

NIGHTINGALE of Cromarty, Michael David, OBE 1960; BSc; BLitt; FSA; Baron of Cromarty; Esquire Bedell, University of London, 1953–94; Chairman, Anglo-Indonesian Corporation plc, since 1971; *b* 6 Dec. 1927; *s* of late Victor Russell John Nightingale, Wormshill, Kent; *m* 1st, 1951, Antonia (marr. diss. 1956), *d* of Stephen Coleby Morland, Glastonbury; 2nd, 1956, Hilary Marion Olwen, *d* of late John Eric Jones, Swansea; two *s* three *d. Educ:* Winchester; Wye Coll.; Magdalen Coll., Oxford. Organised Exhibition from Kent Village Churches, Canterbury, 1951; Asst to Investment Manager, Anglo-Iranian Oil Co., 1951–53; Investment Adviser, Univ. of London, 1954–66; Advr, Kuwait Investment Bd, 1961–62; Dir, Charterhouse Japhet Ltd, 1965–70. Chm., Chillington Corp. plc, 1986–89. Secretary: Museums Assoc. (and Editor of Museums Jl), 1954–60; Museum Cttee, Carnegie UK Trust, 1954–60; Member: Advisory Council on Export of Works of Art, 1954–60; British Cttee of International Council of Museums, 1956–60; Canterbury Diocesan Advisory Cttee, 1964–79; Exec. Cttee, SE Arts Assoc., 1974–77; Area Archaeol. Adv. Cttee for SE England, 1975–79; Investment Cttee, Univs Superannuation Scheme, 1977–84; Mem. Bd, Commonwealth Develt Corp., 1985–92. Mem., Gen. Synod of C of E, 1979–85 (Panel of Chairmen, 1984–85). Member: Kent CC, 1973–77; Maidstone Borough Council, 1973– (Chm., Planning Cttee, 1973–77; Leader, 1976–77; Mayor, 1984–85). Vice-Pres., North Downs Soc.; Chm., Churches Cttee, Kent Archaeological Soc. Dep. Steward, Royal Manor of Wye, 1954–; Asst, Rochester Bridge, 1985– (Warden, 1989–92); a Lord of the Level of Romney Marsh. *Publications:* articles on agrarian and museum subjects. *Address:* Wormshill Court, Sittingbourne, Kent ME9 0TS. *T:* Wormshill (01622) 884235; Perceval House, 21 Dartmouth Row, Greenwich, SE10 8AW. *T:* 0181–692 6033; Cromarty House, Ross and Cromarty IV11 8XS. *T:* Cromarty (01381) 600265.

NIGHTINGALE, Nicholas John; National Secretary, National Council, Young Men's Christian Association, since 1993; *b* 29 Aug. 1942; *s* of late Christopher, (Toby), and of Muriel, (Buster), Nightingale; *m* 1968, Sue Lyth (Rev. Sue Nightingale); one *s* two *d* (and one *d* decd). *Educ:* Brighton, Hove and Sussex GS; Trinity Coll., Dublin (BA, LLB 1964); Harvard Business Sch. (AMP 1983). Qualified as solicitor, 1968; Solicitor, Slaughter & May, 1970–74; Partner, Patterson Glenton & Stracey, 1974; Solicitor and Co. Sec., Rowntree Mackintosh, 1975–85; Exec. Dir, Rowntree plc, 1985–89; Co. Sec., Tate & Lyle, 1989–93. Director: Tom Smith Crackers, 1983–85; Original Cookie Co., 1985–89; Cookie Jar, 1989–; Ellis Patents, 1990–. Chm., Service 9, Bristol Council of Social Service, 1966–70; Treas., YMCA Metropolitan Reg., 1992–93. Vice Chm., Yorks Rural Community Council, 1985–89. *Recreations:* growing trees (especially apple), croquet. *Address:* YMCA, 640 Forest Road, Walthamstow, E17 3DZ. *T:* 0181–520 5599; 31 Shakespeare Tower, Barbican, EC2Y 8DR.

NIGHTINGALE, Roger Daniel; economist and strategist; *b* 5 June 1945; *s* of Douglas Daniel John Nightingale and Edna Kathleen Vincent; one *s* three *d. Educ:* Welwyn Garden City Grammar Sch.; Keele Univ. (BA double hons Maths and Econs); University Coll. London (MSc Stats). Economist, Hoare & Co., 1968; Datastream, 1972, Dir, 1975; Hoare Govett, 1976, Dir, 1980; Head of Economics and Strategy Dept, Smith New Court, 1988–90; founded Roger Nightingale & Associates, consultancy firm, 1990. *Publications:* articles in financial magazines and newspapers. *Recreations:* snooker, collecting dictionaries, European history. *Address:* 22 Lonsdale Road, Chiswick, W4 1ND. *Club:* Reform.

NIGHTINGALE, (William) Benedict (Herbert); theatre critic, The Times, since 1990; *b* 14 May 1939; *s* of late Ronald Nightingale and Hon. Evelyn Nightingale, *d* of 1st Baron Burghclere; *m* 1964, Anne Bryan Redmon; two *s* one *d. Educ:* Charterhouse Sch.; Magdalene College, Cambridge (BA Hons); Univ. of Pennsylvania. General writer and northern drama critic, The Guardian, 1963–66; Literary Editor, New Society, 1966–68; theatre critic, New Statesman, 1968–86; Sunday theatre critic, New York Times, 1983–84; Prof. of English, Theatre and Drama, Univ. of Michigan, 1986–89. *Publications:* Charities, 1973; Fifty Modern British Plays, 1981; Fifth Row Center, 1985. *Address:* 40 Broomhouse Road, SW6 3QX. *Club:* Hurlingham.

NIKLASSON, Frau Bertil; *see* Nilsson, Birgit.

NIKLAUS, Prof. Robert, BA, PhD London; LèsL Lille; DrUniv Rennes *hc* 1963; Hon. DLitt Exon 1981; Officier de l'Ordre National du Mérite, 1972; Professor of French, 1952–75, now Emeritus, also Head of Department of French and Spanish, 1958–64, French and Italian, 1964–75, University of Exeter (formerly University College of the South West); *b* 18 July 1910; *s* of late Jean Rodolphe and Elizabeth Niklaus; *m* 1st, 1935, Thelma (*née* Jones) (*d* 1970); two *s* one *d*; 2nd, 1973, Kathleen (*née* Folta). *Educ:* Lycée Français de Londres; University Coll., London; Univ. of Lille. Sen. Tutor, Toynbee Hall, London, 1931–32; Asst and Asst Lecturer at University Coll., 1932–38; Asst Lecturer, Lecturer, Univ. of Manchester, 1938–52. Dean of the Faculty of Arts, Exeter, 1959–62; Dep. Vice-Chancellor, 1965–67. Visiting Professor: Univ. of Calif., Berkeley, 1963–64; Case Western Reserve Univ., Ohio, 1971; Univ. of British Columbia, 1975–76; Univ. of Natal, Pietermaritzburg, 1978; Rhodes Univ., S Africa, 1990. Hd of Dept of Langs, Univ. of Nigeria, Nsukka, 1977–78. Pres., Assoc. of Univ. Teachers, 1954–55, Mem. Executive Cttee, 1948–62; Pres. Internat. Assoc. of Univ. Profs and Lecturers, 1960–64 (Vice-Pres., 1958–60, 1964–66); Member: Cttee of Modern Humanities Research Association, 1956–71; Cttee, Soc. for French Studies, 1965–72 (Vice-Pres., 1967–68 and 1970–71, Pres. 1968–69); Pres., British Soc. for XVIIIth Century Studies, 1970–72; Treasurer, Internat. Soc. for Eighteenth-century Studies, 1969–79; Post-graduate Awards Cttee of Min. of Education, 1956–61; Management Cttee, British Inst., Paris, 1965–67. Gen. Editor, Textes Français Classiques et Modernes, Hodder & Stoughton. *Publications:* Jean Moréas, Poète Lyrique, 1936; The Nineteenth Century (Post-Romantic) and After (in The Year's Work in Modern Language Studies, VII–XIII), 1937–52; Diderot and Drama, 1942; Beaumarchais, Le Barbier de Séville, 1968; A Literary History of France, the Eighteenth Century, 1970; Beaumarchais, Le Mariage de Figaro, 1983; critical editions of: J.-J. Rousseau, Les Rêveries du Promeneur Solitaire, 1942; Denis Diderot, Pensées Philosophiques, 1950; Denis Diderot, Lettre sur les Aveugles, 1951; Marivaux, Arlequin poli par l'Amour, 1959 (in collab. with Thelma Niklaus); Sedaine, La Gageure imprévue, 1970; (contrib.) Diderot: Œuvres Complètes, vol. II, 1975, vol. IV, 1979; articles in Encyclopaediæ and learned journals; textbooks for schools and universities. *Recreations:* aviculture, the theatre, the cinema. *Address:* 17 Elm Grove Road, Topsham, Exeter, Devon EX3 0EQ. *T:* Topsham (01392) 873627.

NIKOLAYEVA-TERESHKOVA, Valentina Vladimirovna; Hero of the Soviet Union; Order of Lenin; Gold Star Medal; Order of October Revolution; Joliot-Curie Peace Medal; Soviet cosmonaut; Chairman, Russian Association of Internatioanl Co-operation, since 1992; *b* Maslennikovo, 6 March 1937; *d* of late Vladimir and of Elena Fyodorovna Tereshkova; *m* 1963, Andrian Nikolayev (marr. diss.); one *d*. Formerly textile worker, Krasny Perekop mill, Yaroslavl; served on cttees; Sec. of local branch, Young Communist league, 1960; Member: CPSU, 1962–91; Central Cttee, CPSU, 1971; Deputy, 1966, Mem. of Presidium, 1970–90, Supreme Soviet of Russia; Pres., Soviet Women's Cttee, 1968. Joined Yaroslavl Air Sports Club, 1959, and started parachute jumping; joined Cosmonaut Training Unit, 1962; became first woman in the world to enter space when she made 48 orbital flights of the earth in spaceship Vostok VI, 16–19 June 1963. Nile Collar (Egypt), 1971; holds honours and citations from other countries. *Address:* Zvezdny Gorodok, Moscow, Russia.

NILSSON, Birgit, (Fru Bertil Niklasson); Swedish operatic soprano; *b* Karup, Kristianstadslaen, 1922. *Educ:* Stockholm Royal Academy of Music. Debut as singer, 1946; with Stockholm Opera, 1947–51. Has sung at Glyndebourne, 1951; Bayreuth, 1953, 1954, 1957–70; Munich, 1954–58; Hollywood Bowl, Buenos Aires, Florence, 1956; La Scala, Milan, 1958; Covent Garden, 1957, 1960, 1962, 1963, 1973 and 1977; Edinburgh, 1959; Metropolitan, New York, 1959; Moscow, 1964; also in most leading opera houses and festivals of the world. Particularly well-known for her Wagnerian rôles. Austrian Kammersängerin, 1968; Bavarian Kammersängerin, 1970. Hon. RAM, 1970. Hon. Dr: Andover Univ., Mass, 1970; Manhattan Sch. of Music, NY, 1982; East Lansing Univ. of Fine Arts, Mich, 1982. Swedish Royal Acad. of Music's Medal for Promotion of Art of Music, 1968; Swedish Golden Medal (cl. 18 *illis quorum*) (only lady to be so honoured). Comdr of the Vasa Order (1st cl.), Sweden, 1974.

NILSSON, Lars-Åke; Ambassador of Sweden to the Court of St James's, since 1995; *b* 23 May 1943; *s* of Hans and Olga Nilsson; *m* 1974, Charlotte Arnell. *Educ:* Univ. of Lund (MBA 1966). Joined Swedish Diplomatic Service, 1968: Attaché, Paris, 1969; Attaché and Second Sec., Tokyo, 1970–73; 2nd Sec., Washington, 1973–76; 1st Sec., Stockholm, 1976–79; Dep. Asst Under-Sec., Stockholm, 1979–80; Counsellor, London, 1980–84; Minister, Moscow, 1984–88; Ambassador to Czechoslovakia, 1988–91; Perm. Under-Sec., Stockholm, 1991–95. *Publications:* articles and booklets. *Recreations:* reading, talking, spectator sports, especially cricket and football. *Address:* Embassy of Sweden, 11 Montagu Place, W1H 2AL. *T:* 0171–724 2101. *Clubs:* Travellers', Savile; Sällskapet (Stockholm); Swedish Jockey.

NIMMO, Derek Robert; actor, author and producer; *b* 19 Sept. 1932; *s* of Harry Nimmo and Marjorie Sudbury (*née* Hardy); *m* 1955, Patricia Sybil Ann Brown; two *s* one *d*. *Educ:* Quarry School, Liverpool. *Stage:* First appearance, Hippodrome, Bolton, as Ensign Blades in Quality Street, 1952; repertory and variety; Waltz of the Toreadors, Criterion, 1957; Duel of Angels, Apollo, 1958; How Say You?, Aldwych, 1959; The Amorous Prawn, Saville, 1959; The Irregular Verb to Love, Criterion, 1961; See How They Run, Vaudeville, 1964; Charlie Girl, Adelphi, 1965–71 and overseas, 1971–72; Babes in the Wood, Palladium, 1972; Why Not Stay for Breakfast?, Apollo, 1973–75, and overseas tours; Same Time Next Year, Prince of Wales, 1978; Shut Your Eyes and Think of England, Australia, 1979; See How They Run, Shaftesbury, 1984; A Friend Indeed, Shaftesbury, 1984; The Cabinet Minister, Albery, 1991–92; produced and appeared in numerous plays and countries for Intercontinental Entertainment, 1976–; *television: series include:* All Gas and Gaiters; Oh Brother; Oh Father; Sorry I'm Single; The Bed Sit Girl; My Honorable Mrs; The World of Wooster; Blandings Castle; Life Begins at Forty; Third Time Lucky; Hell's Bells; *interview series:* If it's Saturday it must be Nimmo; Just a Nimmo; numerous other appearances; *radio:* Just A Minute, 1968–; *films include:* Casino Royale; The Amorous Prawn; The Bargee; Joey Boy; A Talent for Loving; The Liquidator; Tamahine; One of our Dinosaurs is Missing. RTS Silver Medal, 1970; Variety Club Show Business Personality of the Year, 1971. Freeman, City of London, 1991. *Publications:* Derek Nimmo's Drinking Companion, 1979; Shaken and Stirred, 1984; (ed) Oh, Come On All Ye Faithful!, 1986; Not in Front of the Servants, 1987; Up Mount Everest Without a Paddle, 1988; As the Actress said to the Bishop, 1989; Wonderful Window Boxes, 1990; Table Talk, 1990; Memorable Dinners, 1991. *Recreations:* sailing, collecting English 17th and 18th century walnut furniture and Derby porcelain. *Address:* c/o Michael Whitehall Ltd, 125 Gloucester Road, SW7 4TE. *T:* 0171–244 8466. *Clubs:* Garrick; Beefsteak; Lord's Taverners; Athenæum (Liverpool).

NIMMO, Hon. Sir John (Angus), Kt 1972; CBE 1970; Justice of the Federal Court of Australia, 1977–80; Justice of Australian Industrial Court, 1969–80; *b* 15 Jan. 1909; *s* of John James Nimmo and Grace Nimmo (*née* Mann); *m* 1st, 1935, Teanie Rose Galloway (*d* 1984); two *s*; 2nd, 1985, Maude Pearce. *Educ:* Univ. of Melbourne. Admitted to practise at Victorian Bar, 1933. QC 1957. Mem., Commonwealth Taxation Bd of Review No 2, 1947–54; Actg Supreme Court Justice, Victoria, 1963; Dep. Pres., Commonwealth Conciliation and Arbitration Commn, 1964–69; Chm., Health Insce Cttee of Enquiry, 1968–69. Dep. Pres., Trade Practices Tribunal, 1966–73, also a Justice of Supreme Courts of ACT and NT, 1966–74; on secondment as Chief Justice of Fiji, 1972–74. Royal Comr into future of Norfolk Is, 1975–76; Chm., Commonwealth Legal Aid Commn, 1978–79; Mem., Cttee on Overseas Professional Qualifications, 1978–82. OStJ 1945. *Recreations:* reading, walking. *Address:* 3/9 Dalsten Grove, Mount Eliza, Vic 3930, Australia. *T:* (3) 7877252.

NIMMO SMITH, William Austin, QC (Scot.) 1982; *b* 6 Nov. 1942; *s* of Dr Robert Herman Nimmo Smith and Mrs Ann Nimmo Smith; *m* 1968, Jennifer Main; one *s* one *d*. *Educ:* Eton Coll. (King's Scholar, 1956); Balliol Coll., Oxford (BA Hons Lit. Hum. 1965); Edinburgh Univ. (LLB 1967). Admitted to Faculty of Advocates, 1969; Standing Junior Counsel to Dept of Employment, 1977–82; Advocate-Depute, 1983–86. Chairman: Medical Appeal Tribunals, 1986–91; Vaccine Damage Tribunals, 1986–91; Mem. (part-time), Scottish Law Commn, 1988–. *Recreations:* hill-walking, music. *Address:* 29 Ann Street, Edinburgh EH4 1PL. *Club:* New (Edinburgh).

NIND, Philip Frederick, OBE 1979; TD 1946; Director, Foundation for Management Education, 1968–83; Secretary, Council of Industry for Management Education, 1969–83; *b* 2 Jan. 1918; *s* of W. W. Nind, CIE; *m* 1944, Fay Allardice Crofton (*née* Errington) (*d* 1991); two *d*. *Educ:* Blundell's Sch.; Balliol Coll., Oxford (MA). War service, 1939–46, incl. Special Ops in Greece and Albania (despatches), 1943–44, Mil. Govt Berlin, 1945–46 (Major). Shell Gp of Cos in Venezuela, Cyprus, Lebanon, Jordan and London, 1939–68. Educn and Trng Cttee, CBI (formerly FBI), 1961–68; OECD Working Gp on Management Educn, 1966–69; Nat. Adv. Council on Educn for Industry and Commerce, 1967–70; UGC Management Studies Cttee, 1968–83; NEDO Management Educn Trng and Develt Cttee, 1968–83; Chm., NEDO Management Teacher Panel, 1969–72; Member: Council for Techn. Educn and Trng for Overseas Countries, 1970–75; CNAA Management Studies Bd, 1971–83; Vice-Pres., European Foundn for Management Develt, 1978–83. Member: Oxford Univ. Appts Cttee, 1967–83; Grand Council, Royal Academy of Dancing, 1988– (Mem. Exec. Cttee, 1970–88); Governor: Univ. of Keele, 1961–; Bedford Coll., London Univ., 1967–85. Hon. Fellow, London Business School, 1988. FRSA. Chevalier, Order of Cedars of Lebanon, 1959; Grand Cross, Orders of St Mark and Holy Sepulchre, 1959. *Publications:* (jtly) Management Education and Training Needs of Industry, 1963; Fourth Stockton Lecture, 1973; A Firm Foundation, 1985; Never a Dull Moment, 1991; articles in various jls. *Club:* Special Forces.

NINEHAM, Rev. Prof. Dennis Eric, DD (Oxon); BD (Cantab); Hon. DD (Birmingham); Hon. DD (BDS Yale); Professor of Theology and Head of Theology Department, Bristol University, 1980–86, now Emeritus; Honorary Canon of Bristol Cathedral, 1980–86, now Emeritus; *b* 27 Sept. 1921; *o c* of Stanley Martin and Bessie Edith Nineham, Shirley, Southampton; *m* 1946, Ruth Corfield, *d* of Rev. A. P. Miller; two *s* two *d*. *Educ:* King Edward VI Sch., Southampton; Queen's Coll., Oxford (Hon. Fellow, 1991). Asst Chaplain of Queen's Coll., 1944; Chaplain, 1945; Fellow and Praelector, 1946; Tutor, 1949; Prof. of Biblical and Historical Theology, Univ. of London (King's Coll.), 1954–58; Prof. of Divinity, Univ. of London, 1958–64; Regius Prof. of Divinity, Cambridge Univ., and Fellow, Emmanuel Coll., 1964–69; Warden of Keble Coll., Oxford, 1969–79, Hon. Fellow, 1980. FKC 1963. Examining Chaplain: to Archbishop of York and to Bishop of Ripon; to Bishop of Sheffield, 1947–54; to Bishop of Norwich, 1964–73; to Bishop of Bristol, 1981–. Vis. Prof., Rikkyo Univ., Tokyo, 1994. Select Preacher to Univ. of Oxford, 1954–56, 1971, 1990, 1992, 1994, and to Univ. of Cambridge, 1959; Proctor in Convocation of Canterbury: for London Univ., 1955–64; for Cambridge Univ., 1965–69. Mem. General Synod of Church of England for Oxford Univ., 1970–76; Mem., C of E Doctrine Commn, 1968–76. Roian Fleck Resident-in-Religion, Bryn Mawr Coll., Pa, 1974; Provost's Visitor, Trinity Coll., Toronto, 1992. Governor of Haileybury, 1966–93. *Publications:* The Study of Divinity, 1960; A New Way of Looking at the Gospels, 1962; Commentary on St Mark's Gospel, 1963; The Use and Abuse of the Bible, 1976; Explorations in Theology, no 1, 1977; Christianity Mediaeval and Modern, 1993; (Editor) Studies in the Gospels: Essays in Honour of R. H. Lightfoot, 1955; The Church's Use of the Bible, 1963; The New English Bible Reviewed, 1965; contrib. to: Studies in Ephesians (editor F. L. Cross), 1956; On the Authority of the Bible, 1960; Religious Education, 1944–1984, 1966; Theologians of Our Time, 1966; Christian History and Interpretation, 1967; Christ for us To-day, 1968; Christian Believing, 1976; The Myth of God Incarnate, 1977; Imagination and the Future, 1980; God's Truth, 1988; A Dictionary of Biblical Interpretation, 1990; Resurrection, 1994. *Recreations:* reading, walking. *Address:* 4 Wootten Drive, Iffley Turn, Oxford OX4 4DS. *T:* Oxford (01865) 715941.

See also Very Rev. J. H. Drury.

NINIS, Ven. Richard Betts; Archdeacon of Lichfield (formerly Stafford) and Treasurer of Lichfield Cathedral, since 1974; *b* 25 Oct. 1931; *s* of late George Woodward Ninis and Mary Gertrude Ninis; *m* 1967, Penelope Jane Harwood; two *s* one *d*. *Educ:* Lincoln Coll., Oxford (MA); Bishop's Hostel, Lincoln (GOE). Curate, All Saints, Poplar, 1955–62; Vicar of: St Martins, Hereford, 1962–71; Bullinghope and Dewsall with Callow, 1966–71. Diocesan Missioner for Hereford, 1971–74. Chm., USPG, 1988–91. Chm., Derbyshire Coll. of Higher Educn, 1978–90; Vice Chm., Univ. of Derby, 1992–. *Recreations:* gardening, travel. *Address:* 24 The Close, Lichfield, Staffs WS13 7LD. *T:* Lichfield (01543) 258813.

NIRENBERG, Dr Marshall Warren; Research Biochemist; Chief, Laboratory of Biochemical Genetics, National Heart, Lung and Blood Institute, National Institutes of Health, Bethesda, Md, since 1966; *b* New York, 10 April 1927; *m* 1961, Perola Zaltzman; no *c*. *Educ:* Univs of Florida (BS, MS) and Michigan (PhD). Univ. of Florida: Teaching Asst, Zoology Dept, 1945–50; Res. Associate, Nutrition Lab., 1950–52; Univ. of Michigan: Teaching and Res. Fellow, Biol Chemistry Dept, 1952–57; Nat. Insts of Health, Bethesda: Postdoctoral Fellow of Amer. Cancer Soc., Nat. Inst. Arthritis and Metabolic Diseases, 1957–59, and of Public Health Service, Section of Metabolic Enzymes, 1959–60; Research Biochemist, Section of Metabolic Enzymes, 1960–62 and Section of Biochem. Genetics, 1962–66. Member: Amer. Soc. Biol Chemists; Amer. Chem. Soc.; Amer. Acad. Arts and Sciences; Biophys. Soc.; Nat. Acad. Sciences; Washington Acad. Sciences; Sigma Xi; Soc. for Study of Development and Growth; (Hon.) Harvey Soc.; Leopoldina Deutsche Akademie der Naturforscher; Neurosciences Research Program, MIT; NY Acad. Sciences; Pontifical Acad. Science, 1974. Robbins Lectr, Pomona Coll., 1967; Remsden Mem. Lectr, Johns Hopkins Univ., 1967. Numerous awards and prizes, including Nobel Prize in Medicine or Physiology (jtly), 1968. Hon. Dr Science: Michigan, Yale, and Chicago, 1965; Windsor, 1966; Harvard Med. Sch., 1968; Hon. PhD, Weitzmann Inst. of Science, Israel, 1978. *Publications:* numerous contribs to learned jls and chapters in symposia. *Address:* Laboratory of Biochemical Genetics, National Heart, Lung and Blood Institute, Bethesda, MD 20892, USA; 7001 Orkney Parkway, Bethesda, MD, USA.

NISBET, Prof. Hugh Barr; Professor of Modern Languages, University of Cambridge, since 1982; Professorial Fellow, Sidney Sussex College, since 1982; *b* 24 Aug. 1940; *s* of

Thomas Nisbet and Lucy Mary Hainsworth; *m* 1962, Monika Luise Ingeborg Uecker; two *s*. *Educ:* Dollar Acad.; Univ. of Edinburgh. MA, PhD 1965. University of Bristol: Asst Lectr in German, 1965–67; Lectr, 1967–72; Reader, 1972–73; Prof. of German Lang. and Lit., Univ. of St Andrews, 1974–81. Mem., Gen. Teaching Council for Scotland, 1978–81. Pres., British Soc. for Eighteenth Century Studies, 1986–88. Governor, Dollar Acad., 1978–81. Jt Editor, Cambridge Studies in German, 1983–; Germanic Editor, 1973–80, Gen. Editor, 1981–84, Modern Language Rev. *Publications:* Herder and the Philosophy and History of Science, 1970; (ed with Hans Reiss) Goethe's Die Wahlverwandtschaften, 1971; Goethe and the Scientific Tradition, 1972; (ed) German Aesthetic and Literary Criticism: Winckelmann to Goethe, 1985; (ed with Peter Brooks and Claude Rawson) Cambridge History of Literary Criticism, 9 vols, 1989–; (ed with John Hibberd) Texte, Motive und Gestalten der Goethezeit, 1989; *translations:* Kant, Political Writings, 1970, 2nd edn 1991; Hegel, Lectures on the Philosophy of World History, 1975, 2nd edn 1980; Hegel, Elements of the Philosophy of Right, 1991; articles and reviews on German literature and thought. *Recreations:* music, art history, cycling. *Address:* Sidney Sussex College, Cambridge CB2 3HU. *T:* Cambridge (01223) 338877.

NISBET, Prof. John Donald, OBE 1981; MA, BEd, PhD; FEIS; Professor of Education, Aberdeen University, 1963–88; *b* 17 Oct. 1922; *s* of James Love Nisbet and Isabella Donald; *m* 1952, Brenda Sugden; one *s* one *d*. *Educ:* Dunfermline High Sch.; Edinburgh Univ. (MA, BEd); PhD (Aberdeen); Teacher's Certif. (London). FEIS 1975; Royal Air Force, 1943–46. Teacher, Fife, 1946–48; Lectr, Aberdeen Univ., 1949–63. Editor: British Jl of Educnl Psychology, 1967–74; Studies in Higher Education, 1979–84; Chairman: Educnl Research Bd, SSRC, 1972–75; Cttee on Primary Educn, 1974–80; Scottish Council for Research in Educn, 1975–78; President: British Educnl Research Assoc., 1975; Scottish Inst. of Adult and Continuing Educn, 1991. *Publications:* Family Environment, 1953; Age of Transfer to Secondary Education, 1966; Transition to Secondary Education, 1969; Scottish Education Looks Ahead, 1969; Educational Research Methods, 1970; Educational Research in Action, 1972; Impact of Research, 1980; Towards Community Education, 1980; (ed) World Yearbook of Education, 1985; Learning Strategies, 1986; Educational Disadvantage, 1994; papers in jls on educnl psychology and curriculum develt. *Recreations:* golf, orienteering. *Address:* 7 Lawson Avenue, Banchory AB31 3TW. *T:* Banchory (01330) 823145.
See also S. D. Nisbet.

NISBET, Prof. Robin George Murdoch, FBA 1967; Corpus Christi Professor of Latin, Oxford, 1970–92; Fellow of Corpus Christi College, Oxford, 1952–92, Hon. Fellow 1992; *b* 21 May 1925; *s* of R. G. Nisbet, Univ. Lecturer, and A. T. Husband; *m* 1969, Anne, *d* of Dr J. A. Wood. *Educ:* Glasgow Academy; Glasgow Univ.; Balliol Coll., Oxford (Snell Exhibitioner; Hon. Fellow, 1989). Tutor in Classics, Corpus Christi College, Oxford, 1952–70. *Publications:* Commentary on Cicero, *in Pisonem,* 1961; (with M. Hubbard) on Horace, *Odes I,* 1970; *Odes II,* 1978; Collected Papers on Latin Literature, 1995. *Recreation:* 20th century history. *Address:* 80 Abingdon Road, Cumnor, Oxford OX2 9QW. *T:* Oxford (01865) 862482.

NISBET, Prof. Stanley Donald; Professor of Education, University of Glasgow, 1951–78; *b* 26 July 1912; *s* of Dr J. L. and Isabella Nisbet; *m* 1942, Helen Alison Smith; one *s* one *d*. *Educ:* Dunfermline High Sch., Edinburgh Univ. MA (1st Cl. Hons Classics), 1934; Diploma in Education, 1935; BEd (with distinction in Education and Psychology), 1940. Taught in Moray House Demonstration Sch., Edinburgh, 1935–39. Served War in RAF, 1940–46; research officer at Air Ministry, 1944–46. Lecturer in Education, Univ. of Manchester, Feb.-Sept. 1946; Prof. of Education, Queen's Univ. of Belfast, 1946–51. FRSE 1955; FEIS 1976. *Publications:* Purpose in the Curriculum, 1957; (with B. L. Napier) Promise and Progress, 1970; articles in psychological and educational journals. *Recreations:* walking, sailing. *Address:* 6 Victoria Park Corner, Glasgow G14 9NZ.
See also J. D. Nisbet.

NISBET-SMITH, Dugal; Director, Newspaper Society, since 1983; *b* 6 March 1935; *s* of David and Margaret Homeward Nisbet-Smith; *m* 1959, Dr Ann Patricia Taylor; one *s* two *d*. *Educ:* Southland Boys' High Sch., Invercargill, NZ. Journalist on Southland Daily News, NZ, 1952–56; Features writer and reporter, Beaverbrook Newspapers, London, 1956–60; variously Asst Editor, Gen. Manager and Man. Dir, Barbados Advocate Co., Barbados, WI, Gen. Manager, Sierra Leone Daily Mail Ltd, W Africa, Dep. Gen. Manager, Trinidad Mirror Co., 1960–66; Sen. Industrial Relations Manager, Mirror Gp Newspapers, London, 1966–68; Develt Manager, 1969–71, Production Dir, 1971–73, Man. Dir, 1974–78, Scottish Daily Record and Sunday Mail Ltd, Glasgow; joined Bd, Mirror Gp Newspapers, 1976; Dir/General Manager, 1978–80, Man. Dir, 1980–81, Times Newspapers Ltd; Publishing Advr to HH the Aga Khan, Aiglemont, France, 1981–83. *Recreations:* travel, sculpture, painting. *Address:* The Butterfly, Borough Lane, Great Finborough, Stowmarket, Suffolk IP14 3AS. *T:* Stowmarket (01449) 774286.

NISSAN, Prof. Alfred Heskel, PhD, DSc (Chem. Eng, Birmingham), FIChemE, FAIChE, FAIC; Member Sigma XI; Consultant to WESTVACO (formerly West Virginia Pulp and Paper), New York (Vice-President, 1967–79, and Corporate Director of Research, 1962–79); Professor, College of Environmental Science and Forestry, Syracuse, New York, since 1979; *b* 14 Feb. 1914; *s* of Heskel and Farha Nissan, Baghdad, Iraq; *m* 1940, Zena Gladys Phyllis, *o d* of late Phillip and Lillian Frances Pursehouse-Ahmed, Birmingham; one *d*. *Educ:* The American Sch. for Boys, Baghdad, Iraq; Univ. of Birmingham. Instn of Petroleum Scholarship, 1936; first cl. Hons BSc 1937; Sir John Cadman Medal, 1937; Instn of Petroleum Medal and Prize and Burgess Prize, 1937; Research Fellow, 1937, Lectr, 1940, Univ. of Birmingham; Head of Central Research Laboratories, Bowater Paper Corporation Ltd, 1947; Technical Director in charge of Research, Bowaters Development and Research Ltd, 1950; Research Prof. of Wool Textile Engineering, the Univ. of Leeds, 1953; Prof. of Chemical Engineering, Rensselaer Polytechnic Inst., Troy, NY, USA, 1957. Hon. Vis. Prof., Uppsala Univ., 1974; ERCO Res. Fellow, Univ. of Toronto, 1987. Schwarz Memorial Lectr, Amer. Soc. of Mech. Engrs, 1967; Dow Dist. Lectr, Univ. of British Columbia, 1989. Member: Adv. Council for Advancement of Industrial R&D, State of NY, 1965–; Board of Directors: Technical Assoc. of Pulp & Paper Industry, 1968–71 (R&D Div. Award, 1976); Industrial Res. Inst., 1973–77. Bd of Trustees, Amer. Inst. of Chemists Foundn, 1989–91. Alexander Mitscheslich Medal, Zellcheming, W Germany, 1980; Gold Medal, Technical Assoc. of Pulp and Paper Industry, 1982. *Publications:* (ed) Textile Engineering Processes, 1959; (ed) Future Technical Needs and Trends in the Paper Industry, 1973; Lectures on Fiber Science in Paper, 1977; papers on physical chemistry and chemical engineering problems of petroleum, paper and textile technology in scientific jls. *Address:* 6A Dickel Road, Scarsdale, NY 10583, USA.

NISSEN, David Edgar Joseph; Solicitor to HM Customs and Excise, since 1992; *b* 27 Nov. 1942; *s* of Tunnock Edgar Nissen and Elsie Nissen (*née* Thorne); *m* 1969, Pauline Jennifer (*née* Meaden); two *d*. *Educ:* King's School, Chester; University College London (LLB). Solicitor, admitted 1969. Asst Solicitor, W Midlands Gas Board, 1969–70; Prosecuting Solicitor, Sussex Police Authority, 1970–73; HM Customs and Excise, 1973–90: Asst Solicitor, 1983–87; Principal Asst Solicitor, 1987–90; Legal Advr to Dept of Energy (Principal Asst Treasury Solicitor), 1990–92. *Recreations:* photography, music, gardening. *Address:* c/o HM Customs and Excise, New King's Beam House, SE1 9PJ.

NISSEN, George Maitland, CBE 1987; Chairman, Book Guild Ltd, since 1993; *b* 29 March 1930; *s* of Col Peter Norman Nissen, DSO, and Lauretta Maitland; *m* 1956, Jane Edmunds, *d* of late S. Curtis Bird, New York; two *s* two *d*. *Educ:* Eton; Trinity Coll., Cambridge (MA). National Service, KRRC, 1949–50, 2/Lieut. Sen. Partner, Pember & Boyle, Stockbrokers, 1982–86; Chm., Foreign & Colonial Emerging Markets Trust (formerly CDFC Trust) plc, 1987–; Director: Morgan Grenfell Gp, 1984–87 (Advr, 1987–92); Trades Union Unit Trust Managers Ltd; Govett Strategic Investment Trust; Festiniog Rly, 1993–. Mem., Stock Exchange, 1956–92 (Dep. Chm., 1978–81; Mem. Council, 1973–91); Chairman: Gilt-Edged Market Makers Assoc., 1986–92; IMRO, 1989–92; Dir, The Securities Assoc., 1986–89; Mem., Inflation Accounting Steering Gp, 1976–80. Non-exec. Dir, Ealing, Hammersmith and Hounslow HA, 1993–. Council, GPDST, 1993–. Governor: Reed's Sch., Cobham; Godolphin and Latymer School, Hammersmith; RAM; RSCM; Trustee, Lucy Cavendish Coll., Cambridge, 1994. Hon. FRAM 1994. *Recreations:* railways, music. *Address:* Swan House, Chiswick Mall, W4 2PS. *T:* 0181–994 8203.

NISSEN, Karl Iversen, MD, FRCS; retired Surgeon, Royal National Orthopædic Hospital, W1, 1946–71; Orthopædic Surgeon: Harrow Hospital 1946–71; Peace Memorial Hospital, Watford, 1948–71; *b* 4 April 1906; *s* of Christian and Caroline Nissen; *m* 1935, Margaret Mary Honor Schofield (*d* 1981); one *s* one *d*. *Educ:* Otago Boys' High Sch., Dunedin, NZ; Univ. of Otago, NZ. BSc (NZ) 1927; MB, ChB (NZ) 1932; MD (NZ) 1934; FRCS 1936. Served as Orthopædic Specialist, RNVR, 1943–45. Corresp. mem. Belgian, French, Swiss, German, Scandinavian, Norwegian, Finnish, Danish Socs of Orthopædics. Writes articles and gives talks on the genetics and cure of primary osteoarthrosis of the hip. *Recreation:* human origins. *Address:* Prospect House, The Avenue, Sherborne, Dorset DT9 3AJ. *T:* Sherborne (01935) 813539. *Club:* Naval.

NIVEN, Alastair Neil Robertson, PhD; Literature Director, Arts Council of England (formerly of Great Britain), since 1987; *b* 25 Feb. 1944; *s* of Harold Robertson Niven and Elizabeth Isobel Robertson Niven (*née* Mair); *m* 1970, Helen Margaret Trow; one *s* one *d*. *Educ:* Dulwich Coll.; Gonville and Caius Coll., Cambridge (MA); Univ. of Ghana (Commonwealth Schol.; MA); Univ. of Leeds (PhD). Lecturer in English: Univ. of Ghana, 1968–69; Univ. of Leeds, 1969–70; Lectr in English Studies, Univ. of Stirling, 1970–78; Dir Gen., Africa Centre, London, 1978–84; Chapman Fellow 1984–85, Hon. Fellow 1985, Inst. of Commonwealth Studies; Special Asst to Sec. Gen., ACU, 1985–87. Vis. Prof., Univ. of Aarhus, 1975–76; Vis. Fellow, Aust. Studies Centre, Univ. of London, 1985; Hon. Lectr, SOAS, 1979–85; Hon. Fellow, Univ. of Warwick, 1988. Editor, Jl of Commonwealth Literature, 1979–92. Chairman: Public Schools Debating Assoc. of Eng. and Wales, 1961–62; Literature Panel, GLAA, 1981–84; Sec. and Treas., Assoc. for Commonwealth Lit. and Lang. Studies, 1986–89; Welfare Policy Cttee, 1983–87, Exec. Cttee, 1987–92, UK Council for Overseas Student Affairs; Member: Public Affairs Cttee, Royal Commonwealth Soc., 1979–; Laurence Olivier Awards Theatre Panel, 1989–91; British Library Adv. Cttee for the Centre for the Book, 1990–; Judge, Booker Prize, 1994; Chm., Eurasia Reg., Commonwealth Writers' Prize, 1994, 1995. Mem. Editorial Bd, Annual Register, 1988–. *Publications:* The Commonwealth Writer Overseas (ed), 1976; D. H. Lawrence: the novels, 1978; The Yoke of Pity: the fiction of Mulk Raj Anand, 1978; D. H. Lawrence: the writer and his work, 1980; (with Sir Hugh W. Springer) The Commonwealth of Universities, 1987; (ed) Under Another Sky: the Commonwealth Poetry Prize anthology, 1987; articles in Afr. Affairs, Ariel, Brit. Book News, Jl of Commonwealth Lit., Jl of Indian Writing in English, Jl of RSA, Lit. Half-Yearly, Poetry Review, TES, THES, World Lit. Written in English, etc; study guides on Elechi Amadi, Wm Golding, R. K. Narayan, Raja Rao. *Recreations:* theatre, travel. *Address:* Eden House, 28 Weathercock Lane, Woburn Sands, Bucks MK17 8NT. *T:* Milton Keynes (01908) 582310. *Club:* Commonwealth Trust.
See also C. H. R. Niven.

NIVEN, Dr Colin Harold Robertson; Headmaster, Alleyn's School, Dulwich, since 1992; *b* 29 Sept. 1941; *s* of Harold Robertson Niven and late Elizabeth Isobel Robertson Niven (*née* Mair). *Educ:* Dulwich Coll.; Gonville and Caius Coll., Cambridge (MA); Brasenose Coll., Oxford (DipEd); Nancy Univ. (LèsL); Lille Univ. (Dr de l'Univ.). Lycée Mixte, Châlons-sur-Marne, 1963–64; Samuel Pepys Comprehensive Sch., 1964; Sedbergh Sch., 1964; Housemaster, Fettes Coll., 1965–73; Head of Mod. Langs, Sherborne Sch., 1973–83; Principal: Island Sch., Hong Kong, 1983–87; St George's English Sch., Rome, 1988–91; Vis. Fellow, Westminster Coll., Oxford, 1991; Dir of Internat. Liaison, Sherborne Internat. Study Centre, 1992. Chm., European Div., HMC, 1990–91. FRSA. CCF Medal 1983. *Publications:* Voltaire's Candide, 1978; Thomas Mann's Tonio Kröger, 1980; Vailland's Un jeune homme seul (critical edn), 1983; Island School: the first twenty years, 1987. *Recreations:* theatre, sport, foreign travel, cats. *Address:* Alleyn's School, Dulwich, SE22 8SU; 8 Dulwich Village, SE21 7AL. *T:* 0181–693 2983. *Clubs:* Royal Over-Seas League, Commonwealth Trust, English-Speaking Union.
See also A. N. R. Niven.

NIVEN, Ian; *see* Niven, J. R.

NIVEN, John Robertson, (Ian Niven); Under-Secretary, Department of the Environment, formerly Ministry of Housing and Local Government, 1974–79; *b* 11 May 1919; *s* of Robert Niven and Amelia Mary Hill; *m* 1946, Jane Bicknell; three *s*. *Educ:* Glasgow Academy; Jesus Coll., Oxford. Entered Min. of Town and Country Planning, 1946; Sec., Royal Commn on Local Govt in Greater London, 1957–60. *Address:* White Gates, Parham, Woodbridge, Suffolk IP13 9AA.

NIVEN, Margaret Graeme, ROI 1936; Landscape and Portrait Painter; *b* Marlow, 1906; *yr d* of William Niven, FSA, ARE, JP, Marlow Place, Marlow, Bucks, and Eliza Mary Niven. *Educ:* Prior's Field, Godalming. Studied at Winchester Sch. of Art, Heatherley Sch. of Fine Art, and under Bernard Adams, RP, ROI; Mem. of National Soc. Painters, Sculptors, and Engravers, 1932. Exhibitor at Royal Academy and Royal Soc. of Portrait Painters. Works purchased by Bradford Art Gallery, The Ministry of Works, Homerton Coll., Cambridge, and Bedford Coll., London. Served with WRNS, 1940–45. *Address:* Broomhill, Sandhills, Wormley, near Godalming, Surrey GU8 5UF.

NIVISON, family name of **Baron Glendyne.**

NIX, Prof. John Sydney; Emeritus Professor, University of London, since 1989 (Professor of Farm Business Management, 1982–89, and Head, Farm Business Unit, 1974–89, Wye College); *b* 27 July 1927; *s* of John William Nix and Eleanor Elizabeth (*née* Stears); *m* 1950, Mavis Marian (*née* Cooper); one *s* two *d*. *Educ:* Brockley County Sch.; University Coll. of the South-West. BSc Econ (London), MA Cantab. Instr Lieut, RN, 1948–51. Farm Economics Branch, Sch. of Agriculture, Univ. of Cambridge, 1951–61; Wye College: Farm Management Liaison Officer and Lectr, 1961–70; Sen. Tutor, 1970–72; Sen. Lectr, 1972–75; Reader, 1975–82; apptd to personal chair, the first in Farm Business Management in UK, 1982; Fellow, 1995. Founder Mem., Farm Management Assoc.,

1965; formerly Member: Study Groups etc. for Natural Resources (Tech.) Cttee; Agric. Adv. Council; ARC Tech. Cttee; ADAS Exptl and Develt Cttee; Meat and Livestock Commn; Countryside Commn. Programme Advr, Southern Television, 1966–81; Specialist Advr, Select Cttee on Agric., 1990–91. British Inst. of Management: Chm., Jl Cttee of Centre of Management of Agric., 1971–; Chm., Bd of Farm Management, 1979–81; Nat. Award for outstanding and continuing contrib. to advancement of management in agric. industry, 1982 (1st recipient). President: Agricl Economics Soc., 1990–91; Kingshay Farming Trust, 1991–; Assoc. of Indep. Crop Consultants, 1993–. CIMgt (CBIM 1983). FRSA 1984; FRAgS 1985; FIAgrM 1993. *Publications:* Farm Management Pocketbook, 1966, 26th edn 1995; (with C. S. Barnard) Farm Planning and Control, 1973, 2nd edn 1979, Spanish edn 1984; (with W. Butterworth) Farm Mechanisation for Profit, 1983; (with G. P. Hill and N. T. Williams) Land and Estate Management, 1987, 2nd edn 1989; articles in Jl of Agricl Econs, Jl of RASE, Farm Management, etc. *Recreations:* theatre, cinema, travel, rugby, cricket. *Address:* Wye College, Wye, Ashford, Kent TN25 5AH. *T:* Wye (01233) 812401. *Club:* Farmers'.

NIXON, Sir Edwin (Ronald), Kt 1984; CBE 1974; DL; Deputy Chairman, National Westminster Bank PLC, since 1987 (Director, since 1975); Chairman, Amersham International plc, since 1988 (Director, since 1987); *b* 21 June 1925; *s* of William Archdale Nixon and Ethel (*née* Corrigan); *m* 1952, Joan Lilian (*née* Hill); one *s* one *d*. *Educ:* Alderman Newton's Sch., Leicester; Selwyn Coll., Cambridge (MA; Hon. Fellow 1983). Man. Accountant, Dexion Ltd, 1950–55; IBM United Kingdom Ltd, 1955–90; Chm., IBM UK Hldgs Ltd, 1986–90 (Man. Dir, 1965–78; Chm. and Chief Exec., 1979–86); Director: Royal Insurance PLC, 1980–88; International Westminster Bank PLC, 1987–; UK-Japan 2000 Gp Ltd, 1987–; Partnership Sourcing, 1990–; Natwest Bancorp Inc., 1991–; Natwest Bank USA, 1992–; Alternate Dir, BCH Property Ltd, 1988–; Chm., Natwest Pension Trustees Ltd, 1992–. Member Council: Foundn for Automation and Employment, 1967–77; Electronic Engineering Assoc., 1965–76; CBI, 1971– (Chm. Standing Cttee on Marketing and Consumer Affairs, 1971–78; Mem., Cttee on Industrial Policy, 1978–85; President's Cttee, 1986–88); Foundn for Management Educn, 1973–84. Member: British Cttee of Awards for Harkness Fellowships, 1976–82; Adv. Council, Business Graduates Assoc., 1976–87; Board of Governors, United World Coll. of Atlantic, 1977–; Bd of Trustees, Internat. Inst. for Management Develt, 1990–; Chm. Council, Leicester Univ., 1992–; Member Council: Manchester Business Sch., 1974–86 (Chm., 1979–86); Business in the Community, 1981–88 (Companion, 1992); Westfield Coll., London, 1969–82 (Vice Chm., 1980–82; Hon. Fellow 1983); William Temple Coll., Manchester, 1972–80; Oxford Centre for Management Studies, 1973–83; Open Univ., 1986–92. Member: The Civil Service Coll., 1979–91; Adv. Council, New Oxford English Dictionary, 1985–89; Council for Industry and Higher Educn, 1986–. Trustee, Inst. of Econ. Affairs, 1986–92 (Hon. Trustee, 1992). Member: Chichester Cathedral Develt Trust, 1986–; The Prince's Youth Business Trust, 1987–; Lloyd's of London Tercentary Foundn, 1987–. Pres., Nat. Assoc. for Gifted Children, 1980–91 (Hon. Mem., 1991); Vice-Pres., Opportunities for People with Disabilities (formerly Opportunities for the Disabled), 1980–; Chm., Jt Bd for Pre-Vocational Educn, 1983–87; Mem., Study Commn on the Family, 1979–83. Chm. of Bd of Trustees and a Dir, Royal Opera House, Covent Garden, 1984–87 (Trustee, 1980–87); Chm., Bd of Trustees, Monteverdi Choir and Orch., 1988– (Trustee, 1980–); Vice-Pres., London Internat. String Quartet Competition. Patron, Assoc. Internationale des Etudiantes en Sciences Economiques et Commerciales, 1980–. DL Hampshire, 1987. Hon. Fellow: Inst. of Marketing, 1982 (Hon. Vice-Pres., 1980–); Portsmouth Polytechnic, subseq. Portsmouth Univ., 1986; Leeds Polytechnic, subseq. Leeds Metropolitan Univ., 1991. Hon. DSc Aston, 1985; DUniv Stirling, 1985; Hon. DTech Brunel, 1986; Hon. LLD: Manchester, 1987; Leicester, 1990; Hon. DTech CNAA, 1991. *Recreations:* music, tennis, golf, sailing. *Address:* National Westminster Bank, 41 Lothbury, EC2P 2BP. *T:* 0171–726 1000; Starkes Heath, Rogate, Petersfield, Hants GU31 5EJ. *T:* Rogate (01730) 821504. *Club:* Athenæum.

NIXON, Prof. John Forster, FRS 1994; Professor of Chemistry, University of Sussex, since 1986; *b* 27 Jan. 1937; *s* of late Supt Edward Forster Nixon, MBE and Mary Nixon (*née* Lytton); *m* 1960, Dorothy Joan (Kim) Smith; one *s* one *d*. *Educ:* Univ. of Manchester (BSc 1st Cl. Hons Chem. 1957, MSc 1958; PhD 1960; DSc 1973). Research Associate in Chem., Univ. of Southern Calif., LA, 1960–62; ICI Fellow, Inorganic Chem. Dept, Univ. of Cambridge, 1962–64; Lectr in Inorganic Chem., Univ. of St Andrews, 1964–66; University of Sussex: Lectr in Chem., 1966–76; Reader, 1976–86; Subject Chm. in Chem., 1981–84; Dean, Sch. of Chem. and Molecular Scis, 1989–92. Vis. Associate Prof. in Chem., Univ. of Victoria, BC, Canada, 1970–71; Vis. Prof., Simon Fraser Univ., BC, 1976. Mem., Editl Bd, Phosphorus, Sulfur and Silicon, 1989–. Member: Internat. Cttee on Phosphorus Chem., 1983; IUPAC Commn on Inorganic Nomenclature, 1985–87; Inorganic Chem. Panel, SERC Cttee, 1986–89. Royal Soc. Leverhulme Trust Sen. Res. Fellow, 1993. Mem. Council, Dalton Div., RSC, 1994–. Corday-Morgan Medal and Prize, Chem. Soc., 1973; Main Gp Element Medal, 1985, Tilden Lectr and Medal, 1992, RSC. FRSA 1992. *Publications:* numerous papers in various learned jls. *Recreations:* walking, playing squash, tennis, badminton, watching cricket, theatre. *Address:* School of Chemistry and Molecular Sciences, University of Sussex, Brighton, Sussex BN1 9QJ. *T:* Brighton (01273) 678536; Juggs Barn, The Street, Kingston, Lewes, Sussex BN7 3PB. *T:* Lewes (01273) 483993.

NIXON, Rev. Sir Kenneth Michael John Basil, SJ; 4th Bt *cr* 1906; Teaching Member of the Jesuit Community at St George's College, Harare, since 1954; *b* 22 Feb. 1919; *s* of Sir Christopher William Nixon, 2nd Bt, DSO, and Louise (*d* 1949), *d* of Robert Clery, JP, The Glebe, Athlacca, Limerick; *S* brother, 1978. *Educ:* Beaumont College; Heythrop College, Oxon. Catholic priest and member of the Society of Jesus; ordained, 1952. *Recreation:* cricket. *Heir:* *b* Major Cecil Dominic Henry Joseph Nixon, MC [*b* 5 Feb. 1920; *m* 1953, Brenda, *d* of late Samuel Lycett Lewis and *widow* of Major M. F. McWhor; three *s* one *d*]. *Address:* St George's College, PB 7727, Causeway, Zimbabwe. *T:* Harare (4) 724650.

NIXON, Patrick Michael, CMG 1989; OBE 1984; HM Diplomatic Service; High Commissioner to Zambia, since 1994; *b* 1 Aug. 1944; *s* of John Moylett Gerard Nixon and late Hilary Mary (*née* Paterson); *m* 1968, Elizabeth Rose Carlton; four *s*. *Educ:* Downside; Magdalene Coll., Cambridge (Exhibnr; MA Classical Tripos Pt I and Historical Tripos Pt II). Joined HM Diplomatic Service, 1965; MECAS, Lebanon, 1966; Third Sec., Cairo, 1968; Second Sec. (Commercial), Lima, 1970; First Sec., FCO, 1973; Hd of Chancery, Tripoli, Libya, 1977; Dir, British Inf. Services, New York, 1980; Asst, later Hd, Near East and N Africa Dept, FCO, 1983; Ambassador and Consul-Gen. at Doha, Qatar, 1987–90; Counsellor, FCO, 1990–93. *Address:* c/o Foreign and Commonwealth Office, SW1A 2AH.

NOAKES, Rt. Rev. George; Archbishop of Wales, 1987–91; Bishop of St Davids, 1982–91; *b* 13 Sept. 1924; *s* of David John and Elizabeth Mary Noakes; *m* 1957, Jane Margaretta Davies. *Educ:* Tregaron Secondary School; University Coll. of Wales, Aberystwyth (BA); Wycliffe Hall, Oxford. Curate of Lampeter, 1950–56; Vicar: Eglwyswrw, 1956–59; Tregaron, 1959–67; Dewi Sant, Cardiff, 1967–76; Rector of Aberystwyth, 1976–79; Canon of St Davids Cathedral, 1977–79; Archdeacon of Cardigan, 1979–82; Vicar of Llanychaearn, 1980–82. Hon. DD Wales, 1989. *Recreations:* cricket, angling. *Address:* Hafodlon, Rhydargaeau, Carmarthen, Dyfed SA32 7DT. *T:* Carmarthen (01267) 253302.

NOAKES, John Edward, OBE 1993; FRCGP; Partner, group medical practice in Harrow, since 1961; *b* 27 April 1935; *s* of Edward and Mary Noakes; *m* 1960, Margaret Ann Jenner; two *s* one *d*. *Educ:* Wanstead County High Sch.; Charing Cross Hospital Medical Sch. (MB BS); DObstRCOG. Trainer, Gen. Practice Vocational Trng Scheme, Northwick Park Hosp., 1974–82. Member: Brent Harrow Local Med. Cttee, 1972–; Harrow HA, 1982–90; Chm., Brent Harrow Med. Audit Adv. Gp, 1992–95. Mem. Council, RCGP, 1989– (Vice-Chm., 1990–92; Chairman: NW London Faculty, 1989–91; Maternity Care Task Gp, 1994). *Recreations:* music (mainly opera), horticulture (Alpine plants), exploring Britain's canal system in own Narrow Boat. *Address:* Dykeside Cottage, 113 Rowlands Avenue, Pinner, Middx HA5 4AW. *T:* 0181–428 4289.

NOAKES, Michael, PPROI, RP; portrait and landscape painter; *b* 28 Oct. 1933; *s* of late Basil and Mary Noakes; *m* 1960, Vivien Noakes (*née* Langley), writer; two *s* one *d*. *Educ:* Downside; Royal Academy Schs, London. Nat. Dipl. in Design, 1954; Certificate of Royal Academy Schools, 1960. Commnd: National Service, 1954–56. Has broadcast and appeared on TV on art subjects in UK and USA; Art Correspondent, BBC TV programme Town and Around, 1964–68; subject of BBC films: (with Eric Morley) Portrait, 1977, 1978; (with JAK) Changing Places, 1989. Member Council: ROI, 1964–78 (Vice-Pres. 1968–72; Pres., 1972–78; Hon. Mem. Council, 1978–); RP, 1969–71, 1972–74, 1978–80, 1993–; NS, 1962–76 (Hon. Mem., 1976–); Chm., Contemp. Portrait Soc., 1971; a Dir, Fedn of British Artists, 1981–83 (a Governor, 1972–83). Freeman, City of London; Liveryman, Co. of Woolmen. *Exhibited:* Royal Acad.; Royal Inst. Oil Painters; Royal Soc. Portrait Painters; Contemp. Portrait Soc.; Nat. Society; Young Contemporaries, Grosvenor Galleries, Upper Grosvenor Galls, Woodstock Galls, Royal Glasgow Inst. of Fine Arts, Nat. Portrait Gall.; Roy. Soc. of British Artists; Grafton Gall.; New Grafton Galls; Art Exhibitions Bureau, touring widely in Britain, USA and Canada. Judge, Miss World Contest, 1976. Platinum disc, 1977 (record sleeve design Portrait of Sinatra). *Portraits include:* The Queen (unveiled Silver Jubilee year, for Manchester; Queen's Lancs Regt); Queen Elizabeth The Queen Mother (as Chancellor, Univ. of London; as Patron, RADAR); Prince of Wales (for 2nd KEO Gurkhas); Princess Anne (for Saddlers' Co.; Royal Signals); Duke and Duchess of York; Duchess of Kent; Lord Aberconway; Lord Aldington; Lord Amory; Princess Ashraf; Sir Michael Atiyah; Lord Benson; Lord Barnetson; Lord Boothby; Lord Bowden; Lord Boyd; Lord Butterfield; Lord Carr; FM Lord Carver; Lord Charteris; Lord Chuter-Ede; Lord Craigmyle; Lord Denning; Paul Dirac; Lord Elwyn-Jones; Archbishop Lord Fisher; Dom Charles Fitzgerald-Lombard, Abbot of Downside; Lord Fulton; Sir Alec Guinness; Gen. Sir John Hackett; Gilbert Harding; Robert Hardy; Sir Alan Hodgkin; Cardinal Hume; Lord Kingsdown; AF Lord Lewin; Amb. John J. Louis, USA; Very Rev. Michael Mayne, Dean of Westminster; Cliff Michelmore; Eric Morley; Robert Morley; Malcolm Muggeridge; Sir Gerald Nabarro; Sir David Napley; Max Perutz; Earl of Powis; Ambassador Charles Price, USA; J. B. Priestley; Valerie Profumo; Lord Pym; Sir Ralph Richardson; Dom John Roberts, Abbot of Downside; Sir Martin Roth; Edmund de Rothschild; Lord Runcie; Dame Margaret Rutherford; Lord Selwyn-Lloyd; Sir Roland Smith; Very Rev. M. Sullivan; Margaret Thatcher (as Prime Minister); Lord Todd; Sir Peter Walters; Dennis Wheatley; Sir Mortimer Wheeler; Sir Frank Whittle; Lord Wolfenden; Sir Donald Wolfit; *major group portraits:* Royal Family, with Lord and Lady Mayoress, for Guildhall; Members and Officers, Metropolitan Water Board (47 figures); Lords of Appeal in Ordinary (for Middle Temple); Queen Elizabeth the Queen Mother opening Overlord Embroidery to public view, with Princess Alice, Lord Mountbatten, Duke of Norfolk, etc.; Company of Woolmen showing Princess Royal. *Represented in collections:* The Queen, for Royal Collection Windsor; The Prince of Wales; British Mus.; Nat. Portrait Gall. (incl. Hugill Fund Purchase, RA, 1972); numerous Oxford and Cambridge colleges; County Hall, Westminster; various livery companies and Inns of Court; House of Commons; Univs of London, Nottingham, East Anglia; City Univ.; Frank Sinatra. *Publications:* A Professional Approach to Oil Painting, 1968; contributions to various art journals. *Recreation:* idling. *Address:* 146 Hamilton Terrace, St John's Wood, NW8 9UX. *T:* 0171–328 6754, *Fax:* 0171–625 1220. *Club:* Garrick.

NOAKES, Philip Reuben, OBE 1962; HM Diplomatic Service, retired; *b* 12 Aug. 1915; *y s* of late Charles William and Elizabeth Farey Noakes; *m* 1940, Moragh Jean Dickson; two *s*. *Educ:* Wyggeston Grammar Sch.; Wycliffe Coll.; Queens' Coll., Cambridge (Open Schol.). Mod. Langs Tripos Part I, Hist. Tripos Part II; BA 1937; MA 1945; Pres., Cambridge Union Soc., 1937. Served War, 1940–46; Capt.-Adjt 2nd Fife and Forfar Yeomanry, RAC (despatches). Public Relations Officer, Royal Over-Seas League, 1947–48; Sen. Information Officer, Colonial Office, 1948; Prin. Information Officer, CO, 1953; Information Adviser to Governor of Malta, 1960–61; Chief Information Officer, CO, 1963–66; Commonwealth Office, 1967; Counsellor (Information), Ottawa, 1967–72; Consul-Gen., Seattle, 1973–75. *Recreations:* bird-watching, fishing, shooting, gardening. *Address:* Little St Mary's, St Mary's Lane, Uplyme, Lyme Regis, Dorset DT7 3XH. *T:* Axminster (01297) 33371. *Club:* Royal Over-Seas League.

NOAKES, Sheila Valerie, (Mrs C. B. Noakes); *see* Masters, S. V.

NOBAY, Prof. (Avelino) Robert, PhD; Brunner Professor of Economic Science, University of Liverpool, since 1980; *b* 11 July 1942; *s* of Theodore Anastasio Nobay and Anna Gracia D'Silva; *m* 1st, 1965; two *s*; 2nd, 1987, Carole Ann McPhee. *Educ:* Univ. of Leicester (BA); Univ. of Chicago; PhD Southampton. Jun. Economist, Electricity Council, London, 1964–66; Res. Officer, NIESR, 1966–70; Sen. Lectr, Univ. of Southampton, 1970–80. Vis. Associate Prof., Univ. of Chicago, 1977–79. *Publications:* (with H. G. Johnson) The Current Inflation; (with H. G. Johnson) Issues in Monetary Economics. *Recreations:* sailing, golf, music. *Address:* 33 Chapter Road, SE17 3ES. *T:* 0171–582 9372.

NOBBS, David Gordon; writer; *b* 13 March 1935; *s* of Gordon and Gwen Nobbs; *m* 1968, Mary Blatchford; two step *s* one step *d*. *Educ:* Marlborough; St John's Coll., Cambridge (BA English). Wrote scripts for: That Was the Week That Was, BBC TV, 1963; The Frost Report, The Two Ronnies, The Fall and Rise of Reginald Perrin, 1976–78; BBC TV: The Hello Goodbye Man, 1984; Dogfood Dan and The Carmarthen Cowboy, 1988; Love on a Branch Line, 1994; Yorkshire TV: Sez Les; Cupid's Darts, 1981; A Bit of a Do, 1989, 1990; Rich Tea and Sympathy, 1991; Stalag Luft, 1993; Granada: Our Young Mr Wignall, 1976; The Glamour Girls, 1980, 1982; Channel 4: Fairly Secret Army, 1984, 1986; The Life and Times of Henry Pratt, 1992. *Publications:* The Itinerant Lodger, 1965; Ostrich Country, 1968; A Piece of the Sky is Missing, 1969; The Fall and Rise of Reginald Perrin, 1975; The Return of Reginald Perrin, 1977; The Better World of Reginald Perrin, 1978; Second From Last in the Sack Race, 1983; A Bit of a Do, 1986; Pratt of the Argus, 1988; Fair Do's, 1990; The Cucumber Man, 1994; The Legacy of Reginald Perrin, 1995. *Recreations:* cricket, football, bird-watching, travel, food, drink, bridge, theatre, weeding. *Address:* c/o Jonathan Clowes, Iron Bridge House, Bridge Approach, NW1 8BD. *Club:* Hereford United Football.

NOBES, (Charles) Patrick; retired Headmaster and teacher of English; *b* 17 March 1933; *o c* of Alderman Alfred Robert Nobes, OBE, JP, and Marguerite Violet Vivian (*née* Fathers), Gosport, Hants; *m* 1958, Patricia Jean (*nee* Brand); three *s*. *Educ:* Price's Sch., Fareham, Hants; University Coll., Oxford. MA. With The Times, reporting and editorial, 1956–57; Head of English Dept, King Edward VI Grammar Sch., Bury St Edmunds, 1959–64; Head of English and General Studies and Sixth Form Master, Ashlyns Comprehensive Sch., Berkhamsted, 1964–69; Headmaster: The Ward Freman Sch., Buntingford, Herts, 1969–74; Bedales Sch., 1974–81; Weymouth Grammar Sch., 1981–85, later The Budmouth Sch., 1985–86; St Francis' Coll., Letchworth, 1986–87. Chairman: HMC Co-ed Schs Gp, 1976–80; Soc. of Headmasters of Independent Schs, 1978–80; Mem., SHA Council, 1985–86. General Editor and adapter, Bulls-Eye Books (series for adults and young adults with reading difficulties), 1972–. *Recreations:* writing, cricket and hockey, King Arthur, Hampshire, music, First World War. *Address:* 8 Glen Court, Glenmore Road, Salisbury, Wilts SP1 3HG. *T:* Salisbury (01722) 327363.

NOBES, Peter John, QPM 1986; Chief Constable, West Yorkshire Police, 1989–93; *b* 1 Oct. 1935; *s* of Cornelius James Nobes and Ivy Kathleen (*née* Eke); *m* 1955, Ruth Winifred Barnett; two *d*. *Educ:* Fakenham Modern Secondary Sch.; University Coll. London (Bramshill Scholarship; LLB 1968). Nat. Service, Royal Corps of Signals. W Suffolk (later Suffolk) Constabulary, 1956; Constable to Inspector, Newmarket, Brandon, Ipswich; Police Staff Coll., Bramshill, 1963–64 (Cert. with Dist.); University, 1965–68; Essex and Southend-on-Sea Jt Constabulary (later Essex Police), 1969; Chief Inspector to Chief Supt, Harlow, Basildon, Chelmsford; courses at Police Staff Coll., 1970, 1976; Asst Chief Constable, W Yorks Metropolitan Police, 1977 (management services, criminal investigation, complaints and discipline); Dep. Chief Constable, 1983; Chief Constable, N Yorks Police, 1985. *Publication:* A Policeman's Lot, 1973. *Recreations:* music, gardening, taking exercise.

NOBLE, Adrian Keith; Artistic Director, Royal Shakespeare Company, since 1991; *b* 19 July 1950; *s* of late William John Noble and of Violet Ena (*née* Wells); *m* 1991, Joanne Elizabeth Pearce; one *d*. *Educ:* Chichester High Sch. for Boys; Bristol Univ. (BA); Drama Centre, London. Associate Dir, Bristol Old Vic, 1976–79; Resident Dir, RSC, 1980–82; Guest Dir, Royal Exchange Theatre, Manchester, 1980–81; Associate Dir, RSC, 1982–90. *Stage productions include:* Ubu Rex, A Man's A Man, 1977; A View from the Bridge, Titus Andronicus, The Changeling, 1978; Love for Love, Timon of Athens, Recruiting Officer (Edinburgh Fest.), 1979; Duchess of Malfi, 1980, Paris 1981; Dr Faustus, The Forest, A Doll's House, 1981; King Lear, Antony and Cleopatra, 1982; A New Way to Pay Old Debts, Comedy of Errors, Measure for Measure, 1983; Henry V, The Winter's Tale, The Desert Air, 1984; As You Like It, 1985; Mephisto, The Art of Success (and NY, 1989), Macbeth, 1986; Kiss Me Kate, 1987; The Plantagenets, 1988; The Master Builder, 1989; The Three Sisters, 1990; Henry IV, parts 1 and 2, 1991; The Thebans, 1991; Hamlet, Winter's Tale, 1992; King Lear, Travesties, Macbeth, 1993; A Midsummer Night's Dream, 1994; Romeo and Juliet, The Cherry Orchard, 1995; *opera:* Don Giovanni, Kent Opera, 1983; The Fairy Queen, Aix-en-Provence Fest., 1989. Hon. DLitt Birmingham, 1994. *Address:* Barbican Theatre, EC2Y 8BQ.

NOBLE, Alistair William; Sheriff of North Strathclyde at Dunoon, since 1992; *b* 10 Jan. 1954; *s* of William Alexander Noble and Alexanderina Noble (*née* Fraser); *m* 1986, Olga Helena Marr Wojtas. *Educ:* Aberdeen Grammar Sch.; Aberdeen Univ. (LLB). Admitted Advocate, 1978; Temporary Sheriff, 1986. *Recreation:* reading. *Address:* Sheriff's Chambers, Sheriff Court House, George Street, Dunoon PA23 8BQ. *T:* Dunoon (01369) 704166.

NOBLE, Barrie Paul; Chairman, Civil Service Selection Board Panel, since 1994; *b* 17 Oct. 1938; *s* of late Major and Mrs F. A. Noble; *m* 1965, Alexandra Helene Giddings; one *s*. *Educ:* Hele's, Exeter; New Coll., Oxford (BA Jurisprudence); Univ. of Dakar. RAF, 1957–59. HM Diplomatic Service, 1962–93; Third, later Second Sec., (Leopoldville) Kinshasa, 1965–67; Second Sec. (Commercial), Kaduna, 1967–69; FCO, 1969–72; First Sec., 1972–75 and Head of Chancery, 1975, Warsaw; FCO, 1976–80; Counsellor, UK Mission to UN, Geneva, 1980–84; Counsellor, FCO, 1984–89; Paris, 1989–93. *Publication:* Droit Coutumier, Annales Africaines, 1965. *Recreations:* grass cutting, bridge, skiing. *Clubs:* Royal Air Force, Ski Club of Great Britain; Rolls-Royce Enthusiasts'.

NOBLE, David, WS, JP; Sheriff of North Strathclyde at Oban and Fort William, since 1983; *b* 11 Feb. 1923; *s* of late Donald Noble, Solicitor, Inverness, and Helen Kirk Lynn Melville or Noble; *m* 1947, Marjorie Scott Smith or Noble; two *s* one *d*. *Educ:* Inverness Royal Academy; Edinburgh Univ. (MA, LLB *summa cum laude*). Royal Air Force Bomber Command, 1942–46. Partner in Miller Thomson & Robertson, WS, Edinburgh, 1953–82. JP Midlothian, 1970. *Address:* Woodhouselee, North Connel, Argyll PA37 1QZ. *T:* Connel (01631) 710678.

NOBLE, David, CBE 1989; Under Secretary and Head of Administrative Division, Medical Research Council, 1981–89, retired; *b* 12 June 1929; *s* of late William Ernest Noble and Maggie (*née* Watt); *m* 1969, Margaret Patricia Segal. *Educ:* Buckhurst Hill County High Sch., Essex; University Coll., Oxford (BA Hons English, 1952). Admin. Assistant, UCH, 1952–58; Mem., Operational Res. Unit, Nuffield Provincial Hosps Trust, 1958–61; Project Sec., Northwick Park Hosp. and Clinical Res. Centre, NW Thames RHA and MRC, 1961–68; Medical Research Council: Principal, 1968–72; Asst Sec., 1972–81. Member: Nat. Biological Standards Bd, 1983–90; PHLS Bd, 1990–. *Publications:* contribs to literature on operation and design of hosps and res. labs. *Recreations:* music, reading, travel. *Address:* 173 Bittacy Hill, NW7 1RT. *T:* 0181–346 8005.

NOBLE, Sir David (Brunel), 6th Bt *cr* 1902, of Ardmore and Ardadan Noble, Cardross, Co. Dunbarton; sales consultant, Allied Maples Group Ltd, since 1989; *b* 25 Dec. 1961; *s* of Sir Marc Brunel Noble, 5th Bt, CBE and of Jennifer Lorna, *d* of late John Mein-Austin; *S* father, 1991; *m* 1st, 1987, Virginia Ann (marr. diss. 1993), *yr d* of late Roderick Wetherall; two *s*; 2nd, 1993, Stephanie (*née* Digby); one *s* one *d* (and one *s* decd). *Educ:* Eton Coll.; Cambridge Tutors, Croydon. Sales Exec., Gabriel Communications Ltd, 1986–88. *Recreations:* golf, photography, gardening. *Heir: s* Roderick Lancaster Brunel Noble, *b* 12 Dec. 1988. *Address:* 3 Oast Cottages, Breach Lane, Upchurch, Sittingbourne, Kent ME9 7PH. *Club:* HAC.

NOBLE, Prof. Denis, FRCP; FRS 1979; Burdon Sanderson Professor of Cardiovascular Physiology, Oxford University, since 1984; Tutorial Fellow, 1963–84, Professorial Fellow, since 1984, Balliol College, Oxford; *b* 16 Nov. 1936; *s* of George and Ethel Noble; *m* 1965, Susan Jennifer Barfield, BSc, BA, DPhil; one *s* one *d*. *Educ:* Emanuel Sch., London; University Coll. London (BSc, MA, PhD; Fellow 1985). FRCP 1994. Asst Lectr, UCL, 1961–63; Tutor in Physiology, Balliol Coll., and Univ. Lectr, Oxford Univ., 1963–84; Praefectus of Holywell Manor (Balliol Graduate Centre), 1971–89; Vice-Master, Balliol Coll., 1983–85. Visiting Professor: Alberta, 1969–70; Univs of BC, Calgary, Edmonton, and SUNY at Stonyhook, 1990; Univ. of Auckland, 1990. Lectures: Darwin, British Assoc., 1966; Nahum, Yale, 1977; Bottazzi, Pisa, 1985; Ueda, Tokyo, 1985; Lloyd Roberts, London Med. Soc., 1987; Allerdale Wyld, Northern Industrial and Technical Soc., 1988; Bowden, UMIST, 1988; Annual, Internat. Science Policy Foundn, 1993; Rijlant, Internat. Congress of Electrocardiology, Japan, 1994. Chm., Jt Dental Cttee (MRC, SERC, Depts of Health), 1985–90. Hon. Sec., 1974–80, Foreign Sec., 1986–, Physiol Soc.; Founder Mem., Save British Science; Pres., Med. Section, BAAS, 1991–92; Sec. Gen., IUPS, 1994–. Chm., IUPS Congress, Glasgow, 1993. Hon. MRCP 1988; Hon. FRCP 1994; Mem., Academia Europaea, 1989; Correspondent Etranger (Fellow), Royal Acad. of Medicine, Belgium, 1985. Editor, Progress in Biophysics, 1967–. Scientific Medal, Zoolog. Soc., 1970; Gold Medal, British Heart Foundn, 1985; Pierre Rijlant Prize, Belgian Royal Acad., 1991. *Publications:* Initiation of the Heartbeat, 1975, 2nd edn, 1979; Electric Current Flow in Excitable Cells, 1975; Electrophysiology of Single Cardiac Cells, 1987; Goals, No Goals and Own Goals, 1989; Sodium-Calcium Exchange, 1989; Ionic Channels and the Effect of Taurine on the Heart, 1993; The Logic of Life, 1993; papers mostly in Jl of Physiology; contribs on sci. res. and funding to New Scientist, nat. press, radio and TV. *Recreations:* Indian and French cooking, Occitan language and music, classical guitar. *Address:* 49 Old Road, Oxford OX3 7JZ. *T:* Oxford (01865) 62237.

NOBLE, Sir Fraser; *see* Noble, Sir T. A. F.

NOBLE, Gillian; Deputy Director (Law and Order, Health and Local Government), HM Treasury, since 1995; *b* Edinburgh, 18 Nov. 1947; *d* of John Noble and Jessie Mae Noble (*née* Bonnington). *Educ:* Aberdeen Univ. (MA Hons Econ. Sci. 1969); University Coll. London (MSc Public Sector Econs 1974). Joined MoT, subseq. DoE, as econ., 1969; transf. to HM Treasury, 1976; various posts dealing with: planning and control of public expenditure, 1976–84; pensions and social security, 1984–87; Asst Sec., 1986; Head: Banking Div., 1987–92; Educn Sci. and Nat. Heritage Div., 1992; Under Sec., 1993; Hd, Health, Social Services and Territorial Depts Gp, 1993–95. *Recreations:* listening to music, visiting heritage properties. *Address:* HM Treasury, Parliament Street, SW1P 3AG. *T:* 0171–270 4500.

NOBLE, Sir Iain (Andrew), 3rd Bt *cr* 1923, of Ardkinglas and Eilean Iarmain; OBE 1988; businessman, promoter of good causes; Proprietor: Fearann Eilean Iarmain, Isle of Skye, since 1972; The Gaelic Whiskies; Chairman: Noble and Co. Ltd, merchant bankers, Edinburgh, since 1980; Skye Bridge Ltd, since 1994; Director: Independent Insurance Group PLC (formerly New Scotland Insurance Group), since 1986; Premium Investment Trust PLC, Edinburgh, since 1993, and other companies; *b* 8 Sept. 1935; *s* of Sir Andrew Napier Noble, 2nd Bt, KCMG and of Sigrid, 2nd *d* of Johan Michelet, Norwegian Diplomatic Service; *S* father, 1987; *m* 1990, Lucilla Charlotte James, *d* of late Col H. A. C. Mackenzie, OBE, MC, TD, DL, JP, Dalmore. *Educ:* China, Argentina and England (Eton); University Coll., Oxford (MA 1959). Matthews Wrightson, London, 1959–64; Scottish Council (Develt and Industry), Edinburgh, 1964–69; Jt Founder and Jt Man. Dir, Noble Grossart Ltd, merchant bankers, Edinburgh, 1969–72; Jt Founder and Chm., Seaforth Maritime Ltd, Aberdeen, 1972–78; Chm., Lennox Oil Co. plc, Edinburgh, 1980–85; Co-founder and Dir, Adam and Co. plc, Edinburgh, 1983–93. Dep. Chm., Traverse Theatre, Edinburgh, 1966–68; Mem., Edinburgh Univ. Court, 1970–73; Founder, first Chm., 1973–74, and Trustee, 1974–84, College of Sabhal Mor Ostaig, Isle of Skye; Trustee: Nat. Museums of Scotland, 1987–91; NMS Charitable Trust, 1991–. Chm., Scots Australian Council, 1991–; Pres., Saltire Soc., 1992–. Scotsman of the Year Award, 1981. *Publication:* Sources of Finance, 1968. *Recreations:* Comhradh, beul-aithris is ceol le deagh chompanaich. *Heir: b* Timothy Peter Noble [*b* 21 Dec. 1943; *m* 1976, Elizabeth Mary, *d* of late Alexander Wallace Aitken; two *s* one *d*]. *Address:* (home) 20 Great Stuart Street, Edinburgh EH3 7TN; An Lamraig, Eilean Iarmain, An t-Eilean Sgitheanach IV43 3QR; (office) 5 Darnaway Street, Edinburgh EH3 6DW. *T:* (offices) Isle Ornsay (01471) 833266 and 0131–225 9677. *Club:* New (Edinburgh).

NOBLE, Rt Rev. John Ashley; Bishop of the Northern Region and an Assistant Bishop, Diocese of Brisbane, since 1993; *b* 30 March 1944; *s* of Mowbray Lloyd Noble and Norma June (*née* Shucksmith); *m* 1969, Lorene May Christine Wardrop; one *s* one *d*. *Educ:* St Francis Theological Coll., Brisbane (ThL 1965); Univ. of Queensland (BA 1973); Mt Gravatt Teachers' Coll., Brisbane (Cert. in Teaching, Secondary 1973). Deacon 1965, priest 1968; Asst Curacies, 1965–69; History Subject Master, Queensland Dept of Educn, 1974–78; Asst Chaplain, St Peter's Coll., Adelaide, 1979–81; Chaplain, St Paul's Sch., Brisbane, 1981–82; Diocese of Brisbane: Rector, St John's, Dalby, 1982–84; Rector, St Barnabas', Sunnybank, 1984–88; Lectr, St Francis Theol Coll., 1989–93. *Recreations:* reading, music, computers. *Address:* St Martin's House, 373 Ann Street, Brisbane, Qld 4000, Australia. *T:* (7) 8352213, 52 Denver Road, Carseldine, Qld 4034, Australia.

NOBLE, Kenneth Albert, CBE 1975; Member, Price Commission, 1973–77 (Deputy Chairman, 1973–76); Director, 1954–73, Vice-Chairman, 1966–73, Co-operative Wholesale Society Ltd; Director of associated organisations and subsidiaries. Member: CoID, 1957–65; Post Office Users Nat. Council, 1965–73; Monopolies Commn, 1969–73; London VAT Tribunals Panel, 1977–82. Served War, 1940–46 (despatches); Major RASC. *Publication:* (jtly) Financial Management Handbook, 1977, 2nd edn 1980.

NOBLE, Sir (Thomas Alexander) Fraser, Kt 1971; MBE 1947; Principal and Vice-Chancellor, University of Aberdeen, 1976–81, now Principal Emeritus; *b* 29 April 1918; *s* of late Simon Noble, Grantown-on-Spey and Jeanie Graham, Largs, Ayrshire; *m* 1945, Barbara A. M. Sinclair, Nairn; one *s* one *d*. *Educ:* Nairn Acad; Univ. of Aberdeen. After military service with Black Watch (RHR), entered Indian Civil Service, 1940. Served in NW Frontier Province, 1941–47, successively as Asst Comr, Hazara; Asst Polit. Agent, N Waziristan; Controller of Rationing, Peshawar; Under-Sec., Food Dept and Develt Dept; Sec., Home Dept; Joint Dep. Comr, Peshawar; Civil Aide to Referendum Comr. Lectr in Political Economy, Univ. of Aberdeen, 1948–57; Sec. and Treas., Carnegie Trust for Univs of Scotland, 1957–62; Vice-Chancellor, Leicester Univ., 1962–76. Mem. and Vice-Chm., Bd of Management, Aberdeen Mental Hosp. Group, 1953–57. Sec., Scottish Economic Soc., 1954–58; Vice-Pres., 1962–. Chm., Scottish Standing Conf. of Voluntary Youth Organisations, 1958–62; Vice-Chm., Standing Consultative Council on Youth Service in Scotland, 1959–62. Mem., Departmental Cttee on Probation Service, 1959–62, Chairman: Probation Advisory and Training Board, 1962–65; Television Research Cttee, 1963–69; Advisory Council on Probation and After-Care, 1965–70; Univs Council for Adult Education, 1965–69; Min. of Defence Cttee for Univ. Assistance to Adult Educn in HM Forces, 1965–70; Advisory Board, Overseas Students' Special Fund, 1967–71, Fees Awards Scheme, 1968–75; Cttee of Vice-Chancellors and Principals of Univs of UK, 1970–72; British Council Cttee on Exchanges between UK and USSR, 1973–78; Scottish Council for Community Educn, 1979–80. Member: Academic Advisory Cttee, Univs of St Andrews and Dundee, 1964–66; E Midlands Economic Planning Council, 1965–68; Council, Assoc. Commonwealth Univs, 1970–79; Exec. Cttee, Inter-Univ. Council for Higher Educn Overseas, 1972–79; Exec. Cttee, British Council, 1973–79; British Council Cttee for Commonwealth Univ. Interchange, 1973–79; US-UK Educnl Commn, 1973–76. Hon. LLD: Aberdeen, 1968; Leicester, 1976; Glasgow, 1981; Washington Coll., Maryland, 1981. *Publications:* articles in economic journals and on education. *Recreation:* golf. *Address:* Hedgerley, Victoria Street, Nairn IV12 4HH. *Club:* Nairn Golf.

NODDER, Timothy Edward, CB 1982; Deputy Secretary, Department of Health and Social Security, 1978–84; *b* 18 June 1930; *s* of Edward Nodder. *Educ:* St Paul's Sch.;

Christ's Coll., Cambridge. Under-Sec., DHSS, 1972. *Recreation:* natural history. *Address:* 83 Oakley Street, SW3 5NP.

NOEL, family name of **Earl of Gainsborough.**

NOEL, Rear-Adm. Gambier John Byng, CB 1969; retired; *b* 16 July 1914; *s* of late G. B. E. Noel; *m* 1936, Miss Joan Stevens; four *d. Educ:* Royal Naval Coll., Dartmouth. Joined Royal Navy, 1928; served in War of 1939–45, HMS Aurora and HMS Norfolk (despatches twice); Captain 1959; Imperial Defence Coll., 1962; Staff of Commander Far East Fleet, 1964–67; Rear-Admiral 1967; Chief Staff Officer (Technical) to C-in-C, Western Fleet, 1967–69. *Recreation:* gardening. *Address:* Woodpeckers, Church Lane, Haslemere, Surrey GU27 2BJ. *T:* Haslemere (01428) 643824.

NOEL, Geoffrey Lindsay James; Metropolitan Stipendiary Magistrate, 1975–93; *b* 19 April 1923; *s* of Major James Noel and Maud Noel; *m* 1st, 1947; two *d*; 2nd, 1966, Eileen Pickering (*née* Cooper); two step *s. Educ:* Crewkerne Sch., Somerset. Enlisted Royal Regt of Artillery, 1941; commnd, 1942; attached 9th Para Bn, 6 Airborne Div., 1944, Captain; POW Oflag 79; RWAFF; Major 1957; retd 1960. Called to Bar, Middle Temple, 1962; practised London and SE circuit. Chm., Juvenile Courts, 1977–79; Dep. Circuit Judge, 1980–82. *Recreations:* gardening, golf. *Address:* Loja, Albourne Road, Hurstpierpoint, Hassocks, W Sussex BN6 9ES.

NOEL, Hon. Gerard Eyre Wriothesley; author, publisher and lecturer; Editor, Catholic Herald, 1971–76 and 1982–84, Editorial Director, since 1984; *b* 20 Nov. 1926; *s* of 4th Earl of Gainsborough, OBE, TD, and Alice (*née* Eyre); *m* 1958, Adele Julie Patricia, *d* of Major V. N. B. Were and Dr Josephine Were (*née* Aherne), OBE; two *s* one *d. Educ:* Georgetown, USA; Exeter Coll., Oxford (MA, Modern History). Called to Bar, Inner Temple, 1952. Director: Herder Book Co., 1959–66; Search Press Ltd, 1972–. Literary Editor, Catholic Times, 1958–61; Catholic Herald: Asst Editor, 1968; Editorial Dir, 1976–81. Sen. Res. Fellow, St Anne's Coll., Oxford, 1993–. Lects and lect. tours, UK, USA, Ireland and Spain; Vis. Lectr, Oxford Centre for Jewish Studies, 1992–93. Mem. Exec. Cttee, 1974–, Hon. Treasurer, 1979–81, Council of Christians and Jews. Contested (L) Argyll, 1959. Liveryman, Co. of Stationers and Newspapermakers. Freeman, City of London. Gold Staff Officer at Coronation, 1953. *Publications:* Paul VI, 1963; Harold Wilson, 1964; Goldwater, 1964; The New Britain, 1966; The Path from Rome, 1968; Princess Alice: Queen Victoria's Forgotten Daughter, 1974; contrib. The Prime Ministers, 1974; The Great Lock-Out of 1926, 1976; The Anatomy of the Roman Catholic Church, 1980; Ena: Spain's English Queen, 1984; Cardinal Basil Hume, 1984; (jtly) The Anatomy of the Catholic Church: before and after Pope John Paul II, 1994; *translations:* The Mystery of Love, 1960; The Way to Unity after the Council, 1967; The Holy See and the War in Europe (Official Documents), 1968; articles in: Church Times, Catholic Times, Jewish Chronicle, Baptist Times, Catholic Herald, Literary Review, European, International Mind. *Recreations:* walking, travel, exploring London. *Address:* (office) Herald House, Lamb's Passage, EC1Y 8TQ; Westington Mill, Chipping Campden, Glos GL55 6EB. *Clubs:* Beefsteak, Garrick, White's.

NOEL, Lynton Cosmas; High Commissioner for Grenada in London, 1990–92; *b* 25 Oct. 1928; *m* 1962, Teresa Angela Diamonda; one *s* one *d. Educ:* St Joseph's RC Sch., Grenada; Polytechnic/Holborn Coll. of Law, Languages and Commerce; Inns of Court Sch. of Law (LLB). Asst Head Teacher, 1956–60; Telephone Engr, GPO, 1960–67; called to the Bar, Lincoln's Inn; practised law until 1984; Lectr in Law, Coll. of Law Studies. 1st Sec., Grenada High Commn, London, 1984–85; Chargé d'Affaires, Caracas, 1985–90. *Recreations:* music, chess, languages, logic (elementary). *Address:* 29 Mablethorpe Road, Fulham, SW6 6AQ. *T:* 0171–381 2577.

NOEL-BAKER, Hon. Francis Edward; Director, North Euboean Enterprises Ltd, since 1973; *b* 7 Jan. 1920; *o s* of Baron Noel-Baker, PC, and late Irene, *o d* of Frank Noel, British landowner, of Achmetaga, Greece; *m* 1957, Barbara Christina, *yr d* of late Joseph Sonander, Sweden; four *s* one *d* (and one *s* decd). *Educ:* Westminster Sch.; King's Coll., Cambridge (Exhibitioner; 1st cl. hons History). Founder and Chm., CU Lab. Club, 1939; left Cambridge to join Army, summer 1940, as Trooper, Royal Tank Regt; Commissioned in Intelligence Corps and served in UK, Force 133, Middle East (despatches); returned to fight Brentford and Chiswick Div.; MP (Lab) Brentford and Chiswick Div. of Mddx, 1945–50; Editor, United Nations World/World Horizon, 1945–47, Go! magazine, 1947–48; PPS Admiralty, 1949–50; BBC European Service, 1950–54; MP (Lab) Swindon, 1955–68, resigned from Labour Party, 1969; Sec., 1955–64, Chm., 1964–68, UN Parly Cttee; Vice-Chm., Lab. Cttee for Europe, 1976–78; Member: SDP 1981–83; Conservative Party, 1984–; NUJ, 1946–81. Chm., Advertising Inquiry Council, 1951–68. Chairman: North Euboean Foundation Ltd, 1965–; Candili Craft Centre, Philip Noel-Baker Centre, Euboea, 1983–; Dir, Fini Fisheries, Cyprus, 1976–90; Founder Pres., European Council for Villages and Small Towns, 1984–; Pres., Internat. Campaign for Environmental Health, 1985–; Hon. Pres., Union of Forest Owners of Greece, 1968–. Member: Parochial Church Council, St Martin in the Fields, 1960–68; Freedom from Hunger Campaign UK Cttee Exec. Cttee, 1961; Ecology Party, 1978–; Soil Assoc., 1979–. Governor, Campion Sch., Athens, 1973–78. Archives Fellow Commoner, Churchill Coll., Cambridge, 1989. Wine Constable, Guyenne, 1988–. *Publications:* Greece, the Whole Story, 1946; Spanish Summary, 1948; The Spy Web, 1954; Land and People of Greece, 1957; Nansen, 1958; Looking at Greece, 1967; My Cyprus File, 1985; Book Eight: a taste of hardship, 1987; Three Saints and Poseidon, 1988. *Recreation:* gardening. *Address:* Achmetaga Estate, 340–04 Procopi, Greece. *T:* (227) 41204, *Fax:* (227) 41190; 74 Westbourne Terrace, W2 6QR. *T:* 0171–262 8400, *Fax:* 0171–402 4278. *Clubs:* Travellers, Special Forces; Athens.
See also M. E. F. Chance.

NOEL-BUXTON, family name of **Baron Noel-Buxton.**

NOEL-BUXTON, 3rd Baron *cr* 1930; **Martin Connal Noel-Buxton;** *b* 8 Dec. 1940; *s* of 2nd Baron Noel-Buxton and Helen Nancy (*d* 1949), *yr d* of late Col K. H. M. Connal, CB, OBE, TD; *S* father, 1980; *m* 1st, 1964, Miranda Mary (marr. diss. 1968), *er d* of H. A. Chisenhale-Marsh; 2nd, 1972, Sarah Margaret Surridge (marr. diss. 1982), *o d* of N. C. W. Barrett, TD; one *s* one *d*; 3rd, 1986, Abigail Marie, *yr d* of E. P. R. Clent; one *d. Educ:* Bryanston School; Balliol College, Oxford (MA). Admitted a Solicitor, 1966. *Heir: s* Hon. Charles Connal Noel-Buxton, *b* 17 April 1975.

NOEL-PATON, Hon. (Frederick) Ranald; Group Managing Director, John Menzies, since 1986; *b* 7 Nov. 1938; *s* of late Baron Ferrier, ED and Joane Mary, *d* of Sir Gilbert Wiles, KCIE, CSI; *m* 1973, Patricia Anne Stirling; four *d. Educ:* Rugby School; McGill Univ. (BA). Various posts, British United Airways, 1965–70; various sen. exec. posts, British Caledonian Airways, 1970–86; Director: John Menzies plc, 1986–; Pacific Assets Trust, 1986–; General Accident plc, 1987–; Macallan-Glenlivet plc, 1990–; Royal Bank of Scotland Gp, 1991–93. Hon. DBA Napier, 1992. *Recreations:* fishing, walking, gardening, bird watching, the arts. *Address:* John Menzies, 108 Princes Street, Edinburgh EH2 3AA. *T:* 0131–225 8555. *Clubs:* New (Edinburgh); Shek-O Country, Hong Kong (Hong Kong).

NOEST, Peter John, FRICS; Managing Director, P. H. Gillingham (Investments) Ltd, since 1987; *b* 12 June 1948; *s* of Major A. J. F. Noest and Mrs M. Noest-Gerbrands; *m* 1st, 1972, Lisabeth Penelope Moody (marr. diss. 1993); one *s* one *d*; 2nd, 1993, Jocelyn Claire, *yr d* of A. D. Spencer, *qv. Educ:* St George's Coll., Weybridge; Royal Agricl Coll., Cirencester. FRICS 1978 (ARICS 1973). Joined Knight Frank & Rutley, 1971; Partner i/c Dutch office, Amsterdam, 1972; London Partner, 1977; full equity Partner, 1981; Consultant, 1983, full equity Partner, 1984, Hampton & Sons; Dir, Hampton & Sons Holdings, 1987 (subseq. merged with Lambert Smith to form Lambert Smith Hampton); Dir, Lambert Smith Hampton, 1988–92. *Publication:* (contrib.) Office Development, 1985. *Recreations:* hunting, shooting, farming, travel. *Address:* Dolmans Cottage, Hankerton, Malmesbury, Wilts SN16 9LH. *Clubs:* Turf, Oriental.

NOGUEIRA, Albano Pires Fernandes; Ambassador of Portugal; *b* 8 Nov. 1911; *m* 1937, Alda Maria Marques Xavier da Cunha. *Educ:* Univ. of Coimbra. 3rd Sec., Washington, 1944; 2nd Sec., Pretoria, 1945; 1st Sec., Pretoria, 1948; Head of Mission, Tokyo, 1950; Counsellor, London, 1953; Consul-Gen., Bombay, 1955; Consul-Gen., NY, 1955; Dep. Perm. Rep. UN, NY, 1955; Asst Dir-Gen., Econ. Affairs, Lisbon, 1959; Dir Gen., Econ. Affairs, Lisbon, 1961; Ambassador to: European Communities, Brussels, 1964; NATO, 1970; Court of St James's, 1974–76; Sec.-Gen., Ministry for Foreign Affairs, 1977. Vis. Prof., Univ. of Minho, Braga, 1979, 1980. Mem., Internat. Assoc. of Literary Critics, 1981–. Grand Cross: Merito Civil (Spain), 1961; Order of Infante Dom Henrique (Portugal), 1964; Isabel la Católica (Spain), 1977; Merit (Germany), 1977; St Olav (Norway), 1978; Christ (Portugal), 1981; the Flag with golden palm (Yugoslavia), 1978; Grand Officer: Cruzeiro do Sul (Brazil), 1959; White Elephant (Thailand), 1960. *Publications:* Imagens em Espelho Côncavo (essays); Portugal na Arte Japonesa (essay); Uma Agulha no Céu (novel); contribs to: NATO and the Mediterranean, 1985; NATO's Anxious Birth—the Prophetic Vision of the 1940s, 1985; contrib. leading Portuguese papers and reviews. *Recreations:* reading, writing. *Address:* Avenida Gaspar Corte-Real 18, Apt 4D, 2750 Cascais, Portugal. *T:* 4868264; 5 Rua Alberto de Oliveira, 5–3–E, 3000 Coimbra, Portugal. *T:* (39) 715035. *Clubs:* Grémio Literário, Automóvel de Portugal (Lisbon).

NOLAN, family name of **Baron Nolan.**

NOLAN, Baron *cr* 1994 (Life Peer), of Brasted in the County of Kent; **Michael Patrick Nolan,** Kt 1982; PC 1991; a Lord of Appeal in Ordinary, since 1994; *b* 10 Sept. 1928; *yr s* of James Thomas Nolan and Jane (*née* Walsh); *m* 1953, Margaret, *yr d* of Alfred Noyes, CBE, and Mary (*née* Mayne); one *s* four *d. Educ:* Ampleforth; Wadham Coll., Oxford (Hon. Fellow, 1992). Served RA, 1947–49; TA, 1949–55. Called to Bar, Middle Temple, 1953 (Bencher, 1975); QC 1968; called to Bar, NI, 1974; QC (NI) 1974; a Recorder of the Crown Court, 1975–82; Judge, High Court of Justice, QBD, 1982–91; Presiding Judge, Western Circuit, 1985–88; a Lord Justice of Appeal, 1991–93. Member: Bar Council, 1973–74; Senate of Inns of Court and Bar, 1974–81 (Treasurer, 1977–79). Mem., Sandilands Cttee on Inflation Accounting, 1973–75; Chm., Cttee on Standards in Public Life, 1994–. Mem. Governing Body, Convent of the Sacred Heart, Woldingham, 1973–83; Governor, Combe Bank Sch., 1974–83. *Recreation:* fishing. *Address:* House of Lords, SW1A 0PW. *Clubs:* Army and Navy, Boodle's, MCC.

NOLAN, Benjamin; QC 1992; a Recorder, since 1989; *b* 19 July 1948; *s* of Benjamin Nolan and Jane Nolan (*née* Mercer); *m* 1973, Noreen Frances Kelly; two *d. Educ:* St Joseph's Coll., Blackpool; Newcastle upon Tyne Polytechnic; LLB London, 1970. Called to the Bar, Middle Temple, 1971. *Recreations:* cooking, walking, gardening, swimming. *Address:* 9 Woodhouse Square, Leeds LS3 1AD. *T:* Leeds (0113) 245 1986.

NOLAN, Brig. Eileen Joan, CB 1976; Director, Women's Royal Army Corps, 1973–77; *b* 19 June 1920; *d* of late James John and Ethel Mary Nolan. *Educ:* King's Norton Grammar Sch. for Girls. Joined ATS, Nov. 1942; commissioned, 1945. Lt-Col, 1967; Col, 1970; Brig., 1973. Hon. ADC to the Queen, 1973–77; Chm., NATO Senior Women Officers' Cttee, 1975–77; Dep. Controller Comdt, WRAC, 1977–84. *Address:* c/o Barclays Bank, High Street, Crowthorne, Berkshire.

NONWEILER, Prof. Terence Reginald Forbes, BSc; PhD; CEng; Professor of Mathematics, Victoria University of Wellington, 1975–91, now Emeritus; *b* 8 Feb. 1925; *s* of Ernest James Nonweiler and Lilian Violet Amalie Nonweiler (*née* Holfert); *m* 1949, Patricia Hilda Frances (*née* Neame); four *s* two *d. Educ:* Bethany Sch., Goudhurst, Kent; University of Manchester, BSc 1944, PhD 1960. Scientific Officer, Royal Aircraft Establishment, Farnborough, Hants, 1944–50; Scientific Officer, Scientific Advisor's Dept, Air Ministry, 1950–51; Senior Lecturer in Aerodynamics, College of Aeronautics, Cranfield, Beds, 1951–57; Senior Lecturer in Aeronautical Engineering, The Queen's Univ. of Belfast, 1957–61; Mechan Prof. of Aeronautics and Fluid Mechanics, Glasgow Univ., 1961–75. Consultant: to Admiralty, 1951; to Ministry of Aviation, 1959; to Ministry of Agriculture, 1966; to Wellington City Corp., 1977. Vis. Prof., Cranfield Inst. of Technology, 1991–93. Member, International Academy of Astronautics. *Publications:* Jets and Rockets, 1959; Computational Mathematics, 1984; numerous technical papers on aeronautics, space flight, and submarine motion. *Recreations:* acting and stage production. *Address:* 15 Tui Road, Raumati Beach 6450, New Zealand.

NOONEY, David Matthew; Principal Establishment and Finance Officer, Crown Prosecution Service, since 1993; *b* 2 Aug. 1945; *m* 1973, Maureen Georgina Revell; one adopted *d. Educ:* St Joseph's Acad., Blackheath. FICMA. HM Treasury, 1965–86; on loan to Lord Chancellor's Dept as Management Accounting Advr, 1986–88, transf. to the Dept, 1989; Head, Resources Div., 1988–91; Head, Civil Business, 1991–93; Head, Legal Services and Agencies Div., 1993. *Recreations:* sport, theatre, crosswords, poetry. *Address:* Crown Prosecution Service, 50 Ludgate Hill, EC4M 7EX. *T:* 0171–273 8097.

NOOR, Rusli; Indonesian Order of Satya Lencana Karya Satya, 1974; Secretary General, Association of South East Asian Nations, since 1989; *b* 1 May 1927; *s* of Pangeran Mohamad Noor and Gusti Aminah; *m* 1952, Aji Ratna Kemala Afloes; two *s* five *d. Educ:* Columbia Univ., NY (MA; Cert. Russian Inst.). Indonesian Ministry of Foreign Affairs: served London, Moscow, The Hague, Jakarta, 1951–74; Ambassador to Denmark and Norway, 1974–78; Dir Gen. for Foreign Economic, Social and Cultural Relations, 1978–83; Ambassador to Belgium, Luxembourg and EC, 1983–86; Dir Gen for Foreign Economic Relations, 1986–88; Consultant to Minister for Foreign Affairs, 1988–89. Foreign Orders from Belgium, France, Netherlands and Venezuela. *Recreations:* reading, fishing. *Address:* Jln Imam Bonjol 49, Jakarta, Indonesia. *T:* (21) 334805.

NORBURN, Prof. David, PhD; Director, The Management School, Imperial College of Science, Technology and Medicine, and Professor of Management, University of London, since 1987; Director: Newchurch & Co., since 1985; Whurr Publishing Co. Ltd, since 1994; *b* 18 Feb. 1941; *s* of late Richard Greville and Constance Elizabeth Norburn; *m* 1st, 1962, Veronica Ellis (marr. diss. 1975); one *s* one *d*; 2nd, 1975, Prof. Susan Joyce Birley, *qv. Educ:* Bolton Sch.; LSE (BSc); City Univ. (PhD). Salesman, Burroughs Corp., 1962–66; Management Consultant, Price Waterhouse, 1966–67; Sen. Lectr, Regent Street Polytechnic, 1967–70; Sen. Res. Fellow, City Univ., 1970–72; Lectr, Sen. Lectr, Dir,

MBA programme, London Business Sch., 1972–82; Inaugural Chairholder, Franklin D. Schurz Prof. in Strategic Management, Univ. of Notre Dame, Indiana, 1982–85; Prof. of Strategic Management, Cranfield Inst. of Technology, 1985–87. Freeman, Clockmakers' Co. CIMgt, FRSA. Editor, European Business Journal, 1988–. *Publications:* British Business Policy (with D. Channon and J. Stopford), 1975; articles in professional jls. *Recreations:* antiquarian horology, competitive tennis, carpentry. *Address:* The Management School, Imperial College of Science, Technology and Medicine, 53 Prince's Gate, SW7 2PG. *T:* 0171–589 5111. *Club:* Athenæum.

NORBURN, Susan Joyce, (Mrs David Norburn); *see* Birley, S. J.

NORBURY, 6th Earl of, *cr* 1827; **Noel Terence Graham-Toler;** Baron Norwood, 1797; Baron Norbury, 1800; Viscount Glandine, 1827; *b* 1 Jan. 1939; *s* of 5th Earl and Margaret Greenhalgh (*d* 1984); *S* father 1955; *m* 1965, Anne Mathew; one *s* one *d*. *Heir: s* Viscount Glandine, *qv*. *Address:* The Woodlands, Seer Green, Bucks HP9 2UL.

NORBURY, Brian Martin; Chairman, Opportunities and Networks in Southwark, since 1995; Head of Schools Branch 2, Department for Education (formerly Department of Education and Science), 1988–94; *b* 2 March 1938; *s* of Robert Sidney Norbury and Doris Lilian (*née* Broughton). *Educ:* Churcher's Coll., Petersfield; King's Coll., London (BA; AKC 1959). National Service, RAEC, 1959–61. Asst Principal, WO, 1961; Private Sec. to Under Sec. of State for War, 1962; Asst Private Sec. to Dep. Sec. of State for Defence, 1964; Principal, MoD, 1965, Cabinet Office, 1969; Private Sec. to Sec. of the Cabinet, 1970–73; Asst Sec., MoD, 1973; Principal Private Sec. to Sec. of State for Def., 1979–81; Under Sec., MoD, 1981, DES, later Dept for Educn, 1984–94. Mem. Bd of Visitors, Pentonville Prison, 1994–. FRSA 1992. *Recreation:* riding on top of Routemaster buses. *Address:* 63 Aberdeen Road, N5 2XB. *Club:* Reform.

NORCROSS, Lawrence John Charles, OBE 1986; Headmaster, Highbury Grove School, 1975–87; *b* 14 April 1927; *s* of Frederick Marshall Norcross and Florence Kate (*née* Hedges); *m* 1958, Margaret Wallace; three *s* one *d*. *Educ:* Ruskin Coll., Oxford; Univ. of Leeds (BA Hons English). Training Ship, Arethusa, 1941–42; RN, 1942–49 (E Indies Fleet, 1944–45); clerical asst, 1949–52; Asst Teacher: Singlegate Sch., 1957–61; Abbey Wood Sch., 1961–63; Housemaster, Battersea County Sch., 1963–74; Dep. Headmaster, Highbury Grove Sch., 1974–75. Member: NAS/UWT, 1970–86; Secondary Heads' Assoc., 1975–87; HMC, 1985–87; Trustee and Mem. Exec. Cttee, Nat. Council for Educnl Standards, 1976–89; Trustee: Educnl Res. Trust, 1986–; Ind. Primary and Secondary Educn Trust, 1987–93; Grant Maintained Schools Trust, 1988–; Dir, Choice in Educn, 1989–94; Member: Educn Study Gp, Centre for Policy Studies, 1980–; Univ. Entrance and Schs Examinations Council, Univ. of London, 1980–84; Steering Cttee, Campaign for a Gen. Teaching Council. Mem., Adv. Council, Educn Unit, IEA, 1986–90. Founder and Hon. Sec., John Ireland Soc., 1960–; former Chm., Contemp. Concerts Co-ordination. Occasional broadcasts and television appearances. *Publications:* (with F. Naylor) The ILEA: a case for reform, 1981; (with F. Naylor and J. McIntosh) The ILEA after the Abolition of the GLC, 1983; (contrib.) The Wayward Curriculum, 1986; GCSE: the Egalitarian Fallacy, 1990; occasional articles. *Recreations:* talking to friends, playing bridge badly, watching cricket, listening to music. *Address:* Crockwell Cottage, Crockwell Street, Long Compton, Warwicks CV36 5JN. *T:* Long Compton (01608) 684662; 3 St Nicholas Mansions, 6–8 Trinity Crescent, SW17 7AF. *T:* 0181–767 4299. *Clubs:* St Stephen's Constitutional; Surrey County Cricket.

NORDEN, Denis, CBE 1980; scriptwriter and broadcaster; *b* 6 Feb. 1922; *s* of George Norden and Jenny Lubell; *m* 1943, Avril Rosen; one *s* one *d*. *Educ:* Craven Park Sch., London; City of London Sch. Theatre Manager, 1939–42; served RAF, 1942–45; staff-writer in Variety Agency, 1945–47. With Frank Muir, 1947–64: collaborated for 17 years writing comedy scripts, including: (for radio): Take It From Here, 1947–58; Bedtime with Braden, 1950–54; (for TV): And So To Bentley, 1956; Whack-O!, 1958–60; The Seven Faces of Jim, 1961, and other series with Jimmy Edwards; resident in TV and radio panel-games; collaborated in film scripts, television commercials, and revues; joint Advisors and Consultants to BBC Television Light Entertainment Dept, 1960–64; jointly received Screenwriters Guild Award for Best Contribution to Light Entertainment, 1961; together on panel-games My Word!, 1956–93, and My Music, 1967–. Since 1964, solo writer for television and films; Chm., Looks Familiar (Thames TV), 1973–87; It'll Be Alright on the Night (LWT), 1977–94; It'll be Alright on the Day, 1983; In On The Act, 1988; Pick of the Pilots, 1990; Denis Norden's Laughter File, 1991; Denis Norden's Trailer Cinema, 1992; Laughter by Royal Command, 1993; Legends of Light Music, 1995. Film Credits include: The Bliss of Mrs Blossom; Buona Sera, Mrs Campbell; The Best House in London; Every Home Should Have One; Twelve Plus One; The Statue; The Water Babies. Variety Club of GB Award for Best Radio Personality (with Frank Muir), 1978; Male TV Personality of the Year, 1980. *Publications:* (with Frank Muir): You Can't Have Your Kayak and Heat It, 1973; Upon My Word!, 1974; Take My Word for It, 1978; The Glums, 1979; Oh, My Word!, 1980; The Complete and Utter My Word Stories, 1983; Coming to You Live! behind-the-screen memories of 50s and 60s Television, 1986; You Have My Word, 1989. *Recreations:* reading, loitering. *Address:* 53 Frith Street, W1V 5TE. *Club:* Saturday Morning Odeon.

NORELL, Dr Jacob Solomon, (Jack), FRCGP; principal in general practice, 1956–90; *b* 3 March 1927; *s* of Henry (formerly Habib) Norell and Malka Norell; *m* 1948, Brenda Honeywell (marr. diss. 1973); three *s*. *Educ:* South Devon Technical Coll.; Guy's Hosp. Med. Sch. (MB, BS 1953). MRCS, LRCP 1953; LMSSA 1952; MRCGP 1972, FRCGP 1982. Dean of Studies, RCGP, 1974–81; Exec. Officer, Jt Cttee on Postgrad. Educn for Gen. Practice, 1976–81. Mem. Council, RCGP, 1984–90; Pres., Section of Gen. Practice, RSM, 1989–90. Pres., Balint Soc., 1984–87, Internat. Balint Fedn, 1989–93, ambassadorial rôle in Eastern Europe, 1994–. William Pickles Lectr, RCGP, 1984. Editor, The Practitioner, 1982–83. *Publications:* (co-ed) Six Minutes for the Patient, 1973; Entering General Practice, 1981; papers and chapters on general practice topics: the Balint philosophy, consultation, practice orgn, postgrad. educn, women doctors, measuring quality of med. care, professional self-regulation, doctor-patient relationship. *Recreations:* rural walks, driving open-topped cars, spotting unclad emperors. *Address:* 50 Nottingham Terrace, York Gate, Regent's Park, NW1 4QD. *T:* 0171–486 2979.

NORFOLK, 17th Duke of, *cr* 1483; **Miles Francis Stapleton Fitzalan-Howard,** KG 1983; GCVO 1986; CB 1966; CBE 1960; MC 1944; DL; Earl of Arundel, 1139; Baron Beaumont, 1309; Baron Maltravers, 1330, Earl of Surrey, 1483; Baron FitzAlan, Clun, and Oswaldestre, 1627; Earl of Norfolk, 1644; Baron Howard of Glossop, 1869; Earl Marshal and Hereditary Marshal and Chief Butler of England; Premier Duke and Earl; *b* 21 July 1915; *s* of 3rd Baron Howard of Glossop, MBE, and Baroness Beaumont (11th in line), OBE; *S* to barony of mother, 1971, and of father, 1972, and to dukedom of cousin, 1975; *m* 1949, Anne Mary Teresa, CBE, *e d* of late Wing Commander Gerald Joseph Constable Maxwell, MC, DFC, AFC; two *s* three *d*. *Educ:* Ampleforth Coll.; Christ Church, Oxford (MA; Hon. Student, 1983). 2nd Lieut, Grenadier Guards, 1937. Served War of 1939–45, France, North Africa, Sicily, Italy (despatches, MC), NW Europe. Appointed Head of British Military Mission to Russian Forces in Germany, 1957; Commanded 70 Bde KAR, 1961–63; GOC, 1 Div., 1963–65 (Maj.-Gen.); Dir, Management and Support Intelligence, MoD, 1965–66; Director, Service Intelligence, MoD, 1966–67; retd 1967. Chm., Arundel Castle Trustees, Ltd, 1976–. Pres., Building Socs Assoc., 1982–86. Prime Warden, Fishmongers' Co., 1985–86. Hon. Fellow, St Edmund's Coll., Cambridge, 1983; Hon. Bencher, Inner Temple, 1984. DL West Sussex, 1977. Knight, SMO Malta; Kt Grand Cross, Order of Pius IX. *Heir: s* Earl of Arundel and Surrey, *qv*. *Address:* Arundel Castle, Sussex BN18 9AB. *T:* Arundel (01903) 882173; Carlton Towers, Goole, North Humberside DN14 9LZ. *T:* Goole (01405) 860 243; Bacres House, Hambleden, Henley-on-Thames, Oxfordshire RG9 6RY. *T:* Henley-on-Thames (01491) 571350. *Club:* Pratt's.

See also Lord Michael Fitzalan-Howard, Sir D. P. Frost.

NORFOLK, Lavinia Duchess of, LG 1990; CBE 1971; Lord-Lieutenant of West Sussex, 1975–90; *b* 22 March 1916; *d* of 3rd Baron Belper and of Eva, Countess of Rosebery, DBE; *m* 1937, 16th Duke of Norfolk, KG, PC, GCVO, GBE, TD (*d* 1975); four *d*. *Educ:* Abbotshill, Hemel Hempstead, Herts. President: Nat. Canine Defence League, 1969–; Pony Riding for the Disabled Trust, Chigwell, 1964–; BHS, 1980–82. Vice-President: ASBAH, 1970–; Spastic Soc., 1969–; NSPCC, 1967–. Patron, Riding for the Disabled, 1986– (Pres., 1970–86). Vice Pres., King Edward VII Hosp., Midhurst, 1975–. Steward, Goodwood, 1976–78. BRCS Certificate of Honour and Badge, Class 1, 1969. Silver Jubilee Medal, 1977. *Address:* Arundel Park, Sussex. *T:* Arundel (01903) 882041.

See also Earl of Ancram, Lady Herries of Terregles, Lady Mary Mumford.

NORFOLK, Archdeacon of; *see* Handley, Ven. A. M.

NORFOLK, Ven. Edward Matheson; Archdeacon of St Albans, 1982–87, Emeritus since 1987; *b* 29 Sept. 1921; *s* of Edward and Chrissie Mary Wilson Norfolk; *m* 1947, Mary Louisa Oates; one *s* one *d* (and one *s* decd). *Educ:* Latymer Upper School; Leeds Univ. (BA); College of the Resurrection, Mirfield. Deacon, 1946; priest, 1947; Assistant Curate: Greenford, 1946–47; King Charles the Martyr, South Mymms, 1947–50; Bushey, 1950–53; Vicar: Waltham Cross, 1953–59; Welwyn Garden City, 1959–69; Rector, Great Berkhamsted, 1969–81; Vicar, King's Langley, 1981–82. Hon. Canon of St Albans, 1972–82. *Recreations:* walking, bird-watching. *Address:* 5 Fairlawn Court, Sidmouth, Devon EX10 1UR.

NORFOLK, Leslie William, CBE 1973 (OBE 1944); TD 1946; CEng; Chief Executive, Royal Dockyards, Ministry of Defence, 1969–72; *b* 8 April 1911; *e s* of late Robert and Edith Norfolk, Nottingham; *m* 1944, A. I. E. W. (Nancy) Watson (then WRNS), *d* of late Sir Hugh Watson, IFS (retd); two *s* one *d*. *Educ:* Southwell Minster Grammar Sch., Notts; University Coll., Nottingham (BSc). MICE; MIMechE; MIEE. Assistant and later Partner, E. G. Phillips, Son & Norfolk, consulting engineers, Nottingham, 1932–39. 2nd Lieut 1931, 5 Foresters TA, transferred and served with RE, France, Gibraltar, Home Forces, 1939–45, Lt-Col. Engineer, Dyestuffs Div., ICI Ltd, 1945–53; Resident Engineer, ICI of Canada, Kingston, Ont., 1953–55; Asst Chief Engr, Metals Div., ICI Ltd, 1955–57; Engineering Manager, Severnside Works, ICI Ltd, 1957–59; Engineering Director, Industrias Quimicas Argentinas Duperial SAIC, Buenos Aires, 1959–65; Director, Heavy Organic Chemicals Div., ICI Ltd, 1965–68; retired from ICI, 1968. *Recreations:* home workshop, industrial archaeology. *Address:* Beechwoods, Beechwood Road, Combe Down, Bath, Avon BA2 5JS. *T:* Combe Down (01225) 832104. *Club:* Bath & County (Bath).

NORGARD, John Davey, AO 1982; Chairman, Australian Broadcasting Commission, 1976–81; retired as Executive General Manager, Operations, BHP Co. Ltd, and as Chairman, Associated Tin Smelters, 1970; *b* 3 Feb. 1914; *s* of John Henry and Ida Elizabeth Norgard; *m* 1943, Irena Mary Doffkont; one *s* three *d*. *Educ:* Adelaide Univ. (BE); SA Sch. of Mines (FSASM). Part-time Chm., Metric Conversion Bd, Australia, 1970–81; Chairman: Commonwealth Employment Service Review, 1976–77; Pipeline Authority, 1976–81; Mem., Nat. Energy Adv. Cttee, 1977–80. Dep. Chancellor, La Trobe Univ., 1972–75. Chm., Grad. Careers Council of Australia, 1979–86. *Recreation:* golf. *Address:* 29 Montalto Avenue, Toorak, Victoria 3142, Australia. *T:* (03) 8274937. *Clubs:* Australian, Royal Melbourne Golf, Royal Society of Victoria (Melbourne).

NORLAND, Otto Realf; London representative, Deutsche Schiffsbank (formerly Deutsche Schiffahrtsbank) AG, since 1984; Chairman, Otto Norland Ltd, since 1984; *b* 24 Feb. 1930; *s* of Realph I. O. Norland and Aasta S. Sæther; *m* 1955, Gerd Ellen Andenæs; two *d* (one *s* decd). *Educ:* Norwegian University College of Economics and Business Administration, Bergen. FCIB. Hambros Bank Ltd, 1953–84, Dir, 1964–84. Director: Alcoa of Great Britain Ltd, 1968–84 (Chm., 1978–84); Banque Paribas Norge A/S, Oslo, 1986–88; Northern Navigation International Ltd, USA, 1991–. Dir, Aluminium Fedn Ltd, 1979–84 (Pres., 1982). *Recreations:* tennis, skiing, books (polar explorations). *Address:* Grocers' Hall, Princes Street, EC2R 8AQ. *T:* 0171–726 8726. *Clubs:* Den Norske; Norske Selskab (Oslo).

NORMAN, (Alexander) Vesey (Bethune); Inspector of the Wallace Collection's Armouries, 1977–94; *b* 10 Feb. 1930; *s* of Lt-Col A. M. B. Norman and Sheila M. Maxwell; *m* 1st, 1954, Catherine Margaret Barne (marr. diss. 1987); one *s*; 2nd, 1988, Elizabeth Anne Buddle. *Educ:* Alford Sch.; Trinity Coll., Glenalmond; London Univ. (BA Gen.). FSA; FSAScot. Asst Curator, Scottish United Services Museum, Edinburgh Castle, 1957; Hon. Curator of Arms and Armour, Abbotsford, 1957–63; Asst to Dir, Wallace Collection, 1963; Master of the Armouries, The Royal Armouries, HM Tower of London, 1977–88, retd; Pres., Church Monuments Soc., 1986–91; Vice-President: NADFAS, 1984–89; Arms and Armour Soc., 1983–. Liveryman, Gunmakers' Co., 1981–. *Publications:* Arms & Armour, 1964 (also foreign edns); (with Don Pottinger) Warrior to Soldier, 449–1660, 1966 (USA edn as A History of War and Weapons, 449–1660, reprinted as English Weapons and Warfare, 449–1660, 1979); Small Swords and Military Swords, 1967; The Medieval Soldier, 1971 (also USA); Arms and Armour in the Royal Scottish Museum, 1972; A Catalogue of Ceramics, Wallace Collection, Pt I, 1976; (with C. M. Barne) The Rapier and Small-Sword, 1460–1820, 1980; Catalogue of European Arms and Armour, supplement, Wallace Collection, 1986; articles in learned jls. *Recreation:* study of arms and armour. *Address:* 15 Lansdowne Crescent, Edinburgh EH12 5EH.

NORMAN, Rear-Adm. Anthony Mansfeldt, CB 1989; Bursar and Fellow, St Catharine's College, Cambridge, since 1989; *b* 16 Dec. 1934; *s* of Cecil and Jean Norman; *m* 1961, Judith Pye; one *s* one *d*. *Educ:* Royal Naval Coll., Dartmouth. Graduate ndc. Various sea/shore appts, 1952–73; Staff of Dir Underwater Weapons, 1973–74; student ndc, 1974–75; CO HM Ships Argonaut and Mohawk, 1975–76; Fleet Anti-Submarine Warfare Officer, 1976–78; CO (Captain), HMS Broadsword, 1978–80; Asst Dir Naval Plans, MoD, 1980–83; Captain: 2nd Frigate Sqdn, HMS Broadsword, 1983–85; Sch. of Maritime Ops, HMS Dryad, 1985–86; Dir Gen., Naval Personal Services, MoD (Navy), 1986–89. *Recreations:* tennis, squash, hill walking, travel. *Address:* c/o National Westminster Bank, 208 Piccadilly, W1A 2DG. *Club:* Army and Navy.

NORMAN, Archibald John; Group Chief Executive, Asda Group plc, since 1991; *b* 1 May 1954; *s* of Dr Archibald Percy Norman, *qv*; *m* 1983, Vanessa Mary Peet; one *d*. *Educ:*

Univ. of Minnesota; Emmanuel Coll., Cambridge (BA Hons Econs, MA); Harvard Business Sch. (MBA 1979). Citibank NA, 1975–77; McKinsey & Co. Inc., 1979–86, Principal 1984; Gp Finance Dir, Woolworth Holdings plc, later Kingfisher plc, 1986–91; Chm., Chartwell Land plc, 1987–91; Non-exec. Dir, Geest plc, 1988–91; Member: British Railways Bd, 1992–94; Railtrack Gp Bd, 1994–. Member: DTI Deregulation Taskforce; Anglo-German, Deregulation Taskforce. Pres., W Yorks Business Assoc. Mem. Consultative Cttee, Dulwich Picture Gall., 1990–. *Recreations:* politics, farming, opera, theatre, music, fishing, ski-ing, tennis. *Address:* Asda House, Southbank, Great Wilson Street, Leeds LS11 5AD. *T:* Leeds (0113) 243 5435. *Club:* Vanderbilt.

NORMAN, Archibald Percy, MBE 1945; FRCP; MD; Physician, Hospital for Sick Children, 1950–77, now Hon. Physician; Paediatrician, Queen Charlotte's Maternity Hospital, 1951–77, now Hon. Paediatrician; *b* 19 July 1912; *s* of Dr George Percy Norman and Mary Margaret MacCallum; *m* 1950, Aleida Elisabeth M. M. R. Bisschop; five *s*. *Educ:* Charterhouse; Emmanuel Coll., Cambridge. Served War of 1939–45, in Army, 1940–45. Chairman: Med. and Res. Cttee, Cystic Fibrosis Res. Trust, 1976–84; E Surrey Cttee, Mencap Homes Foundn, 1987–; Mem., Attendance Allowance Appeals Bd, 1978–84. Mem., Bd of Trustees, Tadworth Court Trust, 1988–. *Publications:* (ed) Congenital Abnormalities, 1962, 2nd edn 1971; (ed) Moncreiff's Nursing and Diseases of Sick Children, 1966; (ed) Cystic Fibrosis, 1983; contributions to medical journals. *Address:* White Lodge, Heather Close, Kingswood, Surrey KT20 6NY. *T:* Mogador (01737) 832626.
See also A. J. Norman.

NORMAN, Sir Arthur (Gordon), KBE 1969 (CBE 1966); DFC 1943; and Bar 1944; Chairman, The De La Rue Company, 1964–87; *b* N Petherton, Som, 18 Feb. 1917; *m* 1944, Margaret Doreen Harrington (*d* 1982); three *s* two *d*. *Educ:* Blundell's Sch. Joined Thomas De La Rue & Co., 1934. RAF, 1939–45; Wing-Comdr, 1943. Rejoined Thomas De La Rue & Co., 1946; Director, 1951; Managing Director, 1953–77. Vice-Chm., Sun Life Assurance Society, 1984–87 (Dir, 1966–87); Director: SKF (UK) Ltd, 1970–87; Kleinwort, Benson, Lonsdale plc, subseq. Kleinwort Benson Gp, 1985–88. Pres., CBI, 1968–70. Bd mem., Internat. Inst. for Environment and Develt, 1982–92; Chairman: WWF UK, 1977–84, 1987–90. UK CEED, 1984–; Mem., Nature Conservancy Council, 1980–86. *Recreations:* golf, country life. *Address:* Fir Tree Cottage, Hammoon, Sturminster Newton, Dorset DT10 2DB. *Club:* East India.

NORMAN, Barry (Leslie); author, journalist and broadcaster; *b* 21 Aug. 1933; *s* of late Leslie and Elizabeth Norman; *m* 1957, Diana, *o d* of late A. H. and C. A. Narracott; two *d*. *Educ:* Highgate Sch. Entertainments Editor, Daily Mail, 1969–71, then made redundant; Writer and Presenter of Film, 1973–81, and Film 1983–, BBC1; Presenter of: Today, Radio 4, 1974–76; Going Places, Radio 4, 1977–81; Breakaway, Radio 4, 1979–80; Omnibus, BBC1, 1982; The Chip Shop, Radio 4, 1984; How Far Can You Go?, Radio 4, 1990; Writer and Presenter of: The Hollywood Greats, BBC1, 1977–79, 1984, 1985; The British Greats, 1980; Talking Pictures (series), BBC1, 1988. Weekly columnist: The Guardian, 1971–80; Radio Times. Hon. LittD UEA, 1991. Richard Dimbleby Award, BAFTA, 1981; Columnist of the Year, 1991. *Publications:* The Matter of Mandrake, 1967; The Hounds of Sparta, 1968; Tales of the Redundance Kid, 1975; End Product, 1975; A Series of Defeats, 1977; To Nick a Good Body, 1978; The Hollywood Greats, 1979; The Movie Greats, 1981; Have a Nice Day, 1981; Sticky Wicket, 1984; The Film Greats, 1985; Talking Pictures, 1988; The Birddog Tape, 1992; 100 Best Films of the Century, 1993; The Mickey Mouse Affair, 1995. *Recreation:* playing village cricket. *Address:* c/o Curtis Brown Ltd, 162–168 Regent Street, W1R 5TB.

NORMAN, David Mark; Chairman and Chief Executive, BNB Resources plc, since 1987; Chairman, Norman Broadbent International Ltd, since 1983; *b* 30 Jan. 1941; *s* of late Mark Richard Norman, CBE and of Helen Norman (*née* Bryan); *m* 1966, Diana Sheffield; one *s* three *d*. *Educ:* Eton Coll.; McGill Univ. (BA); Harvard Business Sch. (MBA). Norcros Ltd, 1967–77, Dir of Ops and Main Bd Dir, 1975–77; Russell Reynolds Associates Inc., 1977–82: Exec. Dir, 1977–78; Man. Dir, 1978–82; Chm., Norman Resources Ltd, 1982–83. *Recreations:* golf, tennis, rackets, classical music, opera, ballet. *Address:* BNB Resources plc, 30 Farringdon Street, EC4A 4EA; Burkham House, Alton, Hants GU34 5RS. *T:* Basingstoke (01256) 381211. *Clubs:* Boodle's, Royal Automobile; Queen's, All England Lawn Tennis; New York Racquet and Tennis.

NORMAN, Desmond; *see* Norman, N. D.

NORMAN, Rev. Canon Edward Robert; Canon Residentiary, York Minster, since 1995; *b* 22 Nov. 1938; *o s* of Ernest Edward Norman and Yvonne Louise Norman. *Educ:* Chatham House Sch.; Monoux Sch.; Selwyn Coll., Cambridge (MA, PhD, DD). FRHistS. Lincoln Theological Coll., 1965. Deacon, 1965; Priest, 1971. Asst Master, Beaconsfield Sec. Mod. Sch., Walthamstow, 1957–58; Fellow of Selwyn Coll., Cambridge, 1962–64; Fellow of Jesus Coll., Cambridge, 1964–71; Lectr in History, Univ. of Cambridge, 1965–88; Dean of Peterhouse, Cambridge, 1971–88 (Emeritus Fellow); Dean of Chapel, Christ Church Coll., Canterbury, 1988–95. Wilkinson Prof. of Church History, Wycliffe Coll., Univ. of Toronto, 1981–82; Associated Schol., Ethics and Public Policy Center, Washington, 1986–. NATO Res. Fellow, 1966–68. Asst Chaplain, Addenbrooke's Hosp., Cambridge, 1971–78. Reith Lectr, 1978; Prideaux Lectr, 1980; Suntory-Toyota Lectr, LSE, 1984. Six Preacher in Canterbury Cathedral, 1984–90. FRSA. *Publications:* The Catholic Church and Ireland, 1965; The Conscience of the State in North America, 1968; Anti-Catholicism in Victorian England, 1968; The Early Development of Irish Society, 1969; A History of Modern Ireland, 1971; Church and Society in Modern England, 1976; Christianity and the World Order, 1979; Christianity in the Southern Hemisphere, 1981; The English Catholic Church in the Nineteenth Century, 1983; Roman Catholicism in England, 1985; The Victorian Christian Socialists, 1987; The House of God: church architecture, style and history, 1990; Entering the Darkness: Christianity and its modern substitutes, 1991. *Recreation:* watching television. *Address:* 3 Minster Court, York YO1 2JJ. *Club:* Athenæum.

NORMAN, Ven. Garth; Archdeacon of Bromley, since 1994; *b* 26 Nov. 1938; *s* of Harry and Freda Norman; *m* 1977, Jacqueline Elisabeth (*née* Junge-Bateman); one *s*. *Educ:* Henry Mellish Grammar Sch., Nottingham; Univ. of Durham (BA Hons Theol, DipTh, MA); Univ. of East Anglia (MEd); Univ. of Cambridge (PGCE). Deacon 1963, priest 1964; Curate, St Anne's, Wandsworth, 1963–66; Team Vicar, Trunch, Norfolk, 1966–71; Rector of Gimingham, 1971–77; Team Rector of Trunch, 1977–83; RD, Repps, 1975–83; Principal, Chiltern Christian Trng Scheme, Dio. of Oxford, 1983–88; Dir of Training, Dio. of Rochester, 1988–94; Hon. Canon of Rochester Cathedral, 1991–. *Recreations:* walking, music. *Address:* 6 Horton Way, Farningham, Kent DA4 0DQ. *T:* Farningham (01322) 864522.

NORMAN, Geoffrey, OBE 1995; Deputy Secretary of Commissions (Training), Lord Chancellor's Department, 1990–95; *b* 25 March 1935; *s* of late William Frederick Trafalgar Norman and of Vera May Norman (*née* Goodfellow); *m* 1958, Dorothy Frances King (*d* 1978); two *s* two *d*. *Educ:* Harrow County Sch.; Brasenose Coll., Oxford (MA). Admitted Solicitor, 1959. Deputy Clerk to the Justices, Uxbridge, 1961–66; Clerk to the Justices, N Hertfordshire and Stevenage, 1966–77; Sec., Magistrates' Assoc., 1977–86; Asst Sec. of Commns (Trng), Lord Chancellor's Dept, 1986–90. Member: Duty Solicitor Scheme-making Cttee, 1984–86; Magisterial Cttee, Judicial Studies Bd, 1986–95; Magistrates' Courts Rules Cttee, 1989–93. JP Inner London, 1982–90. Freeman, City of London, 1981; Liveryman, Curriers' Co., 1983. *Publication:* The Magistrate as Chairman (with Lady Ralphs), 1987. *Address:* Easter Cottage, Gosmore, Hitchin, Herts SG4 7QH. *T:* Hitchin (01462) 450783.

NORMAN, George Alfred B.; *see* Bathurst Norman.

NORMAN, Geraldine Lucia; Art Market Correspondent, The Independent, since 1987; *b* 13 May 1940; *d* of Harold Hugh Keen and Catherine Eleanor Lyle Keen (*née* Cummins); *m* 1971, Frank Norman (*d* 1980). *Educ:* St Mary's Sch., Calne; St Anne's Coll., Oxford (MA). Teaching Asst, UCLA, 1961–62; Statistician, The Times, 1962–66; Econ. Writer, FAO, Rome, 1966–67; Sale Room Corresp., The Times, 1969–87. News Reporter of Year, British Press Awards, 1976. *Publications:* (as Geraldine Keen) The Sale of Works of Art, 1971; Nineteenth Century Painters and Painting: a dictionary, 1977; (with Tom Keating and Frank Norman) The Fake's Progress, 1977; (as Florence Place) Mrs Harper's Niece, 1982; Biedermeier Painting, 1987; (with Natsuo Miyashita) Top Collectors of the World, 1993. *Recreations:* transcendental meditation, reading detective stories. *Address:* 5 Seaford Court, 220 Great Portland Street, W1N 5HH. *T:* 0171–387 6067.
See also M. H. Keen.

NORMAN, (Herbert) John (La French), FIMIT, FISOB; writer and organ consultant; *b* 15 Jan. 1932; *s* of Herbert La French Norman, Hon. RCO, FRSA, and Hilda Caroline (*née* West); *m* 1956, Jill Frances Sharp; one *s* two *d*. *Educ:* Tollington Sch.; Imperial Coll., London (BSc 1953). ARCS 1953. Wm Hill & Son and Norman & Beard Ltd (organbuilders by appt to HM Queen), 1953–74; Dir, 1960–74; Man. Dir, 1970–74; Exec., IBM UK Ltd, 1974–90. Work on organs in cathedrals in Gloucester, Norwich, Lichfield, Southwell Minster, Chelmsford and Brisbane, Australia; also Bath Abbey and RCO. Organ Advr, Dio. London, 1975–; Organ Consultant to: Harrow Sch.; Lancing Coll.; Mill Hill Sch.; Sherborne Abbey; Gibraltar Cathedral; Liberal Jewish Synagogue, St John's Wood; St Margaret's, Westminster; St Mary's Pro-cathedral, Dublin; Pershore Abbey. Founding Editor: Musical Instrument Technol., 1969–; The Organbuilder, 1983–; In Sight, 1991–; Columnist, Organists' Rev., 1980–. Member: St Albans Diocesan Synod, 1980–86; Organs Cttee, Council for Care of Churches, 1987–; London DAC for Care of Churches, 1989–; Cathedrals Fabric Commn for England, 1991–. Mem., Music Technol. Adv. Bd, London Guildhall Univ. (formerly City of London Polytechnic), 1990–; Vis. Lectr, RSCM. Past Pres., Inst. of Musical Instrument Technol. Freeman, City of London; Liveryman, Musicians' Co., 1972–. *Publications:* (with Herbert Norman) The Organ today, 1966, 2nd edn 1980; The Organs of Britain, 1984. *Recreations:* writing, music, architecture, travel. *Address:* 15 Baxendale, Whetstone, N20 0EG. *T:* 0181–445 0801.

NORMAN, Jessye; soprano, concert and opera singer; *b* Augusta, Ga, USA, 15 Sept. 1945; *d* of late Silas Norman Sr and Janie King Norman. *Educ:* Howard Univ., Washington, DC (BM *cum laude*). Peabody Conservatory, 1967; Univ. of Michigan, 1967–68 (MMus). Operatic début, Deutsche Oper, Berlin, 1969; La Scala, Milan, 1972; Royal Opera House, Covent Garden, 1972; NY Metropolitan Opera, 1983; American début, Hollywood Bowl, 1972; Lincoln Centre, NYC, 1973. Tours include North and South America, Europe, Middle East, Australia, Israel, Japan. Many international festivals, including Aix-en-Provence, Aldeburgh, Berlin, Edinburgh, Flanders, Helsinki, Lucerne, Salzburg, Tanglewood, Spoleto, Hollywood, Ravinia. Hon. Fellow: Newnham Coll., Cambridge, 1989; Jesus Coll., Cambridge, 1989. Hon. DMus: Howard Univ., 1982; Univ. of the South, Sewanee, 1984; Boston Conservatory, 1984; Univ. of Michigan and Brandeis Univ., Mass, 1987; Harvard Univ., 1988; Cambridge, 1989; Hon DHL Amer. Univ. of Paris, 1989. Hon. RAM 1987. Musician of the Year, Musical America, 1982; prizes include: Grand Prix du Disque (Acad. du Disque Français), 1973, 1976, 1977, 1982, 1984; Grand Prix du Disque (Acad. Charles Cros), 1983; Deutscher Schallplattenpreis, 1975, 1981; Cigale d'Or, Aix-en-Provence Fest., 1977; IRCAM record award, 1982; Grammy, 1984, 1988. Commandeur de l'Ordre des Arts et des Lettres, France, 1984. *Address:* c/o Shaw Concerts Incorporated, 1900 Broadway, New York, NY 10023, USA.

NORMAN, John; *see* Norman, H. J. La F.

NORMAN, Prof. Kenneth Roy, FBA 1985; Professor of Indian Studies, University of Cambridge, 1990–92, Emeritus Professor 1992; *b* 21 July 1925; *s* of Clement and Peggy Norman; *m* 1953, Pamela Raymont; one *s* one *d*. *Educ:* Taunton School; Downing College, Cambridge (MA 1954). Fellow and Tutor, Downing College, Cambridge, 1952–64; Lectr in Indian Studies (Prakrit), 1955–78, Reader, 1978–90, Univ. of Cambridge. Foreign Mem., Royal Danish Acad. of Sciences and Letters, 1983. *Publications:* Elders' Verses I (Theragāthā), 1969; Elders' Verses II (Therīgāthā), 1971; (trans.) Jain Cosmology, 1981; Pāli Literature, 1983; The Group of Discourses (Sutta-nipāta), Vol. I, 1984, Vol. II, 1992; Collected Papers: Vol. I, 1990, Vol. II, 1991, Vol. III, 1992, Vol. IV, 1993, Vol. V, 1994; (ed) Pāli Tipiṭakaṁ Concordance, Vol. II 4–9, 1963–73; (ed) Critical Pāli Dictionary Vol. II 11–17, 1981–90. *Recreations:* reading, walking. *Address:* 6 Huttles Green, Shepreth, Royston, Herts SG8 6PR. *T:* Royston (01763) 260541.

NORMAN, Air Cdre Sir Mark (Annesley), 3rd Bt, *cr* 1915; DL; farmer; *b* 8 Feb. 1927; *s* of Sir Nigel Norman, 2nd Bt, CBE, and Patricia Moyra (*d* 1986) (who *m* 2nd, 1944, Sir Robert Perkins), *e d* of late Colonel J. H. A. Annesley, CMG, DSO; *S* father, 1943; *m* Joanna Camilla, *d* of late Lt-Col I. J. Kilgour; two *s* one *d*. *Educ:* Winchester Coll.; RMC. Coldstream Guards, 1945–47; Flying Officer, 601 (County of London) Sqdn, RAuxAF, 1953–56. Hon. Air Cdre, No 4624 (County of Oxford) Movements Sqdn, RAuxAF; Air Cdre RAuxAF, 1984. Chm., Anglo-US Cttee, RAF Upper Heyford, 1984–91. Director: Gotaas-Larsen Shipping Corp., 1979–88. Chm., IU Europe Ltd, 1973–87. Mem., Council, St Luke's, Oxford, 1985–91 (Chm., 1986–88). Patron and Churchwarden, St Peter's, Wilcote, 1972–. High Sheriff, 1983–84, DL 1985, Oxon. *Recreations:* gardening, workshop, the building of minor follies, offshore cruising. *Heir: s* Nigel James Norman, late Major 13/18th Royal Hussars (Queen Mary's Own) [*b* 5 Feb. 1956; *m* 1994, Mrs Juliet Marriott, *e d* of R. Baxendale; one *s*]. *Address:* Wilcote Manor, Wilcote, Chipping Norton, Oxon OX7 3EB. *T:* Ramsden (01993) 868357, *Fax:* (01993) 868032. *Clubs:* White's, Pratt's, Royal Air Force, MCC; St Moritz Tobogganing; Royal Southern Yacht.
See also N. D. Norman.

NORMAN, (Nigel) Desmond, CBE 1970; CEng; FRAeS; Chairman and Managing Director, AeroNorTec Ltd, since 1988; *b* 13 Aug. 1929; 2nd *s* of Sir Nigel Norman, 2nd Bt (*d* 1943), CBE, and Patricia Moyra (*d* 1987) (who *m* 2nd, 1944, Sir Robert Perkins); *m* 1st, Anne Fogg-Elliott; two *s*; 2nd, 1965, Mrs. Boel Elizabeth Holmsen; two *s* two *d*. *Educ:* Eton; De Havilland Aeronautical Technical Sch. (1946–49). RAF GD Pilot, thereafter 601 Sqdn, RAuxAF Fighter Sqdn, until disbandment, 1948–57. Export Asst at SBAC, 1951–53; Founder of Britten-Norman Ltd with F. R. J. Britten, 1954. *Recreations:* aviation, sailing, shooting. *Address:* Flat 4, 73 Duke Street, W1M 5DH; Le Palland, 87400 St Leonard de Noblat, France. *Clubs:* Royal Air Force, Royal Yacht Squadron.
See also Sir Mark Norman, Bt, W. R. Norman.

NORMAN, Sir Robert (Henry), Kt 1989; OBE 1957; Chairman, Cairns Campus Co-ordinating Committee, James Cook University of North Queensland, since 1987; *b* 30 Jan. 1914; *s* of Robert Moreton Norman and Dora Muriel Hoole; *m* 1942, Betty Merle Kimmins; one *s* three *d*. *Educ:* Christian Brothers' Coll. Joined RAAF, 1941; Dep. Flt Comdr, 1942; 459 Sqdn, 1943; discharged, 1945. Founded Bush Pilot Airways, 1952, retd 1984. Cairns Centenary Co-ordinator, 1976. Past Pres., Rotary Club of Cairns, Marlin Coast; Dist Gov., Dist 9550, Rotary Internat., 1991–92. Hon. DLitt James Cook Univ. of N Qld, 1994. *Publication:* Bush Pilot, 1976. *Recreations:* motoring, reading. *Address:* 12 Gloucester Street, Whitfield, Qld 4870, Australia; PO Box 133, Edge Hill, Qld 4871, Australia.

NORMAN, Sir Robert (Wentworth), Kt 1970; JP; *b* 10 April 1912; *s* of William Henry Norman and Minnie Esther Brown; *m* 1942, Grace Hebden, *d* of Sidney Percy Hebden; one *s* one *d*. *Educ:* Sydney Grammar Sch. Served Army 1940–46: Captain, AIF. Joined Bank of New South Wales, 1928; Manager, Head Office, 1961; Dep. Gen. Manager, 1962; Chief Gen. Manager, 1964–77; Dir, 1977–84. Councillor: Science Foundn for Physics within Univ. of Sydney; Inst. of Public Affairs; Senator and Life Mem., Junior Chamber Internat. Life Mem., Sydney Adv. Bd, Salvation Army. FAIM. JP NSW, 1956. 3rd Order of the Rising Sun (Japan), 1983. *Recreations:* bowls, reading. *Address:* 26/16 Rosemont Avenue, Woollahra, NSW 2025, Australia. *T:* (2) 3631900. *Clubs:* Union, Royal Sydney Golf, Australian Jockey (Sydney).

NORMAN, Sir Ronald, Kt 1995; OBE 1987; CEng; Chairman, Teesside Development Corporation, since 1987; *b* 29 April 1937; *s* of Leonard William Norman and Elsie Louise Norman (*née* Cooke); *m* 1st, 1961, Jennifer Mansfield (marr. diss.); two *s* one *d*; 2nd, 1975, Joyce Lyons. *Educ:* Dulwich Coll.; King's Coll., London (BSc Eng.). CE; CEng, MICE 1966. Man. Dir, then Chm., Cecil M. Yuill Ltd, Developers, Hartlepool, 1965–86; Chm., R. Norman Ltd, Developers, Durham, 1986–93. *Recreations:* mountain climbing, book collecting. *Address:* Hart-on-the-Hill, Dalton-Piercy, Cleveland TS27 3HY. *T:* Hartlepool (01429) 273857.

NORMAN, Vesey; *see* Norman, A. V. B.

NORMAN, Willoughby Rollo; Hon. President, The Boots Co. Ltd, since 1972 (Chairman, 1961–72); Deputy Chairman, English China Clays Ltd; 2nd *s* of Major Rt Hon. Sir Henry Norman, 1st Bt; *m* 1st, 1934, Hon. Barbara Jacqueline Boot, *er d* of 2nd and last Baron Trent, KBE; one *s* two *d*; 2nd, 1973, Caroline Haskard, *d* of William Greville and Lady Diana Worthington. *Educ:* Eton; Magdalen Coll., Oxford. Served War of 1939–45, Major, Grenadier Guards. Director: National Westminster Bank (Chm. Eastern Region), 1963–79; Sheepbridge Engineering Ltd, 1979; Guardian Royal Exchange Assurance, 1961–79. Vice-Chairman Boots Pure Drug Co. Ltd, 1954–61. High Sheriff of Leicestershire, 1960. *Recreations:* shooting, farming, gardening. *Address:* The Grange, South Harting, Petersfield, Hants GU31 5NR; 28 Ranelagh House, Elystan Place, SW3 3LD. *T:* 0171–584 9410. *Clubs:* White's, Pratt's.

See also Sir Mark Norman, Bt, N. D. Norman.

NORMANBY, 5th Marquis of, *cr* 1838; **Constantine Edmund Walter Phipps;** Baron Mulgrave (Ire.) 1767; Baron Mulgrave (GB) 1794; Earl of Mulgrave and Viscount Normanby 1812; *b* 24 Feb. 1954; *e s* of 4th Marquis of Normanby KG, CBE and of Hon. Grania Guinness, *d* of 1st Baron Moyne; *S* father, 1994; *m* 1990, Mrs Nicola St Aubyn, *d* of Milton Shulman, *qv* and Drusilla Beyfus, *qv*; one *s* one *d*. *Educ:* Eton; Worcester Coll., Oxford. *Publications:* Careful with the Sharks, 1985; Among the Thin Ghosts, 1989. *Heir:* *s* Earl of Mulgrave, *qv*. *Address:* Mulgrave Castle, Whitby, N Yorks YO21 3RJ. *Club:* Travellers'.

NORMANTON, 6th Earl of, *cr* 1806; **Shaun James Christian Welbore Ellis Agar;** Baron Mendip, 1794; Baron Somerton, 1795; Viscount Somerton, 1800; Baron Somerton (UK), 1873; Royal Horse Guards, 1965; Blues and Royals, 1969; left Army, 1972, Captain; *b* 21 Aug. 1945; *er s* of 5th Earl of Normanton; *S* father, 1967; *m* 1970, Victoria Susan, *o d* of late J. H. C. Beard; one *s* two *d*. *Educ:* Eton. *Recreations:* shooting, skiing, motor boating. *Heir:* *s* Viscount Somerton, *qv*. *Address:* Somerley, Ringwood, Hants BH24 3PL. *T:* Ringwood (01425) 473253. *Clubs:* White's; Royal Yacht Squadron.

NORMANTON, Sir Tom, Kt 1987; TD; BA (Com); past chairman of a group of companies; *b* 12 March 1917; *m* 1942, Annabel Bettine (*née* Yates); two *s* one *d*. *Educ:* Manchester Grammar Sch.; Manchester Univ. (BA (Com); Chm., Cons. Assoc., 1937–38; Vice-Pres. Students' Union, 1938). Joined family group of textile cos, 1938. Served War of 1939–45: Army (commnd TA 1937) Europe and N Africa; GS appts, GHQ BEF, HQ First and Eighth Armies; HQ 21 Army Gp (wounded, Calais, 1940; despatches, 1944); demob., rank Major, 1946. Chm., Rochdale YC, 1948; Mem. Rochdale CB Council, 1950–53; contested (C) Rochdale, 1959 and 1964. MP (C) Cheadle, 1970–87. Hon. Sec., Cons. Backbencher Industry Cttee, 1972–74; Mem., Expenditure Cttee, 1972–73; opposition front bench spokesman on energy, 1975–79. Contested (C) Cheshire E, European parly elecn, 1989. MEP (C) 1973–89 (elected for Cheshire E, 1979); Member: Cttee on Energy and Research, 1973–79 (Vice-Chm., 1976–79 and (as elected Member), 1979–89)); Cttee on Economic and Monetary Affairs, 1973–79; Budgets Cttee, 1986–89; Pol Affairs Cttee, 1986–89; Jt Africa, Caribbean, Pacific States Standing Conf., 1975–79; spokesman on Competition Policy, 1975; Deleg. to US Congress, 1975–78; Mem., delegn to Turkey, 1987–89; Mem. European Cons. Gp, resp. Indust. Policy; special interests energy and defence; Chm., European All-Party Gp Friends with Israel, 1979–89; Vice-Pres., Pan European Union eV, 1980– (Hon. Treas., 1989–). Mem. Supervisory Bd, European Inst. for Security. Manager, Lancashire Fusiliers Compassionate Fund, 1964–; Trustee, Cotton Industry War Memorial Fund, 1965; apptd Employer panel, NBPI, 1966–68; Member: Council, British Employers Confedn, 1959–64; Council, CBI, 1964–86 (Mem. Europe Cttee, 1964–86, and 1989–, and Econ. Policy Cttee, 1964–70); Stockport Chamber of Commerce, 1970–87; Central Training Council, 1968–74; Exec., UK Automation Council, 1966–73 (Vice-Chm., 1970–73); Cotton and Allied Textiles Ind. Trng Bd, 1966–70; Exec. Council, British Textile Confederation, 1972–76; Mem. Cttee, 1955–, Vice-Chm., 1969–71, Manchester Br. of Inst. of Dirs; Chm., European Textile Industries Cttee; President: British Textile Employers Assoc., 1970–71; Internat. Fedn of Cotton & Allied Textiles Industries, 1970– (Vice-Pres., 1972–76, Pres., 1976–78). Director: Industrial Training Services Ltd, 1972–; N Reg. Bd, Commercial Union Assurance Ltd, 1974–86; Manchester Chamber of Commerce, 1970–89. Consultant, Midland Bank Gp, EEC, Brussels, 1979–91. Mem. Cttee, Anglo-Austrian Soc.; Patron, Assoc. for Free Russia. Pres., New Forest Br., Normandy Veterans Assoc., 1990–; Chairman: British Sect., Confedn of European Ex-servicemen, 1986–90; Hampshire Remembers D-Day Ltd, 1992–. Speaks French and German. AIMgt. *Recreations:* sailing, walking, gardening. *Address:* Nelson House, Nelson Place, Lymington, Hants SO41 9RT. *T:* Lymington (01590) 675095. *Clubs:* Beefsteak; St James's (Manchester); Royal Yacht Squadron; Royal Lymington Yacht.

NORMINGTON, David John; Director of Personnel and Support Services, Department for Education and Employment (formerly Director of Personnel and Development, Department of Employment), since 1992; *b* 18 Oct. 1951; *s* of late Ronald Normington and of Kathleen Normington (*née* Towler); *m* 1985, Winifred Anne Charlotte Harris. *Educ:* Bradford Grammar Sch.; Corpus Christi College, Oxford (BA Hons Mod. Hist.) Department of Employment: joined 1973; Private Sec. to Perm. Sec., 1976–77; Principal Private Sec. to Sec. of State for Employment, 1984–85; Employment Service Regional Dir for London and SE Region, 1987–89; Hd of Strategy and Employment Policy Div., 1990–92. *Recreations:* gardening, ballet, theatre, cricket. *Address:* Department for Education and Employment, Caxton House, Tothill Street, SW1H 9NF. *T:* 0171–273 5766.

NORREYS, Lord; Henry Mark Willoughby Bertie; *b* 6 June 1958; *s* and *heir* of the Earl of Lindsey (14th) and Abingdon (9th), *qv*; *m* 1989, Lucinda, *d* of Christopher Moorsom. *Educ:* Eton; Univ. of Edinburgh. Kt of Honour and Devotion, SMO Malta, 1995. *Address:* Alameda de la Alcaldesa 1, Urbanización La Virginia 16, Camino de Camoján, 29600 Marbella (Málaga), Spain. *Clubs:* Pratt's; Puffin's (Edinburgh).

NORRIE, family name of **Baron Norrie.**

NORRIE, 2nd Baron, *cr* 1957; **George Willoughby Moke Norrie;** Director, Hilliers (Fairfield) Ltd, since 1989; *b* 27 April 1936; *s* of 1st Baron Norrie, GCMG, GCVO, CB, DSO, MC, and Jocelyn Helen (*d* 1938), *d* of late R. H. Gosling; *S* father, 1977; *m* 1964, Celia Marguerite, JP, *d* of John Pelham Mann, MC; one *s* two *d*. *Educ:* Eton College; RMA Sandhurst. Commissioned 11th Hussars (PAO), 1956; ADC to C-in-C Middle East Comd, 1960–61; GSO 3 (Int.) 4th Guards Brigade, 1967–69; retired, 1970. Director: Fairfield Nurseries (Hermitage) Ltd, 1976–89; International Garden Centre (British Gp) Ltd, 1984–86; Conservation Practice Ltd, 1989–91; Advr to S Grundon (Waste) Ltd, 1991–. Mem., H of L EC Cttee, Sub Cttee F (Environment), 1988–92. President: British Trust for Conservation Volunteers, 1987–; Commercial Travellers Benevolent Instn, 1992–; Royal British Legion (Newbury Branch), 1972–; Nat. Kidney Fedn, 1994–; Vice President: Tree Council, 1990–; Council for Nat. Parks, 1990–. Mem., Winston Churchill Meml Trust, 1993–. UK Patron, RLSS, 1994–. *Recreations:* skiing, tennis. *Heir:* *s* Hon. Mark Willoughby John Norrie, *b* 31 March 1972. *Address:* House of Lords, SW1A 0PW. *T:* 0171–219 5353. *Clubs:* Cavalry and Guards, White's, MCC.

NORRIE, Marian Farrow, (Mrs W. G. Walker); Her Honour Judge Norrie; a Circuit Judge, since 1986; *b* 25 April 1940; *d* of Arthur and Edith Jackson; *m* 1st, 1964; two *d*; 2nd, 1983, William Guy Walker; one step *s* two step *d*. *Educ:* Manchester High Sch. for Girls; Nottingham Univ. (LLB). Admitted Solicitor of Supreme Court, 1965; a Recorder, 1979–86. Consultant, Norrie, Bowler & Wrigley, Solicitors, Sheffield, 1983–86 (Sen. Partner, 1968–83). Member: Parole Bd, 1983–85; Appts Commn, Press Council, 1985. *Address:* Croydon Crown Court, Barclay Road, Croydon CR9 3NE.

NORRINGTON, Humphrey Thomas; Vice Chairman (formerly Vice Chairman and Deputy Group Managing Director), Barclays Bank, 1991–93; *b* 8 May 1936; *s* of Sir Arthur Norrington and Edith Joyce, *d* of William Moberly Carver; *m* 1963, Frances Guenn Bateson; two *s* two *d*. *Educ:* Dragon School, Oxford; Winchester; Worcester College, Oxford (MA). Barclays Bank: joined, 1960; general management, 1978–87; Dir, 1985–93; Exec Dir, Overseas Ops, 1987–91. Chm., Exec. Cttee, British Bankers' Assoc., 1990–91. Chm., Southwark Cathedral Develt Trust, 1986–93; Director: City Arts Trust, 1988–93; Mildmay Mission Hosp., 1992–; World Vision UK, 1991–; London Christian Radio, 1994–. Member, Archbishops' Commission: on Rural Areas, 1988–90; on Orgn of the C of E, 1994–95. *Recreations:* music, countryside. *Address:* Hill House, Frithsden Copse, Berkhamsted, Herts HP4 2RQ. *T:* Berkhamsted (01442) 871855. *Club:* United Oxford & Cambridge University.

See also R. A. C. Norrington.

NORRINGTON, Roger Arthur Carver, CBE 1990 (OBE 1980); Associate Chief Guest Conductor, London Philharmonic Orchestra; Musical Director: London Classical Players, since 1978; Schütz Choir of London, since 1962; Co-Director: Early Opera Project, since 1984; Historic Arts, since 1986; *b* 16 March 1934; *s* of late Sir Arthur Norrington and Edith Joyce, *d* of William Moberly Carver; *m* 1st, 1964, Susan Elizabeth McLean May (marr. diss. 1982); one *s* one *d*; 2nd, 1986, Karalyn Mary Lawrence; one *s*. *Educ:* Dragon Sch., Oxford; Westminster; Clare Coll., Cambridge (BA; Hon. Fellow, 1991); Royal Coll. of Music. Freelance singer, 1962–72. Principal Conductor: Kent Opera, 1966–84; Bournemouth Sinfonietta, 1985–89; Music Dir, Orch. of St Luke's, NY, 1990–94. Guest conducts many British, European and American orchestras, appears at Covent Garden, Coliseum, Proms and festivals; broadcasts regularly at home and abroad. Debuts: British, 1962; BBC Radio, 1964; TV 1967; Germany, Austria, Denmark, Finland, 1966; Portugal, 1970; Italy, 1971; France and Belgium, 1972; USA, 1974; Holland, 1975; Switzerland, 1976. Many gramophone recordings. Hon. RAM 1988. FRCM 1992. DUniv York, 1991; Hon. DMus Kent, 1994. Cavaliere, Order al Merito della Repubblica Italiana, 1981. *Publications:* occasional articles in various musical journals. *Recreations:* gardening, reading, walking.

See also H. T. Norrington.

NORRIS, (Alaric) Philip, OBE 1982; **His Honour Judge Norris;** a Circuit Judge, since 1995; *b* 20 Sept. 1942; *yr s* of Charles Henry Norris and Maud Frances Norris; *m* 1967, Pamela Margaret Parker; three *s*. *Educ:* Sir William Turner's Sch., Coatham, Redcar; Queens' Coll., Cambridge (MA). Admitted Solicitor, 1968; commnd Army Legal Services, 1970; retired, in rank of Brig., 1995. *Recreations:* a bit of all sorts, but not golf. *Address:* c/o Woolwich Crown Court, 2 Belmarsh Road, SE28 0EY.

NORRIS, Air Chief Marshal Sir Christopher Neil F.; *see* Foxley-Norris.

NORRIS, Rt. Rev. Mgr David Joseph; Protonotary Apostolic to the Pope; Vicar General of Westminster Diocese, since 1972; General Secretary to RC Bishops' Conference of England and Wales, 1967–83; *b* 17 Aug. 1922; *s* of David William and Anne Norris. *Educ:* Salesian Coll., Battersea; St Edmund's Coll., Ware; Christ's Coll., Cambridge (MA). Priest, 1947; teaching at St Edmund's Coll., Ware, 1948–53; Cambridge, 1953–56; Private Secretary to Cardinal Godfrey, 1956–64; National Chaplain to Catholic Overseas Students, 1964–65; Private Secretary to Cardinal Heenan, 1965–72. *Recreations:* reading, music, sport. *Address:* Cathedral Clergy House, 42 Francis Street, SW1P 1QW. *T:* 0171–798 9055.

NORRIS, David Owen, FRAM, FRCO; pianist and broadcaster; *b* 16 June 1953; *s* of Albert Norris and Margaret Norris (*née* Owen); two *s*. *Educ:* Royal Academy of Music (FRAM 1986); Keble Coll., Oxford (MA). FRCO 1972. Repetiteur, Royal Opera House, 1977–80; Asst Mus. Dir, RSC, 1977–79; Prof., Royal Acad. of Music, 1977–89; Dir, Petworth Fest., 1986–92; Artistic Dir, Cardiff Fest., 1992–; Gresham Prof. of Music, 1993–. Chm., Steans Inst. for Singers, Chicago, 1992–. Concerts world-wide, incl. Tokyo, NY, Chicago, LA, Paris, Zurich, etc. Radio and TV programmes in Britain, Canada and USA. Gilmore Artist Award, 1991. *Recreations:* drinking wine, attending rock concerts. *Address:* 60 Old Oak Lane, NW10 6UB. *T:* 0181–961 4830.

NORRIS, Sir Eric (George), KCMG 1969 (CMG 1963); HM Diplomatic Service, retired; Director: Inchcape & Co., 1977–88 (Deputy Chairman, 1981–86); London Sumatra Plantations Ltd, 1978–88; Gray Mackenzie Ltd, 1978–88; *b* 14 March 1918; *s* of late H. F. Norris, Bengeo, Hertford; *m* 1941, Pamela Crane; three *d*. *Educ:* Hertford Grammar Sch.; St Catharine's Coll., Cambridge. Served Royal Corps of Signals, 1940–46 (Major). Entered Dominions Office, 1946. Served in British Embassy, Dublin, 1948–50; UK High Commission in Pakistan, 1952–55; UK High Commission in Delhi, 1956–57; Dep. High Commissioner for the UK, Bombay, 1957–60; IDC 1961; British Dep. High Comr, Calcutta, 1962–65; Commonwealth Office, 1966–68; High Comr, Kenya, 1968–72; Dep. Under Sec. of State, FCO, 1972–73; High Comr, Malaysia, 1974–77. Chm., Royal Commonwealth Soc., 1980–84. PMN (Malaysia), 1974. *Address:* Tilings, Goring Road, Steyning, W Sussex BN44 3GF. *T:* Steyning (01903) 879064. *Clubs:* East India, Commonwealth Trust.

NORRIS, Gilbert Frank; Chief Road Engineer, Scottish Development Department, 1969–76; *b* 29 May 1916; *s* of Ernest Frank Norris and Ada Norris; *m* 1941, Joan Margaret Catherine Thompson; one *s*. *Educ:* Bemrose Sch., Derby; UC Nottingham. FICE. Served with Notts, Bucks and Lindsey County Councils, 1934–39; Royal Engineers, 1939–46; Min. of Transport: Highways Engr in Nottingham, Edinburgh and Leeds, 1946–63; Asst Chief Engr, 1963–67; Dep. Chief Engr, 1967; Dir, NE Road Construction Unit, 1967–69. *Recreations:* motoring, photography. *Address:* Woodhead Lee, Lamlash, Isle of Arran KA27 8JU.

NORRIS, Col Graham Alexander, OBE (mil.) 1945; JP; Vice Lord-Lieutenant of County of Greater Manchester, 1975–87; *b* 14 April 1913; *er s* of late John O. H. Norris and Beatrice H. Norris (*née* Vlies), Manchester; *m* 1st, 1938, Frances Cicely, *d* of late Walter Gorton, Minchinhampton, Glos; one *d*; 2nd, 1955, Muriel, *d* of late John Corris, Manchester. *Educ:* William Hulme's Grammar Sch.; Coll. of Technology, Manchester; Regent St Polytechnic, London; Merchant Venturers Techn. Coll., Bristol. CEng, FIMechE. Trng as automobile engr, Rolls Royce Ltd, Bristol Motor Co. Ltd; Joseph Cockshoot & Co. Ltd: Works Man., 1937, Works Dir 1946, Jt. Man. Dir 1964, Chm. and Man. Dir, 1968; Dir, Lex Garages Ltd, 1968–70; Dir, Red Garages (N Wales) Ltd, 1973–88. War service, RAOC and REME, UK, ME and Italy, 1940–46 (Lt-Col); Comdr REME 22 (W) Corps Tps (TA), 1947–51; Hon. Col, 1957–61. Mem., NEDC for Motor Vehicle Distrib. and Repair, 1966–74; Pres., Motor Agents Assoc., 1967–68; Vice-Pres., Inst. of Motor Industry, 1973–76; Mem., Industrial Tribunal Panel, 1976–82. Pres., Manchester and Dist Fedn of Boys' Clubs, 1968–74; Vice-Pres., NABC, 1972–; Chm. Council, UMIST, 1971–83; Member Court: Univ. of Manchester; UMIST. Master, Worshipful Co. of Coachmakers and Coach Harness Makers, 1961–62; Freeman, City of London, 1938. JP, Lancashire 1963; DL Co. Palatine of Lancaster, 1962. *Recreations:* walking, social service activities. *Address:* 5 Brook Court, Brook Road, Windermere, Cumbria LA23 2BP.

NORRIS, John Hallam Mercer, CBE 1987; Crown Estate Commissioner, since 1991; Vice Lord-Lieutenant of Essex, since 1992; *b* 30 May 1929; *s* of late William Hallam Norris and Dorothy Edna Norris (*née* Mercer); *m* 1954, Maureen Joy Banyard; two *d*. *Educ:* Brentwood School. Mem., BSES Expedn, Newfoundland, 1947. Partner, W. H. Norris & Sons, 1963–. Chm., Essex River Authy, 1971–74; Member: Anglian Water Authy, 1974–85; Adv. Cttee, 1988, Board, 1989–94, NRA; Adv. Cttee, Envmt Agency, 1994–; Chairman: Essex Land Drainage Cttee, 1974–89; Crouch Harbour Authy, 1981–88. President: CLA, 1985–87 (Mem., Exec. Cttee, 1973–; Chm., 1983–85); Essex Agricl Soc., 1989. FRAgS 1992; Hon. FIWEM 1992. DL Essex, 1989. *Recreations:* fishing, sailing. *Address:* Mountnessing Hall, Brentwood, Essex CM13 1UN. *T:* Brentwood (01277) 352152. *Clubs:* Boodle's, Farmers'.

NORRIS, John Robert, CBE 1991; PhD, DSc; Director, Group Research, Cadbury Schweppes Ltd, 1979–90; *b* 4 March 1932; *s* of Albert Norris and Winifred May Perry; *m* 1956, Barbara Jean Pinder; two *s* one *d* (and one *s* decd). *Educ:* Depts of Bacteriology and Agriculture, Univ. of Leeds (BSc 1st Cl. Hons 1954, PhD 1957, DSc 1987). Lectr in Bacteriology, Univ. of Glasgow, 1957–63; Microbiologist, Shell Research Ltd, 1963–73 (Dir, Borden Microbiol Lab., 1970–73); Dir, Meat Res. Inst., ARC, 1973–79. Editor, Methods in Microbiology, 1969–92. *Publications:* papers in microbiol jls. *Recreations:* walking, wood carving, Yoga. *Address:* Langlands, 10 Langley Road, Bingley, West Yorks BD16 4AB. *T:* Bradford (01274) 510301. *Club:* Farmers'.

NORRIS, Philip; *see* Norris, A. P.

NORRIS, Steven John; MP (C) Epping Forest, since Dec. 1988; Parliamentary Under-Secretary of State, Department of Transport, since 1992; *b* 24 May 1945; *s* of John Francis Birkett Norris and Eileen Winifred (*née* Walsh); *m* 1969, Peta Veronica Cecil-Gibson (separated); two *s*. *Educ:* Liverpool Institute; Worcester College, Oxford. MA. Private company posts, 1967–82. Mem., Berks CC, 1977–85; Dep. Leader, Cons. Group, 1983–85. Mem., Berks AHA, 1979–82; Vice-Chm., W Berks District HA, 1982–85. Contested (C) Oxford E, 1987. MP (C) Oxford E, 1983–87. PPS to Hon. William Waldegrave, MP, Minister of State, DoE, 1985–87, to Rt Hon. Nicholas Ridley, Sec. of State for Trade and Industry, 1990, to Rt Hon. Kenneth Baker, Home Sec., 1991–92. Mem., Select Cttee on Social Services, 1984–85. Chairman: Grant Maintained Schools Trust, 1988–89; Crime Concern Trust, 1988–91; Alcohol and Drug Addiction Prevention and Treatment, 1990–92. Freeman, City of London; Liveryman, Coach and Harness Makers' Co. *Recreations:* reading, not walking. *Address:* House of Commons, SW1A 0AA. *Club:* Brooks's.

NORRIS, Sydney George; Assistant Under Secretary of State, Principal Finance Officer, Home Office, since 1990; *b* 22 Aug. 1937; *s* of late George Samuel Norris, FCA and Agnes Rosa Norris; *m* 1965, Brigid Molyneux FitzGibbon; two *s* one *d*. *Educ:* Liverpool Inst. High Sch. for Boys; University Coll., Oxford (MA); Trinity Hall and Inst. of Criminology, Cambridge (Dip. in Criminology); Univ. of California, Berkeley (MCrim). Intelligence Corps, 1956–58; Home Office, 1963–; Private Sec. to Parly Under Sec. of State, 1966; Harkness Fellow, 1968–70; Sec., Adv. Council on Penal System, 1970–73; Principal Private Sec. to Home Sec., 1973–74; Asst Sec., 1974; seconded to HM Treasury, 1979–81; Asst Under Sec. of State, 1982; seconded to NI Office as Principal Estabt and Finance Officer, 1982–85; Dir of Operational Policy, Prison Dept, 1985–88; Police Dept, 1988–90. *Recreations:* running, fell walking, gardening, piano. *Address:* Home Office, SW1H 9AT. *Club:* Thames Hare and Hounds.

NORRISS, Air Vice-Marshal Peter Coulson, AFC 1977; Director General Aircraft 2, Ministry of Defence (Procurement Executive), since 1991; *b* 22 April 1944; *s* of Arthur Kenworthy Norriss and Marjorie Evelyn Norriss; *m* 1971, Lesley Jean McColl; two *s* one *d*. *Educ:* Beverley Grammar Sch.; Magdalene Coll., Cambridge (MA 1970). Joined RAF, 1966; flying trng, 1966–68; Flying Instruction RAF Coll., Cranwell, 1969–71; Buccaneer Pilot, 1972–76; RAF Staff Coll., 1977; on Staff of RAF Minister, 1977–79; OC, No 16 Sqn, 1980–83; Head, RAF Presentation Team, 1984; Station Comdr, RAF Marham, 1985–87; ADC to the Queen, 1985–87; Higher Comd and Staff Course, 1988; on Staff, Operational Requirements, 1988–91. *Recreations:* golf, squash. *Address:* c/o RAF Personnel Management Centre, RAF Innsworth, Glos GL3 1EZ. *Club:* Royal Air Force.

NORTH, family name of **Earl of Guilford.**

NORTH, Lord; Piers Edward Brownlow North; *b* 9 March 1971; *s* and *heir* of Earl of Guilford, *qv*; *m* 1994, Michèle Desvaux de Marigny. Address: Waldershare Park, Dover, Kent CT15 5BA. *T:* Dover (01304) 820244.

NORTH, Prof. Douglass Cecil, PhD; Professor of Economics, Washington University, since 1983; *b* 6 Nov. 1920; *s* of Henry North and Edith Saitta; *m* 1st, 1944, Lois Heister; three *s*; 2nd, 1972, Elisabeth Case. *Educ:* Univ. of California at Berkeley (BA, PhD). Acting Asst Prof., Asst Prof. and Associate Prof., Univ. of Washington, Seattle, 1950–83; Henry R. Luce Prof. of Law and Liberty and Prof. of Econs and of History, Washington Univ., St Louis, 1983. Peterkin Prof. of Political Economy, Rice Univ., 1979; Pitt Prof. of American Instns, Cambridge, 1981–82. Fellow, Amer. Acad. of Arts and Scis. Hon. Degrees: Cologne 1988; Zürich 1993; Stockholm 1994. (Jtly) Nobel Prize for Economics, 1993. *Publications:* The Economic Growth of the United States 1790–1860, 1961; Growth and Welfare in the American Past, 1966; (with Roger Miller) The Economics of Public Issues, 1971; (with Lance Davis) Institutional Change and American Economic Growth, 1971; (with Robert Thomas) The Rise of the Western World, 1973; Structure and Change in Economic History, 1981; Institutions, Institutional Change and Economic Performance, 1990. *Recreations:* tennis, hiking, music, photography. *Address:* Economics Department, Washington University, Campus Box 1208, 1 Brookings Drive, St Louis, MO 63130–4899, USA.

NORTH, Prof. John David; Professor of History of Philosophy and the Exact Sciences, University of Groningen, Netherlands, since 1977; *b* 19 May 1934; *s* of late J. E. and G. A. North, Cheltenham; *m* 1957, Marion Pizzey; one *s* two *d*. *Educ:* Grammar Sch., Batley; Merton Coll., Oxford (BA 1956, MA 1960, DPhil 1964, DLitt 1993); London Univ. (BSc 1958). University of Oxford: Nuffield Foundn Res. Fellow, 1963–68; Asst Curator, Mus. of Hist. of Sci., 1968–77; University of Groningen: Dean, Central Inter-Faculty, 1981–84; Dean of Faculty, 1991–93. Vis. Prof., Univs in Germany, Denmark and USA. Member: Council, Mus. Boerhaave, Leiden, 1986–; Comité Scientifique, CNRS, Paris, 1985–; Acad. internat. d'histoire des scis, 1967– (Hon. Permanent Sec., 1983–); IAU, 1977 (Pres., Hist. Commn, 1988–92); Royal Netherlands Acad., 1985– (Mem Council, 1990–93); Acad. Leopoldina, 1992–. Corresp. Fellow, British Acad., 1992; Foreign Mem., Royal Danish Acad., 1985. Editor: Archives internat. d'hist. des scis, 1971–84; Travaux de l'Académie, 1984–. *Publications:* The Measure of the Universe, 1965, 2nd edn 1990; Isaac Newton, 1967; (ed) Mid-Nineteenth Century Scientists, 1969; Richard of Wallingford, 3 vols, 1976; (ed with J. Roche) The Light of Nature, 1985; Horoscopes and History, 1986; Chaucer's Universe, 1988, 2nd edn 1990; Stars, Minds and Fate, 1989; The Universal Frame, 1989; Fontana History of Astronomy and Cosmology, 1994. *Recreation:* archaeology. *Address:* Kamperfoelieweg 25, 9765 HJ Paterswolde, Netherlands. *T:* (5907) 91846; 28 Chalfont Road, Oxford OX2 6TH. *T:* Oxford (01865) 58458.

NORTH, John Joseph; Associate, Department of Land Economy, University of Cambridge, since 1992 (Senior Visiting Fellow, 1985–92); *b* 7 Nov. 1926; *s* of Frederick James North and Annie Elizabeth North (*née* Matthews); *m* 1958, Sheila Barbara Mercer; two *s*. *Educ:* Rendcomb College; Univ. of Reading (BSc, DipAgric); Univ. of California (MS). FIBiol 1972. Agricultural Adviser, Nat. Agricultural Advisory Service, 1951; Kellogg Fellowship, USA, 1954–55; Regional Agricultural Officer, Cambridge, 1972; Senior Agricultural Officer, 1976; Chief Agricl Officer, ADAS, MAFF, 1979. *Recreations:* golf, gardening. *Address:* 28 Hauxton Road, Little Shelford, Cambridge CB2 5HJ. *T:* Cambridge (01223) 843369.

NORTH, Sir Jonathan; *see* North, Sir W. J. F.

NORTH, Dr Peter Machin, CBE 1989; DCL; FBA 1990; Principal of Jesus College, Oxford, since 1984; Vice-Chancellor, University of Oxford, since 1993 (Pro-Vice-Chancellor, 1988–93); *b* Nottingham, 30 Aug. 1936; *o s* of late Geoffrey Machin North and Freda Brunt (*née* Smith); *m* 1960, Stephanie Mary, *e d* of T. L. Chadwick; two *s* one *d*. *Educ:* Oakham Sch.; Keble Coll., Oxford (BA 1959, BCL 1960, MA 1963, DCL 1976; Hon. Fellow, 1984). National Service, Royal Leics Regt, 2nd Lieut, 1955–56. Teaching Associate, Northwestern Univ. Sch. of Law, Chicago, 1960–61; Lecturer: University Coll. of Wales, Aberystwyth, 1961–63; Univ. of Nottingham, 1963–65; Tutor in Law, 1965–76, Fellow, 1965–84, Keble Coll., Oxford. Mem., Hebdomadal Council, 1985–. A Law Comr, 1976–84. Vis. Professor: Univ. of Auckland, 1969; Univ. of BC, 1975–76; Dir of Studies, Hague Acad. of Internat. Law, 1970 (general course in private internat. law, 1990); Lectures: Hague Acad. of Internat. Law, 1980; Horace Read Meml, Dalhousie Univ., 1980; Colston, Bristol Univ., 1984; Frances Moran Meml, TCD, 1984; Philip James, Leeds Univ., 1985; James Smart, 1988; MacDermott, QUB, 1991; Graveson, KCL, 1992. Chairman: Road Traffic Law Review, 1985–88; Conciliation Project Adv. Cttee, 1985–88; Management Cttee, Oxford CAB, 1985–88; Appeal Cttee, Assoc. of Certified Accountants, 1990–93 (Mem., 1987–93); Member: Lord Chancellor's Adv. Cttee on Legal Educn, 1973–75; Social Scis and the Law Cttee, ESRC (formerly SSRC), 1982–85; Govt and Law Cttee, ESRC, 1985–87; Council, British Inst. of Internat. and Comparative Law, 1986– (Chm., Private Internat. Law Section, Adv. Bd, 1986–92); Council, Univ. of Reading, 1986–89. Mem., Inst. of Internat. Law, 1985; Associate Mem., Internat. Acad. of Comparative Law, 1990. Hon. Bencher, Inner Temple, 1987; Hon. QC 1993. Hon. Fellow: UCNW, Bangor, 1988; Trinity Coll., Carmarthen, 1995. Hon. LLD Reading, 1992. Mem., Editorial Cttee, British Yearbook of Internat. Law, 1983–; General Editor, Oxford Jl of Legal Studies, 1987–92. *Publications:* (ed jtly) Chitty on Contracts, 23rd edn 1968 - 26th edn 1989; Occupiers' Liability, 1971; The Modern Law of Animals, 1972; Private International Law of Matrimonial Causes, 1977; Cheshire and North's Private International Law, 12th edn 1992; Contract Conflicts, 1982; (with J. H. C. Morris) Cases and Materials on Private International Law, 1984; Private International Law Problems in Common Law Jurisdictions, 1993; Essays in Private International Law, 1993; articles and notes in legal jls. *Recreations:* children, grandchildren, gardening, cricket (both playing and sleeping through). *Address:* Jesus College, Oxford OX1 3DW. *T:* Oxford (01865) 279701; University Offices, Wellington Square, Oxford OX1 2JD. *T:* Oxford (01865) 270242.

NORTH, Dr Richard Alan, FRS 1995; Principal Scientist, Glaxo Institute for Molecular Biology, since 1993; *b* 20 May 1944; *s* of Douglas Abram North and Constance (*née* Ramsden); *m* 1st, 1969, Jean Valerie Aitken Hall; two *d*; 2nd, 1991, Annmarie Surprenant; two *s*. *Educ:* Univ. of Aberdeen (BSc; MB, ChB 1969; PhD 1973). Asst and Associate Prof., Dept of Pharmacol., Loyola Univ., Chicago, 1975–81; Massachusetts Institute of Technology: Associate Prof., Dept of Nutrition and Food Sci., 1981–84; Prof. of Neuropharmacol., Dept of Applied Biol Scis, 1984–86; Sen. Scientist, Vollum Inst., Oregon Health Scis Univ., Portland, 1987–93. Visiting Professor: Flinders Univ., 1983; Bogomoletz Inst., 1984; Frankfurt Univ., 1988. Gaddum Lecture, British Pharmacol Soc., 1988. *Publications:* original res. papers in jls of physiol., pharmacol., neuroscience and biochem. *Recreation:* mountaineering. *Address:* Glaxo Institute for Molecular Biology, 14 chemin des Aulx, Plan-les-Ouates, 1228 Geneva, Switzerland. *T:* (22) 7069942, *Fax:* (22) 7069992.

NORTH, Robert, (Robert North Dodson); dancer and choreographer; Artistic Director, Gothenburg Ballet, since 1991; *b* 1 June 1945; *s* of Charles Dodson and Elizabeth

Thompson; *m* 1978, Janet Smith. *Educ:* Pierrepont Sch. (A levels in Maths, Physics and Art); Central Sch. of Art; Royal Ballet Sch. Dancer and choreographer, London Contemporary Dance Co., 1966–81 (Jt Artistic Dir, 1980–81); seasons with Martha Graham Dance Co., 1967 and 1968; Teacher of Modern Dance, Royal Ballet Sch., 1979–81; Artistic Dir, Ballet Rambert, 1981–86; freelance work, Europe and USA, 1986–90; Ballet Dir, Teatro Regio, Turin, 1990–91. Has choreographed ballets for dance companies throughout the world, including: Royal Ballet; English National Ballet; Dance Theatre of Harlem; Royal Danish Ballet; San Francisco Ballet; Oakland Ballet; Helsinki Ballet; Batsheva; Janet Smith and Dancers; *ballets choreographed* include: Troy Game; Death and the Maiden; The Annunciation; A Stranger I Came; Running Figures; Pribaoutki; Colour Moves; Entre dos Aguas; full-length ballets: Elvira Madigan; Romeo & Juliet; Living in America; Prince Rama and the Demons; Love & Death; The Russian Story; The Snowman; also choreography for films, television (incl. Lonely Town, Lonely Street), theatre and musicals (incl. For My Daughter).

NORTH, Sir Thomas (Lindsay), Kt 1982; FAIM, FRMIA; Chairman, G. J. Coles & Coy Limited, Melbourne, Australia, 1979–83, Hon. Chairman, 1983–84; *b* 11 Dec. 1919; *s* of John North and Jane (*née* Irwin); *m* 1944, Kathleen Jefferis; two *d*. *Educ:* Rutherglen, Vic. FAIM 1972. Joined G. J. Coles & Co. Ltd, 1938; Gen. Man., 1966; Dep. Man. Dir, 1969; Man. Dir, 1975–79; Dir, various G. J. Coles subsid. cos. Dep. Chm., KMart (Australia) Ltd, 1975–; Chairman: Island Cooler Pty Ltd, 1985–; Smurfit Australia Pty Ltd. 1986–. *Recreations:* horse racing, swimming. *Address:* 31 Power Street, Toorak, Vic 3142, Australia. *T:* (3) 8223161. *Clubs:* Athenæum, Royal Automobile Club of Victoria (Melbourne); Australian, Australian Armoured Corps (Sydney); Victorian Amateur Turf (Dep. Chm.), Victorian Racing Club, Moonee Valley Race; Melbourne Cricket.

NORTH, Sir (William) Jonathan (Frederick), 2nd Bt, *cr* 1920; *b* 6 Feb. 1931; *s* of Muriel Norton (*d* 1989), 2nd *d* of Sir William Hicking, 1st Bt, and Hon. John Montagu William North (marr. diss. 1939; he *d* 1987), 2nd *s* of 8th Earl of Guilford; *S* grandfather, 1947 (under special remainder); *m* 1956, Sara Virginia, *d* of Air Chief Marshal Sir Donald Hardman, GBE, KCB, DFC; one *s* two *d*. *Educ:* Marlborough Coll. *Heir: s* Jeremy William Francis North [*b* 5 May 1960; *m* 1986, Lucy, *d* of G. A. van der Meulen, Holland; two *s*]. *Address:* Frogmore, Weston-under-Penyard, Herefordshire HR9 5TQ.

NORTH-EASTERN CARIBBEAN AND ARUBA (formerly **ANTIGUA**), **Bishop of;** *see* West Indies, Archbishop of.

NORTHAMPTON, 7th Marquess of, *cr* 1812; **Spencer Douglas David Compton;** DL; Earl of Northampton, 1618; Earl Compton, Baron Wilmington, 1812; *b* 2 April 1946; *s* of 6th Marquess of Northampton, DSO, and of Virginia, *d* of Lt-Col David Heaton, DSO; *S* father, 1978; *m* 1st, 1967, Henriette Luisa Maria (marr. diss. 1973), *o d* of late Baron Bentinck; one *s* one *d*; 2nd, 1974, Annette Marie (marr. diss. 1977), *er d* of C. A. R. Smallwood; 3rd, 1977, Hon. Mrs Rosemary Dawson-Damer (marr. diss. 1983); one *d*; 4th, 1985, Hon. Mrs Michael Pearson (marr. diss. 1988); one *d*; 5th, 1990, Pamela Martina Raphaela Kyprios. *Educ:* Eton. DL Northants 1979. *Recreation:* freemasonry. *Heir: s* Earl Compton, *qv*. *Address:* Compton Wynyates, Tysoe, Warwicks CV35 0UD. *T:* Tysoe (01295) 680629. *Club:* Turf.

NORTHAMPTON, Bishop of, (RC), since 1990; **Rt. Rev. (Patrick) Leo McCartie;** *b* 5 Sept. 1925; *s* of Patrick Leo and Hannah McCartie. *Educ:* Cotton College; Oscott College. Priest, 1949; on staff of Cotton College, 1950–55; parish work, 1955–63; Director of Religious Education, 1963–68; Administrator of St Chad's Cathedral, Birmingham, 1968–77; Aux. Bp of Birmingham, and Titular Bp of Elmham, 1977–90. Pres., Catholic Commn for Racial Justice, 1978–83; Chm., Cttee for Community Relations, Dept for Christian Responsibility and Citizenship, Bishops' Conf. on Eng. and Wales, 1983–90. Church Representative : Churches Together in England, 1990; Council of Churches for Britain and Ireland, 1990. *Recreations:* music, walking. *Address:* Bishop's House, Marriott Street, Northampton NN2 6AW.

NORTHAMPTON, Archdeacon of; *see* Chapman, Ven. M. R.

NORTHARD, John Henry, CBE 1987 (OBE 1979); FEng 1983; Hon. FIMinE; Director of Operations, 1985–88, Deputy Chairman, 1988–92, British Coal Corporation; Chairman, British Coal Enterprise Ltd, 1991–93; *b* 23 Dec. 1926; *s* of William Henry Northard and Nellie Northard; *m* 1952, Marian Josephine Lay; two *s* two *d*. *Educ:* St Bede's Grammar School, Bradford; Barnsley Mining and Technical College (Certificated Colliery Manager, first class). CEng. Colliery Manager, Yorks, 1955–57, Leics, 1957–63; Group Manager, Leics Collieries, 1963–65; Dep. Chief Mining Engineer, NCB, Staffs Area, 1965–70; Area Dep. Dir (Mining), NCB, N Derbyshire Area, 1970–73; Area Dir, NCB, N Derbyshire Area, 1973–81, Western Area, 1981–85; Bd Mem., NCB, 1986–92. Pres., IMinE, 1982. CIMgt. SBStJ 1981. *Publications:* contribs to mining engineering instns and tech. jls. *Address:* Rydal, 196 Ashgate Road, Chesterfield, Derbyshire S40 4AL. *T:* Chesterfield (01246) 232260.

NORTHBOURNE, 5th Baron *cr* 1884; **Christopher George Walter James;** Bt 1791; FRICS; Chairman, Betteshanger Farms Ltd, since 1975; Deputy Chairman, Center Parcs PLC, since 1988 (Director, since 1988); *b* 18 Feb. 1926; *s* of 4th Baron Northbourne and Katherine Louise (*d* 1980), *d* of late George A. Nickerson, Boston, Mass; *S* father, 1982; *m* 1959, Aliki Louise Hélène Marie Sygne, *e d* of Henri Claudel, Chatou-sur-Seine, and *g d* of late Paul Claudel; three *s* one *d*. *Educ:* Eton; Magdalen Coll., Oxford (MA). Director: Anglo Indonesian Corp., 1971–; Plantation & General (formerly Chillington Corp.) PLC, 1986–. *Heir: s* Hon. Charles Walter Henri James [*b* 14 June 1960; *m* 1987, Catherine Lucy, *d* of Ralph Burrows; one *s* one *d*]. *Address:* 11 Eaton Place, SW1X 8BN. *T:* 0171–235 6790; Coldharbour, Northbourne, Deal, Kent CT14 0NT. *T:* Sandwich (01304) 611277. *Clubs:* Brooks's, Royal Yacht Squadron.

NORTHBROOK, 6th Baron *cr* 1866; **Francis Thomas Baring;** Bt 1793; Investment Manager, Smith and Williamson Securities, since 1993; *b* 21 Feb. 1954; *s* of 5th Baron Northbrook and of Rowena Margaret, 2nd *d* of Brig.-Gen. Sir William Manning, GCMG, KBE, CB; *S* father, 1990; *m* 1987, Amelia Sarah Elizabeth, *er d* of Dr Reginald Taylor; three *d*. *Educ:* Winchester Coll.; Bristol Univ. (BA Hons 1976). Trainee accountant, Dixon Wilson & Co., 1976–80; Baring Brothers and Co. Ltd, 1981–89; Sen. Investment Man., Taylor Young Investment Management Ltd, 1990–93. *Heir:* (to baronetcy) *kinsman* Peter Baring [*b* 12 Sept. 1939; *m* 1973, Rose, *d* of George Nigel Adams; one *s*]. *Address:* House of Lords, SW1A 0PW. *Clubs:* White's, City University.

NORTHCOTE, family name of **Earl of Iddesleigh.**

NORTHCOTE, Prof. Donald Henry, FRS 1968; Fellow of Sidney Sussex College, Cambridge, since 1992 (Master, 1976–92); Professor of Plant Biochemistry, University of Cambridge, 1972–89 (Reader, 1965–72), Emeritus Professor, 1989; *b* 27 Dec. 1921; *m* Eva Marjorie Mayo; two *d*. *Educ:* Sir George Monoux Grammar Sch., London; London Univ.; Cambridge Univ. Fellow, St John's College, Cambridge, 1960–76. Hon. Fellow, Downing Coll., Cambridge, 1976. *Publication:* Differentiation in Higher Plants, 1974, 2nd edn 1980. *Recreations:* sitting and chatting; strolling about. *Address:* Sidney Sussex College, Cambridge CB2 3HU. *T:* Cambridge (01223) 338821; 100 North Street, Burwell, Cambs CB5 0BB. *T:* Newmarket (01638) 743924. *Club:* United Oxford & Cambridge University.

NORTHCOTE, His Honour Peter Colston; a Circuit Judge 1973–89; *b* 23 Oct. 1920; *s* of late William George Northcote and late Edith Mary Northcote; *m* 1947, Patricia Bickley; two *s*. *Educ:* Ellesmere Coll.; Bristol Univ. Called to Bar, Inner Temple, 1948. Chm., Nat. Insce Tribunal; Chm., W Midland Rent Tribunal; Dep. Chm., Agric. Land Tribunal. Commnd KSLI, 1940; served 7th Rajput Regt, Far East (Major). *Recreations:* music, travel, ski-ing. *Address:* Wroxeter Grange, Wroxeter, Shrewsbury, Salop SY5 6HP. *T:* Cross Houses (01743) 761279. *Club:* Army and Navy.

NORTHCOTT, Prof. Douglas Geoffrey, MA, PhD, Cambridge; FRS 1961; Town Trust Professor of Mathematics, University of Sheffield, 1952–82, now Emeritus; *b* London, 1916; *m* 1949, Rose Hilda Austin, Twickenham, Middlesex; two *d*. *Educ:* Christ's Hospital; St John's Coll., Cambridge; Princeton Univ., USA. *Publications:* Ideal Theory, 1953; An Introduction to Homological Algebra, 1960; Lessons on Rings, Modules and Multiplicities, 1968; A First Course of Homological Algebra, 1973; Finite Free Resolutions, 1976; Affine Sets and Affine Groups, 1980; Multilinear Algebra, 1984. *Address:* 25 Parkhead Road, Sheffield S11 9RA.

NORTHERN ARGENTINA, Bishop of, since 1990; **Most Rev. Maurice Walter Sinclair;** Presiding Bishop (Primate) of the Province of the Southern Cone of America, since 1995; *b* 20 Jan. 1937; *s* of Maurice and Dorothea Sinclair; *m* 1962, Gillian (*née* Spooner); four *s*. *Educ:* Chigwell Sch.; Nottingham Univ. (BSc 1959); Leicester Univ. (PGCE 1960); Tyndale Hall, Bristol. Asst Master, Brays Grove County Secondary Sch., Harlow, Essex, 1960–62. Ordained, 1964; Asst Curate, St John's Church, Boscombe, 1964–67; Missionary, South American Missionary Soc., serving in Argentina, 1967–78; Personnel Sec., 1979–83, Asst Gen. Sec., 1983–84, South American Missionary Soc.; Principal, Crowther Hall, Selly Oak Colls, 1984–90. Ibo chief, Nigeria, 1987. *Publications:* Green Finger of God, 1980; Ripening Harvest Gathering Storm, 1988. *Recreations:* gardening, hill walking, veteran football. *Address:* Iglesia Anglicana, Casilla 187, CP 4400 Salta, Argentina. *T:* (87) 310167.

NORTHERN TERRITORY (AUSTRALIA), Bishop of the, since 1992; **Rt. Rev. Richard Franklin Appleby;** *b* 17 Nov. 1940; *s* of Julian Paul Leonard Appleby and Lilian Margaret Appleby (*née* Pragnell); *m* 1966, Elizabeth Clark; two *d*. *Educ:* Eltham High Sch.; Univ. of Melbourne (BSc); St John's Coll., Morpeth (ThL (Hons)). Curate of Glenroy, 1967–68; Curate of N Balwyn and Chaplain to Apprentices and Probation Hostels, 1969–70; Chaplain to Christchurch Grammar Sch., 1970–71; Warden of Wollaston Coll. and Chaplain to the Archbishop of Perth, 1972–75; Rector of Belmont, 1975–80; Dean of Bathurst and Examining Chaplain to the Bishop of Bathurst, 1980–83; Auxiliary Bishop of Newcastle, 1983–92. Pres., NSW Ecumenical Council, 1987–89. *Recreations:* gardening, walking, listening to music. *Address:* Bishop's Lodge, 5 Rankin Street, Nightcliff, NT 0810, Australia. *T:* (89) 852044.

NORTHESK, 14th Earl of *cr* 1647; **David John MacRae Carnegie;** Lord Rosehill and Inglismaldie 1639; estate manager/owner; *b* 3 Nov. 1954; *s* of 13th Earl of Northesk, and Jean Margaret (*d* 1989), *yr d* of Captain (John) Duncan George MacRae; *S* father, 1994; *m* 1979, Jacqueline Reid, *d* of Mrs Elizabeth Reid, Sarasota, Florida, USA; one *s* three *d*. *Educ:* West Hill Park, Titchfield; Eton; Brooke House, Market Harborough; UCL. *Heir: s* Lord Rosehill, *qv*. *Address:* House of Lords, SW1A 0PW.

NORTHFIELD, Baron *cr* 1975 (Life Peer), of Telford, Shropshire; **(William) Donald Chapman;** Chairman: Telford Development Corporation, 1975–87; Consortium Developments Ltd, 1986–92; *b* 25 Nov. 1923; *s* of Wm H. and Norah F. E. Chapman, Barnsley. *Educ:* Barnsley Grammar Sch.; Emmanuel Coll., Cambridge, MA (1st Cl. Hons) Economics, also degree in Agriculture; Senior Scholar of Emmanuel Coll. Research in Agric. Economics, Cambridge, 1943–46. Cambridge City Councillor, 1945–47; Sec., Trades Council and Labour Party, 1945–57; MP (Lab) Birmingham (Northfield), 1951–70. Research Sec. of the Fabian Soc., 1948–49, Gen. Sec., 1949–53. Gwilym Gibbon Fellow, Nuffield Coll., Oxford, 1971–73; Vis. Fellow, Centre for Contemporary European Studies, Sussex Univ., 1973–79. Special Adviser to EEC Commn, 1978–84; Chairman: Rural Develt Commn, 1974–80; Inquiry into recent trends in acquisition and occupancy of agric. land, 1977–79. *Publications:* The European Parliament: the years ahead, 1973; The Road to European Union, 1975; articles and Fabian pamphlets. *Recreation:* travel. *Address:* House of Lords, SW1A 0PW.

NORTHLAND, Viscount; title of heir to Earldom of Ranfurly.

NORTHOLT, Archdeacon of, *see* Broadbent, Ven. P. A.

NORTHUMBERLAND, 11th Duke of, *cr* 1766; **Henry Alan Walter Richard Percy;** Bt 1660; Baron Percy 1722; Earl of Northumberland, Baron Warkworth 1749; Earl Percy 1766; Earl of Beverly 1790; Lord Lovaine, Baron of Alnwick 1784; *b* 1 July 1953; *s* of 10th Duke of Northumberland, KG, GCVO, TD, PC, FRS and of Lady Elizabeth Diana Montagu-Douglas-Scott, *er d* of 8th Duke of Buccleuch and Queensberry, KT, GCVO, PC; *S* father, 1988. *Educ:* Eton; Christ Church, Oxford. President: Alnwick & Dist Cttee for the Disabled; Alnwick Working Men's Club & Inst.; Northumbria Club; Northumbrian Anglers' Fedn; Natural History Soc. of Northumbria; Northumberland Assoc. of Boys Clubs; Northumberland County Victims' Support Scheme; N of England CRC; Craster Br., RNLI; Surrey Farming & Wildlife Adv. Gp; Royal Northumberland Yacht Club; Tyne Mariners' Benevolent Instn; Vice President: Ancient Monuments Soc.; Internat. Sheep Dog Soc.; Patron: Assoc. of Northumberland Local History Socs; Berwick-upon-Tweed Preservation Trust; Internat. Centre for Child Studies; NE Br., Mental Health Foundn; Northumberland Buildings Preservation Trust; Hounslow and Feltham Victim Support Scheme; Hounslow and Twickenham Br., Arthritis Care; Northern Counties Sch. for the Deaf; Royal Northumberland Fusiliers Aid Soc. and Regimental Assoc.; Theatre W4; Tyneside Cinema. MFH 1989; FRSA 1989. *Recreations:* tennis, shooting, movies (film producer and actor). *Heir: b* Lord Ralph George Algernon Percy [*b* 16 Nov. 1956; *m* 1979, Jane, *d* of John W. M. M. Richard; two *s* two *d*]. *Address:* Alnwick Castle, Northumberland NE66 1NQ; Syon House, Brentford, Mddx TW8 8JF.

NORTHUMBERLAND, Archdeacon of; *see* Elliott, Ven. P.

NORTHWAY, Eileen Mary, CBE 1990; RRC 1982 (ARRC 1969); Principal Nursing Officer and Matron-in-Chief, Queen Alexandra's Royal Naval Nursing Service, 1986–90, retired; *b* 22 July 1931; *d* of Ernest and Margaret Northway. *Educ:* St Michael's Convent, Newton Abbot. SRN 1952, SCM 1954; joined QARNNS 1956. QHNS, 1986–90. OStJ 1985. *Recreations:* gardening, reading.

NORTON; *see* Hill-Norton.

NORTON, family name of **Barons Grantley** and **Rathcreedan.**

NORTON, 8th Baron *cr* 1878; **James Nigel Arden Adderley;** *b* 2 June 1947; *er s* of 7th Baron Norton, OBE and of Betty Margaret, *o d* of James McKee Hannah; *S* father, 1993;

m; one *s* one *d*. *Educ:* Downside. FCA 1970. *Heir:* *s* Hon. Edward James Arden Adderley, *b* 19 Oct. 1982. *Address:* 11 Picaterre, Alderney, CI.

NORTON, Donald; Regional Administrator, Oxford Regional Health Authority, 1973–80, retired; *b* 2 May 1920; *s* of Thomas Henry Norton and Dora May Norton (*née* Prentice); *m* 1945, Miriam Joyce, *d* of Herbert and Florence Mann; two *s* one *d*. *Educ:* Nether Edge Grammar Sch., Sheffield; Univs of Sheffield and London. LLB, DPA; FHA. Senior Administrator Sheffield Regional Hosp. Bd, 1948–51; Sec. Supt, Jessop Hosp. for Women and Charles Clifford Dental Hosp., Sheffield, 1951–57; Dep. Sec., Archway Gp of Hosps, London, 1957–60; Gp Sec., Dudley Road Gp of Hosps, Birmingham 1960–70; Sec., Oxford Regional Hosp. Bd, 1970–73. *Recreations:* marriage, golf, gardening. *Address:* The Squirrels, 14 Pullens Field, Headington, Oxford OX3 0BU. *T:* Oxford (01865) 67291. *Clubs:* Victory; Frilford Heath.

NORTON, Captain Gerard Ross, VC 1944; MM; 1/4th Hampshire Regiment; *b* S Africa, 7 Sept. 1915; *m* 1942, Lilia Morris, East London, S Africa; three *d*. *Educ:* Selborne Coll., East London, S Africa. Bank clerk. *Recreations:* Rugger-provincial, tennis, cricket. *Address:* Annandale Farm, Box 112, Banket, Zimbabwe.

NORTON, Hugh Edward; Managing Director, British Petroleum Co. plc, 1989–95; *b* 23 June 1936; *s* of late Lt-Gen. Edward F. Norton, CB, DSO, MC and I. Joyce Norton; *m* 1965, Janet M. Johnson (*d* 1993); one *s*. *Educ:* Winchester Coll.; Trinity Coll., Oxford (BA Hons Lit.Hum.). British Petroleum Co., 1959–95: Regl Co-ordinator, ME, 1977–78; Man. Dir, BP Singapore, 1978–81; Director: Planning, 1981–84; Admin, 1984–86; Chief Exec., BP Exploration Co., 1986–89. *Recreations:* painting, ornithology, tennis, travel. *Club:* Athenæum.

NORTON, James, FCIS; General Secretary, Arthritis and Rheumatism Council for Research, since 1981; *b* 12 July 1931; *s* of James and May Norton; *m* 1956, Dora Ashworth; one *s*. *Educ:* West Hill Sch., Stalybridge. FCIS 1972. Stalybridge, Hyde, Mossley and Dukinfield Tspt Bd, 1947–60; Wing Comdr, RAF, 1961–81. *Recreations:* walking, cricket, Manchester United. *Address:* 665 Chatsworth Road, Chesterfield S40 3PA. *T:* Chesterfield (01246) 566160. *Club:* Royal Air Force.

NORTON, John Lindsey; Senior Partner, Binder Hamlyn, since 1992; *b* 21 May 1935; *s* of Frederick Raymond Norton and Doris Ann Norton; *m* 1959, Judith Ann Bird; three *d*. *Educ:* Winchester College; Cambridge Univ. (MA). Blackburn Robson Coates & Co., 1959–63; BDO Binder Hamlyn, later Binder Hamlyn, 1963–; Chm., BDO Binder, 1988. Hon. Treas., NSPCC, 1991–. *Recreations:* walking, gardening. *Address:* Binder Hamlyn, 20 Old Bailey, EC4M 7BH. *T:* 0171–489 9000. *Club:* Buck's.

NORTON, Michael James; Chief Executive, Radiocommunications Agency, Department of Trade and Industry, since 1993; *b* 15 Dec. 1952; *s* of Christopher Stephen Norton and Lilian Ivy Norton; *m* 1976, Barbara Foster; one *s*. *Educ:* Roan Sch., Blackheath; Sheffield Univ. (BEng Hons (Electronic Engrg) 1974; Mappin Medal, 1974). AMIEE 1974. Post Office (Telecommunications), later British Telecommunications, 1970–87 (lastly, Sen. Man., Internat. Business); Practice Dir, Butler Cox plc, 1987–90; Marketing Dir, Cable & Wireless (Europe), 1990–93. FRSA 1993. *Recreations:* reading, music, amateur radio. *Address:* Radiocommunications Agency, Waterloo Bridge House, Waterloo Road, SE1 8UA. *T:* 0171–215 2339.

NORTON-GRIFFITHS, Sir John, 3rd Bt *cr* 1922; FCA; President and Chief Executive Officer, Main Street Data Services Inc.; *b* 4 Oct. 1938; *s* of Sir Peter Norton-Griffiths, 2nd Bt, and Kathryn (*d* 1980), *e d* of late George F. Schrafft; *S* father, 1983; *m* 1964, Marilyn Margaret, *er d* of Norman Grimley. *Educ:* Eton. FCA 1966. Lately Sub Lieutenant RN. *Heir:* *b* Michael Norton-Griffiths [*b* 11 Jan. 1941; *m* 1965, Ann, *o d* of late Group Captain Blair Alexander Fraser; one *s*]. *Address:* 17 Royal Drive, Bricktown, NJ 08723, USA.

NORWICH, 2nd Viscount, *cr* 1952, of Aldwick; **John Julius Cooper,** CVO 1993; FRSL, FRGS, FSA; writer and broadcaster; *b* 15 Sept. 1929; *s* of 1st Viscount Norwich, PC, GCMG, DSO, and Lady Diana Cooper (*d* 1986), *d* of 8th Duke of Rutland; *S* father, 1954; *m* 1st, 1952, Anne (Frances May) (marr. diss. 1985), *e d* of late Hon. Sir Bede Clifford, GCMG, CB, MVO; one *s* one *d*; 2nd, 1989, Mollie Philipps, *e d* of Baron Sherfield, *qv*. *Educ:* Upper Canada Coll., Toronto, Canada; Eton; University of Strasbourg; New Coll., Oxford. Served 1947–49 as Writer, Royal Navy. Entered Foreign Office, 1952; Third Secretary, British Embassy, Belgrade, 1955–57; Second Secretary, British Embassy, Beirut, 1957–60; worked in Foreign Office (First Secretary from 1961) and in British Delegation to Disarmament Conference, Geneva, from 1960 until resignation from Foreign Service 1964. Chairman: British Theatre Museum, 1966–71; Venice in Peril Fund, 1970–; Colnaghi, 1992–; Jt Chm., World Monuments Fund; Member: Exec. Cttee, National Trust, 1969–95 (Properties Cttee, 1970–87); Franco-British Council, 1972–79; Bd, English Nat. Opera, 1977–81. Curator, Sovereign Exhibn, London, 1992. Director: Heritage Broadcasting Ltd, 1990–93; Robclif Productions Ltd, 1991–94. Has made some thirty documentary films for television, mostly on history and architecture. Commendatore, Ordine al Merito della Repubblica Italiana. *Publications:* (as John Julius Norwich): Mount Athos (with Reresby Sitwell), 1966; The Normans in the South (as The Other Conquest, US), 1967; Sahara, 1968; The Kingdom in The Sun, 1970; A History of Venice, vol. I, The Rise to Empire, 1977, vol. II, The Greatness and the Fall, 1981; Christmas Crackers, 1970–79, 1980; Fifty Years of Glyndebourne, 1985; A Taste for Travel (anthology), 1985; General Editor: Great Architecture of the World, 1975; The Architecture of Southern England, 1985; Byzantium, the early centuries, 1988; (ed) Britain's Heritage, 1982; (ed) The Italian World: history, art and the genius of a people, 1983; More Christmas Crackers 1980–89, 1990, Venice: a traveller's companion, 1990; (ed) The Oxford Illustrated Encyclopaedia of the Arts, 1990; Byzantium: the apogee, 1991; Byzantium: decline and fall, 1995. *Recreations:* sight-seeing, walking at night through Venice. *Heir:* *s* Hon. Jason Charles Duff Bede Cooper, *b* 27 Oct. 1959. *Address:* 24 Blomfield Road, W9 1AD. *T:* 0171–286 5050, *Fax:* 0171–266 2561. *Club:* Beefsteak.

NORWICH, Bishop of, since 1985; **Rt. Rev. Peter John Nott;** *b* 30 Dec. 1933; *s* of Cecil Frederick Wilder Nott and Rosina Mabel Bailey; *m* 1961, Elizabeth May Maingot; one *s* three *d*. *Educ:* Bristol Grammar School; Dulwich Coll.; RMA Sandhurst; Fitzwilliam House, Cambridge; Westcott House, Cambridge (MA). Curate of Harpenden, 1961–64; Chaplain of Fitzwilliam Coll., Cambridge, 1964–69; Fellow of Fitzwilliam Coll., 1967–69, Hon. Fellow, 1993; Chaplain of New Hall, Cambridge, 1966–69; Rector of Beaconsfield, 1969–77; Bishop Suffragan of Taunton, 1977–85. Archbishop's Adviser to HMC, 1980–85; President: SW Region, Mencap, 1978–84; Somerset Rural Music Sch., 1981–85. Vice-Chm., Archbishops' Commn for Rural Areas, 1988–90. *Address:* Bishop's House, Norwich NR3 1SB. *T:* Norwich (01603) 629001.

NORWICH, Dean of; *see* Platten, Very Rev. S. G.

NORWICH, Archdeacon of; *see* Offer, Ven. C. J.

NORWOOD, Her Honour Suzanne Freda, (Mrs John Lexden Stewart); a Circuit Judge, 1973–95; *b* 24 March 1926; *d* of late Frederic Francis Norwood and of Marianne Freda Norwood (*née* Thomas); *m* 1954, John Lexden Stewart (*d* 1972); one *s*. *Educ:* Lowther Coll., Bodelwyddan; St Andrews Univ. MA English, MA Hons History. Called to Bar, Gray's Inn, 1951; practised at Bar, SE Circuit. Member: Parole Bd, 1976–78; Mental Health Review Tribunal, 1983– (Chm., Oxford and Anglia Area, 1994–). Member: Greenwich and Bexley AHA, 1979–82; Greenwich DHA, 1982–85; Bexley DHA, 1985–90. Pres., Medico-Legal Soc., 1990–92. *Recreations:* walking, housekeeping, opera. *Address:* 69 Lee Road, SE3 9EN.

NORWOOD, Sir Walter (Neville), Kt 1971; *b* 14 July 1907; *s* of late Sir Charles Norwood; *m* 1935, Rana Muriel, *d* of David Redpath; two *s* one *d*. *Educ:* Wellington and Wanganui. Trustee: Nuffield Trust for Crippled Children; Laura Fergusson Trust for Disabled Persons; C. J. B. Norwood Crippled Children's Trust; Norwood Cricket Trust. Past President: Wellington Rotary Club; Wellington Racing Club. *Recreations:* racing, farming, sailing. *Address:* Hillcrest, 24 Mataroa Avenue, Northland, Wellington, New Zealand. *Clubs:* Wellesley, Wellington (Wellington, NZ).

NOSS, John Bramble; HM Diplomatic Service, retired; Secretariat, International Primary Aluminium Institute, since 1994; *b* 20 Dec. 1935; *s* of John Noss and Vera Ethel (*née* Mattingly); *m* 1957, Shirley May Andrews; two *s* one *d*. *Educ:* Portsmouth Grammar School. Foreign Office, 1954; RAF, 1955–57; served FO, Beirut, Copenhagen, FCO; Russian language training, 1965; Moscow, 1965–68; Santiago, 1968–70; FCO, 1970–73; First Sec. (Economic), Pretoria, 1974–77; First Sec. (Commercial), Moscow, 1977–78; FCO, 1978–81; Consul (Inward Investment), New York, 1981–85; High Comr, Solomon Is, 1986–88; Dep. Hd of Mission and Commercial Counsellor, Helsinki, 1988–91; Consul-Gen., Perth, 1991–93. *Recreations:* photography, reading, golf. *Address:* 8 Hither Chantlers, Langton Green, Tunbridge Wells, Kent TN3 0BJ. *T:* Tunbridge Wells (01892) 862157.

NOSSAL, Sir Gustav (Joseph Victor), AC 1989; Kt 1977; CBE 1970; FRS 1982; FAA; Director, The Walter and Eliza Hall Institute of Medical Research, Melbourne, since 1965; Professor of Medical Biology, University of Melbourne, since 1965; *b* Austria, 4 June 1931; *m* 1955, Lyn B. Dunnicliff; two *s* two *d*. *Educ:* Sydney Univ. (1st Cl. Hons BScMed (Bacteriology), 1952; 1st Cl. Hons MB, BS 1954 (Mills Prize)); Melbourne Univ. (PhD 1960). FAA 1967; FRACP 1967; Hon. FRCPA 1971; FRACMA 1971; FRCP 1980; FTS 1981; Hon. FRSE 1983. Jun., then Sen. Resident Officer, Royal Prince Alfred Hosp., Sydney, 1955–56; Res. Fellow, Walter and Eliza Hall Inst. of Med. Res., 1957–59; Asst Prof., Dept of Genetics, Stanford Univ. Sch. of Medicine, Calif, 1959–61; Dep. Dir (Immunology), Walter and Eliza Hall Inst. of Med. Res., 1961–65. Vis. scientist and vis. professor to several univs and res. insts; has given many lectures to learned societies, assocs and univs. Dir, CRA Ltd, 1977–. World Health Organisation: Member: Expert Adv. Panel on Immunology, 1967; Adv. Cttee Med. Res., 1973–80; Special Consultant, Tropical Disease Res. Prog., 1976. Chm., West Pac Adv. Co. Med. Res., 1976–80; Member: Aust. Science and Technol. Council, 1975–83; Adv. Bd, John Curtin Sch. of Med. Res., 1981–; Centre for Recombinant DNA Res., Res. Sch. of Biol Sciences, ANU, 1981– (Founder Mem.); Baker Med. Res. Inst., 1982–; Scientific Adv. Cttee, Centenary Res. Inst. of Cancer Medicine and Cell Biol., Sydney, 1983–; Aust. Industrial Res. Develt Incentives Bd, 1983–. Pres., Australian Acad. of Science, 1994–. Mem., Aust. Soc. of Immunology; Hon. Mem., Amer. (1975), French (1979), Indian (1976), Soc. of Immunology; Foreign Hon. Mem., Amer. Acad. of Arts and Scis, 1974. For. Associate, US Nat. Acad. of Scis, 1979; Fellow, New York Acad. of Scis, 1977; For. Fellow, Indian Nat. Sci. Acad., 1980. Hon. MD Johannes Gutenberg Univ., Mainz, 1981. Emil von Behring Prize, Philipps Univ., Marburg, Germany, 1971; Rabbi Shai Shacknai Memorial Prize, Univ. of Jerusalem, 1973; Ciba Foundn Gold Medal, 1978; Burnet Medal, Aust. Acad. of Sci., 1979. Mem. Editorial Bd of several med. jls. *Publications:* Antibodies & Immunity, 1968 (rev. edn 1977); Antigens Lymphoid Cells & The Immune Response, 1971, Medical Science & Human Goals, 1975; Nature's Defences (Boyer Lectures), 1978; Reshaping Life: key issues in genetic engineering, 1984. *Recreations:* golf, literature. *Address:* 46 Fellows Street, Kew, Vic 3101, Australia. *T:* 8618256. *Clubs:* Melbourne (Melbourne); Rosebud Country.

NOSWORTHY, Harold George, CMG 1965; FCCA; FCA; *b* 15 March 1908; *m* 1941, Marjorie Anjelique; two *d*. *Educ:* Kingston Technical High Sch.; private tuition. Entered Jamaica Civil Service, 1929; 2nd class Clerk, 1938; Examiner of Accounts, 1943; Asst Commissioner, Income Tax, 1947; Asst Trade Administrator, 1950; Trade Administrator and Chairman Trade Control Board, 1953; Principal Asst Secretary, Ministry of Finance, 1955; Auditor-General, 1957–66; Dir, Internal Audit Service, UN, 1966–68. Queen's Coronation Medal, 1953; Jamaica Independence Medal, 1962. *Recreations:* reading, billiards, bridge, swimming. *Address:* 18 Hyperion Avenue, PO Box 127, Kingston 6, Jamaica. *T:* 9279889. *Club:* Kingston Cricket (Jamaica).

NOTLEY, Maj.-Gen. Charles Roland Sykes, CB 1994; CBE 1991; President of the Ordnance Board, 1992–94; *b* 5 May 1939; *s* of late Major Henry Sykes Notley, 3rd Carabiniers, and Mrs Stephanie Paterson-Morgan; *m* 1965, Katherine Sonia Bethell; two *d*. *Educ:* Winchester Coll. Commnd 3rd Carabiniers, 1959; Command, Royal Scots Dragoon Guards, 1979–82; Dir, Op. Requirements (Land), MoD, 1986–89; Dir, Logistic Ops (Army), MoD, 1989–90; Vice-Pres., Ordnance Board, 1991–92. *Recreations:* equitation, sailing. *Address:* c/o Royal Bank of Scotland, 67 Lombard Street, EC3 3DL. *Clubs:* Cavalry and Guards, Royal Ocean Racing.

NOTT, Charles Robert Harley, CMG 1959; OBE 1952; retired, New Zealand; *b* 24 Oct. 1904; *e s* of late John Harley Nott, JP, Leominster, Herefordshire and late Mrs Nott, formerly of Bodenham Hall, Herefordshire; *m* 1935, Marion (*née* Macfarlane), Auckland, NZ; one *s* one *d*. *Educ:* Marlborough; Christ's Coll., Cambridge (MA). Colonial Administrative Service: Fiji, 1926; Administrative Officer (Grade II), 1938, (Grade I), 1945. Member of the Legislative Council, Fiji, 1950; HBM's Agent and Consul, Tonga, 1954–57; Sec. for Fijian Affairs, 1957–59; MLC, MEC, retired, 1960. *Recreation:* trout fishing. *Address:* 5 Nigel Street, Havelock North, New Zealand.

NOTT, Rt Hon. Sir John (William Frederic), KCB 1983; PC 1979; Chairman: Hillsdown Holdings, since 1993 (Director, since 1991); Maple Leaf Foods Inc., Canada, since 1993; *b* 1 Feb. 1932; *s* of late Richard Nott, Bideford, Devon, and Phyllis (*née* Francis); *m* 1959, Miloska Sekol, Maribor, Slovenia; two *s* one *d*. *Educ:* King's Mead, Seaford; Bradfield Coll.; Trinity Coll., Cambridge. Lieut, 2nd Gurkha Rifles (regular officer), Malayan emergency, 1952–56; Trinity Coll., Cambridge, 1957–59 (BA Hons Law and Econs); Pres., Cambridge Union, 1959; called to the Bar, Inner Temple, 1959; Gen. Manager, S. G. Warburg & Co. Ltd, Merchant Bankers, 1960–66. MP (C) Cornwall, St Ives, 1966–83; Minister of State, HM Treasury, 1972–74; Cons. front bench spokesman on: Treasury and Economic Affairs, 1975–76; Trade, 1976–79; Sec. of State for Trade, 1979–81; Sec. of State for Defence, 1981–83. Chm and Chief Executive, Lazard Brothers & Co. Ltd, 1985–90 (Dir, 1983–90); Chm., Etam plc, 1991–95; Dep. Chm., Royal Insurance PLC, 1986–89 (Dir, 1985–91); Director: Record Treasury Management plc,

1991–. Adviser: Apax Partners, 1990–; Freshfields, 1991–. *Address:* 32 Hampstead High Street, NW3 1QD. *T:* 0171–794 0677.

NOTT, Kathleen Cecilia, FRSL; author, broadcaster, lecturer and journalist; *d* of Philip and Ellen Nott; *m* Christopher Bailey (marr. diss.). *Educ:* Mary Datchelor Sch., London; Somerville Coll., Oxford (BA Hons, PPE); King's Coll., London. FRSL 1977. President: Progressive League, 1959–61; English PEN, 1974–75. Editor, PEN International (formerly Internat. PEN Bulletin of Selected Books), 1960–88. *Publications: poetry:* Landscapes and Departures, 1947; Poems from the North, 1956; Creatures and Emblems, 1960; Elegies and Other Poems, 1980; *novels:* Mile End, 1938; The Dry Deluge, 1947; Private Fires, 1960; An Elderly Retired Man, 1963; *criticism and philosophy:* The Emperor's Clothes, 1954; A Soul in the Quad, 1969; Philosophy and Human Nature, 1970; The Good Want Power, 1977; *general:* A Clean Well-lighted Place, 1961 (Sweden); contribs to collections of essays, and to periodicals. *Recreations:* playing the piano, gardening. *Address:* Wemyss Lodge Residential Home, Ermin Street, Stratton St Margaret, Swindon, Wilts SN3 4NX. *Clubs:* University Women's, PEN, Society of Authors.

NOTT, Rt. Rev. Peter John; *see* Norwich, Bishop of.

NOTT, Roger Charles L.; *see* Lane-Nott.

NOTTAGE, Raymond Frederick Tritton, CMG 1964; Chairman, Bobath Centre for Children with Cerebral Palsy, since 1987; Deputy Chairman, Association of Lloyd's Members, 1985–91; Treasurer, Arkwright Arts Trust, Hampstead, 1975–92; *b* 1 Aug. 1916; *s* of Frederick and Frances Nottage; *m* 1941, Joyce Evelyn, *d* of Sidney and Edith Philpot; three *d*. *Educ:* Hackney Downs Secondary Sch. Civil servant, Post Office Headquarters, 1936–49; Editor of Civil Service Opinion, and Member Exec. Cttee, Soc. of Civil Servants, 1944–49; Dir-Gen., RIPA, 1949–78. Mem. Hornsey Borough Council, 1945–47. Mem. Cttee on Training in Public Admin. for Overseas Countries, 1961–63; Vice-Pres. Internat. Inst. of Admin. Sciences, 1962–68; Mem. Governing Body, Inst. of Development Studies, Univ. of Sussex, 1966–76; travelled abroad as Consultant and Lectr. *Publications:* Sources of Local Revenue (with S. H. H. Hildersley), 1968; Financing Public Sector Pensions, 1975; (with Gerald Rhodes) Pensions: a plan for the future, 1986; articles on public administration. *Recreations:* music, swimming. *Address:* 119 Haverstock Hill, NW3 4RS.

NOTTINGHAM, Bishop of, (RC), since 1974; **Rt. Rev. James Joseph McGuinness;** *b* 2 Oct. 1925; *s* of Michael and Margaret McGuinness. *Educ:* St Columb's College, Derry; St Patrick's College, Carlow; Oscott College, Birmingham. Ordained, 1950; Curate of St Mary's, Derby, 1950–53; Secretary to Bishop Ellis, 1953–56; Parish Priest, Corpus Christi Parish, Clifton, Nottingham, 1956–72; Vicar General of Nottingham Diocese, 1969; Coadjutor Bishop of Nottingham and Titular Bishop of St Germans, 1972–74. *Recreation:* gardening. *Address:* Bishop's House, 27 Cavendish Road East, The Park, Nottingham NG7 1BB.

NOTTINGHAM, Archdeacon of; *see* Walker, Ven. T. O.

NOULTON, John David; Director of Public Affairs, Eurotunnel, since 1992; *b* 5 Jan. 1939; *s* of John Noulton and Kathleen (*née* Sheehan); *m* 1961, Anne Elizabeth Byrne; three *s* one *d*. *Educ:* Clapham Coll. MCIT; ComplCE 1994. Asst Principal, Dept of Transport, 1970–72; Principal, DoE, 1972–78; Pvte Sec. to Minister of State, DoE, 1976–78; Asst Sec., Depts of the Environment and of Transport, 1978–85; Under Sec., Dept of Transport, 1985–89. British Co-Chm., Channel Tunnel Intergovtl Commn, 1987–89; Dir, Transmanche Link, 1989–92. FRSA 1992. *Recreations:* boating, swimming, walking, reading. *Address:* 12 Ladderstile Ride, Coombe, Surrey KT2 7LP. *T:* 0181–546 3855.

NOURSE, Rt. Hon. Sir Martin (Charles), PC 1985; Kt 1980; **Rt. Hon. Lord Justice Nourse;** a Lord Justice of Appeal, since 1985; *b* 3 April 1932; *yr s* of late Henry Edward Nourse, MD, MRCP, of Cambridge, and Ethel Millicent, *d* of Rt Hon. Sir Charles Henry Sargant, Lord Justice of Appeal; *m* 1972, Lavinia, *yr d* of late Comdr D. W. Malim; one *s* one *d*. *Educ:* Winchester (Fellow, 1993); Corpus Christi Coll., Cambridge (Hon. Fellow, 1988). National Service as 2nd Lieut, Rifle Bde, 1951–52; Lieut, London Rifle Bde Rangers (TA), 1952–55. Called to Bar, Lincoln's Inn, 1956; Bencher, 1978; Mem., General Council of the Bar, 1964–68; a Junior Counsel to BoT in Chancery matters, 1967–70; QC 1970; Attorney Gen., Duchy of Lancaster, 1976–80; a Judge of the Courts of Appeal of Jersey and Guernsey, 1977–80; Judge of the High Court of Justice, Chancery Div., 1980–85. Pres., Council of Inns of Court, 1992–95. *Address:* Royal Courts of Justice, Strand, WC2A 2LL.

See also Sir Edmund Sargant.

NOVA SCOTIA, Bishop of, since 1984; **Rt. Rev. Arthur Gordon Peters;** *b* 21 Dec. 1935; *s* of William Peters and Charlotte Peters (*née* Symes); *m* 1962, Elizabeth Baert; one *s* two *d*. *Educ:* High School, North Sydney, NS; Univ. of King's College, Halifax, NS (BA 1960, BST 1963, BD 1973). Student, Parish of Waverley, 1961–63; deacon 1962, priest 1963, Nova Scotia; Morris Scholar, 1963, at Canterbury (Eng.), Geneva, Jerusalem, Norton (dio. Durham, Eng.); Rector: Weymouth, NS, 1964–68; Annapolis-Granville, NS, 1968–73; Christ Church, Sydney, NS, 1973–82; Bishop Coadjutor of Nova Scotia, 1982–84. Hon. DD Univ. of King's College, 1982. *Recreations:* swimming, ski-ing, reading, skating, photography. *Address:* 5732 College Street, Halifax, NS B3H 1X3, Canada. *T:* (902) 4200717.

NOWELL-SMITH, Prof. Patrick Horace, AM (Harvard); MA (Oxon); Professor of Philosophy, York University, Toronto, 1969–85, now Emeritus; *b* 17 Aug. 1914; *s* of Nowell Charles Smith; *m* 1st, 1946, Perilla Thyme (marr. diss. 1968), *d* of Sir Richard Vynne Southwell; three *s* one *d*; 2nd, 1968, Felicity Margret (marr. diss. 1986), *d* of Dr Richard Leonard Ward; two *d*. *Educ:* Winchester Coll.; New College, Oxford. Commonwealth Fellow, Harvard Univ., 1937–39. Served War of 1939–45, in Army, 1939–45. Fellow and Lecturer, Trinity Coll., Oxford, 1946–57, Estates Bursar, 1951–57; Professor of Philosophy: University of Leicester, 1957–64; University of Kent, 1964–69. *Publications:* Ethics, 1954; articles in Mind, Proc. Aristotelian Soc., Theoria, etc. *Address:* 7 Wyndham House, Plantation Road, Oxford OX2 6JJ.

See also S. H. Nowell-Smith, Sir S. S. T. Young.

NOWELL-SMITH, Simon Harcourt, FSA; *b* 5 Jan. 1909; *s* of late Nowell Charles Smith, sometime Headmaster of Sherborne; *m* 1st, 1938, Marion Sinclair (*d* 1977), *d* of late W. S. Crichton, Liverpool; two *s* one *d*; 2nd, 1986, Judith Adams, *d* of Frederick B. Adams, *qv*. *Educ:* Sherborne; New Coll., Oxford (MA). Editorial Staff of The Times, 1932–44; Assistant Editor, Times Literary Supplement, 1937–39; attached to Intelligence Division, Naval Staff, 1940–45; Secretary and Librarian, The London Library, 1950–56; Secretary, Hospital Library Services Survey, 1958–59; President, Bibliographical Society, 1962–64; Lyell Reader in Bibliography, Oxford Univ., 1965–66. Pres., Oxford Bibliographical Soc., 1972–76. Trustee, Dove Cottage Trust, 1974–82. OStJ. *Publications:* Mark Rutherford, a bibliography, 1930; The Legend of the Master (Henry James), 1947; The House of Cassell, 1958; (ed) Edwardian England, 1964; Letters to Macmillan, 1967; International Copyright Law and the Publisher, 1968; Postscript to Autobiography of William Plomer, 1975. *Address:* St Luke's Nursing Home, 4 Latimer Road, Headington, Oxford OX3 7PF.

See also Prof. P. H. Nowell-Smith.

NOYES, Ralph Norton; writer; *b* 9 June 1923; *s* of late Sidney Ralph Noyes and Nova (*née* Pearce); *m* 1948, Margaret Isaacs; two *s* one *d*. *Educ:* Haberdashers' Aske's Hampstead Sch.; London School of Economics (BScEcon). War service, RAF (aircrew), 1940–46. Air Ministry, 1949–63: Private Sec. to VCAS, 1950–52, and to CAS, 1953; Air Force Dept, 1964–69; idc 1966; Defence Secretariat, 1969–77: Asst Under-Sec. of State (Logistics), 1975–77; UK Rep., NATO Maintenance and Supply Org., 1975–77. Hon. Secretary: SPR, 1990–; Centre for Crop Circle Studies, 1990–92. Member: Folklore Soc., 1987–; British UFO Res. Assoc., 1983–. *Publications:* A Secret Property, 1985; (ed) The Crop Circle Enigma, 1990; several short stories, articles, papers and broadcasts on speculative themes, in Punch, Country Life, Argosy, Fiction Magazine, etc, BBC2, Jl of Soc. for Psych. Res., several times reprinted in anthologies. *Recreations:* travel, research into anomalous topics. *Address:* 9 Oakley Street, SW3 5NN. *T:* 0171–351 6659.

NSEKELA, Amon James, OURT 1985; Director: Tanzania–Zambia Railway Authority, since 1982; Computers and Telecoms Systems, since 1993; *b* 4 Jan. 1930; *s* of Ngonile Reuben Nsekela and Anyambilile Nsekela (*née* Kalinga); *m* 1957, Christina Matilda Nsekela (*née* Kyusa); two *s*. *Educ:* Rungwe Dist Sch.; Malangali Secondary Sch.; Tabora Govt Sen. Sec. Sch.; Makerere UC (DipEd); Univ. of Pacific (Scholar, MA). Schoolteacher, Rungwe Middle Sch. and Alliance Secondary Sch., 1954–57; entered Civil Service as DO, Moshi, 1960; Perm. Sec., Min. of External Affairs and Defence, 1963; Perm. Sec. to Min. of Commerce, 1964; Prin. Sec. to Treasury (also ex-officio Paymaster Gen.), 1966–67. MP 1973–75, and Mem. E African Legis. Assembly, 1967–70. High Comr, UK, 1974–81, and Ambassador Extraordinary and Plenipotentiary to Ireland, 1980–81. Chm. or Dir of many cos and corporations, 1967–, incl.: Chm., Nat. Insurance Corp. of Tanzania, 1967–72; Chm. and Man. Dir, Nat. Bank of Commerce, 1967–74 and 1981–94; Chm., Tanzania Investment Bank, 1982–91; Director: Nat. Develt Corp. (past Chm. when Tanganyika Develt Corp.); Bd of Internal Trade; E African Airways Corp.; Bd, African Medical Res. Fund, 1986–. Mem./Sec., Presidential Commn on Estabt of Democratic One-Party State in Tanzania; Mem., Internat. Council of Trustees, Internat. Defence and Aid Fund for Southern Africa, 1985–. Chairman: Council, Inst. of Finance Management, 1971–; Inst. of Develt Management, 1982–; Public Service Salaries Review Commn, 1985–86. Pres., Tanzania Soc. for Internat. Develt; Past Pres., Economic Assoc. of Tanzania; Chm., Britain–Tanzania Soc., 1982–. Mem., TANU, 1955–. Mem., NEC, Chama Cha Mapinduzi, 1987–. Chm. Council, Univ. of Dar es Salaam; Vice-Chm., Council, Sokoine Univ. of Agriculture, 1982–. *Publications:* Minara ya Historia ya Tanganyika: Tanganyika hadi Tanzania, 1965, new edns 1966 and 1971; Demokrasi Tanzania, 1973; (with A. L. Nhonoli) The Development of Health Services in Mainland Tanzania: Tumetoka Mbali, 1976; Socialism and Social Accountability in a Developing Nation, 1978; (ed) Southern Africa: toward economic liberation, 1981; Towards Rational Alternatives, 1984; A Time to Act, 1984; contribs to Jl of Administration Overseas (ODM), African Review, Development Dialogue. *Recreations:* swimming, darts, reading, writing. *Address:* 9 Lupa Way, Box 722, Mbeya, Tanzania.

NTIWANE, Nkomeni Douglas; Minister for Broadcasting, Information and Tourism, Swaziland, 1992–93; part-time farmer; *b* 16 Feb. 1933; *s* of Isaiah Myotha and Jane Dlamini; *m* 1st, 1960, Sophia Pulane Kali (*d* 1981); three *s*; 2nd, 1983, Phindile T. Mamba. *Educ:* DOT Coll., Middelburg, Transvaal, SA; Columbia Univ. (1967–68; Carnegie Fellow in Dipl.). Certificate Teacher: Mbekelweni Sch., 1962–63; Mhlume Central Sch., 1964–66; Lozitha Central Sch., Jan.-Sept. 1967; High Commissioner for Swaziland in London, 1968–71; Ambassador: Federal Republic of Germany, March 1969; Republic of France, April 1969. Permanent Secretary: Dept of Foreign Affairs, Swaziland, 1971–72; Ministry of Health, 1972–77; Ministry of Commerce, Industry, Mines and Tourism, 1977–80; retired from Civil Service, 1980; Group Personnel, Training and Localisation Manager, Swaki Gp of Cos, 1980–87. Minister for Commerce, Industry and Tourism, 1987–92. Swaziland Independence Medal, 1968; Meritorious Service Medal, Royal Swaziland Umbutfo Defence Force, 1978. *Publications:* Asive Ngwane (Siswati poetry), 1978; (jtly) Takitsi, 1986. *Address:* Emangweni, PO Box 41, Malkerns, Swaziland.

NUGEE, Edward George, TD 1964; QC 1977; *b* 9 Aug. 1928; *o s* of late Brig. George Travers Nugee, CBE, DSO, MC, RA, and of Violet Mary (*née* Richards, now Brooks); *m* 1955, Rachel Elizabeth Makower (*see* R. E. Nugee); four *s*. *Educ:* Brambletye; Radley Coll. (Open Scholar); Worcester Coll., Oxford (Open Exhibnr; Law Mods, Distinction, 1950; 1st Cl. Hons Jurisprudence, 1952; Eldon Law Scholar, 1953; MA 1956). National Service, RA, 1947–49 (Office of COS, GHQ, FARELF); service with 100 Army Photographic Interpretation Unit, TA, 1950–64 (retd Captain, Intell. Corps, 1964). Read as pupil with Lord Templeman and Lord Brightman; called to the Bar, Inner Temple, 1955, Bencher 1976, Reader 1995; *ad eundem* Lincoln's Inn, 1968. Jun. Counsel to Land Commn (Chancery and Conveyancing), 1967–71; Counsel for litigation under Commons Registration Act, 1965, 1968–77; Conveyancing Counsel to Treasury, WO, MAFF, Forestry Commn, MoD (Admiralty), and DoE, 1972–77; Conveyancing Counsel of Court, 1976–77. Poor Man's Lawyer, Lewisham CAB, 1954–72. Member: CAB Adv. Cttee, Family Welfare Assoc., 1969–72; Management Cttee, Greater London Citizens Advice Bureaux Service Ltd, 1972–74; Man. Cttee, Forest Hill Advice Centre, 1972–76; Bar Council, 1962–66 (Mem., External Relations Cttee, 1966–71); Council of Legal Educn, 1967–90 (Vice-Chm. 1976–82, and Chm. of Bd of Studies, 1976–82); Adv. Cttee on Legal Educn, 1971–90; Common Professional Exam. Bd, 1976–89 (Chm., 1981–87); Lord Chancellor's Law Reform Cttee, 1973–; various working parties and consultative groups of Law Commn, 1966–; Inst. of Conveyancers, 1971– (Pres., 1986–87); Chm., Cttee of Inquiry into Management Problems of Privately Owned Blocks of Flats, 1984–85. Church Comr, 1990– (Mem., Bd of Govs, 1993–). Chm. Governors, Brambletye Sch., 1972–77; Mem. Council, Radley Coll., 1975–95. *Publications:* (jtly) Nathan on the Charities Act 1960, 1962; (ed jtly) Halsbury's Laws of England, titles Landlord and Tenant (3rd edn 1958), Real Property (3rd edn 1960, 4th edn 1982); contribs to legal jls. *Recreations:* travel, cooking, the family. *Address:* Wilberforce Chambers, 8 New Square, Lincoln's Inn, WC2A 3QP. *T:* 0171–306 0102; 10 Heath Hurst Road, Hampstead, NW3 2RX. *T:* 0171–435 9204.

NUGEE, Rachel Elizabeth, JP, MA; *b* 15 Aug. 1926; *d* of John Moritz Makower and Adelaide Gertrude Leonaura Makower (*née* Franklin); *m* 1955, Edward George Nugee, *qv*; four *s*. *Educ:* Roedean Sch., Brighton; Lady Margaret Hall, Oxford; MA (EngLang and Lit); Reading Univ. (Dip. Soc. Studies). Joined Mothers' Union, 1956; Diocesan Pres., London Dio., 1974–76; Central Pres., 1977–82; MU rep. on Women's Nat. Commn, 1983–88. Chm., Edmonton Area Social Responsibility Policy Cttee, 1987–90; Member: Royal Free Hosp. (Hampstead Gen. Hosp.) House Cttee and Patients' Services Cttee, 1961–72; London Diocesan Bd for Social Responsibility, 1984–85, 1987–90; Law of Marriage Gp, General Synod, 1985–88; Lord Chancellor's Adv. Cttee on Conscientious Objectors, 1986–. Trustee, One plus One – the Marriage and Partnership res. charity,

to Zimbabwe, 1980–81, in London, 1981–89. *Address:* Tanzanian Mission to UN, 205 E 42nd Street, 13th Floor, New York, NY 10017, USA.

NYE, Prof. John Frederick, FRS 1976; Melville Wills Professor of Physics, University of Bristol, 1985–88 (Professor of Physics, 1969–88), now Professor Emeritus; *b* 26 Feb. 1923; *s* of Haydn Percival Nye and Jessie Mary, *d* of Anderson Hague, painter; *m* 1953, Georgiana Wiebenson; one *s* two *d*. *Educ:* Stowe; King's Coll., Cambridge (Maj. Schol.; MA, PhD 1948). Research, Cavendish Laboratory, Cambridge, 1944–49; Univ. Demonstrator in Mineralogy and Petrology, Cambridge, 1949–51; Bell Telephone Laboratories, NJ, USA, 1952–53; Lectr, 1953, Reader, 1965, Univ. of Bristol; Visiting Professor: in Glaciology, California Inst. of Technol., 1959; of Applied Sciences, Yale Univ., 1964; of Geophysics, Univ. of Washington, 1973. President: Internat. Glaciological Soc., 1966–69; Internat. Commn of Snow and Ice, 1971–75. For. Mem., Royal Swedish Acad. of Scis, 1977. Kirk Bryan Award, Geol. Soc. of Amer., 1961; Seligman Crystal, Internat. Glaciol Soc., 1969; Antarctic Service Medal, USA, 1974; NPL Metrology Award, 1986; Charles Chree Medal, Inst. of Physics, 1989. *Publications:* Physical Properties of Crystals, 1957, rev. edn 1985; papers on physics of crystals, glaciology, optics, and applications of catastrophe theory in scientific jls. *Address:* 45 Canynge Road, Bristol BS8 3LH. *T:* Bristol (0117) 973 3769.
See also P. H. Nye.

NYE, Ven. Nathaniel Kemp; retired; *b* 4 Nov. 1914; *s* of Charles Frederick and Evelyn Nye; *m* 1941, Rosa Jackson; two *s* one *d*. *Educ:* Merchant Taylors' Sch.; King's College London (AKC 1935); Cuddesdon College, Oxford. Ordained 1937 to St Peter's, St Helier Estate, Morden, Surrey; Chaplain RAF, 1940–46 (POW 1941–43; escaped from Italy at liberation); Rector, Holy Trinity, Clapham, 1946–54; Vicar, St Peter's, St Helier Estate, 1954–60; Vicar, All Saints, Maidstone (Parish Church), Canon, and Rural Dean, 1960–66; Tait Missioner, Canterbury Diocese, 1966–72; Archdeacon of Maidstone, 1972–79. Hon. Canon of Canterbury, 1960; Canon Emeritus, 1979; Archdeacon Emeritus, dio. Canterbury, 1982. *Recreations:* woodcraft, sailing, travel; family life! *Address:* Lees Cottage, Boughton Lees, Ashford, Kent TN25 4HX. *T:* Ashford (01233) 626175.

NYE, Peter Hague, FRS 1987; Reader in Soil Science, University of Oxford, 1961–88; Fellow of St Cross College, Oxford, 1966–88 (Senior Fellow, 1982–83), now Emeritus Fellow; *b* 16 Sept. 1921; *s* of Haydn Percival Nye and Jessie Mary (*née* Hague); *m* 1953, Phyllis Mary Quenault; one *s* two *d*. *Educ:* Charterhouse; Balliol Coll., Oxford (MA, BSc (Domus Exhibnr)); Christ's Coll., Cambridge. Agricl Chemist, Gold Coast, 1947–50; Lectr in Soil Science, University Coll. of Ibadan, Nigeria, 1950–52; Sen. Lectr in Soil Science, Univ. of Ghana, 1952–60; Res. Officer, Internat. Atomic Energy Agency, Vienna, 1960–61. Vis. Professor, Cornell Univ., 1974, 1981, Messenger Lectures, 1989; Commonwealth Vis. Prof., Univ. of Western Aust., 1979; Vis. Prof., Royal Vet. and Agricl Univ., Copenhagen, 1990. Pres., British Soc. Soil Science, 1968–69; Mem. Council, Internat. Soc. Soil Science, 1968–74. Governor, Nat. Vegetable Res. Station, 1972–87. *Publications:* The Soil under Shifting Cultivation, 1961; Solute Movement in the Soil-Root System, 1977; articles, mainly in Jl of Soil Science, Plant and Soil, Jl of Agricl Science. *Recreations:* cycling, computing; formerly cricket, tennis, squash. *Address:* Hewel Barn, Common Road, Beckley, Oxon OX3 9UR. *T:* Oxford (01865) 351607.
See also J. F. Nye.

NYE, Robert; writer; *b* 15 March 1939; *s* of Oswald William Nye and Frances Dorothy Weller; *m* 1st, 1959, Judith Pratt (marr. diss. 1967); three *s*; 2nd, 1968, Aileen Campbell; one *d*. *Educ:* Southend High School, Essex. Freelance writer, 1961–. FRSL 1977. *Publications: poetry:* Juvenilia 1, 1961; Juvenilia 2, 1963 (Eric Gregory Award, 1963); Darker Ends, 1969; Agnus Dei, 1973; Two Prayers, 1974; Five Dreams, 1974; Divisions on a Ground, 1976; A Collection of Poems 1955–1988, 1989; 14 Poems, 1994; Henry James and Other Poems, 1995; Collected Poems, 1995; *fiction:* Doubtfire, 1967; Tales I Told My Mother, 1969; Falstaff, 1976 (The Guardian Fiction Prize, 1976; Hawthornden Prize, 1977); Merlin, 1978; Faust, 1980; The Voyage of the Destiny, 1982; The Facts of Life and Other Fictions, 1983; The Memoirs of Lord Byron, 1989; The Life and Death of My Lord Gilles de Rais, 1990; Mrs Shakespeare: the complete works, 1993; *plays:* (with Bill Watson) Sawney Bean, 1970; The Seven Deadly Sins: A Mask, 1974; Penthesilea, Fugue and Sisters, 1976; *children's fiction:* Taliesin, 1966; March Has Horse's Ears, 1966; Wishing Gold, 1970; Poor Pumpkin, 1971; Out of the World and Back Again, 1977; Once Upon Three Times, 1978; The Bird of the Golden Land, 1980; Harry Pay the Pirate, 1981; Three Tales, 1983; Lord Fox and Other Spine-Chilling Tales, 1996; *translation:* Beowulf, 1968; *editions:* A Choice of Sir Walter Ralegh's Verse, 1972; William Barnes: Selected Poems, 1973; A Choice of Swinburne's Verse, 1973; The English Sermon 1750–1850, 1976; The Faber Book of Sonnets, 1976; PEN New Poetry 1, 1986; (jtly) First Awakenings: the early poems of Laura Riding, 1992; A Selection of the Poems of Laura Riding, 1994; contribs to British and American periodicals. *Recreation:* gambling. *Address:* 2 Westbury Crescent, Wilton, Cork, Ireland.

NYERERE, Julius Kambarage; President, United Republic of Tanzania (formerly Tanganyika and Zanzibar), 1964–85; President, Tanganyika African National Union, 1954–77; *b* 1922; *m* 1953, Maria Magige; five *s* two *d*. *Educ:* Tabora Secondary School; Makerere University College; Edinburgh University (MA). Began as Teacher; became President African Association, Dar es Salaam, 1953; formed Tanganyika African National Union, left teaching and campaigned for Nationalist Movement, 1954; addressed Trusteeship Council, 1955, and Cttee of UN Gen. Assembly, 1956. MLC Tanganyika, July-Dec. 1957, resigned in protest; elected Mem. for E Prov. in first elections, 1958, for Dar es Salaam, 1960; Chief Minister, 1960; Prime Minister of Tanganyika, 1961–62; President, Tanganyika Republic, 1962–64. Chm., Chama cha Mapinduzi (The Revolutionary Party) (born of merger between mainland's TANU and Zanzibar Afro-Shiraz Party), 1977–90. Chm., OAU, 1984. First Chancellor, Univ. of East Africa, 1963–70; Chancellor: Univ. of Dar es Salaam, 1970–85; Sokoine Univ. of Agriculture, 1984–92. Chairman: South Commn, 1987–90; South Centre, 1990–. . Holds hon. degrees. *Publications:* Freedom and Unity-Uhuru Na Umoja, 1966; Freedom and Socialism-Uhuru na Ujamaa, 1969; Essays on Socialism, 1969; Freedom and Development, 1973; Swahili trans of Julius Caesar and The Merchant of Venice, 1969. *Address:* PO Box 71000, Dar es Salaam, United Republic of Tanzania; South Centre, Ch. du Champs d'Anier 17, Case postale 228, 1211 Geneva 19, Switzerland.

NYMAN, Michael; composer; *b* 23 March 1944; *s* of Mark and Jeanette Nyman; *m* 1970; two *d*. *Educ:* Royal Academy of Music; King's College London (BMus); Conservatorul Ciprian Porumbescu, Bucharest. FRAM 1991. Music critic, Spectator, New Statesman, The Listener, 1968–78; formed Michael Nyman Band, 1977. *Film scores include:* The Draughtsman's Contract, 1982; Drowning by Numbers, 1988; The Cook, The Thief, His Wife and Her Lover, 1989; Monsieur Hire, 1989; The Hairdresser's Husband, 1990; Prospero's Books, 1991; The Piano, 1992; Carrington, 1994; The Diary of Anne Frank, 1995; *other compositions:* A Broken Set of Rules, Royal Ballet, 1983; The Man Who Mistook his Wife for a Hat (opera), 1986; String Quartets, 1985, 1988, 1990, 1995; Six Celan Songs, 1990–91; Noises, Sounds and Sweet Airs (opera ballet), 1991; Where the Bee Dances, for saxophone and orch., 1991; Songs for Tony, 1993; The Piano Concerto; MGV (Musique à Grand Vitesse), 1995. *Publication:* Experimental Music: Cage and Beyond, 1974, 1995. *Recreation:* QPR. *Club:* Groucho.

O

OAKELEY, Sir John (Digby Atholl), 8th Bt *cr* 1790, of Shrewsbury; Manager, Dehler Yachts UK, since 1988; *b* 27 Nov. 1932; *s* of Sir Atholl Oakeley, 7th Bt and of Mabel, (Patricia), *d* of Lionel H. Birtchnell; *S* father, 1987; *m* 1958, Maureen Frances, *d* of John and Ellen Cox; one *s* one *d*. *Educ:* private tutor. Own charter business, 1958–61; Contracts Manager, Proctor Masts, 1961–72; Managing Director: Freedom Yachts Internat. Ltd, 1981–88; Miller & Whitworth, 1972–81. *Publications:* Winning, 1968; Sailing Manual, 1980; Downwind Sailing, 1981. *Recreation:* yachting (holder of national, international, European and world titles; twice represented Great Britain in Olympic Games). *Heir: s* Robert John Atholl Oakeley [*b* 13 Aug. 1963; *m* 1989, Catherine Amanda, *d* of late William Knowles; one *d*]. *Address:* 10 Bursledon Heights, Long Lane, Bursledon, Hants SO3 8DB. *Club:* Warsash Sailing (Warsash, Hants).

See also M. Oakeley.

OAKELEY, Mary, MA Oxon; Headmistress, St Felix School, Southwold, 1958–78; *b* 2 April 1913; *d* of Maj. Edward Francis Oakeley, S Lancs Regt, and Everilde Anne (*née* Beaumont); *sister* of Sir Atholl Oakeley, 7th Bt. *Educ:* St John's Bexhill-on-Sea; St Hilda's Coll., Oxford. MA Hons History. Asst Mistress: St James's, West Malvern, 1935–38; St George's, Ascot, 1938–39; Headmistress, Craighead Diocesan Sch., Timaru, NZ, 1940–55; Head of American Section, La Châtelainie, St Blaise, Switzerland, 1956–58. *Recreations:* gardening, embroidery. *Address:* 8 Newland Close, Eynsham, Witney, Oxon OX8 1LE. *T:* Oxford (01865) 880759. *Club:* Royal Over-Seas League.

See also Sir J. D. A. Oakeley, Bt.

OAKES, Sir Christopher, 3rd Bt, *cr* 1939; *b* 10 July 1949; *s* of Sir Sydney Oakes, 2nd Bt, and Greta (*d* 1977), *yr d* of Gunnar Victor Hartmann, Copenhagen, Denmark; *S* father, 1966; *m* 1978, Julie Dawn, *d* of Donovan Franklin Cowan, Regina, Canada; one *s* one *d*. *Educ:* Bredon, Tewkesbury; Georgia Mil. Acad., USA. *Heir: s* Victor Oakes, *b* 6 March 1983.

OAKES, Rt. Hon. Gordon James; PC 1979; MP (Lab) Halton, since 1983 (Widnes, Sept. 1971–1983); *b* 22 June 1931; *o s* of late James Oakes and Florence (*née* Hewitt), Widnes, Lancs; *m* 1952, Esther O'Neill, *e d* of late Councillor Joseph O'Neill; three *s*. *Educ:* Wade Deacon Gram. Sch., Widnes; Univ. of Liverpool. BA (Hon.) English, 1952; Admitted Solicitor, 1956. Entered Widnes Borough Council, 1952 (Mayor, 1964–65). Chm. Widnes Constituency Labour Party, 1953–58; contested (Lab): Bebington, 1959; Moss Side (Manchester) by-election, 1961; MP (Lab) Bolton West, 1964–70; PPS, Home Office, 1966–67, DES, 1967–70; Front Bench Opposition spokesman on local govt and the environment, 1970–74; Parly Under-Secretary of State: DoE, 1974–76; Dept of Energy, 1976; Minister of State, DES, 1976–79; Front Bench Opposition spokesman on Environment, 1979–83. British Deleg., NATO Parliamentarians, 1967–70; Member: Select Cttee on Race Relations, 1969–70; Executive, NW Region of Labour Party, 1971–73; Exec. Cttee, CPA, 1979–; Chairman: All-Party Energy Efficiency Gp, 1980–; All-Party Chem. Industry Gp, 1990– (Vice-Chm., 1982–90); Jt Chm., All-Party Gp for the Licensing Trade, 1986–. Vice-President: Rural District Councils Assoc., 1972–74; County Councils Assoc., 1982–; Environmental Officers' Assoc. (formerly Inst. of Public Health Inspectors), 1973–; Building Societies Assoc., 1984–; Jt Chm., Nat. Waste Management Adv. Council, 1974–76. Gov., Commonwealth Inst., 1992–. Hon. Alderman, Borough of Halton. *Publications:* The Management of Higher Education in the Maintained Sector, 1978; various articles. *Recreations:* conversation, motoring with the family, caravanning, maps. *Address:* Upton Bridle Path, Widnes, Cheshire WA8 9HB.

OAKES, Joseph Stewart; barrister-at-law; *b* 7 Jan. 1919; *s* of Laban Oakes and Mary Jane Oakes; *m* 1950, Irene May Peasnall. *Educ:* Royal Masonic Sch., Bushey; Stretford Grammar Sch.; Manchester Univ., 1937–40 (BA Hons). Royal Signals, 1940–48, Captain. Called to Bar, Inner Temple, 1948; practised on Northern Circuit, 1948–91; a Recorder, 1975–82. Presiding Legal Mem., Mental Health Review Tribunal, 1971–91. *Recreations:* horticulture, photography, music. *Address:* 38 Langley Road, Sale, Greater Manchester M33 5AY. *T:* 0161–962 2068.

OAKHAM, Archdeacon of; *see* Fernyhough, Ven. B.

OAKLEY, Brian Wynne, CBE 1981; Director, Logica (Cambridge) Ltd; *b* 10 Oct. 1927; *s* of Bernard and Edna Oakley; *m* 1953, Marian Elizabeth (*née* Woolley); one *s* three *d*. *Educ:* Exeter Coll., Oxford. MA. FInstP, FBCS. Telecommunication Res. Establishment, 1950; Head, Industrial Applications Unit, RRE, 1966–69; Head, Computer Systems Branch, Min. of Technology, 1969–72; Head, Res. Requirements Div., DTI, 1972–78; Sec., SRC, later SERC, 1978–83; Dep. Sec., DTI, and Dir, Alvey Programme, 1983–87. Pres., BCS, 1988. DUniv York, 1988. *Publication:* (with Kenneth Owen) Alvey, 1990. *Recreations:* theatre, sailing. *Address:* 120 Reigate Road, Ewell, Epsom, Surrey KT17 3BX. *T:* 0181–393 4096.

OAKLEY, Christopher John; Group Chief Executive, Midland Independent Newspapers plc, since 1991; Chairman, Birmingham Post & Mail, since 1993; *b* 11 Nov. 1941; *s* of late Ronald Oakley and of Joyce Oakley; *m* 1st, 1962, Linda Margaret Viney (marr. diss. 1986); one *s* two *d*; 2nd, 1990, Moira Jean Martingale; one *s*, and two adopted *d*. *Educ:* Skinners' School, Tunbridge Wells. Kent and Sussex Courier, 1959; Bromley and Kentish Times, 1963; Kent and Sussex Courier, 1963; Evening Argus, Brighton, 1966; Evening Echo, Basildon, 1969; Evening Post, Leeds, 1970; Dep. Editor, Yorkshire Post, 1976; Editor, Lancashire Evening Post, 1981; Dir, Lancashire Evening Post, 1981–83; Editor, Liverpool Echo, 1983–89; Dir, Liverpool Daily Post and Echo Ltd, 1984–89; Editor-in-Chief, 1989–91, Man. Dir, 1990–93, Birmingham Post & Mail.

OAKLEY, John Davidson, CBE 1981; DFC 1944; Chairman: Grosvenor Development Capital, 1981–92; Grosvenor Technology Ltd, 1986–91; Gardners Transformers Ltd, 1986–91 (Deputy Chairman, 1984–86; Director, 1982–91); Third Grosvenor Ltd, 1987–91; *b* 15 June 1921; *s* of Richard Oakley and Nancy Davidson; *m* 1943, Georgina Mary Hare; two *s*. *Educ:* Green Lane Sch. Joined Briggs Motor Bodies Ltd, 1937. Served War in RAF, 1941–46: commissioned 1942; Flt Lt 1943; actg Sqdn Leader 1944; apptd to Air Min. Directorate Staff, 1945. Engrg Buyer, Briggs Motor Bodies Ltd, 1946–53; Dep. Purchase Manager, Body Div., Ford Motor Co. Ltd, 1953–56; Production Dir/General Manager, Standard Triumph (Liverpool) Ltd, until 1962; Managing Director: Copeland & Jenkins Ltd, 1963–71; R. Woolf & Co. Ltd, 1964–67; Gp Man. Dir, L. Sterne & Co., 1967–69; Chairman: General Electric & Mechanical Systems Ltd, 1970–73; Berwick Timpo Ltd, 1970–82; Edgar Allen Balfour Ltd, 1974–79; Australian British Trade Assoc., 1977–81 (Vice-Pres., British Council, 1981–); BOTB Adv. Gp Australia and NZ, 1977–81; Mem., British Overseas Trade Adv. Council, 1977–83. Director: Blairs Ltd, 1976–82; Eagle & Globe Steel Ltd, NSW, 1978–79; Ionian Securities Ltd, 1978–88; Nexos Office Systems Ltd, 1981–82; Isis Gp PLC (formerly Industrial Services plc), 1982–; Beau Brummel Ltd, 1972–85; Robert Jenkins (Hldgs) Ltd, 1976–92 (Dep. Chm., 1978–83, Chm., 1983–90). Oxford Univ. Business Summer School: Dir for 1978; Mem., Steering Cttee, 1981–, Chm., 1984–87. Cons. Mem., Essex CC, 1982–85. Member: Glovers' Co.; Cutlers' Co. in Hallamshire; Inst. of British Carriage & Automobile Manufacturers. CIMgt; FIPS. FRSA. *Recreations:* golf, tennis, walking, bridge. *Address:* 25 Manor Links, Bishop's Stortford, Herts CM23 5RA. *T:* Bishop's Stortford (01279) 507552. *Clubs:* Reform, Royal Air Force; Bishop's Stortford Golf (Bishop's Stortford, Herts).

OAKLEY, Robin Francis Leigh; Political Editor, BBC, since 1992; *b* 20 Aug. 1941; *s* of Joseph Henry Oakley, civil engineer and Alice Barbara Oakley; *m* 1966, Carolyn Susan Germaine Rumball; one *s* one *d*. *Educ:* Wellington College; Brasenose College, Oxford (MA). Liverpool Daily Post, 1964–70; Sunday Express, 1970–79; Assistant Editor: Now! magazine, 1979–81; Daily Mail, 1981–86; Political Editor, The Times, 1986–92. Columnist, People and Politics, BBC World Service, 1986–92; presenter: The Week in Westminster, BBC Radio, 1987–92; Power of Patronage series, BBC, 1991. *Publications:* (with Peter Rose) The Political Year 1970; (with Peter Rose) The Political Year 1971; contribs to educnl series. *Recreations:* theatre, horse racing, sports, bird watching. *Address:* Quarry House, Lynwood Road, Epsom, Surrey KT17 4LD. *Club:* Royal Automobile.

OAKLEY, Wilfrid George, MD, FRCP; Hon. Consulting Physician, King's College Hospital, since 1971; Vice President, British Diabetic Association, since 1971; *b* 23 Aug. 1905; *s* of late Rev. Canon G. D. Oakley and Mrs Oakley; *m* 1931, Hermione Violet Wingate-Saul (*d* 1993); one *s*. *Educ:* Durham School; Gonville and Caius College, Cambridge; St Bartholomew's Hospital. Tancred studentship in Physic, Gonville and Caius Coll., 1923; Bentley Prize and Baly Research Schol., St Bart's Hosp., 1933. Formerly Physician i/c Diabetic Dept, King's College Hosp., 1957–70. Examr, Cambridge and Glasgow Univs. MD (Hon. Mention) Cantab 1934; FRCP 1942. Pres., Med. Soc., London, 1962; Mem. Assoc. of Physicians of Great Britain; Vice-Pres., British Diabetic Assoc., 1971. *Publications:* (jtly) Clinical Diabetes and its Biochemical Basis, 1968; Diabetes and its Management, 1973, 3rd edn 1978; scientific articles and chapters on diabetes in various text-books. *Address:* 12 Courtmead Close, Burbage Road, SE24 9HW. *T:* 0171–737 1920.

OAKSEY, 2nd Baron *cr* 1947 (properly **TREVETHIN,** 4th Baron *cr* 1921, **AND OAKSEY); John Geoffrey Tristram Lawrence,** OBE 1985; JP; Racing Correspondent to Daily Telegraph, 1957–94; racing commentator: ITV, since 1970; Channel Four Racing, since 1984; Director, HTV (West); *b* 21 March 1929; *o s* of 1st Baron Oaksey and 3rd Baron Trevethin and Marjorie (*d* 1984), *d* of late Commander Charles N. Robinson, RN; *S* father, 1971; *m* 1st, 1959, Victoria Mary (marr. diss. 1987), *d* of late Major John Dennistoun, MBE; one *s* one *d*; 2nd, 1988, Rachel Frances Crocker, *d* of late Alan Hunter. *Educ:* Horris Hill; Eton; New College, Oxford (BA); Yale Law School. Racing Correspondent: Horse and Hound, 1959–88; Sunday Telegraph, 1960–88; columnist, Racing Post, 1988–90. Dir, HTV, 1980–91. JP Malmesbury, 1978. *Publications:* History of Steeplechasing (jointly), 1967; The Story of Mill Reef, 1974; Oaksey on Racing, 1991. *Recreations:* skiing, riding. *Heir: s* Hon. Patrick John Tristram Lawrence [*b* 29 June 1960; *m* 1987, Lucinda, *e d* of Demetri Marchessini and Mrs Nicholas Peto; one *s* one *d*]. *Address:* Hill Farm, Oaksey, Malmesbury, Wilts SN16 9HS. *T:* Tetbury (01666) 577303, *Fax:* (01666) 577962. *Club:* Brooks's.

OAKSHOTT, Hon. Sir Anthony (Hendrie), 2nd Bt *cr* 1959; *b* 10 Oct. 1929; *s* of Baron Oakshott, MBE (Life Peer), and Joan (*d* 1986), *d* of Marsden Withington; *S* to baronetcy of father, 1975; *m* 1965, Mrs Valerie de Pret-Roose (marr. diss. 1981; she *d* 1988), *d* of Jack Vlasto. *Educ:* Rugby. *Heir: b* Hon. Michael Arthur John Oakshott [*b* 12 April 1932; *m* 1st, 1957, Christina Rose Methuen (*d* 1985), *d* of late Thomas Banks; three *s*; 2nd, 1988, Mrs (Helen) Clare Jones, *d* of late Edward Ravell]. *Address:* Farmcote, Bledington, Oxfordshire OX7 6UR. *T:* Kingham (01608) 658527. *Club:* White's.

OATES, Prof. (Edward Ernest) David (Michael), FSA; FBA 1974; Professor of Western Asiatic Archaeology, University of London, 1969–82; *b* 25 Feb. 1927; *s* of Thomas Oates and Dora B. Strike; *m* 1956, Joan Louise Lines; one *s* two *d*. *Educ:* Callington County Sch.; Oundle Sch.; Trinity Coll., Cambridge (BA, MA). Fellow of Trinity Coll., Cambridge, 1951–65; Director, British School of Archaeology in Iraq, 1965–69 (Chm., 1988–). Director, British Archaeological Expedition to Tell Brak, Syria, 1976–. FSA 1954. *Publications:* Studies in the Ancient History of N Iraq, 1968; (with J. Oates) The Rise of Civilisation, 1976; contribs to The Dark Ages, ed D. Talbot Rice, 1965; Papers of the British School at Rome, Iraq, etc. *Recreations:* history, carpentry. *Address:* 86 High Street, Barton, Cambridge CB3 7BG. *T:* Cambridge (01223) 262273.

See also Sir Thomas Oates.

OATES, Rev. Canon John; Rector of St Bride's Church, Fleet Street, since 1984; *b* 14 May 1930; *s* of John and Ethel Oates; *m* 1962, Sylvia Mary, *d* of Herbert Charles and Ada Harris; three *s* one *d*. *Educ:* Queen Elizabeth School, Wakefield; SSM, Kelham. Curate, Eton College Mission, Hackney Wick, 1957–60; Development Officer, C of E Youth Council and mem. staff, Bd of Education, 1960–64; Development Sec., C of E Council for Commonwealth Settlement, 1964–65, Gen. Sec. 1965–70; Sec., C of E Cttee on Migration and Internat. Affairs, Bd for Social Responsibility, 1968–71; Vicar of Richmond, Surrey, 1970–84; RD, Richmond and Barnes, 1979–84. Commissary: of Archbishop of Perth and Bishop of NW Australia, 1968–; to Archbishop of Jerusalem, 1969–75; to Bishop of Bunbury, 1969–. Hon. Canon, Bunbury, 1969–. Mem., Unilever Central Ethical Compliance Gp, 1991–. Chapter Clerk, London City Deanery, 1994–. Chaplain: Inst. of Journalists, 1984– (Life FCIJ 1995); Inst. of Public Relations, 1984–; Publicity Club of London, 1984–; London Press Club, 1984–. Chaplain: Co. of Marketors, 1984–; Co. of Stationers and Newspapermakers, 1989–. Freeman, City of London, 1985. *Recreations:* broadcasting, walking, exploring, squash. *Address:* St Bride's Rectory, Fleet Street, EC4Y 8AU. *T:* 0171–353 1301. *Clubs:* Athenæum, Wig and Pen.

OATES, (John) Keith; Managing Director, since 1991 and Deputy Chairman, since 1994, Marks and Spencer plc; a Governor of the BBC, 1988–93; *b* 3 July 1942; *s* of late John Alfred Oates and Katherine Mary (*née* Hole); *m* 1968, Helen Mary (*née* Blake); one *s* three *d*. *Educ:* King's Sch., Chester; Arnold Sch., Blackpool; London School of Economics (BScEcon); Univ. of Manchester Inst. of Sci. and Technology (DipTech Industrial Admin); Bristol Univ. (MSc Management Accounting). FCT 1982. Work Study trainee, Reed Paper Gp, 1965–66; Budgets and Planning Man., IBM (UK) Ltd, 1966–73; Gp Financial Controller, Rolls Royce (1971) Ltd, 1973–74; Controller, Black and Decker Europe, 1974–78; Vice Pres., Finance, Thyssen Bornemisza NV, 1978–84; Finance Dir, Marks and Spencer plc, 1984–91: Founder Chm., Marks and Spencer Financial Services. Non-executive Director: John Laing plc, 1987–89; British Telecom, 1994–; Guinness, 1995–. Member: Council, CBI, 1988–; Bd, London First, 1993–; Sports Council of GB, 1993–; Chm., Europ. Council of Financial Execs, 1984; Mem., 100 Gp Chartered Accountants, 1985–93. Mem. Council, Wycombe Abbey Sch., 1995–. CIMgt 1992. FRSA 1993. *Recreations:* tennis, ski-ing, spectator sports (esp. Association Football, athletics and cricket). *Address:* Michael House, Baker Street, W1A 1DN. *T:* 0171–268 6427.

OATES, Laurence Campbell; Associate Head of Policy Group, Lord Chancellor's Department, since 1995; *b* 14 May 1946; *s* of Stanley Oates and late Norah Christine Oates (*née* Meek); *m* 1968, Brenda Lilian Hardwick; one *s* one *d*. *Educ:* Beckenham and Penge Grammar School; Bristol Univ. (LLB 1967). Called to the Bar, Middle Temple, 1968; Dept. of Employment, 1976–80; Law Officers' Dept, 1980–83; Asst Treasury Solicitor, Dept of Transport, 1983–88; Under Sec. and Hd of Legislation Gp, Lord Chancellor's Dept, 1988–92; Circuit Administrator, Midland and Oxford Circuit, 1992–94. *Recreations:* music, golf. *Address:* (office) Trevelyan House, Great Peter Street, SW1P 4BY.

OATES, Sir Thomas, Kt 1972; CMG 1962; OBE 1958 (MBE 1946); Governor and Commander-in-Chief of St Helena, 1971–76; *b* 5 November 1917; *er s* of late Thomas Oates, Wadebridge, Cornwall; unmarried. *Educ:* Callington Grammar School, Cornwall; Trinity College, Cambridge (MA). Mathematical Tripos (Wrangler). Admiralty Scientific Staff, 1940–46; HMS Vernon, Minesweeping Section, 1940–42; British Admiralty Delegn, Washington, DC, 1942–46; Temp. Lieut, RNVR. Colonial Administrative Service, Nigeria, 1948–55; seconded to HM Treasury, 1953–55; Adviser to UK Delegn to UN Gen. Assembly, 1954. Financial Sec. to Govt of: British Honduras, 1955–59, Aden, 1959–63; Dep. High Comr, Aden, 1963–67; Permanent Sec., Gibraltar, 1968–69; Dep. Governor, Gibraltar, 1969–71. *Recreations:* photography, walking. *Address:* Tristan, Trevone, Padstow, Cornwall PL28 8QX. *Clubs:* East India, Devonshire, Sports and Public Schools, Commonwealth Trust.

See also E. F. D. M. Oates.

OATLEY, Brian; Chairman, Maidstone Priority Care NHS Trust, since 1991; *b* 1 June 1935; *s* of Arnold and Vivian Oatley. *Educ:* Bolton School; King's College, Cambridge. BA, PGCE. Teacher, North Manchester Grammar School, 1959–64; Assistant, Senior Assistant and Deputy County Education Officer, Kent County Council, 1964–84, County Educn Officer, 1984–88. Member: RHS; Kent Trust for Nature Conservation; Detling Singers, Maidstone. Gov., Kent Inst. of Art and Design, 1989–. *Recreations:* music, travel, gardening. *Address:* 45 Beresford Road, Aylesford, Maidstone, Kent ME20 7EP.

OATLEY, Sir Charles (William), Kt 1974; OBE 1956; MA; FRS 1969, FEng, FIEE, FIEEE; Professor of Electrical Engineering, University of Cambridge, 1960–71, now Emeritus; Fellow of Trinity College, Cambridge, since 1945; *b* 14 Feb. 1904; *s* of William Oatley and Ada Mary Dorrington; *m* 1930, (Dorothy) Enid West; two *s*. *Educ:* Bedford Modern Sch.; St John's Coll., Cambridge. Demonstrator, later lecturer, Dept of Physics, KCL, 1927–39. Min. of Supply, Radar Research and Development Establishment, 1939–45. Actg Superintendent in charge of scientific work, 1944–45. Lecturer, later Reader, Dept of Engineering, Cambridge Univ., 1945–60. Director, English Electric Valve Company, 1966–85. Member: Council, Inst. of Electrical Engineers, 1954–56, 1961–64 (Chm. of Radio Section, 1954–55); Council, Royal Society, 1970–72. FEng 1976. Hon. Fellow, Royal Microscopical Soc., 1970; FKC 1976; Foreign Associate, Nat. Acad. of Engineering, USA, 1979. Hon. DSc: Heriot-Watt, 1974; Bath, 1977; Hon. ScD Cambridge, 1990. Achievement Award, Worshipful Co. of Scientific Instrument Makers, 1966; Duddell Medal, Inst. of Physics and Physical Soc., 1969; Royal Medal, Royal Soc., 1969; Faraday Medal, IEE, 1970; Mullard Award, Royal Soc., 1973; James Alfred Ewing Medal, ICE, 1981; Distinguished Scientist Award, Electron Microscopy Soc. of America, 1984; Howard N. Potts Medal, Franklin Inst., 1989. *Publications:* Wireless Receivers, 1932; The Scanning Electron Microscope, 1972; Electric and Magnetic Fields, 1976; papers in scientific and technical journals. *Recreation:* gardening. *Address:* 16 Porson Road, Cambridge CB2 2EU. *T:* Cambridge (01223) 356194.

See also M. C. Oatley.

OATLEY, Michael Charles, CMG 1991; OBE 1975; Joint Managing Director, Ciex Ltd, since 1994; *b* 18 Oct. 1935; *s* of Sir Charles Oatley, *qv* and Lady Oatley (*née* Enid West); *m* 1st, Pippa Howden; two *s* one *d*; 2nd, Mary Jane Laurens; one *s*. *Educ:* The Leys Sch.; Trinity Coll., Cambridge. Served HM Foreign, later Diplomatic, Service, 1959–91; a Man. Dir, Kroll Associates, 1991–94. *Address:* Manor Farmhouse, Caundle Marsh, Sherborne, Dorset DT9 5LX. *Club:* Oriental.

OBAN (St John's Cathedral), Provost of; *see* Maclean of Dochgarroch, Very Rev. A. M.

OBASANJO, Gen. Olusegun; Nigerian Head of State, Head of the Federal Military Government and Commander-in-Chief of the Armed Forces, Nigeria, 1976–79; Member, Advisory Council of State, since 1979; farmer; *b* Abeokuta, Ogun State, Nigeria, 5 March 1937; *m*; two *s* three *d*. *Educ:* Abeokuta Baptist High Sch.; Mons Officers' Cadet Sch., England. Entered Nigerian Army, 1958; commission, 1959; served in Zaire (then, the Congo), 1960. Comdr, Engrg Corps, 1963; Comdr of 2nd (Rear) Div. at Ibadan; GOC 3rd Inf. Div., 1969; Comdr, 3rd Marine Commando Div.; took surrender of forces of Biafra, in Nigerian Civil War, 1969–70; Comdr Engrg Corps, 1970–75. Political post as Federal Comr for Works and Housing, Jan.–July 1975. Chief of Staff, Supreme HQ, July 1975–Feb. 1976. Mem., Internat. Indep. Commn on Disarmament and Security. Part-time Associate, Univ. of Ibadan. *Publications:* My Command (autobiog.), 1980; Africa in Perspective: myths and realities, 1987; Nzeogwu, 1987; Africa Embattled, 1988; Constitution for National Integration and Development, 1989; Not My Will, 1990; Challenge of Leadership in African Development, 1990; Impact of Europe in 1992 on West Africa, 1990; Leadership Challenge of Economic Reforms in Africa, 1991; Challenge of Agricultural Production and Food Security in Africa, 1992. *Recreations:* squash, table tennis, billiards, snooker. *Address:* PO Box 2286, Abeokuta, Ogun State, Nigeria.

OBASI, Godwin Olu Patrick, OFR 1983; Secretary-General, World Meteorological Organization, since 1984; *b* 24 Dec. 1933; *s* of Albert B. Patrick Obasi and Rhoda A. Akande; *m* 1967, Winifred O. Akande; one *s* five *d*. *Educ:* McGill Univ., Canada (BSc Hons Maths and Physics); Massachusetts Inst. of Technology (MSc, DSc Meteorology). Mem., Inst. of Statisticians. University of Nairobi: WMO/UNDP Expert and Sen. Lectr, 1967–74; Acting Head of Dept of Meteorology, 1972–73; Dean, Faculty of Science, Prof. of Meteorology and Chm., Dept of Meteorology, 1974–76; Adviser in Meteorology to Nigerian Govt and Head of Nigerian Inst. for Met. Res. and Training, 1976–78; Dir, Educn and Training Dept, WMO, 1978–83. Fellow of meteorol socs. Dr of Physics *hc* Bucharest, 1991; Hon. LLD Philippines, 1992; Hon DSc: Federal Univ. of Technology, Akure, Nigeria, 1992; Alpine Geophys. Res. Inst., Nal-Chik, 1993. Carl Rossby Award, MIT, 1963; Gold plaque merit award medal, Czechoslovakian Acad. of Sciences, 1986; Medal, Inst. of Meteorol. and Water Management, Poland, 1989; Ogori Merit Award, Nigeria, 1990; Climate Inst. Award, Washington, 1990; Direccion Nacional de Aeronautica Civil Honour of Merit Award, Paraguay, 1992; Gold Medal Award, African Meteorological Soc., 1993; Internat. Global 2000 Award, Centre for Ecol. and Res., India, 1993. Gold Medal, Govt of Paraguay, 1988; Air Force Cross, Venezuela, 1989; Freedom of Ho Chi Minh City, Viet Nam, 1990. Commander, National Order: Côte d'Ivoire, 1992; Niger, 1994. *Publications:* numerous contribs to learned jls. *Recreations:* tennis, gardening. *Address:* Chemin en Vuaracaux, 1297 Founex, Vaud, Switzerland. *T:* (22) 762825.

O'BEIRNE RANELAGH, John, (John Ranelagh), PhD; Consultant, TV 2 Norway, since 1991; Member, Independent Television Commission, since 1994; *b* 3 Nov. 1947; *o s* of James O'Beirne Ranelagh and Elaine Lambert O'Beirne Ranelagh; *m* 1974, Elizabeth Grenville, *y d* of Sir William Hawthorne, *qv*. *Educ:* St Christopher's Sch.; Cambridgeshire Coll. of Arts and Technology; Christ Church, Oxford (MA); Eliot Coll., Univ. of Kent (PhD). Chase Manhattan Bank, 1970; Campaign Dir, Outset Housing Assoc., 1971; Univ. of Kent Studentship, 1972–74; BBC TV, 1974; Conservative Res. Dept, 1975–79; Associate Producer, Ireland: a television history, BBC TV, 1979–81; Commissioning Editor, Channel Four TV Co., 1981–88 (Sec. to the Bd, 1981–83); Dep. Chief Exec. and Dir of Programmes, TV2 Denmark, 1988; Exec. Producer and writer, CIA, BBC TV/NRK/Primetime, 1989–92; Associate, Hydra Associates, 1989–91; Consultant, TVI Portugal, 1992–94. Dir, Broadcasting Research Unit, 1988–90 (Mem., Exec. Cttee, 1984–87). Mem., Political Cttee, UNA, 1978–90. Governor, Daneford Sch., 1977–81. *Publications:* Science, Education and Industry, 1978; (with Richard Luce) Human Rights and Foreign Policy, 1978; Ireland: an illustrated history, 1981; A Short History of Ireland, 1983; The Agency: the rise and decline of the CIA, 1986 (Nat. Intelligence Book Award, and New York Times Notable Book of the Year, 1987); (contrib.) Freedom of Information, ed by Julia Neuberger, 1987; (contrib.) The Revolution in Ireland 1879–1923, ed D. G. Boyce, 1988; Den Anden Kanal, 1989; Thatcher's People, 1991; CIA: a history, 1992 (contrib.) In the Name of Intelligence: essays in honor of Walter Pforzheimer, 1994; (contrib.) The Origin and Development of the CIA in the Administration of Harry S. Truman, 1995. *Recreations:* old Bentley motor cars, quarter horses. *Address:* The Garner Cottages, Mill Way, Grantchester, Cambridge CB3 9NB. *Clubs:* Travellers'; Metropolitan (Washington).

OBOLENSKY, Sir Dimitri, Kt 1984; MA, PhD, DLitt; FBA 1974; FSA; FRHistS; Emeritus Professor, University of Oxford, since 1985 (Professor of Russian and Balkan History, 1961–85, and Student of Christ Church, 1950–85); *b* Petrograd, 1 April 1918; *s* of late Prince Dimitri Obolensky and late Countess Mary Shuvalov; *m* 1947, Elisabeth Lopukhin (marr. diss. 1989). *Educ:* Lycée Pasteur, Paris; Trinity College, Cambridge (Hon. Fellow, 1991). Cambridge: 1st Class Modern and Medieval Langs Tripos Parts I and II; Amy Mary Preston Read and Allen Schol.; Fellow of Trinity Coll., 1942–48; Faculty Asst Lecturer, 1944; Lecturer, Trinity Coll., 1945; Univ. Lecturer in Slavonic Studies, 1946; Reader in Russian and Balkan Medieval History in Univ. of Oxford, 1949–61. Vis. Schol., Dumbarton Oaks Center for Byzantine Studies, Harvard Univ., 1952, 1964, 1977, Vis. Fellow, 1981–82; Vis. Prof. of Russian History, Yale Univ., 1957; Vis. Prof. of European Hist., Univ. of California, Berkeley, 1973; Davis Prof. in Slavic Studies, Wellesley Coll., Mass, 1982; Vis. Mellon Prof., Inst. for Advanced Study, Princeton, 1985–86; Birkbeck Lecturer in Ecclesiastical History, Trinity Coll., Cambridge, 1961; Raleigh Lectr, British Acad., 1981. Vice-Pres., British Acad., 1983–85. Gen. Sec. Thirteenth Internat. Congress of Byzantine Studies, Oxford, 1966; British Co-Chairman: Anglo-Bulgarian Conf. of Historians, 1973; Anglo-Romanian Conf. of Historians, 1975; Chm., British Nat. Cttee, Association Internationale d'Etudes du Sud-Est Européen, 1985–93. Corresp. Mem., Acad. of Athens; Foreign Member: Serbian Acad. of Scis and Arts, 1988; Amer. Philosophical Soc., 1990; Russian Acad. of Scis, 1994. Hon. Dr Univ: Paris, Sorbonne, 1980; Sofia, 1989; Hon. DLitt Birmingham, 1988. *Publications:* The Bogomils, A Study in Balkan Neo-Manichaeism, 1948; (ed) The Penguin Book of Russian Verse, 1962; (jointly) The Christian Centuries, vol. 2: The Middle Ages, 1969; Byzantium and the Slavs, 1971; The Byzantine Commonwealth, 1971; (ed jtly) Companion to Russian Studies, 3 vols, 1976–80; The Byzantine Inheritance of Eastern Europe, 1982; Six Byzantine Portraits, 1988. *Address:* 29 Belsyre Court, Woodstock Road, Oxford OX2 6HU. *T:* Oxford (01865) 56496. *Club:* Athenæum.

OBOTE, Dr (Apollo) Milton; President of Uganda and Minister of Foreign Affairs, 1980–85; former Leader, Uganda People's Congress Party; *b* 1924; *m*; three *s*. Migrated to Kenya and worked as labourer, clerk and salesman, 1950–55; Founder Mem., Kenya Africa Union. Mem., Uganda Nat. Congress, 1952–60; Mem., Uganda Legislative Council, 1957–71; Founder and Mem., Uganda People's Congress, 1960–71; Leader of the Opposition, 1961–62; Prime Minister, 1962–66; Minister of Defence and Foreign Affairs, 1963–65; President of Uganda, 1966–71 (deposed by military coup); in exile in Tanzania, 1971–80; returned to Uganda, 1980. *Address:* c/o Uganda People's Congress, PO Box 1951, Kampala, Uganda.

O'BRIEN, family name of **Barons Inchiquin** and **O'Brien of Lothbury.**

O'BRIEN OF LOTHBURY, Baron *cr* 1973 (Life Peer), of the City of London; **Leslie Kenneth O'Brien,** PC 1970; GBE 1967; President, British Bankers' Association, 1973–80; *b* 8 Feb. 1908; *e s* of late Charles John Grimes O'Brien; *m* 1st, 1932, Isabelle Gertrude Pickett (*d* 1987); one *s*; 2nd, 1989, Marjorie Violet Taylor. *Educ:* Wandsworth School. Entered Bank of England, 1927; Deputy Chief Cashier, 1951; Chief Cashier,

1955; Executive Director, 1962–64; Deputy Governor, 1964–66; Governor, 1966–73; Director: Commonwealth Develt Finance Co. Ltd, 1962–64; The Prudential Assurance Co. Ltd, 1973–80; The Prudential Corp. Ltd, 1979–83; The Rank Organisation, 1974–78; Bank for International Settlements, 1966–73, 1974–83 (Vice-Chm., 1979–83); Saudi Internat. Bank, 1975–84; Vice-Chm., Banque Belge, 1981–88; Mem., Adv. Bd, Unilever Ltd, 1973–78; Consultant to J. P. Morgan & Co., 1973–79; Chm., Internat. Council of Morgan Guaranty Trust Co., NY, 1974–78; Mem. Internat. Adv. Council, Morgan Grenfell & Co. Ltd, 1974–87. Chm., Cttee of Inquiry into export of animals for slaughter, 1973. Member: Finance and Appeal Cttee, RCS, 1973–85; Council, RCM, 1973–90; Bd of National Theatre, 1973–78; Council, Marie Curie Meml Foundn, 1963–78; Investment Adv. Cttee, Mercers' Co., 1973–92; City of London Savings Cttee, 1966–78. A Trustee of Glyndebourne Arts Trust, 1974–78; Hon. Treasurer and Mem. Exec. Cttee, Royal Opera House Develt Appeal, 1977–87. Pres., United Banks' Lawn Tennis Assoc., 1958–81; Vice-Pres., Squash Rackets Assoc., 1972–78. One of HM Lieutenants for City of London, 1966–73; Freeman, City of London in Co. of Mercers; Hon. Liveryman, Leathersellers Co. Hon. DSc City Univ., 1969; Hon. LLD Univ. of Wales, 1973. FRCM 1979. Hon. FCIB. Cavaliere di Gran Croce al Merito della Repubblica Italiana, 1975; Grand Officier, Ordre de la Couronne (Belgium), 1976. *Address:* 3 Peter Avenue, Oxted, Surrey RH8 9LG. *T:* Oxted (01883) 712535. *Clubs:* Boodle's, Grillions, All England Lawn Tennis.

O'BRIEN, Brian Murrough Fergus; Deputy Special Commissioner of Income Tax since 1991; *b* 18 July 1931; *s* of Charles Murrough O'Brien, MB, BCh and late Elizabeth Joyce O'Brien (*née* Peacocke). *Educ:* Bedford Sch.; University Coll., Oxford (BA 1954, MA 1959). Nat. Service, Royal Inniskilling Fusiliers, 1950–51. Called to the Bar, Lincoln's Inn, 1955; Office of Solicitor of Inland Revenue, 1956–70; Asst Solicitor, Law Commn, 1970–80; Secretary, Law Commn, 1980–81. Special Comr of Income Tax, 1981–91. Mem., Senate of Inns of Court and Bar Council, 1977–80; Hon. Gen. Sec., 1962–67 and Chm., 1974–76, CS Legal Soc.; Chm., Assoc. of First Div. Civil Servants, 1979–81. Lay Chm., Westminster (St Margaret's) Deanery Synod, 1978–82. Trustee, St Mary's, Bourne St (Chm. Trustees, 1968–92). *Recreations:* music, travel, light-hearted bridge. *Address:* Rathkeale Cottage, Castlematrix, Rathkeale, Co. Limerick, Ireland. *T:* (069) 64234. *Clubs:* Reform; Kildare Street and University (Dublin).

O'BRIEN, Charles Michael, MA; FIA, FPMI; General Manager (formerly Manager), and Actuary, 1955–84, Council Member, since 1984, Royal National Pension Fund for Nurses; *b* 17 Jan. 1919; *s* of late Richard Alfred O'Brien, CBE, MD, and Nora McKay; *m* 1950, Joy, *d* of late Rupert Henry Prebble and Phyllis Mary Langdon; two *s*. *Educ:* Westminster Sch.; Christ Church, Oxford (MA). Commissioned, Royal Artillery, 1940 (despatches, 1945). Asst Actuary, Equitable Life Assce Soc., 1950; Royal National Pension Fund for Nurses: Asst Manager, 1953; Manager and Actuary, 1955. Director: M & G Assurance Gp Ltd, 1984–91; M & G Life Assurance Co. Ltd, 1991–94. Institute of Actuaries: Fellow, 1949; Hon. Sec., 1961–62; Vice-Pres., 1965–68; Pres., 1976–78. Mem., Governing Body, Westminster Sch., 1970–95. *Address:* The Boundary, Goodley Stock, Crockham Hill, Edenbridge, Kent TN8 6TA. *T:* Edenbridge (01732) 866349.

O'BRIEN, Conor Cruise; Contributing Editor, The Atlantic, Boston; Editor-in-Chief, The Observer, 1979–81; Pro-Chancellor, University of Dublin, since 1973; *b* 3 November 1917; *s* of Francis Cruise O'Brien and Katherine Sheehy; *m* 1st, 1939, Christine Foster (marr. diss. 1962); one *s* two *d*; 2nd, 1962, Máire Mac Entee; one adopted *s* one adopted *d*. *Educ:* Sandford Park School, Dublin; Trinity College, Dublin (BA, PhD). Entered Department of External Affairs of Ireland, 1944; Counsellor, Paris, 1955–56; Head of UN section and Member of Irish Delegation to UN, 1956–60; Asst Sec., Dept of External Affairs, 1960; Rep. of Sec.-Gen. of UN in Katanga, May-Dec. 1961; resigned from UN and Irish service, Dec. 1961. Vice-Chancellor, Univ. of Ghana, 1962–65; Albert Schweitzer Prof. of Humanities, New York Univ., 1965–69. TD (Lab) Dublin North-East, 1969–77; Minister for Posts and Telegraphs, 1973–77. Mem. Senate, Republic of Ireland, 1977–79. Vis. Fellow, Nuffield Coll., Oxford, 1973–75; Fellow, St Catherine's Coll., Oxford, 1978–81; Vis. Prof. and Montgomery Fellow, Dartmouth Coll., USA, 1984–85; Sen. Res. Fellow, Nat. Humanities Center, N Carolina, 1993–94. Member: Royal Irish Acad.; Royal Soc. of Literature. Hon. DLitt: Bradford, 1971; Ghana, 1974; Edinburgh, 1976; Nice, 1978; Coleraine, 1981; QUB, 1984. Valiant for Truth Media Award, 1979. *Publications:* Maria Cross (under pseud. Donat O'Donnell), 1952 (reprinted under own name, 1963); Parnell and his Party, 1957; (ed) The Shaping of Modern Ireland, 1959; To Katanga and Back, 1962; Conflicting Concepts of the UN, 1964; Writers and Politics, 1965; The United Nations: Sacred Drama, 1967 (with drawings by Felix Topolski); Murderous Angels, 1968; (ed) Power and Consciousness, 1969; Conor Cruise O'Brien Introduces Ireland, 1969; (ed) Edmund Burke, Reflections on the Revolution in France, 1969; Camus, 1969; A Concise History of Ireland, 1972; (with Máire Cruise O'Brien) The Suspecting Glance, 1972; States of Ireland, 1972; Herod, 1978; Neighbours: the Ewart-Biggs memorial lectures 1978–79, 1980; The Siege: the saga of Israel and Zionism, 1986; Passion and Cunning, 1988; God Land: reflections on religion and nationalism, 1988; The Great Melody: a thematic biography and commented anthology of Edmund Burke, 1992; Ancestral Voices, 1994. *Recreation:* travelling. *Address:* Whitewater, Howth Summit, Dublin, Ireland. *T:* 322474. *Club:* Athenæum.

O'BRIEN, Prof. Denis Patrick, FBA 1988; Professor of Economics, University of Durham, since 1972; *b* Knebworth, Herts, 24 May 1939; *s* of Patrick Kevin O'Brien and Dorothy Elizabeth Crisp; *m* 1st, 1961, Eileen Patricia O'Brien (*d* 1985); one *s* two *d*; 2nd, 1993, Julia Stapleton. *Educ:* Douai Sch.; University Coll. London (BSc (Econ) 1960); PhD Queen's Univ., Belfast, 1969. In industry, 1960–62; Queen's University, Belfast: Asst Lectr, 1963–65; Lectr, 1965–70; Reader, 1970–72. *Publications:* (with D. Swann) Information Agreements, 1969; J. R. McCulloch, 1970; Correspondence of Lord Overstone, 3 vols, 1971; (jtly) Competition in British Industry, 1974; (ed) J. R. McCulloch: Treatise on Taxation, 1975; The Classical Economists, 1975; Competition Policy, Profitability and Growth, 1979; (with J. Presley) Pioneers of Modern Economics in Britain, 1981; (with A. C. Darnell) Authorship Puzzles in the History of Economics, 1982; (with J. Creedy) Economic Analysis in Historical Perspective, 1984; Lionel Robbins, 1988; Thomas Joplin and Classical Macroeconomics, 1993. *Recreation:* the violin. *Address:* Department of Economics, University of Durham, 23–26 Old Elvet, Durham DH1 3HY. *T:* Durham (0191) 3742274.

O'BRIEN, Dermod Patrick; QC 1983; a Recorder of the Crown Court, since 1978; *b* 23 Nov. 1939; *s* of Lieut D. D. O'Brien, RN, and Mrs O'Brien (*née* O'Connor); *m* 1974, Zoë Susan Norris; two *s*. *Educ:* Ampleforth Coll., York; St Catherine's Coll., Oxford. BA (Jurisprudence); MA. Called to Bar, Inner Temple, 1962, Bencher, 1993; joined Western Circuit, 1963. Governor, Milton Abbey Sch., 1992–. *Recreations:* fishing, shooting, skiing. *Address:* Little Daux Farm, Billingshurst, West Sussex RH14 9DB. *T:* Billingshurst (01403) 784800; (chambers) 2 Temple Gardens, Temple, EC4Y 9AY. *T:* 0171–583 6041.

O'BRIEN, Edna; writer; *b* Ireland; marr. diss.; two *s*. *Educ:* Irish convents; Pharmaceutical Coll. of Ireland. Yorkshire Post Novel Award, 1971. *Publications:* The Country Girls, 1960 (screenplay for film, 1983); The Lonely Girl, 1962; Girls in Their Married Bliss, 1963; August is a Wicked Month, 1964; Casualties of Peace, 1966; The Love Object, 1968; A Pagan Place, 1970; (play) A Pagan Place, 1971; Night, 1972; (short stories) A Scandalous Woman, 1974; Mother Ireland, 1976; Johnnie I hardly knew you, 1977; Mrs Reinhardt and other stories, 1978; Virginia (play), 1979; The Dazzle, 1981; Returning, 1982; A Christmas Treat, 1982; A Fanatic Heart (selected stories), 1985; Tales for the Telling, 1986; Flesh and Blood (play), 1987; Madame Bovary (play), 1987; The High Road, 1988; Lantern Slides (short stories), (Los Angeles Times Award) 1990; Time and Tide, 1992 (Writers' Guild Award, 1993); House of Splendid Isolation, 1994. *Recreations:* walking, meditating. *Address:* c/o Aitken & Stone, 29 Fernshaw Road, SW10. *T:* 0171–351 7561.

O'BRIEN, Sir Frederick (William Fitzgerald), Kt 1984; QC (Scotland) 1960; Sheriff Principal of Lothian and Borders, 1978–89; Sheriff of Chancery in Scotland, 1978–89; Hon. Sheriff at Edinburgh and Paisley, since 1990; *b* 19 July 1917; *s* of Dr Charles Henry Fitzgerald O'Brien and Helen Jane; *m* 1950, Audrey Muriel Owen; two *s* one *d*. *Educ:* Royal High Sch.; Univ. of Edinburgh; MA 1938; LLB 1940. Admitted Faculty of Advocates, 1947. Comr, Mental Welfare Commission of Scotland, 1962–65; Home Advocate Depute, 1964–65; Sheriff-Principal of Caithness, Sutherland, Orkney and Shetland, 1965–75; Interim Sheriff-Principal of Aberdeen, Kincardine and Banff, 1969–71; Sheriff Principal of N Strathclyde, 1975–78; Interim Sheriff Principal of S Strathclyde, 1981. Hon. Mem., Sheriffs' Assoc., 1990–. Member: Scottish Medical Practices Cttee, 1973–76; Scottish Records Adv. Council, 1974–83; Convener of Sheriffs Principal, 1972–89; Chm., Sheriff Court Rules Council, 1975–81. Chm., Northern Lighthouse Bd, 1983–84 and 1986–87. Convener, Gen. Council Business Cttee, Edinburgh Univ., 1980–84. Hon. Pres., Royal High Sch. Former Pupils Club, 1982–92 (Pres. 1975–76); Chm., Edinburgh Sir Walter Scott Club, 1989–92. *Recreations:* golf, music. *Address:* 22 Arboretum Road, Edinburgh EH3 5PN. *T:* 0131–552 1923. *Clubs:* New (Edinburgh); Bruntsfield Golf, Scottish Arts.

O'BRIEN, Rt. Rev. James Joseph; Auxiliary Bishop of Westminster (Bishop in Hertfordshire) (RC), and Titular Bishop of Manaccenser, since 1977; *b* 5 Aug. 1930; *s* of John and Mary Elizabeth O'Brien. *Educ:* St Ignatius College, Stamford Hill; St Edmund's Coll., Ware. Priest, 1954; Assistant, St Lawrence's, Feltham, 1954–62; Catholic Missionary Society, 1962–68; Director of Catholic Enquiry Centre, 1967–68; Rector of Allen Hall, 1968–77. Bishops' Conference of England and Wales: Chm., Dept for Internat. Affairs, 1984–88; Chm., Cttee for Ministerial Formation, 1988–. Prelate of Honour, 1969. *Address:* The Gate House, All Saints Pastoral Centre, London Colney, St Albans, Herts AL2 1AG. *T:* St Albans (01727) 824664.

O'BRIEN, Prof. John W., PhD; Rector Emeritus, Concordia University (incorporating Loyola College and Sir George Williams University, Montreal), since 1984 (Rector and Vice-Chancellor, 1969–84); Professor of Economics, since 1965; *b* 4 Aug. 1931; *s* of Wilfred Edmond O'Brien and Audrey Swain; *m* 1956, Joyce Helen Bennett; two *d*. *Educ:* McGill Univ., Montreal, Que. BA 1953, MA 1955, PhD 1962. Sir George Williams Univ.: Lectr in Economics, 1954; Asst Prof. of Economics, 1957; Associate Prof. of Economics and Asst Dean, 1961; Dean, Faculty of Arts, 1963; Vice-Principal (Academic), 1968–69. Hon. DCL Bishop's Univ., 1976; Hon. LLD McGill Univ., 1976. *Publication:* Canadian Money and Banking, 1964 (2nd edn, with G. Lermer, 1969). *Address:* Concordia University, 1455 de Maisonneuve Boulevard West, Montreal, Que H3G 1M8, Canada. *T:* (514) 8482424.

O'BRIEN, Most Rev. Keith Michael Patrick; *see* St Andrews and Edinburgh, Archbishop of, (RC).

O'BRIEN, Rt. Rev. Kevin; *see* O'Brien, Rt Rev. T. K.

O'BRIEN, Michael; MP (Lab) Warwickshire North, since 1992; *b* 19 June 1954; *s* of Timothy Thomas and Mary O'Brien; *m* 1987, Alison Munro; one *d*. *Educ:* Worcester Tech. Coll.; North Staffs Poly. (BA Hons Hist. and Pol.). Lectr in Law, Colchester Inst., 1981–87; solicitor, 1987–92. Parly Advr, Police Fedn, 1993–. Mem., Treasury Select Cttee, 1993–; Chm., Lab. Home Affairs Cttee. *Address:* House of Commons, SW1A 0AA. *Clubs:* Bedworth Ex-Service Men's (Bedworth); Wood End Social (Kingsbury, N Warwicks).

O'BRIEN, (Michael) Vincent; racehorse trainer, 1943–94; *b* 9 April 1917; *s* of Daniel P. O'Brien and Kathleen (*née* Toomey); *m* 1951, Jacqueline (*née* Wittenoom), Perth, Australia; two *s* three *d*. *Educ:* Mungret Coll., Ireland. Started training in Co. Cork, 1944; moved to Co. Tipperary, 1951. Champion trainer: Nat. Hunt, 1952–53 and 1954–55; Flat, 1966 and 1967. Won all major English and Irish hurdle and steeple-chases, incl. 3 consecutive Grand Nationals, Gold Cups and Champion Hurdles. From 1959 concentrated on flat racing and trained winners of 44 Classics, incl. 6 Epsom Derbys, 6 Irish Derbys and 1 French Derby; also 3 Prix de l'Arc de Triomphe and Washington International; trainer of Nijinsky, first triple crown winner since 1935. Hon. LLD NUI, 1983. *Recreations:* fishing, golf. *Address:* Ballydoyle House, Cashel, Co. Tipperary, Ireland. *T:* (62)61222, *Fax:* (62)61677.

O'BRIEN, Oswald; Director, Workplace Advisory Service, Alcohol Concern (national charity), since 1986 (Director, Education Division, 1984–86); freelance lecturer, since 1983; *b* 6 April 1928; *s* of Thomas and Elizabeth O'Brien; *m* 1950, Freda Rosina Pascoe; one *s*. *Educ:* St Mary's Grammar Sch., Darlington; Fircroft Coll., Birmingham; Durham Univ. BA Hons Politics and Economics. Royal Navy, 1945–48; various posts in industry, 1948–59; College and University, 1959–63; Tutor, WEA, 1963–64; Staff Tutor, Durham Univ., 1964–78; Senior Industrial Relations Officer, Commn on Indust. Relations, 1970–72 (secondment); Dir of Studies and Vice-Principal, Co-operative Coll., 1978–83. Dept of Employment and ACAS Arbitrator in Shipbuilding, 1968–78; Indust. Relations Adviser to various statutary bodies, 1965–78; Chm., Soc. of Indust. Tutors, 1978–82. Mem., Durham CC, 1990–. MP (Lab) Darlington, March-June 1983; contested (Lab) Darlington, 1987. FIMgt. *Publications:* (jtly) Going Comprehensive, 1970; (jtly) Drink and Drugs at Work, 1988; various papers, reports and case studies. *Recreations:* reading, talking, opera. *Address:* 6 Hillclose Avenue, Darlington, Co. Durham DL3 8BH. *T:* Darlington (01325) 315540.

O'BRIEN, Prof. Patrick Karl, DPhil; FBA 1990; Professor of Economic History, University of London, and Director of the Institute of Historical Research, since 1990; *b* 12 Aug. 1932; *s* of William O'Brien and Elizabeth Stockhausen; *m* 1959, Cassy Cobham; one *s* two *d*. *Educ:* London Sch. of Economics (Lilian Knowles Schol.; BSc 1958); Nuffield Coll., Oxford (DPhil). London University: Res. Fellow, 1960–63; Lectr, 1963–70; Reader in Econs and Econ. Hist., 1967–70; Oxford University: Univ. Lectr in Econ. Hist., 1970–84; Reader, 1984–90; Faculty Fellow, 1970–84, Professorial Fellow, 1984–90, Emeritus Fellow, 1991, St Antony's Coll. *Publications:* The Revolution in Egypt's Economic System, 1966; The New Economic History of the Railways, 1977; (with C. Keyder) Economic Growth in Britain and France 1780–1914, 1978; (ed jtly) Productivity in the Economies of Europe in the 19th and 20th Centuries, 1983; (ed) Railways and the Economic Development of Western Europe 1830–1914, 1983; (ed) International Productivity Comparisons 1750–1939, 1986; The Economic Effects of the Civil War,

1988; (ed jtly) The Industrial Revolution and British Society, 1993; contribs to many learned jls. *Recreations:* theatre, Western art, tennis, squash, walking. *Address:* 66 St Bernards Road, Oxford OX2 6EJ. *T:* Oxford (01865) 512004.

O'BRIEN, Patrick William; His Honour Judge O'Brien; a Circuit Judge, since 1991; *b* 20 June 1945; *s* of William C. O'Brien and Ethel M. O'Brien; *m* 1970, Antoinette Wattebot; one *s* two *d. Educ:* St Joseph's Academy, Blackheath; Queens' College, Cambridge (MA, LLM). Called to the Bar, Lincoln's Inn, 1968; practised SE Circuit; a Recorder, 1987. *Recreations:* cricket, choral singing, musical theatre. *Address:* Chelmsford Crown Court, New Street, Chelmsford, Essex CM1 1EL. *T:* Chelmsford (01245) 358222. *Club:* MCC.

O'BRIEN, Raymond Francis; DL; Consultant, The Information Corporation (UK) Ltd, 1993; Chief Executive, Financial Intermediaries, Managers and Brokers Regulatory Association, 1987–90; *b* 13 Feb. 1936; *s* of Ignatius and Anne O'Brien; *m* 1959, Mary Agnes, (Wendy), *d* of late James and of Agnes Alcock; two *s* two *d. Educ:* St Mary's Coll., Great Crosby, Liverpool; St Edmund Hall, Oxford (BA Hons 1959; MA 1962). IPFA. Accountant, Cheshire CC, 1959–65; Head of Data Processing, Staffs CC, 1965–67; Asst County Treas., Notts CC, 1967–70; Dep. Clerk, Notts CC, 1970–73; Clerk of CC and Chief Executive, Notts, 1973–77; Chief Exec., Merseyside MCC, 1978–86; Chief Exec. and Bd Mem., Severn-Trent Water Authy, 1986–87. Mem., Merseyside Area Bd, MSC, 1980–86; Director: Merseyside Economic Development Co. Ltd, 1981–86; Merseyside Cablevision Ltd, 1982–86; Anfield Foundation, 1983–. DL Merseyside, 1980. *Recreations:* sports critic, gardening, music, reading. *Address:* 20 Oldway Drive, Solihull, West Midlands B91 3HP. *T:* 0121–704 4925.

O'BRIEN, Sir Richard, Kt 1980; DSO 1944, MC 1942 (Bar 1944); Chairman, Manpower Services Commission, 1976–82; *b* 15 Feb. 1920; *s* of late Dr Charles O'Brien and of Marjorie Maude O'Brien; *m* 1951, Elizabeth M. D. Craig; two *s* three *d. Educ:* Oundle Sch.; Clare Coll., Cambridge (MA). Served, 1940–45, with Sherwood Foresters and Leicesters, N Africa, ME, Italy and Greece; Personal Asst to Field Marshal Montgomery, 1945–46. Develt Officer, Nat. Assoc. of Boys' Clubs, 1946–48; Richard Sutcliffe Ltd, Wakefield (latterly Prodn Dir), 1948–58; Dir and Gen. Man., Head Wrightson Mineral Engrg Ltd, 1958–61; Dir, Industrial Relns, British Motor Corp., 1961–66; Industrial Adviser (Manpower), DEA, 1966–68; Delta Metal Co. Ltd (subseq. Dir of Manpower, and Dir 1972–76), 1968–76. Chairman: CBI Employment Policy Cttee, 1971–76; Crown Appointments Commn, 1979; Engineering Industry Trng Bd, 1982–85; Archbishop's Commn on Urban Priority Areas, 1983–85; Industrial Participation Assoc., 1983–86; Policy Studies Inst., 1984–90 (Jt Pres., 1991–); Employment Inst. and Charter for Jobs, 1985–87; Community Educn Develt Centre, 1989–94; People for Action, 1991– (Pres., 1994–); Deputy Chairman: AMARC, 1988–91; Church Urban Fund, 1988–94. Member: NEDC, 1977–82; Engrg Council, 1985–88; President: British Inst. of Industrial Therapy, 1982–87; Inst. of Trng and Develt, 1983–84; Nat. Assoc. of Colls of Further and Higher Educn, 1983–85; Concordia (Youth Service Volunteers), 1987– (Chm., 1981–87); Campaign for Work, 1988–92; Employment Policy Inst., 1992–95. Mem. Bd, Community Industry, 1991–; Member Council: Industrial Soc., 1962–86; Univ. of Birmingham, 1969–88; Hymns Ancient & Modern, 1984–. Mem. Ct of Governors, ASC, 1977–83. Hon. DSc Aston, 1979; Hon. LLD: Bath, 1981; Liverpool, 1981; Birmingham, 1982; Hon. DLitt: Warwick, 1983; CNAA (Coll. of St Mark and St John), 1988; DCL Lambeth, 1987; Hon. Fellow Sheffield City Polytech., 1980. JP Wakefield, 1955–61. *Publications:* contrib: Conflict at Work (BBC pubn), 1971; Montgomery at Close Quarters, 1985; Seekers and Finders, 1985; articles in various jls. *Recreations:* reading, theatre, cinema, tennis. *Address:* 53 Abingdon Villas, W8 6XA. *T:* 0171–937 8944.

O'BRIEN, Air Vice-Marshal Robert Peter, OBE 1983; Air Secretary, since 1994; *b* 1 Nov. 1941; *s* of Major Thomas Joseph O'Brien, MC, RE and Doris Winifred O'Brien; *m* 1964, Carole Evelyn Anne Wallace; two *s. Educ:* Salesian College, Farnborough; RAF College, Cranwell. BA (External) London. Commissioned 1962; Pilot 31 Sqn (Canberras), 1963–66; Central Flying Sch./4FTS (Gnats), 1966–67; ADC to AOC 38 Gp, 1967–70; Flt Comdr, 15 Sqn (Buccaneers), 1970–73; Army Staff Coll., 1974; HQ RAF Germany, 1975–77; OC London UAS (Bulldogs), 1977–79; Chief Instr/TTTE (Tornados), 1980–83; Stn Comdr, RAF Marham, 1983–85; Air Staff, MoD, 1985–87; Dep. Comdr/COS HQ BF Cyprus, 1988–91; Dir of Infrastructure (RAF), MoD, 1991–92; Comdt, JSDC, 1992–94. ADC to the Queen, 1983–85. *Recreations:* tennis, golf, walking. *Address:* HQ Personnel and Training Command, Innsworth, Glos GL3 1EZ. *Club:* Royal Air Force.

O'BRIEN, (Robert) Stephen, CBE 1987; Chief Executive: London First, since 1992; London Forum, 1993–94; *b* 14 Aug. 1936; *s* of Robert Henry and Clare Winifred O'Brien; *m* 1st, 1958, Zoë T. O'Brien (marr. diss. 1989); two *s* two *d*; 2nd, 1989, Meriel Barclay. *Educ:* Sherborne Sch., Dorset. Joined Charles Fulton & Co. Ltd, 1956; Dir, 1964; Chm., 1973–82; Chief Exec., 1983–92, Vice-Chm., 1992–, BITC. Chm., Cranstoun, 1969–83 (Pres., 1983–88); Dir, Kirkland-Whittaker Co. Ltd, 1980–82. Chairman: Foreign Exchange and Currency Deposit Brokers Assoc., 1968–72; Project Fullemploy, 1973–91; Home Sec.'s Adv. Bd on Community Radio, 1985–86. Ordained Deacon, 1971; Hon. Curate, St Lawrence Jewry, 1973–80; Chm., Christian Action, 1976–88. Vice-Chm., Church Urban Fund, 1994–. Pres., Esher Assoc. for Prevention of Addiction, 1979–90. Chm., UK 2000, 1988–92 (Mem. Bd, 1986–92); Director: Cities in Schools, 1989–; Prince of Wales' Business Leaders Forum, 1990–; Member: Administrative Council, Royal Jubilee Trusts, 1984–89; Management Cttee, Action Resource Centre, 1986–91; Council, RSA, 1987–91; Trustee: Learning from Experience Trust, 1986–94; Prince's Youth Business Trust, 1987–. Hon. LLD Liverpool, 1994. *Recreations:* causes, gentle gardening. *Address:* 13 Tredegar Square, E3 5AD. *T:* 0181–980 1435.

O'BRIEN, Terence John, CMG 1971; MC 1945; HM Diplomatic Service, retired; *b* 13 Oct. 1921; *s* of Joseph O'Brien; *m* 1950, Phyllis Mitchell (*d* 1952); *m* 1953, Rita Emily Drake Reynolds; one *s* two *d. Educ:* Gresham's Sch., Holt; Merton Coll., Oxford. Ayrshire Yeo., 1942–45. Dominions Office, 1947; CRO, 1947–49; British High Comr's Office, Ceylon, 1950–52; Princ., Treasury, 1953–56; 1st Sec. (Financial), Canberra, 1956–58; Planning Officer, CRO, 1958–60; 1st Sec., Kuala Lumpur, 1960–62; Sec. to Inter-Governmental Cttee, Jesselton, 1962–63; Head of Chancery, New Delhi, 1963–66; Imp. Def. Coll., 1967; Counsellor, FCO (formerly FO), 1968–70; Ambassador: Nepal, 1970–74; Burma, 1974–78; Indonesia, 1978–81. *Address:* Beaufort House, Woodcutts, Dorset SP5 5RP. *T:* Handley (Dorset) (01725) 552234.

O'BRIEN, Rt. Rev. (Thomas) Kevin; Auxiliary Bishop of Middlesbrough, (RC), and Titular Bishop of Ard Carna, since 1981; *b* Cork City, Republic of Ireland, 18 Feb. 1923; *s* of Jack and Mary O'Brien. *Educ:* Christian Brothers Coll., Cork. Ordained, All Hallows College, Dublin, 1948; Curate at Batley, Yorks, 1948–51, and St Anne's Cathedral, Leeds, 1951–56; Catholic Missionary Society, 1956–71, Superior 1960–71; Vicar General, Diocese of Leeds, 1971–81; Parish Priest: St Patrick's, Huddersfield, 1971–79; St Francis, Bradford, 1979–81. Chm., Home Mission Cttee of Bishops' Conference, 1983–; Mem., Co-ordinating Gp for Evangelisation, Churches Together in England, 1986–. *Address:* St Charles Rectory, Jarratt Street, Hull HU1 3HB.

O'BRIEN, Timothy Brian, RDI 1991; designer; Hon. Associate Artist, Royal Shakespeare Company, since 1988 (Associate Artist, 1966–88); *b* 8 March 1929; *s* of Brian Palliser Tiegue O'Brien and Elinor Laura (*née* Mackenzie). *Educ:* Wellington Coll.; Corpus Christi, Cambridge (MA); Yale Univ. Design Dept, BBC TV, 1954; Designer, Associated Rediffusion, 1955–56; Head of Design, ABC Television, 1956–66 (The Flying Dutchman, 1958); partnership in stage design with Tazeena Firth estabd 1961; output incl.: The Bartered Bride, The Girl of the Golden West, 1962; West End prodns of new plays, 1963–64; London scene of Shakespeare Exhibn, 1964; Tango, Days in the Trees, Staircase, RSC, and Trafalgar at Madame Tussaud's, 1966; All's Well that Ends Well, As You Like It, Romeo and Juliet, RSC, 1967; The Merry Wives of Windsor, Troilus and Cressida (also Nat. Theatre, 1976), The Latent Heterosexual, RSC, 1968; Pericles (also Comédie Française, 1974), Women Beware Women, Bartholomew Fair, RSC, 1969; 1970: Measure for Measure, RSC; Madame Tussaud's in Amsterdam; The Knot Garden, Royal Opera; 1971: Enemies, Man of Mode, RSC; 1972: La Cenerentola, Oslo; Lower Depths, The Island of the Mighty, RSC; As You Like It, OCSC; 1973: Richard II, Love's Labour's Lost, RSC; 1974: Next of Kin, NT; Summerfolk, RSC; The Bassarids, ENO; 1975: John Gabriel Borkman, NT; Peter Grimes, Royal Opera (later in Göteborg, Paris); The Marrying of Ann Leete, RSC; 1976: Wozzeck, Adelaide Fest.; The Zykovs, RSC; The Force of Habit, NT; 1977: Tales from the Vienna Woods, Bedroom Farce, NT; Falstaff, Berlin Opera; 1978: The Cunning Little Vixen, Göteborg; Evita, London (later in Australia, Austria, USA); A Midsummer Night's Dream, Sydney Opera House; 1979: The Rake's Progress, Royal Opera; 1981: Lulu, Royal Opera; 1982: La Ronde, RSC; Le Grand Macabre, ENO; 1983: Turandot, Vienna State Opera; 1984: The Mastersingers of Nuremberg, ENO; Tannhäuser, Royal Opera; 1985: Samson, Royal Opera; Sicilian Vespers, Grande Théâtre, Geneva; Old Times, Haymarket; Lucia di Lammermoor, Köln Opera; 1986: The Threepenny Opera, NT; Die Meistersinger von Nürnberg, Netherlands Opera; The American Clock, NT; 1987: Otello (revived 1990), and Die Entführung aus dem Serail, Royal Opera; 1988: Three Sisters, RSC; 1989: Cymbeline, RSC; Exclusive, Strand; 1990: King, Piccadilly; Love's Labours Lost, RSC; 1991: Twelfth Night, Tartuffe, Playhouse; War and Peace, Kirov, Leningrad; Beauty and the Beast, City of Birmingham Touring Opera; 1992: Christopher Columbus, RSC; 1993: Eugene Onegin, Royal Opera; Misha's Party, RSC; 1994: On Approval, Playhouse; The Clandestine Marriage, Queen's; 1995: The Merry Wives of Windsor, NT. Chm., Soc. of British Theatre Designers, 1984–91. (Jtly) Gold Medal for Set Design, Prague Quadriennale, 1975; (jtly) Golden Triga, for Best Nat. Exhibit, Prague Quadriennale, 1991. *Recreation:* sailing. *Address:* 33 Lansdowne Gardens, SW8 2EQ. *T:* 0171–622 5384.

O'BRIEN, Sir Timothy John, 7th Bt *cr* 1849; *b* 6 July 1958; *s* of John David O'Brien (*d* 1980) and of Sheila Winifred, *o d* of Sir Charles Arland Maitland Freake, 4th Bt; *S* grandfather, 1982. *Heir: b* James Patrick O'Brien, *b* 22 Dec. 1964.

O'BRIEN, Turlough Aubrey, CBE 1959; Public Relations Consultant, 1972–82; *b* 30 Sept. 1907; *er s* of late Lieut-Colonel A. J. O'Brien, CIE, CBE; *m* 1945, Phyllis Mary (*d* 1986), twin *d* of late E. G. Tew; two *s* one *d. Educ:* Charterhouse; Christ Church, Oxford. Assistant to Director of Public Relations, Board of Trade, 1946–49; Public Relations Officer: Home Office, 1949–53; Post Office, 1953–64; Chief Public Relations Officer, 1964–66; Director, Public Relations, 1966–68; Public Relations Manager, Bank of London and South America, 1968–72. President, Institute of Public Relations, 1965. *Recreation:* fishing. *Address:* Claremount, 11 Kiln Gardens, Hartley Wintney, Basingstoke, Hants RG27 8RG. *Club:* United Oxford & Cambridge University.

O'BRIEN, Vincent; *see* O'Brien, M. V.

O'BRIEN, William, (Bill), JP; MP (Lab) Normanton, since 1983; *b* 25 Jan. 1929; *m* Jean; three *d. Educ:* state schools; Leeds Univ. Coalminer, 1945–83. Wakefield DC: Mem., 1973–83; former Dep. Leader and Chm., Finance and Gen. Purposes Cttee. Mem., NUM, 1945–; Local Branch Official, 1956–83. Opposition front bench spokesman on the Environment, 1987–92, for Northern Ireland, 1992–. Member: Public Accounts Cttee, 1983–88; Energy Select Cttee, 1986–88. JP Wakefield, 1979. *Recreations:* reading, organising. *Address:* House of Commons, SW1A 0AA. *T:* 0171–219 3000; 29 Limestrees, Ferrybridge Road, Pontefract WF8 2QB.

O'BRIEN, Adm. Sir William (Donough), KCB 1969 (CB 1966); DSC 1942; Commander-in-Chief, Western Fleet, Feb. 1970–Sept. 71, retd Nov. 1971; Vice-Admiral of the United Kingdom and Lieutenant of the Admiralty, 1984–86; *b* 13 Nov. 1916; *s* of late Major W. D. O'Brien, Connaught Rangers and I. R. Caroe (*née* Parnis); *m* 1943, Rita Micallef, Sliema, Malta; one *s* two *d. Educ:* Royal Naval Coll., Dartmouth. Served War of 1939–45: HM Ships Garland, Wolsey, Witherington, Offa, 1939–42; Cottesmore i/c, 1943–44; Arakan Coast, 1945. HMS Venus i/c, 1948–49; Commander 1949; HMS Ceylon, 1952; Admiralty, 1953–55; Captain, 1955; Captain (D) 8th DS in HMS Cheviot, 1958–59; HMS Hermes i/c, 1961–64; Rear-Admiral 1964; Naval Secretary, 1964–66; Flag Officer, Aircraft Carriers, 1966–67; Comdr, Far East Fleet, 1967–69; Admiral 1969. Rear-Admiral of the UK, 1979–84. Chairman: Kennet and Avon Canal Trust, 1974–91; King George's Fund for Sailors, 1974–86. Pres., Assoc. of RN Officers, 1973–88. *Address:* The Black Barn, Steeple Ashton, Trowbridge, Wilts BA14 6EU. *T:* Devizes (01380) 870496. *Club:* Army and Navy.

O'BRIEN QUINN, Hon. James Aiden; *see* Quinn, Hon. J. A. O'B.

O'CATHAIN, Baroness *cr* 1991 (Life Peer), of The Barbican in the City of London; **Detta O'Cathain,** OBE 1983; Managing Director, Barbican Centre, 1990–95; *b* 3 Feb. 1938; *d* of late Caoimhghin O'Cathain and Margaret O'Cathain; *m* 1968, William Bishop. *Educ:* Laurel Hill, Limerick; University College, Dublin (BA). Aer Lingus, Dublin, 1961–66; Group Economist, Tarmac, 1966–69; Economic Advr, Rootes Motors, 1969–72; Sen. Economist, Carrington Vyella, 1972–73; Economic Advr, British Leyland, 1973–74; Dir, Market Planning, Leyland Cars, 1974–76; Corporate Planning Exec., Unigate, 1976–81; Milk Marketing Board: Head of Strategic Planning, 1981–83; Dir and Gen. Manager, 1984; Man. Dir Milk Marketing, 1985–88. Advr on Agricl Marketing to Minister of Agriculture, 1979–83. Director: Midland Bank, 1984–93; Channel 4, 1985–86; Tesco, 1985–; Sears, 1987–94; British Airways, 1993–; BET, 1994–. FCIM 1987; FRSA 1986. *Recreations:* music, reading. *Address:* Eglantine, Tower House Gardens, Arundel, W Sussex BN18 9RU. *T:* Arundel (01903) 883775.

OCKRENT, Michael Robert; film and theatre director; *b* 18 June 1946; *s* of Charles Ockrent and Eve (*née* Edels); *m*; one *s* one *d. Educ:* Highgate Sch.; Edinburgh Univ. (BSc Hons Physics). Trainee dir, Perth Theatre, 1969–73; Artistic Dir, Traverse Theatre, Edinburgh, 1973–76; freelance dir, 1976–; *productions include:* Once a Catholic, Royal Court and Wyndham's, 1977; And a Nightingale Sang, Queen's, 1979; Educating Rita, RSC and Piccadilly, 1980 (Evening Standard Award, Best Play); Passion Play, RSC and Wyndham's, 1984 (Evening Standard Award, Best Comedy); Me and My Girl, 1986 (Olivier Award, Best Musical); Follies, Shaftesbury, 1987 (Olivier Award, Best Musical);

Crazy For You, Prince Edward, 1993 (Olivier Award, Best Musical); Broadway productions: Me and My Girl, 1985; Once a Catholic, 1986; Atkinson at the Atkinson, 1986; Crazy For You, 1992 (Tony Award); A Christmas Carol, 1994; *feature films and television:* Dancin' thru the Dark, 1990; Money For Nothing, 1993. *Publication:* Running Down Broadway, 1992. *Recreation:* tennis, swimming. *Address:* c/o Sara Randall, 265 Liverpool Road, N1 1LX. *T:* 0171–609 5313.

O'CONNELL, Desmond Henry, Jr; Group Managing Director, BOC Group, 1986–90; *b* 22 Feb. 1936; *s* of Desmond H. and Rosemary O'Connell; *m* 1964, Roberta M. Jaeger; two *s* one *d. Educ:* University of Notre Dame, Indiana; Harvard Business School. BS Elec. Eng., MBA. McKinsey & Co., Chicago, 1962–69; Walsh, Killian & Co., 1969–70; Baxter Travenol Labs, Deerfield, 1970–80; Airco, Montvale, NJ, 1980–86. Non-exec. Dir, Lucas Industries, 1988. *Recreations:* golf, ski-ing. *Clubs:* East India; Leander; Indian Hill Country (Winnetka, Ill); Ridgewood Country (Ridgewood, NJ); Harvard (New York); Bay Head Yacht (Bay Head, NJ).

O'CONNELL, John Eugene Anthony, MS (London), FRCS; Consulting Neurological Surgeon, St Bartholomew's Hospital; *b* 16 Sept. 1906; *s* of Thomas Henry and Catherine Mary O'Connell (*née* O'Sullivan); *m* Marjorie Hutchinson Cook, MBE (*d* 1986). *Educ:* Clongowes Wood and Wimbledon Colleges; St Bartholomew's Hospital. Held posts of House Surgeon, Senior Demonstrator of Anatomy, and Surgical Chief Assistant, St Bartholomew's Hospital, 1931–39; Studied at Universities of Michigan and Chicago on Rockefeller Foundation Travelling Fellowship, 1935–36; Surgeon in charge of an EMS Neurosurgical Unit, 1941–46; Surgeon i/c Dept of Neurol Surgery, St Bartholomew's Hosp., 1946–71; Hunterian Professor, Royal College of Surgeons, 1943 and 1950. Emeritus Mem., Soc. of Brit. Neurol Surgeons (ex-Pres.); FRSM (ex-Vice-Pres.); Hon. Member: Neurosurgical Soc. Australasia; Deutsche Gesellschaft für Neurochirurgie; Corresp. Mem., Amer. Assoc. Neurol Surgeons. *Publications:* papers in neurological, surgical and other journals and books. *Recreations:* fly-fishing, bird watching. *Address:* Fishing Cottage, Itchen Abbas, Winchester, Hants SO21 1AT. *T:* Itchen Abbas (01962) 779227.

O'CONNELL, Sir Maurice (James Donagh MacCarthy), 7th Bt *cr* 1869, of Lakeview, Killarney and Ballybeggan, Tralee; *b* 10 June 1958; *s* of Sir Morgan Donal Conail O'Connell, 6th Bt and of Elizabeth, *o d* of late Major John MacCarthy O'Leary; *S* father, 1989; *m* 1993, Francesca, *d* of Clive Raleigh. *Heir: b* John Morgan Ross MacCarthy O'Connell, *b* 17 April 1960. *Address:* Lakeview House, Killarney, Co. Kerry, Ireland.

O'CONNOR, Surgeon Rear-Adm. Anthony, LVO 1967; Director, Red Cross Blood Transfusion Service, Western Australia, 1981–84 (Deputy Director, 1975–81); *b* 8 Nov. 1917; *s* of Armel John O'Connor and Lucy Violet O'Connor (*née* Bullock-Webster); *m* 1946, Catherine Jane (*née* Hayes); three *d. Educ:* Kings Coll., Strand, London; Westminster Hosp. Med. Sch. MRCS, LRCP, MB, BS, FFARCS, MFCM. Qualified Medical Practitioner, 1941; joined Royal Navy (RNVR), 1942; Permanent Commn, 1945; Dep. Medical Director General (Naval), 1969; MO i/c, Inst. of Naval Med. and Dean of Naval Med., 1972–75. QHP 1970–75. *Recreations:* gardening, photography. *Address:* c/o Lloyds Bank, Ludlow, Shropshire.

O'CONNOR, Rev. Canon (Brian) Michael (McDougal); Vicar of Rainham, Kent, since 1979; *b* 20 June 1942; *s* of Brian McDougal O'Connor and Beryl O'Connor; *m* 1968, Alison Margaret Tibbutt; two *s. Educ:* Lancing Coll.; St Catharine's Coll., Cambridge (BA, MA); Cuddesdon Coll., Oxford. Admitted Solicitor, 1964; Asst Curate, St Andrew, Headington, 1969–72; Sec., Oxford Dio. Pastoral Cttee, 1972–79; Rural Dean of Gillingham, 1981–88. Hon. Canon of Rochester Cathedral, 1988–. Member: General Synod, 1975–90 (Mem., Standing Cttee, 1985–90); Crown Appointments Commn, 1987–90; ACC, 1988–92. Deleg., WCC Assembly, Canberra, 1991. *Address:* The Vicarage, 80 Broadview Avenue, Rainham, Gillingham, Kent ME8 9DE. *T:* Medway (01634) 231538. *Club:* National Liberal.

O'CONNOR, Rt. Rev. Cormac Murphy; *see* Murphy-O'Connor.

O'CONNOR, Professor Daniel John; Professor of Philosophy, University of Exeter, 1957–79, now Emeritus; *b* 2 April 1914; *m* 1948, Kathleen Kemsley; no *c. Educ:* Birkbeck Coll., University of London. Entered Civil Service, 1933; Commonwealth Fund Fellow in Philosophy, University of Chicago, 1946–47; Professor of Philosophy, University of Natal, SA, 1949–51; Professor of Philosophy, University of the Witwatersrand, Johannesburg, 1951–52; Lecturer in Philosophy, Univ. Coll. of North Staffordshire, 1952–54; Professor of Philosophy, University of Liverpool, 1954–57. Visiting Professor, University of Pennsylvania, 1961–62. *Publications:* John Locke, 1952; Introduction to Symbolic Logic (with A. H. Basson), 1953; Introduction to the Philosophy of Education, 1957; A Critical History of Western Philosophy (ed), 1964; Aquinas and Natural Law, 1968; Free Will, 1971; (ed jtly) New Essays in the Philosophy of Education, 1973; The Correspondence Theory of Truth, 1975; various papers in philosophical journals. *Address:* 101a Pennsylvania Road, Exeter EX4 6DT.

O'CONNOR, Deirdre Frances; Hon. Justice O'Connor; Judge, Federal Court of Australia, since 1990; President, Australian Industrial Relations Commission, since 1994; *b* 5 Feb. 1941; *d* of D. A. Buff; *m* 1974, Michael Joseph, SC; five *s. Educ:* Bethlehem Coll., Ashfield; Sydney Univ. (BA; LLB 1st Cl. Hons); DipEd New England. Lectr in Law, Univ. of NSW, 1974–75; Sen. Lectr in Law, Macquarie Univ., 1975–78; part-time Lectr on media and law, Aust. Film and TV Sch., 1975–80; admitted NSW Bar, 1980; Comr, NSW Law Reform Commn, 1983–85; Chm., Aust. Broadcasting Tribunal, 1986–90. President: Admin Appeals Tribunal, 1990–94; Nat. Native Title Tribunal, 1993–94. Mem., Aust. Inst. Judicial Admin, 1992–. Trustee, Internat. Inst. of Communications, 1989–92. Member, Council: Order of Australia, 1990–; Univ. of Canberra, 1992–95. *Recreations:* reading, antiques. *Address:* Australian Industrial Relations Commission, 80 William Street, East Sydney, NSW 2011, Australia. *T:* (2) 3320889.

O'CONNOR, Francis Brian, PhD; Director, Enviropower, since 1993; *b* 27 Dec. 1932; *s* of Francis Arthur and Marjorie O'Connor; *m* 1957, Dilys Mary Mathew-Jones; one *s* one *d. Educ:* Quarry Bank High Sch., Liverpool; University Coll. of N Wales, Bangor (BSc, PhD). Univ. of Wales Res. Fellow, 1956–58; Lecturer in Zoology: TCD, 1958–60; UCL, 1960–67; Prof. of Soil Biology, Univ. of Aarhus, Denmark, 1968–69; Dir of Studies in Conservation, UCL, 1969–75; Nature Conservancy Council: Dep. Dir Gen., 1975–84; Dir (England), 1984–90; Dir of Policy, Planning and Services, 1990–91; Chief Officer, Jt Nature Conservation Cttee, 1991–92. *Publications:* numerous scientific. *Recreations:* boating, motoring, restoration of old houses. *Address:* Manor Farm Cottage, 52 Main Street, Ailsworth, Peterborough PE5 7AF. *T:* Peterborough (01733) 380248.

O'CONNOR, Gillian Rose; Personal Finance Editor, Financial Times, since 1994; *b* 11 Aug. 1941; *d* of Thomas McDougall O'Connor and Kathleen Joan O'Connor (*née* Parnell). *Educ:* Sutton High School for Girls; St Hilda's College, Oxford. Editor, Investors Chronicle, 1982–94. *Address:* Financial Times, Number One, Southwark Bridge, SE1 9HL.

O'CONNOR, Rev. Canon Michael; *see* O'Connor, Rev. Canon B. M. McD.

O'CONNOR, Air Vice-Marshal Patrick Joseph, CB 1976; OBE 1943; MD; FRCPE, FRCPsych; Civil Consultant in Neuropsychiatry, Royal Air Force, since 1978; Consultant in Neurology and Psychiatry to Civil Aviation Authority and to British Airways, since 1978; *b* 21 Aug. 1914; *s* of Charles O'Connor, Straffan, Co. Kildare, Eire, farmer; *m* 1946, Elsie, *o d* of David Craven, Leeds, Yorks; one *s* two *d* (and one *d* decd). *Educ:* Roscrea Coll.; University of Dublin. MB, BCh 1938. Joined RAF, 1940; Air Cdre 1966; Air Vice-Marshal 1971; Consultant Adviser in Neurology and Psychiatry to RAF, 1964–78; Senior Consultant to RAF at Central Medical Establishment, 1975–78, Hon. Consultant, 1978–; retired from RAF, 1978. MD 1950; MRCPE 1950; DPM 1953; FRCPE 1960; MRCP 1960; FRCPsych 1970. QHP 1967–78. Member: Med. Council to Migraine Trust; Med. Council on Alcoholism; The EEG Soc.; Assoc. of British Neurologists; Internat. Acad. of Aviation and Space Med., 1977; Internat. League against Epilepsy; Flying Personnel Res. Cttee. Fellow, Aerospace Med. Assoc; FRSM. *Publications:* contrib.: Journal Neurology, Psychiatry and Neurosurgery; British Journal Psychiatry; BMJ. *Recreations:* gardening, shooting. *Address:* 10 Harley Street, W1N 1AA. *T:* 0171–636 6504; St Benedicts, Bacombe Lane, Wendover, Bucks HP22 6EQ. *T:* Aylesbury (01296) 623329. *Club:* Royal Air Force.

O'CONNOR, Rt. Hon. Sir Patrick McCarthy, Kt 1966; PC 1980; a Lord Justice of Appeal, 1980–89; *b* 28 Dec. 1914; *s* of late William Patrick O'Connor; *m* 1938, Mary Garland (*d* 1984), *d* of William Martin Griffin, KC, of Vancouver, BC; two *s* two *d. Educ:* Downside; Merton Coll., Oxford (Hon. Fellow 1987). Called to the Bar, Inner Temple, 1940; Master of the Bench, 1966. Junior Counsel to the Post Office, 1954–60; QC 1960; Recorder: of King's Lynn, 1959–61; of Southend, 1961–66; a Judge of the High Ct of Justice, QBD, 1966–80; Dep. Chairman, IoW QS, 1957–71. Vice-Chm., Parole Bd, 1974–75. A Governor of Guy's Hospital, 1956–60. *Recreation:* golf. *Address:* 210 Rivermead Court, Ranelagh Gardens, SW6 3SG. *T:* 0171–731 3563. *Club:* Hurlingham.

O'CONNOR, Patrick Michael Joseph; QC 1993; *b* 7 Aug. 1949; *s* of Denis Bellew O'Connor and Ingelore Biegel; *m* 1986, Gillian Denise Brasse; two *d. Educ:* St Francis Xavier's Grammar Sch., Liverpool; UCL (LLB Hons). Called to the Bar, Inner Temple, 1970; tenant at 3 Temple Gardens, 1973–84; jt founder mem., 14 Tooks Court Chambers, 1984–. *Publications:* articles in Criminal Law Review and other academic and professional jls. *Address:* 1 Crown Office Row, Temple, EC4Y 7HH. *T:* 0171–797 7111.

O'CONNOR, Rory, CBE 1991; Member, Gibraltar Court of Appeal, since 1991; Judge of the High Court of Hong Kong, 1977–90; *b* Co. Down, 26 Nov. 1925; *s* of late James O'Connor and Mary (*née* Savage); *m* 1963, Elizabeth, *d* of late Frederick Dew; one *s* two *d. Educ:* Blackrock Coll., Dublin; Univ. Coll., Dublin (BCom). Called to Irish Bar, King's Inns, 1949. Resident Magistrate, Kenya, 1956–62; Hong Kong: Magistrate, 1962–70; District Judge, 1970–77. *Address:* 12 Windermere Crescent, Bangor, Co Down, N Ireland.

O'CONNOR, Sandra Day; Associate Justice of the Supreme Court of the United States, since 1981; *b* 26 March 1930; *d* of Harry and Ada Mae Day; *m* 1952, John Jay O'Connor III; three *s. Educ:* Stanford Univ. (BA 1950; LLB 1952). Legal appts in Calif and Frankfurt, 1952–57; in private practice, 1959–65; Asst Attorney-Gen., Arizona, 1965–69; Judge: Maricopa County Superior Ct, 1974–79; Arizona Ct of Appeals, 1979–81. Mem. Senate, Arizona, 1969–74 (majority leader, 1973–74). Director: Nat. Bank of Arizona, Phoenix, 1971–74; Blue Cross/Blue Shield, Arizona, 1975–79. Chm., Maricopa County Juvenile Detention Home, 1966–68; Pres., Heard Museum, Phoenix, 1979–81; Mem. Nat. Bd, Smithsonian Assocs, 1981–82. Trustee, Stanford Univ., 1976–80. Hon. Bencher, Gray's Inn, 1982. *Address:* Supreme Court Building, 1 First Street NE, Washington, DC 20543, USA.

O'CONNOR HOWE, Mrs Josephine Mary; HM Diplomatic Service, retired; *b* 25 March 1924; *d* of late Gerald Frank Claridge and late Dulcie Agnes Claridge (*née* Waldegrave); *m* 1947, John O'Connor Howe (decd); one *d. Educ:* Wychwood Sch., Oxford; Triangle Coll. (course in journalism). Inter-Allied Information Cttee, later, United Nations Information Office, 1942–45; Foreign Office: The Hague, 1945–46; Internat. News Service and freelance, 1946–50; FO, 1952; Counsellor, FCO, 1974–1979. Reader's Digest, 1979–83; Dir, Council for Arms Control, 1983–84; Exec. Editor, Inst. for the Study of Conflict, 1985–89; Freelance Editor specialising in internat. affairs, arms control, etc., 1985–. *Publication:* (ed) Armed Peace—the search for world security, 1984. *Recreations:* theatre, gardening, grandchildren. *Address:* Dering Cottage, Little Chart, Ashford, Kent TN27 0PT. *T:* Pluckley (01233) 840328. *Club:* Commonwealth Trust.

ODDIE, His Honour Christopher Ripley; a Circuit Judge, 1974–94, sitting at Mayor's and City of London Court, 1989–94; *b* Derby, 24 Feb. 1929; *o s* of Dr and Mrs J. R. Oddie, Uttoxeter, Staffs; *m* 1957, Margaret Anne, *d* of Mr and Mrs J. W. Timmis; one *s* three *d. Educ:* Giggleswick Sch.; Oriel Coll., Oxford (MA). Called to Bar, Middle Temple, 1954, Oxford Circuit. Contested (L) Ludlow, Gen. Election, 1970. A Recorder of the Crown Court, 1972–74. Chm., County Court Rule Cttee, 1985–87 (Mem., 1981–87). Member: Judicial Studies Bd, 1989–91; Cttee, Council of Her Majesty's Circuit Judges, 1989–91. Mem. Council, St Mary's Hosp. Med. Sch., 1980–88. Gen. Editor, Butterworth's County Court Precedents and Pleadings, 1988–92. *Recreations:* reading, gossip, opera, walking. *Address:* 89 The Vineyard, Richmond, Surrey TW10 6AT. *T:* 0181–940 4135; Lower Riddings, Woodside, Clun, Shropshire SY7 0JE. *Club:* Reform.

ODDIE, Prof. Guy Barrie, BArch, DipTP; FRIAS; architect; Robert Adam Professor of Architecture, 1968–82, now Emeritus, and Head of Department of Architecture, 1968–80, University of Edinburgh; *b* 1 Jan. 1922; *o s* of Edward Oddie and Eleanor Pinkney; *m* 1952, Mabel Mary Smith (*d* 1990); two step *d. Educ:* state schools in London and Co. Durham; Univ. of Newcastle upon Tyne. Demonstrator, Univ. of Newcastle upon Tyne, 1944–45; Asst, public offices, Glasgow and Coventry, 1945–47; Research Architect, Building Res. Stn, 1947–50; Sen. Lectr, Birmingham Sch. of Architecture, 1950–52; Develt Gp, Min. of Educn, 1952–58; Staff architect, UGC, 1958–63; Consultant to OECD, 1963–66; Dir, Laboratories Investigation Unit, DES, 1966–68. Sen. Advr to OECD Prog. on Educnl Bldg, 1972–84. Participant in and advocate for 1950's architectural movement led by school-designers and aimed at producing quality buildings on time, in the number needed and at a politically acceptable cost. *Publications:* School Building Resources and their Effective Use, 1966; Development and Economy in Educational Building, 1968; Industrialised Building for Schools, 1975; contrib. Architects Jl, Architectural Rev., RIBA Jl. *Recreations:* dry-fly fishing, gardening, company of friends. *Address:* The Causeway, Edinburgh EH15 3QA.

ODDY, Christine Margaret; Member (Lab) European Parliament, Coventry and North Warwickshire, since 1994 (Midlands Central, 1989–94); *b* 20 Sept. 1955; *d* of Eric Lawson Oddy and Audrey Mary Oddy. *Educ:* Stoke Park Sch., Coventry; University Coll. London (LLB Hons); Licence Spéciale en droit européen, Inst. d'Etudes européennes, Brussels; Birkbeck Coll., London (MSc (Econ)). Stagiaire (grad. trainee) in EC, 1979–80; Articled Clerk, Clifford Turner, 1980–82; admitted Solicitor, 1982; Lectr in Law, City of London Poly., 1984–89. European Parliament: Member: Legal Affairs Cttee, 1989–; Social Affairs

Cttee, 1989–; Women's Rights Cttee, 1989–; Central America Delegn, 1989. Member: RIIA, 1990; Law Soc., 1982; ESU, 1987. FRSA 1992. *Recreations:* travel, wine, theatre, cinema. *Address:* 3 Copthall House, Station Square, Coventry CV1 2FZ. *T:* Coventry (01203) 552328.

ODDY, Revel, FSA; Keeper, Department of Art and Archaeology, Royal Scottish Museum, Edinburgh, 1974–83; *b* 11 April 1922; *s* of Sidney Oddy and Muriel Barnfather; *m* 1949, Ariadne Margaret, *d* of late Sir Andrew Gourlay Clow, KCSI, CIE; two *s* two *d. Educ:* Worksop Coll.; Pembroke Coll., Cambridge (MA). FSA 1982. Served War, Loyal Regt and King's African Rifles, 1941–46. Mod. langs master, Dr Challoner's Grammar Sch., Amersham, 1949; Res. Asst, V&A Mus., London, 1950–55; Asst Keeper, Royal Scottish Mus., Edinburgh, 1955–74. *Recreations:* mild gardening, reading. *Address:* 44 Findhorn Place, Edinburgh EH9 2NT. *T:* 0131–667 5815. *Clubs:* Civil Service; University of Edinburgh Staff (Edinburgh).

ODDY, William Andrew, DSc; FSA; Keeper of Conservation, British Museum, since 1985; *b* 6 Jan. 1942; *s* of late William T. Oddy and of Hilda F. Oddy (*née* Dalby); *m* 1965, Patricia Anne Whitaker; one *s* one *d. Educ:* Bradford Grammar Sch.; New Coll., Oxford (BA 1964; BSc 1965; MA 1969; DSc 1994). FSA 1973; FIIC 1974. Joined British Museum Research Lab., 1966, research into conservation and ancient technology; Head of Conservation, 1981. Member: Scientific Cttee, Internat. Congress on Deterioration and Preservation of Stone, 1976–91; Dept of Transport Adv. Cttee on Historic Wrecks, 1981–91; Council, Textile Conservation Centre, 1985–; Cons. Cttee, Council for Care of Churches, 1985–90; Cons. Cttee, Cons. Unit, Mus. and Gall. Commn, 1987–92; Science-based Archaeol. Cttee, SERC, 1990–93; Council, Internat. Inst. for Conservation of Historic and Artistic Works, 1990–; Fabric Adv. Cttee, Cathedral and Abbey Church of St Alban, 1991–. Freeman, Goldsmiths' Co., 1986. *Publications:* editor: Problems in the Conservation of Waterlogged Wood, 1975; Aspects of Early Metallurgy, 1980; Scientific Studies in Numismatics, 1980; Metallurgy in Numismatics 2, 1988; The Art of the Conservator, 1992; Restoration: is it acceptable?, 1994; joint editor: Conservation in Museums and Galleries, 1975; Metallurgy in Numismatics 1, 1980; Aspects of Tibetan Metallurgy, 1981; A Survey of Numismatic Research 1978–1984, 1986; (jtly) Romanesque Metalwork: copper alloys and their decoration, 1986; papers in learned jls. *Recreation:* travel. *Address:* c/o The British Museum, WC1B 3DG.

O'DEA, Sir Patrick Jerad, KCVO 1974; retired public servant, New Zealand; Extra Gentleman Usher to the Queen, since 1981; *b* 18 April 1918; 2nd *s* of late Patrick O'Dea; *m* 1945, Jean Mary, *d* of Hugh Mulholland; one *s* three *d. Educ:* St Paul's Coll. and Univ. of Otago, Dunedin, NZ; Victoria Univ., Wellington, NZ. Joined NZ Public Service, 1936; served in Agriculture Dept, 1936–47. Served War in Royal New Zealand Artillery of 2 NZEF, 1941–45. With Industries and Commerce Dept, 1947–49; subseq. served with Dept of Internal Affairs in various posts interrupted by 2 years' full-time study at Victoria Univ. of Wellington (DPA). Group Exec. Officer, Local Govt, 1959–64; Dep. Sec., 1964–67; Sec. for Internal Affairs, NZ, 1967–78; formerly Sec. for: Local Govt; Civil Defence; Sec. of Recreation and Sport; Clerk of the Writs; NZ Sec. to the Queen, 1969–78, reapptd 1981, for visit of Queen and Duke of Edinburgh to NZ. Chm., Duke of Edinburgh's Award NZ Foundn; Mem., Vicentian Foundn. *Publications:* several papers on local govt in New Zealand. *Recreations:* gardening, golf, bowls. *Address:* 1 Tensing Place, Khandallah, Wellington, New Zealand. *T:* (4) 792424. *Clubs:* Shandon Golf (Petone, NZ); Khandallah Bowling (Khandallah, NZ); Wellesley (Wellington).

ODELL, John William, (Jack), OBE 1969; Chairman, Lledo (London) Ltd, since 1982. Joint Vice-Chairman, Lesney Products & Co. Ltd, Diecasting Engineers, London E9, 1981–82 (Joint Managing Director, 1947–73; Deputy Chairman, 1973–81). *Address:* Lledo (London) Ltd, Woodhall Road, South Street, Ponders End, Enfield, Middx EN3 4ND.

O'DELL, Mrs June Patricia, OBE 1990; Non-Executive Director, Aylesbury Vale Community Healthcare NHS Trust, since 1991; Deputy Chairman, Equal Opportunities Commission, 1986–90; *b* 9 June 1929; *d* of Leonard Vickery, RN and Myra Vickery; *m* 1951 (marr. diss. 1963); one *s* two *d. Educ:* Edgehill Girls College; Plymouth Technical College. Estate Agent. Dir, Eachdale Developments Ltd. Nat. Pres., Fedn of Business and Professional Women, 1983–85; Chm., Employment Cttee, Internat. Fedn of Business Professional Women, 1983–87; Member: Women's Nat. Commn, 1983–85; European Adv. Cttee for Equal Treatment between Women and Men, 1986–90; Authorised Conveyancing Practitioners Bd, 1991–; Legal Aid Adv. Cttee, 1993–94. Mem. Bd, Probus Women's Housing Soc., 1993–; Trustee, Women Returners Network, 1994–. FRSA 1986 (Mem. Council, 1992). *Recreations:* music, particularly opera and choral; writing, literature, the countryside, equestrian events. *Address:* Vale Farm, Kimblewick, Aylesbury, Bucks HP17 8SX. *Club:* University Women's.

ODELL, Prof. Peter Randon; Professor Emeritus, Erasmus University, Rotterdam (Director, Centre for International Energy Studies, 1981–90); *b* 1 July 1930; *s* of late Frank James Odell and late Grace Edna Odell; *m* 1957, Jean Mary McKintosh; two *s* two *d. Educ:* County Grammar Sch., Coalville; Univ. of Birmingham (BA, PhD); Fletcher Sch. of Law and Diplomacy, Cambridge, Mass (AM). FInstPet. RAF 1954–57. Economist, Shell International Petroleum Co., 1958–61; Lectr, LSE, 1961–65; Sen. Lectr, LSE, 1965–68; Prof. of Economic Geography, Erasmus Univ., 1968–81. Visiting Professor: LSE, 1983–; College of Europe, Bruges, 1983–90; Scholar in Residence, Rockefeller Centre, Bellagio, 1984; Killam Vis. Scholar, Univ. of Calgary, 1989. Stamp Meml Lectr, London Univ., 1975. Canadian Council Fellow, 1978. Adviser, Dept of Energy, 1977–78. Contested (Lib Dem) Suffolk, European Elecn, 1989. European Editor, Energy Jl, 1988–90. FRSA 1983. Internat. Assoc. for Energy Econs Prize, for outstanding contribns to energy econs and its literature, 1991; RSGS Centenary Medal, 1993. *Publications:* An Economic Geography of Oil, 1963; Natural Gas in Western Europe, 1969; Oil and World Power, 1970, 8th edn 1986; (with D. A. Preston) Economies and Societies in Latin America, 1973, 2nd edn 1978; Energy: Needs and Resources, 1974, 2nd edn 1977; (with K. E. Rosing) The North Sea Oil Province, 1975; The West European Energy Economy: the case for self-sufficiency, 1976; (with K. E. Rosing) The Optimal Development of the North Sea Oilfields, 1976; (with L. Vallenilla) The Pressures of Oil: a strategy for economic revival, 1978; British Oil Policy: a Radical Alternative, 1980; (with K. E. Rosing) The Future of Oil, 1980–2080, 1980, 2nd edn 1983; (ed with J. Rees) The International Oil Industry: an interdisciplinary perspective, 1986; Global and Regional Energy Supplies: recent fictions and fallacies revisited, 1991. *Address:* 7 Constitution Hill, Ipswich IP1 3RG. *T:* Ipswich (01473) 253376.

ODELL, Sir Stanley (John), Kt 1986; Chairman, South Bedfordshire Community Healthcare NHS Trust, since 1994; *b* 20 Nov. 1929; *s* of George Frederick Odell and Florence May Odell; *m* 1952, Eileen Grace Stuart; four *d. Educ:* Bedford Modern School. Chairman: Mid Beds Young Conservatives, 1953–59; Mid Beds Cons. Assoc., 1964–69 (Pres., 1991–); Beds Cons. European Constituency Council, 1979; E of England Provincial Council, Cons. Party, 1983–86 (Pres., 1991–93); Nat. Union of Cons. and Unionist Assocs, 1989–90 (Vice Chm., 1986–89). Chm., Anglo-American Cttee, RAF Chicksands, 1987–. Mem. Ct, Luton Univ., 1994. Churchwarden, Campton Parish Church, 1993–. *Recreations:* politics, shooting. *Address:* Woodhall Farm, Campton, Shefford, Beds SG17 5PB. *T:* Hitchin (01462) 813230. *Club:* Farmers'.

ODGERS, Graeme David William; Chairman, Monopolies and Mergers Commission, since 1993; *b* 10 March 1934; *s* of late William Arthur Odgers and Elizabeth Minty (*née* Rennie); *m* 1957, Diana Patricia Berge; one *s* two *d* (and one *d* decd). *Educ:* St John's Coll., Johannesburg; Gonville and Caius Coll., Cambridge (Mech. Scis Tripos); Harvard Business Sch. (MBA, Baker Scholar). Investment Officer, Internat. Finance Corp., Washington DC, 1959–62; Management Consultant, Urwick Orr and Partners Ltd, 1962–64; Investment Executive, Hambros Bank Ltd, 1964–65; Director: Keith Shipton and Co. Ltd, 1965–72; C. T. Bowring (Insurance) Holdings Ltd, 1972–74; Chm., Odgers and Co. Ltd (Management Consultants), 1970–74; Dir, Industrial Develt Unit, DoI, 1974–77; Assoc. Dir (Finance), General Electric Co., 1977–78; Gp Finance Dir, 1979–86, Gp Man. Dir, 1983–86, Tarmac; British Telecommunications: pt-time Mem. Bd, 1983–86; Govt Dir, 1984–86; Dep. Chm. and Chief Finance Officer, 1986–87; Gp Man. Dir, 1987–90; Chief Exec., Alfred McAlpine plc, 1990–93. Non-executive Director: Dalgety, 1987–93; Nat. & Provincial Bldg Soc., 1990–93. Mem., Listed Cos' Adv. Cttee, Stock Exchange, 1987–90. *Recreation:* golf. *Address:* Brome House, West Malling, Kent ME19 6NE. *Club:* Wildernesse (Sevenoaks).

ODGERS, Paul Randell, CB 1970; MBE 1945; TD 1949; Deputy Secretary, Department of Education and Science, 1971–75; *b* 30 July 1915; *e s* of late Dr P. N. B. Odgers and Mrs M. A. Odgers (*née* Higgins); *m* 1944, Diana, *d* of late R. E. F. Fawkes, CBE; one *s* one *d. Educ:* Rugby; New Coll., Oxford. Entered CS, Board of Education, 1937. Army Service, UK, Malta, Sicily, Italy, NW Europe, 1939–45 (despatches three times). Asst Secretary: Min. of Educn, 1948; Cabinet Office, 1956; Under-Secretary: Min. of Educn, 1958; Office of First Secretary of State, 1967; Office of Lord President of the Council, 1968; Office of Sec. of State for Social Services, 1968; Cabinet Office, 1970. Vice-Pres., Soc. for Promotion of Roman Studies; Mem. Council, GPDST, 1976–89. *Address:* Stone Walls, Aston Road, Haddenham, Bucks HP17 8AF. *T:* Haddenham (01844) 291830. *Club:* United Oxford & Cambridge University.

See also C. D. Compston.

ODLING, Thomas George, CB 1974; *b* 18 Sept. 1911; *yr s* of late Major W. A. Odling, Paxford, Glos and late Mary Bennett Odling (*née* Case); *m* 1st, Camilla Haldane Paterson (marr. diss.); two *s*; 2nd, Hilary Katharine, *d* of late W. J. Palgrave-Ker, Lilliput, Dorset. *Educ:* Temple Grove; Rugby Sch.; New Coll., Oxford (MA). House of Commons: Asst Clerk, 1935; Clerk of Private Bills, Examr of Petitions for Private Bills and Taxing Officer, 1961–73; Clerk of Select Cttee on Parly Comr for Admin, 1969–73; Clerk of Committees, 1974–76, retired 1976. Temp. attached to Consultative Assembly of Council of Europe during 1949 and later sessions. *Recreations:* music, gardening. *Address:* Paxford, Campden, Glos GL55 6XQ. *Clubs:* Athenæum, MCC.

See also Maj.-Gen. W. Odling.

ODLING, Maj.-Gen. William, CB 1963; OBE 1951; MC; DL; President, English-Speaking Union (Eastern Counties); Chairman: Roman River (Colchester) Conservation Zone; Friends of Essex Churches; Vice-Chairman of School, and Chairman of Hall, Fingringhoe; Treasurer/Secretary, Fingringhoe Ancient Charities; *b* 8 June 1909; *s* of late Major and Mrs W. A. Odling, Paxford, Campden, Glos; *m* 1939, Margaret Marshall (*née* Gardner); one *s* two *d. Educ:* Temple Grove; Wellington Coll.; RMA, Woolwich. Subaltern RHA and RA, chiefly in India until 1938; Captain, 1938; Major, 1946; Lieut-Colonel, 1951; Colonel, 1953; Brigadier 1957; Maj.-General, 1961; Adjutant, TA, 1939; CRA, Madagascar Force, 1942 (MC); GSO 1, RA, COSSAC, Planning Staff for Operation Overlord, 1943; NW Europe Campaign (despatches), 1944; GSO 1, War Office, 1945; GSO 1, Training, GHQMELF, 1948; AQMG, MELF, 1950; AAG Colonel, War Office, 1953; CRA E Anglian Div., 1957; Brig. AQ, HQ E Comd, 1959; Maj.-Gen. i/c Admin, GHQ FELF, 1961–62; COS GHQ FELF 1962–64. DL Essex, 1975. *Recreations:* sailing (Cdre, Atalanta (Yacht) Owners Assoc.), print collecting, gardening, brick building, economising. *Address:* Gun House, Fingringhoe, Colchester CO5 7AL. *T:* Colchester (01206) 735320. *Club:* Army and Navy.

See also T. G. Odling.

ODLING-SMEE, John Charles; Director, European II Department, International Monetary Fund, since 1992; *b* 13 April 1943; *s* of late Rev. Charles William Odling-Smee and of Katharine Hamilton Odling-Smee (*née* Aitchison). *Educ:* Durham School; St John's College, Cambridge. BA Cantab 1964, MA Oxon 1966. Junior Research Officer, Dept of Applied Economics, Cambridge, 1964–65; Asst Research Officer, Inst. of Economics and Statistics, Oxford, 1965–66; Fellow in Economics, Oriel College, Oxford, 1966–70; Research Officer, Inst. of Economics and Statistics, Oxford, 1968–71 and 1972–73; Economic Research Officer, Govt of Ghana, 1971–72; Senior Research Officer, Centre for Urban Economics, LSE, 1973–75; Economic Adviser, Central Policy Review Staff, Cabinet Office, 1975–77; Senior Economic Adviser, HM Treasury, 1977–80; Senior Economist, IMF, 1981–82; Under-Sec., HM Treasury, 1982–89; Dep. Chief Economic Advr, HM Treasury, 1989–90; Sen. Advr, IMF, 1990–91. *Publications:* (with A. Grey and N. P. Hepworth) Housing Rents, Costs and Subsidies, 1978, 2nd edn 1981; (with R. C. O. Matthews and C. H. Feinstein) British Economic Growth 1856–1973, 1982; articles in books and learned jls. *Address:* 3506 Garfield Street NW, Washington, DC 20007, USA. *T:* (202) 6238308.

ODONE, Cristina; Editor, The Catholic Herald, since 1992; *b* 11 Nov. 1960; *d* of Augusto and Ulla Odone. *Educ:* Worcester Coll., Oxford (MA). Freelance journalist, 1983–84; journalist: Catholic Herald, 1985–86; The Times diary, 1987; Vice-Pres., Odone Associates, Washington, 1988–92. *Publication:* The Shrine (novel), 1996. *Recreations:* writing, reading, walking, travelling. *Address:* Catholic Herald, Lamb's Passage, Bunhill Row, EC1Y 8TQ. *T:* 0171–588 3101. *Clubs:* The Keys, Academy.

O'DONNELL, Augustine Thomas, CB 1994; Deputy Director, Macroeconomic Policy and Prospects Directorate, HM Treasury, since 1995; *b* 1 Oct. 1952; *s* of Helen O'Donnell (*née* McClean) and James O'Donnell; *m* 1979, Melanie Joan Elizabeth Timmis; one *d. Educ:* Univ. of Warwick (BA Hons); Nuffield Coll., Oxford (MPhil). Lectr, Dept of Political Economy, Univ. of Glasgow, 1974–79; Econnomist, HM Treasury, 1979–85; First Sec. (Econ.), British Embassy, Washington, 1985–88; Sen. Economic Adviser, 1988–89, Press Sec., 1989–90, HM Treasury; Press Sec. to Prime Minister, 1990–94; Under Sec., Monetary Gp, HM Treasury, 1994–95. *Publications:* articles in economic jls. *Recreations:* football, cricket, tennis. *Address:* HM Treasury, Parliament Street, SW1P 3AG. *Club:* Old Salesians FC.

O'DONNELL, Prof. Barry, FRCS, FRCSI; Professor of Paediatric Surgery, Royal College of Surgeons in Ireland, 1986–93, now Professor Emeritus; Consultant Paediatric Surgeon, Our Lady's Hospital for Sick Children, Dublin, 1957–93; Director, West Deutsche Landesbank, since 1990; *b* 6 Sept. 1926; *e s* of Michael J. O'Donnell and Kathleen O'Donnell (*née* Barry); *m* 1959, Mary Leydon, BA, BComm, BL, *d* of John Leydon, LLD, KCSG; three *s* one *d. Educ:* Christian Brothers College, Cork; Castleknock College, Dublin; University College, Cork (MB Hons 1949). MCh NUI, 1954. FRCS

1953, FRCSI 1953; FRCSEd *ad hominem* 1992. Ainsworth Travelling Scholar, Boston (Lahey Clinic and Boston Floating Hosp., 1955–56); Sen. Registrar, Hosp. for Sick Children, London, 1956–57. Vis. Prof. at many US univs, incl. Harvard, Columbia, Johns Hopkins, Michigan, Pennsylvania; Hunterian Prof., RCS, 1986. Jt Pres., British, Canadian and Irish Med. Assocs, 1976–77; President: British Assoc. of Paediatric Surgeons, 1980–82; Surgical Sect., Royal Acad. of Medicine of Ireland, 1990–92; Mem. Council, RCSI, 1972–77 and 1993–; Chm., Jl Cttee, BMA, 1982–88. Hon. Fellow, Amer. Acad. of Pediatrics, 1974. People of the Year Award, New Ireland Insce Co., 1984; Denis Browne Gold Medal, British Assoc. of Paediatric Surgeons, 1989. *Publications:* Essentials of Paediatric Surgery, 1961, 4th edn 1992; Abdominal Pain in Children, 1985; many other pubns. *Recreations:* talking, golf. *Address:* 28 Merlyn Road, Ballsbridge, Dublin 4, Ireland. *T:* and *Fax:* Dublin 2694000. *Clubs:* Royal Ocean Racing; Royal Irish Yacht; Portmarnock Golf.

O'DONNELL, James Anthony, FRCO; Master of Music, Westminster Cathedral, since 1988 (Assistant Master of Music, 1982–88); *b* 15 Aug. 1961; *s* of Dr James Joseph Gerard O'Donnell and Dr Gillian Anne O'Donnell (*née* Moody). *Educ:* Westcliff High Sch,, Essex; Jesus Coll., Cambridge (Organ Scholar and Open Scholar in Music; BA 1982, MA). Lectr in Church Music Studies, RAM. FRCO 1983 (Performer of the Year, 1987; Mem. Council, 1989–). *Recreations:* opera, food, wine. *Address:* Westminster Cathedral Clergy House, 42 Francis Street, SW1P 1QW. *T:* 0171–798 9066/9057, *Fax:* 0171–798 9090.

See also D. K. *Womersley.*

O'DONNELL, Dr Michael; author and broadcaster; *b* 20 Oct. 1928; *o s* of late James Michael O'Donnell and Nora (*née* O'Sullivan); *m* 1953, Catherine Dorrington Ward; one *s* two *d. Educ:* Stonyhurst; Trinity Hall, Cambridge (Lane Harrington Schol.); St Thomas's Hosp. Med. Sch., London (MB, BChir). FRCGP 1990. Editor, Cambridge Writing, 1948; Scriptwriter, BBC Radio, 1949–52. General Medical Practitioner, 1954–64. Editor, World Medicine, 1966–82. Member: General Medical Council, 1971–; Longman Editorial Adv. Bd, 1978–82. Inaugural lecture, Green Coll., Oxford, 1981. John Rowan Wilson Award, World Medical Journalists Assoc., 1982; John Snow Medal, Assoc. of Anaesthetists of GB and Ireland, 1984. Scientific Adviser: O Lucky Man (film), 1972; Inside Medicine (BBC TV), 1974; Don't Ask Me (Yorkshire TV), 1977; Don't Just Sit There (Yorkshire TV), 1979–80; Where There's Life (Yorkshire TV), 1981–83. *Television plays:* Suggestion of Sabotage, 1963; Dangerous Reunion, 1964; Resolution, 1964; *television documentaries:* You'll Never Believe It, 1962; Cross Your Heart and Hope to Live, 1975; The Presidential Race, 1976; From Europe to the Coast, 1976; Chasing the Dragon, 1979; Second Opinion, 1980; Judgement on Las Vegas, 1981; Is Your Brain Really Necessary, 1982; Plague of Hearts, 1983; Medical Express, 1984; Can You Avoid Cancer?, 1984; O'Donnell Investigates . . . booze, 1985; O'Donnell Investigates . . . food, 1985; O'Donnell Investigates . . . the food business, 1986; O'Donnell Investigates . . . age, 1988; Health, Wealth and Happiness, 1989; What is this thing called health, 1990; The Skin Trade, 1991; Whose Blue Genes?, 1992; Out of Town, Out of Mind, 1993; Beyond belief, 1994; Way beyond belief, 1995; Dads, 1995; *radio:* contributor to Stop the Week (BBC), 1976–92; Chm., My Word (BBC), 1983–92; Presenter, Relative Values (BBC), 1987–; The Bhamjee Beat, 1995. Medical Journalists Assoc. Award, 1973, 1982 and 1990; British Science Writers' Award, 1979. *Publications:* Cambridge Anthology, 1952; The Europe We Want, 1971; My Medical School, 1978; The Devil's Prison, 1982; Doctor! Doctor! an insider's guide to the games doctors play, 1986; The Long Walk Home, 1988; Dr Michael O'Donnell's Executive Health Guide, 1988; Serious Professional Misconduct, 1993; contrib. Punch, New Scientist, The Listener, The Times, The Guardian, Daily Telegraph, Daily Mail. *Recreations:* golf, walking, listening to music, loitering (with and without intent). *Address:* Handon Cottage, Markwick Lane, Loxhill, Godalming, Surrey GU8 4BD. *T:* Hascombe (01483) 208295. *Club:* Garrick.

O'DONNELL, Rt. Hon. Turlough; PC 1979; Lord Justice of Appeal, Supreme Court of Northern Ireland, 1979–89; *b* 5 Aug. 1924; *e s* of Charles and Eileen O'Donnell; *m* 1954, Eileen McKinley; two *s* two *d. Educ:* Abbey Grammar Sch., Newry; Queen's Univ., Belfast (LLB). Called to Bar of Northern Ireland, 1947; called to Inner Bar, 1964; Puisne Judge, NI, 1971–79. Chairman: NI Bar Council, 1970–71, Council of Legal Educn, NI, 1980–90. *Recreations:* golf, folk music. *Address:* c/o Royal Courts of Justice (Ulster), Belfast BT1 3JF.

O'DONOGHUE, His Honour Michael; a Circuit Judge, 1982–94; *b* 10 June 1929; *s* of late Dr James O'Donoghue, MB, ChB and Vera O'Donoghue (*née* Cox). *Educ:* Rhyl Grammar School; Univ. of Liverpool. LLB (Hons) 1950. Called to the Bar, Gray's Inn, 1951; National Service as Flying Officer, RAF, 1951–53; practised at the Chancery Bar, 1954–82; Lectr in Law (part time), Univ. of Liverpool, 1966–82. Mem. (part-time), Lands Tribunal, 1987–94. *Recreations:* music, sailing, photography. *Clubs:* Athenæum (Liverpool); Royal Welsh Yacht (Caernarfon) (Commodore, 1980–82; Pres., 1994–).

O'DONOGHUE, Rt. Rev. Patrick; Auxiliary Bishop of Westminster (Bishop in West London) (RC), since 1993; *b* 4 May 1934; *s* of Daniel O'Donoghue and Sheila O'Donoghue (*née* Twomey). *Educ:* St Edmund's Coll., Ware, Herts. Ordained priest, 1967; Asst priest, Willesden, 1967–70; Mem., Diocesan Mission Team, Westminster, 1970–73; Pastoral Dir, Allen Hall, 1973–78; Asst Administrator, Westminster Cathedral, 1978–85; Rector, Allen Hall, 1985–91; Administrator, Westminster Cathedral, 1991–93. *Recreations:* football, theatre, country walking, the Arts. *Address:* Our Lady and St Bridget, 112 Twickenham Road, Isleworth, Middlesex TW7 6DL. *T:* 0181–568 7371.

O'DONOGHUE, Philip Nicholas, CBiol, FIBiol; General Secretary, Institute of Biology, 1982–89; *b* 9 Oct. 1929; *s* of Terence Frederick O'Donoghue and Ellen Mary (*née* Haynes); *m* 1955, Veronica Florence Campbell; two *d. Educ:* East Barnet Grammar Sch.; Univ. of Nottingham (BSc; MSc 1959). FIBiol 1975. Experimental Officer, ARC's Field Stn, Compton, 1952–55 and Inst. of Animal Physiology, Babraham, 1955–61; Scientific Officer, National Inst. for Res. in Dairying, Shinfield, 1962–66; Lectr in Exptl Vet. Science and later Sen. Lectr in Lab. Animal Science, Royal Postgrad. Med. Sch., Univ. of London, 1966–82. Hume Meml Lect., UFAW, 1990. Vice-Pres., Inst. of Animal Technicians, 1969–; Hon. Sec., Inst. of Biology, 1972–76; Member: TEC, 1973–79 (Chm., Life Sciences Cttee, 1973–80); Council, Section of Comparative Medicine, RSM, 1983– (Pres., 1985–86); President: Lab. Animal Sci. Assoc., 1989–91; Fedn of European Lab. Animal Sci. Assocs, 1990–95. Editor, Laboratory Animals, 1967–82. Lab. Animal Sci. Assoc. Award, 1994. *Publications:* editor of books and author of articles chiefly on the law relating to and the effective use and proper care of laboratory animals. *Recreations:* music, local history, talking, limited gardening. *Address:* 21 Holyrood Road, New Barnet, Herts EN5 1DQ. *T:* 0181–449 3692. *Clubs:* Athenæum, Royal Society of Medicine.

O'DONOVAN, Rev. Canon Oliver Michael Timothy, DPhil; Regius Professor of Moral and Pastoral Theology, University of Oxford, since 1982; Canon of Christ Church, Oxford, since 1982; *b* 28 June 1945; *s* of Michael and Joan M. O'Donovan; *m* 1978, Joan Elizabeth Lockwood; two *s. Educ:* University Coll. Sch., Hampstead; Balliol Coll., Oxford (MA, DPhil); Wycliffe Hall, Oxford; Princeton Univ. Ordained deacon 1972, priest 1973, dio. of Oxford. Tutor, Wycliffe Hall, Oxford, 1972–77; Prof. of Systematic Theology, Wycliffe Coll., Toronto, 1977–82. Member: C of E Bd for Social Responsibility, 1976–77, 1982–85; ARCIC, 1985–90; Anglican-Orthodox Jt Doctrinal Discussions, 1982–84. Hulsean Lectr, Cambridge Univ., 1993–94. *Publications:* The Problem of Self-Love in Saint Augustine, 1980; Begotten or Made?, 1984; Resurrection and Moral Order, 1986; On the Thirty Nine Articles, 1986; Peace and Certainty, 1989; contrib. Jl of Theol Studies, Jl of Religious Ethics, Ethique and Studies in Christian Ethics. *Address:* Christ Church, Oxford OX1 1DP.

O'DOWD, David Joseph, CBE 1995; QPM 1988; HM Inspector of Constabulary, since 1993; *b* 20 Feb. 1942; *s* of late Michael Joseph O'Dowd and Helen (*née* Merrin); *m* 1963, Carole Ann Watson; one *s* one *d. Educ:* Gartree High Sch.; Oadby, Leics; Univ. of Leicester (Dip. Social Studies); Open Univ. (BA); Univ. of Aston (MSc); FBI Nat. Acad., USA. Sgt, Inspector and Chief Inspector, CID, Leicester City Police, 1961–77; Supt, W Midlands Police, Coventry and Birmingham, 1977–84; Hd, Traffic Policing, Dir, Complaints and Discipline Investigation Bureau and Hd, Strategic Planning and Policy Analysis Unit, Metropolitan Police, 1984–86; Chief Constable, Northants Police, 1986–93. British Chief Constables' Rep., Nat. Exec. Inst., FBI Acad., Washington, 1988. Dir, police extended interview scheme, 1992–93. Vis. Teaching Fellow, Mgt Centre, Univ. of Aston, Birmingham, 1988. Fellow, Nene Coll., Northants, 1993. CIMgt 1988. *Recreations:* golf, gardening. *Address:* Block B2, The Westbrook Centre, Milton Road, Cambridge CB4 1YG. *T:* Cambridge (01223) 467115. *Clubs:* Royal Automobile; Northamptonshire County Golf (Church Brampton, Northants).

O'DRISCOLL, Most Rev. Percival Richard; *see* Huron, Archbishop of.

OEHLERS, Maj.-Gen. Gordon Richard, CB 1987; Director, Corps of Commissionaires, since 1994; *b* 19 April 1933; *s* of late Dr Roderic Clarke Oehlers and Hazel Ethne Oehlers (*née* Van Geyzel); *m* 1956, Doreen, (Rosie), Gallant; one *s* one *d. Educ:* St Andrews School, Singapore. CEng, FIEE. Commissioned Royal Corps of Signals, 1958; UK and Middle East, 1958–64; Adjutant, 4th Div. Signals Regt, 1964–66; Instructor, School of Signals, 1966–68; OC 7th Armd Bde HQ and Signals Sqdn, 1968–70; GSO2 (Weapons), 1970–72; CO 7th Signal Regt, 1973–76; Commander Corps Royal Signals, 1st (British) Corps, 1977–79; Dir, Op. Requirements 4 (Army), 1979–84; ACDS (Comd Control, Communications and Inf. Systems), 1984–87. Dir of Security and Investigation, British Telecom, 1987–94. Col Comdt, RCS, 1987–93; Hon. Col 31st (Greater London) Signal Regt (Volunteers), 1988–94. Chm., Royal Signals Instn, 1990–93. Pres., British Wireless Dinner Club, 1986–87. *Recreations:* interested in all games esp. badminton (Captain Warwicks County Badminton Team, 1954–56), lawn tennis (Chm., Army Lawn Tennis Assoc., 1980–86). *Address:* c/o National Westminster Bank, 4 High Street, Petersfield, Hants GU32 3JF.

OESTERHELT, Dr Jürgen; Ambassador of Germany to the Court of St James's, since 1995; *b* 19 Aug. 1935; *s* of Dr Egon Oesterhelt and Trude (*née* Pfohl); *m* 1964, Katharina Galeiski; one *s* one *d. Educ:* Munich Univ. (LLD 1959); State Bar Exam. 1962; Columbia Univ., NY (Master of Comparative Law 1963). Internat. lawyer in Paris, 1963–64; joined German Diplomatic Service, 1964; Moscow, 1965–66, UN, NY, 1967–71; Sofia, 1971–74; Foreign Office, 1974–77; Athens, 1977–80; German Foreign Office: Hd of Div., Legal Dept, 1980–85; Dir, Political Dept, 1985–86; Dir Gen., Legal Dept and Legal Advr to Foreign Minister, 1986–92; Ambassador to Turkey, 1992–95. Cross of Order of Merit (Germany), 1988; Comdr's Cross, Order of Phoenix (Greece), 1982; Comdr's Cross, Order of White Rose (Finland), 1989; Grand Cross 2nd Cl., Order of Merit (Austria), 1990. *Recreations:* sport (ski-ing, tennis), music. *Address:* German Embassy, 23 Belgrave Square, SW1X 8PZ. *T:* 0171–235 5033, 0171–824 1301.

OESTREICHER, Rev. Canon Paul; Director of the International Ministry of Coventry Cathedral, since 1986; Canon Residentiary of Coventry Cathedral, since 1986; Member of the Society of Friends (Quakers), since 1982; journalist; *b* Germany, 29 Sept. 1931; *s* of Paul Oestreicher and Emma (*née* Schnaus); *m* 1958, Lore Feind; two *s* two *d. Educ:* King's High Sch., Dunedin; Otago and Victoria Univs, NZ; Lincoln Theol College. BA Mod. Langs Otago 1953; MA Hons Polit. Sci. Victoria 1955. Ordained 1959. Fled to NZ with refugee parents, 1939; returned to Europe, 1955. Humboldt Res. Fellow, Bonn Univ., 1955–56, Free Univ. of Berlin, 1992–93; fraternal worker with German Lutheran Church at Rüsselsheim, trng in problems of industrial soc. (Opel, Gen. Motors), 1958–59; Curate, Dalston, E London, 1959–61; Producer, Relig. Dept, BBC Radio, 1961–64; Assoc. Sec., Dept of Internat. Affairs, Brit. Council of Churches with special resp. for East-West Relations, 1964–69; Vicar, Church of the Ascension, Blackheath, 1968–81; Asst Gen. Sec. and Sec. for Internat. Affairs, BCC, 1981–86; Dir of (Lay) Trng, Dio. Southwark, 1969–72; Hon. Chaplain to Bp of Southwark, 1975–81; Public Preacher in Dio. Southwark, 1981–86; Hon. Canon of Southwark Cathedral, 1978–83, Canon Emeritus 1983–86. Mem. Gen. Synod of C of E, 1970–86. Member: Brit. Council of Churches working parties on Southern Africa and Eastern Europe; Anglican Pacifist Fellowship (sometime exec. mem.), 1960–; Exec. Mem., Christian Concern for Southern Africa, 1978–81; Chm., of Trustees, Christian Inst. (of Southern Africa) Fund, 1984–95; Chm., British Section, Amnesty International, 1974–79. Mem. Council, Keston Coll. (Centre for the Study of Religion and Communism), 1976–82. Vice-Chm., Campaign for Nuclear Disarmament, 1980–81, Vice-Pres. 1983–; Mem. Alternative Defence Commn, 1981–87; Vice-Chm., Ecumenical Commn for Church and Society in W Europe (Brussels), 1982–86. Shelley Lectr, Radio NZ, 1987. Hon. DLitt Coventry Polytechnic, 1991. Editor, Critic (Otago Univ. newspaper), 1952–53; subseq. free-lance journalist and broadcaster. *Publications:* (ed English edn) Helmut Gollwitzer, The Demands of Freedom, 1965; (trans.) H. J. Schultz, Conversion to the World, 1967; (ed, with J. Klugmann) What Kind of Revolution: A Christian-Communist Dialogue, 1968; (ed) The Christian Marxist Dialogue, 1969; (jtly) The Church and the Bomb, 1983; The Double Cross, 1986. *Address:* Coventry Cathedral Office, 7 Priory Row, Coventry, W Midlands CV1 5ES. *T:* Coventry (01203) 227597, *Fax:* (01203) 631448; 20 Styvechale Avenue, Coventry CV5 6DX. *T:* Coventry (01203) 673704.

O'FERRALL, Very Rev. Basil Arthur, CB 1979; MA; Dean of Jersey, and Rector of St Helier, Jersey, 1985–93; Hon. Canon of Winchester, 1986–93, now Emeritus; *b* 25 Aug. 1924; *s* of Basil James and Mabel Violet O'Ferrall, Dublin; *m* 1952, Joyce Forbes (*née* Taylor); one *s* two *d. Educ:* St Patrick's Cathedral Gram. Sch., Dublin; Trinity Coll., Dublin (BA 1948, MA 1966). Curate Assistant, St Patrick's, Coleraine, 1948; Chaplain RN, 1951; served: HMS Victory, 1951; Ganges, 1952; Gambia, 1952–54; Curlew, 1955; Daedalus, 1956; Amphibious Warfare Sqdn, 1956–58; HMS Adamant, 1958–60; 40 Commando, RM, 1960–62; RN Hosp., Bighi, 1962; HMS Victorious, 1963–64; Condor, 1964–66; Maidstone, 1966–68; St Vincent, 1968; Commando Training Centre, RM, 1969–71; HM Naval Base, Portsmouth, 1971–74; CTC, RM, 1975; Chaplain of the Fleet and Archdeacon of the Royal Navy, 1975–80; Vicar of Ranworth wih Panxworth and Woodbastwick (Norwich) and Bishop's Chaplain for the Broads, 1980–85; Chaplain to the Queen, 1980–85. Hon. Canon of Gibraltar, 1977–80. QHC 1975–80. Mem., Gen. Synod of C of E, 1990–93. *Recreations:* sailing, ornithology. *Address:* The Stone House, Barrack Square, Winchelsea, East Sussex TN36 4EG. *T:* Rye (01797) 223458.

O'FERRALL, Patrick Charles Kenneth, OBE 1989; Chairman, Lloyd's Register of Shipping, since 1993 (Deputy Chairman, 1991–93); *b* 27 May 1934; *s* of late Rev. Kenneth John Spence O'Ferrall and Isoult May O'Ferrall; *m* 1960, Mary Dorothea, 4th *d* of late Maj. C. E. Lugard and Mrs K. I. B. Lugard; one *s* two *d*. *Educ:* Winchester Coll.; New Coll., Oxford (BA Lit.Hum. 1958; MA); Harvard Business Sch. (AMP 1983). Nat. Service, 1952–54, 2nd Lieut, Royal Fusiliers. Iraq Petroleum and associated cos, 1958–70; BP, 1971–73; Total CFP Paris (Total Moyen Orient), 1974–77; Total Oil Marine, London: Commercial Manager, 1977–82; Dir, Gas Gathering Pipelines (N Sea) Ltd, 1977–78; Project Co-ordination Manager, Alwyn N, 1983–85; Projects Co-ordination Manager, 1985–90. Mem., Offshore Industry Adv. Bd, 1992–94. Chm., City of London Outward Bound Assoc., 1993. Master, Coachmakers' and Coach Harness Makers' Co., 1993–94. FRSA 1993; CIMgt 1994. Lay Reader, 1961–. *Recreations:* music (playing violin and singing), tennis, wine, crosswords, travel. *Address:* Lloyd's Register of Shipping, 71 Fenchurch Street, EC3M 4BS. *T:* 0171–709 9166; Ashstead Farmhouse, Ashstead Lane, Godalming, Surrey GU7 1SU. *T:* Godalming (01483) 417601. *Club:* MCC.

OFFALY, Earl of; Thomas FitzGerald; *b* 12 Jan. 1974; *s* of Marquess of Kildare, *qv*.

OFFER, Ven. Clifford Jocelyn; Archdeacon of Norwich and Canon Residentiary of Norwich Cathedral, since 1994; *b* 10 Aug. 1943; *s* of late Rev. Canon Clifford Jesse Offer and Jocelyn Mary Offer; *m* 1980, Dr Catherine Mary Lloyd; two *d*. *Educ:* King's Sch., Canterbury; Exeter Univ. (BA 1967); Westcott House, Cambridge. Ordained deacon, 1969, priest, 1970; Curate, St Peter and St Paul, Bromley, 1969–74; Team Vicar, Southampton City Centre, 1974–83; Team Rector, Hitchin, 1983–94. *Publication:* King Offa in Hitchin, 1992. *Recreations:* collecting naval buttons, ship-modelling, growing chrysanthemums. *Address:* 26 Cathedral Close, Norwich, Norfolk NR1 4DZ. *T:* Norwich (01603) 620375.

OFFORD, Albert Cyril, DSc London; PhD Cantab; FRS 1952; FRSE; Emeritus Professor of Mathematics, University of London; Professor, 1966–73, Hon. Fellow, 1978, London School of Economics and Political Science; *b* 9 June 1906; *s* of Albert Edwin and Hester Louise Offord; *m* 1945, Marguerite Yvonne Pickard; one *d*. *Educ:* Hackney Downs School, London; University Coll. London (Fellow, 1969); St John's Coll., Cambridge. Fellow of St John's Coll., Cambridge, 1937–40; Lectr, UC N Wales, Bangor, 1940–41; Lectr, King's Coll., Newcastle upon Tyne, 1941–45; Professor: King's College, Newcastle upon Tyne, 1945–48; Birkbeck Coll., Univ. of London, 1948–66. *Publications:* papers in various mathematical journals. *Recreation:* early, especially Renaissance, music. *Address:* 24A Norham Gardens, Oxford OX2 6QD. *T:* Oxford (01865) 513703.

O'FLAHERTY, Prof. Coleman Anthony; writer; Deputy Vice-Chancellor, University of Tasmania, Australia, 1991–93; *b* 8 Feb. 1933; *s* of Michael and Agnes O'Flaherty; *m* 1957, Nuala Rose Silke. *Educ:* Nat. Univ. of Ireland (BE); Iowa State Univ. (MS, PhD). FICE; FIE(Aust); FIHT; FCIT. Engineer: Galway Co. Council, Ireland, 1954–55; Canadian Pacific Railway Co., Montreal, 1955–56; M. W. Kellogg Co., USA, 1956–57; Asst Prof., Iowa State Univ., 1957–62; Leeds University: Lectr, 1962–66; Prof. of Transport Engineering, Inst. for Transport Studies and Dept of Civil Engineering, 1966–74; First Asst Comr (Engineering), Nat. Capital Develt Commn, Canberra, 1974–78; Dir and Principal, Tasmanian Coll. of Advanced Educn, subseq. Tasmanian State Inst. of Technology, 1978–90. Vis. Prof., Univ. of Melbourne, 1973. Hon. LLD Tasmania, 1994. *Publications:* Highways, 1967, 2nd edn 1974, vol. I of 3rd edn (Traffic Planning and Engineering), 1986, vol. II of 3rd edn (Highway Engineering), 1988; (jtly) Passenger Conveyors, 1972; (jtly) Introduction to Hovercraft and Hoverports, 1975; contribs to professional jls. *Recreation:* walking. *Address:* 22 Beach Road, Legana, Tasmania 7277, Australia. *T* and *Fax:* (03) 301990. *Club:* Launceston.

O'FLYNN, Rt. Hon. Francis Duncan, (Frank), PC 1987; QC 1968; Chairman, Community Trust, Trust Bank, Wellington, 1988–94 (Director, Trust Bank, 1988–91); *b* 24 Oct. 1918; *s* of Hon. Francis E. O'Flynn, MLC; *m* 1942, Sylvia Elizabeth Hefford; one *s* three *d*. *Educ:* Christchurch Boys' High School; Victoria University of Wellington (BA, LLM). Flight Lieut, RNZAF, 1942–46; Flying Instructor, NZ and 6 Flying Boat Sqdn, Pacific. Barrister and Solicitor, 1948; in practice on own account, 1954–78. MP (Lab): Kapiti, 1972–75; Island Bay, 1978–87. Minister of State and of Defence, NZ, 1984–87. Member: Otaki Borough Council, 1968–71; Wellington City Council, 1977–83. Mem. Council, Wellington District Law Soc., 1970–74. *Recreation:* reading. *Address:* 15 Rosetta Road, Raumati South, Wellington, New Zealand. *T:* (4) 2986631.

of MAR, family name of **Countess of Mar.**

OGATA, Prof. Sadako; United Nations High Commissioner for Refugees, since 1991; *b* 1927; *m*. Director, Inst. of Internat. Relations, Sophia Univ., Japan, later Dean, Faculty of Foreign Studies, to 1990; Minister, Japan Mission to Unicef, 1976–78 (Chm. Exec. Bd); Japanese Rep. on UN Commn on Human Rights, 1982–85. *Address:* United Nations High Commissioner for Refugees, Casa Postale 2500, 1211 Genève 2 dépôt, Switzerland.

OGDEN, Sir (Edward) Michael, Kt 1989; QC 1968; FCIArb; Barrister since 1950; a Recorder (formerly Recorder of Hastings), since 1971; *b* 9 Apr. 1926; *er s* of late Edward Cannon Ogden and Daisy (*née* Paris); *m* 1951, Joan Kathleen, *er d* of late Pius Charles Brodrick and Kathleen (*née* Moran); two *s* two *d*. *Educ:* Downside Sch.; Jesus Coll., Cambridge (MA). FCIArb 1990. Served in RAC (Royal Glos Hussars and 16th/5th Lancers), 1944–47 (Capt.); Inns of Court Regt (TA) 1950–56. Jesus Coll., Cambridge, 1948–49; called to Bar, Lincoln's Inn, 1950; Bencher, 1977. Mem. Bar Council, 1960–64, 1966–70, 1971–78 (responsible for fee negotiations, 1968–72, Treas., 1972–74, Chm., Internat. Relns Cttee, 1974–75); Mem. Senate of the Inns of Court, 1966–70, 1972–78. Leader, SE Circuit, 1975–78. Member: Council of Union Internationale des Avocats, 1962–83; Council of Legal Educn, 1969–74; Council, Internat. Bar Assoc., 1983–87. Chairman: Criminal Injuries Compensation Bd, 1975–89 (Mem., 1968–89); Inter-Professional Wkg Party publishing Actuarial Tables for Personal Injury and Fatal Accident Cases 1982–84, 1992–94 (published 1984, 2nd edn 1994); Disciplinary Appeal Cttee, ICAEW, 1993–; Mem., Lord Chancellor's Adv. on Legal Education, 1972–74. Dir, Internat. Assoc. of Crime Victim Compensation Bds, 1978–89 (Co-Chm. 1983–87). The Independent Assessor for Home Sec. of compensation for miscarriages of justice, 1978–89, and for Minister of Defence, 1986–89. Pres., Sea Fish Licence Tribunal, 1993–94. *Address:* 2 Crown Office Row, Temple, EC4Y 7HJ. *T:* 0171–353 9337. *Club:* Cavalry and Guards.

OGDEN, Eric; *b* 23 Aug. 1923; *s* of Robert and Jane Lillian Ogden, Rhodes, Co. Lancaster; *m*; one *s*; *m* Marjorie (*née* Smith); two *s* two step *d*. *Educ:* Queen Elizabeth's Grammar School, Middleton, Lancs; Leigh Tech. Coll.; Wigan Mining and Tech. Coll. Merchant Service, 1942–46. Textiles, 1946–52; NCB, 1952–64. Mem., Nat. Union of Mineworkers. Councillor, Borough of Middleton, 1958–65. NUM sponsored candidate, West Derby, Liverpool, 1962. MP (Lab 1964–81, SDP 1981–83) Liverpool, Derby W, 1964–83; contested (SDP) Liverpool, Derby W, 1983. Dir, Ogden's, Fotografica & Fulcrum Ltd. Mem., Royal Mail Stamps Adv. Cttee. Chairman: Falkland Islands Assoc., 1983–87; UK Falkland Islands Cttee, 1983–88 (Mem., 1982–); Vice-Pres., Tristan da Cunha Assoc. FRGS 1987. *Recreations:* Central European and Balkan affairs, photography, motoring, heraldry, surviving. *Club:* Europe House.

OGDEN, Sir Michael; *see* Ogden, Sir E. M.

OGILVIE, Sir Alec (Drummond), Kt 1965; Chairman, Powell Duffryn Ltd, 1969–78 (Deputy Chairman, 1967–69); *b* 17 May 1913; *s* of late Sir George Drummond Ogilvie, KCIE, CSI; *m* 1945, Lesley Constance, *d* of E. B. Woollan; two *s*. *Educ:* Cheltenham College. Served War of 1939–45; 2/2nd Gurkha Rifles (Indian Army), 1940–45; Captain 1941; PoW, Singapore, 1942–45. Joined Andrew Yule & Co. Ltd, Calcutta, 1935, Man. Dir, 1956, and Chm., 1962–65. Director: Westinghouse Brake & Signal Co. Ltd, 1966–79; Lindustries Ltd, 1973–79; J. Lyons & Co. Ltd, 1977–78. Pres., Bengal Chamber of Commerce and Industry, 1964–65; Pres., Associated Chambers of Commerce and Industry of India, 1964–65. Member: Council, King Edward VII Hosp. for Officers, 1967–95 (Vice-Pres., 1979–95); Council, Cheltenham Coll., 1973–85 (Dep. Pres., 1983–85). *Recreations:* golf, walking. *Clubs:* Oriental, MCC; Bengal (Calcutta).

OGILVIE, Dr Bridget Margaret; Director, Wellcome Trust, since 1991; *b* 24 March 1938; *er d* of late John Mylne Ogilvie and Margaret Beryl (*née* McRae). *Educ:* New England Girls' Sch., Armidale, NSW; Univ. of New England, Armidale (BRurSc 1960; Distinguished Alumni Award, 1994). PhD 1964, ScD 1981, Cambridge. FIBiol 1985. Parasitology Div., Nat. Inst. for Med. Res., London, 1963–81; Ian McMaster Fellow, CSIRO Div. of Animal Health, Australia, 1971–72; with Wellcome Trust, 1979–: Co-ordinator, Tropical Med. Prog., 1979–81; Dep. Sec. and Asst Dir, 1981–84; Dep. Dir, Science, 1984–89; Dir, Science Progs, 1989–91. Dir, Lloyds Bank, 1995–. Vis. Prof., Dept of Biology, Imperial Coll., London, 1985–92. Member: Council for Science and Technol., 1993–; Commonwealth Scholarship Commn, 1993–. Trustee, Sci. Mus., London, 1992–. Hon. Member: British Soc. for Parasitology, 1990; Amer. Soc. of Parasitologists, 1992; Hon. MRCP 1992; Hon. ARCVS 1993. Hon. Fellow: UCL, 1993; Girton Coll., Cambridge, 1993; Hon. FRVC, 1994. Hon. DSc: Nottingham, Salford, Westminster, 1994; Glasgow, Bristol, ANU, 1995. Lloyd of Kilgerran Prize, 1994. *Publications:* contrib. scientific papers to parasitological and immunological jls. *Recreations:* the company of friends, looking at landscapes, music, gardening. *Address:* The Wellcome Trust, 183 Euston Road, NW1 2BE. *T:* 0171–611 8888. *Club:* Queen's (Sydney).

OGILVIE-GRANT, family name of **Earl of Seafield.**

OGILVIE-LAING of Kinkell, Gerald, NDD; FRBS 1993 (ARBS 1987); sculptor; *b* 11 Feb. 1936; *s* of Gerald Francis Laing and Enid Moody (*née* Foster), and *g s* of Capt. Gerald Ogilvie Laing; adopted name of Ogilvie-Laing by Deed Poll, 1968; *m* 1st, 1962, Jenifer Anne Redway; one *d*; 2nd, 1969, Galina Vassilovna Golikova; two *s*; 3rd, 1988, Adaline Havemeyer Frelinghuysen; two *s*. *Educ:* Berkhamsted Sch.; RMA, Sandhurst; St Martin's Sch. of Art, London (NDD) 1964). Served Royal Northumberland Fusiliers, 1955–60, resigned; lived in NYC, 1964–69; Pop painting, 1962–65, abstract sculpture, 1965–69; Artist in Residence, Aspen Inst., 1966; restored Kinkell Castle, Scotland, 1969–70 (Civic Trust Award, 1971); established Tapestry Workshop, 1970–74; changed to figurative sculpture, 1973. Vis. Prof. of Painting and Sculpture, Univ. of New Mexico, 1976–77; Prof. of Sculpture, Columbia Univ., 1986–87. Installed: Callanish sculpture, Strathclyde Univ., 1971; Frieze of Wise and Foolish Virgins, Edinburgh, 1979; Fountain of Sabrina, Bristol, 1980; Conan Doyle Meml, and Axis Mundi, Edinburgh, 1991; Bank station Dragons, 1995; exhibits frequently; work in many public and private collections worldwide; divides time between Scotland and New York. Member: Art Cttee, Scottish Arts Council, 1978–80; Royal Fine Art Commn for Scotland, 1987–95. Chm., Black Isle Civic Trust, 1991–93. *Publication:* Kinkell—the Reconstruction of a Scottish castle, 1974, 2nd edn 1984. *Address:* Kinkell Castle, Ross and Cromarty IV7 8AT. *T:* Dingwall (01349) 861485; 901 Lexington Avenue, New York, NY 10021, USA. *T:* (212) 7726268. *Club:* Chelsea Arts.

OGILVIE THOMPSON, Julian; Chairman, Anglo American Corporation of SA Ltd, since 1990 (Deputy Chairman, 1983–90); Chairman, De Beers Consolidated Mines Ltd, since 1985 (Deputy Chairman, 1982–85); *b* 27 Jan. 1934; *s* of late Hon. N. Ogilvie Thompson, formerly Chief Justice of S Africa, and of Eve Ogilvie Thompson; *m* 1956, Hon. Tessa Mary Brand, *yr surv. d* of 4th Viscount Hampden, CMG and Leila, Viscountess Hampden; two *s* two *d*. *Educ:* Diocesan Coll., Rondebosch; Univ. of Cape Town; Worcester Coll., Oxford. MA. Diocesan Coll. Rhodes Scholar, 1953. Joined Anglo American Corp. of SA Ltd, 1956; Dir, 1970; Exec. Dir, 1971–82; Chairman: Anglo American Gold Investment Co. Ltd, 1976–90; Minorco SA (formerly Minerals and Resources Corp. Ltd), 1982–; Vice Chairman: First Nat. Bank Ltd, 1977–90; Urban Foundn, 1986–. Hon. LLD Rhodes, 1986. Comdr, Order of the Crown (Belgium), 1993. *Recreations:* shooting, fishing, golf. *Address:* Froome, Froome Street, Athol Extension 3, Sandton, Transvaal, S Africa. *T:* (11) 8843925. *Clubs:* White's; Rand (Johannesburg); Kimberley (Cape Province); The Brook (NY).

See also Baroness Dacre.

OGILVY, family name of **Earl of Airlie.**

OGILVY, Lord; David John Ogilvy; Managing Director, Richard L. Feigen UK Ltd, Art Dealers; *b* 9 March 1958; *s* and *heir* of 13th Earl of Airlie, *qv*; *m* 1st, 1981, Hon. Geraldine Harmsworth (marr. diss. 1991), *d* of Viscount Rothermere, *qv*; one *d*; 2nd, 1991, Tarka Kings; one *s*. *Educ:* Eton and Oxford (MA). *Heir:* *s* Master of Ogilvy, *qv*. *Address:* Airlie Castle, Kirriemuir, Angus DD8 5NG.

OGILVY, Master of; David Huxley Ogilvy; *b* 11 Dec. 1991; *s* and *heir* of Lord Ogilvy, *qv*.

OGILVY, Hon. Sir Angus (James Bruce), KCVO 1989; *b* 14 Sept. 1928; *s* of 12th (*de facto* 9th) Earl of Airlie, KT, GCVO, MC and Lady Alexandra Marie Bridget Coke, *d* of 3rd Earl of Leicester, GCVO, CMG; *m* 1963, HRH Princess Alexandra of Kent; one *s* one *d*. *Educ:* Eton Coll.; Trinity Coll., Oxford (MA). Scots Guards, 1946–48; Mem., HM Body Guard for Scotland (The Royal Company of Archers). President: Imperial Cancer Res. Fund, 1964–94; Youth Clubs UK (formerly NAYC), 1969–89 (Chm. 1964–69); Carr-Gomm Soc., 1983–; Patron: Arthritis Care (formerly British Rheumatism and Arthritis Soc.), 1978– (Chm. 1963–69; Pres., 1969–78); Scottish Wildlife Trust, 1974–90 (Pres., 1969–74); Vice-Patron: Friends of the Elderly & Gentlefolk's Help, 1969– (Treasurer, 1952–63; Chm. 1963–69); Nat. Children's Homes, 1986–. Chm. Adv. Council, and Trustee, Prince's Youth Business Trust, 1986–; Trustee, Prince's Trust, 1993–; Mem. Adv. Council, Prince's Trusts, 1995–. Mem., Governing Council, Society for Promoting Christian Knowledge, 1984–. Trustee, Leeds Castle Foundn, 1975–. Director of various public cos. *Recreations:* architecture, reading, music. *Address:* Thatched House Lodge, Richmond, Surrey TW10 5HP. *T:* 0181–546 8833. *Club:* White's.

See also under Royal Family.

OGILVY, David Mackenzie, CBE 1967; Founder, Ogilvy and Mather, 1948, Chairman to 1973; Chairman, WPP Group, 1989–92; *b* 23 June 1911; *s* of Francis John Longley Ogilvy and Dorothy Fairfield; *m* 1973, Herta Lans; one *s*. *Educ:* Fettes College, Edinburgh;

Christ Church, Oxford (Scholar). British Security Coordination, 1942–45. Dir, NY Philharmonic, 1957–67. Chm., Utd Negro Coll. Fund, 1968. Mem. of Honor, WWF. Dr of letters (*hc*), Adelphi Univ., USA, 1977. Officier, l'Ordre des Arts et des Lettres (France), 1990. *Publications:* Confessions of an Advertising Man, 1963; Blood, Brains and Beer (autobiog.), 1978; Ogilvy On Advertising, 1983. *Recreation:* gardening. *Address:* Château de Touffou, 86300 Bonnes, France.

OGILVY, Sir Francis (Gilbert Arthur), 14th Bt *cr* 1626 (NS), of Inverquharity, Forfarshire; Chartered Surveyor; *b* 22 April 1969; *s* of Sir David John Wilfrid Ogilvy, 13th Bt and of Penelope Mary Ursula, *d* of Captain Arthur Lafone Frank Hills, OBE; *S* father, 1992. *Educ:* Edinburgh Acad.; Glenalmond; RAC, Cirencester (BSc Hons). ARICS. *Heir: cousin* Andrew John Ogilvy, *b* 23 April 1972. *Address:* Winton Cottage, Pencaitland, E Lothian EH34 5AT.

OGILVY-WEDDERBURN, Sir Andrew John Alexander, 13th and 7th Bt *cr* 1704 and 1803; *b* 4 Aug. 1952; *s* of Sir (John) Peter Ogilvy-Wedderburn, 12th and 6th Bt, and of Elizabeth Katharine, *e d* of late John A. Cox, Drumkilbo; *S* father, 1977; *m* 1984, Gillian Meade, *yr d* of Richard Adderley, Pickering, N Yorks; two *s* (twins) one *d* (and one *s* decd). *Educ:* Gordonstoun. *Heir: s* Peter Robert Alexander Ogilvy-Wedderburn, *b* 20 April 1987. *Address:* Silvie, Alyth, Perthshire PH11 8NA.

OGLESBY, Peter Rogerson, CB 1982; *b* 15 July 1922; *s* of late Leonard William Oglesby and late Jessie Oglesby (*née* Rogerson); *m* 1947, Doreen Hilda Hudson; three *d*. *Educ:* Woodhouse Grove Sch., Apperley Bridge. Clerical Officer, Admlty, 1939–47; Exec. Officer, Min. of Nat. Ins., 1947–56; Higher Exec. Officer, MPNI, 1956–62, Principal 1962–64; Principal Private Secretary: to Chancellor of Duchy of Lancaster, 1964–66; to Minister without Portfolio, 1966; to First Sec. of State, 1966–68; to Lord President, 1968; Asst Sec., Cabinet Office, 1968–70, Asst Sec., DHSS, 1970–73; Sec., Occupational Pensions Bd, 1973–74; Under Sec., 1974–79; Dep. Sec., 1979–82, DHSS. Dir, Regency Final Gp, 1983–91. *Address:* 41 Draycot Road, Wanstead, E11 2NX. *T:* 0181–989 5526.

OGLEY, William David; Deputy Controller and Director of Resources, Audit Commission; *b* 26 May 1955; *s* of Thomas William and Olive Ogley; *m* 1976, Anne Dolores Walker; one *d*. *Educ:* Manchester Univ. (BA Hons Physics and Psych.); CIPFA (prize winner). Derbyshire CC, 1976–83 (to Principal Accountant, 1980–83); Group Accountant, Oxfordshire CC, 1983–85; Hertfordshire County Council: Sen. Asst. County Treasurer, 1985–88 (Educn and Social Services); Dep. County Treasurer, 1988–90; Dir, Inf. Systems, 1990–91; Dir of Finance, 1991–93. Member: Bd, Hertford Regl Coll.; Audit Panel, Univ. of Hertfordshire. *Recreations:* tennis, gardening, sailing, family, reading. *Address:* (office) 1 Vincent Square, SW1P 2PN.

OGMORE, 2nd Baron *cr* 1950, of Bridgend; **Gwilym Rees Rees-Williams;** *b* 5 May 1931; *er s* of 1st Baron Ogmore, PC, TD, and of Constance, *er d* of W. R. Wills; *S* father, 1976; *m* 1967, Gillian Mavis, *d* of M. K. Slack; two *d*. *Educ:* Mill Hill School. *Heir: b* Hon. Morgan Rees-Williams [*b* 19 Dec. 1937; *m* 1st, 1964, Patricia (marr. diss. 1970), *o d* of C. Paris Jones; 2nd, 1972, Roberta (marr. diss. 1976), *d* of Captain Alec Cunningham-Reid, DFC; 3rd, 1990, Beata, *o d* of Z. Solski; two *s*]. *Address:* House of Lords, SW1A 0PW.

OGNALL, Sir Harry Henry, Kt 1986; **Hon. Mr Justice Ognall;** a Judge of the High Court of Justice, Queen's Bench Division, since 1986; *b* 9 Jan. 1934; *s* of Leo and Cecilia Ognall; *m* 1977, Elizabeth Young; two step *s* and two *s* one *d* of former marriage. *Educ:* Leeds Grammar Sch.; Lincoln Coll., Oxford (MA (Hons)); Univ. of Virginia, USA (LLM). Called to Bar (Gray's Inn), 1958; Bencher, 1983. Joined NE Circuit; a Recorder, 1972–86; QC 1973. Member: Criminal Injuries Compensation Bd, 1976; Planning Cttee, Senate of Inns of Court and Bar, 1980–83; Professional Conduct Cttee, 1985; Judicial Studies Bd (Chm., Criminal Cttee), 1986–89; Parole Bd, 1989–91 (Vice-Chm., 1990–91). Arbitrator, Motor Insurers' Bureau Agreement, 1979–85. *Recreations:* golf, music, travel. *Address:* Royal Courts of Justice, Strand, WC2A 2LL. *Clubs:* Garrick; Ilkley Golf, Ilkley Bowling.

O'GRADY, Prof. Francis William, CBE 1984; TD 1970; MD, MSc; FRCP, FRCPath, FFPM; Hon. Consultant Microbiologist, Public Health Laboratory Service, since 1974; *b* 7 Nov. 1925; *s* of Francis Joseph O'Grady and Lilian Maud Hitchcock; *m* 1951, Madeleine Marie-Thérèse Becquart; three *d*. *Educ:* Middlesex Hosp. Med. Sch., London (BSc 1st Cl. Hons; MB, BS Hons; MSc; MD). FRCP 1976; FRCPath 1972; FFPM 1989. House Physician, Mddx and North Mddx Hosps, 1951; Asst Pathologist, Bland-Sutton Inst. of Pathol., Mddx Hosp., 1952–53, 1956–58 and 1961–62; Pathologist, RAMC, 1954–55, AER, 1956–72; Asst Prof. of Environmental Medicine, Johns Hopkins Univ., Baltimore, 1959–60; Reader, 1962–66, and Prof. of Bacteriology, 1967–74, Univ. of London; Bacteriologist, St Bartholomew's Hosp., 1962–74; Foundation Prof. of Microbiology, Univ. of Nottingham, 1974–88; Chief Scientist, DHSS, subseq. DoH, 1986–90. Mem., MRC, 1980–84, 1986–90; Chm., MRC Physiol Systems and Disorders Bd, 1980–82 (Mem., 1977–80; Mem., Grants Cttee, 1975–76); Chm., MRC Cttee on Hosp. Infection, 1977–80 (Mem., 1967–77). Member: Antibiotics Panel, Cttee on Med. Aspects of Food Policy, 1968–72; Sub-Cttee on Toxicity, Clin. Trials and Therapeutic Efficacy, 1971–75, and Sub-Cttee on Biol Substances, 1971–81, Cttee on Safety of Medicines; Jt Sub-Cttee on Antimicrobial Substances, Cttee on Safety of Medicines and Vet. Products Cttee, 1973–80; Cttee on Rev. of Medicines, 1975–81; Public Health Lab. Service Bd, 1980–86, 1993–; Nat. Biological Standards Bd, 1983–87. Hon. Consultant Microbiologist to the Army, 1982–91. William N. Creasy Vis. Prof. of Clin. Pharmacology, Duke Univ., NC, 1979. Erasmus Wilson Demonstrator, RCS, 1967; Foundn Lectr, Univ. of Hong Kong, 1974; Sydney Watson Smith Lectr, RCPE, 1975; Jacobson Vis. Lectr, Univ. of Newcastle upon Tyne, 1979; Berk Lectr, British Assoc. of Urol Surgeons, 1980; Garrod Lectr, British Soc. for Antimicrobial Chemotherapy, 1983; Jenner Lectr, St George's Hosp. Med. Sch., 1988. Pres. Council, British Jl of Exper. Pathol., 1980–91 (Mem., 1968–80); Mem. Editorial Boards: Jl of Med. Microbiol., 1970–75; Pathologie Biologie, 1973–78; British Jl of Clin. Pharmacol., 1974–84; Drugs, 1976–88; Gut, 1977–83; Jl of Infection, 1978–83; Revs of Infectious Diseases, 1979–88. *Publications:* Airborne Infection: transmission and control, 1968; Antibiotic and Chemotherapy, 1968, 6th edn 1992; (ed) Urinary Tract Infection, 1968; (ed) Microbial Perturbation of Host Defences, 1981; papers on clin. and exper. infection and on antimicrobial chemotherapy. *Recreation:* watching the vines grow. *Address:* Department of Physiology and Pharmacology, Medical School, Queen's Medical Centre, Nottingham NG7 2UH; des Bouysses, 46700 Puy-l'Evêque, Lot, France.

OGSTON, Alexander George, MA, DSc; FRS 1955; President of Trinity College, Oxford, 1970–78, Hon. Fellow 1978; Fellow, 1937, and Bedford Lecturer, 1950, Balliol College; *b* 30 January 1911; *s* of late Walter Henry Ogston and late Josephine Elizabeth Ogston (*née* Carter); *m* 1934, Elizabeth Wicksteed; one *s* three *d*. *Educ:* Eton College (King's Scholar); Balliol College, Oxford. DPhil 1936, MA 1937, DSc 1970. Demonstrator, Balliol College, 1933; Freedom Research Fellow, London Hospital, 1935; Departmental Demonstrator (Biochemistry), 1938; University Demonstrator, 1944, Oxford; Reader in Biochemistry, University of Oxford, 1955–59; Prof. of Physical Biochemistry, John Curtin School of Medical Research, ANU, 1959–70, Prof. Emeritus, 1970. Vis. Fellow, Inst. for Cancer Research, Philadelphia, Nov. 1978–Jan. 1979 and March–June 1981; Silver Jubilee Vis. Fellow, University House, ANU, March–Aug. 1979. Chairman, Editorial Bd, Biochemical Journal, 1955–59 (Member of Board, 1951–55). Chm., Central Council, Selly Oak Colleges, Birmingham, 1980–84 (Vice-Chm., 1976–80). Fellow, Australian Acad. of Science, 1962; Hon. Fellow: Balliol Coll., Oxford, 1969; Univ. of York, 1980; Selly Oak Colls, 1984; Hon. Mem. American Soc. of Biological Chemists, 1965; Hon. DMed Uppsala, 1977. Davy Medal, Royal Soc., 1986. *Publications:* scientific papers on physical chemistry and biochemistry. *Address:* 6 Dewsbury Terrace, York YO1 1HA.

OGSTON, Prof. Derek, CBE 1995; MD, PhD, DSc; FRCP; FRSE 1982; Professor of Medicine, since 1983, and Vice Principal, since 1987, University of Aberdeen; *b* 31 May 1932; *s* of Frederick John Ogston and Ellen Mary Ogston; *m* 1963, Cecilia Marie Clark; one *s* two *d*. *Educ:* King's Coll. Sch., Wimbledon; Univ. of Aberdeen (MA, MD, PhD, DSc). FRCP Edin 1973; FRCP 1977; FIBiol 1987. University of Aberdeen: Res. Fellow, 1959–62; Lectr in Medicine, 1962–69; Sen. Lectr in Med., 1969–75; Reader in Med., 1975–76; Regius Prof. of Physiology, 1977–83; Dean, Faculty of Medicine, 1984–87. MRC Trav. Fellow, 1967–68. Vice-Chm., Grampian Health Bd, 1993– (Mem., 1991–); Mem., GMC, 1984–94. Mem. Governing Body, Rowett Res. Inst., 1977–92. *Publications:* Physiology of Hemostasis, 1983; Antifibrinolytic Drugs, 1984; Venous Thrombosis, 1987; scientific papers on haemostasis. *Recreation:* home maintenance. *Address:* 64 Rubislaw Den South, Aberdeen AB2 6AX. *T:* Aberdeen (01224) 316587.

O'HAGAN, 4th Baron, *cr* 1870; **Charles Towneley Strachey;** *b* 6 Sept. 1945; *s* of Hon. Thomas Anthony Edward Towneley Strachey (*d* 1955; having assumed by deed poll, 1938, the additional Christian name of Towneley, and his mother's maiden name of Strachey, in lieu of his patronymic) and of Lady Mary (who *m* 1981, St John Gore, *qv*), *d* of 3rd Earl of Selborne, PC, CH; *S* grandfather, 1961; *m* 1st, 1967, Princess Tamara Imeretinsky (marr. diss. 1984); one *d*; 2nd, 1985, Mrs Mary Claire Parsons (*née* Roose-Francis); one *d*. *Educ:* Eton; (Exhibitioner) New College, Oxford. Page to HM the Queen, 1959–62. Independent Member, European Parliament, 1973–75; Junior Opposition Whip, House of Lords, 1977–79; MEP (C) Devon, 1979–94. *Heir: brother* Hon. Richard Towneley Strachey [*b* 29 Dec. 1950; *m* 1983, Sally Anne, *yr d* of Frederick Cecil Cross]. *Address:* The Old Rectory, Weare Giffard, Bideford, Devon EX39 4QP. *Clubs:* Beefsteak, Pratt's.

O'HAGAN, Desmond, CMG 1957; *b* 4 Mar. 1909; *s* of Captain Claud O'Hagan, Nyeri, Kenya and Eva O'Hagan (*née* Napier Magill)); *m* 1942, Pamela, *d* of Major A. H. Symes-Thompson, DSO, Kiambu, Kenya; one *s* two *d*. *Educ:* Wellington Coll.; Clare Coll., Cambridge. Entered Colonial Administrative Service, Kenya, 1931. Called to Bar, Inner Temple, 1935. Private Secretary to British Resident, Zanzibar, 1937; served with E African Forces in N Province, Kenya, 1940–42; Native Courts Adviser, 1948–51; Provincial Commissioner, Coast Province, Kenya, 1952–59; Chairman, Transport Licensing Authority, Tanganyika, 1959–63. *Recreations:* bridge, golf. *Address:* Kianjibbi, Kiambu, Kenya. *Clubs:* East India, Devonshire, Sports and Public Schools; Muthaiga, Nairobi (life mem.).

O'HALLORAN, Michael Joseph; Building and Construction Works Manager; *b* 20 Aug. 1933; British; *m* 1956, Stella Beatrice McDonald; three *d*. *Educ:* Clohanes National School, Eire; self-educated. Railway worker, 1948–63; building works manager, 1963–69; returned to building industry, 1983. MP (Lab 1969–81, SDP 1981–82, Ind. Lab 1983) Islington N, Oct. 1969–1983; contested (Ind. Lab) Islington N, 1983. *Recreation:* football. *Address:* 149 Cheam Road, Cheam, Surrey SM1 2BP. *Club:* Challoner.

O'HARA, Bill, JP; National Governor of the BBC for Northern Ireland, 1973–78; *b* 26 Feb. 1929; *s* of William P. O'Hara and Susanna Agnes O'Hara (*née* Gill); *m* 1953, Anne Marie Finn; two *s* two *d*. *Address:* Summer Cottage, 12 Raglan Road, Bangor, Co. Down, N Ireland BT20 3TL. *Clubs:* Royal Ulster Yacht, Royal Belfast Golf.

O'HARA, Air Vice-Marshal Derek Ive, CB 1981; Manager, Birch Grove Estate, since 1984; *b* 14 Feb. 1928; *s* of late William Edward O'Hara and Daisy Bathurst O'Hara (*née* Ive); *m* 1953, Angela Elizabeth (*née* Marchand); two *s* (one *d* decd). *Educ:* Ardingly Coll., Sussex; RAF Coll., Cranwell. Commnd RAF Coll., 1950; RAF Horsham St Faith and Tuddenham, 1950–54; Egypt, 1954–56; HQ Bomber Comd, 1956–59; Instructor, RAF Coll., 1959–61; RAF Staff Coll., Andover, 1961; Jt Planning HQ ME, Aden, 1962–64; OC Supply, RAF Finningley, 1964; Manchester Univ., 1965; OC Supply, 14 MU RAF Carlisle, 1966–68; Directing Staff, RAF Staff Coll., Andover, 1968–70; Comd of RAF Stafford, 1970–72; Dep. Dir, Supply Management, MoD Harrogate, 1972; RCDS, 1973; Air Commodore Supply and Movements, HQ Strike Comd, 1974–75; Dir, Engrg and Supply Policy, 1975–79; Dir Gen. of Supply, RAF, 1979–82. *Recreations:* sailing, fishing, gardening. *Club:* Royal Air Force.

O'HARA, Edward; MP (Lab) Knowsley South, since Sept. 1990; *b* 1 Oct. 1937; *s* of Robert Edward O'Hara and Clara O'Hara (*née* Davies); *m* 1962, Lillian Hopkins; two *s* one *d*. *Educ:* Magdalen Coll., Oxford (MA 1962); PGCE 1966, DipED (Adv.) 1970, London. Assistant Teacher: Perse Sch., Cambridge, 1962–65; Birkenhead Sch., 1966–70; Lectr and Principal Lectr, C. F. Mott Coll. of Educn, 1970–74; Principal Lectr and Sen. Tutor, Dean of Postgrad. Studies, City of Liverpool Coll. of Higher Educn, 1974–83; Head of Curriculum Studies, Sch. of Educn and Community Studies, Liverpool Polytechnic, 1983–90. Knowsley Borough Council: Mem., 1975–91; Mem., all Standing Cttees; Chm., Libraries and Arts, Finance, Youth, Educn and Econ. Develt and Planning Cttees. Mem., Educn and Planning, and Econ. Develt Cttees, AMA; Member: Bd of Management, NFER, 1986–90; European Assoc. of Teachers; Socialist Educn Assoc.; Hon. Mem. and Parly Advr, Assoc. of Chief Educn Social Workers; Member: Labour Movement in Europe; Communauté de Travail des Régions Européennes de Tradition Industrielle, 1989–90; Perm. Cttee of Assembly of European Regions, 1989–90. Member: Fabian Soc.; Bd of Management, Royal Liverpool Philharmonic Soc., 1987–90; Corresp. Mem., Foundn for Hellenic Culture. Trustee, Community Develt Foundn. Vice-Pres., TS Iron Duke, Huyton. *Recreations:* music (classical, jazz, folk, esp. Rembetiko), reading, theatre, travel, Greek language and culture. *Address:* 69 St Mary's Road, Huyton, Merseyside L36 5SR. *T:* 0151–489 8021. *Clubs:* Halewood Labour, Lyme Grove Labour (Knowsley).

O'HARA, Prof. Michael John, PhD; FRS 1981; FRSE 1969; Distinguished Research Professor, University of Wales College of Cardiff, since 1994; *b* 22 Feb. 1933; *s* of Michael Patrick O'Hara, OBE, and Winifred Dorothy O'Hara; *m* 1st, 1962, Janet Tibbits; one *s* two *d*; 2nd, 1977, Susan Howells; two *s* one *d*. *Educ:* Dulwich Coll. Prep. Sch.; Cranleigh; Peterhouse, Cambridge (MA, PhD). Asst, Lectr, Reader and Prof. (1971), Edinburgh Univ., 1958–78; Prof. of Geology, Univ. of Wales, Aberystwyth, 1978–93. Principal Investigator, NASA Lunar Science Prog., 1968–75; Prof. of Geology, Sultan Qaboos Univ., Oman, 1988–90. Sherman-Fairchild Vis. Scholar, Calif Inst. of Technology, 1984–85; Vis. Prof., Harvard Univ., 1986. Member: Council, NERC, 1986–88; UGC, 1987–89. Associate Mem., Geol Soc. of France. Murchison Medal, Geol Soc., 1983; Bowen Medal, Amer. Geophys. Union, 1984. *Publications:* numerous in learned jls. *Recreation:* mountaineering. *Address:* Department of Earth Sciences, University of Wales College of Cardiff, PO Box 914, Cardiff CF1 3YE. *T:* Cardiff (01222) 874830.

O'HIGGINS, Prof. Paul; Fellow, Christ's College, Cambridge, since 1959 (Vice-Master, 1992–95); Professor of Law, King's College London, 1987–92, now Emeritus; *b* 5 Oct. 1927; *s* of Richard Leo O'Higgins, MC, MRCVS and Elizabeth O'Higgins, MA (*née* Deane); *m* 1952, Rachel Elizabeth Bush; one *s* three *d*. *Educ:* St Ignatius' Coll., Galway; St Columba's Coll., Rathfarnham; Trinity Coll., Dublin (MA, LLB, LLD); MA, PhD, LLD Cantab. MRIA 1986. Called to the Bar, King's Inns, 1957, and Lincoln's Inn, 1959. University of Cambridge: Dir of Studies in Law, Peterhouse, 1960–74; Steward, Christ's Coll., 1964–68; Tutor for Advanced Students, Christ's, 1970–79; University Lectr, 1965–79; Reader in Labour Law, 1979–84; Regius Prof. of Laws, TCD, 1984–87 (Hon. Prof., 1992–). Co-founder, Cambridge Law Surgery, 1969. Lectr in Labour Law, Inns of Court Sch. of Law, 1976–84; Visiting Professor: Univ. of Kent at Canterbury, 1973–74; City Univ., 1992–. Mem. Bureau, European Inst. of Social Security, 1970–95; Mem., Staff Side Panel, Civil Service Arbitration Tribunal, 1972–84; Vice-Pres., Inst. of Shops, Health and Safety Acts Admin, 1973–; Chm., Irish Soc. for Labour Law, 1985–87. Patron, Cambridge Univ. Graduate Union, 1973–84; Trustee, Cambridge Union Soc., 1973–84; Vice-Pres., Haldane Soc., 1976–; Gov., British Inst. of Human Rights, 1988–; Vice-Pres., Inst. of Employment Rights, 1989–; Mem., Acad. of European Private Lawyers, 1994. Mem. Editl Bd, Bibliography of Nineteenth Century Legal Lit., 1991–. Hon. Mem., Grotian Soc., 1968. Gilbert Murray Prize (jt), 1968; Joseph L. Andrews Bibliographical Award, Amer. Assoc. of Law Libraries, 1987. Grand Consul honorifique du consulat de la Vinée de Bergerac, 1983. *Publications:* Bibliography of Periodical Literature relating to Irish Law, 1966, 2nd supp. 1983; (with B. A. Hepple) Public Employee Trade Unionism in the UK: the legal framework, 1971; (with B. A. Hepple) Employment Law, 1971, 4th edn 1981; Censorship in Britain, 1972; Workers' Rights, 1976, 2nd edn 1986; Cases and Materials on Civil Liberties, 1980; Bibliography of Irish Trials, 1986; (with A. D. Dubbins and J. Gennard) Fairness at Work: even-handed industrial relations, 1986; (with M. Partington) Bibliography of Social Security Law, 1986; (ed jtly) The Common Law Tradition: Essays in Irish Legal History, 1990; (ed jtly) Lessons from Northern Ireland, 1991; British and Irish Labour Law, 1979–88: a bibliography, 1993. *Recreations:* wine, talking and travelling, particularly in France and Italy. *Address:* Christ's College, Cambridge CB2 3BU. *T:* Cambridge (01223) 67641. *Club:* Royal Dublin Society (Dublin).

O'HIGGINS, Hon. Thomas Francis, SC (Ireland) 1954; a Judge of the European Court of Justice, 1985–92; *b* 23 July 1916; *e s* of Dr Thomas F. O'Higgins and Agnes McCarthy; *m* 1948, Thérese Keane; five *s* two *d*. *Educ:* St Mary's Coll., Rathmines, Clongowes Wood Coll.; University Coll., Dublin (BA); King's Inns, Dublin (BL). Called to Irish Bar, 1938; Bencher of King's Inns, 1967; Judge of High Court, 1973; Chief Justice of Ireland, 1974–85. Elected to Dail Eireann, 1948; Minister for Health, 1954; contested Presidency, 1966 and 1973. *Recreations:* fishing, golf. *Address:* Glenville Cottage, 75 Monkstown Road, Monkstown, Co. Dublin. *T:* 809119. *Clubs:* Stephen's Green (Dublin); Royal Irish Yacht.

OHLSON, Sir Brian (Eric Christopher), 3rd Bt *cr* 1920; money broker, retired; *b* 27 July 1936; *s* of Sir Eric James Ohlson, 2nd Bt, and of Marjorie Joan, *d* of late C. H. Roosmale-Cocq; *S* father, 1983. *Educ:* Harrow School; RMA Sandhurst. Commissioned into Coldstream Guards, 1956–61. Started money broking, 1961; *Recreations:* sport of kings, cricket, squash, bridge. *Heir: b* Peter Michael Ohlson [*b* 18 May 1939; *m* 1968, Sarah, *o d* of Maj.-Gen. Thomas Brodie, CB, CBE, DSO]. *Address:* 1 Courtfield Gardens, SW5 0PA. *Clubs:* MCC, Hurlingham, Cavalry and Guards.

OISTRAKH, Igor Davidovich; Soviet Violinist; *b* Odessa, 27 April 1931; *s* of late David Oistrakh. *Educ:* Music Sch. and State Conservatoire, Moscow. FRCM. Many foreign tours (USSR, Europe, the Americas, Japan); many gramophone recordings. 1st prize, Violin Competition, Budapest, 1949; 1st prize, Wieniawski Competition, Poznan, 1952; People's Artist of USSR, 1989. Pres., César Franck Soc., Liège; Hon. Pres., Russian Br., Europ. String Teachers Assoc.; Hon. Member: Beethoven Soc., Bonn; Ysaye Foundn, Liège. Mem. jury of major violin competitions; Igor Oistrakh internat. violin competition established Iserlohn, Germany.

OKA, Prof. Takeshi, PhD; FRS 1984; FRSC 1977; Professor of Chemistry, Astronomy and Astrophysics, since 1981, and Robert A. Millikan Distinguished Service Professor, since 1989, University of Chicago; *b* 10 June 1932; *s* of Shumpei and Chiyoko Oka; *m* 1960, Keiko Nukui; two *s* two *d*. *Educ:* University of Tokyo. BSc, PhD. Fellow, Japanese Soc. for Promotion of Science, 1960–63; National Research Council of Canada: Postdoctorate Fellow, 1963–65; Asst Research Physicist, 1965–68; Associate Research Physicist, 1968–71; Senior Research Physicist, 1971–75; Herzberg Inst. of Astrophysics, 1975–81. Centenary Lectr, Royal Soc., 1982; Chancellor's Distinguished Lectr, Univ. of California, 1985–86. Fellow, Amer. Acad. of Arts and Scis, 1987. Steacie Prize, Steacie Fund, NRSC, 1972; Earle K. Plyler Prize, Amer. Physical Soc., 1982. *Recreation:* running. *Address:* 1463 East Park Place, Chicago, IL 60637, USA. *T:* (312) 7525963.

O'KEEFE, John Harold; TV consultant; *b* 25 Dec. 1938; *s* of Terence Harold O'Keefe and Christian Frances (*née* Foot); *m* 1959, Valerie Anne Atkins; two *s* two *d*. *Educ:* Acton County Grammar School. Dir, Newspaper Publishers Assoc., 1974; Hd of Industrial Relations, 1974–81, Production Dir, Central London, 1981, Thames TV, 1982; Man. Dir, Limehouse Studios, 1982–86. *Address:* The White House, Dymock, Glos GL18 2AQ.

O'KEEFFE, (Peter) Laurence, CMG 1983; CVO 1974; HM Diplomatic Service, retired; *b* 9 July 1931; *s* of Richard O'Keeffe and Alice (*née* Chase); *m* 1954, Suzanne Marie Jousse; three *d*. *Educ:* St Francis Xavier's Coll., Liverpool; University Coll., Oxford (schol.). HM Customs and Excise, 1953–62; 2nd, later 1st Sec. (Economic), Bangkok, 1962–65; FO, 1965–68; 1st Sec. and Head of Chancery, Athens, 1968–72; Commercial Counsellor, Jakarta, 1972–75; Head of Hong Kong and Indian Ocean Dept, FCO, 1975–76; Dir-Gen., British Information Services, and Dep. Consul General (Information), New York, 1976–78; Counsellor, Nicosia, 1978–81, Research Associate, Inst. for the Study of Diplomacy, Georgetown Univ., Washington, DC, 1981–82; Ambassador to Senegal, 1982–85, and concurrently (non-resident) to Guinea, Guinea-Bissau, Mali, Mauritania and Cape Verde, 1982–85; Diplomatic Service Chm., CSSB, 1985–86; Head, British Delegn to CSCE Rev. Conf., Vienna, 1986–88; Ambassador to Czechoslovakia, 1988–91. *Publications:* (as Laurence Halley): Simultaneous Equations (novel), 1975; Ancient Affections, 1985; Abiding City (novel), 1986. *Recreation:* gardening. *Address:* Wylye Cottage, Great Wishford, Salisbury, Wilts SP2 0PD.

O'KELLY, Surgeon Rear-Adm. Francis Joseph, OBE 1965; Royal Navy, retired 1980; Occupational Health Consultant, Medical and Health Department, Government of Hong Kong, 1980–86; *b* 24 Dec. 1921; *s* of Francis John O'Kelly and Elizabeth Mary O'Kelly (*née* Rogan); *m* 1954, Winifred Mary Teresa Henry; one *s* three *d*. *Educ:* St Patrick's Coll., Cavan; University Coll., Dublin. MB, BCh 1945; FFCM, FFOM (RCPI), MFOM (RCPE); Hon. FACOM; DPH, DIH. Hosp. appts in Dublin, 1946–48; joined RN 1948; served with RM Commandos, Middle and Far East, 1948–52; HM Ships Unicorn, St Bride's Bay and Centaur, RNB Chatham and RN Air Station, Brawdy, 1952–63; Naval MOH appts, Far East Fleet, Scotland and NI Comd, Portsmouth and Chatham Comd, 1963–72; Dep. Dir, Health and Research, 1972–74; MO i/c RN Hosp. Gibraltar, 1974–77; Surgeon Rear-Adm. (Ships and Establishments), 1977–78; Surg. Rear-Adm. (Naval Hosps), 1978–80; QHP 1977–80. Adviser in Preventive and Industrial Medicine to Med. Dir Gen. (Naval), 1972–77, in Community Medicine, 1977–80. *Publications:* articles in med jls. *Recreations:* reading and travel. *Address:* Breffni, 38 Seamead, Stubbington, Fareham, Hants PO14 2NG.

O'KENNEDY, Michael E.; Senator, Irish Senate, 1965–69 and since 1993; *b* Nenagh, Co. Tipperary, 21 Feb. 1936; *s* of Éamonn and Helena O'Kennedy; *m* 1965, Breda, *d* of late Andrew Heavey and of Mary Heavey; one *s* two *d*. *Educ:* St Flannan's College, Ennis, Co. Clare; Univ. Coll., Dublin. MA 1957. Called to Irish Bar, 1961; Senior Counsel 1973. Mem., Oireachtas Select Constitutional Cttee, 1966. TD (FF) Tipperary N, 1969–80, 1982–93; Parly Sec. to Minister for Educn, 1970–72; Minister without Portfolio, Dec. 1972–Jan. 1973; Minister for Transport and Power, Jan.-March 1973; Opposition spokesman on Foreign Affairs (incl. Anglo-Irish Affairs), 1973–77; Minister for Foreign Affairs, 1977–79; Pres., Council of Ministers of the European Communities, July-Dec. 1979; Minister for Finance, 1979–81; opposition spokesman on finance, 1983–87; Minister for Agriculture and Food, 1987–92; Pres., Council of Agriculture Ministers, EC, Jan.–June 1990. Mem., Commn of the European Communities, 1981–82. Member: All-Party Cttee on Irish Relns, 1973–77; Dáil and Seanad Jt Cttee on Secondary Legislation of the European Communities, 1973–77; Anglo-Irish Parly Body, 1993–; Chm., Inter-Party Cttee on Implications of Irish Unity, 1972–73. *Address:* Gortlandroe, Nenagh, Co. Tipperary, Ireland.

OKEOVER, Sir Peter Ralph Leopold W.; *see* Walker-Okeover.

OKOGIE, Most Rev. Anthony Olubunmi; *see* Lagos, Archbishop of, (RC).

OKOTH, Rt. Rev. Yona; Archbishop of Uganda and Bishop of Kampala, 1984–94; *b* 15 April 1927; *s* of Nasanairi Owora and Tezira Akech; *m* Jessica Naome Okoth; four *s* five *d*. Bishop's clerk, 1947; Ordination Class, 1953–54 (certificate); deacon 1954, priest 1955; Parish Priest, Nagongera, 1956–60; St Augustine's Coll., Canterbury, 1963 (Diploma); Diocesan Treasurer, Mbale Diocese, 1961–65; Provincial Sec., Kampala, 1965–66; studies, Wycliffe Coll., Toronto Univ., 1966–68 (Dip. and LTh); Provincial Sec., Kampala, 1968–72; Diocesan Bishop of Bukedi, 1972–83. Hon. DD Wycliffe Coll., Toronto, 1978. *Recreation:* interest in farming. *Address:* c/o PO Box 255, Tororo, Uganda.

OKRI, Ben; writer; *b* 15 March 1959; *s* of Silver and Grace Okri. *Educ:* Univ. of Essex. Poetry Editor, West Africa, 1983–86; broadcaster and presenter, BBC, 1983–85; Fellow Commoner in Creative Arts, Trinity Coll., Cambridge, 1991–93. Mem., Soc. of Authors, 1986–. Crystal Award, World Econ. Forum, Switzerland, 1995. *Publications:* Flowers and Shadows, 1980; The Landscapes Within, 1982; Incidents at the Shrine, 1986 (Commonwealth Prize for Africa, 1987; Paris Review Aga Khan Prize for fiction, 1987); Stars of the New Curfew, 1988; The Famished Road, 1991 (Booker Prize, 1991; Premio Letterario Internazionale Chianti Ruffino-Antico Fattore, 1993; Premio Grinzane Cavour, 1994); An African Elegy, 1992; Songs of Enchantment, 1993; Astonishing the Gods, 1995; Birds of Heaven, 1995; A Way of Being Free, 1996. *Recreations:* music, chess, theatre, art, martial arts, good conversation, silence. *Address:* c/o Vintage, Random House, 20 Vauxhall Bridge Road, SW1V 2SA. *T:* 0171–973 9700, *Fax:* 0171–932 0077. *Club:* PEN International.

OLAGBEGI II, The Olowo of Owo, (Sir Olateru), Kt 1960; Oba Alaiyeluwa, Olagbegi II, Olowo of Owo, since 1941; Minister of State, Western Region (now Western Provinces) of Nigeria, 1952; President of the House of Chiefs, Western Region (now Western Provinces), 1965; *b* 1910; *s* of Oba Alaiyeluwa, Olagbegi I, Olowo of Owo; married; many *s* and *d* (some decd). *Educ:* Owo Government School. A Teacher in 1934; Treasury Clerk in Owo Native Administration, 1935–41. Queen's Medal, 1957. *Recreations:* lawn tennis, squash racquets. *Address:* PO Box 1, Afin Oba Olowo, Owo, Western Provinces of Nigeria. *T:* Owo 1.

OLANG', Most Rev. Festo Habakkuk; *b* 11 Nov. 1914; *m* 1937, Eseri D. Olang'; four *s* eight *d*. *Educ:* Alliance High School. Teacher, 1936–43; ordained 1945; consecrated Assistant Bishop of Mombasa in Namirembe Cathedral, by Archbishop of Canterbury, 1955; Bishop of Maseno, 1961; Bishop of Nairobi, 1970; Archbishop of Kenya, 1970–79. Hon. DD Univ. of the South Sewanee, USA. *Address:* PO Box 1, Maseno, Kenya.

OLAYAN, Suliman Saleh, Hon. KBE 1987; Founder and Chairman, The Olayan Group, since 1947; *b* 5 Nov. 1918; *s* of Saleh Olayan and Haya Al Ghanim; *m* 1974, Mary Perdikis; one *s* three *d*. *Educ:* Bahrain. Founding Chairman: Arab Commercial Enterprises, 1950–84; Nat. Gas Co., 1951–54; Saudi British Bank, 1978–89; Saudi Spanish Bank, 1979–84; Director: Al Khobar Power Co., 1950–54; Riyad Bank, 1963–78; Saudi Arabian Airlines, 1965–81; Mobil Corp., 1980–83; CS First Boston, 1988–. Member: Internat. Council of Morgan Guaranty Trust Co., 1979–90; Internat. Adv. Bd, Amer. Internat. Gp, 1982–; Adv. Bd, Energy Internat. NV, 1983–92. Chairman: Riyadh Chamber of Commerce and Industry, 1981–89; Council of Saudi Chambers of Commerce and Industry, 1984–87. Member: Internat. Industrial Conf., 1961–; Gp of Thirty, 1984–87; Bd, Inst. for Internat. Econs, 1987–; Internat. Council, INSEAD, 1991–. Mem., Rockefeller Univ. Council, 1974–87 (Alumnus Mem., 1987–). Founding Vice Chm., Handicapped Children's Assoc., Riyadh, 1983–89. Medal of Honour, Madrid Chamber of Commerce and Industry, 1985. Grand Cross, Order of Merit (Spain), 1984; Comdr First Class, Royal Order of Polar Star (Sweden), 1988. *Publications:* contribs on energy to Washington Qly. *Recreations:* swimming, reading, walking. *Address:* PO Box 8772, Riyadh, Saudi Arabia. *Clubs:* Royal Automobile; Equestrian (Riyadh); Knickerbocker (New York); Pacific Union, Bohemian (San Francisco).

OLDENBOURG-IDALIE, Zoë; Chevalier, Légion d'Honneur, 1980; Officier du Mérite des Arts et des Lettres, 1978; writer (as Zoë Oldenbourg); *b* 31 March 1916; *d* of Sergius Oldenbourg, writer and historian, and of Ada (*née* Starynkevitch); *m* 1948, Heinric Idalie; one *s* one *d*. *Educ:* Lycée Molière and Sorbonne, Paris. Prix Fémina, 1953. *Publications:* Argile et cendres, 1946 (The World is Not Enough, 1949); La Pierre angulaire, 1953 (The Cornerstone, 1954); Réveillés de la Vie, 1956 (The Awakened, trans. E. Hyams, 1957); Les Irréductibles, 1958 (The Chains of Love, 1959); Bûcher de Montségur, 1959 (Massacre at Montségur, 1962); Les Brûlés, 1961 (Destiny of Fire, trans. P. Green, 1961); Les Cités charnelles, 1961 (Cities of the Flesh, 1963); Les Croisades: un essai historique, 1963 (The Crusades, trans. Anne Carter, 1966); Catherine de Russie, 1965 (Catherine the Great, 1965); Saint Bernard, 1969; La Joie des pauvres, 1970 (The Heirs of the Kingdom, trans. Anne Carter, 1972); L'Epopée des cathédrales, 1973; Que vous a donc fait Israël?, 1974; Visages d'un autoportrait (autobiog.), 1977; La Joie-Souffrance, 1980; Le Procès du Rêve, 1982; Que nous est Hécube?, 1984; Les Amours égarées, 1987; Déguisements, 1989. *Recreation:* painting. *Address:* c/o Victor Gollancz Ltd, 14 Henrietta Street, WC2; 4 rue de Montmorency, 92100 Boulogne, France.

OLDENBURG, Richard Erik; Chairman, Sotheby's North America, since 1995; *b* 21 Sept. 1933; *s* of Gösta Oldenburg and Sigrid Elisabeth (*née* Lindforss); *m* 1960, Harriet Lisa Turnure. *Educ:* Harvard Coll. (AB 1954). Manager, Design Dept, Doubleday & Co., NYC, 1958–61; Man. Editor, Trade Div., Macmillan Co., NYC, 1961–69; Dir,

Publications, 1969–72, Dir, 1972–94, Museum of Modern Art, NYC, 1969–72. *Address:* c/o Sotheby's, 1334 York Avenue, New York, NY 10021, USA.

OLDFIELD, Bruce, OBE 1990; designer; *b* 14 July 1950; parents unknown; brought up by Dr Barnado's, Ripon, Yorks. *Educ:* Ripon Grammar School; Sheffield City Polytechnic (Hon. Fellow 1987); Ravensbourne College of Art; St Martin's College of Art. Established fashion house, 1975; produced designer collections of high fashion clothes for UK and overseas; began exporting clothes worldwide, 1975; began making couture clothes for individual clients, 1981; opened first Bruce Oldfield retail shop, selling ready to wear and couture to international clientèle, 1984. Exhibitor: British Design Exhibn, Vienna, 1986; Australian Bicentennial Fashion Show, Sydney Opera House, 1988. Lectures: Fashion Inst., NY, 1977; Los Angeles County Museum, 1983; Internat. Design Conf.. Aspen, Colorado, 1986 (Speaker and show). Hon. Fellow RCA, 1990. Designed for films: Jackpot, 1974; The Sentinel, 1976. *Publication:* (with Georgina Howell) Bruce Oldfield's Season, 1987. *Recreations:* music, reading, driving, working. *Address:* 27 Beauchamp Place, SW3 1NJ. *T:* 0171–584 1363.

OLDFIELD, John Richard Anthony; *b* July 1899; *s* of late Major H. E. Oldfield; *m* 1953, Jonnet Elizabeth, *d* of late Maj. H. M. Richards, DL, JP. *Educ:* Eton; Trinity College, Cambridge; Served in: Coldstream Guards, 1918–20; RN, 1939–45. MP (Lab) South-East Essex, 1929–31; Parliamentary Private Secretary to Sec. of State for Air, 1929–30. Mem. LCC, 1931–58 (Vice-Chairman, 1953); CC (C) Kent, 1965–81. *Address:* Doddington Place, near Sittingbourne, Kent ME9 0BB.

OLDFIELD, Michael Gordon, (Mike); musician and composer; *b* 15 May 1953; *s* of Dr Raymond Henry Oldfield and Maureen Bernadine Liston; three *s* two *d*. *Educ:* St Edward's, Reading; Presentation Coll., Reading. Records include: Tubular Bells, 1973 (over 10 million copies sold to date); Hergest Ridge; Ommadawn; Incantations; Platinum; QE2, 1980; Five Miles Out, 1982; Crises, 1983; Discovery, 1984; The Killing Fields (film sound track), 1984; Islands, 1987; The Wind Chimes (video album), 1988; Earthmoving, 1989; Amarok, 1990; Heaven's Open, 1991; Tubular Bells II, 1992; The Songs of Distant Earth, 1994. Extensive world wide concert tours, 1979–. Mem., Assoc. of Professional Composers. Freeman, City of London, 1982. Hon. Pict. *Recreations:* helicopter pilot, squash, ski-ing, cricket. *Address:* c/o Ross, Bennet-Smith, 112 Jermyn Street, SW1Y 6LS. *Club:* Jacobs Larder (Ealing).

OLDHAM, Rev. Canon Arthur Charles Godolphin; *b* 5 Apr. 1905; *s* of late Sidney Godolphin and Lilian Emma Oldham; *m* 1934, Ursula Finch Wigham Richardson (*d* 1984), *d* of late George and Isabel Richardson, Newcastle upon Tyne; one *s* two *d*. *Educ:* King's College School; King's College, London. Business, music and journalism to 1930. Ordained, to Witley, Surrey, 1933; Vicar of Brockham Green, 1936; Rector of Merrow, 1943; Rural Dean of Guildford, 1949; Vicar of Godalming, 1950; Rural Dean of Godalming, 1957; Director of Ordination Training, and Bishop's Examining Chaplain, 1958; Hon. Canon of Guildford, 1959; Canon Residentiary of Guildford Cathedral, 1961–71, retired. *Recreations:* music, sketching. *Address:* The Lawn, Holybourne, Alton, Hants GU34 4ER. *T:* Alton (01420) 544293.

OLDHAM, Prof. (Charles Herbert) Geoffrey, CBE 1990; Professorial Fellow, Science Policy Research Unit, University of Sussex, since 1966 (Director, 1980–92); Science Adviser to President, International Development Research Centre, Ottawa, on secondment, since 1992; *b* 17 Feb. 1929; *s* of Herbert Cecil Oldham and Evelyn Selina Oldham (*née* Brooke); *m* 1951, Brenda Mildred Raven; two *s* one *d* (and one *s* decd). *Educ:* Bingley Grammar Sch.; Reading Univ. (BSc Hons); Toronto Univ. (MA, PhD). Research geophysicist, Chevron Research Corp., 1954–57; Sen. Geophysicist, Standard Oil Co. of California, 1957–60; Fellow, Inst. of Current World Affairs, studying Chinese lang. and sci., 1960–66; Scientific Directorate, OECD, 1965–66; Dep. Dir, Science Policy Res. Unit, 1966–80; Associate Dir, Internat. Develt Res. Centre, Ottawa, 1970–80. Vis. Prof., Stanford Univ., 1979; Vis. Researcher, Aust. Sci. and Tech. Adv. Council, 1988. Chm., UN Adv. Cttee on Sci. and Tech. for Develt, 1991–92; UK Mem., UN Commn on Sci., Technol. and Develt, 1993–. *Publications:* articles in jls on science, technology and Chinese development. *Recreations:* travel, esp. long distance train journeys, golf. *Address:* International Development Research Centre, PO Box 8500, Ottawa, Ont K1G 3H9, Canada; Science Policy Research Unit, University of Sussex, Brighton, Sussex BN1 9RF.

O'LEARY, Michael; barrister; *b* 8 May 1936; *s* of John O'Leary and Margaret McCarthy; unmarried. *Educ:* Presentation Coll., Cork; University Coll., Cork; Columbia Univ., NY. Called to the Bar, King's Inns, Dublin, 1979. Educn Officer, Irish TUC, 1962–65. TD: (Lab) Dublin N Central, 1965–82; (FG) Dublin SW, 1982–87; Minister for Labour, 1973–77; Dep. Leader, Labour Party, 1977–81, Leader, 1981–82 (resigned); Tánaiste (Dep. Prime Minister) and Minister for Industry and Energy, 1981–82; joined Fine Gael, 1982. President, ILO, 1976. Mem. for Ireland, European Parlt, 1979–81. *Address:* Law Library, Four Courts, Dublin 7, Ireland.

O'LEARY, Peter Leslie; Under-Secretary, Inland Revenue, 1978–84; *b* 12 June 1929; *s* of Archibald and Edna O'Leary; *m* 1960, Margaret Elizabeth Debney; four *d*. *Educ:* Portsmouth Southern Grammar Sch.; University Coll., London (BA). Joined Inland Revenue as Inspector, 1952; Sen. Principal Inspector, 1974. *Recreations:* horology, gardening, wine-making. *Address:* 17 Sleaford Road, Heckington, Sleaford, Lincs NG34 9QP. *T:* Sleaford (01529) 461213.

O'LEARY, Terence Daniel, CMG 1982; MA; HM Diplomatic Service, retired 1988; Chairman, Petworth Preservation, since 1989; *b* 18 Aug. 1928; 2nd *s* of late Daniel O'Leary; *m* 1960, Janet Douglas Berney, *d* of Dr H. B. Berney, Masterton, NZ; twin *s* one *d*. *Educ:* Dulwich; St John's Coll., Cambridge. BA 1950. Army, commnd Queen's Royal Regt, 1946–48. Commerce, 1951–53; Asst Principal, CRO, 1953; 2nd Sec., British High Commn, Wellington, 1956–58; Principal, PSO's Dept, CRO, 1958; 1st Sec., New Delhi, 1960–63; 1st Sec., Dar es Salaam, 1963–64; CRO, 1964–65; 1st Sec. and Defence Sec., Canberra, 1965–68; Actg Head, S Asia Dept, FCO, 1969; Asst Sec., Cabinet Office, 1970–72; Counsellor, Pretoria/Cape Town, 1972–74; Dep. High Comr, Wellington, 1974–78; Senior Civil Mem., Directing Staff, Nat. Defence Coll., 1978–81; High Comr in Sierra Leone, 1981–84; High Comr in New Zealand and concurrently to Western Samoa, and Governor of Pitcairn, 1984–87. Mem., EC Monitoring Mission, Yugoslavia, 1991–92. Parish Councillor (Ind.), Petworth, 1993–. *Recreations:* cutting grass, croquet. *Address:* The Old Rectory, Petworth, W Sussex GU28 0DB. *T:* Petworth (01798) 43335. *Clubs:* Travellers'; Wellington (New Zealand).

OLINS, Wallace, (Wally), MA Oxon; FCSD; Chairman, Wolff Olins Ltd; *b* 19 Dec. 1930; *s* of Alfred Olins and Rachel (*née* Muscovitch); *m*1st, 1957, Maria Renate Olga Laura Steinert (marr. diss. 1989); two *s* one *d*; 2nd, 1990, Dornie Watts; one *d*. *Educ:* Highgate Sch.; St Peter's Coll., Oxford (Hons History, MA). National Service, Army, in Germany, 1950–51. S. H. Benson Ltd, London, 1954–57; Benson, India, 1957–62; Caps Design Group, London, 1962–65; Wolff Olins, London, 1965–. Vis. Lectr, Design Management, London Business Sch., 1984–89; Visiting Professor, Management School: Imperial Coll., 1987–89; Lancaster Univ., 1992–; Visiting Professor: Copenhagen Business Sch., 1993; Integer Centro de Excelencia Empresarial, Mexico, 1995–. Vice-Pres., SIAD, 1982–85. Chm., Design Dimension Educnl Trust, 1987–93; Mem. Develt Trust, RPO, 1994–. Mem., Council, RSA, 1989–. *Publications:* The Corporate Personality, 1978; The Wolff Olins Guide to Corporate Identity, 1983; The Wolff Olins Guide to Design Management, 1985; Corporate Identity, 1989; numerous articles in Design and Management publications. *Recreations:* looking at buildings, shopping for books, theatre. *Address:* Wolff Olins, 10 Regents Wharf, All Saints Street, N1 9RL. *T:* 0171–713 7733. *Club:* Groucho.

OLIPHANT, Air Vice-Marshal David Nigel Kington B.; *see* Blair-Oliphant.

OLIPHANT, Sir Mark, (Marcus Laurence Elwin), AC 1977; KBE 1959; FRS 1937; FAA 1954; FTS 1976; Governor of South Australia, 1971–76; *b* Adelaide, 8 Oct. 1901; *e s* of H. G. Oliphant; *m* 1925, Rosa Wilbraham (*d* 1987), Adelaide, S Australia; one *s* one *d*. *Educ:* Unley and Adelaide High Schools; University of Adelaide; Trinity Coll., Cambridge (1851 Exhibitioner, Overseas 1927, Senior 1929; PhD 1929). Messel Research Fellow of Royal Society, 1931; Fellow and Lecturer St John's Coll., 1934. Hon. Fellow, 1952; Assistant Director of Research, Cavendish Laboratory, Cambridge, 1935, Poynting Professor of Physics, University of Birmingham, 1937–50; Dir, Research Sch. of Physical Sciences, ANU, Canberra, 1950–63; Prof. of Physics of Ionised Gases, Inst. of Advanced Studies, ANU, 1964–67, now Professor Emeritus. Pres., Aust. Acad. of Sciences, 1954–57. Hon. DSc (Toronto, Belfast, Melbourne, Birmingham, New South Wales, ANU, Adelaide, Flinders); Hon. LLD (St Andrews). KStJ 1972. *Publications:* Rutherford: recollections of the Cambridge days, 1972; various papers on electricity in gases, surface properties and nuclear physics. *Address:* 28 Carstensz Street, Griffith, ACT 2603, Australia. *Club:* Adelaide (Adelaide).

OLIVE, Prof. David Ian, FRS 1987; Research Professor of Physics, University of Wales Swansea (formerly University College of Swansea), since 1992; *b* 16 April 1937; *s* of Ernest Edward Olive and Lilian Emma Olive (*née* Chambers); *m* 1963, Jenifer Mary Tutton; two *d*. *Educ:* Royal High Sch., Edinburgh; Univ. of Edinburgh (MA); Univ. of Cambridge (BA, PhD). Fellow of Churchill Coll., 1963–70; Lectr, Univ. of Cambridge, 1965–71; Staff Mem., CERN, 1971–77; Imperial College: Lectr, 1977; Reader, 1980; Prof. of Theoretical Physics, 1984–92. Visiting Professor: Univ. of Virginia, 1982–83; Univ. of Geneva, 1986. *Publications:* (jtly) The Analytic S-Matrix, 1966; many articles on theoretical physics in learned jls. *Recreations:* listening to music, golf. *Address:* Department of Physics, University of Wales Swansea, Singleton Park, Swansea SA2 8PP. *T:* Swansea (01792) 295842.

OLIVER, family name of **Baron Oliver of Aylmerton.**

OLIVER OF AYLMERTON, Baron *cr* 1986 (Life Peer), of Aylmerton in the County of Norfolk; **Peter Raymond Oliver;** Kt 1974; PC 1980; a Lord of Appeal in Ordinary, 1986–92; *b* 7 March 1921; *s* of David Thomas Oliver, Fellow of Trinity Hall, Cambridge, and Alice Maud Oliver; *m* 1st, 1945, Mary Chichester Rideal (*d* 1985), *d* of Sir Eric Keightley Rideal, MBE, FRS; one *s* one *d*; 2nd, 1987, Wendy Anne, *widow* of I. Lewis Lloyd Jones. *Educ:* The Leys, Cambridge; Trinity Hall, Cambridge (Hon. Fellow, 1980). Military Service, 1941–45, 12th Bn RTR (despatches). Called to Bar, Lincoln's Inn, 1948, Bencher 1973; QC 1965; Judge of the High Ct of Justice, Chancery Div., 1974–80; a Lord Justice of Appeal, 1980–86. Mem., Restrictive Practices Court, 1976–80; Chm., Review Body on Chancery Div. of High Court, 1979–81. Hon. LLD: City of London Poly., 1989; UEA, 1991. *Recreations:* gardening, music. *Address:* House of Lords, SW1A 0PW.

See also Hon. D. K. R. Oliver.

OLIVER, Benjamin Rhys; Stipendiary Magistrate for Mid-Glamorgan, 1983–95; a Recorder of the Crown Court, 1972–93; *b* 8 June 1928; *m* 1955; one *s* one *d*. *Educ:* Llandovery and Aberystwyth. Called to the Bar, Inner Temple, 1954. *Recreation:* golf.

OLIVER, Hon. David Keightley Rideal; QC 1986; *b* 4 June 1949; *o s* of Baron Oliver of Aylmerton, *qv*; *m* 1st, 1972, Marisa Mirasierras (marr. diss. 1987); two *s*; 2nd, 1988, Judith Britannia Caroline Powell; two *s*. *Educ:* Westminster School; Trinity Hall, Cambridge; Institut d'Etudes Européennes, Brussels. Called to the Bar, Lincoln's Inn, 1972, Bencher, 1994; Junior Counsel to Dir-Gen. of Fair Trading, 1980–86. *Recreations:* gardening, bird watching, shooting. *Address:* 13 Old Square, Lincoln's Inn, WC2A 3UA. *T:* 0171–404 4800.

OLIVER, Dennis Stanley, CBE 1981; PhD, FEng, FIM, FInstP; Director, Pilkington Brothers plc, 1977–86; *b* 19 Sept. 1926; *s* of late James Thomas Oliver and Lilian Mabel Oliver (*née* Bunn); *m* 1st, 1952, Enid Jessie Newcombe (marr. diss. 1984); 2nd, 1988, Elizabeth Emery. *Educ:* Deacon's School, Peterborough; Birmingham Univ. BSc, PhD. Research Fellowship, Univ. of Bristol, 1949–52; Senior Scientific Officer, UKAEA, Culcheth, 1952–55; Head of Metallurgy Div., UKAEA, Dounreay, 1955–63; Chief R & D Officer, Richard Thomas & Baldwin Ltd, 1963–68; Group R & D Dir, Pilkington Brothers plc, 1968–77. Member: Board, British Technology Gp (Member: NEB, 1981–92; NRDC, 1981–92; Court and Council, Cranfield Inst. of Technology, 1976–88. Vis. Prof., Cranfield Inst. of Technology, 1984–88. Director: Anglo-American Venture Fund Ltd, 1980–84; Monotype Corp., 1985–90. Chm., Industrial Experience Projects Ltd, 1981–86; Pres., European Industrial Res. Management Assoc., 1977–81. Patron, Science and Technology Educn on Merseyside, 1982– (Pres., 1978–81); Governor: Liverpool Inst. of Higher Educn, 1979–85; Christ's and Notre Dame Coll., Liverpool, 1979–87; Royal Nat. Coll. for the Blind, 1981–85; Dir, L'Ecole Supérieure du Verre, Belgium, 1971–86; Governor, Community of St Helens Trust Ltd, 1978–86; Founder Trustee, Anfield Foundn, 1983–88. Freeman of City of London; Liveryman: Spectaclemakers Co. (Court of Assts, 1985–88); Co. of Engrs, 1984. FIMgt. KSG 1980. *Publications:* The Use of Glass in Engineering, 1975; Glass for Construction Purposes, 1977; various publications on technical subjects and technology transfer. *Recreations:* music, poetry, cooking. *Address:* Castell Bach, Bodfari, Denbigh, Clwyd LL16 4HT. *T:* Bodfari (01754) 710354.

OLIVER, Dr John Andrew, CB 1968; *b* 25 Oct. 1913; *s* of Robert John Oliver, Limavady, Co. Londonderry and Martha Sherrard, Magilligan, Co. Londonderry; *m* 1943, Stella Ritson; five *s*. *Educ:* Royal Belfast Academical Institution; Queen's Univ., Belfast; Bonn Univ.; Königsberg Univ.; Zimmern School of International Studies, Geneva; Imperial Defence Coll., London. BA 1936; DrPhil, 1951; IDC, 1954. Ministry of Development, NI: Second Sec., 1964–71; Permanent Sec., 1971–74; Permanent Sec., Housing, Local Govt and Planning, NI, 1974–75; Chief Adviser, NI Constitutional Convention, 1975–76. Hon. Sec., Assoc. of Governing Bodies of Voluntary Grammar Schs in NI, 1964–77; Chm., Bd of Governors, Royal Belfast Academical Instn, 1970–77. UK Election Supervisor, Que Que, Rhodesia, 1980. Chm. Management Review, Royal Victoria Hosp. Gp, Belfast, 1981–82. Chm., S Lakeland Council for Voluntary Action, 1980; Vice-Chm., Voluntary Action Cumbria, 1980–. Proposer and interim Governor, new Dallam Schs, Cumbria, 1983–84. Retired deliberately from all cttees and exec. positions on reaching 70, to make way for younger people. Hon. MRTPI, 1964; Hon. Member, Assoc. for Housing and Town Planning, W Germany, 1966. Rhodesia Medal, 1980;

Zimbabwe Independence Medal, 1980. *Publications:* Ulster Today and Tomorrow, 1978; Working at Stormont, 1978; Aspects of Ulster (essays), 1994; short stories; many articles in learned jls on Ulster Admin and on family history. *Recreations:* swimming, maps, languages, family history. *Address:* Laundry Cottage, Hale, Milnthorpe, Cumbria LA7 7BL. *T:* Milnthorpe (015395) 62698. *Club:* Royal Over-Seas League.

OLIVER, Rt. Rev. John Keith; *see* Hereford, Bishop of.

OLIVER, John Laurence; Journalist; *b* 14 Sept. 1910; *s* of late Harold and Teresa Oliver; *m* 1946, Renée Mary Webb; two *s*. *Educ:* Haberdashers' Aske's Hampstead School. Publicity Manager, The Book Society, 1934; Art Editor, The Bystander, 1935–39. War of 1939–45: served in the Field Security Corps; commissioned 1941, The Suffolk Regt (transferred The Cambridgeshire Regt). Joined staff of The Sphere, 1946; Art Editor, 1947; Assistant Editor, 1956; Editor, 1960–64; Editor, The Tatler, 1961–65. *Publications:* Saint John's Wood Church (with Rev. Peter Bradshaw), 1955; Malcolm Morley at the Everyman, 1977; occasional short stories and articles. *Recreations:* reading, theatre going, watching cricket. *Address:* 10 Wellington Place, NW8 9JA. *T:* 0171–286 5891. *Clubs:* Garrick, MCC.

OLIVER, Ven. John Michael; Archdeacon of Leeds, since 1992; *b* 7 Sept. 1939; *s* of Frederick and Mary Oliver; *m* 1964, Anne Elizabeth Barlow; three *d*. *Educ:* Ripon Grammar Sch.; St David's Coll., Lampeter (BA 1962); Ripon Hall, Oxford. Ordained deacon, 1964, priest 1965; Asst Curate, St Peter, Harrogate, 1964–67; Senior Curate, Bramley, Leeds, 1967–72; Vicar: St Mary, Harrogate, 1972–78; St Mary with St David, Beeston, Leeds, 1978–92. Ecumenical Officer for Leeds, 1980–86; Rural Dean of Armley, 1986–92; Hon. Canon of Ripon, 1987–92. *Recreations:* cricket, theatre, cooking, a reluctant gardener. *Address:* 2 Halcyon Hill, Leeds LS7 3PU. *T:* and *Fax:* (home) Leeds (0113) 269 0594, *T:* (office) Leeds (0113) 248 7487.

OLIVER, Group Captain John Oliver William, CB 1950; DSO 1940; DFC 1940; RAF retired; *b* 1911; *e s* of William and Cicely Oliver; *m* 1935, Irene Oxberry (marr. diss. 1951); one *s* two *d*; *m* 1954, Christine Guthrie (marr. diss. 1960); *m* 1962, Anne Fraser Porteous; one *s* two *d* (of whom *s* and *yr d* are twins). *Educ:* Christ's Hospital; Cranwell. Commissioned from Cranwell, General Duties Pilot Branch permanent commn, 1931; served 43 (F) Squadron and 55 (B) Squadron, Iraq; qualified CFS. Served War of 1939–45 (despatches thrice); commanded 85 (F) Squadron, 1940 (BEF, France, 1939–40); Fighter Command and Tactical Air Force; Wing Commander, 1940; Group Captain, 1942 (Trng Fighter Comd, and TAF Plans for Overlord); QS Camberley and Bracknell; Assistant Commandant, RAF Coll., Cranwell, 1948–50; SASO 2 Gp, Germany, CO Kabrit, Egypt, Gp Capt Ops Egypt, and SASO Iraq, 1951–58; ACOS Ops, Allied Forces Northern Europe, 1958–60; retired, 1961. Personnel Officer, ENV (Engineering) Ltd, 1961; Staff Institute Personnel Management, 1962; Personnel Manager, Humber Ltd, 1963; Manager, Training and Administrative Service, Rootes, Coventry, 1965; Senior Training Officer, Engineering Industry Training Board, 1968; Personnel and Trng Manager, Thorn Gp, 1970–76, retired. *Recreations:* painting, sailing.

OLIVER, Prof. Michael Francis, CBE 1985; MD; FRCP, FRCPEd, FFPHM; FRSE; Professor Emeritus, University of Edinburgh, since 1990; *b* 3 July 1925; *s* of late Captain Wilfrid Francis Lenn Oliver, MC (DLI), and Cecilia Beatrice Oliver (*née* Daniel); *m* 1st; two *s* one *d* (and one *s* decd); 2nd, Helen Louise Daniel. *Educ:* Marlborough Coll.; Univ. of Edinburgh. MB, ChB 1947, MD (Gold Medal) 1957. Edinburgh University: Consultant Physician, Royal Infirmary and Sen. Lectr in Medicine, 1961; Reader in Medicine, 1973; Personal Prof. of Cardiology, 1977; Duke of Edinburgh Prof. of Cardiology, 1979–89. Dir, Wynn Inst. for Metabolic Res., 1989–93; Hon. Prof., Nat. Heart and Lung Inst., 1989–93. Mem., Cardiovascular Panel, Govt Cttee on Medical Aspects of Food Policy, 1971–74, 1982–84; UK Rep. Mem., Adv. Panel for Cardiovascular Disease, WHO, 1972–; Chm., BBC-Medical Adv. Gp in Scotland, 1975–81; Mem. Scientific Bd, Internat. Soc. of Cardiology, 1968–78 (Chm., Council on Atherosclerosis and Ischaemic Heart Disease, 1968–75); Chairman: Brit. Atherosclerosis Gp, 1970–75; Science Cttee, Fondation Cardiologique Princess Lilian, Belgium, 1976–85; MoT Panel on driving and cardiovascular disease, 1985–90; Jt Cttee on Higher Medical Training, 1987–90. Convener, Cardiology Cttee, Scottish Royal Colls, 1978–81; Council Mem., Brit. Heart Foundn, 1976–85. Pres., British Cardiac Soc., 1981–85; Pres., RCPEd, 1986–88. FRSE 1987. Hon. FRCPI 1988; Hon. FRACP 1988. Hon. Fellow, Amer. Coll. of Cardiology, 1973. Hon. MD: Karolinska Inst., Stockholm, 1980; Univ. Bologna, 1985. Purkinje Medal, 1981; Polish Cardiac Soc. Medal, 1984. *Publications:* Acute Myocardial Infarction, 1966; Intensive Coronary Care, 1970, 2nd edn 1974; Effect of Acute Ischaemia on Myocardial Function, 1972; Modern Trends in Cardiology, 1975; High-Density Lipoproteins and Atherosclerosis, 1978; Coronary Heart Disease in Young Women, 1978; Strategy for Screening of Coronary Heart Disease, 1986; contribs to sci. and med. jls on causes of coronary heart disease, biochemistry of fats, myocardial metabolism, mechanisms of sudden death, clinical trials of drugs, and population studies of vascular diseases. *Recreations:* Italy and the Italians. *Address:* Barley Mill House, Pencaitland, East Lothian EH34 5EP. *T:* Pencaitland (01875) 340433; 28 Chalcot Road, NW1 8LN. *T:* 0171–722 4460. *Clubs:* Athenæum; New (Edinburgh).

OLIVER, Pauline Ann, (Mrs D. D. Walker); Director of Social Services, Lancashire County Council, since 1990; *b* 17 Nov. 1947; *d* of Percy Leonard Parsons and Doreen Maud Parsons; *m* 1991, David Douglas Walker. *Educ:* Rosebery County Grammar Sch., Epsom; Univ. of Surrey (BSc Hons Human Relns); Goldsmiths' Coll., Univ. of London (CQSW 1972, Dip. Applied Social Studies 1972). Asst Housemother, London Borough of Wandsworth, 1966–67; Social Worker, Surrey CC, 1970–73; social work and managerial posts, London Borough of Lewisham, 1973–83; London Borough of Bexley: Asst Chief Social Services Officer, 1983–87; Chief Social Services Officer, 1987–88; Dep. Dir of Social Services, Lancs CC, 1988–90. Member: Social Care Assoc., British Agencies for Adoption and Fostering; Assoc. of Women Sen. Managers (Personal Social Services). MIMgt. *Recreations:* reading, antiques, gardening. *Address:* Social Services Department, East Cliff County Offices, Preston, Lancs PR1 3EA. *T:* Preston (01772) 264390.

OLIVER, Peter Richard, CMG 1965; HM Diplomatic Service, retired; Ambassador to Uruguay, 1972–77; *b* 3 June 1917; *yr s* of William Henry Oliver and Muriel Daisy Elisabeth Oliver (*née* Widdicombe); *m* 1940, Freda Evelyn Gwyther; two *s* two *d*. *Educ:* Felsted Sch.; Hanover; Berlin; Trinity Hall, Cambridge. Indian Civil Service, 1939–47; served in Punjab and Bahawalpur State. Transferred to HM Foreign (subsequently Diplomatic) Service, 1947; served in Karachi, 1947–49; Foreign Office, 1949–52; The Hague, 1952–56; Havana, 1956–59; Foreign Office, 1959–61; Djakarta, 1961–64; Bonn, 1965–69; Dep. High Comr, Lahore, 1969–72. *Recreations:* publisher-hunting, Bumbloclasm. *Address:* Bridge Cottage, Little Petherick, Wadebridge, Cornwall PL27 7QT. *T:* Rumford (01841) 540358. *Clubs:* Commonwealth Trust; Hawks (Cambridge); Union (Cambridge).

OLIVER, Prof. Emeritus Richard Alexander Cavaye; Professor of Education and Director of the Department of Education in the University of Manchester, 1938–70; Dean of Faculty of Education, 1938–48, 1962–65; Dean of Faculty of Music, 1952–62, 1966–70; *b* 9 Jan. 1904; *s* of Charles Oliver and Elizabeth Smith; *m* 1929, Annabella Margaret White (*d* 1992), MA Edin, MA Oxon; one *s* one *d*. *Educ:* George Heriot's Sch.; University of Edinburgh; Stanford Univ., California, USA. Held Commonwealth Fund Fellowship at Stanford Univ., 1927–29; research educational psychologist in Kenya, 1929–32; Asst Master Abbotsholme Sch. and in Edinburgh, 1933–34; University Extension Lecturer, 1933–34; Asst Director of Education, Wilts Education Cttee, 1934–36; Dep. Secretary, Devon Education Cttee, 1936–38. Director, University of Manchester School of Education, 1947–51; Pro Vice-Chancellor, 1953–57 and 1960–61; Presenter of Hon. Graduands, 1959–64, 1966. Member National Advisory Council on Training and Supply of Teachers, 1949–59; Member, Northern Universities Joint Matriculation Board, 1942–70 (Chm., 1952–55); Member Secondary School Examinations Council, 1958–64. FBPsS. Hon. Research Fellow, Princeton Univ., 1961. Hon. LLD Manchester, 1981. *Publications:* (with others) The Educational Guidance of the School Child, 1936; Research in Education, 1946; The Content of Sixth Form General Studies, 1974; Joint Matriculation Board Occasional Publications; contrib. to East Africa Medical Journal, Africa, British Journal of Psychology, Yearbook of Education, Universities Quarterly, Research in Education, etc. *Recreations:* gardening, painting. *Address:* Waingap, Crook, Kendal, Cumbria LA8 9HT. *T:* Kendal (01539) 821277.

See also H. A. Hetherington.

OLIVER, Prof. Roland Anthony, MA, PhD (Cantab); FBA 1993; Professor of the History of Africa, London University, 1963–86; *b* Srinagar, Kashmir, 30 March 1923; *s* of late Major D. G. Oliver and Lorimer Janet (*née* Donaldson); *m* 1st, 1947, Caroline Florence (*d* 1983), *d* of late Judge John Linehan, KC; one *d*; 2nd, 1990, Suzanne Doyle, *widow* of Brig. Richard Miers. *Educ:* Stowe; King's Coll., Cambridge. Attached to Foreign Office, 1942–45; R. J. Smith Research Studentship, King's Coll., Cambridge, 1946–48; Lecturer, School of Oriental and African Studies, 1948–58, Hon. Fellow, 1992; Reader in African History, University of London, 1958–63. Francqui Prof., University of Brussels, 1961; Visiting Professor: Northwestern Univ., Illinois, 1962; Harvard Univ., 1967; travelled in Africa, 1949–50 and 1957–58; org. international Conferences on African History and Archæology, 1953–61. President: African Studies Assoc., 1967–68; British Inst. in Eastern Africa, 1981–93. Vice-Pres., Royal African Soc., 1965– (Mem. Council, 1959–65); Mem., Perm. Bureau, Internat. Congress of Africanists, 1973–78; Chm., Minority Rights Group, 1973–91. Corresp. Member, Académie Royale des Sciences d'Outremer, Brussels. Editor (with J. D. Fage) Jl of African History, 1960–73. Haile Selassie Prize Trust Award, 1966; Distinguished Africanist Award, American African Studies Assoc., 1989. *Publications:* The Missionary Factor in East Africa, 1952; Sir Harry Johnston and the Scramble for Africa, 1957; (ed) The Dawn of African History, 1961; (with J. D. Fage) A Short History of Africa, 1962; (ed with Gervase Mathew) A History of East Africa, 1963; (with A. E. Atmore) Africa since 1800, 1967; (ed) The Middle Age of African History, 1967; (with B. M. Fagan) Africa in the Iron Age, 1975; (with A. E. Atmore) The African Middle Ages, 1400–1800, 1981; The African Experience, 1991; Gen. Editor (with J. D. Fage), Cambridge History of Africa, 8 vols, 1975–86. *Address:* Frilsham Woodhouse, Thatcham, Berks RG18 9XB. *T:* Hermitage (01635) 201407.

OLIVER, Dr Ronald Martin, CB 1989; RD 1973; Deputy Chief Medical Officer (Deputy Secretary), Department of Health and Social Security, 1985–89, retired; *b* 28 May 1929; *s* of late Cuthbert Hanson Oliver and Cecilia Oliver; *m* 1957, Susanna Treves Blackwell; three *s* one *d*. *Educ:* King's Coll. Sch., Wimbledon; King's Coll., London; St George's Hosp. Med. Sch. (MB, BS 1952). MRCS, LRCP 1952; DCH 1954; DPH 1960; DIH 1961; MD London 1965; MFOM 1978; MRCP 1987; MFCM 1987. Served RNR: Surg. Lieut, 1953–55; Surg. Lt-Comdr, retd 1974. St George's Hosp., London: House Surgeon and Physician, 1952–53; Resident Clin. Pathologist, 1955–56; trainee asst, gen. practice, 1956–57; Asst County MO, Surrey CC, 1957–59; MO, London Transport Exec., 1959–62; MO, later SMO, Treasury Med. Service (later CS Med. Adv. Service), 1962–74; seconded Diplomatic Service as Physician, British Embassy, Moscow, 1964–66; SMO, 1974–79, SPMO, 1979–85, DHSS; Chief Med. Advr, ODA, 1983–85. Gov., Manor House Sch., Little Bookham, 1991– (Chm., 1995). *Publications:* papers in med. jls on epidemiology of heart disease, public health, toxicology, and health service admin. *Recreations:* golf, sailing, gardening, bad bridge. *Address:* Greenhill House, Beech Avenue, Effingham, Surrey KT24 5PH. *T:* Bookham (01372) 452887. *Club:* Effingham Golf.

OLIVER, Rev. Stephen John; Rector of Leeds, since 1991; *b* 7 Jan. 1948; *s* of John Oliver and Nora Oliver (*née* Greenhalgh); *m* 1969, Hilary Joan Barkham; two *s*. *Educ:* St Augustine's Coll., Canterbury; King's Coll. London (AKC 1970). Ordained deacon, 1971, priest, 1972; Asst Curate, Clifton, Nottingham, 1970; Vicar, Christ Church, Newark on Trent, 1975; Rector, St Mary Plumtree, Nottingham, 1979; Producer, Religious Programmes, BBC, 1985, Chief Producer, 1987. Mem., Liturgical Commn, Gen. Synod of C of E, 1991–. Member: Elida Gibbs Ethics Cttee; W Yorks Playhouse Community and Educn Cttee; Leeds Common Purpose Adv. Gp. Chairman, Governors: Leeds Girls' High Sch.; Agnes Stewart High Sch. Pres., Leeds Church Inst. *Publication:* Why Pray?, 1993. *Recreations:* reading, theatre, flying. *Address:* Leeds Rectory, Leeds LS5 3HF. *T:* Leeds (0113) 278 6237. *Club:* Leeds.

OLIVER, His Honour Stephen John Lindsay, QC 1980; Presiding Special Commissioner, and President, VAT and Duties (formerly Value Added Tax) Tribunals, since 1992; *b* 14 Nov. 1938; *s* of Philip Daniel Oliver and Audrey Mary Oliver; *m* 1967, Anne Dawn Harrison Taylor; one *s* two *d*. *Educ:* Rugby Sch.; Oriel Coll., Oxford (MA Jurisprudence). National Service, RN, 1957–59: served submarines; Temp. Sub-Lieut. Called to the Bar, Middle Temple, 1963; Bencher, 1987; a Recorder, 1989–91; Circuit Judge, 1991–92. Asst Boundary Comr, Parly Boundary Commn, 1977. Chm. Blackheath Concert Halls Charity, 1986–92; Mem. Council, London Sinfonietta, 1993–. *Recreations:* music, sailing. *Address:* 15–19 Bedford Avenue, WC1B 3AS. *T:* 0171–631 4242.

OLIVIER, Henry, CMG 1954; Order for Meritorious Service (Gold), 1992, DScEng, PhD London, DEng; FICE, FASCE, Beit Fellow; FRSA; specialist consulting engineer in water resources engineering, Henry Olivier & Associates, since 1974; *b* 25 Jan. 1914; *s* of J. Olivier, Umtali, S Rhodesia; *m* 1st, 1940, Lorna Renée Collier; one *d* (one *s* decd); 2nd, 1979, Johanna Cecilia van der Merwe. *Educ:* Umtali High Sch.; Cape Town Univ. (BSc 1936; MSc 1947); University College, London (PhD 1953); DEng Witwatersrand, 1967. Beit Engineering Schol., 1932–38; Beit Fellow for two Rhodesias, 1939. Engineering post-grad. training with F. E. Kanthack & Partners, Consulting Engineers, Johannesburg, 1937; Sir Alex. Gibb & Partners, Cons. Engineers, London: training 1938, Asst Engineer, 1939. Experience covers design and construction of steam-electric power-stations, hydro-electric, floating harbour, irrigation, and water resources development schemes in UK, Africa, Middle East, and USA; Chief Engineer in charge civil engineering contracts, Owen Falls Hydro-Electric Scheme, Uganda, 1950–54; Partner in firm of Sir Alexander Gibb and Partners (Africa), 1954–55; Resident Director and Chief Engineer (Rhodesia), in firm of Gibb, Coyne & Sogei (Kariba), 1955–60; Consultant (mainly in connection with Indus Basin Project in Pakistan) to Sir Alexander Gibb and Partners, London, 1960–69 (Sen. Consultant, 1967); Partner, Gibb Hawkins and Partners, Johannesburg, 1963–69, associated with design and construction of Hendrik Verwoerd and P. K. le Roux dams on Orange

River, RSA; Chm. LTA Ltd and LTA Engineering Ltd, 1969–73; major projects: Cahora Bassa Hydro-electric Scheme in Mozambique as mem. of Internat. Consortium Zamco; Orange-Fish Tunnel in South Africa; Sen. Partner, Henry Olivier and Associates, 1974–86, acting for Dept of Water Affairs, RSA, on concept plans for water and power projects in Lesotho, Transkei, Swaziland and Botswana; major concept plans accepted and implemented Lesotho Highlands Water Scheme. Mem., Exec. Cttee, SA Nat. Cttee on Large Dams, 1972–81. Hon. Fellow, SA Inst. of Civil Engineers, (Pres., 1979). Hon. DSc: Cape, 1968; Rhodesia, 1977; Orange Free State, 1992. *Publications:* Irrigation and Climate, 1960; Irrigation and Water Resources Engineering, 1972; Damit, 1975; Great Dams in Southern Africa, 1977; Papers to Institution Civil Engineering Journal; Int. Commn on Irrigation and Drainage; Water for Peace Conference, Washington, DC. *Recreation:* bowls. *Address:* PO Box 523, Jeffreys Bay, Cape, 6330, South Africa. *Club:* Country (Johannesburg).

OLIVIER, Lady, (Joan); *see* Plowright, Joan.

OLLARD, Richard Laurence, FRSL, FSA; author and editor; *b* 9 Nov. 1923; *s* of Rev. Dr S. L. Ollard and Mary Ollard (*née* Ward); *m* 1954, Mary, *d* of Sir Walter Buchanan Riddell, 12th Bt; two *s* one *d*. *Educ:* Eton College; New College, Oxford. MA. Lectr in History and English, Royal Naval College, Greenwich, 1948–59; Senior Editor, Collins, 1960–83. Caird Medal, Nat. Maritime Mus., 1992. *Publications:* The Escape of Charles II, 1966; Man of War: Sir Robert Holmes and the Restoration Navy, 1969; Pepys: a biography, 1974, 2nd edn 1991; This War Without an Enemy, 1976; The Image of the King: Charles I and II, 1979; An English Education: a perspective of Eton, 1982; (ed jtly) For Veronica Wedgwood These: studies in Seventeenth-Century History, 1986; Clarendon and his Friends, 1987; (ed) Clarendon's Four Portraits, 1989; Fisher and Cunningham: a study in the personalities of the Churchill era, 1991; Cromwell's Earl: a life of Edward Mountagu, 1st Earl of Sandwich, 1994; Dorset, 1995. *Address:* Norchard Farmhouse, Morcombelake, Bridport, Dorset DT6 6EP; c/o Curtis Brown Ltd, 162–168 Regent Street, W1. *Club:* Brooks's.

OLLERENSHAW, Dame Kathleen (Mary), DBE 1971; DL; MA, DPhil; FIMA, FCP; Freeman of the City of Manchester, 1984; Chairman, Council for St John Ambulance in Greater Manchester, 1974–89; Member, Manchester City Council, 1956–80, Leader of Conservative Opposition, 1977–79; Alderman, 1970–74, Hon. Alderman since 1980; Lord Mayor, 1975–76, Deputy Lord Mayor, 1976–77; *b* 1 Oct. 1912; *d* of late Charles Timpson, JP, and late Mary Elizabeth Timpson (*née* Stops); *m* 1939, Robert Ollerenshaw (*d* 1986); one *s* (one *d* decd). *Educ:* Ladybarn House Sch., Manchester; St Leonards Sch., St Andrews; (open schol. in maths) Somerville Coll., Oxford (Hon. Fellow, 1978). BA (Hons) 1934, MA 1943, DPhil 1945; Foundation Fellow, Institute of Mathematics and its Applications (FIMA), 1964 (Mem. Council, 1973–94, Vice-Pres., 1976–77, Pres., 1978–79; Hon. Fellow 1986). Research Assistant, Shirley Institute, Didsbury, 1937–40. Chairman: Educn Cttee, Assoc. of Municipal Corporations, 1968–71; Assoc. of Governing Bodies of Girls' Public Schs, 1963–69; Manchester Educn Cttee, 1967–70 (Co-opted Mem., 1954–56); Manchester Coll. of Commerce, 1964–69; Council, Science and Technology Insts, 1980–81; first Chm., Court, Royal Northern Coll. of Music, Manchester, 1971–86 (CRNCM, 1978); Member: Central Adv. Council on Educn in England, 1960–63; CNAA, 1964–74; SSRC, 1971–75; Tech. Educn Council, 1973–75; (Vice-Pres.,) British Assoc. for Commercial and Industrial Educn (Mem. Delegn to USSR, 1963); Exec., Assoc. of Educn Cttees, 1967–71; Nat. Adv. Council on Educn for Industry and Commerce, 1963–70; Gen. Adv. Council of BBC, 1966–72; Schools Council, 1968–71; Management Panel, Burnham Cttee, 1968–71; Nat. Foundn of Educnl Res., 1968–71; Layfield Cttee of Inquiry into Local Govt Finance, 1974–76; Court, Univ. of Salford, 1967– (Mem. Council, 1967–89; a Pro-Chancellor, 1983–89); Court, Univ. of Manchester, 1964–; Manchester Polytechnic, 1968–86 (first Chm., 1969–72; Dep.-Chm., 1972–75; Hon. Fellow, 1979); Court, UMIST, 1971–87 (Vice-Pres., 1976–86; Hon. Fellow, 1987); Council, 1975–, Court, 1991–, Lancaster Univ. (a Dep. Pro-Chancellor, 1978–91); Council, CGLI, 1972–84 (Hon. Fellow, 1978; Vice-Pres., 1979–84); Sen. Res. Fellow (part-time), 1972–75, Hon. Res. Fellow, 1975–77, Lancaster Univ.; Rep. Governor, Royal Coll. of Advanced Technol., Salford, 1959–67; Governor: St Leonards Sch., St Andrews, 1950–72 (Pres., 1980–); Manchester High Sch. for Girls, 1959–69; Ladies Coll., Cheltenham, 1966–68; Chethams Hosp. Sch., Manchester, 1967–77; Further Educn Staff Coll., Blagdon, 1960–74; Member: Manchester Statistical Soc., 1950– (Mem. Council, 1977–; Vice-Pres., 1977, Pres., 1981–83); Manchester Astronomical Soc., 1990– (Vice-Pres., 1994–); Hon. Member: Manchester Technology Assoc., 1976– (Pres., 1982); Manchester Literary and Philosophical Soc., 1982–; Hon. Col, Manchester and Salford Univs OTC, 1977–81; Mem., Mil. Educn Cttee, 1979–. Dir, Greater Manchester Independent Radio, Ltd, 1972–83. Winifred Cullis Lecture Fellow to USA, 1965; Fourth Cockroft Lecture, UMIST and Manchester Tech. Assoc., 1977. DStJ 1983 (CStJ 1978) (Mem., Chapter Gen., 1974–). Hon. LLD CNAA, 1975; Hon. DSc Salford, 1975; Hon LLD Manchester, 1976; Hon. DSc Lancaster, 1992; Hon. LLD Liverpool, 1994. DL Greater Manchester, 1987. Mancunian of the Year, Jnr Chamber of Commerce, 1977. *Publications:* Education of Girls, 1958; Education for Girls, 1961; The Girls' Schools, 1967; Returning to Teaching, 1974; The Lord Mayor's Party, 1976; First Citizen, 1977; papers in mathematical journals, 1945–54 and 1977–, incl. Proc. RI 1981 (on form and pattern), Phil. Trans Royal Soc. 1982 (on magic squares), and Proc. Royal Soc. 1986 (on pandiagonal magic squares); articles on education and local govt in national and educational press. *Recreation:* astronomy. *Address:* 2 Pine Road, Didsbury, Manchester M20 6UY. *T:* 0161–445 2948. *Club:* English-Speaking Union.

OLLIS, Prof. William David, BSc, PhD; FRS 1972; CChem; FRSC; Hon. Professor of Organic Chemistry, University of Birmingham, since 1991; *b* 22 Dec. 1924; *s* of Albert George and Beatrice Charlotte Ollis; *m* 1951, Sonia Dorothy Mary Weekes (marr. diss. 1974); two *d*. *Educ:* Cotham Grammar Sch., Bristol; University of Bristol. Assistant Lecturer in Organic Chemistry, University of Bristol, 1946–49, Lecturer, 1949–62, Reader, 1962–63; Prof. of Org. Chem., Univ. of Sheffield, 1963–90. Research Fellow, Harvard, 1952–53; Visiting Professor: UCLA, 1962; University of Texas, 1966; Universidade Federal Rural do Rio de Janeiro, Brasil, 1967–70 (Hon. Prof., 1969); Wesleyan Univ., Conn, 1970–71; Univ. of Sri Lanka, 1974; Univ. of Kuwait, 1986, 1990. Lectures: Robert Gnehm, 1965; Chemical Soc. Tilden, 1969; Peboc, 1982; Irvine, 1984; Syntex, 1985, Pedler, RSC, 1988. Consultant, MoD, 1952–76; Scientific Advr, Home Office, 1954–76; Member: Individual Merit Promotion Panel Scientific CS, 1971–90; Adv. Council for Misuse of Drugs, 1981–. Founder-Chm., Phytochem. Soc., 1966–67; Chm., Publication Cttee, Chem. Soc., 1972–74; Pres., Organic Chem. Div., RSC, 1983–85. Organic Synthesis Medal, RSC, 1982. FRSA. *Publications:* Recent Developments in the Chemistry of Natural Phenolic Compounds, 1961; Structure Determination in Organic Chemistry, 1973; (ed with Sir Derek Barton) Comprehensive Organic Chemistry, vols 1–6, 1979; (contrib.) Advances in Medicinal Phytochemistry, 1986; scientific papers mainly in Jl of Chemical Soc., Perkin TransI, Tetrahedron. *Address:* c/o School of Chemistry, University of Birmingham, Edgbaston, Birmingham B15 2TT. *Club:* Athenæum.

OLNER, William John; MP (Lab) Nuneaton, since 1992; *b* 9 May 1942; *s* of Charles William Olner, miner and Lillian Olner; *m* 1962, Gillian Everitt. *Educ:* Atherstone Secondary Modern Sch.; North Warwicks Tech. Coll. Engineer, Rolls Royce, 1957–92. Nuneaton and Bedworth Borough Council: Cllr, 1972–92; Leader, 1982–87; Mayor, 1987–88; Chm., Envmtl Health Cttee, 1990–92. Mem., Envmt Select Cttee, 1995–. *Recreations:* hospice movement, walking, current affairs. *Address:* c/o House of Commons, SW1A 0AA.

O'LOGHLEN, Sir Colman (Michael), 6th Bt, *cr* 1838; *b* 6 April 1916; *s* of Henry Ross O'Loghlen (*d* 1944; 6th *s* of 3rd Bt) and of Doris Irene, *d* of late Major Percival Horne, RA; *S* uncle 1951; *m* 1939, Margaret, *d* of Francis O'Halloran, Melbourne, Victoria; six *s* two *d*. *Educ:* Xavier Coll., Melbourne; Melbourne Univ. (LLB). Formerly Captain AIF. Sometime Magistrate and Judge of Supreme Court, PNG. *Heir: s* Michael O'Loghlen, *b* 21 May 1945. *Address:* Qld 4077, Australia.

OLSSON, Curt Gunnar; Chairman, Skandinaviska Enskilda Banken, since 1984; *b* 20 Aug. 1927; *s* of N. E. and Anna Olsson; *m* 1954, Asta Engblom; two *d*. *Educ:* Stockholm Sch. of Econs (BSc Econs 1950). Managing Director, Stockholm Group: Skandinaviska Banken, 1970–72; Skandinaviska Enskilda Banken, 1972–76; Man. Dir and Chief Exec., Head Office, 1976–82, and first Dep. Chm., 1982–84, Skandinaviska Enskilda Banken. Director: Atlas Copco AB, 1976–; Fastighets AB Hufvudstaden, 1983–. Hon. Consul Gen. for Finland, 1989. Hon. DEcon, Stockholm, 1992. Kt Order of Vasa, Sweden, 1976; King Carl XVI Gustaf's Gold Medal, Sweden, 1982; Comdr, Royal Norwegian Order of Merit, 1985; Comdr, Order of the Lion, Finland, 1986. *Address:* Skandinaviska Enskilda Banken, 106 40 Stockholm, Sweden. *T:* (8) 221900.

OLSZEWSKI, Jan; MP (Center Civic Alliance), Poland, since 1991; Prime Minister of Poland, 1991–92; *b* Warsaw, 20 Aug. 1930. *Educ:* Warsaw Univ. Mem., underground Boy Scouts during Nazi occupation. Res. Asst, Legal Scis Dept, Polish Acad. Scis, 1954–56; Mem., editorial staff, Po Prostu, 1956–57 (periodical then closed down by authorities); subseq. banned from work as journalist; apprenticeship in legal profession, 1957–62; practised as trial lawyer, specialising in criminal law; served as defense counsel in political trials; suspended from the Bar, 1968 for defending students arrested for anti-communist demonstrations; returned as attorney, 1970. Founder (with Zdzisław Najder), Polish Independence Alliance, 1975–81; Co-Founder, Workers' Defense Cttee, 1976–77; involved in formation of Solidarity, and legal advr, 1980; co-author of statute of Free Trade Union of Coast Workers, 1980, which he personally delivered to Gdansk shipyard; Defense counsel at trials of Solidarity activists, 1980–89; Rep. of Solidarity opposition, Subcommn on legal and judicial reform, 1989; Mem., President Lech Wałęsa's Adv. Cttee, Jan.–Nov. 1991; Pres., Movement for the Republic, 1992–. *Address:* Biuro Poselskie, Al Ujazdowskie 13, 00–567 Warsaw, Poland. *T:* and *Fax:* (2) 6941051.

OLVER, Sir Stephen (John Linley), KBE 1975 (MBE 1947); CMG 1965; HM Diplomatic Service, retired; *b* 16 June 1916; *s* of late Rev. S. E. L. Olver and Mrs Madeleine Olver (*née* Stratton); *m* 1953, Maria Morena, Gubbio, Italy; one *s*. *Educ:* Stowe. Indian Police, 1935–44; Indian Political Service, Delhi, Quetta, Sikkim and Bahrain, 1944–47; Pakistan Foreign Service, Aug.–Oct. 1947; Foreign Service, Karachi, 1947–50; Foreign Office, 1950–53; Berlin, 1953–56; Bangkok, 1956–58; Foreign Office, 1958–61; Washington, 1961–64; Foreign Office, 1964–66; The Hague, 1967–69; High Comr, Freetown, 1969–72; High Comr, Nicosia, 1973–75. *Recreations:* photography, painting. *Address:* 6 Saffrons Court, Compton Place Road, Eastbourne, Sussex BN21 1DX.

OLYOTT, Ven. Leonard Eric; Archdeacon of Taunton and Prebendary of Milverton, 1977–92, Archdeacon Emeritus, 1992; *b* 11 Jan. 1926; *s* of Thomas Olyott and Maude Ann Olyott (*née* Purser); *m* 1951, Yvonne Winifred Kate Keele; two *s* one *d*. *Educ:* Colchester Royal Grammar School; London Univ. (BA 1950); Westcott House, Cambridge. Served RNVR, 1944–47; commissioned, 1945. Asst Curate, St George, Camberwell, 1952–55; Priest-in-Charge, St Michael and All Angels, Birchwood, Hatfield, Herts, 1955–60; Vicar of Chipperfield, Herts, 1960–68; Vicar of Crewkerne, 1968–71; Rector of Crewkerne with Wayford, 1971–77; Rural Dean of Crewkerne, 1972–77; Prebendary of Timberscombe, 1976. Hospital Chaplains Adviser to Bishop of Bath and Wells, 1983–92. *Recreations:* sailing, gardening, music, genealogy. *Address:* 5 Greendale, Ilminster, Somerset TA19 0EB.

O'MALLEY, Stephen Keppel; His Honour Judge O'Malley; a Circuit Judge, since 1989; *b* 21 July 1940; *s* of late D. K. C. O'Malley and Mrs R. O'Malley; *m* 1963, Frances Mary, *e d* of late James Stewart Ryan; four *s* two *d*. *Educ:* Ampleforth Coll.; Wadham Coll., Oxford (MA). Called to Bar, Inner Temple, 1962; Mem. Bar Council, 1968–72; Co-Founder, Bar European Gp, 1977; a Recorder, Western Circuit, 1978–89. Wine Treasurer, Western Circuit, 1986–89. *Publications:* Legal London, a Pictorial History, 1971; European Civil Practice, 1989. *Address:* Heale House, Curry Rivel, Langport, Som TA10 0PN. *T:* Langport (01458) 251220.

OMAN, Julia Trevelyan, (Lady Strong), CBE 1986; RDI 1977; designer; Director, Oman Productions Ltd; *b* 11 July 1930; *d* of late Charles Chichele Oman and Joan Trevelyan; *m* 1971, Sir Roy Colin Strong, *qv*. *Educ:* Royal College of Art, London (Royal Scholar, 1953; Silver Medal, 1955). Designer: BBC Television, 1955–67. Designer: *theatre:* Brief Lives, London and NY, 1967; Country Dance, London and Edinburgh, 1967; 40 Years On, 1968; The Merchant of Venice, NT, 1970; Othello, RSC, 1971; Getting On, Queen's, 1971; The Importance of Being Earnest, Vienna, 1976; Hay Fever and The Wild Duck, Lyric, Hammersmith, 1980; The Shoemakers' Holiday, NT, 1981; Mr and Mrs Nobody, Garrick, 1986; A Man for All Seasons, Chichester and Savoy, 1987; The Best of Friends, Apollo, 1988; *opera:* Mefistofele, WNO, 1957; Eugene Onegin, Covent Garden, 1971; Un Ballo in Maschera, Hamburgische Staatsoper, 1973; La Bohème, Covent Garden, 1974, 1995; Die Fledermaus, Covent Garden, 1977; Die Csardasfürstin, Kassel, 1982; Otello, Stockholm, 1983; Arabella, Glyndebourne, 1984, 1985, 1989; The Consul, Connecticut Grand Opera, USA, 1985; *ballet:* Enigma Variations, Royal Ballet, 1968, Birmingham Royal Ballet, 1994; A Month in the Country, Royal Ballet, 1976, Nat. Ballet of Canada, 1995; Sospiri, 1980; Swan Lake, Boston, 1981; The Nutcracker, 1984; *films:* Alice in Wonderland (BBC TV), 1966 (Designer of the Year Award, 1967); (Art Dir (England)) The Charge of the Light Brigade, 1967; (Art Dir) Laughter in the Dark, 1968; (prodn designer) Julius Caesar, 1969; The Straw Dogs, 1971; *television:* Hay Fever, 1979; Separate Tables, 1982; *exhibitions:* Samuel Pepys, Nat. Portrait Gall., 1971; Mme Tussaud's hist. tableaux, 1979; The Bear's Quest for Ragged Staff, Warwick Castle, 1981. Mem., DES Vis. Cttee for RSA, 1981–85. DesRCA (1st cl.), 1955; FCSD. Hon. DLitt Bristol, 1987. Award for Cable Excellence, for best art direction, NCTA, 1983. *Publications:* Street Children (photographs by Julia Trevelyan Oman; text by B. S. Johnson), 1964; (with Roy Strong) Elizabeth R, 1971; (with Roy Strong) Mary Queen of Scots, 1972; introd. The Merchant of Venice, Folio Soc. edn, 1975; (with Roy Strong) The English Year, 1982; (with Roy Strong) A Celebration of Gardens, 1991; (with Roy Strong) A Country Life, 1994; contrib. Architectural Review (photographs), Vogue (text and photographs). *Address:* c/o Oman Productions Ltd, The Laskett, Much Birch, Hereford HR2 8HZ.

OMAND, David Bruce; Deputy Under Secretary of State (Policy), Ministry of Defence, since 1992; *b* 15 April 1947; *s* of late J. Bruce Omand, JP, and of Esther Omand; *m* 1971,

Elizabeth, *er d* of late Geoffrey Wales, RE, ARCA; one *s* one *d*. *Educ:* Glasgow Acad.; Corpus Christi Coll., Cambridge (BAEcon). Ministry of Defence: Asst Principal, 1970; Private Sec. to Chief Exec. (PE), 1973; Asst Private Sec. to Sec. of State, 1973–75, 1979–80; Principal, 1975; Asst Sec., 1981; Private Sec. to Sec. of State, 1981–82; on loan to FCO as Defence Counsellor, UK Delegn to NATO, Brussels, 1985–88; Asst Under Sec. of State (Management Strategy), 1988–91, (Programmes), 1991–92. *Recreations:* opera, hill-walking. *Address:* Ministry of Defence, Whitehall, SW1. *Club:* Reform.

O'MARA, Margaret; Head of Libraries, Galleries and Museums Group (formerly Arts Group) (Under Secretary), Department of National Heritage, since 1992; *b* 10 May 1951; *d* of Thomas Patrick and Madge O'Mara. *Educ:* St Hilda's Coll., Oxford (1st Cl. Hons Lit.Hum.); University Coll. London (MSc Econs of Public Policy). Entered Treasury, 1973; Private Sec. to Chancellor of Exchequer, 1982–85; Head: Economic Briefing Div., 1985–87; Monetary Policy Div., 1987–90; Public Expenditure Div., monitoring Dept of Employment, 1990–92. *Recreations:* walking, cooking. *Address:* c/o Department of National Heritage, 2–4 Cockspur Street, SW1Y 5DH.

O'MORCHOE, David Nial Creagh, CB 1979; MBE 1967; (The O'Morchoe); Chief of O'Morchoe; sheep farmer; *b* 17 May 1928; *s* of Nial Creagh O'Morchoe and Jessie Elizabeth, *d* of late Charles Jasper Joly, FRS, FRIS, MRIA, Astronomer Royal of Ireland; *S* father as Chief of the Name (O'Morchoe, formerly Oulartleigh and Monamolin), 1970; *m* 1954, Margaret Jane, 3rd *d* of George Francis Brewitt, Cork; two *s* one *d*. *Educ:* St Columba's Coll., Dublin (Fellow 1983; Chm. of Fellows, 1989); RMA Sandhurst. Commissioned Royal Irish Fusiliers, 1948; served in Egypt, Jordan, Gibraltar, Germany, Kenya, Cyprus, Oman; psc 1958, jssc 1966; CO 1st Bn RIrF, later 3rd Bn Royal Irish Rangers, 1967–68; Directing Staff, Staff Coll., Camberley, 1969–71; RCDS 1972; Brigade Comdr, 1973–75; Brig. GS, BAOR, 1975–76; Maj.-Gen. 1977; Comdr, Sultan of Oman's Land Forces, 1977–79, retired. Dep. Col, 1971–76, Col 1977–79, The Royal Irish Rangers. Chm., Republic of Ireland Br., SSAFA/Forces Help Soc., 1987–; Mem. Council, Concern, Dublin, 1984– (Sec., 1989–). Member: Church of Ireland Gen. Synod, 1993–; Rep. Church Body, 1994–. Founder Mem., Standing Council of Irish Chiefs and Chieftans, 1992 (Chm., 1994–). *Recreations:* sailing and an interest in most sports. *Heir:* *s* Dermot Arthur O'Morchoe, *b* 11 Aug. 1956. *Address:* c/o Ulster Bank, Patrick Street, Cork. *Clubs:* Friendly Brothers (Dublin); Irish Cruising.

O'NEIL, Most Rev. Alexander Henry, MA, DD; *b* 23 July 1907; *m* 1931, Marguerite (*née* Roe); one *s*. *Educ:* Univ. of W Ontario (BA 1928; BD 1936; MA 1943; DD 1945); Huron Coll., London, Ont (LTh 1929). Deacon, 1929; Priest, 1930; Principal, Huron Coll., London, Ont, 1941–52; Gen. Sec., British and Foreign Bible Soc. in Canada, 1952–57; Bishop of Fredericton, 1957–63; Archbishop of Fredericton and Metropolitan of the Province of Canada, 1963–71. Hon. DD: Univ. of W Ontario, 1945; Wycliffe Coll., Toronto, 1954; King's Coll., Halifax, 1958; Hon. LLD: W Ontario, 1962; St Thomas Univ., Fredericton, 1970; Hon. DCL Bishop's Univ., Lennoxville, 1964. *Address:* Apt 807 Grosvenor Gates, 1 Grosvenor Street, London, Ont N6A 1Y2, Canada.

O'NEIL, Hon. Sir Desmond (Henry), Kt 1980; Chairman: Western Australia Lotteries Commission, 1981–84; Western Australia Greyhound Racing Association, 1981–84; *b* 27 Sept. 1920; *s* of late Henry McLelland O'Neil and Lilian Francis O'Neil; *m* 1944, Nancy Jean Culver; two *d*. *Educ:* Aquinas Coll., Perth; Claremont Teachers Coll., WA. Served War, Australian Army, 1939–46: Captain, Aust. Corps of Signals. Educn Dept, WA, 1939–58; Mem., Legislative Assembly, WA, 1959–80; Govt Whip, 1962–65; Minister for Housing and Labour, 1965–71; Dep. Leader of Opposition, 1972–73; Minister for: Works and Housing, 1974–75; Works, Housing and the North-West, 1975–77; Dep. Premier, Chief Sec., Minister for Police and Traffic, Minister for Regional Admin and the NW, Western Australia, 1977–80. Col Comdt, Royal Aust. Corps of Signals 5 Mil. Dist, 1980–82. *Recreations:* power boating, fishing. *Address:* 42 Godwin Avenue, South Como, WA 6152, Australia. *T:* 313–2526.

O'NEIL, Roger; Executive Vice President and Member, Executive Committee, Statoil, since 1992; Board Member, Borealis Chemicals, Copenhagen, since 1994; *b* 22 Feb. 1938; *s* of James William O'Neil and Claire Kathryn (*née* Williams); *m* 1976, Joan Mathewson; one *s* one *d*. *Educ:* Univ. of Notre Dame (BS Chemical Engrg, 1959); Cornell Univ. (MBA 1961). Joined Mobil Corp., New York, 1961; Various staff and exec. positions in Japan, Hong Kong, Australia, Paris, Cyprus, London and New York, 1963–73; Chm., Mobil cos in SE Asia, Singapore, 1973–78; Manager, Planning, Mobil Europe Inc., London, 1978–81; Manager, Corporate Econs and Planning, Mobil Corp., New York, 1981–82; Gp Vice Pres., Container Corp. of America, Chicago, 1982–84; Pres., Mobil Oil Italiana SpA, Rome, 1984–87; Chm. and Chief Exec., Mobil Oil Co., London, 1987–91; Dir and Vice Pres., Mobil Europe, 1991–92. Vice-Pres., Inst. of Petroleum, 1989– (FInstPet 1988). Member: President's Council, Asia Soc., NY, 1982–; Adv. Bd, Johnson Business Sch., Cornell Univ., 1990–. FRSA 1988. *Recreations:* archæology, skiing, tennis. *Address:* 3 Ormonde Gate, SW3 4EU. *Clubs:* Royal Automobile, Hurlingham.

O'NEIL, William Andrew; Secretary-General, International Maritime Organization, since 1990; *b* Ottawa, 6 June 1927; *s* of Thomas Wilson and Margaret O'Neil (*née* Swan); *m* 1950, Dorothy Muir; one *s* two *d*. *Educ:* Carleton Univ.; Univ. of Toronto (BASc Civil Engrg 1949). Engrg posts with Fed. Dept of Transport, 1949–55; Div. Engr, Regl Dir and Dir of Construction, St Lawrence Seaway Authy, 1955–71; Federal Department of Transport: Dep. Administrator, Marine Services, 1971–80; also Comr, Canadian Coast Guard, 1975–80; St Lawrence Seaway Authority, 1980–90: Pres. and Chief Exec. Officer; Dir, Canarctic Shipping Co.; Pres., Seaway Internat. Bridge Corp. Council of International Maritime Organization: Canadian Rep., 1972–90; Chm., 1980–90. Chm., Canadian Cttee, Lloyd's Register of Shipping, 1987–88; Mem. Bd, Internat. Maritime Bureau, 1991–. Chancellor, World Maritime Univ., 1991–. Member: Assoc. of Professional Engrs of Ont; ASCE. FCIT; FRSA; Foreign Mem., Royal Acad. of Engrg. LLD (*hc*) Univ. of Malta; Hon. DSc Nottingham Trent. Engrg Medal, Assoc. of Professional Engrs of Ont, 1972; Distinguished Public Service Award (USA), 1980; Admirals' Medal (Canada). *Address:* (office) 4 Albert Embankment, SE1 7SR. *T:* 0171–587 3100; 15 Ropers Orchard, SW3 5AX.

O'NEILL, family name of **Barons O'Neill** and **Rathcavan.**

O'NEILL, 4th Baron *cr* 1868; **Raymond Arthur Clanaboy O'Neill,** TD 1970; Lord-Lieutenant of County Antrim, since 1994; *b* 1 Sept. 1933; *s* of 3rd Baron and Anne Geraldine (she *m* 2nd, 1945, 2nd Viscount Rothermere, and 3rd, 1952, late Ian Fleming, and *d* 1981), *e d* of Hon. Guy Charteris; *S* father, 1944; *m* 1963, Georgina Mary, *er d* of Lord George Montagu Douglas Scott; three *s*. *Educ:* Eton; Royal Agricultural Coll. 2nd Lieut, 11th Hussars, Prince Albert's Own; Major, North Irish Horse, AVR; Lt-Col, RARO; Hon. Colonel: NI Horse Sqn, RYR, 1986–91; 69 Signal Sqn, NI Horse, 1988–93. Chm., Ulster Countryside Cttee, 1971–75. Vice-Chm., Ulster Folk and Transport Mus., 1987–90 (Trustee, 1969–90); Member: NI Tourist Bd, 1973–80 (Chm., 1975–80); NI Nat. Trust Cttee, 1980–91 (Chm., 1981–91); Museums and Galleries Commn, 1987–94; President: NI Assoc. of Youth Clubs, 1965–; Royal Ulster Agricl Soc., 1984–86 (Chm. Finance Cttee, 1974–83). DL Co. Antrim, 1967. *Recreations:* vintage motoring, railways, gardening. *Heir:* *s* Hon. Shane Sebastian Clanaboy O'Neill, *b* 25 July 1965. *Address:* Shanes Castle, Antrim, N Ireland BT41 4NE. *T:* Antrim (018494) 463264. *Club:* Turf.

See also Sir J. A. L. Morgan.

O'NEILL, Dennis James; operatic tenor; *b* 25 Feb. 1948; *s* of late Dr William P. O'Neill and of Eva A. O'Neill (*née* Rees); *m* 1st, 1970, Ruth Collins (marr. diss. 1987); one *s* one *d*; 2nd, 1988, Ellen Folkestad. *Educ:* Gowerton Boys' Grammar Sch. FTCL 1969; ARCM 1971. Specialist in Italian repertoire and works of Verdi in particular; Début: Royal Opera House, Covent Garden, 1979; Vienna State Opera, 1981; Hamburg State Opera, 1981; San Francisco Opera, 1984; Chicago Lyric Opera, 1985; Paris Opera, 1986; Metropolitan Opera, NY, 1986; Bayerische Staatsoper, Munich, 1992; has performed worldwide in opera and concerts. Many recordings. Presenter, Dennis O'Neill, BBC TV, 1987, 1988, 1989. Hon. FWCMD, 1993. *Recreations:* dinner parties, Verdi. *Address:* c/o Ingpen & Williams, 14 Kensington Court, W8 5DN. *T:* 0171–937 5158.

O'NEILL, Martin (John); MP (Lab) Clackmannan, since 1983 (Stirlingshire, East and Clackmannan, 1979–83); *b* 6 Jan. 1945; *s* of John and Minnie O'Neill; *m* 1973, Elaine Marjorie Samuel; two *s*. *Educ:* Trinity Academy, Edinburgh; Heriot Watt Univ. (BA Econ.); Moray House Coll. of Education, Edinburgh. Insurance Clerk, Scottish Widows Fund, 1963–67; Asst Examiner, Estate Duty Office of Scotland, 1971–73; Teacher of Modern Studies: Boroughmuir High School, Edinburgh, 1974–77; Craigmount High School, Edinburgh, 1977–79; Social Science Tutor, Open Univ., 1976–79. Opposition spokesman on Scottish affairs, 1980–84, on defence matters, 1984–88, on energy, 1992–; Chief opposition spokesman on defence, 1988–92. Mem., Select Cttee, Scottish Affairs, 1979–80. Member: GMB; EIS. *Recreations:* watching football, reading, listening to jazz, the cinema. *Address:* House of Commons, SW1A 0AA. *T:* 0171–219 4548; 19 Mar Street, Alloa, Clackmannanshire FK10 1HR. *T:* Alloa (01259) 721536.

O'NEILL, Dr Onora Sylvia, CBE 1995; FBA 1993; Principal, Newnham College, Cambridge, since 1992; *b* 23 Aug. 1941; *d* of Hon. Sir Con O'Neill, GCMG and of Rosemary Margaret (*née* Pritchard) (now Lady Garvey); *m* 1963, Edward John Nell (marr. diss. 1976); two *s*. *Educ:* St Paul's Girls' Sch.; Somerville Coll., Oxford (BA, MA; Hon. Fellow, 1993); Harvard Univ. (PhD). Asst, then Associate Prof., Barnard Coll., Columbia Univ., 1970–77; University of Essex: Lectr, 1977–78; Sen. Lectr, 1978–83; Reader, 1983–87; Prof. of Philosophy, 1987–92. Member: Animal Procedures Cttee, 1990–94; Nuffield Council on Bioethics, 1991–. Fellow, Wissenschaftskolleg, Berlin, 1989–90. Pres., Aristotelian Soc., 1988–89. Foreign Hon. Mem., Amer. Acad. of Arts and Scis, 1993. *Publications:* Acting on Principle, 1976; Faces of Hunger, 1986; Constructions of Reason, 1989; numerous articles on philosophy, esp. political philosophy and ethics in learned jls. *Recreations:* walking, talking. *Address:* Newnham College, Cambridge CB3 9DF. *T:* Cambridge (01223) 335821.

O'NEILL, Prof. Patrick Geoffrey, BA, PhD; Professor of Japanese, School of Oriental and African Studies, University of London, 1968–86, now Emeritus; *b* 9 Aug. 1924; *m* 1951, Diana Howard; one *d*. *Educ:* Rutlish Sch., Merton; Sch. of Oriental and African Studies, Univ. of London. Lectr in Japanese, Sch. of Oriental and African Studies, Univ. of London, 1949. First Sakura Award, Nihon Zenkoku Gakushikai, 1976. Order of the Rising Sun (Japan), 1987. *Publications:* A Guide to Nō, 1954; Early Nō Drama, 1958; (with S. Yanada) Introduction to Written Japanese, 1963; A Programmed Course on Respect Language in Modern Japanese, 1966; Japanese Kana Workbook 1967; A Programmed Introduction to Literary-style Japanese, 1968; Japanese Names, 1972; Essential Kanji, 1973; (ed) Tradition and Modern Japan, 1982; (with H. Inagaki) A Dictionary of Japanese Buddhist Terms, 1984; A Reader of Handwritten Japanese, 1984; (trans.) Japan on Stage, by T. Kawatake, 1990. *Address:* 44 Vine Road, East Molesey, Surrey KT8 9LF.

O'NEILL, Robert James, CMG 1978; HM Diplomatic Service, retired; *b* 17 June 1932; *m* 1958, Helen Juniper; one *s* two *d*. *Educ.* King Edward VI Sch., Chelmsford; Trinity Coll., Cambridge (Schol.). 1st cl. English Tripos Pts I and II. Entered HM Foreign (now Diplomatic) Service, 1955; FO, 1955–57; British Embassy, Ankara, 1957–60; Dakar, 1961–63; FO, 1963–68, Private Sec. to Chancellor of Duchy of Lancaster, 1966, and to Minister of State for Foreign Affairs, 1967–68; British Embassy, Bonn, 1968–72; Counsellor Diplomatic Service, 1972; seconded to Cabinet Office as Asst Sec., 1972–75; FCO, 1975–78; Dep. Governor, Gibraltar, 1978–81; Under Sec., Cabinet Office, 1981–84; Asst Under-Sec. of State, FCO, 1984–86; Ambassador to Austria, and concurrently Head of UK Delegn, MBFR, Vienna, 1986–89; Ambassador to Belgium, 1989–92; EC Presidency Rep. for Macedonia, 1992. *Recreations:* diplomatic history, hill-walking. *Address:* 4 Castle Street, Saffron Walden, Essex CB10 1BP. *T:* Saffron Walden (01799) 520291. *Clubs:* Travellers', Royal Anglo-Belgian.

O'NEILL, Prof. Robert John, AO 1988; FASSA; FIE (Aust); FRHistS; Chichele Professor of the History of War, University of Oxford, since 1987; Fellow, All Souls College, Oxford, since 1987; *b* 5 Nov. 1936; *s* of Joseph Henry and Janet Gibbon O'Neill; *m* 1965, Sally Margaret Burnard; two *d*. *Educ:* Scotch Coll., Melbourne; Royal Military Coll. of Australia; Univ. of Melbourne (BE); Brasenose Coll., Oxford (MA, DPhil 1965; Hon. Fellow, 1990). FASSA 1978; FIE(Aust) 1981; FRHistS 1990. Served Australian Army, 1955–68; Rhodes Scholar, Vic, 1961; Fifth Bn Royal Australian Regt, Vietnam, 1966–67 (mentioned in despatches); Major 1967; resigned 1968. Sen. Lectr in History, Royal Military Coll. of Australia, 1968–69; Australian National University: Sen. Fellow in Internat. Relations, 1969–77, Professorial Fellow, 1977–82; Head, Strategic and Defence Studies Centre, 1971–82; Dir, IISS, 1982–87; Dir of Graduate Studies, Modern History Faculty, Univ. of Oxford, 1990–92. Official Australian Historian for the Korean War, 1969–82. Dir, Shell Transport and Trading, 1992–. Chairman: Management Cttee, Sir Robert Menzies Centre for Australian Studies, Univ. of London, 1990–95; Bd, Centre for Defence Studies, KCL, 1990–95; Vice-Chm. Council, IISS, 1994– (Mem. Council, 1977–82, 1992–). Governor: Ditchley Foundn, 1989–; Internat. Peace Acad., 1990–; Salzburg Seminar, 1992–; Trustee: Imperial War Museum, 1990–; Commonwealth War Graves Commn, 1991–. Mem., Adv. Bd, Investment Co. of America, 1988–; Dir, two Mutual Funds, Capital Group, LA, 1992–. Chm., Round Table Moot, 1986–92. Hon. Col 5th (Volunteer) Royal Green Jackets, 1993–. *Publications:* The German Army and the Nazi Party 1933–1939, 1966; Vietnam Task, 1968; General Giap: politician and strategist, 1969; (ed) The Strategic Nuclear Balance, 1975; (ed) The Defence of Australia: fundamental new aspects, 1977; (ed) Insecurity: the spread of weapons in the Indian and Pacific Oceans, 1978; (ed jtly) Australian Dictionary of Biography, Vols 7–12, 1891–1939, 1979–91; (ed with David Horner) New Directions in Strategic Thinking, 1981; Australia in the Korean War 1950–1953, Vol. I, Strategy and Diplomacy, 1981, Vol. II, Combat Operations, 1985; (ed with David Horner) Australian Defence Policy for the 1980s, 1982; (ed) Security in East Asia, 1984; (ed) The Conduct of East-West Relations in the 1980s, 1985; (ed) New Technology and Western Security Policy, 1985; (ed) Doctrine, the Alliance and Arms Control, 1986; (ed) East Asia, the West and International Security, 1987; (ed) Security in the Mediterranean, 1989; (ed with R. J. Vincent) The West and the Third World, 1990; (ed with Beatrice Heuser) Securing Peace in Europe 1945–62, 1992;

(ed jtly) War, Strategy and International Politics, 1992; articles in many learned jls. *Recreations:* local history, walking. *Address:* All Souls College, Oxford OX1 4AL. *Club:* Garrick.

ONG Teng Cheong; President of Singapore, since 1993; *b* 22 Jan. 1936; *m* 1963, Ling Siew May; two *s*. *Educ:* Chinese High Sch.; Univ. of Adelaide (BArch 1961); Univ. of Liverpool (MCD 1967). Architect, Adelaide and Singapore, 1962–65; town planner in Singapore CS, 1967–71; architect and town planner in private sector, 1971–75. MP: for Kim Keat, 1972–88; Toa Payoh Gp, 1988–93; Sen. Minister of State for Communications, 1975–78; Minister for Communications, 1978–83; Actg Minister for Culture, 1978–80; Minister for Labour, 1980–83; Minister Without Portfolio, 1983–85; 2nd Dep. Prime Minister, 1985–90; Dep. Prime Minister, 1990–93. Chm., People's Action Party Central Exec. Cttee, 1981–93. Sec.-Gen., NTUC, 1983–93. *Address:* Office of the President, Istana, Singapore.

ONGLEY, Hon. Sir Joseph (Augustine), Kt 1987; Judge of the High Court of New Zealand, 1975–86; *b* 5 Feb. 1918; *s* of Arthur Montague Ongley, OBE and Nora Crina Ongley; *m* 1943, Joan Muriel Archer; four *s* one *d*. *Educ:* St Patrick's Coll., Silverstream; Victoria Univ. of Wellington (LLB). Admitted Barrister and Solicitor of Supreme, later High, Court of NZ, 1939; Crown Solicitor, Palmerston North, 1960–75; retired, 1986, then served in temp. capacity until 1995. Life Mem., NZ Cricket Council (former Pres.); Patron, Central Dists Cricket Assoc., NZ, 1995. *Recreations:* formerly cricket (represented NZ), golf. *Address:* 10 Lancaster Street, Karori, Wellington, New Zealand. *T:* Wellington (4) 4769585. *Clubs:* Wellington; Manawatu (Palmerston North).

ÖNHON, Candemir; Ambassador of Turkey to the Court of St James's, 1991–95; *b* Istanbul, 30 Oct. 1933; *s* of Saim and Münire Önhon; *m* 1959, Birsen Kap; one *s* one *d*. *Educ:* Lycée Galatasaray, Istanbul; Faculty of Law, Univ. of Ankara. 3rd Sec., Candidate Officer, Political Dept (i/c Cyprus and Greece), 1956; Military Service, 1956–57; 3rd and 2nd Sec., NATO Dept, 1958–60; 2nd and 1st Sec., Turkish Perm. Delegn to NATO, 1960–64; Consul, Comotini, Greece, 1964–65; Section Director: NATO Dept, 1965–66; Dept of Cyprus and Greece, 1966–67; Counsellor: Nicosia, Cyprus, 1967–69; Athens, 1969–72; Dep. Head, ME Political Dept, 1972; Chief, Cabinet of Presidency of Republic, 1973–76; Rep. of Turkey with rank of Ambassador, Cyprus, 1976–79; Ambassador to Finland, 1979–82; Under-Sec. of Information, PM's Office, 1982–84; Sen. Advr and Inspector, Min. Foreign Affairs, 1984–86; Ambassador to Egypt, 1986–91. *Recreations:* horse-riding, hunting, photography, cinematography. *Address:* Dişisleri Bakanligi, Ankara, Turkey.

O'NIONS, Prof. Robert Keith, PhD; FRS 1983; Professor of the Physics and Chemistry of Minerals, and Fellow of St Hugh's College, University of Oxford, since 1995; *b* 26 Sept. 1944; *s* of William Henry O'Nions and Eva O'Nions; *m* 1967, Rita Margaret Bill; three *d*. *Educ:* Univ. of Nottingham (BSc 1966); Univ. of Alberta (PhD 1969). Post-doctoral Fellow, Oslo Univ., 1970; Demonstr in Petrology, Oxford Univ., 1971–72, Lectr in Geochem., 1972–75; Associate Prof., then Prof., Columbia Univ., NY, 1975–79; Royal Soc. Res. Prof., 1979–95, and Fellow, Clare Hall, 1980–95, Cambridge Univ. Mem., Norwegian Acad. of Sciences, 1980. Macelwane Award, Amer. Geophys. Union, 1979; Bigsby Medal, Geol. Soc. London, 1983; Holmes Medal, Eur. Union of Geosciences, 1995; Lyell Medal, Geol Soc. of London, 1995. *Publications:* contrib. to jls related to earth and planetary sciences. *Address:* Department of Earth Sciences, Oxford University, Oxford OX1 3PR. *T:* Oxford (01865) 272000.

ONSLOW, family name of **Earl of Onslow.**

ONSLOW, 7th Earl of, *cr* 1801; **Michael William Coplestone Dillon Onslow,** Bt 1660; Baron Onslow, 1716; Baron Cranley, 1776; Viscount Cranley, 1801; *b* 28 Feb. 1938; *s* of 6th Earl of Onslow, KBE, MC, TD, and Hon. Pamela Louisa Eleanor Dillon (*d* 1992), *o d* of 19th Viscount Dillon, CMG, DSO; *S* father, 1971; *m* 1964, Robin Lindsay, *o d* of Major Robert Lee Bullard III, US Army, and of Lady Aberconway; one *s* two *d*. *Educ:* Eton; Sorbonne. Life Guards, 1956–60, served Arabian Peninsula. Farmer; director, various cos. Governor, Royal Grammar Sch., Guildford; formerly Governor, University Coll. at Buckingham. Mem., Univ. of Surrey Res. Park Exec. High Steward of Guildford. *Heir:* *s* Viscount Cranley, *qv*. *Address:* Temple Court, Clandon Park, Guildford, Surrey GU4 7RQ. *Clubs:* White's, Beefsteak.
See also A. A. Waugh.

ONSLOW, Rt. Hon. Sir Cranley (Gordon Douglas), KCMG 1993; PC 1988; MP (C) Woking since 1964; *b* 8 June 1926; *s* of late F. R. D. Onslow and Mrs M. Onslow, Effingham House, Bexhill; *m* 1955, Lady June Hay, *yr d* of 13th Earl of Kinnoull; one *s* three *d*. *Educ:* Harrow; Oriel Coll., Oxford; Geneva Univ. Served in RAC, Lieut 7th QO Hussars, 1944–48, and 3rd/4th Co. of London Yeo. (Sharpshooters) (TA) as Captain, 1948–52. Joined HM Foreign Service, 1951; Third Sec. Br. Embassy, Rangoon, 1953–55; Consul at Maymyo, N Burma, 1955–56; resigned, 1960. Served on Dartford RDC, 1960–62, and Kent CC, 1961–64. Parly Under-Sec. of State, Aerospace and Shipping, DTI, 1972–74; an Opposition spokesman on health and social security, 1974–75, on defence, 1975–76; Minister of State, FCO, 1982–83. Chairman: Select Cttee on Defence, 1981–82; Cons. Aviation Cttee, 1970–72, 1979–82; Mem., Select Cttee on Trade and Industry, 1992–. Mem. Exec., 1922 Cttee, 1968–72, 1981–82, 1983–92, Chm., 1984–92. Mem., UK delegn to Council of Europe and WEU, 1977–81. Director: Argyll Group PLC, 1983–93; Redifon Ltd (formerly Rediffusion), 1985– (Chm., 1988–). Chm., Nautical Museums Trust, 1983–. Council Member: Nat. Rifle Assoc.; Salmon & Trout Assoc.; Anglers' Co-operative Assoc.; British Field Sports Soc. MRAeS. Liveryman, Fishmongers' Co., 1991–. *Publication:* Asian Economic Development (ed), 1965. *Recreations:* fishing, shooting, watching cricket. *Address:* Highbuilding, Fernhurst, W Sussex GU27 3NL. *Clubs:* Travellers', Beefsteak, English-Speaking Union.

ONSLOW, Sir John (Roger Wilmot), 8th Bt, *cr* 1797; Captain, Royal Yacht of Saudi Arabia; *b* 21 July 1932; *o s* of Sir Richard Wilmot Onslow, 7th Bt, TD, and Constance (*d* 1960), *o d* of Albert Parker; *S* father, 1963; *m* 1955, Catherine Zoia (marr. diss. 1973), *d* of Henry Atherton Greenway, The Manor, Compton Abdale, near Cheltenham, Gloucestershire; one *s* one *d*; *m* 1976, Susan Fay, *d* of E. M. Hughes, Frankston, Vic, Australia. *Educ:* Cheltenham College. *Heir:* *s* Richard Paul Atherton Onslow, *b* 16 Sept. 1958. *Address:* c/o Barclays Bank, Fowey, Cornwall PL23 1BA.

ONTARIO, Metropolitan of; *see* Huron, Archbishop of.

ONTARIO, Bishop of, since 1992; **Rt. Rev. Peter Ralph Mason;** *b* 30 April 1943; *s* of late Ralph Victor Mason and of Dorothy Ida Mullin; *m* 1965, Carmen Ruth Ruddock; one *s* two *d*. *Educ:* McGill Univ., Montreal (BA 1964; BD 1967; MA 1971); Princeton Univ. (DMin 1983). Ordained, deacon, 1967, priest, 1968; Asst Curate, St Matthew's, Montreal, 1967–69; Incumbent, parish of Hemmingford, 1969–71; Rector: St Clement's, Montreal, 1971–74; St Peter's, Montreal, 1975–80; St Paul's, Halifax, NS, 1980–85; Principal, Wycliffe Theol Coll., Univ. of Toronto, 1985–92. Hon. DD Montreal Diocesan Theol Coll., 1987; Hon. DD: Trinity Coll., Toronto, 1992; Wycliffe Coll., Toronto, 1994. *Recreations:* golf, sailing, ski-ing, opera. *Addresses:* (office) 90 Johnson Street, Kingston, Ontario K7L 1X7, Canada. *T:* (613) 5444774; (home) 73 Seaforth Road, Kingston, Ontario K7M 1E1, Canada.

OPENSHAW, Caroline Jane, (Mrs C. P. L. Openshaw); *see* Swift, C. J.

OPENSHAW, (Charles) Peter (Lawford); QC 1991; a Recorder, since 1988; *b* 21 Dec. 1947; *s* of late Judge William Harrison Openshaw and Elisabeth Joyce Emily Openshaw; *m* 1979, Caroline Jane Swift, *qv*; one *s* one *d*. *Educ:* Harrow; St Catharine's College, Cambridge (MA). Called to the Bar, Inner Temple, 1970; practising on Northern Circuit, Junior 1973; Assistant Recorder, 1985. *Recreations:* fishing, gardening, village life. *Address:* Peel Court Chambers, 45 Hardman Street, Manchester M3 3HA. *T:* 0161–832 3791. *Club:* United Oxford & Cambridge University.

OPIE, Alan John; Principal Baritone with English National Opera, since 1973; *b* 22 March 1945; *s* of Jack and Doris Winifred Opie; *m* 1970, Kathleen Ann Smales; one *s* one *d*. *Educ:* Truro Sch.; Guildhall Sch. of Music (AGSM); London Opera Centre. Principal rôles include: Papageno in The Magic Flute, Sadler's Wells Opera, 1969; Tony in the Globolinks, Santa Fé Opera, 1970; Officer in the Barber of Seville, Covent Garden, 1971; Don Giovanni, Kent Opera, and Demetrius, English Opera Gp, 1972; *English National Opera:* Figaro; Papageno; Gugliemo; Beckmesser; Valentin; Lescaut in Manon; Eisenstein and Falke in Die Fledermaus; Danilo; Silvio; Junius in Rape of Lucretia; Cecil in Gloriana; Faninal in Der Rosenkavalier; Germont in La Traviata; Marcello and Schaunard in La Bohème; Kovalyov in The Nose; Strephon in Iolanthe; Grosvenor in Patience; Tomsky in Queen of Spades; Paolo in Simon Boccanegra; Harlequin in Ariadne auf Naxos; Dr Faust by Busoni; Sharpless in Madame Butterfly; Fiddler in Königskinder; Sancho in Don Quixote, 1994; *Royal Opera, Covent Garden:* Hector in King Priam, 1985; Ping in Turandot, 1986; Mangus in The Knot Garden, 1988; Falke in Die Fledermaus, 1989; Paolo in Simon Boccanegra; rôles in Death in Venice, 1992; Sharpless in Madame Butterfly, 1993; Faninal in Der Rosenkavalier, 1995; *Glyndebourne Festival Opera:* Sid in Albert Herring, 1985, 1990; rôles in Death in Venice, 1989; Figaro in Le Nozze di Figaro, 1991; Balstrode in Peter Grimes, 1992; *Scottish Opera:* Baron in La Vie Parisienne, 1985; Storch in Intermezzo, 1986; Forester in Cunning Little Vixen, 1991; *Opera North:* Diomede in Troilus and Cressida, 1995; *Metropolitan Opera, NY:* Balstrode in Peter Grimes, 1994; has also appeared at Bayreuth Fest., Berlin (Unter den Linden, Berlin Staatsoper, 1990) and in Amsterdam and Munich (rôles include Beckmesser), and at Buxton Fest. and in Brussels, Chicago, Vienna and Paris. *Address:* Quanda, Old Court, Ashtead, Surrey KT21 2TS. *T:* Ashtead (01372) 274038.

OPIE, Geoffrey James; freelance lecturer on 19th and 20th century art and design; *b* 10 July 1939; *s* of Basil Irwin Opie and Florence Mabel Opie (*née* May); *m* 1st, 1964, Pamela Green; one *s* one *d*; 2nd, 1980, Jennifer Hawkins; one *s*. *Educ:* Humphry Davy Grammar School, Penzance; Falmouth Sch. of Art (NDD); Goldsmiths' Coll., London (ATC). Asst Designer, Leacock & Co., 1961; Curator, Nat. Mus. of Antiquities of Scotland, 1963; Designer, Leacock & Co., 1967; Curator, Victoria and Albert Mus., 1969, Educn Dept, 1978–89, Head of Educn Services, 1983–89. *Publications:* The Wireless Cabinet 1930–1956, 1979; contribs to various jls. *Recreations:* painting, literature, music, motorcycling. *Address:* 130 Kingston Road, Teddington, Middx TW11 9JA.

OPIE, Iona Margaret Balfour; folklorist; *b* 13 Oct. 1923; *d* of late Sir Robert Archibald, CMG, DSO, MD, and of Olive Cant; *m* 1943, Peter Mason Opie (*d* 1982); two *s* one *d*. *Educ:* Sandecotes Sch., Parkstone. Served 1941–43, WAAF meteorological section. Hon. Mem., Folklore Soc., 1974. Coote-Lake Medal (jtly with husband), 1960. Hon. MA: Oxon, 1962; OU, 1987; Hon. DLitt: Southampton, 1987; Nottingham, 1991. *Publications:* (all with Peter Opie or using material researched with him): I Saw Esau, 1947, 2nd edn (illus. Maurice Sendak), 1992; The Oxford Dictionary of Nursery Rhymes, 1951; The Oxford Nursery Rhyme Book, 1955; The Lore and Language of Schoolchildren, 1959; Puffin Book of Nursery Rhymes, 1963 (European Prize City of Caorle); Children's Games in Street and Playground, 1969 (Chicago Folklore Prize); The Oxford Book of Children's Verse, 1973; Three Centuries of Nursery Rhymes and Poetry for Children (exhibition catalogue), 1973, enl. edn 1977; The Classic Fairy Tales, 1974; A Nursery Companion, 1980; The Oxford Book of Narrative Verse, 1983; The Singing Game, 1985 (Katharine Briggs Folklore Award; Rose Mary Crawshay Prize; Children's Literature Assoc. Book Award); Tail Feathers from Mother Goose, 1988; (ed jtly) The Treasures of Childhood, 1989; (ed jtly) A Dictionary of Superstitions, 1989; Babies: an unsentimental anthology (from notes assembled with Peter Opie), 1990; (sole author) The People in the Playground, 1993. *Recreation:* opsimathy. *Address:* Westerfield House, West Liss, Hants GU33 6JQ. *T:* Liss (01730) 893309.

OPIE, Roger Gilbert, CBE 1976; Fellow and Lecturer in Economics, New College, Oxford, 1961–92; Emeritus Fellow, since 1992; *b* Adelaide, SA, 23 Feb. 1927; *o s* of late Frank Gilbert Opie and late Fanny Irene Grace Opie (*née* Tregoning); *m* 1955, Norma Mary, *o d* of late Norman and late Mary Canter; two *s* one *d*. *Educ:* Prince Alfred Coll. and Adelaide Univ., SA; Christ Church and Nuffield Coll., Oxford. BA 1st Cl. Hons 1948, MA Adelaide 1950; SA Rhodes Schol., 1951; Boulter Exhibnr, 1952; George Webb Medley Jun. Schol., 1952, Sen. Schol., 1953; PPE 1st Cl. 1953; Nuffield Coll. Studentship, 1954; BPhil 1954. Tutor and Lectr, Adelaide Univ., 1949–51; Asst Lectr and Lectr, LSE, 1954–61; Econ. Adviser, Econ. Section, HM Treasury, 1958–60; Asst Dir, HM Treasury Centre for Administrative Studies, 1964; Asst Dir, Planning Div., Dept of Economic Affairs, 1964–66; Advr, W. Pakistan Planning Commn, 1966; Economic Adviser to Chm., NBPI, 1967–70; Special Univ. Lectr in Econs, Oxford, 1970–75; Tutor and Sen. Tutor, Oxford Univ. Business Summer Sch., 1974–79. Visiting Professor: Brunel Univ., 1975–77; Univ. of Strathclyde, 1984–87. Member: Monopolies and Mergers Commn, 1968–81; Price Commn, 1977–80. Mem., ILO Mission to Ethiopia, 1982. City Councillor, Oxford, 1972–74; Oxford Dist Councillor, 1973–76. Presenter, TV series: Wealth of a Nation; History Today. Economic Correspondent, New Statesman, 1967–71, 1974–76; Editor: The Bankers' Magazine, 1960–64; International Currency Review, 1970–71. Governor, Bryanston Sch. FRSA 1980. *Publications:* co-author of a number of works in applied economics. *Recreations:* sailing, photography, hiding in Cornwall. *Address:* New College, Oxford OX1 3BN. *T:* Oxford (01865) 279555.

OPPÉ, Prof. Thomas Ernest, CBE 1984; FRCP; Professor of Paediatrics, University of London at St Mary's Hospital Medical School, 1969–90, now Emeritus Professor; *b* 7 Feb. 1925; *s* of late Ernest Frederick Oppé and Ethel Nellie (*née* Rackstraw); *m* 1948, Margaret Mary Butcher; three *s* one *d*. *Educ:* University Coll. Sch., Hampstead; Guy's Hosp. Med. Sch. (MB BS, hons dist. in Medicine, 1947). DCH 1950; FRCP 1966. Sir Alfred Fripp Meml Fellow, Guy's Hosp., 1952; Milton Res. Fellow, Harvard Univ., 1954; Lectr in Child Health, Univ. of Bristol, 1956–60; Consultant Paediatrician, United Bristol Hosps, 1960; Asst Dir, 1960–64, Dir, 1964–69, Paediatric Unit, St Mary's Hosp. Med. Sch.; Consultant Paediatrician, St Mary's Hosp., 1960–90. Consultant Adviser in Paediatrics, DHSS, 1971–86; Member, DHSS Committees: Safety of Medicines, 1974–79; Med. Aspects of Food Policy, 1966–88 (Chm., Panel on Child Nutrition); Child Health Services, 1973–76. Royal College of Physicians: Chm., Cttee on Paediatrics, 1970–74; Pro-Censor and Censor, 1975–77; Sen. Censor and Sen. Vice-Pres., 1983–84; University of London: Mem., Bd of Studies in Medicine, 1964–90 (Chm., 1978–80); elected Mem. of Senate, 1981–89; Dean, Faculty of Medicine, 1984–86; Mem. of Court, 1984–89. Member: BMA (Dep. Chm., Bd of Sci. and Educn, 1974–82); British Paediatric Assoc. (Hon. Sec., 1960–63); European Soc. for Paediatric Res., 1969–; GMC, 1984–88; sometime Mem., Governing Bodies, St Mary's Hosp., Inst. of Med. Ethics, Paddington Coll.; Examiner in Paediatrics, Univs of Glasgow, Leicester, Liverpool, London, Sheffield, Wales, Colombo, Singapore. *Publications:* Modern Textbook of Paediatrics for Nurses, 1961; Neurological Examination of Children (with R. Paine), 1966; chapters in books and papers on paediatrics and child health. *Address:* 2 Parkholme Cottages, Fife Road, Sheen Common, SW14 7ER. *T:* 0181–392 1626.

OPPENHEIM, Tan Sri Sir Alexander, Kt 1961; OBE 1955; FRSE; MA, DSc (Oxon); PhD (Chicago); retired; Visiting Professor, University of Benin, Nigeria, 1973–77; Vice-Chancellor, University of Malaya, 1957–65 (Acting Vice-Chancellor, 1955); *b* 4 Feb. 1903; *o s* of late Rev. H. J. and Mrs F. Oppenheim; *m* 1930, Beatrice Templer (marr. diss. 1977), *y d* of Dr Otis B. Nesbit, Indiana, USA; one *d*; and two *s*. *Educ:* Manchester Grammar Sch.; Balliol Coll., Oxford (Scholar). Sen. Mathematical Schol., Oxf., 1926; Commonwealth Fund Fell., Chicago, 1927–30; Lectr, Edinburgh, 1930–31; Prof. of Mathematics, 1931–42, 1945–49; Dep. Principal, 1947, 1949, Raffles Coll., Singapore; Prof. of Mathematics, 1949–57; Dean, Faculty of Arts, 1949, 1951, 1953. L/Bdr, SRA(V), POW (Singapore, Siam), 1942–45; Dean POW University, 1942; Pres. Malayan Mathematical Soc., 1951–55, 1957. Pres. Singapore Chess Club, 1956–60; Pres., Amer. Univs. Club, 1956. Chm. Bd of Management, Tropical Fish Culture Research Institute (Malacca), 1962; Member: Unesco-International Assoc. of Universities Study of Higher Education in Development of Countries of SE Asia, 1962; Academic Adv. Cttee, Univ. of Cape Coast, 1972. Visiting Professor: Univ. of Reading, in Dept of Mathematics, 1965–68; Univ. of Ghana, 1968–73. FIMA 1964. Hon. degrees: DSc (Hong Kong) 1961; LLD: (Singapore) 1962; (Leeds) 1966; DLitt (Malaya) 1965. Alumni Medal, Univ. of Chicago Alumni Assoc., 1977. Panglima Mangku Negara (Fedn of Malaya), 1962; FWA, 1963. *Publications:* papers on mathematics in various periodicals. *Recreations:* chess, bridge. *Address:* Matson House, Remenham, Henley-on-Thames RG9 3HB. *T:* Henley-on-Thames (01491) 572049. *Clubs:* Royal Over-Seas League; Selangor (Kuala Lumpur).

OPPENHEIM, Sir Duncan (Morris), Kt 1960; Adviser to British-American Tobacco Co. Ltd, 1972–74 (Chairman 1953–66, President, 1966–72); Chairman, Tobacco Securities Trust Co. Ltd, 1969–74; Deputy Chairman, Commonwealth Development Finance Co., 1968–74; *b* 6 Aug. 1904; *s* of Watkin Oppenheim, BA, TD, and Helen, 3rd *d* of Duncan McKechnie; *m* 1st, 1932, Joyce Mary (*d* 1933), *d* of Stanley Mitcheson; no *c*; 2nd, 1936, Susan May (*d* 1964), *e d* of Brig.-Gen. E. B. Macnaghten, CMG, DSO; one *s* one *d*. *Educ:* Repton Sch. Admitted Solicitor of the Supreme Court, 1929; Messrs Linklaters & Paines, London, Assistant Solicitor, 1929–34; joined British-American Tobacco Ltd group as a Solicitor, 1934; Director: British-American Tobacco Co. Ltd, 1943; Lloyds Bank Ltd, 1956–75; Equity and Law Life Assurance Society, 1966–80. Chairman: Council, Royal College of Art, 1956–72; Council of Industrial Design, 1960–72 (Mem. 1959); British Nat. Cttee of Internat. Chamber of Commerce, 1963–74; Overseas Investment Cttee CBI, 1964–74; RIIA (Chatham House), 1966–71; Member: Adv. Council, V&A Mus., 1967–79 (Chm. V&A Associates, 1976–81); Crafts Council (formerly Crafts Adv. Cttee), 1972–83 (acting Chm., 1977; Dep. Chm., 1978); Trustee and Mem., Council, 1973–94, Chm. of Council, 1990–, St John's, Smith Square. Governing Body of Repton School, 1959–79; Chm. Court of Governors, Admin. Staff Coll., 1963–71. Hon. Dr and Senior Fellow, Royal College of Art; Hon. FCSD (Hon. FSIAD 1972). Bicentenary Medal, RSA, 1969. *Recreations:* painting, sailing. *Address:* 43 Edwardes Square, Kensington, W8 6HH. *T:* 0171–603 7431. *Clubs:* Athenæum; Royal Yacht Squadron.

OPPENHEIM, Hon. Phillip Anthony Charles Lawrence; MP (C) Amber Valley, since 1983; Parliamentary Under-Secretary of State, Department of Trade and Industry, since 1995; *b* 20 March 1956; *s* of late Henry Oppenheim and of Baroness Oppenheim-Barnes, *qv*. *Educ:* Harrow; Oriel College, Oxford. BA Hons. Company director, author. PPS to Sec. of State for Health, 1988–90, to Sec. of State for Educn and Sci., 1990–92, to Home Sec., 1992–93, to Chancellor of the Exchequer, 1993–94; Parly Under-Sec. of State, Dept of Employment, 1994–95. Co-editor, What to Buy for Business, 1980–85. *Publications:* A Handbook of New Office Technology, 1982; Telecommunications: a user's handbook, 1983; A Word Processing Handbook, 1984; The New Masters: can the West match Japan?, 1991; Trade Wars: Japan versus the West, 1992. *Recreations:* Rugby, tennis, travel, ski-ing, tropical plants. *Address:* House of Commons, SW1A 0AA.

OPPENHEIM-BARNES, Baroness *cr* 1989 (Life Peer), of Gloucester in the county of Gloucestershire; **Sally Oppenheim-Barnes;** PC 1979; *b* 26 July 1930; *d* of Mark and Jeanette Viner; *m* 1st, 1949, Henry M. Oppenheim (*d* 1980); one *s* two *d*; 2nd, 1984, John Barnes. *Educ:* Sheffield High Sch.; Lowther Coll., N Wales. Formerly: Exec. Dir, Industrial & Investment Services Ltd; Social Worker, School Care Dept, ILEA. Trustee, Clergy Rest House Trust. MP (C) Gloucester, 1970–87. Vice Chm., 1971–73, Chm., 1973–74, Cons. Party Parly Prices and Consumer Protection Cttee; Opposition Spokesman on Prices and Consumer Protection, 1974–79; Mem. Shadow Cabinet, 1975–79; Min. of State (Consumer Affairs), Dept of Trade, 1979–82. Chairman: Nat. Consumer Council, 1987–89; Council of Management, Nat. Waterways Museums Trust, 1988–89. Non-executive Director: and Mem., Main Bd, Boots Co., 1982–93; Fleming High Income Trust, 1989–; HFC Bank, 1989–. Nat. Vice-Pres., NUTG, 1973–79 and 1989–90; Pres., Glos Dist Br., BRCS, 1973–. *Recreations:* tennis, bridge. *Address:* Quietways, The Highlands, Painswick, Glos GL6 6SL.

See also Hon. P. A. C. L. Oppenheim.

OPPENHEIMER, Harry Frederick; Chairman: Anglo-American Corporation of SA Ltd, 1957–82 (Director, 1934–82); De Beers Consolidated Mines, Ltd, 1957–84 (Director, 1934–94); *b* Kimberley, S Africa, 28 Oct. 1908; *s* of late Sir Ernest Oppenheimer, DCL, LLD; *m* 1943, Bridget, *d* of late Foster McCall; one *s* one *d*. *Educ:* Charterhouse; Christ Church, Oxford (MA; Hon. Student). MP (SA) Kimberley City, 1948–58. Served 4th SA Armoured Car Regt 1940–45. Chancellor, Univ. of Cape Town, 1967–. Hon. DEcon Natal, 1960; Hon. DLaws: Witwatersrand, 1963; Leeds, 1965; Rhodes, 1965; Hon. DLitt Cape Town, 1985. Instn MM Gold Medal, 1965; Gold Medal, Amer. Inst. of Mining and Metallurgy, 1990. Decoration for Meritorious Service (S Africa), 1985. *Recreations:* horse breeding and racing. *Address:* Brenthurst, Federation Road, Parktown, Johannesburg 2193, South Africa; PO Box 61631, Marshalltown 2107, South Africa. *Clubs:* Brooks's; Rand, Inanda (Johannesburg); Kimberley (SA); Harare (Zimbabwe).

OPPENHEIMER, (Lætitia) Helen, (Lady Oppenheimer); writer on moral and philosophical theology; *b* 30 Dec. 1926; *d* of Sir Hugh Lucas-Tooth (later Munro-Lucas-Tooth), 1st Bt; *m* 1947, Sir Michael Oppenheimer, Bt, *qv*; three *d*. *Educ:* Cheltenham Ladies' Coll.; Lady Margaret Hall, Oxford (Schol.; BPhil, MA). Lectr in Ethics, Cuddesdon Theological Coll., 1964–69. Served on: Archbp of Canterbury's Gp on the law of divorce (report, Putting Asunder, 1966); C of E Marriage Commn (report, Marriage, Divorce and the Church, 1971); Wkg Party, ACCM (report, Teaching Christian Ethics, 1974); C of E Wkg Party on Educn in Personal Relationships (Chm.), 1978–82; Inter-Anglican Theol and Doctrinal Commn (report, For the Sake of the Kingdom, 1986); General Synod Wkg Party on the law of marriage (report, An Honourable Estate, 1988). Pres., Soc. for the Study of Christian Ethics, 1989–91. John Coffin Meml Lectr, London Univ., 1977; First Mary Sumner Lectr, Mothers' Union, 1978; preached University Sermon, Oxford, 1979, Cambridge, 1983. DD Lambeth, 1993. *Publications:* Law and Love, 1962; The Character of Christian Morality, 1965, 2nd edn 1974; Incarnation and Immanence, 1973; The Marriage Bond, 1976; The Hope of Happiness: a sketch for a Christian humanism, 1983; Looking Before and After: The Archbishop of Canterbury's Lent Book for 1988; Marriage, 1990; Finding and Following, 1994; contributor: New Dictionary of Christian Theology, 1983; New Dictionary of Christian Ethics, 1986; Encyclopedia of Theology, 1996; articles in Theology, Religious Studies, etc, and in various collections of essays. *Address:* L'Aiguillon, Grouville, Jersey, CI JE3 9AP. *Club:* Victoria (Jersey).

OPPENHEIMER, Michael Anthony; His Honour Judge Oppenheimer; a Circuit Judge, since 1991; *b* 22 Sept. 1946; *s* of Felix Oppenheimer and Ingeborg Hanna Oppenheimer; *m* 1973, Nicola Anne Brotherton (*see* N. A. Oppenheimer); one *s* one *d*. *Educ:* Westminster Sch.; LSE (LLB). Called to the Bar, Middle Temple, 1970 (Blackstone Exhibnr 1970); Asst Recorder, 1985–89; Recorder, 1989–91. *Recreations:* cinema, theatre, books, performing and listening to music. *Club:* Athenæum.

OPPENHEIMER, Sir Michael (Bernard Grenville), 3rd Bt, *cr* 1921; *b* 27 May 1924; *s* of Sir Michael Oppenheimer, 2nd Bt, and Caroline Magdalen (who *m* 2nd, 1935, Sir Ernest Oppenheimer; she *d* 1972), *d* of Sir Robert G. Harvey, 2nd Bt; *S* father, 1933; *m* 1947, Laetitia Helen Lucas-Tooth (*see* L. H. Oppenheimer); three *d*. *Educ:* Charterhouse; Christ Church, Oxford (BLitt, MA). Served with South African Artillery, 1942–45. Lecturer in Politics: Lincoln Coll., Oxford, 1955–68; Magdalen Coll., Oxford, 1966–68. *Heir:* none. *Address:* L'Aiguillon, Grouville, Jersey, CI JE3 9AP. *Clubs:* Victoria (Jersey); Kimberley (Kimberley).

OPPENHEIMER, Nicola Anne; Principal Establishment and Finance Officer, Lord Chancellor's Department, since 1993; *b* 30 Sept. 1950; *d* of Basil Vincent Brotherton and Joan Pamela Brotherton; *m* 1973, Michael Anthony Oppenheimer, *qv*; one *s* one *d*. *Educ:* St Margaret's Sch., Bushey; Queen's Coll., London; Queen Mary Coll., London Univ. (LLB). Called to the Bar, Middle Temple, 1972. Lord Chancellor's Department, 1973–: Judicial Appts Div., 1985; Head of Personnel Management, 1987; Head of Legal Services and Agencies Div., 1991. *Recreations:* early music, theatre, ski-ing, walking. *Address:* Lord Chancellor's Department, Trevelyan House, 30 Great Peter Street, SW1P 2BY. *T:* 0171–210 8519.

OPPENHEIMER, Peter Morris; Student of Christ Church, Oxford, and University Lecturer in Economics, since 1967; on secondment as Chief Economist, Shell International Petroleum Co., 1985–86; *b* 16 April 1938; *s* of late Friedrich Rudolf and of Charlotte Oppenheimer; *m* 1964, Catherine, *er d* of late Dr Eliot Slater, CBE, FRCP, and Dr Lydia Pasternak; two *s* one *d*. *Educ:* Haberdashers' Aske's Sch.; The Queen's Coll., Oxford (BA 1961). National Service, RN, 1956–58. Bank for International Settlements, Basle, 1961–64; Research Fellow, Nuffield Coll., Oxford, 1964–67. Vis. Prof., London Graduate Sch. of Business Studies, 1976–77; Temp. Econ. Attaché, British Embassy, Moscow, 1991. Mem., Gen. Bd of Faculties, Oxford Univ., 1989–. Director: Panfida plc (formerly Investing in Success Equities Ltd), 1975–92; Target Hldgs, 1982–84; J. Rothschild Investment Management, 1982–86; Jewish Chronicle Ltd, 1986–; Delbanco, Meyer and Co. Ltd, 1986–; Dixons Group plc, 1987–93 (Chm., Audit Cttee, 1987–92). Chm., Caminus Energy Ltd, 1991–93. Delegate, OUP, 1987– (Mem., Finance Cttee, 1989–). Specialist Advr, H of C Expenditure Cttee, 1975–76. Mem., Royal Commn on Legal Services, 1976–79. Mem. Council, Trade Policy Research Centre, 1976–89, and co-Editor, The World Economy, 1977–89; Member: Econ. Adv. Bd, RIIA, 1989–; Editl Bd, International Affairs, 1989–; Exec. Cttee and Chm of Res. Bd, Inst. of Jewish Affairs, 1991–; Renewable Energy Adv. Gp, Dept of Energy, 1991–92; Academic Adv. Council, World ORT Union, 1992–. Governor: St Edward's Sch., Oxford, 1979–; St Clare's Hall, Oxford, 1985–; Haberdashers' Monmouth Schs, 1987–. Freeman, Haberdashers' Co., 1987. Presenter: (BBC radio): File on 4, 1977–80; Third Opinion, 1983; Poles Apart, 1984; (BBC TV) Outlook, 1982–85; (Granada TV) Under Fire, 1988; (participant) Round Britain Quiz, Radio 4, 1979–. *Publications:* (ed) Issues in International Economics, 1980; contribs to symposia, conference procs, prof. jls, bank reviews, etc. *Recreations:* music, opera, amateur dramatics, swimming, ski-ing. *Address:* 6 Linton Road, Oxford OX2 6UG. *T:* Oxford (01865) 58226.

OPPENHEIMER, Sir Philip (Jack), Kt 1970; Chairman, The Diamond Trading Co. (Pty) Ltd, since 1975; *b* 29 Oct. 1911; *s* of Otto and Beatrice Oppenheimer; *m* 1935, Pamela Fenn Stirling; one *s* one *d*. *Educ:* Harrow; Jesus Coll., Cambridge. Dir, De Beers Consolidated Mines Ltd. Bronze Cross of Holland, 1943; Commandeur, Ordre de Léopold, 1977. *Recreations:* golf, horse-racing and breeding. *Address:* (office) 17 Charterhouse Street, EC1N 6RA. *Clubs:* Jockey, Portland, White's.

OPPERMAN, Hon. Sir Hubert (Ferdinand), Kt 1968; OBE 1952; Australian High Commissioner in Malta, 1967–72; *b* 29 May 1904; Australian; *m* 1928, Mavys Paterson Craig; one *s* (one *d* decd). *Educ:* Armadale, Vic.; Bailieston, Vic. Served RAAF 1940–45; commissioned 1942. Commonwealth Public Service: PMG's Dept, 1918–20; Navigation Dept, Trade and Customs, 1920–22. Cyclist: Australian Road Champion, 1924, 1926, 1927, 1929; Winner French Bol d'Or, 1928, and Paris-Brest-Paris, 1931; holder, numerous world's track and road unpaced and motor paced cycling records. Director, Allied Bruce Small Pty Ltd, 1936–60. MHR for Corio, Vic., 1949–67; Mem. Australian Delegn to CPA Conf., Nairobi, 1954; Chief Govt Whip, 1955–60; Minister for Shipping and Transport, 1960–63; Minister for Immigration, 1963–66. Convenor, Commonwealth Jubilee Sporting Sub-Cttee, 1951; Nat. Patron, Aust. Sportsmen's Assoc., 1980–; Chm. Selection Cttee, Aust. Hall of Sporting Fame, 1985–; Hon. Master of Sport, Confedn of Aust. Sport, 1984. Selected as one of 200 People Who Made Australia Great, Heritage 200, 1988. GCSJ 1980 (KSJ 1973); Bailiff Prior, Victoria, 1980–83; Bailiff, Aust. Grand Council, 1983–. Hon. Rotarian, St Kilda Rotary, 1984. Coronation Medal, 1953; Silver medal, 1971, Gold medal, 1991, of City of Paris; Medals of Brest, 1971, Verona, 1972; Médaille Mérite, French Cycling Fedn, 1978; Paul Harris Rotary Award, 1992. *Publication:* Pedals, Politics and People (autobiog.), 1977. *Recreations:* cycling, swimming. *Address:* Apt 243, Salford Park, 100 Harold Street, Wantirna, Vic 3152, Australia. *T:* 8014010. *Clubs:* USI, Air Force (Victoria); Naval and Military (Melbourne).

ORAM, family name of **Baron Oram.**

ORAM, Baron *cr* 1975 (Life Peer), of Brighton, E Sussex; **Albert Edward Oram;** *b* 13 Aug. 1913; *s* of Henry and Ada Edith Oram; *m* Frances Joan, *d* of Charles and Dorothy Barber, Lewes; two *s*. *Educ:* Burgess Hill Element. Sch.; Brighton Grammar Sch.; University of London (London School of Economics and Institute of Education). Formerly a teacher. Served War 1942–45; Royal Artillery, Normandy and Belgium. Research Officer, Co-operative Party, 1946–55. MP (Lab and Co-op) East Ham South, 1955–Feb. 1974; Parly Secretary, ODM, 1964–69; a Lord in Waiting (Govt Whip), 1976–78. Chm.,

Co-op. Develt Agency, 1978–81. Co-ordinator, Develt Programmes, Internat. Co-operative Alliance, 1971–73; Develt Administrator, Intermediate Technol. Develt Gp. Mem., Commonwealth Develt Corp., 1975–76. *Publication:* (with Nora Stettner) Changes in China, 1987. *Recreations:* country walking, cricket, chess. *Address:* 19 Ridgeside Avenue, Patcham, Brighton BN1 8WD. *T:* Brighton (01273) 505333.

ORAM, Rt. Rev. Kenneth Cyril; Assistant Bishop, Diocese of Lichfield, since 1987; *b* 3 March 1919; *s* of Alfred Charles Oram and Sophie Oram; *m* 1943, Kathleen Mary Malcolm; three *s* one *d*. *Educ:* Selhurst Grammar Sch., Croydon; King's Coll., London; Lincoln Theol Coll. BA Hons English, 1st Cl. AKC. Asst Curate: St Dunstan's, Cranbrook, 1942–45; St Mildred's, Croydon, 1945–46; Upington with Prieska, S Africa, 1946–48; Rector of Prieska and Dir of Prieska Mission District, 1949–51; Rector of Mafeking, 1952–59; Dir of Educn, dio. Kimberley and Kuruman, 1953–62; Archdeacon of Bechuanaland, 1953–59; Dean and Archdeacon: of Kimberley, 1960–64; of Grahamstown, 1964–74; Bishop of Grahamstown, 1974–87. *Address:* 10 Sandringham Road, Baswich, Stafford ST17 0AA. *T:* Stafford (01785) 53974.

ORANMORE and BROWNE, 4th Baron (Ireland), *cr* 1836; Baron Mereworth of Mereworth Castle (UK), *cr* 1926; **Dominick Geoffrey Edward Browne;** *b* 21 Oct. 1901; *e s* of 3rd Baron and Lady Olwen Verena Ponsonby (*d* 1927), *e d* of 8th Earl of Bessborough; *S* father, 1927; *m* 1st, 1925, Mildred Helen (who obtained a divorce, 1936; she *d* 1980), *e d* of Hon. Thomas Egerton; two *s* one *d* (and two *d* decd); 2nd, 1936, Oonagh (marr. diss., 1950; she *d* 1995), *d* of late Hon. Ernest Guinness; one *s* (and two *s* decd); 3rd, 1951, Sally Gray, 5b Mount Street, London, W. *Educ:* Eton; Christ Church, Oxford. *Heir: s* Hon. Dominick Geoffrey Thomas Browne [*b* 1 July 1929; *m* 1957, Sara Margaret (marr. diss. 1974), *d* of late Dr Herbert Wright, 59 Merrion Square, Dublin, and late Mrs C. A. West, Cross-in-Hand, Sussex]. *Address:* 52 Eaton Place, SW1X 8AL.

ORCHARD, Edward Eric, CBE 1966 (OBE 1959); *b* 12 Nov. 1920. *Educ:* King's Sch., Grantham; Jesus Coll., Oxford (MA). War Service, 1941–46; FO and HM Embassy, Moscow, 1948–51; Lectr in Russian, Oxford, 1951–52; HM Embassy Moscow and FCO, 1953–76 (Dir of Research, 1970–76). Mem., Waverley Borough Council, 1978–87; Mayor, Haslemere, 1987. *Publications:* articles and reviews. *Recreations:* swimming, gardening, local government and welfare. *Address:* Sturt Meadow House, Haslemere, Surrey GU27 3RT. *T:* Haslemere (01428) 643034.

ORCHARD, Stephen Michael; Chief Executive, since 1989, and Member, since 1992, Legal Aid Board; *b* 5 Aug. 1944; *s* of Stephen Henry Orchard and Ellen Frances Orchard; *m*; one *s* one *d*. *Educ:* Swanage Grammar School. Lord Chancellor's Dept, 1961–89. *Recreations:* walking, food and wine. *Address:* Legal Aid Board, 85 Gray's Inn Road, WC1X 8AA. *T:* 0171–813 1000.

ORCHARD-LISLE, Brig. Paul David, CBE 1988; TD 1961; DL; Senior Partner, Healey & Baker, since 1988; *b* 3 Aug. 1938; *s* of Mervyn and late Phyllis Orchard-Lisle. *Educ:* Marlborough College; Trinity Hall, Cambridge (MA). FRICS. Nat. Service, RA, 1956–58. Joined Healey & Baker, 1961. RA (TA), 1958–88; ADC (TA), 1985–87; Brig. (TA), UKLF, 1985; Chm., TAVRA Greater London, 1988–91. Pres., RICS, 1986–87. Hon. Fellow, Coll. of Estate Management, 1985–. Dep. Chm., Slough Estates plc, 1993– (non-exec. Dir, 1984–). Pres. of Council, Reading Univ., 1994– (Mem. Council, 1989–94); Mem. Council, Marlborough Coll., 1991–; Governor: West Buckland Sch., 1986–; Harrow Sch., 1988–; Nottingham Trent Univ., 1992–94. DL Gtr London, 1987. *Recreations:* golf, squash. *Address:* Bedford House, Bidwell, Houghton Regis, Beds LU5 6JP. *T:* Dunstable (01582) 867317. *Club:* Athenæum.

ORD, Andrew James B.; *see* Blackett-Ord.

ORDE, Denis Alan; His Honour Judge Orde; a Circuit Judge, since 1979; *b* 28 Aug. 1932; *s* of late John Orde, CBE, Littlehoughton Hall, Northumberland, and Charlotte Lilian Orde, County Alderman; *m* 1961, Jennifer Jane, *d* of late Dr John Longworth, Masham, Yorks; two *d*. *Educ:* Oxford Univ. (MA Hons). Served Army, 1950–52, 2nd Lieut 1951; TA, 1952–64 (RA). Pres., Oxford Univ. Conserv. Assoc., 1954; Mem. Cttee, Oxford Union, 1954–55; Vice-Chm., Fedn of Univ. Conserv. Assocs., 1955. Called to Bar, Inner Temple, 1956; Pupil Studentship, 1956; Profumo Prize, 1959. Assistant Recorder: Kingston upon Hull, 1970; Sheffield, 1970–71; a Recorder of the Crown Court, 1972–79; Liaison Judge to Magistrates, 1983–; Resident Judge, Crown Court, 1986–; sits in NE and London. Chm., Criminal Justice Liaison Cttee, Cos of Northumberland, Tyne and Wear and Durham, 1995–; Mem., Lord Chancellor's County Adv. Cttee, 1987–. Contested (C): Consett, 1959; Newcastle upon Tyne West, 1966; Sunderland South, 1970. Mem., Chollerton PCC, 1980–91. Vice-Pres., Northumberland LTA, 1982–. Gov., Christ's Hospital, Sherburn, 1993–. *Recreations:* listening to music, cricket, family history, biography. *Address:* Chollerton Grange, Chollerton, near Hexham, Northumberland NE46 4TG; 11 King's Bench Walk, Temple, EC4. *Club:* Northern Counties (Newcastle).

ORDE, Sir John (Alexander) Campbell-, 6th Bt *cr* 1790, of Morpeth; *b* 11 May 1943; *s* of Sir Simon Arthur Campbell-Orde, 5th Bt, TD, and of Eleanor, *e d* of Col Humphrey Watts, OBE, TD, Haslington Hall, Cheshire; *S* father, 1969; *m* 1973, Lacy Ralls (marr. diss. 1991), *d* of Grady Gallant, Nashville, USA; one *s* three *d*. *Educ:* Gordonstoun. *Heir: s* John Simon Arthur Campbell-Orde, *b* 15 Aug. 1981. *Address:* PO Box 22974, Nashville, TN 37202, USA. *Clubs:* Caledonian, Lansdowne.

ORDE-POWLETT, family name of **Baron Bolton.**

O'REGAN, Hon. Sir (John) Barry; Kt 1984; Judge of the Court of Appeal, Cook Islands, since 1986; *b* 2 Dec. 1915; *s* of John O'Regan; *m* Catherine, *d* of John O'Donnell; four *s* one *d*. *Educ:* Sacred Heart College, Auckland; Victoria University, Wellington (LLB). Army service, 1941–45 (Captain). Partner, Bell O'Regan & Co., 1945–73; Judge of High Court, NZ, 1973–84; Judge of Ct of Appeal, Fiji, 1983–87. Chairman: Prisons Parole Bd, 1977–83; War Pensions Appeal Bd, 1984–90. Member: Council, Wellington Law Soc., 1959–69 (Pres., 1968); Council, NZ Law Soc., 1967–69; Council of Legal Education, 1969–73; Legal Aid Board, 1970–73. Consul-Gen. for Ireland, 1965–73. *Address:* Apt A/4 Lincoln Courts, 1 Washington Avenue, Wellington 2, New Zealand.

O'REILLY, Dr Anthony John Francis, (Dr Tony O'Reilly); Chairman, since 1987, President and Chief Executive Officer, since 1979, H. J. Heinz Co. Inc.; *b* Dublin, 7 May 1936; *o c* of J. P. O'Reilly, former Inspector-General of Customs; *m* 1962, Susan (marr. diss.), *d* of Keith Cameron, Australia; three *s* three *d* (of whom two *s* one *d* are triplets); *m* 1991, Chryss Goulandris. *Educ:* Belvedere Coll., Dublin; University Coll., Dublin (BCL 1958); Bradford Univ. (PhD 1980). Admitted Solicitor, 1958. Industrial Consultant, Weston Evans UK, 1958–60; PA to Chm., Suttons Ltd, Cork, 1960–62; Chief Exec. Officer, Irish Dairy Bd, 1962–66; Man. Dir, Irish Sugar Bd, 1966–69; Man. Dir, Erin Foods Ltd, 1966–69; Jt Man. Dir, Heinz-Erin, 1967–70; Man. Dir, H. J. Heinz Co. Ltd, UK, 1969–71; Sen. Vice-Pres., N America and Pacific, H. J. Heinz Co., 1971–72; Exec. Vice-Pres. and Chief Op. Off., 1972–73, Pres. and Chief Operating Officer, 1973–79, H. J. Heinz Co. Lectr in Business Management, UC Cork, 1960–62. Director: Robt McCowen & Sons Ltd, 1961–62; Agricl Credit Corp. Ltd, 1965–66; Nitrigin Eireann Teoranta, 1965–66; Allied Irish Investment Bank Ltd, 1968–71; Thyssen-Bornemisza Co., 1970–72; Independent Newspapers (Vice Chm., 1973–80; Chm., 1980–); Nat. Mine Service Co., 1973–76; Mobil, 1979–; Bankers Trust Co., 1980–; Allegheny Internat. Inc., 1982–; GEC, 1990–92; Chairman: Fitzwilliam Securities Ltd, 1971–77; Fitzwilton Ltd, 1978– (Dep. Chm., 1972–78); Atlantic Resources PLC, 1981–; Waterford Wedgwood, 1993–. Member: Incorp. Law Soc.; Council, Irish Management Inst.; Hon. LLD: Wheeling Coll., 1974; Rollins Coll., 1978; Trinity Coll., 1978; Allegheny Coll., 1983. *Publications:* Prospect, 1962; Developing Creative Management, 1970; The Conservative Consumer, 1971; Food for Thought, 1972. *Recreations:* Rugby (played for Ireland 29 times), tennis. *Address:* 835 Fox Chapel Road, Pittsburgh, PA 15238, USA; Castlemartin, Kilcullen, Co. Kildare, Ireland. *Clubs:* Reform, Annabels, Les Ambassadeurs; Stephen's Green (Dublin); Union League (New York); Duquesne, Allegheny, Fox Chapel, Pittsburgh Golf (Pittsburgh); Carlton (Chicago); Rolling Rock (Ligonier); Lyford Cay (Bahamas).

O'REILLY, Most Rev. Colm; *see* Ardagh and Clonmacnoise, Bishop of, (RC).

O'REILLY, Francis Joseph; Chancellor, University of Dublin, Trinity College, since 1985 (Pro-Chancellor, 1983–85); Chairman, Ulster Bank Ltd, 1982–89 (Deputy Chairman, 1974–82; Director, 1961–90); Director, National Westminster Bank, 1982–89; *b* 15 Nov. 1922; *s* of Lt-Col Charles J. O'Reilly, DSO, MC, MB, KSG and Dorothy Mary Martin; *m* 1950, Teresa Mary, *e d* of Captain John Williams, MC; three *s* seven *d*. *Educ:* St Gerard's Sch., Bray; Ampleforth Coll., York; Trinity Coll., Dublin (BA, BAI). Served HM Forces, RE, 1943–46. John Power & Son, 1946–66 (Dir, 1952–66, Chm., 1955–66); Chm., Player & Wills (Ire.) Ltd, 1964–81; Chm., 1966–83, Dir, 1983–88, Irish Distillers Gp. President: Marketing Inst. of Ireland, 1983–85; Inst. of Bankers in Ireland, 1985–86. President: Equestrian Fedn of Ireland, 1963–79; Royal Dublin Soc., 1986–89 (Mem. Cttees, 1959–80; Chm. of Soc., 1980–86); Chm., Collège des Irlandais, Paris, 1987–. Hon. Life Delegate, Fédn Equestre Internationale, 1979–. MRIA 1987–. LLD *hc:* Univ. of Dublin, 1978; NUI, 1986. GCLJ 1992. *Recreations:* fox-hunting, racing, gardening. *Address:* Rathmore, Naas, Co. Kildare, Ireland. *T:* Naas 62136. *Clubs:* Kildare Street and University (Dublin); Irish Turf (The Curragh, Co. Kildare).

O'REILLY, William John, CB 1981; OBE 1971; FCPA; Commissioner of Taxation, Australian Taxation Office, 1976–84, retired; *b* 15 June 1919; *s* of William O'Reilly and Ruby (*née* McCrudden). *Educ:* Nudgee Coll., Brisbane, Qld; Univ. of Queensland (AAUQ 1950). FCPA 1990 (FASA 1983). Served RAAF, 1942–44. Joined Australian Public Service, 1946; Australian Taxation Office: Brisbane, 1946–55; Melbourne, 1955–61; Canberra, 1961–84; Asst Comr of Taxation, 1963; First Asst Comr of Taxation, 1964; Second Comr of Taxation (Statutory Office), 1967. *Recreations:* reading, walking. *Address:* 7/48 Glen Road, Toowong, Qld 4066, Australia. *T:* (7) 3710641. *Clubs:* Commonwealth, Canberra (Canberra).

OREJA AGUIRRE, Marcelino; Grand Cross: Order of Charles III, 1980; Order of Isabella the Catholic, 1982; Member, European Commission, since 1995; *b* 13 Feb. 1935; *m* 1967, Silvia Arburua; two *s*. *Educ:* Univ. of Madrid (LLD). Prof. of Internat. Affairs, Diplomatic Sch., Madrid, 1962–70; Dir of Internat. Service, Bank of Spain, 1970–74; Minister of Foreign Affairs, 1976–80; Governor-Gen., Basque Country, 1980–82; Sec. Gen., Council of Europe, 1984–89; Mem. (Partido Popular) European Parlt, 1989–94 (Chm., Institutional Affairs Cttee, 1989–94). Grand Officier de la Légion d'Honneur (France), 1976; Grand Cross: Order of Christ (Portugal), 1978; Order of the Crown (Belgium); (1st Cl.), Order of Service (Austria); (1st Cl.), Order of Merit (Federal Republic of Germany); Order of Orange-Nassau (Netherlands); (1st Cl.) Order of Polar Star (Sweden); Order of Dannebrog (Denmark); Order of Merit (Italy); Order of the Oak Crown (Luxembourg); Order of Merit (Liechtenstein). *Address:* 81 Nunez de Balboa, 28006 Madrid, Spain. *T:* Madrid (1) 5759101; Rue de la Loi 200, 1049 Brussels, Belgium.

ORGAN, (Harold) Bryan; painter; *b* Leicester, 31 Aug. 1935; *o c* of late Harold Victor Organ and Helen Dorothy Organ; *m* (marr. diss. 1981); *m* 1982, Sandra Mary Mills. *Educ:* Wyggeston Sch., Leicester; Coll. of Art, Loughborough; Royal Academy Schs, London. Lectr in Drawing and Painting, Loughborough Coll. of Art, 1959–65. One-man exhibns: Leicester Museum and Art Gallery, 1959; Redfern Gallery, 1967, 1969, 1971, 1973, 1975, 1978, 1980; Leicester 1973, 1976; New York, 1976, 1977; Turin, 1981. Represented: Kunsthalle, Darmstadt, 1968; Mostra Mercatao d'Arte Contemporanea, Florence, 1969; 3rd Internat. Exhibn of Drawing, Germany, 1970; Sao Paolo Museum of Art, Brazil; Baukunst Gallery, Cologne, 1977. Works in public and private collections in England, USA, Germany, France, Canada, Italy. Portraits include: Malcolm Muggeridge, 1966; Sir Michael Tippett, 1966; David Hicks, 1968; Mary Quant, 1969; Nadia Nerina, 1969; Princess Margaret, 1970; Dr Roy Strong, 1971; Elton John, 1973; Lester Piggott, 1973; Lord Ashby, 1975; Sir Rex Richards, 1977; Harold Macmillan, 1980; Prince of Wales, 1981; Lady Diana Spencer, 1981; Lord Denning, 1982; Jim Callaghan, 1982; Duke of Edinburgh, 1983. Hon. MA Loughborough, 1974; Hon. DLitt Leicester, 1985. *Address:* c/o Redfern Gallery, 20 Cork Street, W1X 2HL. *T:* 0171–734 1732.

ORGEL, Prof. Leslie Eleazer, DPhil Oxon, MA; FRS 1962; Senior Fellow and Research Professor, Salk Institute, La Jolla, California, USA, and Adjunct Professor, University of California, San Diego, Calif, since 1964; *b* 12 Jan. 1927; *s* of Simon Orgel; *m* 1950, Hassia Alice Levinson; two *s* one *d*. *Educ:* Dame Alice Owen's Sch., London. Reader, University Chemical Laboratory, Cambridge, 1963–64, and Fellow of Peterhouse, 1957–64. Fellow, Amer. Acad. of Arts and Sciences, 1985; Mem., Nat. Acad. of Scis, USA, 1990. *Publications:* An Introduction to Transition-Metal Chemistry, Ligand-Field Theory, 1960; The Origins of Life: molecules and natural selection, 1973; (with Stanley L. Miller) The Origins of Life on the Earth, 1974. *Address:* Salk Institute, PO Box 85800, San Diego, CA 92186–5800, USA.

ORGILL, Richard Michael James; Director and Deputy Chief Executive, Midland Bank plc, since 1994; *b* 14 Oct. 1938; *m* 1968, Anne Whiteley; two *s* one *d*. *Educ:* Bryanston Sch., Dorset. Gen. Manager and Chief Exec. Officer, Hongkong and Shanghai Banking Corp., Malaysia, 1985–89; Gen. Manager Internat., Hongkong and Shanghai Banking Corp., Hong Kong, 1989–90; Gen. Manager and Chief Exec. Officer, Hongkong Bank of Australia Ltd, 1990–93; Chief Operating Officer, Midland Bank plc, 1993–94. *Address:* Midland Bank, 27–32 Poultry, EC2P 2BX.

O'RIORDAN, Rear-Adm. John Patrick Bruce, CBE 1982; JP; Chief Executive, St Andrew's Hospital, Northampton, since 1990; *b* 15 Jan. 1936; *yr s* of Surgeon Captain Timothy Joseph O'Riordan, RN and Bertha Carson O'Riordan (*née* Young); *m* 1959, Jane, *e d* of John Alexander Mitchell; one *s* two *d*. *Educ:* Kelly College. Nat. Service and transfer to RN, 1954–59; served in submarines, Mediterranean, Home and Far East; HM Ships Porpoise (i/c) and Courageous, NDC, HMS Dreadnought (i/c), MoD, 1960–76; Captain (SM), Submarine Sea Training, 1976–78; RCDS, 1979; HMS Glasgow (i/c), 1980–81; ACOS (Policy), Saclant, USA, 1982–84; Dir, Naval Warfare, MoD, 1984–86; Mil. Dep. Comdt, NATO Defence Coll., Rome, 1986–89. Consultant, Spencer Stuart and Associates, 1989. Director: Workbridge Enterprises Ltd, 1990–; Indep. Healthcare

Assoc., 1993–. JP S Northants, 1991. FIMgt. *Recreations:* sailing, Rugby football, stalking, painting. *Address:* The Little Rectory, Whilton, Daventry, Northants NN11 5NN. *T:* Long Buckby (01327) 843274. *Clubs:* Army and Navy, Royal Navy of 1765 and 1785; Royal Yacht Squadron, Royal Naval Sailing Association.

See also Sir J. A. .N. Graham.

O'RIORDAN, Prof. Timothy; Professor of Environmental Sciences, University of East Anglia, since 1980; *b* 21 Feb. 1942; *s* of Kevin Denis O'Riordan and Norah Joyce O'Riordan (*née* Lucas); *m* 1967, Ann Morison Philip (*d* 1992); two *d. Educ:* Univ. of Edinburgh (MA 1963); Cornell Univ. (MS 1965); Univ. of Cambridge (PhD 1967). Asst Lectr and Associate Prof., Dept of Geography, Simon Fraser Univ., Canada, 1967–74; Reader, Sch. of Environmental Scis, UEA, 1974–80. Gill Meml Award, RGS, 1982. FRSA. *Publications:* Environmentalism 1976, 2nd edn 1981; (jtly) Countryside Conflicts, 1986; (jtly) Sizewell B: an anatomy of the inquiry, 1987; (ed) Environmental Science for Environmental Management, 1994; (ed jtly) Interpreting the Precautionary Principle, 1994; (ed) The politics of climate change in Europe, 1995; (ed) The economics and politics of ecotaxation, 1995. *Recreation:* classical double bass playing. *Address:* Wheatlands, Hethersett Lane, Colney, Norwich NR4 7TT. *T:* Norwich (01603) 810534.

ORKNEY, 8th Earl of, *cr* 1696; **Cecil O'Bryen Fitz-Maurice;** Viscount of Kirkwall and Baron of Dechmont, 1696; *b* 3 July 1919; *s* of Douglas Frederick Harold FitzMaurice (*d* 1937; *g g s* of 5th Earl) and Dorothy Janette (who *m* 2nd, 1939, Commander E. T. Wiggins, DSC, RN), *d* of late Capt. Robert Dickie, RN; *S* kinsman 1951; *m* 1953, Rose Katharine Durk (*d* 1995), *yr d* of late J. W. D. Silley, Brixham. Joined RASC, 1939; served in North Africa, Italy, France and Germany, 1939–46, and in Korea, 1950–51. *Heir: kinsman* Oliver Peter St John [*b* 27 Feb. 1938; *m* 1st, 1963, Mary Juliet (marr. diss. 1985), *d* of late W. G. Scott-Brown, CVO, MD, FRCS, FRCSE; one *s* three *d* (and one *d* decd); 2nd, 1985, Mrs Mary Barbara Huck, *d* of Dr David B. Albertson; one step *s* three step *d*]. *Address:* Ferndown, Dorset BH22 9JG.

ORLEBAR, Sir Michael Keith Orlebar S.; *see* Simpson-Orlebar.

ORMAN, Stanley, PhD; Chief Executive Officer, General Technology Systems Inc., Maryland, since 1990; *b* 6 Feb. 1935; *s* of Jacob and Ettie Orman; *m* 1960, Helen (*née* Hourman); one *s* two *d. Educ:* Hackney Downs Grammar School; King's College London. BSc (1st Cl. Hons) 1957; PhD (Organic Chem.) 1960. MICorrST; FRIC 1969. Research Fellowship, Brandeis Univ., 1960–61; AWRE Aldermaston, research in corrosion and mechano-chemical corrosion, 1961–74, project work, 1974–78; Director Missiles, 1978–81, Chief Weapon System Engineer Polaris, 1981–82, MoD; Minister-Counsellor, Hd of Defence Equip. Staff, British Embassy, Washington, 1982–84; Dep. Dir, AWRE, MoD, 1984–86; Dir Gen., SDI Participation Office, MoD, 1986–90. Founder Chm., Reading Ratepayers' Assoc., 1974; Pres., Reading Hebrew Congregation, 1970–74. *Publications:* Faith in G.O.D.S.: stability in the nuclear age, 1991; numerous papers on free radical chemistry, materials science, mechano-chemical corrosion and ballistic missile defence, in learned jls. *Recreations:* sporting—originally athletics, now tennis and badminton; designing bow ties, woodwork. *Address:* 17825 Stoneridge Drive, Gaithersburg, MD 20878, USA. *T:* (301) 6700685.

ORME, Jeremy David, FCA; Head of Enforcement, Securities and Investments Board, since 1987; *b* 27 Dec. 1943; 2nd *s* of John Samuel Orme, CB, OBE, and of Jean Esther (*née* Harris); *m* 1967, Susan Diane Knights (marr. diss. 1978); two *s. Educ:* Winchester Coll.; Christ Church, Oxford (MA). Robson Rhodes, chartered accountants, 1966–87, Man. Partner, 1982–87; Asst Sec. (on secondment), Dept of Transport, 1979–81. Member: National Bus Co., 1984–86 (Dep. Chm. 1985–86); Audit Commn for Local Authorities and NHS in England and Wales, 1989–. *Address:* c/o Royal Bank of Scotland, Holts, Farnborough, Hants GU14 7NR.

ORME, Prof. Michael Christopher L'Estrange, MD; FRCP; Professor of Pharmacology and Therapeutics, since 1984, and Dean, Faculty of Medicine, since 1991, Liverpool University; *b* 13 June 1940; *s* of Christopher Robert L'Estrange Orme and Muriel Evelyn Janet Orme; *m* 1967, Joan Patricia Abbott; one *s. Educ:* Sherborne Sch.; Sidney Sussex Coll., Cambridge (MB BChir 1964; MA 1965; MD 1975); King's Coll. Hosp. FRCP 1980; FFFP 1994. Sen. Registrar, Hammersmith Hosp., 1970–73, Wellcome Fellowship, Karolinska Inst., Stockholm, 1973–74; Sen. Lectr, 1975–81, Reader in Clinical Pharmacology, 1981–84, Liverpool Univ. *Publications:* Self Help Guide to Medicine, 1988; (ed) Therapeutic Drugs, 1991; contribs to learned jls. *Recreations:* sailing, astronomy, cooking. *Address:* Faculty of Medicine Offices, Duncan Building, Liverpool University, PO Box 169, Liverpool L69 3BX. *T:* 0151–706 4261.

ORME, Robert Thomas Neil; His Honour Judge Orme; a Circuit Judge, since 1992; *b* 25 Jan. 1947; *s* of Thomas Elsmore Orme and Iris Marguerita Orme; *m* 1971, Angela Mary Stokes; one *s* one *d. Educ:* Denstone Coll., Staffs; University Coll. London (LLB Hons). Called to the Bar, Gray's Inn, 1970; Asst Recorder, 1984–88; Recorder, 1988–92. Chm., Moseley Soc., 1993–. *Recreations:* opera, theatre, visiting France, keen interest in conservation. *Address:* Queen Elizabeth II Law Courts, Birmingham B4 7NA. *T:* 0121–236 9751.

ORME, Rt. Hon. Stanley, PC 1974; MP (Lab) Salford East, since 1983 (Salford West, 1964–83); *b* 5 April 1923; *s* of Sherwood Orme, Sale, Cheshire; *m* 1951, Irene Mary, *d* of Vernon Fletcher Harris, Worsley, Lancashire. *Educ:* elementary and technical schools; National Council of Labour Colleges and Workers' Educational Association classes. Warrant Officer, Air-Bomber Navigator, Royal Air Force Bomber Command, 1942–47. Joined the Labour party, 1944; contested (Lab) Stockport South, 1959. Minister of State: NI Office, 1974–76; DHSS, 1976; Minister of State for Social Security, 1976–77, Minister for Social Security, and Mem. Cabinet, 1977–79, Opposition Spokesman on Health and Social Services, June 1979–Dec. 1980, on Industry, 1980–83, on Energy, 1983–87; Chm., PLP, 1987–92. Member of Sale Borough Council, 1958–65; Member: AEU; District Committee, Manchester; shop steward. Hon. DSc Salford, 1985. *Address:* House of Commons, SW1A 0AA; 8 Northwood Grove, Sale, Cheshire M33 3AW. *Club:* ASE (Altrincham).

ORMEROD, Alec William; Metropolitan Stipendiary Magistrate, since 1988; Chairman, Family Court, since 1991; *b* 19 July 1932; *s* of William and Susan Ormerod; *m* 1976, Patricia Mary Large. *Educ:* Nelson Grammar Sch.; Christ's Coll., Cambridge (MA, LLM). Solicitor. Local Govt Service, 1958–64; Sen. Partner, Boyle and Ormerod, Solicitors, Aylesbury, 1964–88. Councillor, Aylesbury Borough Council, 1966–72. Freeman, City of London, 1973. *Recreations:* travel, fine art. *Address:* c/o South Western Magistrates' Court, 176A Lavender Hill, SW11 1JU. *Club:* Naval and Military.

ORMEROD, Pamela Catherine, (Mrs P. A. Ormerod); *see* Meadows, P. C.

ORMESSON, Comte Jean d'; Chevalier des Palmes académiques 1962; Commandeur des Arts et Lettres 1973; Officier de la Légion d'honneur 1988; Officier de l'Ordre national du Mérite, 1978; Membre Académie française 1973; President, International Council for Philosophy and Humanistic Studies (UNESCO), since 1992 (Secretary-General, 1971–92); writer and journalist; *b* 16 June 1925; 2nd *s* of Marquis d'Ormesson, French diplomat and Ambassador; *m* 1962, Françoise Béghin; one *d. Educ:* Ecole Normale Supérieure. MA (History), Agrégé de philosophie. Mem. French delegns to various internat. confs, 1945–48; Mem. staff of various Govt Ministers, 1958–66; Mem. Council ORTF, 1960–62; Mem. Control Cttee of Cinema, 1962–69; Mem. TV Programmes Cttee, ORTF, 1973–74. Mem., Brazilian Acad. of Letters, 1979. Diogenes: Dep. Editor, 1952–72; Mem. Managing Cttee, 1972–80; Editor, 1980–82; Editor-in-Chief, 1982–; Le Figaro: Dir, 1974–77; Editor-in-Chief, 1975–77. *Publications:* L'Amour est un plaisir, 1956; Du côté de chez Jean, 1959; Un amour pour rien, 1960; Au revoir et merci, 1966; Les Illusions de la mer, 1968; La Gloire de l'Empire, 1971 (Grand Prix du Roman de l'Académie française), Amer. edn (The Glory of the Empire), 1975, Eng. edn 1976; Au Plaisir de Dieu, 1974, Amer. edn (At God's Pleasure), 1977, Eng. edn 1978; Le Vagabond qui passe sous une ombrelle trouée, 1978; Dieu, sa vie, son œuvre, 1981; Mon dernier rêve sera pour vous, 1982; Jean qui grogne et Jean qui rit, 1984; Le Vent du soir, 1985; Tous les hommes en sont fous, 1986; Le Bonheur à San Miniato, 1987; Garçon de quoi écrire, 1989; Histoire du Juif errant, 1991; Tant que vous penserez à moi, 1992; articles and essays, columns in Le Figaro, Le Monde, Le Point, La Revue des Deux Mondes, La Nouvelle Revue Française. *Recreation:* ski-navigation. *Address:* CIPSH-UNESCO, 1 rue Miollis, 75732 Paris Cedex 15, France. *T:* 45682685; (home) 10 avenue du Parc Saint-James, 92200 Neuilly-sur-Seine, France.

ORMOND, Sir John (Davies Wilder), Kt 1964; BEM 1940; JP; Chairman: Shipping Corporation of New Zealand Ltd, since 1973; Container Terminals Ltd, since 1975; Exports and Shipping Council, since 1964; *b* 8 Sept. 1905; *s* of J. D. Ormond and Gladys Wilder; *m* 1939, Judith Wall; four *s* one *d. Educ:* Christ's Coll., Christchurch, New Zealand. Chairman, Waipukurau Farmers Union, 1929; President, Waipukurau Jockey Club, 1950; Member, New Zealand Meat Producers Board, 1934–72, Chm., 1951–72. Active Service Overseas (Middle East), 1940. JP, NZ, 1945. DSc (*hc*), 1972. *Recreations:* tennis, polo, Rugby Union football. *Address:* Wallingford, Waipukurau, New Zealand. *T:* (6) 8554701. *Club:* Hawke's Bay (New Zealand).

ORMOND, Richard Louis; Director, National Maritime Museum, since 1986 (Head of Picture Department, 1983–86); *b* 16 Jan. 1939; *s* of late Conrad Eric Ormond and Dorothea (*née* Gibbons); *m* 1963, Leonée Jasper; two *s. Educ:* Oxford University. MA. Assistant Keeper, 1965–75, Dep. Director, 1975–83, Nat. Portrait Gallery. *Publications:* J. S. Sargent, 1970; Catalogue of Early Victorian Portraits in the National Portrait Gallery, 1973; Lord Leighton, 1975; Sir Edwin Landseer, 1982; The Great Age of Sail, 1986; F. X. Winterhalter and the Courts of Europe, 1987. *Recreations:* cycling, opera, theatre. *Address:* 8 Holly Terrace, N6 6LX. *T:* 0181–340 4684. *Club:* Garrick.

ORMONDE, 7th Marquess of, *cr* 1825; **James Hubert Theobald Charles Butler,** MBE 1921; Earl of Ormonde, 1328; Viscount Thurles, 1525; Earl of Ossory, 1527; Baron Ormonde (UK), 1821; 31st Hereditary Chief Butler of Ireland; retired; *b* 19 April 1899; *s* of Lord Theobald Butler (4th *s* of 2nd Marquess) and Annabella Brydon (*d* 1943), *o d* of Rev. Cosmo Reid Gordon, DD; *S* cousin, 1971; *m* 1st, 1935, Nan Gilpin (*d* 1973); two *d*; 2nd, 1976, Elizabeth Liles (*d* 1980). *Educ:* Haileybury College; RMC Sandhurst. Commissioned Dec. 1917, King's Royal Rifle Corps; resigned commission, May 1926 (Lieut). Various business connections in USA. *Heir:* (to earldoms of Ormonde and Ossory) Viscount Mountgarret, *qv*. *Address:* King-Bruwaert House, 6101 South County Line Road, Burr Ridge, IL 60521, USA. *Club:* Naval and Military.

ORMSBY GORE, family name of **Baron Harlech.**

O'RORKE, Richard Charles Colomb; His Honour Judge O'Rorke; a Circuit Judge, since 1994; *b* 4 June 1944; *s* of Charles Howard Colomb O'Rorke and Jacqueline O'Rorke; *m* 1966, Jane Elizabeth Phoebe Harding; one *s* three *d. Educ:* Blundell's Sch.; Exeter Coll., Oxford. Called to the Bar, Inner Temple, 1968; Recorder, Midland and Oxford Circuit, 1987–94. *Recreations:* Japanese literature and culture, gardening. *Address:* c/o Midland and Oxford Circuit Office, 2 Newton Street, Birmingham B4 7LU.

O'ROURKE, Andrew; Ambassador of Ireland to Denmark, since 1991; *b* 7 May 1931; *s* of Joseph O'Rourke and Elizabeth (*née* O'Farrell); *m* 1962, Hanne Stephensen; one *s* two *d. Educ:* Trinity Coll., Dublin (BA, BComm). Joined diplomatic service, 1957; Third Sec., Berne, 1960; First Sec., London, 1964; First Sec., later Counsellor, Dept of Foreign Affairs, Dublin, 1969–73; Counsellor, later Dep. Perm. Rep., Perm. Rep. of Ireland to EEC, 1973–78; Sec.-Gen., Dept of For. Affairs, 1978–81; Perm. Rep. to EEC, 1981–86; Ambassador to: France, OECD and UNESCO, 1986–87; UK, 1987–91. Grand Cross: Order of Civil Merit, Spain, 1985; OM, Luxembourg, 1986; OM, Portugal, 1987. *Recreations:* walking, golf. *Address:* Embassy of Ireland, Østbanegade 21 1 T.H., 2100 Copenhagen, Denmark. *Club:* Kildare Street and University (Dublin).

ORR, Christopher John, RA 1995; RE 1990; artist; *b* 8 April 1943; *s* of Ronald Orr and Violet (*née* Townley); *m* 1984, Catherine Terris; one *s* one *d. Educ:* Royal Coll. of Art (MA; FRCA 1984). Artist and teacher, 1967–. One man touring exhibitions: The Complete Chris Orr, 1976; Many Mansions, 1990. Work in public collections: British Council; Arts Council; V&A Mus.; Science Mus. *Publications:* Many Mansions, 1990; The Small Titanic, 1994. *Recreations:* camping, train-spotting. *Address:* 7 Bristle Hill, Buckingham MK18 1EZ. *T:* Buckingham (01280) 815255. *Club:* Chelsea Arts.

ORR, Sir David (Alexander), Kt 1977; MC and bar 1945; LLB; Chancellor, Queen's University of Belfast, since 1992; *b* 10 May 1922; *s* of late Canon Adrian William Fielder Orr and Grace (*née* Robinson); *m* 1949, Phoebe Rosaleen Davis; three *d. Educ:* High Sch., Dublin; Trinity Coll., Dublin (Hon. LLD 1978). Served Royal Engineers attached QVO Madras Sappers and Miners, 1941–46. With various Unilever companies, 1948–82; Hindustan Lever, 1955–60; Mem. Overseas Cttee, Unilever, 1960–63; Lever Bros Co., New York, 1963, Pres. 1965–67; Dir, 1967–82, Vice-Chm. 1970–74, Chm., 1974–82, Unilever Ltd; Vice-Chm., Unilever NV, 1974–82; Chm., 1983–86, 1991–92, Inchcape (Dep. Chm., 1986–91); Director: Rio Tinto-Zinc Corp., 1981–92; Shell Transport & Trading Co., 1982–92; Mem. Court, Bank of Ireland, 1982–90. Chm., British Council, 1985–92. Chm., Armed Forces Pay Review Body, 1982–84; Member: Cttee to Review Functioning of Financial Instns, 1977–80; Top Salaries Review Body, 1982–85; Adv. Cttee on Business Appointments of Crown Servants, 1984–92. Chairman: Leverhulme Trust, 1982–92; Shakespeare Globe Theatre Trust, 1982–93; Charles Wallace (India) Trust, 1991–; Jt Chm., Anglo-Irish Encounter, 1983–87. Dir, Five Arrows Chile Fund, 1990–; Pres., Children's Medical Charity, 1991–. President: Liverpool Sch. of Tropical Medicine, 1981–89; Coll. of Speech Therapists, 1992–; Governor, LSE, 1980–. FRSA. Hon. LLD: TCD, 1978; Liverpool, 1989; NUI, 1993; DUniv Surrey, 1981. Comdr, Order of Oranje Nassau, 1979. *Recreations:* golf, Rugby, travel. *Address:* 81 Lyall Mews West, SW1X 8DJ; Home Farm House, Shackleford, near Godalming, Surrey GU8 6AH. *Clubs:* Athenæum; Sunningdale Golf.

ORR, Iain Campbell; HM Diplomatic Service; Deputy High Commissioner, Wellington, 1991–94; *b* 6 Dec. 1942; *s* of late Rev. David Campbell Orr and Hilda Dora Moore; *m* 1978, Susan Elizabeth Gunter; one *s* one *d. Educ:* Kirkcaldy High Sch.; St Andrews Univ.

(MA); Linacre Coll., Oxford (BPhil). Asst Lectr, Dept of Politics, Glasgow Univ., 1967–68; entered HM Diplomatic Service, 1968; language student, Hong Kong, 1969–71; Second, later First Sec., Peking, 1971–74; FCO, 1974–78; Asst Political Adviser, Hong Kong, 1978–81; Dublin, 1981–84; FCO, 1984–87; Consul-Gen., Shanghai, 1987–90. *Recreations:* natural history, islands, anthologies, reading poetry. *Address:* c/o Foreign and Commonwealth Office, SW1A 2AH.

ORR, James Bernard Vivian, CVO 1968 (MVO 1962); Secretary, Medical Commission on Accident Prevention, 1970–82; *b* 19 Nov. 1917; *s* of Dr Vivian Bernard Orr and Gladys Constance Orr (*née* Power); unmarried. *Educ:* Harrow; Gordonstoun; RMC, Sandhurst. British South Africa Police, Southern Rhodesia, 1939–46. Attached occupied Enemy Territory Administration in Ethiopia and Eritrea Police Forces, 1941–49; Kenya Police, 1954–57. Private Secretary to HRH The Duke of Edinburgh, 1957–70, an Extra Equerry, 1970–. *Recreations:* horse racing, watching cricket. *Address:* 10 Mulberry Trees, Shepperton, Mddx TW17 8JN. *T:* Walton-on-Thames (01932) 245274.

ORR, Dr James Henry; Consultant in forensic psychiatry, since 1982; *b* 2 Feb. 1927; *s* of Hubert Orr and Ethel Maggs; *m* 1950, Valerie Elizabeth Yates; two *s* one *d*. *Educ:* Bristol Grammar Sch.; Bristol Univ. (MB, ChB 1955). DPM; FRCPsych. Enlisted, 1944; commnd RE, 1947; demobilised, 1949. Hosp. appts, 1955–56; gen. practice, 1956–58; Medical Officer, HM Prison: Leeds, 1958; Winchester, 1962; Lincoln, 1966; SMO, Leeds, 1967; Asst Dir, Prison Med. Services, 1973; Dir, Prison Med. Services, and Mem., Prisons Bd, 1976–82; Mem., Parole Bd, 1983–86. *Recreation:* gardening.

ORR, Jean Fergus Henderson; Director, Office of Manpower Economics, 1973–80; *b* 3 April 1920; *yr d* of late Peter Orr, OBE and Janet Muir Orr (*née* Henderson). *Educ:* privately; University Coll., London (BA; Fellow, 1982). Min. of Aircraft Prodn, temp. Asst Principal, 1942; Min. of Supply: Asst Principal, 1946; Principal, 1949; HM Treasury, 1954: Principal, Official Side Sec. to Civil Service Nat. Whitley Council negotiations on Report of Royal Commn on Civil Service, 1953–55; Asst Sec. 1961; on loan to Office of Manpower Econs as Sec. to Top Salaries Review Body, 1971. *Publication:* (contrib.) Edward Boyle: his life by his friends, ed Ann Gold, 1991. *Recreations:* music, travel, natural history. *Address:* 21 Bathwick Hill, Bath, Avon BA2 6EW. *T:* Bath (01225) 463664. *Club:* United Oxford & Cambridge University.

ORR, Prof. Robin, (Robert Kemsley Orr), CBE 1972; MA, MusD (Cantab); FRCM; Hon. RAM; Hon. FRSAM; Hon. DMus, Hon. LLD; Composer; Professor of Music, Cambridge University, 1965–76, now Professor Emeritus; Fellow of St John's College, Cambridge, 1965–76, Hon. Fellow 1987; *b* Brechin, Scotland, 2 June 1909; *s* of Robert Workman Orr and Florence Mary Kemsley; *m* 1st, 1937, Margaret (marr. diss. 1979), *er d* of A. C. Mace; one *s* two *d*; 2nd, 1979, Doris Winny-Meyer, *d* of Leo Meyer-Bechtler, Zürich. *Educ:* Loretto Sch.; Royal Coll. of Music; Pembroke Coll., Cambridge (Organ Scholar; Hon. Fellow, 1988); Accademia Musicale Chigiana, Siena. Studied privately with Casella and Nadia Boulanger. Dir of Music, Sidcot Sch., Somerset, 1933–36; Asst Lecturer in Music, Univ. of Leeds, 1936–38. Served War of 1939–45, RAFVR, Photographic Intelligence (Flight Lieut). Organist and Dir of Studies in Music, St John's Coll., 1938–51, and Fellow, 1948–56, Univ. Lecturer in Music, 1947–56, Cambridge; Prof. of Theory and Composition, RCM, 1950–56; Gardiner Prof. of Music, Univ. of Glasgow, 1956–65. Mem., Carl Rosa Trust, 1953–70; Chm., Scottish Opera, 1962–76; Director: Arts Theatre, Cambridge, 1970–75; Welsh Nat. Opera, 1977–83. Compositions include: Sonatina for violin and piano, 1941; Three Chinese Songs, 1943; Sonata for viola and piano, 1947; Winter's Tale (Incidental Music), BBC, 1947; Overture, The Prospect of Whitby, 1948; Oedipus at Colonus (Cambridge Univ. Greek Play), 1950; Four Romantic Songs (for Peter Pears), 1950; Festival Te Deum, 1950; Three Pastorals for soprano, flute, viola and piano, 1951; Deirdre of the Sorrows (Incidental Music), BBC, 1951; Italian Overture, 1952; Te Deum and Jubilate in C, 1953; Motet, I was glad, 1955; Spring Cantata, 1955; Sonata for violin and clavier, 1956; Rhapsody for string orchestra; Antigone (Bradfield College Greek Play), 1961; Symphony in one movement, 1963; Full Circle (opera), 1967; From the Book of Philip Sparrow, 1969; Journeys and Places (mezzo-sop. and strings), 1971; Symphony No 2, 1971; Hermiston (opera), 1975; Symphony No 3, 1978; Versus from Ogden Nash for medium voice and strings, 1978; Songs of Zion (choir), 1978; On the Razzle (opera), 1986; Sinfonietta Helvetica, 1990; Rondeau des Oiseaux for recorder, 1993; Three Lyric Pieces for piano, 1994. Hon. DMus Glasgow, 1972; Hon. LLD Dundee, 1976. *Recreations:* gardening, mountain walks. *Address:* 16 Cranmer Road, Cambridge CB3 9BL. *T:* Cambridge (01223) 352858.

ORR-EWING, family name of **Baron Orr-Ewing.**

ORR-EWING, Baron *cr* 1971 (Life Peer), of Little Berkhamsted; **(Charles) Ian Orr-Ewing,** OBE (mil.) 1945; 1st Bt *cr* 1963; Consultant and Director various companies; Chairman, Metrication Board, 1972–77; *b* 10 Feb. 1912; *s* of Archibald Ian Orr Ewing and Gertrude (*née* Runge); *m* 1939, Joan McMinnies; four *s*. *Educ:* Harrow; Trinity Coll., Oxford. MA (Physics). Graduate apprentice, EMI, Hayes, 1934–37; BBC Television Service, 1938–39, 1946–49. Served RAFVR, 1939–46, N Africa, Italy, France and Germany, Wing Comdr, 1941; Chief Radar Officer, Air Staff, SHAEF, 1945 (despatches twice); BBC Television Outside Broadcasts Manager, 1946–48. MP (C) North Hendon, 1950–70; Joint Secretary, Parliamentary Scientific Cttee, 1950; Vice-Pres., Parliamentary and Scientific Cttee, 1965–68; Vice-Chm., 1922 Cttee, 1966–70 (Secretary, 1956); Vice-Chairman, Defence Cttee, 1966–70. PPS to Sir Walter Monckton, Minister of Labour and National Service, Nov. 1951–1955; Parliamentary Under-Secretary of State, for Air, Air Ministry, 1957–59; Parliamentary and Financial Secretary to Admiralty, 1959; Civil Lord of the Admiralty, 1959–63. Dep. Chm., Assoc. of Cons. Peers, 1980–86. Mem., Royal Commn on Standards of Conduct in Public Life, 1975–76. Pres. and Chm. of Council, Electronic Engineering Assoc., 1969–70. Pres., Nat. Ski Fedn of GB, 1972–76. FIEE. *Publication:* (ed) A Celebration of Lords and Commons Cricket 1850–1988, 1989. *Recreations:* tennis, light-hearted cricket and ski-ing. *Heir* (to baronetcy only): *s* Hon. (Alistair) Simon Orr-Ewing [*b* 10 June 1940; *m* 1968, Victoria, *er d* of late Keith Cameron, Fifield House, Milton-under-Wychwood, Oxon; two *s* one *d*]. *Address:* House of Lords, SW1A 0AA. *Clubs:* Boodle's, MCC; All England Lawn Tennis; Vincent's (Oxford).

ORR EWING, Major Edward Stuart; landowner and farmer, since 1969; Lord-Lieutenant of Wigtown, since 1989; *b* 28 Sept. 1931; *s* of late Captain David Orr Ewing, DSO, DL and of Mary Helen Stuart Orr Ewing (*née* Noaks); *m* 1st, 1958, Fiona Anne Bowman (*née* Farquhar) (marr. diss. 1981); one *s* two *d*; 2nd, 1981, Diana Mary Waters. *Educ:* Sherborne; Royal Military Coll. of Science. Regular soldier, The Black Watch, 1950–69. DL Wigtown, 1970. *Recreations:* country sports, ski-ing, painting. *Address:* Dunskey, Portpatrick, Wigtownshire DG9 8TJ. *T:* Portpatrick (01776) 810211. *Club:* New (Edinburgh).

ORR-EWING, Hamish; Chairman, Rank Xerox Ltd, 1980–86; *b* 17 Aug. 1924; *o s* of Hugh Eric Douglas Orr-Ewing and Esme Victoria (*née* Stewart), Strathgarry, Killiecrankie, Perthshire; *m* 1st, 1947, Morar Margaret Kennedy; one *s* (one *d* decd); 2nd, 1954, Ann Mary Teresa Terry. *Educ:* Heatherdown, Ascot; Eton. Served War, Captain Black Watch. Salesman, EMI, 1950; Ford Motor Co., 1954; Ford Light Car Planning Manager, 1959–63; Leyland Motor Corp. Ltd, 1963–65; joined Rank Xerox, 1965; apptd to Bd as Dir of Product Planning, 1968; Dir of Personnel, 1970; Man. Dir, Rank Xerox (UK) Ltd, 1971; Reg. Dir for Rank Xerox Ops in UK, France, Holland, Sweden and Belgium, 1977; Chairman: Jaguar plc, 1984–85; White Horse Hldgs, 1987–91; Dir, Tricentrol PLC, 1975–86. Chairman: Work and Society, 1982–85; European Govt Business Relations Council, 1980–84; Member: MSC, 1983–85; Engrg Council, 1984–87; Envmt Awards Panel, RSA, 1987–; President: Inst. of Manpower Studies, 1986–89; Inst. of Training and Develt, 1987–89. CBI: Member: Bd, Educn Foundn (UBI), 1982–87; Council, 1985–87; Chm., Educn and Trng Cttee, 1985–87. Trustee: Shaw Trust, 1985–; Roman Res. Trust, 1985–. Governor: Interphil, 1985–; New Coll., Swindon, 1984– (Chm. of Govs, 1986–92); Bradon Forest Sch., 1989–92. CIMgt (CBIM 1981). *Recreations:* anything mechanical, country life, the Roman Empire. *Address:* Fox Mill Farm, Purton, near Swindon, Wilts SN5 9EF. *T:* Swindon (01793) 770496.

ORR EWING, Major Sir Ronald Archibald, 5th Bt, *cr* 1886; Major (retired) Scots Guards; *b* 14 May 1912; *e s* of Sir Norman Orr Ewing, 4th Bt, CB, DSO, and Lady Orr Ewing (*née* Robarts), Tile House, Buckingham; *S* father, 1960; *m* 1938, Marion Hester, *yr d* of late Colonel Sir Donald Walter Cameron of Lochiel, KT, CMG, and of Lady Hermione Cameron of Lochiel, *d* of 5th Duke of Montrose, KT; two *s* two *d*. *Educ:* Eton; RMC, Sandhurst. Scots Guards, 1932–53, Major. Served War of 1939–45, Middle East (POW 1942). JP Perthshire, 1956; DL Perthshire, 1963. Grand Master Mason of Scotland, 1965–69. *Recreation:* forestry. *Heir: s* Archibald Donald Orr Ewing [*b* 20 Dec. 1938; *m* 1st, 1965, Venetia Elizabeth (marr. diss. 1972), *y d* of Major and Mrs Richard Turner, Co. Dublin; 2nd, 1972, Nicola Jean-Anne, *d* of Reginald Baron Black, Fovant, near Salisbury; one *s*]. *Address:* Cardross, Port of Menteith, Kippen, Stirling FK8 3JY. *T:* Port of Menteith (01877) 385220. *Club:* New (Edinburgh).

ORREGO-VICUÑA, Prof. Francisco; Professor of International Law, School of Law and Institute of International Studies, University of Chile, since 1969; President, Chilean Council on Foreign Relations, since 1989; *b* 12 April 1942; *s* of Fernando Orrego Vicuña and Raquel Vicuña Viel; *m* 1965, Soledad Bauzá; one *s* two *d*. *Educ:* Univ. of Chile (Degree in Law); LSE (PhD). Admitted to legal practice, 1965. Sen. Legal Advisor, OAS, 1965–69 and 1972–74; Dir, Inst. of Internat. Studies, Univ. of Chile, 1974–83; Ambassador of Chile to UK, 1983–85. Advisor on legal matters to Min. of Foreign Affairs, 1974–83. *Publications:* Derecho de la Integraciòn Latinoamericana, 1969; Los Fondos Marinos, 1976; Antarctic Resources Policy, 1983; The Exclusive Economic Zone, 1984; Antarctic Mineral Exploration, 1988; The Exclusive Economic Zone in International Law, 1989; contrib. Amer. Jl of Internat. Law and Annuaire Français de Droit Internat. *Recreations:* golf, ski-ing. *Address:* Institute of International Studies, University of Chile, PO Box 14187, Suc. 21, Santiago 9, Chile. *T:* (2) 2745377. *Club:* Athenæum.

ORRELL, James Francis Freestone; His Honour Judge Orrell; a Circuit Judge, since 1989; *b* 19 March 1944; *s* of Francis Orrell and late Marion Margaret Orrell; *m* 1970, Margaret Catherine Hawcroft; two *s*. *Educ:* Ratcliffe; Univ. of York (BA History). Called to the Bar, Gray's Inn, 1968; Recorder, Midland and Oxford Circuit, 1988. *Address:* c/o Derby Combined Court Centre, Morledge, Derby DE1 2XE.

ORSON, Rasin Ward, CBE 1985; CompIEE; consultant; Member, The Electricity Council, 1976–89; *b* 16 April 1927; *s* of Rasin Nelson Orson and Blanche Hyre; *m* 1st, 1950, Marie Goodenough; two *s*; 2nd, 1979, Lesley Jean Vallance. *Educ:* Stratford Grammar Sch.; London School of Economics (BScEcon 1948). Asst Statistician, Min. of Civil Aviation, 1948, Statistician, 1953; Electricity Council: Head of Economics and Forecasting Branch, 1963; Dep. Commercial Adviser, 1968; Commercial Adviser, 1972. Dir, Chloride Silent Power, 1974–89. *Recreations:* music, photography. *Address:* The Old Garden, Dunorlan Park, Tunbridge Wells, Kent TN2 3QA. *T:* Tunbridge Wells (01892) 524027.

ORTIZ DE ROZAS, Carlos; Argentine Ambassador to the United States of America, since 1991; *b* 26 April 1926; *m* 1952, María del Carmen Sarobe. *Educ:* School of Diplomacy, Min. of Foreign Affairs, Buenos Aires (grad. 1949). Lawyer, Faculty of Law, Univ. of Buenos Aires, 1950. Entered Argentine Foreign Service, 1948; served Bulgaria, Greece, UAR and UK (Minister); Ambassador to Austria, 1967–70; Permanent Rep. to UN, 1970–77; Pres. UN Security Council, 1971–72; Chairman: First (Polit. and Security) Cttee of 29th Gen. Assembly, 1974; Preparatory Cttee of Special Session on Disarmament, 1977–78; Cttee on Disarmament, Geneva, 1979; Mem. Adv. Bd on Disarmament Studies, New York, 1978–92; Ambassador to UK, 1980–82; Head, Argentine Special Mission to the Holy See, 1982–83; Ambassador to France, 1984–89; Dep. Foreign Minister, 1990. Universidad del Salvador, Buenos Aires: Prof. of History and Constitutional Law, 1958, Prof. of Political Science, 1958–, Faculty of Law; Prof. of Internat. Relations, School of Political Sciences, 1962–, and at School of Diplomacy, 1962–. Holds many foreign decorations incl. Grand Cross, Order of Pius IX, 1985, and Commandeur, Légion d'Honneur, 1985. *Address:* Argentine Embassy, 1600 New Hampshire Avenue NW, Washington, DC 20009, USA. *Clubs:* Jockey, Círculo de Armas (Buenos Aires); Cercle de l'Union Interalliée (Paris).

ORTOLI, François-Xavier; Hon. Chairman, Total, since 1990 (Président Directeur Général, 1984–90); *b* 16 Feb. 1925. *Educ:* Hanoi Faculty of Law; Ecole Nationale d'Administration. Inspector of Finances, 1948–51; Tech. Adv., Office of Minister of Econ. Affairs and Information, 1951–53; Asst Dir to Sec. of State for Econ. Affairs and Sec.-Gen., Franco-Italian Cttee of EEC, 1955; Head, Commercial Politics Service of Sec. of State for Econ. Affairs, 1957; Dir-Gen., Internal Market Div., EEC, 1958; Sec.-Gen., Inter-Ministerial Cttee for Questions of European Econ. Co-operation, Paris, 1961–; Dir of Cabinet to Prime Minister, 1962–66; Comr-Gen. of the Plan, 1966–67; Minister: of Works, 1967–68; of Educn, 1968; of Finance, 1968–69; of Industrial and Scientific Develt, 1969–72; Pres., EEC, 1973–76, a Vice-Pres., with responsibility for econ. and financial affairs, 1977–84. Hon. Fellow, Worcester Coll., Oxford, 1991. Hon. DCL Oxon, 1975; Hon Dr Sch. of Political Scis, Athens, 1975. Commandeur de la Légion d'Honneur; Médaille Militaire; Croix de Guerre, 1945; Médaille de la Résistance. *Address:* 18 rue de Bourgogne, 75007 Paris, France.

OSBORN, Frederic Adrian, (Derek Osborn), CB 1991; Director General (Deputy Secretary), Environmental Protection, Department of the Environment, since 1990; Chairman, European Environment Agency, since 1995; *b* 14 Jan. 1941; *s* of late Rev. George R. Osborn and E. M. Osborn, MBE; *m* 1971, Caroline Niebuhr Tod; one *d* one *s*. *Educ:* Leys School, Cambridge; Balliol College, Oxford. BA Maths 1963, BPhil 1965. Asst Principal, Min. of Housing and Local Govt, 1965; Private Sec. to Minister of State and Perm. Sec., 1967; Royal Commn on Standards of Conduct in Public Life, 1974; Dept of Transport, 1975–77; Department of the Environment, 1977–: Under Sec., Finance, 1982–86, Housing Gp, 1986–87; Dep. Sec., Local Govt and Finance, 1987–89. *Recreations:* music, reading, chess.

OSBORN, Sir John (Holbrook), Kt 1983; semi-retired scientist, soldier, industrialist and politician; *b* 14 Dec. 1922; *s* of late Samuel Eric Osborn and Aileen Decima, *d* of Colonel Sir Arthur Holbrook, KBE, MP; *m* 1st, 1952, Molly Suzanne (*née* Marten) (marr. diss.);

two *d*; 2nd, 1976, Joan Mary MacDermot (*née* Wilkinson) (*d* 1989); 3rd, 1989, Patricia Hine (*née* Read). *Educ:* Rugby; Trinity Hall, Cambridge. MA Cantab; Part 2 Tripos in Metallurgy; Diploma in Foundry Technology, National Foundry Coll., 1949. Served in Royal Corps of Signals, 1943–47 (West Africa, 1944–46; Captain); served in RA (TA) Sheffield, 1948–55, Major. Joined 1947, and Technical Dir, 1951–79, Samuel Osborn & Co. Ltd, and associated companies. Chairman, Hillsborough Divisional Young Conservative and Liberal Association, 1949–53. MP (C) Hallam Div. of Sheffield, 1959–87 (NL and U, 1959–64); PPS to the Secretary of State for Commonwealth Relations and for the Colonies, 1963–64. Chairman: Cons. Parly Transport Cttee, 1970–74; Parly Gp for Energy Studies, 1985–87 (Vice-Chm., Cons. Parly Energy Cttee, 1979–81); Anglo-Swiss Parly Gp, 1981–87; (or Vice-Chm.) Anglo-Soviet Parly Gp, 1968–87; Vice Chm., Parly and Scientific Cttee, 1963–66, 1982 (Officer, 1959–87; Life Mem., 1987); Jt Sec., 1922 Cttee, 1968–87; Member: Science and Technol. Select Cttee, 1970–73; Educn, Science and Arts Select Cttee, 1979–83; Chm., All Party Channel Tunnel Gp, 1985–87. Mem., UK Delegn to Council of Europe and WEU, 1973–75, 1980–87 (Hon. Associate, Council of Europe, 1987–, WEU, 1990–); Council of Europe: Vice Chm., Science and Technol. Cttee, 1981–87; Chm., Eur. Scientific Contact Gp, 1982–87. Chm., Econ. Affairs and Develt Sub-Cttee (North/South: Europe's role), 1985–87. Mem., European Parlt, 1975–79; Mem. Exec., British Br., IPU, 1968–75, 1979–83; Mem. Cttee, European Atlantic Gp, 1990–. Mem., Interim (formerly Voluntary) Licensing Authy, MRC/RCOG, 1987–91. Chairman: Friends of Progress, 1989–95; Business and Develt Cttee, UK Chapter, Soc. for Internat. Develt, 1990–95. Mem., RIIA, 1985–. Freeman Co. of Cutlers in Hallamshire, 1987 (Asst Searcher, 1951–65; Searcher, 1965–70 and 1973–87). Fellow, Institute of British Foundrymen, 1948–72 (Member Council, Sheffield Branch, 1954–64); FIM 1986 (MISI 1947); Fellow, Institute of Directors; Member Council: Sheffield Chamber of Commerce, 1956–89 (Hon. Life Mem., 1989); Assocs British Chambers of Commerce, 1960–62 (Hon. Secretary, 1962–64); British Iron and Steel Res. Association, 1965–68; CBI and Yorks and WR Br., CBI, 1968–79; Industrial Soc., 1963–79 (Life Mem.). Pres., Sheffield Inst. of Advanced Motorists, 1960–; Chm., H of C Motor Club, 1979–84. Mem., Court and Council Sheffield Univ., 1951–79. Chm., Zackery Merton Trust, 1988–. FRSA 1966. Travelled widely in business and politics. *Recreations:* golf, tennis, photography, gardening, ski-ing, gymnasium, swimming. *Address:* Newlands, 147 Hawton Road, Newark, Notts NG24 4QG. *T:* Newark (01636) 704480. *Clubs:* Carlton; Sheffield.

OSBORN, Sir Richard (Henry Danvers), 9th Bt *cr* 1662, of Chicksands Priory, Co. Bedford; fine art consultant; *b* 12 Aug. 1958; surv. *s* of Sir Danvers Lionel Rouse Osborn, 8th Bt, and Constance Violette, JP, OStJ (*d* 1988), *d* of late Major Leonard Frank Rooke, KOSB and RFC; *S* father, 1983. *Educ:* Eton. Christie's, 1978–83; Consultant to P & D Colnaghi Ltd, 1984–86. Dir, Paul Mitchell Ltd (antique frames and picture conservation), 1991–. *Recreations:* cricket, tennis, squash, horse racing, Real tennis. *Heir: kinsman* William Danvers Osborn [*b* 4 June 1909; *m* 1939, Jean Burns, *d* of R. B. Hutchinson, Vancouver; one *d*]. *Address:* 25 Queens Gardens, W2 3BD. *Clubs:* Pratt's, MCC, Turf, Queen's.

OSBORNE, Hon. Lord; Kenneth Hilton Osborne; a Senator of the College of Justice in Scotland, since 1990; *b* 9 July 1937; *s* of Kenneth Osborne and Evelyn Alice (*née* Hilton); *m* 1964, Clare Ann Louise Lewis; one *s* one *d*. *Educ:* Larchfield Sch., Helensburgh; Merchiston Castle Sch., Edinburgh; Edinburgh Univ. (MA, LLB). Admitted to Faculty of Advocates in Scotland, 1962; QC (Scotland) 1976. Standing Junior Counsel to Min. of Defence (Navy) in Scotland, 1974–76; Advocate-Depute, 1982–84. Chairman: Disciplinary Cttee, Potato Marketing Bd, 1975–90; (part-time), VAT Tribunals, 1985–90; Medical Appeal Tribunals, 1987–90; Mem., Lands Tribunal for Scotland, 1985–87. Chm., Local Govt Boundary Commn for Scotland, 1990–. *Recreations:* ski-ing, fishing, gardening, music, cooking. *Address:* 42 India Street, Edinburgh EH3 6HB. *T:* 0131–225 3094; Primrose Cottage, Bridgend of Lintrathen, by Kirriemuir, Angus. *T:* Lintrathen (01575) 560316. *Club:* New (Edinburgh).

OSBORNE, Anthony David, CB 1995; Chief Executive, Government Property Lawyers, 1993–95; *b* 21 March 1935; *s* of Frederick Charles Osborne and Eva Mary Osborne (*née* Tutt); *m* 1958, Ethelwyn Grieve; two *s* one *d*. *Educ:* Brighton College. Articled: Aldrich and Crowther, Brighton; Ashurst, Morris, Crisp & Co., London; admitted Solicitor, 1958; private practice, London, 1958–65; joined Treasury Solicitor's Dept, 1965; Asst Treasury Solicitor, 1975; Solicitor to Health and Safety Commn and Health and Safety Exec., 1985–90; Principal Asst Treasury Solicitor, 1990; Head of Property Div., Taunton, 1990–93. *Recreations:* music, theatre, travel, photography.

OSBORNE, Charles (Thomas); author and critic; *b* 24 Nov. 1927; *s* of Vincent Lloyd Osborne and Elsa Louise Osborne; *m* 1970, Marie Korbelářová (marr. diss. 1975). *Educ:* Brisbane State High Sch. Studied piano and voice, Brisbane and Melbourne; acted in and directed plays, 1944–53; wrote poetry and criticism, published in Aust. and NZ magazines; co-owner, Ballad Bookshop, Brisbane, 1947–51; actor, London, provincial rep. and on tour, also TV and films, 1953–57; Asst Editor, London Magazine, 1958–66; Asst Lit. Dir, Arts Council of GB, 1966–71, Lit. Dir, 1971–86; Chief Theatre Critic, The Daily Telegraph, 1987–91. Broadcaster, musical and literary progs, BBC, 1957–; Dir, Poetry International, 1967–74; Sec., Poetry Book Soc., 1971–84; opera critic, Jewish Chronicle, 1985–. Mem. Editorial Board: Opera, 1970–; Annual Register, 1971–87. Vice Pres., Richard Strauss Soc. DUniv Griffith Univ., Australia, 1994. Gold Medal, Amici di Verdi, 1993. *Publications:* (ed) Australian Stories of Today, 1961; (ed) Opera 66, 1966; (with Brigid Brophy and Michael Levey) Fifty Works of English Literature We Could Do Without, 1967; Kafka, 1967; Swansong (poems), 1968; The Complete Operas of Verdi, 1969 (Italian trans. 1975, French trans. 1989); Ned Kelly, 1970; (ed) Australia, New Zealand and the South Pacific, 1970; (ed) Letters of Giuseppe Verdi, 1971; (ed) The Bram Stoker Bedside Companion, 1973; (ed) Stories and Essays by Richard Wagner, 1973; The Concert Song Companion, 1974; Masterpieces of Nolan, 1976; Masterpieces of Drysdale, 1976; Masterpieces of Dobell, 1976; Wagner and his World, 1977 (USA 1977; trans. Spanish 1985); Verdi, 1977 (trans. Spanish 1985); (ed) Dictionary of Composers, 1977; The Complete Operas of Mozart, 1978 (trans. Ital. 1982); (ed) Masterworks of Opera: Rigoletto, 1979; The Opera House Album, 1979 (trans. Dutch 1981); W. H. Auden: the Life of a Poet, 1980; (ed with Kenneth Thomson) Klemperer Stories, 1980 (trans. German 1981); The Complete Operas of Puccini, 1981; The Life and Crimes of Agatha Christie, 1982; The World Theatre of Wagner, 1982; How to Enjoy Opera, 1983 (trans. Spanish 1985); The Dictionary of Opera, 1983 (trans. Finnish 1984; trans. Portuguese 1987); Letter to W. H. Auden and Other Poems, 1984; Schubert and his Vienna, 1985 (trans. German 1986); Giving It Away (memoirs), 1986; (ed) The Oxford Book of Best-Loved Verse, 1986; Verdi: a life in the theatre, 1987; The Complete Operas of Richard Strauss, 1988; Max Oldaker: last of the matinée idols, 1988; The Complete Operas of Wagner, 1990; The Bel Canto Operas, 1993; The Oxford Opera Guide, 1996; poems in: The Oxford Book of Australian Verse, 1956; Australian Poetry, 1951–52, etc; The Queensland Centenary Anthology, 1959; Australian Writing Today, 1968; various jls; contrib.: TLS, Observer, Sunday Times, Times, Guardian, New Statesman, Spectator, London Mag., Encounter, Opera, Chambers Encyc. Yearbook, and Enciclopedia dello spettacolo; also cassettes. *Recreations:* travelling, planning future projects. *Address:* 125 St George's Road, SE1 6HY. *T:* 0171–928 1534. *Clubs:* Savile; Stardust Slot (Las Vegas).

OSBORNE, Denis Gordon, CMG 1990; Consultant for governance, development and training, since 1992; *b* 17 Sept. 1932; *s* of A. Gordon Osborne and Frances A. Osborne (*née* Watts); *m* 1970, Christine Susannah, *d* of P. Rae Shepherd and C. Elaine Shepherd; two *d*. *Educ:* Dr Challoner's Grammar Sch., Amersham; University Coll., Durham (BSc 1st Cl. Hons Physics, PhD). FInstP 1966. Lectr in Physics, Univ. of Durham, 1957; Lectr, Fourah Bay Coll., Sierra Leone, 1957–58; Lectr, 1958–63, Sen. Lectr, 1963–64, Univ. of Ghana; Reader in Physics, 1964–66, Prof., 1966–71, Dean of Science, 1968–70, Univ. of Dar es Salaam; Res. Fellow, UCL, 1971–72; Cons. for World Bank missions to Malaysia and Ethiopia, 1971, 1972; Overseas Development Administration: Principal, 1972; Multilateral Aid Dept, 1972–75; Mediterranean and Near East Dept, 1975–77; Sci. and Technology Dept, 1977–80; Asst Sec., 1980; Hd of Dept in Natural Resources Div., 1980–84; Hd of E and W Africa Dept, 1984–87; HM Diplomatic Service, High Comr in Malaŵi, 1987–90; RIPA Internat., 1990–92. *Publications:* Way Out: some parables of science and faith, 1977; research papers on geophysics, particularly the equatorial ionosphere; gen. papers on science, technology, educn and develt. *Recreations:* reading, writing, attempts at windsurfing. *Address:* 112 Dulwich Village, SE21 7AQ. *Club:* Athenæum.

OSBORNE, Douglas Leonard, FCIS; Executive Director, Leukaemia Research Fund, since 1989; *b* 19 Oct. 1940; *s* of Leonard Osborne and Gladys Ellen (*née* Ward); *m* 1969, Barbara Helen Bartrop; one *s* one *d*. *Educ:* Royal Masonic Sch. ACIS 1967, FCIS 1985. London Association for the Blind: Asst Sec., 1965–75; Asst Dir, 1975–79; Dir, 1979–83; Administrator, Leukaemia Res. Fund, 1983–89. Mem. Council, Metropolitan Soc. for the Blind, 1979–. *Publication:* (ed jtly) Charities Administration, 1986, and Supplements, 1987–. *Recreations:* listening to music, cooking, travel. *Address:* (office) 43 Great Ormond Street, WC1N 3JJ. *T:* 0171–405 0101.

OSBORNE, Helena; *see* Moore, G. M.

OSBORNE, Kenneth Hilton; *see* Osborne, Rt Hon. Lord.

OSBORNE, Prof. Michael John, FAHA 1985; Vice-Chancellor, La Trobe University, Australia, since 1990; *b* 25 Jan. 1942; *s* of Samuel Osborne and Olive May Osborne (*née* Shove); *m* 1978, Dawn Brindle. *Educ:* Eastbourne Grammar Sch.; Christ Church, Oxford (MA); Catholic Univ. of Leuven (DPhil and Lett.). Lectr, Dept of Classics, Bristol, 1966–67; Lectr, then Sen. Lectr, Dept of Classics and Archaeology, Univ. of Lancaster, 1967–82; University of Melbourne: Prof. and Chm., Dept of Classical and Near Eastern Studies, 1983–90, now Prof. Emeritus; Dep./Associate Dean, Faculty of Arts, 1985–89; Pro-Vice-Chancellor and Vice-Pres., Academic Bd, 1989. Mem., Inst. for Advanced Study, Princeton, 1978–79; Visiting Professor: Maximilians Univ., Munich, 1973; Leuven, 1975, 1988; Vis. Fellow, other univs, 1972–85; Hon. Prof., Yunnan Univ., China. Chm., Victorian Vice-Chancellors' Cttee, 1993–94; Member: Bd of Dirs, Australian Vice-Chancellors' Cttee, 1994 (Chm., Students and Scholarships Cttee); Business/Higher Educn Round Table (Mem., Task Force on Higher Educn); Res. Cttee, Cttee for Econ. Develt of Australia. Laureate, Royal Acad. of Sci., Letters and Fine Arts, Belgium, 1980. *Publications:* Naturalization in Athens, 4 vols, 1981–83; Lexicon of Greek Personal Names, vol. II: Attica, 1994; numerous articles in learned jls on Greek history, Greek epigraphy and Greek archaeology. *Recreations:* tennis, travel, Australian Rules football. *Address:* Office of the Vice-Chancellor, La Trobe University, Bundoora, Vic 3083, Australia. *T:* (3) 94792000. *Club:* Essendon Football.

OSBORNE, Nigel; composer; Professor of Music (part-time), Edinburgh University; *b* 1948. *Educ:* St Edmund Hall, Oxford (Mus. Dir, Oxford Theatre Gp, Exp. Theatre Co., OUDS; Osgood Meml Prize); studied at Warsaw Acad. and Polish Radio Exptl Studio. Staff of Music Dept, Nottingham Univ., 1978; Editor-in-Chief, Contemporary Music Review. *Compositions include:* Seven Words, 1971 (Radio Suisse Romande Prize); Heaventree, 1973 (Gaudeamus Prize); Kinderkreuzzug, 1974; I am Goya, 1977 (Radcliffe Award); Orlando Furioso, 1978; In Camera, 1979; Sinfonia, 1982; Sinfonia II, 1983; Zansa, 1985; The Electrification of the Soviet Union (opera), 1987; Violin Concerto, 1990; Terrible Mouth, 1991; The Sun of Venice, 1991; Hommages, 1993; Art of Fugue, 1993; Sarajevo (opera), 1994; orchestral, choral, instrumental, ballet and electronic music; numerous recordings. *Address:* c/o Universal Edition, 48 Great Marlborough Street, W1V 2BN.

OSBORNE, Sir Peter (George), 17th Bt, *cr* 1629; Chairman and Managing Director, Osborne & Little plc (design company), since 1967; *b* 29 June 1943; *s* of Lt-Col Sir George Osborne, 16th Bt, MC, and Mary (Grace) (*d* 1987), *d* of C. Horn; *S* father, 1960; *m* 1968, Felicity, *d* of Grantley Loxton-Peacock; four *s*. *Educ:* Wellington Coll., Berks; Christ Church Coll., Oxford. *Heir: s* George Gideon Oliver Osborne, *b* 23 May 1971. *Address:* 21 St Petersburgh Place, W2 4LA. *Club:* White's.

OSBORNE, Col Robert; Director, Tree Council, since 1991; *b* 14 March 1936; *s* of Kenneth George Hulbert Osborne and Mary Irene (*née* Daymond); *m* 1st, 1961, Sybil Kathi Gisela Hudson (*née* von Knobloch) (marr. diss. 1988); two *s*; 2nd, 1988, Claudia Downing (*née* Radok); one step *d*. *Educ:* Cheltenham Coll.; RMA, Sandhurst. Commnd RTR, 1955; served BAOR and UK, 1956–72; Staff Coll., Camberley, 1968; US Army, 1972–75; UN Force in Cyprus, 1977–80; Defence and Military Attaché, Cairo, 1983–86; NATO Defence Coll., Rome, 1987; HQ NATO, Brussels, 1987–90, retd. Hon. Citizen, State of Texas, USA, 1974. *Recreations:* antiquities, the countryside, plain cookery. *Address:* 24 Gillespie Road, N5 1LN. *T:* 0171–359 5721.

OSBORNE, Trevor, FRICS; Chairman, Building & Property Management Services plc, since 1993; *b* 7 July 1943; *s* of Alfred Osborne and Annie Edmondson; *m* 1969, Pamela Ann Stephenson; one *s* one *d*. *Educ:* Sunbury Grammar School. South Area Estate Manager, Middx County Council, 1960–65; Partner, A. P. C., 1966–67; Principal, Private Property Interests, 1967–73; Chm., 1973–93, Chief Exec., 1981–93, Speyhawk plc; Chairman: St George, 1985–; Hawk Development Management, 1987–; Lucknam Park Hotels, 1987–94; non-exec. Dir, Redland, 1989–92. Former Pres., British Property Fedn; BPF Vis. Fellow, Land Management, Reading Univ., 1987–90; Chm., Urban Villages Forum; Member: Royal Opera House Develt Bd, 1987–94 (Chm., ROH Development Ltd, 1994); Council of Advrs, Prince of Wales Inst. of Architecture (Trustee, 1991–93); Council, City Property Assoc, 1987–94; Royal Fine Art Commn, 1994–. Leader, Wokingham DC, 1980–82; Trustee, Wokingham Cons. Assoc., 1982–91; Mem. Adv. Cttee, External Relations and Millenium Gp, Westminster CC. Pres., Windsor Arts Centre; Chm., St Sebastian's Playing Field Trust; Dir, London First. Freeman, City of London; Liveryman, Chartered Surveyors' Co. FRSA. *Recreations:* travel, walking, art, theatre, opera, tennis. *Address:* Building & Property House, 19–23 Blackfriars Road, SE1 8NY. *T:* 0171–902 2000, *Fax:* 0171–902 2056; 6 Upper Wimpole Street, W1M 7TD. *Clubs:* Athenæum, Carlton, Arts.

O'SHEA, David Michael; Solicitor to the Metropolitan Police, 1982–87, retired; *b* 27 Jan. 1927; *s* of late Francis Edward O'Shea and Helen O'Shea; *m* 1953, Sheila Winifred Polkinghorne; two *s*. *Educ:* St Ignatius Coll., London; King's Coll., London Univ. (LLB). Served RN, 1946–48. Articled H. C. L. Hanne & Co., London, 1949–52; admitted solicitor, 1952; in practice with H. C. L. Hanne & Co., 1952–56; joined Solicitor's Dept, Metropolitan Police Office, 1956; Dep. Solicitor, 1976–82. *Recreation:* travel. *Address:* c/o New Scotland Yard, SW1H 0BG.

O'SHEA, Michael Kent; Under Secretary, Finance and Resource Management, Department of Trade and Industry, since 1992; *b* 12 March 1951; *s* of Donovan Henry Victor and Joan O'Shea; *m* 1988, Linda Beata Szpala. *Educ:* Bristol Grammar Sch.; Corpus Christi Coll., Cambridge (BA 1st Cl. Hons History). Department of Trade and Industry, 1973–. *Recreations:* playing and watching cricket, listening to Wagner, walking, drinking good beer and wine. *Address:* (office) Ashdown House, 123 Victoria Street, SW1E 6RB. *Clubs:* Mandarins Cricket, Gloucestershire CC.

OSIFELO, Sir Frederick (Aubarua), Kt 1977; MBE 1972; Speaker of Legislative Assembly, Solomon Islands, 1974–78; Chairman: Public Service Commission, since 1975; Police and Prison Service Commission, since 1977; Member, Judicial and Legal Service Commission, since 1977; *b* 15 Oct. 1928; *s* of late Paul Iromea and Joy Ngangale Iromea; *m* 1949, Margaret Tanai; three *s* three *d*. *Educ:* Torquay Technical Coll., England (Dip. Public Admin). Office cleaner, 1945; clerk, 1950; 1st Cl. Magistrate, 1967; Admin. Officer, Cl. B, 1967; Admin. Officer, Cl. A, 1972; District Comr, Eastern Solomons, 1972; Sen. Sec., 1973; Comr of Lands, 1974. Chairman: Cttee of Prerogative of Mercy, 1979; ad hoc cttee on Solomon Islands Honours and Awards, 1979. Pres., Amateur Sports Assoc., 1975–. Lay Canon, 1977. *Address:* PO Box 548, Honiara, Solomon Islands. *T:* (office) 21529, (home) 22018.

OSMAN, Sir (Abdool) Raman (Mahomed), GCMG 1973; CBE 1963; Governor-General of Mauritius, 1972–77; *b* 29 Aug. 1902, of Mauritian parents; unmarried. *Educ:* Royal College, Mauritius; Inns of Court, London. District Magistrate, Mauritius, 1930–38; Additional Substitute Procureur and Advocate General, 1938–50; Actg Procureur and Advocate-General, 1950–51; Actg Chief Justice, Apr.-Nov. 1958; Puisne Judge, Supreme Court of Mauritius, 1950–59, Sen. Puisne Judge, 1959–60, retired. Hon. DCL Mauritius, 1975. *Address:* Le Goulet Terrace, Tombeau Bay, Mauritius. *Club:* Port Louis Gymkhana.

OSMAN, Louis, BA (Arch.); FRIBA; artist, architect, goldsmith, medallist; *b* 30 January 1914; *s* of Charles Osman, Exeter; *m* 1940, Dilys Roberts, *d* of Richard Roberts, Rotherfield, Sussex; one *d*. *Educ:* Hele's School, Exeter; London University (Fellow, UCL, 1984–). Open exhibn at Bartlett School of Architecture, University Coll. London, 1931, and at Slade School; Donaldson Medallist of RIBA, 1935. With British Museum and British School of Archæology Expeditions to Syria, 1936, 1937; designed private and public buildings, 1937–39. Served War of 1939–45, Major in Intelligence Corps: Combined Ops HQ and Special Air Service as specialist in Air Photography, Beach Reconnaissance Cttee, prior to invasion of Europe. Resumed practice in London, 1945, designed buildings, furniture, tapestries, glass, etc; work in Westminster Abbey, Lincoln, Ely, Exeter and Lichfield Cathedrals; Staunton Harold for National Trust; Bridge, Cavendish Square, with Jacob Epstein; Newnham Coll., Cambridge; factory buildings for Cambridge Instrument Co., aluminium Big Top for Billy Smart's Circus, two villages on Dartmoor, etc; consultant architect to British Aluminium Co.; executed commissions as goldsmith and jeweller, 1956–; commissioned by De Beers for 1st Internat. Jewellery Exhibn, 1961; designed and made Prince of Wales' crown for investiture, 1969; British Bicentennial Gift to America housing Magna Carta, 1976; Verulam Medal for Metals Soc., 1975; EAHY Medal, 1975; Olympic Medal, 1976; works in art galleries, museums and private collections in GB, Europe, Canada, USA, S Africa, Australia, Japan, etc; one-man retrospective exhibn, Goldsmiths' Hall, 1971; exhibn, Lisbon, 1990. Mem. Exec. Cttee: The Georgian Group, 1952–56; City Music Soc., 1960–70. *Publications:* reviews and contributions to learned jls. *Recreation:* music. *Address:* Harpton Court, near New Radnor, Presteigne, Powys LD8 2RE. *T:* New Radnor (01544) 350380.

OSMAN, Dr Mohammad Kheir; Member of Foundation Committee, 1981–86, Professor and Dean of Students since 1985, and Educational Advisor to the Vice-Chancellor, Sultan Qaboos University, Muscat, Sultanate of Oman; *b* Gedarif, Sudan, 1928; *s* of Osman Khalifa Taha and Khadija Al Shareef; *m* 1953, Sara Ahmed. *Educ:* Khartoum Univ. (BA); London Univ. (PGCE; AcDip; MA); Univ. of California, LA (PhD). Director: Educational Research and Planning, 1970–71; Sudan/ILO Productivity Centre, Khartoum, 1972; Minister of Education, 1972–75; Mem., Sudan Nat. Assembly, 1972–75; Ambassador to UK, 1975–76; Manager, UNDP/UNESCO Educnl Project, Oman, 1977–84; Adviser to Min. of Educn, Oman, 1984–85. Professional interests include Western educnl experience and indigenous Afro/Arab conditions, and the problems of change through institutional educnl systems. Constitution Decoration, 1973; Two-Niles Decoration for Public Service, 1979; Sultan Qaboos Decoration, 1986. *Address:* Sultan Qaboos University, PO Box 50, Al-Khod, Code 123, Sultanate of Oman. *Club:* Athenæum.

OSMAN, Sir Raman; *see* Osman, Sir A. R. M.

OSMOND, Charles Barry, PhD; FRS 1984; FAA; Director, Research School of Biological Sciences, Australian National University, Canberra, since 1991; *b* 20 Sept. 1939; *s* of Edmund Charles Osmond and Joyce Daphne (*née* Krauss); *m* 1st, 1962, Suzanne Alice Ward; one *s* one *d* (and two *s* decd); 2nd, 1983, Ulla Maria Cornelia Gauhl (*née* Büchen). *Educ:* Morisset Central Sch.; Wyong High Sch.; Univ. of New England, Armidale (University Medal in Botany, 1961; BSc 1961, MSc 1963); Univ. of Adelaide (PhD 1965). FAA 1978. Post-doctoral Res. Associate, Botanical Sciences Dept, Univ. of Calif, LA, 1965; Royal Commn for Exhibn of 1851 and CSIRO Fellow, Botany Sch., Cambridge Univ., 1966; successively Res. Fellow, Fellow and Sen. Fellow, Dept of Environmental Biol., ANU, Canberra, 1967–78, Prof. of Biology, 1978–87 and 1991–; Exec. Dir, Biol Sciences Center, Desert Res. Inst., Reno, 1982–86; Arts and Scis Prof., Duke Univ., USA, 1987–91. Fulbright Sen. Scholar, Univ. of Calif, Santa Cruz, 1973–74; Carnegie Instn Fellow (Plant Biol.), Stanford, 1973–74; Richard Mereton Guest Prof., Technical Univ., Munich, 1974; Overseas Fellow, Churchill Coll., Cambridge, 1980. Goldacre Award, Aust. Soc. of Plant Physiologists, 1972; Edgeworth David Medal, Royal Soc. of NSW, 1974. *Publications:* (ed jtly) Photosynthesis and Photorespiration, 1971; (ed jtly) Photorespiration in Marine Plants, 1976; (jtly) Physiological Processes in Plant Ecology, 1980; (ed jtly) Encyclopedia of Plant Physiology, Vols 12 A-D, Physiological Plant Ecology, 1981–83; (ed jtly) Photoinhibition, 1987; (ed jtly) New Vistas in Measurement of Photosynthesis, 1989; (ed jtly) Plant Biology of the Basin and Range, 1990; (ed jtly) Water and Life, 1992; articles on plant metabolic biology and its ecological implications in learned jls. *Recreations:* biological research, social cricket, music of romantic composers, confections of Continental Europe. *Address:* Research School of Biological Sciences, Australian National University, Box 475, Canberra, ACT 2601, Australia. *T:* (6) 2493841.

OSMOND, Sir Douglas, Kt 1971; CBE 1968 (OBE 1958); QPM 1962; DL; Chief Constable, Shropshire, 1946–62, Hampshire, 1962–77; *b* 27 June 1914. *Educ:* University Coll., London. Metropolitan Police Coll., Metropolitan Police, RN, Control Commn for Germany (Public Safety Branch); Dep. Asst Inspector Gen., 1944–46. Pres., Assoc. of Chief Police Officers of England and Wales, 1967–69; Chm., Police Council for UK, 1972, 1974; Provincial Police Representative, Interpol, 1968–70; Member: Inter-Deptl Cttee on Death Certification and Coroners, 1964–71; Bd of Governors, Police Coll., 1968–72 (Adv. Cttee, 1959–77); Royal Commn on Criminal Procedure, 1978–81. DL Hants, 1981. OStJ 1971. *Address:* Woodbine Cottage, Ovington, Alresford, Hants SO24 0RF. *T:* Winchester (01962) 733729.

OSMOND, Mervyn Victor, OBE 1978; Secretary, Council for the Protection of Rural England, 1966–77 (Assistant Secretary, 1946; Deputy Secretary 1963); *b* 2 July 1912; *s* of Albion Victor Osmond and Florence Isabel (*née* Edwards), Bristol; *m* 1940, Aimée Margaret Moir; one *d*. *Educ:* Clifton Coll. (Schol.); Exeter Coll., Oxford (Schol.). 1st cl. Hon. Class. Mods; 2nd cl. Lit. Hum.; 2nd cl. Jurisprudence; Poland Prizeman (Criminal Law), 1937; called to Bar (Inner Temple), 1938; MA 1939. Practising Barrister, Western Circuit, 1938–40. Joined Gloucestershire Regt, TA, 1931; served war of 1939–45; Royal Fusiliers; DAAG (Major) 352 L of C Sub-Area and 303 L of C Area (Calcutta). *Recreations:* reading, enjoying rural England. *Address:* 39 Stonehill Road, East Sheen, SW14 8RR. *T:* 0181–876 7138.

OSMOND, Michael William Massy, CB 1977; Solicitor to the Department of Health and Social Security, and to the Office of Population Censuses and Surveys, and the General Register Office, 1974–78; *b* 1918; *s* of late Brig. W. R. F. Osmond, CBE, and Mrs C. R. E. Osmond; *m* 1943, Jill Ramsden (*d* 1989); one *s* one *d*. *Educ:* Winchester; Christ Church, Oxford. 2nd Lieut Coldstream Guards, 1939–40. Called to Bar, Inner Temple, 1941; Asst Principal, Min. of Production, 1941–43; Housemaster, HM Borstal Instn, Usk, 1943–45; Legal Asst, Min. of Nat. Insce, 1946; Sen. Legal Asst, 1948; Asst Solicitor, Min. of Pensions and Nat. Insce, 1958; Principal Asst Solicitor, DHSS, 1969. *Recreations:* music, fishing. *Address:* Waylands, Long Newnton, near Tetbury, Glos GL8 8RN. *T:* Tetbury (01666) 503308. *Club:* United Oxford & Cambridge University.

OSMOND, Sir (Stanley) Paul, Kt 1980; CB 1966; *b* 13 May 1917; *o s* of late Stanley C. and Susan Osmond; *m* 1942, Olivia Sybil, JP, *yr d* of late Ernest E. Wells, JP, Kegworth, Leicestershire; two *s*. *Educ:* Bristol Grammar School; Jesus College, Oxford. Served War of 1939–45, in Army (Gloucestershire Regiment and staff), 1940–46. Home Civil Service, 1939–75: Ministry of Education, 1946–48; Private Secretary to Prime Minister, 1948–51; Admiralty, 1951, Asst Secretary, 1954; Under-Secretary, 1959; HM Treasury, 1962, Third Secretary, 1965; Deputy Secretary: Civil Service Dept, 1968–70; Office of the Lord Chancellor, 1970–72; DHSS, 1972–75. Sec. to the Church Commissioners, 1975–80. Member: Lord Chancellor's Cttee on Public Records, 1978–80; Adv. Council on Public Records, 1983–88. Royal Institution: a Manager, 1966–69, 1970–73; Hon. Treas., 1981–86; Vice-Pres., 1981–86, 1989–92; Mem. Council, 1989–92 (Chm., 1989–92). Chm., Nat. Marriage Guidance Council, 1982–88. Mem., Clergy Orphan Corp., 1980–92; Hon. Treasurer, Central London YMCA, 1982–85; Governor, Bristol Grammar Sch., 1972–93 (Vice-Chm., 1984–92); Chm., Lingfield Hosp. Sch., 1981–87. CIMgt (CBIM 1978). *Recreations:* theatre, travel, gardening. *Address:* 20 Beckenham Grove, Bromley, Kent BR2 0JU. *T:* 0181–460 2026. *Club:* Athenæum.

OSMOTHERLY, Edward Benjamin Crofton, CB 1992; Chairman, Commission for Local Administration in England, since 1994; *b* 1 Aug. 1942; *s* of Crofton and Elsie Osmotherly; *m* 1970, Valerie (*née* Mustill); one *d* one *s*. *Educ:* East Ham Grammar School; Fitzwilliam College, Cambridge (MA). Asst Principal, Ministry of Housing and Local Govt, 1963–68 (Private Sec. to Parly Sec., 1966–67, to Minister of State, 1967–68); Principal, 1968–76; Harkness Fellow, 1972–73 (Guest Scholar, Brookings Instn, Washington DC; Exec. Fellow, Univ. of California at Berkeley); Asst Sec., DoE, 1976–79; seconded to British Railways Bd, 1979; Head of Machinery of Govt Div., CSD, 1980–81; Under Sec. (Railways), Dept of Transport, 1982–85; Under Sec., Dir of Personnel, Management and Training, Depts of the Environment and of Transport, 1985–89; Dep. Sec., Public Transport and Res. Dept, 1989–92, Prin. Establishment and Finance Officer, 1992–93, Dept of Transport; Local Govt Ombudsman for SW, E Anglia and Midlands, 1993–94. *Recreation:* reading. *Address:* Commission for Local Administration in England, 21 Queen Anne's Gate, SW1H 9BU.

OSOLA, (Victor) John, (Väinö Juhani), CBE 1980; FEng, FIMechE; Chairman, John Osola & Associates Ltd, since 1983; Director, Cranfield Precision Engineering Ltd, since 1990; *b* 24 Jan. 1926; *s* of Väinö Kaarlo Osola and Violet Agenoria (*née* Jones); *m* 1948, Brenda Lilian Davison; two *s* one *d*. *Educ:* Hymers Coll., Hull; Sunderland Technical Coll., Univ. of Durham (BSc). FEng 1979; FIMechE 1966; Fellow ASME; MInstE. Technical Commn, RE, 1945–48. Gas Turbine Res. Engr, C. A. Parsons & Co. Ltd, 1951–52; Sen. Proj. Design Engr, Procter & Gamble Ltd, 1952–57; Chief Engr, Lankro Chemicals Ltd, 1957–65; Technical Director: Fibreglass Ltd, 1965–72; Triplex Safety Glass Co. Ltd, 1972–79; Chm., Fibreglass Pilkington Ltd, Bombay, 1967–72; Director: Triplex Ireland Ltd, 1976–79; Triclover Safety Glass Co. Ltd, 1976–79; (non-exec.) Kongsberg Systems Technology Ltd, 1983–85; Mem., Pilkington Brothers European Safety Glass Bd, 1977–79; Group Chief Exec., Redman Heenan Internat. plc, 1979–82, non-exec. Dir, 1982–84. Pres., IMechE, 1982–83; Ind. Mem., Mech. Engrg and Machine Tool Requirements Bd, Dept of Industry, 1974–77, Chm. 1977–79; Chm., NEDO Adv. Manufacturing Systems Cttee, 1983–86; Member: Parly and Scientific Cttee, 1983–89; (Founder), Parly Gp for Engrg Develt, 1985–89; Court of Cranfield Inst. of Technol., 1979–85; Policy Bd, Cranfield Product Engrg Centre, 1980–85. Sec., Fellowship of Engrg, 1983–89. Foreign Mem., Finnish Nat. Acad. of Technology, 1989. Associate, St George's House, Windsor, 1980–; Governor, Malvern Coll., 1981–87. Freeman, City of London, 1984; Liveryman, Worshipful Co. of Engineers, 1984–. FRSA 1976. Hon. Fellow, Humberside Coll. of Higher Educn, 1986. MacRobert Award, 1978. *Publications:* papers in specialised engrg jls. *Recreations:* offshore sailing (BoT yachtmaster), music, theatre. *Address:* Whiddon End, Yarhampton Cross, near Stourport-on-Severn, Worcs DY13 0UY. *T:* Great Witley (01299) 896293. *Clubs:* Army and Navy; Royal Dee Yacht (Cheshire); Royal Irish Yacht (Dublin); North West Venturers Yacht (Beaumaris).

OSTLERE, Dr Gordon; *see* Gordon, Richard.

OSTROWSKI, Joan Lorraine; *see* Walley, J. L.

O'SULLEVAN, Peter John, CBE 1991 (OBE 1977); Racing Correspondent: Daily Express, 1950–86; Today, 1986–87; BBC Television Commentator; *b* 3 March 1918; *o s* of late Col John Joseph O'Sullevan, DSO, formerly Resident Magistrate, Killarney, and Vera, *o d* of Sir John Henry, DL, JP; *m* 1951, Patricia, *o d* of Frank Duckworth, Winnipeg, Manitoba, Canada. *Educ:* Hawtreys; Charterhouse; Collège Alpin, Switzerland. Specialised in ill-health in early life and not accepted for fighting forces in 1939–45 war, during which attached to Chelsea Rescue Services. Subsequently worked for John Lane, the Bodley Head, on editorial work and MSS reading. Joined Press Assoc. as Racing Correspondent, 1945, until appointed Daily Express, 1950, in similar capacity. Race-broadcasting 1946– (incl. Australia, S Africa, Italy, France, USA); in 1953 became first regular BBC TV and horse-racing commentator to operate without a race-reader; commentated: first television Grand National, 1960; world's first televised electronic horse race from Atlas computer at Univ. of London, transmitted by BBC TV Grandstand, 1967; first horse race transmitted live via satellite, from NY, to invited audience in London, 1980. Director: Internat. Racing Bureau, 1979–93; Racing Post Ltd, 1985–. Mem., Jockey Club, 1986–. Patron: Brooke Hosp. for Animals; Internat. League for Protection of Horses; Thoroughbred

Rehabilitation Centre. Derby Award for Racing Journalist of the Year, 1971 (with late Clive Graham), 1986; Racehorse Owner of the Year Award, Horserace Writers' Assoc., 1974; Timeform Racing Personality, 1974; Clive Graham Meml Award for services to racing, Press Club, 1978, 1985; Evening News Sports Commentator of the Year, 1978; William Hill Golden Spurs for services to racing, 1985; Par Excellence Award, Racing Club of Ireland, 1993. *Publication:* Calling the Horses: a racing autobiography, 1989. *Recreations:* racehorse owning, in minor way (happiest broadcasting experience commentating success of own horses, Be Friendly, 1966–67, and Attivo, 1974); travel, reading, art, food and wine. *Address:* 37 Cranmer Court, SW3 3HW. *T:* 0171–584 2781.

O'SULLIVAN, (Carrol Austin) John (Naish), CB 1973; LLB (London); Public Trustee, 1971–75; *b* Plaistow, 24 Jan. 1915; *s* of late Dr Carrol Naish O'Sullivan and late Stephanie O'Sullivan (*née* Manning); *m* 1939, Lillian Mary, *y d* of Walter Frank Yate Molineux, Ulverston; one *s* one *d*. *Educ:* Mayfield College. Admitted Solicitor, 1936. Served War of 1939–45, Gordon Highlanders and HQ Special Force SEAC (Captain). Joined Public Trustee Office, 1945; Chief Administrative Officer, 1963–66; Asst Public Trustee, 1966–71. Pres., Holborn Law Soc., 1965–66. Chm. of Governors of St Thomas More High Sch. for Boys, Westcliff-on-Sea, 1964–66. *Publications:* articles in legal jls; short stories. *Recreations:* cricket (watching), wrestling (with crossword puzzles and a computer). *Address:* 13 Orchid Place, South Woodham Ferrers, Essex CM3 5LQ. *T:* Chelmsford (01245) 321530.

O'SULLIVAN, Rt. Rev. Mgr. James, CBE 1973 (MBE 1963); Officiating Chaplain (RC), RAMC Depot and Training Centre, since 1973; *b* 2 Aug. 1917; *s* of Richard O'Sullivan and Ellen (*née* Ahern). *Educ:* St Finnbarr's Coll., Cork; All Hallows Coll., Dublin. Ordained, 1941; joined Royal Army Chaplain's Dept, 1942; 49 Infantry Div., Normandy, 1944; Senior RC Chaplain, Malaya, 1952–54 (despatches 1953); Chaplain Irish Guards, 1954–56; Senior RC Chaplain, Berlin, 1956–59; Staff Chaplain (RC), War Office, 1959–64; Senior RC Chaplain, BAOR, 1965–69; Principal RC Chaplain (Army), 1969–73. *Recreation:* golf. *Address:* Osgil, Vicarage Lane, Ropley, Alresford, Hants SO24 0DU.

O'SULLIVAN, John; *see* O'Sullivan, C. A. J. N.

O'SULLIVAN, Prof. Patrick Edmund, OBE 1988; PhD; CEng; FInstE; Haydon Pilkington Professor of Environmental Design, Head of Bartlett School and Dean of the Faculty of the Built Environment, University College London, since 1989; *b* 28 March 1937; *s* of Daniel O'Sullivan and Margaret Cecilia (*née* Mansfield); *m* 1963, Diana Grimshaw; three *s* one *d*. *Educ:* Finchley Catholic Grammar Sch.; Leeds Univ. (BSc); Durham Univ. (PhD). FCIBSE 1975. University of Newcastle upon Tyne: DSIR Post-Doctoral Res. Fellow, 1963–64; Sen. Res. Fellow in Bldg Sci., 1964–66; Lectr, 1966–70; Sen. Lectr, 1970; Prof. of Architectural Sci., UWIST, 1970–89. Hon. FRIBA. MIOA 1975. *Publications:* Insulation and Fenestration, 1967; Global Warming and the Built Environment, 1994; articles in learned jls. *Recreations:* swimming, riding, walking, theatre, bridge. *Address:* The Bartlett School, University College London, Wates House, 22 Gordon Street, WC1H 0QB. *T:* 0171–380 7503. *Club:* Farmers.

O'SULLIVAN, Sally Angela, (Mrs Charles Wilson); Editor in Chief, Good Housekeeping, since 1991; *b* 26 July 1949; *d* of Lorraine and Joan Connell; *m* 1st, 1973, Thaddeus O'Sullivan (marr. diss.); 2nd, 1980, Charles Martin Wilson, *qv*; one *s* one *d*. *Educ:* Ancaster House Sch.; Trinity Coll., Dublin (BA). Dep. Editor, Woman's World, 1977–78; Women's Editor: Daily Record, 1980; Sunday Standard, 1981; Editor, Options, 1982–88; Launch Editor, Country Homes & Interiors, 1986; Editor: She, 1989; Harpers & Queen, 1989–91. Member: Broadcasting Standards Council, 1994–; Nuffield Council on Bioethics, 1995–. Magazine Editor of the Year, 1986 and 1994. *Recreations:* family, horses. *Address:* National Magazine House, 72 Broadwick Street, W1V 2BP. *T:* 0171–439 5000.

See also Sir M. B. Connell.

OSWALD, Adm. of the Fleet Sir (John) Julian (Robertson), GCB 1989 (KCB 1987); Director: Sema Group PLC, since 1993; James Fisher & Sons plc, since 1993; Marine and General Mutual Life Assurance, since 1994; Vice Chairman, South and West Regional Health Authority, since 1993; *b* 11 Aug. 1933; *s* of George Hamilton Oswald and Margaret Elliot Oswald (*née* Robertson), Newmore, Invergordon; *m* 1958, Veronica Therese Dorette Thompson; two *s* three *d*. *Educ:* Beaudesert Park, Minchinhampton; Britannia RNC, Dartmouth. Junior Officer, 1951; served in HM Ships Devonshire, Vanguard, Verulam, Newfoundland, Jewel, Victorious, Naiad; specialised in Gunnery, 1960; Commanded HMS Yarnton, 1962–63, HMS Bacchante, 1971–72; MoD, 1972–75; RCDS, 1976; Commanded HMS Newcastle, 1977–79; RN Presentation Team, 1979–80; Captain, Britannia RNC, 1980–82; ACDS (Progs), 1982–84; ACDS (Policy and Nuclear), 1985; Flag Officer, Third Flotilla, and Comdr, Anti-Submarine Warfare, Striking Fleet, 1985–87; C-in-C, Fleet, Allied C-in-C, Channel, and C-in-C, E Atlantic, 1987–89; First Sea Lord and Chief of Naval Staff, and First and Principal Naval ADC to the Queen, 1989–93. Vice Pres., RUSI, 1992–; Member: European Atlantic Gp, 1988–; Catholic Union, 1987–; Mensa, 1964–. President: Jellicoe Sea Cadets, Newcastle, 1979–; Invergordon Br., RBL, 1992–; Assoc. of Royal Naval Officers, 1993–; Sea Cadet Assoc., 1994–. Book reviewer for various publications. Hon. DBA CNAA, 1992. *Publications:* The Royal Navy—Today and Tomorrow, 1993; articles on strategy and defence policy. *Recreations:* tennis, gliding, walking, stamp collecting, family. *Address:* c/o Naval Secretary, Victory Building, HM Naval Base, Portsmouth PO1 3LS.

OSWALD, Dr Neville Christopher, TD 1946; MD Cantab 1946; FRCP 1947; retired 1975; formerly: Consultant Physician, St Bartholomew's Hospital; Brompton Hospital; King Edward VII's Hospital for Officers, London; King Edward VII's Hospital, Midhurst; *b* 1 Aug. 1910; *s* of late Col Christopher Percy Oswald, CMG; *m* 1st, 1941, Patricia Rosemary Joyce Cooke (*d* 1947); one *s* one *d*; 2nd, 1948, Marjorie Mary Sinclair; one *d*. *Educ:* Clifton Coll.; Queens' Coll., Cambridge. Research Fellow, USA, 1938–39. Royal Army Medical Corps, 1939–45. Hon. Physician to the Queen, 1956–58; Hon. Consultant in Diseases of the Chest to the Army, 1972–75. Hon. Col, 17th (London) General Hospital RAMC (TA), 1963–70, 217 (Eastern) General Hospital RAMC (V), 1967–70. President: British Tuberculosis Assoc., 1965–67; Thoracic Soc., 1974. DL Greater London, 1973–78. RCP: Mitchell Lectr; Tudor Edwards Lectr. *Publications:* Recent Trends in Chronic Bronchitis, 1958; Diseases of the Respiratory System, 1962; many articles upon respiratory diseases. *Recreations:* travel, golf. *Address:* The Old Rectory, Thurlestone, South Devon TQ7 3NJ. *T:* Kingsbridge (01548) 560555.

OSWALD, Richard Anthony; Deputy Health Service Commissioner, since 1989; *b* 12 Jan. 1941; *s* of Denis Geoffrey Oswald and late Dorothy Lettice Oswald (*née* Shaw); *m* 1963, Janet Iris Penticost; three *s* one *d* (and one *d* decd). *Educ:* The Leys School, Cambridge. DipHSM, MHSM, 1966. NHS admin. posts, 1961–77; Dist Administrator, Leeds West, 1977–84; Gen. Manager, Leeds Western HA, 1985–89. *Recreations:* music, acting, bird-watching, DIY. *Address:* The Orchard Cottage, Cripplegate Lane, Southwater, W Sussex RH13 7HN. *T:* Southwater (01403) 730467.

OSWALD, William Richard Michael, CVO 1988 (LVO 1979); Manager, Royal Studs, since 1970; *b* 21 April 1934; *s* of Lt-Col William Alexander Hugh Oswald, ERD and Rose-Marie (*née* Leahy); *m* 1958, Lady Angela Mary Rose Cecil, LVO, *d* of 6th Marquess of Exeter, KCMG; one *s* one *d*. *Educ:* Eton; King's College, Cambridge (MA). 2nd Lieut The King's Own Royal Regt, 1953; Captain, Royal Fusiliers (TA), 1957. Manager, Lordship and Egerton Studs, 1962–70. Mem. Council, Thoroughbred Breeders' Assoc., 1965–; Chm., Bloodstock Industry Cttee, Animal Health Trust, 1989–. *Recreations:* shooting, painting, military history. *Address:* Flitcham Hall, King's Lynn, Norfolk PE6 3BY. *T:* Hillington (01485) 600319; The Royal Studs, Sandringham, Norfolk PE35 6EF. *T:* Dersingham (01485) 540588. *Club:* White's.

See also Major Sir F. J. Matheson of Matheson, Bt.

O'TOOLE, (Seamus) Peter; actor; *b* 1932; *s* of Patrick Joseph O'Toole; *m* Sian Phillips, *qv* (marr. diss.); two *d*. *Educ:* Royal Academy of Dramatic Art. With Bristol Old Vic Company, 1955–58; first appearance on London stage as Peter Shirley in Major Barbara, Old Vic, 1956. Associate Dir, Old Vic Co., 1980. *Plays include:* Oh, My Papa!, Garrick, 1957; The Long and the Short and the Tall, Royal Court and New, 1959; season with Shakespeare Memorial Theatre Company, Stratford-on-Avon, 1960; Baal, Phœnix, 1963; Hamlet, National Theatre, 1963; Ride a Cock Horse, Piccadilly, 1965; Juno and the Paycock, Man and Superman, Pictures in the Hallway, Gaiety, Dublin, 1966; Waiting for Godot, Happy Days (dir.), Abbey, Dublin, 1969; Uncle Vanya, Plunder, The Apple Cart, Judgement, Bristol Old Vic, 1973; Uncle Vanya, Present Laughter, Chicago, 1978; Macbeth, Old Vic, 1980; Man and Superman, Haymarket, 1982; Pygmalion, Shaftesbury, 1984, Yvonne Arnaud, Guildford, and NY, 1987; The Apple Cart, Haymarket, 1986; Jeffrey Bernard is Unwell, Apollo, 1989, Shaftesbury, 1991; Our Song, Apollo, 1992. *Films include:* Kidnapped, 1959; The Day They Robbed the Bank of England, 1959; The Savage Innocents, 1960; Lawrence of Arabia, 1962; Becket, 1963; Lord Jim, 1964; What's New, Pussycat, 1965; How to Steal a Million, 1966; The Bible . . . in the Beginning, 1966; The Night of the Generals, 1967; Great Catherine, 1968; The Lion in Winter, 1968; Goodbye Mr Chips, 1969; Brotherly Love, 1970; Murphy's War, 1971; Under Milk Wood, 1971; The Ruling Class, 1972; Man of La Mancha, 1972; Rosebud, 1975; Man Friday, 1975; Foxtrot, 1975; The Stunt Man, 1977; Coup d'Etat, 1977; Zulu Dawn, 1978; Power Play, 1978; The Antagonists, 1981; My Favorite Year, 1981; Supergirl, 1983; Club Paradise, 1986; The Last Emperor, 1987; High Spirits, 1988; Creator, 1990; King Ralph, 1991; Wings of Fame, 1991; Rebecca's Daughters, 1992; *television:* Rogue Male, 1976; Strumpet City, 1979; Masada, 1981; Svengali, 1982; Pygmalion, 1983; Kim, 1983; Banshee, 1986; The Dark Angel, 1989; Civvies, 1992. *Publication:* Loitering With Intent, 1992. *Address:* c/o William Morris Agency, 31–32 Soho Square, W1V 5DG. *Club:* Garrick.

OTTAWA, Archbishop of, (RC), since 1989; **Most Rev. Marcel Gervais;** *b* 21 Sept. 1931; *s* of Frédéric Pierre Gervais and Marie-Louise Beaudry. *Educ:* St Peter's Seminary, London, Ont.; Angelicum Athenæum Pontifical Inst., Rome; Pontifical Biblical Inst., Rome; Ecole Biblique et Archéologique Française de Jérusalem. Ordained priest, 1958; Prof. of Sacred Scriptures, St Peter's Seminary, London, 1962–76; Dir of Divine Word Internat. Centre of Religious Educn, London, 1974–80; Auxiliary Bishop of London, Ontario, 1980–85; Bishop of Sault Sainte-Marie, 1985–89; Coadjutor Archbishop of Ottawa, June–Sept. 1989. Pres., Canadian Conf. of Catholic Bishops, 1991. *Address:* Archbishop's Residence, 1247 Kilborn Place, Ottawa, Ont K1H 6K9, Canada. *T:* 738–5025.

OTTAWA, Bishop of, since 1993; **Rt Rev. John Arthur Baycroft;** *b* 2 June 1933; *s* of Robert Baycroft and Mary Alice (*née* Williams); *m* 1955, Joan, *d* of V. Lake; one *s* two *d*. *Educ:* Sir William Turner Sch.; Christ's Coll., Cambridge (Synge Schol.) (BA 1954; MA 1958); Ripon Hall, Oxford; Trinity Coll., Toronto (BD 1959). Ordained deacon, 1955, priest, 1956; Asst Curate, Loughborough, 1955–57; Asst Rector, St Matthew's, Ottawa, 1957–62; Rector: Perth, Ont., 1962–67; St Matthias, Ottawa, 1967–84; Christchurch Cathedral, and Dean of Ottawa, 1984–86; Suffragan Bishop of Ottawa, 1985–93. Hon. DD Montreal Diocesan Theol Coll.; DSL (*jur. dig.*) Thornloe Univ. *Publications:* The Anglican Way, 1980; The Eucharistic Way, 1982; The Way of Prayer, 1983; numerous articles in jls. *Recreations:* theatre, art, ballet. *Address:* (office) 71 Bronson Avenue, Ottawa, Ont K1R 6G6, Canada. *Club:* National Press (Ottawa).

OTTAWAY, Richard Geoffrey James; MP (C) Croydon South, since 1992; Director, Coastal Europe Ltd, since 1990; *b* 24 May 1945; *s* of late Professor Christopher Ottaway, PhD, FRCVS and of Grace Ottaway; *m* 1982, Nicola E. Kisch. *Educ:* Backwell Secondary Modern School, Somerset; Bristol University. LLB (Hons). Entered RN as an Artificer apprentice, 1961; commissioned and entered RNC, Dartmouth, 1966; served with Western Fleet, HM Ships Beechampton, Nubian and Eagle, 1967–70; Bristol Univ., 1971–74; articled to Norton Rose Botterell & Roche, 1974; admitted Solicitor, 1977; specialist in international, maritime and commercial law; Partner, William A. Crump & Son, 1981–87. Contested (C) Nottingham N, 1987; MP (C) Nottingham N, 1983–87. PPS to Ministers of State, FCO, 1985–87, to Pres. of BoT, 1992–95, to Dep. Prime Minister, 1995–. Chm., All-Party Parly Gp on Population and Development, 1992–. *Publications:* (jtly) Road to Reform, 1987; papers on combating internat. maritime fraud, on financial matters and on the environment. *Recreations:* jazz, ski-ing, yacht racing. *Address:* c/o House of Commons, SW1A 0AA. *Club:* Royal Corinthian Yacht.

OTTER, Air Vice-Marshal Victor Charles, CBE 1967 (OBE 1945); Air Officer Engineering, Air Support Command Royal Air Force, 1966–69, retired; *b* 9 February 1914; *s* of Robert and Ada Annie Otter; *m* 1943, Iris Louise Dykes; no *c*. *Educ:* Weymouth Gram. School. RAF Aircraft Apprentice, 1929–32; flying duties, 1935–37; commissioned Engr. Br., 1940; SO (Techn) Controller Research and Development (MAP), 1942–47; Asst Air Attaché, Budapest, 1947–48; Officer Comdg Central Servicing Develt Establt, 1953–55; Chief Engrg Officer, Bomber Comd, 1956–59; OC No 32 Maintenance Unit, 1959–61; STSO Flying Trng Comd, 1961–63; Project Dir, P1154/P1127, 1963–66. CEng, FRAeS, psc. *Address:* Harpenden, 21 Keats Avenue, Littleover, Derby DE23 7EE. *T:* Derby (01332) 512048. *Club:* Royal Air Force.

OTTEWILL, Prof. Ronald Harry, OBE 1989; PhD; FRS 1982; FRSC; Leverhulme Professor of Physical Chemistry, University of Bristol, 1982–92, now Emeritus; *b* 8 Feb. 1927; *m* Ingrid Geraldine Roe; one *s* one *d*. *Educ:* Southall Grammar Sch.; Queen Mary Coll., London (BSc 1948; PhD 1951); Fitzwilliam Coll., Cambridge (MA 1955; PhD 1956). Sen. Asst in Res., 1955–58, Asst Dir of Res., 1958–63, Dept of Colloid Sci., Cambridge Univ.; Bristol University: Lectr, 1964–66; Reader, 1966–70; Prof. of Colloid Science, 1970–82; Head of Dept of Physical Chem., 1973; Dean, Faculty of Science, 1988–90; Head, Sch. of Chem., 1990–92. Chm., SERC Neutron Beam Res. Cttee, 1982–85. Pres., Faraday Soc., 1989– (Hon. Treas., 1985–89; Vice Pres., 1986–89). Lectures: A. E. Alexander, RACI, 1982; Liversidge, RSC, 1985–86; Canadian High Polymer Forum, 1987; Langmuir, ACS, 1988; Rideal, RSC/SCI, 1990. Medal for Surface and Colloid Chemistry, RSC, 1972; Wolfgang Ostwald Medal, Kolloid Gesellschaft, W Germany, 1979; Bude Medal, Collège de France, Paris, 1981; Colloid and Interface

Science Gp Medal, Faraday Div., RSC, 1993. *Publications:* contribs to learned jls. *Address:* School of Chemistry, The University, Bristol BS8 1TS.

OTTON, Sir Geoffrey (John), KCB 1981 (CB 1978); Second Permanent Secretary, Department of Health and Social Security, 1979–86, retired; *b* 10 June 1927; *s.* of late John Alfred Otton and Constance Alma Otton; *m* 1952, Hazel Lomas (*née* White); one *s* one *d. Educ:* Christ's Hosp.; St John's Coll., Cambridge (MA). Home Office, 1950–71: (seconded to Cabinet Office, 1959–61; Principal Private Sec. to Home Sec., 1963–65); Dept of Health and Social Security, 1971–86. Chm., St Piers (Special Sch.), Lingfield, 1987–. *Recreation:* music. *Address:* 72 Cumberland Road, Bromley, Kent BR2 0PW. *T:* 0181–460 9610.

OTTON, Rt Hon. Sir Philip (Howard), Kt 1983; PC 1995; **Rt Hon. Lord Justice Otton;** a Lord Justice of Appeal, since 1995; *b* 28 May 1933; *o s* of late Henry Albert Otton, Kenilworth and Leah Otton; *m* 1965, Helen Margaret, *d* of late P. W. Bates, Stourbridge; two *s* one *d. Educ:* Bablake School, Coventry; Birmingham Univ. LLB 1954. 2nd Lieut, 3rd Dragoon Guards, 1955–57. Called to the Bar, Gray's Inn, 1955, Bencher 1983; QC 1975. Dep. Chm., Beds QS, 1970–72; Junior Counsel to the Treasury (Personal Injuries), 1970–75; a Recorder of the Crown Court, 1972–83; Judge of the High Court, QBD, 1983–95; Presiding Judge, Midland and Oxford Circuit, 1986–88; Judge in Charge of Official Referees Courts, 1991–95. Chairman: Royal Brompton and National Heart and Lung Hospitals SHA, 1991–94; Royal Brompton Heart and Lung NHS Trust, 1994–; Nat. Heart and Lung Inst., 1991–. Governor, Nat. Heart and Chest Hosps, 1979–85. Trustee, Migraine Trust, 1992–. Hon. Mem., Amer. Bar Assoc. FCIArb 1994. *Recreations:* theatre, opera, music. *Address:* Royal Courts of Justice, Strand, WC2A 2LL. *Clubs:* Garrick, Pilgrims.

OTUNGA, HE Cardinal Maurice; *see* Nairobi, Archbishop of, (RC).

OUELLET, Hon. André, PC (Can.); QC (Can.); MP (L) Papineau-St-Michel, since 1988; Minister of Foreign Affairs, Canada, since 1993; *b* St Pascal, Quebec, 6 April 1939; *m* 1965, Édith Pagé; two *s* two *d. Educ:* Univ. of Ottawa (BA); Univ. of Sherbrooke (LLB). Called to the Bar. MP (L) Montreal-Papineau, 1967–84; Parliamentary Secretary: Minister of Ext. Affairs, 1970; Minister of Health and Welfare, 1971; 1972–84, Departments of: Post Office; Consumer and Corporate Affairs; State for Urban Affairs; Public Works; Labour; State for Regl Econ. Develt; Pres., Privy Council and Govt Leader in H of C, 1984. Co-Chm., Nat. Liberal Campaign Cttee, 1992–. *Recreations:* tennis, skiing, reading, theatre. *Address:* Room 314, West Block, House of Commons, Ottawa, Ontario K1A 0A6, Canada. *Club:* Cercle Universitaire (Ottawa).

OUGHTON, John Raymond Charles; Under Secretary, and Head, Prime Minister's Efficiency Unit, Office of Public Service (formerly of Public Service and Science), Cabinet Office, since 1993; *b* 21 Sept. 1952. *Educ:* Reading Sch.; University Coll., Oxford (BA Mod. Hist. 1974). Joined MoD, 1974; Mem. UK Delegn, UN Law of Sea Conf., 1978; Asst Pvte Sec. to Minister of State for Defence, 1978–80; Principal, 1980; on secondment to Canadian Govt, 1980–81; Sales Policy, 1981–83; Office of Personal Advr to Sec. of State for Defence, 1984; Pvte Sec. to Minister for the Armed Forces, 1984–86; Sen. Principal, Directorate of Procurement Policy, 1986–87; Asst Sec., Dir of Procurement Policy, 1988–89; Head of Resources and Progs (Navy), 1990–93. FRSA. *Recreations:* squash, tennis, bridge, watching cricket and football. *Address:* Efficiency Unit, Office of Public Service, Cabinet Office, 70 Whitehall, SW1A 2AS. *T:* 0171–270 0257. *Clubs:* United Oxford & Cambridge University; Tottenham Hotspur Football, Middlesex CC.

OULTON, Sir (Antony) Derek (Maxwell), GCB 1989 (KCB 1984; CB 1979); QC 1985; MA, PhD; Permanent Secretary, Lord Chancellor's Office, and Clerk of the Crown in Chancery, 1982–89; barrister-at-law; Life Fellow, Magdalene College, Cambridge, since 1995 (Fellow, 1990–95); *b* 14 Oct. 1927; *y s* of late Charles Cameron Courtenay Oulton and Elizabeth, *d* of T. H. Maxwell, KC; *m* 1955, Margaret Geraldine (*d* 1989), *d* of late Lt-Col G. S. Oxley, MC, 60th Rifles; one *s* three *d. Educ:* St Edward's Sch., Oxford; King's Coll., Cambridge (scholar; BA (1st Cl.), MA; PhD 1974). Called to Bar, Gray's Inn, 1952, Bencher, 1982; in private practice, Kenya, 1952–60; Private Sec. to Lord Chancellor, 1961–65; Sec., Royal Commn on Assizes and Quarter Sessions, 1966–69; Asst Solicitor, 1969–75. Dep. Sec., 1976–82, and Dep. Clerk of the Crown in Chancery, 1977–82, Lord Chancellor's Office. Vis. Prof. in Law, Bristol Univ., 1990–91. Chm., Mental Health Foundn Cttee on the Mentally Disordered Offender, 1989–92. Trustee, Nat. Gallery, 1989–95. Pres., Electricity Arbitration Assoc., 1990–. Mem., Adv. Council, Inst. of Criminology, Cambridge, 1992–. *Publications:* (jtly) Legal Aid and Advice, 1971; (ed) Lewis, We the Navigators, 2nd edn 1994. *Address:* Magdalene College, Cambridge CB3 0AG. *T:* Cambridge (01223) 332100.

OULTON, Air Vice-Marshal Wilfrid Ewart, CB 1958; CBE 1953; DSO 1943; DFC 1943; FEng; FRIN; FIEE; Chairman, Medsales Executive Ltd, since 1982; *b* 27 July 1911; *s* of Llewellin Oulton, Monks Coppenhall, Cheshire; *m* 1st, 1935, Sarah (*d* 1990), *d* of Rev. E. Davies, Pitsea, Essex; three *s*; 2nd, 1991, Leticia Sara Malcolm. *Educ:* University Coll., Cardiff; Cranwell. Commissioned, 1931; Director, Joint Anti-Submarine School, 1946–48; Joint Services Staff College, 1948–50; Air Attaché, Buenos Aires, Montevideo, Asuncion, 1950–53; idc 1954; Director of Operations, Air Ministry, 1954–56; commanded Joint Task Force "Grapple" for first British megaton weapon tests in the Pacific, 1956–58; Senior Air Staff Officer, RAF Coastal Command, HQ, 1958–60; retd. *Publications:* Christmas Island Cracker, 1987; Technocrat, 1995. *Recreations:* music, travel, grandchildren and great-grandchildren. *Address:* Farthings, Hollywood Lane, Lymington, Hants SO41 9HD. *T:* Lymington (01590) 673498. *Clubs:* Royal Air Force; Royal Lymington Yacht.

OUNSTED, John, MA Cantab; HM Inspector of Schools, 1971–81, retired; *b* London, 24 May 1919; *e s* of late Rev. Laurence J. Ounsted, Dorchester Abbey, Oxon (ordained 1965; formerly with Sun Life Assurance); *m* 1940, Irene, 3rd *d* of late Rev. Alfred Newns; one *s* four *d. Educ:* Winchester (Scholar); Trinity College, Cambridge (Major Scholar). Math. Tripos Part I, 1st Class; Science Tripos Part II, 1st Class; Senior Scholarship, Trinity College. Assistant Master, King Edward's School, Birmingham, 1940–48; Headmaster, Leighton Park School, 1948–70. First layman ever to be Select Preacher, Oxford Univ., 1964. Page Scholarship to visit USA, 1965. Vice-Pres., Botanical Soc. of British Isles, 1989–93. Liveryman, Worshipful Company of Mercers. *Publications:* verses from various languages in the 2 vols of Translation, 1945 and 1947; contributions to Watsonia, The Proceedings of the Botanical Society of the British Isles, and various other educational and botanical periodicals. *Recreations:* botany, camping, being overtaken when motoring. *Address:* Apple Tree Cottage, Woodgreen Common, Fordingbridge, Hants SP6 2BD. *T:* Downton (01725) 512271.

See also Sir A. Foley Newns.

OUSBY, Dr Ian Vaughan Kenneth; writer and broadcaster; *b* 26 June 1947; *s* of Arthur Valentine Ousby and Betty Lettice Grace (*née* Green); *m* 1st 1969, Heather Dubrow (marr. diss. 1979); 2nd, 1984, Mary Dustan Turner (marr. diss. 1993). *Educ:* Bishop's Stortford Coll.; Magdalene Coll., Cambridge (BA 1965); Harvard Univ. (PhD 1973). Temp. Lectr in English, Univ. of Durham, 1974–75; University of Maryland: Asst Prof. of English, 1975–79; Associate Prof., 1979–82. John Simon Guggenheim Meml Foundn Fellow, 1980–81. *Publications:* Bloodhounds of Heaven: the detective in English fiction from Godwin to Doyle, 1976; The Blue Guide to Literary Britain and Ireland, 1985, 2nd edn 1990; (jtly) The Correspondence of John Ruskin and Charles Eliot Norton, 1987; The Cambridge Guide to Literature in English, 1988, 2nd edn 1993, concise edn 1996; The Blue Guide to England, 10th edn 1989, 11th edn 1995; The Englishman's England: taste, travel and the rise of tourism, 1990; James Plumptre's Britain: the journals of a tourist in the 1790's, 1992; The Blue Guide to Burgundy, 1992. *Recreations:* looking at pictures and buildings, listening to music. *Address:* c/o Andrew Lownie Literary Agency, 122 Bedford Court Mansions, Bedford Square, WC1B 3AH. *T:* 0171–636 4917.

OUSELEY, Duncan Brian Walter; QC 1992; a Recorder, since 1994; *b* 24 Feb. 1950; *s* of Maurice and Margaret Ouseley; *m* 1974, Suzannah Price; three *s. Educ:* Trinity Sch., Croydon; Fitzwilliam Coll., Cambridge (MA); University Coll. London (LLM). Called to the Bar, Gray's Inn, 1973 (Atkin Scholar 1972); Junior Counsel to the Crown, Common Law, 1986–92. Chairman, Examination in Public Shropshire Structure Plan, 1985, Hampshire Structure Plan, 1991. *Recreations:* family, sport, music, wine. *Address:* 4/5 Gray's Inn Square, Gray's Inn, WC1R 5AY.

OUTERIÑO, Felix C.; *see* Candela Outeriño.

OUTRAM, Sir Alan James, 5th Bt, *cr* 1858; MA; Under Master, Harrow School (Housemaster, 1979–91); *b* 15 May 1937; *s* of late James Ian Outram and late Evelyn Mary Littlehales; *S* great-uncle, 1945; *m* 1976, Victoria Jean, *d* of late George Dickson Paton, Bexhill-on-Sea; one *s* one *d. Educ:* Spyway, Langton Matravers, Swanage; Marlborough College, Wilts; St Edmund Hall, Oxford. Lt-Col TAVR. *Recreations:* golf, tennis, bridge. *Heir: s* Douglas Benjamin James Outram, *b* 15 March 1979. *Address:* Harrow School, Harrow-on-the-Hill, Middlesex HA1 3HW.

OVENDEN, John Frederick; County Councillor, Kent, since 1985 (Leader, Labour Group, since 1994); *b* 17 Aug. 1942; *s* of late Richard Ovenden and Margaret Louise Ovenden (*née* Lucas); *m* 1963, Maureen (*née* White); one *d. Educ:* Salmestone County Primary Sch., Margate; Chatham House Grammar Sch., Ramsgate. Asst Exec. Engr, Post Office, 1961–74. MP (Lab) Gravesend, Feb. 1974–1979. Contested (Lab) Gravesham, 1983. Manager, Post Office, subseq. British Telecom, 1979–90. *Recreations:* football (as a spectator), cricket (Kent), theatre, gardening, books. *Club:* Gillingham Labour (Gillingham).

OVERALL, Sir John (Wallace), Kt 1968; CBE 1962; MC and Bar; architect, town planner and company director; *b* 15 July 1913; *s* of late W. Overall, Sydney; *m* 1943, Margaret J. (*d* 1988), *d* of C. W. Goodman; four *s. Educ:* Sydney Techn. College. AIF, 1940–45: CO, 1 Aust. Para. Bn (Lt-Col). Chief Architect, S Australian Housing Trust, 1946–48; private practice, Architect and Town Planner, 1949–52; Dir of Architecture, Commonwealth Dept of Works, 1952–57; Comr, Nat. Capital Develt Commn, 1958–72; Chm., Nat. Capital Planning Cttee, 1958–72; Comr, Cities Commn (Chm., Adv. Cttee), 1972–73; Principal, John Overall and Partners, 1973–81; Director: Lend Lease Corp. Ltd, 1973–83; General Property Trust, 1975–83; Alliance Holdings Ltd, 1975–83 (Chm., 1980–83); CSR Ltd, 1973–85. Mem., Parliament House Construction Authority (Commonwealth Govt of Australia), 1979–85; Chm. Assessors, Parlt House Design Competition, 1979–80. Chm. of Olympic Fine Arts Architecture and Sculpture Exhibn, Melb., 1956. Life Fellow, RAIA and API; Hon. Fellow, AIA, 1984; Pres., Austr. Inst. of Urban Studies, 1970–71. Past Pres., Canberra Legacy Club. Sydney Luker Meml Medal, 1970; Sir James Barrett Medal, 1970; Gold Medal, RAIA, 1982. *Publications:* Observations on Redevelopment Western Side of Sydney Cove, 1967; Canberra: yesterday, today and tomorrow, 1995; sundry papers to professional jls. *Recreations:* golf, tennis. *Address:* Unit 1, Kingston Tower, 9 Jardine Street, Kingston, ACT 2604, Australia. *Club:* Commonwealth (Canberra).

OVERBURY, (Henry) Colin (Barry), CBE 1993 (OBE (mil.) 1974); independent lecturer in EC Law; Consultant in EC Law, Allen & Overy, Solicitors; *b* 13 Jan. 1931; *s* of Stanley and Daisy Overbury; *m* 1st, 1954, Dawn Rhodes Dade (marr. diss. 1981); three *s*; 2nd, 1989, Louise Jane Rosewarne. *Educ:* Dragon Sch., Oxford; Eastbourne Coll.; Law Society's Coll. of Law. Admitted Solicitor of the Supreme Court, 1955. HM Army Legal Services, 1955–74: progressively, Captain, Major, Lt-Col; Retired List, Lt-Col, 1974. European Commission: Prin. Administrator, 1974–82; Adviser, 1982–84; Hd of Div., 1984–86; Dir, Directorate-Gen. for Competition, 1986–93, retd; Hon. Dir Gen. Sen. Fellow of the Salzburg Seminar, 1984. *Publications:* articles in Common Market Law Rev., 1977, Fordham Univ. Law Inst. Jl, 1984, 1989. *Recreations:* travel, boating, good living. *Address:* Broke Hall, Nacton, Suffolk IP10 0ET. *Clubs:* Lansdowne; Cercle Royal Gaulois (Brussels); Royal Harwich Yacht.

OVEREND, Prof. (William) George; Professor of Chemistry in the University of London, 1957–87, now Professor Emeritus; Master, Birkbeck College, 1979–87 (Vice-Master, 1974–79; Hon. Fellow, 1988); *b* 16 Nov. 1921; *e s* of late Harold George Overend, Shrewsbury, Shropshire; *m* 1949, Gina Olava, *y d* of late Horace Bertie Cadman, Birmingham; two *s* one *d. Educ:* Priory School, Shrewsbury; Univ. of Birmingham. BSc (Hons) 1943, PhD 1946, DSc 1954, Birmingham; CChem; FRSC (FRIC 1955). Asst Lecturer, Univ. Coll., Nottingham, 1946–47; Research Chemist with Dunlop Rubber Co. Ltd and subsequently British Rubber Producers' Assoc., 1947–49; Hon. Research Fellow, 1947–49, Lecturer in Chemistry, 1949–55, Univ. of Birmingham; Vis. Associate Prof., Pennsylvania State Univ., 1951–52; Reader in Organic Chemistry, Univ. of London, 1955–57; Hd of Dept of Chem., Birkbeck Coll., London, 1957–79. Univ. of London: Mem., Academic Council, 1963–67, 1976–79 and 1984–87; Mem., Collegiate Council, 1979–87; Mem., University Entrance and Schools Examination Council, 1966–67 and 1985–87; Mem., F and GP Cttee, 1976–87; Mem., External Cttee, 1984–87; Chm., Bd of Studies in Chemistry, 1974–76; Mem., Senate, 1976–87; Mem., Jt Cttee of Court and Senate for collective planning, 1976–79; Dean, Faculty of Science, 1978–79; Chm., Acad. Adv. Bd in Sci., 1978–79; Mem., Extra-Mural Council, 1979–87, Chm., 1983–84; Chm., Cttee for Extra-Mural Studies, 1984–87. Mem. Council, Inst. of Educn, 1979–82; Leverhulme Emeritus Fellow, 1987–89. Member Council: National Inst. of Adult Continuing Educn, 1983–88; London and E Anglian Gp for GCSE, 1986–87; Mem. Chem. Bd, 1981–84, Mem. Adv. Bd on Credit Accumulation and Transfer, 1986–87, CNAA. Rep. of South Bank Poly, Assoc. of Colls of Further and Higher Educn, 1981–91. Royal Institute of Chemistry: Examiner, 1958–62; Assessor, 1959–72; Mem., Institutions and Examinations Cttee, 1969–75 (Chm., 1976–85); Mem. Council, 1977–80; Mem. Qual. and Admissions Cttee, 1977–80; Mem. Qual. and Exam. Bd, RSC, 1980–85; Chemical Society (subseq. Royal Society of Chemistry): Mem. Council, 1967–70, 1972–77; Mem. Publications Bd, 1967–78; Hon. Sec. and Hon. Treasurer, Perkin Div., 1972–75; Vice-Pres., 1975–77; Mem., Interdivisional Council, 1972–75; Mem., Educn and Trng Bd, 1972–78; Soc. of Chemical Industry: Mem., Council, 1955–65; Mem., Finance Committee, 1956–65; Mem., Publications Cttee, 1955–65 (Hon. Sec. for publications and Chairman of Publications Committee, 1958–65); Member: Brit. Nat. Cttee for Chemistry, 1961–66, 1973–78; Brit. Nat. Cttee for Biochemistry, 1975–81;

Chemical Council, 1960–63 and 1964–69 (Vice-Chm. 1964–69); European Cttee for Carbohydrate Chemists, 1970–85 (Chm.); Hon. Sec., Internat. Cttee for Carbohydrate Chemistry, 1972–75 (Pres., 1978–80); Mem., Jt IUPAC-IUB Commn on Carbohydrate Nomenclature, 1971–. Jubilee Memorial Lecturer, Society of Chemical Industry, 1959–60; Lampitt Medallist, Society of Chemical Industry, 1965; Member: Pharmacopœia Commission, 1963–81; Home Office Poisons Board, 1973–. Governor: Polytechnic of the South Bank, 1970–91 (Chm., 1980–89; Hon. Fellow 1989); Thomas Huxley Coll., 1971–77; Mem., Council of Governors, Queen Elizabeth Coll., Univ. of London, 1983–85. Mem., Cttee of Management, Inst. of Archaeology, 1980–86. FIMgt (FBIM 1988). Hon. FCollP 1986. DUniv Open, 1988. *Publications:* The Use of Tracer Elements in Biology, 1951; papers in Nature, and Jl of Chemical Soc. *Recreation:* gardening (rose grower). *Address:* Birkbeck College, Gordon House, Gordon Street, WC1. *T:* 0171–380 7479; The Retreat, Nightingales Lane, Chalfont St Giles, Bucks HP8 4SR. *Clubs:* Athenæum, Royal Automobile.

OWEN, family name of **Baron Owen**.

OWEN, Baron *cr* 1992 (Life Peer), of the City of Plymouth; **David Anthony Llewellyn Owen,** CH 1994; PC 1976; European Union Co-Chairman, International Conference on Former Yugoslavia, 1992–95; *b* Plympton, South Devon, 2 July 1938; *s* of Dr John William Morris Owen and Mary Llewellyn; *m* 1968, Deborah Schabert; two *s* one *d*. *Educ:* Bradfield College; Sidney Sussex College, Cambridge (Hon. Fellow, 1977); St Thomas' Hospital. BA 1959; MB, BChir 1962; MA 1963. St Thomas' Hospital: house appts, 1962–64; Neurological and Psychiatric Registrar, 1964–66; Research Fellow, Medical Unit, 1966–68. Contested (Lab) Torrington, 1964; MP (Lab 1966–81, SDP, 1981–92) Plymouth Sutton, 1966–74, Plymouth Devonport, 1974–92. PPS to Minister of Defence, Administration, 1967; Parly Under-Sec. of State for Defence, for RN, 1968–70; Opposition Defence Spokesman, 1970–72, resigned over EEC, 1972; Parly Under-Sec. of State, DHSS, 1974; Minister of State: DHSS, 1974–76; FCO, 1976–77; Sec. of State for Foreign and Commonwealth Affairs, 1977–79; Opposition spokesman on energy, 1979–80. Sponsored 1973 Children's Bill; ministerially responsible for 1975 Children's Act. Co-founder, SDP, 1981; Chm., Parly Cttee, SDP, 1981–82; Dep. Leader, SDP, 1982–83; Leader, SDP, 1983–87, resigned over issue of merger with Liberal Party, re-elected, 1988–92. Chm., Decision Technology Internat., 1970–72. Dir, Coats Viyella plc, 1994–. Member: Independent Commn on Disarmament and Security Issues, 1980–89; Ind. Commn on Internat. Humanitarian Issues, 1983–88. Chm., Humanitas, 1990–. Governor of Charing Cross Hospital, 1966–68; Patron, Disablement Income Group, 1968–. Chairman of SW Regional Sports Council, 1967–71. *Publications:* (ed) A Unified Health Service, 1968; The Politics of Defence, 1972; In Sickness and in Health, 1976; Human Rights, 1978; Face the Future, 1981; A Future That Will Work, 1984; A United Kingdom, 1986; Personally Speaking to Kenneth Harris, 1987; Our NHS, 1988; Time to Declare (autobiog.), 1991; (ed) Seven Ages (anthology of poetry), 1992; articles in Lancet, Neurology, Clinical Science, and Foreign Affairs. *Recreation:* sailing. *Address:* 78 Narrow Street, Limehouse, E14 8BP. *T:* 0171–987 5441.

OWEN, (Alfred) David; Group Chairman, Rubery Owen Holdings Ltd, since 1975; *b* 26 Sept. 1936; *m* 1966, Ethne (*née* Sowman); two *s* one *d*. *Educ:* Brocksford Hall; Oundle; Emmanuel Coll., Cambridge Univ. (MA). Joined Rubery Owen Gp, 1960; Gen. Man., Rubery Owen Motor Div., 1962–67; Dep. Man. Dir, Rubery Owen & Co. Ltd, 1967; Acting Chm. and Man. Dir, Rubery Owen Holdings Ltd, 1969; Director: Brooke Tool Engineering (Holdings) plc, 1968–; Severn Valley Railways (Holdings) plc, 1984–; Blackwell Science Ltd, 1993–. Trustee, Community Develt Foundn (formerly Community Projects Foundn), 1978–; Member: Council, Univ. of Aston, 1981–; Bd, British Library, 1982–90; Bd, Nat. Exhibn Centre, 1982–; Bd, Castle Vale Housing Action Trust, 1993–. President: Comité de Liaison Eur. de la Distrib. Ind. de Pièces de rechange et équipements pour Autos, 1988–90; Commercial Trailer Assoc., 1992–. Hon. DSc Aston, 1988. *Recreations:* walking, photography, music, industrial archaeology, local history, collecting books. *Address:* Mill Dam House, Mill Lane, Aldridge, Walsall, West Midlands WS9 0NB. *T:* (office) 0121–526 3131. *Club:* National.

OWEN, Alun, MC 1945; retired; Under-Secretary, Land Use Planning Group, Welsh Office, 1975–79; *b* 14 March 1919; *m* 1946, Rhona Evelyn Griffiths; one *s* four *d*. *Educ:* West Monmouth Grammar Sch.; Bridgend Grammar Sch.; LSE (BScEcon). Mil. Service, 1939–46: Ches. Regt, 1940–46 (Captain) (despatches, Normandy, 1944); Civil Service, Min. of Labour NW Region, 1946–48; Min. of Fuel and Power, 1948–50; Customs and Excise, 1950–59; Welsh Office, Min. of Housing and Local Govt, 1959–62; Welsh Bd of Health, 1962–69; Welsh Office, 1969–79. *Address:* 12 Knowbury Avenue, Penarth, South Glam CF64 5RX.

OWEN, His Honour Aron, PhD; a Circuit Judge, 1980–92 (Resident Judge, Clerkenwell County Court, 1986–92); Deputy Judge, Clerkenwell County Court, and Family Division, Royal Courts of Justice, 1992–94; *b* 16 Feb. 1919; *m* 1946, Rose (*née* Fishman), JP; one *s* two *d*. *Educ:* Tredegar County Grammar Sch.; Univ. of Wales (BA Hons, PhD). Called to the Bar, Inner Temple, 1948. Freeman, City of London, 1963. *Recreations:* travel, gardening. *Address:* 44 Brampton Grove, Hendon, NW4 4AQ. *T:* 0181–202 8151.

OWEN, Bernard Laurence; a Chairman of Industrial Tribunals, since 1982; *b* 8 Aug. 1925; *s* of Albert Victor Paschal Owen and Dorothy May Owen; *m* 1950, Elsie Yarnold; one *s* two *d*. *Educ:* King Edward's School, Birmingham; solicitor. Commissioned Royal Warwickshire Regt, 1945, service in Sudan, Eritrea, Egypt; staff appts in GHQs Middle East and Palestine, 1946–47; retired 1947 (Major); qualified as solicitor, 1950; a Senior Partner, C. Upfill Jagger Son & Tilley, 1952–82. *Recreations:* gardening, photography, bird watching.

OWEN, David; *see* Owen, A. D.

OWEN, David Harold Owen; Registrar of the Privy Council, since 1983; *b* 24 May 1933; *er* twin *s* of late Lloyd Owen Owen and Margaret Glyn Owen, Machynlleth, Powys; *m* 1st, 1961, Ailsa Ransome Wallis (*d* 1993); three *d*; 2nd, 1995, Julia (*née* Beck), *widow* of W. M. Lowe. *Educ:* Harrow Sch.; Gonville and Caius Coll., Cambridge. Called to the Bar, Gray's Inn, 1958. Served Royal Welch Fusiliers, 1951–53 (2nd Lieut). Campbell's Soups Ltd, King's Lynn, 1958–68; Lord Chancellor's Dept, 1969–80 (Private Sec. to Lord Chancellor, 1971–75); Chief Clerk, Judicial Cttee of Privy Council, 1980–83. *Recreations:* music, travel. *Address:* Judicial Committee of the Privy Council, Downing Street, SW1A 2AJ. *T:* 0171–270 0487. *Club:* Reform.

OWEN, Maj.-Gen. David Lanyon Ll.; *see* Lloyd Owen.

OWEN, Rt. Rev. Edwin, MA; *b* 3 Nov. 1910; *s* of late William Rowland Owen; *m* 1940, Margaret Mary Williams, BA; one *s* one *d*. *Educ:* Royal School, Armagh; Trinity College, Dublin (MA). Deacon 1934, priest 1935, Dublin; Curate of Glenageary, 1934–36; Christ Church, Leeson Park, Dublin, 1936–38; Minor Canon of St Patrick's Cathedral, Dublin, 1935–36; Chancellor's Vicar, 1936–38; Succentor, 1938–42; Incumbent of Birr with Eglish, 1942–57; Canon, Killaloe Cathedral, 1954–57; Rector of Killaloe and Dean of Killaloe Cathedral, 1957–72; Diocesan Secretary of Killaloe and Kilfenora, 1957–72; Bishop of Killaloe, Kilfenora, Clonfert and Kilmacduagh, 1972–76, when diocese amalgamated with Limerick, Ardfert and Aghadoe, and Emly; Bishop of Limerick and Killaloe, 1976–81. *Recreation:* classical music. *Address:* 5 Frankfort Avenue, Rathgar, Dublin 6.

OWEN, Dr Gareth, CBE 1988; DSc; MRIA; CBiol, FIBiol; Principal, University College of Wales, Aberystwyth, 1979–89; Vice-Chancellor, University of Wales, 1985–87; *b* 4 Oct. 1922; *s* of J. R. and B. M. Owen; *m* 1953, Beti Jones; one *s* two *d*. *Educ:* Pontypridd Boys' Grammar Sch.; University Coll., Cardiff (BSc 1950; Fellow, 1982). DSc Glasgow, 1959. FIBiol 1964. Served War, RAF Pilot, 1942–47. Lectr in Zoology, Univ. of Glasgow, 1950–64; Prof. of Zool., 1964–79, and Pro-Vice-Chancellor, 1974–79, Queen's Univ. of Belfast. Welsh Supernumerary, Jesus Coll., Oxford, 1981–82 and 1986–87. Mem., Nature Conservancy Council, 1984–91 (Chm., Adv. Cttee for Wales, 1985–91). Pres., Welsh Centre of Internat. Affairs, 1989–93. Mem., RSPB Adv. Cttee for Wales, 1991–. MRIA 1976. Hon. Fellow: UCW, Cardiff, 1982; AFRC Inst. for Grassland and Envmtl Res., 1991. Hon. Mem. of the Gorsedd, 1983. Hon. DSc QUB, 1982; Hon. LLD Wales, 1989. *Publications:* contrib. Trans Royal Soc., Proc. Malacol. Soc. London, Jl Mar. Biol. Soc., and Qly Jl Micro. Sci. *Recreation:* photography. *Address:* 6A St Margaret's Place, Whitchurch, Cardiff CF4 7AD. *T:* Cardiff (01222) 692199.

OWEN, Sir Geoffrey (David), Kt 1989; Director, Business Policy Programme, Centre for Economic Performance, London School of Economics and Political Science, since 1991; *b* 16 April 1934; *s* of L. G. Owen; *m* 1st, 1961, Dorothy Jane (*d* 1991); two *s* one *d*; 2nd, 1993, Miriam Marianna Gross, *qv*. *Educ:* Rugby Sch.; Balliol Coll., Oxford (MA). Joined Financial Times, 1958, feature writer, industrial correspondent; US Correspondent, 1961; Industrial Editor, 1967; Executive, Industrial Reorganisation Corp., 1967–69; Dir of Admin, Overseas Div., 1969, Dir of Personnel and Admin, 1972, British Leyland Internat.; Dep. Editor, 1974–80, Editor, 1981–90, Financial Times. *Publication:* Industry in the USA, 1966. *Address:* London School of Economics and Political Science, Houghton Street, WC2A 2AE.

OWEN, Gerald Victor; QC 1969; a Recorder of the Crown Court, since 1979; *b* London, 29 Nov. 1922; *m* 1946, Phyllis (*née* Ladsky); one *s* one *d*. *Educ:* Kilburn Grammar Sch.; St Catharine's Coll., Cambridge. Exhibr, St Catharine's Coll., Cambridge, 1940; Drapers' Company Science Schol., Queen Mary Coll., London, 1940. 1st cl. Maths Tripos I, 1941; Senior Optimes Tripos II, 1942; BA 1943, MA 1946, Cantab; Royal Statistical Soc. Certif., 1947; LLB London (Hons) 1949. Research Ballistics, Min. of Supply, 1942–45; Statistical Officer, LCC, 1945–49. Called to Bar, Gray's Inn, 1949; *ad eundem* Inner Temple, 1969. A Dep. Circuit Judge, 1971. Chairman: Dairy Produce Quota Tribunal, 1984–85; Medical Appeals Tribunal, 1984–94. Member, Cttees of Justice on: Legal Aid in Criminal Cases; Complaints against Lawyers, 1970; False Witness, the problem of perjury, 1973. *Address:* 3 Paper Buildings, Temple, EC4Y 7EU. *T:* 0171–797 7000. *Club:* Maccabaeans.

OWEN, Gordon Michael William, CBE 1991; Chairman: Energis Communications Ltd, since 1993; Utility Cable plc, since 1994; *b* 9 Dec. 1937; *s* of Christopher Knowles Owen and late Mrs Margaret Joyce Milward (*née* Spencer); *m* 1963, Jennifer Pearl, (Jane), Bradford; one *s* one *d*. *Educ:* Cranbrook Sch. Cable & Wireless, 1954–91: Dir, 1986–91; Jt Man. Dir, 1987–88; Dep. Chief Exec., 1988–90; Gp Man. Dir, 1990–91; Chairman: Mercury Communications Ltd, 1990–91 (Man. Dir, 1984–90); Peterstar Communications, St Petersburg, 1992–94. Director: Portals Gp, 1988–95; London Electricity, 1989–; Verity (formerly Wharfedale), 1992–; Acorn Computer Group, 1995–. Chm., MacIntyre Care, 1993–. *Recreations:* bee keeping, stamp collecting, sailing, bad golf. *Address:* Little Hawksfold, Vann Road, Fernhurst, W Sussex GU27 3NS.

OWEN, Maj.-Gen. Harry, CB 1972; Chairman, Medical Appeal Tribunal, 1972–84; *b* 17 July 1911; *m* 1952, Maureen (*née* Summers); one *s* one *d*. *Educ:* University Coll., Bangor. BA Hons Philosophy, 1934. Solicitor of Supreme Court, 1939. Commissioned in Queen's Own Cameron Highlanders, 1940–43; joined Mil. Dept of Office of Judge Advocate General, 1943; served in: W Africa, 1945–46; Middle East, 1947–50; Austria, 1952–53; Dep. Dir of Army Legal Services: Far East, 1960–62; HQ, BAOR, 1962–67; Brig. Legal Staff, 1968–69; Maj.-Gen. 1969; Dir, Army Legal Services, 1969–71, retd. *Recreations:* philosophy, history of art, walking, gardening. *Address:* 7 The Chyne, South Park, Gerrards Cross, Bucks SL9 8HZ. *T:* Gerrards Cross (01753) 890701.

OWEN, Sir Hugh (Bernard Pilkington), 5th Bt *cr* 1813; *b* 28 March 1915; *s* of Sir John Arthur Owen, 4th Bt and Lucy Fletcher (*d* 1985), *e d* of F. W. Pilkington; *S* father, 1973. *Educ:* Chillon Coll., Switzerland. *Heir: b* John William Owen [*b* 7 June 1917; *m* 1963, Gwenllian Mary, *er d* of late E. B. Phillips]. *Address:* 63 Dudsbury Road, Ferndown, Dorset BH22 8RD.

OWEN, Sir Hugo Dudley C.; *see* Cunliffe-Owen.

OWEN, Idris Wyn; a director of a company in the construction industry; *b* 1912; *m*. *Educ:* Stockport Sch. and Coll. of Technology; Manchester Sch. of Commerce. Contested (C): Manchester Exchange, 1951; Stalybridge and Hyde, 1955; Stockport North 1966; MP (C) Stockport North, 1970–Feb. 1974; contested (C) Stockport North, Oct. 1974. Member, Stockport Borough Council, 1946; Mayor, 1962–63. Vice-Pres., Nat. Fedn of Building Trades Employers, 1965. FCIOB.

OWEN, Ivor Henri, CBE 1992; CEng, FIMechE; Director General, Design Council, 1988–93; *b* 14 Nov. 1930; *s* of Thomas and Anne Owen; *m* 1954, Jane Frances Graves; two *s* one *d*. *Educ:* Liverpool College of Technology; Manchester College of Science and Technology. Engineering apprentice, later design engineer, Craven Bros (Manchester), Stockport, 1947–57, Manufacturing Develt Engr, Steam Turbine Div., English Electric, Rugby, 1957–62; Manager, Netherton Works, English Electric, Bootle, 1962–66 (hydro electric plant, steam turbine components, condensers, nuclear equipment); Manager, English Electric Computers, Winsford, 1966–69; Manager, Winsford Kidsgrove Works, ICL, 1969–70; Man. Dir, RHP Bearings, 1970–81; Thorn EMI: Chief Exec., Gen. Engineering Div., 1981–83; Chm., Appliance and Lighting Group, 1984–87; Dir, 1984–87. Chm., Ball Roller Bearing Manufrs Assoc., 1978–80; Vice-Pres., Fedn European Bearing Manufrs Assoc., 1978–80. Royal Acad. of Engrg Vis. Prof., Univ. of Bath, 1994–. FRSA. *Recreations:* theatre, reading, running, gardening, motor cycling. *Address:* The Lindens, Back Ends, Chipping Campden, Glos GL55 6AU.

OWEN, Hon. Sir John (Arthur Dalziel), Kt 1986; **Hon. and Rt. Worshipful Mr Justice John Owen;** a Judge of the High Court of Justice, Queen's Bench Division, since 1986; Dean of the Arches Court of Canterbury and Auditor of the Chancery Court of York, since 1980; *b* 22 Nov. 1925; *s* of late R. J. Owen and Mrs O. B. Owen; *m* 1952, Valerie, *d* of W. Ethell; one *s* one *d*. *Educ:* Solihull Sch.; Brasenose Coll., Oxford. MA, BCL 1949. Commnd 2nd King Edward VII's Own Goorkha Rifles, 1944. Called to Bar, Gray's Inn, 1951, Bencher, 1980. Dep. Chm., Warwickshire QS, 1967–71; QC 1970; a Recorder, 1972–84; Dep. Leader, Midland and Oxford Circuit, 1980–84; a Circuit Judge, 1984–86; a Presiding Judge, Midland and Oxford Circuit, 1988–92. Mem. Senate of the Inns of Court and the Bar, 1977–80. Chm., West Midlands Area Mental Health Review

Tribunal, 1972–80. Mem., General Synod of Church of England, Dio. Coventry, 1970–80; Chancellor, Dio. Derby, 1973–80, Dio. Coventry, 1973–80, Dio. Southwell, 1979–80. DCL Lambeth, 1993. *Address:* Royal Courts of Justice, Strand, WC2A 2LL. *Club:* Garrick.

See also Baroness Seccombe.

OWEN, John Aubrey; Director, Regeneration Programmes, Government Office for London, since 1995; *b* 1 Aug. 1945; *s* of late Prebendary Douglas Aubrey Owen and Patricia Joan Owen; *m* 1971, Julia Margaret Jones; one *s* one *d. Educ:* City of London Sch., St Catharine's Coll., Cambridge (MA). Joined Min. of Transport, 1969; Asst Private Sec. to Minister for Transport Industries, 1972; DoE, 1973–75; Dept of Transport, 1975–78; seconded to Cambridgeshire CC, 1978–80; DoE, 1980–; Regional Dir, Northern Regional Office, Depts of the Environment and Transport, 1987–91; Dir, Personnel Management, 1991–95. FRSA. *Recreations:* gardening, opera, reading. *Address:* 33 Valley Road, Welwyn Garden City, Herts AL8 7DH. *T:* Welwyn Garden (01707) 321768.

OWEN, Prof. John Benjamin Brynmor, DSc (Oxon), MSc (Wales); CEng; John William Hughes Professor of Civil Engineering, University of Liverpool, 1950–77, now Emeritus Professor; *b* 2 Sept. 1910; *s* of David Owen, (Degwyl), and Mary Alice Owen; *m* 1938, Beatrice Pearn (*née* Clark); two *d. Educ:* Universities of Oxford and Wales. Drapers Company Scholar, Page Prize and Medal, University College, Cardiff, 1928–31 (Fellow, 1981); Meyricke Scholar, Jesus Coll., Oxford, 1931–32; British Cotton Industry Research Association, 1933–35; Messrs A. V. Roe, Manchester, 1935–36; Royal Aircraft Establishment, Farnborough, 1936–48; Naval Construction Research Establishment, 1948–50. *Publications:* Light Structures, 1965; many contributions to learned journals on design of structures, on helicopters and on investigation of aircraft accidents. *Address:* The University of Liverpool, PO Box 147, Liverpool L69 3BX. *T:* 051–709 6022.

OWEN, John Gethin M.; *see* Morgan-Owen.

OWEN, John Halliwell, OBE 1975; HM Diplomatic Service, retired; *b* 16 June 1935; *e s* of late Arthur Llewellyn Owen, OBE and Doris Spencer (*née* Halliwell); *m* 1st, 1963 (marr. diss. 1971); one *s* one *d*; 2nd, 1972, Dianne Elizabeth (*née* Lowry); one *d. Educ:* Sedbergh School; The Queen's Coll., Oxford (Hastings Scholar). MA. 2nd Lieut, RA, 1954–56; HMOCS, Tanganyika Govt Service, 1960; Dist Officer, Provincial Administration, 1960–61; Dist Comr, 1962; Dist Magistrate and Regional Local Courts Officer, 1963–65; HM Foreign Service, 1966; Second Sec., Dar-es-Salaam, 1968–70; FCO, 1970–73; First Sec., Dacca, 1973–75; FCO 1976; First Sec., Accra, 1976–80; FCO, 1980–82; Counsellor, Pretoria, 1982–86; Counsellor, FCO, 1986–90. *Recreations:* music, travel, wildlife, gardening. *Club:* Dar-es-Salaam Yacht.

OWEN, Maj.-Gen. John Ivor Headon, OBE 1963; *b* 22 Oct. 1922; *s* of Major William H. Owen; *m* 1948, Margaret Jean Hayes; three *d. Educ:* St Edmund's Sch., Canterbury. FBIM; psm, jssc, idc. Joined Royal Marines (as Marine), 1942; temp. 2nd Lieut RM, 1942; 44 Commando RM, Far East, 1942–46; demobilised 1946 (Captain RM); Constable, Metropolitan Police, 1946–47; rejoined Royal Marines as Lieut, 1947; regimental service, 1948–55; Staff Coll., Camberley, 1956; Bde Major, HQ 3 Cdo Bde, 1959–62; Naval Plans, Admty/MoD, 1962–64; 42 Cdo RM, 1964–66; Instructor, Jt Services Staff Coll., 1966–67; CO 45 Cdo RM, 1967–68 (despatches); Col GS, Staff of CGRM, 1969–70; Royal Coll. of Defence Studies, 1971–72; Maj.-Gen, Commando Forces RM, Plymouth, 1972–73. Lt-Col 1966; Col 1970; Maj.-Gen. 1972; Col Comdt, RM, 1983–84, Rep. Col Comdt, 1985–86. UK Partnership Sec. to KMG Thomson McLintock, Chartered Accountants, 1974–87 (the British Mem. of KMG Klynveld Main Goerdeler, 1979–87). Editor, Current Mil. and Political Lit., 1983–91. Chm. Exec. Cttee, Bowles Outdoor Centre, 1984–; a Vice Chm., Clergy Orphan Corp., 1995– (Treas. and Chm., 1980–95); Mem., Ct of Assistants, Sons of the Clergy, 1981–; Chairman of Governors: St Edmund's Sch., Canterbury, 1980–94; St Margaret's Sch., Bushey, 1980–; Chm. of Trustees, Royal Marines Mus., 1989–. *Publications:* Brassey's Infantry Weapons of the World, 1975; contrib. Seaford House Papers, 1971; articles in Contemporary Review and the press. *Recreations:* woodworking, gardening. *Address:* c/o Midland Bank, 62 Hills Road, Cambridge CB2 1LA. *Club:* Army and Navy.

OWEN, Prof. John Joseph Thomas, FRS 1988; Sands Cox Professor and Head of Department of Anatomy, University of Birmingham, since 1978; *b* 7 Jan. 1934; *s* of Thomas and Alice Owen; *m* 1961, Barbara Schofield Forster (marr. diss. 1992); two *s. Educ:* Univ. of Liverpool (BSc, MD); MA Oxon 1963. Lecturer: Univ. of Liverpool, 1960–63; Univ. of Oxford, 1963–72; Fellow, St Cross Coll., Oxford, 1968–72; Sen. Scientist, Imperial Cancer Res. Fund's Tumour Immunology Unit, UCL, 1972–74; Prof. of Anatomy, Univ. of Newcastle upon Tyne 1974–78. Medical Research Council: Mem., Physiol Systems and Disorders Bd, 1978–83; Chm., Grants Cttee, B, 1980–83; Mem., Cell Bd, 1991–94; Member: Wellcome Trust's Biochemistry and Cell Biology Panel, 1987–90; Council, Nat. Kidney Res. Fund, 1987–90; Council, Royal Soc., 1991–93. *Publications:* numerous contribs to sci. literature. *Recreations:* sport, travel. *Address:* Department of Anatomy, Medical School, The University, Birmingham B15 2TT.

OWEN, Prof. John V.; *see* Vallance-Owen.

OWEN, John Wyn, CB 1994; Director General, New South Wales Health Department, Sydney, since 1994; *b* 15 May 1942; *s* of late Idwal Wyn Owen and of Myfi Owen (*née* Hughes); *m* 1967, Elizabeth Ann (*née* MacFarlane); one *s* one *d. Educ:* Friars School, Bangor; St John's Coll., Cambridge (BA 1964, MA 1968); Hosp. Admin. Staff Coll. (DipHA 1967). Trainee, King Edward VII's Hosp. Fund for London, 1964–66; Dep. Hosp. Sec., West Wales Gen. Hosp., Carmarthen, 1966–67; Hosp. Sec., Glantawe HMC, Swansea, 1967–70; Staff Training Officer, Welsh Hosp. Bd, Cardiff, 1968–70; Divl Administrator, Univ. of Wales, Cardiff, HMC, 1970–72; St Thomas' Hospital: Asst Clerk, and King's Fund Fellow, 1972–74; Dist Administrator, St Thomas' Health Dist, Teaching, 1974–79; Trustee, Refresh, 1976–78; Hon. Tutor, Med. Sch., 1974–79; Praeceptor, Sch. of Health Administration, Univ. of Minnesota, 1974–79; Exec. Dir, United Medical Enterprises, London, 1979–85; Dir, NHS Wales, Welsh Office, 1985–94; Chm., Welsh Health Common Services Authy, 1985–94. Member: Strategic Planning and Evaluation Cttee, Nat. Health and MRC, 1994–; Australian Health Ministers' Adv. Council, 1994–. Vis. Fellow, Univ. of NSW, 1979. Trustee, Florence Nightingale Museum Trust, 1983–90; Chm., Health Bldg Educn Gp, British Consultants' Bureau, 1983–85; Mem. Adv. Forum, Personnel Lead Body, 1992–94. FRGS 1968; FHSM 1992; FACHSE 1994; Hon. FFPHM 1991. Hon. Fellow: UCW, Aberystwyth, 1991; UCW, Bangor, 1992. *Publications:* contribs to professional jls. *Recreations:* organ playing, opera, travel. *Address:* Newton Farm, Newton, Cowbridge CF7 7RZ. *T:* Cowbridge (01446) 775113. *Club:* Athenæum.

OWEN, John Wynne, MBE 1979; HM Diplomatic Service; Governor, Cayman Islands, since 1995; *b* 25 April 1939; *s* of Thomas David Owen and Mair Eluned Owen; *m* 1st, 1962, Thelma Margaret Gunton (*d* 1987); one *s* two *d*; 2nd, 1988, Carol Edmunds; one step *d. Educ:* Gowerton Grammar Sch.; Westminster Coll. FO 1956; 2nd Lieut Royal Signals, 1958–60; served Djakarta, Saigon, Paris, San Salvador, to 1967; resigned 1967; business, 1967–70; reinstated 1970; FCO, 1970–73; Tehran, 1973–77; São Paulo, 1978–80; Peking, 1980–82; FCO, 1983; special leave, 1985; Chm., Gunham, Holdings Ltd, 1985–89; Counsellor, FCO, 1989–92; Consul Gen., Boston, 1992–95. Chm., British Laminated Plastics Fabricators' Assoc., 1987–90. Freeman, City of London, 1978; Liveryman, Loriners' Co., 1978. FIMgt. *Recreations:* walking, reading, travel, fly-fishing. *Address:* c/o Foreign and Commonwealth Office, SW1A 2AH. *Clubs:* Royal Automobile, City Livery.

OWEN, Dr Myrfyn; Director General, Wildfowl and Wetlands Trust, since 1992; *b* 8 April 1943; *s* of William Owen and Anne Mary Owen; *m* 1967, Lydia Marian Vaughan (*née* Rees); two *d. Educ:* Sir Hugh Owen Grammar Sch.; University Coll., Aberystwyth (BSc 1964); Univ. of Leeds (PhD 1967). Wildfowl Trust, later Wildfowl and Wetlands Trust: Ecologist, 1967; Conservation Res. Officer, 1974; Asst Dir (Res.), 1979; Head of Res., 1988; Dir, 1991–92. *Publications:* Wildfowl of Europe, 1976; Wild Geese of the World, 1980; Wildfowl in Great Britain, 1986; Waterfowl Ecology, 1990; numerous scientific papers. *Recreations:* gardening, cookery, cycling, wildlife. *Address:* Wildfowl and Wetlands Trust, Slimbridge, Glos GL2 7BT. *T:* Stroud (01453) 890333.

OWEN, Nicholas David Arundel; Presenter, Independent Television News, since 1984; *b* 10 Feb. 1947; *m* 1983, Brenda (*née* Firth); one *s* one *d*, and one step *s* one step *d.* Journalist, 1964; BBC TV, 1981–83. *Publications:* History of the British Trolleybus, 1970; The Brighton Belle, 1972. *Recreations:* reading, walking, golf. *Address:* Independent Television News, 200 Gray's Inn Road, WC1X 8HB. *T:* 0171–430 4750.

OWEN, Patricia, (Mrs Peter Owen); *see* Hodge, P.

OWEN, Peter Francis, CB 1990; Director General for Schools, Department for Education and Employment, since 1995; *b* 4 Sept. 1940; *s* of Arthur Owen and Violet (*née* Morris); *m* 1963, Ann Preece; one *s* one *d. Educ:* The Liverpool Inst.; Liverpool Univ. (BA French). Joined MPBW, 1964; Cabinet Office, 1971–72; Private Sec. to successive Ministers of Housing and Construction, 1972–74; Asst Sec., Housing Policy Review, 1975–77, Local Govt Finance, 1977–80; Under Sec. and Regional Dir of Northern and Yorks and Humberside Regs, Depts of the Environment and of Transport, 1980–82; Under Secretary: Rural Affairs, DoE, 1983; Local Govt Finance Policy, DoE, 1984–86; Dep. Sec., Housing and Construction, DoE, 1986–90; Head of Econ. and Domestic Affairs Secretariat, Cabinet Office, 1990–94; Dep. Sec., Sch. Curriculum and Teachers, DFE, 1994–95. *Recreations:* reading, gardening, French language and literature. *Address:* Department for Education and Employment, Sanctuary Buildings, Great Smith Street, SW1P 3BT.

OWEN, Philip Loscombe Wintringham, TD 1950; QC 1963; *b* 10 Jan. 1920; *er s* of late Rt Hon. Sir Wintringham Stable, MC, and Lucie Haden (*née* Freeman); assumed surname of Owen in lieu of Stable by deed poll, 1942; *m* 1949, Elizabeth Jane, *d* of late Lewis Trelawny Widdicombe, Effingham, Surrey; three *s* two *d. Educ:* Winchester; Christ Church, Oxford (MA). Served War of 1939–45, Royal Welch Fusiliers: W Africa, India, Ceylon, Burma, 1939–47; Major TARO. Received into Roman Catholic Church, 1943. Called to Bar, Middle Temple, 1949; Bencher, 1969; Mem., Gen. Council of the Bar of England and Wales, 1971–77; a Deputy Chairman of Quarter Sessions: Montgomeryshire, 1959–71; Cheshire, 1961–71; Recorder of Merthyr Tydfil, 1971; a Recorder of the Crown Court, 1972–82; Leader, Wales and Chester Circuit, 1975–77. Chm., Adv. Bd constituted under Misuse of Drugs Act, 1974–. Legal Assessor to: Gen. Med. Council, 1970–; Gen. Dental Council, 1970–; RICS, 1970–. Contested (C) Montgomeryshire, 1945. JP Montgomeryshire, 1959; JP Cheshire, 1961. Vice-Pres., Montgomeryshire Cons. and Unionist Assoc.; Pres., Montgomeryshire Soc., 1974–75. Dir, Swansea City AFC Ltd, 1976–87. Trustee, and Mem. Cttee of Mgt, Young Musicians Symphony Orch., 1988–. *Recreations:* shooting, fishing, forestry, music, Association football. *Address:* 15–19 Devereux Court, WC2R 3JJ. *T:* 0171–583 0777; Plas Llwyn Owen, Llanbrynmair, Powys SY19 7BE. *T:* Llanbrynmair (01650) 521542. *Clubs:* Carlton, Pratt's; Cardiff and County; Welshpool and District Conservative; Bristol Channel Yacht (Mumbles).

See also R. O. C. Stable.

OWEN, Rear-Adm. Richard Arthur James, CB 1963; *b* 26 Aug. 1910; *s* of late Captain Leonard E. Owen, OBE, JP; *m* 1941, Jean Sophia (*née* Bluett); one *s* two *d. Educ:* Sevenoaks Sch. Joined RN, 1927; Commander (S) 1945; Captain, 1954; Rear-Admiral, 1961; Director-General, Personal Services, Admiralty, 1962–64; retired. *Address:* Oakridge, Mayfield Road, Fordingbridge, Hants SP6 1DU. *T:* Fordingbridge (01425) 655984.

OWEN, Richard Wilfred, FCA; retired from Touche Ross, 1993; *b* 26 Oct. 1932; *s* of Wilfred Owen and Ivy (*née* Gamble); *m* 1966, Sheila Marie Kerrigan; three adopted *s* one adopted *d*, and one foster *s* one foster *d. Educ:* Gunnersbury Catholic Grammar Sch. Lloyds Bank, 1949–51; RAF Russian translator, 1951–53; accountancy articles, 1953–58; Thomson McLintock, 1958–62; Crompton Parkinson, 1962–64; Touche Ross & Co., Chartered Accountants and Management Consultants, 1964–93: admitted to Partnership, 1969; seconded to Treasury, 1971; Partner-in-Charge, Management Consultancy, 1974–87, Nat. Dir, Personnel, 1987–93; UK Chm., 1988–90; Europ. Dir, Management Consultancy, 1990–92. Pres., Management Consultancies Assoc., 1987. *Address:* High Copse, 92 Harmer Green Lane, Welwyn, Herts AL6 0EP. *T:* Welwyn (01438) 714200.

OWEN, Robert John Richard; Director, European Capital Co. Ltd, since 1992; Deputy Chairman, Nomura International Ltd, Hong Kong, since 1992; *b* 11 Feb. 1940; *s* of Richard Owen and Margaret Owen (*née* Fletcher); *m* 1962, Beatrice; two *s* one *d. Educ:* Repton School; Oxford University. Foreign Office, 1961–68, incl. HM Embassy, Washington, 1965–68; HM Treasury, 1968–70; Morgan Grenfell & Co., 1970–79 (Dir, 1974); Lloyds Bank International, 1979–85 (Dir); Chm. and Chief Exec., Lloyds Merchant Bank, 1985–88; Comr for Securities, Hong Kong, 1988–89; Chm., Securities and Futures Commn, Hong Kong, 1989–92. Mem. Council and Mem. Regulatory Bd, Lloyd's of London, 1993–. *Recreations:* oriental paintings, mountain walking. *Address:* European Capital Co. Ltd, 3 Lombard Street, EC3V 9AA.

OWEN, Robert Michael; QC 1988; a Recorder, since 1987; *b* 19 Sept. 1944; *s* of Gwynne Llewellyn Owen and Phoebe Constance Owen; *m* 1969, Sara Josephine Rumbold; two *s. Educ:* Durham Sch.; Exeter Univ. (LLB). Called to Bar, Inner Temple, 1968, Bencher, 1995; Judicial Mem., Transport Tribunal, 1985. DTI Inspector, 1991. Chm., London Common Law and Commercial Bar Assoc., 1993–. *Address:* 1 Crown Office Row, Temple, EC4Y 7HH. *T:* 0171–797 7500.

OWEN, Robert Penrhyn; Director and Secretary, The Water Companies' Association, 1974–83, retired; *b* 17 Dec. 1918; *s* of late Captain Richard Owen; *m* 1949, Suzanne, *d* of late L. H. West; one *s* one *d. Educ:* Friar's School. War service in Royal Welch Fusiliers, 1939–46, in Madagascar, India, The Arakan and North and Central Burma. Admitted Solicitor, 1947. Asst Solicitor: Berks CC, 1948–50; Leics CC, 1950–54; Chief Asst Solicitor, Lancs CC, 1954–60; 2nd Dep. Clerk and 2nd Dep. Clerk of the Peace, Lancs CC, 1960–63; Gen. Manager, Telford Develt Corp. (New Town), 1963–69; Sec., Chief Exec. Officer and Solicitor, Thames Conservancy, 1969–74. *Recreations:* all sport, gardening, reading. *Address:* Pilgrims Wood, Three Gables Lane, Streatley, Reading RG8 9LJ. *T:* Goring (01491) 874294. *Clubs:* MCC; Phyllis Court (Henley-on-Thames).

OWEN, Samuel Griffith, CBE 1977; MD, FRCP; Second Secretary, Medical Research Council, 1968–82, retired; *b* 3 Sept. 1925; *e s* of late Rev. Evan Lewis Owen and of Marjorie Lawton; *m* 1954, Ruth, *e d* of late Merle W. Tate, Philadelphia, Pa, USA; two *s* two *d*. *Educ:* Dame Allen's Sch.; Durham Univ. MB, BS Dunelm 1948; MRCP 1951; MD Dunelm 1954; FRCP 1965; clinical and research appts at Royal Victoria Infirmary, Newcastle upon Tyne, 1948–49 and 1950–53; RAMC, SMO, HM Troopships, 1949–50; Med. Registrar, Nat. Heart Hosp., 1953–54; Instr in Pharmacology, Univ. of Pennsylvania Sch. of Med., 1954–56; Reader in Med., Univ. of Newcastle upon Tyne, 1964–68 (First Asst, 1956, Lectr, 1960, Sen. Lectr, 1961); Hon. Cons. Physician, Royal Victoria Infirmary, Newcastle upon Tyne, 1960–68; Clin. Sub-Dean of Med. Sch., Univ. of Newcastle upon Tyne, 1966–68 (Academic Sub-Dean, 1964–66); Examr in Med., Univ. of Liverpool, 1966–68; Examr in Membership, RCP, 1967–68 and Mem., Research Cttee, RCP, 1968–76; Member: Brit. Cardiac Soc., 1962–82; Assoc. of Physicians of GB, 1965–; European Molec. Biol. Conf., 1971–82; European Molec. Biol. Lab., 1974–82; Exec. Council, European Science Foundn, 1974–78; Comité de la Recherche Médicale et de la Santé Publique, EEC, 1977–82; Scientific Coordinating Cttee, Arthritis and Rheumatism Council, 1978–82; NW Thames RHA, 1978–82. Consultant to WHO, SE Asia, 1966 and 1967–68; Commonwealth Fund Fellow, Univ. of Illinois, 1966; Fellow, Hunterian Soc., 1978. Chm., Feldberg Foundn, 1974–78; Governor, Queen Charlotte's Hosp. for Women, 1979–82. Liveryman, Soc. of Apothecaries, 1976–. *Publications:* Essentials of Cardiology, 1961 (2nd edn 1968); Electrocardiography, 1966 (2nd edn 1973); contribs to med. jls on heart disease, cerebral circulation, thyroid disease, med. research, etc. *Recreations:* gastronomy, music, theatre. *Address:* Flat 17, 9 Devonhurst Place, Heathfield Terrace, Chiswick, W4 4JB. *T:* 0181–995 3228. *Club:* Royal Society of Medicine.

OWEN, Thomas Arfon; development and funding consultant; Director, Welsh Arts Council, 1984–93; *b* 7 June 1933; *s* of late Hywel Peris Owen and Jennie Owen; *m* 1955, Joy (*née* Phillips); three *s* one *d*. *Educ:* Ystalyfera Grammar School; Magdalen College, Oxford. MA Oxon, MA Wales. Deputy Registrar, 1959, Registrar 1967, UCW Aberystwyth; Chm., Mid-Wales Hosp. Management Cttee, 1972–74; Member: East Dyfed Health Authy, 1982–84; S Glam Health Authy, 1984–87 (Vice-Chm., 1986–87); Consumers' Cttee for GB, 1975–90; Vice-Chm., Coleg Harlech, 1984–; Member Council: UWIST, 1987–88; Univ. of Wales Coll. of Cardiff, 1988–; UCW, Aberystwyth, 1991–; Nat. Library of Wales, 1987– (Vice-Pres., 1992–). Vice-Pres., Llangollen Internat. Eisteddfod, 1984–93; Mem., Gorsedd of Bards, Royal National Eisteddfod, 1984–. FRSA 1991. High Sheriff, Dyfed, 1976–77. *Publications:* articles in educ. jls. *Recreations:* the arts, crossword puzzles. *Address:* Argoed, Ffordd y Fulfran, Borth, Dyfed SY24 5NN. *Club:* Cardiff and County (Cardiff).

OWEN, Trevor Bryan, CBE 1987; Chairman: Bethlem Royal and Maudsley Special Health Authority, 1988–94; Committee of Management, Institute of Psychiatry, since 1990; *b* 3 April 1928; *s* of Leonard Owen, CIE and Dilys (*née* Davies Bryan); *m* 1955, (Jennifer) Gaie (*née* Houston); one *s* one *d*. *Educ:* Rugby Sch.; Trinity Coll., Oxford (Scholar; MA). Sch. Student, British Sch. of Archaeology, Athens, 1953–54; ICI, 1955–78: wide range of jobs culminating in, successively: Chm., J. P. MacDougall Ltd; Dir, Paints, Agricl and Plastics Divs; Co. Personnel Manager; Man. Dir, Remploy Ltd, 1978–88. Member: Higher Educn Review Gp, Govt of NI, 1979–81; CNAA, 1973–79; Continuing Educn Adv. Council, BBC, 1977–85; Council, CBI, 1982–88; Council, Industrial Soc., 1967–88; Council, Inst. of Manpower Studies, 1975–88 (Chm., 1977–78); Chm. Bd of Governors, Nat. Inst. for Social Work, 1985–91 (Mem., 1982–; Mem., Working Party on Role and Tasks of Social Workers, 1981–82). Chm., Phab, 1988–91. *Publications:* Business School Programmes—the requirements of British manufacturing industry (with D. Casey and N. Huskisson), 1971; Making Organisations Work, 1978; The Manager and Industrial Relations, 1979; articles in jls. *Address:* 8 Rochester Terrace, NW1 9JN.

OWEN, Ursula Margaret; Editor and Chief Executive, Index on Censorship, since 1993; *b* 21 Jan. 1937; *d* of Emma Sophie Sachs (*née* Boehm) and Werner Sachs; *m* 1960, Edward Roger John Owen (marr. diss.); one *d*. *Educ:* Putney High Sch.; St Hugh's Coll., Oxford (BA Hons Physiol.); Bedford Coll., London (Dip. Soc. Studies). Lectr, English Lang., Amer. Univ. in Cairo, 1962–63; research work in mental health and physical disabilities, 1964–67; Editor, Frank Cass, 1971–73; Sen. Editor, Barrie & Jenkins, 1973–75; Virago Press: Co-founder, 1974; Director, 1974–; Editl Dir, 1974–90; Jt Man. Dir, 1982–90; Dir, Paul Hamlyn Fund, 1990–92. Cultural Policy Advr to Lab. Party, 1990–92. Dir, New Statesman and Society, 1983–90. Mem., Royal Literary Fund Cttee, 1989–. Gov., Parliament Hill School, 1991–. *Publications:* (ed) Fathers: Reflections by Daughters, 1983; (ed) Whose Cities?, 1991. *Recreations:* music, reading, film, travel. *Address:* Index, 33 Islington High Street, N1 9LH. *T:* 0171–278 2313. *Club:* Groucho.

OWEN, Prof. Walter Shepherd, PhD, DEng; Professor Emeritus of Materials Science, Massachusetts Institute of Technology; *b* 13 March 1920; *s* of Walter Lloyd and Dorothea Elizabeth Owen; *m*; one *d*. *Educ:* Alsop High Sch.; University of Liverpool. Metallurgist, D. Napier and Sons and English Electric Co., 1940–46; Asst Lecturer and Lecturer in Metallurgy, Univ. of Liverpool, 1946–54; Commonwealth Fund Fellow, Metallurgy Dept, Mass Inst. of Technol., 1951–52; on research staff, 1954–57, and Henry Bell Wortley Professor of Metallurgy, 1957–66, Univ. of Liverpool; Thomas R. Briggs Prof. of Engineering and Dir of Materials Science and Engineering, Cornell Univ., 1966–70; Dean of Technological Inst., Northwestern Univ., 1970–71; Vice Pres. for Science and Research, Northwestern Univ., 1971–73; Head of Dept, 1973–82, and Prof. of Physical Metallurgy, 1973–85, Mass Inst. of Technol. Mem., Nat. Acad. of Engineering, USA, 1977. *Publications:* papers in British and American journals on aspects of physical metallurgy. *Recreation:* sailing. *Address:* 1 Marine Terrace, Porthmadog, Gwynedd LL49 9BL; 770 Boylston Street, #7E, Boston, MA 02199, USA. *Club:* St Botolph (Boston).

OWEN-JONES, John Eryl, CBE 1969; JP; DL; Clerk of Caernarvonshire County Council, 1956–74, and Clerk of Lieutenancy; *b* 19 Jan. 1912; *s* of late John Owen-Jones, Hon. FTSC, Rhydwenfa, Old Colwyn; *m* 1944, Mabel Clara, *d* of Grant McIlvride, Ajmer, Rajputana; one *s* one *d*. *Educ:* Portmadoc Grammar Sch.; University Coll. of Wales, Aberystwyth; Gonville and Caius Coll., Cambridge. LLB Wales 1933; MA Cantab 1939. Admitted Solicitor, 1938; Asst Solicitor, Chester Corp., 1939. Sqdn Ldr, RAFVR, 1945; Legal Staff Officer, Judge Advocate General's Dept, Mediterranean. Dep. Clerk, Caernarvonshire CC, 1946; Clerk of the Peace, Caernarvonshire, 1956–71; formerly: Sec., N Wales Combined Probation and After-Care Cttee; Dep. Clerk, Snowdonia Jt Adv. Cttee; Clerk, Gwynedd Police Authority, 1956–67. Member: Central Council, Magistrates' Cts Cttees, 1980–82; Bd, Civic Trust for Wales, 1982–; Bd, Gwynedd Archaeological Trust Ltd, 1982–. Hon. Sec., Caernarvonshire Historical Soc. Mem., Gorsedd of Royal National Eisteddfod of Wales. FRSA 1987. DL Caernarvonshire, 1971; JP 1974, DL 1974, Gwynedd. *Publication:* Caernarvonshire—A Choice of Celebrities: a lecture, with pictorial mementos, 1993. *Recreations:* music, gardening, photography. *Address:* Rhiw Dafnau, Caernarfon, Gwynedd LL55 1LF. *T:* Caernarfon (01286) 673370. *Club:* National Liberal.

OWEN-JONES, Lindsay Harwood; Chairman and Chief Executive Officer, L'Oréal, since 1988; *b* 17 March 1946; *s* of Hugh A. Owen-Jones and Esmee Owen-Jones (*née* Lindsay); *m*; one *d*; *m* 1994, Cristina Furno. *Educ:* Oxford Univ. (BA); European Inst. of Business Admin. Product Manager, L'Oréal, 1969; Head, Public Products Div., Belgium, 1971–74; Manager, SCAD (L'Oréal subsid.), Paris, 1974–76; Marketing Manager, Public Products Div., Paris, 1976–78; Gen. Manager, SAIPO (L'Oréal subsid.), Italy, 1978–81; Pres., 1981–83, Chm., 1991–, COSMAIR (L'Oreal agent), USA; Vice-Pres., L'Oréal Man. Cttee and Mem. Bd of Dirs, 1984; Pres. and Chief Operating Officer, 1984–88. Director: Banque Nationale de Paris, 1989–; LaFarge Coppel, 1993–; Air Liquide, 1994–. *Recreation:* private helicopter pilot. *Address:* L'Oréal, 41 rue Martre, 92117 Clichy, France. *T:* 47567000.

OWENS, Bernard Charles; Director, British Jewellery and Giftware Federation, since 1987 (Vice-President, 1990–91; President, 1991–92; Deputy President, 1992–93); *b* 20 March 1928; *s* of late Charles A. Owens and Sheila (*née* O'Higgins); *m* 1954, Barbara Madeline Murphy; two *s* four *d*. *Educ:* Solihull Sch.; London Sch. of Econs and Pol Science. Commnd 2nd Lieut, RASC, 1947; transf. RARO, 1949 (Lieut). Managing Director: Stanley Bros, 1962–67; Coronet Industrial Securities, 1965–67; Chairman: Unochrome Industries, 1964–79; Silverthorne Group, 1972–79; Director: Hobbs Savill & Bradford, 1957–62; Trinidad Sugar Estates, 1965–67; Cornish Brewery, 1987–93; Local Dir, Alexander Stenhouse UK (formerly Reed Stenhouse UK), 1980–87. Mem. of Lloyd's, 1978–. Mem., Monopolies and Mergers Commn, 1981–93. Chm., Metal Finishing Assoc., 1982–85 (Vice-Chm., 1981–82; Dep. Chm., 1985–88); Treas. and Trustee, British Jewellery Giftware and Leathergoods Benevolent Soc., 1992–; Member: Cttee, Nat. Clayware Fedn, 1962–67; Council, Zoological Society, 1987–90. Mem., Solihull Council, 1953–63 (Chm., Finance Cttee, 1957–63); contested (C) Birmingham, Small Heath, 1959 and March 1961. Freeman, City of London, 1981; Liveryman: Co. of Gardeners, 1982; Basketmakers' Co., 1994; Mem., HAC, 1984–. Life Governor, RNLI, 1984. FRSA 1972. Mem., SMO Malta, 1979. *Recreations:* fine food and wine. *Address:* The Vatch House, Stroud, Glos GL6 7JY. *T:* Stroud (0145376) 3402. *Clubs:* MCC, City Livery, City Livery Yacht (Vice Cdre), Wig and Pen; Stroud Rugby Football (Patron).

OWENS, John Ridland; Chairman, Owens Associates, independent consultancy specialising in strategic advice and government relations, since 1993; Chairman, Haringey Healthcare NHS Trust, since 1993; *b* 21 May 1932; *s* of Dr Ridland Owens and late Elsie Owens; *m* 1st, 1958, Susan Lilian (*née* Pilcher); two *s* one *d*; 2nd, 1985, Cynthia Rose (*née* Forbes); one *s*. *Educ:* Merchant Taylors' Sch.; St John's Coll., Oxford (MA). National Service, RA (Lieut), 1951–52. ICI, 1955–67; Managing Dir, Cape Asbestos Fibres, 1967–73; Dir Gen., Dairy Trade Fedn, 1973–83; Dep. Chm., Assilec, Paris, 1973–83; Exec. Dir, Nat. Dairy Council, 1975–83; Dep. Dir Gen., CBI, 1983–90; Dir Gen., Building Employers Confederation, 1990–92; Dir, UK Skills Ltd, 1990–92. Vice-Chm., EEC Adv. Cttee on Milk and Milk Products; Member: Food and Drink Industry Council, 1973–83; RSA Industry Cttee for Industry Year, 1986; Council, Assoc. of Business Sponsorship of the Arts, 1985–94; RA Adv. Bd, 1987–91; Exec. Cttee, PRONED, 1983–90; Council, CBI, 1990–92. Member: Council, CGLI, 1988–93; Court, City Univ., 1988–. FRSA. Mem. Court, Merchant Taylors' Co., 1982–. *Publications:* Marketing for the NHS —Putting Patients First, 1993; Strategic Procurement for the NHS: working with suppliers, 1995; articles for The Times Review of Industry. *Recreations:* painting, music, walking. *Address:* 40 Blenheim Terrace, NW8 0EG. *T:* 0171–372 7783.

OWER, Dr David Cheyne, TD 1975; Senior Principal Medical Officer, Department of Health and Social Security, 1976–87; *b* 29 July 1931; *s* of Ernest Ower and Helen Edith Cheyne (*née* Irvine); *m* 1954, June Harris; two *s* two *d*. *Educ:* King's Coll. Sch., Wimbledon; King's Coll., London; King's Coll. Hosp. Med. Sch. (MB, BS 1954). DObstRCOG 1959; FFPHM (FFCM 1983; MFCM 1976). Jun. hosp. appts, King's Coll. Hosp. and Kingston Hosp., 1955; RAF Med. Br., 1956–58; gen. practice, 1959–64; DHSS (formerly Min. of Health) Med. Staff, 1965–87. T&AVR, and RAMC(V), 1962–; Lt-Col RAMC(V); CO 221 (Surrey) Field Amb., 1973–75. *Recreations:* music, bridge, thinking about playing golf. *Address:* Merlewood, 94 Coombe Lane West, Kingston-upon-Thames, Surrey KT2 7DB. *T:* 0181–942 8552.

OWERS, Anne Elizabeth; Director, Justice, since 1992; *b* 23 June 1947; *d* of William Spark and Anne Smailes Spark (*née* Knox); *m* 1968, Rev. Ian Humphrey Owers; two *s* one *d*. *Educ:* Washington Grammar Sch., Co. Durham; Univ. of Cambridge (BA Hons). Research and teaching in Zambia, 1968–71; Mem., Southwark Race Relations Commn, 1976–90; work at JCWI, 1981–92 (Gen. Sec., 1986–92). Chm. Bd of Trustees, Refugee Legal Centre, 1994–; Mem., Adv. Council, NCVO, 1994–. *Publications:* chapters and papers on immigration and nationality matters. *Recreations:* theatre, music, books. *Address:* Justice, 59 Carter Lane, EC4V 5AQ.

OWO, The Olowo of; *see* Olagbegi II.

OXBURGH, Sir (Ernest) Ronald, KBE 1992; PhD; FRS 1978; Rector, Imperial College of Science, Technology and Medicine, since 1993; *b* 2 Nov. 1934; *m* Ursula Mary Brown; one *s* two *d*. *Educ:* Liverpool Inst.; Univ. of Oxford (BA 1957, MA 1960); Univ. of Princeton (PhD 1960). Departmental Demonstrator, 1960–61, Lectr in Geology, 1962–78, Univ. of Oxford; Fellow of St Edmund Hall, Oxford, 1964–78, Emeritus Fellow, 1978, Hon. Fellow, 1986; University of Cambridge: Prof. of Mineralogy and Petrology, 1978–91; Hd of Dept of Earth Scis, 1980–88; Fellow of Trinity Hall, 1978–82, Hon. Fellow, 1983; Queens' College: Pres., 1982–89; Professorial Fellow, 1989–91; Hon. Fellow, 1992; Chief Scientific Advr, MoD, 1988–93. Vis. Professor: CIT, 1967–68; Stanford and Cornell Univs, 1973–74; Sherman Fairchild Distinguished Vis. Scholar, CIT, 1985–86. Trustee, Natural History Mus., 1993–. Member: SERC, 1988–; Hong Kong Univ. and Poly. Grants Cttee, 1988–. Pres., Eur. Union of Geosciences, 1985–87 (Hon. Fellow 1993). FGS; Fellow: Geol. Soc. of America; Amer. Geophys. Union. Hon. Mem., Geologists' Assoc.; Foreign Corresp., Geologische Bundesanstalt, Austria and of Geological Soc. of Vienna; For. Mem., Venezuelan Acad. of Scis, 1992. Hon. FIMechE 1993. Hon. Fellow, Univ. Coll., Oxford, 1983. DSc (*hc*): Univ. of Paris, 1986; Leicester, 1990; Loughborough, 1991; Edinburgh, 1994. Bigsby Medal, Geol Soc., 1979. *Publications:* contribs to Nature, Jl Geophys Res., Phil Trans Royal Soc., Annual Reviews, Science, Bull. Geol Soc. America, Jl Fluid Mechanics, Jl Geol Soc. London. *Recreations:* mountaineering, orienteering, reading, theatre. *Address:* Imperial College of Science, Technology and Medicine, Prince Consort Road, SW7 2AZ.

OXBURY, Harold Frederick, CMG 1961; Deputy Director-General, British Council, 1962–66 (Assistant Director-General, 1959); *b* 11 Nov. 1903; *s* of Fredric Thomas Oxbury; *m* 1st, 1928, Violet Bennets (*d* 1954); one *s* one *d*; 2nd, 1954, Helen Shipley (*d* 1975), *d* of Amos Perry, FLS, VMH. *Educ:* Norwich Sch.; Trinity Coll., Cambridge (Senior Scholar). Entered Indian Civil Service, 1928; Chief Collector of Customs, Burma, 1940; in charge of civilian evacuation from N Burma, 1942; Government of Burma Representative, Burma Office, 1942–44; Dep. Controller Finance (Colonel), Military Administration, Burma, 1945; Finance Secretary, Government of Burma, 1946; British Council: Director, Colonies Dept, 1947; Controller Finance, 1956. *Publications:* Great Britons: twentieth century lives, 1985; contrib. number of articles to Dictionary of National Biography, and compiled epitomes for 1961–1985 in Concise edn, 3 vols, 1992. *Recreations:* writing, painting. *Address:* 122B Woodstock Road, Oxford OX2 7NF.

OXENBURY, Dame Shirley (Ann), DBE 1992 (OBE 1987); Personal Assistant to Chairman, Conservative Party, Conservative Central Office; *b* 4 July 1936. *Educ:* Ensham County Sch., London, SW17. Personal Assistant to: Harold Fielding, 1965–70; Katharine Macmillan, Sara Morrison, Baroness Young, 1970–75; Lord Thorneycroft, 1975–81; Cecil Parkinson, 1981–83; John Gummer, 1983–85; Norman Tebbit, 1985–87; Peter Brooke, 1987–89; Kenneth Baker, 1989–90; Christopher Patten, 1990–92; Norman Fowler, 1992–94; Jeremy Hanley, 1994–. Women's Transport Service (FANY), 1979–87. *Recreations:* tennis, swimming, arts, learning languages. *Address:* 106 Duncan House, Dolphin Square, SW1V 3PW. *T:* 0171–222 9000.

OXFORD, Bishop of, since 1987; **Rt. Rev. Richard Douglas Harries;** *b* 2 June 1936; *s* of late Brig. W. D. J. Harries, CBE and Mrs G. M. B. Harries; *m* 1963, Josephine Bottomley, MA, MB, BChir, DCH; one *s* and *d*. *Educ:* Wellington Coll,; RMA, Sandhurst; Selwyn Coll., Cambridge (MA 1965); Cuddesdon Coll., Oxford. Lieut, Royal Corps of Signals, 1955–58. Curate, Hampstead Parish Church, 1963–69; Chaplain, Westfield Coll., 1966–69; Lectr, Wells Theol Coll., 1969–72; Warden of Wells, Salisbury and Wells Theol Coll., 1971–72; Vicar, All Saints, Fulham, 1972–81; Dean, King's Coll., London, 1981–87. GOE examnr in Christian Ethics, 1972–76; Dir, Post Ordination Trng for Kensington Jurisdiction, 1973–79. Vice-Chairman: Council of Christian Action, 1979–87; Council for Arms Control, 1982–87; Member: Home Office Adv. Cttee for reform of law on sexual offences, 1981–85; ACC, 1994–; Bd, Christian Aid, 1994–; Chairman: Southwark Ordination Course, 1982–87; Shalom; ELTSA (End Loans to Southern Africa), 1982–87; Exec. Cttee, CCJ, 1992–. Pres., Johnson Soc., 1988–89. Consultant to Archbishops of Canterbury and York on Interfaith Relns, with special resp. for Jewish Christian relns, 1986–92 (Sir Sigmund Sternberg Award, 1989). Radio and TV work. Lectures: Hockerill, and Drawbridge, London, 1982; Stockton, London Business Sch., 1992; Pall Mall, Inst. of Dirs, 1993; Theological, QUB, 1993; Heslington, York, 1994. FKC 1983. Hon. DD London, 1994. *Publications:* Prayers of Hope, 1975; Turning to Prayer, 1978; Prayers of Grief and Glory, 1979; Being a Christian, 1981; Should Christians Support Guerillas?, 1982; The Authority of Divine Love, 1983; Praying Round the Clock, 1983; Prayer and the Pursuit of Happiness, 1985; Morning has Broken, 1985; Christianity and War in a Nuclear Age, 1986; C. S. Lewis: the man and his God, 1987; Christ is Risen, 1988; Is There a Gospel for the Rich?, 1992; Art and the Beauty of God, 1993; The Real God, 1994; Questioning Faith, 1995; *edited:* (jtly) Seasons of the Spirit, 1984; The One Genius; Through the Year with Austin Farrer, 1987; *edited and contributed:* What Hope in an Armed World?, 1982; Reinhold Niebuhr and the Issues of Our Time, 1986; *contributed to:* Stewards of the Mysteries of God, 1979; Unholy Warfare, 1983; The Cross and the Bomb, 1983; Dropping the Bomb, 1985; Julian, Woman of our Time, 1985; If Christ be not raised, 1986; The Reality of God, 1986; A Necessary End, 1991; articles in Theology, The Times, The Observer and various other periodicals. *Recreations:* theatre, literature, sport. *Address:* Diocesan Church House, North Hinksey, Oxford OX2 0NB. *T:* Oxford (01865) 244566.

OXFORD, Archdeacon of; *see* Weston, Ven. F. V.

OXFORD AND ASQUITH, 2nd Earl of, *cr* 1925; **Julian Edward George Asquith,** KCMG 1964 (CMG 1961); Viscount Asquith, *cr* 1925; Governor and Commander-in-Chief, Seychelles, 1962–67; Commissioner, British Indian Ocean Territory, 1965–67; *b* 22 April 1916; *o s* of late Raymond Asquith and Katharine Frances (*d* 1976), *d* of late Sir John Horner, KCVO; *S* grandfather, 1928; *m* 1947, Anne Mary Celestine, CStJ, *d* of late Sir Michael Palairet, KCMG; two *s* three *d*. *Educ:* Ampleforth; Balliol Coll., Oxford (Scholar), 1st Class Lit. Hum., 1938. Lieut, RE, 1941; Assistant District Commissioner, Palestine, 1942–48; Dep. Chief Secretary, British Administration, Tripolitania, 1949; Director of the Interior, Government of Tripolitania, 1951; Adviser to Prime Minister of Libya, 1952; Administrative Secretary, Zanzibar, 1955; Administrator of St Lucia, WI, 1958. KStJ. *Heir: s* Viscount Asquith, *qv*. *Address:* The Manor House, Mells, Frome, Somerset BA11 3PN. *T:* Mells (01373) 812324. *Club:* Naval and Military.
See also Baron Hylton.

OXFORD, Sir Kenneth (Gordon), Kt 1988; CBE 1981; QPM 1976; DL; Chief Constable, Merseyside Police, 1976–89; Regional Director, Lloyds Bank plc, 1989–91; *b* Lambeth, 25 June 1924; *s* of late Ernest George Oxford and Gladys Violet (*née* Seaman); *m* 1954, Muriel (*née* Panton). *Educ:* Caldecot Sch., Lambeth. RAF, VR Bomber Comd, SEAC, 1942–47. Metropolitan Police, 1947–69, with final rank Det. Ch. Supt, following Intermed. Comd Course, 1966, Sen. Staff Course, 1968, The Police Coll., Bramshill; Asst Chief Constable (Crime), Northumberland Constabulary, 1969; Northumbria Police, 1974; Dep. Chief Constable, Merseyside Police, 1974–75. Member: Forensic Science Soc., 1970; Medico-Legal Soc., 1975; Chairman: Crime Cttee, Assoc. of Chief Police Officers of Eng., Wales and NI, 1977–83; Jt Standing Cttee on Police Use of Firearms, 1979–89; Anti-Terrorist Cttee, 1982–89; Rep., ICPO (Interpol), 1983–86; President: NW Police Benevolent Fund, 1978–89; Assoc. of Chief Police Officers of England, Wales and NI, 1982–83. Pres., Merseyside Br., BIM, 1983–93 (Chm., 1978–81; Vice-Chm., 1975–78); CIMgt (CBIM 1980). Merseyside County Dir, St John Ambulance Assoc., 1976–84 (County Vice Pres., 1985). Chm., Merseyside Community Trust, 1988–. Hon. Colonel: 156 (Liverpool and Greater Manchester) Transport Regt, RCT (Volunteers), 1989–93; 156 (NW) Transport Regt, RLC (V), 1993–95. Freeman, City of London, 1983. FRSA 1983. OStJ 1977. DL Merseyside, 1988. *Publications:* contrib. articles and papers to prof. papers on crime and kindred matters. *Recreations:* shooting, cricket, music, books, roses. *Address:* c/o Chief Constable's Office, PO Box 59, Liverpool L69 1JD. *Clubs:* Commonwealth Trust, Special Forces; Artists (Liverpool); Surrey CC, Lancashire CC, Rainford CC, Liverpool St Helens Rugby Union Football.

OXFUIRD, 13th Viscount of, *cr* 1651; **George Hubbard Makgill;** Bt 1627; Lord Macgill of Cousland, 1651; *b* 7 Jan. 1934; *s* of Richard James Robert Haldane Makgill, RNZAF (*d* 1948) (*yr s* of 11th Bt) and Elizabeth Lyman (*d* 1981), *d* of Gorham Hubbard, Boston, USA; *S* uncle, 1986; *m* 1st, 1967, Alison Campbell (marr. diss. 1977), *er d* of late Neils Max Jensen, Randers, Denmark; three *s* (inc. twin *s*); 2nd, 1980, Venetia Cunitia Mary, *o d* of Major Charles Anthony Steward, Crondall, Farnham, Surrey; one *s*. *Educ:* St Peter's School, Cambridge, NZ; Wanganui Collegiate School. Commissioned RAF, 1955–58. A Deputy Speaker, House of Lords, 1990–. *Recreations:* fishing, gardening, shooting. *Heir: s* Master of Oxfuird, *qv*. *Address:* Hill House, St Mary Bourne, Andover, Hants SP11 6BG. *Club:* Caledonian.

OXFUIRD, Master of; Hon. Ian Arthur Alexander Makgill, MA; *b* 14 Oct. 1969; *s* and *heir* of 13th Viscount of Oxfuird, *qv*.

OXLADE, Zena Elsie, CBE 1984; SRN, RNT; Regional Nursing Officer, East Anglian Regional Health Authority, 1981–87, retired; *b* 26 April 1929; *d* of James and Beatrice May Oxlade. *Educ:* Latymer Grammar Sch., N9. SRN 1950; RNT (London Univ.). Ward Sister, 1952; Theatre Sister 1953; Night Sister, 1954; Sister Tutor, 1956; Principal Tutor, 1963; Principal Nursing Officer, 1969; Chief Nursing Officer, 1973; District Nursing Officer, 1974; Area Nursing Officer, Suffolk AHA, 1978–81. Chm., GNC, 1977–83 (Mem., 1975–83; Chm., GNC Trust, 1983–); Mem., UK Council for Nurses, Midwives and Health Visitors, 1983–89. DUniv Surrey, 1993. *Publication:* Ear, Nose and Throat Nursing, 1972. *Recreations:* motoring, reading, handicrafts. *Address:* 5 Morgan Court, Claydon, Suffolk IP6 0AN. *T:* Ipswich (01473) 831895.

OXLEE, Colin Hamilton; Consultant; Technical Director, Military Division, Defence Research Agency, 1991–92; *b* 14 July 1935; *s* of Leonard William and Margaret Hamilton Oxlee; *m* 1960, Robyn Rosemary Gardner; one *s* one *d*. *Educ:* St Lawrence College, Ramsgate; Univ. of Nottingham (BSc Hons 1959; MScMet 1961). MIM 1960; CEng 1977. Technical apprentice, Appleby-Frodingham Steel Co., 1954–56; Materials Res. Scientist, RARDE, 1961–71; PSO to Chief Scientist (Army), 1971–74; Supt Materials Res., 1974–77, Supt Ammunition, 1977–81, RARDE; Dep. Dir, Scientific and Technical Intell., 1981–84, Dir, Heavy Weapons Projects, 1984–89, MoD; Dep. Dir (Armaments), RARDE, 1989–91. *Publications:* Low Alloy Steels, 1968; procs of Iron and Steel Institute Council of Scientific and Industrial Research, India, 1966, and Iron and Steel Institute of Japan, 1970; official reports. *Recreations:* tennis, jazz, guitar, photography/video, churches, cathedrals, castles and historic houses, travel. *Address:* 9 Springhead, Tunbridge Wells, Kent TN2 3NY.

OXLEY, Humphrey Leslie Malcolm, CMG 1966; OBE 1956; HM Diplomatic Service, retired; *b* 9 Oct. 1909; *s* of W. H. F. Oxley, MRCS, LRCP, FRCOG, and Lily Malcolm; *m* 1945, Frances Olga, *d* of George Bowden, San Jose, Costa Rica; twin *s*. *Educ:* Epsom Coll. Admitted Solicitor, 1933; Junior Legal Assistant, India Office, 1933; Commissioner for Oaths, 1934; Assistant Solicitor, 1944; Commonwealth Relations Office, 1947; Assistant Legal Adviser, 1961; Legal Counsellor, Commonwealth Office, 1965–67; HM Diplomatic Service, 1967; Dep. Legal Adviser, FCO, 1967–69. Legal Consultant to HM Comr, Magistrate, various legal appts, Anguilla, 1971–72. *Recreation:* gardening. *Address:* Sandpipers, Crooked Lane, Birdham, Chichester, West Sussex PO20 7ET. *Club:* Civil Service.

OXLEY, James Keith R.; *see* Rice-Oxley.

OXLEY, Julian Christopher; Director-General, The Guide Dogs for the Blind Association, since 1989; Chairman, International Federation of Guide Dog Schools, since 1990; *b* 23 Nov. 1938; *s* of Horace Oxley and Lilian Oxley (*née* Harris); *m* 1979, Carol (née Heath); one *d*; one *s* two *d* from previous marr. *Educ:* Clifton Coll., Bristol; Oriel Coll., Oxford (Organ Scholar, MA). FCA. Dir and Sec., Williams & James plc, 1970–84; Dir and Sec., Guide Dogs for the Blind Assoc., 1984–89. Mem. Council, Gloucester Civic Trust, 1972–75. Chm. of Govs, Selwyn Sch., Gloucester, 1980–84. *Recreations:* music, old furniture, railways. *Address:* Hillfields, Burghfield, Reading, Berks RG7 3YG. *T:* Reading (01734) 835555. *Clubs:* Kennel; Constitutional (Windsor).

OXMANTOWN, Lord; Laurence Patrick Parsons; Assistant Director, Land and Sky International Group, Beijing and Hong Kong; *b* 31 March 1969; *s* and *heir* of Earl of Rosse, *qv*. *Educ:* Aiglon Coll., Switzerland; Univ. of Beijing Language Inst. *Address:* Lantau Island, Hong Kong.

OZAWA, Seiji; Japanese conductor; Music Director, Boston Symphony Orchestra, since 1973; *b* Shenyang, China, 1 Sept. 1935; *m* 1st, Kyoko Edo; 2nd, Vera Ilyan; one *s* one *d*. *Educ:* Toho School of Music, Tokyo; studied with Hideo Saito, Eugène Bigot, Herbert von Karajan, Leonard Bernstein. Won Besançon Internat. Comp., 1959, Koussevitzky Meml Scholarship, 1960. Asst Conductor, NY Philharmonic Orch., 1961–62 and 1964–65; music dir, Ravinia Fest., Chicago, 1964–68; conductor, Toronto Symph. Orch., 1965–69; music dir, San Francisco Symph. Orch., 1970–76, music advisor, 1976–77; Artistic Advr, Tanglewood Fest., 1970–73. Tours with Boston Symphony Orchestra: Europe, 1976, 1988, 1993; Japan, 1978; China (musical and cultural exchange), 1979; European music festivals, 1979, 1984, 1991; 14 USA cities (orchestra's hundredth birthday), 1982; Japan, 1982 and 1986; Far East, 1989, 1994; S America, 1992; Guest conductor with major orchestras in Canada, Europe, Far East and USA; Conductor, Saito Kinen Orch., Japan (European tours, 1987, 1989, 1991; Carnegie Hall, NY, 1991; Saito Kinen Fest., 1992–). Opera highlights: La Scala, Milan; Covent Garden, London; Paris Opera (incl. world première of Messiaen's Saint François d'Assise); many recordings (awards). Evening at Symphony, PBS television series with Boston Symphony Orch. (Emmy award). Hon. DMus: Univ. of Mass; New England Conservatory of Music; Wheaton Coll., Norton, Mass. Seiji Ozawa Hall inaugurated at Tanglewood, Mass, 1994. Inouye Award (first), for lifetime achievement in the arts, Japan, 1994. *Address:* c/o Ronald A. Wilford, Columbia Artists Management Inc. Conductors Division, 165 West 57th Street, New York, USA; c/o Harold Holt Ltd, 31 Sinclair Road, W14 0NS.

P

PACK, Prof. Donald Cecil, CBE 1978 (OBE 1969); MA, DSc; CMath, FIMA; FEIS, FRSE; Professor of Mathematics, University of Strathclyde, Glasgow, 1953–82, Hon. Professor, 1982–86, Professor Emeritus, 1986 (Vice-Principal, 1968–72); *b* 14 April 1920; *s* of late John Cecil and late Minnie Pack, Higham Ferrers; *m* 1947, Constance Mary Gillam; two *s* one *d*. *Educ:* Wellingborough School; New Coll., Oxford. Lecturer in Mathematics, University College, Dundee, University of St Andrews, 1947–52; Visiting Research Associate, University of Maryland, 1951–52; Lecturer in Mathematics, University of Manchester, 1952–53. Guest Professor: Technische Universität, Berlin, 1967; Bologna Univ. and Politecnico Milano, 1980; Technische Hochschule Darmstadt, 1981; other vis. appts at Warsaw Univ., 1977, Kaiserslautern, 1980, 1984. Member: Dunbartonshire Educn Cttee, 1960–66; Gen. Teaching Council for Scotland, 1966–73; Chairman: Scottish Certificate of Educn Examn Bd, 1969–77; Cttee of Inquiry into Truancy and Indiscipline in Schools in Scotland, 1974–77; Member: various Govt Scientific Cttees, 1952–84; British Nat. Cttee for Theoretical and Applied Mechanics, 1973–78; Internat. Adv. Cttee on Rarefied Gas Dynamics Symposia, 1976–88; Council, Gesellschaft für Angewandte Mathematik und Mechanik, 1977–83; Council, RSE, 1960–63; Scottish Arts Council, 1980–85; Hon. Mem., European Consortium for Mathematics in Industry, 1988. Founder Chm., NYO of Scotland, 1978–88 (Hon. Pres., 1988–); Mem., European Music Year UK Cttee (Chm., Scottish Sub-Cttee), 1982–86; First Hon. Treasurer, IMA, 1964–72; Governor, Hamilton Coll. of Education, 1977–81; Pres., Milngavie Music Club, 1983–93 (Hon. Pres., 1994–). *Publications:* papers on fluid dynamics. *Recreations:* music, gardening, golf. *Address:* 18 Buchanan Drive, Bearsden, Glasgow G61 2EW. *T:* 0141–942 5764.

PACK, Maj.-Gen. Simon James, CBE 1994 (OBE 1990); Royal Marines; Commander, British Forces, Gibraltar, since 1994; *b* 10 July 1944; *s* of Captain A. J. James Pack, OBE, RN and Eloise Pack; *m* 1970, Rosianne Fuller; one *s* one *d*. *Educ:* Fernden Prep. Sch.; Hurstpierpoint Coll. Commnd into RM, 1962; served Malaya, Sarawak, HMS Zulu, ADC to Governor of Queensland, 1969–70; Malta, Army Sch. of Infantry, Norway, Hong Kong, MoD, 1971–80; Directing Staff, Army Staff Coll., 1981–83; MoD, 1984–87; CO 45 Commando Group, 1987–89; COS, HQ Commando Forces, 1989–90; Commitments Staff, MoD, 1990–94; ADC to the Queen, 1991–94. Gov., Oratory Sch., Reading, 1991–. *Recreations:* tennis, sailing, gardening, music. *Address:* HQ British Forces Gibraltar, BFPO 52.

PACKARD, Lt-Gen. Sir (Charles) Douglas, KBE 1957 (CBE 1945; OBE 1942); CB 1949; DSO 1943; retired as GOC-in-C Northern Ireland Command, 1958–61; *b* 17 May 1903; *s* of late Capt. C. T. Packard, MC, Copdock, near Ipswich; *m* 1st, 1937, Marion Lochhead (*d* 1981); one *s* two *d*; 2nd, 1982, Mrs Patricia Miles Sharp. *Educ:* Winchester; Royal Military Academy, Woolwich. 2nd Lieut, RA, 1923; served War of 1939–45, in Middle East and Italy (despatches, OBE, DSO, CBE); Dep.-Chief of Staff, 15th Army Group, 1944–45; Temp. Maj.-Gen. and Chief of Staff, Allied Commission for Austria (British Element), 1945–46; Director of Military Intelligence, WO, 1948–49; Commander British Military Mission in Greece, 1949–51; Chief of Staff, GHQ, MELF, 1951–53; Vice-Quarter-Master-General War Office, 1953–56; Military Adviser to the West African Governments, 1956–58. Lt-Gen. 1957. Col Comdt, RA, 1957–62. Officer Legion of Merit (USA). *Address:* Park Side, Lower Road, Ufford, Woodbridge, Suffolk IP13 6DL. *T:* Eyke (01394) 460418.

PACKARD, Vance (Oakley); Author; *b* 22 May 1914; *s* of Philip and Mabel Packard; *m* 1938, Mamie Virginia Mathews; two *s* one *d*. *Educ:* Pennsylvania State Univ.; Columbia Univ. Reporter, The Boston Record, 1938; Feature Editor, The Associated Press, 1939–42; Editor and Staff Writer, The American Magazine, 1942–56; Staff writer, Colliers, 1956; Distinguished Alumni Award, Pennsylvania State University, 1961; Outstanding Alumni Award, Columbia University Graduate School of Journalism, 1963. LittD Monmouth Coll., 1974. *Publications:* (books on social criticism): The Hidden Persuaders, 1957; The Status Seekers, 1959; The Waste Makers, 1960; The Pyramid Climbers, 1962; The Naked Society, 1964; The Sexual Wilderness, 1968; A Nation of Strangers, 1972; The People Shapers, 1977; Our Endangered Children, 1983; The Ultra Rich, 1989; numerous articles for The Atlantic Monthly. *Recreations:* reading, boating. *Address:* 87 Mill Road, New Canaan, CT 06840, USA. *T:* (203) 9661707.

PACKER, Ven. John Richard; Archdeacon of West Cumberland, since 1991; Priest in-charge of Bridekirk, since 1995; *b* 10 Oct. 1946; *s* of John and Muriel Packer; *m* 1971, Barbara Jack; two *s* one *d*. *Educ:* Manchester Grammar Sch.; Keble Coll., Oxford (MA); Ripon Hall, Oxford; York Univ. (DSA). Ordained deacon, 1970, priest, 1971; Curate, St Peter, St Helier, 1970–73; Director of Pastoral Studies: Ripon Hall, 1973–75; Ripon Coll., Cuddesdon, 1975–77; Chaplain, St Nicolas, Abingdon, 1973–77; Vicar, Wath Upon Dearne with Adwick Upon Dearne, 1977–86; Rural Dean of Wath, 1983–86; Rector, Sheffield Manor, 1986–91; Rural Dean of Attercliffe, 1990–91. Mem., Gen. Synod of C of E, 1985–91 and 1992–. *Recreations:* history, cricket, walking. *Address:* 50 Stainburn Road, Workington, Cumbria CA14 1SN. *T:* Workington (01900) 66190.

PACKER, Prof. Kenneth John, PhD; FRS 1991; CChem, FRSC; Research Professor in Chemistry, Nottingham University, since 1993; *b* 18 May 1938; *s* of late Harry James Packer and Alice Ethel Packer (*née* Purse); *m* 1962, Christine Frances Hart; one *s* one *d*. *Educ:* Harvey Grammar Sch., Folkestone; Imperial Coll., London (BSc Hons Chemistry, 1st cl., 1959); Cambridge Univ. (PhD 1962). CChem 1985, FRSC 1985. Post-doctoral Res. Fellow, Central Res. Dept, E. I. duPont de Nemours, Wilmington, USA, 1962–63; University of East Anglia: SERC Res. Fellow, 1963–64; Lectr in Chemistry, 1964–71; Sen. Lectr, 1971–78; Reader, 1978–82; Prof., 1982–84; BP Research: Sen. Res. Associate, Spectroscopy, 1984–87; Prin. Res. Associate, 1987–90; Chief Res. Associate, Analytical Res. Div., 1990–92; Chief Scientist, Gp Res. and Engrg, BP Internat., 1992–93. Visiting Professor in Chemistry: UEA; Southampton Univ.; KCL; Imperial Coll., London, 1985–92. Science and Engineering Research Council: Member: Physical Chem. Cttee, 1976–81; Chem. Cttee, 1979–82; Sci. Bd, 1988–91; Chm., Central Services Panel, 1980–82; Cttee Mem. and Sec., British Radiofrequency Spectroscopy Gp; Mem. Council, Faraday Div., 1988–91, Mem. Scientific Affairs Bd, 1992–, RSC; Hon. Sec., Royal Instn of GB, 1993–. Gov., Hampton Sch., Hanworth, 1990–93. Ed., Molecular Physics, 1982–88. *Publications:* NMR Spectroscopy of Solid Polymers, 1993; contrib. approx. 120 papers on topics involving develt and application of NMR spectroscopy to internat. jls. *Recreations:* fly-fishing, ski-ing, gardening, music. *Address:* The Coach House, Bunny Hall Lane, Loughborough Road, Bunny, Nottingham NG11 6QT. *T:* Nottingham (0115) 921 2210; Department of Chemistry, University of Nottingham NG7 2RD. *T:* Nottingham (0115) 951 3474.

PACKER, Kerry Francis Bullmore, AC 1983; Chairman, Consolidated Press Holdings Ltd, since 1974; *b* 17 Dec. 1937; *s* of late Sir Douglas Frank Hewson Packer, KBE, and Lady (Gretel Joyce) Packer (*née* Bullmore); *m* 1963, Roslyn Redman Weedon; one *s* one *d*. *Educ:* Cranbrook Sch., Sydney, NSW; Geelong C of E Grammar Sch., Vic. Largest shareholder in: Publishing and Broadcasting Ltd (publisher of magazines and jls for specialist, technical, fashion and trends; major TV broadcaster); Valassis Communications Inc. (producer of free standing coupon inserts in USA newspapers). *Recreations:* golf, tennis, cricket, polo. *Address:* 54 Park Street, Sydney, NSW 2000, Australia. *T:* (2) 2828000. *Clubs:* Athenæum (Melbourne); Royal Sydney Golf, Australian Golf, Elanora Country, Tattersall's (NSW).

PACKER, Richard John; Permanent Secretary, Ministry of Agriculture, Fisheries and Food, since 1993; *b* 18 Aug. 1944; *s* of late George Charles Packer and Dorothy May Packer (*née* Reynolds); *m* 1st, Alison Mary Sellwood; two *s* one *d*; 2nd, Lucy Jeanne Blackett-Ord (*see* L. J. Neville-Rolfe); four *s*. *Educ:* City of London School; Manchester Univ. (BSc 1965, MSc 1966). Ministry of Agriculture, Fisheries and Food, 1967–: on secondment as 1st Sec., Office of Perm Rep. to EEC, 1973–76; Principal Private Sec. to Minister, 1976–78; Asst Sec., 1979; Under Sec., 1985–89; Dep. Sec. (Agricl Commodities, Trade and Food Prodn), 1989–93. *Recreation:* living intensely. *Address:* Ministry of Agriculture, Fisheries and Food, Whitehall Place, SW1A 2HH. *T:* 0171–270 8701.

PACKER, William John; painter and critic; art critic, Financial Times, since 1974; *b* 19 Aug. 1940; *o s* of late Rex Packer and Evelyn Mary Packer (*née* Wornham); *m* 1965, Clare, *er d* of late Thomas Winn and Cecily Philip; three *d*. *Educ:* Windsor Grammar Sch.; Wimbledon Sch. of Art (NDD 1963); Brighton Coll. of Art (ATC 1964). First exhibited, RA, 1963 and continues to exhibit; teaching full-time, 1964–67, part-time in art schs, 1967–77; external assessor, 1980–94. Member: Fine Art Board, CNAA, 1976–83; Adv. Cttee, Govt Art Collection, 1977–84; Crafts Council, 1980–87; Cttee, Nat. Trust Foundn for Art, 1986–. Exhibn selector, incl. first British Art Show, 1979–80. London corrresp., Art & Artists, 1969–74. Inaugural Henry Moore lectr, Florence, 1986. Hon. Fellow, RCA, 1988; Hon. RBA 1992; Ballinglen Artist Fellow, 1995. *Publications:* The Art of Vogue Covers, 1980; Fashion Drawing in Vogue, 1983; Henry Moore: a pictorial biography, 1985; Carl Erickson, and René Bouët-Willaumez, 1989. *Recreations:* hockey, riding, Venice. *Address:* 39 Elms Road, Clapham, SW4 9EP. *T:* 0171–622 1108. *Clubs:* Chelsea Arts, Beak Street Academy.

PACKSHAW, Robin David; Consultant, Sterling Brokers Ltd, since 1993; *b* 20 March 1933; *s* of late Savil Packshaw and Fay Mary Packshaw; *m*; three *s* one *d*. *Educ:* Diocesan Coll., Cape Town; Bradfield Coll., Berks. Served RM, 1951–53; commnd and served in Special Boat Service, 1952; RMFVR, 1953–58. Iraq Petroleum Co. Ltd, 1953–63; Long Till and Colvin Ltd, 1963–69; founded Packshaw & Associates Ltd, Sterling Money Brokers, 1969, became Fulton Packshaw Ltd, 1973; Chm., Charles Fulton (UK) Ltd, Internat. For. Exch. and Currency Deposit Brokers, 1982, subseq. Chm., Internat. City Holdings, Money and Securities Brokers, 1985–89; Chm., Manex Sterling Brokers Ltd, 1993; Consultant: BITC, 1990–92; London First, 1992–93. Chm., Radionics Assoc., 1991–. Chm., Stours Br., N Dorset Conservation Assoc., 1989–95. Church Warden, All Saints, Stour Row, Dorset, 1984–95. Gov., Stower Provost Co. Primary Sch., 1992–95. Freeman, City of London, 1983; Life Mem., Guild of Freemen of City of London. *Recreations:* travel, people, the Church of England. *Address:* 67 King's Road, Chelsea, SW3 4NT. *T:* 0171–730 2587; Duncliffe Hall Farm, Stour Row, Shaftesbury, Dorset SP7 0QH. *T:* East Stour (01747) 838483.

PADFIELD, Nicholas David; QC 1991; a Recorder, since 1995; *b* 5 Aug. 1947; *s* of David Padfield and Sushila, *d* of Sir Samuel Runganadhan; *m* 1st, 1978, Nayana Parekh (*d* 1983); one *d*; 2nd, 1986, Mary Barran, JP, *d* of Sir Edward Playfair, *qv*; two *s*. *Educ:* Charterhouse; University Coll., Oxford (Open Scholar, MA; hockey blue); Trinity Hall, Cambridge (LLB Internat. Law). FCIArb. Called to the Bar, Inner Temple, 1972, Bencher, 1995; Mem. Panel, Treasury Counsel (Common Law), 1985–90. Mem., Panel of Lloyd's Arbitrators, 1991. Mem. Cttee, London Oratory Appeal, 1990–. *Address:* 1 Hare Court, Temple, EC4Y 7BE. *T:* 0171–353 3171. *Clubs:* Garrick, MCC; Vincent's (Oxford).

PADMORE, Elaine Marguirite; Director, Royal Danish Opera, Copenhagen, since 1993; *b* Haworth, Yorks, 3 Feb. 1947; *d* of Alfred and Florence Padmore. *Educ:* Newland High Sch., Hull; Arnold Sch., Blackpool; Birmingham Univ. (MA; BMus); Guildhall Sch. of Music; LTCL. Liberal Studies Lectr, Croydon and Kingston Colls of Art, 1968–70; Books Editor, OUP Music Dept, 1970–71; Producer, BBC Music Div., 1971–76; Announcer, Radio 3, 1982–90. Major BBC Radio 3 series include: Parade, Music of Tchaikovsky's Russia, England's Pleasant Land, Journal de mes Mélodies; Presenter of numerous programmes, incl. Festival Comment, Edinburgh Fest., 1973–81; Chief Producer, Opera, BBC Radio, 1976–83: series incl. complete operas of Richard Strauss and first performances of works by Delius and Havergal Brian; active as professional singer (soprano), particularly of opera; Lectr in Opera, RAM, 1979–87; Artistic Director: Classical Prodns, London, 1990–92; Wexford Festival Opera, 1982–94; DGOS Opera Ireland, 1989–90 and 1991–93; Artistic Consultant, 1992 London Opera Fest. Hon. ARAM. Hungarian Radio Pro Musica Award for prog. Summertime on Bredon, 1973; Prix Musical de Radio Brno for prog. The English Renaissance, 1974; Sunday Independent Award for services to music in Ireland, 1985. Kt, Order of Dannebrog (Denmark), 1994. *Publications:* Wagner (Great Composers' Series), 1970; Music in the Modern Age: chapter on Germany, 1973; contributor to: New Grove Dict. of Music, Proc. of Royal Musical Assoc., Music and Letters, The Listener. *Recreations:* gardening, travel, art exhibitions. *Address:* 11 Lancaster Avenue, Hadley Wood, Barnet, Herts EN4 0EP. *T:* 0181–449 5369.

PADMORE, Sir Thomas, GCB 1965 (KCB 1953; CB 1947); MA; FCIT; *b* 23 April 1909; *e s* of Thomas William Padmore, Sheffield; *m* 1st, 1934, Alice (*d* 1963), *d* of Robert Alcock, Ormskirk; two *d* (one *s* decd); 2nd, 1964, Rosalind Culhane, LVO, OBE (*d* 1995). *Educ:* Central Sch., Sheffield; Queens' Coll., Cambridge (Foundation Scholar; Hon. Fellow, 1961). Secretaries' Office, Board of Inland Revenue, 1931–34; transferred to Treasury, 1934; Principal Private Secretary to Chancellor of Exchequer, 1943–45; Second Secretary, 1952–62; Permanent Sec., Min. of Transport, 1962–68. Dir, Laird Gp Ltd, 1970–79; Dep. Chm., Metropolitan Cammell Ltd, 1969–80. Chairman: Rehearsal Orchestra, 1961–71; Handel Opera Soc., 1963–86. Hon. Treas., Inst. of Cancer Res., 1973–81. *Address:* 39 Cholmeley Crescent, Highgate, N6 5EX. *T:* 0181–340 6587. *Club:* Reform.

PADOVAN, John Mario Faskally; Chairman, AAH, since 1993 (Deputy Chairman, 1992); *b* 7 May 1938; *s* of Umberto Mario Padovan and Mary Nina Liddon Padovan; *m* 1964, Sally Kay (*née* Anderson); three *s*. *Educ:* St George's College, Weybridge; King's College London (LLB); Keble College, Oxford (BCL). FCA. County Bank, 1970–84: Dir, 1971; Dep. Chief Exec., 1974; Chief Exec., 1976; Chm., 1984; Dep. Chm., Hambros Bank and Dir, Hambros, 1984–86; Chm., Merchant Banking Div., Barclays de Zoete Wedd Gp, 1986–91; Dep. Chm., Barclays de Zoete Wedd, 1989–91. Chm., Gardner Merchant, 1993–; Director: Tesco, 1982–; de Zoete & Bevan, 1986–; Mabey Hldgs, 1989– (Chm., 1991–); Hartstone Gp, 1991–; Whitbread, 1992–; Williams Lea Gp, 1992–. Mem. Court, Drapers' Co., 1991–. *Recreations:* golf, walking, contemporary art. *Address:* 15 Lord North Street, SW1P 3LD. *T:* 0171–222 3261. *Clubs:* Royal St George's Golf, West Surrey Golf.

PAFFORD, John Henry Pyle, MA, DLit (London); FSA; FLA; Goldsmiths' Librarian of the University of London, 1945–67; *b* 6 March 1900; *s* of John Pafford and Bessie (*née* Pyle); *m* 1941, Elizabeth Ford, *d* of R. Charles Ford and Margaret Harvey; one *d* (and one *d* decd). *Educ:* Trowbridge High Sch.; University Coll., London (Fellow, 1956). Library Asst, University College, London, 1923–25; Librarian, and Tutor, Selly Oak Colleges, 1925–31 (Hon. Fellow 1985); Sub-Librarian, National Central Library, 1931–45; Lecturer at University of London School of Librarianship, 1937–61. Library Adviser, Inter-Univ. Council for Higher Education Overseas, 1960–68. *Publications:* Bale's King Johan, 1931, and The Sodder'd Citizen, 1936 (Malone Society); Library Co-operation in Europe, 1935; Accounts of Parliamentary Garrisons of Great Chalfield and Malmesbury, 1645–46, 1940; Books and Army Education, 1946; W. P. Ker, A Bibliography, 1950; The Winter's Tale (Arden Shakespeare), 1963; Watts's Divine Songs for Children, 1971; L. Bryskett's Literary Works, 1972; (with E. R. Pafford) Employer and Employed, 1974; John Clavell, 1601–43: highwayman, author, lawyer, doctor, 1993. *Address:* Hillside, Allington Park, Bridport, Dorset DT6 5DD. *T:* Bridport (01308) 422829.

PAGE, family name of **Baron Whaddon.**

PAGE, Annette, (Mrs Ronald Hynd); Ballerina of the Royal Ballet until retirement, 1967; Ballet Mistress, Ballet of the Bayerischestaatsoper, Munich, 1984–86; *b* 18 Dec. 1932; *d* of James Lees and Margaret Page; *m* 1957, Ronald Hynd, *qv*; one *d*. *Educ:* Royal Ballet School. Audition and award of scholarship to Roy. Ballet Sch., 1944. Entry into touring company of Royal Ballet (then Sadler's Wells Theatre Ballet), 1950; promotion to major Royal Ballet Co. (Sadler's Wells Ballet), 1955. Mem., Arts Council of GB, 1976–79. *Roles included:* The Firebird, Princess Aurora in Sleeping Beauty, Odette-Odile in Swan Lake, Giselle, Lise in La Fille Mal Gardée, Juliet in Romeo and Juliet, Cinderella. *Recreations:* music, books, gardening, choral singing.

PAGE, Anthony (Frederick Montague); stage, film and television director; *b* India, 21 Sept. 1935; *s* of Brig. F. G. C. Page, DSO, OBE, and P. V. M. Page. *Educ:* Oakley Hall, Cirencester; Winchester Coll. (Schol.); Magdalen Coll., Oxford (Schol., BA); Neighborhood Playhouse Sch. of the Theater, NY. Asst, Royal Court Theatre, 1958: co-directed Live Like Pigs, directed The Room; Artistic Dir, Dundee Repertory Theatre, 1962; The Caretaker, Oxford and Salisbury; Women Beware Women, and Nil Carborundum, Royal Shakespeare Co., 1963; BBC Directors' Course, then several episodes of Z-Cars, Horror of Darkness and 1st TV prodn Stephen D; Jt Artistic Dir, Royal Court, 1964–65; directed Inadmissible Evidence (later Broadway and film), A Patriot for Me, 1st revival of Waiting for Godot, Cuckoo in the Nest; Diary of a Madman, Duchess, 1966; Artistic Dir, two seasons at Royal Court: Uncle Vanya, 1970; Alpha Beta (also film); Hedda Gabler; Krapp's Last Tape; Not I; Cromwell; other plays transf. from Royal Court to West End: Time Present; Hotel in Amsterdam; revival, Look Back in Anger; West of Suez; directed Hamlet, Nottingham, 1970; Rules of the Game, National Theatre; King Lear, Amer. Shakespeare Fest., 1975; Cowardice, Ambassadors, 1983; Heartbreak House, Broadway, 1984 (televised); Mrs Warren's Profession, Nat. Theatre, 1985; Three Tall Women, Wyndham's, 1994; Absolute Hell, Nat. Theatre, 1995; *television:* The Parachute; Emlyn; Hotel in Amsterdam; Speaking of Murder; You're Free; The Changeling; Headmaster; Sheppey; Absolute Hell, 1991; Middlemarch, 1994; in USA: Missiles of October; Pueblo Incident; FDR, the Last Year; Bill (starring Mickey Rooney (Golden Globe Award); Johnny Belinda; Bill on His Own; The Nightmare Years; Patricia Neal Story; Murder by Reason of Insanity; Second Serve; Pack of Lies; Chernobyl: The Final Warning, 1990; Guests of the Emperor; *films:* Inadmissible Evidence; I Never Promised You a Rose Garden; Absolution; The Lady Vanishes; Forbidden. Directors' and Producers' Award for TV Dir of Year, 1966. *Recreations:* movies, reading, riding, travelling. *Address:* c/o ICM, Oxford House, Oxford Street, W1N 0AX.

PAGE, Sir (Arthur) John, Kt 1984; *b* 16 Sept. 1919; *s* of Sir Arthur Page, QC (late Chief Justice of Burma), and Lady Page, KiH; *m* 1950, Anne, *d* of Charles Micklem, DSO, JP, DL, Longcross House, Surrey; four *s*. *Educ:* Harrow, Magdalene College, Cambridge. Joined RA as Gunner, 1939, commissioned, 1940; served War of 1939–45, Western Desert (wounded), France, Germany; demobilised as Major, comdg 258 Battery Norfolk Yeomanry, 1945; various positions in industry and commerce, 1946–. Chm. Bethnal Green and E London Housing Assoc., 1957–70; contested (C) Eton and Slough, Gen. Election, 1959. MP (C) Harrow W, March 1960–1987. PPS to Parly Under-Sec. of State, Home Office, 1961–63; Conservative Parly Labour Affairs Cttee: Sec., 1960–61, 1964–67, Vice-Chm., 1964–69, Chm., 1970–74; Sec., Conservative Broadcasting Cttee, 1974–76. Pres., Cons. Trade Unionists Nat. Adv. Council, 1967–69; Member: Parly Select Cttee on Race Relations and Immigration, 1970–71; British Delegn to Council of Europe and WEU, 1972–87 (Chm. Budget Cttee, 1973–74, Social and Health Cttee, 1975–78). Mem. Exec., IPU, British Gp, 1970 (Treasurer, 1974–77; Vice-Chm., 1977–79; Chm., 1979–82); Acting Internat. Pres., IPU, 1984 (Dep. Internat. Pres., 1982–84). Vice-Pres., British Insurance Brokers Assoc., 1980–; President: Water Companies Assoc., 1986–89 (Dep. Pres., 1984–86); Independent Schools Assoc., 1971–78; Chm., Council for Indep. Educn, 1974–80. *Recreations:* painting, politics, defending the Monarchy. *Address:* Hitcham Lodge, Taplow, Maidenhead, Berks SL6 0HG. *T:* Burnham (01628) 605056. *Clubs:* Brooks's, MCC.

PAGE, Ashley; Principal Dancer and choreographer, since 1984; *b* 9 Aug. 1956; named Ashley Laverty; *s* of John Henry Laverty and Sheila Rachel Laverty. *Educ:* St Andrew's Sch., Rochester; Royal Ballet Schs. Joined Royal Ballet at Covent Garden, 1976; Soloist, 1980, Principal 1984. Works choreographed for: Royal Ballet; Ballet Rambert, subseq. Rambert Dance Co.; Dutch Nat. Ballet; Dance Umbrella Fest. and other cos in GB and abroad. *Recreations:* interest in all the arts, travel. *Address:* c/o Royal Ballet, Royal Opera House, Covent Garden, WC2. *T:* 0171–240 1200.

PAGE, Bruce; journalist; Director, Direct Image Systems and Communications Ltd, since 1992; *b* 1 Dec. 1936; *s* of Roger and Beatrice Page; *m* 1969, Anne Louise Darnborough; one *s* one *d*. *Educ:* Melbourne High Sch.; Melbourne Univ. The Herald, Melbourne, 1956–60; Evening Standard, 1960–62; Daily Herald, 1962–64; Sunday Times, 1964–76; Daily Express, 1977; Editor, The New Statesman, 1978–82. *Publications:* (jtly) Philby, 1968, 3rd edn 1977; (jtly) An American Melodrama, 1969; (jtly) Do You Sincerely Want to be Rich?, 1971; (jtly) Destination Disaster, 1976; contrib. Ulster, 1972; The Yom Kippur War, 1974; The British Press, 1978. *Recreations:* sailing, reading. *Address:* Beach House, Shingle Street, Shottisham, Suffolk IP12 3BE. *T:* Shottisham (01394) 411427; 32 Lauderdale Tower, Barbican, EC2Y 8BY. *T:* 0171–628 3847.

PAGE, Maj.-Gen. Charles Edward, CB 1974; MBE 1944; DL; *b* 23 Aug. 1920; *s* of late Sir (Charles) Max Page, KBE, CB, DSO, FRCS and Lady (Helen) Page; *m* 1948, Elizabeth Marion, *d* of late Sir William Smith Crawford, KBE; two *s* one *d*. *Educ:* Marlborough Coll.; Trinity Coll., Cambridge. BSc (Eng) London 1949; CEng, FIEE 1968. Commissioned 2nd Lieut Royal Signals from TA, 1941; regimental appts Guards Armd Divisional Signals, 1941–45; CO 19 Indian Div. Signals, 1945–46; psc 1951; GSO2 Staff Coll., 1955–58; GSO1 Combat Develt Directorate, WO, 1960–63; CO 1st Div. Signal Regt, 1963–65; CCR Signals 1 (BR) Corps, 1966–68; Sec., NATO Mil. Cttee, Brussels, 1968–70; DCD(A) MoD, 1971–74; retired 1974. Col Comdt, Royal Corps of Signals, 1974–80. Chm. Adv. Council, Women's Transport Service (FANY), 1994– (Hon. Col, 1976–93). DL W Sussex, 1986. *Recreations:* shooting, golf, fishing. *Address:* 104 Rivermead Court, Ranelagh Gardens, SW6 3SB. *Club:* Royal and Ancient (St Andrews).

PAGE, Dr Christopher Howard; Senior Research Fellow, Sidney Sussex College, Cambridge, since 1985; Lecturer in English, University of Cambridge, since 1989; Director, Gothic Voices, since 1982; *b* 8 April 1952; *s* of Ewart Lacey Page and Marie Victoria (*née* Graham); *m* 1975, Régine Fourcade. *Educ:* Sir George Monoux Grammar Sch.; Balliol Coll., Oxford (BA English 1974; MA); Univ. of York (DPhil). Jun. Res. Fellow, Jesus Coll., Oxford, 1977–80; Lectr in English, New Coll., Oxford, 1980–85. Editor, Plainsong and Medieval Music, 1991–. Presenter, Spirit of the Age, Radio 3, 1992–. Fellow, Fellowship of Makers and Restorers of Historical Instruments, 1982. Chairman: Nat. Early Music Assoc., 1991–; Plainsong and Medieval Music Soc. Dent Medal, Royal Musical Assoc., 1991. *Publications:* Voices and Instruments of the Middle Ages, 1987; The Owl and the Nightingale, 1989; the *Summa Musice*, 1991; Discarding Images, 1993; Songs of the Trouvères, 1995; articles in Early Music, Galpin Soc. Jl, Plainsong and Medieval Music, Musical Times. *Address:* Sidney Sussex College, Cambridge CB2 3HU. *T:* Cambridge (01223) 338800.

PAGE, Cyril Leslie, OBE 1965; Controller, Personnel, Television, BBC Television Service, 1971–76, retired; *b* 20 Oct. 1916; *s* of Cyril Herbert Page and Rosamund Clara Page; *m* 1939, Barbara Mary Rowland; one *s* one *d*. *Educ:* Sherborne Sch. Royal Air Force, 1936–46 (Wing Comdr). British Broadcasting Corporation, 1946–: Asst, Appts Dept, 1947; Asst Admin. Officer, Overseas Services, 1949; Asst Head of TV Admin., 1951; Estabt Officer, TV, 1958; Head of TV Estabt Dept, 1961; Asst Controller, TV Admin., 1964. Dir, Osborne Management Ltd, 1984– (Chm., 1984–92). Mem. Council, Royal Postgrad. Med. Sch., 1975–Sept. 1989. *Recreations:* reading, gardening. *Address:* 95 Fountain Gardens, Windsor, Berks SL4 3SU.

PAGE, David John, FCCA; Director of Finance, Leeds City Council, since 1992; *b* 24 Feb. 1954; *s* of Clifford Page and Evelyn Page (*née* Banks); *m* 1976, Carole Watson; one *s* one *d*. *Educ:* W Leeds Boys' High Sch.; Leeds Poly. FCCA 1976. Trainee accountant, CEGB, 1972–74; Leeds City Council, 1974–: Chief Accountant, 1985–88; Asst Dir of Finance, 1988–89; Sen. Asst Dir of Finance, 1989–92. Gov., Ossett Sch. *Recreations:* music, all sports, caravanning, quizzes. *Address:* 2 King's Close, Ossett, Wakefield, W Yorks WF5 8QU. *T:* Wakefield (01924) 261726. *Club:* Howley Hall Golf (Morley).

PAGE, Rt. Rev. Dennis Fountain; *b* 1 Dec. 1919; *s* of Prebendary Martin Fountain Page and Lilla Fountain Page; *m* 1946, Margaret Bettine Clayton; two *s* one *d*. *Educ:* Shrewsbury Sch.; Gonville and Caius Coll., Cambridge (MA); Lincoln Theological Coll. Curate, Rugby Parish Church, 1943; Priest-in-Charge, St George's Church, Hillmorton, Rugby, 1945; Rector of Hockwold, Vicar of Wilton and Rector of Weeting, Norfolk, 1949; Archdeacon of Huntingdon and Vicar of Yaxley, 1965–75; Hon. Canon of Ely Cathedral, 1968; Bishop Suffragan of Lancaster, 1975–85. *Publication:* Reflections on the Reading for Holy Communion in the Alternative Service Book 1980, 1983. *Recreations:* music, astronomy, gardening. *Address:* Larkrise, Hartest Hill, Hartest, Bury St Edmunds, Suffolk IP29 4ES.

PAGE, Ewan Stafford, PhD, MA, BSc; Vice-Chancellor, University of Reading, 1979–93; *b* 17 Aug. 1928; *s* of late Joseph William Page and Lucy Quayle (*née* Stafford); *m* 1955, Sheila Margaret Smith; three *s* one *d*. *Educ:* Wyggeston Grammar Sch., Leicester; Christ's Coll., Cambridge (MA, PhD, Raleigh Prize 1952); Univ. of London (BSc). Instr, RAF Techn. Coll., 1949–51; Lectr in Statistics, Durham Colls, 1954–57; Director: Durham Univ. Computing Lab., 1957–63; Newcastle Univ. Computing Lab., 1963–78; Visiting Prof., Univ. of N Carolina, Chapel Hill, USA, 1962–63; University of Newcastle upon Tyne: Prof. of Computing and Data Processing, 1965–78; Pro-Vice Chancellor, 1972–78 (Actg Vice-Chancellor, 1976–77). Member: Newcastle AHA, 1976–79; Berks AHA, 1980–82; Oxford RHA, 1982–84; West Berks DHA, 1984–93; Berks HA, 1993–. Mem. Bd, Aycliffe and Peterlee Develt Corp., 1969–78. Chairman: Food Adv. Cttee, 1988–94; Univs' Authorities Panel, 1988–93. Pres., British Computer Soc., 1984–85 (Dep. Pres., 1983–84); Mem., Gen. Optical Council, 1984– (Vice-Chm., 1989–); Hon. Treasurer, Royal Statistical Soc., 1983–89. CIMgt (CBIM 1986); Hon. Fellow, Amer. Statistical Assoc., 1974; Hon. FBCS, 1976; Hon. Fellow, Northumbria Univ. (formerly Newcastle upon Tyne Poly.), 1979. Hon. DSc Reading, 1993. Chevalier, l'Ordre des Palmes Académiques (France), 1991. *Publications:* (jtly) Information Representation and Manipulation in a Computer, 1973, 2nd edn 1978; (jtly) Introduction to Computational

Combinatorics, 1978; papers in statistical and computing jls. *Recreations:* golf, music, reading, vegetable gardening. *Address:* High View, Charlcombe Lane, Bath BA1 5TT.

PAGE, Sir Frederick (William), Kt 1979; CBE 1961; FRS 1978; FEng, Hon. FRAeS; Member of the Board, British Aerospace PLC, 1977–83; Chairman and Chief Executive, Aircraft Group of British Aerospace PLC, 1977–82; retired 1983; *b* 20 Feb. 1917; *s* of Richard Page and Ellen Potter; *m* 1940, Kathleen Edith de Courcy; three *s* one *d*. *Educ:* Rutlish Sch., Merton; St Catharine's Coll., Cambridge (MA). Hawker Aircraft Co., 1938; English Electric, 1945; Chief Engr, 1950, and Dir and Chief Exec. (Aircraft), English Electric Aviation, 1959; Managing Dir, Mil. Aircraft Div. of BAC, 1965–72, Chm., 1967; apptd Managing Dir (Aircraft), BAC, and Chm., Commercial Aircraft Div., 1972. Jt Chm. of SEPECAT, the Anglo-French co. formed for management of Jaguar programme, 1966–73; apptd to Bd of Panavia Aircraft GmbH, 1969, Chm. 1977; apptd Chm. BAC Ltd (a co. of Brit. Aerospace), 1977. Mem. Council, Soc. of Brit. Aerospace Cos Ltd; apptd to Bd of BAC (Operating) Ltd, 1963; Dir, BAC (USA) Inc., 1975–77. FRAeS, 1951–80, Hon. FRAeS, 1980 (Gold Medal, 1974); Fellow, Fellowship of Engrg, 1977. Hon. Fellow, UMIST, 1970. Hon. DSc Cranfield, 1979. British Gold Medal for Aeronautics, 1962. *Recreation:* gardening. *Address:* Renvyle, 60 Waverley Lane, Farnham, Surrey GU9 8BN. *T:* Farnham (01252) 714999. *Club:* United Oxford & Cambridge University.

PAGE, Howard William Barrett; QC 1987; *b* 11 Feb. 1943; *s* of Leslie Herbert Barrett Page and Phyllis Elizabeth Page; *m* 1969, Helen Joanna Shotter; two *s* one *d*. *Educ:* Radley Coll.; Trinity Hall, Cambridge (BA, LLB). Called to the Bar, Lincoln's Inn, 1967 (Mansfield Schol.; Bencher, 1994). *Recreations:* music, walking. *Address:* 1 Hare Court, Temple, EC4Y 7BE.

PAGE, Jennifer Anne, CBE 1994; Chief Executive, Millennium Commission, since 1995; *b* 12 Nov. 1944; *d* of Edward and Olive Page. *Educ:* Barr's Hill Grammar School, Coventry; Royal Holloway College, Univ. of London (BA Hons). Entered Civil Service, 1968; Principal, DoE, 1974; Asst Sec., Dept of Transport, 1980; seconded BNOC, 1981; LDDC, 1983. Senior Vice-Pres., Pallas Invest SA, 1984–89; Chief Exec., English Heritage (Historic Buildings and Monuments Commn), 1989–95. Member, Board: Railtrack Group, 1994–; Equitable Life Assurance Soc., 1994–. *Address:* Millennium Commission, 2 Little Smith Street, SW1P 3DH.

PAGE, Sir John; *see* Page, Sir (Arthur) John and Page, Sir John (Joseph Joffre).

PAGE, John Brangwyn; Chairman, Agricultural Mortgage Corporation, 1982–85; Director: Standard Chartered Bank, 1982–89; Nationwide Building Society, 1982–92; *b* 23 Aug. 1923; *s* of late Sidney John Page, CB, MC; *m* 1948, Gloria Vail; one *s* one *d*. *Educ:* Highgate Sch. (Foundation Schol.); King's Coll., Cambridge (BA). RAF, 1942–46; Cambridge, 1946–48; Bank of England, 1948; seconded to IMF, 1953; Chief Cashier, 1970–80; Exec. Dir, 1980–82. FCIB; CIMgt; FRSA. *Recreations:* gardening, music, travel.

PAGE, Maj.-Gen. John Humphrey, CB 1977; OBE 1967; MC 1952; *b* 5 March 1923; *s* of late Captain W. J. Page, JP, Devizes and late Alice Mary Page (*née* Richards); *m* 1956, Angela Mary Bunting; three *s* one *d*. *Educ:* Stonyhurst. Commnd into RE, 1942; served in NW Europe, India, Korea, Middle East and UK, 1942–60; Instr, Staff Coll., Camberley, 1960–62; comd 32 Armd Engr Regt, 1964–67; idc 1968; CCRE 1st Br. Corps, 1969–70; Asst Comdt, RMA Sandhurst, 1971–74; Dir of Personal Services (Army), MoD, 1974–78, retd. Col Comdt, RE, 1980–85. Dir, London Law Trust, 1979–88. Dir, RBM (Holdings), 1980–86. Member Council: REOWS, 1980– (Chm., 1990–92); Officers' Pension Soc., 1979–; Vice-Chm., SSAFA, 1983–87. Chm. Trustees, Home-Start Consultancy, 1982–90; Mem., Management Cttee, Stackpole Trust, 1981–92. Chm., Bd of Governors, St Mary's Sch., Shaftesbury, 1985–93; Mem., Bd of Governors, Stonyhurst Coll., 1980–90. *Address:* c/o Lloyds Bank, Somerton, Somerset.

PAGE, Sir John (Joseph Joffre), Kt 1979; OBE 1959; Chairman, Christie Hospital NHS Trust, 1991–92; *b* 7 Jan. 1915; 2nd *s* of late William Joseph and Frances Page; *m* 1939, Cynthia Maynard, *d* of late L. M. Swan, CBE; two *s*. *Educ:* Emanuel School. RAF, 1933–38 and 1939–46 (despatches, 1943); Group Captain. Iraq Petroleum Group of Cos, 1938–39 and 1946–70; served in Palestine, Jordan, Lebanon, Syria, Iraq, Qatar, Bahrain and Abu Dhabi; Head Office, London, 1958–61; Gen. Man., 1955–58; Chief Representative, 1961–70. Chm., 1972–77 and 1980–84, Chief Exec., 1975–77, Mersey Docks and Harbour Co.; Dep. Chm., British Ports Assoc., 1974–77; Chm., Nat. Ports Council, 1977–80. Chairman: Chester DHA, 1981–82; North Western RHA, 1982–88. Hon. Fellow, Manchester Metropolitan Univ., 1993. *Recreations:* photography, fishing, music. *Address:* The Cottage, Hockenhull Lane, Tarvin, Chester CH3 8LB. *Clubs:* Oriental, Royal Air Force, MCC.

PAGE, Prof. John Kenneth; energy and environmental consultant; Initiating Director, Cambridge Interdisciplinary Environmental Centre, 1990–92; Professor of Building Science, University of Sheffield, 1960–84, now Emeritus; *b* 3 Nov. 1924; *s* of late Brig. E. K. Page, CBE, DSO, MC; *m* 1954, Anita Bell Lovell; two *s* two *d*. *Educ:* Haileybury College; Pembroke College, Cambridge. Served War of 1939–45, Royal Artillery, 1943–47. Asst Industrial Officer, Council of Industrial Design, 1950–51; taught Westminster School, 1952–53; Sen. Scientific Officer, Tropical Liaison Section, Building Research Station, 1953–56; Chief Research Officer, Nuffield Div. for Architectural Studies, 1956–57; Lecturer, Dept. of Building Science, Univ. of Liverpool, 1957–60. Chm., Environmental Gp, and Mem., Econ. Planning Council, Yorks and Humberside Region, 1965–78; Founding Chm., UK Section, Internat. Solar Energy Soc. Consultant author working with UN internat. agencies on energy use in Third World and on environmental health in tropical bldgs. Farrington Daniels Internat. Award, for distinguished contribs to solar energy studies, 1989. *Publications:* 200 papers on Energy policy, Environmental Design and Planning, Environmental Management, Building Climatology and Solar Energy. *Address:* 15 Brincliffe Gardens, Sheffield S11 9BG. *T:* Sheffield (0114) 255 1570.

PAGE, Prof. Raymond Ian, LittD; Fellow, Corpus Christi College, Cambridge, since 1962; Elrington and Bosworth Professor of Anglo-Saxon, University of Cambridge, 1984–91, now Professor Emeritus; Special Professor in Anglo-Saxon Studies, University of Nottingham, since 1992; *b* 25 Sept. 1924; *s* of Reginald Howard Page and Emily Louise Page; *m* 1953, Elin Benedicte Hustad, *d* of Tormod Kristoffer Hustad and Anne Margarethe Hustad, Oslo; two *d* (one *s* decd). *Educ:* King Edward VII Sch., Sheffield; Rotherham Technical Coll,; Univ. of Sheffield. LittD Cambridge 1974. Assistant Lecturer and Lecturer, Univ. of Nottingham, 1951–61; Cambridge University: successively Lectr, Reader and Professor, Dept of Anglo-Saxon, Norse and Celtic, 1961–91; Sandars Reader in Bibliography, 1989–90; Corpus Christi College: Librarian, 1965–91; Dir, Leverhulme Trust Res. Gp on MS Evidence, Parker Liby, 1989–94. Hon. Sen. Res. Fellow, Dept of Eng. Lang., Univ. of Glasgow, 1993–. Hon. LittD Sheffield, 1994. *Address:* Ashton House, Newnham Road, Cambridge CB3 9EY.

PAGE, Richard Lewis; MP (C) Hertfordshire South West, since Dec. 1979; Parliamentary Under-Secretary of State for Industry and Energy, Department of Trade and Industry, since 1995; *b* 22 Feb. 1941; *s* of Victor Charles and Kathleen Page; *m* 1964, Madeleine Ann Brown; one *s* one *d*. *Educ:* Hurstpierpoint Coll.; Luton Technical Coll. Apprenticeship, Vauxhall Motors, 1959–64; HNC Mech. Engineering; dir of family co., 1964–. Young Conservatives, 1964–66; Councillor, Banstead UDC, 1968–71; contested (C) Workington, Feb. and Oct. 1974; MP (C) Workington, Nov. 1976–1979; PPS: to Sec. of State for Trade, 1981–82; to Leader of the House, 1982–87. Mem., Public Accounts Cttee, 1987–95; Vice-Chm., Cons. Trade and Industry Cttee, 1988–95. Hon. Treasurer, Leukaemia Res. Fund, 1987–95. *Recreation:* most sport. *Address:* House of Commons, SW1A 0AA.

PAGE, Simon Richard; District Judge (formerly Registrar), Guildford, Epsom and Reigate County Courts, and High Court of Justice, since 1980; a Recorder of the Crown Court, since 1980; *b* 7 March 1934; *s* of Eric Rowland Page and Vera (*née* Fenton); *m* 1st, 1963, (marr. diss. 1977); three *s* one *d*; 2nd, 1984. *Educ:* Lancing; LSE (LLB External, 1956). Admitted solicitor (hons), 1957. National Service, Second Lieut RA, 1957–59. Private practice as solicitor, 1959–75; Pres., West Surrey Law Soc., 1972–73; Registrar, Croydon County Court, 1975–80; Pres., Assoc. of County Court and District Registrars, 1983–84. *Recreations:* squash racquets, cricket, bridge. *Address:* c/o The Law Courts, Mary Road, Guildford GU1 4PS.

PAGE WOOD, Sir Anthony John, 8th Bt, *cr* 1837; *b* 6 Feb. 1951; *s* of Sir David (John Hatherley) Page Wood, 7th Bt and Evelyn Hazel Rosemary, *d* of late Captain George Ernest Bellville; *S* father 1955. *Heir: uncle,* Matthew Page Wood [*b* 13 Aug. 1924; *m* 1947; two *d*].

PAGEL, Prof. Bernard Ephraim Julius, FRS 1992; Professor of Astrophysics, NORDITA (Nordic Institute for Theoretical Physics), Copenhagen, since 1990; Visiting Professor of Astronomy, University of Sussex, since 1970; *b* 4 Jan. 1930; *s* of Walter T. U. Pagel and Magdalene M. E. Pagel; *m* 1958, Annabel Ruth Tuby; two *s* one *d*. *Educ:* Merchant Taylors' Sch., Northwood; Sidney Sussex Coll., Cambridge (MA, PhD). Res. Fellow, Sidney Sussex Coll., 1953–56; Radcliffe Student, Pretoria, 1955; PSO, Royal Greenwich Observ., 1955–61; Astrophysicist, Sacramento Peak Observ., New Mexico, 1960; SPSO, 1961–71, DCSO, 1971–89, Royal Greenwich Observ.; Vis. Reader in Astronomy, Univ. of Sussex, 1966–70. Kelvin Lectr, BAAS, 1962; Vice-Pres. and For. Corresp., RAS, 1974–75. Gold Medal, RAS, 1990. *Publications:* Théorie des Atmosphères Stellaires, 1971; articles in Nature, Encycl. Britannica, Monthly Notices of RAS, New Scientist, and procs of astronomical confs. *Recreations:* music, ski-ing, bicycling. *Address:* Groombridge, Lewes Road, Ringmer, East Sussex BN8 5ER. *T:* Ringmer (01273) 812729.

PAGET, family name of **Marquess of Anglesey.**

PAGET DE BEAUDESERT, Lord; Benedict Dashiel Paget; *b* 11 April 1986; *s* and *heir* of Earl of Uxbridge, *qv*.

PAGET, David Christopher John; QC 1994; a Recorder, since 1986; *b* 3 Feb. 1942; *s* of late Henry Paget and of Dorothy Paget (*née* Colenutt), Johannesburg, S Africa; *m* 1968, Dallas Wendy (*née* Hill); two *d*. *Educ:* St John's Coll., Johannesburg. Called to Bar, Inner Temple, 1967; Jun. Prosecuting Counsel to the Crown, 1982–89, Sen. Prosecuting Counsel, 1989–94, CCC. *Recreations:* walking, bird watching, listening to music. *Address:* Queen Elizabeth Building, Temple, EC4Y 9BS. *T:* 0171–583 5766.

PAGET, Lt-Col Sir Julian (Tolver), 4th Bt *cr* 1871; CVO 1984; an Extra Gentleman Usher to the Queen, since 1991 (Gentleman Usher, 1971–91); author; *b* 11 July 1921; *s* of General Sir Bernard Paget, GCB, DSO, MC (*d* 1961) (*g s* of 1st Bt), and Winifred (*d* 1986), *d* of Sir John Paget, 2nd Bt; *S* uncle, Sir James Francis Paget, 3rd Bt, 1972; *m* 1954, Diana Frances, *d* of late F. S. H. Farmer; one *s* one *d*. *Educ:* Radley College; Christ Church, Oxford (MA). Joined Coldstream Guards, 1940; served North West Europe, 1944–45; retired as Lt-Col, 1968. Ed., Guards Magazine, 1976–93. *Publications:* Counter-Insurgency Campaigning, 1967; Last Post: Aden, 1964–67, 1969, The Story of the Guards, 1976; The Pageantry of Britain, 1979; Yeomen of the Guard, 1984; Discovering London's Ceremonial and Traditions, 1989; Wellington's Peninsular War: the battles and battlefields, 1990; Hougoument, The Key to Victory at Waterloo, 1992. *Recreations:* fishing, shooting, travel, writing. *Heir: s* Henry James Paget [*b* 2 Feb. 1959; *m* 1993, Mrs Margrete Varvill (*née* Lynner); one *s*]. *Address:* 4 Trevor Street, SW7 1DU. *T:* 0171–584 3524. *Clubs:* Cavalry and Guards, Flyfishers'.

PAGET, Sir Richard (Herbert), 4th Bt *cr* 1886, of Cranmore Hall, Co. Somerset; independent marketing consultant; *b* 17 Feb. 1957; *s* of Sir John Starr Paget, 3rd Bt and of Nancy Mary, *d* of Lt-Col Francis Parish, DSO, MC; *S* father, 1992; *m* 1985, Richenda Rachel, *d* of Rev. Preb. J. T. C. B. Collins; three *d*. *Educ:* Eton Coll. AES, 1983–87; Nixdorf Computers, 1987–88; Inforem plc, 1988–89; Sales Manager, SAS Inst., 1989–95. *Recreations:* carriage driving, cricket, tennis, parachuting. *Heir: b* David Vernon John Paget [*b* 26 March 1959; *m* 1990, Cluny Macpherson; one *s* one *d*]. *Address:* Burridge Heath Farm, Little Bedwyn, Marlborough, Wilts SN8 3JR.

PAGET-WILKES, Ven. Michael Jocelyn James; Archdeacon of Warwick, since 1990; *b* 11 Dec. 1941; *s* of Arthur Hamilton Paget-Wilkes and Eleanor Bridget Paget-Wilkes; *m* 1969, Ruth Gillian Macnamara; one *s* two *d*. *Educ:* Harper Adams Agricultural Coll. (NDA); London Coll. of Divinity (ALCD). Agricultural Extension Officer, Tanzania, 1964–66; attended London Coll. of Divinity, 1966–69; Curate, All Saints', Wandsworth, 1969–74; Vicar: St James', Hatcham, New Cross, 1974–82; St Matthew's, Rugby, 1982–90. *Publications:* The Church and Rural Development, 1968; Poverty, Revolution and the Church, 1981. *Recreations:* squash, tennis, music, ski-ing, gardening. *Address:* 10 Northumberland Road, Leamington Spa, Warwicks CV32 6HA.

PAGETT, Nicola Mary; actress, *b* 15 June 1945, *d* of Barbara Scott and H. W. F. Scott, took stage name of Pagett; *m* 1977, Graham Swannell; one *d*. *Educ:* St Maurs Convent, Yokohama; The Beehive, Bexhill; RADA. *Stage:* Voyage Round My Father, Haymarket, 1971; Ophelia in Hamlet, Greenwich, 1974; Yahoo, Queen's, 1976; Taking Steps, Lyric, 1980; The Trojan War will not take place, NT, 1983; School for Scandal, Duke of York's, 1984; Aren't We All?, Haymarket, 1984; Old Times, Haymarket, 1985; The Light of Day, Hammersmith, 1987; The Rehearsal, Garrick, 1990; Party Time, Almeida, 1991; The Rules of the Game, Almeida, 1992; What the Butler Saw, NT, 1995; *films:* Seven Men at Daybreak, 1974; Oliver's Story, 1978; Privates on Parade, 1982; *television series:* Upstairs, Downstairs, 1972; Napoleon in Love, 1974; Anna Karenina, 1977; Scoop, 1987; A Bit of a Do, 1988–90; Ain't Misbehavin, 1994–95. *Address:* c/o James Sharkey, 21 Golden Square, W1R 3AG.

PAGNAMENTA, Peter John; television producer; *b* 12 April 1941; *s* of Charles Francis Pagnamenta and Daphne Pagnamenta; *m* 1966, Sybil Healy; one *s* one *d*. *Educ:* Shrewsbury; Trinity Hall, Cambridge (MA). Joined BBC, 1965; Prodn Asst, Tonight and 24 Hours, 1965–67; Asst Editor, 24 Hours, 1967; New York office, 1968–71 (Producer, US Election coverage and Apollo flights); Editor: 24 Hours, 1971; Midweek, 1972–75; Panorama, 1975–77; Dir of News and Current Affairs, Thames Television, 1977–80; Exec. Producer, All Our Working Lives (eleven part series), BBC2, 1984; Editor, Real Lives (documentary strand), BBC 1, 1984–85; Head of Current Affairs Gp, BBC TV, 1985–87; Exec. Producer, BBC TV Documentary Dept, 1981–85, 1987–92; Executive Producer: Nippon (eight parts), BBC 2, 1990; People's Century (26 parts), BBC 1, 1995–96. *Publication:* (with Richard Overy) All Our Working Lives, 1984. *Recreations:* walking, fishing. *Address:* 96 Elgin Crescent, W11 2JL. *T:* 0171–727 9960.

PAIBA, Denis Anthony; His Honour Judge Paiba; a Circuit Judge, since 1982; *b* 10 Dec. 1926; *e s* of late Geoffrey Paiba and Geraldine Paiba; *m* 1955, Lesley Patricia Dresden; two *s. Educ:* University Coll. Sch. (Junior); Magdalen Coll. Sch., Oxford; Jesus Coll., Cambridge. 44 Royal Marine Commando, 1945–47. Financial Times, 1957–58. Called to the Bar, Gray's Inn, 1958; a Recorder of the Crown Court, 1980–82. *Recreations:* theatre, music, gardening, archery, watching rugby and cricket, wining and dining. *Address:* Roehampton, SW15; 3 Temple Gardens, Temple, EC4Y 5BG. *T:* 0171–353 3102.

PAICE, Clifford, FCIT; Member and Group Director, Economic Regulation, Civil Aviation Authority, since 1989; *b* 26 Feb. 1938; *s* of Owen Edward and Dorothy Paice; *m* 1968, Elisabeth Marlin; one *s* two *d. Educ:* Cambridgeshire High Sch.; LSE (BSc Econ.). FCIT 1990. Joined Civil Service, 1959: War Office, 1959–61; MoD, 1962–65; Min. of Econ. Affairs, 1965–68; Treasury, 1968–72; Head, Econ. Divs, CAA, 1972–89. *Address:* Civil Aviation Authority, 45–59 Kingsway, WC2B 6TE. *T:* 0171–832 5785.

PAICE, James Edward Thornton, MP (C) Cambridgeshire South East, since 1987; Parliamentary Under-Secretary of State, Department for Education and Employment (formerly Department of Employment), since 1994; *b* 24 April 1949; *s* of Edward and Winifred Paice; *m* 1973, Ava Barbara Patterson; two *s. Educ:* Framlingham College, Suffolk; Writtle Agricultural College. Farm Manager, 1970–73; farmer, 1973–79; Framlingham Management and Training Services Ltd: Training Officer, 1979–82; Training Manager, 1982–85; Gen. Manager/Exec. Dir, 1985–87; Non-Exec. Dir, 1987–89; Non-Exec. Dir, United Framlingham Farmers, 1989–94. PPS to Minister of State, 1989–91, to Minister, 1991–93, MAFF, to Sec. of State for the Envmt, 1993–94. Mem., Select Cttee on Employment, 1987–89. Chm., All Party Racing and Bloodstock Cttee, 1992–94. Gov., Writtle Agricl Coll., 1991–94. *Recreations:* shooting, windsurfing. *Address:* House of Commons, SW1A 0AA.

PAICE, Karlo Bruce; Assistant Under-Secretary of State, Home Office, 1955–66; *b* 18 August 1906; *s* of H. B. Paice, Horsham, Sussex; *m* 1st, 1935, Islay (*d* 1965), *d* of late Paymaster Comdr Duncan Cook; four *s*; 2nd, 1966, Mrs Gwen Morris (*née* Kenyon) (*d* 1991). *Educ:* Collyer's School, Horsham; Jesus Coll., Cambridge (MA). Second Clerk, Metropolitan Police Courts, 1928; Assistant Principal, Home Office, 1929; Asst Sec. to the Poisons Bd, 1933–35; Private Sec. to successive Parliamentary Under-Secretaries of State for Home Affairs, 1935–39. Principal, 1936; Assistant Secretary, 1941, serving in London Civil Defence Region, Fire Service Department, and Aliens Department. Secretary to the Prison Commission and a Prison Commissioner, 1949–55. *Recreations:* history, music. *Address:* 38 Gretton Court, Girton, Cambridge CB3 0QN. *T:* Cambridge (01223) 277442. *Clubs:* Athenæum; Hove.

PAIGE, Prof. Edward George Sydney, PhD; FRS 1983; Professor of Electrical Engineering, and Fellow of St John's College, University of Oxford, since 1977; *b* 18 July 1930; *s* of Sydney and Maude Paige; *m* 1953, Helen Gill; two *s* two *d. Educ:* Reading University (BSc, PhD). FInstP; FIEE. Junior Research Fellow to DCSO, Royal Radar Establishment, Malvern, 1955–77. *Address:* Department of Engineering Science, University of Oxford, Parks Road, Oxford OX1 3PJ. *T:* Oxford (01865) 273113.

PAIGE, Rear-Adm. Richard Collings, CB 1967; *b* 4 October 1911; *s* of Herbert Collings Paige and Harriet Pering Paige; *m* 1937, Sheila Brambles Ward, *d* of late Dr Ernest Ward, Paignton; two *s. Educ:* Blundell's School, Tiverton; RNE College, Keyham. Joined Navy, 1929. Served in HMS Neptune, Curaçao, Maori, King George V, Superb, Eagle (despatches twice); Captain, 1957; Commanding Officer, RNE College, 1960–62; Commodore Supt, HM Naval Base, Singapore, 1963–65; Admiral Supt HM Dockyard, Portsmouth, 1966–68. Rear-Adm. 1965.

PAIGE, Victor Grellier, CBE 1978; Chairman, National Health Service Management Board, and Second Permanent Secretary, Department of Health and Social Security, 1985–86; *b* 5 June 1925; *s* of Victor Paige and Alice (*née* Grellier); *m* 1948, Kathleen Winifred, 3rd *d* of Arthur and Daisy Harris; one *s* one *d. Educ:* East Ham Grammar Sch.; Univ. of Nottingham. CIPM, FCIT, CBIM, FAIM. Roosevelt Mem. Schol. 1954. Dep. Personnel Manager, Boots Pure Drug Co. Ltd, 1957–67; Controller of Personnel Services, CWS Ltd, 1967–70; Dir of Manpower and Organisation, 1970–74, Exec. Vice-Chm. (Admin), 1974–77, Nat. Freight Corp.; Dep. Chm., Nat. Freight Corp., later Nat. Freight Co., 1977–82; Dir, 1977–88 (non.-exec., 1985–88), and Dep. Chm., 1982–85, Nat. Freight Consortium; Chm., Iveco (UK), 1984–85. Chm., PLA, 1980–85; Member: Manpower Services Commn, 1974–80; Thames Water Authy, 1983–85. Member: Notts Educn Cttee, 1957–63; Secondary Schs Examn Council, 1960–63; UK Adv. Council for Educn in Management, 1962–65; Careers Adv. Bd, Univ. of Nottingham, 1975–81; Chairman: Regional Adv. Council for Further Educn, E Mids, 1967; Exec. Council, British Assoc. for Commercial and Industrial Educn, 1974 (Vice-Pres. 1980); Pres., Inst. of Admin. Management, 1984–90; Vice-Pres., Chartered Inst. of Transport, 1984–85 (Mem. Council, 1976–79); Mem. Council, CBI, 1983–85 (Chm., Educn and Trng Cttee, 1983–85). Mem. Court, Henley, The Management College, 1985–94. Governor, British Liver Foundn, 1990–. Vice-Pres., London Fedn of Boys' Clubs. Freeman, Co. of Watermen and Lightermen of the River Thames; Freeman, City of London, 1981. Commander, Order of Orange Nassau, The Netherlands, 1982. *Publications:* contrib. techn. press on management. *Recreations:* reading, sport generally, athletics in particular (Pres. Notts Athletic Club, 1962–67). *Address:* Queen's Wood, Frithsden, Berkhamsted, Herts HP4 1NW. *T:* Berkhamsted (01442) 865030. *Clubs:* Royal Automobile, MCC.

PAIN, Barry Newton, CBE 1979; QPM 1976; Commandant, Police Staff College, Bramshill, and HM Inspector of Constabulary, 1982–87, retired; *b* 25 Feb. 1931; *s* of Godfrey William Pain and Annie Newton; *m* 1952, Marguerite Agnes King; one *s* one *d. Educ:* Waverley Grammar Sch., Birmingham. Clerk to Prosecuting Solicitor, Birmingham, 1947–51; 2nd Lieut (Actg Captain) RASC, Kenya, 1949–51. Birmingham City Police, 1951–68; Staff Officer to HM Inspector of Constabulary, Birmingham, 1966–68; Asst Chief Constable, Staffordshire and Stoke-on-Trent Constabulary, 1968–74; Chief Constable of Kent, 1974–82; JSSC 1970. Adviser to Turkish Govt on Reorganization of Police, 1972. Pres., Assoc. of Chief Police Officers, 1981–82. *Recreations:* golf, shooting, boating.

PAIN, Gillian Margaret; Chief Reporter, Scottish Office Inquiry Reporters Unit, since 1993; *b* 29 May 1936; *d* of late Geoffrey Ernest Pain and Florence Agnes Pain (*née* Marshall). *Educ:* Felixstowe Coll., Suffolk; Univ. of St Andrews (MA 1957); University Coll. London (DipTP 1965). MRTPI. Asst Teacher of Geography, Northfield Sch., Watford, 1957–58; Photogrammetrist, Hunting Aero Surveys, 1958–60; Asst Map Res. Officer, Directorate of Mil. Surveys, 1960–62; posts with Essex Co. Planning Dept, 1962–73, Asst Chief County Planning Adviser, 1970–73; Department of the Environment: Sen. Housing and Planning Inspector, 1973–77; Principal Planning Inspector, 1977–86; Asst Chief Planning Inspector, 1986–93. Pres., Town and Country Planning Summer Sch., 1992–94. *Publication:* Planning and the Shopkeeper, 1967. *Recreations:* sailing, skiing, classical music. *Address:* Scottish Inquiry Reporters Unit, Room 406, 2 Greenside Lane, Edinburgh EH1 3AG. *T:* 0131–244 5643. *Club:* Blackwater Sailing (Past Commodore) (Essex).

PAIN, Lt-Gen. Sir (Horace) Rollo (Squarey), KCB 1975 (CB 1974); MC 1945; late 4th/7th Royal Dragoon Guards; Head of British Defence Staff, Washington, 1975–78, retired; *b* 11 May 1921; *s* of late Horace Davy Pain, Levenside, Haverthwaite, Ulverston, and late Audrey Pain (*née* Hampson); *m* 1950, Denys Sophia (*née* Chaine-Nickson); one *s* two *d.* Commissioned into Reconnaissance Corps during War of 1939–45: served NW Europe (MC). After War, served for two years in E Africa and Brit. Somaliland before joining 4th/7th Royal Dragoon Gds in Palestine, 1947; attended Staff Coll., Camberley, 1951; subseq. served in Mil. Ops Directorate, in War Office; served with his Regt in BAOR, 1955–56; Mem. Directing Staff, Staff Coll., Camberley, 1957; GSO1, Brit. Army Staff, Washington, DC, 1960; commanded his Regt in BAOR, 1962; commanded one of the three divs, Staff Coll., Camberley, 1964; commanded 5 Inf. Bde in Borneo, 1965; IDC, 1968; ADC to the Queen, 1969; BGS, HQ, BAOR, 1969–70; GOC 2nd Div., 1970–72; Dir of Army Training, MoD, 1972–75; Col Comdt, Mil. Provost Staff Corps, 1974–83; Col. 4th/7th Royal Dragoon Guards, 1979–83. *Address:* Eddlethorpe Hall, Malton, North Yorkshire YO17 9QS. *T:* Malton (01653) 658218. *Club:* Cavalry and Guards.

PAIN, Hon. Sir Peter (Richard), Kt 1975; a Judge of the High Court of Justice, Queen's Bench Division, 1975–88; *b* 6 Sept. 1913; *s* of Arthur Richard Pain and Elizabeth Irene Pain (*née* Benn); *m* 1941, Barbara Florence Maude Riggs; two *s. Educ:* Westminster; Christ Church, Oxford. Called to the Bar, Lincoln's Inn, 1936, Bencher 1972. QC 1965. Chairman: Race Relations Board Conciliation Cttee for Greater London, 1968–71; South Metropolitan Conciliation Cttee, 1971–73; Mem., Parole Bd, 1978–80. Pres., Holiday Fellowship, 1977–83. *Publications:* Manual of Fire Service Law, 1951; The Law Relating to the Motor Trade (with K. C. Johnson-Davies), 1955. *Recreations:* forestry, cricket, mountain walking. *Address:* Loen, St Catherine's Road, Frimley, Surrey GU16 5NJ. *T:* Deepcut (01252) 835639.

PAIN, Sir Rollo; *see* Pain, Sir H. R. S.

PAINE, Sir Christopher Hammon, Kt 1995; DM; FRCP, FRCR; Consultant in Radiotherapy and Oncology, Churchill Hospital, Oxford, since 1970; *b* 28 Aug. 1935; *s* of late Major John Hammon Paine and Joan Frances Shedden; *m* 1959, Susan Martin; two *s* two *d. Educ:* Eton Coll.; Merton Coll., Oxford (BM, BCh 1961; DM 1981); St Bartholomew's Hosp. Med. Sch. FRCP 1976; FRCR (FFR 1969). Junior med. posts, Oxford, London, Paris, 1962–70; Oxford University: Lectr in Radiotherapy and Oncology, 1972–; Dir of Clinical Studies (clinical dean), 1982–85; Dist Gen. Manager, Oxfordshire HA, 1984–88; Chm., Oxford Med. Staff Council, 1991–92. Pres., British Oncological Assoc., 1989–91; Royal College of Radiologists: Dean, Faculty of Clinical Oncology, 1990–92; Vice-Pres., 1991–92; Pres., 1992–95. *Publications:* papers on interstitial and other aspects of radiation therapy. *Recreation:* gardening. *Address:* Kings Farm, Withypool, near Minehead, Somerset TA24 7RE. *T:* Minehead (01643) 831381. *Clubs:* Athenæum, Farmers'.

PAINE, Peter Stanley, CBE 1981; DFC 1944; Chairman, Oracle Teletext Ltd, 1984–93; *b* 19 June 1921; *s* of Arthur Bertram Paine and Dorothy Helen Paine; *m* 1942, Sheila Mary (*d* 1994), *d* of Frederick Wigglesworth, MA; two *s* two *d. Educ:* King's Sch., Canterbury. Served 1940–46, 2 Gp RAF (Flt-Lt). Worked in Punch Publishing Office, 1945–47; Sales Promotion Man., Newnes Pearson, 1948–52, Odhams Press, then Sales Dir and Dir of Tyne Tees Television, 1958–67; Sales Dir and Dir of Yorkshire Television, 1967–74; Managing Director: Tyne Tees Television, 1974–83; Tyne Tees Television Holdings, 1981–84. Director: Trident Television, 1970–81; Independent Television News Ltd, 1982–83; Independent Television Publications Ltd, 1977–83; Broadcasters Audience Res. Bd, 1980–86; Member: Council, Independent Television Companies Assoc., 1974–83 (4 yrs Chm. Marketing Cttee); Cable Authority, 1984–90. *Recreations:* golf, fishing, theatre, music, reading. *Address:* Briarfield, Ashwood Road, Woking, Surrey GU22 7JW. *T:* Woking (01483) 773183. *Club:* Worplesdon Golf.

PAINE, Roger Edward; management consultant; Chief Executive, Cardiff City Council, 1988–94; *b* 20 Oct. 1943; *s* of Ethel May Jones and Edward Paine. *Educ:* Stockport Sch.; Univ. of Wales (BA Hons); Univ. of Manchester (part time; Dip TP); Univ. of Birmingham (MSocSci). Town Planner: Lancs CC, 1964–66; Stockport CB, 1966–68; Lancs CC, 1968–70; Salford City, 1970; Stockport Borough: Corporate Planner, 1971–73; Head of Corporate Planning, 1973–75; Co-ordinator of Central Units, 1975–77; Dep. Chief Exec., Camden, 1977–80; Chief Exec., Wrekin Council, 1980–88. Pres., Solace, 1992–93. Hon. Fellow, Inst. of Local Govt Studies, Birmingham. *Recreations:* music, travel, sport. *Address:* Miravalle, Ballingham Road, Hoarwithy, Hereford HR2 6QG.

PAINTAL, Prof. Autar Singh, Padma Vibhushan 1986; MD, PhD, DSc; FRS 1981; FRSE; Director-General, Indian Council for Medical Research, New Delhi, 1986–91; *b* 24 Sept. 1925; *s* of Dr Man Singh and Rajwans Kaur; *m* 1st; one *s* two *d*; 2nd, 1988, Ashima Anand. *Educ:* SSBS Khalsa High Sch., Lahore; Forman Christian Coll., Lahore; Lucknow Univ. (MB, BS, MD); Edinburgh Univ. (PhD, DSc). Lectr in Physiol., King George's Med. Coll., Lucknow Univ., 1949; Rockefeller Fellow, 1950; Lectr in Physiol., Edinburgh Univ., 1951; Control Officer, Technical Develt Estabt Labs, Min. of Defence, Kanpur, 1952–54; Prof. of Physiology, All-India Inst. of Med. Sciences, New Delhi, 1958–64; Prof. of Physiology and Dir, Vallabhbhai Patel Chest Inst., Delhi Univ., 1964–90 (Asst Dir, 1954–56); Dean, Faculty of Med. Sciences, Delhi Univ., 1966–77. Associate Prof., Albert Einstein Coll. of Medicine, New York, 1956; Vis. Associate Prof. of Physiol., Univ. of Utah, 1957; Commonwealth Vis. Prof., St Bartholomew's Hosp. Med. Sch., London, 1966. FRSE 1966; Fellow: Indian Acad. of Med. Sciences, 1966; Indian National Science Acad., 1971 (Vice Pres., 1981–83; Pres., 1987–88); President: Nat. Coll. of Chest Physicians, 1981–86; Indian Sci. Congress, 1984–85; Member: Physiol Soc., UK, 1953 (Hon. Mem., 1988); Ergonomics Res. Soc., UK, 1954; Foreign Mem., USSR Acad. of Scis, 1988; Hon. Mem., Amer. Physiol. Soc., 1990. B. C. Roy Orator, New Delhi, 1973; Sharpey-Schafer Lectr, Univ. of Edin., 1981; Dr Zakir Husain Meml Lectr, Jawaharlal Nehru Univ., 1984. Hon. FRCP, 1987. Hon. DSc: Benares Hindu Univ., 1982; Delhi Univ., 1984; Aligarh Muslim Univ., 1986; N Bengal Univ., 1990. Basanti Devi Amir Chand Prize, 1967; Silver Jubilee Res. Award, 1978; Barclay Medal, Asiatic Soc., 1982; R. D. Birla Award, 1982; Nehru Sci. Award, 1983; Maharishi Dayanand Centenary Gold Medal, 1983; Acharya J. C. Bose Medal, 1985; C. V. Raman Medal, 1994; Ashutosh Mukherjee Medal, 1994. *Publications:* (ed) Morphology and Mechanisms of Chemoreceptors, 1976; (ed) Respiratory Adaptations, Capillary Exchange and Reflex Mechanisms, 1977; papers in Jl of Physiol. and in other physiol jls. *Recreations:* swimming, rowing, bird watching. *Address:* DST Centre for Visceral Mechanisms, Vallabhbhai Patel

Chest Institute, Delhi University, PO Box 2101, Delhi 110007, India. *T:* Delhi (11) 7257749 and (11) 7257856. *Club:* Roshanara (Delhi).

PAINTER, George Duncan, OBE 1974; biographer and incunabulist; Assistant Keeper in charge of fifteenth-century printed books, British Museum, 1954–74; *b* Birmingham, 5 June 1914; *s* of George Charles Painter and Minnie Rosendale (*née* Taylor); *m* 1942, Isabel Joan, *d* of Samuel Morley Britton, Bristol; two *d. Educ:* King Edward's Sch., Birmingham; Trinity Coll., Cambridge (Schol.). Bell Exhibr; John Stewart of Rannoch Schol.; Porson Schol.; Waddington Schol.; 1st cl. hons Class. Tripos pts I and II; Craven Student; 2nd Chancellor's Class. Medallist, 1936; MA Cantab 1945. Asst Lectr in Latin, Univ. of Liverpool, 1937; joined staff of Dept of Printed Books, BM, 1938. FRSL 1965. Hon. DLitt Edinburgh, 1979. *Publications:* André Gide, A Critical Biography, 1951, rev. edn 1968; The Road to Sinodun, Poems, 1951; André Gide, Marshlands and Prometheus Misbound (trans.), 1953; Marcel Proust, Letters to his Mother (trans.), 1956; Marcel Proust, A Biography, vol. 1, 1959, vol. 2, 1965 (Duff Cooper Memorial Prize), rev. and enl. edn in 1 vol., 1989; The Vinland Map and the Tartar Relation (with R. A. Skelton and T. E. Marston), 1965; André Maurois, The Chelsea Way (trans.), 1966; William Caxton, a Quincentenary Biography, 1976; Chateaubriand, A Biography, vol. 1, The Longed-for Tempests, 1977 (James Tait Black Meml Prize); Studies in Fifteenth-Century Printing, 1984; articles on fifteenth-century printing in The Library, Book Collector, Gutenberg-Jahrbuch. *Recreations:* family life, gardening, music. *Address:* 10 Mansfield Road, Hove, East Sussex BN3 5NN. *T:* Brighton (01273) 416008.

PAINTER, Terence James, CB 1990; a Deputy Chairman and Director General, Board of Inland Revenue, 1986–93; *b* 28 Nov. 1935; *s* of late Edward Lawrence Painter and Ethel Violet (*née* Butler); *m* 1959, Margaret Janet Blackburn; two *s* two *d. Educ:* City of Norwich Sch.; Downing Coll., Cambridge (BA (History)). Nat. Service Commn, Royal Norfolk Regt, 1958–59. Entered Inland Revenue as Asst Principal, 1959; Principal, 1962; seconded to Civil Service Selection Bd, 1967–68; Asst Sec., 1969; seconded to HM Treasury, 1973–75; Under-Sec., 1975–86. *Recreations:* music, books, walking. *Club:* Reform.

PAISLEY, Bishop of (RC), since 1988; **Rt. Rev. John Aloysius Mone;** Auxiliary Bishop of Glasgow, 1984–88; *b* 22 June 1929; *s* of Arthur Mone and Elizabeth Mone (*née* Dunn). *Educ:* Holyrood Secondary School, Glasgow; Séminaire Saint Sulpice, Paris; Institut Catholique, Paris (Faculty of Social Studies). Ordained Priest, Glasgow, 1952; Assistant Priest: St Ninian's, Knightswood, Glasgow, also hosp. and sch. chaplain, 1952–74; Our Lady and St George's, Glasgow, 1975–79; Parish Priest, St Joseph's, Tollcross, Glasgow, 1979–84. Episcopal Vicar, Marriage, 1981–83; Dir, Ministry to Priests Prog., 1982–84. Scottish National Chaplain, Girl Guides, 1971–; Chm., Scottish Catholic Internat. Aid Fund, 1974–75, Pres./Treas., 1985–; Chm., Scottish Catholic Marriage Advisory Council, 1982–84; Pres., Scottish Justice and Peace Commn, 1987–. *Recreations:* watching soccer (attending if possible), playing golf (when time!), playing the piano. *Address:* Bishop's House, 107 Corsebar Road, Paisley, Renfrewshire PA2 9PY. *T:* 0141–889 7200.

PAISLEY, Rev. Ian Richard Kyle; MP (Democratic Unionist) North Antrim, since 1974 (ProtU 1970–74) (resigned seat Dec. 1985 in protest against Anglo-Irish Agreement; re-elected Jan. 1986); Member (DemU) Northern Ireland, European Parliament, since 1979; Minister, Martyrs Memorial Free Presbyterian Church, Belfast, since 1946; *b* 6 April 1926; 2nd *s* of late Rev. J. Kyle Paisley and Mrs Isabella Paisley; *m* 1956, Eileen Emily Cassells; two *s* three *d* (incl. twin *s*). *Educ:* Ballymena Model Sch.; Ballymena Techn. High Sch.; S Wales Bible Coll.; Reformed Presbyterian Theol. Coll., Belfast. Ordained, 1946. Moderator, Free Presbyterian Church of Ulster, 1951; Pres., Whitefield Coll. of the Bible, 1979–. Commenced publishing The Protestant Telegraph, 1966. Contested (Prot U) Bannside, NI Parlt, 1969; MP (Prot U), Bannside, Co. Antrim, NI Parlt, 1970–72; Leader of Opposition, 1972; Chm., Public Accounts Cttee, 1972. Co-Founder, Democratic Unionist Party, NI, 1972. Mem. (Democratic Unionist), N Antrim, NI Assembly, 1973–75; Mem. (UUUC), N Antrim, NI Constitutional Convention, 1975–76; Mem. (DemU) N Antrim, NI Assembly, 1982–86. Hon. DD Bob Jones Univ., SC. FRGS. Mem., Internat. Cultural Soc., Korea, 1977. *Publications:* History of the 1859 Revival, 1959; Christian Foundations, 1960; Ravenhill Pulpit, Vol. 1, 1966, Vol. 2, 1967; Exposition of the Epistle to the Romans, 1968; Billy Graham and the Church of Rome, 1970; The Massacre of St Bartholomew, 1972; America's Debt to Ulster, 1976; (jtly) Ulster—the facts, 1981; No Pope Here, 1982; Dr Kidd, 1982; Those Flaming Tennents, 1983; Mr Protestant, 1985; Be Sure, 1986; Paisley's Pocket Preacher, 1987, vol. II, 1988, vol. III, 1989, vol. IV, 1990; Jonathan Edwards: the theologian of revival, 1987; Union with Rome, 1989; The Soul of the Question, 1990; The Revised English Bible: an exposure, 1990; What a Friend We Have in Jesus, 1994; Understanding Events in Northern Ireland: an introduction for Americans, 1995. *Address:* House of Commons, SW1A 0AA; The Parsonage, 17 Cyprus Avenue, Belfast BT5 5NT.

PAISLEY, Robert, OBE 1977; Life Vice-President, Liverpool Football Club, 1992 (Manager, 1974–83; Board Member, 1983–92; Team Consultant, 1985–87); *b* 23 Jan. 1919; *s* of Samuel and Emily Paisley; *m* 1946, Jessie Chandler; two *s* one *d. Educ:* Eppleton Sen. Mixed Sch., Tyne and Wear. Apprentice bricklayer, 1934; also Hetton Juniors Amateur FC, 1934–37; Bishop Auckland Amateur FC, 1937–39; signed as professional for Liverpool FC, 1939; Army Service, RA, 1939–46; Liverpool FC: 2nd Team Trainer, 1954–59; 1st Team Trainer, 1959–70; Asst Manager, 1970–74. Successes as manager: UEFA Cup, 1976; League Championship, 1976, 1977, 1979, 1980, 1982, 1983; European Cup, 1977, 1978, 1981; League Cup (later known as Milk Cup, then Littlewoods Cup), 1981, 1982, 1983. Manager of the Year Award, 1976, 1977, 1979, 1980, 1982, 1983; Special Merit Award, PFA Award, 1983. Hon. Fellow, Liverpool Polytechnic, 1988. Hon. MSc Liverpool, 1983. Freeman, City of Liverpool, 1983. *Publications:* Bob Paisley's Liverpool Scrap Book, 1979; Bob Paisley: an autobiography, 1983; Bob Paisley's Assessment of the 1986–1987 Liverpool Team, 1987; Fifty Golden Reds, 1990. *Recreations:* all types of sport.

PAJARES, Ramón; Managing Director, Savoy Group of Hotels and Restaurants, since 1994; *b* 6 July 1935; *s* of Juan Antonio Pajares García and Rosario Salazar; *m* 1963, Jean Kathleen Porter; one *s* two *d. Educ:* Madrid Inst. of Hotel and Tourism Studies. Nat. Service, Spanish Navy, 1955–57. Hotel posts: Ritz, Barcelona, 1954–55; San Jorge, Playa de Aro, 1957; Pargue, Llavaneras, 1957–59; Mansion, Eastbourne, 1959–61; Kleiner Reisen, Koblenz, Germany, 1961; Feldbergerhof, Feldberg, 1961–62; Le Vieux Manoir, Morat, Switzerland, 1962; Reina Isabel, Canary Is, 1963–69; Food and Beverage Dir, Inn on the Park, London, 1969–71; Gen. Manager, San Antonio, Lanzarote, Canary Is, 1972–74; Gen. Manager and Vice-Pres., Inn on the Park, later Four Seasons, 1975–94. Member: Assoc. Culinaire Française, 1971; Cookery and Food Assoc., 1973; Leading Hotels of the World Exec. Cttee for UK and Ireland, 1994–. FHCIMA 1982. Freeman, City of London, 1988. Hotelier of Year Award, Brit. Hotel and Catering Ind., 1984; Personalité de l'année for Hotel Ind., 1986. Medals: Mérito Civil (Spain), 1984; Oficial de la Orden de Isabel la Católica (Spain), 1989. *Recreation:* classical music. *Address:* 1 Savoy Hill, WC2R 0BP. *T:* 0171–836 1533. *Clubs:* Annabel's, Les Ambassadeurs.

PAKENHAM, family name of **Earl of Longford.**

PAKENHAM, Elizabeth; *see* Longford, Countess of.

PAKENHAM, Henry Desmond Verner, CBE 1964; HM Diplomatic Service, retired; *b* 5 Nov. 1911; *s* of Hamilton Richard Pakenham and Emilie Willis Stringer; *m* 1st, 1946, Crystal Elizabeth Brooksbank (marr. diss., 1960); one *s* one *d* (and one *s* decd); 2nd, 1963, Venetia Maude; one *s* one *d. Educ:* Monkton Combe; St John Baptist College, Oxford. Taught modern languages at Sevenoaks School, 1933–40. Served in HM Forces, 1940–45. Entered Foreign Service, 1946; served in Madrid, Djakarta, Havana, Singapore, Tel Aviv, Buenos Aires and Sydney; retired 1971. Chm., Suffolk Preservation Soc., 1979–82. Asst Editor, Satow's Guide to Diplomatic Practice, 5th edn, 1979. *Address:* Rose Farm, Brettenham, Suffolk IP7 7QP.

PAKENHAM, Hon. Michael Aidan, CMG 1993; HM Diplomatic Service; Minister, Paris, since 1994; *b* 3 Nov. 1943; *s* of 7th Earl of Longford, *qv* and Countess of Longford, *qv*; *m* 1980, Meta (Mimi) Landreth Doak, *d* of William Conway Doak of Maryland, USA; two *d* two step *d. Educ:* Ampleforth College; Trinity College, Cambridge (MA Classics); Rice University, Texas. Washington Post, 1965; Foreign Office, 1965; Nairobi, 1966; Warsaw, 1967; FCO, 1970; Asst Private Sec., later Private Sec. to Chancellor of Duchy of Lancaster (European Community Affairs), on secondment to Cabinet Office, 1971–74; Geneva (CSCE), 1974; New Delhi, 1974; Washington, 1978; Head of Arms Control and Disarmament Dept, FCO, 1983–87; Counsellor (External Relations), UK Perm. Rep. to EC, Brussels, 1987–91; Ambassador and Consul-Gen., Luxembourg, 1991–94. *Recreations:* tennis, golf, reading history, museums. *Address:* c/o Foreign and Commonwealth Office, SW1A 2AH. *Clubs:* Garrick, MCC; St Nom-la-Breteche Golf.

PAKENHAM, Thomas (Frank Dermot); writer; *b* 14 Aug. 1933; *e s* of 7th Earl of Longford, *qv* and of Countess of Longford, *qv*; (does not use courtesy title); *m* 1964, Valerie, *d* of Major R. G. McNair Scott; two *s* two *d. Educ:* Dragon School, Oxford; Belvedere Coll., Dublin; Ampleforth Coll., York; Magdalen Coll., Oxford (BA Greats 1955). Travelled, Near East and Ethiopia, 1955–56 (discovered unrecorded medieval Ethiopian church at Bethlehem, Begemdir, 1956). Free-lance writing, 1956–58. Editorial staff: Times Educational Supplement, 1958–60; Sunday Telegraph, 1961; The Observer, 1961–64. Founder Mem. 1958, and Member Cttee 1958–64, Victorian Soc.; Founder Mem., and Mem. Cttee 1968–72, Historic Irish Tourist Houses and Gardens Assoc. (HITHA); Treas., British-Irish Assoc., 1972–; Sec. (co-founder), Christopher Ewart-Biggs Memorial Trust, 1976–; Founder and Chm., Irish Tree Soc., 1990–. Chm., Ladbroke Assoc., 1988–. Sen. Associate Mem., St Antony's Coll., Oxford, 1979–81. *Publications:* The Mountains of Rasselas: an Ethiopian adventure, 1959; The Year of Liberty: the story of the Great Irish Rebellion of 1798, 1969; The Boer War, 1979 (Cheltenham Prize, 1980); (selected and introd with Valerie Pakenham) Dublin: a travellers' companion, 1988; The Scramble for Africa, 1991 (W. H. Smith Prize, 1992). *Recreation:* water. *Address:* 111 Elgin Crescent, W11 2JF. *T:* 0171–727 7624; Tullynally, Castlepollard, Westmeath, Ireland. *T:* Mullingar (044) 61159. *Clubs:* Beefsteak; Stephen's Green (Dublin).

PAKENHAM-WALSH, John, CB 1986; Standing Counsel to General Synod of the Church of England, since 1988; *b* 7 Aug. 1928; *s* of late Rev. W. P. Pakenham-Walsh, formerly ICS, and Guendolen (*née* Elliott); *m* 1951, Deryn, *er d* of late Group Captain R. E. G. Fulljames, MC, and Mrs Muriel Fulljames; one *s* four *d. Educ:* Bradfield Coll.; University Coll., Oxford (MA). Called to the Bar, Lincoln's Inn, 1951. Crown Counsel, Hong Kong, 1953–57; Parly Counsel, Fedn of Nigeria, 1958–61; joined Legal Adviser's Br., Home Office, 1961; Under Sec. (Legal), Home Office, 1980–87. Hon. QC 1992. *Address:* Crinken, Weydown Road, Haslemere, Surrey GU27 1DS. *T:* Haslemere (01428) 642033.

PAKINGTON, family name of **Baron Hampton.**

PALADE, Prof. George Emil; scientist, USA; Professor, Division of Cellular and Molecular Medicine and Dean for Scientific Affairs, School of Medicine, University of California at San Diego, since 1990; *b* Iassy, Romania, 19 Nov. 1912; *s* of Emil Palade and Constanta Cantemir; *m* 1st, 1941, Irina Malaxa (decd); one *s* one *d*; 2nd, 1970, Dr Marilyn Farquhar. *Educ:* Liceul Al. Hasdeu, Buzau, Romania; Med. Sch., Univ. of Bucharest (MD). Arrived in US, 1946; naturalized US citizen, 1952. Instructor, Asst Prof., then Lectr in Anatomy, Sch. of Med., Univ. of Bucharest, 1940–45; Visiting Investigator, Rockefeller Inst. for Med. Research, 1946–48; continuing as an Assistant (later the Inst. became Rockefeller Univ., NYC); promoted to Associate, 1951, and Associate Mem., 1953; Prof. of Cell Biology, Rockefeller Univ. and full Member of Rockefeller Inst., 1956; Prof. of Cell Biology, Yale Univ. Med. Sch., 1973; Sen. Res. Scientist, Yale Univ., 1983–90. Fellow, Amer. Acad. of Arts and Sciences; Member: Nat. Acad. of Sciences; Pontifical Acad. of Sciences; Leopoldina Acad.; Romanian Acad.; For. Mem., Royal Soc., 1984. Awards include: Albert Lasker Basic Research, 1966; Gairdner Award, 1967; Hurwitz Prize, 1970; Nobel Prize for Medicine, 1974; Nat. Medal of Science, USA, 1986. *Publications:* Editor: Annual Review of Cell Biology; Jl of Cell Biology (co-founder); Jl of Membrane Biology; numerous contribs med. and sci. jls on structure, biochemistry and function of sub-cellular components. *Address:* School of Medicine, University of California, San Diego, La Jolla, CA 92093–0602, USA. *T:* (619) 5347708, *Fax:* (619) 5346573.

PALETHORPE-TODD, Richard Andrew; *see* Todd, Richard.

PALETTE, John, OBE 1986; Director of Personnel, British Rail, 1982–86; *b* 19 May 1928; *s* of Arthur and Beatrice Palette; *m* 1950, Pamela Mabel Palmer; three *s. Educ:* Alexandra Sch., Hampstead. MCIT. Gen. Railway Admin, 1942–69; Divl Manager, Bristol, 1969–72; Asst Gen. Manager, Western Region, 1972–74; Divl Manager, Manchester, 1974–76; Gen. Manager, Scottish Region, 1976–77, Southern Region, 1977–82, British Railways. Chm., British Transport Ship Management (Scotland) Ltd, 1976. *Recreations:* walking, reading, gardening, watching sport. *Address:* 90 Wargrave Road, Twyford, Reading, Berks RG10 9PJ. *T:* Twyford (Berks) (01734) 340965.

PALIN, Michael Edward; writer and actor; *b* 5 May 1943; *s* of late Edward and Mary Palin; *m* 1966, Helen M. Gibbins; two *s* one *d. Educ:* Birkdale Sch., Sheffield; Shrewsbury; Brasenose Coll., Oxford (BA 2nd Cl. Hons Mod. Hist.). Pres., Transport 2000. Actor and writer: Monty Python's Flying Circus, BBC TV, 1969–74; Ripping Yarns, BBC TV, 1976–80; actor: Three Men in a Boat, BBC, 1975; GBH, Channel 4, 1991; writer: East of Ipswich, BBC TV, 1987; Number 27, BBC1, 1988; *stage play:* The Weekend, Strand, 1994. *Films:* actor and jt author: And Now for Something Completely different, 1970; Monty Python and the Holy Grail, 1974; Monty Python's Life of Brian, 1978; Time Bandits, 1980; Monty Python's "The Meaning of Life," 1982; American Friends, 1991; actor, writer and co-producer: The Missionary, 1982; actor: Jabberwocky, 1976; A Private Function, 1984; Brazil, 1985; A Fish Called Wanda, 1988 (Best Supporting Film Actor, BAFTA Award, 1988). Contributor, Great Railway Journeys of the World, BBC TV, 1980; retraced Phileas Fogg's journey for Around the World in Eighty Days, BBC TV, 1989; travelled from North to South Pole for Pole to Pole, BBC TV, 1992. *Publications:* Monty Python's Big Red Book, 1970; Monty Python's Brand New Bok, 1973; Dr Fegg's Encyclopaedia of *All* World Knowledge, 1984; Limericks, 1985; Around the World in

Eighty Days, 1989; Pole to Pole, 1992 (Travel Writer of the Year, British Book Awards, 1993); Pole to Pole: the photographs, 1994; Hemingway's Chair (novel), 1995; *for children:* Small Harry and the Toothache Pills, 1981; The Mirrorstone, 1986; The Cyril Stories, 1986. *Recreations:* reading, running, railways—preferably all three in a foreign country. *Address:* 68A Delancey Street, NW1 7RY.

PALIN, Air Chief Marshal Sir Roger Hewlett, KCB 1989; OBE 1978; Controller, Royal Air Force Benevolent Fund, since 1993; *b* 8 July 1938; *m* 1967, Kathryn Elizabeth Pye; two *d. Educ:* Canford Sch.; St John's Coll., Cambridge (BA 1967; MA 1979); psc. FRAes; FIPD. Commnd KRRC, 1958; served 3 Para. Bn, 1958–59, 10 Para. Bn (TA), 1959–62; Flight Lieut, 1964; Sqn Leader, 1970; Wing Comdr, 1975; Group Captain, 1980; ADC to the Queen, 1981–82; Air Cdre, 1984; Dir of Defence Progs, MoD, 1984–85; Air Vice-Marshal, 1986; ACDS (Progs), 1986–87; AOC No 11 Gp, 1987–89; Air Marshal, 1989; C-in-C, RAF Germany and Comdr Second Allied Tactical Air Force, 1989–91; Air Chief Marshal, 1991; Air Mem. for Personnel, 1991–93; Air ADC to the Queen, 1991–93; retired 1993. Guest Schol., Woodrow Wilson Internat. Center for Scholars, Washington, 1980; Res. Associate, IISS, 1993. *Recreations:* sport, travel, international relations, defence studies. *Address:* (office) 67 Portland Place, W1N 4AR.

PALING, Helen Elizabeth, (Mrs W. J. S. Kershaw); Her Honour Judge Paling; a Circuit Judge, since 1985; *b* 25 April 1933; *o d* of A. Dale Paling and Mabel Eleanor Thomas; *m* 1961, William John Stanley Kershaw, PhD; one *s* three *d. Educ:* Prince Henry's Grammar Sch., Otley; London Sch. of Economics. LLB London 1954. Called to Bar, Lincoln's Inn, 1955; a Recorder, 1972–85. *Address:* Quayside Law Courts, Newcastle upon Tyne NE1 2LA. *T:* 0191–201 2000.

PALLEY, Dr Claire Dorothea Taylor; Principal of St Anne's College, Oxford, 1984–91, Hon. Fellow, 1992; *b* 17 Feb. 1931; *d* of Arthur Aubrey Swait, Durban; *m* 1952, Ahrn Palley (marr. diss. 1985; he *d* 1993); five *s. Educ:* Durban Girls' Coll.; Univs of Cape Town and London. BA 1950, LLB 1952, Cape Town; PhD London 1965; MA Oxon 1984. Called to Bar, Middle Temple; Advocate, S Africa and Rhodesia. Lecturer: UC Rhodesia and Nyasaland, 1960–65; QUB, 1966–67; Reader, QUB, 1967–70, Prof. of Public Law, 1970–73, and Dean of Faculty of Law, 1971–73; Prof. of Law, 1973–84, and Master of Darwin Coll., 1974–82, Univ. of Kent. Hamlyn Lectr, Reading, 1990. Constitutional Advr, Republic of Cyprus, 1980–94. Member: Council, Minority Rights Group, 1975–94; UN Sub-Commn on Prevention of Discrimination and Protection of Minorities, 1988–; Lord Chancellor's Adv. Cttee on Legal Educn and Conduct, 1991–94. Constitutional Advr to African Nat. Council at Const. Talks on Rhodesia, 1976. Hon. LLD QUB, 1991. *Publications:* The Constitutional History and Law of Southern Rhodesia, 1966; The United Kingdom and Human Rights, 1991; contrib. learned jls. *Address:* Pachna, 4700 Limassol, Cyprus.

PALLISER, Rt. Hon. Sir (Arthur) Michael, GCMG 1977 (KCMG 1973; CMG 1966); PC 1983; HM Diplomatic Service, retired; Chairman, Major Projects Association, since 1994; *b* 9 April 1922; *s* of late Admiral Sir Arthur Palliser, KCB, DSC, and Lady Palliser (*née* Margaret Eva King-Salter); *m* 1948, Marie Marguerite, *d* of late Paul-Henri Spaak; three *s. Educ:* Wellington Coll.; Merton Coll., Oxford (Hon. Fellow 1987). Served with Coldstream Guards, 1942–47; Capt. 1944. Entered HM Diplomatic Service, 1947; SE Asia Dept, Foreign Office, 1947–49; Athens, 1949–51; Second Sec., 1950; Foreign Office: German Finance Dept, 1951–52; Central Dept, 1952–54; Private Sec. to Perm. Under-Sec., 1954–56; First Sec., 1955; Paris, 1956–60; Head of Chancery, Dakar, 1960–62 (Chargé d'Affaires in 1960, 1961 and 1962); Counsellor, and seconded to Imperial Defence College, 1963; Head of Planning Staff, Foreign Office, 1964; a Private Sec. to PM, 1966; Minister, Paris, 1969; Ambassador and Head of UK Deleg. to European Communities, Brussels, 1971; Ambassador and UK Permanent Representative to European Communities, 1973–75; Permanent Under-Sec. of State, FCO and Head of Diplomatic Service, 1975–82. Chm., Samuel Montagu & Co., 1984–85, 1986–93 (Dir, 1983–; Vice Chm., 1984, 1993–95); Deputy Chairman: Midland Montagu (Hldgs), 1987–93; Midland Bank, 1987–91. Director, 1983–92: BAT Industries plc; Booker plc; Eagle Star Hldgs; Shell Transport & Trading Co. plc; Director: United Biscuits (Hldgs), 1983–89; Arbor Acres Farm Inc., 1985–91; UK–Japan 2000 Gp, 1987–; XCL Ltd, 1994–. Dep. Chm., BI (formerly BIEC), 1987–95. Pres., China-Britain Trade Gp, 1992–96; Member: Council, IISS, 1982–91 (Chm., 1983–90); Trilateral Commn, 1982–96; Security Commn, 1983–92; Council, British N American Cttee and Res. Assoc., 1987–95 (British Chm., 1990–92); BOTB, 1993–96. Mem., Royal Nat. Theatre Bd, 1988–. Pres., Internat. Social Service of UK, 1982–96; Chm., City and E London Confedn of Medicine and Dentistry, 1989–95. Trustee, The Tablet, 1989–. Governor, Wellington Coll., 1982–92. FRSA 1983. Fellow, QMW, 1990. Chevalier, Order of Orange Nassau, 1944; Chevalier, Légion d'Honneur, 1957. *Address:* 12B Wedderburn Road, NW3 5QG. *T:* 0171–794 0440. *Club:* Buck's.

PALLOT, Arthur Keith, CB 1981; CMG 1966; Secretary and Director-General, Commonwealth War Graves Commission, 1975–82 (Director of Finance and Establishments, 1956–75); *b* 25 Sept. 1918; *s* of Harold Pallot, La Tourelle, Jersey; *m* 1945, Marjorie, *d* of J. T. Smith, Rugby; two *d. Educ:* Newton College. Royal Navy, 1936; retired as Lt-Comdr, 1947. Commonwealth War Graves Commission, 1947. Awarded the Queen's Commendation for brave conduct, 1958. *Recreations:* walking, squash, cricket, golf.

PALMAR, Sir Derek (James), Kt 1986; FCA; President, Bass PLC, 1987–89 (Chairman, 1976–87; Chairman and Chief Executive, 1976–84; Director, 1970–76); Chairman: Yorkshire Television, 1981–93; Yorkshire–Tyne Tees Television Holdings, 1992–93; Vice President, Brewers' Society, since 1982 (Chairman, 1980–82); *b* 25 July 1919; *o s* of late Lt-Col Frederick James Palmar and Hylda (*née* Smith); *m* 1st, 1946, Edith Brewster (*d* 1990); one *s* one *d*; 2nd, 1992, Shuna, *o d* of late Keith Pyman and Peggy (*née* Hare). *Educ:* Dover College. FCA 1957 (ACA 1947). Served RA and Staff, 1941–46; psc; Lt-Col 1945. Peat, Marwick, Mitchell & Co., 1937–57; Director: Hill Samuel Group, 1957–70; Grindlays Bank, 1970–85. Adviser, Dept of Economic Affairs, 1965–67; Mem., British Railways Bd, 1969–72; Chm., BR Southern Regional Adv. Bd, 1972–79. Chm., Readyhigh, 1986–94; Director: Drayton Consolidated Trust, 1982–93; Consolidated Venture Trust, 1984–93; CM Group Holdings, 1985–92; United Newspapers, 1986–93; Dir, Centre for Policy Studies, 1983–88; Chm., NEDC for Food and Drink Packaging Equipment, 1986–87. Chairman: Zool Soc. of London Develt Trust, 1986–89; Leeds Univ. Foundn, 1986–89; Member: Accounting Standards Cttee, 1982–84; Alcohol Educn and Res. Council, 1982–87. Dir, Business in the Community, 1984–; Mem., Adv. Council, Prince's Youth Business Trust, 1984–. Trustee: Civic Trust, 1979–89; Develt Trust, Queen Elizabeth's Foundn for Disabled People, 1993–. Freeman, City of London; Mem., Ct, Brewers' Co., 1982–89. *Recreations:* shooting, gardening. *Address:* Church Farm, Naunton, Cheltenham, Glos GL54 3AJ. *Club:* Boodle's.

PALMER, family name of **Earl of Selborne, Baron Palmer** and **Baron Lucas of Crudwell.**

PALMER, 4th Baron, *cr* 1933, of Reading; **Adrian Bailie Nottage Palmer;** *b* 8 Oct. 1951; *s* of Col the Hon. Sir Gordon Palmer, KCVO, OBE, TD, MA, FRCM and of the Hon. Lady Palmer, DL; *S* uncle, 1990; *m* 1977, Cornelia Dorothy Katherine, *d* of R. N. Wadham, DFC, Exning, Newmarket; two *s* one *d. Educ:* Eton; Edinburgh Univ. Mem., Exec. Council, HHA, 1981–; Chm., HHA for Scotland, 1994– (Mem., Exec. Council, 1980–; Vice Chm., 1993). Mem., Queen's Body Guard for Scotland (Royal Company of Archers), 1992–. Scottish Rep. to European Landowning Orgn, 1986–92. Sec., The Royal Caledonian Hunt, 1989–. *Recreations:* gardening, shooting, hunting. *Heir: s* Hon. Hugo Bailie Rohan Palmer, *b* 5 Dec. 1980. *Address:* Manderston, Duns, Berwickshire TD11 3PP. *T:* Duns (01361) 883450. *Clubs:* MCC; New (Edinburgh).

PALMER, Adrian Oliver; QC 1992; a Recorder, since 1992; *b* 20 Aug. 1950; *s* of Richard Gilbert Palmer and Patricia Mary Palmer; *m* 1974, Rosemary Shaw; one *s* one *d. Educ:* Clifton Coll., Bristol; St John's Coll., Cambridge (MA). Called to the Bar, Middle Temple, 1972. *Recreations:* gardens, sheep, walking. *Address:* Guildhall Chambers, 23 Broad Street, Bristol BS1 2HG. *T:* Bristol (0117) 927 3366.

PALMER, Andrew Clennel, PhD; FRS 1994; FEng; FICE; Technical Director, SAIC Ltd, since 1993; *b* 26 May 1938; *s* of Gerald Basil Coote Palmer and Muriel Gertrude Palmer (*née* Howes); *m* 1963, Jane Rhiannon Evans; one *d. Educ:* Cambridge Univ. (BA, MA); Brown Univ. (PhD). FICE 1986; FEng 1990. Lectr, Liverpool Univ., 1965–67; Cambridge University: Sen. Asst in Res., 1967–68; Lectr, 1968–75; Fellow, Churchill Coll., 1967–75; Chief Engr, R. J. Brown and Associates, 1975–79; Prof. of Civil Engrg, UMIST, 1979–82; Vice-Pres. Engrg, R. J. Brown and Associates, 1982–85; Man. Dir, Andrew Palmer and Associates, 1985–93. *Publications:* Structural Mechanics, 1976; articles and papers in scientific and engrg jls. *Recreations:* travel, cooking, languages. *Address:* Artillery House, Artillery Row, SW1P 1RT. *T:* 0171–222 8082; 49 Ashley Gardens, Ambrosden Avenue, SW1P 1QF. *T:* 0171–828 8843. *Club:* Athenæum.

PALMER, Andrew Eustace, CMG 1987; CVO 1981; HM Diplomatic Service, retired; Ambassador to the Holy See, 1991–95; *b* 30 Sept. 1937; *s* of late Lt-Col Rodney Howell Palmer, MC, and of Mrs Frances Pauline Ainsworth (*née* Gordon-Duff); *m* 1962, Davina, *d* of Sir Roderick Barclay, *qv*; two *s* one *d. Educ:* Winchester Coll.; Pembroke Coll., Cambridge (MA). Second Lieut. Rifle Bde, 1956–58. Joined HM Foreign (later Diplomatic) Service, 1961; American Dept, FO, 1962–63; Third, later Second, Secretary (Commercial), La Paz, 1963–65; Second Sec., Ottawa, 1965–67; Treasury Centre for Administrative Studies, 1967–68; Central Dept, FO, later Southern European Dept, FCO, 1968–72; First Sec. (Information), Paris, 1972–76; Asst Head of Defence Dept, FCO, 1976–77; RCDS 1978; Counsellor, Head of Chancery and Consul-Gen., Oslo, 1979–82; Hd, Falkland Is Dept, FCO, 1982–85; Fellow, Harvard Center for Internat. Affairs, 1985–86; Ambassador to Cuba, 1986–88; seconded as Pvte Sec. to the Duke and Duchess of Kent, 1988–90. *Recreations:* fishing, tennis, following most sports, photography, ornithology. *Address:* Town Farm Cottage, Little Missenden, Amersham, Bucks HP7 0QX. *Clubs:* Brooks's, MCC.

PALMER, Angela, (Mrs J. D. F. Palmer); journalist; *b* 27 March 1957; *m* 1988, Jeremy David Fletcher Palmer, *er s* of Maj.-Gen. Sir (Joseph) Michael Palmer, *qv*; two *s* one *d. Educ:* George Watson's Ladies' Coll., Edinburgh. Trainee, Evening News, Edinburgh, 1979–82; Peterborough Column, Daily Telegraph, 1982–84; Editor, PHS, The Times, 1984–86; News Editor, Observer, 1986–88; Editor: Observer Mag., 1988–92; Elle, 1992–93. Journalist of the Year, Scotland, 1980. *Recreations:* family, art, travel, horses. *Club:* Reform.

PALMER, Anthony Thomas Richard; *see* Palmer, Tony.

PALMER, Anthony Wheeler, QC 1979; a Recorder of the Crown Court, since 1980; *b* 30 Dec. 1936; *s* of late Philip Palmer and of Doris Palmer; *m* Jacqueline, *d* of Reginald Fortnum, Taunton; one *s* two *d. Educ:* Wrekin Coll., Salop. Called to the Bar, Gray's Inn, 1962. *Address:* 17 Warwick Avenue, Coventry CV5 6DJ. *T:* Coventry (01203) 75340.

PALMER, Arnold Daniel; professional golfer since 1954; golf course designer; *b* 10 Sept. 1929; *s* of Milfred J. and Doris Palmer; *m* 1954, Winifred Walzer; two *d. Educ:* Wake Forest Univ. Winner of numerous tournament titles, including: British Open Championship, 1961, 1962; US Open Championship, 1960; Masters Championship, 1958, 1960, 1962, 1964; Spanish Open Championship, 1975; Professional Golfers' Assoc. Championship, 1975; Canadian PGA, 1980; USA Seniors' Championship, 1981. Hon. Dr of Laws: Wake Forest; Nat. Coll. of Educn; Hon. Dr Hum: Thiel Coll.; Florida Southern College. Hon. Member: Royal and Ancient Golf Club, 1979; Troon Golf Club, 1982; Royal Birkdale Golf Club, 1983. *Publications:* (all jointly) Arnold Palmer Golf Book, 1961; Portrait of a Professional Golfer, 1964; My Game and Yours, 1965; Situation Golf, 1970; Go for Broke, 1973; Arnold Palmer's Best 54 Golf Holes, 1977; Arnold Palmer's Complete Book of Putting, 1986; Play Great Golf, 1987. *Recreations:* aviation (speed record for flying round world in twin-engine jet, 1976), bridge, hunting, fishing. *Address:* PO Box 52, Youngstown, Pa 15696, USA. *T:* (412) 5377751. *Clubs:* (Owner and Pres.) Latrobe Country; (Pres. and Part-Owner) Bay Hill (Orlando, Fla); (Tournament Professional) Laurel Valley Golf; numerous other country, city, golf.

PALMER, Bernard Harold Michael, OBE 1989; MA; Editor of the Church Times, 1968–89; *b* 8 Sept. 1929; *e s* of late Christopher Harold Palmer; *m* 1954, Jane Margaret, *d* of late E. L. Skinner; one *s* one *d. Educ:* St Edmund's School, Hindhead; Eton (King's Scholar); King's College, Cambridge. BA 1952; MA 1956. Member of editorial staff, Church Times, 1952–89; Managing Director, 1957–89; Editor-in-Chief, 1960–68; Chm., 1962–89. DLitt Lambeth, 1988. *Publications:* Gadfly for God: a History of the Church Times, 1991; High and Mitred: a study of prime ministers as bishop-makers, 1992; Reverend Rebels: five Victorian clerics and their fight against authority, 1993; Men of Habit: the Franciscan ideal in action, 1994. *Recreations:* cycling, penmanship. *Address:* Three Corners, 15 East Hill, Charminster, Dorchester, Dorset DT2 9QL. *T:* Dorchester (01305) 260948. *Club:* Commonwealth Trust.

PALMER, Brian Desmond; formerly Under Secretary, Northern Ireland Office; *b* 1 May 1939; *m* 1964, Hilary Eileen Latimer; one *s* one *d. Educ:* Royal Belfast Academical Instn; Queen's Univ. of Belfast (LLB 1962). Joined Northern Ireland Civil Service, 1957: Estate Duty Office, 1957–62; Min. of Home Affairs, 1962–65; Dept of the Environment, 1965–77; Head of Central Secretariat, 1977–81. *Recreation:* golf.

PALMER, Sir (Charles) Mark, 5th Bt, *cr* 1886; *b* 21 Nov. 1941; *s* of Sir Anthony Frederick Mark Palmer, 4th Bt, and of Henriette (*see* Lady Abel Smith); *S* father 1941; *m* 1976, Hon. Catherine Elizabeth Tennant, *y d* of 2nd Baron Glenconner; one *s* one *d. Heir: s* Arthur Morris Palmer, *b* 9 March 1981. *Address:* Mill Hill Farm, Sherborne, Northleach, Glos. *T:* Windrush (014514) 395.

PALMER, Gen. Sir (Charles) Patrick (Ralph), KBE 1987 (CBE 1982; OBE 1974); CIMgt; Constable and Governor of Windsor Castle, since 1992; *b* 29 April 1933; *s* of late Charles Dudley Palmer and Catherine Anne (*née* Hughes-Buller); *m* 1st, 1960, Sonia Hardy Wigglesworth (*d* 1965); one *s*; 2nd, 1966, Joanna Grace Baines; two *d. Educ:* Marlborough Coll.; RMA, Sandhurst. psc 1963. Commnd Argyll and Sutherland Highlanders, 1953; served British Guiana, Berlin, Suez Operation and Cyprus; Instructor,

RMA Sandhurst, 1961–62; BM 153(H) Inf. Bde, 1964–65; 1 Argyll and Sutherland Highlanders, Borneo, Singapore and Aden, 1965–68; MA to Dep. CDS (Intell.), MoD, 1968–70; Instructor, Staff Coll., 1970–72; reformed and commanded 1st Bn Argyll and Sutherland Highlanders, 1972–74; Chief of Staff to Comd British Forces Hong Kong, 1974–76; RCDS, 1977; Comd 7th Armoured Bde, 1977–78; Dep. Comd 1 Armoured Div., 1978–80; Comd British Mil. Adv. and Training Team, Zimbabwe, 1980–82; GOC NE Dist, 1982 and Comd 2nd Inf. Div., 1983; Comdt, Staff Coll., Camberley, 1984–86; Military Sec., 1986–89; C-in-C, AFNORTH, 1989–92. Col of the Argyll and Sutherland Highlanders, 1982–92; Captain of Tarbert Castle, 1982–92. President: Windsor Fest. Soc., 1992–; Royal Windsor Rose and Horticl Soc., 1992–. Patron: King Edward VII Hosp (Windsor) League of Friends, 1992–; E Berks Br., BLESMA, 1993–. *Recreations:* travel, outdoor interests. *Address:* Norman Tower, Windsor Castle, Berks SL4 1NJ. *Clubs:* Army and Navy; Highland Brigade (Pres., 1992).

PALMER, Charles Stuart William, OBE 1973; Vice-President, British Olympic Association, since 1988 (Vice-Chairman, 1977–83; Chairman, 1983–88); President, British Judo Association, since 1977 (Chairman, 1962–85); *b* London, 15 April 1930; *s* of Charles Edward Palmer and Emma Byrne. *Educ:* Drayton Manor County Sch. Represented GB in internat. judo comps, 1949–59; studied judo in Japan, 1951–55; obtained 1st Dan 1948, 4th Dan 1955, 8th Dan 1980, 9th Dan 1989; Mem. 1957, Capt. 1958, 1959, European Judo Champs winning team. Pres., Internat. Judo Fedn, 1965–79 (Hon. Life Pres., 1979–); Vice-Pres., British Schs Judo Assoc., 1967–; Chm., British Univs Judo Assoc., 1968–75. Sec.-Gen., Gen. Assoc of Internat. Sports Fedns, 1975–84; Member: IOC Tripartite Commn, 1974–81; Sports Council, 1983–94; Exec. Council, Assoc. of European Nat. Olympic Cttees, 1985–89 (Pres., Scientific and Medical Commn, 1988–89); Exec. Cttee, CCPR, 1975– (Chm., Games and Sports Div., 1980–; Chm., cttee studying amateurism and eligibility in sport (Palmer Report published, 1988)); Programme Commn, IOC, 1989–. Governor, Sports Aid Foundn, 1979–. Mem., Lloyd's, 1988–. Mem. Council, Royal Albert Hall, 1987–. Manning Award, Sports Writers' Assoc., 1976. Olympic Order (silver), 1980; Gold Medal, European Judo Union, 1982. Key of City of Taipei, 1974, Key of City of Seoul, 1981; Diploma and Bronze Medal, City of Bordeaux, 1970; Distinguished Service Gold Medal (China), 1974; Merito Deportivo Gold Medal (Spain), 1976. *Publications:* technical papers and articles on judo and sports politics. *Recreations:* judo, ski-ing, sport generally, flying light aircraft, orchestral music, opera, languages. *Address:* 4 Hollywood Road, SW10 9HY. *T:* 0171–352 6238. *Clubs:* Budokwai, Kandahar, Ski of Great Britain.

PALMER, Charles William; Sheriff of Tayside, Central and Fife at Dunfermline, since 1992; *b* 17 Dec. 1945; *s* of Charles J. S. Palmer and Patricia Palmer; *m* 1969, Rosemary Ann Holt; one *s* two *d. Educ:* Inverness Royal Academy; Edinburgh University (LLB 1971). Prior to University, short stints in banking and Police Force; Partner, Allan McDougall & Co., SSC, 1975; temporary Sheriff, 1984; Sheriff of N Strathclyde at Dunoon and Dumbarton, 1986–92. *Recreations:* hill walking, ski-ing, amateur opera, choral singing, photography. *Address:* 6 Great Stuart Street, Edinburgh EH3 6AW. *T:* 0131–225 4962.

PALMER, David Erroll Prior; Managing Director, Independent Newspapers (Ireland), since 1994; *b* 20 Feb. 1941; *s* of Sir Otho Prior-Palmer, DSO, and Sheila Peers (*née* Weller-Poley), OBE; *m* 1974, Elizabeth Helen Young; two *s* one *d. Educ:* Eton; Christ Church, Oxford (MA PPE). Joined Financial Times, 1964: New York Correspondent, 1967; Management Editor, 1970; News Editor, 1972; Foreign Editor, 1979; Dep. Editor, 1981; Gen. Manager and Dir, 1983; Dep. Chief Exec., 1989; Chief Exec., 1990–93. Dir and Trustee, Chichester Fest. Theatre, 1991–. First British finisher, seventh over-all, Observer Singlehanded Transatlantic Race, 1976. *Publication:* The Atlantic Challenge, 1977. *Recreations:* sailing, travelling. *Address:* Independent Newspapers, 99 Middle Abbey Street, Dublin 1. *Clubs:* Itchenor Sailing (near Chichester); Royal St George Yacht (Dublin).

PALMER, David Vereker; Chairman, 1982–88, and Chief Executive, 1978–88, Willis Faber plc; Chairman, Syndicate Capital Trust plc, since 1993; *b* 9 Dec. 1926; *s* of late Brig. Julian W. Palmer and Lena Elizabeth (*née* Vereker); *m* 1950, Mildred Elaine O'Neal; three *d. Educ:* Stowe. ACII 1950. Commnd The Life Guards, 1944; served as regular officer in Europe and ME, 1944–49; joined Edward Lumley & Sons, 1949; Manager, New York office, 1953–59; joined Willis, Faber & Dumas Ltd, 1959; Dir, 1961. Mem. Lloyd's, 1953. Chm., British Insurance & Investment Brokers Assoc., 1987–90 (Dep. Chm., 1984–87); Pres., Insurance Inst. of London, 1985–86. Commissioner, Royal Hosp. Chelsea, 1982–88. Master, Worshipful Co. of Insurers, 1982. High Sheriff, Bucks, 1993–94. *Recreations:* farming, shooting. *Address:* Burrow Farm, Hambleden, near Henley-on-Thames, Oxon RG9 6LT. *T:* Henley (01491) 571256. *Clubs:* City of London, Cavalry and Guards.

PALMER, Rev. Canon Derek George; Chaplain to the Queen, since 1990; Team Rector of Dronfield with Holmesfield, since 1987; *b* 24 Jan. 1928; *s* of late George Palmer, MBE and Edna Palmer; *m* 1952, June Cecilie Goddard; two *s* two *d. Educ:* Clifton Coll.; Selwyn Coll., Cambridge (MA); Wells Theological Coll. Deacon 1952, priest 1953; Priest in Charge, Good Shepherd, Bristol, 1954–58; first Vicar of Hartcliffe, 1958–68; Vicar of Christ Church, Swindon, 1968–77; Archdeacon of Rochester and Canon Residentiary of Rochester Cathedral, 1977–83; Home Secretary, Bd for Mission and Unity, 1983–87. Mem., General Synod, 1971–81. Hon. Canon: Rochester Cathedral, 1983–87; Derby Cathedral, 1992–. Chm., Christian Enquiry Agency, 1988–. *Publications:* All Things New, 1963; Quest, 1971; Strangers No Longer, 1990. *Recreation:* canals. *Address:* The Rectory, Church Street, Dronfield, Sheffield S18 6QB.

PALMER, Edward Hurry, CB 1972; retired Civil Servant; *b* 23 Sept. 1912; *s* of late Harold G. Palmer and late Ada S. Palmer; *m* 1940, Phyllis Eagle; no *c. Educ:* Haileybury. Dep. Chief Surveyor of Lands, Admty, 1942; Chief Surveyor of Lands, Admty, 1950; Chief Surveyor of Defence Lands, MoD, 1964; Comptroller of Defence Lands and Claims, MoD, 1968–72; Property Services Agency, DoE: Dir, Defence Lands Services, 1972–73; Dir, Estate Surveying Services, 1973–74. *Recreation:* walking. *Address:* 4 Barrowdene Close, Pinner, Middlesex HA5 3DD. *T:* 0181–866 5961.

PALMER, Felicity Joan, CBE 1993; mezzo-soprano. *Educ:* Erith Grammar Sch.; Guildhall Sch. of Music and Drama. AGSM (Teacher/Performer), FGSM. Kathleen Ferrier Meml Prize, 1970; major appearances at concerts in Britain, America, Belgium, France, Germany, Italy, Russia and Spain, firstly as soprano and then as mezzo-soprano; début as soprano, Dido in Dido and Aeneas, Kent Opera, 1972; début in USA, Marriage of Figaro, Houston, 1973; soprano roles included: Pamina in The Magic Flute, ENO, 1975; Cleopatra in Julius Caesar, Herrenhausen Hanover, and Frankfurt Opera, 1978; title role, Alcina, Bern Opera, 1978; Elektra in Idomeneo, Zurich Opera, 1980; the Countess in The Marriage of Figaro, ENO; Elvira in Don Giovanni, Scottish Opera and ENO; Marguerite in Damnation of Faust, ENO; mezzo-soprano roles include: ENO: Tristan und Isolde, 1981; Rienzi, 1983; Mazeppa, 1984; Herodias in Salome, and The Witch in Hansel and Gretel, 1987; Orfeo, Opera North, 1984; King Priam, Royal Opera, 1985; Albert Herring, Glyndebourne, 1985; Tamburlaine, Opera North, 1985; Katya Kabanova, Chicago Lyric Opera, 1986; début at La Scala, Milan, as Marguerita in world première of Riccardo III by Flavio Testi, 1987; Last Night of the Proms, 1987; début, Netherlands Opera, as Kabanicha in Katya Kabanova, 1988, same role, Glyndebourne, 1988; Mistress Quickly in Falstaff, 1988 and 1990, Marcellina in The Marriage of Figaro, 1989, Glyndebourne; world première of Tippett's New Year, Houston, USA, 1989; The Marriage of Figaro and The Gambler (Prokofiev), Chicago, 1991; Klytemnestra in Elektra, WNO, 1992; Orlando, Aix-en-Provence, 1993; Dialogue des Carmelites, Geneva, 1993; La Fille du Régiment, San Francisco, 1993; Ariodante, WNO, 1994; The Rake's Progress, Chicago, 1994; Ballo in Maschera, Catania, 1995; Elektra, La Scala, Milan, and Japan, 1995; Countess in The Queen of Spades, Glyndebourne, 1995; recitals in Amsterdam, Paris, Vienna, 1976–77, Tokyo, 1991; concert tours with BBC SO, Europe, 1973, 1977 and 1984, Australasia, Far East and Eastern Europe, 1977–; ABC tour of Australia, 1978. Recordings include: Poèmes pour Mi, with Pierre Boulez; Holst Choral Symphony, with Sir Adrian Boult; title role in Gluck's Armide; Elektra in Idomeneo, with Nikolaus Harnoncourt; The Music Makers; Sea Pictures; Britten's Phaedra; recitals, with John Constable, of songs by Poulenc, Ravel and Fauré, and of Victorian ballads. *Address:* c/o Jenny Rose, AOR Management Ltd, Westwood, Lorraine Park, Harrow Weald, Middx HA3 6BX.

PALMER, Rev. Preb. Francis Harvey; Prebendary of Sawley in Lichfield Cathedral, 1986–89; Prebendary Emeritus since 1989; *b* 13 Jan. 1930; *s* of Harry Hereward North Palmer and Ada Wilhelmina Annie Utting; *m* 1955, Mary Susan Lockhart; three *d. Educ:* Nottingham High Sch.; Jesus Coll., Cambridge (Exhibr); Wycliffe Hall, Oxford. MA. Deacon, 1955; Priest, 1956. Asst Curate: Knotty Ash, Liverpool, 1955–57; St Mary, Southgate, Crawley, 1958–60; Chaplain, Fitzwilliam House, Cambridge, 1960–64; Vicar of Holy Trinity, Cambridge and Chaplain to Cambridge Pastorate, 1964–71; Principal, Ridley Hall, Cambridge, 1971–72; Rector of Worplesdon, Surrey, 1972–80; Diocesan Ecumenical Officer, Guildford, 1974–80; Diocesan Missioner, Lichfield, 1980–89. *Publication:* (contrib.) New Bible Dictionary, 1959. *Recreation:* stamp collecting. *Address:* The Old Vicarage, Claverley, Wolverhampton WV5 7DT.

PALMER, Prof. Frank Robert, FBA 1975; Professor and Head of Department of Linguistic Science, University of Reading, 1965–87; *b* 9 April 1922; *s* of George Samuel Palmer and Gertrude Lilian (*née* Newman); *m* 1948, Jean Elisabeth Moore; three *s* two *d. Educ:* Bristol Grammar Sch.; New Coll., Oxford (Ella Stephens Schol., State Schol.) 1942–43 and 1945–48; Merton Coll., Oxford (Harmsworth Sen. Schol.) 1948–49. MA Oxon 1948; Craven Fellow, 1948. Served war, E Africa, 1943–45. Lectr in Linguistics, Sch. of Oriental and African Studies, Univ. of London, 1950–60 (study leave in Ethiopia, 1952–53); Prof. of Linguistics, University Coll. of N Wales, Bangor, 1960–65; Dean of Faculty of Letters and Social Sciences, Univ. of Reading, 1969–72. Linguistic Soc. of America Prof., Buffalo, 1971; Distinguished Visiting Professor: Foreign Languages Inst., Beijung, 1981; Univ. of Delaware, 1983. Professional visits to Canada, USA, Mexico, Venezuela, Peru, Chile, Argentine, Uruguay, Brazil, India, Japan, China, Indonesia, Morocco, Tunisia, Uganda, Kuwait and most countries of Europe. MAE 1991. *Publications:* The Morphology of the Tigre Noun, 1962; A Linguistic Study of the English Verb, 1965; (ed) Selected Papers of J. R. Firth, 1968; (ed) Prosodic Analysis, 1970; Grammar, 1971, 2nd edn 1984; The English Verb, 1974, 2nd edn 1987; Semantics, 1976, 2nd edn 1981; Modality and the English Modals, 1979, 2nd edn 1990; Mood and Modality, 1986; Grammatical Roles and Relations, 1994; articles and reviews on Ethiopian langs, English and linguistic theory, in learned jls. *Recreations:* gardening, crosswords. *Address:* Whitethorns, Roundabout Lane, Winnersh, Wokingham, Berks RG41 5AD. *T:* Wokingham (01734) 786214.

PALMER, Sir Geoffrey (Christopher John), 12th Bt, *cr* 1660; *b* 30 June 1936; *er s* of Lieutenant-Colonel Sir Geoffrey Frederick Neill Palmer, 11th Bt, and Cicely Katherine (who *m* 1952, Robert W. B. Newton; she *d* 1989), *o d* of late Arthur Radmall, Clifton, nr Watford; *S* father 1951; *m* 1957, Clarissa Mary, *er d* of Stephen Villiers-Smith, Knockholt, Kent; four *d. Educ:* Eton. *Recreations:* golf, crossword puzzles, shooting. *Heir: b* Jeremy Charles Palmer [*b* 16 May 1939; *m* 1968, Antonia, *d* of late Ashley Dutton; two *s*]. *Address:* Carlton Curlieu Hall, Leicestershire LE8 0PH. *T:* Great Glen (0153759) 2656. *Clubs:* MCC, I Zingari, Free Foresters, Eton Ramblers, Butterflies, Gentlemen of Leicestershire, Lincolnshire Gentlemen's Cricket, Derbyshire Friars, XL, Frogs, Old Etonian Golfing Society, Old Etonian Racquets and Tennis, Northants Amateurs' CC.

PALMER, Rt. Hon. Sir Geoffrey (Winston Russell), AC 1991; KCMG 1991; PC 1985; Partner, Chen & Palmer, barristers and solicitors, Wellington, since 1995; Professor of Law, Victoria University of Wellington, New Zealand, 1974–79, and since 1991; *b* 21 April 1942; *s* of Leonard Russell and Jessie Patricia Palmer; *m* 1963, Margaret Eleanor Hinchcliff; one *s* one *d. Educ:* Nelson Coll.; Victoria Univ. of Wellington (BA; LLB); Univ. of Chicago (JD). Barrister and Solicitor, High Court of New Zealand. Prof. of Law, Univ. of Iowa, 1969–73, and 1991–95. Vis. Professor of Law, Univ. of Virginia, 1972–73. MP (Lab) Christchurch Central, NZ, 1979–90; Dep. Prime Minister, 1984–89; Attorney-Gen., 1984–89; Minister of Justice, 1984–89; Minister for the Environment, 1987–90; Prime Minister, 1989–90. *Publications:* Unbridled Power?—an interpretation of New Zealand's constitution and government, 1979, 2nd edn 1987; Compensation for Incapacity—a study of law and social change in Australia and New Zealand, 1979; Environmental Politics—a greenprint for New Zealand, 1990; New Zealand's Constitution in Crisis, 1992. *Recreations:* cricket, golf, playing the trumpet. *Address:* 85 Elizabeth Street, Wellington, New Zealand. *T:* (4) 8015185.

PALMER, Horace Anthony, (Tony); Chief Executive, Taylor Woodrow Group, since 1990; *b* 20 Feb. 1937; *s* of Horace Charles and Violet Victoria Palmer; *m* 1961, Beryl Eileen Freakley; two *d. Educ:* Pinner County Grammar School; Hammersmith Sch. of Building. FRICS; FCIOB. Trainee Quantity Surveyor, 1954; Taylor Woodrow: Contracts Manager, 1970; Subsidiary Dir, 1974; Subsidiary Man. Dir, 1987; Man. Dir, 1989. *Recreations:* sports, reading biography. *Address:* Taylor Woodrow Group, 4 Dunraven Street, W1Y 3FG.

PALMER, Joe; *see* Palmer, T. J.

PALMER, John, CB 1986; Chairman, European Passenger Services, British Rail, 1990–94; *b* 13 Nov. 1928; 2nd *s* of late William Nathaniel Palmer and Grace Dorothy May Palmer (*née* Procter); *m* 1958, Lyliane Marthe Jeanjean; two *d. Educ:* Heath Grammar Sch., Halifax; The Queen's Coll., Oxford (Lit. Hum.) (MA). Entered Min. of Housing and Local Govt, 1952; Cabinet Office, 1963–65; Asst Sec., 1965; Under Secretary: DoE, 1971; Dept of Transport, 1976–82; Dep. Sec., Dept of Transport, 1982–89. Liveryman, Carmens' Co., 1987–. FCIT 1987; FRSA 1987. *Address:* 70 College Road, SE21 7LY. *Club:* United Oxford & Cambridge University.

PALMER, Sir John (Chance), Kt 1979; solicitor; Consultant, Bevan Ashford; Vice Lord-Lieutenant of Devon, 1991–95; *b* 21 March 1920; *s* of Ernest Clephan Palmer and Claudine Pattie Sapey; *m* 1945, Mary Winifred, *d* of Arthur Sidney Ellyatt, OBE, and Winifred Mary Ellyatt (*née* East); four *s. Educ:* St Paul's Sch.; St Edmund Hall, Oxford (MA). Served War, RNVR, Atlantic and Mediterranean, 1939–46. Admitted a Solicitor, 1948; Elected Council of Law Society, 1963, President, 1978–79; Member: Criminal

Injuries Compensation Board, 1981–92; SW Region Mental Health Tribunal, 1983–92. Governor, Coll. of Law, 1965–83; Pres., Devon and Exeter Law Society, 1972; Pres., S Western Law Societies, 1973; Chm., Governors of Blundells Sch., 1980–91; Chm., Exmoor Calvert Trust, 1991–94; Chairman, Trustees: London Sailing Project, 1982–92; Internat. Technol Univ., 1988–; Mem. Council, Exeter Univ., 1983–. Hon. Member: Amer. Bar Assoc., 1978; Canadian Bar Assoc., 1979; Florida Defence Lawyers Assoc., 1981. Hon. Sec., Soc. for Protection of Animals in N Africa, 1989–. Hon. Citizen, Texas, 1980. DL Devon, 1984. Hon. LLD Exeter, 1980. *Recreations:* gardening, sailing. *Address:* Lower Withleigh Farmhouse, Tiverton, Devon EX16 8JJ. *T:* Tiverton (01884) 252959. *Clubs:* Athenæum, Royal Over-Seas League, Naval; Western (Glasgow); Royal Yacht Squadron.

PALMER, Sir John (Edward Somerset), 8th Bt, *cr* 1791; retired; Director, W. S. Atkins Agriculture, 1979–88; *b* 27 Oct. 1926; *e s* of Sir John A. Palmer, 7th Bt; *S* father, 1963; *m* 1956, Dione Catharine Skinner; one *s* one *d*. *Educ:* Canford School; Cambridge Univ. (MA); Durham Univ. (MSc). Colonial Service, Northern Nigeria, 1952–61. R. A. Lister & Co. Ltd, Dursley, Glos, 1962–63; Min. Overseas Develt, 1964–68. *Recreations:* fishing, sailing. *Heir: s* Robert John Hudson Palmer [*b* 20 Dec. 1960; *m* 1990, Lucinda Margaret Barker]. *Address:* Court Barton, Feniton, Honiton, Devon EX14 0BD. *T:* Honiton (01404) 851020.

PALMER, Maj.-Gen. Sir (Joseph) Michael, KCVO 1985; Chairman, Copley Marshall & Co. Ltd, since 1980; *b* 17 Oct. 1928; *s* of late Lt-Col William Robert Palmer, DSO, and late Joan Audrey Palmer (*née* Smith); *m* 1953, Jillean Monica Sherston; two *s* one *d*. *Educ:* Wellington College. Commissioned 14th/20th King's Hussars, 1948; Adjutant 14th/20th King's Hussars, 1953–55; Adjutant Duke of Lancaster's Own Yeomanry, 1956–59; psc 1960; jssc 1965; CO 14th/20th King's Hussars, 1969–72; Comdr RAC 1st (BR) Corps, 1974–76; Asst Chief of Staff, Allied Forces Central Europe, 1976–78; Director, Royal Armoured Corps, 1978–81; Defence Services Sec., 1982–85. Col, 14th/20th King's Hussars, 1981–92; Hon. Col, Duke of Lancaster's Own Yeomanry, 1988–92. Director: Alexanders, Laing & Cruickshank Service Co., 1986–89; Credit Lyonnais Construction Co., 1988–90. Chm. of Governors, Sandroyd Sch., 1984–. Liveryman, Salters' Co., 1965 (Master, 1989–90). FBIM. *Recreations:* riding, shooting, music, reading. *Club:* Cavalry and Guards.
See also Angela Palmer.

PALMER, Sir Mark; *see* Palmer, Sir C. M.

PALMER, Maj.-Gen. Sir Michael; *see* Palmer, Maj.-Gen. Sir J. M.

PALMER, Michael Julian Barham, CMG 1990; writer, lecturer and art consultant; Economic Consultant, Institute for East-West Studies, New York and Prague, since 1992; *b* 2 Feb. 1933; *s* of Cecil Barham Palmer and Phyllis Palmer; *m* 1983, Dr Karin Reichel. *Educ:* Corpus Christi College, Oxford (MA). Research Officer, Political and Economic Planning, 1957–61; Sec., Political Cttee, Council of Europe, 1961–66; Councillor for Defence and Armaments, WEU, 1966–68; Dir of Cttees, N Atlantic Assembly, 1968–72; Dir-Gen. of Research European Parlt, 1972–90. Jean Monnet Prof., European Univ. Inst., Florence, 1989. Austrian Order of Merit, 1990; Order of Oak Leaf Crown (Luxembourg), 1990. *Publications:* European Organisations, 1959; European Unity, 1968; Prospects for a European Security Conference, 1971; The European Parliament, 1981; Western Assistance to Central Europe, 1993; From Ensor to Magritte, 1994; Assistance to Transition, 1995; articles in The World Today, Foreign Policy, The Times, Christie's International. *Recreations:* music, art, cooking, climbing. *Address:* 8 rue des Franciscaines, L-1539 Luxembourg Grand Duchy; Glebe House, Easton-on-the-Hill, Stamford, Lincs PE9 2BA.

PALMER, Monroe Edward, OBE 1982; FCA; chartered accountant; *b* 30 Nov. 1938; *s* of William and Sybil Polikoff; *m* 1962, Susette Sandra (*née* Cardash); two *s* one *d*. *Educ:* Orange Hill Grammar Sch. FCA 1963. Chm., Hendon CAB, 1981–83; Vice-Chm., Barnet CAB, 1986–88; Treasurer: Disablement Assoc., London Borough of Barnet, 1971–88; Liberal Parly Party, 1977–83; Jt Treasurer, Liberal Party, 1977–83; Chm., Lib Dem Friends of Israel, 1987–. Councillor (L, then Lib Dem) London Borough of Barnet, 1986–94. Contested: (L) Hendon South, 1979, 1983, 1987; (Lib Dem) Hastings and Rye, 1992. *Recreations:* politics, fishing. *Address:* 31 The Vale, NW11 8SE. *T:* 0181–455 5140; 30 Wellington Square, Hastings. *T:* Hastings (01424) 422095. *Club:* National Liberal.

PALMER, Prof. Nigel Fenton, DPhil; Professor of German Medieval and Linguistic Studies, University of Oxford, since 1992; Professorial Fellow, St Edmund Hall, Oxford, since 1992; *b* 28 Oct. 1946; *s* of James Terence Palmer and Constance May Palmer (*née* Fenton); *m* 1974, Susan Patricia Aldred; one *s* one *d*. *Educ:* Hyde County Grammar Sch.; Worcester Coll., Oxford (MA, DPhil). Lectr in German, Durham Univ., 1970–76; University of Oxford: Univ. Lectr in Medieval German, 1976–90; Reader in German, 1990–92; Fellow, Oriel Coll., 1976–92. Fellow, Humboldt Foundn, 1982. *Publications:* Visio Tnugdali, 1976; Tondolus der Ritter, 1980; (with K. Speckenbach) Träume und Kräuter, 1990; Die Blockbücher der Berlin-Breslauer Sammelbandes, 1992; German Literary Culture in the Twelfth and Thirteenth Centuries, 1993. *Address:* St Edmund Hall, Oxford OX1 4AR. *T:* Oxford (01865) 510487.

PALMER, Prof. Norman Ernest; barrister; Rowe & Maw Professor of Commercial Law, University College London, since 1991; *b* 16 Aug. 1948; *s* of Norman George Palmer and Muriel (*née* Walker); *m* 1970, Judith Ann Weeks (marr. diss.); one *d*; 1994, Ruth Redmond-Cooper. *Educ:* Palmer's Endowed Sch., Grays Thurrock; Magdalen Coll., Oxford (BA Jurisp. 1969; BCL 1971; MA 1974). Called to the Bar, Gray's Inn, 1973; Lectr and Sen. Lectr in Law, Univs of Liverpool, Tasmania and Manchester, 1971–81; Professor of Law: Univ. of Reading, 1981–84 (Head of Dept, 1982–84); Univ. of Essex, 1984–90 (Dean of Faculty, 1985–88); Prof. of English Law, Univ. of Southampton, 1990–91 (Dep. Dean of Faculty). Sec. and a Dir, Internat. Cultural Property Soc., 1990– (Editor, Jl, 1991–). *Publications:* (ed with E. L. G. Tyler) Crossley Vaines on Personal Property, 5th edn, 1973; Bailment, 1979, 2nd edn 1991; (ed jtly) Emden's Construction Law, 1990; (with C. J. Miller) Business Law, 1992; (ed jtly) Interest in Goods, 1993; (with E. McKendrick) Product Liability in the Construction Industry, 1993; Halsbury's Laws of England, 4th edn and re-issue: (ed with H. Street) Titles on Tort; (ed with A. Powell) Bailment; (ed with W. J. Swadling) Carriers. *Recreations:* literature, biography, travel, collecting tombstone verse. *Address:* 2 Field Court, Gray's Inn, WC1R 5BB. *T:* 0171–405 6114.

PALMER, Most Rev. Norman Kitchener, CMG 1981; MBE 1975; *b* 2 Oct 1928; *s* of Philip Sydney and Annie Palmer; *m* 1960, Elizabeth Lucy Gorringe; three *s* one *d*. *Educ:* Kokeqolo, Pawa, Solomon Is; Te Aute, NZ; Ardmore, NZ (Teachers' Cert,); St John's Theological Coll., NZ (LTh; ordained deacon, 1964). Appts in Solomon Islands: Deacon/Teacher, Pawa Secondary (Anglican), 1966; priest, Pawa, 1966; Priest/Headmaster: Alanguala Primary, 1967–69; St Nicholas Primary, 1970–72; Dean, St Barnabas Cathedral, 1973–75; Bishop of Central Melanesia, 1975–87; Archbishop of Melanesia, 1975–87. Member, Public Service Advisory Bd, 1971–75. *Address:* Varei Village, Bauro District, General Post Office, Kira Kira, Makira Province, Solomon Islands.

PALMER, Gen. Sir Patrick; *see* Palmer, Gen. Sir C. P. R.

PALMER, Sir Reginald (Oswald), GCMG 1992; MBE 1973; Governor General, Grenada, since 1992; *b* 15 Feb. 1923; *m* 1954, Judith Juliana Parke; two *s* five *d*. *Educ:* St George's RC Boys' Sch.; Govt Teachers' Trng Coll., Trinidad; Univ. of Birmingham (CertEd); Univ. of Calgary (BEd 1971). Pupil Teacher, 1939–41; pupil teacher scholarship, 1941; Asst Teacher, 1945–56; Headteacher, 1956–68; Tutor, Grenada Teachers' Coll., 1968–72; Asst Educn Officer, 1972–73; Principal, Grenada Teachers' Coll., 1973–74; Chief Educn Officer, 1974–80, retd. Manager, Grenada Teachers' Sch. Supplies Ltd, 1980–87; Pres., Grenada Employers' Fedn, 1987–89. Dir, Grenada Bank of Commerce, 1990–92. Foundn Mem., Grenada Teachers' Social Security and Welfare Assoc. (Sec. 1951–69); Pres., Grenada Union of Teachers, 1962–63. Member: Public Service Commn, 1983–87; Local Adv. Council, Sch. of Continuing Educn, 1978– (Pres. 1989–). Chm., Grenada Drug Avoidance Cttee, 1988–92. Dir, Richmond Fellowship of Grenada, 1991–92. *Recreations:* reading, backyard gardening, walking, sea-bathing. *Address:* Governor General's Office, St George's, Grenada, West Indies.

PALMER, Richard William, OBE 1987; Secretary General, British Olympic Association, since 1977; *b* 13 April 1933; *s* of late Richard Victor Palmer and Mary Ellen Palmer (*née* Sambrook). *Educ:* Haverfordwest Grammar Sch.; Trinity Coll., Carmarthen; The College, Chester (Dip PE); Univ. of Leicester (MEd). Head, PE Dept, Windsor Grammar Sch., 1961–64; Sec., UAU, 1964–69; Gen. Sec., British Univs Sports Fedn, 1969–74; British Olympic Assoc., 1975–. Gen. Sec., Commonwealth Games Council for England, 1977–86; Dep. Chef de Mission, GB, 1976, Chef de Mission, GB, 1980, 1984, 1988, 1992, Olympic Games and Olympic Winter Games; Gen. Team Manager, England, Commonwealth Games, 1978, 1982, 1986. Prix de Merit, Assoc. of Nat. Olympic Cttees, 1990. *Recreations:* golf, sailing, Rugby Union, gardening, fishing. *Address:* British Olympic Association, 1 Wandsworth Plain, SW18 1EH. *T:* 0181–871 2677. *Clubs:* Scribes, East India; Haverfordwest and Fulwell Golf; Llangwm Boat.

PALMER, His Honour Robert Henry Stephen; a Circuit Judge, 1978–93; *b* 13 Nov. 1927; *s* of Henry Alleyn Palmer and Maud (*née* Obbard); *m* 1955, Geraldine Elizabeth Anne Evens; one *s* two *d*. *Educ:* Charterhouse; University Coll., Oxford. Called to the Bar, 1950. Dep. Chm., Berks QS, 1970. A Recorder of the Crown Court, 1972–78. Resident Judge: Acton Crown Court, 1987–91; Harrow Crown Court, 1991–93; Pres., 1983–, S Thames Regl Chm., 1993–, Mental Health Rev. Tribunal. *Publications:* Harris's Criminal Law, 1960; Guide to Divorce, 1965. *Recreation:* self-sufficiency.

PALMER, Sidney John, CB 1972; OBE 1953; Head of Royal Corps of Naval Constructors, 1968–73; *b* 28 Nov. 1913; *m* 1941, Mavis Beatrice Blennerhassett Hallett; four *s*. *Educ:* RNC Greenwich. WhSch 1937. Admty Experiment Works, Haslar, 1938; Portsmouth Dockyard, 1942; Chief Constructor, Sydney, 1945; Constructor Comdr, Hong Kong, 1946; Chief Constructor Aircraft Carriers, 1948; Prof. of Naval Architecture, RNC Greenwich, 1952; Asst Dir Dreadnought Project, 1959; Dep. Dir Polaris Programme, 1963; Dir Naval Ship Production, 1966; Dep. Dir General Ships, 1968–73. Mem. Council, RINA, 1960; Liveryman, Shipwrights' Co., 1968; Hon. Research Fellow, UCL, 1968. Mem., Cttee of Management, RNLI, 1974–78. *Address:* 89 Bloomfield Avenue, Bath, Avon BA2 3AE. *T:* Bath (01225) 312592.

PALMER, Thomas Joseph, (Joe), CBE 1990; Director, National Power plc, since 1991; Chairman, Personal Investment Authority, since 1993; *b* 11 Sept. 1931; *m* 1955, Hilary Westrup; two *s* two *d*. *Educ:* King's School, Bruton; Trinity College, Cambridge. MA. Asst Gen. Man. (Planning), Legal and General Assurance Soc., 1969–72, Dir and Gen. Man. (Admin.), 1972–78; Legal & General Group plc: Dir, 1978–91; Gen. Man. (Internat.), 1978–83; Group Chief Exec., 1984–91. Chm., Laser Richmount, 1991–93; Director: SIB, 1991–93; Halifax BS, 1991–93; Sedgwick Gp, 1992–93; ProShare, 1992–94. Chairman: London Business Sch. Assoc., 1974–78; Assoc. of British Insurers, 1989–91; Pres., Insurance Inst. of London, 1982–83; Dir, Investors' Compensation Scheme, 1992–93. Gov., King's Sch., Bruton, 1989–. Hon. Fellow, London Business Sch., 1990. *Recreations:* gardening, long-distance walking, cross country ski-ing.

PALMER, Tony; *see* Palmer, H. A.

PALMER, Tony; film, television and theatre director; author; brought up by godparents, late Bert Spencer (railway engineer) and Elsie Spencer. *Educ:* Lowestoft Grammar Sch. FRGS 1993. *Films include:* All My Loving, 1968; Farewell Cream, 1968; 200 Motels, 1971 (Gold Record); A Time There Was, 1979 (Italia Prize); At the Haunted End of the Day, 1980 (Italia Prize); Once at a Border, 1981 (Special Jury Prize, San Francisco); Wagner, 1982 (Best Drama, NY Film and TV Fest.); God Rot Tunbridge Wells, 1985 (Best Drama, NY); Maria, 1986 (Gold Medal, NY); Testimony, 1987 (Fellini Prize); The Children, 1989 (Best Director, NY); Menuhin, 1990 (Grand Award, NY); The Symphony of Sorrowful Songs, 1993 (platinum CD; Jury Prize, Chicago Film Fest.); *theatre:* John Osborne's Deja Vu, Comedy, 1992; dir operas, Berlin, Karlsruhe, Munich, Hamburg, Zürich. Numerous BAFTA and Emmy awards. *Publications:* Born Under a Bad Sign, 1970; Trials of Oz, 1971; Electric Revolution, 1972; Biography of Liberace, 1976; All You Need is Love, 1976; Charles II, 1979; A Life on the Road (biog. of Julian Bream), 1982; Menuhin: a family portrait, 1991. *Recreation:* walking. *Address:* Nanjizal, St Levan, Cornwall TR19 6JH. *Club:* Garrick.

PALMER, Maj.-Gen. Tony Brian, CB 1984; CEng, FIMechE; conducted a study on maintenance philosophy and organisation in the Army, 1986; retired 1986; *b* 5 Nov. 1930; *s* of Sidney Bernard Palmer and Ann (*née* Watkins); *m* 1953, Hazel Doris Robinson; two *s*. *Educ:* Wolverton Technical College; Luton College of Technology; General Motors Inst. of Technology, USA. General Motors UK, 1948–51 and 1953–54; commissioned REME 1954; RMCS, 1960–62; Tank Gunnery Trials, Infantry Workshop, staff duties MoD, JSSC, Ops and Plans MoD, 1962–70; Head, DG FVE Secretariat, 1970–72; Comdr REME, 3 Div., 1972–74; Head, Tech. Intell. (Army), 1974–76; Dir, Elect. and Mech. Engineering (Organisation and Training), 1977–79; Comdt, REME Training Centre, 1979–83; Dir-Gen. of Elect. and Mech. Engrg, MoD (Army), 1983–85. Col Comdt, REME, 1986–91. Vice-Pres., S Region, British Sports Assoc. for Disabled, 1980–; Chairman: Somerset Br., Army Benevolent Fund, 1988–; Dorset Cttee for Employment of Disabled People, 1989–91; Somerset Cttee for Employment of People with Disabilities, 1991–94. MIMgt. *Recreations:* history, gardening. *Address:* c/o Barclays Bank, Station Parade, London Road, Sunningdale, Berks SL5 6EW.

PALMES, Peter Manfred Jerome; Principal Assistant Director, Public Prosecutions Department, 1979–81; *b* 28 Feb. 1920; *s* of late Manfred Palmes and Gwendoline Robb; *m* 1st, 1945, Sylvia Theodor (decd); 2nd, 1969, Brenda Laban; one step *d*. *Educ:* Charterhouse; Worcester Coll., Oxford. Served War of 1939–45: Oxford and Bucks LI and 1/8th Gurkha Rifles, 1940–45. Called to Bar, Inner Temple, 1948. Public Prosecutions Dept: Legal Assistant, 1948; Sen. Legal Asst, 1958; Asst Solicitor, 1969; Asst Director, 1977. Jubilee Medal, 1977. *Address:* Chapel Lodge, Cross Colwood Lane, Bolney, West Sussex RH17 5RY.

PALUMBO, family name of **Baron Palumbo.**

PALUMBO, Baron *cr* 1991 (Life Peer), of Walbrook in the City of London; **Peter Garth Palumbo,** MA; Chairman, Arts Council of Great Britain, 1989–94; *b* 20 July 1935; *s* of late Rudolph and of Elsie Palumbo; *m* 1st, 1959, Denia (*d* 1986), *d* of late Major Lionel Wigram; one *s* two *d*; 2nd, 1986, Hayat, *er d* of late Kamel Morowa; one *s* two *d*. *Educ:* Eton College; Worcester College, Oxford. MA Hons Law. Governor, London School of Economics and Political Science, 1976–94; Chairman: Tate Gallery Foundn, 1986–87; Painshill Park Trust Appeal, 1986–; Serpentine Gall., 1994–; Trustee: Mies van der Rohe Archive, 1977–; Tate Gallery, 1978–85; Whitechapel Art Gallery Foundation, 1981–87; Natural History Mus., 1994–; Trustee and Hon. Treas., Writers and Scholars Educnl Trust, 1984–; Mem. Council, Royal Albert Hall, 1995–. Chancellor, Portsmouth Univ., 1992–. Hon. FRIBA; Hon. FFB 1994; Hon. FIStructE 1994. Hon. DLitt Portsmouth, 1993. Nat. Order of Southern Cross (Brazil), 1993. *Recreations:* music, travel, gardening, reading. *Address:* Bagnor Manor, Bagnor, Newbury, Berks RG16 8AG. *T:* Newbury (01635) 40930. *Clubs:* Athenæum, White's, Pratt's; Knickerbocker (New York).

PANAYIDES, Tasos Christou, Hon. GCVO 1990; Ambassador to Iceland, since 1979, and to Sweden, Finland, Norway, Denmark, Latvia, Lithuania and Estonia, since 1994; *b* 9 April 1934; *s* of Christos Panayides and Efrosini Panayides; *m* 1969, Pandora Constantinides; two *s* one *d*. *Educ:* Paphos Gymnasium; Teachers' Training Coll.; Univ. of London (Diploma in Education); Univ. of Indiana, USA (MA Political Science, Diploma in Public Administration). Teacher, 1954–59; First sec. to Pres., 1960–68; Director President's Office, 1969; Ambassador of Cyprus to Federal Republic of Germany, Switzerland, Austria, and Atomic Energy organisation, Vienna, 1969–78; High Comr in UK, and Ambassador to Sweden, Norway and Denmark, 1979–90; Doyen of the Diplomatic Corps in London and Sen. High Comr, 1988–90; Permanent Sec., Min. of Foreign Affairs, Cyprus, 1990–94. Chairman: Commonwealth Foundn Grants Cttee, 1985–88; Commonwealth Fund Tech. Co-operation Bd of Reps, 1986–89; Commonwealth Steering Cttee of Sen. Officials, 1994–95. Hon. Fellow, Ealing Coll. of Higher Educn, 1983. Freeman, City of London, 1984. Hon. LLD Birmingham, 1991. 1st Cl., Grand Order and Grand Cross with Star and Sash, Federal Republic of Germany, 1978; Grand Cross in Gold with Star and Sash, Austria, 1979; Golden Cross of the Archdiocese of Thyateira and Great Britain, 1981; Grand Cross in Gold of Patriarchate of Antioch, 1984. *Publications:* articles in newspapers and magazines. *Recreations:* swimming, reading books. *Address:* Birger Jarlsgatan 37, 4tr, Box 7649, 10394 Stockholm, Sweden; Ministry of Foreign Affairs of the Republic of Cyprus, Nicosia, Cyprus.

PANDEY, Ishwari Raj, Hon. GCVO 1986; Prasiddha Prabala Gorakha-Dakshina Bahu, 1982; Vikhyata Trishakti-Patta, 1974; Additional Foreign Secretary to HM's Government, Kingdom of Nepal, 1988–91; *b* 15 Aug. 1934; *s* of Rajguru Sri Hem Raj Panditgue and Nayab Bada Guruma Khaga Kumari Pandit; *m* 1953, Gita Rajya Laxmi Devi Rana; three *s* two *d*. *Educ:* Bombay Univ. (MA); Univ. of Pittsburgh (MPIA). Planning Officer, Min. of Planning and Develt, 1959; Under Sec., Min. of Finance (Foreign Aid Co-ordination), 1961; Dir, Dept of Industries, 1964; Head of Section for Econ. Relations, Min. of Foreign Affairs, 1966; First Secretary: Royal Nepalese Embassy, London, 1968; Perm. Mission of Kingdom of Nepal to UN, New York, 1972; Head of Section for Neighbouring Countries, Min. of For. Affairs, 1974; Chargé d'Affaires (Counsellor), Royal Nepalese Embassy, Tehran, 1975; Jt Sec., Div for Europe and the Americas, Min. of For. Affairs, 1979; Minister, Royal Nepalese Embassy, New Delhi, 1980; Ambassador to the UK, 1983–88 (concurrently Ambassador to Denmark, Finland, Norway, Iceland and Sweden). Coronation Medal, Bhutan, 1975. *Publications:* The Economic Impact of the Tourist Industry (with special reference to Puerto Rico and Nepal), 1961 (Univ. of Pittsburgh); contrib. to many jls. *Recreations:* reading, travelling. *Address:* Bharatee Bhawan, Dhokatole, Kathmandu, Nepal. *T:* 211297. *Club:* Hurlingham.

PANDOLFI, Filippo Maria; a Vice-President of the Commission of the European Communities, 1989–92; *b* 1 Nov. 1927; *m* 1963, Carola Marziani; three *s* one *d*. *Educ:* Catholic Univ. of Milan (BA in philosophy). Member, Italian Parliament (Christian Democrats), 1968–88; Under Secretary of State, Min. of Finance, 1974–76; Minister of Finance, 1976–78; Minister of the Treasury, 1978–80; Chm. of Interim Cttee of IMF, 1979–80; Minister of Industry, 1980–82; Minister of Agriculture, 1983–88. *Recreations:* music, classical Greek, rock climbing.

PANK, Dorian Christopher L.; *see* Lovell-Pank.

PANK, Maj.-Gen. (John) David (Graham), CB 1989; Chief Executive, Newbury Racecourse plc, since 1990; *b* 2 May 1935; *s* of late Edward Graham Pank and Margaret Sheelah Osborne Pank; *m* 1963, Julia Letitia Matheson; two *s* one *d*. *Educ:* Uppingham Sch. Commnd KSLI, 1958; served in Germany, Borneo, Singapore and Malaya; commanded: 3rd Bn The Light Infantry, 1974–76; 33rd Armoured Bde, 1979–81; Dir Gen. of Personal Services, Army, 1985–88; Dir of Infantry, 1988–90. Col, The LI, 1987–90. President: Army Cricket Assoc., 1987–89; Combined Services Cricket Assoc., 1988. Dir, Racecourse Assoc., 1994–. *Recreations:* racing, fishing, cricket. *Address:* c/o Royal Bank of Scotland, London Drummonds Branch, 49 Charing Cross, SW1A 2DX. *Clubs:* Army and Navy, Victory Services; Mounted Infantry; Free Foresters, I Zingari, Mount Cricket.

PANKHURST, Air Vice-Marshal (Retd) Leonard Thomas, CB 1955; CBE 1944; *b* 26 August 1902; *s* of late Thomas William Pankhurst, Teddington, Middlesex; *m* 1939, Ruth, *d* of late Alexander Phillips, Cromer, Norfolk; one *s* two *d*. *Educ:* Hampton Grammar School. Joined Royal Air Force, 1925; Group Captain, 1942; Air Commodore, 1947; Actg Air Vice-Marshal, 1954. Served War of 1939–45 (despatches, CBE); Directorate of War Organisation, Air Ministry, 1938–41; Coastal Command, 1941–42; Mediterranean Air Forces, 1942–45. Air Officer Commanding 44 Group Transport Command, 1945–46; Asst Comdt RAF Staff Coll., 1946; idc, 1947; Dir Staff Trg, Air Ministry, 1948–50; Air Officer Commanding RAF E Africa, 1950–52; Dir of Postings, Air Ministry, 1953–54; Director-General of Personnel (I), Air Ministry, 1954–57. *Address:* Earl's Eye House, 8 Sandy Lane, Chester CH3 5UL. *T:* Chester (01244) 320993.

PANNETT, Juliet Kathleen, MBE 1993; FRSA; painter; *b* Hove; 2nd *d* of Charles Somers and May (*née* Brice); *m* 1938, Major M. R. D. Pannett (*d* 1980), late the Devonshire Regt; one *s* one *d*. *Educ:* Harvington Sch., Ealing; Wistons Sch., Brighton; Brighton College of Art. Special Artist to Illustrated London News, 1957–64. *Exhibitions:* Royal Festival Hall, 1957, 1958; Qantas Gallery, 1959; New York, 1960; Cleveland, Ohio, 1960; Cooling Gallery, London, 1961; Coventry Cathedral Festival, 1962; Gloucester Three Choirs Festival, 1962; Brighton Corporation Gallery, Rottingdean, 1967; Arun Art Centre, 1967, 1969, 1972; Fine Art Gall., London, 1969; Mignon Gall., Bath, 1970; Brotherton Gall., London, 1980; Pacific and Fringe Clubs, Hong Kong, 1986; Wigmore Hall, 1989, 1991; RNCM, 1989; Stamford Arts Centre, 1995. Exhibitor: Royal Academy; Royal Society of Portrait Painters; Royal Inst. of Painters in Watercolours, etc. Official Artist on Qantas Inaugural Jet Flight, London to Sydney, 1959, London to Hong Kong, 1964; Air Canada Inaugural Flight, London to Vancouver, 1968. Freeman: City of London, 1960; Painter Stainers' Company, 1960. *Work in Permanent Collections:* 22 portraits in National Portrait Gall.; Bodleian Library; Maudsley Hospital; Army Phys. Training Sch., Aldershot; Gurkha Mus., Aldershot; Painter Stainers' Hall, London; Edinburgh Univ.; D Day painting for Devon and Dorset Regt, 1963; Commemorative Stained Glass Window (St Alban), Garrison Church, Munster, 1967; painting of Duke of Kent presenting new colours to Devon and Dorset Regt, 1982; Portraits, many for official bodies, include: HM The Queen, 1989; HRH Princess Alexandra, 1984; HRH Prince Andrew, HRH Prince Edward, for HM The Queen, 1974; HRH Princess Marina, Duchess of Kent, 1968; Lord Alport; Lord Annan; Lord Baden-Powell; Lady Baden-Powell; Group Captain Sir Douglas Bader; Maj.-Gen. T. A. Boam; Sir Denys Buckley; Lord Butler; Lord Caldecote; Lord David Cecil; Group Captain Leonard Cheshire; Lord Dacre; Lord Delfont; Lord Denning; Gen. Sir Martin Farndale; Christopher Fry; Lord Goodman; Lord Hailsham; Lady Heseltine; Ivon Hitchens; Bishop Huddleston; Bishop Hunt; Sir John Kendrew; C. S. Lewis; Dr Quett Masire, President of Botswana; Lord Montagu; Lady Montagu; Patrick Moore; Sir Nevill Mott; Lord Mountbatten of Burma; Sir David Napley; Dr David Newsome; Lavinia Duchess of Norfolk; Lord Sackville; Lord Salmon; Lord Shackleton; Lord Shawcross; Gilbert Spencer; Lord Spencer; Rt Hon. Margaret Thatcher; Col Digby Thompson; Lord Tonypandy; Sir Barnes Wallis. Has broadcast on art subjects on TV in UK and USA. *Publications:* cover portraits for books by Sir Thomas Beecham, Charles Causley, Henry Cecil, Canon Collins, Mary Drewery, Louis Golding, Gerald Pawle and Cyril Scott; drawings reproduced in The Times, Daily Telegraph, Birmingham Mail, Radio Times, The Lancet, Leisure Painter, The Artist, Law Guardian, Guardian Gazette, etc. *Recreation:* painting surgical operations, musicians and old barns. *Address:* Pound House, Roundstone Lane, Angmering Village, Sussex BN16 4AL. *T:* Rustington (01903) 784446.

PANNICK, David Philip; QC 1992; Fellow of All Souls College, Oxford, since 1978; a Recorder, since 1995; *b* 7 March 1956; *s* of Maurice and Rita Pannick; *m* 1978, Denise Sloam; two *s* one *d*. *Educ:* Bancroft's Sch., Woodford Green, Essex; Hertford Coll., Oxford (MA, BCL). Called to the Bar, Gray's Inn, 1979; Jun. Counsel to the Crown (Common Law), 1988–92. Columnist, The Times, 1991–. Mem., Editl Bd, Public Law, 1990–. *Publications:* Judicial Review of the Death Penalty, 1982; Sex Discrimination Law, 1985; Judges, 1987; Advocates, 1992. *Recreations:* reading, watching television, jogging. *Address:* 2 Hare Court, Temple, EC4Y 7BH. *T:* 0171–583 1770.

PANNONE, Rodger John; Senior Partner, Pannone & Partners (formerly Pannone March Pearson), Solicitors, since 1991; Chairman, Employment Relations Associates Ltd, since 1989; President of the Law Society of England and Wales, 1993–94; *b* 20 April 1943; *s* of late Cyril John Alfred Pannone and Violet Maud (*née* Weeks); *m* 1966, Patricia Jane Todd; two *s* one *d*. *Educ:* St Brendan's Coll., Bristol; Coll. of Law, London; Law Sch., Manchester. Articled to Casson & Co., Salford, 1966–69; Asst Solicitor and Partner, W. H. Thompson, 1969–73; Partner, Pannone March Pearson, subseq. Pannone & Partners, 1973–. Member: Lord Chancellor's Adv. Cttee on Civil Justice, 1986–89; Council, Law Soc., 1979– (Vice-Pres., 1992–93). Vice-Pres., British Acad. of Experts, 1994–. FRSA 1992. Fellow, Manchester Metropolitan Univ., 1994. Hon. DLitt Salford, 1993; Hon. LLD Nottingham Trent, 1993. *Publications:* numerous legal pubns. *Recreations:* the Lake District, walking slowly, food and wine. *Address:* 5 Darley Avenue, West Didsbury, Manchester M20 2XE. *T:* 0161–832 3000; 123 Deansgate, Manchester M3 2BU. *Clubs:* St James's, Northern Lawn Tennis (Manchester).

PANTER-DOWNES, Mollie Patricia, (Mrs Clare Robinson); London Correspondent, The New Yorker, 1939–87; *b* 25 Aug. 1906; *o c* of late Major Edward Panter-Downes, Royal Irish Regt and Kathleen Cowley; *m* 1927, Clare, 3rd *s* of late Aubrey Robinson; two *d*. *Educ:* mostly private. Wrote novel, The Shoreless Sea, at age of 16 (published John Murray, 1924); wrote in various English and American publications. *Publications:* Letter from England, 1940; Watling Green (children's book), 1943; One Fine Day, 1947; Ooty Preserved, 1967; At the Pines, 1971; London War Notes, 1972; contributed to The New Yorker Book of War Pieces, 1947.

See also J. M. F. Duer.

PANTIN, Most Rev. Anthony; *see* Port of Spain, Archbishop of.

PANTLIN, Sir Dick (Hurst), Kt 1993; CBE 1977 (OBE 1970); Partner, 1946–52, Co-Managing Director, 1952–68, Henrijean International Insurance Brokers; *b* 8 Dec. 1919; *s* of Albert Ralph Pantlin and Gwendolyn Clara Thomas; *m* 1946, Janine Henrijean; two *s*. *Educ:* Felsted; Alliance Française, Paris. ACIB. War service, Royal Marines, 1940–46, Major (despatches 1944). Founder and Chairman: British Sch., Brussels, 1969–95 (Pres., 1995); Council of British Indep. Schs in EC, 1980–95 (Pres., 1995); Trustee, St George's English Sch., Rome, 1988–; Pres., British Chamber of Commerce, Belgium and Luxembourg, 1975–77; Vice-Pres., Royal Belgo-British Union, 1975–; Founder and first Pres., Council of British Chambers of Commerce in Continental Europe, 1975–78. Chevalier: Ordre de la Couronne (Belgium), 1959; Ordre de Léopold (Belgium), 1969. *Publications:* articles for expatriates on educn, British nationality and voting legislation. *Recreations:* golf, travel, politics, ancestral research. *Address:* 11 Avenue de Mercure, Brussels B1180, Belgium. *T:* and *Fax:* (2) 3752721. *Clubs:* Army and Navy; Royal Golf de Belgique.

PANTLING, Mary; *see* Allen, Mary.

PANTON, Air Cdre Alastair Dyson, CB 1969; OBE 1950; DFC 1939; Provost Marshal and Director of RAF Security, 1968–71; retired; *Educ:* Bedford School; RAF Coll., Cranwell. Pilot Officer, No 53 Sqdn RAF, 1937; POW 1940–45; OC, Nos 58 and 540 Sqdns, 1946–47; Air Staff, Hong Kong, 1948–50; Wing Comdr Flying, RAF Coningsby, 1951–53; Staff Coll., 1953–54; Air Ministry, 1954–57; Station Comdr, RAF Cranwell, 1957–60, RAF Bircham Newton, 1961–62, RAF Tern Hill, 1963–64; HQ Far East Air Force, 1965–67. *Recreations:* gardening, poetry, carpentry. *Address:* Old Post Horns, Belle Hill, Giggleswick, Settle, N Yorks BD24 0BA.

PANTON, (Elizabeth) Jane; Headmistress, Bolton School Girls' Division, since 1994; *b* 20 June 1947; *d* of Richard Henry Panton and Constance Doreen Panton. *Educ:* Clayton Hall Grammar Sch., Newcastle; Merchant Taylors' Sch. for Girls, Liverpool; St Hugh's Coll., Oxford (MA Hons History); West Midlands Coll. of Educn, Walsall (PGCE). Teacher, Moreton Hall, near Oswestry, 1972–73; Third Mistress, Shrewsbury High Sch., 1973–83; Head of History and of Sixth Form, Clifton High Sch., Bristol, 1983–88; Headmistress, Merchant Taylors' Sch. for Girls, Crosby, Liverpool, 1988–94. Member: HMC/GSA Assisted Places Working Party, 1992–; GSA Professional Develt Cttee, 1992–; ISIS North Cttee, 1993–. Mem., Sefton FHSA, 1990–92. Mem. Council, Liverpool Univ., 1990–94. FRSA. *Recreations:* fell walking, UK and abroad, birdwatching, foreign travel, music, art, reading. *Address:* Bolton School Girls' Division, Bolton BL1 4PB. *T:* Bolton (01204) 840201.

PANTON, Dr Francis Harry, MBE 1948; Consultant, Cabinet Office, since 1985; Director, Royal Armament Research and Development Establishment, Ministry of Defence, 1980–83; *b* 25 May 1923; 3rd *s* of George Emerson Panton and Annie Panton; *m* 1952, Audrey Mary Lane (*d* 1989); two *s*; *m* 1995, Pauline Joyce Dean. *Educ:* City Sch., Lincoln; University College and Univ. of Nottingham. PhD Nottingham 1952. Served

War of 1939–45: commissioned, Bomb Disposal, Royal Eng., 1943–47. Pres., Univ. of Nottingham Union, 1950–51; Vice-Pres., Nat. Union of Students, 1952–54; Technical Officer, ICI, Billingham, 1952–53; Permanent Under-Secretary's Dept, FO, 1953–55; Office of Political Adviser, Berlin, 1955–57; Dep. Head, Technical Research Unit, MoD, 1957–58; Attaché, British Embassy, Washington, DC, 1958–59; Technical Adviser, UK Delegn to Conf. on Discontinuance of Nuclear Tests, Geneva, 1959–61; Permanent Under-Secretary's Dept, FO, 1961–63; Counsellor (Defence), British Embassy, Washington, DC, 1963–66; Head of Defence Science 6, MoD, 1966–68; Asst Chief Scientific Adviser (Nuclear), MoD, 1969–76; Dir Gen., Estabs, Resources and Programmes (B), MoD, April–Sept. 1976; Dir, Propellants, Explosives and Rocket Motor Estabt, and Head, Rocket Motor Exec., MoD, 1976–80. FRSC (FRIC 1961); FRSA 1973; FRAeS 1982. *Recreations:* bridge, reading local history. *Address:* Cantis House, 1 St Peter's Lane, Canterbury, Kent CT1 2BP. *T:* Canterbury 452902. *Club:* Reform.

PANTON, Jane; *see* Panton, E. J.

PANTRIDGE, Prof. (James) Frank, CBE 1978; MC 1942; *b* 3 Oct. 1916. *Educ:* Queen's Univ., Belfast (MD). FRCP 1957; FACC 1967. Research Fellow, Univ. of Mich, 1948–49; Dir, Regional Medical Cardiology Centre, NI, 1977–82; Hon. Prof. of Cardiol., QUB. Canadian Heart Foundn Orator; St Cyres Orator, National Heart Hosp., London. Chm., British Cardiac Soc., 1978. Developer of the Portable Defibrillator, and initiator (with J. S. Geddes) of pre-hospital coronary care. Hon. FRCPI. DUniv Open, 1981; Hon. DSc NUU, 1981. *Publications:* The Acute Coronary Attack, 1975; An Unquiet Life (autobiog), 1989, 3rd edn 1991. *Recreation:* fishing. *Address:* Hillsborough, Co. Down, N Ireland BT26 6EH. *T:* Hillsborough (01846) 689976.

PAOLOZZI, Sir Eduardo (Luigi), Kt 1989; CBE 1968; RA 1979 (ARA 1972); sculptor; HM Sculptor in Ordinary for Scotland, since 1986; Visiting Professor, Royal College of Art, since 1989 (Tutor in Ceramics, 1968–89); *b* 7 March 1924; *s* of Rudolpho Antonio Paolozzi and Carmella (*née* Rossi), both Italian; *m* (marr. diss.) three *d*. *Educ:* Edinburgh School of Art; Slade Sch. Worked in Paris, 1947–50; Instructor, Central School of Arts and Crafts, London, 1950–55; Lecturer, St Martin's School of Art, 1955–56; Prof. of Ceramics at Fachhochschule, Cologne, 1977–81; Prof. of Sculpture, Akad. der Bildenden Künste, Munich, 1981–91. Trustee, Nat. Portrait Gall., 1988–. Fellow, UCL, 1986. Hon. Dr RCA, 1979; Hon. RSA; Hon. DLitt: Glasgow, 1980; Heriot-Watt, 1987; London, 1987. British Critics Prize, 1953; David E. Bright Foundn Award, 1960; Watson F. Blaire Prize, 1961; Purchase Prize, Internat. Sculpture Exhibn at Solomon R. Guggenheim Mus., 1967; First Prize for Sculpture, Carnegie Internat. Exhibn, 1967; Sculpture Prize, European Patent Office, Munich, 1978; First Prize, Rhinegarten Cologne comp., 1981; Grand Prix d'Honneur, Print Biennale at Ljubljana, Yugoslavia, 1983. *One-man exhibitions include:* first in London, Mayor Gallery, 1947; first in New York, Betty Parsons Gallery, 1960, also 1962; Tate Gallery, 1971; V&A Mus., 1973, 1977 (print retrospective); Nationalgal., W Berlin, 1975; Fruit Market Gall., Edinburgh, 1976; Kassel, Germany, 1978; Glasgow League of Artists, 1979; Edinburgh Univ., 1979; Cologne, Germany, 1979; Museum for Künste und Gewerbe, Hamburg, 1982; Aedes Gall., Berlin, 1983; Invited artist, 6th Internat. Drawing Biennale, Cleveland (UK), 1983; Architectural Assoc., London; Royal Scottish Acad., Stadische Galerie im Lenbachhaus, Munich; Mus. Ludwig, Cologne; De Beyerd Mus., Breda, Holland; Contemporary Art Centre, Lyon, France; Ivan Dougherty Gall., Sydney, Aust., 1985; Cork, Ireland, 1985; Mus. of Mankind, 1986; RA, 1986; Serpentine Gall., 1987; Nat. Portrait Gall., 1988; Talbot Rice Art Gall., Edinburgh, 1989; Goethe Inst., London, 1991; Fitzwilliam Mus., Cambridge, 1992. Designed: glass mosaics for Tottenham Ct Road Underground Station, London; film sets for Percy Adlon's Herschel and the Music of the Stars, 1984–85. Work in permanent collections: Tate Gallery; Contemporary Art Society; Museum of Modern Art, New York; Kowloon Park, Hong Kong, etc. Work exhibited in: British Pavilion, Venice Biennale, 1952; Documenta 2, Kassel, 1959; New Images of Man, New York, 1959; British Pavilion, 30th Venice Biennale; Open Air Sculpture, Battersea Park, London; British Sculpture in the Sixties, Tate Gallery. Corresponding Mem., Bayerische Akad. der Schöner Künste, 1990. Hon. Member: AA, 1980; RGI, 1993; Hon. RIAS, 1991. Eduardo Paolozzi Art Sch. inaugurated at Ipswich Sch., 1987. Goethe Medal, 1991. Cavalieri Ufficiale, Ordine al Merito (Italy), 1991. *Relevant publications:* Eduardo Paolozzi, by Winfried Konnertz, 1984. *Recreation:* music. *Address:* 107 Dovehouse Street, SW3 6JZ. *Clubs:* Athenæum, Chelsea Arts.

PAPADOPOULOS, Achilles Symeon, CMG 1980; LVO 1972; MBE 1954; HM Diplomatic Service, retired; High Commissioner in the Bahamas, 1981–83; *b* 16 Aug. 1923; *s* of late Symeon Papadopoulos and Polyxene Papadopoulos; *m* 1954, Joyce Martin (*née* Stark); one *s* two *d*. *Educ:* The English School, Nicosia, Cyprus. British Mil. Admin, Eritrea, 1943; HMOCS: Cyprus, 1953; Dar es Salaam, 1959; Malta, 1961; HM Diplomatic Service: Malta, 1965; Nairobi, 1965; FCO, 1968; Colombo, 1971; Washington, 1974; Havana, 1974; Ambassador to El Salvador, 1977–79, to Mozambique, 1979–80; attached UK Mission to UN, Sept.–Dec. 1980. *Recreations:* golf, bridge. *Address:* 14 Mill Close, Great Bookham, Leatherhead, Surrey KT23 3JX.

PAPANDREOU, Dr Andreas George; Prime Minister of Greece, 1981–89 and since 1993; *b* 5 Feb. 1919; *s* of late George Papandreou and Sophia (*née* Mineiko); *m* 2nd, 1951, Margaret Chadd (marr. diss. 1989); three *s* one *d*; *m* 3rd, 1989, Mrs Dimitra Liani. *Educ:* Athens Univ. Law Sch.; Harvard, USA. Associate Professor: Univ. of Minnesota, 1947–50; Northwestern Univ., 1950–51; Professor: Univ. of Minnesota, 1951–55; Univ. of California, 1955–63; Dir, Centre of Econ. Res., Athens, 1961–64; Minister to Prime Minister, Greece, Feb.–Nov. 1964; Minister of Economic Co-ordination, 1965; Deputy for Ahaia, 1965–67; in prison, April–Dec. 1967; Founder and Chm., Pan-Hellenic Liberation Movement, 1968–74; Prof., Univ. of Stockholm, 1968–69; Prof. of Economics, York Univ., Canada, 1969–74; Founder and Pres., Panhellenic Socialist Movement, 1974–; Leader of the Opposition, 1977–81 and 1989–93; Minister of Defence, 1981–86. *Publications:* Economics as a Science, 1958; A Strategy for Greek Economic Development, 1962; Fundamentals of Model Construction in Microeconomics, 1962; The Greek Front, 1970; Man's Freedom, 1970; Democracy at Gunpoint, 1971; Paternalistic Capitalism, 1972; Project Selection for National Plans, 1974; Socialist Transformation, 1977. *Address:* Office of the Prime Minister, Parliament Building, Athens, Greece.

PAPANDREOU, Vasso; MP (Pasok) Athens, since 1993; Member, Commission of the European Communities, 1989–92; *d* of Andreas and Anastasia Papandreou. *Educ:* Athens Economic Univ. (BSc 1969); London Univ. (MSc 1971); Reading Univ. (PhD 1980). Economics Tutor, Exeter Univ., 1971–73; Res. Asst, Oxford Univ., 1973–74; Lectr, High Business and Econs Sch., Athens, 1981–85; MP, Greece, 1985–89; Dep. Minister, 1985–86, Alternate Minister, 1986–88, for Industry, Energy and Technology, 1985–86; Alternate Minister for Trade, 1988–89. Panhellenic Socialist Movement: Mem., Central Cttee, 1981–85; Mem., Exec. Bureau of Central Cttee, 1984–88. Dir, Hellenic Orgn for Small and Medium Size Firms, 1981–85. Mem., Bd of Dirs, Commercial Bank of Greece, 1982–85. Hon. DEd CNAA, 1992; Hon. DLitt Sheffield, 1992; Dr *hc* Paul Sabatier Univ., Toulouse, 1993. Chevalier, Legion of Honour (France), 1993. *Publications:* Multinational Companies and Less Developed Countries: the case of Greece, 1981; numerous papers and articles. *Address:* 15 Omirou Street, 10672 Athens, Greece.

PAPOULIAS, George Dimitrios; Commander, Order of Phoenix; Order of George I; Ambassador to the Court of St James's and (non-resident) to Iceland, 1990–93; *b* 19 May 1927; *s* of Dimitrios G. Papoulias and Caterina Kontopoulou; *m* 1974, Emily Pilavachi; one *d*. *Educ:* Athens Univ. (Law degree; Econ. and Comm. Scis degree). Military service, 2nd Lieut, 1950–51. Entered Greek Diplomatic Service, 1955; served Athens, New Delhi, Bonn; Dep. Perm. Deleg. to UN and to Internat Orgns, Geneva, 1964–69; Counsellor, 1967; Dir, Political Affairs, Min. of N Greece, 1969–70; Minister, Paris and Perm. Rep. to Unesco, 1971–74; Mem., Bd of Dirs, Resettlement Fund, Council of Europe, 1971–74; Ambassador to UN, NY, 1975–79, to Turkey, 1979–83, to USA, 1983–89; Alternate Minister and Minister for Foreign Affairs, 1989, 1990; special envoy of Greek govt to UN talks on former Yugoslav Republic of Macedonia, 1993. Holds foreign orders and decorations. *Recreations:* archaeology, history. *Address:* Rigillis 16, Athens 10674, Greece. *T:* 7229888. *Clubs:* Brooks's; Athenian (Greece).

PAPOUTSIS, Christos; economist; Member, European Commission, since 1995; *b* 11 April 1953. Pres., Nat. Students' Orgn, Students of Greece, 1978–80. Special Advr, Min. of Presidency of Govt, Greece, 1981–84; European Parliament: Mem., 1984–94; Vice Chm., Socialist Gp; Mem., Budgets and Budgetary Control Cttees, 1989–94; Vice-Chm., Canada Delegn, 1984–89; Mem., USA Delegn, 1989–94. Mem., Exec. Bureau and Central Cttee, Pan-Hellenic Socialist Movt (PASOK). *Publication:* European Journeys, 1994. *Address:* European Commission, Rue de la Loi 200, 1049 Brussels, Belgium.

PAPUA NEW GUINEA, Archbishop of, since 1990; **Most Rev. Bevan Meredith;** Primate of the Province of Papua New Guinea, since 1990; Bishop of New Guinea Islands, since 1977; *b* Alstonville, NSW, 14 Aug. 1927; 3rd *c* of Stanley Meredith and Edith Meredith (*née* Witchard). *Educ:* Univ. of Queensland; St Francis Theol Coll., Brisbane. Teacher, Slade Sch., Warwick, Qld and Housemaster, Highfields House, 1948–53; Staff, Martyrs' Meml Sch., PNG, 1954–58; deacon 1961, priest 1962, St Thomas, Toowong; Priest-in-charge, Managalas, PNG, 1963–67; Asst Bp of New Guinea, 1969–77. *Recreations:* music, photography, philately. *Address:* PO Box 159, Rabaul, East New Britain Province, Papua New Guinea.

PAQUET, Dr Jean-Guy, CC 1994 (OC 1984); FRSC; President and Chief Executive Officer, National Optics Institute, since 1994; *b* Montmagny, Qué, 5 Jan. 1938; *s* of Laurent W. Paquet and Louisianne Coulombe. *Educ:* Université Laval (BSc Engrg Physics, 1959; DSc Elec. Engrg, 1963); Ecole Nat. Sup. de l'Aéronautique, Paris (MSc Aeronautics, 1960). FRSC 1978; FAAAS 1981. Université Laval: Asst Prof. of Elec. Engrg, 1962; Associate Prof., 1967; Head, Elec. Engrg Dept, 1967–69; Vice-Dean (Research), Faculty of Science, 1969–72; Prof. of Elec. Engrg, 1971; Vice-Rector (Academic), 1972–77; Rector, 1977–87; Pres., La Laurentienne Vie Inc., 1987–94. Fellowships: French Govt, 1959; NATO, 1962; Nat. Science Foundn, 1964; Québec Govt, 1965. Def. Res. Bd of Canada Grant, 1965–76. National Research Council of Canada: Fellowship, 1961; Grant, 1964–77; Mem., Associate Cttee on Automatic Control, 1964–70; Special Asst to Vice-Pres. (Scientific), 1971–72. Pres., Conf. of Rectors and Principals of Univs of Prov. of Québec, 1979–81. Member: Council, Univs of Prov. of Qué, 1973–77; Bd, Assoc. of Scientific, Engrg and Technol Community of Canada, 1970–77 (Pres., 1975–76); Bd, French Canadian Assoc. for Advancement of Science, 1969–71; Canadian Assoc. of Univ. Res. Administrators; Special Task Force on Res. and Develt, Science Council of Canada, 1976; Order of Engrs, Qué; Amer. Soc. for Engrg Educn; Amer. Management Assoc., 1980; Soc. for Res. Administrators. Member Board: Interamerican Univs Assoc., 1980–87; Assoc. des universités partiellement ou entièrement de langue française, 1981–87 (Vice-Pres., 1983); Assoc. of Commonwealth Univs, 1981–87; Founding Mem., Corporate Higher Educn Forum. Pres., Selection Cttee, Outstanding Achievement Awards, Canada, 1984 (Mem., 1983). DSc *hc* McGill Univ., 1982; DLaw *hc*, York Univ., 1983. *Publications:* (with P. A. Roy) Rapport d'études bibliographiques: l'automation dans la production et la distribution de l'énergie électrique, 1968; (with J. F. Le Maître) Méthodes pratiques d'étude des oscillations non-linéaires: application aux systèmes par plus-ou-moins, 1970; more than fifty pubns in scientific jls, on control systems engrg; articles on research, develt and scientific policy. *Recreations:* jogging, travels, golf. *Address:* National Optics Institute, 369 Franquet Street, Sainte-Foy, Québec, PQ G1P 4N8, Canada. *T:* (418) 6577006, *Fax:* (418) 6577009. *Clubs:* Cercle de la Garnison de Québec, Club de Golf Royal Québec (Québec).

PARAGUAY, Bishop of, since 1988; **Rt. Rev. John Alexander Ellison;** *b* 24 Dec. 1940; *s* of Alexander and Catherine Ellison; *m* 1964, Judith Mary Cox; one *s* two *d*. *Educ:* London College of Divinity (ALCD); Borough Road College (Teacher's Cert.). Secondary school teacher, 1961–64. Deacon 1967, priest 1968; Curate, St Paul, Woking, 1967–71; missionary, church planter, evangelist; Bible school/Bible institute lecturer, 1971–79; Asst to Archdeacon, St Saviour, Belgrano, Dio. Argentina, 1979–82; Rector, Aldridge, Dio. Lichfield, 1983–88. *Recreations:* walking, gardening, family, dining out, club. *Address:* Diocesan Office, Casilla de Correo 1124, Asunción, Paraguay. *Club:* Garden (Asunción).

PARAYRE, Jean-Paul Christophe; Chevalier de la Légion d'Honneur; Officier, l'Ordre National du Mérite, 1978; French building and civil engineering executive; Member, Supervisory Board: Peugeot SA, since 1984; Alcatel NV, since 1992; Vice-Chairman, Group Bolloré, since 1994; *b* Lorient, 5 July 1937; *s* of Louis Parayre and Jehanne Malarde; *m* 1962, Marie-Françoise Chaufour; two *s* two *d*. *Educ:* Lycées in Casablanca and Versailles; Ecole Polytechnique, Paris; Ecole Nationale des Ponts et Chaussées. Engr, Dept of Highways, 1963–67; Technical Adviser: Min. of Social Affairs, 1967; Min. of Economy and Finance, 1968; Dir of Mech. Industries, Min. of Industry and Res., 1970–74; Chief Adviser to Pres. and Gen. Man., Banque Vernes et Commerciale de Paris, 1974; Manager of Planning, Automobile Div. of Peugeot, 1975; Manager, Automobile Div., Peugeot-Citroën, 1976; Chm., Peugeot SA, 1977–84; Mem., Supervisory Bd, 1977–84, Dir-Gen., 1984–88, Chm. and Chief Exec. Officer, 1988–90, Dumez SA. Chm., GIE Trans-Manche Construction, 1986–92; Vice-Chm., Lyonnaise des Eaux-Dumez, 1990–92; Mem., Board of Directors: Crédit National, 1978–; Valeo, 1986–91; GTM, 1986–92; LVMH, 1987–89; Jean Lefebvre, 1988–92; Vallourec, 1989–; McAlpine, 1990–92; Inchcape plc, 1991–94; Indosuez, 1991–94. *Recreations:* tennis, golf. *Address:* (office) Group Bolloré, Tour Delmas, 31/32 Quai de Dion Bouton, 92800 Puteaux, France; 3 Rond-Point Saint-James, 92200 Neuilly-sur-Seine, France. *Clubs:* Polo de Paris, Golf de Morfontaine.

PARBO, Sir Arvi (Hillar), AC 1993; Kt 1978; Non-Executive Chairman, Western Mining Corporation Ltd, since 1990 (Chairman and Managing Director, 1974–86; Executive Chairman, 1986–90); *b* 10 Feb. 1926; *s* of Aado and Hilda Parbo; *m* 1953, Saima Soots; two *s* one *d*. *Educ:* Clausthal Mining Acad., Germany; Univ. of Adelaide (BE Hons). Western Mining Corporation: Underground Surveyor, 1956; Underground Manager, Nevoria Mine, 1958–60; Techn. Asst to Man. Dir, 1960–64; Dep. Gen. Supt, WA, 1964–68; Gen. Manager, 1968–71 (Dir, 1970–); Dep. Man. Dir, 1971; Man. Dir, 1971. Director: Aluminium Co. of America, 1980–; Hoechst Australian Investments Pty Ltd, 1981–; Chase AMP Bank Ltd, 1985–91; Sara Lee Corp., 1991–; Chairman: Munich Reinsurance Company of Australia Ltd, 1984 (Dir, 1983–); Zurich Insurance Australian Group, 1985–; Alcoa of Australia Ltd, 1978–; The Broken Hill Pty Co. Ltd, 1989–92

(Dir, 1987–92). Member: Chase Internat. Adv. Bd; Degussa AG Supervisory Bd, 1988–93. Hon. DSc: Deakin, 1989; Curtin, 1989; Hon. DEng Monash, 1989; DUniv Flinders, 1991. Comdr, Order of Merit, Germany, 1979; Grand Cordon, Order of the Sacred Treasure, Japan, 1990; Australian Achiever, 1990. *Recreations:* reading, carpentry. *Address:* Western Mining Corporation Ltd, 360 Collins Street, Melbourne, Vic 3000, Australia; GPO Box 860K, Melbourne, Vic 3001. *T:* 602 0316. *Clubs:* Melbourne, Australian (both Melbourne); Weld (Perth); Commonwealth (Canberra); Hannans (Kalgoorlie); Duquesne (Pittsburgh, USA).

PARDOE, Alan Douglas William; QC 1988; a Recorder of the Crown Court, since 1990; *b* 16 Aug. 1943; *s* of William Pardoe and Grace Pardoe, DSc, FRSC; *m* 1st, 1972, Mary Ensor (marr. diss. 1976); 2nd, 1991, Catherine Williams (marr. diss. 1994). *Educ:* Oldbury Grammar Sch.; St Catharine's Coll., Cambridge (MA, LLB). Called to the Bar, Lincoln's Inn, 1971 (Hardwicke Schol.). Asst Lectr and Lectr in Law, Univ. of Exeter, 1965–70; Vis. Lectr in Law, Univ. of Auckland, NZ, 1970; Lectr in Law, Univ. of Sussex, 1970–74; began practice at the Bar, 1973. *Publications:* A Practical Guide to the Industrial Relations Act 1971, 1972; articles in legal periodicals. *Recreations:* mountain-walking, cooking. *Address:* 50 Northumberland Place, W2 5AS; Devereux Chambers, Devereux Court, Temple, WC2R 3JJ. *T:* 0171–353 7534. *Club:* Travellers'.

PARDOE, Dr Geoffrey Keith Charles, OBE 1988; PhD; FEng, FRAeS; FBIS; consultant, since 1993; Chairman: General Technology Systems Ltd, 1973–93 (Managing Director, 1973–88); General Technology Systems (Scandinavia) A/S, 1985–93; President: General Technology Systems SA, Belgium, since 1979; General Technology Systems Inc. (USA), since 1986; Director, International Academy of Science, since 1993; *b* 2 Nov. 1928; *s* of James Charles Pardoe and Ada Violet Pardoe; *m* 1953, Dorothy Patricia Gutteridge; one *s* one *d*. *Educ:* Wanstead County High Sch., London; London Univ. (BScEng Hons); Loughborough Coll. (DLC Hons Aeronautics; PhD (Astronautics) Loughborough Univ., 1984). FRAeS 1968; FEng 1988. Sen. Aerodynamicist, Armstrong Whitworth Ltd, 1949–51; Chief Aerodynamicist, Guided Weapons, De Havilland Props Ltd, 1951–56, Proj. Manager, Blue Streak, 1956–60; Hawker Siddeley Dynamics Ltd: Chief Engr, Weapons and Space Research, 1960–63; Chief Proj. Engr, Space Div., 1963–69; Sales Exec., 1969–73; Exec. Dir, British Space Develt Co. Ltd, 1960–74. Chm., Procogen Computer Systems Ltd, 1981–86; Man. Dir, 1985–87, Dep. Chm., 1987–93, Surrey Satellite Technology Ltd; Director: Philip A. Lapp Ltd, Canada, 1973–; Gen. Technology Systems (Netherlands) BV, Den Haag, 1982–; Eurosat SA, Switzerland, 1971–83; Eurotech Develts Ltd, 1981–83; 3 DIS (Europe) Ltd, 1994–. Vice Pres., Eurospace (Paris), 1961–73; Pres., RAeS, 1984–85 (Vice-Pres., 1981–83). Dep. Chm., 1981–86, Chm., 1986–, Watt Cttee on Energy. Mem., Internat. Acad. of Astronautics, 1982. FRSA; FInstD. *Publications:* The Challenge of Space, 1964; Integration of Payload and Stages of Space Carrier Vehicles, 1964; Project Apollo: The way to the Moon, 1969, 2nd edn 1970; The Future for Space Technology, 1984; over 50 main pubns in learned society pubns and jls; about 100 articles; about 2000 TV and radio interviews 1959–. *Recreations:* skiing, flying, badminton, photography, wind-surfing. *Address:* 23 Stewart Road, Harpenden, Herts AL5 4QE. *T:* Harpenden (01582) 460719. *Clubs:* Royal Air Force, Institute of Directors.

PARDOE, John George Magrath, CBE 1975; FRAeS; Director-General, Airworthiness, Civil Aviation Authority, 1972–79. *Educ:* Coll. of Aeronautical Engineering. Entered design work in Aircraft Industry, 1935; joined Accidents Inspection Br. of Air Ministry, 1942; joined Staff, Air Registration Bd, 1945; Chief Technical Officer, 1969. Médaille de l'aéronautique, 1980.

PARDOE, John Wentworth; Chairman, Sight and Sound Education Ltd, 1979–89; *b* 27 July 1934; *s* of Cuthbert B. Pardoe and Marjorie E. W. (*née* Taylor); *m* 1958, Joyce R. Peerman; two *s* one *d*. *Educ:* Sherborne; Corpus Christi Coll., Cambridge (MA). Television Audience Measurement Ltd, 1958–60; Osborne Peacock Co. Ltd, 1960–61; Liberal News, 1961–66. MP (L) Cornwall N, 1966–79; Treasurer of the Liberal Party, 1968–69. Presenter, Look Here, LWT, 1979–81. Sen. Res. Fellow, PSI, 1979–81. Consultant to Nat. Assoc. of Schoolmasters, 1967–73. Director: William Schlackman Ltd, 1968–71; Gerald Metals, 1972–83; Mem. London Metal Exchange, 1973–83. Mem., Youth Trng Bd, 1985–89. *Recreations:* walking, reading, music, carpentry. *Address:* 18 New End Square, NW3 1LN.

PAREKH, Prof. Bhikhu Chhotalal; Professor of Political Theory, University of Hull, since 1982; *b* 4 Jan. 1935; *s* of Chhotalal Parekh and Gajaraben Parekh; *m* 1959, Pramila (*née* Dalal); three *s*. *Educ:* Univ. of Bombay (BA 1954, MA 1956); Univ. of London (PhD 1966). Tutor, LSE, 1962–63; Asst Lectr, Univ. of Glasgow, 1963–64; Univ. of Hull: Lectr, Sen. Lectr and Reader, 1964–82. Vice-Chancellor, Univ. of Baroda, 1981–84. Visiting Professor: Univ. of BC, 1968–69; Concordia Univ., 1974–75; McGill Univ., 1976–77. Mem., Rampton/Swann Cttee of Inquiry into Educnl Problems of Ethnic Minority Children, 1978–82; Mem. Council, PSI, 1985–90; Vice Pres., UK Council for Overseas Students Affairs, 1989–; Chm., British Assoc. of S Asia Scholars, 1989–91. Dep. Chm., CRE, 1985–90; Mem., Commn on Rise of Neo-Fascism in Europe, 1992–. Trustee: Runnymede Trust, 1985–; Inst. for Public Policy Res., 1988–; Gandhi Foundn, 1988–; Anne Frank Educnl Trust, 1992–. FRSA 1988. *Publications:* Politics and Experience, 1968; Dissent and Disorder, 1971; The Morality of Politics, 1972; Knowledge and Belief in Politics, 1973; Bentham's Political Thought, 1973; Colour, Culture and Consciousness, 1974; Jeremy Bentham: ten critical essays, 1974; The Concept of Socialism, 1975; Hannah Arendt and the Search for a New Political Philosophy, 1981; Karl Marx's Theory of Ideology, 1982; Contemporary Political Thinkers, 1982; Political Discourse, 1986; Gandhi's Political Philosophy, 1989; Colonialism, Tradition and Reform, 1989; Jeremy Bentham: critical assessments (4 vols), 1993; The Decolonisation of Imagination, 1995, Crisis and Change in Contemporary India, 1995; articles in learned jls incl. Political Studies, British Jl of Political Science, Social Research, Jl of History of Ideas, Indian Jl of Social Science, Hist. of Pol Thought, TLS. *Recreations:* reading, music. *Address:* 211 Victoria Avenue, Hull HU5 3EF.

PARENT, Hon. Gilbert; MP (L) Welland-St Catharines-Thorold, 1974–85 and since 1988; Speaker of the House of Commons, Canada, since 1994; *b* 25 July 1935; *s* of Joseph Nelson Parent and Marie Delina (*née* Boulanger); *m* 1958, Joan Davis; four *d*. *Educ:* St Joseph's Coll., Rensselear, Ind. (BSc); Niagara Univ., NY (MA); State Univ. of NY (MEd). French teacher: Notre Dame High Sch., Welland, Ont, 1957–59; Dennis Morris High Sch., St Catharines, Ont, 1959–70; Vice-Principal, Thorold Secondary Sch., 1970–74; history teacher, Niagara South Bd of Educn, 1985–89. Hon. LLD: St Joseph's Coll., Ind., 1995; Niagara Univ., NY, 1995. *Recreations:* reading, playing golf, gardening, spending time with grand-children, promoting greater awareness of Parliament among young people. *Address:* Speaker's Office, House of Commons Room 328-N, Centre Block, Ottawa, Ontario K1A 0A6, Canada.

PARFIT, Derek Antony, FBA 1986; Senior Research Fellow, All Souls College, Oxford, since 1984; *b* 11 Dec. 1942; *s* of Norman and Jessie Parfit. *Educ:* Eton; Balliol College, Oxford. BA Modern History, 1964. Fellow of All Souls, 1967–. *Publication:* Reasons and Persons, 1984. *Recreation:* architectural photography. *Address:* All Souls College, Oxford OX1 4AL. *T:* Oxford (01865) 279282.

PARGETER, Edith Mary; OBE 1994; BEM 1944; *b* 28 Sept. 1913; 3rd *c* of Edmund Valentine Pargeter and Edith Hordley; unmarried. *Educ:* Dawley C of E Elementary Sch.; County High School for Girls, Coalbrookdale. Worked as a chemist's assistant, and at twenty succeeded in finding a publisher for first-and unsuccessful-book. WRNS Aug. 1940, teleprinter operator (BEM 1944); dispersed from the Service, Aug. 1945. FIIAL 1962. MA Birmingham, 1994. Gold Medal and Ribbon, Czechoslovak Society for International Relations, 1968. *Publications:* Hortensius, Friend of Nero, Iron Bound, 1936; The City Lies Foursquare, 1939; Ordinary People, 1941; She Goes to War, 1942; The Eighth Champion of Christendom, 1945; Reluctant Odyssey, 1946; Warfare Accomplished, 1947; By Firelight, 1948; The Fair Young Phoenix, 1948; The Coast of Bohemia, 1949; Lost Children, 1950; Fallen Into the Pit, 1951; Holiday with Violence, 1952; This Rough Magic, 1953; Most Loving Mere Folly, 1953; The Soldier at the Door, 1954; A Means of Grace, 1956; Tales of the Little Quarter (trans. from the Czech of Jan Neruda), 1957; Don Juan (trans. from the Czech of Josef Toman), 1958; Assize of the Dying, 1958; The Heaven Tree, 1960; The Green Branch 1962; The Scarlet Seed, 1963; The Terezín Requiem (trans. from the Czech of Josef Bor), 1963; The Lily Hand and other stories, 1965; Close Watch on the Trains (trans from the Czech of Bohumil Hrabal), 1968; Report on my Husband (trans. from the Czech of Josefa Slánská), 1969; A Bloody Field by Shrewsbury, 1972; Sunrise in the West, 1974; The Dragon at Noonday, 1975; The Hounds of Sunset, 1976; Afterglow and Nightfall, 1977; The Marriage of Meggotta, 1979; *as Ellis Peters:* many crime and mystery novels including: Monk's-hood, 1980 (Silver Dagger, Crime Writers Assoc.); Saint Peter's Fair, 1981; The Leper of Saint Giles, 1981; The Virgin in the Ice, 1982; The Sanctuary Sparrow, 1982; The Devil's Novice, 1983; Dead Man's Ransom, 1984; The Pilgrim of Hate, 1984; An Excellent Mystery, 1985; The Raven in the Foregate, 1986; The Rose Rent, 1986; The Hermit of Eyton Forest, 1987; The Confession of Brother Haluin, 1988; The Heretic's Apprentice, 1989; The Potter's Field, 1989; The Summer of the Danes, 1991; The Holy Thief, 1992; Brother Cadfael's Penance, 1994; (with Roy Morgan), non-fiction: Shropshire, 1992; Strongholds and Sanctuaries, 1993. *Recreations:* collecting gramophone records, particularly of voice; reading anything and everything; theatre. *Address:* Troya, 3 Lee Dingle, Madeley, Telford, Salop TF7 5TW. *T:* Telford (01952) 585178.

PARGETER, Rt. Rev. Philip; Auxiliary Bishop of Birmingham, (RC), and Titular Bishop of Valentiniana, since 1989; *b* 13 June 1933; *s* of Philip William Henry Pargeter and Ellen Pargeter. *Educ:* St Bede's Coll., Manchester; Oscott Coll., Sutton Coldfield. Priest, 1959; on staff of Cotton College, 1959–85; Administrator, St Chad's Cathedral, Birmingham, 1985–90; Canon, 1986. *Recreations:* reading, listening to music, walking. *Address:* Grove House, 90 College Road, Sutton Coldfield B73 5AH. *T:* 0121–354 4363.

PARIS, Archbishop of; *see* Lustiger, His Eminence Cardinal J.-M.

PARISH, Sir David (Elmer) W.; *see* Woodbine Parish.

PARISOT, Pierre; Chevalier de l'Ordre du Mérite; Chevalier de la Légion d'Honneur; Deputy Managing Director, Société Générale d'Entreprises, since 1991; Chairman, Transmanche-Link (TML), since 1991; *b* Ambacourt, France, 9 Jan. 1940; *s* of Louis Parisot and Marie (*née* Boye); *m* 1963, Evelyne Treilhou; two *s* two *d*. *Educ:* Ecole Polytechnique; Ecole Nationale des Ponts et Chaussées; Institut d'Etudes Politiques de Paris. Assistant to the Director, Civil Works Department: Réunion Island, 1966–72; Morbihan, Brittany, 1973–76; Dep. Dir, Personnel Policy and Mod. Management Methods, Min. of Civil Works, Transport and Envmt, 1976–77; Technical Advr, French Home Office Cabinet, 1977–80; Internat. Dir, St Gobain subsid., SOBEA, 1980–84; Dir Gen., SOGEA (Group Général des Eaux), 1985–90; Chairman: Supervisory Bd, Société des Tuyaux BONNA (Gp Générale des Eaux), 1990–; Consortium Grand Stade SA, 1995. *Recreations:* sailing, ski-ing. *Address:* Société Générale d'Entreprises, 1 Cours Ferdinand de Lesseps, 92851 Rueil-Malmaison Cedex, France. *T:* (1) 47164000.

PARIZEAU, Jacques, PhD; Member, Québec National Assembly (Parti Québécois) for Assomption, 1976–84 and since 1989; Prime Minister of Québec, since 1994; *b* Montreal, 9 Aug. 1930; *s* of Gerard Parizeau and Germaine Parizeau (*née* Biron), *m* 1st, 1956, Alicja Poznanska (decd); one *s* one *d*; 2nd, 1992, Lisette Lapointe. *Educ:* Ecole des Hautes Etudes Commerciales, Montreal; Institut d'Etudes Politiques, Paris (Dip. 1952); London Sch. of Econs (PhD 1955). Prof., Ecole des Hautes Etudes Commerciales, Montreal, 1955–65, 1967–76 and 1985–89 (Dir, Applied Econs Inst., 1973–75). Econs and financial advr to Prime Minister and Cabinet of Québec, 1961–69; Minister of Finance, 1976–84; also Pres., Treasury Bd and Minister of Revenue and of Financial Instns; Leader, Official Opposition, 1989–94. Parti Québécois: Mem., 1969–; Chm., Nat. Exec., 1970–73; Pres., 1988–. Pres., Québec Financial Instns Task Force, 1967–69; Chm., Québec Municipalities Study Commn, 1985. *Publications:* The Terms of Trade of Canada, 1966; numerous articles. *Recreations:* reading, music, ski-ing. *Address:* Office of the Prime Minister, 855 Grand Allée Est, Edifice J, 3e Etage, Québec, PQ G1A 1A2, Canada.

PARK, family name of **Baroness Park of Monmouth.**

PARK OF MONMOUTH, Baroness *cr* 1990 (Life Peer), of Broadway in the County of Hereford and Worcester; **Daphne Margaret Sybil Désirée Park,** CMG 1971; OBE 1960; HM Diplomatic Service, retired; Principal of Somerville College, Oxford, 1980–89; *b* England, 1 Sept. 1921; British parents; unmarried. *Educ:* Rosa Bassett Sch.; Somerville Coll., Oxford (Hon. Fellow, 1990). WTS (FANY), 1943–47 (Allied Commn for Austria, 1946–48). FO, 1948; UK Delegn to NATO, 1952; 2nd Sec., Moscow, 1954; FO, 1956; Consul and 1st Sec., Leopoldville, 1959; FO, 1961; Lusaka, 1964; FO, 1967; Consul-Gen., Hanoi, 1969–70; Hon. Res. Fellow, Univ. of Kent, 1971–72, on sabbatical leave from FCO; Chargé d'Affaires *ai*, Ulan Bator, Apr.–June 1972; FCO, 1973–79. Gov., BBC, 1982–87. Chm., Legal Aid Adv. Cttee to the Lord Chancellor, 1985–91. Chm., RCHM, 1989–94. Member: British Library Bd, 1983–89; Sheffield Develt Corp. Bd, 1989–92; RIIA; Royal Asiatic Soc.; Mem. Council, VSO, 1981–84; Mem. Council, GB–Sasakawa Foundn, 1994–; Dir, Zoo Develt Trust, 1989–90. Pro-Vice-Chancellor, Univ. of Oxford, 1985–89. Mem., Thatcher Foundn, 1992–; Trustee: Royal Armouries Develt Trust, 1991–92; Jardine Educnl Trust, 1991–. MRSA. Hon. LLD: Bristol, 1988; Mount Holyoke Coll., 1992. *Recreations:* good talk, politics, and difficult places. *Address:* House of Lords, SW1A 0PW. *Clubs:* United Oxford & Cambridge University, Naval and Military, Commonwealth Trust, Special Forces.

PARK, Andrew Edward Wilson, QC 1978; QC (NI) 1992; *b* 27 Jan. 1939; *m* 1962, Ann Margaret Woodhead; two *s* one *d* (and one *s* decd). *Educ:* Leeds Grammar Sch.; University Coll., Oxford. Winter Williams Law Schol., 1959; BA (Jurisp.) 1960, MA 1964. Various academic posts in UK and abroad, 1960–68. Called to the Bar, Lincoln's Inn, 1964, Bencher, 1986; practice at Revenue Bar, 1965–; Chairman: Taxation and Retirement Benefits Cttee of the Bar Council, 1978–82; Revenue Bar Assoc., 1987–92; Treasurer, Senate of the Inns of Court and Bar, 1982–85. *Publications:* The Sources of Nigerian Law, 1963; various articles, notes and reviews in legal periodicals, mainly concerning taxation.

Recreations: tennis, golf. *Address:* Gray's Inn Chambers, Gray's Inn, WC1R 5JA. *T:* 0171–242 2642.

PARK, Hon. Sir Hugh (Eames), Kt 1965; Judge of the High Court of Justice, Queen's Bench Division, 1973–85 (Family Division, 1965–73); retired; *b* 24 April 1910; *er s* of late William Robert and Helen Beatrice Park; *m* 1938, Beryl Josephine, *d* of late Joseph and Margery Coombe; three *d. Educ:* Blundell's; Sidney Sussex Coll., Cambridge (Hon. Fellow, 1968). Called to the Bar, Middle Temple, 1936; QC 1960; Bencher, 1965. Member Western Circuit. Served War, 1940–45; Sqdn Leader, 1945. Recorder of Penzance, 1959–60; of Exeter, 1960–64; of Southampton, 1964–65. Member, Court of Exeter Univ., 1961; Member, Board of Governors, Blundell's Sch., 1961–81. Commn of Assize, North East Circuit, 1963; Judge of the Courts of Appeal, Channel Islands, 1964–65; Chairman, County of Devon Quarter Sessions, 1964–71; Deputy Chairman, Cornwall County Quarter Sessions, 1959–71; Presiding Judge, Western Circuit, 1970–75. Hon. LLD Exeter, 1984. *Recreation:* fishing. *Address:* 34 Ordnance Hill, St John's Wood, NW8 6PU. *T:* 0171–586 0417; 1 Church Street, Gorran Haven, Cornwall PL26 6JH. *T:* Mevagissey (01726) 842333.

See also C. O. Hum.

PARK, Ian Grahame, CBE 1995; Chairman, Northcliffe Newspapers Group Ltd, since 1995 (Managing Director, 1982–95); Director, Associated Newspaper Holdings plc, since 1983; *b* 15 May 1935; *s* of William Park and Christina (*née* Scott); *m* 1965, Anne Turner; one *s. Educ:* Lancaster Royal Grammar Sch.; Queens' Coll., Cambridge. 1st Bn Manchester Regt, Berlin (Nat. Service Commn), 1954–56. Trainee Journalist, Press and Journal, Aberdeen, 1959; Asst Lit. Editor, Sunday Times, 1960–63; various management posts, Thomson Newspapers, 1963–65; Liverpool Daily Post and Echo, 1965–, Man. Dir and Editor in Chief, 1972–82. Dir, Daily Mail & General Trust, 1994–. Mem. Council, Newspaper Soc., 1967– (Pres., 1980–81); Dir, Press Assoc., 1973–83 (Chm., 1978–79 and 1979–80); Dir, Reuters, 1978–82, 1988–94. Mem. Newspaper Panel, Monopolies and Mergers Commn, 1986–95. Dir, Radio City (Sound of Merseyside Ltd), 1973–82; Dir, Liverpool Playhouse, 1973–80; Trustee, Blue Coat Soc. of Arts, Liverpool, 1973–82. FRSA. *Recreations:* eighteenth-century English pottery, twentieth-century English pictures. *Address:* 31 John Street, WC1N 2QB. *Club:* Reform.

PARK, (Ian) Michael (Scott), CBE 1982; Consultant, Paull & Williamsons, Advocates, Aberdeen, since 1991 (Partner, 1964–91); *b* 7 April 1938; *m* 1964, Elizabeth Mary Lamberton Struthers; two *s. Educ:* Aberdeen Grammar Sch.; Aberdeen Univ. (MA, LLB). Admitted Mem. Soc. of Advocates, Aberdeen, 1962 (Treas., 1991–92; Pres., 1992–93). Temp. Sheriff, 1976–94. Law Society of Scotland: Mem. Council, 1974–85; Vice-Pres., 1979–80; Pres., 1980–81. A Chm., Med. Appeal Tribunals, 1991–; Mem., Criminal Injuries Compensation Bd, 1983–. Chm., Aberdeen Citizens Advice Bureau, 1976–88. Frequent broadcaster on legal topics. *Recreations:* golf, gardening. *Address:* Beechwood, 46 Rubislaw Den South, Aberdeen AB2 6AX. *T:* Aberdeen (01224) 313799. *Club:* New (Edinburgh).

PARK, Dame Kiri; *see* Te Kanawa, Dame K.

PARK, Dame Merle (Florence), (Dame Merle Bloch), DBE 1986 (CBE 1974); Principal, Royal Ballet; Director, Royal Ballet School, since 1983; *b* Salisbury, S Rhodesia, 8 Oct. 1937; *d* of P. J. Park, Eastlea, Salisbury, S Rhodesia, C Africa; *m* 1st, 1965, James Monahan, CBE (marr. diss. 1970; he *d* 1985); one *s*; 2nd, 1971, Sidney Bloch. *Educ:* Elmhurst Ballet Sch. Founder, Ballet Sch., St Peter's Sq., W6, 1977–83. Joined Sadler's Wells Ballet, 1955; first rôle, a Mouse (Sleeping Beauty prologue); first solo, Milkmaid (Façzce); principal soloist, 1959. First danced: Blue Bird (Act III, Sleeping Beauty), 1956; Swanhilda (Coppelia), Mamzelle Angot (Mamzelle Angot), 1958; Lise (Fille Mal Gardée), 1960; Cinderella, 1962; Juliet (Romeo and Juliet), 1965; Giselle, Celestial (Shadow Play), 1967; Clara (Nutcracker), Aurora (Sleeping Beauty), 1968; Odette (Swan Lake), 1971; A Walk to Paradise Garden, 1972; Firebird, Odette/Odile (Swan Lake), Dances at a Gathering, 1973; Manon, Emilia (The Moor's Pavane), Aureole, Terpsichore (Apollo), Elite Syncopations, 1974; Lulu, 1976; Kate (The Taming of the Shrew), La Bayadère, Tuesday's Child (Jazz Calendar), Triad, Symphonic Variations, Waltzes of Spring (in Royal Opera Fledermaus), Le Papillon, 1977; Countess Larisch (Mayerling), 1978; La Fin du Jour, 1979; Mary Vetsera (Mayerling), Natalia (A Month in the Country), Adieu, 1980; Chloë (Daphnis and Chloë), Isadora, 1981; Raymonda, 1983. Queen Elizabeth Award, Royal Acad. of Dancing, 1982. *Recreations:* gardening, reading. *Address:* c/o Royal Ballet School, 144 Talgarth Road, W14 9DE.

PARK, Michael; *see* Park, I. M. S.

PARKE, Prof. Dennis Vernon William, PhD, DSc; CChem, FRSC, FIBiol, FRCPath; (first) Professor and Head of Department of Biochemistry, University of Surrey, 1967–87; University Professor of Biochemistry, 1986–90; Emeritus Professor, since 1990; *b* London, 15 Nov. 1922; *e s* of William Parke and Florence Parke; *m* 1943, Doreen Joan Dunn; two *s* one *d. Educ:* West Ham Municipal Secondary Sch. (Gurney Scholar); Chelsea and University Colls, Univ. of London 1940–48; St Mary's Hosp. Med. Sch., London (PhD, DSc). War Service, RA RAMC, 1942–47. Head, Dept of Microbiol Chem., Glaxo Labs Ltd, 1948–49; St Mary's Hosp. Med. Sch., Univ. of London: Res. Asst to Prof. R. T. Williams, FRS, 1949–52; Lectr in Biochem., 1952–58, Sen. Lectr, 1958–62; Reader in Biochem., 1962–67; Dean, Faculty of Biol and Chem. Sciences, Univ. of Surrey, 1971–75. Visiting Professor: Univ. of Calif, Davis, 1978; Edmonton, Canada, 1984. Sometime Examnr, Univs of Dublin (Trinity), Edinburgh, Glasgow, Liverpool, London, Newcastle upon Tyne, Reading, Strathclyde, Wales, Auckland, Ibadan, Nairobi, Singapore, Sydney and Wellington. Sigma Xi Lectr, Univ. of Calif (Davis), 1978. Member: Cttee on Safety of Drugs, 1968–70; Cttee on Safety of Medicines, 1970–83; Cttee on Med. Aspects of Chemicals in Food and Environment, DHSS, 1972–86; Food Additives and Contaminants Cttee, MAFF, 1972–80; WHO Expert Panel on Food Additives, 1975–88; WHO Sci. Gp on Toxicity Evaluation of Chemicals, 1975; WHO Cons. in Indust. Toxicol., 1974, 1979, 1981, 1983; Sci. Dir, NATO Workshop on Ecotoxicology, July–Aug. 1977; Consultant to Environmental Protection Agency, Washington, 1985. Dir, Food and Veterinary Labs Ltd, 1988–92. Mem., Internat. Acad. of Environmental Safety. Scheele Lectr and Medal, Uppsala, 1989. Hon. MRCP 1985; Hon. Member: Polish Soc. of Toxicology, 1984; Biochemical Soc., 1991; Hon. Fellow, Polish Soc. of Occupational Medicine, 1984. MD *hc* Lødz, 1995. Editor, Xenobiotica, 1970–93. *Publications:* The Biochemistry of Foreign Compounds, 1968; (ed) Enzyme Induction, 1975; Drug Metabolism from Microbe to Man, 1977; Mucus in Health and Disease, 1977; Immunotoxicology, 1983; The Future of Predictive Safety Evaluation, 1987; Food, Nutrition and Chemical Toxicity, 1993; chapters in books and res. papers in biochem., pharm. and med. jls. *Recreations:* landscape gardening, music. *Address:* Trevelen, Poyle Road, Guildford, Surrey GU1 3SL. *T:* Guildford (01483) 573667.

PARKER, family name of **Earls of Macclesfield** and **Morley.**

PARKER, A(gnes) Miller, RE; Artist and Wood-engraver; *b* Irvine, Ayrshire, 25 March 1895; *d* of William McCall and Agnes Mitchell Parker; *m* 1918, William McCance, Artist (marr. diss. 1963, and she legally assumed maiden name); no *c. Educ:* Glasgow School of Art (Diploma, Haldane Scholar). Instructress, Glasgow School of Art, 1918–20; Art Mistress, Maltmans Green School, Gerrards Cross, 1920–28; Art Mistress, Clapham High School and Training Coll., 1928–30; Walter Brewster Prize, 1st International Exhibition of Engraving and Lithography, Chicago, 1929; Wood-engraver to Gregynog Press, Newtown, Montgomeryshire, 1930–33. *Publications:* Chief Illustrated Editions; Esopes Fables by Caxton, 1931; Daisy Matthews and three other tales by Rhys Davies, 1932; XXI Welsh Gypsy Folk-Tales, collected by John Sampson, 1933; The House with the Apricot by H. E. Bates, 1933; Forest Giant-translated from the French by J. H. Ross (Colonel T. E. Lawrence), 1935; Through the Woods by H. E. Bates, 1936; Down the River by H. E. Bates, 1937; Gray's Elegy written in a Country Church-yard (Limited Editions Club of NY), 1938; Richard II-Shakespeare (Limited Editions Club of NY), 1940; A Shropshire Lad by A. E. Housman, 1940; The Return of the Native by Thomas Hardy (Limited Editions Club of NY), 1942; Essays in Russet by Herbert Furst, 1944; Spring of the Year by Richard Jefferies, 1946; The Life of the Fields, 1947, Field and Hedgerow, 1948, The Open Air, 1948, The Old House at Coate, 1948, by Richard Jefferies; Animals Under the Rainbow by Aloysius Roche, 1952; The Faerie Queene by Edmund Spenser, vols I and II, 1953; Lucifer by J. C. Powys, 1956; Tess of the D'Urbervilles, 1956, and Far From the Madding Crowd, 1958, by Thomas Hardy (New York); The Tragedies of Shakespeare (New York), 1959; The Mayor of Casterbridge by Thomas Hardy (Limited Editions Club of NY), 1964; Poems of Shakespeare (Limited Editions Club of NY), 1967; Jude the Obscure by Thomas Hardy (Limited Editions Club of NY), 1969. *Recreations:* fishing and cats.

PARKER, Alan William, CBE 1995; film director and writer; *b* 14 Feb. 1944; *s* of William and Elsie Parker; *m* 1966, Annie Inglis (marr. diss. 1992); three *s* one *d. Educ:* Owen's Sch., Islington. Advertising Copywriter, 1965–67; Television Commercials Director, 1968–78. Wrote screenplay, Melody, 1969; wrote and directed: No Hard Feelings, 1972; Our Cissy, 1973; Footsteps, 1973; Bugsy Malone, 1975; A Turnip Head's Guide to the British Cinema, 1985; Angel Heart, 1987; Come See the Paradise, 1990; directed: The Evacuees, 1974; Midnight Express, 1977; Fame, 1979; Shoot the Moon, 1981; The Wall, 1982; Birdy, 1984; Mississippi Burning, 1989; The Commitments, 1991; The Road to Wellville, 1995. Vice-Chm., Directors Guild of Great Britain, 1982–; Mem., British Screen Adv. Council, 1985–. BAFTA Michael Balcon Award for Outstanding Contribution to British Film, 1985. *Publications: novels:* Bugsy Malone, 1976; Puddles in the Lane, 1977; *cartoon:* Hares in the Gate, 1983.

PARKER, Cameron Holdsworth, OBE 1993; DL; Vice-Chairman, Lithgows Ltd, since 1991 (Managing Director, 1984–92); *b* 14 April 1932; *s* of George Cameron Parker and Mary Stevenson Parker; *m* 1st, 1957, Elizabeth Margaret Thomson (*d* 1985); three *s*; 2nd, 1986, Marlyne Honeyman, Mem. Stock Exchange. *Educ:* Morrison's Acad., Crieff; Glasgow Univ. (BSc Hons). John G. Kincaid & Co. Ltd, Greenock: Asst Manager, 1958; Asst Gen. Man., 1961; Dir, 1963; Man. Dir, 1967; Chm., 1976; Chm. and Chief Exec., Scott Lithgow Ltd, Port Glasgow, 1980–83. Bd Mem., British Shipbuilders, 1977–80, 1981–83. Director, 1984–94 (Chairman, 1984–92): Campbeltown Shipyard Ltd; J. Fleming Engrg Ltd; Glasgow Iron & Steel Co. Ltd; Landcatch Ltd; Lithgow Electronics Ltd; Malakoff & Wm Moore Ltd; McKinlay & Blair Ltd; Prosper Engrg Ltd; Director: Lithgows Pty Ltd, 1984–94; Scottish Homes, 1992–; Clyde Shaw Ltd, 1992–94. Mem. Scottish Council, CBI, 1986–92. Mem., Argyll and Clyde Health Bd, 1991–95. Freeman, City of London, 1981; Liveryman, Worshipful Co. of Shipwrights, 1981–. DL Renfrewshire, 1993. *Recreation:* golf. *Address:* Heath House, Rowantreehill Road, Kilmacolm, Renfrewshire PA13 4PE. *T:* Kilmacolm (0150587) 3197.

PARKER, Christopher William Oxley, MA; JP; DL; *b* 28 May 1920; *s* of late Lieut-Col John Oxley Parker, TD, and Mary Monica (*née* Hills); *m* 1947, Jocelyn Frances Adeline, *d* of late Colonel C. G. Arkwright, Southern Rhodesia; one *s* two *d. Educ:* Eton; Trinity Coll., Oxford. Served War of 1939–45, 147th Field Regt (Essex Yeomanry) RA, 1939–42. Director: Strutt and Parker (Farms) Ltd; Local Dir, Chelmsford Bd, Barclays Bank, 1951–83. Mem., Nat. Trust Properties Cttee, 1974–89; Mem. Exec. Cttee, CLA, 1959–73; Pres., Essex CLA, 1987–. JP Essex, 1952; High Sheriff of Essex, 1961; DL Essex 1972. *Recreations:* shooting, golf; estate management. *Address:* Faulkbourne Hall, Witham, Essex CM8 1SP. *T:* Witham (01376) 513385. *Club:* Boodle's.

PARKER, Clifford Frederick, MA, LLB Cantab; Bracton Professor of Law at the University of Exeter, 1957–85 (Deputy Vice-Chancellor, 1963–65, Public Orator, 1977–81); *b* 6 March 1920; *yr s* of late Frederick James Parker and Bertha Isabella (*née* Kemp), Cardiff; *m* 1945, Christine Alice (*née* Knowles); two *d. Educ:* Cardiff High Sch.; Gonville and Caius Coll., Cambridge. Royal Air Force, 1940–43. Solicitor of Supreme Court, 1947–94. Lecturer in Common Law, University of Birmingham, 1951–57; Senior Tutor and Asst Director of Legal Studies, Faculty of Law, University of Birmingham, 1956–57. Pres., Soc. of Public Teachers of Law, 1974–75. Chm., Exeter Area, Supplementary Benefit, later Social Security Appeal Tribunal, 1978–93. JP Devon, 1969–92. *Publications:* contrib. to legal periodicals. *Address:* Lynwood, Exton, Exeter EX3 0PR. *T:* Exeter (01392) 874051.

PARKER, (Diana) Jean, CBE 1989; Director, Goldsborough Healthcare plc, since 1994; *b* 7 June 1932; *d* of Lewis William Reeve Morley and Amy (*née* Southwood); *m* 1959, Dudley Frost Parker (*d* 1971); one *s* one *d. Educ:* Kesteven and Grantham Girls' Sch.; Birmingham Univ. (BCom). CIMgt (CBIM 1986). Director: Vacu-Lug Traction Tyres Ltd, 1957–; Central Independent Television Plc, 1982–; British Steel (Industry) Ltd, 1986–90; Grantham and Dist Hosp. NHS Trust, 1995–. Mem. Bd, E Midlands Electricity, 1983–90; Mem., E Midlands, later Eastern Adv. Bd, National Westminster Bank, 1985–92; Chm., Lincs Jt Develt Cttee, 1983–; Chm., CBI Smaller Firms Council, 1986–88. Chm., N Lincs HA, 1987–90; Non-exec. Dir, Lincs Ambulance and Health Service Trust, 1991–92. *Club:* University Women's.

PARKER, Sir Douglas D.; *see* Dodds-Parker.

PARKER, Rear-Adm. Douglas Granger, CB 1971; DSO 1945; DSC 1945; AFC 1952; Assistant Chief of Naval Staff (Operations and Air), 1969–71, retired; *b* 21 Nov. 1919; *s* of R. K. Parker; *m* 1953, Margaret Susan, *d* of late Col W. Cooper; one *s* one *d. Educ:* W Hartlepool Technical Coll. Joined Royal Navy, 1940; Command Fleet Air Arm Fighter Squadrons, 1948–51; Commanded: HMS Cavendish, 1961–62; RN Air Station, Lossiemouth, 1965–67; HMS Hermes, 1967–69. Captain 1959; Rear-Adm. 1969. *Address:* High Meadow, Walhampton, Lymington, Hants. *T:* Lymington (01590) 673259. *Club:* Royal Lymington Yacht.

PARKER, Sir Eric (Wilson), Kt 1991; FCA; Chairman, Graham Consulting, since 1993; *b* 8 June 1933; *s* of Wilson Parker and Edith Gladys (*née* Wellings); *m* 1955, Marlene Teresa (*née* Neale); two *s* two *d. Educ:* The Priory Grammar Sch. for Boys, Shrewsbury. FCA 1967 (ACA 1956); CIMgt (CBIM 1983). Articled Clerk with Wheeler, Whittingham & Kent, Shrewsbury, 1950–55; National Service, Pay Corps, 1956–58; Taylor Woodrow Gp, 1958–64; Trafalgar House Gp, 1965–93; Finance/Admin Dir, 1969; Dep. Man. Dir, 1973; Gp Man. Dir, 1977; Chief Exec., 1983–92; Dep. Chm., 1988–93. Non-Executive

Director: European Assets Trust NV, 1972–85; Sealink UK Ltd, 1979–81; British Rail Investments Ltd, 1980–84; Evening Standard Co. Ltd, 1982–85; Touche Remnant Hldgs Ltd, 1985–89; Caradon plc (formerly Metal Box plc, then MB-Caradon), 1985–; The Royal Automobile Club (formerly The Automobile Pty Ltd), 1986–; Hardy Oil & Gas plc, 1989–. Advr, Phoenix Develt Capital Fund, 1992–. Dir, Race Horse Owners' Assoc., 1994–. Proprietor, Crimbourne Stud, 1991–. *Recreations:* sports (including golf and horseracing), wines. *Address:* Crimbourne House, Crimbourne Lane, Wisborough Green, Billingshurst, W Sussex RH14 0HR. *Clubs:* Royal Automobile, MCC; West Sussex Golf.

PARKER, Frederick John, (Jack), FICE, FIStructE, FIHT; Chief Highway Engineer (Under Secretary), Department of Transport, 1988–91; *b* 6 Sept. 1927; *s* of Charles Fred Parker and Eleanor Emily (*née* Wright); *m* 1955, Ann Shirley Newnham; three *d*. *Educ:* Shene Grammar School; Univ. of Liverpool (BEng 1948; MEng 1951). Engineer with Scott, Wilson, Kirkpatrick & Partners in London, Hong Kong and elsewhere, 1952–65; Sen. Engineer, then Partner, with Husband & Co., 1965–78; Director, W. S. Atkins & Partners, 1978–88. Institution of Highways and Transportation: Chm., Greater London Br., 1975–77; Vice-Pres., 1985; Pres., 1988. Vice-Chm., Brit. Nat. Cttee of Permanent Internat. Assoc of Road Congresses, 1988–91. *Publications:* professional papers in engineering jls. *Recreations:* athletics (Olympics 1952 and 1956, European silver medallist 1954); local affairs, music. *Address:* 43 York Avenue, East Sheen, SW14 7LQ. *T:* 0181–876 1059. *Club:* South London Harriers.

PARKER, Geoffrey; *see* Parker, James G. and Parker, N. G.

PARKER, Prof. Geoffrey Alan, FRS 1989; Professor in the Department of Environmental and Evolutionary Biology, University of Liverpool, since 1989; *b* 24 May 1944; *s* of late Dr Alan Parker and G. Ethel Parker (*née* Hill); *m* 1967, Susan Mary Wallis (*d* 1994); one *s* one *d*. *Educ:* Stockton Heath Primary Sch.; Lymm Grammar Sch.; Univ. of Bristol (BSc (1st Cl. Hons Zoology; Rose Bracher Prize for Biology); PhD); Univ. of Cambridge (MA). Asst Lectr 1968, Lectr 1969, Sen. Lectr 1976, Reader 1980, Univ. of Liverpool. Fellow of King's Coll., Cambridge, 1978–79; Nuffield Sci. Res. Fellow, 1982–83; BBSRC (formerly SERC) Sen. Res. Fellow, 1990–95. *Publications:* many scientific papers in learned jls. *Recreations:* playing jazz in local bands (clarinet), mainly Dixieland; breeding, showing and judging exhibition bantams (Hon. Sec./Treasurer, Partridge & Pencilled Wyandotte Club, 1987–94; Mem. Council, Poultry Club, 1986–90). *Address:* Saunton, The Runnel, Neston, South Wirral, Cheshire L64 3TG. *T:* 0151–336 4202.

PARKER, Geoffrey John, CBE 1985; Chief Executive, Maritime Transport Services Ltd, since 1989; *b* 20 March 1937; *s* of Stanley John Parker and Alice Ellen Parker; *m* 1957, Hazel Mary Miall; two *s* two *d*. *Educ:* County Grammar Sch., Hendon. Commercial Dir, Townsend Car Ferries Ltd, 1972–74; Man. Dir, Atlantic Steam Navigation Co., 1974–87; Man. Dir, 1976–87, Chm., 1983–87, Felixstowe Dock & Rly Co.; Chairman: Larne Harbour Bd, 1983–87; European Ferries PLC, 1986–87; Chief Exec., Highland Participants, 1987–89. Mem., Nat. Bus Co., 1980–87. FCIT 1982. *Recreation:* golf. *Address:* 101 Valley Road, Ipswich, Suffolk IP1 4NF. *T:* Ipswich (01473) 216003. *Club:* Ipswich Golf (Purdis Heath, Ipswich).

PARKER, Herbert John Harvey; *see* Parker, John.

PARKER, Hugh; Visiting Lecturer, Sloan School of Management, Massachusetts Institute of Technology, since 1992; *b* 12 June 1919; *s* of Ross Parker and Ruth Baker Parker; *m* 1957, Elsa del Carmen Mijares Osorio; one *s* one *d*. *Educ:* Tabor Academy; Trinity Hall, Cambridge; Massachusetts Inst. of Technology. North Carolina Shipbuilding Co., 1941–43; General Electric Co., 1945–46; Ludlow Manufacturing Co., 1947–50; McKinsey & Co. Inc., 1951–84 (Sen. Dir, 1974–84). Pres., American Chamber of Commerce (UK), 1976–79. Governor, Ditchley Foundn. *Publications:* Letters to a New Chairman, 1979; numerous articles on management. *Recreations:* reading, sculling, cooking. *Address:* 2 Redstone Lane, Marblehead, MA 01945, USA. *Clubs:* The Pilgrims, United Oxford & Cambridge University; Leander; Racquet and Tennis (New York); Eastern Yacht (Mass).

PARKER, Jack; *see* Parker, F. J.

PARKER, (James) Geoffrey; High Master, Manchester Grammar School, 1985–94; Chairman, Teacher Training Agency, since 1994; *b* 27 March 1933; *s* of late Ian Sutherland Parker and Kathleen Lilian Parker; *m* 1956, Ruth Major; two *d*. *Educ:* Alderman Newton's Sch., Leicester; Christ's Coll., Cambridge (Exhibnr); Wadham Coll., Oxford. National Service, RA, 1954–56. Asst Master, Bedford Modern Sch., 1957–66; Head of History Dept, Tonbridge Sch., 1966–75; Headmaster, Queen Elizabeth Grammar Sch., Wakefield, 1975–85. Chairman: HMC, 1991; ISIS, 1994–. Gov., Charterhouse, 1993–; Trustee: St George's English Sch., Rome, 1992–; Berlin British Sch., 1994–. *Recreation:* sailing. *Address:* Ty Mawr, Carno, Powys SY17 5LL. *T:* Carno (01686) 420276.

PARKER, Dr James Gordon; Registrar of Public Lending Right, since 1991; *b* 1 June 1952; *s* of James Frank Taylor Parker and Mary Hutchison Gordon; *m* 1975, Catherine Ann Hyndman; one *s* one *d*. *Educ:* Stranraer High Sch.; Edinburgh Univ. (MA 1st Cl. Hons History 1974; PhD 1977). Vans Dunlop Res. Schol., Edinburgh Univ., 1974–77; Carnegie Travelling Schol. to India, 1976. Royal Commission on Historical Manuscripts: Res. Asst, 1977–87; Asst Keeper, resp. for Nat. Register of Archives, 1987–91. *Publications:* (contrib.) The Scots Abroad, 1985; Bibliographies of British Statesmen No 5 (Lord Curzon), 1991; (contrib.) International Directory of Company Histories, vol. 4, 1991; Library & Information Briefings Series No 51 (on PLR), 1994; reviews and contribs to learned jls. *Recreations:* golf, squash, gardening, family. *Address:* Public Lending Right, Bayheath House, Prince Regent Street, Stockton-on-Tees, Cleveland TS18 1DF; 14 Ash Grove, Kirklevington, Yarm, Cleveland TS15 9NQ. *T:* Eaglescliffe (01642) 791445.

PARKER, James Mavin, (Jim Parker); composer and conductor; *b* Hartlepool, 18 Dec. 1934; *s* of James Robertson Parker and Margaret Mavin; *m* 1969, Pauline George; two *d*; one *d* by a previous marriage. *Educ:* various grammar schools; Guildhall Sch. of Music (AGSM 1959; Silver Medal; Hon. GSM 1986). LRAM 1959. Professional oboeist, 1959; joined the Barrow Poets, 1963. Wrote musical settings of Sir John Betjeman's poems, Banana Blush, 1973 (recorded these and subsequent settings with Sir John as speaker); wrote music for Chichester Theatre, 1974–77; music for television and films, 1977–, includes: Credo; Another Six English Towns; Good Behaviour; Wynne and Penkovsky; Mapp and Lucia; Time After Time; Betjeman's Britain; Late Flowering Love; The Miser; España Viva; The Blot (silent film made in 1921); Girl Shy (Harold Lloyd silent film); Wish Me Luck; House of Cards; Parnell and the Englishwoman; The House of Eliott; Soldier Soldier; Body and Soul; To Play the King; Goggle Eyes; Late Flowering Lust. *Compositions* include: with William Bealby-Wright: Moonshine Rock, 1972; Mister Skillicorn Dances, 1974; with Cicely Herbert: Mayhew's London, 1978; La Comédie Humaine, 1986; (with John Betjeman) Poems (ballet), 1981; In The Gold Room (words by Oscar Wilde), 1983; (with Jeremy Lloyd) The Woodland Gospels, 1984, re-written as Heaven's Up, 1990; (with John Edmunds) Pelican Five, 1986. Recordings with Barrow Poets, Keith Michell, Peter Sellers, Harry Secombe, Twiggy, etc. *Publications:* (with Wally K. Daly) Follow the Star, 1975; (with Jeremy Lloyd) Captain Beaky, 1977; with Tom Stanier: The Shepherd King, 1979; The Burning Bush, 1980; All Aboard, 1983; Blast Off, 1986; A Londoner in New York (suite for brass), 1986; (with Tom Stanier and Chris Ellis) BabylonTimes, 1988; English Towns (for flute and piano), 1988; Mississippi Five (woodwind quintet), 1991; Lullingstone (for concert band), 1986; The Golden Section (brass quintet), 1993; Concerto for clarinet and strings, 1994. *Recreations:* literature, 20th Century art. *Address:* 19 Laurel Road, Barnes, SW13 0EE. *T:* 0181–876 8571.

PARKER, James Roland Walter, CMG 1978; OBE 1968; HM Diplomatic Service, retired; Governor and Commander-in-Chief, Falkland Islands and Dependencies, and High Commissioner, British Antarctic Territory, 1976–80; *b* 20 Dec. 1919; *s* of late Alexander Roland Parker, ISM; *m* 1941, Deirdre Mary Ward. Served War of 1939–45: 1st London Scottish, 1940–41. Ministry of Labour, 1938–57; Labour Attaché, Tel Aviv, 1957–60; Labour Adviser: Accra, 1960–62; Lagos, 1962–64; seconded to Foreign Office, 1965–66; Dep. High Comr, Enugu, 1966–67; Commonwealth Office (later FCO), 1968–70; Head of Chancery, Suva, Fiji, 1970–71; High Comr in The Gambia, 1972–75; Consul-Gen., Durban, 1976. *Address:* Crockers Hill, Yarlington, Somerset BA9 8DJ; 1 St Edmund's Court, NW8 7QL.

PARKER, Jean; *see* Parker, D. J.

PARKER, John; *see* Parker, T. J.

PARKER, Sir John; *see* Parker, Sir W. J.

PARKER, Comdr (John) Michael (Avison), CVO 1957 (MVO 1953); RN (retired); *b* 23 June 1920; *s* of late Capt. C. A. Parker, CBE, Royal Australian Navy, Melbourne; *m* 1st, 1943, Eileen Margaret Anne (*née* Allan) (marr. diss. 1958); one *s* one *d*; 2nd, 1962, Carol (marr. diss.; she *d* 1977); one *d* (one *s* decd); 3rd, 1976, Mrs Jean Lavinia Grice Ramsay. *Educ:* Xavier College, Melbourne, Australia. Royal Navy, 1938–47. Equerry-in-Waiting to Princess Elizabeth and the Duke of Edinburgh, 1947–52; Private Sec. to Duke of Edinburgh, 1947–57. Dir., Brain Behavioural Res. Cttee, La Trobe Univ., 1984–. Chm., Australian Dredging and Gen. Services Co., 1987–. Advr, Special Events Cttee for Melbourne, 1993. Member: Aust.-Britain Soc. (Vice-Pres.); Navy League; RSL; Australian Ballet Trust; Chairman: Royal Navy Assoc.; Trustees, Melbourne Maritime Trust; Trustee: World Wildlife Australia; The World Ship Trust (UK). Chm., Plain English Foundn, Aust. *Recreations:* painting, tennis, golf, sailing. *Address:* Santosa, 33 Albany Road, Toorak, Vic 3142, Australia; Lapwing, Robe, SA 5276, Australia. *Clubs:* Melbourne; Sandringham Yacht (Melbourne); Robe Golf (SA).

PARKER, Hon. Sir Jonathan (Frederic), Kt 1991; **Hon. Mr Justice Parker;** Judge of the High Court of Justice, Chancery Division, since 1991; Vice Chancellor of the County Palatine of Lancaster, since 1994; *b* 8 Dec. 1937; *s* of late Sir (Walter) Edmund Parker, CBE and late Elizabeth Mary Butterfield; *m* 1967, Maria-Belen Burns; three *s* one *d*. *Educ:* Winchester College; Magdalene College, Cambridge (MA). Called to Bar, Inner Temple, 1962, Bencher, 1985; QC 1979; a Recorder, 1989–91; Attorney Gen. of Duchy of Lancaster, 1989–91; practising member of the Bar, 1962–91. *Recreations:* painting, gardening. *Address:* Royal Courts of Justice, Strand, WC2A 2LL. *Club:* Garrick.

PARKER, Keith John, OBE 1993; General Manager, Express and Star, Wolverhampton, since 1995 (Editor, 1977–94); Managing Director, Shropshire Newspapers, since 1996; *b* 30 Dec. 1940; *s* of Sydney John Parker and Phyllis Mary Parker; *m* 1962, Marilyn Ann Edwards; one *s*. Various editorial appointments; Editor, Shropshire Star, 1972–77. Pres., Guild of British Newspaper Editors, 1987–88 (Vice-Pres., 1986–87; Chm., Parly and Legal Cttee, 1991–94); Mem., Press Complaints Commn, 1992–94. *Recreations:* reading, travel. *Address:* 94 Wrottesley Road, Tettenhall, Wolverhampton, West Midlands WV6 8SJ. *T:* Wolverhampton (01902) 758595.

PARKER, Kenneth Blades; QC 1992; *b* 20 Nov. 1945; *s* of Rudolph Parker, Capt., Argyll and Sutherland Highlanders and Catherine (*née* Boyd); *m* 1967, Margaretha Constance Beyerman; three *s* one *d*. *Educ:* Kettering Grammar Sch.; Exeter Coll., Oxford (Class. Schol.; 1st cl. Lit. Hum. 1968; 1st cl. BCL 1973; Vinerian Schol.). Lectr in Law, Univ. of Oxford and Fellow, Exeter Coll., Oxford, 1973–76; called to the Bar, Gray's Inn, 1975; Arbitrator, Lloyd's, 1988–. Specialist Advr, H of C Select Cttee for Trade and Ind., 1991. *Publications:* (Asst Ed.) Chitty on Contracts, 23rd edn, 1972; (contrib.) Common Market Law of Competition, 1987. *Recreations:* tennis, ski-ing. *Address:* 4 Raymond Buildings, Gray's Inn, WC1R 5BP. *T:* 0171–405 7211.

PARKER, Lyn; HM Diplomatic Service; Counsellor (Political and Institutional Affairs), UK Permanent Representation to the European Union, Brussels, since 1995; *b* 25 Nov. 1952; *s* of Ronald Arthur Parker and Tjardina Torrenga; *m* 1991, Jane Elizabeth Walker; one *d*. *Educ:* King's Sch., Canterbury; Magdalen Coll., Oxford (BA Jurisprudence); Manchester Univ. (MA European Community Studies). Lectr in Law, Manchester Univ., 1975–78; joined HM Diplomatic Service, 1978; Second, later First, Sec., Athens, 1980–84; FCO, 1984–88; Cabinet Office, 1989–91; Head of Chancery and Political Counsellor, New Delhi, 1992–95. *Recreations:* music, sailing, walking. *Address:* c/o Foreign and Commonwealth Office, King Charles Street, SW1A 2AH.

PARKER, Margaret Annette McCrie Johnston, (Margaret Johnston); actress; *d* of James and Emily Dalrymple Johnston; *m* 1946, Albert E. W. Parker (*d* 1974). *Educ:* North Sydney and Neutral Bay High School; Sydney University, Australia. Student, RADA; studied with Dr Stefan Hock; in repertory and acted as understudies. *Plays:* Murder without Crime, 1943; Fifth Column, 1944; Last of Summer, 1944; Time of Your Life, 1946; Shouting Dies, 1946; Barretts of Wimpole Street, 1947; Always Afternoon, 1949; Summer and Smoke, 1950; Second Threshold, 1951; The Dark is Light Enough, 1954; Sugar in the Morning, 1959; The Ring of Truth, 1959; Masterpiece, 1961. Stratford Memorial Theatre, 1956 season: Othello, The Merchant of Venice, Measure for Measure; Chichester Festival Theatre, 1966 Season. Lady Macbeth. *Films:* Rake's Progress, 1945; Man About the House, 1946; Portrait of Clare, 1949; Magic Box, 1951; Knave of Hearts, 1953; Touch and Go, 1955; Nose on her Face; Life at the Top, 1965; Psychopath; Sebastian. Television plays. *Address:* c/o Al Parker Ltd, 55 Park Lane, W1Y 3DH.

PARKER, Comdr Michael; *see* Parker, Comdr J. M. A.

PARKER, His Honour Michael Clynes, QC 1973; a Circuit Judge, 1978–94; *b* 2 Nov. 1924; *s* of Herbert Parker and Elsie Vera Parker (sometime Pres., NUT); *m* 1950, Molly Leila Franklin; one *s* two *d*. *Educ:* City of London Sch.; Pembroke Coll., Cambridge (BA, LLB). Sec., Cambridge Union, 1943. Flt-Sgt/Air Gunner, RAF, 1943–47. Called to Bar, Gray's Inn, 1949; practised in London and SE Circuit; a Recorder of the Crown Court, 1972–78. Contested (Lab) S Kensington, 1951. *Recreations:* theatre, watching cricket. *Address:* 17 Courtnell Street, W2 5BU. *Clubs:* United Oxford & Cambridge University, MCC.

See also B. Tizard.

PARKER, Major Michael John, CVO 1991; MBE 1968; Producer: Royal Tournament, since 1974; Edinburgh Tattoo, since 1991; *b* 21 Sept. 1941; *s* of Capt. S. J. Wilkins and V. S. M. Wilkins (*née* Parker); name changed by Deed Poll, 1959. *Educ:* Dulwich Coll. Prep. Sch.; Hereford Cathedral Sch.; RMA Sandhurst. Captain, Queen's Own Hussars,

1961–71 (produced Berlin Tattoo, 1965, 1967 and 1971); Major, TA, Special List, attached QOH, 1973–. Producer of international events, 1972–: Berlin Tattoo, 1972–88; Aldershot Army Display, 1974–83; Queen's Bonfire, Windsor and others, Queen's Silver Jubilee, 1977; Wembley Musical Pageant, 1979, 1981, 1985; Great Children's Party for Internat. Year of the Child, 1979; Carols for the Queen, 1979; Royal Fireworks (Prince of Wales's wedding), 1981; Heart of the Nation, son et lumière, Horse Guards, 1983, 1985; America's Cup, Newport, 1983; Great St John Party (180,000 children), Hyde Park, 1985; King Hussein of Jordan's 50th Birthday Celebration, 1985; Finale, Christmas Horse Show, Olympia, 1986–; Jordanian Royal Wedding, 1987, 1993; Coronation Anniversary Celebration, Jordan, 1988; Joy to the World, Royal Albert Hall, 1988–; Royal Equestrian Day, Oman, 1990; Fortress Fantasia, Gibraltar, 1990; Queen Mother's 90th Birthday Celebration, Horse Guards, 1990; Opening Ceremony, World Equestrian Games, 1990; Economic Summit Spectacular, Buckingham Palace, 1991; British Nat. Day Expo '92, Seville, 1992; The Queen's 40th Anniversary Celebration, 1992; Memphis in May Internat. Tattoo, 1992–94; King Hussein of Jordan's 40th Anniversary Celebrations, Unveiling of Queen Elizabeth Gate in Hyde Park, 1993; Channel Tunnel Gala Fireworks Display, D-Day Celebrations in Portsmouth, Normandy Veterans, RAH, Army Benevolent Fund, Drumhead Service, Royal Hosp. Chelsea, Pavarotti, Internat. Horse Show Modena Italy, P&O ship naming, China, 1994; P&O ship naming, Portsmouth, VE Day Celebrations in Hyde Park and Buckingham Palace, VJ Celebrations on Horseguards, Jersey Liberation Fireworks, King Hussain of Jordan's 60th Birthday Celebration, Jordan, Horse Show in Los Angeles, 1995; HM The Sultan of Oman's Silver Jubilee Celebrations, Oman, 50th Anniversary Celebrations of the Independence of the Hashemite Kingdom of Jordan, 1996. Vice-Pres., Morriston Orpheus Choir; Vice-Patron, Internat. Music Centre for Blind Children, Luberadz, Poland. KStJ 1985 (OStJ 1982). Grand Officer, Order of al Istiqlal (Jordan), 1987. *Publication:* The Awful Troop Leaders Gunnery Crib, 1969. *Recreations:* painting, antiques, giving parties. *Club:* Cavalry and Guards.

PARKER, Michael Joseph Bennett; Managing Director since 1970, and Chairman since 1980, Favor Parker Ltd; *b* 22 June 1931; *s* of Henry Gordon Parker and Alice Rose Parker; *m* 1960, Tania Henrietta Tiarks; two *s* one *d*. *Educ:* Eton; Magdalene Coll., Cambridge (BA Agric., MA). Chm., Sovereign Chicken Gp, 1977–. Chm., Land Settlement Assoc., 1982–85; Mem., UKAEA, 1985–88. *Recreations:* country sports, wind-surfing, lying in the sun. *Address:* Gooderstone Manor, King's Lynn, Norfolk PE33 9BP. *T:* Gooderstone (01366) 328255.

PARKER, Michael St J.; *see* St John Parker.

PARKER, Prof. (Noel) Geoffrey, PhD, LittD; FBA 1984; Robert A. Lovett Professor of Military and Naval History, Yale University, since 1993; *b* 25 Dec. 1943; *s* of late Derek Geoffrey Parker and Kathleen Betsy Symon; *m* 1st, Angela Maureen Chapman; one *s* one *d*; 2nd, Jane Helen Ohlmeyer; two *s*. *Educ:* Nottingham High Sch.; Christ's Coll., Cambridge (BA 1965; MA; PhD 1968; LittD 1981). Fellow of Christ's Coll., Cambridge, 1968–72; Lectr in Mod. Hist., 1972–78, Reader in Mod. Hist., 1978–82, and Prof. of Early Mod. Hist., 1982–86, St Andrews Univ. Charles E. Nowell Dist. Prof. of History, Univ. of Illinois at Urbana-Champaign, 1986–93 (Dept Chair, 1989–91). British Acad. Exchange Fellow, Newberry Library, Chicago, 1981; Visiting Professor: Vrije Universiteit, Brussels, 1975 (Dr phil and letters *hc*, 1990); Univ. of BC, Vancouver, Canada, 1979–80; Keio Univ., Tokyo, 1984. Lees Knowles Lectr in Mil. Hist., Univ. of Cambridge, 1984. Television scripts and broadcasts. Corres. Fellow, Spanish Royal Acad. of History, 1988–. Order of Isabel the Catholic (Spain), Kt Grand Cross, 1992 (Encomienda, 1988). *Publications:* The Army of Flanders and the Spanish Road 1567–1659, 1972, 3rd edn 1990; The Dutch Revolt, 1977, 3rd edn 1985; Philip II, 1978, 3rd edn 1995; Europe in Crisis 1598–1648, 1979; Spain and the Netherlands 1559–1659, 1979, 2nd edn 1990; The Thirty Years' War, 1984; (ed) The World: an illustrated history, 1986, 2nd edn 1992; The Military Revolution: military innovation and the rise of the West 1500–1800, 1988, 3rd edn 1995 (Dexter Prize, 1987–90); (with Colin Martin) The Spanish Armada, 1988, 2nd edn 1992; (ed) Cambridge Illustrated History of Warfare, 1996; edited numerous other works; articles and reviews. *Recreations:* travel, archaeology. *Address:* Department of History, Yale University, PO Box 208324, New Haven, CT 06520–8324, USA. *T:* (203) 4321357.

PARKER, Sir Peter; *see* Parker, Sir W. P. B.

PARKER, Sir Peter, KBE 1993; Kt 1978; LVO 1957; Chairman: Mitsubishi Electric UK Ltd, since 1984; Whitehead Mann Group Plc, since 1984; *b* 30 Aug. 1924; *s* of late Tom and Dorothy S. Parker; *m* 1951, Gillian Rowe-Dutton, *d* of late Sir Ernest Rowe-Dutton, KCMG, CB, and of Lady Rowe-Dutton; three *s* one *d*. *Educ:* Bedford Sch.; London Univ.; Lincoln Coll., Oxford (Hon. Fellow, 1980). Major, Intelligence Corps, 1943–47. Commonwealth Fund Fellowship to Cornell and Harvard, 1950–51. Contested (Lab) Bedford, 1951. Phillips Electrical, 1951–53; Head of Overseas Dept, Industrial Soc. 1953–54; Sec., Duke of Edinburgh's Study Conf. on Human Problems of Industry, 1954–56 (Vice-Chm., UK Trustees, Commonwealth Study Confs, 1986–); joined Booker McConnell Ltd, 1956; Chairman: Bookers Engineering & Industrial Holdings Ltd, 1966–70; Associated British Maltsters Ltd, 1971–73; Curtis Brown Ltd, 1971–76; Victoria Deep Water Terminal Ltd, 1971–76; Dawnay Day Group, 1971–76; BRB, 1976–83; Oakland Develt Capital Fund, 1985–93; Horace, Holman Gp Ltd, 1988–93; Evered, subseq. Bardon Gp, 1989–94; Fidelity Japan OTC and Regional Markets Fund, 1990–; Apricot Computers, 1990–; Arcadian Internat., 1990–; Scruttons plc, 1993–; Fidelity Japanese Values, 1994–; Vice-Chm., H. Clarkson & Co. (Hldgs), 1984–93 (Dir, 1976–93; Chm., 1975–76); Director: Booker Bros McConnell & Co. Ltd, 1960–70; Rockware Gp, 1976–92 (Chm., 1971–76, and 1983–92); Group 4 Securitas, 1984–; Rebound IPD Ltd, 1992–. Chm.-designate, Nat. Ports Authority, 1970; Chm., Clothing EDC, 1971–78; Member: British Tourist Authy Bd, 1969–75; British Airways Bd, 1971–81; Royal Nat. Theatre Bd, 1986–91; Political and Econ. Plannning Exec. (Vice-Chm., 1969–70; Hon. Treasurer, 1973–78); Council, BIM (Chm., 1984–86); Foundn on Automation & Human Develt, 1971–; Engineering Industries Council, 1975–76; NEDC, 1980–83. Dir, UK-Japan 2000 Gp, 1986–; Chm., Japan Fest. 1991. Founder Mem., Council of Foundn for Management Educn; Chairman: Westfield College, 1969–76 (Hon. Fellow, 1979); Ct of Governors, LSE, 1988–; Dep. Chm., Ct of London Univ., 1970–; Chm., Adv. Council, Business Graduates Assoc. Vis. Fellow, Nuffield Coll., Oxford, 1980 (Hon. Fellow, 1980). Mem. Council, Oxford Mus. of Modern Art, 1984–; Trustee, British Architecture Library Trust, 1984; Dir, Design Mus., 1989–; Chm., Young Vic, 1993–; Pres., Industry Council for Packaging and Envmt, 1990–. Dimbleby Lecture, BBC TV, 1984. Hon. Fellow: SIAD; SOAS, 1991; London Business Sch., 1991. Hon. LLD: London, 1981; Manchester Polytechnic, 1981; Bath, 1983; Birmingham, 1991. Communicator of the Year Award, British Assoc. of Indust. Editors, 1981; Bicentenary Medal, RSA, 1990. CStJ 1983. Grand Cordon of Order of Sacred Treasure (Japan), 1991. *Publication:* For Starters (autobiog.), 1989. *Recreations:* Rugby (played for Bedford and E Mids); swimming, browsing. *Address:* Fountain House, 130 Fenchurch Street, EC3M 5EE. *T:* 0171–621 1472.

PARKER, Sir Richard (William) Hyde, 12th Bt, *cr* 1681; DL; *b* 5 April 1937; *o s* of Sir William Stephen Hyde Parker, 11th Bt, and Ulla Ditlef, *o d* of C. Ditlef Nielsen, Dr of Philosophy, Copenhagen; *S* father 1951; *m* 1972, Jean, *d* of late Sir Lindores Leslie, 9th Bt; one *s* three *d* (incl. twin *d*). *Educ:* Millfield; Royal Agricultural College. High Sheriff and DL, Suffolk, 1995. *Heir: s* William John Hyde Parker, *b* 10 June 1983. *Address:* Melford Hall, Long Melford, Suffolk CO10 9AA.

PARKER, Robert Stewart; Parliamentary Counsel, since 1992; *b* 13 Jan. 1949; *o s* of Robert Arnold Parker and Edna Parker (*née* Baines). *Educ:* Brentwood School; Trinity College, Oxford (Scholar; First in Mods; MA 1974). Called to the Bar, Middle Temple, 1975 (Harmsworth Exhibnr; Astbury Senior Law Scholarship); Lincoln's Inn *ad eundem*, 1977. Classics Master, Brentwood School, 1971–74; in practice at the Bar, 1975–80; Office of Parly Counsel, 1980; Law Commn, 1985–87; Dep. Parly Counsel, 1987–92. Freeman, City of London, 1984; Liveryman, Wheelwrights' Co., 1984. MIMgt (MBIM 1984). *Publication:* Cases and Statutes on General Principles of Law (with C. R. Newton), 1980. *Recreations:* the Livery, cricket, bridge, books, music. *Address:* Office of the Parliamentary Counsel, 36 Whitehall, SW1A 2AY. *Clubs:* Athenæum, City Livery, Langbourn Ward.

PARKER, Rt. Hon. Sir Roger (Jocelyn), Kt 1977; PC 1983; a Lord Justice of Appeal, 1983–92; *b* 25 Feb. 1923; *s* of Captain Hon. T. T. Parker, DSC, RN (Retired) and Marie Louise Leonie (*née* Kleinwort); *m* 1948, Ann Elizabeth Frederika (*née* White); one *s* three *d*. *Educ:* Eton; King's Coll., Cambridge. Served Rifle Bde, 1941–46. Called to Bar, Lincoln's Inn, 1948, Bencher, 1969; QC 1961. Dep. Chm., Herts QS, 1969–71; Judge of the Courts of Appeal, Jersey and Guernsey, 1974–83; a Judge of the High Court, QBD, 1977–83. Member, Bar Council, 1968–69, Vice-Chm., 1970–72, Chm., 1972–73. Vice-Pres., Senate of Four Inns of Court, 1972–73. Treas., Lincoln's Inn, 1990–91. Conducted Windscale Nuclear Fuel Reprocessing Inquiry, 1977. Chm., Court of Inquiry into Flixborough Explosion, 1974. *Clubs:* Lansdowne; Leander.

PARKER, Ronald William, CBE 1959; JP; *b* 21 Aug. 1909; *s* of late Ernest Edward Parker, MBE, Accountant of Court, and Margaret Parker (*née* Henderson); *m* 1937, Phyllis Mary (*née* Sherren); two *s*. *Educ:* Royal High School, Edinburgh. Chartered Accountant, 1933. Secretary, later Dir, Weston Group of Companies, 1935; Asst Dir of Finance, Ministry of Fuel and Power, 1942; Partner, J. Aikman, Smith & Wells, CA, 1946. National Coal Board: Finance Dir, Scottish Division, 1947; Dep. Chm., North Western Division, 1954; Chm., Scottish Division, 1955–67; Regional Chm., Scottish Region, 1967–68; Chm., Scottish Gas Bd, 1968–72, Scottish Gas Reg., 1972–74. JP City and County of Edinburgh, 1972. *Recreations:* gardening, fishing. *Address:* Claremont, 3 South Lauder Road, Edinburgh EH9 2LL. *T:* 0131–667 7666. *Club:* New (Edinburgh).

PARKER, (Thomas) John, FEng; Chairman,Babcock International Group, since 1994 (Deputy Chairman and Chief Executive, 1993–94); *b* 8 April 1942; *s* of Robert Parker and Margaret Elizabeth Parker (*née* Bell); *m* 1967, Emma Elizabeth (*née* Blair); one *s* one *d*. *Educ:* Belfast Coll. of Technology. FEng 1983; FRINA; FIMarE. Harland & Wolff, Belfast: Student Apprentice Naval Architect, 1958–63; Ship Design Staff, 1963–69 (Nat. Physical Lab. (Ship Hydrodynamics), on secondment, 1964); Numerical Applications Manager, 1969–71; Prodn Drawing Office Manager, 1971–72; Gen. Manager, Sales and Projects, 1972–74; Man. Dir, Austin-Pickersgill Ltd, Sunderland, 1974–78; British Shipbuilders: Dir of Marketing, 1977–78; Bd Mem. for Shipbuilding, 1978–83; Dep. Chief Exec., 1980–83; Chm. and Chief Exec., Harland and Wolff, 1983–93. Mem., British Coal Corp., 1986–93; Non-Exec. Dir, GKN, 1993–. Member: Council, RINA, 1978–80, 1982–; Bd of Governors, Sunderland Polytechnic, 1976–81; Internat. Cttee, Bureau Veritas, Paris, 1979–83; Gen. Cttee, Lloyd's Register of Shipping, 1983–; Industrial Develt Bd of NI, 1983–87. Hon. DSc (Eng) Queen's Univ. Belfast, 1985; Hon. ScD Trinity Coll. Dublin, 1986; Hon. DSc Ulster, 1992. *Publications:* papers to Trans IES, RINA. *Recreations:* reading, motoring in the countryside, ships, sailing, music. *Address:* Babcock International Group, The Lodge, Badminton Court, Church Street, Amersham, Bucks HP7 0DD. *T:* Amersham (01494) 727296.

PARKER, Vice-Adm. Sir (Wilfred) John, KBE 1969 (OBE 1953); CB 1965; DSC 1943; *b* 12 Oct. 1915; *s* of Henry Edmond Parker and Ida Mary (*née* Cole); *m* 1943, Marjorie Stuart Jones, Halifax, NS, Canada; two *d*. *Educ:* RN College, Dartmouth. Joined Royal Navy, 1929; War Service in N Atlantic, N Russia, Mediterranean, Pacific, Korea (OBE); sunk in HMS Edinburgh and HMS Trinidad; mined in HMS Sheffield; torpedoed in HMS Newfoundland; DSC (Capture of Sicily); twice mentioned in despatches (HMS Edinburgh on N Russian convoys, and destruction of an Italian convoy, HMS Aurora 1942); Imperial Defence College, 1957; Commodore West Indies, 1958–60; Captain RNC Dartmouth, 1961–63; an Asst Chief of Defence Staff, Min. of Defence, 1963–66; Flag Officer, Medway, and Adm. Supt HM Dockyard, Chatham, 1966–69, retd 1969. Pres., RN Communication Chief Petty Officers Assoc., 1969–94. *Recreation:* 7 grandchildren (3 Mayo, 3 Panton, 1 Polak). *Address:* Flint Cottage, East Harting, Petersfield, Hants GU31 5LT. *Club:* Royal Navy.

PARKER, Sir (William) Peter (Brian), 5th Bt *cr* 1844, of Shenstone Lodge, Staffordshire; FCA; Partner, Stephenson Nuttall & Co., chartered accountants, Newark, since 1988; *b* 30 Nov. 1950; *s* of Sir (William) Alan Parker, 4th Bt and of Sheelagh Mary, *o d* of late Dr Sinclair Stevenson; *S* father, 1990; *m* 1976, Patricia Ann, *d* of R. Filtness and Mrs D. Filtness; one *s* one *d*. *Educ:* Eton. FCA 1974. *Heir: s* John Malcolm Parker, *b* 14 May 1980. *Address:* Apricot Hall, Sutton-cum-Beckingham, Lincoln LN5 0RE.

PARKER-JERVIS, Roger, DL; Deputy Chairman, CGA plc, 1982–90; *b* 11 Sept. 1931; *s* of George Parker-Jervis and late Ruth, *d* of C. E. Farmer; *m* 1958, Diana, *d* of R. St V. Parker-Jervis; two *s* one *d*. *Educ:* Eton; Magdalene College, Cambridge. Served Rifle Brigade, 1950–51, Queen Victoria Rifles, 1951–54; ADC to Governor of Tasmania, 1954–56. Bucks County Council: Mem., 1967–93; Chm., 1981–85. Mem., Milton Keynes Develt Corp., 1975–92; Pres., Timber Growers of England and Wales, 1981–83; Vice-Chm., Forestry Cttee of GB, 1981–83. Chm., Bucks Historic Buildings Trust, 1983–; Mem., Thames and Chiltern Regl Cttee, NT, 1987–94. Mem., Dutch Barge Assoc. High Sheriff of Bucks, 1973–74, DL Bucks, 1982. *Recreations:* barging on the French canals, painting, shooting. *Address:* The Old Schoolhouse, The Green, Brill, Bucks HP18 9RU. *T:* Brill (01844) 238025. *Clubs:* Farmers', Greenjackets.

PARKES, Sir Edward (Walter), Kt 1983; DL; FEng; Vice-Chancellor, University of Leeds, 1983–91; Chairman, Committee of Vice-Chancellors and Principals of the Universities of the United Kingdom, 1989–91 (Vice-Chairman, 1985–89); *b* 19 May 1926; *o s* of Walter Frederick Parkes; *m* 1950, Margaret Parr (*see* Margaret Parkes); one *s* one *d*. *Educ:* King Edward's, Birmingham; St John's College, Cambridge; Scholar; 1st cl. hons Mech. Sci. Tripos, 1945; MA, PhD, ScD; FIMechE. At RAE and in the aircraft industry, 1945–48; research student and subsequently Univ. Lecturer, Cambridge, 1948–59; Fellow and Tutor of Gonville and Caius College; Vis. Prof., Stanford Univ., 1959–60; Head of the Department of Engineering, Univ. of Leicester, 1960–65; Prof. of Mechanics, Cambridge, and Professorial Fellow, Gonville and Caius Coll., 1965–74 (Mem. Gen. Bd, Dep. head of Dept of Engineering); Vice-Chancellor, City Univ., 1974–78; Chm., UGC, 1978–83. Member: Brynmor Jones Cttee, 1964–65; Adv. Bd for Res. Councils, 1974–83; University and Polytechnic Grants Cttee for Hong Kong, 1974–;

Chm., Clinical Academic Staff Salaries Cttee, 1985–90. Chm., Adv. Panel on Limestone Workings in the W Midlands, 1983–. DL W Yorks, 1990. Hon. FIMechE 1992. Hon. DTech Loughborough, 1984; Hon. DSc: Leicester, 1984; City, 1988; Hon. LLD Wales, 1984. *Publications:* Braced Frameworks, 1965, 2nd edn 1974; papers on elasticity, dynamic plasticity or thermal effects on structures in Proc. and Phil. Trans. Royal Society and other jls. *Address:* The Cottage, Headington Hill, Oxford OX3 0BT. *Club:* Athenæum.

PARKES, John Alan; Chief Executive, Humberside County Council, and Clerk to Humberside Lieutenancy, since 1988; *b* 18 Jan. 1939; *s* of Arthur and Alice Parkes: *m* 1963, Margaret Jill (*née* Clayton); two *d*. *Educ:* Nottingham High Sch.; Oriel Coll., Oxford (MA). IPFA 1965. Various posts from graduate traineeship, Council Finance, Derbyshire, 1961–68; Asst County Treasurer, Glos, 1968–71; Dep., then County Treasurer, Lindsey, 1971–74; Dir of Finance, Humberside, 1974–88. Member: Phildrew Ventures Adv. Cttee, 1986–; Financial Reporting Council, 1990–. Advr, ACC, 1976–; Sec., 1980–86, Pres., 1987–88, Soc. of County Treasurers; Dir, Humberside TEC, 1990–. Freeman, City of London, 1988. Hon. Fellow, Univ. of Humberside, 1991. *Publications:* articles on local govt finance in prof. jls. *Recreations:* walking, cars, railways. *Address:* County Hall, Beverley, North Humberside HU17 9BA. *T:* Hull (01482) 884830. *Clubs:* Royal Over-Seas League; Rotary (Beverley).

PARKES, John Hubert, CB 1984; Permanent Secretary, Department of Education, Northern Ireland, 1979–90; *b* 1 Oct. 1930; 2nd *s* of Frank Hubert Parkes and Mary Edith (*née* Barnes), Birmingham; *m* 1956, Elsie Griffiths Henderson; two *s*. *Educ:* George Dixon Sch., Birmingham; Magdalen Coll., Oxford (MA). Joined NI Civil Service, 1953; Asst Sec. 1966; RCDS 1972; Dep. Sec., 1973. Hon. DLitt Ulster, 1991. *Address:* The New House, Boreham Street, Hailsham, E Sussex BN27 4SF. *Club:* United Oxford & Cambridge University.

PARKES, Dr Malcolm Beckwith, FSA; FRHistS; FBA 1993; Fellow and Tutor, Keble College, Oxford, since 1965; Reader in Palaeography, University of Oxford, since 1993; *b* 26 June 1930; *s* of Edward James Lennard Parkes and Clara Parkes (*née* Beckwith); *m* 1954, Ann Winifred Dodman; two *s*. *Educ:* Colfe's Grammar Sch.; Strasbourg Univ.; Hertford Coll., Oxford (BA Eng. Lang. and Lit. 1953; MA 1957; BLitt 1959; Gordon-Duff Prize 1959; DLitt 1985). FSA 1971; FRHistS 1977. Archivist, Lambeth Palace Library, 1957–58; Lectr in English Lang., Keble and Mansfield Colls, Oxford, 1961–65; Lectr, Faculty of English, 1964–71, Lectr in Palaeography, 1971–93, Univ. of Oxford. Vis. Prof., Universität Konstanz, 1974 and 1980; James J. Hill Prof., Univ. of Minn (Twin Cities), 1991. Special Lecturer: in Palaeography and Diplomatic, Univ. of Durham, 1972; in Palaeography, Univ. of London, 1976; Lectures: Jarrow, 1982; Mont Follick, Univ. of Manchester, 1986; Robert F. Metzdorf, Univ. of Rochester, NY, 1987; James L. Rosier, Univ. of Pennsylvania, 1995. Mem., Standing Conf. of Nat. and Univ. Libraries, Adv. Cttee on MSS, 1977–86. Member: Wolfenbütteler Mediävistenkreis, 1986–; Comité Internat. de Paléographie Latine, 1986–. Corresp. Fellow, Medieval Acad. of America, 1992. *Publications:* English Cursive Book Hands 1250–1500, 1969, rev. edn 1979; (ed with A. G. Watson) Medieval Scribes, Manuscripts and Libraries: essays presented to N. R. Ker, 1978; Medieval Manuscripts of Keble College, Oxford, a descriptive catalogue, 1979; Scribes, Scripts and Readers, 1991; Pause and Effect: an introduction to the history of punctuation in the West, 1992; introductions to facsimile edns of various manuscripts; articles and chapters on topics in palaeography, book production and ownership, and history of reading in learned jls and series. *Recreation:* growing fuchsias. *Address:* Keble College, Oxford OX1 3PG. *T:* Oxford (01865) 272727.

PARKES, Margaret, (Lady Parkes), CBE 1990; JP; President, Christian Education Movement, since 1992; a Governor of the BBC, 1984–89; *b* 26 Sept. 1925; *d* of John and Dorothy Parr; *m* 1950, Sir Edward Walter Parkes, *qv*; one *s* one *d*. *Educ:* Perse School for Girls, Cambridge; Leicester Univ. (MEd). Homerton Coll., Cambridge, 1965–74. Pres., Leeds Marriage and Personal Counselling Service, 1987–91; Chairman: London Diocesan Bd of Educn, 1976–80; Colleges Adv. Cttee, Gen. Synod Bd of Educn, 1982–86; Radio London Adv. Council, 1979–83; Ripon Diocesan Bd of Educn, 1988–91; Leeds Parish Church Commn, 1988. Member: Press Council, 1978–84; Secondary Exams Council, 1983–88; Voluntary Sector Consultative Council, 1984–88; Chairman: Design and Technology Wkg Gp for Nat. Curriculum, 1988–89; NCET, 1991–92. Chm. of Governors, Whitelands Coll., London, 1981–87. JP Inner London 1977. *Address:* The Cottage, Headington Hill, Oxford OX3 0BT.

PARKES, Norman James, CBE 1976 (OBE 1960); Clerk of the Australian House of Representatives, 1971–76, retired; *b* 29 July 1912; *s* of Ernest William Parkes; *m* 1937, Maida Cleave, *d* of James Nicholas Silk; two *s*. *Educ:* Victorian State Schools. AASA. Parliamentary officer, 1934: with Reporting Staff, 1934–37; with House of Representatives, 1937–76. *Recreation:* bowls. *Address:* 1/3 Nuyts Street, Red Hill, Canberra, ACT 2603, Australia. *T:* (6) 2957320. *Clubs:* Canberra Bowling, National Press (Canberra).

PARKES, Terence, (Larry); freelance cartoonist, since 1957; *b* 19 Nov. 1927; *s* of Walter Thomas Parkes and Alice Parkes (*née* Hirons); *m* 1952, Jean Pauline Woodward; one *s* one *d*. *Educ:* Handsworth Grammar Sch., Birmingham; Birmingham Coll. of Art (Art Teacher's Dip.). Regular contributor to Punch, 1954–92; contrib. Private Eye, 1962–94; illustrations in Observer and Daily and Sunday Telegraph; worked for Joan Littlewood's Theatre Workshop, 1973–74; contrib. HMSO and FO pubns. Fellow, Univ. of W Midlands (formerly Birmingham Poly.), 1991. *Publications:* Man in Apron, 1959; Man in Office, 1961; Man at Work, 1962; Man at Large, 1964; Man and Dog, 1965 (US); Man in Garden, 1966; Man and Wife, 1966 (US); Large Economy Man, 1967 (US); Private Eye Cartoon Library, 1974; Art Collection, 1982; Best of Larry, 1985; Larry on Art, 1986; Larry's Great Western, 1987; Garden Lot, 1988; DIY Man, 1989; Larry on Larry (autobiog.), 1994. *Recreations:* ceramic sculpture, Rottweiler dog walking. *Address:* 20 West Street, Stratford-upon-Avon, Warwickshire CV37 6DW. *T:* Stratford-upon-Avon (01789) 293547; Flat 4, 4 Payton Street, Stratford-upon-Avon, Warwickshire CV37 6VA. *T:* Stratford-upon-Avon (01789) 292900.

PARKHOUSE, James, MD, FFARCS; Hon. Director, Medical Careers Research Group, Oxford, since 1989 (Director, 1984–89); *b* 30 March 1927; *s* of Charles Frederick Parkhouse and Mary Alice Sumner; *m* 1952, Hilda Florence Rimmer; three *s* two *d*. *Educ:* Merchant Taylors' Sch., Great Crosby; Liverpool Univ. (MD 1955). MB ChB, 1950; MA Oxon 1960; MSc Manchester 1974. DA; FFARCS 1952. Anaesthetist, RAF Med. Br., 1953–55. Sen. Resident Anaesth., Mayo Clinic, 1957–58; First Asst, Nuffield Dept of Anaesths, Oxford, and Hon. Cons. Anaesth., United Oxford Hosps, 1958–66; Prof. and Head of Dept of Anaesths, Univ. of Manitoba, and Chief Anaesth., Winnipeg Gen. Hosp., 1967–68; Postgrad. Dean, Faculty of Med., Sheffield Univ., and Hon. Cons. Anaesth., United Sheffield Hosps, 1969–70; Prof. of Anaesths, Manchester Univ., and Hon. Cons. Anaesth., Manchester and Salford AHAs (Teaching), 1970–80; Prof. of Postgraduate Med. Educn, Univ. of Newcastle upon Tyne, and Postgrad. Dean and Dir, Northern Postgrad. Inst. for Medicine and Dentistry, 1980–84. Consultant, postgrad. med. trng, WHO, 1969–89; Specialist Adviser, H of C Social Services Cttee, 1980–81, 1984. Member: Sheffield Reg. Hosp. Bd, 1969–70; Bd, Faculty of Anaesthetists, 1971–82; Neurosciences Bd, MRC, 1977–80; GMC, 1979–89; Nat. Trng Council, NHS, 1981–84; North Tyneside HA, 1982–84. *Publications:* A New Look at Anaesthetics, 1965; Medical Manpower in Britain, 1979; Doctors' Careers, 1991; contrib. to The Lancet, BMJ and specialist jls. *Recreations:* music, golf. *Address:* 145 Cumnor Hill, Oxford OX2 9JA. *Club:* Royal Birkdale Golf.

PARKHOUSE, Peter; Chairman, Severn NHS Trust, since 1992; *b* 22 July 1927; *s* of late William Richard Parkhouse, MBE, and late Alice Vera Parkhouse (*née* Clarke); *m* 1st, 1950, Mary Alison Holland (*d* 1987); one *s* one *d*; 2nd, 1994, Sally Isabel Squires. *Educ:* Blundell's Sch.; Peterhouse, Cambridge (organist, 1944–45); Cologne Univ. BA 1947, MA 1950. Instr Lieut, RN, 1947–50; Asst Master, Uppingham Sch., 1951–52; Asst Principal, Min. of Food, 1952; transf. to MAFF, 1955; served in private office of successive Ministers and Parly Secs, 1954–58; Principal 1958; Principal Private Sec. to Minister, 1966–67; Asst Sec. 1967; Under-Sec. 1973; Dir in Directorate-Gen. for Agriculture, Commn of European Communities, 1973–79; Under Sec., 1979–84. Mem., EDC for Agriculture, 1982–84. *Recreations:* music (sub-organist of Tetbury Parish Church), fishing. *Address:* Stafford House, The Chipping, Tetbury, Glos GL8 8ET. *T:* Tetbury (01666) 502540. *Club:* United Oxford & Cambridge University.

PARKIN, Prof. David John, PhD; FBA 1993; Professor of Anthropology with reference to Africa, University of London, at School of Oriental and African Studies, since 1981; *b* 5 Nov. 1940; *s* of Cecil Joseph Parkin and Rose May Parkin (*née* Johnson); *m* 1962, Monica Ann Lacey; two *s* one *d*. *Educ:* London Univ. (BA 1st cl. Hons African Studies 1962); SOAS (PhD Social Anthropol. 1965). FRAI 1966. Res. Associate, E African Inst. of Social Res., Makerere Univ. Coll., Kampala, Uganda, 1962–64 and 1966–67; School of Oriental and African Studies, University of London: Asst Lectr, 1964–65; Lectr, 1965–71; Lecturer: Sussex Univ., 1971–72; SOAS, 1972–76; Reader in Anthropol., SOAS, 1976–81. University of Nairobi: Sen. Res. Fellow, Lang. Survey Unit, 1968–69; Sen. Res. Associate, 1977–78; Vis. Prof., Univ. of Calif, Berkeley, 1980; Directeur d'études Associé, Ecole des Hautes Etudes en Sciences Sociales, Paris, 1986, 1987 and 1993; Chercheur Associé, CNRS, Paris, 1992–93. Hon. Dir, Internat. African Inst., 1992–. Chm., Assoc. of Social Anthropologists of GB and Commonwealth, 1989–93. MAE 1993. Rivers Meml Medal, RAI, 1985. *Publications:* Neighbours and Nationals in an African City Ward, 1969; Palms, Wine and Witnesses, 1972; (ed) Town and Country in Central and Eastern Africa, 1975; The Cultural Definition of Political Response, 1978; The Sacred Void, 1991; edited: Semantic Anthropology, 1982; The Anthropology of Evil, 1985; Swahili Language and Society, 1985; Transformations of African Marriage, 1987; (ed) Social Stratification in Swahili Society, 1989; Bush, Base, Forest, Farm, 1992. *Recreations:* music, voyaging, swimming, squash. *Address:* School of Oriental and African Studies, Thornhaugh Street, Russell Square, WC1H 0XG. *T:* 0171–323 6327/6331.

PARKIN, John Mackintosh; Administrator, Royal Courts of Justice, 1982–85, retired; *b* 18 June 1920; *s* of Thomas and Emily Cecilia Parkin; *m* Biancamaria Giuganino, Rome; two *d*. *Educ:* Nottingham High Sch.; Emmanuel Coll., Cambridge (Sen. Schol.; MA). Royal Artillery, 1939–46 (Captain). Asst Principal, WO, 1949; Registrar, RMCS, 1957–60; Principal Private Sec. to Sec. of State for War, 1960–62; Asst Sec. 1962; Sen. Fellow, Harvard Univ., 1966–67; Comd Sec., BAOR, 1967–70; Asst Under-Sec. of State, MoD, 1974–80. Mem., Royal Patriotic Fund Corpn, 1977–80. *Recreation:* history of architecture and art. *Address:* 18 Dulwich Mead, 48–50 Half Moon Lane, SE24 9HS. *T:* 0171–274 7581.

PARKIN, Sara Lamb; environmentalist; *b* 9 April 1946; *d* of Dr George Lamb McEwan and Marie Munro Rankin; *m* 1969, Dr Donald Maxwell Parkin; two *s*. *Educ:* Barrs Hill School, Coventry; Edinburgh Royal Infirmary (RGN). Ward Sister, Royal Infirmary, Edinburgh, and Res. Asst, Nursing Res. Unit, Univ. of Edinburgh, 1973–74; Council Mem., Brook Adv. Centre, 1974–76; Family Planning Nurse, Brook Clinic, Edinburgh and Leeds AHA, 1976–80. Green Party, UK: Internat. Liaison Sec., 1983–90; Speaker, 1989–92; Chair, Executive, 1992; Co-Sec., European Green Co-ordination, 1985–90; Dir, Forum for the Future. Hon. DSc Ball State Univ., Indiana, 1993. *Publications:* Green Parties: an international guide, 1989; Green Futures: agenda for the twenty first century, 1991; Green Light on Europe, 1991; The Life and Death of Petra Kelly, 1994. *Recreations:* reading, films, theatre, opera, walking, camping, gardening.

PARKINS, Graham Charles; QC 1990; a Recorder, since 1989; *b* 11 Nov. 1942; *s* of John Charles Parkins and Nellie Elizabeth Parkins; *m* 1st, 1964, Carole Ann Rowe (marr. diss. 1977); two *s* one *d*; 2nd, 1977, Susan Ann Poole (*d* 1994); two *d*. *Educ:* Harwich County High Sch.; Mid-Essex Coll. of Law; LLB Hons London. Called to the Bar, Inner Temple, 1972; an Asst Recorder, 1986–89. Mem., FB Soc., Norwich. *Recreations:* golf, sailing, relaxing. *Address:* 24 King Coel Road, Lexden, Colchester CO3 5AQ. *Club:* North Countryman's (Colchester).

PARKINSON, family name of **Baron Parkinson**.

PARKINSON, Baron *cr* 1992 (Life Peer), of Carnforth in the County of Lancashire; **Cecil Edward Parkinson,** PC 1981; *b* 1 Sept. 1931; *s* of Sidney Parkinson, Carnforth, Lancs; *m* 1957, Ann Mary, *d* of F. A. Jarvis, Harpenden, Herts; three *d*. *Educ:* Royal Lancaster Grammar Sch., Lancaster; Emmanuel Coll., Cambridge. BA 1955, MA 1961. Joined Metal Box Company as a Management Trainee; joined West, Wake, Price, Chartered Accountants, 1956; qualified 1959; Partner, 1961–71; founded Parkinson Hart Securities Ltd, 1967; Director of several cos, 1965–79, 1984–87, 1992–. Constituency Chm., Hemel Hempstead Conservative Assoc.; Chm., Herts 100 Club, 1968–69; contested (C) Northampton, 1970. MP (C) Enfield West, Nov. 1970–74, Hertfordshire South, 1974–83, Hertsmere, 1983–92. PPS to Minister for Aerospace and Shipping, DTI, 1972–74; an Asst Govt Whip, 1974; an Opposition Whip, 1974–76; Opposition Spokesman on trade, 1976–79; Minister for Trade, Dept of Trade, 1979–81; Paymaster General, 1981–83; Chancellor, Duchy of Lancaster, 1982–83; Sec. of State for Trade and Industry, June-Oct. 1983, for Energy, 1987–89, for Transport, 1989–90. Chm. of Cons. Party, 1981–83. Sec., Cons. Parly Finance Cttee, 1971–72; Chm., Anglo-Swiss Parly Gp, 1979–82; Pres., Anglo-Polish Cons. Soc., 1986–. *Publication:* Right at the Centre: an autobiography, 1992. *Recreations:* reading, golf, skiing; ran for combined Oxford and Cambridge team against Amer. Univs, 1954 and 1955; ran for Cambridge against Oxford, 1954 and 1955. *Address:* House of Lords, SW1A 0PW. *Clubs:* Beefsteak, Garrick, Pratt's; Hawks (Cambridge).

PARKINSON, Desmond John, OBE 1950; Under-Secretary, Agricultural Research Council, 1971–73; *b* 8 March 1913; *s* of late Frederick A. Parkinson, Rio de Janeiro; *m* 1st, 1940, Leonor Hughes (marr. diss. 1954); 2nd, 1955, Lorna Mary Britton (*née* Wood); no *c*. *Educ:* Hereford Cathedral Sch.; St John's Coll., Cambridge; Brasenose Coll., Oxford. BA Cantab 1935; Colonial Admin. Service, 1936–60 (Gold Coast, Colonial Office, British Guiana, Nigeria); UK MAFF, 1960–63; ARC, 1963–73. *Recreation:* gardening. *Address:* Glebe House, North Cadbury, Yeovil, Somerset BA22 7DW. *T:* North Cadbury (01963) 440181. *Club:* United Oxford & Cambridge University.

PARKINSON, Ewart West, BSc, DPA, CEng, FICE, PPRTPI, FIMunE; OStJ; development adviser in urban regeneration; Director of Environment and County

Engineer, County of South Glamorgan, 1973–85; *b* 9 July 1926; *s* of Thomas Edward Parkinson and Esther Lilian West; *m* 1948, Patricia Joan Wood; two *s* one *d*. *Educ:* Wyggeston Sch., Leicester; Coll. of Technology, Leicester (BSc, DPA). Miller Prize (bridge design), Instn CE, 1953. After working with Leicester, Wakefield, Bristol and Dover Councils, he became Dep. Borough Engr, Chelmsford, 1957–60; Dep. City Surveyor Plymouth, 1960–64; City Planning Officer, Cardiff, 1964–73, specialising in reconstruction of war damaged cities and urban regeneration. Mem. Council, RTPI, 1971–83 (Vice-Pres., 1973–75, Pres., 1975–76, Chm. Internat. Affairs Bd, 1975–80); Member: Sports Council for Wales, 1966–78 (Chm., Facilities Cttee); Internat. Soc. of City and Regional Planners, 1972; Govt Deleg. to UN Conf. on Human Settlements, 1976; Watt Cttee for Energy, 1977–83 (Chm., Working Gp on Energy and Envt, 1980–83); UK mem., Internat. Wkg Party on Urban Land Policy, Internat. Fedn for Housing and Planning, 1979–85; Chairman: Internat. Wkg Party on Energy and the Environment, Internat. Fedn for Housing and Planning, 1982–85 (Life Mem. 1986); Wkg Party on Land Policy, Royal Town Planning Inst., 1983–85; led Study Tours to Soviet Union, 1977, India and Bangladesh, 1979, China, 1980, Kenya, Zimbabwe and Tanzania, 1981; lecture visits to People's Republic of China at invitation of Ministry of Construction, 1982, 1986, 1989, 1990, 1991. Director: Moving Being Theatre Co., 1986–90; W. S. Atkins (Wales), 1988–; Pontypridd Market Co., 1988–. Chairman: STAR Community Trust Ltd, 1979–; Intervol, 1985–89; Wales Sports Centre for the Disabled Trust, 1986–; Norwegian Church Preservation (formerly Rebuilding) Trust, 1992– (Man. Trustee, 1988); Roald Dahl Arts Project Trust, 1995–; Dir, Cardiff Action for the Single Homeless, 1988–; Vice-Pres., Wales Council for the Disabled, 1982–. Diamond Jubilee Silver Medal, Nat. Housing and Town Planning Council, 1978; many urban design awards, from Prince of Wales Cttee, Civic Trust, Concrete Soc., and Cardiff 2000. OStJ 1980 (S Glamorgan Council, 1975–). *Publications:* The Land Question, 1974; And Who is my Neighbour?, 1976; articles in prof. jls on land policy, energy and the environment, and public participation. *Recreations:* working, travelling, being with family, talking with friends. *Address:* 42 South Rise, Llanishen, Cardiff CF4 5RH. *T:* Cardiff (01222) 756 394.

PARKINSON, Graham Edward; Metropolitan Stipendiary Magistrate, since 1982; a Recorder, since 1989; *b* 13 Oct. 1937; *s* of Norman Edward Parkinson and Phyllis (*née* Jaquiss); *m* 1963, Dinah Mary Pyper; one *s* one *d*. *Educ:* Loughborough Grammar Sch. Admitted Solicitor of the Supreme Court, 1961. Articled to J. Tempest Bouskell, Leicester, 1955–60; Asst Solicitor: Slaughter & May, 1961–63; Amery Parkes & Co., 1963–67; Partner, Darlington and Parkinson, Ealing, 1967–82. Pres., Central and S Mddx Law Soc., 1978–79; Mem. Cttee, London Criminal Courts Solicitors Assoc., 1978–80. *Recreations:* going to the opera, reading, piano playing, listening to music. *Address:* Horseferry Road Magistrates' Court, 70 Horseferry Road, SW1P 2AX.

PARKINSON, Howard; HM Diplomatic Service; Consul General, Washington, since 1994; *b* 29 March 1948; *s* of Ronald Parkinson and Doris (*née* Kenyon); *m* 1974, Linda Wood; one *s* one *d*. *Educ:* Openshaw Tech. High Sch., Manchester. BoT, 1967–69; joined HM Diplomatic Service, 1969; Latin American Floater, 1972–74; Vice Consul: Tegucigalpa, 1974–75; Buenos Aires, 1975–78; Second Sec., Maputo, 1978–81; Second, later First Sec., FCO, 1981–85; First Sec. (Commercial), Lisbon, 1985–89; on loan to British Gas, 1989–91; Asst Hd, Migration and Visa Dept, FCO, 1991–94. *Recreations:* travel, music, reading. *Address:* c/o Foreign and Commonwealth Office, King Charles Street, SW1A 2AH.

PARKINSON, Dr James Christopher, MBE 1963; TD 1962; Deputy Director, Brighton Polytechnic, 1970–83, retired; *b* 15 Aug. 1920; *s* of late Charles Myers Parkinson, Pharmacist, Blackburn, Lancs; *m* 1950, Gwyneth Margot, *d* of late Rev. John Raymond Harrison, Macclesfield, Ches; three *s*. *Educ:* Queen Elizabeth's Gram. Sch., Blackburn; Univ. Coll., Nottingham. BPharm, PhD (London), FRPharmS. Served in Mediterranean area, Parachute Regt, 1943–46; Parachute Regt TA: 16 AB Div. and 44 Parachute Bde, 1949–63 (Major). Lectr, Sch. of Pharmacy, Univ. of London, 1948–54; Head of Sch. of Pharmacy, Brighton Coll. of Technology, 1954–64; Dep. Sec., Pharmaceutical Soc. of Gt Britain, 1964–67; Principal, Brighton Coll. of Technology, 1967–70. Mem. various pharmaceutical cttees of British Pharmacopœia, British Pharmaceutical Codex and British Veterinary Codex, 1956–64; Examr, Pharmaceutical Soc. of Gt Britain, 1954–64; Mem. Bds of Studies in Pharmacy and Librarianship, CNAA, 1965–75. Mem., Mid-Downs DHA, 1984–87. Member, Gen. Synod of Church of England, 1970–85. *Publications:* research papers on applied microbiology in Jl Appl. Bact. and Jl Pharm. (London) and on pharmaceutical education in Pharm. Jl. *Recreation:* do-it-yourself. *Address:* 5 Marchants Close, Hurstpierpoint, West Sussex BN6 9XB. *T:* Hurstpierpoint (01273) 833369.

PARKINSON, Michael; interviewer, television presenter, writer; *b* 28 March 1935; *m* Mary Heneghan; three *s*. *Educ:* Barnsley Grammar School. Journalist on local paper; The Guardian; Daily Express; columnist on Sunday Times; radio work; has written for Punch, The Listener, New Statesman; Columnist: Daily Mirror, 1986–90; Daily Telegraph, 1991–; Editor, Catalyst, 1988–; Producer and interviewer: Granada's Scene; Granada in the North; World in Action; What the Papers Say; reporter on 24 Hours (BBC); Exec. producer and presenter, London Weekend Television, 1968; Presenter: Cinema, 1969–70; Tea Break, Where in the World, The Movie Quiz, 1971; host of own chat show, Parkinson, 1971–82; TV-am, 1983–84; Parkinson in Australia, 1979–84; Give Us a Clue, 1984; All Star Secrets, 1984–86; The Skag Kids, 1985; Parkinson One-to-One, 1987–88; Desert Island Discs, BBC Radio 4, 1986–88; LBC Radio, 1990; Help Squad, 1991; Surprise Party, 1993. Founder-Director, Pavilion Books, 1980–. *Publications:* Football Daft, 1968; Cricket Mad, 1969; (with Clyde Jeavons) Pictorial History of Westerns, 1972; Sporting Fever, 1974; (with Willis Hall) Football Classified, 1974; George Best: an intimate biography, 1975; (with Willis Hall) A–Z of Soccer, 1975; Bats in the Pavilion, 1977; The Woofits, 1980; Parkinson's Lore, 1981; The Best of Parkinson, 1982. *Address:* c/o Michael Parkinson Enterprises Ltd, IMG, Media House, 3 Burlington Lane, W4 2TH.

PARKINSON, Sir Nicholas (Fancourt), Kt 1980; consultant; *b* 5 Dec. 1925; *s* of late Rev. C. T. Parkinson, MA Oxon, and Dorothy Fancourt (*née* Mitchell); *m* 1952, Roslyn Sheena Campbell; two *d*. *Educ:* King's Sch., Parramatta, NSW; Univ. of Sydney (BA). Entered Aust. Foreign Service, 1951; Third Sec., Cairo, 1953–56; First Sec., Hong Kong, 1958–61; Counsellor, Moscow, Wellington, Kuala Lumpur, 1963–67; Chm., Jt Intell. Cttee, Dept of Defence, Canberra, 1967–70; High Comr, Singapore, 1970–74; Dep. Sec., Dept of For. Affairs, Canberra, 1974–76; Ambassador to the US, 1976–77 and 1979–82; Sec., Dept of For. Affairs, Canberra, 1977–79. Dir, Sears World Trade (Australia), 1983–86. Mem., ABC Adv. Council, 1991–93. *Recreation:* bridge. *Address:* 62 Collings Street, Pearce, ACT 2607, Australia. *T:* (62) 2861004; Shiloh, Mount Tomah, NSW 2758, Australia. *Club:* Commonwealth (Canberra).

PARKINSON, Ronald Dennis; Assistant Curator, Victoria and Albert Museum, since 1978; *b* 27 April 1945; *s* of Albert Edward Parkinson and Jennie Caroline Clara Meager. *Educ:* St Dunstan's Coll.; Clare Coll., Cambridge (MA). Res. Assistant: Paul Mellon Foundn for British Art, 1971–72; V&A Mus., 1972–74; Asst Keeper, Tate Gall., 1974–78. *Publications:* (ed jtly) Richard Redgrave, 1988; Catalogue of British Oil Paintings 1820–1860 in the Victoria and Albert Museum, 1990; articles in Apollo, Burlington Mag., Cambridge Res., Connoisseur, Country Life, Times Higher Educn Sup. *Recreations:* reading, shopping. *Address:* Victoria and Albert Museum, South Kensington, SW7 2RL. *T:* 0171–938 8474. *Club:* Algonquin.

PARKINSON, Thomas Harry, CBE 1972; DL; Town Clerk, 1960–72, Clerk of the Peace, 1970–72, Birmingham; *b* Bilston, 25 June 1907; *y s* of G. R. J. Parkinson; *m* 1936, Joan Catherine, *d* of C. J. Douglas-Osborn; two *s* one *d*. *Educ:* Bromsgrove; Birmingham University. LLB Hons 1929. Admitted Solicitor, 1930. RAF, 1939–45. Asst Solicitor, Birmingham Corp., 1936–49; Dep. Town Clerk, Birmingham, 1949–60. Pres., Birmingham Law Soc., 1969–70. Sec., W Midlands Passenger Transport Authority, 1969–72; Member: Water Services Staff Adv. Commn, 1973–78; W Midlands Rent Assessment Panel, 1972–78; Sec., Nat Exhibn Centre Ltd, 1972–78; Hon. Member: Birmingham Assoc. of Mech. Engrs; Inst. of Housing. DL Warwickshire, 1970. Hon. DSc Aston, 1972. *Recreations:* walking, sailing, gardening. *Address:* Three Springs Barn, Stanford Bishop, Bringsty, Worcester WR7 5UA. *T:* Suckley (01886) 884314.

PARKYN, Brian (Stewart); General Manager, Training Services, British Caledonian Airways Ltd, 1981–88; *b* 28 April 1923; *o s* of Leslie and Gwen Parkyn, Whetstone, N20; *m* 1951, Janet Anne, *o d* of Charles and Jessie Stormer, Eastbourne; one *s* one *d*. *Educ:* King Edward VI Sch., Chelmsford; technical colleges. Principal, Glacier Inst. of Management (Associated Engineering Ltd), 1976–80. Director: Scott Bader Co. Ltd, 1953–83; Hunting Industrial Plastics Ltd, 1979–83; Halmatic Ltd, 1983–88. British Plastics Federation: Chm., Reinforced Plastics Gp, 1961–63; Mem. Council, 1959–75. Vice Pres., Rubber and Plastics Inst., 1972–75. Has travelled widely and lectured in N and S America, Africa, Australasia, India, Japan, USSR and China, etc.; Plastics Lectr, Worshipful Co. of Horners, 1967. Contested (Lab) Bedford, 1964; MP (Lab) Bedford, 1966–70; Mem., Select Cttee on Science and Technology, 1967–70; Chm., Sub-Cttee on Carbon Fibres, 1969; contested (Lab) Bedford, Oct. 1974. Member: Council, Cranfield Inst. of Technology, 1970–94; Council, RSA, 1976–82 (Hon. Treas., 1977–82). FIM. *Publications:* Democracy, Accountability and Participation in Industry, 1979; various papers and books on polyester resins and reinforced plastics. *Recreations:* writing, industrial democracy. *Address:* 9 Clarendon Square, Leamington Spa, Warwicks CV32 5QJ. *T:* Leamington (01926) 330066.

PARMOOR, 4th Baron *cr* 1914; **Milo Cripps;** *b* 18 June 1929; *s* of 3rd Baron Parmoor, DSO, TD, DL, and Violet Mary Geraldine, *d* of Sir William Nelson, 1st Bt; *S* father, 1977. *Educ:* Ampleforth; Corpus Christi College, Oxford. *Heir: cousin* (Matthew) Anthony Leonard Cripps, *qv*. *Address:* Dairy, Sutton Veny, Wilts BA12 7AL.

PARNABY, Dr John, CBE 1987; FEng 1986; FIMechE; FIEE; Managing Director, Lucas Electronic Systems Products (formerly Lucas Applied Technology Sector), since 1990; Chairman, Lucas Management Systems (formerly Lucas Metier), since 1990; Chairman, Lucas Engineering and Systems Ltd (Managing Director, 1990); *b* 10 July 1937; *s* of John Banks Parnaby and Mary Elizabeth Parnaby; *m* 1959, Lilian Armstrong; three *s* one *d*. *Educ:* Durham Univ. (BSc Mech. Engrg, 1961); Glasgow Univ. (PhD Control Engrg, 1966). FIProdE 1978; FIMechE 1978; MIEE 1966. Technical Apprentice, 1954–58, Ironworks Develt Engr, 1961–62, United Steel Co.; Res. Asst, Univ. of Durham, 1962–63; Lectr in Mech. Engrg, Univ. of Glasgow, 1963–66; Sen. Projects Engr, Albright & Wilson Ltd, 1966–67; Works Man., Solway Chemicals Ltd, 1967–70; University of Bradford: Sen. Lectr, 1970–73; Prof. of Manufg Systems Design, 1973–80 (Chm., Sch. of Manufacturing Systems Engrg, 1975–80); Technical and Marketing Dir, subseq. Jt Man. Dir, Rieter Scragg Ltd, 1980–82; Gen. Man., Dunlop Ltd, 1982–83; Gp Dir, Technology, Lucas Industries, 1983–90. Chm., Link Steering Cttee, DTI/OST, 1993–. Vis. Hon. Prof. of Manufacturing Systems Engrg, Univ. of Birmingham, 1984–. Pres., IProdE, 1989; Dep. Pres., IEE, 1993–; Hon. FIEE 1991; Hon. Fellow: Coventry Poly., 1989; Sheffield Poly., 1991. Hon. DTech: Liverpool Poly., 1990; Loughborough Univ., 1991; Hon. DSc Hull, 1991; DUniv Open, 1992. Gold Medal, Instn of Manufg Engrs, 1987; Faraday Medal, IEE, 1994. *Publications:* Minicomputers and Microcomputers in Engineering and Manufacture, 1986; over 40 papers in engrg and management jls on manufg systems, control engrg, process engrg, business process systems engrg and machinery design. *Recreations:* hockey, sailing. *Address:* Crest Edge, Beechnut Lane, Solihull, W Midlands B91 2NN. *T:* 0121–705 4348.

PARNELL, family name of **Baron Congleton.**

PARR, John Robert; Director-General, Air Transport Users Council, since 1989; *b* 25 Sept. 1934; *s* of Henry George Parr and Hilda Frances Parr (*née* Pattison); *m* 1993, Margaret Dolores O'Reilly. *Educ:* Dulwich Coll.; Merton Coll., Oxford (MA). British Iron and Steel Fedn, 1959–65; Dept of Economic Affairs, 1966–68; British Steel Corp., 1968–73; Dir-Gen., British Footwear Manufacturers' Fedn, 1973–76; Divl Head, Gen. Secretariat, Council of Ministers of EC, 1976–89, Hon. Dir, 1989. *Recreations:* political history of 19th and 20th centuries, opera and other forms of classical music, Irish country life. *Address:* Air Transport Users Council, 103 Kingsway, WC2B 6QX. *T:* 0171–242 3882.

PARR, (Thomas) Donald, CBE 1986; Chairman, William Baird PLC, since 1981; *b* 3 Sept. 1930; *s* of Thomas and Elizabeth Parr; *m* 1954, Gwendoline Mary Chaplin; three *s* one *d*. *Educ:* Burnage Grammar Sch. Own business, 1953–64; Chm., Thomas Marshall Investments Ltd, 1964–76; Director: William Baird PLC, 1976–; Vendôme Luxury Gp (formerly Dunhill Holdings) PLC, 1986–; Hepworth PLC, 1989–; Kwik Save Group, 1991–. Chm., British Clothing Industry Assoc., 1987–91; Member: NW Industrial Develt Bd, 1975–87; Ct of Governors, UMIST, 1984–. *Recreation:* sailing. *Address:* Homestead, Homestead Road, Disley, Stockport, Cheshire SK12 2JP. *T:* Disley (01663) 765211. *Clubs:* Boodle's; Royal Ocean Racing (Admiral); Royal Yacht Squadron (Cowes).

PARRAMATTA, Bishop of; *see* King, Rt Rev. B. F. V.

PARRINDER, Prof. (Edward) Geoffrey (Simons); Professor of Comparative Study of Religions, University of London, at King's College, 1970–77, Professor Emeritus, 1977; *b* 30 April 1910; *s* of William Patrick and Florence Mary Parrinder; *m* 1936, Esther Mary Burt; two *s* one *d*. *Educ:* private sch.; Richmond Coll., London Univ.; Faculté libre de théologie protestante, Montpellier. MA, PhD, DD London. Minister of Methodist Church, Dahomey and Ivory Coast, 1933; ordained 1936; Principal, Séminaire Protestant, Dahomey, 1936–40, 1945–46; Methodist Church: Redruth, 1940; Dahomey, 1943; Guernsey, 1946; Lectr in Religious Studies, 1949, Sen. Lectr, 1950–58, UC Ibadan; Reader in Comparative Study of Religions, Univ. of London, 1958–70; Dean, Faculty of Theology, KCL, 1972–74. Hon. Sec., Internat. Assoc. for History of Religions, British Br., 1960–72, Pres., 1972–77; President: London Soc. for Study of Religion, 1980–82; London Soc. of Jews and Christians, 1981–90 (Hon. Life Pres., 1990). Lectures: Charles Strong (Australian Church), 1964; Wilde, in Natural and Comparative Religion, Oxford Univ., 1966–69; Teape, Delhi, Madras, 1973. Vis. Prof., Internat. Christian Univ., Tokyo, 1977–78; Vis. Lectr, Surrey Univ., 1978–83. FKC 1972; Hon. DLitt Lancaster, 1975. *Publications:* West African Religion, 1949; Bible and Polygamy, 1950; West African Psychology, 1951; Religion in an African City, 1953; African Traditional Religion, 1954; Story of Ketu, 1956; Introduction to Asian Religions, 1957; Witchcraft, 1958; (ed) African

Ideas of God, 1961; Worship in the World's Religions, 1961; Comparative Religion, 1962; Upanishads, Gītā and Bible, 1962; What World Religions Teach, 1963; The Christian Debate, 1964; The World's Living Religions, 1965; A Book of World Religions, 1965; Jesus in the Qur'ān, 1965; African Mythology, 1967; Religion in Africa, 1969, repr. as Africa's Three Religions, 1976; Avatar and Incarnation, 1970; Dictionary of Non-Christian Religions, 1971; (ed) Man and his Gods, 1971, repr. as Illustrated History of the World's Religions, 1983; The Indestructible Soul, 1973; Themes for Living, 1973; The Bhagavad Gita, a Verse Translation, 1974; Something after Death?, 1974; The Wisdom of the Forest, 1975; Mysticism in the World's Religions, 1976; The Wisdom of the Early Buddhists, 1977; Sex in the World's Religions, 1980; Storia Universale delle Religioni, 1984; Encountering World Religions, 1987; A Dictionary of Religious and Spiritual Quotations, 1989; The Sayings of the Buddha, 1991; Son of Joseph, 1992; articles and reviews in jls of theology, African and Asian religions and Annual Register, 1958–. *Recreations:* travel, gardening, literature. *Address:* 31 Charterhouse Road, Orpington, Kent BR6 9EJ. *T:* Orpington (01689) 823887.

See also D. M. Boston.

PARRIS, Matthew Francis; author, journalist and broadcaster; *b* 7 Aug. 1949; *s* of Leslie Francis Parris and Theresa Eunice Parris (*née* Littler). *Educ:* Waterford School, Swaziland; Clare Coll., Cambridge (BA Hons); Yale Univ., USA (Paul Mellon Fellowship). Foreign Office, 1974–76; Conservative Research Dept, 1976–79; MP (C) West Derbyshire, 1979–86; Presenter, Weekend World, LWT, 1986–88. Mem., Broadcasting Standards Council, 1992–. *Publications:* Inca-Kola, 1990; A Traveller's Tale of Peru, 1990; So Far So Good, 1991; Look Behind You!, 1993; (ed) Scorn, 1994; Great Parliamentary Scandals, 1995. *Recreation:* distance running. *Address:* c/o The Times, Pennington Street, E1 9XN.

PARROTT, Andrew Haden; conductor and musicologist; *b* 10 March 1947. *Educ:* Merton Coll., Oxford (schol.; BA 1969). Dir of Music, Merton Coll., Oxford, 1969–71; formerly musical assistant to Sir Michael Tippett. Founded Taverner Choir, 1973, then Taverner Consort and Taverner Players, for performance of music ranging from medieval to late 18th century. Débuts: BBC Prom. concerts, 1977; EBU, 1979; La Scala, 1985; Salzburg, 1987; Guest Conductor worldwide of symphony and chamber orchs, opera and contemporary music. About 50 recordings. *Publications:* (ed jtly) New Oxford Book of Carols, 1992; contrib. learned jls. *Address:* c/o Allied Artists, 42 Montpelier Square, SW7 1JZ.

PARROY, Michael Picton; QC 1991; a Recorder, since 1990; *b* 22 Oct. 1946; *s* of Gerard May and Elizabeth Mary Parroy; *m* 1978, Susan Patricia Blades (*née* Winter). *Educ:* Malvern College; Brasenose College, Oxford (MA). Called to the Bar, Middle Temple, 1969. *Publication:* Road Traffic, in Halsbury's Laws of England, 4th edn. vol. 40, 1983. *Recreations:* gardening, food and wine, dog walking. *Address:* First Floor, 3 Paper Buildings, Temple, EC4Y 7EU.

PARRY, family name of **Baron Parry.**

PARRY, Baron *cr* 1975 (Life Peer), of Neyland, Dyfed; **Gordon Samuel David Parry;** DL; President, Milford Docks Company, since 1991 (Chairman, 1984–91); Chairman, Taylorplan Services, since 1987; *b* 30 Nov. 1925; *s* of Thomas Lewis Parry and Anne Parry (*née* Evans); *m* 1948, Glenys Parry (*née* Incledon); one *d. Educ:* Neyland Board Sch.; Pembroke County Intermediate Sch.; Trinity Coll., Carmarthen; Univ. of Liverpool (Dipl. Advanced Educn). Teacher: Coronation Sch., Pembroke Dock, 1945–46; Llanstadwell Voluntary Primary Sch., Neyland, 1946–47; Barn St Voluntary Sch., Haverfordwest, 1947; County Primary Sch., Neyland, 1947–52; Librarian, Housemaster, County Sec. Sch., Haverfordwest, 1952–62 and 1963–68; Inst. of Educn, Univ. of Liverpool, 1962–63; Warden, Pembs Teachers' Centre, 1969–78. Former member: Welsh Develt Authority; Gen. Adv. Council, IBA; Welsh Arts Council; Schs Council Cttee for Wales; Member: Fac. of Educn, Univ. Coll. of Wales Aberystwyth; Council, Open Univ. (Chm., Adv. Cttee on Studies in Educn, 1978–83); British Tourist Authority, 1978–84; President: Pembs Br., Multiple Sclerosis Soc.; Pembs Spastics Soc.; Spastics Soc., Wales; Commonwealth Games Appeal Cttee for Wales, 1979; Keep Wales Tidy Cttee, 1979– (Chm., 1979–86); BICSc, 1981–91; Tidy Britain (formerly Keep Britain Tidy) Gp, 1991– (Chm., 1986–91); Chairman: Wales Tourist Bd, 1978–84; British Cleaning Council, 1983–; Keep Britain Beautiful Campaign, 1986–; Clean World Internat., 1991–; British Travel Educn Trust; Vice President: Nat. Chamber of Trade, 1980; Internat. Year of Disabled People in Wales, 1979; Nat. Soc. for Mentally Handicapped Children, S Wales Region; Soc. of Handicapped Drivers in Wales; Welsh Nat. Council of YMCAs. Contested (Lab) Monmouth 1959, Pembroke 1970, and Feb. and Oct. 1974. Writer, broadcaster, and TV panel Chm. FRSA; Fellow: Tourism Soc., 1979; HCIMA, 1980; BICSc, 1981; James Cook Univ., N Qld, Aust, 1989. DL Dyfed, 1993. Hon. Fellow: Trinity Coll., Carmarthen, 1990; Polytechnic of Wales, 1991. Hon. Fellow, Inst. of Wastes Management. Hon. DEd Wales, 1992. *Recreations:* travel; watching Welsh Rugby XV win the Grand Slam; reading. *Address:* Willowmead, 52 Port Lion, Llangwm, Haverfordwest, Pembrokeshire, Dyfed SA62 4JT. *T:* Neyland (01646) 600667.

PARRY, Alan; President, Johnson & Higgins Ltd, since 1989 (Chairman, 1987–89); *b* 30 Oct. 1927; *s* of George Henry James Edgar Parry and Jessica Cooke; *m* 1954, Shirley Yeoman; one *s* one *d. Educ:* Reedham School. Leonard Hammond Ltd, 1941; Sedgwick Collins Ltd, 1948, Dir, 1960; Dir, Man. Dir, Dep. Chm. and Chm., Sedgwick companies and subsidiaries, to 1981; Chm., Carter Brito e Cunha, 1982–87. Mem., Lloyd's Insurance Brokers' Assoc., 1961–64, 1970–73, 1975–78 (Chm., 1977); Mem. Council, BIBA, and LIBA and BIBA rep. on Cttee on Invisible Exports, 1977; Mem., Cttee of Lloyd's, 1979–82, 1985–88 (Dep. Chm., 1987–88). *Recreations:* flyfishing, drama. *Address:* The Quarry, Firtoll Road, Mayfield, East Sussex TN20 6NG.

PARRY, Anthony Joseph, QFSM 1990; County Fire Officer, 1985–90, and Chief Executive, County Fire Service, 1986–90, Greater Manchester; *b* 20 May 1935; *s* of Henry Joseph Parry and Mary Elizabeth McShane; *m* 1959, Elizabeth Therese Collins; three *s* one *d. Educ:* St Francis Xavier's Coll., Liverpool. MIFireE. Liverpool Fire Bde, 1958; Fire Service Technical Coll., 1967; Gloucestershire Fire Service, 1969; Avon Fire Service, 1974; Lancashire County Fire Service, 1975. Long Service and Good Conduct Medal, 1978. *Address:* 18 Oakenclough Drive, Bolton BL1 5QY.

PARRY, Prof. Eldryd Hugh Owen, OBE 1982; MD, FRCP; Chairman, Tropical Health and Education Trust, since 1989; *b* 28 Nov. 1930; *s* of Dr Owen Parry and Dr Constance Parry (*née* Griffiths); *m* 1960, Helen Madeline, *d* of Humphry and Madeline House; one *s* three *d. Educ:* Shrewsbury; Emmanuel Coll., Cambridge; Welsh Nat. Sch. of Medicine (BChir 1955; MA; MD). FWACP. Junior posts, Cardiff Royal Infirmary, Nat. Heart Hosp., Hammersmith Hosp., 1956–65; seconded to UCH, Ibadan, 1960–63; Associate Prof., Haile Selassie I Univ., Addis Ababa, 1966–69; Prof. of Medicine, Ahmadu Bello Univ., 1969–77; Foundn Dean, Faculty of Health Sciences, Univ. of Ilorin, Nigeria, 1977–80; Dean and Prof. of Medicine, Sch. of Med. Scis, Kumasi, 1980–85; Dir, Wellcome Tropical Inst., 1985–90; Sen. Res. Fellow, LSHTM, 1990–95. Albert Cook Meml Lectr, Kampala, 1974; Mem., Med. and Dental Council, Ghana, 1980–85; Chm., Council, All Nations Christian Coll., 1986–. Frederick Murgatroyd Prize, RCP, 1973. *Publications:* Principles of Medicine in Africa, 1976; papers on medicine in the tropics in med. jls. *Recreations:* tennis, Wales, old Welsh furniture. *Address:* 21 Edenhurst Avenue, SW6 3PD.

See also J. P. H. House.

PARRY, Emyr J.; *see* Jones Parry.

PARRY, Emyr Owen; solicitor; a Recorder of the Crown Court, since 1979; District Judge at the Caernarfon Group of County Courts and the District Registry of the High Court at Llangefni, Caernarfon and Rhyl, since 1992; *b* 26 May 1933; *s* of Ebenezer Owen Parry and Ellen Parry; *m* 1959, Enid Griffiths; one *s* one *d. Educ:* Caernarfon Grammar Sch.; University Coll. of Wales, Aberystwyth (LLB Hons Wales, 1954). Admitted solicitor, 1957. Estabd own practice in Llangefni, Anglesey, 1958; formed partnership (Emyr Parry & Davies) with Mrs Elinor C. Davies, 1964; Dep. Circuit Judge, 1975. Chairman: Social Security (formerly National Insurance) Appeals Tribunal, Holyhead Area, 1969–92; Medical Appeal Tribunal, 1986–92; Solicitor Mem., Lord Chancellor's County Court Rule Cttee, 1975–80. *Recreations:* cricket, music, theatre.

PARRY, John Alderson, CBE 1985; BBC National Governor for Wales, 1986–91; *b* 3 Jan. 1934; *s* of Albert Parry and Mary Parry (*née* Alderson); *m* 1959, Joan Rathbone; one *s* one *d. Educ:* Leighton Park, Reading; Christ's College, Cambridge (MA, Vet MB). MRCVS; FRAgS 1986. Veterinary practice, Brecon, 1958–. Mem., Agricl Adv. Council, 1969–73; Chairman: Hill Farming Res. Orgn, 1981–87 (Mem., 1971–); Welsh Agricl Adv. Cttee, BBC, 1978–85; Welsh Office Hydatid Control Steering Cttee, 1981–; Member: Sec. of State for Wales' Agricl Adv. Cttee, 1978–; AFRC, 1982–92 (Chm., Animals Res. Cttee, 1983–87); Develt Bd for Rural Wales, 1985–88; Council, Royal Welsh Agricl Soc., 1986–; Dir, Animal Disease Res. Assoc., 1987–. President: BVA, 1976–77; RCVS, 1986–87. Chm., Governing Body, Inst. of Grassland and Animal Prodn, AFRC, 1987–; Gov., McCauley Land Use Res. Inst., 1987–. *Recreations:* field sports. *Address:* Watergate Mill, Brecon, Powys LD3 9AN. *T:* Brecon (01874) 2113. *Clubs:* United Oxford & Cambridge University, Farmers'; Hawks (Cambridge); Cardiff & County (Cardiff).

PARRY, Mrs Margaret Joan; Headmistress of Heathfield School, Ascot, 1973–82; *b* 27 Nov. 1919; *d* of W. J. Tamplin, Llantrisant, Glamorgan; *m* 1946, Raymond Howard Parry; two *s* one *d. Educ:* Howell's Sch., Llandaff, Cardiff; Univ. of Wales. Hons English Cl I. Married to a schoolmaster at Eton; taught and coached interesting people from time to time; Examiner for: Civil Service, LCC, Schools Examination Boards. Patron, Univ. of Buckingham, 1983. *Recreations:* books, music, tapestry. *Address:* Carreg Gwaun, 23a Murray Court, Ascot, Berks SL5 9BP. *T:* Ascot (01344) 26299.

PARRY, Prof. Martin Lewis, PhD; Professor of Environmental Management, Department of Geography, University College London, since 1994; *b* 12 Dec. 1945; *s* of John Fyson Parry and Frances Joan (*née* Stewart); *m* 1968, Cynthia Jane Mueller; two *d. Educ:* Univ. of Durham (BA Hons); Univ. of West Indies (MSc); Univ. of Edinburgh (PhD). Lectr, Univ. of Edinburgh, 1972–73; University of Birmingham: Lectr, 1973–86; Sen. Lectr, 1986–88; Reader, 1988–89; Prof. of Envmtl Management, 1989–91; Prof. of Envmtl Management, and IBM Dir, Envmtl Change Unit, Oxford Univ., 1991–94. *Publications:* Climatic Change, Agriculture and Settlement, 1976; The Impact of Climatic Variations on Agriculture, Vol. 1 1988, Vol. 2 1989; Climate Change and World Agriculture, 1990. *Recreations:* squash, ski-ing, sailing. *Address:* Department of Geography, University College London, Gower Street, WC1E 6BT. *Club:* Oriental.

PARRY, Robert; MP (Lab) Liverpool, Riverside, since 1983 (Liverpool Exchange, 1970–74; Liverpool, Scotland Exchange, 1974–83); *b* 8 Jan. 1933; *s* of Robert and Sarah Parry (*née* Joyce); *m* 1956, Marie (*née* Hesdon) (*d* 1987). *Educ:* Bishop Goss RC School, Liverpool. Became a building trade worker. Full-time organizer for National Union of Public Employees, 1960–67; now sponsored Member, Transport and General Workers' Union. Member of Co-operative Party. Member, Liverpool City Council, 1963–74. Chm., Merseyside Gp of Labour MPs, 1976–87. Mem., UK Delegn to Council of Europe Assembly and WEU, 1984–92. Pres., Assoc. for Democracy in Hong Kong, 1980–; Co-President: Internat. Cttee for Human Rights in S Korea, 1984–; Internat. Cttee for Peaceful and Indep. Reunification of Korea, 1984–; Founder Pres., Human Rights Internat., 1994–. Patron: UNA Hong Kong, 1977–; Rotunda Boxing Club, 1975–; KIND (Kids in Need and Distress); President: Liverpool and Dist Sunday Football League (largest in Europe), 1973–; Liverpool Transport Boxing and Sporting Club, 1982–. Special interests: human rights, peace and disarmament, civil liberties, foreign affairs, particularly Central and SE Asia, overseas aid and the third world. *Address:* House of Commons, SW1A 0AA.

PARRY, Victor Thomas Henry, MA Oxon; FLA; Director of Central Library Services and Goldsmiths' Librarian, University of London, 1983–88; *b* 20 Nov. 1927; *s* of Thomas and Daisy Parry; *m* 1959, Mavis K. Russull; two *s* one *d. Educ:* St Julian's High Sch., Newport; St Edmund Hall, Oxford (MA); University College, London (DipLib). FLA 1959. Manchester Public Libraries, 1950–56; Colonial Office and CRO Library, 1956–60; Librarian, Nature Conservancy, 1960–63; British Museum (Natural History), 1963–74; Chief Librarian and Archivist, Royal Botanic Gdns, Kew, 1974–78; Librarian, SOAS, Univ. of London, 1978–83. Chm., Circle of State Librarians, 1966–68; Mem., Adv. Cttee, British Library Dept of Humanities and Social Scis (formerly Reference Div.), 1983–90; Council Member: Sir Anthony Panizzi Foundn, 1983–89; London Soc., 1984–88. FRSA. *Publications:* contrib. prof. books and jls. *Recreations:* ball games, books, bridge, railways. *Address:* 69 Redway Drive, Twickenham TW2 7NN. *T:* 0181–894 0742.

PARRY, Prof. William, PhD; FRS 1984; Professor of Mathematics, University of Warwick, since 1970; *b* 3 July 1934; *s* of late Richard Parry and Violet Irene Parry; *m* 1958, Benita (*née* Teper); one *d. Educ:* University Coll. London (BSc 1956); Univ. of Liverpool (MSc 1957); Imperial Coll. of Science and Technol., London (PhD 1960). Lectr, Univ. of Birmingham, 1960–65; Sen. Lectr, Univ. of Sussex, 1965–68; Reader, Univ. of Warwick, 1968– 70. Member: Labour Party; NCCL. *Publications:* Entropy and Generators in Ergodic Theory, 1969; Topics in Ergodic Theory, 1981; (with S. Tuncel) Classification Problems in Ergodic Theory, 1982; articles in Trans Amer. Math. Soc., Amer. Jl of Maths, and Annals of Maths. *Recreations:* theatre, concerts, walking. *Address:* Manor House, High Street, Marton CV23 9RR. *T:* Marton (01926) 632501.

PARRY BROWN, Arthur Ivor; *see* Brown, A. I. P.

PARRY-EVANS, Air Chief Marshal Sir David, GCB 1991 (KCB 1985); CBE 1978; Royal Air Force, retired; Chief Commander, St John Ambulance, since 1992; *b* 19 July 1935; *s* of late Group Captain John Parry-Evans, MRCS, LRCP, DLO, and of Dorothy Parry-Evans; *m* 1960, Ann, 2nd *d* of late Charles Reynolds and of Gertrude Reynolds; two *s. Educ:* Berkhamsted School. Joined RAF, 1956; served FEAF, Coastal Command, United States Navy, RN Staff Coll., 1958–70; Headquarters Strike Command, 1970–74; OC 214 Sqn, 1974–75; OC RAF Marham, 1975–77; MoD, 1977–81 (Director of Defence Policy, 1979–81); Comdt, RAF Staff Coll., 1981–82; AOC Nos 1 and 38 Groups, RAF Strike Comd, 1982–85; C-in-C RAF Germany, and Comdr, Second

ATAF, 1985–87; Dep. Chief of Defence Staff (Progs and Personnel), 1987–89; Air Mem. for Personnel, 1989–91. Gov., Royal Star and Garter Home, 1991–. KStJ 1992. *Address:* c/o National Westminster Bank, 26 Spring Street, W2 1WE. *Club:* Royal Air Force.

PARRY EVANS, Mary Alethea, (Lady Hallinan); a Recorder of the Crown Court, since 1978; *b* 31 Oct. 1929; *o c* of Dr Evan Parry Evans, MD, JP, and Dr Lilian Evans; *m* 1955, Sir Adrian Lincoln Hallinan, *qv*; two *s* two *d*. *Educ:* Malvern Girls' Coll.; Somerville Coll., Oxford (BCL, MA). Called to Bar, Inner Temple, 1953; Wales and Chester Circuit. Member: Cardiff City Council, 1961–70; S Glamorgan CC, 1972–81; S Glamorgan Health Authority, 1977–81. Lady Mayoress of Cardiff, 1969–70. *Address:* (chambers) 33 Park Place, Cardiff. *T:* Cardiff (01222) 33313.

PARRY JONES, Terence Graham; *see* Jones, Terry.

PARSLOE, Prof. Phyllida; Professor of Social Work, 1978–July 1996, and Warden of Wills Hall, since 1991, Bristol University; *b* 25 Dec. 1930; *d* of late Charles Guy Parsloe and of Mary Zirphie (*née* Munro). *Educ:* Bristol Univ. (BA, PhD); London Univ. (Cert. in Mental Health). Probation Officer, Devon CC, 1954–59; Psychiatric Social Worker, St George's Hospital, 1959–65; Lectr, London Sch. of Economics, 1965–70; Associate Prof., Sch. of Law, Indiana Univ., 1970–73; Prof. of Social Work, Univ. of Aberdeen, 1973–78; Pro-Vice Chancellor, Bristol Univ., 1988–91. Member: Central Council for Educn and Training in Social Work, 1986–; Commonwealth Scholarships Commn. *Publications:* The Work of the Probation and After Care Officer, 1967; Juvenile Justice in Britain and America, 1978; (with Prof. O. Stevenson) Social Service Teams: the practitioner's view, 1978; Social Service Area Teams, 1981; report to the Sec. of State for Scotland on Social Work in Prisons, 1987; (with S. Macara *et al*) Data Protection in Health and Social Services, 1988; Aiming for Partnership, 1990; contribs to: British Jl of Social Work, Community Care, Social Work Today, British Jl Criminology. *Recreations:* hill walking, crafts, gardening. *Address:* School for Policy Studies, 8 Woodland Road, Bristol BS8 1TN; 15 Elliston Road, Bristol BS6 6QG.

PARSONS, family name of **Earl of Rosse.**

PARSONS, Adrian; *see* Parsons, C. A. H.

PARSONS, Alan; *see* Parsons, T. A.

PARSONS, Alfred Roy, AO 1986; High Commissioner for Australia in the UK, 1984–87, retired; *b* 24 May 1925; *s* of W. G. R. Parsons and R. E. Parsons; *m* 1958, Gillian Tryce Pigot; two *s* one *d*. *Educ:* Hobart High School; Univ. of Tasmania (postgraduate research; BCom); Canberra University College. Dept of Foreign Affairs, 1947; Djakarta, 1950–53, Rangoon, 1956–58, Berlin, 1961–62; Aust. Mission to UN, NY, 1962–64; Counsellor, Djakarta, 1964–66; High Comr, Singapore, 1967–70; First Asst Sec., Canberra, 1970–73; High Comr, Kuala Lumpur, 1973–76; Dep. Sec., periodically Acting Sec., Dept of Foreign Affairs, 1978–83. Chm., Commonwealth Observer Gp on Namibia, 1989. Member: Australia Japan Foundn, 1978–83; Australia China Council. Pres., ACT Br., Lord's Taverners Australia. *Recreations:* golf, reading. *Address:* 11 Hotham Crescent, Deakin, Canberra, ACT 2600, Australia. *Clubs:* Commonwealth (Canberra); Royal Canberra Golf, Canberra Wine and Food.

PARSONS, Sir Anthony (Derrick), GCMG 1982 (KCMG 1975; CMG 1969); LVO 1965; MC 1945; HM Diplomatic Service, retired; Research Fellow, University of Exeter, since 1984 (Lecturer, 1984–87); *b* 9 Sept. 1922; *s* of late Col H. A. J. Parsons, MC; *m* 1948, Sheila Emily Baird; two *s* two *d*. *Educ:* King's Sch., Canterbury; Balliol Coll., Oxford (Hon. Fellow 1984). HM Forces, 1940–54; Asst Mil. Attaché, Baghdad, 1952–54; Foreign Office, 1954–55; HM Embassy: Ankara, 1955–59; Amman, 1959–60; Cairo, 1960–61; FO, 1961–64; HM Embassy, Khartoum, 1964–65; Political Agent, Bahrain, 1965–69; Counsellor, UK Mission to UN, NY, 1969–71; Under-Sec., FCO, 1971–74; Ambassador to Iran, 1974–79; FCO, 1979; UK Perm. Rep. to UN, 1979–82; Special Advr to PM on foreign affairs, 1982–83. Bd Mem., British Council, 1982–86. Order of the Two Niles (Sudan), 1965. *Publications:* The Pride and the Fall, 1984; They Say the Lion, 1986; From Cold War to Hot Peace: UN interventions 1947–1994, 1995. *Recreations:* gardening, golf, tennis. *Address:* Highgrove, Ashburton, South Devon TQ13 7HD. *Club:* Royal Over-Seas League.

PARSONS, (Charles) Adrian (Haythorne); Ombudsman to National Solicitors Network, since 1992; consultant on charity matters, Wilde Sapte, solicitors, since 1989, and to other solicitors; *b* 15 June 1929; *s* of Dr R. A. Parsons and Mrs W. S. Parsons (*née* Haythorne); *m* 1951, Hilary Sharpe; one *d*. *Educ:* Bembridge Sch.; Wadham Coll., Oxford. Called to Bar, Gray's Inn, 1964. Coutts & Co., Bankers, 1952–64; joined Charity Commn, 1964; Dep. Comr, 1972; Comr, 1974–89; Head of Legal Staff, 1981; Unit Trust Ombudsman, 1989–90. Chm., Brompton Business Coll. *Address:* 6 Garrick Close, The Green, Richmond, Surrey TW9 1PF. *T:* 0181–940 3731. *Club:* United Oxford & Cambridge University.

See also Sir R. E. C. F. Parsons.

PARSONS, Colin James, FCA; Group Chairman, Taylor Woodrow plc, since 1992 (Director, since 1987); *b* Neath, Wales, 15 Jan. 1934; *s* of Ivor Parsons and Elsie (*née* Price); *m* 1960, Alice McAuley; two *s*. *Educ:* Haverfordwest and Neath Grammar Schs. CA 1955; FCA 1991. Peat Marwick Mitchell, Toronto, 1957–59; Monarch Development Corp., 1959–92: Pres., 1977–79; Chm., 1992. *Recreations:* running, tennis, golf. *Address:* 4 Dunraven Street, W1Y 3FG. *Clubs:* Albany, Granite, Donalda (Toronto).

PARSONS, David; *see* Parsons, J. D.

PARSONS, John Christopher, LVO 1992; Deputy Keeper of the Privy Purse and Deputy Treasurer to the Queen, since 1988; *b* 21 May 1946; *s* of Arthur Christopher Parsons and Veronica Parsons; *m* 1982, Hon. Anne Manningham-Buller, *d* of 1st Viscount Dilhorne, PC; two *s* one *d*. *Educ:* Harrow; Trinity College, Cambridge. BA (Mech. Scis) 1968. FCA, FIMC. Dowty Group Ltd, 1968–72; Peat, Marwick, Mitchell & Co., 1972–85; Asst Treas. to the Queen, 1985–87; Dep. Dir (Finance), Royal Collection, 1992–93. *Address:* The Old Stables, Kensington Palace, W8 4PU. *Clubs:* Brooks's, Pratt's.

PARSONS, Prof. (John) David, DSc; FEng 1988; FIEE; David Jardine Professor of Electrical Engineering, since 1982, Pro-Vice-Chancellor, since 1990, University of Liverpool; *b* 8 July 1935; *s* of Oswald Parsons and Doris Anita (*née* Roberts); *m* 1969, Mary Winifred Stella Tate. *Educ:* University College of Wales, Cardiff (BSc); King's College London (MSc (Eng), DSc (Eng)). FIEE 1986. GEC Applied Electronics Labs, 1959–62; Regent Street Poly., 1962–66; City of Birmingham Poly., 1966–68; Lectr, Sen. Lectr and Reader in Electronic Engrg, Univ. of Birmingham, 1969–82; University of Liverpool: Head, Dept of Electrical Engrg and Electronics, 1983–86; Dean, Faculty of Engrg, 1986–89. Vis. Prof., Univ. of Auckland, 1982; Vis. Res. Engr, NTT, Japan, 1987. UN Expert in India, 1977; Hon. SPSO, RSRE, Malvern, 1978–82. Member Council: IERE, 1985–88; IEE, 1988–89. *Publications:* Electronic and Switching Circuits, 1975; Mobile Radio Communications, 1989; The Mobile Radio Propagation Channel, 1992; many papers on radio communication systems and radio propagation in learned jls. *Recreations:* golf, bridge, ski-ing. *Address:* Department of Electrical Engineering and Electronics, University of Liverpool, PO Box 147, Liverpool L69 3BX. *T:* 0151–794 4503.

PARSONS, Sir (John) Michael, Kt 1970; Deputy Chairman and Chief Executive, 1979–81, Senior Managing Director, 1976–81, Director, 1971–81, Inchcape & Co. Ltd; *b* 29 Oct. 1915; *s* of late Rt Rev. Richard Godfrey Parsons, DD, Bishop of Hereford; *m* 1st, 1946, Hilda Mary Frewen (marr. diss. 1964); one *s* two *d*; 2nd, 1964, Caroline Inagh Margaret Frewen. *Educ:* Rossall Sch.; University Coll., Oxford. Barry & Co., Calcutta, 1937. Served in Royal Garhwal Rifles (Indian Army), 1939–45: Bde Major, 1942; POW, Singapore, 1942. Macneill & Barry Ltd, Calcutta, 1946–70; Chm. & Managing Dir, 1964–70; Chm., Macdonald Hamilton & Co. Pty Ltd, 1970–72; Chairman and Director: Assam Investments, 1976–81; Paxall Investments Ltd, 1982–84; Dep. Chm. and Dir, Inchcape Insurance Hldgs Ltd, 1979–83; Dir, Commonwealth Develt Finance Co. Ltd, 1973–86. Vice-Chm., Indian Jute Mills Assoc., 1960–61; President: Bengal Chamber of Commerce, 1968–69; Associated Chambers of Commerce of India, 1969; Chm., UK Cttee, Fedn of Commonwealth Chambers of Commerce, 1974; Mem., Advisory Council on Trade, Bd of Trade, India, 1968–69. Chm. Council, Royal Commonwealth Soc., 1976–80, Vice Pres., 1980–; Pres., India, Pakistan and Bangladesh Assoc., 1973–78, Vice Pres., 1978. Dep. Chm., Internat. Bd, United World Colls, 1981–86. *Recreation:* golf. *Address:* Tall Trees, Warren Hill Lane, Aldeburgh, Suffolk IP15 5QB. *T:* Aldeburgh (01728) 452917. *Clubs:* Oriental; Bengal, Tollygunge (Calcutta); Union (Sydney).

PARSONS, Kenneth Charles, CMG 1970; OBE 1962; HM Diplomatic Service, retired; Counsellor, Foreign and Commonwealth Office, 1972–80; *b* 9 Jan. 1921; *m* 1st, 1949, Monica (*née* Howell) (decd); two *d*; 2nd, 1977, Mary Woolhouse. *Educ:* Haverfordwest Grammar Sch.; Exeter Coll., Oxford. Served War of 1939–45: with Oxfordshire and Buckinghamshire LI, 1941–46. 1st Class Hons, Mod. Langs (at Oxford), 1948. Joined Diplomatic Service, 1949; served FO, Moscow, Tokyo, Rangoon and Athens, 1951–72; FCO, 1972–77; Counsellor, with British Forces, Hong Kong, 1977–79. *Recreations:* rowing, swimming, walking. *Address:* 46 Lackford Road, Chipstead, Surrey CR5 3TA. *T:* Downland (01737) 555051. *Club:* Carlton.

PARSONS, Sir Michael; *see* Parsons, Sir J. M.

PARSONS, Patricia, (Mrs J. D. Parsons); *see* Beer, Patricia.

PARSONS, Air Comdt Dame Pauline, (formerly **Air Comdt Dame Pauline Giles**), DBE 1967; RRC; Matron-in-Chief, Princess Mary's Royal Air Force Nursing Service, 1966–70, retired; *b* 17 Sept. 1912; *m* 1987, Daniel G. Parsons, OBE. *Educ:* Sheffield. Joined PMRAFNS, Nov. 1937; later appointments included Principal Matron for Royal Air Force Command in Britain and Western Europe; became Matron-in-Chief, PMRAFNS, Sept. 1966. *Address:* Coma Colat, La Massana, Andorra.

PARSONS, Prof. Peter John, FBA 1977; Regius Professor of Greek, University of Oxford, since 1989; Student of Christ Church, Oxford, since 1964; *b* 24 Sept. 1936; *s* of Robert John Parsons and Ethel Ada (*née* Frary). *Educ:* Raynes Park County Grammar Sch.; Christ Church, Oxford (MA 1961). Oxford University: Craven Scholar, 1955; 1st Cl. Hons Mods and de Paravicini Scholar, 1956; Chancellor's Prize for Latin Verse and Gaisford Prize for Greek Verse, 1st Cl. Lit. Hum., Derby Scholar, Dixon and Sen. Scholar of Christ Church, 1958; Passmore Edwards Scholar, 1959; Lectr in Documentary Papyrology, 1960–65; Lectr in Papyrology, 1965–89. J. H. Gray Lectr, Univ. of Cambridge, 1982; Heller Lectr, Univ. of Calif, Berkeley, 1988. Hon. PhD Bern, 1985; Hon. DLitt Milan, 1994. *Publications:* (jtly) The Oxyrhynchus Papyri XXXI, 1966, XXXIII and XXXIV, 1968, LIV, 1987, LIX, 1992, LX, 1994; The Oxyrhynchus Papyri XLII, 1973; (with H. Lloyd-Jones) Supplementum Hellenisticum, 1983; articles in learned jls. *Recreations:* music, cinema, cooking and eating. *Address:* Christ Church, Oxford OX1 1DP. *T:* Oxford (01865) 276223.

PARSONS, Sir Richard (Edmund Clement Fownes), KCMG 1982 (CMG 1977); HM Diplomatic Service, retired; Ambassador to Sweden, 1984–87; *b* 14 March 1928; *s* of Dr R. A. Parsons; *m* 1960, Jenifer Jane Mathews (*d* 1981); three *s*. *Educ:* Bembridge Sch.; Brasenose Coll., Oxford. Served in Army, 1949–51; joined HM Foreign (subseq. Diplomatic) Service, 1951; FO, 1951–53; 3rd Sec., Washington, 1953–56; 2nd Sec., Vientiane, 1956–58; FO, 1958–60; 1st Sec., Buenos Aires, 1960–63; FO, 1963–65; 1st Sec., Ankara, 1965–67; FO, 1967–69; Counsellor, Lagos, 1969–72; Head of Personnel Ops Dept, FCO, 1972–76; Ambassador to: Hungary, 1976–79; Spain, 1980–84. Plays produced in London, Edinburgh and Brighton. *Publications:* The Moon Pool, 1988; Mortmain and other plays, 1993; *as John Haythorne:* None of Us Cared for Kate, 1968; The Strelsau Dimension, 1981; Mandrake in Granada, 1984; Mandrake in the Monastery, 1985. *Recreations:* reading, writing, music, travel. *Address:* 152 De Beauvoir Road, N1 4DJ. *Club:* Garrick.

See also C. A. H. Parsons.

PARSONS, Roger, PhD, DSc; FRS 1980; FRSC; Professor of Chemistry, University of Southampton, 1985–92, now Emeritus; *b* 31 Oct. 1926; *s* of Robert Harry Ashby Parsons and Ethel Fenton; *m* 1953, Ruby Millicent Turner; three *s* one *d*. *Educ:* King Alfred Sch., Hampstead; Strathcona High Sch., Edmonton, Alta; Imperial Coll. of Science and Technol., (BSc, PhD). DSc Bristol 1962; ARCS 1946; FRIC 1962. Asst Lectr, Imp. Coll. of Science and Technol., 1948–50; Deedes Fellow, UC Dundee, St Andrews Univ., 1950–54; Lectr, then Reader in Electrochem., Bristol Univ., 1954–79; Dir, Lab. d'Electrochimie Interfaciale, Centre Nat. de la Recherche Scientifique, Meudon, France, 1977–84. Unesco Specialist, Buenos Aires, 1961; Vis. Prof., Calif Inst. of Technol., 1966–67. Royal Society of Chemistry: Pres., Faraday Div., 1991–93 (Vice-Pres., 1984–91, 1993–); Liversidge Lectr, 1989–90. Hon. Fellow, Polish Chem. Soc., 1981. Palladium Medal, US Electrochem. Soc., 1979; Bruno Breyer Medal, Electrochem. Div., RACI, 1980; Prix Paul Pascal de l'Acad. des Scis, 1983; Galvani Medal, Electrochem. Div., Italian Chem. Soc., 1986. Editor, Jl of Electroanal. Chem., 1962–. *Publications:* Electrochemical Data, 1956; (with J. Lyklema) Electrical Properties of Interfaces, 1983; (ed jtly) Standard Potentials in Aqueous Solution, 1985; (ed with R. Kalvoda) Electrochemistry in Research and Development, 1985; *circa* 200 papers in scientific jls. *Recreations:* listening to music, going to the opera. *Address:* Department of Chemistry, The University, Southampton SO17 1BJ.

PARSONS, (Thomas) Alan, CB 1984; LLB; Chief Adjudication Officer, Department of Health and Social Security, 1984–86; *b* 25 Nov. 1924; *s* of late Arthur and Laura Parsons; *m* 1st, 1947, Valerie Vambeck; one *s*; 2nd, 1957, Muriel Lewis; two *s*. *Educ:* Clifton Coll.; Bristol Univ. (LLB). Called to the Bar, Middle Temple, 1950. Served, Royal Marines, 1943–46. Legal Asst, Min. of Nat. Insurance, 1950; Sen. Legal Asst, Min. of Pensions and Nat. Insurance, 1955; Asst Solicitor, 1968, Principal Asst Solicitor, 1977, DHSS. *Recreations:* walking, listening to music. *Address:* 11 Northiam Street, Pennethorne Place, E9 7HX. *T:* 0181–986 0930.

PÄRT, Arvo; free-lance composer, since 1982; *b* Estonia, 11 Sept. 1935; *s* of August Pärt and Linda Anette Pärt (*née* Mäll); *m* 1st, 1959, Hille Aasmäe (marr. diss.); one *d*; one *d* by

Marina Nestieva; 2nd, 1972, Nora Supina; two *s*. *Educ:* composition studies with Heino Eller, Conservatory of Music, Tallinn, Estonia. Sound Engr, Estonian broadcasting station, Tallinn, 1958–67; free-lance composer, Tallinn, 1967–80; emigrated to Vienna, 1980; became Austrian citizen, 1981; Scholar, Deutscher Akademischer Austauschdienst, Berlin, 1981. Hon. PhD: Acad. of Music, Tallinn, 1990; Royal Swedish Music Acad., 1991. *Compositions* include: Sinfonie No 1, 1963; Sinfonie No 2, 1966; Credo, 1968; Sinfonie No 3, 1971; Fratres (variations for ensembles, orchestra and various instruments), 1977, 1980, 1983, 1985, 1989, 1990, 1991, 1992; Tabula Rasa (double violin concerto), 1977; Sarah was Ninety Years Old, 1977, 1990; Passio, 1982; Stabat Mater, 1985; Te Deum, 1985; Miserere, 1989; Berliner Messe (choir, soloists and organ), 1990; Berliner Messe (choir, soloists and string orch.), 1991; Sieben Magnificat-Antiphonen, 1991; Litany (soloists, choir and orch.), 1994. *Address:* c/o Universal Edition Ltd, 48 Great Marlborough Street, W1V 2BN.

PARTHIER, Prof. Benno; Director, Institut für Pflanzenbiochemie, Halle, since 1990; President, Deutsche Akademie der Naturforscher Leopoldina, since 1990; *b* 21 Aug. 1932; *s* of Hermann and Helene Parthier; *m* 1967, Christiane Luecke; one *s* two *d*. *Educ:* Martin Luther Univ., Halle-Wittenberg (Dip. Biol. 1958; Dr rer. nat. 1961; Dr habil. 1967). Asst, Botanical Inst., Univ. Halle, 1958–65; Head, Dept of Molecular Biol., Inst. of Plant Biochemistry, Acad. of Scis, GDR, 1967–90. Mem., learned socs, Germany and overseas. *Publications:* (with R. Wollgiehn) Von der Zelle zum Molekül, 1971 (Polish edn 1976); (with L. Nover and M. Luckner) Zell differenzierung, Molekulare Grundlagen und Probleme, 1978 (English edn 1982); numerous papers in sci. jls; Editor or co-Editor 10 sci. jls. *Recreations:* gardening, travelling. *Address:* Institut für Pflanzen-biochemie, Weinberg 3, 06120 Halle, Germany. *T:* (345) 5582160; Deutsche Akademie der Naturforscher Leopoldina, August-Bebel Strasse 50a, 06019 Halle, Germany. *T:* (345) 2026795.

PARTINGTON, Gillian Doreen, (Mrs W. D. Partington); *see* Ruaux, G. D.

PARTINGTON, Prof. Thomas Martin; Professor of Law, since 1987, Pro-Vice Chancellor, since 1995, Bristol University; *b* 5 March 1944; *s* of Thomas Paulett Partington and Alice Emily Mary Partington; *m* 1st, 1970, Marcia Carol Leavey (marr. diss.); one *s*; 2nd, 1978, Daphne Isobel Scharenguivel; one *s* one *d*. *Educ:* King's Sch., Canterbury; Peterhouse, Cambridge (BA 1965; LLB 1966). Called to the Bar, Middle Temple, 1984. Asst Lectr, Bristol Univ., 1966–69; Lectr, Warwick Univ., 1969–73, LSE, 1973–80; Prof. of Law, Brunel Univ., 1980–87 (Dean, Faculty of Soc. Scis, 1985–87); Dean, Faculty of Law, Bristol Univ., 1988–92. Visiting Professor: Osgoode Hall Law Sch., Canada, 1976; Univ. of NSW, 1983. Chm., Cttee of Heads of Univ. Law Schools, 1990–92. Vice-Chm., Legal Action Gp, 1982–83; Member: Lord Chancellor's Adv. Cttee on Legal Aid, 1988–91; Law Society's Trng Cttee, 1989–92; Law Society's Academic Consultative Cttee, 1989–92; Judicial Studies Bd, 1992–95 (Mem., Tribunals Cttee, 1988–95); Trng Cttee, Indep. Tribunal Service Bd, 1993–; Council on Tribunals, 1994–; External Adviser, Educn and Trng Cttee, Inst. of Housing, 1985–89. Part time Chairman: Soc. Security Appeals Tribunal, 1990–94; Med. Appeals Tribunal, 1992–94; Disability Appeals Tribunal, 1992–94. Academic Consultant, Chambers of A. Arden, QC, 1993–. Chm., Socio-Legal Studies Assoc., 1993–. Gen. Editor, Anglo-American Law Review, 1984–. *Publications:* Landlord and Tenant, 1975; Claim in Time, 1978; (with A. Arden) Housing Law, 1983; (with P. O'Higgins) Bibliography of Social Security Law, 1986; Secretary of State's Powers of Adjudication in Social Security Law, 1990; (with J. Hill) Housing Law: cases, materials and commentary, 1991; articles on public law, housing law, social security law, legal educn, Legal Aid and Legal Services. *Recreations:* playing the violin, reading fiction, gardening, cooking. *Address:* Little Court, Grib Lane, Blagdon, Avon BS18 6SA. *T:* Blagdon (01761) 462916.

PARTON, Prof. John Edwin; Professor of Electrical Engineering, University of Nottingham, 1954–78, now Emeritus; *b* Kingswinford, Staffordshire, 26 Dec. 1912; *s* of Edwin and Elizabeth Parton; *m* 1940, Gertrude Brown; one *s* one *d*. *Educ:* Huntington Church of England Sch.; Cannock Chase Mining Coll.; University of Birmingham. BSc (1st Class Hons), 1936, PhD, 1938, Birmingham; DSc Glasgow, 1971. Training: Littleton Collieries, 1934; Electrical Construction Co., 1935; Asst Engineer, PO Engineering Dept, Dollis Hill Research Station, 1938–39; Part-time Lecturer: Cannock Chase Mining Coll., 1931–38; Northampton Polytechnic, 1938–39. Served RNVR Electrical Branch, Sub-Lt, 1939, to Lt-Comdr, 1943–45. Sen. Sci. Officer, British Iron and Steel Research Assoc., 1946; Lecturer, 1946–54, Senior Lecturer, 1954, University of Glasgow. Sen. Vis. Scientist, Nat. Sci. Foundn at Univ. of Tennessee, 1965–66; Vis. Prof., Univ. of W Indies, Trinidad, 1979, 1980. Chairman, East Midland Centre Institution of Electrical Engineers, 1961–62. FIEE 1966; Life MIEEE 1990; FIMechE 1967. *Publications:* Applied Electromagnetics (jtly), 1975; papers in Proc. IEE, Trans. IEEE, Trans. IES, Instrument Practice, International Journal of Electrical Engineering Education, etc. *Recreations:* golf, gardening, bowls, bridge. *Address:* 93 Parkside, Wollaton, Nottingham NG8 2NQ. *T:* Nottingham (0115) 928 6693.

PARTRIDGE, Bernard B.; *see* Brook-Partridge.

PARTRIDGE, Derek William, CMG 1987; HM Diplomatic Service, retired; *b* 15 May 1931; *o s* of late Ernest and Ethel Elizabeth Partridge (*née* Buckingham), Wembley. *Educ:* Preston Manor County Grammar Sch., Wembley. Entered Foreign Service (later Diplomatic Service), 1949. Royal Air Force, 1949–51. Served: Foreign Office, 1951–54; Oslo, 1954–56; Jedda, 1956; Khartoum, 1957–60; Sofia, 1960–62; Bangkok, 1962; Manila, 1962–65; Djakarta, 1965–67; FCO, 1967–70; Diplomatic Service Inspectorate, 1970–72; British Consul-General, Brisbane, 1972–74; First Sec. (Economic and Commercial), Colombo, 1974–77; FCO, 1977–86: Counsellor and Head of Migration and Visa Dept, 1981–83; Counsellor and Head of Nationality and Treaty Dept, 1983–86; High Comr, Sierra Leone, 1986–91. Mem. (Lib Dem) Southwark BC, 1994–. Internat. Consultant, Action in Internat. Medicine; Mem., Royal African Soc. *Address:* 16 Wolfe Crescent, Rotherhithe, SE16 1SF.

PARTRIDGE, Frances Catherine, FRSL; writer and literary journalist; *b* 15 March 1900; *d* of William Cecil Marshall, architect, and Margaret Anna Marshall (*née* Lloyd); *m* 1933, Major Reginald Sherring Partridge, (Ralph Partridge), MC and Bar, Croix de Guerre (*d* 1960); one *s* (Lytton Burgo Partridge, *d* 1963). *Educ:* Bedales Sch.; Newnham Coll., Cambridge (BA). Antiquarian bookseller, 1922–28; translator of numerous books from French and Spanish, to 1965. *Publications:* (ed with husband) The Greville Memoirs, 8 vols, 1938; A Pacifist's War, 1978; Memories, 1981; Julia, 1983; Everything to lose, 1986; Friends in Focus, 1987; Hanging On, 1990; Other People, 1993; Good Company, 1994. *Recreations:* music, reading, botany. *Address:* 15 West Halkin Street, SW1X 8JL. *T:* 0171–235 6998. *Club:* International PEN.

PARTRIDGE, Ian Harold, CBE 1992; concert singer (tenor); *b* 12 June 1938; *s* of late Harold Partridge and Ena Stinson; *m* 1959, Ann Glover; two *s*. *Educ:* New Coll., Oxford (chorister); Clifton Coll. (music scholar); Royal Coll. of Music; Guildhall Sch. of Music (LGSM, singing and teaching). Began as piano accompanist, although sang tenor in Westminster Cath. Choir, 1958–62; full-time concert singer, 1963–; performs in England and all over the world, both in recitals (with sister Jennifer) and in concerts; has worked with many leading conductors, incl. Stokowski, Boult, Giulini, Boulez and Colin Davis. Opera debut at Covent Garden as Iopas in Berlioz, Les Troyens, 1969. Title role, Britten's St Nicolas, Thames Television (Prix Italia, 1977). Over 100 records, *including:* Bach, St John Passion; Handel, Chandos Anthems, and Esther; Schubert, Die Schöne Müllerin, Die Winterreise; Schumann, Dichterliebe; Beethoven, An die ferne Geliebte; Vaughan-Williams, On Wenlock Edge; Warlock, The Curlew; Fauré and Duparc Songs; Britten, Serenade and Winter Words; as conductor (of Pro Cantione Antiqua), The Triumphs of Oriana. Innumerable radio broadcasts, many TV appearances. Governor, Clifton Coll., 1981–. Sir Charles Santley Meml Gift, Musicians' Co., 1992. *Recreations:* bridge, horse racing, theatre, cricket. *Address:* 127 Pepys Road, SW20 8NP. *Club:* Garrick.

PARTRIDGE, John Albert, CBE 1981; RA; FRIBA; architect in private practice; a Senior and Founder Partner, Howell, Killick, Partridge & Amis (HKPA), since 1959; *b* 26 Aug. 1924; *s* of George and Gladys Partridge; *m* 1953, Doris (*née* Foreman); one *s* one *d*. *Educ:* Shooter's Hill Grammar Sch., Woolwich; Polytechnic School of Architecture, Regent Street. FRIBA 1966 (ARIBA 1951); RA 1988 (ARA 1980). London County Council Housing Architects Dept, 1951–59; Design Tutor, Architectural Assoc., 1958–61. The work of HKPA includes universities, colleges, public buildings, housing and leisure buildings; principal commissions include: Wolfson, Rayne and Gatehouse building, St Anne's Coll., Oxford; New Hall and Common Room building, St Antony's Coll., Oxford; Wells Hall, Reading Univ.; Middlesex Polytechnic College of Art, Cat Hill; Medway Magistrates' Court; The Albany, Deptford; Hall of Justice, Trinidad and Tobago; Warrington Court House; Basildon Magistrates' Courthouse; Berlin Mineral Spa; Haywards Heath Magistrates' Courthouse; Japanese University Chaucer Coll., Univ. of Kent, Canterbury. RIBA: Vice-Pres., 1977–79; Hon. Librarian, 1977–81; Chm. Res. Steering Gp, 1977–84. Vice-Pres., Concrete Soc., 1979–81. External Examiner in Architecture: Bath Univ., 1975–78, 1992; Thames Polytechnic, 1978–86; Cambridge Univ., 1979–81; Manchester Univ., 1982–; South Bank Polytechnic, 1982–86; Brighton Polytechnic, 1987–90; RCA, 1991–93. Governor, Building Centre Trust, 1982–; Chm., Assoc. of Consultant Architects, 1983–85. Mem., NEDO Construction Res. Strategy Cttee, 1983–86; Architect Mem., FCO Adv. Bd on the Diplomatic Estate, 1985–. *Publications:* articles in technical press. *Recreations:* looking at buildings, travel, sketching and taking photographs. *Address:* Cudham Court, Cudham, near Sevenoaks, Kent TN14 7QF. *T:* Biggin Hill (01959) 571294. *Club:* Arts.

PARTRIDGE, Prof. Linda, FRSE; Weldon Professor of Biometry, University College London, since 1993; *b* 18 March 1950; *d* of George and Ida Partridge; *m* 1983, Dr V. K. French (marr. diss.). *Educ:* Convent of the Sacred Heart, Tunbridge Wells; St Anne's Coll., Oxford (MA); Wolfson Coll., Oxford (DPhil 1974). FRSE 1992. Post-doctoral Fellow, York Univ., 1974–76; Edinburgh University: Lectr, 1976–87; Reader in Zoology, 1987–92; Prof. of Evolutionary Biol., 1992–93. President: Internat. Soc. for Behavioural Ecology, 1990–92; Assoc. for Study of Animal Behaviour, 1995–. *Publications:* on evolutionary biology in scientific jls. *Recreations:* tennis, hill walking, gardening. *Address:* Department of Genetics and Biometry, University College London, Wolfson House, 4 Stephenson Way, NW1 2HE.

PARTRIDGE, Sir Michael (John Anthony), KCB 1990 (CB 1983); Permanent Secretary, Department of Social Security, 1988–95; *b* 29 Sept. 1935; *s* of late Dr John Henry Partridge, DSc, PhD, and Ethel Green; *m* 1968, Joan Elizabeth Hughes; two *s* one *d*. *Educ:* Merchant Taylors'; St John's Coll., Oxford (BA (1st Cl. Hons Mods and Lit Hum) 1960, MA 1963; Hon. Fellow, 1991). Entered Home Civil Service (Min. of Pensions and Nat. Insce), 1960; Private Sec. to Permanent Sec., 1962–64; Principal, 1964–71 (MPNI, Min. of Social Security and DHSS); DHSS: Asst Sec., 1971–76; Under Sec., 1976–81; Dep. Sec., 1981–83; Dep. Under-Sec. of State, Home Office, 1983–87; Second Permanent Sec., DHSS, 1987–88. Senior Treasurer, Methodist Ch. Finance Div., 1980–. Mem. Court, Univ. of York, 1991–. Gov., Middlesex Univ., 1992–. Liveryman, Merchant Taylors' Co., 1987. *Recreations:* Do-it-Yourself, classical sites, reading, ski-ing. *Address:* 27 High View, Pinner, Middlesex HA5 3NZ. *Club:* United Oxford & Cambridge University.

PASCALL, David Lewis, CBE 1993; Chief Executive, Asia Pacific and Finance Director, Money and Securities Broking, MAI plc, since 1993; *b* 5 Feb. 1949; *s* of Robert Lewis Pascall and Dorothy Pascall (*née* Smith); *m* 1980, Carolyn Judith White; one *s* two *d*. *Educ:* Queen Mary's Grammar Sch., Basingstoke; Univ. of Birmingham (BSc 1st Cl. Hons Chem. Engrg 1970); INSEAD, Fontainebleau (MBA Dist. 1979). With British Petroleum Co. plc, 1967–93: posts in oil refining, trading, finance and business management in UK and, 1974–79, Germany and France; Divl Manager, BP Finance Internat., 1986–89; Manager: Project 1990, 1989–90; Business Simplification, BP Exploration, 1990–93. On secondment to: Central Policy Rev. Staff, Cabinet Office, 1982–83; No 10 Policy Unit, 1983–84. Mem., 1990–91, Chm., 1991–93, Nat. Curriculum Council; Mem. Exec. Cttee, Field Studies Council, 1993–. Foundn Gov., St James' Primary Sch., Muswell Hill, 1989–. Mem., NS, 1994–. *Recreations:* my family, current affairs, golf. *Address:* MAI plc, 8 Montague Close, SE1 9RD. *T:* 0171–800 1917. *Club:* Highgate Golf.

PASCO, Richard Edward, CBE 1977; actor; Hon. Associate Artist, Royal Shakespeare Company; *b* 18 July 1926; *s* of Cecil George Pasco and Phyllis Irene Pasco; *m* 1st, Greta (*née* Watson) (marr. diss.); one *s*; 2nd, 1967, Barbara (*née* Leigh-Hunt). *Educ:* Colet Court; King's Coll. Sch., Wimbledon; Central Sch. of Speech and Drama (Gold Medallist). Served HM Forces, 1944–48. 1st stage appearance, She Stoops to Conquer, 1943; 1st London appearance, Zero Hour, Lyric, 1944; 1st New York appearance, The Entertainer, 1958. London appearances include: leading roles, English Stage Co., Royal Court, 1957; The Entertainer, Palace, 1957; The Lady from the Sea, Queen's, 1961; Teresa of Avila, Vaudeville, 1961; Look Homeward, Angel, Phoenix, 1962; The New Men, Strand, 1962; The Private Ear and the Public Eye, Globe, 1963; Bristol Old Vic: Henry V (title role), Berowne in Love's Labour's Lost, 1964; Peer Gynt (title role), Angelo in Measure for Measure, Hamlet (title role), 1966 (and world tour); Ivanov, Phoenix, 1965; The Italian Girl, Wyndham's, 1968. Joined RSC, 1969; leading roles include: Becket, Murder in the Cathedral, Aldwych, 1972; (alternated with Ian Richardson) Richard and Bolingbroke in Richard II, Stratford-on-Avon, 1973, and Stratford and Aldwych, 1974; Jacques in As You Like It, 1973; tour of Amer. univs; Jack Tanner in Man and Superman, Malvern Festival, tour and Savoy, 1977; Timon in Timon of Athens, Clarence in Richard III, Arkady Schatslivtses in The Forest, Stratford, 1980–81; La Ronde, Aldwych, 1982; National Theatre: The Father in Six Characters in Search of an Author, Pavel in Fathers and Sons, 1987; Rt Rev. Charlie Allen in Racing Demon, 1990, 1993; Sir Peter Edgecombe in Murmuring Judges, 1991, 1993; Birling in An Inspector Calls, 1992; Malcolm Pryce in Absence of War, 1993; Boss Findley in Sweet Bird of Youth, 1994. Many foreign tours; accompanied HSH Princess Grace of Monaco at Edinburgh, Stratford and Aldeburgh Festivals and on tour of USA, 1977–78. Frequent appearances at Aldeburgh, Brighton, Windsor and Harrogate festivals, Stratford-upon-Avon Poetry Festival etc. Recent films: A Watcher in the Woods; Wagner. Countless TV and radio appearances; recent television series: Sorrell & Son; Drummonds; Hannay; Inspector Morse; Absence of War, etc. Many recordings of poems, plays, recitals, etc. Life Trustee, Shakespeare Birthplace Trust, 1992. *Recreations:* music, gardening, reading. *Address:* c/o Michael Whitehall Ltd, 125 Gloucester Road, SW7 4TE. *Club:* Garrick.

PASCO, Rowanne, (Mrs William FitzGerald); writer and broadcaster; *b* 7 Oct. 1938; *d* of John and Ann Pasco; *m* 1994, Rev. William FitzGerald. *Educ:* Dominican Convent, Chingford; Ursuline Convent, Ilford; Open Univ. (BA). Reporter, 1956–57, Editor, 1957–58, Chingford Express; Publicity Officer, NFU, 1958–59; Account Exec., Leslie Frewin PR, 1959–60; Travel Rep., Horizon Holidays, 1960–64; Publicity Asst, Paramount Pictures Corp., Hollywood, 1964–66; Publicity Officer, Religious Progs, Radio and TV, BBC, 1966–71; Reporter, BBC Radio London, 1971–72; TV Editor, Ariel, BBC Staff Newspaper, 1972–74; Radio 4 Reporter, 1974–76; Researcher, Religious Progs, BBC TV, 1976–77; Producer and Presenter, Religious Progs, BBC Radio, 1977–78; Dep. Editor, 1979–81, Editor, 1981–87, The Universe; Religious Editor, TV-am, 1987–92; religious correspondent, GMTV, 1993–94; Editl Advr, CCJ, 1994–. *Publications:* (ed with Fr John Redford) Faith Alive, 1988, New Catechism edn, 1994; One Hundred & One Questions on the Catechism, 1995; Why I am a Catholic, 1995. *Recreations:* gardening, Italy, creative cooking. *Address:* 12 Rickthorne Road, N19 4JS.

PASCOE, Alan Peter, MBE 1975; Chairman: The Sponsorship Group Ltd; Alan Pascoe Associates Ltd (Director, 1976–83; Managing Director, 1983); *b* 11 Oct. 1947; *s* of Ernest George Frank Pascoe and Joan Rosina Pascoe; *m* 1970, Della Patricia (*née* James); one *s* one *d*. *Educ:* Portsmouth Southern Grammar Sch.; Borough Road Coll. (Cert. in Educn); London Univ. (Hons degree in Educn). Master, Dulwich Coll., 1971–74; Lectr in Physical Educn, Borough Road Coll., Isleworth, 1974–80. Chm., Carat Sponsorship, 1987–92; Dir, WCRS, then Aegis Gp, 1986–92. Member: Sports Council, 1974–80; Minister for Sport's Working Party on Centres of Sporting Excellence; BBC Adv. Council, 1975–79. European Indoor Champion, 50m Hurdles, 1969; Europ. Games Silver Medallist, 110m Hurdles, 1971; Silver Medal, Olympic Games, Munich, 4×400m Relay, 1972; Europa Gold Cup Medallist, 400m Hurdles, 1973; Commonwealth Games Gold Medal, 400m Hurdles, and Silver Medal, 4×400m Relay, 1974; Europ. Champion and Gold Medallist in both 400m Hurdles and 4×400m Relay, 1974; Europa Cup Gold Medallist, 400m Hurdles, 1975; Olympic Finalist (injured), Montreal, 1976; Europe's Rep., World Cup Event, 1977. *Publication:* An Autobiography, 1979. *Recreations:* theatre, sport. *Address:* c/o The Sponsorship Group, 141–143 Drury Lane, WC2B 5TB. *T:* 0171–379 5220.

PASCOE, Dr Michael William; Head of Science, Camberwell College of Arts (formerly Camberwell School of Arts and Crafts), 1981–90; *b* 16 June 1930; *s* of Canon W. J. T. Pascoe and Mrs D. Pascoe; *m* 1st, 1956, Janet Clark (marr. diss. 1977); three *d*; 2nd, 1977, Brenda Hale Reed; one *d*. *Educ:* St John's, Leatherhead; Selwyn Coll., Cambridge (BA, PhD). MInstP. Res. Student (Tribology), Cambridge, 1951–55; Physicist: Mount Vernon Hosp., Northwood, 1956–57; British Nylon Spinners Ltd, 1957–60; Chemist/Physicist, ICI Paints Div., 1960–67; Lectr (Polymer Science), Brunel Univ., 1967–77; Principal Scientific Officer, 1976–79, Keeper of Conservation and Technical Services, 1979–81, British Museum. Tutor and Counsellor, Open Univ., 1971–76. Occasional Lectr: Winchester Coll., 1989–90; Univ. of Stirling, 1991–; Camberwell Coll. of Arts; Vis. Lectr in Materials, Univ. of Brunel, 1995. Consultant to: Royal Acad. of Arts (Great Japan exhibn), 1982–; Mary Rose Trust, 1978–83; Council for the Care of Churches, 1980–91; Public Record Office (Domesday exhibn), 1986; Science Museum, 1988; Parliament of Guyana, 1991–. FRSA. *Publications:* contrib. to books on polymer tribol. and technol.; articles in scientific, engrg and conservation jls on tribol., materials technol. and on conservation methods. *Recreations:* painting and drawing *inter alia*. *Address:* 15 Parkfield Road, Ickenham, Uxbridge UB10 8LN. *T:* Uxbridge (01895) 674723.

PASCOE, Nigel Spencer Knight; QC 1988; a Recorder of the Crown Court, since 1979; *b* 18 Aug. 1940; *er s* of late Ernest Sydney Pascoe and of Cynthia Pascoe; *m* 1964, Elizabeth Anne Walter; two *s* four *d*. *Educ:* Epsom Coll. Called to the Bar, Inner Temple, 1966; Leader, Western Circuit, 1995. County Councillor for Lyndhurst, Hants, 1979–84. Founder and Editor, All England Qly Law Cassettes, 1976–85. *Publications:* The Trial of Penn and Mead, 1985; articles in legal jls. *Recreations:* theatre, devising and presenting with Elizabeth Pascoe legal anthologies, after-dinner speaking, cricket, play writing. *Address:* 3 Pump Court, Temple, EC4 7AJ. *T:* 0171–353 0711. *Club:* Garrick.

PASCOE, Gen. Sir Robert (Alan), KCB 1985; MBE 1968; Adjutant General, 1988–90; Aide de Camp General to the Queen, 1989–91, retired; *b* 21 Feb. 1932; *er s* of late C. and Edith Mary Pascoe; *m* 1955, Pauline (*née* Myers); one *s* three *d*. *Educ:* Tavistock Grammar Sch.; RMA, Sandhurst. rcds, psc. Commissioned Oxford and Bucks LI, 1952; served with 1 Oxf. Bucks, 1 DLI and 4 Oxf. Bucks (TA), 1953–57; Middle East Centre for Arab Studies, Lebanon, 1958–59; 1st Cl. Interpretership (Arabic); GSO2 Land Forces Persian Gulf, 1960–62; sc Camberley, 1963; Co. Comd 2RGJ, UK and Malaysia, 1964–66 (despatches (Borneo) 1966); GSO2 HQ 2 Div. BAOR, 1967–68; Co. Comd 1RGJ, UK and UNFICYP, 1968–69; Second in Comd 2RGJ, BAOR, 1969; MA to QMG, 1970–71; Comd 1RGJ, 1971–74, BAOR and NI (despatches (NI) 1974); Col General Staff HQ UKLF, 1974–76; Comd 5 Field Force BAOR, 1976–79; rcds 1979; Asst Chief of Gen. Staff (Operational Requirements), MoD, 1980–83; Chief of Staff, HQ, UKLF, 1983–85; GOC Northern Ireland, 1985–88. Rep. Col Comdt, RGJ, 1988–90; Colonel Commandant: 1st Bn Royal Green Jackets, 1986–91; Army Legal Corps, 1988–90. Hon. Col, Oxfordshire ACF, 1991–. Chm. of Governors, Royal Sch., Bath, 1988– (Governor, 1981–). Mem. Council, King Edward VII Hosp., 1995. President: Army LTA, 1986–91; Army Boxing Assoc., 1989–90. Chairman: Reg. Forces Employment Assoc., 1994–; Ex-Services Resettlement Gp, 1994–. Vice Pres., Royal Patriotic Fund Corp., 1992–; Patron, Retired Officers Assoc., 1991–. Chairman: 43rd and 52nd Club, 1992–; Oxford and Bucks LI Mus. Trustees, 1992–. Freeman, City of London, 1992; Hon. Liveryman, Fruiterers' Co., 1992. *Recreations:* gardening, golf, fishing, tennis, ski-ing. *Clubs:* Army and Navy; Queen's.

PASHLEY, Prof. Donald William, FRS 1968; Professor of Materials, Imperial College of Science, Technology and Medicine, 1979–92, now Professor Emeritus and Senior Research Fellow; *b* 21 April 1927; *s* of late Harold William Pashley and Louise Pashley (*née* Clarke); *m* 1954, Glenys Margaret Ball; one *s* one *d*. *Educ:* Henry Thornton Sch., London; Imperial Coll., London (BSc). 1st cl. hons Physics, 1947; PhD 1950. Research Fellow, Imp. Coll., 1950–55; TI Res. Labs, Hinxton Hall: Res. Scientist, 1956–61; Gp Leader and Div. Head, 1962–67; Asst Dir, 1967–68; Dir, 1968–79 (also Dir of Research, TI Ltd, 1976–79); Imperial College: Hd, Dept of Materials, 1979–90; Dean, Royal Sch. of Mines, 1986–89; Mem. Governing Body, 1986–89. Mem. Council, Royal Soc., 1981–83. Rosenhain Medal, Inst. of Metals, 1968. *Publications:* (jtly) Electron Microscopy of Thin Crystals, 1965; numerous papers on electron microscopy and diffraction, thin films and epitaxy in Phil. Mag., Proc. Roy. Soc., etc. *Address:* 11 The Gables, Oxshott, Leatherhead, Surrey KT22 0SD. *T:* Oxshott (01372) 844518; Department of Materials, Imperial College, SW7 2AZ.

PASLEY, Sir (John) Malcolm (Sabine), 5th Bt *cr* 1794; FBA 1991; Emeritus Fellow, Magdalen College, Oxford; *b* 5 April 1926; *s* of Sir Rodney Marshall Sabine Pasley, 4th Bt, and Aldyth Werge Hamber (*d* 1983); *S* father, 1982; *m* 1965, Virginia Killigrew Wait; two *s*. *Educ:* Sherborne Sch.; Trinity Coll., Oxford (MA). War service, Royal Navy, 1944–46. Laming Travelling Fellow, Queen's Coll., Oxford, 1949–50; Lectr in German, Brasenose and Magdalen Colls, 1950–58; Fellow and Tutor, 1958–86, Vice-Pres., 1979–80, Magdalen Coll. Mem., Deutsche Akademie für Sprache und Dichtung, 1983–. Hon. DPhil Giessen, 1986. Austrian Ehrenkreuz für Wissenschaft und Kunst, 1st cl., 1987. *Publications:* (co-author) Kafka-Symposion, 1965; (ed) Germany: A Companion to German Studies, 1972, 2nd edn 1982; (trans.) Kafka Shorter Works, vol. 1, 1973; (ed) Nietzsche: Imagery and Thought, 1978; (ed) Franz Kafka, Das Schloss, 1982; (ed) Max Brod, Franz Kafka, Reiseaufzeichnungen, 1987; Briefwechsel, 1989; (ed) Franz Kafka, Der Process, 1990; (trans.) Franz Kafka, The Transformation and other stories, 1992; (ed) Franz Kafka, Nachgelassene Schriften und Fragmente I, 1993. *Heir: s* Robert Killigrew Sabine Pasley, *b* 23 Oct. 1965. *Address:* 25 Lathbury Road, Oxford OX2 7AT.

PASMORE, (Edwin John) Victor, CH 1981; CBE 1959; RA 1984; Artist; *b* Chelsham, Surrey, 3 Dec. 1908; *s* of late E. S. Pasmore, MD; *m* 1940, Wendy Blood; one *s* one *d*. *Educ:* Harrow; attended evening classes, LCC Central School of Arts & Crafts. Local government service, LCC County Hall, 1927–37; joined the London Artists' Assoc., 1932–34, and the London Group, 1932–52. Associated with the formation of the Euston Road School, 1937–39, and the first post-war exhibitions of abstract art, 1948–53; joined the Penwith Society, St Ives, 1951–53. Visiting teacher, LCC Camberwell School of Art, 1945–49; Central School of Arts and Crafts, 1949–53. Master of Painting, Durham University, 1954–61; consultant urban and architectural designer, South West Area, Peterlee New Town, 1955–77. Trustee, Tate Gall., 1963–66. Hon. degrees from Newcastle-upon-Tyne, 1967; Surrey, 1969; RCA; Warwick, 1985. *Retrospective exhibitions:* Venice Biennale, 1960; Musée des Arts Décoratifs, Paris, 1961; Stedelijk Museum, Amsterdam, 1961; Palais des Beaux Arts, Brussels, 1961; Louisiana Museum, Copenhagen, 1962; Kestner-Gesellschaft, Hanover, 1962; Kunsthalle, Berne, 1963; Tate Gallery, 1965; São Paolo Biennale, 1965; Cartwright Hall, Bradford, 1980; Royal Acad., London, 1980; Musée des Beaux Arts, Calais, 1985; Yale Center for British Art, USA, 1988; Phillips Mus., Washington, 1988; Center for Internat. Contemp. Art, NY, 1990; Serpentine Gall., 1991. Marlborough Galleries, London, Rome, NY, Zurich, Toronto and Tokyo. *Retrospective graphic exhibitions:* Marlborough Gallery, Tate Gallery, Galleria 2RC, Rome, Milan, Lubjlana, Messina, Oslo, Osaka. Stage backcloth designs for Young Apollo, Royal Ballet, Covent Gdn, 1984. Works represented in: Tate Gallery and other public collections in Gt Britain, Canada, Australia, Holland, Italy, Austria, Switzerland, France and the USA. Carnegie Prize for painting, Pittsburgh International, 1964. Grand Prix d'Honneur, International Graphics Biennale, Lubjlana, 1977; Charles Wollaston Award, Royal Acad., 1983. *Publication:* Monograph and Catalogue Raisonnée, Vol. I 1980, Vol. II 1992. *Address:* Dar Gamri, Gudja, Malta; 12 St Germans Place, Blackheath, SE3. *Club:* Arts.

PASQUA, Charles Victor; President, General Council for Hauts-de-Seine, 1973–76 and since 1988; Minister of State and Minister for the Interior and Town and Country Planning, France, 1993–95; *b* 18 April 1927; *s* of late André Pasqua and Françoise (*née* Rinaldi); *m* 1947; one *s*. *Educ:* Grasse High Sch.; Law Inst., Nice; Univ. of Aix-en-Provence (degree in Law). Sales Rep., then Sales Dir, 1962–63; Dir for sales in France and exports, 1963–68. Deputy (UDR) for Hauts-de-Seine, 1968–73; President: Centre National de la Libre Enterprise; Amicale Parlementaire Présence et Action du Gaullisme, 1972–73; Nat. Sec., then Dep. Gen. Sec., UDR, 1974–76; Senator (RPR) for Hauts-de-Seine, 1977–86 and 1988–93; Pres., RPR in Senate, 1981–86 and 1988–93; Minister of Interior, 1986–88. Croix du Combattant volontaire de la Résistance; Médaille de la France Libre; Chevalier de la Légion d'Honneur. *Publications:* La Libre enterprise un état d'esprit, 1964; L'ardeur nouvelle, 1985; Que demande le peuple, 1992. *Recreation:* travel. *Address:* Conseil Général des Hauts-de-Seine, Hôtel du Département, 2/16 Boulevard Soufflot, 92015 Nanterre, France.

PASTERFIELD, Rt. Rev. Philip John; an Assistant Bishop, Diocese of Exeter, 1984–90; *b* 1920; *s* of Bertie James Pasterfield and Lilian Bishop Pasterfield (*née* Flinn); *m* 1948, Eleanor Maureen, *d* of William John Symons; three *s* one *d*. *Educ:* Denstone Coll., Staffs; Trinity Hall, Cambridge (MA); Cuddesdon Coll., Oxford. Army Service, 1940–46; commnd in Somerset Light Infantry. Deacon 1951, Priest 1952. Curate of Streatham, 1951–54; Vicar of West Lavington, Sussex, and Chaplain, King Edward VII Hosp., Midhurst, 1954–60; Rector of Woolbeding, 1955–60; Vicar of Oxton, Birkenhead, 1960–68; Rural Dean of Birkenhead, 1966–68; Canon Residentiary and Sub Dean of St Albans, 1968–74; Rural Dean of St Albans, 1972–74; Bishop Suffragan of Crediton, 1974–84. *Recreations:* ornithology, music. *Address:* 2 Brixton Court, Brixton, Plymouth PL8 2AH.

PASTINEN, Ilkka, KCMG (Hon.) 1976; Finnish Ambassador to the Court of St James's, 1983–91; *b* 17 March 1928; *s* of Martti and Ilmi Pastinen; *m* 1950, Eeva Marja Viitanen; two *d*. Entered Diplomatic Service, 1952; served Stockholm, 1955; Perm. Mission to UN, 1957–60; Peking, 1962–64; London, 1966–69; Ambassador and Dep. Representative of Finland to UN, 1969–71; Special Representative of Sec. Gen. of UN to Cttee of Disarmament, 1971–75; Ambassador and Perm. Representative of Finland at UN, NY, 1977–83. Kt Comdr of Order of White Rose of Finland, 1984. *Address:* Maneesikatu 1–3B, Helsinki, Finland. *Clubs:* Athenæum, Travellers'; Swinley Forest Golf.

PASTON-BEDINGFELD, Sir Edmund George Felix, 9th Bt, *cr* 1661; Major late Welsh Guards; Managing Director, Handley Walker (Europe) Ltd, 1969–80; *b* 2 June 1915; *s* of 8th Bt and Sybil (*d* 1985), *e d* of late H. Lyne Stephens of Grove House, Roehampton; *S* father, 1941; *m* 1st, 1942, Joan Lynette (*née* Rees) (*d* 1965); one *s* one *d*; 2nd, 1957, Agnes Kathleen (*d* 1974), *d* of late Miklos Gluck, Budapest; 3rd, 1975, Mrs Peggy Hannaford-Hill (*d* 1991), Fort Victoria, Rhodesia; 4th, 1992, Sheila Riddell (*née* Finlayson Douglas). *Educ:* Oratory School; New College, Oxford. Under-Sec., Head of Agricultural Div., RICS, 1966–69. Liveryman, Bowyers' Co., 1988–. *Heir: s* Henry Edgar Paston-Bedingfeld, *qv*. *Address:* The Old Stables, Livermere Road, Great Barton, Bury St Edmunds, Suffolk IP35 2RZ. *T:* Bury St Edmunds (01284) 788160. *Clubs:* Naval and Military, New Cavendish.

PASTON-BEDINGFELD, Henry Edgar; York Herald of Arms, since 1993; *b* 7 Dec. 1943; *s* and *heir* of Sir Edmund Paston-Bedingfeld, Bt, *qv*; *m* 1968, Mary Kathleen, *d* of Brig. R.D. Ambrose, CIE, OBE, MC; two *s* two *d*. *Educ:* Ampleforth College, York. Chartered Surveyor. Rouge Croix Pursuivant of Arms, 1983–93. Genealogist, British Assoc. of SMO Malta, 1995–. Founder Chairman, Norfolk Heraldry Soc., 1975–80, Vice-Pres. 1980–; Member Council: Heraldry Soc., 1976–85, and 1990–; Norfolk Record Soc., 1986–; Sec., Standing Council of the Baronetage, 1984–88; Vice-President: Cambridge Univ. Heraldic and Genealogical Soc., 1988–; Suffolk Family Hist. Soc., 1991–. Rep. of Duke of Norfolk, Commn d'Inf. et de Liaison des Assocs Nobles d'Europe, 1994. Freeman of the City of London; Liveryman: Scriveners' Co; Bowyers' Co. Kt of Sovereign Mil. Order of Malta. *Publications:* Oxburgh Hall, The First 500 Years, 1982; (jtly) Heraldry, 1993. *Address:* The College of Arms, Queen Victoria Street, EC4V 4BT. *T:* 0171–236 6420; Oxburgh Hall, Norfolk PE33 9PS. *T:* Gooderstone (01366) 328269. *Club:* Boodle's.

PASTON BROWN, Dame Beryl, DBE 1967; *b* 7 March 1909; *d* of Paston Charles Brown and Florence May (*née* Henson). *Educ:* Streatham Hill High School; Newnham Coll., Cambridge (MA); London Day Training College. Lecturer: Portsmouth Training

Coll., 1933–37; Goldsmiths' Coll., Univ. of London, 1937–44 and 1946–51. Temp. Asst Lecturer, Newnham Coll., 1944–46. Principal of City of Leicester Training Coll., 1952–61; Principal, Homerton College, Cambridge, 1961–71. Chairman, Assoc. of Teachers in Colleges and Depts of Educn, 1965–66. *Address:* 21 Keere Street, Lewes, East Sussex BN7 1TY. *T:* Lewes (01273) 473608.

PATAKI, George Elmer; Governor, New York State, since 1955; *b* 24 June 1945; *s* of Louis Pataki and Margaret Pataki; *m* Elizabeth (Libby) Rowland; two *s* two *d. Educ:* Peekskill High Sch.; Yale Univ. (BA 1967); Columbia Univ. Sch. of Law (JD 1970). Associate, Dewey, Ballantine, Bushby, Plamer and Wood, 1970–74; Partner, Plunkett & Jaffe, 1974–89. Mem., State Assembly 91st AD, 1985–92; Ranking Minority Member: Assembly Envmtl Conservation Cttee, 1987–90; Assembly Educn Cttee, 1991–92; Mem., State Senate 37th SD, 1993–95; Chm., State Ethics Cttee, 1993–95. Mayor, Peekskill, Westchester City, 1982–84. Co-proprietor, Pataki Farm, Peekskill, NY. *Recreations:* hiking in the woods, ski-ing, basketball, working on the family farm. *Address:* Executive Chamber, State Capitol, Albany, NY 12224, USA. *T:* (518) 4748418.

PATCHETT, Terry; MP (Lab) Barnsley East, since 1983; *b* 11 July 1940; *s* of Wilfred and Kathleen Patchett; *m* 1961, Glenys Veal; one *s* two *d. Educ:* State schools; Sheffield University (Economics and Politics). Miner; NUM Houghton Main Branch Delegate, 1966–83; Mem., Yorkshire Miners' Exec., 1976–83; former Member: Appeals Tribunals; Community Health Council. Mem., Wombwell UDC, 1969–73. Mem., H of C Expenditure Cttee (Social Services Sub-Cttee), 1985–87. *Recreations:* walking, gardening, golf. *Address:* 71 Upperwood Road, Darfield, near Barnsley, S Yorks S73 9RQ. *T:* Barnsley (01226) 757684. *Clubs:* Darfield Working Men's; Darfield Cricket.

PATE, Prof. John Stewart, FRS 1985; FAA 1980; FLS; Professor of Botany, University of Western Australia, since 1974; *b* 15 Jan. 1932; *s* of Henry Stewart Pate and Muriel Margaret Pate; *m* 1959, Elizabeth Lyons Sloan, BSc; three *s. Educ:* Campbell College; Queen's Univ., Belfast (BSc, MSc, PhD, DSc). FLS 1990. Lectr, Sydney Univ., 1956–60; Lectr, Reader, Personal Chair in Plant Physiology, Queen's Univ. Belfast, 1960–73. Vis. Fellow, Univ. of Cape Town, 1973. *Publications:* (ed with J. F. Sutcliffe) Physiology of the Garden Pea, 1977; (ed with A. J. McComb) Biology of Australian Plants, 1981; (with K. W. Dixon) Tuberous, Cormous and Bulbous Plants, 1983; (ed with J. S. Beard) Kwongan: plant life of the sandplain, 1984; reviews on carbon:nitrogen metabolism. *Recreations:* music, nature study, hobby farming. *Address:* 83 Circe Circle, Dalkeith, WA 6009, Australia. *T:* (9) 3866070.

PATEL, Indraprasad Gordhanbhai, Hon. KBE 1990; PhD; Director, London School of Economics and Political Science, 1984–90 (Hon. Fellow, 1990); *b* 11 Nov. 1924; *s* of F. Patel Gordhanbhai Tulsibhai and M. Patel Kashiben Jivabhai; *m* 1958, Alaknanda Dasgupta; one *d. Educ:* Bombay Univ. (BA Hons); King's Coll., Cambridge (BA, PhD; Hon. Fellow, 1986). Prof. of Economics and Principal, Baroda Coll., Maharaja Sayajirao Univ. of Baroda, 1949; Economist, later Asst Chief, IMF, 1950–54; Dep. Economic Adviser, Min. of Finance, India, 1954–58; Alternate Exec. Dir for India, IMF, 1958–61; Chief Economic Adviser, Min. of Finance and Planning Commn, 1962–64, 1965–67; Special Sec. and Sec., Dept of Economic Affairs, 1967–72; Dep. Administrator, UN Develt Programme, 1972–77; Governor, Reserve Bank of India, 1977–82; Dir, Indian Inst. of Management, Ahmedabad, 1982–84. Vis. Prof., Delhi Univ., 1964. Chm., Aga Khan Rural Support Programme, India, 1990–. Hon. DLitt: Sardar Patel Univ.; Maharaja Sayajirao Univ. of Baroda, 1993; Hon. DCL, Univ. of Mauritius, 1990. Padma Vibhushan, 1991. *Publications:* Essays in Economic Policy and Economic Growth, 1986; articles in IMF staff papers etc. on inflation, monetary policy, internat. trade. *Recreations:* music, reading, watching cricket. *Address:* 12 Amee Co-operative Housing Society, Diwali Pura, Old Padra Road, Vadodara 390015, India.

PATEL, Praful Raojibhai Chaturbhai; Company Director, Investment Adviser in UK, since 1962; Hon. Secretary, All-Party Parliamentary Committee on UK Citizenship, since 1968; *b* Jinja, Uganda, 7 March 1939; *s* of Raojibhai Chaturbhai Patel, Sojitra, Gujarat, India, and Maniben Jivabhai Lalaji Patel, Dharmaj, Gujarat; unmarried. *Educ:* Government Sec. Sch., Jinja, Uganda; London Inst. of World Affairs, attached to University Coll., London (Extra Mural Dept). Sec., Uganda Students Union, 1956–58; Deleg. to Internat. Youth Assembly, New Delhi, 1958; awarded two travel bursaries for visits to E, Central and S Africa, and Middle East, to study and lecture on politics and economics; arrived in Britain as student, then commenced commercial activities, 1962; increasingly involved in industrial, cultural and educational projects affecting immigrants in Britain. Spokesman for Asians in UK following restriction of immigration resulting from Commonwealth Immigrants Act 1968; Council Mem., UK Immigrants Advisory Service, 1970–; Mem., Uganda Resettlement Bd, 1972–74; Hon. Sec., Uganda Evacuees Resettlement Advisory Trust, 1974–; Pres., Nava Kala India Socio-Cultural Centre, London, 1962–75; Chm. Bd of Trustees, Swaminarayan Hindu Mission, UK, 1970–76; Jt Convener, Asian Action Cttee, 1976; Convener, Manava Trust, 1979–. Contested (Lab) Brent North, 1987. *Publications:* articles in newspapers and journals regarding immigration and race relations. *Recreations:* cricket; campaigning and lobbying; current affairs; and inter-faith co-operation. *Address:* 60 Bedford Court Mansions, Bedford Avenue, Bedford Square, WC1B 3AD. *T:* 0171–580 0897. *Club:* Commonwealth Trust.

PATEMAN, Jack Edward, CBE 1970; FEng; Chairman, Kent County Engineering Society, since 1989; *b* 29 Nov. 1921; *s* of William Edward Pateman and Lucy Varley (*née* Jetten); *m* 1949, Cicely Hope Turner; one *s* one *d. Educ:* Gt Yarmouth Grammar Sch. Served War of 1939–45, RAF, 1940–46. Research Engineer: Belling & Lee, 1946–48; Elliott Bros (London) Ltd, 1948–51; formed Aviation Div. of EBL at Borehamwood, 1951–62; Dep. Chm. and Jt Man. Dir, Elliott Flight Automation Ltd, 1962–71; Man. Dir, 1971–86, Dep. Chm., 1986–87, GEC Avionics; Director: Canadian Marconi Co., 1971–87; GEC Computers Ltd, 1971–89 (Chm., 1978–82); Elliott Brothers (London) Ltd, 1979–89; Marconi Electronic Devices, 1980–87; GEC Avionics Projects Ltd, 1980–89; GEC Information Systems, 1982–86; GEC Avionics Projects (UK) Ltd, 1984–89; General Electric Co. Plc, 1986–88. GEC-Marconi Ltd, 1987–89. British Gold Medal, RAeS, 1981. *Recreation:* sailing. *Address:* Spindles, Ivy Hatch, Sevenoaks, Kent TN15 0PG. *T:* Plaxtol (01732) 810364.

PATEMAN, Prof. John Arthur Joseph, FRS 1978; FRSE 1974; Emeritus Professor of Genetics, Australian National University; *b* 18 May 1926; *s* of John and Isobel May Pateman; *m* 1952, Mary Phelps; one *s* two *d. Educ:* Clacton County High Sch., Essex; University Coll., Leicester. BSc, PhD(Lond); MA(Cantab). Lectr, Univ. of Sheffield, 1954–58; Sen. Lectr, Univ. of Melbourne, Australia, 1958–60; Lectr, Univ. of Cambridge, 1960–67; Prof., Flinders Univ., S Australia, 1967–70; Prof. of Genetics, Univ. of Glasgow, 1970–79; Prof. of Genetics, ANU, 1979–88 (Exec. Dir, Centre for Recombinant DNA Res., 1982–88). Fellow, Churchill Coll., Cambridge, 1961–67. *Publications:* scientific papers in genetical, biochemical and microbiological jls. *Recreations:* reading, music, walking. *Address:* 1 Abberbury Road, Oxford OX4 4ET. *T:* Oxford (01865) 748275.

PATERSON, Alexander Craig, (Alastair), CBE 1987; FEng 1983; Senior Partner, Bullen and Partners, Consulting Engineers, 1969–88, retired (Partner 1960–69); *b* 15 Jan. 1924; *s* of Duncan McKellar Paterson and Lavinia (*née* Craig); *m* 1947, Betty Hannah Burley; two *s* two *d. Educ:* Glasgow High Sch.; Royal Coll. of Science and Technol. (ARCST); Glasgow Univ. (BSc). FICE 1963; FIMechE 1964; FIStructE 1970; FCIArb 1968. Commd REME, 1944; served India and Burma, attached Indian Army, 1944–47. Engineer: with Merz and McLellan, 1947–58; with Taylor Woodrow, 1958–60. Mem., Overseas Projects Bd, 1984–87. Institution of Structural Engineers: Mem. Council, 1976–89; Vice Pres., 1981–84; Pres., 1984–85; Institution of Civil Engineers: Mem. Council, 1978–81 and 1982–91; Vice-Pres., 1985–88; Pres., 1988–89. Pres., British Section, Société des Ingénieurs et Scientifiques de France, 1980; Chm., British Consultants Bureau, 1978–80; Member: Council, British Bd of Agrément, 1982–95; Engrg Council, 1987–90. Mem. Court, Cranfield Inst. of Technol., 1970–80. Hon. DSc Strathclyde, 1989. *Publications:* professional and technical papers in engrg jls. *Recreations:* sailing, gardening. *Address:* Willows, The Byeway, West Wittering, Chichester, West Sussex PO20 8LJ. *T:* Birdham (01243) 514199. *Club:* Caledonian.

PATERSON, Dame Betty (Fraser Ross), DBE 1981 (CBE 1973); DL; Chairman: NW Thames Regional Health Authority, 1973–84; National Staff Advisory Committee for England and Wales (Nurses and Midwives), 1975–84; *b* 14 March 1916; *d* of Robert Ross Russell and Elsie Marian Russell (*née* Fraser); *m* 1940, Ian Douglas Paterson; one *s* one *d. Educ:* Harrogate Coll.; Western Infirmary, Glasgow. Mem. Chartered Soc. of Physiotherapy (MCSP). County Comr, Herts Girl Guides, 1950–57. Member: Herts CC, 1952–74 (Alderman 1959–74; Chm., 1969–73); NE Metropolitan Regional Hosp. Bd, 1960–74; Governing Body, Royal Hosp. of St Bartholomew, 1960–74; Commn for the New Towns, England and Wales, 1961–75 (Dep. Chm., 1971–75); Governing Body, Bishop's Stortford Coll., 1967–81; Central Health Services Council, 1969–74; Gen. Council, King Edward's Hosp. Fund for London, 1975–84 (Management Cttee, 1975–80); Chm. Trustees, NHS Pensioners' Trust, 1991–; Pres., Herts Assoc. of Local Councils, 1980–90; Vice-Pres., Herts Magistrates' Assoc., 1987–. JP Herts, 1950–86 (Chm. Bishop's Stortford Bench, 1978–86); DL Herts, 1980. *Recreations:* music, cooking, family. *Address:* 52 Free Trade Wharf, The Highway, E1 9ES. *T:* 0171–791 0367.

PATERSON, Bill; *see* Paterson, W. T.

PATERSON, Prof Sir Dennis (Craig), Kt 1976; MB, BS 1953, MD 1983; FRCS, FRACS; Director and Chief Orthopaedic Surgeon, Adelaide Children's Hospital, since 1970; Consultant Orthopaedic Surgeon, Queen Victoria Hospital, since 1968; Clinical Associate Professor, University of Adelaide, since 1990; *b* 14 Oct. 1930; *s* of Gilbert Charles Paterson and Thelma Drysdale Paterson; *m* 1955, Mary, *d* of Frederick Mansell Hardy; one *s* three *d. Educ:* Collegiate Sch. of St Peter; Univ. of Adelaide (MB, BS 1953; MD 1983). FRCS 1958, FRACS 1961. Res. Med. Officer: Royal Adelaide Hosp., 1954; Adelaide Children's Hosp., 1955; Registrar, Robert Jones & Agnes Hunt Orthop. Hosp., Oswestry, Shropshire, 1958–60; Royal Adelaide Hospital: Sen. Registrar, 1960–62; Cons. Orthop. Surg., 1964–86; Cons. Orthop. Surg., Repatriation Gen. Hosp., Adelaide, 1962–70; Adelaide Children's Hospital: Asst Hon. Orthop. Surg., 1964–66; Sen. Hon. Orthop. Surg., 1966–70; Mem. Bd of Management, 1976–84; Chm., Med. Adv. Cttee, 1976–84; Chm., Med. Staff Cttee, 1976–84. Amer./British/Canadian Trav. Prof., 1966. Royal Australasian Coll. of Surgeons: Mem., Bd of Orthop. Surg., 1974–82, 1984–85 (Chm., 1977–82); Mem., Court of Examnrs, 1974–84; Mem., SA Cttee, 1974–78; Fellow: British Orthopaedic Assoc.; RSocMed; Member: Aust. Orthopaedic Assoc. (Censor-in-Chief, 1976–80; Dir, Continuing Educn, 1982–85); AMA; Internat. Scoliosis Res. Soc.; SICOT (Aust. Nat. Delegate, 1975–84, First Vice-Pres., 1984–87; Pres., 1987–90); Paediatric Orthopaedic Soc.; W Pacific Orthopaedic Soc.; Hon. Mem., American Acad. of Orthopaedic Surgeons, 1981. Pres., Crippled Children's Assoc. of South Australia Inc., 1970–84 (Mem. Council, 1966–70). Life Mem., S Aust. Cricket Assoc. Queen's Jubilee Medal, 1977. *Publications:* over 80 articles in Jl of Bone and Joint Surg., Clin. Orthopaedics and Related Res., Aust. and NZ Jl of Surg., Med. Jl of Aust., Western Pacific Jl of Orthop. Surg. *Recreations:* tennis, golf, gardening, vigneron. *Address:* 31 Myall Avenue, Kensington Gardens, SA 5068, Australia. *T:* (8) 3323364. *Clubs:* Adelaide, Royal Adelaide Golf, Kooyonga Golf (Adelaide).

PATERSON, Francis, (Frank), FCIT; General Manager, Eastern Region, British Rail, York, 1978–85; Member, British Railways (Eastern) Board, 1978–85; Chairman, North Yorkshire Family Practitioner Committee, 1987–91; *b* 5 April 1930; *s* of Francis William Paterson and Cecilia Eliza Reid Brownie; *m* 1950, Grace Robertson; two *s* two *d. Educ:* Robert Gordon's Coll., Aberdeen. Joined LNER as Junior Clerk, 1946; clerical and supervisory positions in NE Scotland; management training, Scotland, 1956–59; various man-management, operating and marketing posts, Scotland, Lincs and Yorks, 1960–66; Operating Supt, Glasgow North, 1967–68; Sales Manager, Edinburgh, 1968; Asst Divl Manager, S Wales, 1968–70; Dir, United Welsh Transport, 1968–70; Harbour Comr, Newport Harbour, 1968–70; Divl Manager, Central Div., Southern Region, 1970–75; Director: Southdown Motor Services Ltd, 1970–73; Brighton, Hove & District Omnibus Co., 1970–73; Dep. Gen. Man., Southern Region, 1975–77; Chief Freight Manager, British Railways Bd, 1977–78. Dir, N Yorks Moors Rly plc, 1993–. Vice-Chm., Nat. Railway Mus. Cttee, 1984– (Mem., 1978–); Member: CBI Southern Regional Council, 1975–77; CBI Transport Policy Cttee, 1977–78; BBC NE Adv. Council, 1987–91; Chm., BBC Local Radio Adv. Council, Radio York, 1987–91. Pres., St Andrews Soc. of York, 1989–90. Trustee, Friends of Nat. Railway Museum, 1988–. Mem. Court, Univ. of York, 1981–92. OStJ 1980. FCIT 1978 (Mem. Council, CIT, 1979–84). *Publications:* papers to transport societies. *Recreations:* transport, travel, hill walking, country pursuits, Scottish culture, enjoying grandchildren. *Address:* Alligin, 97 Main Street, Askham Bryan, York YO2 3QS. *T:* York (01904) 708478.

PATERSON, His Honour Frank David; a Circuit Judge (formerly County Court Judge), 1968–93; *b* 10 July 1918; *yr s* of late David Paterson and Dora Paterson, Liverpool; *m* 1953, Barbara Mary, 2nd *d* of late Oswald Ward Gillow and Alice Gillow, Formby; one *s* two *d. Educ:* Calderstones Preparatory Sch. and Quarry Bank High Sch., Liverpool; Univ. of Liverpool (LLB). Called to Bar, Gray's Inn, 1941; Warden, Unity Boys' Club, Liverpool, 1941; Asst Warden, Florence Inst. for Boys, Liverpool, 1943. Practised on Northern Circuit. Chairman: Min. of Pensions and Nat. Insce Tribunal, Liverpool, 1957; Mental Health Review Tribunal for SW Lancashire and Cheshire, 1963. Asst Dep. Coroner, City of Liverpool, 1960. Pres., Merseyside Magistrates' Assoc., 1978–93. Hon. LLD Liverpool, 1993. *Address:* Vailima, 2 West Lane, Formby, Liverpool L37 7BA. *T:* Formby (01704) 874345. *Club:* Athenæum (Liverpool).

PATERSON, Sir George (Mutlow), Kt 1959; OBE 1946; QC (Sierra Leone) 1950; Chairman, Industrial Tribunals, 1965–79; *b* 3 Dec. 1906; *e s* of late Dr G. W. Paterson; *m* 1935, Audrey Anita, *d* of late Major C. C. B. Morris, CBE, MC; one *s* two *d. Educ:* Grenada Boys' School; St John's College, Cambridge. Appointed to Nigerian Administrative Service, 1929. Called to the Bar, Inner Temple, 1933. Magistrate, Nigeria, 1936; Crown Counsel, Tanganyika, 1938. War of 1939–45: served with the King's African Rifles, 1939 (wounded 1940); Occupied Enemy Territories Admin., 1941; Lieutenant-Colonel 1945. Solicitor-General, Tanganyika, 1946; Attorney-General, Sierra Leone, 1949, Ghana, 1954–57; Chief Justice of Northern Rhodesia, 1957–61, retired 1961;

appointed to hold an inquiry into proposed amendments to the Potato Marketing Scheme, 1962; appointed legal chairman (part-time), Pensions Appeal Tribunals, 1962; appointed chairman Industrial Tribunals, South Western Region, 1965. *Recreations:* shooting, gardening, genealogy. *Address:* St George's, Westbury, Sherborne, Dorset DT9 3RA. *T:* Sherborne (01935) 814003. *Club:* Bath and County (Bath).

See also T. P. P. Clifford.

PATERSON, Sqdn-Ldr Ian Veitch, CBE 1969; DL; JP; Deputy Chairman, Local Government Boundary Commission for Scotland, 1974–80; *b* 17 Aug. 1911; *s* of Andrew Wilson Paterson; *m* 1940, Anne Weir, *d* of Thomas Brown; two *s* one *d. Educ:* Lanark Grammar School; Glasgow University. Served RAF, 1940–45. Entered local govt service, Lanark, 1928; Principal Legal Asst, Aberdeen CC; Lanarkshire: Dep. County Clerk, 1949; County Clerk, 1956, resigned 1974. Chm., Working Party which produced The New Scottish Local Authorities Organisation and Management structures, 1973. DL Lanarkshire (Strathclyde), 1963; JP Hamilton (formerly Lanarkshire). *Address:* 12 Fairfield Lodge, Green Street, Bothwell, Glasgow.

PATERSON, James Rupert; HM Diplomatic Service, retired; *b* 7 Aug. 1932; *s* of late Major Robert Paterson, MC, Seaforth Highlanders and Mrs Josephine Paterson; *m* 1956, Kay Dineen; two *s* two *d. Educ:* Nautical Coll., Pangbourne; RMA, Sandhurst. Commnd RA, 1953 (Tombs Meml Prize); Staff Coll., Camberley, 1963; retd from Army with rank of Major, 1970; joined FCO, 1970; First Sec., Pakistan, 1972; Dep. High Comr, Trinidad and Tobago, 1975; Ambassador to the Mongolian People's Republic, 1982; Consul-General, Istanbul, 1985, Geneva, 1989–92. *Recreations:* reading, travel, golf. *Address:* c/o Barclays Bank, Deal, Kent CT14 6EP.

PATERSON, James Veitch; Sheriff of the Lothian and Borders (formerly Roxburgh, Berwick and Selkirk) at Jedburgh, Selkirk and Duns, since 1963; *b* 16 April 1928; *s* of late John Robert Paterson, ophthalmic surgeon, and Jeanie Gouinlock; *m* 1956, Ailie, *o d* of Lt-Comdr Sir (George) Ian Clark Hutchison, *qv*; one *s* one *d. Educ:* Peebles High School; Edinburgh Academy; Lincoln College, Oxford; Edinburgh University. Admitted to Faculty of Advocates, 1953. *Recreations:* fishing, shooting, gardening. *Address:* Sunnyside, Melrose, Roxburghshire TD6 9BE. *T:* Melrose (0189682) 2502. *Club:* New (Edinburgh).

PATERSON, John Mower Alexander, OBE 1985; JP; Vice Lord-Lieutenant of Buckinghamshire, since 1984; *b* 9 Nov. 1920; *s* of Leslie Martin Paterson and Olive Harriette Mower; *m* 1944, Daisy Miriam Ballanger Marshall; one *s* two *d. Educ:* Oundle; Queens' Coll., Cambridge (MA Hons). Served War, RE, 1941–46. Cincinnati Milling Machines, Birmingham, 1946–48; Dir, 1945–87, Chm., 1960–85, Bifurcated Engineering, later BETEC PLC, Aylesbury; Dir and Works Man., Bifurcated & Tubular Rivet Co. Ltd, Aylesbury, 1948–60; Chm., Rickmansworth Water Co., 1988–90 (Dir, 1984–90; Dep. Chm., 1986–88); Dir, Three Valleys Water Services plc, 1991–92. Member: Southern Regional Council, CBI, 1971–85 (Chm., 1974–76); Grand Council, CBI, 1971–84. Gen. Comr of Taxes, Aylesbury Div., 1959–. Mem., Lloyd's, 1960–. Pres., Aylesbury Divl Cons. and Unionist Assoc., 1984–85; Chm., Bucks Council for Voluntary Youth Services, 1978–91 (Pres., 1992–); Member: Management Cttee, Waddesdon Manor (NT), 1980–; Governing Body, Aylesbury Coll. of Further Educn, 1961–88 (Chm., 1977–87); Governing Body, Aylesbury GS, 1974– (Chm., 1984–). JP 1962, High Sheriff 1978, DL 1982, Bucks. KStJ 1991 (Mem., Chapter-Gen., 1992–; Mem., 1980–, Chm., 1981–, Council, Bucks Br.). *Recreations:* sailing, veteran cars, gardening. *Address:* Park Hill, Potter Row, Great Missenden, Bucks HP16 9LT. *T:* Great Missenden (01494) 862995. *Clubs:* Royal Ocean Racing; Royal Yacht Squadron (Cowes); Royal Lymington Yacht (Cdre, 1973–76); Veteran Car of Great Britain.

PATERSON, Very Rev. John Munn Kirk; Minister Emeritus of St Paul's Parish Church, Milngavie (Minister, 1970–87); Moderator of the General Assembly of the Church of Scotland, 1984–85; *b* 8 Oct. 1922; *s* of George Kirk Paterson and Sarah Ferguson Paterson (*née* Wilson); *m* 1946, Geraldine Lilian Parker; two *s* one *d. Educ:* Hillhead High School, Glasgow; Edinburgh Univ. MA, BD. RAF, 1942–46 (Defence and Victory medals, Italy Star, 1945). Insurance Official, 1940–58 (ACII 1951); Assistant Minister, 1958–64; Ordained Minister of Church of Scotland, 1964–. Hon. DD Aberdeen, 1986. *Recreations:* fishing, hill walking. *Club:* Royal Over-Seas League (Edinburgh).

PATERSON, Very Rev. John Thomas Farquhar; Dean of Christ Church, Dublin, since 1989; *b* Portadown, Co. Armagh, 21 Dec. 1938; *s* of Henry Paterson and Margreta Elizabeth Paterson (*née* Bell); unmarried. *Educ:* Portadown College; Trinity College, Dublin (BA, MA, BD). Curate-Assistant: Drumglass (Dungannon), 1963; St Bartholomew, Dublin, 1966; Priest-in-charge, St Mark, Dublin and Asst Chaplain, TCD, 1968; Vicar, St Bartholomew with Christ Church, Leeson Park, Dublin, 1972; Dean and Rector of Kildare, 1978. Lectr in Pastoral Liturgy, Church of Ireland Theol Coll., 1984–91. Hon. Sec., Gen. Synod, Church of Ireland, 1985–91. *Publications:* articles in Irish theological jls (Search, The Furrow, Doctrine and Life). *Recreations:* travel, reading, music. *Address:* The Deanery, St Werburgh Street, Dublin 8, Ireland. *T:* (1) 4781797, (cathedral) (1) 6778099, *Fax:* (1) 6798991. *Club:* Kildare Street and University (Dublin).

PATERSON, Sir John (Valentine) J.; *see* Jardine Paterson.

PATERSON, William Alexander; *see* Alexander, Bill.

PATERSON, William Tulloch, (Bill Paterson); actor since 1968; *b* 3 June 1945; *s* of late John Paris Paterson and of Ann Tulloch Paterson; *m* 1984, Hildegard Bechtler; one *s* one *d. Educ:* Whitehill Sen. Secondary Sch., Glasgow; RSAMD. First professional engagement, Glasgow Citizens' Theatre, 1968; Asst Dir, Citizens' Theatre for Youth, 1970–72; Founder Mem., 7:84 (Scotland) Theatre Co. *Stage:* The Cheviot, the Stag and the Black Black Oil, 1973; Writer's Cramp, 1977; Whose Life is it Anyway?, Savoy, 1978; Guys and Dolls, NT, 1982; Schweyk, NT, 1983; Death and the Maiden, Royal Court, 1992; Misery, Criterion, 1993; Mongrel's Heart, Edinburgh, 1994; *films:* Comfort and Joy, 1984; The Killing Fields, 1984; Defence of the Realm, 1985; A Private Function, 1986; The Adventures of Baron Munchausen, 1987; The Witches, 1989; Truly Madly Deeply, 1991; Chaplin, 1992; *television series and serials:* Smiley's People; The Singing Detective; Auf Wiedersehen Pet; Traffik; Tell Tale Hearts; Hard Times. *Address:* c/o Kerry Gardner Management, 15 Kensington High Street, W8 5NP.

PATERSON-BROWN, Dr June, CBE 1991; DL; Chief Commissioner, Girl Guides Association, and Commonwealth Chief Commissioner, 1985–90; *b* 8 Feb. 1932; *d* of Thomas Clarke Garden and Jean Martha (*née* Mallace); *m* 1957, Dr Peter N. Paterson-Brown; three *s* one *d. Educ:* Esdaile Sch.; Edinburgh Univ. (MB, ChB). MO in Community Health, 1960–85. Scottish Chief Comr, Girl Guides Assoc., 1977–82. Non-Exec. Dir, Border Television, 1980–; Chm., Borders Children's Panel Adv. Cttee, 1982–85; Trustee: Prince's Trust, 1982–94 (Vice-Chm., 1982–92); MacRobert's Trust, 1987–; Chm., Scottish Standing Conf. Voluntary Youth Organisations, 1982–85. DL Roxburgh, Ettrick and Lauderdale, 1990. *Recreations:* ski-ing, golfing, fishing, tennis, music, reading. *Address:* Norwood, Hawick, Roxburghshire TD9 7HP. *T:* Hawick (01450) 72352. *Club:* Lansdowne.

PATEY, Very Rev. Edward Henry; Dean of Liverpool, 1964–82, now Dean Emeritus; *b* 12 Aug. 1915; *s* of Walter Patey, MD, and Dorothy Patey; *m* 1942, Margaret Ruth Olivia Abbott, OBE; one *s* three *d. Educ:* Marlborough College; Hertford College, Oxford; Westcott House, Cambridge. Assistant Curate, St Mary-at-the-Walls, Colchester, 1939; MA (Oxon) 1941; Assistant Curate Bishopwearmouth Parish Church, Sunderland, 1942; Youth Chaplain to the Bishop of Durham, 1946; Vicar of Oldland, with Longwell Green, Bristol, 1950; Secretary, Youth Department, The British Council of Churches, 1952; Assistant Gen. Secretary, The British Council of Churches, 1955; Canon Residentiary of Coventry Cathedral, 1958. Hon. LLD Liverpool, 1980. *Publications:* Religion in the Club, 1956; Boys and Girls Growing Up, 1957; Worship in the Club, 1961; A Doctor's Life of Jesus, 1962; Young People Now, 1964; Enquire Within, 1966; Look out for the Church, 1969; Burning Questions, 1971; Don't Just Sit There, 1974; Christian Lifestyle, 1975; All in Good Faith, 1978; Open the Doors, 1978; Open the Book, 1981; I Give You This Ring, 1982; My Liverpool Life, 1983; Becoming An Anglican, 1985; Preaching on Special Occasions, 1985; Questions For Today, 1986; For the Common Good, 1989; Faith in a Risk-Taking God, 1991. *Recreations:* reading, listening to music, walking. *Address:* 139 High Street, Malmesbury, Wilts SN16 9AL.

PATHAK, Raghunandan Swarup; Judge of the International Court of Justice, The Hague, since 1989; *b* 25 Nov. 1924; *s* of Gopal Swarup Pathak and Prakashwati; *m* 1955, Asha Paranjpe; three *s. Educ:* St Joseph's Coll., Allahabad; Ewing Christian Coll., Allahabad; Allahabad Univ. (BSc 1945; LLB 1947; MA (Pol. Sci.) 1948; Sastri Medal in Internat. Law, 1947). Enrolled Advocate: Allahabad High Court, 1948; Supreme Court of India, 1957; Additional Judge, 1962, Judge, 1963, Allahabad High Court; Chief Justice, Himachal Pradesh High Court, 1972; Judge, Supreme Court of India, 1978; Chief Justice of India, 1986–89. Chm., All India Univ. Professors' Internat. Law Res. Gp, 1969–89; Visitor, Nat. Law Sch. of India, Bangalore, 1986–89; Pro-Chancellor, Univ. of Delhi, 1986–89; Distinguished Vis. Prof., Inst. of Advanced Studies in the Humanities, Edinburgh Univ. President: Indian Law Inst., 1986–89; Indian Council of Legal Aid and Advice; Indian Soc. of Internat. Law, 1989–; International Law Association, London: Mem., 1952–; Pres., India Regl Br., 1986–89; Mem., Cttee on Space Law, and Cttee on Enforcement of Human Rights; Vice-Pres., Indian Acad. of Environmental Law and Research. Chm., World Congress on Law and Medicine, New Delhi, 1985; Member: Indo-Soviet Internat. Law Confs; Indo-W German Internat. Law Colloquia; UN Univ. project on Internat. Law, Common Patrimony and Intergenerational Equity; UN Univ. project on Internat. Law and Global Change, 1989. Lectures worldwide on law and on human rights. Hon. Bencher, Gray's Inn, 1988. Hon. LLD: Agra; Panjab; Hon. DLitt Kashi Vidyapeeth, Varanasi. *Publications:* papers on internat. law, law of the sea, etc, in learned jls. *Recreations:* golf, photography. *Address:* 5 Janpath, New Delhi 110011, India. *T:* (11) 3019224. *Clubs:* Delhi Gymkhana, India International Centre, Delhi Golf (New Delhi).

PATIENCE, Andrew; QC 1990; a Recorder of the Crown Court, since 1986; *b* 28 April 1941; *s* of late William Edmund John Patience and of Louise Mary Patience; *m* 1975, Jean Adèle Williams; one *s* one *d. Educ:* Whitgift School, Croydon; St John's College, Oxford (MA). Called to the Bar, Gray's Inn, 1966. *Recreations:* mimicry, complaining, sleeping. *Address:* 5 Paper Buildings, Temple, EC4Y 7HB. *T:* 0171–353 5638. *Club:* United Oxford & Cambridge University.

PATMORE, Prof. (John) Allan, CBE 1993; JP; Professor of Geography, University of Hull, 1973–91, Professor Emeritus, since 1991; Vice-Chairman, Sports Council, 1988–94 (Member, 1978–94); *b* 14 Nov. 1931; *s* of John Edwin Patmore and Marjorie Patmore; *m* 1956, Barbara Janet Fraser; one *s* two *d. Educ:* Harrogate Grammar Sch.; Pembroke Coll., Oxford (MA, BLitt). Served RAF, Educn Br., 1952–54. Department of Geography, University of Liverpool: Tutor, 1954–55; Asst Lectr, 1955–58; Lectr, 1958–69; Sen. Lectr, 1969–73; University of Hull: Dean of Social Science, 1979–81; Pro-Vice-Chancellor, 1982–85. Visiting Professor: Univ. of Southern Illinois, 1962–63; Univ. of Canterbury, NZ, 1978. Pres. 1979–80, Trustee 1979–88, Hon. Mem., 1991, Geographical Assoc.; Pres., Sect. E, BAAS, 1987–88. Pres., N Yorks Moors Assoc., 1993–; Member: N York Moors National Park Cttee, 1977–92; Nat. Parks Review Panel, 1990–91; Countryside Commn, 1992–; Inland Waterways Amenity Adv. Council, 1993–94. Chm., Friends of Nat. Railway Mus., 1992–; Mem. Adv. Cttee, Nat. Railway Mus., 1988–. JP Hull, 1975. Hon. DLitt Loughborough, 1993. *Publications:* Land and Leisure, 1970; People, Place and Pleasure, 1975; Recreation and Resources, 1983. *Recreations:* pursuing railway history, enjoying the countryside. *Address:* 4 Aston Hall Drive, North Ferriby, North Humberside HU14 3EB. *T:* Hull (01482) 632269.

PATNICK, Sir (Cyril) Irvine, Kt 1994; OBE 1980; MP (C) Sheffield, Hallam, since 1987; *b* Oct. 1929; *m* 1960, Lynda Margaret (*née* Rosenfield); one *s* one *d. Educ:* Sheffield Poly. FCIOB. Member: Sheffield City Council, 1967–70; Sheffield MDC, 1971–88; S Yorks CC, until abolition in 1986 (Opposition Leader, 1973–86); Dep. Chm., S Yorks Residuary Body, 1985–87; Chm., Local Govt Adv. Cttee, 1989–90. Contested (C) Sheffield, Hillsborough, 1970, 1979. An Asst Govt Whip, 1989–90; a Lord Comr of HM Treasury (Govt Whip), 1990–94. Vice-Chm., Cons. Party Back-bench Envmt Cttee, 1988–89. Mem., Cons. Party NEC, 1982–89. Chm., Yorks and Humberside Council for Sport and Recreation, 1979–85; Member: Sheffield Community Health Council, 1974–75; Yorks and Humberside Tourist Bd, 1977–79; Governor, Sports Aid Foundn, Yorks and Humberside, 1980–85. *Address:* House of Commons, SW1A 0AA.

PATON, Alasdair Chalmers, CEng, FICE, FIWEM; Chief Executive, Scottish Environment Protection Agency, since 1995; *b* Paisley, 28 Nov. 1944; *o s* of David Paton and Margaret Elizabeth Paton (*née* Chalmers); *m* 1969, Zona Gertrude Gill; one *s* one *d. Educ:* John Neilson Instn, Paisley; Univ. of Glasgow (BSc). Assistant Engineer: Clyde Port Authy, 1967–71; Dept of Agric. and Fisheries for Scotland, 1971–72; Sen. Engineer, Scottish Develt Dept, 1972–77; Engineer, Public Works Dept, Hong Kong Govt, 1977–80; Scottish Development Department: Sen. Engineer, 1980–84; Principal Engineer, 1984–87; Dep. Chief Engineer, 1987–91; Dir and Chief Engineer, Water and Waste Directorate, Scottish Office Envmt Dept, 1991–95. *Recreations:* Rotary, sailing, golf. *Address:* Scottish Environment Protection Agency, Suite V1, Saughton House, Broomhouse Drive, Edinburgh EH11 3XD. *T:* 0131–455 8680.

PATON, Sir Angus; *see* Paton, Sir T. A. L.

PATON, Ann; QC (Scot.) 1990; *d* of James McCargow and Ann Dunlop or McCargow; *m* 1974, Dr James Y. Paton; no *c. Educ:* Laurel Bank Sch.; Univ. of Glasgow (MA 1972; LLB 1974). Admitted to the Scottish Bar, 1977. Standing Junior Counsel: to the Queen's and Lord Treasurer's Remembrancer (excluding *Ultimus Haeres*), 1979; in Scotland to Office of Fair Trading, 1981; Advocate Depute, 1992–94. Mem., Criminal Injuries Compensation Bd, 1995. *Publications:* Map of Sheriffdoms and Sheriff Court Districts in Scotland, 1977, 2nd edn 1980; (Jt Asst Editor) Gloag and Henderson, Law of Scotland, 8th edn 1980, 9th edn 1987; (with R. G. McEwan) A Casebook on Damages in Scotland, 1983, 2nd edn as Damages in Scotland (sole author), 1989; contrib. Scottish Current Law Statutes, Session Cases, Scots Law Times, and Green's Reparation Bulletin. *Recreations:*

sailing, tennis, golf. *Address:* 23 Drummond Place, Edinburgh EH3 6PN. *Club:* Grange Tennis.

PATON, Douglas Shaw F.; *see* Forrester-Paton.

PATON, Maj.-Gen. Douglas Stuart, CBE 1983 (MBE 1961); FFPHM; Commander Medical HQ BAOR, 1983–85; retired 1986; *b* 3 March 1926; *s* of Stuart Paton and Helen Kathleen Paton (*née* Hooke); *m* 1957, Jennifer Joan Land; two *d.* *Educ:* Sherborne; Bristol University. MB ChB 1951; FFPHM 1989 (FFCM 1982, MFCM 1973). Commissioned RAMC, 1952; served Middle East (Canal Zone), Malaya, Hong Kong and UK, 1952–61; 16 Para Bde, 1961–66; jssc 1966; CO BMH Terendak, Malaysia, 1967–70; MoD, 1970–73; CO Cambridge Mil. Hosp., Aldershot, 1973–76; rcds 1977; DDMS HQ 1 (BR) Corps, 1978–81; Dep. Dir-Gen., Army Med. Services, MoD, 1981–83. QHP 1981–86. Hon. Col 221 (Surrey) Field Amb. RAMC(V), TA, 1988–92. Chm., RAMC Assoc., 1988–. Mem. Bd of Governors, Moorfields Eye Hosp., 1988–91. CStJ 1986. *Publications:* contribs to Jl RAMC. *Recreations:* golf, skiing, travel, opera, gardening. *Address:* Brampton, Springfield Road, Camberley, Surrey GU15 1AB.

PATON, Hon. (Frederick) Ronald N.; *see* Noel-Paton.

PATON, Ven. Michael John Macdonald; Archdeacon of Sheffield, 1978–87, Archdeacon Emeritus since 1988; *b* 25 Nov. 1922; *s* of late Rev. William Paton, DD, and Grace Mackenzie Paton (*née* Macdonald); *m* 1952, Isobel Margaret Hogarth; one *s* four *d.* *Educ:* Repton School; Magdalen Coll., Oxford (MA). Indian Army, 1942–46; HM Foreign Service, 1948–52; Lincoln Theological Coll., 1952–54; Deacon 1954, priest 1955; Curate, All Saints', Gosforth, Newcastle upon Tyne, 1954–57; Vicar, St Chad's, Sheffield, 1957–67; Chaplain, United Sheffield Hosps, 1967–70; Vicar, St Mark's, Broomhill, Sheffield, 1970–78. *Publications:* contrib. to: Essays in Anglican Self-criticism, 1958; More Sermons from Great St Mary's, 1971; Religion and Medicine, 1976; Mud and Stars, 1991. *Recreations:* hill walking, music, birdwatching. *Address:* 947 Abbeydale Road, Sheffield S7 2QD. *T:* Sheffield (0114) 236 6148.

See also Rt. Rev. H. W. Montefiore.

PATON, Sir (Thomas) Angus (Lyall), Kt 1973; CMG 1960; FRS 1969; FEng; Consulting Civil Engineer, since 1984; *b* 10 May 1905; *s* of Thomas Lyall Paton and Janet (*née* Gibb); *m* 1932, Eleanor Joan Delmé-Murray (*d* 1964); two *s* two *d.* *Educ:* Cheltenham Coll.; University College, London. Fellow of University College. Joined Sir Alexander Gibb & Partners as pupil, 1925; after experience in UK, Canada, Burma and Turkey on harbour works, hydro-electric projects and industrial development schemes, was taken into partnership, 1938; Senior Partner, 1955–77; Senior Consultant, 1977–84. Responsible for design and supervision of construction of many large industrial factories and for major hydro-electric and irrigation projects, including Owen Falls and Kariba Schemes, and for overall supervision of Indus Basin Project in W. Pakistan; also for economic surveys in Middle East and Africa on behalf of Dominion and Foreign Governments. Member UK Trade Mission to: Arab States, 1953; Egypt, Sudan and Ethiopia, 1955. Mem. NERC, 1969–72. Pres. ICE, 1970–71; Chm., Council of Engineering Instns, 1973; Past Chairman Assoc. of Consulting Engineers. FICE (Hon. FICE, 1975); FIStructE, Fellow Amer. Soc. of Civil Engineers, Past Pres., British Section, Soc. of Civil Engineers (France); a Vice-Pres., Royal Soc., 1977–78; For. Associate, Nat. Acad. of Engineering, USA, 1979. Founder Fellow, Fellowship of Engineering, 1976; FRSA. Fellow, Imperial Coll., London, 1978. Hon. DSc: London, 1977; Bristol, 1981. *Publications:* Power from Water, 1960; technical articles on engineering subjects. *Address:* L'Epervier, Route Orange, St Brelade, Jersey JE3 8LW. *T:* (01534) 45619.

PATON WALSH, Jill; self-employed author, since 1966; *b* 29 April 1937; *d* of John Llewelyn Bliss and Patricia Paula DuBern; *m* 1961, Antony Paton Walsh (separated); one *s* two *d.* *Educ:* St Michael's Convent, Finchley; St Anne's Coll., Oxford (BA English; MA; DipEd). Schoolteacher, Enfield Girls' Grammar Sch., 1959–62. Arts Council Creative Writing Fellowship, Brighton Poly., 1976–77, 1977–78; Gertrude Clark Whitall Meml Lectr, Library of Congress, 1978; vis. faculty mem., Center for Children's Lit., Simmons Coll., Boston, Mass, 1978–86. A Judge, Whitbread Lit. Award, 1984; Chm., Cambridge Book Assoc., 1987–89; former Mem., Management Cttee, Soc. of Authors; Member: Cttee, Children's Writers' and Illustrators' Gp; Adjunct British Bd, Children's Literature New England. *Publications: fiction:* Farewell, Great King, 1972; Lapsing, 1986; A School for Lovers, 1989; The Wyndham Case, 1993; Knowledge of Angels, 1994; A Piece of Justice, 1995; *for children:* The Island Sunrise: pre-historic Britain, 1975; *fiction:* Hengest's Tale, 1966; The Dolphin Crossing, 1967; (with Kevin Crossley-Holland) Wordhoard, 1969; Fireweed (Book World Fest. Award), 1970; Goldengrove, 1972; Toolmaker, 1973; The Dawnstone, 1973; The Emperor's Winding Sheet (jtly, Whitbread Prize), 1974; The Butty Boy, 1975 (US edn as The Huffler); Unleaving (Boston Globe/Horn Book Award), 1976; Crossing to Salamis, The Walls of Athens, and Persian Gold, 1977–78 (US combined edn as Children of the Fox, 1978); A Chance Child, 1978; The Green Book, 1981 (re-issued as Shine, 1988); Babylon, 1982; Lost & Found, 1984; A Parcel of Patterns (Universe Prize), 1984; Gaffer Samson's Luck, 1985 (Smarties Prize Grand Prix, 1984); Five Tides, 1986; Torch, 1987; Birdy and the Ghosties, 1989; Grace, 1991; When Grandma Came, 1992; Matthew and the Sea-Singer, 1992; Pepi and the Secret Names, 1994. *Recreations:* photography, gardening, reading. *Address:* c/o David Higham Associates, 5–8 Lower John Street, Golden Square, W1R 4HA. *T:* 0171–437 7888.

PATRICK, Gail; *see* Patrick, L. G.

PATRICK, Graham McIntosh, CMG 1968; CVO 1981; DSC 1943; Under Secretary, Department of the Environment, 1971–81, retired; *b* 17 Oct. 1921; *m* 1945, Barbara Worboys; two *s.* *Educ:* Dundee High Sch.; St Andrews Univ. RNVR (Air Branch), 1940–46. Entered Ministry of Works, 1946; Regional Director: Middle East Region, 1965–67; South West Region, DoE, 1971–75; Chm., South West Economic Planning Bd, 1971–75; Dir, Scottish Services, PSA, 1975–81. *Address:* 3 Blueberry Downs, Coastguard Road, Budleigh Salterton, Devon EX9 6NU.

PATRICK, (James) McIntosh, ROI 1949; ARE; RSA 1957 (ARSA 1949); painter and etcher; *b* 4 Feb. 1907; *s* of Andrew G. Patrick and Helen Anderson; *m* 1933, Janet (*d* 1983), *d* of W. Arnot Watterston; one *s* one *d.* *Educ:* Morgan Academy, Dundee; Glasgow School of Art. Awarded Guthrie Award RSA, 1935; painting Winter in Angus purchased under the terms of the Chantrey Bequest, 1935; paintings purchased for Scottish Nat. Gall. of Modern Art; Tate Gall.; National Gallery of South Africa, Cape Town; Art Gallery of South Australia; Scottish Contemp. Art Assoc.; and Municipal collections Manchester, Aberdeen, Hull, Dundee, Liverpool, Glasgow, Greenock, Perth, Southport, Newport (Mon.), Arbroath, also for Lady Leverhulme Art Gallery, etc.; etchings in British Museum and other print collections. Served War of 1939–46, North Africa and Italy; Captain (General List). Fellow: Duncan of Jordanstone Coll. of Art, Dundee, 1987; Glasgow Sch. of Art, 1994. Hon. LLD Dundee, 1973. *Recreations:* gardening, music. *Address:* c/o Fine Art Society, 148 New Bond Street, W1Y 0JT; 67 Magdalen Yard Road, Dundee DD2 1AL. *T:* Dundee (01382) 668561.

PATRICK, John Bowman; Sheriff of North Strathclyde (formerly Renfrew and Argyll) at Greenock, 1968–83; *b* 29 Feb. 1916; *s* of late John Bowman Patrick, Boot and Shoe maker, Greenock, and late Barbara Patrick (*née* James); *m* 1945, Sheina Struthers McCrea (*d* 1993); one *d.* *Educ:* Greenock Academy; Edinburgh Univ. (MA 1937); Glasgow Univ. (LLB 1946). Served War in Royal Navy, Dec. 1940–Dec. 1945; conscripted as Ordinary Seaman, finally Lieut RNVR. LLB Glasgow 1946. Admitted as a Solicitor in Scotland, June 1947; admitted to Faculty of Advocates, July 1956. Sheriff of Inverness, Moray, Nairn, Ross and Cromarty at Fort William and Portree (Skye), 1961–68. *Address:* 107 Springfield Road, Aberdeen AB1 7RT. *T:* Aberdeen (01224) 318979.

PATRICK, (Lilian) Gail; Sheriff of Tayside, Central and Fife at Kirkcaldy, since 1991; *b* 24 Dec. 1941; *d* of Alexander Findlay McFadzean, MA, LLB and Elizabeth Fullerton McFadzean (*née* Fenton); *m* 1967, Spencer Francis Rodger, LLB, WS, *s* of Francis and Isabel Patrick; one *s* three *d.* *Educ:* Radleigh Sch., Glasgow; Marr Coll., Troon; St Andrews Univ. (MA); Edinburgh Univ. (LLB). Enrolled as solicitor, 1966; pt-time practice, 1967–79; Lecturer and Tutor: Glasgow Univ., 1967–82; Edinburgh Univ., 1980–82, 1985–90; pt-time Procurator Fiscal Depute, 1979–80; admitted to Faculty of Advocates, 1981; Standing Jun. Counsel, Scottish Educn Dept, 1986–91; Chm., Social Security Appeal Tribunal, 1986–91; Reporter, Scottish Legal Aid Bd, 1986–91; Temp. Sheriff, 1988–91; called to the Bar, Lincoln's Inn, 1990. *Recreations:* golf, hill-walking, cycling, fishing, music. *Address:* 13 Succoth Place, Edinburgh EH12 6BJ; Old Schoolhouse, Linsidemore, by Lairg, Sutherland IV27 4EU. *Clubs:* Murrayfield Golf (Edinburgh); Ladies' Golf (Troon); Bonar Bridge and Ardgay Golf (Bonar Bridge, Sutherland).

PATRICK, Margaret Kathleen, OBE 1976; District/Superintendent Physiotherapist, Central Birmingham Health Authority (Teaching) (formerly United Birmingham Hospitals Hospital Management Committee), 1951–88, retired; *b* 5 June 1923; *d* of late Roy and Rose Patrick. *Educ:* Godolphin and Latymer Sch., London; Guy's Hosp. Sch. of Physiotherapy. BA, Open Univ., 1980. MCSP (Hon. FCSP). Chm. Physio. Adv. Cttee, and Mem. Health Care Planning for Elderly, Birmingham AHA (T). Member: Exec., Whitley Council PTA, 1960–75 (Chm., PTA Cttee C, 1960–75); Tunbridge Cttee on Rehab. Services, 1971–72; Hosp. Adv. Service on Geriatrics, 1972; DHSS Working Party on Stat. Data in Physio., 1969–76; Council, Chartered Soc. of Physio., 1953–75 (Exec. Mem., 1960–75; Vice Chm., 1971–75); Birmingham AHA (Teaching), 1979–82; Vice-Chm., Bromsgrove and Redditch HA, 1982–90. Assoc. of Supt Chartered Physiotherapists: Chm., 1964–75; Pres., 1971–72. *Publications:* Ultrasound Therapy: a textbook for physiotherapists, 1965; (contrib.) Physiotherapy in some Surgical Conditions, ed Joan Cash, 1977, 2nd edn 1979; contrib. Physiotherapy, and articles on ultrasound therapy, geriatric care, and paediatrics. *Recreation:* gardening.

PATTEN, Brian; poet; *b* 7 Feb. 1946. Regents Lectr, Univ. of Calif (San Diego), 1985. *Publications: poetry:* Penguin Modern Poets, 1967; Little Johnny's Confession, 1967; Notes to the Hurrying Man, 1969; The Irrelevant Song, 1971; The Unreliable Nightingale, 1973; Vanishing Trick, 1976; The Shabby Angel, 1978; Grave Gossip, 1979; Love Poems, 1981; Clare's Countryside: a book on John Clare, 1982; New Volume, 1983; Storm Damage, 1988; Grinning Jack (Selected Poems), 1990; *novel:* Mr Moon's Last Case, 1975 (Mystery Writers of Amer. Special Award, 1976); *for younger readers:* The Elephant and the Flower, 1969; Jumping Mouse, 1971; Emma's Doll, 1976; The Sly Cormorant and the Fish: adaptations of The Aesop Fables, 1977; (ed) Gangsters, Ghosts and Dragonflies, 1981; Gargling with Jelly, 1985; Jimmy Tag-along, 1988; Thawing Frozen Frogs, 1990; (ed) The Puffin Book of Twentieth Century Children's Verse, 1991; Grizzelda Frizzle, 1992; The Magic Bicycle, 1993; Impossible Parents, 1994; The Utter Nutters, 1994; *plays:* The Pig And The Junkle, 1975; (with Roger McGough) The Mouth Trap, 1982; Blind Love, 1983; Gargling with Jelly, 1989; *recordings:* Brian Patten Reading His Own Poetry, 1969; British Poets Of Our Time, 1974; Vanishing Trick, 1976; The Sly Cormorant, 1977. *Address:* c/o Puffin Books, 27 Wrights Lane, W8 5TZ. *Club:* Chelsea Arts.

PATTEN, Rt. Hon. Christopher (Francis), PC 1989; Governor and Commander-in-Chief, Hong Kong, since 1992; *b* 12 May 1944; *s* of late Francis Joseph Patten and Joan McCarthy; *m* 1971, Mary Lavender St Leger Thornton; three *d.* *Educ:* St Benedict's School, Ealing; Balliol College, Oxford. Conservative Research Dept, 1966–70; Cabinet Office, 1970–72; Home Office, 1972; Personal Asst to Chairman of Conservative Party, 1972–74; Director, Conservative Research Dept, 1974–79. Contested (C) Bath, 1992. MP (C) Bath, 1979–92. PPS to Chancellor of Duchy of Lancaster and Leader of House of Commons, 1979–81, to Secretary of State for Social Services, 1981; Parly Under-Sec. of State, NI Office, 1983–1985; Minister of State, DES, 1985–86; Minister of State (Minister for Overseas Develt), FCO, 1986–89; Sec. of State for the Envmt, 1989–90; Chancellor of Duchy of Lancaster, 1990–92; Chm. of Cons. Party, 1990–92. Vice Chm., Cons. Parly Finance Cttee, 1981–83; Mem., Select Cttees on Defence and Procedure, 1982–83. *Publication:* The Tory Case, 1983. *Recreations:* reading, tennis, travelling in France and Spain. *Address:* Government House, Hong Kong. *Clubs:* Beefsteak, Royal Automobile.

PATTEN, Rt. Hon. John (Haggitt Charles), PC 1990; MP (C) Oxford West and Abingdon, since 1983 (City of Oxford, 1979–83); *b* 17 July 1945; *s* of Jack Patten and late Maria Olga (*née* Sikora); *m* 1978, Louise Alexandra Virginia, 2nd *d* of late John Rowe, Norfolk, and Claire Rowe, Oxfordshire; one *d.* *Educ:* Wimbledon Coll.; Sidney Sussex Coll., Cambridge (PhD 1972). University Lectr, 1969–79, Fellow, Hertford Coll., 1972–94, Univ. of Oxford. Oxford City Councillor, 1973–76. PPS to Mr Leon Brittan and Mr Tim Raison, Ministers of State at the Home Office, 1980–81; Parliamentary Under-Secretary of State: NI Office, 1981–83; DHSS, 1983–85; Minister of State for Housing, Urban Affairs and Construction, DoE, 1985–87; Minister of State, Home Office, 1987–92; Sec. of State for Educn, 1992–94. Advr, Charterhouse Bank. *Publications:* The Conservative Opportunity (with Lord Blake), 1976; English Towns, 1500–1700, 1978; Pre-Industrial England, 1979; (ed) The Expanding City, 1983; (with Paul Coones) The Penguin Guide to the Landscape of England and Wales, 1986; Things to Come: the Tories in the 21st Century, 1995. *Recreation:* talking to my wife and daughter. *Address:* House of Commons, SW1A 0AA. *Club:* Beefsteak.

PATTEN, Nicholas John; QC 1988; *b* 7 Aug. 1950; *s* of Peter Grenville Patten and Dorothy Patten (*née* Davenport); *m* 1984, Veronica Mary Schoeneich; two *s* one *d.* *Educ.* Tulse Hill Sch.; Christ Church, Oxford (Open Schol.; MA; BCL (1st Cl. Hons Jurisprudence)). Called to the Bar, Lincoln's Inn, 1974. *Recreations:* gardening, ski-ing, motor cars. *Address:* 9 Old Square, Lincoln's Inn, WC2A 3SR. *T:* 0171–405 4682.

PATTEN, Prof. Tom, CBE 1981; PhD; FEng 1986; FIMechE; FRSE; consultant; Chairman, Marine Technology Directorate Ltd, since 1992 (Director, since 1988); Professor and Head of Department of Mechanical Engineering, Heriot-Watt University, 1967–82, now Emeritus; *b* 1 Jan. 1926; *s* of late William Patten and Isabella (*née* Hall); *m* 1950, Jacqueline McLachlan (*née* Wright); one *s* two *d.* *Educ:* Leith Acad.; Edinburgh Univ. (BSc, PhD). CEng, FIMechE 1965; FRSE 1967. Captain REME, 1946–48: served Palestine and Greece. Barry Ostlere & Shepherd Ltd, Kirkcaldy, 1949; Asst Lectr, Lectr and Sen. Lectr, Dept of Engrg, Univ. of Edinburgh, 1950–67; Dir, Inst. of Offshore Engineering, Heriot-Watt Univ., 1972–79; Vice-Principal, Heriot-Watt Univ., 1978–80,

Acting Principal, 1980–81. Vis. Res. Fellow, McGill Univ., Canada, 1958. Researches in heat transfer, 1950–83; British and foreign patents for heat exchange and fluid separation devices. Man. Dir, Compact Heat Exchange Ltd, 1970–87; Chm., Envmt and Resource Technology Ltd, 1982–91; Director: Pict Petroleum, 1981–93; Melville Street Investments plc, 1983–95; New Darien Oil Trust plc, 1985–88; Seaboard Lloyd Ltd, 1986–87; Brown Brothers & Co. Ltd, 1986–88; Sealand Industries plc, 1987–94 (Chm., 1987–91); Benson Gp plc, 1991–; Edinburgh Petroleum Services Ltd, 1992–. Member: Council, IMechE, 1971–73, 1975–88 and 1989– (Pres., 1991–92); Oil Develt Council for Scotland, 1973–78; SRC Marine Technol. Task Force, 1975–76; Design Council (Scottish Cttee), 1979–82; Offshore Technol. Bd, Dept of Energy, 1985–88; Co-ordinating Cttee on Marine Sci. and Technol., 1987–91; Supervisory Bd, NEL, 1989–91; Pres., Engrg Cttee on Oceanic Resources, 1987–90. Council, RSE, 1969–79 (Vice-Pres. RSE, 1976–79); Pres., Soc. for Underwater Technol., 1985–87. Freeman, City of London, 1991; Liveryman, Engineers' Co., 1992. Hon. Fellow, Napier Univ. (formerly Poly.), 1992. Hon. DEng Heriot-Watt, 1987; Hon. DSc Edinburgh, 1992; Dr *hc* Univ. Politécnica de Madrid, 1993. *Publications:* technical and scientific papers in field of heat transfer in Proc. IMechE, and Internat. Heat Transfer Conf. Proc.; also papers on offshore engineering. *Recreations:* squash, music. *Address:* 67/7 Grange Loan, Edinburgh EH9 2EG. *T:* 0131–662 1101. *Clubs:* Caledonian; New (Edinburgh).

PATTENDEN, Prof. Gerald, FRS 1991; Sir Jesse Boot Professor, and Head of Department of Organic Chemistry, Nottingham University, since 1988; *b* 4 March 1940; *s* of Albert James and Violet Eugene Pattenden; *m* 1969, Christine Frances Doherty; three *d. Educ:* Brunel Univ. (BSc); Queen Mary College London (PhD, DSc). CChem, FRSC. Lectr, UC, Cardiff, 1966–72; Nottingham University: Lectr, 1972–75; Reader, 1975–80; Prof., 1980–88. Chm., Org. Chem. Cttee, SERC, 1992–94. RSC Corday-Morgan Medal and Prize, 1975; Simonsen Lect. and Medal, 1987; Tilden Lect. and Medal, 1991; RSC Award for Synth. Org. Chem., 1992; Pedler Lect. and Medal, 1993; RSC Award for Heterocyclic Chem., 1994. *Publications:* editor of several books and jls. *Recreations:* sport, entertainment, gardening. *Address:* Chemistry Department, The University, Nottingham NG7 2RD. *T:* Nottingham (0115) 951 3530.

PATTERSON, Arthur, CMG 1951; Assistant Secretary, Department of Health and Social Security, 1968–71; *b* 24 June 1906; 2nd *s* of late Alexander Patterson; *m* 1942, Mary Ann Stocks, *er d* of late J. L. Stocks; two *s* one *d. Educ:* Methodist Coll., Belfast; Queen's Univ., Belfast; St John's Coll., Cambridge. Entered Ministry of Labour, 1929; Assistant Secretary, 1941; transferred to Ministry of National Insurance, 1945; lent to Cyprus, 1953; Malta, 1956; Jamaica, 1963; Kuwait, 1971. *Address:* 8 Searles Meadow, Dry Drayton, Cambs CB3 8BU. *T:* Crafts Hill (01954) 789911.

PATTERSON, Maj.-Gen. Arthur Gordon, CB 1969; DSO 1964; OBE 1961; MC 1945; Director of Army Training, 1969–72; retired; *b* 24 July 1917; *s* of late Arthur Abbey Patterson, Indian Civil Service; *m* 1949, Jean Mary Grant; two *s* one *d. Educ:* Tonbridge Sch.; RMC Sandhurst. Commnd, 1938; India and Burma, 1939–45; Staff Coll., Camberley, 1949; jssc 1955; CO 2nd 6th Queen Elizabeth's Own Gurkha Rifles, 1959–61; Comdr 99 Gurkha Inf. Brigade, 1962–64; idc 1965; GOC 17 Div. and Maj.-Gen., Bde of Gurkhas, 1965–69. Col, 6th Queen's Own Gurkha Rifles, 1969–73. *Address:* Burnt House, Benenden, Cranbrook, Kent TN17 4DT. *Club:* Naval and Military.

PATTERSON, Ben; *see* Patterson, G.B.

PATTERSON, Dr Colin, FRS 1993; FLS; Curator of Fossil Fishes, Natural History Museum (formerly British Museum (Natural History)), since 1962; *b* 13 Oct. 1933; *o s* of late Maurice William Patterson and Norah Joan (*née* Elliott); *m* 1955, Rachel Caridwen, *e d* of late Ceri Richards, CBE, DLitt, FRCA and Frances Richards, ARCA; two *d. Educ:* Tonbridge Sch.; Imperial Coll. of Science and Technology (BSc 1957); University Coll. London (PhD 1961). ARCS 1957. Commnd RE, 1952–54. Lectr in Biology, Guy's Hosp. Med. Sch., 1957–62. Research Associate in Ichthyology, Amer. Mus. of Natural History, NY, 1969–; Agassiz Vis. Lectr, Mus. of Comparative Zoology, Harvard Univ., 1970. FLS 1967. Linnean Society: Zool Editor, 1978–82; Editorial Sec., 1982–85; Vice-Pres., 1981. Scientific Medal, Zool Soc. of London, 1972. *Publications:* (ed jtly) Interrelationships of Fishes, 1973; Evolution, 1978; (ed) Molecules and Morphology in Evolution, 1987; papers and monographs on living and fossil fishes, systematics, evolution, etc. *Recreations:* cinema, drink, walking. *Address:* The Natural History Museum, SW7 5BD. *T:* 0171–938 8846; 6 Lonsdale Road, SW13 9EB.

PATTERSON, (Constance) Marie, (Mrs Barrie Devney), CBE 1978 (OBE 1973); National Officer, Transport and General Workers' Union, 1976–84 (National Woman Officer, 1963–76); Member of General Council of TUC 1963–84 (Chairman, 1974–75 and 1977); *b* 1 April 1934; *d* of Dr Richard Swanton Abraham; *m* 1st, 1960, Thomas Michael Valentine Patterson (marr. diss. 1976); 2nd, 1984, Barrie Devney. *Educ:* Pendleton High Sch.; Bedford Coll., Univ. of London (BA). Member: Exec., Confedn of Shipbuilding and Engrg Unions, 1966–84 (Pres., 1977–78); Hotel and Catering Trng Bd, 1966–87; Equal Opportunities Commn, 1975–84; Central Arbitration Commn, 1976–94; Legal Aid Adv. Cttee, 1988–90; Council, Office of Banking Ombudsman, 1992–. Dir of Remploy, 1966–87. Lay Mem., Press Council, 1964–70. Chm. Council, Queen's Coll., Harley St, 1994–. Hon. DSc Salford, 1975. *Recreations:* sight-seeing, jig-saws.

PATTERSON, Eric, MBE 1970; HM Diplomatic Service, retired; Consul-General, 1982–88 and Counsellor (Commercial), 1986–88, Auckland; *b* 2 May 1930; *s* of Richard and Elizabeth Patterson; *m* 1953, Doris (*née* Mason); two *s. Educ:* Hookergate Grammar Sch., Co. Durham. Served Royal Signals, 1948–50. Local govt service, 1947–50; Lord Chancellor's Dept, 1950–52; BoT, 1952–62; Asst Trade Comr, Halifax, NS, 1962–67; Second Sec. (Commercial), Khartoum, 1967–70; First Sec. (Commercial), The Hague, 1970–74; FCO, 1974–76; First Sec. (Commercial), Warsaw, 1976–80; FCO, 1980–82. *Recreations:* golf, sailing, photography, fly-fishing. *Address:* 3 Prebble Place, Auckland 5, New Zealand. *Clubs:* Northern, Auckland, Auckland Golf, Royal New Zealand Yacht Squadron (Auckland).

PATTERSON, George Benjamin, (Ben); Principal Administrator, Internal Market Division, Directorate General for Research, European Parliament, since 1994; *b* 21 April 1939; *s* of late Eric James Patterson and Ethel Patterson; *m* 1970, Felicity Barbara Anne Raybould; one *s* one *d. Educ:* Westminster Sch.; Trinity Coll., Cambridge (MA); London Sch. of Economics. Lecturer, Swinton Conservative Coll., 1961–65; Editor (at Conservative Political Centre), CPC Monthly Report, 1965–74; Dep. Head, London Office of European Parlt, 1974–79. MEP (C) Kent W, 1979–94; contested (C) Kent W, Eur. Parly elecns, 1994. *Publications:* The Character of Conservatism, 1973; Direct Elections to the European Parliament, 1974; Europe and Employment, 1984; Vredeling and All That, 1984; VAT: the zero rate issue, 1988; A Guide to EMU, 1990; A European Currency, 1994. *Recreations:* squash, reading science fiction. *Address:* Elm Hill House, High Street, Hawkhurst, Kent TN18 4XU. *T:* Hawkhurst (01580) 752780; 9 rue de la Chapelle, 8017 Strassen, Luxembourg. T: 310783, *Fax:* 434070. *Club:* Institute of Directors.

PATTERSON, Harry; novelist; *b* 27 July 1929; *s* of Henry Patterson and Rita Higgins Bell; *m* 1st, 1958, Amy Margaret Hewitt (marr. diss. 1984); one *s* three *d*; 2nd, 1985, Denise Lesley Anne Palmer. *Educ:* Roundhay Sch., Leeds; Beckett Park Coll. for Teachers; London Sch. of Economics as external student (BSc(Hons) Sociology). FRSA. NCO, The Blues, 1947–50. 1950–58: tried everything from being a clerk to a circus tent-hand; 1958–72: variously a schoolmaster, Lectr in Liberal Studies, Leeds Polytechnic, Sen. Lectr in Education, James Graham Coll. and Tutor in Sch. Practice, Leeds Univ.; since age of 41, engaged in full-time writing career. Dual citizenship, British/Irish. *Publications include:* (as Jack Higgins): Prayer for the Dying, 1973 (filmed 1985); The Eagle has Landed, 1975 (filmed 1976); Storm Warning, 1976; Day of Judgement, 1978; Solo, 1980; Luciano's Luck, 1981; Touch the Devil, 1982; Exocet, 1983; Confessional, 1985 (filmed 1985); Night of the Fox, 1986 (filmed 1989); A Season in Hell, 1989; Cold Harbour, 1990; The Eagle Has Flown, 1990; Angel of Death, 1995; (as Harry Patterson): The Valhalla Exchange, 1978; To Catch a King, 1979 (filmed 1983); Dillinger, 1983; Walking Wounded (stage play), 1987; and many others (including The Violent Enemy, filmed 1969, and The Wrath of God, filmed 1972) under pseudonyms (Martin Fallon, Hugh Marlowe, Henry Patterson); some books trans. into 42 languages. DUniv Leeds Metropolitan, 1995. *Recreations:* tennis, old movies. *Address:* c/o Ed Victor Ltd, 162 Wardour Street, W1V 3AT.

PATTERSON, Hugh Foggan, MA; Secretary, King's College London, 1977–83; *b* 8 Nov. 1924; *s* of late Sir John Robert Patterson, KBE, CMG, and late Esther Margaret Patterson; *m* 1956, Joan Philippa Abdy Collins (*d* 1994); one *s* two *d. Educ:* Royal Grammar Sch., Newcastle upon Tyne; King's Coll., Cambridge (MA). Served War, Royal Artillery, 1943–47. HMOCS, Nigeria, 1950–61; Universities of: Birmingham, 1962–63; Warwick, 1964–69; London, 1969–83 (Clerk of the Senate, 1976–77). *Recreations:* music, golf.

PATTERSON, John Allan, CB 1989; Panel Chairman, Recruitment and Assessment Services, since 1992; *b* 10 Oct. 1931; *s* of William Gilchrist Patterson and May (*née* Eggie); *m* 1956, Anne Marie Lasson; one *s* two *d. Educ:* Epsom Coll.; Clare Coll., Cambridge (Major Scholar in Classics, Stewart of Rannoch Scholar; BA 1954). HM Diplomatic Service, 1954–65: served in Bangkok, 1957–61 and in Rome, 1961–64 (Private Sec. to the Ambassador); HM Treasury, 1965–81 (on loan to Cabinet Office, 1974–78); Dep. Dir of Savings, Dept for Nat. Savings, 1981–86; Dir of Savings and Head, Dept for Nat. Savings, 1986–91. Chm., Money Management Council, 1991–94. FRSA 1989. *Recreations:* gardening, walking, languages, church, Godalming CAB. *Address:* 5 Nelson Gardens, Guildford GU1 2NZ. *T:* Guildford (01483) 564369.

PATTERSON, Marie; *see* Patterson, C. M.

PATTERSON, Dr Mark Lister; *b* 2 March 1934; *s* of Alfred Patterson and Frederica Georgina Mary Lister Nicholson; *m* 1958, Jane Teresa Scott Stokes; one *s* two *d. Educ:* privately; St Bartholomew's Hosp. Med. Coll., Univ. of London (MB 1959). MRCP. Jun. hosp. appts at St Bartholomew's Hosp., Royal Postgrad. Med. Sch., and MRC Exptl Haematol. Unit; Consultant Haematologist to Nat. Heart and Chest Hosps, 1967–84. Mem., GLC, 1970–73 and 1977–81; Parly Candidate (C) Ealing N, 1974. *Recreations:* medicine, politics. *Address:* Wolverton Manor, Shorwell, Newport, Isle of Wight PO30 3JS. *T:* Isle of Wight (01983) 740609. *Club:* Carlton.

PATTERSON, Paul Leslie; composer; Professor of Composition, since 1970, Head of Composition and Twentieth Century Music, since 1985, Royal Academy of Music; Artistic Director, Exeter Festival, since 1991; formed: Manson Ensemble, 1968; The Patterson Quintet, 1982; *b* 15 June 1947; *s* of Leslie and Lilian Patterson; *m* 1981, Hazel Wilson; one *s* one *d. Educ:* Royal Academy of Music. FRAM 1980. Freelance composer, 1968–; Arts Council Composer in Association, English Sinfonia, 1969–70; Director, Contemporary Music, Warwick Univ., 1974–80; Composer in Residence: SE Arts Assoc., 1980–82; Bedford School, 1984–85; Southwark Fest., 1989–91; James Allen School, Dulwich, 1990–91; Three Spires Fest., Truro, 1992–94; Guest Prof., Yale Univ., 1989–90. Member: Exec. Cttee, Composers Guild, 1972–75; Council, SPNM, 1975–81, 1985–; Adv. Council, BBC Radio London, 1986–; Adv. Cttee, Arts Council's Recordings Panel, 1986–; Artistic Director of RAM Festivals: Lutosławski, 1984; Penderecki, 1986; Messiaen, 1987; Henze, 1988; Berio, 1989; Carter, 1990; Da Capo, 1993; Schnittke, 1994. Featured Composer at: Three Choirs Fest., Patterson at South Bank Fest., 1988; Cheltenham Fest., 1988, 1990; Peterborough Fest., 1989; Exeter Fest, 1991. Performances world wide by leading orchestras and soloists and ensembles; also film and TV music. Numerous recordings. Pres., RAM Club, 1993–94. FRSA 1989. OM, Polish Ministry of Culture, 1987. *Publications:* Rebecca, 1968; Trumpet Concerto, 1969; Time Piece, 1972; Kyrie, 1972; Requiem, 1973; Comedy for Five Winds, 1973; Requiem, 1974; Fluorescences, 1974; Clarinet Concerto, 1976; Cracowian Counterpoints, 1977; Voices of Sleep, 1979; Concerto for Orchestra, 1981; Canterbury Psalms, 1981; Sinfonia, 1982; Mass of the Sea, 1983; Deception Pass, 1983; Duologue, 1984; Mean Time, 1984; Europhony, 1985; Missa Brevis, 1985; Stabat Mater, 1986; String Quartet, 1986; Magnificat and Nunc Dimittis, 1986; Propositions, 1987; Trombone Quartet, 1987; Suite for Cello, 1987; Sorriest Cow, 1987; Tides of Mananan, 1988; Te Deum, 1988; Tunnel of Time, 1989; White Shadows, 1989; Symphony, 1990; The End, 1990; Mighty Voice, 1991; Violin Concerto, 1992; Little Red Riding Hood, 1992; Magnificat, 1993; Music for Opening Channel Tunnel, 1994; Overture: Songs of the West, 1995. *Recreations:* sailing, croquet, swimming, computing. *Address:* 31 Cromwell Avenue, Highgate, N6 5HN. *T:* 0181–348 3711, *Fax:* 0181–340 6489.

PATTERSON, Rt Hon. Percival (Noel James); PC 1992; QC 1984; MP (PNP) South East Westmoreland, 1972–80 and since 1989; Prime Minister of Jamaica, since 1992; Minister of Defence, since 1993; *b* 10 April 1935; *s* of Henry Patterson and Ina James; *m* (marr. diss.); one *s* one *d. Educ:* Somerton Primary; St James Calabar High Sch., Kingston; Univ. of the West Indies (BA Hons English 1959); LSE (LLB 1963). Called to the Bar, Middle Temple, 1963; admitted to Jamaican Bar, 1963; private legal practice, Kingston. Senator, Leader of Opposition Business, 1969–70; Minister of Industry and Tourism, 1972–77; Dep. Prime Minister and Minister of Foreign Affairs and Foreign Trade, 1978–80; Minister of Develt Planning and Production, 1989–90; Minister of Finance and Planning, 1990–91. Order of Liberator Simon Bolivar (Venezuela), 1st Class, 1992; Order of San Martin (Argentina), 1992. *Recreations:* music (jazz/Jamaican), sports (cricket, boxing, track and field, tennis). *Address:* c/o Jamaica House, Hope Road, Kingston 6, Jamaica. *T:* 9279941, 9267863.

PATTERSON, Rev. Canon William James, CBE 1991; Dean of Ely, 1984–90; Vicar of Abbotsley, Everton and Waresley, 1990–93; *b* 25 Sept. 1930; *s* of William Moscrop and Alice Patterson; *m* 1955, Elisabeth Roederer; one *s* two *d. Educ:* Haileybury; Balliol College, Oxon. MA. Asst Curate of St John Baptist, Newcastle upon Tyne, 1955–58; Priest-in-Charge, Rio Claro with Mayaro, Dio. Trinidad, 1958–65; Rector of Esher, 1965–72; RD of Emly, 1968–72; Rector of Little Downham, 1972–80; Priest-in-Charge of Coveney, 1978–80; Archdeacon of Wisbech, 1979–84; Vicar of Wisbech St Mary,

1980–84. Hon. Canon, Ely Cathedral, 1990–. *Recreation:* cycling. *Address:* 1 Watledge Close, Tewkesbury, Glos GL20 5RJ.

PATTIE, Rt. Hon. Sir Geoffrey (Edwin), Kt 1987; PC 1987; MP (C) Chertsey and Walton since Feb. 1974; Vice-Chairman, Conservative Party, since 1990; Joint Chairman, GEC-Marconi, since 1991 (Chairman, 1990); *b* 17 Jan. 1936; *s* of late Alfred Edwin Pattie, LDS, and Ada Clive (*née* Carr); *m* 1960, Tuëma Caroline (*née* Eyre-Maunsell); one *s* (one *d* decd). *Educ:* Durham Sch.; St Catharine's Coll., Cambridge (MA). BA Cantab 1959. Called to Bar, Gray's Inn, 1964. Served: Queen Victoria's Rifles (TA), 1959–61; (on amalgamation) Queen's Royal Rifles (TA), now 4th Royal Green Jackets, 1961–65; Captain, 1964. Mem. GLC, Lambeth, 1967–70; Chm. ILEA Finance Cttee, 1968–70. Chm. of Governors, London Coll. of Printing, 1968–69. Contested (C) Barking, 1966 and 1970. Sec., Cons. Parly Aviation Cttee, 1974–75, 1975–76, Vice Chm., 1976–77, 1977–78; Jt Sec., Cons. Parly Defence Cttee, 1975–76, 1976–77, 1977–78, Vice Chm., 1978–79; Mem., Cttee of Public Accounts, 1976–79; Vice-Chm., All Party Cttee on Mental Health, 1977–79. Parly Under Sec. of State for Defence for the RAF, 1979–81, for Defence Procurement, 1981–83; Minister of State: for Defence Procurement, 1983–84; DTI (Minister for IT), 1984–87. Mem. General Synod of Church of England, 1970–75. Chm., Intellectual Property Inst., 1994–. Trustee, Excalibur Scholarship Scheme, 1992–. FRSA 1990. *Publications:* Towards a New Defence Policy, 1976; (with James Bellini) A New World Role for the Medium Power: the British Opportunity, 1977. *Recreations:* travel, opera, cricket. *Address:* c/o House of Commons, SW1A 0AA. *Clubs:* Reform, Royal Green Jackets, MCC.

PATTINSON, Rev. Sir Derek; *see* Pattinson, Rev. Sir W. D.

PATTINSON, John Mellor, CBE 1943; MA; *b* 1899; *s* of late J. P. Pattinson, JP, Mobberley, Cheshire; *m* 1927, Wilhelmina (*d* 1983), *d* of late W. J. Newth, Cheltenham; two *s*. *Educ:* Rugby Sch.; RMA; Cambridge Univ. RFA with BEF, 1918–19. Anglo-Iranian Oil Co., South Iran, 1922–45, General Manager, 1937–45. Director until 1969: British Petroleum Co. of Canada Ltd; Triad Oil Co. Ltd; BP Germany AG; Dep. Chm. 1960–65, and Man. Dir 1952–65, British Petroleum Co. Ltd; Dir, Chartered Bank, 1965–73.

PATTINSON, Peter L. F.; *see* Foden-Pattinson, P. L.

PATTINSON, Rev. Sir (William) Derek, Kt 1990; Secretary-General, General Synod of Church of England, 1972–90; *b* 31 March 1930; *s* of late Thomas William and Elizabeth Pattinson. *Educ:* Whitehaven Grammar Sch.; Queen's Coll., Oxford (Stanhope Historical Essay Prize, 1951; BA 1952; MA 1956); St Deiniol's Liby, Hawarden; Coll. of Resurrection, Mirfield. Entered Home Civil Service, 1952; Inland Revenue Dept, 1952–62 and 1965–68; HM Treasury, 1962–65 and 1968–70; Assoc. Sec.-Gen., General Synod, 1970–72. Chm., William Temple Assoc., 1966–70; Member: Archbishops' Commn on Church and State, 1966–70; British Council of Churches, 1972–90; London Diocesan Synod, 1972–91. Ordained deacon, 1991, priest, 1992; Asst Curate, St Gabriel's Pimlico, 1991–. Principal, Soc. of the Faith, 1992–. Vice-Chm., Grosvenor Chapel Cttee, 1973–81; Vice-Pres., SPCK; Chm. of Governors, Liddon House, 1972–; Chm., English Friends of Anglican Centre in Rome, 1985; Gov., Sir John Cass Foundn, 1973–92; Vice Chm., Greycoat Hosp., 1988–. Freeman, City of London, 1973; Member: Parish Clerks' Co. (Master, 1986–87); Woolmens' Co. Member: Alcuin Club; Nikaean Club. Parish Clerk, St Luke's, Old Street, 1972–; Churchwarden, St Michael's Cornhill, 1988–91. *Address:* 9 Strutton Court, Great Peter Street, SW1P 2HH. *T:* 0171–222 6307.

PATTISON, Prof. Bruce; Professor of Education, University of London Institute of Education, 1948–76, now Emeritus; *b* 13 Nov. 1908; *s* of Matthew and Catherine Pattison; *m* 1937, Dorothy Graham (*d* 1979). *Educ:* Gateshead Grammar Sch.; King's Coll., Newcastle upon Tyne; Fitzwilliam House, Cambridge. Henry Mellish Sch., Nottingham, 1933–35; Hymers Coll., Hull, 1935–36; Lecturer in English, University College, London, 1936–48 (Reader, 1948). Board of Trade, 1941–43; Ministry of Supply, 1943–45. *Publications:* Music and Poetry of the English Renaissance, 1948, 2nd edn 1970; Special Relations, 1984. *Address:* 62 The Vale, Coulsdon, Surrey CR5 2AW. *T:* 0181–660 2991. *Clubs:* Athenæum, National Liberal.

PATTISON, David Arnold, PhD; Principal Associate, Cobham Resource Consultants, since 1990; *b* 9 Feb. 1941; *s* of David Pattison and Christina Russell Bone; *m* 1967, Anne Ross Wilson; two *s* one *d*. *Educ:* Glasgow Univ. (BSc 1st Cl. Hons, PhD). Planning Assistant, Dunbarton County Council, 1966–67; Lecturer, Strathclyde Univ., 1967–70; Head of Tourism Division, Highlands and Islands Development Board, 1970–81; Chief Exec., Scottish Tourist Board, 1981–85; Dir of Leisure and Tourism Consulting, Arthur Young Group, 1985–90. Hon. Prof., Queen Margaret Coll., Edinburgh, 1992. Hon. Pres., Scottish YHA. *Publications:* Tourism Development Plans for: Argyll, Bute, Ayrshire, Burgh of Ayr, Ulster. *Recreations:* reading, watching soccer and Rugby, golf, gardening. *Address:* 7 Cramond Glebe Gardens, Cramond, Edinburgh EH4 6NZ.

PATTISON, Rev. Dr George Linsley; Dean of Chapel, King's College, Cambridge, since 1991; *b* 25 May 1950; *s* of George William Pattison and Jean Pattison; *m* 1971, Hilary Christine Cochrane; one *s* two *d*. *Educ:* Perse Sch., Cambridge; Edinburgh Univ. (MA, BD); Durham Univ. (PhD). Ordained deacon, 1977, priest, 1978; Curate, St James' Church, Benwell, Newcastle upon Tyne, 1977–80; Priest-in-charge, St Philip and St James' Church, Kimblesworth, Co. Durham, 1980–83; Res. Student, Durham Univ., 1980–83; Rector, Badwell Ash, Great Ashfield, Hunston and Stowlangtoft with Langham, Suffolk, 1983–91. Has broadcast on BBC Radio 4 and World Service on subjects of art and religion. Editor, Modern Believing, 1994–. *Publications:* Art, Modernity and Faith, 1991; Kierkegaard: the aesthetic and the religious, 1992; (ed) Kierkegaard on Art and Communication, 1993; (with Sister Wendy Beckett) Pains of Glass, 1995; articles on theology, philosophy of religion and the arts in specialist and non-specialist jls. *Recreations:* family life, running, music, films, theatre. *Address:* King's College, Cambridge CB2 1ST. *T:* Cambridge (01223) 331100.

PATTISON, Michael Ambrose; Director, Sainsbury Family Charitable Trusts, since 1995; *b* 14 July 1946; *s* of Osmond John Pattison and late Eileen Susanna Pattison (*née* Cullen); *m* 1975, Beverley Jean, *d* of Genevieve and Hugh Webber, Florida, USA; one *d*. *Educ:* Sedbergh School; University of Sussex (BA Hons 1968). Min. of Overseas Develt, 1968; Asst Private Sec. to Minister, 1970; seconded to HM Diplomatic Service as First Sec., Perm. Mission to UN, New York, 1974; ODA, 1977; Private Sec. to successive Prime Ministers, 1979–82; ODA, 1982, Establishment Officer, 1983–85; Chief Exec. and Sec. Gen., RICS, 1985–95; Dir, Surveyors Holdings Ltd, 1985–95. Mem. Council, British Consultants Bureau, 1985–95. Dir, Battersea Arts Centre Trust, 1988–94. Mem., Cambridge Univ. Careers Service Syndicate, 1989–93; Pro-Chancellor, Greenwich Univ., 1994– (Gov., 1989–, when Thames Poly.). Vis. Fellow, City Univ., 1990–. FRSA 1990. *Recreations:* cricket, Real tennis, countryside. *Address:* (office) 9 Red Lion Court, EC4A 3EB. *T:* 0171–410 0330. *Clubs:* Athenæum; Warwickshire CC.

PATTON, Joseph Alexander, CBE 1982; FRAgS; farmer; *b* 17 Jan. 1936; *s* of Marshall Lyons and Bessie Robinson Patton; *m* 1967, Mary Morton Kirkpatrick; one *s* two *d*. Member: Milk Marketing Board, NI, 1982–; Council, Food From Britain, 1983–; Broadcasting Council of NI, 1982–84. President: Young Farmers' Clubs of Ulster, 1969–71; Ulster Farmers' Union, 1980–81. FRAgS 1984. *Address:* Roseyards, 107 Kirk Road, Ballymoney, Co. Antrim, Northern Ireland BT53 8HN. *T:* Dervock (012657) 41263.

PATTULLO, Sir (David) Bruce, Kt 1995; CBE 1989; Group Chief Executive, since 1988, and Governor, since 1991, Bank of Scotland; *b* 2 Jan. 1938; *s* of late Colin Arthur Pattullo and Elizabeth Mary Bruce; *m* 1962, Fiona Jane Nicholson; three *s* one *d*. *Educ:* Rugby Sch.; Hertford Coll., Oxford (BA). FCIBS. Commnd Royal Scots and seconded to Queen's Own Nigeria Regt. Gen. Man., Bank of Scotland Finance Co. Ltd, 1973–77; Dir, 1977–, Chief Exec., 1977–78, British Linen Bank Ltd; Bank of Scotland: Dep. Treas., 1978; Treas. and Gen. Manager (Chief Exec.), 1979–88; Dir, 1980–; Dep. Governor, 1988–91. Director: Melville Street Investments, 1973–90; Bank of Wales, 1986–; NWS Bank plc, 1986–; Standard Life Assurance Co., 1985–. Chm., Cttee, Scottish Clearing Bankers, 1981–83, 1987–89; Pres., Inst. of Bankers in Scotland, 1990–92 (a Vice-Pres., 1977–90). First Prizeman (Bilsland Prize), Inst. of Bankers in Scotland, 1964. FRSE 1990. *Recreation:* tennis. *Address:* 6 Cammo Road, Edinburgh EH4 8EB. *Clubs:* Caledonian; New (Edinburgh).

PAUFFLEY, Anna Evelyn Hamilton; QC 1995; *b* 13 Jan. 1956; *d* of Donald Eric Hamilton Pauffley and Josephine Sybil Pauffley. *Educ:* Godolphin Sch., Salisbury; London Univ. (BA Hons). Called to the Bar, Middle Temple, 1979. *Address:* 4 Paper Buildings, Temple, EC4Y 7EX. *T:* 0171–583 0816.

PAUK, György, Hon. RAM 1990; international concert violinist; Professor at Guildhall School of Music and Drama; Professor, Royal Academy of Music, since 1987; *b* 26 Oct. 1936; *s* of Imre and Magda Pauk; *m* 1959, Susanne Mautner; one *s* one *d*. *Educ:* Franz Liszt Acad. of Music, Budapest. Toured E Europe while still a student; won three internat. violin competitions, Genoa 1956, Munich 1957, Paris 1959; soon after leaving Hungary, settled in London, 1961, and became a British citizen. London début, 1961; seasonal appearances there and in the provinces, with orchestra, in recital and chamber music; also plays at Bath, Cheltenham and Edinburgh Fests and London Promenade Concerts; performs in major European music venues; US début, under Sir George Solti, with Chicago Symph. Orch., 1970, followed by further visits to USA and Canada to appear with major orchs; holds master classes in many US univs, major music schs in Japan and Internat. Mozart Acad., Prague; plays regularly in Hungary following return in 1973; overseas tours to Australia, NZ, S America, S Africa, Middle and Far East; many performances for BBC, incl. Berg and Bartók concertos, with Boulez. As conductor/soloist, has worked with the English, Scottish and Franz Liszt chamber orchs and London Mozart Players; guest dir, Acad. of St Martin-in-the-Fields. Has made many recordings including: Bartok Sonatas (among top records in US, 1982), and Bartok's music for solo violin, with piano, and for two violins; Tippett Concerto (Best Gramophone Record Award, 1983); Berg Concerto (Caecilia Prize, Belgium, 1983); complete sonatas for violin and harpsichord by Handel; all violin concertos and orch. works by Mozart; Brahms Sonatas. With Peter Frankl and Ralph Kirshbaum, formed chamber music trio, 1973; performances at major fests; public concerts in Gt Britain have incl. complete Brahms and Beethoven Cycles; the trio has also made many broadcasts for the BBC. First performances: Penderecki's Violin Concerto, Japan, 1979, UK, 1980; Tippett's Triple Concerto, London, 1980; Lutosawski's Chain 2, with composer conducting, Britain, The Netherlands and Hungary, 1986–87; Sir Peter Maxwell Davies' Violin Concerto, Switzerland, 1988; William Mathias' Violin Concerto, Manchester, 1991. Hon. GSM, 1980. *Address:* c/o Tennant Artists, 39 Tadema Road, SW10 0PY.

PAUL, Alan Roderick; HM Diplomatic Service; Counsellor and Deputy Senior Representative, Joint Liaison Group, Hong Kong, since 1991; *b* 13 May 1950; *s* of late Roderick Ernest Paul and of Hilda May Paul (*née* Choules); *m* 1979, Rosana Yuen Ling Tam; one *s* one *d*. *Educ:* Wallington High Sch. for Boys; Christ Church, Oxford (Scholar; MA Modern Langs, 1st class Hons). FCO, 1972–73; language training, Univs of Cambridge and Hong Kong, 1973–75; FCO, 1975–77; Peking, 1977–80; FCO, 1980–84; Head of Chancery, The Hague, 1984–87; Asst Head, 1987–89, Head, 1989–91, Hong Kong Dept, FCO. *Recreations:* gardening, genealogy, philately, music. *Address:* c/o Foreign and Commonwealth Office, King Charles Street, SW1A 2AH.

PAUL, Geoffrey David, OBE 1991; United States Affairs Editor, Jewish Chronicle, since 1991; *b* 26 March 1929; *s* of Reuben Goldstein and Anne Goldstein; *m* 1st, 1952, Joy Stirling (marr. diss. 1972); one *d*; 2nd, 1974, Rachel Mann; one *s*. *Educ:* Liverpool, Kendal, Dublin. Weekly newspaper and news agency reporter, 1947–57; asst editor, Jewish Observer and Middle East Review, 1957–62; Jewish Chronicle, 1962–: successively sub-editor, foreign editor, Israel corresp., deputy editor; Editor, 1977–90. *Publication:* Living in Jerusalem, 1981. *Address:* 130 Dwight Place, Englewood, NJ 07631, USA. *T:* (201) 8941490.

PAUL, George William; DL; Chairman: Norwich Union, since 1994; Harrisons & Crosfield, since 1994; *b* 25 Feb. 1940; *s* of William Stuart Hamilton Paul and Diana Violet Anne Martin; *m* 1st, 1963, Mary Annette Mitchell (*d* 1989); two *s* one *d*; 2nd, Margaret J. Kilgour (*née* Hedges). *Educ:* Harrow; Wye Coll., Univ. of London (BSc Agric Hons). Pauls & Whites Foods: Marketing Dir, 1968; Managing Dir, 1972; Pauls & Whites: Dir, 1972; Group Managing Dir, 1982; Chm., Pauls, 1985; Harrisons & Crosfield: Dir, 1985; Jt Chief Exec., 1986; Chief Exec., 1987–94; Dir, 1990–, Vice-Chm., 1992–94, Norwich Union. Mem., Jockey Club; Chm., Jockey Club Estates Ltd, 1991–. High Sheriff, Suffolk, 1990, DL Suffolk, 1991. *Recreations:* theatre, country sports, sailing. *Address:* Bluegates, Wherstead, Ipswich, Suffolk IP9 2AU. *T:* Copdock (01473) 730274. *Clubs:* Boodle's, Farmers'.

PAUL, Air Cdre Gerard John Christopher, CB 1956; DFC 1944; MA; FRAeS; *b* 31 Oct. 1907; *s* of E. W. Paul, FRCS; *m* 1st, 1937, Rosemary (*d* 1975), *d* of Rear-Admiral H. G. E. Lane, CB; two *s* one *d*; 2nd, 1987, Mollie Denise Samuels, *d* of Joseph Samuels, MM. *Educ:* Cheltenham Coll.; St John's Coll., Cambridge. Entered Royal Air Force, 1929; Fleet Air Arm, 1931–36; served War of 1939–45 in England and N.W. Europe; Commandant, Central Flying School, 1954–56; retired, 1958. Secretary-General of the Air League, 1958–71. Life Vice-Pres., RAF Gliding and Soaring Assoc.; Pres., Popular Flying Assoc., 1969–78. Croix de Guerre avec Palme (Belgium), 1944; Military Cross (Czechoslovakia), 1945. *Recreations:* dogs, garden. *Address:* Wearne House, Old Alresford, Hants SO24 9DH. *Club:* Royal Air Force.

PAUL, Hugh Glencairn B.; *see* Balfour-Paul.

PAUL, Rev. Canon John Douglas; Dean of Moray, Ross and Caithness, 1991–92; *b* 13 Sept. 1928; *s* of George Anson Moncreiff Paul and Vivian (*née* Ward); *m* 1969, Mary Susan Melody Woodhouse. *Educ:* Winchester Coll.; Edinburgh Univ. (MA); Ely Theol Coll. Asst Curate, Portsmouth, 1954–56; Missionary Priest, Mozambique, 1956–70; Archdeacon, Mozambique, 1965–70; Rector: Castle Douglas, 1970–75; Portobello, 1975–80; Holy Trinity, Elgin, with St Margaret's, Lossiemouth, 1980–92. Hon. Canon and Synod Clerk, Dio. of Moray, Ross and Caithness, 1989–91; Hon. Canon, St Andrew's Cathedral, Inverness, 1992–. *Publication:* Mozambique: Memoirs of a Revolution, 1975. *Recreation:* travel. *Address:* 2 The Avenue, Gifford EH41 4QX. *T:* Gifford (01620) 810547.

PAUL, Sir John (Warburton), GCMG 1965 (KCMG 1962); OBE 1959; MC 1940; Lieutenant Governor, Isle of Man, 1974–80; *b* 29 March 1916; 2nd *s* of Walter George Paul and Phoebe (*née* Bull), Weymouth; *m* 1946, Kathleen Audrey, CStJ 1962, *d* of Dr A. D. Weeden, Weymouth; three *d. Educ:* Weymouth Coll., Dorset; Selwyn Coll., Cambridge (MA; Hon. Fellow, 1982). Secretary, Maddermarket Theatre, Norwich, 1936. Commissioned Royal Tank Regt (Suppl. Res.), 1937; regular commission, RTR, 1938; BEF 1940 (despatches, prisoner-of-war); ADC and Private Secretary to Governor of Sierra Leone, 1945 (seconded). Called to the Bar, Inner Temple, 1947. Colonial Administrative Service, Sierra Leone, 1947; District Commissioner, 1952; Permanent Secretary, 1956; Provincial Commissioner, 1959; Secretary to the Cabinet, 1960; Governor and C-in-C, The Gambia, 1962–65; Governor-General of The Gambia, 1965–66; Governor and C-in-C: British Honduras, 1966–72; The Bahamas, 1972–73; Governor-General, The Bahamas, July–Oct. 1973. Dir, Overseas Relns, St John Ambulance, 1981–89. Member Board, West African Airways Corporation, 1954–56. Chm., St Christopher Motorists' Security Assoc., and associated cos, 1980–93. A Patron, Pain Relief Foundn, 1980–. Mem., Bd of Governors, Pangbourne Coll., 1981–86. KStJ 1962 (Member: Chapter-Gen., 1981–91; St John Council, Hants, 1990–). *Recreation:* painting. *Address:* Sherrens Mead, Sherfield-on-Loddon, Hampshire RG27 0ED. *Clubs:* Athenæum, MCC; Hawks (Cambridge).

PAUL, Noël Strange, CBE 1978; Director, Press Council, 1976–79 (Assistant Secretary, 1964, Secretary, 1968–76), retired; *b* 1914; *y s* of late S. Evan Paul, SSC, and Susan, *d* of Dr Henry Habgood; *m* 1950, Mary, *yr d* of Philip J. Bone, FRSA, MRST, Luton. *Educ:* Kingston Grammar School. Journalist, Press Assoc., 1932; served War of 1939–45, Iran and Italy, Major seconded RAF (despatches). Home Counties Newspapers, 1949; Liverpool Daily Post, 1958. Mem., Steering Cttee on the Mass Media, Council of Europe, 1976–82; Governor, English-Speaking Union, 1980–82. *Publications:* Self-regulation of the Press, 1982; Principles for the Press, 1985. *Recreations:* sailing, photography. *Address:* The Lodge, St Catherine's, Strachur, Argyllshire PA25 8AZ. *T:* Inveraray (01499) 302208.

PAUL, Robert Cameron, FEng 1990; Chief Executive, Albright & Wilson plc, since 1995; *b* 7 July 1935; *m* 1965, Diana Kathleen Bruce; two *d. Educ:* Rugby Sch.; Corpus Christi Coll., Cambridge (MEng). Nat. Service, 2nd Lieut RE, 1953–55. Chemical Engineer, ICI, Runcorn, 1959; Dir, ICI Fibres, 1976; Dep. Chm., Mond Div., ICI, 1979; Dep. Chm. and Man. Dir, Albright & Wilson, 1986–95. Non-Exec. Dir, Courtaulds plc, 1994–. Pres., IChemE, 1990–91. Hon DEng Birmingham, 1990. *Recreations:* music (piano), golf. *Address:* Albright & Wilson, 210–222 Hagley Road West, Oldbury, Warley, West Midlands B68 0NN. *T:* 0121–429 4942. *Clubs:* Oriental; Royal Wimbledon Golf.

PAUL, Roderick Sayers; Chief Executive, Severn Trent Water, 1988–95; *b* 22 April 1935; *s* of late Dr Robert Andrew Patrick Paul and Dr Margaret Louisa Paul; *m* 1965, Ann Broadway; one *s* one *d. Educ:* Wellington College; St Edmund Hall, Oxford (MA Jurisp.). Glynwed plc, 1962; British Oxygen, 1969; British Oxygen, S Africa, 1977; Mitchell Cotts, 1984–88, Chief Exec., 1986–88. *Recreations:* model making, boating, golf. *Address:* Church Cottage, Lower Quinton, Stratford-upon-Avon CV37 8SH.

PAUL, Air Marshal Sir Ronald Ian S.; *see* Stuart-Paul.

PAUL, Swraj; Padma Bhushan; Chairman: Caparo Group Ltd, since 1978; Caparo Industries Plc, since 1981; Caparo Inc., USA, since 1988; Armstrong Equipment Ltd, since 1989; CREMSA, Spain, since 1989; ENSA, Spain, since 1989; *b* 18 Feb. 1931; *s* of Payare and Mongwati Paul; *m* 1956, Aruna Vij; three *s* one *d* (and one *d* decd). *Educ:* Punjab Univ. (BSc); Mass Inst. of Technol. (BSc, MSc (Mech. Engrg)). Began work as Partner in family-owned Apeejay Surrendra Gp, India, 1953; came to UK in 1966 and estabd first business, Natural Gas Tubes Ltd; Caparo Group Ltd formed in 1978 as holding co. for UK businesses involved in engrg, hotel and property develt, investment; Caparo Industries Plc (engrg, metals) formed in 1981. Founder Chm., Indo-British Assoc., 1975–. FRSA. Padma Bhushan (equivalent to British Peerage), 1983. Hon. PhD Amer. Coll. of Switzerland, Leysin, 1986; Hon. DSc (Econ) Hull, 1992. Corporate Leadership Award, MIT, 1987. *Publication:* Indira Gandhi, 1984, 2nd edn 1985. *Address:* Caparo House, 103 Baker Street, W1M 1FD. *T:* 0171–486 1417. *Clubs:* MCC, Royal Automobile; Royal Calcutta Turf, Royal Calcutta Golf (Calcutta); Cricket of India (Bombay).

PAULET, family name of **Marquess of Winchester.**

PAULIN, Prof. Roger Cole, DrPhil, LittD; Schröder Professor of German, University of Cambridge, since 1989; Fellow, Trinity College, Cambridge since 1989; *b* 18 Dec. 1937; *s* of Thomas Gerald Paulin and Paulina (*née* Duff); *m* 1966, Traute Fielitz; one *s* one *d. Educ:* Otago Boys' High Sch., Dunedin, NZ; Univ. of Otago (MA); Heidelberg Univ. (DrPhil); MA, LittD (Cantab). Asst Lectr, Univ. of Birmingham, 1963–64; Lectr, Univ. of Bristol, 1965–73; Fellow and Coll. Lectr in German, Trinity Coll., Cambridge, 1974–87; Univ. Lectr, Univ. of Cambridge, 1975–87; Henry Simon Prof. of German, Univ. of Manchester, 1987–89. Mem., Editl Bd, Literatur-Lexikon, 1988–93. *Publications:* Ludwig Tieck: a literary biography, 1985, 2nd edn 1986 (trans. German, 1988); The Brief Compass, 1985; Ludwig Tieck, 1987; Theodor Storm, 1991. *Recreation:* gardening. *Address:* 45 Fulbrooke Road, Cambridge CB3 9EE. *T:* Cambridge (01223) 322564.

PAULIN, Thomas Neilson; poet and critic; G. M. Young Lecturer in English Literature, University of Oxford, since 1994; Fellow, Hertford College, Oxford, since 1994; *b* 25 Jan. 1949; *s* of Douglas and Mary Paulin; *m* 1973, Munjiet Kaur Khosa; two *s. Educ:* Hull Univ. (BA); Lincoln Coll., Oxford (BLitt). English Department, University of Nottingham: Lectr, 1972–89; Reader in Poetry, 1989–94. Hon. DLitt Saskatchewan, 1987. *Publications:* Thomas Hardy: the poetry of perception, 1975; A State of Justice, 1977; The Strange Museum, 1980; Liberty Tree, 1983; The Riot Act, 1985; Ireland and the English Crisis, 1985; The Faber Book of Political Verse, 1986; The Hillsborough Script, 1987; Fivemiletown, 1987; Seize the Fire, 1989; The Faber Book of Vernacular Verse, 1990; Minotaur: poetry and the nation state, 1992; Walking a Line, 1994. *Address:* c/o Faber & Faber, 3 Queen Square, WC1N 3AU.

PAULUSZ, Jan Gilbert; a Recorder of the Crown Court, since 1980; *b* 18 Nov. 1929; *s* of Jan Hendrik Olivier Paulusz and Edith (*née* Gilbert); *m* 1973, Luigia Maria Attanasio. *Educ:* The Leys Sch., Cambridge. Called to the Bar, Lincoln's Inn, 1957; South Eastern Circuit, 1959–. *Recreations:* mountain walking, photography. *Address:* 50 Royston Gardens, Redbridge, Ilford, Essex IG1 3SY.

PAUNCEFORT, Bernard Edward, OBE 1983; HM Diplomatic Service, retired 1986; Administrator, Tristan da Cunha, South Atlantic, 1989–92; *b* 8 April 1926; *o s* of Frederick George Pauncefort and Eleanor May (*née* Jux); *m* 1956, Patricia Anne, *yr d* of Charles Ernest Leah and Alice (*née* Kendal-Banks). *Educ:* Wandsworth School. RAFVR 1942–44; Royal Fusiliers, 1944–48. Metropolitan Police Civil Staff, 1948–53; HM Colonial Service, 1953; Malaya, 1953–56; Tanganyika, 1956–63; CRO, 1963–67; First Sec., Zambia, 1967–68; Consul, Cape Town, 1969–72; Lord Pearce's staff, Rhodesia, 1971–72; Head of Chancery, Madagascar, 1972–73; FCO, 1973–76; Sec. to Seychelles Electoral Review Commn, 1976; Head of Chancery, Burma, 1976–78; Dir, British Inf. Services, S Africa, 1978–80; Lord Soames' staff, Rhodesia-Zimbabwe, 1979–80; Administrator, Ascension Island, 1980–82; FCO, 1982–83; Counsellor and Chief Sec., Falkland Is, 1983–85; Counsellor, FCO, 1985–86; Under-Sec., Govt of the Turks & Caicos Is. W Indies, 1986–88. Zimbabwe Medal, 1980. *Recreations:* dogs, showing and breeding; birds, waterways. *Address:* 10 New Church Road, Uphill, Weston-super-Mare, Avon BS23 4UY.

PAUNCEFORT-DUNCOMBE, Sir Philip; *see* Duncombe.

PAVAROTTI, Luciano; Italian tenor; *b* 12 Oct. 1935; *s* of Fernando Pavarotti and Adele (*née* Venturi); *m* 1961, Adua Veroni; three *d. Educ:* Istituto Magistrale. Teacher, 1955–57. Professional début, Teatro Municipale, Reggio Emilia, 1961; sang throughout Europe, 1961–64; US début and Australian tour 1965; rôles include Rodolfo in La Bohème, Cavaradossi in Tosca, Duke of Mantua in Rigoletto, Radames in Aïda, Ernani, Alfredo in La Traviata, Manrico in Il Trovatore, Rodolfo in Luisa Miller, Arturo in I Puritani, Elvino in La Sonnambula, Nemorino in L'Elisir d'Amore, Idomeneo, Enzo in La Gioconda, Riccardo (Gustavo) in Un Ballo in Maschera, Don Carlos, etc. Chevalier des Grieux in Manon. Grammy Award for best classical vocal soloist, 1978, 1979, 1981, 1988, 1990. *Publications:* (jtly) Pavarotti: my own story, 1981; Grandissimo Pavarotti, 1986. *Address:* c/o Herbert Breslin, 119 West 57th Street, New York, NY 10019, USA.

PAVEY, Martin Christopher; educational consultant; *b* 2 Dec. 1940; *s* of Archibald Lindsay Pavey and Margaret Alice Pavey (*née* Salsbury); *m* 1969, Louise Margaret (*née* Bird); two *s. Educ:* Magdalen College Sch., Oxford; University Coll., London (Hons English); Nottingham Univ. (MA English); Univ. of Cambridge (Dip. Educn). Wigglesworth & Co., London and E. Africa (Shipping and Finance), 1956–62; Assistant Master: King's Sch., Ely, 1962–64; Lancing Coll., 1968–71; Fairham Comprehensive School, Nottingham: Head of English, 1971–75; Dep. Headmaster, 1975–76; Headmaster, 1976–81; Headmaster: Cranbrook School, 1981–88; Latymer Upper School, Hammersmith, 1988–91. *Recreations:* art architecture, cinema. *Address:* 5 Vineyards, Bath, Avon BA1 5NA.

PAVORD, Anna, (Mrs T. D. O. Ware); Gardening Correspondent, The Independent, since 1986; *b* 1940; *d* of Arthur Vincent Pavord and Christabel Frances (*née* Lewis); *m* 1966, Trevor David Oliver Ware; three *d. Educ:* Univ. of Leicester (BA Hons English). PA/Dir, Line Up, BBC2, 1963–70; contributor, Observer Mag., 1970–92; writer and presenter, Flowering Passions, Channel 4 TV, 1991–92. Associate Editor, Gardens Illustrated, 1993–. *Publications:* Foliage, 1990; The Flowering Year, 1991; Gardening Companion, 1992; Hidcote, 1993; The Border Book, 1994. *Recreations:* sailing, walking, gardening, visiting Dominica. *Address:* c/o The Independent, 1 Canada Square, Canary Wharf, E14 5AP. *T:* 0171–293 3000.

PAWLEY, Prof. Godfrey Stuart, PhD; FRS 1992; FRSE; Professor of Computational Physics, University of Edinburgh, since 1985; *b* 22 June 1937; *s* of George Charles Pawley and Winifred Mary (*née* Wardle); *m* 1961, Anthea Jean Miller; two *s* one *d. Educ:* Bolton Sch.; Corpus Christi Coll., Cambridge (MA, PhD 1962). Chem. Dept, Harvard Univ., 1962–64; University of Edinburgh: Lect, 1964–69; Reader, 1970–85. Guest Prof., Chem. Dept, Århus Univ., Denmark, 1969–70. Principal Investigator, Colloidal Hydrodynamics Computational Grand Challenge. FRSE 1975. *Publications:* (contrib.) An Introduction to OCCAM 2 programming, 2nd edn, 1989; numerous scientific papers. *Recreations:* choral singing, mountain walking. *Address:* 26 Relugas Road, Edinburgh EH9 2ND. *T:* 0131–667 2122.

PAWLEY, Robert John; Head of Profession, Valuation Office Agency, since 1995; *b* 10 Sept. 1939; *s* of Frederick Clifford and Marjorie Pawley; *m* 1965, Simone Elizabeth Tayar; two *s. Educ:* Plymouth Coll.; Exeter Univ. (BA). FRICS. Private practice, Plymouth, 1962–71; joined Valuation Office, 1972; Dist Valuer, Waltham Forest, 1977, Haringey, 1978–81; Suptg Valuer, Chief Valuer's Office, London, 1981–84, Cambridge, 1984–87; Asst Chief Valuer, 1987–88; Dep. Chief Valuer, Inland Revenue Valuation Office, later Dep. Chief Exec. (Technical), Valuation Office Agency, 1989–95. *Recreations:* 18th century English naval history and exploration, period model boats, antiques. *Address:* Chief Executive's Office, Valuation Office Agency, New Court, Carey Street, WC2A 2JE. *T:* 0171–324 1154.

PAWSEY, James Francis; MP (C) Rugby and Kenilworth, since 1983 (Rugby, 1979–83); *b* 21 Aug. 1933; *s* of William Pawsey and Mary Mumford; *m* 1956, Cynthia Margaret Francis; six *s* (including twins twice). *Educ:* Coventry Tech. School; Coventry Tech. Coll. Director: (non-exec.) Autobar Group Ltd, 1983–; St Martins Hosps Ltd, 1989–; Ranelagh Ltd, 1992–. Parliamentary Private Secretary: DES, 1982–83; DHSS, 1983–84; to Minister of State for NI, 1984–86. Member: Parly Scientific Cttee, 1982–; Select Cttee of Parly Comr for Admin, 1983– (Chm., 1993); Select Cttee on Standing Orders, 1987–; Exec., 1922 Cttee, 1989–; Liaison Cttee, 1993–; Ct of Referees, 1993–; Chm., Cons Parly Educn Cttee, 1985–; Mem. Exec., IPU, 1984–; Sec., Cons. Back Bench Social Services and Educn Cttees, 1982–83; Chm., W Midlands Gp of Cons. MPs, 1993–. Member: Rugby RDC, 1965–73; Rugby Borough Council, 1973–75; Warwickshire CC, 1974–79; former Chm. and Pres., Warwickshire Assoc. of Parish Councils. MInstD. KLJ. *Publication:* The Tringo Phenomenon, 1983. *Address:* Rugby and Kenilworth Conservative Association, Albert Buildings, Albert Street, Rugby CV21 5RS. *T:* Rugby (01788) 569556.

PAWSON, Prof. Anthony James, PhD; FRS 1994; FRSC 1994; Senior Scientist, Samuel Lunenfeld Research Institute, Mount Sinai Hospital, Toronto, since 1985; Professor, Department of Molecular and Medical Genetics, University of Toronto, since 1985; *b* 18 Oct. 1952; *s* of Henry Anthony Pawson, OBE and Hilarie Anne Pawson (*née* Bassett); *m* 1975, Margaret Anne Luman; two *s* one *d. Educ:* Clare Coll., Cambridge (BA); London Univ. (PhD). Grad. Student, ICRF, London, 1973–76; Postdoctoral Fellow, Univ. of Calif, Berkeley, 1976–80; Asst Prof., Univ. of BC, 1981–85. Terry Fox Cancer Res. Scientist, Nat. Cancer Inst. of Canada, 1988–; Internat. Res. Schol., Howard Hughes Med. Inst., 1991–; Apotex Prof. of Molecular Oncology, Mt Sinai Hosp., 1991–. Gairdner Foundn Internat. Award, 1994. *Publications:* papers in Nature, Cell, Science, Molecular and Cell Biol., Proc. Nat. Acad. of Sci. (USA), Jl Virology, EMBO Jl, Jl Biol Chem., Oncogene and other learned jls. *Recreations:* reading, theatre, fly-fishing, ski-ing, baseball. *Address:* Samuel Lunenfeld Research Institute, Mount Sinai Hospital, 600 University Avenue, Toronto, Ont M5G 1X5, Canada. *T:* (416) 5868262; 34 Glenwood Avenue, Toronto, Ont M6P 3C6, Canada. *T:* (416) 7632266.

PAWSON, Anthony John Dalby; Assistant Under-Secretary of State (Fleet Support), Ministry of Defence, since 1993; *b* 14 Oct. 1946; *s* of Donald Pawson and Kathleen (*née* Goodwin); *m* 1969, Kathleen Chisholm; one *s* one *d. Educ:* Kent Coll., Canterbury; City Univ. (BSc 1st Class Hons Computer Science). MoD 1967; Private Sec. to Chief of Air Staff, 1978–80; First Sec., UK Delgn to NATO, Brussels, 1981–83; Private Sec. to Sec. of

State for NI, 1990–92; RCDS 1992. *Recreations:* Rugby, cricket. *Address:* Ministry of Defence, Main Building, Whitehall, SW1A 2HB. *Clubs:* Civil Service; Tunbridge Wells RFC.

PAXMAN, Jeremy Dickson; journalist, author and broadcaster; *b* 11 May 1950; *s* of Arthur Keith Paxman and Joan McKay Dickson. *Educ:* Malvern College; St Catharine's College, Cambridge (Exhibnr). Reporter: N Ireland, 1974–77; BBC TV Tonight, 1977–79; Panorama, 1979–85; The Bear Next Door; presenter: Breakfast Time, 1986–89; Newsnight, 1989–; Did You See?, 1991–93; You Decide—with Paxman, 1995; Chm., University Challenge, 1994–. Award for Internat. Current Affairs, RTS, 1985. *Publications:* (jtly) A Higher Form of Killing: the secret story of gas and germ warfare, 1982; Through the Volcanoes: a Central American journey, 1985; Friends in High Places: who runs Britain?, 1990; Fish, Fishing and the Meaning of Life, 1994. *Recreations:* fishing, ski-ing, snoozing. *Address:* c/o BBC TV, W12 7RJ.

PAXMAN, Timothy Giles, LVO 1989; HM Diplomatic Service; Counsellor (Economic and Commercial), Rome, since 1994; *b* 15 Nov. 1951; *s* of Arthur Keith Paxman and Joan McKay Paxman (*née* Dickson); *m* 1980, Segolene Claude Marie Cayol; three *d*. *Educ:* Malvern Coll.; New Coll., Oxford. DoE, 1974–76; Dept of Transport, 1976–78; Ecole Nat. d'Admin, Paris, 1978–79; joined FCO, 1980: 1st Secretary: UK Perm. Rep. to EC, 1980–84; FCO, 1984–88; Head of Chancery, Singapore, 1988–92; on secondment to Cabinet Office, 1992–94. *Recreations:* tennis, ski-ing, jazz and blues music, cinema. *Address:* c/o Foreign and Commonwealth Office, King Charles Street, SW1A 2AH.

See also J. D. Paxman.

PAXTON, John; author, also writing as Jack Cherrill; Editor, The Statesman's Year-Book, 1969–90; *b* 23 Aug. 1923; *m* 1950, Joan Thorne; one *s* one *d*. Head of Economics department, Millfield, 1952–63. Joined The Statesman's Year-Book, 1963, Dep. Ed., 1968; Consultant Editor, The New Illustrated Everyman's Encyclopaedia, 1981–84. Jt Treas., English Centre, Internat. PEN, 1973–78; Chm., West Country Writers' Assoc., 1993–95. *Publications:* (with A. E. Walsh) Trade in the Common Market Countries, 1965; (with A. E. Walsh) The Structure and Development of the Common Market, 1968; (with A. E. Walsh) Trade and Industrial Resources of the Common Market and Efta Countries, 1970; (with John Wroughton) Smuggling, 1971; (with A. E. Walsh) Into Europe, 1972; (ed) Everyman's Dictionary of Abbreviations, 1974, 2nd edn 1986, as Penguin Dictionary of Abbreviations, 1989; World Legislatures, 1974; (with C. Cook) European Political Facts 1789–1990, 3 vols, 1975–92; The Statesman's Year-Book World Gazetteer, 1975, 4th edn, 1991; (with A. E. Walsh) Competition Policy: European and International Trends and Practices, 1975; The Developing Common Market, 1976; A Dictionary of the European Economic Community, 1977, 2nd edn, A Dictionary of the European Communities, 1982 (commended, McColvin Medal Cttee); (with C. Cook) Commonwealth Political Facts, 1979; (with S. Fairfield) Calendar of Creative Man, 1980; Companion to Russian History, 1984, 2nd edn as Encyclopedia of Russian History, 1993; Companion to the French Revolution, 1988; The Statesman's Year-Book Historical Companion, 1988; (with G. Payton) Penguin Dictionary of Proper Names, 1991; European Communities (a bibliography), 1992; Longman Companion to Imperial Russia, 1995; contrib. to Keesing's Contemporary Archives, TLS. *Address:* Moss Cottage, Hardway, Bruton, Somerset BA10 0LN. *T:* Bruton (01749) 813423. *Club:* PEN.

PAXTON, Peter James, FCIS; FCCA; FCIB; Chief Executive Officer, Cambridge and District Co-operative Society Ltd, 1972–86; *b* 27 April 1923; *m* 1st, 1947, Betty Jane Madden (marr. diss. 1980); one *s* one *d*; 2nd, 1985, Sylvia June Stock. *Educ:* Lawrence Sherriff Sch., Rugby. Served RAF, 1941–46. Accountant, Rugby Co-operative Society Ltd, 1949–55; Chief Accountant, Cambridge and District Co-operative Society Ltd, 1955; Chairman: CWS, 1980–86; Co-operative Bank, 1980–86; First Co-op. Finance, 1980–86; Co-op. City Investments, 1983–86; Dep. Chm., Co-op. Insce Soc., 1983–86. *Address:* Harvest Home, 37 Green End, Fen Ditton, Cambridge CB5 8SX.

PAXTON, (Peter) Robin; Managing Director, London Weekend Television Broadcasting Ltd, 1993–94; *b* 14 April 1951; *s* of late Richard Gordon Paxton and of Marion Paxton; *m* 1987, Linda Jane French; two *s*. *Educ:* Leighton Park Sch.; Sussex Univ. (BA Hons); LSE (MScEcon); Nuffield Coll., Oxford. London Weekend Television: joined 1977; producer and programme editor, current affairs, 1977–85; Head, Network Features, 1985–87; Editor, The London Programme, 1987; Head, Regl Progs, 1987–90; Controller, Factual Progs, 1990–93. *Address:* 60 Burnt Ash Road, SE12 8PY. *T:* 0181–318 0935.

PAYE, Jean-Claude; Chevalier de la Légion d'Honneur; Officier de l'Ordre National du Mérite; Chevalier de l'Ordre National du Mérite agricole; Croix de la Valeur militaire; Secretary-General, OECD, 1984–May 1996; *b* 26 Aug. 1934; *s* of late Lucien Paye and of Suzanne Paye (*née* Guignard); *m* 1963, Laurence Hélène Marianne Jeanneney; two *s* two *d*. *Educ:* Lycée Bugeaud, Algiers; Lycée Carnot, Tunis; Faculté de droit, Tunis; Institut d'Etudes Politiques, Paris; Ecole Nationale d'Administration. Government service, 1961–64; Technical Adviser to: Sec. of State for Scientific Research, 1965; Minister of Social Affairs, 1966; Chief Adviser to Vice-Pres., EEC, 1967–73; Adviser, Embassy, Bonn, 1973; Asst Principal Private Sec. to Minister of Foreign Affairs, 1974–76; Diplomatic Advr to Prime Minister, 1976–79; Head of Economic and Financial Affairs, Ministry of Foreign Affairs, 1979–84; Pres., Exec. Cttee in special Session, OECD, 1979–84. *Address:* (until June 1996) OECD, 2 rue André-Pascal, 75775 Paris cedex 16, France; (from June 1996) 1 Place A. Deville, 75006 Paris, France.

PAYKEL, Prof. Eugene Stern, FRCP; FRCPE; FRCPsych; Professor of Psychiatry and Head of Department, University of Cambridge, since 1985; Professorial Fellow, Gonville and Caius College, Cambridge, since 1985; *b* 9 Sept. 1934; *s* of late Joshua Paykel and Eva Stern Paykel; *m* 1969, Margaret, *d* of late John Melrose and Joan Melrose; two *s*. *Educ:* Auckland Grammar Sch.; Univ. of Otago (MB ChB, MD; Stuart Prize, Joseph Pullar Schol., 1956); DPM London. Maudsley Hosp., 1962–65; Asst Prof. of Psychiatry and Co-Dir/Dir, Depression Res. Unit, Yale Univ., 1966–71; Consultant and Sen. Lectr, 1971–75, Reader, 1975–77, Prof. of Psychiatry, 1977–85, St George's Hosp. Med. Sch., Univ. of London. Chief Scientist's Adviser and Mem., Mental Illness Res. Liaison Gp, DHSS, 1984–88; Chm., Jt Cttee on Higher Psychiatric Trng, 1990–95. Previously examiner Univs of Edinburgh, Nottingham, Manchester, London, and RCPsych. Mem., Neurosciences Bd, MRC, 1981–85, 1995–. Mem., Bethlem Royal and Maudsley Hosp. SHA, 1990–94. Vice Pres., RCPsych, 1994–96 (Chm., Social and Community Psych. Sect., 1984–88); Mem. Bd and Chm., Pharmaco-psychiatry Sec., World Psychiatric Assoc., 1993–; Hon. Mem., British Assoc. for Psychopharmacology (Pres., 1982–84); Pres., Marce Soc., 1992–94. Trustee, Mental Health Foundn, 1988–. Foundations Fund Prize for Res. in Psychiatry, 1978; BMA Film Competition Bronze Award, 1981; Anna Monika Stiftung 2nd Prize, 1985. Jt Editor, Jl of Affective Disorders, 1979–93; Editor, Psychological Medicine, 1994–; Member, Editorial Board: Social Psychiatry; Psychopharmacology; Jl of Psychosomatic Research; Acta Psychiatrica Belgica. *Publications:* The Depressed Woman, 1974; Psychopharmacology of Affective Disorders, 1979; Monoamine Oxidase Inhibitors: the state of the art, 1981; Handbook of Affective Disorders, 1982, 2nd edn 1992; Community Psychiatric Nursing for Neurotic Patients, 1983; papers on depression, psychopharmacology, social psychiatry, life events, evaluation of treatment. *Recreations:* opera, music, theatre. *Address:* Department of Psychiatry, University of Cambridge, Addenbrooke's Hospital, Hills Road, Cambridge CB2 2QQ. *T:* Cambridge (01223) 336961.

PAYNE, Alan Jeffrey, CMG 1988; HM Diplomatic Service, retired; Secretary General, International Primary Aluminium Institute, since 1989; *b* 11 May 1933; *s* of Sydney Ellis Payne and Lydia Payne; *m* 1959, Letitia Freeman; three *s*. *Educ:* Enfield Grammar Sch.; Queens' Coll., Cambridge (Exhibnr). FIL 1962. RN, 1955–57. EMI, London, later Paris, 1957–62; Secretariat, NATO, Paris, 1962–64; joined Diplomatic Service, 1965; Commonwealth Relations Office (later FCO), 1965–67; British High Commn, Kuala Lumpur, 1967–70; FCO, 1970–72; British Embassy, Budapest, 1972–75; Counsellor, Mexico City, 1975–79; FCO, 1979–82; Consul-General, Lyons, 1982–87; High Comr, Jamaica, and Ambassador (non-resident) to Haiti, 1987–89. *Recreations:* music, theatre, restoring old cars. *Clubs:* Royal Automobile; Liphook Golf.

PAYNE, Arthur Stanley, OBE 1977; HM Diplomatic Service, retired; Director, then Chief Executive, Southern Africa Association, 1988–92; *b* 17 Nov. 1930; *s* of late Arthur and Lilian Gertrude Payne; *m* 1964, Heather Elizabeth Cavaghan; one *d*. *Educ:* Chatham Tech. Sch.; Gillingham Grammar Sch.; Nat. Defence Coll. HM Forces, 1949–50. Joined BoT, 1949; Raw Materials Dept, Washington, 1951–52; Min. of Materials, London, 1953–55; British Trade Commns, New Delhi, Bombay, Port of Spain, and Georgetown (First Sec.), 1956–67; joined HM Diplomatic Service, 1965; First Sec. (Inf.), Auckland, 1967–70; FCO, 1971–74; Dacca, 1974–76; Bonn, 1976–78; FCO, 1978–79; Dep. High Comr and Head of Chancery, Gabarone, 1980–83; Counsellor and Hd of Commercial Dept, Manila, 1983–87. Hon. Consultant, UK Southern Africa Business Assoc., 1993–95. *Recreations:* bridge, music, computing, cooking. *Address:* Hoders Gate, Woodhurst Park, Oxted, Surrey, RH8 9HA.

PAYNE, Prof. Christopher Charles; Chief Executive, Horticulture Research International, since 1990; *b* 15 May 1946; *s* of Rupert George Payne and Evelyn Violet (*née* Abbott); *m* 1969, Margaret Susan Street; one *s* one *d*. *Educ:* Wadham Coll., Oxford (MA, DPhil). CBiol, MIBiol, FIBiol 1995; FIHort. Post-Doctoral Fellow, Univ. of Otago, NZ, 1972; SSO, NERC, Oxford, 1973–77; PSO, 1977–83, Head, Entomology Dept, 1983–86, Glasshouse Crops Res. Inst., Littlehampton; Head, Crop Protection Div., Inst. of Horticultural Res., E Malling, 1987–90. Hon. Prof., Univ. of Warwick, 1991–. Editor in Chief, Biocontrol Science and Technology, 1991–. *Publications:* (with R. Hull and F. Brown) Virology: directory and dictionary of animal, bacterial and plant viruses, 1989; numerous contribs to books and learned jls. *Recreations:* gardening, walking, cycling. *Address:* 25 Chapel Street, Wellesbourne, Warwick CV35 9QU. *T:* Stratford-upon-Avon (01789) 842562. *Club:* Farmers'.

PAYNE, Christopher Frederick, CBE 1987; QPM 1975; DL; Chief Constable of Cleveland Constabulary, 1976–90; *b* 15 Feb. 1930; *o s* of late Gerald Frederick Payne, OBE, BEM, QPM, and Amy Florence Elizabeth Payne (*née* Parker); *m* 1952, Barbara Janet Saxby; one *s* three *d*. *Educ:* Christ's Coll., Finchley; Hendon Technical Coll. CBIM 1987. Joined Metropolitan Police, 1950; Sen. Comd. course, 1965; Home Office R&D Br., 1968–70; Comdr 'X' Div., 1971–74; Comdr Airport Div., 1974–76. Dep. Chm., Metrop. Police Friendly Soc., 1971–76; Police Advr to ACCs' Social Services Cttee, 1979–90; Chm., Public Order Sub-Cttee, ACPO, 1981–88; Pres., Chief Constables' Club, 1989–90. Sen. Vis. Res. Fellow, Univ. of Bradford, 1991–. Adviser to: Chemical Hazards Unit, Qld Govt, 1989–90; UN Disaster Relief Org. External Services, 1990–; Emergency Planning Advr, BRCS, Cleveland, 1990–. County Dir, St John Ambulance, Cleveland, 1978–85; Comdr, SJAB, Cleveland, 1985–89; Chm., St John Council, Cleveland, 1986–89. Chm., Cleveland Mental Health Support Gp, 1981–86; Vice-Pres., Cleveland Youth Assoc., 1983–; Vice Chm., Royal Jubilee and Prince's Trusts Cttee for Durham and Cleveland, 1984–90. Freeman, City of London, 1988. DL Cleveland 1983. CStJ 1985 (OStJ 1980). *Publications:* various articles on contingency planning and management. *Recreations:* painting, philately, gardening. *Address:* c/o The Chief Constable's Office, PO Box 70, Ladgate Lane, Middlesbrough, Cleveland TS8 9EH. *Club:* Cleveland.

PAYNE, Prof. David Neil, FRS 1992; Deputy Director, Optoelectronics Research Centre, since 1989, and Pirelli Professor of Photonics, since 1991, University of Southampton; *b* 13 Aug. 1944; *s* of Raymond and Maisie Payne. *Educ:* Univ. of Southampton (BSc, PhD). Commissioning Engineer, English Electric Co., 1962; University of Southampton: Research Asst, 1969; Jun. Res. Fellow, 1971; Pirelli Res. Fellow, 1972, Sen. Res. Fellow, 1978, Principal Res. Fellow, 1981; Pirelli Reader, 1984. Fellow, Optical Soc. of America, 1995. Awards include: Rank Prize for Optoelectronics, 1991; IEEE/OSA John Tyndall Award, 1991; Computers and Communications Prize, Foundn for Computer and Communications Promotion in Japan, 1993. *Publications:* numerous contribs to learned jls. *Recreations:* squash, cooking, scuba diving, motorcycling, gardening. *Address:* Optoelectronics Research Centre, The University, Southampton SO17 1BJ. *T:* Southampton (01703) 593583.

PAYNE, Donald Hedley; Chief Executive, Willis Corroon, 1992–95; *b* 14 Nov. 1938; *s* of Norman Kingsley and Elizabeth Payne; *m* 1965, Leonore Maria Beatrice Skjoldebrand; one *s* one *d*. *Educ:* Christ's Hosp.; Durham Univ. (BSc Hons). ACII. Director: Bland Payne Ltd, 1965–79; Willis Faber PLC, 1979–90; Willis Corroon PLC, 1992–95. *Recreations:* travel, opera, ski-ing. *Address:* Latchmoor, Westerham Road, Limpsfield, Surrey RH8 0SW. *T:* Oxted (01883) 722122. *Club:* Royal Automobile.

PAYNE, (Geoffrey John) Nicholas; Director, The Royal Opera, Covent Garden, since 1993; *b* 4 Jan. 1945; *s* of John Laurence Payne and Dorothy Gwendoline Payne (*née* Attenborough); *m* 1986, Linda Jane Adamson; two *s*. *Educ:* Eton Coll. (King's Schol.); Trinity Coll., Cambridge (BA Eng Lit). Finance Assistant, Royal Opera House, 1968–70; Subsidy Officer, Arts Council, 1970–76; Financial Controller, Welsh National Opera, 1976–82; Gen. Adminr, Opera North, 1982–93. *Address:* Royal Opera House, Covent Garden, WC2E 7QA.

PAYNE, Henry Salusbury Legh D.; *see* Dalzell Payne.

PAYNE, Ian; barrister; *b* 15 July 1926; *s* of late Douglas Harold Payne and of Gertrude (*née* Buchanan); *m* 1st, 1951, Babette (marr. diss. 1975), *d* of late Comte Clarence de Chalus; four *s* two *d*; 2nd, 1977, Colette Eugénie, *d* of late Marinus Jacobus van der Eb, Rotterdam. *Educ:* Wellington Coll. Commnd 60th Rifles, 1944–48. Called to the Bar, Lincoln's Inn, 1953, Hong Kong, 1981; Dep. Recorder of Derby, 1969–72; a Recorder, 1972–81. *Address:* 2 Crown Office Row, Temple, EC4; 1415 Prince's Building, Central, Hong Kong. *T:* 5221778. *Clubs:* Garrick; Hong Kong; Refreshers Cricket.

PAYNE, Rev. James Richmond, MBE 1982; ThL; JP; General Secretary, Bible Society in Australia, 1968–88; Chairman, United Bible Societies World Executive Committee, 1976–88; *b* 1 June 1921; *s* of late R. A. Payne, Sydney, New South Wales; *m* 1943, Joan, *d* of late C. S. Elliott; three *s*. *Educ:* Drummoyne High School; Metropolitan Business College, Moore Theological College, Sydney. Served War of 1939–45: AIF, 1941–44. Catechist, St Michael's, Surry Hills, NSW, 1944–47; Curate, St Andrew's, Lismore, NSW,

1947–50; Rector, St Mark's, Nimbin, NSW, 1950–52; Chaplain, RAAF, Malta and Amberley, Qld, 1952–57; Rector, St Stephen's, Coorparoo, Qld, 1957–62; Dean of Perth, Western Australia, 1962–68. Hon. Commissary in Australia for Anglican Bp of Central Tanganyika, E Africa, 1988–. JP, ACT, 1969. *Publications:* Around the World in Seventy Days, 1965; And Now for the Good News, 1982. *Recreations:* sport, walking, reading, family. *Address:* 10/42 Jinka Street, Hawker, ACT 2614, Australia. *T:* (6) 2546722. *Club:* Commonwealth (Canberra).

PAYNE, Jane Marian, (Mrs A. E. Payne); *see* Manning, J. M.

PAYNE, Keith, VC 1969; *b* 30 Aug. 1933; *s* of Henry Thomas Payne and Remilda Payne (*née* Hussey); *m* 1954, Florence Catherine Payne (*née* Plaw); five *s*. *Educ:* State School, Ingham, North Queensland. Soldier, Department of Army, Aug. 1951–75; 1 RAR, Korea, 1952–53; 3 RAR, Malaya, 1963–65; Aust. Army Trng Team, Vietnam, 1969 (Warrant Officer; awarded VC after deliberately exposing himself to enemy fire while trying to cover his outnumbered men); WO Instructor: RMC, Duntroon, ACT, 1970–72; 42 Bn, Royal Qld Regt, Mackay, 1973–75; Captain, Oman Army, 1975–76. Member: VC and GC Assoc.; Legion of Valour, USA; Aust. Army Training Team Vietnam Assoc.; Life Member: Totally and Permanently Disabled Soldiers' Assoc. (Pres., Mackay Centre); Korea & SE Asia Forces Assoc.; Special Operations Assoc., USA; RSL (also Sarina Sub Br.). Patron, TRY-Sponsored Aust. Cadet Corp Units (Victoria). Freeman City of Brisbane and of Shire of Hinchinbrook. Vietnamese Cross of Gallantry, with bronze star, 1969; US Meritorious Unit Citation; Vietnamese Unit Citation Cross of Gallantry with Palm; DSC (US); SSM (US). *Recreations:* football, fishing, hunting. *Address:* 11 Canberra Street, North Mackay, Qld 4740, Australia. *T:* (79) 578497.

PAYNE, Leonard Sidney, CBE 1983; Director, J. Sainsbury Ltd, 1974–86; Adviser on Distribution and Retailing, Coopers & Lybrand, since 1986; *b* 16 Dec. 1925; *s* of Leonard Sydney Payne and Lillian May Leggatt; *m* 1944, Marjorie Vincent; two *s*. *Educ:* Woodhouse Grammar School. FCCA, CIMgt, FCIT. Asst Accountant, Peek Frean & Co. Ltd, 1949–52; Chief Accountant, Administrator of various factory units, head office appts, Philips Electrical Industries, 1952–62; Dep. Gp Comptroller, Morgan Crucible Co. Ltd, 1962–64; British Road Services Ltd: Finance Dir, 1964–67; Asst Man. Dir, 1967–69; Man. Dir, 1969–71; Dir of Techn. Services and Develt, Nat. Freight Corp., 1971–74, Vice-Chm. Executive 1974. President: Freight Transport Assoc., 1980–82; Chartered Inst. of Transport, 1983–84. Chm., CBI Transport Policy Cttee, 1980–86. *Recreations:* gardening, swimming, squash, chess. *Address:* Apartment 5, Evenholme, Green Walk, Bowdon, Altrincham, Cheshire WA14 2SL.

PAYNE, Nicholas; *see* Payne, G. J. N.

PAYNE, Sir Norman (John), Kt 1985; CBE 1976 (OBE 1956; MBE (mil.) 1944); FEng; Chairman, BAA plc (formerly British Airports Authority), 1977–91 (Chief Executive, 1972–77); *b* 9 Oct. 1921; *s* of late F. Payne, Folkestone; *m* 1946, Pamela Vivien Wallis (separated); four *s* one *d*. *Educ:* John Lyon Sch., Harrow; City and Guilds Coll., London. BSc Eng Hons; FCGI, FICE, FCIT. Royal Engrs (Captain), 1939–45 (despatches twice); Imperial Coll. of Science and Technology London (Civil), 1946–49; Sir Frederick Snow & Partners, 1949, Partner 1955; British Airports Authority: Dir of Engrg, 1965; Dir of Planning, 1969, and Mem. Bd 1971. Pres., West European Airports Assoc., 1975–77; Chairman: Airports Assoc. Co-ordinating Council, 1976; Aerodrome Owners' Assoc., 1983–84. Chm., British Sect., Centre for European Public Enterprise, 1979–82. Chm., NICG, 1982–83; Comr, Manpower Services Commn, 1983–85. Pres., CIT, 1984–85. CBIM (FBIM 1975); RAeS 1987. FIC 1989; FRSA 1990. Hon. FIStructE, 1988; Hon. FRIBA 1991. Hon. DTech Loughborough, 1985. *Publications:* various papers on airports and air transport. *Recreations:* travel, gardening. *Address:* L'Abri, La route des Merriennes, St Martin, Guernsey, CI.

PAYNE, Peter Charles John, PhD; MSc(AgrEng); farmer, since 1975; *b* 8 Feb. 1928; *s* of late C. J. Payne, China Clay Merchant, and Mrs F. M. Payne; *m* 1961, Margaret Grover; two *s* one *d*. *Educ:* Plymouth Coll.; Teignmouth Grammar School; Reading University. BSc Reading 1948; Min. of Agriculture Scholar, Durham Univ., MSc(AgrEng) 1950; Scientific Officer, Nat. Institute of Agricultural Engineering, 1950–55; PhD Reading 1954; Lecturer in Farm Mechanisation, Wye College, London Univ., 1955–60; Lecturer in Agricultural Engineering, Durham Univ., 1960–61; Principal, Nat. Coll. of Agricultural Engineering, Silsoe, 1962–75; Visiting Professor: Univ. of Reading, 1969–75; Cranfield Inst. of Technology, 1975–80. Chm., Agricl Panel, Intermed. Technol. Develt Gp, 1979–86; Mem., British Inst. of Agricl Consultants, 1978. Vice-Pres., Section III, Commn Internationale du Génie Rural, 1969. FIAgrE 1968; FRAgSs 1971; CEng 1980; ACIArb 1986. *Publications:* various papers in agricultural and engineering journals. *Recreation:* sailing. *Address:* Garlidna Farm, Porkellis, Helston TR13 0JX. *T:* Falmouth (01326) 40301.

PAYNE, Rt. Rev. (Sidney) Stewart; *see* Newfoundland, Western, Archbishop of.

PAYNE, (Trevor) Ian; *see* Payne, I.

PAYNE-BUTLER, George William; County Treasurer, Surrey County Council, 1973–79 (Assistant, 1962; Deputy, 1970); *b* 7 Oct. 1919; *s* of late George and Letitia Rachel Payne; *m* 1947, Joyce Louise Cockburn; one *s* two *d*. *Educ:* Woking Sch. for Boys. Joined Surrey CC, 1937. Served War, RAF, 1940–45. Chartered Municipal Treasurer, 1950 (CIPFA). *Recreations:* gardening, handicraft work in wood, reading. *Address:* Janston, Hillier Road, Guildford, Surrey GU1 2JQ. *T:* Guildford (01483) 65337.

PAYNE-GALLWEY, Sir Philip (Frankland), 6th Bt, *cr* 1812; Director, British Bloodstock Agency plc, since 1968; *b* 15 March 1935; *s* of late Lt-Col Lowry Philip Payne-Gallwey, OBE, MC and of Janet, *d* of late Albert Philip Payne-Gallwey; *S* cousin, 1964. *Educ:* Eton; Royal Military Academy, Sandhurst. Lieut, 11th Hussars, 1957. *Recreations:* hunting, shooting, golf. *Heir:* none. *Address:* The Little House, Boxford, Newbury, Berks. *T:* Boxford (01488) 608315; 29 Cadogan Street, SW3 2PP. *T:* 0171–589 4231; British Bloodstock Agency plc, 1 Chapel View, High Street, Lambourn, Newbury, Berks RG16 7XL. *T:* Lambourn (01488) 73111. *Clubs:* Cavalry and Guards, White's.

PAYNTER, Prof. John Frederick, OBE 1985; Professor of Music Education, 1982–94, and Head of Department of Music, 1983–94, University of York; *b* 17 July 1931; *s* of late Frederick Albert Paynter and late Rose Alice Paynter; *m* 1956, Elizabeth Hill; one *d*. *Educ:* Emanuel Sch., London; Trinity Coll. of Music, London (GTCL 1952). DPhil York, 1971. Teaching appts, primary and secondary schs, 1954–62; Lectr in Music, City of Liverpool C. F. Mott Coll. of Educn, 1962–65; Principal Lectr (Head of Dept of Music), Bishop Otter Coll., Chichester, 1965–69; Lectr, Dept of Music, Univ. of York, 1969, Sen. Lectr, 1974–82. Composer and writer on music-educn. Dir, Schs Council Proj., Music in the Secondary School Curriculum, 1973–82. Gen. Editor, series, Resources of Music; Jt Editor, British Jl of Music Educn. FRSA 1987. Hon. GSM 1985. *Publications:* (with Peter Aston) Sound and Silence, 1970; Hear and Now, 1972; (with Elizabeth Paynter) The Dance and the Drum, 1974; All Kinds of Music, vols 1–3, 1976, vol. 4, 1979; Sound Tracks, 1978; Music in the Secondary School Curriculum: trends and developments in class music teaching, 1982; Sound and Structure, 1992; (ed) A Companion to Contemporary Musical Thought, 1992; articles and revs in Music in Educn, Music Teacher, Times Educnl Sup., Music Now (Aust. Contemp. Music Qtly), Music Educn Rev., Canadian Music Educator, Muziek en Onderwijs, beQuadro, Kreativ Musik Undervining, Muzikale vorming, Proposte di musica creativa nella scuola, Musikalische Erfahrung, Zwischen Aufklärung und Kulturindustrie, Investigating Music (Australian Broadcasting Commn); scripts and commentaries for schs broadcasts and TV; *musical compositions:* choral and instrumental works including: Landscapes, 1972; The Windhover, 1972; May Magnificat, 1973; God's Grandeur, 1975; Sacraments of Summer, 1975; Galaxies for Orchestra, 1977; The Voyage of Brendan, 1978; The Visionary Hermit, 1979; The Inviolable Voice, 1980; String Quartet no 1, 1981; Cantata for the Waking of Lazarus, 1981; The Laughing Stone, 1982; Contrasts for Orchestra, 1982; Variations for Orchestra and Audience, 1983; Conclaves, 1984; Piano Sonata, 1987; Time After Time, 1991; String Quartet no 2, 1991; Four Sculptures of Austin Wright (for solo violin and orch.), 1991–94. *Address:* Westfield House, Newton upon Derwent, York YO4 5DA.

PAYNTER, Air Cdre Noel Stephen, CB 1946; DL; retired; *b* 26 Dec. 1898; *s* of late Canon F. S. Paynter, sometime Rector of Springfield, Essex; *m* 1925, Barbara Grace Haagensen; one *s* one *d*. *Educ:* Haileybury; RMC, Sandhurst. Flying Brevet, 1917; France and Russia, 1918–19 (St Anne 3rd Class); North-West Frontier, 1919–21; North-West Frontier, 1925–30; Malta, 1934; Directorate of Intelligence, Air Ministry, 1936–39; Chief Intelligence Officer, Middle East, 1939–42 (despatches); Chief Intelligence Officer, Bomber Command, 1942–45 (CB); Directorate of Intelligence, Air Ministry, 1946. Chm. Buckinghamshire Playing Fields Assoc., 1958–65; Chm. Bucks Army Cadet Force (TA), 1962–65. High Sheriff, Bucks, 1965. DL Buckinghamshire, 1963. *Address:* Lawn House, Edgcott, near Aylesbury, Bucks HP18 0TN. *T:* Grendon Underwood (01296) 770238.

PAYTON, Stanley Walden, CMG 1965; Chief of Overseas Department, Bank of England, 1975–80, retired; *b* 29 May 1921; *s* of late Archibald Walden Payton and late Ethel May Payton (*née* Kirtland); *m* 1941, Joan (*née* Starmer); one *s* one *d*. *Educ:* Monoux School. Fleet Air Arm, 1940–46; Entered Bank of England, 1946; UK Alternate on Managing Board of European Payments Union, Paris, 1957–59; First Governor of Bank of Jamaica, 1960–64.

PAZ, Octavio; Mexican author; poet; Director, Revista Vuelta; *b* Mexico City, 31 March 1914; *s* of Octavio Paz and Josefina Lozano; *m* Marie José Tramini; one *d*. *Educ:* National Univ. of Mexico. Founded and directed Mexican literary reviews: Barandal, 1931; Taller, 1938; El Hijo Pródigo, 1943. Guggenheim Fellowship, USA, 1944. Sec., Mexican Embassy, Paris, 1946; New Delhi, 1952; Chargé d'Affaires *ad interim*, Japan, 1952; posted to Secretariat for External Affairs México, 1953–58; Extraordinary and Plenipotentiary Minister to Mexican Embassy, Paris, 1959–62; Ambassador to India, 1962–68; in Oct. 1968 resigned in protest at bloody students' repression in Tlatelolco. Simon Bolivar Prof. of Latin-American Studies, Cambridge, 1970; Vis. Prof. of Spanish American Lit., Univ. of Texas, Austin, and Pittsburgh Univ., 1968–70; Charles Eliot Norton Prof. of Poetry, Harvard Univ., 1971–72. Editor, Plural, Mexico City, 1971–75. Prizes include: Internat. Poetry Grand Prix, 1963; Nat. Prize for Literature, Mexico, 1977; Jerusalem Prize, 1977; Critics' Prize, Spain, 1977; Golden Eagle, Nice, 1978; Ollin Yoliztli, Mexico, 1980; Cervantes, Spain, 1982; Neustadt Internat. Prize for Literature, US, 1982; T. S. Eliot Prize, Ingersoll Foundn, USA, 1987; Nobel Prize for Literature, 1990. *Publications: poetry:* Luna Silvestre, 1933; Bajo tu Clara Sombra y otras poemas sobre Espanã, 1937; Raiz del Hombre, 1937; Entre la Piedra y la Flor, 1941; A la Orilla del Mundo, 1942; Libertad bajo Palabra, 1949; Aguila o Sol?, 1951 (trans. as Eagle or Sun?, 1970); Semillas para un Himno, 1956; Piedra de Sol, 1957 (trans. as Sun Stone, 1960); La Estación Violenta, 1958; Libertad bajo Palabra (poetical works 1935–57), 1960; Salamandra (poetical works 1958–61), 1962; Viento Entero, 1965; Blanco, 1967; Discos Visuales, 1968; Ladera Este, 1969; La Centena, 1969; Topoemas, 1971; Renga, 1971; New Poetry of Mexico (Anthol.), 1972; Pasado en Claro, 1975; Vuelta, 1976; Poemas 1935–1975, 1979; Arbol adentro, 1987; *in English:* Early Poems (1935–57), 1963; Configurations, 1971; A Draft of Shadows and Other Poems, 1979; Airborn/Hijos del Aire, 1981; Selected Poems, 1984; Collected Poems (1957–87), 1987; *prose:* El Laberinto de la soledad, 1950 (trans. as Labyrinth of Solitude, 1961); El Arco y la Lira, 1956 (trans. as The Bow and The Lyre, 1975); Las Peras del Olmo, 1957; Cuadrivio, 1965; Los Signos en Rotación, 1965; Piertas al campo, 1966; Corriente Alterna, 1967 (trans. as Alternating Current, 1972); Claude Lévi-Strauss o el Nuevo Festín de Esopo, 1967 (trans. as On Lévi-Strauss, 1970); Marcel Duchamp o El Castillo de la Pureza, 1968 (trans. as Marcel Duchamp or the Castle of Purity, 1970); Conjunciones y Disyunciones (essay), 1969 (trans. as Conjunctions and Disjunctions, 1974); Postdata, 1970 (trans. as The Other Mexico, 1972); El Mono Gramático, 1971 (trans. as The Monkey Grammarian, 1989); Las Cosas en su Sitio, 1971; Traducción: Literatura y Literalidad, 1971; El Signo y el Garabato, 1973; Los Hijos del Limo, 1974 (trans. as Children of the Mire, 1974); Marcel Duchamp: Apariencia Desnuda, 1978 (trans. as Marcel Duchamp: Appearance Stripped Bare, 1981); Xavier Villaurrutia en Persona y en Obra, 1978; El Ogro Filantrópico, 1979; In mediaciones, 1979; Sombras de Obra, 1983; Tiempo Nublado, 1983 (trans. as One Earth, Four or Five Worlds); Hombres en su siglo, 1984; Pasión Critica, 1985; On poets and others (essays on literature), 1986; Convergences, 1987; Sor Juana: her life and world, 1988; *translations:* Versiones y Diversiones, 1974. *Address:* c/o Revista Vuelta, Presidente Canonza 210, Coyoacán, México 4000 DF, México.

PEACE, David Brian, MBE 1977; FSA; glass engraver; town planner, 1948–82; *b* 13 March 1915; *y s* of Herbert W. F. Peace, Sheffield, and Mabel Peace (*née* Hammond); *m* 1939, Jean Margaret, ARCA (*d* 1989), *d* of Rev. McEwan and Margaret Lawson, Mill Hill; two *d*. *Educ:* Mill Hill; Univ. of Sheffield. ARIBA, FRTPI. RAF Airfield Construction Service, 1942–46, Sqdn Leader. Glass engraver, 1935–; presentation glass, 1952–; 11 one-man shows; work in 14 public collections, including: V&A (4); Kettle's Yard, Cambridge (6); Nat. Glass Mus., Stourbridge (2); Keatley Trust (7); Fitzwilliam Mus.; Corning Mus., USA; windows, screens and doors since 1956 in many churches and colleges, incl. St Nicholas Liverpool, St Albans Cathedral, Manchester Cathedral, St Botolph Aldgate, St Nicholas Whitehaven; Royal Acad. of Music, Waltham Abbey, Gray's Inn Chapel, Great St Mary's, Cambridge, Chapel Royal, Brighton; with Sally Scott: Westminster Abbey, Norwich Cathedral, Lancaster and Sheffield Univs, Lincoln Coll., Oxford, and St John's Coll., Cambridge, Bunwell Church, Cambs, Christ the Cornerstone, Milton Keynes; retrospective exhibn, 1990. Master, Art Workers Guild, 1973; Guild of Glass Engravers: first Chm., 1975; Pres., 1980–86; Liveryman, Glaziers' Co., 1977. Town Planner: Staffs CC, 1948–61; Cambs CC, Dep. County Planning Officer, 1961–75, then head of envtl planning, 1975–80 (MBE); DoE appeals inspectorate, 1980–82. Member: Council for Visual Education, 1960–80; Council, RTPI, 1961–62, 1972–73; Council for British Archæology, 1965–85. President: Surveyors Club, 1984; ASCHB, 1994; Member: Ely DAC for Care of Churches, 1963–; Council, Artists Gen. Benevolent Assoc., 1994. Hon. DSc Tech. Sheffield Univ., 1991. *Publications:* Glass Engraving: lettering and design, 1985; The Engraved Glass of David Peace: the architecture of lettering, 1990; Eric Gill, the Inscriptions: a descriptive catalogue, 1994; various publications on conservation and the law; originator of A Guide to Historic Buildings Law, 1965 (The Cambridgeshire Guide); Historic Buildings: maps and guides to the Peak District and N Wales. *Recreations:*

townscape, heraldry. *Address:* Abbots End, High Street, Hemingford Abbots, Huntingdon PE18 9AA. *T:* Huntingdon (01480) 462472. *Club:* Arts.

See also David Davies.

PEACH, Ceri; *see* Peach, G. C. K.

PEACH, Denis Alan, CB 1985; Chief Charity Commissioner, 1982–88; *b* 10 Jan. 1928; *s* of late Richard Peach and Alice Ellen Peach; *m* 1957, Audrey Hazel Chamberlain. *Educ:* Selhurst Grammar Sch., Croydon. Home Office, 1946–82: Asst Principal, 1951; Private Sec. to Perm. Under Sec of State, 1956; Principal, 1957; Sec. to Anglo-Egyptian Resettlement Bd, 1957–58; Prison Commn, 1958–62; Asst Sec., 1967; Asst Under Sec. of State, 1974–82 (Prin. Finance Officer, 1974–80). *Recreations:* painting, gardening. *Address:* 10 Morkyns Walk, Alleyn Park, SE21 8BG. *T:* 0181–670 5574. *Club:* Reform.

PEACH, Prof. (Guthlac) Ceri (Klaus), DPhil; Professor of Social Geography, since 1992, and Head of Department, School of Geography, since 1995, Oxford University; Fellow and Tutor, St Catherine's College, Oxford, since 1969; *b* 26 Oct. 1939; *s* of Wystan Adams Peach and Charlotte Marianne (*née* Klaus); *m* 1964, Susan Lesley Godfrey; two *s* one *d*. *Educ:* Howardian High Sch., Cardiff; Merton Coll., Oxford (MA, DPhil). Oxford University: Demonstrator, 1964–66; Faculty Lectr in Geography, 1966–92; St Catherine's College: Dean, 1971–73; Sen. Tutor, 1973–77; Finance Bursar, 1981–84; Domestic Bursar, 1986–89; Vice-Master, 1990–92; Pro-Master, 1993–94. Visiting Fellow: Dept of Demography, ANU, 1972; Dept of Sociology, Yale Univ., 1977; Fulbright Vis. Prof., Univ. of Calif, Berkeley, 1985. *Publications:* West Indian Migration to Britain: a social geography, 1968; Urban Social Segregation, 1975; (ed jtly) Ethnic Segregation in Cities, 1981; (ed jtly) Geography and Ethnic Pluralism, 1984; (ed jtly) South Asians Overseas, 1990; The Caribbean in Europe, 1991. *Recreations:* travelling, reading, computing, poetry. *Address:* St Catherine's College, Oxford OX1 3UJ.

PEACH, Sir Leonard (Harry), Kt 1989; Chairman, Police Complaints Authority, since 1992; *b* 17 Dec. 1932; *s* of late Harry and Beatrice Peach; *m* 1958, Doreen Lilian (*née* Barker); two *s*. *Educ:* Queen Mary's Grammar Sch., Walsall; Pembroke Coll., Oxford (MA); LSE (Dip. Personnel Management). Research Asst to Randolph S. Churchill, 1956; personnel management posts, 1956–62; IBM UK Ltd: personnel management posts, 1962–71; Dir of Personnel, 1971–72; Gp Dir, Personnel, IBM Europe, Africa, Middle East (based Paris), 1972–75; Dir, Personnel and Corporate Affairs, 1975–85 and 1989–92; seconded to DHSS, 1985–89: Dir, Personnel, NHS Management Bd, 1985; Chief Exec., NHS Management Bd, 1986–89 (in rank of 2nd Perm. Sec.); Chairman: NHS Training Authy, 1986–91; Skillbase Ltd, 1990–94; Standards Develt Cttee, Management Charter Initiative, 1989–; Development Partnership Consultancy, 1993–; Non-exec. Dir, Royal London Hosp., 1991–94. Chm., PSI, 1991–. Director: IBM UK Rentals, 1971–76; IBM UK Holdings, 1976–85, and 1989–92; IBM UK Pensions Trust, 1989–92; IBM UK Trust, 1989–92; non-exec. Director: Nationwide Anglia Bldg Soc, 1990–93; Coutts Consulting plc, 1993–; Pres., IPM, and Chm., IPM Services Ltd, 1983–85 and 1991– (President's Gold Medal, 1988); Mem., Data Protection Tribunal, 1985–. President: Manpower Soc., 1991–; Assoc. of Business Schs, 1993–. Chm., Univ. of Westminster, 1993–; Vice-Chm., Morley Coll., 1993–; Gov., Portsmouth Grammar Sch., 1976–. CIMgt; CIPM; FRSA. Hon. FFOM, RCP, 1994. Hon. Fellow, Thames Polytechnic, 1990. Hon. DSc Aston, 1991. *Publications:* articles on personnel management and social responsibility. *Recreations:* opera, theatre, cricket, gardening. *Address:* Crossacres, Meadow Road, Wentworth, Virginia Water, Surrey GU25 4NH. *T:* Wentworth (019904) 2258.

PEACOCK, Prof. Sir Alan (Turner), Kt 1987; DSC 1945; MA; FBA 1979; FRSE; Hon. Research Professor in Public Finance, Heriot-Watt University, since 1987; *b* 26 June 1922; *s* of late Professor A. D. Peacock, FRSE and of Clara Mary (*née* Turner); *m* 1944, Margaret Martha Astell Burt; two *s* one *d*. *Educ:* Dundee High School; University of St Andrews (1939–42, 1945–47). Royal Navy, 1942–45 (Lieut RNVR). Lecturer in Economics: Univ. of St Andrews, 1947–48; London Sch. of Economics, 1948–51 (Hon. Fellow, 1980); Reader in Public Finance, Univ. of London, 1951–56; Prof. of Economic Science, Univ. of Edinburgh, 1957–62; Prof. of Economics, Univ. of York, 1962–78; Prof. of Economics, and Principal-designate, University Coll. at Buckingham, 1978–80, Principal, 1980–83; Vice-Chancellor, Univ. of Buckingham, 1983–84, Professor Emeritus, 1985–; Exec. Dir, David Hume Inst., Edinburgh, 1985–90. Seconded from Univ. of York as Chief Economic Adviser, Depts of Industry and Trade, 1973–76. Visiting Prof. of Economics, Johns Hopkins Univ., 1958. Keynes Lectr, British Acad., 1994. Mem., 1959–87, Chm., 1991–93, Adv. Council, IEA (Trustee, 1987–93); Member: Commission of Enquiry into land and population problems of Fiji, 1959; Departmental Committee on Electricity in Scotland, 1961; Council, REconS, 1961–78; Cttee of Enquiry on impact of rates, 1964; Commn on the Constitution, 1970–73; SSRC, 1972–73; Cttee of Inquiry on Retirement Provision, 1984; Chm., Rowntree Inquiry into Corporate Takeovers, 1990–91. Chm., UN Adv. Mission to Russian Fedn on Social Protection, 1992. Pres., Internat. Inst. of Public Finance, 1966–69. Mem., Arts Council, 1986–92; Chairman: Arts Council Enquiry on Orchestral Resources, 1969–70; Cttee on Financing the BBC, 1985–86; Scottish Arts Council, 1986–92. Non-exec. Director: Economist Intelligence Unit Ltd, 1977–84; Caledonian Bank plc. FRSE 1989. DUniv: Stirling, 1974; Brunel, 1989; Hon. DEcon Zürich, 1984; Hon. DSc: Buckingham, 1986; Edinburgh, 1990; Hon. LLD: St Andrews, 1990; Dundee, 1990; Dr *hc* Catania, 1991. *Publications:* Economics of National Insurance, 1952; (ed) Income Redistribution and Social Policy 1954; National Income and Social Accounting (with H. C. Edey), 1954, 3rd imp. 1967; The National Income of Tanganyika (1952–54) (with D. G. M. Dosser), 1958; The Growth of Public Expenditure in the UK, 1890–1955 (with J. Wiseman), 1961; Economic Theory of Fiscal Policy (with G. K. Shaw), 1971, 2nd edn, 1976; The Composer in the Market Place (with R. Weir), 1975; Welfare Economics: a liberal re-interpretation (with C. K. Rowley), 1975; Economic Analysis of Government, 1979; (ed and contrib.) Structural Economic Policies in West Germany and the UK, 1980; (ed jtly) Political Economy of Taxation, 1981; (ed and contrib.) The Regulation Game, 1984; (ed jtly) Public Expenditure and Government Growth, 1985; Waltz Contrasts (for piano solo), 1988; Public Choice Analysis in Historical Perspective, 1992; (with G. Bannock) Corporate Takeovers and the Public Interest, 1991; Paying the Piper, 1993; (ed jtly) Cultural Economics and Cultural Policies, 1994; articles on applied economics in Economic Jl, Economica and other journals. *Recreations:* trying to write music, wine spotting. *Address:* 146/4 Whitehouse Loan, Edinburgh EH9 2AN. *T:* 0131–447 5917. *Clubs:* Reform; New (Edinburgh).

PEACOCK, Hon. Andrew Sharp; company director, since 1994; *b* 13 Feb. 1939; *s* of late A. S. Peacock and Iris Peacock. *Educ:* Scotch Coll., Melbourne, Vic; Melbourne Univ. (LLB). Former Partner, Rigby & Fielding, Solicitors; Chm., Peacock and Smith Pty Ltd, 1962–69. Army Reserve (Captain), 1966–94. Pres., Victorian Liberal Party, 1965–66; MP (L) Kooyong, Australia, 1966–94; Minister for Army and Minister assisting Prime Minister, 1969–71; Minister for Army and Minister asstg Treasurer, 1971–72; Minister for External Territories, Feb.-Dec. 1972; Mem., Opposition Exec., 1973–75; Oppos. Shadow Minister for For. Affairs, 1973–75, 1985–87; Minister for: Foreign Affairs, 1975–80; Industrial Relns, 1980–81; Industry and Commerce, 1982–83; Leader of the Parly Liberal Party, and of the Opposition, 1983–85; Dep. Leader, Liberal Party and Dep. Leader, Opposition, 1987–89; Leader, Parly Liberal Party, and of the Opposition, 1989–90; Shadow Attorney-Gen. and Shadow Minister for Justice, 1990–92; Shadow Minister: for Trade, 1992–93; for Foreign Affairs, 1993–94. Chm., Internat. Democrat Union, 1989–92. *Recreations:* horse racing, sailboarding, Australian Rules football. *Address:* PO Box 18197, Collins Street East, Melbourne, Vic 8003, Australia. *T:* (3) 2040108. *Clubs:* Melbourne, Melbourne Cricket, Victoria Amateur Turf (Melbourne); Victoria Racing, Moonee Valley Racing.

PEACOCK, Elizabeth Joan, JP; MP (C) Batley and Spen, since 1983; *b* 4 Sept. 1937; *d* of late John and Dorothy Gates; *m* 1963, Brian D. Peacock; two *s*. *Educ:* St Monica's Convent, Skipton. Asst to Exec. Dir, York Community Council, 1979–83; Administrator, four charitable trusts, York, 1979–83. County Councillor, N Yorks, 1981–84. PPS to Minister of State, Home Office, 1991–92, to Minister for Social Security and disabled people, 1992. Mem., Select Cttee on Employment, 1983–87. Chairman: All Party Trans Pennine Gp, 1988–94; All Party Wool Textile Gp, 1989–. Hon. Sec., Yorks Cons. MPs, 1983–88; Vice Chm., Cons. Back-bench Party Organisation Cttee, 1985–87; Mem. Exec. Cttee, 1922 Cttee, 1987–91; Mem. Exec., CPA, 1987–92. Mem., BBC Gen. Adv. Council, 1987–93. Vice Pres., Yorks Area Young Conservatives, 1984–87; Pres., Yorks Area Cons. Trade Unionists, 1991– (Vice Pres., 1987–91). FRSA 1990. JP Macclesfield, 1975–79, Bulmer East 1983. *Recreations:* reading, motoring. *Address:* House of Commons, SW1A 0AA. *T:* 0171–219 4092; (constituency office) 27A Northgate, Cleckheaton, West Yorks BD19 3HH. *T:* Cleckheaton (01274) 872968.

PEACOCK, Ian Douglas; Chief Executive, Lawn Tennis Association, since 1986; *b* 9 April 1934; *s* of Andrew Inglis Peacock and Minnie Maria (*née* King); *m* 1962, Joanna Hepburn MacGregor; one *s* one *d*. *Educ:* Sevenoaks Sch. Pilot Officer, RAF, 1953–54. Slazengers Ltd, 1955–83, Man. Dir 1976–83; Sports Marketing Surveys Ltd, 1984–85. Pres., British Sports & Allied Industry Fedn, 1984–85; Director: Golf Foundn, 1982–; LTA Trust, 1988–; Queen's Club Ltd, 1993–. Dir, Golf Foundn (Chm., Golf Ball Cttee, 1976–). Trustee, Torch Trophy Trust, 1993–. *Recreations:* golf, ski-ing, painting. *Address:* Moat End House, Church Lane, Burstow, Surrey RH6 9TG. *T:* Smallfield (01342) 842262. *Clubs:* Queen's, Royal Air Force; Royal Ashdown Forest Golf (Forest Row).

PEACOCK, (Ian) Michael; Chairman: Unique Broadcasting Co. Ltd, since 1989; The Peacock Foundation, since 1990; The Truly Classic Yacht Co. Ltd, since 1994; *b* 14 Sept. 1929; *e s* of Norman Henry and Sara Barbara Peacock; *m* 1956, Daphne Lee; two *s* one *d*. *Educ:* Kimball Union Academy, USA; Welwyn Garden City Grammar School; London School of Economics (BSc Econ.). BBC Television: Producer, 1952–56; Producer Panorama, 1956–58; Asst Head of Television Outside Broadcasts, 1958–59; Editor, Panorama, 1959–61; Editor, BBC Television News, 1961–63; Chief of Programmes, BBC-2, 1963–65; Controller, BBC-1, BBC Television Service, 1965–67; Managing Dir, London Weekend Television Ltd, 1967–69; Chm., Monitor Enterprises Ltd, 1970–89; Man. Dir, Warner Bros TV Ltd, 1972–74; Exec. Vice-Pres., Warner Bros Television Inc., 1974–76. Dir, Video Arts Ltd, 1972–89; Pres., Video Arts Inc., 1976–78; Man. Dir, Dumbarton Films Ltd (formerly Video Arts Television), 1978–87; Chairman: Video Answers, 1989–90; Publishing Projects plc, 1990–92. Dep. Chm., Piccadilly Radio, 1988–89. IPPA: First Chm., 1981–82; Mem. Council, 1981–88. Mem., Ct of Governors, LSE, 1982–. *Recreations:* sailing, gardening. *Address:* 21 Woodlands Road, Barnes, SW13 0JZ. *T:* 0181–876 2025. *Clubs:* Savile, Royal Thames Yacht, Royal Ocean Racing.

PEACOCK, Michael; *see* Peacock, I. M.

PEACOCK, Dr William James, AC 1994; BSc, PhD; FRS 1982; FAA; Chief, Division of Plant Industry, Commonwealth Scientific and Industrial Research Organization, since 1978; *b* 14 Dec. 1937; *m* 1961, Margaret Woodward; one *s* two *d*. *Educ:* Katoomba High Sch.; Univ. of Sydney (BSc, PhD). FAA 1976. CSIRO Postdoctoral Fellow, 1963 and Vis. Associate Prof. of Biology, 1964–65, Univ. of Oregon; Res. Consultant, Oak Ridge National Lab., USA, 1965; res. staff, Div. of Plant Industry, CSIRO, 1965–. Adjunct Prof. of Biology, Univ. of Calif, San Diego, 1969; Vis. Professor: of Biochem., Stanford Univ., 1970; of Molecular Biol., Univ. of Calif, LA, 1977. For. Associate, US Nat. Acad. of Scis, 1990; For. Fellow, Indian Nat. Science Acad., 1990. FTS 1988; FAIAS 1989. Edgeworth David Medal, Royal Soc. of NSW, 1967; Lemberg Medal, Aust. Biochem. Soc., 1978; BHP Bicentennial Prize for Pursuit of Excellence in Science and Technol., 1988; CSIRO Medal for Leadership of Div. of Plant Industry, 1989; Burnet Medal, Aust. Acad. of Sci., 1989. *Publications:* editor of 5 books on genetics and molecular biology; approx. 200 papers. *Recreations:* squash, sailing, bush-walking. *Address:* 16 Brassey Street, Deakin, ACT 2600, Australia. *T:* (home) (6) 2814485, (office) (6) 2465250, *Fax:* (6) 2465530.

PEACOCKE, Rev. Canon Arthur Robert, MBE 1993; DSc, ScD, DD; SOSc; Hon. Chaplain, since 1988, and Hon. Canon, since 1995, Christ Church Cathedral, Oxford; Warden, Society of Ordained Scientists, 1987–92, now Emeritus; *b* 29 Nov. 1924; *s* of Arthur Charles Peacocke and Rose Elizabeth (*née* Lilly); *m* 1948, Rosemary Winifred Mann; one *s* one *d*. *Educ:* Watford Grammar Sch.; Exeter Coll., Oxford (Scholar; BA Chem., BSc 1946; MA, DPhil 1948). DSc Oxon, 1962; ScD Cantab (incorp.), 1973; DD Oxon, 1982. DipTh 1960, BD 1971, Birmingham. Asst Lectr, Lectr and Sen. Lectr in Biophys. Chemistry, Univ. of Birmingham, 1948–59; Lectr in Biochem., Oxford Univ., and Fellow and Tutor in Chem., subseq. in Biochem., St Peter's Coll., 1959–73; Lectr in Chem., Mansfield Coll., Oxford, 1964–73; Dean and Fellow, Clare Coll., Cambridge, 1973–84; Dir, Ian Ramsey Centre, St Cross Coll., Oxford, and Fellow, St Cross Coll., 1985–88; Catechist, Exeter Coll., Oxford, 1989–93. Rockefeller Fellow, Univ. of Calif at Berkeley, and Univ. of Wis, 1951–52; Vis. Fellow, Weizmann Inst., Israel, 1956; Prof. of Judeo-Christian Studies, Tulane Univ., 1984; J. K. Russell Fellow in Religion and Science, Center for Theology and Natural Sci., Berkeley, 1986; Royden Davis Prof., Georgetown Univ., 1994; Lectures: Bampton, Oxford Univ., 1978; Bishop Williams Meml, Rikkyo (St Paul's) Univ., Japan, 1981; Shann, Univ. of Hong Kong, 1982; Mendenhall, DePauw Univ., Indiana, 1983; McNair, Univ. of N Carolina, 1984; Nina Booth Bricker Meml, Tulane Univ., 1986, 1989; Norton, Southern Baptist Seminary, Louisville, 1986; Sprigg, Virginia Theol Seminary, 1987; Rolf Buchdahl, N Carolina State Univ., 1987; Drawbridge, KCL, 1987; Alister Hardy Meml, 1989; Gifford, St Andrews Univ., 1993. Lay Reader, Oxford Dio., 1960–71; ordained, 1971; Mem., Archbps' Commn on Christian Doctrine, 1969–76 (Mem. sub-gp on Man and Nature, 1972–74); Chm., Science and Religion Forum, 1972–78, Vice-Pres., 1981–; Vice-Pres., Inst. of Religion in an Age of Science, USA, 1984–87 (Academic Fellow, 1987). Select Preacher, Oxford Univ., 1973, 1985; Hulsean Preacher, Cambridge Univ., 1976; Judge, Templeton Foundn Prize, 1979–82. Meetings Sec., Sec. and Chm., Brit. Biophys. Soc., 1965–69. Hon. DSc DePauw Univ., Indiana, 1983; Hon. DLitHum Georgetown Univ., Washington, 1991. Mem. Editorial Bd, Biochem. Jl, and Biopolymers, 1966–71, Zygon, 1973–. Editor, Monographs in Physical Biochemistry (OUP), 1967–82. Lecomte du Noüy Prize, 1973. *Publications:* Molecular Basis of Heredity (with J. B. Drysdale), 1965 (repr. 1967); Science and the Christian Experiment, 1971; (with M. P. Tombs) Osmotic Pressure of Biological Macromolecules, 1974; (with J. Dominian) From Cosmos to Love, 1977; Creation and the World of Science, 1979; (ed) The Sciences and Theology in the Twentieth Century, 1982; The Physical Chemistry of Biological Organization, 1983; Intimations of Reality,

1984; (ed) Reductionism in Academic Disciplines, 1985; God and the New Biology, 1986; (ed with G. Gillett) Persons and Personality, 1987; (ed with S. Andersen) Evolution and Creation: a European perspective, 1987; Theology for a Scientific Age, 1990, new edn 1993; articles and papers in scientific and theol jls, and symposia vols. *Recreations:* piano, music, walking, churches. *Address:* 55 St John Street, Oxford OX1 2LQ; Exeter College, Oxford OX1 3DP. *T:* Oxford (01865) 512041, *Fax:* (01865) 54791.

See also C. A. B. Peacocke.

PEACOCKE, Prof. Christopher Arthur Bruce, FBA 1990; Waynflete Professor of Metaphysical Philosophy, University of Oxford and Fellow of Magdalen College, Oxford, since 1989; *b* 22 May 1950; *s* of Rev. Dr Arthur Robert Peacocke, *qv*; *m* 1980, Teresa Anne Rosen; one *s* one *d. Educ:* Magdalen College Sch., Oxford; Exeter Coll., Oxford (MA, BPhil, DPhil). Kennedy Schol., Harvard Univ., 1971; Sen. Schol., Merton Coll., Oxford, 1972; Jun. Res. Fellow, Queen's Coll., Oxford, 1973; Prize Fellow, All Souls Coll., Oxford, 1975; Fellow and Tutor, New Coll., Oxford, and CUF Lectr in Philosophy, 1979–85; Susan Stebbing Prof. of Philosophy, KCL, 1985–88. Visiting Professor: Berkeley, 1975; Ann Arbor, 1978; UCLA, 1981; Maryland, 1987; Vis. Fellow, ANU, 1981; Fellow, Center for Advanced Study in the Behavioral Sciences, Stanford, 1983; Vis. Res. Associate, Center for Study of Language and Information, Stanford, 1984. Pres., Mind Assoc., 1986; Mem., Steering Cttee, European Soc. for Philosophy and Psychology, 1991–. *Publications:* Holistic Explanation: action, space, interpretation, 1979; Sense and Content, 1983; Thoughts: an essay on content, 1986; A Study of Concepts, 1992; papers on philosophy of mind and language, and philosophical logic, in Jl of Philosophy, Philosophical Rev., etc. *Recreations:* music, visual arts. *Address:* Magdalen College, Oxford OX1 4AU. *T:* Oxford (01865) 276000.

PEAKE, family name of **Viscount Ingleby.**

PEAKE, David Alphy Edward Raymond; Director, Kleinwort Benson Group plc, since 1986 (Chairman, 1989–93); *b* 27 Sept. 1934; *s* of Sir Harald Peake, AE and Mrs Resy Peake, OBE; *m* 1962, Susanna Kleinwort; one *s* one *d. Educ:* Ampleforth Coll.; Christ Church, Oxford (MA History, 1958). 2nd Lieut Royal Scots Greys, 1953–55. Banque Lambert, Brussels, 1958–59; J. Henry Schroder Wagg & Co. Ltd, 1959–63; Kleinwort Benson Ltd, 1963–93; Dir, 1971–93; Vice-Chm., 1985–87; Chm., 1988–89; Hargreaves Group, 1964–86: Dir, 1964–86; Vice-Chm., 1967–74; Chm., 1974–86; Director: Banque Nationale de Paris, 1974–; M & G Gp, 1979–87. Pt-time Mem. of Bd, British Liby, 1990–. Chairman: City and Inner London N TEC, 1990–93; Educn 2000 Trust, 1994–; Mem., BOTB, 1993–. Trustee, Harefield Hosp. Fund, 1994–. Mem. Ct of Assts, Goldsmiths' Co., 1992–. *Recreations:* reading, country sports. *Address:* 15 Ilchester Place, W14 8AA. *T:* 0171–602 2375. *Clubs:* Brooks's, Pratt's, Cavalry and Guards.

PEAKE, Air Cdre (retired) Dame Felicity (Hyde), (Lady Peake), DBE 1949 (MBE 1941); AE; *b* 1 May 1913; *d* of late Colonel Humphrey Watts, OBE, TD, and Mrs Simon Orde; *m* 1st, 1935, John Charles Mackenzie Hanbury (killed on active service, 1939); no *c*; 2nd, 1952, Sir Harald Peake, AE (*d* 1978); one *s. Educ:* St Winifreds, Eastbourne; Les Grands Huguenots, Vaucresson, Seine et Oise, France. Joined ATS Company of the RAF, April 1939; commissioned in the WAAF, Aug. 1939; served at home and in the Middle East; Director, Women's Auxiliary Air Force, 1946–49; Director Women's Royal Air Force, from its inception, 1949, until her retirement, 1950; Hon. ADC to King George VI, 1949–50. Member Advisory Cttee, Recruitment for the Forces, 1958. Trustee: Imperial War Museum, 1963–85 (Chm., 1986–88, Pres., 1988–92, Friends of Imperial War Museum); St Clement Danes church, 1989–. Governor, London House, 1958–76, 1978–92; Mem. Council, RAF Benevolent Fund, 1946–94 (a Vice-Pres., 1978–); Mem. Council, Union Jack Club, 1950–78. *Publication:* Pure Chance, 1993.

PEAKE, John Fordyce; consultant; Associate Director (Scientific Development), Natural History Museum, 1989–92; *b* 4 June 1933; *s* of late William Joseph Peake and of Helena (*née* Fordyce); *m* 1963, Pamela Joyce Hollis; two *d. Educ:* City of Norwich Grammar Sch.; University Coll. London (BSc). National Trust, 1955–56; Norwich Technical Coll., 1956–58; Nature Conservancy Studentship, 1958–59; British Museum (Natural History): Research Fellow, 1959–61; Sen. Scientific Officer, 1961–69; PSO, 1969–71; Dep. Keeper, 1971–85; Keeper of Zoology, 1985–89. Hon. Research Associate, Bernice P. Bishop Mus., Honolulu, 1972–. Royal Society: Member: Aldabra Research Cttee, 1972–77; Southern Zones Cttee, 1982–86; Unitas Malacologica: Treas. 1962–63, Mem. Council, 1963–75; Vice Pres., Malacological Soc. of London, 1976–78; Council Mem., Zoological Soc. of London, 1985–88. *Publications:* (editor and contributor with Dr V. Fretter) Pulmonates, 3 vols, 1975–79; papers on taxonomy, biogeography and ecology of terrestrial molluscs in sci. jls. *Recreation:* gardening. *Address:* Spring Cottage, Trycewell Lane, Ightham, Sevenoaks, Kent TN15 9HN. *T:* Borough Green (01732) 882423.

PEAKE, John Morris, CBE 1986; Chairman: Cambridgeshire Careers Guidance Ltd, since 1995; Baker Perkins PLC, 1984–87; *b* 26 Aug. 1924; *s* of late Albert Edward Peake and Ruby Peake (*née* Morris); *m* 1953, Elizabeth Rought; one *s* one *d. Educ:* Repton School; Clare College, Cambridge (Mech. Scis Tripos; MA 1949); Royal Naval College, Greenwich (Dip. Naval Arch.). FIMechE; FIMA; CIMgt. Royal Corps of Naval Constructors, 1944–50; Personnel Administration Ltd, 1950–51; Baker Perkins (BP): joined 1951; Dir, parent co., 1956; Jt Man. Dir, BP Ltd, 1963–66; Man. Dir, BP Pty, 1969–74, in Australia; Pres., BP Inc., 1975–77, in USA; Dep. Man. Dir, BP Holdings, 1978–79, Man. Dir, 1980–85. Member: Chemicals and Minerals Requirements Bd, 1978–81; Council, CBI, 1980–89 (Chairman: Overseas Schols Bd, 1981–87; Educn and Trng Cttee, 1986–88); Council, BTEC, 1986–89 (Chm., Bd for Engineering, 1985–91); MSC, subseq. Trng Commn, 1986–88; RSA Examinations Bd, 1987–93 (Chm., 1989–93); RSA Council, 1989–93; Adv. Council, British Library, 1989–92; Design Council, 1991–93 (Chm. Educn Cttee, 1990–94); Chm., Greater Peterborough Partnership, 1994–95; Vice Chm., Gtr Peterborough TEC, 1990–94. Chm., Nene Park Trust, 1988–93. Hockey Silver Medal, London Olympics, 1948. FRSA. Hon. DTech CNAA, 1986. *Recreations:* sport, travel. *Address:* Old Castle Farmhouse, Stibbington, Peterborough PE8 6LP. *T:* Stamford (01780) 782683. *Clubs:* East India, MCC.

PEAKER, Prof. Malcolm, DSc, PhD; FZS, FLS, FIBiol, FRSE; Director, Hannah Research Institute, Ayr, since 1981; Hannah Professor, University of Glasgow, since 1981; *b* 21 Aug. 1943; *s* of Ronald Smith Peaker and Marian (*née* Tomasin); *m* 1965, Stephanie Jane Large; three *s. Educ:* Henry Mellish Grammar Sch., Nottingham; Univ. of Sheffield (BSc Zoology; DSc); Univ. of Hong Kong (SRC NATO Scholar; PhD). FZS 1969; FIBiol 1979; FRSE 1983; FLS 1989. Inst. of Animal Physiology, ARC, 1968–78; Head, Dept of Physiol., Hannah Res. Inst., 1978–81. Chairman: British Dendrobatid Gp, 1991–; Bd, London Zoo, 1992–93; Vice-Pres., Council, Zoological Soc. of London, 1992–94. Mem. Editorial Board: Jl of Dairy Science, 1975–78; Internat. Zoo Yearbook, 1978–82; Jl of Endocrinology, 1981–91; Procs of RSE, 1989–92; Endocrine Actions, 1991–; Editor: British Jl of Herpetology, 1977–81; Internat. Circle of Dairy Research Leaders, 1982–. *Publications:* Salt Glands in Birds and Reptiles, 1975; (ed) Avian Physiology, 1975; (ed) Comparative Aspects of Lactation, 1977; (ed jtly) Physiological Strategies in Lactation, 1984; papers in physiol, endocrinol, zool, biochem., vet. and agricl science jls. *Recreations:* vertebrate zoology, natural history, golf, grumbling about bureaucrats. *Address:* Hannah Research Institute, Ayr KA6 5HL. *T:* Prestwick (01292) 76013. *Club:* Farmers'.

PEARCE, Andrew; Deputy Head of Tourism Unit, European Commission, Brussels, since 1994; *b* 1 Dec. 1937; *s* of late Henry Pearce, Liverpool cotton broker, and Evelyn Pearce; *m* 1966, Myra Whelan; three *s* one *d. Educ:* Rydal School, Colwyn Bay; University of Durham. BA. Formerly in construction industry; in Customs Dept, EEC, Brussels, 1974–79. Contested (C) Islington North, 1969 and 1970; Mem. (C) Cheshire W, Eur. Parlt, 1979–89; contested (C): Cheshire W, European Parly elecn, 1989; Ellesmere Port and Neston, 1992. Founder and Vice-Pres., British Cons. Assoc. in Belgium; Vice-Pres., Consultative Assembly of Lomé Convention, 1980–89. Chm., Internat. Trade Cttee, British Retail Consortium, 1990–93; Vice Chm., European Business Develt Gp, Liverpool Chamber of Commerce, 1991–93. Governor: Archway Comprehensive School, 1967–70; Woodchurch High Sch., Birkenhead, 1985–90; Nugent Sch., Liverpool, 1992–94. *Address:* Devon House, 13 Lingdale Road, West Kirby, Wirral L48 5DG.

PEARCE, (Ann) Philippa, (Mrs M. J. G. Christie); freelance writer of children's fiction, since 1967; *b* 23 Jan. 1920; *d* of Ernest Alexander Pearce and Gertrude Alice (*née* Ramsden); *m* 1963, Martin James Graham Christie (decd); one *d. Educ:* Perse Girls' Sch., Cambridge; Girton Coll., Cambridge (MA Hons English Pt I, History Pt II). Temp. civil servant, 1942–45; Producer/Scriptwriter, Sch. Broadcasting, BBC Radio, 1945–58; Editor, Educn Dept, Clarendon Press, 1958–60; Children's Editor, André Deutsch Ltd, 1960–67. Also lectures. FRSL 1994. *Publications:* Minnow on the Say, 1955 (3rd edn 1974); Tom's Midnight Garden, 1958 (3rd edn 1976; Carnegie Medal, 1959); Mrs Cockle's Cat, 1961 (2nd edn 1974); A Dog So Small, 1962 (2nd edn 1964); (with Sir Harold Scott) From Inside Scotland Yard, 1963; The Strange Sunflower, 1966; (with Sir Brian Fairfax-Lucy) The Children of the House, 1968 (2nd edn 1970) (reissued as The Children of Charlecote, 1989); The Elm Street Lot, 1969 (enlarged edn, 1979); The Squirrel Wife, 1971 (2nd edn 1992); What the Neighbours Did and other stories, 1972 (2nd edn 1974); (ed) Stories from Hans Christian Andersen, 1972; Beauty and the Beast (re-telling), 1972; The Shadow Cage and other stories of the supernatural, 1977; The Battle of Bubble and Squeak, 1978 (Whitbread Award, 1978); Wings of Courage (trans. and adapted from George Sand's story), 1982; The Way to Sattin Shore, 1983; Lion at School and other stories, 1985; Who's Afraid? and other strange stories, 1986; The Toothball, 1987; Emily's Own Elephant, 1987; Freddy, 1988; Old Belle's Summer Holiday, 1989; Here comes Tod, 1992; (ed) Dread and Delight: a century of children's ghost stories (anthology), 1995; reviews in TLS and Guardian. *Address:* c/o Viking-Kestrel Books, 27 Wright's Lane, W8 5TZ. *T:* 0171–938 2200.

PEARCE, Sir Austin (William), Kt 1980; CBE 1974; PhD; FEng; Chairman, Oxford Instruments Group, 1987–91; *b* 1 Sept. 1921; *s* of William Thomas and Florence Annie Pearce; *m* 1st, 1947, Maglona Winifred Twinn (*d* 1975); three *d*; 2nd, 1979, Dr F. Patricia Grice (*née* Forsythe) (*d* 1993). *Educ:* Devonport High Sch. for Boys; Univ. of Birmingham. BSc (Hons) 1943, PhD 1945; Cadman Medallist. Joined Agwi Petroleum Corp., 1945 (later Esso Petroleum Co., Ltd): Asst Refinery Manager, 1954–56; Gen. Manager Refining, 1956–62; Dir, 1963; Man. Dir, 1968–71; Chm., 1972–80; Chm., British Aerospace, 1980–87; Director: Esso Europe Inc., 1972–80; Esso Africa Inc., 1972–80; Pres., Esso Holding Co. UK Inc., 1971–80; Chairman: Esso Pension Trust Ltd, 1972–80; Irish Refining Co. Ltd, 1965–71; Director: Williams & Glyn's Bank, 1974–85 (a Dep. Chm., 1980–83; Chm., 1983–85); Royal Bank of Scotland Gp (formerly Nat. & Commercial Banking Gp), 1978–92 (a Vice-Chm., 1985–92); Pearl Assurance PLC, 1985–91; Jaguar PLC, 1986–93; Smiths Ind. PLC, 1987–92. Part-time Mem., NRDC, 1973–76; Member: Adv. Council for Energy Conservation, 1974–79; Energy Commn, 1977–79; British Aerospace, 1977–87 (Mem., Organising Cttee, 1976); Standing Commn on Energy and the Environment, 1978–81; Takeover Panel, 1987–92. Chm., UK Petroleum Industry Adv. Cttee, 1977–80; Pres., UK Petroleum Industry Assoc. Ltd, 1979–80; CBI: Chm., Industrial Policy Cttee, 1982–85; Chm., Industrial Steering Policy Gp, 1985–86. President: Inst. of Petroleum, 1968–70; The Pipeline Industries Guild, 1973–75; Oil Industries Club, 1975–77; Pres., SBAC, 1982–83. Mem., Bd of Governors, English-Speaking Union, 1974–80; Chm., Bd of Trustees, Science Museum, 1986–95. Treas., RSA, 1988–93. Chm., Warden Housing Assoc., 1994–. Mem. Council, Surrey Univ., 1981–93 (Pro-Chancellor, 1986–93; Pro Chancellor Emeritus, 1994–). Hon. DSc: Southampton, 1978; Exeter, 1985; Salford, 1987; Cranfield, 1987; Hon. DEng Birmingham, 1986; DUniv Surrey, 1993. *Recreations:* golf, woodwork. *Address:* 25 Caroline Terrace, Belgravia, SW1W 8JT. *Club:* Royal Wimbledon Golf.

PEARCE, Brian; *see* Pearce, J. B.

PEARCE, Sir (Daniel Norton) Idris, Kt 1990; CBE 1982; TD 1972; DL; Consultant, Richard Ellis, Chartered Surveyors and International Property Consultants, since 1992 (Partner, 1961–92; Managing Partner, 1981–87); Deputy Chairman, English Partnerships, since 1993; *b* 28 Nov. 1933; *s* of late Lemuel George Douglas Pearce and Evelyn Mary Pearce; *m* 1963, Ursula Helene Langley; two *d. Educ:* West Buckland Sch.; College of Estate Management. FRICS. Commnd RE, 1958; comd 135 Field Survey Sqdn, RE(TA), 1970–73. Joined Richard Ellis 1959. Chairman: English Estates, 1989–94; Flexit Cos, 1993–; Director: The Phoenix Initiative, 1991; ITC, 1992–94; Nat. Mortgage Bank, 1992–; Higgs & Hill, 1993–; Dusco UK Ltd, 1993–. Royal Instn of Chartered Surveyors: Member: Gen. Council, 1980–94; Management Bd, 1984–91; Chm., Parly and Public Affairs Cttee, 1984–89; Vice Pres., 1986–90; Pres., 1990–91. Chm., Internat. Assets Valuation Standards Cttee, 1981–86. Member: Adv. Panel for Instnl Finance in New Towns, 1974–80; Sec. of State for Health and Social Security Inquiry into Surplus Land in the NHS, 1982; PSA Adv. Bd, 1981–86; FCO Adv. Panel on Diplomatic Estate, 1985–; Financial Reporting Review Panel, 1991–93; Bd, London Forum, 1993–; Property Advr, NHS Management Bd, 1985–90; Dep. Chm., Urban Regeneration Agency, 1993–. Chm., Higher Educn Funding Council for Wales, 1992–; Member: UFC, 1991–93; HEFCE, 1992–. Vice Chm., Greater London TA&VRA, 1991–94 (Mem. 1970–; Chm., Works and Bldgs Sub-Cttee, 1983–90). Chm. Develt Bd, Nat. Art-Collections Fund, 1988–92. Member: Court, City Univ., 1987–; Council, Univ. of Surrey, 1993– (Pro-Chancellor, 1994–). Chm. Governors, Stanway Sch., Dorking, 1982–85. Trustee, Rochester Bridge Trust, 1991–94. Gov., Peabody Trust, 1992–. Contested (C) Neath, 1959. DL Greater London, 1986. Hon. Fellow, Coll. of Estate Management, 1987; Centenary Fellow, Thames Poly., 1991; Companion, De Montfort Univ., 1992. Hon. Col, 135 Indep. Topographic Sqn, RE(V), TA, 1989–94. FRSA 1989. Hon. DSc: City, 1990; Oxford Poly., 1991; Salford Univ., 1991; Hon. DEng West of England, 1994. *Publications:* A Call to Talent, 1993; various articles on valuation and property matters. *Recreations:* reading, opera, ballet, travel. *Clubs:* Brooks's, City of London.

PEARCE, Edward Robin; author and political commentator; Columnist, The Guardian, since 1990; *b* 28 March 1939; *s* of late Frank Pearce and of Olive Pearce (*née* Johnson); *m* 1966, Deanna Maria Stanwell (*née* Singer); one *d. Educ:* Queen Elizabeth Grammar Sch., Darlington; St Peter's Coll., Oxford (MA); Univ. of Stockholm. Res. Asst, Labour Party, Transport Hse, 1964–66; Res. Officer, Police Fedn, 1966–68; with Douglas Mann & Co., solicitors, 1968–70; teacher, S Shields, 1970–75; contributor, Sunday Express, 1975–77;

Leader-writer, Daily Express, 1977–79; Parly sketch-writer, Daily Telegraph, 1979–87; freelance career, 1987–: columnist, Sunday Times, 1987–90; contrib. Sunday Telegraph, Daily Mail, Evening Standard, Wall St Jl, Sunday Tribune (Dublin), New Statesman, Spectator, Punch, Encounter, Tatler, New Republic (Washington), London Rev. of Books, Lit. Rev., TLS, etc. Panel Mem., The Moral Maze, Radio 4, 1991–, and BBC 2, 1994–; contrib. News Talk, LBC, 1989–92. Columnist of Year Award, What the Papers Say, 1987; Peter Wilson Award, League Against Cruel Sports, 1993. *Publications:* The Senate of Lilliput, 1983; Hummingbirds and Hyenas, 1985; Looking Down on Mrs Thatcher (collected Commons sketches), 1987; The Shooting Gallery, 1989; The Quiet Rise of John Major, 1990; Election Rides, 1992; Machiavelli's Children, 1993. *Recreations:* listening to classical music, esp. Schubert, watching cricket, esp. Lancashire, and football, esp. Oldham Athletic, reading history, esp. 18th Century, travel, esp. Italy, wandering around old towns, esp. ones with bookshops. *Address:* c/o The Guardian, 119 Farringdon Road, EC1R 3ER; Press Gallery, House of Commons, SW1A 0AA. *Clubs:* Reform, Academy.

PEARCE, Sir Eric (Herbert), Kt 1979; OBE 1970; Consultant to General Television Corporation, Channel Nine, Melbourne, Australia, since 1990 (Director of Community Affairs, 1979–90); *b* 5 March 1905; *s* of Herbert Clement Pearce and Louise Mary Pearce; *m* 1956, Betty Constance Ham (decd). *Educ:* Raynes Sch., Hants. Served War, FO RAAF, 1942–44. Studio Manager/Chief Announcer, Radio Stn 3DB, Melbourne, 1944–50; Gen. Man., Radio Stns 5KA-AO-RM, SA, 1950–55; Dir of Progs, major broadcasting network, Australia, 1955–56; Chief Announcer/Sen. Newsreader, General TV, Channel Nine, 1957–79. *Recreations:* walking, swimming, golf. *Address:* c/o General Television Corporation, Channel Nine, 22 Bendigo Street, Richmond, Vic 3121, Australia. *Clubs:* Athenæum, Toorak Services (Melbourne).

PEARCE, Most Rev. George; former Archbishop of Suva; *b* 9 Jan. 1921; *s* of George H. Pearce and Marie Louise Duval. *Educ:* Marist Coll. and Seminary, Framingham Center, Mass, USA. Entered Seminary, 1940; Priest, 1947; taught in secondary sch. in New England, USA, 1948–49; assigned as missionary to Samoa, 1949; consecrated Vicar Apostolic of Samoa, 1956; first Bishop of Apia, 1966; Archbishop of Suva, 1967–76, retired 1976. *Address:* Cathedral Rectory, 30 Fenner Street, Providence, RI 02903, USA. *T:* (401) 331–2434.

PEARCE, Howard John Stredder, CVO 1993; HM Diplomatic Service; Counsellor and Deputy Head of Mission, Budapest, since 1995; *b* 13 April 1949; *s* of late Ernest Victor Pearce and Ida (*née* Booth). *Educ:* City of London Sch.; Pembroke Coll., Cambridge (MA, LLB). Joined HM Diplomatic Service, 1972; FCO, 1972–74; Third Sec., Buenos Aires, 1975–78; FCO, 1978–83; First Sec. and Hd of Chancery, Nairobi, 1983–87; FCO, 1987–90; Sen. Associate Mem., St Antony's Coll., Oxford, 1990–91; Dep. Hd of Mission, Budapest, 1991–94; Fellow, Center for Internat. Affairs, Harvard Univ., 1994. Mem., Exec. Cttee, VSO, 1988–90. *Recreations:* classical music, opera, reading, travel. *Address:* c/o Foreign and Commonwealth Office, King Charles Street, SW1A 2AH. *Club:* United Oxford & Cambridge University.

PEARCE, Howard Spencer; Director for Wales, Property Services Agency, Department of Environment, 1977–85; *b* 23 Sept. 1924; *m* 1951, Enid Norma Richards (*d* 1994); one *s*. *Educ:* Barry County Sch.; College of Estate Management. ARICS. Armed Services, Major RE, 1943–47. Ministry of Works: Cardiff, 1953–61; Salisbury Plain, 1961–64; Ministry of Public Building and Works: Hong Kong, 1964–67; Abingdon, 1967–70; Area Officer, Abingdon, 1970–72; Regional Works Officer, SW Region, Bristol, PSA, Dept of Environment, 1972–77. *Recreations:* music, playing golf and watching Rugby football. *Address:* 2 Longhouse Close, Lisvane, Cardiff CF4 5XR. *T:* Cardiff (01222) 762029. *Club:* Cardiff Golf.

PEARCE, Sir Idris; *see* Pearce, Sir D. N. I.

PEARCE, (John) Brian; Director, The Inter Faith Network for the United Kingdom, since 1987; *b* 25 Sept. 1935; *s* of late George Frederic Pearce and Constance Josephine Pearce; *m* 1960, Michelle Etcheverry; four *s*. *Educ:* Queen Elizabeth Grammar Sch., Wakefield; Brasenose Coll., Oxford (BA). Asst Principal: Min. of Power, 1959; Colonial Office, 1960; Private Sec. to Parly Under-Sec. of State, 1963; Principal: Colonial Office, 1964; Dept of Economic Affairs, 1967; Principal Private Sec. to Sec. of State for Economic Affairs, 1968–69; Asst Sec., Civil Service Dept, 1969, Under-Sec., 1976; Under-Sec., HM Treasury, 1981–86, retd. *Recreations:* comparative theology, music, architecture. *Address:* 124 Court Lane, SE21 7EA.

PEARCE, John Trevor Archdall, CMG 1964; *b* 7 May 1916; *s* of late Rev. W. T. L. A. Pearce, Seven Hills, NSW, Australia, and late N. B. Pearce, Prahran, Victoria, Australia; *m* 1st, 1948, Isabel Bundey Rankine(*d* 1983), Hindmarsh Island, S Australia; no *c*; 2nd, 1984, Judith Burland Kingsley-Strack, Sydney, NSW. *Educ:* The King's Sch., Parramatta, Australia; Keble Coll., Oxford. MA. District Officer, Tanganyika, 1939. War Service: Kenya, Abyssinia, Ceylon, India, Burma, 1940–46, Major RE. Tanganyika: District Commissioner, 1950; Provincial Commissioner, 1959; Permanent Secretary (Admin), Office of the Vice-President, 1961; Chairman, Public Service Commn, Basutoland, 1963, Swaziland, 1965; Registrar, Papua and New Guinea Univ. of Technology, 1969–73. *Recreations:* golf, piano music, solitude, travel in remote places. *Address:* Clippings, 14 Golf Street, Buderim, Qld 4556, Australia.

PEARCE, Maj.-Gen. Leslie Arthur, CB 1973; CBE 1971 (OBE 1964; MBE 1956); Chief of General Staff, NZ Army, 1971–73, retd; *b* 22 Jan. 1918; British parents; *m* 1944, Fay Mattocks, Auckland, NZ; two *s* one *d*. *Educ:* in New Zealand. Joined Army, 1937; served War: Greece, Western Desert, Italy, 1939–45. Staff Coll., Camberley, 1948. Directing Staff, Australia Staff Coll., 1958–59; Commandant, Army Schools, NZ, 1960; Comdg Officer, 1 NZ Regt, in NZ and Malaysia, 1961–64; Dep. QMG, NZ Army, 1964–65; Dir of Staff Duties, NZ Army, 1966; IDC, 1967; QMG, 1968–69; Dep. Chief of Defence Staff, 1970. Chm., Vocational Training Council, 1975–81. Company director. Dep. Chm., NZ Council for Educnl Res., 1983–85 (Mem., 1977–85). *Recreations:* golf, fishing, gardening; Provincial and Services Rugby representative, in youth. *Address:* 49/106 Becroft Drive, Forrest Hill, Auckland, New Zealand.

PEARCE, Rev. Neville John Lewis; Priest-in-charge, Swainswick/Woolley, Diocese of Bath and Wells, since 1993; Chief Executive, Avon County Council, 1982–89; *b* 27 Feb. 1933; *s* of John and Ethel Pearce; *m* 1958, Eileen Frances Potter; two *d*. *Educ:* Queen Elizabeth's Hosp., Bristol; Silcoates Sch., Wakefield; Univ. of Leeds (LLB Hons 1953, LLM 1954); Trinity Theol Coll., Bristol. Asst Solicitor: Wakefield CBC, 1957–59; Darlington CBC, 1959–61; Chief Asst Solicitor, Grimsby CBC, 1961–63, Dep. Town Clerk, 1963–65; Dep. Town Clerk, Blackpool CBC, 1965–66; Town Clerk, Bath CBC, 1967–73; Dir of Admin and County Solicitor, Avon CC, 1973–82. Ordained (C of E), 1991; Asst Curate, St Swithin, Walcot, Bath, 1991–93. *Recreations:* home, family, Anglican church affairs. *Address:* Penshurst, Weston Lane, Bath BA1 4AB. *T:* Bath (01225) 426925.

PEARCE, Philippa; *see* Pearce, A. P.

PEARCE, Prof. Robert Penrose, FRMetS; FRSE; Professor of Meteorology and Head of Department of Meteorology, University of Reading, 1970–90, now Emeritus Professor; *b* 21 Nov. 1924; *s* of Arthur Penrose Pearce and Ada Pearce; *m* 1951, Patricia Frances Maureen Curling; one *s* two *d*. *Educ:* Bishop Wordsworth Sch., Salisbury; Imperial Coll., London (BSc, ARCS, DIC, PhD). Asst, Meteorological Office, 1941–43. Served RAF, 1943–47 (commnd 1945). Lectr, then Sen. Lectr in Mathematics, Univ. of St Andrews, 1952–66; Reader in Phys. Climatology, Imperial Coll., 1966–70. Pres., Royal Meteorological Soc., 1972–74; Chm., World Meteorol Org. Working Gp in Trop. Meteorology, 1978–90. *Publications:* Observer's Book of Weather, 1980; (co-ed) Monsoon Dynamics, 1981; sci. papers in meteorol jls. *Recreations:* walking, gardening, bridge, music. *Address:* Schiehallion, 27 Copped Hall Way, Camberley, Surrey GU15 1PB. *T:* Camberley (01276) 63103.

PEARL, David Stephen, PhD; **His Honour Judge Pearl;** a Circuit Judge, since 1994; *b* 11 Aug. 1944; *s* of Chaim Pearl and Anita (*née* Newman); *m* 1st, 1967, Susan Roer (marr. diss.); three *s*; 2nd, 1985, Gillian Maciejewska. *Educ:* George Dixon Grammar Sch., Birmingham; Westminster City Sch.; Birmingham Univ. (LLB); Queens' Coll., Cambridge (Sen. Scholar; LLM, MA, PhD). Called to the Bar, Gray's Inn, 1968; Cambridge University: Asst Lectr in Law, 1967–72; Lectr, 1972–89; Res. Fellow, Queens' Coll., 1967–69; Fellow and Dir of Studies in Law, Fitzwilliam Coll., Cambridge, 1969–89 (Life Fellow, 1989); Prof. of Law and Dean, Sch. of Law, UEA, 1989–94, Hon. Prof., 1995–; a Recorder, 1992–94. Vis. Prof., KCL, 1995–. Immigration Appeals Adjudicator, 1980–92; Chm., Immigration Appeal Tribunal, 1992–; Chief Immigration Adjudicator, 1994–. Vice-Pres., Internat. Soc. for Family Law, 1991–. Yorke Prize, Cambridge, 1972; Shaw Prize, Boston Coll. Law Sch., 1985; Van Heyden de Lancy Prize, Cambridge, 1991. *Publications:* A Textbook on Muslim Personal Law, 1979, 2nd edn 1987; Interpersonal Conflict of Laws in India, Pakistan and Bangladesh, 1980; (with K. Gray) Social Welfare Law, 1980; (with B. Hoggett) Family Law and Society, 1983, 3rd edn 1991; Family Law and Immigrant Communities, 1986; (with A. Grubb) Blood Testing AIDS and DNA Profiling, 1990; (jtly) Butterworth's Immigration Law Service, 1991. *Recreation:* long distance running (rather slowly). *Address:* Immigration Appeals Authority, 231 Strand, WC1R 1DA. *T:* 0171–353 8060.

PEARL, Valerie Louise, DPhil; FRHistS; President, New Hall, Cambridge, 1981–95; *b* 31 Dec. 1926; *d* of late Cyril Raymond Bence and Florence Bence; *m* 1949, Morris Leonard Pearl; one *d*. *Educ:* King Edward VI High Sch., Birmingham; St Anne's Coll., Oxford (Exhibnr; Hon. Fellow, 1994). BA Hons Mod. History; MA, DPhil (Oxon). Allen Research Studentship, St Hugh's Coll., Oxford, 1951; Eileen Power Studentship, 1952; Sen. Research Studentship, Westfield Coll., London, 1962; Leverhulme Research Award, 1962; Graham Res. Fellow and Lectr in History, Somerville Coll., Oxford, 1965; Reader in History of London, 1968–76, Prof. of History of London, 1976–81, University College London. Convenor of conf to found The London Journal, Chm. of Editorial Bd, Editor-in-Chief, 1973–77; McBride Vis. Prof., Cities Program, Bryn Mawr Coll., Pennsylvania, 1974; Woodward Lectr, Yale Univ., New Haven, 1974; Lectr, Indian Council for Soc. Sci., Calcutta, New Delhi, 1977; John Stow Commem. Lectr, City of London, 1979; James Ford Special Lectr, Oxford, 1980; Sir Lionel Denny Lectr, Barber Surgeons' Co., 1981. Literary Dir, Royal Historical Soc., 1975–77; Pres., London and Mddx Archaeol. Soc., 1980–82; Governor, Museum of London, 1978; Comr, Royal Commn on Historical MSS, 1983; Syndic: Cambridge Univ. Library, 1982; Cambridge Univ. Press, 1984. FSA 1976. *Publications:* London and the Outbreak of the Puritan Revolution, 1625–43, 1961; Change and Stability in 17th Century London (inaugural lecture, Univ. of London), 1978; (ed jtly) History and Imagination: essays for Hugh Trevor-Roper, 1981; (ed) J. Stow, The Survey of London, 1987; contribs to: Nuove Questione (ed L. Bulferetti), 1965; Studies in London History (ed W. Kellaway, A. Hollaender), 1969; The Interregnum (ed G. Aylmer), 1972; Puritans and Revolutionaries (ed K. Thomas, D. Pennington), 1978; also to learned jls and other works, including Trans Royal Hist. Soc., Eng. Historical Rev., History of English Speaking Peoples, Past and Present, Archives, Economic Hist. Rev., History, Jl of Eccles. History, Times Literary Supplement, The London Journal, London Rev. of Books, Albion, Listener, BBC, Rev. of English Studies, Proc. Mass. Hist. Soc., DNB Missing Persons, Urban History. *Recreations:* walking and swimming. *Address:* New Hall, Cambridge CB3 0DF. *T:* Cambridge (01223) 351721.

PEARLMAN, Valerie Anne; Her Honour Judge Pearlman; a Circuit Judge, since 1985; *b* 6 Aug. 1936; *d* of Sidney and Marjorie Pearlman; *m* 1972; one *s* one *d*. *Educ:* Wycombe Abbey Sch. Called to the Bar, Lincoln's Inn, 1958; a Recorder, 1982–85. Member: Parole Bd, 1989–94; Civil and Family Cttee, Judicial Studies Bd, 1992–; Chm., Home Sec's Adv. Bd on Restricted Patients, 1991–; Mem., Cttee on Mentally Disordered Offenders, Mental Health Foundn, 1992–. Mem. Council, Marlborough Coll., 1989–. Patron, Suzy Lamplugh Trust, 1987–. *Recreations:* gardening, reading. *Address:* Crown Court at Southwark, English Grounds, SE1 2HU.

PEARS, David Francis, FBA 1970; Student of Christ Church, Oxford, 1960–88, now Emeritus; Professor of Philosophy, Oxford University, 1985–88; *b* 8 Aug. 1921; *s* of late Robert and Gladys Pears; *m* 1963, Anne Drew; one *s* one *d*. *Educ:* Westminster Sch.; Balliol Coll., Oxford. Research Lecturer, Christ Church, 1948–50; Univ. Lectr, Oxford, 1950–72, Reader, 1972–85; Fellow and Tutor, Corpus Christi Coll., 1950–60. Visiting Professor: Harvard, 1959; Univ. of Calif, Berkeley, 1964; Rockefeller Univ., 1967; Los Angeles, 1979; Hill Prof., Univ. of Minnesota, 1970; Humanities Council Res. Fellow, Princeton, 1966. Mem., l'Inst. Internat. de Philosophie, 1978– (Prés., 1988–90). *Publications:* (trans. with B. McGuinness), Wittgenstein, Tractatus Logico-Philosophicus, 1961, repr. 1975; Bertrand Russell and the British Tradition in Philosophy, 1967, 2nd edn 1972; Ludwig Wittgenstein, 1971; What is Knowledge?, 1971; (ed) Russell's Logical Atomism, 1973; Some Questions in the Philosophy of Mind, 1975; Motivated Irrationality, 1984; The False Prison: a study of the development of Wittgenstein's philosophy, vol. I, 1987, vol. II, 1988; Hume's System, 1990. *Address:* 7 Sandford Road, Littlemore, Oxford OX4 4PU. *T:* Oxford (01865) 778768.

PEARSALL, Phyllis Isobel, MBE 1986; FRGS; painter, water colourist, etcher, writer; Founder and Director, since 1936, and Chairman and Managing Director, since 1958, Geographers' A to Z Map Co. Ltd; Founder and Director, since 1966, and Chairman, since 1987, Geographers' Map Trust; *b* 25 Sept. 1906; *d* of Alexander Gross and Isobel (*née* Crowley); *m* 1926, Richard Montague Stack Pearsall (marr. diss. 1938). *Educ:* Roedean; Collège de Jeunes Filles, Fécamp; Sorbonne. One-man shows: continuously 1926–; Little Gall., Arundel, 1983– (1988 exhibn opened by Minister for the Arts); Sally Hunter Fine Art Gall., 1989, 1995; exhibn, New Ashgate Gall., Farnham, 1990. Work in V&A Mus. and Mus. of London. 50th Anniversary Exhibn of A to Z develt at RGS (opened by Speaker of the H of C), 1986. Designer of book jackets and Christmas cards. Hd of Sect., MOI, 1942–45. FRGS 1936. *Publications:* Castilian Ochre, 1934; Fleet Street, Tite Street, Queer Street, 1983; Only the Unexpected Happens, 1985; Women 1939–40, 1985; Women at War, 1990; From Bedsitter to Household Name: the personal story of A to Z Maps, 1990; An Artist's Pilgrimage in Business, 1993; short stories in Cornhill Mag., New Yorker. *Recreations:* cooking, opera, theatre. *Address:* Geographers' A to Z Map Co.

Ltd, Fairfield Road, Borough Green, Sevenoaks, Kent TN15 8PP. *T:* Sevenoaks (01732) 781000. *Clubs:* Arts, University Women's.

PEARSE, Prof. Anthony Guy Everson, MA, MD (Cantab); FRCP, FRCPath; DCP (London); Professor of Histochemistry, University of London, Royal Postgraduate Medical School, 1965–81, now Emeritus; *b* 9 Aug. 1916; *o s* of Captain R. G. Pearse, DSO, MC, Modbury, Devon, and Constance Evelyn Steels, Pocklington, Yorks; *m* 1947, Elizabeth Himmelhoch, MB, BS (Sydney), DCP (London); one *s* three *d. Educ:* Sherborne Sch.; Trinity Coll., Cambridge. Kitchener Scholar. Posts, St Bart's Hospital, 1940–41; Surg.-Lt, RNVR, 1941–45 (21st and 24th Destroyer Flotillas). Registrar, Edgware General Hospital, 1946; Asst Lecturer in Pathol., PG Med. School, London, 1947–51, Lecturer, 1951–57; Cons. Pathol., Hammersmith Hospital, 1951; Fulbright Fellow and Visiting Prof. of Path., University of Alabama, 1953–54; Guest Instructor in Histochemistry: University of Kansas, 1957, 1958; Vanderbilt Univ., 1967; Reader in Histochemistry, University of London, 1957–65; Middleton Goldsmith Lectr, NY Path. Soc., 1976; Feulgen Lectr, Deutsch Ges. Histochem., 1983, Hon. Mem., 1986. Member: Path. Society (GB), 1949 (Hon. Mem., 1990); Biochem. Society (GB), 1957; European Gastro Club, 1969; Hon. Member or Member various foreign societies incl. Deutsche Akademie der Naturforscher Leopoldina, 1973 and Amer. Assoc. Endocrine Surgeons, 1981; Corresp. Mem., Deutsche Gesellschaft für Endokrinologie, 1978; Hon. Fellow, Royal Microscop. Society, 1964 (Vice-Pres., 1970–72; Pres., 1972–74). Hon. Mem., Mark Twain Soc., 1977. Hon. MD: Basel, 1960; Krakow, 1978. Raymond Horton-Smith Prize, Univ. of Cambridge, 1950; John Hunter Medal and Triennial Prize, RCS, 1976–78; Ernest Jung Foundn Prize and Medal for Medicine, 1979; Fred W. Stewart Medal and Prize, Sloan-Kettering Cancer Center, NY, 1979; Jan Swammerdam Medal, Soc. for Advancement of Nat. Scis, Amsterdam, 1988; Schleiden Medal, Deutsche Akademie der Naturforscher Leopoldina, 1989. Member Editorial Board: Histochemie, 1958–73; Jl Histochem. Cytochem., 1959–68; Enzymol. biol. clin., 1961–67; Jl of Royal Microscopical Soc., 1967–69; Histochemical Jl, 1968–; Brain Research, 1968–76; Cardiovascular Research, 1968–75; Virchow's Archiv 'B', 1968–91; Jl Microscopy, 1969–81; Jl of Neuro-visceral Relations, 1969–73; Jl of Molecular and Cellular Cardiology, 1970–79; Scand. Jl Gastroenterol., 1971–81; Jl Neural Transmission, 1973–76; Jl of Pathology, 1973–83; Progress in Histochem. Cytochem., 1973–; Histochemistry, 1974–91; Mikroscopie, 1977–88; Basic and Applied Histochem., 1979–90; Acta Histochem., 1980–; Europ. Jl of Basic and Applied Histochem., 1991–92; European Jl of Hystochem., 1993–; Editor, Medical Biology, 1974–84. *Publications:* Histochemistry Theoretical and Applied, 1953, 2nd edn, 1960; 3rd edn, vol. I, 1968, vol. II, 1972; 4th edn vol. I, 1980, vol. II, 1984, vol. III (with P. J. Stoward), 1991; numerous papers on theoretical and applied histochemistry, esp. endocrinology (The Neuroendocrine System). *Recreations:* horticulture (plant hybridization, Liliaceae, Asclepiadaceae); ship modelling, foreign touring. *Address:* Church Cottage, Church Lane, Cheriton Bishop, Exeter EX6 6HY. *T:* Cheriton Bishop (01647) 24231. *Club:* Naval.

PEARSE, Barbara Mary Frances, (Mrs M. S. Bretscher), PhD; FRS 1988; Staff Scientist, Medical Research Council Laboratory of Molecular Biology, Cambridge, since 1981; *b* 24 March 1948; *d* of Reginald William Blake Pearse and Enid Alice (*née* Mitchell); *m* 1978, Mark Steven Bretscher, *qv*; one *s* one *d. Educ:* The Lady Eleanor Holles Sch., Hampton, Mddx; University Coll. London (BSc Biochemistry, PhD). MRC Res. Fellowship, 1972–74; Beit Meml Fellowship, 1974–77; SRC Advanced Fellowship, 1977–82; CRC Internat. Fellowship Vis. Prof., Stanford Med. Centre, USA, 1984–85. Mem., EMBO, 1982–. EMBO Medal, 1987. *Publications:* contribs to sci. jls. *Recreations:* wild flowers, planting trees, fresh landscapes. *Address:* Ram Cottage, 63 Commercial End, Swaffham Bulbeck, Cambridge CB5 0ND. *T:* Cambridge (01223) 811276.

PEARSE, Sir Brian (Gerald), Kt 1994; FCIB; Chairman: Lucas Industries PLC, since 1994; Housing Corporation, since 1994; *b* 23 Aug. 1933; *s* of Francis and Eileen Pearse; *m* 1959, Patricia M. Callaghan; one *s* two *d. Educ:* St Edward's Coll., Liverpool. Martin's Bank Ltd, 1950; Barclays Bank, 1969–91: Local Dir, Birmingham, 1972; Gen. Man., 1977; Chief Exec. Officer, N America, 1983; Finance Dir, 1987–91; Chief Exec., 1991–94, Dir, 1994–95, Midland Bank. Dir, Smith & Nephew, 1993–; non-exec. Dir, HSBC plc, 1992–94. Chm., Assoc. for Payments Clearing Services, 1987–91. Director: British American Chamber of Commerce, 1987–; Private Finance Panel, 1993–; BOTB, 1994–. Chairman: Young Enterprise, 1992; British Invisibles, 1994–. Mem., Council for Industry of Higher Educn. Treas., KCL, 1992–. Pres., CIB, 1993–94. Governor, St Edward's Coll., Liverpool, 1992. FRSA 1991. CIMgt (CBIM 1992). *Recreations:* Rugby football, opera. *Address:* Lucas Industries PLC, 44–46 Park Street, W1Y 4DJ. *Club:* Royal Automobile.

PEARSE, Rear-Adm. John Roger Southey G.; *see* Gerard-Pearse.

PEARSON, family name of **Viscount Cowdray** and **Baron Pearson of Rannoch.**

PEARSON OF RANNOCH, Baron *cr* 1990 (Life Peer), of Bridge of Gaur in the district of Perth and Kinross; **Malcolm Everard MacLaren Pearson;** Chairman, PWS Holdings plc, since 1988; *b* 20 July 1942; *s* of Col John MacLaren Pearson; *m* 1st, 1965, Francesca Frua De Angeli (marr. diss. 1970); one *d*; 2nd, 1977, Hon. Mary, *d* of Baron Charteris of Amisfield, *qv*; two *d. Educ:* Eton. Founded PWS group of reinsurance brokers, 1964. Member: H of L Select Cttee on Eur. Communities, 1992–; Sub-cttee C on Envmt and Social Affairs, 1992–. Chm., Rannoch Protection Group, 1979–; founded Rannoch Trust, 1984 (Exec. Trustee). Mem., CNAA, 1983–93 (Hon. Treas., 1986–93). Hon. Pres., Nat. Soc. for Mentally Handicapped People in Residential Care, 1994–. *Recreations:* stalking, fishing, golf. *Address:* Rannoch Barracks, Rannoch Station, Perthshire PH17 2QE. *Clubs:* White's; Swinley Forest Golf.

PEARSON, Brig. Alastair Stevenson, CB 1958; DSO; OBE 1953; MC; TD; farmer; Lord Lieutenant of Dunbartonshire, 1979–90; Keeper of Dumbarton Castle, since 1981; *b* 1 June 1915; *m* 1944, Mrs Joan Morgan Weld-Smith; three *d. Educ:* Kelvinside Acad.; Sedbergh. Co. Director, 1936–39; served War of 1939–45 (MC, DSO, and three Bars); embodied 6th Bn Highland LI, TA, 1939; transferred to Parachute Regt, 1941; Lt-Col 1942; CO 1st and 8th Para Bns, 1942–45, CO 15th (Scottish) Bn The Parachute Regt (TA), 1947–53; Dep. Comd 46 Parachute Bde (TA), 1953–59. Comd Scotland Army Cadet Force, Brigadier, 1967–81. ADC to the Queen, 1956–61. Hon. Col, 15th (Scottish) Bn The Parachute Regt (TA), 1963–77 and 1983–90; Hon. Sheriff, Dunbarton, 1991. DL Glasgow, 1951, Dunbartonshire, 1975. KStJ 1980. *Address:* Tullochan, Gartocharn, by Alexandria, Dunbartonshire G83 8ND. *T:* Gartocharn (01389) 830205.

PEARSON, Anthony James; Director of Programmes, Prison Service, since 1993; *b* 2 Nov. 1939; 2nd *s* of Leslie Pearson and Winifred Pearson (*née* Busby); *m* 1964, Sandra Lowe; two *d. Educ:* Saltley Grammar Sch., Birmingham; Exeter Univ. (BA Hons 1961); Oxford Univ. (Dip. Soc. and Public Admin 1962). Assistant Prison Governor: Maidstone, 1963–67; Albany, 1967–69; Parkhurst, 1970–72; Dep. Governor, Wandsworth Prison, 1972–73; Prison Service HQ, 1973–77; Prison Governor: Gartree, 1977–81; Brixton, 1981–85; HM Dep. Chief Inspector of Prisons, 1985–87; Prison Service Headquarters: Hd of Div., 1987–89; Hd, Directorate of Telecommunications, 1989–91; Area Manager, 1991–93. *Recreations:* Rugby, cricket (armchair expert). *Address:* Prison Service, Cleland House, Page Street, SW1P 4LN. *T:* 0171–217 6544.

PEARSON, Rev. Canon Brian William; Archbishop's Officer for Mission and Evangelism and Tait Missioner for Canterbury Diocese, since 1991; *b* 18 Aug. 1949; *s* of Victor William Charles Pearson and Florence Irene (*née* Webster); *m* 1974, Althea Mary Stride; two *s. Educ:* Roan Sch. for Boys, Blackheath; Brighton Polytechnic (BSc Hons); City Univ. (MSc); Ordination Training (Southwark Ordination Course); MTh Oxford 1994. CEng; MBCS; FHSM. Systems Engineer: IBM UK, 1967–71; Rohm and Haas UK, 1971–72; Lectr, Thames Polytechnic, 1972–81; College Head of Dept, Northbrook Coll., W Sussex, 1981–88; Bishop's Research Officer and Communications Officer, Bath and Wells, 1988–91. Hon. Canon, Canterbury Cathedral, 1992. *Publication:* Yes Manager: Management in the local church, 1986. *Recreations:* cricket, theatre, cinema, music, learning about life through the experiences of two young sons, travel, enjoying the humour God has placed in His world. *Address:* c/o The Old Palace, Canterbury, Kent CT1 2EE.

PEARSON, David Compton Froome; Deputy Chairman, Robert Fleming Holdings Ltd, 1986–90 (Director, 1974–90); *b* 28 July 1931; *s* of late Compton Edwin Pearson, OBE and of Marjorie (*née* Froome); *m* 1966, Venetia Jane Lynn (marr. diss. 1994); two *d. Educ:* Haileybury; Downing Coll., Cambridge (MA). Linklaters & Paines, Solicitors, 1957–69 (Partner, 1961–69); Dir, Robert Fleming & Co. Ltd, 1969–90; Chairman: The Fleming Property Unit Trust, 1971–90; Gill & Duffus Group Plc, 1982–85 (Dir, 1973–85); Robert Fleming Securities, 1985–90; River & Mercantile Investment Management Ltd, 1994–; Dep. Chm., Austin Reed Group Plc, 1977– (Dir, 1971–); Director: Blue Circle Industries Plc, 1972–87; Lane Fox and Partners Ltd, 1987–91; River & Mercantile Trust Plc, 1994–; Chesterton International Plc, 1994–. Mem., Finance Act 1960 Tribunal, 1978–84. *Recreations:* gardening, walking. *Address:* The Manor, Berwick St John, Shaftesbury, Dorset SP7 0EX. *T:* Donhead (01747) 828363. *Club:* Brooks's.

PEARSON, Derek Leslie, CB 1978; Deputy Secretary, Overseas Development Administration (formerly Ministry of Overseas Development), 1977–81; *b* 19 Dec. 1921; *s* of late George Frederick Pearson and Edith Maud Pearson (*née* Dent); *m* 1956, Diana Mary, *d* of late Sir Ralph Freeman; no *c. Educ:* William Ellis Sch.; London Sch. of Economics. BSc (Econ). Served War of 1939–45; Lieut (A) (O) RNVR. Colonial Office, 1947; seconded to Kenya, 1954–56; Principal Private Sec. to Sec. of State for Colonies, 1959–61; Dept of Technical Cooperation, 1961; Asst Sec., 1962; ODM, 1964; Under Secretary: CSD, 1970–72; Min. of Overseas Develt, 1972–75; Dep. Sec., Cabinet Office, 1975–77. *Address:* Langata, Little London Road, Horam, Heathfield, East Sussex TN21 0BG. *Clubs:* Naval, Civil Service.

PEARSON, (Edward) John (David); Director, Regional Policies Directorate-General, Commission of the European Communities, since 1991; *b* 1 March 1938; *s* of Sydney Pearson and Hilda Beaumont; *m* 1963, Hilary Stuttard; three *s* two *d. Educ:* Huddersfield Coll.; Emmanuel Coll., Cambridge (MA). Admin. Trainee, London Transport Exec., 1959; Asst Principal, MoT, 1960, Principal 1965; Sen. Principal, DoE, 1971; Commission of the European Communities: Head of Div., Transport Directorate-Gen., 1973–81; Dir, Fisheries Directorate-Gen., 1981–91. *Recreation:* orienteering (Pres., Belgian Orienteering Assoc., 1982–87; Chm., Develt and Promotion Cttee, 1986–88, Mem. Council, 1988–94, Internat. Orienteering Fedn). *Address:* Rue du Repos 56, 1180 Brussels, Belgium. *T:* (2) 3751182.

PEARSON, Sir (Francis) Nicholas (Fraser), 2nd Bt *cr* 1964, of Gressingham, Co. Palatine of Lancaster; Director, Saison Holdings BV, since 1990; *b* 28 Aug. 1943; *s* of Sir Francis Fenwick Pearson, 1st Bt, MBE and of Katharine Mary, *d* of Rev. D. Denholm Fraser; *S* father, 1991; *m* 1978, Henrietta Elizabeth, *d* of Comdr Henry Pasley-Tyler. *Educ:* Radley Coll. Commnd The Rifle Brigade, 1961; active service, Cyprus, Zambia, Borneo, 1961–67; ADC to: Army Comdr, Far East, 1967; C-in-C, Far East, 1968. Dir, Hill & Delamain Ltd, 1970–75; Dep. Chm., Claughton Manor Brickworks, 1978; Chairman: Turner Gp Ltd, 1979; House of Hanover Gp; Director: Intercontinental Hotel Group Ltd, 1989–; Virgin Atlantic Airlines, 1989–; Ecofin Gp; Passport Hotels. Trustee, Ruskin Foundn. Prospective Parly Cand. (C), Oldham West, 1976–79. *Recreations:* walking, poetry, fishing. *Heir:* none. *Address:* c/o National Westminster Bank, 55 Main Street, Kirkby Lonsdale, Cumbria. *Clubs:* Carlton; Vanderbilt Racquet.

PEARSON, Dr Graham Scott, CB 1990; CChem, FRSC; Assistant Chief Scientific Adviser (Non-Proliferation), Ministry of Defence, since 1995; *b* 20 July 1935; *s* of Ernest Reginald Pearson and Alice (*née* Maclachlan); *m* 1960, Susan Elizabeth Meriton Benn; two *s. Educ:* Woodhouse Grove Sch., Bradford; St Salvator's Coll., Univ. of St Andrews (BSc 1st Cl. Hons Chemistry, 1957; PhD 1960). Postdoctoral Fellow, Univ. of Rochester, NY, USA, 1960–62; joined Scientific Civil Service, 1962; Rocket Propulsion Estab., 1962–69; Def. Res. and Develt Staff, Washington, DC, 1969–72; PSO to Dir Gen. Res. Weapons, 1972–73; Asst Dir, Naval Ordnance Services/Scientific, 1973–76; Technical Adviser/Explosives, Materials and Safety (Polaris), 1976–79; Principal Supt, Propellants Explosives and Rocket Motor Estab., Westcott, 1979–80; Dep. Dir 1, 1980–82 and Dep. Dir 2, 1982–83, RARDE, Fort Halstead; Dir Gen., ROF (Res. and Develt), 1983–84; Dir, Chemical Defence Estabt, later Dir Gen., Chemical and Biol Defence Estabt, Porton Down, 1984–95. FRSA 1989. *Publications:* contrib. to: Advances in Photochemistry, vol. 3, 1964; Advances in Inorganic and Radio Chemistry, vol. 8, 1966; Oxidation and Combustion Reviews, vol. 3, 1968 and vol. 4, 1969; Biological Weapons: Weapons of the Future?, 1993; Non-Conventional Weapons Proliferation in the Middle East, 1993; articles on combustion, and on chemical and biological defence and arms control, in scientific jls; official reports. *Recreations:* long distance walking, photography, reading, gardening. *Address:* Ministry of Defence, Main Building, Whitehall, SW1A 2HB. *T:* 0171–218 7312.

PEARSON, Ian Phares, PhD; MP (Lab) Dudley West, since Dec. 1994; *b* 5 April 1959; *m* Annette Pearson; two *d. Educ:* Brierley Hill GS; Balliol Coll., Oxford (BA Hons PPE, MA); Warwick Univ. (PhD). Mem. (Lab) Dudley BC, 1984–87. Local Govt Policy Res. Officer, Lab. Party, 1985–87; Dep. Dir, Urban Trust, 1987–88; Jt Chief Exec., W Midlands Enterprise Bd, 1991–94. *Address:* House of Commons, SW1A 0AA.

PEARSON, Prof. James Douglas; Emeritus Professor of Bibliography, with reference to Asia and Africa, School of Oriental and African Studies, University of London (Professor, 1972–79); *b* 17 Dec. 1911; *m* 1st, Rose Betty Burden (marr. diss.); one *s*; 2nd, Hilda M. Wilkinson; three *s. Educ:* Cambridge Univ. (MA). Asst Under-librarian, Cambridge Univ. Library, 1939–50; Librarian, Sch. of Oriental and African Studies, Univ. of London, 1950–72. Hon. FLA, 1976. Walford Award for services to bibliography, 1992. *Publications:* Index Islamicus, 1958–82; Oriental and Asian Bibliography, 1966; Oriental Manuscripts in Europe and North America, 1971; (ed jtly) Arab Islamic Bibliography, 1977; (ed) South Asia Bibliography, 1978; Creswell's Bibliography of the Architecture, Arts and Crafts of Islam, Supplement II, 1984; A Guide to Manuscripts and Documents in the British Isles relating to South and SE Asia, Vol. I, 1989, Vol. II, 1990; A Guide to Manuscripts and Documents in the British Isles relating to Africa, Vol I, 1993, Vol. II, 1994. *Recreations:* natural history, travel. *Address:* 79 Highsett, Hills Road, Cambridge CB2 1NZ.

PEARSON, John; *see* Pearson, E. J. D.

PEARSON, Captain John William, CBE 1981; Regional Administrator, Mersey Regional Health Authority, 1977–81; *b* 19 Sept. 1920; *s* of Walter and Margaret Jane Pearson; *m* 1945, Audrey Ethel Whitehead; two *s*. *Educ:* Holloway Sch. FCIS, FHA, FCCA, IPFA. Served War, RA (Field), 1939–46. Hospital Service, LCC, 1947–48; NW Metropolitan Regional Hosp. Bd, 1948–49; Northern Gp, HMC, Finance Officer, 1949–62; Treasurer: St Thomas' Bd of Governors, 1962–73; Mersey Regional Health Authority, 1973–77. Pres., Assoc. of Health Service Treasurers, 1970–71. *Recreations:* tennis, golf, gardening, snooker. *Address:* 20 Weare Gifford, Shoeburyness, Essex SS3 8AB. *T:* Southend (01702) 585039.

PEARSON, Keith Philip, MA; FRSE; Headmaster, George Heriot's School, Edinburgh, since 1983; *b* 5 Aug. 1941; *s* of Fred G. and Phyllis Pearson; *m* 1965, Dorothy (*née* Atkinson); two *d*. *Educ:* Madrid Univ. (Dip. de Estudios Hispanicos); Univ. of Cambridge (MA; Cert. of Educn). Teacher, Rossall Sch., 1964–72 (Head of Mod. Langs, 1968–72); George Watson's College: Head of Mod. Langs, 1972–79; Dep. Principal, 1979–83. *Recreations:* sport, mountains, music, DIY. *Address:* 11 Pentland Avenue, Edinburgh EH13 0HZ. *T:* 0131–441 2630.

PEARSON, Sir Nicholas; *see* Pearson, Sir F. N. F.

PEARSON, Maj.-Gen. Ronald Matthew, CB 1985; MBE 1959; Director Army Dental Service, 1982–85, retired; *b* 25 Feb. 1925; *s* of Dr John Pearson and Sheila Pearson (*née* Brown); *m* 1956, Florence Eileen Jack; two *d*. *Educ:* Clifton Hall Sch., Ratho, Midlothian; Glasgow Acad.; Glasgow Univ./Glasgow Dental Hosp. LDS RFPS(Glas) 1948; FBIM 1979. Civilian Dental Practice, 1948–49. Commnd RADC, 1949; served: RWAFF, 1950–53; UK, 1953–57; BAOR, 1957–60; UK, 1961–67; CO No 1 Dental Gp, BAOR, 1967–70; CO Army Dental Centres, Cyprus, 1970–73; CO No 8 Dental Gp, UK, 1973–75; CO No 4 Dental Gp, UK, 1975–76; Dep. Dir Dental Service, UKLF, 1976–78; Dep. Dir Dental Service, BAOR, 1978–82. QHDS, 1978–85. CStJ 1983. *Recreations:* trout fishing, photography, gardening, caravanning. *Address:* c/o Royal Bank of Scotland, Holts Branch, Victoria Road, Farnborough, Hants GU14 7NR.

PEARSON, Sybil Angela Margaret, (Mrs Michael Pearson); *see* Jones, S. A. M.

PEARSON, Gen. Sir Thomas (Cecil Hook), KCB 1967 (CB 1964); CBE 1959 (OBE 1953); DSO 1940, and Bar, 1943; DL; retired 1974; *b* 1 July 1914; *s* of late Vice-Admiral J. L. Pearson, CMG; *m* 1947, Aud, *d* of late Alf Skjelkvale, Oslo; two *s*. *Educ:* Charterhouse; Sandhurst. 2nd Lieutenant Rifle Bde, 1934. Served War of 1939–45, M East and Europe; CO 2nd Bn The Rifle Bde, 1942; Dep. Comdr 2nd Independent Parachute Bde Gp 1944; Dep. Comdr 1st Air-landing Bde 1945; GSO1 1st Airborne Div. 1945; CO 1st Bn The Parachute Regt 1946; CO 7th Bn The Parachute Regt 1947; GSO1 (Land Air Warfare), WO, 1948; JSSC, GSO1, HQ Malaya, 1950; GSO1 (Plans), FARELF, 1951; Directing Staff, JSSC, 1953; Comdr 45 Parachute Bde TA 1955; Nat. Defence Coll., Canada, 1956; Comdr 16 Indep. Parachute Bde 1957; Chief of Staff to Dir of Ops Cyprus, 1960; Head of Brit. Mil. Mission to Soviet Zone of Germany, 1960; Major-General Commanding 1st Division, BAOR, 1961–63; Chief of Staff, Northern Army Group, 1963–67; Comdr, FARELF, 1967–68; Military Sec., MoD, 1968–72; C-in-C, Allied Forces, Northern Europe, 1972–74; psc 1942; jssc 1950; ndc Canada 1957. ADC Gen. to the Queen, 1974. Col Comdt, the Royal Green Jackets, 1973–77. Fisheries Mem., Welsh Water Auth., 1980–83. DL Hereford and Worcester, 1983. Haakon VII Liberty Cross, 1948; Medal of Honour, Norwegian Defence Assoc., 1973. *Recreations:* field sports, yachting. *Clubs:* Naval and Military; Kongelig Norsk Seilforenning.

PEART, Brian; Under-Secretary, Ministry of Agriculture, Fisheries and Food, 1976–85; *b* 17 Aug. 1925; *s* of late Joseph Garfield Peart and Frances Hannah Peart (*née* English); *m* 1952, Dorothy (*née* Thompson); one *s* one *d*. *Educ:* Wolsingham Grammar Sch.; Durham Univ. (BA). Served War, RAF, 1943–47. Agricultural Economist, Edinburgh Sch. of Agric., 1950–57; Sen. Agricultural Economist, 1957–64; Regional Farm Management Adviser, MAFF, West Midlands Region, 1964–67; Chief Farm Management Adviser, MAFF, 1967–71; Regional Manager, MAFF, Yorks/Lancs Region, 1971–74; Head of Intelligence and Trng Div., 1974–76; Chief Administrator, ADAS, 1976–80; Under Sec., Lands Gp, MAFF, 1980–85. *Recreations:* golf, genealogy, bridge, The Times crossword. *Address:* 18 Derwent Close, Claygate, Surrey KT10 0RF. *Club:* Farmers'.

PEART, Michael John, CMG 1995; LVO 1983; HM Diplomatic Service; Ambassador to Fiji and concurrently High Commissioner (non-resident) to Kiribati, Nauru and Tuvalu, since 1995; *b* 15 Dec. 1943; *s* of Joseph Albert William Peart and Thelma Theresa Peart (*née* Rasmussen); *m* 1968, Helena Mary Stuttle; one *s* (one *d* decd). *Educ:* Gillingham County Grammar Sch., Kent. Prison Dept, Home Office, 1960–65; FCO 1966–69; served Blantyre, 1969–71; Warsaw, 1972–75; Mexico City, 1975–80; FCO, 1980–83; Dhaka, 1983–86; FCO, 1987–91; Ambassador, Lithuania, 1991–94. *Recreations:* music, reading, walking. *Address:* c/o Foreign and Commonwealth Office, King Charles Street, SW1A 2AH.

PEART, Prof. Sir (William) Stanley, Kt 1985; MD; FRS 1969; Professor of Medicine, University of London, at St Mary's Hospital Medical School, 1956–87, now Emeritus; *b* 31 March 1922; *s* of J. G. and M. Peart; *m* 1947, Peggy Parkes; one *s* one *d*. *Educ:* King's College School, Wimbledon; Medical School, St Mary's Hospital. MB, BS (Hons), 1945; FRCP, 1959; MD (London), 1949. Lecturer in Medicine, St Mary's Hospital, 1950–56. Master, Hunterian Inst., RCS, 1988–92. Wellcome Trust: Trustee, 1975–94; Dep. Chm., 1991–94; Consultant, 1994–; Beit Trustee, 1986–. Goulstonian Lectr, 1959, Croonian Lectr, 1979, RCP. Hon. For. Mem., Académie Royale de Médicine de Belgique, 1984. Hon. FIC, 1988. Hon. DSc Edinburgh, 1993. Stouffer Prize, Amer. Heart Assoc., 1968. *Publications:* chapters in: Cecil-Loeb, Textbook of Medicine; Renal Disease; Biochemical Disorders in Human Disease; articles in Biochemical Journal, Journal of Physiology, Lancet. *Recreations:* ski-ing, reading, tennis. *Address:* 17 Highgate Close, N6 4SD.

PEASE, family name of **Barons Gainford,** and **Wardington.**

PEASE, Sir (Alfred) Vincent, 4th Bt *cr* 1882; *b* 2 April 1926; *s* of Sir Alfred (Edward) Pease, 2nd Bt (*d* 1939), and of his 3rd wife, Emily Elizabeth (Dowager Lady Pease, JP) (*d* 1979); *S* half-brother, 1963; unmarried. *Educ:* Bootham School, York; Durham Sch. of Agric., Houghall. *Heir: b* Joseph Gurney Pease [*b* 16 Nov. 1927; *m* 1953, Shelagh Munro, *d* of C. G. Bulman; one *s* one *d*]. *Address:* 149 Aldenham Road, Guisborough, Cleveland TS14 8LB. *T:* Guisborough (01287) 636453.

PEASE, Dr Rendel Sebastian, FRS 1977; Programme Director for Fusion, UKAEA, 1981–87; *b* 1922; *s* of Michael Stewart Pease and Helen Bowen (*née* Wedgwood); *m* 1952, Susan Spickernell; two *s* three *d*. *Educ:* Bedales Sch.; Trinity Coll., Cambridge (MA, ScD). Scientific Officer, Min. of Aircraft Prodn at ORS Unit, HQ, RAF Bomber Comd, 1942–46; research at AERE, Harwell, 1947–61; Div. Head, Culham Lab. for Plasma Physics and Nuclear Fusion, UKAEA, 1961–67; Vis. Scientist, Princeton Univ., 1964–65; Asst Dir, UKAEA Research Gp, 1967; Dir, Culham Lab., UKAEA, 1968–81. Gordon Godfrey Vis. Prof. of Theoretical Physics, Univ. NSW, 1984, 1988 and 1991; Visitor, Blackett Lab., Imperial Coll., London, 1992–. Chairman: Adam Hilger Ltd, 1976–77; Plasma Physics Commn, Internat. Union of Pure and Applied Physics, 1975–78; Internat. Fusion Res. Council, Internat. Atomic Energy Agency, 1976–83; British Pugwash Gp, 1988–. Member: Council, Royal Soc., 1985–87 (a Vice-Pres., 1986–87); Fabian Soc.; Inst. of Physics (Vice-Pres., 1973–77; Pres., 1978–80); Amer. Inst. of Physics; IEE. Hon. Fellow, European Nuclear Soc., 1990. DUniv Surrey, 1973; Hon. DSc: Aston, 1981; City Univ., 1987. *Publications:* articles in physics jls, and Pugwash confs on science and world affairs. *Recreation:* music. *Address:* The Poplars, West Ilsley, Newbury, Berks RG16 0AW.

PEASE, Sir Richard Thorn, 3rd Bt *cr* 1920; DL; Chairman, Yorkshire Bank, 1986–90 (Director, since 1977; Deputy Chairman, 1981–86); *b* 20 May 1922; *s* of Sir Richard Arthur Pease, 2nd Bt, and Jeannette Thorn (*d* 1957), *d* of late Gustav Edward Kissel, New York; *S* father, 1969; *m* 1956, Anne, *d* of late Lt-Col Reginald Francis Heyworth; one *s* two *d*. *Educ:* Eton. Served with 60th Rifles, Middle East, Italy and Greece, 1941–46 (Captain). Director: Owners of the Middlesbrough Estate Ltd, 1954–86; Barclays Bank, 1964–89; Bank of Scotland, 1977–85; Grainger Trust PLC, 1986–94; Vice-Chairman: Barclays Bank Ltd, 1970–82; Barclays Bank UK Management, 1971–82; Chm., Foreign and Colonial High Income Trust, 1990–92. DL Northumberland, 1990. *Heir: s* Richard Peter Pease, *b* 4 Sept. 1958. *Address:* Hindley House, Stocksfield-on-Tyne, Northumberland NE43 7SA.

PEASE, Robert John Claude; HM Diplomatic Service, retired; Counsellor (Administration) and Consul-General, British Embassy, Moscow, 1977–80; *b* 24 April 1922; *s* of Frederick Robert Hellier Pease and Eileen Violet Pease (*née* Beer); *m* 1945, Claire Margaretta Whall; one *s* two *d*. *Educ:* Cattedown Road Sch., Plymouth; Sutton High Sch., Plymouth. Served War of 1939–45; Telegraphist, RN, 1942; commnd Sub Lt RNVR, 1944. Clerk, Lord Chancellor's Dept, Plymouth County Court, 1939, Truro County Court, 1946; Foreign Office, 1948; Moscow, 1952; HM Consul, Sarajevo, 1954; 2nd Sec., Bangkok, 1958; HM Consul, Gdynia, 1959, Düsseldorf, 1961; 1st Sec., Pretoria, 1964, Bombay, 1966; FCO, 1969; Dep. High Commissioner, Mauritius, 1973. *Recreations:* golf, opera. *Address:* 5 Springfield Road, Camberley, Surrey GU15 1AB.

PEASE, Rosamund Dorothy Benson; Under Secretary, Department of Health, 1989–95; *b* 20 March 1935; *d* of Helen Bowen (*née* Wedgwood) and Michael Stewart Pease; one *s*. *Educ:* Chester Sch., Nova Scotia; Perse Sch., Cambridge; Mount Sch., York; Newnham Coll., Cambridge (BA Classical Tripos). Asst Principal, Min. of Health, 1958; Principal, 1965; Asst Sec., Pay Board, 1973; Office of Manpower Economics, 1974; Cabinet Office, 1975–76; DHSS, 1976; Office of Population Censuses and Surveys, 1983; Under Sec., NI Office, 1985. *Recreations:* gardening, family.
See also R. S. Pease.

PEASE, Sir Vincent; *see* Pease, Sir A. V.

PEAT, Sir Gerrard (Charles), KCVO 1988; FCA; Partner, KPMG Peat Marwick (formerly Peat Marwick Mitchell, then Peat Marwick McLintock) & Co., Chartered Accountants, 1956–87; Auditor to the Queen's Privy Purse, 1980–88 (Assistant Auditor, 1969–80); *b* 14 June 1920; *s* of Charles Urie Peat, MC, FCA, and Ruth (*née* Pulley); *m* 1949, Margaret Josephine Collingwood; one *s*. *Educ:* Sedbergh Sch. FCA 1961. Served War, RAF and ATA (pilot), 1940–45 (Service Medals); Pilot, 600 City of London Auxiliary Sqdn, 1948–51. Underwriting Mem. of Lloyd's, 1973–; Member: Cttee, Assoc. of Lloyd's Members, 1983–89; Council of Lloyd's, 1989–92. Member: Corp. of City of London, 1973–78; Worshipful Co. of Turners, 1970–. Hon. Treasurer, Assoc. of Conservative Clubs, 1971–78. Jubilee Medal, 1977. *Recreations:* travel, shooting, fishing, golf, flying. *Address:* (office) Britannia House, Glenthorne Road, W6 0LF. *T:* 0181–748 9898; Flat 10, 35 Pont Street, SW1X 0BB. *T:* 0171–245 9736; Home Farm, Upper Basildon, Pangbourne, Berks RG8 8ND. *T:* Upper Basildon (01491) 671241. *Clubs:* Boodle's, MCC.

PEAT, Ven. Lawrence Joseph; Archdeacon of Westmorland and Furness, 1989–95; *b* 29 Aug. 1928; *s* of Joseph Edward and Lilian Edith Peat; *m* 1953, Sheila Shipway; three *s* three *d*. *Educ:* Lincoln Theological College. Curate of Bramley, Leeds, 1958–61; Rector of All Saints', Heaton Norris, Stockport, 1961–65; Vicar of Bramley, Leeds, 1965–73; Team Rector of Southend-on-Sea, 1973–79; Vicar of Skelmsmergh, Selside and Longsleddale, Cumbria, 1979–86; RD of Kendal, 1984–88; Team Vicar of Kirkby Lonsdale, 1986–88. Canon of Carlisle Cathedral, 1988–. *Recreations:* walking, music. *Address:* 17 Railway Terrace, Lindal-in-Furness, Cumbria LA12 0LQ.

PEAT, Michael Charles Gerrard, CVO 1994; FCA; Director of Finance and Property Services, HM Household, since 1990; *b* 16 Nov. 1949; *m* 1976, Deborah Sage (*née* Wood); two *s* two *d* (and one *s* decd). *Educ:* Eton; Trinity Coll., Oxford (MA); INSEAD, Fontainebleau (MBA). FCA 1975. KPMG Peat Marwick, 1972–93. *Recreations:* sport, history, literature.

PEAT, (William Wood) Watson, CBE 1972; FRAgS; JP; farmer; broadcaster; Scottish Governor of the BBC, 1984–89; Chairman, Broadcasting Council for Scotland, 1984–89; *b* 14 Dec. 1922; *o s* of William Peat and Margaret Hillhouse; *m* 1955, Jean Frew Paton McHarrie; two *s* one *d*. *Educ:* Denny Public School. Served with Royal Signals, Europe and India, 1941–46; Lieut 1944. Member: Nat. Council, Scottish Assoc. of Young Farmers' Clubs, 1949– (Chm., 1953–54; Vice-Pres., 1975; Pres., 1979); Stirling CC, 1959–74 (Vice-Convenor, 1967–70); Council, NFU Scotland, 1959–78 (Pres., 1966–67); Scottish River Purification Adv. Cttee, 1960–79; Bd of Management, Royal Scottish Nat. Hosp., 1962–72; Council, Hannah Research Inst., 1963–82; Council, Scottish Agricultural Organisation Soc. Ltd, 1963– (Pres., 1974–77); Bd of Management, British Farm Produce Council, 1964–87 (Vice-Chm., 1980–87); Agric. Marketing Develt Exec. Cttee, 1966–67; Central Council for Agric. and Horticultural Co-operation, 1967–; Food from Britain Co-operative Development Board, 1983–89; Bd of Management, Oatridge Agric. Coll., 1967–75; Gen. Comr of Income Tax, 1962; Governor, West of Scotland Agric. Coll., 1964–90 (Vice Chm., 1975, Chm., 1983–88); Chm. Council, Scottish Agricl Colls, 1984–90; Dir, Agri-Finance (Scotland) Ltd, 1968–79; Chm., BBC Scottish Agric. Adv. Cttee, 1971–75; Chm., Scottish Adv. Cttee, Assoc. of Agriculture, 1974–79, Vice Pres., 1979–; Director: Fedn of Agricultural Co-operatives (UK) Ltd, 1974–77; FMC PLC, 1974–83; Mem., British Agricl Council, 1974–84. FRAgS 1987. JP Stirlingshire, 1963. *Recreations:* amateur radio, flying. *Address:* Carbro, 61 Stirling Road, Larbert, Stirlingshire FK5 4SG. *T:* Larbert (01324) 562420. *Clubs:* Farmers', BBC.

PECK, His Honour David (Edward); a Circuit Judge (formerly Judge of County Courts), 1969–85; *b* 6 April 1917; *m* 1st, 1950, Rosina Seton Glover Marshall (marr. diss.); one *s* three *d*; 2nd, 1973, Frances Deborah Redford (*née* Mackenzie) (marr. diss.); one *s*; 3rd, 1983, Elizabeth Charlotte Beale (*née* Boost). *Educ:* Charterhouse School; Balliol College, Oxford. Served Army (Cheshire Regiment), 1939–46. Called to Bar, Middle Temple, 1949. Mem., County Court Rule Cttee, 1978–84 (Chm., 1981–84); Jt Editor, County Court Practice, 1982–90. *Address:* 2 Gray's Inn Square, WC1R 5JH.

PECK, Sir Edward (Heywood), GCMG 1974 (KCMG 1966; CMG 1957); HM Diplomatic Service, retired; *b* 5 Oct. 1915; *s* of Lt-Col Edward Surman Peck, IMS, and Doris Louise Heywood; *m* 1948, Alison Mary MacInnes; one *s* two *d. Educ:* Clifton College; The Queen's College, Oxford. 1st Cl. Hons (Mod. Langs), 1937; Laming Travelling Fellow, 1937–38. Entered Consular Service, 1938; served in Barcelona, 1938–39; Foreign Office, 1939–40; Sofia, 1940; Ankara, 1940–44; Adana, 1944; Iskenderun, 1945; Salonica, 1945–47; with UK Deleg. to UN Special Commn on the Balkans, 1947; Foreign Office, 1947–50; seconded to UK High Commissioner's Office, Delhi, 1950–52; Counsellor, Foreign Office, 1952–55; Dep. Comdt, Brit. Sector, Berlin, 1955–58; on staff of UK Commissioner-General for S-E Asia, 1959–60; Assistant Under-Secretary of State, Foreign Office, 1961–66; British High Commissioner in Kenya, 1966–68; Dep. Under-Secretary of State, FCO, 1968–70; British Perm. Rep. to N Atlantic Council, 1970–75. Dir, Outward Bound (Loch Eil), 1976–90; Mem. Council, Nat. Trust for Scotland, 1982–87. Hon. Vis. Fellow in Defence Studies, Aberdeen Univ., 1976–85. *Publications:* North-East Scotland (Bartholomew's Guides Series), 1981; Avonside Explored, 1983; The Battle of Glenlivet, 1994. *Recreations:* mountaineering, travel, reading history and writing guide books. *Address:* Easter Torrans, Tomintoul, Banffshire AB37 9HJ. *Club:* Alpine.

PECK, Gregory; film actor, US, since 1943; *b* 5 April 1916; *s* of Gregory P. Peck and Bernice Ayres; *m* 1st, 1942, Greta Konen Rice (marr. diss. 1954); two *s* (and one *s* decd); 2nd, 1955, Veronique Passani; one *s* one *d. Educ:* Calif Public Schools; Univ. of Calif (BA). Broadway stage, 1941–43. *Films:* Days of Glory, 1943; Keys of the Kingdom, Valley of Decision, 1944; Spellbound, 1945; Duel in the Sun, The Yearling, 1946; The Macomber Affair, Gentlemen's Agreement, 1947; The Paradine Case, 1948; Yellow Sky, The Great Sinner, Twelve O'Clock High, 1949; The Gun Fighter, 1950; Only the Valiant, Captain Horatio Hornblower, David and Bathsheba, 1951; The World in his Arms, 1952; The Snows of Kilimanjaro, 1952; Roman Holiday, 1953; The Million Pound Note, 1953; Night People, 1954; The Purple Plain, 1954; The Man in the Grey Flannel Suit, 1956; Moby Dick, 1956; Designing Woman, 1957; The Bravados, 1958; The Big Country (co-producer), 1958; Pork Chop Hill, 1959; On the Beach, 1959; Guns of Navarone, 1960; Cape Fear, 1961; To Kill a Mocking Bird, 1962 (Academy Award for best performance); Captain Newman, MD, 1963; Behold a Pale Horse, 1964; Mirage, 1965; Arabesque, 1965; Mackenna's Gold, 1967; The Chairman, 1968; The Stalking Moon, 1968; Marooned, 1970; I Walk the Line, 1971; Shoot Out, 1971; The Trial of the Catonsville Nine, 1972; Billy Two-Hats, 1974; The Boys From Brazil, 1978; The Sea Wolves, 1980; Amazing Grace and Chuck, 1987; Old Gringo, 1989; Other People's Money, 1991; *television:* The Blue and the Gray, 1982; The Scarlet and the Black, 1983; *produced:* The Dove, 1974; The Omen, 1976; MacArthur, 1977. Nat. Chm., Amer. Cancer Soc., 1966. Mem., Nat. Council on Arts, 1965–67, 1968–; Pres., Acad. Motion Picture Arts and Sciences, 1967–70; Chm., Board of Trustees, Amer. Film Inst., 1967–69. Medal of Freedom Award, 1969; Jean Hersholt Humanitarian Award, Acad. of Motion Picture Arts and Sciences, 1968. *Recreations:* riding, swimming, bicycling, gardening. *Club:* Players (New York).

PECK, Maj.-Gen. Richard Leslie, CB 1991; FRGS; CEng, FICE; Director, The Churches Conservation Trust (formerly Redundant Churches Fund), since 1992; *b* 27 May 1937; *s* of Frank Archibald Peck and late Molly Peck (*née* Eyels); *m* 1962, Elizabeth Ann, *d* of Major Denis James Bradley and Barbara Edith Amy Bradley (*née* Metcalfe); two *s* one *d. Educ:* Wellingborough Sch.; Royal Mil. Acad., Sandhurst; Royal Mil. Coll. of Science, Shrivenham. BScEng. Commnd RE, 1957; served Cyprus, Libya, Germany, UK; psc 1969; Bde Major 5 Inf. Bde, 1969–71; Sqn Comd BAOR, 1972–73; Directing Staff, Staff Coll., 1973–77; CO 21 Engr Regt, 1977–79; Asst Mil. Sec., 1979–81; Comd 19 Inf. Bde, 1981–83; RCDS 1984; Dir Army Service Conditions, MoD, 1985; Dir Personnel, Staff of CDS, 1985–87; Engr-in-Chief (Army), 1988–91. Mem., Lord Kitchener Meml Fund, 1992–. Col Comdt, RE, 1991–; Col, Queen's Gurkha Engineers, 1991–. Freeman, City of London, 1991; Mem., Engineers' Co, 1990–. *Recreations:* Association football, cricket, golf, shooting, ski-ing, Rugby football. *Address:* c/o National Westminster Bank, Rushden, Northamptonshire NN10 0PX. *Clubs:* Army and Navy, MCC; I Zingari, Free Foresters, Band of Brothers, Cryptics; Royal Mid-Surrey Golf.

PECK, Stanley Edwards, CBE 1974; BEM 1954; QPM 1964; DL; HM Inspector of Constabulary, 1964–78; *b* 1916; *er s* of late Harold Edwards Peck, Edgbaston and Shanghai; *m* 1939, Yvonne Sydney Edwards (*d* 1994), *er d* of late John Edwards Jessop, LDS; two *s* two *d. Educ:* Solihull School; Birmingham University. Served with RAF, 1941–45 (Flt-Lt). Joined Metropolitan Police, 1935; Chief Inspector and Supt, New Scotland Yard, 1950–54; Asst Chief Constable, Staffs, 1954–61; Chief Constable, Staffs, 1961–64. DL Staffs, 1962. Pres., Royal Life Saving Soc., UK, 1969–74 (Chm., East Midlands Region, RLSS, 1968–80). OStJ. *Recreations:* golf and dog walking. *Address:* Lodge Gardens, Walnut Grove, Radcliffe-on-Trent, Nottinghamshire NG12 2AD. *Club:* Royal Air Force.

PECKFORD, Hon. (Alfred) Brian; PC (Can.) 1982; Premier of the Province of Newfoundland and Labrador, 1979–89; *b* Whitbourne, Newfoundland, 27 Aug. 1942; *s* of Ewart Peckford and Allison (*née* Young), St John's; *m* 1st, 1969, Marina, *d* of Raymond Dicks and Hope (*née* Adams), Halls Bay; two *d*; 2nd, 1986, Carol Ellsworth; one *s. Educ:* Lewisporte High Sch.; Memorial Univ. of Newfoundland (BAEd). Schoolmaster, 1962–63 and 1966–72. MHA (Progressive C) Green Bay, 1972–89; Special Asst to Premier, 1973; Minister: of Dept of Municipal Affairs and Housing, 1974; of Mines and Energy, 1976, also of Rural Development, 1978. Leader of Progressive Cons. Party, Newfoundland and Labrador, 1979–89. Pres., Peckford Inc., 1989–. Hon. LLD Meml Univ. of Newfoundland, 1986. *Recreations:* reading, sport, swimming, ski-ing.

PECKHAM, Arthur John; UK Permanent Representative, Food and Agriculture Organisation, Rome, 1977–80; *b* 22 Sept. 1920; *s* of Richard William Peckham and Agnes Mercy (*née* Parker); *m* 1949, Margaret Enid Quirk; two *s* one *d. Educ:* The Judd Sch., Tonbridge. RAF (Pilot), 1942–46, 59 Sqdn Coastal Command. Cadet, Min. of Labour and Nat. Service, 1948; Colonial Office: Asst Principal, 1950; Private Sec. to Perm. Under-Sec., 1952; Principal, 1954; Counsellor (Technical Assistance), Lagos, 1964; Asst Sec., Min. of Overseas Devel t, 1966; Minister, FAO, Rome, 1977. *Recreation:* gardening. *Address:* 147A Newmarket Road, Norwich NR4 6SY.

PECKHAM, Prof. Catherine Stevenson, MD, FRCP, FRCOG, FRCPath, FFPHM; Professor of Paediatric Epidemiology, Institute of Child Health, University of London, since 1985; Hon. Consultant, Hospital for Sick Children, Great Ormond Street, since 1985; *b* 7 March 1937; *d* of Alexander King, *qv*; *m* 1958, Sir Michael John Peckham, *qv*; three *s. Educ:* St Paul's Girls' Sch.; University Coll., London (MB BS, MD). FFPHM (FFPM 1980); FRCP 1988; FRCPath 1991; FRCOG 1994. Reader in Community Medicine and Head of Dept, Charing Cross Hosp. Med. Sch., 1980–85. Member: Standing Med. Adv. Cttee, DoH, 1992–; Health Adv. Cttee, British Council, 1992–; Bd, PHLS, 1989–92; Children Nationwide, Scientific Adv. Cttee, 1994–; Chairman: Steering Cttee on Epidemiol Res., Surveillance and Forecasting, WHO Global Prog. on AIDS, 1991–; Exec. Cttee, British Paediatric Surveillance Unit, 1993–. Member: Fulbright Commn, 1987–; Bd of Govs, St Paul's Sch., 1992–; UK Women's Forum, 1990–; ASA, 1993–. Harding Award, Action Research, 1993. *Publications:* The Peckham Report: national immunization study, 1989; chapters and papers on infections in pregnancy and early childhood, national cohort studies and epidemiology of common childhood conditions. *Recreation:* flute.

PECKHAM, Sir Michael John, Kt 1995; FRCP, FRCPGlas, FRCR, FRCPath; Director, Research and Development, Department of Health, since 1991; *b* 2 Aug. 1935; *s* of William Stuart Peckham and Gladys Mary Peckham; *m* 1958, Catherine Stevenson King (*see* Prof. C. S. Peckham); three *s. Educ:* St Catharine's Coll., Cambridge (MA); University College Hosp. Med. Sch., London (MD). MRC Clin. Res. Schol., Inst. Gustav Roussy, Paris, 1965–67; Institute of Cancer Research, London: Lectr, 1967–71; Sen. Lectr, 1971–74; Prof. of Radiotherapy, 1974–86; Dean, 1984–86; Dir, BPMF, 1986–90. Consultant: Royal Marsden Hosp., 1971–86; to Royal Navy, 1974–86. Mem., MRC, 1991–; Mem., MRC Cell Biology and Disorders Bd, 1977–81. Member, Special Health Authority: Gt Ormond St Hosp., 1988–90; Brompton Nat. Heart and London Chest Hosps, 1986–90; Hammersmith and Queen Charlotte's Hosps, 1989–90. President: European Radiotherapy Gp, 1978; European Soc. of Therapeutic Radiology and Oncology, 1983–85; British Oncological Assoc., 1986–88; Fedn of European Cancer Socs, 1989–91 (Pres.-elect, 1987–89); Mem., British Council Scientific Adv. Cttee, 1988–92. Vice-Chm., Council, ICRF, 1988–91. Chm., Ecco V Cancer Trust, 1989–; Founder: Bob Champion Cancer Trust, 1983; British Oncological Assoc., 1985; Co-founder, European Soc. of Therapeutic Radiology and Oncology, 1988. Trustee, Louise Buchanan Meml Trust, 1973–. Editor-in-Chief, European Jl of Cancer, 1989–. FRSA. Dr *hc*: Univ. de Franche-Comté at Besançon, 1991; Catholic Univ. of Louvain, 1993; Hon. DSc Loughborough, 1992. *Publications:* Management of Testicular Tumours, 1981; (jtly) The Biological Basis of Radiotherapy, 1983; (jtly) Primary Management of Early Breast Cancer, 1985; (jt sen. editor) Oxford Textbook of Oncology, 1994; articles on cancer research and cancer treatment, medical education, health research and development. *Recreation:* painting. *Address:* Richmond House, Whitehall, SW1. *Club:* Reform.

PECKOVER, Dr Richard Stuart; Corporate Director of Safety, UK Atomic Energy Authority, since 1992; *b* 5 May 1942; *s* of Rev. Cecil Raymond Peckover and Grace Lucy (*née* Curtis). *Educ:* King Edward VII Sch., King's Lynn; Wadham Coll., Oxford (MA); Corpus Christi Coll., Cambridge (PhD). FInstP, FIMA, FRMetS, FRAS, FSaRS. United Kingdom Atomic Energy Authority: Res. Scientist, Culham Lab., 1969–81; Res. Associate, MIT, 1973–74; Safety and Reliability Directorate, 1982, Br. Head, 1983–87; Asst Dir, AEE Winfrith, 1987, Dep. Dir, 1989, Site Dir, 1990. Mem., Amer. Nucl. Soc. *Recreations:* walking, talking, listening to music. *Address:* Winfrith Technology Centre, Dorchester, Dorset DT2 8DH. *T:* Dorchester (01305) 251888. *Club:* United Oxford & Cambridge University.

PEDDER, Air Marshal Sir Ian (Maurice), KCB 1982; OBE 1963; DFC 1949; Senior Consultant, SAL, international aviation consultants, since 1992; Chairman, Dan-Air Services, 1989–90 (Deputy Chairman, 1986–89); *b* 2 May 1926; *s* of Maurice and Elsie Pedder; *m* 1949, Jean Mary (*née* Kellett); one *s* two *d. Educ:* Royal Grammar Sch., High Wycombe; Queen's Coll., Oxford. Service in Nos 28, 60, 81, 213 Sqdns, CFS, and with Burma Air Force, 1946–59; Staff Coll., Andover, and MoD, 1959–62; Far East, 1962–64; Staff appts, 1965–70; RCDS, 1971; Comdg RAF Chivenor, 1972–74; Nat. Air Traffic Services, 1974–84, Dep. Controller, 1977–81, Controller and Mem. CAA, 1981–84. Dir, Davies & Newman plc, 1989–92. *Publications:* contribs to Service jls, UK and US. *Recreations:* study of Victorian times, photography, riding (a bicycle). *Address:* The Chestnuts, Cheddar, Somerset. *Clubs:* Royal Air Force, Victory Services.

PEDDIE, Hon. Ian James Crofton; QC 1992; an Assistant Recorder, since 1992; *b* 17 Dec. 1945; *s* of Baron Peddie, MBE, JP and Hilda Mary Alice (*née* Bull), (Lady Peddie); *m* 1976, Susan Renée Howes; two *s* two *d. Educ:* Gordonstoun Sch.; University Coll. London (LLB Hons). Called to the Bar, Inner Temple, 1971. *Recreations:* family life, classic cars. *Address:* 22 Old Buildings, Lincoln's Inn, WC2A 3UJ. *T:* 0171–831 0222.

PEDDIE, Robert Allan; general management consultant since 1983; Chairman, Polymeters Response International Ltd, since 1992; *b* 27 Oct. 1921; *s* of Robert Allan Peddie and Elizabeth Elsie (*née* Sharp); *m* 1946, Ilene Ivy Sillcock (*d* 1990); one *d. Educ:* Nottingham Univ. (BSc Eng). Electricity Dept, Hull Corp., 1946; joined nationalised electricity supply industry, 1948, and held various appts; Supt, Bradwell Nuclear Power Stn, 1958; Asst Reg. Dir, NW Region, 1962; Dep. Reg. Dir, Mids Region, 1967; Dir-Gen., SE Region, 1970; Mem. CEGB, 1972–77; part-time Mem., UKAEA, 1972–77; Chm., S Eastern Electricity Bd, 1977–83. *Recreations:* swimming, golf, walking. *Address:* c/o PRI, Moorside Road, Winchester SO23 7RX. *T:* Winchester (01962) 840048.

PEDERSEN, Prof. (Knud) George, OC 1993; PhD; FCCT; FRSA; Professor, The University of Western Ontario, since 1985 (President and Vice-Chancellor, 1985–94); *b* 13 June 1931; *s* of Hjalmar Nielsen Pedersen and Anna Marie (*nee* Jensen); *m* 1st, 1953, Joan Elaine Vanderwarker (*d* 1988); one *s* one *d*; 2nd, 1988, Penny Ann Jones. *Educ:* Vancouver Normal Sch. (Dip. in Teaching 1952); Univ. of BC (BA History and Geography, 1959); Univ. of Washington (MA 1964); Univ. of Chicago (PhD 1969). FCCT 1977; FRSA 1983. Schools in North Vancouver: Teacher, Highlands Elem. Sch., 1952–56; Vice-Principal, North Star Elem. Sch., 1956–59; Principal, Carisbrooke Elem. Sch., 1959–61; Vice-Principal, Handsworth Sec. Sch., 1961–63; Principal, Balmoral Sec. Sch., 1963–65; Univ. of Chicago: Teaching Intern, 1966; Staff Associate, Midwest Admin Center, 1965–66, Res. Associate (Asst Prof.), 1966–68; Asst Prof., Ontario Inst. for Studies in Educn and Univ. of Toronto, 1968–70; Asst Prof. and Associate Dir, Midwest Admin Center, Div. of Social Sciences, Univ. of Chicago, 1970–72; Faculty of Educn, Univ. of Victoria: Associate Prof., 1972–75; Dean, 1972–75; Vice-Pres. (Academic), and Prof., Univ. of Victoria, 1975–79; Pres. and Prof., Simon Fraser Univ., 1979–83; Pres. and Prof., Univ. of British Columbia, 1983–85. Universities Council of British Columbia: Mem., Prog. Co-ordinating Cttee, 1975–78; Mem., Business Affairs Cttee, 1975–78; Mem., Long-range Planning Cttee, 1979—85. Chm., Adv. Cttee on Educnl Planning, Min. of Educn (Prov. of BC), 1977–78; Member: Jt Bd of Teacher Educn, Prov. of BC, 1972–75; Planning Cttee, Canadian Teachers' Fedn, 1974; Planning Cttee, 1973–74, and Bd of Dirs, 1974–75 and 1979–80, BC Council for Leadership in Educn; Interior Univ. Progs Bd, Min. of Educn, 1977–78. Member, Board of Directors: Assoc. of Univs and Colls of Canada, 1979–84 (Mem., Adv. Cttee, Office of Internat. Devel t, 1979–83); Public Employers' Council of BC, 1979–84; Vancouver Bd of Trade, 1983–85; Pulp and Paper Res. Inst. of Canada, 1983–85; President: N Vancouver Teachers' Assoc., 1962–63; N Vancouver Principals' and Vice-Principals' Assoc., 1963–64; Vice-Pres., Inter-American Orgn for Higher Educn, 1992– (Mem. Bd of Dirs, 1979–85); Sec.-Treasurer, Canadian Assoc. of Deans and Directors of Educn, 1972–73 and 1973–74. Member: Amer. Educnl Res. Assoc., 1965–; National Soc. for Study of Educn, 1965–; Canadian Assoc. of Sch. Administrators, 1968–; Canadian Educn Assoc., 1968–; Canadian Educnl Researchers' Assoc., 1968–; Canadian Soc. for Study of Educn, 1968–; Internat. Council on Educn for Teaching, 1968–; Canadian Bureau for Internat. Educn, 1970–; Canadian Foundn for Econ. Educn, 1970–; Canadian Soc. for Study of Higher Educn, 1975–; Inst. of Public Admin. of Canada, 1976–; Internat. Assoc. of Univ. Presidents, 1979–; Assoc. of

Commonwealth Univs, 1979–; Comparative and Internat. Educn Soc., 1980–; Assoc. for Advancement of Scandinavian Studies in Canada, 1981–; Bd of Dirs, Corporate and Higher Educn Forum, 1988–. Member: BoT, Vancouver, 1983–85; Nat. Council, Canadian Human Rights Foundn, 1984–. Mem., Bd of Dirs, MacMillan Bloedel Ltd, 1984–86. Member, Board of Governors: Arts, Sciences and Technol. Centre, 1980–85; Leon and Thea Koerner Foundn, 1981–85; Mem., Bd of Trustees, Discovery Foundn, 1980–85. Confedn of Canada 125th Anniversary Medal, 1992; Officer, Order of Ont, 1994. *Publications:* The Itinerant Schoolmaster: a socio-economic analysis of teacher turnover, 1973; chapters in books on educn; articles in Administrator's Notebook (Univ. of Chicago), Selected Articles for Elem. Sch. Prinicipals, Res. in Educn, Educn and Urban Soc., Educn Canada, Teacher Educn, Resources in Educn, Elem. Sch. Jl, Jl of Educnl Admin, and Canadian Jl of Univ. Continuing Educn; book reviews; proc. of confs and symposia; governmental and institutional studies and reports. *Address:* University of Western Ontario, London, Ont N6A 5B8, Canada. *T:* (519) 6613106; (home) 2232 Spruce Street, Vancouver, BC V6H 2P3, Canada. *T:* (604) 7332400. *Clubs:* London Hunt and Country, London, University (London, Ont.); University (Toronto); Semiahmoo Golf and Country.

PEDLEY, Alan Sydney, DFC 1946; Lord Mayor of Leeds, 1975–1976; District Insurance Manager, 1974–82, retired; *b* 16 Aug. 1917; *s* of Herbert Leonard Pedley and Edith Mary (*née* Skipsey); *m* 1st, 1949, Evelyn Anderson (*née* Scott) (*d* 1977); 2nd, 1981, Shirley Elizabeth, *widow* of Reg Howard. *Educ:* Leeds Modern Sch. Entered Insurance, 1934; retd (Commercial Union), 1971; joined Barclays Insurance Services Co. Ltd, 1971. Member: Leeds City Council, 1951–81; W Yorkshire Metropolitan CC, 1973–81; Dep. Lord Mayor, 1971–72. Hon. Alderman, City of Leeds, 1993. FCII 1949. *Recreations:* cricket, Association football, Rugby League, music, theatre, the Arts, after dinner speaking. *Address:* Whitelea, 8 Bentcliffe Close, Leeds LS17 6QT. *T:* Leeds (0113) 268 5424.

PEDLEY, Rev. Canon (Geoffrey) Stephen; Chaplain to the Queen, since 1984; Residentiary Canon of Durham Cathedral, since 1993; *b* 13 Sept. 1940; *s* of Geoffrey Heber Knight and Muriel Pedley; *m* 1970, Mary Frances Macdonald; two *s* one *d*. *Educ:* Marlborough College; Queens' College, Cambridge (MA); Cuddesdon Theological College. Curate: Liverpool Parish Church, 1966; Holy Trinity, Coventry, 1969; Rector of Kitwe, Zambia, 1971–77; Vicar of St Peter's, Stockton, 1977–88; Rector, Whickham, 1988–93. *Recreations:* architecture, English literature, travel. *Address:* 6A The College, Durham DH1 3EQ. *T:* 0191–384 5489.

PEDLEY, Stephen; *see* Pedley, G. S.

PEDLEY, Prof. Timothy John, PhD, ScD; FRS 1995; Professor of Applied Mathematics, University of Leeds, 1990–April 1996; G. I. Taylor Professor of Fluid Mechanics, University of Cambridge, from April 1996; Fellow of Gonville and Caius College, Cambridge, 1973–89 and from April 1996; *b* 23 March 1942; *s* of Richard Rodman Pedley and Jean Mary Mudie Pedley (*née* Evans); *m* 1965, Avril Jennifer Martin Uden; two *s*. *Educ:* Trinity Coll., Cambridge (BA 1963; MA, PhD 1967; ScD 1982). Post-doctoral Fellow, Johns Hopkins Univ., 1966–68; Res. Associate, then Lectr, Physiol. Flow Studies Unit and Dept of Maths, Imperial Coll. London, 1968–73; Department of Applied Mathematics and Theoretical Physics, University of Cambridge: Asst Dir of Res., 1973–77; Lectr, 1977–89; Reader in Biolog. Fluid Dynamics, 1989. EPSRC Sen. Res. Fellow, 1995–. *Publications:* (ed) Scale Effects in Animal Locomotion, 1977; (jtly) The Mechanics of the Circulation, 1978; The Fluid Mechanics of Large Blood Vessels, 1980; (ed with C. P. Ellington) Biological Fluid Dynamics, 1995; numerous articles in fluid mechanics and biomechanics jls. *Recreations:* bird-watching, running, reading. *Address:* Oakhurst Farm, 375 Shadwell Lane, Leeds LS17 8AH; (from April 1996) Department of Applied Mathematics and Theoretical Physics, Silver Street, Cambridge CB3 9EW. *T:* Cambridge (01223) 337900.

PEEBLES, Prof. Phillip James Edwin, FRS 1982; Professor of Physics, since 1965, and Albert Einstein Professor of Science, since 1984, Princeton University; *b* Winnipeg, 25 April 1935; *s* of Andrew Charles Peebles and Ada Marian (*née* Green); *m* 1958, Jean Alison Peebles, three *d*. *Educ:* Univ. of Manitoba (BSc 1958); Princeton Univ. (Ma 1959; PhD 1962). Member: Amer. Phys. Soc.; Amer. Astron. Soc.; AAAS; Internat. Astron. Union, Fellow: Amer. Physical Soc.; Amer. Acad. of Arts and Scis; Royal Soc. of Canada. Hon. DSc: Univ. of Toronto, 1986; Univ. of Chicago, 1986; McMaster Univ., 1989; Univ. of Manitoba, 1989. *Publications:* Physical Cosmology, 1971; The Large Scale Structure of the Universe, 1979; (ed jtly) Objects of High Redshift, 1980; Quantum Mechanics, 1992; Principles of Physical Cosmology, 1993. *Address:* 24 Markham Road, Princeton, NJ 08540, USA; Department of Physics, Princeton University, Jadwin Hall, PO Box 708, Washington Road, Princeton, NJ 08544–0708, USA.

PEECH, Alan James; *b* 24 August 1905; *s* of late Albert Orlando Peech; *m* 1948, Betty Leese; no *c*. *Educ:* Wellington College; Magdalen College, Oxford (BA). Former Governor, Wellington College, retd 1975. Independent Chm., Cement Makers' Fedn, 1970–76; former Dep. Chm., Steetley Co. Ltd, retd 1976; Pres., British Iron and Steel Fedn, Jan.-June 1967; Jt Man. Dir, United Steel Cos Ltd, 1962–67, Chm., 1962–71; a Dep. Chm., BSC, 1967–70; Man. Dir, Midland Gp BSC, 1967–70. Hon. LLD Sheffield, 1966. *Recreations:* fishing and shooting. *Address:* High House, Blyth, Worksop, Notts S81 8HG. *T:* Blyth (01909) 591255. *Club:* MCC.

PEECH, Neil Malcolm; President, Steetley PLC, 1976–92 (Managing Director, 1935–68, Chairman, 1935–76); *b* 27 Jan. 1908; *s* of Albert Orlando Peech; *m* 1932, Margaret Josephine (*d* 1991), *d* of late R. C. Smallwood, CBE, Worplesdon, Surrey; one *s* one *d*. *Educ:* Wellington College; Magdalen College, Oxford. Developed the production of magnesia from seawater and dolomite, 1939. Consul for Sweden, 1974–76 (Vice Consul, 1949–74). Underwriting member of Lloyd's, 1950–69; Director, Sheepbridge Engineering Ltd, 1949–79, and Albright & Wilson Ltd, 1958–79. Chairman, Ministry of Power Solid Smokeless Fuel Committee, 1959. High Sheriff of Yorkshire, 1959. Chevalier, Order of Vasa, Sweden, 1963. *Recreation:* fishing. *Address:* Park House, Firbeck, Worksop, Notts S81 8JW. *T:* Worksop (01909) 732494.

PEEK, Sir Francis (Henry Grenville), 4th Bt, *cr* 1874; *b* 16 Sept. 1915; *o s* of 3rd Bt and Edwine Warner (*d* 1959), *d* of late W. H. Thornburgh, St Louis, USA; *S* father, 1927; *m* 1st, 1942, Ann (marr. diss., 1949), *d* of late Captain Gordon Duff and *widow* of Sir Charles Mappin, Bt (she *m* 1951, Sir William Rootes, later 1st Baron Rootes); 2nd, Marilyn (marr. diss., 1967), *d* of Dr Norman Kerr, London and Bahamas; one *s* decd; 3rd, Mrs Caroline Kirkwood, *d* of late Sir Robert Kirkwood, KCMG, OJ. *Educ:* Eton; Trinity College, Cambridge. ADC to Governor of Bahamas, 1938–39; served Irish Guards, 1939–46. *Heir: cousin* William Grenville Peek [*b* 15 Dec. 1919; *m* 1950, Lucy Jane, *d* of late Major Edward Dorrien-Smith, DSO; one *s* three *d*]. *Address:* Villa du Parc, 8 Avenue Jean de Noailles, Cannes 06400, France. *Club:* White's.

PEEK, Vice-Adm. Sir Richard (Innes), KBE 1972 (OBE 1944); CB 1971; DSC 1945; pastoralist; *b* 30 July 1914; 2nd *s* of late James Norman and Kate Ethel Peek; *m* 1943, Margaret Seinor (*née* Kendall) (*d* 1946); one *s*; *m* 1952, Mary Catherine Tilley (*née* Stops); two *d*. *Educ:* Royal Australian Naval College. Joined RAN, 1928; served War of 1939–45 in HMS Revenge, HMAS Cerberus, Hobart, Australia, Navy Office; Korean War Service in HMAS Tobruk, 1951; Flag Officer Comdg HMA Fleet, 1967–68; Chief of Naval Staff, Australia, 1970–73. Legion of Merit (US), 1951. *Recreations:* gardening, golf. *Address:* Rothlyn, RMB, Monaro Highway, via Cooma, NSW 2630, Australia. *Clubs:* Royal Automobile (Sydney); Royal Commonwealth Society (Canberra).

PEEL, family name of **Earl Peel.**

PEEL, 3rd Earl *cr* 1929; **William James Robert Peel;** Bt 1800; Viscount Peel, 1895; Viscount Clanfield, 1929; Lord Warden of the Stannaries, Duchy of Cornwall, since 1994; *b* 3 Oct. 1947; *s* of 2nd Earl Peel and Kathleen (*d* 1972), *d* of Michael McGrath; *S* father, 1969; *m* 1st, 1973, Veronica Naomi Livingston (marr. diss. 1987), *d* of Alastair Timpson; one *s* one *d*; 2nd, 1989, Hon. Mrs Charlotte Hambro, *yr d* of Baron Soames, PC, GCMG, GCVO, CH, CBE and of Lady Soames, *qv*; one *d*. *Educ:* Ampleforth; University of Tours; Cirencester Agric. Coll. Mem., Nature Conservancy Council for England, 1991–; Chm., Game Conservancy, 1994–. Mem., Prince's Council, Duchy of Cornwall, 1993–. President: Yorks Wildlife Trust, 1989–; Gun Trade Assoc., 1993–. *Heir: s* Viscount Clanfield, *qv*. *Address:* Kilgram Grange, Jervaulx, Ripon, N Yorks HG4 4PQ. *Clubs:* Turf; Leyburn Market.

PEEL, David Alexander Robert; Under Secretary, Director of Administration Resources, Department of the Environment, since 1990; *b* 12 Nov. 1940; *s* of late Maj. Robert Edmund Peel and Sheila Mary (*née* Slattery); *m* 1971, Patricia Muriel Essery; two *s*. *Educ:* St Edmund's Coll., Ware; University Coll., Oxford. Building labourer, New Scotland Yard develt, 1963; joined MoT, 1964; Private Sec. to Minister of State, 1967; Principal, 1968; DoE, 1970; First Sec., UK Perm. Repn to EC, Brussels, 1972; Private Sec. to Minister for Transport, 1975; Asst Sec., Depts of Transport and the Environment, 1976–90: Nat. Roads Prog. and Highway Policy, 1982; Okehampton Bypass (Confirmation of Orders) Act, 1985; Interdeptl Review on Using Private Enterprise in Govt, 1986; Office Services, 1987–90. *Recreations:* allotment gardening, music, baroque architecture. *Address:* Department of the Environment, 2 Marsham Street, SW1P 3EB. *T:* 0171–276 3544.

PEEL, Sir John; *see* Peel, Sir W. J.

PEEL, John; *see* Ravenscroft, J. R. P.

PEEL, Prof. John David Yeadon, FBA 1991; Professor of Anthropology and Sociology, with reference to Africa, School of Oriental and African Studies, University of London, since 1989; *b* 13 Nov. 1941; *e s* of late Prof. Edwin Arthur Peel and Nora Kathleen Yeadon; *m* 1969, Jennifer Christine Ferial, *d* of K. N. Pare, Leicester; three *s*. *Educ:* King Edward's Sch., Birmingham; Balliol Coll., Oxford (Scholar; BA 1963, MA 1966); LSE (PhD 1966); DLit London 1985. Asst Lectr, then Lectr in Sociology, Nottingham Univ., 1965–70; Lectr in Sociology, LSE, 1970–73; Charles Booth Prof. of Sociology, 1975–89, Dean, Faculty of Social and Envmtl Studies, 1985–88, Univ. of Liverpool; Dean of Undergraduate Studies, SOAS, 1990–94. Vis. Reader in Sociology and Anthropology, Univ of Ife, Nigeria, 1973–75; Vis. Prof. in Anthropology and Sociology, Univ. of Chicago, 1982–83. Associate, Inst. of Develt Studies, 1973–94. Vice-Pres., African Studies Assoc. of UK, 1994–96. Editor, Africa, and Officer, Internat African Inst., 1979–86; Gen. Editor, Internat. African Library, 1986–. Marett Lectr, Univ. of Oxford, 1993. Amaury Talbot Prize for African Anthropology, 1983; Herskovits Award, African Studies Assoc., USA, 1984. *Publications:* Aladura: a religious movement among the Yoruba, 1968; Herbert Spencer: the evolution of a sociologist, 1971; (ed) Herbert Spencer on Social Evolution, 1972; Ijeshas and Nigerians, 1983; articles in anthropological, sociological and Africanist jls. *Recreations:* gardening, fell-walking, old churches. *Address:* 23 Mount Road, Upton, Wirral, Merseyside L49 6JA. *T:* 0151–678 6783.

PEEL, Sir John (Harold), KCVO 1960; MA, BM, BCh; FRCP 1971; FRCS 1933; FRCOG 1944; Surgeon-Gynæcologist to the Queen, 1961–73; Consulting Obstetric and Gynæcological Surgeon, King's College Hospital, since 1969; Emeritus Consulting Gynæcologist, Princess Beatrice Hospital, since 1965; *b* 10 December 1904; *s* of Rev. J. E. Peel; *m* 1st, 1936, Muriel Elaine Pellow; one *d*; *m* 2nd, 1947, Freda Margaret Mellish (*d* 1993). *Educ:* Manchester Grammar Sch.; Queen's Coll., Oxford. MA, BM, BCh Oxon 1932. King's College Hospital Med. Sch., qualified 1930; MRCS, LRCP. Obstetric and Gynæcological Surgeon: King's Coll. Hosp., 1936–69; Princess Beatrice Hosp., 1937–65; Queen Victoria Hosp., East Grinstead, 1941–69; Surgeon EMS, 1939–45. Director of Clinical Studies, King's College Hospital Medical School, 1948–67. Mem., Economic and Social Cttee, EEC, 1973–78. Litchfield Lecturer, Oxford University, 1961 and 1969; Sir Kadar Nath Das Lecturer, Bengal O and G Soc., 1962; Sir A. Mudaliar Lecturer, Madras Univ., 1962; Vis. Prof., Cape Town Univ., 1963; Travelling Prof., S African Council, RCOG, 1968. Past Examiner, Universities of Oxford, Cambridge, London, Liverpool, Bristol, Glasgow, Newcastle, Nat. Univ. of Ireland, Birmingham, Dundee, Sheffield, Conjoint Board, RCOG and CMB. Nuffield visitor to Colonies, 1950 and 1953. President, RCOG, 1966–69 (Hon. Treasurer, 1959–66, Councillor, 1955–); President: Internat. Fedn of Obstetrics and Gynæcology, 1970–73; Chelsea Clinical Society, 1960; BMA 1970 (Chm., Bd of Science and Educn, 1972–76); Family Planning Assoc., 1971–74; Chm., DHSS Cttees of Enquiry: Domiciliary Midwifery and Bed Needs, 1971; The Use of Fetus and Fetal Material for Research, 1972. FKC 1980; Hon. Fellow: American Association of Obstetricians and Gynæcologists, 1962 (Joseph Price Oration, 1961); Edinburgh Obstetrical Soc., 1971; RSM, 1973; Hon. Member: Canadian Assoc. of O and G, 1955; Italian Assoc O and G, 1960; Hon. Treas., GMC, 1972–75; Hon. FRCS (Canada), 1967; Hon. FCOG (SA), 1968; Hon. MMSA 1970; Hon. FACS 1970; Hon. FACOG 1971; Hon. Fellow, American Gynæcological Soc., 1974. Hon. DSc Birmingham, 1972; Hon. DM Southampton, 1974; Hon. DCh Newcastle, 1980. *Publications:* Textbook of Gynæcology, 1943; Lives of the Fellows of Royal College of Obstetricians and Gynaecologists 1929–69, 1976; Biography of William Blain-Bell, 1986; numerous contributions to Medical Journals. *Recreations:* fishing, gardening. *Address:* 11 Harnwood Road, Harnham, Salisbury SP2 8DD. *T:* Salisbury (01722) 334892. *Club:* Naval and Military.

PEEL, Jonathan Sidney, CBE 1994; MC 1957; Vice Lord-Lieutenant of Norfolk, since 1981; Director, Norwich Union Insurance Group, since 1973; *b* 21 June 1937; *s* of Major D. A. Peel (killed in action 1944) and Hon. Mrs David Peel (*née* Vanneck); *m* 1965, Jean Fulton Barnett, *d* of Air Chief Marshal Sir Denis Barnett, GCB, CBE, DFC; one *s* four *d*. *Educ:* Norwich Sch.; Eton; St John's Coll., Cambridge (BA Land Economy; MA 1970). Commnd, Rifle Bde, Royal Green Jackets, 1956; served Malaya, 1956–57; UN forces, Congo (Zaire), 1960–61; Cyprus, 1962–63; resigned, 1966. Chm., Pleasureworld plc, 1986–89. Vice Pres., Norfolk Naturalists Trust, 1984–; National Trust: Mem. Exec. Cttee, 1982–; Mem. Council, 1984–; Dep. Chm., 1992–; Chm., Cttee for East Anglia, 1981–90; Chm., Properties Cttee, 1990–. Norfolk Scouts Association: Dist Comr, 1971–75; Comr for Norwich, 1975–77; County Comr, 1977–81. Chairman: E Anglian Br., Royal Forestry Soc., 1979–81; Norfolk Police Authority, 1983–89; Norfolk Churches Trust, 1983–85; The Broads Authority, 1985–; Norwich Sch., 1985–; How Hill Trust, 1987–; Pres.,

Norfolk Assoc. for the Advancement of Music, 1978–93. Mem., Norfolk CC, 1973– (Chm., Planning and Transportation Cttee, 1990–93). JP North Walsham, 1973–86. High Sheriff, Norfolk, 1984. *Publication:* (with M. J. Sayer) Towards a Rural Policy for Norfolk, 1973. *Recreations:* forestry, music. *Address:* Barton Hall, Barton Turf, Norwich NR12 8AU. *T:* Smallburgh (01692) 536250. *Clubs:* Boodle's; Norfolk (Norwich).

PEEL, Sir (William) John, Kt 1973; *b* 16 June 1912; *s* of late Sir William Peel, KCMG, KBE, and Violet Mary Drake, *er d* of W. D. Laing; *m* 1936, Rosemary Mia Minka, *er d* of Robert Readhead; one *s* three *d*. *Educ:* Wellington College; Queens' College, Cambridge. Colonial Administrative Service, 1933–51; on active service, 1941–45; British Resident, Brunei, 1946–48; Res. Comr, Gilbert and Ellice Is Colony, 1949–51. Personal Asst to Man. Dirs of Rugby Portland Cement Co. Ltd, 1952–54. Contested (C) Meriden Division of Warwickshire, 1955; MP (C) Leicester SE, 1957–Feb. 1974; Parliamentary Private Secretary to: Economic Secretary to the Treasury, 1958–59; Minister of State, Board of Trade, 1959–60; Asst Govt Whip (unpaid), 1960–61; a Lord Comr of the Treasury, Nov. 1961–Oct. 1964. Parly Delegate to: Assemblies of Council of Europe, 1961–74; WEU 1961–74 (Vice-Pres., 1967, Pres. 1972, Chm., Defence and Armaments Cttee, 1970–72, WEU); N Atlantic Assembly, 1959–74 (Leader, 1970–74; Pres., N Atlantic Assembly, Nov. 1972); Mem., British Delegn to European Parlt, Strasbourg, 1973–74; Hon. Dir, Cons. Party Internat. Office, 1975–76. Member Council: Victoria League for Commonwealth Friendship, 1974–83 (Dep. Chm., 1976–81; Chm., 1982–83; Dep. Pres. and Mem., Chairman's Adv. Cttee, 1983–); British Atlantic Cttee; Mem. Central Council, Royal Over-Seas League, 1980–86; Chairman: Hospitality and Branches Cttee of Victoria League, 1974–78, Hospitality Cttee, 1978–81; Overseas Students Adv. Cttee, 1980–81; Jt Standing Cttee of Victoria League and Royal Commonwealth Soc., 1975–83; Westminster for Europe Branch, European Movement, 1974–77. Mem. Ct of Assistants, Framework Knitters' Co. (Master, 1983). Dato Seri Laila Jasa Brunei 1969; Dato Setia Negara Brunei 1971. *Recreations:* varied. *Address:* 51 Cambridge Street, SW1V 4PR. *T:* 0171–834 8762. *Clubs:* Carlton, Hurlingham; Hawks (Cambridge).

PEELER, Joseph; Regional Director for the South-East Region, Departments of the Environment and Transport, and Chairman of Regional Board, 1979–86, retired; *b* 22 April 1930; *s* of late Edward Francis Peeler and Marjorie Cynthia Peeler; *m* 1958, Diana Helen (*née* Wynne); three *s* one *d*. *Educ:* King Edward VI Grammar Sch., Stratford-on-Avon; Wimbledon Coll.; Jesus Coll., Oxford (Scholar, 1948; BA 1st Cl. Hons Modern History, 1951; MA 1955). RAF, 1951–53. Entered Civil Service (Min. of Transport and Civil Aviation), 1953; Private Sec. to Parly Sec., 1956–58; Principal, 1958; seconded to Home Office, 1964–66; Asst Sec., 1966; Under Sec., 1978. Chairman: Burford and Dist Soc., 1990–93 (Vice-Chm., 1993–); Burford Guild of Arts, 1993–. *Recreations:* history, crosswords, bridge, walking. *Address:* Cocklands, Fulbrook, Burford, Oxon OX18 4BE. *T:* Burford (01993) 822612.

PEERS, Most Rev. Michael Geoffrey; Primate of the Anglican Church of Canada, since 1986; *b* 31 July 1934; *s* of Geoffrey Hugh Peers and Dorothy Enid Mantle; *m* 1963, Dorothy Elizabeth Bradley; two *s* one *d*. *Educ:* University of British Columbia (BA Hons); Universität Heidelberg (Zert. Dolm.-Interpreter's Certificate); Trinity Coll., Toronto (LTh). Deacon 1959, priest 1960; Curate: St Thomas', Ottawa, 1959–61; Trinity, Ottawa, 1961–65; University Chaplain, Diocese of Ottawa, 1961–66; Rector: St Bede's, Winnipeg, 1966–72; St Martin's, Winnipeg, with St Paul's Middlechurch, 1972–74; Archdeacon of Winnipeg, 1969–74; Rector, St Paul's Cathedral, Regina, 1974–77; Dean of Qu'Appelle, 1974–77; Bishop of Qu'Appelle, 1977–82; Archbishop of Qu'Appelle and Metropolitan of Rupert's Land, 1982–86. Hon. DD: Trinity Coll., Toronto, 1977; St John's Coll., Winnipeg, 1981; Wycliffe Coll., Toronto, 1987; Univ. of Kent, 1988; Montreal Dio. Coll., 1989; Coll. of Emmanuel and St Chad, Saskatoon, 1990; Vancouver Sch. of Theol., 1991; Thorneloe Univ., 1991; Bishop's Univ., Lennoxville, 1993. *Address:* 600 Jarvis Street, Toronto, Ontario M4Y 2J6, Canada. *T:* (416) 9249192.

PEET, Ronald Hugh, CBE 1974; Chairman: Stockley Plc, 1984–87; PWS Holdings plc, 1987–88; *b* 12 July 1925; *s* of Henry Leonard and Stella Peet; *m* 1st, 1949, Winifred Joy Adamson (*d* 1979); two *s* two *d*; 2nd, 1981, Lynette Judy Burgess Kinsella. *Educ:* Doncaster Grammar Sch.; Queen's Coll., Oxford (MA). Served in HM Forces, Captain RA, 1944–47. Legal and General Assurance Society Limited: joined 1952; emigrated to Australia, 1955; Sec., Australian Branch, 1955–59; Asst Life Manager, 1959–65; Manager and Actuary for Australia, 1965–69; returned to UK as General Manager (Ops), 1969; Dir, 1969–84; Chief Exec., 1972–84; Chm., 1980–84; Dir and Chief Exec., Legal & General Gp Plc, 1980–84. Chm., Aviation & General Insurance Co. Ltd, 1978–80; Director: AMEC Plc, 1984–; Howard Gp plc, 1985–86; Independent Insurance Group plc, 1988–. Director: City Arts Trust Ltd, 1976–90 (Chm., 1980–87); Royal Philharmonic Orchestra Ltd, 1977–88; English National Opera, 1978–84, 1985–. Chm., British Insurance Assoc., 1978–79. FIA. *Recreations:* music, opera. *Address:* 9 Marlowe Court, Petyward, SW3 3PD. *Clubs:* Hurlingham, City of London.

PEGG, Michael Anstice, PhD; University Librarian and Director, John Rylands University Library, University of Manchester, 1981–90; *b* 3 Sept. 1931; *s* of Benjamin and Rose Pegg; *m* 1st, 1955, Jean Williams; three *s*; 2nd, 1986, Margaret Rae. *Educ:* Burton-on-Trent Grammar Sch.; Univ. of Southampton. BA (London); PhD (Southampton); MA (Manchester) 1985. Captain, Royal Army Education Corps, Educn Officer, SHAPE, Paris, 1958–61; Asst Keeper, Nat. Library of Scotland, Edinburgh, 1961–67; Sec. and Estabt Officer, Nat. Library of Scotland, Edinburgh, 1967–76; Librarian, Univ. of Birmingham, 1976–80. Vis Fellow, Beinecke Library, Yale Univ., 1989. Member: British Library Bd, 1981–84; Standing Conference of Nat. and Univ. Libraries' Council, 1981–83. *Publications:* Les Divers Rapports d'Eustorg de Beaulieu (édn critique), 1964 (Geneva); Catalogue of German Reformation Pamphlets in Libraries of Great Britain and Ireland, 1973 (Baden Baden); Catalogue of Sixteenth-century German Pamphlets in Collections in France and England, 1977 (Baden Baden); Catalogue of Reformation Pamphlets in Swiss Libraries, 1983; Catalogue of Sixteenth-century German and Dutch books in the Royal Library Copenhagen, 1989; Catalogue of German Reformation Pamphlets in Swedish Libraries, 1994; occasional papers to learned jls. *Recreations:* travel, reading, railways. *Address:* c/o John Rylands University Library, University of Manchester, Oxford Road, Manchester M13 9PP.

PEGGIE, Robert Galloway Emslie, CBE 1986; Commissioner for Local Administration (Ombudsman) in Scotland, 1986–94; Chairman, Scottish Local Government Staff Commission, since 1994; *b* 5 Jan. 1929; *s* of John and Euphemia Peggie; *m* 1955, Christine Jeanette Simpson; one *s* one *d*. *Educ:* Lasswade High Sch. Certified accountant; Accountancy apprenticeship, 1946–52; Accountant in industry, 1952–57; Public Service, Edinburgh City, 1957–74; Chief Exec., Lothian Regl Council, 1974–86. Chm., Scottish Local Govt Adv. Cttee on Staffing Matters, 1994–. Mem., Gen. Convocation and Court, Heriot-Watt Univ., 1988–. (Convener, Finance Cttee, 1989–). Governor, Edinburgh Coll. of Art, 1989–. *Recreation:* golf. *Address:* 54 Liberton Drive, Edinburgh EH16 6NW. *T:* 0131–664 1631.

PEGLER, Alfred Ernest, OBE 1978; DL; Councillor: Crawley Borough Council, since 1956; West Sussex County Council, since 1959; *b* 18 Jan. 1924; *s* of Frank Walter James Pegler and Violet Maud Pegler; *m* 1944, E. E. McDonald; one *s* one *d*. *Educ:* Cork Street Sch., Peckham; Oliver Goldsmith Sch., Peckham. Engrg apprentice, 1938–42; served War, RAF Air Crew, 1942–46; toolmaker, 1946–62; Civil Service Engrg Inspector, 1963–81. Chm., Crawley Council, 1959 and 1966; Chm. Housing Cttee, 1971–77. Leader, Labour Gp, W Sussex CC, 1977–. Mem., Crawley Cttee, New Towns Commn, 1962– (Chm., 1974–). Mayor, Crawley Borough Council, 1982–83, 1983–84. Mem., Sussex Police Authority, 1973–. Contested (Labour): Horsham, 1959 and 1964; Gloucester, Feb. 1974. DL West Sussex, 1982. *Recreations:* gardening, politics. *Address:* 7 Priors Walk, Three Bridges, Crawley, West Sussex RH10 1NX. *T:* Crawley (01293) 27330.

PEI, Ieoh Ming, FAIA, RIBA; architect; Founding Partner, Pei Cobb Freed & Partners (formerly I. M. Pei & Partners), Architects, New York, since 1955; *b* Canton, China, 26 April 1917; naturalized citizen of USA, 1954; *m* 1942, Eileen Loo; three *s* one *d*. *Educ:* St John's Middle Sch., Shanghai; MIT (BArch 1940); Harvard Grad. Sch. of Design (MArch 1946). FAIA 1964. Nat. Defense Res. Cttee, 1943–45; Asst Prof., Harvard Grad. Sch. of Design, 1945–48; Dir Architecture, Webb & Knapp Inc., 1948–55; Wheelwright Travelling Fellow, Harvard, 1951. Designed Nat. Center for Atmospheric Res., Boulder, Colo, 1961–67; other projects include: John F. Kennedy Library, Boston, 1965–79; E Building, Nat. Gall. of Art, Washington, 1968–78; Morton H. Myerson Symphony Center, Dallas, 1982–89; Regent Hotel, NY, 1989–; also church, hosp., municipal and corporate bldgs, schs, libraries and museums in US; numerous projects worldwide include: Fragrant Hill Hotel, Beijing, 1979–82; Bank of China, Hong Kong, 1982–89; expansion and renovation, The Louvre, Paris, 1983–93. Member: Nat. Council on Humanities, 1966–70; Urban Design Council, NYC, 1967–72; AIA Nat. Urban Policy Task Force, 1970–74; Nat. Council on Arts, 1981–84. Member: Nat. Acad. Design, 1965; Amer. Acad. Arts and Scis, 1967; AAIL, 1975 (Chancellor, 1978–80); Institut de France, 1983. Hon. Degrees include: Pennsylvania, Columbia, NY, Brown, Colorado, Chinese Univ. of Hong Kong, Amer. Univ. of Paris. Numerous awards including: Arnold Brunner Award, Nat. Inst. Arts and Letters, 1961; Medal of Honour, NY Chapter, AIA, 1963; Thomas Jefferson Meml Medal for Architecture, 1976; Gold Medal, AAAL, 1979; Gold Medal, AIA, 1979; La Grande Médaille d'Or L'Académie d'Architecture, France, 1981; Architectural Firm Award, AIA, 1968; Praemium Imperiale, US, 1989. Medal of Liberty, US, 1986; Chevalier de La Légion d'Honneur, 1988; US Medal of Freedom, 1993. *Address:* 600 Madison Avenue, New York, NY 10022, USA. *T:* (212) 7513122.

PEIRCE, Rev. Canon (John) Martin; Canon Residentiary of Christ Church, Oxford, since 1987, and Oxford Diocesan Director of Ordinands, since 1985; *b* 9 July 1936; *s* of Martin Westley and Winifred Mary Peirce; *m* 1968, Rosemary Susan Milne; two *s*. *Educ:* Brentwood Sch.; Jesus Coll., Cambridge; Westcott House, Cambridge. MA Cantab. Served Royal Air Force, 1954–56. Teacher, St Stephen's Coll., Hong Kong, 1960–64; Curate, St John Baptist, Croydon, 1966–70; Team Vicar, St Columba, Fareham, 1970–76; Team Rector, Langley, Slough, 1976–85. *Recreations:* walking, gardening. *Address:* 70 Yarnells Hill, Oxford OX2 9BG. *T:* Oxford (01865) 721330.

PEIRCE, Robert Nigel; HM Diplomatic Service; Political Adviser, Hong Kong, since 1993; *b* 18 March 1955; *s* of Kenneth Frank Peirce and Margaret Peirce; *m* 1978, Christina Anne Skipworth Davis; one *s* one *d*. *Educ:* Taunton Sch.; St Catherine's Coll., Oxford (MA); Faculty of Oriental Studies, Univ. of Cambridge. Joined FCO, 1977; Hong Kong, 1979–80; Peking, 1980–83; FCO, 1983–85; Cabinet Office, 1985–86; Dep. Political Advr, Hong Kong, 1986–88; Private Sec. to Sec. of State for Foreign and Commonwealth Affairs, 1988–90; UK Mission to UN, 1990–93. *Recreations:* family, friends, speculation. *Address:* c/o Foreign and Commonwealth Office, King Charles Street, SW1A 2AH. *Club:* Hong Kong (Hong Kong).

PEIRSE, Sir Henry G. de la P. B.; *see* Beresford-Peirse.

PEIRSE, Air Vice-Marshal Sir Richard (Charles Fairfax), KCVO 1988; CB 1984; Gentleman Usher of the Scarlet Rod, Order of the Bath, since 1990; *b* 16 March 1931; *s* of late Air Chief Marshal Sir Richard Peirse, KCB, DSO, AFC and late Lady Peirse; *m* 1st, 1955, Karalie Grace Cox (marr. diss. 1963); two *d*; 2nd, 1963, Deirdre Mary O'Donovan (*d* 1976); (one *s* decd); 3rd, 1977, Anna Jill Margaret Long (*née* Latey). *Educ:* Bradfield Coll.; RAF Coll., Cranwell. Commnd 1952; 2nd TAF No 266 Sqdn and HQ 2 Gp, 1952; Flying Instructor, Cranwell, 1956; Air Staff No 23 Gp, 1960; Staff Coll., 1962; Flt Comdr No 39 Sqdn and OC Ops Wg, Luqa, Malta, 1963; Air Sec.'s Dept, 1965; jssc 1968; OC No 51 Sqdn, 1968; Dep. Captain, The Queen's Flight, 1969; RCDS 1972; OC RAF Waddington, 1973; Dep. Dir, Op Requirements, 1976; Dir of Personnel (Air), 1977; Dir of Op Requirements, 1980; AOC and Comdt, RAF Coll. Cranwell, 1982; Defence Services Sec., 1985–88, retd. *Recreations:* theatre, archaeology. *Address:* The Old Mill House, Adderbury, near Banbury, Oxon OX17 3LW. *T:* Banbury (01295) 810196. *Club:* Royal Air Force.

PEIRSON, Margaret Ellen; Under Secretary, Department of Social Security (on secondment), since 1990; *b* 28 Nov. 1942; *e d* of late David Edward Herbert Peirson, CBE and of Norah Ellen Peirson (*née* Corney). *Educ:* North London Collegiate Sch.; Somerville Coll., Oxford (MA Maths); Yale Univ. Joined HM Treasury, 1965; secondment to Bank of England, 1982–84; Under Sec., 1986. *Recreations:* choral singing, theatre. *Address:* Department of Social Security, The Adelphi, 1–11 John Adam Street, WC2N 6HT.

PELHAM, family name of **Earls of Chichester** and **Yarborough.**

PELHAM, Hugh Reginald Brentnall, PhD; FRS 1988; Member, Scientific Staff, Medical Research Council Laboratory of Molecular Biology, Cambridge, since 1981; *b* 26 Aug. 1954; *s* of late Reginald A. and of Pauline M. Pelham. *Educ:* Marlborough Coll., Wiltshire; Christ's Coll., Cambridge (MA, PhD). Research Fellow, Christ's Coll., 1978–84; Dept of Embryology, Carnegie Instn of Washington Baltimore, Md, 1979–81; Visitor, Univ. of Zürich, 1987–88. Colworth Medal, Biochemical Soc., 1988; EMBO medal, 1989; Louis Jeantet Prize for Medicine, 1991. *Publications:* papers in sci. jls on molecular and cell biology. *Address:* MRC Laboratory of Molecular Biology, Hills Road, Cambridge CB2 2QH. *T:* Cambridge (01223) 248011.

PELHAM BURN, Angus Maitland; JP; farmer; Vice Lord-Lieutenant for Kincardineshire, since 1978; Director, Bank of Scotland, since 1977 (Director, since 1973, Chairman, since 1977, Aberdeen Local Board); Chairman: Scottish Provident Institution, since 1995 (Director, since 1975; Deputy Chairman, 1991–95); Aberdeen Trust plc, since 1993; *b* 13 Dec. 1931; *s* of late Brig. Gen. H. Pelham Burn, CMG, DSO, and late Mrs K. E. S. Pelham Burn; *m* 1959, Anne R. Pelham Burn (*née* Forbes-Leith); four *d*. *Educ:* Harrow; N of Scotland Coll. of Agriculture. Hudson's Bay Co., 1951–58. Director: Aberdeen and Northern Marts Ltd, 1970–86 (Chm., 1974–86); Jessfield Ltd, 1970–88; Aberdeen Meat Marketing Co. Ltd, 1973–86 (Chm., 1974–86); Prime Space Design (Scotland) Ltd, 1981–87; Status Timber Systems, 1986–90; Skeendale Ltd, 1987–88; Abtrust Scotland Investment Co., 1989–; Chairman and Director: MacRobert Farms (Douneside) Ltd, 1970–87; Pelett Administration Ltd, 1973–94; Taw Meat Co., 1984–86. Chm., Aberdeen Airport Consultative Cttee, 1986–; Mem., Accounts Commn, 1980–94 (Dep. Chm., 1992–94). Mem. Council, Winston Churchill Meml Trust, 1984–93; Dir., Aberdeen

Assoc. for Prevention of Cruelty to Animals, 1975– (Chm., 1984–89). Pres., Aberdeen Br., Inst. of Marketing, 1987–90. Member: Kincardine CC, 1967–75 (Vice Convener, 1973–75); Grampian Regional Council, 1974–94. Member, Queen's Body Guard for Scotland (Royal Co. of Archers), 1968–. Hon. FInstM. JP Kincardine and Deeside, 1984; DL Kincardineshire 1978. OStJ 1978. *Recreations:* fishing, vegetable gardening, photography, stalking. *Address:* Knappach, Banchory, Kincardineshire AB31 3JS. *T:* Crathes (01330) 844555; (office) (01330) 823343, *Fax:* (01330) 823749. *Clubs:* New (Edinburgh); Royal Northern (Aberdeen).

PELIZA, Major Robert John, OBE 1989; ED 1955; company director, since 1962; Speaker, House of Assembly, Gibraltar, since 1989; *b* 16 Nov. 1920; *s* of late Robert Peliza; *m* 1950, Irma Risso; three *s* four *d. Educ:* Christian Brothers' Coll., Gibraltar. Served in Gibraltar Defence Force (now Gibraltar Regt), 1939–61. Founder Mem., Integration with Britain Party (first leader), 1967; Chief Minister, 1969–72, apptd following Gen. Elections, 1969; elected MHA, 1969–84; Leader of the Opposition, 1972–73. Pres., Gibraltar Br, CPA, 1989. Hon. Col, Gibraltar Regt, 1993–. *Recreations:* walking, painting, reading, jogging, cycling, rowing. *Address:* 203 Water Gardens, Gibraltar.

PELLEREAU, Maj.-Gen. Peter John Mitchell, MA, CEng, FIMechE, FIMgt; Secretary, Association of Consulting Engineers, 1977–87; *b* Quetta, British India, 24 April 1921; *s* of late Col J. C. E. Pellereau, OBE and Mrs A. N. V. Pellereau (*née* Betham); *m* 1949, Rosemary, *e d* of late S. R. Garnar; two *s. Educ:* Wellington Coll.; Trinity Coll., Cambridge. BA 1942, MA 1957. Commnd into Royal Engrs, 1942; War Service in NW Europe, 1944–45; OC 26 Armd Engr Sqdn, RE, 1946; ptsc, psc, 1950–51; Sec., Defence Research Policy Cttee, 1960; Asst Mil. Sec., WO, 1961; CO 131 Parachute Engr Regt RE TA, 1963; Mil. Dir of Studies, RMCS, 1965; Asst Dir RE Equipment Develt, 1967; Sen. Mil. Officer, Royal Armament R&D Estabt, 1970; Vice-Pres., 1973–75, Pres., 1975–76, Ordnance Board; retired 1976. Hon. Col, RE (Vol.) (Explosive Ordnance Disposal), 1980–86. Liveryman: Worshipful Co. of Plumbers, 1977–92; Worshipful Co. of Engineers, 1984–92. Mem., Smeatonian Soc. of Civil Engineers, 1981–. Vice-Pres., Surrey Hockey Umpires' Assoc., 1979–85; Pres., Oxted Hockey Club, 1975–84. Mem., Wolfe Soc. Cttee, 1978–; Chm., Westerham Motorway Action Gp, 1993–. *Recreations:* lawn tennis, golf. *Address:* Woodmans Folly, Crockham Hill, Edenbridge, Kent TN8 6RJ. *T:* Edenbridge (01732) 866309.

PELLEW, family name of **Viscount Exmouth.**

PELLEW, Dr Jill Hosford; Director, Development Office, University of Oxford, since 1994; Fellow of Trinity College, Oxford, since 1995; *b* 29 April 1942; *d* of Prof. Frank Thistlethwaite, *qv* and of late Jane (*née* Hosford); *m* 1965, Mark Edward Pellew, *qv*; two *s. Educ:* Cambs High Sch. for Girls; St Hilda's Coll., Oxford (BA 1964; MA 1968); Queen Mary Coll., London (MA 1970); PhD London 1976. MoD, 1964–66; part-time univ. teaching, Univ. of Saigon, Univ. of Sussex, Hollins Coll., Va, American Univ., Washington, 1967–89; Exec. Sec., Chatham Hse Foundn, Washington, 1984–89; Develt Officer, St Hilda's Coll., Oxford, 1989–90; Dir of Develt, Imperial Coll. of Science, Technology and Medicine, London, 1991–94. *Publications:* The Home Office 1848–1914: from clerks to bureaucrats, 1982; (with S. Cassese) The Comparative History of Public Administration: the merit system, 1987; various articles in learned jls on admin. hist. *Recreations:* books, people, music, travel, food. *Address:* 30 Taynton, near Burford, Oxon OX18 4UH. *T:* Burford (01993) 823208. *Club:* Reform.

PELLEW, Mark Edward, LVO 1980; HM Diplomatic Service; Head of North America Department, Foreign and Commonwealth Office, since 1991; *b* 28 Aug. 1942; *e s* of late Comdr Anthony Pownoll Pellew, RN retd, and of Margaret Julia Critchley (*née* Cookson); *m* 1965, Jill Hosford Thistlethwaite (*see* J. H. Pellew); two *s. Educ:* Winchester; Trinity Coll., Oxford (BA). Entered HM Diplomatic Service, 1965; FO, 1965–67; Third Sec., Singapore, 1967–69; Second Sec., Saigon, 1969–70; FCO, 1970–76; First Sec., Rome, 1976–80; Asst Head of Personnel Ops Dept, FCO, 1981–83; Counsellor: Washington, 1983–89; on secondment to Hambros Bank, 1989–91. *Recreations:* singing, playing the horn. *Address:* c/o Foreign and Commonwealth Office, King Charles Street, SW1A 2AH. *Club:* Hurlingham.

See also R. A. Pellew.

PELLEW, Robin Anthony, PhD; Director and Chief Executive, WWF-World Wide Fund for Nature, since 1994; *b* 27 Sept. 1945; *s* of late Comdr Anthony Pownoll Pellew, RN and Margaret Julia Critchley (*née* Cookson); *m* 1974, Pamela Daphne Gibson MacLellan; one *s* one *d. Educ:* Marlborough Coll.; Edinburgh Univ. (BSc 1968); University College London (MSc 1972; PhD 1981). Sen. Res. Scientist, Serengeti Res. Inst., Tanzania, 1973–78; BBC Natural History Unit, 1978–79; Res. Fellow, Physiology Lab., Cambridge, 1979–82; Cambridge University Press: Sen. Editor, 1982–86; Editorial Manager, 1986–87; Dir, Conservation Monitoring Centre, IUCN, 1987–88; Dir, World Conservation Monitoring Centre, Cambridge, 1988–93. Member: Council, RGS, 1988–; Envt Cttee, RSA, 1993–. *Publications:* numerous scientific papers on wild life management and conservation in professional jls. *Recreations:* travelling to exotic places, watching wild life. *Address:* 2 Luard Road, Cambridge CB2 2PJ. *T:* Cambridge (01223) 246935.

See also M. E. Pellew.

PELLING, Anthony Adair; Director, GJW Government Relations Ltd, London and Washington, since 1993; *b* 3 May 1934; *s* of Brian and Alice Pelling; *m* 1st, 1958, Margaret Lightfoot (*d* 1986); one *s* one *d*; 2nd, 1989, Virginia Glen-Calvert. *Educ:* Purley Grammar Sch.; London Sch. of Economics. BSc (Econ); MIPM. National Coal Board, 1957–67; entered MPBW as Principal, 1967; Asst Sec., 1970, Under Sec., 1981, DoE; seconded as Dep. Dir, Business in the Community, 1981–83; Dept of Transport, 1983–85, London Regional Dir, DoE, 1987–91; Dir, Construction Policy, DoE, 1991–93. Director: Croydon FHSA; Croydon Business Venture; Cities in Schools. *Recreations:* music, theatre. *Clubs:* Reform; Surrey CC.

PELLING, Henry Mathison, FBA 1992; Fellow of St John's College, Cambridge, 1966–80 and since 1980 (*socius ejectus*); Supernumerary Fellow, Queen's College, Oxford, 1980; *b* 27 Aug. 1920; *s* of late D. L. Pelling, Prenton, Cheshire, and late Mrs M. M. Pelling; unmarried. *Educ:* Birkenhead School; St John's Coll., Cambridge. Class. Tripos Part I, 1941; History Tripos Part II, 1947 (MA 1945; PhD 1950; LittD 1975). Army service, 1941–45; Commnd RE, 1942; served NW Europe campaign, 1944–45. Fellow, Queen's Coll., Oxford, 1949–65; Tutor, 1950–65; Dean, 1963–64; Asst Dir of Research (History), Cambridge, 1966–76; Reader in Recent British History, Cambridge, 1976–80. Smith-Mundt Schol., University of Wisconsin, USA, 1953–54; Fellow, Woodrow Wilson Center, Washington, DC, 1983. Hon. DHL New Sch. for Social Res., New York, 1983. *Publications:* Origins of the Labour Party, 1954; Challenge of Socialism, 1954; America and the British Left, 1956; British Communist Party, 1958; (with Frank Bealey) Labour and Politics, 1958; American Labor, 1960; Modern Britain, 1885–1955, 1960; Short History of the Labour Party, 1961, 10th edn 1993; History of British Trade Unionism, 1963, 5th edn 1992; Social Geography of British Elections, 1967; Popular Politics and Society in Late Victorian Britain, 1968, 2nd edn 1979; Britain and the Second World War, 1970; Winston Churchill, 1974, 2nd edn 1989; The Labour Governments 1945–51, 1984; Britain and the Marshall Plan, 1988; articles and reviews in learned journals. *Recreations:* theatre, films. *Address:* St John's College, Cambridge CB2 1TP. *T:* Cambridge (01223) 338600. *Clubs:* National Liberal, Commonwealth Trust.

PELLY, Derek Roland, (Derk); Deputy Chairman, Barclays Bank PLC, 1986–88 (Vice Chairman, 1984–85); *b* 12 June 1929; *s* of late Arthur Roland Pelly and late Elsie Pelly; *m* 1953, Susan Roberts; one *s* two *d. Educ:* Marlborough; Trinity Coll., Cambridge. Served RA, 1947–49 (2nd Lieut). Entered Barclays Bank, 1952; Local Director: Chelmsford, 1959; Luton, 1969; Vice Chm., 1977–85, Chm., 1986–87, Barclays Internat. Ltd. Dir, The Private Bank & Trust Co., 1989–94. Member: Milton Keynes Develt Corp., 1976–85; Council, ODI, 1984–89. Mem. Cttee, Family Assce Soc., 1988–91. Dir, Chelmsford Dio. Bd of Finance, 1989–. Governor: London House for Overseas Graduates, 1985–91; Chelmsford Coll., 1994–. *Recreation:* painting. *Address:* The Bowling Green, 8 The Downs, Great Dunmow, Essex CM6 1DT. *T:* Great Dunmow (01371) 872662.

PELLY, Sir Richard (John), 7th Bt *cr* 1840, of Upton, Essex; farmer, since 1991; *b* 10 April 1951; *s* of Richard Heywood Pelly, 2nd *s* of Sir Alwyne Pelly, 5th Bt, MC and of Mary Elizabeth Pelly (*née* Luscombe); *S* uncle, 1993; *m* 1983, Clare Gemma Dove; three *s. Educ:* Wellington Coll., Berks; Wadham Coll., Oxford (BA Agriculture and Forestry Science). ACA 1978–82. Price Waterhouse, London, 1974–78; Birds Eye Foods Ltd, 1978–81; New Century Software Ltd, 1981–. *Recreations:* walking, cycling, windsurfing, shooting. *Heir: s* Anthony Alwyne Pelly, *b* 30 Oct. 1984. *Address:* The Manor House, Preshaw Park, Upham, Southampton SO32 1HP. *T:* Southampton (01962) 771751.

PEMBERTON; *see* Leigh-Pemberton, family name of Baron Kingsdown.

PEMBERTON, Col Alan Brooke, CVO 1988; MBE 1960; *b* 11 Sept. 1923; *s* of Eric Harry Pemberton (Canadian by birth) and Phyllis Edith Pemberton (*née* Brooke-Alder); *m* 1952, Pamela Kirkland Smith, of Winnipeg, Canada; two *s. Educ:* Uppingham School; Trinity College, Cambridge. Commissioned Coldstream Guards, 1942; war service in Italy and NW Europe; ADC to Earl Alexander of Tunis, Governor-General of Canada, 1951–52; ADC to Gen. Sir Gerald Templer, High Comr to Malaya, 1952–53; Commanded 1st Bn Coldstream Guards, 1963–66; Regtl Lt-Col, 1966–67; retired 1967 (Hon. Col). Queen's Body Guard, Yeomen of the Guard: Exon, 1967; Ensign; Clerk of the Cheque; Lieutenant, 1985–93. Chm. and Man. Dir, Diversified Corporate Services Ltd, 1970–85. Special Constable, A Div., Metropolitan Police, 1975–76. *Recreations:* painting, reading, travel. *Address:* Eastfields Farm, Stoke-by-Nayland, Colchester, Essex CO6 4TB. *Club:* Pratt's.

PEMBERTON, Rev. Desmond Valdo; Assistant National Superintendent, Wesleyan Church, since 1990; a President, Churches Together in England, since 1990; *b* 23 March 1927; *s* of Charles and Lilla Pemberton; *m* 1951, Inez Pauline Fieulleteau; six *s* four *d. Educ:* Dept of Education and Ministry, Wesleyan Church HQ, USA. Clergyman, ordained 1969. Voluntary work for Church, 1958–66; Pastoral work, 1966–72; Dist Superintendent, Wesleyan Holiness Church, 1972–Aug. 1990 when Church adopted Nat. status. Distinguished Service Award, Wesleyan Church, 1983. *Publication:* contrib. Faith in The City of Birmingham, 1990. *Recreations:* walking, reading. *Address:* c/o Churches Together in England, Inter-Church House, 35–41 Lower Marsh, SE1 7RL. *T:* 0121–444 3883.

PEMBERTON, Sir Francis (Wingate William), Kt 1976; CBE 1970; DL; FRICS; company director; *b* 1 Oct. 1916; *s* of late Dr William Warburton Wingate (assumed Arms of Pemberton, by Royal Licence, 1921) and Viola Patience Campbell Pemberton; *m* 1941, Diana Patricia, *e d* of late Reginald Salisbury Woods, MD, and Irene Woods, CBE, TD; two *s. Educ:* Eton; Trinity Coll., Cambridge (MA). Senior Consultant, Bidwells, Chartered Surveyors, 1980–89. Director: Agricultural Mortgage Corp. Ltd, 1969–91; Barclays Bank UK Ltd, 1977–81; Severn Trent Property Ltd, 1990–95. Chm. Adv. Cttee, Inst. of Animal Physiology and Genetics Res. (Cambridge and Edinburgh), 1983–90; Hon. Dir, Royal Show, 1963–68; Royal Agricultural Society of England: Mem. Council, 1951– (Pres., 1974–75, Dep. Pres., 1975–76); Chm. Exec. Bd, 1969–71; Trustee, 1969–; Gold Medal for distinguished services to agric., 1989. Trustee, Robinson Coll., Cambridge, 1973–85. Member: Water Resources Board, 1964–74; Winston Churchill Meml Trust, 1965–80; Economic Planning Council for East Anglia, 1965–74; National Water Council, 1974–81; Water Authorities Superannuation Pension Fund (Dep. Chm, Fund Management and Policy Cttee), 1983–89. High Sheriff, Cambridgeshire and Isle of Ely, 1965–66; DL Cambs, 1979. *Address:* Trumpington Hall, Cambridge CB2 2LH. *T:* Cambridge (01223) 841941. *Club:* Farmers'.

PEMBERTON, Prof. John, MD London; FRCP, FFCM; DPH Leeds; Professor of Social and Preventive Medicine, The Queen's University, Belfast, 1958–76; *b* 18 Nov. 1912; British; *m* 1937, Winifred Ethel Gray; three *s. Educ:* Christ's Hospital; University College and UCH, London. House Physician and House Surgeon, University College Hospital, 1936–37; Rowett Research Institute under the late Lord Boyd Orr, 1937–39; Rockefeller Travelling Fellow in Medicine, Harvard, Mass., USA, 1954–55; Director of MRC Group for research on Respiratory Disease and Air Pollution, and Reader in Social Medicine, University of Sheffield, 1955–58. Mem., Health Educn Council, DHSS, 1973–76. Milroy Lectr, RCP, 1976. *Publications:* (with W. Hobson) The Health of the Elderly at Home, 1954; (ed) Recent Studies in Epidemiology, 1958; (ed) Epidemiology: Reports on Research and Teaching, 1963; Will Pickles of Wensleydale, 1970; articles in Lancet, BMJ, etc. *Recreations:* reading, TV, walking, visual arts. *Address:* Iona, Cannon Fields, Hathersage, Sheffield S30 1AG.

PEMBROKE, 17th Earl of, *cr* 1551, **AND MONTGOMERY,** 14th Earl of, *cr* 1605; **Henry George Charles Alexander Herbert;** Baron Herbert of Caerdiff, 1551; Baron Herbert of Shurland, 1605; Baron Herbert of Lea (UK), 1861; DL; Hereditary Grand Visitor of Jesus College, Oxford; *b* 19 May 1939; *s* of 16th Earl of Pembroke and Montgomery, CVO, and Mary Countess of Pembroke, CVO (*d* 1995); *S* father, 1969; *m* 1st, 1966, Claire Rose (marr. diss. 1981), *o d* of Douglas Pelly, Swaynes Hall, Widdington, Essex; one *s* three *d*; 2nd, 1988, Miranda Juliet, *d* of Comdr John Oram, Bulbridge House, Wilton; two *d. Educ:* Eton Coll.; Oxford Univ. Royal Horse Guards, 1958–60 (National Service); Oxford University, 1960–63. DL Wilts 1995. *Recreations:* photography, gardening, horse racing. *Heir: s* Lord Herbert, *qv. Address:* Wilton House, Salisbury, Wilts SP2 0BJ. *T:* Salisbury (01772) 743744.

PEÑA, Paco; musician; flamenco guitar player, since 1954; Professor of Flamenco, Rotterdam Conservatory, since 1985; *b* 1 June 1942; *s* of Antonio Peña and Rosario Perez; *m* 1982, Karin Vaessen; two *d. Educ:* Córdoba, Spain. London début, 1963; founded: Paco Peña Flamenco Co., 1970; Centro Flamenco Paco Peña, Córdoba, 1981; Misa Flamenca, 1991. Ramón Montoya Prize, 1983. *Address:* c/o Wim Visser, Staalstraat 10–12, 1011JL Amsterdam, Netherlands. *T:* (20) 6233700, (20) 6208212; c/o Karin Vaessen, 4 Boscastle Road, NW5 1EG. *Fax:* 0171–485 2320.

PENDER, 3rd Baron, *cr* 1937; **John Willoughby Denison-Pender;** Joint Chairman, Bremar Trust Ltd, 1977–83; Chairman, J. J. L. D. Frost plc, 1983–84; *b* 6 May 1933; *s* of 2nd Baron and of Camilla Lethbridge (*d* 1988), *o d* of late Willoughby Arthur Pemberton;

S father, 1965; *m* 1962, Julia, *yr d* of Richard Nevill Cannon; one *s* two *d*. *Educ:* Eton. Formerly Lieut, 10th Royal Hussars and Captain, City of London Yeomanry (TA). Dir, Globe Investment Trust Ltd, 1969–70. Vice Pres., Royal Sch. for Deaf Children, 1992–. Steward: Folkestone Racecourse, 1985–; Lingfield Park, 1989–. *Heir: s* Hon. Henry John Richard Denison-Pender [*b* 19 March 1968; *m* 1994, Vanessa, *d* of John Eley, NSW, Australia]. *Address:* North Court, Tilmanstone, Kent CT14 0JP. *T:* Sandwich (01304) 611726. *Clubs:* White's, Pratt's.

PENDER, Comr Dinsdale Leslie; Territorial Commander in United Kingdom and Republic of Ireland, Salvation Army, since 1993; *b* 22 March 1932; *s* of William Leslie Pender and Florence Lillian Pender (*née* Widdowson); *m* 1954, Winifred Violet Dale; one *s* two *d*. *Educ:* Colfe's Grammar Sch., Lewisham; Bradford Grammar Sch.; William Booth Meml Trng Coll. Served RAF, 1949–51. Commnd and ordained as Salvation Army Officer, 1952; CO, Manchester, Bath, Coventry and London, 1953–73; Divl Comdr, Northern Div., 1973–77; Asst Field Sec., Nat. HQ, 1977–80; Chief Sec., NZ and Fiji, 1980–84; Territorial Commander: Southern Africa, 1984–86; Scotland, 1986–90; Australia Southern, 1990–93. *Recreations:* music, swimming. *Address:* Salvation Army Territorial Headquarters, 101 Queen Street, EC4P 4EP. *T:* 0171–236 5222.

PENDERECKI, Krzysztof; Rector, State Academy of Music, Kraków, since 1972; Professor of Composition, School of Music, Yale University, New Haven, Conn, 1973–78; *b* Debica, Poland, 23 Nov. 1933; *s* of Tadeusz Penderecki and Zofia Penderecki; *m* 1965, Elzbieta Solecka; one *s* one *d*. *Educ:* State Acad. of Music, Kraków, Poland (Graduate 1958). Compositions include: Threnody to the Victims of Hiroshima, 1959–61 (52 strings); Passion According to St Luke, 1965–66 (oratorio); Utrenja, 1969–71 (oratorio); Devils of Loudun, 1969 (opera); Cello Concerto No 1, 1971–72; First Symphony, 1972; Magnificat, 1974 (oratorio); Awakening of Jacob, 1974 (orchestra); Paradise Lost, 1976–78 (rappresentazione for Chicago Lyric Opera; Milton libretto, Christopher Fry); Violin Concerto, 1977; Te Deum, 1979–80; (Christmas) Symphony No 2, 1980; Lacrimosa, 1980; Agnus Dei (for chorus a cappella), 1981; Cello Concerto No 2, 1982 (Grammy Award, Nat. Acad. of Recording Arts and Scis, 1988); Viola Concerto, 1983; Polish Requiem, 1983–84; Die schwarze Maske, 1986 (opera); Veni creator and Song of Cherubin (for chorus a cappella), 1987; Das unterbrochene Gedanke (for string quartet), 1988; Passacaglia, 1988 (orchestra); Symphony No 3, 1988; Symphony No 4, 1989; Adagio, 1989 (orchestra); Ubu Rex, 1991 (opera); Symphony No 5, 1991–92; Flute Concerto, 1992–93; Quartet for clarinet and string trio, 1993; Violin Concerto No 2, 1995. Hon. Dr: Univ. of Rochester, NY; St Olaf Coll., Northfield, Minn; Katholieke Univ., Leuven; Univ. of Bordeaux; Georgetown Univ., Washington; Univ. of Belgrade; Universidad Autónoma, Madrid; Adam Mickiewicz Univ.; Warsaw Univ.; Acad. of Music, Cracow and Warsaw. Member: RAM (Hon.); Akad. der Künste, Berlin (Extraordinary); Akad. der Künste der DDR, Berlin (Corresp.); Kungl. Musikaliska Akad., Stockholm; Accad. Nazionale di Santa Cecilia, Rome (Hon.); Acad. Nacional de Bellas Artes, Buenos Aires (Corresp.). Grosser Kunstpreis des Landes Nordrhein-Westfalen, 1966; Prix Italia, 1967/68; Gottfried von Herder Preis der Stiftung FvS zu Hamburg, 1977; Prix Arthur Honegger, 1977; Sibelius Prize, Wihouri Foundn, 1983; Premio Lorenzo Magnifico, 1985; Wolf Prize, 1987; Manuel de Falla Gold Medal, Accademia de Bellas Artes, Granada, 1989. Das Grosse Verdienstkreuz des Verdienstordens (Germany), 1990. *Publications:* all works published. *Recreations:* dendrology, gardening. *Address:* Cisowa 22, 30229 Kraków, Poland. *T:* (12) 225760, *Fax:* (12) 365060; ICM Artists Ltd, 8942 Wilshire Boulevard, Beverly Hills, CA 90211, USA. *T:* (310) 5504477.

PENDERED, Richard Geoffrey; Chairman, Bunge & Co., 1987–90; *b* 26 Sept. 1921; *s* of Richard Dudley Pendered and Adèle Pendered (*née* Hall); *m* 1953, Jennifer Preston Mead; two *s* two *d*. *Educ:* Winchester College (Scholar); Magdalene College (Scholar). GCCS Bletchley, 1940–52 (renamed GCHQ); Bunge & Co., 1952–90, Dir, 1957, Man. Dir, 1963–86. *Recreations:* fishing, shooting, golf. *Address:* 41 Sandy Lodge Lane, Northwood, Middx HA6 2HX. *Club:* Moor Park Golf.

PENDLEBURY, Edward; Assistant Under Secretary of State (Sales Administration), Ministry of Defence, 1983–85, retired; *b* 5 March 1925; *s* of Thomas Cecil Pendlebury and Alice (*née* Sumner); *m* 1957, Joan Elizabeth Bell; one *s*. *Educ:* King George V Sch., Southport; Magdalen Coll., Oxford (MA). Served War, RNVR, 1943–46. Asst Principal, Min. of Food, 1949–53; Principal: MAFF, 1953–56; MoD (British Defence Staff, Washington), 1956–60; MAFF, 1960–66; Asst Secretary: DEA, 1966–70; MoD, 1970–80; Exec. Dir (Civilian Management), MoD, 1980–83. *Recreations:* gramophone, gardening, gazing. *Address:* Bosworth House, Draycott, near Moreton-in-Marsh, Glos GL56 9LF. *T:* Blockley (01386) 701059.

PENDOWER, John Edward Hicks, FRCS; Dean, Charing Cross and Westminster Medical School, 1989–93; *b* 6 Aug. 1927; *s* of Thomas Curtis Hicks Pendower and Muriel May Pendower (*née* Newbury); *m* 1st, 1960, Kate Tuohy (*d* 1987); one *s* two *d*; 2nd, 1989, Mrs Paulette Gleave. *Educ:* Dulwich College; King's College London; Charing Cross Hosp. Med. Sch. (MB BS (Hons Med.) 1950). FRCS 1955. Called to the Bar, Inner Temple, 1972. Served RAMC. Charing Cross Hosp. and St Mark's Hosp., 1950–62; Harvey Cushing Fellow, Harvard Med. Sch., 1959–60; Consultant Surgeon: Mayday Hosp., Croydon, 1964–89; Charing Cross Hosp., 1965–87 (Vice Dean, 1979–84; Sub Dean, Charing Cross and Westminster Med. Sch., 1984–87); former examr in surgery, London Univ. Mem., Hammersmith and Fulham, subseq. Riverside, HA, 1983–90. Special Trustee, Charing Cross Hosp.; Trustee, Malcolm Sargent Cancer Fund for Children. *Recreations:* formerly squash rackets, now walking; collecting campaign medals. *Address:* Rosemary, Promenade de Verdun, Purley, Surrey CR8 3LN. *T:* 0181–660 8949.

PENDRED, Piers Loughnan; Special Assistant to Director-General, British Council, since 1994; *b* 24 Aug. 1943; *s* of Loughnan Wildig Pendred and Dulcie Treen Hall; *m* 1973, Carol Ann Haslam; one *s* one *d*. *Educ:* Ardingly College; Trinity Hall, Cambridge (MA Fine Arts and Architecture). VSO teacher, S India, 1965–67; British Council: Television Officer, Sudan, 1967–69, Ethiopia, 1969–71; TV Training Officer, London, 1972–76; Head of Production, 1976–81; Dir, Design, Production and Publishing, 1981–84; Dir, Press and Inf., 1984–87; Controller, later Dir of Finance, 1987–94. Sen. Exec. Programme, London Business Sch., 1987.

PENDRY, Prof. John Brian, PhD; FRS 1984; Professor of Theoretical Solid State Physics, Department of Physics, Imperial College of Science, Technology and Medicine, University of London, since 1981; Dean, Royal College of Science, since 1993; *b* 4 July 1943; *s* of Frank Johnson Pendry and Kathleen (*née* Shaw); *m* 1977, Patricia Gard. *Educ:* Downing Coll., Cambridge (MA; PhD 1969). Res. Fellow in Physics, Downing Coll., Cambridge, 1969–72; Mem. of Technical Staff, Bell Labs, USA, 1972–73; Sen. Asst in Res., Cavendish Lab., Cambridge Univ., and Fellow in Physics and Praelector, Downing Coll., 1973–75; SPSO and Head of Theory Gp, Daresbury Lab., 1975–81. *Publications:* Low Energy Electron Diffraction, 1974; Surface Crystallographic Information Service, 1987; scientific papers. *Recreations:* music, gardening. *Address:* The Blackett Laboratory, Imperial College of Science, Technology and Medicine, SW7 2BZ. *T:* 0171–594 7603, ext. 6901.

PENDRY, Thomas; MP (Lab) Stalybridge and Hyde since 1970; *b* 10 June 1934; *m* 1966, Moira Anne Smith; one *s* one *d*. *Educ:* St Augustine's, Ramsgate; Oxford Univ. RAF, 1955–57. Full time official, Nat. Union of Public Employees, 1960–70; Mem., Paddington Borough Council, 1962–65; Chm., Derby Labour Party, 1966. An Opposition Whip, 1971–74; a Lord Comr of the Treasury and Govt Whip, 1974, resigned 1977; Parly Under-Sec. of State, NI Office, 1978–79; Opposition Spokesman on NI, 1979–81, on overseas development, 1981–82, on regional affairs and devolution, 1982–84, on sport and tourism, 1992–. Member: Select Cttee on Envmt, 1987–92; Select Cttee on Members' Interests, 1987–92. Chairman: All Party Football Cttee, 1980–92; PLP Sports Cttee, 1984–92; Jt Chm., All Party Jazz Gp, 1991–. Member: Speaker's Conf., 1973; UK delegn to WEU and Council of Europe, 1973–75; Industrial Law Soc. Mem., Nat. Adv. Cttee, Duke of Edinburgh's Award Scheme; Steward, British Boxing Bd of Control, 1987–. Pres., Stalybridge Public Band. *Recreations:* sport; football, cricket, boxing (sometime Middleweight Champion, Hong Kong; boxed for Oxford Univ.). *Address:* House of Commons, SW1A 0AA. *Clubs:* Wig and Pen, Lord's Taverners.

PENFOLD, Peter Alfred, CMG 1995; OBE 1986; HM Diplomatic Service; Governor, British Virgin Islands, 1991–95; *b* 27 Feb. 1944; *s* of Alfred Penfold and Florence (*née* Green); *m* 1st, 1972, Margaret Quigley (marr. diss. 1983); 2nd, 1992, Celia Dolores Koenig. *Educ:* Sutton Co. Grammar Sch. Joined Foreign Service, 1963; Bonn, 1965–68; Kaduna, 1968–70; Latin American Floater, 1970–72; Canberra, 1972; FCO, 1972–75; Second Secretary: Addis Ababa, 1975–78; Port of Spain, 1978–81; First Sec., FCO, 1981–84; Dep. High Comr, Kampala, 1984–87; First Sec., FCO, 1987–91. *Recreations:* travel, flying, mountaineering, reading. *Address:* c/o Foreign and Commonwealth Office, King Charles Street, SW1A 2AH.

PENFOLD, Maj.-Gen. Robert Bernard, CB 1969; LVO 1957; *b* 19 Dec. 1916; *s* of late Bernard Hugh Penfold, Selsey, and late Ethel Ives Arnold; *m* 1940, Ursula, *d* of late Lt-Col E. H. Gray; two *d*. *Educ:* Wellington; RMC, Sandhurst. 2nd Lieut, Royal Leics Regt, 1936; commnd into 11th Sikh Regt, Indian Army, 1937; served in NWFP and during War of 1939–45 in Middle East, Central Mediterranean Forces; Instructor, Staff Coll., Quetta, 1946–47; transf. to British Army, RA, 1947; RN Staff Coll., 1953; Secretary, British Joint Services Mission, Washington, 1957–59; comdg 6 King's African Rifles, Tanganyika, 1959–61; Comdr 127 Inf. Bde (TA), 1962–64; Security Ops Adviser to High Commissioner, Aden, 1964–65; Imperial Defence Coll., 1966; Chief of Defence Staff, Kenya, 1966–69; GOC South East District, 1969–72. Gen. Manager and Chief Exec., Royal Hong Kong Jockey Club, 1972–80. Chm., Horseracing Adv. Council, 1980–86. *Recreations:* shooting, golf, gardening. *Address:* Park House, Amport, Andover, Hants SP11 8BW. *Club:* Army and Navy.

PENGELLY, Richard Anthony; Under Secretary, Welsh Office, 1977–85; *b* 18 Aug. 1925; *s* of Richard Francis Pengelly and Ivy Mildred Pengelly; *m* 1st, 1952, Phyllis Mary Rippon; one *s*; 2nd, 1972, Margaret Ruth Crossley; two *s* one *d*. *Educ:* Plymouth Coll.; School of Oriental and African Studies; London Sch. of Economics and Political Science (BScEcon). Served War: Monmouthshire Regt and Intell. Corps, 1943–47. Joined Min. of Supply as Asst Principal, 1950, Principal, 1954; NATO Defence Coll., 1960–61; Asst Sec., Min. of Aviation, 1964; RCDS 1971; Min. of Defence, 1972. *Recreations:* skiing, golf. *Address:* Byways, Wern Goch Road, Cyncoed, Cardiff, S Wales CF2 6SD. *T:* Cardiff (01222) 764418.

PENHALIGON, Dame Annette, DBE 1993; Member, Carrick District Council, Cornwall, 1987–94; *b* 9 Feb. 1946; *d* of late Owen Bennett Lidgey and of Mabel Lidgey; *m* 1968, David Charles Penhaligon, MP (*d* 1986); one *s* one *d*; *m* 1994, Robert William Egerton. *Educ:* Truro Girls' Grammar Sch. Subpostmistress, Chacewater PO, 1967–79; Sec. to husband, David Penhaligon, MP (L) Truro, 1974–86. Non-exec. Dir, Cornwall Independent Radio, 1992–. *Publication:* Penhaligon, 1989. *Recreations:* supporting charities helping people with learning disabilities, most activities which don't involve sport. *Address:* 90 Durnford Street, Stonehouse, Plymouth PL1 3QW. *T:* Plymouth (01752) 226646.

PENINGTON, Prof. David Geoffrey, AC 1988; Vice-Chancellor, University of Melbourne, 1988–95; *b* 4 Feb. 1930; *s* of Geoffrey Alfred Penington and Marjorie Doris (*née* Fricke); *m* 1st, 1956, Audrey Mary Grummitt (marr. diss.); two *s* two *d*; 2nd, 1984, Sonay Hussein. *Educ:* Magdalen Coll., Oxford (BA 1953; BM BCh 1955; MA 1957; DM 1969). MRCP 1957; MRACP 1968; FRCPA 1971; FRCP 1972; FRACP 1972. Consultant physician, London Hosp., 1963–67; Melbourne University: 1st Assistant in Medicine, 1968–70; Prof. and Chm. of Dept of Medicine, 1970–87; Dean, Faculty of Medicine, 1978–85. Vis. Res. Fellow, Wolfson Coll., Oxford, 1975–76; Sims Commonwealth Travelling Prof., RCS, 1981. Mem., Bd of Dirs, Pacific Dunlop, 1991–. Chief Advr, Health Policy & Progs, Health Dept, Victoria, 1986–87; Chairman: Cttee of Inquiry into Rights of Private Practice in Public Hosps, 1984; AIDS Task Force, 1984–87; Nat. Blood Transfusion Cttee of Australian Red Cross Soc., 1976–87. Member of Board: Walter and Eliza Hall Inst. for Med. Res.; Ludwig Inst., Royal Melbourne Hosp. *Publications:* (ed) De Gruchy's Clinical Haematology in Medical Practice, 5th edn, 1989; res. pubns on clin. and exptl haematology. *Recreations:* music, painting, fishing. *Address:* 177 Park Drive, Parkville, Vic 3052, Australia. *Club:* Melbourne (Melbourne).

PENLEY, William Henry, CB 1967; CBE 1961; PhD; FEng; engineering consultant, since 1985; *b* 22 March 1917; *s* of late William Edward Penley and late Clara (*née* Dodgson), Wallasey, Cheshire; *m* 1st, 1943, Raymonde Evelyn (*d* 1975), *d* of late Frederick Richard Gough, Swanage, Dorset; two *s* one *d*; 2nd, 1977, Marion Claytor, *d* of late Joseph Enoch Airey, Swanage, Dorset. *Educ:* Wallasey Grammar Sch.; Liverpool Univ.; BEng, 1937; PhD, 1940. FIEE (MIEE 1964); FRAeS 1967; FRSA 1975; FEng 1978. Head of Guided Weapons Department, Royal Radar Establishment, 1953–61; Director, Royal Radar Establishment, 1961–62; Director-General of Electronics Research and Development, Ministry of Aviation, 1962–64; Deputy Controller of Electronics, Ministry of Aviation, then Ministry of Technology, 1964–67; Dir, Royal Armament R&D Establishment, 1967–70; Chief Scientist (Army), 1970–75, Dep. Controller, Establishments and Res. B, 1971–75, MoD; Controller, R&D Establishments, and Research, MoD, and Professional Head of Science Gp of the Civil Service, 1976–77; Chm., Appleton Lab. Establishment Cttee, 1977–79; Dep. Dir, Under Water Weapons, Marconi Space and Defence Systems Ltd, Stanmore, 1979–82; Engrg Dir, Marconi Underwater Systems Ltd, 1982–85. Sec., Swanage Choral and Operatic Soc., 1986–. Silver Jubilee Medal, 1977. *Address:* 28 Walrond Road, Swanage, Dorset BH19 1PD. *T:* Swanage (01929) 425042. *Club:* Commonwealth Trust.

PENLINGTON, Ross Grange, CBE 1995 (OBE (mil.) 1980); AE 1972 (Clasp 1979); a Judge of the Court of Appeal of Hong Kong, 1988–95; *b* 3 March 1931; *s* of Cedric Grange Penlington and Elsie May Penlington; *m* 1956, Valerie Ann Wacher; two *d*. *Educ:* Christ Coll., NZ; Univ. of Canterbury, NZ. LLB 1954. Barrister and Solicitor, Christchurch, NZ, 1954–59; Legal Officer, Magistrate and Attorney Gen., Western Samoa, 1959–64; Hong Kong: Crown Counsel, 1965–75; Dir of Public Prosecutions, 1976–77; District Court Judge, 1977–80; High Court Judge, 1980–88. Commnd Hong Kong RAuxAF, 1964; Pilot's Brevet, 1965; CO (Wing Comdr), 1975–83; Hon. Air

Cdre, 1983–93. *Recreations:* flying, golf, tennis, fishing, racing. *Address:* 78 Ngamotu Road, Taupo, New Zealand. *Clubs:* Royal Air Force; Hong Kong, Shek-O, Royal Hong Kong Jockey (Hong Kong).

PENMAN, Ian Dalgleish, CB 1987; Deputy Secretary, Central Services, Scottish Office, 1984–91; *b* 1 Aug. 1931; *s* of late John B. Penman and Dorothy Dalgleish; *m* 1963, Elisabeth Stewart Strachan; three *s*. *Educ:* Glasgow Univ. (MA Classics); Balliol Coll., Oxford (MA Lit. Hum.; Snell Exhibnr and Ferguson Scholar). National Service, RAF, 1955–57 (Educn Br.). Asst Principal, HM Treasury, 1957–58; Scottish Office, 1958–91; Private Sec. to Parly Under-Sec. of State, 1960–62; Principal, Scottish Develt Dept, 1962–69; Asst Sec., Estab. Div., 1970–72; Asst Sec., Scottish Home and Health Dept, 1972–78; Under-Sec., Scottish Develt Dept, 1978–84. Member: Chm.'s Panel, CSSB, 1991–95; Sec. of State's Panel of Inquiry Reporters, 1992–94; Council on Tribunals, 1994– (Mem., Scottish Cttee, 1994–); Church of Scotland Cttee on Probationers, 1994–. Chm., Viewpoint Housing Assoc., 1991–95; Chief Exec., Scottish Homes, April–Oct. 1991. *Recreations:* walking, music, swimming. *Address:* 1/3 Fettes Rise, Edinburgh EH4 1QH. *T:* 0131–552 2180. *Club:* New (Edinburgh).

PENN, Richard; Chief Executive, City of Bradford Metropolitan Council, since 1989; *b* 4 Oct. 1945; *s* of George Stanley; *m* 1968, Jillian Mary Elias; three *s* one *d*. *Educ:* Canton High Sch., Cardiff; University Coll., Cardiff (BSc Econs Jt Hons); University Coll., Swansea (DipEd). MBPS. Lectr, University Coll., Cardiff, 1968–70; Glamorgan, then W Glamorgan, CC, 1970–76; Asst Chief Exec., Cleveland CC, 1976–78; Dep. Chief Exec., W Midlands CC, 1978–81; Chief Exec., Knowsley Metropolitan Council, 1981–89. Dep. Chm., Bradford and District TEC; Dir, Bradford Breakthrough. Dir, Public Finance Foundn. Vis. Fellow, Inst. of Local Govt Studies. Dir, Nat Mus. of Photography, Film and Television. FIMgt; FRSA. *Recreations:* family, Rugby Union, theatre, good food. *Address:* City Hall, Bradford, West Yorks BD1 1HY. *T:* Bradford (01274) 752002. *Club:* Royal Over-Seas League.

PENNANT; *see* Douglas-Pennant.

PENNANT, His Honour David Edward Thornton; a Circuit Judge (formerly County Court Judge), 1961–84; *b* 2 Aug. 1912; *s* of David Falconer Pennant, DL, JP, Barrister-at-law, late of Nantlys, St Asaph, N. Wales, and late Lilla Agnes Pennant; *m* 1938, Alice Catherine Stainer; three *s* one *d*. *Educ:* Charterhouse; Trinity Coll., Cambridge. Called to Bar, Inner Temple, 1935. Served, 1939–45, with Royal Signals (TA); OC, Signals Officers' Training Sch., Mhow, India, 1944–45. Chancellor, Dio. Monmouth, 1949–77. Governing, and Representative Bodies, Church in Wales, 1946–83. Chm., Radnorshire QS, 1962–64; Deputy Chairman: Brecknockshire QS, 1956–64; Flintshire QS, 1962–71; Dorset QS, 1971. Joint Chairman, Medical Appeals Tribunal for Wales, 1957–61; Mem., County Court Rule Cttee, 1970–78. *Recreation:* gardening. *Address:* 12 Ettrick Road, Branksome Park, Poole, Dorset BH13 6LG. *T:* Bournemouth (01202) 765614.

PENNANT-REA, Rupert Lascelles; Chairman, Caspian, since 1995; *b* 23 Jan. 1948; *s* of Peter Athelwold Pennant-Rea and Pauline Elizabeth Pennant-Rea; *m* 1st, 1970, Elizabeth Louise Greer (marr. diss. 1975); 2nd, 1979, Jane Trevelyan Hamilton (marr. diss. 1986); one *s* one *d*; 3rd, 1986, Helen Jay; one *s* and two step *d*. *Educ:* Peterhouse, Zimbabwe; Trinity Coll., Dublin (BA); Manchester Univ. (MA). Confedn of Irish Industry, 1970–71; Gen. and Municipal Workers Union, 1972–73; Bank of England, 1973–77; The Economist, 1977–93, Editor, 1986–93; Dep. Gov., Bank of England, 1993–95. Non-executive Director: B.A.T. Industries, 1995–; Gordon House Asset Management, 1995–; Consultant, World Bank. Chm., Steering Gp, Financial Markets Gp, LSE, 1995–; Mem., Gp of Thirty, 1995–. Council: ODI, 1987–; Trinity Foundn, 1995–. Gov., Peterhouse, Zimbabwe, 1994–. *Publications:* Gold Foil, 1979; (jtly) Who Runs the Economy?, 1980; (jtly) The Pocket Economist, 1983; (jtly) The Economist Economics, 1986. *Recreations:* music, tennis, fishing, family. *Address:* Caspian, 4 Temple Place, WC2R 3HP. *T:* 0171–304 8114. *Clubs:* MCC, Reform; Harare (Zimbabwe).

PENNELL, Rev. Canon (James Henry) Leslie, TD and Bar, 1949; Rector of Foxearth and Pentlow (Diocese of Chelmsford), 1965–72, and of Borley and Lyston (Diocese of Chelmsford), 1969–72; Hon. Canon, Inverness Cathedral, since 1965 (Provost, 1949–65); *b* 9 Feb. 1906; *s* of late J. H. L. Pennell and late Elizabeth Esmé Gordon Steel; *m* 1939, Ursula Mary, *d* of Rev. A. E. Gledhill; twin *s* and *d*. *Educ:* Edinburgh Academy; Edinburgh University (BL); Edinburgh Theological College. Precentor, Inverness Cathedral, 1929–32; Rector, St Mary's, Dunblane, and Offic. Chaplain to Queen Victoria School, 1932–49; Officiating Chaplain, Cameron Barracks, 1949–64. TA, 1934; BEF, 1940; SCF, 1943; DACG, 34th Ind. Corps, 1945; SCF Corps Troops, Scottish Comd, 1946–50. *Recreations:* reading and travel. *Address:* The Croft, Hundon, Sudbury, Suffolk CO10 8EW. *T:* Hundon (01440) 786221.

PENNEY, Most Rev. Alphonsus Liguori; Archbishop (RC) of St John's (Newfoundland), 1979–91, now Emeritus; *b* 17 Sept. 1924; *s* of Alphonsus Penney and Catherine Penney (*née* Mullaly). *Educ:* St Bonaventure's Coll., St John's, Newfoundland; University Seminary, Ottawa (LPh, LTh). Assistant Priest: St Joseph's Parish, St John's, 1950–56; St Patrick's Parish, St John's, 1956; Parish Priest: Marystown, Placentia Bay, Newfoundland, 1957; Basilica Parish, St John's, 1969. Prelate of Honour, 1971. Bishop of Grand Falls, Newfoundland, 1972. Hon. LLD, Memorial Univ. of Newfoundland, 1980. Confederation Medal, 1967. *Recreations:* walking, golf. *Address:* PO Box 1029, Almonte, Ont K0A 1A0, Canada.

PENNEY, Jennifer Beverly; Senior Principal, Royal Ballet, retired 1988; *b* 5 April 1946; *d* of Beverley Guy Penney and Gwen Penney. *Educ:* in Canada (grades 1–12). Entered Royal Ballet Sch., 1962; joined Royal Ballet, 1963; became soloist during 1967, principal dancer during 1970, and senior principal dancer during 1974. Evening Standard Award, 1980. *Recreation:* painting (water-colours). *Address:* 245 Mountain Park Drive, Salt Spring Island, British Columbia V8K 1G3, Canada.

PENNEY, Penelope Anne; Headmistress, Haberdashers' Aske's School for Girls, Elstree, since 1991; *b* 30 Sept. 1942; *d* of Richard Chamberlain, *qv*; *m* 1963, Rev. William Affleck Penney; one *s* two *d*. *Educ:* Chatelard Sch., Switzerland; Bristol Univ. (BA Hons 1964). Head of Langs and Communications, Astor of Hever Sch., Maidstone, 1974–79; Headmistress: Prendergast Sch., Catford, 1980–86; Putney High Sch. (GPDST), 1987–91. Pres., GSA, 1994–95. Freeman, City of London, 1993. FIMgt 1995; MInstD 1995. Associate Mem., Inst. of Dirs. FRSA. *Recreation:* fast cars. *Address:* Haberdashers' Aske's School for Girls, Aldenham Road, Elstree, Herts WD6 3BT. *T:* 0181–953 4261.

PENNEY, Reginald John; Assistant Under-Secretary of State, Ministry of Defence, 1964–73, retired; *b* 22 May 1919; *s* of Herbert Penney and Charlotte Penney (*née* Affleck); *m* 1941, Eileen Gardiner; one *s* two *d*. *Educ:* Westminster School. War Service, Royal West Kent Regt, 1939–46. Civil Servant, Air Ministry, until 1964, including service with Far East Air Force, Singapore, 1960–63. Chm., Sherborne Soc., CPRE, 1976. *Recreation:* golf. *Address:* Rumbow Cottage, Acreman Street, Sherborne, Dorset DT9 3NX.

PENNICOTT, Maj.-Gen. Brian Thomas, CVO 1994; Group Personnel Manager, Sun Alliance Group, since 1995 (Group Security Adviser, 1994–95); Gentleman Usher to the Queen, since 1995; *b* 15 Feb. 1938; *s* of Thomas Edward Pennicott and Vera Ethel (*née* Gale); *m* 1962, Patricia Anne Chilcott; two *s* three *d*. *Educ:* Portsmouth Northern Grammar Sch.; RMA, Sandhurst. Commnd, RA, 1957; RMCS, Shrivenham, 1969–70; Staff Coll., Camberley, 1971; GSO2 (W), Project Management Team 155mm Systems, 1972–73; NDC, Latimer, 1976–77; CO 29 Commando Regt, RA, 1977–80; SO1 Mil. Sec.'s Br. 6, MoD, 1980–82; Comdr Artillery, Falkland Is, 1982; Asst Mil. Attaché, Washington, 1982–83; Comdr Artillery, 1 Armd Div., 1983–86; NDC, Canada, 1986–87; Dep. Mil. Sec. (A), 1987–89; Dir, RA, 1989–91; Defence Services Sec., 1991–94 and ACDS (Personnel and Reserves), 1992–94. Col Comdt, RA, 1991–; Hon. Col, 289 Commando Battery, RA(V), 1991–. Chm., Army FA, 1991–94. *Recreations:* tennis, golf, bridge. *Address:* c/o Lloyds Bank, Cox's & King's Branch, PO Box 1190, 7 Pall Mall, SW1Y 5NA. *Club:* Army and Navy.

PENNING-ROWSELL, Edmund Lionel; wine writer; Wine Correspondent: Country Life, 1954–87; Financial Times, since 1964; *b* 16 March 1913; *s* of Edmund Penning-Rowsell and Marguerite Marie-Louise Penning-Rowsell (*née* Egan); *m* 1937, Margaret Wintringham; one *s* two *d*. *Educ:* Marlborough College. Journalist, Morning Post, 1930–35; Book Publisher, Frederick Muller Ltd, 1935–50; Sales Manager, B. T. Batsford, 1952–57; Dir, book publisher, Edward Hulton & Co./Studio-Vista, 1957–63; Manager, World Book Fair, Earl's Court, 1964. Mem. Cttee of Management, Internat. Exhibition Co-op. Wine Soc., 1959–87 (Chm., 1964–87); Chm., Internat. Co-operative Wine Soc., 1964–87; Founder Mem., William Morris Soc., 1953–54 (Vice-Pres.). Chevalier de l'Ordre du Mérite Agricole (France), 1971; Chevalier de l'Ordre du Mérite National (France), 1981. *Publications:* Red, White and Rosé, 1967; The Wines of Bordeaux, 1969, 6th edn 1989; (ed, trans. and updated) Higounet *et al*, Château Latour: the history of a great vineyard 1331–1992, 1993. *Recreation:* drinking wine, particularly claret. *Address:* Yew Trees House, Wootton, Woodstock, Oxford OX20 1EG. *T:* Woodstock (01993) 811281. *Club:* Travellers'.

PENNINGTON, Michael Vivian Fyfe; freelance actor and writer; *b* 7 June 1943; *s* of late Vivian Maynard Cecil Pennington and Euphemia Willock (*née* Fyfe); *m* Katharine Ann Letitia Barker (marr. diss.); one *s*. *Educ:* Marlborough Coll.; Trinity Coll., Cambridge (BA English). RSC, 1964–65; BBC, ITV, Woodfall Films Ltd, West End Theatre, Royal Court Theatre, etc, 1966–74; RSC, 1974–81: roles included Berowne, Angelo and Hamlet; Crime and Punishment, Lyric Hammersmith, 1983; National Theatre: Strider, 1984; Venice Preserv'd, 1984; Anton Chekhov, 1984; The Real Thing, Strand, 1985; Jt Artistic Dir, English Shakespeare Co., 1986–93: three world tours playing Henry V, Richard II, Coriolanus, Leontes, Macbeth, and Dir, Twelfth Night; Playing with Trains, RSC, 1989; Vershinin, The Three Sisters, Gate, Dublin, 1990; The Gift of the Gorgon, Barbican, 1992, Wyndhams, 1993; Dir, Twelfth Night, Tokyo, 1993; Hamlet, Gielgud, 1994; Taking Sides, Chichester, transf. Criterion, 1995; *television* includes: Oedipus the King, 1985; Return of Sherlock Holmes, 1986. *Publications:* Rossya—A Journey Through Siberia, 1977; The English Shakespeare Company, 1990; Hamlet: a user's guide, 1995. *Recreations:* music, literature. *Address:* c/o Marmont Management Ltd, Langham House, 308 Regent Street, W1R 5AL.

PENNINGTON, Prof. Robert Roland; Professor of Commercial Law, Birmingham University, 1968–94, subseq. Professor Emeritus; *b* 22 April 1927; *s* of R. A. Pennington; *m* 1965, Patricia Irene; one *d*. *Educ:* Birmingham Univ. (LLB, LLD). Solicitor. Reader, Law Soc.'s Sch. of Law, 1951–62; Mem. Bd of Management, Coll. of Law, 1962; Sen. Lectr in Commercial Law, 1962–68 and Dean, Faculty of Law, Birmingham Univ., 1979–82. Vis. Prof., QMW, 1995–. Govt Adviser on Company Legislation, Trinidad, 1967 and Seychelles, 1970; UN Adviser on Commercial Law, 1970–; Special Legal Adviser to EEC, 1972–79. Editor, European Commercial Law Library, 1974–. *Publications:* Company Law, 1959, 7th edn 1995; Companies in the Common Market, 1962, 3rd edn as Companies in the European Communities, 1982; The Investor and the Law, 1967; Stannary Law: A History of the Mining Law of Cornwall and Devon, 1973; Commercial Banking Law, 1978; Gesellschaftsrecht des Vereinigten Königreichs, 1981 (in Jura Europae: Gesellschaftsrecht); The Companies Acts 1980 and 1981: a practitioners' manual, 1983; Stock Exchange Listing: the new regulations, 1985; Directors' Personal Liability, 1987; Company Liquidations: the substantive law: the procedure (2 vols), 1987; The Law of the Investment Markets, 1990; Pennington's Corporate Insolvency Law, 1991. *Recreations:* travel, walking, history, archaeology. *Address:* Gryphon House, Langley Road, Claverdon, Warwicks CV35 8QA.

PENNISON, Clifford Francis, CBE 1977; *b* 28 June 1913; *s* of Henry and Alice Pennison; *m* 1940, Joan Margaret Hopkins; three *d*. *Educ:* Taunton Sch.; Bristol Univ. (BA, 1st Cl. Hons, Hist.). Barrister-at-Law, Inner Temple, 1951. Appointed senior management trainee, Unilever Ltd, 1938. Field Security Officer, Army, 1940–46 (Captain). Principal, Home Civil Service, 1946; Assistant Secretary, and Director of Organisation and Methods, Ministry of Food, 1949; Ministry of Agriculture: Director of Statistics Div., 1953; Director of Public Relations Div., 1958; Director of External Relations Div., 1961; FAO: Permanent UK representative, 1963–66; Director, Economic Analysis Div., 1966–67; Asst Dir-Gen., Admin and Finance, 1967–74; Consultant, EEC/FAO relations, 1974–76; retired 1976. Diplôme, Lettres Modernes, and Diplôme, Langue allemande, Univ. of Nice, 1977–81; Final examination (French), Inst. of Linguists, 1984. *Recreations:* reading, foreign languages. *Address:* 9 Arden Drive, Wylde Green, Sutton Coldfield B73 5ND. *T:* 0121–384 2289.

PENNY, family name of **Viscount Marchwood.**

PENNY, (Francis) David, CBE 1982; FRSE; FEng 1980; consulting engineer; *b* 20 May 1918; *s* of late David Penny and Esther Colley; *m* 1949, Betty E. Smith, *d* of late Oswald C. Smith. *Educ:* Bromsgrove County High School; University Coll., London (BSc), Fellow 1973. Engineering Apprenticeship, Cadbury Bros Ltd, 1934–39; Armament Design Establishment, Ministry of Supply, 1939–53; Chief Development Engineer, Fuel Research Station, 1954–58; Dep. Dir, Nat. Engineering Laboratory, 1959–66, Dir, 1967–69; Managing Director: YARD Ltd, 1969–79; Yarrow Public Ltd Co., 1979–83. Chairman: Control Systems Ltd, 1979–83; Automatic Revenue Controls Ltd, 1979–83. Mem. Bd, BSI, 1982–91. FIMarE; FIMechE; Member Council, IMechE, 1964–85 (a Vice-Pres., 1977–81, Pres., 1981–82); Pres., Smeatonian Soc. of Civil Engrs, 1991–92. *Publications:* various technical papers. *Recreations:* gardening, walking. *Address:* The Park, Dundrennan, Kirkcudbright DG6 4RA. *T:* Dundrennan (01557) 500244.

PENNY, Joseph Noel Bailey, QC 1971; *b* 25 Dec. 1916; *s* of Joseph A. Penny, JP and Isabella Downie, JP; *m* 1st, 1947, Celia (*d* 1969), *d* of Mr and Mrs R. H. Roberts; three *s* one *d*; 2nd, 1972, Sara Margaret, *d* of Sir Arnold France, *qv*; one *d*. *Educ:* Worksop College; Christ Church, Oxford; MA (Oxon). Major, Royal Signals, 1939–46 (despatches). Called to Bar, Gray's Inn, 1948. A Social Security (formerly Nat. Ins.) Comr, 1977–89. *Recreations:* wine and song, travel and amateur dramatics. *Address:* Fair Orchard, Camden Road, Lingfield, Surrey RH7 6AF. *T:* Lingfield (01342) 832191.

See also N. B. Penny.

PENNY, Nicholas Beaver, MA, PhD; Clore Curator of Renaissance Painting, National Gallery, since 1990; *b* 21 Dec. 1949; *s* of Joseph Noel Bailey Penny, *qv*; *m* 1971, Anne Philomel Udy (marr. diss.); two *d*. *Educ:* Shrewsbury Sch.; St Catharine's Coll., Cambridge (BA, MA); Courtauld Inst., Univ. of London (MA, PhD). Leverhulme Fellow in the History of Western Art, Clare Hall, Cambridge, 1973–75; Lectr, History of Art Dept, Univ. of Manchester, 1975–82; Sen. Res. Fellow, History of Western Art, King's Coll., Cambridge, 1982–84; Keeper of Western Art, Ashmolean Mus., Oxford, and Professorial Fellow, Balliol Coll., Oxford, 1984–89. Slade Prof. of Fine Art, Univ. of Oxford, 1980–81. Cavaliere nell'Ordine al merito della Repubblica Italiana, 1990. *Publications:* Church Monuments in Romantic England, 1977; Piranesi, 1978; (with Francis Haskell) Taste and the Antique, 1981; Mourning, 1981; (ed jtly) The Arrogant Connoisseur, 1982; (with Roger Jones) Raphael, 1983; (ed) Reynolds, 1986; Alfred and Winifred Turner, 1988; (with Robert Flynn Johnson) Lucian Freud, Works on Paper, 1988; Ruskin's Drawings, 1988; (jtly) From Giotto to Dürer, 1991; Catalogue of European Sculpture in the Ashmolean Museum: 1540 to the present day, 3 vols, 1992; The Materials of Sculpture, 1993; reviews for London Review of Books; articles in Apollo, Burlington Magazine, Connoisseur, Jl of Warburg and Courtauld Insts, Past and Present, and elsewhere. *Address:* The National Gallery, Trafalgar Square, WC2N 5DN.

PENNYCUICK, Prof. Colin James, FRS 1990; Research Professor in Zoology, University of Bristol, since 1993; *b* 11 June 1933; *s* of Brig. James Alexander Charles Pennycuick, DSO and Marjorie Pennycuick; *m* Sandy; one *s*. *Educ:* Wellington College; Merton College, Oxford (MA); Peterhouse, Cambridge (PhD). Lectr in Zoology, 1964–75, Reader, 1975–83, Bristol Univ.; seconded as Lectr in Zoology, Univ. of Nairobi, 1968–71, as Dep. Dir, Serengeti Res. Inst., 1971–73; Maytag Prof. of Ornithology, Univ. of Miami, 1983–92. *Publications:* Animal Flight, 1972; Bird Flight Performance, 1989; Newton Rules Biology, 1992. *Recreation:* gliding. *Address:* School of Biological Sciences, University of Bristol, Woodland Road, Bristol BS8 1UG.

PENRHYN, 6th Baron *cr* 1866; **Malcolm Frank Douglas-Pennant,** DSO 1945; MBE 1943; *b* 11 July 1908; 2nd *s* of 5th Baron Penrhyn and Alice Nellie (*d* 1965), *o d* of Sir William Charles Cooper, 3rd Bt; *S* father 1967; *m* 1954, Elisabeth Rosemary, *d* of late Brig. Sir Percy Laurie, KCVO, CBE, DSO, JP; two *d*. *Educ:* Eton; RMC, Sandhurst. Colonel (retd), KRRC. *Heir:* *b* Hon. Nigel Douglas-Pennant [*b* 22 Dec. 1909; *m* 1st, 1935, Margaret Dorothy (*d* 1938), *d* of T. G. Kirkham; one *s*; 2nd, 1940, Eleanor Stewart (*d* 1987), *d* of late Very Rev. H. N. Craig; one *s* one *d*; 3rd, 1993, Stella Mary, *widow* of Rev. J. R. Wingfield Digby, and *y d* of Stanley Bradwell]. *Address:* Littleton Manor, Winchester, Hants SO22 6QU. *T:* Winchester (01962) 880205. *Clubs:* Naval and Military, Flyfishers'.

See also Sir T. R. Troubridge, Bt.

PENRITH, Bishop Suffragan of, since 1994; **Rt. Rev. Richard Garrard;** *b* 24 May 1937; *s* of Charles John Garrard and Marjorie Louise (*née* Pow); *m* 1961, Elizabeth Ann Sewell; one *s* one *d*. *Educ:* Northampton Grammar Sch.; King's Coll., Univ. of London (BD, AKC). MIMgt. Ordained deacon, 1961, priest, 1962; Assistant Curate: St Mary's, Woolwich, 1961–66; Great St Mary's, Cambridge, 1966–68; Chaplain/Lectr, Keswick Hall Coll. of Educn, Norwich, 1968–74; Principal, Church Army Training Coll., 1974–79; Canon Chancellor, Southwark Cathedral and Dir of Training, dio. of Southwark, 1979–87; Canon Residentiary, St James's Cathedral, Bury St Edmunds and Advr for Clergy Training, dio. of St Edmundsbury and Ipswich, 1987–91; Archdeacon of Sudbury, 1991–94. *Publications:* Picture, Ponder, Pray, Promise, 1991; Lent with St Mark, 1992; A Time to Pray, 1993; Lent with St Matthew, 1995. *Recreations:* cats, crosswords, Italy, the fells. *Address:* Holm Croft, 13 Castle Road, Kendal LA9 7AU. *T:* Kendal (01539) 727836.

PENROSE, Hon. Lord; George William Penrose; a Senator of the College of Justice in Scotland, since 1990; *b* 2 June 1938; *s* of late George W. Penrose and Janet L. Penrose; *m* 1964, Wendy Margaret Cooper; one *s* two *d*. *Educ:* Glasgow Univ. (MA, LLB). CA. Advocate, 1964; QC 1978; Advocate Depute, 1986; Home Advocate Depute, 1988. Procurator to Gen. Assembly of Ch. of Scotland, 1984–90. Pres., Scottish procs of Aircraft and Shipbuilding Industries Arbitration Tribunal, 1977–83; Mem., panel of Chairmen, Financial Services Tribunal, 1988–90. *Recreation:* walking. *Address:* Court of Session, Parliament House, Edinburgh EH1 1RQ.

PENROSE, Anne Josephine, (Mrs J. Penrose); *see* Robinson, A. J.

PENROSE, Prof. Edith Tilton; economic consultant; Professor, 1977–84, Associate Dean for Research and Development, 1982–84, Professor Emeritus, since 1984, Institut Européen d'Administration des Affaires, Fontainebleau; Professor of Economics (with reference to Asia), School of Oriental and African Studies, University of London, 1964–78, Professor Emeritus, since 1978; *b* 29 Nov. 1914; *d* of George Albert Tilton and Hazel Sparling Tilton; *m* 1st, 1934, David Burton Denhardt (*d* 1938); 2nd, 1944, Ernest F. Penrose (*d* 1984); three *s*. *Educ:* Univ. of California, Berkeley (AB); Johns Hopkins Univ. (MA, PhD). Research Assoc., ILO, Geneva and Montreal, 1939–41; Special Asst, US Ambassador, London, 1941–46; US Delegn to UN, NY, 1946–47; research at Johns Hopkins Univ., 1948–50; Lectr and Res. Assoc., Johns Hopkins Univ., 1950–60; Vis. Fellow, Australian Nat. Univ., 1955–56; Assoc. Prof. of Econs, Univ. Baghdad, 1957–59; Reader in Econs, Univ. of London (LSE and SOAS), 1960–64; Head, Dept of Econs, SOAS, 1964–79. Associate Fellow, Oxford Centre of Management Studies, later Templeton College, Oxford, 1982–85; Visiting Professor: Univ. Dar Es Salaam, 1971–72; Univ. of Toronto, 1977; Hon. Vis. Fellow in Management Econs, Bradford Univ., 1989–95. Member: Sainsbury Cttee of Enquiry into Relationship of Pharmaceutical Industry with Nat. Health Service, 1965–67; SSRC, 1974–76 (Econ. Cttee, 1970–76, Chm., 1974–76); Medicines Commn, 1975–78; Dir, Commonwealth Develt Corp., 1975–78; Mem. Council, Royal Economic Soc., 1975–80; Governor, NIESR, 1974–. Dr *hc*: Uppsala, 1984; Helsinki Sch. of Econs, 1991; Hon. DLitt Bradford, 1994. Award: for distinguished contribs to lit. of energy econs, Internat. Assoc. of Energy Economists, 1986; for outstanding contrib. to research, Acad. of Internat. Business, 1993. *Publications:* Food Control in Great Britain, 1940; Economics of the International Patent System, 1951; The Theory of the Growth of the Firm, 1959, new edn 1995; The Large International Firm in Developing Countries: The International Petroleum Industry, 1968; The Growth of Firms, Middle East Oil and Other Essays, 1971; (with E. F. Penrose) Iraq: international relations and national development, 1978; articles and contributions to books. *Recreations:* travel, theatre, gardening. *Address:* The Barn, 30A Station Road, Waterbeach, Cambridge CB5 9HT. *T:* Cambridge (01223) 861618. *Club:* Commonwealth Trust.

PENROSE, George William; *see* Penrose, Hon. Lord.

PENROSE, Maj.-Gen. (retd) John Hubert, OBE 1956; MC 1944; *b* 24 Oct. 1916; *e s* of late Brig. John Penrose, MC and late Mrs M. C. Penrose (*née* Hendrick-Aylmer); *m* 1941, Pamela Elizabeth, *d* of late H. P. Lloyd, Neath, Glam.; four *d*. *Educ:* Winchester Coll.; RMA Woolwich, 2nd Lieut, RA, 1936; war service in European Theatre, BEF, 1939–40, and BLA, 1944; subseq. service in India, Germany, Malaya and UK; idc 1964; Defence Adviser to British High Comr, New Delhi, 1968–71; retired 1972. *Publication:* (with Brigitte Mitchell) Letters from Bath, 1766–1767, by the Rev. John Penrose, 1983. *Address:* West Hoe House, Bishop's Waltham, Southampton SO32 1DT. *T:* Bishop's Waltham (01489) 892363.

PENROSE, Prof. Oliver, FRS 1987; FRSE; Professor of Mathematics, Heriot-Watt University, 1986–94; *b* 6 June 1929; *s* of Lionel S. Penrose, FRS, and Margaret Penrose (*née* Leathes); *m* 1953, Joan Lomas Dilley; two *s* one *d* (and one *s* decd); *Educ:* Central Collegiate Inst., London, Ont; University Coll. London (BSc); Cambridge Univ. (PhD). FRSE 1989. Mathematical Physicist, English Electric Co., Luton, 1952–55; Res. Asst, Yale Univ., 1955–56; Lectr, then Reader, in Mathematics, Imperial Coll., London 1956–69; Prof. of Mathematics, Open Univ., 1969–86. *Publications:* Foundations of Statistical Mechanics, 1970; about 60 papers in physics jls; a few book reviews. *Recreations:* making music, chess. *Address:* 29 Frederick Street, Edinburgh EH2 2ND. *T:* 0131–225 5879.

See also R. Penrose.

PENROSE, Sir Roger, Kt 1994; FRS 1972; Rouse Ball Professor of Mathematics, University of Oxford, since 1973; *b* Colchester, Essex, 8 Aug. 1931; *s* of Lionel Sharples Penrose, FRS; *m* 1959, Joan Isabel Wedge (marr. diss. 1981); three *s*; *m* 1988, Vanessa Dee Thomas. *Educ:* University Coll. Sch.; University Coll., Univ. of London (BSc spec. 1st cl. Mathematics), Fellow 1975; St John's Coll., Cambridge (PhD; Hon. Fellow, 1987). NRDC (temp. post, Feb.-Aug. 1956); Asst Lectr (Pure Mathematics), Bedford Coll., London, 1956–57; Research Fellow, St John's Coll., Cambridge, 1957–60; NATO Research Fellow, Princeton Univ. and Syracuse Univ., 1959–61; Research Associate King's Coll., London, 1961–63; Visiting Associate Prof., Univ. of Texas, Austin, Texas, 1963–64; Reader, 1964–66, Prof. of Applied Mathematics, 1966–73, Birkbeck Coll., London. Visiting Prof., Yeshiva, Princeton, Cornell, 1966–67 and 1969; Lovett Prof., Rice Univ., Houston, 1983–87; Distinguished Prof. of Physics and Maths, Syracuse Univ., NY, 1987–. Member: London Mathematical Soc.; Cambridge Philosophical Soc.; Inst. for Mathematics and its Applications; International Soc. for General Relativity and Gravitation. Adams Prize (Cambridge Univ.), 1966–67; Dannie Heineman Prize (Amer. Phys. Soc. and Amer. Inst. Physics), 1971; Eddington Medal (with S. W. Hawking), RAS, 1975; Royal Medal, Royal Soc., 1985; Wolf Foundn Prize for Physics (with S. W. Hawking), 1988; Dirac Medal and Prize, Inst. of Physics, 1989; Einstein Medal, 1990. *Publications:* Techniques of Differential Topology in Relativity, 1973; (with W. Rindler) Spinors and Space-time, Vol. 1, 1984, Vol. 2, 1986; The Emperor's New Mind, 1989 (Science Book Prize, 1990); Shadows of the Mind, 1994; many articles in scientific jls. *Recreations:* 3 dimensional puzzles, doodling at the piano. *Address:* Mathematical Institute, 24–29 St Giles, Oxford OX1 3LB. *T:* Oxford (0865) 273546.

PENRY-DAVEY, David Herbert; QC 1988; barrister; a Recorder, since 1986; *b* 16 May 1942; *s* of late Watson and of Lorna Penry-Davey; *m* 1970, Judy Walter; two *s* one *d*. *Educ:* Hastings Grammar Sch.; King's Coll., London (LLB Hons). British Univs debating tour of Canada, 1964. Called to the Bar, Inner Temple, 1965, Bencher, 1993; Leader, S Eastern Circuit, 1992–95. Vice-Chm., Gen. Council of the Bar, 1995. *Recreations:* music, golf, cycling, hill-walking. *Address:* 15 Carson Road, SE21 8HT. *T:* 0181–670 4929.

PENTECOST, David Henry; quality management consultant, since 1992; Director, Paragon Consulting Associates Ltd, since 1994; *b* 17 March 1938; *s* of Walter Henry Pentecost and Emily Louisa Pentecost; *m* 1st, 1959, Maureen Monica Taylor (marr. diss. 1979); one *s* one *d*; 2nd, 1980, Ann Carol Ansell (*née* Hills); one *s* one *d*. *Educ:* Battersea Grammar Sch.; Wandsworth Sch.; King's Coll., London (LLB, AKC); FCIPS. Called to Bar, Gray's Inn, 1962. Post Office: Asst Principal, 1962; Asst Private Sec. to Postmaster General, 1969; Dep. Telephone Man., 1972; Dir, Major Systems Procurement, British Telecom, 1982, subseq. British Telecom Plc, 1984; Chief Procurement Officer, 1986–88, Gp Dir of Quality, 1988–90, British Telecom Plc. Exec. Dir, European Foundn for Quality Management, 1990–92. *Recreations:* walking, period house restoration.

PENTREATH, Dr Richard John, CBiol, FIBiol; FSRP; Chief Scientist, and Director of Environmental Strategy, Environment Agency, since 1995; *b* 28 Dec. 1943; *s* of John Alistair Dudley Pentreath and Mary Lena (*née* Gendall); *m* 1965, Elisabeth Amanda Leach; two *d*. *Educ:* Humphry Davy Grammar Sch.; QMC, London (BSc (Special)); DSc London; Univ. of Auckland (PhD). FIBiol 1980; CBiol 1984; FSRP 1989. Commonwealth Schol., 1966–68; SRC Fellow, 1969; Fisheries Radiobiol Lab., MAFF, 1969–89: Hd, Aquatic Envmtl Protection Div. and Dep. Dir, Fisheries Res., 1988–89; Chief Scientist, and Dir Water Quality, NRA, 1989–95. Member: NERC, 1992–; Adv. Bd, Centre for Social and Econ. Res. on Global Envt, 1994–; Res. Ass. Panel, HEFC, 1995–. *Publications:* Nuclear Power, Man and the Environment, 1980; contrib. numerous scientific papers. *Recreations:* Cornish history, crewing tall ships, visual arts. *Address:* 6 Court Gardens, Batheaston, Bath BA1 7PH. *T:* Bath (01225) 859737.

PENZER, Dr Geoffrey Ronald, CChem, FRSC; Partner, Penzer Allen, since 1992; *b* 15 Nov. 1943; *s* of Ronald and Dora Penzer; *m* 1966, Sylvia Elaine (*née* Smith); one *s* one *d*. *Educ:* Merchant Taylors' Sch.; St John's Coll., Oxford (MA; DPhil 1969). CChem, FRSC 1979. Jun. Res. Fellow, Merton Coll., Oxford, 1967–69; Res. Chemist, Univ. of Calif, 1969–70; Lectr in Biol Chem., Univ. of York, 1970–75; British Council: Science Officer, Cairo, 1975–80; Science Officer, Mexico, 1980–84; Dir, Technical Co-operation Training Dept, 1984–87; Dir, Management Div., and Manager, HQ Location Project, 1987–91. Dir, Open Book Inspections, 1993–. Trustee, Outset, 1994–. FIMgt 1993. *Publications:* contrib. scientific books and jls. *Recreations:* music, landscapes, walking. *Address:* Laston House, Heslington, York YO1 5DT; c/o Penzer Allen, 75 Westow Hill, SE19 1TX.

PENZIAS, Dr Arno Allan; Vice-President, Research, AT&T Bell Laboratories, since 1981; Board Director, A. D. Little, since 1992; *b* 26 April 1933; *s* of Karl and Justine Penzias; *m* 1954, Anne Barras Penzias; one *s* two *d*. *Educ:* City Coll. of New York (BS Physics, 1954); Columbia Univ. (MA Physics, 1958; PhD Physics, 1962). Bell Laboratories: Mem., Technical Staff, 1961–72; Head, Radio Physics Res., 1972–76; Dir, Radio Res. Lab., 1976–79; Exec. Dir, Research, Communications Sciences, 1979–81. Lectr, Princeton Univ., 1967–72, Vis. Prof., Astrophysical Scis Dept, 1972–85; Res. Associate, Harvard Univ., 1968–80; Adjunct Prof., State Univ. of NY, Stony Brook, 1974–84; Lee Kuan Yew Dist. Vis., Nat. Univ. of Singapore, 1991. Lectures: Kompfner, Stanford Univ., 1979; Gamow, Colorado Univ., 1980; Jansky, NRAO, 1983; Michelson Meml, Dept US Navy, 1985; Tanner, Southern Utah State Coll., 1987; Klopsteg, Northwestern Univ., 1987; NSF Distinguished, 1987; Regent's, Univ. of Calif., Berkeley, 1990. Member: Sch. of Engrg and Applied Science (Bd Overseers), Univ. Pennsylvania, 1983–86; Union Councils for Soviet Jews Adv. Bd, 1983–; NSF Industrial Panel on Science and Technology, 1982–; CIT Vis. Cttee, 1977–79; NSF Astronomy Adv. Panel, 1978–79; MNAS, 1975–; Wissenschaftliche Fachbeirat, Max-Planck Inst., Bonn, 1978–85 (Chm., 1981–83); Bd of Dirs, IMNET, 1986–92. Vice-Chm., Cttee of Concerned Scientists, 1976– (Mem., 1975–). Mem., National Acad. of Engrg, 1990. Hon. MIEEE, 1990. Trustee, Trenton State Coll., 1977–79. Dir, Grad. Faculties Alumni, Columbia Univ., 1987–. Hon. degrees: Paris Observatory, 1976; Wilkes Coll., City Coll. of NY, Yeshiva Univ., and Rutgers Univ., 1979; Bar Ilan Univ., 1983; Monmouth Coll., 1984; Technion-Israel Inst. of Technology, Pittsburgh Univ., Ball State Univ., Kean Coll., 1986; Ohio

State Univ., Iona Coll., 1988; Drew Univ., 1989; Lafayette Coll., 1990; Columbia Univ., 1990; George Washington Univ., 1992; Rensselaer Polytechnic Inst., 1992; Pennsylvania Univ., 1992; Bloomfield Coll., 1994. Henry Draper Medal, National Acad. of Sciences, 1977; Herschel Medal, RAS, 1977; (jtly) Nobel Prize for Physics, 1978; Townsend Harris Medal, City Coll. NY, 1979; Newman Award, City Coll. NY, 1983; Joseph Handleman Prize in the Scis, 1983; Grad. Faculties Alumni Award, 1984; Big Brothers Inc. of NY, City Achievement in Science Award, 1985; Priestly Award, Dickinson Coll., 1989; Pake Prize, APS, 1990; NJ Literary Hall of Fame, 1991; Pender Award, Pennsylvania Univ., 1992. Mem. Editorial Bd, Annual Revs of Astronomy and Astrophysics, 1974–78; Associate Editor, Astrophysical Jl Letters, 1978–82. *Publications:* Ideas and Information: managing in a high-tech world, 1989; 100 published articles, principally in Astrophysical Jl. *Address:* AT&T Bell Laboratories, 600 Mountain Avenue, Murray Hill, NJ 07974, USA. *T:* (908) 5823361.

PEPPARD, Nadine Sheila, CBE 1970; race relations consultant; *b* 16 Jan. 1922; *d* of late Joseph Anthony Peppard and May Peppard (*née* Barber). *Educ:* Macclesfield High Sch.; Manchester Univ. (BA, Teacher's Dip.). French teacher, Maldon Grammar Sch., 1943–46; Spanish Editor, George G. Harrap & Co. Ltd, 1946–55; Trg Dept, Marks and Spencer, 1955–57; Dep. Gen.-Sec., London Council of Social Service, 1957–64; Nat. Advisory Officer for Commonwealth Immigrants, 1964–65; Gen. Sec., Nat. Cttee for Commonwealth Immigrants, 1965–68; Chief Officer, Community Relations Commn, 1968–72; Adviser on Race Relations, Home Office, 1972–83, retd. *Publications:* (trans.) Primitive India, 1954; (trans.) Toledo, 1955; various professional articles. *Recreations:* cookery, writing. *Address:* 20 Park House, Park Place, Cheltenham, Glos GL50 2RF. *T:* Cheltenham (01242) 242583.

PEPPER, Prof. Gordon Terry, CBE 1990; Director, Centre for Financial Markets, since 1988, and Professor, since 1991, City University Business School (Hon. Visiting Professor, 1987–90); Chairman, Payton Pepper & Sons Ltd, since 1987; *b* 2 June 1934; *s* of Harold Terry Pepper and Jean Margaret Gordon Pepper (*née* Furness); *m* 1958, Gillian Clare Huelin; three *s* one *d.* *Educ:* Repton; Trinity College, Cambridge (MA); FIA, FIIMR. Equity & Law Life Assurance Soc., 1957–60; W. Greenwell & Co.: Partner, 1962; Joint Senior Partner, 1980–86; Chairman, Greenwell Montagu & Co., 1986–87; Dir and Sen. Advr, Midland Montagu, 1985–90. Member: Cttee on Industry and Finance, NEDC, 1988–90; ESRC, 1989–93. *Publications:* Money, Credit and Inflation, 1990; Money, Credit and Asset Prices, 1994; papers to Jl of Inst. of Actuaries. *Recreations:* sailing, tennis, family. *Address:* Staddleden, Sissinghurst, Cranbrook, Kent TN17 2AN. *T:* Cranbrook (01580) 712852. *Clubs:* Reform, Royal Ocean Racing.

PEPPER, Kenneth Bruce, CB 1965; Commissioner of HM Customs and Excise, 1957–73; *b* 11 March 1913; *s* of late E. E. Pepper; *m* 1945, Irene Evelyn Watts; two *s.* *Educ:* County High Sch., Ilford; London Sch. of Economics. Joined HM Customs and Excise, 1932; Asst Sec., 1949; Commissioner, 1957. Lieutenant, Intelligence Corps, 1944. *Address:* Fairfield, Cae Mair, Beaumaris, Gwynedd LL58 8YN.

PEPPER, Prof. Michael, FRS 1983; Professor of Physics, University of Cambridge, since 1987; Professorial Fellow of Trinity College, Cambridge, since 1987 (Senior Research Fellow, 1982–87); Managing Director, Toshiba Cambridge Research Centre Ltd, since 1991; *b* 10 Aug. 1942; *s* of Morris and Ruby Pepper; *m* 1973, Jeannette Denise Josse, MB, BS, MRCPsych; two *d.* *Educ:* St Marylebone Grammar Sch.; Reading Univ. (BSc Physics, 1963; PhD Physics, 1967); MA 1987, ScD 1989, Cantab. FInstP 1991. Res. Physicist, Mullard Ltd, 1967–69; res. in solid state physics, The Plessey Co., Allen Clark Res. Centre, 1969–73; Cavendish Lab., 1973– (in association with The Plessey Co., 1973–82); Warren Res. Fellow of Royal Soc., Cavendish Lab., 1978–86; Principal Res. Fellow, GEC plc, Hirst Res. Centre, 1982–87. Mem., Univ. Council, 1993–, Gen. Bd of Faculties, 1995–, Cambridge. Vis. Prof., Bar-Ilan Univ., Israel, 1984; Lectures: Inaugural Mott, Inst. of Physics, 1985; Royal Soc. Review, 1987; Rankin, Liverpool Univ., 1987; G. I. Taylor, Cambridge Philosophical Soc., 1988; Resnick, Bar-Ilan Univ., 1995. Past and present mem. of various cttees and panels of Inst. of Physics (Editl Bd, Jl of Physics, Condensed Matter), Royal Soc. (Associate Editor, 1983–89), Rutherford Meml Cttee, 1987–91, DTI and SERC (Cttees on Solid State Devices, Semiconductors, 1984–89). Fellow, Amer. Physical Soc., 1992. Hon. DSc Bar-Ilan, 1993. Guthrie Prize and Medal, Inst. of Physics, 1985; Hewlett-Packard Prize, European Physical Soc., 1985; Hughes Medal, Royal Soc., 1987. *Publications:* papers on semiconductors and solid state physics in jls. *Recreations:* whisky tasting, reading, travel, homework with two *d.* *Address:* Cavendish Laboratory, Madingley Road, Cambridge CB3 0HE. *T:* Cambridge (01223) 337330; Toshiba Cambridge Research Centre, 260 Cambridge Science Park, Milton Road, Cambridge CB4 4WE. *T:* Cambridge (01223) 424666. *Clubs:* Athenæum; Arsenal Football.

PEPPER, Michael Peter Gregory, PhD; Head of Business Statistics Division, Central Statistical Office, since 1993; *b* 2 June 1945; *s* of Arthur Pepper and Anne (*née* Panian); *m* 1991, Alice Fox; two *s* one *d.* *Educ:* Dr Challoner's Grammar Sch., Amersham; London Univ. (BSc Maths (Ext.)); Essex Univ. (MSc); PhD Bath. Res. Fellow, Univ. of Bath, 1970–74; Statistician, Dept of Energy, 1974–79; Sen. Statistician, Govt of Botswana, 1979–81; Statistician, Dept of Energy, 1981–86; Chief Statistician and Dir of Stats, Welsh Office, 1986–93. *Recreations:* squash, running, gardening, choral music. *Address:* Central Statistical Office, Government Buildings, Cardiff Road, Newport, Gwent NP9 1XG. *T:* Newport (01633) 812352.

PEPPIATT, Hugh Stephen Kenneth; Chairman, Moorfields Eye Hospital, since 1991; *b* 18 Aug. 1930; *s* of late Sir Leslie Peppiatt, MC and Lady (Cicely) Peppiatt; *m* 1960, Claire, *e d* of late Ian Douglas Davidson, CBE and Claire Davidson; three *s* two *d.* *Educ:* Winchester College; Trinity College, Oxford; Univ. of Wisconsin. Partner, Freshfields, Solicitors, 1960–90: Resident Partner, New York, 1977–81; Sen. Partner, 1982–90. Director: Greig Fester Gp, 1990–; Hardy Oil & Gas, 1992–; Chairman: Butten Trustees, PA Consulting Gp, 1986–; Appeals Cttee, EBRD, 1992–. Mem. Management Cttee, Inst. of Ophthalmology, 1991–. Trustee, Help the Aged, 1991–. *Recreations:* hillwalking, fly fishing, birdwatching. *Address:* 28 Bathgate Road, Wimbledon, SW19 5PN. *T:* 0181–947 2709. *Clubs:* City of London; Royal Wimbledon Golf; Racquet and Tennis, Larchmont Yacht (New York).

PEPPITT, John Raymond, QC 1976; **His Honour Judge Peppitt;** a Circuit Judge, since 1991; *b* 22 Sept. 1931; *s* of late Reginald Peppitt and Phyllis Claire Peppitt; *m* 1960, Judith Penelope James; three *s.* *Educ:* St Paul's Sch.; Jesus Coll., Cambridge (BA Classical Tripos). Called to the Bar, Gray's Inn, 1958, Bencher, 1982; a Recorder, 1976–91. *Recreation:* collecting water-colours. *Address:* Canterbury County Court, Riding Gate House, 37 Old Dover Road, Canterbury CT1 3JB.

PEPYS, family name of **Earl of Cottenham.**

PERAHIA, Murray, FRCM; pianist; co-artistic director, Aldeburgh Festival, 1981–89; *b* New York, 19 April 1947; *s* of David and Flora Perahia; *m* 1980, Naomi Shohet (Ninette); two *s.* *Educ:* High Sch. of Performing Arts; Mannes College (MS); studied piano with Jeanette Haien, M. Horszowski, Arthur Balsam. FRCM 1987; FRAM 1994. Hon. Dir, Britten-Pears Sch. for Advanced Musical Studies, 1981–. Won Kosciusko Chopin Prize, 1965; début Carnegie Recital Hall, 1966; won Leeds Internat. Piano Festival, 1972; Avery Fisher Award, 1975; regular tours of Europe, Asia, USA; numerous recordings include complete Mozart Piano Concertos (as dir and soloist with English Chamber Orch.), complete Beethoven Piano Concertos (with Bernard Haitink and Royal Concertgebouw), Bartók Sonata for Two Pianos and Percussion (Grammy Award, 1989). *Address:* c/o Harold Holt, 31 Sinclair Road, W14 0NS.

PERCEVAL, family name of **Earl of Egmont.**

PERCEVAL, Viscount; Thomas Frederick Gerald Perceval; *b* 17 Aug. 1934; *e s* of 11th Earl of Egmont, *qv.*

PERCEVAL, Michael; HM Diplomatic Service; Consul-General, Barcelona, since 1992; *b* 27 April 1936; *o s* of late Hugh Perceval and Guida Brind; *m* 1968, Alessandra Grandis; one *s* one *d.* *Educ:* Downside Sch.; Christ Church, Oxford (Schol.; 2nd Cl. Hons English Lit.). Served Royal Air Force, Nicosia, 1956–60; film production asst, Athens, 1960; freelance correspondent, Madrid, 1961–69. Joined FCO, 1970; First Sec. (Press), UK Rep. to EC, Brussels, 1972–74; First Sec. and subseq. Head of Chancery, British High Commission, Nicosia, 1974–78; Asst Head of Mexico and Caribbean Dept, FCO, 1978–79; Counsellor, Havana, 1980–82; Counsellor (Political and Economic) and Consul-Gen., Brasilia, 1982–85; Counsellor (Commercial), Rome, 1985–89; Consul-General, São Paulo, 1990–92. *Publication:* The Spaniards, 1969, 2nd edn 1972. *Recreations:* music, walking, the Mediterranean. *Address:* c/o Foreign and Commonwealth Office, King Charles Street, Whitehall, SW1A 2AH.

PERCEVAL, Robert Westby, TD 1968; Clerk Assistant, House of Lords, 1964–74; retired; *b* 28 Aug. 1914; *m* 1948, Hon. J. I. L. Littleton, *er d* of 5th Baron Hatherton; two *s* two *d.* *Educ:* Ampleforth; Balliol College, Oxford. Joined Parliament Office, House of Lords, 1938. Royal Artillery, 1939–44; General Staff, War Office, 1944–45. *Address:* Pillaton Old Hall, Penkridge, Staffs ST19 5RZ. *Clubs:* Beefsteak, Turf.

PERCHARD, Colin William, OBE 1984; Minister (Cultural Affairs), India, British Council, since 1993; *b* 19 Oct. 1940; *m* 1970, Elisabeth Penelope Glynis, *d* of Sir Glyn Jones, GCMG, MBE; three *s.* *Educ:* Victoria Coll., Jersey; Liverpool Univ. (BA Hons History); Internat. Inst. for Educnl Planning, UNESCO, Paris (DipEd Planning and Admin). British Council: Asst Rep., Blantyre, Malawi, 1964–68; Regional Officer, Africa S of the Sahara, 1968–71: Asst Rep., Calcutta, 1971–72; Officer i/c Dhaka, 1972; Rep., Seoul, 1973–76; Dir, Technical Co-operation Trng Dept, 1976–79; Internat. Inst. for Educnl Planning, Paris, 1979–80; Rep., Harare, 1980–86; Controller, Africa Div., 1986–90; Dir and Cultural Counsellor, Turkey, 1990–93. *Recreations:* theatre, music, cooking. *Address:* The British Council, 10 Spring Gardens, SW1A 2BN. *T:* 0171–930 8466.

PERCIVAL, Rt. Hon. Sir Ian, Kt 1979; PC 1983; QC 1963; *b* 11 May 1921; *s* of Eldon and Chrystine Percival; *m* 1942, Madeline Buckingham Cooke; one *s* one *d.* *Educ:* Latymer Upper School; St Catharine's College, Cambridge (MA). Served HM Forces, 1940–46: 2nd Bn the Buffs, N Africa and Burma; Major. Called to the Bar, Inner Temple, 1948, Bencher, 1970, Reader, 1989, Treas., 1990. Recorder of Deal, later of the Crown Court, 1971–. MP (C) Southport, 1959–87. Solicitor-General, 1979–83; Conservative Parly Legal Committee: Sec., 1964–68; Vice-Chm., 1968–70; Chm., 1970–74 and 1983–87. Mem., Sidley & Austin, US and Internat. Attorneys at Law, 1984–92. Fellow, Inst. of Taxation (Chm., Parly Cttee, 1965–71); Mem., Royal Economic Soc.; FCIArb 1983. Pres., Masonic Trust for Girls and Boys, 1989–93. Freeman, City of London, 1987; Master, Co. of Arbitrators, 1993–94. *Recreations:* golf, parachuting, windsurfing, tennis. *Address:* 2 Harcourt Buildings, Temple, EC4Y 9DB. *T:* 0171–583 2939; (chambers) 5 Paper Buildings, Temple, EC4Y 7HB. *T:* 0171–583 9275; Oxenden, Stone-in-Oxney, near Tenterden, Kent TN30 7HD. *Clubs:* Carlton, City Livery, Rye Golf.

PERCIVAL, Prof. Ian Colin, PhD; FRS 1985; Professor of Physics, Queen Mary and Westfield (formerly Queen Mary) College, University of London, since 1992 (Professor of Applied Mathematics, 1974–92); *b* 27 July 1931; *m* 1955, Jill Cuff (*née* Herbert); two *s* one *d.* *Educ:* Ealing County Grammar Sch.; UCL (BSc, PhD; Fellow, 1986). FRAS. Lectr in Physics, UCL, 1957–61; Reader in Applied Maths, QMC, 1961–67; Prof. of Theoret. Physics, Univ. of Stirling, 1967–74. Naylor Prize, London Mathematical Soc., 1985; Alexander von Humboldt Foundn Award, 1993. *Publications:* (with Derek Richards) Introduction to Dynamics, 1983; (with Owen Greene and Irene Ridge) Nuclear Winter, 1985; papers in learned jls on scattering theory, atomic and molecular theory, statistical mechanics, classical dynamics and theory of chaos and foundations of quantum theory. *Address:* Queen Mary and Westfield College, Mile End Road, E1 4NS. *T:* 0171–975 5555.

PERCIVAL, Prof. John, FSA; Professor and Head of School of History and Archaeology, University of Wales College of Cardiff, since 1988; *b* 11 July 1937; *s* of Walter William Percival and Eva Percival (*née* Bowers); *m* 1st, 1962, Carole Ann Labrum (*d* 1977); two *d;* 2nd, 1988, Jacqueline Anne Gibson (*née* Donovan). *Educ:* Colchester Royal Grammar Sch.; Hertford Coll., Oxford (Lucy Schol.; 1st Cl. Lit. Hum.; MA; DPhil). FSA 1977. Harmsworth Sen. Schol., Merton Coll., Oxford, 1961; University College, Cardiff: Asst Lectr in Ancient History, 1962; Lectr, 1964; Sen. Lectr, 1972; Reader, 1979; Dean of Faculty of Arts, 1977–79; Dep. Principal, Univ. of Wales Coll. of Cardiff, 1987–90. Vice-Pres., 1989–, Chm. Council, 1990–95, Classical Assoc. (Jt Sec., 1979–89). Mem. Ct of Govs, Nat. Library of Wales, 1991–. *Publications:* The Reign of Charlemagne (with H. R. Loyn), 1975; The Roman Villa, 1976, 2nd edn 1988; articles in historical and archaeol jls. *Recreations:* music, gardening. *Address:* 26 Church Road, Whitchurch, Cardiff CF4 2EA. *T:* Cardiff (01222) 617869.

PERCIVAL, John; Dance Consultant, The Times, since 1994 (Dance Critic, 1965–94); Editor, Dance & Dancers, since 1981; *b* 16 March 1927; *s* of Cecil Ernest Percival and Mua Phoebe Margaret Mary Percival (*née* Milchard); *m* 1954, Freda Betty Margaret Thorne-Large (marr. diss. 1972); *m* 1972, Judith Alymer Cruickshank. *Educ:* Sir George Monoux Grammar Sch., Walthamstow; St Catherine's Coll., Oxford (MA). On admin. staff, LCC, then GLC and ILEA, 1951–90. Archivist, Ballet Annual, 1960–64; ballet critic, New Daily, 1960–65; Associate Editor, Dance & Dancers, 1964–81; London correspondent: Dance Mag. (NY), 1965–69; German annual, Ballett, 1966–87; London dance critic, NY Times; Chm. and Dir, Dance & Dancers Ltd, 1991–. Advr, Nureyev Foundn, 1993–. Mem. Cttee, Gulbenkian Foundn. Has broadcast on radio and TV in Britain, Europe, America and Australia. *Publications:* Antony Tudor, 1963; Modern Ballet, 1970, rev. edn 1980; The World of Diaghilev, 1971, rev. edn 1979; Experimental Dance, 1971; Nureyev: aspects of the dancer, 1975, rev. edn 1979 (trans. Italian 1981, Japanese 1983); The Facts about a Ballet Company, 1979; Theatre in My Blood: a biography of John Cranko, 1983 (trans. German 1985); (with Alexander Bland) Men Dancing, 1984; The World of Nureyev, 1996; contributed to: Enciclopedia dello Spettacolo, 1966; Marcia Haydee, Ballerina, 1975; Encyclopaedia of Dance and Ballet, 1977; Des Ballett und die Kunste, 1981; John Neumeier und das Hamburger Ballett, 1983, 2nd edn 1993. *Recreations:*

watching dance and writing and talking about it, eating with friends. *Address:* 36 Great James Street, WC1N 3HB. *T:* 0171–405 0267. *Club:* Critics' Circle (Past Pres.).

PERCIVAL, Robert Clarendon, FRCS, FRCOG; Consulting Obstetric Surgeon, The Royal London Hospital; *b* 16 Sept. 1908; British; *m* 1st, 1944, Beryl Mary Ind (*d* 1967); one *d;* 2nd, 1972, Beatrice Myfanwy Evans, FFARCS. *Educ:* Barker College, NSW; Sydney University; The London Hospital (qualified 1933). Resident appointments: Poplar Hospital; Hosp. for Sick Children, Gt Ormond St; The London Hosp.; Southend Gen. Hosp. Obstetric and Gynæcological 1st Asst, The London Hosp., 1937–41; Surgeon-Lt-Comdr, RNVR, 1941–45 (Surgical Specialist); Obstetric Surgeon, The London Hospital, 1947–73, Director, Obstetric Unit, 1968–73. Chm., Obst. Adv. Cttee, NE Region Met. Hosp. Bd, 1967–73; President: Section of Obst. and Gyn., RSocMed, 1973–74; The London Hosp. Clubs' Union, 1965 (Treasurer, 1955–73); United Hosps RFC, 1969–72; London Hosp. Cricket Club, 1946–72. *Publications:* (jtly) Ten Teachers' Midwifery, 1958, new edition as Ten Teachers' Obstetrics, 1972; (jtly) Ten Teachers' Diseases of Women, 1965, new edition as Ten Teachers' Gynæcology, 1971; (jtly) British Obstetric Practice, 1963; (ed) Holland and Brews Obstetrics, 1969, 14th edn 1979; contribs to Lancet, British Jl of Obst. and Gynæcol. *Recreations:* fishing, golf. *Address:* Coker Wood Cottage, Pendomer, near Yeovil, Somerset BA22 9PD. *T:* Corscombe (01935891) 328. *Clubs:* Gynaeological Travellers' of GB and Ireland; Royal Navy Ski.

PERCIVAL, Sir (Walter) Ian; *see* Percival, Sir Ian.

PERCIVAL-PRESCOTT, Westby William, FIIC; practising conservator and painter; *b* 22 Jan. 1923; *s* of William Percival-Prescott and Edith Percival; *m* 1948, Silvia Haswell Miller; one *s. Educ:* Edinburgh Coll. of Art (DA Hons). FIIC 1957. Andrew Grant Scholar, National Gall., 1945; restoration of Rubens Whitehall ceiling, 1947–51; Restorer i/c House of Lords frescos, 1953; worked in National Gall. Conservation Dept, 1954–56; directed restoration of Painted Hall, Greenwich, 1957–60; National Maritime Museum: estabd Picture Conservation Dept, 1961; Keeper and Head of Picture Dept, 1977–83; organised first internat. conf. on Comparative Lining Techniques, 1973 (Ottawa, 1974); produced and designed historical exhibitions: Idea and Illusion, 1960; Four Steps to Longitude, 1963; The Siege of Malta, 1970; Captain Cook and Mr Hodges, 1979; The Art of the Van de Veldes, 1982. Vis. Sen. Lectr, Dept of Fine Art, Univ. of Leeds, 1980. Internat. Council of Museums: Co-ordinator, Conservation Cttee, 1975–84; Mem., Directory Bd, Conservation Cttee, 1981–84. *Publications:* The Coronation Chair, 1957; The Lining Cycle, 1974, Swedish edn 1975; Handbook of Lining Terms, 1974; Thornhill at Greenwich, 1978; Micro X-Ray Techniques, 1978; Techniques of Suction Lining, 1981; The Art of the Van de Veldes, 1982; technical papers. *Recreations:* listening to music, travel. *Address:* 34 Compayne Gardens, NW6 3DP. *T:* 0171–624 4577.

PERCIVAL SMITH, Ven. (Anthony) Michael; Archdeacon of Maidstone, 1979–89; *b* 5 Sept. 1924; *s* of Kenneth and Audrey Smith; *m* 1950, Mildred Elizabeth; two *d. Educ:* Shrewsbury; Gonville and Caius Coll., Cambridge (MA); Westcott House Theological Coll. Served Army, Rifle Brigade, 1942–46. Cambridge, 1946–48; Westcott House, 1948–50. Deacon 1950, priest 1951; Curate, Holy Trinity, Leamington, 1950–53; Domestic Chaplain to Archbishop of Canterbury, 1953–57; Vicar of All Saints, Upper Norwood, 1957–66; Vicar of Yeovil, 1966–72; Prebendary of Wells Cathedral, 1968–72; RD of Murston, 1968–72; Vicar of St Mildred's, Addiscombe, Croydon, 1972–80; Hon. Canon of Canterbury Cathedral, 1980–; Diocesan Dir of Ordinands, 1980–89; RD of Rye, 1991–93. *Recreations:* reading, walking. *Address:* The Garden House, Horseshoe Lane, Beckley, East Sussex TN31 6RZ. *T:* Beckley (01797) 260514.

PERCY, family name of **Duke of Northumberland.**

PERCY, Algernon Eustace Hugh H.; *see* Heber-Percy.

PERCY, John Pitkeathly, (Ian), CA; Scottish Senior Partner, Grant Thornton, since 1991; *b* 16 Jan. 1942; *s* of John Percy and Helen Glass Percy (*née* Pitkeathly); *m* 1965, Sheila Isobel Horn; two *d. Educ:* Edinburgh Acad. Qualified as a Chartered Accountant with Graham Smart & Annan, Edinburgh, 1968; Grant Thornton: Partner, Edinburgh, 1970–78; London, 1978–91; Managing Partner, 1981–88; Sen. Partner, 1988–91. Chairman: MacDonald Orr, 1992–; W & J R Watson (Holdings), 1992–; Deputy Chairman: Caledonian Bank, 1992–; Edinburgh Healthcare Trust, 1994–; Director: Morgan Grenfell (Scotland), 1992–; Edinburgh Acad., 1992–; Scottish Provident Instn, 1993–; William Wilson (Holdings), 1993–. Chm., Accounts Commn, 1992–. Hon. Prof. of Accounting and Auditing, Aberdeen Univ., 1988–. Mem., Convocation, Heriot-Watt Univ., 1992–. Pres., Inst. of Chartered Accountants of Scotland, 1990–91 (Sen. Vice-Pres., 1989–91). Freeman, City of London, 1983; Liveryman, Painter Stainers' Co., 1983. FRSA 1989. *Recreations:* golf, fishing. *Address:* Grant Thornton, 1/4 Atholl Crescent, Edinburgh EH3 8LQ. *T:* 0131–229 9181; 30 Midmar Drive, Edinburgh EH10 6BU. *T:* 0131–447 3645. *Clubs:* Royal Automobile, Institute of Directors, Caledonian; New (Edinburgh); Denham Golf; Royal & Ancient (St Andrews), Hon. Company of Edinburgh Golfers.

PERCY, His Honour Rodney Algernon; a Circuit Judge, 1979–93; caravan site operator, since 1993; *b* 15 May 1924; 3rd *s* of late Hugh James Percy, Solicitor, Alnwick; *m* 1948, Mary Allen, *d* of late J. E. Benbow, Aberystwyth; one *s* three *d. Educ:* Uppingham; Brasenose Coll., Oxford (MA). Lieut, Royal Corps of Signals, 1942–46, served in Burma, India, Malaya, Java. Called to Bar: Middle Temple, 1950; Lincoln's Inn, 1987 (*ad eund*). Dep. Coroner, N Northumberland, 1957; Asst Recorder, Sheffield QS, 1964; Dep. Chm., Co. Durham QS, 1966–71; a Recorder of the Crown Court, 1972–79. Pres., Tyneside Marriage Guidance Council, 1983–87; Founder Mem., Family Conciliation Service for Northumberland and Tyneside, 1982– (Pres., 1988–93). *Publications:* (ed) Charlesworth on Negligence, 4th edn 1962, 5th edn 1971, 6th edn 1977, 7th edn (Charlesworth & Percy on Negligence) 1983, 8th edn 1990; (contrib.) Atkin's Court Forms, 2nd edn, Vol. 20, 1982, rev. edn 1987, 1993 (title Health and Safety at Work), and Vol. 29, 1983, rev. edn 1991 (title Negligence). *Recreations:* golf, gardening, hill walking, King Charles Cavalier spaniels, beach-combing. *Address:* Brookside, Lesbury, Alnwick, Northumberland NE66 3AT. *T:* Alnwick (01665) 830326/830000.

PERDUE, Rt. Rev. Richard Gordon; *b* 13 Feb. 1910; *s* of Richard Perdue; *m* 1943, Evelyn Ruth Curry, BA; two *d. Educ:* Trinity Coll., Dublin. BA 1931; MA and BD 1938. Deacon 1933, priest 1934, Dublin. Curate of Drumcondra with N Strand, 1933–36; Rathmines, 1936–40; Incumbent of Castledermot with Kinneagh, 1940–43; Roscrea, Diocese of Killaloe, 1943–54; Archdeacon of Killaloe and Kilfenora, 1951–54; Examining Chaplain to Bishop of Killaloe, 1951–54; Bishop of Killaloe, Kilfenora, Clonfert and Kilmacduagh, 1953–57; Bishop of Cork, Cloyne and Ross, 1957–78. *Address:* 23 Le Cren Street, Timaru, New Zealand.

PEREGRINE, Gwilym Rhys, DL; Member: Independent Broadcasting Authority, 1982–89 (Chairman, Welsh Advisory Committee, 1982–89); Welsh Fourth Channel Authority, 1982–89; *b* 30 Oct. 1924; *s* of Rev. and Mrs T. J. Peregrine; *m* 1958, Gwyneth Rosemary Williams; one *s* one *d. Educ:* Caterham Sch., Surrey; Gwendraeth Valley Grammar Sch. Admitted Solicitor, 1949. Carmarthenshire County Council: Asst Solicitor, 1949–56; Dep. Clerk, 1956–72 (also Dep. Clerk of the Peace); Clerk and Chief Exec., 1972–74; Chief Exec., Dyfed CC, 1974–81. DL Dyfed, 1974. *Recreations:* golf, cricket, Rugby, music, reading. *Address:* 1 Newnham Crescent, Sketty, Swansea SA2 0RZ. *Clubs:* Fairwood Park Golf (Swansea); Glamorgan Cricket, Bronwydd Cricket.

PEREIRA, Arthur Leonard, FRCS; Consulting Ear, Nose and Throat Surgeon to St George's Hospital, London; *b* 10 March 1906; British; *m* 1973, Mrs Jane Wilson (*née* Lapworth). *Educ:* Merchant Taylors' School. MRCS, LRCP 1929; MB, BS London 1931; FRCS 1936. Otologist to: the Metropolitan Hospital, E8, 1941–47; St George's Hospital, 1946–71. *Address:* Dormers, The Drive, Old Bosham, Sussex PO18 8JG.

PEREIRA, Sir (Herbert) Charles, Kt 1977; DSc; FRS 1969; Consultant, tropical agriculture research; *b* 12 May 1913; *s* of H. J. Pereira and Maud Edith (*née* Machin), both of London; *m* 1941, Irene Beatrice, *d* of David Sloan, Belfast; three *s* one *d. Educ:* Prince Albert Coll., Saskatchewan; St Albans Sch.; London Univ. Attached Rothamsted Expl Stn for PhD (London) 1941. Royal Engineers, 1941–46 (despatches). Colonial Agric. Service, Coffee Research Stn, Kenya, 1946–52; Colonial Research Service, established Physics Div. at East African Agriculture and Forestry Research Org., Kenya, 1952–61; DSc London 1961; Dir, ARC of Rhodesia and Nyasaland, 1961–63; Dir, ARC of Central Africa (Rhodesia, Zambia and Malawi), 1963–67; Dir, East Malling Research Station, 1969–72; Chief Scientist (Dep. Sec.), MAFF, 1972–77. Member: Natural Environment Res. Council, 1971–77; ARC, 1973–77; ABRC, 1973–77; Chm., Sci. Panel, Commonwealth Develt Corp., 1978–91; Pres., Tropical Agric. Assoc., 1990–. Mem. Bd of Trustees, Royal Botanic Gdns, Kew, 1983–86; Trustee, Marie Stopes Internat., 1991–. FInstBiol; FRASE 1977; CompICE, 1971; Hon. DSc Cranfield, 1977. Haile Selassie Prize for Research in Africa, 1966. *Publications:* (jtly) Hydrological Effects of Land Use Changes in East Africa, 1962; Land Use and Water Resources, 1973; Policy and Practice in the Management of Tropical Watersheds, 1989; papers in research jls; Founding Editor, Rhodesian Jl Agric. Research. *Recreations:* swimming, sailing. *Address:* Peartrees, Nestor Court, Teston, Maidstone, Kent ME18 5AD. *T:* Maidstone (01622) 813333. *Clubs:* Athenæum; Harare (Zimbabwe).

PEREIRA, Margaret, CBE 1985; BSc; FIBiol; Controller, Home Office Forensic Science Service, 1982–88; *b* 22 April 1928. *Educ:* La Sainte Union Convent, Bexley Heath; Dartford County Grammar School for Girls; Chelsea Coll. of Science and Technol. BSc 1953. Joined Metropolitan Police Forensic Science Lab., New Scotland Yard, 1947; Dep. Dir, Home Office Forensic Science Central Res. Estab., 1976; Director, Home Office Forensic Science Laboratory: Aldermaston, 1977; Chepstow, 1979. *Address:* 24 Kingswood Close, Englefield Green, Egham, Surrey TW20 0NQ.

PEREIRA GRAY, Denis John; *see* Gray.

PEREIRA-MENDOZA, Vivian, MScTech, CEng, FIEE; Director, Polytechnic of the South Bank, 1970–80; *b* 8 April 1917; *o s* of Rev. Joseph Pereira-Mendoza, Manchester; *m* 1942, Marjorie, *y d* of Edward Lichtenstein; two *d. Educ:* Manchester Central High Sch.; Univ. of Manchester. Asst Lectr, Univ. of Manchester, 1939. Served War, 1940–45, in Royal Corps of Signals; Major, and GSO II (War Office). Sen. Lectr, Woolwich Polytechnic, 1948; Head of Dept: of Electrical Engrg, NW Kent Coll. of Technology, 1954; of Electrical Engrg and Physics, Borough Polytechnic, 1957; Vice-Principal, Borough Polytechnic, 1964; Principal, Borough Polytechnic, 1966–70. Mem. Council, Chelsea Coll., Univ. of London, 1972–85. *Address:* Flat 20, Whitegates, Wilmslow Road, Cheadle, Cheshire SK8 1HG. *T:* 0161–491 2900.

PERES, Shimon; Minister of Foreign Affairs, Israel, since 1992; Member of Knesset, since 1959; *b* 1923; *s* of Yitzhak and Sarah Persky; *m* 1945, Sonia Gelman; two *s* one *d. Educ:* New York Univ.; Harvard Univ. Head of Naval Services, 1948–49; Head of Israel Defense Min. delegn to US, 1949–52; Dep. Dir-Gen., Defense Min., 1953–59; Dep. Defense Minister, 1959–65; Sec. Gen., Rafi Party, 1965–67; Minister: of Immigrant Absorption, 1969–70; of Transport and Communications, 1970–74; of Information, 1974; of Defense, 1974–77; Acting Prime Minister, 1977; Prime Minister, 1984–86; Vice Premier, 1986–90; Minister of Foreign Affairs, 1986–88; Minister of Finance, 1988–90. Chm, Israel Labour Party, 1977–; Vice-Pres., Socialist Internat., 1978–. (Jtly) Nobel Peace Prize, 1994. *Publications:* The Next Phase, 1965; David's Sling, 1970; Tomorrow is Now, 1978; From These Men, 1980; Entebbe Diary, 1991; The New Middle East, 1993; Battling for Peace: memoirs, 1995. *Recreation:* reading. *Address:* Ministry of Foreign Affairs, Jerusalem, Israel. *T:* (2) 303111.

PERETZ, David Lindsay Corbett; Deputy Director, International Finance, HM Treasury, since 1994; *b* 29 May 1943; *s* of Michael and April Peretz; *m* 1966, Jane Wildman; one *s* one *d. Educ:* The Leys Sch., Cambridge; Exeter Coll., Oxford (MA). Asst Principal, Min. of Technol., 1965–69; Head of Public Policy and Institutional Studies, IBRO, 1969–76; HM Treasury: Principal, 1976–80; Asst Sec., External Finance, 1980–84; Principal Pvte Sec. to Chancellor of Exchequer, 1984–85; Under-Secretary: Home Finance, 1985–86; Monetary Gp, Public Finance, 1986–90; UK Exec. Dir, IMF and World Bank, and Economic Minister, Washington, 1990–94. *Recreations:* walking, sailing, listening to music. *Address:* c/o HM Treasury, Parliament Street, SW1P 3AG.

PÉREZ DE CUÉLLAR, Javier, Hon. GCMG; Secretary-General, United Nations, 1982–91; *b* 19 Jan. 1920; *m* Marcela (*née* Temple); one *s* one *d. Educ:* Law Faculty, Catholic Univ., Lima, Perú. Joined Peruvian Foreign Ministry, 1940; Diplomatic Service, 1944; Sec., Peruvian Embassies in France, UK, Bolivia and Brazil and Counsellor, Embassy, Brazil, 1944–60; Mem., Peruvian Delegn to First Session of Gen. Assembly, UN, 1946; Dir, Legal, Personnel, Admin, Protocol and Political Affairs Depts, Min. of Foreign Affairs, Perú, 1961–63; Peruvian Ambassador to Switzerland, 1964–66; Perm. Under-Sec. and Sec.-Gen. of Foreign Office, 1966–69; Ambassador of Perú to USSR and to Poland, 1969–71; Perm. Rep. of Perú to UN, 1971–75 (Rep. to UN Security Council, 1973–74); Special Rep. of UN Sec.-Gen. in Cyprus, 1975–77; Ambassador of Perú to Venezuela, 1978; UN Under-Sec.-Gen. for Special Political Affairs, 1979–81. President: World Commn on Culture and Develt, UN/UNESCO, 1992–; Internat. Disability Foundn, 1992–; Fondation de l'Arche de la Fraternité, 1993–; Chm. Emeritus, Inter-Amer. Dialogue, 1992–. Former Professor: of Diplomatic Law, Academia Diplomática del Perú; of Internat. Relations, Academia de Guerra Aérea del Perú. LLD *hc:* Univ. of Nice, France, 1983; Carleton Univ., Ottawa, 1985; Osnabruck Univ., 1986; Coimbra Univ., 1986; Oxford, 1993; other hon. degrees include: Jagiellonian Univ., Poland, 1984; Charles Univ. Czechoslovakia, 1984; Sofia Univ., Bulgaria, 1984; Universidad Nacional Mayor de San Marcos, Perú, 1984; Vrije Universiteit Brussel, Belgium, 1984; Sorbonne Univ., Paris, 1985; Cambridge Univ., 1989. Various internat. awards including: Prince of Asturias Prize, 1987; Olof Palme Prize, 1989; Jawaharlal Nehru Award, 1989. Grand Cross, Order of El Sol (Perú); foreign decorations include: US Medal of Freedom; Grand Cross, Legion of Honour (France). *Publications:* Manual de Derecho Diplomático, 1964; Anarchy or Order, 1992. *Address:* 18 avenue de la Bourdonnais, 75007 Paris, France; Avenida A. Miro Quesada, 1071 Lima, Perú. *Clubs:* Travellers (Paris); Nacional, Ecuestre Huachipa, Villa, Jockey (Lima, Perú).

PÉREZ ESQUIVEL, Adolfo; sculptor; Hon. President: Servicio Paz y Justicia en América Latina, since 1986; Servicio Paz y Justicia Argentina, since 1973; President, International League for the Rights and Liberation of Peoples, since 1987; *b* 26 Nov. 1931; *m* 1956, Amanda Guerreño; three *s*. *Educ:* Nat. Sch. of Fine Arts, Buenos Aires. Prof. of Art, Manuel Belgrano Nat. Sch. of Fine Arts, Buenos Aires, 1956–76; Prof., Faculty of Architecture and Urban Studies, Univ. Nacional de la Plata, 1969–73; Gen. Co-ordinator, Servicio Paz y Justicia en América Latina, 1974–86. Work in permanent collections: Buenos Aires Mus. of Modern Art; Mus. of Fine Arts, Córdoba; Fine Arts Mus., Rosario. Joined group dedicated to principles of militant non-violence, and engaged in projects to promote self-sufficiency in urban areas, 1971; founded Paz y Justicia magazine, 1973. Co-founder, Ecumenical Movement for Human Rights, Argentina; Pres., Permanent Assembly for Human Rights. Premio la Nación de Escultura; Pope John XXIII prize, Pax Christi Orgn, 1977; Nobel Peace Prize, 1980. *Address:* Servicio Paz y Justicia, Piedras 730, CP 1070, Buenos Aires, Argentina.

PERHAM, Rev. Canon Michael Francis; Canon Residentiary and Precentor of Norwich Cathedral, since 1992; *b* 8 Nov. 1947; *s* of Raymond Maxwell Perham and Marcelle Winifred Perham; *m* 1982, Alison Jane Grove; four *d*. *Educ:* Hardye's Sch., Dorchester; Keble Coll., Oxford (BA 1974; MA 1978); Cuddesdon Theol Coll. Curate, St Mary, Addington, 1976–81; Sec., C of E Doctrine Commn, 1979–84; Chaplain to Bp of Winchester, 1981–84; Team Rector, Oakdale Team Ministry, Poole, 1984–92. Member: Liturgical Commn of C of E, 1986–; Archbishops' Commn on Church Music, 1988–92; Gen. Synod of C of E, 1989–92 and 1993–. Chairman: Praxis, 1990–; Liturgical Cttee, Dio. of Norwich, 1992–; Cathedrals' Liturgy Gp, 1994–; Norfolk Arts Cttee, RSCM, 1994–. *Publications:* The Eucharist, 1978, 2nd edn 1981; The Communion of Saints, 1980; Liturgy Pastoral and Parochial, 1984; (with Kenneth Stevenson) Waiting for the Risen Christ, 1986; (ed) Towards Liturgy 2000, 1989; (ed) Liturgy for a New Century, 1991; (with Kenneth Stevenson) Welcoming the Light of Christ, 1991; Lively Sacrifice, 1992; (ed) The Renewal of Common Prayer, 1993; (ed) Model and Inspiration, 1993; (compiled) Enriching the Christian Year, 1993. *Recreations:* reading, writing, creating liturgical texts, walking in the Yorkshire dales. *Address:* 27 The Close, Norwich, Norfolk NR1 4DZ. *T:* Norwich (01603) 219484.

PERHAM, Prof. Richard Nelson, ScD, FRS 1984; Professor of Structural Biochemistry, since 1989, Head of Department of Biochemistry, since 1985, Cambridge University; Fellow, St John's College, Cambridge, since 1964; *b* 27 April 1937; *s* of Cyril Richard William Perham and Helen Harrow Perham (*née* Thornton); *m* 1969, Nancy Jane, *d* of Temple Haviland Lane, Halifax, Nova Scotia; one *s* one *d*. *Educ:* Latymer Upper School; St John's College, Cambridge; BA 1961, MA 1965, PhD 1965, ScD 1976; Scholar; Slater Studentship, 1961–64; Henry Humphreys Prize, 1963. Nat. Service RN, 1956–58. Cambridge University: MRC Scholar, Lab. of Molecular Biol., 1961–64; Univ. Demonstrator in Biochem., 1964–69, Lectr, 1969–77; Reader in Biochemistry of Macromolecular Structures, 1977–89; Res. Fellow, St John's Coll., 1964–67, Tutor, 1967–77, Pres., 1983–87. Helen Hay Whitney Fellow, Dept of Molecular Biophysics, Yale Univ., 1966–67; EMBO Fellow, Max-Planck-Institut für Medizinische Forschung, Heidelberg, 1971; Drapers' Vis. Prof., Univ. of New South Wales, 1972; Biochem. Soc. Visitor, Aust. and NZ, 1979; Fogarty Internat. Scholar, NIH, USA, 1990–93. Member: EMBO, 1983; SRC Enzyme Chem. and Tech. Cttee, 1973–75; Enzyme Panel, Biol. Scis Cttee, 1975–76; SERC Science Bd, 1985–90; Biochem. Soc. Cttee, 1980–84; British Nat. Cttee for Biochem., 1982–87; Scientific Adv. Cttee, Lister Inst. of Preventive Medicine, 1992–; Dir's Adv. Gp, AFRC Inst. of Animal Physiology, 1983–86; Exec. Council, CIBA Foundn, 1989–; Chm., Biol Scis Cttee, SERC, 1987–90 (Mem., 1983–85); Pres., Section D (Biological Scis), BAAS, 1987–88. Mem., Academia Europaea, 1992. Syndic, CUP, 1988–. FRSA 1988. Max Planck Res. Prize, 1993. *Publications:* (ed) Instrumentation in Amino Acid Sequence Analysis, 1975; papers in sci. jls. *Recreations:* gardening, rowing (Lady Margaret BC), theatre, nosing around in antique shops. *Address:* Department of Biochemistry, Tennis Court Road, Cambridge CB2 1QW. *T:* Cambridge (01223) 333663; St John's College, Cambridge CB2 1TP. *T:* Cambridge (01223) 338600; 107 Barton Road, Cambridge CB3 9LL. *T:* Cambridge (01223) 63752. *Clubs:* United Oxford & Cambridge University; Hawks (Cambridge).

PERKINS, Alice Elizabeth; Deputy Director, Public Spending (Overseas and Agriculture), HM Treasury, since 1995; *b* 24 May 1949; *d* of Derrick Leslie John Perkins and Elsa Rose Perkins, CBE (*née* Rink); *m* 1978, John Whitaker Straw, *qv*; one *s* one *d*. *Educ:* North London Collegiate Sch. for Girls; St Anne's Coll., Oxford (BA Hons Modern Hist. 1971). Joined CS, DHSS, 1971; Principal, 1976–84; Asst Sec., DHSS, then DSS, 1984–90; Dir of Personnel, DSS, 1990–93; Under Sec, Defence Policy and Materiel Gp, HM Treasury, 1993–95. Trustee, Whitehall and Industry Gp, 1993–. *Recreations:* gardening, riding, looking at paintings. *Address:* HM Treasury, Parliament Street, SW1P 3AG.

PERKINS, Bernard James; Chairman, Harlow Development Corporation, 1972–79; *b* 25 Jan. 1928; *y s* of George and Rebecca Perkins; *m* 1956, Patricia (*née* Payne); three *d*. *Educ:* Strand School. Member: Lambeth Council, 1962–71 (Leader, 1968–71); Community Relations Commn, 1970–72; SE Econ. Planning Council, 1971–79; Alderman, GLC, 1971–73; Chm., GLC Housing Cttee, 1972–73. *Recreation:* social service. *Address:* 38 Cedar Close, Dulwich, SE21 8HX. *T:* 0181–761 8695.

PERKINS, Prof. Donald Hill, CBE 1991; FRS 1966; Professor of Elementary Particle Physics, 1965–93, and Fellow of St Catherine's College, since 1965, Oxford University; *b* 15 Oct. 1925; *s* of George W. and Gertrude Perkins; *m* 1955, Dorothy Mary (*née* Maloney); two *d*. *Educ:* Malet Lambert High School, Hull. BSc London 1945; PhD London 1948; 1851 Senior Scholar, 1948–51. G. A. Wills Research Associate in Physics, Univ. of Bristol, 1951–55; Lawrence Radiation Lab., Univ. of California, 1955–56; Lectr in Physics, 1956–60, Reader in Physics, 1960–65, Univ. of Bristol. Mem., SERC, 1985–89. Hon. DSc Sheffield, 1982. Guthrie Medal, Inst. of Physics, 1979; Holweck Medal and Prize, Société Française de Physique, 1992. *Publications:* The Study of Elementary Particles by the Photographic Method (with C. F. Powell and P. H. Fowler), 1959; Introduction to High Energy Physics, 1972, 3rd edn 1986; about 50 papers and review articles in Nature, Physical Review, Philosophical Magazine, Physics Letters, Proc. Royal Soc., Nuovo Cimento, etc. *Recreations:* squash, tennis. *Address:* Birchwood, Bedwells Heath, Boars Hill, Oxford OX1 5JE. *T:* Oxford (01865) 739308.

PERKINS, Air Vice-Marshal Irwyn Morse, MBE 1957; Royal Air Force, retired; Medical Officer, 1981–85 and Hon. Consultant in Medical Computing, 1985–93, Royal Military College of Science; *b* 15 Dec. 1920; *s* of William Lewis Perkins and Gwenllian Perkins, Ystalyfera, Swansea; *m* 1948, Royce Villiers Thompson, *d* of William Stanley Thompson and Zöe Thompson, The Mountain, Tangier; one *s* one *d*. *Educ:* Pontardawe, Swansea; St Mary's Hospital, Paddington, W2. MRCS, LRCP 1945; MFCM 1973. Commnd RAF, 1946; SMO: RAF Gibraltar, 1946–49; several flying stations in UK; DGMS Dept, MoD, 1955–57; RAF Laarbruch, Germany, 1958–61; RAF Khormaksar, Aden, 1964–66; DPMO, Bomber and Strike Commands, 1966–69; CO RAF Hospital, Ely, Cambs, 1969–72; PMO RAF Germany, 1972–75; CO PMRAF Hospital, Halton, 1975–77; PMO, Support Comd, 1977–80. Hon. Surgeon to HM the Queen, 1975–80. *Publication:* (with Prof. R. W. Shephard) Shephard-Perkins Injury Classification, 1990. *Recreations:* study of archival medical records, woodworking, DIY. *Address:* 5 Redlands Close, Highworth, Swindon, Wilts SN6 7SN. *T:* Swindon (01793) 765097. *Club:* Royal Air Force.

PERKINS, James Alfred, MA, PhD; Chairman and Chief Executive Officer, International Council for Educational Development, 1970–90, now Chairman Emeritus; *b* 11 Oct. 1911; *s* of H. Norman Perkins and Emily (*née* Taylor); *m* 1st, 1938, Jean Bredin (*d* 1970); two *s* three *d*; 2nd, 1971, Ruth B. Aall; one step *s* three step *d*. *Educ:* Swarthmore Coll., Pa (AB); Princeton Univ., NJ (MA, PhD). Instructor Polit. Sci., Princeton Univ., 1937–39; Asst Prof. and Asst Dir, Sch. of Public and Internat. Affairs, Princeton, 1939–41; Dir, Pulp and Paper Div., Office of Price Admin., 1941–43; Asst to Administrator, For. Econ. Admin., 1943–45; Vice-Pres. Swarthmore Coll., 1945–50; Exec. Associate, Carnegie Corp. of NY, 1950–51; Dep. Chm. (on leave) Res. and Develt Bd, Dept of Defense, 1951–52; Vice-Pres., Carnegie Corp. of NY, 1951–63; Pres., Cornell Univ., 1963–69. Carnegie Foundn for the Advancement of Teaching: Sec. 1954–55; Vice-Pres., 1955–63. Chm., Pres. Johnson's Gen. Adv. Cttee on Foreign Assistance Prog., 1965–68; Trustee: Rand Corp., 1961–71; United Negro Coll. Fund (Chm. of Bd), 1965–69; Educl Testing Service, 1964–68; Dir Emeritus, Council on Foreign Relations; Mem. Gen. Adv. Cttee of US Arms Control and Disarmament Agency, 1963–66; Chm. NY Regents Adv. Cttee on Educational Leadership, 1963–67. Member: Bd of Directors, Chase Manhattan Bank, 1967–75; Stevenson Memorial Fund, 1966–69; Trustee, Aspen Inst., 1973–; Director: Overseas Develt Council, 1969–; Center for Inter-Amer. Relations, 1969–76; Inst. of Internat. Educn, 1981–87; Vice Chm., Acad. for Educnl Develt. Chm., President Carter's Commn on Foreign Language and Internat. Studies, 1978–79. Mem. Society of Friends, Swarthmore, Pa. Hon. LLD and Hon. LHD 32 colls and univs. *Publications:* The University in Transition, 1966; Higher Education: from Autonomy to Systems, 1972; The University as an Organization, 1973; contrib. to: Public Admin. Review, Amer. Polit. Sci. Review, Educational Record, etc. *Address:* (home) 94 North Road, Princeton, NJ 08540, USA; (office) 20 Nassau Street, Princeton, NJ 08542, USA. *Clubs:* University (NYC); Nassau (Princeton).

PERKINS, Maj.-Gen. Kenneth, CB 1977; MBE 1955; DFC 1953; Commander, Sultan's Armed Forces, Oman, 1975–77 (successfully concluded Dhofar War); *b* 15 Aug. 1926; *s* of George Samuel Perkins and Arabella Sarah Perkins (*née* Wise); *m* 1st, 1949, Anne Theresa Barry (marr. diss. 1984); three *d*; 2nd, 1985, Hon. Celia Sandys, *d* of Rt Hon. Lord Duncan-Sandys, CH, PC and Diana, *d* of Rt Hon. Sir Winston Churchill, KG, OM, CH, FRS; one *s* one *d*. *Educ:* Lewes County Sch. for Boys; New Coll., Oxford. Enlisted 1944; commnd RA 1946; various appts in Middle and Far East, BAOR and UK until 1965, incl. Korean War, Malayan Emergency, and Staff Coll. Quetta 1958; Instructor, Staff Coll. Camberley, 1965–66; CO 1st Regt Royal Horse Artillery, 1967–69; GSO 1 Singapore, 1970; Comdr 24 Bde, 1971–72; RCDS 1973; Central Staff, MoD, 1974; Maj.-Gen., 1975; Asst Chief of Defence Staff (Ops), 1977–80; Dir, Military Assistance Office, MoD, 1980–82. Col Comdt, RA, 1980–85. Vice Pres., Sultan of Oman's Armed Forces Assoc., 1994– (Chm., 1987–94). Mem. Council, Res. Inst. for Study of Conflict, 1992–. Mil. Advr, The Sun newspaper. Chm., Politicians' Complaints Commn, 1992–93. Selangor Distinguished Conduct Medal (Malaya), 1955; Hashemite Order of Independence, first class, 1975; Order of Oman, 1977. *Publications:* Weapons and Warfare, 1987; A Fortunate Soldier (autobiog.), 1988; Khalida (novel), 1991; articles in professional jls. *Recreations:* writing, painting (exhibited RA), cycling, family pursuits. *Address:* 4 Bedwyn Common, Marlborough, Wilts SN8 3HZ. *Club:* Army and Navy.

PERLMAN, Itzhak; violinist; *b* Tel Aviv, 31 Aug. 1945; *s* of Chaim and Shoshana Perlman; *m* 1967, Toby Lynn Friedlander; two *s* three *d*. Studied at Tel Aviv Acad. of Music with Ryvka Goldgart, and at Juilliard Sch., NY, under Dorothy Delay and Ivan Galamian. First solo recital at age of 10 in Israel; New York début, 1958. Leventritt Meml Award, NY, 1964. Tours extensively in USA and plays with all major American symphony orchestras; recital tours of Canada, South America, Europe, Israel, Far East and Australia; recorded numerous works for violin. Has received many Grammy Awards. Hon. degrees: Harvard; Yale; Brandeis. *Recreation:* cooking. *Address:* c/o Harold Holt Ltd, 31 Sinclair Road, W14 0NS.

PERMANAND, Rabindranath; High Commissioner in London for Trinidad and Tobago, since 1993; *b* 17 July 1935; *s* of late Ram Narais Permanand and of Kalawatee Permanand (*née* Capildeo); *m* 1969, Ursel Edda Schmid; one *s* one *d*. *Educ:* Queen's Royal Coll., Trinidad; Univ. of Calcutta (BA Hons); Univ. of Delhi (MA); Univ. of West Indies (Dip. Internat. Relations). History Teacher, Queen's Royal Coll., 1959–66; joined Min. of Foreign Affairs, 1966; Dep. High Comr, Georgetown, Guyana, 1966–69; First Sec., Ottawa, 1969–72; Chief of Protocol, 1973–77; Counsellor and Minister Counsellor, Brussels, 1977–81; Consul-Gen., Toronto, 1981–84; Head, Political Div., 1984–88; Ambassador and Perm. Rep. to UN, Geneva, 1988–93. *Recreations:* reading, music, walking, cricket. *Address:* Trinidad and Tobago High Commission, 42 Belgrave Square, SW1X 8NT. *T:* 0171–245 9351, *Fax:* 0171–823 1065.

PEROWNE, Rear-Adm. James Francis, OBE 1983; Senior Naval Member, Royal College of Defence Studies, since 1995; *b* 29 July 1947; *s* of Lt Comdr John Herbert Francis Perowne and Mary Joy Perowne (*née* Dibb), Saundersfoot, Dyfed; *m* 1st, 1971, Susan Anne Holloway (marr. diss. 1990); four *s*; 2nd, 1992, Caroline Nicola Grimson. *Educ:* Sherborne Sch.; BRNC Dartmouth. CO, HMS Opportune, 1976–77; CO, HMS Superb, 1981–83; Staff of CBNS Washington, 1983–86; CO, HMS Boxer, 1986–88; Asst Dir, Naval Warfare, 1988–90; Captain, Second Submarine Sqdn, 1990–92; Captain, Sixth Frigate Sqdn and CO, HMS Norfolk, 1992–94. MInstD. *Recreations:* golf, gardening, old Jaguar cars. *Address:* Royal College of Defence Studies, Seaford House, 37 Belgrave Square, SW1X 8NS. *T:* 0171–915 4834. *Clubs:* Army and Navy, Royal Navy of 1765 and 1785.

PERRETT, Desmond Seymour; QC 1980; **His Honour Judge Perrett;** a Circuit Judge, since 1992; *b* 22 April 1937; *s* of His Honour John Perrett and of Elizabeth Mary Perrett (*née* Seymour); *m* 1961, Pauline Merriel, *yr d* of late Paul Robert Buchan May, ICS, and of Esme May; one *s* one *d*. *Educ:* Westminster Sch. National Service, RN, 1955–57: midshipman RNVR, 1955; Suez, 1956, and Cyprus, 1957. Called to the Bar, Gray's Inn, 1962, Bencher, 1989; Oxford Circuit, 1963–72; Midland and Oxford Circuit, 1972–; a Recorder, 1978–92; Mem., Senate of the Inns of Court and of the Bar, 1983–87. Chm. Disciplinary Appeals Cttee, Cricket Council, 1986–. Mem. Governing Body, Horris Hill Sch., 1986–. *Recreations:* cricket, fishing, shooting. *Address:* 2 Crown Office Row, Temple, EC4Y 7HJ. *T:* 071–353 9337. *Club:* MCC.

PERRIN, Charles John; Deputy Chairman, Hambros Bank Ltd, since 1986; *b* 1 May 1940; *s* of late Sir Michael Perrin, CBE, and Nancy May, *d* of late Rt Rev. C. E. Curzon; *m* 1966, Gillian Margaret, *d* of late Rev. M. Hughes-Thomas; two *d*. *Educ:* Winchester; New Coll., Oxford (Schol.; MA). British Council Travelling Scholarship, 1962–63; called to the Bar, Inner Temple, 1965. Joined Hambros Bank, 1963, Dir, 1973–; Chm., Hambro Pacific, Hong Kong, 1983–94; Dir, Hambros PLC, 1985–. Non-exec. Dir, Harland and

Wolff, 1984–89. Hon. Treas., UK Assoc. for International Year of the Child, 1979; Vice-Chm., UK Cttee for UNICEF, 1972–91. Member: Royal Brompton Nat. Heart and Lung Hosps SHA, 1993–94; Royal Brompton Hosp. NHS Trust, 1994–. Member Council: Zoological Soc. of London, 1981–88 and 1991; Univ. of London, 1995–. Governor: Queen Anne's Sch., Caversham, 1981–; London Hosp. Med. Coll., 1991–. *Publication:* Darwinism Today (Endeavour Prize Essay, 1958). *Recreation:* sailing. *Address:* 4 Holford Road, Hampstead, NW3 1AD. *T:* 0171–435 8103. *Club:* Athenæum.

PERRIN, John Henry; *b* 14 Jan. 1916; *s* of Walter William Perrin, Faringdon and Sonning, Berks, and Amelia (*née* Honey), Oxford; *m* 1940, Doris Winifred Barrington-Brider; two *s*. *Educ:* Minchenden Sch.; London Univ. HM Customs and Excise; Royal Navy, 1939–46; Min. of Agriculture, 1948–76: Principal Private Sec. to Minister (Lord Amory), 1955–57; Regional Controller, Eastern Region, 1957–68; Under Sec., 1968–76. Dir-Gen., British Agricl Export Council, 1976–77. Inspector, Public Inquiries, Depts of the Environment and Transport, 1978–84. *Clubs:* Naval, Civil Service, Royal Yachting; RNVR Yacht; Cambridge University Cricket.

PERRIN, Air Vice-Marshal Norman Arthur; Secretary General, ECTEL, European Conference of Telecommunications Industry Associations, since 1991; *b* 30 Sept. 1930; *s* of late Albert Arthur and Mona Victoria (*née* Stacey); *m* 1956, Marie (*née* Bannon), *d* of late Peter and Lucy Bannon; one *s*. *Educ:* Liverpool Collegiate School; Hertford College, Oxford; RAF Technical College. BA; CEng, FRAeS. Nat. Service commn, Airfield Construction Branch, RAF, Suez Canal Zone, 1951–53; perm. commn, Tech. Branch, 1953; Advanced GW course, 1956–57; Air Ministry, 1958–61; HQ 11 Group, 1961–62; Staff Coll., 1963; FEAF, 1964–65; OC Eng Wing, RAF Seletar, 1966–67; JSSC 1967; Op. Requirements, SAGW, 1967–70; Chief Instructor, Systems Engineering, RAF Coll., 1970–72; Group Captain Plans, HQ Maintenance Comd, 1972–75; C. Mech. Eng., HQ Strike Comd, 1975–78; RCDS 1979; Dir Air GW MoD (PE), 1980–83; Vice-Pres. (Air), Ordnance Board, 1983: Pres., Ordnance Board, 1984–86. Dir, TEMA, 1987–91. *Recreations:* bridge, crosswords, Liverpool FC watching. *Address:* c/o Barclays Bank, 10 High Street, Marlow, Bucks SL7 1AR. *Club:* Royal Air Force.

PERRING, Franklyn Hugh, OBE 1988; writer; broadcaster; environmental consultant; *b* 1 Aug. 1927; *s* of Frank Arthur and Avelyn Millicent Perring; *m* 1st, 1951, Yvonne Frances Maud Matthews (marr. diss. 1972); one *s*; 2nd, 1972, Margaret Dorothy Barrow; one *d*. *Educ:* Earls Colne Grammar Sch.; Queens' Coll., Cambridge (MA, PhD). FLS; FIBiol 1979. Botanical Society of British Isles Distribution Maps Scheme: Hd, 1954–59; Dir, 1959–64; Hd, Biological Records Centre, Monks Wood Experimental Station, 1964–79; Botanical Sec., Linnean Soc. of London, 1973–78; Gen. Sec., RSNC, 1979–87. Pres., Botanical Soc. of the British Isles, 1993–95. Hon. DSc Leicester, 1989. *Publications:* (jtly) Atlas of the British Flora, 1962; (jtly) A Flora of Cambridgeshire, 1964; Critical Supplement to the Atlas of the British Flora, 1968; (ed) The Flora of a Changing Britain, 1970; (ed jtly) The British Oak, 1974; (jtly) English Names of Wild Flowers, 1974, 2nd edn 1986; (jtly) British Red Data Book of Vascular Plants, 1977, 2nd edn 1983; (ed jtly) Ecological Effects of Pesticides, 1977; RSNC Guide to British Wild Flowers, 1984; (jtly) Ecological Flora of the Shropshire Region, 1985; (ed jtly) Changing Attitudes to Nature Conservation, 1988; (jtly) The Macmillan Guide to British Wildflowers, 1989; (ed jtly) The Nature of Northamptonshire, 1989; (ed jtly) Tomorrow is Too Late, 1990; Britain's Conservation Heritage, 1991; (ed jtly) Insects, Plants and Set-aside, 1995; sci. papers in Jl of Ecology, Watsonia, etc. *Recreations:* opera-going, poetry reading, plant-hunting in the Mediterranean. *Address:* Green Acre, Wood Lane, Oundle, Peterborough PE8 5TP. *T:* Oundle (01832) 273388, *Fax:* (01832) 274568.

PERRING, John Raymond, TD 1965; Chairman, Perrings Finance Ltd, since 1987; *b* 7 July 1931; *e s* and *heir* of Sir Ralph Perring, Bt, *qv*; *m* 1961, Ella Christine, *e d* of late Tony and Ann Pelham; two *s* two *d*. *Educ:* Stowe School. Nat. Service, then TA, RA, 1949–60; Royal Fusiliers (City of London), 1960–65. Joined family business, Perring Furnishings, 1951, Dir 1957, Jt Man. Dir 1964, Vice-Chm., 1972, Chm., 1981–88. Nat. Pres., Nat. Assoc. of Retail Furnishers, 1971–73; Mem. Council, Retail Consortium, 1972–91 (Chm., non-food policy cttee, 1987–91); Mem. EDC (Distributive Trades), 1974–78. City of London: Sheriff, 1991–92; One of HM Lieutenants, 1963–; Assistant, Merchant Taylors' Co., 1980, Master, 1988, 1994; Master, Furniture Makers' Co., 1978. Trustee, Ranyard Meml Charitable Trust, 1983– (Chm., 1990–). FRSA. OStJ 1992. *Recreations:* outdoor pursuits. *Address:* 21 Somerset Road, Wimbledon, SW19 5JZ. *T:* 0181–946 8971. *Clubs:* City Livery, Royal Automobile; Royal Wimbledon Golf; Bembridge Sailing.

PERRING, Sir Ralph (Edgar), 1st Bt *cr* 1963; Kt 1960; Chairman, Perring Furnishings Ltd, 1948–81; *b* 23 March 1905; *yr s* of late Colonel Sir John Perring, DL, JP; *m* 1928, Ethel Mary, OStJ (*d* 1991), *o d* of late Henry T. Johnson, Putney; two *s* (and one *s* decd). *Educ:* University College Sch., London. Lieut, RA (TA) 1938–40, invalided. Member Court of Common Council (Ward of Cripplegate), 1948–51; Alderman of City of London (Langbourn Ward), 1951–75, one of HM Lieutenants of the City of London, and Sheriff, 1958–59. Lord Mayor of London, 1962–63. Chairman, Spitalfields Market Cttee, 1951–52; JP County of London, 1943–; Member: LCC for Cities of London and Westminster, 1952–55; County of London Licensing Planning Cttee; New Guildford Cathedral Council; Consumer Advisory Council, BSI, 1955–59; Bd of Governors, E-SU, 1976–81. Governor: St Bartholomew's Hospital, 1964–69; Imperial College of Science and Technology, 1964–67; Christ's Hospital; Vice-Chairman, BNEC Cttee for Exports to Canada, 1964–67, Chairman, 1968–70; Dir, Confederation Life Insurance Co. of Canada, 1969–81. Vice-President, Royal Bridewell Hospital (King Edward's Sch., Witley, 1964–75); Trustee, Morden Coll., Blackheath, 1970–, Chm. 1979–. Master Worshipful Co. of Tin Plate Workers, 1944–45; Master, Worshipful Co. of Painters-Stainers, 1977–78; Sen. Past Master and Founder Mem., Worshipful Co. of Furniture Makers; Mem. Court, Farmers' Co.; President Langbourn Ward Club, 1951–75. FRSA 1975. KStJ. Grand Cross of Merit (Republic of Germany), 1959; Order of Homayoun (Iran), 1959; Grand Officer, Order of Leopold (Belgium), 1963; Knight Commander, Royal Order of George I (Greece), 1963; Commander de la Valeur Camerounaise, 1963. *Heir:* *s* John Raymond Perring, *qv*. *Address:* 15 Burghley House, Somerset Road, Wimbledon, SW19 5JB. *T:* 0181–946 3433. *Clubs:* Royal Automobile, City Livery (President, 1951–52).

PERRINS, Prof. Christopher Miles, LVO 1987; DPhil; Director, Edward Grey Institute of Field Ornithology, since 1974, and Professor of Ornithology, since 1992, Oxford University; Fellow, 1970–74, Professorial Fellow, since 1974, Wolfson College, Oxford; *b* 11 May 1935; *s* of Leslie Howard Perrins and Violet Amy (*née* Moore); *m* 1963, Mary Ceresole Carslake; two *s*. *Educ:* Charterhouse; QMC (BSc Hons Zool.); Oxford Univ. (DPhil). Edward Grey Institute of Field Ornithology, University of Oxford: Research Officer, 1963–66; Sen. Res. Officer, 1966–84; Reader, 1984–92. Mem., General Bd of Faculties, Oxford Univ., 1983–91, 1995– (Chm., Bldgs Cttee, 1995–). The Queen's Swan Warden, 1993. Pres., Internat. Ornithol Congress, 1990–94; Hon. Corresp. Mem. 1976–83, Hon. Fellow 1983–, Amer. Ornithologists Union; Hon. Fellow: German Ornithologists Union, 1991; Netherlands Ornithologists Union, 1992. Godman-Salvin Medal, British Ornithologists Union, 1988; Conservation Medal, RSPB, 1992. *Publications:* (ed with B. Stonehouse) Evolutionary Ecology, 1977; British Tits, 1979; (with T. R. Birkhead) Avian Ecology, 1983; (ed with A. L. A. Middleton) The Encyclopaedia of Birds, 1985; (with M. E. Birkhead) The Mute Swan, 1986; New Generation Guide: Birds, 1987; (ed with J. D. Lebreton and G. J. M. Hirons) Bird Population Studies, 1991; (Senior Ed.) Birds of the Western Palearctic, vol. VII, 1993, vols VIII and IX, 1994. *Recreations:* photography, walking. *Address:* Edward Grey Institute of Field Ornithology, Department of Zoology, University of Oxford, South Parks Road, Oxford OX1 3PS. *T:* Oxford (01865) 271169.

PERRIS, Sir David (Arthur), Kt 1977; MBE 1970; JP; Secretary, Trades Union Congress West Midlands Regional Council, 1974–94; Chairman, Birmingham Hospital Saturday Fund, since 1985 (Vice-Chairman, 1975–85); *b* 25 May 1929; *s* of Arthur Perris; *m* 1955, Constance Parkes, BPharm, FRPharmS; one *s* one *d*. *Educ:* Sparkhill Commercial Sch., Birmingham. Film distribution industry, 1944–61; Reed Paper Group, 1961–65; Vice-Chm., ATV Midlands Ltd, 1980–81; Dir, Central Independent Television plc, 1982–83 (Vice Chm., W Midlands Bd). Sec., Birmingham Trades Council, 1966–83; a Chm., Greater Birmingham Supplementary Benefits Appeal Tribunal, 1982–89. Chairman: Birmingham Regional Hosp. Bd, 1970–74; West Midlands RHA, 1974–82; NHS National Trng Council, 1975–82; Mem. Bd of Governors, United Birmingham Hosps, 1965–74; Mem., Birmingham Children's Hosp. House Cttee, 1958–71 (Chm. 1967–71). Member: W Mids Econ. Planning Council, 1968–70; Midlands Postal Bd, 1974–81. Chairman: Central Telethon Trust, 1987–; W Midlands Charitable Trust Gp, 1991–93. Life Governor, Univ. of Birmingham, 1972; Elective Gov. Birmingham & Midland Inst., 1989–. Mem. Council, Magistrates' Assoc., 1995– (Chm., 1975–86, Pres., 1986–, Birmingham Br.); Pres., Public Service Announcements Assoc., subseq. Community Media Assoc., 1983–; Vice Pres., British Health Care Assoc., 1994–. Life Fellow, British Fluoridation Soc., 1987. Hon. LLD Birmingham, 1981. JP Birmingham, 1961. *Recreations:* cinema, reading. *Address:* Broadway, 21 Highfield Road, Moseley, Birmingham B13 9HL. *T:* 0121–449 3652.

PERRIS, John Douglas; HM Diplomatic Service, retired; *b* 28 March 1928; *s* of Frank William Perris and Alice Perris; *m* 1954, Kathleen Mary Lewington; one *s* two *d*. *Educ:* St Paul's, Knightsbridge; Westminster City Sch. Entered FO, 1945; Bahrain, 1951; Bucharest, 1953; Hamburg, 1955; FO, 1957; Tehran, 1960; Second Sec. (Admin), Caracas, 1963; Second Sec. (Econ.), Berlin, 1966; First Sec. (Admin), Baghdad, 1969; FCO (Inspectorate), 1972; First Sec./Head of Chancery/Consul, Tegucigalpa, 1974; First Sec. (Consular and Immigration), New Delhi, 1976; FCO, 1979; Counsellor (Admin), Bonn, 1982–86. *Recreations:* sport (non-active), reading (thrillers), bridge, DIY. *Address:* 128 Wakehurst Road, SW11 6BS. *T:* 0171–228 0521.

PERROW, (Joseph) Howard; Chairman, Co-operative Union Ltd, 1975–83; Chief Executive Officer and Secretary, Greater Lancastria Co-operative Society Ltd, 1976–83; *b* 18 Nov. 1923; *s* of Joseph and Mary Elizabeth Perrow; *m* 1947, Lorraine Strick; two *s*. *Educ:* St Just, Penzance, Cornwall; Co-operative Coll., Stanford Hall, Leics (CSD). Joined Penzance Co-operative Soc., 1940. Served RAF, 1943–47. Various managerial positions in Co-operative Movement: in W Cornwall, with CRS N Devon, Carmarthen Soc., Silverdale (Staffs) and Burslem Socs; Mem., Co-operative Union Central Exec., 1966–83, Vice-Chm., 1973–75; Vice-Chm., NW Sectional Bd, 1970–75; Director: CWS, 1970–83; Nat. Co-operative Chemists, 1973–83; Greater Manchester Independent Radio, 1973–83; Mem., Central Cttee, Internat. Co-operative Alliance, 1975–83; Mem. Council (rep. Co-operative Union), Retail Consortium, 1976–83. President, Co-operative Congress, 1979. *Recreations:* football, cricket. *Address:* Blue Seas, Cliff Road, Mousehole, Penzance, Cornwall TR19 6QT. *T:* Penzance (01736) 731330. *Club:* Bolitho's (St Just).

PERRY, family name of **Baroness Perry of Southwark** and **Baron Perry of Walton.**

PERRY OF SOUTHWARK, Baroness *cr* 1991 (Life Peer), of Charlbury in the County of Oxfordshire; **Pauline Perry;** President, Lucy Cavendish College, Cambridge University, since 1994; *b* 15 Oct. 1931; *d* of John George Embleton Welch and Elizabeth Welch; *m* 1952, George Walter Perry; three *s* one *d*. *Educ:* Girton Coll., Cambridge (MA). Teacher in English Secondary Sch., Canadian and American High Schs, 1953–54 and 1959–61; High School Evaluator, New England, USA, 1959–61; Research Fellow, Univ. of Manitoba, 1956–57; Lecturer in Philosophy: Univ. of Manitoba, 1957–59; Univ. of Massachusetts at Salem, 1960–62; Lectr in Education (part-time), Univ. of Exeter, 1962–66; Tutor for In-Service Trng, Berks, 1966–70; Part-time Lectr in Educn, Dept of Educational Studies, Oxford Univ., 1966–70; HM Inspector of Schools, 1970–86; Staff Inspector, 1975; Chief Inspector, 1981. Dir, S Bank Poly., 1987–92; Vice-Chancellor, S Bank Univ., 1992–93. Member: Cttee on Internat. Co-operation in Higher Educn, British Council, 1987–; ESRC, 1988–91; Governing Body, Institute of Develt Studies, Sussex Univ., 1987–94; Bd, South Bank Centre, 1992–94; NI Higher Educn Council, 1993–94; Nat. Adv. Council on Educn and Training Targets, 1993–95; Prime Minister's Adv. Panel on Citizen's Charter, 1993–; Overseas Project Bd, 1993–; H of L Select Cttee on Science and Technol., 1992–. Chm., DTI Export Gp for Educn and Trng Sector, 1993–; Member: Advr on Police Trng to Home Office, 1991–93. Rector's Warden, Southwark Cath., 1990–94. MInstD. Mem., Pedagogical Acad., Swedish Acad. of Sci., 1992. Mem. Court, Univ. of Bath, 1991–. Freeman, City of London, 1992. Liveryman, Bakers' Co., 1992. Hon. FCollP, 1987; Hon. FRSA, 1988. Hon. Fellow, Sunderland Polytechnic, 1990. Hon LLD: Bath, 1991; Aberdeen, 1994; Hon. DLitt: Sussex, 1992; South Bank, 1994; Surrey, 1995; Hon. DEd Wolverhampton, 1994. *Publications:* Case Studies in Teaching, 1969; Case Studies in Adolescence, 1970; Your Guide to the Opposite Sex, 1970; *contributions to:* Advances in Teacher Education, 1989; Women in Education Management, 1992; Public Accountability and Quality Control in Higher Education, 1990; The Future of Higher Education, 1991; What is Quality in Higher Education?, 1993; Education in the Age of Information, 1993; articles in various educnl jls; freelance journalism for radio and TV (incl. appearances on Question Time, Any Questions, Woman's Hour, Newsnight). *Recreations:* music, walking, cooking. *Address:* House of Lords, SW1A 0PW.

PERRY OF WALTON, Baron *cr* 1979 (Life Peer), of Walton, Bucks; **Walter Laing Macdonald Perry,** Kt 1974; OBE 1957; FRS 1985; FRSE 1960; Vice-Chancellor, The Open University, 1969–80, Fellow, since 1981; *b* 16 June 1921; *s* of Fletcher S. Perry and Flora M. Macdonald; *m* 1st, 1946, Anne Elizabeth Grant (marr. diss. 1971); three *s*; 2nd, 1971, Catherine Hilda Crawley; two *s* one *d*. *Educ:* Ayr Acad.; Dundee High Sch. MB, ChB 1943, MD 1948, DSc 1958 (University of St Andrews); MRCP (Edinburgh), 1963; FRCPE 1967; FRCP 1978; Fellow, UCL, 1981–. Medical Officer, Colonial Medical Service (Nigeria), 1944–46; Medical Officer, RAF, 1946–47; Member of Staff, Medical Research Council, 1947–52; Director, Department of Biological Standards, National Institute for Medical Research, 1952–58. Prof. of Pharmacology, University of Edinburgh, 1958–68, Vice-Principal, 1967–68. Member, British Pharmacopœia Commission, 1952–68; Secretary, British Pharmacological Society, 1957–61. Chairman: Community Radio Milton Keynes, 1979–82; Living Tapes Ltd, 1980–; Videotel Marine Internat., 1985–. Chairman: Research Defence Soc., 1979–82 (Pres., 1993–); Delegacy of Goldsmiths' Coll., 1981–84; Standing Cttee on Continuing Educn, UGC and Nat. Adv. Body for Public Sector Higher Educn, 1985–89. Dep. Leader, SDP peers in House of Lords, 1981–83, 1988–89. Hon. DSc Bradford, 1974; Hon. LLD Dundee, 1975; Hon.

DHL: Maryland, 1978; State Univ. of NY, 1982; DUniv: Athabasca, 1979; Stirling, 1980; Open, 1981; Hon. DLitt: Deakin Univ., Australia, 1981; Andhra Pradesh Open Univ., 1987; Hon. DEd Univ. of Victoria, 1992. Wellcome Gold Medal, 1994. *Publications:* Open University, 1976; papers in Journal of Physiology, British Journal of Pharmacology and Chemo-therapy, etc. *Recreations:* making music and playing games. *Address:* The Open University, 10 Drumsheugh Gardens, Edinburgh EH3 7QJ. *Clubs:* Savage; Scottish Arts (Edinburgh).

PERRY, Alan Joseph; Director, Whitehall Strategic Management Consultants Ltd, since 1992; *b* 17 Jan. 1930; *s* of late Joseph and Elsie Perry; *m* 1961, Vivien Anne Ball; two *s*. *Educ:* John Bright Grammar Sch., Llandudno; Dartford Grammar Sch. Served RE, 1948–50. HM Treasury, 1951–68 and 1970–78; CSD, 1968–70; Principal 1968, Asst Sec. 1976; Counsellor (Economic), Washington, 1978–80; Asst Sec., HM Treasury, 1980–86; Advr on Govt Affairs, Ernst & Whinney, 1986–88; Dir, Public Sector Services, Ernst & Young, 1989–92. Chm., Review of BBC External Services, 1984.

PERRY, Charles Bruce; Professor of Medicine, University of Bristol, 1935–69, Emeritus since 1969; *b* 1903; *s* of Charles E. and Sarah Duthie Perry; *m* 1929, Mildred Bernice Harvey; three *d*. *Educ:* Bristol Grammar Sch.; University of Bristol, MB, ChB 1926, MD 1928; FRCP, 1936. Physician, Bristol Royal Hospital for Sick Children and Women, 1928; Physician, Winford Orthopædic Hospital, 1930; Buckston Browne Prize, Harveian Society of London, 1929; Markham Skeritt Memorial Prize, 1931; Asst Physician, Bristol General Hospital, 1933. Lectures: Long Fox Memorial, 1943; Bradshaw, RCP, 1944; Lumleian, RCP, 1969; Carey Coombs, Univ. of Bristol, 1969; Cyril Fernando Meml, Ceylon, 1971. Pro-Vice-Chancellor, University of Bristol, 1958–61 (Hon. Fellow, 1986); President Assoc. of Physicians of Great Britain and Ireland, 1961–62; Chairman, British Cardiac Society, 1961–62; Censor, RCP, 1962–64; Medical Mem., Pensions Appeals Tribunals, 1969–79; Trustee, Jenner Appeal, 1982–. *Publications:* Bacterial Endocarditis, 1936; The Bristol Royal Infirmary 1904–1974, 1981; The Voluntary Medical Institutions of Bristol, 1984; The Bristol Medical School, 1984; Edward Jenner, 1986; various papers in the Medical Press dealing with research in Diseases of the Heart. *Address:* Beechfield, 54 Grove Road, Coombe Dingle, Bristol BS9 2RR. *T:* Bristol (0117) 968 2713.

PERRY, David Gordon; Chairman, John Waddington plc, since 1993 (Chief Executive, 1988–92); *b* 26 Dec. 1937; *s* of late Elliott Gordon Perry and Lois Evelyn Perry; *m* 1961, Dorne Mary Busby; four *d*. *Educ:* Clifton Coll.; Christ's Coll., Cambridge. Management Trainee and Sales Exec., ES&A Robinson Ltd, 1960–66; Sales Dir 1966–69, Man. Dir 1969–78, Fell & Briant Ltd (subsid. of British Printing Corp.); British Printing Corporation: Chm. and Chief Exec., Packaging Div., 1978–80; Dir, 1980–81; John Waddington plc: Dep. Man. Dir, 1981–82; Man. Dir, 1982–88; Non-Executive Director: Whitecroft plc, 1991–; Dewhirst Gp plc, 1992–; National & Provincial Building Soc., 1993–. CIMgt (CBIM 1985). FRSA 1990. *Recreation:* Rugby football (Cambridge Blue 1958, England XV 1963–66, Captain 1965). *Address:* Deighton House, Deighton, near Escrick, York YO4 6HQ. *Club:* United Oxford & Cambridge University.

PERRY, Sir David (Howard), KCB 1986; Chief of Defence Equipment Collaboration, Ministry of Defence, 1985–87, retired; *b* 13 April 1931; *s* of Howard Dace Perry and Annie Evelyn Perry; *m* 1961, Rosemary Grigg; one *s* two *d*. *Educ:* Berkhamsted Sch.; Pembroke Coll., Cambridge (MA). CEng, FRAeS. Joined Aero Dept, RAE, 1954; Aero Flt Div., 1954–66; Aero Projs Div., 1966–71; Head of Dynamics Div., 1971–73; RCDS, 1974; Head of Systems Assessment Dept, RAE, 1975–77; Ministry of Defence (Procurement Executive): Dir-Gen. Future Projects, 1978–80; Dir-Gen. Aircraft 1, 1980–81; Dep. Controller of Aircraft, 1981–82, Controller of Aircraft 1982; Chief of Defence Procurement, 1983–85. *Recreations:* gardening, painting. *Address:* 23 Rectory Road, Farnborough, Hants GU14 7BU.

PERRY, Sir David Norman; *see* Perry, Sir Norman.

PERRY, Ernest George; *b* 25 April 1908; British; *m* 1950, Edna Joyce Perks-Mankelow; one *s*. *Educ:* LCC secondary school. Textiles, 1923–33; Insurance, 1933–64. Member Battersea Borough Council, 1934–65 (Mayor of Battersea, 1955–56); Alderman, London Borough of Wandsworth, 1964–72. MP (Lab) Battersea S, 1964–74, Wandsworth, Battersea S, 1974–79; Asst Govt Whip, 1968–69; Lord Commissioner, HM Treasury, 1969–70; an Opposition Whip, 1970–74; an Asst Govt Whip, 1974–75. Served with Royal Artillery, 1939–46: Indian Army and Indian Artillery (Troop Sgt); Far East, 1942–45. *Recreations:* local government, sport, reading. *Address:* 6 Brinkley Road, Worcester Park, Surrey KT4 8JF. *T:* 0181–337 4679.

PERRY, George Henry; b 24 Aug. 1920; *s* of Arthur and Elizabeth Perry; *m* 1944, Ida Garner; two *d*. *Educ:* elementary sch. and technical college. Engineering Apprentice, 1934–41. Naval Artificer, 1941–46 (Atlantic and Italy Stars; 1939–45 Star). Railway Fitter, 1946–66. Derby Town Councillor, 1955–66. Chairman: Derby Water Cttee, 1957–61; S Derbys Water Board, 1961–66; Derby Labour Party, 1961–62; Secretary, Derby Trades Council, 1961–66. Contested (Lab) Harborough, 1964; MP (Lab) Nottingham South, 1966–70. *Recreation:* walking. *Address:* 123 Hawthorn Street, Derby DE2 8BB. *T:* Derby (01332) 44687.

PERRY, John; *see* Perry, R. J.

PERRY, Rt. Rev. John Freeman; *see* Southampton, Bishop Suffragan of.

PERRY, Rev. John Neville; *b* 29 March 1920; *s* of Robert and Enid Perry; *m* 1946, Rita Dyson Rooke; four *s* four *d*. *Educ:* The Crypt Gram. Sch., Gloucester; Univ. of Leeds (BA 1941), College of the Resurrection, Mirfield. Asst Curate, All Saints', Poplar, 1943–50; Vicar, St Peter De Beauvoir Town, Hackney, 1950–63, Vicar, St Dunstan with St Catherine, Feltham, Mddx, 1963–75; Rural Dean of Hounslow, 1967–75; Archdeacon of Middlesex, 1975–82; Rector of Orlestone with Ruckinge and Warehorne, Kent, 1982–86. Mem. Latey Cttee on the Age of Majority, 1966–67. *Recreation:* relief wood carving. *Address:* 73 Elizabeth Crescent, East Grinstead, West Sussex RH19 3JG.

PERRY, John William; Chairman and Managing Director, Unisys, 1987–94; *b* 23 Sept. 1938; *s* of John and Cecilia Perry; *m* 1961, Gillian Margaret; two *d*. *Educ:* Wallington Grammar Sch.; Brasenose Coll., Oxford (MA). Burroughs: Dir of Marketing, UK, 1967–71, Europe Africa Div., 1977–78; Group Dir, Internat. Marketing, 1978–80; Vice-President: Strategic Planning, 1981; Financial Systems Gp., 1983; Central USA, 1985–86; Man. Dir, Burroughs UK, 1986; Corporate Officer, Unisys Corp., 1990. Director: Sperry; Burroughs Machines; BMX Information Systems; BMX Holdings; Unisys Holdings; Convergent Technologies (UK); non-exec. Dir, Trace Computers, 1994–. Trustee, Information Age Project, 1989. Mem., Bd of Governors, Polytechnic of East London, 1989. *Recreations:* gardening, golf, reading, music. *Address:* The Great Barn, Sandpit Lane, Bledlow, Bucks HP27 9QQ.

PERRY, Rev. Canon Michael Charles, MA; Canon Residentiary, since 1970 and Sub-Dean, since 1985, Durham Cathedral; Senior Chaplain to the Bishop of Durham, since 1993; *b* 5 June 1933; *o s* of late Charlie Perry; *m* 1963, Margaret, *o d* of late John Middleton Adshead; two *s* one *d*. *Educ:* Ashby-de-la-Zouch Boys' Grammar Sch.; Trinity Coll., Cambridge (Sen. Schol.); Westcott House, Cambridge. Asst Curate of Berkswich, Stafford, 1958–60; Chaplain, Ripon Hall, Oxford, 1961–63; Chief Asst for Home Publishing, SPCK, 1963–70; Archdeacon of Durham, 1970–93. Examining Chaplain to Bishop of Lichfield, 1965–74. Sec., Archbishops' Commn on Christian Doctrine, 1967–70. Diocesan Chm., 1970–81, Mem. Council, 1975–81, USPG; Mem., 1981–88, Vice-Chm., 1982–88, Hosp. Chaplaincies Council, Gen. Synod; Mem. Council for the Deaf, Gen. Synod, 1986–90. Mem., Durham HA, 1982–88. Trustee, 1970–May 1996, Chm., 1982–May 1996, Lord Crewe's Charity; Chm., Churches' Fellowship for Psychical and Spiritual Studies, 1986–95. Lectures: Selwyn, NZ, 1976; Marshall Meml, Melbourne, 1976; Beard Meml, London, 1977; Maurice Elliott Meml, London, 1986; Shepherd Meml, Worcester, 1988. Editor, Church Quarterly, 1968–71; Editor, Christian Parapsychologist, 1977–. *Publications:* The Easter Enigma, 1959; The Pattern of Matins and Evensong, 1961; (co-author) The Churchman's Companion, 1963; Meet the Prayer Book, 1963; (contrib.) The Miracles and the Resurrection, 1964; (ed) Crisis for Confirmation, 1967; (co-author) Declaring The Faith: The Printed Word, 1969; Sharing in One Bread, 1973; The Resurrection of Man, 1975; The Paradox of Worship, 1977; A Handbook of Parish Worship, 1977, 2nd edn 1989; (contrib.) Yes to Women Priests, 1978; (co-author) A Handbook of Parish Finance, 1981, 3rd edn 1992; Psychic Studies: a Christian's view, 1984; Miracles Then and Now, 1986; (ed) Deliverance, 1987, 2nd edn 1996; Gods Within: a critical guide to the New Age, 1992. *Address:* 7 The College, Durham DH1 3EQ. *T:* Durham (0191) 3861891.

PERRY, Sir Michael (Sydney), Kt 1994; CBE 1990 (OBE 1978); Chairman, Unilever plc, since 1992; Vice Chairman, Unilever NV, since 1992; *b* 26 Feb. 1934; *s* of Sydney Albert Perry and Jessie Kate (*née* Brooker); *m* 1958, Joan Mary Stallard; one *s* two *d*. *Educ:* King William's Coll., IoM; St John's Coll., Oxford (MA). Unilever, 1957–: Chm., Lever Brothers (Thailand) Ltd, 1973–77; Pres., Lever y Asociados SACIF, Argentina, 1977–81; Chm., Nippon Lever KK, 1981–83; Jt Man. Dir, UAC Internat., 1983–85, Chm., 1985–87; Dir, Unilever plc and Unilever NV, 1985–; Personal Products Co-ordinator, 1987–91; Vice-Chm., Unilever plc, 1991–92; Non-executive Director: Bass plc, 1991–; British Gas plc, 1994–. Mem., BOTB, 1986–92; Jt Chm., Netherlands British Chamber of Commerce, 1989–93; Chairman: Japan Trade Gp, 1991–; Sen. Salaries Rev. Body, 1995–. Member: Council, Prince's Youth Business Trust, 1992–; CBI President's Cttee, 1993–; Council, BESO, 1993–; Governing Body, ICC UK, 1993–. Pres., Advertising Assoc., 1993–. Vice-Pres., Liverpool Sch. of Trop. Med., 1991–; Mem. Council, Atlantic Coll., 1993–. Chm., Shakespeare Globe Trust, 1993–. Trustee, Leverhulme Trust, 1991–. CIMgt (CBIM 1992). FRSA 1992. *Recreations:* music (choral), walking. *Address:* Unilever House, Blackfriars, EC4P 4BQ. *T:* 0171–822 5879. *Clubs:* Oriental; Worcestershire Golf.

PERRY, Sir Norman, Kt 1977; MBE; retired. Knighthood awarded for services to the community and the Maori people, New Zealand. *Address:* Waiotahi, Opotiki, New Zealand.

PERRY, Norman Henry, PhD; Chief Executive and Policy Co-ordinator, Wolverhampton Metropolitan Borough Council, since 1990; *b* 5 March 1944; *s* of late Charles and Josephine Perry; *m* 1970, Barbara Ann Marsden; two *s*. *Educ:* Quintin Sch., NW8; University Coll. London (BA 1965; PhD 1969). Lectr in Geography, UCL, 1965–69; Sen. Res. Officer, GLC, 1969–73; Sen. Res. Fellow, SSRC Survey Unit, 1973–75; joined DoE, 1975; Principal, London and Birmingham, 1975–80; Asst Sec., W Midlands Regl Office, 1980–86; Head of Inner Cities Unit (G4), Dept of Employment, then DTI, 1986–88; Under Sec., and Dir W Midlands, DTI, 1988–90. Dir, Wolverhampton TEC, 1990–; Gov., Univ. of Wolverhampton, 1993–. *Publications:* (contrib.) European Glossary of Legal and Administrative Terminology, 1974, 1979, 1988; contribs to books and learned jls in fields of geography, planning, organisational sociology and urban policy. *Address:* Civic Centre, St Peter's Square, Wolverhampton WV1 1SH. *T:* Wolverhampton (01902) 314000. *Club:* Arden (Solihull).

PERRY, Prof. Roger, FEng 1994; FRSC; Professor of Environmental Control and Waste Management (formerly of Public Health and Water Technology), Imperial College of Science, Technology and Medicine, since 1981; Director, Centre for Environmental Control and Waste Management (formerly for Toxic Waste Management), since 1990; *b* 21 June 1940; *s* of Charles William and Gladys Perry; *m* (marr. diss.); one *s* one *d*. *Educ:* King Edward's Grammar Sch., Birmingham; Univ. of Birmingham (BSc, PhD); DSc London 1992. FRSH, FIWEM, FICE. Held number of industrial appts in chem. industry until 1964; Depts of Chemistry and Chem. Engineering, Univ. of Birmingham, 1964–70; Mem., academic staff, Imperial Coll., 1970–. Cons. to number of major chemical and engrg based industries and govt depts, UK and overseas, also to UNEP and WHO, resulting in involvement in major environmental projects in some 30 countries. Mem., Univ. of London Senate and Academic Council, 1984–. *Publications:* Handbook of Air Pollution Analysis (ed jtly with R. Young), 1977, 2nd edn (ed jtly with R. M. Harrison), 1986; approx. 200 papers in various scientific jls. *Recreations:* travel, gardening, cooking, building. *Address:* Imperial College of Science, Technology and Medicine, Centre for Environmental Control and Waste Management, South Kensington, SW7 2BU. *T:* 0171–589 5111. *Club:* Athenæum.

PERRY, Roy James; Member (C) Wight and Hampshire South, European Parliament, since 1994; *b* 12 Feb. 1943; *s* of George and Dora Perry; *m* 1968, Veronica Haswell; two *d*. *Educ:* Tottenham County Grammar Sch.; Exeter Univ. Marks & Spencer, 1964–66; Lectr in Govt and Politics, 1966–75, Sen. Lectr, 1975–94, Southampton Tech. Coll. Leader, Test Valley Borough Council, 1985–94. *Recreations:* bridge, keep fit, French travel and food. *Address:* Tarrants Farm House, Maurys Lane, Wellow, Romsey, Hants SO51 6DA. *Club:* Royal Naval and Royal Albert Yacht.

PERRY, (Rudolph) John; QC 1989; a Recorder, since 1992; *b* 20 Feb. 1936; *s* of Rudolph Perry and Beatrice (*née* Tingling, now Robertson); *m* (marr. diss.); one *d*. *Educ:* Ruseas High Sch., Lucea, Jamaica; Southgate Technical Coll.; London Sch. of Economics (LLB (Hons), LLM); Univ. of Warwick (MA (Industrial Relations)). Lectr (part-time), LSE, 1970–78; Lectr, 1971, Sen. Lectr, 1974–78, City of London Poly. Called to the Bar, Middle Temple, 1975; in practice, 1976–; an Asst Recorder, 1988. *Recreations:* watching cricket, travel, cinema. *Address:* 3 Gray's Inn Square, Gray's Inn, WC1R 5AH. *T:* 0171–831 2311.

PERRY, Prof. Samuel Victor, BSc (Liverpool), PhD, ScD (Cantab); FRS 1974; Professor of Biochemistry, 1959–85, now Emeritus, and Head of Department of Biochemistry, 1968–85, University of Birmingham; *b* 16 July 1918; *s* of late Samuel and Margaret Perry; *m* 1948, Maureen Tregent Shaw; one *s* two *d*. *Educ:* King George V Sch., Southport; Liverpool Univ.; Trinity Coll., Cambridge. Served in War of 1939–45, home and N. Africa; Royal Artillery, 1940–46, Captain; POW 1942–45. Research Fellow, Trinity Coll., Cambridge, 1947–51; Commonwealth Fund Fellow, University of Rochester, USA, 1948–49; University Lecturer, Dept of Biochemistry, Cambridge, 1950–59. Member: Standing Cttee for Research on Animals, ARC, 1965–72; Biol Scis and Enzyme Cttees, SRC, 1968–71; Medical Res. Cttee, Muscular Dystrophy Gp of GB, 1970–90;

Systems Bd, MRC, 1974–77; Research Funds Cttee, British Heart Foundn, 1974–82; British Nat. Cttee for Biochemistry, 1978–87 (Chm., 1982–87); Council, Royal Soc., 1986–88; Chairman: Cttee of Biochemical Soc., 1980–83; Adv. Bd, Meat Res. Inst., 1980–85. Croonian Lectr, Royal Soc., 1984. FAAAS 1987. Hon. Mem., Amer. Soc. of Biol Chemists, 1978; Corresponding Mem., Société Royale des Sciences, Liège, 1978; Mem., Accad. Virgiliana, Mantova, 1979; Foreign Mem., Accademia Nazionale dei Lincei, 1989. CIBA Medal, Biochemical Soc., 1977. *Publications:* scientific papers in Biochemical Journal, Nature, Biochemica Biophysica Acta, etc. *Recreations:* gardening, building stone walls, Rugby football (Cambridge, 1946, 1947, England, 1947, 1948). *Address:* 41 Selly Wick Drive, Selly Park, Birmingham B29 7JQ. *T:* 0121–472 2100.

PERRY, William Arthur; Command Secretary (Adjutant General, Personnel and Training Command), Ministry of Defence, since 1994; *b* 5 Aug. 1937; *s* of Arthur Perry and Elizabeth Grace (*née* Geller); *m* 1962, Anne Rosemary Dight; two *d. Educ:* St Dunstan's Coll. Min. of Aviation, 1960–61; Second Sec. (Defence Supply), Bonn, 1964–66; Min. of Technology, then MoD, 1966–74; First Sec., UK Delegn to NATO, 1974–77; Head, Defence Secretariat 8, MoD, 1978–80; Counsellor (Defence Supply), Bonn, 1980–84; Regl Marketing Dir, Defence Exports Services Orgn, 1984–88; Asst Sec., MoD (PE), 1988–92; Dir (Finance and Secretariat), Air 1, MoD (PE), 1992–94. Mem., Royal Patriotic Fund Corp., 1994–. *Recreations:* opera, gardening, genealogy. *Address:* c/o Ministry of Defence, Trenchard Lines, Upavon, Pewsey, Wilts SN9 6BE.

PERRY, Dr William James; Secretary of Defense, United States of America, since 1994; *b* Pa, 11 Oct. 1927; *m* Lee; three *s* two *d. Educ:* Butler High Sch., Butler, Pa; Carnegie Tech.; Stanford Univ. (BS Maths, MS); Penn State Univ. (PhD Maths). Served US Army: Fort Belvoir, Japan and Okinawa, 1946–47; Army Reserves, 1950–55. Dir, Electronic Defense Labs, Sylvania/General Telephone; Exec. Vice Pres., Hambrecht and Quist Inc.; Founder, ESL Inc., 1964, Pres., 1964–77; Under-Sec. of Defense for Res. and Engrg, 1977–81; Stanford University: Prof., Sch. of Engrg; Co-Dir, Center for Internat. Security and Arms Control; Chm., Technol. Strategies & Alliances; Dep. Sec. of Defense, 1993–94. Member: President's Foreign Intelligence Adv. Bd; Tech. Rev. Panel, Senate Select Cttee on Intelligence; Carnegie Commn on Sci., Technol. and Govt; Cttee on Internat. Security and Arms Control, NAS. Mem., Nat. Acad. Engrg; Fellow, Amer. Acad. Arts and Scis. Distinguished Public Service Medal, Dept of Defense, 1980 and 1981; Distinguished Service Medal, NASA, 1981; Medal of Achievement, Amer. Electronics Assoc., 1980. *Address:* Office of the Secretary of Defense, Washington, DC 20301, USA.

PERRYMAN, (Francis) Douglas; Director, Homes Assured Corporation, 1989–90; *b* 23 April 1930; *s* of Frank Smyth Perryman and Caroline Mary Anderson; *m* 1955, Margaret Mary Lamb; two *d. Educ:* West Hartlepool Grammar School; Durham Univ. BCom (Hons); FCA. Articled Clerk, 1951–55; Nat. Service, commnd RAPC, 1955–57; National Coal Board: Area Chief Accountant, Fife and Scottish South Areas, 1963–72; Finance Dir, Opencast Exec., 1972; Dir Gen. of Finance, 1978–81; Board Mem. for Finance, PO, 1981; Bd Mem., then Corporate Dir, for Finance, 1981–86, Corporate Commercial Dir, 1986–88, BT. Mem. Council, CBI, 1987–88. *Recreations:* golf, Rugby football, music, Francophile. *Address:* Long Mynd, 69 Copperkins Lane, Amersham, Bucks HP6 5RA. *T:* Amersham (01494) 721611.

PERSSON, Rt. Rev. William Michael Dermot; Suffragan Bishop of Doncaster, 1982–92; an Assistant Bishop, diocese of Bath and Wells, since 1994; *b* 27 Sept. 1927; *s* of Leslie Charles Grenville Alan and Elizabeth Mercer Persson; *m* 1957, Ann Davey; two *s* one *d. Educ:* Monkton Combe School; Oriel Coll., Oxford (MA); Wycliffe Hall Theological Coll. National service, Army, 1945–48; commissioned, Royal Signals. Deacon 1953, priest 1954; Curate: Emmanuel, South Croydon, 1953–55; St John, Tunbridge Wells, 1955–58; Vicar, Christ Church, Barnet, 1958–67; Rector, Bebington, Cheshire, 1967–79; Vicar, Knutsford with Toft, 1979–82. General Synod: Mem., House of Clergy, 1975–82, House of Bishops, 1985–92; Chm., Council for Christian Unity, 1991–92. *Recreations:* gardening, writing poetry. *Address:* Ryall's Cottage, Burton Street, Marnhull, Sturminster Newton, Dorset DT10 1PS.

PERT, Prof. Geoffrey James, PhD; FRS 1995; FInstP; Professor of Computational Physics, University of York, since 1987; *b* 15 Aug. 1941; *s* of Norman James Pert and Grace Winifred Pert (*née* Barnes); *m* 1987, Janice Ann Alexander; one *d. Educ:* Norwich Sch.; Imperial Coll., Univ. of London (BSc; PhD 1967). FInstP 1979. University of Alberta: Fellow, 1967–68; Asst Prof., 1968–69; Associate Prof., 1969–70; University of Hull: Lectr, 1970–74; Sen. Lectr, 1974–78; Reader, 1978–82; Prof., 1982–87. *Publications:* papers in learned scientific jls. *Recreations:* hill-walking, gardening. *Address:* Department of Physics, University of York, Heslington, York YO1 5DD. *T:* York (01904) 432250.

PERT, Michael; QC 1992; a Recorder, since 1988; *b* 17 May 1947; *s* of Lieut Henry McKay Pert (RN, retd) and Noreen (*née* Murphy); *m* 1971, Vivien Victoria Braithwaite (marr. diss. 1993); one *s* two *d. Educ:* St Boniface's Coll., Plymouth; Manchester Univ. (LLB Hons). Called to the Bar, Gray's Inn, 1970. *Recreations:* beekeeping, sailing. *Address:* 1 King's Bench Walk, Temple, EC4Y 7DB. *T:* 0171–353 8436.

PERTH, 17th Earl of, *cr* 1605; **John David Drummond,** PC 1957; Baron Drummond of Cargill, 1488; Baron Maderty, 1609; Baron Drummond, 1686; Lord Drummond of Gilston, 1685; Lord Drummond of Rickertoun and Castlemaine, 1686; Viscount Strathallan, 1686; Hereditary Thane of Lennox, and Hereditary Steward of Menteith and Strathearn; Representative Peer for Scotland, 1952–63; First Crown Estate Commissioner, 1962–77; Chairman, Ditchley Foundation, 1963–66; *b* 13 May 1907; *o s* of 16th Earl of Perth, PC, GCMG, CB, and Hon. Angela Constable-Maxwell (*d* 1965), *y d* of 11th Baron Herries; *S* father 1951; *m* 1934, Nancy Seymour, *d* of Reginald Fincke, New York City; two *s. Educ:* Downside; Cambridge Univ. Lieut, Intelligence Corps, 1940; seconded to War Cabinet Offices, 1942–43, Ministry of Production, 1944–45; Minister of State for Colonial Affairs, 1957–62 (resigned). Chm., Reviewing Cttee on Export of Works of Art, 1972–76. Member: Court of St Andrews Univ., 1967–86; Adv. Council, V&A Museum, 1971–72; Trustee, Nat. Library of Scotland, 1968–. Hon. FRIBA 1978; Hon. FRIAS 1988; Hon. FSA 1994. Hon. LLD St Andrews, 1986. *Heir: s* Viscount Strathallan, *qv. Address:* 14 Hyde Park Gardens Mews, W2 2NU. *T:* 0171–262 4667; Stobhall, by Perth PH2 6DR.

PERTH (Australia), Archbishop of, and Metropolitan of Western Australia, since 1981; **Most Rev. Peter Frederick Carnley;** *b* 17 Oct. 1937; *s* of Frederick Carnley and Gweyenneth Lilian Carnley (*née* Read); *m* 1966, Carol Ann Dunstan; one *s* one *d. Educ:* St John's Coll., Morpeth, NSW (ThL 1st Cl., ACT, 1962); Univ. of Melbourne (BA, 1st Cl. Hons, 1966); Univ. of Cambridge (PhD 1969). Deacon 1962, priest 1964, Bath; Licence to Officiate, dio. Melbourne, 1963–65; Asst Curate of Parkes, 1966; Licence to Officiate, dio. Ely, 1966–69; Chaplain, Mitchell Coll. of Advanced Education, Bath, 1970–72; Research Fellow, St John's Coll., Cambridge, 1971–72; Warden, St John's College, St Lucia, Queensland, 1972–81; Residentiary Canon, St John's Cathedral, Brisbane, 1975–81; Examining Chaplain to Archbishop of Brisbane, 1975–81. DD *hc* Gen. Theological Seminary, NY, 1984. ChStJ 1982 (Sub Prelate, 1991). *Publications:* The Poverty of Historical Scepticism, in Christ, Faith and History (ed S. W. Sykes and J. P. Clayton), 1972; The Structure of Resurrection Belief, 1987. *Recreations:* gardening, swimming. *Address:* 52 Mount Street, Perth, WA 6000, Australia. *T:* (home) (9) 3221253; (office) (9) 3257455. *Clubs:* Western Australian (Perth); St John's (Brisbane).

PERTH (Australia), Archbishop of, (RC), since 1991; **Most Rev. Barry James Hickey;** *b* 16 April 1936; *s* of G. Hickey. *Educ:* Christian Brothers Coll., WA; St Charles Seminary, WA; Propaganda Fide Coll., Rome; Univ. of WA. Dir, Centacare, Perth (Catholic Family Welfare), 1972–82; Episcopal Vicar for Social Welfare, 1982–84; Parish Priest of Highgate, WA, 1983–84; Bishop of Geraldton, WA, 1984–91. Mem., Bd of Inst. of Family Studies, Melbourne, 1980–83; Chm., Australian Catholic Social Welfare Commn, 1984. *Recreations:* tennis, walking. *Address:* Archbishop's House, Victoria Square, Perth, WA 6000, Australia.

PERTH (Australia), Assistant Bishop of; *see* Farran, Rt Rev. B. G.; Murray, Rt Rev. D. O.

PERTH, (St Ninian's Cathedral), Provost of; *see* Franz, Very Rev. K. G.

PERUTZ, Max Ferdinand, OM 1988; CH 1975; CBE 1963; PhD; FRS 1954; Member, scientific staff, Medical Research Council Laboratory of Molecular Biology, 1979– (Chairman, 1962–79); *b* 19 May 1914; *s* of Hugo and Adèle Perutz; *m* 1942, Gisela Peiser; one *s* one *d. Educ:* Theresianum, Vienna; Univ. of Vienna; Univ. of Cambridge (PhD 1940). Hon. Fellow: Peterhouse, Cambridge, 1962; Darwin Coll., Cambridge, 1984. Dir, MRC Unit for Molecular Biology, 1947–62; Chm., European Molecular Biology Orgn, 1963–69. Reader, Davy Faraday Res. Lab., 1954–68, and Fullerian Prof. of Physiology, 1973–79, Royal Instn. Hon. FRSE, 1976; Hon. FRCP 1993; Hon. Member American Academy of Arts and Sciences, 1963; Corresp. Member, Austrian Acad. of Sciences, 1963; Mem., Akademie Leopoldina, Halle, 1964; Foreign Member: American Philosophical Society, 1968; Royal Netherlands Acad., 1972; French Acad. of Sciences, 1976; Bavarian Acad. of Sciences, 1983; National Acad. of Sciences, Rome, 1983; Accademia dei Lincei, Rome, 1984; Acad. of Science of DDR, 1985; For. Associate, Nat. Acad. of Sciences, USA, 1970; Mem., Pontifical Acad. of Sciences, Rome, 1981. Hon. degrees: in philosophy: Vienna, 1965; Salzburg, 1972; in science: Edinburgh, 1965; East Anglia, 1967; Cambridge, 1981; York, 1990; Oxford, 1993; Paris, 1993; in medicine, Rome, 1988. Nobel Prize for Chemistry (jointly), 1962; Ehrenzeichen für Wissenschaft und Kunst (Austria), 1966; Royal Medal, 1971, Copley Medal, 1979, Royal Soc. Actonian Prize, Royal Instn, 1984. Pour le Mérite, FRG, 1988. *Publications:* Proteins and Nucleic Acids, Structure and Function, 1962; (jtly) Atlas of Haemoglobin and Myoglobin, 1981; Is Science Necessary?, 1988; Mechanisms of Co-operativity and Allosteric Control in Proteins, 1990; Protein Structures: new approaches to disease and therapy, 1992. *Address:* 42 Sedley Taylor Road, Cambridge CB2 2PN; Laboratory of Molecular Biology, Hills Road, Cambridge CB2 2QH.

PERY, family name of **Earl of Limerick.**

PESARAN, Prof. (Mohammad) Hashem, PhD; Professor of Economics, Cambridge University, and Fellow of Trinity College, Cambridge, since 1988; *b* 30 March 1946; *s* of Jamal and Effat Pesaran; *m* 1969, Marion Fay Swainston; three *s* two *d. Educ:* Salford Univ. (BSc 1968); Cambridge Univ. (PhD 1972). Jun. Res. Officer, Dept of Applied Econs, Cambridge Univ., and Lektor, Trinity Coll., Cambridge, 1971–73; Asst to Vice-Governor, 1973–74, and Head of Econ. Res. Dept, 1974–76, Central Bank of Iran; Under-Sec., Min. of Educn, Iran, 1977–78; Teaching Fellow, and Dir of Studies in Econs, Trinity Coll., Cambridge, 1979–88; Lectr in Econs, 1979–85, and Reader in Econs, 1985–88, Cambridge Univ. Prof. of Econs, and Dir, Program in Applied Econometrics, UCLA, 1989–93. Visiting Lecturer: Harvard Univ., 1982; Dutch Network for Quantitative Econs, Groningen, 1985; Vis. Fellow, ANU, 1984 and 1988; Visiting Professor: Univ. of Rome, 1986; Univ. of Calif, LA, 1987–88; Univ. of Pennsylvania, 1993. Mem., HM Treasury Academic Panel, 1993–; Outside Mem., Meteorol Office, 1994–. Mem. Adv. Bd, and Res. Fellow, Econ. Res. Forum of Arab Countries, Iran and Turkey, 1993–. Fellow, Econometric Soc., 1990. Founding Ed., Jl of Applied Econometrics, 1985–. Hon. DLitt Salford, 1993. *Publications:* World Economic Prospects and the Iranian Economy—a short term view, 1974 (also Persian); (with L. J. Slater) Dynamic Regression: theory and algorithms, 1980 (trans. Russian, 1984); (ed with T. Lawson) Keynes' Economics: methodological issues, 1985; The Limits to Rational Expectations, 1987; (with B. Pesaran) Data–FIT: an interactive software econometric package, 1987 (paperback edn, as Microfit, 1989); (ed with T. Barker) Disaggregation in Economic Modelling, 1990; (with B. Pesaran) Microfit 3.0, 1991; (ed with S. Potter) Non-Linear Dynamics, Chaos and Econometrics, 1993; scientific papers in econ. and econometric jls. *Recreations:* basketball (half-blue, Cambridge University), squash, swimming. *Address:* Trinity College, Cambridge CB2 1TQ; 283 Hills Road, Cambridge CB2 2RP. *T:* Cambridge (01223) 335216.

PESCOD, Prof. Mainwaring Bainbridge, OBE 1977; CEng, FICE, FCIWEM; Tyne and Wear Professor of Environmental Control Engineering, since 1976, and Head of Department of Civil Engineering, since 1983, University of Newcastle upon Tyne; *b* 6 Jan. 1933; *s* of Bainbridge and Elizabeth Pescod; *m* 1957, Mary Lorenza (*née* Coyle); two *s. Educ:* Stanley Grammar Sch., Co. Durham; King's Coll., Univ. of Durham (BSc); MIT (SM). CEng 1973, FICE 1980; FIWEM 1987 (FIPHE 1971; FIWES 1983; MIWPC 1967); MRSH 1964; MInstWM 1985. Lectr in Engrg, Fourah Bay Coll, Freetown, Sierra Leone, 1957–61; Asst Engr, Babtie, Shaw & Morton, CCE, Glasgow, 1961–64; Asst and Associate Prof. of Environmental Engrg, 1964–72, Prof. and Head of Div. of Environmental Engrg, 1972–76, Asian Inst. of Technol., Bangkok, Thailand. Mem., Northumbrian Water Authority, 1986–89; Director: Northumbrian Water Group, 1989–; Motherwell Bridge Envirotec, 1991–; Chm. and Man. Dir, Envmtl Technology Consultants, 1988–. *Publications:* (ed with D. A. Okun) Water Supply and Wastewater Disposal in Developing Countries, 1971; (ed. with A. Arar) Treatment and Use of Sewage Effluent for Irrigation, 1988; (ed) Urban Solid Waste Management, 1991; pubns on water supply, wastewater treatment, environmental pollution control and management in learned jls and conf. proc. *Recreations:* squash, reading, advisory assignments in developing countries. *Address:* Tall Trees, High Horse Close Wood, Rowlands Gill, Tyne and Wear NE39 1AN. *T:* Rowlands Gill (01207) 542104. *Clubs:* British, Royal Bangkok Sports (Bangkok, Thailand).

PEŠEK, Libor; Music Director, Royal Liverpool Philharmonic Society and Orchestra, since 1987; *b* 22 June 1933. *Educ:* Academy of Musical Arts, Prague (studied conducting, piano, 'cello, trombone). Worked at Pilsen and Prague Opera Houses; Founder Director, Prague Chamber Harmony, 1958–64; Chief Conductor, Slovak Philharmonic, 1980–81; Conductor in residence, Czech Philharmonic, 1982– (tours and fests, Europe, Russia, Far East); guest conductor: Los Angeles Philharmonic, St Louis Symphony and other US orchestras; The Philharmonia, LSO, Orchestre Nat. de France, and other European orchestras; numerous recordings incl. much Czech repertoire. Pres., Prague Spring Fest. Hon. DMus Liverpool Polytechnic, 1989. *Recreations:* physics, Eastern philosophy and literature, particularly Kafka, Dostoyevsky and Tolstoy. *Address:* c/o IMG Artists (Europe), Media House, 3 Burlington Lane, W4 2TH.

PESKETT, Stanley Victor, MA; Principal, Royal Belfast Academical Institution, 1959–78; *b* 9 May 1918; *o s* of Sydney Timber and Mary Havard Peskett; *m* 1948, Prudence Eileen, OBE 1974, *o d* of C. R. A. and M. A. Goatly; two *s* one *d* (and one *d* decd). *Educ:* Whitgift Sch.; St Edmund Hall, Oxford. Served War, 1939–46 (despatches) in Royal Marines, Norway, Shetland, Normandy, India and Java; Lt-Col, 1944; two Admiralty awards for inventions. Senior English Master, 1946–59, Housemaster 1954–59, The Leys School. Mem. Cttee, Headmasters' Conf., 1976; Mem. Council, Headmasters' Assoc., and Pres., Ulster Headmasters' Assoc., 1973–75; Chm., Northern Ireland Cttee, Voluntary Service Overseas, 1969–78; Founder Pres., Irish Schools Swimming Assoc., 1968–69 (Chm., Ulster Branch, 1968–78); Chm., NI Branch, School Library Assoc., 1964–73; Governor, Belfast Sch. of Music, 1974–77; Mem. Adv. Council, UDR, 1975–78. *Publications:* The Metfield Clock, 1980; (contrib.) People, Poverty and Protest in Hoxne Hundred 1780–1880, 1982; Only For a Day, 1984; Our Names, 1985; Wheelock 'Founder of Medfield', 1992; Monumental Inscriptions, Metfield, Suffolk, 1992; Clark's Kin, 1995; articles in educational jls. *Address:* Huntsman and Hounds Cottage, Metfield, Harleston, Norfolk IP20 0LB. *T:* Fressingfield (01379) 586425.
See also R. W. Seymour.

PESKIN, Richard Martin; Chairman, since 1986, and Managing Director, since 1985, Great Portland Estates PLC; *b* 21 May 1944; *s* of Leslie and Hazel Peskin; *m* 1979, Penelope Howard Triebner; one *s* two *d*. *Educ:* Charterhouse; Queens' Coll., Cambridge (MA, LLM). Great Portland Estates, 1967–: Dir, 1968; Asst Man. Dir, 1972. FRSA 1989. CIMgt (CBIM 1989). *Recreations:* racing, golf. *Address:* 41 Circus Road, NW8 9JH. *T:* 0171–289 0492. *Clubs:* Royal Automobile; Wentworth Golf.

PESTELL; *see* Wells-Pestell.

PESTELL, Catherine Eva; *see* Hughes, C. E.

PESTELL, John Edmund; Partnership Secretary, Linklaters & Paines, 1990–94; *b* 8 Dec. 1930; *s* of late Edmund Pestell and Isabella (*née* Sangster); *m* 1958, Muriel Ada (*née* Whitby); three *s*. *Educ:* Roundhay Sch.; New Coll., Oxford (MA). National Service, 1949–50. Jt Intell. Bureau, 1953–57; Asst Principal, WO, 1957–60; Private Sec. to Parly Under Sec. of State for War, 1958–60; Principal, WO and MoD, 1960–70; Admin. Staff Coll., Henley, 1963; Private Sec. to Minister of Defence (Equipment), 1969–70; Asst Sec., MoD, 1970–72; Press Sec. (Co-ordination), Prime Minister's Office, 1972–74; Asst Sec., CSD, 1974–76, Under Sec., 1976–81; Under Sec., HM Treasury, 1981–84; Asst Under-Sec. of State, MoD, 1984–88; Resident Chm., CSSB, 1988–90. Mem., CS Pay Res. Unit Bd, 1978–80. Governor, Cranleigh Sch., 1975–. *Address:* New House, Bridge Road, Cranleigh, Surrey GU6 7HH. *T:* Cranleigh (01483) 273489. *Club:* Athenæum.
See also C. E. Hughes.

PESTELL, Sir John Richard, KCVO 1969; an Adjudicator, Immigration Appeals, Harmondsworth, 1970–87; *b* 21 Nov. 1916; *s* of late Lt-Comdr Frank Lionel Pestell, RN, and Winifred Alice Pestell; *m* 1951, Betty Pestell (*née* Parish); three *d*. *Educ:* Portsmouth Northern Secondary Sch. Joined British South Africa Police, Southern Rhodesia, 1939; retired, 1965, with rank of Asst Commissioner. Served, 1944–47, Gen. List, MELF, in Cyrenaica Defence Force. Secretary/Controller to Governor of S Rhodesia, Rt Hon. Sir H. V. Gibbs, 1965–69. *Recreation:* walking. *Address:* Batch Cottage, North Road, Charlton Horethorne, near Sherborne, Som DT9 4NS.

PESTON, family name of **Baron Peston.**

PESTON, Baron *cr* 1987 (Life Peer), of Mile End in Greater London; **Maurice Harry Peston;** Professor of Economics at Queen Mary College, University of London, 1965–88, now Emeritus; *b* 19 March 1931; *s* of Abraham and Yetta Peston; *m* 1958, Helen Conroy; two *s* one *d*. *Educ:* Belle Vue School, Bradford; Hackney Downs School; London School of Economics (BSc Econ); Princeton Univ., NJ, USA. Scientific Officer, then Sen. Scientific Officer, Army Operational Research Group, 1954–57; Asst Lecturer, Lectr, Reader in Economics, LSE, 1957–65. Economic Adviser: HM Treasury, 1962–64; Min. of Defence, 1964–66; H of C Select Cttee on Nationalised Industries, 1966–70, 1972–73; Special Adviser to Sec. of State for Education, 1974–75, to Sec. of State for Prices 1976–79. Chairman: Pools Panel, 1991–; NFER, 1991–; Member: CNAA (and Chm. of Economics Bd), 1967–73; SSRC (Chm. of Economics Bd), 1976–79; Council of Royal Pharmaceutical Soc. of GB, 1986–. Fellow: Portsmouth Poly., 1987; QMW, 1992. *Publications:* Elementary Matrices for Economics, 1969; Public Goods and the Public Sector, 1972; Theory of Macroeconomic Policy, 1974, 2nd edn 1982; Whatever Happened to Macroeconomics?, 1980; The British Economy, 1982, 2nd edn 1984; ed and contrib. to many other books; articles in economic jls. *Address:* House of Lords, SW1A 0PW. *T:* 0171–219 3000.

PETCH, Barry Irvine, FCA; General Manager, IBM Financing International Ltd, 1989–93; *b* 12 Oct. 1933; *s* of Charles Reginald Petch and Anne (*née* Fryer); *m* 1966, Anne Elisabeth (*née* Johannessen); two *s* one *d*. *Educ:* Doncaster Grammar Sch. FCA 1967. IBM United Kingdom Ltd, 1959–80; Controller, IBM Europe, 1981–83; Vice-Pres., Finance, IBM Europe, 1983–89. Part-time Mem., Price Commn, 1973–77. Dir, Pathfinder NHS Trust, 1995–. *Recreations:* tennis, golf, sailing. *Club:* Reform.

PETERBOROUGH, Bishop of; *no new appointment at time of going to press.*

PETERBOROUGH, Dean of; *see* Bunker, Very Rev. M.

PETERKEN, Laurence Edwin, CBE 1990; Special Projects Director, NHS in Scotland, since 1993; *b* 2 Oct. 1931; *s* of Edwin James Peterken and Constance Fanny (*née* Giffin); *m* 1st, 1955, Hanne Birgithe Von Der Recke (decd); one *s* one *d*; 2nd, 1970, Margaret Raynal Blair; one *s* one *d*. *Educ:* Harrow Sch. (Scholar); Peterhouse, Cambridge (Scholar); MA. Pilot Officer, RAF Regt, Adjt No 20 LAA Sqdn, 1950–52. Service Div. Manager, Hotpoint Ltd, 1961–63, Commercial Dir, 1963–66; Man. Dir, British Domestic Appliances Ltd, 1966–68; Dir, British Printing Corporation Ltd, 1969–73; Debenhams Ltd: Man. Dir, Fashion Multiple Div., 1974–76; Management Auditor, 1976–77; Controller, Operational Services, GLC, 1977–85; Acting Dir, Royal Festival Hall, 1983–85, to implement open foyer policy; Gen. Man., 1986–93, Dir, 1989–93, Gtr Glasgow Health Bd. Chairman: Working Party on Disposal of Clinical Waste in London, 1982–83; GLC Chief Officers' Guild, 1983–85; Member: Scottish Health Management Efficiency Gp, 1986–; Scottish Health Clinical Resources and Audit Gp, 1989–93; Scottish Health Service Adv. Council, 1989–93. Vice Chm., RIPA, W of Scotland, 1991–93; Chm., Glasgow and W of Scotland Inst. of Public Admin, 1993–. Churchwarden, Haslemere Parish Church, 1985–86. *Recreations:* music, golf. *Address:* 25 Kingsborough Gardens, Glasgow G12 9NH. *Club:* Athenæum.

PETERKIEWICZ, Prof. Jerzy; novelist and poet; Professor of Polish Language and Literature, University of London, 1972–79; *b* 29 Sept. 1916; *s* of late Jan Pietrkiewicz and Antonina (*née* Politowska). *Educ:* Dlugosz Sch., Wloclawek; Univ. of Warsaw; Univ. of St Andrews (MA 1944); King's Coll., London (PhD 1947). Freelance writer until 1950; Reader (previously Lectr) in Polish Language and Literature, Sch. of Slavonic and East European Studies, Univ. of London, 1952–72, Head of Dept of E European Lang. and Lit., 1972–77. *Publications:* Prowincja, 1936; Wiersze i poematy, 1938; Pogrzeb Europy, 1946; The Knotted Cord, 1953; Loot and Loyalty, 1955; Polish Prose and Verse, 1956; Antologia liryki angielskiej, 1958; Future to Let, 1958; Isolation, 1959; (with Burns Singer) Five Centuries of Polish Poetry, 1960 (enlarged edn 1970); The Quick and the Dead, 1961; That Angel Burning at my Left Side, 1963; Poematy londynskie, 1965; Inner Circle, 1966; Green Flows the Bile, 1969; The Other Side of Silence (The Poet at the Limits of Language), 1970; The Third Adam, 1975; (ed and trans.) Easter Vigil and other Poems, by Karol Wojtyla (Pope John Paul II), 1979; Kula magiczna (Poems 1934–52), 1980; (ed and trans.) Collected Poems, by Karol Wojtyla (Pope John Paul II), 1982; Poezje wybrane (Selected Poems), 1986; Literatura polska w perspektywie europejskiej (Polish Literature in its European context; essays trans. from English), 1986; Messianic Prophecy: a case for reappraisal, 1991; In the Scales of Fate (autobiog.), 1993; Wiersze dobrzynskie (early poems), 1994; The Place Within: the poetry of Pope John Paul II, 1994; essays, poems and articles in various periodicals; radio plays, BBC Radio 3. *Recreation:* travels, outward and inward. *Address:* 7 Lyndhurst Terrace, NW3 5QA.

PETERKIN, Sir Neville (Allan Mercer), Kt 1981; Chief Justice, West Indies Associated States, 1980–84; *b* 27 Oct. 1915; *s* of Joseph Allan Peterkin and Evelyn Peterkin; *m* 1942, Beryl Thompson; two *s* one *d*. *Educ:* Wellington Sch., Somerset, England. Called to Bar, Middle Temple, 1939. Registrar, St Lucia, 1943; Magistrate, Trinidad and Tobago, 1944; Resident Magistrate, Jamaica, 1954; High Court Judge: Trinidad, 1957; Associated States, 1967; Justice of Appeal, Associated States, 1975. *Recreations:* golf, bridge. *Address:* Reduit, Gros Inlet, St Lucia, West Indies. *T:* 28113.

PETERS, Rt. Rev. Arthur Gordon; *see* Nova Scotia, Bishop of.

PETERS, Sir (David) Keith, Kt 1993; FRCP, FRCPath; FRS 1995; Regius Professor of Physic, University of Cambridge, and Fellow, Christ's College, Cambridge, since 1987; *b* 26 July 1938; *s* of Herbert Lionel and Olive Peters; *m* 1st, 1961, Jean Mair Garfield (marr. diss. 1978); one *s* one *d*; 2nd, 1979, Pamela Wilson Ewan; two *s* one *d*. *Educ:* Welsh National Sch. of Medicine. MB, BCh, 1961; MRCP 1964; FRCP 1975; FRCPath 1991. Junior posts in United Cardiff Hosps, 1961–65; Med. Research Council, Clinical Res. Fellowship, 1965–68; Lectr in Med., Welsh Nat. Sch. of Med., 1968–69; Royal Postgraduate Medical School: Lectr, 1969; Sen. Lectr, 1974; Reader in Med., 1975; Prof. of Medicine and Dir, Dept of Medicine, 1977–87; Consultant Physician, Hammersmith Hosp., 1969–87. Member: MRC, 1984–88 (Chm., MRC Physiological Systems Bd, 1986–88); ACOST, 1987–90; Chm., NRPB, 1994–. Hon. MD Wales, 1987; Hon. DSc Aberdeen, 1994. *Publications:* (ed jtly) Clinical Aspects of Immunology, 4th edn 1982, 5th edn 1993; in various jls on immunology of renal and vascular disease. *Recreations:* tennis, chess. *Address:* 7 Chaucer Road, Cambridge CB2 2EB. *T:* Cambridge (01223) 356117. *Club:* Garrick.

PETERS, Ellis; *see* Pargeter, E.

PETERS, Prof. George Henry; Research Professor in Agricultural Economics and Head of Agricultural Economics Unit, Queen Elizabeth House, University of Oxford, since 1986; Fellow, Wolfson College, Oxford, since 1980 (Vicegerent, 1991–93); *b* 2 Sept. 1934; *s* of William and Mary Peters; *m* 1959, Judith Mary Griffiths; two *d*. *Educ:* Mold Grammar Sch., Clwyd; University Coll. of Wales, Aberystwyth (BSc, MSc); King's Coll., Cambridge. National Service, Educn Br., RAF, 1957–59. Inst. for Res. in Agricl Econs, Univ. of Oxford, 1959–67; University of Liverpool: Lectr in Econs, 1967–69; Sen. Lectr, 1969–70; Brunner Prof. of Economic Science, 1970–79; Hd of Dept of Econs and Commerce, 1976–79; Dir, Inst. of Agricl Econs, Univ. of Oxford, 1980–86. Pres., Agricl Econs Soc., 1991–92. Ed., Procs of Internat. Assoc. of Agricl Economists, 1991–. *Publications:* Cost Benefit Analysis and Public Expenditure (IEA Eaton Paper 8), 1966, 3rd edn 1973; Private and Public Finance, 1971, 2nd edn 1975; ESRC/RSS Reviews of UK Statistical Sources, vol. 23, Agriculture, 1988; (ed with B. F. Stanton) Sustainable Agricultural Development: the role of international co-operation, 1992; (ed) International Library of Critical Writings in Economics, Agricultural Economics, 1995; (ed with D. D. Hedley) Agricultural Competitiveness, 1995; articles in Jl of Agricl Econs, Oxford Agrarian Studies, etc. *Recreations:* all sport, increasingly as a spectator. *Address:* Gable End Cottage, 33 The Moors, Kidlington, Oxford OX5 2AH. *T:* Kidlington (018675) 372232.

PETERS, Sir Keith; *see* Peters, Sir D. K.

PETERS, Kenneth Jamieson, CBE 1979; DL; FSAScot; Member, Peterhead Bay Authority Board, since 1983 (Vice-Chairman, since 1989); *b* 17 Jan. 1923; *s* of William Jamieson Peters and Edna Rosa Peters (*née* Hayman); *m* 1951, Arunda Merle Jane Jones. *Educ:* Aberdeen Grammar Sch.; Aberdeen Univ. Served War of 1939–45: last rank Captain/Adjutant, 2nd Bn King's Own Scottish Borderers. Editorial staff, Daily Record and Evening News Ltd, 1947–51; Asst Editor: Evening Express, Aberdeen, 1951–52; Manchester Evening Chronicle, 1952–53; Editor: Evening Express, Aberdeen, 1953–56; The Press and Journal, Aberdeen, 1956–60; Dir, 1960–90, Man. Dir, 1960–80, Chm., 1980–81, Aberdeen Journals Ltd. Director: Highland Printers Ltd (Inverness), 1968–83; Aberdeen Assoc. of Social Service, 1973–78; Thomson Regional Newspapers, 1974–80; Thomson Scottish Petroleum Ltd, 1981–86; Thomson N Sea, 1981–88; Thomson Forestry Hldgs, 1982–88; Member: Scottish Reg. Bd, BR, 1982–92; Girobank, Scotland Bd, 1984–90. Pres., Scottish Daily Newspaper Soc., 1964–66 and 1974–76; Mem., Press Council, 1974–77; Pres., Publicity Club of Aberdeen, 1972–81; Member: Scottish Adv. Cttee of British Council, 1967–84; Cttee, Films of Scotland, 1970–82; Chm., NE Cttee, 1982–88, Mem. Exec., 1982–88, Fellow, 1988, Scottish Council (Devclt and Industry). FSAScot 1980; FIMgt (FBIM 1980); ACIT 1985; FRSA 1989. JP City of Aberdeen, 1961; DL Aberdeen, 1978. *Publications:* The Northern Lights, 1978; (ed) Great North Memories, vol. 1, 1978, vol. 2, 1981; Burgess of Guild, 1982. *Recreations:* cricket, Rugby football, walking. *Address:* 47 Abergeldie Road, Aberdeen AB1 6ED. *T:* Aberdeen (01224) 587647. *Clubs:* MCC; Royal Northern and University (Aberdeen).

PETERS, Martin Trevor, CB 1991; CEng, FRAeS; Technical Planning Director, British Aerospace plc, 1992–94; *b* 23 Dec. 1936; *s* of Reginald Thomas Peters and Catherine Mary Peters (*née* Ings); *m* 1958, Vera Joan Horton; one *s*. *Educ:* Aylesbury Grammar Sch.; Watford Tech. Coll.; High Wycombe Coll. of Further Educn. MIMechE, CEng 1968; FRAeS 1988. Airtech, 1953–55; RAF, 1955–57; Airtech, 1957–59; RPE Westcott, 1959–64; NGTE Pyestock, 1964–71; MoD, 1971–77; Supt of Engineering, A&AEE Boscombe Down, 1977–79; NAMMA, Munich, 1979–81; Dir, Aircraft Post Design Services, MoD (PE), 1981–83; RCDS, 1984; Dir-Gen. Aircraft, 1984–87; Dep. Controller Aircraft, 1987–89; Dir, RAE, 1989–91; Tech. Dir, BAe Commercial Aircraft Ltd, 1991–92. *Recreations:* ski-ing, walking, music, 18th century ship modelling. *Address:* 96 East Avenue, Talbot Woods, Bournemouth BH3 7DD.

PETERS, Mary Elizabeth, CBE 1990 (MBE 1973); self employed; Managing Director, Mary Peters Sports Ltd, since 1977; *b* 6 July 1939; *d* of Arthur Henry Peters and Hilda Mary Peters. *Educ:* Portadown Coll., Co. Armagh; Belfast Coll. of Domestic Science (DipDomSc). Represented Great Britain: Olympic Games: 4th place, Pentathlon, 1964; 1st, Pentathlon (world record), 1972; Commonwealth Games: 2nd, Shot, 1966; 1st, Shot,

1st Pentathlon, 1970; 1st, Pentathlon, 1974. Member: Sports Council, 1974–80, 1987–94; Northern Ireland Sports Council, 1974–93 (Vice-Chm., 1977–81); Ulster Games Foundn, 1984–93; NI BBC Broadcasting Council, 1981–84; NI Tourist Bd, 1993–. Dir, Churchill Foundn Fellowship Scholarship, Calif, 1972. Asst Sec., Multiple Sclerosis Soc., 1974–78; Pres., Old-Age Pensioners' Coal and Grocery Fund. Hon. Senior Athletic Coach, 1975–; BAAB Pentathlon Coach, 1976; Team Manager: GB women's athletic team, European Cup, 1979; GB women's athletic team, Moscow, 1980 and Los Angeles, 1984. Pres., NIWAAA, 1985–87; Vice-President: Assoc. of Youth Clubs; NI Assoc. of Youth Clubs; Riding for the Disabled; Driving for the Disabled; Trustee, Ulster Sports Trust, 1972; Patron: NIAAA, 1981–; Friends of Royal Victoria Hosp., Belfast, 1988–. Awards: BBC Sports personality, 1972; Athletic Writers', 1972; Sports Writers', 1972; Elizabeth Arden Visible Difference, 1976; Athletics, Dublin (Texaco), 1970 and 1972; British Airways Tourist Endeavour, 1981; Living Action, 1985; Evian Health, 1985. Hon. DSc, New Univ. of Ulster, 1974. *Publication:* Mary P., an autobiography, 1974. *Address:* Willowtree Cottage, River Road, Dunmurry, Belfast, N Ireland BT17 9DP.

PETERS, Prof. Raymond Harry; Professor of Polymer and Fibre Science, University of Manchester, 1955–84, now Emeritus; *b* 19 Feb. 1918. *Educ:* County High Sch., Ilford; King's Coll., London Univ.; Manchester Univ. BSc (London) 1939, PhD (London), 1942, in Chemistry; BSc (Manchester), 1949, BSc (London), 1949, in Mathematics; DSc (London), 1968. Scientist at ICI Ltd, 1941–46 and 1949–55. Visiting Professor: UMIST, 1984–86; Univ. of Strathclyde, 1984–. President, Society of Dyers and Colourists, 1967–68. *Publications:* Textile Chemistry: Vol. I, The Chemistry of Fibres, 1963; Vol. II, Impurities of Fibres: Purification of Fibres, 1967; Vol. III, Physical Chemistry of Dyeing, 1975; contributions to Journals of Chemical Society, Society of Dyers and Colourists, Textile Institute, British Journal of Applied Physics, etc. *Recreation:* gardening. *Address:* 1 Vale Road, Pownall Park, Wilmslow, Cheshire SK9 5QA.

PETERS, Prof. Richard Stanley, BA (Oxon), BA (London), PhD (London); Professor of the Philosophy of Education, University of London Institute of Education, 1962–82, now Emeritus Professor; Dean, Faculty of Education, London University, 1971–74; *b* 31 Oct. 1919; *s* of late Charles Robert and Mabel Georgina Peters; *m* 1943, Margaret Lee Duncan; one *s* two *d*. *Educ:* Clifton Coll., Bristol; Queen's Coll., Oxford; Birkbeck Coll., University of London. War service with Friends' Ambulance Unit and Friends' Relief Service in E. London, 1940–44. Classics Master, Sidcot School, Somerset, 1944–46; Birkbeck Coll., University of London: Studentship and part-time Lecturer in Philos. and Psychol., 1946–49; full-time Lecturer in Philos. and Psychol., 1949–58; Reader in Philosophy, 1958–62. Visiting Prof. of Education: Grad. School of Education, Harvard Univ., 1961; Univ. of Auckland, 1975; Visiting Fellow, Australian National Univ., 1969. Part-time lectureships, Bedford Coll., LSE; Tutor for University of London Tutorial Classes Cttee and Extension Cttee. Member, American National Academy of Education, 1966. *Publications:* (revised) Brett's History of Psychology, 1953; Hobbes, 1956; The Concept of Motivation, 1958; (with S. I. Benn) Social Principles and the Democratic State, 1959; Authority, Responsibility and Education, 1960; Ethics and Education, 1966; (ed) The Concept of Education, 1967; (ed) Perspectives on Plowden, 1969; (with P. H. Hirst) The Logic of Education, 1970; (ed with M. Cranston) Hobbes and Rousseau, 1971; (ed with R. F. Dearden and P. H. Hirst) Education and the Development of Reason, 1972; Reason and Compassion (Lindsay Meml Lectures), 1973; (ed) The Philosophy of Education, 1973; Psychology and Ethical Development, 1974; (ed) Nature and Conduct, 1975; (ed) The Role of the Head, 1976; Education and the Education of Teachers, 1977; (ed) John Dewey Reconsidered, 1977; Essays on Educators, 1981; Moral Development and Moral Education, 1981. *Address:* 16 Shepherd's Hill, N6 5AQ.

PETERS, Air Vice-Marshal Robert Geoffrey, CB 1992; Director of Welfare, RAF Benevolent Fund, since 1993; *b* 22 Aug. 1940; *s* of Geoffrey Ridgeway Peters and Henriette Catharine Peters; *m* 1966, Mary Elizabeth (*née* Fletcher); one *d* three *s*. *Educ:* St Paul's Sch., London; RAF Coll., Cranwell (Gen. Duties/Pilot). Beverley C Mk1 Pilot Nos 34 and 47 Sqdns, Singapore and UK, 1961–66; Flt Comdr, No 46 Sqdn (Andovers), RAF Abingdon, 1967–68; MoD Central Staffs (Asst MA to Chief Adviser Personnel and Logistics), 1968–69; OC Flying Trng Sqdn, Air Electronics and Air Engr Trng Sch., RAF Topcliffe, 1970–72; RAF Staff Coll., Bracknell, 1973; Air Sec.'s Dept, MoD, 1974–76; OC 10 Sqdn (VC10), RAF Brize Norton, 1977–78; Directorate of Forward Policy (RAF), MoD, 1979–81; PSO to Dep. SACEUR(UK), SHAPE, Belgium, 1981–83; OC RAF St Mawgan, 1984–85; RCDS 1986; Comdr, RAF Staff and Air Attaché, Washington, 1987–90. Comdt, RAF Staff Coll., Bracknell, 1990–93. President: RAF Fencing Union, 1986–93; Combined Services Fencing Assoc., 1988–. Freeman, City of London, 1977; Liveryman, Co. of Coachmakers and Coach Harness Makers, 1977. QCVSA 1973. *Recreations:* squash, golf, sailing. *Address:* RAF Benevolent Fund, 67 Portland Place, W1N 4AR. *T:* 0171–580 8343. *Club:* Royal Air Force.

PETERS, Theophilus, CMG 1967; HM Diplomatic Service, retired; freelance lecturer on Chinese Art and History; *b* 7 Aug. 1921; *er s* of late Mark Peters and Dorothy Knapman; *m* 1953, Lucy Bailey Summers, *d* of late Lionel Morgan Summers, Winter Park, Fla; two *s* three *d*. *Educ:* Exeter Sch., Exeter; St John's Coll., Cambridge (MA). Served War of 1939–45: 2nd Lieut, Intelligence Corps, 1942; Captain, 8 Corps HQ, 1944; Normandy, 1944; Holland, 1944–45 (despatches); Germany; Major. Entered HM Foreign (subseq. Diplomatic) Service; Vice-Consul/2nd Secretary, Peking, 1948; FO, 1951–52; Tripoli and Benghazi (Libya), 1953; FO, 1956; Dep. Secretary-General, Cento, 1960; Head of Chancery, Manila, 1962; Counsellor (Commercial), Peking, 1965; Dir, Diplomatic Service Language Centre, 1968–71, and Head of Training Dept, FCO, 1969–71; Counsellor and Consul-Gen., Buenos Aires, 1971–73; Consul-Gen., Antwerp, 1973–78. Dir, Theophilus Knapman & Co., 1979–87. *Address:* Henlopen House, Church Road, Ketton, Stamford, Lincs PE9 3RD.

PETERS, Prof. Wallace, MD, DSc; FRCP; Hon. Research Fellow, International Institute of Parasitology, since 1992; Professor of Medical Protozoology, London School of Hygiene and Tropical Medicine, University of London, 1979–89, now Emeritus; *b* 1 April 1924; *s* of Henry and Fanny Peters; *m* 1954, Ruth (*née* Scheidegger). *Educ:* Haberdashers' Aske's Sch.; St Bartholomew's Hosp., London. MB BS, 1947; MRCS, DTM&H. Served in RAMC, 1947–49; practised tropical medicine in West and East Africa, 1950–52; Staff Mem., WHO, Liberia and Nepal, 1952–55; Asst Dir (Malariology), Health Dept, Territory of Papua and New Guinea, 1956–61; Research Associate, CIBA, Basle, Switzerland, 1961–66; Walter Myers Prof. of Parasitology, Univ. of Liverpool, 1966–79; Dean, Liverpool Sch. of Tropical Medicine, 1975–78; Jt Dir, Malaria Reference Lab., PHLS, 1979–89. Vice-Pres. and Pres., Brit. Soc. Parasit., 1972–76; President: Brit. Sect., Soc. Protozool., 1972–75; Royal Soc. of Trop. Medicine and Hygiene, 1987–89 (Vice-Pres., 1982–83, 1985–87). Chm., WHO Steering Cttee on Chemotherapy of Malaria, 1975–83; Member: Expert Adv. Panel, WHO, 1967–; WHO Steering Cttees on Leishmaniasis, 1979; Editorial Bd, Ann. Trop. Med. Parasit., 1966–79; Trop. Med. Research Bd, MRC, 1973–77; Scientific Council, Inst. of Cellular and Molecular Path., 1981–84; Parasitol. Bd, Institut Pasteur, 1979–87; Sec., European Fedn Parasit., 1979–84 (Vice-Pres., 1975–79). Hon. Consultant on malariology to the Army, 1986–89. Dr *hc*, Univ. Réne Descartes, Paris, 1992. Rudolf Leuckart Medal, German Soc. of Parasitol., 1980; King Faisal Internat. Prize in Medicine, 1983. *Publications:* A Provisional Checklist of Butterflies of the Ethiopian Region, 1952; Chemotherapy and Drug Resistance in Malaria, 1970, 2nd edn 1987; (with H. M. Gilles) A Colour Atlas of Tropical Medicine and Parasitology, 1976, 4th edn 1995; (ed with R. Killick-Kendrick) Rodent Malaria, 1978; (ed with W. H. G. Richards) Antimalarial Drugs, 2 vols, 1984; (ed with R. Killick-Kendrick) The Leishmaniases in Biology and Medicine, 1987; A Colour Atlas of Arthropods in Clinical Medicine, 1992; numerous papers in jls, on trop. med. and parasitology. *Recreation:* photography. *Address:* International Institute of Parasitology, 395A Hatfield Road, St Albans, Herts AL4 0XU. *T:* St Albans (01727) 833151.

PETERS, William, CMG 1981; LVO 1961; MBE 1959; HM Diplomatic Service, retired; Joint Chairman, Jubilee 2000; *b* 28 Sept. 1923; *o s* of John William Peters and Louise (*née* Woodhouse), Morpeth, Northumberland; *m* 1944, Catherine B. Bailey; no *c*. *Educ:* King Edward VI Grammar Sch., Morpeth; Balliol Coll., Oxford (MA Lit. Hum. 1948); LSE and SOAS. War Service, Queen's Royal Rifles, KOSB, and 9th Gurkha Rifles, 1942–46. Joined HMOCS as Asst District Comr, Gold Coast, 1950; served in Cape Coast, Bawku and Tamale; Dep. Sec., Regional Comr, Northern Region, 1958–59; apptd to CRO as Asst Prin., 1959; Prin., 1959; 1st Sec., Dacca, 1960–63; 1st Sec., Cyprus, 1963–67; Head of Zambia and Malawi Dept, CRO, 1967–68; Head of Central African Dept, FCO, 1968–69; Dir, Internat. Affairs Div., Commonwealth Secretariat, 1969–71; Counsellor and Head of Chancery, Canberra, 1971–73; Dep. High Comr, Bombay, 1974–77; Ambassador to Uruguay, 1977–80; High Comr in Malaŵi, 1980–83. Member: Royal African Soc., 1980–85 (Hon. Treas., 1983–85); RSAA, 1987– (Mem., Editl Bd, 1990–); Exec., S Atlantic Council, 1985–; Chairman: Exec. Cttee, Lepra, 1984–92; Ethnic Minorities Sub-Cttee, Abbeyfield Soc., 1991–; Council and Exec. Cttee, USPG, 1991–94 (Council Mem., 1988–; Vice-Pres., 1994–); Tibet Soc. of UK, 1985–93; Trustee, Tibet Relief Fund of UK; President: Downs Br., Royal British Legion, 1986–; Rotary Club of Deal, 1989–90. Governor, Walmer Sch., 1989–. FIMgt (FBIM 1984). *Publications:* Diplomatic Service: Formation and Operation, 1971; contribs to Jls of Asian Affairs and of African Administration; Illustrated Weekly of India; Noticias (Uruguay); Army Qly and Defence Jl; Christian Aid; Asian Affairs; Transmission. *Recreations:* music, carpentry. *Address:* 12 Crown Court, Middle Street, Deal, Kent CT14 7AG. *T:* Dover (01304) 362822. *Clubs:* United Oxford & Cambridge University, Commonwealth Trust.

PETERSEN, Sir Jeffrey (Charles), KCMG 1978 (CMG 1968); HM Diplomatic Service, retired; *b* 20 July 1920; *s* of Charles Petersen and Ruby Petersen (*née* Waple); *m* 1962, Karin Kristina Hayward; two *s* four *d*. *Educ:* Westcliff High Sch.; London School of Economics. Served RN (Lieut, RNVR), 1939–46. Joined Foreign Office, 1948; 2nd Secretary, Madrid, 1949–50; 2nd Secretary, Ankara, 1951–52; 1st Secretary, Brussels, 1953–56; NATO Defence College, 1956–57; FO, 1957–62; 1st Secretary, Djakarta, 1962–64; Counsellor, Athens, 1964–68; Minister (Commercial), Rio de Janeiro, 1968–71; Ambassador to: Republic of Korea, 1971–74; Romania, 1975–77; Sweden, 1977–80. Chairman: Barclays Bank SAE (Spain), 1981–87; GVA Internat. Ltd, 1983–89; North Sea Assets PLC, 1989–94; Ake Larson Ltd, 1990–93; other directorships. Chm., British Materials Handling Bd; President: Anglo Swedish Soc.; Anglo-Korean Soc.; Vice Pres., Swedish Chamber of Commerce for UK. Knight Grand Cross, Order of Polar Star (Sweden), 1984; Order of Diplomatic Merit (Republic of Korea), 1985. *Recreations:* painting, making things, totting. *Address:* 32 Longmoore Street, SW1V 1JF. *T:* 0171–834 8262; Crofts Wood, Petham, Kent CT4 5RX. *T:* Canterbury (01227) 700537. *Clubs:* Travellers'; Kent and Canterbury.

PETERSEN, Hon. Sir Johannes B.; *see* Bjelke-Petersen.

PETERSEN, Niels Helveg; MP (Social Liberal) Denmark, 1966–74, and since 1977; Minister for Foreign Affairs, Denmark, since 1993; *b* 17 Jan. 1939; *s* of Lilly and Kresten Helveg Petersen; *m* 1984, Kirsten Lee, MD; two *s*. *Educ:* Univ. of Copenhagen (LLB 1965); Univ. of Stanford, Calif. Chief of Cabinet, Danish EU Comr, 1974–77; Chm., Parly Group, 1978–88; Minister for Economic Affairs, 1988–90. *Recreations:* chess, tennis, soccer football. *Address:* Ministry of Foreign Affairs, Asiatisk Plads 2, 1448 Copenhagen K, Denmark. *T:* (45) 33920000.

PETERSHAM, Viscount; Charles Henry Leicester Stanhope; *b* 20 July 1945; *s* and *heir* of 11th Earl of Harrington, *qv*; *m* 1966, Virginia Alleyne Freeman Jackson, Mallow (marr. diss. 1983); one *s* one *d*; *m* 1984, Anita Countess of Suffolk and Berkshire. *Educ:* Eton. *Heir:* *s* Hon. William Henry Leicester Stanhope, *b* 14 Oct. 1967. *Address:* Mount St John, Felixkirk, Thirsk, N Yorks YO7 2DT. *T:* Thirsk (01845) 537205.

See also Viscount Linley.

PETERSON, Cathryn Mary; *see* Pope, C. M.

PETERSON, Col Sir Christopher (Matthew), Kt 1994; CBE 1983; TD 1952; Chairman, Cardiff Health Foods Ltd, since 1988; *b* 22 Feb. 1918; *s* of Oscar Peterson and Minnie Dee; *m* 1945, Grace Winifred McNeil; one *s* one *d* (and one *s* decd). *Educ:* St Illtyd's Coll., Cardiff; Cardiff Tech. Coll. Shipbroker Office, Cardiff Docks, 1936–39; served RASC, 1940–46 (Capt.). Joined S Wales India Rubber Co., subseq. SWIRCO-Newton Gp, 1952, Chm., 1968–79; Dir, Dorada Hlgs plc, 1979–83; Chairman: Wales Local Bd, Commercial Union Assce Co., 1972–77; J. McNeil (Cameras), 1983–92; Randall Cox (Photographic), 1984–92; Cox & Tarry Ltd, 1984–89; Stanton-King Orgn, 1985–89; Taff Ely Enterprise Partnership, 1989–91; SWIRCO-Hall, 1990–92. Member: Cardiff City Council, 1968–71; S Glam CC, 1973–85. JP City of Cardiff, 1973; DL 1977, High Sheriff 1981–82, S Glam. Served TA, 1946–65; CO, 1961–65 (Lt-Col), Hon. Col, 1972–77, 157 Regt RCT. OStJ 1991. *Recreation:* walking. *Address:* 51 Rannoch Drive, Cyncoed, Cardiff CF2 6LP. *T:* Cardiff (01222) 754062; 15 Castle Pill Crescent, Steyton, Milford Haven, Dyfed SA73 1HD. *Clubs:* Army and Navy; Cardiff and County.

PETERSON, Colin Vyvyan, CVO 1982; Lay Assistant to Bishop of Winchester, 1985–94; *b* 24 Oct. 1932; *s* of late Sir Maurice Drummond Peterson, GCMG; *m* 1966, Pamela Rosemary Barry; two *s* two *d*. *Educ:* Winchester Coll.; Magdalen Coll., Oxford. Joined HM Treasury, 1959; Sec. for Appointments to PM and Ecclesiastical Sec. to the Lord Chancellor, 1974–82; Under Sec., Cabinet Office (MPO), 1982–85. *Recreation:* fishing. *Address:* Balldown Farmhouse, Sparsholt, Hants SO21 2LZ. *T:* Sparsholt (01962) 776368.

PETERSON, Rev. David Gilbert, PhD; Lecturer, Moore Theological College, Sydney, 1984–Aug. 1996; Principal, Oak Hill Theological College, from Sept. 1996; *b* 29 Oct. 1944; *s* of Gilbert Samuel and Marie Jean Peterson; *m* 1970, Lesley Victoria (*née* Stock); three *s*. *Educ:* Univ. of Sydney (MA); Moore Theol Coll., Sydney (BD (Lond.)); Univ. of Manchester (PhD 1978). Ordained deacon, 1968, priest, 1969; St Matthew's, Manly, dio. of Sydney, 1968–71; Lectr, Moore Theol Coll., 1971–75, 1978–79; Post-grad. study, Univ. of Manchester and Sunday Asst, St Mary's, Cheadle, dio. of Chester, 1975–78; Rector and Sen. Canon, St Michael's, Provisional Cathedral, Wollongong, dio. of Sydney, 1980–83. *Publications:* Hebrews and Perfection, 1982; Engaging with God, 1992; Possessed by God, 1995; The Book of Acts and its Theology, 1995. *Recreations:* golf, swimming, music. *Address:* (until Aug. 1996) Moore Theological College, 1 King Street, Newtown,

NSW 2042, Australia. *T:* (2) 5192644; (from Sept. 1996) Oak Hill Theological College, Chase Side, Southgate, N14 4PS.

PETERSON, Hon. David Robert; PC (Can.) 1992; QC (Can.) 1980; Partner, Cassels, Brock & Blackwell, since 1991; *b* 28 Dec. 1943; *s* of Clarence Marwin Peterson and Laura Marie (*née* Scott); *m* 1974, Shelley Christine Matthews; two *s* one *d.* *Educ:* Univ. of Western Ontario (BA Phil./PolSci); Univ. of Toronto (LLB). Called to Bar, Ontario, 1969. Chm. and Pres., C. M. Peterson Co. Ltd, 1969–75; MLA for London Centre, Ontario, 1975–90. Leader, Liberal Party of Ontario, 1982–90; Leader of the Opposition, 1982–85; Premier of Ontario, 1985–90. *Recreations:* theatre, riding, jogging, ski-ing, tennis, reading, gardening. *Address:* Cassels, Brock & Blackwell, 40 King Street W, Suite 2100, Scotia Plaza, Toronto, Ont M5H 3C2, Canada. *Club:* London (Ontario) Hunt.

PETERSON, Rev. Canon John Louis, ThD; Secretary General, Anglican Consultative Council, since 1995; *b* 17 Dec. 1942; *s* of J. Harold Peterson and Edythe V. Peterson; *m* 1966, Kirsten Ruth Bratlie; two *d.* *Educ:* Concordia Coll. (BA 1965); Harvard Divinity Sch. (STB 1968); Chicago Inst. for Advanced Theol Studies (ThD 1976). Instr, OT and Syro-Palestinian Archaeol., Seabury-Western Theol Seminary, Evanston, 1968–76; Canon Theologian and Admin. Asst to Bishop, dio. of Western Michigan, 1976–82; Vicar, St Stephen's Plainwell, Mich, 1976–82; Dean of St George's Coll., and Canon Residentiary, St George's Cathedral, Jerusalem, 1982–94, Hon. Canon, 1995–. Hon. Canon: Cathedral Ch. of Christ the King, Kalamazoo, Mich, 1982–; Canterbury Cathedral, 1995. Hon. DD, Virginia Theol Seminary, 1993. *Publications:* We Are All Citizens of Jerusalem: The Way of the Cross in the Holy City, 1994; contrib. Anchor Bible Dictionary, 1992. *Address:* Anglican Consultative Council, 157 Waterloo Road, SE1 8UT. *T:* 0171–620 1110.

PETERSON, Rt. Rev. Leslie Ernest; Bishop of Algoma, 1983–94; *b* 4 Nov. 1928; *s* of late Ernest Victor Peterson and of Dorothy Blanche Peterson (*née* Marsh); *m* 1953, Yvonne Hazel Lawton; two *s* three *d.* *Educ:* Univ. of Western Ontario (BA 1952); Huron College (LTh 1954; DD (*jd*) 1984); Teachers' Coll., North Bay, Ont., 1970. Deacon 1954, priest 1955; Incumbent of All Saints', Coniston, Ont., 1954–59; St Peter's Elliot Lake, 1959–63; Rector, Christ Church, North Bay, 1963–78; Teacher, Marshall Park Elem. School, 1970–78; Rector, Trinity Church, Parry Sound, 1978–83; Coadjutor Bishop, June–Sept. 1983. STD (*hc*) Thorneloe, 1992. *Recreations:* canoe tripping, gardening, skiing. *Address:* 615 Santa Monica Road, London, Ontario N6H 3W2, Canada.

PETERSON, Oscar Emmanuel, CC (Canada) 1984 (OC 1972); concert jazz pianist; *b* 15 Aug. 1925; *s* of Daniel Peterson and Kathleen Peterson; *m* 1st, 1947, Lillian Alice Ann; two *s* three *d*; 2nd, 1966, Sandra Cythia, *d* of H. A. King; 3rd, Charlotte; one *s*; 4th, 1990, Kelly Ann Green; one *d.* *Educ:* (academic) Montreal High Sch.; (music) private tutors. 1st prize, amateur show, 1940; Carnegie Hall debut, 1950; 1950–: numerous jazz awards; TV shows; composer and arranger; yearly concert tours in N America, Europe, GB and Japan; has performed also in S America, Mexico, WI, Australia, NZ and Russia. *Television series:* (Canada): Oscar Peterson Presents, 1974; Oscar Peterson and Friends, 1980; (BBC) Oscar Peterson's Piano Party, 1974. Chancellor, York Univ., Ontario, 1991–. Mem., Bd of Govs, Credit Valley Hosp., Mississauga, Ont., 1984–. Oscar Peterson scholarship established, Berklee Coll. of Mus., 1982. Grammy award, 1974, 1975, 1977, 1978, 1979, 1990, 1991. Hon. LLD: Carleton Univ., 1973; Queen's Univ., Kingston, 1976; Concordia, 1979; MacMaster, 1981; Victoria, 1981; York, 1982; Toronto, 1985; Hon. DMus: Sackville, 1980; Laval, 1985; Hon. DFA Northwestern, Ill, 1983. Civic Award of Merit, Toronto, 1972, second mention, 1983; Diplôme d'Honneur, Canadian Conf. of the Arts, 1974; Toronto Arts Awards, Lifetime Achievement, 1991; Gov. General's Award, Lifetime Achievement, 1992; Glenn Gould Prize, 1993. Officer, Order of Arts and Letters (France), 1989; Chevalier, Order of Quebec, 1991; Order of Ontario, 1992. *Publications:* Oscar Peterson New Piano Solos, 1965; Jazz Exercises and Pieces, 1965; Jazz Playbook, vol. 1A, 1991, vol. 1B, 1993. *Recreations:* audio, photography, boating, fishing. *Address:* Regal Recordings Ltd, 2421 Hammond Road, Mississauga, Ont L5K 1T3, Canada. *T:* (416) 8552370, *Fax:* (416) 8551773.

PETHERBRIDGE, Edward; actor and director; *b* 3 Aug. 1936; *s* of late William and Hannah Petherbridge; *m* 1st, 1957, Louise Harris (marr. diss. 1980); one *s*; 2nd, 1981, Emily Richard, actress; one *s* one *d.* *Educ:* Grange Grammar Sch., Bradford; Northern Theatre Sch. Early experience in repertory and on tour; London début, Dumain in Love's Labours Lost and Demetrius in A Midsummer Night's Dream, Regent's Park Open Air Theatre, 1962; All in Good Time, Mermaid, and Phoenix, 1963; with Nat. Theatre Co. at Old Vic, 1964–70, chief appearances in: Trelawny of the Wells, Rosencrantz and Guildenstern are Dead, A Flea in her Ear, Love for Love, Volpone, The Advertisement, The Way of the World, The White Devil; Alceste in The Misanthrope, Nottingham, Lulu, Royal Court, and Apollo, 1970; John Bull's Other Island, Mermaid, Swansong, opening of Crucible, Sheffield, 1971; Founder Mem., Actors' Co., 1972; chief appearances at Edinburgh Fests, NY, and on tour, 1972–75: 'Tis Pity she's a Whore, Rooling the Roost, The Way of the World, Tartuffe, King Lear; also devised, dir. and appeared in Knots (from R. D. Laing's book), The Beanstalk, a wordless pantomime, and dir. The Bacchae; RSC tour of Australia and NZ, 1976; dir. Uncle Vanya, Cambridge Theatre Co., 1977; Chasuble in The Importance of Being Earnest, and dir., devised and appeared in Do You Love Me (from R. D. Laing's book), Actors' Co. tour and Round House, 1977; Crucifer of Blood, Haymarket, 1979; Royal Shakespeare Company: tour, 1978, Twelfth Night; Three Sisters, 1979; Suicide, Newman Noggs in Nicholas Nickleby (Best Supporting Actor, London Drama Critics' Award, 1981), No Limits to Love, 1980; Nicholas Nickleby, Broadway, 1981; Twelfth Night, British Council tour (Philippines, Singapore, Malaysia, China and Japan), followed by season at Warehouse, London, 1982; Peter Pan, Barbican, 1983; Strange Interlude, Duke of York's, 1984, Broadway, 1985 (Olivier Award, 1984); Love's Labours Lost, Stratford, 1984; Busman's Honeymoon, Lyric, Hammersmith, 1988; The Eight O'Clock Muse, one-man show, Riverside Studios, 1989; The Power and the Glory, Chichester, 1990; Cyrano de Bergerac (title rôle), Greenwich, 1990; Point Valaine, and Valentine's Day (musical, from Shaw's You Never Can Tell), Chichester, 1991; Noël & Gertie, Duke of York's, 1991; National Theatre: The Rivals, 1983; Co-Dir, McKellen Petherbridge Co. at NT, 1984–86, acting in Duchess of Malfi, The Cherry Orchard, The Real Inspector Hound, and The Critic, 1985, company appeared at Internat. Theatre Fests, Paris and Chicago, 1986; Alceste in The Misanthrope, co-prodn with Bristol Old Vic, 1989; The Seagull, RNT, 1994. Numerous television appearances include: Vershinin in Three Sisters (from RSC prod.); Lytton Strachey in No Need to Lie; Newman Noggs in Nicholas Nickleby (from RSC prod.); Gower in Pericles; Lord Peter Wimsey; Marsden in Strange Interlude; Uncle in Journey's End; No Strings. Hon. DLitt Bradford, 1989. *Recreations:* listening to music, photography, theatre history. *Address:* c/o Jonathan Altaras Associates, 2 Goodwins Court, WC2N 4LL. *T:* 0171–497 8878.

PETHICK, Brig. Geoffrey Loveston, CBE 1960; DSO 1944; *b* 25 Nov. 1907; *s* of late Captain E. E. Pethick, RN and May (*née* Brook); *m* 1st, 1939, Nancy Veronica Ferrand (*d* 1980); one *d*; 2nd, 1981, Mrs Paula Usborne. *Educ:* Newton College. Commissioned, Royal Artillery, 1927; RHA 1934; served War of 1939–45: Staff Coll., Camberley, 1940; CO, Field Regt, 1942; Far East, 1945; Jt Services Staff Coll., 1946; Dep. Dir, WO, 1948; idc, 1950; Comdr 3 Army Group, RA, 1951; IDC, 1952; Comdr RA 3 Div. 1953; Army Council Staff, 1957; retired, 1960. Dir, British Paper Makers' Association, 1960–74. *Address:* Little Croft, Fireball Hill, Sunningdale, Berks SL5 9PJ. *T:* Ascot (01344) 22018.

PETIT, Sir Dinshaw Manockjee, 4th Bt *cr* 1890; *b* 13 Aug. 1934; *s* of Sir Dinshaw Manockjee Petit, 3rd Bt and Sylla (*d* 1963), *d* of R. D. Tata; *S* father, 1983; *m* 1st, 1964, Nirmala Nanavatty (marr. diss. 1985); two *s*; 2nd, 1986, Elizabeth Maria Tinkelenberg. President: N. M. Petit Charities, 1983–; Sir D. M. Petit Charities, 1983–; F. D. Petit Sanatorium, 1983–; Persian Zoroastrian Amelioration Fund, 1983–; Petit Girls' Orphanage, 1983–; D. M. Petit Gymnasium, 1983–; J. N. Petit Institute, 1983–; Native Gen. Dispensary, 1983–; Trustee, Soc. for Prevention of Cruelty to Animals; Mem., Managing Cttee, B. D. Petit Parsi Gen. Hospital. Pres., Ripon Club, Bombay. *Heir: s* Jehangir Petit, *b* 21 Jan. 1965. *Address:* Petit Hall, 66 Nepean Sea Road, Bombay 400006, India.

PETIT, Roland; Officier de la Légion d'honneur; Chevalier des Arts et des Lettres; Chevalier de l'Ordre National du Mérite; French choreographer and dancer; Artistic Director and Choreographer, Ballet National de Marseille; *b* Villemomble, 13 Jan. 1924; *m* 1954, Renée (Zizi) Jeanmaire; one *d.* *Educ:* Ecole de Ballet de l'Opéra de Paris. L'Opéra de Paris, 1940–44; founded Les Vendredis de la Danse, 1944, Les Ballets des Champs-Elysées, 1945, Les Ballets de Paris de Roland Petit, 1948; Artistic Dir and Choreographer, Ballets de Marseille. Choreographic works include: Les Forains, Le Jeune Homme et la Mort, Les Demoiselles de la nuit, Carmen, Deuil en 24 heures, Le Loup, L'éloge de la Folie, Les Chants de Maldoror, Notre Dame de Paris, Paradise Lost, Les Intermittences du coeur, La Symphonie fantastique, La Dame de Pique, Die Fledermaus, L'Arlésienne, Le Chat Botté, Coppelia, The Blue Angel, Pink Floyd Ballet, Ma Pavlova, Charlot Danse Avec Nous, etc; choreographer and dancer: La Belle au Bois Dormant; Cyrano de Bergerac. Appeared in films Hans Christian Andersen; Un, Deux, Trois, Quatre (arr. ballets, for film, and danced in 3); 4 ballets, Black Tights. *Address:* Ballet National de Marseille, 20 Boulevard Gabès, 13008 Marseille, France.

PETO, Sir Henry (George Morton), 4th Bt *cr* 1855; *b* 29 April 1920; *s* of Comdr Sir Henry Francis Morton Peto, 3rd Bt, RN, and Edith (*d* 1945), *d* of late George Berners Ruck Keene; *S* father, 1978; *m* 1947, Frances Jacqueline, JP, *d* of late Ralph Haldane Evers; two *s.* *Educ:* Sherborne; Corpus Christi College, Cambridge. Served War with Royal Artillery, 1939–46. Manufacturing industry, 1946–80. *Heir: s* Francis Michael Morton Peto [*b* 11 Jan. 1949; *m* 1974, Felicity Margaret, *d* of late Lt-Col John Alan Burns; two *s*]. *Address:* Stream House, Selborne, Alton, Hants GU34 3LE.

PETO, Sir Michael (Henry Basil), 4th Bt *cr* 1927; *b* 6 April 1938; *s* of Brig. Sir Christopher Henry Maxwell Peto, 3rd Bt, DSO, and Barbara (*d* 1992), *yr d* of Edwyn Thomas Close; *S* father, 1980; *m* 1st, 1963, Sarah Susan (marr. diss. 1970), *y d* of Major Sir Dennis Stucley, 5th Bt; one *s* two *d*; 2nd, 1971, Lucinda Mary, *yr d* of Major Sir Charles Douglas Blackett, 9th Bt; two *s.* *Educ:* Eton; Christ Church, Oxford (MA). Called to the Bar, Inner Temple, 1960. Mem., Stock Exchange, 1965–; Dir, Barnett Consulting Gp, 1985–. *Heir: s* Henry Christopher Morton Bampfylde Peto, *b* 8 April 1967. *Address:* Lower Church Cottage, Cliddesden, near Basingstoke, Hants RG25 2JQ. *Club:* Pratt's.

PETO, Prof. Richard, FRS 1989; ICRF Professor of Medical Statistics and Epidemiology, University of Oxford, since 1992; Fellow of Green College, Oxford, since 1979; *b* 14 May 1943; *s* of Leonard Huntley Peto and Carrie Clarinda Peto; *m* 1970, Sallie Messum (marr. diss.); two *s*, and two *s* by Gale Mead. *Educ:* Trinity Coll., Cambridge (MA Natural Sci.); Imperial Coll., London (MSc Statistics). Research Officer: MRC, 1967–69; Univ. of Oxford, 1969–72; Lectr, Dept of Regius Prof. of Medicine, 1972–75, Reader in Cancer Studies, 1975–92, Univ. of Oxford. *Publications:* Natural History of Chronic Bronchitis and Emphysema, 1976; Quantification of Occupational Cancer, 1981; The Causes of Cancer, 1983; Diet, Lifestyle and Mortality in China, 1990; (jtly) Mortality from Smoking in Developed Countries 1950–2000, 1994. *Recreations:* science, children. *Address:* Radcliffe Infirmary, Oxford OX2 6HE. *T:* Oxford (01865) 52830/58379.

PETRE, family name of **Baron Petre.**

PETRE, 18th Baron *cr* 1603; **John Patrick Lionel Petre;** DL; *b* 4 Aug. 1942; *s* of 17th Baron Petre and of Marguerite Eileen, *d* of late Ion Wentworth Hamilton; *S* father, 1989; *m* 1965, Marcia Gwendolyn, *d* of Alfred Plumpton; two *s* one *d.* *Educ:* Eton; Trinity College, Oxford (MA). DL Essex, 1991. OStJ 1994. *Heir: s* Hon. Dominic William Petre, *b* 9 Aug. 1966. *Address:* Writtle Park, Highwood, Chelmsford, Essex CM1 3QF.

PETRE, Francis Herbert Loraine; His Honour Judge Petre; a Circuit Judge, since 1972; Chairman, Police Complaints Authority, 1989–92; *b* 9 March 1927; *s* of late Maj.-Gen. R. L. Petre, CB, DSO, MC and Mrs Katherine Sophia Petre; *m* 1958, Mary Jane, *d* of late Everard C. X. White and Sydney Mary Carleton White (*née* Holmes), three *s* one *d.* *Educ:* Downside; Clare Coll., Cambridge. Called to Bar, Lincoln's Inn, 1952; Dep. Chm., E Suffolk QS, 1970; Dep. Chm., Agricultural Lands Tribunal (Eastern Area), 1972; a Recorder, 1972; Regular Judge, Central Criminal Court, 1982–93. *Address:* The Ferriers, Bures, Suffolk CO8 5DL.

PETRIE, Joan Caroline, (Lady Bathurst); HM Diplomatic Service, retired 1972; *b* 2 Nov. 1920; *d* of late James Alexander Petrie, Barrister-at-law, and Adrienne Johanna (*née* van den Bergh); *m* 1968, Sir Maurice Edward Bathurst, *qv*; one step *s.* *Educ:* Wycombe Abbey Sch.; Newnham Coll., Cambridge (Mary Ewart Schol.). 1st cl. Med. and Mod. Langs Tripos, 1942, MA 1964. Entered HM Foreign Service, 1947: FO, 1947–48; 2nd Sec., The Hague, 1948–50; FO, 1950–54; 1st Sec., 1953; Bonn, 1954–58; FO (later FCO), 1958–71; Counsellor 1969; Head of European Communities Information Unit, FCO, 1969–71. Mem., UK Delegn to Colombo Plan Consultative Cttee, Jogjakarta, 1959. Adviser, British Group, Inter-Parly Union, 1962–68. Officer, Order of Leopold (Belgium), 1966. *Recreations:* music, genealogy, gardening. *Address:* Airlie, The Highlands, East Horsley, Surrey KT24 5BG. *T:* East Horsley (01483) 283269. *Club:* United Oxford & Cambridge University.

PETRIE, Sir Peter (Charles), 5th Bt *cr* 1918, of Carrowcarden; CMG 1980; Adviser on European and Parliamentary Affairs to Governor of Bank of England, since 1989; HM Diplomatic Service, retired; *b* 7 March 1932; *s* of Sir Charles Petrie, 3rd Bt, CBE, FRHistS and Jessie Cecilia (*d* 1987), *d* of Frederick James George Mason; *S* half-brother, 1988; *m* 1958, Countess Lydwine Maria Fortunata v. Oberndorff, *d* of Count v. Oberndorff, The Hague and Paris; two *s* one *d.* *Educ:* Westminster; Christ Church, Oxford. BA Lit. Hum., MA. 2nd Lieut Grenadier Guards, 1954–56. Entered HM Foreign Service, 1956; served in UK Delegn to NATO, Paris 1958–61; UK High Commn, New Delhi (seconded CRO), 1961–64; Chargé d'Affaires, Katmandu, 1963; Cabinet Office, 1965–67; UK Mission to UN, NY, 1969–73; Counsellor (Head of Chancery), Bonn, 1973–76; Head of European Integration Dept (Internal), FCO, 1976–79; Minister, Paris, 1979–85; Ambassador to Belgium, 1985–89. *Recreations:* country pursuits. *Heir: s* Charles James Petrie [*b* 16 Sept. 1959; *m* 1981, France de Hauteclocque; three *s* (one *d* decd)]. *Address:* 16A Cambridge Street, SW1V 4QH; 40 rue Lauriston, 75116 Paris, France; Le Hameau du Jardin, Lestre, 50310 Montebourg, France. *Clubs:* Brooks's, Beefsteak; Jockey (Paris).

PETT, Maj.-Gen. Raymond Austin, CB 1995; MBE 1976; Director of Infantry, since 1994; *b* 23 Sept. 1941; *s* of late Richard John Austin Pett and Jessie Lyle Pett (*née* Adamson); *m* 1965, (Joan) Marie McGrath Price, *d* of FO Bernard Christopher McGrath, RAF (killed in action 1943) and of Mrs Robert Henry Benbow Price; one *s* one *d*. *Educ:* Christ's Coll.; RMA Sandhurst; rcds, psc. Commnd Lancashire Regt (Prince of Wales's Vols), 1961; regtl service in GB, BAOR, Swaziland and Cyprus; seconded 2nd Bn 6th QEO Gurkha Rifles, Malaysia and Hong Kong, 1967–69; Instr, RMA Sandhurst, 1969–72; Staff Coll., 1972–73; DAA&QMG, HQ 48 Gurkha Inf. Bde, 1974–75; 1st Bn, Queen's Lancashire Regt, 1976–78; GSO2 ASD 3, MoD, 1978–80; CO, 1st Bn King's Own Royal Border Regt, 1980–82; Staff Coll. (HQ and Directing Staff), 1983–84; Col ASD 2, MoD, 1984; Col Army Plans, MoD, 1985; Comd Gurkha Field Force, 1985–86, and Comd 48 Gurkha Inf. Bde, 1986–87, Hong Kong; RCDS 1988; Dir, Army Staff Duties, MoD, 1989–91; DCS and Sen. British Officer, HQ AFNORTH, 1991–94. Col, 6th QEO Gurkha Rifles, 1988–94; Col Comdt, King's Div., 1994–. FIMgt. *Recreations:* the arts, military history, house restoration, ski-ing. *Clubs:* Army and Navy, Ronnie Scott's.

PETTIFER, Julian; freelance writer and broadcaster; *b* 21 July 1935; *s* of Stephen Henry Pettifer and Diana Mary (*née* Burton); unmarried. *Educ:* Marlborough; St John's Coll., Cambridge. Television reporter, writer and presenter: Southern TV, 1958–62; Tonight, BBC, 1962–64; 24 Hours, BBC, 1964–69; Panorama, BBC, 1969–75; Presenter, Cuba—25 years of revolution (series), ITV, 1984; Host, Busman's Holiday, ITV, 1985–86. Numerous television documentaries, including: Vietnam, War without End, 1970; The World About Us, 1976; The Spirit of '76, 1976; Diamonds in the Sky, 1979; Nature Watch, 1981–82, 1985–86, 1988, 1990, 1992; Automania, 1984; The Living Isles, 1986; Missionaries, 1990; See for Yourself, 1991; Assignment, 1991; Nature, 1992. Trustee, Royal Botanic Gdns, Kew, 1993–. President: Berks, Bucks and Oxfordshire Naturalists Trust, 1990–; RSPB, 1995–; Vice-Pres., RSNC, 1992–. Reporter of the Year Award, Guild of Television Directors and Producers, 1968; Cherry Kearton Award for Contribution to Wildlife Films, RGS, 1990. *Publications:* (jtly) Diamonds in the Sky: a social history of air travel, 1979; (jtly) Nature Watch, 1981; (jtly) Automania, 1984; (jtly) Missionaries, 1990; (jtly) Nature Watch, 1994. *Recreations:* travel, sport, cinema. *Address:* c/o Curtis Brown, 28–29 Haymarket, SW1Y 4SP. *T:* 0171–396 6600. *Club:* Queen's.

PETTIFOR, Prof. David Godfrey, PhD; FRS 1994; Isaac Wolfson Professor of Metallurgy, since 1992, and Head of Department of Materials, since 1994, Oxford University; Fellow, St Edmund Hall, Oxford, since 1992; *b* 9 March 1945; *s* of Percy Hayward Pettifor and Margaret Cotterill; *m* 1969, Lynda Ann Potgieter (marr. diss. 1989); two *s*. *Educ:* Univ. of Witwatersrand (BSc Hons 1967); PhD Cantab 1970. Lectr, Dept of Physics, Univ. of Dar es Salaam, 1971; Res. Asst, Cavendish Lab., Cambridge, 1974; Vis. Res. Scientist, Bell Labs, USA, 1978; Imperial College, London: Lectr and Reader, Dept of Mathematics, 1978–88; Prof. of Theoretical Solid State Physics, 1988–92. *Publications:* papers incl. Structures maps for pseudo-binary and ternary phases (Inst. of Metals Prize, 1989). *Recreation:* walking. *Address:* Department of Materials, University of Oxford, Parks Road, Oxford OX1 3PH. *T:* Oxford (01865) 273751.

PETTIGREW, Prof. John Douglas, FRS 1987; FAA 1987; Professor of Physiology, since 1983, Director, Vision, Touch and Hearing Research Centre, since 1988, University of Queensland; *b* 2 Oct. 1943; *s* of John James Pettigrew and Enid Dellmere Holt; *m* 1968, Rona Butler; one *s* two *d*. *Educ:* Katoomba High Sch.; Univ. of Sydney (BSc Med., MSc, MB BS). Jun. Resident MO, Royal Prince Alfred Hosp., 1969; Miller Fellow 1970–72, Res. Associate 1973, Univ. of California, Berkeley; Asst Prof. of Biology 1974, Associate Prof. of Biology 1978, CIT; Actg Dir, National Vision Res. Inst. of Aust., 1981. *Publications:* Visual Neuroscience, 1986; numerous pubns in Nature, Science, Jl of Physiol., Jl of Comp. Neurol., Exp. Brain Res., etc. *Recreations:* bird watching, mountaineering. *Address:* 423 Savages Road, Brookfield, Qld 4069, Australia. *T:* (7) 33741561.

PETTIGREW, Sir Russell (Hilton), Kt 1983; FInstD; FCIT; Chairman, Chep Handling Systems NZ Ltd, 1980–93; *b* 10 Sept. 1920; *s* of Albert and Bertha Pettigrew; *m* 1965, Glennis Olive Nicol; one *s* one *d*. *Educ:* Hangatiki Sch., King Country. Served War, Naval Service, 1941–45 (Service Medals). Hawkes Bay Motor Co., 1935–40; Pettigrews Transport, 1946–63; formed Allied Freightways (now Freightways Holdings Ltd), 1964. Chairman: NZ Maritime Holdings Ltd, 1981–89; AGC NZ, 1984–88; Dep. Chm., NZ Forest Products, 1980–88 (Dir, 1975–90). FCIT 1972; Fellow, NZ Inst. of Dirs, 1972; Life Mem., NZ Road Transport Assoc., 1981. Knighthood for services to the Transport Industry. *Publication:* article in The Modern Freight Forwarder and the Road Carrier, 1971. *Recreations:* farming, deer farming, stud breeding (Herefords), Rugby, surfing, jogging, horse racing. *Address:* PO Box 16, Bay View, Napier, New Zealand. *T:* (6) 8366426. *Clubs:* Auckland, Hawkes Bay (New Zealand).

PETTIT, Sir Daniel (Eric Arthur), Kt 1974; Chairman, PosTel Investment Management (formerly Post Office Staff Superannuation Fund), 1979–83; *b* Liverpool, 19 Feb. 1915; *s* of Thomas Edgar Pettit and Pauline Elizabeth Pettit (*née* Kerr); *m* 1940, Winifred, *d* of William and Sarah Bibby; two *s*. *Educ:* Quarry Bank High Sch., Liverpool; Fitzwilliam Coll., Cambridge (MA; Hon. Fellow, 1985). School Master, 1938–40 and 1946–47; War Service, Africa, India, Burma, 1940–46 (Major, RA); Unilever: Management, 1948–57; Associated Company Dir and Chm., 1958–70. Chm., Nat. Freight Corp., 1971–78 (part-time Mem. Bd, 1968–70); Member: Freight Integration Council, 1971–78; National Ports Council, 1971–80; Bd, Foundn of Management Educn, 1973–84; Waste Management Adv. Council, 1971–78; Chm., EDC for Distributive Trades, 1974–78. Chairman: Incpen, 1979–90; RDC Properties, 1987–; Director: Lloyds Bank Ltd, 1977–78 (Chm., Birmingham & W Midlands Bd, 1978–85); Lloyds Bank (UK) Ltd, 1979–85; Black Horse Life Assurance Co. Ltd, 1983–85; Lloyds Bank Unit Trust Managers Ltd, 1981–85; Bransford Farmers Ltd. Mem. Council, British Road Fedn Ltd. Hon. Col, 162 Regt RCT (V). Freeman, City of London, 1971; Liveryman, Worshipful Co. of Carmen, 1971. CBIM; FCIT (Pres. 1971–72); FRSA; FIM; MIPM. *Publications:* various papers on transport and management matters. *Recreations:* cricket, Association football (Olympic Games, 1936; Corinthian FC, 1935–); fly-fishing. *Address:* Bransford Court Farm, Worcester WR6 5JL. *Clubs:* Farmers', MCC; Hawks (Cambridge).

PETTITT, Gordon Charles, OBE 1991; transport management consultant; Managing Director, Regional Railways, British Rail, 1991–92; *b* 12 April 1934; *s* of Charles and Annie Pettitt; *m* 1956, Ursula Margareta Agnes Hokamp; three *d*. *Educ:* St Columba's Coll., St Albans; Pitman's Coll., London. FCIT. British Rail, 1950–92: Freight Sales Manager, Eastern Reg., 1976; Chief Passenger Manager, Western Reg., 1978; Divl Manager, Liverpool Street, Eastern Reg., 1979; Dep. Gen. Manager, 1983, Gen. Manager, 1985, Southern Reg.; Dir, Provincial, 1990–91. Governor, Middlesex Univ. (formerly Polytechnic), 1989–. *Recreations:* walking, foreign travel. *Address:* Beeches Green, Woodham Lane, Woking, Surrey GU21 5SP.

PETTY, Very Rev. John Fitzmaurice; Provost of Coventry Cathedral, since 1988; *b* 1935; *m* 1963, Susan Shakerley; three *s* one *d*. *Educ:* RMA Sandhurst; Trinity Hall, Cambridge (BA 1959, MA 1965); Cuddesdon College. Commnd RE, 1955; seconded Gurkha Engineers, 1959–62; resigned commission as Captain, 1964. Deacon 1966, priest 1967; Curate: St Cuthbert, Sheffield, 1966–69; St Helier, Southwark Dio., 1969–75; Vicar of St John's, Hurst, Ashton-under-Lyne, 1975–87; Area Dean of Ashton-under-Lyne, 1983–87; Hon. Canon of Manchester Cathedral, 1986. *Recreations:* cycling, ski-ing. *Address:* c/o Coventry Cathedral, 7 Priory Row, Coventry CV1 5ES. *T:* Coventry (01203) 227597.

PETTY, William Henry, CBE 1981; County Education Officer, Kent, 1973–84; *b* 7 Sept. 1921; *s* of Henry and Eveline Ann Petty, Bradford; *m* 1948, Margaret Elaine, *o d* of Edward and Lorna Bastow, Baildon, Yorks; one *s* two *d*. *Educ:* Bradford Grammar Sch.; Peterhouse, Cambridge; London Univ. MA 1950, BSc 1953. Served RA, India and Burma, 1941–45. Admin, teaching and lectrg in London, Doncaster and N R Yorks, 1946–57; Sen. Asst Educn Officer, W R Yorks CC 1957–64; Dep. County Educn Officer, Kent CC, 1964–73. Member: Council and Court, Univ. of Kent at Canterbury, 1974–84, 1992–; Local Govt Trng Bd, Careers Service Trng Cttee, 1975–84; Careers Service Adv. Council, 1976–84; Trng and Further Educn Cons. Gp, 1977–83; Vital Skills Task Gp, 1977–78; Manpower Services Commn, SE Counties Area Bd, 1978–83; Bd of Dirs, Industrial Trng Service, 1978–; Exec. Mem. and Sec. for SE Reg., Soc. of Educn Officers, 1978–82; Pres., Soc. of Educn Officers, 1980–81; Chm., Assoc. of Educn Officers, 1979–80 (Vice-Chm., 1978–79); Member: JNC for Chief Officers, Officers' side, 1974–84 (Chm., 1981–84); C of E Bd of Educn, Schs Cttee, 1981–86; County Educn Officers' Soc., 1974–84 (Chm., 1982–83); Youth Trng Task Gp, 1982; National Youth Trng Bd, 1983–84; Kent Area Manpower Bd, 1983–84; Canterbury Diocesan Bd of Educn, 1984–92 (Vice-Chm., 1989–92); Consultant, Further Educn Unit, 1984–90. Dir, Sennocke Services Ltd, 1989–. Governor: Christ Church Coll., Canterbury, 1974–94 (Chm., 1992–94; Vice-Chm., 1988–92); Sevenoaks Sch., 1974–; YMCA Nat. Coll., 1992–94. Hon. DLitt Kent, 1983. Prizewinner: Cheltenham Fest. of Lit., 1968; Camden Fest. of Music and Arts, 1969. Greenwood Prize, 1978; Lake Aske Meml Award, 1980. *Publications:* No Bold Comfort, 1957; Conquest, 1967; (jtly) Educational Administration, 1980; Executive Summaries (booklets), 1984–90; Springfield, 1994; (with Robert Roberts) Genius Loci, 1995; contrib. educnl and lit. jls and anthologies. *Recreations:* literature, travel. *Address:* Willow Bank, Moat Road, Headcorn, Kent TN27 9NT. *T:* Headcorn (01622) 890087. *Club:* United Oxford & Cambridge University.

PETTY-FITZMAURICE; *see* Mercer Nairne Petty-Fitzmaurice, family name of Marquess of Lansdowne.

PEYREFITTE, (Pierre-) Roger; French author; *b* 17 Aug. 1907; *o s* of Jean Peyrefitte, landowner, and Eugénie Jamme; unmarried. *Educ:* Collège St Benoit, Ardouane, Hérault (Lazarist); Collège du Caousou, Toulouse, Hte. Garonne (Jesuit); Lycée de Foix, Ariège; Université de Toulouse; Ecole libre des Sciences Politiques, Paris. Bachelier de l'enseignement secondaire; Diplôme d'études supérieures de langue et de littérature française; Diplômé de l'Ecole libre des Sciences Politiques (major de la section diplomatique). Concours diplomatique, 1931; attached to Ministry of Foreign Affairs, 1931–33; Secretary, French Embassy, Athens, 1933–38; attached to Ministry of Foreign Affairs, 1938–40 and 1943–45. *Publications:* Du Vésuve à l'Etna, 1952; Chevaliers de Malte, 1957; La Nature du Prince, 1963; Les Juifs, 1965; Notre Amour, 1967; Manouche, 1972; Un Musée de l'Amour, 1972; La Muse garçonnière, 1973; Catalogue de la collection de monnaies grecques et romaines de l'auteur, 1974; Tableaux de chasse, ou la vie extraordinaire de Fernand Legros, 1976; Propos secrets, 1977; La Jeunesse d'Alexandre, 1977; L'Enfant de coeur, 1978; Les Conquêtes d'Alexandre, 1980; Propos secrets 2, 1980; Alexandre le Grand, 1981; Henry de Montherlant-Roger Peyrefitte: Correspondence, 1983; Voltaire, Sa Jeunesse et son Temps, 1985; L'Innominato, nouveaux propos secrets, 1989; Réflexion sur De Gaulle, 1992; Voltaire et Frédéric II, 1992; *novels:* Les Amitiés particulières, 1944 (Prix Théophraste Renaudot, 1945); Mademoiselle de Murville, 1947; L'Oracle, 1948; Les Amours singulières, 1949; La Mort d'une mère, 1950; Les Ambassades, 1951; La Fin des Ambassades, 1953; Les Clés de Saint Pierre, 1955; Jeunes proies, 1956; L'Exilé de Capri, 1959; Les Fils de la lumière, 1962; Les Américains, 1968; Des Français, 1970; La Coloquinte, 1971; Roy, 1979; L'Illustre écrivain, 1982; La Soutane rouge, 1983; *plays:* Le Prince des neiges, 1947; Le Spectateur nocturne, 1960; Les Ambassades (adaptation of A. P. Antoine), 1961. *Recreations:* travel, walks, collecting antiques. *Address:* 9 Avenue du Maréchal Maunoury, 75016 Paris, France.

PEYTON, family name of **Baron Peyton of Yeovil.**

PEYTON OF YEOVIL, Baron *cr* 1983 (Life Peer), of Yeovil in the County of Somerset; **John Wynne William Peyton;** PC 1970; Chairman, British Alcan Aluminium, 1987–91; *b* 13 Feb. 1919; *s* of late Ivor Eliot Peyton and Dorothy Helen Peyton; *m* 1947, Diana Clinch (marr. diss., 1966); one *s* one *d* (and one *s* decd); *m* 1966, Mrs Mary Cobbold. *Educ:* Eton; Trinity College, Oxford. Commissioned 15/19 Hussars, 1939; Prisoner of War, Germany, 1940–45. Called to the Bar, Inner Temple, 1945. MP (C) Yeovil, 1951–83; Parly Secretary, Ministry of Power, 1962–64; Minister of Transport, June-Oct. 1970; Minister for Transport Industries, DoE, 1970–74. Chm., Texas Instruments Ltd, 1974–90. Treas., Zoological Society of London, 1984–91. *Address:* The Old Malt House, Hinton St George, Somerset TA17 8SE. *T:* Crewkerne (01460) 73618; 6 Temple West Mews, West Square, SE11 4TJ. *T:* 0171–582 3611. *Club:* Boodle's.

PEYTON, Kathleen Wendy; writer (as K. M. Peyton); *b* 2 Aug. 1929; *d* of William Joseph Herald and Ivy Kathleen Herald; *m* 1950, Michael Peyton; two *d*. *Educ:* Wimbledon High Sch.; Manchester Sch. of Art (ATD). Taught art at Northampton High Sch., 1953–55; started writing seriously after birth of first child, although had already had 4 books published. *Publications: as Kathleen Herald:* Sabre, the Horse from the Sea, 1947, USA 1963; The Mandrake, 1949; Crab the Roan, 1953; *as K. M. Peyton:* North to Adventure, 1959, USA 1965; Stormcock Meets Trouble, 1961; The Hard Way Home, 1962; Windfall, 1963, USA (as Sea Fever), 1963; Brownsea Silver, 1964; The Maplin Bird, 1964, USA 1965 (New York Herald Tribune Award, 1965); The Plan for Birdsmarsh, 1965, USA 1966; Thunder in the Sky, 1966, USA 1967; Flambards Trilogy (Guardian Award, 1970): Flambards, 1967, USA 1968; The Edge of the Cloud, 1969, USA 1969 (Carnegie Medal, 1969); Flambards in Summer, 1969, USA 1970; Fly-by-Night, 1968, USA 1969; Pennington's Seventeenth Summer, 1970, USA (as Pennington's Last Term), 1971; The Beethoven Medal, 1971, USA 1972; The Pattern of Roses, 1972, USA 1973; Pennington's Heir, 1973, USA 1974; The Team, 1975; The Right-Hand Man, 1977; Prove Yourself a Hero, 1977, USA 1978; A Midsummer Night's Death, 1978, USA 1979; Marion's Angels, 1979, USA 1979; Flambards Divided, 1981; Dear Fred, 1981, USA 1981; Going Home, 1983, USA 1983; Who, Sir? Me, Sir?, 1983; The Last Ditch, 1984, USA (as Free Rein), 1983; Froggett's Revenge, 1985; The Sound of Distant Cheering, 1986; Downhill All the Way, 1988; Darkling, 1989, USA 1990; Skylark, 1989; No Roses Round the Door, 1990; Poor Badger, 1991, USA 1991; Late to Smile, 1992; The Boy Who Wasn't There, 1992, USA 1992; The Wild Boy, 1993; Snowfall, 1994. *Recreations:* riding, walking, gardening, sailing. *Address:* Rookery Cottage, North Fambridge, Chelmsford, Essex CM3 6LP.

PEYTON-JONES, Julia; Director, Serpentine Gallery, since 1991; *b* 18 Feb. 1952; *d* of Jeremy Peyton-Jones and Rhona (*née* Wood); *m* 1975, Prosper Riley-Smith (marr. diss.

1985). *Educ:* Tudor Hall; Byam Shaw Sch. of Art (Dip BS; LCAD); Royal Coll. of Art (MA). Started 20th century Picture Dept, Phillips, auctioneers, 1974–75; Lectr, Painting and Humanities Depts, Edinburgh Sch. of Art, 1978–79; Organiser: Atlantis Gall., London, 1980–81; Wapping Artists' Open Studios Exhibn, 1981–82; Tolly Cobbold Eastern Arts 4th Nat. Exhibn, Cambridge and tour, 1982–84; Raoul Dufy 1877–1953 exhibn, Hayward Gall., 1983–84; Linbury Prize for Stage Design (selection and exhibn), 1986–87 (Mem., Exec. Cttee, 1988–); Sponsorship Officer, Arts Council and S Bank Bd, 1984–87; Curator, Hayward Gall., 1988–91. Arts Council: Collection Purchaser, 1989–90; Mem., Visual Arts Projects Cttee, 1991–93; Mem., Visual Arts, Photography and Architecture Panel, 1994–. Trustee: Public Art Develt Trust, 1987–88; Chisenhale Trust, 1987–89; New Contemporaries Exhibn, 1988–90. Painter, 1974–87; exhibitions include: Riverside Studios (individual), 1978; ICA, 1973; John Moores, Liverpool, 1978; Royal Scottish Acad., 1979. *Recreations:* contemporary arts in general, visual arts in particular. *Address:* 25 Sudeley Street, N1 8HW.

PFIRTER, Rogelio (Francisco Emilio); Ambassador of the Argentine Republic to the Court of St James's, since 1995; *b* 25 Aug. 1948; *s* of Rogelio and Amanda Pfirter von Mayenfisch; *m* 1980, Isabel Serantes Braun. *Educ:* Colegio Inmaculada SJ, Argentina; Universidad de Litoral (grad as lawyer); Inst. of Foreign Service, Argentina. Third Sec., S America Dept, 1974; Second, then First Sec., Perm. Mission to UN, 1975–80; Counsellor: Undersecretariat of Foreign Affairs, 1980–81; London, 1982; Minister Counsellor, then Minister Plenipotentiary, Perm. Mission to UN, 1982–90; Alternate Perm. Rep. to UN, 1989; Dep. Hd, Foreign Minister's Cabinet, 1990–91; Dir, Internat. Security, Nuclear and Space Affairs, 1991; Under-Sec., Foreign Policy, 1992; Mem., Posting and Promotion Bd, 1993–95. Mem., Bd of Dirs, Argentine Nat. Commn for Space Activities, 1994–95. Mem., UN Adv. Bd on Disarmament Matters, 1993–96. Order of Merit, Cavaliere di Gran Croce (Italy), 1992; Order of Merit (Chile), 1992; Order of Isabel la Católica (Spain), 1994. *Publications:* (jtly) Cuentos Originales, 1965; articles on policy, in particular on security and nuclear affairs. *Address:* The Argentine Embassy, 53 Hans Place, SW1A 0LA. *T:* 0171–584 6494. *Club:* Los Pingüinos (Buenos Aires).

PFLEGER, Martin Charles; Assistant Auditor General (Principal Establishment Officer and Principal Finance Officer), National Audit Office, since 1993; *b* 5 May 1948; *m*; two *s* one *d*; *m* 1995, Amanda Jane Dolphin. *Educ:* CIPFA. National Audit Office: Dir, IT Audit, 1986; Dir, Corporate Policy and Finance, 1988. MInstD, 1991. Editor, IntoIT; Mem. Editl Bd, Government Computing and AudIT. *Publications:* articles on IT and business management in the public sector. *Recreations:* golf, hill walking, bridge. *Address:* National Audit Office, 157–197 Buckingham Palace Road, SW1W 9SP. *T:* 0171–798 7314.

PFLIMLIN, Pierre; *b* 5 Feb. 1907; *s* of Jules Pflimlin and Léonie Schwartz; *m* 1939, Marie-Odile Heinrich; one *s* two *d*. *Educ:* Mulhouse; University of Strasbourg. Dr of Laws, 1932. Mem. for Bas-Rhin Dept, French Parliament (Nat. Assembly), 1945–67; Under Sec. of State, Ministries for Public Health and for Economics, 1946; Minister: of Agriculture, 1947–49 and 1950–51; of Trade and External Economic Relations, 1951–52; of State in charge of relations with Council of Europe, 1952; for Overseas Territories, 1952–53; of Finance and Economics, 1955–56 and 1957–58; Prime Minister, May-June 1958; Minister of State in de Gaulle Govt, 1958–59; Minister of State for Co-operation with Overseas Countries, 1962. Mem., Consultative Assembly of Council of Europe (President, 1963–66) and of European Parliament, 1959–67; European Parliament: Mem., 1979–89; Vice-Pres., 1979–84; Pres., 1984–87. Mayor, City of Strasbourg, 1959–83. *Publications:* Industry in Mulhouse, 1932; The Economic Structure of the Third Reich, 1938; Alsace: destiny and will, 1963; The Europe of the Communities, 1966; Mémoires d'un Européen de la IVe à la Ve République, 1991. *Address:* 24 avenue de la Paix, 67000 Strasbourg, France. *T:* 88373235.

PHAROAH, Prof. Peter Oswald Derrick, MD, FFCM; Professor of Public Health (formerly of Community Health), University of Liverpool, since 1979; *b* 19 May 1934; *s* of Oswald Higgins Pharoah and Phyllis Christine Gahan; *m* 1960, Margaret Rose McMinn; three *s* one *d*. *Educ:* Lawrence Memorial Royal Military School, Lovedale, India; Palmers School, Grays, Essex; St Mary's Hospital Medical School. MD, MSc. Graduated, 1958; Med. House Officer and Med. Registrar appointments at various London Hosps, 1958–63; MO and Research MO, Dept of Public Health, Papua New Guinea, 1963–74; Sen. Lectr in Community Health, London School of Hygiene and Tropical Medicine, 1974–79. *Publication:* Endemic Cretinism, 1971. *Recreations:* squash, walking, philately. *Address:* 11 Fawley Road, Liverpool L18 9TE. *T:* 0151–724 4896.

PHELAN, His Honour Andrew James; a Circuit Judge, 1974–95; *b* 25 July 1923; *e s* of Cornelius Phelan, Kilganey House, Clonmel, Eire; *m* 1950, Joan Robertson McLagan; one *s* two *d*. *Educ:* Clongoweswood, Co. Kildare; National Univ. of Ireland (MA); Trinity Coll., Cambridge. Called to: Irish Bar, King's Inn, 1945; English Bar, Gray's Inn, 1949. Jun. Fellow, Univ. of Bristol, 1948–50; in practice at English Bar, 1950–74. *Publication:* The Law for Small Boats, 2nd edn, 1970. *Recreations:* sailing, mountain walking. *Address:* 17 Hartington Road, Chiswick, W4 3TL. *T:* 0181–994 6109. *Clubs:* Royal Cruising, Bar Yacht.

PHELPS, Anthony John, CB 1976; Deputy Chairman, Board of Customs and Excise, 1973–82; *b* 14 Oct. 1922; *s* of John Francis and Dorothy Phelps, Oxford; *m* 1st, 1949, Sheila Nan Rait (*d* 1967), *d* of late Colin Benton Rait, Edinburgh; one *s* two *d*; 2nd, 1971, Janet M. T., *d* of late Charles R. Dawson, Edinburgh. *Educ:* City of Oxford High Sch.; University Coll., Oxford. HM Treasury, 1946; Jun. Private Sec. to Chancellor of the Exchequer, 1949–50; Principal, 1950; Treasury Rep. in Far East, 1953–55; Private Sec. to the Prime Minister, 1958–61; Asst Sec., 1961; Under-Sec., 1968. Freeman, City of Oxford, 1971. *Publication:* (with Sir Richard Hayward) A History of Civil Service Cricket, 1993. *Recreations:* music, watching sport. *Address:* 1 Woodsyre, Sydenham Hill, SE26 6SS. *T:* 0181–670 0735. *Clubs:* City Livery, MCC.

PHELPS, Charles Frederick, DPhil, DSc; educational consultant; Consultant to Rector on International Affairs, Imperial College of Science, Technology and Medicine, 1990–92; *b* 18 Jan. 1934; *s* of Seth Phelps and Rigmor Kaae; *m* 1960, Joanna Lingeman; one *s* one *d*. *Educ:* Bromsgrove Sch.; Oxford Univ. (MA, DPhil; DSc 1990). Lecturer, Univ. of Bristol: in Chemical Physiology, 1960–63; in Biochemistry, 1963–70; Reader in Biochemistry, Univ. of Bristol, 1970–74; Prof. of Biochemistry, Univ. of Lancaster, 1974–80; Principal, Chelsea Coll., London, 1981–84; Pro-Rector (Internat. Affairs), Imperial Coll., 1984–89. Visiting Fellow, Univ. of Rome, 1968–69. Consultant, World Bank Educational Mission to China, 1980 and to Korea, 1982. Mem. Senate, 1980–84, Mem., F and GP Cttee, 1983–88, Chm., Univ. Trng Cttee, 1984–92, London Univ. Member: Cttee, Biochemical Soc., 1980–84; Cttee, British Biophysical Soc., 1974–84 (Chm., 1983–84); Research Cttee of Arthritis and Rheumatism Council, 1974–78. Trustee, America European Community Assoc. Trust, 1986–. Mem. Governing Body, Royal Postgraduate Med. Fedn, 1986–92; Mem. Council, Queen Elizabeth Coll., 1983–85; Governor: Furzedown Sch., 1980–85; King Edward Sch., Witley, 1984–; Mill Hill Sch., 1985–; Royal Grammar Sch., Guildford, 1989–. FKC 1985. Editorial Board: Biochim. Biophys. Acta, 1976–80, 1983–84; Internat. Research Communications Systems Jl of Med. Scis, 1980–. *Publications:* numerous papers in medical and science jls. *Recreations:* enjoying things Italian, 17th Century science, landscape gardening. *Address:* Brockhurst, The Green, Chiddingfold, near Guildford, Surrey GU8 4TU. *T:* Wormley (01428) 683092. *Club:* Athenæum.

PHELPS, Howard Thomas Henry Middleton; Chairman, Brewery Court Ltd, 1990–94; *b* 20 Oct. 1926; *s* of Ernest Henry Phelps, Gloucester, and Harriet (*née* Middleton); *m* 1949, Audrey (*née* Ellis); one *d*. *Educ:* Crypt Grammar Sch., Gloucester; Hatfield Coll.; Durham Univ. BA Hons Politics and Econs 1951. National Coal Board, Lancs, Durham and London, 1951–72, finally Dep. Dir-Gen. of Industrial Relations; Personnel Dir, BOAC, 1972; British Airways: Gp Personnel Dir, 1972; Bd Mem., 1973–83; Dir of Operations, 1979–86. Chairman: Sutcliffe Catering Gp, 1986–88; Sterling Guards Ltd, 1986–89; Earls Court and Olympia Ltd, 1986–89; Niccol Centre Ltd, 1989–90. Non-Exec. Chm., QA Training Ltd, Cirencester, 1989–94; Dir, P&OSN Co., 1986–89; Non-Exec. Dir, Alden Press Ltd, Oxford, 1990–. FRAeS; FCIT; CBIM. Chm., Alice Ruston Housing Assoc., 1973–84; President: Durham Univ. Soc., 1988– (Chm., 1975–88); Pres., Hatfield Assoc., 1983–. Chm. Council, Durham Univ., 1992– (Mem., 1985–88); Dep. Chm., Governing Body, Middlesex Polytechnic, 1987–89 (Vis. Prof., 1987–); Chm., Cirencester Tertiary Coll., 1990–; Gov., Rendcomb Coll., Cirencester. *Recreations:* gardening, musical appreciation. *Address:* Tall Trees, Chedworth, near Cheltenham, Glos GL54 4AB. *T:* Fossebridge (01285) 720324. *Club:* Royal Over-Seas League.

PHELPS, Maj.-Gen. Leonard Thomas Herbert, CB 1973; OBE 1963; *b* 9 Sept. 1917; *s* of Abijah and Jane Phelps; *m* 1945, Jean Irene, *d* of R. Price Dixon; one *s* one *d*. CIMgt (CBIM 1980; FBIM 1973). Served War, Hong Kong, 1940–41; India/Burma, 1941–47. Student, Staff Coll., Quetta, 1946; DAQMG, HQ Land Forces Hong Kong, 1951–53; Second in Command, 4th Trng Bn, RAOC, 1955–57; War Office: DAAG, 1957–59; ADOS, 1961–63; AA & QMG Singapore Mil. Forces, 1963; Chief of Staff and Dep Comdr, 4th Malaysian Inf. Bde, 1964; ADOS, WO, 1965–67; Chief Inspector, Land Service Ammunition, 1967–70; Comdr, Base Organisation, RAOC, 1970; Dir, Ordnance Services, MoD (Army), 1971–73; retired 1973; Col Comdt, RAOC, 1976–78. Man. Dir, The Warrior Gp, 1975–78; Director: Leon Davis & Co., 1975–82; Debenhams Business Systems Ltd, 1982–84. Parchment Award for life saving, Royal Humane Soc., 1936. *Publication:* A History of the Royal Army Ordnance Corps 1945–1982, 1991.

PHELPS, Maurice Arthur; human resource consultant, since 1989; Managing Partner, Emslie Phelps Consultancy Group; *b* 17 May 1935; *s* of H. T. Phelps; *m* 1960, Elizabeth Anne Hurley; two *s* one *d*. *Educ:* Wandsworth School; Corpus Christi College, Oxford Univ. BA Hons Modern History. Shell Chemical Co. Ltd, 1959–68; Group Personnel Planning Adviser, Pilkington Bros Ltd, 1968–70; Group Personnel Dir, Unicorn Industries Ltd, 1970–72; Dir of Labour and Staff Relations, W Midland Passenger Transport Exec., 1973–77; Dir of Personnel, Heavy Vehicle Div., Leyland Vehicles Ltd, 1977–80; Bd Mem. for Personnel and Industrial Relations, 1980–87, non-exec. Bd Mem., 1987–, British Shipbuilders; Dir of Personnel and Employee Relations, Sealink UK Ltd, 1987–89. Human Resource Consultant: Maurice Phelps Associates, 1989–; Emslie Phelps Associates, 1989–; Value Through People Ltd, 1991–; Saratoga (Europe), 1993–. Freeman: City of London; Co. of Watermen and Lightermen. *Address:* Abbotsfield, Goring Heath, S Oxon RG8 7SA.

PHELPS, Richard Wintour, CBE 1986; General Manager, Central Lancashire New Town Development Corporation, 1971–86; consultant in management of urban development and housing, since 1986; *b* 26 July 1925; *s* of Rev. H. Phelps; *m* 1955, Pamela Marie Lawson; two *d*. *Educ:* Kingswood Sch.; Merton Coll., Oxford (MA). 14th Punjab Regt, IA, 1944–46. Colonial Admin. Service, Northern Region and Fed. Govt. of Nigeria, 1948–57 and 1959–61; Prin., HM Treasury, 1957–59 and 1961–65; Sen. Administrator, Hants CC, 1965–67; Gen. Manager, Skelmersdale New Town Develt Corp., 1967–71. Advr (part-time) on housing to Govt of Vanuatu, 1986–89; Consultant on housing policy to Falkland Is Govt, 1988–89; Chm., Examn in Public Replacement Structure Plan, Derbys CC, 1989, Notts CC and Northants CC, 1990, West Sussex CC, 1991, Leics CC, 1992, Cambs CC, 1994. Contested (SDP) Barrow and Furness, 1987. Winston Churchill Trust Travelling Fellowship, 1971. *Recreations:* reading, travel. *Address:* c/o Midland Bank, New Market Street, Ulverston, Cumbria. *Club:* Commonwealth Trust.

PHILIP, Hon. Lord; Alexander Morrison Philip; Chairman, Scottish Land Court, since 1993; President, Lands Tribunal for Scotland, since 1993; *b* 3 Aug. 1942; *s* of late Alexander Philip, OBE and of Isobel Thomson Morrison; *m* 1971, Shona Mary Macrae; three *s*. *Educ:* High School of Glasgow; St Andrews University (MA 1963); Glasgow University (LLB 1965). Solicitor, 1967–72; Advocate 1973; Standing Junior Counsel to Scottish Education Dept, 1982; Advocate-Depute, 1982–85. QC (Scotland), 1984. Chm., Medical Appeal Tribunals, 1988–92. *Recreations:* golf, piping. *Address:* Scottish Land Court, 1 Grosvenor Crescent, Edinburgh EH12 5ER. *T:* 0131–225 3595. *Clubs:* Scottish Arts, Royal Scottish Pipers' Society (Edinburgh).

PHILIP, Alexander Morrison; *see* Philip, Hon. Lord.

PHILIP, John Robert, DSc; FRS 1974; FAA 1967; Fellow, Commonwealth Scientific and Industrial Research Organization, Australia, 1991–92, now Emeritus; *b* 18 Jan. 1927; *e s* of late Percival Norman Philip and Ruth (*née* Osborne), formerly of Ballarat and Maldon, Vic., Australia; *m* 1949, Frances Julia, *o d* of late E. Hilton Long; two *s* one *d*. *Educ:* Scotch Coll., Melbourne; Univ. of Melbourne (Queen's Coll.). BCE 1946, DSc 1960. Research Asst, Melb. Univ., 1947; Engr, Qld Irrig. Commn, 1948–51; Research Staff, CSIRO, 1951–, Sen. Prin. Res. Scientist, 1961–63; Chief Res. Scientist and Asst Chief, Div. of Plant Industry, 1963–71; Chief, Dir. of Envmtl Mechanics, subseq. Centre for Envmtl Mechanics, 1971–80 and 1983–91; Associate Mem., CSIRO Exec., 1978; Dir, Inst. of Physical Scis, 1980–83. Visiting Scientist, Cambridge Univ., 1954–55; Res. Fellow, Calif. Inst. Techn., 1957–58; Vis. Prof., Univ. of Illinois, 1958 and 1961; Nuffield Foundn Fellow, Cambridge Univ., 1961–62; Res. Fellow, Harvard Univ., 1966–67; Vis. Prof., Univ. of Florida, 1969; Vinton-Hayes Fellow, Harvard Univ., 1972; Vis. Res. Fellow, Cornell Univ., 1979; Vis. Fellow Commoner, Trinity Coll., Cambridge, 1994. Mem. Council, Australian Acad. of Sci., 1972–78 (Biol. Sec., 1974–78); ANZAAS: Pres. Section 1 (Physics), 1970; Pres. Sect. 8 (Maths), 1971. FRMetS; Fellow, Amer. Geophys. Union, 1981; Foreign Mem., All-Union (subseq. Russian) Acad. of Agricl Scis, 1991; For. Associate, NAE, USA, 1995. Hon. DEng Melbourne, 1983; Hon. DPh Agricl Univ. of Athens, 1991; Hon. DSc Guelph, 1995. Horton Award, 1957, Horton Medal, 1982, Amer. Geophys. Union; David Rivett Medal, 1966; Thomas Ranken Lyle Medal, 1981; Eminent Researcher Award, Aust. Water Res. Adv. Council, 1990; University Medal, Agricl Univ. of Athens, 1993. *Publications:* papers in scientific jls on soil and porous medium physics, fluid mechanics, hydrology, micrometeorology, mathematical and physical aspects of physiology and ecology. *Recreations:* reading, writing, architecture. *Address:* CSIRO Centre for Environmental Mechanics, GPO Box 821, Canberra, ACT

2601, Australia. *T:* (6) 2465645; 42 Vasey Crescent, Campbell, ACT 2601, Australia. *T:* (6) 2478958.

PHILIPPE, André J., Hon. GCVO 1972; Luxembourg Ambassador to the United States of America, 1987–91; *b* Luxembourg City, 28 June 1926. Dr-en-Droit. Barrister-at-Law, Luxembourg, 1951–52. Joined Luxembourg Diplomatic Service, 1952; Dep. to Dir of Polit. Affairs, Min. of Foreign Affairs, 1952–54; Dep. Perm. Rep. to NATO, 1954–61 and to OECD, 1959–61; Dir of Protocol and Legal Adviser, Min. of For. Affairs, 1961–68; Ambassador and Perm. Rep. to UN and Consul-Gen., New York, 1968–72 (Vice-Pres., 24th Session of Gen. Assembly of UN, 1969); Ambassador to UK, Perm. Rep. to Council of WEU, and concurrently Ambassador to Ireland and Iceland, 1972–78; Ambassador to France, 1978–84; Ambassador to UN, NY, 1984–87. Commander: Order of Adolphe Nassau (Luxembourg); Légion d'Honneur (France); Grand Officer: Order of Merit (Luxembourg), 1983; Order of Oaken Crown (Luxembourg), 1988. *Address:* 25 rue Adolphe, 1116 Luxembourg.

PHILIPPS, family name of **Viscount St Davids** and **Baron Milford.**

PHILIPPS, Hon. Hanning; *see* Philipps, Hon. R. H.

PHILIPPS, Hon. (Richard) Hanning, MBE 1945; JP; Hon. Major Welsh Guards; Lord-Lieutenant of Dyfed, 1974–79 (HM Lieutenant of Pembrokeshire, 1958–74); *b* 14 Feb. 1904; 2nd *s* of 1st Baron and *b* of 2nd Baron Milford; *m* 1930, Lady Marion Violet Dalrymple, FRAgS (*d* 1995), *d* of 12th Earl of Stair, KT, DSO; one *s* one *d. Educ:* Eton. Contested (Nat) Brecon and Radnor, 1939. Served War of 1939–45, NW Europe, 1944–45 (MBE). Vice-Lieutenant of Pembrokeshire, 1957. Hon. Colonel Pembroke Yeomanry, 1959. Chairman: Dun & Bradstreet Ltd, 1946–69; Milford Haven Conservancy Bd, 1963–75; Northern Securities Trust Ltd, 1950–80; Hon. Pres. (former Chm.) Schweppes Ltd; Dir, Picton Land and Investment Pty Ltd, W Australia; Trustee, Picton Castle Trust, Graham and Kathleen Sutherland Foundn. Pres., Order of St John, Pembrokeshire, 1958–. CStJ. *Recreations:* painting, forestry, gardening. *Address:* Picton Castle, Haverfordwest, Pembrokeshire, Dyfed SA62 4AS. *T:* Rhos (01437) 751201. *Club:* Boodle's.

PHILIPS, Prof. Sir Cyril (Henry), Kt 1974; Professor of Oriental History, University of London, 1946–80; Director, School of Oriental and African Studies, London, 1957–76; Vice-Chancellor, University of London, 1972–76 (Deputy Vice-Chancellor, 1969–70); *b* Worcester, 27 Dec. 1912; *s* of William Henry Philips; *m* 1st, 1939, Dorcas (*d* 1974), *d* of John Rose, Wallasey; one *d* (one *s* decd); 2nd, 1975, Joan Rosemary, *d* of William George Marshall. *Educ:* Rock Ferry High School; Univs of Liverpool (MA) and London (PhD). Bishop Chavasse Prizeman; Gladstone Memorial Fellow. Frewen Lord Prizeman (Royal Empire Soc.), 1935; Alexander Prizeman (Royal Hist. Soc.), 1938; Sir Percy Sykes Meml Medal (RSAA), 1976; Asst Lectr, Sch. of Oriental Studies, 1936. Served in Suffolk Infantry, Army Education Corps, 1940–43; Col Commandant, Army School of Education, 1945. Chief Instructor, Dept of Training, HM Treasury, 1945–46. Colonial Office Mission on Community Development, Africa, 1947. Lectures: Montague Burton, Univ. of Leeds, 1966; Creighton, Univ. of London, 1972; James Smart, on Police, 1979; Home Office Bicentenary, 1982; Police, Univ. of Bristol, 1982; Dawtry Meml, Univ. of Leeds, 1983. Chairman: UGC Cttee on Oriental, African and Slavonic Studies, 1965–70; UGC Cttee on Latin American Studies, 1966–70; India Cttee of Inter-University Council and British Council, 1972–; Royal Commn on Criminal Procedure, 1978–80; Police Complaints Bd, 1980–85; Council on Tribunals, 1986–89; Inst. of Archaeology, 1979–85, Inst. of Latin American Studies, 1978–87 (Univ. of London); Member: Social Development Cttee, Colonial Office, 1947–55; Colonial Office Research Council, 1955–57; University Grants Cttee, 1960–69; Commonwealth Education Commn, 1961–70; Postgraduate Awards Cttee (Min. of Education), 1962–64; Modern Languages Cttee (Min. of Education), 1964–67; Inter-Univ. Council, 1967–77; Court, London Univ., 1970–76; Governor: Chinese Univ. of Hong Kong, 1965–75; Mill Hill Sch., 1980–91 (Chm., 1982); Governor and Trustee, Richmond Coll., 1979–84. Pres., Royal Asiatic Soc., 1979–82, 1985–88. Hon. Fellow, Asiatic Soc., Bengal, 1995. Hon. DLitt: Warwick, 1967; Bristol, 1983; Sri Lanka, 1986; Hon. LLD Hong Kong, 1971. India Tagore Medal, 1968; Bombay Freedom Medal, 1977. *Publications:* The East India Company, 1940 (2nd edn 1961); India, 1949; Handbook of Oriental History, 1951 (2nd edn 1962); Correspondence of David Scott, 1951; Historians of India, Pakistan and Ceylon, 1961; The Evolution of India and Pakistan, 1962; Politics and Society in India, 1963; Fort William–India House Correspondence, 1964; History of the School of Oriental and African Studies, 1917–67, 1967; The Partition of India, 1970; The Correspondence of Lord William Bentinck, Governor General of India 1828–35, 1977; Beyond the Ivory Tower, 1995. *Address:* School of Oriental and African Studies, Malet Street, WC1E 7HP. *T:* 0171–637 2388. *Club:* Athenæum.

PHILIPS, Justin Robin Drew; Metropolitan Stipendiary Magistrate, since 1989; *b* 18 July 1948; *s* of late Albert Lewis Philips, Solicitor and of Henrietta Philips (*née* Woolfson). *Educ:* John Lyon School, Harrow; College of Law, London. Called to the Bar, Gray's Inn, 1969; practised criminal bar, 1970–89; Chm., Youth Court, 1993–; an Asst Recorder, 1994–. Hon. Sec., Hendon Reform Synagogue, 1990–94 (Mem. Council, 1979–90). *Recreations:* music, reading, attempting to keep fit. *Address:* c/o Tower Bridge Magistrates' Court, 211 Tooley Street, SE1 2JY. *T:* 0171–407 4232.

PHILIPSON, Garry, DFC 1944; Managing Director, Aycliffe and Peterlee Development Corporation, 1974–85; *b* 27 Nov. 1921; *s* of George and Marian Philipson; *m* 1949, June Mary Miller Somerville; one *d. Educ:* Stockton Grammar Sch.; Durham Univ. (BA(Hons)). Jubilee Prize, 1947. Served War, RAFVR (2 Gp Bomber Comd), 1940–46. Colonial Service and Overseas Civil Service, 1949–60. Various Dist and Secretariat posts, incl. Clerk, Exec. Council and Cabinet Sec., Sierra Leone; Principal, Scottish Develt Dept, 1961–66; Under Sec., RICS, 1966–67; Dir, Smith and Ritchie Ltd, 1967–70; Sec., New Towns Assoc., 1970–74; Vice-Chm. (NE), North Housing Assoc., 1985–92. Trustee, Dales-Care, 1988–91. *Publications:* Aycliffe and Peterlee New Towns 1946–88, 1988; Press articles and contribs to various jls. *Recreations:* country pursuits, history. *Address:* Little Lodge Farm, Lane End Common, North Chailey, East Sussex BN8 4JH. *T:* Newick (01825) 723027. *Club:* Royal Air Force.

PHILIPSON, John Trevor Graham; QC 1989; *b* 3 March 1948; *s* of William Arnold Philipson and Rosalind Philipson; *m* 1974, Victoria Caroline Haskard (marr. diss. 1983). *Educ:* Newcastle Royal Grammar Sch.; Wadham Coll., Oxford (BA Jurisprudence 1970; BCL 1st cl. 1971). Called to the Bar, Middle Temple, 1972, Sen. Harmsworth Schol. *Recreations:* walking, gardening, travel. *Address:* Fountain Court, Temple, EC4Y 9DH. *T:* 0171–583 3335; 239 Knightsbridge, SW7 1DJ. *Clubs:* Savile, Royal Automobile.

PHILIPSON-STOW, Sir Christopher, 5th Bt *cr* 1907; DFC 1944; retired; *b* 13 Sept. 1920; *s* of Henry Matthew Philipson-Stow (*d* 1953) (3rd *s* of 1st Bt) and Elizabeth Willes (*d* 1979), *d* of Sir Thomas Willes Chitty, 1st Bt; *S* cousin, 1982; *m* 1952, Elizabeth Nairn, *d* of late James Dixon Trees and *widow* of Major F. G. McLaren, 48th Highlanders of Canada; two *s. Educ:* Winchester. *Heir: er s* Robert Matthew Philipson-Stow, *b* 29 Aug. 1953. *Address:* SS 1 Site 2 Comp 51, 92 Cambridge Street, Penetanguishene, Ontario L0K 1P0, Canada.

PHILLIMORE, family name of **Baron Phillimore.**

PHILLIMORE, 5th Baron *cr* 1918, of Shiplake, Oxfordshire; **Francis Stephen Phillimore;** Bt 1881; barrister; *b* 25 Nov. 1944; *o s* of 4th Baron Phillimore and Anne Elizabeth Phillimore (*d* 1995), *e d* of Major Arthur Algernon Dorrien-Smith, DSO; *S* father, 1994; *m* 1971, Nathalie Berthe Louisa Pequin; two *s* one *d. Educ:* Eton Coll.; Trinity Coll., Cambridge (BA). Called to the Bar, Middle Temple, 1972. *Recreations:* polo, sailing, shooting. *Heir: er s* Tristan Anthony Stephen Phillimore, *b* 18 Aug. 1977. *Address:* Coppid Hall, Binfield Heath, Henley-on-Thames, Oxon RG9 4JR. *T:* Henley-on-Thames (01491) 573174. *Clubs:* Brooks's, Pratt's; Royal Yacht Squadron.

PHILLIMORE, John Gore, CMG 1946; a Managing Director of Baring Brothers & Co. Ltd, 1949–72; *b* 16 April 1908; 2nd *s* of late Adm. Sir Richard and Lady Phillimore, Shedfield, Hants; *m* 1951, Jill, *d* of late Captain Mason Scott, Royal Navy retd, Buckland Manor, Broadway, Worcs, and of Hon. Mrs Scott; two *s* two *d. Educ:* Winchester College; Christ Church, Oxford. Partner of Roberts, Meynell & Co., Buenos Aires, 1936–48; Representative of HM Treasury and Bank of England in South America, 1940–45. Prime Warden, Fishmongers' Co., 1974–75. High Sheriff of Kent, 1975, DL Kent, 1979–84. Condor de los Andes (Bolivia), 1940; Commander, Orden de Mayo (Argentina), 1961. *Address:* Brooklyn House, Kingsclere, near Newbury, Berks RG15 8QY. *T:* Newbury (01635) 298321. *Club:* White's.

PHILLIPS, family name of **Baron Phillips of Ellesmere.**

PHILLIPS OF ELLESMERE, Baron *cr* 1994 (Life Peer), of Ellesmere in the County of Shropshire; **David Chilton Phillips,** KBE 1989; Kt 1979; BSc, PhD (Wales); FRS 1967; FInstP; Chairman, Finsbury Communications Ltd, since 1992; Professor of Molecular Biophysics and Fellow of Corpus Christi College, Oxford, 1966–90, now Emeritus Professor and Hon. Fellow; *b* 7 March 1924; *o s* of late Charles Harry Phillips and Edith Harriet Phillips (*née* Finney), Ellesmere, Shropshire; *m* 1960, Diana Kathleen (*née* Hutchinson); one *d. Educ:* Ellesmere C of E Schools; Oswestry Boys' High Sch.; UC, Cardiff. Radar Officer, RNVR, 1944–47. UC, Cardiff, 1942–44 and 1947–51. Post-doctoral Fellow, National Research Council of Canada, 1951–53; Research Officer, National Research Laboratories, Ottawa, 1953–55; Research Worker, Davy Faraday Research Lab., Royal Institution, London, 1955–66. Fullerian (Vis.) Prof. of Physiology, Royal Institution, 1979–85, Christmas lectures, 1980. Chm., ABRC, 1983–93 (part-time, 1983–90); Mem., MRC, 1974–78; Royal Soc. Assessor, MRC, 1978–83; Member: ACARD, 1983–87; Technology Requirements Bd, 1985–88; ACOST, 1987–93; HEFCE, 1992–93. Dir, Celltech Ltd, 1982–. UK Co-ordinator, Internat. Science Hall, Brussels Exhibition, 1958; Member, European Molecular Biology Organization (EMBO), 1964, Mem. Council, 1972–78; Royal Society: Vice-Pres., 1972–73, 1976–83; Biological Sec., 1976–83; Vice Pres., Foundn for Sci. and Technology, 1995–. Trustee, Wolfson Foundn, 1988–; Gov., De Montfort Univ., 1993–; Mem. Council, John Innes Centre, 1994–. Foreign Hon. Member: Amer. Academy of Arts and Sciences, 1968; Royal Swedish Acad. of Scis, 1989; Hon. Mem., Amer. Society of Biological Chemists, 1969 (Lecturer, 1965); For. Associate, Amer. Nat. Acad. of Science, 1985; Mem., Academia Europaea, 1989 (Vice-Pres., 1994–). Lectures: Almroth Wright Meml, 1966; Plenary, Internat. Biochem. Congress, Tokyo, 1967, Hamburg, 1976, Internat. Crystallography Congress, Kyoto, 1972; Hassel, Oslo, 1968; Harvey, NY, 1971; Ramsden, Manchester, 1973; Edward Clark Lee, Chicago, 1978; A. L. Patterson, Philadelphia, 1979; W. H. Stein, NY, 1983; Bragg, Leeds and London, 1985; Chancellor's, Salford, 1988; Dunham, Harvard Med. Sch., 1989; Romanes, Edinburgh, 1990; Rutherford, Royal Soc. UK–Canada, 1990; Irvine, St Andrews, 1991; Krebs Lecture and Medal, FEBS, 1971; Feldberg Prize, 1968; CIBA Medal, Biochem. Soc., 1971; Royal Medal, Royal Society, 1975; (jtly) Prix Charles Léopold Mayer, French Académie des Sciences, 1979; (jtly) Wolf Prize for Chemistry, Wolf Foundn, Israel, 1987; Gregoric Aminoff Prize, Swedish Royal Acad., 1991; Actonian Prize, Royal Instn, 1991; President's Medal, Royal Acad. of Engrg, 1994. Hon. FRSE 1991; Hon. FRCP 1991. Hon. DSc: Leicester, 1974; Univ. of Wales, 1975; Chicago, 1978; Exeter, 1982; Warwick, 1982; Birmingham, 1987; Glasgow, 1990; Glamorgan, 1994; Bath, 1994; Hon. PhD Weizmann Inst. of Science, 1990; DUniv: Essex, 1983; Stirling, 1995. Member, Ed. Board, Journal of Molecular Biology, 1966–76. *Publications:* papers in Acta Cryst. and other journals. *Address:* 35 Addisland Court, Holland Villas Road, W14 8DA. *T:* 0171–602 0738. *Club:* Athenæum.

PHILLIPS, Adrian Alexander Christian; freelance environmental consultant; Professor of Countryside and Environmental Planning, City and Regional Planning Department, University of Wales College of Cardiff, since 1992; *b* 11 Jan. 1940; *s* of Eric Lawrance Phillips, *qv*; *m* 1963, Cassandra Frances Elaïs Hubback, MA Oxon, *d* of D. F. Hubback, CB; two *s. Educ:* The Hall, Hampstead; Westminster Sch.; Christ Church, Oxford (1st Cl. Hons MA Geography). MRTPI; FRSA; FRGS. Planning Services, Min. of Housing and Local Govt, 1962–68; Sen. Research Officer and Asst Director, Countryside Commission, 1968–74; Special Asst, Executive Director, United Nations Environment Programme (UNEP), Nairobi, Kenya, 1974–75; Head, Programme Coordination Unit, UNEP, Nairobi, 1975–78; Director of Programmes, IUCN, Switzerland, 1978–81; Dir, then Dir Gen., Countryside Commn, 1981–92. Chm., Commn on Nat. Parks and Protected Areas, IUCN, 1994– (Dep. Chm., 1988–94). Hon. FLI. *Publications:* articles and chapters on envmtl and conservation topics. *Recreations:* walking, stroking the cat. *Address:* 2 The Old Rectory, Dumbleton, near Evesham, Worcs WR11 6TG. *T:* Evesham (01386) 882094. *Club:* Royal Over-Seas League.

PHILLIPS, Alan; *see* Phillips, D. A.

PHILLIPS, Andrew Bassett; Director, Humanities and Social Sciences, British Library, since 1990; *b* 26 Sept. 1945; *s* of William Phillips and Doreen (*née* Harris); *m* 1976, Valerie Cuthbert; two *s* one *d. Educ:* Newport High Sch.; Reading Univ. (BA). ALA. British Nat. Bibliography Ltd, 1969–70; Research Officer, Nat. Libraries ADP Study, 1970–71; Admin. Officer, Nat. Council for Educnl Technol., 1971–73; British Library: various posts in Bibliographic Servs and Ref. (subseq. Humanities and Social Scis) Divs, 1973–86; Dir, Public Services and Planning and Admin, 1987–90. Part-time Lectr, West London Coll, 1972–75. Director: Cedar Audio Ltd, 1992–94; Saga Continuation Ltd, 1993–. Trustee, Shakespeare's Birthplace, 1991–. *Publications:* various reviews, articles. *Address:* 23 Meynell Road, E9 7AP. *T:* 0181–985 7413.

PHILLIPS, Anne, (Mrs Basil Phillips); *see* Dickinson, V. A.

PHILLIPS, Rev. Canon Anthony Charles Julian; Headmaster, King's School, Canterbury, 1986–Aug. 1996; Canon Theologian, Diocese of Truro, since 1986; Hon. Canon, Canterbury Cathedral, 1987–Aug. 1996; *b* 2 June 1936; *s* of Arthur Reginald Phillips and Esmée Mary Phillips; *m* 1970, Victoria Ann Stainton; two *s* one *d. Educ:* Kelly Coll., Tavistock (schol.); King's Coll., London (BD, 1st cl.; AKC, 1st cl.; Archibald Robertson Prize, 1962; Jun. McCaul Hebrew Prize, 1963); Gonville and Caius Coll., Cambridge (PhD 1967); College of the Resurrection, Mirfield. Ordained priest, 1967;

Curate, Good Shepherd, Cambridge, 1966–69; Dean, Chaplain and Fellow, Trinity Hall, Cambridge, 1969–74; Chaplain and Fellow, 1975–86, Domestic Bursar, 1982–84, St John's Coll., Oxford; Lecturer in Theology: Jesus Coll., Oxford, 1975–86; Hertford Coll., Oxford, 1984–86; S. A. Cook Bye Fellow, Gonville and Caius Coll., 1984. Hon. Chaplain to Bishop of Norwich, 1970–71; Examining Chaplain to: Bp of Oxford, 1979–86; Bp of Manchester, 1980–86; Bp of Wakefield, 1984–86. Archbps of Canterbury and York Interfaith Cons. for Judaism, 1984–86. *Publications:* Ancient Israel's Criminal Law, 1970; Deuteronomy (Cambridge Bible Commentary), 1973; God BC, 1977; (ed) Israel's Prophetic Tradition, 1982; Lower Than the Angels, 1983; Preaching from the Psalter, 1987; The Passion of God, 1995; contrib. to: Words and Meanings (ed P. R. Ackroyd and B. Lindars), 1968; Witness to the Spirit (ed W. Harrington), 1979; The Ministry of the Word (ed G. Cuming), 1979; Heaven and Earth (ed A. Linzey and P. Wexler), 1986; Tradition and Unity (ed Dan Cohn-Sherbok), 1991; Glimpses of God (ed Dan Cohn-Sherbolz), 1993; articles in theol jls, The Times, Expository Times, etc. *Recreations:* gardening, beachcombing. *Address:* (until Aug. 1996) The King's School, Canterbury, Kent CT1 2ES. *T:* Canterbury (01227) 475501; (from Aug. 1996) The Old Vicarage, 10 St Peter's Road, Flushing, Falmouth, Cornwall TR11 5TT.

PHILLIPS, Prof. Calbert Inglis, FRCS, FRCSE; Professor of Ophthalmology, University of Edinburgh and Ophthalmic Surgeon, Royal Infirmary, Edinburgh, 1972–90, now Professor Emeritus; *b* 20 March 1925; *o s* of Rev. David Horner Phillips and Margaret Calbert Phillips; *m* 1962, Christina Anne Fulton, MB, FRCSE; one *s. Educ:* Glasgow High Sch.; Robert Gordon's Coll., Aberdeen; Aberdeen Univ. MB, ChB Aberdeen 1946; DPH Edinburgh 1950; FRCS 1955; MD Aberdeen 1957; PhD Bristol 1961; MSc Manchester 1969; FRCSE 1973. Lieut and Captain, RAMC, 1947–49. House Surgeon: Aberdeen Royal Infirmary, 1946–47 (House Phys., 1951); Aberdeen Maternity Hosp., 1949; Glasgow Eye Infirmary, 1950–51; Asst, Anatomy Dept, Glasgow Univ., 1951–52; Resident Registrar, Moorfields Eye Hosp., 1953–54; Sen. Registrar, St Thomas' Hosp. and Moorfields Eye Hosp., and Res. Asst, Inst. of Ophthalmology, 1954–58; Consultant Surg., Bristol Eye Hosp., 1958–63; Alexander Piggott Wernher Trav. Fellow, Dept of Ophthal., Harvard Univ., 1960–61; Consultant Ophthalmic Surg., St George's Hosp., 1963–65; Prof. of Ophthal., Manchester Univ., and Hon. Consultant Ophthalmic Surg. to United Manchester Hosps, 1965–72. Hon. FBOA 1975. *Publications:* (ed jtly) Clinical Practice and Economics, 1977; Basic Clinical Ophthalmology, 1984; Logic in Medicine, 1988, 2nd edn 1995; (jtly) Ophthalmology: a Primer for medical students and practitioners, 1994; papers in Eur., Amer., and Japanese Jls of Ophthal., Nature, Brain, BMJ, etc, mainly on intra-ocular pressure and glaucoma, retinal detachments, ocular surgery and hereditary diseases. *Address:* 5 Braid Mount Crest, Edinburgh EH10 6JN.

PHILLIPS, Caryl; writer; *b* 13 March 1958. *Educ:* Queen's Coll., Oxford (BA English 1979). Writer in Residence: Literary Criterion Centre, Mysore, India, 1987; Univ. of Stockholm, Sweden, 1989; Nat. Inst. of Educn, Singapore, 1994; Amherst College, Massachusetts: Vis. Writer, 1990–92; Writer in Residence, 1992–94; Prof. of English and Writer in Residence, 1994–; Vis. Prof., Univ. of NY, 1993. British Council Fiftieth Anniversary Fellow, 1984; Guggenheim Fellow, 1992; Rockefeller Foundn (Bellagio) Residency, 1993. Giles Cooper Award, BBC, 1984; Bursary in Drama, Arts Council of GB, 1984; Martin Luther King Meml Prize, 1987; James Tait Black Meml Prize, 1994; Lannan Foundn Literary Award, 1994. *Publications: plays:* Strange Fruit, 1981; Where there is Darkness, 1982; The Shelter, 1984; *novels:* The Final Passage, 1985; A State of Independence, 1986; Higher Ground, 1989; Cambridge, 1991; Crossing the River, 1993; *screenplay:* Playing Away, 1987; *non-fiction:* The European Tribe, 1987. *Recreations:* running, tennis. *Address:* c/o Aitken, Stone and Wylie Ltd, 29 Fernshaw Road, SW10 0TG.

PHILLIPS, David; *see* Phillips, J. D.

PHILLIPS, Prof. David; Professor of Physical Chemistry, since 1989 and Head of Department of Chemistry, since 1992, Imperial College of Science, Technology and Medicine; *b* 3 Dec. 1939; *s* of Stanley and Daphne Ivy Phillips; *m* 1970, Caroline Lucy Scoble; one *d. Educ:* South Shields Grammar-Technical Sch.; Univ. of Birmingham (BSc, PhD). Post doctoral Fellow, Univ. of Texas, 1964–66; Vis. Scientist, Inst. of Chemical Physics, Acad. of Scis of USSR, Moscow, 1966–67; Lectr 1967–73, Sen. Lectr 1973–76, Reader 1976–80, in Phys. Chem., Univ. of Southampton; Royal Institution of Great Britain: Wolfson Prof. of Natural Philosophy, 1980–89; Actg Dir, Jan.–Oct. 1986; Dep. Dir, 1986–89. Vice-Pres. and Gen. Officer, BAAS, 1988–89. Mem., Faraday Council, RSC, 1990–93. Nyholm Lectr, RSC, 1994. *Publications:* (jtly) Time-Correlated Single-Photon Counting, 1984; Polymer Photophysics, 1985; (jtly) Jet Spectroscopy and Dynamics, 1995; over 385 res. papers and revs in sci. lit. on photochem., photophys. and lasers. *Recreations:* music, travel. *Address:* 195 Barnett Wood Lane, Ashtead, Surrey KT21 2LP. *T:* Ashtead (01372) 274385. *Club:* Athenæum.

PHILLIPS, His Honour (David) Alan; a Circuit Judge, 1983–95; Chancellor, diocese of Bangor, 1988–95; *b* 21 July 1926; *s* of Stephen Thomas Phillips, MC and Elizabeth Mary Phillips; *m* 1960, Jean Louise (*née* Godsell); two *s. Educ:* Llanelli Grammar Sch.; University Coll., Oxford (MA). Left school, 1944. Served War, Army, 1944; commnd, 1946, RWF; Captain (GS), 1947; demobilised, 1948. Oxford, 1948–51. Lectr, 1952–59. Called to Bar, Gray's Inn, 1960. Stipendiary Magistrate for Mid-Glamorgan, 1975–83; a Recorder of the Crown Court, 1974–83. *Recreations:* music, chess, swimming.

PHILLIPS, Prof. Dewi Zephaniah; Professor of Philosophy, University College, Swansea, since 1971; Danforth Professor of the Philosophy of Religion, Claremont Graduate School, California, since 1992; *b* 24 Nov. 1934; *s* of David Oakley Phillips and Alice Frances Phillips; *m* 1959, Margaret Monica Hanford; three *s. Educ:* Swansea Grammar Sch.; UC Swansea (MA); St Catherine's Society, Oxford (BLitt). Asst Lectr, Queen's Coll., Dundee, Univ. of St Andrews, 1961–62; Lectr at Queen's Coll., Dundee, 1962–63; UC Bangor, 1963–65; University College, Swansea: Lectr, 1965–67; Sen. Lectr, 1967–71; Dean of the Faculty of Arts, 1982–85; Vice-Principal, 1989–92. Visiting Professor: Yale Univ., 1985; Claremont Graduate Sch., 1986. Hintz Meml Lectr, Univ. of Arizona, Tucson, 1975; Vis. Prof. and McMartin Lectr, Univ. of Carleton, 1976; Agnes Cuming Visitor, Univ. Coll. Dublin, 1982; Lectures: William James, Lousiana State Univ., 1982; Marett, Oxford, 1983; Riddell Meml, Newcastle, 1986; Aquinas, Oxford, 1987; Cardinal Mercier, Leuven, 1988. Editor, Philosophical Investigations, 1982–. *Publications:* The Concept of Prayer, 1965; (ed) Religion and Understanding, 1967; (ed) Saith Ysgrif Ar Grefydd, 1967; (with H. O. Mounce) Moral Practices, 1970; Death and Immortality, 1970; Faith and Philosophical Enquiry, 1970; (with Ilham Dilman) Sense and Delusion, 1971; Athronyddu Am Grefydd, 1974; Religion Without Explanation, 1976; Through A Darkening Glass: Philosophy, Literature and Cultural Change, 1981; Dramau Gwenlyn Parry, 1981; Belief, Change and Forms of Life, 1986; R. S. Thomas: poet of the hidden God, 1986; Faith after Foundationalism, 1988; From Fantasy to Faith, 1991; Interventions in Ethics, 1992; Wittgenstein and Religion, 1993; Writers of Wales: J. R. Jones, 1995; General Editor: Studies in Ethics and the Philosophy of Religion, 1968–74; Values and Philosophical Enquiry, 1976–86; Swansea Studies in Philosophy, 1989; Claremont Studies in the Philosophy of Religion, 1993–; papers in philosophical jls. *Recreations:* lawn tennis and supporting Swansea City AFC. *Address:* 45 Queen's Road, Sketty, Swansea SA2 0SB. *T:* Swansea (01792) 203935.

PHILLIPS, Diane Susan; Director, Housing Resources and Management, Department of the Environment, since 1994; *b* 29 Aug. 1942; *d* of Michael Keogh and Jessie (*née* Tite); *m* 1967, John Phillips; two *d. Educ:* Univ. of Wales. NEDO, 1967–72; Civil Service, 1972–: Principal, DoE, 1972–77, Cabinet Office, 1977–78; Asst Sec., Dept of Transport, 1978–80; DoE, 1981–: Grade 4, Local Govt Finance, 1988–90; Under Sec. (Grade 3) and Principal Finance Officer, Property Hldgs, 1990–94. *Address:* Department of the Environment, 2 Marsham Street, SW1P 3EB.

PHILLIPS, Edward Thomas John, (Jack), CBE 1985; Controller, English Language and Literature Division, British Council, 1985–89; Consultant, British Executive Service Overseas, since 1990; *b* 5 Feb. 1930; *s* of late Edward Emery Kent Phillips and of Margaret Elsie Phillips; *m* 1952, Sheila May (*née* Abbott); two *s* two *d. Educ:* Exmouth Grammar Sch., University Coll. London; Inst. of Education, London; School of Oriental and African Studies London (BA Hons; postgraduate Cert. of Educn; Dip. in linguistics). RAF, 1948–49. HMOCS, Educn Officer, Nigeria, 1953–62; British Council: Head, Cultural and Educn Unit, Overseas Students' Dept, 1962–65; English Lang. Officer, Enugu, Nigeria, 1966–67; Sen. Lectr, Coll. of Educn, Lagos Univ., Nigeria, 1967–70; English Lang. Teaching Advr, Min. of Educn, Cyprus, 1970–72; Chief Inspector, English Teaching Div., London, 1972–75; Rep., Bangladesh, Dacca, 1975–77; Dir, Personnel Dept and Dep. Controller Personnel Staff Recruitment Div., 1977–80; Rep, Malaysia, 1980–85. Dir, Project Mala (India), 1992–. Member: British-Malaysia Soc.; Anti-Slavery Soc.; Britain-Nigeria Assoc. *Publications:* (ed jtly) Organised English, Books I and II, 1973; contribs to English Language Teaching Jl. *Recreations:* music, theatre, tennis, golf, swimming. *Address:* 1 Bredune, off Church Road, Kenley, Surrey CR8 5DU. *T:* 0181–660 1929.

PHILLIPS, Edwin William, MBE 1946; Chairman: Friends Provident Life Office, 1968–88; United Kingdom Provident Institution, 1986–88; Director, Lazard Bros & Co. Ltd, 1960–83; *b* 29 Jan. 1918; *s* of C. E. Phillips, Chiswick; *m* 1951, P. M. Matusch; two *s. Educ:* Latymer Upper Sch. Joined Edward de Stein & Co., Merchant Bankers, 1934. Army, 1939–46; Major, Sherwood Rangers Yeomanry. Rejoined Edward de Stein & Co., 1946, Partner, 1954; merged into Lazard Bros & Co. Ltd, 1960. Director: British Rail Property Bd, 1970–87; Phoenix Assurance, 1975–85; Woolwich Equitable Building Soc., 1977 (Vice-Chm., 1984–86; Sen. Vice-Chm., 1986–88); Chm., Higgs and Hill, 1975–82. *Recreation:* cricket. *Address:* Down House, Downsway, Merrow, Surrey GU1 2YA. *T:* Guildford (01483) 301196. *Club:* MCC.

PHILLIPS, Eric Lawrance, CMG 1963; retired; *b* 23 July 1909; *s* of L. Stanley Phillips and Maudie Phillips (*née* Elkan), London, NW1; *m* 1938, Phyllis Bray (*d* 1991), artist; two *s* one step *d. Educ:* Haileybury Coll.; Balliol Coll., Oxford (Scholar, BA). With Erlangers Ltd, 1932–39. Served War of 1939–45, Captain, RA. Principal, Bd of Trade, 1945, Monopolies Commn, 1949; Asst Secretary, Monopolies Commn, 1951, Bd of Trade, 1952; Under-Sec., Bd of Trade, 1964–69; Sec., Monopolies Commn, 1969–74; consultant to Monopolies and Mergers Commn, 1974–75. Hon. Chm., Abbeyfield West London Soc., 1980–86. *Recreations:* looking at pictures, places and buildings. *Address:* 46 Platts Lane, NW3 7NT. *T:* 0171–435 7873. *Club:* Royal Automobile.

See also A. A. C. Phillips.

PHILLIPS, Sir Fred (Albert), Kt 1967; CVO 1966; QC (Barbados) 1991; Government Relations Consultant, Cable and Wireless (Caribbean); *b* 14 May 1918; *s* of Wilbert A. Phillips, Brighton, St Vincent. *Educ:* London Univ. (LLB); Toronto Univ.; McGill Univ. (MCL); Hague Acad. of International Law. Called to the Bar, Middle Temple. Legal Clerk to Attorney-General of St Vincent, 1942–45; Principal Officer, Secretariat, 1945–47; Windward Island: Chief Clerk, Governor's Office, 1948–49; District Officer/Magistrate of District III, 1949–53; Magistrate, Grenada, and Comr of Carriacou, 1953–56; Asst Administrator and MEC, Grenada, 1957–58 (Officer Administrating the Govt, April 1958); Senior Asst Sec., Secretariat, Fedn of W Indies (dealing with constitutional development), 1958–60; Permanent Sec. (Sec. to Cabinet), 1960–62 (when Fedn dissolved); actg Administrator of Montserrat, 1961–62; Sen. Lectr, Univ. of W Indies and Sen. Resident Tutor, Dept of Extra-mural Studies, Barbados, 1962–63; Registrar, Coll. of Arts and Science, Univ. of W Indies, 1963–64; Sen. Res. Fellow, Faculty of Law and Centre for Developing Area Studies, McGill Univ., 1964–65; Guggenheim Fellow, 1965; Administrator of St Kitts, 1966–67; Governor, St Kitts/Nevis/Anguilla, 1967–69. Has attended numerous conferences as a Legal or Constitutional Adviser. KStJ 1968. Hon. LLD West Indies, 1989. *Publications:* Freedom in the Caribbean: a study in constitutional change, 1977; The Evolving Legal Profession in the Commonwealth, 1978; West Indian Constitutions: post-Independence reforms, 1985; Caribbean Life and Culture: a citizen reflects, 1991; papers in various jls. *Recreations:* reading, bridge. *Address:* Chambers, PO Box 262, Kingstown, St Vincent, West Indies; PO Box 206, Bridgetown, Barbados.

PHILLIPS, (Gerald) Hayden, CB 1989; Permanent Secretary, Department of National Heritage, since 1992; *b* 9 Feb. 1943; *s* of Gerald Phillips and Dorothy Phillips; *m* 1st, 1967, Dr Ann Watkins (marr. diss.); one *s* one *d*; 2nd, 1980, Hon. Laura Grenfell; one *s* two *d. Educ:* Cambridgeshire High Sch.; Clare Coll., Cambridge (MA); Yale Univ., USA (MA). Home Office: Asst Principal, 1967; Economic Adviser, 1970–72; Principal, 1972–74; Asst Sec., and Principal Private Sec. to Sec. of State for Home Dept, 1974–76; Dep. Chef de Cabinet to Pres., Commn of European Communities, 1977–79; Asst Sec., Home Office, 1979–81, Asst Under-Sec. of State, 1981–86; Dep. Sec., Cabinet Office (MPO, subseq. Office of the Minister for the Civil Service), 1986–88; Dep. Sec., HM Treasury, 1988–92. Member: Council, KCL, 1993–; Ct of Govs, Henley Mgt Coll., 1993–. *Recreations:* fishing, other arts and sports, India. *Address:* c/o Department of National Heritage, 2–4 Cockspur Street, SW1Y 5DH. *Club:* Brooks's.

PHILLIPS, Hayden; *see* Phillips, G. H.

PHILLIPS, Sir Henry (Ellis Isidore), Kt 1964; CMG 1960; MBE 1946; Hon. Vice-Chairman, SIFIDA Investment Co. (SA); Chairman, Assured Property Trust plc; director of other companies; *b* 30 Aug. 1914; *s* of late Harry J. Phillips, MBE; *m* 1st, 1941, Vivien Hyamson (marr. diss., 1965); two *s* one *d*; 2nd, 1966, Philippa Cohen. *Educ:* Haberdashers' Sch., Hampstead; University College London (BA 1936; MA 1939; Fellow 1991). FRHistS 1965. Inst. of Historical Research, 1936–39. Commissioned in Beds and Herts Regt, 1939; served War of 1939–45, with 5th Bn, becoming Adjutant; POW, Singapore, 1942. Joined Colonial Administrative Service and appointed to Nyasaland, 1946 (until retirement in 1965); Development Secretary, 1952; seconded to Federal Treasury of Rhodesia and Nyasaland, 1953–57, Dep. Sec., 1956; Financial Sec., Nyasaland Govt, 1957–64, and Minister of Finance, 1961–64. Man. Dir, Standard Bank Finance and Development Corp., 1966–72. Dir, Nat. Bank of Malaŵi, 1983–88; Chm., Ashley Industrial Trust plc, 1986–88. Member: Civil Aviation Authority, 1975–80; Finance Cttee, UCL, 1985–. Chm., Urbanaid Africa, 1993–; Hon. Vice-Pres., Stonham Housing Assoc., 1992– (Vice Chm., 1984–92); Hon. Treasurer: Stonham Meml Trust, 1977–; SOS

Sahel Internat. (UK), 1987–. Hon. Vice-Pres., Friends of University Coll., 1992–. *Address:* 34 Ross Court, Putney Hill, SW15 3NZ. *T:* 0181–789 1404. *Club:* MCC.

PHILLIPS, Sir Horace, KCMG 1973 (CMG 1963); HM Diplomatic Service, retired; *b* 31 May 1917; *s* of Samuel Phillips and Polly Yaffie; *m* 1944, Idina Doreen Morgan; one *s* one *d*. *Educ:* Hillhead High Sch., Glasgow. Joined Board of Inland Revenue, 1935. Served War of 1939–45, Dorsetshire and 1st Punjab Regts, 1940–47. Transf. to FO, Oct. 1947; Acting Vice-Consul, Shiraz, Nov. 1947; Vice-Consul, Bushire, 1948; Consul, Shiraz, 1949; 1st Secretary, Kabul, Oct. 1949; Foreign Office, 1951; 1st Secretary, and Consul, Jedda, 1953; Counsellor, 1956; seconded to Colonial Office, Dec. 1956, as Protectorate Secretary, Aden, until Aug. 1960; Counsellor, British Embassy, Tehran, Oct. 1960; Deputy Political Resident in the Persian Gulf, at Bahrain, 1964–66; Ambassador to Indonesia, 1966–68; High Comr in Tanzania, 1968–72; Ambassador to Turkey, 1973–77. Resident Rep., Taylor Woodrow Internat. Ltd: Iran, 1978–79, Hong Kong, 1979–84, Bahrain, 1984–85, China (at Peking), 1985–87. Lecturer in International Relations: Bilkent Univ., Ankara, 1988–92; Erciyes Univ., Kayseri, Turkey, 1993–94. Hon. LLD Glasgow, 1977. Order of the Taj (Iran), 1961. *Publications:* Envoy Extraordinary, 1995; articles of topical political and diplomatic interest in Asian Wall Street Jl, 1980–86. *Recreations:* languages, long-distance car driving. *Address:* 34a Sheridan Road, Merton Park, SW19 3HP. *T:* 0181–542 3836. *Clubs:* Travellers'; Hong Kong (Hong Kong).

PHILLIPS, Ian, FCA; Chief Executive, BBC Pension Services Ltd, since 1990; *b* 16 July 1938; *s* of Wilfrid and Dorothy Phillips; *m* 1961, Fay Rosemary Stoner; two *s*. *Educ:* Whitgift Sch., South Croydon. Articled clerk, Hatfield Dixon Roberts Wright & Co., Accountants, 1955–61; Senior Asst, Robert J. Ward & Co., Accountants, 1961–65; Management Services Dept, John Lewis' Partnership, 1965–69; London Transport Executive: Director of Corporate Planning, 1969–75; Chief Business Planning Officer, 1975–78; Group Planning Director, 1978–80; Mem. Board, LTE, later LRT, 1980–84; Dir, Finance and Planning, BRB, 1985–88; Dir, Finance, BBC, 1988–93; Chm., BBC Enterprises Ltd, 1991–93. *Recreations:* playing golf, watching sport, the country, my family. *Address:* Glebe Cottage, Duntisbourne Abbots, Cirencester, Glos GL7 7JN.

PHILLIPS, Prof. Ian, MD; FRCP, FRCPath; Professor of Medical Microbiology, since 1974, and Clinical Dean, since 1992, United Medical and Dental Schools of Guy's and St Thomas's Hospitals; *b* 10 April 1936; *s* of late Stanley Phillips and Emma (*née* Price). *Educ:* St John's Coll., Cambridge (MA, MD); St Thomas's Hosp. Med. Sch. (MB BCh). FRCPath 1981; FRCP 1983; MFPHM 1992. Chm., Pathology, Guy's and St Thomas's Hosp. NHS Trust, 1990–. Civilian Consultant, RAF, 1979–. Chm., Dist Mgt Team, 1978–79. Mem., Veterinary Products Cttee, 1981–85. Mem. Council, RCPath, 1974–76 asnd 1987–90. Chairman: Brit. Soc. for Antimicrobial Chemotherapy, 1979–82; Assoc. of Med. Microbiologists, 1989–93; Pres., European Soc. for Clinical Microbiol. and Infectious Diseases, 1955–96. Mem., S London Botanical Inst. Mem., Victorian Soc. Freeman, City of London, 1975; Liveryman, Soc. of Apothecaries, 1975. *Publications:* (ed jtly) Laboratory Methods in Antimicrobial Chemotherapy, 1978; (jtly) Microbial Disease, 1979; contrib. chapters and papers. *Recreations:* botany, music, opera. *Address:* Department of Microbiology, United Medical and Dental School, St Thomas Hospital, SE1 7EH. *T:* 0171–928 9292, *Fax:* 0171–928 0730. *Clubs:* Athenæum, Royal Society of Medicine.

PHILLIPS, Jack; *see* Phillips, E. T. J.

PHILLIPS, Jeremy Patrick Manfred, QC 1980; *b* 27 Feb. 1941; *s* of late Manfred Henry Phillips, CA, and late Irene Margaret (*née* Symondson); *m* 1968, Virginia Gwendoline (*née* Dwyer) (marr. diss. 1974); one *s* (and one *s* decd); *m* 1976, Judith Gaskell (*née* Hetherington); two *s* two *d*. *Educ:* St Edmund's Sch., Hindhead, Surrey; Charterhouse. Apprentice Accountant, Thomson McLintock & Co., 1957–61. Called to Bar, Gray's Inn, 1964; in practice, 1964–. Owner of Kentwell Hall, Long Melford, Suffolk, 1971–; organizer of Kentwell's Annual Historical Re-Creations of Tudor Domestic Life. Dir, CARE Britain. *Publications:* contrib. Cooper's Students' Manual of Auditing, Cooper's Manual of Auditing and various pamphlets, papers, guides, etc, on Kentwell Hall and Tudor period. *Recreations:* Kentwell Hall, historic buildings, Tudor history and Tudor domestic life. *Address:* Kentwell Hall, Long Melford, Suffolk CO10 9BA.

PHILLIPS, John, RIBA; architect in private practice, since 1955; *b* 25 Nov. 1926; *s* of John Tudor Phillips and Bessie Maud Phillips; *m* 1955, Eileen Margaret Fryer. *Educ:* Christ's Coll., Finchley; Northern Polytechnic, Holloway. ARIBA 1954. Studied under Romilly B. Craze, Architect, 1948–52. Surveyor to the Fabric: Truro Cathedral, 1961 (Consultant Architect, 1979–); Westminster Cathedral, 1976–; RIBA 1979–; Consultant Architect to Brisbane Cathedral, 1988–. Pres., Ecclesiastical Architects' and Surveyors' Assoc., 1982. *Recreations:* looking at churches, choral singing. *Address:* (home) 8 Friary Way, North Finchley, N12 9PH. *T:* 0181–445 3414; (office) 1 Greenland Place, NW1 0AP. *T:* 0171–284 0077.

PHILLIPS, (John) David, QPM 1994; Chief Constable of Kent, since 1993; *b* 22 April 1944; *s* of late Percy Phillips and of Alfreda Phillips; *m* 1970, Nancy Wynn Rothwell; one *s*. *Educ:* Leigh Grammar Sch.; Manchester Univ. (BA 1st Cl. Hons Econs). Served: Lancs Constabulary, 1963–84; Gtr Manchester Constabulary, 1984–89; Dep. Chief Constable, Devon and Cornwall, 1989–93. *Recreations:* history, golf. *Address:* Police Headquarters, Sutton Road, Maidstone, Kent ME15 9BZ.

PHILLIPS, John Fleetwood Stewart, CMG 1965; HM Diplomatic Service, retired; *b* 16 Dec. 1917; *e s* of late Major Herbert Stewart Phillips, 27th Light Cavalry, and Violet Gordon, *d* of late Sir Alexander Pinhey, KCSI; *m* 1948, Mary Gordon Shaw, MB, BS; two *s* two *d*. *Educ:* Brighton; Worcester Coll., Oxford (Open Exhibition in Classics, MA). Represented Univ. and County intermittently at Rugby football, 1938–39. Served with 1st Bn, Argyll and Sutherland Highlanders in N Africa and Crete (wounded and captured, 1941). Appointed to Sudan Political Service, 1945; served in Kordofan and Blue Nile Provinces. HM Diplomatic Service, 1955, served in Foreign Office; Oriental Secretary in Libya, 1957; Consul-General at Muscat, 1960–63; Counsellor, British Embassy, Amman, 1963–66; Imperial Defence Coll., 1967; Dep. High Comr, Cyprus, 1968; Ambassador to Southern Yemen, 1969–70, to Jordan, 1970–72, to Sudan, 1973–77. *Recreations:* gardening and feuding. *Address:* Southwood, Gordon Road, Horsham, Sussex RH12 2EF. *T:* Horsham (01403) 252894.

PHILLIPS, John Francis, CBE 1977 (OBE 1957); QC 1981; arbitrator; Chairman: London Court of International Arbitration, 1984–87; Private Patients Plan (formerly Provident Association for Medical Care), 1977–84, now President (Vice-Chairman, 1972–77; Director, since 1958); *b* 1911; *e s* of late F. W. Phillips and late Margaret (*née* Gillan); *m* 1937, Olive M. Royer; one *s* two *d*. *Educ:* Cardinal Vaughan Sch.; London Univ.; Trinity Hall, Cambridge. LLB (Hons) London; LLB (1st Cl. Hons), LLM Cantab. Barrister-at-law, Gray's Inn, 1944. Civil Servant (Lord Chancellor's Dept, Royal Courts of Justice), 1933–44; Parly Sec. and Asst Gen. Sec., Nat. Farmers' Union of England and Wales, 1945–57; Institute of Chartered Secretaries and Administrators: Sec. and Chief Exec., 1957–76; Mem. Council, 1976–81; Pres., 1977. Member: Council, Chartered Inst. of Arbitrators, 1969–83 (Vice-Pres., 1974–76; Pres., 1976–77); Gen. Cttee, Bar Assoc. for Commerce, Finance and Industry, 1967–88 (Vice-Chm., 1976–78 and 1980–81; Chm., 1978–80; Vice-Pres., 1982–88; Hon. Mem., 1989–); Senate of the Inns of Court and the Bar; Bar Council; Cttees of Senate and Council, 1978–83; Council for Accreditation of Correspondence Colls, 1969–80 (Hon. Treas., 1969–74; Chm., 1975–80); British Egg Marketing Bd, 1969–71; Departmental Cttee of Enquiry into Fowl Pest, 1971; Vice-Chm. and Mem., Business Educn Council, 1974–80; Chairman: Jt Cttee for Awards in Business Studies and Public Admin, 1968–75 (Mem. Jt Cttee for Awards, 1960–75); Houghton Poultry Res. Station, 1976–82 (Governor, 1973–82); Dep. Chm., Eggs Authority, 1971–80; Pres., Associated Examining Bd, GCE, 1992– (Mem., 1958–; Vice-Chm., 1973–76; Chm., 1976–92). Governor: Christ's Hospital, 1957–; Crossways Trust, 1959–71 (Financial Advisor, 1966–71); Nuffield Nursing Homes Trust, 1975–81 (Vice-Pres., 1981–84); Mem. Council and Exec. Cttee, Animal Health Trust, 1976–95; Deleg. to Internat. Labour Conf., 1950–56. FCIS 1958; FCIArb (FIArb 1966); CIMgt (Council, BIM, 1969–74); FRSA 1983. Hon. Mem. CGLI, 1992. Master, Co. of Chartered Secretaries and Administrators, 1978 and 1986–87; Founder Master, Worshipful Co. of Arbitrators, 1980–82; Master, Co. of Scriveners, 1982–83. OStJ. DCL City Univ., 1985. *Publications:* The Agriculture Act, 1947, 1948; Heywood and Massey's Lunacy Practice, 1939; Arbitration: Law, Practice and Precedents, 1988; many articles on aspects of law relating to land, agriculture and arbitration. *Recreation:* travel. *Address:* 17 Ossulton Way, Hampstead Garden Suburb, N2 0DT. *T:* 0181–455 8460; (office) Private Patients Plan, Phillips House, Tunbridge Wells, Kent TN1 2PL; (chambers) Verulam Chambers, Peer House, Verulam Street, Gray's Inn Road, WC1X 8LZ. *Clubs:* Athenæum, United Oxford & Cambridge University, City Livery.

PHILLIPS, Hon. John Harber; Hon. Mr Justice Phillips; Chief Justice of Victoria, since 1991; *b* 18 Oct. 1933; *s* of Anthony and I. Muriel Phillips; *m* 1962, Helen Isobel Rogers; two *s* one *d*. *Educ:* De La Salle Coll., Malvern; Univ. of Melbourne (LLB). Called to the Bar: Victoria, 1959; Middle Temple, 1979; practised at Victorian Bar, 1959–84; Justice: Supreme Court of Victoria, 1984–90; Federal Court of Australia, 1990–91. Mem., Victorian Bar Council, 1974–84; Chairman: Criminal Bar Assoc., 1982, 1983; Nat. Crime Authy, 1990–91; Victorian Council of Legal Educn, 1991–; Victoria Law Foundn, 1991–. Chairman: Victorian Inst. of Forensic Pathol., 1985–; Nat. Inst. of Forensic Sci., 1991. Vis. Prof. of Advocacy, Monash Univ., 1988–89. Hellenic Dist. for Service to Greek community of Victoria, 1992. *Publications:* (jtly) Forensic Science and the Expert Witness, 1985; Advocacy with Honour, 1986; The Trial of Ned Kelly, 1987; Poet of the Colours: the life of John Shaw Neilson, 1988; *plays:* By a Simple Majority: the trial of Socrates, 1990; Conference with Counsel, 1991. *Address:* Chief Justice's Chambers, Supreme Court of Victoria, 210 William Street, Melbourne, Vic 3000, Australia. *T:* (3) 96036139.

PHILLIPS, John Randall; Principal Officer, Mid Glamorgan County Council, since 1994; Chairman, since 1995, Lord Mayor, from April 1996, Cardiff County Council; *b* 22 April 1940; *s* of James Phillips and Charlotte Phillips (*née* Phelps); *m* 1967, Margaret Ray Davies; one *s* one *d*. *Educ:* Cardiff High Sch.; University Coll., Cardiff (BA Econ. 1961). Dip. Soc. Studies 1967. Cardiff City Council, 1963–66; Glam CC, 1967–74; Mid Glam CC, 1974–: Principal Trng Officer, 1974–82; Principal Asst (Child Abuse), 1982–89; Dist Social Services Officer, Cynon Valley, 1989–94. Cardiff City Council, 1972–96: Chm. of Personnel, 1974–76 and 1979–83; Dep. Leader, Labour Gp, 1986, Ldr, 1990–94; Vice Chm., 1987, Chm., 1990, Policy; Leader, 1990–94; Dep. Lord Mayor, 1994–95. Mem., Cardiff Bay Develt Corp., 1990–. *Recreations:* politics, listening to music, wine making. *Address:* 15 Kyle Crescent, Whitchurch, Cardiff CF4 1ST. *T:* Cardiff (01222) 624878.

PHILLIPS, Jonathan, PhD; Director, Executive Agencies, Department of Transport, since 1993; *b* 21 May 1952; *s* of Gilbert Reginald Phillips and Ruby May Phillips (*née* Hughes); *m* 1974, Amanda Rosemary Broomhead; two *s*. *Educ:* Queen Mary's Grammar Sch., Walsall; St John's Coll., Cambridge (BA 1973; PhD 1978); London Univ. Inst. of Educn (PGCE 1974). Department of Trade, later Department of Trade and Industry, 1977–93: seconded: to CBI econs directorate, 1982–83; as Sec., Cttee of Inquiry into regulatory arrangements at Lloyd's, 1986–87; Asst Sec., 1987–93; Under-Sec., 1993. *Recreations:* music, walking. *Address:* Department of Transport, Great Minster House, 76 Marsham Street, SW1P 4DR. *T:* 0171–271 5948.

PHILLIPS, Marisa, DLitt; President, Mental Health Review Tribunal, since 1990; *b* 14 April 1932; *d* of Dr and Mrs J. Fargion; *m* 1956, Philip Harold Phillips; one *s* one *d*. *Educ:* Henrietta Barnet Sch., London; Univ. of Redlands, California (Fulbright Schol.; BA Hons); Rome Univ. (DLitt). Called to Bar, Lincoln's Inn, 1963. On return from Redlands Univ., worked for US Inf. Service, Rome, 1954–56; spent one year in Berlin, as husband then in Army; period of work with Penguin Books; read for the Bar, joining DPP as Legal Asst, 1964; Legal Adviser, Police Complaints Bd, 1977; returned to DPP, 1979; Asst Dir, DPP, 1981; Principal Asst DPP, 1985; Asst Hd of Legal Services, 1986–87, Dir of Legal Casework, 1987–90, Crown Prosecution Service. Sen. Legal Advr, Banking Ombudsman, 1990–. Comr, Mental Health Act Commn, 1991–; Chm., Rent Assessment Panel, 1992–. *Recreations:* music, theatre, foreign travel.

PHILLIPS, Captain Mark Anthony Peter, CVO 1974; ADC(P); Consultant, Gleneagles Mark Phillips Equestrian Centre, since 1992; *b* 22 Sept. 1948; *s* of P. W. G. Phillips, MC, and late Anne Patricia (*née* Tiarks); *m* 1973, HRH The Princess Anne (marr. diss. 1992); one *s* one *d*. *Educ:* Marlborough Coll.; RMA Sandhurst. Joined 1st The Queen's Dragoon Guards, July 1969; Regimental duty, 1969–74; Company Instructor, RMA Sandhurst, 1974–77; Army Trng Directorate, MoD, 1977–78, retired. Personal ADC to HM the Queen, 1974–. Student, RAC Cirencester, 1978. Chm., British Olympic Equestrian Fund, 1989–; Chef d'Equipe and Coach, US Three Day Event Team, 1993–Nov. 1996. In Three Day Equestrian Event, GB winning teams: Team Championships: World, 1970; European, 1971; Olympic Gold Medallists (Team), Olympic Games, Munich, 1972; Olympic Silver Medallists (Team), Olympic Games, Seoul, 1988; Mem., Equestrian Team (Reserve), Olympic Games, Mexico, 1968 and Montreal, 1976. Winner, Badminton Three Day Event, 1971, 1972, 1974, 1981. Chm., Glos Youth Assoc.; Dir, Glos TEC, 1991–; Patron: BAFPA; Everyman Theatre, Cheltenham. Liveryman: Farriers' Co.; Farmers' Co; Carmen's Co.; Loriners' Co.; Freeman: Loriners Co.; City of London; Yeoman, Saddlers' Co. *Recreations:* riding, Rugby football, athletics. *Address:* Aston Farm, Cherington, Tetbury, Glos GL8 8SW. *Club:* (Hon. Mem.) Buck's.
See also under Royal Family.

PHILLIPS, Max; Assistant Under Secretary of State, Ministry of Defence, 1977–84; *b* 31 March 1924; *m* 1953, Patricia Moore; two *s* two *d*. *Educ:* Colston's Sch., Bristol; Christ's Hospital; Magdalene Coll., Cambridge (Schol.; 1st cl. Hist. Tripos, pts I and II; MA). Served War, RA, 1943–46. Appointed to Home Civil Service, 1949; Colonial Office, 1949–59; Sec., Nigeria Fiscal Commn, 1957–58; UKAEA, 1959–73; Procurement Exec., MoD, 1973–74; HM Treasury, 1974–77; retired 1984, re-employed as Asst Sec., MoD, 1984–87. Gov., Christ's Hospital, 1979– (Almoner, 1981–92). *Recreations:* modern myths, exploring the imagination and the countryside. *Address:* 2 Wilderness Farmhouse, Onslow Village, Guildford, Surrey GU2 5QP. *T:* Guildford (01483) 61308.

PHILLIPS, Mervyn John, AM 1987; FAIB; Chairman, I.B.J. Australia Bank Ltd, since 1992; *b* 1 April 1930; *m* 1956, Moya, *d* of A. C. Bleazard; one *s* one *d*. *Educ:* De La Salle

Coll., Ashfield; Univ. of Sydney (BEc). FAIB 1990. Commonwealth Bank of Australia, 1946–60; Reserve Bank of Australia, 1960–92: Manager for PNG, 1962–64; Chief Manager, Internat. Dept, 1976–79, Securities Markets Dept, 1980–82, Financial Markets Group, 1983–85; Adviser, 1982; Chief Admin. Officer, 1985–87; Dep. Gov. and Dep. Chm., 1987–92. Dir, CBOA Credit Union, 1964–73 (Chm., 1967–72); Chm., Note Printing Australia, 1990–93; Director: QBE Insurance Gp, 1992–; Alcoa of Australia, 1992–; Aust. Gas Light Co., 1992–; O'Connell Street Associates Pty, 1992–; GRW Property Ltd, 1994–. Member: PNG Currency Conversion Commn, 1965–66; NSW Credit Union Adv. Cttee, 1968–72; Govt Cttees on PNG Banking, 1971–73; Off-shore Banking in Australia, 1984. Nat. Treas., Australian Catholic Relief, 1993–. Member: Senate, Australian Catholic Univ., 1991–; Adv. Council, Australian Grad. Sch. of Management, 1991–. Mem., Pontifical Council, Cor Unum, 1994–. *Address:* O'Connell Street Associates Pty Ltd, 2 O'Connell Street, Sydney, NSW 2000, Australia. *T:* (2) 2231822.

PHILLIPS, Prof. Neville Crompton, CMG 1973; Vice-Chancellor and Rector, University of Canterbury, Christchurch, New Zealand 1966–77; retired; *b* 7 March 1916; 2nd *s* of Samuel and Clara Phillips, Christchurch, NZ; *m* 1940, Pauline Beatrice, 3rd *d* of Selby and Dorothy Palmer, Te Aratipi, Havelock North, NZ; one *s* two *d*. *Educ:* Dannevirke High Sch.; Palmerston North Boys' High Sch.; Canterbury University College; Merton Coll., Oxford. BA (NZ) 1936; MA 1938; Hon. LittD (Cantuar) 1977; NZ University Post-Grad. Schol. in Arts, Arnold Atkinson Prizeman, 1938; Journalist, Sun and Press, Christchurch, 1932–38; read PPE at Oxford, 1938–39; RA (Gunner, subseq. Major), 1939–46; service in Tunisia and Italy (despatches). Lecturer in History and Political Science, Canterbury University College, 1946–47; Senior Lecturer, 1948; Prof. of History and Political Science, 1949–62; Prof. of History, 1962–66; Emeritus Prof., 1966; presented with Festschrift, 1984. Chairman: Canterbury Centennial Provincial Historical Cttee, 1948–66; Management Cttee, Canterbury Archaeological Trust, Kent, 1980–83; 1st Pres., Canterbury Historical Assoc., 1953; Editorial Adviser, NZ War Histories, 1957–67; US Dept of State Leader Grantee, 1966; Member: Council, Canterbury Manufacturers' Assoc., 1967–77; Christchurch Teachers' Coll. Council, 1968–76; NZ Vice-Chancellors' Cttee, 1966–77 (Chm., 1973–74); Council, Assoc. of Commonwealth Univs, 1973–74; NZ Council Educational Research, 1973–77. *Publications:* Italy, vol. 1 (The Sangro to Cassino), 1957 (New Zealand War Histories); Yorkshire and English National Politics, 1783–84, 1961; The Role of the University in Professional Education, 1970; (ed) A History of the University of Canterbury, 1873–1973, 1973; articles, mainly on eighteenth-century English politics, in English and NZ jls. *Recreations:* walking, watching cricket, things Italian. *Address:* Tyle House, Hackington Road, Tyler Hill, Canterbury, Kent CT2 9NF. *T:* Canterbury (01227) 471708.

PHILLIPS, Hon. Sir Nicholas (Addison), Kt 1987; **Hon. Mr Justice Phillips;** a Judge of the High Court of Justice, Queen's Bench Division, since 1987; *b* 21 Jan. 1938; *m* 1972, Christylle Marie-Thérèse Rouffiac (*née* Doreau); two *d*, and one step *s* one step *d*. *Educ:* Bryanston Sch.; King's Coll., Cambridge (MA). Nat. Service with RN; commnd RNVR, 1956–58. Called to Bar, Middle Temple (Harmsworth Scholar), 1962, Bencher, 1984. In practice at Bar, 1962–87; Jun. Counsel to Minister of Defence and to Treasury in Admiralty matters, 1973–78; QC 1978; a Recorder, 1982–87. Mem., Panel of Wreck Comrs, 1979. Chm., Law Adv. Cttee, British Council, 1991–; Chm., Council of Legal Educn, 1992–; Vice Pres., British Maritime Law Assoc., 1993–. Governor, Bryanston Sch., 1975– (Chm. of Governors, 1981–). *Recreations:* sea, mountains, Mauzac. *Address:* Royal Courts of Justice, Strand, WC2A 2LL. *Club:* Brooks's.

PHILLIPS, Prof. Owen Martin, FRS 1968; Decker Professor of Science and Engineering, Johns Hopkins University, since 1975; *b* 30 Dec. 1930; *s* of Richard Keith Phillips and Madeline Lofts; *m* 1953, Merle Winifred Simons; two *s* two *d*. *Educ:* University of Sydney; Trinity Coll., Cambridge Univ. ICI Fellow, Cambridge, 1955–57; Fellow, St John's Coll., Cambridge, 1957–60; Asst Prof., 1957–60, Assoc. Prof., 1960–63, Johns Hopkins Univ.; Asst Director of Research, Cambridge, 1961–64; Prof. of Geophysical Mechanics, Johns Hopkins Univ., 1963–68, of Geophysics, 1968–75. Assoc. Editor Jl of Fluid Mechanics, 1964–; Mem. Council, Nat. Center of Atmospheric Research, Boulder, Colorado, 1964–68; Member: US Nat. Cttee Global Atmospheric Research Project, 1968; Res. Co-ord. Panel, Gas Research Inst., 1981–85; Principal Staff, Applied Phys. Lab., 1982–. Mem.-at-large, Amer. Meteorol. Soc. Publications Commn, 1971–75; Pres., Maryland Acad. of Scis, 1979–85. Sec., Bd of Trustees, Chesapeake Res. Consortium, 1973–74 (Trustee, 1972–75). Adams Prize, Univ. of Cambridge, 1965; Sverdrup Gold Medal, Amer. Metereol. Soc., 1975. *Publications:* The Dynamics of the Upper Ocean, 1966, 3rd edn 1976, Russian edn 1968; The Heart of the Earth, 1968, Italian edns 1970, 1975; The Last Chance Energy Book, 1979; (ed) Wave Dynamics and Radio Probing of the Ocean Surface, 1985; Flow and Reactions in Permeable Rocks, 1990; various scientific papers in Jl Fluid Mechanics, Proc. Cambridge Philos. Soc., Jl Marine Research, Proc. Royal Society, Deep Sea Research, Journal Geophys. Research. *Address:* 23 Merrymount Road, Baltimore, MD 21210, USA. *T:* (410) 4337195. *Clubs:* Johns Hopkins (Baltimore), Hamilton Street (Baltimore); Quissett Yacht (Mass).

PHILLIPS, Sir Peter (John), Kt 1990; OBE 1983; Chairman, Principality Building Society, since 1991 (Deputy Chairman, 1988–91); *b* 18 June 1930; *s* of Walter Alfred Phillips and Victoria Mary Phillips; *m* 1956, Jean Gwendoline Williams; one *s* one *d*. *Educ:* Radley College; Pembroke College, Oxford (MA). Joined Aberthaw and Bristol Channel Portland Cement Co., 1956, Jt Man. Dir, 1964–83; Western Area Dir, Blue Circle Industries, 1983–84; Dep. Chm., 1985, Chm., 1987–93, A. B. Electronic Products Gp. *Recreations:* walking, fishing, reading. *Address:* Great House, Llanblethian, near Cowbridge, South Glam CF7 7JG. *T:* Cowbridge (01446) 775163. *Club:* Cardiff and County.

PHILLIPS, Peter Sayer; Founder and Musical Director, The Tallis Scholars, since 1973; Music Critic, The Spectator, since 1983; *b* 15 Oct. 1953; *s* of Nigel Sayer Phillips and Patricia Ann Witchell (*née* Wyatt); *m* 1987, Clio (marr. diss. 1993), *d* of D. O. Lloyd-Jacob, *qv*. *Educ:* Winchester Coll.; St John's Coll., Oxford (Organ Scholar). Teacher: Oxford Univ., 1976–81; Trinity Coll. of Music, 1980–84; RCM, 1981–88. Co-founder and Dir, Gimell Records, 1981–. Mem., Early Music Cttee, Arts Council, 1987–88. Ed., Early Music Gazette, 1980–82; cricket correspondent, Spectator, 1989; Prop. and Adv. Ed., Musical Times, 1995–. Many awards for recordings made by Tallis Scholars, incl. Gramophone Record of the Year, 1987, and Early Music Record of the Year, 1991, Gramophone magazine. *Publications:* English Sacred Music 1549–1649, 1991; (contrib.) Companion to Medieval and Renaissance Music, 1992; contrib. Spectator, Guardian, Musical Times, New Republic, Listener, Early Music, Music and Letters, Music and Musicians. *Recreations:* Romantic music, cricket, philology, Arabia. *Address:* 22 Gibson Square, N1 0RD. *T:* 0171–354 0627, 0171–226 8047, *Fax:* 0171–704 1007; 48 rue des Francs Bourgeois, 75003 Paris, France. *T:* 42724461. *Clubs:* Athenæum, Chelsea Arts, MCC.

PHILLIPS, Surgeon Rear-Adm. Rex Philip, CB 1972; OBE 1963; Medical Officer-in-Charge, Royal Naval Hospital, Plymouth, 1969–72, retired; *b* 17 May 1913; 2nd *s* of William John Phillips, late Consultant Anaesthetist at Royal Victoria Infirmary, Newcastle upon Tyne, and Nora Graham Phillips; *m* 1939, Gill Foley; two *s*. *Educ:* Epsom Coll.; Coll. of Med., Newcastle upon Tyne, Univ. of Durham (now Univ. of Newcastle upon Tyne). Qual. MB, BS 1937; Ho. Surg., Ingham Infirmary, S Shields, 1938. Joined RN, 1939; served War of 1939–45: HMS Rochester, 1939–41; Royal Marines, 1941–43; HMS Simba, 1943–45. HMS Excellent, 1945–47; qual. Dip. in Ophthalmology (London), 1948; HMS Implacable, Fleet MO, 1949–51; Specialist in Ophthalmology: HMS Ganges, 1951–53; Central Air Med. Bd, 1953–55; RN Hosp., Malta (Senior), 1955–57; Admty Adv. in Ophth. to Med. Dir-Gen., 1957–65; Surg. Captain 1963; SMO, RN Hosp., Malta, 1965–68; Staff MO to Flag Officer Submarines, 1968–69. QHS 1969–72. CStJ 1970. *Recreations:* golf, bridge. *Address:* Langstone House, 25 Langstone High Street, Havant, Hants PO9 1RY. *T:* Havant (01705) 484668.

PHILLIPS, Richard Charles Jonathan; QC 1990; *b* 8 Aug. 1947; *yr s* of Air Commodore M. N. Phillips, MD, ChB, DMRD and Dorothy E. Phillips; *m* 1978, Alison Jane Francis (OBE 1991); one *d*. *Educ:* King's School, Ely; Sidney Sussex College, Cambridge (Exhibnr). Called to the Bar, Inner Temple, 1970. Asst Parly Boundary Comr, 1992–. *Recreations:* travel, natural history, photography, walking. *Address:* 2 Harcourt Buildings, Temple, EC4Y 9DB. *T:* 0171–353 8415.

PHILLIPS, Robin; actor and director; *b* 28 Feb. 1942; *s* of James William Phillips and Ellen Anne (*née* Barfoot). *Educ:* Midhurst Grammar School, Sussex. Trained as director, actor and designer, Bristol Old Vic Co.; first appearance, Bristol, as Mr Puff in The Critic, 1959; Associate Dir, Bristol Old Vic, 1960–61; played at Lyric, Hammersmith, 1961, Chichester Fest., 1962, and with Oxford Playhouse Co., 1964. Asst Dir, Timon of Athens and Hamlet, Royal Shakespeare Co., Stratford upon Avon, 1965; Dir or Associate Dir, Hampstead, Exeter, (Thorndike) Leatherhead, 1966–69; Artistic Dir, Stratford Festival, Canada, 1974–80; Artistic Dir, Grand Theatre Co., London, Ontario, 1982; Dir, Young Company, Stratford Festival Theatre, 1986; Dir Gen., The Citadel Theatre, Edmonton, Canada, 1990–95. Hon. Dr Univ. of Western Ontario, 1982. Guild Shield, Conestoga Coll., 1982. *London prodns include:* Tiny Alice, RSC, Aldwych, 1970; Abelard and Heloise, Wyndhams and Broadway; The Two Gentlemen of Verona, Stratford and Aldwych, 1970; Miss Julie, for RSC (also directed film); Virginia, Haymarket, 1981; *Chichester:* Caesar and Cleopatra and Dear Antoine, 1971; played Dubedat in The Doctor's Dilemma and directed The Lady's Not for Burning and The Beggar's Opera, 1972; The Jeweller's Shop, 1982; Antony and Cleopatra, 1985; *Greenwich:* formed Company Theatre and apptd Artistic Dir, 1973: plays directed include: The Three Sisters, Rosmerholm, Zorba; *Stratford Festival prodns incl.:* 1975: The Two Gentlemen of Verona and The Comedy of Errors (both also Nat. tour), Measure for Measure, Trumpets and Drums and The Importance of Being Earnest; 1976–78: Hamlet, The Tempest, Antony and Cleopatra, A Midsummer Night's Dream, The Way of the World, Richard III, The Guardsman, As You Like It, Macbeth, The Winter's Tale, Uncle Vanya, The Devils, Private Lives, Hay Fever, Judgement; 1979: Love's Labours Lost, The Importance of Being Earnest, King Lear; 1980: Virginia, Long Day's Journey into Night; 1986: Cymbeline; 1987: The School for Scandal, As You Like It, Romeo and Juliet, Journey's End; 1988: Twelfth Night, King Lear, Oedipus, The Critic; 1993: King John; *Edmonton prodns incl.:* A Midsummer Night's Dream, The Crucible, 1989; The Philadelphia Story, 1990; Never the Sinner, The Mousetrap, Romeo and Juliet, Democracy, 1991; Lend Me A Tenor, Fallen Angels, Oedipus, Man of La Mancha (also Toronto, 1993), Black Comedy, Invisible Friends, The Royal Hunt of the Sun, Hamlet, As You Like It, 1992; La Bête, The Two of Us, She Stoops to Conquer, Saint Joan, Oliver!, Aspects of Love (also Toronto, US tour), 1993; Cyrano de Bergerac, Macbeth, Hay Fever (also Winnipeg), 1994; *other prodns incl.:* The Marriage of Figaro, Canadian Opera Co., Toronto, 1993. *Films:* as actor: Decline and Fall, David Copperfield (title part), Tales from the Crypt; as director: The Wars, Miss Julie, Waiting for the Parade. *TV:* Wilfred Desert in The Forsyte Saga, Constantin in The Seagull. *Address:* Wildwood House, RR3, Lakeside, Ontario N0M 2G0, Canada.

PHILLIPS, Sir Robin Francis, 3rd Bt, *cr* 1912; Owner and Principal, Ravenscourt Theatre School, London; *b* 29 July 1940; *s* of Sir Lionel Francis Phillips, 2nd Bt, and Camilla Mary, *er d* of late Hugh Parker, 22 Chapel Street, Belgrave Square, SW1; *S* father, 1944. *Educ:* Aiglon Coll., Switzerland. Chief Air Traffic Control Officer, Biggin Hill, 1970–78; Hazel Malaone Management, 1978–81; Devonair Radio, 1981–83; Radio Luxembourg, 1984; Hd of Casting, Corona Stage School, 1985–89. *Heir:* none. *Address:* 12 Manson Mews, Queens Gate, SW7 5AF.

PHILLIPS, (Ronald) William, JP; Director, NB Selection Ltd, since 1991; *b* 21 April 1949; *s* of Ronald Phillips and Phoebe Nora Haynes; *m* 1979, Dorothy Parsons. *Educ:* Steyning Grammar Sch.; University College of Wales, Aberystwyth (BScEcon). Joined CS, 1971; served in Dept of Transport, PSA, DoE, Develt Commn (Private Sec. to Lord Northfield); Asst County Sec., Kent CC, 1979–80; UK Expert to EC Council of Ministers Wkg Party on Environmental Impact Assessment, 1980–83; Greater London Reg. Office, DoE (Local Govt Reorganisation), 1983–86; Head of Policy Unit, 1986–87, Man. Dir, 1987–91, Westminster CC. FRSA 1990; FIMgt (FBIM 1990). JP Maidstone, 1992. *Recreation:* travel. *Address:* Livesey Cottage, Livesey Street, Teston, Kent ME18 5AY.

PHILLIPS, Siân; actress; *d* of D. Phillips and Sally Phillips; *m* 1st, 1960, Peter O'Toole, *qv* (marr. diss. 1979); two *d*; 2nd, 1979, Robin Sachs (marr. diss. 1992). *Educ:* Pontardawe Grammar Sch.; Univ. of Wales (Cardiff Coll.) (BA Hons English; Fellow, 1982); RADA (Maggie Albanesi Scholarship, 1956; Bancroft Gold Medal, 1958). BBC Radio Wales, mid 1940s–, and BBC TV Wales, early 1950s–; Newsreader and Announcer, and Mem. Rep. Co., BBC, 1953–55; toured for Welsh Arts Council with National Theatre Co., 1953–55; Arts Council Bursary to study drama outside Wales, 1955. Mem., Arts Council Drama Cttee, 1970–75. Governor: St David's Trust, 1970–73; Welsh Coll. of Music and Drama, 1992–. *Theatre:* London: Hedda Gabler, 1959; Ondine, and the Duchess of Malfi, 1960–61 (1st RSC season at Aldwych); The Lizard on the Rock, 1961; Gentle Jack, Maxibules, and The Night of the Iguana, 1964; Ride a Cock Horse, 1965; Man and Superman, and Man of Destiny, 1966; The Burglar, 1967; Epitaph for George Dillon, 1972; A Nightingale in Bloomsbury Square, 1973; The Gay Lord Quex, 1975; Spinechiller, 1978; You Never Can Tell, Lyric, Hammersmith, 1979; Pal Joey, Half Moon, 1980 and Albery, 1981; Dear Liar, Mermaid, 1982; Major Barbara, NT, 1982; Peg, Phoenix, 1984; Gigi, Lyric, Shaftesbury Ave., 1985; Thursday's Ladies, Apollo, 1987; Brel, Donmar, 1987; Paris Match, Garrick, 1989; Vanilla, Lyric, 1990; The Manchurian Candidate, Lyric, Hammersmith, and nat. tour, 1991; Painting Churches, Playhouse, 1992; The Glass Menagerie, Cambridge Theatre Co. nat. tour, 1989; Ghosts, Welsh Arts Council tour, and Sherman Theatre, Wales, 1993; The Lion in Winter, UK nat. tour, 1994; An Inspector Calls, NY, 1995. *TV drama series* include: Shoulder to Shoulder, 1974; How Green was my Valley, 1975; I, Claudius, 1976; Boudicca, and Off to Philadelphia in the Morning, 1977; The Oresteia of Aeschylus, 1978; Crime and Punishment, 1979; Sean O'Casey (RTE), 1980; Winston Churchill, The Wilderness Years, 1981; Language and Landscape (6 bilingual films, Welsh and English), 1985; The Snow Spider, 1988; Shadow of the Noose, 1989; Emlyn's Moon, 1990; Perfect Scoundrels, 1990; Tonight at 8.30: Hands Across the Sea; The Astonished Heart; Ways and Means, 1991; The Borrowers, 1992, 1993; *TV films* include: A Painful Case (RTE), 1985; While Reason Sleeps; Return to

Endor, 1986 (USA); Siân (biographical), 1987; Heidi, 1993; Mind to Kill (also in Welsh); Summer Silence (musical, also in Welsh). *Films* include: Becket, 1963; Goodbye Mr Chips, and Laughter in the Dark, 1968; Murphy's War, 1970; Under Milk Wood, 1971; The Clash of the Titans, 1979; Dune, 1984; Ewocks Again, and The Doctor and the Devils, 1985; Valmont, 1989; Age of Innocence, 1994. Has made recordings, incl. Peg, Gigi, I remember Mama, Pal Joey, Bewitched, Bothered and Bewildered, and A Little Night Music. RTS Annual Lecture (Eng. and Welsh transmissions), 1993. FWNCMD, 1991; Fellow, Cardiff Coll., Univ. of Wales, 1983; Hon. Fellow, Polytechnic of Wales, 1988. Hon. DLitt Wales, 1984. Critics Circle Award, New York Critics Award, and Famous 7 Critics Award, for Goodbye Mr Chips, 1969; BAFTA Award for How Green was my Valley and I, Claudius, 1978; Royal Television Soc. Award for I, Claudius (Best Performer), 1978. Mem., Gorsedd of Bards, 1960 (for services to drama in Wales). *Publications:* Siân Phillips' Needlepoint, 1987; gen. journalism (Vogue, Cosmopolitan, Daily Mail, 3 years for Radio Times, Country Living, Options). *Recreations:* gardening, needlepoint, drawing. *Address:* c/o Saraband Ltd, 265 Liverpool Road, Barnsbury, N1 1HS.

PHILLIPS, Tom, RA 1989 (ARA 1984); RE 1987; painter, writer and composer; *b* 25 May 1937; *s* of David John Phillips and Margaret Agnes (*née* Arnold); *m* 1961, Jill Purdy (marr. diss. 1988); one *s* one *d*; *m* 1995, Fiona Maddocks. *Educ:* St Catherine's College, Oxford (MA; Hon. Fellow, 1992); Camberwell School of Art. NDD. One man shows: AIA Galleries, 1965; Angela Flowers Gall., 1970–71; Marlborough Fine Art, 1973–75; Dante Works, Waddington Galleries, 1983; retrospective exhibitions: Gemeente Museum, The Hague, 1975; Kunsthalle, Basel, 1975; Serpentine, 1975; 50 years of Tom Phillips, Angela Flowers Gall., 1987; Mappin Art Gall., Sheffield, 1987; Nat. Gall., Jamaica, 1987; Bass Mus., Miami, 1988; Nat. Gall., Australia, 1988; City Art Inst., Sydney, 1988; Nat. Portrait Gall., 1989; N Carolina Mus., 1990; Royal Acad., 1992; V&A, 1992; Ulster Mus., 1993; Yale Center, USA, 1993; work in collections: British Museum, Tate Gall., V&A, Nat. Portrait Gall., Imperial War Mus., Ashmolean Mus., Oxford, Mus. Fine Arts, Budapest, MOMA NY, Philadelphia Museum, Bibliothèque Nationale, Paris, Gemeente Museum, Boymans Museum, Rotterdam, Nat. Museum, Stockholm, Nat. Gall. of Australia; designed tapestries for St Catherine's, Oxford; music: first perf. opera Irma, 1973; York, 1974; ICA, 1983; recordings incl. Irma, 1980 (new version, 1988); Intervalles/Music of Tom Phillips 1982; television: collaborated on Dante series, 1984–89 (1st prize Montreal Fest., 1990; Prix Italia, 1991); film scripts: Tom Phillips (Grierson Award, BFI, 1976; Golden Palm Award, Chicago, 1976); The Artist's Eye (TV film), 1988; Twenty Sites (TV film), 1989. Chairman: RA Library, 1987–95; RA Exhibns Cttee, 1995; Vice-Chm., British Copyright Council, 1984–88. Hon. Pres., S London Artists, 1987–. Francis Williams Prize, V&A 1983; First Prize, Hunting Gp of Cos, 1988. *Publications:* Trailer, 1971; A Humument, 1980, rev. edn 1987; illustr. trans. Dante's Inferno, 1982; Works/Texts to 1974, 1975; Heart of a Humument, 1985; The Class of Forty-Seven, 1990; Works/Texts vol. II, 1992; Humument Supplement, 1992; Plato's Symposium, 1992; (with Salman Rushdie) Merely Connect, 1994; (ed) Africa: the art of a continent, 1995. *Recreation:* collecting African sculpture. *Address:* 57 Talfourd Road, SE15 5NN. *T:* 0171–701 3978, *Fax:* 0171–703 2800. *Clubs:* Chelsea Arts, Groucho; Surrey County Cricket.

PHILLIPS, Vernon Francis, CIPFA; FCA; Chief Executive, Bedfordshire County Council, 1989–92, retired; *b* 7 July 1930; *s* of Charles and May Phillips; *m* 1955, Valerie P. Jones; two *s* one *d*. *Educ:* Wilson Sch., Reading. CIPFA (Hons) 1954; ASAA 1958; FCA 1970. Berkshire CC, 1946–53; Swindon BC, 1953–55; Bristol City Council, 1955–58; Coventry City Council, 1958–61; Dep. Borough Treas., Luton CB, 1962–73; County Treas., Bedfordshire CC, 1973–89. Adviser to ACC, 1985–92. Member: Soc. of County Treas, 1973–; Assoc. of County Chief Execs, 1989–; SOLACE, 1989–. Mem., Bedford Rotary Club. *Recreations:* reading, music (listening), dancing, walking, paperweights, stained glass windows, photography. *Address:* 5 Troon Close, Bedford MK41 8AY. *T:* Bedford (01234) 345628.

PHILLIPS, William; *see* Phillips, R. W.

PHILLIPS GRIFFITHS, Allen; *see* Griffiths.

PHILLIS, Robert Weston; Deputy Director-General, BBC, since 1993; Chairman, BBC Worldwide, since 1994; *b* 3 Dec. 1945; *s* of Francis William Phillis and Gertrude Grace Phillis; *m* 1966, Jean (*née* Derham); three *s*. *Educ:* John Ruskin Grammar Sch.; Nottingham Univ. (BA Industrial Econs 1968). Apprentice, printing industry, 1961–65; Thomson Regional Newspapers Ltd, 1968–69; British Printing Corp. Ltd, 1969–71; Lectr in Industrial Relations, Edinburgh Univ. and Scottish Business Sch., 1971–75; Vis. Fellow, Univ. of Nairobi, 1974; Personnel Dir, later Man. Dir, Sun Printers Ltd, 1976–79; Managing Director: Independent Television Publications Ltd, 1979–82 (Dir, 1979–87); Central Independent Television plc, 1981–87 (non-exec. Dir, 1987–91); Gp Man. Dir, Carlton Communications, 1987–91; Chief Exec., ITN, 1991–93; Man. Dir, BBC World Service, 1993–94; Chm., BBC Enterprises Bd, 1993–94. Chairman: ITV Network Programming Cttee, 1984–86; ITV Film Purchase Gp, 1985–87; Zenith Productions Ltd, 1984–91. Director: ITN Ltd, 1982–87 and 1991–93; Periodical Publishers Assoc., 1979–82; Ind. Television Cos Assoc., 1982–87; Internat. Council, Nat. Acad. of Television Arts and Scis, 1985– (Vice Chm. (Internat.), 1994–); Worldwide Television News Corp., 1991–93. Dir and Trustee, Television Trust for the Environment, 1985–. FRSA 1984; FRTS 1988 (Chm., 1989–92; Vice Pres., 1994). *Recreations:* family, sport, news. *Address:* BBC, Broadcasting House, W1A 1AA. *Clubs:* Reform, Groucho.

PHILLPOTTS, (Mary) Adelaide Eden, (Mrs Nicholas Ross); writer; *b* Ealing, Middlesex, 23 April 1896; *d* of late Eden Phillpotts; *m* 1951, Nicholas Ross. *Publications: novels:* The Friend, 1923; Lodgers in London, 1926; Tomek, the Sculptor, 1927; A Marriage, 1928; The Atoning Years, 1929; Yellow Sands, 1930; The Youth of Jacob Ackner, 1931; The Founder of Shandon, 1932; The Growing World, 1934; Onward Journey, 1936; Broken Allegiance, 1937; What's Happened to Rankin?, 1938; The Gallant Heart, 1939; The Round of Life, 1940; Laugh with Me, 1941; Our Little Town, 1942; From Jane to John, 1943; The Adventurers, 1944; The Lodestar, 1946; The Fosterling, 1949; Stubborn Earth, 1951; Village Love, 1988; The Beacon of Memory, 1990; *plays:* Arachne, 1920; Savitri the Faithful, 1923; Camillus and the Schoolmaster, 1923; Akhnaton, 1926; (with Eden Phillpotts) Yellow Sands, 1926; Laugh With Me, 1938; *poetry:* Illyrion, and other Poems, 1916; A Song of Man, 1959; *travel:* Panorama of the World, 1969; *miscellaneous:* Man, a Fable, 1922; (selected with Nicholas Ross) Letters to Nicholas Ross from J. C. Powys (ed A. Uphill), 1971; A Wild Flower Wreath, 1975; Reverie: An Autobiography, 1981. *Address:* Trelana Home, Poughill, near Bude, Cornwall EX23 9EL.

PHILO, Gordon Charles George, CMG 1970; MC 1944; HM Diplomatic Service, retired; *b* 8 Jan. 1920; *s* of Charles Gilbert Philo and Nellie Philo (*née* Pinnock); *m* 1952, Mavis (Vicky) Ella (*d* 1986), *d* of John Ford Galsworthy and Sybel Victoria Galsworthy (*née* Strachan). *Educ:* Haberdashers' Aske's Hampstead Sch.; Wadham Coll., Oxford. Methuen Scholar in Modern History, Wadham Coll., 1938. Served War, HM Forces, 1940–46: Royal West African Frontier Force, 1942–43; Airborne Forces, Normandy and Europe, 1944–45; India 1945–46. Alexander Korda Scholar, The Sorbonne, 1948–49; Lectr in Modern History, Wadham Coll., 1949–50; Foundn Mem., St Antony's Coll., Oxford, 1950–51. Foreign Office, 1951; Russian course, Christ's Coll., Cambridge, 1952–53; Istanbul, Third Sec., 1954–57; Ankara, Second Sec., 1957–58; FO, 1958–63; Kuala Lumpur, First Sec., 1963–67; FO, 1968; Consul-Gen., Hanoi, 1968–69; FCO, 1969–78. Extended Interview Assessor, Home Office Unit, CSSB, 1978–90. Chm. Council, Kipling Soc., 1986–88. Kesatria Mangku Negara (Hon.), Order of Malaysia, 1968. *Publications:* (jtly with wife, as Charles Forsyte): Diplomatic Death, 1960; Diving Death, 1962; Double Death, 1965; Murder with Minarets, 1968; The Decoding of Edwin Drood, 1980; articles in various jls. *Recreations:* travel, writing. *Address:* 10 Abercorn Close, NW8 9XS. *Club:* Athenæum.

PHILPOT, Nicholas Anthony John; His Honour Judge Philpot; a Circuit Judge, since 1992; *b* 19 Dec. 1944; *s* of late Oliver Lawrence Spurling Philpot, MC, DFC, and of Margaret Nathalie Forsyth (*née* Owen); two *s*. *Educ:* Winchester Coll.; New Coll., Oxford (BA PPE 1966). VSO, Bolivia, 1966–67. Called to the Bar, Lincoln's Inn, 1970; Asst Recorder, 1987–90; Recorder, 1990–92. *Address:* c/o Inner London Crown Court, Newington Causeway, SE1 6AZ.

PHILPS, Dr Frank Richard, MBE (mil.) 1946; retired; Consultant in Exfoliative Cytology, University College Hospital, WC1, 1960–73; Director, Joint Royal Free and University College Hospitals, Department of Cytology, 1972–73; *b* 9 March 1914; *s* of Francis John Philps and Matilda Ann Philps (*née* Healey); *m* 1941, Emma L. F. M. Schmidt; two *s* one *d*. *Educ:* Christ's Hospital, Horsham, Sussex. MRCS, LRCP, 1939; MB, BS, 1939; DPH 1947; MD London, 1952; FRCPath, 1966; Fellow, International Academy of Cytology, 1967. RAF Medical Service, 1940–46; Japanese POW, 1942–45. Junior Hospital Appointments, UCH, 1950–54; Consultant Pathologist, Eastbourne, 1954–64; Research Asst, UCH, 1955–60. Hon. Cons. in Cytology, Royal Free Hosp., 1972–73. Producer, with wife, Wild Life Series of Educational Nature Films and films on pottery making, for Educational Foundation for Visual Aids; made BBC films, The Magic of a Dartmoor Stream, 1977, The Magic of a Dartmoor Wood, 1979. Exhibitor in the annual exhibition of the Royal Inst. of Painters in Watercolours, 1980–84. BBC Nature Film Prize, 1963; Council for Nature Film Prize, 1966. *Publications:* A Short Manual of Respiratory Cytology, 1964; Watching Wild Life, 1968, 3rd edn 1984; papers on Cytology to several medical journals, 1954–67. *Recreations:* living in the country; watching wild animals and filming them, painting. *Address:* Woodlands, Sydenham Wood, Lewdown, Okehampton EX20 4PP. *T:* Chillaton (01822) 860347.

PHIPPS, family name of **Marquess of Normanby.**

PHIPPS, Colin Barry, PhD; Chairman: Clyde Petroleum plc, since 1983 (Deputy Chairman and Chief Executive, 1979–83); Greenwich Resources plc, since 1989; *b* 23 July 1934; *s* of Edgar Reeves Phipps and Winifred Elsie Phipps (*née* Carroll); *m* 1956, Marion May Phipps (*née* Lawrey); two *s* two *d*. *Educ:* Townfield Elem. Sch., Hayes, Mddx; Acton County; Swansea Grammar; University Coll. London; Birmingham Univ. BSc, 1st cl. Hons Geol. London 1955; PhD, Geol. Birm. 1957. Royal Dutch/Shell Geologist: Holland, Venezuela, USA, 1957–64; Consultant Petroleum Geologist, 1964–79. Chm., Brindex (Assoc. of British Independent Oil Exploration Cos), 1983–86. MP (Lab) Dudley W, Feb. 1974–1979. Mem., Council of Europe/WEU, 1976–79. Contested: (Lab) Walthamstow E, 1969; (SDP/L Alliance) Worcester, 1983; (SDP/L Alliance) Stafford, 1987. Founder mem., SDP; Mem. SDP Nat. Cttee, 1984–89; Chm., W Midland Regional council, SDP, 1986–89. FGS 1956; FInstPet 1972; CGeol 1991; Mem. Instn of Geologists, 1978. Chairman: Twentieth Century British Art Fair, 1988–93; Falklands Conservation (formerly Falkland Islands Foundn), 1990–92 (Trustee, 1983–); English String Orch., 1990–92 (Dir, 1985–92). *Publications:* (co-ed) Energy and the Environment: democratic decision-making, 1978; What Future for the Falklands?, 1977 (Fabian tract 450); contrib.: Qly Jl Geol Sci., Geol. Mag., Geol. Jl, etc. *Recreations:* various and changing with age. *Address:* Mathon Court, Mathon, Malvern WR13 5NZ. *T:* Malvern (01684) 892267; 38 Cheyne Walk, SW3 5HJ. *T:* 0171–352 5381. *Clubs:* Reform, Chelsea Arts.

PHIPPS, Air Vice-Marshal Leslie William, CB 1983; AFC 1959; *b* 17 April 1930; *s* of late Frank Walter Phipps and Beatrice Kate (*née* Bearman). *Educ:* SS Philip and James Sch., Oxford. Commnd RAF, 1950; served, 1951–69: Fighter Sqdns; Stn Comdr, RAF Aqaba, Jordan; OC No 19 (F) Sqdn; Central Fighter Estab.; RN Staff Coll.; HQ 1 (British) Corps; Stn Comdr, RAF Labuan, Borneo; OC No 29 (F) Sqdn; Jt Services Staff Coll.; Dir, RAF Staff Coll., 1970–72; Comdr, Sultan of Oman's Air Force, 1973–74; RCDS, 1975; Comdr, UK Team to Kingdom of Saudi Arabia, 1976–78; Dir of Air Def. and Overseas Ops, 1978–79; Air Sec., (RAF), 1980–82; Sen. Directing Staff, RCDS, 1983; retired. BAe (Mil. Aircraft Div.), 1984–91. Service with nat. and local charities, 1991–. *Recreations:* sailing, squash, music. *Address:* 33 Knole Wood, Devenish Road, Sunningdale, Berks SL5 9QR. *Clubs:* Royal Air Force; Royal Air Force Yacht (Hamble).

PHIPPS, Rt. Rev. Simon Wilton, MC 1945; Assistant Bishop, Dioceses of Chichester and Southwark, since 1986; *b* 6 July 1921; *s* of late Captain William Duncan Phipps, CVO, RN, and late Pamela May Ross; *m* 1973, Mary, *widow* of Rev. Dr James Welch and *d* of late Sir Charles Eric Palmer. *Educ:* Eton; Trinity Coll., Cambridge; Westcott House, Cambridge. Joined Coldstream Guards, 1940; commnd, 1941; Capt., 1944; ADC to GOC-in-C Northern Comd India, Nov. 1945; Mil. Asst to Adjt Gen. to the Forces, War Office, 1946; Major, 1946. BA (History) Cantab, 1948; MA 1953; Pres., Cambridge Univ. Footlights Club, 1949. Ordained 1950. Asst Curate, Huddersfield Parish Church, 1950; Chaplain, Trinity Coll., Cambridge, 1953; Industrial Chaplain, Coventry Dio., 1958; Hon. Canon, Coventry Cath., 1965; Bishop Suffragan of Horsham, 1968–74; Bishop of Lincoln, 1974–86. Chm. Council, William Temple Foundation, 1985–89; Pres., Assoc. of Pastoral Care and Counselling, 1985–94; Mem., Home Sec's Cttee of Inquiry into Liquor Licensing Laws, 1971–72; formerly Mem. Council, Industrial Soc. *Publication:* God on Monday, 1966. *Recreations:* gardening, painting, cooking. *Address:* Sarsens, Shipley, W Sussex RH13 8PX. *T:* Coolham (01403) 741354. *Club:* Army and Navy.

PHIZACKERLEY, Ven. Gerald Robert; Archdeacon of Chesterfield, 1978–March 1996; *b* 3 Oct. 1929; *s* of John Dawson and Lilian Mabel Ruthven Phizackerley; *m* 1959, Annette Catherine, *d* of Cecil Frank and Inez Florence Margaret Baker; one *s* one *d*. *Educ:* Queen Elizabeth Grammar School, Penrith; University Coll., Oxford (MA); Wells Theological Coll. Curate of St Barnabas Church, Carlisle, 1954–57; Chaplain of Abingdon School, 1957–64; Rector of Gaywood, Norfolk, 1964–78; Rural Dean of Lynn, 1968–78; Hon. Canon of Norwich Cathedral, 1975, of Derby Cathedral, 1978; Priest-in-charge, Ashford-in-the-Water with Sheldon, 1978–90. Fellow, Woodard Corporation, 1981. JP Norfolk, 1972. *Recreations:* books, theatre, Border collies. *Address:* The Old Parsonage, Taddington, Buxton, Derbys SK17 9TW. *T:* Taddington (01298) 85607, *Fax:* (01298) 85583; (from April 1996) Archway Cottage, Hall Road, Leamington Spa, Warwickshire CV32 5RA. *T:* Leamington Spa (01926) 332740.

PHYSICK, John Frederick, CBE 1984; DrRCA; FSA; Deputy Director, Victoria and Albert Museum, 1983; *b* 31 Dec. 1923; *s* of Nino William Physick and Gladys (*née* Elliott);

m 1954, Eileen Mary Walsh; two *s* one *d*. *Educ:* Battersea Grammar Sch. Royal Navy, 1942–46 (Petty Officer Airman). Joined Victoria and Albert Museum, as Museum Asst, Dept of Engraving, Illustration and Design, 1948; Research Asst, 1949; Sen. Research Asst, 1965; Asst Keeper, Dept of Public Relations and Educn, 1967; Keeper, Dept of Museum Services, 1975–83; Sec. to Adv. Council, 1973–83; Asst to Dir, 1974–83. Leverhulme Trust Emeritus Fellow, 1984–86. Pres., Church Monument Soc., 1984–86; Member: Rochester Dio. Adv. Cttee for the Care of Churches, 1964–91 (Vice-Chm., 1987–91); RIBA Drawings Cttee, 1975; Cathedrals Adv. Cttee, 1977–81; Council for Care of Churches Monuments Sub-Cttee, 1978– (Chm., 1984–); Council for Care of Churches Conservation Cttee, 1984– (Chm., 1993–); Council, British Archaeol Assoc., 1985–88; Westminster Abbey Architectural Adv. Panel, 1985–; Rochester Cathedral Fabric Cttee, 1987– (Vice-Chm., 1992–); Council, Soc. of Antiquaries, 1991–93; Adv. Cttee, Public Monuments and Sculpture Assoc., 1991–. Trustee, London Scottish Regt, 1977–87. *Publications:* Catalogue of the Engravings of Eric Gill, 1963; (ed) Handbook to the Departments Prints and Drawings and Paintings, 1964; The Duke of Wellington in caricature, 1965; Designs for English Sculpture 1680–1860, 1969; The Wellington Monument, 1970; (jtly) Victorian Church Art, 1971; Five Monuments from Eastwell, 1973; (with M. D. Darby) Marble Halls, 1973; Photography and the South Kensington Museum, 1975; (with Sir Roy Strong) V&A Souvenir Guide, 1977; The Victoria and Albert Museum—the history of its building, 1982; (ed) V&A Album II, 1983; (ed) Sculpture in Britain 1530–1830, 2nd edn 1988; (contrib.) Change and Decay, the Future of our Churches, 1977; (contrib.) Westminster Abbey, 1986; (contrib.) The Royal College of Art, 1987; (introd.) Westminster Abbey: the monuments, 1989. *Recreations:* photography, looking at church monuments. *Address:* 49 New Road, Meopham, Kent DA13 0LS. *T:* Meopham (01474) 812301; 14 Park Street, Deal, Kent CT14 6AG. *T:* Deal (01304) 381621.

PIACHAUD, Prof. David François James; Professor of Social Policy (formerly Social Administration), London School of Economics, since 1987; *b* 2 Oct. 1945; *s* of Rev. Preb. François A. Piachaud and Mary R. Piachaud; *m* 1988, Louise K. Carpenter; one *s* one *d*. *Educ:* Westminster Sch.; Christ Church, Oxford (MA); Univ. of Michigan (MPA). Economic Asst, DHSS, 1968–70; Lectr, 1970–83, Reader, 1983–87, LSE. Policy Advr, Prime Minister's Policy Unit, 1974–79. *Publications:* The Causes of Poverty (jtly), 1978; The Cost of a Child, 1979; (jtly) Child Support in the European Community, 1980; The Distribution and Redistribution of Incomes, 1982; (jtly) The Fields and Methods of Social Planning, 1984; (jtly) The Goals of Social Policy, 1989; contribs to learned jls. *Recreations:* carpentry, travelling. *Address:* London School of Economics, Houghton Street, WC2A 2AE. *T:* 0171–405 7686.

PIANO, Renzo; architect; *b* 14 Sept. 1937; *m* 1962, Magda Ardnino; two *s* one *d*. *Educ:* Milan Poly. Sch. of Architecture. Works include: Pompidou Centre, Paris (with Sir Richard Rogers); De Menil art gallery, Houston; Schlumberger research labs, Paris; redevelopment of Potsdamer Platz, Berlin; refurbishment of Fiat Lingotto factory, Turin; Kansai International Airport, Osaka. RIBA Gold Medal, 1989. *Address:* 14 rue St Croix de la Bretonnerie, 75004 Paris, France.

PICARDA, Hubert Alistair Paul; QC 1992; *b* 4 March 1936; *s* of late Pierre Adrien Picarda, Docteur en Droit (Paris), Avocat à la Cour d'Appel de Paris, Barrister, Middle Temple, and Winifred Laura (*née* Kemp); *m* 1976, Ann Hulse; one *s* one *d*. *Educ:* Westminster Sch.; Magdalen Coll., Oxford (Open Exhibnr in Classics; BA Jurisprudence 1961; MA; BCL 1963); University Coll. London (Bunnell Lewis Prize for Latin Verse, 1962). Called to the Bar, Inner Temple, 1962, *ad eundem* Lincoln's Inn and Gray's Inn, 1965; in practice at Chancery Bar, 1964–; Night Lawyer, Daily Express, 1964–72; Lectr, Holborn Coll. Law, Langs and Commerce, 1965–68. Mem., Senate and Bar Council, 1978–81. Pres., Charity Law Assoc., 1992–. Pres., Hardwicke Soc., 1968–72. Mem., Inst. Conveyancers. Member: Classical Assoc.; Horatian Soc. Managing Editor: Charity Law and Practice Rev., 1992–; Receivers, Administrators and Liquidators Qly, 1994–; Mem., Editl Bd, Butterworths Jl of Internat. Banking and Financial Law, 1995–. *Publications:* Law and Practice Relating to Charities, 1977, 2nd edn 1995; Law Relating to Receivers, Managers and Administrators, 1984, 2nd edn 1990; contrib. legal periodicals and The Spectator. *Recreations:* Andalusia, Latin. *Address:* 10 Old Square, Lincoln's Inn, WC2A 3SU. *T:* 0171–405 0758. *Clubs:* Beefsteak, Pratt's.

PICCARD, Dr Jacques; scientist; President, Foundation for the Study and Preservation of Seas and Lakes; *b* Belgium, 1922; Swiss Citizen; *s* of late Prof. Auguste Piccard (explorer of the stratosphere, in lighter-than-air craft, and of the ocean depths, in vehicles of his own design); *m* 1953, Marie Claude (*née* Maillard); two *s* one *d*. *Educ:* Brussels; Switzerland. Grad., Univ. of Geneva, 1946; Dip. from Grad. Inst. of Internat. Studies. Asst Prof., Univ. of Geneva, 1946–48. With his father, he participated in design and operation of the first deep diving vessels, which they named the bathyscaph (deep ship); this vessel, like its successor, operated independently of a mother ship; they first constructed the FNRS-2 (later turned over to the French Navy) then the Trieste (ultimately purchased by US Navy); Dr J. Piccard piloted the Trieste on 65 successive dives (the last, 23 Jan. 1960, was the record-breaking descent to 35,800 feet in the Marianas Trench, off Guam in the Pacific Ocean). He built in 1963, the mesoscaph Auguste Piccard, the first civilian submarine, which made, in 1964–65, over 1,100 dives carrying 33,000 people into the depths of Lake Geneva; built (with Grumman) 2nd mesoscaph, Ben Franklin, and in 1969 made 1.500 miles/30 days drift dive in Gulf Stream. Founded: Fondation pour l'Etude et la Protection de la Mer et des Lacs, 1966 (built research submersible, F. A.-FOREL, 1978); Institut International d'Ecologie, 1972. Hon. doctorate in Science, Amer. Internat. Coll., Springfield, Mass, 1962; Hon. DSc, Hofstra Univ., 1970. Holds Distinguished Public Service Award, etc. *Publications:* The Sun beneath the Sea, 1971; technical papers and a popularized account (trans. many langs) of the Trieste, Seven Miles Down (with Robert S. Dietz). *Address:* (home) 19 avenue de l'Avenir, 1009 Pully-Lausanne, Switzerland. *T:* (21) 7288083; (office) Fondation pour l'Etude et la Protection de la Mer et des Lacs, 1096 Cully, Switzerland. *T:* (21) 7992565.

PICK, Charles Samuel; Managing Director, Heinemann Group of Publishers, 1979–85; Founder, Charles Pick Consultancy, 1985; Consultant to Wilbur Smith; *b* 22 March 1917; *s* of Samuel and Ethel Pick; *m* 1938, Hilda Beryl Hobbs; one *s* one *d*. *Educ:* Masonic School, Bushey. Started in publishing with Victor Gollancz, 1933; founder member, Michael Joseph Ltd, 1935. Served War, 1939–46; commnd RA, AA Command; apptd Staff Captain; served ALFSEA, India, Ceylon and Singapore. Jt Man. Director, Michael Joseph Ltd, 1959; resigned, 1962; joined William Heinemann Ltd as Man. Director, 1962; Director, Heinemann Group of Publishers, 1962; Director, Pan Books, 1968–85; Chairman: Secker & Warburg, 1973–80; William Heinemann, 1973–80; William Heinemann, Australia and South Africa, 1973–80; William Heinemann International, 1979–85; Heinemann Educational Books International, 1979–85; Heinemann Inc., 1980–85; Heinemann Distribution Ltd, 1980–85; Chm. and Pres., Heinemann Holdings Inc., 1980–85. Mem. Council, Publishers' Assoc., 1980–83. *Recreations:* walking, reading, theatre. *Address:* Littlecot, 28 Compton Road, Lindfield, Sussex RH16 2JZ *T:* Lindfield (01444) 482218; 3 Bryanston Place, W1H 7FN. *T:* 0171–402 8043. *Clubs:* Savile, MCC.

PICKARD, Prof. Huia Masters, FDSRCS; Professor of Conservative Dentistry, University of London, 1963–74, now Emeritus; *b* 25 March 1909; *o s* of late Ernest Pickard and Sophie Elizabeth Robins; *m* 1945, Daphne Evelyn (*d* 1995), *d* of Hugh F. Marriott; two *d*. *Educ:* Latymer Sch.; Royal Dental Hosp. of London Sch. of Dental Surgery; Charing Cross Hosp. MRCS, LRCP, FDSRCS. Private dental practice, pre-1940; EMS, East Grinstead, 1939. Served War, in RAMC, 8th Army (despatches), 1940–45. Dental practice and teaching, 1945; Dir, Dept of Conservative Dentistry, Royal Dental Hosp., and Consultant, 1955; Reader, London Univ., 1957–63; Dir of Dept of Restorative Dentistry, Royal Dental Hosp., 1965–74. Mem. Bd of Governors, St George's Hosp., 1969; First Pres., British Soc. for Restorative Dentistry, 1969; Pres., Odontological Section of Royal Soc. Med., 1971; Examr for Univs of London, Newcastle, Glasgow, Birmingham, Wales; also RCS. Governor, Latymer Sch., Edmonton, 1968–84 (Chm., 1980–83). Tomes Medal, BDA, 1983. *Publications:* Manual of Operative Dentistry, 1961, 6th edn 1990; contribs: Dental Record, Brit. Dental Jl, Internat. Dental Jl. *Address:* 14 Kingsdown, 115A Ridgway, Wimbledon, SW19 4RL. *T:* 0181–879 1790.

PICKARD, John Anthony, (Tony Pickard); professional tennis coach to Stefan Edberg, 1985–94; *b* 13 Sept. 1934; *s* of John William Pickard and Harriet Haywood Pickard; *m* 1958, Janet Sisson; one *s* twin *d*. *Educ:* Ripley Sch.; Diocesan Sch., Derby; Derby Tech. Coll. Worked under Harry Hopman, Australia (LTA), 1953–54; Sherwood Foresters, 1954–56; Mem., British Davis Cup team, 1958–63; Dir, Chellaston Brick Co., Derby, 1965; Dir, 1967, Man. Dir, 1971, F. Sisson & Sons and subsidiaries, Langley Mill; Captain, under-21 tennis team, winning Galea Cup, 1972; non-playing Captain, British Davis Cup team, 1973–76, 1991–94. GB Coach of the Year, 1988. *Recreations:* golf, walking, cars, spending time at home, football. *Address:* Whitemoor House, Blyth Road, Perlethorpe, Notts NG22 9ED. *T:* Mansfield (01623) 822369. *Clubs:* All England Lawn Tennis; International Tennis Clubs of GB, America, Germany, Sweden; Ripley Tennis; Lindrick Golf.

PICKARD, Prof. John Douglas, FRCS, FRCSE; Bayer Professor of Neurosurgery, University of Cambridge, since 1991; Consultant Neurosurgeon, Addenbrooke's Hospital, Cambridge, since 1991; Professorial Fellow, St Catharine's College, Cambridge, since 1991; *b* 21 March 1946; *s* of late Reginald James Pickard and Eileen Muriel Pickard (*née* Alexander); *m* 1971, Charlotte Mary, *d* of late Robert Stuart Townshend and Maureen Charlotte Townshend (*née* Moran); one *s* two *d* (and one *s* decd). *Educ:* King George V Grammar Sch., Southport; St Catharine's Coll., Cambridge (BA 1st Class 1967; MA); King's Coll. Hosp. Med. Sch., London (MB BChir 1970; MChir 1981 (distinction)). KCH, 1970–72; Inst. of Neurol Sci., Glasgow, 1972–73; Falkirk Hosp., 1973–74; Univ. of Pennsylvania Hosp., 1974–75; Registrar, Sen. Registrar, Lectr in Neurosurgery, Inst. of Neurol Sci., Glasgow, 1976–79; Consultant Neurosurgeon, Wessex Neurol Centre, Southampton, 1979–91; Sen. Lectr, 1979, Reader, 1984, Prof. of Clin. Neurol Scis, 1987–91, Univ. of Southampton. Mem. Council, Soc. of British Neurol Surgeons. Founder Trustee, British Brain and Spine Foundn; Dir, Internat. Soc. Cerebral Blood Flow and Metabolism. *Publications:* numerous articles in med. and sci. jls. *Recreation:* family life. *Address:* Academic Neurosurgical Unit, Addenbrooke's Hospital, Cambridge CB2 2QQ. *T:* Cambridge (01223) 336946.

PICKARD, (John) Michael, FCA; Chairman, London Docklands Development Corporation, since 1992 (Deputy Chairman, 1991–92); *b* 29 July 1932; *s* of John Stanley Pickard and Winifred Joan Pickard; *m* 1959, Penelope Jane (*née* Catterall); three *s* one *d*. *Educ:* Oundle School. Finance Dir, British Printing Corp., 1965–68; Man. Dir, Trusthouses Ltd/Trusthouse Forte Ltd, 1968–71; Founder Chm., Happy Eater Ltd, 1972–86; Dep. Chief Exec., 1986–88, Chief Exec., 1988–92, Sears plc; Chairman: Grattan plc, 1978–84; Courage Ltd and Imperial Brewing & Leisure Ltd, 1981–86; Dep. Chief Exec., Imperial Gp plc, 1985–86. Director: Brown Shipley Hlgs, 1986–93; Electra Investment Trust, 1989–; Nationwide Building Soc., 1991–94; Bentalls, 1993–; United Racecourses (Holdings) Ltd, 1995–. Chm. Council, Roedean Sch., 1980–91. Member: Bd, BTA, 1968–71; Cttee, AA, 1994–. Mem., Court of Assistants, Co. of Grocers, 1990. *Recreations:* cricket, tennis, golf. *Address:* 16 Grosvenor Hill Court, Bourdon Street, W1X 9HG. *Clubs:* Pilgrims, MCC; Walton Heath Golf; Headley Cricket.

PICKARD, Hon. Neil Edward William; Agent General for New South Wales, 1991–92; *b* 13 Feb. 1929; *s* of Edward Henry Pickard and Ruby (*née* McGilvray); *m* 1983, Sally Anne Egan. *Educ:* Sydney Univ. (BA, MEd, DipEd); Leigh Coll. (LTh). Mem., World Student Conf., Strasbourg, 1960. Minister, Methodist Ch., 1952–65; High Sch. teacher, 1966–69; Chm., Far W Ambulance Service, 1969–70; Sydney University: Lectr in Educn, 1970–73; Member: House Cttee, Wesley Coll.; Univ. Educn Res. Cttee. Alderman: Peak Hill Council, 1964–65; Dubbo CC, 1968–70. Liberal Party: Western Regl Chm., 1966–72; Mem., Central Exec., NSW, 1966–72; Chm., Educn and Agenda Cttees, 1966–72. New South Wales Parliament: MP (Lib) Hornsby, 1973–91; Chm., Parly Educn Cttee; Mem., Select Cttee on NSW Sch. Cert. Assessment Procedures, 1979–81; Minister for Educn, 1976; Shadow Minister for Educn, Develt, Mineral Resources and Energy, 1976–88; Minister for Minerals and Energy, 1988–91. Freeman, City of London, 1992. *Recreations:* music, international relations, travel, tennis, cricket, bowls, soccer. *Address:* 11 Woolcott Avenue, Wahroonga, NSW 2076, Australia. *Clubs:* Royal Automobile, East India; Australian (Sydney).

PICKARD, Tony; *see* Pickard, J. A.

PICKEN, Dr Laurence Ernest Rowland, FBA 1973; Fellow of Jesus College, Cambridge, 1944–76, now Emeritus (Hon. Fellow, 1989); *b* 1909. *Educ:* Oldknow Road and Waverley Road, Birmingham; Trinity Coll., Cambridge (Hon. Fellow, 1991). BA 1931; PhD 1935; ScD 1952. Asst Dir of Research (Zoology), Cambridge Univ., 1946–66; Asst Dir of Research (Oriental Music), Cambridge Univ., 1966–76. Editor: Musica Asiatica, 1977–84; Music from the Tang Court, 1981–. FIBiol. Hon. Fellow, SOAS, 1991. DLitt *hc* 1988. Trail Award, Linnean Soc., 1960; Curt Sachs Award, Amer. Musical Instrument Soc., 1995. *Publications:* The Organization of Cells and Other Organisms, 1960; Folk Musical Instruments of Turkey, 1975; contribs to many learned jls. *Address:* Jesus College, Cambridge CB5 8BL.

PICKERING, Prof. Brian Thomas; Deputy Vice-Chancellor, University of Bristol, since 1992; *b* 24 May 1936; *s* of Thomas Pickering and Dorothy May Pickering; *m* 1965, Joan Perry; two *d*. *Educ:* Haberdashers' Aske's Hatcham Boys' Sch.; Univ. of Bristol (BSc 1958; PhD 1961; DSc 1974). Research Biochemist, Hormone Res. Lab., Univ. of California, 1961–62; Scientific Staff, NIMR, MRC, 1963–65; University of Bristol: Lectr in Biochem. and Pharmacol., 1965–70 (Mem., MRC Gp for Res. in Neurosecretion); Lectr in Anatomy and Biochem., 1970–72; Reader in Anatomy and Biochem., 1972–78; Prof. of Anatomy and Head of Dept, 1978–92; Dean, Faculty of Medicine, 1985–87. Vis. Prof., Univ. of Geneva, 1977. Mem., Bristol & Weston HA, 1988–90; Non-Exec. Dir, United Bristol Healthcare NHS Trust, 1990–. Mem., Animal Grants Bd, AFRC, 1988–94 (Chm., 1991–94). Associate Editor, Jl of Endocrinology, 1972–77. European Society for Comparative Endocrinology: Sec. and Treasurer, 1971–77; Vice-Pres., 1986–90; Pres., 1990–94; Sec., British Neuroendocrine Gp, 1986–92; mem., other learned bodies. Hon.

Fellow, Romanian Acad. of Med. Sci., 1991. Hon. MD Carol Davila, Bucharest. Medal, Soc. for Endocrinology, 1977. *Publications:* contribs to professional jls. *Address:* The University, Bristol BS8 1TH.

PICKERING, Sir Edward (Davies), Kt 1977; Executive Vice-Chairman, Times Newspapers Ltd, since 1982; Chairman, The Times Supplements Ltd, since 1989; *b* 4 May 1912; 3rd *s* of George and Louie Pickering; *m* 1st, 1936, Margaret Soutter (marr. diss., 1947); one *d*; 2nd, 1955, Rosemary Whitton; two *s* one *d*. *Educ:* Middlesbrough High Sch. Chief Sub-Editor Daily Mail, 1939. Served Royal Artillery 1940–44; Staff of Supreme Headquarters Allied Expeditionary Force, 1944–45. Managing Editor: Daily Mail, 1947–49; Daily Express, 1951–57; Editor, Daily Express, 1957–62; Dir, Beaverbrook Newspapers, 1956–64; Editorial Dir, The Daily Mirror Newspapers Ltd, 1964–68, Chm., 1968–70; Director: Scottish Daily Record and Sunday Mail Ltd, 1966–69; IPC, 1966–75; Chairman: International Publishing Corporation Newspaper Div., 1968–70; IPC Magazines, 1970–74; Mirror Group Newspapers, 1975–77; Director: Times Newspapers Holdings Ltd, 1981–; William Collins Sons & Co. Ltd, 1981–89; Harper Collins Publishers Ltd, 1989–. Member: Press Council, 1964–69, 1970–82 (Vice-Chm., 1976–82); Press Complaints Commn, 1991–94 (Consultant, 1994–). Treasurer, Fédération Internationale de la Presse Periodique, 1971–75; Chm. Council, Commonwealth Press Union, 1977–86. Hon. Freeman, Stationers' and Newspaper Makers' Co., 1985. Master, Guild of St Bride, 1981–. Astor Award for distinguished service to Commonwealth Press, CPU, 1986. Hon. DLitt City, 1986. *Club:* Garrick.

PICKERING, Errol Neil, PhD; Director General, International Hospital Federation, since 1987; *b* 5 May 1938; *s* of Russell Gordon and Sylvia Mary Pickering. *Educ:* York Univ., Canada (BA Hons); Univ. of Toronto (DipHA); Univ. of New South Wales (PhD). Asst Administrator, St Michael's Hosp., Toronto, 1971–73; Executive Director: Aust. Council on Hosp. Standards, 1973–80; Aust. Hosp. Assoc., 1980–87. Dir, Health Care Risk Solutions Ltd. Pres., UNICEF Australia, 1984–86. Chm., Internat. Assoc. Forum, 1990–92. Mem., European Soc. of Assoc. Execs. *Publications:* many articles on hosp. and health policy issues. *Recreations:* classical music, bridge. *Address:* 4 Abbot's Place, NW6 4NP. *T:* 0171–372 7181. *Club:* Royal Society of Medicine.

PICKERING, Ven. Fred; Archdeacon of Hampstead, 1974–84; Archdeacon Emeritus since 1984; *b* 18 Nov. 1919; *s* of Arthur and Elizabeth Pickering; *m* 1948, Mabel Constance Threlfall; one *s* one *d*. *Educ:* Preston Grammar Sch.; St Peter's Coll., Oxford; St Aidan's Theol Coll., Birkenhead. BA 1941 (PPE), MA 1945. Curate: St Andrew's, Leyland, 1943–46; St Mary's, Islington, 1946–48; Organising Sec. for Church Pastoral Aid Soc. in NE England, 1948–51; Vicar: All Saints, Burton-on-Trent, 1951–56; St John's, Carlisle, 1956–63; St Cuthbert's, Wood Green, 1963–74; Rural Dean of East Haringey, 1968–73; Exam. Chaplain to Bp of Edmonton, 1973–84. *Address:* 11 Gracey Court, Woodland Road, Broadclyst, Exeter EX5 3LP. *T:* Exeter (01392) 460988.

PICKERING, Prof. John Frederick; Deputy Vice Chancellor, University of Portsmouth, since 1992; (Vice-President (Business and Finance), 1988–90, acting President, 1990–91, Deputy President, 1991–92, Portsmouth Polytechnic); *b* 26 Dec. 1939; *er s* of William Frederick and Jean Mary Pickering; *m* 1967, Jane Rosamund Day; two *d*. *Educ:* Slough Grammar Sch.; University Coll. London (BSc Econ; PhD; DSc Econ); MSc Manchester. In indust. market res., 1961–62; Lectr, Univ. of Durham, 1964–66, Univ. of Sussex, 1966–73; Sen. Directing Staff, Admin. Staff Coll., Henley, 1974–75. UMIST: Prof. of Industrial Economics, 1975–88; Vice-Principal, 1983–85; Dep. Principal, 1984–85; Dean, 1985–87. Mem., UGC Business and Management Studies sub-cttee, 1985–88. Dir, Staniland Hall Ltd, 1988–94; Dir and Chm., Univ. of Portsmouth (formerly Portsmouth Polytechnic) Enterprise Ltd, 1989–. Mem., Gen. Synod of Church of England, 1980–90; Church Comr for England, 1983–90; Mem., Archbishop's Commn on Urban Priority Areas, 1983–85; Pres., BCMS-Crosslink (formerly BCMS), 1986–92. Member: Council of Management, Consumers' Assoc., 1969–73, 1980–83; Retail Prices Index Adv. Cttee, 1974–; Monopolies and Mergers Commn, 1990–. *Publications:* Resale Price Maintenance in Practice, 1966; (jtly) The Small Firm in the Hotel and Catering Industry, 1971; Industrial Structure and Market Conduct, 1974; The Acquisition of Consumer Durables, 1977; (jtly) The Economic Management of the Firm, 1984; papers and articles in learned jls in economics and management. *Recreations:* music, cricket, theatre. *Address:* c/o University of Portsmouth, University House, Winston Churchill Avenue, Portsmouth PO1 2UP. *T:* Portsmouth (01705) 843203. *Club:* Commonwealth Trust.

PICKERING, Richard Edward Ingram; His Honour Judge Richard Pickering; a Circuit Judge, since 1981; *b* 16 Aug. 1929; *s* of late Richard and Dorothy Pickering; *m* 1962, Jean Margaret Eley; two *s*. *Educ:* Birkenhead Sch.; Magdalene Coll., Cambridge (MA). Called to the Bar, Lincoln's Inn, 1953; has practised on Northern Circuit, 1955–81; a Recorder of the Crown Court, 1977–81. Admitted as advocate in Manx Courts (Summerland Fire Inquiry), 1973–74. Councillor, Hoylake UDC, 1961–64; Legal Chm., Min. of Pensions and Nat. Insurance Tribunal, Liverpool, 1967–77; pt-time Chm., Liverpool Industrial Tribunal, 1977–79; Nominated Judicial Mem., Merseyside Mental Health Rev. Tribunal, 1984 (Legal Mem., 1967–79; Regional Chm., 1979–81); Northern Circuit Rep., Cttee, Council of Circuit Judges, 1984–89. *Recreations:* walking, gardening, study of military history. *Address:* c/o The Crown Court, Liverpool L2 1XA. *Clubs:* United Oxford & Cambridge University; Athenæum (Liverpool); Union (Cambridge).

PICKERING, Thomas Reeve; Ambassador of the United States of America to Russia, since 1993; *b* Orange, NJ, 5 Nov. 1931; *s* of Hamilton R. Pickering and Sarah C. (*née* Chasteney); *m* 1955, Alice J. Stover; one *s* one *d*. *Educ:* Bowdoin Coll. (AB); Fletcher Sch. of Law and Diplomacy (MA); Univ. of Melbourne (MA). Served to Lt-Comdr, USNR, 1956–59. Joined US For. Service, 1959; For. Affairs Officer, Arms Control and Disarmament Agency, 1961; Political Advr, US Delegn to 18 Nation Disarmament Conf., Geneva, 1962–64; Consul, Zanzibar, 1965–67; Counselor, Dep. Chief of Mission, Amer. Embassy, Dar-es-Salaam, 1967–69; Dep. Dir Bureau, Politico-Mil. Affairs, State Dept, 1969–73; Special Asst to Sec. of State and Exec. Sec., Dept of State, 1973–74; Amb. to Jordan, 1974–78; Asst Sec. for Bureau of Oceans, Internat. Environmental and Sci. Affairs, Washington, 1978–81; Ambassador: to Nigeria, 1981–83; to El Salvador, 1983–85; to Israel, 1986–88; Ambassador and US Perm. Rep. to UN, 1989–92; Ambassador to India, 1992–93. Mem. Council, For. Relns, IISS, 1973–. Phi Beta Kappa. Hon. LLD: Bowdoin Coll., 1984; Atlantic Union Coll., 1990; Tufts Univ., 1990; Hebrew Union Coll., 1991; Willamette Univ., 1991; Drew Univ., 1991; Franklin Pierce Coll., 1991; Hofstra, 1992; Lafayette Coll., 1992. *Address:* American Embassy, Novinsky Bul., 19/23 Moscow, Russia. *Club:* Cosmos (Washington).

PICKETT, Thomas, CBE 1972; retired,1986; Senior Regional Chairman, North West Area, Industrial Tribunals (England and Wales), 1975–85 (Chairman for Manchester, 1972); *b* 22 November 1912; *s* of John Joseph Pickett and Caroline Pickett (*née* Brunt); *m* 1940, Winifred Irene Buckley (*d* 1993), *yr d* of late Benjamin Buckley; no *c*. *Educ:* Glossop Grammar School; London University (LLB). Barrister-at-Law, Lincoln's Inn; called to Bar, 1948. Served in Army, 1939–50, retiring with permanent rank of Major. Dep. Asst Dir of Army Legal Services, 1948; Dist Magistrate, Gold Coast, 1950; Resident Magistrate, Northern Rhodesia 1955; Sen. Res. Magistrate, 1956; Acting Puisne Judge, 1960; Puisne Judge, High Courts of Northern Rhodesia, 1961–64, Zambia, 1964–69; Justice of Appeal, 1969–71, Acting Chief Justice, 1970, Judge President, Court of Appeal, 1971, Zambia. Chairman: Tribunal on Detainees, 1967; Electoral Commn (Supervisory); Delimitation Commn for Zambia, 1968; Referendum Commn, 1969; Local Govt Commn, 1970. *Recreations:* walking, swimming. *Address:* Bryn Awelon, Aber Place, Craigside, Llandudno, Gwynedd LL30 3AR. *T:* Llandudno (01492) 544244. *Clubs:* Royal Over-Seas League; Victoria (Llandudno).

PICKETT-HEAPS, Prof. Jeremy David, PhD; FRS 1995; FAA; Professor, School of Botany, University of Melbourne, since 1988; *b* 5 June 1940; *s* of Harold Arthur Pickett-Heaps and Edna Azura (*née* May); *m* 1st, 1965, Daphne Charmian Scott (*d* 1970); one *s* one *d*; 2nd, 1977, Julianne Francis Jack; two *s*. *Educ:* Clare Coll., Cambridge (BA; PhD 1965). Fellow, Research Sch. of Biol Sci., ANU, 1965–70; Prof., Dept of Molecular, Cellular and Developmental Biol., Univ. of Colorado, 1970–88. FAA 1992. *Publications:* Green Algae, 1972; numerous scientific res. papers. *Recreations:* various. *Address:* 47 St Leonards Road, Ascot Vale, Vic 3032, Australia. *T:* (3) 3444519.

PICKFORD, David Michael, FRICS; Chairman, Committee of Management: Lilliput Property Unit Trust, since 1984; Gulliver Developments Property Unit Trust, since 1987; Swift Balanced Property Unit Trust, since 1993; *b* 25 Aug. 1926; *s* of Aston Charles Corpe Pickford and Gladys Ethel Pickford; *m* 1956, Elizabeth Gwendoline Hooson; one *s* two *d*. *Educ:* Emanuel Sch., London; Coll. of Estate Management. FRICS 1953. Hillier Parker May & Rowden, 1943–46; LCC, 1946–48; London Investment & Mortgage Co., 1948–57; Haslemere Estates plc, 1957–86: Man. Dir, 1968–83; Chm., 1983–86; Dir, City & Metropolitan Building Soc., 1986–90; Chairman: Exeter Park Estates, 1986–91; Luis Palau Europe Ltd, 1980–; Dabet Ltd, 1986–; Compco Hldgs PLC, 1987–; Louth Estates (No 2) Ltd, 1989–; Brushfield Properties Ltd, 1990–; Stonechange Ltd, 1990–; Wigmore Property Investment Trust Plc, 1993–. President: London Dist, The Boys' Bde, 1967–86 (Hon. Life Pres., 1986); Christians in Property, 1990– (Chm., 1978–90); Chm., Drug and Alcohol Foundn, 1987–90 (Vice-Pres., 1990–92); Director: Mission to London, 1980–; London and Nationwide Missions, 1982–; Billy Graham Evangelistic Assoc., 1986–; CARE Campaigns Ltd (also Trustee), 1987–; Youth with a Mission, 1986–; Trustee: David Pickford Charitable Foundn, 1968–; Pickford Trust, 1972–; Prison Fellowship, 1989– (Chm. Trustees, 1990–93); London Prison Creative and Counselling Trust, 1991–93; Genesis Arts Trust, 1994–. *Recreations:* sheep farming, youth work, gardening. *Address:* 33 Grosvenor Square, Mayfair, W1X 9LL. *T:* 0171–493 1156; Elm Tree Farm, Mersham, near Ashford, Kent TN25 7HS. *Fax:* Aldington (01233) 720522.

PICKFORD, Prof. (Lillian) Mary, DSc; FRS 1966; Professor, Department of Physiology, University of Edinburgh, 1966–72 (Reader in Physiology, 1952–66); retired 1972, now Emeritus Professor; *b* 14 Aug. 1902; *d* of Herbert Arthur Pickford and Lillian Alice Minnie Wintle. *Educ:* Wycombe Abbey Sch.; Bedford and University Colls, Univ. of London. BSc (1st cl., Gen.) 1924; BSc (2nd cl., Physiology Special) 1925; MSc (Physiology) 1926; MRCS, LRCP 1933; DSc London 1951. FRSE 1954; FRCPE 1977. House Physician and Casualty Officer, Stafford Gen. Infirmary, 1935; Jun. Beit Memorial Research Fellow, 1936–39; Lectr, Dept of Physiology, Univ. of Edinburgh, 1939; Personal Chair, Dept of Physiology, Univ. of Edinburgh, 1966. Special Prof. of Endocrinology, Nottingham Univ., 1973–83. Fellow, University Coll., London, 1968–. Hon. DSc Heriot-Watt, 1991. *Publications:* The Central Role of Hormones, 1969; papers in Jl Physiology, British Jl Pharmacology, Jl Endocrinology. *Recreations:* walking, travel, painting. *Address:* 12 Ormidale Terrace, Edinburgh EH12 6EQ.

PICKFORD, Prof. Mary; *see* Pickford, Prof. L. M.

PICKFORD, Michael Alan, CB 1994; FIA; Directing Actuary, Supervision of Insurance Companies and Friendly Societies, Government Actuary's Department, since 1989; *b* 22 Aug. 1937. *Educ:* City of Oxford Sch. Govt Actuary's Dept, 1958–. *Address:* Government Actuary's Department, 22 Kingsway, WC2B 6LE.

PICKLES, Eric Jack; MP (C) Brentwood and Ongar, since 1992; a Vice-Chairman, Conservative Party, since 1993; *b* 20 April 1952; *m* 1976, Irene. *Educ:* Greenhead Grammar Sch.; Leeds Polytechnic. Joined Conservative Party, 1968; Young Conservatives: Area Chm., 1976–78; Nat. Vice-Chm., 1978–80; Nat. Chm., 1980–81; Conservative Party: Member: Nat. Union Exec. Cttee, 1975–91; One Nation Forum, 1987–91; Nat. Local Govt Adv. Cttee, 1985– (Chm., 1992–); Lectr, Cons. Agents Examination Courses, 1988–; Local Govt Editor, Newsline, 1990–. Bradford Council: Councillor, 1979–91; Chm., Social Services, 1982–84; Chm., Educn, 1984–86; Leader, Cons. Gp, 1987–91; Leader of Council, 1988–90. Dep. Leader, Cons. Gp, AMA, 1989–91. PPS to Minister for Industry, 1993–. Mem., Yorks Area RHA, 1982–90. *Recreations:* film buff, opera, serious walking. *Address:* House of Commons, SW1A 0AA.

PICKLES, His Honour James; a Circuit Judge, 1976–91; *b* 18 March 1925. Practised at Bradford, 1949–76; a Recorder of the Crown Court, 1972–76. *Publications:* Straight from the Bench, 1987; Judge for Yourself, 1992; Off the Record (novel), 1993. *Address:* Hazelwood, Heath Road, Halifax, West Yorks HX3 0BA.

PICKTHALL, Colin; MP (Lab) Lancashire West, since 1992; *b* 13 Sept. 1944; *s* of Frank Pickthall and Edith (*née* Bonser), Dalton-in-Furness; *m* 1973, Judith Ann Tranter; two *d*. *Educ:* Univ. of Wales (BA); Univ. of Lancaster (MA). Teacher, Ruffwood Comprehensive Sch., Kirkby, 1967–70; Edge Hill College of Higher Education: Sen. Lectr in English Lit., 1970–83; Head, European Studies, 1983–92. County Councillor, Ormskirk, Lancs CC, 1989–93. *Recreations:* fell-walking, gardening, cricket, theatre. *Address:* 237 Prescot Road, Aughton, Ormskirk, Lancs L39 5AE. *T:* (office) Ormskirk (01695) 570094.

PICKTHORN, Sir James (Francis Mann), 3rd Bt *cr* 1959, of Orford, Suffolk; Partner, Pickthorn, estate agents and chartered surveyors, since 1994; *b* 18 Feb. 1955; *o s* of Sir Charles William Richards Pickthorn, 2nd Bt and of Helen Antonia, *o d* of Sir James Gow Mann, KCVO; *S* father, 1995. *Educ:* Eton; Reading Univ. (BSc Estate Management). With Healey & Baker, 1977–82; Debenham Tewson & Chinnocks, 1982–86; Kinney & Green, 1986–94 (Partner, 1991–94); founded Pickthorn, 1994. TA (HAC), 1978–. *Recreation:* sailing. *Heir: uncle* Henry Gabriel Richards Pickthorn [*b* 29 Sept. 1928; *m* 1955, Mary, *d* of C. J. J. T. Barton, CMG, OBE; three *s* one *d*]. *Address:* 45 Ringmer Avenue, SW6 5LP; (office) Pickthorn, 24 Lime Street, EC3M 7HR. *T:* 0171–621 1380.

PICKUP, David Cunliffe; Chief Executive, Sports Council Trust Company, 1993–94; Director General, Sports Council, 1988–93; *b* 17 Sept. 1936; *s* of Robert and Florence Pickup; *m* 1960, Patricia Moira Aileen (*née* Neill); three *s*. *Educ:* Bacup and Rawtenstall Grammar Sch. Min. of Education, 1955–63; MPBW, 1964–71 (incl. periods as Pvte Sec. to four Ministers); Department of the Environment: Prin. Pvte Sec. to Minister for Housing and Construction, 1971–72; Asst Sec., 1972; Housing, 1972–75; Personnel, 1975–77; Under Sec., 1977; Regl Dir, Northern Reg., 1977–80; Housing, 1980–84; Local Govt, 1984–85; Dep. Sec., Assoc. of Dist Councils, 1986–88. FRSA 1992. *Recreations:* reading, music, sport, walking. *Address:* 15 Sandford Road, Bromley, Kent BR2 9AL. *T:* 0181–402 2354.

PICKUP, David Francis William; Principal Assistant Treasury Solicitor, and Legal Adviser to the Ministry of Defence, since 1991; *b* 28 May 1953; *s* of Joseph and Muriel Pickup; *m* 1975, Anne Elizabeth Round. *Educ:* Poole Grammar Sch.; Polytechnic of Central London (Univ. of London External LLB Hons). Called to the Bar, Lincoln's Inn, 1976, Gibraltar, 1988. Joined Treasury Solicitor's Dept as Legal Asst, 1978, Sen. Legal Asst, 1981; Grade 5 1987; Estabt Finance and Security Officer, 1988–90; Grade 3, Chancery Litigation Div., 1990. *Recreations:* playing and watching cricket, ski-ing, listening to music, food and wine, travel. *Address:* Queen Anne's Chambers, 28 Broadway, SW1H 9JS. *T:* 0171–218 0723. *Club:* Pyrford Cricket.

PICKUP, Ronald Alfred; actor; *b* 7 June 1940; *s* of Eric and Daisy Pickup; *m* 1964, Lans Traverse, USA; one *s* one *d*. *Educ:* King's Sch., Chester; Leeds Univ. (BA); Royal Academy of Dramatic Art. Repertory, Leicester, 1964; Royal Court, 1964 and 1965–66; National Theatre, 1965, 1966–73, 1977: appearances include: Rosalind, in all-male As You Like It, 1967; Richard II, 1972; Edmund, in Long Day's Journey into Night, 1971; Cassius, in Julius Caesar, 1977; Philip Madras, in The Madras House, 1977; Norman, in Norman Conquests, Globe, 1974; Play, Royal Court, 1976; Hobson's Choice, Lyric, Hammersmith, 1981; Astrov, in Uncle Vanya, Haymarket, 1982; Allmers in Little Eyolf, Lyric, Hammersmith, 1985; Gayev, in The Cherry Orchard, Aldwych, 1989; *films:* Three Sisters, 1969; Day of the Jackal, 1972; Joseph Andrews, 1976; 39 Steps, Zulu Dawn, 1978; Nijinsky, 1979; Never Say Never Again, John Paul II, 1983; Eleni, Camille (remake), 1984; The Mission, 1985; The Fourth Protocol, 1986; *television:* series and serials: Dragon's Opponent, 1973; Jennie, Fight Against Slavery, 1974; Tropic, 1979; Life of Giuseppe Verdi, 1982; Wagner, 1982; Life of Einstein, 1983; Moving, 1984; The Fortunes of War, 1987; Behaving Badly, 1988; A Time to Dance, 1992; My Friend Walter, 1992; The Riff Raff Element, 1993, 1994; other: The Philanthropist, Ghost Trio, The Discretion of Dominic Ayres, 1977; Memories, Henry VIII, 1978; England's Green and Pleasant Land, Christ Hero, 1979; The Letter, Ivanhoe, 1981; Orwell on Jura, 1983; The Rivals, 1986; The Attic, Chekov in Yalta, 1988; A Murder of Quality, 1990; Absolute Hell, 1991; The War that Never Ends, 1991; The Golden Years, 1992; In the Cold Light of Day, 1994; Milner, 1994; Ruth Rendell Mysteries, 1994; A Very Open Prison, 1995. *Recreations:* listening to music, walking, reading.

PICTET, François-Charles; Ambassador of Switzerland to Austria, 1990–94, and on Special Mission to the Holy See, since 1993; *b* Geneva, 21 July 1929; *e s* of Charles Pictet, Geneva, and Elisabeth (*née* Decazes), France; *m* 1st, 1954, Elisabeth Choisy (*d* 1980), Geneva; three *s*; 2nd, 1983, Countess Marie-Thérèse Althann, Austria. *Educ:* College Calvin, Geneva; Univ. of Geneva (Faculty of Law). Called to the Swiss Bar, 1954. Joined Swiss Federal Dept of Foreign Affairs, 1956; Attaché, Vienna, 1957; Sec., Moscow, 1958–60; 1st Sec., Ankara, 1961–66; Dep. Dir, Internat. Orgns, Dept of For. Affairs, Berne, 1966–75; Minister Plenipotentiary, 1975; Ambassador to Canada and (non-resident) to the Bahamas, 1975–79; Ambassador, Perm. Rep. to Internat. Orgns in Geneva, 1980–84; Ambassador to UK, 1984–89, to the Netherlands, 1989–90; Hd of Swiss Delgn to CSCE, Vienna, 1991–93. *Address:* 6 rue Robert-de-Traz, 1206 Geneva, Switzerland. *T:* (22) 7890086.

PICTON, Jacob Glyndwr, (Glyn Picton), CBE 1972; Senior Lecturer in Industrial Economics, University of Birmingham, 1947–79; *b* Aberdare, Glam, 28 Feb. 1912; *s* of David Picton and Ellen (*née* Evans); *m* 1939, Rhiannon Mary James (Merch Megan), LRAM, ARCM (*d* 1978); one *s* one *d*. *Educ:* Aberdare Boys' County Sch.; Birmingham Univ. (MCom). Chance Bros Ltd, 1933–47, Asst Sec. 1945–47. Pres., W Midland Rent Assessment Panel, 1965–72 (Chm. Cttee 1973–81); Governor, United Birmingham Hosps, 1953–74; Chm., Children's Hosp., 1956–66; Teaching Hosps Rep. Professional and Techn. Whitley Council, 1955–61; Mem., Birmingham Regional Hosp. Bd, 1958–74 (Vice-Chm. 1971–74); Mem., NHS Nat. Staff Cttee, 1964–73 (Vice-Chm. 1968–73); Chm., Birmingham Hosp. Region Staff Cttee, 1964–74; Vice-Chm., W Mids RHA, 1973–79 (Mem., 1979–82); Vice-Chm., NHS Nat. Staff Cttee (Admin. and Clerical), 1973–82; NHS Nat. Assessor (Admin), 1973. Chm., Birmingham Industrial Therapy Assoc. Ltd, 1965–79 and W Bromwich Industrial Therapy Assoc. Ltd, 1969–79; Indep. Mem., Estate Agents Council, 1967–69; Chm. of Wages Councils, 1953–82; Dep. Chm., Commn of Inquiry concerning Sugar Confectionery and Food Preserving Wages Council, 1961; Chm., Commn of Inquiry concerning Licensed Residential Estabts and Restaurants Wages Council, 1963–64; sole Comr of Inquiry into S Wales Coalfield Dispute, 1965 (report published, 1965, introducing concept of constructive tension into industrial relns inspired by wife's analogy with the harp which produces harmony under tension); Dep. Chm., Commn of Inquiry concerning Industrial and Staff Canteens Wages Council, 1975; Independent Arbitrator, Lock Industry, 1976–81. Has donated working papers: on Picton family to Nat. Liby of Wales; on academic and public service to Univ. of Birmingham. *Publications:* various articles and official reports. *Recreations:* music, gardening, Pembrokeshire history. *Address:* Maes y Tannau, 54 Chesterwood Road, Kings Heath, Birmingham B13 0QE. *T:* 0121–444 3959.

PIDDINGTON, Philip Michael, CBE 1988; HM Diplomatic Service, retired; Counsellor, Foreign and Commonwealth Office, 1987–90; *b* 27 March 1931; *s* of Percy Howard Piddington and Florence Emma (*née* Pearson); *m* 1955, Sylvia Mary Price; one *s* one *d*. *Educ:* Waverley Grammar Sch., Birmingham. Served HM Forces, 1949–51. Entered Min. of Works, 1947; FO, 1952; Jedda, 1956; Tokyo, 1962–66; First Sec., Lagos, 1969–71; Consul: NY, 1971–73; Istanbul, 1973–77; First Sec., FCO, 1978–83; Counsellor and Consul-Gen., Brussels, 1983–87. *Recreations:* riding, walking, photography. *Address:* The Pump House, St Mary's Road, East Claydon, Bucks MK18 2NA. *T:* Aylesbury (01296) 712302.

PIDGEON, Sir John (Allan Stewart), Kt 1989; Chairman, since 1980, and Managing Director, since 1960, F. A. Pidgeon & Son and associated companies; *b* 15 July 1926; *s* of Frederick Allan Pidgeon and Margaret Ellen Pidgeon, MBE; *m* 1st, 1952, Sylvia Dawn (*d* 1991); one *s* four *d*; 2nd, 1993, Mrs Pamela Barbara Howell. *Educ:* Church of England Grammar Sch., Brisbane. Fellow, Aust. Inst. of Building; FIDA. Served 2nd AIF, 1944–45. Joined F. A. Pidgeon & Son Pty, 1946. Director: Suncorp Building Soc., 1976–91; Folkestone Ltd, 1985–. Chm., Builders' Registration Bd of Qld, 1985–93. Pres., Qld Master Builders' Assoc., 1970 72 (Trustee, 1978–). Chm., Salvation Army Adv. Bd., 1988–93. FAICD. *Recreations:* ski-ing, tennis, swimming. *Address:* 43 Beesley Street, West End, Brisbane, Qld 4101, Australia. *T:* (7) 38448001. *Clubs:* Brisbane, Tattersalls, Polo, Brisbane Amateur Turf (Brisbane); Brisbane Yacht.

PIËCH, Ferdinand; Chairman, Board of Management, Volkswagen AG, since 1993 (Member, since 1992); *b* Vienna, 17 April 1937; *s* of Dr jur Anton Piëch and Louise (*née* Porsche). *Educ:* in Switzerland; Tech. Univ. of Zurich. Mem., Management Bd i/c R and D, Audi NSU Auto Union AG/Audi AG, 1975–88; Chm., Bd of Management, Audi AG, 1988–92. Dr *hc* Vienna Technical Univ., 1984. *Address:* c/o Volkswagen AG, Postfach, 38436 Wolfsburg, Germany. *T:* (5361) 923596.

PIEŃKOWSKI, Jan Michał; author and illustrator, since 1958; Founder Director, Gallery Five Ltd, 1961; *b* 8 Aug. 1936; *s* of late Jerzy Dominik Pieńkowski and Wanda Maria Pieńkowska. *Educ:* Cardinal Vaughan Sch., London; King's Coll., Cambridge (MA Classics and English). Art Dir, J. Walter Thompson, William Collins, and Time and Tide, London, 1958–61. Work includes graphics and murals, posters and greeting cards, children's TV, and book illustration. *Stage designs:* Meg and Mog Show, 1981–88; Beauty and the Beast, Royal Opera House, 1986; Théâtre de Complicité, 1988; Sleeping Beauty, Euro Disney, 1992. Kate Greenaway Medal, Library Assoc., 1972 and 1979. *Publications:* illustrator: The Kingdom under the Sea, 1971; Meg and Mog series, 1973–90; Tale of a One Way Street, 1978; Past Eight O'Clock, 1986; A Foot in the Grave, 1989; M.O.L.E., 1993, etc; illustrator/author: Nursery series, 1973–91; Haunted House, 1979; Robot, 1981; Dinner Time, 1981; Christmas, 1984; Little Monsters, 1986; Small Talk, 1988; Easter, 1989; Fancy That, 1990; Phone Book, 1991; Door Bell, 1992; Road Hog, 1993; ABC Dinosaurs, 1993; Toilet Book, 1994; 1001 Words, 1994; Furrytails series, 1994; Nursery Cloth Books series, 1994. *Recreations:* movies, ski-ing, gardening, painting. *Address:* Oakgates, Barnes. *Clubs:* Chelsea Arts, Polish Hearth.

PIERCE, Francis William, MA (Belfast and Dublin); Hughes Professor of Spanish, University of Sheffield, 1953–80, now Emeritus Professor; Dean of the Faculty of Arts, 1964–67; *b* 21 Sept. 1915; *s* of late Robert Pierce, JP and Catherine Ismay Pierce; *m* 1944, Mary Charlotte Una, *o d* of late Rev. J. C. Black, Asyut, Upper Egypt; three *s*. *Educ:* Royal Belfast Academical Institution; Queen's University, Belfast. BA, 1st Cl. Hons, Spanish studies, QUB, 1938; Postgrad. Schol., Columbia Univ., New York, 1938–39; MA, QUB, 1939; Asst Lectr in Spanish, Univ. of Liverpool, 1939–40. Dep. to Prof. of Spanish, TCD, 1940–45; MA *jure officii*, Univ. of Dublin, 1943; Hughes Lectr in Spanish, Univ. of Sheffield, 1946. Visiting Professor: Brown Univ., Providence, RI, 1968; Case Western Reserve Univ., Cleveland, O, 1968. President: Anglo-Catalan Soc., 1955–57; Assoc. of Hispanists of GB and Ireland, 1971–73. Commander, Orden de Isabel la Católica (Spain), 1986. *Publications:* The Heroic Poem of the Spanish Golden Age: Selections, chosen with Introduction and Notes, 1947; Hispanic Studies: Review and Revision, 1954; (ed) Hispanic Studies in Honour of I. González Llubera, 1959; La poesía épica del siglo de oro, 1961 (Madrid), 2nd edn 1968; The Historie of Aravcana, transcribed with introd. and notes, 1964; (ed with C. A. Jones) Actas del Primer Congreso Internacional de Hispanistas, 1964; (ed) Two Cervantes Short Novels, 1970, 2nd edn 1976; (ed) La Cristiada by Diego de Hojeda, 1971; (ed) Luís de Camões: Os Lusíadas, 1973, 2nd edn 1981; Amadís de Gaula, 1976; Alonso de Ercilla y Zúñiga, 1984; (ed) Repertorio de Hispanistas de Gran Bretaña e Irlanda, 1984; Asociación Internacional de Hispanistas: fundación e historia, 1986; (ed A. Bernat) Narrativa española de los siglos XVI y XVII: cuatro lecciones, 1991; articles and reviews in Hispanic Review, Mod. Language Review, Bulletin of Hispanic Studies, Bulletin Hispanique, Ocidente, Estudis Romànics, Quaderni Ibero-Americani. *Address:* 357 Fulwood Road, Sheffield S10 3BQ. *T:* Sheffield (0114) 266 4239.

PIERCE, Hugh Humphrey; *b* 13 Oct. 1931; *s* of Dr Gwilym Pierce, Abercynon, Glam; *m* 1958, Rachel Margaret Procter; two *s*. *Educ:* Clifton; King's Coll., Univ. of London. LLB Hons 1954; Pres. Faculty of Laws Soc.; Pres. Union. Called to Bar, Lincoln's Inn, 1955. Diploma Personnel Management, 1962; MIPM 1963. Army Service, 2nd Lieut Intell. Corps (Cyprus), 1955–57; Kodak Ltd, legal and personnel work, 1957–63; joined BBC, 1963, personnel and industrial relations; Admin. Officer, Local Radio, 1967–68; Local Radio Develt Manager, 1968–69; General Manager, Local Radio, 1970–74; Asst Controller, Staff Admin, 1974–78; Asst Controller, Employment Policy and Appts, 1978–80. Chm., First Framework Ltd, 1988–93; Member: Indep. Cttee for Supervision of Telephone Information Standards, 1987–93; Indep. Manpower Commn, Coll. of Occupational Therapists, 1988–89; Exec. Cttee, Howard League, 1979–90; Treas., Prisoners' Advice and Law Service, 1986–89; Member: Justice; Amnesty; Trustee: Community Develt Trust; Nat. Council for the Welfare of Prisoners Abroad. *Recreations:* chamber music, narrow boats. *Address:* 13 Southwood Hall, Muswell Hill Road, N6 5UF. *T:* 0181–444 6001; Pant y Bryn, Llanwnog, Caersws, Powys. *T:* Newtown (01686) 688229.

PIERCY, family name of **Baron Piercy.**

PIERCY, 3rd Baron *cr* 1945, of Burford; **James William Piercy;** *b* 19 Jan. 1946; *s* of 2nd Baron Piercy and Oonagh Lavinia (*d* 1990), *d* of late Major Edward John Lake Baylay, DSO; *S* father, 1981. *Educ:* Shrewsbury; Edinburgh Univ. (BSc 1968). AMIEE; FCCA. *Heir: b* Hon. Mark Edward Pelham Piercy [*b* 30 June 1953; *m* 1979, Vivien Angela, *d* of His Honour Judge Evelyn Faithfull Monier-Williams, *qv*; one *s* three *d*]. *Address:* 13 Arnold Mansions, Queen's Club Gardens, W14 9RD.

PIERCY, Hon. Joanna Elizabeth; *see* Turner, Hon. J. E.

PIERCY, Hon. Penelope Katherine, CBE 1968; Under-Secretary, Ministry of Technology, 1965–68; *b* 15 Apr. 1916; *d* of 1st Baron Piercy, CBE. *Educ:* St Paul's Girls' School; Somerville College, Oxford. War of 1939–45, various appointments, Military Intelligence. Foreign Office, 1945–47; Economist, Colonial Development Corp., 1948–54; Department of Scientific and Industrial Research, 1955–65 (Sen. Prin. Scientific Officer, 1960). *Address:* Charlton Cottage, Tarrant Rushton, Blandford Forum, Dorset DT11 8SD.

PIERRE, Abbé; (Henri Antoine Grouès); Officier de la Légion d'Honneur, 1980; French priest; Founder of the Companions of Emmaüs; *b* Lyon, 5 Aug. 1912; 5th *c* of Antoine Grouès, Soyeux. *Educ:* Collège des Jésuites, Lyon. Entered Capuchin Monastery, 1930; studied at Capuchin seminary, Crest, Drôme, and Faculté de Théologie, Lyon. Secular priest, St Joseph Basilica, Grenoble. Served war of 1939–45 (Officier de la Légion d'Honneur, Croix de Guerre, Médaille de la Résistance); Alsatian and Alpine fronts; Vicar of the Cathedral, Grenoble; assumed name of Abbé Pierre and joined resistance movement, 1942; Chaplain of French Navy at Casablanca, 1944; of whole Free French Navy, 1945. Elected (Indep.) to 1st Constituent Assembly of 4th French Republic, 1945; elected as candidate of Mouvement Républicain Populaire to 2nd Constituent Assembly; re-elected 1946; contested (Indep.), 1951. Président de l'Exécutif du Mouvement Universel pour une Confédération Mondiale, 1947–51. Founded the Companions of Emmaüs, a movement to provide a roof for the "sanslogis" of Paris, 1949. *Publications:* 23 Mois de Vie Clandestine; L'Abbé Pierre vous Parle; Vers l'Homme; Feuilles Eparses; Emmaüs ou Venger l'homme. *Address:* 2 avenue de la Liberté, 94220 Charenton-le-Pont, Val de Marne, France. *T:* 43686244.

PIERS, Sir Charles Robert Fitzmaurice, 10th Bt, *cr* 1660; Lt-Comdr RCNVR; *b* 30 Aug. 1903; *s* of Sir Charles Piers, 9th Bt, and Hester Constance (Stella) (*d* 1936), *e d* of late S. R. Brewis of Ibstone House, Ibstone; *S* father, 1945; *m* 1936, Ann Blanche Scott (*d* 1975), *o d* of late Capt. Thomas Ferguson (The Royal Highlanders); one *s* (one *d* decd). *Educ:* RN Colleges, Osborne and Dartmouth. Served European War, 1939–45. *Heir: s* James Desmond Piers, [*b* 24 July 1947; *m* 1975, Sandra Mae Dixon; one *s* one *d*]. *Address:* 6709 Chisholm Trail RR1, Duncan, BC V9L 1M3, Canada.

PIERS, Rear-Adm. Desmond William, DSC 1943; CM 1982; CD; RCN, retd; Agent General of Nova Scotia in the United Kingdom and Europe, 1977–79; *b* 12 June 1913; *s* of William Harrington Piers and Florence Maud Piers (*née* O'Donnell), MD; *m* 1941,

Janet, *d* of Dr and Mrs Murray Macneill, Halifax, NS; one step *d*. *Educ:* Halifax County Acad.; RMC of Canada; RN Staff Coll.; Nat. Defence Coll. of Canada. Joined RCN as cadet, 1932; CO, HMC Destroyer Restigouche, and Sen. Officer, Fourth Canadian Escort Gp on N Atlantic convoy routes, 1941–43 (DSC); CO, HMC Destroyer Algonquin with Brit. Home Fleet, Scapa Flow, and participated in invasion of Normandy and convoys to N Russia, 1944–45, Comdr 1945; Exec. Officer, HMC Aircraft Carrier Magnificent (Comdr), 1947–48; Dir, Naval Plans and Ops, Naval Headquarters, Ottawa (Captain), 1949–50; Asst COS (Personnel and Admin.) to SACLANT, 1952–53; CO, HMC Cruiser Quebec, 1955–56; Sen. Canadian Offr Afloat (Atlantic), 1956–57; Comdt, RMC Canada, and Hon. ADC to the Governor General (Cdre), 1957–60; Asst Chief of Naval Staff (Plans), Naval HQ, 1960–62; Chm., Can. Def. Liaison Staff, Washington DC, and Can. Rep. on NATO Mil. Cttee (Rear-Adm.), 1962–66; retd 1967. Chm., NS Div. Can. Corps of Commissionaires, 1988–91. Hon. Life Mem., Nat. Trust for Scotland, 1984. Hon. DScMil, RMC of Canada, 1978. Freeman of City of London, 1978; KCLJ 1989. *Recreations:* golf, tennis, figure skating, photography. *Address:* The Quarter Deck, Chester, Nova Scotia B0J 1J0, Canada. *T:* (902) 2754462. *Clubs:* Halifax (Halifax); Halifax Golf and Country, Chester Golf, Chester Tennis, Chester Curling (Nova Scotia).

PIGGOTT, Donald James; Director-General, British Red Cross Society, 1980–85; *b* 1 Sept. 1920; *s* of James Piggott and Edith Piggott (*née* Tempest); *m* 1974, Kathryn Courtenay-Evans (*née* Eckford). *Educ:* Bradford Grammar School; Christ's College, Cambridge (MA); London School of Economics. Served Army in NW Europe and India, 1941–46. PA to Finance and Supply Director, London Transport, 1947–50; Shell-Mex and BP Ltd, 1951–58; Manager Development Div., Marketing Dept, British Petroleum Co. Ltd, 1958–73; BRCS: Dir, Internat. Affairs, 1973; Head of Internat. Div., 1975; Asst Dir-Gen. International, 1980. Member: Central Appeals Adv. Cttee, BBC and IBA, 1980–83; Jt Cttee, St John and Red Cross, 1980–91; Dep. Pres., Suffolk Br., BRCS, 1987–93. Liveryman, Co. of Carmen, 1988–. FRSocMed 1993. OStJ 1983. *Recreations:* music, theatre. *Address:* Beech Tree House, The Green, Tostock, Bury St Edmunds, Suffolk IP30 9NY. *T:* Beyton (01359) 270589; 6 Pier House, Cheyne Walk, SW3 5HG. *T:* 0171–352 1520. *Clubs:* City Livery; Hawks (Cambridge); Achilles.

PIGGOTT, Maj.-Gen. Francis James Claude, CB 1963; CBE 1961; DSO 1945; *b* Tokyo, Japan, 11 Oct. 1910; *s* of late Maj.-Gen. F. S. G. Piggott, CB, DSO; *m* 1940, Muriel Joan, *d* of late Wilfred E. Cottam, Rotherham, Yorks; one *s* one *d*. *Educ:* Cheltenham; RMC Sandhurst. 2nd Lieut The Queen's Royal Regt, 1931; Language Officer, Japan, 1935–37; Captain, 1939; served 1939–45 in France (despatches), New Zealand, India and Burma (DSO); in Japan, UK and Egypt (OBE and Bt Lt-Col), 1946–52; attended 1st Course, Joint Services Staff Coll., 1947; Lt-Col comdg 1st Bn The Queen's Royal Regt, 1952, BAOR and Malaya; Colonel, War Office, 1954; Comd 161 Infantry Bde (TA), 1956; Dep. Director of Military Intelligence, War Office (Brigadier), 1958; Major-General, 1961; Assistant Chief of Staff (Intelligence), SHAPE, 1961–64; retired, 1964; served in Civil Service (Security), 1965–75. Col, The Queen's Royal Surrey Regt, 1964–66; Dep. Col (Surrey) The Queen's Regt, 1967–69. *Recreations:* cricket and foreign travel. *Address:* Meeting House Farm, Long Lane, Wrington, Avon BS15 7SP. *Clubs:* Army and Navy, Free Foresters.

PIGGOTT, Lester Keith; jockey, 1948–85 and 1990–95; trainer, 1985–87; *b* 5 Nov. 1935; *s* of late Keith Piggott and Iris Rickaby; *m* 1960, Susan Armstrong; two *d*. Selection of races won: the Derby (9 times): 1954 (on Never Say Die); 1957 (on Crepello); 1960 (on St Paddy); 1968 (on Sir Ivor); 1970 (on Nijinsky); 1972 (on Roberto); 1976 (on Empery); 1977 (on The Minstrel); 1983 (on Teenoso); St Leger (8 times); The Oaks (6 times); 2,000 guineas (5 times); 1,000 guineas (twice). In many seasons 1955–85 he rode well over 100 winners a year, in this country alone; rode 4,000th winner in Britain, 14 Aug. 1982; record 30th classic win, 1 May 1992; Champion Jockey 11 times, 1960, 1964–71, 1981, 1982; rode frequently in France; won Prix de l'Arc de Triomphe on Rheingold, 1973, on Alleged, 1977 and 1978; won Washington, DC, International on Sir Ivor, 1968 (first time since 1922 an English Derby winner raced in USA), on Karabas, 1969, on Argument, 1980. *Relevant publication:* Lester, the Official Biography, by Dick Francis, 1986. *Recreations:* swimming, water skiing, golf. *Address:* Florizel, Newmarket, Suffolk CB8 0NY. *T:* Newmarket (01638) 662584.

PIGGOTT, Prof. Stuart, CBE 1972; FBA 1953; Abercromby Professor of Prehistoric Archæology, University of Edinburgh, 1946–77; *b* 28 May 1910; *s* of G. H. O. Piggott. *Educ:* Churchers Coll., Petersfield; St John's Coll., Oxford (Hon. Fellow, 1979). On staff on Royal Commn on Ancient Monuments (Wales), 1929–34; Asst Dir of Avebury excavations, 1934–38; from 1939 in ranks and later as Intelligence Officer in Army in charge of military air photograph interpretation, South-East Asia. Conducted archæological excavations in southern England and carried out research on European prehistory up to 1942; in India, 1942–45; studied Oriental prehistory. FRSE; FSA (Gold Medal, 1983); Fellow, UCL, 1985. Mem. German Archæolog. Inst., 1953; Hon. Mem. Royal Irish Acad., 1956; Foreign Hon. Member: American Academy of Arts and Sciences, 1960; Archæolog. Inst. of America, 1990. Trustee, British Museum, 1968–74. Travelled in Europe and Asia. Hon. DLittHum, Columbia, 1954; Hon. DLitt Edinburgh, 1984. Grahame Clark Medal, British Acad., 1993. *Publications:* Some Ancient Cities of India, 1946; Fire Among the Ruins, 1948; British Prehistory, 1949; William Stukeley: an XVIII Century Antiquary, 1950; Prehistoric India, 1950; A Picture Book of Ancient British Art (with G. E. Daniel), 1951; Neolithic Cultures of British Isles, 1954; Scotland before History, 1958; Approach to Archæology, 1959; (ed) The Dawn of Civilization, 1961; The West Kennet Long Barrow, 1962; Ancient Europe, 1965; Prehistoric Societies (with J. G. D. Clark), 1965; The Druids, 1968; Introduction to Camden's Britannia of 1695, 1971; (ed jtly) France Before the Romans, 1974; Ruins in a Landscape, 1977; Antiquity Depicted, 1978; (ed and contrib.) Agrarian History of England and Wales Ii, 1981; The Earliest Wheeled Transport, 1983; Ancient Britons and the Antiquarian Imagination, 1989; Wagon, Chariot and Carriage, 1992; numerous technical papers in archæological jls. *Recreation:* reading. *Address:* The Cottage, West Challow, Wantage, Oxon OX12 9TN.

PIGNATELLI, Frank; Director of Education, Strathclyde Region, 1988–April 1996; *b* 22 Dec. 1946; *s* of Frank and Elizabeth Pignatelli; *m* 1969, Rosetta Anne McFadyen; one *s* one *d*. *Educ:* Univ. of Glasgow (MA; DipEd, MEd); Jordanhill Coll. of Educn (Secondary Teachers Cert.). Teacher, St Mungo's Acad., Glasgow, 1970; Hd of Dept, St Gregory's Secondary Sch., Glasgow, 1974; Asst Headteacher, St Margaret Mary's Secondary Sch, Glasgow, 1977; Strathclyde Region: Educn Officer, Renfrew Div., 1978; Asst Dir of Educn, 1983; Depute Dir of Educn, 1985. Hon. Lectr in Educn, 1988–90, Vis. Prof., 1990–, Univ. of Glasgow. Chm., RIPA (West of Scotland), 1990–93; Member: Adv. Scottish Council for Educn and Trng Targets, 1993–; Bd, SCOTVEC, 1993–. FIMgt (FBIM 1989; Pres., Renfrewshire, 1991–93). FRSA 1992. DUniv Paisley, 1993. *Publications:* Basic Knowledge 'O' French, 1974; Higher French Past Papers, 1975; contributor, World Year Book in Education, TES. *Recreations:* swimming, genealogy, do-it-yourself, reading. *Address:* 10 Whittingehame Drive, Glasgow G12 0XX. *T:* 0141–334 3458.

PIGOT, Sir George (Hugh), 8th Bt *cr* 1764, of Patshull, Staffs; management consultant, since 1995; *b* 28 Nov. 1946; *s* of Maj.-Gen. Sir Robert Pigot, 7th Bt, CB, OBE, DL, and Honor (*d* 1966), *d* of Captain Wilfred St Martin Gibbon; *S* father, 1986; *m* 1st, 1967, Judith Sandeman-Allen (marr. diss. 1973); one *d*; 2nd, 1980, Lucinda Jane (marr. diss. 1993), *d* of D. C. Spandler; two *s*. *Educ:* Stowe. Dir, Southern Trout Ltd, 1993–95 (Man. Dir, 1994–95). Hon. Treas., British Trout Assoc., 1990–92. *Recreations:* classic cars, golf. *Heir: s* George Douglas Hugh Pigot, *b* 17 Sept. 1982. *Address:* Mill House, Mill Lane, Padworth, near Reading, Berks RG7 4JX.

PIGOT, His Honour Thomas Herbert, QC 1967; a Circuit Judge, 1972–90; Common Serjeant in the City of London, 1984–90; Senior Judge (non-resident), Sovereign Base Area, Cyprus, 1984–90 (Deputy Senior Judge, 1971–84); *b* 19 May 1921; *e s* of late Thomas Pigot and of Martha Ann Pigot; *m* 1950, Zena Marguerite, *yr d* of late Tom and Dorothy Gladys Wall; three *d*. *Educ:* Manchester Gram. Sch. (Schol.); Brasenose Coll., Oxford (Somerset Schol.). BA (1st cl. hons Jurisprudence) 1941; MA 1946; BCL 1947. Commissioned Welch Regt, 1942; served N Africa with Royal Lincs Regt; wounded and taken prisoner, 1943; released, 1945. Called to Bar, Inner Temple, 1947, Bencher, 1985; practised in Liverpool on Northern Circuit until 1967. Mem., Bar Council, 1970. One of HM Comrs of Lieutenancy, City of London, 1984–90. Hon. Liveryman, Cutlers' Co. *Recreation:* golf. *Clubs:* Vincent's (Oxford); Huntercombe Golf.

PIGOTT, Sir (Berkeley) Henry (Sebastian), 5th Bt *cr* 1808; farmer; *b* 24 June 1925; *s* of Sir Berkeley Pigott, 4th Bt, and Christabel (*d* 1974), *d* of late Rev. F. H. Bowden-Smith; *S* father, 1982; *m* 1954, (Olive) Jean, *d* of John William Balls; two *s* one *d*. *Educ:* Ampleforth College. Served War with Royal Marines, 1944–45. *Recreation:* sailing (blue water). *Heir: er s* David John Berkeley Pigott [*b* 16 Aug. 1955; *m* 1st, 1981 (marr. diss.); 2nd, 1986, Julie Wiffen]. *Address:* Brook Farm, Shobley, Ringwood, Hants BH24 3HT. *T:* Ringwood (01425) 3268.

PIGOTT, Dr Christopher Donald; Director, University Botanic Garden, Cambridge, 1984–95; *b* 7 April 1928; *s* of John Richards Pigott and Helen Constance Pigott (*née* Lee); *m* 1st, 1954, Margaret Elsie Beatson (*d* 1981); one *d*; 2nd, 1986, Sheila Lloyd (*née* Megaw). *Educ:* Mill Hill School; University of Cambridge. MA, PhD. Asst Lectr, and Lectr, Univ. of Sheffield, 1951–60; Univ. Lectr, Cambridge, 1960–64; Fellow of Emmanuel Coll., Cambridge, 1962–64; Prof. of Biology, Univ. of Lancaster, 1964–84; Professorial Fellow, Emmanuel Coll., Cambridge, 1984–95; Member: Nature Conservancy, 1971–73; Nature Conservancy Council, 1979–82; Council, 1980–92, Properties Cttee, 1990–, Nat. Trust; Res. Users Adv. Gp, Forestry Commn, 1993– (Mem., Home Grown Timber Adv. Cttee, 1987–94); Foreign Mem., Acad. d'Agriculture de France (Silviculture), 1982–. *Publications:* contribs to sci. jls (ecology and physiology of plants). *Recreations:* walking, travelling. *Address:* Greenbank, Ayresome Lane, Cartmel LA11 7SQ.

PIGOTT, Ronald Wellesley, FRCS, FRCSI; Consultant Plastic Surgeon, Frenchay Hospital, Bristol, 1969–93, Hon. Consultant, since 1993; *b* 16 Sept. 1932; *s* of Thomas Ian Wellesley Pigott and Kathleen Muriel (*née* Parsons); *m* 1958, Sheila King; four *s*. *Educ:* Oakham Sch., Rutland; Univ. of Dublin (BA, MB, BCh, BAO). FRCSI 1960; FRCS 1962. Short service commn, Parachute Field Ambulance, 1960–62. Sen. Registrar, Plastic Surgery, Stoke Mandeville Hosp., 1962–68; Robert Johnson Fellow, Univ. of Miami, 1967. Pioneered endoscopy of velopharyngeal isthmus in the condition of velopharyngeal incompetence; developed split screen recording of endoscopic and radiological examn of velopharyngeal isthmus with A. P. W. Makepeace; pioneered computer-based assessment of symmetry for application to cleft lip and nose deformity with B. Coghlan and D. Matthews. President: Eur. Assoc. of Plastic Surgeons, 1992–93; British Assoc. of Aesthetic Plastic Surgeons, 1993. James Halloran Bennet Medal in Surgery, 1956; James Berry Prize 1979, Jacksonian Prize 1979, RCS; Mowlem Award, Brit. Assoc. Plastic Surgeons, 1982. *Publications:* chapters regarding investigation and treatment of cleft lip and palate in: Advances in the Management of Cleft Lip and Palate, 1980; Clinics in Plastic Surgery, 1985; Scott Brown's Paediatric Otolaryngology, 5th edn 1987; Current Therapy in Plastic and Reconstructive Surgery, 1989; article on develt of endoscopy of palatopharyngeal isthmus, Proc. Royal Soc., 1977; articles in Lancet, Brit. Jl Plastic Surgery, Plastic Reconstructive Surgery, Annals Plastic Surgery, Scandinavian Jl Plastic Reconstructive Surgery. *Recreations:* formerly hockey (represented Ireland, University of Dublin and Army and Combined Services), tennis (represented Univ. of Dublin), painting, sculpture, gardening. *Address:* Department of Plastic Surgery, Frenchay Hospital, Bristol BS16 1LE. *T:* Bristol (0117) 970 1212; 2 Clifton Park, Bristol BS8 3BS. *T:* Bristol (0117) 973 6504. *Club:* Royal Society of Medicine.

PIGOTT-BROWN, Sir William Brian, 3rd Bt, *cr* 1902; *b* 20 Jan. 1941; *s* of Sir John Pigott-Brown, 2nd Bt (killed in action, 1942) and Helen (who *m* 1948, Capt. Charles Raymond Radclyffe), *o d* of Major Gilbert Egerton Cotton, Priestland, Tarporley, Cheshire; *S* father, 1942. *Heir:* none. *Address:* 47 Eaton Mews North, SW1X 8LL.

PIGOTT-SMITH, Timothy Peter; actor and director; *b* 13 May 1946; *s* of Harry Thomas Pigott-Smith and Margaret Muriel (*née* Goodman); *m* 1972, Pamela Miles; one *s*. *Educ:* Bristol Univ. (BA Hons 1967); Bristol Old Vic Theatre Sch. Bristol Old Vic, 1969–70; Prospect Th. Co., 1970–71; RSC, 1972–75; Birmingham, Cambridge, Nottingham and Royal Court Th., 1975–77; Benefactors, Vaudeville, 1984; Bengal Lancer (one-man show), Leicester, transf. Lyric, Hammersmith, 1985; Antony and Cleopatra, Entertaining Strangers, Winter's Tale, Cymbeline, and Tempest, NT, 1986–88; dir, Samuel Beckett's Company, Donmar Warehouse (Edinburgh Fest. Fringe award), 1987; Artistic Dir, Compass Th., 1989–92; Brutus in Julius Caesar, 1990; Salieri in Amadeus, 1991; Saki—an anthology, 1991; Mr Rochester in Jane Eyre, Playhouse, 1993; The Picture of Dorian Gray, Lyric, 1994; Retreat, Orange Tree, Richmond, 1995; The Letter, Lyric, 1995; director: Royal Hunt of the Sun, 1989; Playing the Wife, 1992; Hamlet, Regent's Park, 1994. *Films:* Aces High, 1975; Joseph Andrews, 1977; Sweet William, 1978; The Day Christ Died, 1979; Richard's Things, 1981; Clash of the Titans, 1981; Escape to Victory, 1981; Hunchback of Notre Dame, 1982; State of Emergency, 1985; Life Story (Best TV Film, BAFTA), 1987; The True Adventures of Christopher Columbus, 1992; The Remains of the Day, 1993; The Bullion Boys, 1993; The Shadowy Third, 1994; *television: series and serials:* Dr Who, 1970; Glittering Prizes, 1975; North and South, 1975; Wings, 1976; Eustace and Hilda, 1977; The Lost Boys, 1978; The Wilderness Years, 1982; Fame is the Spur, 1982; The Jewel in the Crown (Best TV Actor, BAFTA; TV Times Best Actor; BPG Best Actor), 1984; The Chief, 1989–91; *plays:* School Play, 1979; No Mama No, 1986. *Publication:* Out of India, 1987. *Recreations:* music, sport. *Address:* c/o Michael Whitehall, 125 Gloucester Road, SW7 4TE.

PIHL, Brig. Hon. Dame Mary Mackenzie, DBE 1970 (MBE 1958); Director, Women's Royal Army Corps, 1967–Aug. 1970, retired; *b* 3 Feb. 1916; *d* of Sir John Anderson, later 1st Viscount Waverley, PC, GCB, OM, GCSI, GCIE, FRS, and Christina Mackenzie Anderson; *m* 1973, Frithjof Pihl (*d* 1988). *Educ:* Sutton High Sch.; Villa Brillantmont, Lausanne. Joined Auxiliary Territorial Service, 1941; transferred to Women's Royal Army Corps, 1949. Hon. ADC to the Queen, 1967–70. *Clubs:* English-Speaking Union, Naval.

PIKE, Baroness *cr* 1974 (Life Peer), of Melton, Leics; **Irene Mervyn Parnicott Pike,** DBE 1981; Chairman, Broadcasting Complaints Commission, 1981–85; *b* 16 Sept. 1918; *d* of I. S. Pike, Company Director, Okehampton, Devonshire. *Educ:* Hunmanby Hall; Reading

University. BA Hons Economics and Psychology, 1941. Served WAAF, 1941–46. Mem., WRCC, 1955–57. Contested (C): Pontefract, 1951; Leek, Staffordshire, 1955. MP (C) Melton, Leics, Dec. 1956–Feb. 1974; Assistant Postmaster-General, 1959–63; Joint Parliamentary Under-Secretary of State, Home Office, 1963–64. Mem., Robens Cttee on Safety and Health of People at their Place of Work, 1970–72. Director: Watts, Blake, Bearne & Co. Ltd; Dunderdale Investments. Chairman: IBA Gen. Adv. Council, 1974–79; WRVS, 1974–81. *Recreations:* gardening, walking. *Address:* Hownam, near Kelso, Roxburgh TD5 8AL.

PIKE, Prof. (Edward) Roy, PhD; FRS 1981; Clerk Maxwell Professor of Theoretical Physics, University of London at King's College, since 1986 (Head of School of Physical Sciences and Engineering, 1991–94); *b* 4 Dec. 1929; *s* of Anthony Pike and Rosalind Irene Pike (*née* Davies); *m* 1955, Pamela Sawtell; one *s* two *d*. *Educ:* Southfield Grammar Sch., Oxford; University Coll., Cardiff (BSc, PhD; Fellow, 1981). CPhys, FInstP, CMath, FIMA. Served Royal Corps of Signals, 1948–50. Fulbright Schol., Physics Dept, MIT, 1958–60; Royal Signals and Radar Estabt Physics Group, 1960: theoretical and experimental research condensed matter physics and optics; Individual Merit: SPSO 1967; DCSO 1973; CSO, 1984–90. Vis. Prof. of Maths, Imperial Coll., London, 1985–86. Chm., Oval (114) Ltd, 1984–85; non-exec. Dir, Richard Clay plc, 1985–86. Govt assessor, SRC Physics Cttee, 1973–76. Mem. Council: Inst. of Physics, 1976–85; European Physical Soc., 1981–83; Vice-Pres. for Publications and Chm., Adam Hilger Ltd, 1981–85; Director: NATO Advanced Study Insts, 1973, 1976; NATO Advanced Res. Workshops, 1987–88 and 1991. Hon. Editor: Journal of Physics A, 1973–78; Optica Acta, 1978–83; Quantum Optics, 1989–94. Nat. Science Foundn Vis. Lectr, USA, 1959; Lectures: Univ. of Rome, 1976; Univ. of Bordeaux, 1977; Simon Fraser Univ., 1978; Univ. of Genoa, 1980. FKC 1993. Royal Society Charles Parsons medal and lecture, 1975; MacRobert award (jtly) and lecture, 1977; Worshipful Co. of Scientific Instrument Makers Annual Achievement award (jtly), 1978; Committee on Awards to Inventors award, 1980; Confrérie St-Etienne, 1980–. *Publications:* (jtly) Introduction to High Temperature Superconductivity Theory, 1995; (jtly) The Quantum Theory of Radiation, 1995; (ed) High Power Gas Lasers, 1975; edited jointly: Photon Correlation and Light Beating Spectroscopy, 1974; Photon Correlation Spectroscopy and Velocimetry, 1977; Frontiers in Quantum Optics, 1986; Fractals, Noise and Chaos, 1987; Quantum Measurement and Chaos, 1987; Squeezed and Non-classical Light, 1988; Photons and Quantum Fluctuations, 1988; Inverse Problems in Scattering and Imaging, 1991; numerous papers in scientific jls. *Recreations:* music, languages, woodwork. *Address:* 3a Golborne Mews, North Kensington, W10 5SB.

PIKE, Rt Rev. Eric; *see* Port Elizabeth, Bishop of.

PIKE, Lt-Gen. Hew William Royston, DSO 1982; MBE 1977; Deputy Commander-in-Chief, and Field Army Commander, HQ Land Command, since 1995; *b* 24 April 1943; *s* of Lt-Gen. Sir William Pike, KCB, CBE, DSO; *m* 1966, Jean Matheson; one *s* two *d*. *Educ:* Winchester Coll.; RMA Sandhurst. Commissioned Parachute Regt, 1962; 3 Para, Middle East, Africa, Guyana, 1963–66; ADC, UK and Norway, 1966–67; 1 Para, Middle East, UK, 1967–70; Sch. of Infantry, 44 Para Bde (V), 1970–74; Staff College, 1975; Brigade Major, 16 Para Bde, 1976–77; Co. Comdr, 3 Para Germany and UK, 1978–79; CO, 3 Para, UK and Falkland Is Campaign, 1980–83 (despatches 1981); Comd 22 Armd Bde, Bergen-Hohne, 1987–90; RCDS 1990; GOC 3rd (UK) Div., 1992–94; Comdt, RMA, Sandhurst, 1994–95. *Recreations:* walking, ski-ing, gardening. *Address:* c/o Lloyds Bank, Castle Street, Farnham, Surrey.

PIKE, Air Cdre James Maitland Nicholson, CB 1963; DSO 1942; DFC 1941; RAF, retired; with Ministry of Defence, 1969–78; *b* 8 Feb. 1916; *s* of late Frank Pike, Glendarary, Achill Island, Co. Mayo, Eire, and Daphne (*née* Kenyon Stow), Worcester; *m* 1st, 1942, Mary Bettina Dell; one *d*; 2nd, 1955, Amber Pauline Bettesworth Hellard; one *s* one step *d*; 3rd, 1972, Dorothy May Dawson (*née* Holland) (*d* 1994); one step *d*. *Educ:* Stowe; RAF Coll., Cranwell. Commnd 1937; War Service: Aden, Middle East, UK (Coastal Command), Malta and Azores. Directing staff, RAF Staff Coll., 1945–47; Group Capt. 1955; Comd RAF Station, St Mawgan and RAF Station, Kinloss, 1955–57; SASO, RAF Malta, 1958–60; Air Cdre 1961; AOC, RAF Gibraltar, 1961–62; Imperial Defence College, 1963; Air Cdre Intelligence (B), Ministry of Defence, 1964; Dir of Security, RAF, 1965–69. *Recreations:* shooting, fishing, gundog training. *Address:* The Hyde, 31 Brookside, Watlington, Oxford OX9 5AQ.

PIKE, Sir Michael (Edmund), KCVO 1989; CMG 1984; HM Diplomatic Service, retired; *b* 4 Oct. 1931; *s* of Henry Pike and Eleanor Pike; *m* 1962, Catherine (*née* Lim); one *s* two *d*. *Educ:* Wimbledon Coll.; London Sch. of Econs and Polit. Science; Brasenose Coll., Oxford (MA 1956). Service in HM Armed Forces, 1950–52. Editor, Cherwell, Oxford Univ., 1954; part-time News Reporter, Sunday Express, 1954–55; Feature Writer and Film Critic, Surrey Comet, 1955–56; joined HM Foreign (now Diplomatic) Service, 1956; Third Secretary: FO, 1956–57; Seoul, 1957–59; Second Secretary: Office of Comr Gen. for Singapore and SE Asia, 1960–62; Seoul, 1962–64; FO, 1964–68; First Sec., Warsaw, 1968–70; FCO, 1970–73; First Sec., Washington, 1973–75; Counsellor: Washington, 1975–78; Tel Aviv, 1978–82; RCDS, 1982; Ambassador to Vietnam, 1982–85; Minister and Dep. UK Perm. Rep. to NATO, Brussels, 1985–87; High Comr, Singapore, 1987–90. Political Affairs Advr, Sun Internat. Exploration and Production Co., 1991–93; Dir, Govett Asian Smaller Cos Investment Trust Ltd. Member: Bid Cttee, British Olympic Bid: Manchester 2000, 1991–93; Bid Cttee, English Commonwealth Games Bid, Manchester 2002, 1994–; Sensitivity Review Unit, FCO, 1992–. Special Rep. of Sec. of State for Foreign and Commonwealth Affairs, 1992–; HM Govt Co-ordinator, Conf., Britain in the World, 1995. Pres., Union of Catholic Students of GB, 1955–56; Dir, Catholic Housing Aid Soc., 1995–; Member: Greenwich Town Centre Management Agency, 1993–; Greenwich and Lewisham Br. Management Cttee, New Parent and Infant Network, 1993 . *Recreations:* reading, running, contemplating London. *Address:* c/o Library and Records Department, Foreign and Commonwealth Office, SW1A 2AH.

PIKE, Peter Leslie; MP (Lab) Burnley, since 1983; *b* 26 June 1937; *s* of Leslie Henry Pike and Gladys (*née* Cunliffe); *m* 1962, Sheila Lillian Bull; two *d*. *Educ:* Hinchley Wood County Secondary Sch. (Commercial Dept); Kingston Technical Coll. Pt 1 Exam., Inst. of Bankers. National Service, RM, 1956–58. Midland Bank, 1954–62; Twinings Tea, 1962–63; Organiser/Agent, Labour Party, 1963–73; Mullard (Simonstone) Ltd, 1973–83. Mem., GMBATU (Shop Steward, 1976–83). Member: Merton and Morden UDC, 1962–63; Burnley Bor. Council, 1976–84 (Leader, Labour Gp, 1980–83; Gp Sec., 1976–80). Opposition frontbench spokesperson: on Rural Affairs, 1990–92; on Housing, 1992–94. Member: Envmt Select Cttee, 1985–90; Procedural Select Cttee, 1995–; Deregulation Select Cttee, 1995–; Chairman: PLP Environment Cttee, 1987–90; All Party Romanian Gp, 1994–; Jt-Chm., All Party Transport Forum, 1995–; Vice-Chm., All Party Gp on Homelessness, 1995–. Member: Nat. Trust, 1974–; CND; Anti-Apartheid. *Recreation:* Burnley Football Club supporter. *Address:* 73 Ormerod Road, Burnley, Lancs BB11 2RU. *T:* Burnley (01282) 34719. *Clubs:* Byerden House Socialist; Philips Sports and Social.

PIKE, Sir Philip Ernest Housden, Kt 1969; Chief Justice of Swaziland, 1970–72, retired; *b* 6 March 1914; *s* of Rev. Ernest Benjamin Pike and Dora Case Pike (*née* Lillie); *m* 2nd, 1959, Millicent Locke Staples; one *s* one *d* of 1st marriage. *Educ:* De Carteret School, and Munro Coll., Jamaica; Middle Temple, London. Barrister at Law, 1938. Crown Counsel, Jamaica, 1947–49; Legal Draftsman, Kenya, 1949–52; Solicitor General, Uganda, 1952–58; QC (Uganda) 1953; Attorney General, Sarawak, 1958–65; QC (Sarawak) 1958; Chief Justice, High Court in Borneo, 1965–68; Judge, High Court of Malawi, 1969–70, Actg Chief Justice, 1970. Coronation Medal, 1953. PNBS-Sarawak, 1965; Malaysia Commemorative Medal, 1967; PMN Malaysia 1968. *Recreations:* golf, gardening. *Address:* 3 Earlewood Court, 180/184 Ron Penhaligon Way, Robina Waters, Qld 4226, Australia.

PIKE, Dr Richard Andrew, CEng, FIMechE; FIChemE; FInstPet; Director General, Institution of Mechanical Engineers, since 1993; *b* 2 April 1950; *s* of Tudor Morgan Pike and Eileen Mary (*née* Oxley); *m* 1986, Fiona Elizabeth Henry; one *s* two *d*. *Educ:* Gosport Co. Grammar Sch.; Downing Coll., Cambridge (BA 1st Cl. Engrg; MA; PhD 1977). CEng 1987; FIMechE 1988; FIChemE 1991; FInstPet 1992. Joined British Petroleum as univ. apprentice, 1968; Maintenance Engr, BP Llandarcy, 1971–72; res. student, Cambridge, 1972–75; Develt Engr, BP Engrg, London, 1975–80; Area Commissioning Engr, Sullom Voe Terminal, Shetland, 1980–82; Business Develt Co-ordinator, Jt Ventures, London, 1982–83; Develt Supt, Pipelines and Facilities, Aberdeen, 1984–85; Offshore Prodn Engr, Forties, North Sea, 1985–86; Manager Technical, Sullom Voe Terminal, 1986–88; Manager, Jt Venture, Japan, 1988–89; Gen. Manager, Chems, BP Far East, Tokyo, 1989–93; Pres., BP Chems, Japan, 1991–93; Dir, Samsung-BP Chems, S Korea, 1989–91. *Recreations:* reading, swimming, languages, travel. *Address:* Institution of Mechanical Engineers, 1 Birdcage Walk, SW1H 9JJ. *T:* 0171–222 7899.

PIKE, Roy; *see* Pike, E. R.

PILBROW, Richard Hugh; Chairman, Theatre Projects Consultants, since 1957; *b* 28 April 1933; *s* of Arthur Gordon Pilbrow and Marjorie Pilbrow; *m* 1st, 1958, Viki Brinton; one *s* one *d*; 2nd, 1974, Molly Friedel; one *d*. *Educ:* Cranbrook Sch.; Central Sch. of Speech and Drama. Stage Manager, Teahouse of the August Moon, 1954; founded Theatre Projects, 1957. Lighting Designer for over 200 prodns in London, New York, Paris and Moscow, incl.: Brand, 1959; Blitz, 1962; Zorba, 1968; Annie, 1978; Oklahoma!, 1980; The Little Foxes, Windy City, 1982; Singin' In the Rain, 1983; Heliotrope Bouquet, 1991; Four Baboons Adoring the Sun, 1992; The Magic Flute, LA, 1993; Showboat, 1993; for Nat. Theatre Co., 1963–, incl. Hamlet, 1963, Rosencrantz and Guildenstern are Dead, 1966; Heartbreak House, 1975; Love for Love, 1985. Theatrical Producer in London of prodns incl.: A Funny Thing Happened on the Way to the Forum, 1963, 1986; Cabaret, 1968; Company, 1972; A Little Night Music, 1975; West Side Story, 1984; The Mysteries, Lyceum, 1985; I'm Not Rappaport, 1986. Film Prod., Swallows and Amazons, 1973; TV Productions: All You Need is Love—the story of popular music, 1975; Swallows and Amazons for Ever, 1984; Dir, Mister, 1971. Theatre Projects Consultants have been consultants on many theatres incl. Disney Concert Hall, LA, Nat. Theatre of GB, Barbican Theatre, Royal Opera House, and theatres and arts centres in Canada, Iran, Hong Kong, Saudi Arabia, Mexico, Iceland, Nigeria, Norway, USA, etc. Vice President: Assoc. of British Theatre Technicians: Nat. Youth Theatre; Co-founder, Soc. of Brit. Theatre Designers, 1975; Mem., Assoc. of Lighting Designers (Chm., 1982–85); Member: Drama Panel, Arts Council of GB, 1968–70; Soc. of West End Theatre; Council, London Acad. of Music and Drama. FRSA. *Publication:* Stage Lighting, 1970, 3rd edn 1991. *Recreations:* The Hebrides, cooking, dogs. *Address:* Theatre Projects Consultants Inc., 871 Ethan Allen Highway, Ridgefield, CT 06877, USA. *Club:* Garrick.

PILDITCH, Sir Richard (Edward), 4th Bt, *cr* 1929; *b* 8 Sept. 1926; *s* of Sir Philip Harold Pilditch, 2nd Bt, and Frances Isabella, *d* of J. G. Weeks, JP, Bedlington, Northumberland; *S* brother (Sir Philip John Frederick Pilditch, 3rd Bt) 1954; *m* 1950, Pauline Elizabeth Smith; one *s* one *d*. *Educ:* Charterhouse. Served War of 1939–45, with Royal Navy, in India and Ceylon, 1944–45. *Recreations:* shooting, fishing. *Heir:* *s* John Richard Pilditch, *b* 24 Sept. 1955. *Address:* 4 Fishermans Bank, Mudeford, Christchurch, Dorset BH23 3NP.

PILE, Colonel Sir Frederick (Devereux), 3rd Bt *cr* 1900; MC 1945; *b* 10 Dec. 1915; *s* of Gen. Sir Frederick Alfred Pile, 2nd Bt, GCB, DSO, MC; *S* father, 1976; *m* 1st, 1940, Pamela (*d* 1983), *d* of late Philip Henstock; two *d*; 2nd, 1984, Mrs Josephine Culverwell. *Educ:* Weymouth; RMC, Sandhurst. Joined Royal Tank Regt, 1935; served War of 1939–45, Egypt and NW Europe; commanded Leeds Rifles, 1955–56; Colonel GS, BJSM, Washington, DC, 1957–60; Commander, RAC Driving and Maintenance School, 1960–62. Secretary, Royal Soldiers' Daughters' School, 1965–71. *Publication:* Better than Riches, 1993. Recreations: fishing, cricket, travelling. *Heir:* *nephew* Anthony John Devereux Pile [*b* 7 June 1947; *m* 1977, Jennifer Clare Youngman; two *s* one *d*]. *Club:* MCC.

PILE, Sir William (Dennis), GCB 1978 (KCB 1971; CB 1968); MBE 1944; Chairman, Board of Inland Revenue, 1976–79; *b* 1 Dec. 1919; *s* of James Edward Pile and Jean Elizabeth Pile; *m* 1948, Joan Marguerite Crafter; one *s* two *d*. *Educ:* Royal Masonic School; St Catharine's College, Cambridge. Served Border Regt, 1940–45. Ministry of Education, 1947–50, 1951–66; Cabinet Office, 1950; Asst Under-Sec. of State: Dept of Education and Science, 1962; Ministry of Health, 1966; Dep. Under-Sec. of State, Home Office, 1967–70; Director-General, Prison Service, 1969–70; Permanent Under-Sec. of State, DES, 1970–76. Director: Nationwide Building Soc., 1980–88; Distillers' Co. Ltd, 1980–85. *Address:* The Manor House, Riverhead, near Sevenoaks, Kent TN13 2AS. *T:* Sevenoaks (01732) 54498. *Clubs:* United Oxford & Cambridge University; Hawks (Cambridge).

PILGER, John Richard; journalist, author and film-maker; *b* 9 Oct. 1939; *s* of Claude Pilger and Elsie (*née* Marheine); *m* Scarth Flett; one *s*; one *d* by Yvonne Roberts. *Educ:* Sydney High Sch. Cadet journalist, Sydney Daily Telegraph, Australia, qualified, 1961; freelance journalist, Italy, 1962; Reuter, London, 1962; feature writer, chief foreign correspondent, Daily Mirror, London, 1962–86 (reporter, Vietnam War, 1966–75, Cambodia, 1979–91, etc). Campaigns incl. Thalidomide 'X list' victims, and Australian Aboriginal land rights. Films include: The Quiet Mutiny, 1970; A Faraway Country (Czechoslovakia), 1977; Year Zero: the silent death of Cambodia, 1979; The Last Dream, 1988; Death of a Nation: the Timor conspiracy, 1994. Hon. DLitt Staffordshire; DPhil *hc* Dublin City. Awards include: Descriptive Writer of the Year, 1966; Reporter of the Year, 1967; Journalist of the Year, 1967, 1979; Internat. Reporter of the Year, 1970; News Reporter of the Year, 1974; Campaigning Journalist of the Year, 1977; UN Media Peace Prize and Gold Medal, 1979–80; George Foster Peabody Award, USA, 1990; Reporters Sans Frontiers Award, France, 1990; Richard Dimbleby Award, 1991; US TV Academy Award (Emmy), 1991. *Publications:* The Last Day, 1975; Aftermath: the struggle of Cambodia and Vietnam, 1981; The Outsiders, 1984; Heroes, 1986; A Secret Country, 1989; Distant Voices, 1992. *Recreations:* swimming, sunning, mulling. *Address:* 57 Hambalt Road, SW4 9EQ. *T:* 0181–673 2848.

PILGRIM, Cecil Stanley, CCH 1986; High Commissioner for Guyana in London, 1986–92, and concurrently Ambassador (non-resident) to France, the Netherlands and Yugoslavia; *b* 1 Feb. 1932; *s* of Errol Pilgrim and Edith Pilgrim; *m* 1979, Cita I. Pilgrim; one *d*. *Educ:* Queen's Coll., Guyana; Univ. of Guyana (BSc; post graduate course in Internat. Relations). Diplomatic Cadet, Guyana, 1967; Second Sec., Jamaica, 1969; First Sec., China, 1974; Counsellor, USSR, 1978; Ambassador, Cuba, 1979. *Recreations:* reading, music, badminton, walking, cricket, enjoys sports of all types. *Address:* Norlyn, Brighton, Black Rock, Barbados, West Indies.

PILKINGTON, Sir Antony (Richard), Kt 1990; DL; Chairman, Pilkington plc (formerly Pilkington Brothers plc), 1980–95; *b* 20 June 1935; *s* of Arthur Cope Pilkington and Otilia Dolores Pilkington; *m* 1960, Alice Kirsty, *er d* of Sir Thomas Dundas, 7th Bt, MBE and of Lady Dundas; three *s* one *d*. *Educ:* Ampleforth Coll.; Trinity Coll., Cambridge (MA History). Coldstream Guards, 1953–55. Joined Pilkington Brothers, 1959; Dir, 1973–95; Dep. Chm., 1979–80. Director: BSN Gervais Danone (France), 1975–80 (Mem., Internat. Consultative Cttee, 1982–94); GKN, 1982–91; National Westminster Bank, 1984–94; Libbey-Owens-Ford Co. (USA), 1984–89; ICI, 1991–. Mem., European Round Table, 1984–95. Chm., Community of St Helens Trust, 1978–. Mem. Council, Liverpool Univ., 1977–79. Hon. LLD Liverpool, 1987. DL Merseyside, 1988. *Recreations:* interesting motor cars, ski-ing, sailing, P. G. Wodehouse. *Address:* Pilkington plc, Prescot Road, St Helens, Lancs WA10 3TT. *T:* St Helens (01744) 28882. *Clubs:* Pratt's, MCC.

PILKINGTON, Godfrey; *see* Pilkington, R. G.

PILKINGTON, Lawrence Herbert Austin, CBE 1964; JP; Director, Pilkington Brothers Ltd, 1943–81; *b* 13 Oct. 1911; 2nd *s* of Richard Austin and Hon. Hope Pilkington; *m* 1936, Norah Holden (*d* 1992), Whitby, Ont., Canada; two *d*. *Educ:* Bromsgrove School; Magdalene College, Cambridge. Volunteer with Grenfell Mission, 1933–34. Joined Pilkington Brothers Limited, 1935. Chairman: Glass Delegacy, 1949–54; Glass Industry Research Assoc., 1954–58; British Coal Utilisation Research Assoc., 1963–68; Soc. of Acoustic Technology, 1963–; Member: Building Research Board, 1958–62; Wilson Cttee on Noise, 1960–63; Adv. Council on R&D for Fuel and Power, 1973–75. President, Soc. of Glass Technology, 1960–64. JP Lancs, 1942. Hon. LLD Sheffield, 1956; Hon. DSc Salford, 1970. *Publications:* mainly on glass in various technical jls. *Recreations:* sailing, climbing, amateur radio, shooting. *Address:* Coppice End, Colborne Road, St Peter Port, Guernsey GY1 1EP. *Club:* Royal Dee Yacht.

PILKINGTON, Air Vice-Marshal Michael John, CB 1991; CBE 1982; Air Officer Commanding Training Units, Royal Air Force Support Command, 1989–92, retired; *b* 9 Oct. 1937; *s* of David and Mary Pilkington; *m* 1960, Janet Rayner; one *d*. *Educ:* Bromley Grammar Sch. psc rcds. Commnd Royal Air Force, 1956; Bomber Sqdns, No 35, No 83, No 27, 1959–70; RAF sc 1971; HQ Near East Air Force, 1972–73; CO No 230 Vulcan OCU, 1974–75; Defence Policy Staff, 1977–78; CO RAF Waddington, 1979–81; RCDS 1982; Branch Chief Policy, SHAPE, 1982–85; DG of Trng, RAF, 1986–89. *Recreations:* golf, tennis, gardening, theatre, wine. *Club:* Royal Air Force.

PILKINGTON, Muriel Norma, MA; Headteacher, Wycombe High School, since 1986; *b* 1 Jan. 1941; *d* of Norman Herbert Fosbury and Lilian Alice Fosbury; *m* 1st, 1962, Anthony Leonard Andrews; one *s*; 2nd, 1983, Derek Brogden Pilkington; one step *s* one step *d*. *Educ:* Woking County Grammar Sch.; Helene Lange Hochschule, Hamburg; Lady Margaret Hall, Oxford (BA 1962; MA 1970). Asst Teacher, Shephalbury Sch., Stevenage, 1962–64; 2nd in Dept, Hatfield Girls' Grammar Sch., 1964–66; Head of Dept/Faculty, Sir James Altham Sch., Watford, 1970–81; Dep. Head, Francis Bacon Sch., St Albans, 1981–86. Chm., Area 6 SHA, 1993–95. Trustee, Whitmore Vale Housing Assoc. Governor: Bucks Coll., Brunel Univ.; London Arts Schs; Chiltern Gate Sch. FRSA 1990. *Recreations:* music, jogging, gastronomy, travel. *Address:* Wycombe High School, Marlow Hill, High Wycombe, Bucks HP11 1TB.

PILKINGTON, Rev. Canon Peter; Chairman, Broadcasting Complaints Commission, since 1992; Hon. Canon of Canterbury Cathedral, 1975–90, now Canon Emeritus; *b* 5 Sept. 1933; *s* of Frank and Doris Pilkington; *m* 1966, Helen, *d* of Charles and Maria Wilson; two *d*. *Educ:* Dame Allans Sch., Newcastle upon Tyne; Jesus Coll., Cambridge. BA 1955, MA 1958. Schoolmaster, St Joseph's Coll., Chidya, Tanganyika, 1955–57; ordained 1959; Curate in Bakewell, Derbs, 1959–62; Schoolmaster, Eton College, 1962–75, Master in College, 1965–75; Headmaster, King's Sch., Canterbury, 1975–86; High Master, St Paul's Sch., 1986–92. Mem., Parole Bd, 1990–95. *Address:* Oxenford House, near Ilminster, Somerset TA19 0PP. *T:* Ilminster (01460) 52813. *Clubs:* Beefsteak, Garrick.

PILKINGTON, (Richard) Godfrey; Partner and Director, Piccadilly Gallery, since 1953; *b* 8 Nov. 1918; *e s* of Col Guy R. Pilkington, DSO and Margery (*née* Frost); *m* 1950, Evelyn Edith (Eve) Vincent; two *s* two *d*. *Educ:* Clifton; Trinity Coll., Cambridge (MA). Lieut, RA, N Africa and Central Mediterranean, 1940–46. Joined Frost & Reed, art dealers, 1947; edited Pictures and Prints, 1951–60; founded Piccadilly Gallery, 1953. Master, Fine Art Trade Guild, 1964–66; Chm., Soc. of London Art Dealers, 1974–77. Governor, Wimbledon Sch. of Art, 1990–. *Publications:* numerous exhibn catalogues and magazine articles. *Recreations:* walking, boating, tennis, golf. *Address:* 45 Barons Court Road, W14 9DZ. *Clubs:* Athenæum, Garrick, Hurlingham.

PILKINGTON, Dr Roger Windle; author; *b* 17 Jan. 1915; 3rd *s* of Richard Austin Pilkington and Hon. Hope (*née* Cozens-Hardy); *m* 1st, 1937, Theodora Miriam Jaboor; one *d* (and one *s* decd); 2nd, 1973, Fru Ingrid Geijer, Stockholm. *Educ:* Rugby; Freiburg, Germany; Magdalene Coll., Cambridge (MA, PhD). Research, genetics, 1937; Chm., London Missionary Soc., 1962; Chm. of Trustees, Homerton Coll., Cambridge, 1962; Chm. of Govs, Hall Sch., 1962; jt author, Sex and Morality Report, Brit. Council of Churches, 1966; Vice-Pres., River Thames Soc., 1967; Master, Glass Sellers' Co., 1967. *Publications:* Males and Females, 1948; Stringer's Folly, Biology, Man and God, Sons and Daughters, 1951; How Your Life Began, 1953; Revelation Through Science, 1954; Jan's Treasure, In the Beginning, 1955; Thames Waters, The Facts of Life, 1956; Small Boat Through Belgium, The Chesterfield Gold, The Great South Sea, The Ways of the Sea, 1957; The Missing Panel, 1958; Small Boat Through Holland, Robert Boyle: Father of Chemistry, How Boats Go Uphill, 1959; Small Boat to the Skagerrak, World Without End, The Dahlia's Cargo, Don John's Ducats, 1960; Small Boat to Sweden, Small Boat to Alsace, The Ways of the Air, Who's Who and Why, 1961; Small Boat to Bavaria, Nepomuk of the River, Boats Overland, How Boats are Navigated, 1962; The River, (with Noel Streatfeild) Confirmation and After, Facts of Life for Parents, Small Boat to Germany, The Eisenbart Mystery, 1963; Heavens Alive, Small Boat Through France, 1964; Small Boat in Southern France, Glass, 1965; Small Boat on the Thames, The Boy from Stink Alley, 1966; Small Boat on the Meuse, Small Boat to Luxembourg, 1967; Small Boat on the Moselle, 1968; Small Boat to Elsinore, 1968; Small Boat in Northern Germany, 1969; Small Boat on the Lower Rhine, 1970; Small Boat on the Upper Rhine, 1971; Waterways in Europe, 1972; The Ormering Tide, 1974; The Face in the River, 1976; Geijer in England, 1983; Small Boat Down the Years, 1987; Small Boat in the Midi, 1989; I Sailed on the Mayflower, 1990; One Foot in France, 1992; View from the Shore, 1995; contribs to Guardian, Daily Telegraph, Times, Family Doctor, Yachting World, etc. *Recreations:* inland waterways, walking. *Address:* 4 Links Court, Grouville, Jersey JE3 9DD.

PILKINGTON, Sir Thomas Henry Milborne-Swinnerton-, 14th Bt, *cr* 1635; Chairman, Thos & James Harrison Ltd, since 1980 (Director, since 1963); Chairman, Charente Steamship Co. Ltd, since 1977; Deputy Chairman, Cluff Resources plc, since 1988; *b* 10 Mar. 1934; *s* of Sir Arthur W. Milborne-Swinnerton-Pilkington, 13th Bt and Elizabeth Mary (she *m* 1950, A. Burke), *d* of late Major J. F. Harrison, King's Walden Bury, Hitchin; *S* father 1952; *m* 1961, Susan, *e d* of N. S. R. Adamson, Durban, South Africa; one *s* two *d*. *Educ:* Eton College. Sen. Steward, Jockey Club, 1994–. *Recreations:* golf, racing. *Heir:* *s* Richard Arthur Milborne-Swinnerton-Pilkington [*b* 4 Sept. 1964; *m* 1994, Katya, *d* of T. J. Clemence; one *d*]. *Address:* King's Walden Bury, Hitchin, Herts SG4 8JU. *Club:* White's.

PILL, Rt Hon. Sir Malcolm (Thomas), Kt 1988; PC 1995; **Rt Hon. Lord Justice Pill;** a Lord Justice of Appeal, since 1995; *b* 11 March 1938; *s* of late Reginald Thomas Pill, MBE and Anne Pill (*née* Wright); *m* 1966, Roisin Pill (*née* Riordan); two *s* one *d*. *Educ:* Whitchurch Grammar Sch.; Trinity Coll., Cambridge. MA, LLM, Dip. Hague Acad. of Internat. Law. Served RA, 1956–58; Glamorgan Yeomanry (TA), 1958–67. Called to Bar, Gray's Inn, 1962, Bencher, 1987; Wales and Chester Circuit, 1963 (Treas., 1985–87; Presiding Judge, 1989–93); a Recorder, 1976–87; QC 1978; a Judge of the High Court, QBD, 1988–95; a Judge, Employment Appeal Tribunal, 1992–95. 3rd Sec., Foreign Office, 1963–64. Dep. Chm., Parly Boundary Commn for Wales, 1993–95. Chairman: UNA (Welsh Centre) Trust, 1969–77, 1980–87; Welsh Centre for Internat. Affairs, 1973–76; Eur Parly Cttee for Wales, 1993. Chm., UK Cttee, Freedom from Hunger Campaign, 1978–87. *Address:* Royal Courts of Justice, Strand, WC2A 2LL. *Clubs:* Army and Navy; Cardiff and County.

PILLAR, Rt. Rev. Kenneth Harold; Bishop Suffragan of Hertford, 1982–89; an Assistant Bishop, diocese of Sheffield, since 1990; *b* 10 Oct. 1924; *s* of Harold and Mary Pillar; *m* 1955, Margaret Elizabeth Davies; one *s* three *d*. *Educ:* Devonport High School; Queens' Coll., Cambridge (MA); Ridley Hall, Cambridge. Asst Curate, Childwall, Liverpool, 1950–53; Chaplain, Lee Abbey, Lynton, N Devon, 1953–57; Vicar: St Paul's, Beckenham, 1957–62; St Mary Bredin, Canterbury, 1962–65; Warden of Lee Abbey, Lynton, N Devon, 1965–70; Vicar of Waltham Abbey, Essex, 1970–82; RD of Epping Forest, 1976–82. *Recreation:* walking. *Address:* 75 Dobcroft Road, Millhouses, Sheffield S7 2LS. *T:* Sheffield (0114) 236 7902.

PILLAR, Adm. Sir William (Thomas), GBE 1983; KCB 1980; CEng, FIMechE; FIMarE; Lieutenant-Governor and Commander-in-Chief, Jersey, 1985–90; *b* 24 Feb. 1924; *s* of William Pillar and Lily Pillar; *m* 1946, Ursula, *d* of Arthur B. Ransley, MC; three *s* one *d*. *Educ:* Blundells Sch., Tiverton; RNEC. FIMechE 1969, FIMarE 1972. Entered RN, 1942; HMS Illustrious, 1946–48; staff RNEC, 1948–51; HMS Alert, 1951–53; HM Dockyard, Gibraltar, 1954–57; HMS Corunna, 1957–59; BEO, HMS Lochinvar, 1959–61; staff of C-in-C, SASA, Cape Town, 1961–64; HMS Tiger, 1964–65; staff of Dir of Naval Officer Appts (Eng), 1965–67; Sowc 1967; Naval Ship Prodn Overseer, Scotland and NI, 1967–69, IDC 1970; Asst Dir, DG Ships, 1971–73; Captain RNEC, 1973–75; Port Adm., Rosyth, 1976–77; Asst Chief of Fleet Support, 1977–79; Chief of Fleet Support (Mem., Admiralty Bd of Defence Council), 1979–81; Comdt, RCDS, 1982–83. Cdre, RNSA, 1980–83 (Life Vice Cdre, 1990). Mem. Council, RUSI, 1984–87 (Vice Chm., 1986–87). President: RN Modern Pentathlon Assoc., 1978–83; Square Rigger Club (Support of Trng Ship Royalist), 1988–; RNVR Youth Sail Training Trust, 1993–; Forces Help Soc. and Lord Roberts Workshops, 1991–. Chm., Zeals Parish Council, 1992–. KStJ 1985. *Recreations:* sailing, rough gardening and fixing things. *Address:* Selwood, Zeals Row, Zeals, Warminster, Wilts BA12 6PE. *Clubs:* Naval (Pres., 1991–); Royal Yacht Squadron, Royal Naval Sailing Association (Portsmouth).

PILLING, Joseph Grant, CB 1995; Principal Establishment and Finance Officer, Department of Health, since 1993; *b* 8 July 1945; *s* of late Fred and Eva Pilling; *m* 1968, Ann Cheetham; two *s*. *Educ:* Rochdale Grammar Sch.; King's Coll., London; Harvard. Asst Principal, 1966, Pvte Sec. to Minister of State, 1970, Home Office; Asst. Pvte Sec. to Home Sec., 1970–71; NI Office, 1972; Harkness Fellow, Harvard Univ. and Univ. of Calif at Berkeley, 1972–74; Home Office, 1974–78; Pvte Sec. to Sec. of State for NI, 1978–79; Home Office, 1979–84; Under Sec., DHSS, 1984–87; Dir of Personnel and Finance, HM Prison Service, Home Office, 1987–90; Dep. Under Sec. of State, NI Office, 1990–91; Dir-Gen., HM Prison Service, Home Office, 1991–92. *Address:* Department of Health, 79 Whitehall, SW1A 2NS. *Club:* Athenæum.

PILLINGER, Prof. Colin Trevor, PhD; FRS 1993; Professor of Planetary Science, Open University, since 1990; *b* 9 May 1943; *s* of Alfred Pillinger and Florence (*née* Honour); *m* 1975, Judith Mary Hay; one *s* one *d*. *Educ:* Kingswood Grammar Sch.; University Coll. Swansea, Univ. of Wales (BSc Hons Chem. 1965; PhD 1968). Department of Chemistry, University of Bristol: Post Doctoral Fellow, 1968–72; BSC Fellow, 1972–74; Res. Associate, 1974–76; Res. Associate and Sen. Res. Associate, Dept of Earth Sci., Cambridge, 1976–84; Sen. Res. Fellow, Dept of Earth Sci., Open Univ., 1984–90. FRAS 1981 (Mem. Council, 1989–91); Fellow, Meteoritical Soc., 1986; FRGS 1993; Mem., British Mass Spectrometry Soc. Hon. DSc Bristol, 1985. *Publications:* numerous papers in learned jls and contribs to radio and TV, UK and abroad. *Recreations:* farming, animals, soccer. *Address:* Planetary Sciences Unit, Open University, Milton Keynes MK7 6AA. *T:* Milton Keynes (01908) 652119, *Fax:* (01908) 655910.

PIMENTA, His Eminence Simon Ignatius Cardinal; *see* Bombay, Archbishop of, (RC).

PIMLOTT, Prof. Benjamin John; Professor of Politics and Contemporary History, Birkbeck College, University of London, since 1987; *b* 4 July 1945; *s* of late John Alfred Ralph Pimlott, CB, and Ellen Dench Howes Pimlott; *m* 1977, Jean Ann Seaton; three *s*. *Educ:* Rokeby Sch., Wimbledon; Marlborough Coll., Wilts; Worcester Coll., Oxford (Open Schol.; MA, BPhil); PhD Newcastle. FRHistS 1993. Lectr, Newcastle Univ., 1970–79; Res. Associate, LSE, 1979–81; Lectr 1981–86, Reader 1986–87, Birkbeck Coll., London Univ. British Acad. Thank Offering to Britain Fellow, 1972–73; Nuffield Foundn Res. Fellow, 1977–78. Chm., ESRC Whitehall Prog. Commng Panel, 1993–94, Steering Cttee, 1994–. Contested (Lab): Arundel, Feb. 1974; Cleveland and Whitby, Oct. 1974, and 1979. Mem. Exec., Fabian Soc., 1987– (Chm., 1993–94). Political columnist: Today, 1986–87; The Times, 1987–88; New Statesman (political editor), 1987–88; Sunday Times, 1988–89. Editor, Samizdat, 1988–90. *Publications:* Labour and the Left in the 1930s, 1977, 2nd edn 1986; (ed with Chris Cook) Trade Unions in British Politics, 1982, 2nd edn 1991; (ed) Fabian Essays in Socialist Thought, 1984; Hugh Dalton, 1985, 2nd edn 1986 (Whitbread Biography Prize, 1985); (ed) The Second World War Diary of Hugh Dalton 1940–45, 1986; (ed) The Political Diary of Hugh Dalton 1918–40, 1945–60, 1987; (ed with Jean Seaton) The Media in British Politics, 1987; (ed with A. Wright and T. Flower) The Alternative, 1990; (ed with S. MacGregor) Tackling the Inner Cities, 1990; Harold Wilson, 1992; Frustrate Their Knavish Tricks, 1994; articles in learned jls and articles and reviews in Guardian, Independent, Independent on Sunday, Observer, TLS, etc. *Address:* 9 Milner Place, Islington, N1 1TN. *T:* 0171–609 1793.

PINA-CABRAL, Rt Rev. Daniel (Pereira dos Santos) de; an Auxiliary Bishop, Diocese of Gibraltar in Europe, since 1976; Archdeacon of Gibraltar, 1986–94; *b* 27 Jan. 1924; *m* 1951, Ana Avelina Pina-Cabral; two *s* two *d*. *Educ:* University of Lisbon (Licentiate in Law). Archdeacon of the North in the Lusitanian Church, 1965; Suffragan Bishop of Lebombo (Mozambique), Church of the Province of Southern Africa, 1967; Diocesan Bishop of Lebombo, 1968; Canon of Gibraltar, 1976–. *Address:* Rua Henrique Lopes de Mendonça 253-4 °Dto-Hab. 42, 4150 Porto, Portugal. *T:* (2) 6177772.

PINCHAM, Roger James, CBE 1982; Chairman, Venture Consultants Ltd, since 1980; Associate Director, Gerrard Vivian Gray, since 1988; *b* 19 Oct. 1935; *y s* of late Sam and of Bessie Pincham; *m* 1965, Gisela von Ulardt (*d* 1974); one *s* two *d*. *Educ:* Kingston Grammar School. National Service, RAF, 1954–56. With Phillips & Drew, 1956–88, Partner, 1967–76, consultant, 1976–88. Mem., London Stock Exchange, 1963–91; MSI, 1992–. Director: Market Access Internat., then Europ. Political Consultancy Gp., 1985–94; CFI Ltd, 1987–; Cornwall Independent Radio Ltd, 1991–; ICOR(LPG) Internat. Ltd, 1992–; UK Radio Holdings Ltd, 1992–. Contested (L) Leominster, 1970, Feb. and Oct. 1974, 1979, 1983. Liberal Party: Nat. Exec., 1974–75 and 1978–87; Assembly Cttee, 1974–87; Standing Cttee, 1975–83; Chm. of Liberal Party, 1979–82; Jt Negotiating Cttee with SDP, and signatory to A Fresh Start for Britain, 1981. Founder Chm., Gladstone Club, 1973–; First Chairman: Indep. Educnl Assoc., 1974–; St James and St Vedast Schools, 1974–; Mem. Council, City Appeal for Eng. Coll. in Prague, 1991–; Gov., Sidney Perry Foundn, 1993–; Founder Trustee, John Stuart Mill Inst., 1992–; Trustee, Princess Margarita of Romania Trust, 1994–. Pres., Kington Eisteddfod, 1978. FRSA 1994. Freeman, City of London. Liveryman: Barbers' Co. (Master, 1993–94); Founders' Co.; Freeman, Co. of Watermen and Lightermen. *Publications:* (jtly) New Deal for Rural Britain, 1977; (ed) New Deal for British Farmers, 1978. *Recreations:* gardening, cricket, theatre, music. *Address:* 7 The Postern, Wood Street, Barbican, EC2Y 8BJ. *T:* 0171–638 8154. *Clubs:* Reform, National Liberal, City of London, Royal Automobile; Surrey County Cricket, Woolhope Naturalists' Field.

PINCHER, (Henry) Chapman; freelance journalist, novelist and business consultant; Assistant Editor, Daily Express, and Chief Defence Correspondent, Beaverbrook Newspapers, 1972–79; *b* Ambala, India, 29 March 1914; *s* of Major Richard Chapman Pincher, E Surrey Regt, and Helen (*née* Foster), Pontefract; *m* 1965, Constance, (Billee), Wolstenholme; one *s* one *d* (by previous *m*). *Educ:* Darlington Gram. Sch.; King's Coll., London (FKC 1979); Inst. Educn; Mil. Coll. of Science. Carter Medallist, London, 1934; BSc (hons Botany, Zoology), 1935. Staff Liverpool Inst., 1936–40. Joined Royal Armoured Corps, 1940; Techn SO, Rocket Div., Min. of Supply, 1943–46; Defence, Science and Medical Editor, Daily Express, 1946–73. Hon. DLitt Newcastle upon Tyne, 1979. Granada Award, Journalist of the Year, 1964; Reporter of the Decade, 1966. *Publications:* Breeding of Farm Animals, 1946; A Study of Fishes, 1947; Into the Atomic Age, 1947; Spotlight on Animals, 1950; Evolution, 1950; (with Bernard Wicksteed) It's Fun Finding Out, 1950; Sleep, and how to get more of it, 1954; Sex in Our Time, 1973; Inside Story, 1978; (jtly) Their Trade is Treachery, 1981; Too Secret Too Long, 1984; The Secret Offensive, 1985; Traitors—the Labyrinths of Treason, 1987; A Web of Deception, 1987; The Truth about Dirty Tricks, 1991; One Dog and Her Man, 1991; Pastoral Symphony (autobiog.), 1993; A Box of Chocolates, 1993; As It Was In The Beginning, 1995; *novels:* Not with a Bang, 1965; The Giantkiller, 1967; The Penthouse Conspirators, 1970; The Skeleton at the Villa Wolkonsky, 1975; The Eye of the Tornado, 1976; The Four Horses, 1978; Dirty Tricks, 1980; The Private World of St John Terrapin, 1982; Contamination, 1989; original researches in genetics, numerous articles in scientific, agricultural and sporting jls. *Recreations:* fishing, shooting, natural history, country life; spy-hunting, ferreting in Whitehall and bolting politicians. *Address:* The Church House, 16 Church Street, Kintbury, near Hungerford, Berks RG17 9TR. *T:* Kintbury (01488) 658855.

PINCHIN, Malcolm Cyril; County Education Officer, Surrey, 1982–93; *b* 4 May 1933; *s* of Cyril Pinchin and Catherine Pinchin; *m* 1957, Diana Elizabeth Dawson; three *s*. *Educ:* Cheltenham Grammar Sch.; Univ. of Bristol (BSc). Education Officer, HMOCS, Malawi, 1958–67; Asst Educn Officer, Northampton, 1967–70; Asst Dir of Educn, 1970–74, Asst Dep. Dir of Educn, 1974–76, Leicestershire; Dep. Chief Educn Officer, Devon, 1976–82. Mem., Dio. of Westminster Educn Bd, 1993–. Trustee: Duke of Edinburgh Award, 1989–; Children's Trust, Tadworth, 1993–. FRSA 1986. *Recreations:* gardening, fly fishing, bee keeping, opera. *Address:* Firbank, 41 Knoll Road, Dorking, Surrey RH4 3ES. *T:* Dorking (01306) 882768.

PINCOTT, Leslie Rundell, CBE 1978; Managing Director, Esso Petroleum Co. Ltd, 1970–78; *b* 27 March 1923; *s* of Hubert George Pincott and Gertrude Elizabeth Rundell; *m* 1944, Mary Mae Tuffin; two *s* one *d*. *Educ:* Mercers' Sch., Holborn. Served War, Royal Navy, 1942–46. Broads Paterson & Co. (Chartered Accountants), 1946–50; joined Esso Petroleum Co. Ltd, 1950; Comptroller, 1958–61; Asst Gen. Manager (Marketing), 1961–65; Dir and Gen. Manager, Cleveland Petroleum Co. Ltd, 1966–68; Standard Oil Co. (NJ): Exec. Asst to Pres., and later, to Chm., 1968–70; Vice-Chm., Remploy Ltd, 1979–87 (Dir, 1975–87); Chairman: Canada Permanent Trust Co. (UK) Ltd, 1978–80; Stone-Platt Industries PLC, 1980–82; Edman Communications Gp PLC, 1982–87; Investment Cttee, London Development Capital Fund (Guinness Mahon), 1985–; BR Southern Bd, 1986–89 (Dir, 1977–89). Director: George Wimpey PLC, 1978–85; Highlands Fabricators Ltd, 1984–91. A Dep. Chm., 1978–79, Chm., 1979–80, Price Commn; Chairman: Hundred Gp of Chartered Accountants, 1978–79; Oxford Univ. Business Summer Sch., 1975–78; Printing Industries EDC, NEDO, 1982–88. Pres., District Heating Assoc., 1977–79. Vice-Pres., English Schs Athletics Assoc., 1977–; Mem. Council, ISCO, 1982–. Mem., The Pilgrims, 1971–. FCA; CIMgt. *Recreation:* tennis. *Address:* 6 Lambourne Avenue, Wimbledon, SW19 7DW. *Club:* Hurlingham (Chm., 1988–92).

PINDER, Andrew; *see* Pinder, J. A.

PINDER, Ven. Charles; Archdeacon of Lambeth, 1986–88, now Archdeacon Emeritus; *b* 5 May 1921; *s* of Ernest and Gertrude Pinder; *m* 1943, Ethel, *d* of Albert and Emma Milke; four *d*. *Educ:* King's College London (AKC). Ordained, 1950; Curate, St Saviour, Raynes Park, 1950–53; Vicar: All Saints, Hatcham Park, 1953–60; St Laurence, Catford, 1960–73; Sub-Dean of Lewisham, 1968–73; Borough Dean of Lambeth, 1973–86. Hon. Chaplain to Bishop of Southwark, 1963–80; Hon. Canon of Southwark, 1973–86. Member of Parole Board, 1976–80; Chm., Brixton Prison Bd of Visitors, 1983–86. *Recreations:* most outdoor sports and selective indoor games; listening to music. *Address:* 22 Somerstown, Chichester, West Sussex PO19 4AG. *T:* Chichester (01243) 779708.

PINDER, (John) Andrew; Head of European Operations and Technology, Global Finance, Citibank NA, since 1995; *b* 5 May 1947; *s* of Norah Joan Pinder and William Gordon Pinder; *m* 1st, 1970, Patricia Munyard (marr. diss. 1980); one *d*; 2nd, 1981, Susan Ellen Tyrrell; one *d* and one step *s*. *Educ:* De La Salle Coll., Sheffield; Coleshill Grammar Sch., Warwicks; Univ. of Liverpool (BA Hons Social Studies). Inspector of Taxes, 1972–76; Board of Inland Revenue: Policy Div., 1976–79; Management Div., 1979–90, Under Sec., Dir of IT, 1989; Prudential Corporation: Dir of Systems, 1990–92; Dir, Gp Management Services, 1991–92; Dir, Systems and Business Ops, 1992–94. FRSA. Freeman, City of London; Mem., Co. of Information Technologists. *Recreations:* music, walking, gardening, reading, fly-fishing. *Address:* 61 Andrewes House, Barbican, EC2Y 8AY. *Club:* Institute of Directors.

PINDLING, Rt. Hon. Sir Lynden Oscar, KCMG 1983; PC 1976; Member, House of Assembly, Commonwealth of the Bahamas; Leader of the Opposition, since 1992; *b* 22 March 1930; *s* of Arnold Franklin and Viola Pindling; *m* 1956, Marguerite McKenzie; two *s* two *d*. *Educ:* Western Senior Sch., Nassau Govt High Sch.; London Univ. (LLB 1952; LLD 1970; DHL 1978). Called to the Bar, Middle Temple, 1953. Practised as Lawyer, 1952–67. Leader of Progressive Liberal Party, 1956; elected to Bahamas House of Assembly, 1956, re-elected 1962, 1967, 1968, 1972, 1977, 1982, 1987, 1992. Worked for human rights and self-determination in the Bahamas; Mem., several delegns to Colonial Office, 1956–66; took part in Constitutional Conf., May 1963; Leader of Opposition, 1964; Mem., Delegns to UN Special Cttee of Twenty-four, 1965, 1966; Premier of the Bahamas and Minister of Tourism and Development, 1967; led Bahamian Delegn to Constitutional Conf., London, 1968; to Independence Conf., 1972; Prime Minister and Minister of Econ. Affairs, 1969–92 (first Prime Minister after Independence, 1973–92). Chm., Commonwealth Parly Assoc., 1968. *Recreations:* swimming, boating, travel. *Address:* Leader of the Opposition, PO Box N-8174, Nassau, Bahamas.

PINHEIRO, João de Deus, PhD, DSc; Member, European Commission (formerly Commission of European Communities), since 1993; *b* Lisbon, 11 July 1945; *s* of Agostinho de Matos Salvador Pinheiro and Maria de Lurdes Rogado Pereira Salvador Pinheiro; *m* 1970, Maria Manuela Vieira Paisana; three *s* one *d*. *Educ:* Technol High Inst., Portugal (Licentiate in Chem. Engrg); Univ. of Birmingham (MSc Chem. Engrg, PhD Engrg Scis, DSc Engrg). University of Minho, Portugal: Dir, Dept of Planning, 1978–81; Dir, Sch. of Engrg, 1979–80; Prof., Engrg Scis, 1981; Associate Vice-Chancellor, 1981–82; Vice-Chancellor, 1984–85; Sec. of State for Educn and Schs Admin, 1982–83; Minister of Educn, then Minister of Educn and Culture, then Minister for Foreign Affairs, 1985–92; Mem., Nat. Parliament, for Viano do Castelo, 1985–87, for Porto, 1987–95; Mem., Nat. Council, Social Democratic Party, 1987; Pres., Cttee of Ministers, Council of Europe, 1991; Hon. Pres., Council of Ministers, NATO, 1990–91; Pres., Council of Ministers, EC, 1992. Mem. 1979–83, Vice-Pres., 1983–84, Nat. Council for Scientific and Technol Res. Grã-Cruz, Ordem Militar de Cristo (Portugal), 1993; numerous foreign decorations. *Recreations:* golf, tennis, reading, cinema, music, etc. *Address:* c/o European Commission, Breydel 10/16, 200 rue de la Loi, 1049 Brussels, Belgium. *T:* (2) 2991111. *Clubs:* Aroeira Golf, Quinta da Marinha Golf and Tennis, VilaSol, Quinta do Lago, S Lourenço, Pinheiros Altos, Vilamoura (Portugal); Brabantse Golf (Brussels).

PININFARINA, Sergio; Cavaliere del Lavoro, 1976; engineer; Member, European Parliament (Liberal and Democratic Group), 1979–88; President, Pininfarina SpA; *b* 8 Sept. 1926; *s* of Battista Pininfarina and Rosa Copasso; *m* 1951, Giorgia Gianolio; two *s* one *d*. *Educ:* Polytechnic of Turin; graduated in Mech. Eng., 1950. President: Federpiemonte, 1983–88; OICA, 1987–89; Confindustria, 1988–92; Comitato Promotore Alta Velocità, 1991–; Vice-Pres., UNICE, 1990–94. Board Member: Ferrari; Banca Passadore; Banca Brignone; LUISS; Toro Assicurazioni. Foreign Mem., Royal Swedish Acad. of Engrg Scis, 1988. Hon. Dr Econs and Commerce, LUISS, Rome, 1993. Légion d'Honneur, 1979. Hon. RDI 1983. Compasso d'Oro, 1995. *Recreation:* golf. *Address:* PO Box 295, 10100 Turin, Italy. *T:* (11) 70911. *Clubs:* Società Whist Accademia Filarmonica, Rotary, Subalpino, Artisti (Turin); Golf Torino, Golf Garlenda, Associazione Sportiva I Roveri.

PINKER, Sir George (Douglas), KCVO 1990 (CVO 1983); FRCS, FRCSEd, FRCOG; Surgeon-Gynaecologist to the Queen, 1973–90; Consulting Gynaecological Surgeon and Obstetrician, St Mary's Hospital, Paddington and Samaritan Hospital, since 1958; Consulting Gynaecological Surgeon, Middlesex and Soho Hospitals, since 1969; Consultant Gynæcologist, King Edward VII Hospital for Officers, since 1974; *b* 6 Dec. 1924; *s* of late Ronald Douglas Pinker and of Queenie Elizabeth Pinker (*née* Dix); *m* Dorothy Emma (*née* Russell); three *s* one *d* (incl. twin *s* and *d*). *Educ:* Reading Sch.; St Mary's Hosp., London Univ. MB BS London 1947; DObst 1949; MRCOG 1954; FRCS(Ed) 1957; FRCOG 1964; FRCS 1989. Late Cons. Gyn. Surg., Bolingbroke Hosp., and Res. Off., Nuffield Dept of Obst., Radcliffe Infirmary, Oxford; late Cons. Gyn. Surg., Queen Charlotte's Hosp. Arthur Wilson Orator, 1972 and 1989, Turnbull Scholar, and Hon. Consultant Obstetrician and Gynaecologist, 1972, Royal Women's Hosp., Melbourne. Examiner in Obst. and Gynae.: Univs of Cambridge, Dundee, London, and FRCS Edinburgh; formerly also in RCOG, and Univs of Birmingham, Glasgow and Dublin. Sims Black Travelling Prof., RCOG, 1979; Vis. Prof., SA Regional Council, RCOG, 1980. Pres., RCOG, 1987–90 (Hon. Treas., 1970–77; Vice-Pres., 1980–83). Pres., British Fertility Soc., 1987; Mem. Council, Winston Churchill Trust, 1979–95; Mem., Blair Bell Res. Soc.; FRSocMed (Pres., 1992–94); Hon. Mem., British Paediatric Assoc., 1988. Hon. FRCSI 1987; Hon. FRACOG 1989; Hon. FACOG 1990; Hon. Fellow, S African Soc. of Obstetricians and Gynaecologists, 1990; Hon. FCMSA 1991. Chm., Editorial Bd, Modern Medicine (Obs. and Gynae.), 1989–91 (Mem., 1980–91). *Publications:* (all jtly) Ten Teachers Diseases of Women, 1964; Ten Teachers Obstetrics, 1966; A Short Textbook of Obstetrics and Gynaecology, 1967. *Recreations:* music, gardening, sailing, skiing, fell walking. *Address:* 96 Harley Street, W1N 1AF. *T:* 0171–935 7254; Sycamore House, Willersey, Broadway, Worcs WR12 7PJ. *Club:* Garrick.

PINKER, Prof. Robert Arthur; Professor of Social Administration, London School of Economics and Political Science, since 1993; Member, since 1991, and Privacy Commissioner, since 1994, Press Complaints Commission; *b* 27 May 1931; *s* of Dora Elizabeth and Joseph Pinker; *m* 1955, Jennifer Farrington Boulton (*d* 1994); two *d*. *Educ:* Holloway County Sch.; LSE (Cert. in Social Sci. and Admin. 1959; BSc Sociology 1962; MSc Econ 1965). University of London: Head of Sociology Dept, Goldsmiths' Coll., 1964–72; Lewisham Prof. of Social Admin, Goldsmiths' Coll. and Bedford Coll., 1972–74; Prof. of Social Studies, Chelsea Coll., 1974–78; Prof. of Social Work Studies, LSE, 1978–93; Pro-Director, LSE, 1985–88; Pro Vice Chancellor for Social Scis, London Univ., 1989–90. Chm., British Library Project on Family and Social Research, 1983–86; Member: Council, Advertising Standards Authority, 1988–; Direct Mail Accreditation Centre, 1995–. Chm. Governors, Centre for Policy on Ageing, 1988–94; Gov., BPMF, 1990–94. Chm., Editl Bd, Jl of Social Policy, 1981–86. *Publications:* English Hospital Statistics 1861–1938, 1964; Social Theory and Social Policy, 1971; The Idea of Welfare, 1979; Social Work in an Enterprise Society, 1990. *Recreations:* reading, writing, travel, unskilled gardening. *Address:* 76 Coleraine Road, Blackheath, SE3 7PE. *Tel:* 081–858 5320.

PINKERTON, Prof. John Henry McKnight, CBE 1983; Professor of Midwifery and Gynæcology, Queen's University, Belfast, 1963–85, now Emeritus; Gynæcologist: Royal Victoria and City Hospitals, Belfast, 1963–85; Ulster Hospital for Women and Children, 1963–85; Surgeon, Royal Maternity Hospital, Belfast, 1963–85; *b* 5 June 1920; *s* of late

William R. and Eva Pinkerton; *m* 1947, Florence McKinstry, MB, BCh, BAO; four *s*. *Educ:* Royal Belfast Academical Institution; Queen's Univ., Belfast. Hyndman Univ. Entrance Scholar, 1939; MB, BCh, BAO Hons; Magrath Scholar in Obstetrics and Gynæcology, 1943. Active service in HM Ships as Surg.-Lt, RNVR, 1945–47. MD 1948; MRCOG 1949; FRCOG 1960; FZS 1960; FRCPI 1977. Sen. Lectr in Obstetrics and Gynæcology, University Coll. of the West Indies, and Consultant Obstetrician and Gynæcologist to University Coll. Hosp. of the West Indies, 1953–59; Rockefeller Research Fellow at Harvard Medical Sch., 1956–57; Prof. of Obstetrics and Gynæcology, Univ. of London, at Queen Charlotte's and Chelsea Hosps and the Inst. of Obstetrics and Gynæcology, 1959–63; Obstetric Surgeon to Queen Charlotte's Hosp.; Surgeon to Chelsea Hosp. for Women. Vice-Pres., RCOG, 1977–80; Chm., Inst. of Obstetrics and Gynæcol., RCPI, 1984–87. Hon. DSc NUI, 1986. *Publications:* various papers on obstetrical and gynæcological subjects. *Address:* 41c Sans Souci Park, Belfast BT9 5BZ. *T:* Belfast (01232) 682956.

See also W. R. Pinkerton.

PINKERTON, William Ross, CBE 1977; JP; HM Nominee for Northern Ireland on General Medical Council, 1979–83, retired; a director of companies; *b* 10 April 1913; *s* of William Ross Pinkerton and Eva Pinkerton; *m* 1943, Anna Isobel Lyness; two *d*. Managing Director, H. Stevenson & Co. Ltd, Londonderry, 1941–76. Mem., Baking Wages Council (NI), 1957–74. Mem. later Chm, Londonderry/Gransha Psychiatric HMC, 1951–69; Vice-Chm., then Chm., North West HMC, 1969–72; Chm., Western Health and Social Services Board, 1972–79; Member: Central Services Agency (NI), 1972–79; NI Health and Social Services Council, 1975–79; Lay Mem., Health and Personal Social Services Tribunal, NI, 1978–. Member, New Ulster Univ. Court, 1973–85, Council, 1979–85. Hon. Life Governor: Altnagelvin, Gransha, Waterside, St Columb's, Roe Valley, Strabane, Foyle and Stradreagh Hosps. JP Co. Londonderry, 1965–84, Div. of Ards, 1984–91, Div. of Craigavon, 1991. *Recreations:* yachting, fishing. *Address:* 9 Harwich Mews, Culcavey Road, Hillsborough, Co. Down, Northern Ireland BT26 6RH. *T:* Hillsborough (01846) 682421. *Club:* Royal Highland Yacht (Oban).

See also J. H. McK. Pinkerton.

PINNER, Hayim, OBE 1989; consultant, administrator, linguist, educator, lecturer, journalist, broadcaster; Director, Sternberg Charitable Trust, since 1991; *b* London, 25 May 1925; *s* of late Simon Pinner and Annie Pinner (*née* Wagner); *m* 1956, Rita Reuben, Cape Town (marr. diss. 1980); one *s* one *d*. *Educ:* Davenant Foundation School; London University; Yeshivah Etz Hayim; Bet Berl College, Israel. Served RAOC, 1944–48; Editor, Jewish Vanguard, 1950–74; Exec. Dir, B'nai B'rith, 1957–77; Sec. Gen., Board of Deputies of British Jews, 1977–91. Hon. Vice-Pres., Zionist Fedn of GB and Ireland, 1975– (Hon. Treasurer, 1971–75); Vice-Pres., Labour Zionist Movement; Hon. Sec., CCJ; Member: Jewish Agency and World Zionist Orgn; Adv. Council, World Congress of Faiths; Trades Adv. Council; Hillel Foundn; Jt Israel Appeal; Lab. Party Middle East Cttee; 'B' List of Parly Candidates; UNA; Founder Mem. Exec., Inter-Faith. FRSA. Freeman, City of London. Contribs to Radio 4, Radio London, London Broadcasting, BBC TV. Encomienda de la Orden del Mérito Civil (Spain), 1993. *Publications:* contribs to UK and foreign periodicals, Isra-Kit. *Recreations:* travelling, swimming, reading, talking. *Address:* 62 Grosvenor Street, W1X 9DA.

PINNER, Ruth Margaret, (Mrs M. J. Pinner); *see* Kempson, R. M.

PINNINGTON, Geoffrey Charles; Editor, Sunday People, 1972–82; *b* 21 March 1919; *s* of Charles and Beatrice Pinnington; *m* 1941, Beryl, *d* of Edward and Lilian Clark; two *d*. *Educ:* Harrow County Sch.; Rock Ferry High Sch., Birkenhead; King's Coll., Univ. of London. Served War as Air Navigator, RAF Bomber and Middle East Commands, 1940–45 (Sqdn Ldr, 1943). On staff of (successively): Middlesex Independent; Kensington Post (Editor); Daily Herald: Dep. News Editor, 1955; Northern Editor, 1957; Dep. Editor, 1958; Daily Mirror: Night Editor, 1961, Assistant Editor, 1964, Dep. Editor, 1968; Dir, Mirror Group Newspapers, 1976–82. Mem., Press Council, 1982–86 (Jt Vice-Chm., 1983–86). *Recreations:* his family, travel, reading, music, theatre and the arts, amateur cine-photography. *Address:* 23 Lauderdale Drive, Richmond, Surrey TW10 7BS.

PINNINGTON, Roger Adrian, TD 1967; Chairman: Jenbacher Holdings (UK) PLC (formerly Telfos Holdings), since 1991; Lynx Holdings PLC, since 1992; Cortworth PLC, since 1994; Huntingdon International Holdings plc, since 1994; British World Aviation Ltd, since 1994; *b* 27 Aug. 1932; *s* of William Austin Pinnington and Elsie Amy Pinnington; *m* 1974, Marjorie Ann Pearson; one *s* three *d*. *Educ:* Rydal Sch., Colwyn Bay; Lincoln Coll., Oxford (MA). Marketing Dir, Jonas Woodhead & Sons, 1963–74; 1975–82: Vice Pres., TRW Europe Inc.; Man. Dir, CAM Gears Ltd; Pres., TRW Italia SpA; Dir Gen., Gemmer France; Pres., Torfinasa; Dep. Chm. and Ch. Exec., UBM Group, 1982–85; Dir, Norcros, 1985–86; Dir and Chief Exec., Royal Ordnance PLC, 1986–87; Dir and Gp Chief Exec., RHP, subseq. Pilgrim House Gp, 1987–89. *Recreations:* gardening, arguing with Sally, collecting sad irons and sauce bottle labels. *Address:* 15 Lennox Gardens Mews, SW1X 0DP. *T:* 0171–581 9684. *Clubs:* Royal Automobile; Vincent's (Oxford).

PINNINGTON-HUGHES, John; *see* Hughes.

PINNOCK, Comdr Harry James, RN retd; Director, Cement Makers' Federation, 1979–87; *b* 6 April 1927; *s* of Frederick Walter Pinnock and Kate Ada (*née* Shepherd); *m* 1962, Fru Inger Connie Åhgren (*d* 1978); one *d*. *Educ:* Sutton Valence Sch. Joined RN, 1945; Midshipman, HMS Nelson, 1945–47; Sub-Lieut/Lieut, HMS Belfast, Far East, 1948–50; RN Rhine Flotilla, 1951–52; Staff of First Sea Lord, 1952–55; Lt-Comdr, Mediterranean Minesweepers, 1955–57; HMS Ceylon, E of Suez, 1957–59; Staff of C-in-C Plymouth, 1960–61; HQ Allied Naval Forces, Northern Europe, Oslo, 1961–63; Comdr, MoD, 1964–67, retd. Cement Makers' Fedn, 1970–87. *Recreations:* ski-ing, gardening, travel.

PINNOCK, Trevor, CBE 1992; ARCM; harpsichordist; conductor; Director, The English Concert, since 1973; Artistic Director and Principal Conductor, National Arts Centre Orchestra, Ottawa, since 1991; *b* Canterbury, 16 Dec. 1946. *Educ:* Canterbury Cathedral Choir Sch.; Simon Langton Grammar Sch., Canterbury; Royal Coll. of Music, London (Foundn Scholar; Harpsichord and Organ Prizes). ARCM Hons (organ) 1965. London début with Galliard Harpsichord Trio (Jt Founder with Stephen Preston, flute and Anthony Pleeth, 'cello), 1966; solo début, Purcell Room, London, 1968. Formed The English Concert for purpose of performing music of baroque period on instruments in original condition or good modern copies, 1972, making its London début in English Bach Festival, Purcell Room, 1973. NY début at Metropolitan Opera, conducting Handel Giulio Cesare, 1988. Recordings of complete keyboard works of Rameau; Bach Toccatas, Partitas, Goldberg Variations, Concerti, Handel Messiah and Suites, Purcell Dido and Aeneas, orchestral and choral works of Bach, Handel, Vivaldi, complete symphonies of Mozart, etc. Hon. doctorates: Ottawa, 1993; Kent, 1995. *Address:* c/o Ms Jan Burnett, 8 St George's Terrace, NW1 8XJ. *T:* 0171–911 0901, *Fax:* 0171–911 0903.

PINSENT, Sir Christopher (Roy), 3rd Bt *cr* 1938; Lecturer and Tutor, Camberwell School of Art, 1962–86, retired; *b* 2 Aug. 1922; *s* of Sir Roy Pinsent, 2nd Bt, and Mary Tirzah Pinsent (*d* 1951), *d* of Dr Edward Geoffrey Walls, Spilsby, Lincs; *S* father, 1978; *m* 1951, Susan Mary, *d* of John Norton Scorer, Fotheringhay; one *s* two *d*. *Educ:* Winchester College. *Heir: s* Thomas Benjamin Roy Pinsent, *b* 21 July 1967. *Address:* The Chestnuts, Castle Hill, Guildford, Surrey GU1 3SX.

PINSENT, Matthew Clive, MBE 1992; oarsman; *b* 10 Oct. 1970; *s* of Ewen and Jean Pinsent. *Educ:* Eton College; St Catherine's College, Oxford (BA Hons Geography 1993). Winner, coxless pairs championships: (with Tim Foster) Junior World, 1988; (with Steven Redgrave): World, 1991, 1993, 1994 and 1995; Olympics, 1992; Mem., Oxford Boat Race winning crew, 1990, 1991. *Recreations:* golf, flying. *Club:* Leander (Henley-on-Thames).

PINSENT, Roger Philip; HM Diplomatic Service, retired; *b* 30 Dec. 1916; *s* of late Sidney Hume Pinsent; *m* 1941, Suzanne Smalley; one *s* two *d*. *Educ:* Downside Sch.; Lausanne, London and Grenoble Univs. London Univ. French Scholar, 1938; BA Hons London, 1940. HM Forces, 1940–46; HM Diplomatic Service, May 1946; 1st Sec., HM Legation, Havana, 1948–50; HM Consul, Tangier, 1950–52; 1st Sec., HM Embassy, Madrid, 1952–53; FO, 1953–56; 1st Sec., Head of Chancery, HM Embassy, Lima (Chargé d'Affaires, 1958, 1959), 1956–59; Dep. Head of UK Delegation to the European Communities, Luxembourg, 1959–63; HM Ambassador to Nicaragua, 1963–67; Counsellor (Commercial), Ankara, 1967–70; Consul-Gen., São Paulo, 1970–73. Mem., Inst. of Linguists, 1976–79. Mem., Stow Probus Club, 1974–. *Recreations:* music, photography, book-binding, golf. *Address:* Cranfield Cottage, Maugersbury, Stow-on-the-Wold, Glos GL54 1HR. *T:* Cotswold (01451) 830992. *Clubs:* Broadway Golf; Stow on the Wold RFC.

PINSON, Barry, QC 1973; *b* 18 Dec. 1925; *s* of Thomas Alfred Pinson and Alice Cicily Pinson; *m* 1950, Miriam Mary; one *s* one *d*; *m* 1977, Anne Kathleen Golby. *Educ:* King Edward's Sch., Birmingham; Univ. of Birmingham. LLB Hons 1945. Fellow Inst. Taxation. Mil. Service, 1944–47. Called to Bar, Gray's Inn, 1949, Bencher 1981. Trustee, RAF Museums, 1980–; Chm., Addington Soc., 1987–90. *Publications:* Revenue Law, 17 edns. *Recreations:* music, photography. *T:* 0171–798 8450. *Club:* Arts.

PINTER, Lady Antonia; *see* Fraser, Antonia.

PINTER, Harold, CBE 1966; FRSL; actor, playwright and director; Associate Director, National Theatre, 1973–83; *b* 10 Oct. 1930; *s* of J. Pinter; *m* 1st, 1956, Vivien Merchant (marr. diss. 1980; she *d* 1982); one *s*; 2nd, 1980, Lady Antonia Fraser, *qv*. *Educ:* Hackney Downs Grammar Sch. Actor (mainly repertory), 1949–57. *Directed:* The Collection (co-dir with Peter Hall), Aldwych, 1962; The Birthday Party, Aldwych, 1964; The Lover, The Dwarfs, Arts, 1966; Exiles, Mermaid, 1970; Butley, Criterion, 1971; Butley (film), 1973; Next of Kin, Nat. Theatre, 1974; Otherwise Engaged, Queen's, 1975, NY 1977; Blithe Spirit, Nat. Theatre, 1977; The Rear Column, Globe, 1978; Close of Play, Nat. Theatre, 1979; The Hothouse, Hampstead, 1980 (for TV, 1982); Quartermaine's Terms, Queen's, 1981; Incident at Tulse Hill, Hampstead, 1982; The Trojan War Will Not Take Place, Nat. Theatre, 1983; The Common Pursuit, Lyric Hammersmith, 1984; Sweet Bird of Youth, Haymarket, 1985; Circe and Bravo, Wyndham's, 1986; Vanilla, Lyric, 1990; The New World Order, Royal Court, 1991; Party Time, Almeida, 1991 (for TV, 1992); Oleanna, Royal Court, 1993; Taking Sides, Minerva, Chichester, 1995. Hon. DLitt: Reading, 1970; Birmingham, 1971; Glasgow, 1974; East Anglia, 1974; Stirling, 1979; Brown, 1982; Hull, 1986; Sussex, 1990; E London, 1994; Sofia, 1995. Shakespeare Prize, Hamburg, 1970; Austrian State Prize for European Literature, 1973; Pirandello Prize, 1980; Donatello Prize, 1982; Elmer Holmes Bobst Award, 1984; British Literary Prize, 1995. *Plays:* The Room (stage 1957, television 1965); The Birthday Party, 1957 (stage 1958, television 1960 and 1987, film 1968); The Dumb Waiter, 1957 (stage 1960, television 1964 and 1987); The Hothouse, 1958 (stage 1980, television 1981); A Slight Ache, 1958 (radio 1959, stage 1961, television 1966); A Night Out, 1959 (radio and television, 1960); The Caretaker, 1959 (stage 1960 and 1991, film 1963, television 1966 and 1982); Night School, 1960 (television 1960 and 1982, radio 1966); The Dwarfs (radio 1960, stage 1963); The Collection (television 1961 and 1979, stage 1962); The Lover (television 1962 (Italia Prize) and 1977, stage 1963); Tea Party, 1964 (television 1965, stage 1970); The Homecoming, 1964 (stage 1965, film 1973); The Basement, 1966 (television 1967, stage 1970); Landscape, 1967 (radio 1968, stage 1969); Silence, 1968 (stage 1968); Night, 1969; Old Times, 1970 (stage 1971, television 1975); Monologue, 1972 (television 1973); No Man's Land, 1974 (stage 1975 and 1992, television 1978); Betrayal (stage 1978 (SWET Award, 1979) and 1991, film 1983); Family Voices, 1980 (radio 1981 (Giles Cooper Award, 1982), stage 1981); A Kind of Alaska, 1982 (stage and television 1984); Victoria Station (stage 1982); One for the Road (stage and television 1984); Mountain Language (stage 1988); The New World Order (stage 1991); Party Time (stage 1991, television 1992); Moonlight (stage 1993). *Screenplays:* The Caretaker, The Servant, 1962; The Pumpkin Eater, 1963; The Quiller Memorandum, 1966; Accident, 1967; The Birthday Party, The Homecoming, 1968; The Go-Between, 1969; Langrishe, Go Down, 1970 (adapted for television, 1978); A la Recherche du Temps Perdu, 1972; The Last Tycoon, 1974; The French Lieutenant's Woman, 1981; Betrayal, 1981; Victory, 1982; Turtle Diary, 1985; The Handmaid's Tale, 1987; The Heat of the Day, 1988; Reunion, 1989; The Trial, 1989; The Comfort of Strangers, 1990. *Publications:* The Caretaker, 1960; The Birthday Party, and other plays, 1960; A Slight Ache, 1961; The Collection, 1963; The Lover, 1963; The Homecoming, 1965; Tea Party, and, The Basement, 1967; (co-ed) PEN Anthology of New Poems, 1967; Mac, 1968; Landscape, and, Silence, 1969; Five Screenplays, 1971; Old Times, 1971; Poems, 1971; No Man's Land, 1975; The Proust Screenplay: A la Recherche du Temps Perdu, 1978; Betrayal, 1978; Poems and Prose 1949–1977, 1978; I Know the Place, 1979; Family Voices, 1981; Other Places, 1982; French Lieutenant's Woman and other screenplays, 1982; One For The Road, 1984; Collected Poems and Prose, 1986; (co-ed) 100 Poems by 100 Poets, 1986; Mountain Language, 1988; The Heat of the Day, 1989; The Dwarfs (novel), 1990; Party Time, 1991; Moonlight, 1993; (ed jtly) 99 Poems in Translation, 1994. *Recreation:* cricket. *Address:* c/o Judy Daish Associates Ltd, 2 St Charles Place, W10 6EG.

PIPE, Martin Charles; racehorse trainer, National Hunt and flat racing; *b* 29 May 1945; *m* 1971, Mary Caroline; one *s*. First trainer's licence, 1977; jt founder, Pipe-Scudamore Racing Club PLC, 1989; only British trainer to saddle 200 winners in a season, 1989. *Publication:* (with Richard Pitman) Martin Pipe: the champion trainer's story, 1992. *Address:* Pond Farm House, Nicholashayne, near Wellington, Somerset TA21 9QY.

PIPER, Rt Rev. Dr Reginald John; Bishop of Wollongong, and an Assistant Bishop, Diocese of Sydney, since 1993; *b* 25 Feb. 1942; *s* of Leslie and Myra Elaine Piper; *m* 1967, Dorothy Patricia Lock; one *s* two *d*. *Educ:* Australian Nat. Univ. (BSc 1963); Moore Coll., Sydney (Theol. Schol. 1970); Melbourne Coll. of Divinity (BD 1975); Fuller Theol Seminary, LA (DMin 1992). Ordained deacon, 1966, priest, 1967; Curate: St Stephen's, Willougby, 1966–69; St Clement's, Lalor Park, 1970–71; Rector: St Aidan's, Hurstville

Grove, 1972–75; Christ Church, Kiama, 1975–79; Holy Trinity, Adelaide, 1980–93. *Address:* Anglican Church Centre, 74 Church Street, Wollongong, NSW 2500, Australia.

PIPPARD, Prof. Sir (Alfred) Brian, Kt 1975; FRS 1956; Cavendish Professor of Physics, University of Cambridge, 1971–82, now Emeritus; *b* 7 Sept. 1920; *s* of late Prof. A. J. S. Pippard; *m* 1955, Charlotte Frances Dyer; three *d.* *Educ:* Clifton Coll.; Clare Coll., Cambridge (Hon. Fellow 1973). BA (Cantab) 1941, MA 1945. PhD 1949; ScD 1966. Scientific Officer, Radar Research and Development Establishment, Great Malvern, 1941–45; Stokes Student, Pembroke Coll., Cambridge, 1945–46; Demonstrator in Physics, University of Cambridge, 1946; Lecturer in Physics, 1950; Reader in Physics, 1959–60; John Humphrey Plummer Prof. of Physics, 1960–71; Pres., Clare Hall, Cambridge, 1966–73 (Hon. Fellow, 1993). Visiting Prof., Institute for the Study of Metals, University of Chicago, 1955–56. Fellow of Clare Coll., Cambridge, 1947–66. Cherwell-Simon Memorial Lectr, Oxford, 1968–69; Eddington Meml Lectr, Cambridge, 1988. Pres., Inst. of Physics, 1974–76. Hughes Medal of the Royal Soc., 1959; Holweck Medal, 1961; Dannie-Heineman Prize, 1969; Guthrie Prize, 1970. *Publications:* Elements of Classical Thermodynamics, 1957; Dynamics of Conduction Electrons, 1962; Forces and Particles, 1972; The Physics of Vibration, vol. 1, 1978, vol. 2, 1983; Response and Stability, 1985; Magnetoresistance, 1989; (ed and contrib.) 20th Century Physics, 1995; papers in Proc. Royal Soc., etc. *Recreation:* music. *Address:* 30 Porson Road, Cambridge CB2 2EU. *T:* Cambridge (01223) 358713.

PIRATIN, Philip; *b* 15 May 1907; *m* 1929, Celia Fund; one *s* two *d.* *Educ:* Davenant Foundation Sch., London, E1. Was a Member of Stepney Borough Council, 1937–49; MP (Com) Mile End Division of Stepney, 1945–50.

PIRELLI, Leopoldo; Knight, Order of Labour Merit, 1977; engineer; Chairman, Pirelli SpA, since 1965; *b* 27 Aug. 1925; *s* of Alberto Pirelli and Ludovica Zambeletti; *m* 1947, Giulia Ferlito; one *s* one *d.* *Educ:* Milan University (Politecnico); graduated in Mech. Eng. 1950. Mem., Bd of Dirs, 1954, Vice-Chm., 1956, Pirelli SpA; Partner, Pirelli & Co., 1957–; Mem., Bd of Dirs, 1956, Vice-Chm., 1979–, Soc. Internat. Pirelli. Member, Board of Directors: Generale Industrie Metallurgiche, 1949–; Mediobanca, 1958–; Riunione Adriatica Sicurtà, 1959–; Banca Commerciale Italiana, 1982–; Società Metallurgica Italiana, 1983–; Compagnia Finanziaria De Benedetti, 1987–. Mem., Exec. Council, Confedn of Italian Industries, 1957– (Dep. Chm., 1974–80; Mem. Bd, 1974–82). *Address:* Piazza Cadorna 5, 20123 Milan, Italy. *T:* (2) 85351. *Clubs:* Dadi, Rotary, Unione (Milan); Yacht Club Italiano.

PIRIE, Group Captain Sir Gordon (Hamish Martin), Kt 1984; CVO 1987; CBE 1946; JP; DL; Deputy High Bailiff of Westminster, 1978–87; Member, Westminster City Council, 1949–82 (Mayor, 1959–60; Leader of Council, 1961–69; Alderman, 1963–78; Lord Mayor, 1974–75); Director, Parker Gallery; *b* 10 Feb. 1918; *s* of Harold Victor Campbell Pirie and Irene Gordon Hogarth; *m* 1st, 1953, Margaret Joan Bomford (*d* 1972); no *c*; 2nd, 1982, Joanna, *widow* of John C. Hugill. *Educ:* Eton (King's scholar); RAF Coll., Cranwell. Permanent Commission, RAF, 1938. Served War of 1939–45: Dir of Ops, RNZAF, Atlantic and Pacific (despatches, CBE); retired as Group Captain, 1946. Comr No 1 (POW) Dist SJAB, 1960–69; Comdr St John Ambulance, London, 1969–75; Chm., St John Council for London, 1975–85. Vice-Pres., Services Sound and Vision Corp., 1990– (Chm., 1979–90). A Governor of Westminster Sch., 1962–94; Mem., Bd of Green Cloth Verge of Palaces, 1962–87; Vice-Pres., Engineering Industries Assoc., 1966–69; Mem., Council of Royal Albert Hall, 1965–92 (a Vice-Pres., 1985–92); a Trustee: RAF Museum, 1965–; Dolphin Square Trust Ltd, 1971–; Vice-Chm., London Boroughs Assoc., 1968–71; Pres., Conf. of Local and Regional Authorities of Europe, 1978–80 (Vice-Pres., 1974–75, 1977–78, 1980–82); a Vice-Pres., British Sect., IULA/CEM, 1980–88; Mem. Solicitors' Disciplinary Tribunal, 1975–93. Contested (LNat&U) Dundee West, 1955. DL, JP Co. of London, 1962; Mem., Inner London Adv. Cttee on appointment of Magistrates, 1969–87; Chm., S Westminster PSD, 1974–77. Liveryman, Worshipful Company of Girdlers. FRSA. KStJ 1969. Pro Merito Medal, Council of Europe, 1982. Comdr, Legion of Honour, 1960, Comdr, Cross of Merit, SMO Malta, 1971; JSM Malaysia, 1974. *Recreations:* motoring, bird-watching. *Address:* Cottage Row, Tarrant Gunville, Blandford, Dorset DT11 8JJ. *T:* Tarrant Hinton (01258) 830212. *Clubs:* Carlton, Royal Air Force.

PIRIE, Henry Ward; crossword compiler, journalist and broadcaster; Sheriff (formerly Sheriff-Substitute) of Lanarkshire at Glasgow, 1955–74; *b* 13 Feb. 1922; *o* surv. *s* of late William Pirie, Merchant, Leith; *m* 1948, Jean Marion (*d* 1992), *y d* of late Frank Jardine, sometime President of RCS of Edinburgh; four *s.* *Educ:* Watson's Coll., Edinburgh; Edinburgh Univ. MA 1944; LLB 1947. Served with Royal Scots; commnd Indian Army, 1944; Lieut, Bombay Grenadiers, 1944–46. Called to Scottish Bar, 1947. Sheriff-Substitute of Lanarkshire at Airdrie, 1954–55. OStJ 1967. *Recreations:* curling, golf, bridge. *Address:* 16 Poplar Drive, Lenzie, Kirkintilloch, Dunbartonshire G66 4DN. *T:* 0141–776 2494.

PIRIE, Iain Gordon; Sheriff of Glasgow and Strathkelvin, since 1982; *b* 15 Jan. 1933; *s* of Charles Fox Pirie and Mary Ann Gordon; *m* 1960, Sheila Brown Forbes, MB, ChB; two *s* one *d.* *Educ:* Harris Acad., Dundee; St Andrews Univ. (MA, LLB). Legal Asst, Stirling, Eunson & Belford, Solicitors, Dunfermline, 1958–60; Depute Procurator Fiscal, Paisley, 1960–67; Sen. Depute Procurator Fiscal, Glasgow, 1967–71; Procurator Fiscal: Dumfries, 1971–76; Ayr, 1976–79; Sheriff of S Strathclyde, Dumfries and Galloway, 1979–82. *Recreations:* golf, tennis, reading, gardening, playing the violin.

PIRIE, Madsen (Duncan), PhD; President, Adam Smith Institute, since 1978; *b* 24 Aug. 1940; *s* of Douglas Gordon Pirie and Eva (*née* Madsen). *Educ:* Univ. of Edinburgh (MA Hons 1970); Univ. of St Andrews (PhD 1974). Distinguished Vis. Prof. of Philosophy, Hillsdale Coll., Michigan, 1975–78. Mem., Adv. Panel on Citizen's Charter, 1991–95. *Publications:* Trial and Error and the Idea of Progress, 1978; The Book of the Fallacy, 1985; Privatization, 1988, Micropolitics, 1988, (with Eamonn Butler) The Sherlock Holmes IQ Book, 1995. *Recreation:* calligraphy. *Address:* PO Box 316, London SW1P 3DJ.

PIRIE, Norman Wingate, FRS 1949; *b* 1 July 1907; *yr s* of late Sir George Pirie, RSA, painter, Torrance, Stirlingshire; one *s* one *d.* *Educ:* Emmanuel Coll., Cambridge. Demonstrator in Biochemical Laboratory, Cambridge, 1932–40; Virus Physiologist, 1940–46, Head of Biochemistry Dept, 1947–73, Rothamsted Experimental Station, Harpenden. Copley Medal, 1971; Rank Prize for Nutrition, 1976. *Publications:* Food Resources: conventional and novel, 1969, 2nd edn 1976; Leaf Protein and other aspects of fodder fractionation, 1978, 2nd edn, Leaf Protein and its by-products in human and animal nutrition, 1987; ed several works on world food supplies; scientific papers on various aspects of Biochemistry but especially on separation and properties of macromolecules; articles on viruses, the origins of life, biochemical engineering, and the need for greatly extended research on food production and contraception. *Address:* Rothamsted Experimental Station, Harpenden, Herts AL5 2JQ. *T:* Harpenden (01582) 763133.

PIRNIE, Graham John Campbell; HM Diplomatic Service; Ambassador to Paraguay, since 1995; *b* 9 Aug. 1941; *s* of late Ian Campbell Pirnie and of Emily Elizabeth Pirnie; *m* 1967, Kathleen Gunstone; two *s* one *d.* *Educ:* Surbiton Grammar Sch.; Birmingham Univ. (BSocSc). Graduate VSO, 1963–64; joined Foreign and Commonwealth Office, 1965: Information Res. Dept, 1965; FCO, 1966–68; Third Sec. and Vice Consul, Phnom Penh, 1968–70; Commercial Officer, Paris, 1970–74; Second Sec. (Commercial), The Hague, 1974–77; FCO, 1977–82; First Sec. and Consul, Geneva, 1982–86; JSDC 1986; FCO, 1986–89; Dep. Head of Mission and Consul, Quito, 1989–93; FCO, 1993–95. *Recreations:* fell-walking, natural history, antiques restoration, reading (political autobiographies), cross country ski-ing. *Address:* c/o Foreign and Commonwealth Office, King Charles Street, SW1A 2AH.

PIRNIE, Rear Adm. Ian Hugh, CB 1992; FIEE; Chairman: Furness Enterprise Ltd, since 1993; Morecambe Bay Health Authority, since 1994; *b* 17 June 1935; *s* of late Hugh and Linda Pirnie; *m* 1958, Sally Patricia (*née* Duckworth); three *d.* *Educ:* Christ's Hosp., Horsham; Pembroke Coll., Cambridge (MA). FIEE 1986. Qualified in submarines, 1964; post-graduate educn, RMCS, Shrivenham, 1964–65; sea service in aircraft carriers, destroyers and submarines; commanded RNEC, Manadon, 1986–88; Chief, Strategic Systems Exec., MoD, 1988–92, RN retd, 1993. Non-exec. Dir, Cumbria Ambulance Service, 1992–94. *Recreations:* fell walking, bird watching, opera, classical music, topiary. *Club:* Army and Navy.

PIRRIE, David Blair, FCIB; Director of International and of Private Banking and Financial Services, Lloyds Bank Plc, since 1992; *b* 15 Dec. 1938; *s* of John and Sylvia Pirrie; *m* 1966, Angela Sellos; three *s* one *d.* *Educ:* Strathallen Sch., Perthshire; Harvard Univ. (Management Develt). FCIB 1987. Lloyds Bank: Gen. Man., Brazil, 1975–81; Dir, Lloyds Bank International, 1981–83; Gen. Man., Gp HQ, 1983–85; Sen. Dir, Internat. Banking, 1985–87; Sen. Gen. Man., UK Retail Banking, 1987–89; Dir, UK Retail Banking, 1989–92. *Recreations:* golf, theatre, music. *Address:* Lloyds Bank Plc, 71 Lombard Street, EC3P 3BS.

PIRZADA, Syed Sharifuddin, SPk 1964; Attorney-General of Pakistan, 1965–66, 1968–71 and 1977–89; Ambassador-at-Large with status of Federal Minister, 1989–93; Chairman, Heritage Council, 1989–93; *b* 12 June 1923; *s* of Syed Vilayat Ali Pirzada; *m* 1960; two *s* two *d.* *Educ:* University of Bombay. LLB 1945; barrister-at-law. Secretary, Provincial Muslim League, 1946; Managing Editor, Morning Herald, 1946; Prof., Sind Muslim Law Coll., 1947–55; Advocate: Bombay High Court, 1946; Sind Chief Court, 1947; West Pakistan High Court, 1955; Supreme Court of Pakistan, 1961; Senior Advocate Supreme Court of Pakistan; Foreign Minister of Pakistan, 1966–68; Minister for Law and Parly Affairs, 1979–85; Advr to Chief Martial Law Administrator and Federal Minister, 1978. Sec.-Gen., Orgn of the Islamic Conf., 1984–88 (Chm. Cttee of Experts for drafting statute of Islamic Internat. Ct of Justice, 1980). Represented Pakistan: before International Tribunal on Rann of Kutch, 1965; before Internat. Ct of Justice regarding Namibia, SW Africa, 1971; Pakistan Chief Counsel before ICAO Montreal in complaint concerning overflights over Indian territory; Leader of Pakistan delegations to Commonwealth Conf. and General Assembly of UN, 1966; Mem., UN Sub-Commn on Prevention of Discrimination and Protection of Minorities, 1972– (Chm., 1968). Hon. Advisor, Constitutional Commn, 1961; Chm., Pakistan Company Law Commn, 1962; Mem., Internat. River Cttee, 1961–68; President: Pakistan Br., Internat. Law Assoc., 1964–67; Karachi Bar Assoc., 1964; Pakistan Bar Council, 1966; Inst. of Internat. Affairs. Led Pakistan Delegn to Law of the Sea Conferences, NY, 1978 and 1979, and Geneva, 1980. Member: Pakistan Nat. Gp, Panel of the Permanent Ct of Arbitration; Panel of Arbitrators and Umpires, Council of Internat. Civil Aviation Organisation; Panel of Arbitrators, Internat. Centre for Settlement of Investment Disputes, Washington; Internat. Law Commn, 1981–. *Publications:* Pakistan at a Glance, 1941; Jinnah on Pakistan, 1943; Leaders Correspondence with Jinnah, 1944, 3rd edn 1978; Evolution of Pakistan, 1962 (also published in Urdu and Arabic); Fundamental Rights and Constitutional Remedies in Pakistan, 1966; The Pakistan Resolution and the Historic Lahore Session, 1970; Foundations of Pakistan, vol. I, 1969, vol. II, 1970; Some Aspects of Quaid-i-Azam's Life, 1978, Collected Works of Quaid-i-Azam Mohammad Ali Jinnah, vol. I, 1985, vol. II, 1986. *Recreation:* bridge. *Address:* First Floor, Press Centre Building, Shahrah-E-Kamal Attaturk Road, Karachi, Pakistan. *Clubs:* Sind (Karachi); Karachi Boat, Karachi Gymkhana.

PISANI, Edgard (Edouard Marie Victor); Chevalier de la Légion d'honneur; *b* Tunis, 9 Oct. 1918; *s* of François and Zoë Pisani; *m* Isola Chazereau (decd); three *s* one *d*; *m* 1984, Carmen Berndt; one *s.* *Educ:* Lycée Carnot, Tunis; Lycée Louis-le-Grand, Paris. LèsL. War of 1939–45 (Croix de Guerre; Médaille de la Résistance). Chef du Cabinet, later Dir, Office of Prefect of Police, Paris, 1944; Dir, Office of Minister of Interior, 1946; Prefect: of Haute-Loire, 1946; of Haute-Marne, 1947; Senator (democratic left) from Haute-Marne, 1954; Minister of Agriculture, 1961; (first) Minister of Equipment, 1966; Deputy, Maine et Loire, 1967–68; Minister of Equipment and Housing, 1967; Conseiller Général, Maine et Loire, 1964–73; Mayor of Montreuil Bellay, 1965–75; Senator (socialist) from Haute-Marne, 1974–81; Mem., European Parlt, 1978–79 (Pres., Econ. and Monetary Affairs Cttee); Mem. for France, EEC, 1981–84; High Comr and Special Envoy to New Caledonia, 1984–85; Minister for New Caledonia, 1985–86. Member: Commn on Develt Issues (Brandt Commn), 1978–80; Economic and Social Cttee. Mem., Club of Rome, 1975. President: Inst. du Monde Arabe, 1988–; Centre Internat. des Hautes Etudes Agronomiques Mediterranenes, 1991–95. Dir, L'Evénement Européen, 1988–94. *Publications:* La région: pourquoi faire?, 1969; Le général indivis, 1974; Utopie foncière, 1977; Socialiste de raison, 1978; Défi du monde, campagne d'Europe, 1979; (contrib.) Pour la science, 1980; La main et l'outil, 1984; Pour l'Afrique, 1988; Persiste et Signe, 1992. *Address:* (home) 225 rue du Faubourg St Honoré, 75008 Paris, France.

PISCHETSRIEDER, Bernd; Chairman, Executive Board, BMW AG, since 1993; *b* 15 Feb. 1948. *Educ:* Munich Technical Univ. (Diplom-Ingenieur). BMW, 1973–: Production Planning Engineer, Munich, 1973–75; Head, Ops Control Dept, Munich factory, 1975–77; Head, Work Preparation Div., Dingolfing factory, 1978–81; Dir of Production, Develt, Purchasing and Logistics, S Africa, 1982–85; Head, Quality Assurance, 1985–87; Head, Technical Planning, 1987–90; Dep. Mem., Exec. Bd, 1990 (Production); Mem., Exec. Bd, 1991 (Production). *Address:* BMW AG, Petuelring 130, Postfach 40 02 40, 80788 Munich, Germany.

PITAKAKA, Sir (Puibangara) Moses, GCMG 1995; Governor-General, Solomon Islands, since 1994; *b* 24 Jan. 1945; *s* of Isaiah Puibangara and Lilian Tanaquana; *m* 1967, Lois Qilariava; three *s* four *d.* *Educ:* Goldie Coll., Western Prov., Solomon Is; Solomon Is Teachers' Coll.; Univ. of Birmingham; Univ. of S Pacific, Fiji; Univ. of Manchester; Queen Elizabeth House, Oxford Univ. School teacher, Solomon Is, 1964–66; Educn Officer, 1969–71; Dist Officer, Lands Officer and Magistrate, 1972–75; Honiara Town Clerk, Jan.–May 1976; Hd of Foreign Affairs, Prime Minister's Office, 1977–79; managed family business, 1980–81; Chm., N New Georgia Timber Co-op. Commn of Inquiry, 1982; Human Resources Develt Manager, Unilever Gp in Solomon Is, 1983–85; Leadership Code Commission: Comr, 1987–88; Chm., 1989–94. Chairman: Solomon Is Citizenship Commn, 1978–88; Nat. Educn Bd, 1980–86; Comr to Judicial and Legal Services Commn, 1981–83. Deacon, World Wide Church of God, 1993–. *Recreations:*

reading, canoeing, swimming, jogging, table tennis. *Address:* Government House, PO Box 252, Honiara, Solomon Islands. *T:* 21777.

PITBLADO, Sir David (Bruce), KCB 1967 (CB 1955); CVO 1953; *b* 18 Aug. 1912; *o s* of Robert Bruce and Mary Jane Pitblado; *m* 1941, Edith (*d* 1978), *yr d* of Captain J. T. and Mrs Rees Evans, Cardigan; one *s* one *d*. *Educ:* Strand Sch.; Emmanuel Coll., Cambridge (Hon. Fellow 1972); Middle Temple. Entered Dominions Office, 1935; Asst Private Secretary to Secretary of State, 1937–39; served in War Cabinet Office, 1942; transferred to Treasury, 1942; deleg. to UN Conf., San Francisco, 1945; Under-Secretary, Treasury, 1949; Principal Private Secretary to the Prime Minister (Mr Clement Attlee, Mr Winston Churchill, and Sir Anthony Eden), 1951–56; Vice Chm., Managing Bd, European Payments Union, 1958; Third Secretary, Treasury, 1960; Economic Minister and Head of Treasury Delegation, Washington, and Executive Dir for the UK, IMF and World Bank, 1961–63; Permanent Sec., Min. of Power, 1966–69, Permanent Sec. (Industry), Min. of Technology, 1969–70; Civil Service Dept, 1970–71; Comptroller and Auditor-General, 1971–76. Advr on non-exec. directorships, Inst. of Dirs, 1977–81. Chm., Davies's Educnl Trust, 1979–89. Member: Data Protection Cttee, 1976–78; Victoria County Histories Cttee, 1974–; Finance Cttee, RPMS, 1980–; Council, SSAFA, 1976–90 (Hon. Treasurer). Jt Editor, The Shetland Report, 1978. Companion Inst. of Fuel. *Address:* 23 Cadogan Street, SW3 2PP; Pengoitan, Borth, Dyfed SY24 5LN. *Club:* Athenæum.

PITCHER, Sir Desmond (Henry), Kt 1992; DL; CEng, FIEE, FBCS; Chairman: Mersey Barrage Co., since 1986; Merseyside Development Corporation, since 1991; North West Water Group, since 1993 (Director, since 1990; Deputy Chairman, 1991–93); *b* 23 March 1935; *s* of George Charles and Alice Marion Pitcher; *m* 1st 1961 (marr. diss.); twin *d*; 2nd, 1978 (marr. diss.); two *s*; 3rd, 1991, Norma Barbara Niven. *Educ:* Liverpool Coll. of Technology. MIEEE (USA). A. V. Roe & Co., Develt Engr, 1955; Automatic Telephone and Elec. Co. (now Plessey), Systems Engr, 1958; Univac Remington Rand (now Sperry Rand Ltd), Systems Engr, 1961; Sperry Univac: Dir, Systems, 1966; Managing Dir, 1971; Vice-Pres., 1974; Dir, Sperry Rand, 1971–76, Dep. Chm., 1974–76; Man. Dir, Leyland Vehicles Ltd, 1976–78; Dir, British Leyland, 1976–78; Man. Dir, Plessey Telecommunications and Office Systems, 1978–83; Dir, Plessey Co., 1979–83; Director: The Littlewoods Orgn, 1983–95 (Gp Chief Exec., 1983–93; Vice-Chm., 1993–95); National Westminster Bank, 1994–. Mem., Northern Adv. Bd, Nat. Westminster Bank, 1989–92. Vis. Prof. of Business Policy, Univ. of Manchester, 1993–. Dir, CEI, 1979; Pres., TEMA, 1981–83. Dep. Chm., Everton Football Club, 1990– (Dir, 1987–). DL Merseyside, 1992. Freeman, City of London, 1987; Liveryman, Co. of Information Technologists, 1992–. CIMgt; FRIAS; FRSA 1987; Hon. FIDE; Hon. Fellow, Liverpool John Moores Univ., 1993. Knight, Order of St Hubert (Austria), 1991. *Publications:* Institution of Electrical Engineers Faraday Lectures, 1974–75; various lectures on social implications of computers and micro-electronics. *Recreations:* golf, music. *Address:* Onston Hall, Onston, Cheshire CW8 2RG. *Clubs:* Brooks's, Royal Automobile; Royal Birkdale Golf; Delamere Golf; Moor Park Golf; Lancs CC.

PITCHER, Prof. Wallace Spencer, PhD, DSc, DIC; George Herdman Professor of Geology, 1962–81, now Emeritus, and Leverhulme Emeritus Research Fellow, 1981–83, University of Liverpool; *b* 3 March 1919; *s* of Harry George and Irene Bertha Pitcher; *m* 1947, Stella Ann (*née* Scutt); two *s* two *d*. *Educ:* Acton Tech. Coll., Chelsea Coll. Asst Analytical Chemist, Geo. T. Holloway & Co., 1937–39. Served War, RAMC, 1939–44. Chelsea Coll., 1944–47; Imperial College: Demonstrator, 1947–48; Asst Lectr, 1948–50; Lectr, 1950–55; Reader in Geology, King's Coll., London, 1955–62. Geological Society London: Hon. Sec., 1970–73; Foreign Sec., 1974–75; Pres., 1976–77; Pres., Section C, British Assoc., 1979. FGS; FIMM. Hon. MRIA 1977; Hon. FRSE 1993. Hon. Member: GA, 1972; Geol Soc. America, 1982. Hon. ScD Dublin, 1983; Hon. DSc Paris-Sud, 1993. Lyell Fund, 1956, Bigsby Medal, 1963, Murchison Medal, 1979, Geol Soc. of London; Liverpool Geol Soc. Silver Medal, 1969; Aberconway Medal, Instn of Geologists, 1983; Univ. Helsinki Medal, 1986. *Publications:* ed (with G. W. Flinn) Controls of Metamorphism, 1965; (with A. R. Berger) Geology of Donegal: a study of granite emplacement and unroofing, 1972; (with E. J. Cobbing) Geology of Western Cordillera of Northern Peru, 1981; (jtly) Magmatism at a Plate Edge: the Peruvian Andes, 1985; Nature and Origin of Granite, 1993; many papers on late Precambrian stratigraphy, tillites, Caledonian and Andean granites, structure of the Andes. *Address:* 14 Church Road, Upton, Wirral, Merseyside L49 6JZ. *T:* 0151–677 6896.

PITCHERS, Christopher John; His Honour Judge Pitchers; a Circuit Judge, since 1986; *b* 2 Oct. 1942; *s* of Thomas and Melissa Pitchers; *m* 1965, Judith Stevenson; two *s*. *Educ:* Uppingham Sch.; Worcester Coll., Oxford. MA. Called to the Bar, Inner Temple, 1965; a Recorder, 1981–86. Mem., Criminal Cttee, Judicial Studies Bd, 1991–95. Hon. Sec., Council of HM Circuit Judges, 1992–. Vice-Pres., NACRO, 1994–. *Address:* The Crown Court, Wellington Street, Leicester LE1 6HG.

PITCHFORD; *see* Watkins-Pitchford.

PITCHFORD, His Honour Charles Neville; a Circuit Judge, Wales and Chester Circuit, 1972–87. Called to the Bar, Middle Temple, 1948. *Address:* Llanynant, Kennel Lane, Coed Morgan, Abergavenny, Gwent NP7 9UR.
See also C. J. Pitchford.

PITCHFORD, Christopher John; QC 1987; a Recorder, since 1987; *b* 28 March 1947; *s* of Charles Neville Pitchford, *qv*; *m* 1st, 1970, Rosalind (*née* Eaton) (marr. diss. 1991); two *d*; 2nd, 1991, Denise (*née* James). *Educ:* Duffryn Comprehensive Sch., Newport, Gwent; Queen's Coll., Taunton, Somerset; Queen Mary Coll., London (LLB). Called to the Bar, Middle Temple, 1969; practised London, 1969–72 and Cardiff, 1972–87; an Asst Recorder, 1984–87. Arbitrator, Motor Insurers Bureau, 1994. *Recreation:* fishing. *Address:* Garth Gynydd, Bedlinog, Mid Glam CF46 6TH; Farrar's Building, Temple, EC4Y 7BD. *Clubs:* Cardiff and County (Cardiff); Bedlinog Racing.

PITCHFORTH, Harry; General Manager, Home Grown Cereals Authority, 1974–78, retired; *b* 17 Jan. 1917; *s* of John William Pitchforth and Alice Hollas; *m* 1941, Edna May Blakebrough; one *s* one *d*. *Educ:* Heath Sch., Halifax; Queen's Coll., Oxford. 1st class Hons, School of Modern History, Oxford, 1939. Served War, 1940–45, Captain, RASC, and later Education Officer, 5 Guards Brigade. Ministry of Food, 1945; Principal Private Secretary, to Minister, Major G. Lloyd-George, 1952–54; seconded to National Coal Board, 1955–58; Ministry of Agriculture, Fisheries and Food: Regional Controller, 1957–61; Director of Establishments and Organisation, 1961–65; Under-Sec., HM Treasury, 1965–67; Controller of HM Stationery Office and the Queen's Printer of Acts of Parliament, 1967–69; Chief Executive, Metropolitan Water Bd, 1969–74. *Recreations:* walking, music. *Address:* 93 George V Avenue, Pinner, Mddx HA5 5SU. *T:* 0181–863 1229.

PITFIELD, Hon. (Peter) Michael, CVO 1982; PC (Can.) 1984; QC (Can.) 1972; Senator, Canada, since Dec. 1982; *b* Montreal, 18 June 1937; *s* of Ward Chipman Pitfield and Grace Edith (*née* MacDougall); *m* 1971, Nancy Snow; one *s* two *d*. *Educ:* Lower Canada Coll., Montreal; Sedbergh Sch., Montebello; St Lawrence Univ. (BASc; Hon. DLitt 1979); McGill Univ. (BCL); Univ. of Ottawa (DESD). Lieut, RCNR. Read Law with Mathewson Lafleur & Brown, Montreal (associated with firm, 1958–59); called to Quebec Bar, 1962; QC (Fed.) 1972; Admin. Asst to Minister of Justice and Attorney-Gen. of Canada, 1959–61; Sec. and Exec. Dir, Royal Commn on Pubns, Ottawa, 1961–62; Attaché to Gov.-Gen. of Canada, 1962–65; Sec. and Res. Supervisor of Royal Commn on Taxation, 1963–66; entered Privy Council Office and Cabinet Secretariat of Govt of Canada, 1965; Asst Sec. to Cabinet, 1966; Dep. Sec. to Cabinet (Plans), and Dep. Clerk to Council, 1969; Dep. Minister, Consumer and Corporate Affairs, 1973; Clerk of Privy Council and Sec. to Cabinet, 1975–79 and 1980–Nov. 1982; Sen. Adviser to Privy Council Office, Nov.–Dec. 1982. Rep., UN Gen. Assembly, 1983; Chm., Senate Cttee on Security and Intelligence, 1983. Director: Power Corp., Montreal; Trust Co., LaPresse; Great West Life Assurance Co.; Investor's Gp Ltd, Winnipeg; Fellow, Harvard Univ., 1974; Mackenzie King Vis. Prof., Kennedy Sch. of Govt, Harvard, 1979–80. Member: Canadian, Quebec and Montreal Bar Assocs; Can. Inst. of Public Admin; Can. Hist. Assoc.; Can. Polit. Sci. Assoc.; Amer. Soc. Polit. and Social Sci.; Internat. Commn of Jurists; Beta Theta Pi. Trustee, Twentieth Century Fund, NY; Member Council: Canadian Inst. for Advanced Res., Toronto; IISS. *Recreations:* squash, ski-ing, reading. *Address:* (office) The Senate, Ottawa, Ont K1A 0K4, Canada. *Clubs:* University, Mount Royal, Racket (Montreal).

PITKEATHLEY, Jill Elizabeth, OBE 1993; Chief Executive, Carers National Association, since 1988; *b* 4 Jan. 1940; *d* of Roland Wilfred Bisson and Edith May Bisson (*née* Muston); *m* 1961, W. Pitkeathley (marr. diss. 1978); one *s* one *d*. *Educ:* Ladies' Coll., Guernsey; Bristol Univ. (BA Econ). Social worker, 1961–64; Voluntary Service Co-ordinator, Manchester and Essex, 1970–83; Nat. Consumer Council, 1983–86; Dir, Nat. Council for Carers, 1986 until merger with Assoc. of Carers, 1988. Advr to Griffith's Rev. of Community Care, 1986–88; Mem., Health Adv. Service, 1993–. Vice-Pres., Community Council for Berks, 1990–. Mem., RSA, 1992–. *Publications:* When I Went Home, 1978; Mobilising Voluntary Resources, 1982; Volunteers in Hospitals, 1984; Supporting Volunteers, 1985; It's my duty, isn't it?, 1989; Only Child, 1994; (with David Emerson) Age Gap Relationships, 1996. *Recreations:* gardening, grand-children, writing. *T:* Reading (01734) 471067; (office) 0171–490 8818.

PITMAN, Sir Brian (Ivor), Kt 1994; Chief Executive and Director, Lloyds Bank Plc, since 1983; *b* 13 Dec. 1931; *s* of late Ronald Ivor Pitman and of Doris Ivy Pitman (*née* Short); *m* 1954, Barbara Mildred Ann (*née* Darby); two *s* one *d*. *Educ:* Cheltenham Grammar School. FCIB. Entered Lloyds Bank, 1952, Jt Gen. Manager, 1975; Exec. Dir, Lloyds Bank International, 1976, Dep. Chief Exec., 1978; Dep. Group Chief Exec., Lloyds Bank Plc, 1982. Chm., Lloyds First Western Corp., 1983–; Director: Lloyds Bank California, 1982–86; Nat. Bank of New Zealand Ltd, 1982–; Lloyds and Scottish Plc, 1983; Lloyds Bank International Ltd, 1985–87; Lloyds Merchant Bank Holdings Ltd, 1985–88; NBNZ Holdings Ltd, 1990–. *Recreations:* golf, cricket, music. *Address:* Lloyds Bank Plc, 71 Lombard Street, EC3P 3BS. *Clubs:* MCC, St George's Hill Golf.

PITMAN, David Christian; His Honour Judge Pitman; a Circuit Judge, since 1986; *b* 1 Dec. 1936; 3rd *s* of Sir (Isaac) James Pitman, KBE, and Hon. Margaret Beaufort Pitman (*née* Lawson-Johnston); *m* 1971, Christina Mary Malone-Lee; one *s* two *d*. *Educ:* Eton Coll.; Christ Church, Oxford (BA (PPE) 1961, MA 1964). Editorial role in publishing books in Initial Teaching Alphabet, 1960–63; called to Bar, Middle Temple,1963; commenced practice, 1964; a Recorder, 1986. National Service: 2nd Lieut, 60th Rifles, 1955–57; Territorial Army: Lieut Queen's Westminsters, KRRC, 1957–61; Captain, then Major, Queen's Royal Rifles (TA), 1961–67; Major, 5th (T) Bn RGJ, 1967–69. *Recreations:* music, the open air. *Address:* c/o The Crown Court, Snaresbrook, Hollybush Hill, E11 1QW.

PITMAN, Jennifer Susan; professional racehorse trainer (National Hunt), since 1975; Director, Jenny Pitman Racing Ltd, since 1975; *b* 11 June 1946; *d* of George and Mary Harvey; *m* 1965, Richard Pitman (marr. diss.); two *s*. *Educ:* Sarson Secondary Girls' School. Training of major race winners includes: Midlands National, 1977 (Watafella); Massey Ferguson Gold Cup, Cheltenham, 1980 (Bueche Giorod); Welsh National, 1982 (Corbiere), 1983 (Burrough Hill Lad), 1986 (Stearsby); Grand National, 1983 (Corbiere); Cheltenham Gold Cup, 1984 (Burrough Hill Lad), 1991 (Garrison Savannah); Welsh Champion Hurdle, 1991 (Wonderman), 1992 (Don Valentino); King George VI Gold Cup, 1984 (Burrough Hill Lad); Hennessey Gold Cup, Newbury, 1984 (Burrough Hill Lad); Whitbread Trophy, 1985 (Smith's Man); Ritz Club National Hunt Handicap, Cheltenham, 1987 (Gainsay), 1989 (Golden Freeze), 1991 (Smith's Cracker); Sporting Life Weekend Chase, Liverpool, 1987 (Gainsay); Philip Cornes Saddle of Gold Final, Newbury, 1988 (Crumpet Delite). Trainer of the Year, 1983/84, 1990. *Publication:* Glorious Uncertainty (autobiog.), 1984. *Address:* Weathercock House, Upper Lambourn, near Newbury, Berks RG16 7QT. *T:* Lambourn (01488) 71714. *Club:* International Sporting.

PITOI, Sir Sere, Kt 1977; CBE 1975; MACE; Chairman, Public Services Commission of Papua New Guinea, since 1971; *b* Kapa Kapa Village, SE of Port Moresby, 11 Nov. 1935; *s* of Pitoi Sere and Laka Orira; *m* 1957, Daga Leva; two *s* three *d*. *Educ:* Sogeri (Teachers' Cert.); Queensland Univ. (Cert. in Diagnostic Testing and Remedial Teaching); Univ. of Birmingham, UK (Cert. for Headmasters and Administrators). Held a number of posts as teacher, 1955–57, and headmaster, 1958–68, in Port Moresby, the Gulf district of Papua, Eastern Highlands, New Britain. Apptd a District Inspector of Schools, 1968. Chm., Public Service Bd, Papua New Guinea, 1969–76. Fellow, PNG Inst. of Management. *Recreation:* fishing. *Address:* PO Box 6029, Boroko, Papua New Guinea. *Clubs:* Rotary (Port Moresby); Cheshire Home (PNG).

PITT, Barrie (William Edward); author and editor of military histories; *b* Galway, 7 July 1918; *y s* of John Pitt and Ethel May Pitt (*née* Pennell); *m* 1st, 1943, Phyllis Kate (*née* Edwards); one *s* (decd); 2nd, 1953, Sonia Deirdre (*née* Hoskins) (marr. diss., 1971); 3rd, 1983, Frances Mary (*née* Moore). *Educ:* Portsmouth Southern Grammar Sch. Bank Clerk, 1935. Served War of 1939–45, in Army. Surveyor, 1946. Began writing, 1954. Information Officer, Atomic Energy Authority, 1961; Historical Consultant to BBC Series, The Great War, 1963; Editor, Purnell's History of the Second World War, 1964; Editor-in-Chief: Ballantine's Illustrated History of World War 2, 1967 (US Book Series); Ballantine's Illustrated History of the Violent Century, 1971; Editor: Purnell's History of the First World War, 1969; British History Illustrated, 1974–78; Consultant Editor, The Military History of World War II, 1986. *Publications:* The Edge of Battle, 1958; Zeebrugge, St George's Day, 1918, 1958; Coronel and Falkland, 1960; 1918 The Last Act, 1962; The Battle of the Atlantic, 1977; The Crucible of War: Western Desert 1941, 1980; Churchill and the Generals, 1981; The Crucible of War: Year of Alamein 1942, 1982; Special Boat Squadron, 1983; (with Frances Pitt) The Chronological Atlas of World War II, 1989; contrib. to: Encyclopaedia Britannica; The Sunday Times. *Recreations:* reading, listening to classical music. *Address:* 10 Wellington Road, Taunton, Somerset TA1 4EG. *T:* Taunton (01823) 337188. *Club:* Savage.

PITT, Desmond Gordon; Commissioner of HM Customs and Excise, 1979–83; *b* 27 Dec. 1922; *s* of Archibald and Amy Pitt; *m* 1946, Barbara Irene; one *s* two *d*. *Educ:*

Bournemouth Sch. FCCA, ACIS, AIB. Officer, HM Customs and Excise, 1947; Inspector, 1958; Asst Sec., 1973; Under Sec., 1979. Hon. Treasurer, Wessex Autistic Soc. *Recreations:* travel, sailing. *Address:* 4 Ken Road, Southbourne, Bournemouth, Dorset BH6 3ET. *Club:* Thorpe Bay Yacht.

PITT, Rt. Rev. Mgr George Edward, CBE 1965; *b* 10 Oct. 1916; *s* of Francis Pitt and Anna Christina Oviedo. *Educ:* St Brendan's Coll., Bristol; Ven. English College, Rome. Priest, 1939; worked in Diocese of Clifton, 1940–43; joined Royal Navy as Chaplain, 1943; Principal Roman Catholic Chaplain, RN, 1963–69; Parish Priest, St Joseph's, Wroughton, Wilts, 1969–86. Nominated a Domestic Prelate, 1963. *Recreation:* music. *Address:* 5 West Mall, Bristol BS8 4BH. *T:* Bristol (0117) 973 3235.

PITT, Sir Harry (Raymond), Kt 1978; BA, PhD; FRS 1957; Vice-Chancellor, Reading University, 1964–79; *b* 3 June 1914; *s* of H. Pitt; *m* 1940, Clemency Catherine, *d* of H. C. E. Jacoby, MIEE; four *s*. *Educ:* King Edward's Sch., Stourbridge; Peterhouse, Cambridge. Bye-Fellow, Peterhouse, Cambridge, 1936–39; Choate Memorial Fellow, Harvard Univ., 1937–38; Univ. of Aberdeen, 1939–42. Air Min. and Min. of Aircraft Production, 1942–45. Prof. of Mathematics, Queen's Univ., Belfast, 1945–50; Deputy Vice-Chancellor, Univ. of Nottingham, 1959–62; Prof. of Pure Mathematics, Univ. of Nottingham, 1950–64. Visiting Prof., Yale Univ., 1962–63. Chm., Universities Central Council on Admissions, 1975–78. Pres., IMA, 1984–85. Hon. LLD: Aberdeen 1970; Nottingham 1970; Hon. DSc: Reading, 1978; Belfast, 1981. *Publications:* Tauberian Theorems, 1957; Measure, Integration and Probability, 1963; Measure and Integration for Use, 1986; mathematical papers in scientific journals. *Address:* 46 Shinfield Road, Reading, Berks RG2 7BW. *T:* Reading (01734) 872962.

PITT, Michael Edward, CEng, FICE; Chief Executive, Cheshire County Council, since 1990; *b* 2 Feb. 1949; *s* of Albert and Doris Joan Pitt; *m* 1969, Anna Maria Di Claudio; two *d*. *Educ:* University College London (first class Hons BSc Engrg). CEng 1974; FICE 1989. Civil Servant, 1970–72; motorway design and construction, 1972–75; transportation planner in private sector and local govt, 1975–80; Asst County Surveyor, Northumberland CC, 1980–84; Dep. Dir, Dir of Property Services and Dir of Tech. Services, Humberside CC, 1984–90. *Publications:* papers in technical jls. *Recreations:* family life, walking the Yorkshire moors. *Address:* County Hall, Chester CH1 1SF. *T:* Chester (01244) 602101.

PITT, William Henry; management consultant, construction industry; *b* 17 July 1937; *m* 1961, Janet Pitt (*née* Wearn); one *d*. *Educ:* Heath Clark Sch., Croydon; London Nautical Sch.; Polytechnic of South Bank; Polytechnic of N London (BA Philos./Classics). Lighting Engineer, 1955–75; Housing Officer, Lambeth Borough Council, 1975–81. Chm., Lambeth Br., NALGO, 1979–81. Joined Liberal Party, 1959; contested: (L) Croydon NW, Feb. and Oct. 1974, 1979, 1983; Thanet South (L/Alliance), 1987, (Lib. Dem.), 1992. MP (L) Croydon NW, Oct. 1981–1983; first L and SDP Alliance cand. to be elected MP. *Recreations:* photography, choral singing, listening to music, reading, walking. *Address:* 10 Inverness Terrace, Broadstairs, Kent CT10 1QZ. *Club:* National Liberal.

PITT-BROOKE, John Stephen; Command Secretary, Land Command, Ministry of Defence, since 1995; *b* 9 Sept. 1950; *s* of late Reginald Pitt-Brooke and of Hilda (*née* Wright); *m* 1986, Rosalind, *d* of Prof. William Mulligan, *qv*; two *s*. *Educ:* Salford Grammar Sch.; Queens' Coll., Cambridge (MA). MoD, 1971–74; NI Office, 1974–77; Private Sec. to Minister of State for NI, 1975–77; MoD, 1978; NATO Defence Coll., 1980; Private Sec. to Permanent Under Sec., MoD, 1984–87; Cabinet Office, 1988–89; Private Sec. to Sec. of State for Defence, 1992–94. *Recreations:* family life, literature, cricket, supporting Manchester City Football Club. *Address:* c/o Land Command, Wilton, Wilts SP2 0AG. *Clubs:* London Salfordians Amateur Rugby League; Lancashire County Cricket.

PITTS, Sir Cyril (Alfred), Kt 1968; Governor, University of Westminster (formerly Polytechnic of Central London), 1984–95 (Chairman of Governors, 1985–93); *b* 21 March 1916; *m* 1942, Barbara; two *s* one *d*. *Educ:* St Olave's; Jesus Coll., Cambridge. Chairman of ICI Companies in India, 1964–68; Chm., ICI (Export) Ltd and Gen. Manager, Internat. Coordination, ICI Ltd, 1968–78; Dir, ICI Americas Ltd, 1974–77; Dep. Chm., Ozalid Gp Holdings Ltd, 1975–77. Chairman: Process Plant EDC, 1979–83; Peter Brotherhood, 1980–83. President: Bengal Chamber of Commerce and Industry, and Associated Chambers of Commerce and Industry of India, 1967–68; British and S Asian Trade Assoc., 1978–83. Councillor, RIIA, 1968–77. Hon. DLitt Westminster, 1993. *Address:* 11 Middle Avenue, Farnham, Surrey GU9 8JL. *T:* Farnham (01252) 715864. *Clubs:* Oriental; Bengal (Calcutta).

PITTS, John Kennedy; Chairman, Legal Aid Board, 1988–95; *b* 6 Oct. 1925; *s* of Thomas Alwyn Pitts and Kathleen Margaret Pitts (*née* Kennedy); *m* 1st, 1957, Joan Iris Light (*d* 1986); 2nd, 1990, Julia Bentall. *Educ:* Bristol Univ. (BSc). Res. Officer, British Cotton Industry Res. Assoc., 1948–53; ICI, 1953–78; Dir, ICI Mond Div., 1969–71; Dep. Chm., ICI Agricl Div., 1972–77; Chairman: Richardsons Fertilizers, 1972–76; Hargreaves Fertilizers, 1975–77; Vice-Pres., Cie Neerlandaise de l'Azote, 1975–77. Chm. and Chief Exec., Tioxide Group, 1978–87. Mem., Tees and Hartlepool Port Authy, 1976–78; Chm., SASDA (formerly Shildon & Sedgefield Develt Agency), 1991–94. Pres., Chem. Industries Assoc., 1984–86. *Address:* Hall Garth House, Carthorpe, Bedale, N Yorks DL8 2LD. *Club:* Royal Automobile.

PITTS CRICK, R.; *see* Crick, Ronald P.

PIX WESTON, John; *see* Weston, J. P.

PIZZEY, Erin Patria Margaret; Founder of first Shelter for Battered Wives and their children, 1971; therapeutic consultant and fund-raiser, Women's Aid Ltd; *b* 19 Feb. 1939; *d* of Cyril Edward Antony Carney and Ruth Patricia Balfour-Last; *m* 1961, John Leo Pizzey (marr. diss. 1979); one *s* one *d*. *Educ:* St Antony's; Leweston Manor, Sherborne, Dorset. Somewhat chequered career as pioneering attracts frequent clashes with the law; appearances at such places as Acton Magistrates Court and the House of Lords could be considered milestones in the fulfilment of a career dedicated to defending women and children. Member: Soc. of Authors; AFI; Smithsonian Instn. Diploma of Honour, Internat. order of volunteers for peace, 1981; Distinguished Leadership Award, World Congress of Victimology, 1987; San Valentino d'Oro prize for lit., 1994. *Publications:* (as Erin Pizzey) Scream Quietly or the Neighbours Will Hear, 1974 (paperback), 2nd edn 1978; Infernal Child (autobiog.), 1978; The Slut's Cookbook, 1981; Prone to Violence, 1982; Erin Pizzey Collects, 1983; *novels:* The Watershed, 1983; In the Shadow of the Castle, 1984; The Pleasure Palace, 1986; First Lady, 1987; The Consul General's Daughter, 1988; The Snow Leopard of Shanghai, 1989; Other Lovers, 1991; Morning Star, 1991; Swimming with Dolphins, 1992; For the Love of a Stranger, 1993; Kisses, 1995; The Wicked World of Women, 1996; poems and short stories. *Recreations:* wine, books, travel. *Address:* Il Molino di Trove, 23 San Giovanni d'Asso, Siena 53020, Italy. *T:* and *Fax:* 577823170; Cayman Islands.

PLAISTOWE, (William) Ian (David), FCA; Director of Audit and Business Advisory Practice for Europe, Arthur Andersen, since 1993; *b* 18 Nov. 1942; *s* of David William Plaistowe and Julia (*née* Ross Smith); *m* 1968, Carolyn Anne Noble Wilson; two *s* one *d*. *Educ:* Marlborough Coll., Queens' Coll., Cambridge. Joined Arthur Andersen & Co., 1964; Partner, 1976; Head of Accounting and Audit practice, London, 1984–87; Dir of Acctg and Audit for UK and Ireland, 1987–93. Chm., Auditing Practices Bd of UK and Ireland, 1994–. Institute of Chartered Accountants in England and Wales: Chairman: London Soc. of Chartered Accountants, 1981–82; Post Qualification Cttee, 1985–86; Practice Regulation Directorate, 1987–90; Mem. Council, 1985–; Vice-Pres., 1990–91; Dep. Pres., 1991–92; Pres., 1992–93. *Publications:* articles in learned jls. *Recreations:* golf, tennis, squash, ski-ing, gardening. *Address:* Heybote, Ellesborough, Aylesbury, Bucks HP17 0XF. *T:* Aylesbury (01296) 622758. *Clubs:* Carlton; Moor Park Golf.

PLANT, family name of **Baron Plant of Highfield.**

PLANT OF HIGHFIELD, Baron *cr* 1992 (Life Peer), of Weelsby in the County of Humberside; **Raymond Plant,** PhD; DLitt; Master of St Catherine's College, Oxford, since 1994; *b* 19 March 1945; *s* of Stanley and Marjorie Plant; *m* 1967, Katherine Sylvia Dixon; three *s*. *Educ:* Havelock Sch., Grimsby; King's Coll. London (BA); Hull Univ. (PhD 1971). Lectr, then Sen. Lectr in Philosophy, Univ. of Manchester, 1967–79; Prof. of Politics, Univ. of Southampton, 1979–94. Lectures: Stevenson, Univ. of Glasgow, 1981; Agnes Cumming, UC Dublin, 1987; Stanton, Univ. of Cambridge, 1989–90 and 1990–91; Sarum, Univ. of Oxford, 1991; Ferguson, Manchester Univ., 1994; Scott Holland, 1995; Charles Gore, 1995. Chair, Labour Party Commn on Electoral Systems, 1991–93. Times columnist, 1988–92. Hon. DLitt: London Guildhall Univ., 1993; Hull, 1994. *Publications:* Hegel, 1974, 2nd edn 1984; Community and Ideology, 1974; Political Philosophy and Social Welfare, 1981; Philosophy, Politics and Citizenship, 1984; Conservative Capitalism in Britain and the United States: a critical appraisal, 1988; Modern Political Thought, 1991. *Recreations:* music, opera, thinking about the garden, listening to my wife playing the piano, reading. *Address:* The Master's Lodgings, St Catherine's College, Oxford OX1 3UJ. *T:* Oxford (01865) 271762.

PLANTIN, Marcus; ITV Network Director, since 1992; *b* 23 Oct. 1945; *s* of Charles P. Plantin and Vera H. Plantin; *m* 1980, Kate Benfield; two *s*. *Educ:* Surbiton County Grammar Sch.; Guildford Sch. of Acting. Producer, BBC TV, 1978–84; London Weekend Television: Head of Light Entertainment, 1985–87; Controller of Entertainment, 1987–90; Dir of Progs, 1990–92; Dir, London Weekend Productions and LWT Holdings, 1990–92. *Recreations:* gardening, swimming, reading. *Address:* ITV Network Centre, 200 Gray's Inn Road, WC1X 8HF.

PLASKETT, Maj.-Gen. Frederick Joseph, CB 1980; MBE 1966; FCIT; Director General and Chief Executive, Road Haulage Association, 1981–88; *b* 23 Oct. 1926; *s* of Frederick Joseph Plaskett and Grace Mary Plaskett; *m* 1st, 1950, Heather (*née* Kington) (*d* 1982); four *d*; 2nd, 1984, Mrs Patricia Joan Healy. Commnd infantry, 1946; RASC, 1951; RCT, 1965; regimental and staff appts, India, Korea, Nigeria, Malaya, Germany and UK; Student, Staff Coll., Camberley, 1958; Jt Services Staff Coll., 1964; Instr, Staff Coll., Camberley, 1966–68; Management Coll., Henley, 1969; RCDS, 1975; Dir of Movements (Army), 1975–78; Dir Gen., Transport and Movements (Army), 1978–81, retired. Col Comdt, RCT, 1981–91 (Rep. Col Comdt, 1989). Chm., British Railways Bd, London Midland Region, 1989–92 (Mem., 1986–88). Director: Foden Trucks (Paccar UK) (formerly Sandbach Engrg Co.), 1981–; RHA Insce Services Ltd, 1982–88; British Road Federation, 1982–88. Comr, Royal Hosp., Chelsea, 1985–88. Freeman, City of London, 1979; Liveryman, Co. of Carmen, 1979–. *Recreations:* fishing, sailing, gardening. *Address:* c/o National Westminster Bank, The Commons, Shaftesbury, Dorset SP7 8JY. *Clubs:* Army and Navy; Royal Motor Yacht.

PLASTOW, Sir David (Arnold Stuart), Kt 1986; Chairman, Medical Research Council, since 1990; Deputy Chairman, TSB Group Plc, since 1991; *b* Grimsby, 9 May 1932; *s* of late James Stuart Plastow and Marie Plastow; *m* 1954, Barbara Ann May; one *s* one *d*. *Educ:* Culford Sch., Bury St Edmunds. Apprentice, Vauxhall Motors Ltd, 1950; joined Rolls-Royce Ltd, Motor Car Div., Crewe, Sept. 1958; apptd Marketing Dir, Motor Car Div., 1967; Managing Director: Motor Car Div., 1971; Rolls-Royce Motors Ltd, 1972 (Gp Man. Dir, 1974–80); Vickers Plc: Dir, 1975–92; Man. Dir, 1980–86; Chief Exec., 1980–92; Chm., 1987–92. Dep. Chm., 1987–89, Jt Dep. Chm., 1989–94, Guinness PLC; Chm., Inchcape plc, 1992–95; Regional Dir, Lloyds Bank, 1974–76; non-executive Director: GKN, 1978–84; Legal & General Gp Plc, 1985–87; Cable & Wireless, 1991–93. Trustee, Royal Opera House Trust, 1992– (Chm., 1992–93). Mem., European Adv. Council, Tenneco, 1984–86; Bd Mem., Tenneco Inc. (Houston), 1985–92. Vice-Pres., Inst. of Motor Industry, 1974–82; Pres., SMMT, 1976–77, 1977–78 (Dep. Pres., 1978–79, 1979–80); Pres., Motor Industry Res. Assoc., 1978–81; Chm., Grand Council, Motor and Cycle Trades Benevolent Fund, 1976–82. Patron, Coll. of Aeronautical and Automobile Engrg, 1972–79. Chm., Industrial Soc., 1983–87 (Mem., 1981); Dep. Chm., Listed Cos Adv. Cttee, 1987–90; Member: Council, CBI; BOTB, 1980–83; Engineering Council, 1980–83; Offshore Energy Technology Bd, 1985–86; Bd of Companions, BIM (Pres. S Cheshire Br.); Council, Regular Forces Employment Assoc. Patron, The Samaritans, 1987–; Chm., 40th Anniversary Appeal Cttee, Mental Health Foundn, 1988–; Gov., BUPA, 1990– (Dep. Chm., 1992–). Chancellor, Univ. of Luton, 1993–. Chm. Governors, Culford Sch., 1979–. Pres., Crewe Alexandra FC, 1975–82. Liveryman, Worshipful Co. of Coachmakers & Coach Harness Makers. FRSA. Young Business Man of the Year Award, The Guardian, 1976. Hon. DSc Cranfield, 1978. *Recreations:* golf, music. *Clubs:* Buck's; Royal and Ancient (St Andrews); Royal St George's (Sandwich).

PLATER, Alan Frederick, FRSL 1985; freelance writer, since 1960; *b* 15 April 1935; *s* of Herbert Richard Plater and Isabella Scott Plater; *m* 1st, 1958, Shirley Johnson (marr. diss. 1985); two *s* one *d*; 2nd, 1986, Shirley Rubinstein; three step *s*. *Educ:* Pickering Road Jun. Sch., Hull; Kingston High Sch., Hull; King's Coll., Newcastle upon Tyne. ARIBA (now lapsed). Trained as architect and worked for short time in the profession before becoming full-time writer in 1960; has written extensively for radio, television, films and theatre, also for The Guardian, Listener, New Statesman, etc. Pres., Writers' Guild of GB, 1991–95 (Co-chair, 1986–87). FRSA 1991. Works include: *theatre:* A Smashing Day (also televised); Close the Coalhouse Door (Writers' Guild Radio Award, 1972); And a Little Love Besides; Swallows on the Water; Trinity Tales; The Fosdyke Saga; Fosdyke Two; On Your Way, Riley!; Skyhooks; A Foot on the Earth; Prez; Rent Party (musical); Sweet Sorrow; Going Home; I Thought I Heard a Rustling; *films:* The Virgin and the Gypsy; It Shouldn't Happen to a Vet; Priest of Love; *television:* plays: So Long Charlie; See the Pretty Lights; To See How Far It Is (trilogy); Land of Green Ginger; Willow Cabins; The Party of the First Part; The Blacktoft Diaries; Thank You, Mrs Clinkscales; Doggin' Around; biographies: The Crystal Spirit; Pride of our Alley; Edward Lear—at the edge of the sand; Coming Through; series and serials: Z Cars; Softly Softly; Shoulder to Shoulder; Trinity Tales; The Good Companions; The Consultant; Barchester Chronicles (adaptation of The Warden, and Barchester Towers, by Trollope); The Beiderbecke Affair; The Fortunes of War (adaptation of Balkan and Levant trilogies by Olivia Manning); A Very British Coup (International Emmy; Golden Fleece of Georgia (USSR); Best Series BAFTA Award; Best Series RTS Award; Best Series Broadcasting Press Guild Award; Best Series and Grand Prix, Banff Internat. TV Fest., Canada); The Beiderbecke Connection; Campion (adapted from Margery Allingham); A Day in Summer (adaptation of J. L. Carr novel); Misterioso; A Few Selected Exits (adapted from Gwyn Thomas; Cymru Writing Award, BAFTA, Regl Programme Award, RTS, 1993); Oliver's Travels; *radio:* The Journal of Vasilije Bogdanovic (Sony Radio Award, 1983). Hon. Fellow, Humberside Coll. of Higher Educn, 1983; Hon. DLitt Hull, 1985. RTS Writer's Award, 1984/85; Broadcasting Press Guild Award, 1987; Writer's Award, BAFTA, 1988; Northern Personality Award, Variety Club of GB, 1989. *Publications:* The Beiderbecke Affair, 1985; The Beiderbecke Tapes, 1986; Misterioso, 1987; The Beiderbecke Connection, 1992; Oliver's Travels, 1994; plays and shorter pieces in various anthologies. *Recreations:* reading, theatre, snooker, jazz, grandchildren, talking and listening. *Address:* c/o Alexandra Cann Representation, 337 Fulham Road, SW10 9TW. *T:* 0171-352 6266. *Clubs:* Dramatists', Ronnie Scott's.

PLATT, family name of **Baroness Platt of Writtle.**

PLATT OF WRITTLE, Baroness *cr* 1981 (Life Peer), of Writtle in the County of Essex; **Beryl Catherine Platt,** CBE 1978; FEng 1987; DL; Chairman, Equal Opportunities Commission, 1983–88; *b* 18 April 1923; *d* of Ernest and Dorothy Myatt; *m* 1949, Stewart Sydney Platt; one *s* one *d. Educ:* Westcliff High School; Girton Coll., Cambridge (MA; Fellow, 1988). CEng, FRAeS; Hon. FRAeS 1994. Technical Assistant, Hawker Aircraft, 1943–46; BEA, 1946–49. Mem. Bd, British Gas, 1988–94. Member: Engineering Council, 1981–90; Engrg Training Authy, 1990–92; Meteorological Office Adv. Cttee (UK), 1992– (Chm., 1995). Member, Chelmsford RDC, 1958–74. Member, Essex CC, 1965–85: Alderman, 1969–74; Vice-Chm., 1980–83; Chm., Education Cttee, 1971–80. Mem., H of L Select Cttee for Science and Technology, 1982–85 and 1990–94. Mem., Adv. Cttee on Women's Employment, 1984–88. Vice-Chairman: Technician Education Council, 1979–81; London Regional Adv. Council for Technology Education, 1975–81. President: Chelmsford Engrg Soc., 1979–80; Cambridge Univ. Engrs Assoc., 1987–; Assoc. for Sci. Educn, 1988; Pipeline Industries Guild, 1994–; Vice-President: UMIST, 1985–92; Engrg Section, BAAS (Pres., 1988); ACC, 1992 (Mem. Educn Cttee, 1974–80); Member: CNAA, 1973–79; Council, CGLI, 1974–94; Cambridge Univ. Appointments Bd, 1975–79; Council, Careers Research and Adv. Centre, 1983–93; Council, RSA, 1983–88; COPUS, 1990–93; Council, Foundn for Sci. and Technology, 1991–. Member of Court: Essex Univ., 1964–; City Univ., 1969–78; Brunel Univ., 1985–92; Cranfield Inst. of Technology, 1989–; Chancellor, Middlesex Univ., 1993–. Trustee, Homerton Coll., 1970–81. Liveryman, Engineers' Co., 1988. DL Essex 1983. Freeman, City of London, 1988. Fellow, 1987, Dir, 1989–94, Smallpeice Trust; Fellow, Manchester Polytechnic, 1989. FIGasE 1990; FRSA. Hon. FIMechE 1984; Hon. FITD 1994; Hon. FCP 1987; Hon. FIStructE 1991; Hon. FICE 1991; Hon. Fellow: Polytechnic of Wales, 1985; Women's Engrg Soc., 1988; UMIST, 1992. Hon. DSc: City, 1984; Salford, 1984; Cranfield, 1985; Nottingham Trent, 1993; DUniv: Open Univ., 1985; Essex, 1985; Middlesex, 1993; Hon. DEng Bradford, 1985; Hon. DTech: Brunel, 1986; Loughborough, 1993; Hon. LLD Cantab, 1988. European Engr, FEANI, 1987; Insignia Award *hc*, CGLI, 1988. *Recreations:* cooking, reading. *Address:* House of Lords, SW1A 0PW. *Club:* United Oxford & Cambridge University.

PLATT, Anthony Michael Westlake, CBE 1991; Chief Executive, London Chamber of Commerce and Industry, 1984–91; *b* 28 Sept. 1928; *s* of late James Westlake Platt, CBE and Veronica Norma Hope Platt (*née* Arnold); *m* 1st, 1952, Jennifer Susan Scott-Fox; three *s*; 2nd, 1984, Heather Mary Stubbs; one step *s* one step *d*; 3rd, 1987, Sarah Elizabeth Russell. *Educ:* Stowe School; Balliol College, Oxford (PPE 1951). Foreign Office, 1951, served Prague, 1953–54, NY, 1955–56; Shell Group of Cos: Switzerland, 1957; Guatemala, 1959; S Africa, 1961; Venezuela, 1963; London, 1969; The Hague, 1972; London, 1975–77 (Billiton UK); The Hague, 1977–78 (Billiton Internat.); London, 1979–84. Advr, Council of British Chambers in Europe, 1992–. *Recreations:* gliding, opera, languages. *Address:* 114 Castelnau, Barnes, SW13 9EU.

See also C. P. S. Platt.

PLATT, Prof. Colin Peter Sherard; Professor of History, Southampton University, since 1983; *b* 11 Nov. 1934; twin *s* of late James Westlake Platt and Veronica Norma Hope Arnold; *m* 1963, Valerie Ashforth; two *s* two *d. Educ:* Collyers Grammar School, Horsham; Balliol College, Oxford (BA 1st cl., MA); Leeds University (PhD). Research Assistant in Medieval Archaeology, Leeds Univ., 1960–62, Lectr, 1962–64; Lectr, Sen. Lectr and Reader in History, Southampton Univ., 1964–83. *Publications:* The Monastic Grange in Medieval England, 1969; Medieval Southampton: the port and trading community AD 1000–1600, 1973; (with Richard Coleman-Smith) Excavations in Medieval Southampton 1953–1969, 2 vols, 1975; The English Medieval Town, 1976; Medieval England: a social history and archaeology from the Conquest to 1600 AD, 1978; The Atlas of Medieval Man, 1979; The Parish Churches of Medieval England, 1981; The Castle in Medieval England and Wales, 1982; The Abbeys and Priories of Medieval England, 1984; Medieval Britain from the Air, 1984; The Traveller's Guide to Medieval England, 1985; The National Trust Guide to late Medieval and Renaissance Britain, 1986; The Architecture of Medieval Britain: a social history (Wolfson History Award), 1990; The Great Rebuildings of Tudor and Stuart England: revolutions in architectural taste, 1994; After the Black Death: plague and social change in late medieval England, 1996. *Recreations:* reading novels, visiting medieval antiquities. *Address:* Department of History, University of Southampton, Southampton SO17 1BJ. *T:* Southampton (01703) 592211.

See also A. M. W. Platt.

PLATT, Eleanor Frances, QC 1982; a Recorder of the Crown Court, since 1982; *b* 6 May 1938; *er d* of late Dr Maurice Leon Platt and Sara Platt (*née* Stein), Hove, Sussex; *m* 1963; two *c.* Educ: Hove County School for Girls; University College London. LLB 1959. Called to the Bar, Gray's Inn, 1960. Mem., Matrimonial Causes Rule Cttee, 1986–90. Treas., Family Law Bar Assoc., 1990– (Acting Chm., 1995). Chairman: Law, Parly and Gen. Purposes Cttee, Bd of Deputies of British Jews, 1988–94; New London Synagogue, 1994–. *Recreations:* the arts, travel, skiing. *Address:* 1 Garden Court, Temple EC4Y 9BJ. *T:* 0171-797 7900.

PLATT, Sir (Frank) Lindsey, 2nd Bt *cr* 1958; *S* father, 1986; *m* 1951, Johanna Magdalena Elisabeth Laenger (*d* 1995); one *d* (and one *d* decd). *Heir:* none.

PLATT, John Richard; His Honour Judge Platt; a Circuit Judge, since 1992; *b* 21 Nov. 1942; *s* of Arthur James Platt and Joan Platt; *m* 1986, Jayne Mary Webb; two *d. Educ:* Sherborne Sch.; Trinity Hall, Cambridge. Partner, Lee Davies & Co., Solicitors, 1969–82; Registrar and District Judge, Bow County Court, 1982–92. *Publication:* contrib. New Law Jl. *Recreations:* wine and food, music, travel.

PLATT, Margaret; *see* Wright, M.

PLATT, Michael Edward Horsfall; Pensions Ombudsman, 1991–94; *b* 24 Aug. 1934; *s* of Fred Horsfall Platt and Alice Martha Taylor Platt (*née* Wilde). *Educ:* Taunton Sch.; The Queen's Coll., Oxford. Nat. Service, RAF, 1952–54. Min. of Labour, 1959; Min. of Pensions and Nat. Insurance, 1960; Min. of Social Security, 1966; Private Sec. to Minister of State, DHSS, 1968–70; Cabinet Office, 1970–71; DHSS, 1971–86; Chief Adjudication Officer, 1986–90. *Recreations:* theatre, music. *Address:* c/o Office of the Pensions Ombudsman, 11 Belgrave Road, SW1V 1RB. *T:* 0171-834 9144.

PLATT, Norman, OBE 1985; opera director and writer; Artistic Director, Kent Opera, 1969–89 and since 1991; *b* 29 Aug. 1920; *s* of Edward Turner Platt and Emily Jane Platt; *m* 1st, 1942, Diana Franklin Clay; one *s* one *d*; 2nd, 1963, Johanna Sigrid Bishop; one *s* two *d. Educ:* Bury Grammar Sch.; King's Coll., Cambridge (BA). Principal: Sadler's Wells Opera, 1946–48; English Opera Group, 1948; Mem. Deller Consort, and freelance singer, actor, teacher and producer in Britain and Western Europe; founded Kent Opera, 1969; co-founded Canterbury Theatre and Festival Trust, 1983; re-founded Kent Opera, 1991. His many prodns for Kent Opera include: The Return of Ulysses; Agrippina; The Seraglio; Dido and Aeneas; Peter Grimes. Hon. DCL Kent, 1981. *Publications:* translations of numerous songs and operas, incl. L'Incoronazione di Poppea, Don Giovanni and Fidelio; articles on musical subjects. *Recreations:* reading, theatre, music. *Address:* Pembles Cross, Egerton, Ashford, Kent TN27 9EN. *T:* Egerton (0123376) 237.

PLATT, Hon. Sir Peter, 2nd Bt *cr* 1959; Professor of Music, University of Sydney, 1975–89; *b* 6 July 1924; *s* of Baron Platt (Life Peer), and Margaret Irene (*d* 1987), *d* of Arthur Charles Cannon; *S* to baronetcy of father, 1978; *m* 1948, Jean Halliday, *d* of late Charles Philip Brentnall, MC; one *s* two *d. Educ:* Abbotsholme School, Derbyshire; Magdalen Coll., Oxford; Royal College of Music. BMus 1950, MA, BLitt 1954, Oxon; FGSM 1973. Lectr and Sen. Lectr in Music, Univ. of Sydney, 1952–57; Professor of Music, Univ. of Otago, NZ, 1957–75. Served War of 1939–45 with RNVR (despatches). *Heir: s* Martin Philip Platt [*b* 9 March 1952; *m* 1971, Frances Corinne Moana, *d* of Trevor Samuel Conley; two *s* two *d*]. *Address:* 1 Ellison Place, Pymble, NSW 2073, Australia.

PLATT, Stephen; Editor, New Statesman and Society, since 1991; *b* 29 Sept. 1954; *s* of Kenneth Norman Platt and Joyce (*née* Pritchard); one *d* by Diane Louise Paice; partner, Anna Elizabeth Sutton. *Educ:* Longton High Sch., Stoke-on-Trent; Wade Deacon Sch., Widnes; LSE (BSc (Econ)). Teacher, Moss Brook Special Sch., Widnes, 1972–73; Dir, Self Help Housing Resource Library, Poly. of N London, 1977–80; Co-ordinator, Islington Community Housing, 1980–83; freelance writer and journalist, 1983–; News Editor, subseq. Acting Editor, New Society, 1985–88; columnist and writer, 1988–91; Editor: Midweek, 1988–89; Enjoying the Countryside, 1988–. *Publications:* various. *Recreations:* football, walking, countryside, gardening, breeding frogs, Paddington Bear. *Address:* 46 Tufnell Park Road, N7 0DT. *T:* 0171-263 4185. *Clubs:* Red Rose; Port Vale.

PLATT, Terence Charles; Deputy Under-Secretary of State and Principal Establishment Officer, Home Office, since 1992; *b* 22 Sept. 1936; *yr s* of Bertram Reginald Platt, QPM and Nina Platt; *m* 1959, Margaret Anne Cotmore; two *s. Educ:* St Olave's and St Saviour's Grammar School; Joint Services School for Linguists; Russian Interpreter. HM Immigration Officer, 1957; Asst Principal, Home Office, 1962; Principal, 1966; Cabinet Office, 1970; Principal Private Sec. to Sec. of State for NI (Rt Hon. William Whitelaw), 1972–73; Asst Sec., Home Office, 1973–81; Asst Under-Sec. of State and Princ. Estabt and Finance Officer, NI Office, 1981–82; Asst Under-Sec. of State and Dir of Regimes and Services, Prison Dept, Home Office, 1982–86; Asst Under-Sec. of State (Ops and Resources), Immigration and Nationality Dept, Home Office, 1986–92; Chief Inspector, Immigration Service, 1991–92. *Publication:* New Directions in Prison Design (Wkg Party Report), 1985. *Recreations:* growing roses, photography, butterflies. *Address:* c/o Home Office, 50 Queen Anne's Gate, SW1H 9AT.

PLATTEN, Very Rev. Stephen George; Dean of Norwich, since 1995; *b* 17 May 1947; *s* of George Henry and Marjory Platten; *m* 1972, Rosslie Thompson; two *s. Educ:* Stationers' Company's Sch.; Univ. of London (BEd Hons 1972); Trinity Coll., Oxford (Dip. Theol. 1974); Cuddesdon Theol Coll. Deacon 1975, Priest 1976; Asst Curate, St Andrew, Headington, Oxford, 1975–78; Chaplain and Tutor, Lincoln Theol Coll., 1978–82; Diocesan Dir of Ordinands and Canon Residentiary, Portsmouth Cathedral, 1983–89; Dir, post-ordination trng and continuing ministerial educn, Dio. Portsmouth, 1984–89; Archbishop of Canterbury's Sec. for Ecumenical Affairs, 1990–95. Hon. Canon of Canterbury Cathedral, 1990–. Anglican Sec., ARCIC (II), 1990–95. Chm., Soc. for Study of Christian Ethics, 1983–88. Minister Provincial, European Province, Third Order, SSF, 1991–. Dir, SCM Press, 1990–. Guestmaster, Nikaean Club, 1990–95. *Publications:* (contrib.) Deacons in the Ministry of the Church, 1987; (series editor) Ethics and Our Choices, 1990–; (contrib.) Spirituality and Psychology, 1990; (contrib.) Say One for Me, 1991; contribs to theol and educnl jls. *Recreations:* walking, music, literature, Northumberland. *Address:* The Deanery, Norwich, Norfolk NR1 4EG. *T:* Norwich (01603) 760140. *Club:* Athenæum.

PLATTS-MILLS, John Faithful Fortescue, QC 1964; Barrister; *b* 4 Oct. 1906; *s* of John F. W. Mills and Dr Daisy Platts-Mills, Karori, Wellington, NZ; *m* 1936, Janet Katherine Cree (*d* 1992); six *s. Educ:* Nelson College, NZ; Victoria University, NZ (LLB 1st Cl. 1927, LLM 1st Cl. 1928); Balliol College, Oxford (Rhodes Scholar; BA 1st Cl. 1930, BCL 1931, MA 1948). MP (Lab) Finsbury, 1945–48, (Lab Ind) 1948–50. Pilot Officer, RAF, 1940; "Bevin Boy", 1944; collier, 1945. Bencher, Inner Temple, 1970. President: Haldane Soc.; Soc. for Cultural Relations with the USSR; Vice-Pres., Internat. Assoc. of Democratic Lawyers. *Address:* Cloisters, Temple, EC4Y 7AA. *T:* 0171-583 0303. *Clubs:* Athenæum; Vincent's (Oxford); Leander (Henley-on-Thames).

See also M. F. Platts-Mills.

PLATTS-MILLS, Mark Fortescue; QC 1995; *b* 17 Jan. 1951; *s* of John Faithful Fortescue Platts-Mills, *qv*; *m* 1982, Dr Juliet Anne Britton; one *s. Educ:* Bryanston Sch.; Balliol Coll., Oxford (BA Eng. Sci. and Econ.). Called to the Bar, Inner Temple, 1974. *Recreations:* gardening, hockey, cricket. *Address:* 8 New Square, Lincoln's Inn, WC2A 3QP.

PLAYER, Dr David Arnott, FRCPE, FRCPsych, FFCM; District Medical Officer, South Birmingham Health Authority, 1987–91; *b* 2 April 1927; *s* of John Player and Agnes Gray; *m* 1955, Anne Darragh; two *s. Educ:* Calder Street Sch.; Bellahouston Acad., Glasgow; Glasgow Univ. MB, ChB, DPH, DPM. House Surgeon, Dumfries and Galloway Royal Infirmary, 1950; Consultant in Dermatology and VD, RAMC (Far East), 1950–52; House Surgeon, Western Infirmary, Glasgow, 1952; House Physician, Bridge of Earn Hosp., 1952–53; House Surgeon (Obst., Gyn. and Paed.), Halifax Royal Infirmary, 1953–54; GP, W Cumberland and Dumfriesshire, 1954–59; Registrar (Infectious Diseases), Paisley Infectious Diseases Hosp., 1959–60; Asst MOH, Dumfriesshire, 1960–62; Registrar (Psychiatry), Crighton Royal Hosp., Dumfries, 1962–64; MOH, Dumfries Burgh, 1964–70; MO (Mental Health Div.), SHHD and Med. and Psych. Adviser to Sec. of State for Scotland on Scottish Prison and Borstal Service, 1970–73; Dir, Scottish Health Educn Group, 1973–82; Dir Gen., Health Educn Council, 1982–87. Hon. Vis. Prof., Dept of Clinical Epidemiology and Gen. Practice, Royal Free Hosp. Sch. of Medicine, 1983–. *Publications:* articles in Health Bulletin, Internat. Jl of Health Educn, Scottish Trade Union Review. *Recreations:* golf, cycling. *Address:* 7 Ann Street, Edinburgh EH4 1PL.

PLAYER, Gary (Jim); professional golfer, since 1953; *b* Johannesburg, 1 Nov. 1935; *s* of Francis Harry Audley Player and late Muriel Marie Ferguson; *m* 1957, Vivienne, *d* of Jacob Wynand Verwey; two *s* four *d. Educ:* King Edward Sch., Johannesburg. Won first,

Dunlop tournament, 1956; major championship wins include: British Open, 1959, 1968, 1974; US Masters, 1961, 1974, 1978; US PGA, 1962, 1972; US Open, 1965; S African Open, thirteen times, 1956–81; S African PGA, 1959, 1960, 1969, 1979, 1982; Australian Open, seven times, 1958–74; Tooth Gold Coast Classic, Australia, 1981; Johnnie Walker Trophy, Spain, 1984; World Match Play Tournament, 1965, 1966, 1968, 1971, 1973. *Publications:* Golf Begins at 50 (with Desmond Tolhurst), 1988; To Be the Best, 1991. *Address:* c/o IMG, 1 Erieview Plaza, Suite 1300, Cleveland, OH 44114, USA.

PLAYFAIR, Sir Edward (Wilder), KCB 1957 (CB 1949); *b* 17 May 1909; *s* of late Dr Ernest Playfair; *m* 1941, Dr Mary Lois Rae; three *d. Educ:* Eton; King's Coll., Cambridge (Hon. Fellow, 1986). Inland Revenue, 1931–34; HM Treasury, 1934–46 and 1947–56 (Control Office for Germany and Austria, 1946–47); Permanent Under-Secretary of State for War, 1956–59; Permanent Sec., Ministry of Defence, 1960–61. Chairman, International Computers and Tabulators Ltd, 1961–65; Director: National Westminster Bank Ltd, 1961–79; Glaxo Hldgs Ltd, 1961–79; Tunnel Holdings Ltd, 1966–80; Equity and Law Life Assce Soc. plc, 1968–83. Governor, Imperial Coll. of Science and Technology, 1958–83 (Fellow, 1972); College Cttee of UCL, 1961–77 (Hon. Fellow, UCL, 1969); Chm., National Gallery, 1972–74 (Trustee, 1967–74). Hon. FBCS. *Address:* 62 Coniger Road, Fulham, SW6 3TA. *T:* 0171–736 3194. *Club:* Brooks's.
See also N. D. Padfield.

PLAYFORD, Jonathan Richard; QC 1982; a Recorder, since 1985; *b* 6 Aug. 1940; *s* of Cecil R. B. Playford and Euphrasia J. Playford; *m* 1978, Jill Margaret Dunlop; one *s* one *d. Educ:* Eton Coll.; London Univ. (LLB). Called to the Bar, Inner Temple, 1962, Bencher, 1991. *Recreations:* music, sheep farming, beekeeping, woodworking. *Address:* 2 Harcourt Buildings, Temple, EC4Y 9DB. *T:* 0171–583 9020. *Clubs:* Garrick, Royal Automobile; Huntercombe Golf (Henley).

PLAYLE, Colin; Project Director, Retail, British Gas, since 1994; *b* 13 May 1933; *s* of James and Florence Playle; *m* 1st, 1957, Reena Mary Cuppleditch (marr. diss. 1975); two *d*; 2nd, 1976, Patricia Margaret Golds. *Educ:* University College London (BA Hons). CompIGasE. British Gas: Marketing and Customer Service, E Midlands Gas Bd, 1957–75; Regl Marketing Manager, E Midlands, 1975–78; Dir of Marketing, British Gas NE, 1978–86; Sen. Mem., British Gas Privatisation Team, 1986; HQ Dir, Industrial and Commercial Gas, London, 1988–91; Regl Chm., British Gas Scotland, 1991–94. Chm., Combined Heat and Power Assoc., 1991–93. *Recreations:* ski-ing, ornithology, modern literature. *Address:* Upton Barn, Main Street, Upton, Newark, Notts SG23 5SY.

PLEETH, William, OBE 1989; FGSM; FRCM; Professor of 'Cello, Guildhall School of Music, 1948–78; *b* 12 Jan. 1916; *s* of John Pleeth and Edith Pleeth; *m* 1944, Margaret Good; one *s* one *d. Educ:* London until 1929; Leipzig Conservatoire, 1930–32. Internat. concert 'cellist in duos, trios, string quartets and concertos; début: Leipzig, 1931; London, 1933; broadcasting and recording, 1933–80; 'cello master classes in Europe, Canada, USA; frequent member, internat. music juries. *Publication:* Cello (Menuhin series), 1982. *Recreations:* gardening, reading, researching into old English furniture. *Address:* 19 Holly Park, N3 3JB. *T:* 0181–346 0277.

PLEMING, Nigel Peter; QC 1992; *b* 13 March 1946; *s* of late Rev. Percy Francis Pleming and of Cynthia Myra Pleming (now Mrs Leslie Tuxworth); *m* 1979, Evelyn Carol Joan Hoffmann; one *s* two *d. Educ:* King Edward VI Grammar Sch., Spilsby; Kingston Polytechnic (LLB); University Coll. London (LLM). Lectr, Kingston Poly, 1969–73; called to the Bar, Inner Temple, 1971; in practice at the Bar, 1974–; Junior Counsel to the Crown (Common Law), 1987–92. *Recreations:* cricket, tennis, painting, blues guitar. *Address:* 39 Essex Street, WC2R 3AT. *T:* 0171–583 1111. *Club:* National Liberal.

PLENDER, Richard Owen; QC 1989; barrister; *b* 9 Oct. 1945; *s* of George Plender and Louise Mary (*née* Savage); *m* 1978, Patricia Clare (*née* Ward); two *d. Educ:* Dulwich Coll.; Queens' Coll., Cambridge (MA, LLB; Rebecca Squire Prize; LLD 1993); Univ. of Illinois (LLM; JSD 1972, College of Law Prize); Univ. of Sheffield (PhD 1973). Called to the Bar, Inner Temple, 1972 (Berridale-Keith Prize); in practice at the Bar, 1974–. Consultant, UN Law and Population Programme, 1972–74; Consultant Legal Adviser, UN High Comr for Refugees, 1974–78; Legal Sec., Court of Justice of European Communities, 1980–83; Dir of Studies, 1987, Dir of Res., 1988, Hague Acad. of Internat. Law; Dir, Centre of European Law, KCL, 1988–91; Special Legal Advr to States of Jersey, 1988–. Leverhulme Fellow, Yale Law Sch., 1980; British Acad. Fellow, Soviet Acad. of Sciences, 1985; Sen. Mem., Robinson Coll., Cambridge, 1983–; Associate Prof., Univ. de Paris II (Univ. de Droit, d'Economie et des Sciences Sociales), 1989–90; Hon. Vis. Prof., City Univ., 1991–. *Publications:* International Migration Law, 1972, 2nd edn 1988; (ed and contrib.) Fundamental Rights, 1973; Cases and Materials on the Law of the European Communities, 1980 (with J. Usher), 3rd edn 1993; A Practical Introduction to European Community Law, 1980; (with J. Peres Santos) Introducción al Derecho Comunitario Europeo, 1984; (ed and contrib.) Legal History and Comparative Law: essays in honour of Albert Kiralfy, 1990; The European Contracts Convention: the Rome convention on the choice of law for contracts, 1991; contribs in English, French, German and Spanish to jls and encyclopedias. *Recreations:* writing light verse, classical music (especially late nineteenth century orchestral). *Address:* 20 Essex Street, WC2R 3AL. *T:* 0171–583 9294; Forrester Norall and Sutton, 1 Place Madon, 1130 Brussels, Belgium. *T:* (2) 2191620.

PLENDERLEITH, Harold James, CBE 1959; MC 1918; BSc, PhD; FRSE; FBA 1973; FSA; FMA; Director, International Centre for the Study of the Preservation and Restoration of Cultural Property (created by UNESCO), 1959–71, now Emeritus; Vice-President, International Institute for the Conservation of Museum Objects, 1958 (President, 1965–67, Hon. Fellow 1971); *b* 19 Sept. 1898; *s* of Robert James Plenderleith, FEIS; *m* 1926, Elizabeth K. S. Smyth (*d* 1982). *Educ:* Dundee Harris Acad.; St Andrews Univ. Scientific Asst, Dept of Scientific and Indust. Res., attached to British Museum, Bloomsbury, 1924; Asst Keeper, British Museum, 1927; Keeper, Research Lab., British Museum, 1949–59. Mem., Hon. Scientific Adv. Cttee, Nat. Gallery, 1935–81 (Chm., 1944–58); Professor of Chemistry, Royal Academy of Arts, London, 1936–58. Hon. Treas. Internat. Inst. for Conservation of Museum Objects, 1950–58; Hon. Mem., Internat. Council of Museums; Hon. Chm., Scottish Soc. for Conservation and Restoration, 1984. Rhind Lecturer (Edinburgh) 1954. Gold Medal, Society of Antiquaries of London, 1964; Gold Medal, Univ. of Young Nam, Tae Gu, Korea, 1970; Bronze Medal, UNESCO, 1971; Conservation Service Award, US Dept of the Interior, 1976; ICCROM International Oscar, Rome, 1979. Hon. LLD St Andrews. *Publications:* The Preservation of Antiquities, 1934; The Conservation of Prints, Drawings and Manuscripts, 1937; The Preservation of Leather Bookbindings, 1946; The Conservation of Antiquities and Works of Art, 1956 (2nd edn with A. E. A. Werner, 1971); papers on allied subjects and on technical examinations of museum specimens in museum and scientific journals. *Recreations:* art and music. *Address:* Riverside, 17 Rockfield Crescent, Dundee DD2 1JF. *T:* Dundee (01382) 641552. *Club:* Athenæum.

PLENDERLEITH, Ian; Executive Director, Bank of England, since 1994; Senior Broker to Commissioners for Reduction of National Debt, since 1989; *b* 27 Sept. 1943; *s* of Raymond William Plenderleith and Louise Helen Plenderleith (*née* Martin); *m* 1967, Kristina Mary Bentley; one *s* two *d. Educ:* King Edward's Sch., Birmingham; Christ Church, Oxford (MA); Columbia Business Sch., NY (MBA; Beta Gamma Sigma Medal, 1971). Joined Bank of England, 1965; seconded to IMF, Washington DC, 1972–74; Private Sec. to Governor, 1976–79; Alternate Dir, EIB, 1980–86; Hd of Gilt-Edged Div., 1982–90; Asst Dir, 1986–90; Associate Dir, 1990–94. Dir, Bank of England Nominees Ltd, 1994–; Alternate Dir, BIS, 1994–. Dir, London Stock Exchange (formerly Mem., Stock Exchange Council), 1989–. Chairman: Stock Borrowing and Lending Cttee, 1990–95; Editl Cttee, OECD Study on Debt Management, 1990–93; Co-Chm., Gilt Borrowers Forum, 1991–94; Member: Legal Risk Rev. Cttee, 1991–92; Financial Law Panel, 1992–94. Member: Adv. Bd, Inst. of Archaeology Develt Trust, UCL, 1987–; Eur. Bd of Overseers, Columbia Business Sch., 1991–; Fund-raising Planning Gp, St Bartholomew's Hosp., 1992–94; Council, British Mus. Soc., 1993–. Fellow, ACT, 1989. Liveryman, Innholders' Co., 1977. *Recreations:* archaeology, theatre, cricket, ski-ing. *Address:* Bank of England, EC2R 8AH. *T:* 071–601 4444. *Club:* Tillington Cricket (Hon. Sec, 1983–).

PLENDERLEITH, Thomas Donald; Hon. Fellow, Royal Society of Painter-Etchers and Engravers, 1987 (RE 1961 (retd); ARE 1951); Senior Art Master, St Nicholas Grammar School, Northwood, 1956–85, retired; *b* 11 March 1921; *s* of James Plenderleith and Georgina Ellis; *m* 1949, Joyce Rogers; one *s. Educ:* St Clement Danes; Ealing Sch. of Art; Hornsey Sch. of Art. Pilot, Bomber Command, RAF, 1941–46. Art Master, Pinner County Grammar Sch., 1948–56. Art Teacher's Diploma, 1947. *Recreations:* cricket, badminton. *Address:* Homelea, Tresean, Cubert, Newquay, Cornwall TR8 5HN.

PLEYDELL-BOUVERIE, family name of **Earl of Radnor.**

PLIATZKY, Sir Leo, KCB 1977 (CB 1972); Civil Service, 1947–80; *b* 1919; *m* 1948, Marian Jean Elias (*d* 1979); one *s* one *d. Educ:* Manchester Grammar Sch.; City of London Sch.; Corpus Christi Coll., Oxford (Hon. Fellow, 1980). First Cl. Classical Honour Mods, 1939. Served in RAOC and REME, 1940–45 (despatches). First Cl. Philosophy, Politics and Economics, 1946. Research Sec., Fabian Soc., 1946–47; Min. of Food, 1947–50; HM Treasury, 1950–77; Under-Sec., 1967; Dep. Sec., 1971; Second Permanent Sec., 1976; Permanent Sec., Dept of Trade, 1977; retired 1979, retained for special duties, 1979–80. Mem., British Airways Bd, 1980–84 (Non-exec. Dir, 1984–85); Director: Associated Communications Corporation Ltd, 1980–82; Central Independent Television plc, 1981–89; Ultramar plc, 1981–90. Chm., Industry Wkg Pty on Production of Television Commercials, 1986–89 (report published, 1987). Vis. Prof., City Univ., 1980–84; Associate Fellow, LSE, 1982–85; Sen. Res. Fellow, PSI, 1983–84. Trustee, History of Parliament Trust, 1982–, Treasurer 1983–94. Hon. DLitt Salford, 1986. *Publications:* Getting and Spending, 1982, rev. edn 1984; Paying and Choosing, 1985; The Treasury under Mrs Thatcher, 1989. *Address:* 27 River Court, Upper Ground, SE1 9PE. *T:* 0171–928 3667. *Club:* Reform.

PLOTKIN, Prof. Gordon David, PhD; FRS 1992; FRSE; Professor of Computation Theory, Edinburgh University, since 1986; *b* 9 Sept. 1946; *s* of Manuel Plotkin and Mary (*née* Levin); *m* 1984, Lynda (*née* Stephenson) (marr. diss.); one *s*; *m* 1994, Hephzibah (*née* Kolban). *Educ:* Univ. of Glasgow (BSc 1967); Univ. of Edinburgh (PhD 1972). University of Edinburgh: Res. Associate and Res. Fellow, 1971–72; Lectr, 1975; Reader, 1982–86. BP Venture Res. Fellow, 1981–87; SERC Sen. Res. Fellow, 1992. MAE 1989. *Publications:* (ed with G. Kahn) Semantics of Data Types, 1984; (ed with G. Huet) Logical Frameworks, 1991; (ed with J.-L. Lassez) Computational Logic: essays in honour of Alan Robinson, 1991; (ed jtly) Situation Theory and its Applications, 1991; (ed with G. Huet) Logical Environments, 1993; (ed with M. Dezani-Ciancaglini) Typed Lambda Calculi and Applications, 1995; contribs to jls of computer science and logic. *Recreations:* hill-walking, chess. *Address:* Department of Computer Science, University of Edinburgh, The King's Buildings, Edinburgh EH9 3JZ. *T:* 0131–650 5158.

PLOURDE, Most Rev. Joseph Aurèle; Archbishop of Ottawa (RC), 1967–89, now Emeritus; *b* 12 Jan. 1915; *s* of Antoine Plourde and Suzanne Albert. *Educ:* Bathurst Coll.; Bourget Coll., Rigaud; Major Seminary of Halifax; Inst. Catholique, Paris; Gregorian Univ., Rome. Auxiliary Bishop of Alexandria, Ont., 1964. Hon. DEducn, Moncton Univ., 1969. *Address:* Jean-Paul II Residence, 1243 Kilborn Place, Ottawa, Ont K1H 6K9, Canada.

PLOUVIEZ, Peter William; General Secretary, British Actors' Equity Association, 1974–91; *b* 30 July 1931; *s* of Charles and Emma Plouviez; *m* 1978, Alison Dorothy Macrae; two *d* by previous marr. *Educ:* Sir George Monoux Grammar Sch.; Hastings Grammar Sch. Greater London Organiser, NUBE, 1955–60; Asst Sec., 1960, Asst Gen. Sec., 1964, Equity. Contested (Lab), St Marylebone bye-election, 1963; Councillor, St Pancras, 1962–65. Chairman: Nat. Council for Drama Trng, 1991–; Equity Trust Fund, 1991– (Dir, 1989–); The Dancers' Trust, 1992–; Cttee for Protection of Artistic Freedom, 1992–, and Cttee for Live Performance, 1992–, Internat. Fedn of Actors; Vice-Chm., Theatres Trust, 1992– (Trustee, 1977–). Director: Children's Film and TV Foundn; Dance Companies Resettlement Fund, 1992–; Trustee: Evelyn Norris Trust, 1975–; Carl Rosa Trust Ltd, 1980–. FRSA 1992. *Recreation:* drawing. *Address:* c/o National Council for Drama Training, 5 Tavistock Place, WC1H 9SS. *Club:* Green Room.

PLOWDEN, family name of **Baron Plowden.**

PLOWDEN, Baron, *cr* 1959, of Plowden (Life Peer); **Edwin Noel Plowden,** GBE 1987 (KBE 1946); KCB 1951; *b* 6 Jan. 1907; 4th *s* of late Roger H. Plowden; *m* 1933, Bridget Horatia (*see* Lady Plowden); two *s* two *d. Educ:* Switzerland; Pembroke College, Cambridge (Hon. Fellow, 1958). Temporary Civil Servant Ministry of Economic Warfare, 1939–40; Ministry of Aircraft Production, 1940–46; Chief Executive, and Member of Aircraft Supply Council, 1945–46; Vice-Chairman Temporary Council Cttee of NATO, 1951–52; Cabinet Office, 1947; Treasury, 1947–53, as Chief Planning Officer and Chairman of Economic Planning Board. Adviser on Atomic Energy Organization, 1953–54; Chairman, Atomic Energy Authority, 1954–59; Visiting Fellow, Nuffield College, 1956–64; Chm. Cttee of Enquiry: Treasury control of Public Expenditure, 1959–61; organisation of Representational Services Overseas, 1963–64; Aircraft Industry, 1964–65; Structure of Electricity Supply Industry in England and Wales, 1974–75; into CBI's aims and organisation, 1974–75; Dep. Chm., Cttee of Inquiry on Police, 1977–79; Chm., Police Complaints Bd, 1976–81; Independent Chm., Police Negotiating Bd, 1979–82; Chm., Top Salaries Review Body, 1981–89 (Mem., 1977–). Pres., TI Gp (formerly Tube Investments Ltd), 1976–90 (Chm., 1963–76); Director: Commercial Union Assurance Co. Ltd, 1946–78; National Westminster Bank Ltd, 1960–77; Chm., Equity Capital for Industry Ltd, 1976–82; Mem., Internat. Adv. Bd, Southeast Bank NA, 1982–86. Chm., CBI Companies Cttee, 1976–80; Vice-Chm., CBI Pres.'s Cttee, 1977–80. Pres., London Graduate Sch. of Business Studies, 1976–90 (Chm. 1964–76); Chm., Standing Adv. Cttee on Pay of Higher Civil Service, 1968–70; Member: Civil Service Coll. Adv. Council, 1970–76; Engineering Industries Council, 1976; Ford European Adv. Council, 1976–83. Hon. Fellow, London Business Sch., 1988. Hon. DSc: Pennsylvania State Univ., 1958; Univ. of Aston, 1972; Hon. DLitt, Loughborough, 1976. *Publication:* An Industrialist in the Treasury: the post war years (autobiog.), 1989. *Address:* Martels Manor, Dunmow,

Essex CM6 1NB. *T:* Great Dunmow (01371) 872141; 11 Abingdon Gardens, 40 Abingdon Villas, W8 6BY. *T:* 0171–937 4238.

See also W. J. L. Plowden.

PLOWDEN, Lady, (Bridget Horatia), DBE 1972; Chairman: Independent Broadcasting Authority, 1975–80; Training Commission (formerly Manpower Services Commission) Area Manpower Board, North London, 1983–88; 2nd *d* of late Admiral Sir H. W. Richmond, KCB, and of Lady Richmond (Elsa, *née* Bell); *m* 1933, Baron Plowden, *qv*; two *s* two *d*. *Educ:* Downe House. Dir, Trust Houses Forte Ltd, 1961–72. A Governor and Vice-Chm., BBC, 1970–75. Chairman: Mary Feilding Guild (formerly Working Ladies Guild), 1945–88 (Pres., 1992–) Professional Classes Aid Council, 1958–73 (Pres., 1973–86); Central Adv. Council for Educn (England), 1963–66; Metropolitan Architectural Consortium for Educn, 1968–79; Member: (Co-opted) Educn Cttee, ILEA, 1967–73 (Vice-Chm., ILEA Schs Sub-Cttee, 1967–70); Houghton Inquiry into Pay of Teachers, 1974; President: Relate (formerly Nat. Marriage Guidance Council), 1983–93; Adv. Cttee for Educn of Romany and other Travellers, 1983– (Chm., 1973–83); Voluntary Orgns Liaison Council for Under-Fives, 1985– (Founder and Chm., 1978); Pre-School Playgroups Assoc., 1972–82 (Vice-Pres., 1982–); Nat. Inst. of Continuing Adult Educn, 1981–88; Coll. of Preceptors, 1987–94 (Vice-Pres., 1983; Hon. Fellow, 1973); Harding House Assoc.; Delves House, 1961–88 (formerly Chm.). Member: Nat. Theatre Bd, 1976–88; Drake Fellowship, 1981–87; Fairbridge/Drake Soc., 1988–89. Chairman: Governors, Philippa Fawcett Coll. of Educn, 1967–76; Robert Montefiore Comprehensive Sch., 1968–78. Liveryman, Goldsmiths' Co., 1979–. JP Inner London Area Juvenile Panel, 1962–71. FRTS 1980. Hon. LLD: Leicester, 1968; Reading, 1970; London, 1976; Hon. DLitt Loughborough, 1976; DUniv Open, 1974. *Address:* Martels Manor, Dunmow, Essex CM6 1NB. *T:* Great Dunmow (01371) 872141; 11 Abingdon Gardens, 40 Abingdon Villas, W8 6BY. *T:* 0171–937 4238.

See also W. J. L. Plowden.

PLOWDEN, William Julius Lowthian, PhD; independent consultant; Senior Adviser, Harkness Fellowships, London, since 1991; Associate Director, Atlantic Fellowships, since 1995; *b* 7 Feb. 1935; *s* of Lord and Lady Plowden, *qqv*; *m* 1960, Veronica Gascoigne; two *s* two *d*. *Educ:* Eton; King's Coll., Cambridge (BA, PhD); Univ. of Calif, Berkeley. Staff Writer, Economist, 1959–60; BoT, 1960–65; Lectr in Govt, LSE, 1965–71; Central Policy Review Staff, Cabinet Office, 1971–77; Under Sec., Dept of Industry, 1977–78; Dir-Gen., RIPA, 1978–88; Exec. Dir, UK Harkness Fellowships, NY, 1988–91. Hon. Prof., Dept of Politics, Univ. of Warwick, 1977–82; Vis. Prof. in Govt, LSE, 1982–88; Vis. Prof., Univ. of Bath, 1992–; Sen. Res. Associate, IPPR, 1992–94; Vis. Sen. Res. Fellow, London Business Sch., 1993–94. Mem., W Lambeth DHA, 1982–87. Trustee: CSV, 1984–; Public Mgt Foundn, 1992–; Southern Africa Advanced Educn Project, 1986–. Mem. Ct of Govs, LSE, 1987–. *Publications:* The Motor Car and Politics in Britain, 1971; (with Tessa Blackstone) Inside the Think Tank: advising the Cabinet 1971–1983, 1988; Mandarins and Ministers, 1994. *Address:* 49 Stockwell Park Road, SW9 0DD. *T:* 0171–274 4535.

PLOWDEN ROBERTS, Hugh Martin; Director, Argyll Group plc, since 1983; *b* 6 Aug. 1932; *s* of Stanley and Joan Plowden Roberts; *m* 1956, Susan Jane Patrick; two *d*. *Educ:* St Edward's School, Oxford; St Edmund Hall, Oxford. BA 1954, MA 1956. FIGD 1980. Payne & Son Meat Group, 1954–60 (Dir, 1958); Asst Gen. Manager (Meat Group), Co-operative Wholesale Society, 1960–67; Allied Suppliers Ltd, 1967–82: Dir, 1971; Dep. Man. Dir, 1974; Man. Dir, 1978; Chm., 1980–82; Dir, Cavenham Ltd, 1979, Chm., 1981–82; Dep. Chm., Argyll Stores Ltd, 1983–85; Chm., Dairy Crest Foods, subseq. Dairy Crest Ltd, 1985–88; Dir, Lawson Mardon Group Ltd, 1987–91. Comr, Meat and Livestock Commn, 1975–79; Mem., MMB, 1983–89. *Recreations:* country pursuits. *Address:* Barn Cottage, Fulking, Henfield, W Sussex BN5 9NH. *T:* Brighton (01273) 857622. *Club:* Farmers'.

PLOWMAN, John Patrick; Director, Wildlife and Countryside, Department of the Environment, since 1994; *b* 20 March 1944; *s* of late Robert and of Ruth Plowman, Bolter End, Bucks; *m* 1973, Daphne Margaret Brock Kennett; two *s* one *d*. *Educ:* St Edward's Sch., Oxford; Grenoble Univ.; University Coll., Univ. of Durham (BA). MoD, 1967–75: Private Office, Minister of State for Defence, 1969–71; Resident Observer, CSSB, 1975; Cabinet Office, 1976–78; MoD and UK Delegn to UN Law of Sea Conf., 1979–81; Asst Sec., DoE, 1982–86; Counsellor, UK Repn to EC, 1986–90; Head, Envmtl Protection (Europe), 1990–93; Regl Dir for NW, DoE and Dept of Transport, 1993–94. Served Royal Marines Reserve, 1968–71. *Recreations:* music, fishing, tennis, cricket. *Address:* (office) 2 Marsham Street, SW1. *T:* 0171–276 3682. *Club:* Royal Over-Seas League.

PLOWMAN, Hon. Sir John (Robin), Kt 1979; CBE 1970 (OBE 1949); Member of the Legislative Council, later Senator, Bermuda, 1966–82, Government Leader in the Senate, 1968–82; Minister of Government and Commercial Services, Bermuda, 1980–82; *b* Bermuda, 18 Sept. 1908; *s* of Owen and Elizabeth Plowman; *m* 1936, Marjorie Hardwick (*d* 1990); two *s*. *Educ:* Bermuda and England. Member, Ealing Borough Council, 1931–35; returned to Bermuda, 1935; Bermuda Volunteer Engineers, 1939–42; Dep. Dir, Dir and later Chm. of Bermuda Supplies Commission, 1942–47; Man. Director of Holmes, Williams & Purvey Ltd, 1947–78, Chairman of Board, 1961–. Chm. or Mem. of various govt commns and bds, including Training and Employment, Ports Facilities, Transport Control and Civil Service; Minister of Organisation, 1968–77; Minister of Marine and Air Services, 1977–80. Attached to UK negotiating team for Bermuda II Civil Aviation agreement, 1977. Chm. Bd of Governors, Warwick Academy, 1946–73; Life Vice-Pres. Bermuda Olympic Assoc. and Bermuda Football Assoc. *Recreations:* golf, sports administration. *Address:* Chiswick, Paget, Bermuda. *Clubs:* Carlton; Royal Hamilton Dinghy and Mid-Ocean (Bermuda).

PLOWRIGHT, David Ernest; international television production and broadcasting consultant; Chairman, Granada Television Ltd, 1987–92; Deputy Chairman, Channel Four Television, since 1992; Visiting Professor in Media Studies, Salford University, since 1992; *b* 11 Dec. 1930; *s* of late William Ernest Plowright and of Daisy Margaret Plowright; *m* 1953, Brenda Mary (*née* Key); one *s* two *d*. *Educ:* Scunthorpe Grammar Sch.; on local weekly newspaper and during National Service, Germany. Reporter, Scunthorpe Star, 1950; freelance corresp. and sports writer, 1952; Reporter, Feature Writer and briefly Equestrian Corresp., Yorkshire Post, 1954; Granada Television: News Editor, 1957; Producer, Current Affairs, 1960; Editor, World in Action, 1966; Head of Current Affairs, 1968; Controller of Programmes, 1969–79; Jt Man. Dir, 1975–81; Man. Dir, 1981–87; Director: Granada Internat., 1975–92; Granada Gp, 1981–92. Chm., Network Programme Cttee, ITV, 1980–82. Chm., ITCA, 1984–86. Director: Superchannel, 1986–89; Merseyside Tourism Board, 1986–88; British Satellite Broadcasting, 1987–90; British Screen, 1988–92; Tate Gall., Liverpool, 1988–91. Vice Pres., RTS, 1982–94; Member: Steering Cttee, European Film and TV Forum, 1988–91; Internat. Council, Nat. Acad. for TV Arts and Scis, 1988–92; Manchester Olympic Bid Cttee, 1988; Chm. Develt Cttee, Manchester City of Drama 1994, 1992–94. Trustee, BAFTA (Fellow, 1992). Gov., Manchester Polytechnic, 1988–90. Hon. DLitt Salford, 1989; Hon. DArt Liverpool Poly., 1991. *Recreations:* television, watching sport, messing about in a boat. *Address:* Westways, Wilmslow Road, Mottram St Andrew, Cheshire SK10 4QT. *T:* Wilmslow (01625) 820948.

See also J. A. Plowright.

PLOWRIGHT, Joan Ann, (The Lady Olivier), CBE 1970; leading actress with the National Theatre, 1963–74; Member of the RADA Council; *b* 28 Oct. 1929; *d* of late William Ernest Plowright and of Daisy Margaret (*née* Burton); *m* 1st, 1953, Roger Gage (marr. diss.); 2nd, 1961, (as Sir Laurence Olivier) Baron Olivier, OM (*d* 1989); one *s* two *d*. *Educ:* Scunthorpe Grammar School; Laban Art of Movement Studio; Old Vic Theatre School. First stage appearance in If Four Walls Told, Croydon Rep. Theatre, 1948; Bristol Old Vic and Mem. Old Vic Co., S Africa tour, 1952; first London appearance in The Duenna, Westminster, 1954; Moby Dick, Duke of York's, 1955; season of leading parts, Nottingham Playhouse, 1955–56; English Stage Co., Royal Court, 1956; The Crucible, Don Juan, The Death of Satan, Cards of Identity, The Good Woman of Setzuan, The Country Wife (transferred to Adelphi, 1957); The Chairs, The Making of Moo, Royal Court, 1957; The Entertainer, Palace, 1957; The Chairs, The Lesson, Phoenix, NY, 1958; The Entertainer, Royale, NY, 1958; The Chairs, The Lesson, Major Barbara, Royal Court, 1958; Hook, Line and Sinker, Piccadilly, 1958; Roots, Royal Court, Duke of York's, 1959; Rhinoceros, Royal Court, 1960; A Taste of Honey, Lyceum, NY, 1960 (Best Actress Tony Award); Rosmersholm, Greenwich, 1973; Saturday, Sunday, Monday, Queen's, 1974–75; The Sea Gull, Lyric, 1975; The Bed Before Yesterday, Lyric, 1975 (Variety Club of GB Award, 1977); Filumena, Lyric, 1977 (Soc. of West End Theatre Award, 1978); Enjoy, Vaudeville, 1980; The Cherry Orchard, Haymarket, 1983; The House of Bernada Alba, Globe, 1986; Time and the Conways, Old Vic, 1990; If We are Women, Greenwich, 1995; Chichester Festival: Uncle Vanya, The Chances, 1962; St Joan (Best Actress Evening Standard Award), Uncle Vanya, 1963; The Doctor's Dilemma, The Taming of the Shrew, 1972; Cavell, 1982; The Way of the World, 1984; National Theatre: St Joan, Uncle Vanya, Hobson's Choice, opening season, 1963; The Master Builder, 1964; Much Ado About Nothing, 1967, 1968; Three Sisters, 1967, 1968; Tartuffe, 1967, 1968; The Advertisement, 1968; Love's Labour's Lost, 1968; The Merchant of Venice, 1970; A Woman Killed With Kindness, 1971; The Rules of the Game, 1971; Eden End, 1974; Mrs Warren's Profession, 1985. Produced, The Travails of Sancho Panza, 1969; directed: Rites, 1969; A Prayer for Wings, 1985; Married Love, 1988; Time and the Conways, 1990. *Films include:* The Entertainer, 1960; Three Sisters, 1970; Equus; Britannia Hospital, 1982; Wagner, Revolution, 1985; Drowning by Numbers, The Dressmaker, 1988; I Love You to Death, Avalon, 1989; Stalin, 1992 (Golden Globe Award, 1993); Enchanted April, 1993 (Golden Globe Award, 1993); Denis the Menace, A Place for Annie, A Pin for the Butterfly, Widow's Peak, Last Action Hero, 1993; On Promised Land, Hotel Sorrento, A Pyromaniac's Love Story, The Scarlett Letter, 1994; *films for TV:* The Merchant of Venice, Brimstone and Treacle, A Dedicated Man; other *television* appearances include: Daphne Laureola, 1976; The Birthday Party, 1987; The Importance of Being Earnest, 1988; And a Nightingale Sang, 1989; House of Bernada Alba, 1991; Clothes in the Wardrobe, 1992. 18th annual Crystal Award, Women in Film, USA. *Recreations:* reading, music, entertaining. *Address:* c/o Write On Cue, Third Floor, 15 New Row, WC2N 4LA; ICM, 76 Oxford Street, W1R 1RB.

See also D. E. Plowright.

PLOWRIGHT, Rosalind Anne, (Mrs J. A. Kaye); soprano; *b* 21 May 1949; *d* of Robert Arthur Plowright and Celia Adelaide Plowright; *m* 1984, James Anthony Kaye; one *s* one *d*. *Educ:* Notre Dame High Sch., Wigan; Royal Northern Coll. of Music, Manchester. LRAM. London Opera Centre, 1974–75; Glyndebourne Chorus and Touring Co., début as Agathe in Der Freischutz, 1975; WNO, ENO, Kent Opera, 1975–78; Miss Jessel in Turn of the Screw, ENO, 1979 (SWET award); début at Covent Garden as Ortlinde in Die Walküre, 1980; with Bern Opera, 1980–81, Frankfurt Opera and Munich Opera, 1981; débuts: in USA (Philadelphia and San Diego), Paris, Madrid and Hamburg, 1982; at La Scala, Milan, Edinburgh Fest., San Francisco and New York (Carnegie Hall), 1983; in Berlin, 1984; in Houston, Pittsburgh, Verona, Montpellier and Venice, 1985; in Rome, Florence and Holland, 1986; in Tulsa, Buenos Aires, Santiago di Chile, Israel and Bonn, 1987; with NY Phil. and Paris Opera, 1987; in Lausanne, Geneva, Oviedo and Bilbao, 1988; in Zurich, Copenhagen, Lisbon and Torre del Lago, 1989; with Vienna State Opera, 1990; in Nice, 1991; in Wiesbaden, 1992; in Leeds, 1993; in Athens and Bregenz, 1994. Principal rôles include: Ariadne; Aida; Amelia in Un Ballo in Maschera; Leonora in Il Trovatore; Leonora in La Forza del Destino; Desdemona in Otello; Violetta in La Traviata; Elena in I Vespri Siciliani; Abigaille in Nabucco; Elisabetta in Don Carlos; Lady Macbeth; Manon Lescaut; Giorgetta in Il Tabarro; Suor Angelica; Norma; Alceste; Médée; Maddalena in Andrea Chénier; La Gioconda; Tatyana in Eugene Onegin; Tosca. Has given recitals and concerts in UK, USA and Europe, made opera and concert recordings, and opera telecasts; acting début, House of Elliott, TV serial, 1993. First prize, 7th Internat. Comp. for Opera Singers, Sofia, 1979; Prix Fondation Fanny Heldy, Acad. Nat. du Disque Lyrique, 1985. *Recreation:* fell walking. *Address:* c/o Artists Management Ltd, 2 Fir Hill Villas, Hollywater Road, Bordon, Hants GU35 0AG.

PLOWRIGHT, Walter, CMG 1974; DVSc; FRS 1981; FRCVS; Head, Department of Microbiology, ARC Institute for Research on Animal Diseases, Compton, Berks, 1978–83; *b* 20 July 1923; 2nd *s* of Jonathan and Mahala Plowright, Holbeach, Lincs; *m* 1959, Dorothy Joy (*née* Bell). *Educ:* Moulton and Spalding Grammar Schs; Royal Veterinary Coll., London. DVSc (Pret.) 1964; MRCVS 1944; FRCVS 1977; FRVC 1987. Commissioned, RAVC, 1945–48; Colonial Service, 1950–64; Animal Virus Research Inst., Pirbright, 1964–71 (seconded E Africa, 1966–71); Prof. of Vet. Microbiology, RVC, 1971–78. Hon. Mem., Acad. Royale des Sciences d'Outre-Mer, Brussels, 1986. Hon. DSc: Univ. of Nairobi, 1984; Reading, 1986. J. T. Edwards Memorial Prize, 1964; R. B. Bennett Commonwealth Prize of RSA, 1972; Bledisloe Vet. Award, RASE, 1979; King Baudouin Internat. Develt Prize, 1984; Dalrymple-Champneys Cup, BVA, 1984; Gold Award, Office Internat. des Epizooties, Paris, 1988; Outstanding Scientific Achievement Award, Animal Health Trust, 1991; Theiler Meml Trust Award, South Africa, 1994. *Publications:* numerous contribs to scientific jls relating to virus diseases of animals. *Recreations:* gardening, travel. *Address:* Whitehill Lodge, Goring-on-Thames, Reading RG8 0LL. *T:* Goring (01491) 872891.

PLUM, Patrick; *see* McConville, M. A.

PLUMB, family name of **Baron Plumb**.

PLUMB, Baron *cr* 1987 (Life Peer), of Coleshill in the County of Warwickshire; **Charles Henry Plumb;** Kt 1973; DL; Member (C) The Cotswolds, European Parliament, since 1979; *b* 27 March 1925; *s* of Charles and Louise Plumb; *m* 1947, Marjorie Dorothy Dunn; one *s* two *d*. *Educ:* King Edward VI School, Nuneaton. National Farmers Union: Member Council, 1959; Vice-President, 1964, 1965; Deputy-President, 1966, 1967, 1968, 1969; President, 1970–79. European Parliament: Chm., Agricl Cttee, 1979–82; Leader, EDG, 1982–87; Pres., 1987–89. Chm., British Agricl Council, 1975–79. Chm., Agricultural Mortgage Corp., 1994–95. Mem., Duke of Northumberland's Cttee of Enquiry on Foot and Mouth Disease, 1967–68; Member Council: CBI; Animal Health Trust. Chm.,

Internat. Agricl Trng Programme, 1987–. Pres., Royal Agric. Soc. of England, 1977, Dep. Pres. 1978; President: Internat. Fedn of Agricl Producers, 1979–82; Comité des Organisations Professionels Agricoles de la CEE (COPA), 1975–77. Pres., Nat. Fedn of Young Farmers' Clubs, 1976–; Patron, Warwicks Co. Fedn of YFC, 1974–; Hon. Pres., Ayrshire Cattle Soc. Liveryman, Farmers' Co. FRSA 1970; FRAgS 1974. DL Warwick 1977. Hon. DSc Cranfield, 1983. Order of Merit (FRG), 1979. *Recreations:* country pursuits, fishing. *Address:* The Dairy Farm, Maxstoke, Coleshill, Warwicks B46 2QJ. *T:* Coleshill (01675) 463133, *Fax:* Coleshill (01675) 464156; 2 Queen Anne's Gate, SW1H 9AA. *T:* 0171–222 0411. *Clubs:* St Stephen's Constitutional, Farmers', Coleshill Rotary (Hon. Member).

PLUMB, Sir John (Harold), Kt 1982; FBA 1968; historian; Master of Christ's College, Cambridge, 1978–82; Professor of Modern English History, University of Cambridge, 1966–74, now Emeritus; *b* 20 Aug. 1911; 3rd *s* of late James Plumb, Leicester. *Educ:* Alderman Newton's Sch., Leicester; University Coll., Leicester; Christ's Coll., Cambridge. BA London, 1st Class Hons History, 1933; PhD Cambridge, 1936; LittD Cambridge, 1957. Ehrman Research Fellow, King's Coll., Cambridge, 1939–46; FO, 1940–45; Fellow of Christ's Coll., 1946–, Steward, 1948–50, Tutor, 1950–59. Vice-Master, 1964–68. Univ. Lectr in History, 1946–62; Reader in Modern English History, 1962–65; Chm. of History Faculty, 1966–68, Univ. of Cambridge. Trustee: National Portrait Gallery, 1961–82; Fitzwilliam Museum, 1985–92 (Syndic, 1960–77); Member: Wine Standards Bd, 1973–75; Council, British Acad., 1977–80; Chm., Centre of E Anglian Studies, 1979–82. FRHistS; FSA; FRSL 1969. Visiting Prof., Columbia Univ., 1960; Distinguished Vis. Prof., NYC Univ., 1971–72, 1976; Cecil and Ida Green Honors Chair, Texas Christian Univ., 1974; Dist. Vis. Prof., Washington Univ., 1977; Lectures: Ford's, Oxford Univ., 1965–66; Saposnekov, City College, NY, 1968; Guy Stanton Ford, Univ. of Minnesota, 1969; Stenton, Reading, 1972; George Rogers Clark, Soc. of the Cincinnati, 1977. Chm., British Inst. of America, 1982–90; Hon. For. Mem., Amer. Acad. for Arts and Sciences, 1970; Hon. Member: Soc. of Amer. Historians, 1976; Amer. Historical Assoc., 1981. Hon. DLitt: Leicester, 1968; East Anglia, 1973; Bowdoin Coll., 1974; S California, 1978; Westminster Coll., 1983; Washington Univ., St Louis, 1983; Bard Coll., NY, 1988. Editor, History of Human Society, 1959–; Sen. Editor to American Heritage Co. Historical Adviser, Penguin Books, 1960–92; Editor, Pelican Social History of Britain, 1982–. *Publications:* England in the Eighteenth Century, 1950; (with C. Howard) West African Explorers, 1952; Chatham, 1953; (ed) Studies in Social History, 1955; Sir Robert Walpole, Vol. I, 1956, Vol. II, 1960, both vols repr. 1972; The First Four Georges, 1956; The Renaissance, 1961; Men and Places, 1962; Crisis in the Humanities, 1964; The Growth of Political Stability in England, 1675–1725, 1967; Death of the Past, 1969; In the Light of History, 1972; The Commercialisation of Leisure, 1974; Royal Heritage, 1977; New Light on the Tyrant, George III, 1978; Georgian Delights, 1980; Royal Heritage: The Reign of Elizabeth II, 1980; (with Neil McKendrick and John Brewer) The Birth of a Consumer Society, 1982; Collected Essays: Vol. I, The Making of a Historian, 1988; Vol. II, The American Experience, 1989; *contrib. to:* Man versus Society in Eighteenth Century Britain, 1968; Churchill Revised, 1969 (Churchill, the historian); *festschrift:* Historical Perspectives: Essays in Honour of J. H. Plumb, 1974. *Address:* Christ's College, Cambridge CB2 3BU. *T:* Cambridge (01223) 334900. *Club:* Brooks's.

PLUMBLY, Derek John, CMG 1991; HM Diplomatic Service; Head of Chancery, UK Mission to the United Nations, New York, since 1992; *b* 15 May 1948; *s* of late John C. Plumbly and Jean Elizabeth (*née* Baker); *m* 1979, Nadia Gohar; two *s* one *d*. *Educ:* Brockenhurst Grammar Sch.; Magdalen Coll., Oxford (BA PPE). VSO, Pakistan, 1970; Third Sec., FCO, 1972; MECAS, 1973; Second Sec., Jedda, 1975; First Sec., Cairo, 1977; FCO, 1980; First Sec., Washington, 1984; Dep. Head of Mission, Riyadh, 1988. *Address:* c/o Foreign and Commonwealth Office, King Charles Street, SW1A 2AL.

PLUME, John Trevor; Regional Chairman, Industrial Tribunals (London North), 1984–87, *b* 5 Oct. 1914; *s* of William Thomas and Gertrude Plume; *m* 1948, Christine Mary Wells; one *d*. *Educ:* City of London School; Inns of Court School of Law. Called to the Bar, Gray's Inn, 1936, Bencher, 1969. Legal Associate Mem., Town Planning Inst., 1939; served Royal Artillery, 1940–46 (Captain). Practiced at Bar, specialising in property law, 1936–76; Chm., Industrial Tribunals, 1976–87. Liveryman, Clockmakers' Co. *Recreations:* beekeeping, carpentry, gardening, fishing. *Address:* Mulberry Cottage, Forest Side, Epping, Essex CM16 4ED. *T:* Epping (01992) 572389.

PLUMLEY, Rev. Prof. Jack Martin; Herbert Thompson Professor of Egyptology, 1957–77, and Fellow of Selwyn College, since 1957, University of Cambridge; Priest-in-Charge, Longstowe, Cambs, 1981–95; *b* 2 Sept. 1910; *e s* of Arthur Henry Plumley and Lily Plumley (*née* Martin); *m* 1st, 1938, Gwendolen Alice Darling (*d* 1984); three *s*; 2nd, 1986, Ursula Clara Dowle. *Educ:* Merchant Taylors' Sch., London; St John's Coll., Durham (BA, Univ. Hebrew Schol., MLitt); King's Coll., Cambridge (MA). Deacon 1933; Priest 1934; curacies, 1933–41; Vicar of Christ Church, Hoxton, 1942–45, of St Paul's, Tottenham, 1945–47; Rector and Vicar of All Saints', Milton, Cambridge, 1948–57; Cambridge University: Associate Lectr in Coptic, 1949–57; Acting Dean, Pembroke Coll., 1981–82; Mem. Council of Senate, 1965–70. Stephen Glanville Meml Lectr, Fitzwilliam Mus., Cambridge, 1982. Dir of excavations on behalf of Egypt Exploration Soc. at Qasr Ibrim, Nubia, 1963, 1964, 1966, 1969, 1972, 1974, 1976; Chm., British Cttee of Internat. Critical Greek New Testament Project, 1963–87. Pres., Internat. Soc. for Nubian Studies, 1978–82, Patron, 1982–. FSA 1966; Fellow, Inst. of Coptic Studies, United Egyptian Repub., 1966; Corresp. Mem., German Inst. of Archaeology, 1966. *Recreations:* music, rowing, photography, travel. *Address:* Selwyn College, Cambridge CB3 9DQ; 13 Lyndewode Road, Cambridge CB1 2HL. *T:* Cambridge (01223) 350328.

PLUMMER, family name of **Baron Plummer of St Marylebone.**

PLUMMER OF ST MARYLEBONE, Baron *cr* 1981 (Life Peer), of the City of Westminster; **(Arthur) Desmond (Herne) Plummer;** Kt 1971; TD 1950; JP; DL; President, Portman Building Society, since 1990 (Chairman, 1983–90); *b* 25 May 1914; *s* of late Arthur Herne Plummer and Janet (*née* McCormick); *m* 1941, Pat Holloway (Pres., Cons. Women's Adv. Cttee, Greater London Area, 1967–71); one *d*. *Educ:* Hurstpierpoint Coll.; Coll. of Estate Management. Served 1939–46, Royal Engineers. Member: TA Sports Bd, 1953–79; London Electricity Consultative Council, 1955–66; St Marylebone Borough Council, 1952–65 (Mayor, 1958–59); LCC, for St Marylebone, 1960–65; Inner London Educn Authority, 1964–76. Greater London Council: Mem. for Cities of London and Westminster, 1964–73, for St Marylebone, 1973–76; Leader of Opposition, 1966–67 and 1973–74; Leader of Council, 1967–73. Member: South Bank Theatre Board, 1967–74; Standing Conf. on SE Planning, 1967–74; Transport Co-ordinating Council for London, 1967–69; Local Authorities Conditions of Service Adv. Bd, 1967–71; Exec. Cttee, British Section of Internat. Union of Local Authorities, 1967–74; St John Council for London, 1971–94; Exec. Cttee, Nat. Union Cons. and Unionist Assocs, 1967–76; Chm., St Marylebone Conservative Assoc., 1965–66. Chm., Horserace Betting Levy Bd, 1974–82; Dep. Chm., Nat. Employers' Mutual Gen. Insurance Assoc., 1973–86; Chm., Nat. Employers' Life Assce, 1983–89; Pres., Met. Assoc. of Bldg Socs, 1983–89. Member of Lloyd's. Mem. Court, Univ. of London, 1967–77. Chairman: Epsom and Walton Downs Trng Grounds Man. Bd, 1974–82; National Stud, 1975–82; President: London Anglers' Assoc., 1976–; Thames Angling Preservation Soc., 1970–. Liveryman, Worshipful Co. of Tin Plateworkers. FAI 1948; FRICS 1970; FRSA 1974; Hon. FFAS 1966. JP, Co. London, 1958; DL Greater London, 1970. KStJ 1986. *Publications:* Time for Change in Greater London, 1966; Report to London, 1970; Planning and Participation, 1973. *Recreations:* swimming (Capt. Otter Swimming Club, 1952–53); growing things, horse racing, swimming. *Address:* 4 The Lane, St Johns Wood, NW8 0PN. *Clubs:* Carlton (Chm., Political Cttee, 1979–84; Pres., 1984–), Royal Automobile, MCC.

PLUMMER, (Arthur) Christopher (Orme), CC (Canada) 1968; actor; *b* Toronto, 13 Dec. 1929; *m* 1st, 1956, Tammy Lee Grimes; one *d*; 2nd, 1962, Patricia Audrey Lewis (marr. diss. 1966); 3rd, 1970, Elaine Regina Taylor. *Educ:* public and private schs, Montreal. French and English radio, Canada, 1949–52; Ottawa Rep. Theatre; Broadway: Starcross Story, 1951–52; Home is the Hero, 1953; The Dark is Light Enough, 1954 (Theatre World Award); The Lark, 1955; J. B., 1958 (Tony nomination); Arturo Ui, 1963; Royal Hunt of the Sun, 1965–66; Stratford, Conn, 1955: Mark Antony, Ferdinand; leading actor, Stratford Festival, Canada, 1956–67: Henry V, The Bastard, Hamlet, Leontes, Mercutio, Macbeth, Cyrano de Bergerac, Benedic, Aguecheek, Antony; Royal Shakespeare Co., Stratford-on-Avon, 1961–62: Benedic, Richard III; London debut as Henry II in Becket, Aldwych and Globe, 1961 (Evening Standard Best Actor Award, 1961); National Theatre, 1971–72: Amphytrion 38, Danton's Death; Broadway musical, Cyrano, 1973 (Outer Critics Circle Award and Tony Award for Best Actor in a Musical, NY Drama Desk Award); The Good Doctor, NY, 1974; Iago in Othello, NY, 1982 (Drama Desk Award); Macbeth, NY, 1988; No Man's Land, NY, 1994. *Films:* Stage-Struck, 1956; Across the Everglades, 1957; The Fall of the Roman Empire, 1963; The Sound of Music, 1964 (Golden Badge of Honour, Austria); Daisy Clover, 1964; Triple Cross, 1966; Oedipus Rex, 1967; The Battle of Britain, 1968; Royal Hunt of the Sun, 1969; The Pyx, 1973; The Man Who Would Be King, 1975; Aces High, 1976; The Moneychangers, 1976 (Emmy Award); International Velvet, 1978; The Silent Partner, 1978; Hanover Street, 1979; Murder by Decree, 1980 (Genie Award, Canada); The Disappearance, 1981; The Janitor, 1981; The Amateur, 1982; Dreamscape, 1984; Playing for Keeps, 1985; Lily in Love, 1985; Souvenir, 1989; Where The Heart Is, 1990, and others. TV appearances, Britain, Denmark, and major N American networks, incl. Hamlet at Elsinore, BBC and Danish TV, 1964 (4 Emmy Award nominations). First entertainer to win Maple Leaf Award (Arts and Letters), 1982. *Recreations:* tennis, ski-ing, piano. *Clubs:* Players, River (New York).

PLUMMER, Christopher; *see* Plummer, A. C. O.

PLUMMER, Maj.-Gen. Leo Heathcote, CBE 1974; retired 1979; *b* 11 June 1923; *s* of Lt-Col Edmund Waller Plummer and Mary Dorothy Brookesmith; *m* 1955, Judyth Ann Dolby; three *d*. *Educ:* Canford Sch.; Queens' Coll., Cambridge. Commnd RA, 1943; War Service, N Africa, Sicily, Italy, 1943–45 (mentioned in despatches, 1945); Adjt, TA, 1947–49; Staff Coll., Camberley, 1952, Directing Staff, 1961–63; Comdt, Sudan Staff Coll., 1963–65; CO, 20 Heavy Regt, 1965–67; Col, Gen. Staff, MoD, 1967; Brig., 1967; Comdr, 1st Artillery Bde, 1967–70; Dep. Dir Manning (Army), 1971–74; Asst Chief of Staff Ops, HQ Northern Army Gp, 1974–76; Chief, Jt Service Liaison Orgn, Bonn, 1976–78. ADC to HM The Queen, 1974–76; Col Comdt, RA, 1981–86. Chm., Civil Service Commn Selection Bd, 1983–91. *Recreation:* gardening. *Address:* Vivers Lodge, Old Road, Kirkbymoorside, York YO6 6BD. *Club:* Army and Navy.

PLUMMER, Peter Edward; Deputy Director, Department for National Savings, 1972–79; *b* 4 Nov. 1919; *s* of Arthur William John and Ethel May Plummer; *m* 1949, Pauline Wheelwright; one *s* one *d*. *Educ:* Watford Grammar Sch. Served War, REME, 1941–46. Customs and Excise, 1936–38; Dept for National Savings, 1938–79; Principal, 1956; Assistant Sec., 1964; seconded to Nat. Giro, 1970–71; Under-Sec., 1972. *Recreations:* gardening, photography. *Address:* Old Timbers, Farm Lane, Nutbourne, Chichester, W Sussex P018 8SA. *T:* Emsworth (01243) 77450.

PLUMPTON, Alan, CBE 1980; BSc, FEng 1991; FIEE; Chairman: Schlumberger plc, since 1992; Beaufort Management Consultants, since 1992; Manx Electricity Authority, since 1986; *b* 24 Nov. 1926; *s* of late John Plumpton and of Doris Plumpton; *m* 1950, Audrey Smith; one *s* one *d*. *Educ:* Sunderland Technical Sch.; Durham Univ. (BSc Elec. Eng). Pupil Engr, Sunderland Corp. Elec. Undertaking, 1942; various engrg and commercial appts, NEEB, 1948–61; Dist Manager, E Monmouthshire Dist, S Wales Electricity Bd, 1961–64. Admin. Staff Coll., Henley, 1963; Dep. Chief Commercial Engr, S Wales Elec. Bd, 1964–67; Chief Commercial Engr, S Wales Elec. Bd, 1967–72; Dep. Chm., London Elec. Bd, 1972–76, Chm., 1976–81; Dep. Chm., Electricity Council, 1981–86. Chairman: Ewbank Preece Group, 1986–92; Schlumberger Measurement and Systems, 1988–92; Dir, Eleco Holdings, 1993–. MInstD 1986; CIMgt. Liveryman, Gardeners' Co. JP Mon, 1971–72. *Recreations:* golf, gardening. *Address:* Lockhill, Stubbs Wood, Amersham, Bucks HP6 6EX. *T:* Amersham (01494) 433791. *Clubs:* City Livery; Harewood Downs Golf (Dir, 1992–).

PLUMPTRE, family name of **Baron Fitzwalter.**

PLUMSTEAD, Isobel Mary, (Mrs N. J. Coleman); District Judge, Principal Registry, Family Division of the High Court, since 1990; *b* 19 July 1947; *d* of John Archibald Plumstead, DFM, MA and Nancy Plumstead (*née* Drummond); *m* 1971, Nicholas John Coleman; one *s* two *d*. *Educ:* Norwich High Sch. for Girls (GPDST); St Hugh's College, Oxford (BA 1969; MA 1985); Inns of Court Sch. of Law. Blackstone Entrance Scholar, 1967, Colombos Prize for Internat. Law, 1970, Harmsworth Scholar, 1970–73, Middle Temple. Called to the Bar, Middle Temple, 1970; Registrar, Principal Registry, Family Div. of High Court, 1990; Asst Recorder, 1994–. Mem., Civil and Family Cttee, Judicial Studies Bd, 1993–. Trustee: New Parents' Infant Network (Newpin), 1989–; Hackney and E London Family Mediation Service, 1993–. Gov., St Margaret's Sch., Hampstead, 1993–. *Recreations:* family, food, fine and foul wines. *Address:* Principal Registry of Family Division, Somerset House, WC2R 1LP; Francis Taylor Building, Temple, EC4Y 7BY. *Club:* Aldeburgh Yacht.

PLUNKET, family name of **Baron Plunket.**

PLUNKET, 8th Baron *cr* 1827; **Robin Rathmore Plunket;** *b* 3 Dec. 1925; *s* of 6th Baron Plunket (*d* 1938) and Dorothé Mabel (*d* 1938), *d* of late Joseph Lewis and *widow* of Captain Jack Barnato, RAF; *S* brother, 1975; *m* 1951, Jennifer, *d* of late Bailey Southwell, Olivenhoutpoort, S Africa. *Educ:* Eton. Formerly Captain, Rifle Brigade. *Heir:* *b* Hon. Shaun Albert Frederick Sheridan Plunket [*b* 5 April 1931; *m* 1961, Judith Ann, *e d* of late G. P. Power; one *s* one *d*; *m* 1980, Mrs Elizabeth de Sancha (*d* 1986); *m* 1989, Mrs Andrea Reynolds]. *Address:* Rathmore, Chimanimani, Zimbabwe; 39 Lansdowne Gardens, SW8 2EL. *Club:* Boodle's.

PLUNKET GREENE, Mary, (Mrs Alexander Plunket Greene); *see* Quant, Mary.

PLUNKETT, family name of **Baron Dunsany,** and of **Baron Louth.**

PLUNKETT, William Joseph; Valuer and Estates Surveyor, Greater London Council, 1977–81; *b* 8 Nov. 1921; *s* of John Joseph Archer and Marjorie Martin Plunkett; *m* 1949, Gwendoline Innes Barron; two *s* five *d*. *Educ:* Finchley Catholic Grammar Sch.; Coll. of Estate Management. BSc(Est. Man.). FRICS. RN, 1941–46; commnd, 1942; Lt RNVR. Dep. County Valuer, Middlesex CC, 1962–65; Asst Valuer, Valuation and Estates Dept, GLC, 1965–73; Dep. Valuer and Estates Surveyor, GLC, 1973–74; Dir of Valuation and Estates Dept, GLC, 1974–77. Mem., South Bank Polytechnic Adv. Cttee on Estate Management, 1973–76; Chm., Covent Garden Officers' Steering Gp, 1977–81. Mem. General Council, RICS, 1978–80 (Pres. Planning and Develt Div., 1978–79; Chm., S London Br. Cttee, 1976–77); Pres., Assoc. of Local Authority Valuers and Estate Surveyors, 1980–81. *Publications:* articles on Compensation, Valuation and Development. *Address:* 63 Radnor Cliff, Folkestone, Kent CT20 2JL. *T:* Folkestone (01303) 248868.

PLYMOUTH, 3rd Earl of, *cr* 1905; **Other Robert Ivor Windsor-Clive;** Viscount Windsor (UK 1905); 15th Baron Windsor (England, *cr* 1529); DL; FRSA 1953; *b* 9 October 1923; *e s* of 2nd Earl and Lady Irene Charteris (*d* 1989), *d* of 11th Earl of Wemyss; *S* father, 1943; *m* 1950, Caroline Helen, *o d* of Edward Rice, Dane Court, Eastry, Kent; three *s* one *d*. *Educ:* Eton. Mem., Museums and Galls Commn (formerly Standing Commn on Museums and Galls), 1972–82; Chm., Reviewing Cttee on Export of Works of Art, 1982–85. DL County of Salop, 1961. *Heir: s* Viscount Windsor, *qv*. *Address:* Oakly Park, Ludlow, Salop SY8 2JW.

See also Sir Alan Glyn.

PLYMOUTH, Bishop Suffragan of, since 1988; **Rt. Rev. Richard Stephen Hawkins;** *b* 2 April 1939; *s* of late Ven. Canon John Stanley Hawkins and Elsie Hawkins (*née* Briggs); *m* 1966, Valerie Ann Herneman; one *s* one *d* (and one *s* one *d* decd). *Educ:* Exeter School; Exeter Coll., Oxford; St Stephen's House, Oxford. MA (Oxon); BPhil (Exeter Univ.); CQSW. Asst Curate, St Thomas, Exeter, 1963–66; Team Vicar of Clyst St Mary, Clyst Valley Team Ministry, 1966–78; Bishop's Officer for Ministry and Joint Director, Exeter-Truro Ministry Training Scheme, 1978–81; Team Vicar, Central Exeter Team Ministry, 1978–81; Diocesan Director of Ordinands, 1979–81; Priest-in-charge, Whitestone with Oldridge, 1981–87; Archdeacon of Totnes, 1981–88. *Address:* 31 Riverside Walk, Tamerton Foliot, Plymouth PL5 4AQ. *T:* Plymouth (01752) 769836.

PLYMOUTH, Bishop of, (RC), since 1986; **Rt. Rev. Mgr. Hugh Christopher Budd;** *b* 27 May 1937; *s* of John Alfred and Phyllis Mary Budd. *Educ:* St Mary's Primary School, Hornchurch, Essex; Salesian Coll., Chertsey, Surrey; Cotton Coll., North Staffs; English Coll., Rome. PhL; STD. Ordained Priest, 1962; post-ordination studies, 1963–65; Tutor, English Coll., Rome, 1965–71; Lectr at Newman Coll., Birmingham and part-time Asst Priest, Northfield, Birmingham, 1971–76; Head of Training, Catholic Marriage Advisory Council, National HQ, London, 1976–79; Rector, St John's Seminary, Wonersh, Surrey, 1979–85; Administrator, Brentwood Cathedral, Essex, Nov. 1985–Jan. 1986. *Recreations:* walking, cricket (watching), music (listening). *Address:* The Cathedral House, Cecil Street, Plymouth, Devon PL1 5HW; Bishop's House, 31 Wyndham Street West, Plymouth, Devon PL1 5RZ.

PLYMOUTH, Archdeacon of; *see* Ellis, Ven. R. G.

POANANGA, Maj.-Gen. Brian Matauru, CB 1980; CBE 1977 (OBE 1967; MBE 1962); Chief of General Staff, New Zealand Army, 1978–81, retired; *b* 2 Dec. 1924; *s* of Henare and Atareta Poananga; *m* 1949, Doreen Mary Porter (formerly QAIMNS/R); two *s* one *d*. *Educ:* Royal Military College, Duntroon, Australia. Graduated RMC, 1946; served BCOF, Japan, 1947–48; Commonwealth Div., Korea, 1952–53; (mentioned in despatches, 1952); Staff Coll., Camberley, 1957; 28 Commonwealth Inf. Bde, Malaya, 1959–61; Jt Services Staff Coll., Latimer, 1964; CO 1RNZIR, Malaysia, 1965–67 (mentioned in despatches, Sarawak, 1966); Dir of Army Training, 1968–69; Dir of Services Intelligence, 1969–70; Comdr Army Training Gp, 1970–72; RCDS, 1973; Comdr 1st (NZ) Inf. Bde Gp, 1974; NZ High Commissioner to Papua New Guinea, 1974–76; Deputy Chief of General Staff, 1977–78. *Recreations:* golf and fishing. *Address:* PO Box 397, Taupo, New Zealand. *T:* Taupo 48296. *Club:* Taupo (NZ).

POCOCK, Air Vice-Marshal Donald Arthur, CBE 1975 (OBE 1957); Director, British Metallurgical Plant Constructors Association, 1980–85; *b* 5 July 1920; *s* of late A. Pocock and of E. Broad; *m* 1947, Dorothy Monica Griffiths; two *s* three *d*. *Educ:* Crouch End. Served War of 1939–45: commissioned, 1941; Middle East, 1941–48. Transport Command, 1948–50; commanded RAF Regt Sqdn, 1950–52; Staff Coll., 1953; Staff Officer, HQ 2nd Allied TAF, 1954–57; comd RAF Regt Wing, 1957–58; MoD, 1958–59; HQ Allied Air Forces Central Europe, 1959–62; Sen. Ground Defence SO, NEAF, 1962–63; MoD, 1963–66; Sen. Ground Defence SO, FEAF, 1966–68; ADC to the Queen, 1967; Commandant, RAF Catterick, 1968–69; Dir of Ground Defence, 1970–73; Comdt-Gen. RAF Regt, 1973–75. Gen. Man., Iran, British Aerospace Dynamics Gp, 1976–79. *Address:* 16 Dence Park, Herne Bay, Kent CT6 6BQ. *T:* Herne Bay (01227) 374773. *Club:* Royal Air Force.

POCOCK, Gordon James; Director, Communications Educational Services Ltd, 1983–87; *b* 27 March 1933; *s* of late Leslie and Elizabeth Maud Pocock; *m* 1959, Audrey Singleton (*d* 1990). *Educ:* Royal Liberty Sch., Romford; Keble Coll., Oxford. Joined PO, 1954; Private Sec. to Dir Gen., 1958–59; Principal, 1960–68; Asst Sec., 1968–72; Dep. Dir, 1972–76; Dir, Ext. Telecommns, 1976–79; Dir, Telecommns Marketing, 1979, Sen. Dir, 1979–81; Chief Exec., Merlin Business Systems, BT, 1981–84. Fellow, Nolan Norton & Co., 1985–87. *Publications:* Corneille and Racine, 1973; Boileau and the Nature of Neo-Classicism, 1980; article on Nation, Community, Devolution and Sovereignty. *Recreations:* travel, theatre, local history. *Address:* Friars Lodge, Friars Lane, Richmond, Surrey TW9 1NL. *T:* 0181–940 7118.

POCOCK, Kenneth Walter, MBE 1993; *b* 20 June 1913; *s* of Walter Dunsdon Pocock and Emily Marion Pocock; *m* 1939, Anne Tidmarsh; one *s* one *d*. *Educ:* Canford School. United Dairies (London) Ltd, 1930; Armed Forces, 1942–46; Man. Dir, Edinburgh and Dumfriesshire Dairy Co. Ltd, 1946; Dir, United Dairies Ltd, 1948; Pres., Scottish Milk Trade Fedn, 1956–59; Dir, Unigate Ltd, 1959; Man. Dir, Unigate Ltd and United Dairies Ltd, 1963; Chm. of Milk Div., Unigate Ltd, 1968; Dep. Chm., Unigate Ltd, 1970–75; Life Pres., Unigate Long Service Corps (40 years), 1992 (Pres., 1971–92); Governor, Nat. Dairymen's Benevolent Instn, 1962– (Chm., 1977–81). *Recreations:* motoring, shooting, photography, gardening. *Address:* 4 Dorchester House, Marsham Lane, Gerrards Cross, Bucks SL9 8HA. *T:* Gerrards Cross (01753) 889278.

POCOCK, Leslie Frederick, CBE 1985; Chairman, Liverpool Health Authority, 1982–86; *b* 22 June 1918; *s* of Frederick Pocock and Alice Helena Pocock; *m* 1946, Eileen Horton; two *s*. *Educ:* Emanuel School. FCCA. Chief Accountant: London & Lancashire Insurance Co. Ltd, 1959; Royal Insurance Co. Ltd, 1966; Chief Accountant and Taxation Manager, 1971, Dep. Gp Comptroller, 1974, Royal Insurance Gp; retired 1981. Gen. Comr of Income Tax, 1982–93. Dir, Federated Pension Services (Guarantee) Ltd, 1995–. Pres., Assoc. of Certified Accountants, 1977–78. Mem., UK Central Council for Nursing, Midwifery and Health Visiting, 1983–87; Chm., Merseyside Residuary Body, 1985; Hon. Treas., Merseyside Improved Houses, 1986–. Chm. Governors, Sandown Coll., Liverpool, 1989–91. *Recreations:* countryside, golf. *Address:* Barn Lee, Tithebarn Close, Lower Heswall, Wirral, Merseyside L60 0EY. *T:* 0151–342 2917.

PODDAR, Prof. Ramendra Kumar, PhD; Professor of Biophysics, Calcutta University, since 1973 (Vice-Chancellor, 1979–83); Member of Parliament (Rajya Sabha), since 1985 (Vice-Chairman, 1987–89); *b* 9 Nov. 1930; *m* 1955, Srimati Jharna Poddar; two *s* one *d*. *Educ:* Univ. of Calcutta (BSc Hons Physics, MSc Physics; PhD Biophysics); Associateship Dip., Saha Inst. of Nuclear Physics. Progressively, Research Asst, Lecturer, Reader, Associate Prof., Biophysics Div., Saha Inst. of Nuclear Physics, 1953–73. IAEA Advr to Govt of Mali, 1962. Study visits to Univ. of California, Berkeley, 1958–60, Cold Spring Harbor Biological Lab., 1960, Purdue Univ., 1960–61, California Inst. of Technology, 1970, CNRS, Paris, 1978. Advr, West Bengal Pollution Control Bd. Vice-Pres., West Bengal Acad. of Science and Technol.; Chm., Inst. of Wetland Management and Ecological Design. *Publications:* more than 50 research papers in the fields of biophysics, molecular biology and photobiology. *Address:* Department of Biophysics, Molecular Biology and Genetics, University College of Science, Calcutta 700009, India. *T:* (office) (11) 508386, (home) (33) 375656 (Calcutta); (33) 3782193.

PODGER, Geoffrey John Freeman; Under Secretary for Health Promotion, Department of Health, since 1993; *b* 3 Aug. 1952; *s* of Leonard Podger and Beryl (*née* Freeman). *Educ:* Worthing High Sch. for Boys; Pembroke Coll., Oxford (Open Scholar; BA Medieval and Modern Langs 1974; MA 1977). MoD, 1974–82; Internat. Staff, NATO HQ, Brussels, 1977–79; Department of Health and Social Security, subseq. Department of Health, 1982–; loaned to Falkland Islands Govt as Sec. to Port Stanley Hosp. Fire Inquiry, 1985; Private Sec. to Chm. (subseq. Chief Exec.), NHS Management Bd and Sec. to Bd, 1985–87; Principal Private Sec. to Sec. of State for Social Services, 1987–88; Head, Internat. Relations Unit, 1992–93. *Address:* Department of Health, Wellington House, 133–155 Waterloo Road, SE1 8UG. *T:* 0171–972 4148.

PODMORE, Ian Laing; Chief Executive, Sheffield City Council, 1974–89; *b* 6 Oct. 1933; *s* of Harry Samuel Podmore and Annie Marion (*née* Laing); *m* 1961, Kathleen Margaret (*née* Langton); one *s* one *d*. *Educ:* Birkenhead School. Admitted Solicitor 1960. Asst Solicitor, Wallasey County Borough, 1960–63; Sen. Asst Solicitor, Southport Co. Borough, 1963–66; Deputy Town Clerk: Southport, 1966–70; Sheffield, 1970–74. *Recreations:* golf, gardening, watching football. *Address:* 55 Devonshire Road, Sheffield S17 3NU. *Club:* Abbeydale Golf.

PODRO, Prof. Michael Isaac, PhD; FBA 1992; Professor, Department of Art History and Theory, University of Essex, since 1973; *b* 13 March 1931; *s* of Joshua Podro and Fanny Podro; *m* 1961, Charlotte Booth; two *d*. *Educ:* Berkhamsted Sch.; Jesus Coll., Cambridge (MA); University Coll. London (PhD). Hd of Dept of Art History, Camberwell Sch. of Art and Crafts, 1961–67; Lectr in the Philosophy of Art, Warburg Inst., Univ. of London, 1967–69; Reader, Dept of Art History and Theory, Univ. of Essex, 1969–73. Trustee, V&A Mus., 1987–. *Publications:* Manifold in Perception: theories of art from Kant to Hildebrand, 1972; Critical Historians of Art, 1982. *Address:* 1 Provost Road, NW3 4ST. *T:* 0171–722 7435.

POGO, Most Rev. Ellison Leslie; *see* Melanesia, Archbishop of.

PÖHL, Karl Otto; Gross Kreuz des Verdienstordens der Bundesrepublik Deutschland; Partner, Sal. Oppenheim Jr & Cie, since 1991; Governor, Deutsche Bundesbank and German Governor, International Monetary Fund and Bank for International Settlements, 1980–91; *b* 1 Dec. 1929; *m* 1974; two *s* two *d*. *Educ:* Göttingen Univ. (Econs; Diplom.-Volkswirt). Div. Chief for Econ. Res., IFO-Institut, Munich, 1955–60; econ. journalist, Bonn, 1961–67; Mem. Exec., Fed. Assoc. of German Bank, Cologne, 1968–69; Div. Chief in Fed. Min. of Econs, Bonn, 1970–71; Dept Chief in Fed. Chancellery (Head, Dept for Econ. and Fiscal Policy), Bonn, 1971–72; Sec. of State in Fed. Min. of Finance, 1972–77; Dep. Governor, Deutsche Bundesbank, 1977–79; Chairman: EEC Monetary Cttee, 1976–77; Deputies of Gp of Ten, 1978–80; Gp of Ten, 1983–89; Cttee of Governors, Central Banks of EC Member States, 1990–91. Hon. DHL Georgetown Univ., 1983; Hon. DEconSc Ruhr Univ., 1985; Hon. DPhil Tel Aviv, 1986; Hon. Dr of Laws Univ. of Md, 1987; Hon. DSc: Buckingham, 1992; London, 1992. *Publications:* miscellaneous. *Address:* Sal. Oppenheim Jr & Cie, Bockenheimer Landstrasse 20, 60323 Frankfurt, Germany.

POITIER, Sidney, KBE (Hon.) 1974; actor, film and stage; director; Board Member, Walt Disney Company, since 1994; *b* Miami, Florida, 20 Feb. 1927; *s* of Reginald Poitier and Evelyn (*née* Outten); *m* 1950, Juanita Hardy (marr. diss.); four *d*; *m* 1975, Joanna Shimkus; two *d*. *Educ:* private tutors; Western Senior High Sch., Nassau; Governor's High Sch., Nassau. Served War of 1941–45 with 1267th Medical Detachment, United States Army. Started acting with American Negro Theatre, 1946. *Plays include:* Anna Lucasta, Broadway, 1948; A Raisin in the Sun, Broadway, 1959; *films include:* Cry, the Beloved Country, 1952; Red Ball Express, 1952; Go, Man, Go, 1954; Blackboard Jungle, 1955; Goodbye, My Lady, 1956; Edge of the City, 1957; Band of Angels, 1957; Something of Value, 1957; The Mark of the Hawk, 1958; The Defiant Ones, 1958 (Silver Bear Award, Berlin Film Festival, and New York Critics Award, 1958); Porgy and Bess, 1959; A Raisin in the Sun, 1960; Paris Blues, 1960; Lilies of the Field, 1963 (award for Best Actor of 1963, Motion Picture Academy of Arts and Sciences); The Bedford Incident, 1965; The Slender Thread, 1966; A Patch of Blue, 1966; Duel at Diablo, 1966; To Sir With Love, 1967; In the Heat of the Night, 1967; Guess Who's Coming to Dinner, 1968; For Love of Ivy, 1968; They Call Me Mister Tibbs, 1971; The Organization, 1971; The Wilby Conspiracy, 1975; Deadly Pursuit, 1988; Sneakers, 1992; director and actor: Buck and the Preacher, 1972; A Warm December, 1973; Uptown Saturday Night, 1975; Let's Do It Again, 1976; A Piece of the Action, 1977; *director:* Stir Crazy, 1981; Hanky Panky, 1982. *Publication:* This Life (autobiography), 1980. *Address:* c/o Walt Disney Company, 500 South Buena Vista Street, Burbank, CA 91521, USA.

POLAK, Cornelia Julia, OBE 1964 (MBE 1956); HM Diplomatic Service, retired; *b* 2 Dec. 1908; *d* of late Solomon Polak and late Georgina Polak (*née* Pozner). Foreign Office, 1925–38; Asst Archivist, British Embassy, Paris, 1938–40; Foreign Office, 1940–47; Vice-Consul, Bergen, 1947–49; Consul, Washington, 1949–51; Foreign Office, 1951–55; Consul, Paris, 1955–57; Consul, Brussels, 1957–60; Foreign Office, 1960–63; Head of Treaty and Nationality Department, Foreign Office, 1963–67; Consul General, Geneva, 1967–69, retired; re-employed at FCO, 1969–70. *Address:* 24 Belsize Court, NW3 5QJ.

POLAK, Prof. Julia Margaret, (Mrs Daniel Catovsky), FRCPath; Professor of Endocrine Pathology, Royal Postgraduate Medical School, London University, since 1984, and Deputy Director, Department of Histopathology, Hammersmith Hospital, since 1988; *b* 26 June 1939; *d* of Carlos and Rebeca Polak; *m* 1961, Daniel Catovsky, *qv*; two *s* one *d*. *Educ:* Univ. of Buenos Aires (MD 1964; Dip Histopath. 1966); DSc London, 1980. Hospital appts, Buenos Aires, 1961–67; Royal Postgraduate Medical School, London: Research Assistant in Histochemistry, 1968–69; Asst Lectr, Lectr, and Sen. Lectr, 1970–82; Reader, 1982–84; Member: Exec. Cttee, Acad. Bd, 1990–; Med. Exec. Unit,

Hammersmith Hosp., 1990–; Sub-Cttee in Biotech., London Univ., 1988–. Chm., British Endocrine Pathologists Gp, 1988–; Mem., Exec. Cttee of Council, Amer. Heart Assoc., 1989–. Mem., editl bds of med. jls. Benito de Udaondo Cardiology Prize, 1967; Medal, Soc. of Endocrinology, 1984; Sir Eric Sharpe Prize for Oncology, Cable and Wireless, 1986–87. *Publications:* contribs to Nature and numerous professional jls. *Address:* Department of Histochemistry, Royal Postgraduate Medical School, Du Cane Road, W12 0NN. *T:* 0181–740 3231.

POLAND, Rear-Adm. Edmund Nicholas, CB 1967; CBE 1962; *b* 19 Feb. 1917; 2nd *s* of late Major Raymond A. Poland, RMLI; *m* 1941, Pauline Ruth Margaret Pechell; three *s* one *d* (and one *d* decd). *Educ:* Royal Naval Coll., Dartmouth. Served at sea during Abyssinian and Palestine crises, Spanish Civil War; War of 1939–45: convoy duties, Norwegian waters; Motor Torpedo Boats, Channel and Mediterranean; Torpedo Specialist, 1943; Staff Officer Ops to Naval Force Comdr, Burma; Sqdn T. Officer, HMS Royalist; HMS Hornet, 1946; Flotilla Torpedo and Anti-Submarine Officer of Third Submarine Flotilla, HMS Montclare; Air Warfare Div., Admiralty, 1950; British Naval Staff, Washington, 1953; jssc 1955; Directorate of Tactics and Ship Requirements, Admiralty; comd RN Air Station, Abbotsinch, 1956; Nato Standing Gp, Washington; Director of Under Sea Warfare (Naval), Ministry of Defence, 1962; Chief of Staff to C-in-C Home Fleet, 1965–68; retired. Commander, 1950; Capt., 1956; Rear-Adm., 1965. Vice-Pres., Internat. Prisoners' Aid Assoc., 1978, Chm. (UK), 1979; Vice-Pres., Scottish Assoc. for Care and Resettlement of Offenders, 1979 (Dir, 1974–79). *Publications:* The Torpedomen, 1992; Majumba's Survival Trail, 1992. *Recreations:* golf, fishing, gardening. *Address:* 39 Limmer Lane, Felpham, Bognor Regis, West Sussex PO22 7HD.

See also R. D. Poland.

POLAND, Richard Domville, CB 1973; *b* 22 Oct. 1914; *er s* of late Major R. A. Poland, RMLI, and late Mrs F. O. Bayly-Jones; *m* 1948, Rosalind Frances, *y d* of late Surgeon-Captain H. C. Devas; one *s* one *d*. *Educ:* RN Coll., Dartmouth. Traffic Trainee, Imperial Airways, 1932; Traffic Clerk, British Continental Airways and North Eastern Airways, 1934–39. Ops Officer, Air Ministry, Civil Aviation Dept, 1939; Civil Aviation Dept Rep., W Africa, 1942–44; Private Secretary to Minister of Civil Aviation, 1944–48; Principal, 1946; Asst Secretary, 1953; Shipping Attaché, British Embassy, Washington, DC, 1957–60; Under-Secretary: Min. of Transport, 1964–70; DoE, 1970–74. Sec., Internat. Maritime Industry Forum, 1976–78. Chm., Kent Branch, CPRE, 1980. *Address:* 63 Alexandra Road, Kew, Surrey TW9 2BT. *T:* 0181–948 5039.

See also Rear-Admiral E. N. Poland.

POLANI, Prof. Paul Emanuel, MD, DCH; FRCP, FRCOG; FRS 1973; Prince Philip Professor of Pædiatric Research in the University of London, 1960–80, now Professor Emeritus; Geneticist, Pædiatric Research Unit, Guy's Hospital, London, since 1983 (in Division of Medical and Molecular Genetics of United Medical and Dental Schools of Guy's and St Thomas' Hospitals); Children's Physician, and Consultant Emeritus, Guy's Hospital; Geneticist, Italian Hospital; Director, SE Thames Regional Genetics Centre, 1976–82; *b* 1 Jan. 1914; first *s* of Enrico Polani and Elsa Zennaro; *m* 1944, Nina Ester Sullam; no *c*. *Educ:* Trieste, Siena and Pisa (Scuola Normale Superiore, Italy). CM; MD (Pisa) 1938; DCH 1945; MRCP 1948; FRCP 1961; FRCOG *ad eund* 1979. National Birthday Trust Fund Fellow in Pædiatric Research, 1948; Assistant to Director, Dept of Child Health, Guy's Hospital Medical School, 1950–55; Research Physician on Cerebral Palsy and Director, Medical Research Unit, National Spastic Society, 1955–60; Dir, Paediatric Res. Unit, Guy's Hosp. Med. Sch., 1960–83. Consultant to WHO (Regional Office for Europe) on Pregnancy Wastage, 1959; Consultant, Nat. Inst. Neurol. Disease and Blindness, Nat. Insts of Health, USA, 1959–61. Chm., Mutagenesis Cttee, UK, 1975–86. Vis. Prof. of Human Genetics and Develt, Columbia Univ., 1977–86. Harveian Orator, 1988. Hon. FRCPath 1985; Hon. FRCPI 1989; Hon. Fellow, UMDS of Guy's and St Thomas' Hospital, 1994. Sanremo Internat. Award and Prize for Genetic Res., 1984; Baly Medal, RCP, 1985, Gold Medal, International Cerebral Palsy Society, 1988. Commendatore, Order of Merit of the Republic, Italy, 1981. *Publications:* The Impact of Genetics on Medicine, 1990; chapters in books on human genetics, mental deficiency, psychiatry and pædiatrics; papers on human genetics, cytogenetics, experimental meiosis, congenital malformations and neurological disorders of children. *Recreations:* reading, riding, ski-ing. *Address:* Little Meadow, West Clandon, Surrey GU4 7TL. *T:* Guildford (01483) 222436. *Club:* Athenæum.

POLANYI, Prof. Hon. John Charles, PC (Can.) 1992; CC (Canada) 1979 (OC 1974); FRS 1971; FRSC 1966 (Hon. FRSC 1991); University Professor, since 1974 and Professor of Chemistry, University of Toronto, since 1962; *b* 23 Jan. 1929; *m* 1958, Anne Ferrar Davidson; one *s* one *d*. *Educ:* Manchester Grammar Sch.; Victoria Univ., Manchester (BSc, PhD, DSc). Research Fellow: Nat. Research Council, Ottawa, 1952–54; Princeton Univ., 1954–56; Univ. of Toronto: Lectr, 1956; Asst Prof., 1957–60; Assoc. Prof., 1960–62. Mem., Scientific Adv. Bd, Max Planck Inst. for Quantum Optics, Garching, Germany, 1982–92. Sloan Foundn Fellow, 1959–63; Guggenheim Meml Fellow, 1970–71, 1979–80; Sherman Fairchild Distinguished Scholar, CIT, 1982; Vis. Prof. of Chem., Texas A & M Univ., 1986; John W. Cowper Dist. Vis. Lectr, SUNY at Buffalo, 1986; Dist. Vis. Speaker, Univ. of Calgary, 1987; Consolidated Bathurst Vis. Lectr, Concordia Univ., 1988; Beam Dist. Vis. Prof., Iowa Univ., 1992; Hitchcock Prof., Calif Univ., Berkeley, 1994; Lectures include: Centennial, Chem. Soc., 1965; Ohio State Univ., 1969 (and Mack Award); Reilly, Univ. of Notre Dame, 1970; Harkins Meml, Univ. of Chicago, 1971; Purves, McGill Univ., 1971; Killam Meml Schol., 1974, 1975; F. J. Toole, Univ. of New Brunswick, 1974; Philips, Haverford Coll., 1974; Kistiakowsky, Harvard Univ., 1975; Camille and Henry Dreyfus, Kansas, 1975; J. W. T. Spinks, Saskatchewan, 1976; Laird, Western Ontario, 1976; CIL Dist., Simon Fraser Univ., 1977; Gucker, Indiana Univ., 1977; Jacob Bronowski Meml, Toronto Univ., 1978; Hutchison, Rochester Univ., 1979; Priestley, Penn State Univ., 1980; Barré, Univ. of Montreal, 1982; Chute, Dalhousie, and Redman, McMaster, 1983; Wiegand, Toronto Univ., Condon, Colorado Univ., Allan, Alberta Univ., and Willard, Wisconsin Univ., 1984; Holmes, Lethbridge Univ., 1985; Walker-Ames, Univ. of Washington, 1986; Morino, Japan, J. T. Wilson, Ont Sci. Centre, Welsh, Univ. of Toronto, and Spiers Meml, Faraday Div., RSChem., 1987; Polanyi, IUPAC, W. B. Lewis, Atomic Energy of Canada Ltd, Priestman, Univ. of New Brunswick, Killam, Univ. of Windsor, Herzberg, Carleton Univ., and Falconbridge, Laurentian Univ., 1988; Dupont, Indiana Univ., and C. R. Mueller, Purdue Univ., 1989; Laurier, Wilfrid Laurier Univ., and Goodrich, Case Western Reserve Univ., 1990; Phillips, Pittsburgh, 1991; Dove Meml, Toronto, 1992; Fritz London, Duke Univ., 1993; Linus Pavling, CIT, 1994; Hagey, Waterloo Univ., 1995. Hon. FRSE 1988; Hon. For. Mem., Amer. Acad. of Arts and Sciences, 1976; For. Associate, Nat. Acad. of Sciences, USA, 1978; Mem., Pontifical Acad. of Scis, 1986. Hon. DSc: Waterloo, 1970; Memorial, 1976; McMaster, 1977; Carleton, 1981; Harvard, 1982; Rensselaer, Brock, 1984; Lethbridge, Victoria, Ottawa, Sherbrooke, Laval, 1987; Manchester, York, 1988; Acadia, Univ. de Montréal, and Weizmann Inst. of Science, Israel, 1989; Univ. of Bari, Italy, Univ. of BC, and McGill Univ., 1990; Queen's, 1992; Free Univ., Berlin, 1993; Laurentian, Toronto, Liverpool, 1995; Hon. LLD: Trent, 1977; Dalhousie, 1983; St Francis Xavier, 1984; Concordia Univ., 1990; Calgary, 1994. Marlow Medal, Faraday Soc., 1963; Steacie Prize for Natural Scis, 1965; Chem. Inst. Canada Medal, 1976 (Noranda Award, 1967); Chem. Soc. Award, 1970; Henry Marshall Tory Medal, 1977, Michael Polanyi Medal, 1989, RSC; Remsen Award, Amer. Chem. Soc., 1978; (jtly) Wolf Prize in Chemistry, Wolf Foundn, Israel, 1982; (jtly) Nobel Prize for Chemistry, 1986; Killam Meml Prize, Canada Council, 1988; Royal Medal, 1989, Bakerian Prize, 1994, Royal Soc.; eponymous award, Canadian Soc. for Chem., 1992. KStJ 1987. *Film:* Concept in Reaction Dynamics, 1970. *Publications:* (with F. G. Griffiths) The Dangers of Nuclear War, 1979; papers in scientific jls, articles on science policy and on control of armaments. *Address:* 142 Collier Street, Toronto, Ont M4W 1M3, Canada.

POLE, Prof. Jack Richon, PhD; FBA 1985; FRHistS; Rhodes Professor of American History and Institutions, Oxford University, 1979–89; Fellow of St Catherine's College, since 1979; *b* 14 March 1922; *s* of Joseph Pole and Phœbe (*née* Rickards); *m* 1952, Marilyn Louise Mitchell (marr. diss. 1988); one *s* two *d*. *Educ:* Oxford Univ. (BA 1949); Princeton Univ. (PhD 1953). MA Cantab 1963. FRHistS 1970. Instr in History, Princeton Univ., 1952–53; Asst Lectr/Lectr in Amer. History, UCL, 1953–63; Cambridge University: Reader in Amer. History and Govt, 1963–79; Fellow, Churchill Coll., 1963–79 (Vice-Master, 1975–78); Mem., Council of Senate, 1970–74. Vis. Professor: Berkeley, 1960–61; Ghana, 1966; Chicago, 1969; Peking, 1984. Commonwealth Fund Amer. Studies Fellowship, 1956; Fellow, Center for Advanced Study in Behavioral Sciences, 1969–70; Guest Schol., Wilson Internat. Center, Washington, 1978–79; Goleib Fellow, NY Univ. Law Sch., 1990; Sen. Res. Fellow, Coll. of William & Mary, Va, 1991; Leverhulme Trust Emeritus Fellow, 1991–93. Jefferson Meml Lectr, Berkeley, 1971; Richard B. Russell Lectr, Ga, 1981. Vice-Pres., Internat. Commn for History of Representative and Parly Instns, 1990–; Member: Council, Inst. for Early Amer. History and Culture, 1973–76; Acad. Européenne d'Histoire, 1981. Hon. Fellow, Hist. Soc. of Ghana. *Publications:* Abraham Lincoln and the Working Classes of Britain, 1959; Abraham Lincoln, 1964; Political Representation in England and the Origins of the American Republic, 1966 (also USA); (ed) The Advance of Democracy, USA 1967; The Seventeenth Century: the origins of legislative power, USA 1969; (ed) The Revolution in America: documents of the internal development of America in the revolutionary era, 1971 (also USA); (co-ed) The Meanings of American History, USA 1971; Foundations of American Independence, 1763–1815, 1973 (USA 1972); (Gen. Editor) American Historical Documents (ed, Slavery, Secession and Civil War), 1975; The Decision for American Independence, USA 1975; The Idea of Union, USA 1977; The Pursuit of Equality in American History, USA 1978, 2nd edn 1993; Paths to the American Past, 1979 (also USA); The Gift of Government: political responsibility from the English Restoration to American Independence, USA 1983; (co-ed) Colonial British America: essays in the new history of the early modern era, USA 1983; (ed) The American Constitution: For and Against: the Federalist and Anti-Federalist papers, USA 1987; (co-ed) The Blackwell Encyclopedia of the American Revolution, 1991 (also USA); articles in Amer. Hist. Rev., William and Mary Qly, Jl of Southern Hist., Enc. Brit., Enc. of Amer. Congress. *Recreations:* cricket, painting, writing. *Address:* 20 Divinity Road, Oxford OX4 1LJ; St Catherine's College, Oxford OX1 3UJ. *Clubs:* MCC; Trojan Wanderers Cricket (Co-founder, 1957).

POLE, Sir Peter Van Notten, 5th Bt, *cr* 1791; FASA; ACIS; accountant, retired; *b* 6 Nov. 1921; *s* of late Arthur Chandos Pole and late Marjorie, *d* of late Charles Hargrave, Glen Forrest, W Australia; *S* kinsman, 1948; *m* 1949, Jean Emily, *d* of late Charles Douglas Stone, Borden, WA; one *s* one *d*. *Educ:* Guildford Grammar Sch. *Recreations:* reading, travel. *Heir:* *s* Peter John Chandos Pole [*b* 27 April 1952; *m* 1973, Suzanne Norah, BAppSc(MT), *d* of Harold Raymond and Gwendoline Maude Hughes; two *s* one *d*]. *Address:* 130/60 Kalinda Drive, City Beach, WA 6015, Australia.

POLGE, Prof. (Ernest John) Christopher, CBE 1992; FRS 1983; Director, Mastercalf Ltd, since 1994; Hon. Professor of Animal Reproductive Biotechnology, University of Cambridge, since 1989; Fellow, Wolfson College, Cambridge, since 1984; *b* 16 Aug. 1926; *s* of late Ernest Thomas Ella Polge and Joan Gillet Polge (*née* Thorne); *m* 1954, Olive Sylvia Kitson; two *s* two *d*. *Educ:* Bootham Sch., York; Reading Univ. (BSc Agric.); PhD London 1955. Dept of Agricl Econs, Bristol Univ., 1947–48; Nat. Inst. for Med. Res., London, 1948–54; ARC Unit of Reproductive Physiology and Biochem., later Animal Res. Station, 1954–86, Officer-in-Charge, 1979–86; Scientific Dir, Animal Biotechnology Cambridge Ltd, Animal Res. Stn, Cambridge, 1986–93. Lalor Foundn Fellow, Worcester Foundn for Exptl Biol., Shrewsbury, Mass and Univ. of Illinois, 1967–68. Consultant: WHO, Geneva, 1965; FAO, Rome, 1983 and 1987. Member Committee: Soc. for Study of Fertility, 1955–64, 1976–83 (Sec., 1960–63; Chm., 1978–81); Soc. for Low Temp. Biol., 1974–79 (Chm., 1976–79). Chm., Journals of Reproduction and Fertility Ltd, 1982–87 (Mem., Council of Management and Exec. Cttee, 1972–79). Lectures: Sir John Hammond Meml, Soc. for Study of Fertility, 1974; Blackman, Oxford, 1979; Cameron-Gifford, Newcastle, 1984; E. H. W. Wilmott, Bristol, 1986; Clive Behrens, Leeds, 1988; Sir John Hammond Meml, British Soc. of Animal Production, 1989. FRAgS 1991; Hon. FRASE 1984; Hon. ARCVS 1986. Prof. *hc* and Dr *hc*, Ecological Univ. of Romania, 1991. Hon. DSc: Univ. of Illinois, 1990; Guelph, 1994. (Jtly) John Scott Award, City of Philadelphia, 1969; Sir John Hammond Meml Prize, British Soc. of Animal Prodn, 1971; Pioneer Award, Internat. Embryo Transfer Soc., 1986; Marshall Medal, Soc. for Study of Fertility, 1988; Internat. Prize for Agriculture, Wolf Foundn, 1988; Japan Prize for Science and Technology for Biological Prodn, 1992. *Publications:* papers on reproduction in domestic animals and low temp. biol., in biological jls. *Recreations:* gardening, fishing. *Address:* The Willows, 137 Waterbeach Road, Landbeach, Cambridge CB4 4EA. *T:* Cambridge (01223) 860075.

POLIAKOFF, Stephen; playwright and film director; *s* of Alexander Poliakoff and late Ina Montagu; *m* 1983, Sandy Welch; one *s* one *d*. *Educ:* Westminster Sch.; Cambridge Univ. *Plays:* Clever Soldiers, 1974; The Carnation Gang, 1974; Hitting Town, 1975; City Sugar, 1976, Strawberry Fields, NT, Shout Across the River, RSC, 1978; The Summer Party, 1980; Favourite Nights, 1981; Breaking the Silence, RSC, 1984; Coming in to Land, NT, 1987; Playing With Trains, RSC, 1989; Sienna Red, nat. tour, 1992; *films:* Hidden City; Close My Eyes; Century; *TV plays include:* Caught on a Train (BAFTA Award); She's Been Away (Venice Film Festival Prize). *Publications:* all plays; Plays One, 1989. *Recreations:* watching cricket, going to the cinema. *Address:* 33 Devonia Road, N1 8JQ. *T:* 0171–354 2695.

POLIZZI, Hon. Olga, (Hon. Mrs William Shawcross), CBE 1990; Director, since 1983, and Managing Director, Building and Design Department, since 1980, Forte PLC; *d* of Baron Forte, *qv*; *m* 1st, 1966, Alessandro Polizzi di Sorrentino (*d* 1980); two *d*; 2nd, 1993, Hon. William Hartley Hume Shawcross, *qv*. *Educ:* St Mary's Sch., Ascot. Westminster City Councillor, 1989–94. Co-Chm., Grosvenor House Antiques Fair, 1980–; Mem. Council, RCM, 1992–. Gov., St Mary's Sch., Ascot, 1988–. *Recreations:* walking, ski-ing, opera. *Address:* Forte PLC, 166 High Holborn, WC1V 6TT. *T:* 0171–836 7744.

See also Hon. Sir R. J. V. Forte.

POLKINGHORNE, Rev. Canon John Charlton, PhD, ScD; FRS 1974; President, Queens' College, Cambridge, since 1989; *b* 16 Oct. 1930; *s* of George Baulkwill

Polkinghorne and Dorothy Evelyn Polkinghorne (*née* Charlton); *m* 1955, Ruth Isobel Martin; two *s* one *d*. *Educ:* Elmhurst Grammar Sch.; Perse Sch.; Trinity Coll., Cambridge (MA 1956; PhD 1955; ScD 1974); Westcott House, Cambridge, 1979–81. Deacon, 1981; Priest, 1982. Fellow, Trinity Coll., Cambridge, 1954–86; Commonwealth Fund Fellow, California Institute of Technology, 1955–56; Lecturer in Mathematical Physics, Univ. of Edinburgh, 1956–58; Cambridge University: Lecturer in Applied Mathematics, 1958–65; Reader in Theoretical Physics, 1965–68; Prof. of Mathematical Physics, 1968–79; Fellow, Dean and Chaplain of Trinity Hall, Cambridge, 1986–89 (Hon. Fellow, 1989). Hon. Prof. of Theoretical Physics, Univ. of Kent at Canterbury, 1985. Curate: St Andrew's, Chesterton, 1981–82; St Michael's, Bedminster, 1982–84; Vicar of St Cosmus and St Damian in the Blean, 1984–86; Canon Theologian, Liverpool Cathedral, 1994–. Mem. SRC, 1975–79; Chairman: Nuclear Phys Bd, 1978–79; Cttee to Review the Research Use of Fetuses and Fetal Material, 1988–89; Task Force to Review Services for Drugs Misusers, 1994–. Member: C of E Doctrine Commn, 1989–; Gen. Synod of C of E, 1990–. Chm. of Governors, Perse Sch., 1972–81; Governor, SPCK, 1984–. Licensed Reader, Diocese of Ely, 1975. Hon. DD Kent, 1994; Hon. DSc Exeter, 1994. *Publications:* (jointly) The Analytic S-Matrix, 1966; The Particle Play, 1979; Models of High Energy Processes, 1980; The Way the World Is, 1983; The Quantum World, 1984; One World, 1986; Science and Creation, 1988; Science and Providence, 1989; Rochester Roundabout, 1989; Reason and Reality, 1991; Science and Christian Belief, 1994; Quarks, Chaos and Christianity, 1994; many articles on elementary particle physics in learned journals. *Recreation:* gardening. *Address:* The President's Lodge, Queens' College, Cambridge CB3 9ET. *T:* Cambridge (01223) 335532.

POLLACK, Anita Jean; Member (Lab) London SW, European Parliament, since 1989; *b* NSW, Australia, 3 June 1946; *d* of John and Kathleen Pollack; *m* 1986, Philip Bradbury; one *d*. *Educ:* City of London Polytechnic (BA 1979); Birkbeck Coll., Univ. of London (MSc Polit. Sociology 1981). Advertising copy writer, Australia, 1963–69; book editor, 1970–75; student, 1976–79; Research Asst to Rt Hon. Barbara Castle, MEP, 1981–89. *Recreations:* family, cinema, rock music. *Address:* 177 Lavender Hill, SW11 5TE.

POLLARD, Maj.-Gen. Anthony John Griffin, CB 1992; CBE 1985; General Officer Commanding, South West District, 1990–92, retired; *b* 8 April 1937; *s* of William Pollard and Anne Irene Griffin; *m* Marie-Luise; four *s*. *Educ:* Oakham Sch.; Jesus Coll., Cambridge. Commnd Royal Leics Regt, 1956; served Cyprus, Germany, Hong Kong, Borneo, Malta; Staff Coll., 1969; Staff 7 Armd Bde, 1970–72; Instr, Staff Coll., 1975–77; CO 1st Bn Royal Anglian Regt, 1977–79; (Norway, NI, Germany); QMG's Secretariat, 1980; Col, Tactical Doctrine, BAOR, 1981; Col, Ops and Tactical Doctrine, 1(BR) Corps, 1982; Comdr, British Forces, Belize, 1983–84; Comdt, Sch. of Infantry, 1984–87; Comdr, British Mil. Mission to Uganda, 1985–86; Dir Gen., Trng and Doctrine (Army), 1987–90. Dep. Col, Royal Anglian Regt, 1986–92; Colonel Commandant: Small Arms Sch. Corps, 1987–92; Queen's Div., 1990–92; Hon. Col Suffolk ACF, 1992–. Governor, Framlingham Coll., 1993–. *Recreations:* fishing, gardening, archaeology, ancient buildings. *Club:* Army and Navy.

POLLARD, Maj.-Gen. Barry; *see* Pollard, Maj.-Gen. C. B.

POLLARD, Bernard, CB 1988; Deputy Secretary and Director General (Technical), Board of Inland Revenue, 1985–88; *b* 24 Oct. 1927; *m* 1961, Regina (*née* Stone); one *s* one *d*. *Educ:* Tottenham Grammar Sch.; London Univ. (BSc Econ; Gladstone Meml Prize (Econs), 1949). Called to the Bar, Middle Temple, 1968. Served RAF (Flying Officer), 1949–53. Entered Tax Inspectorate, Inland Revenue, 1953; Principal Inspector of Taxes, 1969; Asst Sec., 1973; Under Sec., 1979; Dir of Counter Avoidance and Evasion Div., 1981–85. *Recreations:* reading biographies, watching cricket and National Hunt racing. *Address:* 10 Merrows Close, Northwood, Mddx HA6 2RT. *T:* Northwood (01923) 824762.

POLLARD, Charles; QPM 1990; Chief Constable of Thames Valley Police, since 1991; *b* 4 Feb. 1945; *s* of Humphrey Charles Pollard and Margaret Isobel Pollard (*née* Philpott); *m* 1972, Erica Jane Allison Jack; two *s* one *d*. *Educ:* Oundle Sch.; Bristol Univ. (LLB). Metropolitan Police, 1964; Sussex Police, 1980; Asst Chief Constable, Thames Valley Police, 1985–88; Dep. Asst Comr, i/c No 5 (SW) Area of London, Metropolitan Police, 1988–91. Chm., Quality of Service Cttee, ACPO, 1993–94; Vice-Chm., Thames Valley Partnership (working for safer communities), 1992–. Vis. Fellow, Nuffield Coll., Oxford, 1993–. *Recreations:* tennis, walking, family pursuits. *Address:* Thames Valley Police HQ, Kidlington, Oxon OX5 2NX. *T:* Kidlington (01865) 846000.

POLLARD, Maj.-Gen. (Charles) Barry; Chairman, Haig Homes, since 1987; *b* 20 April 1927; *s* of Leonard Charles Pollard and Rose Constance (*née* Fletcher); *m* 1954, Mary Heyes; three *d*. *Educ:* Ardingly Coll.; Selwyn Coll., Cambridge. Commnd, Corps of RE, 1947; served in ME, Korea and UK, 1947–58; Student, Staff Coll., Camberley, 1958; GSO 2 (Trng), HQ Eastern Comd, 1959–61; Liaison Officer, Ecole du Genie, France, 1961–63; OC 5 Field Sqdn, 1963–65; JSSC, 1965; Mil. Asst to DCOS, Allied Forces Central Europe, 1966; GSO 1 MoD, 1967; GSO 1 (DS), Staff Coll., Camberley, 1968; CRE 3 Div., 1969–71; Col GS 3 Div., 1971–72; CCRE 1st British Corps, 1972–74; RCDS, 1975; Chief Engr, BAOR, 1976–79. Col Comdt, RE, 1982–87. National Dir, Trident Trust, 1980–84; Gen. Man., Solent Business Fund, 1984–91. *Recreations:* sailing, golf. *Address:* Yateley, Coombe Road, Salisbury, Wilts SP2 8BT.

POLLARD, Christopher Charles; Editorial Director, Gramophone, since 1993; *b* 30April 1957; s of Anthony Cecil and Margaret Noelle Pollard; *m* 1984, Margaret Ann Langlois; three *d*. *Educ:* Merchant Taylors' Sch., Northwood; Newland Park Coll. Joined Gramophone, 1981; Man. Editor, 1986. Editor, The Good CD Guide, 1988–. *Recreations:* Rugby football, cricket, cars, music. *Address:* Beechcroft, Hotley Bottom, Great Missenden, Bucks HP16 9PL.

POLLARD, Eve, (Lady Lloyd); Editor, Sunday Express and Sunday Express Magazine, 1991–94; *d* of late Ivor and Mimi Pollard; *m* 1st, 1968, Barry Winkleman (marr. diss. 1979); one *d*; 2nd, 1979, Sir Nicholas Lloyd, *qv*; one *s*. Fashion Editor: Honey, 1967–68; Daily Mirror Magazine, 1968–69; Women's Editor: Observer Magazine, 1970–71; Sunday Mirror, 1971–81; Asst Ed., Sunday People, 1981–83; Features Ed. and presenter, TV-am, 1983–85; Editor: Elle USA (launched magazine in NY), 1985–86; Sunday magazine, News of the World, 1986; You magazine, Mail on Sunday, 1986–88; Sunday Mirror and Sunday Mirror Magazine, 1988–91. Formerly contributor to Sunday Times. Mem., English Tourist Bd, 1993–. *Publications:* Jackie: biography of Mrs J. K. Onassis, 1971; (jtly) Splash!, 1995. *Address:* c/o Simpson-Fox Associates, 52 Shaftesbury Avenue, W1V 7DE. *T:* 0171–434 9167.

POLLARD, George Neil; Taxing Master of the Supreme Court, since 1994; *b* 25 Nov. 1935; *s* of Rev. George Pollard and Elizabeth Beatrice Pollard (*née* Briggs). *Educ:* Queen's Coll., Taunton; Law Society Sch. of Law. Admitted Solicitor, 1958; Solicitor, E. W. Nickerson & Son, 1958–59, J. Clayton & Co., 1959–61; Partner, Duthie Hart & Duthie, 1962–94. President: W Essex Law Soc., 1984–85; London Criminal Court Solicitors' Assoc., 1988–89; Mem. Cttee, No 1 Legal Aid Area, 1978–94. *Recreations:* reading, sailing, music. *Address:* 17 John Spencer Square, Canonbury, N1 2LZ. *T:* 0171–359 1220. *Club:* Royal Corinthian Yacht.

POLLARD, Richard Frederick David; His Honour Judge Pollard; a Circuit Judge, since 1990; *b* 26 April 1941; *s* of William Pollard and Anne Irene Pollard (*née* Griffin), CBE; *m* 1964, Angela Susan Hardy; one *s* two *d*. *Educ:* Oakham School; Trinity College Dublin (BA); Univ. of Cambridge (Dip. Crim.). Called to the Bar, Gray's Inn, 1967. *Recreations:* walking, art nouveau, looking out of the window. *Address:* c/o Midland and Oxford Circuit, 2 Newton Street, Birmingham B4 7LU.

POLLARD, Prof. Sidney; Professor of Economic History, University of Bielefeld, 1980–90, Emeritus Professor since 1990; *b* 21 April 1925; *s* of Moses and Leontine Pollak; *m* 1st, 1949, Eileen Andrews; two *s* one *d*; 2nd, 1982, Helen Trippett. *Educ:* London School of Economics. University of Sheffield: Knoop Fellow, 1950–52; Asst Lecturer, 1952–55; Lecturer, 1955–60; Senior Lecturer, 1960–63; Prof. of Economic History, 1963–80. Corresp. Fellow, British Acad., 1989. Hon. DLitt Sheffield, 1992. *Publications:* Three Centuries of Sheffield Steel, 1954; A History of Labour in Sheffield 1850–1939, 1959; The Development of the British Economy 1914–1950, 1962, 3rd edn, 1914–1980, 1983; The Genesis of Modern Management, 1965; The Idea of Progress, 1968; (with D. W. Crossley) The Wealth of Britain, 1086–1966, 1968; (ed) The Gold Standard and Employment Policies between the Wars, 1970; (ed, with others) Aspects of Capital Investment in Great Britain, 1750–1850, 1971; (ed) The Trades Unions Commission: the Sheffield outrages, 1971; (ed with J. Salt) Robert Owen, prophet of the poor, 1971; (ed with C. Holmes) Documents of European Economic History, vol. 1, 1968, vols 2 and 3, 1972; The Economic Integration of Europe, 1815–1970, 1974; (ed with C. Holmes) Essays in the Economic and Social History of South Yorkshire, 1977; (with Paul Robertson) The British Shipbuilding Industry 1870–1914, 1979; Peaceful Conquest, 1981; The Wasting of the British Economy, 1982; (with C. H. Feinstein) Studies in Capital Formation in Great Britain, 1988; Britain's Prime and Britain's Decline, 1988; Wealth and Poverty, 1990; Typology of Industrialization Processes in the 19th Century, 1990; (ed with Karl Ditt) Von der Heimarbeit in die Fabrik, 1992; (ed with D. Ziegler) Markt, Staat, Planung, 1992; articles in learned journals in field of economics, economic history and history. *Recreations:* walking, music. *Address:* 34 Bents Road, Sheffield S11 9RJ. *T:* Sheffield (0114) 236 8543.

POLLEN, Sir John Michael Hungerford, 7th Bt of Redenham, Hampshire, *cr* 1795; *b* 6 April 1919; *s* of late Lieut-Commander John Francis Hungerford Pollen, RN; *S* kinsman, Sir John Lancelot Hungerford Pollen, 6th Bt, 1959; *m* 1st, 1941, Angela Mary Oriana Russi (marr. diss., 1956); one *s* one *d*; 2nd, 1957, Mrs Diana Jubb. *Educ:* Downside; Merton Coll., Oxford. Served War of 1939–45 (despatches). *Heir:* *s* Richard John Hungerford Pollen [*b* 3 Nov. 1946; *m* 1971, Christianne, *d* of Sir Godfrey Agnew, *qv*; four *s* three *d*]. *Address:* Manor House, Rodbourne, Malmesbury, Wiltshire SN16 0EX; Lochportain, Isle of North Uist, Outer Hebrides.

POLLEN, Peregrine Michael Hungerford; Executive Deputy Chairman, 1975–77, Deputy Chairman, 1977–82, Sotheby Parke Bernet and Co.; *b* 24 Jan. 1931; *s* of late Sir Walter Michael Hungerford Pollen, MC, JP, and Lady Pollen; *m* 1958, Patricia Helen Barry; one *s* two *d*. *Educ:* Eton Coll.; Christ Church, Oxford. National Service, 1949–51. ADC to Sir Evelyn Baring, Governor of Kenya, 1955–57; Sotheby's, 1957–82: Dir, 1961; Pres., Sotheby Parke Bernet, New York, 1965–72. *Address:* Norton Hall, Mickleton, Glos GL55 6PU. *T:* Mickleton (01386) 438218. *Clubs:* Brooks's, Beefsteak.

POLLINGTON, Viscount; John Andrew Bruce Savile; *b* 30 Nov. 1959; *s* and *heir* of 8th Earl of Mexborough, *qv*.

POLLOCK, family name of **Viscount Hanworth.**

POLLOCK, Alexander; Sheriff of Grampian, Highland and Islands at Aberdeen and Stonehaven, since 1993; *b* 21 July 1944; *s* of Robert Faulds Pollock, OBE, and Margaret Findlay Pollock; *m* 1975, Verena Francesca Gertraud Alice Ursula Critchley; one *s* one *d*. *Educ:* Rutherglen Academy; Glasgow Academy; Brasenose Coll., Oxford (Domus Exhibnr; MA); Edinburgh Univ. (LLB); Perugia Univ. Solicitor, Bonar Mackenzie & Kermack, WS, 1970–73; passed advocate, 1973; Advocate Depute, 1990–91; Sheriff (floating) of Tayside, Central and Fife at Stirling, 1991–93. Contested (C) Moray, 1987. MP (C): Moray and Nairn, 1979–83; Moray, 1983–87. PPS to Sec. of State for Scotland, 1982–86, to Sec. of State for Defence, 1986–87. Mem., Commons Select Cttee on Scottish Affairs, 1979–82, 1986–87. Sec., British-Austrian Parly Gp, 1979–87. Mem., Queen's Body Guard for Scotland, Royal Co. of Archers, 1984–. *Recreations:* music, cycling, dogs. *Address:* Drumdarrach, Forres, Moray, Scotland IV36 0DW. *Clubs:* New (Edinburgh); Highland (Inverness); Forres Golf.

POLLOCK, Prof. Christopher John, PhD, DSc; Director, Institute of Grassland and Environmental Research, since 1993; *b* 28 March 1947; *s* of Neil Cunningham Pollock and Margaret Pollock (*née* Charlton); *m* 1970, Elizabeth Anne Bates; one *s* one *d*. *Educ:* Trinity Hall, Cambridge (MA); Birmingham Univ. (PhD, DSc). Post-Doctoral Fellow, Botany Sch., Cambridge, 1971–74; joined Welsh Plant Breeding Station, now Inst. of Grassland and Envmtl Res., 1974; Head, Res. Gp, 1985; Head, Envmtl Biology Dept, 1989. Fulbright Fellow, Univ. of California, Davis, 1978–79; NATO Sen. Res. Fellow, Purdue Univ., 1987–92; Prof., Univ. of Wales, Aberystwyth, 1993; Prof., Nottingham Univ., 1994. *Publications:* (jtly) Carbon Partitioning Within and Between Organisms, 1992; (with J. F. Farrar) The Biology of Fructans, 1993; reviews; papers in sci. jls. *Recreations:* golf, walking, woodwork. *Address:* Institute of Grassland and Environmental Research, Plas Gogerddan, Aberystwyth SY23 3EB. *T:* Aberystwyth (01970) 828255. *Club:* St David's (Aberystwyth).

POLLOCK, David John Frederick; Director, Action on Smoking and Health, 1991–94; *b* 3 Feb. 1942; *s* of Leslie William Pollock and late Dorothy Emily (*née* Holt); *m* 1976, Lois Jaques (marr. diss. 1991); one *s*. *Educ:* Beckenham and Penge Grammar Sch.; Keble Coll., Oxford (BA Lit. Hum. 1964); London Business Sch. British Coal Corporation, 1964–90: Head of Central Secretariat, 1972–78; Head of Staff Planning and Orgn, 1980–90. Mem., Hackney BC, 1974–78. Sec., Charity Law Reform Cttee, 1972–77. Chairman: British Humanist Assoc., 1970–72; Rationalist Press Assoc., 1989–. Treasurer, Hackney North Labour Party, 1989–92. *Publications:* articles in humanist, health and other jls. *Recreations:* theatre, gardening. *Address:* 13 Dunsmure Road, N16 5PU. *T:* 0181–800 3542.

POLLOCK, Ellen Clara; actress and director; President, The Shaw Society; Professor at RADA and Webber Douglas School of Acting; *b* 29 June 1902; *m* 1st, 1929, Lt-Col L. F. Hancock, OBE, RE (decd); one *s*; 2nd, 1945, James Proudfoot (*d* 1971). *Educ:* St Mary's College, W2; Convent of The Blessed Sacrament, Brighton. First appeared, Everyman, 1920, as page in Romeo and Juliet. Accompanied Lady Forbes-Robertson on her S. African tour, and later visited Australia as Moscovitch's leading lady. West End successes include: Hit the Deck, Hippodrome, 1927; Her First Affaire, Kingsway, and Duke of York's, 1930; The Good Companions, Her Majesty's, 1931; Too True to be Good, New, 1933; Finished Abroad, Savoy, 1934; French Salad, Westminster and Royalty, 1934; The Dominant Sex, Shaftesbury and Aldwych, 1935. Open Air Theatre: Lysistrata; As You

Like It. Seasons of Shaw's plays: at Lyric, Hammersmith, 1944, and with late Sir Donald Wolfit at King's, Hammersmith, 1953; three seasons of Grand Guignol plays at The Irving and Granville, Walham Green; Six Characters in Search of an Author, New Mayfair Theatre, 1963; Lady Frederick, Vaudeville and Duke of York's, 1969–70; Ambassador, Her Majesty's, 1971; Pygmalion, Albery, 1974; Tales from the Vienna Woods, Nat. Theatre, 1976; The Dark Lady of the Sonnets, Nat. Theatre, 1977; The Woman I Love, Churchill, 1979; Country Life, Lyric, Hammersmith, 1980; Harlequinade, and Playbill, Nat. Theatre, 1980. Has acted in numerous films and TV, incl. Forsyte Saga, The Pallisers, World's End and The Nightingale Saga; also radio broadcasts. *Productions include:* Summer in December, Comedy Theatre, 1949; Miss Turner's Husband, St Martin's, 1949; The Third Visitor, Duke of York's, 1949; Shavings, St Martin's, 1951; Mrs Warren's Profession, Royal Court, 1956; A Matter of Choice, Arts, 1967. *Recreations:* motoring, antiques and cooking. *Address:* 9 Tedworth Square, SW3 4DU. *T:* 0171–352 5082.

POLLOCK, Sir George F(rederick), 5th Bt, *cr* 1866; Artist-Photographer since 1963; *b* 13 Aug. 1928; *s* of Sir (Frederick) John Pollock, 4th Bt and Alix l'Estom (*née* Soubiran); *S* father, 1963; *m* 1951, Doreen Mumford, *o d* of N. E. K. Nash, CMG; one *s* two *d*. *Educ:* Eton; Trinity Coll., Cambridge. BA 1953, MA 1957. 2nd Lieut, 17/21 Lancers, 1948–49. Admitted Solicitor, 1956, retd. Hon. FRPS (Past Pres.). FRSA. Past Chm., London Salon of Photography. *Heir:* *s* David Frederick Pollock [*b* 13 April 1959; *m* 1985, Helena, *o d* of L. J. Tompsett]. *Address:* 83 Minster Way, Bathwick, Bath BA2 6RL. *T:* Bath (01225) 464692. *Club:* DHO (Wengen).

POLLOCK, Sir Giles (Hampden) Montagu-, 5th Bt *cr* 1872; management consultant, since 1974; Associate of Korn/Ferry Carré/Orban International Ltd, since 1989; *b* 19 Oct. 1928; *s* of Sir George Seymour Montagu-Pollock, 4th Bt, and Karen-Sofie (*d* 1991), *d* of Hans Ludwig Dedekam, Oslo; *S* father, 1985; *m* 1963, Caroline Veronica, *d* of Richard F. Russell; one *s* one *d*. *Educ:* Eton; de Havilland Aeronautical Technical School. de Havilland Enterprise, 1949–56; Bristol Aeroplane Co. Ltd, 1956–59; Bristol Siddeley Engines Ltd, 1959–61; Associate Dir, J. Walter Thompson Co. Ltd, 1961–69; Director: C. Vernon & Sons Ltd, 1969–71; Acumen Marketing Group Ltd, 1971–74; 119 Pall Mall Ltd, 1972–78; Associate, John Stork & Partners, subseq. John Stork Internat., 1980–89. *Recreations:* bicycling, water-skiing, walking. *Heir:* *s* Guy Maximilian Montagu-Pollock, *b* 27 Aug. 1966. *Address:* The White House, 7 Washington Road, SW13 9BG. *T:* 0181–748 8491. *Club:* Institute of Directors.

POLLOCK, John Denton; General Secretary, Educational Institute of Scotland, 1975–88; a Forestry Commissioner, 1978–91; *b* 21 April 1926; *s* of John Pollock and Elizabeth (*née* Crawford); *m* 1961, Joyce Margaret Sharpe; one *s* one *d*. *Educ:* Ayr Academy; Royal Technical Coll., Glasgow; Glasgow Univ.; Jordanhill Coll. of Education. BSc (Pure Science). FEIS 1971. RE, 1945–48 (commnd). Teacher, Mauchline Secondary Sch., 1951–59; Head Teacher, Kilmaurs Secondary Sch., 1959–65; Rector, Mainholm Acad., 1965–74. Chm., Scottish Labour Party, 1959 and 1971. Vice-Chm., Scottish TUC, 1980–81, Chm., 1981–82 (Mem., Gen. Council, 1975–87). Member: (Annan) Cttee on Future of Broadcasting, 1974–77; Gen. Adv. Council, BBC, 1981–84; Broadcasting Council for Scotland, 1985–89; Manpower Services Cttee Scotland, 1977–88; Employment Appeal Tribunal, 1991–; Council for Tertiary Educn in Scotland, 1979–83; Exec. Bd, European Trade Union Cttee for Educn, 1980–90 (Vice-Pres., 1986–87 and 1989–90); Chm., European Cttee, World Conf. of Orgns of Teaching Profession, 1980–90; Mem. World Exec., World Conf. of Orgns of Teaching Profession, 1986–90. Chm., Network Scotland, 1992– (Dir, 1991–92). Russell Award, for services to internat. educn, Stockholm, 1993. *Address:* 52 Douglas Road, Longniddry, East Lothian, Scotland EH32 0LJ. *T:* Longniddry (01875) 52082.

POLLOCK, Martin Rivers, FRS 1962; Professor of Biology, University of Edinburgh, 1965–76, now Emeritus; *b* 10 Dec. 1914; *s* of Hamilton Rivers Pollock and Eveline Morton Pollock (*née* Bell); *m* 1st, 1941, Jean Ilsley Paradise (marr. diss.); two *s* two *d*; 2nd, 1979, Janet Frances Machen. *Educ:* Winchester Coll., Trinity Coll., Cambridge; University College Hospital, London. BA Cantab, 1936; Senior Scholar, Trinity Coll., Cambridge, 1936; MRCS, LRCP 1939; MB, BCh Cantab 1940. House Appointments at UCH and Brompton Hospital, 1940–41; Bacteriologist, Emergency Public Health Laboratory Service, 1941–45; seconded to work on Infective Hepatitis with MRC Unit, 1943–45; apppointment to scientific staff, Medical Research Council, under Sir Paul Fildes, FRS, 1945–; Head of Division of Bacterial Physiology, Nat. Inst. for Medical Research, Mill Hill (MRC), 1949–65. *Publications:* (ed) Report of Conference on Common Denominators in Art and Science, 1983; articles in British Journal of Experimental Pathology, Biochemical Journal, Journal of General Microbiology, etc. *Recreation:* contemplating, planning but no longer undertaking various forms of mildly adventurous travel through deserts, painting. *Address:* Marsh Farm House, Margaret Marsh, Shaftesbury, Dorset SP7 0AZ. *T:* Marnhull (01258) 820479.

POLLOCK, Adm. of the Fleet Sir Michael (Patrick), GCB 1971 (KCB 1969; CB 1966); LVO 1952; DSC 1944; *b* 19 Oct. 1916; *s* of late C. A. Pollock and Mrs G. Pollock; *m* 1st, 1940, Margaret Steacy (*d* 1951), Bermuda; two *s* one *d*; 2nd, 1954, Marjory Helen Reece (*née* Bisset); one step *d*. *Educ:* RNC Dartmouth. Entered Navy, 1930; specialised in Gunnery, 1941. Served War of 1939–45 in Warspite, Vanessa, Arethusa and Norfolk, N. Atlantic, Mediterranean and Indian Ocean. Captain, Plans Div. of Admiralty and Director of Surface Weapons; comd HMS Vigo and Portsmouth Sqdn, 1958–59; comd HMS Ark Royal, 1963–64; Asst Chief of Naval Staff, 1964–66; Flag Officer Second in Command, Home Fleet, 1966–67; Flag Officer Submarines and Nato Commander Submarines, Eastern Atlantic, 1967–69; Controller of the Navy, 1970–71; Chief of Naval Staff and First Sea Lord, 1971–74; First and Principal Naval Aide-de-Camp to the Queen, 1972–74. Comdr, 1950; Capt., 1955; Rear-Adm., 1964; Vice-Adm., 1968; Adm., 1970. Bath King of Arms, 1976–85. *Recreations:* sailing, shooting, travel. *Address:* The Ivy House, Churchstoke, Montgomery, Powys SY15 6DU.

POLLOCK, Peter Brian; His Honour Judge Pollock; a Circuit Judge, since 1987; *b* 27 April 1936; *s* of late Brian Treherne Pollock and Helen Evelyn Pollock (*née* Holt-Wilson); *m* 1st, 1966, Joan Maryon Leggett (marr. diss. 1981); two *s* (and one *s* decd); 2nd, 1988, Jeannette Mary Nightingale. *Educ:* St Lawrence College. Called to the Bar, Middle Temple, 1958. A Recorder of the Crown Court, 1986–87. *Recreations:* playing tennis, watching cricket, travel, walking, cooking, gardening. *Address:* Croydon Crown Court, Altyre Road, Croydon CR9 5AB. *T:* 0181–681 2533. *Clubs:* MCC, Roehampton.

POLTIMORE, 7th Baron *cr* 1831; **Mark Coplestone Bampfylde;** Bt 1641; Director, Christie's, since 1987 (Associate Director, 1984–87); *b* 8 June 1957; *s* of Captain the Hon. Anthony Gerard Hugh Bampfylde (*d* 1969) (*er s* of 6th Baron) and of Brita Yvonne (who *m* 2nd, 1975, Guy Elmes), *o d* of late Baron Rudolph Cederström; *S* grandfather, 1978; *m* 1982, Sally Anne, *d* of Dr Norman Miles; two *s* one *d*. *Publication:* (with Philip Hook) Popular Nineteenth Century Painting: a dictionary of European genre painters, 1986. *Heir:* *s* Hon. Henry Anthony Warwick Bampfylde, *b* 3 June 1985. *Address:* Ridgemoor Farm House, West Street, Burghclere, Newbury, Berks RG15 9LD. *Club:* White's.

POLUNIN, Nicholas, CBE 1976; MS (Yale); MA, DPhil, DSc (Oxon.); FLS; FRGS; Editor (founding), Environmental Conservation, since 1974; Co-Editor, Environmental Challenges, since 1993; President: The Foundation for Environmental Conservation, since 1975; World Council for the Biosphere, since 1984; *b* Hammonds Farm, Checkendon, Oxon; *e s* of late Vladimir and Elizabeth Violet (*née* Hart) Polunin; *m* 1st, 1939, Helen Lovat Fraser (*d* 1973); one *s*; 2nd, 1948, Helen Eugenie Campbell; two *s* one *d*. *Educ:* The Hall, Weybridge; Latymer Upper and privately; Oxford, Yale and Harvard Univs. Open Scholar of Christ Church, Oxford, 1928–32; First Class Hons Nat. Sci. Final Examination, Botany and Ecology; Goldsmiths' Senior Studentship for Research, 1932–33; Botanical tutor in various Oxford Colls, 1932–47; Henry Fellowship at Pierson Coll., Yale Univ., USA, 1933–34 (Sigma Xi); Departmental Demonstrator in Botany 1934–35, and Senior (Research) Scholar of New Coll., Oxford, 1934–36; Dept of Scientific and Industrial Research, Senior Research Award, 1935–38; Rolleston Memorial Prize, 1938; DSIR Special Investigator, 1938; Research Associate, Gray Herbarium, Harvard Univ., USA, 1936–37, and subs. Foreign Research Associate; Fielding Curator and Keeper of the Univ. Herbaria, Oxford, and Univ. Demonstrator and Lectr in Botany, 1939–47; Oxford Univ. Botanical Moderator, 1941–45; Macdonald Prof. of Botany, McGill Univ., Canada, 1947–52 (Visiting Prof., 1946–47); Research Fellow, Harvard Univ., 1950–53; Lectr in Plant Science and Research Associate, Yale Univ., 1953–55; Project Dir, US Air Force, 1953–55, and Consultant to US Army Corps of Engineers; formerly Sen. Research Fell. and Lectr, New Coll., Oxford; Prof. of Plant Ecology and Taxonomy, Head of Dept of Botany, and Dir of Univ. Herbarium, etc., Baghdad, Iraq, Jan. 1956–58 (revolution); Founding Prof. of Botany and Head of Dept, Faculty of Science (which he established as Dean), Univ. of Ife, Nigeria, 1962–66 (revolutions, etc). Leverhulme Res. Award, 1941–43; Arctic Inst. Res. Fellowship, 1946–48; Guggenheim Mem. Fellowship, 1950–52. Haley Lectr, Acadia Univ., NS, 1950; Visiting Lectr and Adviser on Biology, Brandeis Univ., Waltham, Mass, 1953–54; Guest Prof., Univ. of Geneva, 1959–61 and 1975–76. FRHS; Fellow: AAAS, Arctic Inst. NA. Vice Pres., Internat. Soc. of Naturalists. Member or Leader, numerous scientific expeditions from 1930, particularly in arctic or sub-arctic regions, including Spitsbergen (widely, including crossing alone), Lapland (3 times), Iceland, Greenland, Canadian Eastern Arctic (5 times, including confirmation of Spicer Islands in Foxe Basin north of Hudson Bay and discovery in 1946 of last major islands to be added to world map following their naming in 1949 as Prince Charles Is. and Air Force Is.), Labrador-Ungava (many times), Canadian Western Arctic (including Magnetic Pole), Alaska, summer and winter flights over geographical North Pole; subsequently in Middle East and West Africa; Ford Foundation Award, Scandinavia and USSR, 1966–67. International Botanical Congresses: VII (Stockholm, 1950); VIII (Paris, 1954); X (Edinburgh, 1964); XI (Seattle, 1969, symposium chm., etc); XII (Leningrad, 1975, Conservation Section 1st chm., etc.); XIII (Sydney, 1981); International Congresses of Ecology: I (The Hague, 1974); II (Jerusalem, 1978); IV (Syracuse, NY, 1986, contrib. paper *in absentia* with E. P. Odum). Convener and Gen. Ed., Envmtl Monographs and Symposia, 1979–88; Founding Editor: Biological Conservation, 1967–74; Plant Science Monographs, 1954–78; World Crops Books, 1954–69; Chm. Editl Bd, Cambridge Studies in Environmental Policy; Member, Advisory Board: The Environmentalist, 1981–95; Environmental Awareness, 1989–, and other jls. International Conferences on Environmental Future, 1971–91: Chm., Internat. Steering Cttee, and Editor of Proceedings, 1st Conf. Finland, 1971; Secretary-General and Editor: 2nd Conf., Iceland, 1978, 3rd Conf., Edinburgh, 1987, 4th Conf., Budapest, 1990; Founding Chm. Foundn for Environmental Conservation, 1973 (consolidated and placed under Geneva cantonal and Swiss federal surveillance, 1975; Life Pres., 1975). Initiated annual Biosphere Day, 21 Sept. 1991. US Order of Polaris; Marie-Victorin Medal for services to Canadian botany; Ramdeo Medal for Environmental Scis, India, 1986; Internat. Sasakawa Environment Prize, 1987; Academia Sinica Medal, China, 1988; USSR Vernadsky Medal, 1988; Hungarian Acad. of Sciences' Founder's (Zéchenyi) Medal, 1990. Elected to Global 500 Roll of Honour, UN Envmt Programme, 1991. Officer, Order of Golden Ark (Netherlands), 1990. *Publications:* Russian Waters, 1931; The Isle of Auks, 1932; Botany of the Canadian Eastern Arctic, vol. I, Pteridophyta and Spermatophyta, 1940; (ed) vol. II, Thallophyta and Bryophyta, 1947; vol. III, Vegetation and Ecology, 1948; Arctic Unfolding, 1949; Circumpolar Arctic Flora, 1959; Introduction to Plant Geography, 1960 (subseq. Amer., Indonesian and other edns); Eléments de Géographie botanique, 1967; (ed) The Environmental Future, 1972; Growth Without Ecodisasters?, 1980; Ecosystem Theory and Application, 1986; (with Sir John Burnett) Maintenance of The Biosphere, 1990; Surviving With The Biosphere, 1993; (with Mohammad Nazim) Environmental Challenges, vol. I, 1993, vol. II, 1994; World Who's Who and Does What in Environment and Conservation, 1996; papers chiefly on arctic and boreal flora, phytogeography, ecology, vegetation, aerobiology, and conservation; editor of International Industry, 1943–46; contrib. Encyclopædia Britannica, Encyclopedia of the Biological Scis, etc., and some 650 other scientific papers, editorials, reviews, etc, to various jls. *Recreations:* travel and scientific exploration, nature conservation, stock-markets. *Address:* 7 Chemin Taverney, 1218 Grand-Saconnex, Geneva, Switzerland. *T:* (022) 7982383/4, *Fax:* (022) 7982344; c/o New College, Oxford. *Clubs:* Reform (life); Harvard (life), Torrey Botanical (New York City); Canadian Field Naturalists' (Ottawa).

POLWARTH, 10th Lord, *cr* 1690 (Scot.); **Henry Alexander Hepburne-Scott,** TD; DL; Vice-Lord-Lieutenant, Borders Region (Roxburgh, Ettrick and Lauderdale), since 1975; Member, Royal Company of Archers; a Scots Representative Peer, 1945–63; Chartered Accountant; *b* 17 Nov. 1916; *s* of late Hon. Walter Thomas Hepburne-Scott (*d* 1942); *S* grandfather, 1944; *m* 1st, 1943, Caroline Margaret (marr. diss. 1969; she *d* 1982), 2nd *d* of late Captain R. A. Hay, Marlefield, Roxburghshire, and Helmsley, Yorks; one *s* three *d*; 2nd, 1969, Jean, *d* of late Adm. Sir Angus Cunninghame Graham of Gartmore, KBE, CB, and formerly wife of C. E. Jauncey, QC (now Rt Hon. Lord Jauncey); two step *s* one step *d*. *Educ:* Eton Coll.; King's Coll., Cambridge. Served War of 1939–45, Captain, Lothians and Border Yeomanry. Former Partner, firm of Chiene and Tait, CA, Edinburgh; Governor, Bank of Scotland, 1966–72, Director, 1950–72 and 1974–87; Chm., General Accident, Fire & Life Assurance Corp., 1968–72; Director: ICI Ltd, 1969–72, 1974–81; Halliburton Co., 1974–87; Canadian Pacific Ltd, 1975–86; Sun Life Assurance Co. of Canada, 1975–84. Minister of State, Scottish Office, 1972–74. Chm., later Pres., Scottish Council (Develt and Industry), 1955–72. Member: Franco-British Council, 1981–90; H of L Select Cttee on Trade, 1984–85. Chairman: Scottish Nat. Orchestra Soc., 1975–79; Scottish Forestry Trust, 1987–90. Murrayfield Hosp., 1982–90. Chancellor, Aberdeen Univ., 1966–86. Hon. LLD: St Andrews; Aberdeen; Hon. DLitt Heriot-Watt; DUniv Stirling. FRSE; FRSA; Hon. FRIAS. DL Roxburgh, 1962. *Heir:* *s* Master of Polwarth, *qv*. *Address:* Easter Harden, Hawick, Roxburghshire TD9 7LP. *T:* Hawick (01450) 72069. *Clubs:* Army and Navy; New (Edinburgh).

See also Baron Moran.

POLWARTH, Master of; Hon. Andrew Walter Hepburne-Scott; *b* 30 Nov. 1947; *s* and *heir* of 10th Lord Polwarth, *qv*; *m* 1971, Isabel Anna, *e d* of Maj. J. F. H. Surtees, OBE, MC; two *s* two *d*. *Educ:* Eton; Trinity Hall, Cambridge. *Address:* Harden, Hawick, Roxburghshire TD9 7LP. *Clubs:* New (Edinburgh); Knickerbocker (New York).

POLYNESIA, Bishop in, since 1975; **Rt. Rev. Jabez Leslie Bryce;** *b* 25 Jan. 1935. *Educ:* St John's College, Auckland, NZ (LTh); St Andrew's Seminary, Manila, Phillipines (BTh).

Deacon 1960, priest 1962, Polynesia; Curate of Suva, 1960–63; Priest-in-charge: Tonga, 1964; St Peter's Chinese Congregation, Manila, 1965–67; Archdeacon of Suva, 1967–69; Deputy Vicar-General, Holy Trinity Cathedral, Suva, 1967–72; Lectr, St John Baptist Theological Coll., Suva, 1967–69; Vicar of Viti Levu W, 1969–75; Archdeacon in Polynesia, 1969–75; Vicar-General of Polynesia, 1972–75. Chm., Pacific Conf. of Churches, 1976–86. *Recreations:* tennis, golf. *Address:* Bishop's House, PO Box 35, Suva, Fiji Islands. *T:* (office) 304716, (home) 302553, *Fax:* 302 152.

POMEROY, family name of **Viscount Harberton.**

POMEROY, Anthony Michael John, FCIT; Director of Education Training and Membership, Chartered Institute of Transport, since 1989; *b* 11 Oct. 1930; *s* of Jack Pomeroy and Margaret (*née* Tyler); *m* 1957, Joan Olive Beard (*d* 1993); one *s* one *d*. *Educ:* Univ. of Nottingham (BA Hist. 1954). FCIT 1967. Traffic Manager, Grey Green Coaches, 1954–57; Claims Manager, N. Francis & Co., 1957–59; Distribn Controller then Trng Exec., Advance Linen Services, 1959–63; Dir of Transport, Louis Reece (Kent) Ltd, 1963–85; freelance lectr in transport studies and transport consultant, 1985–89. Dir, Transport Tutorial Assoc., 1985–89. FRSA 1991. *Publications:* contrib. various distance learning courses in transport hist., operations and policy. *Recreations:* family genealogy, music and theatre, transport, local history. *Address:* 182 Kings Hall Road, Beckenham, Kent BR3 1LJ. *T:* 0181–778 6382.

PONCET, Jean André F.; *see* François-Poncet.

POND, Carole; *see* Tongue, C.

POND, Christopher; Director, Low Pay Unit, since 1980; *b* 25 Sept. 1952; *s* of Charles Richard Pond and Doris Violet Pond; *m* 1990, Carole Tongue, *qv*; one *d*. *Educ:* Univ. of Sussex (BA Hons Econs). Research Asst in Econs, Birkbeck Coll., Univ. of London, 1974–75; Res. Officer, Low Pay Unit, 1975–78; Lectr in Econs, CS Coll., 1978–79. Vis. Lectr in Econs, Univ. of Kent, 1983–84; Hon. Vis. Prof. and Res. Fellow, Univ. of Surrey, 1984–86; Hon. Vis. Prof., Univ. of Middlesex. Consultant, Open Univ., 1987–88 and 1991–92. Contested (Lab) Welwyn Hatfield, 1987. FRSA 1992. *Publications:* (jtly) To Him Who Hath, 1977; (jtly) Taxation and Social Policy, 1981. *Recreations:* running, reading, amusing my daughter. *Address:* 123 Richmond Avenue, N1 0LR. *T:* 0171–609 0878.

PONDER, Prof. Bruce Anthony John, PhD; FRCP; Cancer Research Campaign Professor of Human Cancer Genetics, University of Cambridge, since 1992; Fellow, Jesus College, Cambridge, since 1993; *b* 25 April 1944; *s* of Anthony West Ponder and Dorothy Mary Ponder (*née* Peachey); *m* 1969, Margaret Ann Hickinbotham; one *s* three *d*. *Educ:* Charterhouse Sch.; Cambridge Univ.; St Thomas's Hosp. Med. Sch. MA, MB BChir (Cambridge); PhD (London); FRCP 1987; NHS hosp. appts, 1968–73; Clinical Research Fellow, ICRF, 1973–76; first Hamilton Fairley Fellow, CRC at Harvard Med. Sch., 1977–78; Clinical Scientific Officer, ICRF, St Bartholomew's Hosp., 1978–80; Institute of Cancer Research: CRC Fellow and Sen. Lectr in Med., Royal Marsden Hosp., 1980–87; Reader in Human Cancer Genetics and Head, Section of Cancer Genetics, 1987–89; Dir, CRC Human Cancer Genetics Gp, Univ. of Cambridge, 1989–. Hon. Consultant Physician: Royal Marsden Hosp., 1980–; Addenbrooke's Hosp., Cambridge, 1989–. Gibb Fellow, CRC, 1990. Internat. Public Service Award, Nat. Neurofibromatosis Foundn, USA, 1992. *Publications:* papers on genetics, cancer, developmental biology. *Recreations:* gardening, travel, golf, sailboarding, wine. *Address:* Addenbrooke's Hospital, Hills Road, Cambridge CB2 2QQ. *T:* Cambridge (01223) 336900, *Fax:* (01223) 336902; 43 High Street, Cottenham, Cambridge CB4 4SA. *Club:* Royal Ashdown Forest Golf (Forest Row).

PONSONBY, family name of **Earl of Bessborough** and of **Barons de Mauley, Ponsonby of Shulbrede,** and **Sysonby.**

PONSONBY OF SHULBREDE, 4th Baron *cr* 1930, of Shulbrede; **Frederick Matthew Thomas Ponsonby;** *b* 27 Oct. 1958; *o s* of 3rd Baron and of Ursula Mary, *yr d* of Comdr Thomas Stanley Lane Fox-Pitt, OBE, RN; *S* father, 1990. *Educ:* Holland Park Comprehensive Sch.; University Coll., Cardiff; Imperial Coll., London. Councillor (Lab), London Borough of Wandsworth, 1990–94. Opposition frontbench spokesman on educn, H of L, 1992–. *Heir:* none. *Address:* House of Lords, SW1A 0PW.

PONSONBY, Sir Ashley (Charles Gibbs), 2nd Bt *cr* 1956; KCVO 1993; MC 1945; Director, J. Henry Schroder, Wagg & Co. Ltd, 1962–80; Lord-Lieutenant of Oxfordshire, since 1980; *b* 21 Feb. 1921; *o s* of Col Sir Charles Edward Ponsonby, 1st Bt, TD, and Hon. Winifred (*d* 1984), *d* of 1st Baron Hunsdon; *S* father, 1976; *m* 1950, Lady Martha Butler, *yr d* of 6th Marquess of Ormonde, CVO, MC; four *s*. *Educ:* Eton; Balliol College, Oxford. 2nd Lieut Coldstream Guards, 1941; served war 1942–45 (North Africa and Italy, wounded); Captain 1943; on staff Bermuda Garrison, 1945–46. A Church Commissioner, 1963–80; Mem., Council of Duchy of Lancaster, 1977–92. DL Oxon, 1974–80. *Heir: e s* Charles Ashley Ponsonby [*b* 10 June 1951; *m* 1983, Mary P., *yr d* of late A. R. Bromley Davenport and of Mrs A. R. Bromley Davenport, Over Peover, Knutsford, Cheshire; two *s* one *d*]. *Address:* Woodleys, Woodstock, Oxon OX20 1HJ. *T:* Woodstock (01993) 811422. *Club:* Pratt's.

PONSONBY, Myles Walter, CBE 1966; HM Diplomatic Service, retired; County Councillor, Idmiston Division, Wiltshire County Council, 1988–93; *b* 12 Sept. 1924; *s* of late Victor Coope Ponsonby, MC and Gladys Edith Ponsonby (*née* Walter); *m* 1951, Anne Veronica Theresa Maynard, *y d* of Brig. Francis Herbert Maynard, CB, DSO, MC, and of Ethel Maynard (*née* Bates); one *s* two *d*. *Educ:* St Aubyn's, Rottingdean; Eton College. HM Forces (Captain, KRRC), 1942–49. Entered Foreign (subseq. Diplomatic) Service, 1951; served in: Egypt, 1951; Cyprus, 1952–53; Beirut, 1953–56; Djakarta, 1958–61; Nairobi, 1963–64; Hanoi (Consul-Gen.), 1964–65; FO, 1966–69; Rome, 1969–71; FCO, 1972–74; Ambassador to Mongolian People's Republic, 1974–77; FCO, 1977–80. *Recreation:* exploring the British Isles. *Address:* The Old Vicarage, Porton, near Salisbury, Wilts SP4 0LH. *T:* Idmiston (01980) 610914. *Clubs:* Army and Navy, Travellers.

PONSONBY, Robert Noel, CBE 1985; Consultant, Musicians Benevolent Fund, since 1993; Controller of Music, BBC, 1972–85; *b* 19 Dec. 1926; *o s* of late Noel Ponsonby, BMus, Organist Christ Church Cathedral, Oxford, and Mary White-Thomson; *m* 1st, 1957, Una Mary (marr. diss.), *er d* of late W. J. Kenny; 2nd, 1977, Lesley Margaret Black (marr. diss.), *o d* of late G. T. Black. *Educ:* Eton; Trinity Coll., Oxford. MA Oxon, Eng. Litt. Commissioned Scots Guards, 1945–47. Organ Scholar, Trinity Coll., Oxford, 1948–50; staff of Glyndebourne Opera, 1951–55; Artistic Director of the Edinburgh International Festival, 1955–60; with Independent Television Authority, 1962–64; Gen. Administrator, Scottish Nat. Orchestra, 1964–72. Adminr, Friends of the Musicians Benevolent Fund, 1987–93. Director: Commonwealth Arts Festival, Glasgow, 1965; Henry Wood Promenade Concerts, 1974–86; Artistic Dir, Canterbury Fest., 1987–88. Artistic Adviser to Internat. Arts Guild of Bahamas, 1960–72. Chm., London Choral Soc., 1990–94; Programme Consultant, RPO, 1993–. Mem., Music Adv. Panel, Arts Council of GB, 1986–89. Trustee, Young Concert Artists Trust, 1984–89. Governor, Purcell Sch., 1985–88. Hon. RAM 1975; Hon. Mem., ISM, 1992. FRSA 1979. *Publication:* Short History of Oxford University Opera Club, 1950. *Recreations:* fell-walking, English and Scottish painting, music. *Address:* 11 St Cuthbert's Road, NW2 3QJ.

PONTECORVO, Guido, FRS 1955; FRSE 1946; FLS 1971; PhD; DrAgr; *b* Pisa, Italy, 29 Nov. 1907; *s* of Massimo Pontecorvo and Maria (*née* Maroni); *m* 1939, Leonore Freyenmuth, Frauenfeld (*d* 1986), Switzerland; one *d*. *Educ:* Univ. of Pisa (DrAgr 1928); Univ. of Edinburgh (PhD 1941). Ispettorato Agrario per la Toscana, Florence, 1931–38; Inst. of Animal Genetics, Univ. of Edinburgh, 1938–40 and 1944–45; Dept of Zoology, Univ. of Glasgow, 1941–44; Dept of Genetics, Univ. of Glasgow, 1945–68 (Prof. 1956–68); Hon. Dir, MRC Unit of Cell Genetics, 1966–68; Mem. Res. Staff, Imperial Cancer Res. Fund, 1968–75, Hon. Consultant Geneticist, 1975–80. Visiting Prof., Albert Einstein Coll. Med., 1965, 1966; Vis. Lectr, Washington State Univ., 1967; Royal Society, Leverhulme Overseas Vis. Prof., Inst. of Biophysics, Rio de Janeiro, 1969 and Dept of Biology, Pahlavi Univ., 1974; Sloane Foundn Vis. Prof., Vermont, 1971; Visiting Professor: UCL, 1968–75; King's Coll., London, 1970–71; Biology Dept, Tehran Univ., 1975; Prof. Ospite Linceo, Scuola Normale Superiore, Pisa, 1976–81; Raman Prof., Indian Acad. of Scis, 1982–83. Lectures: Jesup, Columbia Univ., 1956; Messenger, Cornell Univ., 1957; Leeuwenhoek, Royal Soc., 1962; L. C. Dunn, NY Blood Center, 1976; J. Weigle Meml, CIT, 1984; Gandhi Meml, Raman Inst., 1983. Pres., Genetical Soc., 1964–66; Vice-Pres., Inst. of Biology, 1969–71. Emeritus Mem., Academia Europaea, 1989; For. Hon. Member: Amer. Acad. Arts and Sciences, 1958; Danish Royal Acad. Sci. and Letters, 1966; Peruvian Soc. of Medical Genetics, 1969; Indian National Science Acad., 1983; Indian Acad. of Scis, 1984; Accademia dei XL, 1993; For. Associate, Nat. Acad. of Scis, USA, 1983. Hon. DSc: Leicester, 1968; Camerino, 1974; East Anglia, 1974; Hon. LLD Glasgow, 1978. Hansen Prize, Carlsberg Foundn, 1961; Darwin Medal, Royal Soc., 1978. Campano d'Oro, Pisa, 1979. *Publications:* Ricerche sull' economia montana dell' Appennino Toscano, 1933 (Florence); Trends in Genetic Analysis, 1958; Topics in Genetic Analysis, 1985; numerous papers on genetics and high mountain botany. *Recreation:* alpine plants photography. *Address:* 60 Thornhill Square, N1 1BE. *T:* 0171–700 5320.

PONTEFRACT, Bishop Suffragan of, since 1993; **Rt. Rev. John Thornley Finney;** *b* 1 May 1932; *s* of Arthur Frederick and Elaine Mary Finney; *m* 1959, Sheila Elizabeth Russell; three *d*. *Educ:* Charterhouse; Hertford College, Oxford (BA Jurisp.; Dip. Theol.). Ordained 1958; Curate, All Saints, Headington, 1958–61; Curate in Charge, Aylesbury, 1961–65; Rector, Tollerton, Notts, 1965–71; Vicar, St Margaret's, Aspley, Nottingham, 1971–80; Adviser in Evangelism to Bishop of Southwell, 1980–89; Officer for Decade of Evangelism, 1990–93. Manager, Research Project in Evangelism, BCC, 1989–92. *Publications:* Saints Alive!, 1983; Understanding Leadership, 1989; The Well Church Book, 1991; Church on the Move, 1992; Finding Faith Today, 1992; Stories of Faith, 1995. *Recreations:* golf, growing old gracefully. *Address:* Pontefract House, 181a Manygates Lane, Wakefield WF2 7DR.

PONTEFRACT, Archdeacon of; *see* Flack, Ken. J. R.

PONTI, Signora Carlo; *see* Loren, Sophia.

PONTIFEX, Brig. David More, CBE 1977 (OBE 1965; MBE 1956); General Secretary, Army Cadet Force Association and Secretary, Combined Cadet Force Association, 1977–87; *b* 16 Sept. 1922; *s* of Comdr John Weddall Pontifex, RN, and Monica Pontifex; *m* 1968, Kathleen Betsy (*née* Matheson); one *s* four *d*. *Educ:* Worth Preparatory Sch.; Downside Sch. Commnd The Rifle Brigade, 1942; served War, Italy (despatches); Staff Coll., Camberley, 1951; HQ Parachute Brigade, 1952–54; Kenya, 1954–56; War Office, 1956–58; Armed Forces Staff Coll., USA, 1958–59; Brigade Major, 63 Gurkha Brigade, 1961–62; CO 1st Bn Federal Regular Army, Aden, 1963–64; GSO1 2nd Div., BAOR, 1965–66; Col GS, Staff Coll., Camberley, 1967–69; Divisional Brig., The Light Div., 1969–73; Dep. Dir, Army Staff Duties, MoD, 1973–75; Dep. Comdr and COS, SE District, 1975–77, retired 1977. ADC to the Queen, 1975–77. *Address:* 68 Shortheath Road, Farnham, Surrey GU9 8SQ. *T:* Farnham (01252) 723284. *Club:* Naval and Military.

PONTIN, Sir Frederick William, (Sir Fred Pontin), Kt 1976; Founder: Pontin's Ltd, 1946; Pontinental Ltd, 1963; Chairman and Joint Managing Director of Pontin's Ltd, 1946–79 (Hon. President, since 1987), and Pontinental (HS) Ltd, 1972–79; Chairman, 1983–85, Deputy Chairman, 1985–87, Kunick Leisure; Chairman, Ponti's, 1988, retired; *b* 24 Oct. 1906; *m* Dorothy Beatrice Mortimer; one *d*. *Educ:* Sir George Monoux Grammar Sch., Walthamstow. Began career on London Stock Exchange, 1920. Catering and welfare work for Admiralty, Orkney Is, 1939–46. Acquired: Industrial Catering Bristol, 1946; Brean Sands Holiday Village, 1946. Chief Barker, Variety Club of GB (Raising £1,000,000 for charity), 1968; Mem. Exec. Bd, Variety Club, 1968–, Pres. 1969–75, formed 15 regional centres of club; Companion Mem., Grand Order of Water Rats. Prescot Band. Life Mem., BRCS (Hon. Vice Pres., Dorset Branch). Freeman of Christchurch, Dorset. *Recreations:* racing (owner of Specify, winner of 1971 Grand National, and Cala Mesquida, winner of 1971 Schweppes Gold Trophy); connected with Walthamstow Avenue FC for many years prior to 1939–45 war; interested in all sporting activities. *Address:* Flat 127, 3 Whitehall Court, SW1A 2EL. *T:* 0171–839 5251. *Clubs:* Farmers', Lord's Taverners, Saints and Sinners, Institute of Directors, Variety of GB.

PONTIN, John Graham; Chairman: JT Group Ltd, since 1961; Dartington Hall Trust, since 1984 (Trustee, since 1980); *b* 2 June 1937; *s* of Charles Cyril Pontin and Phyllis (*née* Frieze); *m* 1st, 1966, Gillian Margaret Harris (marr. diss. 1971); one *s* one *d*; 2nd, 1977, Sylviane Marie-Louise Aubel. *Educ:* Bristol Tech. Sch. (Building). Founder, JT Group, 1961; Director: GWR Radio, 1979–92; Avery's of Bristol, 1982–94; Dartington & Co., 1986–95; Chm., Dartington Glass, 1986–88. Trustee, Gtr Bristol Foundn (formerly Gtr Bristol Community Trust), 1987–. *Recreations:* gardening, walking. *Address:* 8 High Street, Chew Magna, Bristol BS18 8PW. *T:* Bristol (0117) 929 7127. *Club:* Reform.

POOLE, family name of **Baron Poole.**

POOLE, 2nd Baron *cr* 1958, of Aldgate; **David Charles Poole;** Group Chief Executive, Ockham (formerly Sturge) Holdings PLC, since 1994; *b* 6 Jan. 1945; *s* of 1st Baron Poole, PC, CBE, TD and Betty Margaret Gilkison (*d* 1988); *S* father, 1993; *m* 1967; one *s*; *m* 1995, Mrs Lucinda Edsell. *Educ:* Dragon Sch., Oxford; Gordonstoun; Christ Church, Oxford (MA); INSEAD, Fontainebleau (MBA). Samuel Montagu & Co. Ltd, 1967–74; Bland Payne & Co. Ltd, 1974–78; Capel-Cure Myers, 1978–87; Bonomi Group, 1987–90; James Capel, 1990–94; Mem., Prime Minister's Policy Unit (on secondment), 1992–94. *Recreations:* cruising, ballet. *Heir: s* Hon. Oliver John Poole, *b* 30 May 1972. *Address:* 53 The Chase, SW4 0NY. *Clubs:* Brooks's, Groucho; Royal Yacht Squadron, Island Sailing.

POOLE, Dame Anne; *see* Poole, Dame Avril A. B.

POOLE, Anthony Cecil James; Head of Administration Department, House of Commons, 1985–88, retired; *b* 9 Oct. 1927; *s* of Walter James Poole and Daisy Poole (*née* Voyle); *m* 1951, Amelia Keziah (*née* Pracy); one *d*. *Educ:* Headlands Grammar School, Swindon. Served RN, 1945–47; Department of Employment, 1947–76; Principal Establishments

Officer, Manpower Services Commn, 1976–80; House of Commons, 1980, Head of Establishments Office, 1981. *Recreations:* golf, gardening.

POOLE, Dame (Avril) Anne (Barker), DBE 1992; Chief Nursing Officer, Department of Health (formerly of Health and Social Security), 1982–92; non-executive Director, South West Surrey Health Authority, since 1993; *b* 11 April 1934; *d* of Arthur George and Norah Heritage; *m* 1959, John Percy Poole. *Educ:* High Sch., Southampton. SRN 1955, SCM 1957, Health Visitors Cert., 1958. Asst Chief Nursing Officer, City of Westminster, 1967–69; Chief Nursing Officer, London Borough of Merton, 1969–73; Area Nursing Officer, Surrey AHA, 1974–81; Dep. Chief Nursing Officer, DHSS, 1981–82. Trustee, Marie Curie Meml Foundn, 1992–. FRSocMed 1993; CIMgt (CBIM 1984). *Address:* Ancaster House, Church Hill, Merstham, Surrey RH1 3BL.

POOLE, Hon. Sir David Anthony, Kt 1995; **Hon. Mr Justice Poole;** a Judge of the High Court of Justice, Queen's Bench Division, since 1995; *b* 8 June 1938; *s* of William Joseph Poole and Lena (*née* Thomas); *m* 1974, Pauline Ann O'Flaherty; four *s*. *Educ:* Ampleforth; Jesus Coll., Oxford (Meyricke Exhibnr in Classics; MA); Univ. of Manchester Inst. of Science and Technology (DipTechSc). Called to the Bar, Middle Temple, 1968 (Bencher, 1992); QC 1984; a Recorder, 1983–95. Chm., Assoc. of Lawyers for the Defence of the Unborn, 1985–92. *Address:* Royal Courts of Justice, Strand, WC2A 2LL. *Clubs:* London Irish Rugby Football, Vincent's.

POOLE, David Arthur Ramsay; Managing Director, Blue Circle Industries, 1987–89; *b* 30 Sept. 1935; *s* of late Arthur Poole and Viola Isbol (*née* Ramsay); *m* 1961, Jean Mary Male; three *d*. *Educ:* King's Sch., Canterbury; St Edmund Hall, Oxford (MA Jurisprudence). Nat. service, 2nd Lieut, RA, 1955–57. Baring Bros & Co., 1960–65; APCM Ltd (now BCI), 1965–70; Wm Brandts & Co., 1970–73; British Caledonian Gp, 1973–75; Blue Circle Industries, 1976–89. *Recreations:* shooting, ski-ing, travel. *Address:* Fairhaven, 23 Fairmile Avenue, Cobham, Surrey KT11 2JA. *T:* Cobham (01932) 864830. *Clubs:* East India, Royal Automobile.

POOLE, David James, PPRP (RP 1969); ARCA; artist; *b* 5 June 1931; *s* of Thomas Herbert Poole and Catherine Poole; *m* 1958, Iris Mary Toomer; three *s*. *Educ:* Stoneleigh Secondary Sch.; Wimbledon Sch. of Art; Royal Coll. of Art. National Service, RE, 1949–51. Sen. Lectr in Painting and Drawing, Wimbledon Sch. of Art, 1962–77. Pres., Royal Soc. of Portrait Painters, 1983–91. One-man exhibns, Zurich and London. Portraits include: The Queen, The Duke of Edinburgh, The Queen Mother, Prince Charles, Princess Anne, Princess Margaret, Earl Mountbatten of Burma and The Duke of Kent; also distinguished members of govt, industry, commerce, medicine, the academic and legal professions. Work in private collections of the Queen and the Duke of Edinburgh, and in Australia, S Africa, Bermuda, France, W Germany, Switzerland, Saudi Arabia and USA. *Recreations:* painting, drawing. *Address:* Trinity Flint Barn, Weston Lane, Weston, Petersfield, Hants GU32 3NN. *T:* Petersfield (01730) 265075; Studio 6, Burlington Lodge, Rigault Road, Fulham, SW6 4JJ. *T:* 0171–736 9288.

POOLE, Isobel Anne; Sheriff of the Lothian and Borders, since 1979, at Edinburgh, since 1986; *b* 9 Dec. 1941; *d* of late John Cecil Findlay Poole, DM Oxon, and Constance Mary (*née* Gilkes), SRN. *Educ:* Oxford High Sch. for Girls; Edinburgh Univ. (LLB). Admitted to Faculty of Advocates, 1964. Formerly Standing Jun. Counsel to Registrar Gen. for Scotland. Member: Sheriffs' Council, 1980–85; Scottish Lawyers European Gp, 1977–. *Recreations:* country, arts, houses, gardens, friends. *Address:* Sheriff's Chambers, Sheriff Court House, Chambers Street, Edinburgh EH1 1LB. *Club:* Scottish Arts (Edinburgh).

POOLE, Col Peter Michael, CBE 1992; TD 1964; Vice Lord-Lieutenant, County of Merseyside, since 1994; Partner, Denton Clark & Co., since 1991; *b* 29 Sept. 1929; *s* of Reginald and Madeline Isobel Poole; *m* 1956, Diana Rosemary Hiam Wilson; three *s* one *d*. *Educ:* Sedbergh Sch.; Gonville and Caius Coll., Cambridge. FRICS (Ryde Meml Prizewinner, 1955); Fellow, CAAV. Univ. Officer, Cambridge, 1954–60; Chartered Surveyor and Land Agent; Principal, Poole & Partners, Liverpool, 1960–91. Mem., Lord Chancellor's Panel of Arbitrators, 1977; Chm., Merseyside Adv. Cttee on Gen. Comrs of Income Tax, 1993–. Dir, Merseyside Youth Assoc., 1973–. Liveryman and Mem., Chartered Surveyors' Co., 1980–. JP Liverpool 1976; DL Merseyside 1975. CO, 107 Corps Engr Regt, RE (TA), 1965–67; Brevet Col, 1967; Hon. Col, 75 Engr Regt, RE (V), 1972–80; Chm., North West TA&VRA, 1990–92. *Publication:* The Valuation of Pipeline Easements and Wayleaves, 1962. *Recreations:* ornithology, golf, travel, photography. *Address:* Shelford, 3 Heron Court, Parkgate, South Wirral L64 6TB. *T:* 0151–336 2529. *Club:* Athenæum (Liverpool).

POOLE, Richard John; Director, Defence Operational Analysis Establishment, Ministry of Defence, 1986–89, retired; *b* 20 Feb. 1929; *s* of Leonard Richard Poole and Merrie Wyn Poole; *m* 1st, 1953, Jean Doreena Poole (*née* Welch) (*d* 1991); two *d*; 2nd, 1993, Jane Amelia (*née* Alan). *Educ:* Univ. of Adelaide, SA (BEng 1st Cl. Hons). Long Range Weapons Estabt, Aust. Dept of Defence, 1951; Ministry of Defence, UK: Admiralty Signals and Radar Estabt, 1957; Head of Div., 1971; Scientific Adviser, 1980, Dir Gen. (Estabts), 1984. *Recreations:* radio, cars, photography.

POOLE-WILSON, Prof. Philip Alexander, MD, FRCP; Simon Marks British Heart Foundation Professor of Cardiology, National Heart and Lung Institute (formerly Cardiothoracic Institute), University of London, since 1988; *b* 26 April 1943; *s* of Denis Smith Poole-Wilson, CBE, MCh, FRCS and Monique Michelle Poole-Wilson; *m* 1969, Mary Elizabeth, *d* of William Tattersall MD and Joan Tattersall; two *s* one *d*. *Educ:* Marlborough Coll.; Trinity Coll., Cambridge (Major Scholar; MA, MD); St Thomas's Hosp. Med. Sch. FRCP 1983; FACC 1992. House appts, St Thomas' Hosp., Brompton Hosp., Hammersmith Hosp.; Lectr, St Thomas' Hosp.; British-American Travelling Fellowship from British Heart Foundn at UCLA, 1973–74; Cardiothoracic Institute, London University: Senior Lectr and Reader, 1976–83; Vice-Dean, 1981–84; apptd Prof. of Cardiology, 1983; Hon. Consultant Physician, Royal Brompton Nat. Heart and Lung Hosp. (formerly at Nat. Heart Hosp.), 1976–. Chm., Cardiac Muscle Research Group, 1984–87; Mem. Council, British Heart Foundn, 1985–. European Society of Cardiology: Fellow, 1988; Mem. Bd, 1988–90; Sec., 1990–92; Pres.-elect, 1992–94; Pres., 1994–96. Strickland-Goodall Lectr, 1983 and Bradshaw Lectr, 1993, British Cardiac Soc. *Publications:* articles and contribs to books on physiology and biochemistry of normal and diseased heart. *Recreations:* sailing, gardening. *Address:* 174 Burbage Road, SE21 7AG. *T:* 0171–274 6742. *Clubs:* Athenæum; Parkstone Yacht.

POOLEY, Dr Derek, CBE 1995; Chief Executive, UKAEA Government Division, since 1994; *b* 28 Oct. 1937; *s* of Richard Pike Pooley and Evelyn Pooley; *m* 1961; Jennifer Mary Davey; two *s* one *d*. *Educ:* Sir James Smith's Sch., Camelford, Cornwall; Birmingham Univ. (BSc 1958; PhD 1961). FInstP 1979. A. A. Noyes Res. Fellow, Calif Inst. of Technol., Pasadena, 1961–62; UKAEA, Harwell: Res. Scientist, 1962–68; Leader of Defects Gp, later of Physics Applications Gp, 1968–76; Head of Materials Devel Div., 1976–81; Dir of Non-nuclear Energy Res., 1981–83; Chief Scientist, Dept of Energy, 1983–86; Dep. Dir, 1986–89, Dir, 1989–90, Atomic Energy Estabt, Winfrith, later AEA Technol.; Dir, AEA Thermal Reactor Services, 1990–91; Man. Dir, Nuclear Business Gp, AEA Technol., 1991–94. Non-exec. Dir, UK Nirex Ltd, 1995–. Pres., British Nuclear Energy Soc., 1992–94; Chm., Scientific and Technical Cttee, Euratom, 1994–. *Publications:* Real Solids and Radiation, 1975; chapters in: Radiation Damage Processes in Materials, 1975; Shaping Tomorrow, 1981; Energy and Feedstocks in the Chemical Industry, 1983; Energy Technologies for the UK, 1986. *Recreations:* photography, gardening, walking. *Address:* 11 Halls Close, Drayton, Abingdon, Oxon OX14 4LU. *T:* Abingdon (01235) 559454.

POOLEY, Frederick Bernard, CBE 1968; PPRIBA; Architect to Greater London Council, 1978–80, Controller of Planning and Transportation, 1974–80, and Superintending Architect of Metropolitan Buildings, 1978–80; *b* 18 April 1916; *s* of George Pooley and Elizabeth Pawley; *m* 1944, Hilda Olive Williams; three *d*. *Educ:* West Ham Grammar Sch.; RIBA, FRICS, FRTPI, MIStructE, FCIArb. Served war, RE, 1940–45. Deputy Borough Architect and Planning Officer, County Borough of West Ham, 1949–51; Deputy City Architect and Planning Officer, Coventry, 1951–54; County Architect and Planning Officer, Bucks, 1954–74. Major projects include: public and sch. bldg programme; scheme for public acquisition of bldgs of arch. or hist. interest for preservation and resale; new methods for assembling and servicing land; early planning work for new Milton Keynes. RIBA: Mem. Council, 1962–; Treasurer, 1972; Pres., 1973–75. *Publications:* contribs on planning, transport and architecture. *Address:* Long Ridge, Whiteleaf, Aylesbury, Bucks HP17 0LZ. *T:* Princes Risborough (01844) 346151.

POOLEY, Peter; Hon. Director General, European Commission, since 1995; *b* 19 June 1936; *er* (twin) *s* of late W. M. Pooley, OBE, Truro, and of Grace Lidbury; *m* 1966, Janet Mary, *er d* of Jack Pearson, Banbury; one *s* one *d*. *Educ:* Brentwood Sch.; Clare Coll., Cambridge (BA); Royal Tank Regt. Joined MAFF as Asst Principal, 1959; seconded to: Diplomatic Service, 1961–63 (served in Brussels) and 1979–82 (Minister (Agric.), Office of UK Perm. Rep. to EEC, Brussels); CSD, 1977–79; Under-Sec., 1979, Fisheries Sec., 1982, MAFF; Dep. Dir Gen., Agric., EC, 1983–89; Dep. Dir Gen., 1989–92, Actg Dir Gen., 1993–94, Develt, EC. Chm., Bd of Management, British Sch. of Brussels, 1991–94. *Recreation:* playing cricket. *Address:* 53 Dereymaekerlaan, 3080 Tervuren, Belgium.
See also R. Pooley.

POOLEY, Robin; Managing Director: Anglian Produce Ltd, since 1988; Anglian Potato Services Ltd, since 1988; Chairman, Pseedco Ltd, since 1995; Member, British Agricultural Council, since 1981; *b* 19 June 1936; *yr* (twin) *s* of late W. Melville Pooley, OBE and of Grace M. Pooley (*née* Lidbury); *m* 1972, Margaret Anne, *yr d* of Jack Pearson, Banbury; one *d*. *Educ:* Brentwood School. Various posts, Towers & Co. Ltd, 1954–71; Gen. Manager, CWS Gp, 1971–76; Man. Dir, Buxted Poultry Ltd, 1976–81; Chief Exec., Potato Marketing Bd, 1981–88. Director: Butchers' Co. Estates Ltd, 1977–; Solanex Ltd, 1981–; UPB Porcofram plc, 1995–. Master, Co. of Butchers, 1987. *Recreations:* country pursuits, freemasonry. *Address:* Barn Hill, Strumpshaw, Norfolk NR13 4NS. *T:* Norwich (01603) 715992. *Clubs:* Farmers', City Livery.
See also P. Pooley.

POORE, Duncan; *see* Poore, M. E. D.

POORE, Sir Herbert Edward, 6th Bt, *cr* 1795; *b* April 1930; *s* of Sir Edward Poore, 5th Bt, and Amelia Guliemone; *S* father 1938. *Heir: u* Nasionceno Poore [*b* 1900; *m* Juana Borda (*d* 1943); three *s* three *d*]. *Address:* Curuzu Cuatia, Corrientes, Argentine Republic.

POORE, Dr (Martin Edward) Duncan, MA, PhD; FIBiol, FRGS; Senior Consultant (formerly Director), Forestry and Land Use Programme, International Institute for Environment and Development, and consultant in conservation and land use, since 1983; *b* 25 May 1925; *s* of T. E. D. Poore and Elizabeth McMartin; *m* 1948, Judith Ursula, *d* of Lt-Gen. Sir Treffry Thompson, KCSI, CB, CBE, and late Mary Emily, *d* of Rev. Canon Medd; two *s*. *Educ:* Trinity Coll., Glenalmond; Edinburgh Univ.; Clare Coll., Cambridge. MA, PhD Cantab.; MA Oxon. MICFor; MIEEM. Japanese interpreter, 1943–45. Nature Conservancy, 1953–56; Consultant Ecologist, Hunting Technical Services, 1956–59; Prof. of Botany, Univ. of Malaya, Kuala Lumpur, 1959–65; Dean of Science, Univ. of Malaya, 1964–65; Lectr, Forestry Dept, Oxford, 1965–66; Dir, Nature Conservancy, 1966–73; Scientific Dir, Internat. Union for Conservation of Nature and Natural Resources, Switzerland, 1974–78; Prof. of Forest Science and Dir, Commonwealth Forestry Inst., Oxford Univ., 1980–83; Fellow of St John's Coll., Oxford, 1980–83. Member: Thames Water Authority, 1981–83; Nature Conservancy Council, 1981–84. Pres., British Assoc. of Nature Conservationists, 1984–92 (Vice Pres., 1993–); Vice-Pres., Commonwealth Forestry Assoc., 1989–; Hon. Member: Botanical Soc. of Scotland, 1992; IUCN (World Conservation Union), 1978 (Hon. Mem., and Fred M. Packard Award, 1990, Commn for Nat. Parks and Protected Areas). FRSA. *Publications:* The Vanishing Forest, 1986; No Timber without Trees, 1990; (with Jeffrey Sayer) The Management of Tropical Moist Forest Lands, 1991; Guidelines for Mountain Protected Areas, 1992; (with Judy Poore) Protected Landscapes in the United Kingdom, 1992; papers on ecology and land use in various jls and scientific periodicals. *Recreations:* hill walking, natural history, music, gardening, photography. *Address:* Balnacarn, Glenmoriston, Inverness-shire IV3 6YJ. *T:* Glenmoriston (01320) 340261. *Club:* Royal Over-Seas League.

POOT, Anton, Hon. CBE 1989; Managing Director, 1984–88, Chairman, 1984–89, Philips Electronics & Associated Industries Ltd; Chairman, Philips UK Ltd, 1985–89; *b* 23 Nov. 1929; *m* 1983, Jesmond Masters; one *s* one *d* by a former marriage. *Educ:* High School in Holland; electronics and economics, Holland and Johannesburg. NV Philips' Gloeilampenfabrieken, Hilversum, Utrecht, Eindhoven, 1946–51; Philips S Africa, Fedn of Rhodesia and Nyasaland, 1951–63; NV Philips' Gloeilampenfabrieken, Eindhoven, 1963–66; Chairman and Man. Dir, Philips East Africa, 1967–71; Man. Dir, Ada (Halifax) Ltd and Philips Electrical Ltd UK, 1971–76; Man. Dir, NV Philips' Gloeilampenfabrieken, Eindhoven, 1976–78; Chm. and Man. Dir, Philips Appliances Div., 1978–83. A Dir, LSO, 1988–. Hon. Freeman, Co. of Information Technologists, 1988. FInstD; FRSA. Officer, Order of Oranje-Nassau (Netherlands), 1989. *Recreations:* music, golf, orchids, ski-ing. *Address:* Priors Corner, Priorsfield Road, Godalming, Surrey GU7 2RQ.

POPE, His Holiness the; *see* John Paul II.

POPE, Cathryn Mary; soprano; *b* 6 July 1957; *m* 1982, Stuart Petersen. *Educ:* Royal College of Music (ARCM); National Opera Studio. Début, ENO: Sophie, in Werther, 1983; Anna, in Moses, 1986; Susanna, in Marriage of Figaro, 1987; Gretel, in Hansel and Gretel, 1987; Oksana, in Christmas Eve, 1988; Despina, in Così fan tutte, 1988; Pamina, in Die Zauberflöte, 1989; Micaëla, in Carmen, 1993; Tatyana, in Eugene Onegin, 1994; Amsterdam: début, Gretel, 1990; Mélisande, in Pelléas et Mélisande, 1991; Elvira, in Don Giovanni, and Susanna, 1991; Opera Europa: Nedda, in Pagliacci, 1995. Numerous recordings.

POPE, Dudley Bernard Egerton; Naval historian and author; *b* 29 Dec. 1925; *s* of late Sydney Broughton Pope and late Alice Pope (*née* Meehan); *m* 1954, Kathleen Patricia Hall; one *d*. *Educ:* Ashford (Kent). Served War of 1939–45: Midshipman, MN, 1941–43 (wounded and invalided). The Evening News: naval and defence correspondent, 1944–57, Dep. Foreign Editor, 1957–59; resigned to take up full-time authorship, 1959. Counsellor,

Navy Record Soc., 1964–68. Cruising trans-Atlantic and Caribbean in own yacht, doing naval historical research, 1965–87. Created: "Lt Ramage RN" series of historical novels covering life of naval officer in Nelson's day, 1965; series of novels portraying sea life of Yorke family, 1979. Hon. Mem., Mark Twain Soc., 1976. *Publications: non-fiction:* Flag 4, the Battle of Coastal Forces in the Mediterranean, 1954; The Battle of the River Plate, 1956, repr. 1987; 73 North, 1958; England Expects, 1959; At 12 Mr Byng was Shot, 1962, repr. 1987; The Black Ship, 1963; Guns, 1965; The Great Gamble, 1972; Harry Morgan's Way, 1977; Life in Nelson's Navy, 1981; The Devil Himself, 1987; *fiction: the Ramage series:* Ramage (Book Society Choice) 1965; Ramage and the Drum Beat (Book Society Alternative Choice), 1967; Ramage and the Freebooters (Book of the Month Club Alt. Choice), 1969; Governor Ramage, RN, 1973; Ramage's Prize, 1974; Ramage and the Guillotine, 1975; Ramage's Diamond, 1976; Ramage's Mutiny, 1977; Ramage and the Rebels, 1978; The Ramage Touch, 1979; Ramage's Signal, 1980; Ramage and the Renegades, 1981; Ramage's Devil, 1982; Ramage's Trial, 1984; Ramage's Challenge, 1985; Ramage at Trafalgar, 1986; Ramage and the Saracens, 1988; Ramage and the Dido, 1989; *the Yorke series:* Convoy (Book Club Associates' Choice), 1979; Buccaneer, 1981; Admiral, 1982; Decoy, (World Book Club Choice), 1983; Galleon, 1986; Corsair, 1987. *Recreations:* ocean cruising, skin-diving. *Address:* c/o Campbell Thomson & McLaughlin, 1 King's Mews, WC1N 2JA.

POPE, Sir Ernle; *see* Pope, Sir J. E.

POPE, Geoffrey George, CB 1986; PhD; FEng 1988; FRAeS; aerospace technology consultant; *b* 17 April 1934; *s* of Sir George Reginald Pope and of Susie (*née* Hendy); *m* 1st, 1961, Rosemary Frances Harnden (*d* 1989); two *s*; 2nd, 1991, Helen Vernon Brewis. *Educ:* Epsom Coll.; Imperial Coll., London. MSc (Eng) 1959, DIC 1959, PhD 1963. FRAeS 1970; FCGI 1982. Junior Technical Asst, Hawker Aircraft Ltd, 1952–53; Student, Imperial Coll., 1953–58; Royal Aircraft Establishment: Structures Dept, 1958–73 (Head, Research Div., 1969–73); Aerodynamics Dept, 1973–77 (Head, 1974–77); Gp Head, Aerodynamics, Structures and Materials Depts, 1978–79; Dep. Dir (Weapons), 1979–81; Asst Chief Scientific Advr (Projects), MoD, 1981–82; Dep. Controller and Adviser (Res. and Technol.), MoD, 1982–84; Dir, RAE, 1984–89; Dep. Chief Scientific Advr, MoD, 1989–94. Pres., RAeS, 1993–94. *Publications:* papers on aeronautical technology in various technical jls. *Recreations:* music, photography, walking. *Address:* 3 Silver Street, Thorverton, Exeter EX5 5LT. *T:* Exeter (01392) 860159.

POPE, Gregory James; MP (Lab) Hyndburn, since 1992; *b* 29 Aug. 1960; *s* of Samuel J. Pope and Sheila M. (*née* Day); *m* 1985, Catherine M. Fallon; two *s* one *d*. *Educ:* St Mary's Coll., Blackburn; Univ. of Hull (BA Hons). Local govt officer, 1987–92. *Recreations:* walking, football, squash, chess, music. *Address:* House of Commons, SW1A 0AA. *T:* 0171–219 5842. *Club:* Old Band (Accrington).

POPE, Jeremy James Richard, OBE 1985; Managing Director, Eldridge, Pope & Co. plc, since 1988 (Joint Managing Director, 1982–88); *b* 15 July 1943; *s* of Philip William Rolph Pope and Joyce Winifred Harcourt Pope (*née* Slade); *m* 1969, Hon. Jacqueline Best; three *s*. *Educ:* Charterhouse; Trinity Coll., Cambridge. Law tripos, MA. Solicitor. Joined Eldridge, Pope & Co., 1969, Finance and Planning Dir, 1972–82. Chm., Smaller Firms Council, CBI, 1981–83; Member: NEDC, 1981–85; Top Salaries Review Body, 1986–93; Exec. Cttee, Food and Drinks Fedn, 1986–89 (Dep. Pres., 1987–89). Mem., Royal Commn on Environmental Pollution, 1984–92. Wessex Regl Rivers Adv. Cttee, NRA, 1994. Chairman: Winterbourne Hosp. plc, 1981–89; Wessex Medical Trust, 1993–. Gov., Forres Sch., Swanage, 1984–92. Trustee, Devonshire and Dorset Regtl Charity, 1994. FRSA. *Recreations:* shooting, fishing, gardening, cooking the resultant produce. *Address:* (office) Dorchester Brewery, Dorchester, Dorset DT1 1QT. *T:* Dorchester (01305) 251251; (home) Field Cottage, West Compton, Dorchester, Dorset DT2 0EY. *T:* Maiden Newton (01300) 20469.

POPE, Air Vice-Marshal John Clifford, CB 1963; CBE 1959; CEng, FIMechE; FRAeS; RAF (retired); *b* 27 April 1911; *s* of George Newcombe-Pope; *m* 1950, Christine Agnes (*d* 1982), *d* of Alfred Hames, Chichester; one *s* two *d*. *Educ:* Tiverton Boys' Middle Sch.; RAF Technical Training Sch., Halton (aircraft apprentice); RAF Coll., Cranwell (cadet; Sir Charles Wakefield Scholar). Graduated as pilot and commnd, 1932; served with No 3 Sqdn, 1933, Nos 27 and 39, on NW Frontier, 1933–36. War of 1939–45; Comd RAF Station, Cleave, 1940–42; served in Egypt and Palestine, 1943–46; Asst Dir Research and Develt, Min. of Supply, 1947–50; Dir of Engineering, RNZAF, 1951–53; Comd RAF Station, Stoke Heath, 1954–57; Sen. Tech. Staff Officer, No 3 Gp Bomber Comd, 1957–59 and Flying Trng Comd, 1960–61; AOC and Comdt, RAF Technical College, 1961–63; Senior Technical Staff Officer, Transport Command, 1963–66. Life Vice-Pres., RAF Boxing Assoc. *Recreation:* scale model steam engineering. *Address:* Dilston, 47 Oxford Road, Stone, near Aylesbury, Bucks HP17 8PD. *T:* Aylesbury (01296) 748467. *Club:* Royal Air Force.

POPE, Vice-Adm. Sir (John) Ernle, KCB 1976; *b* 22 May 1921; *s* of Comdr R. K. C. Pope, Homme House, Herefordshire. *Educ:* RN Coll., Dartmouth. Royal Navy, 1935. Served throughout War of 1939–45, in Destroyers. CO, HMS Decoy, 1962–64; Dir, Naval Equipment, 1964–66; CO, HMS Eagle, 1966–68; Flag Officer, Western Fleet Flotillas, 1969–71; C of S to C-in-C Western Fleet, 1971–74; Comdr, Allied Naval Forces, S Europe, 1974–76; Rear-Adm. 1969; Vice-Adm. 1972. Dep. Pres., Royal Naval Assoc. *Recreations:* sailing, shooting. *Address:* Homme House, Much Marcle, Herefordshire. *Club:* Army and Navy.

See also Rear-Adm. M. D. Kyrle Pope.

POPE, Sir Joseph (Albert), Kt 1980; DSc, PhD (Belfast), WhSc; Director, since 1960, Consultant, since 1988, TQ International (formerly TecQuipment Group), Nottingham (Chairman, 1974–88); *b* 18 October 1914; *s* of Albert Henry and Mary Pope; *m* 1940, Evelyn Alice Gallagher; one *s* two *d*. *Educ:* School of Arts and Crafts, Cambridge; King's College, London. Apprentice, Boulton & Pauls, Norwich, 1930–35. Whitworth Scholarship, 1935. Assistant Lecturer in Engineering, Queen's Univ., Belfast, 1938–44; Assistant Lecturer in Engineering, Univ. of Manchester, 1944–45; Lecturer, then Senior Lecturer, Univ. of Sheffield, 1945–49; Professor of Mechanical Engineering, Nottingham University, 1949–60; Research Dir, Mirrlees Nat. Research Div., Stockport, and Dir, Mirrlees National Ltd 1960–69; Vice-Chancellor, Univ. of Aston in Birmingham, 1969–79. Director: John Brown & Co. Ltd, 1970–82; Midlands Electricity Bd, 1975–80; Royal Worcester Ltd, 1979–83; Chm., W Midlands Econ. Planning Council, 1977–79. Gen. Treasurer, British Assoc., 1975–82; Pres., Whitworth Soc., 1978–79; Chm., Birmingham Civic Soc., 1978–79. Hon. LLD Birmingham, 1979; Hon. DUniv Heriot-Watt, 1979; Hon. DSc: Aston, 1979; Belfast, 1980; Salford, 1980; Nottingham, 1987. *Publications:* papers on the impact of metals and metal fatigue published in Proc. of Inst. of Mech. Engineers and Jl of Iron and Steel Inst. *Address:* 3 Mapperley Hall Drive, Nottingham NG3 5EP. *T:* Nottingham (0115) 962 1146.

POPE, Rear-Adm. Michael Donald K.; *see* Kyrle Pope.

POPE, Very Rev. Robert William, OBE 1971; Dean of Gibraltar, 1977–82; *b* 20 May 1916; *s* of late Rev. Jonas George Pope and Marjorie Mary Pope (*née* Coates); *m* 1940, Elizabeth Beatrice Matilda (*née* Bressey); two *s* one *d*. *Educ:* English College, Temuco, Chile; Harvey Grammar Sch., Folkestone; Maidstone Grammar Sch.; St Augustine's Coll., Canterbury; Durham Univ. (LTh). Deacon 1939, priest, 1940, Rochester; Curate: Holy Trinity, Gravesend, 1939–41; St Nicholas, Guildford, 1942–43; Priest in charge, Peaslake, 1943–44; Chaplain, Royal Navy, 1944–71; Vicar of Whitchurch with Tufton and Litchfield, Dio. Winchester, 1971–77. Member of Sion College. Minister Provincial of European Province, 1985–91, and Minister Gen., 1987–90, Third Order of Soc. of St Francis. *Address:* 5 Wreath Green, Tatworth, Chard, Somerset TA20 2SN. *T:* Chard (01460) 220987.

POPHAM, Maj.-Gen. Christopher John, CB 1982; Director, British Atlantic Committee, 1982–92; *b* 2 April 1927; *s* of late Gordon F. B. Popham and Dorothy A. L. Popham (*née* Yull); *m* 1950, Heather Margaret, *y d* of late Lt-Col and Mrs H. R. W. Dawson; two *s*. *Educ:* Merchant Taylors' School. Commnd Royal Engineers, 1946; served with King George V's Own Bengal Sappers and Miners, RIE and Royal Pakistan Engineers, 1946–48; UK and Germany, 1948–57; Staff Coll., 1958; Cyprus, 1959–62; OC 4 Field Sqdn, 1963–65; JSSC 1965; Mil. Asst to QMG, 1966–68; CO 36 Engineer Regt, 1968–70; CRE 4 Div., 1971–73; Comd 12 Engineer Bde, 1973–75; BGS Intelligence and Security, HQ BAOR and ACOS G-2 HQ Northern Army Group, 1976–79; Asst Chief of Staff (Intell.), SHAPE, 1979–82. Col Comdt, RE, 1982–87. FIMgt. *Recreations:* music, photography, railways. *Address:* c/o Barclays Bank, High Street, Andover, Hants SP10 1LN.

POPHAM, Mervyn Reddaway, FBA 1988; FSA; Lecturer in Aegean Archaeology, Oxford, since 1972; *b* 14 July 1927; *s* of Richard and Lilly Popham. *Educ:* Exeter Sch.; Univ. of St Andrews (MA); Univ. of Oxford (DipArch). FSA 1960. Colonial Administrative Service, Cyprus, 1951–58 (Comr, Troodos Dist., 1955–56); Macmillan Student, 1961–63 and Asst Dir, 1963–70, British Sch. of Archaeology at Athens; Asst Prof., Univ. of Cincinnati, 1970–72. *Publications:* The Last Days of the Palace at Knossos, 1964; The Destruction of the Palace at Knossos, 1970; Lefkandi I: the iron age settlement and cemeteries, 1980; The Unexplored Mansion at Knossos, 1984; Lefkandi II, 1992–93; articles and excavation reports in learned jls. *Recreations:* music, photography. *Address:* 110 Woodstock Road, Oxford OX2 7NF. *T:* Oxford (01865) 512605.

POPJÁK, George Joseph, DSc (London), MD; FRS 1961; FRSC; Professor of Biochemistry at University of California in Los Angeles, 1968–84, now Emeritus; *b* 5 May 1914; *s* of late George and Maria Popják, Szeged, Hungary; *m* 1941, Hasel Marjorie, *d* of Duncan and Mabel Hammond, Beckenham, Kent. *Educ:* Royal Hungarian Francis Joseph University, Szeged. Demonstrator at Department of Morbid Anatomy and Histology, University of Szeged, 1938–39; Br. Council Scholar, Postgraduate Med. School of London, 1939–41; Demonstrator in Pathology, Dept of Pathology, St Thomas's Hosp. Med. School, London, 1941–43; Beit Mem. Fellow for medical research at St Thomas's Hosp. Med. School, London, 1943–47; Member scientific staff of Med. Research Council at Nat. Inst. for Med. Research, 1947–53; Director of Medical Research Council Experimental Radiopathology Research Unit, Hammersmith Hosp., 1953–62; Jt Dir, Chemical Enzymology Lab., Shell Res. Ltd, 1962–68; Assoc. Prof. in Molecular Sciences, Warwick Univ., 1965–68. Foreign member of Belgian Roy. Flemish Acad. of Science, Literature and Fine Arts, 1955; Hon. Member: Amer. Soc. of Biological Chemists, 1968; Alpha-Omega-Alpha, 1970; Mem., Amer. Acad. of Arts and Sciences, 1971. (With Dr J. W. Cornforth, FRS) CIBA Medal of Biochemical Soc., 1965 (first award); Stouffer Prize, 1967; Davy Medal, Royal Soc., 1968; Award in Lipid Chem., Amer. Oil Chem. Soc., 1977; Distinguished Scientific Achievement award, Amer. Heart Assoc., 1978. *Publications:* Chemistry, Biochemistry and Isotopic Tracer Technique (Roy. Inst. of Chemistry monograph), 1955; (jtly) Lipids, Chemistry, Biochemistry and Nutrition, 1986; articles on fat metabolism in Jl Path. Bact., Jl Physiol., Biochemical Jl, etc. *Recreations:* music, modelling and gardening. *Address:* Departments of Medicine and Biological Chemistry, University of California at Los Angeles, Center for the Health Sciences 47–123 CHS, Los Angeles, CA 90024–1679, USA.

POPLE, John Anthony, FRS 1961; Trustees' Professor of Chemistry, Northwestern University, Evanston, since 1993; *b* 31 Oct. 1925; *e s* of Herbert Keith Pople and Mary Frances Jones, Burnham-on-Sea, Som.; *m* 1952, Joy Cynthia Bowers; three *s* one *d*. *Educ:* Bristol Grammar School; Cambridge University, MA, PhD. Mayhew Prize, 1948, Smith Prize, 1950, Cambridge; Fellow, Trinity College, 1951–58, Lecturer in Mathematics, 1954–58, Cambridge; Superintendent of Basic Physics Division, National Physical Laboratory, 1958–64; Prof. of Chem. Physics, subseq. John Christian Warner Univ. Prof. of Natural Scis, Carnegie-Mellon Univ., Pittsburgh, 1964–93; Adjunct Prof. of Chemistry, Northwestern Univ., 1986–93. Ford Visiting Professor, Carnegie Inst. of Technology, Pittsburgh, 1961–62. Fellow: Amer. Physical Soc., 1970; Amer. Acad. of Arts and Scis, 1971; AAAS, 1980. For. Associate, Nat. Acad. of Sci., 1977. Marlow Medal, Faraday Soc., 1958; ACS Pauling Award, 1977; Awards from American Chemical Society: Langmuir, 1970; Harrison Howe, 1971; Gilbert Newton Lewis, 1973; Pittsburgh, 1975; Computers in Chemistry, 1991. Sen. US Scientist Award, Alexander von Humboldt Foundn, 1981; G. Willard Wheland Award, Univ. of Chicago, 1981; Evans Award, Ohio State Univ., 1982; Oesper Award, Univ. of Cincinnati, 1984; Davy Medal, Royal Soc., 1988; Wolf Prize in Chemistry, Israel, 1991. *Publications:* High Resolution nuclear magnetic resonance, 1959; Approximate Molecular Orbital Theory, 1970; Ab initio Molecular Orbital Theory, 1986; scientific papers on molecular physics and theoretical chemistry. *Recreations:* music, travel. *Address:* Northwestern University, 2145 Sheridan Road, Evanston, IL 60208–3113, USA; #7K, 1500 Sheridan Road, Wilmette, IL 60091, USA.

POPOV, Viktor Ivanovich; Counsellor, Foreign Ministry, Russia, 1986–90; *b* 19 May 1918; *m* Natalia Aleksandrovna Popova; two *s*. *Educ:* Moscow Inst. of History and Philosophy; Higher Diplomatic Sch. of USSR. Entered Min. of Foreign Affairs, 1954; Vietnam, 1960–61; Australia, 1967–68; UK, 1968; Ambassador on special assignments, UN and Unesco, and Rector, Diplomatic Acad. of USSR, 1968–80; Ambassador to UK, 1980–86. Many Soviet and foreign awards. *Publications:* Anglo-Soviet Relations 1927–29; Anglo-Soviet Relations 1929–39; (jtly) History of Diplomacy series III.

POPPLEWELL, Catharine Margaret, (Lady Popplewell); JP; DL; Member, Independent Television Commission, 1991–95; *b* 30 July 1929; *d* of Alfred John Storey and Gladys Mabel Storey; *m* 1954, Hon. Sir Oliver Bury Popplewell, *qv*; four *s* (and one *s* decd). *Educ:* Malvern Girls' College; Newnham College, Cambridge (MA Hons); Hughes Hall, Cambridge (PGCE). Mem., Bd of Visitors, Aylesbury Prison, 1974–79; Chm., Bucks County Probation Cttee, 1981–91; Mem., Bucks County Council, 1977–85 (Chm., Educn Cttee, 1981–85). Mem., IBA, 1987–90. Chm., Oxford Dio. Council for the Deaf, 1987–91; Trustee, Bucks Historic Churches Trust, 1985–. Chm., Thames Valley Partnership, 1993–. Mem. Council, Open Univ., 1985–95; Chm. Governors, Amersham and Wycombe Coll., 1981–; School Governor: Godstowe; Winchester House; Ashfold; Sir William Borlase's Grammar. Buckinghamshire: JP, 1968; High Sheriff, 1992–93; DL, 1993. *Recreations:* sailing, theatre.

POPPLEWELL, Hon. Sir Oliver (Bury), Kt 1983; **Hon. Mr Justice Popplewell;** Judge of the High Court of Justice, Queen's Bench Division, since 1983; *b* 15 Aug. 1927; *s* of late Frank and Nina Popplewell; *m* 1954, Catharine Margaret Storey (*see* C. M. Popplewell); four *s* (and one *s* decd). *Educ:* Charterhouse (Schol.); Queens' Coll., Cambridge (Class. exhibnr). BA 1950; LLB 1951; MA. CUCC, 1949–51. Called to the Bar, Inner Temple, 1951, Bencher, 1978; QC 1969. Recorder, Burton-on-Trent, 1970–71; Dep. Chm., Oxon QS, 1970–71; a Recorder of the Crown Court, 1972–82. Indep. Mem., Wages Councils, 1962–82, Chm. 1973–82; Mem., Home Office Adv. Bd on Restricted Patients, 1981–82; Vice-Chm., Parole Bd, 1986–87 (Mem., 1985–87); Mem., Parole Review Cttee, 1987–88; Chm., Inquiry into Crowd Safety and Control at sports grounds, 1985–86; Pres., Employment Appeal Tribunal, 1986–88 (Mem., 1984–85). MCC: Mem. Cttee, 1971–74, 1976–79, 1980–; Trustee, 1983–94; Pres., 1994–. Gov., Sutton's Hosp. in Charterhouse, 1986–88. *Recreations:* sailing, cricket, tennis. *Address:* Royal Courts of Justice, Strand, WC2A 2LL. *Clubs:* Garrick, MCC; Hawks (Cambridge), Blakeney Sailing.

PORCHESTER, Lord; George Reginald Oliver Molyneux Herbert; *b* 10 Nov. 1956; *s* and *heir* of Earl of Carnarvon, *qv*; *m* 1989, Jayne, *d* of K. A. Wilby, Cheshire; one *s* one *d*. *Educ:* St John's Coll., Oxford (BA). A Page of Honour to the Queen, 1969–73. *Heir: s* Hon. George Kenneth Oliver Molyneux Herbert, *b* 13 Oct. 1992. *Address:* Dairy Farm Cottage, Highclere Park, Newbury RG15 9RN. *Club:* White's.

PORRITT, Hon. Sir Jonathon (Espie), 2nd Bt *cr* 1963, of Hampstead, co. London; freelance writer and broadcaster; Director, Friends of The Earth, 1984–90; *b* 6 July 1950; *s* of Baron Porritt, GCMG, GCVO, CBE and of Kathleen Mary, 2nd *d* of A. S. Peck; *S* to Btcy of father, 1994; *m* 1986, Sarah, *d* of Malcolm Staniforth, Malvern; two *d*. *Educ:* Eton; Magdalen Coll., Oxford (BA (First Cl.) Modern Languages). ILEA Teacher, 1975–84: Head of English and Drama, Burlington Danes School, W12, 1980–84. Presenter, Where on earth are we going?, BBC TV, 1990. Ecology Party: candidate: General Elections, 79 and 1983; European Elections, 1979 and 1984; Local Elections, 1977, 1978, 1982; Party Council Member, 1978–80, 1982–84; Chairman, 1979–80, 1982–84. *Publications:* Seeing Green—the Politics of Ecology, 1984; Friends of the Earth Handbook, 1987; The Coming of the Greens, 1988; Where on Earth are We Going?, 1991; (ed) Save the Earth, 1991; Captain Eco (for children), 1991. *Recreation:* walking. *Heir: b* Hon. Jeremy Charles Porritt [*b* 19 Jan. 1953; *m* 1980, Penny, *d* of J. H. Moore; two *s*]. *Address:* 9 Lypiatt Terrace, Cheltenham, Glos GL50 2SX.

PORT ELIZABETH, Bishop of, since 1993; **Rt Rev. Eric Pike;** *b* 11 Nov. 1936; *s* of Eric and Elizabeth Pike; *m* 1st, 1963, Wendy Anne Walker; one *s* one *d*; 2nd, 1977, Joyce Davidson; two step *s* three step *d*. *Educ:* Graaff Reinet TC (Primary Teachers Cert. 1957); St Paul's Theol Coll., Grahamstown (DipTh 1968). Worked in Govt Service, Transkei, SA, 1955; taught at Queen's Coll. Boys' High Sch., 1958–65; ordained deacon, 1968, priest, 1969; Asst Priest, St John's, E London, 1969–71; Rector: St Paul's, Komga, 1971–72; St Mark's, E London, 1972–77; Archdeacon of E London and Operation Outreach, 1978–87; Rector, St Alban's, E London, 1987–89; Suffragan Bishop of Grahamstown, 1989–93. *Recreations:* jogging, walking, gardening, bird watching. *Address:* PO Box 7109, Newton Park, Port Elizabeth 6055, South Africa. *T:* (41) 351387.

PORT OF SPAIN, Archbishop of, since 1968; **Most Rev. Anthony Pantin,** CSSp; *b* 27 Aug. 1929; *s* of Julian and Agnes Pantin, both of Trinidad. *Educ:* Sacred Heart Private Sch., Belmont Boys' Intermediate Sch., St Mary's Coll., Port of Spain; Seminary of Philosophy, Montreal; Holy Ghost Missionary Coll., Dublin. Ordained Dublin, 1955; Guadeloupe, French West Indies, 1956–59; Fatima College, Port of Spain, 1959–64; Superior, St Mary's Coll., Port of Spain, 1965–68. Member: Vatican Secretariat for Christian Unity, 1971–83; Vatican Congregation for Evangelisation of Peoples, 1989–. Vice-Pres., Antilles Episcopal Conference, 1990–93 (Pres., 1979–84). Hon. FCP 1982. *Address:* Archbishop's House, 27 Maraval Road, Port of Spain, Trinidad. *T:* 6221103.

PORTAL, Sir Jonathan (Francis), 6th Bt *cr* 1901; FCA; freelance accountant, since 1993; *b* 13 Jan. 1953; *s* of Sir Francis Spencer Portal, 5th Bt, and of Jane Mary, *d* of late Albert Henry Williams, OBE; *S* father, 1984; *m* 1982, Louisa Caroline, *er d* of F. J. C. G. Hervey-Bathurst, Somborne Park, near Stockbridge, Hants; three *s*. *Educ:* Marlborough; Univ. of Edinburgh (BCom). FCA (ACA 1977). Gp Financial Controller, Henderson Admin, 1989–91; Finance Dir, Grosvenor Ventures Ltd, 1992–93. Mem., Clothworkers' Co. *Heir: s* William Jonathan Francis Portal, *b* 1 Jan. 1987. 7 *Address:* Burley Wood, Ashe, Basingstoke, Hants RG25 3AG.

PORTARLINGTON, 7th Earl of, *cr* 1785; **George Lionel Yuill Seymour Dawson-Damer;** Baron Dawson 1770; Viscount Carlow 1776; *b* 10 Aug. 1938; *er s* of Air Commodore Viscount Carlow (killed on active service, 1944) and Peggy (who *m* 2nd, 1945, Peter Nugent; she *d* 1963), *yr d* of late Charles Cambie; *S* grandfather, 1959; *m* 1961, Davina, *e d* of Sir Edward Windley, KCMG, KCVO; three *s* one *d*. *Educ:* Eton. Page of Honour to the Queen, 1953–55. Director: G. S. Yuill & Co. Ltd, Sydney, 1964; Yuills Australia, Sydney, 1983–; John Swire & Sons Pty Ltd, Sydney, 1988–; Australian Stock Breeders Co. Ltd, Brisbane, 1966. *Heir: s* Viscount Carlow, *qv*. *Recreations:* fishing, ski-ing, books. *Address:* 118 Wolseley Road, Point Piper, NSW 2027, Australia. *T:* Sydney (2) 3639725. *Clubs:* Union, Australian (Sydney); Royal Sydney Golf.

PORTEN, Anthony Ralph; QC 1988; a Recorder, since 1993; *b* 1 March 1947; *s* of late Ralph Charles Porten and of Joan Porten (*née* Edden); *m* 1970, Kathryn Mary (*née* Edwards); two *d*. *Educ:* Epsom Coll.; Emmanuel Coll., Cambridge (BA; Athletics Blue, 1967). Called to the Bar, Inner Temple, 1969; joined Lincoln's Inn (*ad eund.*), 1973. Practising mainly in town and country planning and local government work. *Recreations:* walking the dog, cleaning the car. *Address:* Clive Cottage, Claremont Drive, Esher, Surrey KT10 9LU. *T:* Esher (01372) 467513; 2–3 Gray's Inn Square, WC1R 5JH. *T:* 0171–242 4986. *Clubs:* Royal Automobile; Hawks (Cambridge).

PORTEOUS, Christopher, MA; Headmaster of Eltham College, 1959–83; *b* 2 April 1921; *e s* of late Rev. Gilbert Porteous; *m* 1944, Amy Clunis, *d* of Theodore J. Biggs; one *s* three *d*. *Educ:* Nottingham High Sch. (Foundation Scholar); Emmanuel Coll., Cambridge (Senior Scholar). First Classes, with distinction, in Classical Tripos. Master of Classical Sixth, Mill Hill Sch., 1947–55; Asst Director, HM Civil Service Commission, 1955–59. Mem., Admiralty Interview Bd, 1975–94. *Publication:* Eltham College, Past and Present, 1992. *Recreations:* travel, writing, the countryside. *Address:* Little Thatch, Edwardstone, Sudbury, Suffolk CO10 5PR.

PORTEOUS, Christopher Selwyn, CBE 1993; Solicitor to Commissioner of Police for the Metropolis, since 1987; *b* 8 Nov. 1935; *s* of Selwyn Berkeley Porteous (*né* Potous) and Marjorie Irene Porteous; *m* 1960, Brenda Jacqueline Wallis; four *d*. *Educ:* Dulwich Coll.; Law Society Sch. of Law. Articled to Clerk to Malling RDC, 1954–60; qual. as solicitor, 1960; LCC, 1960–62; Legal Asst with Scotland Yard, 1962–68; Sen. Legal Asst, 1968–76; Asst Solicitor, 1976–87. Mem., Solicitors European Gp, 1991–. Anglican Reader, 1958–; Mem., Pastoral Cttee, Rochester Dio., 1984–88. Hon. Mem., ACPO, 1995. *Recreations:* reading, poetry, hymn writing, walking. *Address:* c/o Solicitor's Department, New Scotland Yard, Broadway, SW1H 0BG. *T:* 0171–230 7353.

PORTEOUS, James, DL; FEng 1986; FIEE; FInstE; FSS; Chairman and Chief Executive, Yorkshire Electricity Group plc, 1990–92; *b* 29 Dec. 1926; *e s* of James and Isabella Porteous; *m* 1960, Sheila Beatrice (*née* Klotz); two *d*. *Educ:* Jarrow Grammar School; King's College, Durham University. BSc Hons. NESCo Ltd, NE Electricity Bd, NE Div., BEA, 1945–62; Central Electricity Generating Board: Operations Dept, HQ, 1962–66; System Op. Eng., Midlands Region, 1966–70; Dir, Operational Planning, SE Region, 1970–72; NE Region, 1972–75; Dir-Gen., Midlands Region, 1975–84; Chm., Yorks Electricity Bd, 1984–90. Mem., Electricity Council, 1984–90; Director: Electricity Association Ltd, 1990–92; National Grid Company (Holdings) plc, 1990–92. Chm., BR (Eastern) Board, 1990–92 (Mem., 1986–90); Mem., E Midlands Economic Planning Council, 1976–79. Director: Peter Peregrinus Ltd, 1981–92, 1993–; Merz and McLellan Ltd, 1992–. Vice-Pres., IEE, 1992–93; National Vice-President: Opportunities for People with Disabilities, 1990–92; Neighbourhood Energy Action, 1992–. Hon. DSc Aston, 1990; Hon. DEng Bradford, 1991. CIMgt. DL N Yorks, 1991. *Recreations:* highland life, railways. *Club:* Caledonian.

PORTEOUS, Rev. Prof. Norman Walker, MA Edinburgh et Oxon, BD Edinburgh, DD St Andrews; Professor Emeritus, University of Edinburgh, since 1968; *b* Haddington, 9 Sept. 1898; *yr s* of late John Dow Porteous, MA, formerly Rector of Knox Memorial Inst, Haddington, and Agnes Paton Walker; *m* 1929, May Hadwen (*d* 1981), *y d* of late John Cook Robertson, Kirkcaldy; three *s* three *d*. *Educ:* Knox Memorial Institute, Haddington; Universities of Edinburgh, Oxford (Trinity College), Berlin, Tübingen and Münster; New Coll., Edinburgh. MA Edinburgh with 1st Class Honours in Classics; MA Oxon with 1st Class in Literæ Humaniores; BD Edinburgh with distinction in Old Testament; 1st Bursar at Edinburgh University, 1916; C. B. Black Scholar in New Testament Greek, 1920; John Edward Baxter Scholar in Classics, 1923; Ferguson Scholar in Classics, 1923; Senior Cunningham Fellow at New College and Kerr Travelling Scholar, 1927; served in army, 1917–19, commissioned 2nd Lieut, March 1918, served overseas with 13th Royal Scots; Ordained to Ministry of United Free Church of Scotland, 1929; Minister of Crossgates Church, Church of Scotland, 1929–31; Regius Professor of Hebrew and Oriental Languages in the University of St Andrews, 1931–35; University of Edinburgh: Professor of Old Testament Language, Literature and Theology, 1935–37; Prof. of Hebrew and Semitic Languages, 1937–68; Principal of New Coll., and Dean of Faculty of Divinity, 1964–68; retd, 1968. Hon. DD St Andrews, 1944; Lectures: Stone, Princeton Theological Seminary, 1953; Montague Burton, Leeds, 1974. President, Soc. for Old Testament Study, 1954. *Publications:* Das Alte Testament Deutsch 23: Das Danielbuch, 1962, 4th edn 1985 (English edition, 1965, 2nd, 1979); Living the Mystery: Collected Essays, 1967; Old Testament and History, 5 lectures in Annual of Swedish Theological Inst., vol. VIII, 1970–71; contributions to: Theologische Aufsätze Karl Barth zum 50 Geburtstag, 1936; Record and Revelation, 1938; The Old Testament and Modern Study, 1951; Peake's Commentary on the Bible, 1962. *Address:* 3 Hermitage Gardens, Edinburgh EH10 6DL. *T:* 0131–447 4632.

PORTEOUS, Colonel Patrick Anthony, VC 1942; RA, retired 1970; *b* 1 Jan. 1918; *s* of late Brig.-General C. McL. Porteous, 9th Ghurkas, and late Mrs Porteous, Fleet, Hampshire; *m* 1st, 1943, Lois Mary (*d* 1953), *d* of late Maj.-General Sir H. E. Roome, KCIE; one *s* one *d*; 2nd, 1955, Deirdre, *d* of late Eric King; three *d*. *Educ:* Wellington Coll.; Royal Military Acad., Woolwich. BEF France, Sept. 1939–May 1940, with 6th AA Regt, RA; Dieppe, Aug. 1942 (VC); No 4 Commando, Dec. 1940–Oct. 1944; BLA June-Sept. 1944; 1st Airborne Div. Dec. 1944–July 1945; 6th Airborne Div., July 1945–March 1946; Staff Coll., Camberley, May-Nov. 1946; 16 Airborne Div. TA, Jan. 1947–Feb. 1948; 33 Airborne Lt Regt, RA, Feb. 1948–April 1949; No 1 Regular Commission Board, 1949; Instructor, RMA, Sandhurst, July 1950–July 1953; GHQ, Far East Land Forces, Singapore, Sept. 1953–July 1955; 1st Singapore Regt, RA, July-Dec. 1955; 14 Field Regt, RA, 1956–58; RAF Staff Coll., Jan. 1958–Dec. 1958; AMS, HQ Southern Comd, 1959–60; Colonel Junior Leaders Regt, RA, 1960–63; Colonel, General Staff War Office, later Ministry of Defence, 1963–66; Comdr Rheindahlen Garrison, 1966–69. *Recreation:* sailing. *Address:* Christmas Cottage, Church Lane, Funtington, W Sussex PO18 9LQ. *T:* Bosham (01243) 575315.

PORTER, family name of **Baron Porter of Luddenham.**

PORTER OF LUDDENHAM, Baron *cr* 1990 (Life Peer), of Luddenham in the County of Kent; **George Porter,** OM 1989; Kt 1972; BSc (Leeds); MA, PhD, ScD (Cambridge); FRS 1960; Professor, since 1987, and Chairman of the Centre for Photomolecular Sciences, Imperial College of Science, Technology and Medicine, London, since 1990; Chancellor of Leicester University, since 1986; Emeritus Professor, Royal Institution, since 1988; *b* 6 Dec. 1920; *m* 1949, Stella Jean Brooke; two *s*. *Educ:* Thorne Grammar Sch.; Leeds Univ.; Emmanuel Coll., Cambridge. Ackroyd Scholar, Leeds Univ., 1938–41. Served RNVR, Radar Officer, in Western Approaches and Mediterranean, 1941–45. Cambridge: Demonstrator in Physical Chemistry, 1949–52, Fellow of Emmanuel Coll., 1952–54; Hon. Fellow, 1967; Asst Director of Research in Physical Chemistry, 1952–54; Asst Director of British Rayon Research Assoc., 1954–55; Prof. of Physical Chemistry, 1955–63, Firth Prof. of Chemistry, 1963–66, Univ. of Sheffield; Resident Prof. and Dir, Royal Institution of Great Britain, 1966–85, Hon. Mem., 1988–. Member: ARC, 1964–66; Adv. Scientific Cttee, Nat. Gall., 1966–68; BBC Sci. Consultative Gp, 1967–75; Open Univ. Council, 1969–75; Science Mus. Adv. Council, 1970–73; Council and Science Bd, SRC, 1976–80; ACOST, 1987–91. Trustee, BM, 1972–74. President: Chemical Soc., 1970–72 (Pres. Faraday Div., 1973–74); Comité Internat. de photobiologie, 1968–72; Nat. Assoc. for Gifted Children, 1975–80; R&D Soc., 1977–82; Assoc. for Science Educn, 1985; BAAS, 1985–86; Royal Soc., 1985–90; Internat. Youth Sci. Fortnight, 1987–89. Counsellor, Inst. for Molecular Sci., Okasaki, Japan, 1980–83. Master, Salters' Co., 1993–94 (Hon. Liveryman, 1981–). Fairchild Scholar, CIT, 1974; Hitchcock Prof., Univ. of Calif at Berkeley, 1978; Gresham Prof. of Astronomy, Gresham Coll., 1990–94. Lectures: Bakerian, 1977, Humphry Davy, 1985, Royal Soc.; Romanes, Oxford, 1978; Robertson Meml, Nat. Acad. of Scis, USA, 1978; Dimbleby, 1988; many other named lectures. Mem., Academia Europaea, 1987; Foreign Associate: Nat. Acad. of Scis; Amer. Acad. of Arts and Scis; Amer. Philos. Soc.; Pontifical Acad.; Japan Acad.; Accad. dei Lincei; Indian Nat. Science Acad.; Indian Acad. of Scis; acads of Madrid, Lisbon, Göttingen, Leopoldina, Hungary and NY; Foreign Mem., USSR Acad. of Sciences, 1988. Hon. Professor: Univ. of Kent; Beijing Tech. Univ.; Chinese Acad. of Scis; Hon. Fellow: Emmanuel Coll., Cambridge; QMC; Imperial Coll., London; Hon. FRSE 1983; Hon. FRSC 1991. Hon. Doctorates: Utah, Sheffield, East Anglia, Durham, Leeds, Leicester, Heriot-Watt, City, Manchester, St Andrews, London, Kent, Oxon, Hull, Instituto Quimica de Sarria, Barcelona, Pennsylvania, Coimbra, Lille, Open, Surrey, Bristol, Notre Dame, Reading, Loughborough, Brunel, Bologna, Rio de Janeiro, Philippines, Córdoba, Liverpool, Cambridge, Central Lancashire, Mangalore, Buckingham. Royal Society of Chemistry: Corday-Morgan Medal, 1955; Tilden Medal, 1958; Liversidge Medal, 1970; Faraday Medal, 1980; Longstaff Medal, 1981; (jtly) Nobel Prize for Chemistry, 1967;

Silvanus Thompson Medal, 1969; Royal Society: Davy Medal, 1971; Rumford Medal, 1978; Michael Faraday Award, 1991; Copley Medal, 1992; Kalinga Prize, UNESCO, 1977; first Porter Medal for photochemistry, Eur., Japanese and Inter-Amer. Photochemical Socs, 1988. *Publications:* Chemistry for the Modern World, 1962; scientific papers in Proc. Royal Society, Trans. Faraday Society, etc. TV Series: Laws of Disorder, 1965–66; Young Scientist of the Year, 1966–81; Time Machines, 1969–70; Controversy, 1971–75; Natural History of a Sunbeam, 1976–77. *Recreation:* sailing. *Address:* Departments of Chemistry and Biochemistry, Imperial College, SW7 2AY.

PORTER, Alastair Robert Wilson, CBE 1985; Secretary and Registrar, Royal College of Veterinary Surgeons, 1966–91, retired; barrister; *b* 28 Sept. 1928; *s* of late James and Olivia Porter (*née* Duncan); *m* 1954, Jennifer Mary Priaulx Forman; two *s* one *d*. *Educ:* Irvine Royal Academy; Glasgow Academy; Merton Coll., Oxford (MA). Called to Bar, Gray's Inn, 1952. Resident Magistrate, N Rhodesia, 1954; Registrar of High Court of N Rhodesia, 1961; Permanent Secretary: Min. of Justice, N Rhodesia, 1964; Min. of Justice, Govt of Republic of Zambia, Oct. 1964. Mem., Fedn (formerly Liaison Cttee) of Veterinarians of the EEC, 1966–86, Sec.-Gen., 1973–79; Chm., EEC's Adv. Cttee on Veterinary Trng, 1986–87 (Vice-Chm., 1981–86). Lectures: Wooldridge Meml, BVA Congress, 1976; MacKellar Meml, Western Counties Veterinary Assoc., Tavistock, 1978; Weipers, Glasgow Univ., 1985; Keith Entwhistle Meml, Cambridge Univ., 1987. Hon. Member: BVA, 1978; British Small Animals Vet. Assoc., 1991; Australian Vet. Assoc., 1991; Hon. Associate, RCVS, 1979. Chm. Bd of Govs, Blue Cross, 1995–. Hon. DVMS Glasgow, 1994. Centenary Prize, 1981, and Victory Medal, 1991, Central Vet. Soc.; Akademische Ehrenbürger, Hannover Veterinary Sch., 1988. *Publication:* (jtly) An Anatomy of Veterinary Europe, 1972. *Address:* 4 Savill Road, Lindfield, Haywards Heath, West Sussex RH16 2NX. *T:* Lindfield (01444) 482001.

PORTER, Andrew Brian; Music Critic, The Observer, since 1992; *b* 26 Aug. 1928; *s* of Andrew Ferdinand Porter and Vera Sybil (*née* Bloxham). *Educ:* University Coll., Oxford (MA). Music Critic, Financial Times, 1952–72; Editor, Musical Times, 1960–67; Music Critic, New Yorker, 1972–92. Vis. Fellow, All Souls Coll., Oxford, 1972–73; Bloch Prof., Univ. of Calif, Berkeley, 1980–81. Corresp. Mem., Amer. Musicol Soc., 1994. *Publications:* A Musical Season, 1974; The Ring of the Nibelung, 1976; Music of Three Seasons, 1978; Music of Three More Seasons, 1981; (ed with D. Rosen) Verdi's Macbeth: a sourcebook, 1984; The Tempest (opera libretto), 1985; Musical Events 1980–1983, 1987; Musical Events 1983–1986, 1989; The Song of Majnun (opera libretto), 1991; contrib. Music & Letters, Musical Qly, etc. *Recreation:* cooking. *Address:* The Observer, 119 Farringdon Road, EC1R 3ER. *T:* 0171–713 4293.

PORTER, Prof. Arthur, OC 1983; MSc, PhD (Manchester); FIEE; FCAE; FRSC 1970; Professor of Industrial Engineering, and Chairman of Department, University of Toronto, Toronto, 1961–76, now Emeritus Professor; President, Arthur Porter Associates Ltd, since 1973; Associate, Institute for Environmental Studies, University of Toronto, since 1981; *b* 8 Dec. 1910; *s* of late John William Porter and Mary Anne Harris; *m* 1941, Phyllis Patricia Dixon; one *s*. *Educ:* The Grammar Sch., Ulverston; University of Manchester. Asst Lecturer, University of Manchester, 1936–37; Commonwealth Fund Fellow, Massachusetts Inst. of Technology, USA, 1937–39; Scientific Officer, Admiralty, 1939–45; Principal Scientific Officer, National Physical Laboratory, 1946; Prof. of Instrument Technology, Royal Military Coll. of Science, 1946–49; Head, Research Division, Ferranti Electric Ltd, Toronto, Canada, 1949–55; Professor of Light Electrical Engineering, Imperial College of Science and Technology, University of London, 1955–58; Dean of the College of Engineering, Saskatchewan Univ., Saskatoon, 1958; Acting Dir, Centre for Culture and Technology, Toronto Univ., 1967–68; Academic Comr, Univ. of W Ontario, 1969–71. Dir and Founding Chm., Scientists and Engineers for Energy and Environment Inc., 1981–84. Chairman: Canadian Environmental Adv. Council, 1972–75; Ontario Royal Commn on Electric Power Planning, 1975–80. *Publications:* An Introduction to Servomechanisms, 1950; Cybernetics Simplified, 1969; Towards a Community University, 1971; articles in Trans. Royal Society, Proc. Royal Society, Phil. Mag., Proc. Inst. Mech. Eng, Proc. IEE, Nature, etc. *Recreations:* tennis, travel, energy conservation. *Address:* Apt 603, Imperial Club, 3399 Gulf Shore Boulevard N, Naples, FL 33940, USA. *T:* (813) 2632540. *Clubs:* Athenæum; Arts and Letters, National (Toronto); Wyndemere (Naples, Florida).

PORTER, Arthur Thomas, MRSL 1979; MA, PhD; Pro-Chancellor and Chairman of Court, University of Sierra Leone, Freetown, Sierra Leone, since 1992 (Vice-Chancellor, 1974–84); *b* 26 Jan. 1924; *m* 1953, Rigmor Sondergaard (*née* Rasmussen); one *s* one *d*. *Educ:* Fourah Bay Coll. (BA Dunelm); Cambridge Univ. (BA (Hist Tripos), MA); Boston Univ. (PhD). Asst, Dept of Social Anthropology, Edinburgh Univ., UK, 1951–52. Prof. of History and Head of Dept of Hist., also Dir of Inst. of African Studies, Fourah Bay Coll., 1963–64; Principal, University Coll., Nairobi, Univ. of E Africa, 1964–70; UNESCO Field Staff Officer; Educl Planning Adviser, Min. of Educn, Kenya, 1970–74. Mem. Exec. Bd, UNESCO, 1976–80. Africanus Horton Meml Lectr, Edinburgh Univ., 1983; Fulbright Schol.-in-Residence, Bethany Coll., Kansas, 1986–87. Chm., Bd of Dirs, Sierra Leone Nat. Diamond Mining Co., 1976–85. Hon. LHD Boston 1969; Hon. LLD Royal Univ. of Malta 1969; Hon. DLitt Univ. of Sierra Leone, 1988. Phi Beta Kappa 1972. Symonds Medal, ACU, 1985. *Publications:* Creoledom, a Study of the Development of Freetown Society, 1963; contribs to The Times, Africa, African Affairs. *Recreation:* photography. *Address:* 26b Spur Road, Wilberforce, PO Box 1363, Freetown, Sierra Leone, West Africa. *T:* (22) 31736; 81 Fitzjohn Avenue, Barnet, Herts EN5 2HN. *T:* 0181–441 1551.

PORTER, Barry; *see* Porter, G. B.

PORTER, David John; MP (C) Waveney, since 1987; *b* 16 April 1948; *s* of late George Porter and of Margaret Porter; *m* 1978, Sarah Jane Shaw; two *s* two *d*. *Educ:* Lowestoft Grammar School; New College of Speech and Drama, London. Teacher, London, 1970–72; Dir and Co-Founder, Vivid Children's Theatre, 1972–78; Head of Drama, Benjamin Britten High School, Lowestoft, 1978–81; Conservative Party Agent: Eltham, 1982–83; Norwich North, 1983–84; Waveney, 1985–87. Member, Select Committee: on Social Security, 1991–92; for Educn, 1992–. *Recreations:* family, Waveney area—past, present and future. *Address:* House of Commons, Westminster, SW1A 0AA. *T:* 0171–219 6235/3516.

PORTER, Dorothea Noelle Naomi, (Thea Porter); fashion designer, since 1967; *b* 24 Dec. 1927; *d* of Rev. Dr M. S. Seale and Renée Seale; *m* 1953, Robert S. Porter (marr. diss. 1967); one *d*. *Educ:* Lycée français, Damascus; Fernhill Manor; Royal Holloway Coll., London Univ. Embassy wife, Beirut; fashion designer, 1967–, interior and fabric designer. *Recreations:* cooking, travelling, music, painting, collecting antique Islamic fabrics and objets; consulting clairvoyants. *Address:* 13 Bolton Street, W1Y 7PA. *Club:* Colony Room.

PORTER, George Barrington, (Barry); MP (C) Wirral South, since 1983 (Bebington and Ellesmere Port, 1979–83); *b* 11 June 1939; *s* of Kenneth William Porter and Vera Porter; *m* 1965, Susan Carolyn James; two *s* three *d*. *Educ:* Birkenhead Sch.; University Coll., Oxford (BA Hons). Admitted solicitor, 1965. Councillor: Birkenhead County Bor. Council, 1967–74; Wirral Bor., 1975–79 (Chm., Housing Cttee, 1976–77, and Educn Cttee, 1977–79). Mem., Select Cttee on Trade and Industry; Sec., All Party Parly Solicitors Gp. *Recreations:* golf, Rugby Union football, watching cricket, real ale. *Address:* House of Commons, SW1A 0AA. *Clubs:* Royal Commonwealth Society, Royal Automobile; Oxton Conservative, Ellesmere Port Conservative; Birkenhead Park Football, Wirral Ladies Golf, Birkenhead Squash Racquets, Oxton Cricket.

PORTER, Ivor Forsyth, CMG 1963; OBE 1944; HM Diplomatic Service, retired; *b* 12 Nov. 1913; *s* of Herbert and Evelyn Porter; *m* 1951, Ann, *o d* of late Dr John Speares (marr. diss., 1961); *m* 1961, Katerina, *o c* of A. T. Cholerton; one *s* one *d*. *Educ:* Barrow Grammar Sch.; Leeds Univ. (BA, PhD). Lecturer at Bucharest Univ., 1939–40; Temp. Secretary, at Bucharest Legation, 1940–41; Raiding Forces, 1941–45 (Major). Joined Foreign (subseq. Diplomatic) Service, May 1946, as 2nd Secretary in Sen. Branch; 1st Secretary 1948; transferred to Washington, 1951; Foreign Office, 1953; UK Delegation to NATO Paris as Counsellor and Head of Chancery, 1956; Nicosia, 1959 (Deputy Head UK Mission), Deputy High Commissioner, 1961–62, Cyprus; Permanent Rep. to Council of Europe, Strasbourg, 1962–65 (with personal rank of Minister); Dep. High Commissioner, Eastern India, 1965–66; Ambassador, UK Delegn to Geneva Disarmament Conf., 1968–71 (Minister, 1967–68); Ambassador to Senegal, Guinea, Mali and Mauritania, 1971–73; later Dir, Atlantic Region, Research Dept, FCO, retired. *Publications:* (as Ivor Crane) The Think Trap (novel), 1972; Operation Autonomous: with SOE in wartime Roumania, 1989. *Recreations:* writing, walking. *Address:* 17 Redcliffe Road, SW10 9NP. *Clubs:* Travellers', PEN.

PORTER, James Forrest, CBE 1991; Director General (formerly Director) of the Commonwealth Institute, 1978–91; Leverhulme Research Fellow, and Visiting Fellow, London University Institute of Education, since 1991; *b* Frodsham, Cheshire, 2 Oct. 1928; *s* of Ernest Porter and Mary Violetta Porter; *m* 1952, Dymphna, *d* of Leo Francis Powell, London; two *d*. *Educ:* Salford Grammar Sch.; LSE (BSc Sociol.); Univ. of London Inst. of Educn (MA). Asst Master, St George in the East Sec. Sch., Stepney, 1948–50; Leverhulme Scholar, Univ. of London, 1950–55; Lectr in Sociol. and Educn, Worcester Coll., 1955–60; Head of Educn Dept, Chorley Coll., 1960–62; Dep. Principal, Coventry Coll., 1962–67; Principal, Bulmershe Coll. of Higher Educn, Reading, 1967–78. Director: bi-annual internat. courses on teacher educn, Brit. Council, 1975, 1977, 1979, on Museum Educn, 1982; Adult Literacy Support Services Fund, 1977–81. Consultant: Finland, 1976; Unesco, Paris, 1979–; Commonwealth Fellow, Australia, 1977. Chm., Newsconcern Foundn, 1984–91; Member: Nat. Cttee of Inquiry into Teacher Educn and Trng (James Cttee), 1971; Educn Cttee, UGC, 1970–78; Educnl Adv. Council, IBA, 1970–80; Nat. Council for Dance Educn, 1978; Exec. Cttee, Internat. Council of Museums, 1981–87; Educn Council, BBC, 1987–92; President: British Comparative Educn Soc., 1983–84; World Educn Fellowship, 1989– (Chm., 1979–82). Member: UK Delegn to Unesco, Geneva, 1975 (Vice-Pres., Commn on Changing Role of Teacher); Unesco Missions to Morocco and Senegal, 1982, to Jordan, 1983. Mem., Educn Council, Royal Opera House, Covent Garden, 1985–91. Mem., Editorial Bd, Higher Education Review, 1974–; Chm., Editorial Bd, Commonwealth Today, 1985–89 (Mem., 1982). FRSA 1978; Hon. FCP 1978; FRGS 1984. *Publications:* (ed) Rural Development and the Changing Countries of the World, 1969; (with N. Goble) The Changing Role of the Teacher, Paris 1977. *Recreations:* writing, river watching. *Address:* House by the Water, Bolney Avenue, Shiplake, Oxon RG9 3NS; Institute of Education, University of London, 20 Bedford Way, WC1H 0AL.

PORTER, Janet S.; *see* Street-Porter.

PORTER, Air Vice-Marshal John Alan, OBE 1973; CEng, FRAeS, FIEE; Deputy Vice-Chancellor, University of Glamorgan, since 1994; *b* 29 Sept. 1934; *s* of late Alan and Etta Porter; *m* 1961, Sandra Rose (marr. diss.); two *s*. *Educ:* Lawrence Sheriff School, Rugby; Bristol Univ. (BSc); Southampton Univ. (Dip Soton). Commissioned in Engineer Branch, RAF, 1953; appts in UK, USA and Cyprus, 1953–79; Royal College of Defence Studies, 1980; Dep. Gen. Manager, NATO MRCA Develt and Production Agency (NAMMA), Munich, 1981–84; Dir-Gen. Aircraft 2, MoD(PE), 1984–88; Dir-Gen., Communications, Inf. Systems and Orgn (RAF), 1988–89; RAF retd, 1989. Dir, Communications-Electronics Security Gp, 1989–91; Dir, Sci. and Technol., 1991–94, GCHQ. *Recreations:* music, horology. *Address:* University of Glamorgan, Pontypridd, Mid Glam CF37 1DC. *Club:* Royal Air Force.

PORTER, John Andrew, TD; JP; DL; Partner, Porter and Cobb, as Chartered Surveyor, 1940–81; *b* 18 May 1916; *s* of late Horace Augustus Porter, DFC, JP, and Vera Marion Porter; *m* 1941, Margaret Isobel Wisnom; two *d*. *Educ:* Radley Coll.; Sidney Sussex Coll., Cambridge (MA). Commissioned RA, TA, 1938; served War, 1939–46, Lt-Col. Director: Kent County Building Soc., 1947 (Chm., 1965–68); Hastings and Thanet Building Soc., 1968–78 (Chm., 1972–78); Anglia, Hastings and Thanet, later Anglia, Building Soc., 1978–87 (Chm., 1978–81). JP Gravesham PSD, 1952, Chm., Gravesham Div., 1976–83, Dep. Chm., 1983–85. Pres., Gravesend Cons. Assoc., 1965–77. Chm., Bd of Govs, Cobham Hall Sch., 1987–91. General Commissioner of Taxes, 1970–90. DL Kent, 1984. *Recreations:* cricket, reading, golf. *Address:* Leaders, Hodsoll Street, near Wrotham, Kent TN15 7LH. *T:* Fairseat (01732) 822260. *Clubs:* Royal Automobile, MCC; Hawks (Cambridge); Kent CC (Pres., 1985–86).

PORTER, Sir John Simon H.; *see* Horsbrugh-Porter.

PORTER, Prof. Rev. Canon (Joshua) Roy; Professor of Theology, University of Exeter, 1962–86 (Head of Department, 1962–85), now Professor Emeritus; *b* 7 May 1921; *s* of Joshua Porter and Bessie Evelyn (*née* Earlam). *Educ:* King's Sch., Macclesfield; Merton Coll., Oxford (Exhibnr); S Stephen's House, Oxford. BA: Mod. Hist. (Cl. I), Theology (Cl. I), MA Oxon. Liddon Student, 1942; Deacon 1945, Priest 1946; Curate of S Mary, Portsea, 1945–47; Resident Chaplain to Bp of Chichester, 1947–49; Hon. Chaplain, 1949–50; Examining Chaplain from 1950; Fellow, Chaplain and Lectr, Oriel Coll., Oxford, 1949–62; Tutor, 1950–62; Kennicott Hebrew Fellow, 1955; Sen. Denyer and Johnson Schol., 1958; Select Preacher: Univs of Oxford, 1953–55, Cambridge, 1957, TCD, 1958; Canon and Preb. of Wightring and Theol Lectr in Chichester Cath., 1965–88; Wiccamical Canon and Preb. of Exceit, 1988–; Vis. Prof., Southeastern Seminary, Wake Forest, N Carolina, 1967; Dean of Arts, Univ. of Exeter, 1968–71; Proctor in Convocation of Canterbury for dio. of Exeter, 1964–75; for Other Univs (Canterbury), 1975–; Examining Chaplain to Bps of Peterborough, 1973–86, of Truro, 1973–81, of London, 1981–91, and of Gibraltar in Europe, 1989–93. Ethel M. Wood Lectr, Univ. of London 1979; Michael Harrah Wood Lectr, Univ. of the South, Sewanee, Tenn, 1984; Lectr in Old Testament Studies, Holyrood Seminary, NY, 1987–. Member: Gen. Synod, 1970–90 (Panel of Chairmen, 1984–86); ACCM, 1975–86; Council of Management, Coll. of St Mark and St John, 1980–85; Vice-Pres., Folklore Soc., 1979–83 (Pres., 1976–79; Hon. Mem., 1983); President: SOTS, 1983; Anglican Assoc., 1986–; Vice-Chm., Prayer Book Soc., 1987–. FAMS. *Publications:* World in the Heart, 1944; Moses and Monarchy, 1963; The Extended Family in the Old Testament, 1967; Proclamation and Presence, 1970, 2nd rev. edn, 1983; The Non-Juring Bishops, 1973;

Leviticus, 1976, Japanese edn 1984; Animals in Folklore, 1978; The Crown and the Church, 1978; Folklore and the Old Testament, 1981; trans. C. Westermann, The Living Psalms, 1989; Synodical Government in the Church of England, 1990; An Illustrated Key to the Bible, 1995; *contributor to:* Promise and Fulfilment, 1963; A Source Book of the Bible for Teachers, 1970; The Journey to the Other World, 1975; Tradition and Interpretation, 1979; A Basic Introduction to the Old Testament, 1980; Divination and Oracles, 1981; Folklore Studies in the Twentieth Century, 1981; The Folklore of Ghosts, 1981; Israel's Prophetic Tradition, 1982; Tracts for Our Times, 1983; The Hero in Tradition and Folklore, 1984; Harper's Bible Dictionary, 1985, new edn 1995; Arabia and the Gulf: from traditional society to modern states, 1986; The Seer in Celtic and Other Traditions, 1989; Schöpfung und Befreiung, 1989; A Dictionary of Biblical Interpretation, 1990; Christianity and Conservatism, 1990; The Oil of Gladness, 1993; Boundaries and Thresholds, 1993; The Oxford Companion to the Bible, 1993; World Mythology, 1993; numerous articles in learned jls and dictionaries. *Recreations:* theatre and opera, book-collecting, travel. *Address:* 36 Theberton Street, Barnsbury, N1 0QX. *T:* 0171–354 5861; 68 Sand Street, Longbridge Deverill, near Warminster, Wilts BA12 7DS. *T:* Warminster (01985) 40311. *Club:* Athenæum.

PORTER, Air Marshal Sir Kenneth; *see* Porter, Air Marshal Sir M. K. D.

PORTER, Sir Leslie, Kt 1983; President, Tesco PLC, 1985–90 (Chairman, 1973–85; Deputy Chairman and Managing Director, 1972–73); *b* 10 July 1920; *s* of late Henry Alfred and Jane Porter; *m* 1949, Shirley Cohen (*see* Dame Shirley Porter); one *s* one *d*. *Educ:* Holloway County Sch. Joined family textile business (J. Porter & Co), 1938. Served War: Techn. Quartermaster Sergt, 1st Bn The Rangers, KRRC, in Egypt, Greece, Crete, Libya, Tunisia, Algeria, Italy, 1939–46. Re-joined J. Porter & Co, 1946; became Managing Dir, 1955. Joined Tesco Stores (Holdings) Ltd: Dir, 1959; Asst Managing Dir, 1964; Dep. Chm., 1970. Member of Lloyd's, 1964–. Pres., Inst. of Grocery Distribution, 1977–80. Vice-Pres., NPFA; Chm., Sports Aid Foundn, 1985–88 (Hon. Vice Pres., 1988–). Internat. Vice-Pres., Mus. of the Diaspora, 1984–. Hon. Chm., Bd of Governors, 1989–, Chancellor, 1993–, Tel Aviv Univ.; Governor, Hong Kong Baptist Coll.; Hon. PhD (Business Management), Tel Aviv Univ., 1973. OStJ 1992. *Recreations:* golf, yachting, bridge. *Clubs:* Royal Automobile, City Livery, Rugby; Dyrham Park Country (Barnet, Herts); Coombe Hill Golf (Kingston Hill, Surrey).

PORTER, Marguerite Ann, (Mrs Nicky Henson); Guest Artist, Royal Ballet Co., since 1986 (Senior Principal Dancer, 1976–85); *b* 30 Nov. 1948; *d* of William Albert and Mary Porter; *m* (marr. diss.); *m* 1986, Nicky Henson, *qv*; one *s*. *Educ:* Doncaster. Joined Royal Ballet School, 1964; graduated to Royal Ballet Co., 1966; soloist, 1972; Principal, 1976; favourite roles include: Juliet in Romeo and Juliet, Manon, Natalia in A Month in the Country. *Film:* Comrade Lady. *Publication:* Ballerina: a dancer's life, 1989. *Recreations:* my family, friends. *Address:* c/o Richard Stone Partnership, 25 Whitehall, SW1A 2BS.

PORTER, Air Marshal Sir (Melvin) Kenneth (Drowley), KCB 1967 (CB 1959); CBE 1945 (OBE 1942); Royal Air Force, retired; *b* 19 Nov. 1912; *s* of late Flt Lieut Edward Ernest Porter, MBE, DCM and late Helen Porter; *m* 1940, Elena (*d* 1993), *d* of F. W. Sinclair; two *s* one *d*. *Educ:* No. 1 School of Technical Training, Halton; RAF Coll., Cranwell. Commissioned, 1932; Army Co-operation Sqdn, Fleet Air Arm, 1933–36, as PO and FO; specialised on Signals, 1936–37, Flt-Lieut; Sqdn Leader, 1939. Served War of 1939–45 (despatches thrice, OBE, CBE, Legion of Merit, USA); Chief Signals Officer, Balloon Command, 1939; DCSO and CSO, HQ No 11 Group, 1940–42; Temp. Wing Comdr, 1941; CSO, HQ 2nd TAF, 1943–45; CSO HQ No 83 Gp, Temp Gp Captain, 1943; Actg Air Commodore, 1944–45; CSO, HQ Bomber Command, 1945; Air Min. Tech. Plans, 1946–47, Gp Captain, 1946; Member Directing Staff, RAF Staff Coll., Andover, 1947–49; Senior Tech. Staff Officer, HQ No. 205 Group, 1950–52; Comdg Nos 1 and 2 Air Signallers Schools, 1952–54; CSO HQ 2nd ATAF, 1954–55; CSO, HQ Fighter Command, Actg Air Commodore, 1955–58, Air Cdr, 1958; Student Imperial Defence Coll., 1959; Commandant of No 4 School of Technical Training, RAF St Athan, Glamorgan, and Air Officer Wales, 1960–61; Actg Air Vice-Marshal, 1961; Air Vice-Marshal, 1962; Director-General: Ground Training, 1961–63; of Signals (Air), Ministry of Defence, 1964–66; AOC-in-C, Maintenance Command, 1966–70; Hd of RAF Engineer Branch, 1968–70; Actg Air Marshal, 1966; Air Marshal, 1967. Dir of Tech. Educn Projects, UC Cardiff, 1970–74. CEng 1966; FIEE; FRAeS; CIMgt. *Recreation:* reading. *Address:* c/o Lloyds Bank, 12 Durdham Park, Bristol BS6 6XA.

PORTER, Peter Neville Frederick, FRSL; freelance writer, poet; *b* Brisbane, 16 Feb. 1929; *s* of William Ronald Porter and Marion Main; *m* 1st, 1961, Jannice Henry (*d* 1974); two *d*; 2nd, 1991, Christine Berg. *Educ:* Church of England Grammar Sch., Brisbane; Toowoomba Grammar Sch. Worked as journalist in Brisbane before coming to England in 1951; clerk, bookseller and advertising writer, before becoming full-time poet, journalist, reviewer and broadcaster in 1968. Chief work done in poetry and English literature. Hon. DLitt: Melbourne, 1985; Loughborough, 1987. *Publications:* Once Bitten, Twice Bitten, 1961; Penguin Modern Poets No 2, 1962; Poems, Ancient and Modern, 1964; A Porter Folio, 1969; The Last of England, 1970; Preaching to the Converted, 1972; (trans.) After Martial, 1972; (with Arthur Boyd) Jonah, 1973; (with Arthur Boyd) The Lady and the Unicorn, 1975; Living in a Calm Country, 1975; (jt ed) New Poetry 1, 1975; The Cost of Seriousness, 1978; English Subtitles, 1981; Collected Poems, 1983 (Duff Cooper Prize); Fast Forward, 1984; (with Arthur Boyd) Narcissus, 1985; The Automatic Oracle, 1987 (Whitbread Poetry Award, 1988); (with Arthur Boyd) Mars, 1988; A Porter Selected, 1989; Possible Worlds, 1989; The Chair of Babel, 1992; Millennial Fables, 1995. *Recreations:* buying records and listening to music; travelling in Italy. *Address:* 42 Cleveland Square, W2 6DA. *T:* 0171–262 4289.

PORTER, Prof. Robert, DM, FRACP, FAA; Dean, Faculty of Medicine, Monash University, Victoria, since 1989 (Deputy Vice Chancellor (Research), 1992–93); *b* 10 Sept. 1932; *s* of William John Porter and late Amy Porter (*née* Tottman); *m* 1961, Anne Dorothy Steell; two *s* two *d*. *Educ:* Univ. of Adelaide (BMedSc, DSc); Univ. of Oxford (MA, BCh, DM). Rhodes Scholarship, South Australia, 1954; Radcliffe Travelling Fellowship in Med. Sci., University Coll., Oxford, 1962; Lectr, Univ. Lab. of Physiology, Oxford, 1960–67; Fellow, St Catherine's Coll., and Medical Tutor, Oxford, 1963–67; Prof. of Physiology and Chm., Dept of Physiology, Monash Univ., 1967–79; Howard Florey Prof. of Med. Res., and Dir, John Curtin Sch. of Med. Res., ANU, 1980–89; Fogarty Scholar-in-Residence, NIH, 1986–87. Member: Bd of Dirs, Alfred Gp of Hosps and Monash Med. Centre, 1989–; Bd of Govs, Menzies Sch. of Health Res., Darwin, 1985–; Bd of Management, Baker Med. Res. Inst., 1980–. *Publications:* (with C. G. Phillips) Cortico-Spinal Neurones: their role in movement, 1977; (with R. N. Lemon) Corticospinal function and voluntary movement, 1993; articles on neurophysiology and control of movement by the brain. *Recreations:* outdoor sports. *Address:* 7 Beach Street, Balnarring Beach, Vic 3926, Australia. *T:* (home) (59) 831518; (office) (3) 99054318.

PORTER, Rt. Rev. Robert George, OBE 1952; Bishop of The Murray, 1970–89; *b* 7 Jan. 1924; *s* of Herbert James and Eileen Kathleen Porter; *m* 1954, Elizabeth Mary Williams; two *d*. *Educ:* Canterbury Boys' High School; St John's Theological Coll., Morpeth, NSW; Moore College, Sydney (ThL Hons). Served with AIF, 1942–44. Deacon 1947, priest 1948; Assistant Curate, Christ Church Cathedral, Ballarat, Victoria, 1947–49; Assistant Curate, St Paul's, Burwood, Sydney, 1949–50; Priest in charge of Isivita and Agenehambo, Diocese of New Guinea, 1950–57; Archdeacon of Ballarat, 1957–70; Assistant Bishop of Ballarat, 1967–70. KSJ 1992. *Recreations:* gardening, reading. *Address:* 75 Lambert Road, Joslin, SA 5070, Australia.

PORTER, Robert Stanley, CB 1972; OBE 1959; Deputy Secretary (Chief Economist), Overseas Development Administration, Foreign and Commonwealth Office (formerly Ministry of Overseas Development), 1980–84; retired; *b* 17 Sept. 1924; *s* of S. R. Porter; *m* 1st, 1953, Dorothea Naomi (marr. diss. 1967), *d* of Rev. Morris Seale; one *d*; 2nd, 1967, Julia Karen (*d* 1992), *d* of late Edmund A. Davies; 3rd, 1993, Mary Napiorkowska (*née* Woolley). *Educ:* St Clement Danes, Holborn Estate, Grammar Sch.; New Coll., Oxford. Research Economist, US Economic Cooperation Administration Special Mission to the UK, 1949; British Middle East Development Division: Asst Statistical Adviser, Cairo, 1951; Statistical Adviser and Economist, Beirut, 1955; Min. of Overseas Development: Dir, Geographical Div., Economic Planning Staff, 1965; Dep. Dir-Gen. of Economic Planning, 1967; Dir-Gen. of Economic Planning, 1969. Vis. Prof., David Livingstone Inst. for Overseas Develt Studies, 1984–87. *Publications:* articles in Oxford Economic Papers, Kyklos, Review of Income and Wealth, ODI Development Policy Review. *Recreations:* music, theatre. *Address:* Lower Saunders, Cheriton Fitzpaine, Crediton, Devon EX17 4JA. *T:* Cheriton Fitzpaine (01363) 866645. *Club:* Athenæum.

PORTER, Rt. Hon. Sir Robert (Wilson), Kt 1971; PC (NI) 1969; QC (NI) 1965; County Court Judge, Northern Ireland, 1978–95; *b* 23 Dec. 1923; *s* of late Joseph Wilson Porter and late Letitia Mary (*née* Wasson); *m* 1953, Margaret Adelaide, *y d* of late F. W. Lynas; one *s* one *d* (and one *d* decd). *Educ:* Model Sch. and Foyle Coll., Londonderry; Queen's Univ., Belfast. RAFVR, 1943–46; Royal Artillery (TA), 1950–56. Foundation Schol., Queen's Univ., 1947 and 1948; LLB 1949. Called to Bar: N Ireland, 1950; Ireland, 1975; Middle Temple, 1988. Lecturer in Contract and Sale of Goods, Queen's Univ., 1950–51; Jun. Crown Counsel, Co. Londonderry, 1960–63, Co. Down, 1964–65; Counsel to Attorney-General for N Ireland, 1963–64 and 1965; Recorder: of Londonderry, 1979–81; of Belfast, 1993–95. Vice-Chairman, 1959–61, Chairman, 1961–66, War Pensions Appeal Tribunal for N Ireland. MP (U) Queen's Univ. of Belfast, 1966–69, Lagan Valley, 1969–73, Parlt of N Ireland; Minister of Health and Social Services, N Ireland, 1969; Parly Sec., Min. of Home Affairs, 1969; Minister of Home Affairs, Govt of NI, 1969–70. *Recreations:* gardening, golf. *Address:* Larch Hill, Church Close, Ballylesson, Belfast, N Ireland BT8 8JX. *Club:* Royal Air Force.

PORTER, Rev. Canon Roy; *see* Porter, Rev. Canon J. R.

PORTER, Prof. Roy Sydney, PhD; FBA 1994; Professor in the Social History of Medicine, Wellcome Institute for the History of Medicine, since 1993; *b* 31 Dec. 1946; *m* 1st, 1970, Susan Limb (marr. diss.); 2nd, 1983, J. Rainfray (marr. diss.); 3rd, 1987, Dorothy Watkins (marr. diss.). *Educ:* Christ's Coll., Cambridge (BA 1968; PhD 1974). Cambridge University: Res. Fellow, Christ's Coll.,1970–72; Fellow and Dir of Studies in History, 1972–79, Dean, 1977–79, Churchill Coll.; Asst Lectr, 1974–77, Lectr, 1977–79, in European Hist.; Sen. Lectr, 1979–91, Reader, 1991–93, Wellcome Inst. Vis. Prof., UCLA, 1988–89; Visiting Fellow: Princeton Univ., 1989; Stanford Univ., 1989. *Publications:* The Making of Geology, 1977; William Hobbs's The Earth Generated and Anatomized, 1981; English Society in the Eighteenth Century, 1982, 2nd edn 1990; (jtly) Documents of the Early Industrial Revolution, 1983; The Earth Sciences: an annotated bibliography, 1983; Mind Forg'd Manacles: madness and psychiatry in England from Restoration to Regency, 1987; Disease, Medicine and Society in England 1550–1860, 1987; A Social History of Madness, 1987; Edward Gibbon: making history, 1988; (jtly) In Sickness and in Health: the British Experience 1650–1850, 1988; Health for Sale: quackery in England 1650–1850, 1989; (jtly) Patient's Progress: doctors and doctoring in eighteenth century England, 1989; The Enlightenment, 1990; Doctor of Society: Thomas Beddoes and the sick trade in late Enlightenment England, 1991; (jtly) Consumption and Culture in the Seventeenth and Eighteenth Centuries: a bibliography, 1991; Hysteria Beyond Fraud, 1993; London: a social history, 1994; (jtly) The Facts of Life: the creation of sexual knowledge in Britain 1650–1950, 1995; also edited and contrib. to many other books. *Address:* The Wellcome Institute for the History of Medicine, 183 Euston Road, NW1 2BE.

PORTER, Dame Shirley, (Lady Porter), DBE 1991; DL; Councillor, Hyde Park Ward, 1974–93, Leader, 1983–91, Westminster City Council; Lord Mayor of Westminster, 1991–92; *b* 29 Nov. 1930; *d* of late Sir John (Edward) Cohen and Lady (Sarah) Cohen; *m* 1949, Sir Leslie Porter, *qv*; one *s* one *d*. *Educ:* Warren Sch., Worthing, Sussex; La Ramée, Lausanne, Switzerland. Founded Designers' Guild, 1970; Sec., Porter Investments, 1970–; Chairman: Neurotech Medical Systems, 1992–94; LBC, 1993–94; Dir, Capital Radio, 1982–88. Westminster City Council: Conservative Whip, 1974–77; Road Safety Cttee, 1974–82; Member: Co-ordinating Cttee, 1981–82; Chairman: Highways and Works Cttee, 1978–82 (Vice-Chm., 1977–78); Gen. Purposes Cttee, 1982–83; Policy Review Cttee, 1982–83; Policy and Resources Cttee, 1983–91. Chairman: (also Founder), WARS Campaign (Westminster Against Reckless Spending), 1981–84; Cleaner City Campaign, 1979–81; Pres., Eur. Conf. on Tourism and the Envmt, 1992–; Vice-Pres., Cleaner London Campaign, 1979–81; Mem. Exec., Keep Britain Tidy Gp, 1977–81. Pres., British Inst. of Cleaning Science, 1991–; Mem. Ct, Guild of Cleaners, 1976–. Member: Bd, London Festival Ballet, 1988–89; Trustee, London Philharmonic Trust, 1991–93. Hon. Mem., London Community Cricket Assoc., 1989–. Governor, Tel Aviv Univ., 1982. JP Inner London, 1972–84; DL Greater London, 1988. FRSA 1989. *Recreations:* golf, tennis, ballet, promoting London. *Address:* 63 Chester Square, SW1W 9EA. *Clubs:* Royal Automobile, Queen's, Racquets; Frilford Heath Golf (Oxford); Coombe Hill Golf, Dyrham Park Golf.

PORTER, Stanley; *see* Porter, W. S.

PORTER, Thea; *see* Porter, D. N. N.

PORTER, (Walter) Stanley, TD 1950; MA (Cantab); Headmaster of Framlingham College, 1955–71; *b* 28 Sept. 1909; *s* of late Walter Porter, Rugby; *m* 1937, Doreen (*d* 1992), *o d* of B. Haynes, Rugby; one *d*. *Educ:* Rugby Sch.; Gonville and Caius Coll., Cambridge. Assistant Master and Officer Commanding Training Corps, Trent Coll., 1933–36; Felsted Sch., 1936–43; Radley Coll., 1944–55. FRSA 1968. *Recreations:* travel, amateur dramatics; formerly Rugby football, hockey. *Address:* The Hermitage, 29 Cumberland Street, Woodbridge, Suffolk IP12 4AH. *T:* Woodbridge (01394) 382340.

PORTERFIELD, Dr James Stuart; retired; Reader in Bacteriology, Sir William Dunn School of Pathology, Oxford University, and Senior Research Fellow, Wadham College, Oxford, 1977–89; now Emeritus Fellow; *b* 17 Jan. 1924; *yr s* of late Dr Samuel Porterfield and Mrs Lilian Porterfield, Widnes, Lancs, and Portstewart, Co. Londonderry, NI; *m* 1950, Betty Mary Burch; one *d* (one *s* decd). *Educ:* Wade Deacon Grammar Sch., Widnes; King's Sch., Chester; Liverpool Univ. MB, ChB 1947, MD 1949. Asst Lectr in Bacteriology, Univ. of Liverpool, 1947–49; Bacteriologist and Virologist, Common Cold

Res. Unit, Salisbury, Wilts, 1949–51; Pathologist, RAF Inst. of Pathology and Tropical Med., Halton, Aylesbury, Bucks, 1952–53; seconded to W African Council for Med. Res. Labs, Lagos, Nigeria, 1953–57; Mem. Scientific Staff, Nat. Inst. for Med. Res., Mill Hill, 1949–77; WHO Regional Ref. Centre for Arthropod-borne Viruses, 1961–65; WHO Collaborating Lab., 1965–89; Ref. Expert on Arboviruses, Public Health Lab. Service, 1967–76. Chm., Arbovirus Study Gp, Internat. Cttee for Nomenclature of Viruses, 1968–78; Meetings Sec., Soc. for General Microbiology, 1972–77; Vice-Pres., Royal Soc. for Tropical Med. and Hygiene, 1980–81 (Councillor, 1973–76); Secretary and Vice-Pres., Royal Institution, 1973–78. *Publications:* (ed) Andrewes' Viruses of Vertebrates, 5th edn, 1989; (ed) Exotic Viral Infections, 1995; contribs to medical and scientific jls. *Recreations:* fell-walking, gardening. *Address:* Green Valleys, Goodleigh, Barnstaple, Devon EX32 7NH.

PORTES, Prof. Richard David, DPhil; Professor of Economics, London Business School, since 1995; Director, Centre for Economic Policy Research, since 1983; *b* 10 Dec. 1941; *s* of Herbert Portes and Abra Halperin Portes; *m* 1963, Bobbi Frank; one *s* one *d*. *Educ:* Yale Univ. (BA 1962 *summa cum laude* maths and philosophy); Balliol and Nuffield Colls, Oxford (Rhodes Schol., Woodrow Wilson Fellow, Danforth Fellow; MA 1965; DPhil 1969). Official Fellow and Tutor in Econs, Balliol Coll., Oxford, 1965–69; Asst Prof. of Econs and Internat. Affairs, Princeton Univ., 1969–72; Prof. of Econs, Birkbeck Coll., Univ. of London, 1972–94 (Head, Dept of Econs, 1975–77 and 1980–83). Dir d'Etudes, Ecole des Hautes Etudes en Sciences Sociales, Paris, 1978–. Guggenheim Fellow, 1977–78; British Acad. Overseas Vis. Fellow, 1977–78; Res. Associate, Nat. Bureau of Econ. Res., Cambridge, Mass, 1980–; Vis. Prof., Harvard Univ., 1977–78. Vice-Chm., Econs Cttee, SSRC, 1981–84. Member: Bd of Dirs, Soc. for Econ. Analysis (Rev. of Econ. Studies), 1967–69, 1972–80 (Sec. 1974–77); RIIA, 1973– (Res. Cttee, 1982–); Council on Foreign Relations, 1978–; Hon. Degrees Cttee, Univ. of London, 1984–89. Fellow, Econometric Soc., 1983–; Sec.-Gen., Royal Econ. Soc., 1992– (Council, 1986–92; Exec. Cttee, 1987–); Council, European Econ. Assoc., 1992–. Co-Chm., Bd of Governors, and Sen. Editor, Economic Policy, 1985–. *Publications:* (ed) Planning and Market Relations, 1971; The Polish Crisis, 1981; Deficits and Détente, 1983; (ed) Threats to International Financial Stability, 1987; (ed) Global Macroeconomics: policy conflict and cooperation, 1987; (ed) Blueprints for Exchange Rate Management, 1989; (ed) Macroeconomic Policies in an Interdependent World, 1989; (ed) Economic Transformation in Hungary and Poland, 1990; (ed) External Constraints on Macroeconomic Policy: the experience of Europe, 1991; (ed) The Path of Reform in Central and Eastern Europe, 1991; (ed) Economic Transformation in Central Europe, 1993; (ed) European Union Trade with Eastern Europe, 1995; (ed) Economic Transformation: the next stage in Central Europe, 1995; contribs to many learned jls. *Recreation:* living beyond my means. *Address:* Centre for Economic Policy Research, 25–28 Old Burlington Street, W1X 1LB. *T:* 0171–734 9190. *Club:* Groucho.

PORTILLO, Rt. Hon. Michael (Denzil Xavier); PC 1992; MP (C) Enfield, Southgate, since December 1984; Secretary of State for Defence, since 1995; *b* 26 May 1953; *s* of late Luis Gabriel Portillo and of Cora Waldegrave Blyth; *m* 1982, Carolyn Claire Eadie. *Educ:* Harrow County Boys' School; Peterhouse, Cambridge (1st cl. Hons MA History). Ocean Transport & Trading Co., 1975–76; Conservative Res. Dept., 1976–79; Special Advr, Sec. of State for Energy, 1979–81; Kerr McGee Oil (UK) Ltd, 1981–83; Special Adviser: to Sec. of State for Trade and Industry, 1983; to Chancellor of the Exchequer, 1983–84; an Asst Govt Whip, 1986–87; Parly Under Sec. of State, DHSS, 1987–88; Minister of State, Dept of Transport, 1988–90; Minister of State for Local Govt, DoE, 1990–92; Chief Sec. to HM Treasury, 1992–94; Sec. of State for Employment, 1994–95. *Address:* House of Commons, SW1A 0AA. *Club:* Carlton.

PORTLAND, 11th Earl of, *cr* 1689; **Henry Noel Bentinck;** Viscount Woodstock, Baron Cirencester, 1689; Count of the Holy Roman Empire; *b* 2 Oct. 1919; *s* of Capt. Count Robert Bentinck (*d* 1932) and Lady Norah Ida Emily Noel (*d* 1939), *d* of 3rd Earl of Gainsborough; *S* to Earldom of kinsman, 9th Duke of Portland, CMG, 1990; *m* 1st, 1940, Pauline (*d* 1967), *y d* of late Frederick William Mellowes; one *s* two *d*; 2nd, 1974, Jenifer, *d* of late Reginald Hopkins. *Heir: s* Viscount Woodstock, *qv*.

PORTMAN, family name of **Viscount Portman.**

PORTMAN, 9th Viscount, *cr* 1873; **Edward Henry Berkeley Portman;** Baron 1873; *b* 22 April 1934; *s* of late Hon. Michael Berkeley Portman (*d* 1959) (*yr s* of 7th Viscount), and June Charles (*d* 1947); *S* uncle, 1967; *m* 1st, 1956, Rosemary Farris (marr. diss., 1965); one *s* one *d*; 2nd, 1966, Penelope Allin; three *s* (and one *s* decd). *Educ:* Canford; Royal Agricultural College. Farmer. *Recreations:* shooting, fishing, music. *Heir: s* Hon. Christopher Edward Berkeley Portman [*b* 30 July 1958; *m* 1983, Caroline Steenson (marr. diss.); one *s*; *m* 1987, Patricia Martins Pim, *er d* of Senhor Bernardino Pim; one *s*]. *Address:* Clock Mill, Clifford, Herefordshire HR3 5HB. *T:* Clifford (01497) 831235. *Club:* White's.

PORTSMOUTH, 10th Earl of, *cr* 1743; **Quentin Gerard Carew Wallop;** Viscount Lymington, Baron Wallop, 1720; Hereditary Bailiff of Burley, New Forest; Director, Grainger Trust plc; *b* 25 July 1954; *s* of Oliver Kintzing Wallop (Viscount Lymington) (*d* 1984) and Ruth Violet (*d* 1978), *yr d* of Brig.-Gen. G. C. Sladen, CB, CMG, DSO, MC; *S* grandfather, 1984; *m* 1st, 1981, Candia (*née* McWilliam) (marr. diss. 1984); one *s* one *d*; 2nd, 1990, Annabel, *d* of Dr and Mrs Ian Fergusson; one *d*. *Educ:* Eton; Millfield. Pres., Basingstoke Cons. Assoc., 1992–. *Heir: s* Viscount Lymington, *qv*. *Address:* Farleigh House, Farleigh Wallop, Basingstoke, Hants RG25 2HT.

PORTSMOUTH, Bishop of, since 1995; **Rt Rev. Kenneth William Stevenson,** PhD, DD, FRHistS; *b* 9 Nov. 1949; *s* of Frederik Robert and Margrete Stevenson; *m* 1970, Sarah Julia Mary (*née* Glover); one *s* three *d*. *Educ:* Edinburgh Acad.; Edinburgh Univ. (MA 1970); Southampton Univ. (PhD 1975); Manchester Univ. (DD 1987). FRHistS 1990. Ordained deacon, 1973, priest, 1974; Asst Curate, Grantham with Manthorpe, 1973–76; Lectr, Boston, 1976–80; part-time Lectr, Lincoln Theol Coll., 1975–80; Chaplain and Lectr, Manchester Univ., 1980–86; Team Vicar, 1980–82, Team Rector, 1982–86, Whitworth, Manchester; Rector, Holy Trinity and St Mary's, Guildford, 1986–95. Member: C of E Liturgical Commn, 1986–; Faith and Order Advisory Gp, 1991–. Vis. Prof., Univ. of Notre Dame, Indiana, 1983. *Publications:* Nuptial Blessing, 1982; Eucharist and Offering, 1986; Jerusalem Revisited, 1988; The First Rites, 1989; Covenant of Grace Renewed, 1994; Handing On, 1996. *Recreations:* historical biographies, thrillers, walking, butterflies, piano, horn. *Address:* Bishopswood, The Avenue, Fareham, Hants PO14 1NT. *T:* Fareham (01329) 280247.

PORTSMOUTH, Bishop of, (RC), since 1988; **Rt. Rev. (Roger Francis) Crispian Hollis;** *b* 17 Nov. 1936; *s* of Christopher and Madeleine Hollis. *Educ:* Stonyhurst College; Balliol Coll., Oxford (MA); Venerable English College, Rome (STL). National Service as 2nd Lt, Somerset Light Infantry, 1954–56. Ordained priest, 1965; Assistant in Amesbury, 1966–67; RC Chaplain, Oxford Univ., 1967–77; RC Assistant to Head of Religious Broadcasting, BBC, 1977–81; Administrator, Clifton Cathedral, Bristol, 1981–87; Auxiliary Bishop of Birmingham (Bishop in Oxfordshire), 1987–88. *Recreations:* occasional golf, walking, cricket watching. *Address:* Bishop's House, Edinburgh Road, Portsmouth PO1 3HG.

PORTSMOUTH, Archdeacon of; *see* Knowles, Ven. G. P.

PORTSMOUTH, Provost of; *see* Yorke, Very Rev. M. L.

POSKITT, Prof. Trevor John, DSc, PhD; Professor of Civil Engineering, Queen Mary and Westfield College (formerly Queen Mary College), University of London, 1972–94; *b* 26 May 1934; *s* of late William Albert Poskitt, Worthing, and Mrs D. M. Poskitt, Lincoln; *m* 1968, Gillian Mary, *d* of L. S. Martin, MBE, Romiley, Cheshire; one *s* one *d*. *Educ:* Corby Technical Sch.; Huddersfield Technical Coll.; Univ. of Leeds; Univ. of Cambridge. HND (Mech. Eng.); BSc Leeds, PhD Cambridge, DSc Manchester; CEng, FICE, FIStructE. Apprentice Engineer to Thos. Broadbent & Sons, Huddersfield, 1949–53; Graduate Assistant, English Electric Co. Ltd, 1958–60; Whitworth Fellow, 1960–63; Lectr, 1963–71, Senior Lectr, 1971–72, in Civil Engineering, Univ. of Manchester. *Publications:* numerous on civil engineering topics. *Recreations:* tennis, music. *Address:* Tanglewood, Lunghurst Road, Woldingham, Surrey CR3 7EJ. *T:* Woldingham (01883) 653101.

POSNANSKY, Jeremy Ross Leon; QC 1994; *b* 8 March 1951; *s* of Anthony Posnansky and Evelyn Davis (*née* Leon), JP; *m* 1974, Julia Sadler, *d* of late Richard Sadler, MBE; two *d*. *Educ:* St Paul's Sch.; Coll. of Law. Called to the Bar, Gray's Inn, 1972, Antigua and Barbuda, 1995; Asst Recorder, 1993–. Mem., Family Courts Business and Service Cttees, Inner London, 1991–94. *Recreations:* scuba diving, travels with my family, computers. *Address:* 1 Mitre Court Buildings, Temple, EC4Y 7BS. *T:* 0171–797 7070.

POSNER, Michael Vivian, CBE 1983; a Director, Railways (formerly British Rail) Pension Trustee Company, since 1986; Secretary-General, European Science Foundation, 1986–93; *b* 25 Aug. 1931; *s* of Jack Posner; *m* 1953, Rebecca Posner, *qv*; one *s* one *d*. *Educ:* Whitgift Sch.; Balliol Coll., Oxford. Research Officer, Oxford Inst. of Statistics, 1953–57; University of Cambridge: Asst Lecturer, Lecturer, then Reader in Economics, 1958–79; Fellow, Pembroke Coll., 1960–83; Chm., Faculty Bd of Economics, 1974–75. Vis. Prof., Brookings Instn, Washington, 1971–72. Director of Economics, Ministry of Power, 1966–67; Economic Adviser to Treasury, 1967–69; Economic Consultant to Treasury, 1969–71; Consultant to IMF, 1971–72; Energy Adviser, NEDO, 1973–74; Econ. Adviser, Dept of Energy, 1974–75; Dep. Chief Econ. Adviser, HM Treasury, 1975–76. Chm., SSRC, 1979–83; Econ. Dir, NEDO, 1984–86. Member: BRB, 1976–84; Post Office Bd, 1978–79; Member: Adv. Council for Energy Conservation, 1974–82; Standing Commn on Energy and the Environment, 1978–81. Mem. Council, PSI, 1978–83 (Senior Res. Fellow, 1983–84). DEd (*hc*) CNAA, 1989; Hon. LLD Bristol, 1992. *Publications:* (co-author) Italian Public Enterprise, 1966; Fuel Policy: a study in applied economics, 1973; (ed) Resource Allocation in the Public Sector, 1977; (ed) Demand Management, 1978; (co-author) Energy Economics, 1981; (ed) Problems of International Money 1972–1985, 1986; books and articles on economics. *Recreation:* country life. *Address:* Rushwood, Jack Straw's Lane, Oxford OX3 0DN. *T:* Oxford (01865) 63578. *Club:* United Oxford & Cambridge University.

POSNER, Prof. Rebecca; Professor of the Romance Languages, University of Oxford, 1978–Oct. 1996; Fellow, St Hugh's College, Oxford, since 1978; *b* 17 Aug. 1929; *d* of William and Rebecca Reynolds; *m* 1953, Michael Vivian Posner, *qv*; one *s* one *d*. *Educ:* Somerville Coll., Oxford. MA, DPhil (Oxon); PhD (Cantab). Fellow, Girton Coll., Cambridge, 1960–63; Prof. of French Studies, Univ. of Ghana, 1963–65; Reader in Language, Univ. of York, 1965–78. Vis. Prof. of Romance Philology, Columbia Univ., NY, 1971–72; Vis. Senior Fellow, Princeton Univ., 1983. *Publications:* Consonantal Dissimilation in the Romance Languages, 1961; The Romance Languages, 1966; (with J. Orr and I. Iordan) Introduction to Romance Linguistics, 1970; (ed with J. N. Green) Trends in Romance Linguistics and Philology: vol. 1, Romance Comparative and Historical Linguistics, 1980; vol. 2, Synchronic Romance Linguistics, 1981; vol. 3, Language and Philology in Romance, 1982; vol. 4, National and Regional Trends in Romance Linguistics and Philology, 1982; vol. 5, Bilingualism and Conflict in Romance, 1993; (contrib.) Legacy of Latin, ed R. Jenkyns, 1992; numerous articles. *Recreations:* walking, gardening, theatre, music. *Address:* St Hugh's College, Oxford OX2 6LE. *T:* Oxford (01865) 274995 and 270488; Rushwood, Jack Straw's Lane, Oxford OX3 0DN. *T:* Oxford (01865) 63578.

POSNETT, Sir Richard (Neil), KBE 1980 (OBE 1963); CMG 1976; HM Diplomatic Service, retired; *b* 19 July 1919; *s* of Rev. Charles Walker Posnett, K-i-H, Medak, S India, and Phyllis (*née* Barker); *m* 1st; two *s* one *d*; 2nd, 1959, Shirley Margaret Hudson; two *s* one *d*. *Educ:* Kingswood; St John's Coll., Cambridge (won 120 yards hurdles for Cambridge *v* Oxford, 1940). BA 1940, MA 1947. Called to the Bar, Gray's Inn, 1951. HM Colonial Administrative Service in Uganda, 1941; Chm., Uganda Olympic Cttee, 1956; Colonial Office, London, 1958; Judicial Adviser, Buganda, 1960; Perm. Sec. for External Affairs, Uganda, 1962; Perm. Sec. for Trade and Industry, 1963; joined Foreign (subseq. Diplomatic) Service, 1964; FO, 1964; served on UK Mission to UN, NY, 1966–70; briefly HM Comr in Anguilla, 1969; Head of W Indian Dept, FCO, 1970–71; Governor and C-in-C of Belize, 1972–76; Special Mission to Ocean Island, 1977; Dependent Territories Adviser, FCO, 1977–79; British High Comr, Kampala, 1979. UK Comr, British Phosphate Comrs, 1978–81. Governor and C-in-C, Bermuda, 1981–83. Mem., Lord Chancellor's Panel of Ind. Inspectors, 1983–89. First ascent of South Portal Peak on Ruwenzori, 1942. Member: RIIA; Royal Forestry Soc.; Royal African Soc. President: Kingswood Assoc., 1980; Godalming Joigny Friendship Assoc., 1987– (Chm., 1984–87). Gov., Kingswood Sch., 1985–93. KStJ 1972. *Publications:* articles in Uganda Journal, World Today. *Recreations:* ski-ing, golf, trees. *Address:* Bahati, Old Kiln Close, Churt, Surrey GU10 2JH. *Clubs:* Commonwealth Trust, Achilles; West Surrey Golf; Hankley Common Golf; Privateers Hockey.

POSNETTE, Prof. Adrian Frank, CBE 1976; FRS 1971; VMH 1982; Director, East Malling Research Station, Kent, 1972–79 (Deputy Director, 1969–72, and Head of Plant Pathology Section, 1957–72); *b* 11 Jan. 1914; *e s* of late Frank William Posnette and Edith (*née* Webber), Cheltenham; *m* 1937, Isabelle, *d* of Dr Montgomery La Roche, New York; one *s* two *d*. *Educ:* Cheltenham Grammar Sch.; Christ's Coll., Cambridge. MA, ScD Cantab; PhD London; AICTA Trinidad; FIBiol. Research at Imperial Coll. of Tropical Agriculture, Trinidad, 1936–37; Colonial Agric. Service, Gold Coast, 1937; Head of Botany and Plant Pathology Dept, W African Cacao Research Inst., 1944; research at East Malling Research Stn, 1949–. Vis. Prof. in Plant Sciences, Wye Coll., Univ. of London, 1971–78. *Publications:* Virus Diseases of Apples and Pears, 1963; numerous research papers in Annals of Applied Biology, Jl of Horticultural Science, Nature, Tropical Agriculture. *Recreations:* ornithology, sailing, gardening. *Address:* Gwyn, Sutton Valence, Maidstone, Kent ME17 3AD. *T:* Maidstone (01622) 843234. *Club:* Hawks (Cambridge).

POST, Herschel; Chief Executive and Deputy Chairman, Coutts & Co., since 1995 (Chief Operating Officer, 1994–95); Member of Council, London Stock Exchange (formerly International Stock Exchange), since 1988 (Deputy Chairman, 1989–95); *b* 9 Oct. 1939; *s* of Herschel E. and Marie C. Post; *m* 1963, Peggy Mayne; one *s* three *d*. *Educ:* Yale Univ. (AB); Oxford Univ. (BA, MA); Harvard Law Sch. (LLB). Associate, Davis Polk & Wardwell, attorneys, 1966–69; Exec. Dir, Parks Council of NY, 1969–72; Dep. Adminr and Comr, Parks, Recreation and Cultural Affairs Admin, NYC, 1973; Vice-Pres., Morgan Guaranty Trust Co., 1974–83; Chief Operaing Officer, Lehman Brothers Internat. (Europe) and Lehman Brothers Securities Ltd, 1990–94. President: Shearson Lehman Global Asset Management, 1984–90; Posthorn Global Asset Management, 1984–90. Trustee, Earthwatch Europe, 1988–. *Address:* Coutts & Co., 440 Strand, WC2R 0QS. *T:* 0171–753 1000.

POST, Col Kenneth Graham, CBE 1945; TD; *b* 21 Jan. 1908; *s* of Donnell Post and Hon. Mrs Post; *m* 1st, 1944, Stephanie Bonté Wood (marr. diss., 1963); one *s* two *d*; 2nd, 1963, Diane Allen; two *s*. *Educ:* Winchester; Magdalen, Oxford. London Stock Exchange, 1929–37; 2nd Lieut, RA (TA) 1937; Norway, 1940; War Office, 1941–42; Ministry of Supply, 1943–44; Ministry of Works, 1945–47; Ministry of Housing, 1956–57; Ministry of Defence, 1957–59. Member Corby New Town Development Corporation, 1955–62; Director, Civic Trust, 1957–63. *Address:* 3 Shepherds Walk, Pembury Road, Tunbridge Wells, Kent TN2 3QR. *T:* Tunbridge Wells (01892) 548560. *Club:* Pratt's.

POSTGATE, Prof. John Nicholas, FBA 1993; Professor of Assyriology, University of Cambridge, since 1994; Fellow, Trinity College, Cambridge, since 1982; *b* 5 Nov. 1945; *s* of Ormond Oliver Postgate and Patricia Mary Postgate (*née* Peet); *m* 1968, Carolyn June Prater; one *s* one *d*. *Educ:* Winchester Coll.; Trinity Coll., Cambridge (BA Oriental Studies 1967; MA 1970). Lectr in Akkadian, SOAS, 1967–71; Fellow, Trinity Coll., Cambridge, 1970–74; Asst Dir, British Sch. of Archaeology, Iraq, 1971–75; Dir, British Archaeol. Expedn to Iraq, 1975–81; Lectr in Hist. and Archaeol. of Ancient Near East, 1981–85, Reader in Mesopotamian Studies, 1985–94, Univ. of Cambridge. Director of excavations: Abu Salabikh, S Iraq, 1975–89; Kilise Tepe, S Turkey, 1994–. *Publications:* Neo-Assyrian Royal Grants and Decrees, 1969; The Governor's Palace Archive, 1973; Taxation and Conscription in the Assyrian Empire, 1974; Fifty Neo-Assyrian Legal Documents, 1976; The First Empires, 1977; (ed) Abu Salabikh Excavations, vols 1–4, 1983–93; (with S. M. Dalley) Tablets from Fort Shalmaneser, 1984; The archive of Urad-Šerua and his family, 1988; Early Mesopotamia: society and economy at the dawn of history, 1992; (with F. M. Fales) Imperial administrative records, pt I 1992, pt II 1995; (with B. K. Ismail) Texts from Niniveh, 1993; articles in Iraq and other learned jls. *Address:* Trinity College, Cambridge CB2 1TQ. *T:* Cambridge (01223) 338443.

POSTGATE, Prof. John Raymond, FRS 1977; FIBiol; Director, AFRC Unit of Nitrogen Fixation, 1980–87 (Assistant Director, 1963–80), and Professor of Microbiology, University of Sussex, 1965–87, now Emeritus; *b* 24 June 1922; *s* of Raymond William Postgate and Daisy Postgate (*née* Lansbury); *m* 1948, Mary Stewart; three *d*. *Educ:* principally Woodstock Sch., Golders Green; Kingsbury County Sch., Mddx; Balliol Coll., Oxford. BA, MA, DPhil, DSc. Research in chemical microbiology: with D. D. Woods on action of sulfonamide drugs, 1946–48, with K. R. Butlin on sulphate-reducing bacteria, 1948–59. Research on bacterial death, 1959–63, incl. Visiting Professor: Univ. of Illinois, 1962–63, working on sulphate-reducing bacteria; Oregon State Univ., 1977–78. President: Inst. of Biology, 1982–84; Soc. for Gen. Microbiology, 1984–87. Hon. DSc Bath, 1990. *Publications:* Microbes and Man, 1969, 3rd edn 1992; Biological Nitrogen Fixation, 1972; A Plain Man's Guide to Jazz, 1973; Nitrogen Fixation, 1978; The Sulphate-Reducing Bacteria, 1979, 2nd edn 1984; The Fundamentals of Nitrogen Fixation, 1982; The Outer Reaches of Life, 1994; (with Mary Postgate) A Stomach for Dissent: the life of Raymond Postgate, 1994; ed, 4 scientific symposia; regular columnist in Jazz Monthly, 1952–72; numerous scientific papers in microbiol/biochem. jls; many jazz record reviews in specialist magazines; articles on jazz. *Recreations:* listening to jazz and attempting to play it. *Address:* 1 Houndean Rise, Lewes, Sussex BN7 1EG. *T:* Lewes (01273) 472675.

POSWILLO, Prof. David Ernest, CBE 1989; FDSRCS, FRACDS, FIBiol, FRCPath; Emeritus Professor of Oral and Maxillofacial Surgery, University of London, since 1992 (Professor of Oral and Maxillofacial Surgery, United Medical and Dental Schools of Guy's and St Thomas' Hospitals, 1983–92); *b* 1 Jan. 1927; *s* of Ernest and Amelia Poswillo, Gisborne, NZ; *m* 1956, Elizabeth Alison, *d* of Whitworth and Alice Russell, Nelson, NZ; two *s* two *d*. *Educ:* Gisborne Boys' High, NZ; Univ. of Otago. BDS 1948, DDS 1962, DSc 1975, Westminster Hosp.; FDSRCS 1952, FRACDS 1966, FIBiol 1974, FRCPath 1981. OC S District Hosp., RNZDC, 1949–51; Hill End Hosp., St Albans, 1952; Dir of Oral Surgery, Christchurch Hosp., NZ, 1953–68; Prof. of Teratology, RCS, 1969–77; Consultant Oral Surgeon, Queen Victoria Hosp., East Grinstead, 1969–77; Prof. of Oral Path. and Oral Surgery, Univ. of Adelaide, and Sen. Oral and Maxillofacial Surgeon, Royal Adelaide and Childrens' Hosps, 1977–79; Prof. of Oral Surgery, and Mem. Council, Royal Dental Hosp., London, 1977–83. Consultant Adviser to Chief MO, DHSS, 1979–86; Chairman: Wkg Pty on Anaesthesia, Sedation and Resuscitation in Dentistry (Poswillo Report), DoH, 1990; Cttee on Dental and Surgical Materials, DoH, 1993–; Scientific Cttee on Tobacco and Health, DoH, 1994–. Mem., Bd of Faculty of Dental Surgery, RCS, 1981–89. Medical Defence Union: Council Mem., 1983–; Chm., Dental Cttee, 1983–88; Mem., Bd of Management, 1992. Sec. Gen., Internat. Assoc. of Oral and Maxillofacial Surgeons, 1983–89 (Hon. Fellow, 1992); President: BAOMS, 1990–91; Section of Odontology, RSM, 1989–90 (Hon. Treas., 1994–). Trustee, Tobacco Products Research Trust, 1980–95; Human Task Force, WHO, 1976–78. Mem. Council of Govs, UMDS of Guy's and St Thomas' Hosps, 1983–92. Hunterian Trustee, RCS, 1994–. Hunterian Prof., RCS, 1968, 1976; Regents' Prof., Univ. of California, 1987. Lectures: Arnott Demonstrator, 1972; Erasmus Wilson, 1973; Darwin-Lincoln, Johns Hopkins, 1975; Waldron, Harvard, 1976; Richardson, Harvard, 1981; Tomes, RCS, 1982; President's, BAOMS, 1985; Friel Meml, European Orthodontic Soc., 1987; Sarnat, UCLA, 1989; William Guy, RCSE, 1990. Fellow, German Acad. of Nat. Scis (Leopoldina), 1988, Foreign Associate, Inst. of Medicine, Nat. Acad. of Scis, USA, 1989. Hon. FFDRCSI, 1984; Hon. FIMFT, 1985; Hon. FRSocMed 1995. Hon. MD Zürich, 1983. RNZADC Prize, 1948; Tomes Prize, 1966; Down Medal, 1973; Kay-Kilner Prize, 1975; ASOMS Research Award, 1976; Hunter Medal and Triennial Prize, 1976; 2nd Orthog. Surg. Award, Univ. of Texas, 1982; Edison Award, Univ. of Michigan, 1987; Colyer Gold Medal, RCS, 1990; Goldman Medal and Lecture, BPMF, 1992. Por Cristo Medal (Ecuador), 1989. *Publications:* (with C. L. Berry) Teratology, 1975; (with B. Cohen and D. K. Mason) Oral Surgery and Pathology, 1978; (with B. Cohen and D. K. Mason) Oral Medicine and Diagnosis, 1978; (with D. J. Simpson and D. David) The Craniosynostoses, 1982; (with D. Henderson) Atlas of Orthognathic Surgery, 1984; (jtly) Dental, Oral and Maxillofacial Surgery, 1986; (jtly) The Effects of Smoking on the Foetus, Neonate and Child, 1992; papers on surgery, pathology and teratology in dental, medical and sci jls. *Recreations:* art, reading, gardening. *Address:* Ferndale, Oldfield Road, Bickley BR1 2LE *T:* 0181–467 1578.

POTTER, Prof. Allen Meyers, PhD; James Bryce Professor of Politics, University of Glasgow, 1970–84, retired; *b* 7 March 1924; *s* of Maurice A. and Irene M. Potter; *m* 1949, Joan Elizabeth Yeo; two *d*. *Educ:* Wesleyan Univ., Conn (BA 1947, MA 1948); Columbia Univ., NY (PhD 1955). FSS 1967. Instructor, College of William and Mary, 1949–51; Lectr/Sen. Lectr, Univ. of Manchester, 1951–62; Vis. Professor, Univ. of Texas, 1960; Professor: Univ. of Strathclyde, 1963–65; Univ. of Essex, 1965–70; Pro-Vice-Chancellor, Univ. of Essex, 1969–70; Vice-Principal, Univ. of Glasgow, 1979–82. Dir, SSRC Data Bank, 1967–70. Member, US-UK Educational Commn, 1979–84. Governor, Glasgow Sch. of Art, 1979–82. *Publications:* American Government and Politics, 1955, 2nd edn 1978; Organised Groups in British National Politics, 1961; articles in American and British social science jls. *Recreation:* inventing table games. *Address:* 14 Severn Drive, Malvern, Worcs WR14 2SZ. *T:* Malvern (01684) 569315.

POTTER, Arthur Kingscote, CMG 1957; CBE (mil.) 1946; *b* 7 April 1905; *s* of late Richard Ellis Potter, Ridgewood, Almondsbury, Glos and Harriott Isabel Potter (*née* Kingscote, of Kingscote, Glos); *m* 1950, Hilda, *d* of late W. A. Butterfield, OBE; one *d*. *Educ:* Charterhouse; New Coll., Oxford (BA). Entered Indian CS, 1928; posted to Burma; in charge of Pegu earthquake relief, 1930–31; District Comr, 1934; Controller of Finance ('reserved' subjects), 1937; Financial Adviser, Army in Burma, 1942 (despatches); Finance Secretary, Government of Burma (in Simla), 1942–43; Financial Adviser (Brigadier), 11th Army Group, 1943, and Allied Land Forces, South-East Asia, 1943–44; Chief Financial Officer (Brig.), Military Administration of Burma, 1944–47; HM Treasury Representative in India, Pakistan and Burma, 1947–50; Asst Secretary, HM Treasury, 1950–56; Counsellor, UK Delegation to NATO, Paris, 1956–65. *Address:* Lower House Barns, Bepton, Midhurst, W Sussex GU29 0JB.

POTTER, Dr David Edwin; Founder, and Chairman, since 1980, Psion plc; *b* 4 July 1943; *s* of Paul James Potter and Mary Agnes (*née* Snape); *m* 1969, Elaine Goldberg; three *s*. *Educ:* Trinity Coll., Cambridge (Exhibnr; MA); Imperial Coll., London (PhD 1970). Lectr, Blackett Lab., Imperial Coll., London, 1970–80. Commonwealth Schol., 1966–69; Asst Prof., UCLA, 1974. Director: Charterhouse Venture Fund Management Ltd, 1985–94; Press Assoc. Ltd, 1994– (Vice-Chm., 1995–); London First Centre, 1994–. Mem., London Regl Council, CBI, 1993–. Mountbatten Medal for Outstanding Services to Electronics Industry, Nat. Electronics Council, 1994. *Publications:* Computational Physics, 1972; contribs to various physics jls. *Recreations:* tennis, flute-playing, reading, gardening.

POTTER, David Roger William; Group Chief Executive, Guinness Mahon Holdings, since 1990; Chairman and Chief Executive, Guinness Mahon & Co. Ltd, Merchant Bankers, since 1990; *b* 27 July 1944; *s* of William Edward Potter and Joan Louise (*née* Frost); *m* 1966, Joanna Trollope, *qv* (marr. diss. 1983); two *d*; *m* 1991, Teresa Jill Benson; one *d*. *Educ:* Bryanston Sch.; University Coll., Oxford (MA). Nat. Discount Co., 1965–69; Managing Director: Credit Suisse First Boston and Credit Suisse White Weld, 1969–81; Samuel Montagu & Co. Ltd, 1981–89; Midland Montagu Corporate Banking, 1986–89; Director: Thomas Cook, 1989–91; Tyndal plc, 1989–91. Governor: Bryanston Sch., 1982–; UMDS Guy's and St Thomas' Hosps, 1988– (Chm., Finance Cttee). Trustee: ORBIS, 1991–; Youth for Britain, 1994–. FInstD. *Recreations:* shooting, gardening, golf. *Address:* (office) 32 St Mary at Hill, EC3P 3AJ. *T:* 0171–772 7401. *Clubs:* United Oxford & Cambridge University, City; Vincent's (Oxford).

POTTER, Donald Charles, QC 1972; *b* 24 May 1922; *s* of late Charles Potter, Shortlands, Kent. *Educ:* St Dunstan's Coll.; London Sch. of Economics. RAC (Westminster Dragoons), 1942–46 (Lieut); served England, NW Europe (D-day), Germany; mentioned in despatches; Croix de Guerre (France). LLB London 1947; called to Bar, Middle Temple, 1948; Bencher, Lincoln's Inn, 1979. Asst Lectr in Law, LSE, 1947–49; practised at Bar, 1950–95. Chm., Revenue Bar Assoc., 1978–88. Special Comr of Income Tax (part-time), 1986–95; Chm. (part-time), VAT Tribunal, 1986–95. *Publications:* (with H. H. Monroe) Tax Planning with Precedents, 1954; (with K. J. Prosser) Tax Appeals, 1991. *Recreations:* music, theatre, reading. *Address:* 27 Old Buildings, Lincoln's Inn, WC2A 3UJ; Compass Cottage, East Portlemouth, Devon TQ8 8PE. *Club:* Garrick.

POTTER, Ernest Frank; Director, Finance, Cable & Wireless plc, 1979–87 (Director of Finance and Corporate Planning, 1977–79); *b* 29 April 1923; *s* of Frank William and Edith Mary Potter; *m* 1st, 1945, Madge (*née* Arrowsmith) (*d* 1990); one *s*; 2nd, 1992, Barbara (*née* Brewis-Levie). *Educ:* Dr Challoner's Grammar Sch., Amersham. FCMA, FCIS, MIMC. Commissioned Pilot and Navigator, RAF, 1941–49. Chief Accountant, Bulmer & Lumb Ltd, 1950–58; Director, Management Consulting, Coopers & Lybrand, 1959–71; British Steel Corporation, Cammell Laird Shipbuilders Ltd, 1972–77; Director (non-executive): Cable & Wireless (West Indies) Ltd, 1977–87; Bahrain Telecommunications Corp., 1982–89; Cable & Wireless North America Inc, 1980–87; Cable & Wireless Hongkong Ltd, 1982–87; Cable & Wireless (Leasing) Ltd, 1982–87; Bahrain Telecommunications Corp., 1982–89; Cable & Wireless Marine Ltd, 1984–87; Mercury Communications Ltd, 1985–87; Cable & Wireless (Bermuda) Ltd, 1986–87; General Hybrid Ltd, 1987–91; Cable Corp. Ltd, 1988–; Windsor Cable Ltd, 1988–; Telephone Corp. Ltd, 1988–92; Micrelec Gp, 1989–92; Chairman: Clebern Internat. Ltd, 1988–89; Holmes Protection Inc., 1990–91; Themes Internat., 1991–92. Mem., Accounting Standards Cttee, 1985–90. *Recreations:* golf, sailing. *Address:* Long Meadow, Gorse Hill Road, Virginia Water, Surrey GU25 4AS. *T:* Wentworth (01344) 842178. *Clubs:* Royal Air Force; Foxhills (Surrey); St Mawes Sailing.

POTTER, Francis Malcolm; His Honour Judge Malcolm Potter; a Circuit Judge, since 1978; *b* 28 July 1932; *s* of Francis Martin Potter and Zilpah Jane Potter; *m* 1970, Bertha Villamil; one *s* one *d*. *Educ:* Rugby Sch.; Jesus Coll., Oxford. Called to Bar, Lincoln's Inn, 1956. A Recorder of the Crown Court, 1974–78. *Recreation:* painting. *Address:* The Priory Courts, 33 Bull Street, Birmingham B4 6DS. *Club:* Army and Navy.

POTTER, Jeremy; *see* Potter, R. J.

POTTER, Jeremy Patrick L.; *see* Lee-Potter.

POTTER, Maj.-Gen. Sir John, KBE 1968 (CBE 1963; OBE 1951); CB 1966; Chairman, Traffic Commissioners and Licensing Authority, Western Traffic Area, 1973–83; *b* 18 April 1913; *s* of late Major Benjamin Henry Potter, OBE, MC; *m* 1st, 1943, Vivienne Madge (*d* 1973), *d* of late Captain Henry D'Arcy Medlicott Cooke; one *s* one *d*; 2nd, 1974, Mrs D. Ella Purkis; one step *s* one step *d*. Served War of 1939–45. Major-General, 1962; Colonel Comdt: RAOC, 1965–69; RCT, 1968–73. Director of Supplies and Transport, 1963–65; Transport Officer in Chief (Army), 1965–66; Dir of Movements (Army), MoD, 1966–68; retired. *Address:* Orchard Cottage, The Orchard, Freshford, Bath, Avon BA3 6EW.

POTTER, John Herbert, MBE 1974; HM Diplomatic Service, retired; *b* 11 Jan. 1928; *s* of Herbert George and Winifred Eva Potter; *m* 1953, Winifred Susan Florence Hall; one *d*. *Educ:* elementary education at various state schools. Electrical Engineering jobs, 1942–45; served HM Forces, 1945–48; GPO, 1948–53; Foreign Office, 1953–55; Commercial Attaché, Bangkok, 1955–57; FO, 1957–60; Istanbul, 1960; Ankara, 1960–64; Second Secretary, Information, 1962; Second Sec., Information, Addis Ababa, 1964; Vice-Consul, Information, Johannesburg, 1964–66; DSAO, later FCO, 1966–70; First Sec. (Administration): Brussels, 1970–74; Warsaw, 1974–76; FCO (Inspectorate), 1976–80; Counsellor (Admin.) and Consul-Gen., Moscow, 1980–81; Counsellor (Administration),

Bonn, 1981–82. *Recreations:* reading, languages, walking, gardening. *Address:* 6 Salvington Crescent, Bexhill-on-Sea, E Sussex TN39 3NP.

POTTER, John McEwen, DM, FRCS; Emeritus Fellow and Dean of Degrees, Wadham College, Oxford; Director of Postgraduate Medical Education and Training, University of Oxford, 1972–87; *b* 28 Feb. 1920; *er s* of Alistair Richardson Potter and Mairi Chalmers Potter (*née* Dick); *m* 1943, Kathleen Gerrard; three *s*. *Educ:* Clifton Coll.; Emmanuel Coll., Cambridge; St Bartholomew's Hosp. BA, MB, BChir Cantab, 1943; MA 1945; FRCS 1951; MA, BM, BCh Oxon, 1963, DM 1964. Active service (Captain, RAMC), Europe, India and Burma, 1944–47. Lectr in Physiol. and Jun. Chief Asst, Surg. Professorial Unit, St Bart's Hosp., 1948–51; Graduate Asst to Nuffield Prof. of Surgery, Oxford, 1951–56; E. G. Fearnsides Scholar, Cambridge, 1954–56; Hunterian Prof., 1955; Cons. Neurosurgeon: Manchester Royal Infirmary, 1956–61; Radcliffe Infirm., Oxford, 1961–72; Hon. Cons. Neurosurgeon, Oxford RHA and Oxfordshire HA, 1972–87. Vis. Prof., UCLA, 1967; University of Oxford: Clin. Lectr in Neurosurgery, 1962–68; Univ. Lectr, 1968–87; Mem., Gen. Bd of Faculties, 1975–83; Hebdomadal Council, 1983–89; Fellow: Linacre Coll., 1967–69; Wadham Coll., 1969–87 (Professorial Fellow, 1974–87; Sub-Warden, 1978–81). Governor, United Oxford Hosps, 1973. Cairns Lectr, Adelaide, 1974. Examr for Final BM, BCh Oxon; Ext. Examr, Med. Sciences Tripos Pt II, Cambridge Univ. FRSM (Pres., Sect. of Neurol., 1975–76); Member: GMC, 1973–89 (Chm., Registration Cttee, 1979–89); Oxfordshire HA, 1982–89; Medical Appeal Tribunal, 1987–92; Soc. of British Neurol Surgeons (formerly Hon. Sec. and Archivist); Vice-Pres., 4th Internat. Congress of Neurol Surgery. Corres. Member: Amer. Assoc. of Neurol Surgeons; Deutsche Gesellschaft für Neurochirurgie; Sociedad Luso-Espanhola de Neurocirurgia; Hon. Mem., Egyptian Soc. of Neurol Surgeons. *Publications:* The Practical Management of Head Injuries, 1961, 4th edn 1984; contrib. to books and jls on subjects relating mostly to neurology and med. educn. *Recreation:* fishing. *Address:* 47 Park Town, Oxford OX2 6SL. *T:* Oxford (01865) 57875; Myredykes, Newcastleton, Roxburghshire TD9 0SR.

See also R. J. Potter.

POTTER, Malcolm; *see* Potter, F. M.

POTTER, Hon. Sir Mark Howard, Kt 1988; **Hon. Mr Justice Potter;** a Judge of the High Court of Justice, Queen's Bench Division (Commercial Court), since 1988; *b* 27 Aug. 1937; *s* of Prof. Harold Potter, LLD, PhD, and Beatrice Spencer Potter (*née* Crowder); *m* 1962, Undine Amanda Fay, *d* of Major James Miller, 5/6th Rajputana Rifles, and Bunty Miller, painter; two *s*. *Educ:* Perse Sch., Cambridge; Gonville and Caius Coll., Cambridge (Schol.; BA (Law Tripos) 1960, MA 1963). National Service, 15 Med. Regt RA, 1955–57 (commnd 1956); 289 Lt Parachute Regt RHA(TA), 1958–64. Asst Supervisor, Legal Studies, Girton, Gonville and Caius, Queens' and Sidney Sussex Colls, 1961–68; called to Bar, Gray's Inn, 1961, Bencher, 1987; in practice, 1962–88; QC 1980; a Recorder, 1986–88; a Presiding Judge, Northern Circuit, 1991–94; Judge i/c of Commercial Court, 1994–95. Member: Supreme Ct Rule Cttee, 1980–84; Lord Chancellor's Civil Justice Review Cttee, 1985–88; Chm., Bar Public Affairs Cttee, 1987; Vice-Chm., Council of Legal Educn, 1989–91. *Recreations:* family and sporting. *Address:* Royal Courts of Justice, Strand, WC2A 2LL. *Club:* Garrick.

POTTER, Rev. Philip Alford; General Secretary, World Council of Churches, 1972–84; *b* 19 Aug. 1921; *s* of Clement Potter and Violet Peters, Roseau, Dominica, Windward Is, WI; *m* 1st, 1956, Ethel Olive Doreen Cousins (*d* 1980), Jamaica, WI; 2nd, 1984, Rev. Barbel von Wartenberg, FRG. *Educ:* Dominica Grammar Sch.; United Theological Coll., Jamaica; London Univ. BD, MTh. Methodist Minister. Overseas Sec., British SCM, 1948–50; Superintendent, Cap Haitien Circuit, Methodist Church, Haiti, 1950–54; Sec., later Dir, Youth Dept, WCC, 1954–60; Sec. for WI and W Africa, Methodist Missionary Society, London, 1961–66; Dir, Commn on World Mission and Evangelism, and Associate Gen. Sec., WCC, 1967–72. Chaplain, Univ. of WI and Lectr, United Theol Coll. of WI, 1985–90. Mem., then Chm., Youth Dept Cttee, WCC, 1948–54; Chm., World Student Christian Fedn, 1960–68. Editor: Internat. Review of Mission, 1967–72; Ecumenical Rev., 1972–84. Hon. Doctor of Theology: Hamburg Univ., Germany, 1971; Geneva, 1976; Theol Inst. of Rumanian Orthodox Church, 1977; Humboldt Univ., Berlin, 1982; Uppsala, 1984; Hon. LLD W Indies, 1974; Hon. DD Birmingham, 1985. Niwano Peace Prize, Japan, 1986. *Publications:* (with Prof. Hendrik Berkhof) Key Words of the Gospel, 1964; The Love of Power or the Power of Love, 1974; Life in all its Fullness, 1981; chapter in Explosives Lateinamerika (ed by T. Tschuy), 1969; essays in various symposia; contrib. various jls, incl. Ecumenical Rev., Internat. Rev. of Mission, Student World. *Recreations:* swimming, hiking, music, geology. *Address:* Kauffmannstrasse 40, 70195 Stuttgart, Germany.

POTTER, Raymond, CB 1990; Deputy Secretary, 1986–93 (Courts and Legal Services, 1986–91), Head of the Court Service and Deputy Clerk of the Crown in Chancery, 1989–93, Lord Chancellor's Department; *b* 26 March 1933; *s* of William Thomas Potter and Elsie May Potter; *m* 1959, Jennifer Mary Quicke; one *s*. *Educ:* Henry Thornton Grammar School. Called to the Bar, Inner Temple, 1971, Bencher, 1989. Central Office, Royal Courts of Justice, 1950; Western Circuit, 1963; Chief Clerk, Bristol Crown Court, 1972; Dep. Circuit Administrator, Western Circuit, 1976; Circuit Administrator, Northern Circuit, 1982–86. Pres., S Western Rent Assessment Panel, 1995. *Recreation:* painting. *Address:* 8 Robinson Way, Backwell, Bristol BS19 3BP. *Club:* Athenæum.

POTTER, (Ronald) Jeremy; Director, Constable & Co. (Publishers), since 1980; *b* 25 April 1922; *s* of Alistair Richardson Potter and Mairi Chalmers (*née* Dick); *m* 1950, Margaret, *d* of Bernard Newman; one *s* one *d*. *Educ:* Clifton Coll.; Queen's Coll., Oxford (Neale Exhibnr, MA). Served War, Intell. Officer, Indian Army. Manager, subseq. Man. Dir, Dep. Chm., New Statesman, 1951–69; Man. Dir, Independent Television Publications Ltd, 1970–79; Chm., Independent Television Books Ltd, 1971–79; Chm., Hutchinson Ltd, 1982–84 (Dir, 1978–84; Dep. Chm., 1980–82); Director: Page and Moy (Holdings) plc, 1979–88; LWT (Holdings) plc, 1979–92. Pres., Periodical Publishers Assoc., 1978–79; Appeals Chm., Newsvendors' Benevolent Instn, 1979; Chairman: Twickenham Arts Council, 1967–68; Richard III Soc., 1971–89; Oxford Playhouse Trust, 1990–92. FRSA. Captain, Hampstead Hockey Club, 1954–57; World Amateur over 60s Champion, Real tennis, 1986–88. *Publications:* Good King Richard?, 1983; Pretenders, 1986; Independent Television in Britain, Vol. 3: Politics and Control 1968–80, 1989, Vol. 4: Companies and Programmes 1968–80, 1990; Tennis and Oxford, 1994; *novels:* Hazard Chase, 1964; Death in Office, 1965; Foul Play, 1967; The Dance of Death, 1968; A Trail of Blood, 1970; Going West, 1972; Disgrace and Favour, 1975; Death in the Forest, 1977; The Primrose Hill Murder, 1992; The Mystery of the Campden Wonder, 1995. *Recreations:* reading, writing, Real tennis. *Address:* The Old Pottery, Larkins Lane, Headington, Oxford OX3 9DW. *Clubs:* Garrick, MCC, Puritans Hockey.

See also J. McE. Potter.

POTTER, Ronald Stanley James; Director of Social Services, Surrey County Council, 1970–81; *b* 29 April 1921; *e s* of late Stanley Potter and Gertrude Mary Keable, Chelmsford; *m* 1954, Ann (Louisa Eleanor) Burnett; one *s* one *d*. *Educ:* King Edward VI Grammar Sch., Chelmsford. MISW. Territorial Army, 1939, War Service, 1939–47; commnd RA, 1942; Captain 1946. Area Welfare Officer, Essex CC, 1953–61; Dep. Co. Welfare Officer, Lindsey CC, 1962; County Welfare Officer: Lindsey CC, 1962–64; Herts CC, 1964–70. Dir, Watford Sheltered Workshop Ltd, 1964–70; Mem. Cttee of Enquiry into Voluntary Workers in Social Services, 1966–69; Dir, Industrial Advisers to Blind Ltd, 1969–74; Vice Pres., SE Regional Assoc. for Deaf, 1984–88 (Vice-Chm., 1968–76; Chm., 1976–84); Member: Council of Management, RNID, 1968–71, 1976–84; Nat. Jt Council for Workshops for the Blind, 1970–81; Adv. Council, Nat. Corp. for Care of Old People, 1974–77; Local Authorities Adv. Cttee on Conditions of Service of Blind Workers, 1974–81; Exec. Council, RNIB, 1975–81; Nat. Adv. Council on Employment of Disabled People, 1978–81; Dir, Remploy Ltd, 1974–86. *Recreations:* walking, swimming, caravanning, bowls. *Address:* Ridge Cottage, 16 Howard Ridge, Burpham Lane, Guildford, Surrey GU4 7LY. *T:* Guildford (01483) 504272.

POTTER, Maj.-Gen. Sir Wilfrid John; *see* Potter, Maj.-Gen. Sir John.

POTTERTON, Homan, FSA; art historian and writer; Editor, Irish Arts Review, since 1993; Director, National Gallery of Ireland, 1980–88; *b* 9 May 1946; sixth *s* of late Thomas Edward Potterton and Eileen Potterton (*née* Tong). *Educ:* Kilkenny Coll.; Trinity Coll., Dublin (BA 1968, MA 1973); Edinburgh Univ. (Dip. Hist. Art 1971). FSA 1981. Cataloguer, National Gall. of Ireland, 1971–73; Asst Keeper, National Gall., London, 1974–80. Mem. Bd, GPA Dublin Internat. Piano Competition, 1987–92. HRHA 1982. *Publications:* Irish Church Monuments 1570–1880, 1975; A Guide to the National Gallery, 1976, rev. edn 1980 (German, French, Italian and Japanese edns 1977); The National Gallery, London, 1977; Reynolds and Gainsborough: themes and painters in the National Gallery, 1976; Pageant and Panorama: the elegant world of Canaletto, 1978; (jtly) Irish Art and Architecture, 1978; Venetian Seventeenth Century Painting (National Gallery Exhibn Catalogue), 1979; introd. to National Gallery of Ireland Illustrated Summary Catalogue of Paintings, 1981; (jtly) National Gallery of Ireland, 50 Pictures, 1981; Dutch 17th and 18th Century Paintings in the National Gallery of Ireland: a complete catalogue, 1986; contrib. Burlington Mag., Apollo, Connoisseur, FT and Country Life. *Recreations:* America, Italy. *Address:* 119 West 71st Street, New York, NY 10023, USA. *T:* (212) 7210510; 3 Westmoreland Terrace, SW1V 4AG. *T:* 0171–834 8279. *Club:* St Stephen's Green (Dublin).

POTTINGER, (William) George; *b* 11 June 1916; *e s* of late Rev. William Pottinger, MA, Orkney, and Janet Woodcock; *m* 1946, Margaret Rutherfurd Clark McGregor; one *s*. *Educ:* George Watson's; High School of Glasgow; Edinburgh Univ.; Heidelberg; Queens' Coll., Cambridge (Major Scholar). Entered Scottish Home Dept, as Assistant Principal, 1939. Served War of 1939–45, RFA; France, N Africa, Italy (despatches), Lieut-Col RA. Principal, 1945; Private Secretary to successive Secretaries of State for Scotland, 1950–52; Asst Secretary, Scottish Home Dept, 1952; Secretary, Royal Commn on Scottish Affairs, 1952–54; Under-Secretary: Scottish Home Dept, 1959–62; Scottish Home and Health Dept, 1962–63; Scottish Development Dept, 1963–64; Scottish Office, 1964–68; Dept of Agriculture and Fisheries for Scotland, 1968–71; Secretary, Dept of Agriculture and Fisheries for Scotland, 1971. *Publications:* The Winning Counter, 1971; Muirfield and the Honourable Company, 1972; St Moritz: an Alpine caprice, 1972; The Court of the Medici, 1977; The Secretaries of State for Scotland 1926–76, 1979; Whisky Sour, 1979; The Afghan Connection, 1983; Mayo, Disraeli's Viceroy, 1990; (with Sir Patrick Macrory) The Ten Rupee Jezail, 1993; Heirs of the Enlightenment, 1993; The Real Admirable Crichton, 1995; papers and reviews. *Recreations:* real tennis, golf, fishing. *Address:* West Lodge, Balsham, Cambridge CB1 6EP. *T:* Cambridge (01223) 892958. *Club:* Savile.

POTTS, Archibold; Director, Bewick Press, since 1989; *b* 27 Jan. 1932; *s* of late Ernest W. Potts and Ellen Potts; *m* 1957, Marguerite Elsie (*née* Elliott) (*d* 1983); one *s* one *d*. *Educ:* Monkwearmouth Central Sch., Sunderland; Ruskin and Oriel Colls, Oxford (Dip. Econ. and Pol. Sci., 1958; BA PPE 2nd cl. hons, 1960); ext. postgrad. student, London Univ. (Postgrad. CertEd 1964) and Durham Univ. (MEd 1969). Nat. Service, RAF, 1950–53. Railway Clerk, 1947–50 and 1953–56. Lecturer: N Oxfordshire Tech. Coll., 1961; York Tech. Coll., 1962–65; Rutherford Coll. of Technology and Newcastle upon Tyne Polytechnic, 1965–80; Head of Sch. of Business Admin, 1980–87, Associate Dean, Faculty of Business and Professional Studies, 1988, Newcastle upon Tyne Polytechnic. Moderator, local history courses, Tyneside Open Coll. Fedn, 1992–. Tyne and Wear County Council: Councillor, 1979–86; Vice-Chm., Planning Cttee, 1981–86; Vice-Chm., Council, 1983–84; Chm., Council, 1984–85. Contested (Lab) Westmorland, 1979. Chm., NE Labour History Soc., 1990–; Mem., Exec. Cttee, Soc. for Study of Labour History, 1987–. *Publications:* Stand True, 1976; Bibliography of Northern Labour History, 1982–; (ed) Shipbuilders and Engineers, 1987; Jack Casey, the Sunderland Assassin, 1991; The Wearside Champions, 1993; contribs to Dictionary of Labour Biography, vol. 2 1974, vol. 4 1977, vol. 5 1979, vol. 9 1993; articles on economics and history. *Recreations:* local history, watching old films. *Address:* 47 Graham Park Road, Gosforth, Newcastle upon Tyne NE3 4BJ. *T:* 0191–284 5132. *Club:* Victory Service.

POTTS, Hon. Sir (Francis) Humphrey, Kt 1986; **Hon. Mr Justice Potts;** a Judge of the High Court of Justice, Queen's Bench Division, since 1986; *b* 18 Aug. 1931; *er s* of late Francis William Potts and Elizabeth Hannah (*née* Humphrey), Penshaw, Co. Durham; *m* 1971, Philippa Margaret Campbell, *d* of the late J. C. H. Le B. Croke and Mrs J. F. G. Downes; two *s* and two step *s*. *Educ:* Royal Grammar Sch., Newcastle upon Tyne; St Catherine's Society, Oxford. BCL 1954, MA 1957. Barrister-at-Law, Lincoln's Inn, 1955 (Tancred Student, 1953; Cholmeley Scholar, 1954), Bencher, 1979; North Eastern Circuit, 1955; practised in Newcastle upon Tyne, 1955–71; QC 1971; a Recorder, 1972–86; admitted to Hong Kong Bar, 1984; Presiding Judge, NE Circuit, 1988–91. Member: Mental Health Review Tribunal, 1984–86; Criminal Injuries Compensation Bd, 1985–86; Parole Bd, 1992– (Vice-Chm., 1995–). *Address:* Royal Courts of Justice, Strand, WC2A 2LL.

POTTS, Paul John; Editor, PA News, since 1995; *b* 21 Jan. 1950; *s* of late Michael Henry Potts and of Sylvia Brenda Potts; *m* 1st, 1976, Gabrielle Jane Fagan (marr. diss.); one *s* two *d*; 2nd, 1994, Judith Anne Fielding. *Educ:* Worksop Coll. Gen. Reporter, Sheffield Star, 1968–74; Lobby Corresp., Yorkshire Post, 1974–78; General Reporter: Daily Telegraph, 1978–81; Mail on Sunday, 1981–82; Political Ed., News of the World, 1982–86; Political Ed., then Asst Ed., later Dep. Ed., Daily Express, 1986–95. *Recreations:* all sports, walking. *Address:* PA News Ltd, PA NewsCentre, 292 Vauxhall Bridge Road, SW1V 1AE. *T:* 0171–963 7000.

POTTS, Peter; JP; General Secretary, General Federation of Trade Unions, 1977–94; *b* 29 June 1935; *s* of late John Peter Potts and of Margaret (*née* Combs); *m* 1st, 1956, Mary Longden (*d* 1972); two *s* one *d*; 2nd, 1974, Angela Elouise van Lieshout (*née* Liddelow); one step *s* one step *d*. *Educ:* Chorlton High Sch., Manchester; Ruskin Coll., Oxford; Oxford Univ. (Dip. in Econs and Pol. Science). Served RAF, 1953–55. USDAW, 1951–65; Res. Officer, Union of Tailors and Garment Workers, 1965–74; National Officer, Clerical and Supervisory Staffs, 1974–77. Member: Clothing EDC, 1970–77 (Trade Union Advisor, 1966–70); Jt Textile Cttee, NEDO, 1970–77; Trade Union Unit

Trust Investors Cttee, 1977–94 (Chm., 1984–94); Trade Union Res. Unit, 1975– (Chm., 1984–); Trade Union Internat. Res. and Educn Gp, 1979– (Chm., 1994–); Press Council, 1987–90; Governing Council, Ruskin Coll., 1977– (Mem. Exec. Cttee, 1977–; Vice-Chm., 1984–). JP N Beds, 1983. *Recreations:* do-it-yourself hobbies, art, listening to jazz. *Address:* 3 Tadmere, Two Mile Ash, Milton Keynes, Bucks MK8 8DG.

POTTS, Robin, QC 1982; barrister; *b* 2 July 1944; *s* of William and Elaine Potts; *m*; one *s*; *m* Helen Elizabeth Sharp; two *s* one *d*. *Educ:* Wolstanton Grammar Sch.; Magdalen Coll., Oxford (BA, BCL). Called to the Bar, Gray's Inn, 1968, Bencher, 1993. *Publication:* (contrib.) Gore-Browne on Companies, 43rd edn. *Address:* The Grange, Church Lane, Pinner, Mddx HA5 3AB. *T:* 0181–866 9013.

POULTER, Brian Henry; Secretary, Northern Ireland Audit Office, since 1989; *b* 1 Sept. 1941; *s* of William Henry Poulter, PhC, MPS, and Marjorie Elizabeth Everett McBride; *m* 1968, Margaret Ann Dodds; one *s* twin *d*. *Educ:* Regent House Grammar Sch., Newtownards. Qual. as certified accountant, 1966. Hill, Vellacott and Bailey, Chartered Accountants, 1959–62; entered NICS, 1962; Min. of Health and Local Govt, 1962–65; Min. of Health and Social Services, 1965–71; Deputy Principal: Local Enterprise Develt Unit, 1971–74; Dept of Commerce, 1974–75; Chief Auditor 1975–81, Dep. Dir 1981–82, Dir 1982–87, Exchequer and Audit Dept; Dir, NI Audit Office, 1987–88. *Recreations:* reading, walking, cricket. *Address:* Northern Ireland Audit Office, 106 University Street, Belfast BT7 1EU. *T:* Belfast (01232) 251129.

POULTER, Jane Anne Marie; *see* Bonvin, J. A. M.

POULTON, Richard Christopher, MA; Head Master, Christ's Hospital, Horsham, 1987–July 1996; *b* 21 June 1938; *e s* of Rev. Christopher Poulton and Aileen (*née* Sparrow); *m* 1965, Zara, *o d* of Prof. P. and Mrs J. Crossley-Holland; two *s* one *d*. *Educ:* King's Coll., Taunton; Wesleyan Univ., Middletown, Conn, USA; Pembroke Coll., Cambridge (BA 1961, CertEd 1962, MA 1965). Asst Master: Bedford Sch., 1962–63; Beckenham and Penge Grammar Sch., 1963–66; Bryanston School: Asst Master, 1966–80; Head of History Dept, 1971–76; Housemaster, 1972–80; Headmaster, Wycliffe Coll., 1980–86. Gov., Oxford and Cambridge Examinations Bd, 1987–90. JP S Glos, 1985–86. Freeman, City of London, 1987; Yeoman, 1990, Liveryman, 1993, Co. of Ironmongers. FRSA 1994. *Publications:* Victoria, Queen of a Changing Land, 1975; Kings and Commoners, 1977; A History of the Modern World, 1980. *Recreations:* writing, hill walking, choral music. *Address:* (until July 1996) The Head Master's House, Christ's Hospital, Horsham, W Sussex RH13 7LS. *T:* Horsham (01403) 252547.

POULTON, William Dacres Campbell; His Honour Judge Poulton; a Circuit Judge, since 1994; *b* 15 Dec. 1937; *o s* of late Arthur Stanley Poulton and Winifred Evelyn Poulton (*née* Montgomery Campbell); *m* 1970, Carolyn Frances Macken; two *s* one *d*. *Educ:* Dover Coll.; New Coll., Oxford (BA 1961; MA 1964). Called to the Bar, Middle Temple, 1965; Recorder 1992–94. *Publications:* contribs to Law Quarterly Review and Halsbury's Laws of England (Landlord and Tenant). *Recreations:* ski-ing, gardening, walking.

POUNCEY, Denys Duncan Rivers, MA, MusB Cantab; FRCO; Organist and Master of the Choristers, Wells Cathedral, 1936–70; Conductor of Wells Cathedral Oratorio Chorus and Orchestra, 1946–66; Hon. Diocesan Choirmaster, Bath and Wells Choral Association, 1946–70; *b* 23 Dec. 1906; *s* of late Rev. George Ernest Pouncey and late Madeline Mary Roberts; *m* 1937, Evelyn Cottier. *Educ:* Marlborough College; Queens' College, Cambridge. Asst to Dr Cyril Rootham, Organist and Choirmaster of St John's Coll., Cambridge, 1928–34; Organist and Choirmaster, St Matthew's, Northampton, 1934–36; Founder Conductor of Northampton Bach Choir. *Address:* Waverley Hotel, 10 Tregonwell Road, Minehead, Somerset TA24 5DJ. *T:* Minehead (01643) 704764.

POUND, Sir John David, 5th Bt *cr* 1905; *b* 1 Nov. 1946; *s* of Sir Derek Allen Pound, 4th Bt; *S* father, 1980; *m* 1st, 1968 (marr. diss.); one *s*; 2nd, 1978, Penelope Ann, *er d* of Grahame Arthur Rayden, Bramhall, Cheshire; two *s*. Liveryman, Leathersellers' Co. *Heir:* *s* Robert John Pound, *b* 12 Feb. 1973.

POUND, Rev. Canon Keith Salisbury; Chaplain to HM Prison, Grendon and Spring Hill, since 1993; a Chaplain to the Queen since 1988; *b* 3 April 1933; *s* of Percy Salisbury Pound and Annie Florence Pound. *Educ:* Roan School, Blackheath; St Catharine's Coll., Cambridge (BA 1954, MA 1958); Cuddesdon Coll., Oxford. Curate, St Peter, St Helier, Dio. Southwark, 1957–61; Training Officer, Hollowford Training and Conference Centre, Sheffield, 1961–64, Warden 1964–67; Rector of Holy Trinity, Southwark, with St Matthew, Newington, 1968–78; RD, Southwark and Newington, 1973–78; Rector of Thamesmead, 1978–86; Sub-Dean of Woolwich, 1984–86; Dean of Greenwich, 1985–86; Chaplain-Gen. and Archdeacon to Prison Service, 1986–93. Hon. Canon of Southwark Cathedral, 1985–. *Publication:* Creeds and Controversies, 1976. *Recreations:* theatre, music, books, crosswords. *Address:* HM Prison, Grendon and Spring Hill, Grendon Underwood, Aylesbury, Bucks HP18 0TD. *T:* Aylesbury (01296) 770494. *Club:* Civil Service.

POUNDS, Maj.-Gen. Edgar George Derek, CB 1975; retired; *b* 13 Oct. 1922; *s* of Edgar Henry Pounds, MBE, MSM, and Caroline Beatrice Pounds; *m* 1944, Barbara Winifred May Evans; one *s* one *d*. *Educ:* Reading Sch. War of 1939–45: enlisted, RM, 1940 (King's Badge, trng); HMS Kent, 1941–42 (Atlantic); commissioned as Reg. Off., Sept. 1942 (sword for dist., trng); HMS Berwick, 1943–44 (Atlantic and Russia). Co. Comdr, RM, 1945–51: Far East, Palestine, Malta, UK (Sniping Wing), Korea (US Bronze Star, 1950); Captain 1952. Instr, RM Officers' Trng Wing, UK, 1952–54; Adjt, 45 Commando, RM, 1954–57, Malta, Cyprus (despatches), Suez; RAF Staff Coll., Bracknell, 1958; Staff Captain, Dept of CGRM, London, 1959–60; Major 1960; Amphibious Ops Officer, HMS Bulwark, 1961–62, Kuwait, Aden, E Africa, Borneo; Corps Drafting Off., UK, 1962–64; 40 Commando RM: 2nd in Comd, 1964–65, Borneo, and CO, 1966–67, Borneo and Far East; CO, 43 Commando, RM, 1967–68, UK based; GSO1 Dept CGRM, 1969–70; Col 1970; Naval Staff, MoD, 1970–72; Comdt Commando Trng Centre, RM, 1972–73; Actg Maj.-Gen. 1973; Maj.-Gen., RM, 1974; Commanding Commando Forces, RM, 1973–76, retired. Chief Exec., British Friesian Cattle Soc., 1976–87; Chm., RM Officers' Widows Pension Funds, 1987–92. Agricl Cons. (Europe), 1987. *Publications:* articles on strategy, amphibious warfare, and tactics in professional jls, on cattle breeding and dairying in farming jls, and on computing in computer jls. *Recreations:* target rifle shooting, gardening, computer usages, reading. *Clubs:* Army and Navy, Farmers'.

POUNDS, Prof. Kenneth Alwyne, CBE 1984; FRS 1981; Chief Executive, Particle Physics and Astronomy Research Council, since 1994; Professor of Space Physics, and Director, X-ray Astronomy Group, since 1973, and Head of Department of Physics and Astronomy, since 1986, University of Leicester (on leave of absence); *b* 17 Nov. 1934; *s* of Harry and Dorothy Pounds; *m* 1st, 1961, Margaret Mary (*née* Connell); two *s* one *d*; 2nd, 1982, Joan Mary (*née* Millit); one *s* one *d*. *Educ:* Salt Sch., Shipley, Yorkshire; University Coll. London (BSc, PhD; Fellow, 1993). Department of Physics, University of Leicester: Asst Lectr, 1960; Lecturer, 1961; Sen. Lectr, 1969. Member: SERC, 1980–84 (Chm., Astronomy, Space and Radio Bd); Management Bd, British Nat. Space Centre, 1986–88; Pres., RAS, 1990–92. DUniv York, 1984; Hon. DSc Loughborough, 1992. Gold Medal, RAS, 1989. *Publications:* many, in Monthly Notices, Nature, Astrophysical Jl, etc. *Recreations:* sport, music. *Address:* 12 Swale Close, Oadby, Leicester LE2 4GF. *T:* Leicester (0116) 271 9370.

POUNTAIN, Sir Eric (John), Kt 1985; DL; Chairman: Tarmac PLC, 1983–94 (Group Chief Executive, 1979–92); James Beattie PLC, since 1987 (Deputy Chairman, 1985–87; Director, since 1984); IMI PLC, since 1989 (Director, since 1988); *b* 5 Aug. 1933; *s* of Horace Pountain and Elsie Pountain; *m* 1960, Joan Patricia Sutton; one *s* one *d*. *Educ:* Queen Mary Grammar Sch., Walsall. CIMgt; FFB, FIHE, FCIB; FRSA. Joined F. Maitland Selwyn & Co., auctioneers and estate agents, 1956, joint principal, 1959; founded Midland & General Develts, 1964, acquired by John McLean & Sons Ltd, 1969; Chief Exec., John McLean & Sons, 1969, acquired by Tarmac PLC, 1974; Chief Exec., newly formed Tarmac Housing Div., until 1979. Director: Tarmac PLC, 1977–94; Midland Bank, 1986–92; United Newspapers, 1992–; Lloyds Chemists plc, 1993–; John Maunders Gp, 1994–. Member: Financial Develt Bd, NSPCC, 1985–; Adv. Council, Prince's Youth Business Trust, 1988–; President's Appeal Cttee, Age Concern, 1991–; Trustee, Lichfield Cathedral Trustees, 1995–. President: Haflinger Soc. of GB; Shropshire Enterprise Trust; Midlands Industrial Council, 1988–; Patron, Staffs Agricl Soc. DL Stafford, 1985. *Recreations:* golf, shooting, tennis. *Address:* Edial House, Edial, Lichfield WS7 0ZT; James Beattie PLC, 71/78 Victoria Street, Wolverhampton WV1 3PQ.

POUNTNEY, David Willoughby, CBE 1994; freelance director; *b* 10 Sept. 1947; *s* of Dorothy and Willoughby Pountney; *m* 1980, Jane Henderson; one *s* one *d*. *Educ:* St John's College Choir School, Cambridge; Radley College; St John's College, Cambridge (MA). Joined Scottish Opera, 1970; 1st major production Katya Kabanova (Janacek), Wexford Fest., 1972; Dir of Productions, Scottish Opera, 1976–80; individual guest productions for all British Opera companies, also USA (Metropolitan Opera début, world première of The Voyage by Philip Glass, 1992), Aust., Italy, Germany, The Netherlands; Dir of Prodns, ENO, 1982–93; productions for ENO include: Rusalka (Dvorak); Osud (Janacek); Dr Faust (Busoni); Lady Macbeth of Mtsensk (Shostakovich); Wozzeck (Berg); Pelléas and Mélisande (Debussy); Don Carlos (Verdi); Falstaff (Verdi); The Adventures of Mr Broucek (Janacek); Inquest of Love (Jonathan Harvey). Chevalier de l'Ordre des Arts et des Lettres (France), 1993. *Publications:* (with Mark Elder and Peter Jonas) Power House, 1992; numerous trans. of opera, esp. Czech and Russian repertoire. *Recreations:* croquet, food and wine. *Address:* 35 Brookfield, Highgate West Hill, N6 6AT. *T:* 0181–342 8900. *Club:* Garrick.

POUT, Harry Wilfrid, CB 1978; OBE 1959; CEng, FIEE; Marconi Underwater Systems Ltd, 1982–86, Defence Consultant, since 1986; *b* 11 April 1920; British; *m* 1949, Margaret Elizabeth (*née* Nelson); three *d*. *Educ:* East Ham Grammar Sch.; Imperial Coll., London. BSc (Eng); ACGI 1940. RN Scientific Service, 1940; Admty Signal Estab. (later Admty Signal and Radar Estab.), 1940–54; Dept of Operational Research, Admty, 1954–59; idc 1959; Head of Guided Weapon Projects, Admty, 1960–65; Asst Chief Scientific Adviser (Projects), MoD, 1965–69; Dir, Admiralty Surface Weapons Estabt, 1969–72; Dep. Controller, Guided Weapons, 1973, Guided Weapons and Electronics, 1973–75, Air Systems, 1975–79, Aircraft Weapons and Electronics, 1979–80, MoD. Defence consultant, 1980–82. FCGI 1972; FIMgt. *Publications:* (jtly) The New Scientists, 1971; (contrib.) Radar at Sea—the Royal Navy in World War 2, 1993; (contrib.) The Applications of Radar in the Royal Navy in World War 2, 1995; classified books; contribs to jls of IEE, RAeS, RUSI, Jl of Naval Sci., etc. *Recreations:* mountaineering, gardening and do-it-yourself activities, amateur geology. *Address:* Oakmead, Fox Corner, Worplesdon, near Guildford, Surrey GU3 3PP. *T:* Worplesdon (01483) 232223.

POVER, Alan John, CMG 1990; HM Diplomatic Service, retired; High Commissioner to the Republic of Gambia, 1990–93; *b* 16 Dec. 1933; *s* of John Pover and Anne (*née* Hession); *m* 1964, Doreen Elizabeth Dawson; one *s* two *d*. *Educ:* Salesian College, Thornleigh, Bolton. Served HM Forces, 1953–55; Min. of Pensions and Nat. Insce, 1955–61; Commonwealth Relations Office, 1961; Second Secretary: Lagos, 1962–66; Tel Aviv, 1966–69; Second, later First, Sec., Karachi/Islamabad, 1969–73; First Sec., FCO, 1973–76; Consul, Cape Town, 1976–80; Counsellor, Diplomatic Service Inspector, 1983–86; Counsellor and Consul-Gen., Washington, 1986–90. *Recreations:* cricket, golf, gardening. *Address:* 11 Farriers Lane, East Ilsley, Berks RG20 7JB. *Club:* Commonwealth Trust.

POVEY, Keith, QPM 1991; Chief Constable, Leicestershire, since 1993; *b* 30 April 1943; *s* of late Trevor Roberts Povey and Dorothy (*née* Parsonnage); *m* 1964, Carol Ann Harvey; two *d*. *Educ:* Abbeydale Grammar Sch., Sheffield; Sheffield Univ. (BA Law). Joined Sheffield City Police, 1962; Chief Superintendent, S Yorks, seconded as Staff Officer to Sir Lawrence Byford, HMCIC, 1984–86; Asst Chief Constable, Humberside, 1986–90; Dep. Chief Constable, Northants, 1990–93. Hon. Secretary: ACPO General Purposes Cttee, 1994–; ACPO Crime Prevention Sub-cttee, 1994–. Chm., British Police Flying Assoc., 1989–. *Recreations:* jogging, flying (private pilot's licence). *Address:* Leicestershire Constabulary, PO Box 999, Leicester LE99 1AZ. *T:* Leicester (0116) 253 0066.

POWDITCH, Alan (Cecil Robert), MC 1944; JP; District Administrator, NW District, Kensington and Chelsea and Westminster Area Health Authority, 1974–77, retired; *b* 14 April 1912; *s* of Cecil John and Annis Maudie Powditch; *m* 1942, Barbara Leggat (*d* 1992); one *s* one *d*. *Educ:* Mercers School. Entered Hospital Service, 1933; Accountant, St Mary's Hospital, W2, 1938. Served War of 1939–45, with 51st Royal Tank Regt, 1941–46. Dep. House Governor, St Mary's Hospital, 1947–50, Sec. to Bd of Governors, 1950–74. Mem. Nat. Staff Cttee (Min. of Health) 1964–72; Chm., Juvenile Panel, Gore Div., 1973–76. Mem. Council, Sue Ryder Foundn, 1977–85; Mem. Magistrates' Courts Cttee, 1979–81. JP Co. Middlesex 1965, supp. List 1982. *Recreations:* golf; interested in gardening when necessary. *Address:* 27 Gateway Close, Northwood, Mddx HA6 2RW.

POWELL; *see* Baden-Powell.

POWELL, Albert Edward, JP; General President of Society of Graphical and Allied Trades, 1973–82, of SOGAT '82 1982–83; *b* 20 May 1927; *s* of Albert and Mary Powell; *m* 1947, Margaret Neville; one *s* two *d*. *Educ:* Holy Family Elementary Sch., Morden. FIWSP. London Organiser, SOGAT, 1957, Organising Secretary, 1967. Has served on various Committees and Boards, including: past Chairman, Croydon College of Art, past Governor, London College of Printing. Chairman, Paper & Paper Products Industry Trng Bd, 1975– (Mem. Central Arbitration Cttee, 1976–); Member: TUC Printing Industries Cttee, 1971–; NEDO Printing Industries Sector Working Party, 1980–; Methods-Time Measurement Assoc., 1966–. Member: Industrial Tribunal, 1983–; Social Security Appeal Tribunal, 1984–; Parole Bd, 1986–. JP: Wimbledon, 1961–75; Southend-on-Sea, 1975–80; Bexley, 1980–. Queen's Silver Jubilee Medal, 1977. *Recreations:* gardening reading (science fiction), music. *Address:* 31 Red House Lane, Bexleyheath, Kent DA6 8JF. *T:* 0181–304 7480.

POWELL, Anthony Dymoke, CH 1988; CBE 1956; *b* 21 Dec. 1905; *o s* of late Lt-Col P. L. W. Powell, CBE, DSO; *m* 1934, Lady Violet Pakenham, 3rd *d* of 5th Earl of

Longford, KP; two *s. Educ:* Eton; Balliol College, Oxford, MA; Hon. Fellow, 1974. Served War of 1939–45, Welch Regt and Intelligence Corps, Major. A Trustee, National Portrait Gallery, 1962–76. Hon. Mem., Amer. Acad. of Arts and Letters, 1977; Hon. Fellow, Mod. Lang. Assoc. of Amer., 1981. Hon. DLitt: Sussex, 1971; Leicester, 1976; Kent, 1976; Oxon, 1980; Bristol, 1982; Wales, 1992. Hudson Review Bennett Prize, 1984; T. S. Eliot Prize for Creative Lit., Ingersoll Foundn, 1984. Orders of: the White Lion, (Czechoslovakia); the Oaken Crown and Croix de Guerre (Luxembourg); Leopold II (Belgium). *Publications:* Afternoon Men, 1931; Venusberg, 1932; From a View to a Death, 1933; Agents and Patients, 1936; What's become of Waring, 1939; John Aubrey and His Friends, 1948, rev. edn 1988; Selections from John Aubrey, 1949; A Dance to the Music of Time, 12 vol. sequence, 1951–75: A Question of Upbringing, 1951; A Buyer's Market, 1952; The Acceptance World, 1955; At Lady Molly's, 1957 (James Tait Black Memorial Prize); Casanova's Chinese Restaurant, 1960; The Kindly Ones, 1962; The Valley of Bones, 1964; The Soldier's Art, 1966; The Military Philosophers, 1968; Books do Furnish a Room, 1971; Temporary Kings, 1973 (W. H. Smith Prize, 1974); Hearing Secret Harmonies, 1975; O, How The Wheel Becomes It!, 1983; The Fisher King, 1986; The Album of Anthony Powell's Dance to the Music of Time (ed. V. Powell), 1987; Miscellaneous Verdicts (criticism), 1990; Under Review (criticism), 1992; *memoirs:* To Keep the Ball Rolling, 4 vols, 1976–82 (abridged one vol. edn 1983): Infants of the Spring, 1976; Messengers of Day, 1978; Faces In My Time, 1980; The Strangers All are Gone, 1982; Journals 1982–1986, 1995; *plays:* Afternoon Men (adapted by Riccardo Aragno), Arts Theatre Club, 1963; The Garden God, 1971; The Rest I'll Whistle, 1971. *Address:* The Chantry, near Frome, Somerset BA11 3LJ. *T:* Frome (01373) 836314. *Clubs:* Travellers', Pratt's.

POWELL, Sir Arnold Joseph Philip; *see* Powell, Sir Philip.

POWELL, Arthur Barrington, CMG 1967; *b* 24 April 1918; *er s* of late Thomas and Dorothy Powell, Maesteg, Glam; *m* 1945, Jane, *d* of late Gen. Sir George Weir, KCB, CMG, DSO; four *s* one *d. Educ:* Cowbridge; Jesus Coll. Oxford. Indian Civil Service, 1939–47; served in Province of Bihar. Asst Princ., Min. of Fuel and Power, 1947; Princ. Private Sec. to Minister, 1949–51; Asst Sec., 1955; Petroleum Div., 1957–68; Petroleum Attaché, HM Embassy, Washington, 1962–64; Gas Div., 1968–72; Reg. Finance Div., DoI, 1972–76; Exec. Dir, Welsh Develt Agency, 1976–83. *Address:* Mulberry House, Pwllmeyric, Chepstow, Gwent NP6 6LA. *Clubs:* United Oxford & Cambridge University; Royal Porthcawl Golf; St Pierre Golf & Country (Chepstow).

POWELL, Sir Charles (David), KCMG 1990; Director: Jardine Matheson Holdings and associated companies, since 1991; National Westminster Bank, since 1991 (Chairman, International Advisory Board); Trafalgar House, since 1993 (Deputy Chairman, since 1994); Arjo-Wiggins Appleton, since 1993; Christian Dior, since 1994; *b* 6 July 1941; *s* of Air Vice Marshal John Frederick Powell, *qv*; *m* 1964, Carla Bonardi; two *s. Educ:* King's Sch., Canterbury; New Coll., Oxford (BA). Entered Diplomatic Service, 1963; Third Sec., FO, 1963–65; Second Sec., Helsinki, 1965–67; FCO, 1968–71; First Sec. and Private Sec. to HM Ambassador, Washington, 1971–74; First Sec., Bonn, 1974–77; FCO, 1977–80 (Counsellor, 1979; Special Counsellor for Rhodesia negotiations, 1979–80); Counsellor, UK Perm. Repn to European Communities, 1980–84; Private Sec. to the Prime Minister, 1984–91. Vice-Pres., China-Britain Trade Gp, 1993–; Chm., Singapore British Business Council, 1994–. Chm., Schizophrenia Res. Appeal, 1993–. *Recreation:* walking. *Address:* c/o Matheson & Co., 3 Lombard Street, EC3V 9AQ. *Clubs:* Turf, Beefsteak.
See also J. Powell.

POWELL, Gen. Colin Luther, Hon. KCB 1993; Legion of Merit, Bronze Star, Air Medal, Purple Heart; Chairman, Joint Chiefs of Staff, USA, 1989–93; *b* 5 April 1937; *s* of late Luther Powell and Maud Ariel Powell (*née* McKoy); *m* 1962, Alma V. Johnson; one *s* two *d. Educ:* City Univ. of New York (BS Geology); George Washington Univ. (MBA). Commissioned 2nd Lieut, US Army, 1958; White House Fellow, 1972–73; Comdr, 2nd Brigade, 101st Airborne Div., 1976–77; exec. asst to Sec. of Energy, 1979; sen. mil. asst to Dep. Sec. of Defense, 1979–81; Asst Div. Comdr, 4th Inf. Div., Fort Carson, 1981–83; sen. mil. asst to Sec. of Defense, 1983–86; US V Corps, Europe, 1986–87; dep. asst to President 1987, asst 1987–89, for Nat. Security Affairs; General 1989; C-in-C, US Forces Command, Fort McPherson, April–Sept. 1989. *Publication:* My American Journey (autobiog.), 1995. *Recreations:* racquetball, restoring old Volvos. *Address:* 1317 Ballantrae Farm Drive, McLean, VA 22101, USA.

POWELL, His Honour (Dewi) Watkin, JP; a Circuit Judge, and Official Referee for Wales, 1972–92; *b* Aberdare, 29 July 1920; *o s* of W. H. Powell, AMICE and of M. A. Powell, Radyr, Glam; *m* 1951, Alice, *e d* of William and Mary Williams, Nantmor, Caerns; one *d. Educ:* Penarth Grammar Sch.; Jesus Coll., Oxford (MA). Called to Bar, Inner Temple, 1949. Dep. Chm., Merioneth and Cardigan QS, 1966–71; Dep. Recorder of Cardiff, Birkenhead, Merthyr Tydfil and Swansea, 1965–71; Junior, Wales and Chester Circuit, 1968; Liaison Judge for Dyfed, 1974–84, for Mid Glamorgan, 1984–91. Vice-Pres., South and Mid Glamorgan and Gwynedd branches of Magistrates' Assoc. Mem. Exec. Cttee, Plaid Cymru, 1943–55, Chm., Constitutional Cttee, 1967–71; Mem. Council, Hon. Soc. of Cymmrodorion, 1965– (Chm., 1978–84; Vice Pres., 1984–). Member, Court and Council: Univ. of Wales; Univ. of Wales Coll. of Cardiff (Vice Pres. and Vice Chm. of Council; Hon. Fellow); Univ. of Wales Coll. of Medicine. Hon. Mem., Gorsedd of Bards. President: Cymdeithas Theatr Cymru, 1984–89; Baptist Union of Wales, 1993–94; Vice-Pres., Free Church Council of Wales, 1993–. JP Mid Glamorgan. *Recreations:* gardening, reading theology, Welsh history and literature. *Address:* Nanmor, Moranedd, Cricieth, Gwynedd.

POWELL, Earl Alexander, III, PhD; Director, National Gallery of Art, Washington, since 1992; *b* 24 Oct. 1943; *s* of Earl Alexander Powell and Elizabeth Powell; *m* 1971, Nancy Landry; three *d. Educ:* A. B. Williams Coll.; Harvard Univ. (PhD 1974); A. M. Fogg Art Mus. Teaching Fellow in Fine Arts, Harvard Univ., 1970–74 (Travelling Fellowship, 1973–74); Curator, Michener Collection and Asst Prof. of Art History, Univ. of Texas at Austin, 1974–76; National Gallery of Art, Washington: Mus. Curator, Sen. Staff Asst to Asst Director and Chief Curator, 1976–78; Exec. Curator, 1979–80; Dir, LA County Mus. of Art, 1980–92. Hon. DFA: Otis Parsons, 1987; Williams, 1993. King Olav Medal (Norway), 1978; Chevalier of Arts and Letters (France), 1985. *Publication:* Thomas Cole, 1990. *Address:* National Gallery of Art, 6th and Constitution Avenue NW, Washington, DC 20565, USA. *T:* (202) 8426001. *Club:* Metropolitan (Washington).

POWELL, Rt. Hon. Enoch; *see* Powell, Rt Hon. J. E.

POWELL, Francis Turner, MBE 1945; Chairman, Laing & Cruickshank, Stockbrokers, 1978–80; *b* 15 April 1914; *s* of Francis Arthur and Dorothy May Powell; *m* 1940, Joan Audrey Bartlett; one *s* one *d. Educ:* Lancing College. Served War, Queen's Royal Regt (TA), 1939–45 (Major). Joined L. Powell Sons & Co. (Stockbrokers), 1932, Partner, 1939; merged with Laing & Cruickshank, 1976. Mem. Council, Stock Exchange, 1963–78 (Dep. Chm., 1976–78). *Recreations:* golf, gardening. *Address:* Tanglewood, Oak Grange Road, West Clandon, Surrey GU4 7UB. *T:* Guildford (01483) 222698.

POWELL, Geoffrey; *see* Powell, J. G.

POWELL, Geoffry Charles Hamilton; Founding Partner, Chamberlin, Powell & Bon, 1952–85, retired; Consultant, Chamberlin, Powell, Bon and Woods, since 1985; *b* 7 Nov. 1920; *s* of late Col D. H. Powell and Violet (*née* Timins); *m* 1st, Philippa Cooper; two *d*; 2nd, Dorothy Grenfell Williams (head, African Service, BBC) (*d* 1994); one *s. Educ:* Wellington College; AA School of Architecture. RIBA; AA Dipl. Asst to Frederick Gibberd, 1944, to Brian O'Rorke, 1946; teaching at Kingston School of Art (School of Architecture), 1949. Work includes: Golden Lane Estate; expansion of Leeds Univ.; schools, houses, commercial buildings; Barbican. Member: Council, Architectural Assoc., 1969–75; SE Economic Planning Council, 1967–69. *Recreations:* travel, painting. *Address:* Glen Cottage, River Lane, Petersham, Surrey TW10 7AG. *T:* 0181–940 6286.

POWELL, Prof. James Alfred, PhD; FIOA; Lucas Professor of Informing Design Technology and Director, Graduate School, Salford University, since 1994; *b* Sutton, 30 Oct. 1945; *s* of James Herbert Powell and Eileen Powell (*née* Newell); *m* 1969, Jennifer Elizabeth Morton; one *s. Educ:* De Burgh Sch., Tadworth; UMIST (BSc, MSc; AUMIST); Salford Univ. (PhD). FIOA 1984. ICI Schol., Salford Univ., 1970–71; Lectr, then Sen. Res. Associate, Sch. of Architecture, Dundee Univ., 1971–74; School of Architecture, Portsmouth Polytechnic: Reader in Building Utilisation, 1975–84; Prof. of Design Studies, 1984–91; Hd of Dept, 1990–91; Dep. Dean of Technol., Hd of Dept of Engrg and Mfg Systems and Lucas Prof. of Design Systems, Brunel Univ., 1991–94. Science and Engineering Research Council: IT Applications Co-ordinator, 1988–93; Mem., Engrg Bd, 1988–93; Chm., Educn and Trng Cttee, 1988–93; IT Awareness in Engrg Co-ordinator, EPSRC, 1994. Designer, Menuhin Auditorium for Portsmouth String Quartet Fest., 1980. Award for Interactive Audio in Multi Media, European Multi Media Assoc., 1992. *Publications:* Design: Science: Methods, 1981; Changing Design, 1982; Designing for Building Utilisation, 1984; Noise at Work Regulations, 1990, 2nd edn 1994; Intelligent Command and Control Acquisition and Review using Simulation, 1992; The Powell Report: review of SERC engineering education and training, 1993; Informing Technologies for Construction, Civil Engineering and Transport, 1993; Neural Computing, 1994; Engineering Decision Support, 1995; Virtual Reality and Rapid Prototyping, 1995. *Recreations:* meditation, cycling, squash, yoga, boating, painting. *Address:* Graduate School, Research and Graduate College, University of Salford, Salford M5 4WT. *T:* 0161–745 5464.

POWELL, John Alfred, MA, DPhil, CEng, FIEE, FRSE; consultant; *b* 4 Nov. 1923; *s* of Algernon Powell and Constance Elsie (*née* Honour); *m* 1949, Zena Beatrice (*née* Steventon); one *s* one *d. Educ:* Bicester County Sch.; The Queen's Coll., Oxford. No 1 Sch. of Technical Trng, RAF Halton, 1940–42. The Queen's Coll., Oxford, 1945–48. DPhil, Clarendon Lab., Oxford, 1948–51; Post-Doctorate Research Fellowship, Nat. Research Council, Ottawa, Canada, 1952–54; Marconi Research Labs, 1954–57; Texas Instruments Ltd: joined, 1957; Gen. Manager, 1959; Man. Dir, 1963; Asst Vice-Pres., TI Inc. (US), 1968; EMI Ltd: Main Bd Dir, Group Tech. Dir, 1971; Dir, Commercial Electronics, 1972; Dep. Man. Dir, 1973; Gp Man. Dir, 1974–78; Vice Chm., 1978–79. Mem., Honeywell Adv. Council, 1978–82. Faraday Lectr, 1978–79. CBIM (FBIM 1974); FRSA 1975; SMIEE (US). Member: Electronic Components Bd, 1968–71; Court of Cranfield Coll. of Technology, 1968–72; Electronics Research Council, 1972–74; Cttee of Inquiry into Engrg Profession, 1977–80; Physical Scis Sub-Cttee, UGC, 1980–85. Hon. Mem., BIR, 1980. *Recreations:* arts, sports, the rural scene. *Address:* Kym House, 21 Buccleuch Road, Branksome Park, Poole, Dorset BH13 6LF.

POWELL, Rt. Hon. (John) Enoch, PC 1960; MBE 1943; MA (Cantab); *b* 16 June 1912; *s* of Albert Enoch Powell and Ellen Mary Breese; *m* 1952, Margaret Pamela, *d* of Lt-Col L. E. Wilson, IA; two *d. Educ:* King Edwards, Birmingham; Trinity College, Cambridge. Craven Scholar, 1931; First Chancellor's Classical Medallist; Porson Prizeman; Browne Medallist, 1932; BA (Cantab); Craven Travelling Student, 1933; Fellow of Trinity College, Cambridge, 1934–38; MA (Cantab) 1937; Professor of Greek in the University of Sydney, NSW, 1937–39; Pte and L/Cpl R Warwickshire Regt, 1939–40; 2nd Lieut General List, 1940; Captain, General Staff, 1940–41; Major, General Staff, 1941; Lieut-Col, GS, 1942; Col, GS, 1944; Brig. 1944; Diploma in Oriental and African Studies. Contested (UU) South Down, 1987. MP: (C) Wolverhampton SW, 1950–Feb. 1974; (UU) Down South Oct. 1974–83, South Down, 1983–87 (resigned seat Dec. 1985 in protest against Anglo-Irish Agreement; re-elected Jan. 1986). Parly Sec., Ministry of Housing and Local Government, Dec. 1955–Jan. 1957; Financial Secretary to the Treasury, 1957–58; Minister of Health, July 1960–Oct. 1963. *Publications:* The Rendel Harris Papyri, 1936; First Poems, 1937; A Lexicon to Herodotus, 1938; The History of Herodotus, 1939; Casting-off, and other poems, 1939; Herodotus, Book VIII, 1939; Llyfr Blegywryd, 1942; Thucydidis Historia, 1942; Herodotus (translation), 1949; Dancer's End and The Wedding Gift (poems), 1951; The Social Services; Needs and Means, 1952; (jointly) One Nation, 1950; Change is our Ally, 1954; Biography of a Nation (with Angus Maude), 1955, 2nd edn 1970; Great Parliamentary Occasions, 1960; Saving in a Free Society, 1960; A Nation not Afraid, 1965; Medicine and Politics, 1966, rev. edn 1976; The House of Lords in the Middle Ages (with Keith Wallis), 1968; Freedom and Reality, 1969; Common Market: the case against, 1971; Still to Decide, 1972; Common Market: renegotiate or come out, 1973; No Easy Answers, 1973; Wrestling with the Angel, 1977; Joseph Chamberlain, 1977; A Nation or No Nation (ed R. Ritchie), 1978; Enoch Powell on 1992 (ed R. Ritchie), 1989; Collected Poems, 1990; The Evolution of the Gospel, 1994; numerous political pamphlets. *Address:* 33 South Eaton Place, SW1W 9EN. *T:* 0171–730 0988. *Club:* Athenæum.

POWELL, Air Vice-Marshal John Frederick, OBE 1956; Warden and Director of Studies, Moor Park College, 1972–77; *b* 12 June 1915; *y s* of Rev. Morgan Powell, Limpley Stoke, Bath; *m* 1939, Geraldine Ysolda, *e d* of late Sir John Fitzgerald Moylan, CB, CBE; four *s. Educ:* Lancing; King's Coll., Cambridge (MA). Joined RAF Educnl Service, 1937; Lectr, RAF College, 1938–39; RAFVR (Admin. and Special Duties) ops room duties, Coastal Comd, 1939–45 (despatches); RAF Educn Br., 1946; Sen. Instructor in History, RAF Coll., 1946–49; RAF Staff Coll., 1950; Air Min., 1951–53; Sen. Tutor, RAF Coll., 1953–59; Educn Staff, HQ FEAF, 1959–62; MoD, 1962–64; Comd Educn Officer, HQ Bomber Comd, 1964–66; OC, RAF Sch. of Educn, 1966–67; Dir of Educational Services, RAF, 1967–72; Air Commodore, 1967; Air Vice-Marshal, 1968. *Recreations:* choral music, tennis, gardening. *Address:* Barker's Hill Cottage, Donhead St Andrew, Shaftesbury, Dorest SP7 9EB. *T:* Donhead (01747) 828505. *Club:* Royal Air Force.
See also Sir C. D. Powell, J. Powell.

POWELL, (John) Geoffrey, CBE 1987; Deputy Chairman, Local Government Boundary Commission for England, 1984–90; *b* 13 Jan. 1928; *s* of H. W. J. and W. A. S. Powell. *Educ:* Shrewsbury. FRICS; FSVA; ACIArb. Lieut, Welsh Guards, 1945–48. Chm., Property Adv. Gp, DoE, 1982–86 (Chm., New Towns Sub-Gp, 1982–86); Member: Skelmersdale New Town Corp., 1978–85; Review Cttee of Govt Valuation Services, 1982; British Rail Property Board, 1985–91; NCB Pension Fund Adv. Panel, 1985–90. Sec.-Gen., European Group of Valuers of Fixed Assets, 1982–87; European Rep., Internat.

Assets Valuation Standards Cttee, 1984–87. Chm., RICS Cttees, 1960–83, incl. Assets Valuation Standards Cttee, 1981–83. External Examr, Reading Univ., 1986–88; Member: Liverpool Univ. Dept. of Civic Design Adv. Cttee, 1986–90; Adv. Panel, Law Center, USC, 1987–. Mem. Editl Bd, Rent Review and Lease Renewal, 1985–89. *Address:* Whites Farmhouse, Mickleton, near Chipping Campden, Glos GL55 6PU. *T:* Mickleton (01386) 438146.

POWELL, John Lewis; QC 1990; *b* 14 Sept. 1950; *s* of Gwyn Powell and Lilian Mary Powell (*née* Griffiths); *m* 1973, Eva Zofia Lomnicka; one *s* two *d. Educ:* Christ Coll., Brecon; Amman Valley Grammar Sch.; Trinity Hall, Cambridge (MA, LLB). Called to the Bar, Middle Temple, 1974 (Harmsworth Schol.). In practice, 1974–. Pres., Soc. of Construction Law, 1991–. Contested (Lab) Cardigan, 1979. *Publications:* (with R. Jackson, QC) Professional Negligence, 1982, 3rd edn 1992; (with Eva Lomnicka) Encyclopedia of Financial Services Law, 1987; (ed jtly) Palmer's Company Law, 24th edn 1987, 25th edn 1992; Issues and Offers of Company Securities: the new regimes, 1988. *Recreations:* travel, walking, sheep farming. *Address:* 2 Crown Office Row, Temple, EC4Y 7HJ. *T:* 0171–797 8000.

POWELL, Jonathan; Chief of Staff to the Leader of Opposition, since 1995; *b* 14 Aug. 1956; *s* of Air Vice-Marshal John Frederick Powell, *qv* and Geraldine Ysolda Powell (*née* Moylan); *m* 1980, Karen Elizabeth Drayne; two *s. Educ:* University Coll., Oxford (MA Hist.); Univ. of Pennsylvania (MA Hist.). With BBC, 1978; Granada TV, 1978–79; joined FCO, 1979; Lisbon, 1980–83; FCO, 1983–85; Member, British Delegation to: CDE, Stockholm, 1985; CSCE, Vienna, 1985–89; FCO, 1989–91; Washington, 1991–95. *Recreations:* walking, ski-ing. *Address:* House of Commons, SW1A 0AA. *T:* 0171–219 4354.

See also Sir C. D. Powell.

POWELL, Jonathan Leslie; Director of Drama and Co-production, Carlton UK Television, since 1993; *b* 25 April 1947; *s* of James Dawson Powell and Phyllis Nora Sylvester (*née* Doubleday); *m* 1990, Sally Jane Brampton, *qv*; one *d. Educ:* Sherborne; University of East Anglia. BA Hons (English and American Studies). Script editor and producer of drama, Granada TV, 1970–77; BBC TV: Producer, drama serials, 1977–83; Hd of Drama Series and Serials, 1983–87; Hd of Drama, 1987; Controller, BBC1, 1988–92. *TV serials include:* Testament of Youth, 1979 (BAFTA award); Tinker Tailor Soldier Spy, 1979; Pride and Prejudice, 1980; Thérèse Raquin, 1980; The Bell, 1982; Smiley's People, 1982 (Peabody Medal, USA); The Old Men at the Zoo, 1983; Bleak House, 1985; Tender is the Night, 1985; A Perfect Spy, 1987. Royal Television Soc. Silver Award for outstanding achievement, 1979–80. *Address:* c/o Carlton UK Television, 35–38 Portman Square, W1H 9FU. *T:* 0171–486 6688.

POWELL, Prof. Lawrie William, AC 1990; MD, PhD; FRACP, FRCP; Professor of Medicine, University of Queensland, since 1975; Director, Queensland Institute of Medical Research, since 1990; *b* 4 Dec. 1934; *s* of Victor Alexander Powell and Ellen Evelyn (*née* Davidson); *m* 1958, Margaret Emily Ingram; two *s* three *d. Educ:* Univ. of Queensland (MB BS 1958; MD 1965; PhD 1973); Univ. of London; Harvard Medical Sch. FRACP 1975; FRCP 1991. Hon. Lectr, Royal Free Hosp. and Univ. of London, 1963–65; Vis. Prof., Harvard Medical Sch., 1972–73. *Publications:* Metals and the Liver, 1978; Fundamentals of Gastroenterology, 1975, 6th edn 1995. *Recreations:* music, chess, bushwalking. *Address:* 22 Paten Road, The Gap, Brisbane, Qld 4061, Australia.

POWELL, Lewis Franklin, Jr; Associate Justice of US Supreme Court, 1971–87, retired; *b* Suffolk, Va, USA, 19 Sept. 1907; *s* of Lewis Franklin Powell and Mary Lewis (*née* Gwathmey); *m* 1936, Josephine Pierce Rucker; one *s* three *d. Educ:* McGuire's Univ. Sch., Richmond, Va; Washington and Lee Univ., Lexington, Va (BS *magnum cum laude,* LLB); Harvard Law Sch. (LLM). Admitted to practice, Bar of Virginia, 1931; subseq. practised law; partner in firm of Hunton, Williams, Gay, Powell and Gibson, in Richmond, 1938–71. Served War, May 1942–Feb. 1946, USAAF, overseas, to rank Col; subseq. Col. US Reserve. Legion of Merit and Bronze Star (US), also Croix de Guerre with Palms (France). Member: Nat. Commn on Law Enforcement and Admin of Justice, 1965–67; Blue Ribbon Defence Panel, 1969–70. Chairman or Dir of companies. Pres., Virginia State Bd of Educn; Past Chm. and Trustee, Colonial Williamsburg Foundn; Trustee, Washington and Lee Univ., etc. Mem., Amer. Bar Assoc. (Pres. 1964–65); Fellow, Amer. Bar Foundn (Pres. 1969–71); Pres. or Mem. various Bar Assocs and other legal and social instns; Hon. Bencher, Lincoln's Inn. Holds several hon. degrees. Phi Beta Kappa. Is a Democrat. *Publications:* contribs to legal periodicals, etc. *Address:* c/o Supreme Court Building, Washington, DC 20543, USA. *Club:* University (NYC).

POWELL, Prof. Michael James David, FRS 1983; John Humphrey Plummer Professor of Applied Numerical Analysis, University of Cambridge, since 1976; Professorial Fellow of Pembroke College, Cambridge, since 1978; *b* 29 July 1936; *s* of William James David Powell and Beatrice Margaret (*née* Page); *m* 1959, Caroline Mary Henderson; two *d* (one *s* decd). *Educ:* Eastbourne Coll.; Peterhouse, Cambridge (Schol.; BA 1959; ScD 1979). Mathematician at Atomic Energy Research Estabt, Harwell, 1959–76; special merit research appt to banded level, 1969, and to senior level, 1975. George B. Dantzig prize in Mathematical Programming, 1982; Naylor Prize, London Math. Soc., 1983. *Publications:* Approximation Theory and Methods, 1981; papers on numerical mathematics, especially approximation and optimization calculations. *Recreations:* canals, golf, walking. *Address:* 134 Milton Road, Cambridge CB4 1LE.

POWELL, Sir Nicholas (Folliott Douglas), 4th Bt *cr* 1897; Company Director; *b* 17 July 1935; *s* of Sir Richard George Douglas Powell, 3rd Bt, MC, and Elizabeth Josephine (*d* 1979), *d* of late Lt-Col O. R. McMullen, CMG; *S* father, 1980; *m* 1st, 1960, Daphne Jean (marr. diss. 1987), 2nd *d* of G. H. Errington, MC; one *s* one *d*; 2nd, 1987, Davina Allsopp; two *s* one *d. Educ:* Gordonstoun. Lieut Welsh Guards, 1953–57. *Heir: s* James Richard Douglas Powell [*b* 17 Oct. 1962; *m* 1991, Susanna, *e d* of David Murray Threipland, one *s* one *d*]. *Address:* Hillside Estate, Bromley, Zimbabwe.

POWELL, Prof. Percival Hugh, MA, DLitt, Dr Phil.; Professor of German, Indiana University, 1970–83, now Emeritus; *b* 4 Sept. 1912; 3rd *s* of late Thomas Powell and late Marie Sophia Roeser; *m* 1944, Dorothy Mavis Pattison (*née* Donald) (marr. diss. 1964); two *s* one adopted *d*; *m* 1966, Mary Kathleen (*née* Wilson); one *s. Educ:* University College, Cardiff (Fellow 1981); Univs of Rostock, Zürich, Bonn. 1st Class Hons German (Wales), 1933; Univ. Teachers' Diploma in Education, 1934; MA (Wales) Dist. 1936; Research Fellow of Univ. of Wales, 1936–38; Modern Languages Master, Towyn School, 1934–36; Dr Phil. (Rostock) 1938; Lektor in English, Univ. of Bonn, 1938–39; Asst Lectr, Univ. Coll., Cardiff, 1939–40; War Service, 1940–46 (Capt. Intelligence Corps); Lecturer in German, Univ. Coll., Leicester, 1946, Head of Department of German, 1954; Prof. of German, Univ. of Leicester, 1958–69. Barclay Acheson Prof. of Internat. Studies at Macalester Coll., Minn., USA, 1965–66. DLitt (Wales) 1962. British Academy award, 1963; Fritz Thyssen Foundation Award, 1964; Leverhulme Trust Award, 1968. *Publications:* Pierre Corneilles Dramen in Deutschen Bearbeitungen, 1939; critical editions of dramas of Andreas Gryphius, 1955–72; critical edn of J. G. Schoch's Comœdia vom Studentenleben, 1976; Trammels of Tradition, 1988; Louise von Gall, 1993; Therese, 1996; articles and reviews in English and foreign literary jls. *Recreation:* music. *Address:* c/o Department of Germanic Studies, Ballantine Hall, Indiana University, Bloomington, IN 47405, USA.

POWELL, Sir Philip, CH 1984; Kt 1975; OBE 1957; RA 1977 (ARA 1972); FRIBA; Partner of Powell and Moya, Architects, since 1946, and Powell, Moya and Partners, 1976–92; *b* 15 March 1921; *yr s* of late Canon A. C. Powell and late Mary Winnifred (*née* Walker), Epsom and Chichester; *m* 1953, Philippa, *d* of Lt-Col C. C. Eccles, Tunbridge Wells; one *s* one *d. Educ:* Epsom Coll.; AA Sch. of Architecture (Hons Diploma). *Works include:* Churchill Gdns flats, Westminster, 1948–62 (won in open competition); houses and flats at Gospel Oak, St Pancras, 1954, Vauxhall Park, Lambeth, 1972, Covent Garden, 1983; houses at: Chichester, 1950; Toys Hill, 1954; Oxshott, 1954; Baughurst, Hants, 1954; Skylon for Fest. of Britain, 1951 (won in open competition); British Pavilion, Expo 70, Osaka, Japan, 1970; Mayfield Sch., Putney, 1955; Plumstead Manor Sch., Woolwich, 1970; Dining Rooms at Bath Acad. of Art, Corsham, 1970, and Eton Coll., 1974; extensions, Brasenose Coll., Oxford, 1961, and Corpus Christi Coll., Oxford, 1969; picture gall. and undergrad. rooms, Christ Church, Oxford, 1967; Wolfson Coll., Oxford, 1974; Cripps Building, St John's Coll., Cambridge, 1967; Cripps Court, Queens' Coll., Cambridge, 1976; Chichester Fest. Theatre, 1961; Swimming Baths, Putney, 1967; Hosps at Swindon, Slough, High Wycombe, Wythenshawe, Woolwich, Maidstone, Hastings, Ashington, Great Ormond Street, 1959–93; Museum of London, 1976; London and Manchester Assurance HQ, near Exeter, 1978; Sch. for Advanced Urban Studies, Bristol Univ., 1981; NatWest Bank, Shaftesbury Ave, London, 1982; labs etc, and Queen's Building, RHBNC, Egham, 1986–90; Queen Elizabeth II Conf. Centre, Westminster, 1986. Has won numerous medals and awards for architectural work, inc. Royal Gold Medal for Architecture, RIBA, 1974. Mem. Royal Fine Art Commn, 1969–94; Treas. RA, 1985–95. Trustee, Sir John Soane's Museum, 1984–. *Recreations:* travel, listening to music. *Address:* 16 The Little Boltons, SW10 9LP. *T:* 0171–373 8620.

POWELL, Raymond; MP (Lab) Ogmore, since 1979; *b* 19 June 1928; *s* of Albert and Lucy Powell; *m* 1950, Marion Grace Evans; one *s* one *d. Educ:* Pentre Grammar Sch.; National Council of Labour Colls; London School of Economics. British Rail, 1945–50; Shop Manager, 1950–66; Secretary/Agent to Walter Padley, MP, 1967–69, voluntarily, 1969–79; Sen. Administrative Officer, Welsh Water Authority, 1969–79. Welsh Regl Opposition Whip, Opposition Pairing Whip. Member: Select Cttee, Employment, 1979–82; Welsh Select Cttee, 1982–85; Select Cttee, H of C Services, 1987–; Cttee of Selection, 1987–; Chm., Parly New Building Cttee, 1987–. Chairman: Labour Party Wales, 1977–78; S Wales Euro-Constituency Labour Party, 1979–. Secretary: Welsh PLP, 1984–; Welsh Parly Party; Anglo-Bulgarian All Party Gp, 1984–; Treas., Anglo-Romanian All Party Gp, 1984–; Vice-Chm., Parly Agric. Cttee, 1987. *Recreations:* gardening, sport, music. *Address:* 8 Brynteg Gardens, Bridgend, Mid-Glam CF31 3EW. *T:* Bridgend (01656) 652159. *Club:* Ogmore Constituency Labour Party Social.

POWELL, Sir Richard (Royle), GCB 1967 (KCB 1961; CB 1951); KBE 1954; CMG 1946; Deputy Chairman, Permanent Committee on Invisible Exports, 1968–76; Chairman, Alusuisse (UK) Ltd and subsidiary companies, 1969–84; *b* 30 July 1909; *er s* of Ernest Hartley and Florence Powell; unmarried. *Educ:* Queen Mary's Grammar Sch., Walsall; Sidney Sussex Coll., Cambridge (Hon. Fellow, 1972). Entered Civil Service, 1931 and apptd to Admiralty; Private Sec. to First Lord, 1934–37; Member of British Admiralty Technical Mission, Canada, and of British Merchant Shipbuilding Mission, and later of British Merchant Shipping Mission in USA, 1940–44; Civil Adviser to Commander-in-Chief, British Pacific Fleet, 1944–45; Under-Secretary, Ministry of Defence, 1946–48. Dep. Sec., Admiralty, 1948–50; Dep. Sec., Min. of Defence, 1950–56; Permanent Secretary, Board of Trade, 1960–68 (Min. of Defence, 1956–59). Dir, Philip Hill Investment Trust, 1968–81; Director: Whessoe Ltd, 1968–88; Hill Samuel Group, 1970–79; Sandoz Gp of Cos, 1972–87 (Chm.); Clerical, Medical and General Life Assurance Soc., 1972–85; BPB Industries PLC, 1973–83; Ladbroke Gp, 1980–86; Bridgewater Paper Co. Ltd, 1984–90. Pres., Inst. for Fiscal Studies, 1970–78. *Address:* 56 Montagu Square, W1H 1TG. *T:* 0171–262 0911. *Club:* Athenæum.

POWELL, Robert William; Headmaster of Sherborne, 1950–70; retired; *b* 29 October 1909; *s* of late William Powell and Agnes Emma Powell; *m* 1938, Charity Rosamond Collard; one *s. Educ:* Bristol Grammar School; Christ Church, Oxford. Assistant Master, Repton, May–Dec. 1934; Assistant Master, Charterhouse, 1935. Served War of 1939–45, 1940–45. Housemaster of Gownboys, Charterhouse, 1946–50. *Recreations:* fishing, music. *Address:* Manor Farm House, Child Okeford, near Blandford, Dorset DT11 8EE. *T:* Child Okeford (01258) 860648.

POWELL, Sally Jane, (Mrs Jonathan Powell); *see* Brampton, S. J.

POWELL, Victor George Edward; Senior Partner, Victor G. Powell Associates, Management Consultants, 1963–88; Professor of Management, ILO International Centre for Advanced Training, 1982–88; Director, Mosscare Housing Association Ltd, 1974–88; retired; *b* London, 1 Jan. 1929; *s* of George Richard Powell and Kate Hughes Powell, London; *m* 1956, Patricia Copeland Allen; three *s* one *d. Educ:* Beckenham Grammar Sch.; Univs of Durham and Manchester. BA 1st cl. hons Econs 1954, MA Econ. Studies 1957, Dunelm; PhD Manchester 1963. RN Engrg Apprentice, 1944–48. Central Work Study Dept, ICI, London, 1954–56; Chief Work Study Engr, Ind Coope Ltd, 1956–58; Lectr in Industrial Administration, Manchester Univ., 1959, Hon. Lectr 1959–63; Asst Gen. Manager, Louis C. Edwards & Sons Ltd, 1959–63; Chm., Food Production & Processing Ltd, 1971–74. Sen. Advr, 1976, Dir and Chief Advr, 1977–82, ILO. Gen. Sec., 1970–72, Dir, 1972–73, War on Want. MBIM 1957; Mem. Inst. Management Consultants, 1968. *Publications:* Economics of Plant Investment and Replacement Decisions, 1964; Techniques for Improving Distribution Management, 1968; Warehousing, 1976; Improving the Performance of Public Enterprises, 1986; various articles. *Recreations:* music, walking. *Address:* Knowles House, Hollin Lane, Sutton, Macclesfield, Cheshire SK11 0HR. *T:* Sutton (01260) 252334.

POWELL, William Rhys; MP (C) Corby, since 1983; *b* 3 Aug. 1948; *s* of late Rev. Canon Edward Powell and Anne Powell; *m* 1973, Elizabeth Vaudin; three *d. Educ:* Lancing College; Emmanuel College, Cambridge. BA 1970, MA 1973. Called to the Bar, Lincoln's Inn, 1971; Barrister, South Eastern Circuit, 1971–87. PPS to Minister for Overseas Develt, 1985–86, to Sec. of State for the Envmt, 1990–92. Member, Select Committee: on Procedure, 1987–90; on Foreign Affairs, 1990–91; on Sci. and Technol., 1992–; Mem., Jt Parly Ecclesiastical Cttee, 1987–; Joint Secretary: Cons. Back-bench For. Affairs Cttee, 1985 and 1987–90; Cons. Back-bench Defence Cttee, 1988–90; Chairman: All-Party Parly Gp for the Gulf, 1993–; British-Italian Parly Gp, 1992–; British-Taiwan Parly Gp, 1992–; British-Mongolia Parly Gp, 1993–; British-Tunisia Parly Gp, 1995–. Jt Chm., CAABU, 1992–; Mem. Council, British Atlantic Cttee, 1985–90. Fellow, Industry and Parlt Trust, 1991. As Private Mem. piloted Copyright (Computer Software) Amendment Act, 1985. *Address:* House of Commons, SW1A 0AA. *Club:* Corby Conservative.

POWELL-COTTON, Christopher, CMG 1961; MBE 1951; MC 1945; JP; Uganda CS, retired; *b* 23 Feb. 1918; *s* of Major P. H. G. Powell-Cotton and Mrs H. B. Powell-Cotton (*née* Slater); unmarried. *Educ:* Harrow School; Trinity College, Cambridge. Army Service, 1939–45: commissioned Buffs, 1940; seconded KAR, Oct. 1940; T/Major, 1943. Apptd to Uganda Administration, 1940, and released for Mil. Service. District Commissioner, 1950; Provincial Commissioner, 1955; Minister of Security and External Relations, 1961. Landowner in SE Kent. Dir, Powell-Cotton Museum of Nat. History and Ethnography. *Address:* Quex Park, Birchington, Kent CT7 0BH. *T:* Thanet (01843) 841836. *Club:* MCC.

POWELL-JONES, John Ernest, CMG 1974; HM Diplomatic Service, retired; Ambassador to Switzerland, 1982–85; *b* 14 April 1925; *s* of late Walter James Powell-Jones and Gladys Margaret (*née* Taylor); *m* 1st, 1949, Ann Murray (marr. diss. 1967); two *s* one *d*; 2nd, 1968, Pamela Sale. *Educ:* Charterhouse; University Coll., Oxford (1st cl. Modern Hist.). Served with Rifle Bde, 1943–46. HM Foreign (now Diplomatic) Service, 1949; 3rd Sec. and Vice-Consul, Bogota, 1950–52; Eastern and later Levant Dept, FO, 1952–55; 2nd, later 1st Sec., Athens, 1955–59; News Dept, FO, 1959–60; 1st Sec., Leopoldville, 1961–62; UN Dept, FO, 1963–67; ndc Canada 1967–68; Counsellor, Political Adviser's Office, Singapore, 1968–69; Counsellor and Consul-General, Athens, 1970–73; Ambassador at Phnom Penh, 1973–75; RCDS 1975; Ambassador to Senegal, Guinea, Mali, Mauritania and Guinea-Bissau, 1976–79, to Cape Verde, 1977–79; Ambassador and Perm. Rep., UN Conf. on Law of the Sea, 1979–82. Chm., Inter Counsel UK Ltd, 1986–93. Mem., Waverley BC, 1987–95. Member: Bd, Surrey Historic Bldgs Trust, 1989–92; Council, SE England Agricl Soc., 1991–95. *Recreations:* gardening, walking. *Address:* Gascons, Gaston Gate, Cranleigh, Surrey GU6 8QY. *T:* Cranleigh (01483) 274313. *Club:* Travellers'.
See also M. E. P. Jones.

POWER, Sir Alastair John Cecil, 4th Bt *cr* 1924, of Newlands Manor; *b* 15 Aug. 1958; *s* of Sir John Patrick McLannahan Power, 3rd Bt and of Melanie, *d* of Hon. Alastair Erskine; *S* father, 1984. *Heir: b* Adam Patrick Cecil Power, *b* 22 March 1963.

POWER, Mrs Brian St Quentin; *see* Stack, (Ann) Prunella.

POWER, Michael George; Director, Greenwich Hospital, 1982–87; *b* 2 April 1924; *s* of Admiral of the Fleet Sir Arthur Power, GCB, GBE, CVO, and Amy Isabel (*née* Bingham); *m* 1954, Kathleen Maeve (*née* McCaul); one *s* two *d* and two step *d*. *Educ:* Rugby Sch.; Corpus Christi Coll., Cambridge. Served War, Rifle Bde, 1942–46 (Captain); ME Centre of Arab Studies (Jerusalem), 1946–47; Colonial Admin. Service, 1947–63: District Officer: Kenya, 1948–53; Malaya, 1953–57; Kenya, 1957–63; Home Civil Service, 1963–81; Under-Sec., MoD, 1973–81. Almoner, Christ's Hosp., 1983–88. *Recreations:* carpentry, gardening. *Address:* Wancom Way, Puttenham Heath Road, Compton, Guildford GU3 1DU. *T:* Guildford (01483) 810470.

POWER, Hon. Noel Plunkett; Hon. Mr Justice Power; a Vice-President of the Court of Appeal of the Supreme Court of Hong Kong, since 1993 (a Judge of Appeal, 1987–93); *b* 4 Dec. 1929; *s* of John Joseph Power and Hilda Power; *m* 1965, Irma Maroya; two *s* one *d*. *Educ:* Downlands Coll.; Univ. of Queensland (BA, LLB). Called to the Bar, Supreme Court of Queensland and High Court of Australia, 1955; Magistrate, Hong Kong, 1965–76; Pres., Lands Tribunal, Hong Kong, 1976–79; a Judge of the Supreme Court of Hong Kong, 1979–87. Chm., Internat. Wine and Food Soc., Hong Kong Island, 1984–. Chm. Editl Bd, Hong Kong Law Reports. *Publications:* (ed) Lands Tribunal Law Reports, 1976–79. *Recreations:* travel, cooking, reading. *Address:* 76 G Peak Road, Hong Kong. *T:* 8496798. *Clubs:* Hong Kong (Hong Kong); Queensland (Brisbane).

POWERSCOURT, 10th Viscount *cr* 1743; **Mervyn Niall Wingfield;** Baron Wingfield, 1743; Baron Powerscourt (UK), 1885; *b* 3 Sept. 1935; *s* of 9th Viscount Powerscourt and Sheila Claude (*d* 1992), *d* of late Lt-Col Claude Beddington; *S* father, 1973; *m* 1962, Wendy Ann Pauline (marr. diss. 1974), *d* of R. C. G. Slazenger; one *s* one *d*; *m* 1978, Pauline, *d* of W. P. Vann, San Francisco. *Educ:* Stowe; Trinity Coll., Cambridge. Formerly Irish Guards. *Heir: s* Hon. Mervyn Anthony Wingfield, *b* 21 Aug. 1963.
See also Sir H. R. H. Langrishe, Bt.

POWIS, 8th Earl of *cr* 1804; **John George Herbert;** Baron Clive (Ire.), 1762; Baron Clive (GB), 1794; Viscount Clive, Baron Herbert of Chirbury, Baron Powis, 1804; Assistant Professor, Redeemer College, Ontario, Canada, 1990–92; *b* 19 May 1952; *s* of 7th Earl of Powis and of Hon. Katharine Odeyne de Grey, *d* of 8th Baron Walsingham, DSO, OBE; *S* father, 1993; *m* 1977, Marijke Sophia, *d* of Maarten Nanne Guther, Ancaster, Canada; two *s* two *d*. *Educ:* Wellington; McMaster Univ., Ontario, Canada (MA; PhD 1994). Formerly Lectr, McMaster Univ. *Heir: s* Viscount Clive, *qv*. *Address:* Walcot, Chirbury, Montgomery, Powys SY15 6BP.

POWLES, Stephen Robert; QC 1995; *b* 7 June 1948; *s* of Andrew Frederick Arthur Powles and Nora (*née* Bristol); *m* 1975, Geraldine Patricia Hilda Adamson; one *s* one *d*. *Educ:* Westminster Sch.; University Coll., Oxford (MA). Called to the Bar: Middle Temple, 1972 (Harmsworth Maj. Exhibnr, 1971; Astbury Law Schol., 1972); Lincoln's Inn (*ad eundem*), 1977. *Recreations:* hill-walking, sailing, my border terrier. *Address:* 2 Harcourt Buildings, Temple, EC4Y 9DB. *T:* 0171–583 9020. *Club:* Royal Solent Yacht.

POWLETT; *see* Orde-Powlett.

POWLEY, John Albert; Enquiry Officer, Post Office, since 1991; *b* 3 Aug. 1936; *s* of Albert and Evelyn Powley; *m* 1957, Jill (*née* Palmer); two *s* one *d*. *Educ:* Cambridge Grammar Sch.; Cambridgeshire Coll. of Arts and Technology. Apprenticeship, Pye Ltd, 1952–57; RAF, 1957–59; retail shop selling and servicing radio, television and electrical goods, 1960–84. Cambs CC, 1967–77; Cambridge City Council, 1967–79; Leader, Cons. Group, 1973–79; Chm., Housing Cttee, 1972–74, 1976–79; Leader of Council, 1976–79. Contested (C): Harlow, 1979; Norwich S, 1987. MP (C) Norwich S, 1983–87. Chm., Soham Cons. Assoc., 1991–. Sec./Manager, Wensum Valley Golf Club, Taverham, Norfolk, 1989–90. *Recreations:* golf, cricket, football. *Address:* Kyte End, 70A Brook Street, Soham, Ely, Cambs CB7 5AE. *T:* Ely (01353) 624552.

POWNALL, Henry Charles; QC 1979; **His Honour Judge Pownall;** a Circuit Judge, since 1984; *b* 25 Feb. 1927; *er s* of late John Cecil Glossop Pownall, CB, and Margaret Nina Pownall (*née* Jesson); *m* 1955, Sarah Bettine, *d* of late Major John Deverell; one *s* one *d* (and one *d* decd). *Educ:* Rugby Sch.; Trinity Coll., Cambridge; BA 1950, MA 1963; LLB 1951. Served War, Royal Navy, 1945–48. Called to Bar, Inner Temple, 1954, Bencher, 1976; joined South-Eastern Circuit, 1954. Junior Prosecuting Counsel to the Crown at the Central Criminal Court, 1964–71; a Sen., subseq. 2nd, Prosecuting Counsel, 1971–79; a Recorder of the Crown Court, 1972–84; Sen. Resident Judge, Knightsbridge Crown Court, 1984–88; a Judge, Courts of Appeal of Jersey and Guernsey, 1980–86. Mem. Cttee: Orders and Medals Research Soc., 1961–69, and 1970– (Pres., 1971–75, 1977–81); Nat. Benevolent Instn, 1964–. Hon. Legal Advr, ABA, 1976–89. Freeman, City of London, 1989. *Publication:* Korean Campaign Medals, 1950–53, 1957. *Recreations:* travel; medals and medal ribbons. *Address:* Central Criminal Court, Old Bailey, EC4M 7EH. *Clubs:* Pratt's, Hurlingham; Ebury Court.
See also J. L. Pownall, Sir D. M. Mountain.

POWNALL, John Harvey; Director, DTI-North West, 1988–93; *b* 24 Oct. 1933; *s* of Eric Pownall and Gladys M. Pownall (*née* Baily); *m* 1958, Pauline M. Marsden, *o d* of William Denton Marsden; one *s* two *d*. *Educ:* Tonbridge School; Imperial College, London (BSc Eng Met). ARSM. Scientific Officer, Atomic Energy Research Estab., Harwell, 1955–59; Warren Spring Lab., DSIR, 1959–64; Dept of Economic Affairs, 1964–66; Board of Trade/Dept of Trade and Industry, 1966–83; Dir-Gen., Council of Mechanical and Metal Trade Assocs, 1983–85; Hd of Electricity Div., Dept of Energy, 1985–87; Under Sec., DTI, 1987, on secondment to CEGB, 1987–88. Mem. Council, Salford Univ., 1989– (Chm., Estates and Bldgs Cttee, 1993–). *Publications:* papers in professional jls. *Address:* The West House, Arley Hall, Northwich, Cheshire CW9 6LZ. *T:* Arley (01565) 777448. *Club:* St James's (Manchester).

POWNALL, Brig. John Lionel, OBE 1972; Deputy Chairman, Police Complaints Authority, 1986–93 (Member, 1985–86); *b* 10 May 1929; *yr s* of late John Cecil Glossop Pownall, CB and Margaret Nina Pownall (*née* Jesson); *m* 1962, Sylvia Joan Cameron Conn, *d* of late J. Cameron Conn, WS and Florence Conn (*née* Lennox); two *s*. *Educ:* Rugby School; RMA Sandhurst. Commissioned 16th/5th Lancers, 1949; served Egypt, Cyrenaica, Tripolitania, BAOR, Hong Kong, Cyprus; psc, jssc; Comd 16th/5th The Queen's Royal Lancers, 1969–71; Adjutant-Gen.'s Secretariat, 1971–72; Officer i/c RAC Manning and Records, 1973–75; Col, GS Near East Land Forces/Land Forces Cyprus, 1975–78; Asst Dir, Defence Policy Staff, MoD, 1978–79; Brig. RAC, UKLF, 1979–82; Brig. GS, MoD, 1982–84; retired 1984. Col, 16th/5th The Queen's Royal Lancers, 1985–90. *Recreations:* country pursuits, arts. *Address:* Sweatmans, Milland, Liphook, Hampshire GU30 7JT. *Club:* Cavalry and Guards.
See also H. C. Pownall.

POWNALL, Leslie Leigh, MA, PhD; Chairman, NSW Planning and Environment Commission, 1974–77, retired; *b* 1 Nov. 1921; *y s* of A. de S. Pownall, Wanganui, New Zealand; *m* 1943, Judith, *d* of late Harold Whittaker, Palmerston North. *Educ:* Palmerston North Boys' High Sch.; Victoria University College, University of Canterbury, University of Wisconsin. Asst Master, Christchurch Boys' High Sch., 1941–46; Lecturer in Geography: Christchurch Teachers' Coll., 1946–47; Ardmore Teachers' Coll., 1948–49; Auckland University College, 1949–51; Senior Lecturer in Geography, 1951–60, Prof. of Geography, 1960–61, Vice-Chancellor and Rector, 1961–66, University of Canterbury; Clerk of the University Senate, Univ. of London, 1966–74. Consultant, Inter-University Council for Higher Educn Overseas, London, 1963; Consultant to Chm. of Working Party on Higher Educn in E Africa, 1968–69. Member Meeting, Council on World Tensions on Social and Economic Development (S Asia and Pacific), Kuala Lumpur, Malaysia, 1964; Governor, Internat. Students Trust, London, 1967–74; Member: Central Governing Body, City Parochial Foundation, London, 1967–74 (Mem., Grants Sub-Cttee; Chm., Finance and Gen. Purposes Cttee); UK Commonwealth Scholarship Commn, 1979–80. *Publications:* New Zealand, 1951 (New York); geographic contrib. in academic journals of America, Netherlands and New Zealand. *Recreations:* music, literature. *Clubs:* Canterbury, University (Christchurch, NZ).

POWNALL, Michael Graham; Principal Clerk, Overseas Office, since 1988, and Clerk of Committees, since 1991, House of Lords; *b* 11 Oct. 1949; *s* of Raymond Pownall and Elisabeth Mary Pownall (*née* Robinson); *m* 1974, Deborah Ann, *e d* of T. H. McQueen; two *d*. *Educ:* Repton Sch.; Exeter Univ. Joined Parliament Office, House of Lords, 1971: seconded to CSD as Private Sec. to Leader of House and Govt Chief Whip, 1980–83; Estabt Officer and Sec. to Chm. of Cttees, 1983–88; Principal Clerk of Private Bills, 1988–90. *Recreation:* bird-watching. *Address:* 13 Flanders Road, Chiswick, W4 1NQ. *T:* 0181–994 0797. *Club:* Riverside Racquet.

POWNALL, (Stephen) Orlando (Fletcher); Senior Treasury Counsel, Central Criminal Court, since 1995; *b* 13 Nov. 1952; *s* of Alan Pownall and Carola Pownall (*née* Thielker); *m* 1978, Katherine Higgins; one *s* two *d*. *Educ:* Oundle Sch.; Faculté de Droit, Paris. Called to the Bar, Middle Temple, 1975; Jun. Treasury Counsel, 1991–95. *Recreations:* Rugby, golf, painting, gardening. *Address:* 1 Crown Office Row, Temple, EC4Y 7HH. *T:* 0171–797 7111.

POWYS, family name of **Baron Lilford.**

POYNTON, Sir (Arthur) Hilton, GCMG 1964 (KCMG 1949; CMG 1946); *b* 20 April 1905; *y s* of late Arthur Blackburne Poynton, formerly Master of University College, Oxford; *m* 1946, Elisabeth Joan, *d* of late Rev. Edmund Williams; two *s* one *d*. *Educ:* Marlborough Coll.; Brasenose Coll., Oxford (Hon. Fellow 1964). Entered Civil Service, Department of Scientific and Industrial Research, 1927; transferred to Colonial Office, 1929; Private Secretary to Minister of Supply and Minister of Production 1941–43; reverted to Colonial Office, 1943; Permanent Under-Secretary of State, CO, 1959–66. Mem. Governing Body, SPCK, 1967–72. Mem., Ct of Governors, London Sch. Hygiene and Tropical Med., 1965–77; Treas., Soc. Promotion Roman Studies, 1967–76; Dir, Overseas Branch, St John Ambulance, 1968–75. KStJ 1968. *Recreations:* music, travel. *Address:* Craigmillar, 47 Stanhope Road, Croydon CR0 5NS. *T:* 0181–688 3729.

POYNTON, (John) Orde, CMG 1961; MD; Consulting Bibliographer, University of Melbourne, 1962–74; Fellow of Graduate House, University of Melbourne, 1971–84; *b* 9 April 1906; *o s* of Frederick John Poynton, MD, FRCP, and Alice Constance, *d* of Sir John William Powlett Campbell-Orde, 3rd Bt, of Kilmory; *m* 1965, Lola, *widow* of Group Captain T. S. Horry, DFC, AFC. *Educ:* Marlborough Coll.; Gonville and Caius Coll., Cambridge; Charing Cross Hospital (Univ. Schol. 1927–30). MA, MD (Cambridge); MD (Adelaide) 1948; MRCS, LRCP; Horton-Smith prize, University of Cambridge, 1940. Sen. Resident MO, Charing Cross Hosp., 1932–33; Health Officer, Fed. Malay States, 1936–37; Res. Officer Inst. for Med. Research, FMS, 1937–38, Pathologist, 1938–46; Lectr in Pathology, Univ. of Adelaide, 1947–50; Pathologist, Inst. of Med. and Veterinary Science, S Australia, 1948–50, Director, 1950–61. Dir, Commercial Finance Co., 1960–70. Life Gov., Nat. Gallery of Australia, 1990. Hon. LLD Melbourne, 1977. *Publications:* monographs and papers relating to medicine and bibliography. *Recreation:* bibliognostics. *Address:* The Terraces, 2 Mount Eliza Way, Mount Eliza, Victoria 3930, Australia. *T:* (3) 97873660. *Club:* MCC.

POYNTZ, Rt Rev. Samuel Greenfield; Bishop of Connor, 1987–95; *b* 4 March 1926; *s* of James and Katharine Jane Poyntz; *m* 1952, Noreen Henrietta Armstrong; one *s* two *d*. *Educ:* Portora Royal School, Enniskillen; Univ. of Dublin. Mod., Mental and Moral Sci. and Oriental Langs, 1948; 1st cl. Div. Test., 1950; MA 1951; BD 1953; PhD 1960. Deacon 1950, priest 1951; Curate Assistant: St George's, Dublin, 1950–52; Bray, 1952–55; St Michan and St Paul, Dublin, 1955–59; Rector of St Stephen's, Dublin, 1959–67; Vicar of St Ann's, Dublin, 1967–78; Archdeacon of Dublin, 1974–78; Exam. Chaplain to Archbishop of Dublin, 1974–78; Bishop of Cork, Cloyne and Ross, 1978–87. Chairman: Youth Dept, British Council of Churches, 1965–69; Irish Council of Churches, 1986–88; Vice-Pres., BCC, 1987–90. *Publications:* The Exaltation of the Blessed Virgin Mary, 1953; St Stephen's—One Hundred and Fifty Years of Worship and Witness, 1974; Journey towards Unity, 1975; St Ann's—the Church in the heart of the City, 1976; (ed) Church the Way, the Truth, and Your Life, 1955; Our Church—Praying with our Church

Family, 1983. *Recreations:* interest in Rugby football, travel, stamp collecting. *Address:* 10 Harmony Hill, Lisburn, Co. Antrim, N Ireland BT2 4ER. *T:* Lisburn (01846) 679013.

POZNANSKY, Dulcie Vivien; *see* Coleman, D. V.

PRACY, Robert, FRCS; Dean of the Institute of Laryngology and Otology, University of London, 1981–85, retired; a Medical Chairman, Pensions Appeal Tribunals, since 1984 (Medical Member, since 1982); *b* 19 Sept. 1921; *s* of Douglas Sherrin Pracy and Gwendoline Blanche Power; *m* 1946, Elizabeth Patricia Spicer; one *s* two *d* (and one *s* decd). *Educ:* Berkhamsted Sch.; St Bartholomew's Hosp. Med. Coll. (MB BS 1945); MPhil (Lond.) 1984. LRCP 1944; MRCS, FRCS 1953. Former Captain, RAMC. House Surgeon appts, St Bartholomew's Hosp.; formerly: Registrar, Royal Nat. Throat, Nose and Ear Hosp.; Consultant Surgeon: Liverpool Regional Board, 1954; United Liverpool Hosps, 1959; Alder Hey Childrens' Hosp., 1960; Royal Nat. Throat, Nose and Ear Hosp.; Hosp. for Sick Children, Gt Ormond St; Dir, Dept of Otolaryngology, Liverpool Univ. Mem. Ct of Examnrs, RCS and RCSI. Lectures: Yearsley, 1976; Joshi, 1978; Wilde, 1979; Semon, London Univ., 1980. Pres., British Assoc. of Otolaryngologists; FRSocMed (Pres., Sect. of Laryngology, 1982–83). Hon. FRCSI 1982; Hon. Fellow: Irish Otolaryngol Assoc.; Assoc. of Otolaryngologists of India; Polish Otolaryngological Assoc. *Publications:* (jtly) Short Textbook: Ear, Nose and Throat, 1970, 2nd edn 1974 (trans. Italian, Portuguese, Spanish); (jtly) Ear, Nose and Throat Surgery and Nursing, 1977; contribs to learned jls. *Recreations:* cabinet making, painting, engraving, reading, theatre. *Address:* Ginkgo House, New Road, Moreton-in-Marsh, Glos GL56 0AS. *T:* Moreton-in-Marsh (01608) 650740.

PRAG, (Andrew) John (Nicholas Warburg), MA, DPhil; FSA; Keeper of Archaeology, Manchester Museum, University of Manchester, since 1969; *b* 28 Aug. 1941; *s* of Adolf Prag and Frede Charlotte (*née* Warburg); *m* 1969, Kay (*née* Wright); one *s* one *d*. *Educ:* Westminster Sch. (Queen's Scholar); Brasenose Coll., Oxford (Domus Exhibnr 1960; Hon. Scholar 1962; BA 1964; Dip. Classical Archaeol. 1966; Sen. Hulme Scholar, 1967; MA 1967; DPhil 1975). FSA 1977. Temp. Asst Keeper, Ashmolean Museum, Oxford, 1966–67; Hon. Lectr, Dept of History, 1977–83, Dept of Archaeology, 1984–, Univ. of Manchester. Vis. Prof. of Classics, McMaster Univ., 1978; Vis. Fellow, British Sch. at Athens, 1994. Editor, Archaeological Reports, 1975–87. *Publications:* The Oresteia: iconographic and narrative tradition, 1985; articles on Greek art and archaeology in learned jls. *Recreations:* travel, walking, cooking, music. *Address:* Manchester Museum, The University, Manchester M13 9PL. *T:* 0161–275 2665.

PRAG, Derek; Member (C) Hertfordshire, European Parliament, 1979–94; *b* 6 Aug. 1923; *s* of late Abraham J. Prag and Edith Prag; *m* 1948, Dora Weiner; three *s*. *Educ:* Bolton Sch.; Emmanuel Coll., Univ. of Cambridge (MA; Cert. of Competent Knowledge in Russian). Served War, Intelligence Corps, England, Egypt, Italy, Austria, 1942–47. Economic journalist with Reuters News Agency in London, Brussels and Madrid, 1950–55; Information Service of High Authority, European Coal and Steel Community, 1955–59; Head of Division, Jt Information Service of European Communities, 1959–65; Director, London Information Office of European Communities, 1965–73; ran own consultancy company on relations with EEC, 1973–79. Mem., 1982–94, Dep. Chm., 1989–94, Institutional Cttee (EDG spokesman, 1982–84 and 1987–92; EPP dep. spokesman, and British Cons. spokesman, 1992–94); Political spokesman for European Democratic (Cons.) Group, 1984–87; Chm., European Parlt All-Party Disablement Gp, 1980–94; Vice-Pres., Eur. Parlt-Israel Intergroup, 1990–94. Associate Mem., RIIA, 1973–. Hon. Dir, EEC Commn, 1974; Hon. Mem., EP, 1994. Hon. DLitt Hertfordshire, 1993. Silver Medal of European Merit, Fondation du Mérite Européen, 1974. *Publications:* (with E. D. Nicholson) Businessman's Guide to the Common Market, 1973; various reports on Europe's internat. role, and booklets and articles on European integration. *Recreations:* reading, theatre, music, walking, swimming, gardening; speaks seven languages. *Address:* 47 New Road, Digswell, Welwyn, Herts AL6 0AQ. *Clubs:* Carlton, Royal Over-Seas League; Royal Automobile (Brussels).

PRAG, John; *see* Prag, A. J. N. W.

PRAGNELL, Anthony William, CBE 1982 (OBE 1960); DFC 1944; Deputy Director-General, Independent Broadcasting Authority (formerly Independent Television Authority), 1961–83; Director, Channel Four Television, 1983–88; *b* 15 Feb. 1921; *s* of William Hendley Pragnell and Silvia Pragnell; *m* 1955, Teresa Mary (*d* 1988), *d* of Leo and Anne Monaghan, Maidstone; one *s* one *d*. *Educ:* Cardinal Vaughan Sch., London. Asst Examiner, Estate Duty Office, 1939. Served RAF, 1942–46. Examiner, Estate Duty Office, 1946. LLB London Univ., 1949. Asst Principal, General Post Office, 1950; Asst Secretary, ITA, 1954; Secretary, ITA, 1955. Vis. Fellow, European Inst. for the Media, Univ. of Manchester, 1983–92, Düsseldorf, 1992–. Fellow, Royal Television Soc., 1980. Emile Noël European Prize, 1987. *Publications:* Television in Europe: quality and values in a time of change, 1985; (ed) Opening up the Media, 1993. *Recreations:* reading, music. *Address:* Ashley, Grassy Lane, Sevenoaks, Kent TN13 1PL. *T:* Sevenoaks (01732) 451463. *Club:* Royal Air Force.

PRAIS, Prof. Sigbert Jon, FBA 1985; Senior Research Fellow, National Institute of Economic and Social Research, London, since 1970; Visiting Professor of Economics, City University, since 1975; *b* 19 Dec. 1928; *s* of Samuel and Bertha Prais; *m* 1971, Vivien Hennessy, LLM, solicitor; one *s* three *d*. *Educ:* King Edward's School, Birmingham; Univ. of Birmingham (MCom); Univ. of Cambridge (PhD, ScD); Univ. of Chicago. Dept of Applied Economics, Cambridge, 1950–57; research officer, NIESR, 1953–59; UN Tech. Assistance Orgn, 1959–60; IMF Washington, 1960–61; Finance Dir, Elbief Co., 1961–70. Mem. Council, Royal Economic Soc., 1979–83. Mem. Council, City Univ., 1990–94. Hon. DLitt City Univ., 1989. *Publications:* Analysis of Family Budgets (jtly), 1955, 2nd edn 1971; Evolution of Giant Firms in Britain, 1976, 2nd edn 1981; Productivity and Industrial Structure, 1981; Productivity, Education and Training, 1995; articles in economic and statistical jls, esp. on influence of educn on economic progress. *Address:* 83 West Heath Road, NW3 7TN. *T:* 0181–458 4428; (office) 0171–222 7665.

PRANCE, Sir Ghillean (Tolmie), Kt 1995; DPhil; FRS 1993; FLS, FIBiol; FRGS; Director, Royal Botanic Gardens, Kew, since 1988; *b* 13 July 1937; *s* of Basil Camden Prance, CIE, OBE and Margaret Hope Prance (*née* Tolmie); *m* 1961, Anne Elizabeth Hay; two *d*. *Educ:* Malvern Coll.; Keble Coll., Oxford (BA, MA, DPhil). FLS 1961; FIBiol 1988. New York Botanical Garden: Res. Asst, 1963–66; Associate Curator, 1966–68; B. A. Krukoff Curator of Amazonian Botany, 1968–75; Dir of Research, 1975–81; Vice-Pres., 1977–81; Senior Vice-Pres., 1981–88. Adjunct Prof., City Univ. of NY, 1968–; Vis. Prof. in Tropical Studies, Yale, 1983–89; Vis. Prof., Reading Univ., 1988–; Dir of Graduate Studies, Instituto Nacional de Pesquisas da Amazônia, Manaus, Brazil, 1973–75; 14 botanical expedns to Amazonia. President: Assoc. of Tropical Biol., 1979–80; Amer. Assoc. of Plant Taxonomists, 1984–85; Systematics Assoc., 1989–91; Mem. Council, RHS, 1990–. FRGS 1989; Fellow, AAAS, 1990; Corresponding Member: Brazilian Acad. of Scis, 1976; Botanical Soc. of America, 1994; Foreign Member: Royal Danish Acad. of Scis and Letters, 1988; Royal Swedish Acad. of Scis, 1989; Associate Mem., Third World Acad. of Scis, 1993. Fil Dr *hc* Univ. Göteborgs, Sweden, 1983; Hon. DSc: Kent, 1994; Portsmouth, 1994; Kingston, 1994; St Andrews, 1995. Henry Shaw Medal, Missouri Botanical Garden, St Louis, 1988; Linnean Medal, 1990; Patron's Medal, RGS, 1994. *Publications:* Arvores de Manaus, 1975; Algumas Flores da Amazonia, 1976; Extinction is Forever, 1977; Biological Diversification in the Tropics, 1981; Amazonia: key environments, 1985; Leaves, 1986; Manual de Botânica Econômica do Maranhão, 1988; Flowers for all Seasons, 1989; Out of the Amazon, 1992; Bark, 1993. *Recreations:* squash, flower stamp collecting, bird watching. *Address:* 49 Kew Green, Richmond, Surrey TW9 3AA. *T:* 0181–332 5112. *Club:* Explorers (New York) (Fellow).

PRANKERD, Thomas Arthur John, FRCP; Professor of Clinical Haematology, 1965–79 and Dean, 1972–77, University College Hospital Medical School; Hon. Consultant Physician: University College Hospital; Whittington Hospital; *b* 11 Sept. 1924; *s* of late H. A. Prankerd, Barrister-at-Law, and J. D. Shorthose; *m* 1950, Margaret Vera Harrison Cripps; two *s* (and one *s* one *d* decd). *Educ:* Charterhouse Sch.; St Bartholomew's Hospital Med. Sch. MD (London) Gold Medal 1949; FRCP 1962. Jnr med. appts, St Bart's and University Coll. Hosp., 1947–60. Major, RAMC, 1948–50. Univ. Travelling Fellow, USA, 1953–54; Consultant Physician, University Coll. Hosp., 1960–65. Goulstonian Lectr, RCP, 1963; Examr, RCP, and various univs. Visiting Professor: Univ. of Perth, WA, 1972; Univ. of Cape Town, 1973. Mem., NE Thames RHA, 1976–79. Mem. Bd of Governors, UCH, 1972–74. *Publications:* The Red Cell, 1961; Haematology in Medical Practice, 1968; articles in med. jls. *Recreations:* fishing, gardening, music. *Address:* Milton Lake, Milton Abbas, Blandford, Dorset DT11 0BJ. *T:* Milton Abbas (01822) 880278.

PRASASVINITCHAI, Sudhee; Kt Grand Cordon, Order of the Crown of Thailand, 1982; Kt Grand Cordon, Order of the White Elephant, 1986; Ambassador of Thailand to the Court of St James's, 1986–91; Advisor to Foreign Ministry, 1991–92; *b* 17 March 1931; *s* of Phra and Nang Prasasvinitchai; *m* 1964, Ponglak (*née* Sriyanonda); one *s* two *d*. *Educ:* Thammasat Univ., Bangkok (LLB); Magdalene Coll., Cambridge (MA, LLB); Univ. of Paris (DUP); National Defence Coll., Thailand. Joined Min. of Foreign Affairs, Thailand, 1950; Chief of S Asia Div., Political Dept, 1966; First Sec., Jakarta, 1968–70; Chief of Legal Div., Treaty and Legal Dept, 1970; Dep. Dir-Gen., Political Dept, 1973; Minister-Counsellor, Washington, DC, 1974–75; Ambassador and Perm. Rep. to UN, Geneva, 1976; Ambassador to Fed. Republic of Germany, 1979–82; Dir-Gen., Political Dept, 1982–84; Dep. Perm. Sec., Min. of Foreign Affairs, 1984–86. Chakrabarti Mala Medal, 1975. *Address:* 99 Phaholyothin Road 5, Bangkok 10400, Thailand. *T:* (2) 2791997.

PRASHAR, Usha Kumari, (Mrs V. K. Sharma), CBE 1995; a part-time Civil Service Commissioner, since 1990; Non-executive Director, Channel 4, since 1992; Deputy Chairman, National Literacy Trust, since 1992; *b* 29 June 1948; *d* of Nauhria Lal Prashar and Durga Devi Prashar; *m* 1973, Vijay Kumar Sharma. *Educ:* Duchess of Gloucester Sch., Nairobi; Wakefield Girls' High Sch. (Head Girl, 1966–67); Univ. of Leeds (BA Hons Pol. Studies); Univ. of Glasgow (postgrad. Dip. Social Admin). Race Relations Bd, 1971–75; Asst Dir, Runnymede Trust, 1976–77, Dir, 1977–84; Res. Fellow, PSI, 1984–86; Dir, NCVO, 1986–91. Vice-Chm., British Refugee Council, 1987–89. Member: Arts Council of GB, 1979–81, Arts Council of England, 1994–; Study Commn on the Family, 1980–83; Social Security Adv. Cttee, 1980–83; Exec. Cttee, Child Poverty Action Gp, 1984–85; GLAA, 1984–86; London Food Commn, 1984–90; BBC Educnl Broadcasting Council, 1987–89; Adv. Council, Open College, 1987–89; Solicitors' Complaints Bureau, 1989–90; Royal Commn on Criminal Justice, 1991–93; Lord Chancellor's Adv. Cttee on Legal Educn and Conduct, 1991–; Council, PSI, 1992–; Bd, Energy Saving Trust, 1992–. Hon. Vice-Pres., Council for Overseas Student Affairs, 1986–. Trustee: Thames Help Trust, 1984–86; Charities Aid Foundn, 1986–91; Independent Broadcasting Telethon Trust, 1987–; Acad. of Indian Dance, 1987–91; Chm., English Adv. Cttee, Nat. AIDS Trust, 1988–89; Patron: Sickle Cell Soc., 1986–; Elfrida Rathbone Soc., 1988–. Mem., Royal Holloway Coll., 1992. FRSA. Hon. Fellow, Goldsmiths' Coll., Univ. of London, 1992. Hon. LLD: De Montfort, 1994; South Bank Univ., 1994. *Publications:* *contributed to:* Britain's Black Population, 1980; The System: a study of Lambeth Borough Council's race relations unit, 1981; Scarman and After, 1984; Sickle Cell Anaemia, Who Cares? a survey of screening, counselling, training and educational facilities in England, 1985; Routes or Road Blocks, a study of consultation arrangements between local authorities and local communities, 1985; Acheson and After: primary health care in the inner city, 1986. *Recreations:* reading, country walks, music, golf. *Address:* National Literacy Trust, 1A Grosvenor Gardens, SW1W 0BD. *Club:* Reform.

PRATCHETT, Terence David John; author; *b* 28 April 1948; *s* of David and Eileen Pratchett; *m* 1968, Lyn Purves; one *d*. *Educ:* High Wycombe Tech. High Sch.; Beaconsfield Public Library. Assorted journalism, 1965–80; Press Officer, CEGB, 1980–87. *Publications:* The Carpet People, 1971; The Dark Side of the Sun, 1976; Strata, 1981; The Colour of Magic, 1983; The Light Fantastic, 1986; Equal Rites, 1987; Mort, 1987; Sourcery, 1988; Wyrd Sisters, 1988; Pyramids, 1989; Truckers, 1989; Guards! Guards!, 1989; The Unadulterated Cat, 1989; Eric, 1989; (with N. Gaiman) Good Omens, 1990; Moving Pictures, 1990; Diggers, 1990; Wings, 1990; Reaper Man, 1991; Witches Abroad, 1991; Small Gods, 1992; Only You Can Save Mankind, 1992; Lords and Ladies, 1992; Johnny and the Dead, 1993; Men At Arms, 1993; Soul Music, 1994; Interesting Times, 1994. *Recreation:* letting the mind wander. *Address:* c/o Colin Smythe, PO Box 6, Gerrards Cross, Bucks SL9 7HA. *T:* Gerrards Cross (01753) 886000.

PRATLEY, Alan Sawyer; Deputy Financial Controller, Commission of the European Communities, since 1990 (Director, Financial Control, 1986–90); *b* 25 Nov. 1933; *s* of Frederick Pratley and Hannah Pratley (*née* Sawyer); *m* 1st, 1960, Dorothea Rohland (marr. diss. 1979); two *d*; 2nd, 1979, Josette Kairis; one *d*. *Educ:* Latymer Upper School; Sidney Sussex Coll., Cambridge. BA Modern Languages (German, Russian). Head, German Dept, Stratford Grammar Sch., West Ham, 1958–60; Asst Dir, Examinations, Civil Service Commn, 1960–68; Home Office, 1968–73; Commission of the European Communities: Head, Individual Rights Div., 1973–79; Dep. Chef de cabinet to Christopher Tugendhat, 1979–80; Adviser to Michael O'Kennedy, 1980–81; Dir of Admin, 1981–86. *Recreations:* tennis, gardening. *Address:* Commission des Communautés Européennes, 200 rue de la Loi, 1049 Brussels, Belgium. *Club:* Travellers'.

PRATLEY, Clive William; Under Secretary, Lord Chancellor's Department, 1976–85; Circuit Administrator: Midland and Oxford Circuit, 1976–82; North-Eastern Circuit, 1982–85; a Reference Secretary (reserve panel), Monopolies and Mergers Commission, 1990–92; *b* 23 Jan. 1929; *s* of late F. W. Pratley and late Minnie Pratley (*née* Hood); *m* 1962, Eva, *d* of late Nils and of Kerstin Kellgren, Stockholm; one *s* one *d*. *Educ:* RMA Sandhurst; and after retirement from Army, at Univs of Stockholm, 1961–62, and Hull, 1962–65 (LLB Hons). Commissioned into Royal Tank Regt, 1949; active list, 1949–61; Adjt, 2nd RTR, 1959–61; reserve list, 1961–79; Hon. Captain, 1979–. Entered Administrative Class of Home Civil Service as Principal, 1966; Lord Chancellor's Department: Sen. Principal, 1971; Asst Sec., 1974; Under Sec., 1976. *Recreations:* (before disablement) offshore and ocean sailing (RYA coastal skipper; Cape Horner, 1992), the countryside, badminton, music. *Address:* The Old Chapel, Aldfield, near Ripon, North Yorkshire HG4 3BE. *T:* Sawley (01765) 620277.

PRATLEY, David Illingworth; Director of Leisure, Tourism and Economic Development, Bath City Council, since 1992; *b* 24 Dec. 1948; *s* of Arthur George Pratley and Olive Constance Illingworth. *Educ:* Westminster Abbey Choir Sch.; Westminster Sch.; Univ. of Bristol (LLB). PRO, Thorndike Theatre, Leatherhead, 1970–71; Gen. Asst, Queen's Univ. Festival, Belfast, 1971–73; Dep. Dir, Merseyside Arts Assoc., 1973–76; Dir, Greater London Arts Assoc., 1976–81; Regl Dir, Arts Council of GB, 1981–86; Chief Exec., Royal Liverpool Philharmonic Soc., 1987–88; Man. Dir, Trinity Coll. of Music, 1988–91. Chm., Alliance Arts Panel, 1987–88; Council Mem., Nat. Campaign for the Arts, 1986–92 (Chm., 1988–92); Dir, Dance Umbrella Ltd, 1986– (Chm., 1990–92). FRSA. *Publications:* (co-ed) Culture for All, 1981; reports: The Pursuit of Competence—the Arts and the European Community, 1987; Cumbria County Arts Strategy, 1987; Musicians Go To School, 1993. *Recreations:* music, theatre, art, countryside, travel. *Address:* 16 Guinea Lane, Lansdown, Bath BA1 5NB. *Club:* Athenæum.

PRATT, family name of **Marquess Camden.**

PRATT, Anthony Malcolm G.; *see* Galliers-Pratt.

PRATT, (Arthur) Geoffrey, CBE 1981; Hon. Secretary, Institution of Gas Engineers, 1982–87; *b* 19 Aug. 1922; *s* of William Pratt, Willington, Co. Durham; *m* 1946, Ethel Luck; two *s* twin *d*. *Educ:* King James I Grammar Sch., Bishop Auckland. CEng, FIGasE. Joined E Mids Gas Bd, 1951: Chief Engr, 1964; Dir of Engrg, 1967; Dep. Chm., S Eastern Gas Bd, 1970–72; Chm., SE Gas Region, 1972–81; part-time Mem., British Gas Corp., 1981–82. Chm., Metrogas Building Soc., 1977–85. Pres., IGasE, 1974–75; Hon. FIGasE 1987. *Recreations:* keep-fit, swimming. *Address:* 3 Hither Chantlers, Langton Green, Tunbridge Wells, Kent TN3 0BJ.

PRATT, Camden; *see* Pratt, R. C.

PRATT, Christopher Leslie; Metropolitan Stipendiary Magistrate, since 1990; *b* 15 Dec. 1947; *s* of late Leslie Arthur Cottrell Pratt and of Phyllis Elizabeth Eleanor Pratt; *m* 1973, Jill Rosemary Hodges; two *s*. *Educ:* Highgate Sch. Admitted Solicitor, 1972. Court Clerk, Hendon, Harrow and Uxbridge Courts, 1967–72; Dep. Clerk to the Justices, Wimbledon and Uxbridge, 1972–76; Clerk to the Justices, Highgate, Barnet and S Mimms, 1976–90; Clerk to Barnet Magistrates' Courts Cttee and Trng Officer, Justices and staff, 1986–90. Mem. Council, Justices' Clerks' Soc., 1983–90 (Chm., Parly Cttee, Chm., Conf. and Social Cttee). *Recreation:* conjuring (Hon. Sec., The Magic Circle). *Address:* Old Street Magistrates' Court, 335 Old Street, EC1V 9LJ. *Club:* Magic Circle.

PRATT, (Ewart) George, CVO 1986; Trustee: The Prince's Trust, since 1976 (Chairman, 1978–86; Hon. Administrator, 1976–78); REACT, since 1990; *b* 10 Oct. 1917; *s* of George William Pratt and Florence (*née* Redding); *m* 1948, Margaret Heath; two *s*. *Educ:* an independent sch.; London Sch. of Economics and Political Science (Dip. Social Sci. and Public Admin). Successively, probation officer, sen. probation officer, asst chief and, from 1970, dep. chief probation officer, Inner London Probation Service, 1949–81. Mem. numerous govtl, professional and charitable adv. gps, including: Cttee on the Voluntary Worker in the Social Services, 1966–69; Home Office Working Party on Community Service by Offenders, 1971–72; Social Responsibility Cttees of the Baptist Union and BCC, and Sec., a church-related housing assoc., 1964–81. Chm., Assoc. of Social Workers, 1959–70; Founder-Gov., Nat. Inst. for Social Work, 1961–71; Treas., BASW, 1970–73. Elder, URC. Silver Jubilee Medal, 1977. *Publications:* essays and articles on issues relating to field of criminal justice and treatment of offenders. *Recreations:* music, theatre, travel. *Address:* 14 The Squirrels, The Avenue, Branksome Park, Poole BH13 6AF. *T:* Poole (01202) 767552. *Club:* Royal Automobile.

PRATT, Michael John; QC 1976; a Recorder of the Crown Court, since 1974; *b* 23 May 1933; *o s* of W. Brownlow Pratt; *m* 1960, Elizabeth Jean Hendry; two *s* three *d*. *Educ:* West House Sch., Edgbaston; Malvern Coll. LLB (Birmingham). Army service, 2nd Lieut, 3rd Carabiniers (Prince of Wales's Dragoon Guards); Staff Captain. Called to the Bar, Middle Temple, 1954, Bencher, 1986. *Recreations:* music, theatre, sport generally. *Address:* 9 Moorland Road, Edgbaston, Birmingham B16 9JP. *T:* 0121–454 1071. *Clubs:* Cavalry and Guards; Birmingham Conservative.

PRATT, (Richard) Camden; QC 1992; a Recorder, since 1993; *b* 14 Dec. 1947; *s* of Richard Sheldon Pratt, MA Oxon, and late Irene Gladys Pratt; *m* 1973, (Dorothy Jane) Marchia Allsebrook. *Educ:* Boston Grammar Sch.; Westcliff High Sch.; Lincoln Coll., Oxford (MA Jurisp). Called to the Bar, Gray's Inn, 1970. Chm., Sussex Courts Liaison Cttee, 1993–. *Recreations:* walking, sailing, travel, people. *Address:* 1 King's Bench Walk, Temple, EC4Y 7DB. *T:* 0171–583 6266, *Fax:* 0171–583 2068.

PRATT, Roger Allan; Director, Conservative Party in Scotland, since 1993; *b* 28 Dec. 1950; *s* of Allan Pratt and Joyce Isobel Pratt (*née* Dodds); *m* 1st, 1975, Ann Heaton (marr. diss. 1993); one *s* one *d*; 2nd, 1993, Lynn Mary Tomlinson; one step-*s* one step-*d*. *Educ:* King Edward's Fiveways Sch., Birmingham. Organiser, E. Midlands Area YC, 1971–72; NW Area Youth Develt Officer, 1972–74; Agent, Liverpool Wavertree Cons. Assoc., 1975–76; Nat. YC Organiser, 1976–79; Agent, Pendle, Burnley and Hyndburn Cons. Assocs, 1980–84; North West Area, then NW Region: Dep. Central Office Agent, 1984–89; Central Office Agent, 1989–93; Regl Dir, 1993. *Recreation:* cricket. *Address:* Suite 1/1, 14 Links Place, Leith, Edinburgh EH6 7EZ. *T:* 0131–555 2900.

PRATT, Timothy Jean Geoffrey, CB 1993; Counsel to the Speaker (European Legislation), House of Commons, since 1993; *b* 25 Nov. 1934; *s* of Geoffrey Cheeseborough Pratt and Elinor Jean (*née* Thomson); *m* 1963, Pamela Ann Blake; two *d*. *Educ:* Brighton College; Trinity Hall, Cambridge (MA). Called to the Bar, Middle Temple, 1959; in practice, 1959–61; joined Treasury Solicitor's Dept, 1961; Law Officers' Dept, 1972; DTI, 1974; Legal Advisor: Dir-Gen. of Fair Trading, 1979; Cabinet Office (European Secretariat), 1985; Dep. Treasury Solicitor, 1990–93. *Address:* House of Commons, SW1A 0AA. *Club:* United Oxford & Cambridge University.

PRAWER, Prof. Siegbert Salomon, FBA 1981; Taylor Professor of German Language and Literature, University of Oxford, 1969–86, now Professor Emeritus; Professorial Fellow, 1969–86, Supernumerary Fellow, 1986–90, Hon. Fellow, 1990, The Queen's College, Oxford (Dean of Degrees, 1978–93); *b* 15 Feb. 1925; *s* of Marcus and Eleonora Prawer; *m* 1949, Helga Alice (*née* Schaefer); one *s* two *d* (and one *s* decd). *Educ:* King Henry VIII Sch., Coventry; Jesus Coll. (Schol.) and Christ's Coll., Cambridge. Charles Oldham Shakespeare Scholar, 1945, MA 1950, LittD 1962, Cantab; PhD Birmingham, 1953; MA 1969, DLitt 1969, Oxon. Adelaide Stoll Res. Student, Christ's Coll., Cambridge, 1947–48; Asst Lecturer, Lecturer, Sen. Lecturer, University of Birmingham, 1948–63; Prof. of German, Westfield Coll., London Univ., 1964–69. Visiting Professor: City Coll., NY, 1956–57; University of Chicago, 1963–64; Harvard Univ., 1968; Hamburg Univ., 1969; Univ. of Calif, Irvine, 1975; Otago Univ., 1976; Pittsburgh Univ., 1977; Visiting Fellow: Knox Coll., Dunedin, 1976; Humanities Research Centre, ANU, 1980; Tauber Inst., Brandeis Univ., 1981–82; Russell Sage Foundn, NY, 1988. Hon. Director, London Univ. Inst. of Germanic Studies, 1966–68. President: British Comp. Lit. Assoc., 1984–87 (Hon. Fellow, 1989); English Goethe Soc., 1990–94. Hon. Fellow, London Univ. Inst. Germanic Studies, 1987; Fellow, Deutsche Akademie für Sprache und Dichtung, 1989. Hon. Mem., Modern Language Assoc. of America, 1986. Hon. Dr. phil. Cologne, 1984; Hon. DLitt Birmingham, 1988. Goethe Medal, 1973; Friedrich Gundolf Prize, 1986; Gold Medal, German Goethe Soc., 1995. Co-editor: Oxford German Studies, 1971–75; Anglica Germanica, 1973–79. *Publications:* German Lyric Poetry, 1952; Mörike und seine Leser, 1960; Heine's Buch der Lieder: A Critical Study, 1960; Heine: The Tragic Satirist, 1962; The Penguin Book of Lieder, 1964; The Uncanny in Literature (inaug. lect.), 1965; (ed, with R. H. Thomas and L. W. Forster) Essays in German Language, Culture and Society, 1969; (ed) The Romantic Period in Germany, 1970; Heine's Shakespeare, a Study in Contexts (inaug. lect.), 1970; (ed) Seventeen Modern German Poets, 1971; Comparative Literary Studies: an Introduction, 1973; Karl Marx and World Literature, 1976 (Isaac Deutscher Meml Prize, 1977); Caligari's Children: the film as tale of terror, 1980; Heine's Jewish Comedy: a study of his portraits of Jews and Judaism, 1983; A. N. Stencl: poet of Whitechapel (Stencl Meml Lect.), 1984; Coalsmoke and Englishmen (Bithell Meml Lecture), 1984; Frankenstein's Island: England and the English in the writings of Heinrich Heine, 1986; Israel at Vanity Fair: Jews and Judaism in the writings of W. M. Thackeray, 1992; articles on German, English and comparative literature in many specialist periodicals and symposia. *Recreation:* portrait drawing. *Address:* 9 Hawkswell Gardens, Oxford OX2 7EX.

See also Mrs R. P. Jhabvala.

PRAWER JHABVALA, Mrs Ruth; *see* Jhabvala.

PREBBLE, David Lawrence; Master, Queen's Bench Division, Supreme Court of Justice, since 1981; *b* 21 Aug. 1932; *s* of late George Wilson Prebble and Margaret Jessie Prebble (*née* Cuthbertson); *m* 1959, Fiona W. Melville; three *d*. *Educ:* Cranleigh; Christ Church, Oxford. MA. National Service, 1950–52; commissioned in 3rd Carabiniers (Prince of Wales's Dragoon Guards); served TA, 1952–61, City of London Yeomanry (Rough Riders) TA (Captain). Called to the Bar, Middle Temple, 1957; practised at Bar, 1957–81. *Recreations:* reading; operetta; wine and food; hounds and dogs; friends' horses; own wife and family; (not necessarily in foregoing order as to precedence). *Address:* 16 Wool Road, Wimbledon, SW20 0HW. *T:* 0181–946 1804. *Club:* Royal Wimbledon Golf.

PREBBLE, John Edward Curtis, FRSL; Writer; *b* 23 June 1915; *o s* of late John William Prebble, Petty Officer, RN, and Florence (*née* Wood); *m* 1st, 1936, Betty (*d* 1993), *d* of late Ernest Golby; two *s* one *d*; 2nd, 1994, Jan, *d* of late Andrew Reid. *Educ:* Sutherland Public Sch., Saskatchewan; Latymer Upper Sch., London. Entered journalism, 1934; in ranks with RA, 1940–45; Sergeant-reporter with No 1 British Army Newspaper Unit (Hamburg), 1945–46; reporter, columnist and feature-writer for British newspapers and magazines, 1946–60; novelist, historian, film-writer and author of many plays and dramatised documentaries for radio and TV. *Publications: novels:* Where the Sea Breaks, 1944; The Edge of Darkness, 1948; Age Without Pity, 1950; The Mather Story, 1954; The Brute Streets, 1954; The Buffalo Soldiers, 1959; *short stories:* My Great Aunt Appearing Day, 1958; Spanish Stirrup, 1972; *biography:* (with J. A. Jordan) Mongaso, 1956; *history:* The High Girders, 1956; Culloden, 1961; The Highland Clearances, 1963; Glencoe, 1966; The Darien Disaster, 1968; The Lion in the North, 1971; Mutiny: Highland Regiments in Revolt, 1975; John Prebble's Scotland, 1984; The King's Jaunt: George IV in Edinburgh, 1988; *autobiography:* Landscapes and Memories, 1993. *Recreation:* serendipity. *Address:* 905 Nelson House, Dolphin Square, SW1V 3PA. *T:* 0171–798 8253.

PREBBLE, Stuart Colin; Controller, ITV Network Factual Programmes, since 1993; *b* 15 April 1951; *s* of Dennis Stanley Prebble and Jean Margaret Prebble; *m* 1978, Marilyn Anne Charlton; two *d*. *Educ:* Univ. of Newcastle upon Tyne (BA Hons English Lang. and Lit.). Reporter, BBC TV News, 1975–80; Presenter, Granada TV, 1981; Producer, 1983–88, Editor, 1988–89, World in Action; Head of Regl Progs, Granada, 1989–90; Man. Dir, North East TV, 1990–91; Head of Factual Progs, Granada, 1992. *Publications:* A Power in the Land, 1988; The Lazarus File, 1989. *Recreations:* cycling, cinema, music. *Address:* ITV Network Centre, 200 Gray's Inn Road, WC1X 8HF. *T:* 0171–843 8107.

PRELOG, Prof. Dr Vladimir; Professor of Organic Chemistry, Swiss Federal Institute of Technology, 1950–76, retired; *b* 23 July 1906; *m* 1933, Kamila Vitek; one *s*. *Educ:* Inst. of Technology, Prague. Chemist, Prague, 1929–34; Lecturer and Professor, University of Zagreb, 1935–41. Privatdozent, Swiss Federal Inst. of Technology, Zürich, 1941; Associate Professor, 1947, Full Professor, 1950. Mem. Bd, CIBA-GEIGY Ltd, Basel, 1960–78. Vis. Prof. of Chemistry, Univ. of Cambridge, 1974. Mem. Leopoldina, Halle/Saale, 1963; Hon. Member: American Acad. of Arts and Sciences, 1960; Chem. Society, 1960; Nat. Acad. of Sciences, Washington, 1961; Royal Irish Acad., Dublin, 1971; Foreign Member: Royal Society, 1962; Acad. of Sciences, USSR, 1966; Acad. dei Lincei, Roma 1965; Istituto Lombardo, Milano, 1964; Royal Danish Acad. of Sciences, 1971; Amer. Philosophical Soc. Philadelphia, 1976; Acad. Sciences, Paris, 1981; Mem., Papal Acad. of Science, 1986–. Dr *hc*: Universities of: Zagreb, 1954; Liverpool, 1963; Paris, 1963; Bruxelles, 1969; Weizmann Inst., Rehovot, 1985. Hon. DSc: Cambridge, 1969; Manchester, 1977; Inst. Quimico Sarria, Barcelona, 1978; Edvard Kardelj Univ. of Ljubljana, 1989; Univ. of Osijek, 1989; Prague Inst. of Chemical Technol., 1992. Davy Medal, Royal Society, 1967; A. W. Hofmann Medal, Gesell. deutscher Chem., 1967; Marcel Benoist Prize, 1965; Roger Adams Award, 1969; (jtly) Nobel Prize for Chemistry, 1975. Order of Rising Sun, Japan, 1977; Order of Yugoslav Star, 1977; Order of Yugoslav Banner with Golden Wreath, 1986. *Publications:* numerous scientific papers, mainly in Helvetica chimica acta. *Address:* (office) Laboratorium für organische Chemie, ETH-Zentrum, Universitätstrasse 16, 8092 Zürich, Switzerland; (home) Bellariastrasse 33, 8002 Zürich. *T:* (1) 2021781.

PRENDERGAST, (Christopher) Anthony, CBE 1981; DL; Chairman, Dolphin Square Trust Ltd, since 1967; Director General, Location of Industry Bureau Ltd, since 1983; an Underwriting Member of Lloyd's; *b* 4 May 1931; *s* of Maurice Prendergast, AINA, and Winifred Mary Prendergast, Falmouth; *m* 1959, Simone Ruth Laski (*see* Dame S. R. Prendergast); one *s*. *Educ:* Falmouth Grammar School. Westminster City Council: Mem., 1959–90; Chairman: Housing Cttee, 1962–65; Health Cttee, 1965–68; Town Planning Cttee, 1972–75, 1976–78; Gen. Purposes Cttee, 1978–80; Management Services, 1981–83; Licensing Sub Cttee, 1983–90; Lord Mayor and Dep. High Steward of Westminster, 1968–69; High Sheriff of Greater London, 1980. Additional Mem., GLC (Covent Garden Cttee), 1971–75; Member: London Boroughs Trng Cttee, 1965–68; Docklands Develt Cttee, 1974; AMA Cttee, 1976–89; Nat Jt Council (Manual Workers), 1978–82, 1983–89; Conf. of Regl and Local Auths of Europe, 1983–89. Chairman: Location of Offices Bureau, 1971–79; LACSAB, 1983–89; Joint Negotiating Cttee for Chief Execs of Local Authorities, 1984–89, for Chief Officers of Local Authorities, 1984–89; Gen. Purposes Cttee, London Boroughs Assoc., 1986–90. Mem., LEB, 1983–89; Dir, LE plc, 1990–94. Governor, Westminster Sch., 1974–. Master, Pattenmakers' Co., 1983–84. DL Greater London, 1988. FRSA 1984. *Recreations:* fishing, shooting, photography. *Address:* 52 Warwick Square, SW1V 2AJ. *T:* 0171–821 7653. *Clubs:* Carlton, Brooks's, Irish; MCC.

PRENDERGAST, Sir Kieran; *see* Prendergast, Sir W. K.

PRENDERGAST, Robert James Christie Vereker; His Honour Judge Prendergast; a Circuit Judge, since 1989; *b* 21 Oct. 1941; *s* of Richard Henry Prendergast and Jean (*née* Christie); *m* 1971, Berit, (Bibi), Thauland; one *d. Educ:* Downside; Trinity Coll., Cambridge (BA (Hons) Law; MA). Called to the Bar, Middle Temple, 1964; Harmsworth Law Schol.; S Eastern Circuit, 1964–89; an Asst Recorder, 1984–87; a Recorder, 1987–89. Chm., NE London Crown Court Liaison Cttee, 1984–89. Mem., S Eastern Circuit Wine Cttee, 1987–89. *Recreations:* most gentle pursuits. *Address:* 9 King's Bench Walk, Temple, EC4Y 7DX. *T:* 071–353 5638.

PRENDERGAST, Dame Simone (Ruth), DBE 1986 (OBE 1981); JP, DL; *b* 2 July 1930; *d* of late Mrs Neville Blond, OBE and late Norman Laski; *m* 1st, 1953, Albert Kaplan (marr. diss. 1957); 2nd, 1959, Christopher Anthony Prendergast, *qv*; one *s. Educ:* Queen's College; Cheltenham Ladies' College. Lady Mayoress of Westminster, 1968–69; Member: Lord Chancellor's Adv. Cttee for Inner London, 1981–91; Solicitors' Disciplinary Tribunal, 1986–; E London and Bethnal Green Housing Assoc., 1988–90; Exec. Cttee, Westminster Children's Soc., 1970– (Chm., 1980–90); Chairman: Greater London Area Nat. Union of Conservative Assocs, 1984–87; Blond McIndoe Centre for Med. Research, 1986–; Jewish Refugees Cttee, 1980–; Vice-Chm., Age Concern, Westminster, 1989–; Mem. Council, 1969–, Jt Treas., 1991–, Central British Fund for World Jewish Relief. Mem. Court of Patrons, RCS, 1987. FRSA 1988. JP Inner London 1971; DL Greater London 1982. Associate CStJ 1982. *Recreation:* gardening. *Address:* 52 Warwick Square, SW1V 2AJ. *T:* 071–821 7653.

PRENDERGAST, Sir (Walter) Kieran, KCVO 1991; CMG 1990; HM Diplomatic Service; Ambassador to Turkey, since 1995; *b* 2 July 1942; *s* of late Lt-Comdr J. H. Prendergast and Mai Hennessy; *m* 1967, Joan Reynolds; two *s* two *d. Educ:* St Patrick's College, Strathfield, Sydney, NSW; Salesian College, Chertsey; St Edmund Hall, Oxford. Turkish language student Istanbul, 1964; Ankara, 1965; FO (later FCO), 1967; 2nd Sec. Nicosia, 1969; Civil Service Coll., 1972; 1st Sec. FCO, 1972; The Hague, 1973; Asst Private Sec. to Foreign and Commonwealth Sec. (Rt Hon. Anthony Crosland, Rt Hon. Dr David Owen), 1976; UK Mission to UN, NY, 1979 (detached for duty Jan.–March 1980 at Govt House, Salisbury); Counsellor, Tel Aviv, 1982; Head of Southern African Dept, FCO, 1986–89; High Comr to Zimbabwe, 1989–92; High Comr to Kenya, 1992–95. Rhodesia Medal, 1980; Zimbabwe Independence Medal, 1980. *Recreations:* family, walking, reading, shooting, wine. *Address:* c/o Foreign and Commonwealth Office, SW1A 2AH. *Clubs:* Beefsteak; Muthaiga (Nairobi).

PRENTICE, family name of **Baron Prentice.**

PRENTICE, Baron *cr* 1992 (Life Peer), of Daventry in the County of Northamptonshire; **Reginald Ernest Prentice,** Kt 1987; PC 1966; JP; company director and public affairs consultant; *b* 16 July 1923; *s* of Ernest George and Elizabeth Prentice; *m* 1948, Joan Godwin; one *d. Educ:* Whitgift Sch.; London School of Economics. Temporary Civil Servant, 1940–42; RA, 1942–46; commissioned 1943; served in Italy and Austria, 1944–46. Student at LSE, 1946–49. BSc (Econ). Member staff of Transport and General Workers' Union, Asst to Legal Secretary; in charge of Union's Advice and Service Bureau, 1950–57. MP (Lab): E Ham N, May 1957–1974, Newham NE, 1974–Oct. 1977; MP (C): Newham NE, Oct. 1977–1979; Daventry, 1979–87; Minister of State, Department of Education and Science, 1964–66; Minister of Public Building and Works, 1966–67; Minister of Overseas Develt, 1967–69; Opposition Spokesman on Employment, 1972–74; Sec. of State for Educn and Science, 1974–75; Minister for Overseas Develt, 1975–76; Minister of State (Minister for Social Security), DHSS, 1979–81. Exec. Mem. Cttee, Nat. Union of Cons. Assocs, 1988–90. Alderman, GLC, 1970–71. JP County Borough of Croydon, 1961. *Publications:* (jt) Social Welfare and the Citizen, 1957; Right Turn, 1978. *Recreations:* walking, golf. *Address:* Wansdyke, Church Lane, Mildenhall, Marlborough, Wilts SN8 2LU. *Club:* Carlton.

PRENTICE, Bridget Theresa, JP; MP (Lab) Lewisham East, since 1992; *b* 28 Dec. 1952; *d* of James and Bridget Corr; *m* 1975, Gordon Prentice, *qv. Educ:* Glasgow Univ. (MA English Lit. and Mod. Hist.); London University: Avery Hill Coll. (PGCE); Southlands Coll. (Adv. Dip. in Careers Educn and Guidance); South Bank Univ. (LLB 1992). Teacher, ILEA, 1974–88. Councillor, Hammersmith and Fulham London BC, 1986–92. JP Inner London, 1985. *Recreations:* music, reading, crosswords, knitting, my two cats. *Address:* 37 Chalcroft Road, SE13 5RE. *T:* 0181–318 2711.

PRENTICE, Prof. Daniel David; Allen & Overy Professor of Corporate Law, Oxford University, since 1991; Fellow of Pembroke College, Oxford; *b* 7 Aug. 1941; *s* of Thomas James Prentice and Agnes Prentice (*née* Fox); *m* 1965, Judith Mary Keane; one *s* one *d. Educ:* St Malachy's Coll., Belfast; Queen's Univ., Belfast (LLB); Univ. of Chicago (JD); MA Oxford (by special resolution). Called to the Bar, Lincoln's Inn, 1982. Associate Prof., Univ. of Ontario, 1966–68; Lectr, UCL, 1968–73; Lectr, 1973–90, Reader, 1991, Univ. of Oxford. Vis. Prof., various univs. Asst. Editor, Law Qly Rev., 1988–. *Publication:* (ed) Chitty, Law of Contracts, 25th edn 1983, 26th edn 1989. *Recreation:* squash. *Address:* Pembroke College, Oxford OX1 1DW. *T:* Oxford (01865) 276438.

PRENTICE, Gordon; MP (Lab) Pendle, since 1992; *b* 28 Jan. 1951; *s* of Esther and William Prentice; *m* 1975, Bridget Theresa Prentice, *qv. Educ:* Univ. of Glasgow (MA; Pres., Glasgow Univ. Union, 1972–73). Mercury House Publications, 1974–78; Local Govt Officer, 1978–81; Labour Party Policy Directorate, 1982–92 (Asst Local Govt Officer and Local Govt Officer). Mem. Council, London Borough of Hammersmith and Fulham, 1982–90 (Leader of Council, 1986–88). *Recreations:* cooking, gardening. *Address:* House of Commons, SW1A 0AA. *T:* 0171–219 3000.

PRENTICE, (Hubert Archibald) John, CEng; FInstP; consultant on manufacturing and management strategies to several UK and USA companies; *b* 5 Feb. 1920; *s* of Charles Herbert Prentice and Rose Prentice; *m* 1947, Sylvia Doreen Elias; one *s. Educ:* Woolwich Polytechnic, London; Salford Univ. (BSc, MSc). CEng; MRAeS 1962; FInstP 1967. Min. of Supply, 1939–56; R&D posts, res. estabts and prodn, MoD, 1956–60; Space Dept, RAE, Min. of Aviation, 1960–67; Head, Road User Characteristics Res., 1967–70, and Head, Driver Aids and Abilities Res., 1970–72, MoT; Head, Road User Dynamics Res., DoE, 1972–75; Counsellor (Sci. and Technol.), British Embassy, Tokyo, 1975–80. *Recreations:* walking, climbing. *Address:* 5 Foxhill Crescent, Camberley, Surrey GU15 1PR. *T:* Camberley (01276) 66373.

PRENTICE, Thomas, MC 1945; Life President, Harrisons & Crosfield plc, since 1988 (Chairman, 1977–88); *b* 14 Oct. 1919; *s* of Alexander and Jean Young Prentice; *m* 1949, Peggy Ann Lloyd; two *s* two *d. Educ:* McLaren High Sch., Callander, Perthshire. Served Army, 1939–46. Harrisons & Crosfield (Sabah) Sdn. Bhd., Malaysia, 1947–67; Harrisons & Crosfield plc, 1967–. *Recreations:* golf, gardening. *Address:* Harrisons & Crosfield plc, One Great Tower Street, EC3R 5AH. *Club:* East India, Devonshire, Sports and Public Schools.

PRENTICE, Hon. Sir William (Thomas), Kt 1977; MBE 1945; Senior Member, Administrative Appeals Tribunal, Australia, 1981–87; *b* 1 June 1919; *s* of Claud Stanley and Pauline Prentice; *m* 1946, Mary Elizabeth, *d* of F. B. Dignam; three *s* one *d. Educ:* St Joseph's College, Hunters Hill; Sydney Univ. (BA, LLB). AIF, Middle East and New Guinea, 2–33 Inf. Bn and Staff Captain 25 Aust. Inf. Bde, Owen Stanleys and Lae Ramu campaigns; Staff Course, Duntroon, 1944; Staff Captain, 7 Aust. Inf. Bde, Bougainville campaign, 1944–45. Resumed law studies, 1946; admitted Bar, NSW, 1947; Judge, Supreme Court, PNG, 1970; Senior Puisne Judge, 1975; Deputy Chief Justice on independence, PNG, 1975, Chief Justice 1978–80. *Recreations:* bush walking, swimming, reading. *Address:* 16 Olympia Road, Naremburn, NSW 2065, Australia. *Clubs:* Tattersall's, Cricketers' (Sydney).

PRENTICE, Dame Winifred (Eva), DBE 1977 (OBE 1972); SRN; President, Royal College of Nursing, 1972–76; *b* 2 Dec. 1910; *d* of Percy John Prentice and Anna Eva Prentice. *Educ:* Northgate Sch. for Girls, Ipswich; E Suffolk and Ipswich Hosp. (SRN); W Mddx Hosp. (SCM Pt I); Queen Elizabeth Coll., London Univ. (RNT); Dip. in Nursing, London Univ. Ward Sister: E Suffolk and Ipswich Hosp., 1936–39; Essex County Hosp., 1941–43; Nurse Tutor, King's Lynn Hosp., 1944–46; Principal Tutor, Stracathro Hosp., Brechin, Angus, 1947–61, Matron, 1961–72. *Publications:* articles in Nursing Times and Nursing Mirror. *Recreations:* music, amateur dramatics, gardening. *Address:* Marleish, 4 Duke Street, Brechin, Angus DD9 6JY. *T:* Brechin (013562) 2606. *Club:* New Cavendish.

PRESCOTT, John Barry; Managing Director and Chief Executive Officer, The Broken Hill Pty Co. Ltd, since 1991; *b* 22 Oct. 1940; *s* of late John Norman Prescott and Margaret Ellen (*née* Brownie); *m* 1985, Jennifer Cahill; one *s* three *d. Educ:* N Sydney Boys' High Sch.; Univ. of NSW (BComm Industrial Relns). Joined The Broken Hill Pty Co. Ltd as Industrial Relns Trainee, 1958: various industrial relns positions, 1958–69; Superintendent, Industrial Relns, Shipping and Stevedoring, Newcastle and Sydney, 1969–74; Asst Fleet Manager, Ops, Newcastle, 1974–79; Exec. Asst to Gen. Manager, Transport, 1979–80; Manager Ops, Transport, 1980–82; Gen. Manager, Transport, 1982–87; Exec. Gen. Manager and Chief Exec. Officer, BHP Steel, 1987–91. Hon. LLD Monash, 1994. *Recreations:* tennis, golf, carpentry. *Address:* The Broken Hill Pty Co. Ltd, BHP Tower, Bourke Place, 600 Bourke Street, Melbourne, Vic 3000, Australia. *T:* (3) 96093333. *Clubs:* Australian, Melbourne, Huntingdale Golf (Melbourne); Newcastle (Newcastle).

PRESCOTT, Prof. John Herbert Dudley, PhD; FIBiol; FRAgS; Principal, Wye College, University of London, since 1988; *b* 21 Feb. 1937; *s* of Herbert Prescott and Edith Vera Prescott; *m* 1960, Diana Margaret Mullock; two *s* two *d. Educ:* Haileybury; Univ. of Nottingham (BSc (Agric), PhD). FIBiol 1983; FRAgS 1986. Lectr in Animal Prodn, Univ. of Newcastle upon Tyne, 1963–72; Animal Prodn Officer in Argentina, FAO, UN, 1972–74; Head of Animal Prodn Advisory and Develt, E of Scotland Coll. of Agric., 1974–78; Prof. of Animal Prodn, 1978–84, and Head of Animal Div., 1978–84, Sch. of Agric., Univ. of Edinburgh; Dir, Grassland, later Animal and Grassland, Res. Inst., 1984–86; Dir, Grassland and Animal Prodn Res., AFRC, 1986–88. Vis. Prof., Univ. of Reading, 1985–88; Vis. Prof., UCW, Aberystwyth, 1988. *Publications:* scientific papers in Animal Prodn and Agricultural Science; technical articles. *Recreations:* farming, walking, wildlife, the countryside. *Address:* Wye College, University of London, Wye, Ashford, Kent TN25 5AH.

PRESCOTT, Rt. Hon. John (Leslie); PC 1994; MP (Lab) Hull East, since 1983 (Kingston upon Hull (East), 1970–83); Deputy Leader of the Labour Party, since 1994; *b* 31 May 1938; *s* of John Herbert Prescott, JP, and Phyllis Prescott; *m* 1961, Pauline Tilston; two *s. Educ:* Ellesmere Port Secondary Modern Sch.; WEA; correspondence courses; Ruskin Coll., Oxford (DipEcon/Pol Oxon); Hull Univ. (BSc Econ). Trainee Chef, 1953–55; Steward, Passenger Lines, Merchant Navy, 1955–63; Ruskin Coll., Oxford, 1963–65; Recruitment Officer, General and Municipal Workers Union (temp.), 1965; Hull Univ., 1965–68. Contested (Lab) Southport, 1966; Full-time Official, National Union of Seamen, 1968–70. PPS to Sec. of State for Trade, 1974–76; opposition spokesman on Transport, 1979–81; opposition front bench spokesman on Regional Affairs and Devolution, 1981–83, on Transport, 1983–84 and 1988–93, on Employment, 1984–87 and 1993–94, on Energy, 1987–88; Mem., Shadow Cabinet, 1983–. Member: Select Cttee Nationalized Industries, 1973–79; Council of Europe, 1972–75; European Parlt, 1975–79 (Leader, Labour Party Delegn, 1976–79). Mem., NEC, Labour Party, 1989–. *Publication:* Not Wanted on Voyage, 1966. *Address:* House of Commons, SW1A 0AA.

PRESCOTT, Sir Mark, 3rd Bt, *cr* 1938, of Godmanchester; Racehorse Trainer, in Newmarket; *b* 3 March 1948; *s* of late Major W. R. Stanley Prescott (MP for Darwen Div., 1943–51; 2nd *s* of Colonel Sir William Prescott, 1st Bt) and Gwendolen (who *m* 2nd, 1952, Daniel Orme (*d* 1972); she *d* 1992), *o c* of late Leonard Aldridge, CBE; *S* uncle, Sir Richard Stanley Prescott, 2nd Bt, 1965. *Educ:* Harrow. *Address:* Heath House, Moulton Road, Newmarket, Suffolk CB8 8DU. *T:* Newmarket (01638) 662117.

PRESCOTT, Brig. Peter George Addington, MC 1944; Secretary, National Rifle Association, 1980–88; *b* 22 Sept. 1924; *s* of Col and Mrs John Prescott; *m* 1953, June Marian Louise Wendell; one *s* one *d. Educ:* Eton Coll.; Staff Coll. (psc 1957); Royal Coll. of Defence Studies (rcds 1973). Commnd Grenadier Guards, 1943; 2nd Armoured Bn Gren. Gds, 1944–45; comd 2nd Bn Gren. Gds, 1966–69; Comdr 51st Inf. Bde, 1970–72; Dep. Comdr NE Dist, 1974–77; Dep. Dir of Army Trng, 1977–79, retd. Chevalier, Royal Order of the Sword, Sweden, 1954. *Recreations:* sailing, painting, gardening. *Address:* The Bourne, Church Lane, Holybourne, Alton, Hants GU34 4HD.

PRESCOTT, Peter John; Director, Arts Division, British Council, 1990–93, retired; *b* 6 April 1936; *s* of Wentworth James Prescott and Ellen Marie (*née* Burrows); *m* 1971, Gillian Eileen Lowe. *Educ:* Windsor Grammar School; Pembroke College, Oxford (MA). Joined British Council, 1963; Asst Cultural Attaché, Egypt, 1963–67; London, 1967–70; Sussex Univ., 1970–71; France, 1971–75; London, 1975–79; on secondment to Dept of Education and Science, 1979–81; Australia, 1981–84; Rep., France, and Cultural Counsellor, British Embassy, Paris, 1984–90. *Recreations:* reading, music, theatre, walking, swimming, travel. *Address:* 6/22 Greville Place, NW6 5JG. *T:* 0171–624 6269.

PRESCOTT, Peter Richard Kyle; QC 1990; *b* 23 Jan. 1943; *s* of Richard Stanley Prescott and Sarah Aitchison Shand; *m* 1967, Frances Rosemary Bland; two *s* one *d. Educ:* St George's Coll., Argentina; Dulwich Coll.; University Coll. London (BSc); Queen Mary Coll., London (MSc). Called to the Bar, Lincoln's Inn, 1970. *Publication:* The Modern Law of Copyright (with Hugh Laddie, QC, and Mary Vitoria), 1980, 2nd edn 1995. *Recreations:* music, flying, reading, cooking. *Address:* 8 New Square, Lincoln's Inn, WC2A 3QP. *T:* 0171–405 4321.

PRESCOTT, Westby William P.; *see* Percival-Prescott.

PRESS, Dr Frank; Cecil and Ida Green Senior Fellow, Carnegie Institution of Washington, since 1993; *b* 4 Dec. 1924; *m* 1946, Billie Kallick; one *s* one *d. Educ:* City Coll., NY (BS 1944); Columbia Univ. (MA 1946; PhD 1949). Columbia University: Res. Associate, 1946–49; Instr in Geology, 1949–51; Asst Prof. of Geology, 1951–52; Associate Prof., 1952–55; Prof. of Geophysics, 1955–65 and Dir, Seismol. Lab., 1957–65, CIT; Prof. of Geophysics and Chm., Dept of Earth and Planetary Scis, MIT, 1965–77; Sci. Advisor to Pres. and Dir, Office of Sci. and Tech. Policy, 1977–80; Prof., MIT, 1981; Pres., NAS, 1981–93. Member: President's Sci. Adv. Commn, 1961–64; Nat. Sci. Bd, 1970–; Lunar and Planetary Missions Bd, NASA; participant, bilateral scis agreement with Peoples Republic of China and USSR; US Deleg. to Nuclear Test Ban Negotiations, Geneva and Moscow. Mem., Acad. of Arts and Scis, and other US and internat. bodies. Numerous awards, incl. Japan Prize, Sci. and Technol. Foundn of Japan, 1993, US Nat. Medal of Science, 1994, and hon. degrees. Officer, Legion of Honour, 1989. *Publications:* (jtly) Propagation of Elastic Waves in Layered Media, 1957; (ed jtly) Physics and Chemistry of the Earth, 1957; (jtly) Earth, 1986; Understanding Earth, 1994; numerous papers. *Address:* c/o Carnegie Institution of Washington, 5241 Broad Branch Road, NW, Washington, DC 20015, USA.

PRESS, John Bryant, FRSL; author and poet; *b* 11 Jan. 1920; *s* of late Edward Kenneth Press and late Gladys (*née* Cooper); *m* 1947, Janet Crompton; one *s* one *d*. *Educ:* King Edward VI Sch., Norwich; Corpus Christi Coll., Cambridge, 1938–40 and 1945–46. Served War of 1939–45: RA, 1940–45. British Council, 1946–79: Athens, 1946–47; Salonika, 1947–50; Madras, 1950–51; Colombo, 1951–52; Birmingham, 1952–54; Cambridge, 1955–62; London, 1962–65; Paris, 1966–71 (also Cultural Attaché, British Embassy); Regional Dir, Oxford, 1972–78; Literature Advr, London, 1978–79. Mem. Council, RSL, 1961–88. Gave George Elliston Poetry Foundation Lectures at Univ. of Cincinnati, 1962; Vis. Prof., Univ. of Paris, 1981–82. *Publications:* The Fire and the Fountain, 1955; Uncertainties, 1956; (ed) Poetic Heritage, 1957; The Chequer'd Shade, 1958 (RSL Heinemann Award); Andrew Marvell, 1958; Guy Fawkes Night, 1959; Herrick, 1961; Rule and Energy, 1963; Louis MacNeice, 1964; (ed) Palgrave's Golden Treasury, Book V, 1964, Book VI, 1994; A Map of Modern English Verse, 1969; The Lengthening Shadows, 1971; John Betjeman, 1974; Spring at St Clair, 1974; Aspects of Paris, (with illus by Gordon Bradshaw), 1975; (with Edward Lowbury and Michael Riviere) Troika, 1977; Poets of World War I, 1983; Poets of World War II, 1984; A Girl with Beehive Hair, 1986. Libretto, new version of Bluebeard's Castle, for Michael Powell's colour television film of Bartok's opera, 1963. *Recreations:* travel (especially in France), theatre, opera, concerts, cinema; architecture and visual arts; watching football and cricket. *Address:* 5 South Parade, Frome BA11 1EJ. *T:* Frome (01373) 461142.

PRESSMAN, Mrs J. J.; *see* Colbert, Claudette.

PRESTON; *see* Campbell-Preston.

PRESTON, family name of **Viscount Gormanston.**

PRESTON, Geoffrey Averill; Assistant Counsel to Chairman of Committees, House of Lords, 1982–89; *b* 19 May 1924; *s* of George and Winifred Preston; *m* 1953, Catherine Wright. *Educ:* St Marylebone Grammar Sch. Barrister-at-Law. Served, RNVR, 1942–46. Called to Bar, Gray's Inn, 1950. Treasury Solicitor's Dept, 1952–71; Solicitor's Department: Dept of Environment, 1971–74; Dept of Trade, 1974–75; Under-Sec. (Legal), Dept of Trade, 1975–82. *Recreations:* gardening, carpentry, chess. *Address:* Ledsham, Glaziers Lane, Normandy, Surrey GU3 2DQ. *T:* Guildford (01483) 811250.

PRESTON, Dr Ian Mathieson Hamilton, CBE 1993; FEng 1982; FIEE; Chairman: Mining Scotland, since 1995; (designate) East of Scotland Water Authority, since 1995; *b* 18 July 1932; *s* of John Hamilton Preston and Edna Irene Paul; *m* 1958, Sheila Hope Pringle; two *s*. *Educ:* Univ. of Glasgow (BSc 1st cl. Hons; PhD). MInstP 1959; FIEE 1974. Asst Lectr, Univ. of Glasgow, 1959–65; joined SSEB, 1965, Chief Engineer, Generator Design and Construction, 1972–77; Dir Gen., Generation Develt and Construction Div., CEGB, 1977–83; Dep. Chm., SSEB, 1983–90; Chief Exec., Scottish Power, 1990–95. Director: Morgan Grenfell (Scotland), 1994–; Clydeport plc, 1994–; Motherwell Bridge, 1995–. Chm., Scottish Council Develt and Industry, 1992–. *Recreations:* fishing, gardening. *Address:* 10 Cameron Crescent, Carmunnock, Glasgow G76 9DX.

PRESTON, Jeffrey William, CB 1989; Deputy Director General, Office of Fair Trading, since 1990 (Acting Director General, 1995); *b* 28 Jan. 1940; *s* of William and Sybil Grace Preston (*née* Lawson). *Educ:* Liverpool Collegiate Sch.; Hertford Coll., Oxford (MA 1966). Asst Principal, Min. of Aviation, 1963; Private Sec. to Permanent Sec., BoT, 1966; Principal: BoT, 1967; HM Treasury, 1970; DTI, 1973; Asst Sec., Dept of Trade, 1975–82; Under Sec. and Regional Dir, Yorks and Humberside Region, DTI, 1982–85; Dep. Sec., Industrial and Economic Affairs, Welsh Office, 1985–90. Chm., Hertford Soc., 1987–. *Recreations:* motoring, opera, swimming. *Address:* Office of Fair Trading, Field House, Bream's Buildings, EC4A 1PR. *T:* 0171–269 8921. *Clubs:* United Oxford & Cambridge University.

PRESTON, Kieran Thomas, FCIT; Director General, West Yorkshire Passenger Transport Executive, since 1993; *b* 30 Nov. 1950; *s* of Charles Edward Preston and Mary Kate Preston; *m* 1974, Denise Marie Gregory; two *s*. *Educ:* Leeds Poly. (BA Hons Mgt and Admin). FCIT 1994. Local Govt Officer, various appts, 1972–89; Leeds City Council: Projects Dir, 1989–91; Actg Dir of Admin, 1991–92; Chief Services Officer, 1992–93. FIPD 1992. *Recreations:* keeping fit, horse riding, playing and watching football, cricket. *Address:* West Yorkshire Passenger Transport Executive, Wellington House, 40–50 Wellington Street, Leeds LS1 2DE; 15 Morritt Avenue, Leeds LS15 7EP. *T:* Leeds (0113) 260 9093.

PRESTON, Michael Richard, ATD; FCSD; consultant designer; *b* 15 Oct. 1927; *s* of Major Frederick Allan Preston, MC and Winifred Gertrude (*née* Archer); *m* 1st, 1955, Anne Gillespie Smith; 2nd, 1980, Judith Gaye James. *Educ:* Whitgift Sch.; Guildford Sch. of Art; Goldsmiths' Coll., London Univ. (NDD 1953; ATD 1954); Dip. in Humanities (London) 1964. FCSD (FSIAD 1972; MSIAD 1953). Served HM Forces, Queen's Royal Regt, 1944–48, Queen's Royal Regt, TA & HAC, 1948–61. Asst Art Master, Whitgift Sch., 1954–55; Drawing Master, Dulwich Coll., 1955–64; Science Mus., 1964–87; Head of Design, 1964–86; Keeper, Dept of Museum Services, 1987; designed exhibitions, including: Centenary of Charles Babbage, 1971; A Word to the Mermaids, 1973; Tower Bridge Observed, 1974; The Breath of Life, 1974; Nat. Rly Mus., York, 1975; Sci. and Technol. of Islam, 1976; Nat. Mus. of Photography, Bradford, 1977–83; Stanley Spencer in the Shipyard, 1979; Wellcome Mus. of Hist. of Medicine, 1980; Sci. and Technol. of India, 1982; The Great Cover-up Show, 1982; Beads of Glass, 1983; Louis Pasteur and Rabies, 1985. Advisory Assignments on Museum Projects: Iran, 1976–79; Spain, 1977–80; Germany, 1978–79; Canada, 1979–82, 1984–86; Trinidad, 1982–83; Turkey, 1984–94; Hong Kong, 1985; consultant to: Dean and Chapter of Canterbury, 1987–; Wellcome Foundn, 1987–; TAVRA Greater London, 1988–94; Mus. of East Asian Art (formerly Mus. of Far Eastern Antiquities), Bath, 1988–93; Design Expo '89, Nagoya; Bank of England Museum, 1989; Norwich Tourism Agency, 1989–91; Tricycle Theatre, 1989–90; Nat. Theatre, 1989–90; Scottish Office, 1990; English Heritage, 1990; Richmond Theatre, 1990; Accademia Italiana, 1990–94; Société Générale, 1992–; Castrol Internat., 1994–95. Mem., BTEC Validation Panel, 1986–92. Chm., Greenwich Soc., 1961–64. Society of Industrial Artists and Designers: Vice-Pres., 1976, 1979–81; Chm., Membership Bd, 1976–79; Chm., Design Management Panel, 1976–80. Mem., ICOM, 1964–. Trustee, Vivat Trust, 1989–92. Hon. Keeper of Pictures, Arts Club, 1992–. Vis. Prof., NID, Ahmedabad, 1989–. Guild of Glass Engravers: Hon. FGGE 1980; Pres., 1986–92. FRSA 1955–68. *Recreations:* travel, food, conversation, jazz. *Address:* 37 Walham Grove, SW6 1QR. *T:* 0171–381 4363. *Club:* Arts.

PRESTON, Myles Park; HM Diplomatic Service, retired; *b* 4 April 1927; *s* of Robert and Marie Preston; *m* 1st, 1951, Ann Betten (marr. diss.); one *s* one *d*; 2nd, 1981, Joy Moore (*née* Fisher). *Educ:* Sudley Road Council Sch.; Liverpool Inst. High Sch.; Clare Coll., Cambridge. Instructor Lieut, RN, 1948–51; Asst Principal, Admty, 1951–53; CRO, 1953–54; 2nd Sec., British High Commn, New Delhi, 1954–56; 1st Sec., CRO, 1956–59; 1st Sec., Governor-General's Office and British High Commn, Lagos, 1959–62; CRO, 1962–64; 1st Sec., British High Commn, Kampala, 1964–67; Commonwealth Office and FCO, 1967–69; Counsellor and Consul-Gen., Djakarta, 1969–72; Canadian Nat. Defence Coll., 1972–73; FCO, 1973–77; Dep. Governor, Solomon Islands, 1977–78; Consul-Gen., Vancouver, 1978–79. *Address:* 20 Prince Edwards Road, Lewes, East Sussex BN7 1BE. *T:* Lewes (01273) 475809.

PRESTON, Prof. Paul, FRHistS; FBA 1994; Professor of International History, London School of Economics, since 1991; *b* 21 July 1946; *s* of Charles Ronald Preston and Alice Hoskisson; *m* 1983, Gabrielle Patricia Ashford-Hodges; two *s*. *Educ:* St Edward's Coll., Liverpool; Oriel Coll., Oxford. Lectr in Modern History, Univ. of Reading, 1974–75; Queen Mary College, University of London: Lectr and Reader in Modern History, 1975–85; Prof. of History, 1985–91. Comendador de la Orden de Mérito Civil (Spain), 1986. *Publications:* (ed) Spain in Crisis, 1976; The Coming of the Spanish Civil War, 1978, 2nd edn 1994; (ed) Revolution and War in Spain 1931–1939, 1984; (with Denis Smyth) Spain, the EEC and NATO, 1984; The Triumph of Democracy in Spain, 1986; The Spanish Civil War 1936–1939, 1986; The Politics of Revenge, 1990; Franco, 1993. *Recreations:* classical music, opera, modern fiction, wine. *Address:* Department of International History, London School of Economics, Houghton Street, WC2A 2AE. *T:* 0171–955 7107.

PRESTON, Peter John; Editor-in-chief and Chairman, The Guardian and The Observer, since 1995; *b* 23 May 1938; *s* of John Whittle Preston and Kathlyn (*née* Chell); *m* 1962, Jean Mary Burrell; two *s* two *d*. *Educ:* Loughborough Grammar Sch.; St John's Coll., Oxford (MA EngLit). Editorial trainee, Liverpool Daily Post, 1960–63; Guardian: Political Reporter, 1963–64; Education Correspondent, 1965–66; Diary Editor, 1966–68; Features Editor, 1968–72; Production Editor, 1972–75; Editor, 1975–95. British Exec. Chm., IPI, 1988–. Hon. DLitt Loughborough, 1982; DU Essex, 1994. *Recreations:* football, films; four children. *Address:* The Guardian, 119 Farringdon Road, EC1R 3ER.

PRESTON, Sir Peter (Sansome), KCB 1978 (CB 1973); Permanent Secretary, Overseas Development Administration, Foreign and Commonwealth Office (formerly Ministry of Overseas Development), 1976–82; *b* Nottingham, 18 Jan. 1922; *s* of Charles Guy Preston, Solicitor; *m* 1951, Marjory Harrison; two *s* three *d*. *Educ:* Nottingham High School. War Service, RAF, 1942–46; Board of Trade: Exec. Officer, 1947; Higher Exec. Off., 1950; Asst Principal, 1951; Principal, 1953; Trade Comr, New Delhi, 1959; Asst Sec., 1964; idc 1968; Under-Sec., BoT later DTI, 1969–72; Dep. Sec., Dept of Trade, 1972–76. Mem., BOTB, 1975–76. Dir, Wellcome Internat. Trading Co. Ltd, 1985–92; Dep. Chm., CARE Britain, 1985–95. *Address:* 5 Greville Park Avenue, Ashtead, Surrey KT21 2QS. *T:* Ashtead (01372) 272099.

PRESTON, Prof. Reginald Dawson, FRS 1954; retired; Professor of Plant Biophysics, 1953–73 (now Professor Emeritus), and Head, Astbury Department of Biophysics, 1962–73, University of Leeds; Chairman, School of Biological Sciences, 1970–73; Dean of the Faculty of Science, 1955–58; *b* 21 July 1908; *s* of late Walter C. Preston, builder, and late Eliza Preston; *m* 1935, Sarah J. Pollard (decd); two *d* (one *s* decd); *m* 1963, Dr Eva Frei. *Educ:* Leeds University; Cornell University, USA. BSc (Hons Physics, Class I), 1929; PhD (Botany), 1931; 1851 Exhibition Fellowship, 1932–35; Rockefeller Foundation Fellowship, 1935–36. Lecturer, Botany Dept, Univ. of Leeds, 1936–46; Sen. Lectr, 1946–49; Reader, 1949–53. Vis. Prof. of Botany, Imperial Coll., London, 1976–79. Mem. NY Acad. Sci., 1960. Hon. Mem., Internat. Assoc. of Wood Anatomists, 1981. DSc 1943; CPhys (FInstP 1944); FLS 1958; FIWSc 1960; FIAWS 1973. Anselme Payen Award, Amer. Chem. Soc., 1983; Disting. Service Medal, Leeds Phil. Lit. Soc., 1983. Editor: Proc. Leeds Phil. Soc. Sci. Sec., 1950–74; Advances in Botanical Research, 1968–77; Associate Editor, Jl Exp. Bot., 1950–77. *Publications:* Molecular Architecture of Plant Cell Walls, 1952; Physical Biology of Plant Cell Walls, 1974; about 180 articles in Proc. Roy. Soc., Nature, Ann. Bot., Biochem. Biophys Acta, Jl Exp. Bot., etc. *Recreations:* walking, climbing, music. *Address:* 117 St Anne's Road, Leeds, West Yorks LS6 3NZ. *T:* Leeds (0113) 278 5248.

PRESTON, Sir Ronald (Douglas Hildebrand), 7th Bt *cr* 1815; country landowner and journalist; *b* 9 Oct. 1916; *s* of Sir Thomas Hildebrand Preston, 6th Bt, OBE, and Ella Henrietta (*d* 1989), *d* of F. von Schickendantz; *S* father, 1976; *m* 1st, 1954, Smilya Stefanovic (marr. diss.); 2nd, 1972, Pauleen Jane, *d* of late Paul Lurcott. *Educ:* Westminster School; Trinity Coll., Cambridge (Hons History and Economics, MA); Ecole des Sciences Politiques, Paris. Served War, 1940–46, in Intelligence Corps, reaching rank of Major: Western Desert, Middle East, Italy, Austria, Allied Control Commn, Bulgaria. Reuter's Correspondent, Belgrade, Yugoslavia, 1948–53; The Times Correspondent: Vienna and E Europe, 1953–60; Tokyo and Far East, 1960–63. HM Diplomatic Service, 1963–76; retired, 1976. *Recreations:* shooting, tennis, picture frame making. *Heir: cousin* Philip Charles Henry Hulton Preston [*b* 31 Aug. 1946; *m* 1980, Kirsi Sylvi Annikk, *d* of late Eino Yrjö Pullinen; one *s* two *d*]. *Clubs:* Travellers; Norfolk (Norwich); Tokyo (Tokyo).

PRESTON, Rev. Prof. Ronald Haydn, DD; Professor of Social and Pastoral Theology in the University of Manchester, 1970–80, now Emeritus; *b* 12 March 1913; *o s* of Haydn and Eleanor Jane Preston; *m* 1948, Edith Mary Lindley; one *s* two *d*. *Educ:* London School of Economics, University of London; St Catherine's Coll., Oxford. BSc (Econ.) 1935, Cl. II, Div. I; Industrial Secretary of Student Christian Movement, 1935–38; BA Cl. I Theology, 1940; MA 1944; MA Manchester 1974; BD, DD Oxon 1983. Curate, St John, Park, Sheffield, 1940–43; Study Secretary, Student Christian Movement, 1943–48; Warden of St Anselm Hall, University of Manchester, 1948–63; Lectr in Christian Ethics, Univ. of Manchester, 1948–70; Examining Chaplain: to Bishop of Manchester, 1948–; to Bishop of Sheffield, 1971–80; Canon Residentiary of Manchester Cathedral, 1957–71, Sub-Dean 1970–71, Hon. Canon 1971, Canon Emeritus, 1980. Editor, The Student Movement, 1943–48. *Publications:* (jointly) Christians in Society, 1939; (jointly) The Revelation of St John the Divine, 1949; Technology and Social Justice, 1971; (ed) Industrial Conflicts and their Place in Modern Society, 1974; (ed) Perspectives on Strikes, 1975; (ed) Theology and Change, 1975; Religion and the Persistence of Capitalism, 1979; (ed jtly) The Crisis in British Penology, 1980; Explorations in Theology, No 9, 1981; Church and Society in the late Twentieth Century, 1983; The Future of Christian Ethics, 1987; Religion and the Ambiguities of Capitalism, 1991; (jtly) Christian Capitalism or Christian Socialism?, 1994; Confusions in Christian Social Ethics, 1994; reviews, etc in The Guardian, Theology, etc. *Address:* 161 Old Hall Lane, Manchester M14 6HJ. *T:* 0161–225 3291.

PRESTON, Rosalind, OBE 1993; Vice President, Board of Deputies of British Jews, 1991–94; *b* 29 Dec. 1935; *d* of Benjamin and Marie Morris; *m* 1958, Ronald Preston; one *s* one *d*. *Educ:* Talbot Heath Sch., Bournemouth. Voluntary sector activity, 1960–; Nat. Pres., Nat. Council of Women, 1988–90; Vice Pres., British Br., Women's Internat. Zionist Orgn, 1993–; Co-Vice-Chm., Inter Faith Network for UK, 1994–. Dir (non-exec.), Harrow and Hillingdon Healthcare NHS Trust, 1994–March 1996. FRSA 1990. Paul Harris Fellow, Rotary Internat., 1992. *Recreations:* walking, reading newspapers, family and friends. *Address:* c/o National Council of Women, 36 Danbury Street, N1 8JU.

PRESTON, Simon John; Organist and Master of the Choristers, Westminster Abbey, 1981–87; *b* 4 Aug. 1938. *Educ:* Canford Sch.; King's Coll., Cambridge (Dr Mann Organ Student). BA 1961, MusB 1962, MA 1964. ARCM, FRAM. Sub Organist, Westminster Abbey, 1962–67; Acting Organist, St Albans Abbey, 1968–69; Organist and Lecturer in Music, Christ Church, Oxford, 1970–81. Conductor, Oxford Bach Choir, 1971–74. FRSA. Hon. FRCO 1975; Hon. FRCCO 1986; Hon. FRCM 1986. Edison Award, 1971; Grand Prix du Disque, 1979; Performer of the Year Award, NY Chapter, Amer. Guild of Organists, 1987. *Recreations:* croquet, theatre. *Address:* Little Hardwick, Langton Green, Tunbridge Wells, Kent TN3 0EY. *T:* Tunbridge Wells (01892) 862042.

PRESTON, Timothy William; QC 1982; a Recorder of the Crown Court, since 1979; *b* 3 Nov. 1935; *s* of Charles Frank Preston, LDS, RCS and Frances Mary, *o d* of Captain W. Peters, 5th Lancers; *m* 1965, Barbara Mary Haygarth. *Educ:* Haileybury; Jesus Coll., Oxford (BA 1960). 2/Lieut 16/5 Lancers, 1955; Captain, Staffs Yeomanry, retd. Called to the Bar, Inner Temple, 1964. *Recreations:* hunting, golf. *Address:* 2 Temple Gardens, EC4Y 9AY. *T:* 0171–583 6041. *Club:* Cavalry and Guards.

PRESTON, Walter James, FRICS; Partner, Jones Lang Wootton, 1957–87, Consultant since 1987; *b* 20 March 1925; *s* of Walter Ronald and Agnes Ann McNeil Preston; *m* 1956, Joy Dorothea Ashton; two *s* one *d*. *Educ:* Dollar Academy, Perthshire. Served Royal Engineers, 1943–47. Jones Lang Wootton, 1948–, Staff, 1948–57. Dir (non-exec.), Lynton Property and Reversionary plc, 1985–88. Liveryman: Chartered Surveyors' Co., 1977–; Vintners' Co., 1990–. *Recreation:* golf. *Address:* Barry Lodge, Pond Road, Hook Heath, Woking, Surrey GU22 0JY. *T:* Woking (01483) 763420. *Clubs:* Carlton; Phyllis Court (Henley); Woking Golf; Trevose Golf and Country, St Enodoc Golf (North Cornwall).

PRESTT, His Honour Arthur Miller, QC 1970; a Circuit Judge (formerly Judge of County Courts), 1971–90; Hon. Recorder of Manchester and Senior Circuit Judge, Manchester, 1982–90; *b* 23 April 1925; *s* of Arthur Prestt and Jessie (*née* Miller), Wigan; *m* 1949, Jill Mary, *d* of late Graham Dawbarn, CBE, FRIBA, FRAeS, and of Olive Dawbarn (*née* Topham); one *s* one *d*. *Educ:* Bootham Sch., York; Trinity Hall, Cambridge (MA). Served 13th Bn Parachute Regt, France, Belgium, India, Malaya, Java, 1944–46; Major Legal Staff and War Crimes Prosecutor, 1946–47. Called to Bar, Middle Temple, 1949. Chm., Mental Health Review Tribunal, 1963–70; Dep. Chm., Cumberland QS, 1966–69, Chm., 1970–71. Has held various appts in Scout Assoc. (Silver Acorn, 1970). Pres., SW Lancs Parachute Regt Assoc., 1980–91. JP Cumberland, 1966. 5 years Medal, Ampleforth Lourdes Hospitalite, 1976. *Recreations:* gardening, golf. *Address:* 10 Heigham Grove, Norwich NR2 3DQ. *Club:* Norfolk (Norwich).

PRESTWICH, Prof. Michael Charles, FRHistS; FSA; Professor of History, since 1986, and Pro-Vice-Chancellor, since 1992, University of Durham; *b* 30 Jan. 1943; *s* of John Oswald Prestwich and late Menna Prestwich; *m* 1973, Margaret Joan Daniel; two *s* one *d*. *Educ:* Charterhouse; Magdalen Coll., Oxford (MA, DPhil). FSA 1980. Res. Lectr, Christ Church, Oxford, 1965–69; Lectr in Mediaeval History, Univ. of St Andrews, 1969–79; Reader in Medieval History, Univ. of Durham, 1979–86. *Publications:* War, Politics and Finance under Edward I, 1972; The Three Edwards: war and state in England 1272–1377, 1980; Documents illustrating the Crisis of 1297–98 in England, 1980; Edward I, 1988; English Politics in the Thirteenth Century, 1990; English Armies in the Middle Ages, 1996; articles in learned jls. *Recreation:* ski-ing. *Address:* 46 Albert Street, Western Hill, Durham DH1 4RJ. *T:* Durham (0191) 3862539.

PRETORIA, Bishop of, since 1982; **Rt. Rev. Richard Austin Kraft;** *b* 3 June 1936; *s* of Arthur Austin Kraft and Mary Roberta Hudson Kraft; *m* 1958, Phyllis Marie Schaffer; three *s* one *d*. *Educ:* Ripon Coll., Ripon, Wisconsin, USA (BA); General Theolog. Seminary, New York (MDiv; Hon. DD 1983). Deacon then priest, 1961; Asst priest, St Alphege's, Scottsville, dio. Natal, 1961–63; Asst priest and Rector, St Chad's Mission, Klip River, 1963–67; Dir of Christian Education, Diocese of Zululand, 1968–76; Rector, All Saints Parish, Melmoth, 1974–76; Dir of Education Dept, Church of Province of S Africa, 1977–79; Dean and Rector, St Alban's Cathedral, Diocese of Pretoria, 1979–82. Canon, Dio. of Zululand, 1971; Canon Emeritus, 1977. *Recreation:* woodwork. *Address:* Bishop's House, 414 Albert Street, Waterkloof, Pretoria 0181, S Africa. *T:* (home) (12) 462401, (office) (12) 3222218, *Fax:* (12) 3229411.

PRETTY, Dr Katharine Bridget; Principal, Homerton College, Cambridge, since 1991; *b* 18 Oct. 1945; *d* of M. W. and B. E. W. Hughes; *m* 1988, Prof. Tjeerd Hendrik van Andel. *Educ:* King Edward VI High Sch. for Girls, Birmingham; New Hall, Cambridge (MA, PhD). New Hall, Cambridge: College Lectr and Fellow in Archaeology, 1972–91; Admissions Tutor, 1979–85; Sen. Tutor, 1985–91. Member: Council of Senate, Univ. of Cambridge, 1981–89; Financial Bd, Univ. of Cambridge, 1986–. *Recreations:* archaeology, botany, Arctic travel. *Address:* Homerton College, Cambridge CB2 2PH. *T:* Cambridge (01223) 411141.

PREVIN, André (George); conductor and composer; Conductor Laureate, London Symphony Orchestra, since 1992; *b* Berlin, Germany, 6 April 1929; *s* of Jack Previn and Charlotte Epstein; *m* 1970; three *s* (inc. twin *s*), three *d*; *m* 1982, Heather, *d* of Robert Sneddon; one *s*. *Educ:* Berlin and Paris Conservatoires; private study with Pierre Monteux, Castelnuovo-Tedesco. Composer of film scores, 1950–62 (four Academy Awards). Music Dir, Houston Symphony Orchestra, 1967–69; Principal Conductor, London Symphony Orchestra, 1968–79, Conductor Emeritus, 1979; Music Director: Pittsburgh Symphony Orchestra, 1976–84; Los Angeles Phil. Orch., 1986–89; Music Dir, 1985–86, Prin. Conductor, 1987–91, RPO; Guest Conductor, most major orchestras, US and Europe, Covent Garden Opera, Salzburg Festival, Edinburgh Festival, Osaka Festival; Music Dir, London South Bank Summer Festival, 1972–74. Member: Composers Guild of GB; Amer. Composers League; Dramatists League. Recording artist. Principal compositions: Cello Sonata; Violin Sonata, 1994; Guitar Concerto; Wind Quintet; Serenades for Violin; piano preludes; Piano Concerto, 1984; Trio for piano, oboe and bassoon, 1994; Symphony for Strings; overtures; Principals, Reflections (for orchestra); Every Good Boy Deserves Favour (text by Tom Stoppard); Six Songs Mezzo-Soprano (text by Philip Larkin); Honey and Rue (text by Toni Morrison); Sally Chisum Remembers Billy the Kid (text by Michael Ondaatje); Four Songs for soprano, cello and piano (text by Toni Morrison), 1994. Annual TV series: specials for BBC; PBS (USA). *Publications:* Music Face to Face, 1971; (ed) Orchestra, 1979; André Previn's Guide to Music, 1983; No Minor Chords (autobiog.), 1992; *relevant publications:* André Previn, by Edward Greenfield, 1973; Previn, by H. Ruttencutter, 1985. *Address:* c/o Harrison/Parrott Ltd, 12 Penzance Place, W11 4PA. *Club:* Garrick.

PREVITE, John Edward; QC 1989; **His Honour Judge Previte;** a Circuit Judge, since 1992; *b* 11 May 1934; *s* of late Lt Col K. E. Previte, OBE and Edith Frances (*née* Capper); *m* 1959, Hon. Phyllida Browne, *d* of 6th Baron Kilmaine, CBE; two *s*. *Educ:* Wellington Coll.; Christ Church, Oxford (MA). Called to the Bar, Inner Temple, 1959, Bencher, 1986; a Recorder, Western Circuit, 1987–92. *Recreation:* sailing. *Address:* c/o Inner Temple, EC4Y 7HL.

PREVOST, Sir Christopher (Gerald), 6th Bt *cr* 1805; *b* 25 July 1935; *s* of Sir George James Augustine Prevost, 5th Bt and Muriel Emily (*d* 1939), *d* of late Lewis William Oram; *S* father, 1985; *m* 1964, Dolores Nelly, *o d* of Dezo Hoffmann; one *s* one *d*. *Educ:* Cranleigh School. Served 60th Regt (formed by Prevost family) and Rifle Bde; Kenya Service Medal, 1955. IBM, 1955–61; Pitney-Bowes, 1963–76; founder of Mailtronic Ltd, manufacturers and suppliers of mailroom equipment, 1977. Lord of the Manor, Stinchcombe, Glos. *Recreations:* squash; skiing (Member of British Jetski Assoc. and Team sponsor). *Heir:* *s* Nicholas Marc Prevost, *b* 13 March 1971. *Address:* Highway Cottage, Berrygrove Lane, Watford, Herts WD2 8AE. *Club:* Cloisters Wood (Stanmore, Middx).

PREY, Hermann; baritone; *b* Berlin, 11 July 1929; *s* of Hermann Prey; *m* Barbara Pniok; one *s* two *d*. *Educ:* Humanistisches Gymnasium, Berlin; Staatliche Musikhochschule, Berlin. With State Opera, Wiesbaden, 1952; appearances in Germany, Vienna, (La Scala) Milan, (Metropolitan Opera) New York, Buenos Aires, San Francisco, Covent Garden, etc. Festivals include: Salzburg, Bayreuth, Edinburgh, Vienna, Tokyo, Aix-en-Provence, Perugia, Berlin. *Address:* 82152 Krailling vor München, Fichtenstrasse 14, Germany; c/o Kristian Lange, Ludwig Behr Strasse 7, 82327 Tutzing, Germany; c/o Lies Askonas, 6 Henrietta Street, WC2E 8LA.

PRICE, (Alan) Anthony; author and journalist; Editor, The Oxford Times, 1972–88; *b* 16 Aug. 1928; *s* of Walter Longsdon Price and Kathleen Price (*née* Lawrence); *m* 1953, Yvonne Ann Stone; two *s* one *d*. *Educ:* King's Sch., Canterbury; Merton Coll., Oxford (Exbnr; MA). Oxford & County Newspapers, 1952–88. *Publications:* The Labyrinth Makers, 1970 (CWA Silver Dagger); The Alamut Ambush, 1971; Colonel Butler's Wolf, 1972; October Men, 1973; Other Paths to Glory, 1974 (CWA Gold Dagger, 1974; Swedish Acad. of Detection Prize, 1978); Our Man in Camelot, 1975; War Game, 1976; The '44 Vintage, 1978; Tomorrow's Ghost, 1979; The Hour of the Donkey, 1980; Soldier No More, 1981; The Old Vengeful, 1982; Gunner Kelly, 1983; Sion Crossing, 1984; Here Be Monsters, 1985; For the Good of the State, 1986; A New Kind of War, 1987; A Prospect of Vengeance, 1988; The Memory Trap, 1989; Eyes of the Fleet, 1990. *Recreations:* military history, travelling, gardening. *Address:* Wayside Cottage, Horton-cum-Studley, Oxford OX33 1AW. *T:* Oxford (01865) 351326.

PRICE, (Arthur) Leolin; QC 1968; *b* 11 May 1924; 3rd *s* of late Evan Price and Ceridwen Price (*née* Price), Hawkhurst, Kent; *m* 1963, Hon. Rosalind Helen Penrose Lewis, CBE, *er d* of 1st Baron Brecon, PC, and of Mabel, Baroness Brecon, CBE, JP; two *s* two *d*. *Educ:* Judd Sch., Tonbridge; Keble Coll., Oxford (Schol.; MA). War service, 1943–46 with Army: Capt., RA; Adjt, Indian Mountain Artillery Trng Centre and Depot, Ambala, Punjab, 1946. Treas., Oxford Union, 1948; Pres., Oxford Univ. Conserv. Assoc., 1948. Tutor, Keble Coll., Oxford, 1951–59. Called to Bar, Middle Temple, 1949, Bencher, 1970–, Treas. 1990; Barrister of Lincoln's Inn, 1959. QC (Bahamas) 1969; QC (NSW) 1987. Member: Editorial Cttee, Modern Law Review, 1954–65; Bar Council Law Reform Cttee, 1969–75; Cttee, Soc. of Cons. Lawyers, 1971– (Vice-Chm., 1987–90); Cttee of Management, Inst. of Child Health, 1972– (Chm., 1976–). Director: Thornton Pan-European Investment Trust (formerly Child Health Res. Investment Trust), 1980– (Chm., 1987–); Marine Adventure Sailing Trust plc, 1981–89; Thornton Asian Emerging Markets Investment Trust plc, 1989–. Governor, Gt Ormond St Hosp. for Sick Children, 1972–; Mem., Falkland Islands Cttee, 1972–. Governor, Christ Coll., Brecon, 1977–. Chancellor, Diocese of Swansea and Brecon, 1982–. *Publications:* articles and notes in legal jls. *Address:* 32 Hampstead Grove, NW3 6SR. *T:* 0171–435 9843; 10 Old Square, Lincoln's Inn, WC2A 3SU. *T:* 0171–405 0758; Moor Park, Llanbedr, near Crickhowell, Powys NP8 1SS. *T:* Crickhowell (01873) 810443; Selborne Chambers, 174 Phillip Street, Sydney, NSW 2000, Australia. *T:* (2) 2335188. *Club:* Carlton.

See also V. W. C. Price.

PRICE, Barry; *see* Price, W. F. B.

PRICE, Barry David Keith, CBE 1991; QPM 1981; intelligence consultant, since 1993; Co-ordinator, National Drugs Intelligence Unit, 1987–92; *b* 28 June 1933; *s* of John Leslie Price and Lena Price; *m* 1953, Evelyne Jean Horlick; three *d*. *Educ:* Southall Grammar Sch. FBIM 1975. Metropolitan Police, 1954–75: Constable, uniform and CID, then through ranks to Det. Chief Supt; Asst Chief Constable, Northumbria Police, 1975–78; Dep. Chief Constable, Essex Police, 1978–80; Chief Constable, Cumbria Constabulary, 1980–87. Member: Adv. Council on the Misuse of Drugs, 1982–87; Drugs Intelligence Steering Gp, 1987–; Advr to ACPO Crime Cttee on drugs matters, 1985–88 (past Chm. and Sec.). President: English Police Golf Assoc., 1981–92; Northern Police Cricket League, 1983–87; Patron, NW Counties Schoolboys ABA, 1980–87. SBStJ 1982 (County Dir, St John Amb. Assoc., 1981–87). Police Long Service and Good Conduct Medal, 1976. *Publications:* various articles in law enforcement and med. pubns. *Recreations:* golf, painting, gardening.

PRICE, (Benjamin) Terence; Secretary-General, Uranium Institute, 1974–86; *b* 7 January 1921; *er s* of Benjamin and Nellie Price; *m* 1947, Jean Stella Vidal; one *s* one *d*. *Educ:* Crypt School, Gloucester; Queens' College, Cambridge (Scholar). Naval electronics res., 1942–46; Lieut RNVR, 1945–46; Atomic Energy Research Establishment, Harwell (Nuclear Physics Division), 1947–59; Head of Reactor Development Division, Atomic Energy Estabt, Winfrith, 1959–60; Chief Scientific Officer, Ministry of Defence, 1960–63; Assistant Chief Scientific Adviser (Studies), Ministry of Defence, 1963–65; Director, Defence Operational Analysis Establishment, MoD, 1965–68, Chief Scientific Adviser, Min. of Transport, 1968–71; Dir of Planning and Development, Vickers Ltd, 1971–73. Chm., NEDO Mechanical Handling Sector Working Party, 1976–80. Reviewer, CET, 1984–85. *Publications:* Radiation Shielding, 1957; Political Electricity, 1990. *Recreations:* making music, writing, ski-ing. *Address:* Seers Bough, Wilton Lane, Jordans, Beaconsfield, Bucks HP9 2RG. *T:* Chalfont St Giles (01494) 874589. *Club:* Athenæum.

PRICE, Bernard Albert; County Clerk and Chief Executive, Staffordshire County Council, and Clerk to the Lieutenancy, since 1983; *b* 6 Jan. 1944; *s* of Albert and Doris Price; *m* 1966, Christine Mary, *d* of Roy William Henry Combes; two *s* one *d*. *Educ:* Whitchurch Grammar Sch., Salop; King's Sch., Rochester, Kent; Merton Coll., Oxford (BA 1965, MA 1970). DMS, Wolverhampton Polytechnic, 1972. Articled, later Asst Solicitor, Worcs CC, 1966–70; Asst Solicitor, subseq. Dep. Dir of Admin, Staffs CC, 1970–80; Sen. Dep. Clerk, Staffs CC, 1980–83. *Recreations:* sailing, walking. *Address:* The Cottage, Yeatsall Lane, Abbots Bromley, Rugeley, Staffs WS15 3DY. *T:* Burton on Trent (01283) 840269.

PRICE, Rear-Adm. Cecil Ernest, CB 1978; AFC 1953; Deputy Assistant Chief of Staff (Operations), SHAPE, 1976–80, retired; *b* 29 Oct. 1921; *s* of Ernest C. Price and Phyllis

M. Price; *m* 1946, Megan Morgan; one *s* one *d*. *Educ:* Bungay Grammar Sch. Joined Royal Navy, 1941; Captain 1966; idc 1970; Director: Naval Air Warfare, 1971–72; Naval Operational Requirements, 1972–73; CO RNAS, Culdrose, 1973–75; Rear-Adm. 1976. *Recreations:* golf, fishing, gardening. *Address:* 17 Harefield Road, Croxton, Thetford IP24 1NE.

PRICE, Hon. Charles H., II; Chairman of Board, Mercantile Bank of Kansas City, since 1990; Director, Mercantile Bancorporation, St Louis; non-executive Director, since 1989: British Airways PLC; Hanson PLC; New York Times Co.; Texaco Inc.; Sprint, Inc.; *b* 1 April 1931; *s* of Charles Harry Price and Virginia (*née* Ogden); *m* 1969, Carol Ann Swanson; two *s* three *d*. *Educ:* University of Missouri. Chairman: Price Candy Co., 1969–81; American Bancorpn, 1973–81; American Bank & Trust Co., 1973–81; American Mortgage Co., 1973–81; Ambassador: to Belgium, 1981–83; to UK, 1983–89. Chm., Midwest Res. Inst., 1990– (Vice-Chm. and Mem. Exec. Cttee, 1978–81); Mem. Bd of Dirs, Civic Council, Greater Kansas City, 1979–80. Member: Young Presidents Orgn; IISS; World Business Council. Hon. Fellow, Regent's Coll., London, 1986. Hon. Dr Westminster Coll., Missouri, 1984; Hon. Dr of Laws Missouri, 1988. Salvation Army's William Booth Award, 1985; Kansas City Mayor's World Citizen of the Year, 1985, Trustee Citation Award, Midwest Res. Inst., 1987; Distinguished Service Award, Internat. Relations Council, 1989; Mankind Award, Cystic Fibrosis Foundn, 1990; Gold Good Citizen Award, Sons of the American Revolution, 1991. *Recreations:* tennis, golf, shooting. *Address:* 1 West Armour Boulevard, Ste 300, Kansas City, Mo 64111, USA. *Clubs:* White's, Mark's; Swinley Forest Golf; Metropolitan (Washington); Eldorado Country (Palm Springs); Castle Pines Country (Denver); Kansas City Country, River (Kansas City); Mill Reef (Antigua).

PRICE, Sir Charles (Keith Napier) Rugge-, 9th Bt *cr* 1804; Senior Management Consultant, City of Edmonton, 1982–89; *b* 7 Aug. 1936; *s* of Lt-Col Sir Charles James Napier Rugge-Price, 8th Bt, and of Lady (Maeve Marguerite) Rugge-Price (*née* de la Peña); *S* father, 1966; *m* 1965, Jacqueline Mary (*née* Loranger); two *s*. *Educ:* Middleton College, Eire. 5th Regt Royal Horse Artillery, Germany and Wales, 1954–59. Actuarial Dept, William Mercers Ltd, Canada, 1959–60; Alexander and Alexander Services Ltd, Montreal, Canada, 1960–67; with Domtar Ltd, 1968–71; Manager, Tomenson Alexander Ltd, Toronto, 1971–76; Supervisor, Compensation, City of Edmonton, 1976–81. *Heir:* *s* James Keith Peter Rugge-Price, *b* 8 April 1967. *Address:* 2 Lorne Crescent, St Albert, Alberta T8N 3R2, Canada.

PRICE, Christopher; Principal, Leeds Metropolitan University, 1992–94, now Principal Emeritus (Director, Leeds Polytechnic, 1986–92); Chairman, Statesman & Nation Publishing Co. Ltd, since 1994 (Director, since 1991); freelance journalist and broadcaster; *b* 26 Jan. 1932; *s* of Stanley Price; *m* 1956, Annie Grierson Ross; two *s* one *d*. *Educ:* Leeds Grammar School; Queen's College, Oxford. Sec., Oxford Univ. Labour Club, 1953; Chm., Nat. Assoc. of Labour Student Organisations, 1955–56. Sheffield City Councillor, 1962–66; Dep. Chm., Sheffield Educn Cttee, 1963–66. Contested (Lab): Shipley, 1964; Birmingham, Perry Barr, 1970; Lewisham W, 1983. MP (Lab): Perry Barr Division of Birmingham, 1966–70; Lewisham W, Feb. 1974–1983; PPS to Secretary of State for Education and Science, 1966–67 and 1975–76; Chm., H of C Select Cttee on Educn, Science and the Arts, 1980–83. Mem., European Parlt, 1977–78. Dir, London Internat. Festival of Theatre Ltd, 1982–86; Pro-Asst Dir, The Polytechnic of the South Bank, 1983–86. Chm., Council, Nat. Youth Bureau, 1977–80; Member: Council, Inst. for Study of Drug Dependence, 1984–86; Bd, Phoenix House Ltd (Britain's largest gp of drug rehabilitation houses), 1986–87 (Chm., 1980–86). Mem. Bd, Yorks and Humberside Arts, 1994–. Co-Chm., Campaign for Freedom of Information, 1990–94; Pres., BEMAS, 1992–94; Member: Delegacy, Univ. of London Goldsmiths' Coll., 1981–86; Court, Polytechnic of Central London, 1982–86; London Centre for Biotechnology Trust, 1984–86; Fellow, Internat. Inst. of Biotechnology, 1984. Vis. Sen. Fellow, Office of Public Management, 1994–; Vis. Fellow, Centre for Policy Studies in Educn, Univ. of Leeds, 1994–. FRSA 1988. Editor, New Education, 1967–68; Educn corresp., New Statesman, 1969–74; Columnist: TES, 1983–85; THES, 1990–92. DUniv Leeds Metropolitan, 1994. *Publications:* (contrib.) A Radical Future, 1967; Crisis in the Classroom, 1968; (ed) Your Child and School, 1968; Which Way?, 1969; (contrib.) Life and Death of the Schools Council, 1985; (contrib.) Police, the Constitution and the Community, 1985. *Address:* 17 Albert Hill, Settle, N Yorks BD24 9HE. *Club:* Athenæum.
See also H. M. Jackson.

PRICE, Curtis Alexander, PhD; Principal, Royal Academy of Music, since 1995; *b* 7 Sept. 1945; *s* of Dalias Price and Lillian Price (*née* Alexander); *m* 1981, Rhian Samuel; one step *s*. *Educ:* Southern Illinois Univ. (BA 1967); Harvard Univ. (AM 1970; PhD 1974). Washington University, St Louis: Asst Prof., 1974–79; Associate Prof., 1979–82; King's College London: Lectr, 1982–85; Reader in Historical Musicology, 1985–88; King Edward Prof. and Head of Dept of Music, 1988–95; FKC 1994. Guggenheim Fellow, 1982–83; FRSA. Hon. RAM, 1993. Einstein Award, Amer. Musicol. Soc., 1979; Dent Medal, Royal Musical Assoc., 1985. *Publications:* Music in the Restoration Theatre, 1979; Henry Purcell and the London Stage, 1984; Dido and Aeneas: a critical score, 1986; The Impresario's Ten Commandments, 1992. *Address:* Royal Academy of Music, Marylebone Road, NW1 5HT; 7 Haven Lane, W5 2HZ. *T:* 0181–991 1395.

PRICE, Maj.-Gen. David; *see* Price, Maj.-Gen. M. D.

PRICE, Sir David (Ernest Campbell), Kt 1980; DL; *b* 20 Nov. 1924; *o s* of Major Villiers Price; *m* 1960, Rosemary Eugénie Evelyn, *o d* of late Cyril F. Johnston, OBE; one *d*. *Educ:* Eton; Trinity College, Cambridge; Yale University, USA; Rosebery Schol., Eton; Open History Schol., Trinity College, Cambridge. Served with 1st Battalion Scots Guards, CMF; subsequently Staff Captain (Intelligence) HQ, 56 London Div., Trieste, 1942–46. Trin. Coll., Cambridge, BA Hons, MA. Pres. Cambridge Union; Vice-Pres. Fedn of Univ. Conservative and Unionist Assocs, 1946–48; Henry Fellow of Yale Univ., USA, 1948–49. Industrial Consultant. Held various appts in Imperial Chemical Industries Ltd, 1949–62. MP (C) Eastleigh Div. of Hampshire, 1955–92; Parly Sec., Board of Trade, 1962–64; Opposition Front-Bench spokesman on Science and Technology, 1964–70; Parly Sec., Min. of Technology, June-Oct. 1970; Parly Sec., Min. of Aviation Supply, 1970–71; Parly Under-Sec. of State, Aerospace, DTI, 1971–72. Member: Public Accounts Cttee, 1974–75; Select Cttee on Transport, 1979–83; Select Cttee on Social Services, 1983–90; Select Cttee on Health, 1990–92; Vice-Pres., Parly and Scientific Cttee, 1975–79 and 1982–86 (Vice-Chm., 1965–70, Chm., 1973–75 and 1979–82). Vice-Chm., Cons. Arts and Heritage Cttee, 1979–81 and 1983–87; Chm., Cons. Shipping and Ship-Building Cttee, 1985–91; President: Wessex Area Cons. and Unionist Party, 1986–89 (Life Vice-Pres., 1991); Romsey and Waterside Cons. Assoc., 1993–; Itchen Test and Avon Cons. Euro-Forum, 1994–. British Representative to Consultative Assembly of the Council of Europe, 1958–61. Dir, Assoc. British Maltsters, 1966–70. Gen. Cons. to IIM (formerly IWM), 1973–90; Cons. to Union International Ltd, 1974–92; Non-exec. Dir, Southampton Univ. Hosps Trust, 1993–. Vice-Pres., IIM, 1980–92. Pres., Wessex Rehabilitation Assoc., 1990–; Chm., Hants CC Community Care Forum, 1993–; Trustee: Wessex Medical Trust, 1990–; Nuffield Theatre, 1990–. Governor, Middlesex Hospital, 1956–60. DL Hants, 1982. *Recreations:* swimming, arts and heritage, wine, cooking, gardening. *Address:* Forest Lodge, Moonhills Lane, Beaulieu, Hampshire SO42 7YW. *T:* Beaulieu (01590) 612537. *Clubs:* Athenæum, Beefsteak.

PRICE, Eric Hardiman Mockford; Proprietor, Energy Economics Consultancy, since 1995; Director, Robinson Brothers (Ryders Green) Ltd, since 1985; *b* 14 Nov. 1931; *s* of Frederick H. Price and Florence N. H. Price (*née* Mockford); *m* 1963, Diana M. S. Robinson; one *s* three *d*. *Educ:* St Marylebone Grammar Sch.; Christ's Coll., Cambridge. Econs Tripos, 1955; MA 1958. FREconS, 1956; FSS 1958; MInstPet 1992. Army service, 1950–52; HAC, 1952–57. Supply Dept, Esso Petroleum Co. Ltd, 1955–56; Economist: Central Electricity Authority, 1956–57; Electricity Council, 1957–58; British Iron & Steel Fedn, 1958–62; Chief Economist, Port of London Authority, 1962–67; Sen. Econ. Adviser, Min. of Transport, 1966–69; Chief Econ. Adviser, Min. of Transport, 1969–71; Dir of Econs, 1971–75, Under Sec., 1972–76, Dir of Econs and Stats, 1975–76, DoE; Under Sec., Econs and Stats Div., Depts of Industry, Trade and Consumer Protection, 1977–80; Head of Econs and Stats Div., Dept of Energy, 1980–92; Chief Econ. Advr, Dept of Energy, later DTI, 1980–93. Special Consultant, Nat. Econ. Res. Associates, 1993–. Member: Soc. of Business Economists, 1961; Expert Adv. Gp on Entry into Freight Transport Market, EEC, 1973–75; Northern Regional Strategy Steering Gp, 1976–77; Expert Gp on Venture Capital for Industrial Innovation, EEC, 1978–79; Soc. of Strategic and Long-range Planning, 1980–; Council, Internat. Assoc. of Energy Economists, 1981–85; Energy Panel, SSRC, 1980–83; Council, British Inst. of Energy Economics, 1986 (Mem., 1980–; Vice-Chm., 1981–82 and 1988–89; Chm., 1982–85); Steering Cttee, Jt Energy Programme, RIIA, 1981–89, Steering Cttee, Energy and Envmtl Prog., 1989–; Adv. Council, Energy Econs Centre, Univ. of Surrey, 1989–. UK rep., Econ. Res. Cttee, European Council of Ministers of Transport, 1968–76; UK rep. on Six Nations' Prog. on Govt Policies towards Technological Innovation in Industry, 1977–80; Mem., World Bank's Groupe des Sages on Econs of Global Warming, 1990–. Member, Advisory Board: Transport Studies Unit, Oxford Univ., 1973–75; Centre for Res. in Industrial, Business and Admin Studies, Univ. of Warwick, 1977–80. FInstD 1990. *Publications:* various articles in learned jls on transport and industrial economics, energy and energy efficiency, investment, public sector industries, technological innovation in industry, regional planning, environmental abatement policies, and East European energy issues. *Recreations:* tennis, squash, local history. *Address:* Batchworth Heath Farm, London Road, Rickmansworth, Herts WD3 1QB. *Clubs:* Moor Park Golf; Northwood Squash.

PRICE, Sir Francis (Caradoc Rose), 7th Bt *cr* 1815; QC (Can.) 1992; barrister and solicitor; *b* 9 Sept. 1950; *s* of Sir Rose Francis Price, 6th Bt and of Kathleen June, *d* of late Norman W. Hutchinson, Melbourne; *S* father, 1979; *m* 1975, Marguerite Jean Trussler, Justice, Court of Queen's Bench, Alberta, *d* of Roy S. Trussler, Victoria, BC; three *d*. *Educ:* Eton; Trinity College, Melbourne Univ. (Sen. Student 1971, LLB Hons 1973); Univ. of Alberta (LLM 1975); Canadian Petroleum Law Foundn Fellow, 1974–75. Admitted barrister and solicitor, Province of Alberta 1976, Northwest Territories 1978, Canada; Bencher, Law Soc. of Alberta, 1990–94. Lectr, 1979–89, and Course Head, 1983–89, Alberta Bar Admission Course. Chartered Arbitrator, Arbitration and Mediation Inst. of Canada, 1994. OLJ 1991. *Publications:* Pipelines in Western Canada, 1975; Mortgage Actions in Alberta, 1985; contribs to Alberta and Melbourne Univ. Law Revs, etc. *Recreations:* cricket, opera, running, theatre. *Heir:* *b* Norman William Rose Price, [*b* 17 March 1953; *m* 1987, Charlotte Louise, *yr d* of R. R. B. Baker]. *Address:* 9626 95th Avenue, Edmonton, Alberta T6C 2A4, Canada. *Clubs:* Centre, Faculty (Edmonton).

PRICE, Sir Frank (Leslie), Kt 1966; DL; Chairman, Sir Frank Price Associates SA, since 1986; *b* 26 July 1922; *s* of G. F. Price; marr. diss.; one *s*; *m* Daphne Ling. *Educ:* St Matthias Church Sch., Birmingham; Vittoria Street Arts Sch. Elected to Birmingham City Council, 1949; Alderman, 1958–74; Lord Mayor, 1964–65. Member: Council, Town and Country Planning Assoc., 1958–74; W Midlands Economic Planning Council, 1965–72; Nat. Water Council, 1975–79; Chm., British Waterways Bd, 1968–84. Founder/Chm., Midlands Art Centre for Young People, 1960–71; Chairman: W Midlands Sports Council, 1965–69; Telford Development Corporation, 1968–71; Dir, National Exhibn Centre, 1968–74. Member: Minister of Transport's Cttee of Inquiry into Major Ports, 1961; English Tourist Board, 1976–83; President: BAIE, 1979–83; Mojacar Assoc. of Commerce, 1994–. Livery Co. of Basketmakers. FSVA; FCIT; Mem., Fédn Internat. des Professions Immobilières. FRSA. DL: Warwicks, 1970–77; West Midlands, 1974–77; Herefordshire and Worcestershire, 1977–84. Freeman, City of London. *Publications:* various pamphlets and articles on town planning, transport and public affairs. *Recreations:* painting, cruising. *Address:* Casa Non Such, Apartado 534, Mojacar, Almeria 04638, Spain. *Club:* Reform.

PRICE, Gareth; Director, Thomson Foundation, since 1993; *b* 30 Aug. 1939; *s* of Rowena and Morgan Price; *m* 1962, Mari Griffiths; two *s* one *d*. *Educ:* Aberaeron Grammar School and Ardwyn Grammar School, Aberystwyth; University College of Wales, Aberystwyth (BA Econ; Hon. Fellow, 1987). Asst Lectr in Economics, Queen's Univ., Belfast, 1962–64; BBC Wales: Radio Producer, Current Affairs, 1964–66; Television Producer, Features and Documentaries, 1966–74; Dep. Head of Programmes, 1974–81; Head of Programmes, 1981–85; Controller, 1986–90. Controller of Broadcasting, Thomson Foundn, 1990–93. Hon. Prof. of Communication, Univ. of Wales, Cardiff, 1994–. Consultant to UNESCO and broadcasting corps of Kazakhstan, Bulgaria, Namibia, South Africa. *Publication:* David Lloyd George (with Emyr Price and Bryn Parry), 1981. *Recreation:* travel. *Address:* 98 Pencisely Road, Llandaff, Cardiff, South Glamorgan CF5 1DQ. *T:* Cardiff (01222) 568332. *Club:* Cardiff and County (Cardiff).

PRICE, Geoffrey Alan; DL; IPFA, CIMgt; Chief Executive and County Treasurer, Hereford and Worcester County Council, 1983–93; Clerk: to Lord Lieutenant, Hereford and Worcester, 1983–93; to West Mercia Police Authority, 1983–93. Non-exec. Dir, Herefordshire HA; Consultant, Local Govt Financial Management. Formerly County Treasurer, Hants CC; previous appts in: Gloucester CC; Southend-on-Sea; Cheshire CC; West Sussex CC. DL Hereford and Worcester, 1993. *Address:* Grovesend, Old Church Road, Colwall, Herefordshire WR13 6EZ.

PRICE, Rt. Hon. George (Cadle), PC 1982; Prime Minister of Belize, 1981–84, and 1989–93 (Premier from 1964 until Independence, 1981); *b* 15 Jan. 1919; *s* of William Cadle Price and Irene Cecilia Escalante de Price. *Educ:* Holy Redeemer Primary Sch., Belize City; St John's Coll., Belize City. Private Sec. to late Robert S. Turton; entered politics, 1944; City Councillor, 1947–65 (Mayor of Belize City several times); founding Mem., People's United Party, 1950; Party Sec., 1950–56; became Leader, 1956; elected to National Assembly, 1954; under 1961 Ministerial System, led People's United Party to 100% victory at polls and became First Minister; under 1964 Self-Govt Constitution, title changed to Premier; has led delegns to Central American and Caribbean countries; spearheaded internationalization of Belize problem at internat. forums; addressed UN's Fourth Cttee, 1975, paving way for overwhelming victory at UN when majority of nations voted in favour of Belize's right to self-determination and territorial integrity. *Address:* c/o House of Representatives, Belmopan, Belize.

PRICE, Geraint; *see* Price, W. G.

PRICE, Gerald Alexander Lewin; QC 1992; a Recorder of the Crown Court, since 1990; *b* 13 Sept. 1948; *s* of Denis Lewin Price and Patricia Rosemary (*née* Metcalfe); *m* 1974, Theresa Elisabeth Iremonger-Watts; two *s*. *Educ:* Haileybury Coll.; College of Law; Inns of Court Law Sch. Called to the Bar, Middle Temple, 1969; in private practice, Cardiff, 1970–77; Bermuda: Resident Stipendiary Magistrate, 1977–81; Chief Stipendiary Magistrate and Sen. Coroner, 1981–84; in private practice, Cardiff, 1984–. Chairman: Liquor Licence Authority, Land Valuation Appeals Tribunal, Price Control Commn and Jury Revising Tribunal, 1981–84. Mem., Commonwealth Magistrates and Judges Assoc., 1984–. Mem., RYA. *Recreations:* travel, classical music, sunshine, tennis. *Clubs:* Commonwealth Trust; Glamorgan Lawn Tennis and Croquet (Merthyr Mawr).

PRICE, Very Rev. Hilary Martin Connop; Rector and Provost of Chelmsford, 1967–77, now Provost Emeritus; *b* 1912; *s* of late Rev. Connop Lewis Price and late Shirley (*née* Lewis); *m* 1939, Dorothea (*née* Beaty-Pownall); one *s* two *d*. *Educ:* Cheltenham Coll.; Queens' Coll., Cambridge (MA); Ridley Hall, Cambridge. Asst Curate, St Peter's, Hersham, Surrey, 1936–40; Sen. Chaplain, Portsmouth Cathedral, 1940–41; Asst Curate, Holy Trinity, Cambridge, 1941–46; Chaplain, RAFVR, 1943–46; Vicar, St Gabriel's, Bishopwearmouth, 1946–56; Rector and Rural Dean, Newcastle-under-Lyme, 1956–67. Prebendary of Lichfield, 1964–67. Proctor in Convocation: of York for Durham Dio., 1954–56; of Canterbury for Lichfield Dio., 1962–67. Mem., General Synod, 1970–75. *Address:* 98 St James Street, Shaftesbury, Dorset SP7 8HF. *T:* Shaftesbury (01747) 852118.

PRICE, James Richard Kenrick; QC 1995; *b* 14 Sept. 1948; *s* of Lt-Col Kenrick Jack Price, DSO, MC, 9th Lancers and Juliet Hermione, *d* of Marshal of the Royal Air Force Sir John Cotesworth Slessor, GCB, DSO, MC; *m* 1983, Hon. Virginia Yvonne, *d* of Baron Mostyn, *qv*. *Educ:* Eton College; St Edmund Hall, Oxford. Called to the Bar, Inner Temple, 1974. *Recreations:* fine and decorative arts, mountains, ski-ing. *Address:* 5 Raymond Buildings, Gray's Inn, WC1R 5BP. *T:* 0171–242 2902. *Clubs:* Brooks's, Beefsteak.

PRICE, Sir (James) Robert, KBE 1976; FAA 1959; Chairman of the Executive, Commonwealth Scientific and Industrial Research Organization, 1970–77; *b* 25 March 1912; *s* of Edgar James Price and Mary Katherine Price (*née* Hughes); *m* 1940, Joyce Ethel (*née* Brooke); one *s* two *d*. *Educ:* St Peter's Coll., Adelaide; Univ. of Adelaide (BSc Hons, MSc, DSc); Univ. of Oxford (DPhil). Head, Chemistry Section, John Innes Horticultural Inst., London, 1937–40; (UK) Min. of Supply, 1941–45; Div. of Industrial Chemistry, Council for Scientific and Industrial Research (CSIR), Australia, from 1945; CSIRO: Officer-in-Charge, Organic Chem. Section, 1960, subseq. Chief of Div. of Organic Chem.; Mem., Executive, 1966. Pres., Royal Aust. Chemical Inst., 1963–64. *Publications:* numerous scientific papers in learned jls. *Recreations:* squash; growing Australian native plants. *Address:* Yangoora, 2 Ocean View Avenue, Red Hill South, Victoria 3937, Australia. *Club:* Sciences (Melb.).

PRICE, John Alan, QC 1980; a Recorder of the Crown Court, since 1980; a Deputy Circuit Judge, since 1975; *b* 11 Sept. 1938; *s* of Frederick Leslie Price and Gertrude Davilda Alice Price; *m* 1964, Elizabeth Myra (*née* Priest) (marr. diss. 1982); one *s* one *d*; *m* 1984, Alison Elizabeth Curran (*née* Ward); two step *d*. *Educ:* Stretford Grammar Sch.; Manchester Univ. (LLB Hons 1959). Called to the Bar, Gray's Inn, 1961; in practice on Northern Circuit; Head of 60 King St Chambers, Manchester, 1978–80. *Recreations:* tennis, squash, football, golf. *Address:* 61 Fleet Street, EC4Y 1JU; 25 Byrom Street, Manchester M3 4PF. *Club:* Wilmslow Rugby Union Football.

PRICE, Air Vice-Marshal John Walter, CBE 1979 (OBE 1973); oil and gas exploration consultant; *b* Birmingham, 26 Jan. 1930; *s* of late Henry Walter Price and Myrza Price (*née* Griffiths); *m* 1956, Margaret Sinclair McIntyre (*d* 1989), Sydney, Aust. *Educ:* Solihull Sch.; RAF Coll., Cranwell. MRAeS 1971; MInstPet; FIMgt (FBIM 1979). Joined RAF, 1948; Adjutant, No 11 (Vampire) Sqn, 1950–52; No 77 (Meteor) Sqn, RAAF, Korea, 1952–53 (mentioned in despatches, 1953); No 98 Sqn (Venoms and Vampires), 1953–54; No 2 (F) Op. Trng Unit (Vampires) and No 75 (F) Sqn (Meteors), RAAF, 1954–56; Cadet Wing Adjutant, RAF Tech. Coll., Henlow, 1956–60; RAF Staff Coll., 1960; Air Ministry (Ops Overseas), 1961–64; Comd No 110 Sqn (Sycamore and Whirlwind), 1964–66; Directing Staff, RAF Staff Coll., 1966–68; PSO to Chief of Air Staff, 1968–70; Comd No 72 (Wessex) Sqn, 1970–72; Air Warfare Course, 1973; Dep. Dir Ops (Offensive Support and Jt Warfare), MoD (Air), 1973–75; sowc 1975–76; Comd RAF Laarbruch, 1976–78; Gp Capt. Ops, HQ Strike Comd, 1979; Dir of Ops (Strike), MoD (Air), 1980–82; ACAS (Ops), 1982–84, retd. Clyde Petroleum plc, 1984–95 (Manager, External Affairs and Exploration Admin, 1986–95). Mem. Council, Inst. of Management, 1994–. Governor, Solihull Sch., 1979–, Chm., 1983–. *Recreations:* motorcycling, golf, cabinet making. *Address:* 2 Palace Yard, Hereford HR4 9BJ. *Club:* Royal Air Force.

PRICE, Leolin; *see* Price, A. L.

PRICE, Leonard Sidney, OBE 1974; HM Diplomatic Service, retired 1981; *b* 19 Oct. 1922; *s* of late William Price and late Dorothy Price; *m* 1958, Adrienne Mary (*née* Wilkinson); two *s* one *d*. *Educ:* Central Foundation Sch., EC1. Served War, 1942–45. Foreign Office, 1939–42 and 1945–48; Chungking, later Vice-Consul, 1948; Mexico City, 1950; Rome, 1953; Vice-Consul, later Second Sec., Katmandu, 1954; FO, 1957; Consul, Split, 1960; Consul and First Sec., Copenhagen, 1963; FO, later FCO, 1967; First Sec. i/c, Kuching, 1970; Suva, 1972; Parly Clerk, FCO, 1975; Counsellor (Admin), Canberra, 1977–81. Dep. Dir, St John Ambulance Assoc., Somerset, 1982–84; Hon. Treas., Council of Order of St John, Somerset, 1983–88. *Recreation:* reading ancient, medieval and military history. *Address:* 5 Staplegrove Manor, Taunton, Somerset TA2 6EG. *T:* Taunton (01823) 337093. *Club:* Civil Service.

PRICE, Leontyne; Opera Prima Donna (Soprano), United States; *b* 10 Feb. 1927. *Educ:* Public Schools, Laurel, Mississippi; Central State College, Wilberforce, Ohio (BA); Juilliard Sch. of Music, NY. Four Saints, 1952; Porgy and Bess, 1952–54. Operatic Debut on TV, 1955, as Tosca; Concerts in America, England, Australia, Europe. Operatic debut as Madame Lidouine in Dialogues of Carmelites, San Francisco, 1957; Covent Garden, Verona Arena, Vienna Staatsoper, 1958; five roles, inc. Leonora in Il Trovatore, Madame Butterfly, Donna Anna in Don Giovanni, Metropolitan, 1960–61; Salzburg debut singing soprano lead in Missa Solemnis, 1959; Aida in Aida, Liu in Turandot, La Scala, 1960; opened season at Metropolitan in 1961 as Minnie in Fanciulla del West; opened new Metropolitan Opera House, 1966, as Cleopatra in world premiere of Samuel Barber's Antony and Cleopatra; debut Teatre Dell'Opera, Rome, in Aida, 1967; debut Paris Opera, in Aida, 1968; debut Teatro Colon, Buenos Aires, as Leonora in Il Trovatore, 1969; opened season at Metropolitan Opera, in Aida, 1969. Numerous recordings. Vice-Chm., Nat. Inst. for Music Theatre. Member: Metropolitan Opera Assoc.; Bd of Dirs, Dance Theatre of Harlem; Bd of Trustees, NY Univ. Life Mem., NAACP. Fellow, Amer. Acad. of Arts and Sciences. Hon. Dr of Music: Howard Univ., Washington, DC, 1962; Central State Coll., Wilberforce, Ohio, 1968; Hon. DHL, Dartmouth Univ., 1962; Hon. Dr of Humanities, Rust Coll., Holly Springs, Miss, 1968; Hon. Dr of Humane Letters, Fordham Univ., New York, 1969. Hon. Mem. Bd of Dirs, Campfire Girls, 1966. Presidential Medal of Freedom, 1965; Spingarn Medal, NAACP, 1965; Nat. Medal of Arts, 1985; 18 Grammy Awards, Nat. Acad. Recording Arts and Scis. Order of Merit (Italy), 1966; Commandeur, Ordre des Arts et des Lettres (France), 1986. *Recreations:* cooking, dancing, shopping for clothes, etc, antiques for homes in Rome and New York. *Address:* c/o Columbia Artists Management Inc., 165 W 57th Street, New York, NY 10019, USA.

PRICE, Sir Leslie Victor, Kt 1976; OBE 1971; Chairman, Australian Wheat Board, 1977–86 (Member, 1971–86); *b* Toowoomba, Qld, 30 Oct. 1920; *s* of late H. V. L. Price; *m* Lorna Collins; one *s* two *d*. President: Queensland Graingrowers Assoc., 1966–77; Australian Wheatgrowers Fedn, 1970–72; Mem., Queensland State Wheat Bd, 1968–77. *Recreation:* clay target shooting. *Address:* 20 Muir Street, Richmond, Vic 3121, Australia. *Clubs:* Queensland; Melbourne.

PRICE, (Llewelyn) Ralph, CBE 1972; Director, Honeywell, since 1971 (Chairman, 1971–81); *b* 23 Oct. 1912; *s* of late L. D. Price, schoolmaster, and late Lena Elizabeth (*née* Dixon); *m* 1939, Vera Patricia Harrison; one *s* two *d*. *Educ:* Quarry Bank Sch., Liverpool. Chartered Accountant, 1935; Sec. to Honeywell Ltd, 1936; Cost Investigator, Min. of Supply, 1943–46; Dir of Manufacturing (Scotland), Honeywell Ltd, 1947; Financial Dir, Honeywell Europe, 1957; Dir, Computer Div., Honeywell, 1960; Managing Dir, Honeywell Ltd, 1965; Chm., Honeywell UK Adv. Council, 1981–. Chm., ML Hldgs Ltd, 1976–87. Pres., British Industrial, Measuring & Control Apparatus Manufrs Assoc., 1971–76. CIMgt. *Recreations:* golf, bridge, music. *Address:* Nascot, Pinkneys Drive, Pinkneys Green, Maidenhead, Berks SL6 6QD. *T:* Maidenhead (01628) 28270. *Clubs:* Royal Automobile; Temple Golf (Maidenhead).

PRICE, Dame Margaret (Berenice), DBE 1993 (CBE 1982); opera singer; *b* Tredegar, Wales, 13 April 1941; *d* of late Thomas Glyn Price and of Lilian Myfanwy Richards. *Educ:* Pontllanfraith Secondary Sch.; Trinity Coll. of Music, London. Debut as Cherubino in Marriage of Figaro, Welsh Nat. Opera Co., 1962; debut, in same rôle, at Royal Opera House, Covent Garden, 1963; has subseq. sung many principal rôles at Glyndebourne, San Francisco Opera Co., Cologne Opera House, Munich State Opera, Hamburg State Opera, Vienna State Opera, Lyric Opera, Chicago, Paris Opera; La Scala, Milan; Metropolitan Opera House, NY. Major rôles include: Countess in Marriage of Figaro; Pamina in The Magic Flute; Fiordiligi in Cosi Fan Tutte; Donna Anna in Don Giovanni; Konstanze in Die Entführung; Amelia in Simone Boccanegra; Agathe in Freischütz; Desdemona in Otello; Elisabetta in Don Carlo; Amelia in Un Ballo In Maschera; title rôles in Aida, Norma and Ariadne auf Naxos. BBC recitals and concerts, also TV appearances. Has made recordings. Hon. FTCL; Hon. DMus Wales, 1983. Elisabeth Schumann Prize for Lieder; Ricordi Prize for Opera; Silver Medal, Worshipful Co. of Musicians; Bayerische Kammersängerin. *Recreations:* cooking, driving, reading, walking, swimming. *Address:* c/o Bayerische Staatsoper München, Max Josef Platz 2, 80539 München, Germany.

PRICE, Maj.-Gen. (Maurice) David, CB 1970; OBE 1956; *b* 13 Feb. 1915; *s* of Edward Allan Price and Edna Marion Price (*née* Turner); *m* 1st, 1938, Ella Lacy (*d* 1971), *d* of late H. L. Day; two *s* two *d*; 2nd, 1972, Mrs Olga Marion Oclee (*d* 1989). *Educ:* Marlborough; RMA, Woolwich. 2nd Lt R Signals, 1935; Vice-Quartermaster-Gen., MoD (Army), 1967–70, retired. Col Comdt, Royal Corps of Signals, 1967–74. *Recreation:* fishing. *Address:* The Cross, Chilmark, Salisbury, Wiltshire SP3 5AR. *T:* Teffont (01722) 716212.

PRICE, Michael Anthony, LVO 1991; HM Diplomatic Service; Counsellor, Paris, since 1995; *b* 13 Aug. 1944; *s* of Francis George and Lena Beatrice Price; *m* 1968, Elizabeth Anne Cook; one *s* one *d*. *Educ:* Forest Grammar Sch. Bd of Trade, 1964; Diplomatic Service, 1966–; served New Delhi, Freetown, Paris, Montreal; Dep. Head of News Dept, FCO, 1984; First Sec. (Press and Public Affairs), Washington, 1988; Counsellor and HM Consul-Gen., Tokyo, 1992; on loan to No 10 Downing St, 1994–95. *Recreations:* cricket, Gilbert and Sullivan, cooking. *Address:* c/o Foreign and Commonwealth Office, SW1A 2AH; 8 Robert Wallace Close, Bishop's Stortford, Herts CM23 2TG.

PRICE, Nicholas Peter Lees; QC 1992; a Recorder of the Crown Court, since 1987; *b* 29 Sept. 1944; *s* of Frank Henry Edmund Price, MBE (mil.) and Agnes Lees Price; *m* 1969, Wilma Ann Alison (*née* Steel); one *s* one *d*. *Educ.* Prince of Wales Sch., Nairobi; Edinburgh Univ. (LLB). Called to the Bar, Gray's Inn, 1968. Mem., Gen. Council of the Bar, 1993– (Jt Vice Chm., Legal Services Cttee, 1994; Vice Chm., Public Affairs Cttee, 1995); Associate Mem., Criminal Bar Assoc., 1993–. *Recreations:* reading, crosswords, destructive gardening. *Address:* 3 Raymond Buildings, Gray's Inn, WC1R 5BH. *T:* 0171–831 3833.

PRICE, Sir Norman (Charles), KCB 1975 (CB 1969); Member, European Court of Auditors, 1977–83; Chairman, Board of Inland Revenue, 1973–76 (Deputy Chairman, 1968–73); *b* 5 Jan. 1915; *s* of Charles William and Ethel Mary Price; *m* 1940, Kathleen Beatrice (*née* Elston); two *d*. *Educ:* Plaistow Grammar School. Entered Civil Service as Executive Officer, Customs and Excise, 1933; Inspector of Taxes, Inland Revenue, 1939; Secretaries' Office, Inland Revenue, 1951; Board of Inland Revenue, 1965. *Recreations:* music, history. *Address:* 73 Linkswood, Compton Place Road, Eastbourne BN21 1EF. *T:* Eastbourne (01323) 25941.

PRICE, Rev. Canon Peter Bryan; General Secretary, United Society for the Propagation of the Gospel, since 1992; *b* 17 May 1944; *s* of Alec Henry Price and Phyllis Evelyn Mary Price; *m* 1967, Edith Margaret Burns; four *s*. *Educ:* Redland Coll., Bristol (Cert Ed 1966); Oak Hill Theol Coll. (Dip. in Pastoral Studies, 1974). Asst Master, Ashton Park Sch., Bristol, 1966–70; Tutor, Lindley Lodge, Nuneaton, 1970; Head of Religious Studies, Cordeaux Sch., Louth, 1970–72; ordained, 1974; Community Chaplain, Crookhorn, Portsmouth and Asst Curate, Christ Church, Portsdown, 1974–78; Chaplain, Scargill House, Kettlewell, 1978–80; Vicar, St Mary Magdalene, Addiscombe, Croydon, 1980–88; Canon Residentiary and Chancellor, Southwark Cathedral, 1988–91, Canon Emeritus, 1992. *Publications:* The Church as Kingdom, 1987; Seeds of the Word, 1996. *Recreations:* painting, swimming, walking, conversation. *Address:* 14 Oakwood Road, SW20 0PW. *T:* 0181–946 3814.

PRICE, Peter Nicholas; Member (C) London South East, 1984–94 (Lancashire West, 1979–84), European Parliament; *b* 19 Feb. 1942; *s* of Rev. Dewi Emlyn Price and Kate Mary Price (*née* Thomas). *Educ:* Worcester Royal Grammar Sch.; Aberdare Boys' Grammar Sch.; Univ. of Southampton (BA (Law)); Coll. of Law, Guildford. Solicitor. Interviewer and current affairs freelance broadcaster, 1962–67; Asst Solicitor, Glamorgan CC, 1967–68; solicitor in private practice, 1966–67 and 1968–85. Contested (C) Gen. Elecs: Aberdare 1964, 1966; Caerphilly 1970; Nat. Vice-Chm., Young Conservatives, 1971–72; Mem., Nat. Union Exec. Cttee, 1969–72 and 1978–79; Vice-Chm., Cons. Pol. Centre Nat. Cttee, 1978–79; Hon. Sec., For. Affairs Forum, 1977–79; Vice-Chm., Cons. Gp for Europe, 1979–81; Mem. Council, Europ. Movement, 1971–81. Chm., European Parliament: Budgetary Control Cttee, 1989–94 (Vice-Chm., 1979–84, and its Rapporteur for series of 4 major reports on Community finances, 1985–86); spokesman for Europ. Democratic Gp: Legal Affairs Cttee, 1984–87; Budgets Cttee, 1986–89; Mem., ACP/EEC Jt Assembly, 1981–94. Fellow, Industry and Parlt Trust, 1981–82; Vice-Pres., UK Cttee, Europ. Year of Small and Med.-sized Enterprises, 1983. Vice-Pres., Llangollen Internat. Eisteddfod, 1981–. *Publications:* misc. pol. pamplets and newspaper articles. *Recreations:*

theatre, music, photography. *Address:* 60 Marlings Park Avenue, Chislehurst, Kent BR7 6RD. *T:* Orpington (01689) 820681, *Fax:* (01689) 890622.

PRICE, Rev. Peter Owen, CBE 1983; BA; FPhS; RN retired; Minister of Blantyre Old Parish Church, Glasgow, since 1985; *b* Swansea, 18 April 1930; *e s* of late Idwal Price and Florence Price; *m* 1st, 1957, Margaret Trevan (*d* 1977); three *d*; 2nd, 1982, Marilyn Lorne Campbell (*née* Murray) (marr. diss. 1992). *Educ:* Wyggeston Sch., Leicester; Didsbury Theol Coll., Bristol. BA Open Univ. Ordained, 1960, Methodist Minister, Birmingham; commnd RN as Chaplain, 1960; served: HMS Collingwood, 1960; RM, 1963–64; Staff of C-in-C Med., 1964–68; RNAS Brawdy, 1968–69; RM, 1970–73; HMS Raleigh, 1973; HMS Drake, 1974–78; BRNC Dartmouth, 1978–80; Principal Chaplain, Church of Scotland and Free Churches (Naval), MoD, 1981–84. Hon. Chaplain to the Queen, 1981–84. *Recreations:* warm water sailing, music. *Address:* The Manse of Blantyre Old, High Blantyre, Glasgow G72 9UA.

PRICE, Peter S.; *see* Stanley Price.

PRICE, Philip John; His Honour Judge Price; QC 1989; a Circuit Judge, since 1993; *b* 16 May 1943; *s* of Ernest Price and Eunice Price (*née* Morgan); *m* 1967, Mari Josephine Davies; one *s* two *d*. *Educ:* Cardiff High Sch.; Pembroke Coll., Oxford (MA). Lectr in Law, Univ. of Leeds, 1966–70; called to the Bar, Gray's Inn, 1969; in practise: on Wales and Chester Circuit, 1971–90, 1993–; London, 1990–93. Chancellor, Dio. Monmouth, 1992–. Mem., Governing Body, Church in Wales, 1993–. *Recreations:* architecture, books, cricket. *Address:* The Law Courts, Cathays Park, Cardiff CF1 3PG. *T:* Cardiff (01222) 345931. *Clubs:* Cardiff and County; Glamorgan CC.

PRICE, Ralph; *see* Price, L. R.

PRICE, Sir Robert; *see* Price, Sir J. R.

PRICE, Air Vice-Marshal Robert George, CB 1983; *b* 18 July 1928; *s* of Charles and Agnes Price, Hale, Cheshire; *m* 1st, 1958, Celia Anne Mary Talamo (*d* 1987); one *s* four *d*; 2nd, 1989, Edith Barbara Dye. *Educ:* Oundle Sch.; RAF Coll., Cranwell. 74 Sqn, 1950; Central Flying Sch., 1952; 60 Sqn, 1956; Guided Weapons Trials Sqn, 1958; Staff Coll., 1960; Bomber Comd, 1961; JSSC 1964; CO 31 Sqn, 1965; PSO to Dep. SACEUR, 1968; CO RAF Linton-on-Ouse, 1970; RCDS 1973; Dep. Dir Operations, 1974; Group Captain Flying Trng, Support Comd, 1978; Dep. Chief of Staff, Support HQ, 2nd Allied Tactical Air Force, 1979; AOA, RAF Germany, 1980; AOA, HQ Strike Comd, 1981–83. *Recreations:* golf, ski-ing, bridge. *Address:* c/o Barclays Bank, Easingwold, Yorkshire YO6 3AE. *Club:* Royal Air Force.

PRICE, Sir Robert (John) G.; *see* Green-Price.

PRICE, Roy Kenneth, CB 1980; Under-Secretary (Legal), in office of HM Treasury Solicitor, 1972–81; *b* 16 May 1916; *s* of Ernest Price and Margaret Chapman Price (*née* Scott); *m* 1948, Martha (*née* Dannhauser); one *s* one *d*. *Educ:* Eltham Coll. Qualified as Solicitor, 1937. Town Clerk, Borough of Pembroke, and Clerk to Castlemartin Justices, 1939–40. Served War, Army, 1940–46. Officer in Charge, Legal Aid (Welfare), Northern Command, 1946 (Lt-Col). Joined HM Treasury Solicitor, as Legal Asst, 1946; Sen. Legal Asst, 1950; Asst Solicitor, 1962. Mem. Exec. Council, RNIB, 1981–; Pres., Richmond Assoc., Nat. Trust, 1985–; Trustee, Richmond Almshouse Charities, 1987–; Chm., Portcullis Trust, 1980–90. *Recreations:* theatre, travel. *Address:* 16 Queensberry House, Friars Lane, Richmond, Surrey TW9 1NT. *T:* 0181–940 6685. *Club:* Law Society.

PRICE, Terence; *see* Price, B. T.

PRICE, Vivian William Cecil; QC 1972; *b* 14 April 1926; 4th *s* of late Evan Price, Hawkhurst, Kent; *m* 1961, Elizabeth Anne, *o c* of late Arthur Rawlins and Georgina (*née* Guinness); three *s* two *d*. *Educ:* Judd Sch., Tonbridge, Kent; Trinity Coll., Cambridge (BA); Balliol Coll., Oxford (BA). Royal Navy, 1946–49, Instructor Lieut. Called to the Bar: Middle Temple, 1954 (Bencher, 1979); Hong Kong, 1975; Singapore, 1979. Dep. High Court Judge (Chancery Div.), 1975–85; a Recorder of the Crown Court, 1984. Sec., Lord Denning's Cttee on Legal Educn for Students from Africa, 1960; Junior Counsel (Patents) to the Board of Trade, 1967–72; Mem., Patents Procedure Cttee, 1973. Mem., Incorporated Council of Law Reporting for England and Wales, 1980–85. *Address:* Redwall Farmhouse, Linton, Kent ME17 4AX. *T:* Maidstone (01622) 743682. *Club:* Travellers'.

See also A. L. Price.

PRICE, (William Frederick) Barry, OBE 1977; HM Diplomatic Service, retired; Consul-General, Amsterdam, 1983–85; *b* 12 Feb. 1925; *s* of William Thomas and Vera Price; *m* 1948, Lorraine Elisabeth Suzanne Hoather; three *s* two *d*. *Educ:* Worcester Royal Grammar Sch.; St Paul's Training Coll., Cheltenham; Open Univ. (BA Hons 1994). Served War: Armed Forces, 1944–47: commissioned Royal Warwicks, 1945; demobilised, 1947. Primary Sch. Teacher, 1948. Joined Bd of Trade, 1950; Asst Trade Comr: in Delhi, 1954; in Nairobi, 1957; Trade Commissioner, Accra, 1963; transferred to HM Diplomatic Service, 1966; 1st Sec., Sofia, 1967; seconded to East European Trade Council, 1971; Consul-Gen., Rotterdam, 1973–77; Consul, Houston, 1978–81; Counsellor (Commercial and Economic), Bangkok, 1981–82; Kuala Lumpur, 1982. Chm., Anglo-Netherlands Soc., 1989–94. Comdr, Order of Orange-Nassau (Netherlands), 1989. *Recreation:* Dutch studies. *Address:* 46 Finchley Park, N12 9JL. *T:* 0181–445 4642. *Club:* Oriental.

PRICE, William George; *b* 15 June 1934; *s* of George and Lillian Price; *m* 1963, Joy Thomas (marr. diss. 1978); two *s*. *Educ:* Forest of Dene Technical Coll.; Gloucester Technical Coll. Staff Journalist: Three Forest Newspapers, Cinderford, until 1959; Coventry Evening Telegraph, 1959–62; Birmingham Post & Mail, 1962–66. Consultant, Nat. Fedn of Licensed Victuallers, 1979. MP (Lab) Rugby, Warks, 1966–79; PPS: to Sec. of State for Educn and Science, 1968–70; to Dep. Leader, Labour Party, 1972–74; Parliamentary Secretary: ODM, March-Oct. 1974; Privy Council Office, 1974–79. Contested (Lab): Rugby, 1979; Dudley W, 1983. *Recreation:* sport. *Address:* 53 West Heath Court, Northend Road, NW11.

PRICE, Prof. (William) Geraint, FRS 1988; FEng 1986; FIMechE; FRINA; Professor of Ship Science, Department of Ship Science, University of Southampton, since 1990; *b* 1 Aug. 1943; *s* of Thomas Price and Ursula Maude Price (*née* Roberts); *m* 1967, Jennifer Mary Whitten; two *d*. *Educ:* Merthyr Tydfil County Grammar Sch.; University Coll. Cardiff (Univ. of Wales) (G. H. Latham Open Sci. Scholar; BSc, PhD); Univ. of London (DSc(Eng)). FRINA 1980; FIMechE 1989. Res. Asst, later Lectr, UCL, 1969–81; Reader in Applied Mechanics, Univ. of London, 1981–82; Prof. of Applied Mechanics, Brunel Univ., 1982–90. Fellow, Japan Soc. for Promotion of Science, 1987. *Publications:* Probabilistic Theory of Ship Dynamics, 1974; Hydroelasticity of Ships, 1979. *Recreations:* walking, sailing, rugby, squash, barbecueing. *Address:* Tŷ Gwyn, 45 Palmerston Way, Alverstoke, Gosport, Hants PO12 2LY. *T:* Gosport (01705) 351719.

PRICE, William John R.; *see* Rea Price.

PRICE, Winford Hugh Protheroe, OBE 1983; FCA; City Treasurer, Cardiff City Council, 1975–83; *b* 5 Feb. 1926; *s* of Martin Price and Doris Blanche Price. *Educ:* Cardiff High Sch. IPFA 1952; FCA 1954. Served War, RAFVR, 1944–48. City Treasurer's and Controller's Dept, Cardiff, 1942; Dep. City Treasurer, Cardiff, 1973–75. Public Works Loan Comr, 1979–83. Treasurer and Financial Adviser, Council for the Principality, 1975–83; Financial Adviser, Assoc. of Dist Councils Cttee for Wales, 1975–83; Treasurer: The Queen's Silver Jubilee Trust (S Glam), 1976–83; Royal National Eisteddfod of Wales (Cardiff), 1978. Occasional lectr on local govt topics. *Publications:* contrib. to jls. *Recreation:* chess. *Address:* 3 Oakfield Street, Roath, Cardiff CF2 3RD. *T:* Cardiff (01222) 494635.

PRICE EVANS, David Alan; *see* Evans.

PRICHARD, David Colville Mostyn; Headmaster, Wycliffe College, since 1994; *b* 26 May 1934; *s* of Rev. George Mostyn Prichard and Joan Mary Mostyn Prichard; *m* 1992, Catherine Elizabeth Major (Headmistress, Warwick Prep. Sch.). *Educ:* Radley Coll.; Pembroke Coll., Oxford (Captain of Boats; MA). FCollP. Asst Master, Monkton Combe Sch., 1955–68 (Dir, Centenary Appeal, 1962; Founder, GB 1st Vol. Police Cadets, 1964; CO, CCF, 1964–68); Headmaster, Port Regis, Motcombe Park, 1969–93. Founder, Nat. Conf. for Govs, Bursars and Heads, 1981–93; Chm., IAPS, 1989–90. Trustee, Smallpeice Trust, 1980–; Chm., Smallpeice Enterprises, 1986–95; Co-Chm., Operation New World, 1992–; Mem. Council, CTC Trust, 1994–; Vice Pres., Glos Pied Piper Appeal, 1995. Governor: Swanbourne House Sch.; Holmewood House Sch., 1987–; Orwell Park Sch., 1995–. Freeman, City of London, 1990; Liveryman, Lorimers' Co., 1990–. FIMgt; FRSA. *Publication:* Training for Service, 1967. *Recreations:* education, travel, gardening, rowing (OUBC Isis VIII). *Address:* Headmaster's House, Wycliffe College, Stonehouse, Glos GL10 2JQ; Castleton House, Sherborne, Dorset DT9 3SA. *T:* Sherborne (01935) 816539. *Clubs:* National, Carlton, East India; Leander.

PRICHARD, Mathew Caradoc Thomas, CBE 1992; DL; Chairman: Agatha Christie Ltd, since 1971; Booker Entertainment (formerly Authors' Division, Booker McConnell PLC), since 1985; *b* 21 Sept. 1943; *s* of late Major H. de B. Prichard and of Rosalind Hicks; *m* 1967, Angela Caroline Maples; one *s* two *d*. *Educ:* Eton College; New College, Oxford. BA (PPE). Penguin Books, 1965–69. Vice-Pres., Nat. Mus. of Wales, 1992– (Mem. Court of Governors and Council, 1975–); Member: Welsh Arts Council, 1980–94 (Chm., 1988–94); Arts Council of GB, 1983–94. High Sheriff, Glamorgan, 1972–73; DL S Glam, 1994. *Recreations:* golf, cricket, bridge. *Address:* Pwllywrach, Colwinston, Cowbridge, South Glamorgan CF71 7NJ. *T:* Cowbridge (01446) 772256. *Clubs:* Boodle's, MCC; Cardiff and County; Royal & Ancient Golf (St Andrews); Royal Porthcawl Golf.

PRICHARD, Air Vice-Marshal Richard Augustin R.; *see* Riseley-Prichard.

PRICHARD, Air Commodore Richard Julian Paget, CB 1963; CBE 1958; DFC 1942; AFC 1941; *b* 4 Oct. 1915; *o s* of Major W. O. Prichard, 24th Regt; unmarried. *Educ:* Harrow; St Catharine's Coll., Cambridge. Entered RAF, 1937; Air Armament Sch., Eastchurch and Manby, 1937–39; Flying Instructor, South Cerney, 1939–41; No. 21 (LB) Squadron, 1942–43; Staff Coll. (psa), 1943; AEAF, 1943–45; Chief Intelligence Officer, Burma and FEAF, 1946–47; Chief Flying Instructor, RAF Coll., Cranwell, 1947–49; Ministry of Defence, 1949–52; Instructor, RAF Staff Coll., 1953–55; Station Comdr, RAF Tengah, Singapore, 1956–58. IDC, 1959; Director Air Plans, Air Ministry, 1960–63; AOC No 13 Scottish Sector, Fighter Command, 1963–64; AOC Northern Sector of Fighter Command, 1965–66; retired, 1966. US Legion of Merit, 1944. *Recreation:* fishing. *Club:* Royal Air Force.

PRICHARD-JONES, Sir John, 2nd Bt, *cr* 1910; barrister; farmer and bloodstock breeder; *b* 20 Jan. 1913; *s* of 1st Bt and Marie, *y d* of late Charles Read, solicitor; *S* father, 1917; *m* 1937, Heather, (from whom he obtained a divorce, 1950), *er d* of late Sir Walter Nugent, 4th Bt; one *s*; *m* 1959, Helen Marie Thérèse, *e d* of J. F. Liddy, dental surgeon, 20 Laurence Street, Drogheda; one *d*. *Educ:* Eton; Christ Church, Oxford (BA Hons; MA). Called to Bar, Gray's Inn, 1936. Commnd, Queen's Bays, 1939, and served throughout War. *Heir:* *s* David John Walter Prichard-Jones, BA (Hons) Oxon, *b* 14 March 1943. *Address:* Allenswood House, Lucan, Co. Dublin.

PRICKETT, Prof. (Alexander Thomas) Stephen, PhD; Regius Professor of English Language and Literature, University of Glasgow, since 1990; *b* 4 June 1939; *s* of Rev. William Ewart Prickett and Barbara Browning (*née* Lyne); *m* 1st, 1967, Diana Joan Mabbutt; one *s* one *d*; 2nd, 1983, Maria Angelica Alvarez. *Educ:* Kent Coll., Canterbury; Trinity Hall, Cambridge (BA 1961; PhD 1968); University Coll., Oxford (DipEd). FAHA 1986. English teacher, Uzuakoli, E Nigeria, 1962–64; Asst Lectr, Lectr, and Reader, Univ. of Sussex, 1967–82; Prof. of English, ANU, Canberra, 1983–89. Vis. Lectr, Smith Coll., Mass, USA, 1970–71; Vis. Fulbright Prof., Univ. of Minnesota, 1979–80. Fellow, Soc. for Values in Higher Educn, USA, 1992; FRSA 1993. *Publications:* Do It Yourself Doom, 1962; Coleridge and Wordsworth: the poetry of growth, 1970, 2nd edn 1980; Romanticism and Religion, 1976; Victorian Fantasy, 1979, 2nd edn 1982; Words and the Word: language poetics and biblical interpretation, 1986, 2nd edn 1988; England and the French Revolution, 1988; Reading the Text: biblical criticism and literary theory, 1991; (jtly) The Bible, 1991. *Recreations:* walking, ski-ing, drama. *Address:* Department of English, University of Glasgow, Glasgow G12 8QQ.

PRICKETT, Air Chief Marshal Sir Thomas (Other), KCB 1965 (CB 1957); DSO 1943; DFC 1942; RAF retired; *b* 31 July 1913; *s* of late E. G. Prickett; *m* 1st, 1942, Elizabeth Gratian, (*d* 1984), *d* of late William Galbally, Laguna Beach, Calif, USA; one *s* one *d*; 2nd, 1985, Shirley Westerman. *Educ:* Stubbington House Sch.; Haileybury Coll. Assistant, later Manager, sugar estates, India with Begg Sutherland Ltd, 1932–37. Served Bihar Light Horse, Indian Army (Auxiliary). Joined RAF, 1937; Desert Air Force, Bomber Comd, 1939–45; commanded RAF Tangmere, 1949–51; Group Captain operations, HQ Middle East Air Force, 1951–54; commanded RAF Jever, 1954–55; attended Imperial Defence Coll., 1956; Chief of Staff Air Task Force, 1956; Director of Policy, Air Ministry, 1957–58; SASO, HQ No 1 Group, 1958–60; ACAS (Ops) Air Ministry, 1960–63; ACAS (Policy and Planning) Air Ministry, 1963–64; AOC-in-C, NEAF, Comdr British Forces Near East, and Administrator, Sovereign Base Area, 1964–66; AOC-in-C, RAF Air Support Command, 1967–68; Air Mem. for Supply and Organisation, MoD, 1968–70; Dir, Goodwood Estate, 1970–78; Man. Dir, Goodwood Terrena, 1970–78. *Recreations:* polo, sailing, golf. *Address:* 46 Kingston Hill Place, Kingston upon Thames KT2 7QY. *Club:* Royal Air Force.

PRIDDLE, Robert John, CB 1994; Executive Director, International Energy Agency, since 1994; *b* 9 Sept. 1938; *s* of late Albert Leslie Priddle and of Alberta Edith Priddle; *m* 1962, Janice Elizabeth Gorham; two *s*. *Educ:* King's Coll. Sch., Wimbledon; Peterhouse, Cambridge (MA). Asst Principal, Min. of Aviation, 1960, Principal 1965; Private Sec. to Minister for Aerospace, 1971–73; Asst Sec., DTI, 1973, and Dept of Energy, 1974; Under Sec., Dept of Energy, 1977–85; Under Sec., DTI, 1985–89; Dep. Sec. and Dir Gen. of Energy Resources, Dept of Energy, subseq. DTI, 1989–92; Dep. Sec., Corporate and Consumer Affairs, DTI, 1992–94. Pres., Conf. of European Posts and Telecommunications Administrations, 1987–89; Chm. Governing Bd, Internat. Energy Agency, 1991–92.

Mem., Financial Reporting Council, 1992–94. *Publication:* Victoriana, 1959, 2nd edn 1963. *Address:* International Energy Agency, 2 rue André Pascal, 75775 Paris, France.

PRIDEAUX, Sir Humphrey (Povah Treverbian), Kt 1971; OBE 1945; DL; Chairman, Morland & Co., 1983–93 (Director, 1981–93; Vice Chairman, 1982); Chairman, Lord Wandsworth Foundation, 1966–92; *b* 13 Dec. 1915; 3rd *s* of Walter Treverbian Prideaux and Marion Fenn (*née* Arbuthnot); *m* 1939, Cynthia, *er d* of late Lt-Col H. Birch Reynardson, CMG; four *s*. *Educ:* St Aubyns, Rottingdean; Eton; Trinity Coll., Oxford (MA). Commissioned 3rd Carabiniers (Prince of Wales's Dragoon Guards) 1936; DAQMG Guards Armd Div., 1941; Instructor, Staff Coll., 1942; AQMG 21 Army Gp, 1943; AA QMG Guards Armd Div., 1944; Joint Planning Staff, War Office, 1945; Naval Staff Coll., 1948; Commandant School of Administration, 1948; Chiefs of Staff Secretariat, 1950; retired, 1953. Director, NAAFI, 1956–73 (Man. Dir, 1961–65; Chm., 1963–73); Dir, London Life Association Ltd, 1964–88 (Vice-Pres., 1965–72; Pres., 1973–84); Chm., Brooke Bond Liebig Ltd, 1972–80 (Dir, 1968; Dep. Chm., 1969–71); Vice-Chm., W. H. Smith & Son Ltd, 1977–81 (Dir, 1969–77); Dir, Grindlays, 1982–85. DL Hants 1983. *Recreations:* country pursuits. *Address:* Kings Cottage, Buryfields, Odiham, Hants RG29 1NE. *T:* Basingstoke (01256) 703658. *Club:* Cavalry and Guards.

See also *J. H. Prideaux, W. A. Prideaux.*

PRIDEAUX, John Denys Charles Anstice, CBE 1994; PhD; Director, Docklands Light Railway, since 1994; Chairman, Prideaux and Associates, since 1994; *b* 8 Aug. 1944; *s* of Denys Robert Anstice-Prideaux and Frances Hester Dorothy Anstice-Prideaux (*née* Glaze); *m* 1972, Philippa Mary (*née* Morgan); one *s* one *d*. *Educ:* St Paul's; Univ. of Nottingham (BSc, PhD). British Railways: Operational Research, 1965; Area Manager, Newton Abbot, 1972; Strategic Planning Officer, 1974; Divl Manager, Birmingham, 1980; Dir, Policy Unit, 1983–86; Dir, 1986–91, Man. Dir, 1991, InterCity; Man. Dir, New Ventures, 1992–94; Chm., Union Railways, 1992–93; Dir, Green Arrow, 1994–. Member: Adv. Cttee on Trunk Road Assessment, 1977; Transport Cttee, SERC and ESRC, 1982; Planning and Envmt Cttee, ESRC, 1985. Mem, Council, Manchester Business School, 1987. *Publications:* railway histories, papers on management and transport. *Recreations:* riding, hunting, shooting, sailing, ski-ing, design. *Address:* 17 Highgate West Hill, N6 6NP.

PRIDEAUX, Julian Humphrey, OBE 1995; Chief Agent, National Trust, since 1987; *b* 19 June 1942; 2nd *s* of Sir Humphrey Povah Treverbian Prideaux, *qv*; *m* 1967, Jill, 3rd *d* of R. P. Roney-Dougal; two *s*. *Educ:* St Aubyns, Rottingdean; Eton; Royal Agricultural Coll. (Dip. Estate Management). ARICS 1966, FRICS 1974. Land Agent with Burd & Evans, Shrewsbury, 1964–67; Agent to Col Hon. C. G. Cubitt and others, 1967–69; Land Agent, Cornwall Region, NT, 1969–77; Dir, Thames and Chilterns Region, NT, 1978–86. *Recreations:* walking, fishing. *Address:* Steps House, West Wycombe, High Wycombe, Bucks HP14 3AG. *T:* High Wycombe (01494) 443319. *Club:* Farmers'.

PRIDEAUX, Walter Arbuthnot, CBE 1973; MC 1945; TD 1948; *b* 4 Jan. 1910; *e s* of Walter Treverbian Prideaux and Marion Fenn (*née* Arbuthnot); *m* 1937, Anne, *d* of Francis Stewart Cokayne; two *s* two *d*. *Educ:* Eton; Trinity Coll., Cambridge. Solicitor, 1934. Assistant Clerk of the Goldsmiths' Company, 1939–53, Clerk 1953–75. Chm., City Parochial Foundn, 1972–80. Kent Yeomanry, 1936–48. *Recreation:* rowed for Cambridge, 1930, 1931.

See also *Sir H. P. T. Prideaux.*

PRIDHAM, Brian Robert; HM Diplomatic Service, retired; Research Fellow, since 1983, and Director, 1985–86 and since 1987, Centre for Arab Gulf Studies (Deputy Director, 1984–85), and Lecturer in Arabic, Department of Arabic and Islamic Studies, 1984–87, University of Exeter; *b* 22 Feb. 1934; *s* of Reginald Buller Pridham and Emily Pridham (*née* Winser); *m* 1954, Fay Coles; three *s*. *Educ:* Hele's Sch., Exeter. MA Exon, 1984. RWAFF (Nigeria Regt), 1952–54; Foreign Office, 1954–57; MECAS, 1957–59; Bahrain, 1959; Vice-Consul, Muscat, 1959–62; Foreign Office, 1962–64; 2nd Sec., Algiers, 1964–66, 1st Sec., 1966–67; Foreign Office, 1967–70; Head of Chancery: La Paz, 1970–73; Abu Dhabi, 1973–75; Dir of MECAS, Shemlan, Lebanon, 1975–76; Counsellor, Khartoum, 1976–79; Head of Communications Ops Dept, FCO, 1979–81. *Publications:* (ed) Contemporary Yemen: politics and historical background, 1984; (ed) Economy, Society and Culture in Contemporary Yemen, 1984; (ed) The Arab Gulf and the West, 1985; (ed) Oman: economic, social and strategic developments, 1986; The Arab Gulf and the Arab World, 1987. *Recreations:* sailing, old roses. *Address:* c/o Barclays Bank, Exeter EX4 3LL.

PRIDHAM, Kenneth Robert Comyn, CMG 1976; HM Diplomatic Service, retired; *b* 28 July 1922; *s* of late Colonel G. R. Pridham, CBE, DSO, and Mignonne, *d* of late Charles Cumming, ICS; *m* 1965, Ann Rosalind, *d* of late E. Gilbert Woodward, Metropolitan Magistrate, and of Mrs Woodward. *Educ:* Winchester; Oriel Coll., Oxford. Lieut, 60th Rifles, 1942–46; served North Africa, Italy, Middle East (despatches). Entered Foreign (subseq. Diplomatic) Service, 1946; served at Berlin, Washington, Belgrade and Khartoum, and at the Foreign Office; Counsellor: Copenhagen, 1968–72; FCO, 1972–74; Asst Under Sec. of State, FCO, 1974–78; Ambassador to Poland, 1978–81. Vis. Res. Fellow, RIIA, 1981–82. *Address:* c/o Lloyds Bank, 8/10 Waterloo Place, SW1Y 4BE. *Club:* Travellers'.

PRIEST, Rear-Adm. Colin Herbert Dickinson C.; *see* Cooke-Priest.

PRIEST, Prof. Robert George, MD, FRCPsych; Professor of Psychiatry, University of London and Head of Department of Psychiatry at St Mary's Hospital Medical School, Imperial College of Science, Technology and Medicine, since 1973; Hon. Consultant Psychiatrist, St Mary's Hospital, London, since 1973; *b* 28 Sept. 1933; *er s* of late James Priest and of Phoebe Priest; *m* 1955, Marilyn, *er d* of late Baden Roberts Baker and of Evelyn Baker; two *s*. *Educ:* University Coll., London and University Coll. Hosp. Med. Sch. MB, BS 1956; DPM 1963; MRCPE 1964; MD 1970; MRCPsych 1971 (Foundn Mem.); FRCPE 1974; FRCPsych 1974. Lectr in Psychiatry, Univ. of Edinburgh, 1964–67; Exchange Lectr, Univ. of Chicago, 1966; Consultant, Illinois State Psychiatric Inst., Chicago, 1966; Sen. Lectr, St George's Hosp. Med. Sch., London, 1967–73; Hon. Consultant: St George's Hosp., London, 1967–73; Springfield Hosp., London, 1967–73. University of London: Recognised Teacher, 1968–; Mem., Bd of Studies in Medicine, 1968–93 (Chm., 1987–89); Mem., Academic Adv. Bd in Medicine, 1987–90; Mem. Senate, 1989–93; Mem., Academic Council, 1989–93. Examiner in Psychiatry, NUI, 1975–78, 1980–83. Chm., Psychiatric Adv. Sub-Cttee, NW Thames RHA, 1976–79 (Vice-Chm., Reg. Manpower Cttee, 1980–83). Member: Council (Chm. Membership Cttee), British Assoc. for Psychopharmacology, 1977–81; World Psychiatric Assoc., 1980–93 (Mem. Cttee, 1985–93, Mem. Council, 1989–93); Central Cttee for Hosp. Med. Services, 1983–89 (Chm., Psych. Sub-Cttee, 1983–87); Pres., Soc. for Psychosomatic Res., 1980–81 (Vice-Pres., 1978–80); Chm., Mental Health Gp Cttee, BMA, 1982–85 (Mem. 1978–85, 1990–); Internat. Coll. of Psychosomatic Medicine: Fellow, 1977; Mem. Gov. Body and UK Delegate, 1978–81; Treasurer, 1981–83; Secretary, 1981–85; Vice-Pres., 1985–87; Royal College of Psychiatrists: Mem., Public Policy Cttee, 1972–80, 1983– (Chm., 1983–88); Mem. Council, 1982–88; Registrar, 1983–88; Chm., Gen. Psych. Cttee, 1985–89; Mem., Court of Electors, 1983–88 (Chm., Fellowship Sub-Cttee, 1984–88). A. E. Bennett Award, Soc. for Biol Psychiatry, USA (jtly), 1965; Doris Odlum Prize (BMA), 1968; Gutheil Von Domarus Award, Assoc. for Advancement of Psychotherapy and Amer. Jl of Psychotherapy, NY, 1970. *Publications:* Insanity: A Study of Major Psychiatric Disorders, 1977; (ed jtly) Sleep Research, 1979; (ed jtly) Benzodiazepines Today and Tomorrow, 1980; (ed) Psychiatry in Medical Practice, 1982; Anxiety and Depression, 1983; (ed) Sleep, 1984; (ed) Psychological Disorders in Obstetrics and Gynaecology, 1985 (Spanish edn 1987); (jtly) Minski's Handbook of Psychiatry, 7th edn, 1978, 8th edn as Handbook of Psychiatry, 1986; Anxiety and Depression, 1988; (jtly) Sleepless Nights, 1990; (jtly) Depression and Anxiety, 1992 (Spanish edn 1992); chapters in: Current Themes in Psychiatry, 1978; Mental Illness in Pregnancy and the Puerperium, 1978; Psychiatry in General Practice, 1981; Modern Emergency Department Practice, 1983; The Scientific Basis of Psychiatry, 1983, 2nd edn 1992; The Psychosomatic Approach: contemporary practice of wholeperson care, 1986; articles in BMJ, Brit. Jl of Psychiatry, Amer. Jl of Psychotherapy and other learned jls. *Recreations:* squash, tennis, foreign languages, nature study. *Address:* Woodeaves, 29 Old Slade Lane, Richings Park, Iver, Bucks SL0 9DY. *T:* Iver (01753) 653178.

PRIESTLEY, Prof. Charles Henry Brian, AO 1976; FAA 1954; FRS 1967; Professor of Meteorology, Monash University, Australia, 1978–80; *b* 8 July 1915; *s* of late T. G. Priestley; *m* 1946, Constance, *d* of H. Tweedy; one *s* two *d*. *Educ:* Mill Hill Sch.; St John's Coll., Cambridge. MA 1942, ScD 1953. Served in Meteorological Office, Air Ministry, 1939–46; subseq. with CSIRO, Australia; Chief of Div. of Meteorological Physics, 1946–71; Chm., Environmental Physics Res., 1971–78. David Syme Prize, University of Melbourne, 1956. Member Exec. Cttee, International Assoc. of Meteorology, 1954–60, Vice-Pres., 1967–75; Vice-Pres., Australian Acad. of Science, 1959–60; Mem., Adv. Cttee, World Meteorological Organisation, 1964–68 (Chm., 1967; Internat. Met. Orgn Prize, 1973). FRMetSoc (Hon. Life Fellow, 1978; Buchan Prize, 1950 and Symons Medal, 1967, of Society); FInstP. Hon. Mem., Amer. Met. Soc., 1978 (Rossby Medal, 1975). Hon. DSc Monash, 1981. *Publications:* Turbulent Transfer in the Lower Atmosphere, 1959; about 60 papers in scientific journals. *Recreation:* golf. *Address:* Unit 7, 4 Fraser Street, Malvern, Vic 3144, Australia.

PRIESTLEY, Clive, CB 1983; *b* 12 July 1935; *s* of late Albert Ernest and Annie May Priestley; *m* 1st, 1961, Barbara Anne Wells (marr. diss. 1984); two *d*; 2nd, 1985, Daphne June Challis Loasby, JP, DL, *o d* of late W. Challis and Dorothy Franks. *Educ:* Loughborough Grammar Sch.; Nottingham Univ. BA 1956; MA 1958. Nat. Service, 1958–60. Joined HM Home Civil Service, 1960; Min. of Educn, later DES, 1960–65; Schools Council, 1965–67; Harkness Commonwealth Fund Fellow, Harvard Univ., 1967–68; CSD, 1969–79; Prime Minister's Office, 1979–83 (Chief of Staff to Sir Derek Rayner); Under Sec., 1979–83; MPO, 1982–83; Dir, British Telecom plc, 1983–88. Consultant: Corp. of London, 1988–90; Metropolitan Police Comr, 1989–91; LDDC, 1990–91; NEDC, 1992–93. Chm., Review of structure of arts funding in NI for govt, 1992, of responsibilities and gradings of chief officers of nat. museums, galleries and libraries, 1994; Assessor, Review of museums policy in NI, 1995. Member: Council, Univ. of Reading, 1984–86; Philharmonia Trust, 1985–87; Univ. of Cambridge Careers Service Syndicate, 1986–90; Adv. Council, Buxton Festival, 1987–; Arts Council, of GB, 1991–94, of England, 1994–95; Chm., London Arts Bd, 1991–; Vice-Pres., St Bartholomew's Hosp. Med. Coll., 1993– (Mem. Council, 1990–). Governor: Royal Shakespeare Co., 1984–; City Lit. Inst., 1995–. Wandsman, St Paul's Cathedral, 1983–. Freeman, City of London, 1989; Liveryman, Worshipful Co. of Glaziers and Painters of Glass, 1989. *Publications:* financial scrutinies of the Royal Opera House, Covent Garden Ltd, and of the Royal Shakespeare Co., 1984. *Address:* c/o London Arts Board, 133 Long Acre, WC2E 9AF. *T:* 0171-240 1313. *Club:* Army and Navy.

PRIESTLEY, Mrs J. B.; *see* Hawkes, Jacquetta.

PRIESTLEY, Rev. John Christopher; Vicar of Christ Church, Colne, since 1975; Chaplain to the Queen, since 1990; *b* 23 May 1939; *s* of Ronald Edmund Priestley and Winifred Mary Priestley (*née* Hughes); *m* 1964, Margaret Ida Machan; one *s* one *d*. *Educ:* William Hulme Grammar Sch.; Trinity Coll., Oxford (MA); Wells Theol Coll.; MMin Sheffield, 1993. Asst Master, St James Sch., Clitheroe, 1961–64; Dep. Headmaster, Green Sch., Padiham, 1964–70; ordained, Blackburn Cathedral, 1968; Asst Curate: All Saints, Habergham, Burnley, 1968–70; St Leonard's, Padiham, 1970–75. Convenor, Pastoral Auxiliaries, Dio. Blackburn, 1987–91; Rural Dean of Pendle, 1991–. *Publications:* contribs to Church Times, Church of England Newspaper. *Recreation:* music, reading, long-distance walking. *Address:* Christ Church Vicarage, Colne, Lancs BB8 7HF. *T:* Colne (01282) 863511.

PRIESTLEY, Leslie William, TD 1974; FCIB; CIMgt; FCIM; Board Member, Civil Aviation Authority, since 1990; *b* 22 Sept. 1933; *s* of Winifred and George Priestley; *m* 1960, Audrey Elizabeth (*née* Humber); one *s* one *d*. *Educ:* Shooters Hill Grammar School. Head of Marketing, Barclaycard, 1966–73; Asst Gen. Manager, Barclays Bank, 1974–77, Local Dir, 1978–79; Sec. Gen., Cttee of London Clearing Bankers, 1979–83; Dir, Bankers' Automated Clearing Services, 1979–83; Man. Dir, Barclays Insurance Services Co., 1983–84; Regional Gen. Manager, Barclays Bank, 1984–85; Dir and Chief Exec., TSB England & Wales plc (formerly TSB England and Wales and Central Trustee Savings Bank), 1985–89; Director: TSB Gp plc, 1986–89; Hill Samuel Bank, 1988–89; Pearce Gp Hldgs, 1989–. Director: London Electricity plc (formerly London Electricity Board), 1984–; Pinnacle Insurance, 1990–; Omnia/ICL, 1991–94; London Chamber of Commerce and Industry, 1993–; Expatriate Management Ltd, 1994–. Banking Advr, Touche Ross & Co., 1990–; Financial Services Advr, ICL, 1991–. Mem., Monopolies and Mergers Commn, 1990–. Member of Council: Chartered Inst. of Bankers, 1988–89; Assoc. for Payment Clearing Services, 1988–89. Vis. Fellow, UCNW, 1989–95. Consultant Editor, Bankers' Magazine, 1972–81. FCIM (FInstM 1987). FRSA. *Publication:* (ed) Bank Lending with Management Accounts, 1981. *Recreations:* reading, gardening, swimming, golf. *Address:* CAA House, 45–59 Kingsway, WC2B 6TE. *Clubs:* Royal Automobile, Wig and Pen; Sundridge Park Golf.

PRIESTLEY, Prof. Maurice Bertram, MA, PhD; Professor of Statistics, University of Manchester Institute of Science and Technology, since 1970 and Head of Department of Mathematics, 1973–75, 1977–78, 1980–85 and 1987–89; *b* 15 March 1933; *s* of Jack and Rose Priestley; *m* 1959, Nancy, *d* of late Ralph and Hilda Nelson; one *s* one *d*. *Educ:* Manchester Grammar Sch.; Jesus Coll., Cambridge. BA (Wrangler, 1954), MA, DipMathStat (Cambridge); PhD (Manchester). Scientific Officer, RAE, 1955–56; Asst Lectr, Univ. of Manchester, 1957–60, Lectr, 1960–65; Vis. Professor, Princeton and Stanford Univs, USA, 1961–62; Sen. Lectr, UMIST, 1965–70; Dir, Manchester-Sheffield Sch. of Probability and Stats, and Hon. Prof. of Probability and Stats, Sheffield Univ., 1976–79, 1988–89, 1991–92. Mem. Court and Council, UMIST, 1971–74 and 1989–. FIMS; FSS; Member Council: Royal Statistical Soc., 1971–75; Manchester Statistical Soc., 1986–; Mem., ISI. Editor-in-chief, Jl of Time Series Analysis, 1980–. *Publications:* Spectral Analysis and Time Series, Vols I and II, 1981; Non-linear and non-stationary time series analysis, 1988; papers and articles in Jl RSS, Biometrika, Technom., Automatica, Jl of

Sound and Vibration. *Recreations:* music, hi-fi and audio, golf. *Address:* Department of Mathematics, University of Manchester Institute of Science and Technology, PO Box 88, Manchester M60 1QD. *T:* 0161–236 3311.

PRIESTLEY, Philip John; HM Diplomatic Service; Consul-General, Geneva, since 1992; *b* 29 Aug. 1946; *s* of late Frederick Priestley and Caroline (*née* Rolfe); *m* 1972, Christine Rainforth; one *s* one *d*. *Educ:* Boston Grammar Sch.; Univ. of East Anglia (BA Hons). FCO 1969; served Sofia and Kinshasa; First Sec., FCO, 1976; Wellington, 1979–83; FCO, 1984–87; Commercial Counsellor and Dep. Head of Mission, Manila, 1987–90; Ambassador to Gabon, 1990–91; Fellow, Center for Internat. Affairs, Harvard Univ., 1991–92. *Recreations:* golf, tennis, bridge, Rotary, theatre. *Address:* c/o Foreign and Commonwealth Office, King Charles Street, SW1A 2AH.

PRIESTLEY, Dr Robert Henry, CBiol, FIBiol; General Secretary, Institute of Biology, since 1989; *b* 19 March 1946; *s* of Henry Benjamin Priestley, MA, BSc and Margaret Alice (*née* Lambert); *m* 1970, Penelope Ann Fox, BSc; two *d*. *Educ:* Brunts Grammar Sch., Mansfield; Univ. of Southampton (BSc 1967); Univ. of Exeter (PhD 1972). FIBiol 1988. Plant Pathologist, Lord Rank Res. Centre, Rank Hovis McDougall, 1970–73; National Institute of Agricultural Botany: Cereal Pathologist, 1973–78; Head of Cereal Path. Section, 1978–82; Head of Plant Path. Dept, 1982–88. Sec., UK Cereal Pathogen Virulence Survey, 1974–82; Member: Council Fedn of British Plant Pathologists, 1980–81; Internat. Soc. for Plant Path., 1988–92; Treasurer, British Soc. for Plant Path., 1981–87; Member: British Nat. Cttee for Microbiology, 1982–89; Cttee of Management, Biol. Council, 1989–91; Bd, CSTI, 1989–; Parly and Sci. Cttee, 1989–; Chm., European Communities Biol. Assoc., 1992–. *Publications:* papers on diseases of crops; articles in Biologist. *Recreation:* music, gardening, collecting, football, swimming. *Address:* Institute of Biology, 20–22 Queensberry Place, SW7 2DZ. *T:* 0171–581 8333.

PRIESTMAN, Jane, OBE 1991; FCSD; design management consultant; *b* 7 April 1930; *d* of late Reuben Stanley Herbert and Mary Elizabeth Herbert (*née* Ramply); *m* 1954, Arthur Martin Priestman (marr. diss. 1986); two *s*. *Educ:* Northwood College; Liverpool Coll. of Art (NDD, ATD). Design practice, 1954–75; Design Manager, Gen. Manager, Architecture and Design, BAA, 1975–86; Dir, Architecture and Design, BRB, 1986–91. Advr, Art Center Europe, 1987–. Member: LRT Design Panel, 1985–88; Jaguar Styling Panel, 1988–91; Percentage for Art Steering Gp, Arts Council, 1989–91. Governor: Commonwealth Inst., 1987–; Kingston Univ. (formerly Kingston Polytechnic), 1988–95. Hon. FRIBA; FRSA. Hon. DDes De Montfort, 1994. *Recreations:* textiles, city architecture, opera, travel. *Address:* 30 Duncan Terrace, N1 8BS. *T:* 0171–837 4525. *Club:* Architecture.

PRIESTMAN, John David; Clerk of the Parliamentary Assembly of the Council of Europe, 1971–86; *b* 29 March 1926; *s* of Bernard Priestman and Hermine Bréal; *m* 1951, Nada Valić; two *s* two *d*. *Educ:* private sch. in Paris; Westminster Sch.; Merton Coll. and Christ Church, Oxford (Hon. Mods, Lit. Hum.). Served Coldstream Guards, 1944–47, Temp. Captain. Third, subseq. Second, Sec., Belgrade, 1949–53; Asst Private Sec. to Rt Hon. Anthony Eden, 1953–55; joined Secretariat, Council of Europe, 1955; Head of Sec. Gen's Private Office, 1961; Sec., Cttee of Ministers, 1966; Dep. Clerk of Parly Assembly, 1968–71. Hon. Life Mem., Assoc. of Secretaries General of Parlt, 1986. Rep. in Alpes Maritimes, French Nat. Assoc. of Prison Visitors. *Recreations:* off-piste Alpine ski-ing, music, competition bridge, gastronomic research. *Address:* 13 chemin de la Colle, 06160 Antibes, France. *T:* 93617724; 6 rue Adolphe Wurtz, 67000 Strasbourg, France. *T:* 88354049.

PRIGOGINE, Vicomte Ilya; Grand-Croix de l'Ordre de Léopold II, Belgium; Professor, Université Libre de Bruxelles, 1951–87, now Emeritus; Director, Instituts Internationaux de Physique et de Chimie, since 1959; Director, Ilya Prigogine Center of Statistical Mechanics, Thermodynamics and Complex Systems, since 1967 and Ashbel Smith Regental Professor, since 1984, University of Texas at Austin; *b* Moscow, 25 Jan. 1917; created Viscount, 1989; *m* 1961, Marina Prokopowicz; two *s*. *Educ:* Univ. of Brussels (Lic. Sc. Physiques, 1939; Dr en Sciences Chimiques, 1941). Prof., Dept of Chemistry, Enrico Fermi Inst. for Nuclear Studies, and Inst. for Study of Metals, Univ. of Chicago, 1961–66. Associate Dir of Studies, l'Ecole des Hautes Etudes en Sciences Sociales, France, 1987; Hon. Prof., Banaras Hindu Univ., Varanasi, 1988; RGK Foundn Centennial Fellow, Univ. of Texas, 1989–90; Dist. Visitor, Inst. for Advanced Study, Princeton, 1993. Special Advr, EEC, 1993. Pres. elect, Internat. Soc. for Gen. Systems Res., Louisville, Ky, USA, 1988. Mem. Sci. Adv. Bd, Internat. Acad. for Biomedical Drug Res., 1990. Hon. Pres., Université Philosophique Européenne, Paris; Member: Académie Royale de Belgique, 1958; Royal Soc. of Sciences, Uppsala, Sweden, 1967; German Acad. Naturforscher Leopoldina, GDR, 1970; Acad. Internat. de Philosophie des Sciences, 1973; Acad. Européenne des Scis, des Arts et des Lettres, Paris, 1980 (Vice-Pres., 1980); Accademia Mediterranea delle Scienze, Catania, 1982; Internat. Acad. of Social Perspective, Geneva, 1983; Haut Conseil de la Francophonie, Paris, 1984; Max-Planck Foundn, Fed. Republic of Germany, 1984; World Inst. of Sci., 1992; Assoc. Descartes, 1992; Academia Scientiarium et Artium Europaea, Salzburg, 1993; Hon. Member: Amer. Acad. of Arts and Sciences, 1960; Chem. Soc., Warsaw, 1971; Soc. for Studies on Entropy, Japan, 1983; Biophys. Soc., China, 1986; Royal Soc. of Chemistry, Belgium, 1987. Fellow: Acad. of Sciences, New York, 1962; World Acad. of Art and Science, 1986; Centennial Foreign Fellow, Amer. Chem. Soc., 1976; Foreign Fellow: Indian Nat. Sci. Acad., 1979; Acad. das Ciencias de Lisbõa; Foreign Associate, Nat. Acad. of Sciences, USA, 1967; Hon. Fellow, Nat. Acad. of Scis of India, 1992; Foreign Member: Akad. der Wissenschaften der DDR, Berlin, 1980; USSR Acad. of Scis, 1982; Corresponding Member: Acad. of Romania, 1965; Soc. Royale des Sciences, Liège, 1967; Section of Phys. and Math., Akad. der Wissenschaften, Göttingen, 1970; Akad. der Wissenschaften, Vienna, 1971; Rheinish-Westfählische Akad. der Wissenschaften, Düsseldorf, 1980; Archives de Psychologie, Univ. of Geneva, 1982; Accad. Nazionale di Scienze, Lettere e Arti, Modena, 1992. Dr (*hc*): Newcastle upon Tyne, 1966; Poitiers, 1966; Chicago, 1969; Bordeaux, 1972; Uppsala, 1977; Liège, 1978; Aix-Marseille, 1979; Georgetown, 1980; Rio de Janeiro, 1981; Cracow, 1981; Stevens Inst. of Technology, Hoboken, 1981; Tours, France, 1984; Heriot-Watt, 1985; Universidad Nacional de Educación a Distancia, Madrid, 1985; Nanking Univ., China, 1986; Peking Univ., China, 1986; Buenos Aires, 1989; Facolta di Magistero, Cagliari Univ., 1990; Univ. of Siena, 1990; Nice, France, 1991; Univ. of the Philippines, 1991; Univ. of Santiago, Chile, 1991; Univ. of Tucumán, Argentina, 1991; Moscow Lomonosov Univ., 1993; 'Al.I. Cuza' Iaşi, Romania, 1994. Prizes: Van Laar, Société Chimique de Belgique, 1947; A. Wetrems 1950, and Annual (jtly) 1952, Acad. Royale de Belgique; Francqui, 1955; E. J. Solvay, 1965; Nobel Prize for Chemistry, 1977; Southwest Science Forum, New York Acad. of Science; Honda, Honda Foundn, Tokyo, 1983; Umberto Biancamano, Pavia, Italy, 1987; (jtly) Gravity Res. Foundn Award, 1988. Gold Medals: Swante Arrhenius, Royal Acad. of Sciences, Sweden, 1969; Cothenius, German Acad. Naturforscher Leopoldina, 1975; Rumford, Royal Soc., 1976; Ostend, 1987. Bourke Medal, Chem. Soc., 1972; Medal, Assoc. for the Advancement of Sciences, Paris, 1975; Karcher Medal, Amer. Crystallographic Assoc., 1978; Descartes Medal, Univ. Descartes, Paris, 1979; Médaille d'Or de la Ville de Pavie, 1987; Médaille d'Or de la Ville d'Ostende, 1987; Médaille d'Or de l'Université de Padoue, 1988; Distinguished Service Medal, Austin, Texas, 1989. Hon. Citizen: Dallas, USA, 1983; Montpellier, France, 1983; Uccle, Belgium, 1987. Commandeur, l'Ordre du Mérite, France; Commandeur, l'Ordre des Arts et des Lettres, France, 1984; Commandeur de la Légion d'Honneur, France, 1989. *Publications:* (with R. Defay) Traité de Thermodynamique, conformément aux méthodes de Gibbs et de Donder: Vol. I, Thermodynamique Chimique, 1944 (Eng. trans. 1954); Vol. II, Tension Superficielle et Adsorption, 1951 (Eng. trans. 1965); Etude Thermodynamique des Phénomènes Irreversibles, 1947; Introduction to Thermodynamics of Irreversible Processes, New York 1954 (3rd edn 1967); (with A. Bellemans and V. Mathot) The Molecular Theory of Solutions, Amsterdam 1957; Non. Equilibrium Statistical Mechanics, 1962 (also New York); (with R. Herman) Kinetic Theory of Vehicular Traffic, New York 1971; (with P. Glansdorff) Thermodynamic Theory of Structure, Stability and Fluctuations, London and New York 1971 (also French edn); (with G. Nicolis) Self-Organization in Non Equilibrium Systems, 1977 (also New York); From Being to Becoming: time and complexity in the physical sciences, 1980 (also French, German, Japanese, Russian, Italian and Chinese edns); (with I. Stengers) La Nouvelle Alliance: les métamorphoses de la science, 1981 (Prix du Haut Comité de la langue française, Paris, 1981) (also English, German, Italian, Yugoslavian, Spanish, Rumanian, Swedish, Dutch, Danish, Portuguese, Russian, Japanese, Chinese, Bulgarian, Korean and Polish edns); (with I. Stengers) Entre le temps et l'éternité, 1988 (also Dutch, Italian, Portuguese and Spanish edns); (with G. Nicolis) Exploring Complexity, 1989 (also German, Chinese, Russian, Italian and French edns). *Recreations:* art, music. *Address:* avenue Fond'Roy 67, 1180 Bruxelles, Belgium. *T:* (2)3742952.

PRIMAROLO, Dawn; MP (Lab) Bristol South, since 1987; *b* 2 May 1954; *m* 1972 (marr. diss.); one *s*; *m* 1990, Thomas Ian Ducat. *Educ:* Thomas Bennett Comprehensive Sch., Crawley; Bristol Poly.; Bristol Univ. Mem., Avon CC, 1985–87. Opposition front bench spokesman on health, 1992–94, on Treasury affairs, 1994–. Mem., Select Cttee on Members' Interests, 1988–92. *Address:* House of Commons, SW1A 0AA; (office) Transport House, Victoria Street, Bristol BS1 6AY. *T:* Bristol (0117) 929 3298.

PRIME, Prof. Henry Ashworth, CEng, FIEE; Professor of Electronic and Electrical Engineering, University of Birmingham, 1963–86, now Professor Emeritus; *b* 11 March 1921; *s* of late E. V. Prime and Elsie (*née* Ashworth); *m* 1943, Ella Stewart Reid; one *s* one *d*. *Educ:* N Manchester High Sch.; Manchester Univ. (MSc). CEng, FIEE 1964. Scientific Officer, Admiralty Signal and Radar Estab., 1942–46; Lectr, Univ. of Liverpool, 1946–50; Sen. Lectr, Univ. of Adelaide, 1950–55; Chief Electronic Engr and Manager Control Div., Brush Elec. Engrg Co., 1955–63. Pro-Vice-Chancellor, Univ. of Birmingham, 1978–82. Vis. Professor: Univ. of Teheran, 1971; Univ. of Hanover, 1978; Univ. of Cape Town, 1984. Chm., IFAC Technical Cttee on Terminology, 1987–93. Member: CNAA Elec. Engrg Bd, 1970–74; Naval Educn Adv. Cttee, 1973–79 (Chm., 1978–79). Mem. Council, IEE, 1974–77, 1980–84, 1985–88; Chm., Computing and Control Divl Bd, IEE, 1982–83. *Publications:* (contrib.) Telecommunication Satellites, ed Gatland, 1964; Modern Concepts in Control Theory, 1970; papers in scientific jls on electrical discharges, microwave interaction with ionised gases, and control systems. *Address:* 2 Oakdene Drive, Birmingham B45 8LQ. *T:* 0121–445 2545.

PRIMROSE, family name of **Earl of Rosebery.**

PRIMROSE, Sir John Ure, 5th Bt *cr* 1903, of Redholme, Dumbreck, Govan; *b* 28 May 1960; *s* of Sir Alasdair Neil Primrose, 4th Bt and of Elaine Noreen, *d* of Edmund Cecil Lowndes, Buenos Aires; *S* father, 1986; *m* 1983, Marion Cecilia (marr. diss. 1987), *d* of Hans Otto Altgelt; two *d*. *Heir:* *b* Andrew Richard Primrose, *b* 19 Jan. 1966. *Educ:* St Peter's School and Military Acad. BA.

PRIMUS, The; *see* Holloway, Most Rev. R. F.

PRINCE, David; Chief Executive, District Audit Service, Audit Commission for Local Authorities and NHS in England and Wales, since 1994; *b* 31 May 1948; *s* of Charles and Phyllis Grace Prince; *m* 1973, Davina Ann Pugh. *Educ:* Exeter Univ. (BA Hons English). MCIPFA. Hants CC Grad. Trainee, 1969–71; finance posts, Berks CC, 1971–76; Chief Accountant, Cambs CC, 1976–81, and Asst Co. Treasurer; Dep. Co. Treasurer, Herts CC, 1981–86; Dir, Finance and Admin, Cambs CC, 1986–91; Chief Exec., Leics CC, 1991–94. FRSA. *Recreations:* theatre, music, gardening. *Address:* Audit Commission, 1 Vincent Square, SW1P 2PN.

PRINCE, Prof. Frank Templeton, MA (Oxon); *b* Kimberley, South Africa, 13 Sept. 1912; 2nd *s* of late H. Prince and Margaret Templeton (*née* Hetherington); *m* 1943, Pauline Elizabeth, *d* of late H. F. Bush; two *d*. *Educ:* Christian Brothers' Coll., Kimberley, South Africa; Balliol Coll., Oxford. Visiting Fellow, Graduate Coll., Princeton, NJ, 1935–36. Study Groups Department, Chatham House, 1937–40. Served Army, Intelligence Corps, 1940–46. Department of English, 1946–57, Prof. of English, 1957–74, Southampton Univ.; Prof. of English, Univ. of WI, Jamaica, 1975–78. Hurst Vis. Prof., Brandeis Univ., 1978–80; Vis. Prof., Washington Univ., St Louis, 1980–81, Sana'a Univ., N Yemen, 1981–83; Visiting Fellow, All Souls Coll., 1968–69. Clark Lectr, Cambridge, 1972–73. Pres., English Assoc., 1985–86. Hon. DLitt Southampton, 1981; DUniv York, 1982. *Publications:* Poems, 1938; Soldiers Bathing (poems), 1954; The Italian Element in Milton's Verse, 1954; The Doors of Stone (poems), 1963; Memoirs in Oxford (verse), 1970; Drypoints of the Hasidim (verse), 1975; Collected Poems, 1979; Later On (poems), 1983; Walks in Rome (verse), 1987; Collected Poems, 1993. *Recreations:* music, etc. *Address:* 32 Brookvale Road, Southampton SO17 1QR. *T:* Southampton (01703) 555457.

PRINCE, Harold Smith; theatrical director/producer; *b* NYC, 30 Jan. 1928; *s* of Milton A. Prince and Blanche (*née* Stern); *m* 1962, Judith Chaplin; two *d*. *Educ:* Univ. of Pennsylvania (AB 1948). Co-Producer: The Pajama Game, 1954–56 (co-prod film, 1957); Damn Yankees, 1955–57 (co-prod film, 1958); New Girl in Town, 1957–58; West Side Story, 1957–59; Fiorello!, 1959–61 (Pulitzer Prize); Tenderloin, 1960–61; A Call on Kuprin, 1961; They Might Be Giants, London 1961; Side By Side By Sondheim, 1977–78. Producer: Take Her She's Mine, 1961–62; A Funny Thing Happened on the Way to the Forum, 1962–64; Fiddler on the Roof, 1964–72; Poor Bitos, 1964; Flora the Red Menace, 1965. Director-Producer: She Loves Me, 1963–64, London 1964; Superman, 1966; Cabaret, 1966–69, London 1968, tour and NY, 1987; Zorba, 1968–69; Company, 1970–72, London 1972; A Little Night Music, 1973–74, London 1975 (dir. film, 1977); Pacific Overtures, 1976. Director: A Family Affair, 1962; Baker Street, 1965; Something For Everyone (film), 1970; New Phoenix Rep. prodns of Great God Brown, 1972–73, The Visit, 1973–74, and Love for Love, 1974–75; Some of my Best Friends, 1977; On the Twentieth Century, 1978; Evita, London 1978, USA 1979–83, Australia, Vienna, 1980, Mexico City, 1981; Sweeney Todd, 1979, London 1980; Girl of the Golden West, San Francisco Op., 1979; world première, Willie Stark, Houston Grand Opera, 1981; Merrily We Roll Along (musical) 1981; A Doll's Life (musical), 1982; Madame Butterfly, Chicago Lyric Op., 1982; Turandot, Vienna state Op., 1983; Play Memory, 1984; End of the World, 1984; Diamonds, 1985; The Phantom of the Opera, London, 1986, NY, 1988, Los Angeles, 1989, Canada, 1989; Roza, USA, 1987; Cabaret (20th anniversary revival), tour and Broadway, 1987; Kiss of the Spider Woman, 1990, Toronto, London, Broadway, 1993; (also adapted) Grandchild of Kings, 1992; Showboat, Toronto, 1993,

NY, 1994. Directed for NY City Opera: Ashmedai, 1976; Kurt Weill's Silverlake, 1980; Candide, 1982; Don Giovanni, 1989; Faust, Metropolitan Opera, 1990; co-Director-Producer, Follies, 1971–72; co-Producer-Director: Candide, 1974–75; Merrily We Roll Along, 1981; A Doll's Life, 1982; Grind (musical), 1985. Antoinette Perry Awards for: The Pajama Game; Damn Yankees; Fiorello!; A Funny Thing Happened on the Way to the Forum; Fiddler on the Roof; Cabaret; Company; A Little Night Music; Candide; Sweeney Todd; Evita; The Phantom of the Opera; SWET award: Evita, 1977–78. Member: League of New York Theatres (Pres., 1964–65); Council for National Endowment for the Arts. Hon. DLit, Emerson College, 1971; Hon. Dr of Fine Arts, Univ. of Pennsylvania, 1971. Drama Critics' Circle Awards; Best Musical Award, London Evening Standard, 1955–58, 1972 and 1992. Kennedy Center Honoree, 1994. *Publication:* Contradictions: notes on twenty-six years in the theatre, 1974. *Recreation:* tennis. *Address:* Suite 1009, 10 Rockefeller Plaza, New York, NY 10020, USA. *T:* (212) 3990960.

PRINCE, Maj.-Gen. Hugh Anthony, CBE 1960; retired as Chief, Military Planning Office, SEATO, Bangkok; *b* 11 Aug. 1911; *s* of H. T. Prince, FRCS, LRCP; *m* 1st, 1938, Elizabeth (*d* 1959), *d* of Dr Walter Bapty, Victoria, BC; two *s*; 2nd, 1959, Claude-Andrée, *d* of André Romanet, Château-de-Tholot, Beaujeu, Rhône; one *s*. *Educ:* Eastbourne Coll.; RMC, Sandhurst. Commissioned, 1931; served in 6th Gurkha Rifles until 1947; The King's Regt (Liverpool), 1947. *Recreations:* golf, gardening, antiques. *Address:* 36 Route de la Crau, 13280 Raphèle-les-Arles, France. *T:* 90984693.

PRINCE-SMITH, Sir (William) Richard, 4th Bt, *cr* 1911; *b* 27 Dec. 1928; *s* of Sir William Prince-Smith, 3rd Bt, OBE, MC, and Marjorie, Lady Prince-Smith (*d* 1970); *S* father, 1964; *m* 1st, 1955, Margaret Ann Carter; one *s* one *d*; 2nd, 1975, Ann Christina Faulds. *Educ:* Charterhouse; Clare Coll., Cambridge (MA). BA (Agric.) 1951. *Recreations:* music, photography, travel. *Heir:* *s* James William Prince-Smith, Capt. 13th/18th Royal Hussars (QMO), *b* 2 July 1959. *Address:* 40–735 Paxton Drive, Rancho Mirage, CA 92270–3519, USA. *T:* (619) 3211975. *Club:* Springs Country (Rancho Mirage).

PRINDL, Dr Andreas Robert; Chairman, Nomura Bank International, since 1990; *b* 25 Nov. 1939; *s* of Frank Joseph Prindl and Vivian Prindl (*née* Mitchell); *m* 1963, Veronica Maria Koerber; one *s* one *d*. *Educ:* Princeton Univ. (BA); Univ. of Kentucky (MA, PhD). Morgan Guaranty Trust Company: NY and Frankfurt, 1964–70; Vice-Pres., IMM, London, 1970–76; Gen. Manager, Tokyo, 1976–80; CEO Saudi Internat. Bank, London, 1980–82; Vice-Pres., Mergers and Acquisitions, Morgan Guaranty, 1982–84; Managing Director: Nomura Internat., 1984–86; Nomura Bank Internat., 1986–90. Pres., Chartered Inst. of Bankers, 1994–. *Publications:* (jtly) International Money Management, 1972; Foreign Exchange Risk, 1976; Japanese Finance, 1981; Money in the Far East, 1986; (ed) Banking and Finance in Eastern Europe, 1992; (ed jtly) Ethical Conflicts in Finance, 1994. *Recreations:* classical music (member, Brighton Festival Chorus), attempting to run one marathon each year. *Address:* Nomura Bank International, Nomura House, 1 St Martin's-le-Grand, EC1A 4NP. *T:* 0171–929 2366. *Club:* Reform.

PRING, Prof. Richard Anthony; Professor of Educational Studies, University of Oxford, since 1989; Fellow of Green College, Oxford, since 1989; *b* 20 April 1938; *s* of Joseph Edwin and Anne-Marie Pring; *m* 1970, Helen Faye Evans; three *d*. *Educ:* Gregorian Univ. and English College, Rome (PhL); University Coll. London (BA Hons Philosophy); Univ. of London Inst. of Education (PhD); College of St Mark and St John (PGCE). Asst Principal, Dept of Educn and Science, 1962–64; teacher in London comprehensive schools, 1965–67, 1973–78; Lectr in Education: Goldsmiths' Coll., 1967–70; Univ. of London Inst. of Educn, 1972–78; Prof. of Educn, Univ. of Exeter, 1978–89. Hon. DLitt Kent, 1995. Editor, British Jl of Educational Studies, 1986–. *Publications:* Knowledge and Schooling, 1976; Personal and Social Education, 1984; The New Curriculum, 1989; Closing the Gap, 1995. *Recreations:* running half marathons, cycling, writing, campaigning for comprehensive schools. *Address:* Green College, Oxford OX2 6HG.

PRING-MILL, Robert Duguid Forrest, DLitt; FBA 1988; Fellow of St Catherine's College, Oxford, since 1965; *b* 11 Sept. 1924; *o s* of late Major Richard Pring-Mill, RA and Nellie (*née* Duguid); *m* 1950, Maria Brigitte Heinsheimer; one *s* one *d*. *Educ:* Colegio de Montesión, Palma de Mallorca; New Coll., Oxford (BA 1st cl. Mod. Langs, 1949; DLitt 1986). Enlisted, 1941; commnd The Black Watch, RHR, 1942; temp. Capt., 1945. Oxford University: Sen. Demy, Magdalen Coll., 1950–52; Univ. Lectr in Spanish, 1952–88; Lectr, New Coll., 1956–88, Exeter Coll., 1963–81; Tutor, St Catherine's Coll., 1965–88. English Editor: Romanistisches Jahrbuch, 1953–; Estudios Lulianos, 1957–; Commissió Editora Lul·liana, 1960–. Magister, Maioricensis Schola Lullistica, 1957; Corresp. Mem., Inst. d'Estudis Catalans, 1966. Premi Pompeu Fabra, 1956; Premi Ciutat de Palma, 1979; Premi Catalònia, 1991. Cross of St George (Generalitat de Catalunya), 1990; Commander, Order of Isabel la Católica (Spain), 1990; Officer, Order of Bernardo O'Higgins (Chile), 1992. *Publications:* Chinese Triad Societies, 1946; (ed) Lope de Vega: Five Plays, 1961; El Microcosmos Lul·lià, 1961; Ramón Llull y el Número Primitivo de las Dignidades, 1963; (with N. Tarn) The Heights of Macchu Picchu, 1966; (with Katya Kohn) Neruda Poems, 1969; (ed) Raymundus Lullus, Quattuor Libri Principiorum, 1969; Neruda: A Basic Anthology, 1975; Cardenal: Marilyn Monroe & Other Poems, 1975; The Scope of Spanish-American Committed Poetry, 1977; (with Donald Walsh) Cardenal: Apocalypse and Other Poems, 1977; Spanish American Committed Poetry: canciones de lucha y esperanza, 1978; (ed jtly) Studies in Honour of P. E. Russell, 1981; (ed jtly) Hacia Calderón, 1982; Cantas-Canto-Cantemos, 1983; Gracias a la vida: the power and poetry of song, 1990; Estudis sobre Ramón Llull, 1991 (Premi Crítica Serra d'Or, 1992); Neruda exhibn catalogue, 1993; articles in learned jls, Encyc. Britannica, etc, on Ramón Llull, Calderón, modern poetry and Spanish-American protest song. *Recreations:* glass engraving; travel, photography and field recording in Latin America. *Address:* 11 North Hills, Brill, Bucks HP18 9TH. *T:* Brill (01844) 237481.

PRINGLE, Air Marshal Sir Charles (Norman Seton), KBE 1973 (CBE 1967); MA, FEng 1977; *b* 6 June 1919; *s* of late Seton Pringle, OBE, FRCSI, Dublin; *m* 1946, Margaret, *d* of late B. Sharp, Baildon, Yorkshire; one *s*. *Educ:* Repton; St John's Coll., Cambridge. Commissioned, RAF, 1941; served India and Ceylon, 1942–46. Air Ministry, 1946–48; RAE, Farnborough, 1949–50; attached to USAF, 1950–52; appts in UK, 1952–60; STSO No 3 Group, Bomber Comd, 1960–62, and Air Forces Middle East, 1962–64; Comdt RAF St Athan and Air Officer Wales, 1964–66; MoD, 1967; IDC, 1968. Dir-Gen. of Engineering (RAF) MoD, 1969–70; Air Officer Engineering, Strike Command, 1970–73; Dir-Gen. Engineering (RAF), 1973; Controller, Engrg and Supply (RAF), 1973–76; Sen. Exec., Rolls Royce Ltd, 1976–78; Dir, Hunting Engineering Ltd, 1976–78; Dir and Chief Exec., SBAC, 1979–84. Dir, FR Group plc, 1985–89. Pres., RAeS, 1975–76; Vice-Chm., 1976–77, Chm., 1977–78, CEI. Mem. Council, RSA, 1978–83 and 1986–92. Chm. Governors, Repton Sch., 1985–92. Hon. FRAeS, 1989. CIMgt. *Recreations:* photography, ornithology, motor sport. *Address:* Appleyards, Fordingbridge, Hants SP6 3BP; K9 Sloane Avenue Mansions, SW3 3JP. *T:* 0171–584 3432. *Clubs:* Royal Air Force, Buck's.

PRINGLE, Hon. Sir John (Kenneth), Kt 1993; **Hon. Mr Justice Pringle;** Justice of the High Court of Northern Ireland, since 1993; *b* 23 June 1929; *s* of late Kenneth Pringle and Katie (*née* Batchen); *m* 1960, Ruth Henry; two *s* one *d*. *Educ:* Campbell Coll., Belfast; Queen's Univ., Belfast (BSc 1st Cl. Hons 1950; LLB 1st Cl. Hons 1953). Called to the Bar, NI, 1953, Bencher, 1973; QC (NI), 1970; Recorder of Belfast, 1984–93. Chm., Bar Council of NI, 1975–80. *Recreations:* gardening, being outdoors. *Address:* Royal Courts of Justice, Belfast BT1 3JF.

PRINGLE, John Martin Douglas; *b* 1912; *s* of late J. Douglas Pringle, Hawick, Scotland; *m* 1936, Celia, *d* of E. A. Carroll; one *s* two *d*. *Educ:* Shrewsbury Sch.; Lincoln Coll., Oxford. First Class Literae Humaniores, 1934. Editorial Staff of Manchester Guardian, 1934–39. Served War of 1939–45 with King's Own Scottish Borderers, 1940–44; Assistant Editor, Manchester Guardian, 1944–48; Special Writer on The Times, 1948–52; Editor of The Sydney Morning Herald, 1952–57; Deputy Editor of The Observer, 1958–63; Managing Editor, Canberra Times, 1964–65; Editor, Sydney Morning Herald, 1965–70. *Publications:* China Struggles for Unity, 1938; Australian Accent, 1958; Australian Painting Today, 1963; On Second Thoughts, 1971; Have Pen, Will Travel, 1973; The Last Shenachie, 1976; The Shorebirds of Australia, 1987. *Address:* 8/105A Darling Point Road, Darling Point, NSW 2027, Australia.

PRINGLE, Margaret Ann; Head of Holland Park School, 1986–94; *b* 28 Sept. 1946. *Educ:* Holton Park Girls' Grammar Sch.; Somerville College, Oxford (MA, BLitt English Lang. and Lit.). English Teacher, Selhurst High School, Croydon, 1972–76; Head of English, Thomas Calton School, Peckham, 1976–81; Dep. Head, George Green's School, Isle of Dogs, 1981–86. *Recreations:* all food, all music, most dancing, and occasionally not thinking about education.

PRINGLE, Dr Robert William, OBE 1967; BSc, PhD; CPhys; FRSE; FRS(Can); President, Nuclear Enterprises Ltd, Edinburgh, since 1976; *b* 2 May 1920; *s* of late Robert Pringle and late Lillias Dalgleish Hair; *m* 1948, Carol Stokes; three *s* one *d*. *Educ:* George Heriot's Sch., Edinburgh; Edinburgh Univ. (Vans Dunlop Scholar in Natural Philosophy). Lecturer, Natural Philosophy, Edinburgh, 1945; Mem. Bd, Manitoba Cancer Inst., 1949–55; Associate Professor of Physics, Manitoba, 1949; Prof. and Chairman of Physics, Manitoba, 1953–56; Chm. and Man. Dir, Nuclear Enterprises Ltd, 1956–76 (Queen's Award to Industry, 1966, 1979); Dir, N Sea Assets Ltd, 1977–78. Member: Scottish Council, CBI (Cttee), 1966–72; Scottish Univs Industry Liaison Cttee, 1968–75; Bd, Royal Observatory (Edinburgh), 1968–79; Council, SRC, 1972–76; Bd, Astronomy, Space and Radio (SRC), 1970–72; Bd, Nuclear Physics (SRC), 1972–76; Economic Council for Scotland, 1971–75; Bd, Scottish Sch. Business Studies, 1972–83. University of Edinburgh: Mem. Court, 1967–75; Mem., Finance Cttee, 1967–75; Mem. Bd, Centre for Indust. Liaison and Consultancy, 1968–84; Mem., Press Cttee, 1977–78. Trustee: Scottish Hospitals Endowments Res. Trust, 1976–88; Scottish Trust for the Physically Disabled, 1977–84. Hon. Adviser, Nat. Museum of Antiquities of Scotland, 1969–. FInstP 1948; Fellow, American Physical Soc., 1950; FRS(Can) 1955; FRSE 1964; Hon. Fellow, Royal Scottish Soc. Arts, 1972; CPhys 1985; Sen. Life Mem., IEEE, 1990. *Publications:* (with James Douglas) 20th Century Scottish Banknotes, Vol. II, 1986; papers on nuclear spectroscopy and nuclear geophysics in UK and US scientific journals. *Recreations:* golf, book-collecting, Rugby (Edinburgh, Edinburgh and Glasgow, Rest of Scotland, 1945–48; Pres., Manitoba RU, 1952–55; organiser, first Monte Carlo Internat. Rugby Sevens, 1987). *Address:* 27 avenue Princesse Grace, Monaco. *Clubs:* Athenæum; New (Edinburgh); Yacht Club de Monaco, Golf de Monte Carlo.

PRINGLE, Lt Gen. Sir Steuart (Robert), 10th Bt, *cr* 1683, Stichill, Roxburghshire; KCB 1982; Commandant General Royal Marines 1981–84; Chairman and Chief Executive, Chatham Historic Dockyard Trust, 1984–91; *b* 21 July 1928; *s* of Sir Norman H. Pringle, 9th Bt and Lady (Oonagh) Pringle (*née* Curran) (*d* 1975); *S* father, 1961; *m* 1953, Jacqueline Marie Gladwell; two *s* two *d*. *Educ:* Sherborne. Royal Marines: 2nd Lieut, 1946; 42 Commando, 1950–52; 40 Commando, 1957–59; Chief Instructor, Signal Trng Wing, RM, 1959–61; Bde Signal Officer, 3 Commando Bde, RM, 1961–63; Defence Planning Staff, 1964–67; Chief Signal Officer, RM, 1967–69; 40 Commando, Far East, 1969–71; CO 45 Commando Group, 1971–74; HQ Commando Forces, 1974–76; RCDS, 1977; Maj.-Gen. RM Commando Forces, 1978–79; Chief of Staff to Comdt Gen., RM, 1979–81. Col Comdt, RM, 1989–90, Representative Col Comdt, 1991–92. President: St Loye's Coll., 1984–; City of London Br., RM Assoc., 1984–; Vice-Pres., Officers Pensions Soc., 1984–; Mem. Council, Union Jack Club, 1982–85; Vice-Patron, Royal Naval Benevolent Trust, 1984–. CIMgt. Liveryman, Plaisterers' Co., 1984. Hon. DSc City, 1982; Hon. LLD Exeter, 1994. Hon. Admiral, Texas Navy; Hon. Mem., Co. of Bear Tamers. *Publications:* (contrib) Peace and the Bomb, 1982; The Future of British Seapower, 1984; contribs to RUSI Jl, Navy International, etc. *Heir:* *s* Simon Robert Pringle [*b* 6 Jan. 1959; *m* 1992, Pamela Margaret, *d* of George Hunter; one *d*]. *Address:* 76 South Croxted Road, Dulwich, SE21 8BD. *Clubs:* Army and Navy; Royal Thames Yacht, MCC.

PRIOR, family name of **Baron Prior.**

PRIOR, Baron *cr* 1987 (Life Peer), of Brampton in the County of Suffolk; **James Michael Leathes Prior;** PC 1970; Chairman, The General Electric Company plc, since 1984; *b* 11 Oct. 1927; 2nd *s* of late C. B. L. and A. S. M. Prior, Norwich; *m* 1954, Jane Primrose Gifford, 2nd *d* of late Air Vice-Marshal O. G. Lywood, CB, CBE; three *s* one *d*. *Educ:* Charterhouse; Pembroke College, Cambridge (1st class degree in Estate Management, 1950; Hon. Fellow, 1992). Commissioned in Royal Norfolk Regt, 1946; served in India and Germany; farmer and land agent in Norfolk and Suffolk. MP (C): Lowestoft, Suffolk, 1959–83; Waveney, 1983–87. PPS to Pres. of Bd of Trade, 1963, to Minister of Power, 1963–64, to Mr Edward Heath, Leader of the Opposition, 1965–70; Minister of Agriculture, Fisheries and Food, 1970–72; Lord Pres. of Council and Leader of House of Commons, 1972–74; Opposition front bench spokesman on Employment, 1974–79; Sec. of State for Employment, 1979–81; Sec. of State for NI, 1981–84. A Dep. Chm., Cons. Party, 1972–74 (Vice-Chm., 1965). Chairman: Allders, 1989–94; East Anglian Radio PLC, 1992–; Director: United Biscuits (Holdings), 1984–; Barclays Bank, 1984–89; Barclays International, 1984–89; J. Sainsbury, 1984–92; Member: Tenneco European Adv. Bd, 1986–; Internat. Adv. Bd, Amer. Internat. Gp, 1988–. Chancellor, Anglia Poly. Univ., 1992– (Hon. PhD 1992). Chairman: Council of Industry and Higher Educn, 1986–91; Archibishops' Commn on Rural Areas, 1988–91; Great Ormond Street Wishing Well Appeal, 1985–89; Special Trustees, Great Ormond Street, 1989–; Industry and Parliament Trust, 1990–94; Rural Housing Trust, 1990–; Royal Veterinary Coll., 1990–; Trustee, Internat. Centre for Child Studies, 1987–91. *Publications:* (jtly) The Right Approach to the Economy, 1977; A Balance of Power, 1986. *Recreations:* cricket, tennis, golf, gardening. *Address:* House of Lords, SW1A 0PW. *Clubs:* Garrick, MCC; Butterflies Cricket.

PRIOR, Ven. Christopher, CB 1968; Archdeacon of Portsmouth, 1969–77, Archdeacon Emeritus since 1977; *b* 2 July 1912; *s* of late Ven. W. H. Prior; *m* 1945, Althea Stafford (*née* Coode); two *d*. *Educ:* King's Coll., Taunton; Keble Coll., Oxford; Cuddesdon Coll. Curate of Hornsea, 1938–41; Chaplain RN from 1941, Chaplain of the Fleet, 1966–69. Served in: HMS Royal Arthur, 1941; HMHS Maine, 1941–43; HMS Scylla, 1943–44;

HMS Owl, 1944–46; various ships, 1946–58; Britannia RNC, Dartmouth, 1958–61; HMS Blake, 1961–62; HM Dockyard, Portsmouth, 1963–66; QHC, 1966–69. *Recreation:* walking. *Address:* Ponies End, West Melbury, Shaftesbury, Dorset SP7 0LY. *T:* Shaftesbury (01747) 811239.

PRIOR, Peter James, CBE 1980; DL; Chairman, H. P. Bulmer Holdings PLC, 1977–82 (Director, 1977–85; Managing Director, H. P. Bulmer Ltd, 1966–77); *b* 1 Sept. 1919; *s* of Percy Prior; *m* 1957, Prinia Mary, *d* of late R. E. Moreau, Berrick Prior, Oxon; two *s*. *Educ:* Royal Grammar Sch., High Wycombe; London Univ. BSc(Econ). FCA, FIMC, FIMgt, FRSA. Royal Berks Regt, 1939; Intell. Corps, 1944–46 (Captain) (Croix-de-Guerre 1944). Company Sec., Saunders-Roe (Anglesey) Ltd, 1948; Consultant, Urwick, Orr & Partners, 1951; Financial Dir, International Chemical Co., 1956; Financial Dir, British Aluminium Co., 1961; Dep. Chm., Holden Hydroman, 1984–88; Dir, Trebor, 1982–86. Member: English Tourist Bd, 1969–75; Midlands Electricity Bd, 1973–83; Chairman: Inquiry into Potato Processing Industry, 1971; Motorway Service Area Inquiry, 1977–78; Home Office Deptl Inquiry into Prison Discipline, 1984–85. Pres., Incorp. Soc. of British Advertisers' Council, 1980–83; Mem. Council, BIM, 1974–82. Chm. Trustees, Leadership Trust, 1975–79; Member: Council, Regular Forces Employment Assoc., 1981–86; Council, Operation Raleigh, 1984–89. DL Hereford and Worcester, 1983. Communicator of the Year Award, British Assoc. of Industrial Editors, 1982. *Publications:* Leadership is not a Bowler Hat, 1977; articles on management and leadership. *Recreations:* flying, motor-cycling, swimming, mountain walking, formerly parachuting (UK record for longest delayed drop (civilian), 1981). *Address:* Highland, Holbach Lane, Sutton St Nicholas, Hereford HR1 3DF. *T:* Bodenham (01568) 797222. *Clubs:* Army and Navy, Special Forces.

PRIOR, William Johnson, CBE 1979; CEng, FIEE; Chairman, Manx Electricity Authority, 1984–85; retired; *b* 28 Jan. 1924; *s* of Ernest Stanley and Lilian Prior; *m* 1945, Mariel (*née* Irving); two *s* one *d*. *Educ:* Goole and Barnsley Grammar Schs. Barugh, Mexborough, Stuart Street (Manchester) and Stockport Power Stations, 1944–52; Keadby, 1952–56, Supt, 1954–56; Supt, Berkeley, 1957–58; Supt, Hinkley Point Generating Station, 1959–66; CEGB and predecessors: Asst Reg. Dir (Generation), NW Region, 1967–70; Dir (Generation), SW Region, 1970–72; Dir-Gen., SE Region, 1972–76; Mem., Electricity Council, 1976–79; Chm., Yorks Electricity Bd, 1979–84. Member: NCB, 1977–83; Adv. Cttee on Safety of Nuclear Installations, 1980–87. *Recreation:* country walking. *Address:* Highfield House, Lime Kiln Lane, Kirk Deighton, Wetherby, W Yorks LS22 4EA. *T:* Wetherby (01937) 584434.

PRITCHARD, family name of **Baron Pritchard.**

PRITCHARD, Baron *cr* 1975 (Life Peer), of West Haddon, Northamptonshire; **Derek Wilbraham Pritchard;** Kt 1968; DL; *b* 8 June 1910; *s* of Frank Wheelton Pritchard and Ethel Annie Pritchard (*née* Cheetham); *m* 1941, Denise Arfor Pritchard (*née* Huntbach); two *d*. *Educ:* Clifton College, Bristol. Took over family business of E. Halliday & Son, Wine Merchants, 1929, Man. Dir, 1930–51, Chm., 1947. Called up in TA and served War of 1939–45; demob. as Col and joined Bd of E. K. Cole, Ltd, 1946. Joined Ind Coope Ltd, as Man. Dir of Grants of St James's Ltd, 1949, Chm., 1960–69; Chm., Victoria Wine Co. Ltd, 1959–64. Director: Ind Coope Ltd, 1951; Ind Coope Tetley Ansell Ltd on merger of those companies, 1961, subseq. renamed Allied Breweries Ltd, 1961–80 (Chm., 1968–70); Allied Breweries Investments Ltd, 1961–80; Licences & General Assurance Ltd, 1952–56, subseq. merged with Guardian Assurance Ltd, 1956–80; Guardian Royal Exchange Assurance Ltd, 1956–80; George Sandeman Sons & Co. Ltd, 1952–80; J. & W. Nicholson (Holdings), 1962–82; Carreras Ltd, 1970–72 (Chm.); Dorchester Hotel Ltd, 1976–80 (Chm.); Rothmans of Pall Mall Canada Ltd, 1972–77; Rothmans of Pall Mall (Australia) Ltd, 1972–77; Rothmans of Pall Mall (Malaysia) Berhad, 1972–77; Rothmans of Pall Mall (Singapore) Ltd, 1972–77; Deltec International, 1975–77; London-American Finance Corp., 1976–78; Midland Bank Ltd, 1968–85; Samuel Montagu Ltd, 1969–86; Adelaide Associates Ltd, 1970–; Rothmans International Ltd, 1972–86 (Chm., 1972–75); Rothmans Group Services SA, 1972–86; Rothmans of Pall Mall (London) Ltd, 1972–86; Rothmans Tobacco Hldgs Ltd, 1972–86; Carreras Group (Jamaica) Ltd, 1972–86; Paterson, Zochonis & Co. Ltd, 1977–89; Philips Electronic & Associated Industries Ltd, 1978–85; Lyford Cay Property Owners Assoc. Ltd, 1980–; Tiedmann-Goodnow Internat. Capital Corp., 1980–89 (Chm., 1980–86); Matterhorn Investment Co. Ltd (Chm., 1980–85); Thoroughbred Holdings Internat. Ltd, 1982– (Chm.); Euro-Canadian Bank Inc., 1984–89; Templeton Foundn Adv. Bd, 1980– (Chm., 1984–85); Templeton, Galbraith & Hansberger Ltd, 1987–; Templeton Investments Management Ltd, 1980–; Best Investments Inc.; Chalk International Airlines, 1984–; Equator Hldgs, 1985–; Equator Bank, 1985–; Dextra Bank & Trust Co., 1986–89 (Chm.). Chairman: Dorchester Hotel Bd of Trustees, 1976–87; Dorchester Pension Fund, 1976–86; Rothmans Internat. Adv. Bd, 1986–89; Mem., Salomon Bros Adv. Bd, USA, 1980–83; Dep Chm., British National Export Council, 1965–66, Chm. 1966–68; Member: Nat. Inds Appts Bd, 1973–82; Top Salaries Review Body, 1975–78; House of Lords EEC Cttee, 1975–79, EEC Sub-Cttee A, 1975–80; Cttee, British Foundn for Age Research, 1975–84; British Overseas Trade Adv. Council, 1976–84; Fund Raising Cttee, RCS, 1976–87; Chancellor of the Duchy of Lancaster's Cttee on Business Sponsorship of the Arts, 1980–87; Amer. European Community Assoc., 1981–88; President: British Export Houses Assoc., 1976–83; Northants Co. Branch, Royal Agricl Benevolent Instn, 1981–87; Patron: Northants British Red Cross Soc., 1982– (Pres., 1975–83); Inst. of Directors, 1966– (Pres., 1968–74); Vice-President: Inst. of Export, 1976– (Pres., 1974–76); Wine and Spirit Assoc. of GB, 1964– (Pres., 1962–64); Northants Youth Club Assoc., 1965–; East of England Agricl Soc., 1974–; Co-Chm., UK-Jamaica Cttee, 1981–87; Trustee: Age Action Trust, 1975–80; St Giles Church, Northampton, 1976–86; Patron: Northampton and County Chamber of Commerce, 1978–; Three Shires Indept Hosp., 1978–; Abbeyfield Soc. for the Aged, 1979– (Pres., 1970–79); Governor: Clifton Coll., Bristol; Nene Coll., Northampton. DL Northants, 1974. *Recreations:* farming, tennis, golf, hunting. *Address:* West Haddon Hall, Northampton NN6 7AU. *T:* West Haddon (01788) 510210.

PRITCHARD, Arthur Alan, CB 1979; JP; formerly Deputy Under Secretary of State, Ministry of Defence; *b* 3 March 1922; *s* of Arthur Henry Standfast Pritchard and Sarah Bessie Myra Pritchard (*née* Mundy); *m* 1949, Betty Rona Nevard (*née* Little); two *s* one *d*. *Educ:* Wanstead High Sch., Essex. Board of Trade, 1939. RAFVR Pilot, 1941–52. Joined Admiralty, 1952; Asst Sec., 1964; Royal College of Defence Studies, 1972; Asst Under-Sec. of State, Naval Personnel and Op. Requirements, MoD, 1972–76; seconded as Dep. Sec., NI Office, 1976–78; Secretary to the Admiralty Bd, 1978–81. Management consultant, 1984–89. Chm., Fordingbridge and Dist Community Assoc., 1990–95. JP Ringwood, 1986 (Totton and New Forest, 1981–86; Chm., Ringwood Bench, 1991–92). *Recreations:* caravanning, walking. *Address:* Courtlands, Manor Farm Road, Fordingbridge, Hants. SP6 1DY. *Club:* Royal Air Force.

PRITCHARD, Rear-Adm. Gwynedd Idris, CB 1981; *b* 18 June 1924; *s* of Cyril Idris Pritchard and Lily Pritchard; *m* 1975, Mary Thérèsa (*née* Curtin); three *s* (by previous marriage). *Educ:* Wyggeston Sch., Leicester. FBIM, MNI. Joined Royal Navy, 1942; Sub-Lieut 1944; Lieut 1946; Lt-Comdr 1954; Comdr 1959; Captain 1967; Rear-Adm. 1976; Flag Officer Sea Training, 1976–78; Flag Officer Gibraltar, 1979–81; retired list, 1981. Chm., SW Regl Planning Conf., 1990–93. Mem., Dorset CC, 1985–. *Recreations:* riding, caravanning. *Address:* Hoofprints, Beach Road, Burton Bradstock, Dorset DT6 4RF.

PRITCHARD, Gwynn; *see* Pritchard, I. G.

PRITCHARD, Hugh Wentworth, CBE 1969; Member of Council of Law Society, 1947–66; *b* 15 March 1903; *s* of late Sir Harry G. Pritchard; *m* 1934, Barbara Stableforth (*d* 1987); two *s*. *Educ:* Charterhouse; Balliol College, Oxford. Admitted a solicitor, 1927; partner in Sharpe Pritchard & Co., 1928–80. Pres. Soc. of Parliamentary Agents, 1952–55; Member: Statute Law Committee, 1954–81; Committee on Administrative Tribunals and Enquiries, 1955; Council on Tribunals, 1958–70. Lay Reader, 1947. Served War of 1939–45, in England, France, Belgium and Germany; joined The Queen's as a private; commissioned in RAOC, attaining rank of Lt-Col. *Address:* 128 Foxley Lane, Purley, Surrey CR8 3NE. *T:* 0181-660 9029.

PRITCHARD, (Iorwerth) Gwynn; Head of Welsh Programmes, BBC Cymru/Wales, since 1992; *b* 1 Feb. 1946; *s* of Rev. Islwyn Pritchard and Megan Mair Pritchard; *m* 1970, Marilyn Bartholomew (*d* 1994); two *s* one *d*. *Educ:* King's Coll., Cambridge (MA). Producer and Director: BBC Television, London, 1969–78; BBC Wales, 1979–81; HTV Wales, 1982–85; Commissioning Editor, 1985–88, Sen. Commissioning Editor for Educn, 1989–92, Channel 4. Pres., INPUT Internat. Bd, 1988–93. Trustee: Welsh Writers Trust, 1990–; Broadcasting Support Services, 1990–92; Nat. Inst. for Adult and Contg Educn, 1990–92. Sheffield Internat. Documentary Fest., 1993–; Aberystwyth Internat. Film Fest., 1993–. Mem. Council, Coleg Harlech, 1992–; Gov., Ysgol Gynradd Pencae, 1992–. Winston Churchill Fellow, Winston Churchill Meml Trust, 1973; Huw Weldon Fellow, UCNW, Bangor, 1990–91. Chevalier de l'Ordre des Arts et des Lettres (France), 1990. *Recreations:* swimming, walking, cinema, reading. *Address:* Pennaeth Rhaglenni Cymraeg, BBC Cymru/Wales, Broadcasting House, Llandaff, Cardiff CF5 2YQ.

PRITCHARD, Kenneth John, CB 1982; Director, Greenwich Hospital, 1987–92; *b* 18 March 1926; *s* of William Edward Pritchard and Ethel Mary Pritchard (*née* Cornfield); *m* 1st, 1949, Elizabeth Margaret Bradshaw (*d* 1978); two *d*; 2nd, 1979, Angela Madeleine Palmer; one *s* two *d*. *Educ:* Newport High Sch.; St Catherine's Coll., Oxford (MA 1951). Served Army, 1944–48; Indian Mil. Acad., Dehra Dun, 1945; served with 8th/12th Frontier Force Regt and 2nd Royal W Kent Regt. Asst Principal, Admiralty, 1951; Private Sec. to Sec. of State for Wales, 1964; Asst Sec., Min. of Aviation, 1966; RCDS, 1972; Principal Supply and Transport Officer (Naval), Portsmouth, 1978, Exec. Dir 1980; Dir Gen. of Supplies and Transport (Naval), MoD, 1981–86, retd. FCIPS (FInstPS 1986). *Recreations:* squash, tennis. *Address:* Pickford House, Beckington, Som BA3 6SJ. *T:* Frome (01373) 830329. *Club:* Bath and County (Bath).

PRITCHARD, Kenneth William, OBE 1992; WS; Secretary of the Law Society of Scotland, since 1976; *b* 14 Nov. 1933; *s* of Dr Kenneth Pritchard, MB, BS, DPH, and Isobel Pritchard, LDS (*née* Broom); *m* 1962, Gretta (*née* Murray), BL, WS; two *s* one *d*. *Educ:* Dundee High Sch.; Fettes Coll.; St Andrews Univ. (BL). National Service, Argyll and Sutherland Highlanders, 1955–57; commnd 2nd Lieut, 1956; TA 1957–62 (Captain). Joined J. & J. Scrimgeour, Solicitors, Dundee, 1957, Sen. Partner, 1970–76. WS 1984. Hon. Sheriff, Dundee, 1978–; Temp. Sheriff, 1995–. Member: Sheriff Court Rules Council, 1973–76; Lord Dunpark's Cttee Considering Reparation upon Criminal Conviction, 1973–77; Secretary, Scottish Council of Law Reporting, 1976. Governor, Moray House Coll. of Educn, 1982–84; Mem. Ct, Univ. of Dundee, 1990–93. Mem., National Trust for Scotland Jubilee Appeal Cttee, 1980–82. Pres., Dundee High Sch. Old Boys Club, 1975–76; Captain of the Former Pupil RFC, Dundee High Sch., 1959–62. Hon. Prof. of Law, Strathclyde Univ., 1986–94. *Recreation:* golf. *Address:* 36 Ravelston Dykes, Edinburgh EH4 3EB. *T:* 0131-332 8584. *Clubs:* New, Bruntsfield Links Golfing Association (Edinburgh); Hon. Company of Edinburgh Golfers (Muirfield).

PRITCHARD, Sir Neil, KCMG 1962 (CMG 1952); HM Diplomatic Service, retired; Ambassador in Bangkok, 1967–70; *b* 14 January 1911; *s* of late Joseph and Lillian Pritchard; *m* 1943, Mary Burroughes (*d* 1988), Pretoria, S Africa; one *s*. *Educ:* Liverpool Coll.; Worcester Coll., Oxford. Dominions Office, 1933; Private Secretary to Permanent Under-Sec., 1936–38; Assistant Secretary, Rhodesia-Nyasaland Royal Commission, 1938; Secretary, Office of UK High Commissioner, Pretoria, 1941–45; Principal Secretary, Office of UK Representative, Dublin, 1948–49; Assistant Under-Secretary of State, Commonwealth Relations Office, 1951–54; Dep. UK High Commissioner: Canada, 1954–57; Australia, 1957–60; Actg Dep. Under-Sec. of State, CRO, 1961; British High Comr in Tanganyika, 1961–63; Deputy Under-Secretary of State, Commonwealth Office (formerly CRO), 1963–67. *Recreation:* golf. *Address:* Little Garth, Daglingworth, Cirencester, Glos GL7 7AQ.

PRITCHARD, Prof. Thomas Owen, JP; Chairman, Cynefin Environmental Ltd, consultants in sustainable development, since 1991; Professorial Fellow, Institute of Earth Studies, University of Wales, Aberystwyth; *b* 13 May 1932; *s* of late Owen and Mary Pritchard; *m* 1957, Enyd Ashton; one *s* one *d*. *Educ:* Botwnnog Grammar Sch.; Univ. of Wales (BSc Hons Botany and Agric. Botany); Univ. of Leeds (PhD Genetics). Midlands Regl Officer and Head of Educn, Nature Conservancy, 1957–67; Dep. Dir for Wales, Nature Conservancy—NERC 1967–73; Dir for Wales, NCC, 1973–91. Consultant, Council of Europe, 1968. Vis. Prof., Dept of Forestry and Resource Management, Univ. of California, Berkeley, 1981–. Dir, CTF Training Ltd, 1982–91; Chairman: Coed Cymru Ltd, 1983–92; Bardsey Island Trust, 1987–93; Welsh Historic Gdns Trust, 1994–; Exec., POW Cttee, 1971–73; Vice Chm. (Educn), IUCN, 1966–73; former Chm. and Mem., conservation and envtl bodies, nat. and internat. Member: Genetical Soc.; British Ecological Soc. Member: Ct of Govs and Council: UC, Bangor, 1981–; Nat. Museum of Wales, 1981–91. Member: Gorsedd of Bards, Royal Nat. Eisteddfod; Hon. Soc. of Cymmrodorion. FRSA. JP Bangor, 1978. *Publications:* Cynefin y Cymro, 1989; numerous contribs to sci. and educn jls. *Recreation:* sailing. *Address:* Graig Lwyd, 134 Ffordd Penrhos, Bangor, Gwynedd LL57 2BX. *T:* Bangor (01248) 370401.

PRITCHETT, Sir Victor (Sawdon), CH 1993; Kt 1975; CBE 1968; CLit 1988; author and critic; *b* 16 Dec. 1900; *s* of Sawdon Pritchett and Beatrice Martin; *m* Dorothy, *d* of Richard Samuel Roberts, Welshpool, Montgomeryshire; one *s* one *d*. *Educ:* Alleyn's School. Christian Gauss Lectr, Princeton Univ., 1953; Beckman Prof., Univ. California, Berkeley, 1962; Writer-in-Residence, Smith Coll., Mass, 1966; Vanderbilt Univ., Tenn., 1981; Visiting Professor: Brandeis Univ., Mass; Columbia Univ.; Clark Lectr, 1969. Foreign Member: Amer. Acad. and Inst., 1971; Amer. Acad. Arts and Sciences, 1971. Pres., Internat. PEN, 1974–76; Soc. of Authors, 1977–. Hon. LittD Leeds, 1972; Hon. DLitt: Columbia, 1978; Sussex, 1980; Harvard, 1985. *Publications:* Marching Spain, 1928, repr. 1988; Clare Drummer, 1929; The Spanish Virgin, 1930; Shirley Sanz, 1932; Nothing Like Leather, 1935; Dead Man Leading, 1937; You Make Your Own Life, 1938; In My Good Books, 1942; It May Never Happen, 1946; The Living Novel, 1946; Why Do I Write?, 1948; Mr Beluncle, 1951; Books in General, 1953; The Spanish Temper, 1954; Collected Stories, 1956; When My Girl Comes Home, 1961; London Perceived, 1962; The Key to My Heart, 1963; Foreign Faces, 1964; New York Proclaimed, 1965; The

Working Novelist, 1965; Dublin: A Portrait, 1967; A Cab at the Door (autobiog.), 1968 (RSL Award); Blind Love, 1969; George Meredith and English Comedy, 1970; Midnight Oil (autobiog.), 1971; Balzac, 1973; The Camberwell Beauty, 1974; The Gentle Barbarian, 1977; Selected Stories, 1978; The Myth Makers, 1979; On the Edge of the Cliff, 1980; The Tale Bearers, 1980; (ed) The Oxford Book of Short Stories, 1981; (with Reynolds Stone) The Turn of the Years, 1982; Collected Stories, 1982; More Collected Stories, 1983; The Other Side of a Frontier, 1984; Man of Letters, 1985; Chekhov, 1988; A Careless Widow and Other Stories, 1989; At Home and Abroad, 1990; The Complete Short Stories, 1990; Lasting Impressions, 1990; The Complete Essays, 1991. *Address:* 12 Regent's Park Terrace, NW1 7ED. *Clubs:* Savile, Beefsteak.

PRITTIE, family name of **Baron Dunalley.**

PROBERT, David Henry, FCIS, FCMA, FCCA; Chairman, W. Canning plc, since 1986 (Director, 1976; Chief Executive, 1979–86); Chairman, Crown Agents for Oversea Governments and Administrations, since 1990 (Deputy Chairman, 1985–90; Crown Agent since 1981); Crown Agent for Holdings and Realisation Board, since 1981; *b* 11 April 1938; *s* of William David Thomas Probert and Doris Mabel Probert; *m* 1968, Sandra Mary Prince; one *s* one *d. Educ:* Bromsgrove High School. Director: BSA Ltd, 1971–73; Mills and Allen International Ltd, 1974–76; HB Electronics plc, 1977–86; British Hallmarking Council, 1983–91; Linread Public Limited Company, 1983–90; ASD plc, 1985–90; Sandvik Ltd, 1985–90; Rockwool Ltd, 1988–90, 1992–; Private Patients Plan Ltd, 1988–; Richard Burbidge Ltd, 1990–91; William Sinclair plc, 1994–; Hampson Industries plc, 1994–. Pres., Birmingham Chamber of Commerce and Industry, 1994–May 1995 (Vice Pres., 1992–94). CIMgt. *Recreations:* theatre, music, sport. *Address:* 4 Blakes Field Drive, Barnt Green, Worcs B45 8JT. *Clubs:* Royal Automobile, Lord's Taverners.

PROBERT, (William) Ronald; Managing Director, Business Development, 1992–93, Member of the Board, 1985–93, Group Executive Member, 1989–93, British Gas plc (formerly British Gas Corporation), retired; *b* 11 Aug. 1934; *s* of William and Florence Probert; *m* 1957, Jean (*née* Howard); three *s. Educ:* Grammar Sch., Ashton-under-Lyne; Univ. of Leeds (BA). FIGasE; CIMgt. Entered gas industry, 1957; various marketing appts in E Midlands Gas Bd, 1957–67; Conversion Manager, 1967, Service Manager, 1971, Marketing Dir, 1973, E Midlands Gas Bd; Asst Dir of Marketing, 1975, Dir of Sales, 1977, British Gas Corp.; Man. Dir Marketing, British Gas, 1982–89; Man. Dir, Gas Supply and Strategy, 1989–92. Dir, E Berks NHS Trust, 1991–. *Recreations:* narrowboats, music, winemaking. *Address:* 32 Austen Way, Gerrards Cross, Bucks SL9 8NW. *T:* Gerrards Cross (01753) 888527.

PROBINE, Dr Mervyn Charles, CB 1986; FRSNZ; FInstP; FNZIM; company director and consultant, since 1986; *b* 30 April 1924; *s* of Frederick Charles and Ann Kathleen Probine; *m* 1949, Marjorie Walker; one *s* one *d. Educ:* Univ. of Auckland (BSc); Victoria Univ. of Wellington (MSc); Univ. of Leeds (PhD). Physicist, DSIR, 1946–67; Dir, Physics and Engineering Lab., 1967–77; Asst Dir-Gen., DSIR, 1977–79; State Services Commission: Comr, 1979–80; Dep. Chm., 1980–81; Chm., 1981–86, retired. Chm., GEC (NZ), 1986–95; Dir, Fujitsu (NZ), 1986–. Chairman: Legislation Adv. Cttee, 1991–; Insurance and Savings Ombudsman Commn, 1994–. Trustee, Nat. Library of NZ, 1992–. *Publications:* numerous scientific research papers and papers on application of science in industry. *Recreations:* bridge, sailing, angling. *Address:* 24 Bloomfield Terrace, Lower Hutt, New Zealand. *T:* (4) 5663492. *Club:* Wellington (Wellington, NZ).

PROBY, Sir Peter, 2nd Bt *cr* 1952; FRICS; Lord-Lieutenant of Cambridgeshire, 1981–85; *b* 4 Dec. 1911; *s* of Sir Richard George Proby, 1st Bt, MC, and Betty Monica (*d* 1967), *d* of A. H. Hallam Murray; *S* father, 1979; *m* 1944, Blanche Harrison, *o d* of Col Henry Harrison Cripps, DSO; one *s* three *d* (and one *s* decd). *Educ:* Eton; Trinity College, Oxford. BA 1934. Served War of 1939–45, Captain, Irish Guards. Bursar of Eton College, 1953–71. *Heir: s* William Henry Proby, MA, FCA [*b* 13 June 1949; *m* 1974, Meredyth Anne Brentnall; four *d. Educ:* Eton; Lincoln Coll., Oxford (MA)]. *Address:* Pottle Green, Elton, Peterborough PE8 6SG. *T:* Oundle (01832) 280434.

PROCHASKA, Dr Alice Marjorie Sheila, FRHistS; Director of Special Collections, British Library, since 1992; *b* 12 July 1947; *d* of John Harold Barwell and Hon. Sheila McNair; *m* 1971, Dr Franklyn Kimmel Prochaska; one *s* one *d. Educ:* Perse Sch. for Girls, Cambridge; Somerville Coll., Oxford (BA 1968; MA 1973; DPhil 1975). Assistant Keeper: London Museum, 1971–73; Public Record Office, 1975–84; Sec. and Librarian, Inst. of Historical Res., 1984–92. Chm., Nat. Council on Archives, 1991–95; Member: History Working Gp on Nat. Curriculum, DES, 1989–90; Council, RHistS, 1991–95; Heritage Educn Trust, 1992–; Hereford Mappa Mundi Trust, 1992–95; Bd, Inst. of Historical Res., 1992–; Library Panel, Wellcome Inst., 1993–; Adv. Panel, Qualidator, Univ. of Essex, 1995–. *Publications:* London in the Thirties, 1973; History of the General Federation of Trade Unions 1899–1980, 1982; Irish History from 1700: a guide to sources in the Public Record Office, 1986; (ed jtly with F. K. Prochaska), Margaretta Acworth's Georgian Cookery Book, 1987; contribs to learned jls. *Recreations:* family life, historical cookery, collecting watercolours. *Address:* British Library, Great Russell Street, WC1B 3DG. *T:* 0171–323 7501.

PROCKTOR, Patrick, RWS 1981; RE 1991; painter since 1962; *b* 12 March 1936; 2nd *s* of Eric Christopher Procktor and Barbara Winifred (*née* Hopkins); *m* 1973, Kirsten Bo (*née* Andersen) (*d* 1984); one *s. Educ:* Highgate; Slade Sch. (Diploma). Many one-man exhibns, Redfern Gallery, from 1963. Designed windows for AIDS Recreation Centre, St Stephen's Hosp., Fulham, 1988. Retrospective tour, England and Wales, 1990. *Publications:* One Window in Venice, 1974; Coleridge's Rime of the Ancient Mariner (new illustrated edn), 1976; A Chinese Journey (aquatint landscapes), 1980; (illustrated) Sailing through China, by Paul Theroux, 1983; Patrick Procktor Prints 1959–85 (catalogue raisonné), 1985; A Shropshire Lad, by A. E. Housman (new illustrated edn), 1986; Self-Portrait (autobiog.), 1991; *relevant publication:* Patrick Procktor (monograph by Patrick Kinmonth), 1985. *Recreation:* Russian ballet. *Address:* 26 Manchester Street, W1M 5PG. *T:* 0171–486 1763. *Club:* Garrick.

PROCTER, Jane Hilary; Editor, Tatler, since 1990; *m* 1985, Thomas Charles Goldstaub; one *s* one *d. Educ:* Queen's Coll., Harley St. Fashion Asst, Vogue, 1974–75; Asst Fashion Editor, Good Housekeeping, 1975–77; Actg Fashion Editor, Woman's Jl, 1977–78; Fashion Writer, Country Life, 1978–80; Freelance Fashion Editor, The Times, Sunday Times and Daily Express, 1980–87; Editor, British W, 1987–88. *Publication:* Dress Your Best, 1983. *Recreations:* sailing, ski-ing. *Address:* Tatler, Vogue House, 1 Hanover Square, W1R 0AD. *T:* 0171–499 9080.

PROCTER, (Mary) Norma; contralto; international concert singer; *b* Cleethorpes, Lincolnshire, 15 Feb. 1928. *Educ:* Wintringham Secondary Sch. Vocal studies with Roy Henderson, musicianship with Alec Redshaw, lieder with Hans Oppenheim and Paul Hamburger. London début, Southwark Cathedral, 1948; operatic début, Lucretia, in Britten's Rape of Lucretia, Aldeburgh Festival, 1957; Covent Garden début, Gluck's Orpheus, 1960. Specialist in concert works, oratorios and recitals; appeared with all major conductors and orchestras, and in all major festivals, UK and Europe; performed in Germany, France, Spain, Italy, Portugal, Holland, Belgium, Norway, Denmark, Sweden, Finland, Austria, Luxembourg, Israel, S America; BBC Last Night of the Proms, 1974. Many recordings. Hon. RAM 1974. *Address:* 194 Clee Road, Grimsby, South Humberside, DN32 8NG.

PROCTER, Robert John Dudley; Chief Executive, Lincolnshire County Council, 1983–95; *b* 19 Oct. 1935; *s* of Luther Donald Procter and Edith Muriel Procter; *m* 1962, Adrienne Allen; one *s* one *d. Educ:* Cheltenham Grammar School. Admitted Solicitor, 1961. Articled Clerk, Glos CC, 1956–61; Assistant Solicitor: Bath City, 1961–63; Cumberland CC, 1963–65; Lindsey County Council: Sen. Asst Solicitor, 1965–69; Asst Clerk, 1969–71; Dep. Clerk, Kesteven CC, 1971–73; Dir of Personnel, 1973–77, Dir of Admin, 1977–83, Lincolnshire CC. Chm., Assoc. of County Chief Execs, 1994–95. Mem., Warner Cttee of Inquiry into recruitment and selection of staff in children's homes, 1992. *Recreations:* horse racing, swimming, keyboard playing, freemasonry. *Address:* Pas Seul, The Paddock, Sudbrooke, Lincoln LN2 2QS. *T:* Lincoln (01522) 750313.

PROCTER, Sidney, CBE 1986; FCIB; Commissioner, Building Societies Commission, 1986–93; company director; *b* 10 March 1925; *s* of Robert and Georgina Margaret Procter; *m* 1952, Isabel (*née* Simmons); one *d. Educ:* Ormskirk Grammar School. Served RAF, 1943–47. Entered former Williams Deacon's Bank, 1941; Asst General Manager, 1969; Dep. Dir, Williams & Glyn's Bank, 1970; Divl Dir, 1975; Exec. Dir, 1976–85; Asst Chief Executive, 1976; Dep. Chief Executive, 1977; Chief Exec., 1978–82; Dep. Gp Man. Dir, Royal Bank of Scotland Gp, 1979–82; Gp Chief Exec., 1982–85; Vice Chm., 1986; Director: Royal Bank of Scotland, 1978–86 (Vice Chm., 1986); Provincial Insurance Co., 1985–86; Dep. Chm., Provincial Group, 1991–94 (Dir, 1986–94); Chairman: Exeter Bank, 1991–; Provincial Group Holdings, 1994–. Adviser to Governor, Bank of England, 1985–87. Chm., Exeter Trust, 1986– (Dir, 1985–). *Address:* The Piece House, Bourton-on-the-Water, Glos GL54 2AZ. *T:* Cotswold (01451) 820425.

PROCTOR, Anthony James; His Honour Judge Proctor; a Circuit Judge, since 1988; *b* 18 Sept. 1931; *s* of James Proctor and Savina Maud (*née* Horsfield); *m* 1964, Patricia Mary Bryan; one *d. Educ:* Mexborough Grammar Sch., Yorkshire; St Catharine's Coll., Cambridge (MA, LLM). Flying Officer, RAF, 1953–55. Articled to Sir Bernard Kenyon, County Hall, Wakefield, 1955–58; admitted Solicitor 1958. Sen. Prosecuting Solicitor, Sheffield Corp., 1959–64; Partner, Broomhead & Neals, Solicitors, Sheffield, 1964–74; Dist Registrar and County Court Registrar, Barrow in Furness, Lancaster, Preston, 1974–88; a Recorder, 1985. Pres., Assoc. of Dist and Court Registrars, 1985–86. *Recreations:* fell walking, travel, genealogy. *Address:* The Sessions House, Lancaster Road, Preston PR1 2PD. *T:* Preston (01772) 821451.

PROCTOR, David Victor; Research Associate and Consultant, National Maritime Museum, since 1989; *b* 1 March 1930; *s* of Comdr Victor William Lake Proctor, RN and Marjorie Proctor (*née* Weeks); *m* 1st, 1959, Margaret Graham (marr. diss. 1984); three *s*; 2nd, 1984, Marion Clara Calver; one step *s* five step *d. Educ:* Dauntsey's Sch.; Clare Coll., Cambridge (MA; DipEd 1955); Imperial Coll., London (DIC). Shipbroking, 1953–54; Teacher: Lycée de Brest, France, 1955–56; Clifton Coll., Bristol, 1956–62; National Maritime Museum: Educn Officer, 1962–72; Sec. and Educn Officer, 1972–74; Head of Educn and Res. Facilities, 1974–76; Head of Printed Books and Manuscripts Dept, 1976–87; Head of Printed, Manuscript and Technical Records Dept, 1987–89. Internat. Congress of Maritime Museums: Sec. Gen., 1972–78; Mem. Exec. Council, 1978–81; Vice-Pres., 1981–84; Trustee, 1984–. Chm., Gp for Educnl Services in Museums, 1971–75; Mem., Adv. Council, Internat. Council of Museums, 1983–; Vice Pres., Internat. Commn for Maritime Hist., 1990– (Sec. Gen., 1980–85; Mem., Exec. Council, 1985–90); Trustee: Madeleine Mainstone Trust, 1980–; Jane Austen Centre, 1987–94. Fellow, Huguenot Soc. of London, 1986–. *Publications:* Child of War, 1972; Music of the Sea, 1992; contribs to jls on museums, museum educn and hist. of science. *Recreations:* sailing, piano, walking, travel, DIY. *Address:* 6 Vange Mews, Rochester, Kent ME1 1RA. *T:* Medway (01634) 849592. *Clubs:* Royal Cruising; Rochester Cruising.

PROCTOR, Harvey; *see* Proctor, K. H.

PROCTOR, Ven. Jesse Heighton, MA (London); Archdeacon of Warwick, 1958–74, now Emeritus; Vicar of Sherbourne, Warwick, 1958–69; *b* 26 May 1908; *s* of Thomas and Sophia Proctor, Melton Mowbray; *m* 1938, Helena Mary Wood (*d* 1992), *d* of John Thomas and Jessie Wood, Melton Mowbray; one *s* two *d. Educ:* County Grammar Sch. of King Edward VII, Melton Mowbray; Coll. of St Mark and St John, Chelsea, Univ. of London; St Andrew's Theological Training House, Whittlesford. Asst Master, Winterbourne Sch., Croydon, 1929–32; Sen. History Master, Melton Mowbray Gram. Sch., 1932–35; Deacon 1935, Priest 1936; Chap. and Tutor, St Andrew's, Whittlesford, 1935–38; Curate, St Philip's, Leicester, 1938–39; Vicar, Glen Parva and South Wigston, and Chap., Glen Parva Barracks, Leicester, 1939–46; Precentor of Coventry Cath., 1946–58; Hon. Canon of Coventry, 1947; Chaplain, Gulson Hosp., 1953–58; Sen. Examining Chap. to Bishop of Coventry, 1947–65; Canon Theologian of Coventry, 1954–59; Vice-Pres. CMS. Governor: Univ. of Warwick, 1966–68; City of Coventry Coll. of Educn, 1966–70. Barnabas of Coventry Evening Telegraph, 1955–75. *Publication:* contrib. to Neville Gorton (SPCK), 1957. *Recreations:* study of theology and history; the countryside. *Address:* Dilkusha, 22 Bank Crescent, Ledbury, Herefordshire HR8 1AA. *T:* Ledbury (01531) 2241.

PROCTOR, (Keith) Harvey; Director, Proctor's Shirts and Ties, since 1992; *b* 16 Jan. 1947; *s* of late Albert Proctor and Hilda Tegerdine. *Educ:* High School for Boys, Scarborough; Univ. of York. BA History Hons, 1969. Asst Director, Monday Club, 1969–71; Research Officer, Conservative 1970s Parliamentary Gp, 1971–72; Exec. Director, Parliamentary Digest Ltd, 1972–74; British Paper & Board Industry Federation: Asst Sec., 1974–78; Secretary, 1978–79; Consultant, 1979–87. MP (C): Basildon, 1979–83; Billericay, 1983–87. Mem., Exec. Council, Monday Club, 1983–87. Pres., Richmond Chamber of Commerce, 1992–94 (Vice-Pres., 1990–92). Trustee, SW London Community Foundn, 1993–. Editor, News and Views, 1991–. *Publication:* Billericay in Old Picture Postcards, 1985. *Recreations:* tennis, collecting British contemporary art. *Address:* 11 Brewers Lane, Richmond Upon Thames, Surrey TW9 1HH. *T:* 0181–332 1099.

PROCTOR-BEAUCHAMP, Sir Christopher Radstock P.; *see* Beauchamp.

PROFUMO, John Dennis, CBE 1975 (OBE (mil.) 1944); 5th Baron of Italy (*cr* 1903); *b* 30 Jan. 1915; *e s* of late Baron Albert Profumo, KC; *m* 1954, Valerie Hobson, *qv*; one *s. Educ:* Harrow; Brasenose College, Oxford. 1st Northamptonshire Yeomanry, 1939 (despatches); Brigadier, Chief of Staff UK Mission in Japan, 1945. MP (C) Kettering Division, Northamptonshire, 1940–45; MP (C) Stratford-on-Avon Division of Warwickshire, 1950–63; Parliamentary Secretary, Ministry of Transport and Civil Aviation, Nov. 1952–Jan. 1957; Parliamentary Under-Secretary of State for the Colonies, 1957–58; Parliamentary Under-Sec. of State, Foreign Affairs, Nov. 1958–Jan. 1959; Minister of State for Foreign Affairs, 1959–60; Secretary of State for War, July 1960–June 1963. Dir, Provident Life Assoc. of London, 1975– (Dep. Chm., 1978–82). Mem., Bd of

Visitors, HM Prison, Grendon, 1968–75. Chm., Toynbee Hall, 1982–85, Pres. 1985–. *Recreations:* fishing, gardening, DIY. *Heir: s* David Profumo [*b* 30 Oct. 1955; *m* 1980, Helen, *o d* of Alasdair Fraser; two *s* one *d*]. *Club:* Boodle's.

PROKHOROV, Prof. Alexander Mikhailovich; Hero of Socialist Labour, 1969, 1986; Order of Lenin (five-fold); Physicist; Director, General Physics Institute, Russian Academy of Sciences (formerly Academy of Sciences of the USSR), Moscow, since 1983; Editor-in-Chief, Bolshaya Sovetskaya Encyclopedia Publishing House, since 1970; *b* Atherton, Australia, 11 July 1916; *s* of Mikhail Prokhorov; *m* 1941, Galina Alexeyevna (*née* Shelepina); one *s*. *Educ:* Leningrad State University; Lebedev Inst. of Physics. Corresp. Mem., Academy of Sciences of the USSR (Department of General Physics and Astronomy), 1960–66, Full Mem., 1966–, Mem. Presidial Body, 1970, Academician-Secretary, 1973–. Chm., Nat. Commn of Soviet Physicists, 1973–. Professor, Moscow University, 1958–. Hon. Professor: Delhi Univ.; Bucharest Univ., 1971; Cluz Univ., 1977; Praha Politechnical Inst., 1980. Member: European Phys. Soc., 1977; European Acad. of Scis, Art and Literature, 1986; Hon. Member: Amer. Acad. of Arts and Sciences, 1972; Acad. of Sciences of Hungary, 1976; Acad. of Sciences, German Democratic Republic, 1977; Acad. of Scis of Czechoslavakia, 1982; Acad. of Scis Leopoldina, 1984. Joined Communist Party of the Soviet Union, 1950. Awarded Lenin Prize, 1959; Nobel Prize for Physics (jointly with Prof. N. G. Basov and Prof. C. H. Townes), 1964. *Publications:* contributions on non-linear oscillations, radiospectroscopy and quantum radio-physics. *Address:* General Physics Institute, Russian Academy of Sciences, Vavilov Street 38, 117942, GSP-1 Moscow, Russia.

PROKHOROVA, Violetta; *see* Elvin, V.

PROOM, Major William Arthur, TD 1953; *b* 18 Dec. 1916; *s* of Arthur Henry Proom and Nesta Proom; *m* 1941, Nellie Lister; one *s* one *d*. *Educ:* Richmond Sch., Yorks; Keighley Technical Coll. Commnd TA, 1/6 Bn Duke of Wellington's Regt, 1938; served War: Iceland, 1940–42; REME/IEME, India and Burma, 1943–46; Major, retd. Mayor of Keighley, 1973; Member: W Yorks Metropolitan CC, 1974–81 (Chm., 1979–80); City of Bradford Metrop. Dist Council, 1975–79. Chm., NE Gas Consumers' Council, 1973–77. *Recreations:* gardening, reading. *Address:* 7 Cragside Avenue, Belford, Northumberland NE70 7NA.

PROOPS, Mrs Marjorie, OBE 1969; journalist; *d* of Alfred and Martha Rayle; *m* 1935; one *s*. *Educ:* Dalston Secondary Sch. Daily Mirror, 1939–45; Daily Herald, 1945–54; Daily Mirror, 1954–; Sunday Mirror, 1992–. Broadcaster, Television, 1960–. Member: Royal Commn on Gambling, 1976–78; Council for One Parent Families. Woman Journalist of the Year, 1969; Chairman's Award, British Press Awards, 1994. *Publications:* Pride, Prejudice & Proops, 1975; Dear Marje, 1976; *relevant publication:* Marje: the guilt and the gingerbread, by Angela Patmore, 1993. *Address:* Sherwood Close, SW13 0JD.

PROPHET, Prof. Arthur Shelley, CBE 1980; DDS; DpBact; FDSRCS; FFDRCSI; Professor of Dental Surgery, University of London, 1956–83, now Emeritus; *b* 11 Jan. 1918; *s* of Eric Prophet and Mabel Wightman; *m* 1942, Vivienne Mary Bell; two *s*. *Educ:* Sedbergh School; University of Manchester. BDS Hons (Preston Prize and Medal), 1940; Diploma in Bacteriology (Manchester), 1948; DDS (Manchester) 1950; FDSRCS 1958; FFDRCS Ireland, 1964. RNVR (Dental Branch), 1941–46; Nuffield Dental Fellow, 1946–48; Lecturer in Dental Bacteriology, University of Manchester, 1948–54; Lecturer in Dental Surgery, QUB, 1954–56; Dir of Dental Studies, 1956–74, Dean of Dental Studies, 1974–77, UCH Dental Sch.; Dean, UCH Medical Sch., 1977–80; Dean, 1980–82, Vice-Dean, 1982–83, Faculty of Clinical Scis, UCL. Lectures: Charles Tomes, RCS, 1977; Wilkinson, Univ. of Manchester, 1978; Elwood, QUB, 1979; Shefford, UCL, 1983. Rep. of University of London on Gen. Dental Council, 1964–84. Elected Mem. Bd, Faculty of Dental Surgery, RCS, 1964–80 (Vice-Dean, 1972–73); Member: Cttee of Management, Inst. of Dental Surgery, 1963–83; Dental Sub-Cttee, UGC, 1968–78; Bd of Governors, UCH, 1957–74; Camden and Islington AHA(T), 1974–82; Bloomsbury HA, 1982–83. WHO Consultant, 1966; Consultant Dental Advr, DHSS, 1977–83. DSc *hc* Malta, 1987. *Publications:* contrib. to medical and dental journals. *Recreations:* golf, gardening. *Address:* Little Orchard, Minstead, Lyndhurst, Hants SO43 7FW. *T:* Southampton (01703) 814003.

PROPHET, John; Regional Chairman of Industrial Tribunals, Yorkshire and Humberside, since 1988; *b* 19 Nov. 1931; *s* of Benjamin and Elsie Prophet; *m* 1961, Pauline Newby; three *d*. *Educ:* Trinity Coll., Cambridge (MA). Called to the Bar, Lincoln's Inn, 1956; Shell International, 1956–60; private practice at the Bar, 1960–; Sen. Lectr, Law Faculty, Leeds Univ., 1968–76; full-time Chm. of Industrial Tribunals, 1976–88. Consultant, Nat. Assoc. of Local Councils, 1968–89. *Publications:* The Structure of Government, 1968; The Parish Councillor's Guide, 1974, 17th edn 1993; Fair Rents, 1976. *Recreations:* tennis, chess, gardening.

PROPHIT, Prof. Penny Pauline; Professor of Nursing Studies, University of Edinburgh, 1983–92 (Head of Department, 1983–88); *b* 7 Feb. 1939; *d* of C. Alston Prophit and Hortense Callahan. *Educ:* Marillac Coll., St Louis Univ., USA (BSN); Catholic Univ. of America (MSN, BNSc, PhD). Asst Prof., Catholic Univ. of America, 1975; Associate Professor: Univ. of Southern Mississippi, 1975; Louisiana State Univ. Med. Center, 1975; Cons., WHO, Europ. Office, Copenhagen, 1977–; Prof., Katholieke Univ., Leuven, Belgium, 1977. Mental Welfare Comr for Scotland, 1985–; Mem., UK Central Council for Nursing, Midwifery and Health Visiting, 1988–. Delta Epsilon Sigma, Nat. Catholic Scholastic Honor Soc., 1966; Sigma Theta Tau, Internat. Nursing Scholastic Honor Soc., 1970; Sigma Epsilon Phi, Catholic Univ. of Amer. Honor Soc., 1975. *Publications:* Understanding/Responding, 1982; res. articles on nursing care of the elderly, stress in nursing, interdisciplinary collaboration, etc. *Recreations:* jogging, reading and writing poetry and short stories, playing piano and listening to music of all kinds. *Address:* 2 Garvald Grange Cottages, Haddington, East Lothian EH41 4LL. *T:* Garvald (01620) 830222.

PROSSER, Hon. Lord; William David Prosser; a Senator of the College of Justice in Scotland and Lord of Session, since 1986; *b* 23 Nov. 1934; *yr s* of David G. Prosser, MC, WS, Edinburgh; *m* 1964, Vanessa, *er d* of Sir William O'Brien Lindsay, KBE, Nairobi; two *s* two *d*. *Educ:* Edinburgh Academy; Corpus Christi Coll., Oxford (MA); Edinburgh Univ. (LLB). Advocate, 1962; QC (Scotland) 1974; Standing Junior Counsel in Scotland, Board of Inland Revenue, 1969–74; Advocate-Depute, 1978–79; Vice-Dean, Faculty of Advocates, 1979–83; Dean of Faculty, 1983–86. Mem., Scottish Cttee, Council on Tribunals, 1977–84. Chm., Royal Fine Art Commn for Scotland, 1990–95. Chairman: Royal Lyceum Theatre Co., 1987–92; Scottish Historic Buildings Trust, 1988–; Chamber Gp of Scotland, 1993–; Edinburgh Sir Walter Scott Club, 1993–; Scottish Architectural Educn Trust, 1994–. Hon. FRIAS 1995. *Address:* 7 Randolph Crescent, Edinburgh EH3 7TH. *T:* 0131–225 2709; Netherfoodie, Dairsie, Fife. *T:* Balmullo (01334) 870438. *Clubs:* New, Scottish Arts (Edinburgh).

PROSSER, David John, FIA; Chief Executive, Legal & General Group, since 1991; *b* 26 March 1944; *s* of Ronald and Dorothy Prosser; *m* 1971, Rosemary Margaret Snuggs; two *d*. *Educ:* Univ. of Wales (BSc). Sun Alliance Group, 1965–69; Hoare Govett, 1969–73; CIN Management, 1973–88; Legal & General, 1988–. Dir, SWALEC, 1991–. Mem. of Bd, ABI. *Recreation:* watching the children grow up. *Address:* Legal & General Group, Temple Court, 11 Queen Victoria Street, EC4N 4TP. *Club:* Royal Automobile.

PROSSER, (Elvet) John; QC 1978; **His Honour Judge Prosser;** a Circuit Judge, since 1988; *b* 10 July 1932; *s* of David and Hannah Prosser; *m* 1957, Mary Louise Cowdry; two *d*. *Educ:* Pontypridd Grammar Sch.; King's Coll., London Univ. LLB. Flt Lt, RAF, 1957–59. Called to the Bar, Gray's Inn, 1956, Bencher, 1986; Mem., Senate of Inns of Court and the Bar, 1980–87; a Recorder, 1972–88; Leader, Wales and Chester Circuit, 1984–87. Part-time Chm. of Industrial Tribunals, 1975–81. An Asst Boundary Comr for Wales, 1977–. *Recreations:* watching cricket and television. *Address:* Crown Court, Cathays Park, Cardiff. *Clubs:* East India, Devonshire, Sports and Public Schools; Cardiff and County (Cardiff).

PROSSER, Sir Ian (Maurice Gray), Kt 1995; FCA; Chairman and Chief Executive, Bass PLC, since 1987 (Vice Chairman, 1982–87; Group Managing Director, 1984–87); *b* 5 July 1943; *s* of late Maurice and of Freda Prosser; *m* 1964, Elizabeth Herman; two *d*. *Educ:* King Edward's School, Bath; Watford Grammar School; Birmingham Univ. (BComm). Coopers & Lybrand, 1964–69; Bass Charrington Ltd, later Bass PLC, 1969–; Financial Dir, 1978. Director: Boots Co., 1984–; Lloyds Bank, 1988–. Chm., Stock Exchange Listed Cos Adv. Cttee, 1992– (Mem., 1990–). Chm., Brewers and Licensed Retailers Assoc. (formerly Brewers' Soc.), 1992–94 (Dir, 1983–). *Recreations:* bridge, gardening. *Address:* Bass PLC, 20 North Audley Street, W1Y 1WE. *T:* 0171–409 1919. *Club:* Royal Automobile.

PROSSER, Margaret Theresa; National Organiser, Transport and General Workers' Union, since 1992 (National Secretary, 1984–92); *b* 22 Aug. 1937; *d* of Frederick James and Lillian (*née* Barry); *m* (marr. diss.); one *s* two *d*. *Educ:* St Philomena's Convent, Carshalton; North East London Polytechnic (Post Grad. Dip. in Advice and Inf. Studies, 1977). Associate Mem., Inst. of Legal Execs, 1982. Advice Centre Organiser, Southwark Community Develt Project, 1974–76; Advr, Southwark Law Project, 1976–83; Trade Union Official, 1983–; Pres., TUC, 1995. Member: Equal Opportunities Commn, 1987–93; Employment Appeal Tribunal, 1995–. *Recreations:* walking, gardening, reading. *Address:* 154 Moffat Road, Thornton Heath, Surrey CR7 8PX. *T:* 0181–771 5487.

PROSSER, Raymond Frederick, CB 1973; MC 1942; *b* 12 Sept. 1919; *s* of Frederick Charles Prosser and Jane Prosser (*née* Lawless); *m* 1949, Fay Newmarch Holmes; two *s* three *d*. *Educ:* Wimbledon Coll.; The Queen's Coll., Oxford (1938–39 and 1946). Served Royal Artillery (Field), 1939–45 (MC, despatches): service in Egypt, Libya, India and Burma; Temp. Major. Asst Principal, Min. of Civil Aviation, 1947; Sec., Air Transport Advisory Council, 1952–57; Private Sec. to Minister of Transport and Civil Aviation, 1959, and to Minister of Aviation, 1959–61; Counsellor (Civil Aviation), HM Embassy, Washington, DC, 1965–68; Under-Sec., Marine Div., BoT, later DTI, 1968–72; Deputy Sec., Regional Industrial Organisation and Policy, DTI, later DoI, 1972–77; Principal Estabt and Finance Officer, Depts of Industry, Trade, and Prices and Consumer Protection, 1977–79, retired. Dir, European Investment Bank, 1973–77. Mem. (part-time), CAA, 1980–85. *Address:* Juniper House, Shalford Common, Shalford, Guildford, Surrey GU4 8DF. *T:* Guildford (01483) 566498.

PROSSER, William David; *see* Prosser, Hon. Lord.

PROTHEROE, Alan Hackford, CBE (mil.) 1991 (MBE (mil.) 1980); TD 1981; DL; journalist and media consultant; Managing Director, Services Sound and Vision Corporation, 1988–94; *b* 10 Jan. 1934; *s* of Rev. B. P. Protheroe and R. C. M. Protheroe; *m* 1956, Anne Miller; two *s*. *Educ:* Maesteg Grammar Sch., Glamorgan. FBIM; MIPR. Nat. Service, 2nd Lieut The Welch Regt, 1954–56; Lt-Col, Royal Regt of Wales (TA), 1979–84; Col, 1984–90. Reporter, Glamorgan Gazette, 1951–53; BBC Wales: Reporter, 1957–59; Industrial Correspondent, 1959–64; Editor, News and Current Affairs, 1964–70; BBC TV News: Asst Editor, 1970–72; Dep. Editor, 1972–77; Editor, 1977–80; Asst Dir, BBC News and Current Affairs, 1980–82; Asst Dir Gen., BBC, 1982–87. During BBC career wrote, produced, directed and presented films and radio programmes, reported wars, and travelled widely; seconded to Greek Govt to assist in reorganisation of Greek TV, 1973. Mem., Steering Cttee, EBU News Gp, 1977–87; Director: Visnews Ltd, 1982–87; Defence Public Affairs Consultants Ltd, 1987–; Chm., Europac Gp Ltd, 1990– (Dir, 1989–). Mem. Council, RUSI, 1984–87; Association of British Editors: Founder Mem., 1984–; Dep. Chm., 1984–87; Chm., 1987. Chm., Eastern Wessex Reserve Forces Assoc., 1991– (Dep. Chm., 1990–91). St James's Vice Pres., 1990–, and Mem. Bd of Mgt, 1992–, RBL; Dir, RBL Training, 1992–. Hon. Col, TA Information Officers, 1991–. DL Bucks, 1993. *Publications:* contribs to newspapers and specialist jls on industrial, media and defence affairs. *Recreations:* pistol and rifle shooting. *Address:* Amberleigh House, 60 Chapman Lane, Flackwell Heath, Bucks HP10 9BD. *T* and *Fax:* Bourne End (01628) 528492. *Club:* Savile.

PROUD, Sir John (Seymour), Kt 1978; mining engineer; director and chairman of companies; *b* 9 Aug. 1907; *s* of William James Proud and Hannah Seymour; *m* 1964, Laurine, *d* of M. Ferran. *Educ:* Univ. of Sydney (Bachelor of Engrg, Mining and Metallurgy). CEng, FIMM, FIE(Aust), F(Aus)IMM. Chm., Newcastle Wallsend Coal Co., which merged with Peko Mines NL, 1960; Chm., Peko-Wallsend Investments Ltd, then Chm., Peko-Wallsend Ltd; retd from chair, 1978; Dir/Consultant, 1978–82. Chairman: Electrical Equipment Ltd (Group), 1978–82 (Dir, 1943–83); Oil Search Ltd, 1978–88 (Dir, 1974–); Oil Co. of Australia NL, 1979–83; Dir, CSR Ltd, 1974–79. Fellow of Senate, Univ. of Sydney, 1974–83. Chm. Trustees, Lizard Island Reef Res. Foundn, 1978–87; Trustee, Aust. Museum, 1971–77. Hon. DEng Sydney, 1984. *Recreations:* yachting, pastoral activity. *Address:* 9 Finlay Road, Turramurra, NSW 2074, Australia. *Clubs:* Union, Royal Sydney Yacht Squadron, Royal Prince Alfred Yacht, American (Sydney).

PROUDFOOT, Bruce; *see* Proudfoot, V. B.

PROUDFOOT, (George) Wilfred; owner, self-service stores; consultant in distribution; professsional hypnotist and hypnotherapist, Master Practitioner of Neuro-Linguistic Programming; owner, Proudfoot School of Hypnosis and Hypnotherapy; *b* 19 December 1921; *m* 1950, Margaret Mary, *d* of Percy Clifford Jackson, Pontefract, Yorks; two *s* one *d*. *Educ:* Crook Council Sch.; Scarborough Coll. Served War of 1939–45, NCO Fitter in RAF, 1940–46. Served Scarborough Town Council, 1950–58 (Chm. Health Cttee, 1952–58). MP (C) Cleveland Division of Yorkshire, Oct. 1959–Sept. 1964; PPS to Minister of State, Board of Trade, Apr.-July 1962, to Minister of Housing and Local Govt and Minister for Welsh Affairs (Rt Hon. Sir Keith Joseph, Bt, MP), 1962–64; MP (C) Brighouse and Spenborough, 1970–Feb. 1974; Minister of State, Dept of Employment, 1970; contested (C) Brighouse and Spenborough, Oct. 1974. Man. Dir, Radio 270, 1965–. Chm., Scarborough Cons. Assoc., 1978–80; Chm., Cleveland European Constituency Cons. Assoc., 1979–. Professional hypnotist; face lifted by Dr John Williams, USA, 1978. Chm., British Council of Hypnotist Examiners, 1983–; Mem., Virginia Satir Internat. Avanta Network, 1987–. *Publications:* The Two Factor Nation, or How to make the people rich, 1977; The Consumer Guide to Hypnosis, 1990. *Recreations:* reading, photography, caravanning, travel, walking, jogging. *Address:* 278 Scalby Road, Scarborough, North Yorkshire YO12 6EA. *T:* Scarborough (01723) 367027.

PROUDFOOT, Prof. (Vincent) Bruce, FSA 1963; FRSE 1979; FRSGS; Professor of Geography, University of St Andrews, 1974–93, Emeritus 1993; *b* 24 Sept. 1930; *s* of late Bruce Falconer Proudfoot; *m* 1961, Edwina Valmai Windram Field; two *s*. *Educ:* Royal Belfast Academical Instn; Queen's Univ., Belfast (BA, PhD). Research Officer, Nuffield Quaternary Research Unit, QUB, 1954–58; Lectr in Geography, QUB, 1958–59, Durham Univ., 1959–67; Tutor, 1960–63, Librarian, 1963–65, Hatfield Coll., Durham; Visiting Fellow, Univ. of Auckland, NZ, and Commonwealth Vis. Fellow, Australia, 1966; Associate Prof., 1967–70, Prof., 1970–74, Univ. of Alberta, Edmonton, Canada; Acting Chm., Dept of Geography, Univ. of Alberta, 1970–71; Co-ordinator, Socio-Economic Opportunity Studies, and Staff Consultant, Alberta Human Resources Research Council, 1971–72. Trustee, Nat. Mus. of Antiquities of Scotland, 1982–85. Chairman: Rural Geog. Study Gp, Inst. of British Geographers, 1980–84; Soc. for Landscape Studies, 1979–83. Royal Society of Edinburgh: Mem. Council, 1982–85 and 1990–91; Vice-Pres., 1985–88; Gen. Sec., 1991–. Vice-Pres., Soc. of Antiquaries of Scotland, 1982–85; Pres., Section H (Anthrop. and Archaeol.), BAAS, 1985; Hon. Pres., Scottish Assoc. of Geography Teachers, 1982–84; Royal Scottish Geographical Society: Mem. Council, 1975–78, 1992–93; Chm. Council, 1993–; Vice-Pres., 1993–; Hon. Editor, 1978–93; Fellow, 1991; Chm., Dundee Centre, 1993– (Mem., Cttee, 1976–93). Lectures: Lister, BAAS, 1964; Annual, Soc. for Landscape Studies, 1983; Estyn Evans, QUB, 1985. *Publications:* The Downpatrick Gold Find, 1955; (with R. G. Ironside *et al*) Frontier Settlement Studies, 1974; (ed) Site, Environment and Economy, 1983; numerous papers in geographical, archaeological and soils jls. *Recreation:* gardening. *Address:* Westgate, Wardlaw Gardens, St Andrews, Scotland KY16 9DW. *T:* St Andrews (01334) 473293. *Club:* New (Edinburgh).

PROUDFOOT, Wilfred; *see* Proudfoot, G. W.

PROUDMAN, Sonia Rosemary Susan, (Mrs C. Cartwright); QC 1994; *b* 30 July 1949; *d* of Kenneth Oliphant Proudman and Sati Proudman (*née* Hekimian); *m* 1987, Crispian Cartwright; one *d*. *Educ:* St Paul's Girls' Sch. (Foundn Schol.); Lady Margaret Hall, Oxford (Open Schol.; BA 1st Cl. Hons Jurisprudence 1971; MA 1973). Called to the Bar, Lincoln's Inn, 1972 (Kennedy Schol., Buchanan Prize); Oxford Univ. Eldon Law Schol., 1973; in practice at Chancery Bar, 1974–. *Address:* 11 New Square, Lincoln's Inn, WC2A 3QB. *Clubs:* Hurlingham, CWIL.

PROUT, family name of **Baron Kingsland.**

PROVAN, James Lyal Clark; Member (C) South Downs West, European Parliament, since 1994; farmer; *b* 19 Dec. 1936; *s* of John Provan and Jean (*née* Clark); *m* 1960, Roweena Adele Lewis; twin *s* one *d*. *Educ:* Ardvreck Sch., Crieff; Oundle Sch., Northants; Royal Agricultural Coll., Cirencester. Member: Tayside Regional Council, 1978–82; Tay River Purification Bd, 1978–82. Chairman: McIntosh Donald Ltd, 1989–94; James McIntosh & Co., 1990–94. MEP (C) NE Scotland, 1979–89; Quaestor, 1987–89; Member: Agriculture and Fisheries Cttee, 1979–89 (EDG spokesman on agricl and fisheries affairs, 1982–87); Environment, Consumer Affairs and Public Health Cttee, 1979–89. Exec. Dir, Scottish Financial Enterprise, 1990–91. Mem., AFRC, 1990–94. Chm., Rowett Res. Inst., 1992–. Area President, Scottish NFU, 1965 and 1971; Treasurer, Perth and E Perthshire Conservative Assoc., 1975–77; Member, Lord Lieutenant's Queen's Jubilee Appeal Cttee, 1977. FRSA 1987. *Publication:* The European Community: an ever closer union?, 1989. *Recreations:* country pursuits, sailing, flying, musical appreciation, travel. *Address:* Middle Lodge, Barns Green, Horsham, West Sussex RH13 7NL. *T:* Horsham (01403) 733700, *Fax:* (01403) 733588. *Clubs:* Farmers', East India; Royal Perth Golfing Society.

PROVAN, Marie; *see* Staunton, M.

PROWSE, Florence Irene; *see* Calvert, F. I.

PROWSE, Philip (John); theatre director and designer; Co-director, Glasgow Citizens' Theatre, since 1970; Head of Theatre Design Department, Slade School of Fine Art, since 1995; *b* 29 Dec. 1937; *s* of late Alan William Auger Prowse and Violet Beatrice (*née* Williamson). *Educ:* King's Sch., Worcester; Malvern Coll. of Art; Slade Sch. of Fine Art. Professional début: Diversions for Royal Ballet, Royal Opera House, 1961; subsequent prodns and designs for opera, ballet and drama including: Glasgow Citizens' Theatre; rep. theatres; West End theatres; Royal Nat. Theatre; RSC, Barbican; Old Vic Theatre; Royal Opera; Royal Ballet; ENO; Sadler's Wells Royal Ballet; WNO; Scottish Opera; Opera North; English Nat. Ballet (Festival Ballet); Scottish Ballet; prodns in Europe and US; festival appearances: Rome, Wiesbaden, Holland, Warsaw, Zurich, Belgrade, Edinburgh, Cologne, Hamburg, Venice, Parma, E Berlin, Halle, Caracas. *Recreation:* work. *Address:* Citizens' Theatre, 119 Gorbals Street, Glasgow G5 9DS. *T:* 0141–429 5561.

PRYCE, (George) Terry, CBE 1994; Chairman, Horticulture Research International (formerly British Society for Horticultural Research), since 1990; *b* 26 March 1934; *s* of Edwin Pryce and Hilda Florence (*née* Price); *m* 1957, Thurza Elizabeth Tatham, JP; two *s* one *d*. *Educ:* Welshpool Grammar Sch.; National Coll. of Food Technol. MFC, FIFST, CIMgt. Dir, various food cos in THF Gp, 1965–70; Asst Man. Dir, Dalgety (UK) Ltd, 1970–72; Man. Dir, Dalgety (UK) and Dir, DPLC, 1972–78; Man. Dir, 1978–81, Chief Exec., 1981–89, Dalgety PLC. Chm., Solway Foods Ltd, 1990–94; Director: H. P. Bulmer Holdings, 1984–94; Jas Bowman and Sons Ltd, 1991–. Council Member: AFRC, 1986–94; UK Food and Drink Fedn, 1987–89; Mem. Adv. Bd, Inst. of Food Res., 1988–94. Chm., UK Food Assoc., 1986–88. *Recreations:* sport, esp. golf; reading. *Address:* 89 Brookmans Avenue, Brookmans Park, Hatfield, Herts AL9 7QG. *T:* Hatfield (01707) 42039. *Club:* Athenæum.

PRYCE, Rt. Rev. James Taylor; a Suffragan Bishop of Toronto (Area Bishop of York-Simcoe), since 1985; *b* 3 May 1936; *s* of James Pryce and Florence Jane (*née* Taylor); *m* 1962, Marie Louise Connor; two *s* one *d* (and one *s* decd). *Educ:* Bishop's Univ., Lennoxville, Quebec (BA, LST). Ordained Deacon, 1962, priest, 1963; Asst Curate, Church of the Ascension, Don Mills, 1962–65; Incumbent: St Thomas' Church, Brooklin, Ont, 1965–70; St Paul's, Lorne Park, 1970–75; Christ Church, Scarborough, 1975–81; St Leonard's, North Toronto, 1981–85. Hon. DD, Wycliffe Coll., 1986. *Address:* 8 Pinehurst Court, Aurora, Ontario L4G 6B2, Canada. *T:* (905) 7277863.

PRYCE, Jonathan; actor; *b* 1 June 1947; lives with partner, Kate Fahy; two *s* one *d*. *Educ:* RADA. FWCMD. Patron, Friends United Network, 1992–. *Theatre includes:* The Comedians, Nottingham Old Vic, 1975, NY 1976 (Tony Award); title rôle, Hamlet, Royal Court, 1980 (Olivier Award); The Caretaker, Nat. Th., 1981; Accidental Death of an Anarchist, Broadway, 1984; The Seagull, Queen's, 1985; title rôle, Macbeth, RSC, 1986; Uncle Vanya, Vaudeville, 1988; Miss Saigon, Drury Lane, 1989 (Olivier Award and Variety Club Award), NY, 1991 (Tony Award for Best Actor in Musical, 1991); Oliver!, Palladium, 1994; *television includes:* Roger Doesn't Live Here Anymore (series), 1981; Timon of Athens, 1981; Martin Luther, 1983; Praying Mantis, 1983; Whose Line Is It Anyway?, 1988–; The Man from the Pru, 1990; Selling Hitler, 1991; Mr Wroe's Virgins, 1993; Thicker Than Water, 1993; *films include:* Something wicked this way comes, 1982; The Ploughman's Lunch, 1983; Brazil, 1985; The Doctor and the Devils, 1986; Haunted Honeymoon, 1986; Jumpin' Jack Flash, 1987; Consuming Passions, 1988; The Adventures of Baron Munchausen, 1988; The Rachel Papers, 1989; Glengarry Glen Ross, 1992; The Age of Innocence, 1992; Barbarians at the Gate, 1992; Great Moments in Aviation, 1993; A Business Affair, 1993; Shopping, 1994; Carrington, 1995 (Best Actor Award, Cannes, 1995); *recordings include:* Miss Saigon; Nine—the Concert; Under Milk Wood; Cabaret. *Address:* c/o James Sharkey Associates Ltd, 21 Golden Square, W1R 3PA; c/o Duva Flack Associates, 200 W 57th Street, Suite 1407, New York, NY 10019, USA.

PRYCE, Maurice Henry Lecorney, FRS 1951; Professor of Physics, University of British Columbia, 1968–78, now Emeritus Professor; *b* 24 Jan. 1913; *e s* of William John Pryce and Hortense Lecorney; *m* 1939, Susanne Margarete Born (marr. diss., 1959); one *s* three *d*; *m* 1961, Freda Mary Kinsey. *Educ:* Royal Grammar Sch., Guildford; Trinity Coll., Cambridge. Commonwealth Fund Fellow at Princeton, NJ, USA, 1935–37; Fellow of Trinity Coll., Cambridge, and Faculty Asst Lecturer, University of Cambridge, 1937–39; Reader in Theoretical Physics, University of Liverpool, 1939–45. Engaged on Radar research with Admiralty Signal Establishment, 1941–44, and on Atomic Energy Research with National Research Council of Canada, Montreal, 1944–45. University Lecturer in Mathematics and Fellow of Trinity Coll., Cambridge, 1945–46; Wykeham Professor of Physics, University of Oxford, 1946–54; Henry Overton Wills Professor of Physics, University of Bristol, 1954–64; Prof. of Physics, University of Southern California, 1964–68. Visiting Professor: Princeton Univ., NJ, USA, 1950–51; Duke Univ., NC, USA, 1958; Univ. of Sussex, 1976–77. Mem., Technical Adv. Cttee to Atomic Energy of Canada Ltd on Nuclear Fuel Waste Management Program, 1979–96. *Publications:* various on Theoretical Physics, in learned journals. *Recreations:* theoretical scientific research, reading, music. *Address:* 4754 West 6th Avenue, Vancouver, BC V6T 1C5, Canada; Physics Department, University of British Columbia, 6224 Agriculture Road, Vancouver, BC V6T 1Z1, Canada. *Club:* Athenæum.

PRYCE, Prof. Roy; Director, Federal Trust for Education and Research, 1983–90, Senior Research Fellow, since 1990; *b* 4 Oct. 1928; *s* of Thomas and Madeleine Pryce; *m* 1954, Sheila Rose, *d* of Rt Hon. James Griffiths, CH; three *d*. *Educ:* Grammar Sch., Burton-on-Trent; Emmanuel Coll., Cambridge (MA, PhD). MA Oxon. Research Fellow: Emmanuel Coll., Cambridge, 1953–55; St Antony's Coll., Oxford, 1955–57; Head of London Information Office of High Authority of European Coal and Steel Community, 1957–60; Head of London Inf. Office, Jt Inf. Service of European Communities, 1960–64; Rockefeller Foundn Res. Fellow, 1964–65; Dir, Centre for Contemp. European Studies, Univ. of Sussex, 1965–73; Directorate General for Information, Commission of the European Communities: Dir, 1973–78; Sen. Advr for Direct Elections, 1978–79; Chief Advr for Programming, 1979–81. Vis. Professorial Fellow, Centre for Contemporary European Studies, Univ. of Sussex, 1973–81; Vis. Professor: Coll. of Europe, Bruges, 1965–72; Eur. Univ. Inst., Florence, 1981–83; Eur. Inst. for Public Admin, Maastricht, 1983–88. *Publications:* The Italian Local Elections 1956, 1957; The Political Future of the European Community, 1962; (with John Pinder) Europe After de Gaulle, 1969, German and Ital. edns 1970; The Politics of the European Community, 1973; (ed) The Dynamics of European Union, 1987; (ed jtly) Maastricht and Beyond, 1994; contrib. Enc. Brit., Jl Common Market Studies, etc. *Recreations:* gardening, collecting water colours and prints.

PRYCE, Terry; *see* Pryce, G. T.

PRYCE-JONES, Alan Payan, TD; book critic, author and journalist; *b* 18 Nov. 1908; *s* of late Colonel Henry Morris Pryce-Jones, CB; *m* 1934, Thérèse (*d* 1953), *d* of late Baron Fould-Springer and of Mrs Frank Wooster, Paris; one *s*; *m* 1968, Mrs Mary Jean Kempner Thorne (*d* 1969), *d* of late Daniel Kempner. *Educ:* Eton; Magdalen Coll., Oxford. Formerly Asst Editor, The London Mercury, 1928–32; subseq. Times Literary Supplement; Editor, Times Literary Supplement, 1948–59; Book critic: New York Herald Tribune, 1963–66; World Journal Tribune, 1967–68; Newsday, 1969–71; Theatre Critic, Theatre Arts, 1963–. Trustee, National Portrait Gallery, 1950–61; Director, Old Vic Trust, 1950–61; Member Council, Royal College of Music, 1956–61; Program Associate, The Humanities and Arts Program, Ford Foundation, NY, 1961–63. Served War of 1939–45, France, Italy, Austria; Lieut-Colonel, 1945. *Publications:* The Spring Journey, 1931; People in the South, 1932; Beethoven, 1933; 27 Poems, 1935; Private Opinion, 1936; Nelson, an opera, 1954; Vanity Fair, a musical play (with Robin Miller and Julian Slade), 1962; The Bonus of Laughter (autobiog.), 1987. *Recreations:* music, travelling. *Address:* 46 John Street, Newport, RI 02840, USA. *Clubs:* Travellers', Garrick, Beefsteak, Pratt's; Knickerbocker, Century (New York); Artillery (Galveston, Texas).

PRYER, (Eric) John, CB 1986; Chief Land Registrar, 1983–90; Assistant Secretary, Council for Licensed Conveyancers, 1991–92; *b* 5 Sept. 1929; *s* of late Edward John and Edith Blanche Pryer; *m* 1962, Moyra Helena Cross; one *s* one *d*. *Educ:* Beckenham and Penge County Grammar Sch.; Birkbeck Coll., London Univ. (BA Hons). Called to the Bar, Gray's Inn, 1957. Exec. Officer, Treasury Solicitor's Dept, 1948; Legal Asst, HM Land Registry, 1959; Asst Land Registrar, 1965; Dist Land Registrar, Durham, 1976; Dep. Chief Land Registrar, 1981–83. Hon. Associate Mem., RICS, 1986. *Publications:* (ed) Ruoff and Roper, The Law and Practice of Registered Conveyancing, 5th edn 1986, 6th edn 1991; Land Registration Handbook, 1990; official pubns; articles in jls. *Recreation:* reading.

PRYKE, Sir David Dudley, 3rd Bt *cr* 1926; *b* 16 July 1912; *s* of Sir William Robert Dudley Pryke, 2nd Bt; *S* father 1959; *m* 1945, Doreen Winifred, *er d* of late Ralph Bernard Wilkins; two *d*. *Educ:* St Lawrence Coll., Ramsgate. Liveryman Turners' Company, 1961 (Master, 1985–86). *Heir: nephew* Christopher Dudley Pryke *b* 17 April 1946. *Address:* 27 Wantz Haven, Princes Road, Maldon, Essex CM9 7HA.

PRYKE, Roy Thomas; Director of Education Services, Kent County Council, since 1989; *b* 30 Nov. 1940; *s* of Thomas George and Nellie Matilda Pryke; *m* 1962, Susan Pauline Andrew; one *s* three *d*. *Educ:* Univ. of Wales (BA Hons); Univ. of Manchester (PGCE). Teacher, Manchester, 1963–71; Education Officer, Devon, 1971–79; Deputy Chief Education Officer: Somerset, 1980–82; Devon, 1983–87; Dep. Chief Educn Officer and Head of Operations, Cambridgeshire, 1987–89. Adviser to: Council of Local Educn Authorities, 1992–; ACC, 1994–; Sec. and Hon. Treas., Standing Conference of Chief Educn Officers, 1994–. FRSA 1988; Hon. FCP 1991. Chevalier, Ordre des Palmes Académiques (France), 1994. *Publications:* contributor to: Open Plan Schools, 1978; The Head's Legal Guide, 1984; The Revolution in Education and Training, 1986; articles in Education Jl on curriculum and on education management. *Recreations:* foreign travel and languages, photography, tennis, running. *Address:* South House, Lambden Thorne, Pluckley, Kent TN27 0RB. *T:* Pluckley (01233) 84720.

PRYN, Maj.-Gen. William John, OBE 1973; MB, BS; FRCS, FRCSEd; Director of Army Surgery, and Consulting Surgeon to the Army, 1982–86, retired; *b* 25 Jan. 1928; *s* of late Col Richard Harold Cotter Pryn, FRCS, late RAMC and Una St George Ormsby (*née* Roe); *m* 1st, 1952, Alison Lynette (marr. diss.), 2nd *d* of Captain Norman Arthur Cyril Hardy, RN; two *s* one *d*; 2nd, 1982, June de Medina, *d* of Surg. Comdr Norman Bernard de Medina Greenstreet, RN; one step *s* one step *d*. *Educ:* Malvern Coll.; Guy's Hosp. Med. Sch., London Univ. (MB, BS 1951). MRCS, LRCP 1951; FRCS 1958; FRCSEd 1984. Trooper, 21st SAS Regt (Artists Rifles), TA, 1948–50. House appts, Gen. Hosp., Ramsgate and Royal Berks Hosp., Reading, 1951–52; commnd into RAMC, 1952; Regtl MO to No 9 Training Regt RE, 1952–53; surg. appts in mil. hosps in UK, Cyprus and N Africa, 1953–58; seconded as Surg. Registrar, Royal Postgrad. Med. Sch., Hammersmith Hosp., 1958–59; Officer i/c Surg. Div. and Consultant Surgeon to mil. hosps, Malaya, Singapore, N Borneo and UK, 1959–69; CO BMH Dhekelia, 1969–72; Sen. Consultant Surgeon in mil. hosps, UK and NI, 1972–77; Consulting Surgeon to BAOR, 1977–82; Consultant in Surgery to Royal Hosp., Chelsea, 1982–86; Hon. Consultant to S Dist, Kensington and Chelsea and Westminster AHA (T), 1981. Member: EUROMED Gp on Emergency Medicine, 1980–86; Specialty Bd in Surgery, and Reg. Trng Cttee in Gen. Surgery, Defence Medical Services, 1982–86; Med. Cttee, Defence Scientific Adv. Council, 1982–86; BMA, 1950–; Wessex Surgeons Club, 1976–. Member Council: RAMC, 1982–86; Mil. Surgical Soc., 1982–. Fellow, Assoc. of Surgeons of GB and Ireland, 1960 (Mem., Educn Adv. Cttee, 1982–86). QHS 1981–86. OStJ 1984. Mem., Editorial Bd, Injury, 1982–86. *Publications:* (contrib.) Field Surgery Pocket Book, 1981; original articles in the Lancet and British Jl of Surgery. *Recreations:* fishing, shooting and other country pursuits, golf, tennis, sailing, gardening, joinery, house maintenance.

PRYNNE, Andrew Geoffrey Lockyer; QC 1995; *b* 28 May 1953; *s* of late Maj.-Gen. Michael Whitworth Prynne, CB, CBE and Jean Violet Prynne; *m* 1977, Catriona Mary Brougham; three *d*. *Educ:* Marlborough Coll.; Univ. of Southampton (LLB Hons). Called to the Bar, Middle Temple, 1975. *Recreations:* sailing, shooting, ski-ing. *Address:* 2 Harcourt Buildings, Temple, EC4Y 9DB. *T:* 0171–583 9020. *Clubs:* Royal Yacht Squadron; Royal Solent Yacht; Island Sailing (IoW).

PRYOR, Arthur John, PhD; Head, Competition Policy Division, Department of Trade and Industry, since 1993; *b* 7 March 1939; *s* of late Quinton Arthur Pryor, FRICS and Elsie Margaret (*née* Luscombe); *m* 1964, Marilyn Kay Petley; one *s* one *d*. *Educ:* Harrow County Grammar Sch.; Downing Coll., Cambridge (MA; PhD). Asst Lectr, then Lectr, in Spanish and Portuguese, UC Cardiff, 1963–66; Asst Principal, BoT and ECGD, 1966–69; Principal, DTI, 1970–73; First Sec., British Embassy, Washington, 1973–75; Principal, Dept of Trade, 1975–77; Assistant Secretary: Shipping Policy Div., Dept of Trade, 1977–80; Air Div., DoI, 1980–83; Department of Trade and Industry: Asst Sec., Internat. Trade Policy Div., 1984–85; Under Sec. and Regional Dir, W Midlands Region, 1985–88; Dir Gen., BNSC, 1988–93. *Publications:* contribs to modern lang. jls. *Recreations:* tennis, golf, book collecting. *Address:* Competition Policy Division, Department of Trade and Industry, Ashdown House, 123 Victoria Street, SW1E 6RB.

PRYOR, Brian Hugh; QC 1982; **His Honour Judge Brian Pryor;** a Circuit Judge, since 1986; *b* 11 March 1931; *s* of Lt-Col Ronald Ernest Pryor, Royal Sussex Regt, and Violet Kathleen Pryor (*née* Steele); *m* 1955, Jane Mary Smith; one *s* two *d*. *Educ:* Chichester High Sch.; University Coll., Oxford (Open Exhibnr Mod. History; BA Jurisprudence). Called to the Bar, Lincoln's Inn, 1956; Sir Thomas More Bursary, Lincoln's Inn, 1958. Member: SE Circuit Bar Mess, 1957; Kent County Bar Mess, 1957; Chm., Kent Bar Mess, 1979–82; Mem., SE Circuit Bar Mess Wine Cttee, 1979–82. A Recorder, 1981–86. Mem., Camberwell HA Res. Ethics Cttee, 1990–. *Recreation:* gardening.

PRYOR, John Pembro, MS; FRCS; Consultant Urological Surgeon to St Peter's Hospital, since 1975; Dean, Institute of Urology, London University, 1978–85; *b* 25 Aug. 1937; *s* of William Benjamin Pryor and Kathleen Pryor; *m* 1959, Marion Hopkins; four *s*. *Educ:* Reading Sch.; King's Coll. and King's Coll. Hosp. Med. Sch. (MB, BS). AKC 1961; FRCS 1967; MS London 1971. Training appointments: Doncaster Royal Infirm., 1965–66; Univ. of Calif, San Francisco, 1968–69; King's Coll. Hosp. and St Paul's Hosp., 1971–72. Hunterian Prof., RCS, 1971 and 1995. Chm. (first), British Andrology Soc., 1979–84; Chm., European Assoc. of Genital Microsurgeons, 1992–. Treas., British Jl of Urology, 1991–. St Peter's Medal, British Assoc. of Urol Surgeons, 1995. *Publications:* (ed jtly) Andrology, 1987; (ed) Urological prostheses, appliances and catheters, 1992; (jtly) Impotence: an integrated approach to clinical practice, 1992; articles on urology and andrology in scientific jls. *Address:* Andrology Unit, Lister Hospital, Chelsea Bridge Road, SW1W 8RH. *T:* 0171–730 3417.

PRYOR, Robert Charles, QC 1983; **His Honour Judge Pryor;** a Circuit Judge, since 1991; *b* 10 Dec. 1938; *s* of Charles Selwyn Pryor and Olive Woodall Pryor; *m* 1969, Virginia Sykes; one *s* one *d*. *Educ:* Eton; Trinity Coll., Cambridge (BA). National Service, KRRC, 2nd Lieut 1958. Called to the Bar, Inner Temple, 1963; a Recorder, 1989–91. Director, Sun Life Corp. (formerly Sun Life Assurance) plc, 1977–91. *Address:* Falcon Chambers, Falcon Court, EC4Y 1AA.

PRYS-DAVIES, family name of **Baron Prys-Davies.**

PRYS-DAVIES, Baron *cr* 1982 (Life Peer), of Llanegryn in the County of Gwynedd; **Gwilym Prys Prys-Davies;** Consultant, Morgan Bruce & Nicholas, Solicitors, Cardiff, Pontypridd and Porth, since 1987 (Partner, 1957–87); *b* 8 Dec. 1923; *s* of William and Mary Matilda Davies; *m* 1951, Llinos Evans; three *d*. *Educ:* Towyn Sch., Towyn, Merioneth; University College of Wales, Aberystwyth. Served RN, 1942–46. Faculty of Law, UCW, Aberystwyth, 1946–52; President of Debates, Union UCW, 1949; President Students' Rep. Council, 1950; LLB 1949; LLM 1952. Admitted Solicitor, 1956. Contested (Lab) Carmarthen, 1966. Special Adviser to Sec. of State for Wales, 1974–78. Official opposition spokesman: on health, 1983–89; on N Ireland, 1982–93; on Welsh Office, 1987–. Member: H of L Select Cttee on Parochial Charities Bill and Small Charities Bill, 1983–84; H of L Select Cttee on murder and life imprisonment, 1988–89; British-Irish Inter-Parly Body, 1990–. Chm., Welsh Hosps Bd, 1968–74; Member: Welsh Council, 1967–69; Welsh Adv. Cttee, ITA, 1966–69; Working Party on 4th TV Service in Wales, Home Office and Welsh Office, 1975–; Adv. Gp, Use of Fetuses and Fetal Material for Res., DHSS and Welsh Office, 1972; Econ. and Social Cttee, EEC, 1978–82. Vice-Pres., Coleg Harlech, 1989–. OStJ. *Publications:* A Central Welsh Council, 1963; Y Ffermwr a'r Gyfraith, 1967. *Address:* Lluest, 78 Church Road, Tonteg, Pontypridd, Mid Glam CF38 1EN. *T:* Newtown Llantwit (01443) 2462.

PRYS-ROBERTS, Prof. Cedric, DM; FRCA; Professor of Anaesthesia, University of Bristol, since 1976; President, Royal College of Anaesthetists, since 1994; *b* 8 Aug. 1935; *s* of late William Prys Roberts and Winifred Prys Roberts (*née* Osborne Jones); *m* 1961, Linda Joyce Bickerstaff; two *s* two *d*. *Educ:* Dulwich Coll.; St Bartholomew's Hosp. Med. Sch. (MB BS London); MA, DM Oxon; PhD Leeds. FANZCA. Research Fellow, Univ. of Leeds, 1964–67; Clinical Reader in Anaesthetics, Oxford Univ., 1967–76; Fellow, Worcester Coll., Oxford, 1970–76; Hon Cons. Anaesthetist, Radcliffe Infirmary, 1967–76; Prof. of Anaesthesia, Univ. of California, San Diego, 1974; Hon. Consultant Anaesthetist, Bristol Royal Infirmary and Bristol Royal Hosp. for Sick Children, 1976–. Hunterian Prof., RCS, 1978. *Publications:* (ed) The Circulation in Anaesthesia, 1980; (ed) Pharmacokinetics of Anaesthesia, 1984; (ed) Monitoring in Anaesthesia and Intensive Care, 1994; (ed) International Practice of Anaesthesia, 2 vols, 1995; contribs to learned jls. *Recreations:* mountaineering, ski-ing, philately, music (playing trumpet). *Address:* Foxes Mead, Cleeve Hill Road, Cleeve, Bristol BS19 4PG; Flat 2, 54 Russell Square, WC1B 4HP.

PUDDEPHATT, Andrew Charles; General Secretary, Liberty (formerly National Council for Civil Liberties), since 1989; *b* 2 April 1950; *s* of Andrew Ross Puddephatt and Margaret McGuire; two *d*. *Educ:* Sidney Sussex College, Cambridge (BA 1971). Worked as teacher in 1970s; computer programmer, 1978–81. Councillor, Hackney Council, 1982–90 (Leader, 1986–89). *Recreations:* literature, music. *Address:* Liberty, 21 Tabard Street, SE1 4LA. *T:* 0171–403 3888.

PUGH, Alastair Tarrant, CBE 1986; Consultant, Goldman Sachs International Ltd, since 1988; Executive Vice Chairman/Director of Strategy, British Caledonian Group plc, 1985–88; *b* 16 Sept. 1928; *s* of Sqdn Leader Rev. Herbert Cecil Pugh, GC, MA, and Amy Lilian Pugh; *m* 1957, Sylvia Victoria Marlow; two *s* one *d*. *Educ:* Tettenhall Coll., Staffs; De Havilland Aeronautical Tech. Sch. FRAeS; FCIT; FIFF; CBIM. Design Dept, De Havilland Aircraft Co., 1949–52; Sen. Designer, H. M. Hobson, 1952–55; journalist, Flight, 1955–61; Channel Air Bridge, 1961–63; British United Airways, 1963–70: Planning Dir, 1968; British Caledonian Airways: Dir, R&D, 1970; Production Dir, 1973–74; Corporate Planning Dir, 1974–77; Dep. Chief Exec., 1977–78; Man. Dir, 1978–85. President: Inst. of Freight Forwarders, 1981–82; CIT, 1988–89. *Recreation:* the chain-driven Frazer Nash. *Address:* England's Cottage, Sidlow Bridge, Reigate, Surrey RH2 8PN. *T:* Reigate (01737) 43456.

PUGH, Andrew Cartwright; QC 1988; a Recorder, since 1990; *b* 6 June 1937; *s* of late Lewis Gordon Pugh and of Erica Pugh; *m* 1984, Chantal Hélène Langevin; two *d*. *Educ:* Tonbridge; New Coll. Oxford (MA). Served Royal Sussex Regt, 1956–57. Bigelow Teaching Fellow, Law Sch., Univ. of Chicago, 1960–61. Called to the Bar, Inner Temple, 1961, Bencher, 1989. Legal Assessor, GMC and GDC, 1991–. *Recreations:* gardening, reading, tennis. *Address:* 2 Hare Court, Temple, EC4Y 7BH. *T:* 0171–583 1770. *Club:* United Oxford & Cambridge University.

PUGH, Charles Edward, (Ted Pugh), CBE 1988; Managing Director, National Nuclear Corporation Ltd, 1984–87; *b* 17 Sept. 1922; *s* of Gwilym Arthur and Elsie Doris Pugh; *m* 1945, Edna Wilkinson; two *s* and *d*. *Educ:* Bolton and Salford Technical Colleges. CEng, MIMechE; FInstE 1987. Lancashire Electric Power Co., 1941–48; CEGB Project Manager responsible for construction of 6 power stations, 1951–71; Chief Electrical and Control and Instrumentation Engineer, CEGB, Barnwood, 1971–73; Special Services, CEGB, 1973–76; Dir of Projects, CEGB, 1976–82; PWR Project Dir, NNC, 1982–84. Pres., Inst. of Energy, 1988–89. Hon. FINucE 1984. *Recreations:* power stations, sculpture, painting, music, gardening and walking.

PUGH, Edward Clevely; Director, British Council, Poland, since 1994; *b* 14 Sept. 1937; *s* of Edgar Pallister Pugh and late Dora Lois Pugh (*née* Clevely); *m* 1962, Thirza Carolyn Browning; one *s* one *d*. *Educ:* Exeter Univ. (BA Econs and Govt 1962); SOAS, Univ. of London. Nat. Service, RN, 1955–57. Robinson Waxed Paper Co. Ltd, 1955 and 1962; British Council, 1963–: Lectr, Tehran, 1963–67; Asst Rep., Tripoli, 1967–71; Regl Dir, Ndola, Zambia, 1971–74; Dep. Rep., 1974–75, Rep., 1975–77, Ethiopia; seconded to ODM, 1977–79; Dir, FE and Pacific Dept, London, 1979–80; Rep., Tanzania, 1980–83; Dep. Rep., Delhi, 1983–86; Rep., Thailand, 1986–90; Americas, Pacific and Asia Division: Asst Dir, 1990–91; Dep. Dir, 1991–92; Dir, 1992–93; Regl Dir, S Asia and Oceania, 1993–94. *Recreations:* reading, music, theatre, art, walking, swimming. *Address:* 43 Offham Road, W Malling, Maidstone, Kent ME19 6RB. *T:* Maidstone (01732) 843317.

PUGH, Harold Valentine, CBE 1964; Chairman, Northern Ireland Joint Electricity Authority, 1967–70, retired; *b* 18 Oct. 1899; *s* of Henry John Valentine Pugh and Martha (*née* Bott); *m* 1934, Elizabeth Mary (*née* Harwood); two *s* one *d*. *Educ:* The High Sch., Murree, India; Manchester College of Technology. Trained Metropolitan-Vickers (asst engineer erection, 1925–30). Chief Engineer, Cory Bros, 1930–35; Deputy Superintendent and later Superintendent, Upper Boat Power Station, 1935–43; Generation Engineer, South Wales Power Company, 1943–44; Deputy Chief Engineer, Manchester Corporation Electricity Dept, 1944–48; Controller, British Electricity Authority, South Wales Division, 1948; Controller, British (later Central) Electricity Authority, London Division, 1951; Chairman: Eastern Electricity Board, 1957–63; South-Eastern Electricity Board, 1963–66. Director: Aberdare Holdings, 1966–70. AMCT; FIEE; FIMechE. *Recreations:* gardening, golf. *Address:* Clontaff, Doggetts Wood Lane, Chalfont St Giles, Bucks HP8 4TH. *T:* Little Chalfont (01494) 2330.

PUGH, Sir Idwal (Vaughan), KCB 1972 (CB 1967); Chairman, Chartered Trust Ltd, 1979–88; Director: Standard Chartered Bank, 1979–88; Halifax Building Society, 1979–88; *b* 10 Feb. 1918; *s* of late Rhys Pugh and Elizabeth Pugh; *m* 1946, Mair Lewis (*d* 1985); one *s* one *d*. *Educ:* Cowbridge Grammar Sch.; St John's Coll., Oxford (Hon. Fellow, 1979). Army Service, 1940–46. Entered Min. of Civil Aviation, 1946; Alternate UK Rep. at International Civil Aviation Organisation, Montreal, 1950–53; Asst Secretary, 1956; Civil Air Attaché, Washington, 1957–59; Under Secretary, Min. of Transport, 1959; Min. of Housing and Local Govt, 1961; Dep. Sec., Min. of Housing and Local Govt, 1966–69; Permanent Sec., Welsh Office, 1969–71; Second Permanent Sec., DoE, 1971–76. Parly Comr for Administration and Health Service Comr for England, Wales and Scotland, 1976–79. Chm., Develt Corp. of Wales, 1980–83. Chm., RNCM, 1988–92 (Hon. Mem., 1992); Vice-Pres, UC Swansea, 1988–94 (Hon. Fellow, 1995); President: Coleg Harlech, 1990–; Cardiff Business Club, 1991–. Hon. LLD Wales, 1988. *Address:* 5 Murray Court, 80 Banbury Road, Oxford OX2 6LQ. *Club:* Brooks's.

PUGH, John Arthur, OBE 1968; HM Diplomatic Service, retired; British High Commissioner to Seychelles, 1976–80; *b* 17 July 1920; *er s* of late Thomas Pugh and Dorothy Baker Pugh. *Educ:* Brecon Grammar Sch.; Bristol Univ. RN, 1941–45. Home CS, 1950–54; Gold Coast Admin. Service, 1955–58; Adviser to Ghana Govt, 1958–60; First Sec., British High Commn, Lagos, 1962–65; First Sec. (Economic), Bangkok, and British Perm. Rep. to Economic Commn for Asia and Far East, 1965–68; British Dep. High Comr, Ibadan, 1971–73; Diplomatic Service Inspector, 1973–76. *Publications:* The Friday Man, 1992; editorial and other contributions to jls etc on political affairs, travel and history. *Recreations:* Oriental ceramics, travel. *Address:* Pennybrin, Hay on Wye, Hereford HR3 5RS. *T:* Hay on Wye (01497) 820695. *Club:* Commonwealth Trust.

PUGH, John Stanley; Editor, Liverpool Echo, 1978–82; *b* 9 Dec. 1927; *s* of John Albert and Winifred Lloyd Pugh; *m* 1953, Kathleen Mary; two *s* one *d*. *Educ:* Wallasey Grammar School. Editor, Liverpool Daily Post, 1969–78. *Recreation:* golf. *Address:* 26 Westwood Road, Noctorum, Birkenhead, Merseyside L43 9RQ. *Club:* Royal Liverpool (Hoylake).

PUGH, Lionel Roger Price, CBE 1975; VRD 1953; Executive Member, British Steel Corporation, 1972–77; *b* 9 May 1916; *s* of late Henry George Pugh, Cardiff; *m* 1942, Joyce Norma Nash; one *s* one *d*. *Educ:* Clifton. FCA. Supply Officer, RNVR, 1938–60; war service mainly in Mediterranean, 1939–46; retired as Lt Comdr, RNR, 1960. With

Deloitte & Co., 1933–47; joined Guest Keen Bladwins Iron & Steel Co. Ltd, 1947; Dir 1955; Man. Dir 1960; Chm. 1962; Jt Man. Dir, GKN Steel, 1964. Dir, Product Co-ordination, British Steel Corp., 1967; Dep. Commercial Man. Dir, 1969; Man. Dir, Ops and Supplies, 1970; Mem., Corporate Finance and Planning, 1972; Chairman: BSC (UK) Ltd, 1974–77; BSC Chemicals Ltd, 1974–77; Redpath Dorman Long Ltd, 1974–77. Dir, 1973, Dep. Chm., 1977–86, Bridon plc; Dir, Ryan Internat., 1979–85. Pres., Iron and Steel Inst., 1973; Hon. Member: American Iron and Steel Inst. 1973; Metals Soc., 1976; Inst. of Metals, 1985; Inst. of Materials, 1992. Mem., Civil Aviation Council for Wales, 1962–66; part-time Mem., S Wales Electricity Bd, 1963–67. DL S Glamorgan (formerly Glamorgan), 1963–78. Gold Cross of Merit (Poland), 1942. *Address:* Brook Cottage, Bournes Green, Oakridge, Glos GL6 7NL. *T:* Gloucester (01452) 770554. *Clubs:* Naval and Military; Cirencester Golf.

PUGH, Peter David S.; *see* Storie-Pugh.

PUGH, Roger Courtenay Beckwith, MD; Pathologist to St Peter's Hospitals and the Institute of Urology, London, 1955–82; *b* 23 July 1917; *y s* of late Dr Robert Pugh, Talgarth, Breconshire, and of late Margaret Louise Pugh (*née* Gough); *m* 1942, Winifred Dorothy, *yr d* of late Alfred Cooper and late Margaret Cooper (*née* Evans); one *s* one *d*. *Educ:* Gresham's Sch., Holt; St Mary's Hospital (University of London). MRCS, LRCP 1940; MB, BS, 1941; MD 1948; MCPath 1964, FRCPath 1967; FRCS 1983. House Surgeon, St Mary's Hospital and Sector Hospitals, 1940–42; War Service in RAF (Mediterranean theatre), 1942–46, Sqdn Leader; Registrar, Department of Pathology, St Mary's Hospital, 1946–48; Asst Pathologist and Lecturer in Pathology, St Mary's Hospital, 1948–51; Asst Morbid Anatomist, The Hospital for Sick Children, Great Ormond Street, 1951–54. Erasmus Wilson Demonstrator, RCS, 1959, 1961; Member: Board of Governors, St Peter's Hospitals, 1961–82; Pathological Society of Great Britain and Ireland; Assoc. of Clin. Pathologists (Marshall Medal, 1982); Internat. Society of Urology; Internat. Acad. of Pathology (former Pres., British Div.; Cunningham Medal, 1993); Hon. Member British Assoc. of Urological Surgeons (St Peter's Medal, 1981); FRSocMed (Hon. Mem., and former Pres., Sect. of Urology). *Publications:* (ed) Pathology of the Testis, 1976; various contributions to Pathological, Urological and Paediatric Journals. *Recreations:* gardening, photography. *Address:* 3 Waldron Gardens, Shortlands Road, Bromley, Kent BR2 0JR. *T:* 0181–464 4240.

PUGH, Ted; *see* Pugh, C. E.

PUGH, William David, CBE 1965; FIM; CIMgt; JP; retired; Deputy Chairman, English Steel Corporation Ltd, 1965–67 (Managing Director, 1955–65); Director of Personnel, British Steel Corporation (Midland Group), 1967–70; *b* 21 Nov. 1904; *s* of late Sir Arthur and Lady Pugh; *m* 1936, Mary Dorothea Barber; one *d*. *Educ:* Regent Street Polytechnic; Sheffield Univ. Joined Research Dept, Vickers Ltd, Sheffield, 1926, Director, Vickers Ltd, 1962–67; Chairman: The Darlington Forge Ltd, 1957–66; Taylor Bros & Co. Ltd, 1959–66; Director: (and alternate Chairman), Firth Vickers Stainless Steels Ltd, 1948–67; High Speed Steel Alloys Ltd, 1953–68; Industrial Training Council Service, 1960–67; British Iron and Steel Corp. Ltd, 1962–67; Sheffield Boy Scouts Holdings Ltd, 1965–85 (Scout Silver Wolf, 1983); Sheffield Centre for Environmental Research Ltd. Associate of Metallurgy (Sheffield University; Mappin Medallist). Hon. Fellow, Sheffield Hallam Univ. (formerly Sheffield Poly.), 1969. Hon. DMet Sheffield, 1966. *Recreations:* gardening, golf, reading, voluntary work, drystone-walling. *Address:* Weirholme, Derwent Drive, Baslow, Bakewell, Derbys DE45 1RS. *T:* Baslow (01246) 582210. *Club:* Sheffield (Sheffield).

PUGSLEY, Sir Alfred Grenvile, Kt 1956; OBE 1944; DSc; FRS 1952; FEng; Professor of Civil Engineering, University of Bristol, 1944–68, now Emeritus; Pro-Vice-Chancellor, 1961–64; *b* May 1903; *s* of H. W. Pugsley, BA, FLS, London; *m* 1928, Kathleen M. Warner (*d* 1974); no *c*. *Educ:* Rutlish Sch.; London Univ. Civil Engineering Apprenticeship at Royal Arsenal, Woolwich, 1923–26; Technical Officer, at the Royal Airship Works, Cardington, 1926–31; Member scientific and technical staff at Royal Aircraft Establishment, Farnborough, 1931–45, being Head of Structural and Mechanical Engineering Dept there, 1941–45. Visiting Lecturer on aircraft structures at Imperial Coll., London, 1938–40. Chairman of Aeronautical Research Council, 1952–57; Member: Advisory Council on Scientific Policy, 1956–59; Tribunal of Inquiry on Ronan Point, 1968; Member of various scientific and professional institutions and cttees; President: IStructE, 1957–58; Section G, British Assoc. for Advancement of Science, 1960; a Vice-Pres., ICE, 1971–73. Emeritus Mem., Smeatonian Soc. of Civil Engrs, 1989. Hon. FRAeS 1963; Hon. FICE 1981. Hon. Fellow, Bristol Univ., 1986. Hon. DSc: Belfast, 1965; Cranfield, 1978; Birmingham, 1982; Hon. DUniv Surrey, 1968. Structural Engineers' Gold Medal, 1968; Civil Engineers' Ewing Gold Medal, 1979. *Publications:* The Theory of Suspension Bridges, 1957 (2nd edn 1968); The Safety of Structures, 1966; (ed and contrib.) The Works of Isambard Kingdom Brunel, 1976; numerous Reports and Memoranda of Aeronautical Research Council; papers in scientific journals and publications of professional engineering bodies; articles and reviews in engineering press. *Address:* 4 Harley Court, Clifton Down, Bristol BS8 3JU. *Club:* Athenæum.

PUGSLEY, David Philip; His Honour Judge Pugsley; a Circuit Judge, since 1992; *b* 11 Dec. 1944; *s* of Rev. Clement Pugsley and Edith (*née* Schofield); *m* 1966, Judith Mary Mappin; two *d*. *Educ:* Shebbear College; St Catharine's College, Cambridge (MA). Called to the Bar, Middle Temple, 1968; practised Midland and Oxford Circuit until 1985; Chm. of Industrial Tribunals, Birmingham Reg., 1985–92; a Recorder, 1991–92. Pres., Council of Industrial Tribunal Chairmen, 1991–92. *Publication:* (jtly) Industrial Tribunals Compensation for Loss of Pension Rights, 1990. *Recreations:* golf, fly fishing, theatre. *Address:* 3 Fountain Court, Steelhouse Lane, Birmingham B4 6DR.

PUIG de la BELLACASA, José Joaquín, Hon. GCVO 1986; Grand Cross of Isabel la Católica; Grand Cross of Merito Naval; Encomienda de Numero de Carlos III; Chairman, Council for Foreign Affairs, Spain, since 1995; *b* 5 June 1931; *s* of José Maria Puig de la Bellacasa and Consuelo de Urdampilleta; *m* 1960, Paz de Aznar Ybarra; four *s* two *d*. *Educ:* Areneros Jesuit Coll., Madrid; Madrid Univ. Barrister-at-law. Entered Diplomatic Service, 1959; Dirección General Politica Exterior, 1961–62; Minister's Cabinet, 1962–69; Counsellor, Spanish Embassy, London, 1971–74; Private Sec. to Prince of Spain, 1974–75, to HM King Juan Carlos, 1975–76; Director-General: Co-op. Tecnica Internacional, 1976; Servicio Exterior, 1977–78; Under-Sec. of State for Foreign Affairs, 1978–80; Ambassador to Holy See, 1980–83; Ambassador to UK, 1983–90; Sec.-Gen., Spanish Royal Household, 1990–91; Ambassador to Portugal, 1991–95. Hon. Fellow, QMC, 1987. Holds several foreign decorations. *Address:* Felipe IV 7, Madrid 28014, Spain. *Clubs:* Beefsteak, White's; Nuevo, Golf de Puerta de Hierro (Madrid).

PULFORD, Richard Charles; writer and consultant; *b* 14 July 1944; *s* of late Charles Edgar Pulford and Grace Mary Pulford (*née* Vickors). *Educ:* Royal Grammar Sch., Newcastle upon Tyne; St Catherine's Coll., Oxford (BA Jurisprudence). Voluntary service in the Sudan, 1966–67; Home Civil Service, 1967–79: Department of Education and Science: Asst Principal, 1967–72, Principal, 1972–75; HM Treasury, 1975–77; Asst Secretary, DES, 1977–79. Arts Council of GB: Dep. Sec.-Gen., 1979–85; South Bank Planning Dir, 1985–86; Gen. Dir (Admin), South Bank Centre, 1986–92. Bd Mem., Internat. Soc. of Performing Arts Administrators, 1988–92 (Pres., 1990–91); Member: South Bank Theatre Bd, 1985–92; Council, English Stage Co., 1989–; Chm., Nat. Campaign for the Arts, 1992–; Vice Pres., Mid-Northumberland Arts Gp, 1985–. Trustee, Crusaid and STAR Foundn, 1993–. *Publications:* articles in various newspapers and specialist magazines. *Recreations:* entertaining at home, idling in the tropics, primary smoking. *Address:* 905 Beatty House, Dolphin Square, SW1V 3PN. *T:* 0171–798 8308, *Fax:* 0171–932 0119.

PULLAN, Prof. Brian Sebastian, PhD; FBA 1985; Professor of Modern History, University of Manchester, since 1973; *b* 10 Dec. 1935; *s* of late Horace William Virgo Pullan and of Ella Lister Pullan; *m* 1962, Janet Elizabeth Maltby; two *s*. *Educ:* Epsom Coll.; Trinity Coll., Cambridge (MA, PhD); MA Manchester. Nat. Service, RA, 1954–56. Cambridge University: Res. Fellow, Trinity Coll., 1961–63; Official Fellow, Queens' Coll., 1963–72; Univ. Asst Lectr in History, 1964–67; Lectr, 1967–72; Dean, Faculty of Arts, Manchester Univ., 1982–84. Feoffee of Chetham's Hosp. and Library, Manchester, 1981–. Corresp. Fellow, Ateneo Veneto, 1986. Serena Medal, British Academy, 1991. *Publications:* (ed) Sources for the History of Medieval Europe, 1966; (ed) Crisis and Change in the Venetian Economy in the Sixteenth and Seventeenth Centuries, 1968; Rich and Poor in Renaissance Venice, 1971; A History of Early Renaissance Italy, 1973; The Jews of Europe and the Inquisition of Venice, 1983; (ed with Susan Reynolds) Towns and Townspeople in Medieval and Renaissance Europe: essays in memory of Kenneth Hyde, 1990; (ed with David Chambers) Venice: a documentary history 1450–1630, 1992; Poverty and Charity: Europe, Italy, Venice, 1400–1700, 1994; articles and reviews in learned jls and collections. *Recreations:* dogs, theatre. *Address:* 30 Sandhurst Road, Didsbury, Manchester M20 0LR. *T:* 0161–445 3665.

PULLAN, John Marshall, MChir, FRCS; Hon. Surgeon, St Thomas' Hospital, London; late of King Edward VII Hospital, Bolingbroke Hospital, London and Royal Masonic Hospital, London; *b* 1 Aug. 1915; *e s* of late William Greaves Pullan and Kathleen, *d* of Alfred Marshall, Otley, Yorkshire; *m* 1940, Leila Diana, *d* of H. C. Craven-Veitch, Surgeon; one *s* three *d*. *Educ:* Shrewsbury; King's Coll., Cambridge; St Thomas' Hospital, London. MA Cantab (1st Cl. Nat. Sc. Tripos) 1937; MB, BChir 1940; FRCS, 1942; MChir 1945. Teacher in Surgery, Univ. of London; Examiner in Surgery, Univs of: London, 1956; Cambridge. Member: Court of Examiners, RCS, 1964; Board of Governors, St Thomas' Hospital. *Publications:* Section on Diseases of the Liver, Gall Bladder and Bile Ducts, in Textbook of British Surgery, ed Sir Henry Souttar, 1956; articles in surgical journals. *Address:* Palings, Warboys Road, Kingston Hill, Surrey KT2 7LS. *T:* 0181–546 5310. *Clubs:* White's, Flyfishers', Boodle's.

PULLÉE, Ernest Edward, CBE 1967; ARCA, ACSD, FSAE, NEAC; painter; Chief Officer, National Council for Diplomas in Art and Design, 1967–74; retired; *b* 19 Feb. 1907; *s* of Ernest and Caroline Elizabeth Pullée; *m* 1933, Margaret Fisher, ARCA, NEAC; one *s*. *Educ:* St Martin's Sch., Dover; Royal Coll. of Art, London. Principal: Gloucester Coll. of Art, 1934–39; Portsmouth Coll. of Art, 1939–45; Leeds Coll. of Art, 1945–56; Leicester Coll. of Art and Design, 1956–67. Regular exhibitor, RA summer exhibns and at London and provincial galls. Pres., Nat. Soc. for Art Educn, 1945, 1959; Chm., Assoc. of Art Instns, 1959; Mem., Nat. Adv. Coun. for Art Educn, 1959; Mem., Nat. Coun. for Diplomas in Art and Design, 1961. FRSA 1952. Hon. Life Mem., NEAC, 1986. Hon. Fellow: Portsmouth Polytechnic, 1976; Leicester Polytechnic, 1977. Hon. DA (Manchester), 1961. *Publications:* contribs to professional and academic jls. *Recreation:* travel. *Address:* 3 March Square, The Drive, Summersdale, Chichester, W Sussex PO19 4AN. *Club:* Chelsea Arts.

PULLEIN-THOMPSON, Denis; *see* Cannan, D.

PULLEIN-THOMPSON, Josephine Mary Wedderburn, MBE 1984; writer; General Secretary, English Centre, International PEN, 1976–93; *e d* of H. J. Pullein-Thompson, MC and Joanna Cannan, novelist. *Educ:* briefly at Wychwood Sch., Oxford. Horsewoman and writer; Vis. Comr, 1960–68, Dist Comr, 1970–76, Pony Club; Member: Cttee, Crime Writers' Assoc., 1971–73; Cttee, Children's Writers' Gp, Soc. of Authors, 1973–79 (Dep. Chm., 1978–79); English Centre of International PEN: Cttee, 1974–76; Pres., 1993. *Publications:* How Horses are Trained, 1961; (jtly) Ponies in Colour, 1962; Learn to Ride Well, 1966; Horses and Their Owners (anthology), 1970; Ride Better and Better, 1974; *fiction:* It Began with Picotee (with sisters), 1946; Six Ponies, 1946; I had Two Ponies, 1947; Plenty of Ponies, 1949; Pony Club Team, 1950; The Radney Riding Club, 1951; Prince Among Ponies, 1952; One Day Event, 1954; Show Jumping Secret, 1955; Patrick's Pony, 1956; Pony Club Camp, 1957; The Trickjumpers, 1958; All Change, 1961; Race Horse Holiday, 1971; Proud Riders, 1973; Black Ebony, 1975; Star Riders of the Moor, 1976; Fear Treks the Moor, 1978; Black Nightshade, 1978; Ride to the Rescue, 1979; Ghost Horse on the Moor, 1980; The No Good Pony, 1981; Treasure on the Moor, 1982; The Prize Pony, 1982; Black Raven, 1982; Pony Club Cup, 1982; Save the Ponies, 1984; Mystery on the Moor, 1984; Pony Club Challenge, 1984; Pony Club Trek, 1985; Suspicion Stalks the Moor, 1986; Black Swift, 1991; A Job with Horses, 1994; *crime:* Gin and Murder, 1959; They Died in the Spring, 1960; Murder Strikes Pink, 1963; (as J Mann) A Place with Two Faces, 1972. *Recreations:* travelling, gardening, reading, theatre going. *Address:* 16 Knivet Road, SW6 1JH.

See also D. Cannan, D. L. A. Farr.

PULLEN, Dr Roderick Allen; HM Diplomatic Service; Deputy High Commissioner, Nairobi, since 1994; *b* 11 April 1949; *s* of Derrick Brian Pullen and Celia Ada Pullen (*née* Wood); *m* 1971, Karen Lesley Sketchley; two *s* one *d*. *Educ:* Maidstone Grammar Sch.; Mansfield Coll., Oxford (BA); Sussex Univ. (DPhil). MoD, 1975–78; Second Sec., UK Delegn to NATO, 1978–80; MoD, 1980–81; First Sec., UK Delegn to CSCE, 1981–82; FCO, 1982–84; Dep. High Comr, Suva, 1984–88; FCO, 1988–90; Counsellor, Paris, 1990–94. *Recreations:* riding, travel. *Address:* c/o Foreign and Commonwealth Office, King Charles Street, SW1A 2AH. *Club:* Muthaiga Country (Nairobi).

PULLEN, Sir (William) Reginald (James), KCVO 1987 (CVO 1975; MVO 1966); LLB; FCIS; JP; Clerk to the Trustees, United Westminser Almshouses, since 1987; Deputy High Bailiff of Westminster, since 1988; *b* 17 Feb. 1922; *er s* of late William Pullen and Lillian Pullen (*née* Chinn), Falmouth; *m* 1948, Doreen Angela Hebron; two *d*. *Educ:* Falmouth Gram. School; King's College, London; private study. Served War of 1939–45; Flt Lt, RAFVR (admin and special duties) SE Asia. Westminster Abbey: Asst to Chief Accountant, 1947; Dep. Registrar, 1951; Receiver-Gen., 1959–87; Chapter Clerk, 1963–87; Registrar, 1964–84; Sec. Westminster Abbey Appeal, 1953. Westminster City Council, 1962–65. Jt. Hon. Treas., CCJ, 1988–91. Trustee: The Passage (RC) Day Centre for Homeless People, 1983–94; Abbey Community Centre, 1990–. JP Inner London, 1967. Liveryman, Worshipful Co. of Fishmongers; Freeman, Worshipful Co. of Wax Chandlers. KStJ 1987 (CStJ 1981; OStJ 1969). *Publication:* contrib. A House of Kings, 1966. *Recreations:* travel, dogwalking, gerentology. *Address:* 42 Rochester Row, SW1P 1BU. *T:* 0171–828 3210. *Clubs:* Royal Air Force, MCC; Hurlingham.

PULLEYBLANK, Prof. Edwin George, PhD; FRSC; Professor of Chinese, University of British Columbia, 1966–87, now Emeritus; *b* Calgary, Alberta, 7 Aug. 1922; *s* of W. G.

E. Pulleyblank, Calgary; *m* 1945, Winona Ruth Relyea (decd), Arnprior, Ont; one *s* two *d. Educ:* Central High School, Calgary; University of Alberta; University of London. BA Hons Classics, Univ. of Alberta, 1942; Nat. Research Council of Canada, 1943–46. School of Oriental and African Studies, Univ. of London: Chinese Govt Schol., 1946; Lectr in Classical Chinese, 1948; PhD in Classical Chinese, 1951; Lectr in Far Eastern History, 1952; Professor of Chinese, University of Cambridge, 1953; Head, Dept of Asian Studies, Univ. of British Columbia, 1968–75. Fellow of Downing Coll., Cambridge, 1955–66. *Publications:* The Background of the Rebellion of An Lu-Shan, 1955; Middle Chinese, 1984; Lexicon of Reconstructed Pronunciation in Early Middle Chinese, Late Middle Chinese and Early Mandarin, 1991; Outline of Classical Chinese Grammar, 1995; articles in Asia Major, Bulletin of School of Oriental and African Studies, etc. *Address:* c/o Department of Asian Studies, University of British Columbia, Vancouver, BC V6T 1Z2, Canada.

PULLINGER, Sir (Francis) Alan, Kt 1977; CBE 1970; DL; Chairman, Haden Carrier Ltd, 1961–79; *b* 22 May 1913; *s* of William Pullinger; *m* 1st, 1946, Felicity Charmian Gotch Hobson (decd); two *s* one *d*; 2nd, 1966, Jacqueline Louise Anne Durin (decd). *Educ:* Marlborough Coll.; Balliol Coll., Oxford (MA). Pres., IHVE, 1972–73. Chm., Hertfordshire Scouts, 1976–91. Vice Chm. Council, Benenden Sch., 1980–. Hon. FCIBSE, 1977. DL Herts, 1982. *Recreations:* mountaineering, sailing, beagling. *Address:* Barnhorn, Meadway, Berkhamsted, Herts HP4 2PL. *T:* Berkhamsted (01442) 863206. *Clubs:* Alpine, Travellers'.

PULLINGER, John Elphick; His Honour Judge Pullinger; a Circuit Judge, since 1982; *b* 27 Aug. 1930; *s* of late Reginald Edward Pullinger and of Elsie Florence Pullinger; *m* (separated); one *s* one *d*; partner, Natasha Aghdas Pullinger (*née* Tavoosi); one *s. Educ:* Friern Barnet Grammar Sch.; Quintin Sch.; London Sch. of Econs and Pol. Science (LLB 1955). Official Solicitor's Office, 1948. Nat. Service, 1949–50. British Inst., Florence, 1953. Min. of Educn qualified teacher, 1955. Called to the Bar, Lincoln's Inn, 1958; Sir Thomas More Bursary, 1958. Legal Sec. to Lord Shrewsbury's Commn of Enquiry into the Infantile Paralysis Fellowship, 1958–59; Dep. Judge Advocate, 1965; AJAG, 1972–82; Judge Advocate to NZ Force SE Asia, 1973–75; served on JAG's staff in Germany, Mediterranean, Near East, ME and Far East. Member: NSRA, 1977–; NRA, 1979–; Historical Breechloading Smallarms Assoc., 1984–; Internat. Soc. for Military Law and the Law of War, UK Gp, 1988–; HAC, 1950–; Burrswood Internat. Fellowship, 1994ldi. Vis. Lectr in Law, Coll. of Estate Management, Univ. of London, 1961–63. *Publication:* The Position of the British Serviceman under the Army and Air Force Acts 1955, 1975. *Recreations:* shottist, bibliophile. *Address:* 1 Essex Court, Temple, EC4Y 9AR.

PULVERTAFT, Rear-Adm. David Martin, CB 1990; Secretary, Defence, Press and Broadcasting Advisory Committee, since 1992; *b* 26 March 1938; *s* of late Captain William Godfrey Pulvertaft, OBE, RN and Annie Joan Pulvertaft (*née* Martin); *m* 1961, Mary Rose Jeacock; one *s* two *d. Educ:* Canford Sch., Dorset; Britannia RN Coll., Dartmouth; RN Engineering Coll., Manadon. BSc (Eng) 1962. FIMechE 1989 (MIMechE 1974). HMS Ceylon, 1958–59; HMS Anchorite, Singapore, 1963–66; HMS Dreadnought, 1967–71; 10th Submarine Sqdn, 1971–72; HM Dockyard, Devonport, 1973–75; Nat. Defence Coll., Latimer, 1975–76; MoD 1976–78; HM Dockyard, Devonport, 1979–82; RCDS, 1983; MoD, 1984–87; Dir Gen. Aircraft (Navy), 1987–90; Dir Gen., Procurement and Support Orgn (Navy), 1990–92. FIMgt (FBIM 1990). *Recreations:* genealogy, printing, bookbinding. *Address:* Ministry of Defence, Main Building, SW1A 2HB. *Club:* Naval.

PULZER, Prof. Peter George Julius, PhD; FRHistS; Gladstone Professor of Government and Public Administration, University of Oxford, 1985–Sept. 1996; Fellow of All Souls College, 1985–Sept. 1996; *b* 20 May 1929; *s* of Felix and Margaret Pulzer; *m* 1962, Gillian Mary Marshall; two *s. Educ:* Surbiton County Grammar Sch.; King's Coll., Cambridge (1st Cl. Hons Historical Tripos 1950; PhD 1960); London Univ. (1st Cl. Hons BSc Econ 1954). FRHistS 1971. Lectr in Politics, Magdalen Coll. and Christ Church, Oxford, 1957–62; University Lectr in Politics, Oxford, 1960–84; Official Student and Tutor in Politics, Christ Church 1962–84. Visiting Professor: Univ. of Wisconsin, 1965; Sch. of Advanced Internat. Studies, Johns Hopkins Univ., 1972; Univ. of Calif, LA, 1972; Eric Voegelin, Munich Univ., 1988; Potsdam Univ., 1993. Mem. Governing Body, Historisches Kolleg, Munich, 1993–. *Publications:* The Rise of Political Anti-Semitism in Germany and Austria, 1964, 2nd edn 1988 (German edn 1966); Political Representation and Elections in Britain, 1967, 3rd edn 1975; Jews and the German State, 1992; German Politics 1945–1995, 1995; contrib. to jls, year books and symposia. *Recreations:* opera, walking. *Address:* All Souls College, Oxford OX1 4AL. *T:* (until Sept. 1996) Oxford (01865) 279348.

PUMFREY, Nicholas Richard; QC 1990; *b* 22 May 1951; *s* of Peter and Maureen Pumfrey. *Educ:* St Edward's Sch., Oxford; St Edmund Hall, Oxford (BA Physics, 1972, Law, 1974). Called to the Bar, Middle Temple, 1975; Jun. Counsel to HM Treasury (Patents), 1987–90. *Recreation:* cycling. *Address:* 11 South Square, Gray's Inn, WC1R 5EU.

PUMPHREY, Sir (John) Laurence, KCMG 1973 (CMG 1963); HM Diplomatic Service, retired; Ambassador to Pakistan (formerly High Commissioner), 1971–76; *b* 22 July 1916; *s* of late Charles Ernest Pumphrey and Iris Mary (*née* Moberly-Bell); *m* 1945, Jean, *e d* of Sir Walter Buchanan Riddell, 12th Bt; four *s* one *d. Educ:* Winchester; New College, Oxford. Served War of 1939–45 in Army. Foreign Service from 1945. Head of Establishment and Organisation Department, Foreign Office, 1955–60; Counsellor, Staff of British Commissioner-General for SE Asia, Singapore, 1960–63; Counsellor, HM Embassy, Belgrade, 1963–65; Deputy High Commissioner, Nairobi, 1965–67; British High Comr, Zambia, 1967–71. Military Cross, 3rd Class (Greece), 1941. *Address:* Caistron, Thropton, Morpeth, Northumberland NE65 7LG.

PURCELL, Prof. Edward Mills, PhD; Gerhard Gade University Professor, Harvard University, 1960–80, now Emeritus; *b* 30 Aug. 1912; *s* of Edward A. Purcell and Mary Elizabeth Mills; *m* 1937, Beth C. Busser; two *s. Educ:* Purdue University; Harvard University. PhD Harvard, 1938. Instructor in Physics, Harvard, 1938–40; Radiation Laboratory, Mass. Inst. of Technology, 1940–45; Associate Professor of Physics, Harvard, 1945–49; Professor of Physics, 1949–60. Senior Fellow, Society of Fellows, Harvard, 1950–71. Halley Lectr, Oxford Univ., 1982. Foreign Mem., Royal Soc., 1989. Hon. DEng Purdue, 1953; Hon. DSci Washington Univ., St Louis, 1963. (Jointly) Nobel Prize in Physics, 1952; Nat. Medal of Science, 1979. *Publications:* Principles of Microwave Circuits, 1948; Physics for Students of Science and Engineering, 1952; Electricity and Magnetism, 1965; papers in Physical Review, Astrophys. Jl, Biophys. Jl. *Address:* 5 Wright Street, Cambridge, MA 02138, USA. *T:* 547–9317.

PURCELL, Harry, CBE 1982; Member (C) for Chaddesley Corbett, Hereford and Worcester County Council, since 1974 (Vice-Chairman, 1989–90); *b* 2 Dec. 1919; *s* of Charles and Lucy Purcell; *m* 1941, Eunice Mary Price; three *s* one *d. Educ:* Bewdley C of E Sch.; Kidderminster Coll. Joined TA, 1938; served War, 1939–46, Queen's Own Worcester Hussars; Transport Officer, Berlin, 1946–48. Carpet industry, 1949–60; self-employed, 1961. Formerly Mem., Kidderminster Bor. Council; Mayor of Kidderminster, 1967–68. Chairman: West Mercia Police Authority, 1979–82; National Police Negotiating Bd, 1978–82; Vice-Chm., ACC, 1982–85 (Chm., Police Cttee, 1977–81; Vice Chm., Personnel Cttee, 1990–); Mem., Home Office Race Relations Cttee, 1981–. Chm., Local Authorities Mutual Investment Trust, 1987–93; non-exec. Dir, Charities Official Investment Fund, 1988–93. *Recreations:* theatre, tennis, public service. *Address:* Meadowsmead, Woodrow, Chaddesley Corbett, near Kidderminster, Worcs DY10 4QG. *T:* Chaddesley Corbett (01562) 777347. *Club:* Carlton.

PURCELL, (Robert) Michael, CMG 1983; HM Diplomatic Service, retired; Adviser and Secretary, East Africa Association, 1984–87; *b* 22 Oct. 1923; *s* of late Lt-Col Walter Purcell and Constance (*née* Fendick); *m* 1965, Julia Evelyn, *o d* of late Brig. Edward Marsh-Kellett; two *d. Educ:* Ampleforth Coll. Commnd 60th Rifles (Greenjackets), 1943–47. Colonial Service, later HMOCS, Uganda, 1949–62, retd; 1st Sec., CRO, later FCO, 1964–68; 1st Sec. (Commercial/Economic), Colombo, 1968–69; FCO, 1969–71; 1st Sec. (Aid), Singapore, 1971–73; Head of Chancery, HM Legation to the Holy See, 1973–76; Counsellor and Dep. High Comr, Malta, 1977–80; Ambassador to Somali Democratic Republic, 1980–83. KCSG 1976. *Recreations:* country life, books. *Address:* French Mill Cottage, Shaftesbury, Dorset SP7 0LT. *T:* Shaftesbury (01747) 53615. *Club:* Naval and Military.

PURCELL, Rev. Canon William Ernest; author and broadcaster; Residentiary Canon of Worcester Cathedral, 1966–76; *b* 25 May 1909; *s* of Will and Gwladys Purcell; *m* 1939, Margaret Clegg; two *s* one *d. Educ:* Keble Coll., Oxford (MA); Univ. of Wales (BA); Queens Coll., Birmingham. Curate: St. John's Church, Keighley, 1938; Dover Parish Church, 1939–43; Vicar: St. Peter's, Maidstone, 1944–47; Sutton Valence, 1947–53; Chaplain, HM Borstal Instn, East Sutton, 1947–53; Religious Broadcasting Organiser, BBC Midlands, 1953–66. *Publications:* These Thy Gods, 1950; Pilgrim's Programme, 1957; Onward Christian Soldier (biog. of S. Baring Gould), 1957; A Plain Man Looks At Himself, 1962; Woodbine Willie (biog. of G. Studdert Kennedy), 1962; This Is My Story, 1963; The Plain Man Looks At The Commandments, 1966; Fisher of Lambeth (biog. of Archbp of Canterbury), 1969; Portrait of Soper (biog. of Lord Soper), 1972; British Police in a Changing Society, 1974; A Time to Die, 1979; Pilgrim's England, 1981; The Christian in Retirement, 1982; Martyrs of Our Time, 1983; Seekers and Finders, 1985; The Anglican Spiritual Tradition, 1988. *Address:* 14 Conifer Close, Cumnor Hill, Oxford OX2 9HP. *Club:* National Liberal.

PURCHAS, Christopher Patrick Brooks; QC 1990; a Recorder, since 1986; *b* 20 June 1943; *s* of Rt Hon. Sir Francis Purchas, *qv*; *m* 1974, Bronwen Mary Vaughan; two *d. Educ:* Summerfield Sch.; Marlborough Coll.; Trinity Coll., Cambridge (MA). Called to the Bar, Inner Temple, 1966, Bencher, 1995. *Recreations:* tennis, shooting. *Address:* 2 Crown Office Row, Temple, EC4Y 7HJ. *T:* 0171–353 9337.

See also R. M. Purchas.

PURCHAS, Rt. Hon. Sir Francis (Brooks), Kt 1974; PC 1982; a Lord Justice of Appeal, 1982–93; *b* 19 June 1919; *s* of late Captain Francis Purchas, 5th Royal Irish Lancers and late Millicent Purchas (*née* Brooks); *m* 1942, Patricia Mona Kathleen, *d* of Lieut Milburn; two *s. Educ:* Summerfields Sch., Oxford; Marlborough Coll.; Trinity Coll., Cambridge. Served RE, 1940–46: North Africa, 1943 (despatches); Hon. Lt-Col retd (Africa Star, Italy Star, 1939–45 Medal; Defence Medal). Allied Mil. Commission, Vienna. Called to Bar, Inner Temple, 1948, QC 1965, Bencher, 1972; practised at Bar, 1948–74; Leader, SE Circuit, 1972–74; Dep. Chm., E Sussex QS, 1966–71; Recorder of Canterbury, 1969–71 (Hon. Recorder of Canterbury, 1972–74); Recorder of the Crown Court, 1972–74; a Judge of the High Court of Justice, Family Div., 1974–82; Presiding Judge, SE Circuit, 1977–82. Comr, Central Criminal Court, 1970–71. Mem., Bar Council, 1966–68, 1969–71, 1972–74. Judicial Mem., City Disputes Panel, 1994–; Dep. Appeal Comr, PIA, 1994–. FCIArb. Mem. of Livery, Worshipful Co. of Broderers, 1962. *Recreations:* shooting, golf, fishing. *Address:* Parkhurst House, near Haslemere, Surrey GU27 3BY. *T:* North Chapel (01428) 707280; 1 Temple Gardens, Temple, EC4Y 9BB. *T:* 0171–353 5124. *Clubs:* Boodle's; Hawks (Cambridge).

See also C. P. B. Purchas, R. M. Purchas.

PURCHAS, Robin Michael; QC 1987; a Recorder, since 1989; *b* 12 June 1946; *s* of Rt Hon. Sir Francis Brooks Purchas, *qv*; *m* 1970, Denise Anne Kerr Finlay; one *s* one *d. Educ:* Summerfields; Marlborough College; Trinity College, Cambridge (MA). Called to the Bar, Inner Temple, 1968; practised principally in local govt, administrative and parliamentary work, 1969–; Assistant Recorder, 1985. *Recreations:* opera, music, fishing, tennis, swimming, ski-ing, sailing, shooting, golf. *Address:* (chambers) 2 Harcourt Buildings, Temple, EC4Y 9DB. *T:* 071–353 8415. *Clubs:* Lansdowne, Queen's; Royal West Norfolk Golf; Royal Worlington and Newmarket Golf; Brancaster Staithe Sailing.

See also C. P. B. Purchas.

PURCHASE, Kenneth; MP (Lab) Wolverhampton North East, since 1992; *b* 8 Jan. 1939; *m* 1960, Brenda Sanders; two *d. Educ:* Springfield Secondary Modern Sch.; Wolverhampton Polytechnic (BA). Toolmaker: Lucas, 1960–68; Ever Ready, 1968–76; with Telford Development Corp., 1977–80; with Walsall MBC, 1981–82; Business Development Advr and Company Sec., Black Country CDA Ltd, 1982–92. Mem. (Lab) Wolverhampton CBC, subseq. MBC, 1970–90. Contested (Lab) Wolverhampton North East, 1987. Mem., Select Cttee on Trade and Industry; Jt Chm., All Party Exports Gp; Chm., PLP Trade and Industry Cttee, 1992–. *Address:* House of Commons, SW1A 0AA.

PURDEN, Roma Laurette, (Laurie Purden; Mrs J. K. Kotch), MBE 1973; journalist and writer; *b* 30 Sept. 1928; *d* of George Cecil Arnold Purden and Constance Mary Sheppard; *m* 1957, John Keith Kotch (*d* 1979); two *d. Educ:* Harecroft Sch., Tunbridge Wells. Fiction Editor, Home Notes, 1948–51; Asst Editor, Home Notes, 1951–52; Asst Editor, Woman's Own, 1952; Sen. Asst Editor, Girl, 1952–54; Editor of: Housewife, 1954–57; Home, 1957–62; House Beautiful, 1963–65; Good Housekeeping, 1965–73; Editor-in-Chief: Good Housekeeping, and Womancraft, 1973–77; Woman's Journal, 1978–88; Woman & Home, 1982–83. Dir, Brickfield Publications Ltd, 1978–80. Magazine Editor of the Year, 1979, British Soc. of Magazine Editors; Consumer Magazine of the Year awarded by Periodical Publishers Assoc. to Woman's Journal, 1985. *Address:* 174 Pavilion Road, SW1X 0AW. *T:* 0171–730 4021.

PURDON, Maj.-Gen. Corran William Brooke, CBE 1970; MC 1945; CPM 1982; *b* 4 May 1921; *s* of Maj.-Gen. William Brooke Purdon, DSO, OBE, MC, KHS, and Dorothy Myrtle Coates; *m* 1945, Maureen Patricia, *d* of Major J. F. Petrie, Guides Infantry, IA; two *s* one *d. Educ:* Rokeby, Wimbledon; Campbell Coll., Belfast; RMC Sandhurst. MBIM. Commnd into Royal Ulster Rifles, 1939; service with Army Commandos, France and Germany, 1940–45 (wounded; MC); 1st Bn RU Rifles, Palestine, 1945–46; GHQ MELF, 1949–51; psc 1955; Staff, Malayan Emergency, 1956–58; Co. Comdr, 1 RU Rifles, Cyprus Emergency, 1958; CO, 1st Bn RU Rifles, BAOR and Borneo War, 1962–64; GSO1 and Chief Instructor, Sch. of Infantry, Warminster, 1965–67; Comdr, Sultan's Armed Forces, Oman, and Dir of Ops, Dhofar War, 1967–70 (Sultan's Bravery Medal, 1968 and Distinguished Service Medal for Gallantry, 1969, Oman; CBE); Commandant: Sch. of Infantry, Warminster, 1970–72; Small Arms Sch. Corps, 1970–72; GOC, NW

Dist, 1972–74; GOC Near East Land Forces, 1974–76, retired. Dep. Comr, Royal Hong Kong Police Force, 1978–81; St John Ambulance: Comdr, Wilts, 1981–84; Mem. Council, 1981–86; Pres., Devizes Div., 1993–. Hon. Colonel: Queen's Univ. Belfast OTC, 1975–78; D (London Irish Rifles), 4th Bn Royal Irish Rangers, 1986–93. Pres. Army Gymnastic Union, 1973–76; Patron, Small Arms Sch. Corps Assoc., 1985–90; Governor, Royal Humane Soc., 1985–. KStJ 1983. Commendation Medal (Oman), 1992. *Publications:* List the Bugle: reminiscences of an Irish soldier, 1993; articles in military jls. *Recreations:* physical training, swimming, dogs (English bull terriers, German shepherds). *Address:* Old Park House, Devizes, Wilts SN10 5JR. *Clubs:* Army and Navy; Hong Kong.

PURDY, Robert John, CMG 1963; OBE 1954; Bursar, Gresham's School, Holt, 1965–81; retired from HM Overseas Civil Service, 1963; *b* 2 March 1916; 2nd *s* of late Lt-Col T. W. Purdy, Woodgate House, Aylsham, Norfolk; *m* 1957, Elizabeth (*née* Sharp); two *s* one *d*. *Educ:* Haileybury College; Jesus College, Cambridge (BA). Served 1940–46 with 81 West African Division Reconnaissance Regt, 3rd and 4th Burma Campaigns (despatches, Major). Appointed to Colonial Administrative Service, Northern Nigeria, 1939; promoted Resident, 1956; Senior Resident, Staff Grade, 1957. Resident, Adamawa Province, 1956; Senior Resident, Plateau Province, 1958–61; Senior Resident, Sokoto Province, 1961–63, retd. *Recreations:* shooting, fishing, gardening. *Address:* Spratt's Green House, Aylsham, Norwich NR11 6TX. *T:* Aylsham (01263) 732147.

PURKIS, Dr Andrew James; Public Affairs Adviser to the Archbishop of Canterbury, since 1992; *b* 24 Jan. 1949; *s* of late Clifford Henry Purkis and Mildred Jeannie Purkis; *m* 1980, Jennifer Harwood Smith; one *s* one *d*. *Educ:* Highgate Sch.; Corpus Christi Coll., Oxford; St Antony's Coll., Oxford. 1st class Hons MA Mod. Hist. 1970; DPhil 1978. Home Civil Service, N Ireland Office, 1974; Private Sec. to Perm. Under-Sec. of State, NI Office, 1976–77; Head of Policy Unit, 1980, Asst Dir, 1986, NCVO; Dir, CPRE, 1987–91. Member: Bd, Contact a Family (charity), 1986–93; Bd, Green Alliance, 1992–. *Publications:* (with Paul Hodson) Housing and Community Care, 1982; (with Rosemary Allen) Health in the Round, 1983. *Recreations:* walking, surf-riding, bird-watching, music, theatre. *Address:* 38 Endlesham Road, Balham, SW12 8JL. *T:* 0181–675 2439.

PURLE, Charles Lambert; QC 1989; *b* 9 Feb. 1947; *s* of Robert Herbert Purle and Doreen Florence (*née* Button); *m* 1st, 1969, Lorna Barbara Brown (marr. diss. 1990); one *s* one *d*; 2nd, 1991, Virginia Dabney Hopkins Rylatt; two *s*. *Educ:* Nottingham Univ. (LLB 1969); Worcester Coll., Oxford (BCL 1971). Called to the Bar, Gray's Inn, 1970; in practice, 1972–. *Recreations:* opera, music, food and wine, my children. *Address:* 12 New Square, Lincoln's Inn, WC2A 3SW. *T:* 0171–405 3808.

PURNELL, Nicholas Robert; QC 1985; a Recorder, since 1986; *b* 29 Jan. 1944; *s* of late Oliver Cuthbert Purnell and of Pauline Purnell; *m* 1970, Melanie Stanway; four *s*. *Educ:* Oratory Sch.; King's Coll. Cambridge (Open Exhibnr; MA). Called to the Bar, Middle Temple, 1968 (Astbury Schol.), Bencher 1990; Junior of Central Criminal Court Bar Mess, 1972–75; Prosecuting Counsel to Inland Revenue, 1977–79; Jun. Treasury Counsel, 1979–85. Mem., Bar Council and Senate, 1973–77, 1982–85, 1989–91 (Chm., Legal Aid Fees Cttee, 1989–90); Member: Lord Chancellor's and Home Secretary's Working Party on the Training of the Judiciary, 1975–78; Crown Court Rules Cttee, 1982–88; Lord Chancellor's Adv. Cttee on Educn and Conduct, 1991–; Criminal Cttee, Judicial Studies Bd, 1991–. Chm., Criminal Bar Assoc., 1990–91. Governor, The Oratory Sch., 1994–. *Recreations:* living in France as much as possible, watching Wimbledon FC. *Address:* 36 Essex Street, WC2R 3AS. *T:* 0171–413 0353.

See also P. O. Purnell.

PURNELL, Paul Oliver; QC 1982; a Recorder, since 1985; *b* 13 July 1936; *s* of Oliver Cuthbert and Pauline Purnell; *m* 1966, Celia Consuelo Ocampo; one *s* two *d*. *Educ:* The Oratory Sch.; Jesus Coll., Oxford (MA). Served 4th/7th Royal Dragoon Guards, 1958–62. Called to the Bar, Inner Temple, 1962, Bencher, 1991. Jun. Treasury Counsel at Central Criminal Court, 1976–82. *Recreations:* windsurfing, tennis. *Address:* 1 Crown Office Row, Temple, EC4Y 7HH. *T:* 0171–583 3724. *Club:* Cavalry and Guards.

See also N. R. Purnell.

PURSE, Hugh Robert Leslie; Legal Adviser, Department of Employment and Principal Assistant Treasury Solicitor, since 1988; *b* 22 Oct. 1940; *s* of Robert Purse and Elsie Purse (*née* Kemp). *Educ:* St Peter's School, York; King's College London (LLB). Called to the Bar, Gray's Inn, 1964 (Atkin Scholar). Legal Asst, Dept of Employment, 1969; Legal Adviser to Price Commission, 1978–79; Govt legal service, 1979–. *Address:* Department of Employment, Caxton House, Tothill Street, SW1H 9NF. *T:* 0171–273 5849.

PURSSELL, Anthony John Richard; Member, Board, Civil Aviation Authority, 1984–90; Chairman, Thames Valley and South Midlands Regional Board, Lloyds Bank plc, 1989–91 (Regional Director, 1982–91); *b* 5 July 1926; *m* 1952, Ann Margaret Batchelor; two *s* one *d*. *Educ:* Oriel Coll., Oxford (MA Hons Chemistry). Managing Director: Arthur Guinness Son & Co. (Park Royal) Ltd, 1968; Arthur Guinness Son & Co. (Dublin) Ltd, 1973; Arthur Guinness & Sons plc, 1975–81; Jt Dep. Chm., 1981–83. Mem., IBA, 1976–81. Trustee and Hon. Treas., Oxfam, 1985–92. *Recreations:* travel, golf, sailing, books. *Address:* Allendale, Bulstrode Way, Gerrards Cross, Bucks SL9 7QT. *Club:* Leander (Henley).

PURVES, Dame Daphne (Helen), DBE 1979; Senior Lecturer in French, Dunedin Teachers College, 1967–73, retired (Lecturer, 1963–66); *b* 8 Nov. 1908; *d* of Irvine Watson Cowie and Helen Jean Cowie; *m* 1939, Herbert Dudley Purves; one *s* two *d*. *Educ:* Otago Girls' High Sch., Dunedin, NZ; Univ. of Otago, Dunedin (MA 1st Cl. Hons English and French). Secondary sch. teacher, 1931–40 and 1957–63. Pres., NZ Fedn of University Women, 1962–64; Internat. Fedn of University Women: Mem., Cultural Relations Cttee, 1965–68, Convener, 1968–71; 3rd Vice-Pres., 1971–74; 1st Vice-Pres., 1974–77; Pres., 1977–80. Chm., National Theme Cttee, The Child in the World, NZ Nat. Commn for Internat. Year of the Child, 1978–80; Mem., Internat. Year of the Child Telethon Trust, 1978–81; Exec. Mem., NZ Cttee for Children (IYC) Inc., 1980–82. Mem., NZ Nat. Commn, Unesco, 1964–68. Pres., Friends of Olveston Inc., 1986–88. Mem., Theomin Gall. Management Cttee, 1986–91. *Recreations:* reading, croquet, bridge, travel, heraldry. *Address:* 12 Grendon Court, 36 Drivers Road, Dunedin, New Zealand. *T:* (4) 4675105. *Clubs:* Punga Croquet (Pres., 1988–90); Dunedin Bridge.

PURVES, Elizabeth Mary, (Libby), (Mrs Paul Heiney); writer and broadcaster; *b* 2 Feb. 1950; *d* of late James Grant Purves, CMG; *m* 1980, Paul Heiney; one *s* one *d*. *Educ:* Convent of the Sacred Heart, Tunbridge Wells; St Anne's Coll., Oxford (1st Cl. Hons Eng. Lang. and Lit.). BBC Local Radio (Oxford), 1972–76; Today, Radio 4: Reporter, 1976–79; Presenter, 1979–81; freelance writer, broadcaster; BBC TV Choices, 1982, Midweek (Presenter, 1984–), documentaries; writer for The Times, Sunday Express, Good Housekeeping, She, *et al*; Editor, Tatler, March-Oct. 1983, resigned. *Publications:* (ed) The Happy Unicorns, 1971; (ed) Adventures Under Sail, H. W. Tilman, 1982; Britain At Play, 1982; Sailing Weekend Book, 1985; How Not to be a Perfect Mother, 1986; Where Did You Leave the Admiral, 1987; (jtly) The English and their Horses, 1988; The Hurricane Tree, 1988; One Summer's Grace, 1989; How Not to Raise a Perfect Child, 1991; Getting the Story, 1993; Working Times, 1993; How Not to be a Perfect Family, 1994; Casting Off (novel), 1995. *Recreations:* sailing, walking, writing, radio. *Address:* c/o A. P. Watt Ltd, 20 John Street, WC1N 2DL. *Club:* Royal Cruising.

PURVES, Sir William, Kt 1993; CBE 1988; DSO 1951; Chairman: HSBC Holdings plc, since 1990 (Chief Executive, 1990–92); Midland Bank Plc, since 1994 (Director, since 1987); British Bank of the Middle East, since 1986; *b* 27 Dec. 1931; *s* of Andrew and Ida Purves; *m* 1st, 1958, Diana Troutbeck Richardson (marr. diss. 1988); two *s* two *d*; 2nd, 1989, Rebecca Jane Lewellen. *Educ:* Kelso High School. FIBScot; FCIB. National Service, with Commonwealth Div. in Korea (Subaltern; DSO). National Bank of Scotland, 1948–54; Hongkong and Shanghai Banking Corporation: Germany, Hong Kong, Malaysia, Singapore, Sri Lanka, Japan, 1954–70; Chief Accountant, Hong Kong, 1970; Manager, Tokyo, 1974; Sen. Manager Overseas Operations, 1976; Asst General Manager, Overseas Operations, 1978; General Manager, 1979; Executive Director, 1982; Dep. Chm., 1984–86; Chm. and Chief Exec., 1986–92; non-exec. Dir, 1993–. Dir, Marine Midland Banks Inc., 1982–; non-exec. Director: Shell Transport and Trading, 1993–; East Asiatic Co., 1995–. Hon. Dr Stirling, 1987; Hon. LLD: Sheffield, 1993; Hong Kong, 1994; Hon. DBA Hong Kong Poly., 1993. *Recreations:* golf, Rugby. *Address:* 10 Lower Thames Street, EC3R 6AE. *Clubs:* Royal Automobile; New (Edinburgh); Royal Hong Kong Jockey.

PURVIS, Air Vice-Marshal Henry R.; *see* Reed-Purvis.

PURVIS, John Robert, CBE 1990; Senior Partner, Purvis & Co., since 1986; *b* 6 July 1938; *s* of Lt-Col R. W. B. Purvis, MC, JP, and Mrs R. W. B. Purvis, JP; *m* 1962, Louise S. Durham; one *s* two *d*. *Educ:* Cargilfield, Barnton, Edinburgh; Trinity Coll., Glenalmond, Perthshire; St Salvator's Coll., Univ. of St Andrews (MA Hons). National Service, Lieut Scots Guards, 1956–58. First National City Bank, New York, 1962–69: London, 1962–63; New York, 1963–65; Milan, 1965–69; Treasurer, Noble Grossart Ltd, Edinburgh, 1969–73; Man. Dir, Gilmerton Management Services Ltd, 1973–92. Mem. (C) Mid-Scotland and Fife, European Parlt, 1979–84, contested same seat, 1984; European Democratic Group, European Parliament: whip, 1980–82; spokesman on energy, research and technology, 1982–84. Vice Pres., Scottish Cons. and Unionist Assoc., 1987–89 (Chm., Industry Cttee, 1986–); Mem., IBA, 1985–89 (Chm., Scottish Adv. Cttee, 1985–89); Mem., Scottish Adv. Cttee on Telecommunications, 1990–. Director: James River Fine Papers Ltd, 1984–; Edgar Astaire & Co. Ltd, 1993–94; Jamont NV, 1994–; Johnson Fry European Utilities Trust, 1994–. *Publication:* (section 'Money') in Power and Manoeuvrability, 1978. *Address:* Gilmerton, Dunino, St Andrews, Fife, Scotland KY16 8NB. *T:* St Andrews (01334) 473275. *Clubs:* Cavalry and Guards, Farmers'; New (Edinburgh); Royal and Ancient (St Andrews).

PURVIS, Sir Neville, KCB 1992; Vice Admiral, retired; Chief Executive, British Standards Institution, since 1994; *b* 8 May 1936; *s* of Charles Geoffrey and Sylvia Rose Purvis; *m* 1970, Alice Margaret (*née* Hill); two *s*. *Educ:* Charterhouse; Selwyn College, Cambridge (MA). BRNC Dartmouth, 1953; reading engineering at Cambridge, 1954–57; joined submarine service, 1959; served in HM Ships Turpin, 1960, Dreadnought, 1963, Repulse, 1967; Naval Staff, 1970; Sqdn Engineer Officer, 3rd Submarine Sqdn, 1973; Staff of Flag Officer, Submarines, 1975; RCDS 1980; in Command, HMS Collingwood, 1985–87; Dir Gen., Future Material Projects (Naval), 1987–88; Dir Gen., Naval Manpower and Trng, 1988–90; Mem., Admiralty Bd, and Chief of Fleet Support, 1991–94. FInstD 1993; FRSA 1992. *Recreations:* gardening, chess. *Address:* Dilton Farm, Shere, Guildford, Surrey GU5 9JN.

PURVIS, Stewart Peter; Chief Executive, Independent Television News Ltd, since 1995; *b* 28 Oct. 1947; *s* of Peter and Lydia Purvis; *m* 1972 (marr. diss. 1993); one *d*; one *s*. *Educ:* Dulwich Coll.; Univ. of Exeter (BA). Presenter, Harlech TV, 1968–69; BBC News trainee, 1969; ITN journalist, 1972; Programme Editor, News At Ten, 1980; Editor, Channel Four News, ITN, 1983; Dep. Editor, 1986, Editor, 1989, Editor-in-Chief, 1991, ITN. FRTS 1991. BAFTA Award for Best News or Outside Broadcast, 1986, 1987; BPG Award for Best News or Current Affairs Prog., 1988. *Address:* ITN Ltd, 200 Gray's Inn Road, WC1X 8XZ. *T:* 0171–833 3000.

PUSACK, George Williams, MS; Chief Executive, Mobil Oil Australia Ltd, 1980–85, retired; *b* 26 Sept. 1920; *s* of George F. Pusack and Winifred (*née* Williams); *m* 1942, Marian Preston; two *s* one *d*. *Educ:* Univ. of Michigan; Univ. of Pennsylvania. BSE (AeroEng), BSE (Eng.Math), MS (MechEng). Aero Engr, US Navy, 1942–45; Corporal, US Air Force, 1945–46; Mobil Oil Corp.: Tech. Service and Research Manager, USA, 1946–53; Product Engrg Manager, USA, 1953–59; International Supply Manager, USA, 1959–69; Vice-Pres., N Amer. Div., USA, 1969–73; Regional Exec., Mobil Europe, London, 1973–76; Chm. and Chief Exec, Mobil Oil Co. Ltd, 1976–80. Pres., County Hospice, York, SC, 1989–91. Trustee, Victorian State Opera Foundn, 1983–85. Teacher, layreader, vestryman and warden of Episcopal Church (Trustee, York, SC, 1992–). *Recreations:* golf, travel. *Address:* 400 Avinger Lane #431, Davidson, NC 28036, USA. *T:* (704) 8961431. *Clubs:* River Hills Country (Pres., 1991) (Clover, USA); Australian, Royal Melbourne Golf (Melbourne).

PUSEY, Nathan Marsh, PhD; President Emeritus, Harvard University; *b* Council Bluffs, Iowa, 4 April 1907; *s* of John Marsh Pusey and Rosa Pusey (*née* Drake); *m* 1936, Anne Woodward; two *s* one *d*. *Educ:* Harvard University, USA. AB 1928, AM 1932, PhD, 1937. Assistant, Harvard, 1933–34; Sophomore tutor, Lawrence Coll., 1935–38; Asst Prof., history and literature, Scripps Coll., Claremont, Calif., 1938–40; Wesleyan Univ.: Asst Prof., Classics, 1940–43, Assoc. Prof., 1943–44; President: Lawrence Coll., Appleton, Wisconsin, 1944–53; Harvard Univ., 1953–71; Andrew Mellon Foundn, 1971–75. Pres., United Bd for Christian Higher Educn in Asia, 1979–83. Holds many hon. degrees from Universities and colleges in USA and other countries. Officier de la Légion d'Honneur, 1958. *Publications:* The Age of the Scholar, 1963; American Higher Education 1945–1970, 1978. *Address:* 200 East 66th Street, New York, NY 10021, USA.

PUSINELLI, (Frederick) Nigel (Molière), CMG 1966; OBE 1963; MC 1940; HM Overseas Civil Service, retired; *b* 28 April 1919; second *s* of late S. Jacques and T. May Pusinelli, Frettenham, Norfolk and Fowey, Cornwall; *m* 1941, Joan Mary Chaloner, *d* of late Cuthbert B. and Mildred H. Smith, Cromer, Norfolk and Bexhill-on-Sea, Sussex; one *s* one *d*. *Educ:* Aldenham School; Pembroke College, Cambridge (BA Hons in law). Commissioned RA 1939; served BEF, 1940; India/Burma, 1942–45; Major, 1942; Staff College, Quetta, 1945. Administrative officer, Gilbert and Ellice Islands Colony, 1946–57. Transferred to Aden, 1958; Dep. Financial Sec. and frequently Actg Financial Sec. till 1962; Director of Establishments, 1962–68, and Assistant High Commissioner, 1963–68, Aden and Federation of South Arabia. Member E African Currency Board, 1960–62. Salaries Commissioner various territories in West Indies, 1968–70. Chm., Overseas Service Pensioners' Assoc., 1978–. Chairman: Chichester Harbour Conservancy, 1987–90 (Vice-Chm., 1985–87; Mem., Adv. Cttee, 1971–); RYA Southern Region, 1979–; Chichester Harbour Fedn of sailing clubs and yachting orgns, 1980–87. *Publication:* Report on Census of Population of Gilbert and Ellice Islands Colony, 1947. *Recreation:* dinghy racing. *Address:* Routledge Cottage, Westbourne, Emsworth, Hants PO10 8SE. *T:* Emsworth (01243)

372915. *Clubs:* Commonwealth Trust; Royal Yachting Assoc., Cambridge University Cruising, Emsworth Sailing.

PUTTICK, Richard George; Chairman, 1974–85 and Chief Executive, 1978–85, Taylor Woodrow plc, retired; *b* Kingston, Surrey, 16 March 1916; *e s* of late George Frederick Puttick and Dorothea (*née* Bowerman); *m* 1943, Betty Grace Folbigg; two *s*. *Educ:* St Mark's, Teddington. Joined Taylor Woodrow Construction Ltd, 1940 (the Taylor Woodrow Group's largest contracting subsidiary co.); Dir, 1955; Asst Managing Dir, 1968; Dir, Taylor Woodrow Ltd, 1969; Jt Dep. Chm., 1972. Mem. Council, CBI, July 1967–Dec. 1969; Pres., NW Mddx Branch, BIM, 1976–85. FCIOB; CIMgt. Liveryman, Worshipful Co. of Joiners and Ceilers. *Recreations:* music, reading, gardening, supporting sports. *Address:* Woodlawn, Hanger Hill, Weybridge, Surrey KT13 9XU. *T:* Weybridge (01932) 845131.

PUTTNAM, Sir David (Terence), Kt 1995; CBE 1983; film producer; Chairman, Enigma Productions Ltd, since 1978; *b* 25 Feb. 1941; *s* of Leonard Arthur Puttnam and Marie Beatrix Puttnam; *m* 1961, Patricia Mary (*née* Jones); one *s* one *d*. *Educ:* Minchenden Grammar Sch., London. Advertising, 1958–66; photography, 1966–68; film prodn, 1968–. Producer of feature films including: Bugsy Malone, 1976 (four BAFTA awards); The Duellists, 1977 (Jury Prize, Cannes); Midnight Express, 1978 (two Acad. Awards, three BAFTA Awards); Chariots of Fire, 1981 (four Acad. Awards, three BAFTA Awards, incl. awards for best film); Local Hero, 1982 (two BAFTA Awards); Cal, 1984 (Acting Prize, Cannes); The Killing Fields, 1985 (three Acad. Awards, eight BAFTA Awards incl. Best Film); The Mission, 1986 (Palme d'Or, Cannes, 1986, one Acad. Award, three BAFTA awards, 1987); Memphis Belle, 1990; Meeting Venus, 1991; Being Human, 1993; War of the Buttons, 1994. Chm. and Chief Exec. Officer, Columbia Pictures, 1986–88. Producer of films and series for television. Vis. Industrial Prof., Drama Dept, Bristol Univ., 1986–. Director: National Film Finance Corp., 1980–85; Anglia Television Gp, 1982–; Village Roadshow Corp., 1989–; Survival Anglia, 1989–; Chrysalis Group, 1993–; Chm., Internat. Television Enterprises Ltd, 1988–; Governor, National Film and Television Sch., 1974–, Chm., 1988–. Vice Pres., BAFTA, 1993; Mem., British Screen Adv. Council, 1988. Pres., CPRE, 1985–92. Trustee, Tate Gall., 1986–93. FRGS; FRSA; FRPS. Hon. Fellow, Manchester Polytechnic, 1990; Hon. FCSD 1990; Hon. FLI. Hon. LLD Bristol, 1983; Hon. DLitt: Leicester, 1986; Bradford, 1993; Hon. LittD Leeds, 1992. Michael Balcon Award for outstanding contribn to British Film Industry, BAFTA, 1982. Officier de l'Ordre des Arts et des Lettres (France), 1992. *Recreations:* reading, going to the cinema. *Clubs:* Chelsea Arts, MCC.

PUXON, (Christine) Margaret, (Mrs Margaret Williams); QC 1982; MD, FRCOG; medical/legal consultant; practising barrister, 1954–93; *b* 25 July 1915; *d* of Reginald Wood Hale and Clara Lilian Hale; *m* 1955, F. Morris Williams (*d* 1986), MBE; two *s* one *d*. *Educ:* Abbey Sch., Malvern Wells; Birmingham Univ. (MB, ChB; MD Obstetrics 1944). MRCS, LRCP 1942; FRCOG 1976. Gynaecological Registrar, Queen Elizabeth Hosp., Birmingham, and later Consultant Gynaecologist, Essex CC, 1942–49. Called to the Bar, Inner Temple, 1954. A Dep. Circuit Judge, 1970–86; a Recorder, 1986–88. Privy Council Member, Council of Royal Pharmaceutical Soc., 1975–90; Member: Genetic Manipulation Adv. Gp, 1979–84; Ethical Cttee, RCGP, 1981–. Consultant Editor, Medical Law Reports, 1993–. Liveryman, Worshipful Soc. of Apothecaries, 1982–. *Publications:* The Family and the Law, 1963, 2nd edn 1971; contributed to: Progress in Obstetrics and Gynaecology, 1983; In Vitro Fertilisation: Past, Present and Future, 1986; Gynaecology (ed Shaw, Souter and Stanton), 1991; Safe Practice in Obstetrics and Gynaecology (ed Clements), 1994; contrib. med. and legal jls, incl. Proc. RSM, Practitioner, New Law Jl and Solicitors' Jl. *Recreations:* cooking, travel, opera, gardening. *Address:* 19 Clarence Gate Gardens, Glentworth Street, NW1 6AY. *T:* 0171–723 7922.

PYATT, Rt. Rev. William Allan, CBE 1985; MA; formerly Bishop of Christchurch, retired; *b* Gisborne, NZ, 4 Nov. 1916; *e s* of A. E. Pyatt; *m* 1942, Mary Lilian Carey; two *s* one *d*. *Educ:* Gisborne High Sch.; Auckland Univ.; St John's Coll., Auckland; Westcott House, Cambridge. BA 1938 (Senior Schol. in Hist.); MA 1939. Served War of 1939–45: combatant service with 2 NZEF; Major, 2 IC 20 NZ Armd Regt 1945. Ordained, 1946; Curate, Cannock, Staffs, 1946–48; Vicar: Brooklyn, Wellington, NZ, 1948–52; Hawera, 1952–58; St Peter's, Wellington, 1958–62; Dean of Christchurch, 1962–66; Bishop of Christchurch, 1966–83. *Publications:* contribs to NZ Jl of Theology. *Recreations:* Rugby referee; political comment on radio; golf, wood turning, caravanning; lecturing on current affairs, study of Maori language and racial issues in New Zealand. *Address:* 55a Celia Street, Christchurch 8, New Zealand.

PYBUS, William Michael; Chairman, Homeowners Friendly Society Ltd, since 1991 (Director, since 1980); *b* 7 May 1923; *s* of Sydney James Pybus and Evelyn Mary (*née* Wood); *m* 1959, Elizabeth Janet Whitley; two *s* two *d*. *Educ:* Bedford Sch.; New College, Oxford (1st cl. hons Jurisprudence). Served War, 1942–46: commissioned 1st King's Dragoon Guards; Lieut attached XIth Hussars in Normandy (wounded); King's Dragoon Guards, Egypt, Palestine, Syria, Lebanon; Prosecutor, Mil. Courts, Palestine, 1946 (Major). Admitted Solicitor (Scott Schol.), 1950; Partner, Herbert Oppenheimer, Nathan & Vandyk, Solicitors, 1953–88. Consultant, Denton Hall Burgin & Warrens, later Denton Hall, 1988–94. Chairman: AAH Holdings plc, 1968–92; British Fuel Co., 1968–87; Inter-Continental Fuels Ltd, 1975–88; Siebe (formerly Siebe Gorman Hldgs), 1980–90 (Dir, 1972–); Leigh Interests, 1982–89; Dep. Chm., R. Mansell Ltd, 1980–85; Director: National Westminster Bank (Outer London Region), 1977–88; Cornhill Insurance PLC, 1977–; Overseas Coal Developments Ltd, 1979–88; Bradford & Bingley Building Soc., 1983–94; Vestric Ltd, 1985–91; Conservation Foundn, 1991–; Conservation Foundn Enterprise Ltd, 1991–. Part-time Member: British Railways (London Midland) Bd, 1974; British Railways (Midlands and West) Bd, 1975–77; Chm., BR (London Midland) Bd, 1977–89. Dir, Coal Trade Benevolent Assoc., 1969–; Vice-Pres., Coal Industry Soc., 1981– (Pres., 1976–81). Governor, Harpur Trust, 1979–87. Master: Pattenmakers' Co., 1972–73; Fuellers' Co., 1994–95. Chairman: Ashdown House School Trust Ltd, 1975–89; City Univ. Club, 1975–76. CIMgt (CBIM 1974); FCIM (FInstM 1974); FRSA 1984. *Recreation:* fishing. *Address:* 5 Chancery Lane, Clifford's Inn, EC4A 1BU. *T:* 0171–430 2678. *Clubs:* Cavalry and Guards, MCC; Yorkshire CC.

PYE, Prof. John David, FLS; Professor of Zoology, Queen Mary and Westfield College (formerly Queen Mary College), University of London, 1973–91, now Emeritus; *b* 14 May 1932; *s* of Wilfred Frank Pye and Gwenllian Pye (*née* Davies); *m* 1958, Dr Ade Pye (*née* Kuku), Sen. Lectr, UCL. *Educ:* Queen Elizabeth's Grammar School for Boys, Mansfield; University Coll. of Wales, Aberystwyth (BSc 1954, Hons 1955); Bedford Coll., London Univ. (PhD 1961). Research Asst, Inst. of Laryngology and Otology, London Univ., 1958–64; Lectr in Zoology, 1964–70, Reader, 1970–73, King's Coll. London; Head of Dept of Zoology and Comparative Physiology, Queen Mary Coll., 1977–82. A founder Dir, QMC Instruments Ltd, 1976–89. Linnean Society: Editor, Zoological Jl, 1981–85; Editl Sec. and Mem. Council, 1985–91; Vice-Pres., 1987–90; Mem., IEE Professional Gp Cttee E15, Radar, Sonar, Navigation and Avionics, 1983–86. Mem., RHS, 1988–. Member Editorial Boards: Zoolog. Soc., 1972–77, 1978–83, 1985–90; Jl of Exper. Biol., 1974–78; Jl of Comp. Physiol. A, 1978–; Bioacoustics, 1987–. MRI 1992– (Associate Mem., 1979–92; delivered Friday discourses 1979, 1983, and televised Christmas Lects for Children, 1985–86; co-organizer, discussion evenings, 1994–). *Publications:* Bats, 1968; (with G. D. Sales) Ultrasonic Communication by Animals, 1974; (ed with R. J. Bench and A. Pye) Sound Reception in Mammals, 1975; articles and research papers. *Recreations:* viticulture and vinification, travelling in warm climates. *Address:* Woodside, 24 St Mary's Avenue, Finchley, N3 1SN. *T:* 0181–346 6869; (office) 0171–775 3293.

PYE, Prof. Norman; Professor of Geography, University of Leicester, 1954–79, now Emeritus; Pro-Vice-Chancellor, 1963–66; Dean, Faculty of Science, 1957–60; Chairman of Convocation, 1982–85; *b* 2 Nov. 1913; *s* of John Whittaker Pye and Hilda Constance (*née* Platt); *m* 1940, Isabella Jane (*née* Currie); two *s*. *Educ:* Wigan Grammar School; Manchester University. Manchester University: BA Hons Geography Class I, 1935, Diploma in Education Class I, 1936. Asst Lecturer in Geography, Manchester Univ., 1936–37 and 1938–46; Mem., Cambridge Univ. Spitsbergen Expedn, 1938. Seconded to Hydrographic Dept, Admiralty, for War Service, 1940–46; pt-time lectr, Univ. of Bristol Cttee on Educn in HM Forces, 1941–45. Lecturer in Geography, 1946–53, Sen. Lecturer, 1953–54, Manchester Univ; Mem. Expedn to US Sonora and Mojave Deserts, 1952. Chm., Conf. of Heads of Depts of Geography in British Univs, 1968–70. Vis. Professor: Univ. of Ghana, 1958, 1960; Univ. of BC, 1964, 1983; Univ. of Alberta, Edmonton, 1967, 1968, 1969, 1973, 1974, 1975, 1978; External Examnr: Univ. of E Africa, 1964–67; Univ. of Guyana, 1974–78. Editor, "Geography", 1965–80. Member Corby Development Corp., 1965–80. Governor, Up Holland Grammar Sch., 1953–74; Member: Northants CC Educn Cttee, 1956–74; Court, Nottingham Univ., 1964–79; Standing Conf. on Univ. Entrance, 1966–79; Schools Council, 1967–78. Member: Council, RMetS, 1953–56; Council, Inst. of Brit. Geographers, 1954, 1955; Council, RGS, 1967–70 (Hon. Fellow, 1991); Council for Urban Studies Centres, 1974–81; Brit. Nat. Cttee for Geography, 1970–75; Civic Trust Educn Gp (formerly Heritage Educn Gp), 1976–90; Young Enterprise Leics Area Bd, 1983–; Hon. Mem., Geographical Assoc., 1983– (Mem. Council, 1965–83; Hon. Vice-Pres., 1979–83). *Publications:* The Land Utilisation Survey of Britain: Part 44, Isle of Man, 1941; Leicester and its Region (ed and contrib.), 1972; research papers and articles in learned journals. *Recreations:* travel, oenology, music, gardening. *Address:* 127 Spencefield Lane, Evington, Leicester LE5 6GG. *T:* Leicester (0116) 241 5167. *Club:* Geographical.

PYKE, David Alan, CBE 1986; MD, FRCP; Registrar, Royal College of Physicians of London, 1975–92; Physician-in-charge, Diabetic Department, King's College Hospital, London, 1971–86; *b* 16 May 1921; *s* of Geoffrey and Margaret Pyke; *m* 1948, Janet, *d* of Dr J. Gough Stewart; one *s* two *d*. *Educ:* Leighton Park Sch., Reading; Cambridge Univ.; University Coll. Hosp. Med. Sch., London. MD Cantab; FRCP. Junior med. appts in London and Oxford, 1945–59. Service in RAMC, 1946–48. Apptd to staff of King's Coll. Hosp., 1959. Hon. Sec.: Assoc. of Physicians of GB and Ire., 1968–73; Royal Soc. of Med., 1972–74. *Publications:* (jt ed) Clinical Diabetes and its Biochemical Basis, 1968; (ed) Clinics in Endocrinology and Metabolism, Vol. 1, No 3, 1972; (jtly) Diabetes and its Management, 1973, 3rd edn 1978; articles in med. and sci. jls. *Recreations:* golf, opera. *Address:* 17 College Road, SE21 7BG. *T:* 0181–693 2313.

PYM, family name of **Baron Pym.**

PYM, Baron *cr* 1987 (Life Peer), of Sandy in the County of Bedfordshire; **Francis Leslie Pym;** PC 1970; MC 1945; DL; *b* 13 Feb. 1922; *s* of late Leslie Ruthven Pym, MP, and Iris, *d* of Charles Orde; *m* 1949, Valerie Fortune Daglish; two *s* two *d*. *Educ:* Eton; Magdalene Coll., Cambridge (Hon. Fellow 1979). Served War of 1939–45 (despatches, 1944 and 1945, MC): 9th Lancers, 1942–46; African and Italian campaigns. Contested (C) Rhondda West, 1959; MP (C): Cambridgeshire, 1961–83; Cambridgeshire South East, 1983–87. Asst Govt Whip (unpaid), Oct. 1962–64; Opposition Whip, 1964–67; Opposition Dep. Chief Whip, 1967–70; Parly Sec. to the Treasury and Govt Chief Whip, 1970–73; Sec. of State for NI, 1973–74; Opposition spokesman on: agriculture, 1974–76; H of C affairs and devolution, 1976–78; Foreign and Commonwealth affairs, 1978–79; Sec. of State for Defence, 1979–81; Chancellor of the Duchy of Lancaster and Paymaster Gen., and Leader of the House of Commons, 1981; Lord Pres. of the Council and Leader of the House of Commons, 1981–82; Sec. of State for Foreign and Commonwealth Affairs, 1982–83. Chm., Diamond Cable Communications plc, 1995–; Dir, Christie Brockbank Shipton Ltd, 1994–. Pres., Atlantic Treaty Assoc., 1985–87. Chm., E-SU, 1987–92. Member: Council, BESO; Bd, The Landscape Foundn; Vice-Pres., Registered Engineers for Disaster Relief. Mem. Herefordshire County Council, 1958–61. DL Cambs, 1973. *Publication:* The Politics of Consent, 1984. *Recreation:* touching life at many points. *Address:* Everton Park, Sandy, Beds SG19 2DE. *Clubs:* Buck's, Cavalry and Guards.

PYMAN, Lancelot Frank Lee, CMG 1961; HM Diplomatic Service, retired; *b* 8 August 1910; *s* of late Dr F. L. Pyman, FRS, and Mrs I. C. Pyman; *m* 1936, Sarah Woods Gamble (*d* 1981). *Educ:* Dover College; King's College, Cambridge (Exhibitioner). Entered Levant Consular Service, 1933; various posts in Persia, 1933–38; Consul, Cernauti, Roumania, 1939–40; Vice-Consul, Beirut, Lebanon, 1940–41. Served with HM Forces in Levant States, 1941. Asst Oriental Secretary, HM Embassy, Tehran, Dec. 1941–44; Foreign Office, 1944–48; Consul, St Louis, Missouri, Dec. 1948–49; Oriental Counsellor, Tehran, Dec. 1949–Sept. 1952; Counsellor, British Embassy, Rio de Janeiro, 1952–53; Consul-General, Tetuan, 1953–56; Counsellor, British Embassy, Rabat, 1956–57; HM Consul-General: Zagreb, 1957–61; Basra, March–Dec. 1961; Ambassador to the Somali Republic, 1961–63; Consul-General, San Francisco, 1963–66. *Recreation:* duplicate bridge. *Address:* Knockroe, Delgany, Co. Wicklow, Ireland.

PYPER, Mark Christopher Spring-Rice; Headmaster, Gordonstoun School, since 1990; *b* 13 Aug. 1947; *s* of late Arthur Spring-Rice Pyper and of Rosemary Isabel Pyper; *m* 1979, Jennifer Lindsay Gilderson; one *s* two *d*. *Educ:* Winchester College; Balliol College, Oxford (BA Mod. Hist.). Asst Master, Stoke Brunswick Sch., East Grinstead, 1966–68; Asst Master, then Joint Headmaster, St Wilfrid's Sch., Seaford, 1969–79; Registrar, Housemaster, then Dep. Headmaster, Sevenoaks Sch., 1979–90. Dir, Sevenoaks Summer Festival, 1979–90. *Address:* Headmaster's House, Gordonstoun School, Elgin, Moray IV30 2RF. *T:* Hopeman (01343) 830445. *Club:* MCC.

PYTCHES, Rt. Rev. (George Edward) David; Vicar of St Andrew's, Chorleywood, Rickmansworth, since 1977; *b* 9 Jan. 1931; 9th *c* and 6th *s* of late Rev. Thomas Arthur Pytches and late Eirene Mildred Pytches (*née* Welldon); *m* 1958, Mary Trevisick; four *d*. *Educ:* Old Buckenham Hall, Norfolk; Framlingham Coll., Suffolk; Univ. of Bristol (BA); Trinity Coll., Bristol. MPhil Nottingham, 1984. Deacon 1955, priest 1956; Asst Curate, St Ebbe's, Oxford, 1955–58; Asst Curate, Holy Trinity, Wallington, 1958–59; Missionary Priest in Chol Chol, Chile, 1959–62; in Valparaiso, Chile, 1962–68; Rural Dean, Valparaiso, 1966–70; Diocese of Chile, Bolivia and Peru: Asst Bishop, 1970–72; Vicar General, 1971–72; Bishop, 1972–77. Co-ordinator: New Wine Family Conf., 1984–; Fellowship of Ind. Anglican Churches, 1992–; Soul Survivor Youth Conf., 1993–. Dir, Kingdom Power Trust, 1987–. *Publications:* Come Holy Spirit, 1985; Does God Speak Today?, 1989; Some Said It Thundered, 1990; (jtly) New Wineskins, 1991; Prophecy in the Local Church, 1993. *Recreations:* collecting semi-precious stones, walking. *Address:* The Vicarage, Quickley Lane, Chorleywood, Rickmansworth, Herts WD3 5AE. *T:* Chorleywood (01923) 447111, *Fax:* (01923) 447200.

Q

QESKU, Pavli; Ambassador of the Republic of Albania to the Court of St James's, since 1993; *b* 16 June 1943; *s* of Mihal and Vasilika Qesku; *m* 1973, Lidia Daka; one *s* one *d*. *Educ:* Tirana State Univ. (English Language). Translator at State publishing house, 1968; English teaching, 1975; translator and editor at publishing house, 1978; Ministry of Foreign Affairs, 1993. *Recreations:* reading, writing, music. *Address:* Albanian Embassy, 6 Wilton Court, 59–60 Eccleston Square, SW1V 1PH. *T:* 0171–976 5295.

QUANT, Mary, (Mrs A. Plunket Greene), OBE 1966; RDI 1969; Director of Mary Quant Group of companies since 1955; *b* 11 Feb. 1934; *d* of Jack and Mildred Quant; *m* 1957, Alexander Plunket Greene (*d* 1990); one *s*. *Educ:* 13 schools; Goldsmiths' College of Art. Fashion Designer. Mem., Design Council, 1971–74. Member: British/USA Bicentennial Liaison Cttee, 1973; Adv. Council, V&A Museum, 1976–78. Exhibition, Mary Quant's London, London Museum, 1973–74. FCSD (FSIA 1967). Maison Blanche Rex Award (US), 1964; Sunday Times Internat. Award, 1964; Piavola d'Oro Award (Italy), 1966; Annual Design Medal, Inst. of Industrial Artists and Designers, 1966; Hall of Fame Award, British Fashion Council, 1990. *Publication:* Quant by Quant, 1966. *Address:* 3 Ives Street, SW3 2NE. *T:* 0171–584 8781.

QUANTRILL, Prof. Malcolm, RIBA; architect, author and critic; Distinguished Professor of Architecture, Texas A&M University, since 1986; *b* Norwich, Norfolk, 25 May 1931; *s* of Arthur William Quantrill and Alice May Newstead; *m* 1971, Esther Maeve, *d* of James Brignell Dand and Winifred Dand, Chester; two *s* two *d*. *Educ:* City of Norwich Sch.; Liverpool Univ. (BArch); Univ. of Pennsylvania (MArch); Univ. of Wroclaw (Doc. Ing Arch). RIBA 1961. Fulbright Scholar and Albert Kahn Meml Fellow, Univ. of Pennsylvania, 1954–55; Asst Prof., Louisiana State Univ., 1955–60; Lecturer: Univ. of Wales, Cardiff, 1962–65; UCL, 1965–66; Asst to Dir, Architectural Assoc., 1966–67, Dir, 1967–69; Lectr, Univ. of Liverpool, 1970–73; Dean, Sch. of Environmental Design, Polytechnic of N London, 1973–80; Prof. of Architecture and Urban Design, Univ. of Jordan, Amman-Jordan, 1980–83. Vis. Professor: Univ. of Illinois, Chicago, 1973–75; Carleton Univ., Ottawa, 1978; Gastprofessor, Technische Universität, Wien, 1975–77; Fellow, Graham Foundn for Advanced Studies in the Fine Arts, Chicago, 1984. Sir William Dobell Meml Lectr in Modern Art, Sydney, NSW, 1978; Thomas Cubitt Lectr, London, 1993. Knight Commander, Order of Finnish Lion (Finland), 1988. *Plays performed:* Honeymoon, 1968; Life Class, 1968 (TV); Bust, 1990; radio plays include: The Fence, 1964; Let's Get This Straight, 1977; Immortal Bite, 1982. *Publications:* The Gotobed Trilogy (novels), 1962–64; Ritual and Response in Architecture, 1974; Monuments of Another Age, 1975; On the Home Front (novel), 1977; The Art of Government and the Government of Art, 1978; Alvar Aalto—a critical study, 1983; Reima Pietilä—architecture, context and modernism, 1985; The Environmental Memory, 1987; Reima Pietilä: one man's odyssey in search of Finnish architecture, 1988; (ed) Constancy and Change in Architecture, 1991; (ed) Urban Forms, Suburban Dreams, 1993; Finnish Architecture and the Modernist Tradition, 1995; articles in RIBA Jl, Arch. Assoc. Qly, Arch. Design, and Art Internat. *Address:* College of Architecture, Texas A&M University, College Station, TX 77843–3137, USA. *Club:* Garrick.

QUANTRILL, William Ernest; HM Diplomatic Service, retired; Ambassador to the Republic of Cameroon, and concurrently to the Central African Republic, Equatorial Guinea and the Republic of Chad, 1991–95; *b* 4 May 1939; *s* of late Ronald Frederick Quantrill and Norah Elsie Quantrill (*née* Matthews); *m* 1964, Rowena Mary Collins; three *s* one *d*. *Educ:* Colston's Sch., Bristol; Hatfield Coll., Univ. of Durham (BA Hons French). Entered FO, 1962; served Brussels, Havana, Manila, Lagos, 1964–80; Head of Training Dept, FCO, 1980–81; Dep. Head of Personnel Ops Dept, FCO, 1981–84; Counsellor and Hd of Chancery, Caracas, 1984–88; Dep. Gov., Gibraltar, 1988–90. *Recreations:* wild life, travel. *Address:* 145 Knights Croft, New Ash Green, Longfield, Kent DA3 8HZ. *T:* Ash Green (01474) 873615.

QU'APPELLE, Bishop of, since 1986; **Rt. Rev. Eric Bays;** *b* 10 Aug. 1932; *s* of Rev. Canon P. C. Bays and Hilda (*née* Harper); *m* 1967, Patricia Ann Earle; one *s* one *d*. *Educ:* Univ. of Manitoba (BSc 1955); Univ. of Saskatchewan (BA 1959): Univ. of Emmanuel College (LTh 1959); Christian Theological Seminary (MMin 1974). Flight Lieut, RCAF (Reserve), 1955. Asst Curate, All Saints', Winnipeg, 1959–61; Lecturer, Emmanuel Coll., 1961–62; Priest-in-charge: Burns Lake, BC, 1962–63; Masset, BC, 1963–64; Novice, Community of the Resurrection, Yorks, 1964–65; Vicar, St Saviour's, Winnipeg with Bird's Hill, 1965–68; Rector, All Saints', Winnipeg, 1968–76; Professor, Coll. of Emmanuel and St Chad, 1976–86, Vice-Principal 1981–86. Canon of St John's Cathedral, Winnipeg, 1971–86. Hon. DD Coll. of Emmanuel and St Chad, 1987. *Recreations:* golf, curling. *Address:* Bishop's Court, 1701 College Avenue, Regina, Saskatchewan S4P 1B8, Canada. *T:* (306) 522 8898.

QUARMBY, David Anthony, MA, PhD; FCIT; FILog; Joint Managing Director, J. Sainsbury plc, since 1988 (Director, since 1984); *b* 22 July 1941; *s* of Frank Reginald and Dorothy Margaret Quarmby; *m* 1968, Hilmary Hunter; four *d*. *Educ:* Shrewsbury Sch.; King's Coll., Cambridge (MA); Leeds Univ. (PhD, Dip. Industrial Management). Asst Lectr, then Lectr, Dept of Management Studies, Leeds Univ., 1963; Economic Adviser, Economic Planning Directorate, Min. of Transport, 1966; London Transport Executive: Dir of Operational Research, 1970; Chief Commercial and Planning Officer, 1974; Mem., 1975–84; Man. Dir (Buses), 1978–84; Mem., London Regional Transport, 1984; Director: Homebase Ltd, 1987–89; Shaw's Supermarkets Inc., 1987–92. Vice-President: Bus and Coach Council, 1981–84; CIT, 1987–91; Mem., Nat. Council, Freight Transport Assoc., 1985–88. Member: London Educn Business Partnership, 1988–92; Sch. Curriculum and Assessment Authy, 1993–; Southwark Diocesan Synod, 1982–85; London Adv. Bd, Salvation Army, 1982–87. Dir, and Chm. Develt Cttee, Blackheath Concert Halls, 1990–94. Gov., 1987– (Chm., 1995–), Chm., Finance Cttee, 1991–, James Allen's Girls' Sch., London. CompOR; CIMgt; FRSA. *Publications:* Factors Affecting Commuter Travel Behaviour (PhD Thesis, Leeds), 1967; contribs to Jl of Transport Economics and Policy, Regional Studies, Enterprise Management, and to books on transport, distribution, economics and operational research. *Recreations:* music, singing, walking, family life. *Address:* J. Sainsbury plc, Stamford Street, SE1 9LL. *T:* 0171–921 6000.

QUARREN EVANS, (John) Kerry; His Honour Judge Quarren Evans; a Circuit Judge, on South Eastern circuit, since 1980; *b* 4 July 1926; *s* of late Hubert Royston Quarren Evans, MC and Violet Soule Quarren Evans (*née* George); *m* 1958, Janet Shaw Lawson; one *s* one *d*. *Educ:* King Henry VIII Sch., Coventry; Cardiff High Sch.; Trinity Hall, Cambridge, 1948–51 (MA, LLM). 21st Glam. (Cardiff) Bn Home Guard, 1943–44; enlisted, Grenadier Gds, 1944; commnd Royal Welch Fusiliers, 1946, from OTS Bangalore; att. 2nd Bn The Welch Regt, Burma, 1946–47; Captain 1947. Admitted solicitor, 1953; Partner: Lyndon Moore & Co., Newport, 1954–71; T. S. Edwards & Son, Newport, 1971–80; Recorder, Wales and Chester Circuit, 1974–80. Clerk to Gen. Comrs of Income Tax, Dinas Powis Div., 1960–80; Chm., Newport Nat. Insurance Local Tribunal, 1968–71. *Recreations:* golf, Rugby football, oenology, staurologosophy, old things. *Address:* 2 Mount Park Crescent, Ealing, W5 2RN. *Clubs:* Denham Golf, Royal Porthcawl Golf, Crawshay's Welsh Rugby Football.

QUARTA, Roberto; Director and Group Chief Executive, BBA Group, since 1993; *b* 10 May 1949; *m* 1970, Maureen O'Hearn; one *s* one *d*. *Educ:* Italy and USA; Coll. of the Holy Cross, Mass, USA (BA). Management Trainee, David Gessner, 1971–73; Worcester Controls Corp., 1973–78: Manager, Purchasing and Production Control; Vice-Pres., Internat. Procurement; BTR, 1979–85: Manufacturing Dir, Worcester Controls Corp.; Man. Dir, Worcester Controls UK; Group Man. Dir, Valves Group; Chief Exec., Hitchener Manufacturing Corp., 1985–89; a Chief Divl Exec., BTR, 1989–93. *Recreations:* tennis, music. *Address:* BBA Group, 70 Fleet Street, EC4Y 1EU. *T:* 0171–842 4900.

QUARTANO, Ralph Nicholas, CBE 1987; CEng, MIChemE; Chairman, PosTel Investment Management Ltd, 1987–91 (Chief Executive, 1983–87); Director, The Laird Group PLC, since 1991; *b* 3 Aug. 1927; *s* of late Charles and Vivienne Mary Quartano; *m* 1954, Cornelia Johanna de Gunst; two *d*. *Educ:* Sherborne Sch.; Pembroke Coll., Cambridge (MA). Bataafsche Petroleum Mij, 1952–58; The Lummus Co, 1958–59; Temple Press, 1959–65; Man. Director: Heywood Temple Industrial Publications, 1965–68; Engineering Chemical and Marine Press, 1968–70. The Post Office, 1971–74; Sen. Dir, Central Finance, 1973–74; Chief Exec., Post Office Staff Superannuation Fund, 1974–83. Dir, 1985–93, Dep. Chm., 1987–93, SIB. Director: London American Energy NV, 1981–88; Britoil plc, 1982–88; 3i Group plc (formerly Investors in Industry), 1986–; John Lewis Partnership Pensions Trust, 1986–89; Clerical Medical Investment Group, 1987–; Booker plc, 1988–; British Maritime Technology Ltd, 1988– (Chm., 1995–); Enterprise Oil, 1991–; Heitman Financial, 1991–93; Chm., Murray Emerging Economies Trust plc, 1994–. Member: Engrg Council, 1981–83; City Capital Markets Cttee, 1985–93; Investment Cttee, Pensioen Fonds PGGM, Netherlands, 1986–; Investment Cttee, PTT Pensioen, Netherlands, 1988–; Financial Reporting Council, 1990–. City Advr to Dir-Gen., CBI, 1985–93. Sloan Fellow of London Business School. Gov., BUPA, 1987–. Mem. Council, RSA, 1993–. Trustee, Monteverdi Trust, 1986–93. *Address:* 20 Oakcroft Road, SE13 7ED. *T:* 0181–852 1607.

QUAYLE, James Danforth, (Dan), JD; Vice-President of the United States of America, 1989–93; *b* 4 Feb. 1947; *m* 1972, Marilyn Tucker; two *s* one *d*. *Educ:* DePauw Univ. (BS 1969); Indiana Univ. (JD 1974). Admitted to Indiana Bar, 1974. Court reporter, 1965–69, Associate Publisher and Gen. Manager, 1974–76, Huntington Herald Press; Investigator, Consumer Protection Div., Office of the Attorney General, Indiana, 1970–71; Admin. Assistant to Gov. of Indiana, 1971–73; Dir, Inheritance Tax Div., Indiana, 1973–74; professor of business law, Huntington Coll., 1975. Mem. of Congress, 1976–80; Mem. for Indiana, US Senate, 1981–88. Chairman: Circle Investors, Inc., 1993–; Competitiveness Center, Hudson Inst., 1993–. *Publication:* Standing Firm, 1994. *Address:* 11711 N Pennsylvania, Suite 100, Carmel, IN 46032, USA.

QUAYLE, Prof. John Rodney, PhD; FRS 1978; Vice-Chancellor, University of Bath, 1983–92; *b* 18 Nov. 1926; *s* of John Martin Quayle and Mary Doris Quayle (*née* Thorp); *m* 1951, Yvonne Mabel (*née* Sanderson); one *s* one *d*. *Educ:* Alun Grammar Sch., Mold; University Coll. of North Wales, Bangor (BSc, PhD); Univ. of Cambridge (PhD); MA Oxon. Res. Fellow, Radiation Lab., Univ. of California, 1953–55; Sen. Scientific Officer, Tropical Products Institute, London, 1955–56; Mem. Scientific Staff, MRC Cell Metabolism Res. Unit, Univ. of Oxford, 1956–63; Lectr, Oriel Coll., Oxford, 1957–63; Sen. Lectr in Biochemistry, 1963–65, West Riding Prof. of Microbiol., 1965–83, Sheffield Univ. Vis. Res. Prof. of Gesellschaft für Strahlen und Umweltforschung, Institut für Mikrobiologie, Universität Göttingen, 1973–74; Walker-Ames Vis. Prof., Univ. of Washington, Seattle, 1981. Chm., British Nat. Cttee for Microbiol., 1985–90; Member: AFRC, 1982–84; Adv. Council, RMCS, 1983–92; Council, Royal Soc., 1982–84; Biol Sciences Cttee, SERC, 1981–84; Pres., Soc. for General Microbiology, 1990–93. Member: Council of Management, Bath Festival Soc., 1992–93 (Trustee, 1984–89); Bd, Bath Festivals Trust, 1993–. Korrespondierendes Mitglied, Akademie der Wissenschaften, Göttingen, 1976. Hon. Dr *rer. nat.*, Göttingen, 1989; Hon. DSc: Bath, 1992; Sheffield, 1992. Ciba Medal, Biochem. Soc., 1978. *Publications:* articles in scientific jls. *Recreations:* hill-walking, gardening, bread-making. *Address:* The Coach House, Vicarage Lane, Compton Dando, Bristol BS18 4LA. *T:* Compton Dando (01761) 490399.

QUAYLE, Maj.-Gen. Thomas David Graham, CB 1990; Ombudsman for Corporate Estate Agents, since 1990; *b* 7 April 1936; *s* of Thomas Quayle and Phyllis Gwendolen

Johnson; *m* 1962, Susan Jean Bradford; three *d*. *Educ:* Repton; Trinity College, Oxford. Commissioned RA 1958; Student, Indian Staff Coll., 1968; Comdr, The Chestnut Troop, 1971–72; Instructor, Staff Coll., Camberley, 1974–76; Comdr, 40 Field Regt (The Lowland Gunners), 1976–79; Comdr Artillery, 4th Armoured Div., 1981–83; Defence Attaché, Bonn, 1983–86; Comdr Artillery, 1st British Corps, 1987–90, retd. *Recreations:* shooting, fishing, bridge. *Address:* c/o National Westminster Bank, Salisbury, Wilts SP1 1DF.

QUEBEC, Archbishop of, (RC), and Primate of Canada, since 1990; **Most Rev. Maurice Couture;** *b* 3 Nov. 1926. Perpetual vows with Vincentian Fathers, 1948; ordained priest, 1951; Patro de la Baie, Plessisville, Port Alfred and Bagotville, 1952–55; in charge of Minor Seminary of his Congregation, 1955–65; founder and Rector, Inter-Congregational Seminary, Cap-Rouge, 1965–70; Provincial Superior, 1970–76, Superior General of Congregation, 1976–82; Titular Bishop of Talattula and Auxiliary Bishop of Quebec, 1982–88; Bishop of Baie-Corneau, 1988–90. *Address:* Office of the Archbishop of Quebec, 1073 Boulevard René Levesque Ouest, Quebec, PQ G1S 4R5, Canada.

QUEBEC, Bishop of, since 1991; **Rt Rev. Alexander Bruce Stavert;** *b* 1 April 1940; *s* of Ewart and Kathleen Stavert; *m* 1982, Diana Greig; one *s* two *d*. *Educ:* Lower Canada Coll., Montreal; Bishop's Univ., Lennoxville, PQ (BA 1961): Trinity Coll., Univ. of Toronto (STB 1964; MTh, 1976). Incumbent of Schefferville, Quebec, 1964–69; Fellow, 1969–70, Chaplain, 1970–76, Trinity Coll., Univ. of Toronto; Incumbent, St Clement's Mission East, St Paul's River, PQ, 1976–81; Chaplain, Bishop's Univ., Lennoxville, 1981–84; Dean and Rector, St Alban's Cathedral, Prince Albert, Sask., 1984–91. Hon. DD Toronto, 1986. *Recreations:* swimming, ski-ing. *Address:* 31 rue des Jardins, Québec, PQ G1R 4L6, Canada. *T:* (418) 6923858. *Club:* Garrison (Québec).

QUEENSBERRY, 12th Marquess of, *cr* 1682; **David Harrington Angus Douglas;** late Royal Horse Guards; Viscount Drumlanrig and Baron Douglas, 1628; Earl of Queensberry, 1633; Bt (Nova Scotia), 1668; Professor of Ceramics, Royal College of Art, 1959–83; Partner, Queensberry Hunt Levien design group; *b* 19 Dec. 1929; *s* of 11th Marquess of Queensberry and late Cathleen Mann; *S* father, 1954; *m* 1st, 1956, Mrs Ann Radford; two *d*; 2nd, 1969, Alexandra (marr. diss. 1986), *d* of Guy Wyndham Sich; three *s* one *d*. *Educ:* Eton. Mem. Council, Crafts Council; Pres., Design and Industries Assoc., 1976–78. FCSD; Sen. FRCA, 1990. Hon. DDes Staffordshire, 1993. *Heir: s* Viscount Drumlanrig, *qv*.

QUEGUINER, Jean; Légion d'Honneur, 1970; Administrateur Général des Affaires Maritimes, France; maritime consultant, since 1985; *b* 2 June 1921; *s* of Etienne Quéguiner and Anne Trehin; *m* 1952, Marguerite Gaillard; one *s* one *d*. *Educ:* Lycée Buffon, Collège Stanislas and Faculté de Droit, Paris; Coll. of Administration of Maritime Affairs, St Malo. Docteur en Droit (maritime), Bordeaux. Head of Maritime Dist of Caen, 1953; Dep. Head of Coll. of Admin. of Maritime Affairs, 1955; Head of Safety of Navigation Section, 1963; Vice-Chm. of Maritime Safety Cttee, 1965–68, Dep. Sec.-Gen., 1968–77, IMCO; Chm., Chantiers Navals de l'Esterel, 1981–85. Maritime expert to the Courts, 1986–. Mem., Chambre d'Arbitrage de la Rochelle, 1992–. *Publications:* Législation et réglementation maritime, 1955; Le code de la mer, 1965; La croisière cotière, 1967; Le code fluvial à l'usage des plaisanciers, 1970. *Recreation:* sailing. *Address:* 13 rue de l'Horizon, 17480 Le Château d'Oléron, France.

QUENNELL, Joan Mary, MBE 1958; *b* 23 Dec. 1923; *o c* of late Walter Quennell, Dangstein, Rogate. *Educ:* Dunhurst and Bedales Schools. War Service, WLA and BRCS. Vice-Chairman, Horsham Division Cons. Assoc., 1949 (Chairman, 1958–61); W Sussex CC, 1951–61. Served on Finance, Local Government, Selection and Education Cttees, etc; also as Governor various schools and colleges; Governor, Crawley Coll., Further Education, 1956–69; Member: Southern Reg. Council for Further Education, 1959–61; Reg. Adv. Council, Technological Education (London and Home Counties), 1959–61. MP (C) Petersfield, 1960–Sept. 1974; PPS to the Minister of Transport, 1962–64; Member: Select Cttee on Public Accounts, 1970–74; Speaker's Panel of Temporary Chairmen of House of Commons, 1970–74; Cttee of Selection, House of Commons, 1970–74; Select Cttee on European Secondary Legislation, 1973–74. Chm., EUW, Hampshire, 1978–80. JP W Sussex, 1959–80. *Recreations:* reading, gardening. *Address:* Dangstein, Rogate, near Petersfield, Hants GU31 5BZ.

QUEREJAZU CALVO, Roberto; Cross of the Chaco and Award of Military Merit (Bolivia); Bolivian Ambassador to the Court of St James's 1966–70, and to the Court of The Hague, 1966–70; *b* 24 Nov. 1913; *m* 1944, Dorothy Allman-Lewis; one *s* one *d*. *Educ:* Sucre Univ., Bolivia. Director of Minister's Cabinet, Legal Dept, and Political Dept, Bolivian Foreign Service, 1939–42; First Secretary, Embassy in Brazil, 1943; Secretary-General, Bolivian Delegn to UN, 1946; Bolivian Embassy, London: Counsellor, 1947; Chargé d'Affaires, 1948–52; Bolivian Rep.: to UN Conference on Tin, 1951; to Interamerican Conference for De-Nuclearization of Latin America, Mexico, 1964; Bolivian Delegate: XX UN General Assembly, 1965; 2nd Interamerican Conference Extraord., Rio de Janeiro, 1965; Under-Secretary of State for Foreign Affairs, Bolivia, 1966. Holds foreign awards. *Publications:* Masamaclay (history of Chaco War), 1966; Bolivia and the English, 1973; Llallagua (history of a mountain), 1976; Guano, Salitre, Sangre (history of the Pacific War), 1979; Adolfo Costa du Rels (biography of a diplomat and writer), 1981; Chuquisaca 1539–1825 (colonial history of the capital of Bolivia), 1987; Historia de la Iglesia Católica en Charcas (colonial history of the Catholic Church), 1992. *Address:* Casilla 4243, Cochabamba, Bolivia.

QUICK, Anthony Oliver Hebert; Headmaster of Bradfield College, 1971–85, retired; *b* 26 May 1924; *er s* of late Canon O. C. Quick, sometime Regius Prof. of Divinity at Oxford, and late Mrs F. W. Quick; *m* 1955, Eva Jean, *er d* of late W. C. Sellar and of Mrs Hope Sellar; three *s* one *d*. *Educ:* Shrewsbury Sch.; Corpus Christi Coll., Oxford; Sch. of Oriental and African Studies, Univ. of London (Govt Schol.). 2nd cl. hons Mod. History, Oxford. Lieut, RNVR, serving mainly on East Indies Stn, 1943–46. Asst Master, Charterhouse, 1949–61; Headmaster, Rendcomb Coll., Cirencester, 1961–71. *Publications:* (jtly) Britain 1714–1851, 1961; Britain 1851–1945, 1967; Twentieth Century Britain, 1968; Charterhouse: a history of the school, 1990; (contrib.) A History of Rendcomb College, vol. 2, 1995. *Recreations:* walking, gardening, sailing, fishing. *Address:* Corbin, Scorriton, Buckfastleigh, Devon TQ11 0HU.

QUICK, Dorothy, (Mrs Charles Denis Scanlan); Metropolitan Stipendiary Magistrate, since 1986; *b* 10 Dec. 1944; *d* of Frederick and Doris Quick; *m* 1971, Charles Denis Scanlan; two *s*. *Educ:* Glanafan Grammar Sch., Port Talbot; University Coll. London (LLB). Called to the Bar, Inner Temple, 1969; barrister-at-law, 1969–86. Mem., British Acad. of Forensic Sciences, 1987–. *Recreations:* gardening, theatre, books. *Address:* c/o Highbury Corner Magistrates' Court, 51 Holloway Road, N7 8JA.

QUICK, Norman, CBE 1984; DL; Life President, Quicks Group (formerly H. & J. Quick Group) plc, 1993 (Chairman, 1965–92; Managing Director, 1965–84); *b* 19 Nov. 1922; *s* of James and Jessie Quick; *m* 1949, Maureen Cynthia Chancellor; four *d*. *Educ:* Arnold Sch., Blackpool. FIMI. H. & J. Quick Ltd to H. & J. Quick Group plc, 1939–; served RNVR, Lieut 1941–46 (despatches Mediterranean, 1943); Non Executive Director: Williams & Glyn's Bank, 1979–85; Royal Bank of Scotland, 1985–90; Dir, Piccadilly Radio (formerly Greater Manchester Independent Radio), 1972–89 (Chm., 1980–88). Mem., NW Indust. Council. Pres., Stretford Cons. Assoc., 1974– (formerly Chm.). Mem., Lancs CC, 1954–57. Treasurer, 1975–80, Chm., 1980–83, Univ. of Manchester Council; Mem., Bd of Governors, Arnold Sch. Ltd, Blackpool, 1980–90. DL Greater Manchester, 1987, High Sheriff, 1990. Hon. MA Manchester, 1977; Hon. LLD Manchester, 1984. *Recreation:* Rugby. *Address:* Birkin House, Ashley, Altrincham, Cheshire WA14 3QL. *T:* Bucklow Hill (01565) 830175. *Clubs:* Royal Automobile; St James's (Manchester).

QUICKE, Sir John (Godolphin), Kt 1988; CBE 1978; DL; *b* 20 April 1922; *s* of Captain Noel Arthur Godolphin Quicke and Constance May Quicke; *m* 1953, Prudence Tinné Berthon, *d* of Rear-Adm. (E) C. P. E. Berthon; three *s* three *d*. *Educ:* Eton; New Coll., Oxford. Vice-Chm., North Devon Meat, 1982–86; Mem., SW Reg. Bd, National Westminster Bank, 1974–92. Chairman: Minister of Agriculture's SW Regional Panel, 1972–75; Agricl EDC, NEDO, 1983–88, Agricl Sector Gp, 1988–90; RURAL, 1983–; Estates Panel, NT, 1984–92; Member: Consultative Bd for R&D in Food and Agric., 1981–84; Severn Barrage Cttee, 1978–80; Countryside Commn, 1981–88 (Chm., Countryside Policy Review Panel, 1986–87); Properties Cttee, NT, 1984–. President: CLA, 1975–77; Royal Bath & West of England Soc., 1989–90. Mem. Bd of Governors, Univ. of Plymouth (formerly Polytechnic SW), 1989–93. DL Devon, 1985. Hon. FRASE, 1989. Hon. DSc: Exeter, 1989; Polytechnic South West, 1991. Bledisloe Gold Medal for Landowners, RASE, 1985. *Recreations:* reading, music, gardening. *Address:* Sherwood, Newton St Cyres, near Exeter, Devon EX5 5BT. *T:* Exeter (01392) 851216. *Club:* Boodle's.

QUICKE, Rev. Michael John; Principal, Spurgeon's College, since 1993; *b* 30 July 1945; *s* of George and Joan Quicke; *m* 1968, Carol Bentall; two *s*. *Educ:* Jesus Coll., Cambridge (MA); Regent's Park Coll., Oxford (MA). Nat. Sec. for Student Work, Baptist Union, 1967–69; Minister: Leamington Road Baptist Church, Blackburn, 1972–80; St Andrew's Street Baptist Church, Cambridge, 1980–93. Religious Advr, ITV, 1987–88. Mem. Council, Baptist Union of GB, 1976–; Vice Chm., Doctrine Commn, 1990–95, Worship Commn, 1995–, Baptist World Alliance. Mem., Acad. of Homiletics, 1995–. Hon. DD William Jewell Coll., Liberty, USA, 1994. *Publication:* Christian Apologetics, 1976. *Recreations:* listening to sermons, music, travel. *Address:* Principal's Lodge, Spurgeon's College, South Norwood Hill, SE25 6DJ. *T:* 0181–653 1235.

QUIGLEY, Anthony Leslie Coupland, CEng, FIEE; Under Secretary, Office of Science and Technology, since 1995; *b* 14 July 1946; *s* of late Leslie Quigley and of Vera Barbara Rodaway (*née* Martin); *m* 1968, Monica Dean; one *s* two *d*. *Educ:* Apsley Grammar Sch.; Queen Mary Coll., Univ. of London (BSc Eng). Command Control and Computer Divs, ASWE, 1967–81 (Exchange Scientist, US Naval Surface Weapons Center, 1976–79); Supt, Command and Control Div., 1981–84, Hd, Command, Control and Assessment Gp, 1984–87, RARDE; Dep. Head, Science and Technology Assessment Office, Cabinet Office, 1987–90; Dir, SDI Participation Office, 1990–93, Asst Chief Scientific Advr (Nuclear), 1993–95, MoD. *Publications:* technical papers on radar tracking and command and control. *Recreations:* umpiring cricket, golf, flying models. *Address:* Albany House, 84–86 Petty France, SW1H 9ST. *T:* 0171–271 2071. *Club:* Sweetwoods Park Golf.

QUIGLEY, Sir George; *see* Quigley, Sir W. G. H.

QUIGLEY, Johanna Mary, (Mrs D. F. C. Quigley); *see* Foley, J. M.

QUIGLEY, Sir (William) George (Henry), Kt 1993; CB 1982; PhD; Chairman, Ulster Bank Ltd, since 1989 (Deputy Chairman, 1988–89); Director, National Westminster Bank, since 1990; *b* 26 Nov. 1929; *s* of William George Cunningham Quigley and Sarah Hanson Martin; *m* 1971, Moyra Alice Munn, LLB. *Educ:* Ballymena Academy; Queen's Univ., Belfast, BA (1st Cl. Hons), 1951; PhD, 1955. Apptd Asst Principal, Northern Ireland Civil Service, 1955; Permanent Secretary: Dept of Manpower Services, NI, 1974–76; Dept of Commerce, NI, 1976–79; Dept of Finance, NI, 1979–82; Dept of Finance and Personnel, NI, 1982–88. Director: Irish-American Partnership, 1989–; Short Brothers, 1989–. Chm., Royal Group of Hospitals Trust, NI, 1992–. Chm., NI Div., Inst. of Dirs, 1990–; Member: Fair Employment Commn for NI, 1989–; Council, NI Chamber of Commerce and Industry, 1989–92; Council, NI Div., CBI, 1990–. Professorial Fellow, QUB, 1989–93. Fellow, Inst. of Bankers in Ireland, 1989. CIMgt. *Publication:* (ed with E. F. D. Roberts) Registrum Iohannis Mey: The Register of John Mey, Archbishop of Armagh, 1443–1456, 1972. *Recreations:* historical research, reading, music, gardening. *Address:* Ulster Bank Ltd, 47 Donegall Place, Belfast BT1 5AU.

QUILLEY, Denis Clifford; actor; *b* 26 Dec. 1927; *s* of Clifford Charles Quilley and Ada Winifred (*née* Stanley); *m* 1949, Stella Chapman; one *s* two *d*. *Educ:* Bancroft's, Woodford, Essex. First appearance, Birmingham Rep. Theatre, 1945; The Lady's not for Burning, Globe, 1949; Old Vic and Young Vic Cos, 1950–51: parts included: Fabian in Twelfth Night (on tour, Italy), Gratiano in Merchant of Venice; Revue, Airs on a Shoe String (exceeded 700 perfs), Royal Court, 1953; first leading rôle in West End as Geoffrey Morris in Wild Thyme, Duke of York's, 1955; subseq. parts incl.: Tom Wilson in Grab Me a Gondola (over 600 perfs), Lyric; Captain Brassbound, and Orlando, Bristol Old Vic; Candide, Saville; Benedick in Much Ado about Nothing, Open Air Th.; Archie Rice in The Entertainer, Nottingham Playhouse; Krogstad in A Doll's House, Brighton; Nat. Theatre, 1971–76: Aufidius (Coriolanus); Macbeth; Bolingbroke (Richard II); Caliban (The Tempest); Lopakin (Cherry Orchard); Jamie (Long Day's Journey into Night); Claudius (Hamlet); Hector (Troilus and Cressida); Bajazeth (Tamburlaine); Privates on Parade, Aldwych, 1977, Piccadilly, 1978 (SWET award, 1977); Morell in Candida, Albery Theatre, 1977; Deathtrap, Garrick, 1978; title rôle in Sweeney Todd, Theatre Royal Drury Lane (SWET award), 1980; Molokov in Chess, Barbican, 1985; Antony, in Antony and Cleopatra, Chichester, 1985; Fatal Attraction, Haymarket, 1985; La Cage aux Folles, Palladium, 1986; Pizarro in Royal Hunt of the Sun, UK tour, 1989; The School for Scandal, NT, 1990; Brachiano, The White Devil, NT, 1991; Venus Observed, She Stoops to Conquer, Chichester, 1992; Sweeney Todd, RNT, 1993; The Merry Wives of Windsor, RNT, 1995; has played in NY, Melbourne and Sydney. *Films:* Life at the Top, 1965; Anne of the Thousand Days, 1969; Murder on the Orient Express, 1974; The Black Windmill, 1974; The Antagonists, 1980; Evil Under the Sun, 1981; Privates on Parade, 1982; King David, 1985; Foreign Body, 1986; The Shell-seekers, 1989; Mr Johnson, 1990; A Dangerous Man, 1991. *TV plays and series* incl.: Merchant of Venice; The Father; Henry IV (Pirandello); Murder in the Cathedral; Time Slip; Contrabandits (Aust.); Clayhanger; The Serpent Son; The Crucible; Gladstone, in No 10; Masada; Anno Domini; Murder of a Moderate Man, 1988; Rich Tea and Sympathy, 1991. *Recreations:* playing the piano, flute and cello, walking. *Address:* 22 Willow Road, Hampstead, NW3 1TL. *T:* 0171–435 5976.

QUILLIAM, Hon. Sir (James) Peter, Kt 1988; **Hon. Mr Justice Quilliam;** Judge of the High Court and Court of Appeal, Cook Islands, since 1988; Chief Justice of the Cook Islands, since 1995; *b* 23 March 1920; *s* of Ronald Henry Quilliam, CBE and Gwendoline Minnie Quilliam; *m* 1945, Ellison Jean Gill; two *s* one *d*. *Educ:* Wanganui Collegiate Sch.;

Victoria Univ. of Wellington (LLB). Private practice as barrister and solicitor, 1945–69; Crown Prosecutor, New Plymouth, NZ, 1955–69; Judge, High Court of NZ, 1969–88, and Senior Puisne Judge, 1985–88; Judge of the Ct of Appeal, Fiji, 1992. NZ Police Complaints Authy, 1989–92. Pres., Taranaki Dist Law Soc., 1965–67. *Recreations:* golf, fishing, gardening, reading. *Address:* 9 Puketiro Avenue, Northland, Wellington 5, New Zealand. *T:* (4) 758166. *Clubs:* Wellington, Wellington Golf (NZ).

QUILLIAM, Prof. Juan Pete, (Peter), OBE 1986; DSc; FRCP; Professor of Pharmacology, University of London, at St Bartholomew's Hospital Medical College, 1962–83, now Emeritus; Chairman of Convocation of the University of London, 1973–90; *b* 20 Nov. 1915; *e s* of late Thomas Quilliam, Peel, IoM and Maude (*née* Pavitt); *m* 1st, 1946, Melita Kelly (*d* 1957); one *s* one *d*; 2nd, 1958, Barbara Lucy Marion, *y d* of late Rev. William Kelly, Pelynt, Cornwall. *Educ:* University Coll. Sch.; UCL (exhibnr); UCH Med. Sch. MSc 1938, MB BS 1941; DSc 1969; FRCP 1975. Vice-Pres., London Univ. Athletic Union, 1938; Pres., London Univ. Boat Club, 1939–40 (rowing purple 1938). Sharpey Physiol Schol., UCL, 1939–41; House Phys. and House Surg., UCH, 1941; House Phys., Brompton Hosp. for Diseases of Chest, 1941–42; Asst TB Officer, Chelsea, 1941–42; Exptl Officer, Min. of Supply, 1942–43; served RAFVR Med. Br. (Central Fighter Estabt), 1943–46; Lectr in Pharmacol., KCL, 1945–55; London Univ. Travelling Fellow, 1949–50; Fellow, Johns Hopkins Hosp. Med. Sch., 1949–50; Sen. Lectr and Head of Pharmacol. Dept, 1956, Reader, 1958, St Bartholomew's Hosp. Med. Coll. Gresham Prof. of Physic, 1967–68. Formerly Hon. Clinical Asst, St Bartholomew's Hosp. London University Convocation: Mem. Standing Cttee, 1966–74; Senator, Medicine, 1968–74; Chm., Trust, 1973–90; Mem. Ct and Senate, London Univ. Examiner in Pharmacol. and Clinical Pharmacol. to Univs of London, Edinburgh, Cambridge, Dundee, Liverpool, Manchester, TCD, NUI and Cardiff, also to Fac. of Anaesthetists and Apothecaries Soc. Mem., 1960–88, Dep. Chm., 1975–88, Gen. Optical Council; Gen. Sec., British Pharmacol Soc., 1968–71; British Medical Association: Mem. Council, 1971–85; Chairman: Med. Academic Staff Cttee, 1978, 1980, 1982; Bd of Sci. and Educn, 1982–85; Fellow, 1981; Vice-Pres., 1988. Member: CMO's Academic Forum, 1980–81; Academic Medicine Gp, RCP, 1982–. Member: IBA Advertising Adv. Cttee, 1984–92; Joint BBC/IBA Central Appeals Adv. Cttee, 1987–92. Crouch Harbour Authority: Mem., 1987; Vice-Chm., 1988; Chm., 1989–94; Mem., 1974, Chm., 1987–, Crouch Area Yachting Fedn; Associate Mem., Burnham Week Regatta Jt Clubs Cttee, 1984–. Trustee: City Parochial Foundn, 1977–89; Trust for London, 1986–89; Nat. Forum for Coronary Heart Disease Prevention, 1989– (Hon. Treas., 1990–94); Founder Trustee, 1984–, Chm., 1993–, Help the Hospices Trust (Co-Chm., 1984–93); Mem., Grants Council, Charities Aid Foundn, 1990–. Press Editor, British Jl of Pharmacol., 1957–60. *Publications: jointly:* Medical Effects of Nuclear War, 1983; Boxing, 1984; Young People and Alcohol, 1986; Long term environment effects of nuclear war, 1986; Alternative Therapy, 1986; The Torture Report, 1986; papers on visual purple, blood/acqueous humour barrier permability, intra-ocular fluid, DFP and synaptic transmission in heart and muscle, action drugs on the iris, the ocular critical flicker fusion frequency, the auditory flutter fusion frequency, the electro-pharmacology of sedatives, general anaesthetics on autonomic ganglia as a model of brain synapses, GABA-like actions on lobster muscle, effects of staphylococcal α-toxin on intestine, the ultrastructural effects in autonomic ganglia in the presence of chemical substances, World Medicine, University "Cuts" 1983. *Recreations:* work, sailing. *Address:* Hornbeams, 34 Totteridge Common, Totteridge, N20 8NE. *Club:* United Hospitals Sailing (Burnham-on-Crouch) (Cdre, 1974–).

QUILLIAM, Hon. Sir Peter; *see* Quilliam, Hon. Sir J. P.

QUILLIAM, Peter; *see* Quilliam, J. P.

QUILTER, Sir Anthony (Raymond Leopold Cuthbert), 4th Bt, *cr* 1897; landowner since 1959; *b* 25 March 1937; *s* of Sir (John) Raymond (Cuthbert) Quilter, 3rd Bt and Margery Marianne (*née* Cooke); *S* father 1959; *m* 1964, Mary Elise, *er d* of late Colonel Brian (Sherlock) Gooch, DSO, TD; one *s* one *d*. *Educ:* Harrow. Is engaged in farming. *Recreations:* shooting, golf. *Heir: s* Guy Raymond Cuthbert Quilter [*b* 13 April 1967; *m* 1992, Jenifer, *o d* of John Redvers-Cox]. *Address:* Sutton Hall, Sutton, Woodbridge, Suffolk IP12 3EQ. *T:* Shottisham (01394) 411246.

QUILTER, David (Cuthbert) Tudway; Vice Lord-Lieutenant of Somerset, since 1978; Local Director, Barclays Bank, Bristol, 1962–84 (Director, Barclays Bank UK Ltd, 1971–81); *b* 26 March 1921; *o s* of Percy Cuthbert Quilter and Clare Tudway; *m* 1953, Elizabeth Mary, *er d* of Sir John Carew Pole, 12th Bt, DSO, TD; one *s* two *d*. *Educ:* Eton. Served War of 1939–45, Coldstream Guards, 1940–46. Dir, Bristol Evening Post, 1982–91. JP London Juvenile Courts, 1959–62. Mayor of Wells, 1974–75; Chm. of Trustees, Wells Cathedral Preservation Trust, 1976–; Chm., Somerset Gardens Trust, 1991–; Treasurer, Bristol Univ., 1976–88; Governor, Wells Cathedral Sch., 1968–; Member: Council, Outward Bound Trust, 1959–92; Garden Soc., 1973–; Life Trustee, Carnegie UK Trust, 1981–. Master, Soc. of Merchant Venturers, 1984–85. DL 1970, High Sheriff 1974–75, Somerset. Hon. LLD Bristol, 1989. *Publications:* No Dishonourable Name, 1947; A History of Wells Cathedral School, 1985. *Recreations:* gardening, music, tennis, golf, shooting. *Address:* Milton Lodge, Wells, Somerset BA5 3AQ. *T:* Wells (01749) 672168. *Clubs:* Boodle's, Pratt's.

QUIN; *see* Wyndham-Quin, family name of **Earl of Dunraven.**

QUIN, Joyce Gwendolen; MP (Lab) Gateshead East, since 1987; *b* 26 Nov. 1944; *d* of Basil Godfrey Quin and Ida (*née* Ritson). *Educ:* Univ. of Newcastle upon Tyne (BA French, 1st Cl. Hons); Univ. of London (MSc Internat. Relns). Research Asst, Internat. Dept, Labour Party Headquarters, Transport House, 1969–72; Lecturer in French, Univ. of Bath, 1972–76; Resident Tutor, St Mary's Coll., and Lectr in French and Politics, Univ. of Durham, 1977–79. Mem. (Lab) European Parliament, S Tyne and Wear, 1979–84, Tyne and Wear, 1984–89. Opposition front bench spokesman on trade and industry, 1989–92, on employment, 1992–93, on European affairs, 1993–. Mem., Select Cttee on Treasury and Civil Service, 1987–89. Hon. Fellow: Sunderland Polytechnic, subseq. Univ. of Sunderland, 1986; St Mary's Coll., Durham Univ., 1994. *Publications:* various articles in newspapers and journals. *Recreations:* North-East local history (Newcastle upon Tyne City Guide), music, theatre, walking, cycling. *Address:* House of Commons, SW1A 0AA; (office) Old Bank, Swinburne Street, Gateshead, Tyne & Wear NE8 1AN. *T:* 0191–490 0117.

QUINCE, Peter; *see* Thompson, John W. McW.

QUINE, Prof. Willard Van Orman; American author; Professor of Philosophy, 1948, and Edgar Pierce Professor of Philosophy, 1956–78, Harvard University, now Emeritus Professor; *b* Akron, Ohio, 25 June 1908; *s* of Cloyd Robert and Hattie Van Orman Quine; *m* 1st, 1930, Naomi Clayton; two *d*; 2nd, 1948, Marjorie Boynton; one *s* one *d*. *Educ:* Oberlin Coll., Ohio (AB); Harvard Univ. (AM, PhD). Harvard: Sheldon Travelling Fellow, 1932–33 (Vienna, Prague, Warsaw); Jun. Fellow, Society of Fellows, 1933–36 (Sen. Fellow, 1949–78, Chairman, 1957–58); Instructor and Tutor in Philosophy, 1936–41; Assoc. Professor of Philosophy, 1941–48; Chairman, Dept of Philosophy, 1952–53. Visiting Professor, Universidade de São Paulo, Brazil, 1942. Lieut, then Lieut-Commander, USNR, active duty, 1942–46. Consulting editor, Journal of Symbolic Logic, 1936–52; Vice-President, Association for Symbolic Logic, 1938–40; President, 1953–55; Vice-President, Eastern Division, American Philosophical Assoc., 1950, President, 1957; Member: Amer. Philos. Soc., 1957– (Councillor, 1966–68, 1982–); Acad. Internat. de Philosophie de Science, 1960; Institut International de Philosophie, 1983–. FAAAS, 1945– (Councillor, 1950–53); Fellow, Nat. Acad. of Sciences, 1977–. Corres. Member: Instituto Brasileiro de Filosofia, 1963–; Institut de France, 1978–; Corres. Fellow: British Acad., 1959–; Norwegian Acad. of Scis, 1979–; Trustee, Institute for Unity of Science, 1949–56; Syndic, Harvard University Press: 1951–53; 1954–56, 1959–60, 1962–66. George Eastman Visiting Prof., Oxford Univ., 1953–54; Vis. Professor: Univ. of Tokyo, 1959; Rockefeller Univ., 1968; Collège de France, 1969. A. T. Shearman Lecturer, University of London, 1954; Gavin David Young Lectr in Philosophy, Univ. of Adelaide, 1959; John Dewey Lectr, Columbia Univ., 1968; Paul Carus Lectr, Amer. Philos. Assoc., 1971; Hägerström Lectr, Uppsala, 1973; Vis. Lectr, Calcutta, 1983. Member Institute for Advanced Study, Princeton, USA, 1956–57. Fellow: Centre for Advanced Study in the Behavioural Sciences, Palo Alto, California, 1958–59; Centre for Advanced Studies, Wesleyan Univ., Conn, 1965; Sir Henry Saville Fellow, Merton Coll., Oxford, 1973–74. Hon. degrees: MA Oxon, 1953; DLitt Oxon, 1970; LittD: Oberlin, 1955; Akron, 1965; Washington, 1966; Temple, 1970; Cambridge, 1978; Ripon, 1983; LLD: Ohio State, 1957; Harvard, 1979; DèsL Lille, 1965; LHD: Chicago, 1967; Syracuse, 1981; DPh: Uppsala, 1980; Berne, 1982; Granada, 1986. N. M. Butler Gold Medal, 1970; F. Polacky Gold Medal, Prague, 1991; Charles Univ. Silver Medal, 1993; R. Schock Prize, Sweden, 1993. *Publications:* A System of Logistic, 1934; Mathematical Logic, 1940, rev. edn 1951; Elementary Logic, 1941, rev. edn 1965; O sentido da nova logica, 1944 (São Paulo); Methods of Logic, 1950, rev. edn 1982; From a Logical Point of View, 1953, rev. edn 1961; Word and Object, 1960; Set Theory and its Logic, 1963, revised edn 1969; Ways of Paradox and Other Essays, 1966, rev. edn 1976; Selected Logic Papers, 1966, rev. edn 1995; Ontological Relativity and Other Essays, 1969; Philosophy of Logic, 1970; (with J. S. Ullian) The Web of Belief, 1970; The Roots of Reference, 1974; Theories and Things, 1981; The Time of My Life, 1985; (jtly) The Philosophy of W. V. Quine, 1986; La Scienza e i Dati di Senso, 1987; Quiddities, 1987; Pursuit of Truth, 1989; (jtly) Perspectives on Quine, 1989; The Logic of Sequences, 1990; From Stimulus to Science, 1995; contribs to Journal of Symbolic Logic; Journal of Philosophy; Philosophical Review; Mind; Rivista di Filosofia; Scientific American; NY Review of Books; Library of Living Philosophers. *Recreation:* travel. *Address:* 38 Chestnut Street, Boston, MA 02108, USA. *T:* (617) 7236754.

QUINLAN, Rt. Rev. Alan Geoffrey; A Bishop Suffragan, Diocese of Cape Town, since 1988; *b* 20 Aug. 1933; *s* of late Robert Quinlan and of Eileen Beatrice Quinlan; *m* 1963, Rosalind Arlen Sallie (*née* Reed); three *s* one *d*. *Educ:* Kelham Theological College. RAF, 1952–54. Deacon 1958, Priest 1959; Asst Curate, St Thomas's, Leigh, Lancs, 1958–61; Rector: St Margaret's, Bloemfontein, 1962–68; St Michael and All Angels, Sasolburg, OFS, 1968–72; Warden, Community of Resurrection, Grahamstown and Chaplain, Grahamstown Training Coll., 1972–76; Priest-in-Charge of Training in Ministries and Discipleship, Cape Town Diocese, 1976–80; Rector, All Saints, Plumstead, Cape Town, 1980–88. Canon, St George's Cathedral, Cape Town, 1980. *Publications:* A Manual for Worship Leaders; Discipleship and the Alternative Society; Church-wardens' Handbook. *Recreations:* chess, reading, bird-watching, computers, music. *Address:* 79 Kildare Road, Newlands, Cape Town, 7700, South Africa. *T:* (21) 642444.

QUINLAN, Maj.-Gen. Henry, CB 1960; *b* 5 Jan. 1906; *s* of Dr Denis Quinlan, LRCP, LRCS (Edinburgh), of Castletownroche, Co. Cork; *m* 1936, Euphemia Nancy, *d* of John Tallents Wynyard Brooke of Shanghai, and Altrincham, Cheshire; two *s* two *d*. *Educ:* Clongowes Wood Coll., Sallins, Co. Kildare. BDS 1926; FFD RCS (I) 1964. Royal Army Dental Corps; Lieut, 1927; Captain, Dec. 1930; Major, 1937; Lieut-Colonel, Dec. 1947; Colonel, 1953; Maj.-General, Oct. 1958; Director Army Dental Service, 1958–63; QHDS 1954–64, retired; Colonel Comdt Royal Army Dental Corps, 1964–71. Officer OStJ 1958. *Address:* White Bridges, Redlands Lane, Crondall, Hants GU10 5RF. *T:* Aldershot (01252) 850239.

QUINLAN, Sir Michael (Edward), GCB 1991 (KCB 1985; CB 1980); Director, Ditchley Foundation, since 1992; *b* 11 Aug. 1930; *s* of late Gerald and Roseanne Quinlan; *m* 1965, (Margaret) Mary Finlay; two *s* two *d*. *Educ:* Wimbledon Coll.; Merton Coll., Oxford. (1st Cl. Hon. Mods, 1st Cl. LitHum; MA; Hon. Fellow, 1989). RAF, 1952–54. Asst Principal, Air Ministry, 1954; Private Sec. to Parly Under-Sec. of State for Air, 1956–58; Principal, Air Min., 1958; Private Sec. to Chief of Air Staff, 1962–65; Asst Sec., MoD, 1968; Defence Counsellor, UK Delegn to NATO, 1970–73; Under-Sec., Cabinet Office, 1974–77; Dep. Under-Sec. of State (Policy), MoD, 1977–81; Dep. Sec. (Industry), HM Treasury, 1981–82; Perm. Sec., Dept of Employment, 1983–88; Perm. Under-Sec. of State, MoD, 1988–92. Chm., Civil Service Sports Council, 1985–89; Pres., CS Cricket Assoc., 1992–. Vis. Prof., KCL, 1992–. Director: Lloyds Bank, 1992–; Pilkington, 1992–. Trustee, Science Mus., 1992–. Governor, Henley Management Coll., 1983–88. Pres., Merton Soc., 1992–95. CIMgt (CBIM 1983). *Publications:* many articles on defence and public admin and ethics. *Recreations:* golf, watching cricket, listening to music. *Address:* c/o Ditchley Foundation, Ditchley Park, Enstone, Chipping Norton, Oxon OX7 4ER. *Clubs:* Royal Air Force, MCC.

QUINN, Andrew; Chief Executive, ITV, since 1992; *b* 29 March 1937. Granada TV, 1964–92: Gen. Manager, 1977; Man. Dir, Granada Cable and Satellite, 1983; Man. Dir, 1987; Chief Exec., 1992. *Address:* ITV, 200 Gray's Inn Road, WC1X 8HF.

QUINN, Brian; Executive Director, Bank of England, since 1988; *b* 18 Nov. 1936; *s* of Thomas Quinn and Margaret (*née* Cairns); *m* 1961, Mary Bradley; two *s* one *d*. *Educ:* Glasgow Univ. (MA Hons); Manchester Univ. (MA Econs); Cornell Univ. (PhD). Economist, African Dept, IMF, 1964–70, Rep., Sierra Leone, 1966–68; joined Bank of England, 1970; Economic Div., 1970–74; Chief Cashier's Dept, 1974–77; Head of Information Div., 1977–82; Asst Dir, 1982–88; Head of Banking Supervision, 1986–88. FRSA. *Publications:* (contrib.) Surveys of African Economies, vol. 4, 1971; (contrib.) The New Inflation, 1976; articles in learned jls. *Recreations:* fishing, golf, cycling. *Club:* Bankers'.

QUINN, Brian; *see* Quinn, J. S. B.

QUINN, Prof. David Beers, DLit (QUB), PhD (London), MRIA, FRHistS; Andrew Geddes and John Rankin Professor of Modern History, University of Liverpool, 1957–76; *b* 24 April 1909; *o s* of late David Quinn, Omagh and Belfast, and Albertina Devine, Cork; *m* 1937, Alison Moffat Robertson, MA, *d* of late John Ireland Robertson, Edinburgh; two *s* one *d*. *Educ:* Clara (Offaly) No 2 National Sch.; Royal Belfast Academical Institution; Queen's Univ., Belfast; King's Coll., University of London. University Schol., QUB, 1928–31 (1st Class Hons in Medieval and Modern History, 1931); PhD London, 1934. Asst Lecturer, 1934, and Lecturer, 1937, University College, Southampton; Lecturer in History, QUB, 1939–44; seconded to BBC European Service, 1943; Prof. of History, University College, Swansea, 1944–57; DLit (QUB), 1958. Secretary, Ulster Society for Irish Historical Studies, 1939–44; Member: Council of Hakluyt Society, 1950–54,

1957–60 (Vice-Pres., 1960–82, 1987–, Pres., 1982–87); Council of Royal Historical Society, 1951–55, 1956–60 (Vice-Pres., 1964–68, Hon. Vice-Pres., 1983); Fellow, Folger Shakespeare Lib. (Washington, DC), 1957, 1959, 1963–64; Fellow, John Carter Brown Lib., 1970, 1982; Leverhulme Res. Fellow, 1963; British Council Visiting Scholar, NZ, 1967; Hungary, 1972; Fellow, Huntington Library, 1980; Fellow, Nat. Inst. for the Humanities, 1983; Fulbright Fortieth Anniversary Dist. Fellow, 1986–87; Harrison Vis. Prof., Coll. of William and Mary, Williamsburg, Va, 1969–70; Visiting Professor: St Mary's Coll., St Mary's City, Md, 1976–78, 1980–82, 1984; Michigan Univ., 1979. Hon. Mem. American Historical Assoc., 1986. Hon. FBA 1984. Hon. DLitt: Newfoundland, 1964; New Univ. of Ulster, 1975; NUI, 1981; Hon. DHL: St Mary's Coll., 1978; Coll. of William and Mary, 1995; Hon. LLD Univ. of N Carolina, 1980. Hon. Phi Beta Kappa, 1984. *Publications:* The Port Books or Petty Customs Accounts of Southampton for the Reign of Edward IV, 2 vols, 1937–38; The Voyages and Colonising Enterprises of Sir Humphrey Gilbert, 2 vols, 1940; Raleigh and the British Empire, 1947; The Roanoke Voyages, 1584–90, 2 vols, 1955; (with Paul Hulton) The American Drawings of John White, 1577–1590, 1964; (with R. A. Skelton) R. Hakluyt's Principall Navigations (1589), 1965; The Elizabethans and the Irish, 1966; Richard Hakluyt, Editor, 1967; North American Discovery, 1971; (with W. P. Cumming and R. A. Skelton) The Discovery of North America, 1972; (with N. M. Cheshire) The New Found Land of Stephen Parmenius, 1972; (with A. M. Quinn) Virginia Voyages from Hakluyt, 1973; England and the Discovery of America 1481–1620, 1974; The Hakluyt Handbook, 2 vols, 1974; (with W. P. Cumming, S. E. Hillier and G. Williams) The Exploration of North America, 1630–1776, 1974; The Last Voyage of Thomas Cavendish, 1975; North America from First Discovery to Early Settlements, 1977; (with A. M. Quinn and S. Hillier) New American World, 5 vols, 1979; Early Maryland and a Wider World, 1982; (with A. M. Quinn) The First Settlers, 1982; (with A. M. Quinn) English New England Voyages 1602–1608, 1983; (with A. N. Ryan) England's Sea Empire, 1550–1642, 1983; Set Fair for Roanoke, 1985; (ed) John Derricke, The Image of Ireland, 1986; contrib. to A New History of Ireland, vol. 2, ed A. Cosgrove, 1987; Raleigh and Quinn: the explorer and his Boswell, ed H. G. Jones, 1988; Explorers and Colonies: America 1500–1625, 1990; Ireland and America 1500–1640, 1991; Thomas Harriot and the Problem of America, 1992; (ed with A. M. Quinn) Richard Hakluyt, Discourse of Western Planting, 1994; contribs on Irish history and the discovery and settlement of N America in historical journals. *Address:* 9 Knowsley Road, Cressington Park, Liverpool L19 0PF. *T:* 0151–427 2041.

QUINN, James Aiden O'Brien; QC (Seychelles) 1973; Adjudicator, since 1990, and Special Adjudicator, Immigration Appeals (part-time Adjudicator, 1990–92); part-time legal member, Immigration Appeals Tribunal, 1995; *b* 3 Jan. 1932; *s* of late William Patrick Quinn (Comr, Gárda Siochána) and Helen Mary (*née* Walshe); *m* 1960, Christel Tyner; two *s* one *d. Educ:* Presentation Coll., Bray, Co. Wicklow, Ireland; University Coll., Dublin, NUI (BA, LLB Hons). Called to the Bar: Kings' Inns, Dublin, 1957; Inner Temple, 1967. National City Bank, Dublin, 1949–53; in practice at the Bar, under Colonial Office Scheme, 1958–60; Crown Counsel and Actg Sen. Crown Counsel, Nyasaland, 1960–64; Asst Attorney Gen. and Actg Attorney Gen., West Cameroon, 1964–66; Procureur Général, West Cameroon, and Avocat Général, Fed. Republic of Cameroon, 1966–68; Fed. Republic of Cameroon, 1968–72: Conseiller, Cour Fédérale de Justice; Judge, W Cameroon Supreme Court; Conseiller Technique (Harmonisation des Lois), Ministère de la Justice, Yaoundé; Président, Tribunal Administratif, Cameroun Occidental; Chargé de Cours, Ecole Nationale de l'Administration et de la Magistrature, Yaoundé; Republic of Seychelles: Attorney Gen., also of British Indian Ocean Territory, 1972–76; MLC, MEC and Mem. Parlt, 1972–76; Chief Justice, 1976–77; Actg Dep. Governor, 1974; Mem., Official Delegn on Self-Govt, 1975, and on Independence Constitutions, 1976; collab. with Prof. A. G. Chloros on translation and up-dating of Code Napoleon, 1975–76; Chm., Judicial Service Commn, 1976–77; Gilbert Islands (Kiribati): Chief Justice, 1977–81; Chm., Judicial Service Commn, 1977–81; set up new Courts' system, 1978; Mem., Council of State, 1979–81; Judge, High Court of Solomon Is, 1977–79; Special Prosecutor, Falkland Is, 1981; Botswana: Chief Justice, 1981–87; Chm., Judicial Service Commn, 1981–87; retired, 1987–89; Investment Advr, 1989–90. Mem., Panel of Experts of UN on Prevention of Crime and Treatment of Offenders, 1985–87. Chevalier, Ordre de la Valeur, Republic of Cameroon, 1967; Kiribati Independence Medal, 1979. *Publications:* Magistrates' Courts Handbook: West Cameroon, 1968; Kiribati, 1979; edited: West Cameroon Law Reports, 1961–68; Gilbert Islands Law Reports, 1977–79; Kiribati Law Reports, 1977–79; articles in Commonwealth Law Jl, The Magistrate, etc. *Recreations:* languages, travel, reading, swimming. *Address:* 9 Lorane Court, Langley Road, Watford, Herts WD1 3LZ. *Clubs:* Commonwealth Trust, Royal Over-Seas League.

QUINN, James Charles Frederick; film producer and exhibitor; Chairman, The Minema, 1984–94; *b* 23 Aug. 1919; *y s* of Rev. Chancellor James Quinn and Muriel Alice May (*née* MaGuire); *m* 1942, Hannah, 2nd *d* of Rev. R. M. Gwynn, BD (Sen. Fellow and Vice-Provost, TCD), and Dr Eileen Gwynn; one *s* one *d. Educ:* Shrewsbury Sch.; TCD (Classical Exhibnr); Christ Church, Oxford (MA; Dip. in Econ. and Polit. Sci.). Served War, Irish Guards, Italy, NW Europe; British Army Staff, France, and Town Major, Paris, 1945–46. Courtaulds Ltd, 1949–55. Dir, BFI, 1955–64: National Film Theatre built, London Film Festival inaugurated, 1st Univ. Lectureship in Film Studies in UK estabd at Slade Sch. of Fine Art, University Coll., London and BFI's terms of ref. enld to incl. television. Council of Europe Fellowship, 1966. Chairman: Internat. Short Film Conf., 1971–78 (Life Pres., 1979); National Panel for Film Festivals, 1974–83. Member: Gen. Adv. Council, BBC, 1960–64; Bd, Gardner Arts Centre, Sussex Univ., 1968–71; British Council Film Television and Video Adv. Cttee, 1983–90. Trustee: Imperial War Museum, 1968–78; Grierson Meml Trust, 1975–; Nat. Life Story Collection, 1986–91. Invited to stand by New Ulster Movement as Indep. Unionist Parly candidate, S Down, 1968. Foreign Leader Award, US State Dept, 1962. Films: co-producer, Herostratus, 1966; Producer, Overlord, 1975. Silver Bear Award, Berlin Internat. Film Festival, 1975; Special Award, London Evening News British Film Awards, 1976. Chevalier de l'Ordre des Arts et des Lettres, France, 1979. *Publications:* Outside London, 1965; The Film and Television as an Aspect of European Culture, 1968; contrib. Chambers's Encyclopaedia (cinema), 1956–59. *Recreations:* lawn tennis; formerly Eton Fives. *Address:* Crescent Cottage, 108 Marine Parade, Brighton, E Sussex BN2 1AT. *Clubs:* Cavalry and Guards; Vincent's (Oxford).

QUINN, (James Steven) Brian; Director, since 1985, Chairman, since 1992, Digital Computer Services (Chief Executive, 1989–92); *b* 16 June 1936; *s* of James and Elizabeth Quinn; *m* 1962, Blanche Cecilia James; two *s* one *d. Educ:* St Mary's Coll., Crosby; Waterpark Coll., Ireland; University Coll., Dublin (BCL, LLB). Kings Inn, Dublin. Director: Johnson Radley, 1966–68; United Glass Containers, 1968–69; Head of Industrial Activities, Prices and Incomes Board, 1969–71; Dir, M. L. H. Consultants, 1971–79; Corporate Develt Advr, Midland Bank Internat., 1977–80; Chief Industrial Advr, Price Commn, 1977–78. Chairman: BrightStar Communications, 1983–85; BAJ Holdings, 1985–87; Harmer Holbrook, 1987–88; Man. Dir, Visnews, 1980–86; Dir, Telematique Services, 1985–. Institute of Management (formerly British Institute of Management): CIMgt (CBIM 1985; FBIM 1978); Mem. Council, 1981–87, 1990–; Mem. Finance Cttee, 1981–84; Chm., City of London Branch, 1981–83; Vice Pres., 1983–; Chm., Gtr London Regl Council, 1990–. International Institute of Communications: Trustee, 1982–88, 1992–; Chm., Exec. Cttee, 1984–88; Pres., 1988–91. Mem., Exec. Cttee, Inst. of European Trade and Technology, 1983–. Trustee: Internat. Center of Communications, San Diego State Univ., 1990–. Chm., Finance Cttee, Great Japan Exhbn, 1979–82. Chm., Editl Bd, Professional Manager. *Recreations:* golf, reading, veteran vehicles. *Address:* Craiglea House, Austenwood Lane, Gerrards Cross, Bucks SL9 9DA. *Club:* Athenæum.

QUINN, Dame Sheila (Margaret Imelda), DBE 1987 (CBE 1978); FHSM; FRCN; President, Royal College of Nursing, 1982–86; *b* 16 Sept. 1920; *d* of late Wilfred Amos Quinn and Ada Mazella (*née* Bottomley). *Educ:* Convent of Holy Child, Blackpool; London Univ. (BScEcon Hons); Royal Lancaster Infirmary (SRN 1947); Birmingham (SCM); Royal Coll. of Nursing, London (RNT). FHSM 1971; FRCN 1978. Admin. Sister, then Principal Sister Tutor, Prince of Wales' Gen. Hosp., London, 1950–61; Internat. Council of Nurses, Geneva: Dir, Social and Econ. Welfare Div., 1961–66; Exec. Dir, 1967–70; Chief Nursing Officer, Southampton Univ. Hosps, 1970–74; Area Nursing Officer, Hampshire AHA (Teaching), 1974–78; Regional Nursing Officer, Wessex RHA, 1978–83. Member: E Dorset DHA, 1987–90; Dorset FHSA, 1990–. Nursing Advr, BRCS, 1983–88. Pres., Standing Cttee of Nurses of EEC, 1983–91; Member: Council, Royal Coll. of Nursing, 1971–79 (Chm. Council, 1974–79; Dep. Pres., 1980–82); Bd of Dirs, Internat. Council of Nurses, 1977–85 (first Vice-Pres., 1981–85); Mem., EEC Adv. Cttee on Trng in Nursing, 1978–90. Hon. DSc (Social Sciences) Southampton, 1986. *Publications:* Nursing in The European Community, 1980; Caring for the Carers, 1981; ICN Past and Present, 1989; Nursing, the EC Dimension, 1993; articles, mainly on internat. nursing and EEC, in national and internat. jls. *Recreations:* travel, gardening. *Address:* 31 Albany Park Court, Winn Road, Southampton SO17 1EN. *T:* Southampton (01703) 676592. *Clubs:* New Cavendish, St John's House, Royal Society of Medicine.

QUINN, Terence James; Editor, Daily Record, since 1994; *b* 17 Nov. 1951; *s* of Thomas Quinn and Shirley (*née* Anderson); *m* 1973, Patricia Anna-Maria Gillespie; one *s* one *d* (and one *s* decd). *Educ:* St Aloysius Coll., Glasgow. Editor: Telegraph & Argus, Bradford, 1984–89; Evening News, Edinburgh, 1989–92; Dep. Editl Dir, 1992–94; Editl Dir, 1994, Thomson Regl Newspapers. *Recreations:* tennis, reading, newspapers. *Address:* c/o Daily Record, Anderston Quay, Glasgow G3 8DA. *T:* 0141–248 7000.

QUINNEN, Peter John; Chairman, Frew Macmaster, since 1990; Director, Gold Greenlees Trott, since 1994; *b* 4 April 1945; *s* of John Norman Quinnen and Elisabeth Clark; *m* 1972, Pammy Urquhart; two *s. Educ:* St Benedict's School, Ealing; Christ Church, Oxford (MA Jurisp). FCA. Peat, Marwick, Mitchell & Co., 1966–72; James Capel & Co., 1972–90, Dir, 1982, Chm., and Chief Exec., 1986–90. *Recreations:* golf, opera, music, ballet, sport. *Clubs:* Royal Automobile; Royal Mid-Surrey Golf, St George's Hill, Wednesday Golf.

QUINTON, family name of **Baron Quinton.**

QUINTON, Baron *cr* 1982 (Life Peer), of Holywell in the City of Oxford and County of Oxfordshire; **Anthony Meredith Quinton,** FBA 1977; Chairman of the Board, British Library, 1985–90; *b* 25 March 1925; *s* of late Richard Frith Quinton, Surgeon Captain, RN, and late Gwenllyan Letitia Quinton; *m* 1952, Marcelle Wegier; one *s* one *d. Educ:* Stowe Sch.; Christ Church, Oxford (St Cyres Scholar; BA 1st Cl. Hons PPE 1948). Served War, RAF, 1943–46: flying officer and navigator. Fellow: All Souls Coll., Oxford, 1949–55; New Coll., Oxford, 1955–78 (Emeritus Fellow, 1980); Pres., Trinity Coll., Oxford, 1978–87 (Hon. Fellow, 1987). Delegate, OUP, 1970–76. Mem., Arts Council, 1979–81; Vice Pres., British Acad., 1985–86. Visiting Professor: Swarthmore Coll., Pa, 1960; Stanford Univ., Calif, 1964; New Sch. for Social Res., New York, 1976–77; Brown Univ., 1994. Lecturer: Dawes Hicks, British Acad., 1971; Gregynog, Univ. of Wales, Aberystwyth, 1973; T. S. Eliot, Univ. of Kent, Canterbury, 1976; Robbins, Univ. of Stirling, 1987; Hobhouse, LSE, 1988; Tanner, Warsaw, 1988; R. M. Jones, QUB, 1988; Carter, Lancaster, 1989. President: Aristotelian Soc., 1975–76; Soc. for Applied Philosophy, 1988–91; Royal Inst. of Philosophy, 1990–; Assoc. of Indep. Libraries, 1991–; Friends of Wellcome Inst., 1992–. Chm., Kennedy Meml Trust, 1990–. Governor, Stowe Sch., 1963–84 (Chm. Governors, 1969–75); Fellow, Winchester Coll., 1970–85. DHumLit NY Univ., 1987; DHum Ball State Univ., 1990. Order of Leopold II, Belgium, 1984. *Publications:* Political Philosophy (ed), 1967; The Nature of Things, 1973; Utilitarian Ethics, 1973; (trans.) K. Ajdukiewicz (with H. Skolimowski) Problems and Theories of Philosophy, 1973; The Politics of Imperfection, 1978; Francis Bacon, 1980; Thoughts and Thinkers, 1982. *Recreations:* sedentary pursuits. *Address:* A11 Albany, Piccadilly, W1V 9RD; Mill House, Turville, Henley-on-Thames, Oxford RG9 6QL. *Club:* Garrick.

QUINTON, Sir John (Grand), Kt 1990; Chairman: Barclays Bank PLC, 1987–92 (Deputy Chairman, 1985–87); Football Association Premier League, since 1992; Metropolitan Police Committee, since 1995; *b* 21 Dec. 1929; *s* of William Grand Quinton and Norah May (*née* Nunn); *m* 1954, Jean Margaret Chastney; one *s* one *d. Educ:* Norwich Sch.; St John's Coll., Cambridge (MA 1954); FCIB (FIB 1964). Joined Barclays Bank, 1953: Manager, King's Cross, 1965; seconded to Min. of Health as Principal, Internat. Div. and UK Deleg., World Health Assembly, 1966; Asst Gen. Manager, 1968; Local Dir, Nottingham, 1969; Reg. Gen. Manager, 1971; Gen. Manager, 1975; Dir and Sen. Gen. Man., 1982–84; Vice-Chm., 1985. Dep. Chm., Mercantile Credit Co. Ltd, 1975–79; non-exec. Chm., Wimpey PLC, 1993–95; non-exec. Dir, Norwich and Peterborough BS, 1993–. Chairman: Chief Exec. Officers, Cttee of London Clearing Bankers, 1982–83; Adv. Council, London Enterprise Agency, 1986–90; Office of the Banking Ombudsman, 1987–92; Cttee of London and Scottish Bankers, 1989–91. Member: City Capital Markets Cttee, 1981–86; NE Thames RHA, 1974–87; Accounting Standards Cttee, 1982–85; Econ. and Financial Policy Cttee, CBI, 1985–88 (Chm., 1987–88). Chm., Motability Finance Ltd, 1978–85; Treasurer, Chartered Inst. of Bankers, 1980–86 (Pres., 1989–90); Hon. Treas. and Bd Mem., Business in the Community, 1986–91. Chairman: British Olympic Appeal, 1988; Royal Anniversary Trust Appeal, 1992. Trustee: Royal Acad. Trust, 1987–93; Westminster Abbey Trust, 1991–; Thrombosis Res. Inst., 1993–; Chm. Bd of Trustees, Botanic Gdns Conservation Internat. Pres., East of England Show, 1992. Governor: Motability, 1985–; Ditchley Foundn, 1987–92; Member: Court of Governors, Royal Shakespeare Theatre, 1986–; Court, Henley Coll., 1987–92. FRSA 1988. *Recreations:* gardening, music, golf. *Address:* Chenies Place, Chenies, Bucks WD3 6EU. *Club:* Reform.

QUIRK, family name of **Baron Quirk.**

QUIRK, Baron *cr* 1994 (Life Peer), of Bloomsbury in the London Borough of Camden; **Charles Randolph Quirk,** Kt 1985; CBE 1976; FBA 1975; President, British Academy, 1985–89; Fellow of University College London; *b* 12 July 1920; *s* of late Thomas and Amy Randolph Quirk, Lambfell, Isle of Man; *m* 1st, 1946, Jean (marr. diss. 1979; she *d* 1995), *d* of Ellis Gauntlett Williams; two *s*; 2nd, 1984, Gabriele, *d* of Judge Helmut Stein. *Educ:* Cronk y Voddy Sch.; Douglas High Sch., IOM; University College London. MA, PhD, DLit London. Served RAF, 1940–45. Lecturer in English, University College

London, 1947–54; Commonwealth Fund Fellow, Yale Univ. and University of Michigan, 1951–52; Reader in English Language and Literature, University of Durham, 1954–58; Professor of English Language in the University of Durham, 1958–60, in the University of London, 1960–68; Quain Prof. of English Language and Literature, University Coll. London, 1968–81; Vice-Chancellor, Univ. of London, 1981–85. Dir, Survey of English Usage, 1959–81. Member: Senate, Univ. of London, 1970–85 (Chm., Acad. Council, 1972–75); Ct, Univ. of London, 1972–85; Bd, British Council, 1983–91; BBC Archives Cttee, 1975–81; RADA Council, 1985–. President: Inst. of Linguists, 1982–85; Coll. of Speech Therapists, 1987–91; North of England Educn Conf., 1989; Vice-Pres., Foundn for Science and Technology, 1986–90; Governor: British Inst. of Recorded Sound, 1975–80; E-SU, 1980–85; Richmond Coll., London, 1981–; City Technology Colls, 1986–. Chairman: Cttee of Enquiry into Speech Therapy Services, 1969–72; Hornby Educnl Trust, 1979–; Anglo-Spanish Foundn, 1983–85; British Library Adv. Cttee, 1984–; Vice-Chm., English Language Cttee, E-SU, 1985–. Trustee: Wolfson Foundn, 1987–; American Sch. in London, 1987–89; Royal Comr, 1851 Exhibn, 1987–. Mem., Academia Europaea, 1988. Foreign Fellow: Royal Belgian Acad. of Scis, 1975; Royal Swedish Acad., 1987; Finnish Acad. of Scis, 1991. Hon. FCST; Hon. FIL; Hon. Fellow: Imperial Coll., 1985; QMC, 1986; Goldsmiths' Coll., 1987; King's Coll., 1990; RHBNC, 1990. Hon. Bencher, Gray's Inn, 1982. Hon. Fil. Dr Lund and Uppsala; Hon. DU: Essex; Bar Ilan; Brunel; DUniv Open; Hon. DHC: Liège; Paris; Hon. DLitt: Reading; Newcastle upon Tyne; Durham; Bath; Salford; California; Sheffield; Glasgow; Poznan; Nijmegen; Richmond Coll.; Hon. DCL Westminster; Hon. LLD: Leicester; London; Hon. DSc Aston. Jubilee Medal, Inst. of Linguists, 1973. *Publications:* The Concessive Relation in Old English Poetry, 1954; Studies in Communication (with A. J. Ayer and others), 1955; An Old English Grammar (with C. L. Wrenn), 1955, enlarged edn (with S. E. Deskis), 1994; Charles Dickens and Appropriate Language, 1959; The Teaching of English (with A. H. Smith), 1959, revised edn, 1964; The Study of the Mother-Tongue, 1961; The Use of English (with Supplements by A. C. Gimson and J. Warburg), 1962, enlarged edn, 1968; Prosodic and Paralinguistic Features in English (with D. Crystal), 1964; A Common Language (with A. H. Marckwardt), 1964; Investigating Linguistic Acceptability (with J. Svartvik), 1966; Essays on the English Language—Mediaeval and Modern, 1968; (with S. Greenbaum) Elicitation Experiments in English, 1970; (with S. Greenbaum, G. Leech, J. Svartvik) A Grammar of Contemporary English, 1972; The English Language and Images of Matter, 1972; (with S. Greenbaum) A University Grammar of English, 1973; The Linguist and the English Language, 1974; (with V. Adams, D. Davy) Old English Literature: a practical introduction, 1975; (with J. Svartvik) A Corpus of English Conversation, 1980; Style and Communication in the English Language, 1982; (with S. Greenbaum, G. Leech, J. Svartvik) A Comprehensive Grammar of the English Language, 1985; (with H. Widdowson) English in the World, 1985; Words at Work: lectures on textual structure, 1986; (with G. Stein) English in Use, 1990; (with S. Greenbaum) A Student's Grammar of the English Language, 1990; (with G. Stein) An Introduction to Standard English, 1993; Grammatical and Lexical Variance in English, 1995; contrib. to: conf. proceedings and volumes of studies; papers in linguistic and literary journals. *Address:* University College London, Gower Street, WC1E 6BT. *T:* 0171–387 7050. *Club:* Athenæum.

QUIRK, John Stanton S.; *see* Shirley-Quirk.

R

RABAN, Jonathan, FRSL; author; *b* 14 June 1942; *s* of Rev. Peter J. C. P. Raban and Monica (*née* Sandison); *m* 1985, Caroline Cuthbert (marr. diss. 1992); *m* 1992, Jean Lenihan; one *d*. *Educ:* Univ. of Hull (BA Hons English). FRSL 1975. Lecturer in English and American Literature: UCW, Aberystwyth, 1965–67; Univ. of E Anglia, 1967–69; professional writer, 1969–. *Publications:* The Technique of Modern Fiction, 1969; Mark Twain: Huckleberry Finn, 1969; The Society of the Poem, 1971; Soft City, 1973; Arabia Through the Looking Glass, 1979; Old Glory, 1981 (Heinemann Award, RSL, 1982; Thomas Cook Award, 1982); Foreign Land, 1985; Coasting, 1986; For Love and Money, 1987; God, Man & Mrs Thatcher, 1989; Hunting Mister Heartbreak, 1990 (Thomas Cook Award, 1991); (ed) The Oxford Book of the Sea, 1992. *Recreation:* sailing. *Address:* c/o Aitken & Stone Ltd, 29 Fernshaw Road, SW10 0TG. *Clubs:* Groucho, Cruising Association; Shilshole Bay Yacht (Seattle).

RABBI, The Chief; *see* Sacks, Rabbi Dr J. H.

RABBITTS, Dr Terence Howard, FRS 1987; Member, Scientific Staff, since 1973, Joint Head of Protein and Nucleic Acid Division, since 1988, MRC Laboratory of Molecular Biology, Cambridge; *b* 17 June 1946; *s* of Joan and Frederick Rabbitts; *m* 1984, Pamela Gage; one *d*. *Educ:* John Ruskin Grammar School; Univ. of East Anglia (BSc); Nat. Inst. for Medical Research (PhD). Research Fellow, Dept of Genetics, Univ. of Edinburgh, 1971–73. Colworth Medal, 1981, Ciba Medal and Prize, 1993, Biochemical Soc. *Publications:* papers in scientific jls. *Address:* MRC Laboratory of Molecular Biology, Hills Road, Cambridge CB2 2QH. *T:* Cambridge (01223) 248011.

RABIN, Prof. Brian Robert; Professor of Biochemistry, 1988–93, now Emeritus, Fellow since 1984, University College, London; *b* 4 Nov. 1927; *s* of Emanuel and Sophia Rabin, both British; *m* 1954; one *s* one *d*. *Educ:* Latymer Sch., Edmonton; University Coll., London. BSc 1951, MSc 1952, PhD 1956. University College, London: Asst Lectr, 1954–57; Lectr, 1957–63; Reader, 1963–67; Prof. of Enzymology, 1967–70; Hd of Dept of Biochemistry, 1970–88. Rockefeller Fellow, Univ. of California, 1956–57. Founder Dir, London Biotechnology Ltd, 1985–. *Publications:* numerous in Biochem. Jl, European Jl of Biochem., Nature, Proc. Nat. Acad. Sciences US, etc. *Recreations:* travel, listening to music, carpentry. *Address:* 34 Grangewood, Potters Bar, Herts EN6 1SL. *T:* Potters Bar (01707) 654576. *Club:* Athenæum.

RABIN, Yitzhak; Prime Minister and Minister of Defence, Israel, since 1992; *b* Jerusalem, 1 March 1922; *m* Lea Schlossberg; one *s* one *d*. *Educ:* Staff Coll., England; Kedoorie Coll., Israel. Palmach Bde, 1941–48, incl. War of Independence; rep. Israel Defence Forces at Rhodes armistice negotiations; Israel Defence Forces: Head, Trng Dept, 1953–56; C-in-C, Northern Comd, 1956–59; Dep. COS and Chief of Ops Br., 1959–63; Maj.-Gen.; COS, 1964–68; Ambassador to USA, 1968–73. Mem., Knesset, 1974–; Chm., Labour Party, 1974–77; Minister of Labour, 1974; Prime Minister, 1974–77; Minister of Defence, 1984–90. Hon. PhD. (Jtly) Nobel Peace Prize, 1994. *Publication:* Service Notebook: the Rabin memoirs, 1979. *Address:* c/o Prime Minister's Office, Jerusalem, Israel.

RABINOVITCH, Prof. Benton Seymour, FRS 1987; Professor of Chemistry, University of Washington, Seattle, 1957–86, now Emeritus; *b* 19 Feb. 1919; *s* of Samuel Rabinovitch and Rachel Schachter; *m* 1st, 1949, Marilyn Werby; two *s* two *d*; 2nd, 1980, Flora Reitman. *Educ:* McGill Univ. (BSc, PhD). Served Canadian Army overseas, Captain, 1942–46. Milton Fellow, Harvard Univ., 1946–48; University of Washington: Asst Prof., 1948–53; Associate Prof., 1953–57. Guggenheim Fellow, 1961–62. Fellow, Amer. Acad. of Arts and Scis. Hon. DSc Technion, Haifa, 1991. Sigma Xi Dist. Res. Award, 1981; Peter Debye Award, ACS, 1984; Michael Polanyi Medal, RSC, 1984. *Publications:* Physical Chemistry, 1964; Antique Silver Servers, 1990; (ed) annual reviews Phys. Chem., 1975–85; over 200 contribs to jls. *Recreation:* silversmithing. *Address:* Department of Chemistry BG–10, University of Washington, Seattle, WA 98195, USA. *T:* (206) 5431636.

RABINOWITZ, Harry, MBE 1977; freelance conductor and composer; *b* 26 March 1916; *s* of Israel and Eva Rabinowitz; *m* 1944, Lorna Thurlow Anderson; one *s* two *d*. *Educ:* Athlone High Sch., S Africa; Witwatersrand Univ.; Guildhall Sch. of Music. Conductor, BBC Radio, 1953–60; Musical Dir, BBC TV Light Entertainment, 1960–68; Head of Music, LWT, 1968–77; freelance film, TV, radio and disc activities, 1977–. Conductor: Cats, New London Th., 1981; Song and Dance, Palace Th., 1982; Hollywood Bowl Concerts, 1983 and 1984; Boston "Pops" concerts, 1985, 1986, 1988–92; concerts with RPO, LSO and London Concert Orch.; *films:* conductor: La Dentellière, 1977; Mon Oncle d'Amérique, 1980; The Time Bandits, 1980; Chariots of Fire, 1981; Heat and Dust, 1982; The Missionary, 1983; Electric Dreams (actor/conductor), 1984; The Bostonians, 1984; Return to Oz, Lady Jane Grey, and Revolution—1776, 1985; F/X, and Manhattan Project, 1986; Masters of the Universe, Maurice, 1987; Simon Wiesenthal, Camille Claudet, 1988; Shirley Valentine (jt composer/conductor), Queen of Hearts, 1989; Music Box, Lord of the Flies, La Fille des Collines, 1990; Jalousie, La Tribu, Jesuit Joe, Iran Day of Crisis, Ballad of the Sad Café, J'embrasse pas, Pour Sascha, 1991; Howards End, The Ark and the Flood, 1992; The Remains of the Day, Taxi de Nuit, Moonfish, Petite Apocalypse, 1993; Grosse Fatigue, The Flemish Board, Mantegna & Sons, 1994; Jefferson in Paris, 1995; Jenny et Mr Arnaud, 1995; *television:* composer-conductor: Agatha Christie Hour, 1982; Reilly Ace of Spies, 1983; Glorious Day, 1985; Land of the Eagle, 1990; D. W. Griffiths Father of Film, Memento Mori, 1993; Project Ayrton Senna, 1995. Gold Badge of Merit, British Acad. of Songwriters, Composers and Authors, 1985; award for lifetime contribution to Wavendon Allmusic, 1990. *Recreations:* listening to others making music, gathering edible fungi, wine tasting. *Address:* Yellow Cottage, Walking Bottom, Peaslake, Surrey GU5 9RR. *T:* Dorking (01306) 730605.

RACE, (Denys Alan) Reg; management and policy consultant; *b* 23 June 1947; *s* of Denys and Elsie Race. *Educ:* Sale Grammar School; Univ. of Kent. BA (Politics and Sociology), PhD (Politics). Senior Research Officer, National Union of Public Employees, 1972. MP (Lab) Haringey, Wood Green, 1979–83; Head of Programme Office, GLC, 1983–86; Special Res. Officer, ACTT, 1986; County Dir, Derbys County Council, 1988. Advr, Health Policy Adv. Unit, 1989–93; Partner, Quality Health management consultants, 1993–. *Publications:* The Challenge Now (report on management and organisation of ACTT), 1986; numerous pamphlets and articles in Labour Movement press.

RACE, Ruth Ann; *see* Sanger, Dr R. A.

RACE, Steve, (Stephen Russell Race), OBE 1992; broadcaster, musician and author; *b* Lincoln, 1 April 1921; *s* of Russell Tinniswood Race and Robina Race (*née* Hurley); *m* 1st, Marjorie Clair Leng (*d* 1969); one *d*; 2nd, Léonie Rebecca Govier Mather. *Educ:* Lincoln Sch. (now Christ's Hospital Sch.); Royal Academy of Music. FRAM 1978. Served War, RAF, 1941–46; free-lance pianist, arranger and composer, 1946–55; Light Music Adviser to Associated-Rediffusion Ltd, 1955–60; conductor for many TV series incl. Tony Hancock and Peter Sellers Shows. Appearances in radio and TV shows include: My Music, A Good Read, Jazz in Perspective, Any Questions?, Music Now, Music Weekly, Kaleidoscope, Musician at Large, Captain Pepper's Autograph Album, Jazz Revisited, With Great Pleasure, Desert Island Discs, Steve Race Presents the Radio Orchestra Show, Gershwin Among Friends, Irving Berlin Among Friends, The Two Worlds of Joseph Race; radio reviews in The Listener, 1975–80; long-playing records and commentary for Nat. Gall., London, Glasgow Art Gall. and Nat. Mus. of Wales, 1977–80. Dep. Chm., PRS, 1973–76. Member: Council, Royal Albert Hall of Arts and Scis, 1976–95; Exec. Council, Musicians' Benevolent Fund, 1985–. FRSA 1975. Freeman, City of London, 1982. Governor of Tokyo Metropolis Prize for Radio, 1979; Wavendon Allmusic Media Personality of the Year, 1987; Radio Prog. of the Year, TV and Radio Industries Club Awards, 1988; Gold Badge of Merit for services to British music, BASCA, 1991. *Principal compositions:* Nicola (Ivor Novello Award); Faraway Music; The Pied Piper; incidental music for Richard The Third, Cyrano de Bergerac, Twelfth Night (BBC); Cantatas: Song of King David; The Day of the Donkey; Song of Praise; My Music—My Songs; misc. works incl. ITV advertising sound-tracks (Venice Award, 1962; Cannes Award, 1963); film scores include: Calling Paul Temple, Three Roads to Rome, Against The Tide, Land of Three Rivers. *Publications:* Musician at Large: an autobiography, 1979; My Music, 1979; Dear Music Lover, 1981; Steve Race's Music Quiz, 1983; You Can't be Serious, 1985; The Penguin Masterquiz, 1985; With Great Pleasure, 1986; The Two Worlds of Joseph Race, 1988; (contrib.) The Illustrated Counties of England, 1984; contribs to DNB, Punch, Literary Review, Times, Daily Telegraph, Daily Mail, Independent, Listener, Country Living. *Recreations:* avoiding smokers, studying art history, walking in the woods. *Address:* Martins End Lane, Great Missenden, Bucks HP16 9HS.

RACEY, Prof. Paul Adrian, FRSE; FIBiol; Regius Professor of Natural History, University of Aberdeen, since 1993; *b* 7 May 1944; *s* of Albert and Esme Racey; *m* 1968, Anna Priscilla Notcutt; three *s*. *Educ:* Ratcliffe Coll.; Downing Coll. Cambridge (MA); London Univ. (PhD); Univ. of Aberdeen (DSc). FIBiol 1987; FRSE 1992. Rothamsted Experimental Station, 1965–66; Zoological Soc. of London, 1966–71; Res. Fellow, Univ. of Liverpool, 1971–73; University of Aberdeen: Lectr and Sen. Lectr in Zoology, 1973–85; Prof. of Zoology, 1985–. Chairman: Chiroptera Specialist Gp, IUCN Species Survival Commn, 1986–; Bat Conservation Trust, 1990–; Member: Management Cttee, Scottish Univs Res. and Reactor Centre, 1991– (Mem. Sci. Adv. Bd, 1986–); Council, Fauna & Flora Preservation Soc., 1990– (Chm., Conservation Cttee, 1993–); Bd of Govs, Macaulay Land Use Res. Inst., 1990–; Terrestrial and Freshwater Sci. Cttee, NERC, 1991–94; Exec. Cttee, Mammal Soc., 1991–; Res. Bd, 1992, 1994, Scientific Adv. Cttee, 1994–, Scottish Natural Heritage; former appts with Scottish Examn Bd; NCC for Scotland; NERC. *Publications:* numerous res. papers in professional jls. *Recreations:* riding, sailing, walking, farming. *Address:* Chapelhouses, Oldmeldrum, AB51 OAW. *T:* Oldmeldrum (01651) 872769. *Club:* Commonwealth Trust.

RADCLIFFE, Anthony Frank, FSA; Keeper Emeritus, Victoria and Albert Museum, since 1990; *b* Wivenhoe, Essex, 23 Feb. 1933; *s* of Dr Walter Radcliffe and Murielle Laure Radcliffe (*née* Brée); *m* 1960, Enid Clair Cawkwell; two *s*. *Educ:* Oundle Sch.; Gonville and Caius Coll., Cambridge (MA). Victoria and Albert Museum: joined Dept of Circulation, 1958; transferred to Dept of Architecture and Sculpture, 1960; Res. Asst, Dept of Circulation, 1961–67; Asst to Dir, 1967–74; Asst Keeper, Dept of Architecture and Sculpture, 1974–79; Keeper of Sculpture, 1979–89; Head of Res., 1989–90. Mellon Sen. Vis. Curator, Nat. Gall. of Art, Washington, 1990; Guest Scholar, J. Paul Getty Mus., 1991, 1995; Samuel H. Kress Prof., CASVA, Nat. Gall. of Art, Washington, 1993–94. Medal, Accademia delle Arti del Disegno, Florence, 1986. *Publications:* European Bronze Statuettes, 1966; Jean-Baptiste Carpeaux, 1968; (with J. Pope-Hennessy and T. Hodgkinson) The Frick Collection: an illustrated catalogue, III, IV, 1970; (with C. Avery) Giambologna, sculptor to the Medici, 1978; (with M. Baker and M. Maek Gérard) The Thyssen-Bornemisza Collection: Renaissance and later sculpture, 1992; The Robert H. Smith Collection: Bronzes 1500–1650, 1994; contribs to Burlington Mag., Apollo, Connoisseur, etc. *Address:* Shirley Cottage, 5 Kennylands Road, Sonning Common, Reading RG4 9JR. *T:* Kidmore End (01734) 722182.

RADCLIFFE, Francis Charles Joseph; *b* 23 Oct. 1939; *s* of Charles Joseph Basil Nicholas Radcliffe and Norah Radcliffe (*née* Percy); *m* 1968, Nicolette, *e d* of Eugene Randag; one *s* two *d*. *Educ:* Ampleforth Coll.; Gonville and Caius Coll., Cambridge (MA). Called to the Bar, Gray's Inn, 1962; a Recorder of the Crown Court, 1979. Mem., Assoc. of Lawyers for the Defence of the Unborn. Contested (Christian: stop abortion candidate)

York, 1979; founded York Christian Party, 1981. *Recreations:* shooting, beagling, gardening, etc. *Address:* 11 King's Bench Walk, Temple, EC4Y 7EQ.

RADCLIFFE, Sir Sebastian Everard, 7th Bt *cr* 1813; *b* 8 June 1972; *s* of Sir Joseph Benedict Everard Henry Radcliffe, 6th Bt, MC and of Marcia Anne Helen (who *m* 1988, H. M. S. Tanner), *y d* of Major David Turville Constable Maxwell, Bosworth Hall, Husbands Bosworth, Rugby; *S* father, 1975. *Heir: cousin* Mark Hugh Joseph Radcliffe [*b* 22 April 1938; *m* 1963, Anne, twin *d* of Maj.-Gen. Arthur Evers Brocklehurst, *qv*; three *d*]. *Address:* Le Château de Cheseaux, 1033 Cheseaux, Vaud, Switzerland.

RADCLIFFE, Most Rev. Timothy Peter Joseph, OP; Master of the Order of Preachers (Dominicans), since 1992; *b* 22 Aug. 1945; 3rd *s* of late Hugh John Reginald Joseph Radcliffe, MBE. *Educ:* Downside; St John's College, Oxford (MA; Hon. Fellow, 1993). Entered Dominican Order, 1965; Chaplain to Imperial Coll., 1976–78; taught theology at Blackfriars, Oxford, 1978–88; Prior of Blackfriars, 1982–88; Faculty of Theology, Oxford Univ., 1985–88; Provincial of the English Province, OP, 1988–92. John Toohey Schol. in Residence, Sydney Univ., 1984. Grand Chancellor: Pontifical Univ. of St Thomas (Angelicum), Rome, 1992–; Univ. of Santo Tomas, Manilla, 1992–; Theol. Faculty, Fribourg, 1992–. Pres., Conf. of Major Religious Superiors, 1991–. Chm. Editl Bd, New Blackfriars, 1983–88. Hon. STD Providence Coll., RI, 1993. *Publications:* articles in books and periodicals. *Recreations:* walking and talking with friends, reading Dickens. *Address:* Convento di S Sabina, Piazza Pietro d'Illiria 1, Aventino, 00153 Rome, Italy. *T:* (6) 57941.

See also Sir S. E. Radcliffe, Bt.

RADDA, Prof. George Karoly, CBE 1993; MA, DPhil; FRS 1980; British Heart Foundation Professor of Molecular Cardiology, since 1984, and Head of Department of Biochemistry, since 1991, University of Oxford; Professorial Fellow, Merton College, Oxford, since 1984; Hon. Director, Medical Research Council Unit of Biochemical and Clinical Magnetic Resonance, since 1988; *b* 9 June 1936; *s* of Dr Gyula Radda and Dr Anna Bernolak; *m* 1st, 1961, Mary O'Brien (marr. diss. 1995); two *s* one *d*; 2nd, 1995, Sue Bailey. *Educ:* Pannonhalma, Hungary; Eötvös Univ., Budapest, Hungary; Merton Coll., Oxford (BA Cl. 1, Chem., 1960; DPhil 1962). Res. Associate, Univ. of California, 1962–63; Lectr in Organic Chemistry, St John's Coll., Oxford, 1963–64; Fellow and Tutor in Organic Chem., Merton Coll., Oxford, 1964–84; University Lectr in Biochem., Oxford Univ., 1966–84. Vis. Prof., Cleveland Clinic, 1987. Medical Research Council: Mem. Council, 1988–92; Chm., Cell Biology and Disorders Bd, 1988–92; Chm., Human Genome Directed Programme Cttee, 1992–; Member of Council: Royal Soc., 1990–92; ICRF, 1991– (Chm., Scientific Adv. Cttee, 1994–). Mem., various Editorial Bds of scientific jls including: Editor, Biochemical and Biophysical Research Communications, 1977–85; Man. Editor, Biochimica et Biophysica Acta, 1977–94 (Chm. Editl Bd, 1989–94). Founder Mem., Oxford Enzyme Gp, 1970–86; Pres., Soc. for Magnetic Resonance in Medicine, 1985–86. Mem., Fachbeirat, Max Planck Inst. für Systemphysiologie, Dortmund, 1987–93. Fellow, Soc. of Magnetic Resonance, 1994. Hon. FRCR 1985; Hon. MRCP 1987; Hon. Fellow, Amer. Heart Assoc., 1988. Hon. DM Bern, 1985; Hon. DSc (Med) London, 1991. Colworth Medal, Biochem. Soc., 1969; Feldberg Prize, Feldberg Foundn, 1982; British Heart Foundn Prize and Gold Medal for cardiovascular research, 1982; CIBA Medal and Prize, Biochem. Soc., 1983; Gold Medal, Soc. for Magnetic Resonance in Medicine, 1984; Buchanan Medal, Royal Soc., 1987; Internat. Lectr and Citation, Amer. Heart Assoc., 1987; Skinner Lecture and Medal, RCR, 1989; Rank Prize in Nutrition, 1991. *Publications:* articles in books and in jls of biochemistry and medicine. *Recreations:* opera, swimming, jazz. *Address:* Merton College, Oxford; Department of Biochemistry, Oxford University, South Parks Road, Oxford OX1 3QU. *T:* Oxford (01865) 275272.

RADEGONDE, Sylvestre Louis; Ambassador of The Seychelles to EEC and Belgium, since 1993, concurrently to Germany, The Netherlands and Luxembourg; *b* 16 March 1956. *Educ:* Seychelles Coll.; Polytechnic of Central London (MA Diplomatic Studies). Seychelles Police Force, 1974–85; Dir, Nat. Council for Children, 1985–86; Personnel Manager, Seychelles Hotels, 1986–87; Chief of Protocol and Desk Officer for Americas, Min. Planning and Ext. Relns, 1987–89; Counsellor and Actg High Comr, 1989–92, High Comr, 1992–93, London. *Recreations:* cooking, swimming. *Address:* Seychelles Embassy, 157 Boulevard du Jubile, 1210 Brussels, Belgium. *T:* (2) 4256236.

RADER, Gen. Paul Alexander; General of the Salvation Army, since 1994; *b* 14 March 1934; *s* of Lt-Col Lyell Rader and Gladys (*née* Damon); *m* 1956, (Frances) Kay Fuller; one *s* two *d*. *Educ:* Asbury Coll. and Seminary, USA (BA, BD); Southern Baptist Seminary (MTh); Fuller Theol Seminary (DMiss). Salvation Army: trng work in Korea, 1962–73; Trng Principal, 1973; Educn Sec., 1974–76; Asst Chief Sec., 1976, Chief Sec., 1977–84, Korea; Trng Principal, USA Eastern Territory, 1984–87; Divl Comdr, 1987–89; Chief Sec., 1989; Territorial Comdr, USA Western, 1989–94. Hon. LLD Asbury Coll., USA, 1984. *Recreations:* jogging, reading, music. *Address:* 101 Queen Victoria Street, EC4P 4EP. *T:* 0171–236 5222.

RADFORD, (Courtenay Arthur) Ralegh, FBA 1956; *b* 7 Nov. 1900; *o s* of late Arthur Lock and Ada M. Radford; unmarried. *Educ:* St George's School, Harpenden; Exeter College, Oxford. BA 1921; MA 1937; Inspector of Ancient Monuments in Wales and Monmouthshire, 1929–34; Director of the British School at Rome, 1936–39; Member of Royal Commission on Ancient Monuments in Wales and Monmouthshire, 1935–46; Member of Royal Commission on Historical Monuments (England), 1953–76; supervised excavations at Tintagel, Ditchley, Castle Dore, the Hurlers, Whithorn, Glastonbury, Birsay and elsewhere; FSA 1928 (Vice-Pres. 1954–58; Gold Medal, 1972); FRHistS 1930; President: Prehistoric Soc., 1954–58; Roy. Archæological Inst., 1960–63; Cambrian Archæological Assoc., 1961; Soc. of Medieval Archæology, 1969–71. Hon. DLitt Glasgow, 1963; Univ. of Wales, 1963; Exeter, 1973; *Publications:* Reports on the Excavations at Tintagel, Ditchley, Whithorn, etc.; various articles on archæological subjects. *Address:* Culmcott, Uffculme, Devon EX15 3AT. *Club:* Athenæum.

RADFORD, Joseph; Public Trustee, 1978–80; *b* 7 April 1918; *s* of Thomas Radford and Elizabeth Ann Radford (*née* Sanders); *m* 1976, Rosemary Ellen Murphy. *Educ:* Herbert Strutt, Belper; Nottingham Univ. Admitted solicitor, 1940. First Cl. Hons, Law Soc. Intermediate, 1937; Dist., Law Soc. Final, 1940. Served War, 1940–47, RA; 41st (5th North Staffordshire) RA; 1st Maritime Regt, RA; Staff, MELF (Major). Joined Public Trustee Office, 1949; Chief Admin. Officer, 1973–75; Asst Public Trustee, 1975–78. Mem., Law Soc., 1945– (Hon. Auditor, 1963–65). Freeman, City of London, 1983. Silver Jubilee Medal, 1977. *Address:* 80 Cunningham Park, Harrow, Mddx HA1 4QJ.

RADFORD, Prof. Peter Frank, PhD; Executive Chairman, British Athletic Federation, since 1994; *b* 20 Sept. 1939; *s* of Frank Radford and Lillian E. Radford (*née* Marks); *m* 1961, Margaret M. (*née* Beard); one *d*. *Educ:* Tettenhall Coll.; Cardiff Coll. of Educn (Dip. of Physical Educn); Purdue Univ., USA (MSc); Univ. of Glasgow (PhD 1978). Mem., GB Athletics Teams, 1958–64: held British 100m record, 1958–78; World Records: Jun. 100m and Jun. 200m, 1958; Indoor 50m, 1959; 200m, 1960; 4 × 110 yards Relay, 1963; Bronze Medals, 100m and 4 × 100m Relay, Olympic Games, Rome, 1960. Lectr and Asst Prof., Sch. of Physical Educn and Athletics, McMaster Univ., 1967–75; University of Glasgow: Professor and Head of Departments of: Physical Educn and Recreation, 1976–87; Physical Educn and Sports Sci., 1987–94. Vice-Chm., 1992–93, Chm., 1993–94, British Athletic Fedn Sports Council: Mem., 1983–90; Mem., 1988–91, Chm., 1991–95, Drug Adv. Gp; Chm., Rev. of Coaching in Sport, 1991–93. Mem., Internat. Wkg Gp on Anti-Doping in Sport, 1991–93; Vice-Chm., 1992–94, Chm., 1994–95, Internat. Doping Convention, Council of Europe. *Publications:* contrib. to various jls, conf. proc. and books on topics of sport, educn, sports science, sports history and doping control. *Recreations:* sports history 1650–1850, 18th and 19th century sporting art, gardening. *Address:* Athletics House, 225A Bristol Road, Edgbaston, Birmingham B5 7UB. *T:* 0121–440 5000.

RADFORD, Ralegh; *see* Radford, C. A. R.

RADFORD, Robert Edwin, CB 1979; Assistant Director General, St John Ambulance Association, 1981–84; Deputy Secretary and Principal Finance Officer, Department of Health and Social Security, 1977–81; *b* 1 April 1921; *s* of late Richard James Radford and late May Eleanor Radford (*née* Briant); *m* 1945, Eleanor Margaret, *d* of late John Idwal Jones; one *s* one *d*. *Educ:* Royal Grammar Sch., Guildford. Board of Educn, 1938. Served War, Lieut, RNVR, 1940–46. Colonial Office: Asst Principal, 1947; Private Sec. to Permanent Under-Sec. of State for the Colonies, 1950–51; Principal, 1951; First Sec., UK Commn, Singapore, 1961–63; Asst Sec., Dept of Techn. Co-op., 1963; transferred to ODM, 1964; Counsellor, British Embassy, Washington, and UK Alternate Exec. Dir, IBRD, 1965–67; Under Secretary: FCO (ODA), 1973; DHSS, 1974–76. Mem., SW Surrey HA, 1982–89. *Recreations:* walking, reading. *Address:* 10 Edgeborough Court, Upper Edgeborough Road, Guildford, Surrey GU1 2BL. *T:* Guildford (01483) 61822.

RADICE, Edward Albert, CBE 1946; *b* 2 Jan. 1907; *s* of C. A. Radice, ICS and Alice Effie (*née* Murray), DSc (Econ); *m* 1936, Joan Keeling (*d* 1991); one *s* one *d*. *Educ:* Winchester Coll.; Magdalen Coll., Oxford (1st in Maths Mods; 1st in Lit. Hum.; DPhil). Commonwealth Fund Fellow, Columbia Univ., New York, 1933–35; Assistant Professor of Economics, Wesleyan University, Middletown, Conn., 1937–39; League of Nations Secretariat, 1939; Ministry of Economic Warfare, 1940–44; HM Foreign Service, 1945–53; Min. of Defence, 1953–70 (Dir of Economic Intelligence, 1966–70); Senior Research Fellow, St Antony's Coll., Oxford, 1970–73. *Publications:* (jt) An American Experiment, 1936; Fundamental Issues in the United States, 1936; Savings in Great Britain, 1922–35, 1939; (contrib.) Communist Power in Europe 1944–1949, 1977; (jtly, also co-ed) The Economic History of Eastern Europe 1919–1975, Vols I and II, 1986; papers in Econometrica, Oxford Economic Papers, Economic History Review. *Address:* 2 Talbot Road, Oxford OX2 8LL. *T:* Oxford (01865) 515573.

See also I. de L. Radice.

RADICE, Giles Heneage; MP (Lab) Durham North, since 1983 (Chester-le-Street, March 1973–1983); *b* 4 Oct. 1936. *Educ:* Winchester; Magdalen Coll., Oxford. Head of Research Dept, General and Municipal Workers' Union (GMWU), 1966–73. Front Bench Spokesman on foreign affairs, 1981, on employment, 1981–83, on education, 1983–87; Mem., Treasury and Civil Service Select Cttee, 1987–. Mem., Council, Policy Studies Inst., 1978–83. Vice Chm., British Assoc. for Central and Eastern Europe, 1991–; Chm., European Movt, 1995–. Parly Fellow, St Antony's Coll., Oxford, 1994–95. *Publications:* Democratic Socialism, 1965; (ed jointly) More Power to People, 1968; (co-author) Will Thorne, 1974; The Industrial Democrats, 1978; (co-author) Socialists in Recession, 1986; Labour's Path to Power: the new revisionism, 1989; Offshore: Britain and the European idea, 1992; The New Germans, 1995. *Recreations:* reading, tennis. *Address:* 58A Dartmouth Park Road, NW5 1SN.

RADICE, Italo de Lisle, CB 1969; Secretary and Comptroller General, National Dept Office, 1969–76; Appointed Member, Royal Patriotic Fund Corporation, 1969–91; *b* 2 March 1911; *s* of Charles Albert Radice, ICS, and Alice Effie (*née* Murray); *m* 1st, 1935, Betty Dawson (*d* 1985); three *s* (and one *d* decd); 2nd, 1993, Marie Guise, SRCh. *Educ:* Blundell's School; Magdalen College, Oxford (demy). Admitted Solicitor, 1938, Public Trustee Office, 1939; Military Government East and North Africa, Italy, and Germany, 1941–46; Treasury, 1946, Under-Secretary, 1961–68; Dir, Central Trustee Savings Bank Ltd, 1976–80. Comr for Income Tax, City of London, 1972–86. Cavaliere Ufficiale dell'Ordine al Merito (Italy), 1981. *Address:* Flat 2, Hamilton Terrace, NW8 9QS. *T:* 0171–624 3785.

See also E. A. Radice.

RADJI, Parviz Camran; diplomat; Ambassador of Iran to the Court of St James's, 1976–79; *b* 1936; *m* 1986, Golgoun Partovi. *Educ:* Trinity Hall, Cambridge (MA Econs). National Iranian Oil Co., 1959–62; Private Sec. to Minister of Foreign Affairs, 1962–65; Private Sec. to Prime Minister, subseq. Personal Asst, 1965–72; Special Adviser to Prime Minister, 1972–76. *Publication:* In the Service of the Peacock Throne: the diaries of the Shah's last Ambassador to London, 1983. *Address:* 21 Pembroke Gardens, W8 6HT.

RADLEY-SMITH, Eric John, MS; FRCS; Surgeon: Royal Free Hospital, London; Brentford Hospital; Epsom Hospital; Neurosurgeon, Royal National Throat, Nose and Ear Hospital. *Educ:* Paston; King's College, London; King's College Hospital. MB, BS (Hons, Distinction in Medicine, Surgery, Forensic Medicine and Hygiene), 1933; MS, London, 1936; LRCP, 1933; FRCS 1935 (MRCS 1933). Served War of 1939–45, Wing Comdr i/c Surgical Div. RAFVR. Formerly: Surgical Registrar, King's Coll. Hosp.; House Surgeon, National Hosp. for Nervous Diseases, Queen Square. Examnr in Surgery, Univs of London and West Indies. Mem. Court, RCS. Mem. Assoc. of British Neurosurgeons; Fellow, Assoc. of Surgeons of Great Britain. *Publications:* papers in medical journals. *Recreations:* football and farming.

RADNOR, 8th Earl of, *cr* 1765; **Jacob Pleydell-Bouverie;** Bt 1713–14; Viscount Folkestone, Baron Longford, 1747; Baron Pleydell-Bouverie, 1765; *b* 10 Nov. 1927; *e s* of 7th Earl of Radnor, KG, KCVO, and Helen Olivia, *d* of late Charles R. W. Adeane, CB; *S* father, 1968; *m* 1st, 1953, Anne (marr. diss. 1962), *d* of Donald Seth-Smith, Njoro, Kenya and Whitsbury Cross, near Fordingbridge, Hants; two *s*; 2nd, 1963, Margaret Robin (marr. diss. 1985), *d* of late Robin Fleming, Catter House, Drymen; four *d*; 3rd, 1986, Mary Jillean Gwenellan Pettit. *Educ:* Harrow; Trinity Coll., Cambridge (BA Agriculture). *Heir: s* Viscount Folkestone, *qv*. *Address:* Longford Castle, Salisbury, Wilts SP5 4EF. *T:* Salisbury (01722) 411515.

RADZINOWICZ, Sir Leon, Kt 1970; MA, LLD; FBA 1973; Fellow of Trinity College, Cambridge, since 1948; Wolfson Professor of Criminology, University of Cambridge, 1959–73, and Director of the Institute of Criminology, 1960–72; Associate Fellow, Silliman College, Yale, since 1966; Adjunct Professor of Law and Criminology, Columbia Law School, 1966–75; *b* Poland, 15 Aug. 1906; *m* 1st, 1933, Irene Szereszewski (marr. diss., 1955); 2nd, 1958, Mary Ann (marr. diss. 1979), *d* of Gen. Nevins, Gettysburg, Pa, USA; one *s* one *d*; 3rd, 1979, Isolde Klarmann, *d* of late Prof. Emil and Elfriede Doernenburg, and *widow* of Prof. Adolf Klarmann, Philadelphia; naturalised British subject, 1947. *Educ:* Cracow, Paris, Geneva and Rome. University of Paris, 1924–25; Licencié en Droit, Univ. of Geneva, 1927; Doctor of Law, Rome, 1928; LLD Cambridge, 1951.

Lectr, Univ. of Geneva, 1928–31; Doctor of Law, Cracow, 1929; Reported on working of penal system in Belgium, 1930; Lectr, Free Univ. of Warsaw, 1932–36. Came to England on behalf of Polish Ministry of Justice to report on working of English penal system, 1938; Asst Dir of Research, Univ. of Cambridge, 1946–49; Dir, Dept of Criminal Science, Univ. of Cambridge, 1949–59; Walter E. Meyer Research Prof. of Law, Yale Law Sch., 1962–63; Adj. Prof. in Law of Criminology, Columbia Law Sch, 1964–74; Visiting Professor: Virginia Law Sch., 1968–75; Rutgers Univ., 1968–72, 1979–81; Univ. of Pennsylvania, 1970–73; John Jay Coll., CUNY, 1978–79; Benjamin Cardozo Law Sch., Yeshiva Univ., 1979–81; Univ. of Minnesota Law Sch., 1979; Overseer, Pennsylvania Law Sch. and Associate Trustee, Pennsylvania Univ., 1978–82. Mem., Conseil de Direction de l'Assoc. Intern. de Droit Pénal, Paris, 1947–; Vice-Pres. Internat. Soc. of Social Defence, 1956–; Head of Social Defence Section, UN, New York, 1947–48. Member: Roy. Commn on Capital Punishment, 1949–53; Advisory Council on the Treatment of Offenders, Home Office, 1950–63; Adv. Council on the Penal System, Home Office, 1966–74; Jt Chm., Second UN Congress on Crime, 1955; Chief Rapporteur, 4th UN Congress on Crime, Kyoto, 1970; Chm. Sub-Cttee on Maximum Security in Prisons, 1967–68; Mem. Advisory Coun. on the Penal System, 1966–74; first Pres., Brit. Acad. of Forensic Sciences, 1960–61, Hon. Vice-Pres., 1961–; First Chm. Council of Europe Sci. Cttee, Problems of Crime, 1963–70; Mem. Royal Commn on Penal System in Eng. and Wales, 1964–66; Consultant: Ford Foundn and Bar Assoc., NYC, on teaching and res. in criminol., 1964–65; President's Nat. Commn on Violence, Washington, 1968–69; Min. of Justice, NSW, and Nat. Inst. of Criminology, Canberra, 1973; Hon. Vice-Chm., Fifth UN Congress on Crime, Geneva, 1975; Hon. Vice-Pres., British Soc. of Criminology, 1978. For. Hon. Mem., Amer. Acad. of Arts and Sciences, 1973; Hon. Mem., Amer. Law Inst., 1981; Hon. Fellow, Imperial Police Coll., 1968. Hon. LLD: Leicester, 1965; Edinburgh, 1988. James Barr Ames Prize and Medal, Faculty of Harvard Law School, 1950; Bruce Smith Sr award, Amer. Acad. Criminal Justice Sciences, 1976; Sellin-Glueck Award, Amer. Assoc. of Criminology, 1976. Coronation Medal, 1953. Chevalier de l'Ordre de Léopold, Belgium, 1930. *Publications:* Sir James Fitzjames Stephen (Selden Soc. Lect.), 1957; In Search of Criminology, 1961 (Italian edn 1965; French edn 1965; Spanish edn 1971); The Need for Criminology, 1965; Ideology and Crime (Carpentier Lectures), 1966, (Italian edn 1968); The Dangerous Offender (Frank Newsam Memorial Lecture), 1968; History of English Criminal Law, Vol. I, 1948 (under auspices of Pilgrim Trust), Vols II and III, 1956, Vol. IV, 1968 (under auspices of Rockefeller Foundation), Vol. V (with R. Hood), 1986 (under auspices of Home Office and MacArthur Foundn); (ed with Prof. M. E. Wolfgang) Crime and Justice, 3 vols, 1971, 2nd edn 1977; (with Joan King) The Growth of Crime, 1977 (trans. Italian, 1981); (with R. Hood) Criminology and the Administration of Criminal Justice: a Bibliography (Joseph L. Andrews Award, Amer. Assoc. of Law Libraries 1977), 1976; The Cambridge Institute of Criminology: the background and scope, 1988; The Roots of the International Association of Criminal Law and their Significance, 1991; (ed) English Studies in Criminal Science, now Cambridge Studies in Criminology, 52 vols (Vols I–VII with J. W. C. Turner); numerous articles in English and foreign periodicals. *Address:* Trinity College, Cambridge CB2 1TQ; Rittenhouse Claridge, Apt 2416, Rittenhouse Square, Philadelphia, PA 19103, USA. *Club:* Athenæum.

RAE, Allan Alexander Sinclair, CBE 1973; Chairman, CIBA-GEIGY PLC, 1972–90; *b* 26 Nov. 1925; *s* of John Rae and Rachel Margaret Sinclair; *m* 1st, 1955, Sheila Grace (*née* Saunders) (*d* 1985); two *s* one *d*; 2nd, 1986, Gertrud (*née* Dollinger). *Educ:* Ayr Acad.; Glasgow Univ. LLB. Admitted Solicitor, 1948. Served Army, RA then JAG's Dept (Staff Captain), 1944–47. Partner, 1950, Sen. Partner, 1959, Crawford Bayley & Co., Bombay (Solicitors); Dir and Hd of Legal and Patents Dept, CIBA Ltd, Basle, 1964, Mem. Management Cttee, 1969; Mem. Exec. Cttee, CIBA-GEIGY Ltd, Basle and Chm., CIBA-GEIGY Gp of Cos in UK, 1972–90; Chm., Ilford Ltd, 1972–88; Director: The Clayton Aniline Co. Ltd, 1965–90 (Chm., 1965–87); CIBA-GEIGY Chemicals Ltd, 1965–90 (Chm., 1965–87); Gretag Ltd (formerly Gretag-CX Ltd), 1978–89 (Chm. 1978–87); ABB Power Ltd (formerly British Brown-Boveri Ltd), 1973–89; T & N plc (formerly Turner & Newall PLC), 1979–94; Brown Boveri Kent (Hldgs) Ltd, 1980–94; Mettler Instruments Ltd, 1985–89; Riggs AP Bank Ltd (formerly AP Bank Ltd), 1986–91. Internat. Consultant, Loxleys, Solicitors, 1990–. Member of Council: Chemical Industries Assoc., 1976–91 (Pres., 1986–88); CBI, 1980–; British Swiss Chamber of Commerce, 1965– (Pres., 1969–72). Vice-Chm., Business and Industry Adv. Cttee to OECD, 1986–94. *Recreations:* sailing, golf, ski-ing. *Address:* Bryn Dulas House, Llanddulas, Clwyd LL22 8NA. *Clubs:* Buck's; Royal Thames Yacht.

RAE, Barbara Davis, RSA 1992 (ARSA 1980); RSW 1975; RGI; artist; Lecturer in Drawing and Painting, Glasgow School of Art, since 1975; *b* 10 Dec. 1943; *d* of James Rae and Mary (*née* Young); *m* twice; one *s*. *Educ:* Morrison's Acad., Crieff; Edinburgh Coll. of Art (Dip.; Postgrad. Travelling Schol.); Moray House Coll. of Education. Art Teacher: Ainsley Park Comprehensive, Edinburgh, 1968–69; Portobello Secondary Sch., Edinburgh, 1969–72; Lectr in Drawing, Painting and Printmaking, Aberdeen Coll. of Educn, 1972–75; exchange teacher, Fine Art Dept, Univ. of Md, 1984. Member: Art Panel, CNAA, 1986–93; Bd of Friends, Royal Scottish Acad.; Royal Fine Art Commn for Scotland, 1995–; Trustee, Arts Educnl Trust, 1986–90. Mem., SSA (Pres., 1983); Mem. Council, RSW, 1986–90, Vice-Pres. (E), 1991–. Solo exhibitions include: New '57 Gall., Edinburgh, 1967, 1971; Univ. of York, 1969; Univ. of Aberdeen and Aberdeen Art Gall., 1974; Peterloo Gall., Manchester, 1975; Stirling Gall. and Greenock Arts Guild, 1976; Univ. of Edinburgh, 1978, 1979; Gilbert Parr Gall., London, 1977; Scottish Gall., Edinburgh, 1979, 1983, 1987, 1988, 1990, 1995; Wright Gall., Dallas, 1988; Leinster Fine Art, London, 1986; Glasgow Print Studio, 1987, 1992; Scottish Gall., London, 1989, 1990; Wm Jackson Gall., London, 1990, 1992; Perth Mus. and Art Gall., 1991; Clive Jennings Gall., London, 1992; Gorgensen Fine Art, Dublin, 1993, 1995; Edinburgh Festival, 1995; touring exhibn, Scotland and Leeds, 1993–94; numerous gp exhibitions in Britain, Europe, USA, S America and Australia; works in public and private collections in Britain, Europe and America; tapestry commissioned for Festival Theatre, Edinburgh, 1994. Awards: Arts Council, 1968; Major Arts Council, 1975–81; Guthrie Medal, RSA, 1977; May Marshall Brown, RSW Centenary Exhibn, 1979; RSA Sir Wm Gillies Travel, 1983; Calouste Gulbenkian Printmaking, 1983; Alexander Graham Munro, RSW, 1989; Hunting Gp Prizewinner, 1990; Scottish PO Bd, RSA, 1990; Scottish Amicable, RGI, 1990; W. J. Burness, Royal Scottish Acad., 1990. *Recreations:* collecting art deco china and patchwork quilts. *Address:* Glasgow School of Art, 167 Renfrew Street, Glasgow G3 6RQ. *T:* 0141–353 4500; c/o Art First, 9 Cork Street, W1X 1PD. *Club:* Glasgow Art.

RAE, Gordon Hamilton; Director General, Royal Horticultural Society, since 1993; *b* 12 Sept. 1938; *s* of Peter and Gwendoline Elizabeth Rae; *m* 1965, Judith Elizabeth Pickup; one *s* two *d*. *Educ:* Bablake Sch., Coventry; Wye Coll., Univ. of London (BSc Agric. Hons); Clare Coll., Cambridge (Dip. Agric.); Imperial Coll. of Tropical Agric., Trinidad (DTA). Agricl and Dist Agricl Officer, HM Colonial Service, Kenya, 1962–65; ICI, 1965–93: Gen. Manager, Agricl Chemicals Div., ICI do Brasil, São Paulo, 1980–84; Gen. Manager, ICI Garden and Professional Products, 1989–92. *Recreations:* gardening, fly fishing, photography. *Address:* New House, Church Lane, Grayshott, Hindhead, Surrey GU26 6LY. *T:* Hindhead (01428) 606025.

RAE, Henry Edward Grant, JP; Lord Provost, City of Aberdeen, 1984–88; Lord Lieutenant, City of Aberdeen, 1984–88; *b* 17 Aug. 1925; *s* of late James and Rachel Rae; *m* 1955, Margaret Raffan Burns; one *d*. *Educ:* Queen's Cross School, Aberdeen; Ruthrieston School, Aberdeen. Chairman: Aberdeen Dist Cttee, TGWU, 1969–82; Grampian and Northern Isles Dist Cttee, 1982–85. Councillor, Aberdeen City Council, 1974–96 (Convener, Libraries Cttee, 1977–80, Manpower Cttee, 1980–84). JP Aberdeen 1984 (Chm., Justices' Cttee). OStJ 1987. *Address:* 78 Thistle Court, Aberdeen AB1 1ST. *T:* Aberdeen (01224) 630201.

RAE, Dr John; Business Development Director, since 1993, Director, National Environmental Technology Centre, since 1994, AEA Technology; *b* 29 Sept. 1942; *s* of late John Rae and of Marion Rae (*née* Dow); *m* 1968, Irene (*née* Cassells); one *s* one *d*. *Educ:* Rutherglen Academy; University of Glasgow (BSc 1964, PhD 1967). FInstE 1987. Lecturing and research in physics: Univ. of Glasgow, 1967–68; Univ. of Texas, 1968–70; Univ. Libre, Brussels, 1970–72; Queen Mary College London, 1972–74; Theoretical Physics Div., Harwell: Industrial Fellow, 1974–76; Leader, Theory of Fluids Group, 1976–85; Acting Div. Head, 1985; Chief Scientist, Dept of Energy, 1986–89; Chief Exec., AEA Envmt & Energy, 1990–93. Member: SERC, 1986–89; NERC, 1986–89. *Publications:* scientific papers in professional jls. *Recreations:* music, especially singing; gardening, astronomy. *Address:* AEA Technology, E4 Culham, Abingdon, Oxfordshire OX14 3DB. *T:* Abingdon (01235) 463160.

RAE, Dr John (Malcolm); Director: Portman Group, since 1989; The Observer Ltd, 1986–93; *b* 20 March 1931; *s* of late Dr L. John Rae, radiologist, London Hospital, and Blodwen Rae; *m* 1955, Daphné Ray Simpson, *d* of John Phimester Simpson; two *s* four *d*. *Educ:* Bishop's Stortford Coll.; Sidney Sussex Coll., Cambridge. MA Cantab 1958; PhD 1965. 2nd Lieut Royal Fusiliers, 1950–51. Asst Master, Harrow School, 1955–66; Dept of War Studies, King's Coll., London, 1962–65; Headmaster: Taunton School, 1966–70; Westminster School, 1970–86; Dir, Laura Ashley Foundn, 1986–89. Gresham Prof. of Rhetoric, 1988–90. Chairman: HMC, 1977; Council for Educn in World Citizenship, 1983–87. Member: Nat. Bd for Crime Prevention, 1993–; Council, Nat. Cttee for Electoral Reform; Council, King's Coll. London, 1981–84. Trustee: Children's Film Unit, 1979–; Imperial War Mus., 1980–85. Gov. Highgate Sch., 1989–. Judge, Whitbread Prize, 1980. Freeman, City of London. JP Middlesex, 1961–66. Hon. FCP 1982. *Publications:* The Custard Boys, 1960 (filmed 1979); (jtly, film) Reach for Glory (UN Award); Conscience and Politics, 1970; The Golden Crucifix, 1974; The Treasure of Westminster Abbey, 1975; Christmas is Coming, 1976; Return to the Winter Palace, 1978; The Third Twin: a ghost story, 1980; The Public School Revolution: Britain's independent schools, 1964–1979, 1981; Letters from School, 1987; Too Little, Too Late?, 1989; Delusions of Grandeur: a headmaster's life 1966–1986, 1993; articles in The Times, Encounter; columnist in Times Ed. Supp. *Recreations:* writing, swimming, children, cinema. *Address:* The Portman Group, 2d Wimpole Street, W1M 7AA. *T:* 0171–499 1010; 101 Millbank Court, 24 John Islip Street, Westminster, SW1P 4LG. *T:* 0171–828 1842. *Clubs:* Royal Automobile; Hawks (Cambridge).

RAE, Rita Emilia Anna; QC (Scot.) 1992; *b* 20 June 1950; *d* of Alexander Smith Cowie Rae and Bianca Bruno. *Educ:* Univ. of Edinburgh (LLB Hons). Apprentice, 1972–74, Asst Solicitor, 1974–76, Biggart Baillie & Gifford, Glasgow; Asst Solicitor and Partner, Ross Harper & Murphy, Glasgow, 1976–81; Advocate, 1982–; Temporary Sheriff, 1988–. *Recreations:* classical music, opera, theatre, walking, cycling. *Address:* 73 Fotheringay Road, Glasgow G41 4LQ. *T:* 0141–423 0781.

RAE, Hon. Robert Keith; MPP (New Dem.) for York South, Ontario, since 1982; Premier of Ontario, since 1990; *b* 2 Aug. 1948; *s* of Saul Rae and Lois (*née* George); *m* 1980, Arlene Perly; three *d*. *Educ:* Ecole Internationale, Geneva; Univ. of Toronto (BA Hons 1969; LLB 1977); Balliol Coll., Oxford (BPhil 1971). MP for Broadview-Greenwood, Ontario, 1978–82; Finance Critic, New Democratic Party, 1979–82; Leader, Ontario New Democrats, 1982–; Leader, Official Opposition, Ontario legislature, 1987–90. *Recreations:* tennis, golf, ski-ing, fishing, reading. *Address:* Legislative Building, Queen's Park, Toronto, Ont M7A 1A1, Canada. *T:* (416) 3251941.

RAE, Robert Wright; Civil Service, retired; Clerk to the General Commissioners of Income Tax, Blackheath Division, 1977–88 (Clerk, Bromley Division, 1977–85); *b* 27 March 1914; *s* of Walter Rae and Rachel Scott; *m* 1st, 1945, Joan McKenzie (*d* 1966); two *s*; 2nd, 1977, Marjorie Ann Collyer. *Educ:* George Heriot's Sch., Edinburgh; Edinburgh Univ. MA 1st cl. hons. Asst Inspector of Taxes, 1936; Dep. Chief Inspector of Taxes, 1973–75; Dir Personnel, Inland Revenue, 1975–77. *Recreations:* gardening, walking. *Address:* Oak Lodge, Blackbrook Lane, Bickley, Bromley BR1 2LP. *T:* 0181–467 2377.

RAE, Hon. Sir Wallace (Alexander Ramsay), Kt 1976; Agent-General for Queensland, in London, 1974–80; formerly grazier, Ramsay Park, Blackall, Queensland; *b* 31 March 1914; *s* of George Ramsay Rae and Alice Ramsay Rae. *Educ:* Sydney, Australia. Served War: RAAF Coastal Command, 1939; Pilot, Flt Lt, UK, then OC Test Flight, Amberley, Qld. Mem., Legislative Assembly (Nat. Party of Australia) for Gregory, Qld, 1957–74; Minister for: Local Govt and Electricity, 1969–74; Lands and Forestry, Qld, 1974. Founder Pres., Pony Club Assoc. of Queensland. *Recreations:* music, bowls. *Address:* 94 Garden Village, Findlay Avenue, Port Macquarie, NSW 2444, Australia. *Clubs:* United Service, Tattersall's (Brisbane); Longreach (Longreach).

RAE, Air Vice-Marshal William McCulloch, CB 1993; Senior Directing Staff (Air), Royal College of Defence Studies, 1992–95; *b* 22 June 1940; *s* of William Brewster Rae and Margaret Rae; *m* 1964, Helen, *d* of Thomas and Eileen Reading; two *d*. *Educ:* Aberdeen Grammar School; psc, ndc, rcds. RAF 1958; Nos 213, 10, 55 Sqns, 1960–64; CFS (helicopter element), 1965–67; Radar Res. Flying Unit, Pershore, 1968–70; Sqn Comdr, 6 FTS, 1970–72; Inspectorate of Recruiting, 1973; RAF Staff Coll., 1974; Air Sec's Dept, 1975–77; NDC, 1978; OC 360 Sqn, 1979–81; CDS Staff, 1981–82; Central Policy Staff, MoD, 1982–85; Station Comdr, RAF Finningley, 1985–87; RCDS, 1988; Branch Chief, Policy, SHAPE, 1989–91. *Recreations:* antiques, wine, golf. *Club:* Royal Air Force.

RAE SMITH, David Douglas, CBE 1976; MC 1946; MA; FCA; Senior Partner, Deloitte Haskins & Sells, Chartered Accountants, 1973–82 (Partner, 1954); *b* 15 Nov. 1919; *s* of Sir Alan Rae Smith, KBE, and Lady (Mabel Grace) Rae Smith; *m* 1947, Margaret Alison Watson, *d* of James Watson; three *s* one *d*. *Educ:* Radley Coll.; Christ Church, Oxford (MA). FCA 1959. Served War, RA, 1939–46: ME, N Africa and NW Europe; Captain; MC and mentioned in despatches. Chartered accountant, 1950. Hon. Treasurer, RIIA, 1961–81. Director: Thomas Tilling Ltd, 1982–83; Sandoz Products Ltd, 1983–92; Dep. Chm., Bankers Trustee Co., 1984–91. Member: Licensed Dealers Tribunal, 1974–88; Council, Radley Coll., 1966–92 (Chm., 1976–92). *Recreations:* horse racing, golf, travel. *Address:* Oakdale, Crockham Hill, Edenbridge, Kent TN8 6RL. *T:* Edenbridge (01732) 866220.

RAEBURN, David Antony; Grammatikos (tutor in Ancient Greek Language), Faculty of Literae Humaniores, 1991–Sept. 1996, Grocyn Lecturer, 1992–Sept. 1996, University of

Oxford; *b* 22 May 1927; *e s* of late Walter Augustus Leopold Raeburn, QC; *m* 1961, Mary Faith, *d* of Arthur Hubbard, Salisbury, Rhodesia; two *s* one *d*. *Educ:* Charterhouse; Christ Church, Oxford (Schol., MA). 1st cl. hons Hon. Mods, 2nd in Greats. Nat. Service, 1949–51: Temp. Captain, RAEC. Asst Master: Bristol Grammar Sch., 1951–54; Bradfield Coll., 1955–58 (prod. Greek Play, 1955 and 1958); Senior Classics Master, Alleyn's Sch., Dulwich, 1958–62; Headmaster: Beckenham and Penge Grammar Sch., 1963–70 (school's name changed to Langley Park School for Boys, Beckenham in 1969); Whitgift Sch., Croydon, 1970–91. Schoolteacher Fellow-Commoner, Jesus Coll., Cambridge, 1980. Chm. Classics Cttee, Schs Council, 1974–80; Pres., Jt Assoc. of Classical Teachers, 1983–85; Treas., HMC, 1984–89. FRSA 1969. *Publications:* articles on Greek play production. *Recreation:* play production (produced Cambridge Greek Play, 1980, 1983). *Address:* 13A St Anne's Road, Eastbourne, Sussex BN21 2AJ. *T:* Eastbourne (01323) 24696; Christ Church, Oxford OX1 1DP.

RAEBURN, Maj.-Gen. Sir Digby; *see* Raeburn, Maj.-Gen. Sir W. D. M.

RAEBURN, Prof. John Ross, CBE 1972; BSc (Agric.), PhD, MS; FRSE; FIBiol; Strathcona-Fordyce Professor of Agriculture, Aberdeen University, 1959–78; Principal, North of Scotland College of Agriculture, 1963–78; *b* 20 Nov. 1912; *s* of late Charles Raeburn and Margaret (*née* Ross); *m* 1941, Mary, *o d* of Alfred and Kathrine Roberts; one *s* three *d*. *Educ:* Manchester Grammar School; Edinburgh and Cornell Universities. Professor of Agricultural Economics, Nanking University, 1936–37; Research Officer, Oxford University, 1938–39; Ministry of Food Divisional statistician, 1939–41, Head Agricultural Plans Branch, 1941–46; Senior research officer, Oxford University, 1946–49; Reader in Agricultural Economics, London University, 1949–59. Visiting Professor: Cornell, 1950; Wuhan, 1983. Consultant to UN. Member: Agricultural Mission to Yugoslavia, 1951; Mission of Enquiry into Rubber Industry, Malaya, 1954; Colonial Economic Research Committee, 1949–61; Scottish Agricultural Improvement Council, 1960–71; Scottish Agricultural Develt Council, 1971–76; Verdon-Smith Committee, 1962–64; Council, Scottish Agricultural Colls, 1974–78. Hon. MA Oxford, 1946. FRSE 1961; FIBiol 1968. Vice-President, International Association of Agricultural Economists, 1964–70 (Hon. Life Mem., 1976–); President, Agric. Econ. Society, 1966–67 (Hon. Life Mem., 1981–). *Publications:* Preliminary economic survey of the Northern Territories of the Gold Coast, 1950; (jtly) Problems in the mechanisation of native agriculture in tropical African Territories, 1950; Agriculture: foundations, principles and development, 1984; (jtly) History of the IAAE, 1990; research bulletins and contributions to agricultural economic journals. *Recreation:* gardening. *Address:* 30 Morningfield Road, Aberdeen AB2 4AQ.

RAEBURN, Michael Edward Norman; (4th Bt, *cr* 1923, but does not use the title); *b* 12 Nov. 1954; *s* of Sir Edward Alfred Raeburn, 3rd Bt, and of Joan, *d* of Frederick Hill; *S* father, 1977; *m* 1979, Penelope Henrietta Theodora, *d* of Alfred Louis Penn; two *s* three *d*. *Heir: s* Christopher Edward Alfred Raeburn, *b* 4 Dec. 1981. *Address:* 1 Spring Cottages, Fletching Street, Mayfield, E Sussex TN20 6TN.

RAEBURN, Susan Adiel Ogilvie; QC (Scot.) 1991; Sheriff of Glasgow and Strathkelvin, since 1993; *b* 23 April 1954; *d* of George Ferguson Raeburn and Rose Anne Bainbridge (*née* Morison). *Educ:* St Margaret's Sch. for Girls, Aberdeen; Edinburgh Univ. (LLB). Admitted to Faculty of Advocates, 1977; temp. Sheriff, 1988–93. Part-time Chairman: Social Security Appeal Tribunals, 1986–92; Med. Appeal Tribunals, 1992–93. *Recreations:* travel, the arts. *Address:* Sheriff's Chambers, Sheriff Court House, 1 Carlton Place, Glasgow G5 9OA. *T:* 0141–429 8888. *Club:* Scottish Arts.

RAEBURN, Maj.-Gen. Sir (William) Digby (Manifold), KCVO 1979; CB 1966; DSO 1945; MBE 1941; Major and Resident Governor, HM Tower of London, and Keeper of the Jewel House, 1971–79; *b* 6 Aug. 1915; *s* of late Sir Ernest Manifold Raeburn, KBE, and Lady Raeburn; *m* 1960, Adeline Margaret (*née* Pryor). *Educ:* Winchester; Magdalene College, Cambridge (MA). Commnd into Scots Guards, 1936; despatches, 1942; comd 2nd Bn Scots Guards, 1953; Lieut-Col Comdg Scots Guards, 1958; Comdr, 1st Guards Bde Group, 1959; Comdr, 51st Infty Bde Group, 1960; Director of Combat Development (Army), 1963–65; Chief of Staff to C-in-C, Allied Forces, N Europe, 1965–68; Chief Instructor (Army), Imperial Defence College, 1968–70. Freeman of City of London, 1972. *Recreation:* shooting. *Address:* 25 St Ann's Terrace, NW8 6PH. *Clubs:* Pratt's, Cavalry and Guards; Royal Yacht Squadron.

RAFAEL, Gideon; Ambassador of Israel, retired 1978; *b* Berlin, 5 March 1913; *s* of Max Rafael; *m* 1940, Nurit Weissberg; one *s* one *d*. *Educ:* Berlin Univ. Went to Israel, 1934; Member, kibbutz, 1934–43; Jewish Agency Polit. Dept, 1943; in charge of prep. of Jewish case for JA Polit. Dept, Nuremberg War Crimes Trial, 1945–46; Member: JA Commn to Anglo-American Commn of Enquiry, 1946, and of JA Mission to UN Special Commn for Palestine, 1947; Israel Perm. Deleg. to UN, 1951–52; Alt. Rep. to UN, 1953; Rep. at UN Gen. Assemblies, 1947–67; Counsellor in charge of ME and UN Affairs, Min. for Foreign Affairs, 1953–57; Ambassador to Belgium and Luxembourg, 1957–60, and to the European Economic Community, 1959; Head, Israel Delegn to 2nd Geneva Conf. on Maritime Law, 1960; Dep. Dir-Gen., Min. of Foreign Affairs, 1960–65; Perm. Rep. to UN and Internat. Organizations in Geneva, Sept. 1965–April 1966; Special Ambassador and Adviser to Foreign Minister, 1966–67; Perm. Rep. to UN, 1967; Dir-Gen., Min. for Foreign Affairs, 1967–71; Head, Israel Delegn to UNCTAD III, 1972; Sen. Polit. Adviser, Foreign Ministry, 1972–73; Ambassador to the Court of St James's, 1973–77, and non-resident Ambassador to Ireland, 1975–77; Sen. Advr to Foreign Minister, 1977–78. Visiting Professor: Woodrow Wilson Sch., Princeton Univ., 1988; Hamilton Coll., Clinton, NY, 1989. Bd Mem., Israel Cancer Soc., 1985–. *Publications:* Destination Peace: three decades of Israeli foreign policy, 1981; The Impact of the Six Day War, 1990; articles on foreign affairs in Israel and internat. periodicals. *Address:* Ministry for Foreign Affairs, Jerusalem, Israel.

RAFF, Prof. Martin Charles, FRS 1985; Professor of Biology, University College London, since 1979; *b* 15 Jan. 1938; *s* of David and Reba Raff; *m* 1979, Carol Winter; two *s* one *d*. *Educ:* McGill Univ. (BSc; MD; CM). House Officer, Royal Victoria Hosp., Montreal, 1963–65; Resident in Neurology, Massachusetts General Hosp., 1965–68; Postdoctoral Fellow, Nat. Inst. for Med. Res., 1968–71; Co-director, MRC Develtl Neurobiology Programme, 1971–. Pres., British Soc. of Cell Biology, 1991–. *Publications:* (jtly) T and B Lymphocytes, 1973; (jtly) Molecular Biology of the Cell, 1983, 3rd edn 1994. *Address:* 67 Upper Park Road, NW3 2UL. *T:* 0171–722 5610.

RAFFAN, Keith William Twort; *b* 21 June 1949; *s* of A. W. Raffan, TD, MB, ChB, FFARCS. *Educ:* Robert Gordon's Coll., Aberdeen; Trinity Coll., Glenalmond; Corpus Christi Coll., Cambridge (BA 1971; MA 1977). Parly Correspondent, Daily Express, 1981–83. Contested (C) Dulwich, Feb. 1974, and East Aberdeenshire, Oct. 1974; MP (C) Delyn, 1983–92. Mem., Select Cttee on Welsh Affairs, 1983–92. Introduced Controlled Drugs (Penalties) Act (Private Member's Bill, 1985). Candidate's Parly Aide, by-elections of: Cynon Valley, 1984; Brecon and Radnor, 1985. Vice-Chm., Cons. Party Orgn Cttee, 1985–89; President: Wales Cons. Trade Unionists, 1984–87; Wales Young Conservatives, 1987–90 (Vice-Pres., 1984). Nat. Chm., PEST, 1970–74; Vice-President: Clwyd Pre-School Playgroups Assoc., 1983–; Delyn and Deeside Multiple Sclerosis Soc. Mem. NUJ, 1976–. *Clubs:* Carlton, Chelsea Arts, Royal Automobile; Flint Conservative; Prestatyn Conservative.

RAFFERTY, Anne Judith, (Mrs B. J. Barker); QC 1990; a Recorder, since 1991; *m* 1977, Brian John Barker, *qv*; three *d* (and one *d* decd). *Educ:* Univ. of Sheffield (LLB). Criminal Bar Association: Mem. Cttee, 1986–91; Sec., 1989–91; Vice-Chm., 1993–95; Chm., 1995–; Chm., Bar Conf., 1992. Mem., Royal Commn on Criminal Justice, 1991–93. Chm., Criminal Bar Assoc., 1995– (Vice Chm., 1993–95). Member: SE Circuit Wine Cttee, 1987–90; Pigot Cttee, 1988–89; Circuit Cttee, SE Circuit, 1991–94. Gov., St Andrew's Prep. Sch., Eastbourne; Mem. Council, Eastbourne Coll. FRSA 1993. *Address:* 4 Brick Court, Temple, EC4Y 9AD. *T:* 0171–583 8455. *Club:* Roehampton.

RAFFERTY, Hon. Joseph Anstice, BA; FAIM, FID; JP; Agent General for Victoria in London, 1979–83; investor and primary producer, Australia, since 1983; *b* 10 Jan. 1911; *s* of late Col Rupert A. Rafferty, DSO, and Rose Sarah Anne Rafferty; *m* 1st, 1940, Miriam K. (decd), *d* of late Frank Richards, Devonport, Tas; two *s*; 2nd, 1973, Lyn, *d* of Grace Jones, Brisbane, Qld. *Educ:* Christ Coll., Univ. of Tas (BA); Univ. of Melbourne. FAIM 1954; FID 1960. Commonwealth Public Service, 1934–45; Personnel Manager, Australian National Airways, 1945–53; Personnel Management and Indust. Relations Consultant, 1953–70 (own practice; co. dir). MP (Lib) for: Caulfield, Vic, 1955–58; Ormond, Vic, 1958–67; Glenhuntly, Vic, 1967–79; Chm. Cttees and Dep. Speaker, Victorian Legislative Assembly, 1961–65; Parly Sec. for Cabinet, 1965–70; Minister for Labour and Industry, 1970–76; Asst Minister for Educn, 1970–72; Minister for Consumer Affairs, 1972–76; Minister for Fed. Affairs, 1974–76; Minister for Transport, 1976–78; Chief Sec., 1978–79; Leader, Aust. Delegn to ILO Conf., Geneva, 1974. Pres., Melbourne Jun. Chamber of Commerce, 1950; Treasurer, Nat. Assoc. of Jun. Chambers of Commerce of Australia, 1951; Councillor: Melbourne Chamber of Commerce, 1950–76; Victorian Employers' Fedn, 1952–65. Dep. Leader, Aust. Delegn, 5th World Congress, Jun. Chamber of Commerce, Manila, 1950; Aust. Delegate, 6th World Congress, Jun. Chamber of Industry, Montreal, 1951; Delegate, 17th Triennial Congress, British Empire Chambers of Commerce, London, 1951. Mem. Council, La Trobe Univ., Vic, 1964–70; Trustee, Caulfield Racecourse Reserve, 1965–. JP Victoria, 1970. *Recreations:* golf, swimming, walking, world travel, public speaking. *Address:* 8 Matlock Court, Caulfield North, Vic 3161, Australia. *T:* (3) 95000282. *Clubs:* Royal Wimbledon Golf; Athenæum, Metropolitan Golf, MCC (Melbourne).

RAFFERTY, Rt. Rev. Mgr. Kevin Lawrence; Titular Bishop of Ausuaga and Bishop Auxiliary to Archbishop of St Andrews and Edinburgh, since 1990; Parish Priest of SS John Cantius and Nicholas, Broxburn, since 1986; *b* 24 June 1933; *s* of John Rafferty and Catherine Quigg. *Educ:* Lisnascreaghog and St Adamnan's primary schs; St Columb's Coll., Derry; St Kieran's Coll., Kilkenny. Priest 1957; Assistant Priest: Linlithgow, 1957–67; St David's, Dalkieth, 1967–77; Chaplain, St David's High Sch., Dalkieth, 1967–73; Parish priest, Our Lady, Star of the Sea, North Berwick, 1977–86; Dean of Midlothian and East Lothian, 1982–86; Mem., Coll. of Consultors of archdio., 1984; Vicar-General, archdio. St Andrews and Edinburgh, 1989–. Prelate of Honour to the Pope, 1989. *Recreations:* golf, football, music, reading. *Address:* SS John Cantius and Nicholas, 34 West Main Street, Broxburn, West Lothian EH52 5RJ. *T:* Broxburn (01506) 852040.

RAFFERTY, Kevin Robert; Managing Editor, International Media Partners, New York, since 1989; *b* 5 Nov. 1944; *s* of Leo and Thérèse Rafferty; *m* 1985, Michelle Misquitta. *Educ:* Marist Coll., Kingston upon Hull; Queen's Coll., Oxford (MA). Journalistic training, The Guardian, Sun, 1966–69; Financial Times, 1970–76; Founder Editor, Business Times Malaysia, 1976–77; Consultant Editor, Indian Express Gp, 1978–79; Foreign Correspondent, Financial Times, 1980; Asia Pacific Editor, Institutional Investor, 1981–87; Ed., The Universe, 1987–88. Founder Editor, then Associate Editor, Asia and Pacific Review, Saffron Walden, 1980–. *Publication:* City on the Rocks: Hong Kong's uncertain future, 1989. *Recreations:* travelling, meeting ordinary people, reading. *Address:* International Media Partners, The Cable Building, 611 Broadway, Suite 322, New York, NY 10012, USA. *T:* (212) 995 9595. *Clubs:* United Oxford & Cambridge University; Foreign Correspondents (Hong Kong).

RAFTERY, Peter Albert, CVO 1984 (MVO 1979); MBE 1972; HM Diplomatic Service, retired; *b* 8 June 1929; *s* of John Raftery and Mary (*née* Glynn); *m* 1st, 1949, Margaret Frances Hulse (decd); four *d*; 2nd, 1975, Fenella Jones. *Educ:* St Ignatius Coll., London. Nat. Service, 1947–49. India Office, 1946; CRO, 1949; New Delhi, 1950; Peshawar, 1956; Cape Town, 1959; Kuala Lumpur, 1963; Nairobi, 1964; Asst Political Agent, Bahrain, 1968; First Sec., FCO, 1973; Head of Chancery, Gaborone, 1976; Asst Head, E Africa Dept, FCO, 1980; Counsellor and Consul Gen., Amman, 1982–85; High Comr to Botswana, 1986–89. *Recreation:* tennis. *Address:* PO Box 170, Gaborone, Botswana.

RAGG, Rt. Rev. Theodore David Butler, DD; *b* 23 Nov. 1919; *s* of late Rt Rev. Harry Richard Ragg and Winifred Mary Ragg (*née* Groves); *m* 1945, Dorothy Mary Lee; one *s* two *d*. *Educ:* Univ. of Manitoba; Trinity Coll., Univ. of Toronto (BA, LTh); General Synod (BD). Deacon, 1949; priest, 1950; Asst Curate, St Michael and All Angels, Toronto, 1949; Rector: Nokomis, 1951; Wolseley, 1953; St Clement's N Vancouver, 1955; St Luke's, Victoria, 1957; Bishop Cronyn Memorial, London, 1962; St George's, Owen Sound, 1967. Examining Chaplain to Bishop of Huron, 1964–67; Archdeacon of Saugeen, 1967; elected Suffragan Bishop of Huron, 1973; Bishop of Huron, 1974–84, retired. Hon. DD: Huron Coll., London, Ont., 1975; Trinity Coll., Toronto, Ont., 1975. *Recreations:* woodworking, golf. *Address:* 1771 McRae Avenue, Victoria, BC V8P 1J2, Canada.

RAGGATT, Timothy Walter Harold; QC 1993; a Recorder, since 1994; *b* 13 April 1950; *s* of late Walter George and Norah Margaret Raggatt; *m* 1991, Carol Marion Allison; two *s* one *d*. *Educ:* Redditch County High Sch.; King's Coll. London (LLB 1971). Called to the Bar, Inner Temple, 1972, Tutor, Inns of Court Sch. of Law, 1972–73; in practice on Midland and Oxford Circuit, 1974–; an Asst Recorder, 1991–94. Mem., Professional Assoc. of Diving Instructors, 1992–. *Recreations:* golf, scuba diving, bridge and snooker. *Address:* 1 King's Bench Walk, Temple, EC4Y 7DB; 3 Fountain Court, Steelhouse Lane, Birmingham B4 6DR. *Clubs:* Birmingham, Edgbaston Priory (Birmingham); Edgbaston Golf.

RAGLAN, 5th Baron, *cr* 1852; **FitzRoy John Somerset;** JP; DL; Chairman, Cwmbran New Town Development Corporation, 1970–83; *b* 8 Nov. 1927; *er s* of 4th Baron and Hon. Julia Hamilton, CStJ (*d* 1971), *d* of 11th Baron Belhaven and Stenton, CIE; *S* father, 1964; *m* 1973, Alice Baily (marr. diss. 1981), *yr d* of Peter Baily, Great Whittington, Northumberland. *Educ:* Westminster; Magdalen College, Oxford; Royal Agricultural College, Cirencester. Captain, Welsh Guards, RARO. Crown Estate Comr, 1970–74. Mem., Agriculture and Consumer Affairs sub-cttee, House of Lords Select Cttee on the European Community, 1974–83, 1985–90 (Chm., 1975–77). President: UK Housing Trust, 1983–89 (Chm., S Wales Region, 1976–89); United Welsh Housing Assoc., 1989–. Pres., Pre Retirement Assoc., 1970–77, Vice-Pres. 1977–, Hon. Treas., 1987–. Chairman: Bath Preservation Trust, 1975–77; The Bath Soc., 1977–; Bugatti Owners' Club, 1988–.

President: Gwent Foundn Concert Soc.; Usk Civic Soc.; Usk Farmers Club; Bath Centre of Nat. Trust; S Wales Reg., RSMHCA, 1971–; Mem., Distinguished Members Panel, National Secular Soc.; Patron, The Raglan Baroque Players. JP 1958, DL 1971, Gwent (formerly Monmouthshire). *Recreation:* being mechanic to a Bugatti. *Heir: b* Hon. Geoffrey Somerset [*b* 29 Aug. 1932; *m* 1956, Caroline Rachel, *d* of Col E. R. Hill, *qv*; one *s* two *d*]. *Address:* Cefntilla, Usk, Gwent NP5 1DG. *T:* Usk (01291) 672050. *Clubs:* Beefsteak, Vintage Sports Car; Usk Farmers'.

RAHTZ, Prof. Philip Arthur; Professor of Archaeology, University of York, 1978–86, now Emeritus; *b* 11 March 1921; *s* of Frederick John Rahtz and Ethel May Rahtz; *m* 1st, 1940, Wendy Hewgill Smith (*d* 1977); three *s* two *d*; 2nd, 1978, Lorna Rosemary Jane Watts; one *s*. *Educ:* Bristol Grammar Sch. MA Bristol 1964. FSA. Served RAF, 1941–46. Articled to accountant, 1937–41; photographer (Studio Rahtz), 1946–49; schoolteacher, 1950–53; archaeological consultant, 1953–63; Univ. of Birmingham: Lectr, 1963–75; Sen. Lectr, later Reader, 1975–78. Pres., Council for British Archaeology, 1986–89. Hon. MIFA. *Publications:* Rescue Archaeology, 1973; Chew Valley Lake Excavations, 1978; Saxon and Medieval Palaces at Cheddar, 1979; Invitation to Archaeology, 1985, 2nd edn 1991; Tamworth Saxon Watermill, 1992; Glastonbury, 1993; contrib. nat. and regional jls in England, W Africa and Poland. *Recreations:* swimming, sunbathing, music, travel. *Address:* The Old School, Harome, Helmsley, North Yorkshire YO4 4JE. *T:* Helmsley (01439) 770862.

RAIKES, Vice-Adm. Sir Iwan (Geoffrey), KCB 1976; CBE 1967; DSC 1943; DL; Flag Officer Submarines, and Commander Submarines, Eastern Atlantic Area, 1974–76; retired 1977; *b* 21 April 1921; *s* of late Adm. Sir Robert Henry Taunton Raikes, KCB, CVO, DSO, and Lady (Ida Guinevere) Raikes; *m* 1947, Cecilla Primrose Hunt; one *s* one *d*. *Educ:* RNC Dartmouth. Entered Royal Navy, 1935; specialised in Submarines, 1941; comd HM Submarines: H43, 1943; Varne, 1944; Virtue, 1946; Talent, 1948–49; Aeneas, 1952; comd HM Ships: Loch Insh, 1961; Kent, 1968; Exec. Officer, HMS Newcastle, 1955–57; Dep. Dir, Undersurface Warfare, 1962–64; Dir, Plans & Operations, Staff of C-in-C Far East, 1965–66; JSSC, 1957; IDC, 1967. Rear-Adm., 1970; Naval Sec., 1970–72; Vice-Adm., 1973; Flag Officer, First Flotilla, 1973–74. Chm., United Usk Fishermens' Assoc., 1978–93. Mem., Governing Body, 1979–93, Rep. Body, 1982–93, Church in Wales. DL Powys, 1983. *Recreations:* shooting, fishing, gardening. *Address:* Aberyscir Court, Brecon, Powys LD3 9NW. *Club:* Naval and Military.

RAILTON, Dame Ruth, DBE 1966 (OBE 1954); Founder and Musical Director of the National Youth Orchestra and National Junior Music School, 1947–65; *b* 14 Dec. 1915; *m* 1962, Cecil Harmsworth King (*d* 1987). Educ: St Mary's School, Wantage; Royal Academy of Music, London. Director of Music or Choral work for many schools and societies, 1937–49; Adjudicator, Fedn of Music Festivals, 1946–74; Pres., Ulster Coll. of Music, 1960–; Governor, Royal Ballet School, 1966–74. Founder and Pres., Irish Children's Theatre, 1978–; Vice-Pres., Cork Internat. Fest., 1960–85; Chm., Nat. Children's Orchestra, 1989–; Mem., Bd of Dirs, Nat. Concert Hall, Dublin, 1981–86. Hon. Professor: Chopin Conservatoire, Warsaw, 1960; Conservatoire of Azores, 1972. FRAM 1956; Hon. RMCM 1959; Hon. FRCM 1965; Hon. FTCL 1969. Hon. LLD Aberdeen Univ., 1960. Harriet Cohen Medal for Bach, 1955. *Publication:* Daring to Excel, 1992. *Recreations:* interested in everything. *Address:* 54 Ardoyne House, Pembroke Park, Dublin 4. *T:* Dublin 6617262; 34 Elizabeth Court, Milmans Street, Chelsea, SW10 0DA. *Club:* University Women's.

RAINBOW, (James) Conrad (Douglas), CBE 1979; Chairman, Sovereign Country House Ltd, since 1979; *b* 25 Sept. 1926; *s* of Jack Conrad Rainbow and Winifred Edna (*née* Mears); *m* 1974, Kathleen Margaret (*née* Holmes); one *s* one *d*. *Educ:* William Ellis Sch., Highgate; Selwyn Coll., Cambridge (MA). Asst Master, St Paul's Sch., London, 1951–60; HM Inspector of Schools, 1960–69; Dep. Chief Educn Officer, Lancashire, 1969–74, Chief Educn Officer, 1974–79. Vis. Prof., Univ. of Wisconsin, 1979. Education Consultant: ICI, 1980–85; Shell Petroleum Co. Ltd, 1980–; Advr to H of C Select Cttee on Educn, 1980–82. Mem., Exec. Cttee, Council of British Internat. Schs in EEC, 1975–91. Chairman of Governors: Northcliffe Sch., Hants, 1984–90; Elmslie Sch., Blackpool, 1994–. *Publications:* various articles in educnl jls. *Recreations:* rowing (now as an observer), music, reading. *Address:* Erlesmere, 171 Newton Drive, Blackpool, Lancs FY3 8ND. *T:* Blackpool (01253) 302831. *Club:* Leander.

RAINE, Craig Anthony; poet; Fellow of New College, Oxford, since 1991; *b* 3 Dec. 1944; *s* of Norman Edward Raine and Olive Marie Raine; *m* 1972, Ann Pasternak Slater; one *d* three *s*. *Educ:* Barnard Castle Sch.; Exeter Coll., Oxford (BA Hons in English; BPhil). College Lecturer, Oxford University: Exeter Coll., 1971–72; Lincoln Coll., 1974–75; Exeter Coll., 1975–76; Christ Church, 1976–79. Books Editor, New Review, 1977–78; Editor, Quarto, 1979–80; Poetry Editor: New Statesman, 1981; Faber & Faber, 1981–91. Cholmondeley Poetry Award, 1983. *Publications:* The Onion, Memory, 1978, 5th edn 1986; A Martian Sends a Postcard Home, 1979, 8th edn 1990; A Free Translation, 1981, 2nd edn 1981; Rich, 1984, 3rd edn 1985; The Electrification of the Soviet Union, 1986; (ed) A Choice of Kipling's Prose, 1987; The Prophetic Book, 1988; '1953', 1990; Haydn and the Valve Trumpet (essays), 1990; (ed) Rudyard Kipling: Selected Poetry, 1992; History: The Home Movie, 1994. *Recreation:* music. *Address:* c/o New College, Oxford OX1 3BN.

RAINE, John Stephen; County Director, Derbyshire County Council, since 1989; *b* 13 April 1941; *s* of Alan and Ruby Raine; *m* 1961, Josephine Marlow; two *s*. *Educ:* Sir Joseph Williamson's Mathematical School, Rochester. MIPR. Journalist; Kent Messenger, Sheffield Morning Telegraph, Sheffield Star, Raymond's News Agency, 1957–70; Derbyshire County Council: County Public Relations Officer, 1973–79; Asst to Clerk and Chief Exec., 1979–81; Asst Chief Exec., 1981–88; Dep. County Dir, 1988–89. *Recreations:* walking, travel, smallholding. *Address:* Far Hill Farm, Far Hill, Ashover, Chesterfield, Derbyshire S45 0BB. *T:* Chesterfield (01246) 590501.

RAINE, Kathleen Jessie, (Mrs Madge), FRSL; poet; *b* 1908; *o d* of late George Raine, schoolmaster, and Jessie Raine; *m* Charles Madge (marr. diss.); one *s* one *d*. *Educ:* Girton College, Cambridge. Founder, Temenos Acad. of Integral Studies, 1990. Hon. DLitt: Leicester, 1974; Durham, 1979; Caen, 1987. Queen's Gold Medal for Poetry, 1992. Officier, Ordre des Arts et des Lettres (France), 1995. *Publications:* Stone and Flower, 1943; Living in Time, 1946; The Pythoness, 1949; The Year One, 1952; Collected Poems, 1956; The Hollow Hill (poems), 1965; Defending Ancient Springs (criticism), 1967, 1985; Blake and Tradition (Andrew Mellon Lectures, Washington, 1962), Princeton 1968, London 1969 (abridged version, Blake and Antiquity, Princeton 1978, London 1979, trans. Japanese, 1988); (with George Mills Harper) Selected Writings of Thomas Taylor the Platonist, Princeton and London, 1969; William Blake, 1970; The Lost Country (verse), 1971 (W. H. Smith & Son Award, 1972); On a Deserted Shore (verse), 1973; Yeats, the Tarot and The Golden Dawn (criticism), 1973; Faces of Day and Night, 1973; Farewell Happy Fields (autobiog.), 1973 (French trans. as Adieu prairies heureuses, 1978; Prix du meilleur livre étranger); Death in Life and Life in Death (criticism), 1974; The Land Unknown (autobiog.), 1975 (French trans. as Le royaume inconnu, 1978), The Oval Portrait (verse), 1977; The Lion's Mouth (autobiography), 1977 (French trans. as La Gueul du Lion, 1987); David Jones and the Actually Loved and Known (criticism), 1978; From Blake to a Vision (criticism), 1979; The Oracle in the Heart (verse), 1979; Blake and the New Age (criticism), 1979; Collected Poems, 1981; The Human Face of God, 1982; The Inner Journey of the Poet and other papers (criticism), 1982; L'Imagination Créatrice de William Blake; Yeats the Initiate, 1986; The Presence (verse), 1988; Selected Poems, 1988; Visages du Jour et de la Nuit, 1989; India Seen Afar, 1990; Golgonooza, City of the Imagination, 1991; Living with Mystery (verse), 1992; French trans. of verse: Isis errante, 1978; Sur un rivage désert, 1978; Le Premier Jour, 1980; Le Royaume Invisible, 1991; Spanish trans.: En una desierta orilla, 1980; Swedish trans.: Den Osedda Rosen (selected poetry), 1988; Editor, Temenos, a bi-annual Review devoted to the Arts of the Imagination, 1982–93 (Jt Editor, 1981–82) (10th issue 1989); contributions to literary journals. *Address:* 47 Paultons Square, SW3 5DT. *Club:* University Women's.

RAINER, Luise; actress and painter; *b* Vienna, 12 Jan.; *d* of Heinz Rainer; *m* 1937, Clifford Odets (from whom she obtained a divorce, 1940; he *d* 1963); *m* 1945, Robert (*d* 1989), *s* of late John Knittel; one *d*. *Educ:* Austria, France, Switzerland and Italy. Started stage career at age of sixteen under Max Reinhardt in Vienna; later was discovered by Metro-Goldwyn-Mayer talent scout in Vienna; came to Hollywood; starred in: Escapade, The Great Ziegfeld, The Good Earth, Emperor's Candlesticks, Big City, Toy Wife (Frou Frou), The Great Waltz, Dramatic School; received Motion Picture Academy of Arts and Sciences Award for the best feminine performance in 1936 and 1937. One-man exhibn of paintings at Patrick Seale Gallery, SW1, 1978. US tour in dramatised recitation of Tennyson's Enoch Arden with music by Richard Strauss, 1983–84. George Eastman Award, George Eastman Inst., Rochester, NY, 1982. Grand Cross 1st class, Order of Merit (Federal Republic of Germany), 1985. *Recreation:* mountain climbing. *Address:* 54 Eaton Square, SW1.

RAINGER, Peter, CBE 1978; FRS 1982; FEng; Deputy Director of Engineering, British Broadcasting Corporation, 1978–84, retired; *b* 17 May 1924; *s* of Cyril and Ethel Rainger; *m* 1st, 1953, Josephine Campbell (decd); two *s*; 2nd, 1972, Barbara Gibson. *Educ:* Northampton Engrg Coll.; London Univ. (BSc(Eng)). CEng, FIEE; FEng 1979. British Broadcasting Corporation: Head of Designs Dept, 1968–71; Head of Research Dept, 1971–76; Asst Dir of Engrg, 1976–78. Chairman: Professional Gp E14, IEE, 1973–76; various working parties, EBU, 1971–84. Fellow, Royal Television Soc., 1969. Geoffrey Parr Award, Royal TV Soc., 1964; J. J. Thompson Premium, IEE, 1966; TV Acad. Award, Nat. Acad. of Arts and Scis, 1968; David Sarnoff Gold Medal, SMPTE, 1972. *Publications:* Satellite Broadcasting, 1985; technical papers in IEE, Royal TV Soc. and SMPTE jls. *Recreations:* sculpture, model engineering. *Address:* 22 Mill Meadow, Milford on Sea, Hants SO41 0UG.

RAINS, Prof. Anthony John Harding, CBE 1986; MS, FRCS; Hunterian Trustee, Royal College of Surgeons of England, since 1982; *b* 5 Nov. 1920; *s* of late Dr Robert Harding Rains and Mrs Florence Harding Rains; *m* 1943, Mary Adelaide Lillywhite; three *d*. *Educ:* Christ's Hospital School, Horsham; St Mary's Hospital, London. MB, BS London 1943; MS London 1952; MRCS; LRCP 1943; FRCS 1948. Ho. Surg. and Ho. Phys. St Mary's, 1943. RAF, 1944–47. Ex-Service Registrar to Mr Handfield-Jones and Lord Porritt, 1947–48; Res. Surgical Officer, Bedford County Hosp., 1948–50; Lectr in Surgery, Univ. of Birmingham, 1950–54, Sen. Lectr, 1955–59; Prof. of Surgery, Charing Cross Hosp. Medical Sch., Univ. of London, and Hon. Consultant Surgeon, Charing Cross Hosp., 1959–81; Asst Dir, BPMF, Univ. of London, and Postgraduate Dean, SW Thames RHA, 1981–85. Hon. Consulting Surgeon, United Birmingham Hospitals, 1954–59; Hon. Consultant Surgeon to the Army, 1972–82. Royal College of Surgeons of England: Mem. Court of Examiners, 1968–74; Mem. Council, 1972–84; Dean, Inst. of Basic Med. Scis, 1976–82; Vice-President, 1983–84; Hon. Librarian, 1984–. Chm., Med. Commn on Accident Prevention, 1974–83. Pres., Nat. Assoc. of Theatre Nurses, 1979–81. Trustee, Smith and Nephew Foundn, 1972–. Sir Arthur Keith medal, RCS. Editor: Annals of RCS; Jl of RSocMed, 1985–94. *Publications:* (ed with Dr P. B. Kunkler) The Treatment of Cancer in Clinical Practice, 1959; Gallstones: Causes and Treatment, 1964; (ed) Bailey and Love's Short Practice of Surgery, 13th edn (ed with W, M. Capper), 1965, 20th edn (ed with C. V. Mann), 1988; Edward Jenner and Vaccination, 1975; Emergency and Acute Care, 1976; Lister and Antisepsis, 1977; 1,001 Multiple Choice Questions and Answers in Surgery, 1978, 3rd edn 1991; articles on the surgery of the gall bladder, on the formation of gall stones, inguinal hernia and arterial disease. *Recreations:* rough work, painting. *Address:* 39A St Cross Road, Winchester, Hants SO23 9PR. *T:* Winchester (01962) 869419.

RAISER, Rev. Dr Konrad; General Secretary, World Council of Churches, since 1993; *b* Magdeburg, 25 Jan. 1938; *m* 1967, Elisabeth von Weizsäcker; four *s*. *Educ:* Univ. of Tübingen (DTheol 1970). Ordained into German Evangelical Ch., 1964; Asst Pastor, Württemberg, 1963–65; Lectr, Prostestant Theol. Faculty, Tübingen, 1967–69; World Council of Churches: Study Sec., Commn on Faith and Order, 1969–73; Dep. Gen. Sec., 1973–83; Prof. of Systematic Theol. and Ecumenics, and Dir, Ecumenical Inst., Protestant Theol. Faculty, Univ. of Ruhr, 1983–93. *Publications:* Identität und Sozialität, 1971; Ökumene im Ubergang, 1989 (Ecumenism in Transition, 1991); (contrib.) Dictionary of the Ecumenical Movement, 1991; many essays and articles. *Address:* World Council of Churches, 150 Route de Ferney, PO Box 2100, 1211 Geneva 2, Switzerland.

RAISMAN, John Michael, CBE 1983; Chairman, Council for Industry and Higher Education, since 1991 (Member, since 1988); Chairman, British Biotech plc, since 1995 (Director, since 1993); *b* 12 Feb. 1929; *er s* of Sir Jeremy Raisman, GCMG, GCIE, KCSI, and late Renee Mary Raisman; *m* 1953, Evelyn Anne, *d* of Brig. J. I. Muirhead, CIE, MC; one *s* three *d*. *Educ:* Dragon Sch., Oxford; Rugby Sch.; The Queen's Coll., Oxford (Jodrell Schol., MA Lit Hum). CIMgt (CBIM 1980). Joined Royal Dutch/Shell Group, 1953; served in Brazil, 1954–60; General Manager, Shell Panama, 1961–62; Asst to Exploration and Production Coordinator, The Hague, 1963–65; Gen. Man., Shell Co. of Turkey, 1966–69; President, Shell Sekiyu K. K. Japan, 1970–73; Head, European Supply and Marketing, 1974–77; Man. Dir, Shell UK Oil, 1977–78; Regional Coordinator, UK and Eire, Shell Internat. Pet. Co. Ltd, 1978–85; Shell UK Ltd: Dep. Chm., 1978–79; Chief Exec., 1978–85; Chm., 1979–85; Govt Dir, 1984–87, Dep. Chm., 1987–91, British Telecom. Director: Vickers PLC, 1981–90; Glaxo Hldgs PLC, 1982–90; Lloyds Bank Plc, 1985–; Lloyds Merchant Bank Hldgs Ltd, 1985–87; Candover Investments PLC, 1990–; Tandem Computers Ltd, 1991–. Chairman: Adv. Council, London Enterprise Agency, 1979–85; UK Oil Industry Emergency Cttee, 1980–85; Council of Industry for Management Educn, 1981–85; Investment Bd, Electra-Candover Partners, 1985–. Member: Council, CBI, 1979– (Chm., CBI Europe Cttee, 1980–88); Mem., President's Cttee, 1980–88); Council, Inst. of Petroleum, 1979–81; Council, Inst. for Fiscal Studies, 1982–; Governing Council, Business in the Community, 1982–85; Council, UK Centre for Econ. and Environmental Develt, 1985–89; Royal Commn on Environmental Pollution, 1986–87; Chm., Electronics Industry EDC, 1986–87. Chm., Langs Lead Body, 1990–; Dep. Chm., Nat. Commn on Educn, 1991–. Mem., Council for Charitable Support, 1986–91; Chm., RA Trust, 1987–, Trustee, RA, 1983–; Governor, National

Inst. of Econ. and Social Res., 1983–92; Pro-Chancellor, Aston Univ., 1987–93. DUniv Stirling, 1983; Hon. LLD: Aberdeen, 1985; Manchester, 1986; Hon. DSc Aston, 1992. *Recreations:* golf, skiing, music, theatre, travel. *Address:* Netheravon House, Netheravon Road South, W4 2PY. *Clubs:* Brooks's; Royal Mid-Surrey; Sunningdale Golf.

RAISON, Dr John Charles Anthony, MA, MD; FFPHM; Consultant in Public Health Medicine, Wessex Regional Health Authority, 1982–91, retired; *b* 13 May 1926; *s* of late Cyril A. Raison, FRCS, Edgbaston, Birmingham, and of Ceres Raison; *m* 1st, 1951 (marr. diss. 1982); one *s* two *d*; 2nd, 1983, Ann Alexander, *d* of Captain Faulkner, MM and Mrs J. H. R. Faulkner, Southampton; three step *d*. *Educ:* Malvern Coll.; Trinity Hall, Cambridge; Birmingham Univ. Consultant Clinical Physiologist in Cardiac Surgery, Birmingham Reg. Hosp. Bd, 1962; Hon. Associate Consultant Clinical Physiologist, United Birmingham Hosps, 1963; Sen. Physiologist, Dir of Clinical Res. and Chief Planner, Heart Research Inst., Presbyterian-Pacific Medical Center, San Francisco, 1966; Chief Scientific Officer and Sen. Princ. Medical Officer, Scientific Services, DHSS, 1974–78; Dep. Dir, Nat. Radiological Protection Bd, 1978–81. Vis. Consultant, Civic Hosps, Lisbon (Gulbenkian Foundn), 1962; Arris and Gale Lectr, Royal College of Surgeons, 1965. Councillor, Southam RDC, 1955–59. *Publications:* chapters in books, and papers in medical jls on open-heart surgery, extracorporeal circulation, intensive care, scientific services in health care, and computers in medicine. *Recreations:* gardening, golf, singing. *Address:* Broom Cottage, Easton, near Winchester, Hants SO21 1EF. *T:* Itchen Abbas (01962) 779723.

RAISON, Rt. Hon. Sir Timothy (Hugh Francis), Kt 1991; PC 1982; Chairman: Advertising Standards Authority, 1991–94; Aylesbury Vale Community Healthcare NHS Trust, since 1992; *b* 3 Nov. 1929; *s* of late Maxwell and Celia Raison; *m* 1956, Veldes Julia Charrington; one *s* three *d*. *Educ:* Dragon Sch., Oxford; Eton (King's Schol.); Christ Church, Oxford (Open History Schol.). Editorial Staff: Picture Post, 1953–56; New Scientist, 1956–61; Editor: Crossbow, 1958–60; New Society, 1962–68. Member: Youth Service Develt Council, 1960–63; Central Adv. Council for Educn, 1963–66; Adv. Cttee on Drug Dependence, 1966–70; Home Office Adv, Council on Penal System, 1970–74; (co-opted) Inner London Educn Authority Educn Cttee, 1967–70; Richmond upon Thames Council, 1967–71. MP (C) Aylesbury, 1970–92; PPS to Sec. of State for N Ireland, 1972–73; Parly Under-Sec. of State, DES, 1973–74; Opposition spokesman on the Environment, 1975–76; Minister of State, Home Office, 1979–83; Minister of State, FCO, and Minister for Overseas Develt, 1983–86. Chm., Select Cttee on Educn, Science and the Arts, 1987–89. Sen. Fellow, Centre for Studies in Soc. Policy, 1974–77; Mem. Council, PSI, 1978–79; Vice-Chm. Bd, British Council, 1987–92. Nansen Medal (for share in originating World Refugee Year), 1960. *Publications:* Why Conservative?, 1964; (ed) Youth in New Society, 1966; (ed) Founding Fathers of Social Science, 1969; Power and Parliament, 1979; Tories and the Welfare State, 1990; various political pamphlets. *Recreations:* golf, gardening, history of art. *Club:* Beefsteak.

RAITT, Prof. Alan William, DPhil; FBA 1992; FRSL; Professor of French Literature, Oxford University, since 1992; Fellow, Magdalen College, Oxford, since 1966; *b* 21 Sept. 1930; *s* of William Raitt, MBE, BSc and May (*née* Davison); *m* 1st, 1959, Janet Taylor (marr. diss. 1971); two *d*; 2nd, 1974, Lia Noémia Rodrigues Correia. *Educ:* King Edward VI Grammar Sch. Morpeth; Magdalen Coll., Oxford (MA 1955; DPhil 1957). Oxford University: Fellow (by Examn), Magdalen Coll., 1953–55; Fellow and Lectr in French, Exeter Coll., 1955–66; Lectr in French, Magdalen Coll., 1966–; Reader in French Lit., 1979–92. Vis. Lectr, Univ. of Georgia, 1986; Vis. Prof., Sorbonne, Paris, 1987–88. Gen. Editor, French Studies, 1987–. FRSL 1971. Médaille d'Argent, Grand Prix du Rayonnement de la Langue Française, French Acad., 1987. Officier dans l'Ordre des Palmes Académiques, 1987. *Publications:* Villiers de l'Isle-Adam et le Mouvement symboliste, 1965; Life and Letters in France: the nineteenth century, 1966; Prosper Mérimée, 1970; The Life of Villiers de l'Isle-Adam, 1981; (ed jtly) Villiers de l'Isle-Adam: Œuvres complètes, 1986; Villiers de l'Isle-Adam exorciste du réel, 1987; Flaubert: Trois Contes, 1991; (ed) Mallarmé, Villiers de l'Isle-Adam, 1993; (ed) Villiers de l'Isle-Adam, L'Eve future, 1993; (ed) Flaubert, Pour Louis Bouilhet, 1994; A. C. Friedel et 'Le Nouveau Théâtre allemand': un intermédiaire méconnu, 1995. *Recreation:* watching football. *Address:* Magdalen College, Oxford OX1 4AU. *T:* Oxford (01865) 276024.

RAITZ, Vladimir Gavrilovich; airline and travel consultant; *b* 23 May 1922; *s* of Dr Gavril Raitz and Cecilia Raitz; *m* 1954, Helen Antonia (*née* Corkrey); three *d*. *Educ:* Mill Hill Sch.; London University. BSc(Econ.), Econ. History, 1942. British United Press, 1942–43; Reuters, 1943–48; Chm., Horizon Holidays, 1949–74. Member: NEDC for Hotels and Catering Industry, 1968–74; Cinematograph Films Council, 1969–74; Ct of Governors, LSE, 1971–. Cavaliere Ufficiale, Order of Merit (Italy), 1971. *Recreations:* reading, ski-ing. *Address:* 32 Dudley Court, Upper Berkeley Street, W1H 7PH. *T:* 0171-262 2592; The Coach House, Oakdale Road, Tunbridge Wells, Kent TN4 8DS. *T:* Tunbridge Wells (01892) 547619. *Club:* Reform.

RAJ, Prof. Kakkadan Nandanath; Hon. Emeritus Fellow, Centre for Development Studies, Trivandrum, Kerala State, since 1983 (Fellow, 1973–84); National Professor, since 1992; *b* 13 May 1924; *s* of K. N. Gopalan and Karthiayani Gopalan; *m* 1957, Dr Sarasamma Narayanan; two *s*. *Educ:* Madras Christian Coll., Tambaram (BA (Hons), MA, in Economics); London Sch. of Economics (PhD (Econ); Hon. Fellow, 1982). Asst Editor, Associated Newspapers of Ceylon, Nov. 1947–July 1948; Research Officer, Dept of Research, Reserve Bank of India, Aug. 1948–Feb. 1950; Asst Chief, Economic Div., Planning Commn, Govt of India, 1950–53; University of Delhi: Prof. of Economics, Delhi Sch. of Economics, 1953–73; Vice-Chancellor, 1969–70; Nat. Fellow in Economics, 1971–73; Jawaharlal Nehru Fellow, 1987–88. Mem., Economic Adv. Council to Prime Minister of India, 1983–91. Visiting Prof., Johns Hopkins Univ., Jan.–June, 1958; Vis. Fellow, Nuffield Coll., Oxford, Jan.–June, 1960. Corresp. Fellow, British Academy, 1972. Hon. Fellow, Amer. Economic Assoc. *Publications:* The Monetary Policy of the Reserve Bank of India, 1948; Employment Aspects of Planning in Underdeveloped Economies, 1956; Some Economic Aspects of the Bhakra-Nangal Project, 1960; Indian Economic Growth-Performance and Prospects, 1964; India, Pakistan and China-Economic Growth and Outlook, 1966; Investment in Livestock in Agrarian Economies, 1969; (ed jtly) Essays on the Commercialization of Indian Agriculture, 1985; Organizational Issues in Indian Agriculture, 1990; also articles in Economic Weekly, Economic and Political Weekly, Indian Economic Review, Oxford Economic Papers. *Address:* Nandavan, Kumarapuram, Trivandrum 695011, Kerala State, India. *T:* (home) (471) 443309, (office) (471) 448881, 448412.

RAJAH, Arumugam Ponnu; a Judge of the Supreme Court, Singapore, 1976–90; *b* Negri Sembilan, Malaysia, 23 July 1911; *m* Vijaya Lakshmi; one *s* one *d*. *Educ:* St Paul's Inst., Seremban; Raffles Instn and Raffles Coll., Singapore; Lincoln Coll., Oxford Univ. (BA). Barrister-at-law, Lincoln's Inn. City Councillor, Singapore: nominated, 1947–49; elected, 1949–57; MLA for Farrer Park, Singapore, 1959–66, Chm., Public Accounts Cttee, 1959–63, Speaker, 1964–66; first High Comr for Singapore to UK, 1966–71; High Comr to Australia, 1971–73; practised law, Tan Rajah & Cheah, Singapore, 1973–76. Mem. Bd of Trustees, Singapore Improvement Trust, 1949–57; Mem., Raffles Coll. Council and Univ. of Malaya Council, 1955–63; Chm., Inst. of SE Asian Studies, 1975–84; Pro-Chancellor, Nat. Univ. of Singapore, 1975–. Hon. Dr Laws Nat. Univ. of Singapore, 1984. *Address:* 7–D Balmoral Road, Singapore 1025.

RALEIGH, Dr Jean Margaret Macdonald C.; *see* Curtis-Raleigh.

RALLI, Sir Godfrey (Victor), 3rd Bt, *cr* 1912; TD; *b* 9 Sept. 1915; *s* of Sir Strati Ralli, 2nd Bt, MC; *S* father 1964; *m* 1st, 1937, Nora Margaret Forman (marriage dissolved, 1947); one *s* two *d*; 2nd, 1949, Jean, *er d* of late Keith Barlow. *Educ:* Eton. Joined Ralli Bros Ltd, 1936. Served War of 1939–45 (despatches), Captain, Berkshire Yeomanry RA. Dir and Vice-Pres., Ralli Bros Ltd, 1946–62; Chm., Greater London Fund for the Blind, 1962–82. *Recreations:* fishing, golf. *Heir:* *s* David Charles Ralli [*b* 5 April 1946; *m* 1975, Jacqueline Cecilia, *d* of late David Smith; one *s* one *d*]. *Address:* Great Walton, Eastry, Sandwich, Kent CT13 0DN. *T:* Sandwich (01304) 611355. *Club:* Naval and Military.

RALLING, (Antony) Christopher, OBE 1992; FRGS; freelance writer/director; *b* 12 April 1929; *s* of Harold St George Ralling and Dorothy Blanche Ralling; *m* 1963, Angela Norma (*née* Gardner); one *d*. *Educ:* Charterhouse; Wadham Coll., Oxford (BA 2nd Cl. Hons English). Joined BBC External Services, Scriptwriter, 1955; British Meml Foundn Fellowship to Australia, 1959; Dep. Editor, Panorama, BBC TV, 1964; joined BBC TV Documentaries, 1966; directed The Search for the Nile, 1972 (Amer. Acad. Award, 1972; Peabody Award, 1972); Mem., British Everest Expedn, 1975; produced The Voyage of Charles Darwin, 1978 (British Acad. Award, 1978; Desmond Davies British Acad. Award, 1978; RTS Silver Medal, 1979); Hd of Documentaries, BBC TV, 1980; left BBC to start Dolphin Productions, 1982; directed: The History of Africa, 1984; Chasing a Rainbow (Josephine Baker), 1986 (Amer. Acad. Award, 1986); Prince Charles at Forty, LWT, 1988; The Kon-Tiki Man, BBC, 1989; The Buried Mirror, BBC, 1992. FRGS 1978. *Publications:* Muggeridge Through the Microphone, 1967; The Voyage of Charles Darwin, 1978; Shackleton, 1983; The Kon-Tiki Man, 1990; A Diplomat in Japan, 1992; Return to Everest, 1993. *Recreations:* tennis, ski-ing. *Address:* The Coach House, Tankerville, Kingston Hill, Surrey KT2 7JH. *Club:* Alpine.

RALPH, Colin John, MPhil; RN; DN; Registrar and Chief Executive, United Kingdom Central Council for Nursing, Midwifery and Health Visiting, 1987–94; *b* 16 June 1951; *s* of Harold Ernest Ralph and Vining Bromley. *Educ:* Royal West Sussex Hosp. (RGN); RCN/Univ. of London (DN); Brunel Univ. (MPhil). Staff Nurse and Student, Nat. Heart Hosp., 1974; Charge Nurse, Royal Free Hosp., 1974–77; Nursing Officer, London Hosp., 1978–83; Dir of Nursing, Westminster Hosp. and Westminster Children's Hosp., 1983–86; Chief Nursing Adviser, Gloucester HA, 1986–87. Vis. Sen. Res. Fellow, Dept of Nursing, KCL, 1992–. British Red Cross Society: Mem., Nat. Exec. Cttee, 1974–76; Nursing Adviser, 1975–. Member: Standing Nursing and Midwifery Adv. Cttee, 1986–; Professional Services Cttee, RCN, 1986–87; EC Adv. Cttee on Trng in Nursing, 1990–; Internat. Cttee, RCN, 1991–; National Florence Nightingale Memorial Committee: Florence Nightingale Scholar, 1981; Mem., Council of Management, 1983–. *Publications:* contribs to nursing profession jls and books. *Recreations:* friends, the arts, travel.

RALPH, Richard Peter, CVO 1991; HM Diplomatic Service; Ambassador to Latvia, since 1993; *b* 27 April 1946; *s* of Peter and Marion Ralph; *m* 1970, Margaret Elisabeth Coulthurst; one *s* one *d*. *Educ:* King's Sch., Canterbury; Edinburgh Univ. (MSc). Third Sec., FCO, 1969–70; Third, later Second, Sec., Vientiane, Laos, 1970–73; Second, later First, Sec., Lisbon, 1974–77; FCO, 1977–81; Head of Chancery, Harare, Zimbabwe, 1981–85; Counsellor, FCO, 1985–89; Head of Chancery and Congressional Counsellor, Washington, 1989–93. *Recreation:* motorcycles. *Address:* c/o Foreign and Commonwealth Office, King Charles Street, SW1A 2AH.

RALPHS, Enid Mary, (Lady Ralphs), CBE 1984; JP; DL; Chairman of the Council, Magistrates' Association, 1981–84; *b* 20 Jan. 1915; *d* of Percy William Cowlin and Annie Louise Cowlin (*née* Willoughby); *m* 1938, Sir (Frederick) Lincoln Ralphs, Kt 1973 (*d* 1978); one *s* two *d*. *Educ:* Camborne Grammar Sch.; University Coll., Exeter (BA); DipEd Cambridge. Pres., Guild of Undergrads, Exeter, 1936–37; Vice-Pres., NUS, 1937–38. Teacher, Penzance Grammar Sch., 1937–38; Staff Tutor, Oxford Univ. Tutorial Classes Cttee, 1942–44; pt-time Sen. Lectr, Keswick Hall Coll. of Educn, 1948–80. Member: Working Party on Children and Young Persons Act 1969, 1977–78; Steering Cttee on Community Alternatives for Young Offenders, NACRO, 1979–82; Consultative Cttee on Educn in Norwich Prison, 1982–87; Home Office Adv. Bd on Restricted Patients, 1985–91. Member: Religious Adv. Council, BBC Midland Reg., 1963–66; Guide Council for GB, 1965–68. President: Norwich and Dist Br., UNA, 1973–; Norfolk Girl Guides, 1987–. Governor: Norwich Sch.; Culford Sch.; Visitor, Wymondham Coll., 1991–. Trustee, Norfolk Children's Projects, 1982–. JP Norwich 1958; Chairman: Norwich Juvenile Panel, 1964–79; Norwich Bench, 1977–85; former Mem., Licensing Cttee; Mem., Domestic Panel, 1981–85; Chm., Norfolk Br., Magistrates' Assoc.; Dep. Chm., Norfolk Magistrates' Courts Cttee, 1978–85 (Chm., Trng Sub-Cttee); Mem., Central Council, Magistrates' Courts Cttees, 1974–81. DL Norfolk 1981. Hon. DCL East Anglia, 1989. *Publications:* (jtly) The Magistrate as Chairman, 1987; contribs to various jls. *Recreations:* gardening, travel. *Address:* Jesselton, 218 Unthank Road, Norwich NR2 2AH. *T:* Norwich (01603) 453382. *Clubs:* Royal Over-Seas League; Norfolk (Norwich).

RAMA RAU, Santha; free-lance writer since 1945; English teacher at Sarah Lawrence College, Bronxville, NY, since 1971; *b* Madras, India, 24 Jan. 1923; *d* of late Sir Benegal Rama Rau, CIE and Lady Dhanvanthi Rama Rau; *m* 1st, 1951, Faubion Bowers (marr. diss. 1966); one *s*; 2nd, Gurdon W. Wattles. *Educ:* St Paul's Girls' School, London, England; Wellesley College, Mass., USA. Feature writer for the Office of War Information, New York, USA, during vacations from college, 1942–45. Hon. doctorate: Bates College, USA, 1961; Russell Sage College, 1965; Phi Beta Kappa, Wellesley College, 1960; Roosevelt Coll., 1962; Brandeis Univ., 1963; Bard Coll., NY, 1964. *Publications:* Home to India, 1945; East of Home, 1950; This is India, 1953; Remember the House, 1955; View to the South-East, 1957, My Russian Journey, 1959; A Passage to India (dramatization), 1962; Gifts of Passage, 1962; The Adventuress, 1971; Cooking of India, 1971 (2 vols); A Princess Remembers (with Rajmata Gayatri Devi of Jaipur), 1976; An Inheritance (with Dhanvanthi Rama Rau), 1977; many articles and short stories in New Yorker, Art News, Horizon, Saturday Evening Post, Reader's Digest, etc. *Address:* RR1, Box 200, Amenia, NY 12501, USA.

RAMACHANDRAN, Prof. Gopalasamudram Narayana, FRS 1977; Indian National Science Academy Albert Einstein National Professor, 1984–89; retired; specialist in molecular biology, biophysics and mathematical logic; *b* 8 Oct. 1922; *s* of G. R. Narayana Iyer and Lakshmi Ammal; *m* 1945, Rajalakshmi Sankaran; two *s* one *d*. *Educ:* Maharaja's Coll., Ernakulam, Cochin; Indian Inst. of Science; Univ. of Madras (MA, MSc, DSc); Univ. of Cambridge (PhD). Lectr in Physics, Indian Inst. of Science, 1946–47, Asst Prof., 1949–52; 1851 Exhibn Scholar, Univ. of Cambridge, 1947–49; Prof., Univ. of Madras, 1952–70 (Dean, Faculty of Science, 1964–67); Indian Institute of Science: Prof. of Biophysics, 1970–78; Prof. of Mathematical Philosophy, 1978–81; Hon. Fellow, 1984; Dist. Scientist, Centre for Cellular and Molecular Biology, Hyderabad, 1981–83. Dir, Univ. Grants Commn Centre of Advanced Study in Biophysics, 1962–70; part-time Prof.

of Biophysics, Univ. of Chicago, 1967–78. Member: Physical Res. Cttee, 1959–69; Nat. Cttee for Biophysics, 1961–; Bd of Sci. and Ind. Res., India, 1962–65; Council, Internat. Union of Pure and Applied Biophysics, 1969–72; Commn on Macromolecular Biophysics, 1969; Chm., Nat. Cttee for Crystallography, 1963–70; Senior Vis. Prof., Univ. of Michigan, 1965–66; Jawaharlal Nehru Fellow, 1968–70; Fogarty Internat. Schol., NIH, 1977–78. Fellow, Indian Acad. of Sciences, 1950 (Mem. Council, 1953–70; Sec., 1956–58; Vice-Pres., 1962–64); Fellow, Indian Nat. Sci. Acad., 1963; FRSA 1971. Hon. Mem., Amer. Soc. of Molecular Biology, 1965; Hon. Foreign Mem., Amer. Acad. of Arts and Scis; Founder Member: Indian Acad. of Yoga, 1980; Third World Acad., Rome, 1982. Hon. DSc: Roorkee, 1979; Indian Inst. Technology, Madras, 1985; Hyderabad, 1989; Banaras Hindu, 1991. Bhatnagar Meml Prize, 1961; Watumull Prize, 1964; John Arthur Wilson Award, 1967; Ramanujan Medal, 1971; Maghnad Saha Medal, 1971; J. C. Bose Gold Medal and Prize of Bose Inst., 1975; Fogarty Medal, 1978; Distinguished Alumni Award, Indian Inst. of Sci., 1978; C. V. Raman Award, 1982; Birla Award for Medical Science, 1984. Editor: Current Science, 1950–58; Jl Indian Inst. of Sci., 1973–77; Member Editorial Board: Jl Molecular Biol., 1959–66; Biochimica et Biophysica Acta, 1965–72; Indian Jl Pure and Applied Physics, 1963–80; Internat. Jl Peptide and Protein Res., 1969–82; Indian Jl Biochem. and Biophys., 1970–78; Connective Tissue Research 1972–84; Biopolymers, 1973–86; Jl Biomolecular Structure and Dynamics, 1984–. *Publications:* Crystal Optics, in Handbuch der Physik, vol. 25; Molecular Structure of Collagen, in Internat. Review of Connective Tissue Research, vol. 1; Conformation of Polypeptides and Proteins, in Advances in Protein Chemistry, vol. 23; Conformation Polypeptide Chains, in Annual Reviews in Biochemistry, vol. 39; Fourier Methods in Crystallography, 1970; (ed) Advanced Methods of Crystallography; (ed) Aspects of Protein Structure; (ed) Treatise on Collagen, 2 vols, 1967; (ed) Conformation of Biopolymers, vols 1 and 2, 1967; (ed) Crystallography and Crystal Perfection; (ed) Biochemistry of Collagen. *Recreations:* Indian and Western music; detective fiction. *Address:* Gita, 5, 10–A Main Road, Malleswaram West, Bangalore 560055, India. *T:* (812) 3340362.

RAMADHANI, Most Rev. John Acland; *see* Tanzania, Archbishop of.

RAMAGE, (James) Granville (William), CMG 1975; HM Diplomatic Service, retired; *b* 19 Nov. 1919; *s* of late Rev. George Granville Ramage and Helen Marion (*née* Middlemass); *m* 1947, Eileen Mary Smith; one *s* two *d. Educ:* Glasgow Acad.; Glasgow University. Served in HM Forces, 1940–46 (despatches). Entered HM Foreign Service, 1947; seconded for service at Bombay, 1947–49; transf. to Foreign Office, 1950; First Sec. and Consul at Manila, 1952–56; South-East Asia Dept, FO, 1956–58; Consul at Atlanta, Ga, 1958–62; Gen. Dept, FO, 1962–63; Consul-General, Tangier, 1963–67; High Comr in The Gambia, 1968–71; Ambassador, People's Democratic Republic of Yemen, 1972–75; Consul General at Boston, Massachusetts, 1975–77. *Recreations:* music, golf. *Address:* 4 Merton Hall Road, Wimbledon, SW19 3PP. *T:* 0181–715 7939.

RAMAGE, Prof. Robert, DSc; FRS 1992; CChem, FRSC; FRSE; Forbes Professor of Organic Chemistry, University of Edinburgh, since 1984; *b* 4 Oct. 1935; *s* of Robert Bain Ramage and Jessie Boag Ramage; *m* 1961, Joan Fraser Paterson; three *d. Educ:* Whitehill Sen. Secondary Sch., Glasgow; Univ. of Glasgow (BSc Hons 1958; PhD 1961; DSc 1982). Fulbright Fellow and Fellow of Harvard Coll., 1961–63; Research at Woodward Res. Inst., 1963–64; Lectr then Sen. Lectr, Univ. of Liverpool, 1964–77; Prof., 1977–84, Head of Dept, 1979–84, UMIST; Head, Dept of Chem., Univ. of Edinburgh, 1987–90. FRSE 1986; FRSA 1990. *Recreations:* sport, gardening, current affairs. *Address:* Department of Chemistry, University of Edinburgh, West Mains Road, Edinburgh EH9 3JJ. *T:* 0131–650 4721.

RAMBAHADUR LIMBU, Captain, VC 1966; MVO 1984; HM the Queen's Gurkha Orderly Officer, 1983–84; employed in Sultanate of Negara Brunei Darussalam, 1985–92; *b* Nov. 1939; *s* of late Tekbir Limbu; *m* 1st, 1960, Tikamaya Limbuni (*d* 1966); two *s*; 2nd, 1967, Punimaya Limbuni; three *s*. Army Cert. of Educn 1st cl. Enlisted 10th Princess Mary's Own Gurkha Rifles, 1957; served on ops in Borneo (VC); promoted Sergeant, 1971; WOII, 1976; commissioned, 1977. Hon. Captain (Gurkha Commnd Officer), 1985. *Publication:* My Life Story, 1978. *Recreations:* football, volley-ball, badminton, basketball. *Address:* Ward No 13 Damak, Nagar Palika, PO Box Damak, District Jhapa, Mechi Zone, East Nepal. *Clubs:* VC and GC Association, Royal Society of St George (England).

RAMIN, Mme Manfred; *see* Cotrubas, I.

RAMM, Rev. Canon (Norwyn) MacDonald; Vicar of St Michael at the North Gate with St Martin and All Saints, Oxford, 1961–88 (Curate, 1957–61); City Rector, Oxford, 1961–89; Chaplain to the Queen, 1985–94; *b* 8 June 1924; *s* of Rev. Ezra Edward and Dorothy Mary Ramm; *m* 1962, Ruth Ellen, *d* of late Robert James Kirton, CBE, FIA; two *s* one *d. Educ:* Berkhamsted School; St Peter's Theological College, Jamaica; Lincoln College, Oxford. Jamaica appointments: Curate, St James, Montego Bay, 1951–53, deacon 1951, priest, 1952; Master, Cornwall College; Rector, St Jude's, Stony Hill with Mount James, 1953–57; Master, Wolmers Girls' School; Chaplain to Approved Sch., Stony Hill; Priest in charge, St Martin and All Saints, Oxford, 1961–71; Hon. Canon, Christ Church Cathedral, Oxford, 1985–88, now Emeritus. Chaplain to: HM Prison, Oxford, 1975–88; British Fire Services Assoc., 1980–; RTR, Para Regtl Assoc., Desert Forces (all Oxford branches). Pres., Isis Dist Scout Assoc., 1984–; Chm. Council, Headington Sch., 1984–93 (Patron, 1994); Founder and Pres., Samaritans of Oxford, 1963–. *Publication:* Graces Old and New from Oxford, 1990. *Recreations:* ski-ing, gardening, collecting Graces. *Address:* Fairlawn, Church Lane, Harwell, Abingdon, Oxon OX11 0EZ. *T:* Abingdon (01235) 835454. *Clubs:* Clarendon, Frewen (Oxford), Oxford Rotary.

RAMPAL, Jean-Pierre Louis; Commandeur de la Légion d'Honneur et de l'Ordre National du Mérite; Commandeur des Arts et Lettres; musician, concert flautist, conductor; *b* Marseilles, 7 Jan. 1922; *s* of Joseph Rampal and Andrée Roggero; *m* 1947, Françoise Bacqueyrisse; one *s* one *d. Educ:* Lycée Thiers; Facultés des Sciences et de Médecine, Marseilles; Conservatoire Nat. Sup. de Musique, Paris. Flute Prizes, Marseilles and Paris. Professional flautist, 1945–; numerous internat. festivals, world wide tours; Prof. of Flute, Conservatoire Nat. Sup. de Musique, 1969–82; research in ancient music; conducting début, French Provinces, 1948, Paris, 1967; conducting career mostly in USA, parallel to soloist performances. Prix Edison, Prix Léonie Sonning, 1978; Prix d'Honneur de Montreux, 1980. *Publication:* Music, My Love, 1989. *Recreations:* amateur cinema, tennis, diving. *Address:* (home) 15 avenue Mozart, 75016 Paris, France; (business) Bureau de Concerts de Valmalete, 75008 Paris, France.

RAMPHAL, Sir Shridath Surendranath, OE 1983; GCMG 1990 (CMG 1966); OM (Jamaica) 1990; OCC 1991; Kt 1970; QC (Guyana) 1965, SC 1966; President, World Conservation Union (formerly International Union for Conservation of Nature), 1991–93; Secretary-General of the Commonwealth, 1975–90; *b* 1928; *m. Educ:* King's Coll., London (LLM 1952). FKC 1975; Fellow, London Sch. of Econs, 1979. Called to the Bar, Gray's Inn, 1951 (Hon. Bencher 1981). Colonial Legal Probationer, 1951; Arden and Atkin Prize, 1952; John Simon Guggenheim Fellow, Harvard Law Sch., 1962. Crown Counsel, British Guiana, 1953–54; Asst to Attorney-Gen., 1954–56; Legal Draftsman, 1956–58; First Legal Draftsman, West Indies, 1958–59; Solicitor-Gen., British Guiana, 1959–61; Asst Attorney-Gen., West Indies, 1961–62, Attorney-Gen., Guyana, 1965–73; Minister of State for External Affairs, Guyana, 1967–72; Foreign Minister and Attorney General, Guyana, 1972–73; Minister, Foreign Affairs and Justice, 1973–75; Mem., National Assembly, Guyana, 1965–75. Member: Hon. Adv. Cttee, Center for Internat. Studies, NY Univ., 1966–; Internat. Commn of Jurists, 1970–; Bd, Vienna Inst. of Develt, 1973–; Internat. Hon. Cttee, Dag Hammarskjold Foundn, 1977–; Independent (Brandt) Commn on International Development Issues, 1977–; Ind. (Palme) Commn on Disarmament and Security Issues, 1980–89; Ind. Commn on Internat. Humanitarian Issues, 1983–; World Commn on Environment and Develt, 1984–; Indep. Commn of the South on Develt Issues, 1987–; Brandt Conf. Wkg Gp, 1990; Council, Television Trust for the Environment, 1984–; Internat. Bd, United World Colls, 1984–94; Bd of Governors, World Maritime Univ., Oslo, 1984–; Commonwealth of Learning, 1988–; Carnegie Commn on Preventing Deadly Conflict, 1994–; Bd, Internat. Develt Res. Centre, Ottawa. Vice Pres., Royal Over-Seas League. Chairman: UN Cttee on Develt Planning, 1984–87; W Indian Commn, 1990–92; Leadership Develt Prog., Rockefeller Foundn, 1991–; Adv. Cttee, Future Generations Alliance Foundn, Kyoto, 1994–; Bd, Internat. Inst. for Democracy and Electoral Assistance, 1995–; Co-Chm., Internat. Commn on Global Governance, 1992–. Vice-Chm., Centre for Research on New Internat. Econ. Order, Oxford, 1977–. Mem., Council of Internat. Negotiation Network, Carter Centre, Georgia, 1991–. Advr, Sec. Gen., UN Conf. on Envmt and Develt, 1992. Chancellor: Univ. of Guyana, 1988–92; Univ. of Warwick, 1989; Univ. of WI, 1989. Visiting Professor: Exeter Univ., 1988; Faculty of Laws, KCL, 1988. FRSA 1981; CBIM 1986. Hon. Fellow, Magdalen Coll., Oxford, 1982; Companion, Leicester Poly., 1991. Hon. LLD: Panjab, 1975; Southampton, 1976; St Francis Xavier, NS, 1978; Univ. of WI, 1978; Aberdeen, 1979; Cape Coast, Ghana, 1980; London, 1981; Benin, Nigeria, 1982; Hull, 1983; Yale, 1985; Cambridge, 1985; Warwick, 1988; York, Ont, 1988; Malta, 1989; Otago, 1990; DUniv: Surrey, 1979; Essex, 1980; Hon. DHL: Simmons Coll., Boston, 1982; Duke Univ., 1985; Hon. DCL: Oxon, 1982; E Anglia, 1983; Durham, 1985; Hon. DLitt: Bradford, 1985; Indira Gandhi Nat. Open Univ., New Delhi, 1989; Hon. DSc Cranfield Inst. of Technology, 1987. Albert Medal, RSA, 1988; Internat. Educn Award, Richmond Coll., 1988; Rene Dubos Human Envmt Award, 1993. AC 1982; ONZ 1990; Comdr, Order of Golden Ark (Netherlands), 1994. *Publications:* One World to Share: selected speeches of the Commonwealth Secretary-General 1975–79, 1979; Nkrumah and the Eighties: Kwame Nkrumah Memorial Lectures, 1980; Sovereignty and Solidarity: Callander Memorial Lectures, 1981; Some in Light and Some in Darkness: the long shadow of slavery (Wilberforce Lecture), 1983; The Message not the Messenger (STC Communication Lecture), 1985; The Trampling of the Grass (Economic Commn for Africa Silver Jubilee Lecture), 1985; Inseparable Humanity: an anthology of reflections of Shridath Ramphal (ed Ron Sanders), 1988; An End to Otherness (eight speeches by the Commonwealth Secretary-General), 1990; Our Country, The Planet, 1992; contrib. various political, legal and other jls incl. International and Comparative Law Qly, Caribbean Qly, Public Law, Guyana Jl, Round Table, Foreign Policy, Third World Qly, RSA Jl Internat. Affairs. *Address:* 31 St Matthew's Lodge, 50 Oakley Square, NW1 1NB. *Clubs:* Athenæum, Royal Automobile, Travellers'.

RAMPHUL, Sir Indurduth, Kt 1991; Governor, Bank of Mauritius, since 1982; *b* 10 Oct. 1931; *m* 1962, Taramatee Seedoyal; one *s* one *d. Educ:* Univ. of Exeter (Dip. Public Admin). Asst Sec., Min. of Finance, 1966–67; Bank of Mauritius: Manager, 1967; Chief Manager, 1970; Man. Dir, 1973. Alternate Governor, IMF for Mauritius. *Recreations:* reading, swimming. *Address:* (home) 9 Buswell Avenue, Quatre Bornes, Mauritius. *T:* 4541643; (office) Bank of Mauritius, PO Box 29, Port Louis, Mauritius. *T:* 2084293 and 2126127, *Fax:* 2089204. *Clubs:* Mauritius Turf; Cadets.

RAMSAY, family name of **Earl of Dalhousie.**

RAMSAY, Lord; James Hubert Ramsay, DL; Director, Jamestown Investments Ltd, since 1987; Chairman, William Evans Ltd, since 1994; *b* 17 Jan. 1948; *er s* and *heir* of 16th Earl of Dalhousie, *qv*; *m* 1973, Marilyn, *yr d* of Major Sir David Butter, *qv*; one *s* two *d. Educ:* Ampleforth. 2nd Bn Coldstream Guards, commnd 1968–71, RARO 1971. Director: Hambros Bank Ltd, 1981–82; (exec.) Enskilda Securities, 1982–87; Capel-Cure Myers Capital Management Ltd, 1988–91; Dunedin Smaller Cos Investment Trust, 1993–; Dunedin Japan Investment Trust, 1993–; Scottish Woodlands Ltd, 1993–. Mem., Royal Co. of Archers (The Queen's Body Guard for Scotland), 1979–. Vice Chm., Game Conservancy Trust; Pres., British Deer Soc., 1987–. DL Angus, 1993. *Heir: s* Hon. Simon David Ramsay, *b* 18 April 1981. *Address:* Dalhousie Lodge, Edzell, Angus DD9 7TU; 3 Vicarage Gardens, W8 4AH. *Clubs:* White's, Pratt's, Caledonian (Pres., 1990–), Turf.

RAMSAY, Sir Alexander William Burnett, 7th Bt, *cr* 1806, of Balmain (also *heir-pres* to Btcy of Burnett, *cr* 1626 (Nova Scotia), of Leys, Kincardineshire, which became dormant, 1959, on death of Sir Alexander Edwin Burnett of Leys, and was not claimed by Sir Alexander Burnett Ramsay, 6th Bt, of Balmain); *b* 4 Aug. 1938; *s* of Sir Alexander Burnett Ramsay, 6th Bt and Isabel Ellice, *e d* of late William Whitney, Woodstock, New South Wales; *S* father, 1965; *m* 1963, Neryl Eileen, *d* of J. C. Smith Thornton, Trangie, NSW; three *s. Heir: s* Alexander David Ramsay [*b* 20 Aug. 1966; *m* 1990, Annette Yvonne, *d* of H. M. Plummer]. *Address:* Bulbah, Warren, NSW 2824, Australia.

RAMSAY, Sir Allan (John Heppel Ramsay), KBE 1992; CMG 1989; HM Diplomatic Service; Ambassador to the Kingdom of Morocco, since 1992; *b* 19 Oct. 1937; *s* of Norman Ramsay Ramsay and Faith Evelyn Sorel-Cameron; *m* 1966, Pauline Therese Lescher; two *s* one *d. Educ:* Bedford Sch.; RMA Sandhurst; Durham Univ. Served Army, 1957–70: Somerset Light Infantry, 1957–65; DLI, 1965–70. Entered FCO, 1970; Ambassador: to Lebanon, 1988–90; to Sudan, 1990–91. *Address:* c/o Foreign and Commonwealth Office, SW1A 2AH.

RAMSAY, Andrew Charles Bruce; Under Secretary and Head of Arts and Lottery Group, Department of National Heritage, since 1993; *b* 30 May 1951; *s* of Norman Bruce Ramsay and Marysha Octavia Ramsay; *m* 1983, Katharine Celia Marsh; two *d. Educ:* Winchester Coll.; Bedford Coll., London Univ. (BA). Joined DoE, 1974; Private Sec. to Parly Sec., Dept of Transport, 1978–80; Principal, DoE and Dept of Transport, 1980–85; Asst Sec., DoE, 1986–93. *Recreations:* gardening, opera, birds. *Address:* Department of National Heritage, 2–4 Cockspur Street, SW1Y 5DH; West Hall, Sedgeford, Hunstanton, Norfolk PE36 5LY.

RAMSAY, Maj.-Gen. Charles Alexander, CB 1989; OBE 1979; landowner and farmer; *b* 12 Oct. 1936; *s* of Adm. Sir Bertram Home Ramsay, KCB, KBE, MVO, Allied Naval C-in-C, Invasion of Europe, 1944 (killed on active service, 1945), and Helen Margaret Menzies; *m* 1967, Hon. Mary MacAndrew, *d* of 1st Baron MacAndrew, PC, TD; two *s* two *d. Educ:* Eton; Sandhurst. Commissioned Royal Scots Greys, 1956; attended Canadian Army Staff Coll., 1967–68; served abroad in Germany, Middle East and Far East; Mil. Asst to VCDS, 1974–77; commanded Royal Scots Dragoon Guards, 1977–79; Colonel General Staff, MoD, 1979–80; Comdr 12th Armoured Bde, BAOR and Osnabrück Garrison, 1980–82; Dep. Dir of Mil. Ops, MoD, 1983–84; GOC Eastern District, 1984–87; Dir

Gen., Army Orgn and TA, 1987–89; resigned from Army. Col, Royal Scots Dragoon Guards, 1992–. Director: John Menzies plc, 1990–; Potomac Hldgs Inc., USA; Morningside Developments Ltd USA, and other cos; Chairman: Eagle Enterprises Ltd, Bermuda, 1991–; Cockburns of Leith Ltd, 1992–. Member, Queen's Body Guard for Scotland, Royal Company of Archers. *Recreations:* field sports, equitation, travel, motoring, aviation. *Address:* Bughtrig, Coldstream, Berwickshire TD12 4JP. *T:* Leitholm (01890) 840678; Chesthill, Glenlyon, Perthshire PH15 2NH. *T:* Glenlyon (01887) 877224. *Clubs:* Boodle's, Cavalry and Guards, Pratt's; New (Edinburgh).

RAMSAY, Donald Allan, ScD; FRS 1978; FRSC 1966; Principal Research Officer, National Research Council of Canada, 1968–87; *b* 11 July 1922; *s* of Norman Ramsay and Thirza Elizabeth Beckley; *m* 1946, Nancy Brayshaw; four *d*. *Educ:* Latymer Upper Sch.; St Catharine's Coll., Cambridge. BA 1943, MA 1947, PhD 1947, ScD 1976 (all Cantab). Research Scientist (Div. of Chemistry, 1947, Div. of Physics, 1949, Herzberg Inst. of Astrophysics, 1975), Nat. Research Council of Canada. Fellow, Amer. Phys. Soc., 1964; FCIC 1970 (CIC Medal, 1992); Vice-Pres., Acad. of Science, 1975–76; Hon. Treas., RSC, 1976–79, 1988–91 (Centennial Medal, 1982). Dr *hc* Reims, 1969; Fil.Hed. Stockholm, 1982. Queen Elizabeth II Silver Jubilee Medal, 1977; Commemorative Medal for 125th anniversary of Canadian Confederation, 1992; Alexander von Humboldt Res. Award, 1993, 1995. *Publications:* numerous articles on molecular spectroscopy and molecular structure, espec. free radicals. *Recreations:* sailing, fishing, organ playing. *Address:* 1578 Drake Avenue, Ottawa, Ontario K1G 0L8, Canada. *T:* (613) 7338899. *Club:* Leander (Henley).

RAMSAY, Henry Thomas, CBE 1960; Director, Safety in Mines Research Establishment, Ministry of Technology (formerly Ministry of Power), Sheffield, 1954–70, retired; *b* 7 Dec. 1907; *s* of Henry Thomas and Florence Emily Ramsay, Gravesend, Kent; *m* 1953, Dora Gwenllian Burgoyne Davies (*d* 1979); one *s* one *d*; *m* 1983, Vivian Ducatel Prague, Bay St Louis, Miss. *Educ:* MSc London. On scientific staff, Research Labs, GEC, 1928–48; RAE, 1948–54. Chartered engineer; FInstP; FIMinE; Pres., Midland Inst. Mining Engrs, 1970–71. *Publications:* contrib. to: Trans of Instn of Electrical Engrs; Jl of Inst. of Mining Engrs; other technical jls. *Recreations:* reading, walking.

RAMSAY, Prof. John Graham, CBE 1992; FRS 1973; Professor of Geology, Eidgenössische Technische Hochschule and University of Zürich, 1977–92, Hon. Professor, 1992; *b* 17 June 1931; *s* of Robert William Ramsay and Kathleen May Ramsay; *m* 1st, 1952, Sylvia Hiorns (marr. diss. 1957); 2nd, 1960, Christine Marden (marr. diss. 1987); three *d* (and one *d* decd); 3rd, 1990, Dorothee Dietrich. *Educ:* Edmonton County Grammar Sch.; Imperial Coll., London. DSc, PhD, DIC, BSc, ARCS, FGS. Musician, Corps of Royal Engineers, 1955–57; academic staff Imperial Coll., London, 1957–73: Prof. of Geology, 1966–73; Prof. of Earth Sciences, Leeds Univ., 1973–76. Mem., NERC, 1989–92. Vice-Pres., Société Géologique de France, 1973. For. Associate, US Nat. Acad. of Scis, 1985. Dr *hc* Rennes, 1978. *Publications:* Folding and Fracturing of Rocks, 1967; The Techniques of Modern Structural Geology, 1983. *Recreations:* chamber music, mountaineering, ski-ing. *Address:* Hädeliweg 30, 8044 Zürich, Switzerland.

RAMSAY, Norman James Gemmill; Sheriff of South Strathclyde, Dumfries and Galloway at Kirkcudbright, Stranraer and Dumfries (formerly Dumfries and Galloway, Western Division), 1971–85, now Hon. Sheriff; *b* 26 Aug. 1916; *s* of late James Ramsay and late Mrs Christina Emma Ramsay; *m* 1952, Rachael Mary Berkeley Cox, *d* of late Sir Herbert Charles Fahie Cox; two *s*. *Educ:* Merchiston Castle Sch.; Edinburgh Univ. (MA, LLB). Writer to the Signet, 1939; Advocate, Scotland, 1956. War Service, RN, 1940–46; Lt (S), RNVR. Colonial Legal Service, Northern Rhodesia: Administrator-General, 1947; Resident Magistrate, 1956; Sen. Resident Magistrate, 1958; Puisne Judge of High Court, Northern Rhodesia, later Zambia, 1964–68. Mem., Victoria Falls Trust, 1950–58. *Address:* Mill of Borgue, Kirkcudbright DG6 4SY.

RAMSAY, Patrick George Alexander; Controller, BBC Scotland, 1979–83; retired; *b* 14 April 1926; *yr s* of late Rt Rev. Ronald Erskine Ramsay, sometime Bishop of Malmesbury, and Winifred Constance Ramsay (*née* Partridge); *m* 1948, Hope Seymour Dorothy, *y d* of late Rt Rev. Algernon Markham, sometime Bishop of Grantham, and Winifred Edith Markham (*née* Barne); two *s*. *Educ:* Marlborough Coll.; Jesus Coll., Cambridge (MA). Served War, Royal Navy (Fleet Air Arm), 1944–46. Joined BBC as Report Writer, Eastern European Desk, Monitoring Service, 1949; Liaison Officer, US Foreign Broadcasts Information Service, Cyprus, 1951–52; Asst, Appts Dept, 1953–56; Sen. Admin. Asst, External Broadcasting, 1956–58; Admin. Officer News and Head of News Administration, 1958–64; Planning Manager, Television Programme Planning, 1964–66; Asst Controller: Programme Services, 1966–69; Programme Planning, 1969–72; Controller, Programme Services, 1972–79. General Managerial Advr, Oman Broadcasting Service, 1984–85. A Dir, Windsor Festival Soc., 1973–76. Councillor and Alderman, Royal Borough of New Windsor, 1962–67; Chm., Windsor and Eton Soc., 1971–76. FRSA. *Recreations:* fellwalking, gardening, foreign travel, history, looking in junk shops, thwarting bureaucrats. *Address:* Abcott Manor, Clungunford, Shropshire SY7 0PX.

RAMSAY, Richard Alexander McGregor; Director, Ivory & Sime Investment Management Plc, since 1994; *b* 27 Dec. 1949; *s* of Alexander John McGregor Ramsay and Beatrice Kent Lanauze; *m* 1975, Elizabeth Catherine Margaret Blackwood; one *s* one *d*. *Educ:* Dalhousie Sch.; Trinity Coll., Glenalmond; Aberdeen Univ. (MA Hons in Politics and Sociology). ACA 1975; FCA. Price Waterhouse & Co., 1972–75; Grindlay Brandts, 1976–78; Hill Samuel & Co. Ltd, 1979–87 (Dir, 1984–87); on secondment as Dir, Industrial Devélt Unit, DTI, 1984–86; Dir, 1988–93, Man. Dir, Corporate Finance Div., 1991–93, Barclays De Zoete Wedd; Dir, Ivory & Sime, 1993–94. *Recreations:* hill walking, ski-ing, classic cars, gardening. *Address:* The Little Priory, Sandy Lane, South Nutfield, Surrey RH1 4EJ. *T:* Nutfield Ridge (01737) 822329.

RAMSAY, Thomas Anderson; retired; Post-Graduate Dean and Professor of Post-Graduate Medicine, University of Aberdeen, 1972–76; *b* 9 Feb. 1920; *s* of David Mitchell Ramsay and Ruth Bramfitt Ramsay; *m* 1949, Margaret Lilian Leggat Donald; one *s* two *d*. *Educ:* Glasgow Univ. BSc, MB, ChB. FRCSGlas; FFCM; FRSH; FRCP. Surg. Lieut, RNVR, 1945–47. Various posts in general and clinical hospital practice (mainly paediatric and orthopaedic surg.), 1943–56; Asst, later Dep. Sen. Admin. Med. Officer, NI Hospitals Authority, 1957–58; Dep. Sen., later Sen. Admin. Med. Officer, NE Metropolitan Reg. Hospital Bd, 1958–72; Dir of Post-Grad. Med. Educn, NE Region (Scotland), 1972–76; Regl Med. Officer, W Midlands RHA, 1976–79; Prof. of Post Graduate Med. Educn, Univ. of Warwick, 1980–83; Dir, Post Graduate Med. Educn, Coventry AHA, Warwicks Post Graduate Med. Centre, 1980–85. Vis. Prof. of Health Services Admin, London Sch. of Hygiene and Tropical Medicine, 1971–72; Vis. Prof., Health Services Admin., Univ. of Aston, 1979–. Mem. Bd, Faculty of Community Medicine, 1972–. Governor, London Hosp., 1965–72. *Publications:* several papers in learned jls regarding post-graduate medical educn and community medicine. *Recreations:* travel, photography. *Address:* 26 Pinnaclehill Park, Kelso, Roxburghshire TD5 8HA. *T:* Kelso (01573) 226178.

RAMSAY-FAIRFAX-LUCY, Sir Edmund J. W. H. C.; *see* Fairfax-Lucy.

RAMSBOTHAM, family name of **Viscount Soulbury.**

RAMSBOTHAM, Gen. Sir David (John), GCB 1993 (KCB 1987); CBE 1980 (OBE 1974); Director of International Affairs, DSL Ltd, since 1994; Chairman, Hillingdon Hospital NHS Trust, since 1995; *b* 6 Nov. 1934; *s* of Rt Rev. J. A. Ramsbotham; *m* 1958, Susan Caroline (*née* Dickinson); two *s*. *Educ:* Haileybury Coll.; Corpus Christi Coll., Cambridge (BA 1957, MA 1973). Nat. Service, 1952–54; Rifle Bde, UK and BAOR, 1958–62; seconded to KAR, 1962–63; Staff Coll., 1964; Rifle Bde, Far East, 1965; Staff, 7 Armoured Bde, 1966–68; 3 and 2 Green Jackets (BAOR), 1968–71; MA to CGS (Lt-Col), 1971–73; CO, 2 RGJ, 1974–76; Staff, 4 Armd Div., BAOR, 1976–78; Comd, 39 Infantry Bde, 1978–80; RCDS, 1981; Dir of Public Relns (Army), 1982–84; Comdr, 3 Armd Div., 1984–87; Comdr, UK Field Army and Inspector Gen., TA, 1987–90; Adjt Gen., 1990–93; ADC Gen. to the Queen, 1990–93. Col Comdt, 2nd Battalion, The Royal Green Jackets, 1987–92. Hon. Col, Cambridge Univ. OTC, 1987–93. *Recreations:* sailing, shooting, gardening. *Address:* c/o Lloyds Bank, Grey Street, Newcastle upon Tyne NE99 1SL. *Club:* MCC.

RAMSBOTHAM, Hon. Sir Peter (Edward), GCMG 1978 (KCMG 1972; CMG 1964); GCVO 1976; DL; HM Diplomatic Service, retired; *b* 8 Oct. 1919; *yr s* of 1st Viscount Soulbury, PC, GCMG, GCVO, OBE, MC; *b* and *heir pres.* to 2nd Viscount Soulbury, *qv*; *m* 1st, 1941, Frances Blomfield (*d* 1982); two *s* (one *d* decd); 2nd, 1985, Dr Zaida Hall, *widow* of Ruthven Hall. *Educ:* Eton College; Magdalen College, Oxford (Hon. Fellow, 1991). Intelligence Corps, Europe, 1943–46 (Lt-Col; despatches; Croix de Guerre, 1945). Control Office for Germany and Austria from 1947; Regional Political Officer in Hamburg; entered Foreign Service, Oct. 1948; Political Division of Allied Control Commission, Berlin, Nov. 1948; transferred to Foreign Office, 1950; 1st Secretary, 1950; Head of Chancery, UK Delegation, New York, 1953; Foreign Office, 1957; Counsellor, 1961, Head of Western Organisations and Planning Dept; Head of Chancery, British Embassy, Paris, 1963–67; Foreign Office, 1967–69 (Sabbatical year, Inst. of Strategic Studies, 1968); High Comr, Nicosia, 1969–71; Ambassador to Iran, 1971–74; Ambassador to the United States, 1974–77; Governor and C-in-C of Bermuda, 1977–80. Director: Lloyds Bank, 1981–90; Lloyds Bank Internat., 1981–83; Southern Regl Bd, Lloyds Bank, 1981–90 (Chm., 1983–90); Commercial Union Assurance Co., 1981–90. Trustee, Leonard Cheshire Foundn, 1981–94; Chairman: Ryder-Cheshire Foundn for the Relief of Suffering, 1982–; World Meml Fund for Disaster Relief, 1992– (Trustee, 1989–). Pres., British-American-Canadian Associates, 1994–. Governor, King's Sch., Canterbury, 1981–90. DL Hants, 1992. Hon. LLD: Akron Univ., 1975; Coll. of William and Mary, 1975; Maryland Univ., 1976; Yale Univ., 1977. KStJ 1976. *Recreations:* gardening, fishing. *Address:* East Lane, Ovington, near Alresford, Hants SO24 0RA. *T:* Alresford (01962) 732515. *Clubs:* Garrick; Metropolitan (Washington).

RAMSBURY, Area Bishop of, since 1989; **Rt. Rev. Peter St George Vaughan;** *b* 27 Nov. 1930; *s* of late Dr Victor St George Vaughan and Dorothy Marguerite Vaughan; *m* 1961, Elisabeth Fielding Parker; one *s* two *d*. *Educ:* Charterhouse; Selwyn Coll., Cambridge (MA Theology); Ridley Hall, Cambridge. Deacon 1957, priest 1958; Asst Curate, Birmingham Parish Church, 1957–62; Chaplain to Oxford Pastorate, 1963–67; Asst Chaplain, Brasenose Coll., Oxford, 1963–67; Vicar of Christ Church, Galle Face, Colombo, 1967–72; Precentor of Holy Trinity Cathedral, Auckland, NZ, 1972–75; Principal of Crowther Hall, CMS Training Coll., Selly Oak Colleges, Birmingham, 1975–83; Archdeacon of Westmorland and Furness, 1983–89. Hon. Canon, Salisbury Cathedral, 1989–. Commisary for Bishop of Colombo. MA Oxon (By Incorporation). *Recreations:* gardening, reading, people. *Address:* Bishop's House, High Street, Urchfont, Devizes, Wilts SN10 4QH. *T:* Devizes (01380) 840373.

RAMSDEN, Prof. Herbert, MA, Dr en Filosofía y Letras; Professor of Spanish Language and Literature, University of Manchester, 1961–82, now Emeritus; *b* 20 April 1927; *s* of Herbert and Ann Ramsden; *m* 1953, Joyce Robina Hall, SRN, ONC, CMB; three *s* (incl. twin *s*) twin *d*. *Educ:* Sale Grammar Sch.; Univs of Manchester, Strasbourg, Madrid and Sorbonne. National Service, Inf. and Intell. Corps, 1949–51 (commnd). Travel, study and research abroad (Kemsley Travelling Fellow, etc), 1951–54; University of Manchester: Asst Lectr in Spanish, 1954–57; Lectr in Spanish, 1957–61; Pres., Philological Club, 1966–68. British Hispanists' rep., Nat. Council for Modern Languages, 1972–73; British rep., Asociación Europea de Profesores de Español, 1975–80. *Publications:* An Essential Course in Modern Spanish, 1959; Weak-Pronoun Position in the Early Romance Languages, 1963; (ed with critical study) Azorín, La ruta de Don Quijote, 1966; Angel Ganivet's Idearium español: A Critical Study, 1967; The Spanish Generation of 1898, 1974; The 1898 Movement in Spain, 1974; (ed with critical study) Lorca, Bodas de sangre, 1980; Pío Baroja: La busca, 1982; Pío Baroja: La busca 1903 to La busca 1904, 1982; (ed with critical study) Lorca, La casa de Bernarda Alba, 1983; Lorca's Romancero gitano, 1988; (ed, with critical study) Lorca, Romancero gitano, 1988; articles in Bulletin of Hispanic Studies, Modern Language Review, Modern Languages, etc. *Recreations:* family, hill-walking, foreign travel. *Address:* 7 Burford Avenue, Bramhall, Stockport, Cheshire SK7 1BL. *T:* 0161–439 4306.

RAMSDEN, Rt. Hon. James Edward, PC 1963; Director, since 1973, Chairman, since 1984, the London Clinic; *b* 1 Nov. 1923; *s* of late Capt. Edward Ramsden, MC, and Geraldine Ramsden, OBE, Breckamore Hall, Ripon; *m* 1949, Juliet Barbara Anna, *y d* of late Col Sir Charles Ponsonby, 1st Bt, TD, and Hon. Lady Ponsonby, *d* of 1st Baron Hunsdon; three *s* two *d*. *Educ:* Eton; Trinity College, Oxford (MA). Commnd KRRC, 1942; served North-West Europe with Rifle Brigade, 1944–45. MP (C) Harrogate, WR Yorks, March 1954–Feb. 1974; PPS to Home Secretary, Nov. 1959–Oct. 1960; Under-Sec. and Financial Sec., War Office, Oct. 1960–Oct. 1963; Sec. of State for War, 1963–64; Minister of Defence for the Army, April–Oct. 1964. Director: UK Board, Colonial Mutual Life Assurance Society, 1966–72; Standard Telephones and Cables, 1971–81; Prudential Assurance Co. Ltd, 1972–91 (Dep. Chm., 1976–82); Prudential Corp. Ltd, 1979–91 (Dep. Chm., 1979–82). Mem., Historic Buildings Council for England, 1971–72. *Address:* Old Sleningford Hall, Ripon, North Yorks HG4 3JD. *T:* Ripon (01765) 635229, *Fax:* (01765) 635485. *Club:* Pratt's.

RAMSDEN, Sir John (Charles Josslyn), 9th Bt *cr* 1689, of Byrom, Yorks; HM Diplomatic Service; Head of Information Department, Foreign and Commonwealth Office, since 1993; *b* 19 Aug. 1950; *s* of Sir Caryl Oliver Imbert Ramsden, 8th Bt, CMG, CVO, and of Anne, *d* of Sir Charles Wickham, KCMG, KBE, DSO; *S* father, 1987; *m* 1985, (Jennifer) Jane Bevan; two *d*. *Educ:* Eton; Trinity Coll., Cambridge (MA). With merchant bank, Dawnay, Day & Co. Ltd, 1972–74. Entered FCO, 1975; 2nd Sec., Dakar, 1976; 1st Sec., MBFR, Vienna, 1978; 1st Sec., Head of Chancery and Consul, Hanoi, 1980; FCO, 1982–90; Counsellor, E Berlin, 1990; Counsellor and Dep. Hd of Mission, Berlin, 1991–93. *Address:* c/o Foreign and Commonwealth Office, King Charles Street, SW1A 2AH.

RAMSDEN, (John) Michael; Editorial Contributor, Royal Aeronautical Society (Editor of Publications, 1989–93); *b* 2 Oct. 1928; *s* of John Leonard Ramsden and Edith Alexandra Ramsden; *m* 1953, Angela Mary Mortimer; one *s* one *d*. *Educ:* Bedford Sch.; de Havilland

Aeronautical Tech. Sch. CEng, FRAeS. With de Havilland Aircraft Co. Ltd, 1946–55; Flight, 1955–89: Air Transport Editor, 1961–64; Editor, 1964–81; Editor-in-Chief, Flight International, 1981–89. Chm., Press and Broadcasting Side, Defence Press and Broadcasting Cttee, 1983–89. Dir, de Havilland Aircraft Mus., 1970–. Trustee, Geoffrey de Havilland Flying Foundn, 1992–. Queen's Silver Jubilee Medal, 1977. *Publications:* The Safe Airline, 1976, 2nd edn 1978; Caring for the Mature Jet, 1981. *Recreations:* light-aircraft flying, water-colour painting. *Club:* London School of Flying (Elstree).

RAMSDEN, Michael; *see* Ramsden, J. M.

RAMSDEN, Sally, OBE 1981; Director, North East Broadcasting Co. Ltd (Metro Radio), 1973–81; *d* of John Parkin and Hannah Bentley; *m* 1948, Allan Ramsden. *Educ:* Ryhope Grammar Sch.; Neville's Cross Coll., Durham (Teaching Diploma). Teacher, 1930–47; Headmistress, 1947–69; Asst. Group Officer (part time), Nat. Fire Service, 1941–45; Hon. Organiser, Citizens' Advice Bureau, 1971–73; Pres., UK Fedn of Business and Professional Women, 1972–75 (Hon. Mem., NE Div., 1988–); Member: Women's Nat. Commn, 1972–75; Women's Internat. Year Cttee, 1974–75; VAT Tribunals, 1973–84; Royal Commn on Legal Services, 1976–79; Durham Posts and Telecom Adv. Cttee, 1980–. *Recreations:* fly fishing, gardening, reading. *Address:* 1 Westcott Drive, Durham Moor, Durham City DH1 5AG. *T:* Durham (0191) 3842989.

RAMSEY, Sir Alfred (Ernest), Kt 1967; *b* Dagenham, 1920; *m* 1951, Victoria Phyllis Answorth, *d* of William Welch. *Educ:* Becontree Heath School. Started playing for Southampton and was an International with them; transferred to Tottenham Hotspur, 1949; with Spurs (right back), 1949–51; they won the 2nd and 1st Division titles in successive seasons. Manager of Ipswich Town Football Club, which rose from 3rd Division to Championship of the League, 1955–63; Manager, FA World Cup Team, 1963–74. Played 31 times for England. *Address:* 41 Valley Road, Ipswich, Suffolk IP1 4EE.

RAMSEY, Basil Albert Rowland; Editor, Choir & Organ, since 1993; *b* 26 April 1929; *s* of Florence Lily Ramsey (*née* Childs) and Alfred John Rowland Ramsey; *m* 1953, Violet Mary Simpson; one *s* two *d*. *Educ:* State schools. ARCO. Novello & Co.: Music Editor, 1949; Head of Publishing, 1963; established own publishing Co., 1976; Serious Music Publishing Consultant, Filmtrax plc, 1987–90. Editor: Organists' Review, 1972–84; Music & Musicians, 1989–90; The Musical Times, 1990–92. *Publications:* The Music of Charles Camilleri, 1996; articles and reviews in Musical Times, 1955–93; occasional contributor to weekly and daily press on musical matters. *Recreations:* walking, reading, calligraphy. *Address:* 604 Rayleigh Road, Eastwood, Leigh-on-Sea, Essex SS9 5HU. *T:* Southend-on-Sea (01702) 524305.

RAMSEY, Brig. Gael Kathleen, CBE 1992 (MBE 1976); Director, National Centre for Leadership, since 1995; *b* 8 June 1942; *d* of Lt Col William Hammond, MBE and Kathleen Hammond; *m* 1977 (marr. diss. 1995). *Educ:* Convent of Good Shepherd, Singapore; High Sch. for Girls, Worcester, Gloucester and Dover. Commissioned, WRAC, 1968; Dir, WRAC, 1989–92; Dir Women (Army), 1992; Comdr, Aldershot Bde Area, 1992–95, retd. ADC to the Queen, 1989–92. Freeman, City of London, 1991; Member: Guild of Freemen of City of London, 1992–; Council, Victory Services Club, 1992–; Council, WRAC Assoc., 1989–. Gov., Royal Sch., Hampstead, 1993–. FInstD 1995. *Recreations:* golf, tennis, reading, needlework, travel, messing about with plants. *Address:* c/o Lloyds Bank, Cox's & King's Branch, PO Box 1190, 7 Pall Mall, SW1Y 5NA. *Club:* Queen's.

RAMSEY, Prof. Norman Foster; Higgins Professor of Physics, Harvard University, since 1947; Senior Fellow, Harvard Society of Fellows, since 1971; *b* 27 Aug. 1915; *s* of Brig.-Gen. and Mrs Norman F. Ramsey; *m* 1940, Elinor Stedman Jameson (*d* 1983); four *d*; *m* 1985, Ellie A. Welch. *Educ:* Columbia Univ.; Cambridge Univ. (England). Carnegie Fellow, Carnegie Instn of Washington, 1939–40; Assoc., Univ. of Ill, 1940–42; Asst Prof., Columbia Univ., 1942–45; Research Assoc., MIT Radiation Laboratory, 1940–43; Cons. to Nat. Defense Research Cttee, 1940–45; Expert Consultant to Sec. of War, 1942–45; Grp Leader and Assoc. Div. Head, Los Alamos Lab. of Atomic Energy Project, 1943–45; Chief Scientist of Atomic Energy Lab. at Tinian, 1945; Assoc. Prof., Columbia Univ., 1945–47; Head of Physics Dept, Brookhaven Nat. Lab., 1946–47; Assoc. Prof., Harvard Univ., 1947–50; John Simon Guggenheim Fell., Oxford Univ., 1953–54; George Eastman Vis. Prof., Oxford Univ., 1973–74; Luce Prof. of Cosmology, Mt Holyoke, 1982–83; Prof., Univ. of Virginia, 1983–84. Dir Harvard Nuclear Lab., 1948–50, 1952; Chm., Harvard Nuclear Physics Cttee, 1948–60; Science Adviser, NATO, 1958–59; Fell. Amer. Phys. Soc. and Amer. Acad. of Arts and Sciences; Nat. Acad. of Sciences; Amer. Philos. Soc.; Foreign Associate, French Acad. of Science; Sigma Xi; Phi Beta Kappa; Amer. Assoc. for Advancement of Science, 1940– (Chm., Phys. Sect., 1976). Bd of Directors, Varian Associates, 1964–66; Bd of Trustees: Associated Univs; Brookhaven Nat. Lab., 1952–55; Carnegie Endowment for Internat. Peace; Univ. Research Assoc. (Pres., 1966–81, Pres. Emeritus 1981–); Rockefeller Univ., 1976–; Air Force Sci. Adv. Bd, 1948–54; Dept of Defense Panel on Atomic Energy, 1953–59; Bd of Editors of Review of Modern Physics, 1953–56; Chm. Exec. Cttee for Camb. Electron Accelerator, 1956–63; Coun. Amer. Phys. Soc., 1956–60 (Vice-Pres., 1977; Pres., 1978); Chm., Bd of Governors, Amer. Inst. of Physics, 1980–86. Gen. Adv. Cttee, Atomic Energy Commn, 1960–72. Chm., High Energy Accelerator Panel of President's Sci. Adv. Cttee and AEC, 1963. Chm. Bd, Physics and Astronomy Nat. Res. Council, 1986–89. Pres., Phi Beta Kappa, 1985 (Vice-Pres., 1982). Presidential Certificate of Merit, 1947; E. O. Lawrence Award, 1960; Davisson-Germer Prize, 1974; Award for Excellence, Columbia Univ. Graduate Alumni, 1980; Medal of Honor, IEEE, 1984; Rabi Prize, Frequency Control Symposium, IEEE, 1985; Monie Ferst Prize, Sigma Xi, 1985; Compton Award, Amer. Inst. of Physics, 1985; Rumford Premium, Amer. Acad. of Arts and Scis, 1985; Oersted Medal, Amer. Assoc. of Physics Teachers, 1988; Nat. Medal of Science, 1988; (jtly) Nobel Prize for Physics, 1989; Pupin Medal, Columbia Univ., 1992; Einstein Medal, Optical and Quantum Electronics Soc., 1993; Vannevar Bush Award, 1995. Hon. MA Harvard, 1947; Hon. ScD Cambridge, 1953; Hon. DSc: Case Western Reserve, 1968; Middlebury Coll., 1969; Oxford, 1973; Rockefeller Univ., 1986; Chicago, 1989; Houston, 1992; Michigan, 1993; Hon. DCL Oxford, 1990. *Publications:* Experimental Nuclear Physics, 1952; Nuclear Moments, 1953; Molecular Beams, 1956; Quick Calculus, 1965; and numerous articles in Physical Review and other scientific jls. *Recreations:* tennis, ski-ing, walking, sailing, etc. *Address:* 24 Monmouth Court, Brookline, MA 02146, USA. *T:* (617) 2772313.

RAMSEY, Vivian Arthur; QC 1992; *b* 24 May 1950; *s* of Rt Rev. Ian Thomas Ramsey and Margretta Ramsey (*née* McKay); *m* 1974, Barbara Walker; two *s* two *d*. *Educ:* Harley Sch., Rochester, NY; Abingdon Sch., Oxon; Oriel Coll., Oxford (MA); City Univ. (Dip. Law). CEng, MICE 1977. Civil and Structural Engineer, Ove Arup & Partners, 1972–77, 1979–80; called to the Bar, Middle Temple, 1979; Barrister and Arbitrator, 1981–. Special Prof., Dept of Civil Engineering, Nottingham Univ., 1990–. Chm., Swanley Action Gp, 1989–. Editor, Construction Law Jl, 1984–. *Recreation:* building renovation. *Address:* Keating Chambers, 10 Essex Street, WC2R 3AA. *T:* 0171–240 6981, *Fax:* 0171–240 7722.

RAMSEY, Waldo Emerson W.; *see* Waldron-Ramsey.

RANASINGHE, (Kulatilaka Arthanayake) Parinda; Chief Justice of Sri Lanka, 1988–91; *b* 20 Aug. 1926; *s* of Solomon Ranasinghe and Somawathie Ranasinghe; *m* 1956, Chitra (*née* Mapaguneratne); one *s* three *d*. *Educ:* Royal Coll., Colombo. Advocate of the Supreme Court; appointed Magistrate, 1958; District Judge, 1966–74; High Court Judge, 1974–78; Judge, Court of Appeal, 1978–82, Pres. 1982; Judge, Supreme Court, 1982–88. *Recreation:* walking. *Address:* 18/48 Dabare Mawatha, Colombo 5, Sri Lanka. *T:* (1) 508310.

RANATUNGA, Gen. Sugathapala Cyril; High Commissioner for Sri Lanka in London, 1993–95; *b* 19 Feb. 1930; *m* 1957, Myrtle Sumanasekera; two *s*. *Educ:* St Sylvester's Coll., Kandy; RMA Sandhurst. Joined Sri Lanka Army, as Officer Cadet, 1950; commnd Ceylon LI, 1952; Staff Coll., 1962–63; RCDS, 1974–75; COS, Sri Lanka Army, 1982–85; Sen. Exec. Dir, Airport and Aviation Services Ltd, 1983–85; Lt-Gen. 1985; GOC, Jt Ops Comd, 1985–88; Gen. 1986; Security Advr to Pres. and Sec. to Minister of State for Defence, 1989–90; Sec. to Min. of Defence, 1990–93. Chancellor, Sir John Kotelawela Defence Acad., 1990–. *Recreations:* reading, bridge, golf. *Address:* Erabububela Estate, Mawanella, Sri Lanka. *Clubs:* Colombo Cricket, Colombo Football (Colombo).

RANCE, Gerald Francis, OBE 1985 (MBE 1968); HM Diplomatic Service, retired; *b* 20 Feb. 1927; *s* of Cecil Henry and Jane Carmel Rance; *m* 1949, Dorothy (*née* Keegan); one *d*. *Educ:* Brompton Oratory. HM Forces (RCMP), 1945–48; joined Foreign Service, 1948; Foreign Office, 1948–51; served Belgrade, Rome, Bucharest, Istanbul, Munich, Kabul, New York and Dallas; Inspectorate, FCO, 1973–77; Head of Chancery, Mbabane, 1977–79; First Sec. (Comm.), Nicosia, 1980–83; High Comr to Tonga, 1984–87. *Recreations:* golf, tennis, reading. *Address:* 1 Bruton Close, Chislehurst, Kent BR7 5SF. *Clubs:* Commonwealth Trust; Chislehurst Golf.

RANCHHODLAL, Sir Chinubhai Madhowlal, 3rd Bt *cr* 1913, of Shahpur, Ahmedabad, India; *b* 25 July 1929; *s* of 2nd Bt and Tanumati (*d* 1970), *d* of Javerilal Mehta; *S* father, 1990; grandfather, 1st Bt, was only member of Hindu Community to receive a baronetcy; *m* 1953, Muneera Khodad Fozdar; one *s* three *d*. Arjuna Award, 1972. *Heir: s* Prashant Ranchhodlal [*b* 15 Dec. 1955; *m* 1977, Swati Hrishikesh Mehta; three *d*]. *Address:* Shantikunj, Shahibaug, Ahmedabad-380004, India. *T:* 387531. *Clubs:* Willingdon, Cricket Club of India (Bombay).

RANDALL, Col Charles Richard, OBE 1969; TD 1947; Vice Lord-Lieutenant for the County of Bedfordshire, 1978–91; *b* 21 Jan. 1920; *s* of Charles Randall and Elizabeth Brierley; *m* 1945, Peggy Dennis; one *s* one *d*. *Educ:* Bedford Sch. Served War, 1939–45: commissioned Bedfordshire Yeomanry, 1939. High Sheriff, Bedfordshire, 1974–75. *Recreations:* shooting, fishing, gardening. *Address:* The Rookery, Aspley Guise, Milton Keynes MK17 8HP. *T:* Milton Keynes (01908) 582188. *Clubs:* Naval and Military, MCC.

RANDALL, Rev. Edmund Laurence, AM 1980; Warden, St Barnabas' Theological College, 1964–85, retired; Scholar in Residence, Diocese of Wangaratta, since 1986; *b* 2 June 1920; *s* of Robert Leonard Randall and Grace Annie Randall (*née* Young); unmarried. *Educ:* Dulwich College; Corpus Christi College, Cambridge. BA 1941. MA 1947. Served War, 1940–45, with Royal Artillery (AA). Corpus Christi Coll., 1938–40 and 1945–47. Wells Theological College, 1947–49. Deacon, 1949; Priest, 1950. Assistant Curate at St Luke's, Bournemouth, 1949–52; Fellow of Selwyn College, Cambridge, 1952–57; Chaplain, 1953–57; Residentiary Canon of Ely and Principal of Ely Theological Coll., 1957–59; Chaplain, St Francis Theological Coll., Brisbane, 1960–64; Hon. Canon of Adelaide, 1979–86, of Wangaratta, 1989–. Vis Lectr, St Barnabas' Theol Coll., and Lectr in Theology, Flinders Univ. of SA, Feb–July 1990. *Recreations:* travel, motoring, swimming. *Address:* 44 Mackay Street, Wangaratta, Vic 3677, Australia. *T:* (57) 219007.

RANDALL, Jeff William; Deputy Chairman, Financial Dynamics Ltd, since 1995; *b* 3 Oct. 1954; *s* of Jeffrey Charles Randall and Grace Annie (*née* Hawkridge); *m* 1986, Susan Diane Fidler; one *d*. *Educ:* Royal Liberty Grammar Sch., Romford; Nottingham Univ. (BA Hons Econs); Univ. of Florida. Hawkins Publishers, 1982–85; Asst Editor, Financial Weekly, 1985–86; City Corresp., Sunday Telegraph, 1986–88; The Sunday Times: Dep. City Editor, 1988–89; City Editor, 1989–94; City and Business Editor, 1994–95. Dir, Times Newspapers, 1994–95. Financial Journalist of the Year, FT-Analysis, 1991. *Recreations:* golf, horseracing. *Address:* 4 Crossways, Shenfield, Essex CM15 8QX. *Clubs:* Clermont; Wentworth.

RANDALL, John Paul; Director, Professional Standards and Development, Law Society, since 1987; *b* 23 Nov. 1947; *s* of late E. T. (Ted) Randall and of Mollie Randall (*née* Macrae); *m* 1st, 1972, Hillary Geldard (marr. diss. 1992); one *s* one *d*; 2nd, 1993, Marie Catherine Hague. *Educ:* Wallington County Grammar Sch. for Boys; Univ. of York (BA Hons Biol and Educn 1971). National Union of Students: Dep. Pres., 1971–73; Pres., 1973–75; Civil Service Union: Asst Sec., 1975–77; Asst Gen. Sec., 1977–81; Dep. Gen. Sec., 1981–87. Mem. Council, NCVQ, 1992– (Chm., Accreditation Cttee, 1993–). *Publications:* articles in educnl and legal jls. *Recreations:* running, walking, music, wine, travel. *Address:* Orchard Cottage, The Rampings, Longdon, Worcs GL20 6AL. *Clubs:* South London Harriers, Orion Harriers.

RANDALL, John Yeoman; QC 1995; an Assistant Recorder, since 1995; *b* 26 April 1956; *s* of Richard and Jean Randall; *m* 1982, Christine Robinson; one *s* one *d*. *Educ:* Rugby Sch.; Loomis Inst., USA; Jesus Coll., Cambridge (MA). Called to the Bar: Lincoln's Inn, 1978; NSW, 1979; in practice at English Bar, 1980–. *Recreations:* travel, sports, music. *Address:* 7 Fountain Court, Steelhouse Lane, Birmingham B4 6DR. *T:* 0121–236 8531.

RANDALL, Stuart; MP (Lab) Kingston upon Hull West, since 1983; *b* 22 June 1938; *m* 1963, Gillian Michael; three *d*. *Educ:* University Coll., Cardiff (BSc Elect. Engrg). English Electric Computers and Radio Corp. of America, USA, 1963–66; Marconi Automation, 1966–68; Inter-Bank Res. Orgn, 1968–71; BSC, 1971–76; BL, 1976–80; Nexos Office Systems, 1980–81; Plessey Communications Systems, 1981–83. PPS to Shadow Chancellor of the Exchequer, 1984–85; Opposition front bench spokesman on Agricl, Food and Fisheries Affairs, 1985–87, on home affairs, 1987–92. *Recreation:* sailing. *Address:* House of Commons, SW1A 0AA. *T:* 0171–219 3000.

RANDALL, William Edward, CBE 1978; DFC 1944; AFC 1945; Chairman, Chubb & Son Ltd, 1981–84 (Managing Director, 1971–81, Deputy Chairman, 1976–81); *b* 15 Dec. 1920; *s* of William George Randall and Jane Longdon (*née* Pannell); *m* 1st, 1943, Joan Dorothea Way; two *s* one *d*; 2nd, 1975, Iris Joyce Roads. *Educ:* Tollington Sch., London. FRSA. Served RAF, Flt Lieut, 1941–46. Commercial Union Assce Co., 1946–50; Chubb & Sons Lock and Safe Co., 1950, Man. Dir, 1965; Dir, Chubb & Son Ltd, 1965; Dir, Metal Closures Gp, 1976–86. Member: Home Office Standing Cttee on Crime Prevention, 1967–85; Exec. Cttee, British Digestive Foundn, 1982–86; Chairman: Council, British Security Industry Assoc., 1981–85; Airport Export Gp, NEDO, 1983. *Recreations:* reading, playing bridge. *Address:* Flat 8, Woodhouse, 10 The Avenue, Poole, Dorset BH13 6AG.

RANDELL, Peter Neil; Head of Finance and Administration, Institute of Metals, 1984–89; *b* 18 Nov. 1933; *s* of Donald Randell and Dorothy (*née* Anthonisz); *m* 1962, Anne Loraine

Mudie; one *s* one *d*. *Educ:* Bradfield Coll.; Wye Coll., Univ. of London (BSc (Agric) Hons). FCIS. Farming and other employments, Rhodesia, 1955–61; Asst to Sec., British Insulated Callenders Cables Ltd, 1962–65; Asst Sec., NRDC, 1965–73, Sec. 1973–83, Board Member 1980–81; Sec. Admin and Personnel, British Technology Gp (NRDC and NEB), 1981–83. *Recreations:* the outdoors, reading. *Address:* Wood Dene, Golf Club Road, Hook Heath, Woking, Surrey GU22 0LS. *T:* Woking (01483) 763824.

RANDLE, James Neville, FEng; RDI 1994; Director, Automotive Engineering Centre, University of Birmingham, since 1993; Chairman, Randle Engineering and Design, since 1994; *b* Birmingham, 24 April 1938; *s* of James Randle and Florence (*née* Wilkins); *m* 1963, Jean Violet Allen; one *s* one *d*. *Educ:* Waverley Grammar Sch., Birmingham. MIMechE 1969, FIMechE 1980; FEng 1988. Rover Car Company: apprentice, 1954–59; design and develt engr, 1959–63; Project Manager, 1963–65; Jaguar: R&D Engr, 1965–72; Chief Res. Engr, 1972–78; Vehicle Engrg Dir, 1978–80; Product Engrg Dir, 1980–91. Hon. Prof., Univ. of Birmingham, 1992–. Dir, Volvo Aero Turbines, 1992–. Institution of Mechanical Engineers: Mem. Bd, 1979–88, Chm., 1986–87, Automobile Div.; Mem. Council, 1986–93. Mem., Prince Philip Design Prize Cttee, 1992–95. Pres., Engrg Div., BAAS, 1995–96. FInstD 1986. FRAS 1989. James Clayton Prize, 1986, Crompton Lanchester Medal, 1986, IMechE. *Publications:* technical papers on automobile engrg design. *Recreations:* flying powered aircraft (private pilot's licence), sailing (yacht master's certificate), ski-ing, hill walking, designing automobiles. *Address:* Downwind House, Ryton Road, Bubbenhall, near Coventry CV8 3BH. *T:* Coventry (01203) 306730.

RANDLE, Prof. Sir Philip (John), Kt 1985; MD, FRCP; FRS 1983; Professor of Clinical Biochemistry, University of Oxford, 1975–93, now Emeritus; Fellow of Hertford College, Oxford, 1975–93, now Emeritus; *b* 16 July 1926; *s* of Alfred John and Nora Anne Randle; *m* 1952, Elizabeth Ann Harrison; three *d* (one *s* decd). *Educ:* King Edward VI Grammar Sch., Nuneaton; Sidney Sussex Coll., Cambridge (MA, PhD, MD); UCH, London (Fellow, UCL, 1990). Med. and Surg. Officer, UCH, 1951; Res. Fellow in Biochem., Cambridge, 1952–55; Univ. Lectr, Biochem., Cambridge, 1955–64; Fellow of Trinity Hall and Dir of Med. Studies, 1957–64 (Hon. Fellow, Trinity Hall, 1988); Prof. of Biochem., Univ. of Bristol, 1964–75. Member: Board of Governors, United Cambridge Hospitals, 1960–64; Clinical Endocrinology Cttee, MRC, 1957–64; Chm., Grants Cttee, MRC, 1975–77; Pres., European Assoc. for Study of Diabetes, 1977–80; Chairman, Research Committee: British Diabetic Assoc., 1971–78; British Heart Foundn, 1987–92. DHSS: Mem. Cttee on Med. Aspects Food Policy, 1981–89; Chm., COMA Panel on Diet and Cardiovascular Disease, 1981–84; Consultant Adviser in Biochemistry to CMO, 1981–89. Member: General Medical Council, 1967–75; Gen. Dental Council, 1971–75; Council, Royal Soc., 1987–89 (Vice Pres., 1988–89). Lectures: Banting, British Diabetic Assoc., 1965; Minkowski, European Assoc. for Study of Diabetes, 1966; Copp, La Jolla, 1972; Humphry Davy Rolleston, RCP, 1983; Ciba Medal and Lectr, Biochem. Soc., 1984; Kroc, San Diego, 1992. Corresp. Mem. of many foreign medical and scientific bodies. *Publications:* numerous contribs to books and med. sci. jls on diabetes mellitus, control of metabolism and related topics. *Recreations:* travel, swimming, bricklaying. *Address:* 11 Fitzherbert Close, Iffley, Oxford OX4 4EN; Department of Clinical Biochemistry, Radcliffe Infirmary, Oxford OX2 6HE.

RANDOLPH, Denys, BSc; CEng, MRAeS, FIProdE, FIEE, FInstD, CIMgt; Proprietor, Clapcot Vineyards, since 1986; *b* 6 Feb. 1926; *s* of late Harry Beckham Randolph and Margaret Isabel Randolph; *m* 1951, Marjorie Hales; two *d*. *Educ:* St Paul's School: Queen's Univ., Belfast (BSc). Served Royal Engineers, 1944–48 (Captain). Queen's Univ., Belfast, 1948–52; post-grad. apprenticeship, Short Bros & Harland, 1952–55; Wilkinson Sword Ltd: Prod. Engr/Prod. Dir, Graviner Div., 1955–66; Man. Dir, Hand Tools Div., 1966–69; Chm., Graviner Div., 1969–79; Chm., 1972–79; Pres., 1980–85; Wilkinson Match Ltd: Dir, 1974–80; Chm., 1976–79. Chairman: Woodrush Investments Ltd, 1980–93; Poitires Eyots Ltd, 1972–93; Dir, Henley Distance Learning Ltd, 1985–94. Institute of Directors: Chm., 1976–79; Vice-Pres., 1979–. Past Master: Worshipful Co. of Scientific Instrument Makers, 1977; Cutlers' Co., 1986. Mem. Council, Brunel Univ., 1986 91; Governor, Henley Admin. Staff Coll., 1979–91. FRSA (Manufactures and Commerce). *Publication:* From Rapiers to Razor Blades—The Development of the Light Metals Industry (paper, RSA). *Recreations:* yachting, golf, viticulture. *Address:* Clapcot House, Rush Court, Wallingford OX10 8LJ. *T:* Wallingford (01491) 36586. *Clubs:* Army and Navy, Royal Automobile, City Livery, Little Ship.

RANDOLPH, His Honour John Hugh Edward; a Circuit Judge, 1972–87; *b* 14 Oct. 1913; *s* of late Charles Edward Randolph and Phyllis Randolph; *m* 1959, Anna Marjorie (*née* Thomson). *Educ:* Bradford Grammar Sch.; Leeds University. RAF, 1940–46. Called to Bar, Middle Temple, 1946; practised on NE Circuit until 1965; Stipendiary Magistrate of Leeds, 1965–71. Deputy Chairman: E Riding QS, 1958–63; W Riding QS, 1963–71. *Recreation:* golf. *Address:* Crown Court, Leeds. *Club:* Leeds (Leeds).

RANDOLPH, Rev. Michael Richard Spencer; Editor-in-Chief, Reader's Digest (British Edition), 1957–88; *b* 2 Jan. 1925; *s* of late Leslie Richard Randolph and late Gladys (*née* Keen); *m* 1952, Jenefer Scawen Blunt; two *s* two *d*. *Educ:* Merchant Taylors' Sch.; New Rochelle High Sch., NY, USA; Queen's Coll., Oxford; Canterbury Sch. of Ministry. Served RNVR, Intell. Staff Eastern Fleet, 1944–46, Sub-Lieut. Editorial staff, Amalgamated Press, 1948–52; Odham's Press, 1952–56; Reader's Digest, 1956–88. Press Mem., Press Council, 1975–88; Chm., Soc. of Magazine Editors, 1973. Ordained: deacon, 1990; priest, 1991. Asst Curate (Local NSM), 1990–94, Hon. Asst Priest, 1995–, Biddenden and Smarden. Pres., Weald of Kent Preservation Soc., 1988–. Mem. Smarden Parish Council, 1987–. FRSA 1962. *Recreation:* grandparenthood. *Address:* Little Smarden House, Smarden, Kent TN27 8NB. *Club:* Savile.

RANELAGH, John O'B.; *see* O'Beirne Ranelagh.

RANFURLY, 7th Earl of, *cr* 1831 (Ire.); **Gerald François Needham Knox;** Baron Welles 1781; Viscount Northland 1791; Baron Ranfurly (UK) 1826; *b* 4 Jan. 1929; *s* of Captain John Needham Knox, RN (*d* 1967) (*g g g s* of 1st Earl) and Monica B. H. (*d* 1975), *d* of Maj.-Gen. Sir Gerald Kitson, KCVO, CB, CMG; *S* cousin, 1988; *m* 1955, Rosemary, *o d* of Air Vice-Marshal Felton Vesey Holt, CMG, DSO; two *s* two *d*. *Educ:* Wellington College. Served RN, 1947–60; retired as Lieut Comdr. Member of Stock Exchange, 1964; Partner in Brewin & Co., 1965; Senior Partner, 1982, Chm., 1987–95, Brewin Dolphin & Co. *Recreation:* foxhunting. *Heir: s* Edward John Knox, *b* 21 May 1957. *Address:* Maltings Chase, Nayland, Colchester, Essex CO6 4LZ.

RANG, Prof. Humphrey Peter, DPhil; FRS 1980; Director, Sandoz Institute for Medical Research, since 1983, and Professor of Pharmacology, 1979–83 and since 1995, University College London; *b* 13 June 1936; *s* of Charles Rang and Sybil Rang; *m* 1992, Isobel Heyman. *Educ:* University Coll. Sch.; University Coll. London (MSc 1960); UCH Med. Sch. (MB, BS 1961); Balliol Coll., Oxford (DPhil 1965). J. H. Burn Res. Fellow, Dept of Pharmacol., Oxford, 1961–65; Vis. Res. Associate, Albert Einstein Coll. of Medicine, NY, 1966–67; Univ. Lectr in Pharmacol., Oxford, 1966–72; Fellow and Tutor in Physiol., Lincoln Coll., Oxford, 1967–72; Prof. of Pharmacology: Univ. of Southampton, 1972–74; St George's Hosp. Med. Sch., London, 1974–79; Fellow, 1983, and Vis. Prof., 1983–95, UCL. *Publications:* Drug Receptors, 1973; Pharmacology, 1987. *Recreations:* sailing, music. *Address:* 1 Willow Road, NW3 1TH.

RANGER, Sir Douglas, Kt 1978; FRCS; Otolaryngologist, The Middlesex Hospital, 1950–82; Dean, The Middlesex Hospital Medical School, 1974–83; Hon. Civil Consultant in Otolaryngology, RAF, since 1983; *b* 5 Oct. 1916; *s* of William and Hatton Thomasina Ranger; *m* 1943, Betty, *d* of Captain Sydney Harold Draper and Elsie Draper; two *s*. *Educ:* Church of England Grammar Sch., Brisbane; The Middlesex Hosp. Med. Sch. MB BS 1941, FRCS 1943. Surgical Registrar, The Mddx Hosp., 1942–44. Served War, Temp. Maj. RAMC and Surgical Specialist, 1945–48 (SEAC and MELF). Otolaryngologist, Mount Vernon Hosp., 1958–74; Hon. Sec., Brit. Assoc. of Otolaryngologists, 1965–71. RCS: Mem. Court of Examiners, 1966–72; Mem. Council, 1967–72; Pres., Assoc. of Head and Neck Oncologists of GB, 1974–77. Civil Consultant in Otolaryngology, RAF, 1965–83. Dir, Ferens Inst. of Otolaryngology, 1965–83; Cons. Adviser in Otolaryngology, DHSS, 1971–82. *Publications:* The Middlesex Hospital Medical School, Centenary to Sesquicentenary, 1985; papers and lectures on otolaryngological subjects, esp. with ref. to malignant disease. *Address:* Wisteria House, Bayshill Lane, Cheltenham, Glos GL50 3AX. *T:* Cheltenham (01242) 222865.

RANGER, Prof. Terence Osborn, DPhil; FBA 1988; Rhodes Professor of Race Relations, and Fellow of St Antony's College, University of Oxford, since 1987; *b* 29 Nov. 1929; *s* of Leslie and Anna Ranger; *m* 1954, Shelagh Campbell Clark; three *d*. *Educ:* Highgate Sch.; Univ. of Oxford (BA, MA; DPhil 1960). Lecturer: RNC, Dartmouth, 1955–56; Coll. of Rhodesia and Nyasaland, 1957–63; Prof. of History, Univ. of Dar es Salaam, 1963–69; Prof. of African History, Univ. of Calif, LA, 1969–74; Prof. of Modern History, Univ. of Manchester, 1974–87; Chm., Oxford Univ. Cttee on African Studies, 1987–. Chm., Jl of Southern African Studies, 1976–; Vice-Chm., Past and Present, 1987–. *Publications:* Revolt in Southern Rhodesia 1896–7, 1967; The African Voice in Southern Rhodesia 1898–1930, 1970; Dance and Society in Eastern Africa, 1975; Peasant Consciousness and Guerrilla War in Zimbabwe, 1985. *Recreations:* theatre, opera, walking. *Address:* St Antony's College, Oxford OX2 6JF. *Club:* Commonwealth Trust.

RANK, Sir Benjamin (Keith), Kt 1972; CMG 1955; MS, FRCS; FRACS; FACS; Consulting Plastic Surgeon, Royal Melbourne Hospital, Repatriation Department, Victoria Eye and Ear Hospital; *b* 14 Jan. 1911; *s* of Wreghitt Rank and Bessie Rank (*née* Smith); *m* 1938, Barbara Lyle Facy; one *s* three *d*. *Educ:* Scotch College, Melbourne; Ormond College, University of Melbourne. MB, BS Melbourne, 1934; Resident Medical Officer, Royal Melbourne Hospital, 1935–36; MS (Melb.), 1937; MRCS, LRCP 1938; Resident Surgical Officer, London County Council, 1938–39 (St James' Hospital, Balham); FRCS 1938; Assistant Plastic Surgeon (EMS) at Hill End (Bart's), 1939–40; AAMC, 1940–45; Officer i/c AIF Plastic Surgery Unit in Egypt, and later at Heidelberg Military Hospital, Victoria, Australia (Lt-Col); Hon. Plastic Surgeon, Royal Melbourne Hosp., 1946–66. Carnegie Fellow, 1947. Member: Dental Board of Victoria 1949–73, Joske Orator 1974; BMA State Council, 1950–60; Chm. Exec. Cttee, RACS (Pres., 1966–68); Chm., Cttee of Management, Victorian Plastic Surgery Unit (Preston Hosp.), 1966–85; Member: Bd of Management, Royal Melbourne Hosp., 1976–82 (Vice-Pres., 1979–82); Motor Accident Bd, Victoria, 1972–82. Chm., Consult. Council on Casualty Services, Victoria Health Council; Pres., St John's Ambulance Council, Victoria, 1983–88 (Chm. 1978–83). Sir Arthur Sims Commonwealth Travelling Prof., RCS, 1958; Moynihan Lectr, 1972; Vis. Prof., Harvard Med. Sch., 1976. Syme Orator, RACS, 1976; Stawell Orator, 1977. 87th Mem., James IV Assoc. of Surgeons; Pres., British Assoc. of Plastic Surgeons, 1965. Pres., 5th Internat. Congress of Plastic Surgery, Melbourne, 1971. FRACS 1943; Hon. FACST 1952; Hon. FRCS Canada; Hon. FRCSE 1973; Hon. FACS. Hon. DSc Punjabi Univ., 1970; Hon. Member: Société Française de Chirurgie Plastique; Indian Association of Surgeons. KStJ 1988 (CStJ 1982). *Publications:* (jointly) Surgery of Repair as applied to Hand Injuries, 1953; Jerry Moore, 1975; Head and Hands, 1987; The Family Story, 1992; papers in British, American and Australian Surgical Jls. *Recreations:* golf, gardening, painting. *Address:* 12 Jerula Avenue, Mount Eliza, Victoria 3930, Australia. *Clubs:* Melbourne (Melbourne); Peninsula Golf.

RANK, Joseph McArthur; President, Ranks Hovis McDougall Ltd, 1981–93; *b* 24 April 1918; *s* of late Rowland Rank and of Margaret McArthur; *m* 1946, Hon. Moira (who *m* 1940, Peter Anthony Stanley Woodwark, killed in action, 1943; one *d*), *d* of 3rd Baron Southborough; one *s* one *d*. *Educ:* Loretto. Joined Mark Mayhew Ltd, 1936. Served RAF, 1940–46. Personal Pilot to Air C-in-C, SEAC, 1945; Jt Man. Dir, Joseph Rank Ltd, 1955–65; Dep. Chm. and Chief Exec., Ranks Hovis McDougall Ltd, 1965–69, Chm., 1969–81. Pres., Nat. Assoc. of British and Irish Millers, 1957–58, Centenary Pres., 1978. Hon. Pres., Millers Mutual Assoc., 1991– (Chm., 1969–81); Chm. Council, British Nutrition Foundation, 1968–69; Dir, Royal Alexandra and Albert Sch., 1952–, Chm., Governing Body, 1975–84; Friend of the Royal Coll. of Physicians, 1967–; Council, Royal Warrant Holders Assoc., 1968–71. Mem., Shrievalty Assoc., 1974. First High Sheriff of East Sussex, 1974. Hon. FRCP 1978. *Recreations:* boating, travelling.

RANKEILLOUR, 4th Baron *cr* 1932, of Buxted; **Peter St Thomas More Henry Hope;** farmer and landowner; *b* 29 May 1935; *s* of 3rd Baron Rankeillour and Mary Sibyl, *d* of late Col Wilfrid Ricardo, DSO; *S* father, 1967; unmarried. *Educ:* Ampleforth College; privately. *Recreations:* shooting, architecture, grand-scale landscaping; agricultural equipment inventor. *Heir: cousin* Michael Richard Hope [*b* 21 Oct. 1940; *m* 1964, Elizabeth Rosemary, *e d* of Col F. H. Fuller; one *s* two *d*]. *Address:* Achaderry House, Roy Bridge, West Inverness-shire PH31 4AN. *T:* Spean Bridge (01397) 712206.

RANKIN, Sir Alick (Michael), Kt 1992; CBE 1987; Chairman: Scottish & Newcastle plc (formerly Scottish & Newcastle Breweries), since 1989 (Chief Executive, 1983–91); Christian Salvesen, since 1992 (Director, since 1986); Scottish Financial Enterprise, since 1992; *b* 23 Jan. 1935; *s* of late Lt-Col (Arthur) Niall (Talbot) Rankin, FRPS, FRGS and of Lady Jean Rankin, *qv*; *m* 1st, 1958, Susan Margaret Dewhurst (marr. diss. 1976); one *s* three *d*: 2nd, 1976, Suzetta Barber (*née* Nelson). *Educ:* Ludgrove; Eton College. Scots Guards, 1954–56. Wood Gundy & Co., Investment Dealers, Toronto, 1956–59; Scottish & Newcastle Breweries: joined, 1960; Dir, Retail, Scottish Brewers, 1965–69; Chm. and Man. Dir, Waverley Vintners, 1969–76; Director, 1974; Marketing Dir, 1977–82; Chm., Scottish Brewers, 1982–83; Dep. Chm., 1987–89. Dep. Chm., General Accident, 1995–; Non-Executive Director: Bank of Scotland plc, 1987–; Sears plc, 1991–; Securities Trust of Scotland, 1991–; BAT Industries, 1993–95; James Finlay, 1994–. Chm., The Brewers' Soc., 1989–90. FRSA 1992. *Recreations:* fishing, shooting, golf, tennis, ornithology, oenology. *Address:* 3 Saxe-Coburg Place, Edinburgh EH3 5BR. *T:* 0131–332 3684; 49 Pont Street, SW1X 0BD. *T:* 0171–581 1086. *Clubs:* Boodle's; New (Edinburgh); Hon. Co. of Edinburgh Golfers (Muirfield), Royal and Ancient Golf (St Andrews); I Zingari, Eton Ramblers Cricket; Vanderbilt Tennis.

See also Sir I. N. Rankin, Bt.

RANKIN, Andrew, QC 1968; a Recorder of the Crown Court, 1972–94; *b* 3 Aug. 1924; *s* of William Locke Rankin and Mary Ann McArdle, Edinburgh; *m* 1st, 1944, Winifred (marr. diss. 1963), *d* of Frank McAdam, Edinburgh; two *s* two *d* (and one *s* decd); 2nd,

1964, Veronica (*d* 1990), *d* of George Aloysius Martin, Liverpool; 3rd, 1991, Jenifer Margaret, *d* of Alfred George Hodges Bebington, Wirral. *Educ:* Royal High Sch., Edinburgh; Univ. of Edinburgh; Downing Coll., Cambridge. Served War of 1939–45: Sub-Lt, RNVR, 1943. BL (Edin.) 1946; BA, 1st cl. hons Law Tripos (Cantab), 1948. Royal Commonwealth Soc. Medal, 1942; Cecil Peace Prize, 1946; Lord Justice Holker Exhibn, Gray's Inn, 1947–50; Lord Justice Holker Schol., Gray's Inn, 1950–53; Univ. Blue, Edin., 1943 and 1946 and Camb., 1948. Lectr in Law, Univ. of Liverpool, 1948–52. Called to Bar, Gray's Inn, 1950. *Publications:* (ed, 4th edn) Levie's Law of Bankruptcy in Scotland, 1950; various articles in UK and foreign legal jls. *Recreations:* swimming, travel by sea, racing (both codes), watching soccer (especially Liverpool FC). *Address:* Chelwood, Pine Walks, Prenton, Birkenhead, Merseyside L42 8LQ. *T:* 0151–608 2987; 69 Cliffords Inn, EC4 1BX. *T:* 0171–405 2932; Queen Elizabeth Building, Temple, EC4Y 9BS. *T:* 0171–353 7825/9153.

RANKIN, Sir Ian (Niall), 4th Bt *cr* 1898, of Bryngwyn, Much Dewchurch, Co. Hereford; Chairman, I. N. Rankin Oil Ltd, since 1981; *b* 19 Dec. 1932; *s* of Lt-Col Arthur Niall Rankin (*d* 1965) (*yr s* of 2nd Bt) and of Lady Jean Rankin, *qv*; *S* uncle, 1988; *m* 1st, 1959, Alexandra (marr. diss.), *d* of Adm. Sir Laurence Durlacher, KCB, OBE, DSC; one *s* one *d*; 2nd, 1980, Mrs June Norman, *d* of late Captain Thomas Marsham-Townshend; one *s*. *Educ:* Eton College; Christ Church, Oxford (MA). Lieut, Scots Guards. Chairman, I. N. Rankin Sales Ltd, 1961–; Director: Lindsay and Williams Ltd, 1973; Bayfine Ltd and subsidiaries, 1974–85 (Jt Chm., 1974–81); Highgate Optical and Industrial Co. Ltd and subsidiary, 1976–84 (Jt Chm., 1976–81); New Arcadia Explorations Ltd, 1987–; Bristol Scotts, 1993–. *Recreations:* shooting, tennis, ski-ing, chess. *Heir: s* Gavin Niall Rankin, *b* 19 May 1962. *Address:* 63 Marlborough Place, NW8 0PT. *T:* (office) 0171–286 0251, (home) 0171–625 5330. *Clubs:* White's, Beefsteak, Pratt's; Royal Yacht Squadron.

See also Sir A. M. Rankin.

RANKIN, James Deans, CBE 1983; PhD; Chief Inspector, Cruelty to Animals Act (1876), Home Office, 1976–83; *b* 17 Jan. 1918; *s* of late Andrew Christian Fleming Rankin and Catherine Sutherland (*née* Russell); *m* 1950, Hilary Jacqueline Bradshaw; two *d*. *Educ:* Hamilton Acad.; Glasgow Veterinary Coll. (MRCVS); Reading Univ. (PhD Microbiology). FIBiol. Gen. practice, 1941; Res. Officer, Min. of Agriculture and Fisheries, 1942; Principal Res. Officer, ARC, 1952; Inspector, Home Office, 1969. *Publications:* scientific contribs in standard works and in med. and veterinary jls. *Club:* Farmers'.

RANKIN, Lady Jean (Margaret), DCVO 1969 (CVO 1957); Woman of the Bedchamber to Queen Elizabeth The Queen Mother, 1947–81, Extra Woman of the Bedchamber, since 1982; *b* 15 Aug. 1905; *d* of 12th Earl of Stair; *m* 1931, Niall Rankin (*d* 1965), *s* of Sir Reginald Rankin, 2nd Bt; two *s*. Governor: Thomas Coram Foundation; Magdalen Hosp. Trust. *Address:* House of Treshnish, Dervaig, Isle of Mull PA75 6QX. *T:* Dervaig (01688) 400249.

See also Sir A. M. Rankin, Sir I. N. Rankin, Bt.

RANKIN, Rear-Adm. Neil Erskine, CB 1995; CBE 1988; Flag Officer, Portsmouth, since 1993; *b* 24 Dec. 1940; *s* of late James Hall Rankin and of Jean Laura Rankin (*née* Honeyman); *m* 1969, Jillian Mary Cobb; one *s* one *d*. *Educ:* HMS Conway; BRNC Dartmouth. Joined RN 1958; pilot's wings, 1963; CO HMS Achilles, 1977; CO HMS Bacchante, 1978; Comdr (Air), RNAS Yeovilton, 1979, HMS Invincible, 1981; Naval Air Warfare, MoD, 1982; COS, Flag Officer Third Flotilla, 1984; CO, Captain F8, HMS Andromeda, 1985; Sen. Naval Officer, Middle East, 1985; Dep. Dir, Naval Warfare, MoD, 1987; CO HMS Ark Royal, 1990; Comdr, British Forces Falkland Is, 1992–93. Liveryman, Shipwrights' Co.; Younger Brother, Trinity House. *Recreations:* Rugby (Pres., RNRU), sailing, golf. *Address:* c/o Lloyds Bank, Cox's & King's Branch, Pall Mall, SW1Y 5NA. *Clubs:* Royal Navy of 1765 and 1785, Naval; Royal Naval Golfing; North Berwick Golf; East Lothian Yacht.

RANKIN, Prof. Robert Alexander, MA, PhD, ScD; FRSE, FRSAMD; Professor Emeritus, Glasgow University, since 1982 (Professor of Mathematics, 1954–82; Clerk of the Senate, 1971–78; Dean, Faculty of Science, 1967–69, Dean of Faculties, 1986–88); *b* 27 Oct. 1915; *s* of late Rev. Prof. Oliver Shaw Rankin, DD, and late Olivia Theresa Shaw; *m* 1942, Mary Ferrier Llewellyn, *d* of late W. M. Llewellyn and late K. F. Llewellyn, JP; one *s* three *d*. *Educ:* Fettes; Clare Coll., Cambridge. Wrangler, 1936; Fellow of Clare College, 1939–51; Vis. Fellow, Clare Hall, 1971. Ministry of Supply (work on rockets), 1940–45; Faculty Asst Lecturer, Cambridge Univ., 1945–48; Univ. Lecturer, Cambridge, 1948–51; Asst Tutor, Clare Coll., 1947–51; Praelector, Clare Coll., 1949–51; Mason Professor of Pure Mathematics at Birmingham University, 1951–54. Mathematical Sec. and Editor of Proceedings of Cambridge Philosophical Soc., 1947–51; Hon. Pres. Glasgow Gaelic Soc., 1957–; Pres. Edinburgh Mathematical Soc., 1957–58, 1978–79; Mem., Special Cttee, Advisory Coun. on Educn in Scotland, 1959–61; Vis. Prof., Indiana Univ., 1963–64; Vice-Pres. Roy. Soc. of Edinburgh, 1960–63; Vice-Pres., Scottish Gaelic Texts Soc., 1967–; Founder Mem., and Chm., Scottish Mathematical Council, 1967–73; Chm., Clyde Estuary Amenity Council, 1969–82. Hon. Mem., Edinburgh Mathematical Soc., 1990. Keith Prize, RSE, 1961–63; Senior Whitehead Prize, London Mathematical Soc., 1987. *Publications:* Matematicheskaya Teorija Dvizhenija Neupravljaemykh Raket, 1951; An Introduction to Mathematical Analysis, 1963; The Modular Group and its Subgroups, 1969; Modular Forms and Functions, 1977; (ed) Modular Forms, 1985; papers on the Theory of Numbers, Theory of Functions, Rocket Ballistics and Gaelic Subjects in various journals. *Recreations:* hill-walking, Gaelic studies, organ music. *Address:* 98 Kelvin Court, Glasgow G12 0AH. *T:* 0141–339 2641.

RANKIN, Robert Craig McPherson, CompICE; Chairman, BKR Financial Ltd, since 1988; Director, British Shipbuilders, 1985–91; *b* 15 Aug. 1937; *s* of Robert Craig Rankin and Julia Rankin (*née* Duff); *m* 1963, Alison Barbara Black Douglas; one *s* one *d*. *Educ:* The Academy, Ayr; Royal College of Science and Technology, Glasgow. CompICE 1987; CIMgt (CBIM 1987). Dir, Balfour Beatty Construction (Scotland) Ltd, 1973–74; Dir 1974–83, Exec. Dir 1983–85, Balfour Beatty Construction Ltd; Balfour Beatty Ltd: Dir, 1983–85; Dep. Man. Dir, 1985–86; Man. Dir, 1986–87; Chief Exec., 1986–88; Dir, BICC PLC, 1987–88; Non-executive Director: London & Edinburgh Trust PLC, 1988–91; LDDC, 1989–93. *Recreations:* opera, music, golf, field sports.

RANKINE, Jean Morag, (Mrs N. A. Hall); Deputy Director of the British Museum, since 1983; *b* 5 Sept. 1941; *d* of Alan Rankine and Margaret Mary Sloan Rankine (*née* Reid); *m* 1992, Norman Anthony Hall. *Educ:* Central Newcastle High Sch.; University College London (BA, MPhil; Fellow, 1990); Univ. of Copenhagen. Grad. Assistant, Durham Univ. Library, 1966–67; British Museum: Res. Assistant, Dept of Printed Books, 1967–73; Asst Keeper, Director's Office, 1973–78; Dep. Keeper, Public Services, 1978–83. *Recreations:* sculling, ski-ing, fell-walking, opera, motorcycling. *Address:* British Museum, WC1B 3DG. *Clubs:* Thames Rowing; Clydesdale Amateur Rowing (Glasgow).

RANNIE, Prof. Ian; FRCPath 1964; FIBiol 1964; Professor of Pathology (Dental School), University of Newcastle upon Tyne, 1960–81, Professor Emeritus 1981; *b* 29 Oct. 1915; *o s* of James Rannie, MA, and Nicholas Denniston McMeekan; *m* 1943, Flora Welch; two *s*. *Educ:* Ayr Academy; Glasgow University. BSc (Glas), 1935; MB, ChB (Glas), 1938; BSc Hons Pathology and Bacteriology (Glas), 1939; Hutcheson Research Schol. (Pathology), 1940. Assistant to Professor of Bacteriology, Glasgow, 1940–42; Lecturer in Pathology, 1942–60, King's College, Univ. of Durham. Consultant Pathologist, United Newcastle upon Tyne Hospitals, 1948–81, Hon. Consultant 1981–. Pres., International Soc. of Geographical Pathology, 1969–72; Vice-President: Assoc. of Clinical Pathologists, 1978–80; Internat. Union of Angiology. Hon. Mem., Hungarian Arteriosclerosis Res. Soc. *Publications:* papers on various subjects in medical journals. *Recreation:* golf. *Address:* 5 Osborne Villas, Newcastle upon Tyne NE2 1JU. *T:* Tyneside 0191–281 3163. *Clubs:* East India, Royal Over-Seas League.

RANSFORD, John Anthony; Chief Executive, North Yorkshire County Council, since 1994; *b* 19 Sept. 1948; *s* of Sydney George Ransford and Ethel Alice Ransford (*née* Peters); *m* 1971, Liz Hainsworth; one *s* one *d*. *Educ:* Letchworth Grammar Sch.; Univ. of Sussex (BA Hons Sociol.; MSocWork). CQSW 1972. Probation Officer, SE London Probation and After-Care Service, 1972–74; Kirklees Metropolitan Council: Trng Officer, Social Services Dept, 1974–77; Health Liaison Officer, 1977–79; Asst Dir, Social Services, 1979–82, Dir, 1982–87; Actg Chief Exec., 1987; Dir, Social Services, N Yorks CC, 1988–94. Hon. Sec., Assoc. of Dirs of Social Services, 1993–. *Recreations:* theatre, foreign travel, current affairs. *Address:* County Hall, Northallerton, N Yorks DL7 8AD. *T:* Northallerton (01609) 780780.

RANT, James William, CB 1995; QC 1980; **His Honour Judge Rant;** a Circuit Judge, since 1984, at Central Criminal Court, since 1986; Judge Advocate General of the Army and Royal Air Force, since 1991; *b* 16 April 1936; *s* of late Harry George Rant, FZS and Barbara Rant; *m* 1963, Helen Rant (*née* Adnams), BA; one *s* two *d* (and one *s* decd). *Educ:* Stowe Sch.; Selwyn Coll., Cambridge (MA, LLM). Called to the Bar, Gray's Inn, 1961; pupillage with late James N. Dunlop, 1962–63; a Dep. Circuit Judge, 1975–79; a Recorder, 1979–84. Freeman: City of London, 1986; Clockmakers' Co., 1989. *Recreations:* cookery, music, family life. *Address:* 3 Temple Gardens, Middle Temple Lane, EC4Y 9AA.

RANTZEN, Esther Louise, (Mrs Desmond Wilcox), OBE 1991; Television Producer/Presenter, since 1968; *b* 22 June 1940; *d* of late Harry Rantzen and of Katherine Rantzen; *m* 1977, Desmond Wilcox, *qv*; one *s* two *d*. *Educ:* North London Collegiate Sch.; Somerville Coll., Oxford (MA). Studio manager making dramatic sound effects, BBC Radio, 1963; BBC TV: Researcher, 1965; Dir, 1967; Reporter, Braden's Week, 1968–72; Producer/Presenter, That's Life, 1973–94, scriptwriter, 1976–94; Producer, documentary series, The Big Time, 1976; Presenter: Esther Interviews . . ., 1988; Hearts of Gold, 1988; Esther, 1994–; Producer/Presenter, Drugwatch, Childwatch, The Lost Babies and other progs on social issues; reporter/producer, various documentaries, religious and current affairs TV progs. Member: Nat. Consumer Council, 1981–90; Health Educn Authority, 1989–; Task Force to review services for drug misusers, DoH, 1994. Chm., Childline; Pres., Meet-a-Mum Assoc.; a Vice-President: ASBAH; Health Visitors' Assoc.; Spastics Soc.; Nat. Deaf Children's Soc.; Iain Rennie Hospice at Home; Patron: Addenbrookes Kidney Patients Assoc.; Contact-a-Family (families of disabled children); DEMAND (furniture for the disabled); Downs Children's Assoc.; Children with Aids; Jewels for Children; Scope; Headway; Children Head Injuries Trust; Hesley Foundn; Komso Children's Hosp. Trustee, Ben Hardwick Meml Fund. Hon. Mem., NSPCC, 1989. FRTVS 1995. Hon. DLitt, Southampton Inst. for FE, 1994. Personality of 1974, RTS award; BBC TV Personality of 1975, Variety Club of GB; European Soc. for Organ Transplant Award, 1985; Richard Dimbleby Award, BAFTA, 1988. SSStJ. *Publications:* (with Desmond Wilcox) Kill the Chocolate Biscuit, 1981; Baby Love, 1985; (with Shaun Woodward) Ben: the story of Ben Hardwick, 1985. *Recreations:* family life, the countryside, appearing in pantomime. *Address:* BBC TV, White City, 201 Wood Lane, W12 7RJ. *T:* 0181–752 5252; Noel Gay Artists, 6th Floor, 76 Oxford Street, W1N 0AT. *T:* 0171–412 0400.

RAO, Calyampudi Radhakrishna, FRS 1967; Eberly Professor of Statistics, Penn State University, since 1988; Adjunct Professor, University of Pittsburgh, since 1988 (University Professor, 1979–88); *b* 10 Sept. 1920; *s* of C. D. Naidu and A. Laksmikantamma; *m* 1948, C. Bhargavi Rao; one *s* one *d*. *Educ:* Andhra Univ. (MA, 1st Class Maths); Calcutta Univ. (MA, 1st Class Statistics; Gold Medal); PhD, ScD, Cambridge (Hon. Fellow, King's Coll., Cambridge, 1975). Indian Statistical Institute: Superintending Statistician, 1943–49; Professor and Head of Division of Theoretical Research and Training, 1949–64; Dir, Res. and Training Sch., 1964–76 (Sec., 1972–76); Jawaharlal Nehru Professor, 1976–84. Nat. Prof., India, 1987–92. Co-editor, Sankhya, Indian Jl of Statistics, 1964–72, Editor, 1972–. Member, Internat. Statistical Inst., 1951 (Mem. Statistical Educn Cttee, 1958–; Treasurer, 1962–65; Pres.-elect, 1975–77, Pres., 1977–79, Hon. Mem. 1982); Chm., Indian Nat. Cttee for Statistics, 1962–; President: Biometric Soc., 1973–75 (Hon. Life Mem., 1986); Indian Econometric Soc., 1971–76; Forum for Interdisciplinary Mathematics, 1982–84. Fellow: Indian Nat. Sci. Acad., 1953 (Vice-Pres., 1973, 1974); Inst. of Math. Statistics, USA, 1958 (Pres., 1976–77); Amer. Statistical Assoc., 1972; Econometric Soc., 1972; Indian Acad. of Sciences, 1974; Founder Fellow: Third World Science Acad., 1983; Nat. Acad. of Scis, India, 1988. Hon. Fellow: Royal Stat. Soc., 1969; Amer. Acad. of Arts and Sciences, 1975; Calcutta Stat. Assoc., 1985; Biometric Soc., 1986; Finnish Statistical Soc., 1990. Shanti Swarup Bhatnagar Memorial Award, 1963; Guy Medal in Silver, Royal Stat. Soc., 1965; Padma Bhushan, 1968; Meghnad Saha Medal, 1969; J. C. Bose Gold Medal, 1979; S. S. Wilke's Meml Medal, 1989. Hon. DSc: Andhra; Leningrad; Athens; Osmania; Ohio State; Philippines; Tampere; Neuchatel; Poznan; Indian Statistical Inst.; Colorado State; Hyderabad; Barcelona; Guelph; Hon. DLitt Delhi. Hon. Prof., Univ. of San Marcos, Lima. *Publications:* (with Mahalanobis and Majumdar) Anthropometric Survey of the United Provinces, 1941, a statistical study, 1949; Advanced Statistical Methods in Biometric Research, 1952; (with Mukherjee and Trevor) The Ancient Inhabitants of Jebal Moya, 1955; (with Majumdar) Bengal Anthropometric Survey, 1945, a statistical study, 1959; Linear Statistical Inference and its Applications, 1965; (with A. Matthai and S. K. Mitra) Formulae and Tables for Statistical Work, 1966; Computers and the Future of Human Society, 1968; (with S. K. Mitra) The Generalised Inverse of Matrices and its Applications, 1971; (with A. M. Kagan and Yu. V. Linnik) Characterization Problems of Mathematical Statistics, 1973; (with J. Kleffe) Estimation of Variance Components and its Applications, 1988; Statistics and Truth, 1989; (with D. N. Shaubhag) Choquet-Deny Type Functional Equations with Applications to Stochastic Models. *Address:* Department of Statistics, 326 Classroom Building, Penn State University, University Park, PA 16802–2111, USA.

RAO, Prof. Chintamani Nagesa Ramachandra, Padma Shri, 1974; Padma Vibhushan, 1985; FRS 1982; CChem, FRSC; President, Jawaharlal Nehru Centre for Advanced Scientific Research, since 1994, and Albert Einstein Research Professor, Indian Institute of Science, Bangalore, India; *b* 30 June 1934; *s* of H. Nagesa Rao; *m* 1960, Indumati; one *s* one *d*. *Educ:* Univ. of Mysore (DSc); Univ. of Purdue, USA (PhD). Research Chemist, Univ. of California, Berkeley, 1958–59; Lectr, Indian Inst. of Science, 1959–63; Prof., Indian Inst. of Technology, Kanpur, 1963–76, Head of Chemistry Dept, 1964–68, Dean of Research, 1969–72; Jawaharlal Nehru Fellow, 1973–75; Indian Institute of Science,

Bangalore: Chm., Solid State and Structural Chemistry Unit and Materials Res. Laboratory, 1976–84; Dir, 1984–94. Commonwealth Vis. Prof., Univ. of Oxford, and Fellow, St Catherine's Coll., 1974–75; Jawaharlal Nehru Vis. Prof., Univ. of Cambridge, and Professorial Fellow, Kings' Coll., Cambridge, 1983–84. US Nat. Acad. of Sci. Lect., 1993. President: INSA, 1985–87; IUPAC, 1985–87; Indian Sci. Congress, 1987–88; Indian Acad, of Scis, 1989–91; Materials Res. Soc. of India, 1989–91. Member: First Nat. Cttee of Science and Technology, Govt of India, 1971–74; Science Adv. Cttee to Union Cabinet of India, 1981–86; Chm., Science Adv. Council to Prime Minister, 1986–90. Mem. Gen. Council, ICSU. Foreign Member: Slovenian Acad. of Scis, 1983; Serbian Acad. of Scis, 1986; Amer. Acad. of Arts and Scis, 1986; USSR Acad. of Scis, 1988; Czechoslovak Acad. of Scis, 1988; Polish Acad. of Scis, 1988; US Nat. Acad. of Scis, 1990; Pontifical Acad. of Scis, 1990; Amer. Philosophical Soc., 1995; Founder Mem., Third World Acad. Sci. (Vice-Pres.). Blackett Lectr, Royal Soc., 1991. Hon. DSc: Purdue, 1982; Bordeaux, 1983; Sri Venkateswara, 1984; Roorkee, 1985; Banaras, Osmania, Mangalore and Manipur, 1987; Anna, Mysore, Burdwan, 1988; Wroclaw, 1989; Andhra, Karnatak, 1990; Bangalore, Hyderabad, Indian Inst. of Technology, Kharagpur, 1991. Many awards and medals, incl.: Marlow Medal of Faraday Soc. (London), 1967; Royal Soc. of Chemistry (London) Medal, 1981; Centennial For. Fellowship of Amer. Chemical Soc., 1976; Hevrovsky Gold Medal, Czech. Acad. of Scis, 1989; Golden Jubilee Prize, CSIR, 1992; P. C. Ray Meml Award, 1994; Sahabdeen Award for Sci., Sri Lanka, 1994. *Publications:* 30 books including: Ultraviolet and Visible Spectroscopy, 1960, 3rd edn 1975; Chemical Applications of Infrared Spectroscopy, 1964; Spectroscopy in Inorganic Chemistry, 1970; Modern Aspects of Solid State Chemistry, 1970; University General Chemistry, 1973; Solid State Chemistry, 1974; Phase Transitions in Solids, 1978; Preparation and Characterization of Materials, 1981; The Metallic and the Non-metallic States of Matter, 1985; New Directions in Solid State Chemistry, 1986; Chemistry of Oxide Superconductors, 1988; Chemical and Structural Aspects of High Temperature Oxide Superconductors, 1988; Bismuth and Thallium Superconductors, 1989; Advances in Catalyst Design, 1991; Chemistry of High Temperature Superconductivity, 1991; Superconductivity Today, 1992; Chemistry of Advanced Materials, 1992; Chemical Approaches to the Synthesis of Inorganic Materials, 1994; Transition Metal Oxides, 1995; 800 research papers. *Recreations:* gourmet cooking, gardening. *Address:* JNC President's House, Indian Institute of Science, Bangalore 560012, India. *T:* (80) 3345491.

RAO, P. V. Narasimha; Prime Minister of India and Leader of the Congress (I) Party, since 1991; *b* Karimnagar, Andhra Pradesh, 28 June 1921; widower; three *s* five *d. Educ:* Osmania Univ., Hyderabad; Bombay Univ.; Nagpur Univ. (BSc, LLB). Career as leader, writer, poet, agriculturalist, advocate and administrator. Member, Andhra Pradesh Legislative Assembly, 1957–77; Minister in Andhra Pradesh Govt, 1962–71; Chief Minister of the State, 1971–73. Chm., Telugu Academy, Andhra Pradesh, 1968–74; Vice-Pres., Dakshin Bharat Hindi Prachar Sabha, Madras, 1972; Gen. Sec., All India Congress Cttee, 1975–76. Elected to Lok Sabha (from Hanamkonda, Andhra Pradesh) 1972, 1977 and 1980, (from Ramtek) 1984; 1991; Minister: for External Affairs, 1980–84; for Home Affairs, 1984; of Defence, 1985; of Human Resources Develt, 1985–88; of Health and Family Welfare, 1986–88; of External Affairs, 1988–89. Chairman: Public Accounts Cttee, 1978–79; Bharatiya Vidya Bhavan's Andhra Centre. Has lectured on political matters in univs in USA and Federal Republic of Germany, and has visited many countries. *Publications:* many, including Sahasra Phan (Hindi trans.). *Recreations:* music, cinema, theatre. *Address:* Prime Minister's Office, South Block, New Delhi 110011, India; Vangara Post, Karimnagar District, Andhra Pradesh, India.

RAPER, (Alfred) Graham, CBE 1988; PhD; FEng; Chairman, Projecta, consulting engineers, since 1987; Chief Executive and Deputy Chairman, Davy Corporation, 1985–87; *b* 15 May 1932; *s* of Hilda and Alfred William Raper; *m* 1st, Elizabeth Williams (marr. diss. 1975); two *s* one *d*; 2nd, Valerie Benson; one *s. Educ:* Lady Manners School, Bakewell; Univ. of Sheffield (BScTech Hons, PhD). FIChemE, FIM. Asst Lectr, Univ. of Sheffield, 1955–57; Research Engineer, Head Wrightson Co., 1957–59; Technical Manager, Davy United Engineering, 1959–65; Steel Plant Manager, Highveld Steel & Vanadium, S Africa, 1965–69; joined Davy Corp., 1969. *Publications:* articles in jls of Iron & Steel Institute and British Association. *Recreations:* golf, gardening. *Address:* 54 Golf Links Road, Ferndown, Wimborne, Dorset BH22 8BZ. *T:* Wimborne (01202) 873512.

RAPHAEL, Adam Eliot Geoffrey; writer on Home Affairs, The Economist, since 1994, *b* 22 April 1938; *s* of Geoffrey George Raphael and Nancy Raphael (*née* Rose); *m* 1970, Caroline Rayner Ellis; one *s* one *d. Educ:* Arnold House, Charterhouse; Oriel Coll., Oxford (BA Hons History). 2nd Lieut Royal Artillery, 1956–58. Copy Boy, Washington Post, USA, 1961; Swindon Evening Advertiser, 1962–63; Film Critic, Bath Evening Chronicle, 1963–64; The Guardian: Reporter, 1965; Motoring Correspondent, 1967–68; Foreign Correspondent, Washington and S Africa, 1969–73; Consumer Affairs Columnist, 1974–76; Political Correspondent, The Observer, 1976–81, Political Editor, 1981–86; Presenter, Newsnight, BBC TV, 1987–88; an Asst Editor, 1988, Exec. Editor, 1988–93, The Observer. Awards include: Granada Investigative Journalist of the Year, 1973; British Press Awards, Journalist of the Year, 1973. *Publications:* My Learned Friends, 1989; Ultimate Risk: the inside story of the Lloyd's catastrophe, 1994. *Recreations:* tennis, skiing. *Address:* 50 Addison Avenue, W11 4QP. *T:* 0171–603 9133. *Clubs:* Hurlingham, Royal Automobile, Ski Club of Great Britain.

RAPHAEL, Caroline Sarah; Head of Drama, BBC Radio, since 1994; *b* 15 Jan. 1958; *d* of Arnold Raphael and Lily Suzanne (*née* Shaffer); *m* 1982, Michael Eaves; one *s. Educ:* Putney High Sch.; Manchester Univ. (BA Hons Drama). Theatre director: Nuffield Theatre, 1980–81; Bristol Old Vic, 1981–83; Gate Theatre, London, 1983; Literary Agent and Publisher, Chappels Music, 1983; joined BBC Radio, 1984: Script Reader, Producer, Editor Drama, 1984–90; Editor Drama, Features, Youth Programmes, Radio 5, 1990–94. *Recreations:* listening to radio, watching television. *Address:* Broadcasting House, W1A 1AA. *T:* 0171–580 4465.

RAPHAEL, Prof. David Daiches, DPhil, MA; Emeritus Professor of Philosophy, University of London, since 1983; *b* 25 Jan. 1916; 2nd *s* of late Jacob Raphael and Sarah Warshawsky, Liverpool; *m* 1942, Sylvia, *er d* of late Rabbi Dr Salis Daiches and Flora Levin, Edinburgh; two *d. Educ:* Liverpool Collegiate School; University College, Oxford (scholar). 1st Class, Classical Moderations, 1936; Hall-Houghton Junior Septuagint Prizeman, 1937; 1st Class, Literae Humaniores, 1938; Robinson Senior Scholar of Oriel College, Oxford, 1938–40; Passmore Edwards Scholar, 1939. Served in Army, 1940–41. Temporary Assistant Principal, Ministry of Labour and National Service, 1941–44; temp. Principal, 1944–46. Professor of Philosophy, University of Otago, Dunedin, NZ, 1946–49; Lecturer in Moral Philosophy, Univ. of Glasgow, 1949–51; Senior Lecturer, 1951–60; Edward Caird Prof. of Political and Social Philosophy, Univ. of Glasgow, 1960–70; Prof. of Philosophy, Univ. of Reading, 1970–73; Prof. of Philosophy, Imperial Coll., Univ. of London, 1973–83 (Acad. Dir of Associated Studies, 1973–80; Head of Dept of Humanities, 1980–83; Hon. Fellow 1987). Visiting Professor of Philosophy, Hamilton Coll., Clinton, NY (under Chauncey S. Truax Foundation), and Univ. of Southern California, 1959; Mahlon Powell Lectr, Indiana Univ., 1959; Vis. Fellow, All Souls Coll., Oxford, 1967–68; John Hinkley Vis. Prof. of Political Sci., Johns Hopkins Univ., 1984. Independent Member: Cttee on Teaching Profession in Scotland (Wheatley Cttee), 1961–63; Scottish Agricultural Wages Board, 1962–84; Agricultural Wages Bd for England and Wales, 1972–78. Mem. Academic Adv. Cttee, Heriot-Watt Univ., Edinburgh, 1964–71; Mem. Cttee on Distribution of Teachers in Scotland (Roberts Cttee), 1965–66; Independent Member Police Advisory Board for Scotland, 1965–70; Member Social Sciences Adv. Cttee, UK Nat. Commission, UNESCO, 1966–74; Vice-Pres., Internat. Assoc. Philosophy of Law and Social Philosophy, 1971–87; Pres., Aristotelian Soc., 1974–75. Academic Mem., Bd of Governors, Hebrew Univ. of Jerusalem, 1969–81, Hon. Governor 1981–. *Publications:* The Moral Sense, 1947; Edition of Richard Price's Review of Morals, 1948; Moral Judgement, 1955; The Paradox of Tragedy, 1960; Political Theory and the Rights of Man, 1967; British Moralists 1650–1800, 1969; Problems of Political Philosophy, 1970, 2nd edn 1990; (ed jtly) Adam Smith's Theory of Moral Sentiments, 1976; Hobbes: Morals and Politics, 1977; (ed jtly) Adam Smith's Lectures on Jurisprudence, 1978; (ed jtly) Adam Smith's Essays on Philosophical Subjects, 1980; Justice and Liberty, 1980; Moral Philosophy, 1981, 2nd edn 1994; (trans. jtly with Sylvia Raphael) Richard Price as Moral Philosopher and Political Theorist, by Henri Laboucheix, 1982; Adam Smith, 1985; articles in jls of philosophy and of political studies. *Address:* 54 Sandy Lane, Petersham, Richmond, Surrey TW10 7EL.

RAPHAEL, Frederic Michael; author; *b* 14 Aug. 1931; *s* of late Cedric Michael Raphael and of Irene Rose (*née* Mauser); *m* 1955, Sylvia Betty Glatt; two *s* one *d. Educ:* Charterhouse; St John's Coll., Cambridge (MA (Hons)). FRSL 1964. *Publications: novels:* Obbligato, 1956; The Earlsdon Way, 1958; The Limits of Love, 1960; A Wild Surmise, 1961; The Graduate Wife, 1962; The Trouble with England, 1962; Lindmann, 1963; Orchestra and Beginners, 1967; Like Men Betrayed, 1970; Who Were You With Last Night?, 1971; April, June and November, 1972; Richard's Things, 1973; California Time, 1975; The Glittering Prizes, 1976; Heaven and Earth, 1985; After the War, 1988 (adapted for television, 1989); The Hidden I, 1990; A Double Life, 1993; Old Scores, 1995; *short stories:* Sleeps Six, 1979; Oxbridge Blues, 1980 (also pubd as scripts of TV plays, 1984); Think of England, 1986; The Latin Lover, 1994; *biography:* Somerset Maugham and his World, 1977; Byron, 1982; *essays:* Bookmarks (ed), 1975; Cracks in the Ice, 1979; Of Gods and Men, 1992; France, the Four Seasons, 1994; *screenplays:* Nothing but the Best, 1964; Darling, 1965 (Academy Award); Two For The Road, 1967; Far From the Madding Crowd, 1967; A Severed Head, 1972; Daisy Miller, 1974; The Glittering Prizes, 1976 (sequence of TV plays) (Writer of the Year 1976, Royal TV Soc.); Rogue Male, 1976; (and directed) Something's Wrong (TV), 1978; School Play (TV), 1979; The Best of Friends (TV), 1979; Richard's Things, 1981; After the War (TV series), 1989; (and directed) The Man In The Brooks Brothers Shirt, 1991 (ACE Award); *plays:* From The Greek, Arts, Cambridge, 1979; The Daedalus Dimension (radio), 1982; The Thought of Lydia (radio), 1988; The Empty Jew (radio), 1993; *translations:* (with Kenneth McLeish): Poems of Catullus, 1976; The Oresteia, 1978 (televised as The Serpent Son, BBC, 1979); The Complete Plays of Aeschylus, 1991; Medea, 1994. *Recreations:* tennis, having gardened. *Address:* c/o Deborah Rogers, 20 Powis Mews, W11 1JN. *Clubs:* Savile, The Queen's.

RAPHAEL, Prof. Ralph Alexander, CBE 1982; PhD, DSc (London), ARCS, DIC; FRS 1962; FRSE, FRSC; Fellow of Christ's College, Professor of Organic Chemistry, and Head of Department of Organic and Inorganic Chemistry, Cambridge University, 1972–88, now Hon. Fellow and Professor Emeritus; *b* 1 Jan. 1921; *s* of Jack Raphael; *m* 1944, Prudence Marguerite Anne, *d* of Col P. J. Gaffikin, MC, MD; one *s* one *d. Educ:* Wesley College, Dublin; Tottenham County School; Imperial College of Science and Technology (FIC 1991). Chemist, May & Baker Ltd, 1943–46. ICI Research Fellow, Univ. of London, 1946–49; Lecturer in Organic Chemistry, Univ. of Glasgow, 1949–54; Professor of Organic Chemistry, Queen's University, Belfast, 1954–57; Regius Prof. of Chemistry, Glasgow Univ., 1957–72. Tilden Lectr, Chem. Soc., 1960, Corday-Morgan Vis. Lectr, 1963; Roy. Soc. Vis. Prof., 1967; Pedler Lectr, Chem. Soc., 1973; Pacific Coast Lectr, West Coast Univs tour from LA to Vancouver, 1979; Lady Davis Vis. Prof., Hebrew Univ. of Jerusalem, 1980; Sandin Lectr, Univ. of Alberta, 1985; Andrews Lectr, Univ. of NSW, 1985; Royal Soc. Kan Tong-Po Vis. Prof., Hong Kong Univ., 1989; Emilio Noelting Vis. Prof., Univ. de Haute Alsace, 1990. Vice-Pres. Chemical Soc., 1967–70; Member: Academic Adv. Bd, Warwick Univ., 1962–; Scientific Adv. Cttee, National Gall., 1986–. Hon. MRIA 1987. DUniv Stirling, 1982; Hon. DSc: East Anglia, 1986; QUB, 1989. Meldola Medallist, RIC, 1948; Chem. Soc. Ciba-Geigy Award for Synthetic Chemistry, 1975; Davy Medal, Royal Soc., 1981. *Publications:* Chemistry of Carbon Compounds, Vol. IIA, 1953; Acetylenic Compounds in Organic Synthesis, 1955; papers in Journal of Chemical Society. *Recreations:* music, bridge. *Address:* University Chemical Laboratory, Lensfield Road, Cambridge CB2 1EW. *T:* Cambridge (01223) 336328; 4 Ivy Field, High Street, Barton, Cambs CB3 7BJ. *Club:* Athenæum.

RAPHAEL, Ven. Timothy John; Archdeacon of Middlesex, since 1983; *b* 26 Sept. 1929; *s* of Hector and Alix Raphael; *m* 1957, Anne Elizabeth Shepherd; one *s* two *d. Educ:* Christ's College, Christchurch, NZ; Leeds Univ. (BA). Asst Curate, St Stephen, Westminster, 1955–60; Vicar of St Mary, Welling, Kent, 1960–63; Vicar of St Michael, Christchurch, NZ, 1963–65; Dean of Dunedin, 1965–73; Vicar, St John's Wood, London, 1973–83. *Recreations:* contemporary poetry, theatre, beach-combing. *Address:* 12 St Ann's Villas, W11 4RS. *T:* 0171–603 0856.

RAPHOE, Bishop of, (RC); *no new appointment at time of going to press.*

RASCH, Sir Richard Guy Carne, 3rd Bt, *cr* 1903; a Member of HM Body Guard, Honourable Corps of Gentlemen-at-Arms, 1968–88; *b* 10 Oct. 1918; *s* of Brigadier G. E. C. Rasch, CVO, DSO (*d* 1955); *S* uncle, 1963; *m* 1st, 1947, Anne Mary (*d* 1989), *d* of late Major J. H. Dent-Brocklehurst; one *s* one *d*; 2nd, 1961, Fiona Mary, *d* of Robert Douglas Shaw. *Educ:* Eton; RMC, Sandhurst. Major, late Grenadier Guards. Served War of 1939–45; retired, 1951. *Recreations:* shooting, fishing. *Heir: s* Simon Anthony Carne Rasch [*b* 26 Feb. 1948; *m* 1987, Julia, *er d* of Major Michael Stourton; one *s* one *d. Educ:* Eton; Royal Agric. Coll., Cirencester]. *Address:* 30 Ovington Square, SW3 1LR. *T:* 0171–589 9973; The Manor House, Lower Woodford, near Salisbury, Wilts SP4 6NQ. *Clubs:* White's, Pratt's, Cavalry and Guards.

RASHBASS, Dr Barbara, FRCP; Director and Secretary: Wolfson Foundation, since 1990; Wolfson Family Charitable Trust; *d* of late Leonard Cramer and Sarina (*née* Klinger); *m* 1956, Cyril Rashbass (*d* 1982); two *s* one *d. Educ:* Godolphin Sch., Salisbury; University Coll. London (MB, BS). DCH 1961; DPH 1968; FRCP 1995. FRSM 1989. Called to the Bar, Middle Temple, 1969. PMO, MRC, 1983–87. Dep. Chm., Harrow HA, 1982–84. Mem., Med. Legal Soc., 1970–. *Recreations:* tennis, 'cello, gardening. *Address:* (office) 18/22 Haymarket, SW1Y 4DQ. *T:* 0171–930 1057.

RASHLEIGH, Sir Richard (Harry), 6th Bt *cr* 1831; management accountant; self-employed, since 1990; *b* 8 July 1958; *s* of Sir Harry Evelyn Battie Rashleigh, 5th Bt and Honora Elizabeth (*d* 1987), *d* of George Stuart Sneyd; *S* father, 1984. *Educ:* Allhallows School, Dorset. Management Accountant with Arthur Guinness Son & Co., 1980–82; Dexion-Comino International Ltd, 1982–84; United Biscuits, 1985–88; Wessex Housing,

1988–90. *Recreations:* sailing, tennis, shooting. *Heir:* none. *Address:* Menabilly, Par, Cornwall PL24 2TN. *T:* Par (01726) 815432. *Club:* Royal Fowey Yacht.

RASHLEIGH BELCHER, John; *see* Belcher, J. R.

RASMINSKY, Louis, CC (Canada), 1968; CBE 1946; Governor, Bank of Canada, 1961–73; *b* 1 Feb. 1908; *s* of David and Etta Rasminsky; *m* 1930, Lyla Rotenberg; one *s* one *d. Educ:* University of Toronto; London School of Economics. Financial Section, League of Nations, 1930–39; Chairman, Foreign Exchange Control Board, Canada, 1940–51; Deputy Governor, Bank of Canada, 1956–61. Executive Director: IMF, 1946–62; International Bank, 1950–62; Alternate Governor for Canada, IMF, 1969–73. Chm., Bd of Governors, Internat. Develt Res. Centre, 1973–78. Hon. Fellow, LSE, 1960. Hon. LLD: Univ. of Toronto, 1953; Queen's Univ., 1967; Bishop's Univ., 1968; McMaster Univ., 1969; Yeshiva Univ., 1970; Trent Univ., 1972; Concordia Univ., 1975; Univ. of Western Ontario, 1978; Univ. of British Columbia, 1979; Carleton Univ., 1987; Hon. DHL Hebrew Union Coll., 1963. Outstanding Achievement Award of Public Service of Canada, 1968; Vanier Medal, Inst. of Public Admin, 1974. *Recreations:* golf, fishing. *Address:* 20 Driveway, Apt 1006, Ottawa, Ont K2P 1C8, Canada. *T:* (613) 5940150. *Clubs:* Rideau, Cercle Universitaire d'Ottawa (Ottawa); Five Lakes (Wakefield, PQ).

RASMUSSEN, Poul Nyrup; MP (SDP) Herning-Kredsen, Denmark, since 1988; Prime Minister of Denmark, since 1993; *b* 15 June 1943; *s* of Oluf Nyrup Rasmussen and Vera Nyrup Rasmussen; *m* 1st (marr. diss.); 2nd (marr. diss.); 3rd, 1994, Lone Dybkjær, MEP; (one *c* decd). *Educ:* Esbjerg Statsskole; Univ. of Copenhagen (MA Econs). With Danish Trade Union Council, 1980–86: in Brussels, 1980–81; Chief Economist, 1981–86; Man. Dir, Employees' Capital Pension Fund, 1986–88. Dep. Chm., SDP, 1987–92, Chm., 1992–. *Address:* Office of the Prime Minister, Christiansborg, Prins Jørgens Gaard 11, 1218 Copenhagen K, Denmark. *T:* 33923300.

RATCLIFF, Antony Robin Napier; Director, Eagle Star Holdings plc, since 1980; Deputy Chairman and Chief Executive, Eagle Star Insurance, 1985–87; Visiting Professor, City University Business School, since 1987; *b* 26 Sept. 1925; *m* 1956, Helga Belohlawek, Vienna; one *s.* FIA 1953; ASA. Nat. Correspondent for England, Internat. Actuarial Assoc., 1965–70; Mem. Council, Assoc. of British Insurers (formerly British Insurance Assoc.), 1969–87. Pres., Inst. of Actuaries, 1980–82; Vice-Pres., London Insce Inst., 1964–87. Vice-Pres., Assoc. internat. pour l'Etude de l'Economie de l'Assurance, 1986–90. Corresponding Member: Deutsche Gesellschaft für Versicherungsmathematik; Verein zur Förderung der Versicherungswirtschaft. FRSA. Hon. Treasurer, German Christ Church, London. Messenger and Brown Prize-Winner, Inst. of Actuaries, 1963. Hon. DLitt City, 1986. *Publications:* (jtly) Lessons from Central Forecasting, 1965; (jtly) Strategic Planning for Financial Institutions, 1974; (jtly) A House in Town, 1984; contribs to Jl of Inst. of Actuaries, Trans of Internat. Congress of Actuaries, Jl London Insce Inst., Jl Chartered Insce Inst., Blätter der Deutschen Gesellschaft für Versicherungsmathematik. *Address:* 60 St Mary Axe, EC3A 8JQ. *T:* 0171–929 1111. *Clubs:* Actuaries, Roehampton, Anglo-Austrian Society.

RATCLIFFE, Frederick William, CBE 1994; MA, PhD; JP; University Librarian, University of Cambridge, 1980–94, now Emeritus; Life Fellow, Corpus Christi College, Cambridge, since 1994 (Fellow, 1980–94); *b* 28 May 1927; *y s* of late Sydney and Dora Ratcliffe, Leek, Staffs; *m* 1952, Joyce Brierley; two *s* one *d. Educ:* Leek High Sch., Staffs; Manchester Univ. (MA, PhD); MA Cantab. Served in N Staffs Regt, 1945–48. Manchester University: Graduate Res. Scholarship, 1951; Res. Studentship in Arts, 1952; Asst Cataloguer and Cataloguer, 1954–62; Sub-Librarian, Glasgow Univ., 1962–63; Dep. Librarian, Univ. of Newcastle upon Tyne, 1963–65; University Librarian, 1965–80, Dir, John Rylands University Library, 1972–80, Manchester University. Trustee, St Deiniol's Library, Hawarden, 1975–. Hon. Lectr in Historical Bibliography, Manchester Univ., 1970–80; External Prof., Dept of Library and Inf. Studies, Loughborough Univ., 1981–86; Hon. Res. Fellow, Dept of Library, Archive and Inf. Studies, UCL, 1987–; Sandars Reader in Bibliography, Cambridge Univ., 1988–89. Chm., Library Panel, The Wellcome Trust, 1988–94. Fellow, Chapter of Woodard Schools (Eastern Div.), 1981–. Chm., Adv. Cttee, Nat. Preservation Office, 1984–. Trustee, Cambridge Foundn, 1989–. Hon. FLA 1986. JP Stockport, 1972–80, Cambridge, 1981. Encomienda de la Orden del Merito Civil (Spain), 1988. *Publications:* Preservation Policies and Conservation in British Libraries, 1984; many articles in learned journals. *Recreations:* book collecting, hand printing, cricket. *Address:* 84 Church Lane, Girton, Cambs CB3 0JP. *T:* Cambridge (01223) 277512; Ridge House, The Street, Rickinghall Superior, Diss, Norfolk IP22 1DY. *T:* Diss (01379) 898232.

RATCLIFFE, (John) Michael; Literary Editor, The Observer, since 1989; *b* 15 June 1935; *s* of Donald Ratcliffe and Joyce Lilian Dilks. *Educ:* Cheadle Hulme Sch.; Christ's Coll., Cambridge (MA). Trainee journalist, Sheffield Telegraph, 1959–61; Asst Literary and Arts Editor, Sunday Times, 1962–67; Literary Editor, 1967–72, chief book reviewer, 1972–82, The Times; freelance writer, 1982–83; theatre critic, Observer, 1984–89. Commended Critic of the Year, British Press Awards, 1989. *Publications:* The Novel Today, 1968; The Bodley Head 1887–1987 (completed for J. W. Lambert), 1987. *Recreations:* music, travel, architecture, walking, gardening, cycling. *Address:* 4 Elia Street, N1 8DE. *T:* 0171–837 1687.

RATFORD, Sir David (John Edward), KCMG 1994 (CMG 1984); CVO 1979; HM Diplomatic Service, retired; *b* 22 April 1934; *s* of George Ratford and Lilian (*née* Jones); *m* 1960, Ulla Monica, *d* of Oskar and Gurli Jerneck, Stockholm; two *d. Educ:* Whitgift Middle Sch.; Selwyn Coll., Cambridge (1st Cl. Hons Mod. and Med. Langs). National Service (Intell. Corps), 1953–55. Exchequer and Audit Dept, 1952; FO, 1955; 3rd Sec., Prague, 1959–61; 2nd Sec., Mogadishu, 1961–63; 2nd, later 1st Sec., FO, 1963–68; 1st Sec. (Commercial), Moscow, 1968–71; FCO, 1971–74; Counsellor (Agric. and Econ.), Paris, 1974–78; Counsellor, Copenhagen, 1978–82; Minister, Moscow, 1983–85; Asst Under-Sec., of State (Europe), 1986–90, and Dep. Political Dir, 1987–90, FCO; UK Rep., Permanent Council of WEU, 1986–90; Ambassador to Norway, 1990–94. Comdr, Order of the Dannebrog, Denmark, 1979. *Recreations:* music, tennis. *Address:* Wisborough Cottage, Wisborough Green, West Sussex RH14 0DZ; Käringön, Bohuslän, Sweden. *Club:* Travellers'.

RATHBONE, John Rankin, (Tim Rathbone); MP (C) Lewes since Feb. 1974; *b* 17 March 1933; *s* of J. R. Rathbone, MP (killed in action 1940) and Lady Wright (*see* Beatrice Wright); *m* 1st, 1960, Margarita Sanchez y Sanchez (marr. diss. 1981); two *s* one *d*; 2nd, 1982, Mrs Susan Jenkin Stopford Sackville. *Educ:* Eton; Christ Church, Oxford; Harvard Business School. 2nd Lieut KRRC, 1951–53. Robert Benson Lonsdale & Co., Merchant Bankers, 1956–58; Trainee to Vice-Pres., Ogilvy & Mather Inc., NY, 1958–66; Chief Publicity and Public Relations Officer, Conservative Central Office, 1966–68; Director: Charles Barker Group, 1968–87; Ayer Barker Ltd, 1971–87 (Man. Dir 1971–73; Dep. Chm., 1973–79); Charles Barker City, 1981–87; Charles Barker Manchester, 1983–87 (Chm., 1983–86). PPS to Minister of Health, 1979–82, to Minister for Trade (Consumer Affairs), 1982–83, to Minister for the Arts, 1985. Founder Member: All Party Parly Drugs Misuse Gp, 1984 (Chm., 1987–); Parly Engrg Develt Gp, 1987 (Chm., 1992–); Conservatives for Fundamental Change in South Africa, 1986; All-Party Groups: British-Amer.; British-Latin Amer.; British-Cuban; British-Southern Africa (Chm.); British-Japanese; British-China; British-Jordan; British-Spanish; British-Lebanon (Chm.); British-UAE; British-Iraqi Shias; European Movt; Sane Planning. Deleg. to Council of Europe and WEU, 1987–; Mem., Cons. ME Council. Member Council: Nat. Cttee for Electoral Reform; RSA, 1985–88. FRSA 1979. *Publications:* It's my problem as well: drugs prevention and education, 1992; pamphlet on nursery schooling. *Recreation:* family. *Address:* House of Commons, SW1A 0AA. *T:* 0171–219 3460. *Clubs:* Brooks's, Pratt's; Sussex; Society of Sussex Downsmen.

RATHBONE, Tim; *see* Rathbone, J. R.

RATHCAVAN, 3rd Baron *cr* 1953, of The Braid, Co. Antrim; **Hugh Detmar Torrens O'Neill;** Bt 1929; Director, Lamont Holdings; Chairman: Northern Ireland Tourist Board, since 1988; FRX International, since 1988; *b* 14 June 1939; *o s* of 2nd Baron Rathcavan, PC (NI) and his 1st wife, Clare Désirée (*d* 1956), *d* of late Detmar Blow; *S* father, 1994; *m* 1983, Sylvie Marie-Thérèse Wichard; one *s. Educ:* Eton. Captain, Irish Guards. Financial journalism, Observer, Irish Times, FT; Dep. Chm., IPEC Europe, 1978–82; Chm., Northern Ireland Airports, 1986–92; Director: St Quentin, 1980–94; The Spectator, 1982–84; Old Bushmills Distillery Co., 1988–; Savoy Management, 1989–94; Northern Bank Ltd, 1991–; Berkeley Hotel Co. Ltd, 1995–. *Recreations:* food, travel. *Heir: s* Hon. François Hugh Nial O'Neill, *b* 26 June 1984. *Address:* Cleggan Lodge, Ballymena, Co. Antrim BT43 7JW; 14 Thurloe Place, SW7 2RZ. *Clubs:* Beefsteak, Garrick.

RATHCREEDAN, 3rd Baron *cr* 1916; **Christopher John Norton;** Partner, Norton & Brooksbank, Pedigree Livestock Auctioneers, since 1983; *b* 3 June 1949; *er s* of 2nd Baron Rathcreedan, TD and of Ann Pauline, *d* of late Surg.-Capt. William Bastian, RN; *S* father, 1990; *m* 1978, Lavinia Anne Ross, *d* of A. G. R. Ormiston; two *d. Educ:* Wellington Coll.; RAC Cirencester. Partner, Hobsons, Pedigree Livestock Auctioneers; founded Norton & Brooksbank, 1983. *Recreations:* horse racing, gardening. *Heir: b* Hon. Adam Gregory Norton [*b* 2 April 1952; *m* 1980, Hilary Shelton, *d* of Edmond Ryan; two *d*.]. *Address:* Stoke Common House, Purton Stoke, Swindon, Wilts SN5 9LL. *T:* Swindon (01793) 772492. *Club:* Turf.

RATHDONNELL, 5th Baron, *cr* 1868; **Thomas Benjamin McClintock Bunbury;** *b* 17 Sept. 1938; *o s* of William, 4th Baron Rathdonnell and Pamela (*d* 1989), *e d* of late John Malcolm Drew; *S* father 1959; *m* 1965, Jessica Harriet, *d* of George Gilbert Butler, Scatorish, Bennettsbridge, Co. Kilkenny; three *s* one *d. Educ:* Charterhouse; Royal Naval College, Dartmouth. Lieutenant RN. *Heir: s* Hon. William Leopold McClintock Bunbury, *b* 6 July 1966. *Address:* Lisnavagh, Rathvilly, County Carlow, Ireland. *T:* Carlow (0503) 61104.

RATLEDGE, Prof. Colin, PhD; CChem, FRSC; CBiol, FIBiol; Professor of Microbial Biochemistry, University of Hull, since 1983; *b* 9 Oct. 1936; *s* of Fred Ratledge and Freda Smith Ratledge (*née* Proudlock); *m* 1961, Janet Vivien Bottomley; one *s* two *d. Educ:* Bury High Sch.; Manchester Univ. (BSc Tech, PhD). AMCST; CChem, FRSC 1970; CBiol, FIBiol 1982. Res. Fellowship, MRC Ireland, 1960–64; Res. Scientist, Unilever plc, 1964–67; Hull University, 1967–: Lectr, 1967–73; Sen. Lectr, 1973–77; Reader, 1977–83; Head of Dept of Biochemistry, 1986–88. Visiting Lecturer: Australian Soc. of Microbiol., 1986; NZ Soc. of Microbiol., 1986; Kathleen Barton Wright Meml Lectr (Inst. of Biol./Soc. Gen. Microbiol.), 1995. Mem., AFRC Food Res. Cttee, 1989–92; Chairman: AFRC Food Res. Grants Bd, 1989–92; AFRC Food-borne Pathogens Co-ord. Prog.; Brit. Co-ordinating Cttee for Biotechnology, 1989–91; Inst. of Biol. Industrial Biol. Cttee, 1992–; Vice-Pres., SCI, 1993– (Chm. Biotechnol. Gp, 1990–91; Mem. Council, 1991–93); Sec., Internat. Cttee of Envmtl and Applied Microbiology, 1991–94; Mem., Biotechnology Cttee, Internat. Union of Biochemistry, 1984–. Fellow, Internat. Inst. of Biotechnology, 1993. Editor-in-Chief, World Jl of Microbiol. and Biotechnol., 1987–; Exec. Editor, Biotechnology Techniques, 1988–. *Publications:* The Mycobacteria, 1977; Co-Editor: Microbial Technology: current state, future prospects, 1979; The Biology of the Mycobacteria, vol. 1 1982, vol. 2 1983, vol. 3 1989; Biotechnology for the Oils and Fats Industry, 1984; Microbial Technology in the Developing World, 1987; Microbial Lipids, vol. 1 1988, vol. 2 1989; Microbial Physiology and Manufacturing Industry, 1988; Biotechnology: Social and Economic Impact, 1992; Industrial Application of Single Cell Oils, 1992; Biochemistry of Microbial Degradation, 1993; numerous scientific papers in biol science jls. *Recreations:* walking, gardening. *Address:* Department of Applied Biology, University of Hull, Hull HU6 7RX; 49 Church Drive, Leven, Beverley, E Yorks HU17 5LH. *T:* Hornsea (01964) 542690.

RATNER, Gerald Irving; Chief Executive, Ratners Group, 1986–92; consultant, Tobacco Dock, since 1993; *b* 1 Nov. 1949; *s* of Leslie and Rachelle Ratner; *m* 1st (marr. diss. 1989); two *d*; 2nd, 1989, Moira Day; one *s* one *d. Educ:* Town and Country School, London NW3. Ratners (Jewellers), subseq. Ratners Group: Jt Man. Dir, 1978–84, Man. Dir, 1984–92; Chm., 1986–92. *Recreations:* keeping fit, art, chess. *T:* 0171–702 9681.

RATTEE, Hon. Sir Donald (Keith), Kt 1989; **Hon. Mr Justice Rattee;** a Judge of the High Court of Justice, Chancery Division, since 1993 (Family Division, 1989–93);*b* 9 March 1937; *s* of Charles Ronald and Dorothy Rattee; *m* 1964, Diana Mary, *d* of John Leslie and Florence Elizabeth Howl; four *d. Educ:* Clacton County High School; Trinity Hall, Cambridge (MA, LLB). Called to Bar, Lincoln's Inn, 1962, Bencher, 1985; Second Junior Counsel to the Inland Revenue (Chancery), 1972–77; QC 1977; Attorney Gen. of the Duchy of Lancaster, 1986–89; a Recorder, 1989. Liaison Judge, Family Div. (NE Circuit), 1990–93; Mem., Gen. Council of the Bar, 1970–74. *Recreations:* golf, walking, music, gardening. *Address:* Royal Courts of Justice, Strand, WC2A 2LL. *Clubs:* Royal Automobile; Banstead Downs Golf (Banstead).

RATTLE, Sir Simon, Kt 1994; CBE 1987; Music Director, City of Birmingham Symphony Orchestra, since 1991 (Principal Conductor, 1980–91); Principal Conductor, Orchestra of the Age of Enlightenment, since 1992; *b* Liverpool, 19 Jan. 1955; *m* 1980, Elise Ross, American soprano; two *s.* Won Bournemouth John Player Internat. Conducting Comp., when aged 19. Has conducted: Bournemouth Sinfonietta; Philharmonia; Northern Sinfonia; London Philharmonic; London Sinfonietta; Berlin Philharmonic; Boston Symphony; Chicago Symphony; Cleveland; Concertgebouw; Stockholm Philharmonic; Toronto Symphony, etc. Débuts: Festival Hall, 1976; ENO, 1985; Royal Opera, 1990; Vienna Philharmonic, 1993; Philadelphia, 1993. Royal Albert Hall (Proms. etc.), 1976–; Asst Conductor, BBC Scottish Symphony Orch., 1977–80; Associate Conductor, Royal Liverpool Philharmonic Soc., 1977–80; Glyndebourne début, 1977; Principal Conductor, London Choral Soc., 1979–84; Artistic Dir, South Bank Summer Music, 1981–83; Principal Guest Conductor: Rotterdam Philharmonic, 1981–84; Los Angeles Philharmonic, 1981–92. Exclusive contract with EMI Records. Hon. Fellow, St Anne's Coll., Oxford, 1991. Hon. DMus: Birmingham, 1985; Birmingham Poly., 1985. Chevalier des Arts et des Lettres (France), 1995. *Address:* c/o Harold Holt Ltd, 31 Sinclair Road, W14 0NS. *T:* 0171–603 4600.

RAU, Santha Rama; *see* Rama Rau, S.

RAUSING, Dr Hans A.; Hon. Chairman, Tetra Laval Group, since 1993; *b* 25 March 1926; *s* of Ruben and Elisabeth Rausing; *m* 1958, Märit Norrby; one *s* two *d*. *Educ:* Univ. of Lund, Sweden. Tetra Pak: Man. Dir, 1954–83; Exec. Chm. and Chief Exec. Officer, 1983–91; Chm., Gp Bd, 1985–91; Chm. and Chief Exec. Officer, Tetra Laval Gp, 1991–93. Member, Board: Stockholms Enskilda Bank, Sweden, 1970–72; Skandinaviska Enskilda Banken, Sweden, 1973–82; South-Swedish Univs, Sweden, 1975–80; Business Internat., NY, 1975–79. Mem., Co-ordination Council for Foreign Investments, Russia, 1995–. Mem., Royal Swedish Acad. of Engrg Scis, 1984–94 (Hon. Mem., 1994). Hon. Mem., Acad. of Natural Scis, Russia, 1994. Hon. doctorates: Econs, Lund, 1979; DTech Royal Inst. of Technol., Stockholm, 1985; Econs, Stockholm Sch. of Econs, 1987. *Address:* c/o Tetra Pak Ltd, 1 Longwalk Road, Stockley Park, Uxbridge, Middx UB11 1DL. *T:* Uxbridge (01895) 868000.

RAVEN, Prof. John Albert, FRS 1990; FRSE; Boyd Baxter Professor of Biology, University of Dundee, since 1990; *b* 25 June 1941; *s* of John Harold Edward Raven and Evelyn Raven; *m* 1985, Linda Lea Handley. *Educ:* Wimbish County Primary Sch.; Friends' Sch., Saffron Walden; St John's College, Cambridge (MA, PhD). FRSE 1981. University of Cambridge: Research Fellow, and Official Fellow, St John's Coll., 1966–71; Univ. Demonstrator in Botany, 1968–71; Lectr, and Reader, 1971–80, Prof. (personal chair), 1980–90, Dept of Biol Scis, Univ. of Dundee. *Publications:* Energetics and Transport in Aquatic Plants, 1984; numerous papers in learned jls and chapters in multi-author vols. *Recreations:* aviation, jogging, literature. *Address:* Spital Beag, Waterside, Invergowrie, Dundee DD2 5DQ. *T:* Dundee (01382) 562292.

RAVEN, John Armstrong, CBE 1982; Director-General, International Express Carriers' Conference, 1991–93 and since 1995 (Director (Facilitation), 1993–94); Consultant, World Bank, since 1983; *b* 23 April 1920; *s* of late John Colbeck Raven; *m* 1st, 1945, Megan Humphreys (*d* 1963); one *s* one *d*; 2nd, 1965, Joy Nesbitt (*d* 1983); one step *d*. *Educ:* High Sch., Cardiff; Downing Coll., Cambridge (MA). Called to Bar, Gray's Inn, 1955. Dir, British Coal Exporters' Fedn, 1947–68; Section Head, Nat. Economic Develt Office, 1968–70. Dir-Gen., Assoc. of British Chambers of Commerce, 1972–74; Vice-Chm., SITPRO, 1974–82. *Recreation:* wondering. *Address:* 215 Avenue de Messidor, 1180 Brussels, Belgium. *T:* (2) 3457620. *Club:* United Oxford & Cambridge University.

RAVEN, Dame Kathleen, (Dame Kathleen Annie Ingram), DBE 1968; FRCN 1986; SRN 1936; SCM 1938; Chief Nursing Officer in the Department of Health and Social Security (formerly Ministry of Health), 1958–72; *b* 9 Nov. 1910; *o d* of late Fredric William Raven and late Annie Williams Raven (*née* Mason); *m* 1959, Prof. John Thornton Ingram, MD, FRCP (*d* 1972). *Educ:* Ulverston Grammar School; privately; St Bartholomew's Hosp., London; City of London Maternity Hospital. St Bartholomew's Hospital: Night Superintendent, Ward Sister, Administrative Sister, Assistant Matron, 1936–49; Matron, Gen. Infirmary, Leeds, 1949–57; Dep. Chief Nursing Officer, Min. of Health, 1957–58. Mem. Gen. Nursing Council for England and Wales, 1950–57; Mem. Council and Chm. Yorkshire Br., Roy. Coll. of Nursing, 1950–57; Mem. Central Area Advisory Bd for Secondary Education, Leeds, 1953–57; Area Nursing Officer, Order of St John, 1953–57; Mem. Exec. Cttee Assoc. of Hospital Matrons for England and Wales, 1955–57; Mem. Advisory Cttee for Sister Tutor's Diploma, Univ. of Hull, 1955–57; Internal Examr for Diploma of Nursing, Univ. of Leeds, 1950–57; Member: Area Nurse Trg Cttee, 1951–57; Area Cttee Nat. Hosp. Service Reserve, 1950–57; Central Health Services Council, 1957–58; Council and Nursing Advisory Bd, British Red Cross Soc., 1958–72; Cttee of St John Ambulance Assoc., 1958–72; National Florence Nightingale Memorial Cttee of Great Britain and Northern Ireland, 1958–72; WHO Expert Advisory Panel on Nursing, 1961–79; WHO Fellow, 1960; a Vice-Pres., Royal Coll. of Nursing, 1972–. Civil Service Comr, 1972–80. Chief Nursing Adviser, Allied Med. Gp, 1974–86. Nursing missions to Saudi Arabia and Egypt, 1972–86. Member: Council, Distressed Gentlefolk's Aid Assoc., 1974–89 (Chm., F and GP Cttee 1981–87); Court of Patrons, RCS, 1993–. Founder Gov., Aylesbury GS, 1985. Vice Pres. and Mem. Council, Med. Foundn, Epsom Coll., 1992–. Freedom, City of London, 1986. Hon. Freewoman, Worshipful Co. of Barbers, 1981. FRSA 1970. Hon. DLitt Keele, 1992. Officer (Sister) Order of St John, 1963. *Recreations:* painting, reading, travel. *Address:* Jesmond, Burcott, Wing, Leighton Buzzard, Bedfordshire LU7 0JU. *T:* Aylesbury (01296) 688244. *Club:* Commonwealth Trust.

RAVEN, Simon (Arthur Noël), FRSL; author, critic and dramatist since 1957; *b* 28 Dec. 1927; *s* of Arthur Godart Raven and Esther Kate Raven (*née* Christmas); *m* 1951, Susan Mandeville Kilner (marriage dissolved); one *s*. *Educ:* Charterhouse; King's Coll., Cambridge (MA). Research, 1951–52; regular commn, King's Shropshire Light Inf., 1953–57 (Capt.): served in Kenya; resigned, 1957. Member, Horatian Society. FRSL 1993. *Publications: novels:* The Feathers of Death, 1959; Brother Cain, 1959; Doctors Wear Scarlet, 1960; Close of Play, 1962; The Roses of Picardie, 1980; An Inch of Fortune, 1980; September Castle, 1983. The Alms for Oblivion sequence: The Rich Pay Late, 1964; Friends in Low Places, 1965; The Sabre Squadron, 1966; Fielding Gray, 1967; The Judas Boy, 1968; Places Where They Sing, 1970; Sound the Retreat, 1971; Come like Shadows, 1972; Bring Forth the Body, 1974; The Survivors, 1976; The First-born of Egypt sequence: Morning Star, 1984; The Face of the Waters, 1985; Before the Cock Crow, 1986; New Seed for Old, 1988; Blood of My Bone, 1989; In the Image of God, 1990; The Troubadour, 1992; The Islands of Sorrow, 1994; *short stories:* The Fortunes of Fingel, 1976; *memoirs:* Shadows on the Grass, 1982; The Old School, 1986; The Old Gang, 1988; Bird of Ill Omen, 1989; Is There Anybody There? Said the Traveller: memories of a private nuisance, 1991; *general:* The English Gentleman, 1961; Boys Will be Boys, 1963; Royal Foundation and Other Plays, 1965; contribs to Observer, Spectator, Punch, etc. *Plays and dramatisations for broadcasting:* BBC TV: Royal Foundation, 1961; The Scapegoat, 1964; Sir Jocelyn, 1965; Huxley's Point Counter-Point, 1968; Trollope's The Way We Live Now, 1969; The Pallisers, a serial in 26 episodes based on the six Palliser novels of Anthony Trollope, 1974; Iris Murdoch's An Unofficial Rose, 1975; Sexton Blake, 1978; ABC TV: The Gaming Book, 1965; Thames TV: Edward and Mrs Simpson, a serial based on Edward VIII by Frances Donaldson, 1978; Love in a Cold Climate, a dramatisation of Nancy Mitford's Pursuit of Love and Love in a Cold Climate, 1980; Central TV: Julian Symons's The Blackheath Poisonings, 1993; BBC Radio: Triad, a trilogy loosely based on Thucydides' History of the Peloponnesian War, 1965–68. *Recreations:* cricket, travel, reading, the turf. *Address:* c/o Curtis Brown Ltd, 162–168 Regent Street, W1R 5TB. *Clubs:* MCC, Butterflies Cricket, Trogs' Cricket.

RAVENSCROFT, John Robert Parker, (John Peel); broadcaster/journalist, since 1961; *b* 30 Aug. 1939; *s* of Robert Leslie and Joan Mary Ravenscroft; *m* 1974, Sheila Mary Gilhooly; two *s* two *d*. *Educ:* Woodlands Sch., Deganwy, N Wales; Shrewsbury. National Service, Royal Artillery (B2 Radar Operator), 1957–59. Mill operative, Rochdale, 1959–60; office boy, Dallas, Texas, 1960–65; part-time disc-jockey, 1961–; computer programmer, 1965; Pirate Radio, London, 1967; BBC Radio 1, 1967–. Hon. MA East Anglia, 1989. *Recreations:* making plans to go and live in France, staring out of the window. *Address:* c/o BBC Radio 1, W1A 4DJ. *T:* 0171–580 4468. *Clubs:* Liverpool Supporters; Eddie Grundy Fan (Sutton).

RAVENSCROFT, Ven. Raymond Lockwood; Archdeacon of Cornwall and Canon Librarian of Truro Cathedral, since 1988; *b* 15 Sept. 1931; *s* of Cecil and Amy Ravenscroft; *m* 1957, Ann (*née* Stockwell); one *s* one *d*. *Educ:* Sea Point Boys' High School, Cape Town, SA; Leeds Univ. (BA Gen. 1953); College of the Resurrection, Mirfield. Assistant Curate: St Alban's, Goodwood, Cape, SA, 1955–58; St John's Pro-Cathedral, Bulawayo, S Rhodesia, 1958–59; Rector of Francistown, Bechuanaland, 1959–62; Asst Curate, St Ives, Cornwall, 1962–64; Vicar: All Saints, Falmouth, 1964–68; St Stephen by Launceston with St Thomas, 1968–74; Team Rector of Probus Team Ministry, 1974–88; RD of Powder, 1977–81; Hon. Canon of Truro Cathedral, 1982–88. *Recreations:* walking, reading, local history. *Address:* Archdeacon's House, Knights Hill, Kenwyn, Truro, Cornwall TR1 3UY. *T:* Truro (01872) 72866.

RAVENSDALE, 3rd Baron *cr* 1911; **Nicholas Mosley,** MC 1944; Bt 1781; *b* 25 June 1923; *e s* of Sir Oswald Mosley, 6th Bt (*d* 1980) and Lady Cynthia (*d* 1933), *d* of 1st Marquess Curzon of Kedleston; *S* to barony of aunt, who was also Baroness Ravensdale of Kedleston (Life Peer), 1966, and to baronetcy of father, 1980; *m* 1st, 1947, Rosemary Laura Salmond (marr. diss. 1974; she *d* 1991); three *s* one *d*; 2nd, 1974, Mrs Verity Bailey; one *s*. *Educ:* Eton; Balliol College, Oxford. Served in the Rifle Brigade, Captain, 1942–46. *Publications:* (as Nicholas Mosley): Spaces of the Dark, 1951; The Rainbearers, 1955; Corruption, 1957; African Switchback, 1958; The Life of Raymond Raynes, 1961; Meeting Place, 1962; Accident, 1964; Experience and Religion, 1964; Assassins, 1966; Impossible Object, 1968; Natalie Natalia, 1971; The Assassination of Trotsky, 1972; Julian Grenfell: His Life and the Times of his Death, 1888–1915, 1976; The Rules of the Game: Sir Oswald and Lady Cynthia Mosley 1896–1933, 1982; Beyond the Pale: Sir Oswald Mosley 1933–1980, 1983; Efforts at Truth (autobiog.), 1995; *novels* (series): Catastrophe Practice, 1979; Imago Bird, 1980; Serpent, 1981; Judith, 1986; Hopeful Monsters (Whitbread Prize), 1990. *Heir: s* Hon. Shaun Nicholas Mosley [*b* 5 August 1949; *m* 1978, Theresa Clifford; four *s*]. *Address:* 2 Gloucester Crescent, NW1 7DS. *T:* 0171–485 4514.

RAVENSWORTH, 8th Baron *cr* 1821; **Arthur Waller Liddell,** Bt 1642; JP; *b* 25 July 1924; *s* of late Hon. Cyril Arthur Liddell (2nd *s* of 5th Baron) and Dorothy L., *d* of William Brown, Slinfold, Sussex; *S* cousin 1950; *m* 1950, Wendy, *d* of J. S. Bell, Cookham, Berks; one *s* one *d*. *Educ:* Harrow. Radio Engineer, BBC, 1944–50. JP Northumberland, 1959. *Heir: s* Hon. Thomas Arthur Hamish Liddell [*b* 27 Oct. 1954; *m* 1983, Linda, *d* of H. Thompson; one *s* one *d*]. *Address:* Eslington Park, Whittingham, Alnwick, Northumberland NE66 4UR. *T:* Whittingham (01665) 574239.

RAVIV, Moshe; Ambassador of Israel to the Court of St James's, since 1993; *b* Romania, 23 April 1935; *s* of David and Elka Raviv; *m* 1955, Hanna Kaspi; two *s* one *d*. *Educ:* Hebrew Univ., Jerusalem; Univ. of London (grad. Internat. Relations). Israel Ministry of Foreign Affairs: 2nd Sec., London, 1961–63; Office of Foreign Minister, Mrs Golda Meir, 1964–65; Political Sec. to Foreign Minister, Abba Eban, 1966–68; Counsellor, Washington, 1968–74; Dir, E European Div., 1974–76; Dir, N American Div., 1976–78; Ambassador to the Phillipines, 1978–81; Dir, Economic Div., 1981–83; Minister, London, 1983–88; Dep. Dir Gen., i/c Information, 1988–93. *Recreations:* reading, chess, jogging. *Address:* Embassy of Israel, 2 Palace Green, W8 4QB.

RAWBONE, Rear-Adm. Alfred Raymond, CB 1976; AFC 1951; *b* 19 April 1923; *s* of A. Rawbone and Mrs E. D. Rawbone (*née* Wall); *m* 1943, Iris Alicia (*née* Willshaw); one *s* one *d*. *Educ:* Saltley Grammar Sch., Birmingham. Joined RN, 1942; 809 Sqdn War Service, 1943; CO 736 Sqdn, 1953; CO 897 Sqdn, 1955; CO Loch Killisport, 1959–60; Comdr (Air) Lossiemouth and HMS Ark Royal, 1961–63; Chief Staff Officer to Flag Officer Naval Air Comd, 1965–67; CO HMS Dido, 1968–69; CO RNAS Yeovilton, 1970–72; CO HMS Kent, 1972–73; Dep. ACOS (Operations), SHAPE, 1974–76. Comdr 1958; Captain 1964; Rear-Adm. 1974. Director: Vincents of Yeovil, 1983–86; Vindata, 1984–86; Vincents (Bridgewater) Ltd, 1984–86. *Address:* Halstock Leigh, Halstock, near Yeovil, Somerset BA22 9QU.

RAWCLIFFE, Rt. Rev. Derek Alec, OBE 1971; Assistant Bishop, Diocese of Ripon, since 1991; *b* 8 July 1921; *s* of James Alec and Gwendoline Rawcliffe; *m* 1977, Susan Speight (*d* 1987). *Educ:* Sir Thomas Rich's School, Gloucester; Univ. of Leeds (BA, 1st cl. Hons English); College of the Resurrection, Mirfield. Deacon 1944, priest 1945, Worcester; Assistant Priest, Claines St George, Worcester, 1944–47; Asst master, All Hallows School, Pawa, Solomon Islands, 1947–53; Headmaster, 1953–56; Headmaster, S Mary's School, Maravovo, Solomon Is, 1956–58; Archdeacon of Southern Melanesia, New Hebrides, 1959–74; Assistant Bishop, Diocese of Melanesia, 1974–75; First Bishop of the New Hebrides, 1975–80; Bishop of Glasgow and Galloway, 1981–91. New Hebrides Medal, 1980; Vanuatu Independence Medal, 1980. *Recreations:* music, poetry, numismatics. *Address:* Kitkatts, Wetherby Road, Bardsey, Leeds LS17 9BB. *T:* Wetherby (01937) 572201.

RAWES, Francis Roderick, MBE 1944; MA; *b* 28 Jan. 1916; *e s* of late Prescott Rawes and Susanna May Dockery; *m* 1940, Dorothy Joyce, *d* of E. M. Hundley, Oswestry; two *s* one *d*. *Educ:* Charterhouse; St Edmund Hall, Oxford. Served in Intelligence Corps, 1940–46; GSO3(I) 13 Corps; GSO1 (I) HQ 15 Army Group and MI14 WO. Asst Master at Westminster School, 1938–40 and 1946–64; Housemaster, 1947–64; Headmaster, St Edmund's School, Canterbury, 1964–78. Chm. Governing Body, Westonbirt Sch., 1983–91 (Governor, 1979–95). *Address:* Peyton House, Chipping Campden, Glos GL55 6AL.

RAWLEY, Alan David, QC 1977; a Recorder of the Crown Court, since 1972; Fellow Commoner, Magdalene College, Cambridge, since 1991; *b* 28 Sept. 1934; *er s* of late Cecil David Rawley and of Theresa Rawley (*née* Pack); *m* 1964, Ione Jane Ellis; two *s* one *d*. *Educ:* Wimbledon Coll.; Brasenose Coll., Oxford. Nat. Service, 1956–58; commnd Royal Tank Regt. Called to the Bar, Middle Temple, 1958; Bencher, 1985. Dep. Chairman, Cornwall Quarter Sessions, 1971. *Address:* Lamb Building, Temple, EC4Y 7AS. *T:* 0171–353 6381. *Clubs:* Garrick, Pilgrims, MCC; Hampshire (Winchester).

RAWLINGS, Baroness *cr* 1994 (Life Peer), of Burnham Westgate in the County of Norfolk; **Patricia Elizabeth Rawlings;** *b* 27 Jan. 1939; *d* of Louis Rawlings and Mary (*née* Boas de Winter); *m* 1962, David Wolfson (*see* Baron Wolfson of Sunningdale) (marr. diss. 1967). *Educ:* Oak Hall, Haselmere, Surrey; Le Manoir, Lausanne; Florence Univ.; University Coll. London (BA Hons); London School of Economics (post grad. diploma course, Internat. Relns). Children's Care Cttee, LCC, 1959–61; WNHR Nursing, Westminister Hosp., until 1968. MEP (C) Essex SW, 1989–94; contested (C) Essex West and Hertfordshire East, Eur. parly elecns, 1994. European Parliament, 1989–94: EPP British Section Rep. on Conservative Nat. Union; Albanian, Bulgarian and Romanian Delegn; EDG spokesman on Culture Cttee, substitute on Foreign Affairs Cttee. British Red Cross Society: Mem., 1964–; Chm., Appeals, London Br., until 1988; Nat. Badge of Honour, 1981, Hon. Vice Pres., 1988. Member Council: British Bd of Video Classification, 1986–89; Peace through NATO; British Assoc. for Central and Eastern Europe, 1994–;

Special Advr to Ministry on Inner Cities, DoE, 1987–88. Member: IISS; RIIA; EUW. Dir, English Chamber Orch. and Music Soc. Contested (C): Sheffield Central, 1983; Doncaster Central, 1987. Order of the Rose, Silver Class (Bulgaria), 1991. *Recreations:* music, art, golf, skiing, travel. *Address:* House of Lords, SW1A 0PW. *Clubs:* Queen's; Royal West Norfolk Golf.

RAWLINGS, Flt Lieut Jerry John; President, Republic of Ghana, since 1992; *b* 22 June 1947; *s* of John Rawlings and Victoria Agbotui; *m* 1977, Nana Konadu Agyeman; one *s* three *d.* *Educ:* Achimota Sch., Accra; Ghana Military Acad. Enlisted in Ghana Air Force, 1967; commnd Pilot Officer, 1969; tried for mutiny, May 1979; forcibly released from cell, June 1979, by popular uprising; became Chm., Armed Forces Revolutionary Council; handed over to democratically elected Govt, Sept. 1979; overthrew Govt, Dec. 1981; Chm., Provisional Nat. Defence Council, 1982–92. *Recreations:* flying, swimming, riding, reading. *Address:* Office of the President, PO Box 1627, Accra, Ghana. *T:* (21) 665415.

RAWLINGS, Margaret; actress; *b* Osaka, Japan, 5 June 1906; *d* of Rev. G. W. Rawlings and Lilian Boddington; *m* 1st, 1927, Gabriel Toyne, actor (marr. diss. 1938); no *c*; 2nd, 1942, Robert Barlow (knighted 1943; *d* 1976); one *d.* *Educ:* Oxford High School for Girls; Lady Margaret Hall, Oxford. Left Oxford after one year, and joined the Macdona Players Bernard Shaw Repertory Company on tour, 1927; played Jennifer in the Doctor's Dilemma and many other parts; toured Canada with Maurice Colbourne, 1929; First London engagement Bianca Capello in The Venetian at Little Theatre in 1931, followed by New York; played Elizabeth Barrett Browning, in The Barretts of Wimpole Street in Australia and New Zealand; Oscar Wilde's Salome at Gate Theatre; Liza Kingdom, The Old Folks at Home, Queen's; Mary Fitton in This Side Idolatry, Lyric; Jean in The Greeks had a word for it, Liza Doolittle in Pygmalion and Ann in Man and Superman, Cambridge Theatre, 1935; Katie O'Shea in Parnell, Ethel Barrymore Theatre, New York 1935, later at New, London; Lady Macbeth for OUDS 1936; Mary and Lily in Black Limelight, St James's and Duke of York's, 1937–38; Helen in Trojan Women, Karen Selby in The Flashing Stream, Lyric, 1938–39, and in New York; Revival of Liza in Pygmalion, Haymarket, 1939; You of all People, Apollo, 1939; A House in the Square, St Martin's, 1940; Mrs Dearth in Dear Brutus, 1941–42; Gwendolen Fairfax in the Importance of Being Earnest, Royal Command Perf., Haymarket, 1946; Titania in Purcell's Fairy Queen, Covent Garden, 1946; Vittoria Corombona in Webster's The White Devil, Duchess, 1947; Marceline in Jean-Jacques Bernard's The Unquiet Spirit, Arts, 1949; Germaine in A Woman in Love, tour and Embassy, 1949; The Purple Fig Tree, Piccadilly, 1950; Lady Macbeth, Arts, 1950; Spring at Marino, Arts, 1951; Zabina in Tamburlaine, Old Vic, 1951–52; Lysistrata in The Apple Cart, Haymarket, 1953; Countess in The Dark is Light Enough, Salisbury and Windsor Repertory, 1955; Paulina and Mistress Ford, Old Vic, 1955–56; Title Rôle in Racine's Phèdre, Theatre in the Round, London and tour, 1957–58; Sappho in Sappho, Lyceum, Edinburgh, 1961; Ask Me No More, Windsor, 1962; Title role in Racine's Phèdre, Cambridge Arts, 1963; Ella Rentheim in John Gabriel Borkman, Duchess, 1963; Jocasta in Œdipus, Playhouse (Nottingham), 1964; Gertrude in Hamlet, Ludlow Festival, 1965; Madame Torpe in Torpe's Hotel, Yvonne Arnaud Theatre, Guildford, 1965; Mrs Bridgenorth, in Getting Married, Strand, 1967; Carlotta, in A Song at Twilight, Windsor, 1968; Cats Play, Greenwich, 1973; Mixed Economy, King's Head Islington, 1977; Lord Arthur Saville's Crime, Malvern Fest. and tour, 1980; Uncle Vanya, Haymarket, 1982. One-woman performance, Empress Eugénie, May Fair, London, transf. to Vaudeville, UK tour and Dublin Fest., 1979; repeated at King's Lynn Fest., Riverside Theatre, London, New Univ. of Ulster, 1980; Cologne, Horsham, MacRobert Arts Centre, Stirling, Pitlochry Fest., New Univ. of Ulster, 1981; Spoleto Fest., Charleston, SC, 1983. *Films:* Roman Holiday; Beautiful Stranger; No Road Back; Hands of the Ripper; Dr Jekyll and Mr Hyde, 1989. *Television:* Criss Cross Quiz; Somerset Maugham Hour; Sunday Break; Compact; Maigret; Planemakers; solo performance, Black Limelight, Armchair Theatre, 1969; Wives and Daughters, 1971; Folio, 1983. Innumerable radio broadcasts, incl. We Beg to Differ, Brains Trust, Desert Island Discs (an early castaway), plays (Tumbledown Dick, 1986; Golovliovo, 1988; Crown House (serial), 1988 (and on Radio 4, 1991, 1992)), poetry recitals; recordings of: Keats, Gerard Manley Hopkins, Alice in Wonderland; (Marlowe Soc.) King Lear, Pericles; New English Bible Gospels. *Publication:* (trans.) Racine's Phèdre, 1961 (US, 1962) (first professional prodn at Pearl Theatre, NY, 1993). *Recreation:* poetry. *Address:* Rocketer, Wendover, Aylesbury, Bucks HP22 6PR. *T:* Wendover (01296) 622234.

RAWLINS, Colin Guy Champion, OBE 1965; DFC 1941; Director of Zoos and Chief Executive, Zoological Society of London, 1966–84; *b* 5 June 1919; *s* of R. S. C. Rawlins and Yvonne Blanche Andrews; *m* 1946, Rosemary Jensen; two *s* one *d.* *Educ:* Prince of Wales Sch., Nairobi; Charterhouse; Queen's Coll., Oxford (MA). Served with RAF, 1939–46: Bomber Comd, NW Europe; POW, 1941–45; Sqdn-Leader. HM Overseas Civil Service, 1946–66: Administrative Officer, Northern Rhodesia (later Zambia); appointments at Headquarters and in field; Provincial Commissioner, Resident Secretary. Mem., Pearce Commn on Rhodesian Opinion, 1972. Past Pres., Internat. Union of Dirs of Zool. Gardens. Chm. of Trustees, Zimbabwe Trust, 1993–. FCIS 1967. *Recreations:* aviation, travel, gardening. *Address:* Riverain, Gossmore Lane, Marlow, Bucks SL7 1QF. *T:* Marlow (01628) 472796.

RAWLINS, Brig. Gordon John, OBE 1986; Deputy Secretary, Institution of Electrical Engineers, since 1991; *b* 22 April 1944; *s* of Arthur and Joyce Rawlins; *m* 1st, 1965, Ann Beard (*d* 1986); one *s*; 2nd, 1986, Margaret Anne Ravenscroft; one step *s* one step *d.* *Educ:* Peter Symond's, Winchester; Welbeck College; RMA Sandhurst; RMCS Shrivenham (BSc Eng). CEng, FIEE, psc. Commissioned REME, 1964; served Aden, Oman, Jordan, Hong Kong, BAOR, UK, 1964–77; Staff Coll., 1978; MoD 1978–80; 2 i/c 5 Armd Wksp, REME, BAOR, 1981–82; CO 7 Armd Wksp, REME, BAOR, 1982–84; MoD, 1984–87 (Sec. to COS Cttee, 1987); Comd Maint., 1 (BR) Corps, BAOR, 1988. Sec., Instn of Production, subseq. Manufacturing, Engrs, 1988–91. Liveryman, Turners' Co., 1991. *Recreations:* opera, blues music, Rugby, cricket, compiling general knowledge quizzes. *Address:* c/o Royal Bank of Scotland, Holt's Farnborough Branch, Victoria Road, Farnborough, Hants GU14 7NR. *Club:* Army & Navy.

RAWLINS, Surg. Vice-Adm. Sir John (Stuart Pepys), KBE 1978 (OBE 1960; MBE 1956); *b* 12 May 1922; *s* of Col S. W. H. Rawlins, CB, CMG, DSO and Dorothy Pepys Cockerell; *m* 1944, Diana Colbeck (*d* 1992); one *s* three *d.* *Educ:* Wellington Coll.; University Coll., Oxford (Hon. Fellow, 1991); St Bartholomew's Hospital. BM, BCh 1945; MA, FRCP, FFCM, FRAeS. Surg. Lieut RNVR, HMS Triumph, 1947; Surg. Lieut RN, RAF Inst. Aviation Med., 1951; RN Physiol Lab., 1957; Surg. Comdr RAF Inst., Aviation Med., 1961; HMS Ark Royal, 1964; US Navy Medical Research Inst., 1967; Surg. Captain 1969; Surg. Cdre, Dir of Health and Research (Naval), 1973; Surg. Rear-Adm. 1975; Dean of Naval Medicine and MO i/c, Inst. of Naval Medicine, 1975–77; Actg Surg. Vice-Adm. 1977; Medical Dir-Gen. (Navy), 1977–80. QHP 1975. Chairman: Deep Ocean Engineering Inc., 1983–89; Medical Express Ltd, 1984–; Trident Underwater Engrg (Systems) Ltd, 1985–; General Offshore Corp. (UK) Ltd, 1988–91; Director: Diving Unlimited International Ltd, 1980–; Deep Ocean Technology Inc., 1989– (Chm., 1983–89); Deep Ocean Engrg, 1989–91. Pres., Soc. for Underwater Technology, 1980–84 (Hon. Fellow, 1986); Vice-Pres., Underseas Med. Soc.; Hon. Life Mem., British Sub-Aqua Club, 1983; Founder-Mem. European Underseas Biomed. Soc.; Fellow Aerospace Med. Soc. (Armstrong Lectr, 1980); FRAeS 1973; FRSM. Hon. Fellow, Lancaster Univ., 1986. Hon. DTech Robert Gordon's Inst. of Technology, 1991. Erroll-Eldridge Prize 1967; Sec. of US Navy's Commendation 1971; Gilbert Blane Medal 1971; Tuttle Meml Award 1973; Chadwick Medal and Prize 1975; Nobel Award, Inst. of Explosives Engrs, 1987; Man of the Year, British Council for Rehabilitation of the Disabled, 1964. *Publications:* papers in fields of aviation and diving medicine. *Recreations:* diving, fishing, stalking, riding. *Address:* Little Cross, Holne, Newton Abbot, S Devon TQ13 7RS. *T:* Poundsgate (01364) 631249, *Fax:* (01364) 631400. *Club:* Vincent's (Oxford).

RAWLINS, Prof. Michael David, MD; FRCP, FRCPE, FFPM; Ruth and Lionel Jacobson Professor of Clinical Pharmacology, University of Newcastle upon Tyne, since 1973; *b* 28 March 1941; *s* of Rev. Jack and Evelyn Daphne Rawlins; *m* 1963, Elizabeth Cadbury Hambly; three *d.* *Educ:* St Thomas's Hosp. Med. Sch., London (BSc 1962; MB BS 1965); MD London 1973. FRCP 1977; FRCPE 1987; FFPM 1989. Lectr in Medicine, St Thomas's Hosp., London, 1967–71; Sen. Registrar, Hammersmith Hosp., London, 1971–72; Vis. Res. Fellow, Karolinska Inst., Stockholm, Sweden, 1972–73; Public Orator, Univ. of Newcastle upon Tyne, 1990–93. Pres., NE Council on Addictions, 1991–; Vice-Chm., Northern RHA, 1990–94; Member: Nat. Cttee on Pharmacology, 1977–83; Cttee on the Safety of Medicines, 1980– (Chm., 1993–); Cttee on Toxicity, 1989–92; Standing Gp on Health Technology Assessment, 1993–. Chm., Newcastle SDP, 1981–84. Bradshaw Lectr, RCP, 1986. FRSM 1972. William Withering Medal, RCP, 1994; Dixon Medal, Ulster Med. Soc., 1995. *Publications:* Variability in Human Drug Response, 1973; (ed) Textbook of Pharmaceutical Medicine, 1994; articles on clinical pharmacology in med. and scientific jls. *Recreations:* music, golf. *Address:* 29 The Grove, Gosforth, Newcastle upon Tyne NE3 1NE. *T:* 0191–285 5581; Shoreston House, Shoreston, near Seahouses, Northumberland NE68 7SX. *T:* Seahouses (01665) 720203. *Clubs:* Royal Society of Medicine; Bamburgh Castle Golf.

RAWLINS, Peter Jonathan, FCA; business development consultant, since 1994; *b* 30 April 1951; *e s* of late Kenneth Raymond Ivan Rawlins and of Constance Amande Rawlins (*née* Malzy); *m* 1973, Louise Langton; one *s* one *d.* *Educ:* Arnold House Sch.; St Edward's Sch., Oxford; Keble Coll., Oxford (Hons English Lang. and Lit.; MA). Arthur Andersen & Co., 1972–85: Audit Manager, 1977; Partner, 1983; UK Practice Develt Partner, 1984; full-time secondment to Lloyd's of London as PA to Chief Exec. and Dep, Chm., 1983–84; Dir, Sturge Holdings, and Man. Dir, R. W. Sturge & Co., 1985–89; Chief Exec., Internat., subseq. London, Stock Exchange, 1989–93; Director: Sturge Lloyd's Agencies, 1986–89; Wise Speke Holdings, 1987–89; non-exec. Dir, Lloyd-Roberts & Gilkes, 1989–94. Mem., Cttee, Lloyd's Underwriting Agents Assoc., 1986–89 (Treasurer, 1986–87; Dep. Chm., 1988); Mem., standing cttees, Council of Lloyd's, 1985–89. Director: London Sinfonietta Trust, 1985–88; Half Moon Theatre, 1986–88; Mem. Council and Dir, ABSA, 1982–; Dir and Trustee, London City Ballet Trust, 1986–93; Mem., Develt Council, Royal NT, 1991–. Chm., London First Neighbourhood Approach, 1993–. FRSA 1990. *Recreations:* family, performing arts, tennis, squash, clay pigeon shooting, travelling. *Address:* 19 Spencer Hill, Wimbledon, SW19 4PA. *Clubs:* City of London, MCC.

RAWLINSON, family name of **Baron Rawlinson of Ewell.**

RAWLINSON OF EWELL, Baron *cr* 1978 (Life Peer), of Ewell in the County of Surrey; **Peter Anthony Grayson Rawlinson,** PC 1964; Kt 1962; QC 1959; QC (NI) 1972; *b* 26 June 1919; *o* surv. *s* of late Lt-Col A. R. Rawlinson, OBE, and Ailsa, *e d* of Sir Henry Mulleneux Grayson, Bt, KBE; *m* 1st, 1940, Haidee Kavanagh; three *d*; 2nd, 1954, Elaine Dominguez, Newport, Rhode Island, USA; two *s* one *d.* *Educ:* Downside; Christ's Coll., Cambridge (Exhibitioner 1938, Hon. Fellow 1980). Officer Cadet Sandhurst, 1939; served in Irish Guards, 1940–46; N Africa, 1943 (despatches); demobilized with rank of Major, 1946. Called to Bar, Inner Temple, 1946, Bencher, 1962, Reader, 1983, Treas., 1984; Recorder of Salisbury, 1961–62; called to Bar, Northern Ireland, 1972; Recorder of Kingston upon Thames, 1975–; Leader, Western Circuit, 1975–82; retired from practice at the Bar, 1985. Contested (C) Hackney South, 1951; MP(C) Surrey, Epsom, 1955–74, Epsom and Ewell, 1974–78. Solicitor-General, July 1962–Oct. 1964; Opposition Spokesman: for Law, 1964–65, 1968–70; for Broadcasting, 1965; Attorney-General, 1970–74; Attorney-General for NI, 1972–74. Chm., Parly Legal Cttee, 1967–70. Member of Council, Justice, 1960–62, 1964; Trustee of Amnesty, 1960–62; Member, Bar Council, 1966–68; Mem. Senate, Inns of Court, 1968, Vice-Chm., 1974; Vice-Chm., Bar, 1974–75; Chairman of the Bar and Senate, 1975–76; Pres., Senate of Inns of Court and Bar, 1986–87; Chm., Enquiry into Constitution of the Senate, 1985–86. Chm. of Stewards, RAC, 1985–. Director: Pioneer International (formerly Pioneer Concrete Services) Ltd, Sydney, 1985–91 (Chm., UK subsidiary); Daily Telegraph plc, 1985–; STC plc, 1986–91; Mem., London Adv. Cttee, Hongkong and Shanghai Banking Corp., 1984–90. Chm., London Oratory Appeal, 1983–94; Gov., London Oratory Sch., 1985–95. Hon. Fellow, Amer. Coll. of Trial Lawyers, 1973; Hon. Mem., Amer. Bar Assoc., 1976. SMO Malta. *Publications:* War Poems and Poetry today, 1943; Public Duty and Personal Faith—the example of Thomas More, 1978; A Price Too High (autobiog.), 1989; The Jesuit Factor, 1990; *novels:* The Colombia Syndicate, 1991; Hatred and Contempt (Rumpole Award, CWA), 1992; His Brother's Keeper, 1993; Indictment for Murder, 1994; articles and essays in law jls. *Recreations:* the theatre and painting. *Address:* 9 Priory Walk, SW10 9SP. *Clubs:* White's, Pratt's, Royal Automobile, MCC.

RAWLINSON, Sir Anthony Henry John, 5th Bt *cr* 1891; photographer and inventor; *b* 1 May 1936; *s* of Sir Alfred Frederick Rawlinson, 4th Bt and of Bessie Ford Taylor, *d* of Frank Raymond Emmatt, Harrogate; *S* father, 1969; *m* 1st, 1960, Penelope Byng Noel (marr. diss. 1967), 2nd *d* of Rear-Adm. G. J. B. Noel, RN; one *s* one *d*; 2nd, 1967, Pauline Strickland (marr. diss. 1976), *d* of J. H. Hardy, Sydney; one *s*; 3rd, 1977, Helen Leone (separated), *d* of T. M. Kennedy, Scotland; one *s.* *Educ:* Millfield School. Coldstream Guards, 1954–56. *Recreations:* tennis, sailing. *Heir:* *s* Alexander Noel Rawlinson, *b* 15 July 1964. *Address:* Heath Farm, Guist, Dereham, Norfolk NR20 5PG.

RAWLINSON, Charles Frederick Melville; Senior Adviser, West Merchant Bank, since 1993; Chairman, Boxford Suffolk Holdings, since 1992; *b* 18 March 1934; *s* of Rowland Henry Rawlinson and Olivia Melville Rawlinson; *m* 1962, Jill Rosalind Wesley; three *d.* *Educ:* Canford Sch.; Jesus Coll., Cambridge (MA). FCA, FCT. With A. E. Limehouse & Co., Chartered Accts, 1955–58; Peat Marwick Mitchell & Co., 1958–62; Morgan Grenfell & Co. Ltd, Bankers, 1962–87: Dir, 1970–87; Jt Chm., 1985–87; Morgan Grenfell Group PLC: Dir, 1985–88; Vice-Chm., 1987–88; Sen. Advr, 1988–93; Hon. Pres., Morgan Grenfell (Asia), Singapore, 1989–93; seconded as Man. Dir, Investment Bank of Ireland Ltd, Dublin, 1966–68; Director: Associated Paper Industries plc, 1972–91 (Chm., 1979–91); Willis Faber plc, 1981–89. Chairman: The Hundred Gp of Finance Dirs, 1984–86; Industrial Mems Adv. Cttee on Ethics, ICA, 1991–; Member: Chartered Accountants' Jt Ethics Cttee, 1994–; Council, ICAEW, 1995–. Dir, Britten Sinfonia, 1988–. Chm., Peache Trustees, 1980–; Hon. Vice Pres., NABC—Clubs for Young

People, 1995– (Jt Hon. Treas., 1983–91; Dep. Chm., 1989–92; Chm., 1992–94). *Recreations:* music, sailing, shooting, walking in the hills. *Address:* (office) 33 Gracechurch Street, EC3V 0AX. *Club:* Brooks's.

See also under Royal Family.

RAWLINSON, Dennis George Fielding, OBE 1978; JP; FCIT; Member, Transport Tribunal, since 1986; Company Director, since 1964; *b* 3 Sept. 1919; *s* of George and Mary Jane Rawlinson; *m* 1943, Lilian Mary; one *s* one *d*. *Educ:* Grocers' Co.'s Sch. Army, 1939–46. Various progressive positions in omnibus industry. JP Darlington, 1971. *Recreations:* theatre, music, golf and various lesser sports. *Address:* 62 Cleveland Avenue, Darlington, Co. Durham DL3 7HG. *T:* Darlington (01325) 461254. *Club:* Army and Navy.

RAWLINSON, Ivor Jon, OBE 1988; HM Diplomatic Service; Consul-General, Montreal, since 1993; *b* 24 Jan. 1942; *s* of Vivian Hugh Rawlinson and Hermione (*née* Curry); *m* 1976, Catherine Paule Caudal; one *s* two *d*. *Educ:* Christ Church, Oxford (MA). Joined FO, 1964; Polish lang. student, 1965–66; Warsaw, 1966–69; Bridgetown, 1969–71 (course at Univ. of W Indies); Second Sec., News Dept, FCO, 1971–73; Asst Private Sec. to Minister of State, FCO, 1973–74; Second Sec. (Econ.), Paris, 1974–78; First Secretary: FCO, 1978–80; (Commercial), Mexico City, 1980–84; Consul, Florence and Consul-Gen., San Marino, 1984–88; First Sec., later Counsellor (Inspectorate), FCO, 1988–93; RCDS 1993. *Recreations:* painting, tennis, winter sports, collecting books, restoring farmhouse in France. *Address:* c/o Foreign and Commonwealth Office, King Charles Street, SW1A 2AH. *Clubs:* Hurlingham; Mount Royal, St James' (Montreal).

RAWSON, Christopher Selwyn Priestley; JP; *b* 25 March 1928; *e s* of late Comdr Selwyn Gerald Caygill Rawson, OBE, RN (retd) and late Dr Doris Rawson, MB, ChB (*née* Brown); *m* 1959, Rosemary Ann Focke; two *d*. *Educ:* The Elms Sch., Colwall, near Malvern, Worcs; The Nautical College, Pangbourne, Berks. Navigating Apprentice, Merchant Service, T. & J. Brocklebank Ltd, 1945–48. Sheriff of the City of London, 1961–62; Member of Court of Common Council (Ward of Bread Street), 1963–72; Alderman, City of London, (Ward of Lime Street), 1972–83; one of HM Lieutenants of City of London, 1980–83. A Younger Brother of Trinity House, 1988–. Chairman: Governors, The Elms Sch., Colwall, near Malvern, Worcs, 1965–84; Port and City of London Health Cttee, 1967–70; Billingsgate and Leadenhall Mkt Cttee, 1972–75. Silver Medal for Woollen and Worsted Raw Materials, City and Guilds of London Institute, 1951; Livery of Clothworkers' Company, 1952 (Mem. Court of Assistants, 1977; Master, 1988–89); Freeman, Company of Watermen and Lightermen, 1966 (Mem. Ct of Assts, 1974, Master, 1982–84). Hon. Mem., London Metal Exchange, 1979. ATI 1953; AIMarE 1962. CStJ 1985. JP City of London, 1967. Commander: National Order of Senegal, 1961; Order of the Ivory Coast, 1962; Star of Africa, Liberia, 1962. *Recreations:* shooting, sailing. *Address:* 23 Cristowe Road, SW6 3QF. *Clubs:* Garrick, Royal London Yacht (Cdre, 1990–91), City Livery Yacht (Cdre, 1987–90).

RAWSON, Jessica Mary, CBE 1994; FBA 1990; Warden, Merton College, Oxford, since 1994; *b* 20 Jan. 1943; *d* of Roger Nathaniel Quirk and Paula Quirk; *m* 1968, John Rawson; one *d*. *Educ:* New Hall, Cambridge (BA Hons History; LittD 1991); London Univ. (BA Hons Chinese Lang. and Lit.). Asst Principal, Min. of Health, 1965–67; Department of Oriental Antiquities, British Museum: Asst Keeper II, 1967–71; Asst Keeper I, 1971–76; Dep. Keeper, 1976–87; Keeper, 1987–94. Visiting Professor: Kunsthistorisches Inst., Heidelberg, 1989; Dept of Art, Univ. of Chicago, 1994. Lectures: Barlow, Sussex Univ., 1979; Levintvitt Meml., Harvard, 1989; A. J. Pope, Smithsonian Instn, 1991; Harvey Buchanan, Cleveland Mus. of Art, 1993. Chm., Oriental Ceramic Soc., 1993–; Vice-Chm., Exec. Cttee, GB-China Centre, 1985–87. *Publications:* Chinese Jade Throughout the Ages (with John Ayers), 1975; Animals in Art, 1977; Ancient China, Art and Archaeology, 1980; Chinese Ornament: the lotus and the dragon, 1984; Chinese Bronzes: art and ritual, 1987; The Bella and P. P. Chiu Collection of Ancient Chinese Bronzes, 1988; Western Zhou Ritual Bronzes from the Arthur M. Sackler Collections, 1990; (with Emma Bunker) Ancient Chinese and Ordos Bronzes, 1990; (ed) The British Museum Book of Chinese Art, 1992; Chinese Jade from the Neolithic to the Qing, 1995. *Address:* Merton College, Oxford OX1 4JD. *T:* Oxford (01865) 276352, 276368, *Fax:* (01865) 276282; 3 Downshire Hill, NW3 1NR. *T:* 0171–794 4002.

RAWSON, Prof. Kenneth John, MSc; FEng; RCNC; consultant; Professor and Head of Department of Design and Technology, 1983–89, Dean of Education and Design, 1983–89, Brunel University; *b* 27 Oct. 1926; *s* of late Arthur William Rawson and Beatrice Anne Rawson; *m* 1950, Rhona Florence Gill; two *s* one *d*. *Educ:* Northern Grammar Sch., Portsmouth; HM Dockyard Technical Coll., Portsmouth; RN Colls, Keyham and Greenwich. RCNC; FEng 1984; FRINA; FCSD. WhSch. At sea, 1950–51; Naval Construction Res. Estabt, Dunfermline, 1951–53; Ship Design, Admiralty, 1953–57; Lloyd's Register of Shipping, 1957–59; Ship and Weapons Design, MoD, Bath, 1959–69; Naval Staff, London, 1969–72; Prof. of Naval Architecture, University Coll., Univ. of London, 1972–77; Ministry of Defence, Bath: Head of Forward Design, Ship Dept, 1977–79; Dep. Dir, Ship Design and Chief Naval Architect (Under Sec.), 1979–83. FRSA. *Publications:* Photoelasticity and the Engineer, 1953; (with E. C. Tupper) Basic Ship Theory, 1968, 4th edn 1994; contrib. numerous technical publications. *Recreations:* cabinet making, wine making, gardening, walking. *Address:* Moorlands, The Street, Chilcompton, Bath BA3 4HB. *T:* Mendip (01761) 232793.

RAWSTHORNE, Anthony Robert; Assistant Under-Secretary, Immigration and Nationality Department, Home Office, since 1991; *b* 25 Jan. 1943; *s* of Frederic Leslie and Nora Rawsthorne; *m* 1967, Beverley Jean Osborne; one *s* two *d*. *Educ:* Ampleforth College; Wadham College, Oxford (MA). Home Office, 1966; Asst Sec., 1977; Crime Policy Planning Unit, 1977–79; Establishment Dept, 1979–82; Sec., Falkland Islands Review Cttee, 1982; Principal Private Sec., 1983; Immigration and Nationality Dept, 1983–86; Assistant Under Secretary: Establishment Dept, 1986–91; Equal Opportunities and Gen. Dept, 1991. *Recreations:* bridge, cycling, squash, holidays in France. *Address:* c/o Home Office, Lunar House, 40 Wellesley Road, Croydon CR9 2BY.

RAWSTHORNE, Rt. Rev. John; Titular Bishop of Rotdon and an Auxiliary Bishop of Liverpool, (RC), since 1981; President, St Joseph's College, since 1982; *b* Crosby, Merseyside, 12 Nov. 1936. Priest, 1962. Administrator, St Mary's, Highfield, 1982. *Address:* St Joseph's, Hall Lane, Wrightington, Wigan WN6 9PA.

RAY, Hon. Ajit Nath; Chief Justice of India, Supreme Court of India, 1973–77; *b* Calcutta, 29 Jan. 1912; *s* of Sati Nath Ray and Kali Kumari Debi; *m* 1944, Himani Mukherjee; one *s*. *Educ:* Presidency Coll., Calcutta; Calcutta Univ. (Hindu Coll. Foundn Schol., MA); Oriel College, Oxford (MA; Hon. Fellow, 1975). Called to Bar, Gray's Inn, 1939; practised at Calcutta High Court, 1940–57; Judge, Calcutta High Court, 1957–69; Judge, Supreme Court of India, 1969–73. Pres., Governing Body, Presidency Coll., Calcutta, 1959–70; Vice-President: Asiatic Soc., 1963–65 (Hon. Treas. 1960–63); Internat. Law Assoc., 1977– (Pres., 1974–76; Pres., Indian Br., 1973–77); Indian Law Inst., New Delhi, 1973–77; Ramakrishna Mission Inst. of Culture, 1981–; Mem., Internat. Court of Arbitration, 1976–; Pres., Soc. for Welfare of Blind, Narendrapur, 1959–80; Member: Karma Samiti (Exec. Council), 1963–67 and 1969–72, and Samsad (Court), 1967–71, Visva-Bharati Univ., Santiniketan. *Address:* 15 Panditia Place, Calcutta 700029, India. *T:* (33) 4755213. *Club:* Calcutta (Calcutta).

RAY, Edward Ernest, CBE 1988; Senior Partner, Spicer and Pegler, Chartered Accountants, 1984–88 (Partner, 1957); *b* 6 Nov. 1924; *s* of Walter James Ray and Cecilia May Ray; *m* 1949, Margaret Elizabeth, *d* of George Bull; two *s*. *Educ:* Holloway Co. Sch.; London Univ. (External) (BCom). Served RN, 1943–46. Qualified, Inst. of Chartered Accountants: Mem., 1950; FCA 1955; Council Mem., 1973; Vice Pres., 1980; Dep. Pres., 1981; Pres., 1982, 1983. Chm., London Chartered Accountants, 1972–73. Dir, SIB, 1985–90; Chm., Investors' Compensation Scheme Ltd, 1988–91; Member: City Capital Markets Cttee, 1984–88; Marketing of Investments Bd Organising Cttee, 1984–88. *Publications:* Partnership Taxation, 1972, 3rd edn 1987; (jtly) VAT for Accountants and Businessmen, 1972; contrib. accountancy magazines. *Recreations:* walking, birdwatching, golf. *Address:* 1 Brooklands Court, Bush Hill, N21 2BZ. *Club:* City of London.

RAY, Kenneth Richard, FDSRCS, FRCS; Dean, Faculty of Dental Surgery, Royal College of Surgeons of England, since 1992; *b* 25 Jan. 1930; *s* of late John Thomas Ray and Edith Rose (*née* Hobbs); *m* 1958, Pamela Ann Thomas; one *s* two *d*. *Educ:* City of Oxford High Sch.; Univ. of Birmingham (LDS, BDS). FDSRCS 1959; FRCS 1995; FRACDS 1995. Hse Surgeon, Gen. Hosp., Birmingham, 1955; Sen. Hse Officer, Midlands Regl Plastic and Jaw Surgery Centre, 1956; Registrar, then Sen. Registrar, Royal Dental Hosp. of London and St George's Hosp., 1957–60; Sen. Lectr and Hon. Cons. in Oral Surgery, Univ. of London at Royal Dental Hosp. Sch. of Dental Surgery, 1960–73; Cons. in Oral Surgery, Royal Berks Hosp., Reading and Oxford RHA, 1963–92. Mem., GDC, 1993–95. Chm., Central Cttee for Hosp. Dental Services, 1979–86; Mem., Jt Consultants Cttee, 1979–86 and 1992–95. Royal College of Surgeons: Mem. Bd, Fac. of Dental Surgery, 1981–95; Vice-Dean, 1989; British Dental Association: Mem. Council, 1979–87; Pres., Berks, Bucks and Oxon Br., 1978; Pres., Hosp. Gp, 1979; Pres., BAOMS, 1985. UK Rep., EC Dental Liaison Cttee, 1981–89; UK Rep., EC Adv. Cttee on Trng of Dental Practitioners, 1981–84. Hon. Fellow, BDA, 1990. *Publications:* articles in learned jls and contrib. to textbooks on oral and maxillofacial surgery, local analgesia and health service planning. *Recreations:* fell-walking, natural history, English inns. *Address:* Jacobs Spinney, Rag Hill, Aldermaston, Berks RG7 4NS. *T:* Reading (01734) 712550. *Clubs:* Savage, Royal Society of Medicine.

RAY, Philip Bicknell, CMG 1969; Ministry of Defence 1947–76, retired; *b* 10 July 1917; *s* of late Basil Ray and Clare (*née* Everett); *m* 1946, Bridget Mary Robertson (decd); two *s* one *d*. *Educ:* Felsted Sch.; Selwyn Coll., Cambridge (MA). Indian Police, 1939–47. *Address:* 3 South Green Road, Newnham, Cambridge CB3 9JP.

RAY, Hon. Robert Francis; Senator for Victoria, since 1981; Minister for Defence, Australia, since 1990, and Deputy Leader of Government in the Senate, since 1993; *b* Melbourne, 8 April 1947; *m* Jane. *Educ:* Monash Univ.; Rusden State Coll. Former technical sch. teacher. Australian Labor Party: Mem., 1966–; Deleg., Vic. State Conf., 1970–; Mem., Nat. Exec., 1983–; Minister for Home Affairs and Dep. Manager of Govt Business in the Senate, 1987; Minister assisting the Minister for Transport and Communications, 1988; Minister for Immigration, Local Govt and Ethnic Affairs, 1988–90; Manager of Govt Business in the Senate, 1988–91. *Address:* Parliament House, Canberra, ACT 2600, Australia.

RAY, Robin; freelance broadcaster and writer; *s* of Ted Ray and Sybil (*née* Stevens); *m* 1960, Susan Stranks; one *s*. *Educ:* Highgate Sch.; RADA. London stage debut, The Changeling, 1960. Chief Technical Instructor, RADA, 1961–65; Associate Dir, Meadowbrook Theatre, Detroit, USA, 1965–66. Writer and broadcaster of over 1000 progs for BBC, commercial radio and television, including: Music Now; The Lively Arts; Face the Music; Film Buff of the Year, etc, 1966–85. Drama Critic, Punch, 1986–87; music adviser Classic FM Radio, 1988–. Deviser, Tomfoolery, Criterion Theatre, 1980; author, Café Puccini, Wyndham's Theatre, 1986; co-author/narrator, Let's Do It!, Chichester Fest., 1994. *Publications:* Time For Lovers (anthology), 1975; Robin Ray's Music Quiz, 1978; Favourite Hymns and Carols, 1982; Words on Music, 1984. *Recreations:* music, cinema, reading, shopping. *Address:* c/o David Wilkinson Associates, 115 Hazlebury Road, SW6 2LX. *T.* 0171–371 5188.

RAYANANONDA, Vidhya; Ambassador for Thailand to the Court of St James's and concurrently to the Republic of Ireland, since 1994; *b* 2 March 1942; *s* of Adm. Thavil Rayananonda and M. L. Penari Rayananonda; *m* 1971, Nantana; two *d*. *Educ:* Thammasat Univ., Thailand (BA Internat. Relns); USA (MA Pol Sci.); Nat. Defence Coll., Thailand. Joined Thai Diplomatic Service; Third Sec., Washington; Second Sec., SE Asian Div., Pol Affairs Dept; First Sec., Manila; Ministry of Foreign Affairs: Dir, FE Div., Pol Affairs Dept; Dep. Dir-Gen., Inf. Dept; Consul-Gen., LA, USA; Ambassador attached to Min. of Foreign Affairs; Dep. Sec.-Gen., then Sec.-Gen., to Prime Minister; Dir-Gen., Protocol Dept; Ambassador to Switzerland and Holy See. Kt Grand Cordon, Most Noble Order of Crown (Thailand), 1992; Kt Grand Cross (1st Cl.), Most Exalted Order of White Elephant (Thailand); Order of Sacred Treasure (Gold and Silver Star) (Japan). *Recreation:* playing golf. *Address:* Royal Thai Embassy, 30 Queen's Gate, SW7 5JB; 9 Tregunter Road, SW10 9LS. *T:* 0171–244 6799, 0171–373 8701.

RAYCHAUDHURI, Prof. Tapan Kumar, DPhil, DLitt; Professor of Indian History and Civilisation, University of Oxford, 1992–93; Fellow, St Antony's College, Oxford, 1973–93, now Emeritus; *b* 8 May 1926; *s* of Amiya Kumar and Prativa Raychaudhuri; *m* 1960, Pratima Sen-Roy; one *d*. *Educ:* Presidency Coll., Calcutta; Balliol Coll., Oxford. MA, DPhil Calcutta; MA, DPhil, DLitt Oxon. Lectr, Calcutta Univ., 1948–55; Dep. Dir, Nat. Archives of India, 1957–59 (Acting Dir, 1957–58); Delhi School of Economics: Reader in Econ. History, 1959–64; Prof., 1964–70; Dir, 1965–67; Prof. of History, Delhi Univ., 1971–72; Reader in Mod. S Asian History, Univ. of Oxford, 1973–92. Visiting Professor: Duke Univ., 1964; Univ. of Calif., Berkeley, 1964; Univ. of Penn., 1969; Harvard, 1969–70; El Colegio de Mexico, 1981; Univ. of Sydney, 1986. Gen. Ed (with D. Kumar), Cambridge Economic History of India, 1982–83. *Publications:* Bengal under Akbar and Jahangir: an introductory study in social history, 1953, 2nd edn 1969; Jan Company in Coromandel 1605–1690: European trade and Asia's traditional economics, 1962; (ed with I. Habib) Cambridge Economic History of India, vol. I, 1982, vol. II, 1983; Europe Reconsidered: perceptions of the West in Nineteenth Century Bengal, 1986. *Recreations:* travel, cinema, reading. *Address:* 16 Cavendish Road, Oxford OX2 7TW. *T:* Oxford (01865) 59421.

RAYLEIGH, 6th Baron *cr* 1821; **John Gerald Strutt;** Company Chairman, since 1988; *b* 4 June 1960; *s* of Hon. Charles Richard Strutt (*d* 1981) (2nd *s* of 4th Baron) and of Hon. Jean Elizabeth, *d* of 1st Viscount Davidson, PC, GCVO, CH, CB; *S* uncle, 1988; *m* 1991, Annabel Kate, *d* of W. G. Patterson; two *s*. *Educ:* Eton College; Royal Agricultural College, Cirencester. Lieut, Welsh Guards, 1980–84. Chairman: Lord Rayleigh's Dairies Ltd, 1987–; Lord Rayleigh's Farms Inc., 1988–. MRI. *Recreations:* cricket, gardening,

shooting, silviculture. *Heir:* *s* Hon. John Frederick Strutt, *b* 29 March 1993. *Address:* Terling Place, Chelmsford, Essex CM3 2PJ. *Clubs:* Brooks's, MCC.
See also Hon. B. C. Jenkin.

RAYMER, Michael Robert, OBE 1951; Assistant Secretary, Royal Hospital, Chelsea, 1975–82; *b* 22 July 1917; surv. *s* of late Rev. W. H. Raymer, MA; *m* 1948, Joyce Marion Scott; two *s* one *d*. *Educ:* Marlborough College (Foundation Scholar); Jesus College, Cambridge (Rustat Schol.). BA (Hons) 1939. Administrative Officer, Nigeria, 1940–49 and 1952–55. Served in Royal W African Frontier Force, 1940–43. Colonial Sec. to Govt of the Falkland Islands, 1949–52; Prin. Estab. Officer, N Nigeria, 1954; Controller of Organisation and Establishments, to Government of Fiji, 1955–62; retired, 1962; Principal, MoD, 1962–75. *Recreation:* gardening. *Address:* The Stable House, Manor Farm, Apethorpe, Northants PE8 5DG.

RAYMOND, Robert Jacques; Director General, European Monetary Institute, since 1994; *b* 30 June 1933; *s* of Henri Raymond and Andrée (*née* Aubrière); *m* 1970, Monique Brémond, MD. *Educ:* Sorbonne (Masters Econs 1955). With Bank of France, 1951–94: Audit Dept, 1958–66; Rep. in NY, 1966–67; Hd, Balance of Payments Div., 1969–73; Director: Internat. Affairs, 1973–75; Monetary Stats and Analysis, 1975–76; Dep. Sec. Gen., Conseil Nat. du Crédit, 1975–81; Dep. Hd, 1976–82, Dir Gen., 1982–90, Res. Dept; Dir Gen., Credit Dept, 1990–94. Mem. Bd, various public financial instns in Paris, 1981–94. Chm., monetary experts, Cttee of Govs of EEC, 1981–91. Chevalier de la Légion d'Honneur (France), 1984; Officier, Ordre national du Mérite (France), 1988. *Publications:* La Monnaie, 1976; (jtly) Les relations économiques et monétaires internationales, 1982, 3rd edn 1986; Les institutions monétaires en France, 1991, 2nd edn 1994; L'unification monétaire en Europe, 1993. *Address:* European Monetary Institute, Eurotower, Kaiserstrasse 29, 60311 Frankfurt am Main, Germany. *T:* (69) 27227310.

RAYMOND, William Francis, CBE 1978; FRSC; Agricultural Science Consultant; *b* 25 Feb. 1922; *m* 1949, Amy Elizabeth Kelk; three *s* one *d*. *Educ:* Bristol Grammar Sch.; The Queen's Coll., Oxford (MA). Research Officer, MRC, 1943–45; Head of Animal Science Div. and later Asst Dir, Grassland Research Inst., Hurley, 1945–72; Dep. Chief Scientist, 1972–81, Chief Scientist (Agriculture and Horticulture), 1981–82, MAFF. Mem., ARC, 1981–82. Sec., 8th Internat. Grassland Congress, 1960; President: Brit. Grassland Soc., 1974–75; Brit. Soc. Animal Production, 1981–82. Vis. Prof. in Agriculture, Wye Coll., 1978–83. Chm., Stapledon Meml Trust, 1983–93; Mem., Policy Cttee, CPRE, 1993–; Hon. Treas., RURAL, 1984–; Chm., Internat. Agricl Res. Review, Council for Res. Policy, Denmark, 1992. *Publications:* (with Shepperson and Waltham) Forage Conservation and Feeding, 1972, 4th edn (with Redman and Waltham), 1986; EEC Agricultural Research Framework Programme, 1983; Research in Support of Agricultural Policies in Europe, FAO Regional Conf., Reykjavik, 1984; over 250 papers in scientific jls. *Recreation:* gardening. *Address:* Periwinkle Cottage, Christmas Common, Watlington OX9 5HR. *T:* Watlington (01491) 612942. *Club:* Farmers'.

RAYNE, family name of **Baron Rayne.**

RAYNE, Baron *cr* 1976 (Life Peer), of Prince's Meadow in Greater London; **Max Rayne,** Kt 1969; Chairman, London Merchant Securities plc, since 1960; *b* 8 Feb. 1918; *er s* of Phillip and Deborah Rayne; *m* 1st, 1941, Margaret Marco (marr. diss., 1960); one *s* two *d*; 2nd, 1965, Lady Jane Antonia Frances Vane-Tempest-Stewart, *er d* of 8th Marquess of Londonderry; two *s* two *d*. *Educ:* Central Foundation Sch. and University Coll., London. Served RAF 1940–45. Dir, First Leisure Corp. plc, 1984– (Dep. Chm., 1984–92; Chm., 1992–95); Dep. Chm., British Lion Films, 1967–72; Dir, Housing Corp. (1974) Ltd, 1974–78; Dir, other companies. Gov., 1962–74, Special Trustee, 1974–92, St Thomas' Hosp.; Governor: Royal Ballet Sch., 1966–79; Malvern Coll., 1966–; Centre for Environmental Studies, 1967–73; Member: Gen. Council, King Edward VII's Hosp. Fund for London, 1966–; RADA Council, 1973–; South Bank Bd, 1986–92; Council, St Thomas's Hospital Medical School, 1965–82; Council of Governors, UMDS of Guy's and St Thomas's Hosps, 1982–89. Vice-Pres., Yehudi Menuhin Sch., 1987– (Gov., 1966–87); Hon. Vice-Pres., Jewish Care, 1966–; Chairman: London Festival Ballet Trust, 1967–75; Nat. Theatre Board, 1971–88; Founder Patron, The Rayne Foundation, 1962–. Hon. Fellow: Darwin Coll., Cambridge, 1966; UCL, 1966; LSE 1974; RCPsych, 1977; King's Coll. Hosp. Med. Sch., 1980; UC, Oxford, 1982; King's Coll. London, 1983; Westminster Sch., 1989; RCP, 1992; UMDS, 1992. Hon. LLD London, 1968. Officier, Légion d'Honneur, 1987 (Chevalier 1973). *Address:* 33 Robert Adam Street, W1M 5AH. *T:* 0171–935 3555.

RAYNER, family name of **Baron Rayner.**

RAYNER, Baron *cr* 1983 (Life Peer), of Crowborough in the County of East Sussex; **Derek George Rayner;** Kt 1973; Chairman, 1984–91, Joint Managing Director, 1973–91, Marks and Spencer plc; *b* 30 March 1926; *o s* of George William Rayner and Hilda Jane (*née* Rant); unmarried. *Educ:* City Coll., Norwich; Selwyn Coll., Cambridge (Hon. Fellow 1983). Fellow, Inst. Purchasing and Supply, 1970. Nat. Service, commnd RAF Regt, 1946–48. Joined Marks & Spencer, 1953; Dir, 1967; Chief Exec., 1983–88. Special Adviser to HM Govt, 1970; Chief Exec., Procurement Executive, MoD, 1971–72. Mem., UK Permanent Security Commn, 1977–80. Dep. Chm., Civil Service Pay Bd, 1978–80. Member: Design Council, 1973–75; Council RCA, 1973–76. Adviser to Prime Minister on improving efficiency and eliminating waste in Government, 1979–83. Chm., Coronary Artery Disease Res. Assoc. (CORDA), 1985–91. Pres., St Bartholomew's Hosp. Med. Coll., 1988–93. Trustee, Royal Botanic Gardens, Kew, Foundn, 1992–. Hon. DPhil Bar Ilan Univ., Israel, 1986; DUniv Surrey, 1991. Alexis de Tocqueville Gold Medal, Europ. Inst. of Public Admin, 1988. *Recreations:* music, food, travel. *Address:* c/o Michael House, 47 Baker Street, W1A 1DN. *Club:* Athenæum.

RAYNER, Bryan Roy, CB 1987; Deputy Secretary, Department of Health (formerly of Health and Social Security), 1984–91; *b* 29 Jan. 1932; *s* of Harold and Florence Rayner; *m* 1957, Eleanora Whittaker; one *d*. *Educ:* Stationers' Company's School, N8. Clerical Officer, Customs and Excise, 1948; Asst Private Sec. to Minister of Health, 1960–62; Principal, 1965, Asst Sec., 1970, Under Sec., 1975, DHSS. *Recreation:* listening to music. *Address:* 31 Craigweil Lane, Aldwick, W Sussex PO21 4AN.

RAYNER, Claire Berenice; writer and broadcaster; *b* 22 Jan. 1931; *m* 1957, Desmond Rayner; two *s* one *d*. *Educ:* City of London Sch. for Girls; Royal Northern Hosp. Sch. of Nursing, London (Gold Medal; SRN 1954); Guy's Hosp. (midwifery). Formerly: Nurse, Royal Free Hosp.; Sister, Paediatric Dept, Whittington Hosp. Woman's Own: Med. Correspondent, as Ruth Martin, 1966–75, as Claire Rayner, 1975–87; advice column: The Sun, 1973–80; The Sunday Mirror, 1980–88; Today, 1988–91; columnist, Woman, 1988–92. Radio and television broadcasts include: family advice, Pebble Mill at One, BBC, 1972–74; (co-presenter) Kitchen Garden, ITV, 1974–77; Contact, BBC Radio, Wales, 1974–77; Claire Rayner's Casebook (series), BBC, 1980, 1983, 1984; TV-am Advice Spot, 1985–92; A Problem Shared, Sky TV Series, 1989; Good Morning with Anne and Nick, BBC, 1992–. Non-exec. Dir, Northwick Park and St Mark's NHS Trust, 1995–. FRSM. Pres., Gingerbread; Patron: Terrence Higgins Trust; Turning Point; Royal Philanthropic Soc.; Down's Syndrome Assoc., and others. Hon. Fellow, Polytechnic of N London, 1988. Freeman, City of London, 1981. Med. Journalist of the Year, 1987; Best Specialist Consumer Columnist Award, 1988. *Publications:* Mothers and Midwives, 1962; What Happens in Hospital, 1963; The Calendar of Childhood, 1964; Your Baby, 1965; Careers with Children, 1966; Essentials of Out-Patient Nursing, 1967; For Children, 1967; Shall I be a Nurse, 1967; 101 Facts an Expectant Mother should know, 1967; 101 Key Facts of Practical Baby Care, 1967; Housework - The Easy Way, 1967; Home Nursing and Family Health, 1967; A Parent's Guide to Sex Education, 1968; People in Love, 1968 (subseq. publd as About Sex, 1972); Protecting Your Baby, 1971; Woman's Medical Dictionary, 1971; When to Call the Doctor - What to Do Whilst Waiting, 1972; The Shy Person's Book, 1973; Childcare Made Simple, 1973; Where Do I Come From?, 1975; (ed and contrib.) Atlas of the Body and Mind, 1976; (with Keith Fordyce) Kitchen Garden, 1976; (with Keith Fordyce) More Kitchen Garden, 1977; Family Feelings, 1977; Claire Rayner answers your 100 Questions on Pregnancy, 1977; (with Keith Fordyce) Claire and Keith's Kitchen Garden, 1978; The Body Book, 1978; Related to Sex, 1979; (with Keith Fordyce) Greenhouse Gardening, 1979; Everything your Doctor would Tell You if He Had the Time, 1980; Claire Rayner's Lifeguide, 1980; Baby and Young Child Care, 1981; Growing Pains, 1984; Claire Rayner's Marriage Guide, 1984; The Getting Better Book, 1985; Woman, 1986; When I Grow Up, 1986; Safe Sex, 1987; The Don't Spoil Your Body Book, 1989; Life and Love and Everything: children's questions, 1993; *fiction:* Shilling a Pound Pears, 1964; The House on the Fen, 1967; Starch of Aprons, 1967 (subseq. publd as The Hive, 1968); Lady Mislaid, 1968; Death on the Table, 1969; The Meddlers, 1970; A Time to Heal, 1972; The Burning Summer, 1972; Sisters, 1978; Reprise, 1980; The Running Years, 1981; Family Chorus, 1984; The Virus Man, 1985; Lunching at Laura's, 1986; Maddie, 1988; Clinical Judgements, 1989; Postscripts, 1991; Dangerous Things, 1993; First Blood, 1993; Second Opinion, 1994; Third Degree, 1995; The Performers: Book 1, Gower Street, 1973; Book 2, The Haymarket, 1974; Book 3, Paddington Green, 1975; Book 4, Soho Square, 1976; Book 5, Bedford Row, 1977; Book 6, Long Acre, 1978; Book 7, Charing Cross, 1979; Book 8, The Strand, 1980; Book 9, Chelsea Reach, 1982; Book 10, Shaftesbury Avenue, 1983; Book 11, Piccadilly, 1985; Book 12, Seven Dials, 1986; Poppy Chronicle: Book 1, Jubilee, 1987; Book 2, Flanders, 1988; Book 3, Flapper, 1989; Book 4, Blitz, 1990; Book 5, Festival, 1992; Book 6, Sixties, 1992; Quentin Quartet: Book 1, London Lodgings, 1994; Paying Guests, 1995; *as Sheila Brandon: fiction:* The Final Year, 1962; Cottage Hospital, 1963; Children's Ward, 1964; The Lonely One, 1965; The Doctors of Downlands, 1968; The Private Wing, 1971; Nurse in the Sun, 1972; *as Ann Lynton:* Mothercraft, 1967; contrib. Lancet, Med. World, Nursing Times, Nursing Mirror, and national newspapers and magazines, incl. Design. *Recreations:* talking, cooking, party-giving, theatre-going. *Address:* PO Box 125, Harrow, Mddx HA1 3XE.

RAYNER, David Edward, CBE 1992; FCIT; Board Member, Railtrack Group PLC, since 1994; Director Safety and Standards, Railtrack PLC, since 1994; *b* 26 Jan. 1940; *s* of Marjory and Gilbert Rayner; *m* 1966, Enid Cutty; two *d*. *Educ:* St Peter's School, York; Durham University (BSc Hons). Joined British Railways, 1963; Passenger Marketing Manager, BR Board, 1982; Dep. Gen. Manager, BR, London Midland Region, 1984–86; Gen. Manager, BR, Eastern Region, 1986–87; British Railways Board: Mem., 1987–94; Jt Man. Dir, 1987–89; Man. Dir, Engrg and Operations, 1989–92; Man. Dir, Safety and Operations, 1992–94. Chm., Rail Industry Training Council, 1992–. Hon. Col, Railway Sqn, RLC (TA), 1992. *Recreation:* collector.

RAYNER, Edward John, CBE 1990; Controller, Europe (formerly Europe and North Asia) Division, British Council, 1986–89; *b* 27 Feb. 1936; *s* of Edward Harold Rayner and Edith Rayner; *m* 1960, Valerie Anne Billon; one *s* one *d*. *Educ:* Slough Grammar Sch.; London Univ. (BSc Econs). British Council: Asst Regional Rep., Lahore, Pakistan, 1959–62; Asst Rep., Lagos, Nigeria, 1962–65; Inspector, Complements Unit, 1965–67; Head, Overseas Careers, Personnel Dept, 1967–70; Dep. Rep., Pakistan, 1970–71; Regional Dir, Sao Paulo, Brazil, 1972–75; Controller, Estabts Div., 1975–78; Secretary, 1978–82; Rep., Brazil, 1983–86. *Recreations:* sport, theatre, music.

RAYNER, Rabbi John Desmond, CBE 1993; Minister, Liberal Jewish Synagogue, 1957–89, now Rabbi Emeritus; *b* 30 May 1924; *s* of Ferdinand and Charlotte Rahmer; *m* 1955, Jane Priscilla Heilbronn; two *s* one *d*. *Educ:* Durham Sch.; Emmanuel Coll., Cambridge (MA); Hebrew Union Coll.-Jewish Inst. of Religion, Cincinnati (Hon. DD). Minister, S London Liberal Synagogue, 1953–57; Sen. Minister, Liberal Jewish Synagogue, 1961–89; Leo Baeck College: Lectr in Liturgy and Rabbinic Literature, 1966– (Vice-Pres., 1969–). Hon. Life Pres., Union of Liberal and Progressive Synagogues, 1994; Co-Pres., London Soc. of Jews and Christians, 1990; Chm., Council of Reform and Liberal Rabbis, 1969–71, 1982–84, 1989–92. *Publications:* The Practices of Liberal Judaism, 1958; Towards Mutual Understanding between Jews and Christians, 1960; (ed jtly) Service of the Heart, 1967; Guide to Jewish Marriage, 1975; (ed jtly) Gate of Repentance, 1977; (jtly) Judaism for Today, 1978; (jtly) The Jewish People: their history and their religion, 1987; (ed jtly) Siddur Lev Chadash, 1995. *Recreations:* reading, walking. *Address:* 37 Walmington Fold, N12 7LD. *T:* 0181–446 6196.

RAYNER, Most Rev. Keith; *see* Melbourne, Archbishop of.

RAYNER JAMES, Jonathan Elwyn; *see* James.

RAYNES, Prof. Edward Peter, FRS 1987; Chief Scientist, Sharp Laboratories of Europe Ltd, Oxford, since 1992; *b* 4 July 1945; *s* of Edward Gordon and Ethel Mary Raynes; *m* 1970, Madeline Ord; two *s*. *Educ:* St Peter's School, York; Gonville and Caius College, Cambridge (MA, PhD). CPhys, FInstP. Royal Signals and Radar Establishment, 1971–92: SPSO, 1981; DCSO, 1988–92. Hon. Prof., Sch. of Chemistry, Univ. of Hull, 1990. Rank Prize for Opto-electronics, 1980; Paterson Medal, Inst. of Physics, 1986; Special Recognition Award, Soc. for Information Display, 1987. *Publications:* (ed jtly) Liquid Crystals: their physics, chemistry and applications, 1983; numerous scientific papers and patents. *Recreation:* choral and solo singing. *Address:* Sharp Laboratories of Europe, Oxford Science Park, Oxford OX4 4GA. *T:* Oxford (01865) 747711, *Fax:* (01865) 747717.

RAYNHAM, Viscount; Charles George Townshend; *b* 26 Sept. 1945; *s* and *heir* of 7th Marquess Townshend, *qv*; *m* 1st, 1975, Hermione (*d* 1985), *d* of Lt-Cdr R. M. D. Ponsonby and Mrs Dorothy Ponsonby; one *s* one *d*; 2nd, 1990, Mrs Alison Marshall, *yr d* of Sir Willis Combs, KCVO, CMG. *Educ:* Eton; Royal Agricultural College, Cirencester. Chm. and Dir, AIMS Ltd, 1977–87; Man. Dir, Raynham Workshops Ltd, 1986–; Chm., Pera International, 1988–. Member Council: Design Gp Great Britain Ltd, 1984–90 (Chm., 1988); Norfolk Br., RASE, 1982–. *Heir:* *s* Hon. Thomas Charles Townshend, *b* 2 Nov. 1977. *Address:* Pattesley House, Fakenham, Norfolk NR21 7HT. *T:* Fakenham (01328) 701818. *Club:* White's.

RAYNOR, Philip Ronald; QC 1994; a Recorder, since 1993; *b* 20 Jan. 1950; *s* of Wilfred Raynor and Sheila (*née* Zermansky); *m* 1974, Judith Braunsberg; one *s* one *d*. *Educ:* Roundhay Sch., Leeds; Christ's Coll., Cambridge (Schol., MA). Lectr in Law, Univ. of Manchester, 1971–74; called to the Bar, Inner Temple, 1973; in practice on Northern

Circuit, 1973–. *Recreations:* travel, opera, dining out. *Address:* 40 King Street, Manchester M2 6BA. *T:* 0161–832 9082.

RAYNSFORD, Nick; *see* Raynsford, W. R. N.

RAYNSFORD, Wyvill Richard Nicolls, (Nick); MP (Lab) Greenwich, since 1992; *b* 28 Jan. 1945; *s* of Wyvill Raynsford and Patricia Raynsford (*née* Dunn); *m* 1968, Anne Raynsford (*née* Jelley); three *d*. *Educ:* Repton Sch.; Sidney Sussex Coll., Cambridge (MA); Chelsea Sch. of Art (DipAD). Market research, A. C. Nielsen Co. Ltd, 1966–68; Gen. Sec., Soc. for Co-operative Dwellings, 1972–73; SHAC: Emergency Officer, 1973–74; Research Officer, 1974–76; Dir, 1976–86; Partner, 1987–90, Dir, 1990–92, Raynsford and Morris, housing consultants; Dir, Raynsford Dallison Associates, housing consultants, 1992–93; Consultant, HACAS, 1993–. Councillor (Lab) London Borough of Hammersmith & Fulham, 1971–75 (Chm., Leisure and Recreation Cttee, 1972–74). Contested (Lab) Fulham, 1987. MP (Lab) Fulham, April 1986–1987. Opposition front bench spokesman on London, 1993–, on housing, 1994–. Mem., Envmt Select Cttee, 1992–93. *Publication:* A Guide to Housing Benefit, 1982, 7th edn 1986. *Recreation:* photography. *Address:* 10 Charlton Road, Blackheath, SE3 7HG.

RAZ, Prof. Joseph, FBA 1987; Professor of the Philosophy of Law, Oxford, since 1985, and Fellow of Balliol College, Oxford; *b* 21 March 1939. *Educ:* Hebrew University, Jerusalem (MJur 1963); University Coll., Oxford (DPhil 1967). Lectr, Hebrew Univ., Jerusalem, 1967–70; Research Fellow, Nuffield Coll., Oxford, 1970–72; Tutorial Fellow, Balliol Coll., Oxford, 1972–85. For. Hon. Mem., Amer. Acad. of Arts and Scis, 1992. Hon. Dr Catholic Univ., Brussels, 1993. *Publications:* The Concept of a Legal System, 1970, 2nd edn 1980; Practical Reason and Norms, 1975, 2nd edn 1990; The Authority of Law, 1979; The Morality of Freedom, 1986; Ethics in the Public Domain, 1994. *Address:* Balliol College, Oxford OX1 3BJ. *T:* Oxford (01865) 277721.

RAZZALL, Edward Timothy, (Tim), CBE 1993; Partner, Frere Cholmeley Bischoff, solicitors, since 1973; *b* 12 June 1943; *s* of Leonard Humphrey Razzall, *qv*; *m* 1982, Deirdre Bourke; two *s* two *d*. *Educ:* St Paul's Sch.; Worcester Coll., Oxford (BA). Teaching Associate, Northwestern Univ., Chicago, 1965–66; with Frere Cholmeley Bischoff, 1966–. Councillor (L), Mortlake Ward, London Borough of Richmond, 1974–; Dep. Leader, Richmond Council, 1983–. Treasurer: Liberal Party, 1986–87; Liberal Democrats, 1987–; Pres., Assoc. of Lib Dem Councillors, 1990–. Chm., Abaco Investments plc, 1974–90; Director: Cala plc, 1973–; Star Mining Corp. NL, 1993–; Speciality Shops plc, 1994–. European Lawyer of Year, Inst. of Lawyers in Europe, 1992. *Recreations:* all sports, food and wine. *Address:* 4 John Carpenter Street, EC4Y 0NM. *T:* 0171–615 8000. *Clubs:* National Liberal, MCC.

RAZZALL, Leonard Humphrey; a Master of the Supreme Court (Taxing), 1954–81; *b* 13 Nov. 1912; *s* of Horace Razzall and Sarah Thompson, Scarborough; *m* 1936, Muriel (*d* 1968), *yr d* of late Pearson Knowles; two *s*. *Educ:* Scarborough High Sch. Admitted solicitor, 1935; founded firm Humphrey Razzall & Co., 1938. Served in Royal Marines, 1941–46, Staff Captain; Staff Coll., Camberley (jsc). Contested (L) Scarborough and Whitby Division, 1945. Sometime Examr in High Court practice and procedure for solicitors final examination. *Publications:* A Man of Law's Tale, 1982; Law, Love and Laughter, 1984. *Recreations:* travel, cricket, book-collecting and book-selling, writing letters to The Times. *Address:* Lyle Park, 53 Putney Hill, SW15. *T:* 0181–788 0471. *Clubs:* English-Speaking Union; Scarborough and Pickering Liberal.
See also E. T. Razzall.

RAZZALL, Tim; *see* Razzall, E. T.

REA, family name of **Baron Rea.**

REA, 3rd Baron *cr* 1937, of Eskdale; **John Nicolas Rea,** MD; Bt 1935; General Medical Practitioner, Kentish Town, NW5, 1957–62 and 1968–94; *b* 6 June 1928; *s* of Hon. James Russell Rea (*d* 1954) (2nd *s* of 1st Baron) and Betty Marion (*d* 1965), *d* of Arthur Bevan, MD; *S* uncle, 1981; *m* 1st, 1951, Elizabeth Anne (marr. diss. 1991), *d* of late William Hensman Robinson; four *s*; two *d*; 2nd, 1991, Judith Mary, *d* of late Norman Powell. *Educ:* Dartington Hall School; Belmont Hill School, Mass, USA; Dauntsey's School; Christ's Coll., Cambridge Univ.; UCH Medical School. MA, MD (Cantab); FRCGP; DPH, DCH, DObstRCOG. Research Fellow in Paediatrics, Lagos, Nigeria, 1962–65; Lecturer in Social Medicine, St Thomas's Hosp. Medical School, 1966–68. Vice-Chm., Nat. Forum for Prevention of Coronary Heart Disease, 1985–; Chm., Appropriate Health Resources and Technology Action Gp, 1992–. Opposition spokesman on health, devel and co-operation, H of L, 1992–. FRSocMed (Pres., Section of Gen. Practice, 1985–86). *Publications:* Interactions of Infection and Nutrition (MD Thesis, Cambridge Univ.), 1969; (jtly) Learning Teaching—an evaluation of a course for GP Teachers, 1980; articles on epidemiology and medical education in various journals. *Recreations:* music (bassoon), fishing, sailing, foreign travel, walking. *Heir:* *s* Hon. Matthew James Rea, *b* 28 March 1956. *Address:* 11 Anson Road, N7 0RB. *T:* 0171–607 0546.

REA, Rev. Ernest; Head of Religious Broadcasting, since 1989, and Head of Religious Programmes, Radio, since 1993, BBC; *b* 6 Sept. 1945; *s* of Ernest Rea and Mary Wylie (*née* Blue). *Educ:* Methodist Coll., Belfast; Queen's Univ., Belfast; Union Theological Coll., Belfast. Asst Minister, Woodvale Park Presb. Ch., Belfast, 1971–74; Minister, Bannside Presb. Ch., Banbridge, Co. Down, 1974–79; Religious Broadcasting Producer, BBC Belfast, 1979–84; Sen. Religious Broadcasting Producer, BBC S and W, 1984–88; Editor, Network Radio, BBC S and W, 1988–89. *Recreations:* reading, watching cricket, playing tennis and golf, theatre, music. *Address:* 24 Duke Street, Alderley Edge, Cheshire. *T:* Alderley Edge (01625) 582938.

REA, James Taylor, CMG 1958; HM Overseas Civil Service, retired; *b* 19 Oct. 1907; *s* of Rev. Martin Rea, Presbyterian Minister, and Mary Rea (*née* Fisher); *m* 1934, Catharine (*d* 1990), *d* of Dr W. H. Bleakney, Whitman College, Walla Walla, Washington, USA; one *s* one *d*. *Educ:* Royal School, Dungannon; Queen's University, Belfast (BA); St John's College, Cambridge (MA). HM Colonial Administrative Service (now known as HM Overseas Civil Service) serving throughout in Malaya and Singapore, 1931–58; Principal offices held: Asst Sec., Chinese Affairs, Fedn of Malaya, 1948; Dep. Comr for Labour, Fedn of Malaya, 1949; Dep. Malayan Establishment Officer, 1950; Dep. Pres., 1952–55, Pres., 1955–58, City Council, Singapore. Retired, 1958. Chairman: Hotel Grants Adv. Cttee, NI, 1963–75; NI Training Exec., 1972–75; Down District Cttee, Eastern Health and Social Services Bd, 1974–78; Mem., NI Housing Trust, 1959–71, Vice Chm., 1970–71. Indep. Mem.: Catering Wages Council, N Ireland, 1965–82; Retail Bespoke Tailoring Wages Council, 1965–82; Laundry Wages Council, 1965–82; Shirtmaking Wages Council, 1965–82. Nominated Member General Dental Council, under Dentist Act, 1957, 1961–79. Mem. Downpatrick HMC, 1966–73, Chm., 1971–73. *Address:* Craigduff, 29 Downpatrick Road, Clough, Downpatrick, N Ireland BT30 8NL. *T:* Seaforde (01396) 811258.

REA, Dr John Rowland, FBA 1981; Lecturer in Documentary Papyrology, University of Oxford, since 1965; Senior Research Fellow, Balliol College, Oxford, since 1969; *b* 28 Oct. 1933; *s* of Thomas Arthur Rea and Elsie Rea (*née* Ward); *m* 1959, Mary Ogden. *Educ:* Methodist Coll., Belfast; Queen's Univ., Belfast (BA); University Coll. London (PhD). Asst Keeper, Public Record Office, 1957–61; Res. Lectr, Christ Church, Oxford, 1961–65. *Publications:* The Oxyrhynchus Papyri, Vol. XL, 1972, Vol. XLVI, 1978, Vol. LI, 1984, Vol LV, 1988, Vol. LVIII, 1991, LXIII, 1996, also contribs to Vols XXVII, XXXI, XXXIII, XXXIV, XXXVI, XLI, XLIII, XLIX, L; (with P. J. Sijpesteijn) Corpus Papyrorum Raineri V, 1976; articles in classical jls. *Address:* Balliol College, Oxford OX1 3BJ.

REA, Rupert Lascelles P.; *see* Pennant-Rea.

REA PRICE, (William) John, OBE 1991; Director, National Children's Bureau, since 1991; *b* 15 March 1937; *s* of late John Caxton Rea Price and of Mary Hilda Rea Price; *m* 1962, Maryrose Wingate Miller; two *s* one *d*. *Educ:* University College Sch.; Corpus Christi Coll., Cambridge (MA); LSE (DSA; Cert. Applied Social Studies). London Probation Service, 1962–65; London Borough of Islington Children's Dept, 1965–68; Nat. Inst. for Social Work, 1968–69; Home Office, Community Develt Project, 1969–72; Dir of Social Services, London Borough of Islington, 1972–90. Pres., Assoc. of Dirs of Social Services, 1989–90. *Recreations:* cycling, archaeology, history of landscape. *Address:* National Children's Bureau, 8 Wakley Street, EC1V 7QE. *T:* 0171–843 6000. *Club:* Reform.

READ, Miss; *see* Saint, D. J.

READ, Rt. Rev. Allan Alexander; Bishop of Ontario, 1981–92; *b* 19 Sept. 1923; *s* of Alex P. Read and Lillice M. Matthews; *m* 1949, Mary Beverly Roberts; two *s* two *d*. *Educ:* Trinity Coll., Univ. of Toronto (BA, LTh). Incumbent, Mono East and Mono West, 1947–54; Rector, Trinity Church, Barrie, 1954–71; Canon of St James Cathedral, Toronto, 1957; Archdeacon of Simcoe, 1961–72; Bishop Suffragan of Toronto, 1972–81; priest-in-charge: St Patrick's Cathedral, Meath and Kildare, 1992; Dunster, dio. of Bath and Wells, 1993. Member: Gen. Synod, Anglican Church of Canada, 1959–89; Provincial Synod of Ontario, 1955–91; Hon. Pres., Rural Workers Fellowship, Episcopal Church, with members from USA and Anglican Church of Canada, 1981–; Hon. Mem., Toronto and Metropolitan Region Conservation Authy, 1977–. Hon. DD: Trinity Coll., Toronto, 1972; Wycliffe Coll., Toronto, 1972; Hon. STD Thornloe Coll., Sudbury, 1982. Citizen of the Year, Barrie, 1966; Honorary Reeve, Black Creek, Toronto, 1980; Govt of Ontario citizenship awards. *Publications:* Shepherds in Green Pastures, 1952; Unto the Hills, 1954. *Recreations:* organ music, reading, Canadian history, 1837 Rebellion Upper Canada. *Address:* 39 Riverside Drive, RR1, Kingston, Ont K7L 4V1, Canada.

READ, Gen. Sir Antony; *see* Read, Gen. Sir J. A. J.

READ, Air Marshal Sir Charles (Frederick), KBE 1976 (CBE 1964); CB 1972; DFC 1942; AFC 1958; Chief of the Air Staff, RAAF, 1972–75, retired; *b* Sydney, NSW, 9 Oct. 1918; *s* of J. F. Read, Bristol, England; *m* 1946, Betty E., *d* of A. V. Bradshaw; three *s*. *Educ:* Sydney Grammar Sch. Former posts include: OC, RAAF Base, Point Cook, Vic., 1965–68; OC, RAAF, Richmond, NSW, 1968–70; Dep. Chief of Air Staff, 1969–72. *Recreation:* yachting. *Address:* 2007 Pittwater Road, Bayview, NSW 2104, Australia. *T:* (2) 99971686.

READ, Rev. David Haxton Carswell, MA, DD; Minister of Madison Avenue Presbyterian Church, New York City, USA, 1956–89, now Minister Emeritus; *b* Cupar, Fife, 2 Jan. 1910; *s* of John Alexander Read and Catherine Haxton Carswell; *m* 1936, Dorothy Florence Patricia Gilbert; one *s*. *Educ:* Daniel Stewart's College, Edinburgh; Edinburgh Univ.; Univs of Montpellier, Strasbourg, Paris, and Marburg; New Coll., Edinburgh. MA Edin. (first class Hons in Lit.) 1932; BD (dist. in Dogmatics) 1936. Ordained Minister of the Church of Scotland, 1936; Minister of Coldstream West Church, 1936–39. CF, 1939–45 (despatches; POW, 1940–45, Germany). Minister of Greenbank Parish, Edinburgh, 1939–49; first Chaplain, Univ. of Edinburgh, 1949–55; Chaplain to the Queen in Scotland, 1952–55. Senior Editor, The Living Pulpit, 1991. Guest Lectr and Preacher in USA, Scotland, Canada, Australia. Hon. DD: Edinburgh, 1956; Yale, 1959; Lafayette Coll., 1965; Hope Coll., 1969; Knox Coll., Canada, 1979; Hon. LHD: Hobart Coll., 1972; Trinity Univ., 1972; Hon. LittD Coll. of Wooster, 1966; Hon. DHL: Japan Internat. Christian Univ., 1979; Rockford Coll., 1982. *Publications:* The Spirit of Life, 1939; The Church to Come (trans. from German), 1939; Prisoners' Quest, Lectures on Christian doctrine in a POW Camp, 1944; The Communication of The Gospel, Warrack Lectures, 1952; The Christian Faith, 1955 (NY 1956); I am Persuaded, 1961 (NY 1962); Sons of Anak, 1964 (NY); God's Mobile Family, 1966 (NY); Whose God is Dead?, 1966 (Cin); Holy Common Sense, 1966 (Tenn); The Pattern of Christ, 1967 (NY); The Presence of Christ, 1968 (NJ); Christian Ethics, 1968 (NY 1969); Virginia Woolfe Meets Charlie Brown, 1968 (Mich); Giants Cut Down To Size, 1970; Religion Without Wrappings, 1970; Overheard, 1971; Curious Christians, 1972; Sent from God, 1974; Good News in the Letters of Paul, 1975; Go and make Disciples, 1978; Unfinished Easter, 1978; The Faith is Still There, 1980; Preaching About the Needs of Real People, 1988; *autobiography:* This Grace Given, 1984; Grace Thus Far, 1986; articles and sermons in Atlantic Monthly, Scottish Jl of Theology, Expository Times, etc. *Recreations:* languages; drama; travel, especially in France. *Address:* 258 Riverside Drive, #9A, New York, NY 10025-6161, USA. *Clubs:* Pilgrims of the US, The Century (New York).

READ, Prof. David John, PhD; FRS 1990; Professor of Plant Science, Sheffield University, since 1990; *b* 20 Jan. 1939; *s* of O. Read; *m* (marr. diss.); one *s*. *Educ:* Sexey's Sch., Bruton, Som; Hull Univ. (BSc 1960; PhD 1963). Sheffield University: Jun. Res. Fellow, 1963–66; Asst Lectr, 1966–69; Lectr, 1969–79; Sen. Lectr, 1979–81; Reader in Plant Sci., 1981–90. *Publications:* editor of numerous books and author of papers in learned jls mostly on subject of symbiosis, specifically the mycorrhizal symbiosis between plant roots and fungi. *Recreations:* walking, botany. *Address:* Milestone Cottage, Youlgrave, Bakewell, Derbys DE4 1WD. *T:* Bakewell (01629) 636360.

READ, Prof. Frank Henry, FRS 1984; Professor of Physics, Victoria University of Manchester, since 1975; *b* 6 Oct. 1934; *s* of late Frank Charles Read and Florence Louise (*née* Wright); *m* 1961, Anne Stuart (*née* Wallace); two *s* two *d*. *Educ:* Haberdashers' Aske's Hampstead Sch. (Foundn Scholar, 1946); Royal Coll. of Science, Univ. of London (Royal Scholar, 1952; ARCS 1955; BSc 1955). PhD 1959, DSc 1975, Victoria Univ. of Manchester. FInstP 1968; MIEE 1982; CEng; CPhys. University of Manchester: Lectr, 1959; Sen. Lectr, 1969; Reader, 1974; Res. Dean, Faculty of Sci., 1993–95. Vis. Scientist: Univ. of Paris, 1974; Univ. of Colorado, 1974–75; Inst. for Atomic and Molecular Physics, Amsterdam, 1979–80. Consultant to industry, 1976–. Vice Pres., Inst. of Physics, 1985–89 (Chm., IOP Publishing Ltd, 1985–89); Member: Science Bd, SERC, 1987–90; Council, Royal Soc., 1987–89. Hon. Editor, Jl of Physics B, Atomic and Molecular Physics, 1980–84. *Publications:* (with E. Harting) Electrostatic Lenses, 1976; Electromagnetic Radiation, 1980; papers in physics jls. *Recreations:* stone-masonry, farming. *Address:* Hardingland Farm, Macclesfield Forest, Cheshire SK11 0ND. *T:* Macclesfield (01625) 425759.

READ, Harry; British Commissioner, Salvation Army, 1987–90; Editor, Words of Life, since 1990; *b* 17 May 1924; *s* of Robert and Florence Read; *m* 1950, Winifred Humphries; one *s* one *d*. *Educ:* Sir William Worsley Sch., Grange Town, Middlesbrough. Served RCS, 1942–47 (6th Airborne Div., 1943–45). Commnd Salvation Army Officer, 1948; pastoral work, 1948–54; Lectr, Internat. Training Coll., 1954–62; pastoral work, 1962–64; Divl Youth Sec., 1964–66; Lectr, Internat. Training Coll., 1966–72; Dir, Information Services, 1972–75; Divl Comdr, 1975–78; Principal, Internat. Training Coll., 1978–81; Chief Sec., Canada Territory, 1981–84; Territorial Comdr, Australia Eastern Territory, 1984–87. *Recreations:* writing, hymns, poetry. *Address:* 5 Kingates Court, 43 Wickham Road, Beckenham, Kent BR3 2NB. *T:* 0181–650 4187.

See also J. L. Read.

READ, Imelda Mary, (Mel); Member (Lab) European Parliament, Nottingham and Leicestershire North West, since 1994 (Leicester, 1989–94); *b* Hillingdon, 8 Jan. 1939; *d* of Robert Alan Hocking and Teresa Mary Hocking; *m*; one *s* one *d*, and one step *s*. *Educ:* Bishopshalt Sch., Hillingdon, Mddx; Nottingham Univ. (BA Hons 1977). Laboratory technician, Plessey, 1963–74; researcher, Trent Polytechnic, 1977–80; Lectr, Trent Polytechnic and other instns, 1980–84; Employment Officer, Nottingham Community Relations Council, 1984–89. European Parliament: Chair, British Labour Gp, 1990–92; Quastor, 1992–94. Contested (Lab): Melton, 1979; Leicestershire NW, 1983. Member: Nat Exec. Council, ASTMS, 1975; NEC, MSF; TUC Women's Adv. Cttee; Chair, Regl TUC Women's Cttee. *Publication:* (jtly) Against a Rising Tide, 1992. *Recreations:* beekeeping, gardening. *Address:* Marlene Reid Centre, 85 Belvoir Road, Coalville, Leics LE67 3PH.

READ, Gen. Sir (John) Antony (Jervis), GCB 1972 (KCB 1967; CB 1965); CBE 1959 (OBE 1957); DSO 1945; MC 1941; Governor of Royal Hospital, Chelsea, 1975–81; *b* 10 Sept. 1913; *e s* of late John Dale Read, Heathfield, Sussex; *m* 1947, Sheila, *e d* of late F. G. C. Morris, London, NW8; three *d*. *Educ:* Winchester; Sandhurst. Commissioned Oxford and Bucks Lt Inf., 1934; seconded to Gold Coast Regt, RWAFF, 1936; comd 81 (WA) Div. Reconnaissance Regt, 1943; comd 1 Gambia Regt, 1944; war service Kenya, Abyssinia, Somaliland, Burma; DAMS, War Office, 1947–49; Company Comd RMA Sandhurst, 1949–52; AA&QMG 11 Armd Div., 1953–54; comd 1 Oxford and Bucks Lt Inf., 1955–57; comd 3 Inf. Bde Gp, 1957–59; Comdt School of Infantry, 1959–62; GOC Northumbrian Area and 50 (Northumbrian) Division (TA), 1962–64; Vice-Quarter-Master-General, Min. of Defence, 1964–66; GOC-in-C, Western Comd, 1966–69; Quartermaster-General, 1969–72; Comdt, Royal Coll. of Defence Studies, 1973. ADC (Gen.) to the Queen, 1971–73. Colonel Commandant: Army Catering Corps, 1966–76; The Light Division, 1968–73; Small Arms School Corps, 1969–74; Hon. Col, Oxfordshire Royal Green Jackets Bn ACF, 1983–92. President: TA Rifle Assoc., 1972–90; Ex-Services Fellowship Centres, 1975–91; ACF Assoc., 1983–92 (Chm., 1973–82). Treas., Lord Kitchener Nat. Meml Fund, 1980–87. Governor: Royal Sch. for Daughters of Officers of the Army, 1966–83 (Chm., 1975–81); St Edward's Sch., Oxford, 1972–86; Special Comr, Duke of York's Royal Mil. Sch., 1974–90. *Address:* Brackles, Little Chesterton, near Bicester, Oxon OX6 8PD. *T:* Bicester (01869) 252189. *Club:* Army and Navy.

READ, Sir John (Emms), Kt 1976; FCA 1947; President, Charities Aid Foundation, since 1994 (Trustee, since 1985; Chairman of Trustees, 1990–94); *b* 29 March 1918; *s* of late William Emms Read and of Daysie Elizabeth (*née* Cooper); *m* 1942, Dorothy Millicent Berry; two *s*. *Educ:* Brighton, Hove and Sussex Grammar Sch. Served Royal Navy, 1939–46 (rank of Comdr (S) RNVR); Admiral's Secretary: to Asst Chief of Naval Staff, Admty, 1942–45; to Brit. Admty Technical Mission, Ottawa, Canada, 1945–46. Ford Motor Co. Ltd, 1946–64 (Admin. Staff Coll., Henley, 1952), Dir of Sales, 1961–64; Dir, Electric and Musical Industries Ltd, 1965–87; EMI Group: Jt Man. Dir, 1967; Chief Exec., 1969–79; Dep. Chm., 1973–74; Chm., 1974–79; Thorn EMI: Dep. Chm., 1979–81, Dir, 1981–87. Director: Capitol Industries-EMI Inc., 1970–83; Dunlop Holdings Ltd, 1971–84; Thames Television, 1973–88 (Dep. Chm., 1981–88); Wonderworld plc, 1984–; Hill Samuel Gp, 1987–88; Cafman Ltd, 1990–; Chairman: TSB Holdings Ltd, 1980–86; Trustee Savings Banks Central Bd, 1980–88; Central TSB Ltd, 1983–86; TSB England and Wales, 1983–86; TSB Gp plc, 1986–88; UDT, 1981–85; Target Gp plc, 1987–88; FI Group plc, 1989–93. Chm., EDC for Electronics Industry, 1977–80. Member: (part time), PO Bd, 1975–77; Engineering Industries Council, 1975–80; BOTB, 1976–79; Armed Forces Pay Review Body, 1976–83; Nat. Electronics Council, 1977–80; Groupe des Présidents des Grandes Enterprises Européennes, 1977–80. Vice-Pres., Inst. of Bankers, 1982–89. Member: RN Film Corp., 1975–83; Brighton Festival Soc. Council of Management, 1977–82; CBI Council, 1977–90 (Mem., Presidents' Cttee, 1977–84; Chm., F&GP Cttee, 1978–84); White Ensign Assoc. Council of Management, 1979–; Council, The Prince's Youth Business Trust, 1987–89; Nat. Theatre Devel Council, 1987–90; Court, Surrey Univ., 1986–; Governing Body and F&GP Cttee, BPMF, London Univ., 1982– (Dep. Chm., 1987–); Governing Council, Business in the Community, 1985–89; Council, British Heart Foundn, 1986–89; Chm., Inst. of Neurology Council of Management, 1980–; Trustee: Westminster Abbey Trust, 1978–85; Brain Res. Trust, 1982– (Chm., 1986–); Dir and Trustee, Brighton Fest. Trust, 1977–92; Dir, NCVO Ltd, 1990–94. President: Sussex Assoc. of Boys' Clubs, 1982–; Cheshire Homes, Seven Rivers, Essex, 1979–85; Governor, Admin. Staff Coll., Henley, 1974–92 (Hon. Fellow 1993). CIMgt (FBIM 1974); CompIERE 1974; FIB 1982. DUniv. Surrey, 1989; Hon. DBA Internat. Management Centre, Buckingham, 1990. *Recreations:* music, arts, sports. *Address:* Muster House, 12 Muster Green North, Haywards Heath, W Sussex RH16 4AG. *Clubs:* Royal Over-Seas League, MCC.

READ, John Leslie, FCA; Chairman, Carvent Inc., since 1988; *b* 21 March 1935; *s* of Robert and Florence Read; *m* 1958, Eugenie Ida (*née* Knight); one *s* one *d*. *Educ:* Sir William Turner's School. Partner, Price Waterhouse & Co., 1966–75; Finance Dir, then Jt Chief Exec., Unigate plc, 1975–80; Chairman: Macarthy plc, 1989–92 (Dir, 1986–92); LEP Gp, 1982–91; Director: MB-Caradon Group (formerly Metal Box) plc, 1979–92; Equity Law Life Assurance Soc. plc, 1980–87; Border and Southern Stockholders Investment Trust, later Govett Strategic Investment Trust, 1985–92. Chm., Audit Commn for Local Authorities in England and Wales, 1983–86. *Recreations:* music, sport, reading, photography. *Address:* 2 Milbrook, Esher, Surrey KT10 9EJ. *Club:* Royal Automobile.

See also H. Read.

READ, Leonard Ernest, (Nipper), QPM 1976; National Security Adviser to the Museums and Galleries Commission, 1978–86; *b* 31 March 1925; *m* 1st, 1951, Marion Alexandra Millar (marr. diss. 1979); one *d*; 2nd, 1980, Patricia Margaret Allen. *Educ:* elementary schools. Worked at Players Tobacco factory, Nottingham, 1939–43; Petty Officer, RN, 1943–46; joined Metropolitan Police, 1947; served in all ranks of CID; Det. Chief Supt on Murder Squad, 1967; Asst Chief Constable, Notts Combined Constabulary, 1970; National Co-ordinator of Regional Crime Squads for England and Wales, 1972–76. Vice-President: British Boxing Bd of Control, 1991– (Mem. Council, 1976–82; Vice-Chm., 1988); World Boxing Assoc., 1989–. Freeman, City of London, 1983. *Publication:* Nipper (autobiog.), 1991. *Recreations:* home computing, playing the keyboard. *Address:* 23 North Barn, Broxbourne, Herts EN10 6RR.

READ, Lionel Frank, QC 1973; a Recorder of the Crown Court, since 1974; a Deputy High Court Judge, since 1989; *b* 7 Sept. 1929; *s* of late F. W. C. Read and Lilian (*née* Chatwin); *m* 1956, Shirley Greenhalgh; two *s* one *d*. *Educ:* Oundle Sch.; St John's Coll., Cambridge (MA). Mons OCS Stick of Honour; commnd 4 RHA, 1949. Called to Bar, Gray's Inn, 1954, Bencher, 1981; Mem., Senate of the Inns of Court and the Bar, 1974–77. A Gen. Comr of Income Tax, Gray's Inn Div., 1986–90. Chm., Local Government and Planning Bar Assoc., 1990–94 (Vice-Chm., 1986–90); Member: Bar Council, 1990–94; Council on Tribunals, 1990–. *Recreations:* golf, gardening. *Address:* Cedarwood, Church Road, Ham Common, Surrey TW10 5HG. *T:* 0181–940 5247. *Clubs:* Garrick; Hawks (Cambridge).

READ, Malcolm James; Metropolitan Stipendiary Magistrate, since 1993; *b* 4 May 1948; *s* of Frank James Cruickshank Read and Anne Elizabeth (*née* Oldershaw); divorced; one *s*. *Educ:* Wallington Independent Grammar Sch.; Council of Legal Educn. Called to the Bar, Gray's Inn, 1979; Clerk to Justices, Lewes Magistrates' Court, 1980–81; Clerk to: Hastings, Bexhill, Battle and Rye Justices, 1981–91; E Sussex Magistrates' Courts Cttee, 1981–91; in private practice, Brighton, 1991–93. *Recreations:* motor-cycling, golf (occasionally), dog and cat maintenance. *Address:* Thames Magistrates' Court, 58 Bow Road, E3 4DJ. *T:* 0181–980 1000.

READ, Mel; *see* Read, I. M.

READ, Piers Paul, FRSL; author; *b* 7 March 1941; 3rd *s* of Sir Herbert Read, DSO, MC and Margaret Read, Stonegrave, York; *m* 1967, Emily Albertine, *o d* of Evelyn Basil Boothby, CMG and of Susan Asquith; two *s* two *d*. *Educ:* Ampleforth Coll.; St John's Coll., Cambridge (MA). Artist-in-residence, Ford Foundn, Berlin, 1963–64; Sub-Editor, Times Literary Supplement, 1965; Harkness Fellow, Commonwealth Fund, NY, 1967–68. Member: Council, Inst. of Contemporary Arts, 1971–75; Cttee of Management, Soc. of Authors, 1973–76; Literature Panel, Arts Council, 1975–77. Adjunct Prof. of Writing, Columbia Univ., NY, 1980. Bd Mem., Aid to the Church in Need, 1988–. Governor, Cardinal Manning Boys' Sch., 1985–91. Chm., Catholic Writers' Guild (the Keys), 1992–. TV plays: Coincidence, 1968; The House on Highbury Hill, 1972; The Childhood Friend, 1974; radio play: The Family Firm, 1970. *Publications: novels:* Game in Heaven with Tussy Marx, 1966; The Junkers, 1968 (Sir Geoffrey Faber Meml Prize); Monk Dawson, 1969 (Hawthornden Prize and Somerset Maugham Award); The Professor's Daughter, 1971; The Upstart, 1973; Polonaise, 1976; A Married Man, 1979 (televised 1983); The Villa Golitsyn, 1981; The Free Frenchman, 1986 (televised 1989); A Season in the West, 1988 (James Tait Black Meml Prize); On the Third Day, 1990; A Patriot in Berlin, 1995; *non-fiction:* Alive, 1974 (filmed 1992); The Train Robbers, 1978; Quo Vadis? the subversion of the Catholic Church, 1991; Ablaze: the story of Chernobyl, 1993. *Address:* 50 Portland Road, W11 4LG.

READE, Brian Anthony; HM Diplomatic Service, retired; *b* 5 Feb. 1940; *s* of Stanley Robert Reade and Emily Doris (*née* Lee); *m* 1964, Averille van Eugen; one *s* one *d*. *Educ:* King Henry VIII Sch., Coventry; Univ. of Leeds (BA Hons 1963). Interlang Ltd, 1963–64; Lectr, City of Westminster Coll., 1964–65; 2nd Sec., FCO, 1965–69; 2nd Sec., Bangkok, 1970–71, 1st Sec., 1971–74; FCO, 1974–77; Consul (Econ.), Consulate-General, Düsseldorf, 1977–81; FCO, 1981–82; 1st Sec., Bangkok, 1982–84; Counsellor (ESCAP), Bangkok, 1984–86; Counsellor, FCO, 1986–93. *Recreations:* watching sport, conversation, reading. *Clubs:* Coventry Rugby Football; Royal Bangkok Sports (Thailand).

READE, Sir Kenneth Roy, 13th Bt *cr* 1661, of Barton, Berkshire; *b* 23 March 1926; *s* of Leverne Elton Reade (*d* 1943; 5th *s* of Sir George Compton Reade, 9th Bt), and Norma B. Ward; *S* cousin, 1982; *m* 1944, Doreen D. Vinsant; three *d*. *Heir:* none. *Address:* 1198 Paddock Place, Apt 106, Ann Arbor, MI 48108, USA.

READER HARRIS, Dame (Muriel) Diana, DBE 1972; Headmistress, Sherborne School for Girls, Dorset, 1950–75; *b* Hong Kong, 11 Oct. 1912; *er d* of late Montgomery Reader Harris. *Educ:* Sherborne School for Girls; University of London (external student). BA 1st Class Honours (English), 1934. Asst Mistress, Sherborne School for Girls, 1934, and House Mistress, 1938. Organised Public Schools and Clubs Camps for Girls, 1937–39; in charge of group evacuated from Sherborne to Canada, 1940; joined staff of National Association of Girls' Clubs, 1943; Chm. Christian Consultative Cttee Nat. Assoc. of Mixed Clubs and Girls' Clubs, 1952–68, Vice-Pres., 1968; Chm. Outward Bound Girls' Courses, 1954–59; Mem. Council, Outward Bound Trust, 1956–64. Member: Women's Consultative Cttee, Min. of Labour, 1958–77; Women's Nat. Commn, 1976–78. Member: Dorset Educn Cttee, 1952–70; Exec. Cttee, Assoc. of Headmistresses, 1953–58, 1960 (Pres., 1964–66); Pres., Assoc. of Headmistresses of Boarding Schs, 1960–62; Member: Cttee on Agricl Colls, Min. of Agric., 1961–64; Schs Council, 1966–75. Member: Archbishop's Council on Evangelism, 1966–68; Panel on Broadcasting, Synod of C of E, 1975–86; Bd, Christian Aid, 1976–83 (Chm., 1978–83); Exec. Cttee and Assembly, BCC, 1977–83. Pres., CMS, 1969–82 (Mem., 1953–82, Chm., 1960–63, Exec. Cttee). Lay Canon, Salisbury Cathedral, 1987–92. King George's Jubilee Trust: Mem., Standing Res. and Adv. Cttee, 1949; Mem., Admin. Council, 1955–67; Member: Council, 1951–62, Exec. and Council, 1976–79, Nat. Youth Orch. of GB; ITA, 1956–60; Council, Westminster Abbey Choir Sch., 1976–88; Court, Royal Foundn of St Katharine, 1979–90 (Chm., 1981–88). Patron, Jt Educational Trust, 1986– (Chm., 1982–84, Trustee, 1975–86); President: Sch. Mistresses and Governesses Benevolent Instn, 1980–90; Time and Talents Assoc., 1981–92; British and For. Sch. Soc., 1982–91; Churches' Commn on Overseas Students, 1984–91. Governor: Godolphin Sch., Salisbury, 1975–86; St Michael's Sch., Limpsfield, 1975–83 (Chm., 1977–83). FRSA 1964 (Mem. Council, RSA, 1975–89; Chm., 1979–81; Vice-Pres., 1981–89; Vice-Pres. Emerita, 1989–); Mem., The Pilgrims, 1979–. Hon. FCP 1975. *Address:* 35 The Close, Salisbury, Wilts SP1 2EL. *T:* Salisbury (01722) 326889.

READING, 4th Marquess of, *cr* 1926; **Simon Charles Henry Rufus Isaacs;** Baron 1914; Viscount 1916; Earl 1917; Viscount Erleigh 1917; waste management consultant; *b* 18 May 1942; *e s* of 3rd Marquess of Reading, MBE, MC, and of Margot Irene, *yr d* of late Percy Duke, OBE; *S* father, 1980; *m* 1979, Melinda Victoria, *yr d* of Richard Dewar, Hay Hedge, Bisley, Glos; one *s* two *d*. *Educ:* Eton. Short service commission, 1st Queen's Dragoon Guards, 1961–64. Member of Stock Exchange, 1970–74; Dir, VDA. New Era Fellow, Templeton Foundn. Chm. of Govs, Dean Close Sch., 1990–. Hon. Dr Soka, Tokyo, 1989. *Heir: s* Viscount Erleigh, *qv*. *Address:* Jaynes Court, Bisley, Glos GL6 7BE. *Clubs:* Cavalry and Guards, Queen's, All England Lawn Tennis and Croquet.

READING, Area Bishop of, since 1989; **Rt. Rev. John Frank Ewan Bone;** *b* 28 Aug. 1930; *s* of Jack and Herberta Blanche Bone; *m* 1954, Ruth Margaret Crudgington; two *s* two *d* and one adopted *s*. *Educ:* Monkton Combe School, Bath; St Peter's Coll., Oxford (MA); Ely Theological Coll.; Whitelands Coll. of Education (Grad. Cert. in Education). Ordained, 1956; Assistant Curate: St Gabriel's, Warwick Square, 1956–60; St Mary's, Henley on Thames, 1960–63; Vicar of Datchet, 1963–76; Rector of Slough, 1976–78; Rural Dean of Burnham, 1974–77; Archdeacon of Buckingham, 1978–89. Mem. of General Synod, 1980–85. *Recreations:* collecting antique maps and prints, classical music, coarse gardening, walking. *Address:* Greenbanks, 25 Old Bath Road, Sonning, Reading RG4 6SY.

REAGAN, Ronald, Hon. GCB 1989; President of the United States of America, 1981–89; *b* Tampico, Ill, 6 Feb. 1911; *m* 1st, 1940, Jane Wyman (marr. diss. 1948); one *s* one *d*; 2nd, 1952, Nancy Davis; one *s* one *d*. *Educ:* public schools in Tampico, Monmouth, Galesburg, and Dixon, Ill; Eureka Coll., Ill (AB). Sports Announcer, WHO, Des Moines, 1932–37; actor, films and television, 1937–66; Host and Program Superviser, Gen. Electric Theater (TV), 1954–62; Host, Death Valley Days (TV), 1962–65. Pres., Screen Actors' Guild, 1947–52, 1959–60; Chm., Motion Picture Industry Council, 1949. Served with USAAF, 1942–45. Governor, State of California, 1967–74; Chairman, State Governors' Assoc., 1969. Republican Candidate for nomination for the Presidency, 1976. Operates horsebreeding and cattle ranch. Hon. Fellow, Keble Coll., Oxford, 1994. Presidential Medal of Freedom, USA, 1992. *Publications:* Where's the Rest of Me? (autobiog.), 1965 (repr. 1981 as My Early Life); Abortion and the Conscience of the Nation, 1984; An American Life (autobiog.), 1990. *Address:* 668 St Cloud Road, Bel Air, Los Angeles, CA 90077, USA.

REAMSBOTTOM, Barry Arthur; General Secretary, Civil and Public Services Association, since 1992; *b* 4 April 1949; *s* of Agnes Reamsbottom. *Educ:* St Peter's RC Secondary Sch., Aberdeen; Aberdeen Academy. Scientific Asst, Isaac Spencer & Co., Aberdeen, 1966–69; Social Security Officer, DHSS, Aberdeen, 1969–76; Area Officer, NUPE, Edinburgh, 1976–79; Head of Educn Dept, CPSA, 1979–87; Editor, Press Officer, CPSA, 1987–92. *Recreations:* reading, golf, politics, music, taking photographs, watching Coronation Street. *Address:* Civil and Public Services Association, 160 Falcon Road, SW11 2LN. *T:* 0171–924 2727.

REARDON, Rev. John Patrick; General Secretary, Council of Churches for Britain and Ireland, since 1990; Moderator, General Assembly of the United Reformed Church, 1995–96; *b* 15 June 1933; *s* of John Samuel Reardon and Ivy Hilda Reardon; *m* 1957, Molly Pamela Young; four *s* one *d*. *Educ:* Gravesend Grammar Sch. for Boys; University College London (BA Hons English); King's College London (postgraduate Cert. in Educn). Teacher, London and Gravesend, 1958–61; Minister, Horsham Congregational Church, 1961–68 (Chm., Sussex Congregational Union, 1967); Minister, Trinity Congregational Church, St Albans, 1968–72 (Chm., Herts Congregational Union, 1971–72); Sec., Church and Society Dept, 1972–90, and Dep. Gen. Sec., 1983–90, URC. *Publications:* More Everyday Prayers (contrib.), 1982; (ed) Leaves from the Tree of Peace, 1986; (ed) Threads of Creation, 1989. *Recreations:* modern literature, photography, philately, travel. *Address:* Inter-Church House, 35–41 Lower Marsh, SE1 7RL. *T:* 0171–620 4444.

REARDON, Rev. Canon Martin Alan; General Secretary, Churches Together in England, since 1990; *b* 3 Oct. 1932; *s* of Ernest William Reardon, CBE and Gertrude Mary; *m* 1964, Ruth Maxim Slade; one *s* one *d*. *Educ:* Cumnor House Sch.; St Edward's Sch., Oxford; Selwyn Coll., Cambridge (MA); Cuddesdon Coll., Oxford; Univ. of Geneva; Univ. of Louvain. Asst Curate, Rugby Parish Church, 1958–61; Sec., Sheffield Council of Churches, 1962–71; Sub-Warden, Lincoln Theol Coll., 1971–78; Sec., Bd for Mission and Unity, Gen. Synod of C of E, 1978–89; Rector, Plumpton with East Chiltington, 1989–90. *Publications:* Christian Unity in Sheffield, 1967; (with Kenneth Greet) Social Questions, 1964; What on Earth is the Church For?, 1985; Christian Initiation, 1991; contribs to One in Christ, Theology, Clergy Review, etc. *Recreations:* walking, sketching. *Address:* Inter-Church House, 35–41 Lower Marsh, SE1 7RL.

REARDON SMITH, Sir William (Antony John), 4th Bt *cr* 1920, of Appledore, Devon; management and charities consultant; Trustee and Chairman, Joseph Strong Frazer Trust, since 1980; Chairman, North Eastern Rubber Company Ltd, since 1980; *b* 20 June 1937; *e s* of Sir William Reardon Reardon-Smith, 3rd Bt and his 1st wife, Nesta Florence Phillips (*d* 1959); *S* father, 1995; *m* 1962, Susan Wight, *d* of Henry Wight Gibson; three *s* one *d*. *Educ:* Wycliffe Coll. Nat. Service, RN, Suez, 1956. Sir William Reardon Smith & Sons Ltd and Reardon Smith Line plc, 1957–85 (Dir, 1959–85); Director: London World Trade Centre, 1986–87; Milford Haven Port Authority, 1988–; Marine and Port Services Ltd, 1990–. Member: Baltic Exchange, 1959–87 (Dir, 1982–87; Assoc. Mem., 1990–92); Chamber of Shipping Documentary Cttee, 1963–72 (Chm., 1968–72); Documentary Council, Baltic and Internat. Conf., 1964–82. Dir, UK Protection and Indemnity Club and Freight, Demurrage and Defence Assoc., 1968–80. Trustee and Vice-President: Royal Merchant Navy Sch. Foundn; Bearwood Coll.; Member: Council, King George's Fund for Sailors; City of London Cttee, RNLI. Liveryman: Shipwrights' Co; Poulters' Co. *Recreations:* golf, shooting. *Heir: s* William Nicolas Henry Reardon Smith, *b* 10 June 1963. *Address:* 26 Merrick Square, SE1 4JB. *T:* 0171–403 5723. *Clubs:* Cardiff and County; Royal Porthcawl Golf.

REAY, 14th Lord, *cr* 1628, of Reay, Caithness; **Hugh William Mackay;** Bt of Nova Scotia, 1627; Baron Mackay of Ophemert and Zennewijnen, Holland; Chief of Clan Mackay; *b* 19 July 1937; *s* of 13th Lord Reay and Charlotte Mary Younger; *S* father, 1963; *m* 1st, 1964, Hon. Annabel Thérèse Fraser (marr. diss. 1978; she *m* 1985, Henry Neville Lindley Keswick, *qv*), *y d* of 17th Baron Lovat, DSO, MC; two *s* one *d*; 2nd, 1980, Hon. Victoria Isabella Warrender, *d* of 1st Baron Bruntisfield, MC; two *d*. *Educ:* Eton; Christ Church. Mem., European Parlt, 1973–79 (Vice-Chm., Cons. Gp); Delegate, Council of Europe and WEU, 1979–86. Lord in Waiting (Govt Whip), 1989–91; Parly Under-Sec. of State, DTI, 1991–92. Mem., Select Cttee on European Communities, H of L, 1993–. *Heir: s* The Master of Reay, *qv*. *Address:* House of Lords, SW1A 0PW.

REAY, Master of; Aeneas Simon Mackay, *b* 20 March 1965; *s* and *heir* of 14th Lord Reay, *qv*. *Educ:* Westminster School; Brown Univ., USA. *Recreations:* most sports, especially football, cricket and shooting.

REAY, Lt-Gen. Sir Alan; *see* Reay, Lt-Gen. Sir H. A. J.

REAY, David William, CEng, FIEE; CPhys, FInstP; Chairman, Northumberland Mental Health NHS Trust, since 1992; *b* 28 May 1940; *s* of late Stanley Reay and Madge Reay (*née* Hall); *m* 1964, Constance Susan Gibney; two *d*. *Educ:* Monkwearmouth Grammar School, Sunderland; Newcastle upon Tyne Polytechnic. Independent Television Authority, 1960–62; Alpha Television (ATV and ABC) Services Ltd, 1962–64; Tyne Tees Television Ltd, 1964–72; HTV Ltd: Engineering Manager, 1972–75; Chief Engineer, 1975–79; Dir of Engineering, 1979–84; Man. Dir, 1984–91, Chief Exec., 1991, Tyne Tees Television Hldgs. Chairman: Hadrian Television Ltd, 1988–91; Legend Television Ltd, 1989–91; Man. Dir, Tyne Tees Television Ltd, 1984–91; Director: Tyne Tees Music, 1984–91; Tyne Tees Enterprises, 1984–91; ITCA, now ITVA, 1984–91; Independent Television Publications, 1984–89; Tube Productions, 1986–91; ITN, 1990–91; Tyne and Wear Develt Corp., 1986–88; The Wearside Opportunity Ltd, 1988–91. Mem. Council, Univ. of Newcastle upon Tyne, 1989–94. CIMgt (CBIM 1987); FRTS 1984; FRSA 1992. *Recreations:* walking, reading, music, watching soccer (particularly Sunderland AFC). *Address:* Warreners House, Northgate, Morpeth, Northumberland NE61 3BX.

REAY, Lt-Gen. Sir (Hubert) Alan (John), KBE 1981; FRCP, FRCP(Edin); Chairman, West Lambeth Community Care NHS Trust, since 1992; Director General, Army Medical Services, 1981–85; *b* 19 March 1925; *s* of Rev. John Reay; *m* 1960, Ferelith Haslewood Deane; two *s* two *d* (and one *s* decd). *Educ:* Lancing College; Edinburgh Univ. MB, DTM&H, DCH. Field Medical Services, Malaya, 1949–52 (despatches); Exchange Physician, Brooke Hosp., San Antonio, Texas, 1957; Command Paediatrician: Far East, 1962; BAOR, 1965; Adviser in Paediatrics, MoD (Army), 1968; Hon. Out-patient Consultant, Great Ormond Street Hosp., 1975–79, 1985–87; QHP 1976–85; Postgraduate Dean and Comdt, Royal Army Med. Coll., 1977–79; DMS, HQ BAOR, 1979–81. Hon. Col, 217 (London) General Hosp. RAMC (Volunteers) TA, 1986–90. Chm., Med. Cttee, Royal Star and Garter Home, 1986–92. Member Council: SSAFA, 1986–93; RSocMed, 1987–91 (Pres., Paediatric Section, 1984–85). Pres., Friends of St Thomas' Hosp., 1993–. Vice-Chm., Thames Reach Homelessness Project, 1992–94; Trustee: Children's Hospice for Eastern Reg., Cambridge, 1988–; Buttle Trust, 1991–. Chief Hon. Steward, Westminster Abbey, 1985–. Inaugural Lectr, Soc. of Armed Forces Med. Consultants, Univ. of Health Scis, Bethesda, 1984. Hon. Mem., BPA, 1988. Hon. FRCGP 1985. CStJ 1981 (OStJ 1979). *Publications:* paediatric articles in med. jls. *Address:* c/o National Westminster Bank, PO Box 2, 27–29 Horseferry Road, SW1P 2AZ.

REAY, Dr John Sinclair Shewan; Director, Warren Spring Laboratory, Department of Trade and Industry, 1985–92; *b* Aberdeen, 8 June 1932; *s* of late George Reay, CBE and Tina (*née* Shewan); *m* 1958, Rhoda Donald Robertson; two *s* one *d*. *Educ:* Robert Gordon's College, Aberdeen; Univ. of Aberdeen; Imperial College, London (Beit Fellow). BSc, PhD, DIC. CChem, FRSC. Joined Scottish Agricultural Industries, 1958; Warren Spring Lab., Min of Technology, 1968; Head of Air Pollution Div., DoI, 1972–77; Head, Policy and Perspectives Unit, DTI, 1977–79; Head of Branch, Research Technology Div., DoI, 1979–81; Dep. Dir, Warren Spring Lab., 1981–85. *Publications:* papers on surface chemistry and air pollution. *Recreations:* playing violin, listening to music. *Address:* 13 Grange Hill, Welwyn, Herts AL6 9RH. *T:* Welwyn (01438) 715587.

REAY-SMITH, Richard Philip Morley; Director, Personal Sector, UK Banking Services, Barclays Bank, since 1995; *b* 24 Nov. 1941; *m* 1972, Susan Margaret Hill; two *s*. *Educ:* Stowe Sch.; Durham Univ. (LLB); Harvard Business Sch. (AMP). Barclays Bank 1963–: Local Dir, Shrewsbury, 1984–87; Dep. Chief Exec., Central Retail Services Div., 1987–91; Chief Exec., Barclaycard, 1991–94. Dir, Visa Internat. Services Assoc., 1991–; Chm., APACS Card Payments Gp, 1991–95. First Chm., 1980–85, Vice-Chm., 1985–, Painshill Park Trust. FRSA. *Recreations:* sailing, flying, music. *Address:* Barclays Bank, 54 Lombard Street, EC3P 3AH.

REBUCK, Gail Ruth, (Mrs Philip Gould); Chairman and Chief Executive, Random House UK Ltd, since 1991; *b* 10 Feb. 1952; *d* of Gordon and Mavis Rebuck; *m* 1985, Philip Gould; two *d*. *Educ:* Lycée Français de Londres; Univ. of Sussex (BA). Production Asst, Grisewood & Dempsey, 1975–76; Editor, then Publisher, Robert Nicholson Publications, 1976–78; Publisher, Hamlyn Paperbacks, 1978–82; Publishing Dir, Century Publishing, 1982–85; Publisher, Century Hutchinson, 1985–89; Chm., Random House Div., Random Century, 1989–91. FRSA. *Recreations:* reading, travel. *Address:* Random House UK Ltd, 20 Vauxhall Bridge Road, SW1V 2SA. *T:* 0171–973 9000. *Clubs:* Groucho.

RECKERT, Prof. (Frederick) Stephen, FBA 1994; Camoens Prof. of Portuguese, University of London, King's College, 1967–82, now Emeritus Professor; Founder Member, Institute for Study of Symbology, New University of Lisbon, since 1980; *b* 31 May 1923; *s* of Frederick Carl Reckert and Aileen Templeton Adams Reckert; *m* 1st, 1946, Olwen Roberts (*d* 1963); two *s* one *d*; 2nd, 1965, Dídia Mateus Marques. *Educ:* Exeter Acad., USA; Saybrook Coll., Yale (BA *summa cum laude* 1945); Trinity Coll., Cambridge (MLitt 1948); Berkeley Coll., Yale (PhD 1950). Japanese translator, with RAF Bletchley, 1943–45; Fellow, Berkeley Coll. and Asst Prof. of Spanish, Yale, 1948–58; Prof. and Head of Hispanic Studies, Univ. of Wales, 1958–66; Head, Portuguese and Brazilian Studies, Univ. of London, 1967–82. Visiting Professor: Madrid, 1971; New Univ., Lisbon, 1974–78; Univ. of Rome, 1985; Guest Lectr, Univs of Lisbon, Oporto, Evora, Seville, Warsaw, Jagiellonian Univ. of Cracow. Corresp. Fellow: Hispanic Soc. of America; Portuguese Acad. of Scis.; Royal Spanish Acad. Nobiling Medal for Medieval Studies, Brazil, 1978. Order of Southern Cross (Brazil), 1979; Order of Henry the Navigator (Portugal), 1990. *Publications:* (with Dámaso Alonso) Vida y Obra de Medrano, 1958; (with Helder Macedo) Do Cancioneiro de Amigo, 1976; Gil Vicente, 1977; (with Y. K. Centeno) Fernando Pessoa, 1978; Um Ramalhete para Cesário, 1987; Beyond Chrysanthemums, 1993; Gil Vicente: Espírito, Letra, Texto, 1996; as Frederick Carlson: A Perfeição, Musée de l'Homme, Contos da Palma da Mão, 1994; contribs to jls and collective vols. *Recreations:* poetry, music, conviviality. *Address:* Rua das Janelas Verdes 17-4°, 1200 Lisbon, Portugal. *T:* 3962292; Ayot Weir, Weybridge, Surrey KT 13 8HR. *T:* Weybridge (01932) 843589. *Clubs:* United Oxford & Cambridge University; PEN (English and Portuguese centres).

RECKITT, Lt-Col Basil Norman, TD 1946; Director, Reckitt and Colman Ltd, retired 1972 (Chairman, 1966–70); *b* 12 Aug. 1905; *s* of Frank Norman Reckitt, Architect, and Beatrice Margaret Hewett; *m* 1st, 1928, Virginia Carre-Smith (*d* 1961); three *d*; 2nd, 1966, Mary Holmes (*née* Peirce), *widow* of Paul Holmes, Malham Tarn, near Settle. *Educ:* Uppingham; King's Coll., Cambridge (MA). Joined Reckitt & Sons Ltd, 1927; Dir, Reckitt & Colman Ltd, 1938. 2nd Lieut, 62nd HAA Regt (TA), 1939; Bde Major, 39th AA Brigade, 1940; CO 141 HAA (M) Regt, 1942; Military Government, Germany, 1944–45. Hull University: Chm. Council, 1971–80; Pro-Chancellor, 1971–93, now Emeritus. Sheriff of Hull, 1970–71. Chm., Friends of Abbot Hall Art Gall. and Museums, Kendal, 1982–87; Vice-Chm., YMCA Nat. Centre, Lakeside, Windermere, 1982–87. Hon. LLD, Hull University, 1967. *Publications:* History of Reckitt & Sons Ltd, 1951; Charles I and Hull, 1952; The Lindley Affair, 1972; Diary of Military Government in Germany, 1989; The Journeys of William Reckitt, 1989; Diary of Anti-Aircraft Defence, 1990; Brothers at War, 1991; Petronella, 1994; The Death Hole, 1994; Sibella, 1994. *Recreations:* riding, walking. *Address:* Haverbrack, Milnthorpe, Cumbria LA7 7AH. *T:* Milnthorpe (015395) 63142.

REDDAWAY, Brian; *see* Reddaway, W. B.

REDDAWAY, David Norman, CMG 1993; MBE 1980; HM Diplomatic Service; Minister, Buenos Aires, since 1993; *b* 26 April 1953; *s* of George Frank Norman Reddaway, *qv* and Jean Reddaway, OBE (*née* Brett); *m* 1981, Roshan Taliyeh Firouz; one *s* one *d*. *Educ:* Oundle Sch. (Schol.); Fitzwilliam Coll., Cambridge (Exhibnr; MA Hist.). Joined FCO, 1975; language student, SOAS, 1976 and Iran, 1977; Tehran: Third Sec. later Second Sec. (Commercial), 1977–78; Second Sec. later First Sec. (Chancery), 1978–80; First Secretary: (Chancery), Madrid, 1980–84; FCO, 1985–86; Private Sec. to Minister of State, 1986–88; (Chancery), New Delhi, 1988–90; Chargé d'Affaires, Tehran, 1990–93 (Counsellor, 1991). *Recreations:* ski-ing, tennis, Persian carpets and art. *Address:* c/o Foreign and Commonwealth Office, King Charles Street, SW1A 2AH. *Clubs:* Commonwealth Trust; Hawks (Cambridge); Leander (Henley-on-Thames).

REDDAWAY, (George Frank) Norman, CBE 1965 (MBE 1946); HM Diplomatic Service, retired; *b* 2 May 1918; *s* of late William Fiddian Reddaway and late Kate Waterland Reddaway (*née* Sills); *m* 1944, Jean Brett, OBE; two *s* three *d*. *Educ:* Oundle

School; King's College, Cambridge. Scholar Modern Langs, 1935; 1st Class Hons Mod. Langs Tripos Parts 1 and 2, 1937 and 1939. Served in Army, 1939–46; psc Camberley, 1944. Foreign Office, 1946; Private Sec. to Parly Under Sec. of State, 1947–49; Rome, 1949; Ottawa, 1952; Foreign Office, 1955; Imperial Defence College, 1960; Counsellor, Beirut, 1961; Counsellor, Office of the Political Adviser to the C-in-C, Far East, Singapore, 1965–66; Counsellor (Commercial), Khartoum, 1967–69; Asst Under-Sec. of State, FCO, 1970–74; Ambassador to Poland, 1974–78. Chm., International House (formerly English International), 1978–; Dir, Catalytic International, 1978–89; Consultant: Badger Catalytic, 1989–94; Raytheon Engineers and Constructors, 1994–. Trustee, Thomson Foundn, 1978–. Commander, Order of Merit, Polish People's Republic, 1985. *Recreations:* international affairs, gardening, family history. *Address:* 51 Carlton Hill, NW8 0EL. *T:* 0171–624 9238. *Clubs:* Athenæum, United Oxford & Cambridge University, Commonwealth Trust.

See also D. N. Reddaway, J. S. Wall.

REDDAWAY, Norman; *see* Reddaway, G. F. N.

REDDAWAY, Prof. (William) Brian, CBE 1971; FBA 1967; Professor of Political Economy, University of Cambridge, 1969–80, now Emeritus; Fellow of Clare College, Cambridge, since 1938; Economic Consultant to the World Bank, since 1966; *b* 8 Jan. 1913; *s* of late William Fiddian Reddaway and late Kate Waterland Reddaway (*née* Sills); *m* 1938, Barbara Augusta Bennett; three *s* one *d*. *Educ:* Oundle Sch.; King's Coll., Cambridge; Maj. schol. natural science; 1st cl. Maths tripos, part I, 1st cl. 1st div. Economics tripos, part II; Adam Smith Prize; MA. Assistant, Bank of England, 1934–35; Research Fellow in Economics, University of Melbourne, 1936–37; Statistics Division, Board of Trade (final rank Chief Statistician), 1940–47; University Lectr in Economics, 1939–55, Reader in Applied Economics, 1957–65, Dir of Dept of Applied Economics, 1955–69, Univ. of Cambridge. Economic Adviser to OEEC, 1951–52; Visiting Economist, Center for International Studies, New Delhi, 1959–60; Vis. Lectr, Economic Develt Inst. (Washington), 1966–67; Consultant, Harvard Develt Adv. Service (in Ghana), 1967; Vis. Prof., Bangladesh Inst. of Develt Studies, 1974–75. Economic Consultant to CBI, 1972–83. Regional Adviser, Economic Commn for Western Asia, 1979–80; Consultant to World Bank on Nigerian economy, 1983–87. Member: Royal Commn on the Press, 1961–62; NBPI, 1967–71; Chm., Inquiry into Consulting Engineering Firms' Costs and Earnings, 1971–72. Editor, Economic Jl, 1971–76. *Publications:* Russian Financial System, 1935; Economics of a Declining Population, 1939; (with C. F. Carter, Richard Stone) Measurement of Production Movements, 1948; The Development of the Indian Economy, 962; Effects of UK Direct Investment Overseas, Interim Report, 1967, Final Report, 968; Effects of the Selective Employment Tax, First Report, 1970, Final Report, 1973; ith G. C. Fiegehen) Companies, Incentives and Senior Managers, 1981; Some Key es for the Development of the Economy of Papua New Guinea, 1986; articles in erous economic journals. *Recreations:* skating, walking. *Address:* 12 Manor Court, ge Road, Cambridge CB3 9BE. *T:* Cambridge (01223) 350041.

CLIFFE, Paul; HM Diplomatic Service; Ambassador to the Kingdom of Cambodia, since 1994; *b* 17 March 1945; *s* of Donald Reddicliffe and Vera Irene (*née* Elleby); *m* 1974, Wee Siok Boi; two *s*. *Educ:* Bedford Mod. Sch.; Jesus Coll., Oxford (MA Lit. Hum. 1967); Sch. of Oriental and African Studies, Univ. of London (MA SE Asian Studies 1973); Univ. of Kent. VSO, Vientiane, Laos, 1968–70 and 1971–72; joined HM Diplomatic Service, 1977; Indochina Analyst, Res. Dept, FCO, 1977–85; First Sec., Canberra, 1985–89; Indochina Analyst, 1989–92, Hd, S and SE Asia Section, 1992–94; Res. later Res. and Analysis, Dept, FCO. *Recreations:* bird-watching, books, collecting foreign bank-notes. *Address:* c/o Foreign and Commonwealth Office, King Charles Street, SW1A 2AH.

REDDINGTON, (Clifford) Michael; Chief Executive, Liverpool City Council, 1986–88; *b* 14 Sept. 1932; *s* of Thomas Reddington and Gertrude (*née* Kenny); *m* 1968 Ursula Moor. *Educ:* St Michael's Coll., Leeds; St Edward's Coll., Liverpool; Liverpool Univ. BCom 1953; IPFA 1958; MBCS 1964. Served RAF, 1958–60. City Treasury, Liverpool, 1953–58 and 1960–86; Dep. City Treasurer, 1974, City Treasurer, 1982–86. Mem., Indep. Inquiry into Capital Market Activities of London Borough of Hammersmith and Fulham, 1990. Chairman: Liverpool Welsh Choral Union, 1990–93; Convocation, Univ. of Liverpool, 1993–; Trust Fund Manager, Hillsborough Disaster Appeal Fund, 1989–; Chm., James Bulger Meml Trust, 1993–. *Recreations:* fell-walking, choral singing, cooking. *Address:* Entwood, Westwood Road, Noctorum, Birkenhead L43 9RQ. *T:* 0151–652 6081. *Club:* Athenæum (Liverpool).

REDDISH, Prof. Vincent Cartledge, OBE 1974; Professor Emeritus, Edinburgh University, 1980; *b* 28 April 1926; *s* of William H. M. Reddish and Evelyn Reddish; *m* 1951, Elizabeth Waltho; two *s*. *Educ:* Wigan Techn. Coll.; London Univ. BSc Hons, PhD, DSc. Lectr in Astronomy, Edinburgh Univ., 1954; Lectr in Radio Astronomy, Manchester Univ., 1959; Royal Observatory, Edinburgh: Principal Scientific Officer, 1962; Sen. Principal Sci. Off., 1966; Dep. Chief Sci. Off., 1974; Regius Prof. of Astronomy, Edinburgh Univ., Dir, Royal Observatory, Edinburgh, and Astronomer Royal for Scotland, 1975–80. Governor, Rannoch Sch., 1981–. *Publications:* Evolution of the Galaxies, 1967; The Physics of Stellar Interiors, 1974; Stellar Formation, 1978; The D-Force, 1993; numerous sci. papers in Monthly Notices RAS, Nature and other jls. *Recreations:* hill walking, sailing, ornithology, do-it-yourself. *Address:* 11 Greenhill Terrace, Edinburgh EH10 4BS. *T:* 0131–447 8935.

REDDY, (Neelam) Sanjiva; farmer and lemon grower; President of India, 1977–82; *b* 13 May 1913; *m* Nagaratnamma; one *s* three *d*. *Educ:* Adyar Arts Coll., Anantapur. Andhra Provincial Congress: Sec., Congress Cttee, 1936–46; Pres., 1951–; Leader, Congress Legislature Party, 1953–; Mem. and Sec., Madras Legislative Assembly, 1946; Mem., Indian Constituent Assembly, 1947; Minister for Prohibition, Housing and Forests, Madras Govt, 1949–51; Mem., Rajya Sabha, 1952–53; Andhra Pradesh: Mem., Legislative Assembly, 1953–64; Dep. Chief Minister, 1953–56; Chief Minister, 1956–57 and 1962–64; Pres., All-India Congress Party, 1960–62; Member: Rajya Sabha, 1964–67; Lok Sabha, 1967–71, and 1977; Minister: of Steel and Mines, 1964–65; of Transport, Aviation, Shipping and Tourism, 1966–67; Speaker of Lok Sabha, 1967–69, 1977. *Address:* Illure, Anantapur, Andhra Pradesh, India.

REDESDALE, 6th Baron *cr* 1902; **Rupert Bertram Mitford;** *b* 18 July 1967; *s* of 5th Baron and of Sarah Georgina Cranstoun, *d* of Brig. Alston Cranstoun Todd, OBE; *S* father, 1991. *Educ:* Highgate Sch.; Newcastle Univ. (BA Hons Archaeology). Outdoor instructor, Fernwood Adventure Centre, South Africa, 1990–91. *Recreations:* caving, climbing, ski-ing. *Address:* 2 St Mark's Square, NW1 7TP. *T:* 0171–722 1965. *Club:* Newcastle University Caving.

REDFERN, Michael Howard; QC 1993; *b* 30 Nov. 1943; *s* of Lionel William Redfern and Kathleen Roylance Redfern (*née* Brownston); *m* 1st, 1966, Sylvia Newlands (marr. diss. 1989); one *d*; 2nd, 1991, Diana Barbara Eaglestone; one *d*, and two step *d*. *Educ:* Stretford Grammar Sch. for Boys; Leeds Univ. (LLB Hons). Teacher, 1967–68; Lectr in Law, 1968–69; called to the Bar, Inner Temple, 1970. *Recreations:* music, sport (preferably participating), travel, history. *Address:* 28 St John Street, Manchester M3 4DJ. *T:* 0161–834 8418.

REDFERN, Philip, CB 1983; Deputy Director, Office of Population Censuses and Surveys, 1970–82; *b* 14 Dec. 1922; *m* 1951, Gwendoline Mary Phillips; three *d*. *Educ:* Bemrose Sch., Derby; St John's Coll., Cambridge. Wrangler, Mathematical Tripos, Cambridge, 1942. Asst Statistician, Central Statistical Office, 1947; Chief Statistician, Min. of Education, 1960; Dir of Statistics and Jt Head of Planning Branch, Dept of Educn and Science, 1967. *Recreation:* walking from Yorkshire to Wester Ross.

REDFORD, (Charles) Robert; American actor and director; *b* 18 Aug. 1937; *s* of Charles Redford and Martha (*née* Hart); *m* 1958, Lola Jean Van Wagenen; one *s* two *d*. *Educ:* Van Nuys High Sch.; Univ. of Colorado; Pratt Inst., Brooklyn; Amer. Acad. of Dramatic Arts. *Theatre:* appearances include: Tall Story, Broadway, 1959; Sunday in New York, Broadway, 1961–62; Barefoot in the Park, Biltmore, NY, 1963–64; *television:* appearances include, The Iceman Cometh, 1960; *films* include: as actor: War Hunt, 1962; Inside Daisy Clover, 1965; Barefoot in the Park, 1967; Butch Cassidy and the Sundance Kid, 1969; The Candidate, 1972; The Way We Were, 1973; The Sting, 1973; The Great Gatsby, 1974; All the President's Men, 1976; The Electric Horseman, 1979; The Natural, 1984; Out of Africa, 1985; Legal Eagles, 1986; Havana, 1990; Sneakers, 1992; as director: Ordinary People, 1980 (Acad. Award for Best Dir, 1981); Milagro Beanfield War (also prod.), 1988; A River Runs Through It, 1992; Indecent Proposal, 1993; The River Wild, 1995. *Publication:* The Outlaw Trail, 1978. *Address:* c/o Wildwood Enterprises, 100 Universal City Plaza, Universal City, CA 91608, USA.

REDFORD, Donald Kirkman, CBE 1980; DL; President, The Manchester Ship Canal Company, since 1986 (Managing Director, 1970–80; Chairman, 1972–86); *b* 18 Feb. 1919; *er s* of T. J. and S. A. Redford; *m* 1942, Mabel (*née* Wilkinson), Humberstone, Lincs; one *s* one *d*. *Educ:* Culford Sch.; King's Coll., Univ. of London (LLB). Served, 1937–39, and War until 1945, in RAFVR (retd as Wing Comdr). Practice at the Bar until end of 1946, when joined The Manchester Ship Canal Company, with which Company has since remained. Chairman, Nat. Assoc. of Port Employers, 1972–74; Dep. Chm., British Ports Assoc., 1973–74, Chm. 1974–78. Member: Cttee of Management, RNLI, 1977– (Chm., Search and Research Cttee, 1984–89); Court, Manchester Univ., 1977– (Dep. Treas., 1980–82, Treas., 1982–83, Mem. of Council, 1977–92, Chm. of Council, 1983–87). CIMgt; FRSA. DL Lancs 1983. Hon. LLD Manchester, 1988. *Recreations:* reading, history, sailing, golf. *Address:* North Cotes, 8 Harrod Drive, Birkdale, Southport PR8 2HA. *T:* Southport (01704) 67406. *Clubs:* Oriental; Union (Southport).

REDFORD, Robert; *see* Redford, C. R.

REDGRAVE, Adrian Robert Frank; QC 1992; a Recorder of the Crown Court, since 1985; *b* 1 Sept. 1944; *s* of Cecil Frank Redgrave and Doris Edith Redgrave (*née* Goss); *m* 1967, Ann Cooper; two *s* one *d*. *Educ:* Abingdon Sch.; Univ. of Exeter (LLB 1966). Called to the Bar, Inner Temple, 1968. *Recreations:* tennis, wine, garden, France, Bangalore Phall. *Address:* 1 Serjeants' Inn, Fleet Street, EC4Y 1LL. *T:* 0171–353 9901.

REDGRAVE, Lynn; actress; *b* 8 March 1943; *d* of late Sir Michael Redgrave, CBE, and of Rachel Kempson, *qv*; *m* 1967, John Clark; one *s* two *d*. *Educ:* Queensgate Sch.; Central Sch. of Speech and Drama. Nat. Theatre of GB, 1963–66 (Tulip Tree, Mother Courage, Andorra, Hay Fever, etc); Black Comedy, Broadway 1966; The Two of Us, Slag, Zoo Zoo Widdershins Zoo, Born Yesterday, London 1968–71; A Better Place, Dublin 1972; My Fat Friend, Knock Knock, Mrs Warren's Profession, Broadway 1973–76; The Two of Us, California Suite, Hellzapoppin, US tours 1976–77; Saint Joan, Chicago and NY 1977; Twelfth Night, Amer. Shakespeare Festival, Conn, 1978; Les Dames du Jeudi, LA, 1981; Sister Mary Ignatius Explains It All For You, LA, 1983; The King and I, N American Tour, 1983; Aren't We All, 1985, Sweet Sue, 1987, Love Letters, 1989, Broadway; Les Liaisons Dangereuses, Don Juan in Hell, LA, 1989–91; Three Sisters, Queen's, 1990; A Little Hotel on the Side, The Master Builder, Broadway, 1991–92. One-woman show, Shakspeare for my Father, NY and US tour, 1993. *Films include:* Tom Jones, Girl with Green Eyes, Georgy Girl (NY Film Critics, Golden Globe and IFIDA awards, Academy nomination Best Actress), Deadly Affair, Smashing Time, Virgin Soldiers, Last of the Mobile Hotshots, Every Little Crook and Nanny, National Health, Happy Hooker, Everything You Always Wanted to Know about Sex, The Big Bus, Sunday Lovers, Morgan Stewart's Coming Home, Getting it Right, Midnight. *Television includes:* USA: Co-host of nationally televised talk-show, Not For Women Only, appearances in documentaries, plays, The Muppets, Centennial, Beggarman Thief, The Seduction of Miss Leona, Rehearsal for Murder, The Old Reliable, Jury Duty, Whatever Happened to Baby Jane?, and series: Housecalls (CBS); Teachers Only (NBC); Chicken Soup (ABC); BBC: A Woman Alone, 1988; Death of a Son, 1989; Calling the Shots, 1994. *Publication:* Diet for Life (autobiog.) (US as This is Living), 1991. *Recreations:* cooking, gardening, horse riding. *Address:* PO Box 1207, Topanga, CA 90290, USA. *T:* (310) 4551334, *Fax:* (310) 4551032.

REDGRAVE, Rachel, (Lady Redgrave); *see* Kempson, R.

REDGRAVE, Maj.-Gen. Sir Roy Michael Frederick, KBE 1979; MC 1945; FRGS; *b* 16 Sept. 1925; *s* of late Robin Roy Redgrave and Michelene Jean Capsa; *m* 1953, Caroline Margaret Valerie, *d* of Major Arthur Wellesley and Margaret Baker-Kirby; two *s*. *Educ:* Sherborne Sch. Served War of 1939–45: enlisted Trooper, Royal Horse Guards, 1943; Lieut, 1st Household Cavalry Regt, NW Europe, 1944–45. GSO III Intell., HQ Rhine Army, 1950; Canadian Army Staff Coll., 1955; GSO II Ops HQ, London Dist, 1956; Recce, Sqn Ldr, Cyprus, 1959 (despatches); Mil. Assistant to Dep. SACEUR, Paris, 1960–62; JSSC 1962; Comd Household Cavalry Regt (Mounted), 1963–64; Comd Royal Horse Guards (The Blues), 1965–67; AAG PS12, MoD, 1967–68; Chief of Staff, HQ 2nd Div., 1968–70; Comdr, Royal Armoured Corps, 3rd Div., 1970–72; Nat. Defence Coll., Canada, 1973; Comdt Royal Armoured Corps Centre, 1974–75; British Comdt, Berlin, 1975–78; Comdr, British Forces, Hong Kong, and Maj.-Gen. Brigade of Gurkhas, 1978–80. Hon. Col 31st (RR) Signal Regt (V), 1983–88. Dir Gen., Winston Churchill Meml Trust, 1980–82. Member: Council, Charing Cross and Westminster Med. Sch., 1981–; Hammersmith SHA, 1981–85; Council, Victoria League for Commonwealth Friendship; Britain Nepal Soc., 1982–. Chairman: Hammersmith and Fulham HA, 1981–85; Lambrook Appeal, 1984–85; Charing Cross and West London Hosps, 1988– (Special Trustee, 1981–87); Trustee: Westminster and Roehampton Hosps, 1988–93; Governor General's Horse Guards, Canada, 1987–; Chelsea and Westminster Hosp., 1993–; Governor, Commonwealth Trust, 1989–. Grand Prior, Grand Priory of England, Order of Knights Templar, 1990–. *Recreations:* walking, archaeology, philately. *Address:* c/o Lloyds Bank, Wareham, Dorset BH20 4LX. *Club:* Cavalry and Guards.

REDGRAVE, Steven Geoffrey, MBE 1987; oarsman; sports consultant; *b* 23 March 1962; *m* 1988, Elizabeth Ann Callaway; two *d*. *Educ:* Great Marlow Sch. Represents: Marlow Rowing Club, 1976–; Leander, 1987–. Rowed coxless pairs with Andrew Holmes, to 1989, with Matthew Pinsent, 1990–; winner: Commonwealth Games, 1986 (single sculls, coxed fours, coxless pairs); World Championships, coxless pairs, 1987, 1991,

1993, 1994 and 1995; Gold Medallist, Olympic Games, 1984 (coxed fours), 1988 and 1992 (coxless pairs). *Publication:* Steven Redgrave's Complete Book of Rowing, 1992. *Club:* Leander (Henley-on-Thames).

REDGRAVE, Vanessa, CBE 1967; Actress since 1957; *b* 30 Jan. 1937; *d* of late Sir Michael Redgrave, CBE, and of Rachel Kempson, *qv*; *m* 1962, Tony Richardson (marr. diss., 1967; he *d* 1991); two *d*. *Educ:* Queensgate School; Central School of Speech and Drama. Frinton Summer Repertory, 1957; Touch of the Sun, Saville, 1958; Midsummer Night's Dream, Stratford, 1959; Look on Tempests, 1960; The Tiger and the Horse, 1960; Lady from the Sea, 1960; Royal Shakespeare Theatre Company: As You Like It, 1961, Taming of the Shrew, 1961, Cymbeline, 1962; The Seagull, 1964; The Prime of Miss Jean Brodie, Wyndham's, 1966; Daniel Deronda, 1969; Cato Street, 1971; The Threepenny Opera, Prince of Wales, 1972; Twelfth Night, Shaw Theatre, 1972; Antony and Cleopatra, Bankside Globe, 1973; Design for Living, Phoenix, 1973; Macbeth, LA, 1974; Lady from the Sea, NY, 1976, Roundhouse, 1979; The Aspern Papers, Haymarket, 1984; The Seagull, Queen's, 1985; Chekhov's Women, Lyric, 1985; The Taming of the Shrew and Antony and Cleopatra, Haymarket, 1986; Ghosts, Young Vic, transf. Wyndham's, 1986; Touch of the Poet, Young Vic, transf. Comedy, 1988; Orpheus Descending, Haymarket, 1988, NY, 1989; A Madhouse in Goa, Lyric, Hammersmith, 1989; Three Sisters, Queen's, 1990; When She Danced, Globe, 1991; Heartbreak House, Haymarket, 1992; The Liberation of Skopje, Antony and Cleopatra, Riverside, 1995. *Films:* Morgan—A Suitable Case for Treatment, 1966 (Cannes Fest. Award, Best Actress 1966); The Sailor from Gibraltar, 1967; Blow-Up, 1967; Camelot, 1967; Red White and Zero, 1967; Charge of the Light Brigade, 1968; Isadora, 1968; A Quiet Place in the Country, 1968; The Seagull, 1969; Drop-Out, 1970; La Vacanza, 1970; The Trojan Women, 1971; The Devils, 1971; Mary, Queen of Scots, 1972; Murder on the Orient Express, 1974; Out of Season, 1975; Seven Per Cent Solution, 1975; Julia, 1976 (Academy Award, 1977; Golden Globe Award); Agatha, 1978; Yanks, 1978; Bear Island, 1978; Playing for Time, 1980; My Body, My Child, 1981; Wagner, 1983; The Bostonians, 1984; Wetherby, 1985; Steaming, 1985; Comrades, 1987; Prick Up Your Ears, 1987; Consuming Passions, 1988; A Man For All Seasons, 1988; Orpheus Descending, 1990; Young Catherine, 1990; Whatever Happened to Baby Jane, 1990; The Ballad of the Sad Café, 1991; Howards End, 1992; The House of the Spirits, 1994; Mother's Boys, 1994; Little Odessa, 1995. Has appeared on TV. *Publications:* Pussies and Tigers (anthology of writings of school children), 1963; Vanessa Redgrave: an autobiography, 1991. *Address:* c/o James Sharkey Associates, 15 Golden Square, W1R 3AG.

See also N. J. Richardson.

REDGROVE, Peter William, FRSL; poet, analytical psychologist; Resident Author, Falmouth School of Art, 1966–83; *b* 2 Jan. 1932; *s* of late Gordon James Redgrove and Nancy Lena Cestrilli-Bell; *m* Penelope Shuttle, *qv*; one *d*; (two *s* one *d* by former marr.). *Educ:* Taunton Sch.; Queens' Coll., Cambridge. Scientific journalist and copywriter, 1954–61; Visiting Poet, Buffalo Univ., NY, 1961–62; Gregory Fellow in Poetry, Leeds Univ., 1962–65; study with John Layard, 1968–69. O'Connor Prof. of Literature, Colgate Univ., NY, 1974–75; Leverhulme Emeritus Fellow, 1985–87; Writer at large, N Cornwall Arts, 1988. George Rylands' Verse-speaking Prize, 1954; Fulbright Award, 1961; Poetry Book Society Choices, 1961, 1966, 1979, 1981; Arts Council Awards, 1969, 1970, 1973, 1975, 1977, 1982; Guardian Fiction Prize, 1973; Prudence Farmer Poetry Award, 1977; Cholmondeley Award, 1985. FRSL 1982. *Publications: poetry:* The Collector, 1960; The Nature of Cold Weather, 1961; At the White Monument, 1963; The Force, 1966; Penguin Modern Poets 11, 1968; Work in Progress, 1969; Dr Faust's Sea-Spiral Spirit, 1972; Three Pieces for Voices, 1972; The Hermaphrodite Album (with Penelope Shuttle), 1973; Sons of My Skin: Selected Poems, 1975; From Every Chink of the Ark, 1977; Ten Poems, 1977; The Weddings at Nether Powers, 1979; The Apple-Broadcast, 1981; The Working of Water, 1984; The Man Named East, 1985; The Mudlark Poems and Grand Buveur, 1986; In the Hall of the Saurians, 1987; The Moon Disposes, 1987; Poems 1954–1987, 1989; The First Earthquake, 1989; Dressed as for a Tarot Pack, 1990; Under the Reservoir, 1992; The Laborators, 1993; My Father's Trapdoors, 1994; Abyssophone, 1995; *prose fiction:* In the Country of the Skin, 1973; The Terrors of Dr Treviles (with Penelope Shuttle), 1974; The Glass Cottage, 1976; The Sleep of the Great Hypnotist, 1979; The God of Glass, 1979; The Beekeepers, 1980; The Facilitators, 1982; The One Who Set out to Study Fear, 1989; The Cyclopean Mistress, 1993; *plays:* Miss Carstairs Dressed for Blooding (play-book containing several dramatic pieces), 1976; (for radio): In the Country of the Skin, 1973; The Holy Sinner, 1975; Dance the Putrefact, 1975; The God of Glass, 1977 (Imperial Tobacco Award 1978); Martyr of the Hives, 1980 (Giles Cooper Award 1981); Florent and the Tuxedo Millions, 1982 (Prix Italia); The Sin-Doctor, 1983; Dracula in White, 1984; The Scientists of the Strange, 1984; Time for the Cat-Scene, 1985; Trelamia, 1986; Six Tales from Grimm, 1987; Six Views to a Haunt, 1992; (for television): The Sermon, 1963; Jack Be Nimble, 1980; *non-fiction:* The Wise Wound (with Penelope Shuttle), 1978, rev. edn 1986; The Black Goddess and the Sixth Sense, 1987; Alchemy for Women, 1995. *Recreations:* work, photography, judo (1st Kyu Judo: Otani and Brit. Judo Assoc.), yoga. *Address:* c/o David Higham Associates, 5–8 Lower John Street, Golden Square, W1R 4HA.

REDHEAD, Prof. Michael Logan Gonne, FBA 1991; Professor, since 1987, and Chairman of Department of History and Philosophy of Science, since 1993, Cambridge University; Fellow, since 1988, Vice-President, since 1992, Wolfson College, Cambridge; *b* 30 Dec. 1929; *s* of Robert Arthur Redhead and Christabel Lucy Gonne Browning; *m* 1964, Jennifer Anne Hill; three *s*. *Educ:* Westminster Sch.; University College London (BSc 1st Cl. Hons Physics 1950; PhD Mathematical Phys. 1970). FInstP 1982. Dir, Redhead Properties Ltd, 1962; Partner, Galveston Estates, 1970; Lectr, Sen. Lectr in Philosophy of Science, 1981–84, Prof., Philosophy of Physics, 1984–85, Chelsea Coll., Univ. of London; Prof. of Philosophy of Physics, King's College London, 1985–87; Hd of Dept of Hist. and Philosophy of Sci., Cambridge Univ., 1987–93. Tarner Lectr, Trinity Coll., Cambridge, 1991–94; Visiting Fellow: Pittsburgh Univ., 1985; Princeton Univ., 1991; LSE, 1994; All Souls Coll., Oxford, 1995. Pres., British Soc. for Philos. of Sci., 1989–91. Lakatos Award in Philosophy of Science, 1988. Editor, Studies in History and Philosophy of Modern Physics, 1993–. *Publications:* Incompleteness, Nonlocality and Realism, 1987; From Physics to Metaphysics, 1994; papers in learned jls. *Recreations:* tennis, poetry, music. *Address:* 1 Orchard Court, Orchard Street, Cambridge CB1 1PR. *T:* Cambridge (01223) 321226. *Clubs:* Athenæum, Hurlingham, Queen's.

REDMAN, Prof. Christopher Willard George, FRCP, FRCOG; Consultant and Clinical Professor of Obstetric Medicine, Nuffield Department of Obstetrics and Gynaecology, Oxford University, since 1992; Fellow of Lady Margaret Hall, Oxford; *b* 30 Nov. 1941; *s* of Roderick Oliver Redman and Annie Kathleen Redman (*née* Bancroft); *m* 1964, Corinna Susan Page; four *s* one *d*. *Educ:* St John's Coll., Cambridge (MA; MB, BChir). FRCP 1981; FRCOG (*ad eund*) 1993. Oxford University: Clinical Lectr, Dept of Regius Prof. of Medicine, 1970–76; Univ. Lectr and Consultant, Nuffield Dept of Obstetrics and Gynaecol., 1976–89; Clinical Reader and Cons., 1989–92. *Publications:* scientific articles about pre-eclampsia in med. jls. *Recreation:* hill-walking. *Address:* Nuffield Department of Obstetrics and Gynaecology, John Radcliffe Maternity Hospital, Headington, Oxford OX3 9DU. *T:* Oxford (01865) 221009.

REDMAN, Maj.-Gen. Denis Arthur Kay, CB 1963; OBE 1942; retired; Colonel Commandant, REME, 1963–68; Director, Electrical and Mechanical Engineering, War Office, 1960–63; *b* 8 April 1910; *s* of late Brig. A. S. Redman, CB; *m* 1943, Penelope, *d* of A. S. Kay; one *s* one *d*. *Educ:* Wellington Coll.; London Univ. BSc (Eng) 1st class Hons (London); FCGI, MIMechE, AMIEE. Commissioned in RAOC, 1934; served in Middle East, 1936–43; transferred to REME, 1942; Temp. Brig., 1944; DDME 1st Corps, 1951; Comdt REME Training Centre 1957–59. Graduate of Staff Coll., Joint Services Staff Coll. and Imperial Defence Coll. *Recreations:* normal. *Club:* Army and Navy.

REDMAN, Maurice; Chairman, Scottish Region, British Gas Corporation, 1974–82 (Deputy Chairman, 1970–74); *b* 30 Aug. 1922; *s* of Herbert Redman and Olive (*née* Dyson); *m* 1960, Dorothy (*née* Appleton); two *d*. *Educ:* Hulme Grammar Sch., Oldham; Manchester Univ. BSc(Tech), 1st cl. Hons. Joined staff of Co. Borough of Oldham Gas Dept, 1943; Asst, later Dep. Production Engr, North Western Gas Bd, 1951; Chief Develt Engr, NW Gas Bd, 1957; Chief Engr, Southern Gas Bd, 1966; Dir of Engrg, Southern Gas Bd, 1970. Mem., Internat. Gas Union Cttee on Manufactured Gases, 1961–82. *Publications:* papers to Instn of Gas Engrs, Inst. of Fuel, various overseas conferences, etc. *Recreations:* gardening, music, photography. *Address:* Avington, 3 Cramond Regis, Edinburgh EH4 6LW. *T:* 0131–312 6178. *Club:* New (Edinburgh).

REDMAN, Sydney, CB 1961; *b* 12 Feb. 1914; *s* of John Barritt Redman and Annie Meech; *m* 1939, Barbara Mary Grey; one *s* two *d*. *Educ:* Manchester Gram. Sch.; Corpus Christi Coll., Oxford. Asst Principal, WO, 1936; Principal Private Sec. to Secretary of State for War, 1942–44; Asst Under-Sec. of State: War Office, 1957–63; Ministry of Defence, 1963–64; Dep. Under-Sec. of State (Navy), MoD, 1964–73. Dir-Gen., Timber Trade Fedn, 1973–82. *Address:* Littlehurst, Birch Avenue, Haywards Heath, West Sussex RH17 7SL. *T:* Haywards Heath (01444) 413738.

REDMAYNE, Clive; aeronautical engineering consultant; *b* 27 July 1927; *s* of late Procter Hubert Redmayne and Emma (*née* Torkington) *m* 1952, Vera Muriel, *d* of late Wilfred Toplis and Elsie Maud Toplis; one *s* one *d*. *Educ:* Stockport Sch. BSc (Hons Maths) London External. CEng, MIMechE; FRAeS. Fairey Aviation Co.: apprentice, 1944–48; Stress Office, 1948–50; English Electric Co., Warton: Stress Office, 1950–51; A. V. Roe & Co., Chadderton: Stress Office, 1951–55; A. V. Roe & Co., Weapons Research Div., Woodford: Head of Structural Analysis, 1955–62; Structures Dept, RAE, 1962–67; Asst Director, Project Time and Cost Analysis, Min. of Technology, 1967–70; Sen. Officers' War Course, RNC, Greenwich, 1970; Asst Dir, MRCA, MoD(PE), 1970–74; Division Leader, Systems Engrg, NATO MRCA Management Agency (NAMMA), Munich, 1974–76; Chief Supt, A&AEE, Boscombe Down, 1976–78; Dir, Harrier Projects, MoD(PE), 1978–80; Director General, Future Projects, MoD(PE), 1980–81; Dir Gen. Aircraft 3, Procurement Exec., MoD, 1981–84. *Recreations:* reading, chess, ski-ing, sailing, caravanning. *Address:* Bowstones, 5 Westbrook View, Stottingway Street, Upwey, Weymouth, Dorset DT3 5QA. *T:* Weymouth (01305) 814691.

REDMAYNE, Hon. Sir Nicholas (John), 2nd Bt *cr* 1964; Chairman and Managing Director, Kleinwort Benson Securities, since 1990; Director, since 1987, and Chief Executive, since 1994, Kleinwort Benson Ltd; Director, Kleinwort Benson Group, since 1989; *b* 1 Feb. 1938; *s* of Baron Redmayne, DSO, PC (Life Peer) and Anne (*d* 1982), *d* of John Griffiths; *S* to baronetcy of father, 1983; *m* 1st, 1963, Ann Saunders (marr. diss. 1976; she *d* 1985); one *s* one *d*; 2nd, 1978, Christine Diane Wood Hewitt (*née* Fazakerley); two step *s*. *Educ:* Radley College; RMA Sandhurst. Grenadier Guards, 1957–62. Joined Grieveson, Grant, later Kleinwort Benson Securities, 1963. *Recreations:* shooting, skiing. *Heir:* *s* Giles Martin Redmayne, *b* 1 Dec. 1968. *Address:* Walcote Lodge, Walcote, Lutterworth, Leics LE17 4JR.

REDMOND, Sir James, Kt 1979; FEng, FIEE; Director of Engineering, BBC, 1968–78; *b* 8 Nov. 1918; *s* of Patrick and Marion Redmond; *m* 1942, Joan Morris; one *s* one *d*. *Educ:* Graeme High Sch., Falkirk. Radio Officer, Merchant Navy, 1935–37 and 1939–45; BBC Television, Alexandra Palace, 1937–39; BBC: Installation Engr, 1949; Supt Engr Television Recording, 1960; Sen. Supt Engr TV, 1963; Asst Dir of Engrg, 1967. Pres., Soc. of Electronic and Radio Technicians, 1970–75; Pres., IEE, 1978–79. Mem. Bd, Services Sound and Vision Corporation, 1983–90. Member: Council, Brunel Univ., 1980–88; Council, Open Univ., 1981–94. Hon. FIEE, 1989. Hon. DTech Brunel, 1991; DUniv Open, 1995. *Recreation:* golf. *Address:* 43 Cholmeley Crescent, Highgate, N6 5EX. *T:* 0181–340 1611. *Club:* Athenæum.

REDMOND, Martin; MP (Lab) Don Valley, since 1983; *b* 15 Aug. 1937. *Educ:* Woodlands RC Sch.; Sheffield Univ. Mem., Doncaster Borough Council, 1975–83 (Chm. of Labour Gp and Leader of Council, 1982–83). Vice-Chm., Doncaster AHA. Mem., NUM. *Address:* House of Commons, SW1A 0AA.

REDMOND, Robert Spencer, TD 1953; Director and Chief Executive, National Federation of Clay Industries, 1976–84; *b* 10 Sept. 1919; *m* 1949, Marjorie Helen Heyes; one *s*. *Educ:* Liverpool Coll. Commissioned The Liverpool Scottish (TA), 1938; served War, Army and Special Ops Exec.; released, rank of Major, 1946. Conservative Agent, 1947–56 (Wigan, 1947–49, Knutsford, 1949–56). Managing Dir, Heyes & Co. Ltd, Wigan, 1956–66; Ashley Associates Ltd: Commercial Manager, 1966–69; Managing Dir, 1969–70; Dir, 1970–72. Dir, Manchester Chamber of Commerce, 1969–74. MP (C) Bolton West, 1970–Sept. 1974; Vice-Chm., Cons. Parly Employment Cttee, 1972–74 (Sec., 1971–72). Pres., Alderley Edge Royal British Legion, 1968–76; Chairman: Knutsford and Dist Royal British Legion, 1990–; (and Founder), NW Export Club, 1958–60. *Publication:* How to Recruit Good Managers, 1989. *Address:* 194 Grove Park, Knutsford, Cheshire WA16 8QE. *T:* Knutsford (01565) 632657. *Club:* Army and Navy.

REDPATH, John Thomas, CB 1969; MBE 1944; FRIBA; Director General of Research and Development, Department of the Environment, 1967–71; architect in private practice, 1977–87; *b* 24 Jan. 1915; *m* 1st, 1939, Kate (*née* Francis) (*d* 1949); one *d*; 2nd, 1949, Claesina (*née* van der Vlerk); three *s* one *d*. *Educ:* Price's Sch.; Southern Coll. of Art. Served with RE, 1940–47. Asst Architect: Kent CC, 1936–38; Oxford City Coun., 1938–40; Princ. Asst Architect, Herts, CC, 1948–55; Dep. County Architect, Somerset CC, 1955–59; Chief Architect (Abroad), War Office, 1959–63; MPBW later DoE: Dir of Development, 1963–67; Dir Gen. of Develt, 1971–72; Dep. Chief Executive, PSA, 1972–75; Man. Dir, Millbank Technical Services Educn Ltd, 1975–77. *Publications:* various articles in architectural jls. *Recreation:* golf. *Address:* Pines Edge, Sandy Lane, Cobham, Surrey KT11 2EU. *Club:* Arts.

REDSHAW, Peter Robert Gransden; HM Diplomatic Service; Counsellor, Foreign and Commonwealth Office, since 1992; *b* 16 April 1942; *s* of Robert Henry Gransden Redshaw and Audrey Nita Redshaw (*née* Ward); *m* 1970, Margaret Shaun (*née* Mizon); one *s* two *d*. *Educ:* Boxgrove School; Charterhouse; Trinity College, Cambridge (MA). ACA. Price Waterhouse, 1964–67; FCO, 1968; Kampala, 1970–73; 1st Sec., 1971; FCO, 1973; Lagos, 1982–85; Counsellor, 1985; FCO, 1985–88; Kuala Lumpur, 1988–91. *Recreations:* books, sailing, models, travel. *Address:* c/o Foreign and Commonwealth Office, SW1A 2AH. *Clubs:* Bosham Sailing; Kampala, Royal Lake (Kuala Lumpur).

REDWOOD, Rt. Hon. John (Alan); PC 1993; DPhil; MP (C) Wokingham, since 1987; *b* 15 June 1951; *s* of William Charles Redwood and Amy Emma Redwood (*née* Champion); *m* 1974, Gail Felicity Chippington; one *s* one *d*. *Educ:* Kent Coll., Canterbury; Magdalen and St Antony's Colls, Oxford. MA, DPhil Oxon. Fellow, All Souls Coll., 1972–87. Investment Adviser, Robert Fleming & Co., 1973–77; Investment Manager and Dir, N. M. Rothschild & Sons, 1977–87; Norcros plc: Dir, 1985–89; Jt Dep. Chm., 1986–87; non-exec. Chm., 1987–89. Adviser, Treasury and Civil Service Select Cttee, 1981; Head of PM's Policy Unit, 1983–85. Councillor, Oxfordshire CC, 1973–77. Parly Under Sec. of State, DTI, 1989–90; Minister of State: DTI, 1990–92; DoE, 1992–93; Sec. of State for Wales, 1993–95. Governor of various schools, 1974–83. *Publications:* Reason, Ridicule and Religion, 1976; Public Enterprise in Crisis, 1980; (with John Hatch) Value for Money Audits, 1981; (with John Hatch) Controlling Public Industries, 1982; Going for Broke, 1984; Equity for Everyman, 1986; Popular Capitalism, 1988; The Global Marketplace, 1994. *Recreations:* water sports, village cricket. *Address:* House of Commons, SW1A 0AA. *T:* (office) 0171–219 4205; (home) 0171–976 6603.

REDWOOD, Sir Peter (Boverton), 3rd Bt *cr* 1911; Director, SERCO-IAL Ltd, since 1992; Colonel, late King's Own Scottish Borderers, retired 1987; *b* 1 Dec. 1937; *o s* of Sir Thomas Boverton Redwood, 2nd Bt, TD, and Ruth Mary Redwood (*née* Creighton, then Blair); *S* father, 1974; *m* 1964, Gilian, *o d* of John Lee Waddington Wood, Limuru, Kenya; three *d*. *Educ:* Gordonstoun. National Service, 1956–58, 2nd Lieut, Seaforth Highlanders; regular commn, KOSB, 1959; served in UK (despatches 1972), BAOR, Netherlands, ME, Africa and Far East; Staff Coll., Camberley, 1970; Nat. Defence Coll., Latimer, 1978–79. Mem., Queen's Body Guard for Scotland (Royal Co. of Archers). Liveryman, Goldsmiths' Co. *Recreations:* shooting, silver and silversmithing. *Heir: half-b* Robert Boverton Redwood [*b* 24 June 1953; *m* 1978, Mary Elizabeth Wright; one *s* one *d*]. *Address:* c/o National Westminster Bank, Warminster, Wilts BA12 9AW. *Club:* Army and Navy.

REECE, Sir Charles (Hugh), Kt 1988; Research and Technology Director, Imperial Chemical Industries, 1979–89; *b* 2 Jan. 1927; *s* of Charles Hugh Reece and Helen Youlle; *m* 1951, Betty Linford; two *d*. *Educ:* Pocklington Sch., E Riding; Huddersfield Coll.; Leeds Univ. (PhD, BSc Hons). FRSC 1981. ICI: joined Dyestuffs Div., 1949; Head of Medicinal Process Develt Dept, Dyestuffs Div., 1959; Manager, Works R&D Dept, 1965; Jt Research Manager, Mond Div., 1967; Dir, R&D, Mond Div., 1969; Dep. Chm., Mond Div., 1972; Chm., Plant Protection Div., 1975. Dir, Finnish Chemicals, 1971–75; Chm., Teijin Agricultural Chemicals, 1975–78; non-executive Director: APV plc (formerly APV Holdings), 1984–; British Biotechnology Gp, 1989–. Chm., Univ. of Surrey Robens Inst. of Indust. and Envtl Health and Safety Cttee, 1985–92; Member: ACARD, 1983–87, ACOST, 1987–89; Adv. Cttee on Industry, Cttee of Vice-Chancellors and Principals, 1983–; Council, RSC, 1985–86; SERC, 1985–89; ABRC, 1989–91; UFC, 1989–93; Royal Instn of GB, 1979–92 (Mem. Council, 1985–88); SCI; Parly and Sci. Cttee, 1979– (Vice-Chm., 1986). Hon. DSc: St Andrews, 1986; Queen's, 1988; Bristol, 1989; South West Poly., 1991; DUniv Surrey, 1989. FRSA 1988. *Publications:* reports and papers in learned jls. *Recreations:* sailing, gardening. *Address:* Heath Ridge, Graffham, Petworth, W Sussex GU28 0PT.

REECE, (Edward Vans) Paynter; His Honour Judge Paynter Reece; a Circuit Judge, since 1982; *b* 17 May 1936; *s* of Clifford Mansel Reece and Catherine Barbara Reece (*née* Hathorn); *m* 1967, Rosamund Mary Reece (*née* Roberts); three *s* one *d*. *Educ:* Blundell's Sch.; Magdalene Coll., Cambridge (MA). Called to the Bar, Inner Temple, 1960; a Recorder of the Crown Court, 1980–82. *Recreations:* fishing, golf. *Clubs:* Garrick; New Zealand Golf.

REECE, Sir (James) Gordon, Kt 1986; public affairs consultant, since 1985; *b* 1930; *m* (marr. diss.); six *c*. *Educ:* Ratcliffe Coll.; Downing Coll., Cambridge (Associate Fellow, 1986). Formerly: reporter, Liverpool Daily Post and Echo, then Sunday Express; television producer, ITV, 1960–70; Jt Man. Dir, RM EMI Ltd, 1970–74; Advr to Rt Hon. Margaret Thatcher, 1975–79; Dir of Publicity, Cons. Central Office, 1978–80; a Vice-Pres., Occidental Petroleum Corp., 1980–85. *Recreations:* racing, bridge, books. *Address:* c/o Wells Fargo Bank, 10850 Wilshire Boulevard, Los Angeles, CA 90025, USA. *Clubs:* Portland, Garrick, Buck's; California (Los Angeles); Beach (Santa Monica).

REECE, Paynter; *see* Reece, E. V. P.

REED, Adrian Harbottle, CMG 1981; HM Diplomatic Service, retired; Consul-General, Munich, 1973–80; *b* 5 Jan. 1921; *s* of Harbottle Reed, MBE, FRIBA, and Winifred Reed (*née* Rowland); *m* 1st, 1947, Doris Davidson Duthie (marr. diss. 1975); one *s* one *d*; 2nd, 1975, Maria-Louise, *d* of Dr and Mrs A. J. Boekelman, Zeist, Netherlands. *Educ:* Hele's Sch., Exeter; Emmanuel Coll., Cambridge. Royal Artillery, 1941–47. India Office, 1947; Commonwealth Relations Office, 1947; served in UK High Commission: Pakistan, 1948–50; Fedn of Rhodesia and Nyasaland, 1953–56; British Embassy, Dublin, 1960–62; Commonwealth Office, 1962–68; Counsellor (Commercial), and Consul-Gen., Helsinki, 1968–70; Economic Counsellor, Pretoria, 1971–73. Chairman: Cold Harbour Working Wool Mus., 1983–86; Devon and Exeter Instn, 1989–; SW Maritime Hist. Soc., 1994–; Devon Hist. Soc., 1994–. Bavarian Order of Merit, 1980. *Publications:* articles and reviews on historical (mainly maritime) subjects. *Recreations:* maritime history, the English countryside. *Address:* Old Bridge House, Uffculme, Cullompton, Devon EX15 3AX. *T:* Craddock (01884) 840595.

REED, Prof. Alec Edward, CBE 1994; Founder, 1960, and Executive Chairman, Reed Executive PLC; *b* 16 Feb. 1934; *s* of Leonard Reed and Anne Underwood; *m* 1961, Adrianne Mary Eyre; two *s* one *d*. *Educ:* Grammar School. FCMA, FCIM, FIPD. Founded: Reed Executive; Medicare; Inter-Company Comparison Ltd (now ICC PLC); Reed College of Accountancy; Womankind Worldwide; Ethiopiaid. President: Inst. of Employment Consultants, 1974–78; Internat. Confedn of Private Employment Agency Assocs, 1978–81; Hon. Chm. and Chief Exec., Andrews & Partners, 1985–89 (charity-owned); Mem. Exec. Cttee and Council, CIMA, 1991–95. Mem., Oxfam Fundraising Cttee, 1989–92. Prof., Enterprise and Innovation, Royal Holloway, Univ. of London, 1993– (Fellow, RHBNC, 1988). Mem. Council, RHC, 1979–85 (Chm., Finance and Investment Cttees, 1982–85). *Publication:* Returning to Work, 1989. *Recreations:* family, cinema, tennis, riding, portrait painting. *Address:* Reed Executive, 114 Peascod Street, Windsor, Berks SL4 1DN.

REED, Air Cdre April Anne, RRC 1981; Director of RAF Nursing Services, 1984–85, retired; *b* 25 Jan. 1930; *d* of Captain Basil Duck Reed, RN, and Nancy Mignon Ethel Reed. *Educ:* Channing Sch., Highgate. SRN, SCM. SRN training, Middlesex Hosp., 1948–52; midwifery training, Royal Maternity Hosp., Belfast, 1953; joined Royal Air Force, 1954; Dep. Matron, 1970; Sen. Matron, 1976; Principal Matron, 1981; Matron in Chief (Director), 1984. *Recreations:* sailing, ornithology, antiques, gardening, interest in oriental carpets. *Address:* 3 Edieham Cottages, Angle Lane, Shepreth, Royston, Herts SG8 6QJ. *T:* Royston (01763) 261329. *Club:* Royal Air Force.

REED, Barry St George Austin, CBE 1988; MC 1951; DL; Chairman, Austin Reed Group PLC, since 1973; *b* 5 May 1931; *s* of late Douglas Austin Reed and Mary Ellen (*née* Philpott); *m* 1956, Patricia (*née* Bristow); one *s* one *d*. *Educ:* Rugby Sch. Commnd Middlesex Regt (DCO), 1950; served Korea, 1950–51; TA, 1951–60. Joined Austin Reed Group, 1953; Dir, 1958–; Man. Dir, 1966–85. National Westminster Bank: Dir, City and West End Regions, 1980–87; Dir, 1987–90; Chm., Eastern Regl Adv. Bd, 1987–92; Dir, UK Adv. Bd, 1990–92. Pres., Menswear Assoc. of Britain, 1966–67; Chairman: Retail Alliance, 1967–70; British Knitting and Clothing Export Council, 1985–89; Dir, British Apparel and Textile Confedn, 1992–; Member: Bd, Retail Trading-Standards Assoc., 1964–78; Consumer Protection Adv. Cttee, 1973–79; European Trade Cttee, 1975–84; Cttee, Fleming American Exempt Fund, 1979–94; Council, Royal Warrant Holders Assoc., 1980– (Pres., 1990). Dir, Independent Broadcasting Telethon Trust Ltd, 1991–94. Chm., Queen Elizabeth Scholarship Trust, 1990–95; Trustee, Third Age Challenge Trust. Freeman, City of London, 1963; Liveryman: Glovers' Co., 1963– (Master 1980–81); Guild of Freemen, 1983. DL Greater London, 1977; Rep. DL, London Borough of Hackney, 1980–86. FRSA; CIMgt. *Publications:* papers in clothing, textile and banking jls. *Recreations:* travel, gardens, reading. *Address:* Crakehall House, Crakehall, Bedale, North Yorks DL8 1HS. *T:* Bedale (0677) 422743; 103 Regent Street, W1A 2AJ. *T:* 0171–734 6789. *Clubs:* Naval and Military, Pilgrims, MCC.

See also L. D. Reed.

REED, David; Director of Corporate Communications, Whitbread plc, since 1990; *b* 24 April 1945; *s* of Wilfred Reed and Elsie Swindon; *m* 1973, Susan Garrett, MA Oxon, MScEcon. *Educ:* West Hartlepool Grammar Sch. Former journalist and public relations adviser to Investors in Industry, Rank Xerox, Ernst & Whinney, Hewlett-Packard. Dir and Hd of Corporate and Financial PR, Ogilvy and Mather. MP (Lab) Sedgefield, Co. Durham, 1970–Feb. 1974. *Publications:* many articles in national newspapers and other jls. *Recreations:* theatre, music, walking the dog. *Address:* St Luke's Cottage, Stonor, Oxon RG9 6HE.

REED, Edward John; Clerk to the Clothworkers' Company of the City of London, 1963–78; *b* 2 Sept. 1913; *o c* of late Edward Reed; *m* 1939, Rita Isabel Venus Cheston-Porter; one *s* one *d*. *Educ:* St Paul's School. Admitted Solicitor, 1938. Territorial Service with HAC; commnd 1940; served BEF and BAOR with 63 (WR) Medium Regt RA; Capt. 1942. Clerk to Governors of Mary Datchelor Girls' Sch., 1963–78. Vice Pres., Metropolitan Soc. for the Blind, 1979– (Chm., 1965–79); Chm., Indigent Blind Visiting Society, 1965–79; Vice-Pres., N London District, St John Ambulance, 1969–81. Chm., City Side, Joint Grand Gresham Cttee, 1984. Member: Court of Common Council, City of London, for Tower Ward, 1978–86; Lloyds, 1979–. Clothworkers' Co.: Liveryman, 1964; Sen. Warden, 1981; Mem., Ct of Assistants, 1982–. Governor: Christ's Hosp., 1981–86; City of London Freemen's Sch., 1982–86. Hon. MA Leeds, 1979. CStJ 1968. Chevalier, Order of Leopold with Palm, and Croix de Guerre with Palm, Belgium, 1944. *Recreations:* sailing, photography. *Address:* 54 Hillcrest Gardens, Hinchley Wood, Esher, Surrey KT10 0BX. *T:* 0181–398 3904. *Club:* City Livery.

REED, Gavin Barras; Chairman: Wainhomes plc, since 1994; Ivory & Sime Trustlink Ltd; Milburn Estates Ltd; *b* 13 Nov. 1934; *s* of late Lt-Col Edward Reed and Greta Milburn (*née* Pybus); *m* 1957, Muriel Joyce, *d* of late Humphrey Vaughan Rowlands; one *s* three *d*. *Educ:* Eton; Trinity Coll., Cambridge (BA). National Service, Fleet Air Arm Pilot, 1953–55. Joined Newcastle Breweries Ltd, 1958; took charge of Scottish & Newcastle Breweries Gp Hotels, 1963 (Man. Dir, 1965, Chm., 1970, Thistle Hotels); Dir, Scottish & Newcastle Breweries Ltd, 1970–94; Man. Dir (Develt and Retail), 1974, Man. Dir, 1988–91, Chm., 1991–94, S&NB; Gp Vice-Chm., Scottish & Newcastle plc, 1991–94; Chairman: Newcastle Breweries, 1982–94; McEwan Younger, 1983–94; Matthew Brown (acquired by S&NB), 1987–94. Director: John Menzies, 1992–; Ivory & Sime Enterprise Capital. Chm., N Region, CBI, 1987–88. *Recreations:* shooting, tennis. *Address:* Whitehill, Aberdour, Burntisland, Fife KY3 0RW; Broadgate, West Woodburn, Northumberland NE48 2RN. *Clubs:* Naval; New (Edinburgh).

REED, Jane Barbara; Director of Corporate Affairs, News International plc, since 1989; 2nd *d* of late William and Gwendoline Reed, Letchworth, Herts. *Educ:* Royal Masonic Sch.; sundry further educational establishments. Worked on numerous magazines; returned to Woman's Own, 1965; Editor, 1970–79; Publisher, IPC Women's Monthly Group, 1979–81; Editor-in-Chief, Woman magazine, 1981–82; IPC Magazines: Asst Man. Dir, Specialist Educn and Leisure Gp, 1983; Man. Dir, Holborn Publishing Gp, 1983–85; Man. Editor (Features), Today, News (UK) Ltd, 1985–86; Man. Editor, Today, 1986–89. Pres., Media Soc., 1995. Member: Royal Soc. COPUS, 1986–; Exec. Cttee, Nat. Literacy Trust, 1992–. *Publications:* Girl About Town, 1964; (jtly) Kitchen Sink—or Swim?, 1982. *Address:* 1 Virginia Street, E1 9XY.

REED, Dr John Langdale, CB 1993; FRCP, FRCPsych; Special Advisor, Mental Health (Medical), Department of Health, since 1993; *b* 16 Sept. 1931; *s* of John Thompson Reed and Elsie May Abbott; *m* 1959, Hilary Allin; one *s* one *d*. *Educ:* Oundle Sch.; Cambridge Univ.; Guy's Hosp. Med. Sch. FRCP 1974; FRCPsych 1974. Maudsley Hosp., 1960–67; Consultant Psychiatrist and Sen. Lectr in Psychol Medicine, St Bartholomew's Hosp., 1967–. SPMO, Health Care Div. (Medical), DHSS, subseq. DoH, 1986–93. Special Advr in Forensic Psychiatry, DoH, 1993–. Chairman: DoH/Home Office Rev. of Services for Mentally Disordered Offenders, 1991–92; DoH Wkg Gp on High Security Psychiatric Care, 1992–93; DoH Wkg Gp on Psychopathic Disorder, 1992–93; Adv. Cttee on Mentally Disordered Offenders, 1993–. QHP 1990–93. *Publications:* (with G. Lomas) Psychiatric Services in the Community, 1984; papers on psychiatric services in the community and on drug abuse. *Recreations:* genealogy, opera, bridge, walking (preferably in the Lake District). *Address:* Department of Health, Wellington House, 133–135 Waterloo Road, SE1 8UG.

REED, Laurance Douglas; *b* 4 Dec. 1937; *s* of late Douglas Austin Reed and Mary Ellen Reed (*née* Philpott). *Educ:* Gresham's Sch., Holt; University Coll., Oxford (MA). Nat. Service, RN, 1956–58; worked and studied on Continent (Brussels, Bruges, Leyden, Luxembourg, Strasbourg, Paris, Rome, Bologna, Geneva), 1963–66; Public Sector Research Unit, 1967–69. MP (C) Bolton East, 1970–Feb. 1974; PPS to Chancellor of Duchy of Lancaster, 1973–74. Jt Sec., Parly and Scientific Cttee, 1971–74; Member: Soc. for Underwater Technology; Select Cttee on Science and Technology, 1971–74. *Publications:* Europe in a Shrinking World, 1967; An Ocean of Waste, 1972; Political Consequences of North Sea Oil, 1973; The Soay of Our Forefathers, 1986; Philpott of Fordingbridge, 1994. *Recreations:* gardening, historical research. *Address:* 1 Disraeli Park, Beaconsfield, Bucks HP9 2QE. *T:* Beaconsfield (01494) 673153. *Club:* Carlton.

See also B. St G. A. Reed.

REED, Leslie Edwin, PhD; Chief Industrial Air Pollution Inspector, Health and Safety Executive, 1981–85; *b* 6 Feb. 1925; *s* of Edwin George and Maud Gladys Reed; *m* 1947, Ruby; two *s*. *Educ:* Sir George Monoux Grammar Sch., Walthamstow; University Coll. London (BScEng, MScEng, PhD). Engineering Officer, RNVR, 1945–47; Fuel Research Station, 1950–58; Warren Spring Laboratory, 1958–70; Central Unit on Environmental

Pollution, DoE, 1970–79; Head, Air and Noise Div., DoE, 1979–81. *Address:* 20 Deards Wood, Knebworth, Herts SG3 6PG. *T:* Stevenage (01438) 813272.

REED, Sir Nigel (Vernon), Kt 1970; CBE 1967 (MBE (mil.) 1945); TD 1950; Chief Justice of the Northern States of Nigeria, 1968–75; *b* 31 Oct. 1913; *s* of Vernon Herbert Reed, formerly MP and MLC New Zealand, and of Eila Mabel Reed; *m* 1945, Ellen Elizabeth Langstaff; one *s* two *d*. *Educ:* Wanganui Collegiate School, NZ; Victoria University College, NZ; Jesus College, Cambridge. LLB (NZ) and LLB (Cantab). Called to the Bar, Lincoln's Inn, 1939. Military Service, 1939–45, Lt-Col 1944. Appointed to Colonial Legal Service, 1946; Magistrate, Nigeria, 1946; Chief Magistrate, Nigeria, 1951; Chief Registrar, High Court of the Northern Region of Nigeria, 1955; Judge, High Court of the Northern Region of Nigeria, 1956; Sen. Puisne Judge, High Court of Northern Nigeria, 1964. Comr for Law Revision in States of N Nigeria, 1988–. *Address:* 33 Bayview Road, Paihia, Bay of Islands, New Zealand.

REED, (Robert) Oliver; actor; *b* 13 Feb. 1938; *s* of Peter and Marcia Reed; one *s* one *d*; *m* 1985, Josephine Burge. *Educ:* Ewel Castle. Films include: Oliver, 1967; Women In Love, 1969; The Devils, 1971; Three Musketeers, 1974; Tommy, 1975; The Prince and the Pauper, 1977; Lion of the Desert, Condorman, 1981; Venom, The Sting II, 1982; Second Chance, 1983; Captive, Castaway, 1986; The Adventures of Baron Munchausen, 1989; The Return of the Musketeers, 1989; Treasure Island, 1990; Prisoners of Honour, 1991; Funny Bones, 1995. Return to Lonesome Dove (television series), 1993. *Publication:* Reed All About Me, 1979. *Recreations:* Rugby, racing. *Address:* c/o ICM, Oxford House, 76 Oxford Street, W1N 0AX.

REED, Stanley William; Director, British Film Institute, 1964–72, Consultant on Regional Development, 1972–76; *b* 21 Jan. 1911; *s* of Sidney James Reed and Ellen Maria Patient; *m* 1937, Alicia Mary Chapman; three *d*. *Educ:* Stratford Grammar Sch.; Coll. of St Mark and St John, Chelsea. Teacher in E London schools, 1931–39. In charge of school evacuation parties, 1939–45. Teacher and Visual Aids Officer, West Ham Education Cttee, 1939–50. British Film Institute: Educn Officer, 1950–56; Sec., 1956–64. *Publications:* The Cinema, 1952; How Films are Made, 1955; A Guide to Good Viewing, 1961. Neighbourhood 15 (film, also Dir). *Recreations:* opera and exploring London's suburbs. *Address:* 54 Felstead Road, Wanstead, E11 2QL. *T:* 0181–989 6021.

REED, Prof. Terence James, FBA 1987; Taylor Professor of the German Language and Literature, and Fellow, Queen's College, Oxford, since 1989; *b* 16 April 1937; *s* of William Reed and Ellen (*née* Silcox); *m* 1960, Ann Macpherson; one *s* one *d*. *Educ:* Shooters' Hill Grammar Sch., Woolwich; Brasenose Coll., Oxford (MA). Sen. Scholar, Christ Church, Oxford, 1960–61; Jun. Res. Fellow, Brasenose Coll., Oxford, 1961–63; Fellow and Tutor in Mod. Langs, St John's Coll., Oxford, 1963–88. Pres., English Goethe Soc., 1995–. Co-founder and Editor, Oxford German Studies, 1965–; Editor, Oxford Magazine, 1985–. *Publications:* (ed) Death in Venice, 1972, German edn 1983; Thomas Mann, The Uses of Tradition, 1974; The Classical Centre: Goethe and Weimar 1775–1832, 1980, German edn 1982; Goethe, 1984; (trans.) Heinrich Heine: Deutschland, a not so sentimental journey, 1986; Schiller, 1991; Death in Venice: making and unmaking a master, 1994. *Recreation:* hill walking. *Address:* 14 Crick Road, Oxford OX2 6QL. *T:* Oxford (01865) 58511.

REED, Most Rev. Thomas Thornton, CBE 1980; MA, DLitt, ThD; *b* Eastwood, South Australia, 9 Sept. 1902; *s* of Alfred Ernest Reed, Avoca, Vic; *m* 1932, Audrey Airlie, *d* of Major Harry Lort Spencer Balfour-Ogilvy, MBE, DCM, Tannadice, Renmark, South Australia; two *d* (and one *d* decd). *Educ:* Collegiate Sch. of St Peter, Adelaide; Trinity College, University of Melbourne (Hon. Schol., BA, MA); St Barnabas' Theol. Coll., Adelaide. ThL, ATC, 1st cl. hons. Fred Johns Schol. for Biography, Univ. of Adelaide, 1950. Deacon, 1926; Priest, 1927; Curate, St Augustine's, Unley, 1926–28; Priest in Charge, Berri Mission, 1928–29; Resident Tutor, St Mark's Coll., Univ. of Adelaide, and Area Padre, Toc H, 1929–31; Asst Chaplain, Melbourne Grammar Sch., 1932–36; Rector, St Michael's, Henley Beach, 1936–44; Rector, St Theodore's, Rose Park, 1944–54; Chaplain, Australian Mil. Forces, 1939–57; Chaplain, AIF with HQ, New Guinea Force, 1944–45; Asst Tutor, St Barnabas' Coll., 1940–46; Senior Chaplain, RAAChD, HQ, C Command, South Australia, 1953–56; Editor, Adelaide Church Guardian, 1940–44; Rural Dean, Western Suburbs, 1944; Priest Comr, Adelaide Dio. Centenary, 1947; Canon of Adelaide, 1947–49; Archdeacon of Adelaide, 1949–53; Dean of Adelaide, 1953–57; Bishop of Adelaide, 1957–73; Archbishop of Adelaide, and Metropolitan of S Australia, 1973–75. Pres., Toc H, S Aust., 1960; Pres., St Mark's Coll., Univ. of Adelaide, 1961–74, Hon. Fellow, 1973. Hon. ThD, Australian Coll. of Theology, 1955; DLitt, Univ. of Adelaide, 1954. Chaplain and Sub Prelate of Venerable Order of St John of Jerusalem, 1965. *Publications:* Henry Kendall: A Critical Appreciation, 1960; Sonnets and Songs, 1962; (ed) The Poetical Works of Henry Kendall, 1966; A History of the Cathedral Church of St Peter, Adelaide, 1969; Historic Churches of Australia, 1978. *Recreations:* golf, research on Australian literature, heraldry, and genealogy. *Address:* 44 Jeffcott Street, North Adelaide, SA 5006, Australia. *T:* 2674841; PO Box 130, North Adelaide, SA 5006, Australia. *Clubs:* Adelaide, Naval, Military and Air Force, Royal Adelaide Golf (Adelaide).

REED-PURVIS, Air Vice-Marshal Henry, CB 1982; OBE 1972; Sales Director, British Aerospace Dynamics Group, 1983–89; *b* 1 July 1928; *s* of late Henry Reed and of Nancy Reed-Purvis; *m* 1951, Isabel Price; three *d*. *Educ:* King James I School, Durham; Durham Univ. BSc Hons 1950. Entered RAF, 1950; various Op. Sqdns, 1951–58; Instr, Jt Nuclear Biological and Chemical Sch., 1958–60; RMCS Shrivenham (Nuclear Sci. and Tech.), 1961; MoD Staff, 1962–64; OC No 63 Sqdn, RAF Regt, Malaya, 1964–66; Exchange Duties, USAF, 1966–69; USAF War Coll., 1969–70; OC No 5 Wing RAF Regt, 1970–72; Gp Capt. Regt, HQ Strike Comd, 1972–74, HQ RAF Germany, 1974–76; ADC to the Queen, 1974–76; Dir, RAF Regt, 1976–79; Comdt Gen. RAF Regt and Dir Gen. of Security (RAF) 1979–83. Mem. Exec. Cttee, Forces Help Soc. and Lord Roberts Workshops, 1986–; Vice Pres., Council for Cadet Rifle Shooting, 1985–. *Recreations:* golf, bridge and music. *Address:* Cobb House, Bampton, Oxon OX18 2LW. *T:* Bampton Castle (01993) 851032. *Club:* Royal Air Force.

REEDER, John; QC 1989; a Recorder, since 1991; *b* 18 Jan. 1949; *s* of Frederick and Barbara Reeder; *m* 1971, Barbara Kotlarz (marr. diss. 1994); *m* 1995, Pauline Madden. *Educ:* Catholic Coll., Preston; University Coll. London (LLM); PhD Birmingham 1976. Called to the Bar, Gray's Inn, 1971, NSW 1986. Lectr in Law, Univ. of Birmingham, 1971–76; commenced practice, 1976; Junior Counsel to the Treasury (Admiralty), 1981–89. Lawyer, PNG, 1984. *Recreations:* sailing, travel. *Address:* Queen Elizabeth Building, 1st Floor, Temple, EC4Y 9BS. *T:* 0171–353 9153; Gannets, Kelvedon Road, Tolleshunt D'Arcy, Essex CM9 8TE. *Club:* Royal Corinthian Yacht.

REEDIE, Craig Collins; Chairman, British Olympic Association, since 1992; Member, International Olympic Committee, since 1994; *b* 6 May 1941; *s* of late Robert Lindsay Reedie and Anne Reedie; *m* 1967, Rosemary Jane Biggart; one *s* one *d*. *Educ:* High Sch., Stirling; Univ. of Glasgow (MA, LLB). Partner, D. L. Bloomer & Partners, Glasgow, 1966–. Pres., Scottish Badminton Union, Internat. Badminton Fedn, 1981–84; Mem. Council and Treas., Gen. Assoc. of Internat. Sports Fedns, 1984–92. *Recreations:* reading, golf, sport, sport and more sport. *Address:* 53 Bothwell Street, Glasgow G2 6TS. *T:* 0141–248 7268. *Clubs:* Royal & Ancient Golf (St Andrews), Western Gailes Golf, Ranfurly Castle Golf.

REEDY, Norris John, (Jack); media consultant, since 1994: Haslimann-Taylor Ltd; Institute of Directors (Midlands); Prince's Youth Business Trust (West Midlands); *b* 1934; *s* of John Reedy; *m* 1964, Sheila Campbell McGregor; one *d*. *Educ:* Chorlton High Sch., Manchester; Univ. of Sheffield. Sheffield Telegraph, 1956; Sunday Times, 1961; Lancashire Evening Telegraph, 1962; Guardian, 1964; Birmingham Post, 1964–82 (Editor, 1974–82); Regl Officer, Midlands, 1983–88, Sen. Nat. and Regl Officer, 1988–94, IBA, subseq. ITC. Former Chm. and Nat. Vice-Pres., W Midlands Region, Guild of British Newspaper Editors; Secretary: Birmingham Press Club Ltd; Midlands Centre, Royal Television Soc.; Council Mem., Rotary Club of Birmingham. Chm., Recruitment and Publicity, TA & VRA. *Recreations:* astronomy, natural history, painting, photography. *Address:* The Old Manor, Rowington, near Warwick CV35 7DJ. *T:* Lapworth (015643) 3129.

REEKIE, Henry Enfield; Headmaster of Felsted School, 1951–68; *b* Hayfield, Derbyshire, 17 Oct. 1907; *s* of John Albert Reekie and Edith Dowson; *m* 1936, Pauline Rosalind, *d* of Eric W. Seeman; one *s* three *d*. *Educ:* Oundle; Clare College, Cambridge. Asst Master, Felsted School, 1929, Housemaster, 1933, Senior Science Master, 1945; Headmaster, St Bees School, 1946. *Recreations:* ski-ing, gardening, travel. *Address:* Tarn House, Mark Cross, Crowborough, East Sussex TN6 3NT. *T:* Mayfield (01435) 873100. *Club:* East India, Devonshire, Sports and Public Schools.

REES; *see* Merlyn-Rees.

REES, family name of **Baron Rees.**

REES, Baron *cr* 1987 (Life Peer), of Goytre in the County of Gwent; **Peter Wynford Innes Rees;** PC 1983; QC 1969; Deputy Chairman, Leopold Joseph Holdings Plc, since 1985; director of companies; *b* 9 Dec. 1926; *s* of late Maj.-Gen. T. W. Rees, Indian Army, Goytre Hall, Abergavenny; *m* 1969, Mrs Anthea Wendell, *d* of late Major H. J. M. Hyslop, Argyll and Sutherland Highlanders. *Educ:* Stowe; Christ Church, Oxford. Served Scots Guards, 1945–48. Called to the Bar, 1953, Bencher, Inner Temple, 1976; Oxford Circuit. Contested (C): Abertillery, 1964 and 1965; Liverpool, West Derby, 1966. MP (C): Dover, 1970–74 and 1983–87; Dover and Deal, 1974–83; PPS to Solicitor General, 1972; Minister of State, HM Treasury, 1979–81; Minister for Trade, 1981–83; Chief Sec. to HM Treasury, 1983–85. Chairman: General Cable Ltd, 1990–95; Westminster Industrial Brief, 1990–92; General Mobile Communications, 1991–; Quadrant Group, 1992–; London and Scottish Marine Oil plc, subseq. LASMO, 1988–94; Director: James Finlay, 1986–92; Fleming Mercantile Investment Trust, 1987–; Bradford Cable Communications Ltd, 1990–92; Cable Corp., 1990–95; Talkland International, 1991–; Yorkshire Cable Communications Ltd, 1992–95; Sheffield Cable Media Ltd, 1992–95. Chm., Economic Forestry Group, 1989–93. Chm., Duty Free Confedn, 1987–. Member: Council and Court of Governors, Museum of Wales, 1987–; Museums and Galleries Commn, 1988–. *Address:* 39 Headfort Place, SW1X 7DE; Goytre Hall, Abergavenny, Gwent NP7 9DL. *Clubs:* Boodle's, Beefsteak, White's, Pratt's.

REES, Prof. Andrew Jackson; Regius Professor of Medicine, University of Aberdeen, since 1994; *b* 11 June 1946; *s* of Gordon Jackson Rees and Elisabeth Rees; *m* 1st, 1972, Ann Duncan (marr. diss. 1974); 2nd, 1979, Daphne Elizabeth Wood (marr. diss. 1985); two *d*. *Educ:* King William's Coll., Isle of Man; Liverpool Univ. (MB ChB 1969); London Univ. (MSc). Trained in gen. medicine and nephrology, at Liverpool, Guy's, and Hammersmith Hosps, 1969–79; Consultant Physician, Hammersmith Hosp., 1979–90; Prof. of Nephrology, RPMS, 1990–94. Vis. Prof., Nat. Jewish Hosp., Denver, 1983–84; Goulstonian Lectr, RCP, 1984. Pres., Nephrology Section, RSocMed, 1994–95. Chm., Nat. Kidney Res. Fund, 1995. *Publications:* papers on pathogenesis and treatment of glomerulonephritis. *Recreations:* contemporary theatre and music, ski-ing. *Address:* 2 Thom's Place, Old Aberdeen AB2 3EW. *T:* Aberdeen (01224) 480521.

REES, (Anthony) John (David); Director, Harrow Development Trust, since 1995; *b* 20 July 1943; *s* of Richard Frederick and Betty Rees; *m* 1967, Carol Stubbens; one *s* one *d* (and one *d* decd). *Educ:* Newcastle Royal Grammar Sch.; Clare Coll., Cambridge (Exhibr; BA 2nd Cl. Hons Geog.); PGCE 1966. Head of Economics, Harrow Sch., 1966–80; Head Master, Blundell's Sch., Tiverton, Devon, 1980–92; Rector, Edinburgh Acad., 1992–95. Established Notting Dale Urban Study Centre, 1972; Vis. Tutor, London Inst. of Education, 1973–. Member Executive Committee: Queen's Silver Jubilee Appeal, 1976–82; and Admin. Council, Royal Jubilee Trusts, 1978–82; Chairman: Prince's Trust for Devon, 1981–83; Youth Clubs UK, 1987–89; Founder Dir, Mid Devon Enterprise Agency, 1984–91; Member: CoSIRA Cttee for Devon, 1981–83; Council, Drake Fellowship, 1981–; Cttee, HMC, 1986–91; Bd, Youth Business Initiatives, 1984–; Prince of Wales Community Venture, 1985–; Board: Devon and Cornwall Prince's Youth Business Trust, 1987–92; Fairbridge in Scotland, 1992–95. *Publications:* articles on economics and community service in many jls incl. Economics, Youth in Society, etc. *Recreations:* hill walking, family and friends. *Address:* 5 High Street, Harrow-on-the-Hill, Mddx HA1 3HT.

REES, Arthur Morgan, CBE 1974 (OBE 1963); QPM 1970; DL; Chairman, St John's Staffordshire, since 1974; *b* 20 Nov. 1912; *s* of Thomas and Jane Rees, The Limes, Llangadog; *m* 1943, Dorothy Webb (*d* 1988); one *d*. *Educ:* Llandovery Coll.; St Catharine's Coll., Cambridge. BA 1935, MA 1939. Metropolitan Police, 1935–41; RAF (Pilot), 1941–46 (Subst. Sqdn Ldr; Actg Wing Comdr); Metropolitan Police, 1946–57; Chief Constable: Denbighshire, 1957–64; Staffordshire, 1964–77. Consultant Director: for Wales, Britannia Building Soc., 1983–88; Inter-Globe Security Services Ltd, 1986–88. Chm. (Founder), EPIC, ExPolice in Industry and Commerce, 1978–. Life Mem., Midlands Sports Adv. Cttee, 1981; Chm., Queen's Silver Jubilee Appeal (Sport), 1976–; Mem., King George's Jubilee Trust Council, 1973–; Chm., The Prince's Trust Cttee (Sport and Leisure), 1981–88. Chm., British Karate Fedn, 1982–; President: Welsh Karate Fedn; Staffs Playing Fields Assoc., 1985–; Dep. Pres., Staffs Assoc. of Boys' Clubs, 1975–; Chm., Staffs St John Ambulance Brigade, 1970. Trustee and Board of Governors, Llandovery College; Mem. Court, Univ. of Keele, 1981–84. Founder Pres., Eccleshall Rugby Football Club, 1980–; Founder and Life Pres., EPIC (Ex Police in Industry and Commerce), 1988. DL Staffs, 1967. KStJ 1977 (CStJ 1969). *Recreations:* former Rugby International for Wales (14 caps), Cambridge Rugby Blue, 1933 and 1934; played Welsh Schs Hockey Internationals, 1930; Pres., Crawshays Welsh Rugby XV, 1992– (Chm., 1960–92). *Address:* National Westminster Bank, Eccleshall, near Stafford ST21 6BP. *Clubs:* Royal Air Force; Hawks (Cambridge) (Vice-Chm. 1985, Chm. 1986).

REES, Brian, MA Cantab; Headmaster, Rugby School, 1981–84; *b* 20 Aug. 1929; *s* of late Frederick T. Rees; *m* 1st, 1959, Julia (*d* 1978), *d* of Sir Robert Birley, KCMG; two *s* three *d*; 2nd, 1987, Juliet Akehurst. *Educ:* Bede Grammar Sch., Sunderland; Trinity Coll., Cambridge (Scholar). 1st cl. Historical Tripos, Part I, 1951; Part II, 1952. Eton College: Asst Master, 1952–65; Housemaster, 1963–65; Headmaster: Merchant Taylors' Sch., 1965–73; Charterhouse, 1973–81. Pres., Conference for Independent Further Education,

1973–82; Chm., ISIS, 1982–84. Res. Fellow, City Univ., 1989–90. Patron, UC of Buckingham, 1973–91. Liveryman, Merchant Taylors' Co., 1981. *Publications:* A Musical Peacemaker: biography of Sir Edward German, 1987; (ed) History and Idealism: essays, addresses and letters, by Sir Robert Birley, 1990. *Recreations:* music, painting. *Address:* 52 Spring Lane, Flore, Northants NN7 4LS. *T:* Weedon (01327) 340621.

REES, Prof. Brinley Roderick, MA Oxon; PhD, Hon. LLD Wales; Principal, Saint David's University College, Lampeter, 1975–80; *b* 27 Dec. 1919; *s* of John David Rees and Mary Ann (*née* Roderick); *m* 1951, Zena Muriel Stella Mayall; two *s*. *Educ:* Christ Coll., Brecon; Merton Coll., Oxford (Postmaster). 1st Cl., Class. Hons Mods and Hon. Mention, Craven and Ireland Schols, 1946. Welch Regt, 1940–45. Asst Classics Master, Christ Coll., Brecon, 1947; Cardiff High Sch., 1947–48; Asst Lectr in Classics, University Coll. of Wales Aberystwyth, 1948–49; Lectr 1949–56; Sen. Lectr in Greek, Univ. of Manchester, 1956–58; UC Cardiff: Prof. of Greek, 1958–70; Dean of Faculty of Arts, 1963–65; Dean of Students, 1967–68; Hon. Lectr, 1980–88; Prof. Emeritus, 1981; Vice-Pres., 1986–88; University of Birmingham: Prof. of Greek, 1970–75; Dean of Faculty of Arts, 1973–75; Hon. Life Mem. of Court, 1983. Welsh Supernumerary Fellow, Jesus Coll., Oxford, 1975–76; Leverhulme Emeritus Fellow, 1984–86. Hon. Secretary, Classical Association, 1963–69, Vice-Pres., 1969–78, 1979–, Pres., 1978–79. Hon. LLD Wales, 1981. *Publications:* The Merton Papyri, Vol. II (with H. I. Bell and J. W. B. Barns), 1959; The Use of Greek, 1961; Papyri from Hermopolis and other Byzantine Documents, 1964; (with M. E. Jervis) Lampas: a new approach to Greek, 1970; Classics: an outline for intending students, 1970; Aristotle's Theory and Milton's Practice, 1972; Strength in What Remains, 1980; Pelagius: a reluctant heretic, 1988; Letters of Pelagius and his Followers, 1991; articles and reviews in various classical and other jls. *Address:* 31 Stephenson Court, Wordsworth Avenue, Cardiff CF2 1AX. *T:* Cardiff (01222) 472058.

REES, Prof. Charles Wayne, CBE 1995; DSc; FRS 1974; FRSC; Hofmann Professor of Organic Chemistry, Imperial College, London, 1978–93, now Emeritus Professor; *b* 15 Oct. 1927; *s* of Percival Charles Rees and Daisy Alice Beck; *m* 1953, Patricia Mary Francis; three *s*. *Educ:* Farnham Grammar Sch.; University Coll., Southampton (BSc, PhD). Lectr in Organic Chem.: Birkbeck Coll., Univ. of London, 1955–57; King's Coll., Univ. of London, 1957–63, Reader, 1963–65; Prof. of Organic Chem., Univ. of Leicester, 1965–69; Prof. of Organic Chem., 1969–77, Heath Harrison Prof. of Organic Chem., 1977–78, Univ. of Liverpool. Visiting Prof., Univ. of Würzburg, 1968. Royal Society of Chemistry (formerly Chemical Society): Tilden Lectr, 1973–74; Award in Heterocyclic Chem., 1980; Pres., Perkin Div., 1981–83; Pedler Lectr, 1984–85; Pres., 1992–94; Pres., Chemistry Sect., BAAS, 1984. Hon. DSc Leicester, 1994. *Publications:* Organic Reaction Mechanism (8 annual vols), 1965–72; Carbenes, Nitrenes, Arynes, 1969; (ed jtly) Comprehensive Heterocyclic Chemistry (8 vols), 1984; about 330 research papers and reviews, mostly in jls of Chemical Soc. *Recreations:* music, theatre, London. *Address:* Department of Chemistry, Imperial College of Science, Technology and Medicine, South Kensington, SW7 2AY. *T:* 0171–594 5768, *Fax:* 0171–594 5800.

REES, Sir (Charles William) Stanley, Kt 1962; TD 1949; DL; Judge of High Court of Justice, Family Division (formerly Probate, Divorce and Admiralty Division), 1962–77; *b* 30 Nov. 1907; *s* of Dr David Charles Rees, MRCS, LRCP, and Myrtle May (*née* Dolley); *m* 1934, Jean Isabel Munro Wheildon (*d* 1985); one *s*. *Educ:* St Andrew's College, Grahamstown, S Africa; University College, Oxford. BA, BCL (Oxon). Called to the Bar, 1931; Bencher, Inner Temple, 1962. 2nd Lt 99th Regt AA RA (London Welsh), 1939; JAG's office in Home Commands, 1940–43; Lt-Col in charge JAG's Branch, HQ Palestine Command, 1944–45; released from military service as Hon. Lt-Col, 1945. QC 1957; Recorder of Croydon, 1961–62; Commissioner of Assize, Stafford, Dec. 1961; Dep. Chm., 1959–64, Chm., 1964–71, E Sussex QS. DL E Sussex (formerly Sussex), 1968. Chm., Statutory Cttee, Pharmaceutical Soc. of GB, 1980–81. Governor, Brighton College, 1954–83 (Pres., 1973–83; Vice Patron, 1983). *Recreation:* mountain walking. *Address:* Lark Rise, Lyoth Lane, Lindfield, Haywards Heath, W Sussex RH16 2QA. *Clubs:* United Oxford & Cambridge University, Sussex.
See also Harland Rees.

REES, Sir Dai; *see* Rees, Sir David A.

REES, Prof. David, FRS 1968; Emeritus Professor of Pure Mathematics, University of Exeter (Professor, 1958–83); *b* 29 May 1918; *s* of David and Florence Gertrude Rees; *m* 1952, Joan Sybil Cushen; four *d*. *Educ:* King Henry VIII Grammar School, Abergavenny; Sidney Sussex College, Cambridge. Manchester University: Assistant Lecturer, 1945–46, Lecturer, 1946–49; Cambridge University: Lecturer, 1949–58; Fellow of Downing College, Cambridge, 1950–58, Hon. Fellow, 1970–. Mem. Council, Royal Soc., 1979–81. Hon. DSc Exeter, 1993. Polya Prize, London Mathematical Soc., 1993. *Publications:* papers on Algebraic topics in British and foreign mathematical journals. *Recreations:* reading and listening to music. *Address:* 6 Hillcrest Park, Exeter EX4 4SH. *T:* Exeter (01392) 59398.

REES, Sir David Allan, (Sir Dai Rees), Kt 1993; BSc, PhD, DSc; FRCPath; FRS 1981; FRSC, FIBiol; Secretary, Medical Research Council, since 1987; *b* 28 April 1936; *s* of James Allan Rees and Elsie Bolam; *m* 1959, Myfanwy Margaret Parry Owen; two *s* one *d*. *Educ:* Hawarden Grammar Sch., Clwyd; University Coll. of N Wales, Bangor, Gwynedd (BSc 1956; PhD 1959; Hon. Fellow, 1988). DSc Edinburgh, 1970. FRCPath 1992. DSIR Res. Fellow, University Coll., Bangor, 1959, and Univ. of Edinburgh, 1960; Asst Lectr in Chem., 1961, Lectr, 1962–70, Univ. of Edinburgh; Section Manager, 1970–72, Principal Scientist, 1972–82, and Sci. Policy Exec., 1978–82, Unilever Res., Colworth Lab.; Chm., Science Policy Gp for Unilever Res., 1979–82. Associate Dir (pt-time), MRC Unit for Cell Biophysics, KCL, 1980–82; Dir, Nat. Inst. for Med. Res., Mill Hill, 1982–87. Vis. Professorial Fellow, University Coll., Cardiff, 1972–77. Philips Lecture, Royal Soc., 1984. Member: MRC, 1984–; Council, Royal Soc., 1985–87. Pres., ESF, 1994–. FKC 1989. Hon. FRCP 1986. Hon. DSc: Edinburgh, 1989; Wales, 1991; Stirling, 1995. Colworth Medal, Biochemical Soc., 1970; Carbohydrate Award, Chemical Soc., 1970. *Publications:* various, on carbohydrate chem. and biochem. and cell biology. *Recreations:* river boats, reading, listening to music.

REES, Eleri Mair; Metropolitan Stipendiary Magistrate, since 1994; *b* 7 July 1953; *d* of late Ieuan Morgan and Sarah Alice Morgan (*née* James); *m* 1975, Alan Rees. *Educ:* Ardwyn Grammar Sch., Aberystwyth; Univ. of Liverpool (LLB Hons). Called to the Bar, Gray's Inn, 1975. Court Clerk, Cardiff Magistrates' Court, 1975–82; Bexley Magistrates' Court: Dep. Clerk to Justices, 1982–83; Clerk to Justices, 1983–94. Editor, Family Court Reporter, 1992–94. Mem., Magisterial Cttee, Judicial Studies Bd, 1989–94. *Publications:* contrib. various jls on subject of family law. *Recreations:* travel, cookery, ski-ing. *Address:* Inner London Magistrates' Courts Service, 65 Romney Street, SW1P 3RD.

REES, Harland, MA, MCh, FRCS; Hon. Consultant Urological Surgeon, King's College Hospital; Hon. Consultant Surgeon and Urological Surgeon, Royal Free Hospital; *b* 21 Sept. 1909; *yr s* of Dr David Charles Rees, MRCS, LRCP, and Myrtle May (*née* Dolley); *m* 1950, Helen Marie Tarver; two *s* (one *d* decd). *Educ:* St Andrew's Coll., Grahamstown, S Africa; University Coll., Oxford; Charing Cross Hospital. Rhodes Scholar, Oxford University. Served RAMC, 1942–46; OC Surgical Div. 53, Indian General Hospital. Adviser in Surgery, Siam (Thailand). Examiner in Surgery, University of Cambridge, 1963–73. Councillor (C), S Beds DC, 1978– (Chm., 1986–87). *Publications:* articles and chapters in various books and journals, 1952–63. *Recreations:* walking, cultivation of trees; Rugby football, Oxford *v* Cambridge, 1932–33. *Address:* Kensworth Gorse, Kensworth, near Dunstable, Beds LU6 3RF. *T:* Whipsnade (01582) 872411. *Club:* Vincent's (Oxford).
See also Hon. Sir C. W. S. Rees.

REES, Haydn; *see* Rees, T. M. H.

REES, Helen Blodwen; Assistant Director and Head of Public Affairs, National Art Collections Fund, since 1992; *b* 23 Aug. 1960; *d* of Edward Elgar Rees and Dorothy Rees (*née* Banham). *Educ:* Gaisford High Sch. for Girls, Worthing; New Hall, Cambridge (MA); City Univ. Information Officer, Conran Foundn, 1984–86; Curator, 1986–89, Dir, 1989–92, Design Mus.; Communications Dir, Eureka!, The Mus. for Children, 1992. Member: Adv. Panel, Arts Council of England, 1992–95; Design Adv. Cttee, RSA, 1990–94. Gov., Design Dimension Educnl Trust, 1990–. Editor (and contrib.) Design Museum Publications, 1989–92. *Publications:* 14:24 British Youth Culture, 1986; (contrib.) The Authority of the Consumer, ed Nigel Whiteley, 1993. *Recreations:* friends, films, books. *Address:* 70 Amsterdam Road, E14 3JB. *T:* 0171–538 3230.

REES, Prof. Hubert, DFC 1945; PhD, DSc; FRS 1976; Professor of Agricultural Botany, University College of Wales, Aberystwyth, 1968–91, now Emeritus; *b* 2 Oct. 1923; *s* of Owen Rees and Tugela Rees, Llangennech, Carmarthenshire; *m* 1946, Mavis Hill; two *s* two *d*. *Educ:* Llandovery and Llanelli Grammar Schs; University Coll. of Wales, Aberystwyth (BSc). PhD, DSc Birmingham. Served RAF, 1942–46. Student, Aberystwyth, 1946–50; Lectr in Cytology, Univ. of Birmingham, 1950–58; Sen. Lectr in Agric. Botany, University Coll. of Wales, Aberystwyth, 1958, Reader 1966. *Publications:* Chromosome Genetics, 1977; B Chromosomes, 1982; articles on genetic control of chromosomes and on evolutionary changes in chromosome organisation. *Recreation:* fishing. *Address:* Irfon, Llanbadarn Road, Aberystwyth, Dyfed SY23 1EY. *T:* Aberystwyth (01970) 623668.

REES, Hugh; *see* Rees, J. E. H.

REES, Hugh Francis E.; *see* Ellis-Rees.

REES, Rt. Rev. Ivor; *see* Rees, Rt Rev. J. I.

REES, John; *see* Rees, A. J. D.

REES, John Charles; QC 1991; *b* 22 May 1949; *s* of Ronald Leslie Rees and Martha Therese Rees; *m* 1970, Dianne Elizabeth Kirby; three *s* one *d*. *Educ:* St Illtyd's College, Cardiff; Jesus College, Cambridge (double first class Hons; BA (Law), LLB (Internat. Law), MA, LLM; repr. Univ. in boxing and Association Football; boxing Blue). Called to the Bar, Lincoln's Inn, 1972. Trustee and Governor, St John's College, Cardiff, 1987–. Representative Steward, and Chm., Welsh Area Council, BBB of C. *Recreations:* all sport, esp. boxing and Association Football; theatre. *Address:* Marleigh Lodge, Druidstone Road, Old St Mellons, Cardiff CF3 9XD. *T:* Cardiff (01222) 794918; 33 Park Place, Cardiff CF1 3BA. *Club:* Hawks (Cambridge).

REES, (John Edward) Hugh; Chartered Surveyor; *b* 8 Jan. 1928; *s* of David Emlyn Rees, Swansea; *m* 1961, Gillian Dian Milo-Jones (decd); two *s*. MP (C) Swansea, West Division, Oct. 1959–64; Assistant Government Whip, 1962–64. UK Rep., Econ. and Soc. Cttee, EEC, 1972–78. Dir, Abbey National plc (formerly Abbey National Building Soc.), 1976–91; Chm., Abbey Housing Association Ltd., 1980–92. Mem., Welsh Develt Agency, 1980–86. Trustee, Ffynone House Sch. Trust, 1973– (Chm. 1977–85). Formerly Governor, Nat. Mus. of Wales. FRICS. *Address:* Sherwood, 35 Caswell Road, Newton, Mumbles, Swansea, W Glamorgan SA3 4SD.

REES, Rt Rev. (John) Ivor; Bishop of St Davids, 1991–95; *b* 19 Feb. 1926; *o s* of David Morgan Rees and Cecilia Perrott Rees; *m* 1954, Beverley Richards; three *s*. *Educ:* Llanelli Gram. Sch.; University Coll. of Wales (BA 1950); Westcott House, Cambridge. Served RN, Coastal Forces and British Pacific Fleet, 1943–47. Deacon 1952, priest 1953, Dio. St David's; Curate: Fishguard, 1952–55; Llangathen, 1955–57; Priest-in-Charge, Uzmaston, 1957–59; Vicar: Slebech and Uzmaston, 1959–65; Llangollen, 1965–74; Rural Dean of Llangollen, 1970–74; Rector of Wrexham, 1974–76; Dean of Bangor, 1976–88; Vicar of Cathedral Parish of Bangor, 1979–88; Archdeacon of St Davids and Asst Bp, Dio. of St Davids, 1988–91. Canon of St Asaph, 1975–76; Chaplain, Order of St John for County of Clwyd, 1974–76, County of Gwynedd, 1976–88. SBStJ 1975, OStJ 1981, Sub-Prelate, 1993. *Publications:* Monograph—The Parish of Llangollen and its Churches, 1971; Keeping 40 Days—Sermons for Lent, 1989. *Recreations:* music and good light reading. *Address:* Llys Dewi, 45 Clover Park, Uzmaston Road, Haverfordwest, Dyfed SA61 1UE. *T:* Haverfordwest (01437) 764846.

REES, John Samuel; editorial consultant; Editor, Western Mail, 1981–87; *b* 23 Oct. 1931; *s* of John Richard Rees and Mary Jane Rees; *m* 1957, Ruth Jewell; one *s* one *d*. *Educ:* Cyfarthfa Castle Grammar Sch., Merthyr Tydfil. Nat. Service, Welch Regt and RAEC, 1950–52. Reporter, 1948–50, Sports Editor, 1952–54, Merthyr Express; The Star, ,Sheffield: Reporter, 1954–56; Sub Editor, 1956–58; Dep. Chief Sub Editor, 1958–59; Dep. Sports Editor, 1959–61; Asst Editor, 1961–66; Dep. Editor, Evening Echo, Hemel Hempstead, 1966–69; Editor: Evening Mail, Slough and Hounslow, 1969–72; The Journal, Newcastle upon Tyne, 1972–76; Evening Post-Echo, Hemel Hempstead, 1976–79, Asst Man. Dir, Evening Post-Echo Ltd, 1979–81. Lectr, Centre for Journalism Studies, Univ. of Wales Coll. of Cardiff, 1988–92. *Recreations:* marquetry, watching cricket and rugby, walking, gardening. *Address:* 2 Alton Close, Whirlowdale Park, Sheffield S11 9QQ. *T:* Sheffield (0114) 235 1028.

REES, Prof. Lesley Howard, FRCP; FRCPath; Professor of Chemical Endocrinology, since 1978, Dean since 1989, St Bartholomew's Hospital Medical College; *b* 17 Nov. 1942; *d* of Howard Leslie Davis and Charlotte Patricia Siegrid Young; *m* 1969, Gareth Mervyn Rees. *Educ:* Pates Girls' Grammar Sch., Cheltenham; Malvern Girls' Coll.; London Univ. (MB BS 1965; MD 1972; MSc 1974; DSc 1989). MRCP 1967, FRCP 1979; MRCPath 1976, FRCPath 1988. Editor, Clinical Endocrinology, 1979–84; Subdean, St Bartholomew's Hosp. Med. Coll., 1983–88; Public Orator, London Univ., 1984–86. Chm., Soc. for Endocrinology, 1984–87; Sec.-Gen., Internat. Soc. of Endocrinology, 1984–. Mem., Press Complaints Commn, 1991–94. *Recreations:* music, poetry, reading, ski-ing, administrative gardening. *Address:* 23 Church Row, Hampstead, NW3 6UP. *T:* 0171–794 4936. *Club:* Mosimann's.

REES, Rt. Rev. Leslie Lloyd; Assistant Bishop, Diocese of Winchester, since 1987; *b* 14 April 1919; *s* of Rees Thomas and Elizabeth Rees; *m* 1944, Rosamond Smith (*d* 1989); two *s*. *Educ:* Pontardawe Grammar Sch.; Kelham Theological College. Asst Curate, St Saviour, Roath, 1942; Asst Chaplain, HM Prison, Cardiff, 1942; Chaplain, HM Prison; Durham, 1945; Dartmoor, 1948; Vicar of Princetown, 1948; Chaplain, HM Prison, Winchester, 1955; Chaplain General of Prisons, Home Office Prison Dept, 1962–80; Bishop Suffragan of Shrewsbury, 1980–86. Chaplain to the Queen, 1971–80. Hon. Canon of Canterbury, 1966–80, of Lichfield, 1980–. Freeman, City of London. ChStJ. *Recreation:* music. *Address:* Kingfisher Lodge, Arle Gardens, Alresford, Hants SO24 9BA.

REES, Linford; *see* Rees, W. L. L.

REES, Sir Martin (John), Kt 1992; FRS 1979; Royal Society Research Professor, Cambridge University, since 1992; Fellow, King's College, Cambridge, since 1973 (and 1969–72); Astronomer Royal, since 1995; *b* 23 June 1942; *s* of late Reginald J. and Joan Rees; *m* 1986, Dr Caroline Humphrey, *d* of late Prof. C. H. Waddington. *Educ:* Shrewsbury Sch.; Trinity Coll., Cambridge. MA, PhD (Cantab). Fellow, Jesus Coll., Cambridge, 1967–69; Research Associate, California Inst. of Technology, 1967–68 and 1971; Mem., Inst. for Advanced Study, Princeton, 1969–70; Prof., Univ. of Sussex, 1972–73; Cambridge University: Plumian Prof. of Astronomy and Experimental Philosophy, 1973–91; Dir, Inst. of Astronomy, 1977–82 and 1987–91. Visiting Professor: Harvard Univ., 1972, 1986–88; Inst. for Advanced Studies, Princeton, 1982, 1995; Regents Fellow of Smithsonian Instn, Washington, 1984–88; Fairchild Vis. Scholar, CIT, 1992. President: RAS, 1992–94; BAAS, 1994–95; Chm., Science Adv. Cttee, ESA, 1976–78; Member: Council, Royal Soc., 1983–85 and 1993–95; PPARC, 1994–. Lectures: H. P. Robertson Meml, US Nat. Acad. Sci, 1975; George Darwin, Royal Astron. Soc., 1976; Halley, Oxford, 1978; Milne, Oxford, 1980; Bakerian, Royal Soc., 1982; Danz, Univ. of Washington, 1984; Lauritsen, CIT, 1987; Hitchcock, UC Berkeley, 1994. Member: Academia Europaea, 1989; Pontifical Acad. of Sci., 1990; For. Hon. Mem., Amer. Acad. of Arts and Sciences, 1975; Foreign Associate, Nat. Acad. of Sciences, USA, 1982; Foreign Member: Amer. Phil. Soc., 1993; Royal Swedish Acad. Sci., 1993; Russian Acad. of Sci., 1994. Hon. Fellow, Indian Acad. of Sci., 1990. Hon. DSc: Sussex, 1990; Leicester, 1993; Copenhagen, 1994; Keele, Newcastle and Uppsala, 1995. Hopkins Prize, Cambridge Phil. Soc., 1982; Heinemann Prize, Amer. Inst. Physics, 1984; Bappu Award, Indian Nat. Science Acad., 1986; Gold Medal, RAS, 1987; Guthrie Medal and Prize, Inst. of Physics, 1989; Balzan Prize, Balzan Foundn, 1989; Schwarzschild Medal, Astron. ges., 1989; Robinson Prize for Cosmology, Univ. of Newcastle upon Tyne, 1990; Bruce Gold Medal, Astron. Soc. of Pacific, 1993. Officier, Ordre des Arts et des Lettres (France), 1991. *Publications:* mainly articles and reviews in scientific jls. *Address:* c/o King's College, Cambridge CB2 1ST. *T:* Cambridge (01223) 350411; (office) Cambridge (01223) 337548.

REES, Meuric; *see* Rees, R. E. M.

REES, Rev. Canon Michael; *see* Rees, Rev. Canon R. M.

REES, Owen, CB 1991; Under Secretary, Welsh Office, 1977–94; *b* 26 Dec. 1934; *s* of late John Trevor and Esther Rees, Trimsaran, Dyfed; *m* 1958, Elizabeth Gosby (*d* 1991); one *s* two *d*. *Educ:* Llanelli Grammar Sch.; Univ. of Manchester. BA(Econ). Bank of London and South America, 1957; regional development work in Cardiff, Birmingham and London, BoT, 1959–69; Cabinet Office, 1969–71; Welsh Office, 1971–94; Asst Sec. (European Div.), 1972; Sec. for Welsh Educn, 1977–78; Head, Educn Dept, 1978–80; Dir, Industry Dept, 1980–85; Head, Economic and Regl Policy Gp, 1985–90; Head, Agriculture Dept, 1990–94. *Address:* 4 Llandennis Green, Cyncoed, Cardiff CF2 6JX. *T:* Cardiff (01222) 759712.

REES, Peter Magnall; a Senior Clerk, House of Lords, 1981–84; *b* 17 March 1921; *s* of late Edward Saunders Rees and Gertrude Rees (*née* Magnall); *m* 1949, Moya Mildred Carroll. *Educ:* Manchester Grammar Sch.; Jesus Coll., Oxford. Served War, RA, 1941–46 (SE Asia, 1942–45). HM Overseas Service, Nigeria, 1948; Dep. Govt Statistician, Kenya, 1956; Dir of Economics and Statistics, Kenya, 1961; HM Treasury, 1964; Chief Statistician, 1966; Under-Sec., DTI later Dept of Industry, 1973–81. Consultant, OECD, 1981. *Publications:* articles in statistical jls. *Recreations:* choral singing, music, studying architecture. *Address:* The Old Orchard, Sandford Orcas, Sherborne, Dorset DT9 4RP. *T:* Corton Denham (01963) 220244. *Club:* Commonwealth Trust.

REES, Peter Wynne, RIBA; FRTPI; City Planning Officer, Corporation of London, since 1987; *b* 26 Sept. 1948; *s* of Gwynne Rees, MM, CEng, MIMechE, FMES, and late Elizabeth Rodda Rees (*née* Hynam). *Educ:* Pontardawe Grammar Sch.; Whitchurch Grammar Sch., Cardiff; Bartlett Sch. of Architecture, UCL (BSc Hons); Welsh Sch. of Architecture, Univ. of Wales (BArch); Polytechnic of the South Bank (BTP). Architectural Asst, Historic Bldgs Div., GLC, 1971–72; Asst to Gordon Cullen, CBE, RDI, FSIA, 1973–75; Architect, Historic Areas Conservation, DoE, 1975–79; UK Rep., Council of Europe Wkg Parties studying New Uses for Historic Buildings and The Economics of Building Conservation, 1977–78; Asst Chief Planning Officer, London Bor. of Lambeth, 1979–85; Controller of Planning, Corp. of London, 1985–87. Trustee, Building Conservation Trust, 1985–91. Founder Mem. and Dir, British Council for Offices, 1989. London Rep., EC (formerly European) Working Party on Technological Impact on Future Urban Change, 1989–92; Member: Steering Gp, London World City Study, 1990–91; Officers' Gp, London Pride Partnership, 1994. FRSA 1988. *Publications:* City of London Local Plan, 1989; City of London Unitary Development Plan, 1994; contribs to professional studies and jls. *Recreations:* swimming, Nordic ski-ing, playing the viola, music, tidying. *Address:* City Planning Officer, Guildhall, EC2P 2EJ. *T:* 0171–332 1700. *Clubs:* Guildhall; Cottons.

REES, Philip; a Recorder of the Crown Court, since 1983; *b* 1 Dec. 1941; *s* of John Trevor Rees and Olwen Muriel Rees; *m* 1969, Catherine Good; one *s* one *d*. *Educ:* Monmouth Sch.; Bristol Univ. (LLB Hons). Called to the Bar, Middle Temple, 1965. *Recreations:* music, sport. *Address:* 9 Park Place, Cardiff CF1 3DP. *T:* Cardiff (01222) 382731. *Club:* Cardiff and County (Cardiff).

REES, Prof. Ray; Professor of Economics, University of Munich, since 1993; *b* 19 Sept. 1943; *s* of Gwyn Rees and Violet May (*née* Powell); *m* 1976, Denise Sylvia (*née* Stinson); two *s*. *Educ:* Dyffryn Grammar Sch., Port Talbot; London School of Economics and Political Science (MScEcon). Lectr 1966–76, Reader 1976–78, Queen Mary Coll., Univ. of London; Economic Advr, HM Treasury (on secondment), 1968–72; Prof. of Econs, UC, Cardiff, 1978–87; Prof. of Econs, Univ. of Guelph, Ont, 1987–93. Member (part-time), Monopolies and Mergers Commn, 1985–87. *Publications:* A Dictionary of Economics, 1968, 3rd edn 1984; Public Enterprise Economics, 1975, 3rd edn 1992; Microeconomics, 1981, 2nd edn 1992; Economics: a mathematical introduction, 1991; The Theory of Principal and Agent, 1992; Introduction to Game Theory, 1992; articles in Economic Jl, Amer. Econ. Rev., Jl of Political Econ., Jl of Public Econs, Economica, and others. *Recreations:* playing the guitar, losing chess games. *Address:* Oettingenstr. 2, 80538 Munich, Germany. *T:* (89) 295693.

REES, (Richard Ellis) Meuric, CBE 1982; JP; FRAgS; Lord Lieutenant for Gwynedd, since 1990; Member, Countryside Commission, since 1981 (Chairman, Committee for Wales); Vice Chairman, Hill Farming Advisory Committee (Chairman, Committee for Wales); *b* Pantydwr, Radnorshire, 1924; *m*; three *d*. President: YFC in Wales, 1961; Merioneth Agricl Soc., 1972; Royal Welsh Agricl Show, 1978; former Chm., Welsh Council of NFU; Mem., CLA. Mem., Agricl Trng Bd, 1974 (Chm., Cttee for Wales). Governor: Welsh Agricl Coll., Aberystwyth; Coleg Meirionnydd, Dolgellau. Mem., Tywyn UDC, 1967–73. Chm., N Wales Police Authority, 1982–84. JP Tywyn, 1957 (Chm. of Bench, 1974–); High Sheriff of Gwynedd, 1982–83; DL Gwynedd, 1988. FRAgS 1973. *Address:* Escuan Hall, Tywyn, Gwynedd.

REES, Dr Richard John William, CMG 1979; FRCP, FRCPath; Head, Laboratory for Leprosy and Mycobacterial Research, and WHO Collaborating Centre for Reference and Research on *M. leprae*, National Institute for Medical Research, London, 1969–82; *b* 11 Aug. 1917; *s* of William and Gertrude Rees; *m* 1942, Kathleen Harris; three *d*. *Educ:* East Sheen County Sch., London; Guy's Hosp., London (BSc 1939; MB, BS 1942). MRCS, LRCP 1941, FRCP 1983; MRCPath 1963, FRCPath 1964. Served War, 1942–46: Captain, RAMC Army Blood Transfusion Service, N Africa and Italy campaigns. House Surg. and Phys., Southern Hosp., Kent, 1941–42; Asst Clin. Pathologist, Guy's Hosp., 1946–49; Mem. of Scientific Staff, NIMR, 1949–69. Sec., MRC Leprosy Cttee, 1959–88; Consultant, US Japanese Co-op. Scientific Prog. on Leprosy, 1969–73. Chairman: LEPRA Med. Adv. Bd, 1963–87 (Mem. Exec. Cttee, 1964–87; Vice-Pres., 1987–); Acid Fast Club, 1960; Pres., Section of Comparative Medicine, RSM, 1975. Vice-Pres., Internat. Leprosy Assoc., 1988– (Mem. Council, 1963–88). Member: Trop. Medicine Res. Bd, 1968–72; 3rd WHO Expert Cttee on Leprosy, 1965; WHO IMMLEP Steering Cttee, 1974–90; WHO THELEP Steering Cttee, 1977–82. Almoth Wright Lectr, 1971; Erasmus Wilson Demonstration, RCS, 1973; 1st Clayton Meml Lectr, 1974; BMA Film, Silver Award, Leprosy, 1974. Mem. Editorial Boards: Leprosy Review; Internat. Jl of Leprosy. Hon. Mem., RSM Comparative Medicine Section, 1982. Manson Medal, 1980. *Publications:* scientific papers on basic and applied studies in animals and man relevant to pathogenesis, immunology and chemotherapy of leprosy and tuberculosis. *Address:* Highfield, Highwood Hill, Mill Hill, NW7 4EU. *T:* 0181–959 2021.

REES, Rev. Canon (Richard) Michael; Residentiary Canon, Chester Cathedral, and Canon Missioner, Diocese of Chester, since 1990; Vice-Dean, Chester Cathedral, since 1993; Cheshire County Ecumenical Officer, since 1991; *b* 31 July 1935; *s* of Richard and Margaret Rees; *m* 1958, Yoma Patricia; one *s* one *d*. *Educ:* Brighton College; St Peter's College, Oxford (MA Theol); Tyndale Hall, Bristol. Curate: Crowborough, 1959–62; Christ Church, Clifton, Bristol, 1962–64; Vicar: Christ Church, Clevedon, 1964–72; Holy Trinity, Cambridge, 1972–84; Proctor, General Synod for Ely Diocese, 1975–85; Chief Sec., Church Army, 1984–90. C of E Rep., BCC, 1983–90 (Moderator, Evangelism Cttee, 1986–90). Editor, Missionary Mandate, 1955–68. *Recreations:* photography, filling waste paper baskets. *Address:* 5 Abbey Green, Chester CH1 2JH. *T:* Chester (01244) 347500.

REES, Sir Stanley; *see* Rees, Sir C. W. S.

REES, (Thomas Morgan) Haydn, CBE 1975; JP; DL; Chairman, Welsh Water Authority, 1977–82; Member: National Water Council, 1977–82; Water Space Amenity Commission, 1977–82; *b* 22 May 1915; *y s* of late Thomas Rees and Mary Rees, Gorseinon, Swansea; *m* 1941, Marion, *y d* of A. B. Beer, Mumbles, Swansea; one *d*. *Educ:* Swansea Business Coll. Served War, 1939–45. Admitted solicitor, 1946; Sen. Asst Solicitor, Caernarvonshire CC, 1947; Flints County Council, 1948–65: Dep. Clerk, Dep. Clerk of the Peace, Police Authority, Magistrates Courts Cttee, and of Probation Cttee; 1966–74: Chief Exec.; Clerk of Peace (until office abolished, 1971); Clerk, Flints Police Authority (until merger with N Wales Police Authority, 1967); Clerk of Probation, Magistrates Courts, and of Justices Adv. Cttees; Clerk to Lieutenancy; Chief Exec., Clwyd CC, and Clerk, Magistrates Courts Cttee, 1974–77; Clerk to Lieutenancy and of Justices Adv. Cttee, Clwyd, 1974–77. Clerk, N Wales Police Authority, 1967–77; Secretary: Welsh Counties Cttee, 1968–77; (Corresp.) Rep. Body (Ombudsman) Cttee for Wales, 1974–77; Mem., Severn Barrage Cttee, 1978–81. Asst Comr, Royal Commn on Constitution, 1969–73. Chm., New Jobs Team, Shotton Steelworks, 1977–82; part-time Mem. Bd, BSC (Industry) Ltd, 1979–83. Chm., N Wales Arts Assoc., 1981–93. Member: Lord Chancellor's Circuit Cttee for Wales and Chester Circuit, 1972–77, Welsh Council, 1968–79; Welsh Arts Council, 1968–77 (Mem. Regional Cttee 1981–94); Gorsedd, Royal National Eisteddfod for Wales; Prince of Wales Cttee, 1976–79; Welsh Political Archive Adv. Cttee, Nat. Library of Wales, 1989–92; N Wales Music Festival Cttee, 1983–. Clerk, 1974–77, Mem., 1983–, Theatr Clwyd Governors. Chairman: Govt Quality of Life Experiment in Clwyd, 1974–76; Deeside Enterprise Trust Ltd, 1982–89; President: Clwyd Voluntary Services Council, 1980–; Clwyd Pre-Retirement Assoc., 1986–92. DL Flints 1969, Clwyd 1974; JP Mold, 1977 (Dep. Chm., 1978–84; Chm., 1985). *Recreation:* golf. *Address:* Cefn Bryn, Gwernaffield Road, Mold, Clwyd CH7 1RQ. *T:* Mold (01352) 752421.

REES, William Howard Guest, CB 1988; Chief Veterinary Officer, State Veterinary Service, 1980–88; *b* 21 May 1928; *s* of Walter Guest Rees and Margaret Elizabeth Rees; *m* 1952, Charlotte Mollie (*née* Collins); three *s* one *d*. *Educ:* Llanelli Grammar Sch.; Royal Veterinary Coll., London (BSc). MRCVS; DVSM. Private practice, Deal, Kent, 1952–53; joined MAFF as Veterinary Officer, 1953; stationed Stafford, 1953–66; Divl Vet. Officer, Vet. Service HQ, Tolworth, 1966–69; Divl Vet. Officer, Berks, 1969–71; Dep. Regional Vet. Officer, SE Reg., 1971–73; Regional Vet. Officer, Tolworth, 1973–76, Asst Chief Vet. Officer, 1976–80. Mem., AFRC, 1980–88. FRASE, 1988. Bledisloe Award, RASE, 1988; Gold Medal, Office Internat. des Epizooties, 1994. *Recreations:* Rugby and cricket follower, golf.

REES, William Hurst; Member of Lands Tribunal, 1973–89; *b* 12 April 1917; *s* of Richard and Florence A. Rees; *m* 1941, Elizabeth Mary Wight; two *s* one *d*. *Educ:* College of Estate Management, Univ. of London (BSc (Est. Man.)). FRICS. Served War, RA and RE (SO2), 1940–46; Liaison Officer, Belgian Army Engrs. Head of Valuation Dept, Coll. of Estate Management, 1948–51. Principal in Private Practice as Chartered Surveyor: City of London, Richard Ellis & Son, 1951–61; East Grinstead, Sx, Turner, Rudge & Turner, 1961–73. Gov., Coll. of Estate Management, 1965–72; Mem. Council, RICS, 1967–70; Chm. Bd of Studies in Estate Management, Univ. of London, 1970–74; Chm., Surveying Bd, CNAA, 1976–77; Hon. Mem., Rating Surveyors Assoc. Pres., BSc (Estate Management) Club, 1961–62; Chm., Exams Bd, Incorporated Soc. of Valuers and Auctioneers, 1984–. Hon. FSVA, 1987. *Publications:* Modern Methods of Valuation, 1943, (jointly) 6th edn 1971; (ed) Valuations: Principles into Practice, 1980, 4th edn 1992. *Recreation:* music, mainly opera. *Address:* Brendon, Carlton Road, South Godstone, Godstone, Surrey RH9 8LD. *T:* South Godstone (01342) 892109.

REES, (William) Linford (Llewelyn), CBE 1978; FRCP; FRCPsych; Emeritus Professor of Psychiatry, University of London, 1980; Consulting Physician, St Bartholomew's Hospital, since 1981; Lecturer in Psychological Medicine, St Bartholomew's Medical College, since 1958; Recognised Clinical Teacher in Mental Diseases, Institute of Psychiatry, University of London, since 1956; Chairman: University of London Teachers of Psychiatry Committee; Armed Services Consultant Advisory Board in Psychiatry, since 1979; *b* 24 Oct. 1914; *e s* of late Edward Parry Rees and Mary Rees, Llanelli, Carmathenshire; *m* 1940, Catherine (*d* 1993), *y d* of late David Thomas, and of Angharad Thomas, Alltwen, Glam; two *s* two *d*. *Educ:* Llanelli Grammar School; University Coll., Cardiff; Welsh Nat. Sch. of Medicine; The Maudsley Hosp.; Univ. of London. BSc 1935; MB, BCh 1938; DPM 1940; DSc London, 1978; MRCP 1942; MD 1943; FRCP 1950;

FRCPsych 1971 (Pres., 1975–78); Hon. FRCPsych 1978. David Hepburn Medal and Alfred Hughes Medal in Anatomy, 1935; John Maclean Medal and Prize in Obstetrics and Gynaecology, 1937, etc. Specialist, EMS, 1942; Dep. Med. Supt, Mill Hill Emergency Hosp., 1945; Asst Physician and Postgrad. Teacher in Clinical Psychiatry, The Maudsley Hosp., 1946; Dep. Physician Supt, Whitchurch Hosp., 1947; Regional Psychiatrist for Wales and Mon, 1948; Consultant Physician, The Bethlem Royal Hosp. and The Maudsley Hosp., 1954–66; Med. Dir, Charter Clinic, London, 1980–; Chief Psychiatrist and Exec. Med. Dir, Charter Medical, 1984–89; Dir and Med. Advr, Huntercombe Manor Hosp., and Rehabilitation Gp Ltd, 1989– (Pres., 1992–). Consultant Advisor in Psychiatry to RAF; WHO Consultant to Sri Lanka, 1973; Hon. Consultant, Royal Sch. for Deaf Children. Lectures to Univs and Learned Socs in Europe, USA, Asia, Australia and S America. Examiner: Diploma Psychological Medicine, RCP, 1964–69; MRCP, RCP, RCPE and RCPGlas, 1969–; MB and DPM, Univ. of Leeds, 1969–. President: Soc. for Psychosomatic Research, 1957–58; Royal Coll. of Psychiatrists, 1975–78 (Vice-Pres., 1972–75; Chm., E Anglian Region); Section of Psychiatry, RSM, 1971–72 (Vice-Pres., 1968; Hon. Mem., 1982); BMA, 1978– (Fellow, 1981); Psychiatric Rehabilitation Assoc., 1995 (Vice-Pres., 1988); Vice-Pres., Stress Foundn, 1984–; Chm., Medico-Pharmaceutical Forum, 1982 (Vice-Chm., 1981). Treasurer, World Psychiatric Assoc., 1966– (Hon. Mem., 1982). Member: Clinical Psychiatry Cttee, MRC, 1959–; Council, Royal Medico-Psychological Assoc. (Chm., Research and Clinical Section, 1957–63); Soc. for Study of Human Biology; Asthma Research Council; Cttee on Safety of Medicines (also Toxicity and Clinical Trials Sub-Cttee), 1971–; Psychological Medicine Group, BMA, 1967–; Bd of Advanced Med. Studies, Univ. of London, 1966–69; Higher Degrees Cttee, Univ. of London; Acad. Council Standing Sub-Cttee in Medicine, Univ. of London; Cttee of Management, Inst. of Psychiatry, Maudsley Hosp., 1968–; Council and Exec. Cttee, St Bartholomew's Hosp. Med. Coll., 1972–; Jt Policy Cttee, QMC, St Bartholomew's Hosp. and London Hosp., 1973–; Cttee on Review of Medicines (Chm., Psychotropic Drugs Sub-Cttee); Central Health Services Council; Standing Medical Adv. Cttee; Jt Consultants Cttee; Conference of Presidents of Royal Colls; GMC, 1980–84 (Mem., Educn Cttee, Preliminary Health Cttee and Prof. Conduct Cttee). Founder Mem., Internat. Coll. of Neuro-psychopharmacology. Hon. Mem. Learned Socs in USA, Sweden, Venezuela, East Germany, Spain and Greece. FRSM; Fellow: Eugenics Soc.; and Vice-Pres., Internat. Coll. of Psychosomatic Medicine, 1973; University Coll., Cardiff, 1980 (Governor, 1984–); Distinguished Fellow, Amer. Psychiatric Assoc., 1968; Hon. Fellow: Amer. Soc. of Physician Analysts; Amer. Coll. Psychiatrists; Hon. Member: Biological Psychiatry Assoc., USA; Hong Kong Psychiatric Soc., 1982. Chm. Bd of Trustees, Stress Syndrome Foundn, 1981– (Chm., Scientific Adv. Council). Governor: The Bethlem Royal Hosp. and The Maudsley Hosp.; Med. Coll. of St Bartholomew's Hosp., 1980–. President: Extend, 1976; Golden Jubilee Appeal, Welsh Nat. Sch. of Med., 1980. Co-Editor, Jl of Psychosomatic Research. Liveryman: Barber Surgeons; Apothecaries. Hon. LLD Wales, 1981. Bard of Welsh Gorsedd. *Publications:* (with Eysenck and Himmelweit) Dimensions of Personality, 1947; Short Textbook of Psychiatry, 1967. Chapters in: Modern Treatment in General Practice, 1947; Recent Progress in Psychiatry, 1950; Schizophrenia: Somatic Aspects, 1957; Psychoendocrinology, 1958; Recent Progress in Psychosomatic Research, 1960; Stress and Psychiatric Disorders, 1960. Papers in: Nature, BMJ, Jl of Mental Sci., Jl of Psychosomatic Research, Eugenics Review, etc. Contribs to Med. Annual, 1958–68. *Recreations:* swimming, photography, amusing grandchildren. *Address:* Penbryn, 62 Oakwood Avenue, Purley, Surrey CR8 1AQ. *Club:* Athenæum.

REES-JONES, Geoffrey Rippon, MA Oxon; Principal, King William's College, Isle of Man, 1958–79; *b* 8 July 1914; *er s* of W. Rees-Jones, BA, Ipswich; *m* 1950, Unity Margaret McConnell (*d* 1982), *d* of Major P. M. Sanders, Hampstead; one *s* one *d*. *Educ:* Ipswich School (scholar); University College, Oxford (open scholar). Assistant Master, Eastbourne College, 1936–38, Marlborough College, 1938–54 (Housemaster, C2, 1946–54); Headmaster, Bembridge School, 1954–58. Served War mainly in Commandos, 1940–45; Commandant, Commando Mountain Warfare School, 1943; Staff College, Camberley, 1944 (sc); Brigade Major, 4 Commando Bde, 1944–45 (despatches). *Recreations:* sailing, cricket, golf, fives; Oxford Rugby blue, 1933–35, Wales XV, 1934–36. *Address:* Red Lion Cottage, Braaid, Isle of Man IM4 2AJ. *T:* Castletown (01624) 851360.

REES-MOGG, family name of **Baron Rees-Mogg**.

REES-MOGG, Baron *cr* 1988 (Life Peer), of Hinton Blewitt in the County of Avon; **William Rees-Mogg;** Kt 1981; Chairman: Pickering & Chatto (Publishers) Ltd, since 1983; International Business Communications Plc, since 1994; Director: General Electric Co., since 1981; Private Bank and Trust Co.; *b* 14 July 1928; *s* of late Edmund Fletcher Rees-Mogg and late Beatrice Rees-Mogg (*née* Warren), Temple Cloud, Somerset; *m* 1962, Gillian Shakespeare Morris, *d* of T. R. Morris; two *s* three *d*. *Educ:* Charterhouse; Balliol Coll., Oxford (Brackenbury Scholar). President, Oxford Union, 1951. Financial Times, 1952–60, Chief Leader Writer, 1955–60; Asst Editor, 1957–60; Sunday Times, City Editor, 1960–61; Political and Economic Editor, 1961–63; Deputy Editor, 1964–67; Editor, The Times, 1967–81; columnist, 1992–; Mem., Exec. Bd, Times Newspapers Ltd, 1968–81; Director: The Times Ltd, 1968–81; Times Newspapers Ltd, 1978–81. Chm., Sidgwick & Jackson, 1985–89. Vice-Chm., Bd of Governors, BBC, 1981–86; Chairman: Arts Council of GB, 1982–89; Broadcasting Standards Council, 1988–93. Contested (C) Chester-le-Street, Co. Durham, By-election 1956; General Election, 1959. Treasurer, Institute of Journalists, 1960–63, 1966–68, Pres., 1963–64; Vice-Chm. Cons. Party's Nat. Advisory Cttee on Political Education, 1961–63. Pres., English Assoc., 1983–84. Mem., Internat. Cttee, Pontifical Council for Culture, 1983–87. Vis. Fellow, Nuffield Coll., Oxford, 1968–72. High Sheriff, Somerset, 1978. Hon. LLD Bath, 1977. *Publications:* The Reigning Error: the crisis of world inflation, 1974; An Humbler Heaven, 1977; How to Buy Rare Books, 1985; Picnics on Vesuvius: steps toward the millenium, 1992; (with James Dale Davidson): Blood in the Streets, 1988; The Great Reckoning, 1991. *Recreation:* collecting. *Address:* 17 Pall Mall, SW1Y 5NB. *Club:* Garrick.

REES-WILLIAMS, family name of **Baron Ogmore.**

REES-WILLIAMS, Jonathan, FRCO; Organist and Master of the Choristers, St George's Chapel, Windsor Castle, since 1991; *b* 10 Feb. 1949; *s* of Ivor and Barbara Rees-Williams; *m* 1985, Helen Patricia Harling; one *s* two *d*. *Educ:* Kilburn Grammar Sch.; Royal Academy of Music; New Coll., Oxford (Organ Scholar; MA 1972). LRAM, DipRAM 1969; ARAM 1984; FRCO 1968. Organist: St Edmund, Yeading, 1967; Church of the Ascension, Wembley, 1968; Actg Organist, New Coll., Oxford, 1972; Assistant Organist: Hampstead Parish Church and St Clement Danes, 1972–74; Salisbury Cathedral, 1974–78; Dir of Music, Salisbury Cathedral Sch., 1974–78; Organist and Master of Choristers, Lichfield Cathedral, 1978–91; Conductor, Lichfield Cathedral Special Choir, 1978–91. Chorusmaster, Portsmouth Festival Choir, 1974–78; Accompanist and Asst Dir, Salisbury Musical Soc., 1974–78. *Recreations:* cycling, wine, railways, vintage model railways. *Address:* 25 The Cloisters, Windsor Castle, Windsor, Berks SL4 1NJ. *T:* Windsor (01753) 864529.

REESE, Prof. Colin Bernard, PhD, ScD; FRS 1981; FRSC; Daniell Professor of Chemistry, King's College London, University of London, since 1973; *b* 29 July 1930; *s* of Joseph and Emily Reese; *m* 1968, Susanne Bird; one *s* one *d*. *Educ:* Dartington Hall Sch.; Clare Coll., Cambridge (BA 1953, PhD 1956, MA 1957, ScD 1972). 1851 Sen. Student, 1956–58; Research Fellow: Clare Coll., Cambridge, 1956–59; Harvard Univ., 1957–58; Official Fellow and Dir of Studies in Chem., Clare Coll., 1959–73; Cambridge University: Univ. Demonstrator in Chem., 1959–63; Asst Dir of Res., 1963–64; Univ. Lectr in Chem., 1964–73. FKC 1989. *Publications:* scientific papers, mainly in chemical jls. *Address:* Department of Chemistry, King's College London, Strand, WC2R 2LS. *T:* 0171–873 2260.

REESE, Colin Edward; QC 1987; a Recorder, since 1994; *b* 28 March 1950; *s* of Robert Edward Reese and late Katharine Reese (*née* Moore); *m* 1978, Diana Janet Anderson; two *s* one *d*. *Educ:* Hawarden Grammar School; King Edward VI School, Southampton; Fitzwilliam College, Cambridge (BA 1972; MA 1976). Called to the Bar, Gray's Inn, 1973 (Mould Schol., 1974); admitted, *ad eund.*, Lincoln's Inn, 1976; in practice, 1975–. An Asst Parly Boundary Comr, 1992–. Pres., Cambridge Univ. Law Soc., 1971–72. Liveryman, Bakers' Co., 1991–. *Address:* 1 Atkin Building, Gray's Inn, WC1R 5AT. *T:* 0171–404 0102.

REESE, Surg. Rear-Adm. (John) Mansel, CB 1962; OBE 1953; *b* 3 July 1906; *s* of late Dr D. W. Reese, and late Mrs A. M. Reese; *m* 1946, Beryl (*née* Dunn) (*d* 1973); two *d* (and one *s* decd). *Educ:* Epsom Coll.; St Mary's Hosp. Med. Sch., London University. MRCS, LRCP 1930; DPH 1934. Entered Royal Navy, Jan. 1931; Naval Medical Officer of Health, Orkney and Shetland Comd, 1942–44; Naval MOH, Ceylon, 1944–46; Admiralty, 1947–53; Medical Officer-in-Charge RN Hospital, Plymouth, 1960–63; QHP 1960–63. Surgeon Comdr, 1943; Surgeon Captain, 1954; Surgeon Rear-Adm., 1960; retd 1963. FRSTM&H. Sir Gilbert Blane Gold Medal, 1939. Member Gray's Inn, 1953. CStJ 1961. *Address:* 4 Meldon Court, East Budleigh Road, Budleigh Salterton, Devon EX9 6HE.

REESE, (John) Terence; bridge expert, author and journalist; *b* 28 Aug. 1913; *s* of John and Anne Reese; *m* 1970, Alwyn Sherrington. *Educ:* Bilton Grange; Bradfield Coll. (top scholar); New Coll., Oxford (top class. scholar). Worked at Harrods, 1935–36; left to follow career as bridge expert and journalist. Became bridge correspondent of the London Evening News, 1948, the Observer, 1950, the Lady, 1954, and the London Evening Standard, 1981. Winner of Championships, including: European Champion, 1948, 1949, 1954, 1963; World Champion Bridge Player, 1955; World Team Olympiad, 1960; World Pair Champion, 1961; World Pair Olympiad, 1962; winner of all top British Championships, including Gold Cup eight times and Masters Pairs seven times. Hon. Life Mem., English Bridge Union, 1993. *Publications include:* Reese on Play, 1948; The Expert Game, 1958; Play Bridge with Reese, 1960; Practical Bidding and Practical Play, 1973; (with Albert Dormer) The Complete Book of Bridge, 1973; Play These Hands With Me, 1976; Bridge at the Top (autobiog.), 1977; Teach Yourself Bridge, 1980; Bridge Tips by World Masters, 1980; (with Jeremy Flint) Trick 13 (fiction), 1980; (with David Bird) Miracles of Card Play, 1982; (with Roger Trézel) The Mistakes You Make in Bridge, 1984; (with Martin Hoffman) Play it again Sam, 1985; (with Julian Pottage) Positive Declarer's Play, 1986; Bridge for Ambitious Players, 1988; (with David Bird) Tricks of the Trade, 1989; (with Jeremy Flint) Bridge with the Professional Touch, 1991; Learn Bridge in Five Days, 1995; articles on bridge in magazines and periodicals. *Recreation:* golf.

REESE, Mansel; *see* Reese, J. M.

REEVE, Sir Anthony, KCMG 1992 (CMG 1986); KCVO 1995; HM Diplomatic Service; High Commissioner (formerly Ambassador) to South Africa, since 1991; *b* 20 Oct. 1938; *s* of Sidney Reeve and Dorothy (*née* Mitchell); *m* 1964, Pamela Margaret Angus (marr. diss. 1988); one *s* two *d*. *Educ:* Queen Elizabeth Grammar Sch., Wakefield; Marling Sch., Stroud; Merton Coll., Oxford (MA). Lever Brothers & Associates, 1962–65; joined HM Diplomatic Service, 1965; Middle East Centre for Arab Studies, 1966–68; Asst Political Agent, Abu Dhabi, 1968–70; First Secretary, FCO, 1970–73; First Sec., later Counsellor, Washington, 1973–78; Head of Arms Control and Disarmament Dept, FCO, 1979–81; Counsellor, Cairo, 1981–84; Head of Southern Africa Dept, FCO, 1984–86; Asst Under Sec. of State (Africa), FCO, 1986–87; Ambassador to Jordan, 1988–91. *Recreations:* writing, music. *Address:* c/o Foreign and Commonwealth Office, SW1A 2AH. *Clubs:* United Oxford & Cambridge University; Leander (Henley-on-Thames); Minchinhampton Golf.

REEVE, James Ernest, CMG 1982; HM Diplomatic Service, retired; international management consultant, since 1992; *b* 8 June 1926; *s* of Ernest and Anthea Reeve; *m* 1947, Lillian Irene Watkins; one *s* one *d*. *Educ:* Bishop's Stortford Coll. Vice-Consul, Ahwaz and Khorramshahr, Iran, 1949–51; UN General Assembly, Paris, 1951; Asst Private Sec. to Rt Hon. Selwyn Lloyd, Foreign Office, 1951–53; 2nd Secretary: Brit. Embassy, Washington, 1953–57; Brit. Embassy, Bangkok, 1957–59; FO, 1959–61; HM Consul, Frankfurt, 1961–65; 1st Secretary: Brit. Embassy in Libya, 1965–69; Brit. Embassy, Budapest, 1970–72; Chargé d'Affaires, Budapest, 1972; Counsellor (Commercial), East Berlin, 1973–75; Consul-Gen., Zurich and Principality of Liechtenstein, 1975–80; HM Minister and Consul-Gen., Milan, 1980–83. Secretariat, Internat. Primary Aluminium Inst., London, 1985–93. Dir, Sprester Investments Ltd, 1986–91. *Recreations:* theatre, tennis, skiing, travel. *Address:* Sultan's Gate, 10 Montpellier Parade, Cheltenham, Glos GL50 1UD. *Clubs:* Royal Automobile; East Gloucestershire (Cheltenham).

REEVE, John; Managing Director, Sun Life Corporation plc, since 1989; *b* 13 July 1944; *s* of Clifford Alfred Reeve and Irene Mary Turnidge Reeve; *m* 1st, 1968, Patricia Mary Tomkins; 2nd, 1974, Sally Diane Welton; one *d*. *Educ:* Westcliff High School (Grammar). FCA; CIMgt. Selbey Smith & Earle, 1962–67; Peat Marwick McLintock, 1967–68; Vickers, Roneo Vickers Group: Commercial Dir, Furniture & Systems Div., subseq. Manager, Group Financial Evaluation & Planning, 1968–76; Dir, Accounting Services, Wilkinson Match, 1976–77; Amalgamated Metal Corp.: Controller, Physical Trading Div., subseq. Corporate Controller, 1977–80; Group Finance Director: British Aluminium Co., 1980–83; Mercantile House Holdings, 1983–87; Dep. Man. Dir, 1988–89, Man. Dir, 1989–, Sun Life Assurance Society. Director: The English Concert, 1987– (Chm., 1993–); HMC Group plc, 1988–94; Temple Bar Investment Trust, 1992–. Dep. Pres., Inst. of Business Ethics, 1991–; Member: E London Partnership Bd, 1991–; Life Insce Council, 1991–94, Bd, 1994–, ABI. Gov., Res. into Ageing, 1991–. *Recreations:* yachting, music, theatre. *Address:* Cliff Dene, 24 Cliff Parade, Leigh-on-Sea, Essex SS9 1BB. *Clubs:* National Liberal; Essex Yacht.

REEVE, Mrs Marjorie Frances, CBE 1944; TD 1950; JP; *d* of late Charles Fry, Bedford; *m* 1st, Lieutenant-Commander J. K. Laughton, Royal Navy (*d* 1925); (one *s* decd); 2nd, Major-General C. M. Wagstaff, CB, CMG, CIE, DSO (*d* 1934); 3rd, 1950, Major-General J. T. W. Reeve, CB, CBE, DSO (*d* 1983). Joined ATS, 1938; served with BEF, and in Middle East and BAOR; late Controller ATS. Was i/c Public Welfare Section of Control Commission for Germany (BE); Principal in Board of Trade (Overseas) till 1950; Swedish Red Cross Medal in Silver, 1950; County Director, BRCS, 1953–57; Dep. Pres. Suffolk BRCS, 1957, Hon. Vice-Pres., 1977. Badge of Honour (2nd Class) BRCS, 1970. JP (W Suffolk), 1954. *Address:* Moorhouse Nursing Home, Hindhead, Surrey GU26 6RA. *T:* Hindhead (01428) 735313.

REEVE, Prof. Michael David, FBA 1984; Kennedy Professor of Latin, and Fellow of Pembroke College, University of Cambridge, since 1984; *b* 11 Jan. 1943; *s* of Arthur Reeve and Edith Mary Barrett; *m* 1970, Elizabeth Klingaman; two *s* one *d*. *Educ:* King Edward's Sch., Birmingham; Balliol Coll., Oxford (MA). Harmsworth Senior Scholar, Merton Coll., Oxford, 1964–65; Woodhouse Research Fellow, St John's Coll., Oxford, 1965–66; Tutorial Fellow, Exeter Coll., Oxford, 1966–84, now Emeritus Fellow. Visiting Professor: Univ. of Hamburg, 1976; McMaster Univ., 1979; Univ. of Toronto, 1982–83. Corresp. Mem., Akademie der Wissenschaften, Göttingen, 1990; For. Mem., Istituto Lombardo, Milan, 1993. Editor, Classical Quarterly, 1981–86. *Publications:* Longus, Daphnis and Chloe, 1982; contribs to Texts and Transmission, ed L. D. Reynolds, 1983; Cicero, Pro Quinctio, 1992; articles in European and transatlantic jls. *Recreations:* chess, music, gardening, mountain walking. *Address:* Pembroke College, Cambridge CB2 1RF.

REEVE, Robin Martin, MA; Head Master, King's College School, Wimbledon, since 1980; *b* 22 Nov. 1934; *s* of Percy Martin Reeve and Cicely Nora Parker; *m* 1959, Brianne Ruth Hall; one *s* two *d*. *Educ:* Hampton Sch.; Gonville and Caius Coll., Cambridge (Foundation Schol.; BA cl. 1 Hist. Tripos, 1957; MA). Asst Master, King's Coll. Sch., Wimbledon, 1958–62; Head of History Dept, 1962–80, and Dir of Studies, 1975–80, Lancing Coll. Mem., CATE, 1993–. *Publication:* The Industrial Revolution 1750–1850, 1971. *Recreations:* English history and architecture, gardening. *Address:* Rushmere, South Side, Wimbledon Common, SW19 4TL; The Old Rectory, Coombes, Lancing, W Sussex BN15 0RS. *Club:* East India, Devonshire, Sports and Public Schools.

REEVE, Roy Stephen; HM Diplomatic Service; Ambassador to Ukraine, since 1995; *b* 20 Aug. 1941; *s* of Ernest Arthur Reeve and Joan Elizabeth (*née* Thomas); *m* 1964, Gill Lee; two *d*. *Educ:* Dulwich Coll.; LSE (BSc Econs 1965; MSc 1966). Joined FCO, 1966; Moscow, 1968–71; First Secretary: FCO, 1973–78; (Commercial) Moscow, 1978–80; Counsellor on loan to Home Civil Service, 1983–85; Dep. Consul-General, Johannesburg, 1985–88; Hd, Commercial Management and Export Dept, FCO, 1988–91; Consul-Gen., Sydney, 1991–95. *Recreations:* Rugby Union, scuba diving. *Address:* c/o Foreign and Commonwealth Office, King Charles Street, SW1A 2AH.

REEVE, Suzanne Elizabeth; *see* Warner, S. E.

REEVES, Christopher Reginald; Chairman, Merrill Lynch Europe and Merrill Lynch International Ltd, since 1993; Group Chief Executive, 1980–87, and Deputy Chairman, 1984–87, Morgan Grenfell Group PLC; Joint Chairman, Morgan Grenfell & Co. Ltd, 1984–87; *b* 14 Jan. 1936; *s* of Reginald and Dora Reeves; *m* 1965, Stella, *d* of Patrick and Maria Whinney; three *s*. *Educ:* Malvern College. National Service, Rifle Bde, 1955–57. Bank of England, 1958–63; Hill Samuel & Co. Ltd, 1963–67; joined Morgan Grenfell & Co. Ltd, 1968; Dir, 1970. Sen. Advr to Pres., Merrill Lynch, 1988–89; Vice Chm., Merrill Lynch Internat., 1989–93. Director: London Board, Westpac Banking Corp. (formerly Commercial Bank of Australia Ltd) 1972–90 (Chm., 1976–82, Dep. Chm., 1982–89); Midland and International Banks Ltd, 1976–83; BICC, 1982–; Andrew Weir & Co., 1982–92; Cornhill Insurance PLC (formerly Allianz Internat. Insurance Co. Ltd), 1983–; Oman Internat. Bank, 1984–; International Freehold Properties SARL, 1988–. Dir, Exec. Cttee, Amer. Chamber of Commerce (UK), 1992–. Member: Adv. Panel, City University Business Sch., 1972–81 (Chm., 1979–81); Council, City Univ. Business Sch., 1986–93; Council, Inst. for Fiscal Studies, 1982–87; Treas., Council, City Univ., 1992–; Governor: Stowe Sch., 1976–81; Dulwich College Prep. Sch., 1977–; Mermaid Theatre Trust, 1981–85; Trustee, Chichester Fest. Theatre Trust, 1992–. *Recreations:* sailing, shooting, ski-ing. *Address:* 64 Flood Street, SW3 5TE. *Clubs:* Boodle's; Royal Southern Yacht (Southampton).

REEVES, Dr Colin Leslie; Director of Finance, National Health Service Executive, since 1994; *b* 4 April 1949; *s* of Leslie and Isabelle Reeves; *m* 1978, Christine Lloyd; two *d*. *Educ:* Birkenhead Sch.; Clare Coll., Cambridge (BA 1970; MA); UCNW, Bangor (MSc 1971; PhD 1973); DBA Cornell Univ. 1990. IPFA 1976. Lectr, UCNW, Bangor, 1971–73; Accountancy and Audit Assistant, Warrington County Borough, 1973–75; Asst Treas., Ellesmere Port and Neston BC, 1975–80; Deputy Director of Finance: Stratford-on-Avon DC, 1980–84; NW Thames RHA, 1984–85; Director of Finance: Paddington and N Kensington DHA, 1985–86; NW Thames RHA, 1986–94. Member: Adv. Cttee on Mentally Disordered Offenders, 1993–; Culyer Cttee on R&D, 1993–; NHS Steering Gps on Capitation and on Capital, 1993–; Chancellor of Exchequer's Pvte Finance Panel, 1994–. *Publications:* The Applicability of the Monetary Base Hypothesis to the UK, the USA, France and West Germany, 1974; contrib. professional jls. *Recreations:* sport, especially cricket and golf, history of Test Match cricket, hockey (former regl internat. and county player). *Address:* Hillcrest, 82 Wallingford Road, Goring-on-Thames, Oxon RG8 0HN. *T:* Goring-on-Thames (01491) 872166. *Clubs:* Royal Automobile; Mapledurham Golf.

REEVES, Rev. Donald St John; Rector, St James's Church, Piccadilly, since 1980; *b* 18 May 1934; *s* of Henry and Barbara Reeves. *Educ:* Sherborne; Queens' Coll., Cambridge (BA Hons 1957); Cuddesdon Theol Coll. 2nd Lieut, Royal Sussex Regt, 1952–54. Lectr, British Council, Beirut, 1957–60; Tutor, Brasted Theol Coll., 1960–61; Cuddesdon Theol Coll., 1961–63; deacon, 1963, priest, 1964; Curate, All Saints, Maidstone, 1963–65; Chaplain to Bishop of Southwark, 1965–68; Vicar of St Peter's, Morden, 1969–80. Mem., Gen. Synod of C of E, 1990–. *Publications:* (ed) Church and State, 1984; For God's Sake, 1988; Making Sense of Religion, 1989; Down to Earth: a new vision, 1995. *Recreations:* playing the organ, bee-keeping, watching TV soap operas. *Address:* St James's Church, 197 Piccadilly, W1V 9LF. *T:* 0171–734 4511. *Clubs:* Arts (Hon.), Royal Automobile.

REEVES, Gordon; *see* Reeves, W. G.

REEVES, Helen May, OBE 1986; Director, National Association of Victims Support Schemes, since 1980; *b* 22 Aug. 1945; *d* of Leslie Percival William Reeves and Helen Edith Reeves (*née* Brown). *Educ:* Dartford Grammar School for Girls; Nottingham University (BA Hons Social Admin. 1966). Probation Officer, Inner London Probation Service, 1967–79 (Senior Probation Officer, 1975–79). Mem., Nat. Bd for Crime Prevention, 1993–; Exec. Cttee, World Soc. of Victimology, 1994–; Sec., Eur. Forum for Victim Services, 1994–. Trustee, Kidscape, 1993–. *Recreations:* social and local history and architecture, food, gardens. *Address:* Cranmer House, 39 Brixton Road, SW9 6DZ. *T:* 0171–735 9166.

REEVES, Marjorie Ethel, MA (Oxon), PhD (London), DLitt (Oxon); FRHistS; FBA 1974; Vice-Principal, St Anne's College, Oxford, 1951–62, 1964–67; *b* 17 July 1905; *d* of Robert J. W. Reeves and Edith Saffery Whitaker. *Educ:* The High School for Girls, Trowbridge, Wilts; St Hugh's Coll., Oxford; Westfield Coll., London. Asst Mistress, Roan School, Greenwich, 1927–29; Research Fellow, Westfield Coll., London, 1929–31; Lecturer, St Gabriel's Trng Coll., London, 1931–38; Tutor, later Fellow of St Anne's College, 1938–72, Hon. Fellow, 1973. Member: Central Advisory Council, Min. of Educn, 1947–61; Academic Planning Bd, Univ. of Kent; Academic Advisory Cttee, University of Surrey; formerly Member: Educn Council, ITA; British Council of Churches; School Broadcasting Council. Corresp. Fellow, Medieval Acad. of America, 1979. Hon. DLitt Bath, 1992. Medlicott Medal, Historical Assoc., 1993. *Publications:* Growing Up in a Modern Society, 1946; (ed, with L. Tondelli, B. Hirsch-Reich) Il Libro delle Figure dell'Abate Gioachino da Fiore, 1953; Three Questions in Higher Education (Hazen Foundation, USA), 1955; Moral Education in a Changing Society (ed W. Niblett), 1963; ed, Eighteen Plus: Unity and Diversity in Higher Education, 1965; The Influence of Prophecy in the later Middle Ages: a study in Joachimism, 1969; Higher Education: demand and response (ed W. R. Niblett), 1969; (with B. Hirsch-Reich) The Figurae of Joachim of Fiore, 1972; Joachim of Fiore and the Prophetic Future, 1976; Sheep Bell and Ploughshare, 1978; Why History, 1980; (with W. Gould) Joachim of Fiore and the Myth of the Eternal Evangel in the Nineteenth Century, 1987; Competence, Delight and the Common Good: reflections on the crisis in higher education, 1988; (with J. Morrison) The Diaries of Jeffery Whitaker, 1989; (ed) Prophetic Rome in the High Renaissance period, 1992; Then and There Series: The Medieval Town, 1954, The Medieval Village, 1954, Elizabethan Court, 1956, The Medieval Monastery, 1957, The Norman Conquest, 1958, Alfred and the Danes, 1959; The Medieval Castle, 1960, Elizabethan Citizen, 1961; A Medieval King Governs, 1971; Explorers of the Elizabethan Age, 1977; Elizabethan Country House, 1984; The Spanish Armada, 1988; contributions on history in Speculum, Medieval and Renaissance Studies, Traditio, Sophia, Recherches de Théologie, etc, and on education in Times Educational Supplement, New Era, etc. *Recreations:* music, gardening, bird-watching. *Address:* 38 Norham Road, Oxford OX2 6SQ. *T:* Oxford (01865) 57039. *Club:* University Women's.

REEVES, Prof. Nigel Barrie Reginald, OBE 1987; DPhil; FIL; Professor of German and Head of Department of Modern Languages, Aston University, since 1990; *b* 9 Nov. 1939; *s* of Reginald Arthur Reeves and Marjorie Joyce Reeves; *m* 1982, Minou (*née* Samimi); one *s* one *d*. *Educ:* Merchant Taylors' Sch.; Worcester Coll., Oxford (MA); St John's Coll., Oxford (DPhil 1970). FIL 1981. Lectr in English, Univ. of Lund, Sweden, 1964–66; Lectr in German, Univ. of Reading, 1968–74; Alexander von Humboldt Fellow, Univ. of Tübingen, 1974–75; University of Surrey: Prof. of German, 1975–90; Hd of Dept of Linguistic and Internat. Studies, 1979–90; Dean, Faculty of Human Studies, 1986–90. Guest Prof. of German, Royal Holloway Coll., London Univ., 1976; Vis. Prof., European Business Sch., 1981–88; Sen. Alexander von Humboldt Fellow, Univ. of Hamburg, 1986. Chm., Nat. Congress on Langs in Educn, 1986–90; President: Nat. Assoc. of Language Advisers, 1986–91; Assoc. of Teachers of German, 1988–89; Vice-President: Conf. of University Teachers of German, 1995– (Vice-Chm., 1988–91); Inst. of Linguists, 1990– (Chm. Council, 1985–88); Member: Academic Adv. Council, Linguaphone Inst., 1991–; Modern Langs Steering Cttee, Open Univ., 1991–; Gov., Germanic Inst., Univ. of London, 1989–94. FRSA 1986; CIEx 1987. Goethe Medal, Goethe Inst., Munich, 1989. *Publications:* Merkantil-Tekniska Stilar, 2 Vols, 1965–66; Heinrich Heine: poetry and politics, 1974; (with K. Dewhurst) Friedrich Schiller: medicine, psychology and literature, 1978; (with D. Liston) Business Studies, Languages and Overseas Trade, 1985; (jtly) Making Your Mark: effective business communication in Germany, 1988; (with D. Liston) The Invisible Economy: a profile of Britain's invisible exports, 1988; (jtly) Franc Exchange, effective business communication in France, 1991; (jtly) Spanish Venture, basic business communication in Spain, 1992; (with C. Wright) Linguistic Auditing, 1995; (ed) The German Business Environment, 1996; over 70 articles in learned jls on language, language educn, literature and overseas trade. *Recreations:* gardening, walking. *Address:* Department of Languages and European Studies, Aston University, Aston Triangle, Birmingham B4 7ET.

REEVES, Rt Rev. Sir Paul Alfred, GCMG 1985; GCVO 1986; QSO 1990; Kt 1985; Chair, Fijian Constitutional Review Commission, 1995; *b* 6 Dec. 1932; 2nd *s* of D'Arcy Lionel and Hilda Mary Reeves; *m* 1959, Beverley Gwendolen Watkins; three *d*. *Educ:* Wellington Coll., New Zealand; Victoria Univ. of Wellington (MA); St John's Theol. Coll., Auckland (LTh); St Peter's Coll., Univ. of Oxford (MA; Hon. Fellow, 1980). Deacon, 1958; Priest, 1960; Curate: Tokoroa, NZ, 1958–59; St Mary the Virgin, Oxford, 1959–61; Kirkley St Peter, Lowestoft, 1961–63; Vicar, St Paul, Okato, NZ, 1964–66; Lectr in Church History, St John's Coll., Auckland, NZ, 1966–69; Dir of Christian Educn, Dio. Auckland, 1969–71; Bishop of Waiapu, 1971–79; Bishop of Auckland, 1979–85; Primate and Archbishop of New Zealand, 1980–85; Governor-General, NZ, 1985–90; Rep. of ACC at UN, and Assisting Bishop, Episcopal Dio. of NY, 1991–93; Dean, Te Rau Kahikatea Theol Coll., Auckland, 1994–95. Chm., Environmental Council, 1974–76. KStJ 1986. Hon. DCL Oxford, 1985; Hon LLD Wellington, 1989; Hon. DD: Gen. Theol Seminary, NY, 1992; CDSP San Francisco, 1994; Hon. Dr Edinburgh, 1994. *Recreations:* jogging, sailing, swimming. *Address:* 16E Cathedral Place, Parnell, Auckland, New Zealand.

REEVES, Philip Thomas Langford, RSA 1976 (ARSA 1971); artist in etching and other mediums; Senior Lecturer, Glasgow School of Art, 1973–91; *b* 7 July 1931; *s* of Herbert Reeves and Lilian; *m* 1964, Christine MacLaren (decd); one *d*. *Educ:* Naunton Park Sch., Cheltenham. Student, Cheltenham Sch. of Art, 1947–49. Army service, 4th/7th Royal Dragoon Guards, Middle East, 1949–51. RCA, 1951–54 (ARCA 1st Cl.); Lectr, Glasgow Sch. of Art, 1954–73. Associate, Royal Soc. of Painter Etchers, 1954, Fellow 1964; RSW 1962; RGI 1981. Works in permanent collections: Arts Council; V&A; Gall. of Modern Art, Edinburgh; Glasgow Art Gall.; Glasgow Univ. Print Collection; Hunterian Art Gall., Glasgow; Manchester City Art Gall.; Royal Scottish Acad.; Aberdeen Art Gall.; Paisley Art Gall.; Inverness Art Gall.; Milngavie Art Gall.; Dept of the Environment; Dundee Art Gall.; Scottish Develt Agency; Stirling and Strathclyde Univs; Contemporary Art Soc. *Recreation:* walking. *Address:* 13 Hamilton Drive, Glasgow G12 8DN. *Club:* Traverse (Edinburgh).

REEVES, William Desmond, CB 1993; Partnership Secretary, Coopers & Lybrand, since 1994; *b* 26 May 1937; *s* of late Thomas Norman and Anne Reeves; *m* 1967, Aase Birte Christensen; two *d*. *Educ:* Darwen Grammar Sch.; King's Coll., Cambridge (BA Hist.). National service, RAEC, 1959–61. Joined Admiralty as Asst Principal, 1961; MoD, 1964; Asst Sec., 1973; seconded to Pay Board, 1973–74; Asst Under Sec. of State, Air, MoD (PE), 1982–84, Resources and Progs, MoD, 1984, Systems, Office of Management and Budget, MoD, 1985–88; Under Sec., Cabinet Office, 1989–92; Asst Under Sec. of State (Commitments), MoD, 1992–94. *Address:* Coopers & Lybrand, 1 Embankment Place, WC2N 6NN.

REEVES, Prof. (William) Gordon, FRCP, FRCPath; Professor and Head of Department of Microbiology and Immunology, College of Medicine, Sultan Qaboos University, Muscat, Oman, since 1993; Visiting Professor in the Immunology of Infectious Disease, St Mary's Hospital Medical School, since 1992; *b* 9 July 1938; *s* of Rev. W. H. and Mrs E. L. Reeves; *m* 1970, Elizabeth Susan, *d* of Surg.-Comdr L. A. and Mrs P. Moules; one *s* one *d*. *Educ:* Perse Sch., Cambridge; Guy's Hosp. Med. Sch. (BSc, MB BS). MRCS, LRCP 1964; MRCP 1966; FRCP 1978; FRCPath 1985. Editor, Guy's Hosp. Gazette, 1962–63. HO and Med. Registrar appts at Guy's, Central Middx, Brompton, National, Middx, and University Coll. Hosps, 1964–68; Lecturer: Clinical Pharmacology, Guy's Hosp. Med. Sch., 1968–71; Immunology and Medicine, Royal Postgrad. Med. Sch., 1971–73; Consultant Immunologist, Nottingham HA, 1973–88; Nottingham University:

Sen. Lectr, 1975–85; Prof. of Immunology, 1985–88; Editor, The Lancet, 1989–90; Med. Editor and Consultant, Communicable Disease Surveillance Centre, PHLS, 1991–93. Chm. Cttee, British Soc. for Immunology, 1984–85; Member: Research Cttee, British Diabetic Assoc., 1985–88; Specialty Adv. Cttee on Immunology, RCPath, 1986–88; Hon. Sec., Cttee on Clinical Immunology and Allergy, RCP, 1986–88. *Publications:* (with E. J. Holborow) Immunology in Medicine: a comprehensive guide to clinical immunology, 1977, 2nd edn 1983; Lecture Notes on Immunology, 1987, 3rd edn 1996; contribs to med. and scientific books and jls on immunology and infectious diseases. *Recreations:* music, sailing, tennis. *Address:* College of Medicine, Sultan Qaboos University, PO Box 35, Al-Khod, Muscat 123, Sultanate of Oman.

REFFELL, Adm. Sir Derek (Roy), KCB 1984; Governor and Commander-in-Chief, Gibraltar, 1989–93; *b* 6 Oct. 1928; *s* of late Edward (Roy) and Murielle Reffell; *m* 1956, Janne Gronow Davis; one *s* one *d.* *Educ:* Culford Sch., Suffolk; Royal Naval Coll., Dartmouth. FNI; CIMgt. Various ships at Home, Mediterranean, West Indies and Far East, 1946–63; qualified Navigating Officer, 1954; Comdr 1963; Comd HMS Sirius, 1966–67; Comdr BRNC Dartmouth, 1968–69; Captain 1970; Naval Staff, 1971–74; Comd HMS Hermes, 1974–76; Director Naval Warfare, 1976–78; Commodore Amphibious Warfare, 1978–79; Asst Chief of Naval Staff (Policy), 1979–82; Flag Officer Third Flotilla and Comdr Anti-Submarine Group Two, 1982–83; Flag Officer, Naval Air Comd, 1983–84; Controller of the Navy, 1984–89, retd. Chairman: Bd of Govs, Royal Naval Sch. for Girls, 1989–95; Friends of Gibraltar Heritage Soc., 1994–. Jun. Warden, Coachmakers Company, 1995–96. KStJ 1989. *Recreations:* golf, wine-making.

REFSHAUGE, Maj.-Gen. Sir William (Dudley), AC 1980; Kt 1966; CBE 1959 (OBE 1944); ED 1965; Secretary-General, World Medical Association, 1973–76; Hon. Consultant to Australian Foundation on Alcoholism and Drugs of Dependence, since 1979; *b* 3 April 1913; *s* of late F. C. Refshauge, Melbourne; *m* 1942, Helen Elizabeth, *d* of late R. E. Allwright, Tasmania; four *s* one *d.* *Educ:* Hampton High Sch.; Scotch Coll., Melbourne; Melbourne University. MB, BS (Melbourne) 1938; FRCOG 1961; FRACS 1962; FRACP 1963; Hon. FRSH 1967; FACMA 1967; FRACOG 1978. Served with AIF, 1939–46; Lt-Col, RAAMC (despatches four times). Medical Supt, Royal Women's Hosp., Melbourne, 1948–51; Col, and Dep. DGAMS, Aust., 1951–55; Maj.-Gen., and DGAMS, Aust., 1955–60; QHP, 1955–64. Commonwealth Dir-Gen. of Health, Australia, 1960–73. Chairman: Council, Aust. Coll. of Nursing, 1958–60 (Chm. Educn Cttee, 1951–58); Nat. Health and MRC, 1960–73; Nat. Fitness Council, 1960–73; Nat. Tuberculosis Adv. Council, 1960–73; Prog. and Budget Cttee, 15th World Health Assembly, 1962; Admin., Fin. and Legal Cttee 19th World Health Assembly (Pres., 24th Assembly, 1971); Exec. Bd, WHO, 1969–70 (Mem., 1967–70). Member: Council, Aust. Red Cross Soc., 1954–60; Mem. Nat. Blood Transfusion Cttee, ARCS 1955–60; Nat. Trustee, Returned Services League Aust., 1961–73, 1976–; Mem. Bd of Management, Canberra Grammar Sch., 1963–68; Mem. Bd of Trustees, Walter and Eliza Hall Inst. of Med. Res., Melbourne, 1977–86 (Chm., Ethics Cttee, 1983–88); Chm., Governing Bd, Menzies Sch. of Health Research, Darwin, 1983–87. Chm., ACT Cttee, Mem., Nat. Cttee and Mem. Nat. Exec., Sir Robert Menzies Foundn, 1979–84; Chm., Australian-Hellenic Meml Cttee, 1986–88. Hon. Life Mem., Australian Dental Assoc., 1966. Patron: Australian Sports Medicine Assoc., 1971–; ACT Br., Aust. Sports Medicine Fedn, 1980–; Totally and Permanently Incapacitated Assoc., ACT, 1982–; 2/2 (2nd AIF) Field Regtl Assoc., 1984–; Medical Assoc. for Prevention of War (MAPW), 1989–; ACT Hospice Soc., 1991–; 15 Field Ambulance Assoc., 1991–. Leader, Commemorative Tour of Europe for 60th anniversary, RSL. Nat. Pres., 1st Pan Pacific Conf. on alcohol and drugs, 1980. Hon MD Sydney, 1988. Anzac Peace Prize, 1990, Meritorious Medal, 1992, RSL. *Publications:* contribs to Australian Med. Jl, NZ Med. Jl, etc. *Recreations:* bowls, rug-making, gardening. *Address:* 26 Birdwood Street, Hughes, Canberra, ACT 2605, Australia. *Clubs:* Royal Society of Medicine (London); Naval and Military, Cricket (Melbourne); Commonwealth (Canberra); Bowling (Canberra); Royal Automobile (Victoria).

REGAN, Charles Maurice; Clerk to the Trustees, Hampstead Wells and Campden Trust, 1985–93; Under-Secretary, Department of Health and Social Security, 1972–79 and 1981–85; *b* 31 Oct. 1925; *m* 1961, Susan (*née* Littmann) (*d* 1972); one *s* one *d.* *Educ:* Taunton Sch.; London Sch. of Economics and Political Science (BSc(Econ)). Academic research, 1950–52. Asst Principal, Min. of National Insurance, 1952; Principal Private Sec. to Minister of Pensions and National Insurance, 1962–64; Asst Sec., 1964; Treasury/Civil Service Dept, 1967–70; Under-Sec., DES, 1979–81. *Recreations:* walking, travel. *Address:* 35 Crediton Hill, NW6 1HS. *T:* 0171–794 6404. *Club:* Athenæum.

REGAN, Hon. Donald Thomas; financier, author; Chief of Staff to the President of the United States, 1985–87; *b* 21 Dec. 1918; *s* of late William F. Regan and Kathleen A. Regan; *m* 1942, Ann Gordon Buchanan; two *s* two *d.* *Educ:* Cambridge Latin Sch.; Harvard Univ. (BA). Served War, US Marine Corps, 1940–46; retd as Lt Col, Marine Corps Reserve. Merrill Lynch, Pierce, Fenner & Smith Inc., 1946–81: Vice Pres., 1959–64; Exec. Vice Pres., 1964–68; Pres., 1968–71; Chm. of Bd, 1971–80; Chm. of Bd, Merrill Lynch & Co., Inc., 1973–81; Sec. of the Treasury, US Treasury Dept, 1981–85. Hon. LLD: Hahnemann Med. Coll. and Hosp., 1968; Tri-State Coll., 1969; Univ. of Penn., 1972; Hon. Dr of Commercial Science, Pace Univ., 1973; Hon DHL Colgate Univ., 1984. Fortune magazine's Hall of Fame for business leadership, 1981. Legion of Honour, 1982. *Publications:* A View from the Street, 1972; For the Record: from Wall Street to Washington, 1988. *Recreations:* golf, reading, boating. *Address:* 240 McLaws Circle, Suite 142, Williamsburg, VA 23185, USA. *Clubs:* Army-Navy (Washington, DC); Burning Tree (Bethesda, Md).

REGAN, Rt Rev. Edwin; *see* Wrexham, Bishop of, (RC).

REGAN, Hon. Gerald Augustine, PC (Can.) 1980; QC (Can.) 1970; President, Hawthorne Developments, since 1984; lawyer; *b* Windsor, NS, 13 Feb. 1929; *s* of Walter E. Regan and Rose M. Greene; *m* 1956, A. Carole, *d* of John H. Harrison; three *s* three *d.* *Educ:* Windsor Academy; St Mary's and Dalhousie Univs, Canada; Dalhousie Law Sch. (LLB). Called to Bar of Nova Scotia, 1954. Liberal candidate in Provincial gen. elecs, 1956 and 1960, and in Fed. gen. elec., 1962. MP for Halifax, NS, House of Commons of Canada, 1963–65; Leader, Liberal Party of Nova Scotia, 1965–80; MLA for Halifax-Needham, Provincial gen. elec., 1967, re-elected, 1970–74 and 1978; Premier of Nova Scotia, 1970–78, Leader of the Opposition 1978–80; Minister of Labour, Govt of Canada, 1980–81, Minister responsible for Fitness and Amateur Sport 1980–82; Secretary of State for Canada, 1981–82; Minister for International Trade, 1982–84; Minister of Energy, Mines and Resources, June–Sept. 1984. Mem., NS Barristers Soc.; Chm. Exec. Cttee, Commonwealth Parly Assoc., 1973–76; Mem., Canadian Delegn, UN, 1965. Chm., Trenton Works Inc.; former Chm., Canadian Exporters Assoc.; Director: United Financial Management; Canadian Surety Co.; Air Atlantic; Sceptre Resources; Roman Corp.; Provigo Inc. Governor, Olympic Trust of Canada; Vice-Chm., Tennis Canada. *Recreations:* tennis, ski-ing. *Address:* PO Box 828 Station B, Ottawa, Ontario K1P 5P9, Canada; (home) 2332 Georgina Drive, Ottawa, K2B 7M4, Canada. *Club:* Halifax (Halifax, NS).

REGAN, Maj.-Gen. Michael Dalrymple, OBE 1985; Chief of Staff HQ Adjutant General, since 1995, and Director General Adjutant General's Corps, since 1994; *b* 6 Jan. 1942; *s* of M. L. R. Regan and G. I. Regan (*née* Dalrymple); *m* 1974, Victoria Grenfell; two *d.* *Educ:* St Boniface's Coll.; RMA, Sandhurst. Commnd 1st KSLI, 1962; Instructor, Sch. of Infantry, 1968–70; Adjutant, 3rd LI, 1971–73; Staff Coll., Camberley, 1973–74; BM, 12th Mech. Bde, 1975–76; Company Comdr, 1st LI, 1977–78; MA to C-in-C, UKLF, 1979–82; CO, 3rd LI, 1982–84; Col MS 2, MoD, 1985; Comdr, 20th Armd Bde, 1986–87; RCDS, 1988; DCOS, HQ UKLF, 1989–91; GOC Wales and Western Dist, 1991–94. Col, LI, 1992–. *Recreations:* tennis, golf, ski-ing, sailing, gardening. *Club:* Army and Navy.

REGO, (Maria) Paula (Figueiroa), (Mrs Victor Willing); artist; *b* 26 Jan. 1935; *d* of José Fernandes Figueiroa Rego and Maria de S José Pavva Figueiroa Rego; *m* 1959, Victor Willing (*d* 1988); one *s* two *d.* *Educ:* St Julian's Sch., Carcavelos, Portugal; Slade School of Fine Art, UCL. First Associate Artist, Nat. Gall., Jan.–Dec. 1990. Selected solo exhibitions: (1st at) Soc. Nat. de Belas Artes, Lisbon, 1965; Gal. S Mamede, Lisbon, 1971; Gal. Modulo, Porto, 1977; Gal. III, Lisbon, 1978; Air Gall., London, 1981; Edward Totah Gall., 1982, 1985, 1987; Arnolfini, 1983; Art Palace, NY, 1985; Gulbenkian Foundn (retrospective), 1988; Serpentine Gall. (retrospective), 1988; Marlborough Graphics (nursery rhymes), 1989; Nat. Gall., 1991–92; Marlborough Gall., 1992, 1994. Many collective shows include: ICA, 1965; S Paulo Biennale, 1969, 1985; British Art Show, 1985; Hayward Gall., 1994; also in Japan, Australia, all over Europe. Large painting, Crivelli's Garden, in restaurant of Sainsbury Wing, Nat. Gall., 1992. Sen. Fellow, RCA, 1989–. *Relevant Publication:* Paula Rego, by John McEwen, 1992. *Recreations:* going to the movies, plays. *Address:* c/o Marlborough Fine Art, 6 Albemarle Street, W1X 4BY. *T:* 0171–629 5161.

REHNQUIST, William H.; Chief Justice of the United States, since 1986; *b* 1 Oct. 1924; *s* of William Benjamin and Margery Peck Rehnquist; *m* 1953, Natalie Cornell; one *s* two *d.* *Educ:* Stanford and Harvard Univs. BA, MA 1948, LLB 1952, Stanford; MA Harvard 1949. Law Clerk for Mr Justice Robert H. Jackson, 1952–53; Partner, Phoenix, Ariz: Evans, Kitchell & Jenckes, 1953–55; Ragan & Rehnquist, 1956–57; Cunningham, Carson & Messenger, 1957–60; Powers & Rehnquist, 1960–69; Asst Attorney-Gen., Office of Legal Counsel, Dept of Justice, 1969–72; Associate Justice, Supreme Court, 1972–86. Phi Beta Kappa; Order of the Coif. *Publications:* contrib. US News and World Report, Jl of Amer. Bar Assoc., Arizona Law Review. *Recreations:* swimming, tennis, reading, hiking. *Address:* Supreme Court of the United States, Washington, DC 20543, USA. *Club:* National Lawyers (Washington, DC).

REICH, Peter Gordon; Assistant Chief Scientist (G), Royal Air Force, 1984–85; *b* 16 Sept. 1926; *s* of Douglas Gordon Reich and Josephine Grace Reich; *m* 1948, Kathleen, *d* of Alan and Florence Lessiter, Banstead; three *d.* *Educ:* Sutton Grammar Sch.; London Univ. (BSc). FRIN 1967 (Bronze Medal, 1967). Served RN, 1944–47. Entered Civil Service as Scientific Officer, 1952; Armament Res. Estab., 1952–54; Opl Res. Br., Min. of Transport and Civil Aviation, 1955–60; RAE, 1960–68; Asst Dir of Electronics Res. and Develt (2), Min. of Technol., 1968–70; Asst Dir of Res. (Avionics, Space and Air Traffic), Min. of Aviation Supply, 1971–73; Supt, Def. Opl Analysis Estab., MoD, 1973–76; Mem., Reliability and Costing Study Gp, MoD, 1976–79; Counsellor (Defence Res.), Canberra, and Head of British Defence Res. and Supply Staffs, Australia, 1979–83. *Publications:* papers in Jl of Inst. of Nav., and Jl of Opl Res. Soc. *Recreations:* racquet games, walking, aural pleasures.

REICH, Steve; composer; *b* 3 Oct. 1936; *s* of Leonard Reich and June (*née* Carroll); *m* 1976, Beryl Korot; one *s*, and one *s* from previous *m.* *Educ:* Cornell Univ. (BA Hons Philos. 1957); Juilliard Sch. of Music; Mills Coll. (MA Music 1963); Inst. for African Studies, Univ. of Ghana. Guggenheim Fellow, 1978. Mem., AAAL, 1994. Founded ensemble, Steve Reich and Musicians, 1966, toured the world, 1971–. Music performed by major orchestras, including: NY Philharmonic; San Francisco Symphony; St Louis Symphony; Brooklyn Philharmonic; LA Philharmonic; BBC Symphony; Brooklyn Symphony; commissions received include: Fest. d'Automne, Paris for 200th Anniv. of French Revolution, 1989; BBC Proms in honour of centennial, 1995. *Compositions include:* Drumming, 1971; Music for 18 Musicians, 1976; Eight Lines, 1979–83; Tehillim, 1981; The Desert Music, 1984; Sextet, 1985; Different Trains, 1988 (Grammy Award for Best Contemporary Composition, 1990); The Cave, 1993; City Life, 1995. *Publications:* Writings About Music, 1974. *Address:* c/o Andrew Rosner Allieds Artists, 42 Montpelier Square, SW7 1JZ.

REICHSTEIN, Prof. Tadeus, Dr ing chem; Ordentlicher Professor, Head of Department of Organic Chemistry, University of Basel, 1946–60, now Emeritus; *b* Wloclawek, Poland, 20 July 1897; *s* of Isidor Reichstein and Gustava Brockmann; *m* 1927, Henriette Louise Quarles van Ufford; two *d.* *Educ:* Oberrealschule and Eidgenössische Technische Hochschule, Department of Chemistry, Zürich. Assistant, ETH, Zürich, 1922–34; professor of organic chemistry, ETH, Zürich, 1934; head of department of pharmacy, University of Basel, 1938. Dr *hc* Sorbonne, Paris, 1947, Basel 1951, Geneva, 1967, ETH, Zürich, 1967, Abidjan 1967, London 1968, Leeds 1970. Marcel Benoît Prize, 1948; (jointly) Nobel Prize for Medicine, 1950; Cameron Prize, 1951; Copley Medal, Royal Soc., 1968; Dale Medal, Soc. for Endocrinology, 1975. Foreign Member: Royal Society, 1952; Linnean Society, 1974. Hon. Member: British Pteridological Soc., 1967; Amer. Fern Soc., 1974; Deutsche Botanische Gesellschaft, 1976; Schweizerische Botanische Gesellschaft, 1977. *Publications:* numerous papers. *Recreations:* botany (ferns), devoted gardener, mountain-climber. *Address:* Institut für Organische Chemie der Universität, St Johanns-Ring 19, 4056 Basel, Switzerland. *T:* (061) 3226060.

REID, Dr Alexander Arthur Luttrell; Director-General, Royal Institute of British Architects, since 1994; *b* 11 Jan. 1941; *s* of late Capt. Philip Reid, RN and of Louisa (*née* Luttrell); *m* 1st, 1964, Sara Louise Coleridge (marr. diss. 1987); two *d*; 2nd, 1988, Sian Tudor Roberts; one *s* one *d.* *Educ:* Winchester Coll. (Schol.); Trinity Coll., Cambridge (MA); University Coll., London (MSc; PhD 1974). Served RN, Lieut (helicopter pilot), 1962–67. Post Office Telecommunications: Hd, Long Range Studies, 1972–77; Director: Prestel, 1977–80; Business Systems, 1980–83; Acorn Computer Gp PLC, 1984–85; Octagon Investment Mgt Ltd, 1984–; Chief Exec., DEGW Ltd, 1991–94. Royal College of Art: Council Mem., 1988–90; Chm., 1990–93. Has invented a spanner (for gripping large inaccessible nuts) and audio-conferencing system. *Recreations:* carpentry, sailing. *Address:* 64 Kensington Park Road, W11 3BJ. *T:* 0171–727 2998.

REID, Sir Alexander (James), 3rd Bt *cr* 1897; JP; DL; *b* 6 Dec. 1932; *s* of Sir Edward James Reid, 2nd Bt, KBE, and Tatiana (*d* 1992), *d* of Col Alexander Fenoult, formerly of Russian Imperial Guard; *S* father, 1972; *m* 1955, Michaela Ann, *d* of late Olaf Kier, CBE; one *s* three *d.* *Educ:* Eton; Magdalene Coll., Cambridge. Nat. Certificate Agriculture (NCA). 2nd Lieut, 1st Bn Gordon Highlanders, 1951; served Malaya; Captain, 3rd Bn Gordon Highlanders (TA), retired 1964. Director: Ellon Castle Estates Co. Ltd, 1965–; Cristina Securities Ltd, 1970–. Chm., Clan Donnachaidh Soc., 1994–. Governor, Heath Mount Prep. Sch., Hertford, 1970, Chm., 1976–92. JP Cambridgeshire and Isle of Ely, 1971, DL 1973; High Sheriff, Cambridgeshire, 1987–88. *Recreations:* shooting, travel. *Heir:* *s* Charles Edward James Reid, *b* 24 June 1956. *Address:* Lanton Tower, Jedburgh,

Roxburghshire TD8 6SU. *T:* Jedburgh (01835) 863443. *Clubs:* Caledonian; New (Edinburgh).

REID, Andrew Milton; Deputy Chairman, Imperial Group, 1986–89; *b* 21 July 1929; *s* of late Rev. A. R. R. Reid, DD and of Lilias Symington Tindal; *m* 1953, Norma Mackenzie Davidson (*d* 1993); two *s*; *m* 1995, Audrey Janet Wilson Bruell. *Educ:* Glasgow Academy; Jesus Coll., Oxford. Imperial Tobacco Management Pupil, 1952; Asst Managing Director, John Player & Sons, 1975; Director Imperial Group Ltd, 1978; Chm., Imperial Tobacco Ltd, 1979–86. Dep. Chm., Trade Indemnity plc, 1994– (Dir, 1982–); Dir, Renold PLC, 1983–. Member, Tobacco Adv. Council, 1977–86. Member: Bath and Wells Diocesan Synod, 1986–92; Council, RSCM, 1987–89; Court and Council, Bristol Univ., 1986–; Board, Bristol Develt Corp., 1989– (Dep. Chm., 1993–). Chm. Governors, Colston's Collegiate Sch., 1986–94. Master, Soc. of Merchant Venturers of Bristol, 1991–92. High Sheriff of Avon, 1991. *Recreations:* sailing, golf, fishing. *Address:* Parsonage Farm, Publow, Pensford, near Bristol BS18 4JD. *Club:* United Oxford & Cambridge University.

REID, Beryl, OBE 1986; actress; *b* 17 June 1920. *Educ:* Lady Barne House Sch.; Withington High Sch.; Levenshulme High Sch., Manchester. First stage appearance, Bridlington, 1936; on London stage, 1951; appeared in variety, numerous sketches, revues and pantomimes, 1951–64. *Plays:* The Killing of Sister George, Duke of York's, 1965, NY, 1966 (Tony Award for Best Actress); Blithe Spirit, Globe, 1970; Entertaining Mr Sloane, Royal Court, Duke of York's, 1975; National Theatre: Spring Awakening, Romeo and Juliet, 1974; Il Campiello, Counting the Ways, 1976; The Way of the World, RSC, Aldwych, 1978; Born in the Gardens, Bristol Old Vic, 1979, Globe (SWET Award), 1980; The School for Scandal, Haymarket, and Duke of York's, 1983; A Little Bit on the Side, Yvonne Arnaud, Guildford, 1983; Gigi, Lyric, 1985. *Films include:* The Belles of St Trinians, Star, The Killing of Sister George, Entertaining Mr Sloane, No Sex Please—We're British!, Joseph Andrews, Carry On Emmanuelle, Yellowbeard, The Doctor and the Devils, Duel of Hearts, Comic Strip: Didn't You Kill My Brother? Frequent television and radio performances, including This is Your Life, and her own series on several occasions; Best TV actress award, BAFTA, 1983 (for Smiley's People). *Publications:* So Much Love (autobiog.), 1984; (with Eric Braun) The Cats Whiskers, 1986; (with Eric Braun) Beryl, Food and Friends, 1987; The Kingfisher Jump, 1991. *Recreations:* gardening, cooking. *Address:* Robert Luff, 294 Earls Court Road, SW5 9BB. *T:* 0171–373 7003; James Sharkey Associates, 3rd Floor, 15 Golden Square, W1R 3AG.

REID, Derek Donald; Chief Executive, Scottish Tourist Board, since 1994; *b* 30 Nov. 1944; *s* of Robert Slorach Reid and Selina Mons Lewis Reid (*née* Donald); *m* 1977, Janice Anne Reid; one *s* one *d*. *Educ:* Inverurie Acad., Aberdeen; Aberdeen Univ. (MA); Robert Gordon Inst. of Technol. (Dip. Personnel Mgt). Cadbury Schweppes: mgt trainee, 1968; Divl Dir, 1982–86; Founder Mem., Premier Brands and Dir, Tea Business after mgt buy-out, 1986–89; Man. Dir, Tea Business, 1989–90; dir, various small cos, 1990–94. *Recreations:* golf, cricket, fishing, art appreciation, classical music. *Address:* Bonhard House, by Scone, Perth PH2 7PQ. *T:* Perth (01738) 52471. *Clubs:* Oriental; Murrayshall Golf (Perth), Gleneagles.

REID, Dougal Gordon, CMG 1983; HM Diplomatic Service, retired; Director of Studies, Royal Institute of Public Administration International Ltd, 1985–92; *b* Hong Kong, 31 Dec. 1925; *e s* of late Douglas Reid and Catherine Jean (*née* Lowson), Forfar; *m* 1950, Georgina Elizabeth Johnston; one *s* (and one *s* decd). *Educ:* Sedbergh Sch.; Trinity Hall, Cambridge; LSE. Served in Royal Marines, 1944–46. Cadet, Colonial Admin. Service (later HMOCS), Sierra Leone, 1949; District Comr 1956; retd as Perm. Sec., Min. of Natural Resources, 1962. Arthur Guinness Son & Co. Ltd, 1962–63. Entered CRO, later FCO, 1963; served in: Accra, 1964–65; CO, 1966; Accra, 1966–68 (concurrently Lomé, 1967–68); Seoul, 1968–71; FCO, 1971–74; Kinshasa (and concurrently at Brazzaville, Bujumbura and Kigali), 1974–77; New Delhi, 1977–78; Singapore, 1979–80; Ambassador to Liberia, 1980–85. Mem., Internat. Cttee, Leonard Cheshire Foundn, 1985–92. *Recreations:* military history, jazz, watching sport. *Clubs:* Travellers', Commonwealth Trust, MCC; London Scottish Football; Sadan Pubin (Seoul).

REID, Very Rev. Douglas William John; Dean of Glasgow and Galloway, since 1987; Rector of St Ninian's Episcopal Church, Glasgow, since 1973; *b* 15 Feb. 1934; *s* of Thomas Wood Reid and Catherine Henrietta Reid (*née* Ramsay); *m* 1964, Janet Cicely Nash; two *s*. *Educ:* Trinity Academy, Edinburgh; Episcopal Theological Coll., Edinburgh. Solicitor's clerk, Edinburgh, 1950–53; Army, 1953–55; industrial banking, 1956–60; theol coll., 1960–63; Asst Curate, Holy Trinity, Ayr, 1963–68; Rector, St James, Glasgow, 1968–73. *Recreations:* gardening, hill-walking, steam railways, reading. *Address:* St Ninian's Rectory, 32 Glencairn Drive, Glasgow G41 4PW. *T:* 0141–423 1247.

REID, Elizabeth Margaret, (Mrs M. J. Monk); Director of Education, City of Edinburgh Council, from April 1996 (Director-designate, since 1995); *b* 16 April 1947; *d* of John A. McConachie, MB ChB, FRCPE and J. Margaret McConachie, MB ChB; *m* 1st, 1970, Robin Reid, MA (marr. diss. 1975); 2nd, 1982, Martin J. Monk, BA Hons Oxon. *Educ:* Aberdeen Univ. (MA Hons 1969); London Univ. (MA Educnl Admin 1980). Asst Principal, CS, 1969–70; Inner London Education Authority: schoolteacher, 1970–78; Advr for 16–19 educn, 1978–79; Professional Asst, London Borough of Ealing, 1979–80; Asst Educn Officer, London Borough of Haringey, 1980–83; Sen. Principal Officer (Educn), AMA, 1983–85; Inner London Education Authority: Admin. Head, Further and Higher Educn Br., 1985–88; Dep. Dir of Educn (Further and Higher Educn), 1988–89; Dep. Provost, London Guildhall Univ. (formerly City of London Poly.), 1989–93; Dir of Educn, Lothian Regional Council, 1993–95. FRSA 1989. *Publications:* (contrib.) Central and Local Control of Education After the Education Reform Act 1988, ed R. Morris, 1990; (contrib.) The Future of Higher Education, ed T. Schuller, 1991; (with R. Morris and J. Fowler) Education Act 93: a critical guide, 1993. *Recreations:* theatre, opera, music, reading. *Address:* Department of Education, City of Edinburgh Council, 40 Torphichen Street, Edinburgh EH3 8JJ. *T:* 0131–229 9166.

REID, Rt. Rev. Gavin Hunter; *see* Maidstone, Bishop Suffragan of.

REID, George Newlands; Director (International Promotion), International Red Cross and Red Crescent Movement, since 1990; *b* 4 June 1939; *s* of late George Reid, company director, and of Margaret Forsyth; *m* 1968, Daphne Ann MacColl; two *d*. *Educ:* Tullibody Sch.; Dollar Academy; Univ. of St Andrews (MA Hons). Pres., Students' Representative Council. Features Writer, Scottish Daily Express, 1962; Reporter, Scottish Television, 1964; Producer, Granada Television, 1965; Head of News and Current Affairs (Scottish Television), 1968; freelance broadcaster and journalist, 1972–84; presenter, political and documentary progs, BBC. Head of Inf., 1984–86, Dir of Public Affairs, 1986–90, League of Red Cross and Red Crescent Socs, Geneva. MP (SNP) Stirlingshire E and Clackmannan, Feb. 1974–1979; Member, Select Committee on: Assistance to Private Members, 1975–76; Direct Elections to European Assembly, 1976–77; Mem., British Parly Delegn to Council of Europe and WEU, 1977–79. Dir, Scottish Council Res. Inst., 1974–77. Chief Red Cross deleg. to Armenia, Dec. 1988–Jan. 1989 (awarded Pirogov Gold Medal of Soviet Red Cross). *Address:* 23 Avenue du Bouchet, 1209 Petit Saconnex, Geneva, Switzerland. *T:* (22) 7346705.

REID, Gordon; *see* Reid, J. G.

REID, Rev. Canon Gordon; *see* Reid, Rev. Canon W. G.

REID, Graham Livingstone, CB 1991; Director General of Strategy, International and Analytical Services, Department for Education and Employment, since 1995; *b* 30 June 1937; *s* of late William L. Reid and of Louise M. Reid; *m* 1st, 1973, Eileen M. Loudfoot (marr. diss. 1983); 2nd, 1985, Sheila Rothwell. *Educ:* Univ. of St Andrews (MA); Queen's Univ., Kingston, Canada (MA). Dept of Social and Economic Res., Univ. of Glasgow: Asst Lectr in Applied Economics, 1960, Lectr 1963, Sen. Lectr 1968, Reader 1971; Sen. Econ. Adviser and Head of Econs and Statistics Unit, Scottish Office, 1973–75; Dir, Manpower Intelligence and Planning Div., MSC, 1975–84; Department of Employment: Chief Economic Adviser and Hd, Economic and Social Div., 1984–88 and Dir, Enterprise and Deregulation Unit, 1987; Dep. Sec., Manpower Policy, 1988–90, Resources and Strategy, 1991, Indust. Relns and Internat. Directorate, 1991–95. Vis. Associate Prof., Mich State Univ., 1967; Vis. Res. Fellow, Queen's Univ., Canada, 1969. *Publications:* Fringe Benefits, Labour Costs and Social Security (ed with D. J. Robertson), 1965; (with K. J. Allen) Nationalised Industries, 1970 (3rd edn 1975); (with L. C. Hunter and D. Boddy) Labour Problems of Technological Change, 1970; (with K. J. Allen and D. J. Harris) The Nationalised Fuel Industries, 1973; contrib. to Econ. Jl, Brit. Jl of Indust. Relations, Scot. Jl of Polit. Econ., Indust & Lab. Relns Rev. *Recreations:* golf, music, gardening. *Address:* Department for Education and Employment, Sanctuary Buildings, 20 Great Smith Street, SW1P 3BT. *Club:* Commonwealth Trust.

REID, Sir (Harold) Martin (Smith), KBE 1987; CMG 1978; HM Diplomatic Service, retired; *b* 27 Aug. 1928; *s* of late Marcus Reid and late Winifred Mary Reid (*née* Stephens); *m* 1956, Jane Elizabeth Harwood; one *s* three *d*. *Educ:* Merchant Taylors' Sch.; Brasenose Coll., Oxford (Open Scholar). RN, 1947–49. Entered HM Foreign Service, 1953; served in: FO, 1953–54; Paris, 1954–57; Rangoon, 1958–61; FO, 1961–65; Georgetown, 1965–68; Bucharest, 1968–70; Dep. High Comr, Malaŵi, 1970–73; Private Sec. to successive Secs of State for NI, 1973–74; Head of Central and Southern Africa Dept, FCO, 1974–78; Minister, British Embassy, Pretoria/Cape Town, 1979–82; Resident Chm. (Dip. Service) CS Selection Bd, 1983–84; High Comr to Jamaica, and Ambassador (non-resident) to Haiti, 1984–87; Research Advr, FCO, 1987–88. Hon. Sec., Friends of Student Christian Movement, 1989–92. One-man exhibitions: London, 1983; Kingston, Jamaica, 1987; Dulwich, 1989, 1991, 1994. *Publication:* Pissarro, 1993. *Recreation:* painting. *Address:* 43 Carson Road, SE21 8HT. *T:* 0181–670 6151.

See also M. H. M. Reid.

REID, Sir Hugh, 3rd Bt *cr* 1922; farmer; *b* 27 Nov. 1933; *s* of Sir Douglas Neilson Reid, 2nd Bt, and Margaret Brighton Young (*d* 1992), *d* of Robert Young Maxtone, MBE, JP; *S* father, 1971. *Educ:* Loretto. Royal Air Force, 1952–56; RAFVR, 1956–78 (Flying Officer, Training Branch, 1965–78). *Recreations:* skiing, travel. *Heir:* none. *Address:* Caheronaun Park, Loughrea, Co. Galway.

REID, Iain; Director of Combined Arts, Arts Council of England, since 1994; *b* 27 March 1942; *s* of Jean Reid (*née* Money) and George Aitken Reid; *m* 1st, 1968, Judith Coke; 2nd, 1982, Kay Barlow; one *s* one *d*. *Educ:* Uppingham; RADA; Lancaster Univ. (MA). Actor, 1963–73; theatre administrator, 1973–77; Drama Officer, Greater London Arts, 1977–82; Dir of Arts, Calouste Gulbenkian Foundn (UK), 1982–89; Dir, Arts Co-ordination, later Arts Develt, Arts Council of GB, 1989–94. FRSA 1992. *Recreations:* skating, sailing. *Address:* Arts Council of England, 14 Great Peter Street, SW1P 3NQ.

REID, Ian George; Director, Centre for European Agricultural Studies, Wye College, University of London, 1974–86; *b* 12 May 1921; 2nd *s* of James John Reid and Margaret Jane Reid; *m* 1946, Peggy Eileen Bridgman. *Educ:* Merchant Taylors' Sch.; London Sch. of Econs (BScEcon); Christ's Coll., Cambridge (Dip. Agric.). Lectr, Reading Univ., 1945–53; Lectr, 1953–63, and Sen. Lectr, 1963–86, Wye Coll. Pres., Agricultural Econs Soc., 1981–82. *Recreations:* enjoying music, gardening, art. *Address:* 20 Bridge Street, Wye, Ashford, Kent TN25 5EA. *T:* Wye (Kent) (01233) 812388. *Club:* Farmers'.

REID, James, OBE (mil.) 1968; VRD 1967; Director, Investments and Loans, Commission of European Communities, 1973–76; *b* 23 Nov. 1921; *s* of William Reid, MBE, and Dora Louisa Reid (*née* Smith); *m* 1949, Margaret James (*d* 1987); two *d*. *Educ:* City of London Sch.; Emmanuel Coll., Cambridge (MA). Served War, RN: RNVR (Sub. Lieut), 1942–45. Served RNVR and RNR (Comdr), 1953–72. Entered Northern Ireland Civil Service, 1948 (Asst Principal); Min. of Finance, 1948–61 and 1963–73; Min. of Commerce, 1961–63; Principal, 1953; Asst Sec., 1963; Sen. Asst Sec., 1971; Dep. Sec., 1972. *Recreations:* reading, music. *Address:* 4 Old School Court, King's Lynn, Norfolk PE30 1DB.

REID, (James) Gordon; QC (Scot) 1993; *b* 24 July 1952; *s* of James R. Reid and Constance M. Lawrie or Reid; *m* 1984, Hannah Hogg Hopkins; three *s* one *d*. *Educ:* Melville Coll., Edinburgh; Edinburgh Univ. (LLB Hons). Solicitor, 1976–80; Advocate, 1980–; called to the Bar, Inner Temple, 1991. *Recreations:* music, classical guitar, physical fitness. *Address:* Lower Bunzion, by Pitlessie, Cupar, Fife KY15 7TE. *T:* Ladybank (01337) 830844.

REID, James Robert; QC 1980; a Recorder, since 1985; *b* 23 Jan. 1943; *s* of late Judge J. A. Reid, MC and Jean Ethel Reid; *m* 1974, Anne Prudence Wakefield; two *s* one *d*. *Educ:* Marlborough Coll.; New Coll., Oxford (MA). Called to the Bar, Lincoln's Inn, 1965, Bencher, 1988. Mem., Senate of Inns of Court and the Bar, 1977–80; Mem., Gen. Council of the Bar, 1990–. Chm., Barristers Benevolent Assoc., 1995– (Hon. Jt Treas., 1986–91; Dep. Chm., 1991–95). *Recreations:* fencing, cricket. *Address:* 9 Old Square, Lincoln's Inn, WC2A 3SR.

REID, Dr John; MP (Lab) Motherwell North, since 1987; *b* 8 May 1947; *s* of late Thomas Reid and of Mary Reid; *m* 1969, Catherine (*née* McGowan); two *s*. *Educ:* St Patrick's Senior Secondary Sch., Coatbridge; Stirling Univ. (BA History, PhD Economic History). Scottish Research Officer, Labour Party, 1979–83; Political Adviser to Rt Hon. Neil Kinnock, 1983–85; Scottish Organiser, Trades Unionists for Labour, 1985–87. Opposition spokesman on children, 1989–90, on defence, 1990–. Mem., Public Accounts Cttee, 1988–89. *Recreations:* football, reading, crossword puzzles. *Address:* House of Commons, SW1A 0AA; (office) 114 Manse Road, Newmains, Strathclyde ML2 9BD. *T:* Cambusnethan (01698) 383866, *Fax:* (01698) 381243.

REID, John Boyd, AO 1980; LLB; FAIM; Chairman, James Hardie Industries Ltd, since 1973; *b* 27 Dec. 1929; *s* of Sir John Thyne Reid, CMG. *Educ:* Scotch College; Melbourne Univ. Chm., Comsteel Vickers Ltd, 1983–86; Vice-Chm., Qantas Airways, 1981–86 (Dir, 1977–86); Director: Broken Hill Pty Co., 1972–; Barclays Internat. Australia, 1982–85; Bell Resources Ltd, 1987–88; Peregrine Capital Australia Ltd, 1991–95; Focus Publishing, 1991–. Chm., Australian Bicentennial Authy, 1979–85; Dir, World Expo 88, 1986–89; Member: Admin. Review Cttee, 1975–76; Indep. Inquiry into Commonwealth Serum Labs, 1978; Patron, Australia Indonesia Business Co-operation Cttee, 1979–88 (Pres., 1973–79); Dir, Thailand-Australia Foundn Ltd, 1993–; Mem., Internat. Adv. Bd,

Swiss Banking Corp., 1986–; Chm., Review of Commonwealth Admin, 1981–82. Trustee and Internat. Counsellor, Conference Bd USA; Internat. Council, Stanford Res. Inst., USA. Chairman: NSW Educn and Trng Foundn, 1989–93; Cttee, Aust. Scout Educn and Trng Foundn, 1991; Museum of Contemp. Art, 1994–. Chm. Council, Pymble Ladies Coll., 1975–82 (Mem., 1965–75); Governor, Ian Clunies Ross Meml Foundn, 1975–; Chm., Sydney Adv. Cttee, 1995–, and Red Shield Appeal, 1993–, Salvation Army. Mem., Inst. of Company Dirs. Life Governor, AIM (Sydney Div.). Melbourne Univ. Graduate Sch. of Business Admin Award, 1983; John Storey Medal, AIM, 1985. *Address:* c/o James Hardie Industries Ltd, GPO Box 3935, Sydney, NSW 2001, Australia. *Clubs:* Australian (Sydney); Royal Sydney Yacht Squadron.

REID, Rev. Prof. John Kelman Sutherland, CBE 1970; TD 1961; Professor of Christian Dogmatics, 1961–70, of Systematic Theology 1970–76, University of Aberdeen; *b* 31 March 1910; *y s* of late Reverend Dr David Reid, Calcutta and Leith, and of late Mrs G. T. Reid (*née* Stuart); *m* 1950, Margaret Winifrid Brookes (*d* 1989). *Educ:* George Watson's Boys' College, Edinburgh; Universities of Edinburgh (MA and BD), Heidelberg, Marburg, Basel, and Strasbourg. MA 1st Cl. Hons Philosophy, 1933. Prof. of Philosophy in Scottish Church Coll., Univ. of Calcutta, 1935–37; BD (dist. in Theol.), 1938, and Cunningham Fellow. Ordained into Church of Scotland and inducted into Parish of Craigmillar Park, Edinburgh, 1939. CF, chiefly with Parachute Regt, 1942–46. Jt Ed. Scot. Jl Theol. since inception, 1947; Hon. Sec. Jt Cttee on New Translation of the Bible, 1949–82; Prof. of Theology and Head of Department of Theology, University of Leeds, 1952–61. Hon. DD (Edinburgh), 1957. *Publications:* The Authority of Scripture, 1957; Our Life in Christ, 1963; Christian Apologetics, 1969. Translation of: Oscar Cullmann's The Earliest Christian Confessions, 1949; Baptism in the New Testament, 1952; Calvin's Theological Treatises, ed and trans. 1954; Jean Bosc's The Kingly Office of the Lord Jesus Christ, 1959; Calvin's Concerning the Eternal Pre-destination of God, ed and trans., 1961, repr. 1982. *Address:* 8 Abbotsford Court, 18 Colinton Road, Edinburgh EH10 5EH. *Club:* Mortonhall Golf (Edinburgh).

REID, Prof. John Low, DM; Regius Professor of Medicine and Therapeutics, since 1989, and Clinical Director, Acute Medicine, since 1993, University of Glasgow; *b* 1 Oct. 1943; *s* of Dr James Reid and Irene M. Dale; *m* 1964, Randa Pharaon; one *s* one *d*. *Educ:* Fettes Coll., Edinburgh; Magdalen Coll., Oxford. MA; DM; FRCP, FRCPGlas; FRSE 1995. House Officer, Radcliffe Infirmary, Oxford, and Brompton Hosp., 1967–70; Res. Fellow, RPMS, 1970–73; Vis. Fellow, Nat. Inst. of Mental Health, USA, 1973–74; Royal Postgraduate Medical School: Sen. Lectr in Clin. Pharmacol., and Consultant Physician, 1975–77; Reader in Clin. Pharmacol., 1977–78; Regius Prof. of Materia Medica, Univ. of Glasgow, 1978–89. *Publications:* Central Action of Drugs in Regulation of Blood Pressure, 1975; Lecture Notes in Clinical Pharmacology, 1982; Handbook of Hypertension, 1983; papers on cardiovascular and neurological diseases in clinical and pharmacological journals. *Recreations:* books, gardening, the outdoors. *Address:* Department of Medicine, Western Infirmary, Glasgow G11 6NT. *T:* 0141–211 2886.

REID, Rt. Rev. John Robert; United Mission to Nepal, since 1995; Bishop of South Sydney, 1983–93 (Assistant Bishop, Diocese of Sydney, 1972–93); *b* 15 July 1928; *s* of John and Edna Reid; *m* 1955, Alison Gertrude Dunn; two *s* four *d*. *Educ:* Melbourne Univ. (BA); Moore Coll., Sydney (ThL). Deacon 1955, Priest 1955; Curate, Manly, 1955–56; Rector, Christ Church, Gladesville, NSW, 1956–69; Archdeacon of Cumberland, NSW, 1969–72. *Recreation:* walking. *Address:* c/o United Mission to Nepal, PO Box 126, Kathmandu, Nepal.

REID, Prof. Kenneth Bannerman Milne, PhD; Professor of Immunochemistry, University of Oxford, since 1993; Fellow, Green College, Oxford, since 1986; Director, MRC Immunochemistry Unit, Oxford University, since 1985; *b* 22 Sept. 1943; *s* of John McBean Reid and Maria Anderson (*née* Smith); *m* 1969, Margery Robertson Gilmour; one *s* two *d*. *Educ:* Univ. of Aberdeen (BSc 1965; PhD 1968). SO, Fisheries Res. Unit, Aberdeen Univ., 1968–69; ICI Res. Fellowship, Dept Biochem., Univ. of Oxford, 1969–70; Mem., Scientific Staff, 1970–84, Dep. Dir, 1984–85, MRC Immunochemistry Unit, Dept of Biochemistry, Univ of Oxford. Fellow, EMBO, 1991. Second Wellcome Trust Lecture Award, 1981. *Publications:* Complement, 1988, 2nd edn 1995; author or co-author of numerous papers in jls such as Nature, Biochem. Jl, Jl Immunology. *Recreations:* hill-walking, racket sports (squash, tennis). *Address:* MRC Immunochemistry Unit, Department of Biochemistry, University of Oxford, South Parks Road, Oxford OX1 3QU. *T:* Oxford (01865) 275353.

REID, Leslie, CBE 1978; HM Diplomatic Service, retired; Director General, The Association of British Mining Equipment Companies, 1980–83; *b* 24 May 1919; *s* of late Frederick Sharples and Mary Reid; *m* 1942, Norah Moorcroft; three *d*. *Educ:* King George V Sch., Southport, Lancs. Served War of 1939–45, W Europe and SEAC, Major, XX The Lancashire Fusiliers. Board of Trade, 1947–49; Asst Trade Commissioner: Salisbury, Rhodesia, 1949–55; Edmonton, Alberta, 1955–56; Trade Comr, Vancouver, 1956–60; Principal, BoT, 1960–62; Trade Comr and Economic Advisor, British High Commn, Cyprus, 1962–64; BoT, 1964–66; 1st Sec., FCO, 1966–68; Sen. Commercial Sec., British High Commn, Jamaica, and 1st Sec., British Embassy, Port-au-Prince, Haiti, 1968–70; Commercial and Economic Counsellor, Ghana, 1970–73; Consul Gen., Cleveland, Ohio, 1973–79. *Recreations:* golf, reading. *Address:* Kingsdowne, Albert Terrace, Norwich NR2 2JD.

REID, Prof. Lynne McArthur; Simeon Burt Wolbach Professor of Pathology, Harvard Medical School, since 1976; Pathologist-in-Chief, Children's Hospital, Boston, 1976–90, now Pathologist-in-Chief Emeritus; *b* Melbourne, 12 Nov. 1923; *er d* of Robert Muir Reid and Violet Annie Reid (*née* McArthur). *Educ:* Wimbledon Girls' Sch. (GPDST); Janet Clarke Hall, Trinity Coll., Melbourne Univ.; Royal Melbourne Hosp. MB, BS Melb. 1946; MRACP 1950; MRCP 1951; FRACP, MRCPath (Foundn Mem.) 1964; FRCPath 1966; FRCP 1969; MD Melb. 1969. House Staff, Royal Melb. Hosp., 1946–49; Res. Fellow, Nat. Health and MRC, Royal Melb. Hosp. and Eliza Hall, 1949–51; Res. Asst, Inst. Diseases of Chest, 1951–55; Sen. Lectr founding Res. Dept of Path., Inst. Diseases of Chest, 1955; Reader in Exper. Path., London Univ., 1964; Prof. of Exper. Path., Inst. of Diseases of Chest (later Cardiothoracic Inst.), 1967–76; Hon. Lectr, UC Med. Sch., 1971–76; Hon. Consultant in Exper. Path., Brompton Hosp., 1963–76; Dean, Cardiothoracic Inst. (British Postgrad. Med. Fedn), 1973–76. 1st Hastings Vis. Prof. in Path., Univ. of California, 1965; Holme Lectr, UC Med. Sch., 1969; Walker-Ames Prof., Univ. of Washington, 1971; Neuhauser Lectr, 1976; Fleischner Lectr, 1976; Waring Prof., Stanford and Denver, 1977; Amberson Lectr, Amer. Thoracic Soc., 1978. Mem. Fleischner Soc., 1971 (Pres., 1977); 1st Hon. Fellow, Canadian Thoracic Soc., 1973; Chm., Cystic Fibrosis Res. Trust, 1974 (Mem. Med. Adv. Cttee 1964); Royal Soc. Medicine (Sect. Pathology): Vice-Pres. 1974; Standing Liaison Cttee on Sci. Aspects of Smoking and Health, 1971; Commn of European Cttees (Industrial Safety and Medicine), 1972; Mem. Bd of Governors, Nat. Heart and Chest Hosps, 1974; Manager, Royal Instn of Gt Britain, 1973 (Vice-Pres. 1974); Mem. Gov. Body, British Postgrad. Med. Fedn, 1974. *Publications:* The Pathology of Emphysema, 1967; numerous papers in sci. jls. *Recreations:* music, travel, reading. *Address:* Department of Pathology, Children's Hospital, 300 Longwood Avenue, Boston, MA 02115, USA. *T:* (617) 7357440, *Fax:* (617) 7310554; 50 Longwood Avenue, #216, Brookline, MA 02146, USA. *Clubs:* University Women's; Harvard (Boston).

REID, Malcolm Herbert Marcus; Director, Mercury Life Assurance Co. Ltd, since 1989; *b* 2 March 1927; *s* of late Marcus Reid and Winifred Stephens; *m* 1st, 1956, Eleanor (*d* 1974), *d* of late H. G. Evans, MC; four *s*; 2nd, 1975, Daphne, *e d* of Sir John Griffin, QC. *Educ:* Merchant Taylors' Sch.; St John's Coll., Oxford. Served in Navy, 1945–48 and in RNVR, 1949–53. Entered Board of Trade, 1951; Private Secretary to Permanent Secretary, 1954–57; Trade Comr in Ottawa, 1957–60; Board of Trade, 1960–63; Private Secretary to successive Prime Ministers, 1963–66; Commercial Counsellor, Madrid, 1967–71; Asst Sec., DTI, 1972–74; Under Sec., Dept of Industry, 1974–78, of Trade, 1978–83, DTI, 1983–84; Registrar, Registry of Life Assurance Commn, 1984–86; Chief Exec., Lautro, 1986–89. Mem., Appeal Cttee, ICA, 1990–. *Recreations:* National Hunt racing, inland waterways. *Address:* 7 Church Street, St Ives, Cambs PE17 4DG. *T:* St Ives (01480) 469753. *Club:* United Oxford & Cambridge University.

See also Sir H. M. S. Reid.

REID, Sir Martin; *see* Reid, Sir H. M. S.

REID, Sir Norman (Robert), Kt 1970; DA (Edinburgh); FMA; FIIC; Director, the Tate Gallery, 1964–79; *b* 27 December 1915; *o s* of Edward Daniel Reid and Blanche, *d* of Richard Drouet; *m* 1941, Jean Lindsay Bertram; one *s* one *d*. *Educ:* Wilson's Grammar School; Edinburgh Coll. of Art; Edinburgh Univ. Served War of 1939–46, Major, Argyll and Sutherland Highlanders. Joined staff of Tate Gallery, 1946; Deputy Director, 1954; Keeper, 1959. Fellow, International Institute for Conservation (IIC) (Secretary General, 1963–65; Vice-Chm., 1966); British Rep. Internat. Committee on Museums and Galleries of Modern Art, 1963–79; President, Penwith Society of Arts; Member: Council, Friends of the Tate Gall., 1958–79 (Founder Mem.); Arts Council Art Panel, 1964–74; Inst. of Contemporary Arts Adv. Panel, 1965–; Contemporary Art Soc. Cttee, 1965–72, 1973–77; "Paintings in Hospitals" Adv. Cttee, 1965–69; British Council Fine Arts Cttee, 1965–77 (Chm. 1968–75); Culture Adv. Cttee of UK Nat. Commn for Unesco, 1966–70; Univ. of London, Bd of Studies in History of Art, 1968; Cttee, The Rome Centre, 1969–77 (Pres. 1975–77); Adv. Council, Paul Mellon Centre, 1971–78; Council of Management, Inst. of Contemp. Prints, 1972–78; Council, RCA, 1974–77. Mem. Bd, Burlington Magazine, 1971–75. Trustee, Graham and Kathleen Sutherland Foundn, 1980–85. Represented in collections: Scottish Nat. Gall. of Modern Art; Tate Gall. Hon. LittD East Anglia, 1970. Officer of the Mexican Order of the Aztec Eagle. *Address:* 50 Brabourne Rise, Park Langley, Beckenham, Kent BR3 2SH. *Club:* Arts.

REID, Maj.-Gen. Peter Daer, CB 1981; *b* 5 Aug. 1925; *s* of Col S. D. Reid and Dorothy Hungerford (*née* Jackson) *m* 1958, Catherine Fleetwood (*née* Boodle); two *s* two *d*. *Educ:* Cheltenham College; Wadham Coll., Oxford. Commissioned into Coldstream Guards, 1945; transferred Royal Dragoons, 1947; served: Germany, Egypt, Malaya, Gibraltar, Morocco; Staff Coll., 1959; Comdg Officer, The Royal Dragoons, 1965–68; student, Royal College of Defence Studies, 1973; Commander RAC, 3rd Div., 1974–76; Dir, RAC, 1976–78; Chief Exec., Main Battle Tank 80 Proj., 1979–80; Dir, Armoured Warfare Studies, 1981; Defence Advr, GKN, 1983–88; Mil. Advr, Howden Airdynamics, 1982–88; Associate Mem., Burdeshaw Associates Ltd (USA), 1982–94; Defence Consultant, Vickers Defence Systems Ltd, 1989–94. *Recreations:* sailing, ski-ing, fishing, bird watching. *Address:* The Border House, Cholderton, near Salisbury, Wilts SP4 0DU. *Clubs:* Army and Navy; Royal Western Yacht; Kandahar Ski.

REID, Philip; *see under* Ingrams, R. R.

REID, Sir Robert Paul, (Sir Bob), Kt 1990; Chairman: London Electricity plc, since 1994; Sears plc, since 1995; *b* 1 May 1934; *m* 1958, Joan Mary; three *s*. *Educ:* St Andrews Univ. (MA Pol. Econ. and Mod. Hist.). Joined Shell, 1956; Sarawak Oilfields and Brunei, 1956–59; Nigeria 1959–67 (Head of Personnel); Africa and S Asia Regional Orgn, 1967–68; PA and Planning Adviser to Chairman, Shell & BP Services, Kenya, 1968–70; Man. Dir, Nigeria, 1970–74; Man. Dir, Thailand, 1974–78; Vice-Pres., Internat. Aviation and Products Trading, 1978–80; Exec. Dir, Downstream Oil, Shell Co. of Australia, 1980–83; Co-Ordinator for Supply and Marketing, London, 1983; Dir, Shell International Petroleum Co., 1984–90; Chm. and Chief Exec., Shell UK, 1985–90; Chm., BRB, 1990–95. Director: Bank of Scotland, 1987–; British Borneo Petroleum, 1993–. Chairman: Foundn for Management Educn, 1986–; BIM, 1988–90; Council, London Enterprise Agency, 1990–. Trustee, Science Museum, 1987–92. Chancellor, Robert Gordon Univ., 1993–. Hon. LLD: St Andrews, 1987; Aberdeen, 1988. *Recreations:* golf, sailing. *Clubs:* MCC; Royal and Ancient Golf; Royal Melbourne (Melbourne); Frilford Heath Golf. *Address:* London Electricity plc, Templar House, 81–87 High Holborn, WC1V 6NU. *T:* 0171–242 9050.

REID, Seona Elizabeth; Director, Scottish Arts Council, since 1990; *b* 21 Jan. 1950; *d* of George Robert Hall and Isobel Margaret Reid. *Educ:* Park Sch., Glasgow; Strathclyde Univ. (BA Hons Sociology); Liverpool Univ. (DBA). Business Manager, Lincoln Theatre Royal, 1972–73; Press and Publicity Officer, Northern Dance Theatre, 1973–76; Press and PRO, Ballet Rambert, 1976–79; freelance Arts consultant, 1979–80; Dir, Shape, 1980–87; Asst Dir, Strategy and Regl Devel t, Greater London Arts, 1987–90. FRSA 1991. *Recreations:* walking, travel, food, arts. *Address:* Scottish Arts Council, 12 Manor Place, Edinburgh EH3 7DD. *T:* 0131–226 6051.

REID, Whitelaw; President, Reid Enterprises; *b* 26 July 1913; *s* of late Ogden M. Reid and Mrs Ogden M. Reid; *m* 1st, 1948, Joan Brandon (marr. diss., 1959); two *s*; 2nd, 1959, Elizabeth Ann Brooks; one *s* one *d*. *Educ:* Lincoln Sch., NYC; St Paul's Sch., Concord, New Hampshire; Yale Univ. (BA). New York Herald Tribune: in various departments, 1938–40; foreign correspondent, England, 1940; Assistant to Editor, 1946; Editor, 1947–55; Pres., 1953–55; Chm. of Bd, 1955–58; Director, 1946–65; Dir, 1946–65, Pres., 1946–62, Herald Tribune Fresh Air Fund. Served War of 1939–45, 1st Lieut naval aviator, USNR. Formerly Director: Farfield Foundn; Freedom House; Golden's Bridge Hounds Inc., 1970–83; Dir, Yale Westchester Alumni Assoc. Chm., NY State Cttee on Public Employee Security Procedures, 1956–57. Ambassador to inauguration of President Ponce, Ecuador, 1956. Member: Nat. Commn for Unesco, 1955–60; President's Citizen Advisers on the Mutual Security Program, 1956–57; Yale Alumni Board (Vice-Chm., 1962–64), Yale Univ. Council (Chm., Publications Cttee, 1965–70; Sec., Class of Yale 1936, 1986–91); Nat. Inst. of Social Sciences; formerly Mem., Council on Foreign Relations. District Comr, Purchase Pony Club, 1964–70; Pres., New York State Horse Council (formerly Empire State Horsemen's Assoc.), 1975–80. Fellow, Pierson Coll., Yale, 1949–. *Address:* (home and office) Reid Enterprises, Ophir Farm North, 73 West Patent Road, Bedford Hills, NY 10507, USA. *Clubs:* Century, Overseas Press, Silurians, Pilgrims, Yale, Amateur Ski (New York); Metropolitan (Washington); Windermere Island (Eleuthera, Bahamas); Bedford Golf and Tennis; St Regis Yacht.

REID, Flight Lt William, VC 1943; agricultural consultant; Agriculture Adviser, The MacRobert Trust, Douneside, Tarland, Aberdeenshire, since 1950; *b* 21 Dec. 1921; *s* of late William Reid, Baillieston, Glasgow; *m* 1952, Violet Gallagher, 11 Dryburgh Gdns,

Glasgow, NW1; one *s* one *d.* *Educ:* Coatbridge Secondary Sch.; Glasgow Univ.; West of Scotland Coll. of Agriculture. Student of Metallurgy, Sept. 1940; BSc (Agric.), 1949; Post-Graduate World Travelling Scholarship for 6 months, to study Agric. and Installations in India, Australia, NZ, USA and Canada, 1949–50. Joined RAF 1941; trained in Lancaster, Calif, USA. Won VC during a trip to Düsseldorf, 3 Nov. 1943, when member of 61 Squadron; pilot RAFVR, 617 Squadron (prisoner); demobilised, 1946; recalled to RAF for 3 months, Dec. 1951. Joined RAFVR, commissioned Jan. 1949, 103 Reserve Centre, Perth. Nat. Cattle and Sheep Advr, Spillers Ltd, 1959–81. Freedom of City of London, 1988. *Recreations:* golf, shooting, fishing, etc. *Address:* Cranford, Ferntower Place, Crieff, Perthshire PH7 3DD. *T:* Crieff (01764) 652462. *Club:* Royal Air Force.

REID, William, CBE 1987; FSA; Director, National Army Museum, 1970–87; Consultative Director, The Herald Museum, since 1988; *b* Glasgow, 8 Nov. 1926; *o s* of Colin Colquhoun Reid and Mary Evelyn Bingham; *m* 1958, Nina Frances Brigden. *Educ:* Glasgow and Oxford. Commnd RAF Regt, 1946–48. Joined staff of Armouries, Tower of London, 1956. Organising Sec., 3rd Internat. Congress of Museums of Arms and Military History, London, Glasgow and Edinburgh, 1963; Sec.-Gen., Internat. Assoc. of Museums of Arms and Military History, 1969–81, Pres., 1981–87, Hon. Life Pres., 1987; Member: British Nat. Cttee, ICOM, 1973–88; Council, Chelsea Soc., 1979–85; Founding Council, Army Records Soc., 1983–88. FSA 1965 (Mem. Council, 1975–76); FMA 1974–88, resigned. Trustee: The Tank Museum, 1970–87; RAEC Museum, 1985–; Museum of Richmond, 1987–; Florence Nightingale Museum Trust, 1987–; Royal Hants Regt Mus., 1990–; Twickenham Mus. Gp, 1993–; Lord Brock Meml Trust, 1994–; Mem., Conservative Adv. Cttee on the Arts and Heritage, 1988–. Hon. Life Mem., Friends of the Nat. Army Mus., 1987; Hon. Member: Amer. Soc. of Arms Collectors, 1975; Indian Army Assoc., 1981. Freeman, Scriveners' Co., 1989 (Liveryman, 1990); Freeman, City of London, 1989. *Publications:* (with A. R. Dufty) European Armour in the Tower of London, 1968; The Lore of Arms, 1976 (Military Book Society choice) (also trans. French, German, Danish, Italian, Spanish and Swedish); contribs to British and foreign jls. *Recreations:* the study of armour and arms, military history, music, bird-watching. *Address:* 66 Ennerdale Road, Richmond, Surrey TW9 2DL. *T:* 0181–940 0904. *Club:* Athenæum.

REID, Rev. Canon William Gordon; Vicar-General, Diocese of Gibraltar in Europe, and Canon of Gibraltar Cathedral, since 1992; *b* 28 Jan. 1943; *s* of William Albert Reid and Elizabeth Jean Inglis. *Educ:* Galashiels Academy; Edinburgh Univ. (MA); Keble Coll., Oxford (MA); Cuddesdon College. Deacon 1967, priest 1968; Curate, St Salvador's, Edinburgh, 1967–69; Chaplain and Tutor, Salisbury Theological Coll., 1969–72; Rector, St Michael and All Saints, Edinburgh, 1972–84; Provost of St Andrew's Cathedral, Inverness, 1984–88; Chaplain of St Nicolas, Ankara, 1988–89, of St Peter and St Sigfrid's Church, Stockholm, 1989–92. Councillor, Lothian Regional Council, 1974–84; Chm., Lothian and Borders Police Bd, 1982–84. *Publication:* (ed) The Wind from the Stars, 1992. *Recreations:* travel and languages, Church and politics. *Address:* 4 The Courtyard, Barnsbury Terrace, N1 1JZ. *T:* 0171–607 3834. *Club:* New (Edinburgh).

REID, William Kennedy, CB 1981; Parliamentary Commissioner for Administration, and Health Service Commissioner for England, Scotland and Wales, since 1990; *b* 15 Feb. 1931; 3rd *s* of late James and Elspet Reid; *m* 1959, Ann, *d* of Rev. Donald Campbell; two *s* one *d.* *Educ:* Robert Gordon's Coll.; George Watson's Coll.; Univ. of Edinburgh; Trinity Coll., Cambridge. MA 1st cl. Classics Edinburgh and Cantab. Ferguson scholar 1952; Craven scholar 1956. Nat. service, 1952–54. Min. of Educn, 1956; Cabinet Office, 1964; Private Sec. to Sec. of Cabinet, 1965–67; Sec., Council for Scientific Policy, 1967–72; Under Sec., 1974–78, Accountant-General, 1976–78, DES; Dep. Sec. (Central Services), Scottish Office, 1978–84; Sec., SHHD, 1984–90. Chm. of Govs, Scottish Police Coll., 1984–90. Member: Council on Tribunals, 1990–; Commns for Local Administration in England and in Wales, 1990–. A Dir, Internat. Ombudsman Inst., 1992–Oct. 1996. Lectures: Crookshank, RCR, 1994; Sydenham, Soc. of Apothecaries, 1994. *Recreation:* hill walking. *Address:* Church House, Great Smith Street, SW1P 3BW; 11 Inverleith Terrace, Edinburgh EH3 5NS. *Clubs:* United Oxford & Cambridge University; New (Edinburgh).

REID, William Macpherson; Sheriff of Tayside, Central and Fife, since 1983; *b* 6 April 1938; *s* of William Andrew Reid and Mabel McLeod; *m* 1971, Vivien Anne Eddy; three *d.* *Educ:* Elgin Academy; Aberdeen Univ.; Edinburgh Univ. MA; LLB. Admitted Advocate, 1963; Sheriff of: Lothian and Borders, 1978; Glasgow and Strathkelvin, 1978–83. *Address:* Sheriffs' Chambers, Sheriff Court House, Mar Street, Alloa FK10 1HR.

REID BANKS, Lynne; *see* Banks.

REIDHAVEN, Viscount, (Master of Seafield); James Andrew Ogilvie-Grant; *b* 30 Nov. 1963; *s* and *heir* of Earl of Seafield, *qv*.

REIGATE, Archdeacon of; *no new appointment at time of going to press.*

REIHER, Sir Frederick (Bernard Carl), KBE 1992; CMG 1982; Investment and finance consultant, 1992; Director, Harrisons & Crosfield (PNG) Ltd, 1982–91; Chairman, Harcos Trading (PNG) Ltd, 1982–91; *b* 7 Feb. 1945; *s* of William and Ruth Reiher; *m* 1974, Helen Perpetua; two *s* two *d.* *Educ:* Chanel Coll., Rabaul; Holy Spirit National Seminary, Port Moresby; Univ. of Papua New Guinea (BD). Private Sec. to Minister for Finance, PNG, 1973–76. Joined Diplomatic Service, 1976; established Diplomatic Mission for PNG in London, 1977; High Comr for PNG in London, 1978–80, concurrently accredited Ambassador to FRG, Belgium, EEC and Israel; Sec. of Dept of Prime Minister, PNG, 1980–82. Chairman: PNG Agriculture Bank, 1986–91; PNG Nat. Airline Commn, 1992. *Address:* PO Box 7500, Boroko, Papua New Guinea. *Clubs:* Aviat Social & Sporting, South Pacific Motor Sports, Royal Yacht, PNG Pistol.

REILLY, Sir (D'Arcy) Patrick, GCMG 1968 (KCMG 1957; CMG 1949); OBE 1942; Chairman, Banque Nationale de Paris Ltd (formerly British and French Bank), 1969–80; *b* 17 March 1909; *s* of late Sir D'Arcy Reilly, Indian Civil Service; *m* 1st, 1938, Rachel Mary (*d* 1984), *d* of late Brigadier-General Sir Percy Sykes, KCIE, CB, CMG; two *d*; 2nd, 1987, Ruth, *widow* of Sir Arthur Norvington. *Educ:* Winchester; New Coll., Oxford. (1st class Hon. Mods, 1930, Lit Hum 1932), Hon. Fellow 1972. Laming Travelling Fellow, Queen's College, 1932; Fellow of All Souls College, 1932–39, 1969–; Diplomatic Service, 1933; Third Secretary, Tehran, 1935–38; Ministry of Economic Warfare, 1939–42; First Secretary, Algiers, 1943; Paris, 1944; Athens, 1945. Counsellor, HM Foreign Service, 1947; Counsellor at Athens, 1947–48; Imperial Defence College, 1949; Assistant Under-Secretary of State, Foreign Office, 1950–53; Minister in Paris, 1953–56; Dep. Under-Sec. of State, Foreign Office, Oct. 1956; Ambassador to the USSR, 1957–60; Dep. Under-Sec. of State, Foreign Office, 1960–64; Official Head of UK Delegation to UN Conference on Trade and Development, 1964; Ambassador to France, 1965–68. Pres., 1972–75, Vice-Pres., 1975–, London Chamber of Commerce and Industry. Chairman: London Chamber of Commerce Standing Cttee for Common Market countries, 1969–72; Overseas Policy Cttee, Assoc. of British Chambers of Commerce, 1970–72; London Univ. Management Cttee, British Inst. in Paris, 1970–79; Council, Bedford Coll., London Univ., 1970–75. Hon. DLitt Bath, 1982. Comdr Légion d'Honneur, 1979. *Address:* 75 Warrington Crescent, W9 1EH. *T:* 0171–289 5384. *Club:* Athenæum.

REILLY, Lt-Gen. Sir Jeremy (Calcott), KCB 1987; DSO 1973; Commander Training and Arms Directors, 1986–89, retired; *b* 7 April 1934; *s* of late Lt-Col J. F. C. Reilly and of E. N. Reilly (*née* Moreton); *m* 1960, Julia Elizabeth (*née* Forrester); two *d* (and one *d* decd). *Educ:* Uppingham; RMA Sandhurst. Commissioned Royal Warwickshire Regt, 1954; served Egypt, Cyprus (Despatches), Ireland, Hong Kong, Germany, Borneo, BJSM Washington DC; psc 1965; Brigade Major, BAOR, 1967–69; Chief Instructor, RMA, 1969–71; CO 2nd Bn Royal Regt of Fusiliers, 1971–73 (DSO); Instructor, Staff Coll., 1974–75; Col GS (Army Deployment), MoD, 1975–77; PSO to Field Marshal Lord Carver and attached FCO (Rhodesia), 1977–79; Comdr 6 Field Force and UK Mobile Force, 1979–81; Comdr 4th Armoured Div., BAOR, 1981–83; Dir Battle Develt, MoD, 1983–84; ACDS (Concepts), MoD, 1985–86. Dep. Col, RRF (Warwickshire), 1981–86; Col, RRF, 1986–; Col Comdt, The Queen's Div., 1988–90. *Publications:* minor articles in various jls. *Address:* RHQ RRF, HM Tower of London, EC3N 4AB.

REILLY, Sir Patrick; *see* Reilly, Sir D. P.

REIMAN, Dr Donald Henry; Editor, Shelley and his Circle, Carl H. Pforzheimer Collection, New York Public Library, since 1986; Adjunct Professor of English, University of Delaware, since 1992; *b* 17 May 1934; *s* of Mildred A. (Pearce) Reiman and Henry Ward Reiman; *m* 1st, 1958, Mary A. Warner (marr. diss. 1974); one *d*; 2nd, 1975, Hélène Dworzan. *Educ:* Coll. of Wooster, Ohio (BA 1956; Hon. LittD 1981); Univ. of Illinois (MA 1957; PhD 1960). Instructor, 1960–62, Asst Prof. 1962–64, Duke Univ.; Associate Prof., Univ. of Wisconsin, Milwaukee, 1964–65; Editor, Shelley and his Circle, Carl H. Pforzheimer Liby, 1965–86. James P. R. Lyell Reader in Bibliography, Oxford Univ., 1988–89. Gen. Editor, Manuscripts of the Younger Romantics, 1984– (24 vols); Editor-in-Chief, Bodleian Shelley MSS, 1984– (19 vols). *Publications:* Shelley's The Triumph of Life, 1965; Percy Bysshe Shelley, 1969, 2nd edn 1990; (ed) The Romantics Reviewed, 9 Vols, 1972; (ed) Shelley and his Circle, vols V–VI, 1973, Vols VII–VIII, 1986; (with D. D. Fischer) Byron on the Continent, 1974; (ed with S. B. Powers) Shelley's Poetry and Prose, 1977; (ed) The Romantic Context: Poetry, 128 vols, 1976–79; (ed jtly) The Evidence of the Imagination, 1978; English Romantic Poetry 1800–1835, 1979; Romantic Texts and Contexts, 1987; Intervals of Inspiration, 1988; The Study of Modern Manuscripts, 1993; contribs to reviews and learned jls. *Address:* 907 Aster Avenue, Newark, DE 19711, USA. *T:* (302) 3687199.

REINERS, William Joseph; Director of Research Policy, Departments of the Environment and Transport, 1977–78, retired 1978; *b* 19 May 1923; *s* of late William and Hannah Reiners; *m* 1952, Catharine Anne Palmer; three *s* one *d.* *Educ:* Liverpool Collegiate Sch.; Liverpool Univ. RAE Farnborough, 1944–46; Min. of Works, 1946–50; Head, Building Operations and Economics Div., Building Research Station, 1950–63; Dir of Research and Information, MPBW, 1963–71; Dir of Research Requirements, DoE, 1971–77. Chm., Aldwych Housing Assoc., 1993– (Mem. Bd, 1980–). *Publications:* various on building operations and economics. *Address:* Valais, Berks Hill, Chorleywood, Herts WD3 5AQ. *T:* Chorleywood (01923) 283293.

REINHARDT, Max; Chairman: Reinhardt Books Ltd (formerly HFL (Publishers) Ltd), since 1947; The Nonesuch Press Ltd, since 1986; *b* 30 Nov. 1915; *s* of Ernest Reinhardt and Frieda Reinhardt (*née* Darr); *m* 1st, 1947, Margaret Leighton, CBE (marr. diss. 1955; she *d* 1976); 2nd, 1957, Joan, *d* of Carlisle and Dorothy MacDonald, New York City; two *d.* *Educ:* English High Sch. for Boys, Istanbul; Ecole des Hautes Etudes Commerciales, Paris; London School of Economics. Acquired HFL (Publishers) Ltd, 1947; founded Max Reinhardt Ltd, 1948, which bought: The Bodley Head Ltd, 1956 (Man. Dir, 1957–81; Chm., 1981–87); Putnam & Co., 1963; Jt Chm., Chatto, Bodley Head and Jonathan Cape Ltd, 1973–87. Mem. Council; Publishers' Assoc., 1963–69; Royal Academy of Dramatic Art, 1965–; The Pilgrims, 1966–. *Recreations:* reading for pleasure, swimming, bridge. *Address:* Flat 2, 43 Onslow Square, SW7 3LR. *T:* 0171–589 5527. *Clubs:* Beefsteak, Garrick, Royal Automobile.

REISS, John Henry, OBE 1972; British Ambassador to Liberia, 1973–78, retired; *b* 26 March 1918; *s* of late Rev. Leopold Reiss and Dora Lillian (*née* Twisden-Bedford); *m* 1943, Dora Lily (*née* York); one *s* two *d.* *Educ:* Bradfield Coll.; St Thomas' Hosp. Served War, Army, 1939–42. Kenya Govt, 1945–59; Dir of Information, 1954–59; Commonwealth Office, 1959; Dir of Information Services: Johannesburg, 1961–63; Wellington, New Zealand, 1963–65. Foreign and Commonwealth Office, 1966–69; Dep. British Govt Representative, Antigua/St Kitts, 1969–73. *Recreations:* bridge, computing. *Address:* 1 Manor Crescent, Tytherington, Macclesfield, Cheshire SK10 2EN.

REISZ, Karel; film director; *b* 21 July 1926; *s* of Joseph Reisz and Frederika; *m* 1963, Betsy Blair; three *s.* *Educ:* Leighton Park Sch., Reading; Emmanuel Coll., Cambridge (BA). Formerly: co-ed with Lindsay Anderson, film magazine, Sequence; worked for BFI; first Programme Dir, National Film Theatre. Co-directed, with Tony Richardson, Momma Don't Allow, 1956; produced: Every Day Except Christmas, 1957; This Sporting Life, 1960; directed: We Are the Lambeth Boys, 1958; Saturday Night and Sunday Morning, 1959; Night Must Fall, 1963; Morgan, a Suitable Case for Treatment, 1965; Isadora, 1967; The Gambler, 1975; Dog Soldiers, 1978; The French Lieutenant's Woman, 1981; Sweet Dreams, 1986; Everybody Wins, 1991; *stage plays:* Gardenia, Manhattan Theatre Club, 1991; The Gigli Concert, The Deep Blue Sea, Almeida, 1992; A Doll's House, Gate, Dublin, 1993. *Publication:* The Technique of Film Editing (also ed), 1953.

REITH, Barony of (*cr* 1940); title disclaimed by 2nd Baron; *see under* Reith, Christopher John.

REITH, Christopher John; farmer; *b* 27 May 1928; *s* of 1st Baron Reith, KT, PC, GCVO, GBE, CB, TD, of Stonehaven, and Muriel Katharine, *y d* of late John Lynch Odhams; *S* father, 1971, as 2nd Baron Reith, but disclaimed his peerage for life, 1972; *m* 1969, Penelope Margaret Ann, *er d* of late H. R. Morris; one *s* one *d.* *Educ:* Eton; Worcester College, Oxford (MA Agriculture). Served in Royal Navy, 1946–48; farming thereafter. *Recreations:* fishing, gardening, forestry. *Heir (to disclaimed peerage):* *s* Hon. James Harry John Reith, *b* 2 June 1971. *Address:* Whitebank Farm, Methven, Perthshire PH1 3QU. *T:* Methven (01738) 840333.

REITH, Douglas, CBE 1994; TD 1994; QC (Scotland) 1957; a Social Security (formerly National Insurance) Commissioner, 1960–92; *b* 29 June 1919; *s* of William Reith and Jessie McAllan; *m* 1949, Elizabeth Archer Stewart; one *s* one *d.* *Educ:* Aberdeen Grammar School; Aberdeen University (MA, LLB). Became Member of Faculty of Advocates in Scotland, 1946. Served in Royal Signals, 1939–46. Standing Junior Counsel in Scotland to Customs and Excise, 1949–51; Advocate-Depute, Crown Office, Scotland, 1953–57; Pres., Pensions Appeal Tribunal (Scotland), 1958–64; Chm., Nat. Health Service Tribunal (Scotland), 1963–65. *Address:* 2 Ravelston Court, Ravelston Dykes, Edinburgh EH12 6HQ. *T:* 0131–337 0332. *Club:* New (Edinburgh).

REITH, Martin; HM Diplomatic Service, retired; *b* 6 Dec. 1935; *s* of late James Reith and of Christian (*née* Innes); *m* 1964, Ann Purves; four *s*. *Educ:* Royal High Sch. of Edinburgh. Served: India (Calcutta), 1957–59; Uganda, 1962–66; Scottish Office, Edinburgh, 1966–68; Australia (Canberra), 1969–72; Asst Head of Central and Southern Africa Dept, FCO, 1974–77; Commercial Sec., Beirut, 1977–78; UN Dept, FCO, 1979; Counsellor, NATO Def. Coll., Rome, 1980; Dep. High Comr, Malta, 1980–83; High Comr, Swaziland, 1983–87; Ambassador, Republic of Cameroon, 1987–91. *Recreations:* hill-walking, bridge, Scottish literature. *Address:* Ardnagaul House, Strathtay, by Pitlochry, Perthshire PH9 0PG.

RELLIE, Alastair James Carl Euan, CMG 1987; HM Diplomatic Service, retired; Vice-President, Market Relations, British Aerospace Ltd, since 1993; *b* 5 April 1935; *s* of William and Lucy Rellie; *m* 1961, Annalisa (*née* Modin); one *s* two *d*. *Educ:* Michaelhouse, SA; Harvard Univ., USA (BA). Rifle Bde, 1958–60. Second Sec., FCO, 1963–64; Vice-Consul, Geneva, 1964–67; First Secretary: FCO, 1967–68; (Commercial), Cairo, 1968–70; Kinshasa, 1970–72; FCO, 1972–74; (and later Counsellor), UK Mission to UN, New York, 1974–79; FCO, 1979–92. Member: Bd, Eur. Defence Industries Gp, 1994–; Bd, NATO Industrial Adv. Gp, 1994–; Council, UK Defence Manufrs Assoc., 1994–. *Address:* 50 Smith Street, SW3 4EP. *T:* 0171–352 5734. *Clubs:* Brooks's, Greenjackets.

RELLY, Gavin Walter Hamilton; Executive Director, Anglo American Corporation of South Africa Ltd, since 1966 (Deputy Chairman, 1977–82; Chairman, 1983–90); *b* 6 Feb. 1926; *s* of Cullis Hamilton Relly and Helen Relly; *m* 1951, Jane Margaret Glenton; one *s* two *d*. *Educ:* Diocesan Coll., Cape Town; Trinity Coll., Oxford (MA). Joined Anglo American Corp., 1949 (Sec. to H. F. Oppenheimer and then to Sir Ernest Oppenheimer); Manager, Chm.'s Office, 1958; elected to Bd of Corp., 1965; Chm., Exec. Cttee, 1978; Mem. Bd, Anglo American Industrial Corp., 1973–90 (Chm., 1973–83). Chm., AECI Ltd, 1983–93; Dir, Minerals & Resources Corp. Ltd, 1974–. Member: South Africa Foundn, 1975– (Pres., 1981–82); Bd of Governors, Urban Foundn, 1985. Chm., Bd of Trustees, SA Nature Foundn, 1987–; Trustee: Univ. of S Africa Foundn, 1975–; Univ. of the Witwatersrand Foundn, 1984–. Hon. LLD Rhodes, 1991; Hon. DComm Stellenbosch, 1993. *Recreations:* fishing, golf. *Address:* PO Box 61587, Marshalltown, 2107, South Africa. *T:* (11) 6383234. *Clubs:* Rand, Country (Johannesburg).

RELPH, Michael Leighton George; film producer, director, designer, writer; *s* of late George Relph and Deborah Relph (later Harker); *m* 1st, 1939, Doris Gosden (marr. diss.); one *s*; 2nd, 1950, Maria Barry; one *d*. *Educ:* Bembridge Sch. Stage designer, 1940–50: West-end prodns include: Indoor Fireworks; The Doctor's Dilemma; Up and Doing; Watch on the Rhine; The Man Who Came to Dinner; Frieda; Saloon Bar; Old Acquaintance; Quiet Week-end; Heartbreak House; Relative Values; A Month in the Country; The Last of Summer; Love in Idleness; The White Carnation; The Petrified Forest; The Banbury Nose; They Came to a City. Began film career as apprentice, then Asst Art Dir, Gaumont British Studios; Art Dir, Warner Brothers Studios; Art Dir, Ealing Studios, 1942–45: prodns include: The Bells Go Down; Dead of Night; Champagne Charley; Nicholas Nickleby; Saraband for Dead Lovers (nominated Hollywood Oscar); Associate Producer to Michael Balcon, 1945; subseq. Producer with Basil Dearden as Dir until Dearden's death, 1972: prodns include: The Captive Heart; Kind Hearts and Coronets; The Blue Lamp (Best British Film Award, Brit. Film Acad.); Frieda; Saraband for Dead Lovers; I Believe in You (co-author); The Ship that Died of Shame; The Rainbow Jacket; The Square Ring; The Gentle Gunman; Cage of Gold; Pool of London. Director: Davy, 1957; Rockets Galore, 1958; Producer: Violent Playground; Sapphire (Best British Film Award, Brit. Film Acad.); All Night Long; The Smallest Show on Earth. Founder Dir, Allied Film Makers: produced: League of Gentlemen; Victim; Man in the Moon (co-author); Life for Ruth; The Mind Benders; Woman of Straw; Masquerade (co-author); The Assassination Bureau (also author and designer); The Man Who Haunted Himself (co-author); in charge of production, Boyd's Company, 1978–82: Scum (exec. producer), 1979; An Unsuitable Job for a Woman (co-producer), 1982; Treasure Houses of Britain (TV; exec. producer), 1985; Heavenly Pursuits, 1986; The Torrents of Spring, 1988 (production consultant). Chm., Film Prodn Assoc. of GB, 1971–76; Mem., Cinematograph Films Council, 1971–76; Governor, BFI, 1972–79 (Chm., Prodn Bd, 1972–79). *Recreations:* reading, theatre going, painting. *Address:* The Lodge, Primrose Hill Studios, Fitzroy Road, NW1 8JP. *T:* 0171–586 0249.

See also S. G. M. Relph.

RELPH, Simon George Michael; independent film producer; Director: Skreba Films, since 1980; Greenpoint Films, since 1980; *b* 13 April 1940; *s* of Michael Leighton George Relph, *qv*; *m* 1963, Amanda, *d* of Anthony Grinling, MC; one *s* one *d*. *Educ:* Bryanston School; King's College, Cambridge (MA Mech. Scis). Asst Dir, Feature Films, 1961–73; Production Administrator, Nat. Theatre, 1974–78; Chief Exec., British Screen Finance Ltd, 1985–90. Gov., BFI, 1991–. *Films* include: Production Supervisor, Yanks, 1978; Executive Producer: Reds, 1980; Laughterhouse, 1984; Enchanted April, 1991; Producer/Co-Producer: The Return of the Soldier, 1981; Privates on Parade, 1982; Ploughman's Lunch, 1983; Secret Places, 1984; Wetherby, 1985; Comrades, 1986; Damage, 1992; The Secret Rapture, 1992; Camilla, 1993; Look Me in the Eye, 1994; Blue Juice, 1995. Chevalier, Ordre des Arts et des Lettres (France), 1992. *Recreations:* gardening, photography, golf. *Address:* The Old Malt House, Westwood, Bradford-on-Avon, Wilts BA15 2AG.

RELTON, Stanley; HM Diplomatic Service, retired; Counsellor (Administration), British Embassy, Brussels, 1978–83; *b* 19 May 1923; *m* 1953, José Shakespeare; four *d*. Army, 1942–47. Joined HM Diplomatic Service, 1948: Haifa, 1949; Seoul, 1950; Tokyo, 1951; FCO, 1952–53; Vice-Consul, Stuttgart, 1954–57; Bremen, 1957–59; Consul, Rotterdam, 1959–61; Budapest, 1961–64; Second Sec., Buenos Aires, 1964–68; First Sec., Algiers, 1968–71; FCO, 1971–75; First Sec., Blantyre, Malaŵi, 1975–78. *Recreations:* music, chess. *Address:* 20A Waldegrave Park, Twickenham, Mddx TW1 4TQ.

REMEDIOS, Alberto Telisforo, CBE 1981; opera and concert singer; *b* 27 Feb. 1935; *s* of Albert and Ida Remedios; *m* 1965, Judith Annette Hosken; two *s* one *d*. *Educ:* studied with Edwin Francis, Liverpool. Début with Sadler's Wells Opera, 1956; sings regularly: English Nat. Opera; Royal Opera House, Covent Garden; Welsh Nat. Opera; Metropolitan NY, San Francisco, San Diego, Seattle, Australia, NZ, S Africa, Frankfurt, Bonn, France, Spain; sang Peter Grimes, Teatro Colon, Buenos Aires, 1979; also with major English orchestras. Recordings include Wagner's Ring; Tippett: A Midsummer Marriage. Queen's Prize, RCM, 1958; 1st prize, Union of Bulgarian Composers, 1963. *Recreations:* soccer, motoring, record collecting. *Address:* c/o Judith Newton Opera and Concert Artists, 75 Aberdare Gardens, NW6 3AN. *T:* 0171–328 3097.

REMNANT, family name of **Baron Remnant.**

REMNANT, 3rd Baron *cr* 1928, of Wenhaston; **James Wogan Remnant,** Bt 1917; CVO 1979; FCA; Director, Bank of Scotland, since 1989 (Director since 1973, and Chairman, 1979–92, London Board); Chairman, National Provident Institution, 1990–95 (Director, 1963–95); *b* 23 October 1930; *s* of 2nd Baron and Dowager Lady Remnant (*d* 1990); *S* father, 1967; *m* 1953, Serena Jane Loehnis, *o d* of Sir Clive Loehnis, KCMG; three *s* one *d*. *Educ:* Eton. FCA 1955. Nat. Service, Coldstream Guards, 1948–50 (Lt). Partner, Touche Ross & Co., 1958–70; Man. Dir, 1970–80, Chm., 1981–89, Touche, Remnant & Co.; Chairman: TR City of London Trust, 1978–90 (Dir, 1973–90); TR Pacific Investment Trust, 1987–94. Dep. Chm., Ultramar, 1981–91 (Dir, 1970–91); Director: Australia and New Zealand Banking Group, 1968–81 (Mem., Internat. Bd of Advice, 1987–91); Union Discount Co. of London, 1968–92 (Dep. Chm., 1970–86); Bank of Scotland, 1989– (Dir, 1973–, Chm., 1979–92, London Bd); London Merchant Securities, 1994–, and other cos. Chm., Assoc. of Investment Trust Cos, 1977–79. A Church Comr, 1976–84. Chm., Institutional Shareholders Cttee 1977–78. Trustee, Royal Jubilee Trusts, 1980– (Hon. Treasurer, 1972–80; Chm., 1980–89); President: Wokingham Constituency Cons. Assoc., 1981–95; Nat. Council of YMCAs, 1983–; Florence Nightingale Foundn (formerly Nat. Florence Nightingale Meml Cttee), 1987–; Chm., Learning Through Landscapes Trust, 1989–. Master, Salters' Co., 1995–96. GCStJ (Bailiff of Egle, 1993–). *Heir: s* Hon. Philip John Remnant [*b* 20 December 1954; *m* 1977, Caroline Elizabeth Clare, *yr d* of late Godfrey H. R. Cavendish; one *s* two *d*]. *Address:* Bear Ash, Hare Hatch, Reading RG10 9XR.

RENALS, Sir Stanley, 4th Bt, *cr* 1895; formerly in the Merchant Navy; *b* 20 May 1923; 2nd *s* of Sir James Herbert Renals, 2nd Bt; *S* brother, Sir Herbert Renals, 3rd Bt, 1961; *m* 1957, Maria Dolores Rodriguez Pinto, *d* of late José Rodriguez Ruiz; one *s*. *Educ:* City of London Freemen's School. *Heir: s* Stanley Michael Renals, BSc, CEng, MIMechE, MIProdE [*b* 14 January 1958; *m* 1982, Jacqueline Riley; one *s* one *d*]. *Address:* 52 North Lane, Portslade, East Sussex BN4 2HG.

RENDALL, Peter Godfrey; Headmaster, Bembridge School, Isle of Wight, 1959–74; *b* 25 April 1909; *s* of Godfrey A. H. Rendall and Mary Whishaw Rendall (*née* Wilson); *m* 1944, Ann McKnight Kauffer; two *s* one *d*. *Educ:* Rugby School; Corpus Christi College, Oxford. Assistant Master: Felsted School, Essex, 1931–34; Upper Canada College, Toronto, 1934–35; Felsted School, Essex, 1935–43. Served War of 1939–45, RAF, 1943–46, Flight-Lieut. Second Master, St Bees School, Cumberland, 1946–48; Headmaster Achimota School, Gold Coast, 1949–54; Assistant Master, Lancing College, 1954–59. Clerk to Burford Town Council, 1977–85. Coronation Medal, 1953. *Recreations:* reading, gardening, carpentry, painting. *Address:* Chippings, The Hill, Burford, Oxon OX18 4RE. *T:* Burford (01993) 822459. *Clubs:* Commonwealth Trust; Oxford Union Society.

RENDEL, David Digby; MP (Lib Dem) Newbury, since May 1993; *b* 15 April 1949; *s* of Alexander Rendel and Elizabeth (*née* Williams); *m* 1974, Dr Susan Taylor; three *s*. *Educ:* Eton (schol.); Magdalen Coll., Oxford (BA); St Cross Coll., Oxford. Shell Internat., 1974–77; British Gas, 1977–78; Esso Petroleum, 1978–90. Mem., Newbury DC, 1987–95. *Address:* House of Commons, SW1A 0AA. *T:* 0171–219 3000; Tudor Lodge, Stroud Green, Newbury, Berks RG14 7JA. *T:* Newbury (01635) 581048.

RENDELL, Ruth Barbara; crime novelist, since 1964; *b* 17 Feb. 1930; *d* of Arthur Grasemann and Ebba Kruse; *m* 1950, Donald Rendell; marr. diss. 1975; remarried Donald Rendell, 1977; one *s*. *Educ:* Loughton County High School. FRSL. Arts Council National Book Award for Genre Fiction, 1981; Sunday Times Award for Literary Excellence, 1990. *Publications:* From Doon with Death, 1964; To Fear a Painted Devil, 1965; Vanity Dies Hard, 1966; A New Lease of Death, 1967; Wolf to the Slaughter, 1967 (televised 1987); The Secret House of Death, 1968; The Best Man to Die, 1969; A Guilty Thing Surprised, 1970; One Across Two Down, 1971; No More Dying Then, 1971; Murder Being Once Done, 1972; Some Lie and Some Die, 1973; The Face of Trespass, 1974 (televised, as An Affair in Mind, 1988); Shake Hands for Ever, 1975; A Demon in my View, 1976 (film 1991); A Judgement in Stone, 1977; A Sleeping Life, 1978; Make Death Love Me, 1979; The Lake of Darkness, 1980 (televised, as Dead Lucky, 1988); Put on by Cunning, 1981; Master of the Moor, 1982 (televised 1994); The Speaker of Mandarin, 1983; The Killing Doll, 1984; The Tree of Hands, 1984 (film 1989); An Unkindness of Ravens, 1985; Live Flesh, 1986; Heartstones, 1987; Talking to Strange Men, 1987; (ed) A Warning to the Curious—The Ghost Stories of M. R. James, 1987; The Veiled One, 1988 (televised 1989); The Bridesmaid, 1989; Ruth Rendell's Suffolk, 1989; (with Colin Ward) Undermining the Central Line, 1989; Going Wrong, 1990; Kissing the Gunner's Daughter, 1992; The Crocodile Bird, 1993; Simisola, 1994; *short stories:* The Fallen Curtain, 1976; Means of Evil, 1979; The Fever Tree, 1982; The New Girl Friend, 1985; Collected Short Stories, 1987; The Copper Peacock, 1991; Blood Linen, 1995; (as Barbara Vine): A Dark-Adapted Eye, 1986 (televised 1994); A Fatal Inversion, 1987 (televised 1992); The House of Stairs, 1988; Gallowglass, 1990; King Solomon's Carpet, 1991; Asta's Book, 1993; No Night Is Too Long, 1994. *Recreations:* reading, walking, opera. *Address:* Nussteads, Polstead, Suffolk CO6 5DN; 26 Cornwall Terrace Mews, NW1 5LL. *Clubs:* Groucho, Detection.

RENDLE, Michael Russel; Managing Director, British Petroleum plc, 1981–86; Chairman, OIS International Inspection, PLC, since 1995 (Director, since 1993); Deputy Chairman, British-Borneo Petroleum Syndicate plc, since 1986; Director, Willis Corroon (formerly Willis Faber) plc, since 1985; *b* 20 Feb. 1931; *s* of late H. C. R. Rendle and Valerie Patricia (*née* Gleeson); *m* 1957, Heather, *d* of J. W. J. Rinkel; two *s* two *d*. *Educ:* Marlborough; New College, Oxford. MA. Joined Anglo-Iranian Oil Co. (now BP), 1954; Man. Dir, BP Trinidad, 1967–70; Man. Dir, BP Australia, 1974–78; Dir, BP Trading Ltd, 1978–81; Chairman: BP Chemicals Int., 1981–83; BP Coal, 1983–86; BP Nutrition, 1981–86. Chm., Forestry Investment Management, 1992– (Dir, 1989–); Deputy Chairman: Imperial Continental Gas Assoc., 1986–87; Tace, 1991; Chm., Markheath, later TBI, 1991–95; Director: London Adv. Bd, Westpac Banking Corp. (formerly Commercial Bank of Australia), 1978–89; Petrofina SA, 1986–87; Campbell & Armstrong, 1992–; Mem. BOTB, 1982–86; Chm., European Trade Cttee, 1982–86. Chm. Social Affairs Cttee, UNICE, 1984–87; Mem. Internat. Council and UK Adv. Bd, INSEAD, 1984–86. Mem. Council, Marlborough Coll., 1987–95. *Recreations:* golf, music, outdoor sports, gardening. *Address:* c/o Willis Corroon plc, 10 Trinity Square, EC3P 3AX. *T:* 0171–481 7152. *Clubs:* Vincent's (Oxford); Australian, Royal Melbourne Golf (Melbourne).

RENDLE, Peter Critchfield; Under-Secretary (Principal Finance Officer), Scottish Office, 1978–80, retired; *b* Truro, 31 July 1919; *s* of late Martyn and Florence Rendle; *m* 1944, Helen Barbara Moyes; three *s*. *Educ:* Queen Elizabeth's Sch., Hartlebury. Clerical Officer, Min. of Transport, 1936–49. Served War, Royal Navy, 1940–46 (Lieut RNVR). Min. of Town and Country Planning, 1949; Dept of Health for Scotland, 1950–59 (Sec., Guest Cttee on Bldg Legislation in Scotland); Scottish Home and Health Dept, 1959–63 and 1972–73; Scottish Educn Dept, 1963–72; Under Sec., Housing, Scottish Development Dept, 1973–78. Member: Legal Aid Central Cttee for Scotland, 1980–87; Scottish Is Councils Cttee of Inquiry, 1982–84; Scottish Legal Aid Bd, 1987–89. *Publication:* Rayner Report, Scrutiny of HM Inspectors of Schools in Scotland, 1981. *Recreations:* theatre, taking photographs. *Address:* 3/6 Caithness Place, Clark Road, Edinburgh EH5 3AE. *T:* 0131–552 8024. *Club:* Scottish Arts (Edinburgh).

RENDLESHAM, 8th Baron, *cr* 1806; **Charles Anthony Hugh Thellusson;** Royal Corps of Signals; *b* 15 March 1915; *s* of Lt-Col Hon. Hugh Edmund Thellusson, DSO (3rd *s* of 5th Baron); *S* uncle, 1943; *m* 1st, 1940, Margaret Elizabeth (marr. diss. 1947; she *m* 1962, Patrick P. C. Barthropp), *d* of Lt-Col Robin Rome, Monk's Hall, Glemsford; one *d*; 2nd, 1947, Clare (*d* 1987), *d* of Lt-Col D. H. G. McCririck; one *s* three *d*. *Educ:* Eton. *Heir: s*

Hon. Charles William Brooke Thellusson [*b* 10 Jan. 1954; *m* 1983, Susan Fielding]. *Address:* 498 King's Road, SW10 0LE.

See also Sir William Goring, Bt.

RENÉ, (France) Albert; barrister-at-law; President of the Republic of Seychelles since 1977 (elected, 1979, 1984, 1989, 1993); *b* Mahé, Seychelles, 16 Nov. 1935; *s* of Price René and Louisa Morgan; *m* 1st, 1956, Karen Handlay; one *d*; 2nd, 1975, Geva Adam; one *s*; 3rd, 1993, Sarah Zarqani; one *s*. *Educ:* St Louis Coll., Seychelles; St Maurice, Yalais, Switzerland; St Mary's Coll., Southampton, England; King's Coll., Univ. of London; Council of Legal Educn, 1956; LSE, 1961. Called to Bar, 1957. Leader, Founder, Pres., 1964–78, Seychelles People's United Party (first effective political party and liberation movement in Seychelles); MP, 1965; Mem. in Governing Council, 1967; Mem., Legal Assembly, 1970 and 1974; Minister of Works and Land Development, 1975; Prime Minister, 1976–77; Minister: of Transport, 1984–86; of Admin, Finance and Industries, Planning and External Relns, 1984–89; of Defence, 1986–92. Founder, Leader and Sec.-Gen., Seychelles People's Progressive Front, 1978. Order of the Golden Ark (1st cl.), 1982. *Address:* President's Office, State House, Republic of Seychelles.

RENFREW, family name of **Baron Renfrew of Kaimsthorn.**

RENFREW OF KAIMSTHORN, Baron *cr* 1991 (Life Peer), of Hurlet in the District of Renfrew; **Andrew Colin Renfrew,** FBA 1980; Disney Professor of Archaeology, University of Cambridge, since 1981; Master of Jesus College, Cambridge, since 1986; *b* 25 July 1937; *s* of late Archibald Renfrew and Helena Douglas Renfrew (*née* Savage); *m* 1965, Jane Margaret, *d* of Ven. Walter F. Ewbank, *qv*; two *s* one *d*. *Educ:* St Albans Sch.; St John's Coll., Cambridge (Exhibr); British Sch. of Archaeology, Athens. Pt I Nat. Scis Tripos 1960; BA 1st cl. hons Archaeol. and Anthrop. Tripos 1962; MA 1964; PhD 1965; ScD 1976. Pres., Cambridge Union Soc., 1961; Sir Joseph Larmor Award 1961. Nat. Service, Flying Officer (Signals), RAF, 1956–58. Res. Fellow, St John's Coll., Cambridge, 1965, Professorial Fellow, 1981–86; Bulgarian Govt Schol., 1966; Univ. of Sheffield: Lectr in Prehistory and Archaeol., 1965–70; Sen. Lectr, 1970–72; Reader, 1972; Prof. of Archaeology, Southampton Univ., 1972–81. Vis. Lectr, Univ. of Calif at Los Angeles, 1967. Contested (C) Sheffield Brightside, 1968; Chm., Sheffield Brightside Conserv. Assoc., 1968–72. Member: Ancient Monuments Bd for England, 1974–84; Royal Commn on Historical Monuments (England), 1977–87; Historic Buildings and Monuments Commn for England, 1984–86; Ancient Monuments Adv. Cttee, 1984–; UK Nat. Commn for UNESCO, 1984–86 (Mem. Culture Adv. Cttee, 1984–86); Trustee: Antiquity Trust, 1974–; British Mus., 1991–; Chm., Hants Archaeol Cttee, 1974–81; a Vice-Pres., RAI, 1982–85. Chm., Governors, The Leys, 1984–92. Lectures: Dalrymple in Archaeol., Univ. of Glasgow, 1975; George Grant MacCurdy, Harvard, 1977; Patten, Indiana Univ., 1982; Harvey, New Mexico Univ., 1982; Hill, Univ. of Minnesota, 1987; Tanner, Stanford Univ., 1993. Excavations: Saliagos near Antiparos, 1964–65; Sitagroi, Macedonia, 1968–70; Phylakopi in Melos, 1974–76; Quanterness, Orkney, 1972–74; Maes Howe, 1973–74; Ring of Brodgar, 1974; Liddle Farm, 1973–74. FSA 1968 (Vice-Pres., 1987–92); FSAScot 1970. Freeman, City of London, 1987. Hon. LittD: Sheffield, 1987; Southampton, 1995; Dr *hc* Athens, 1991. Rivers Meml Medal, 1979, Huxley Meml Medal, 1991, RAI. *Publications:* (with J. D. Evans) Excavations at Saliagos near Antiparos, 1968; The Emergence of Civilisation, 1972; (ed) The Explanation of Culture Change, 1973; Before Civilisation, 1973; (ed) British Prehistory, a New Outline, 1974; Investigations in Orkney, 1979; (ed) Transformations: Mathematical Approaches to Culture Change, 1979; Problems in European Prehistory, 1979; (with J. M. Wagstaff) An Island Polity, 1982; (ed) Theory and Explanation in Archaeology, 1982; Approaches to Social Archaeology, 1984; The Prehistory of Orkney, 1985; The Archaeology of Cult, 1985; Archaeology and Language, 1987; (with G. Daniel) The Idea of Prehistory, 1988; The Cycladic Spirit, 1991; (with P. Bahn) Archaeology, 1991; articles in archaeol jls. *Recreations:* modern art, numismatics, travel. *Address:* Master's Lodge, Jesus College, Cambridge CB5 8BL. *T:* Cambridge (01223) 323934; Department of Archaeology, Downing Street, Cambridge CB2 3DZ. *T:* Cambridge (01223) 333521. *Club:* Athenæum.

RENFREW, Glen McGarvie; Managing Director and Chief Executive, Reuters Ltd, 1981–91; *b* 15 Sept. 1928; *s* of Robert Renfrew and Jane Grey Watson; *m* 1954, Daphne Ann Hailey; one *s* two *d* (and one *d* decd). *Educ:* Sydney Univ., NSW, Australia (BA). Joined Reuters, London, 1952; reporting and/or management assignments in Asia, Africa and Europe, 1956–64; London management posts in computer and economic information services, 1964–70; Manager, Reuters N America, 1971–80. *Recreation:* sailing. *Address:* c/o Reuters, 85 Fleet Street, EC4Y 1DY. *Clubs:* Manhasset Bay Yacht (Long Island, NY); National Press (Washington).

RENFREY, Rt. Rev. Lionel Edward William; Dean of Adelaide, since 1966; Assistant Bishop of Adelaide, 1969–89; *b* Adelaide, SA, 26 March 1916; *s* of late Alfred Cyril Marinus Renfrey and Catherine Elizabeth Rose Frerichs (*née* Dickson); *m* 1948, Joan Anne, *d* of Donald Smith, Cooke's Plains, SA; one *s* five *d*. *Educ:* Unley High School; St Mark's Coll., Univ. of Adelaide; St Barnabas' Theological Coll., Adelaide. BA (First Cl. Hons English), ThL (ACT) (Second Cl. Hons). Deacon 1940, priest 1941, Dio. Adelaide; Curate, St Cuthbert's, Prospect, 1940–43; Mission Chaplain, Mid Yorke Peninsula, 1943–44; Warden, Brotherhood of St John Baptist, 1944–47; Priest-in-charge: Berri-Barmera, 1948–50; Kensington Gardens, 1950–57; Rector, St James', Mile End, 1957–63; Rural Dean, Western Suburbs, 1962–63; Organising Chaplain, Bishop's Home Mission Soc., 1963–66; Editor, Adelaide Church Guardian, 1961–66; Archdeacon of Adelaide, 1965–66; Examining Chaplain to Bishop of Adelaide, 1965–85; Administrator (*sede vacante*), Diocese of Adelaide, 1974–75; Rector, Mallala and Two Wells, 1981–88. Patron: Prayer Book Soc. in Australia, 1980–; Monarchist League, 1994–. OStJ 1981 (SBStJ 1969). *Publications:* Father Wise: a Memoir, 1951; Short History of St Barnabas' Theological College, 1965; What Mean Ye By This Service?, 1978; (ed) Catholic Prayers, 1980; (ed) SS Peter and Paul Prayer Book, 1982; Arthur Nutter Thomas, Bishop of Adelaide 1906–1940, 1988. *Recreation:* reading. *Address:* The Deanery, 13 Northcote Terrace, Medindie, SA 5081, Australia. *Club:* Adelaide (Adelaide).

RENNELL, 3rd Baron *cr* 1933, of Rodd, Herefordshire; **John Adrian Tremayne Rodd;** *b* 28 June 1935; *s* of Hon. Gustaf Guthrie Rennell Rodd (*d* 1974) (*yr s* of 1st Baron) and Yvonne Mary Rodd (*d* 1982), *d* of late Sir Charles Murray Marling, GCMG, CB; *S* uncle, 1978; *m* 1977, Phyllis, *d* of T. D. Neill; one *s* three *d*. *Educ:* Downside; RNC, Dartmouth. Served Royal Navy, 1952–62. With Morgan Grenfell & Co. Ltd, 1963–66; free-lance journalist, 1966–67; Marks of Distinction Ltd, 1968–79; Dir, Tremayne Ltd, 1980–91. *Recreations:* Scotland Rugby XV, 1958–65; golf, Real tennis. *Heir: s* Hon. James Roderick David Tremayne Rodd, *b* 9 March 1978. *Clubs:* White's, Portland; Sunningdale (Ascot).

RENNIE, Alexander Allan, CBE 1980; QPM 1971; Chief Constable, West Mercia Constabulary, 1975–81, retired; *b* 13 June 1917; *s* of Charles Rennie and Susan Parsons Rennie; *m* 1941, Lucy Brunt; one *s* one *d*. *Educ:* Ellon Acad., Aberdeenshire. Armed Services, 1941–45: commnd 30 Corps Royal Northumberland Fusiliers; active service in Europe (mentioned in despatches, 1945). Joined Durham County Constab., 1937; Chief Supt, 1963; Dep. Chief Constable, Shropshire, 1963–67; Dir, Sen. Comd Course, Police Coll., Bramshill, 1967–69; Asst Chief Constable, West Mercia, 1969–72, Dep. Chief Constable, 1973–75. OStJ 1975. *Recreations:* golf, hill walking. *Address:* 14 Minter Avenue, Droitwich, Worcs WR9 8RP.

RENNIE, Archibald Louden, CB 1980; Secretary, Scottish Home and Health Department, 1977–84, retired; *b* 4 June 1924; *s* of John and Isabella Rennie; *m* 1950, Kathleen Harkess; four *s*. *Educ:* Madras Coll.; St Andrews University. Minesweeping Res. Div., Admty, 1944–47; Dept of Health for Scotland, 1947–62; Private Sec. to Sec. of State for Scotland, 1962–63; Asst Sec., SHHD, 1963–69; Registrar Gen. for Scotland, 1969–73; Under-Sec., Scottish Office, 1973–77. Member: Scottish Records Adv. Council, 1985–94; Council on Tribunals, 1987–88. Gen. Council Assessor, St Andrews Univ. Court, 1984–85; Chancellor's Assessor and Finance Convener, 1985–89; Vice-Chm., Adv. Cttee on Distinction Awards for Consultants, 1985–; Chm., Disciplined Services Pay Review Cttee, Hong Kong, 1988. Dir, 1989–, Chm., 1994–, Elie Harbour Trust; Trustee, Lockerbie Air Disaster Trust, 1988–91. Mem. Bd, Madras Coll., 1994–. Cdre, Elie and Earlsferry Sailing Club, 1991–93. Hon. FDSRCS 1995. Hon. LLD St Andrews, 1990. *Recreations:* Scottish literature, sailing, firth-watching. *Address:* Well Wynd House, South Street, Elie, Fife KY9 1DN. *T:* Elie (01333) 330741. *Club:* Scottish Arts (Edinburgh).

RENNIE, James Douglas Milne, CB 1986; Parliamentary Counsel, 1976–92; *b* 2 Nov. 1931; *s* of Douglas Frederick Milne Rennie and Margaret Wilson Fleming Rennie (*née* Keanie); *m* 1962, Patricia Margaret Calhoun Watson; one *s* one *d*. *Educ:* Charterhouse; New Coll., Oxford (Schol.). 1st cl. Hon. Mods 1953; 2nd cl. Lit. Hum. 1955; 2nd cl. Jurisprudence 1957; MA. Called to Bar, Lincoln's Inn, 1958 (Cholmeley Schol.). Asst Lectr, UCW Aberystwyth, 1957; practised at Chancery Bar, 1958–65; Asst Parly Counsel, HM Treasury, 1965; Sen. Asst Parly Counsel, 1972; Dep. Parly Counsel, 1973–75. *Recreations:* opera, travel. *Address:* 8 Wellesley Road, W4 4BL. *T:* 0181–994 6627.

RENNIE, John Chalmers; Town Clerk of Aberdeen, 1946–68; retired; *b* 16 April 1907; *s* of late John Chalmers Rennie, Pharmacist, Wishaw; *m* 1937, Georgina Stoddart, *d* of late Henry Bell, Engineer and Ironfounder, Wishaw; one *s*. *Educ:* University of Glasgow (BL). Admitted solicitor, 1929. Town Clerk Depute, Motherwell and Wishaw, 1929–43; Town Clerk Depute, Aberdeen, 1943–46. Dep. Controller, Civil Defence Servs, Motherwell and Wishaw, 1939–43; Secretary: Aberdeen Harbour Bd, 1946–60; NE Fire Area Jt Bd, 1948–68. Mem. Council, Law Soc. of Scotland, 1958–61. Hon. Solicitor (Scotland), NALGO, 1949–64. *Recreation:* surviving. *Address:* 77 Forest Road, Aberdeen AB2 4BJ. *T:* Aberdeen (01224) 638635.

RENNIE, Sir John Shaw, GCMG 1968 (KCMG 1962; CMG 1958); OBE 1955; Commissioner-General, United Nations Relief and Works Agency for Palestine Refugees, 1971–77 (Deputy Commissioner-General, 1968–71); *b* 12 Jan. 1917; *s* of late John Shaw Rennie, Saskatoon, Sask, Canada; *m* 1946, Mary Winifred Macalpine Robertson; one *s*. *Educ:* Hillhead High School; Glasgow University; Balliol College, Oxford. Cadet, Tanganyika, 1940; Asst District Officer, 1942; District Officer, 1949; Deputy Colonial Secretary, Mauritius, 1951; British Resident Comr, New Hebrides, 1955–62; Governor and C-in-C of Mauritius, 1962–March 1968, Governor-General, March-Aug. 1968. Hon. LLD Glasgow, 1972. *Address:* 26 College Cross, N1 1PR; via Roma 37, 06050 Collazzone (PG), Italy. *Club:* Commonwealth Trust.

RENO, Janet; Attorney General of the United States of America, since 1993; *b* 21 July 1938. *Educ:* Cornell Univ. (AB Chem. 1960); Harvard Law Sch. (LLB 1963). Started legal career in private practice; asst state attorney, Florida; Staff Dir, Judiciary Cttee, Florida House of Reps; Partner, Steel, Hector & Davis, Miami, 1976–78; State Attorney, Miami, 1978–93. Pres., Fla Prosecuting Attorneys Assoc., 1984–85; American Bar Association: Member: Special Cttee on Criminal Justice in a Free Soc., 1986–88; Task Force on Minorities and the Justice System, 1992. Herbert Harley Award, Amer. Judicature Soc., 1981; Medal of Honor, Fla Bar Assoc., 1990. *Address:* Department of Justice, Room 4400, 10th & Constitution Avenue NW, Washington, DC 20530, USA. *T:* (202) 5142001.

RENOUF, Sir Francis (Henry), Kt 1987; company chairman; *b* Wellington, NZ, 31 July 1918; *m* 1954, Ann Marie Harkin (marr. diss. 1985); one *s* three *d*; *m* 1985, Susan Sangster (marr. diss. 1989); *m* 1991, Michele Suzanne Ivan-Zadeh-Griaznoff. *Educ:* Wellington Coll.; Victoria Univ. Coll., Wellington (Levin Schol., 1932; MCom 1940); Oxford Univ. (DipEcon 1949). Served 2 NZEF, 1940–46 (Capt.). Stockbroker, 1950–87; Chairman: NZ United Corp. Ltd, 1960–83; Renouf Gp, 1960–87; Renouf Corp. Ltd, 1983–87; Renouf Underwriters Pty. Officer's Cross, Order of Merit, Federal Republic of Germany, 1986. *Recreation:* lawn tennis (represented NZ Univs, 1938–40, Oxford Univ., 1948–49 (Oxford Blue); Pres., NZ LTA, 1985, 1986). *Address:* 37 Eaton Square, SW1W 9DH.

RENOWDEN, Very Rev. Charles Raymond; Dean of St Asaph, 1971–92, now Dean Emeritus; *b* 27 Oct. 1923; *s* of Rev. Canon Charles Renowden; *m* 1951, Ruth Cecil Mary Collis; one *s* two *d*. *Educ:* Llandysil Grammar Sch.; St David's Univ. Coll., Lampeter; Selwyn Coll., Cambridge. BA (Hons Philosophy, cl. I), Lampeter; BA, MA (Hons Theology, cl. I), Cambridge. Served War, Army, Intelligence Corps, in India and Japan, 1944–47. Cambridge Ordination Course; Deacon, 1951, Priest, 1952, Wales. Asst Curate, Hubberston, Milford Haven, 1951–55. St David's Univ. Coll., Lampeter: Lectr in Philosophy and Theology, 1955–57; Head of Dept of Philosophy, 1957–69; Sen. Lectr in Philosophy and Theology, 1969–71. *Publications:* (monograph) The Idea of Unity, 1965; New Patterns of Ministry, 1973; The Rôle of a Cathedral Today and Tomorrow, 1974; contributor to: Theology, The Modern Churchman, Church Quarterly Review, Trivium, Province. *Recreations:* music, gardening, ornithology. *Address:* 17 Llys Idris, Elwy Park, St Asaph, Clwyd LL17 0AJ. *T:* St Asaph (01745) 584591.

RENOWDEN, Ven. Glyndwr Rhys, CB 1987; Chaplain in Chief, Royal Air Force, 1983–88; *b* 13 Aug. 1929; *s* of Charles and Mary Elizabeth Renowden; *m* 1956, Mary Kinsey-Jones; one *d*. *Educ:* Llanelli Grammar Sch.; St David's Coll., Lampeter (BA, LTh). Curate: St Mary's, Tenby, 1952–55; St Mary's, Chepstow, 1955–58; Chaplain, RAF, 1958–88; Asst Chaplain in Chief, 1975–83. QHC, 1980–88. *Recreations:* Rugby football, bridge. *Address:* Red Cedars, Kenystyle, Penally, near Tenby, Dyfed SA70 7PJ.

RENSHAW, Sir (Charles) Maurice (Bine), 3rd Bt *cr* 1903; *b* 7 Oct. 1912; *s* of Sir (Charles) Stephen (Bine) Renshaw, 2nd Bt and of Edith Mary, *d* of Rear-Adm. Sir Edward Chichester, 9th Bt, CB, CMG; *S* father, 1976; *m* 1942, Isabel Bassett (marr. diss. 1947), *d* of late Rev. John L. T. Popkin; one *s* one *d* (and one *s* decd); *m* 2nd, Winifred May, *d* of H. F. Gliddon, Ashwater, Devon, and formerly wife of James H. T. Sheldon; three *s* three *d*. *Educ:* Eton. Served as Flying Officer, RAF (invalided). *Heir: s* John David Renshaw [*b* 9 Oct. 1945; *m* 1970, Jennifer (marr. diss. 1988), *d* of Group Captain F. Murray, RAF; one *s* two *d*]. *Address:* Tam-na-Marghaidh, Balquhidder, Perthshire FK19 8PB; Linwood, Instow, N Devon EX2 7HZ.

RENTON, family name of **Baron Renton.**

RENTON, Baron *cr* 1979 (Life Peer), of Huntingdon in the County of Cambridgeshire; **David Lockhart-Mure Renton,** KBE 1964; TD; PC 1962; QC 1954; MA; BCL; DL; a Deputy Speaker of the House of Lords, 1982–88; *b* 12 Aug. 1908; *s* of late Dr Maurice

Waugh Renton, The Bridge House, Dartford, Kent, and Eszma Olivia, *d* of late Allen Walter Borman, Alexandria; *m* 1947, Claire Cicely Duncan (*d* 1986); three *d*. *Educ:* Stubbington; Oundle; University College, Oxford (BA (Hons Jurisprudence), 1930; BCL, 1931; MA; Hon. Fellow, 1990). Called to Bar, Lincoln's Inn, 1933; South-Eastern Circuit; elected to General Council of the Bar, 1939; Bencher, Lincoln's Inn, 1962, Treasurer, 1979. Commnd RE (TA), 1938; transferred to RA 1940; served throughout War of 1939–45; Capt. 1941; Major, 1943; served in Egypt and Libya, 1942–45. MP (Nat L) 1945–50, (Nat L and C) 1950–68, (C) 1968–79, Huntingdonshire; Parly Sec., Min. of Fuel and Power, 1955–57, Ministry of Power, 1957–58; Joint Parly Under-Sec. of State, Home Office, 1958–61; Minister of State, Home Office, 1961–62; Chm., Select Cttee for Revision of Standing Orders, House of Commons, 1963 and 1970; Dep. Chm., Special Select Cttee on H of C Procedure, 1976–78; Mem., Cttee of Privileges, 1973–79. Recorder of Rochester, 1963–68, of Guildford, 1968–71; Vice-Chm., Council of Legal Educn, 1968–70, 1971–73. Member: Senate of Inns of Court, 1967–69, 1970–71, 1975–79; Royal Commn on the Constitution, 1971–73; Chm., Cttee on Preparation of Legislation, 1973–75. Pres., Statute Law Soc., 1980–. Pres., Mencap (Royal Soc. for Mentally Handicapped Children), 1982–88 (Hon. Treas., 1976–78; Chm., 1978–82). President: Conservation Soc., 1970–71; Nat. Council for Civil Protection (formerly Nat. Council for Civil Defence), 1980–91; Jt Pres., All Party Arts and Heritage Gp, 1989–. Patron: Nat. Law Library, 1979–; Huntingdonshire Conservative Assoc., 1979–; Ravenswood Foundn, 1979–; Gtr London Assoc. for the Disabled, 1986–; DEMAND (Design and Manufacture for Disablement), 1986–. DL Huntingdonshire, 1962, Huntingdon and Peterborough, 1964, Cambs, 1974. Coronation and Jubilee Medals. *Recreations:* outdoor sports and games, gardening. *Address:* Moat House, Abbots Ripton, Huntingdon, Cambs PE17 2PE. *T:* Abbots Ripton (01487) 773227; 16 Old Buildings, Lincoln's Inn, WC2A 3TL. *T:* 0171–242 8986. *Clubs:* Carlton, Pratt's.

RENTON, Gordon Pearson; Chairman, R & D Communications Ltd, since 1990; Director, Mediajet Ltd, since 1987; Assistant Under-Secretary of State, Department of Trade and Industry, 1983–84; *b* 12 Dec. 1928; *s* of Herbert Renton and Annie (*née* Pearson); *m* 1st, 1952, Joan Mary Lucas (marr. diss. 1971); two *s*; 2nd, 1978, Sylvia Jones. *Educ:* King Edward VII Sch., Sheffield; Lincoln Coll., Oxford (Scholar, BA Lit. Hum.). Served Royal Signals, 1951–53. Teacher, W Riding, 1953–54; Asst Principal, Home Office, 1954; Asst Private Sec. to Home Sec. and Lord Privy Seal, 1959–60; Principal, 1960; Asst Sec., 1967; Asst Under-Sec. of State, 1978. Mem., Parole Bd, 1985–88. *Recreations:* music, gardening, sailing. *Address:* Ship Cottage, Pwll Du, Bishopston, Swansea SA3 2AU. *T:* Bishopston (01441) 283796. *Club:* Bristol Channel Yacht.

RENTON, Air Cdre Helen Ferguson, CB 1982; Director, Women's Royal Air Force, 1980–86; *b* 13 March 1931; *d* of late John Paul Renton and Sarah Graham Renton (*née* Cook). *Educ:* Stirling High Sch.; Glasgow Univ. (MA). Joined WRAF, 1954; commnd, 1955; served in UK, 1955–60; Cyprus, 1960–62; HQ Staff, Germany, 1967; MoD Staff, 1968–71; NEAF, 1971–73; Training Comd, 1973–76; MoD Staff, 1976–78. Hon. LLD Glasgow, 1981. *Publications:* (jtly) Service Women, 1977. *Recreations:* needlework, gardening, reading. *Club:* Royal Air Force.

RENTON, Rt. Hon. Ronald Timothy, PC 1989; MP (C) Mid-Sussex since Feb. 1974; *b* 28 May 1932; *yr s* of R. K. D. Renton, CBE, and Mrs Renton, MBE; *m* 1960, Alice Fergusson of Kilkerran, Ayrshire; two *s* three *d*. *Educ:* Eton Coll. (King's Schol.); Magdalen Coll., Oxford (Roberts Gawen Schol.). First cl. degree in History, MA Oxon. Joined C. Tennant Sons & Co. Ltd, London, 1954; with Tennants' subsidiaries in Canada, 1957–62; Dir, C. Tennant Sons & Co. Ltd and Managing Dir of Tennant Trading Ltd, 1964–73; Director: Silvermines Ltd, 1967–84; Australia & New Zealand Banking Group, 1967–76; Fleming Continental European Investment Trust, 1992–, and other cos. Mem., BBC Gen. Adv. Council, 1982–84; Vice Chm., British Council, 1992–. Contested (C) Sheffield Park Div., 1970; PPS to Rt Hon. John Biffen, MP, 1979–81, to Rt Hon. Geoffrey Howe, MP, 1983–84; Parly Under Sec. of State, FCO, 1984–85; Minister of State: FCO, 1985–87; Home Office, 1987–89; Parly Sec. to HM Treasury and Govt Chief Whip, 1989–90; Minister of State, Privy Council Office (Minister for the Arts), 1990–92. Mem., Select Cttee on Nationalised Industries, 1974–79; Vice-Chm., Cons. Parly Trade Cttee, 1974–79; Chairman: Parly British–Hong Kong All-Party Gp, 1992–; Cons. Foreign and Commonwealth Council, 1982–84; Vice-Pres., 1978–80, Pres., 1980–84, Cons. Trade Unionists; Fellow, Industry and Parlt Trust, 1977–79. Member: Adv. Bd, Know-How Fund for Central and Eastern Europe, 1992–; Develt Council, Parnham Trust, 1992–; Criterion Theatre Trust, 1992–; APEX. Mem. Council, Roedean Sch., 1982–. Trustee, Mental Health Foundn, 1985–89. Founding Pres. (with Mick Jagger), Nat. Music Day, 1992–; Chm., Outsider Art Archive, 1995–. *Publications:* The Dangerous Edge (novel), 1994. *Recreations:* writing, mucking about in boats, listening to opera, off-piste bicycling. *Address:* House of Commons, SW1A 0AA. *Club:* Garrick.

RENWICK, family name of **Baron Renwick.**

RENWICK, 2nd Baron *cr* 1964, of Coombe; **Harry Andrew Renwick;** Bt 1927; *b* 10 Oct. 1935; *s* of 1st Baron Renwick, KBE, and of Mrs John Ormiston, Miserden House, Stroud, *er d* of late Major Harold Parkes, Alveston, Stratford-on-Avon; *S* father, 1973; *m* 1st, 1965, Susan Jane (marr. diss. 1989), *d* of late Captain Kenneth S. B. Lucking and of Mrs Moir P. Stormonth-Darling, Lednathie, Glen Prosen, Angus; two *s*; 2nd, 1989, Mrs Homayoun Mazandi, *d* of late Col Mahmoud Yazdanparst Pakzad. *Educ:* Eton. Grenadier Guards (National Service), 1955–56. Partner, W. Greenwell & Co., 1964–80; Dir, General Technology Systems Ltd, 1975–93; Chm., European Informatics Markets, 1994–. Mem., H of L Select Cttee on the European Communities, 1988–92, on Science and Technology, 1992–; Hon. Sec., Parly Information Technology Cttee, 1991–. Vice-Pres., British Dyslexia Assoc., 1982– (Chm., 1977–82); Chm., Dyslexia Educnl Trust, 1986–. *Heir: s* Hon. Robert James Renwick, *b* 19 Aug. 1966. *Address:* House of Lords, SW1A 0PW. *Clubs:* White's, Turf.

RENWICK, Sir Richard Eustace, 4th Bt *cr* 1921; *b* 13 Jan. 1938; *er s* of Sir Eustace Deuchar Renwick, 3rd Bt, and of Diana Mary, *e d* of Colonel Bernard Cruddas, DSO; *S* father, 1973; *m* 1966, Caroline Anne, *er d* of Major Rupert Milburn; three *s*. *Educ:* Eton. *Heir: s* Charles Richard Renwick, [*b* 10 April 1967; *m* 1993, Jane Ann Lyles (*née* Bush); one *s*]. *Address:* Whalton House, Whalton, Morpeth, Northumberland NE61 3UZ. *T:* Whalton (01670) 775383. *Club:* Northern Counties (Newcastle).

RENWICK, Sir Robin (William), KCMG 1989 (CMG 1980); Director, Robert Fleming Holdings Ltd, since 1995; *b* 13 Dec. 1937; *s* of Richard Renwick, Edinburgh, and Clarice (*née* Henderson); *m* 1965, Annie Colette Giudicelli; one *s* one *d*. *Educ:* St Paul's Sch.; Jesus Coll., Cambridge (Hon. Fellow, 1992); Univ. of Paris (Sorbonne). Army, 1956–58. Entered Foreign Service, 1963; Dakar, 1963–64; FO, 1964–66; New Delhi, 1966–69; Private Sec. to Minister of State, FCO, 1970–72; First Sec., Paris, 1972–76; Counsellor, Cabinet Office, 1976–78; Rhodesia Dept, FCO, 1978–80; Political Adviser to Governor of Rhodesia, 1980; Vis. Fellow, Center for Internat. Affairs, Harvard, 1980–81; Head of Chancery, Washington, 1981–84; Asst Under Sec. of State, FCO, 1984–87; Ambassador to S Africa, 1987–91; Ambassador to Washington, 1991–95. FRSA. Hon. LLD: Wits Univ., 1990; Amer. Univ. in London, 1993; Hon. DLitt: Coll. of William and Mary, 1993; Oglethorpe Univ., 1995. *Publications:* Economic Sanctions, 1981; The Special Relationship: myth or reality?, 1995. *Recreations:* tennis, trout fishing. *Address:* Robert Fleming & Co. Ltd, 25 Copthall Avenue, EC3R 7DR. *Clubs:* Brooks's, Hurlingham, Travellers'.

REPORTER, Sir Shapoor (Ardeshirji), KBE 1973 (OBE 1969); Consultant on Economic and Political Matters concerning Iran, since 1962; *b* 26 Feb. 1921; *s* of Ardeshirji Reporter and Shirin Reporter; *m* 1952, Assia Alexandra; one *s* one *d*. *Educ:* Zoroastrian Public Sch., Teheran; matriculated in Bombay (specially designed course in Political Science under Cambridge Univ. Tutors, UK). PRO, British Legation, Teheran, 1941–43; in charge of Persian Unit of All India Radio, New Delhi, 1943–45; Teaching English, Imperial Staff Coll., Teheran, 1945–48; Political Adviser, US Embassy, Teheran, 1948–54; Free-lance Correspondent, 1954–62; Economic Consultant to major British interests in Iran, 1962–73. *Publications:* English-Persian Phrases, 1945 (Delhi); Dictionary of English-Persian Idioms, 1956 (Teheran); Dictionary of Persian-English Idioms, 1972 (Teheran Univ.). *Recreations:* tennis, walking, travelling.

REPP, Richard Cooper, DPhil; Master, St Cross College, Oxford, since 1987; *b* 1 April 1936; *s* of Robert Mathias Repp, Jun., and Martha Repp (*née* Cooper); *m* 1972, Catherine Ross MacLennan; one *s* one *d*. *Educ:* Shady Side Acad., Pittsburgh; Williams Coll., Mass (BA); Worcester Coll., Oxford (1st Cl. Hons Oriental Studies, MA, DPhil; Hon. Fellow 1989). Instr in Humanities, Robert Coll., Istanbul, 1959–62; Oxford University: Univ. Lectr in Turkish History, 1963–; Sen. Proctor, 1979–80; Vice-Chm., Staff Cttee, 1982–84; Member: Gen. Bd of the Faculties, 1982–84, 1985–89; Hebdomadal Council, 1991–; Pro-Vice-Chancellor, 1994–; Linacre College: Fellow, 1964–87, Hon. Fellow, 1987; Sen. Tutor, 1985–87. *Publications:* The Müfti of Istanbul, 1986; various articles on Ottoman history. *Recreations:* gardening, music. *Address:* St Cross College, Oxford OX1 3LZ. *T:* Oxford (01865) 278493. *Club:* Williams (New York).

REPTON, Bishop Suffragan of, since 1986; **Rt. Rev. Francis Henry Arthur Richmond,** MA; *b* 6 Jan. 1936; *s* of Frank and Lena Richmond; *m* 1966, Caroline Mary Berent; two *s* one *d*. *Educ:* Portora Royal School, Enniskillen; Trinity Coll., Dublin (MA); Univ. of Strasbourg (BTh); Linacre Coll., Oxford (MLitt); Wycliffe Hall, Oxford. Deacon, 1963; Priest, 1964; Asst Curate, Woodlands, Doncaster, 1963–66; Sir Henry Stephenson Research Fellow, Sheffield Univ. and Chaplain, Sheffield Cathedral, 1966–69; Vicar, St George's, Sheffield, 1969–77; Anglican Chaplain to Sheffield Univ. and Mem. Sheffield Chaplaincy for Higher Education, 1974–77; Warden, Lincoln Theolog. Coll., and Canon and Prebendary of Lincoln Cathedral, 1977–86. Examng Chaplain to Bishop of Lincoln; Proctor in Convocation for Lincoln, 1980. Select Preacher, Univ. of Oxford, 1985. *Recreations:* listening to classical music, reading, theatre, walking, gardening. *Address:* Repton House, Lea, Matlock, Derbys DE4 5JP. *T:* Dethick (01629) 534644.

RESNAIS, Alain; French film director; *b* Vannes, 3 June 1922; *s* of Pierre Resnais and Jeanne (*née* Gachet); *m* 1969, Florence Mairaux. *Educ:* Collège St François-Xavier, Vannes; Institut des hautes études cinématographiques. Assistant to Nicole Védrée for film Paris 1900, 1947–48; has directed his own films (many of which have won prizes), since 1948. Short films, 1948–59, include: Van Gogh, 1948; Guernica (jtly with Robert Hessens), 1950; Les statues meurent aussi (jtly with Chris Marker), 1952; Nuit et brouillard, 1955. Full length films include: Hiroshima mon amour, 1959; L'année dernière à Marienbad, 1961; Muriel, 1963; La guerre est finie, 1966; Je t'aime, je t'aime, 1968; Stavisky, 1974; Providence, 1977; Mon Oncle d'Amérique, 1980; La vie est un roman, 1983; L'amour à Mort, 1984; Mélo, 1986; Je veux rentrer à la maison, 1989; Smoking, 1993; No Smoking, 1993. *Address:* Artmedia, 10 Avenue George V, 75008 Paris, France.

RESTIEAUX, Rt. Rev. Cyril Edward; *b* 25 Feb. 1910; *s* of Joseph and Edith Restieaux. *Educ:* English Coll., Rome; Gregorian University. Ordained, 1932; Curate at Nottingham, 1933; Parish Priest at Matlock, 1936; Hon. Canon of Nottingham, 1948; Vicar-General of Nottingham, 1951; Provost and Domestic Prelate to HH Pope Pius XII, 1955; Bishop of Plymouth, 1955–86. *Publication:* Dedicated to Christ, 1989. *Address:* Stoodley Knowle, Anstey's Cove Road, Torquay TQ1 2JB.

RESTREPO-LONDOÑO, Andrés; Order of Boyacá, Colombia; private financial consultant, since 1993; President, Empresa Colombiana de Petróleos-ECOPETROL, 1988–92; *b* 20 Jan. 1942; *m* 1968, Ghislaine Ibiza; one *s* three *d*. *Educ:* Universidad de Antioquia; Université de Paris (postgraduate courses, 1966). Professor and Head of Economic Dept., Univ. de Antioquia, 1967–68; Gen. Man., La Primavera chain of stores, 1969–76; Finance Man., Empresas Públicas de Medellín, 1976–79; Gen. Man., Carbones de Colombia (Colombian Coal Bd), 1979–80; Minister for Economic Develt, 1980–81; Ambassador to UK, 1981–82. Chm., Proban SA (Banana Exporting Co.), 1983–84; Pres., Industrias e Inversiones Samper SA (Cement Co.), 1985–88. Order Sol of Perú; Order Cruzeiro do Sul, Brazil. *Publications:* Carbones Térmicos en Colombia, Bases para una Política Contractual, 1981; several articles in El Colombiano, daily newspaper of Medellín, Colombia. *Recreations:* fishing, tennis. *Address:* Calle 136A No 57B-17, Bogotá, DE, Colombia; (office) Calle 93B No 12–28 Of. 303, Santafé de Bogotá, DC, Colombia. *T:* (1) 6217905, 6217954. *Club:* Lagartos (Bogotá).

RETTIE, (James) Philip, CBE 1987; TD 1962; farmer, since 1964; Director: Edinburgh and Glasgow Investment Co., since 1989; Rettie & Co., since 1992; *b* 7 Dec. 1926; *s* of James Rettie and Rachel Buist; *m* 1st, 1955, Helen Grant; two *s* one *d*; 2nd, 1980, Mrs Diana Harvey (*née* Ballantyne). *Educ:* Trinity College, Glenalmond. Royal Engineers, 1945–48; RE (TA), 1949–65. Wm Low & Co. plc, 1948–85 (Chm., 1980–85); Mem., TSB Scotland Area Bd, 1983–88. Chm., Sea Fish Industry Authority, 1981–87. Trustee, Scottish Civic Trust, 1983–. Hon. Colonel: 117 (Highland) Field Support Squadron, RE, TAVR, 1982–87; 277 Airfield Damage Repair Sqdn, RE(T), 1984–89. FRSA. *Recreations:* shooting, gardening, hill-walking. *Address:* Hill House, Ballindean, Inchture, Perthshire PH14 9QS. *T:* Inchture (01828) 686337.

REUPKE, Michael; business consultant, since 1990; *b* Potsdam, Germany, 20 Nov. 1936; *s* of Dr Willm Reupke and Dr Frances G. Reupke (*née* Kinnear); *m* 1963, (Helen) Elizabeth Restrick; one *s* two *d*. *Educ:* Latymer Upper Sch., London; Jesus Coll., Cambridge (MA Mod. Langs); Collège d'Europe, Bruges. Commnd RAF (Technical Training Comd), 1957–58. Joined Reuters, 1962; reporter, France, Switzerland, Guinea and West Germany, 1962–69; Asst European Manager, Gen. News Div., 1970–72; Chief Rep., West Germany, 1973–74; Manager, Latin America and the Caribbean, 1975–77; Editor-in-Chief, 1978–89; Gen. Manager, 1989. Director: Visnews, 1985–89; Internat. Business Information Services SA, 1991–93; Company Information Exchange Ltd, 1992–; Staria Ltd, 1993–94. Member: IPI, 1978–; Internat. Inst. of Communications, 1987–; Radio Authy, 1994–. Trustee, Reuter Foundn, 1982–89. *Recreation:* sailing. *Address:* Tippings, The Common, Stokenchurch, Bucks HP14 3UD. *T:* High Wycombe (01494) 482341; 60 rue St Georges, 75009 Paris, France. *T:* 42805459. *Clubs:* Royal Automobile; Leander (Henley-on-Thames).

REUTER, Edzard; Chairman of Board of Management, Daimler-Benz AG, 1987–95. *Educ:* Univs of Berlin and Göttingen (maths and physics); Free Univ. of Berlin (law). Research Asst, Free Univ. of Berlin Law Faculty, 1953–56; Universum Film, 1957–62; Manager, TV prod. section, Bertelsmann Group, Munich, 1962–64; exec., finance dept, Daimler-Benz, 1964; responsible for management planning and organization, 1971; Dep. Mem., Bd, 1973; Full Mem., Exec. Bd, 1976. *Publications:* Vom Geist der Wirtschaft, 1986; Horizonte der Wirtschaft, 1993.

REVANS, Prof. Reginald William, PhD; MIMinE; Founder, Action Learning Trust, 1977; Professorial Fellow in Action Learning, University of Manchester, since 1986; *b* 14 May 1907; *s* of Thomas William Revans, Principal Ship Surveyor, Board of Trade; *m* 1st, 1932, Annida Aquist, Gothenburg (marriage dissolved, 1947); three *d*; 2nd, 1955, Norah Mary Merritt, Chelmsford; one *s*. *Educ:* Battersea Grammar School; University Coll., London; Emmanuel Coll., Cambridge. BSc London, PhD Cantab. Commonwealth Fund Fellow, Univ. of Michigan, 1930–32; Research Fellow, Emmanuel Coll., Cambridge, 1932–35; Dep. Chief Education Officer, Essex CC, 1935–45; Dir of Education, Mining Assoc. of Gt Britain, 1945–47 and NCB, 1947–50; Research on management of coalmines, 1950–55; Prof., Industrial Admin., Univ. of Manchester, 1955–65; Res. Fellow, Guy's Hosp. Med. Sch., 1965–68; External Prof., Management Studies, Leeds Univ., 1976–78. Dist. Vis. Scholar, Southern Methodist Univ., USA, 1972. Pres., European Assoc. of Univ. Management Centres, 1962–64. Hon. DSc Bath, 1969. Chevalier, Order of Leopold, Belgium, 1971. *Publications:* Report on Education for Mining Industry, 1945; Education of the Young Worker, 1949; Standards for Morale, 1964; Science and the Manager, 1965; The Theory and Practice of Management, 1965; Developing Effective Managers, 1971; (ed) Hospitals, Communication, Choice and Change, 1972; Workers' Attitudes and Motivation (OECD Report), 1972; Childhood and Maturity, 1973; Action Learning in Hospitals, 1976; The ABC of Action Learning, 1978; Action Learning, 1979; The Origins and Growth of Action Learning, 1982; various in professional magazines upon application of analytical methods to understanding of industrial morale. *Recreations:* British Olympic Team, 1928; holder of Cambridge undergraduate long jump record, 1929–62. *Address:* 8 Higher Downs, Altrincham, Cheshire WA14 2QL.

REVELL, Surg. Vice-Adm. Anthony Leslie, QHS 1989; FRCA; Surgeon General, Ministry of Defence, since 1994; *b* 26 April 1935; *s* of Leslie Frederick Revell and Florence Mabel (*née* Styles). *Educ:* King's Coll. Sch., Wimbledon; Ashford and Eastbourne Grammar Schs; Univ. of Birmingham Med. Sch. (MB, ChB); DA 1968. FRCA (FFARCS 1969); FRSM 1970. Joined RN, 1960; HMS Troubridge, 1960–62; HMS Dampier, 1962; HMS Loch Fada and 5th Frigate Sqdn, 1963; Anæsthetist, RN Hosp., Plymouth, 1964–65; HMS Eagle, 1965–67; Clin. Assistant, Radcliffe Infy, Oxford, Alder Hey Children's Hosp., Liverpool, and various courses, 1967–69; Anæsthetist, RN Hosp., Plymouth, 1969–70; RAF Hosps Nocton Hall and Akrotiri, Cyprus, 1970–72; ANZUK Mil. Hosp., Singapore, 1972–74; Cons. Anæsthetist, RN Hosp., Haslar, 1974–79; *ndc*, Latimer, 1979–80; Recruiter, MoD, 1980; Dir of Studies, Inst. of Naval Medicine, 1980–82; on staff, Surg. Rear-Adm. (Naval Hosps), 1982–84; Dir, Med. Personnel, 1984–86; RCDS, 1986; MO i/c, RN Hosp., Plymouth, 1987–88; on staff., C-in-C Fleet, 1988–90; Dir, Clinical Services, Defence Med. Directorate, 1990–91; Surg. Rear-Adm., Operational Med. Services, 1991–92; CSO (Med. and Dental) to C-in-C Fleet, 1992–93; Med. Dir Gen. (Navy), 1993–94. CStJ 1993. *Publications:* Haslar: the Royal Hospital, 1979; (ed jtly) Proc. World Assoc. Anæsthetists, 1970. *Recreation:* choral music. *Address:* 29 Little Green, Alverstoke, Gosport, Hants PO12 2EX. *Club:* Naval and Military.

REVELL, Anthony William; Chief Executive, AAH plc (formerly Holdings), since 1991; *b* 28 June 1938. *Address:* AAH plc, 76 South Park, Lincoln, LN5 8ES. *T:* (01522) 546577.

REVELSTOKE, 5th Baron *cr* 1885, of Membland, Devon; **John Baring;** *b* 2 Dec. 1934; *er s* of 4th Baron Revelstoke and Hon. Florence Fermor-Hesketh (*d* 1971), 2nd *d* of 1st Baron Hesketh; *S* father, 1994. *Edu:* Eton. *Heir:* *b* Hon. James Cecil Baring [*b* 16 Aug 1938; *m* 1st, 1968, Aneta, *yr d* of Erskine A. H. Fisher; two *s*; 2nd, 1983, Sarah, *d* of William Edward Stubbs, MBE; one *d*]. *Address:* House of Lords, SW1A 0PW.

REVERDIN, Prof. Olivier, DrLitt; Professor of Greek, University of Geneva, 1958–83 (Hon. Professor, since 1983); Member, Consultative Assembly of Council of Europe, 1963–74 (President, 1969–72); Deputy (Liberal) for Geneva, Swiss National Council, 1955–71, Council of States (Senate), 1971–79; *b* 15 July 1913; *m* 1936, Renée Chaponnière; two *s* one *d*. *Educ:* Geneva, Paris and Athens. LicLitt 1935; DrLitt Geneva, 1945. Foreign Mem., French Sch. of Archaeology, Athens, 1936–38; Attaché Swiss Legation, Service of Foreign Interests, Rome, 1941–43; Privatdocent of Greek, Univ. of Geneva, 1945–57; Parly Redactor, 1945–54; Chief Editor 1954–59, Manager 1954–67, Pres., 1972–79, Journal de Genève. Mem. 1963–80, Pres. 1968–80, Swiss National Research Council; Mem., Swiss Science Council, 1958–80; Président: Fondation Hardt pour l'étude de l'antiquité classique, Geneva, 1959–; Fondation Archives Jean Piaget, 1973–87; Vice-Pres., European Science Foundn, 1974–77, Mem. Exec. Council, 1977–80; Chm., Collections Baur, Geneva, 1984–. *Publications:* La religion de la cité platonicienne, 1945; La guerre du Sonderbund, 1947, 2nd edn 1987; La Crète, berceau de la civilisation occidentale, 1960; Connaissance de la Suisse, 1966; Les premiers cours de Grec au Collège de France, 1984; Henri Estienne à Genève, 1988; Impressions grecques en Suisse au XVIe et XVIIe siècles, 1991. *Address:* 8 rue des Granges, 1204 Geneva, Switzerland. *T:* (22) 3115191.

REW, Paul Francis, FCA; Partner, Price Waterhouse, since 1987; *b* 20 May 1953; *s* of Lt Col Peter Rew and Diana Edith Rew (*née* Moore); *m* 1982, Mary Ellen Pleasant; two *d*. *Educ:* Churcher's Coll., Petersfield; Exeter Univ. (BSc Engrg Sci.). ACA 1977; FCA 1983. Price Waterhouse: articled, London, 1974; Johannesburg office, 1982–84; Partner, 1987; on secondment to DTI as Under Sec. and Dir, Industrial Develt Unit, 1992–94. Mem., Steering Bd, Insolvency Service, 1992–94. Mem., Bd of Mgt, St Bartholomew's and Queen Alexandra's Coll. of Nursing and Midwifery, 1990–95. *Recreations:* golf, humanistic psychology. *Address:* Price Waterhouse, Southwark Towers, 32 London Bridge Street, SE1 9SY. *T:* 0171–939 3000; Clayton, Ruxley Crescent, Claygate, Surrey KT10 0TX.

REX, Prof. John Arderne; Research Professor on Ethnic Relations, 1984–90, now Emeritus, and Associate Director, Centre for Research in Ethnic Relations, 1974–90, University of Warwick; *b* 5 March 1925; *s* of Frederick Edward George Rex and Winifred Natalie Rex; *m* 1st, 1949, Pamela Margaret Rutherford (marr. diss. 1963); two *d*; 2nd, 1965, Margaret Ellen Biggs; two *s*. *Educ:* Grey Institute High Sch. and Rhodes University Coll., S Africa. BA (S Africa), PhD (Leeds). Served War, Royal Navy (Able Seaman), 1943–45. Graduated, 1948; Lecturer: Univ. of Leeds, 1949–62; Birmingham, 1962–64; Prof. of Social Theory and Institutions, Durham, 1964–70; Prof. of Sociology, Univ. of Warwick, 1970–79; Dir, SSRC Research Unit on Ethnic Relations, Univ. of Aston in Birmingham, 1979–84. Vis. Prof., Univ. of Toronto, 1974–75. *Publications:* Key Problems of Sociological Theory, 1961; (with Robert Moore) Race Community and Conflict, 1967, 2nd edn 1973; Race Relations in Sociological Theory, 1970; Discovering Sociology, 1973; Race, Colonialism and the City, 1974; (ed) Approaches to Sociology, 1974; Sociology and the Demystification of the Modern World, 1974; (with Sally Tomlinson) Colonial Immigrants in a British City, 1979; Social Conflict, 1980; (ed) Apartheid and Social Research, 1981; Race and Ethnicity, 1986; The Ghetto and the Underclass, 1988; Ethnic Identity and Ethnic Organisation in Britain, 1991. *Recreations:* politics, race relations work. *Address:* 33 Arlington Avenue, Leamington Spa, Warwicks CV32 5UD.

REYES, Narciso G., Bintang Mahaputera, 1964; Order of Diplomatic Service Merit, 1972; President, Philippine Council for Foreign Relations, 1986–87; *b* Manila, 6 Feb. 1914; *m*. *Educ:* Univ. of Sto Tomas (AB). Mem., English Faculty, Univ. of Sto Tomas, 1935–36; Assoc. Ed., Philippines Commonweal, 1935–41; Nat. Language Faculty, Ateneo de Manila, 1939–41; Assoc. Ed., Manila Post, 1945–47; Assoc. News Ed., Evening News, Manila, 1947–48; Man. Ed., Philippine Newspaper Guild Organ, 1947–48; Dir, Philippine Information Agency, 1954–55; Minister-Counsellor, Bangkok, 1956; Public Relations Dir, SEATO, 1956–58; Minister, later Amb., Burma, 1958–62; Ambassador to: Indonesia, 1962–67; London, Stockholm, Oslo, Copenhagen, 1967–70; Permanent Rep. to UN, 1970–77; Philippine Ambassador to People's Republic of China, 1977–80; Sec. Gen., ASEAN, 1980–82. Mem. various delegns and missions, incl. sessions of UN; Philippine Rep. to UN Commn for Social Devt, 1967–72 (Vice-Chm., 1967; Chm., 1968); Special UN Rep. on Social Develt, 1968; Rep. to UN Human Rights Commn, 1970–72; Chairman: UNICEF Exec. Bd, 1972–74; UN Gen. Assembly Finance and Economic Cttee, 1971; Pres., UNDP Governing Council, 1974; Vice-Pres., UN Environment Governing Council, 1975. Chm., External Educn Plans, 1988–89. Vice-Chm., Philippine Futuristics Soc. Editor, Foreign Relations Jl, 1986–. Outstanding Alumnus, Univ. of Sto Tomas, 1969. Dr of Laws (*hc*), Philippine Women's Univ., 1977. Gawad Mabini Award, Philippines, 1994. *Publications:* essays, poems and short stories. *Address:* 8 Lipa Road, Philamlife Homes, Quezon City, Manila, Philippines.

REYNOLD, Frederic; QC 1982; *b* 7 Jan. 1936; *s* of late Henry and Regina Reynold. *Educ:* Battersea Grammar School; Magdalen College, Oxford. BA Hons Jurisprudence. Called to the Bar, Gray's Inn, 1960, Bencher, 1991; commenced practice, 1963. *Publication:* The Judge as Lawmaker, 1967. *Recreations:* music, the arts, association croquet, dining out among friends. *Address:* 5 Hillcrest, 51 Ladbroke Grove, W11 3AX. *T:* 0171–229 3848. *Club:* Sussex County Croquet.

REYNOLDS, Alan (Munro); painter, maker of reliefs, and printmaker; *b* 27 April 1926; *m* 1957, Vona Darby. *Educ:* Woolwich Polytechnic Art School; Royal College of Art (Scholarship and Medal). One man exhibitions: Redfern Gall., 1952, 1953, 1954, 1956, 1960, 1962, 1964, 1966, 1970, 1972, 1974; Durlacher Gall., New York, 1954, 1959; Leicester Galleries, 1958; Aldeburgh, Suffolk, 1965; Arnolfini Gall., Bristol, 1971 (graphics); Annely Juda Fine Art, 1978, 1991; Juda Rowan Gall., 1982, 1986; Thomas Agnew, Albemarle Street Gall., 1982; Gall. Wack, Kaiserslautern, 1986, 1990; Galerie Lalumière, Paris, 1990; Galerie Art, Nürnberg, 1992. Work in exhibitions: Carnegie (Pittsburgh) Internat., USA, 1952, 1955, 1958, 1961; Internat. Exhibn, Rome, (awarded one of the three equal prizes), subsequently Musée d'Art Moderne, Paris, and Brussels; British Council Exhibn, Oslo and Copenhagen, 1956; Redfern Gall., 1971; Spectrum, Arts Council of GB, 1971; British Painting 1952–77, Royal Academy, 1977; Galerie Loyse Oppenheim, Nyon, Switzerland, 1977; Galerie Renée Ziegler, Zürich, 1981; group exhibitions: Scottish Nat. Gall. of Modern Art, Edinburgh, 1984; Annely Juda Fine Art and Juda Rowan Gall., London, 1985; Galeries Renée Ziegler, Zürich, 1985–86; Annely Juda Fine Art, 1986; Wilhelm-Hack Mus., Ludwigshafen am Rhein, 1987; Stiftung für Konkrete Kunst, Reutlingen, 1992–93. Works acquired by: Tate Gall.; V&A; National Galleries of: S Aust.; Felton Bequest, Vic., Aust.; NZ; Canada; City Art Galleries of: Birmingham; Bristol; Manchester; Wakefield; Mus. of Modern Art, NY; Contemporary Art Soc.; British Council; Arts Council of GB; Rothschild Foundn; The Graves Art Gall., Sheffield; Nottingham Castle Mus.; Fitzwilliam Mus., Cambridge; Mus. of Modern Art, São Paulo, Brazil; Leeds Art Gall.; Toledo Art Gall., Ohio, USA; Oriel Coll., Oxford; Warwick Univ.; Mus. and Art Galls, Brighton and Plymouth; Texas Univ., Austin, USA; Berlin Nat. Gall.; McCrory Corp., NY; Wilhelm-Hack Mus., Ludwigshafen am Rhein; Louisiana Mus., Denmark; Tel Aviv Mus., Israel; Musée des Beaux Arts de Grenoble; Mus. Pfalzgalerie, Kaiserslautern, W Germany; Inst. für Kultur, Nordhein Westfalen. CoID Award, 1965; Arts Council of GB Purchase Award, 1967. *Relevant Publication:* The Painter, Alan Reynolds, by J. P. Hodin, 1962. *Address:* Briar Cottage, High Street, Cranbrook, Kent TN17 3EN.

REYNOLDS, Albert; Member of the Dáil (TD) (FF), since 1977; Taoiseach (Prime Minister of Ireland), 1992–94; President, Fianna Fáil, 1992–94 (Vice-President, 1983–92); *b* Rooskey, Co. Roscommon, 3 Nov. 1932; *m* Kathleen Coen; two *s* five *d*. *Educ:* Summerhill Coll., Sligo. Minister: for Posts and Telegraphs, and for Transport, 1979–81; for Industry and Energy, March–Dec. 1982; Opposition spokesperson: for Industry and Employment, 1983–85; for Energy, 1985–87; Minister for: Industry and Commerce, 1987–88; Finance, 1988–91. Mem., Oireachtas Jt Cttee on Commercial State-Sponsored Bodies, 1983–87. Member: Longford CC, 1974–79; Longford County Cttee of Agric., 1974–79; Longford Health Cttee, 1974–79. Pres., Longford Chamber of Commerce, 1974–78; Chm., Longford Recreational Develt Centre. *Address:* Government Buildings, Upper Merrion Street, Dublin 2, Ireland. *T:* Dublin 6685333.

REYNOLDS, (Arthur) Graham, OBE 1984; FBA 1993; Keeper of the Department of Prints and Drawings, 1961–74 (of Engraving, Illustration and Design, 1959–61), and of Paintings, Victoria and Albert Museum, 1959–74; *b* Highgate, 10 Jan. 1914; *o s* of late Arthur T. Reynolds and Eva Mullins; *m* 1943, Daphne, *d* of late Thomas Dent, Huddersfield. *Educ:* Highgate School; Queens' College, Cambridge. Joined staff of Victoria and Albert Museum, 1937. Seconded to Ministry of Home Security, 1939–45. Hon. Keeper of Portrait Miniatures, Fitzwilliam Mus., Cambridge, 1994. Member: Adv. Council, Paul Mellon Centre for Studies in British Art, 1977–84; Reviewing Cttee on the Export of Works of Art, 1984–90. Trustee, William Morris Gallery, Walthamstow, 1972–75; Chm., Gainsborough's House Soc., Sudbury, 1977–79. Leverhulme Emeritus Fellowship, 1980–81. *Publications:* Twentieth Century Drawings, 1946; Nicholas Hilliard and Isaac Oliver, 1947, 2nd edn 1971; Van Gogh, 1947; Nineteenth Century Drawings, 1949; Thomas Bewick, 1949; An Introduction to English Water-Colour Painting, 1950, rev. edn 1988; Gastronomic Pleasures, 1950; Elizabethan and Jacobean Costume, 1951; English Portrait Miniatures, 1952, rev. edn 1988; Painters of the Victorian Scene, 1953; Catalogue of the Constable Collection, Victoria and Albert Museum, 1960, rev. edn 1973; Constable, the Natural Painter, 1965; Victorian Painting, 1966, 2nd edn 1987; Turner, 1969; A Concise History of Water Colour Painting, 1972; Catalogue of Portrait Miniatures, Wallace Collection, 1980; Constable's England, 1983; The Later Paintings and Drawings of John Constable, 2 vols, 1984 (Mitchell Prize); The Earlier Paintings and Drawings of John Constable, 1995; Editor of series English Masters of Black and White; contribs to Burlington Magazine, Apollo, etc. *Address:* The Old Manse, Bradfield St George, Bury St Edmunds, Suffolk IP30 0AZ. *T:* Sicklesmere (01284) 386610. *Club:* Athenæum.

REYNOLDS, Barbara, MA Cantab; BA (Hons), PhD London; author, lexicographer; Reader in Italian Studies, University of Nottingham, 1966–78; *b* 13 June 1914; *d* of late Alfred Charles Reynolds; *m* 1st, 1939, Prof. Lewis Thorpe (*d* 1977); one *s* one *d*; 2nd, 1982, Kenneth Imeson(*d* 1994). *Educ:* St Paul's Girls' Sch.; UCL. Asst Lectr in Italian, LSE

1937–40. Chief Exec. and Gen. Editor, The Cambridge Italian Dictionary, 1948–81; Man. Editor, Seven, an Anglo-American Literary Review, 1980–. Mem. Coun. Senate, Cambridge Univ., 1961–62. University Lecturer in Italian Literature and Language, Cambridge, 1945–62 (Faculty Assistant Lecturer, 1940–45); Warden of Willoughby Hall, Univ. of Nottingham, 1963–69. Vis. Professor: Univ. of Calif., Berkeley, 1974–75; Wheaton Coll., Illinois, 1977–78, 1982; Trinity Coll., Dublin, 1980, 1981; Hope Coll., Mich., 1982. Hon. Reader in Italian, Univ. of Warwick, 1975–80. Chm., Dorothy L. Sayers Soc., 1986–. Hon. DLitt: Wheaton Coll., Illinois, 1979; Hope Coll., Mich., 1982; Durham Univ., 1995. Silver Medal for Services to Italian culture (Italian Govt), 1964; Edmund Gardner Prize, 1964; Silver Medal for services to Anglo-Veneto cultural relations, Prov. Admin of Vicenza, 1971; Cavaliere Ufficiale al Merito della Repubblica Italiana, 1978. *Publications:* (with K. T. Butler) Tredici Novelle Moderne, 1947; The Linguistic Writings of Alessandro Manzoni: a Textual and Chronological Reconstruction, 1950; rev. edn with introd., Dante and the Early Astronomers, by M. A. Orr, 1956; The Cambridge Italian Dictionary, Vol. I, Italian-English, 1962, Vol. II, English-Italian, 1981; (with Dorothy L. Sayers) Paradise: a translation into English triple rhyme, from the Italian of Dante Alighieri, 1962; (with Lewis Thorpe) Guido Farina, Painter of Verona, 1967; La Vita Nuova (Poems of Youth); trans. of Dante's Vita Nuova, 1969; Concise Cambridge Italian Dictionary, 1975; Orlando Furioso, trans. into rhymed octaves of Ariosto's epic, Vol. I, 1975 (Internat. Literary Prize, Monselice, Italy, 1976) Vol. II, 1977; (ed) Cambridge-Signorelli Dizionario Italiano-Inglese, Inglese-Italiano, 1986; (ed jtly) The Translator's Art, 1987; The Passionate Intellect: Dorothy L. Sayers' encounter with Dante, 1989; Dorothy L. Sayers: her life and soul, 1993; The Letters of Dorothy L. Sayers, Vol. I, 1995; numerous articles on Italian literature in learned jls. *Address:* 220 Milton Road, Cambridge CB4 1LQ. *T:* Cambridge (01223) 565380. *Clubs:* University Women's (Chm., 1988–90), Authors'.

See also A. C. Thorpe.

REYNOLDS, Sir David James, 3rd Bt, *cr* 1923; Member of Lloyd's Insurance; *b* 26 Jan. 1924; *er s* of Sir John Francis Roskell Reynolds, 2nd Bt, MBE, JP and Milicent (*d* 1931), *d* of late Major James Orr-Ewing and late Lady Margaret Orr-Ewing, *d* of 7th Duke of Roxburghe; *S* father 1956; *m* 1966, Charlotte Baumgartner; one *s* two *d*. *Educ:* Downside. Active service in Army, 1942–47, Italy, etc; on demobilisation, Captain 15/19 Hussars. *Recreation:* sport. *Heir: s* James Francis Reynolds, *b* 10 July 1971. *Address:* Blanche Pierre House, St Lawrence, Jersey, CI.

REYNOLDS, Prof. Edward Osmund Royle, CBE 1995; MD; FRCP, FRCOG; FRS 1993; Professor of Neonatal Paediatrics, University College London (formerly University College Hospital) Medical School, since 1976; *b* 3 Feb. 1933; *s* of Edward Royle Reynolds and Edna Reynolds; *m* 1956, Margaret Lindsay Ballard; two *s*. *Educ:* St Paul's Sch.; St Thomas's Hosp. Med. Sch. (Henry Myers Exhbn, 1958). BSc, MD London; DCH; FRCP 1975; FRCOG (*ad eundem*) 1983. Posts at St Thomas' Hosp., 1959–62; Research Fellow in Pediatrics: Harvard Med. Sch., 1962–64; Yale Med. Sch., 1964; Res. Asst, then Lectr and Sen. Lectr, UCH Med. Sch., 1964–76; Hd, Dept of Paediatrics, UCMSM, 1987–93. Consultant Paediatrician, UCH, 1969–94. Hon. Prof. of Paediatrics, Inst. of Child Health, 1994; William Julius Mickle fellow, Univ. of London, 1976–77. Numerous visiting professorships, incl. RSocMed Foundn Vis. Prof. to Amer. Acad. of Pediatrics, 1989. Specialist Advr (perinatal medicine), H of C Social Services and Health Select Cttees, 1978–92; Member: Scientific Adv. Panel, Foundn for Study of Infant Deaths, 1990–; Bd of Management, Inst. of Child Health, 1990–. President: BLISS (Baby Life Support Systems), 1982–; Neonatal Soc., 1991–94; Mem., Hooke Cttee, Royal Soc., 1993–. Hon. Member: Argentine Paediatric Assoc.; Italian Soc. for Perinatal Medicine; British Assoc. of Perinatal Medicine, 1992 (Founder's Lectr, 1992). Lectures: Charles West, RCP, 1989; George Frederic Still Meml, BPA, 1995. Dawson Williams Meml Prize, BMA, 1992; James Spence Medal, BPA, 1994; Maternité Prize, Europ. Assoc. of Perinatal Medicine, 1994; Harding Award, Action Research, 1995. *Publications:* numerous chapters and papers on neonatal physiology and medicine. *Recreations:* countryside, travel, music, photography, archæology, sport (particularly fencing, in the past; mem., British foil team, 3rd World Championship, Rome, 1955). *Address:* 72 Barrowgate Road, Chiswick, W4 4QU. *T:* 0181–994 3326; 4 Ginge, Oxon OX12 8QR. *Club:* Royal Society of Medicine.

REYNOLDS, Eva Mary Barbara; *see* Reynolds, Barbara.

REYNOLDS, Fiona Claire, (Mrs R. W. T. Merrill); Director, Council for the Protection of Rural England, since 1992; *b* 29 March 1958; *d* of Jeffrey Alan Reynolds and Margaret Mary (*née* Watson); *m* 1981, Robert William Tinsley Merrill; two *d*. *Educ:* Rugby High Sch. for Girls; Newnham Coll., Cambridge (MA, MPhil 1980). Sec., Council for Nat. Parks, 1980–87; Asst Dir, CPRE, 1987–91. Global 500 Award, UN Envmt Programme, 1990. *Recreations:* hillwalking, classical music and opera, reading. *Address:* Council for the Protection of Rural England, 25 Buckingham Palace Road, SW1W 0PP. *T:* 0171–976 6433; 13 Ferntower Road, Highbury, N5 2JE.

REYNOLDS, Prof. Francis Martin Baillie, DCL; FBA 1988; Professor of Law, University of Oxford, since 1992; Fellow of Worcester College, Oxford, since 1960; *b* 11 Nov. 1932; *s* of Eustace Baillie Reynolds and Emma Margaret Hanby Reynolds (*née* Holmes); *m* 1965, Susan Claire Shillito; two *s* one *d*. *Educ:* Winchester Coll.; Worcester Coll., Oxford (BA 1956; BCL 1957; MA 1960; DCL 1986). Bigelow Teaching Fellow, Chicago Univ., 1957–58. Called to the Bar, Inner Temple, 1960, Hon. Bencher 1979. Reader in Law, Oxford Univ., 1977–92. Visiting Professor, Nat. Univ. of Singapore, UCL, Univ. of Melbourne, Monash Univ., Otago Univ., Univ. of Sydney, Univ. of Auckland. Hon. QC 1993. Gen. Editor, Lloyd's Maritime and Commercial Law Qly, 1983–87; Editor, Law Qly Review, 1987–. *Publications:* (ed jtly) Chitty on Contracts, 24th edn 1977, to 26th edn 1989; (ed jtly) Benjamin's Sale of Goods, 1974, 4th edn 1992; Bowstead on Agency, (ed jtly) 13th edn 1968, 14th edn 1976, (ed) 15th edn 1985; contribs to legal jls. *Recreations:* music, walking. *Address:* Worcester College, Oxford OX1 2HB. *T:* Oxford (01865) 278300.

REYNOLDS, Gillian; Radio Critic, The Daily Telegraph, since 1975; *b* 15 Nov. 1935; *d* of Charles Morton and Ada (*née* Kelly); *m* 1958, Stanley Reynolds (marr. diss. 1982); three *s*. *Educ:* St Anne's Coll., Oxford (BA); Mount Holyoke Coll., South Hadley, Mass, USA. TV journalist, 1964–; Radio Critic, The Guardian, 1967–74; Programme Controller, Radio City, Liverpool, 1974–75. Fellow (first to be apptd), Radio Acad., 1990; FRSA. *Recreation:* listening to the radio. *Address:* Flat 3, 1 Linden Gardens, W2 4HA. *T:* 0171–229 1893.

REYNOLDS, Graham; *see* Reynolds, A. G.

REYNOLDS, Guy Edwin K.; *see* King-Reynolds.

REYNOLDS, Maj.-Gen. Jack Raymond, CB 1971; OBE 1945; ERD 1948; DL; Director of Movements (Army), Ministry of Defence, 1968–71, retired; *b* 10 June 1916; *s* of Walter Reynolds and Evelyn Marion (*née* Burrows); *m* 1940, Joan Howe Taylor; one *s* one *d*. *Educ:* Haberdashers' Aske's. Student Apprentice, AEC Ltd, 1934. Commissioned RASC (SR), 1936. Served War of 1939–45, France, Middle East and Italy (despatches). CRASC 7th Armoured Div., 1955–57; GSO 1 War Office, 1958–60; Col GS; UK Delegn to NATO Standing Group, Washington, DC, 1960–62; DDST, Southern Command, 1962–64; Commandant, RASC Training Centre, 1964–65; Imperial Defence College, 1966; Dep. Quarter-Master-General, BAOR, 1967–68. Col Comdt, Royal Corps of Transport, 1972–78. Dir-Gen., BHS, 1971–75; Dir-Gen., 1975–85, Pres., 1985–88, BEF. FCIT. DL Northants, 1984. *Recreation:* fishing. *Address:* Old Mill House, Hellidon, near Daventry, Northants NN11 6LG.

REYNOLDS, James; Judge of the High Court, Eastern Region of Nigeria, 1956–63; *b* Belfast, May, 1908; *yr s* of late James Reynolds and late Agnes Forde (*née* Cully); *m* 1946, Alexandra Mary Erskine Strain; two *s* two *d*. *Educ:* Belfast Roy. Acad.; Queen's Univ., Belfast. Called to Bar of N Ire., 1931; practised at N Ire Bar, 1931–40. Colonial Legal Service as Crown Counsel in Hong Kong, 1940. Prisoner-of-war in Japanese hands, 1941–45. Returned to Hong Kong, 1946; apptd District Judge, 1953. Chairman: Local Tribunal under Nat. Insce Acts, 1964–83; Industrial Tribunal, 1969–81.

See also J. K. Reynolds.

REYNOLDS, (James) Kirk; QC 1993; *b* 24 March 1951; *s* of James Reynolds, *qv* and Alexandra Mary (*née* Strain). *Educ:* Campbell Coll., Belfast; Peterhouse, Cambridge (MA). Called to the Bar, Middle Temple, 1974. *Publications:* The Handbook of Rent Review, 1981; The Renewal of Business Tenancies, 1985. *Address:* Falcon Chambers, Falcon Court, EC4Y 1AA. *T:* 0171–353 2484.

REYNOLDS, Joyce Maire, FBA 1982; Fellow of Newnham College, 1951–84, now Hon. Fellow, and Reader in Roman Historical Epigraphy, 1983–84, University of Cambridge; *b* 18 Dec. 1918; *d* of late William Howe Reynolds and Nellie Farmer Reynolds. *Educ:* Walthamstow County High Sch. for Girls; St Paul's Girls' Sch., Hammersmith; Somerville Coll., Oxford (Hon. Fellow, 1988). Temp. Civil Servant, BoT, 1941–46; Rome Scholar, British Sch. at Rome, 1946–48; Lectr in Ancient History, King's Coll., Newcastle upon Tyne, 1948–51; Cambridge University: Asst Lectr in Classics, 1952–57; Univ. Lectr 1957–83; Dir of Studies in Classics, 1951–79 and Lectr in Classics, 1951–84, Newnham Coll. Woolley Travelling Fellow, Somerville Coll., Oxford, 1961; Mem., Inst. for Advanced Study, Princeton, USA, 1984–85; Vis. Prof., Univ. of Calif at Berkeley, 1987. President: Soc. for Libyan Studies, 1981–86; Soc. for the Promotion of Roman Studies, 1986–89. Corresponding Member: German Archaeol Inst., 1971–; Austrian Archaeol Inst., 1991–. Hon. DLitt Newcastle upon Tyne, 1984. *Publications:* (with J. B. Ward Perkins) The Inscriptions of Roman Tripolitania, 1952; Aphrodisias and Rome, 1982; (with R. Tannenbaum) Jews and Godfearers at Aphrodisias, 1987; articles on Roman history and epigraphy in jls, 1951–. *Recreation:* walking. *Address:* Newnham College, Cambridge CB3 9DF. *T:* Cambridge (01223) 335700.

REYNOLDS, Kirk; *see* Reynolds, J. K.

REYNOLDS, Leighton Durham, FBA 1987; Fellow and Tutor in Classics, Brasenose College, Oxford, since 1957; *b* 11 Feb. 1930; *s* of Edgar James Reynolds and Hester Ann Reynolds (*née* Hale); *m* 1962, Susan Mary Buchanan, *d* of Prof. Sir Colin Buchanan, *qv*; one *s* two *d*. *Educ:* Caerphilly Grammar Sch.; University Coll., Cardiff (BA 1st cl. Hons 1950); St John's Coll., Cambridge (BA 1st cl. Hons 1952; Craven Student, 1952; MA 1956); MA Oxon 1956. Flying Officer, RAF, 1952–54. Jun. Res. Fellow, Queen's Coll., Oxford, 1954–57. Visiting Professor: Cornell Univ., 1960, 1971; Univ. of Texas at Austin, 1967. Mem., Inst. for Advanced Study, Princeton, 1965, 1987. Editor, Classical Review, 1975–87. *Publications:* The Medieval Tradition of Seneca's Letters, 1965; (ed) Seneca, Epistulae Morales, 1965; (with N. G. Wilson) Scribes and Scholars, 1968, 3rd edn 1991; (ed) Seneca, Dialogi, 1977; (ed) Texts and Transmission: a survey of the Latin classics, 1983; (ed) Sallust, 1991. *Recreations:* walking, camping, gardening, plant-hunting. *Address:* Winterslow Cottage, Lincombe Lane, Boars Hill, Oxford OX1 5DZ. *T:* Oxford (01865) 735741.

REYNOLDS, Martin Paul; His Honour Judge Reynolds; a Circuit Judge, since 1995; *b* 25 Dec. 1936; *s* of Cedric Hinton Fleetwood Reynolds and Doris Margaret (*née* Bryan); *m* 1961, Gaynor Margaret Phillips; three *s*. *Educ:* University College Sch., Hampstead; St Edmund Hall, Oxford (MA). ACIArb 1982. Called to the Bar, Inner Temple, 1962. Councillor, London Borough of Islington, 1968–71 and 1972–82. Contested (Lab) Harrow West, Oct. 1994. *Recreations:* navigating European waterways in a Dutch barge, gastronomy, music. *Address:* Hamilton Lodge, 3 Mountfort Crescent, N1 1JW. *T:* 0171–607 7357. *Clubs:* Savage; Brandyhole Yacht (Hullbridge).

REYNOLDS, Dr Martin Richard Finch; Associate Director of Health Policy and Public Health, East Riding Health Authority, since 1993; *b* 26 July 1943; 2nd *s* of Gerald Finch Reynolds and Frances Bertha (*née* Locke); *m* 1965, Shelagh (*née* Gray); two *d*. *Educ:* Newton Abbot Grammar Sch.; Univ. of Bristol. MB ChB, DPH; FFPHM. House posts in medicine, surgery, infectious diseases and paediatrics, 1966–67; Dep. Med. Officer, Glos CC, 1967–70; Sen. Dep. Med. Officer, Bristol City and Asst Sen. Med. Officer, SW Regional Hosp. Bd, 1970–74; Dist Community Physician, Southmead Dist of Avon AHA (Teaching) and Med. Officer for Environmental Health, Northavon Dist Council, 1974–79; Area Med. Officer, Wilts AHA, 1979–80; Regional MO/Chief Med. Advr, South Western RHA, 1980–86; Specialist in Community Medicine, 1986–89, Consultant in Public Health Medicine, 1989–93, Hull HA. *Publications:* contrib. various articles in professional jls on subjects in community medicine. *Address:* Knights Cottage, Callas, Bishop Burton, Beverley, N Humberside HU17 8QL.

REYNOLDS, Michael Emanuel, CBE 1977; Founder/Owner, Susan Reynolds Books Ltd, 1977–84; *b* 22 April 1931; *s* of Isaac Mark and Henrietta Rosenberg; *m* 1964, Susan Geraldine Yates; two *d*. *Educ:* Haberdashers' Aske's (HSC). Marks & Spencer Ltd, 1951–61; Food Controller, British Home Stores Ltd, 1961–64; Spar (UK) Ltd, 1964–77: Trading Controller, 1964–67; Chm. and Managing Dir, 1967–77; BV Intergroup Trading (IGT), 1974–77: Founder Mem., Bd of Admin.; Dir, 1974–75; Chm. and Dir, 1975–77. FRSA. *Recreations:* tennis, squash, bridge. *Address:* 55 Newlands Terrace, 155 Queenstown Road, SW8 3RN. *T:* 0171–627 5862.

REYNOLDS, Maj.-Gen. Michael Frank, CB 1983; author and lecturer (military history); *b* 3 June 1930; *s* of Frank Reynolds and Gwendolen Reynolds (*née* Griffiths); *m* 1955, Anne Bernice (*née* Truman); three *d*. *Educ:* Cranleigh; RMA, Sandhurst (Infantry prize). Commnd Queen's Royal Regt, 1950 (last serving Adjt, 1959); served Germany, Korea (severely wounded), Cyprus (EOKA emergency), Canada (exchange officer), Persian Gulf, Netherlands, Belgium; psc 1960; GSO 1 Ops, HQ AFCENT, 1970–71; CO 2 Queen's, BAOR and Ulster, 1971–73; GSO 1 Ops, N Ireland, 1973–74; Comdr 12 (Mech) Bde, BAOR, 1974–76; RCDS, 1977; Dep. Adjt Gen., BAOR, 1978–80; Comdr, Allied Command Europe Mobile Force (Land), 1980–83; Asst Dir, IMS (Plans and Policy), HQ NATO, 1983–86, retired. (Last) Col Comdt, Queen's Division, 1984–86; Col, The Queen's Regt, 1989–92. Pres., Queen's Assoc., 1992–95. Comdr First Cl., Order of the Dannebrog (Denmark), 1990; Grand Cross, Order of Orange-Nassau (Netherlands), 1992. *Publication:* The Devil's Adjutant, 1995. *Recreations:* military history (especially Battle of the Ardennes, 1944), writing.

REYNOLDS, Sir Peter (William John), Kt 1985; CBE 1975; Director: Boots Co. plc, since 1986; Guardian Royal Exchange plc, since 1986; Avis Europe Ltd, since 1988; Cilva Holdings plc, since 1989; *b* 10 Sept. 1929; *s* of Harry and Gladys Victoria Reynolds; *m* 1955, Barbara Anne, *d* of Vincent Kenneth Johnson, OBE; two *s*. *Educ:* Haileybury Coll., Herts. National Service, 2nd Lieut, RA, 1948–50. Unilever Ltd, 1950–70: Trainee; Managing Dir, then Chm., Walls (Meat & Handy Foods) Ltd. Ranks Hovis McDougall: Asst Gp Managing Dir, 1971; Gp Man. Dir, 1972–81; Chm., 1981–89; Dep. Chm., 1989–93. Director: Guardian Royal Exchange Assurance plc, 1986–; Pioneer Concrete (Hldgs), 1990–; Nationwide Anglia Building Soc., 1990–92. Chairman: EDC Employment and Trng Cttee, 1982–87; Resources Cttee, Food and Drink Fedn (formerly Food and Drink Industries Council), 1983–86; Member: EDC for Food and Drink Manufg Industry, 1976–87; Consultative Bd for Resources Develt in Agriculture, 1982–84; Covent Garden Market Authority, 1989–; Dir, Industrial Develt Bd for NI, 1982–89; Mem., Peacock Cttee on Financing the BBC, 1985–86. Dir, Freemantle Trust (formerly Bucks Comm. Housing Trust), 1992–. Gov., Berkhamsted Sch., 1985–; Life Gov., Haileybury, 1985. High Sheriff, Bucks, 1990–91. *Address:* Rignall Farm, Rignall Road, Great Missenden, Bucks HP16 9PE. *T:* Great Missenden (01240) 64714. *Club:* Naval and Military.

REYNOLDS, Prof. Philip Alan, CBE 1986; DL; Vice-Chancellor, University of Lancaster, 1980–85; *b* 15 May 1920; *s* of Harry Reynolds and Ethel (*née* Scott); *m* 1946, Mollie Patricia (*née* Horton); two *s* one *d*. *Educ:* Worthing High Sch.; Queen's Coll., Oxford (BA 1940, 1st Cl. Mod. Hist.; MA 1950). Served War, 1940–46: HAA and Staff, UK, ME and Greece; Major 1945. Asst Lectr, then Lectr in Internat. History, LSE, 1946–50; Woodrow Wilson Prof. of Internat. Politics, UCW Aberystwyth, 1950–64 (Vice-Principal, 1961–63); Prof. of Politics and Pro-Vice-Chancellor, Univ. of Lancaster, 1964–80. Vis. Professor: in Internat. Relations, Toronto, 1953; in Commonwealth History and Instns, Indian Sch. of Internat. Studies, New Delhi, 1958; Anspach Fellow, Univ. of Pa, 1971; Vis. Res. Fellow, ANU Canberra, 1977. Vice-Chm., Cttee of Vice-Chancellors and Principals, 1984–85; Chm., Brit. Internat. Studies Assoc., 1976, Hon. Pres., 1981–84; Mem. Council, RIIA, 1975–80. DL Lancs, 1982. Hon. DLitt Lancaster, 1985; DUniv Open, 1994. *Publications:* War in the Twentieth Century, 1951; Die Britische Aussenpolitik zwischen den beiden Weltkriegen, 1952 (rev. edn, 1954, as British Foreign Policy in the Inter-War Years); An Introduction to International Relations, 1971, rev. edn 1994 (Japanese edn 1977, Spanish edn 1978); (with E. J. Hughes) The Historian as Diplomat: Charles Kingsley Webster and the United Nations 1939–46, 1976; contrib. New Cambridge Mod. Hist., History, Slavonic Rev., Pol. Qly, Pol. Studies, Internat. Jl, Internat. Studies, Brit. Jl of Internat. Studies, Educn Policy Bulletin, Higher Educn, Univs Qly, Minerva. *Recreations:* music, bridge, eating and drinking. *Address:* Lattice Cottage, Borwick, Carnforth, Lancs LA6 1JR. *T:* Carnforth (01524) 732518.

REYNOLDS, Dr Roy Gregory; Chief Executive, Commonwealth Development Corporation, since 1994; *b* 4 May 1939; *s* of Henry Herbert Reynolds and Alice Emily Reynolds; *m* 1963, Monica Cecelia; one *s* one *d*. *Educ:* George Dixon Grammar Sch., Birmingham; Birmingham Univ. (BSc Chem. Eng 1960); Imperial Coll., London (PhD 1964). Shell Internat. Petroleum Co., 1964–92. *Recreations:* keeping fit, golf, general reading. *Address:* Commonwealth Development Corporation, 1 Bessborough Gardens, SW1V 2JQ. *Club:* Royal Automobile.

REYNOLDS, Susan Mary Grace, FRHistS; FBA 1993; Fellow and Tutor in Modern History, Lady Margaret Hall, Oxford, 1964–86, now Fellow Emeritus; Lecturer in Modern History, Oxford University, 1965–86; Hon. Research Fellow, History Department, University College London; *b* 27 Jan. 1929; *d* of Hugh Reynolds and Maisie Reynolds (*née* Morten). *Educ:* The Study, Montreal; Howell's Sch., Denbigh; Lady Margaret Hall, Oxford (History Cl. II, MA); Dip. Archive Admin, UCL. FRHistS 1968. Archive Asst, 1951–52; Victoria County Histories, 1952–59; school teacher, 1959–64. Visiting Professor: Dartmouth Coll., USA, 1986–87; Central European Univ., Budapest, 1994. *Publications:* (ed) Register of Roger Martival, Bishop of Salisbury, vol. 3, 1965; Introduction to the History of English Medieval Towns, 1977; Kingdoms and Communities in Western Europe 900–1300, 1984; Fiefs and Vassals, 1994; articles in historical jls. *Address:* Flat 3, 26 Lennox Gardens, SW1X 0DQ. *T:* 0171–584 2505.

REYNOLDS, William Oliver, OBE 1973 (MBE 1944); *b* 2 Nov. 1915; General Manager, Eastern Region, British Rail, 1973–76; *s* of Edgar Ernest Reynolds and Elizabeth Wilson Biesterfield; *m* 1944, Eleanor Gill; two *s*. *Educ:* Royal Grammar Sch., Newcastle upon Tyne. LNER Traffic apprentice, 1936. Served War, with Royal Engineers, 1940–46: despatches, 1942 and 1944; Lt-Col, 1944. Lt-Col, Engineer and Railway Staff Corps, RE (T&AVR IV), 1971–. Divisional Manager, London Midland, BR, 1960; Asst Gen. Manager, Scottish Region, 1964; Chief Operating Manager, BR Bd, 1968; Exec. Dir, BR Bd, 1969. Mem., Adv. Council, Science Mus. 1975–84; Chm., Friends of Nat. Railway Mus. 1984–93. FCIT. *Recreations:* fishing, golf, gardening. *Address:* Oak House, Follifoot, Harrogate, N Yorks HG3 1DR. *Club:* Oriental.

REYNTIENS, Nicholas Patrick, OBE 1976; Head of Fine Art, Central School of Art and Design, London, 1976–86; *b* 11 Dec. 1925; *s* of Nicholas Serge Reyntiens, OBE, and Janet MacRae; *m* 1953, Anne Bruce; two *s* two *d*. *Educ:* Ampleforth; Edinburgh Coll. of Art (DA). Served Scots Guards, 1943–47. St Marylebone Sch. of Art, 1947–50; Edinburgh Coll. of Art, 1950–51. Founder (with wife, Anne Bruce, the painter), Reyntiens Trust, which ran art sch., Burleighfield, where pupils from UK, Ireland, France, Germany, Japan, Canada, Australia, New Zealand, US and Iceland learned art of stained glass, and which had facilities for tapestry design and teaching, a printing house for editioning in lithography, etching and silkscreen, as well as workshops for stained glass, ceramics, drawing and painting. Has lectured in USA, Spain, Mexico, France and Switzerland; occasional Vis. Prof., Pilchuck Sch. of Glass, Washington State, USA. Many commissions, including glass for Liverpool RC Metropolitan Cathedral; for 35 years interpreted painters' designs into stained glass, as well as own commissions for stained glass, 1953 , including baptistery window, Coventry Cathedral, Eton Coll. Chapel, Robinson Coll., Cambridge, St Margaret's Westminster (all with John Piper), Derby Cathedral and Liverpool Metropolitan Cathedral (with Ceri Richards), All Saints Basingstoke (with Cecil Collins); completed glazing of Christ Church Hall, Oxford, 1980–84. Retrospective exhibn of autonomous panels, Ontario, 1990. Member: Court, RCA; Adv. Cttee in Decoration, Brompton Oratory; Adv. Cttee in Decoration, Westminster Cathedral; Adv. Cttee, Westminster Abbey, 1981–. Art Critic, The Tablet. *Publications:* Technique of Stained Glass, 1967, 2nd edn 1977; The Beauty of Stained Glass, 1990; has written for architectural, art, literary and political magazines and on cooking for Harpers & Queen. *Address:* Ilford Bridges Farm, Close Stocklinch, Ilminster, Som TA19 9HZ. *T:* Ilminster (01460) 52241, *Fax:* Ilminster (01460) 57150.

RHEA, Alexander Dodson, III; *b* 10 May 1919; *s* of Alexander D. Rhea, Jr and Annie Rhea; *m* 1945, Suzanne Menocal; one *s*. *Educ:* Princeton Univ. BA Econs and Social Instns. Active service as Lt-Comdr USNR, 1941–45. Vice-Pres., Govt Employees Ins. Corp., Washington, DC, 1946–48; Treas. and Man. Dir, General Motors de Venezuela, Caracas, 1949–55; Vice-Pres., General Motors Overseas Corp., 1960–68; Regional Gp Dir, NY, 1960–66, Staff Man., 1966–67, General Motors Overseas Operations; Chm. and Man. Dir, General Motors-Holden's, Melbourne, 1968–70; Chm. and Man. Dir., Vauxhall Motors Ltd, 1970–74; Chm., General Motors Corp. European Adv. Council, 1974–77; Exec. Vice-Pres. and Dir, General Motors Overseas Corp., 1974–77. *Recreations:* reading, golf. *Address:* 580 Park Avenue, New York, NY 10021, USA. *Clubs:* Knickerbocker, Princeton, Colony (New York); Fort Worth, River Crest Country (Fort Worth, Texas); Melbourne (Melbourne); Greenbrier Golf and Tennis (White Sulphur Springs, West Virginia).

RHIND, Prof. David William; Director General and Chief Executive, Ordnance Survey, since 1992; *b* 29 Nov. 1943; *s* of late William Rhind and of Christina Rhind; *m* 1966, Christine Young; one *s* two *d*. *Educ:* Berwick Grammar School; Bristol Univ. (BSc); Edinburgh Univ. (PhD); London Univ. (DSc). FRGS; FRICS 1991. Research Fellow, Royal College of Art, 1969–73; Lectr then Reader, Univ. of Durham, 1973–81; Birkbeck College, London University: Prof. of Geography, 1982–91; Dean, Faculty of Economics, 1984–86; Co-ordinator for IT, 1985–88; Governor, 1986–90; Head, Resource Centre for Economics, Geography and Statistics, 1987–91, also for Computer Science and Maths, 1989–91. Visiting Fellow: Internat. Trng Centre, Netherlands, 1975; ANU, 1979. Vice-Pres., Internat. Cartographic Assoc., 1984–91; Mem., Govt Cttee on Enquiry into handling of geographic inf., 1985–87; Advisor, H of L Select Cttee on Sci. and Tech., 1983–84; Chairman: Bloomsbury Computing Consortium Management Cttee, 1988–91; Royal Soc. Ordnance Survey Scientific Cttee, 1989–91. Hon. Sec., RGS, 1988–91. Hon. DSc Bristol, 1993. *Publications:* (jtly) Land Use, 1980; The Census User's Handbook, 1983; (jtly) Atlas of EEC Affairs, 1984; (jtly) Geographical Information Systems, 1991; (jtly) Postcodes: the new geography, 1992; numerous papers on map-making and computerised databases. *Recreations:* travelling, home decorating. *Address:* Ordnance Survey, Romsey Road, Maybush, Southampton SO16 4GU. *T:* Southampton (01703) 792000.

RHODES, Col Sir Basil (Edward), Kt 1987; CBE 1981 (OBE (mil.) 1945; MBE (mil.) 1944); TD 1946; DL; Partner, Gichard & Co., solicitors, since 1946; *b* Rotherham, 8 Dec. 1915; *s* of late Col Harry Rhodes and of Astri Rhodes (*née* Natvig); *m* 1962, Joëlle, *er d* of Robert Vilgard, Paris; one *s*. *Educ:* St Edward's Sch., Oxford. Served War of 1939–45, Western Desert, Greece, Crete and Burma (wounded; mentioned in despatches). Admitted solicitor, 1946. Director: Carlton Main Brickworks, 1972–; Duncan Millar & Associates; Wessex Fare; Yorkshire Merchant Securities. Mem. (C) Town Council, Rotherham, 1949–74, Mayor, 1970–71; Chm., 1949–75, Pres., 1975–, Rotherham Cons. Assoc.; Chm., S Yorks Cons. Fedn, 1964–; Treas., Cons. Central Office Yorks Area, 1983–88. DL 1975, High Sheriff, 1982–83, S Yorks. *Recreations:* fieldsports, ski-ing, gardening. *Address:* Bubnell Hall, Baslow, Bakewell, Derbys DE4 1RL. *T:* Baslow (01246) 583266. *Clubs:* Cavalry and Guards; Sheffield (Sheffield).

RHODES, George Harold Lancashire, TD 1946; Regional Chairman of Industrial Tribunals: Manchester, 1985–88; Liverpool, 1987–88; *b* 29 Feb. 1916; *er s* of Judge Harold and Ena Rhodes of Bowdon, Cheshire. *Educ:* Shrewsbury School; The Queen's College, Oxford (MA 1941). Commissioned 52nd Field Regt RA TA, 1938; war service, BEF, 1940, Middle East, 1942, Italy, 1943–46 (Major). Called to the Bar, Gray's Inn, 1947; practised on N Circuit; the Junior, 1948; Office of Judge Advocate General (Army and RAF), 1953; Asst Judge Advocate General, 1967; Chm., Industrial Tribunals (Manchester), 1974, Dep. Regional Chm., 1975. *Recreations:* walking, golf. *Address:* 8 Newington Court, The Firs, Bowdon, Cheshire WA14 2UA. *T:* 0161–928 1200.

RHODES, John Andrew, FCIT; Director, Passenger Services Regulation, Office of the Rail Regulator, since 1993; *b* 22 May 1949; *s* of George and Elsie Rhodes; *m* 1985, Marie Catherine Carleton. *Educ:* Queen Elizabeth Sch., Barnet; Wadham Coll., Oxford (MA Mod. History). Civil Service: various posts in DoE, Cabinet Office, Dept of Transport, 1971–87; Dir Gen., W Yorks PTE, 1988–92; Strategy and Planning Advr, BRB, 1992–93. *Recreations:* music, transport history, gardening. *Address:* 26 Warwick Road, Bishop's Stortford, Herts CM23 5NW. *T:* Bishop's Stortford (01279) 656482.

See also P. J. Rhodes.

RHODES, Sir John (Christopher Douglas), 4th Bt, *cr* 1919; *b* 24 May 1946; *s* of Sir Christopher Rhodes, 3rd Bt, and of Mary Florence, *d* of late Dr Douglas Wardleworth; *S* father, 1964. *Heir: b* Michael Philip James Rhodes [*b* 3 April 1948; *m* 1973, Susan, *d* of Patrick Roney-Dougal; one *d*].

RHODES, Prof. John David, OBE 1992; PhD, DSc; FRS 1993; FEng; Chairman and Chief Executive Officer, Filtronic Ltd, since 1977; Industrial Professor, Leeds University, since 1981; *b* 9 Oct. 1943; *s* of Jack and Florence Rhodes; *m* 1965, Barbara Margaret Pearce; one *s* one *d*. *Educ:* Univ. of Leeds (BSc, PhD, DSc). FIEEE 1980; FIEE 1984; FEng 1987. Leeds University: Res. Asst, 1964–66; Res. Fellow, 1966–67; Sen. Res. Engr, Microwave Develt Labs, USA, 1967–69; Leeds University: Lectr, 1969–72; Reader, 1972–75; Prof., 1975–81. Hon. DEng Bradford, 1988. *Publication:* Theory of Electrical Filters, 1976. *Recreation:* cricket. *Address:* Boodles, Thorpe Lane, Guiseley, Leeds LS20 8JH. *T:* Guiseley (01943) 874573.

RHODES, John Ivor McKinnon, CMG 1971; *b* 6 March 1914; *s* of late Joseph Thomas Rhodes and late Hilda (*née* McKinnon); *m* 1939, Eden Annetta Clark (*d* 1990); one *s* one *d*. *Educ:* Leeds Modern School. Exec. Officer, WO, 1933; Financial Adviser's Office, HQ British Forces in Palestine, 1938; Major 1940; Asst Comd Sec., Southern Comd, 1944; Financial Adviser, London District, 1946; Principal 1947, Asst Sec. 1959, HM Treasury; Minister, UK Mission to UN, 1966–74. Member: UN Pension Board, 1966–71; UN Cttee on Contributions, 1966–71, 1975–77; Chm., UN Adv. Cttee on Admin. and Budgetary Questions, 1971–74; Senior Adviser (Asst Sec.-Gen.) to Administrator, UNDP, 1979–80. *Recreations:* gardening, playing the electronic organ. *Address:* Quintins, Watersfield, Pulborough, W Sussex RH20 1NE. *T:* Bury (01798) 831634.

RHODES, Marion, RE 1953 (ARE 1941); etcher, painter in water colour and oils; *b* Huddersfield, Yorks, 1907; *d* of Samuel Rhodes and Mary Jane Mallinson. *Educ:* Greenhead High School, Huddersfield; Huddersfield Art School; Leeds College of Art; The Central School of Arts and Crafts, London. Art Teachers' Certificate (Univ. of Oxford), 1930; teaching posts, 1930–67; pt-time lecturer in Art at Berridge House Training Coll., 1947–55. SGA 1936, Hon. Life Mem., 1969; FRSA 1944; Member, Manchester Acad. of Fine Art, 1955–81; Paris Salon: Honourable Mention, 1952; Bronze Medal, 1956; Silver Medal 1961; Gold Medal, 1967. Exhibited from 1934 at: Royal Academy, Royal Scottish Academy, Mall Gall., The Paris Salon, Walker Art Gall., Towner Art Gall., Atkinson Art Gall., Southport, Brighton, Bradford, Leeds, Manchester and other provincial Art Galls, also USA and S Africa. Etching of Jordans' Hostel and drawing of The Meeting House purchased by Contemporary Art Soc. and presented to British Museum; other works in the Print Room, BM, and Print Room, V&A; work also purchased by Bradford Corp. Art Gall., Brighouse Art Gall., Huddersfield Art Gall., Stoke-on-Trent Educn Cttee's Loan Scheme, and South London (Camberwell) Library Committee; works reproduced. Fellow, Ancient Monuments Soc.; Associate, Artistes Français, 1971–79; Hon. Mem., Tommasso Campanella Acad., Rome (Silver Medal, 1970). Cert. of Merit, Dictionary of Internat. Biography, 1972. Mem., Accademia delle

Arti e de Lavoro (Parma), 1979–82; Academic of Italy with Gold Medal, 1979. *Publication:* illustrations for Robert Harding's Snettisham, 1982. *Recreations:* gardening and geology. *Address:* 2 Goodwyn Avenue, Mill Hill, NW7 3RG. *T:* 0181–959 2280. *Club:* English-Speaking Union.

RHODES, Sir Peregrine (Alexander), KCMG 1984 (CMG 1976); HM Diplomatic Service, retired; Director-General, British Property Federation, 1986–93; *b* 14 May 1925; *s* of Cyril Edmunds Rhodes and Elizabeth Jocelyn Rhodes; *m* 1st, 1951, Jane Marion Hassell (marr. diss.); two *s* one *d*; 2nd, 1969, Margaret Rosemary Page. *Educ:* Winchester Coll.; New Coll., Oxford (BA Lit. Hum. (1st cl)). Served with Coldstream Guards, 1944–47. Joined FO, 1950; 2nd Sec., Rangoon, 1953–56; Private Sec. to Minister of State, 1956–59; 1st Sec., Vienna, 1959–62; 1st Sec., Helsinki, 1962–65; FCO, 1965–68, Counsellor 1967; Inst. for Study of Internat. Organisation, Sussex Univ., 1968–69; Counsellor, Rome, 1970–73; Chargé d'Affaires, E Berlin, 1973–75; on secondment as Under Sec., Cabinet Office (Chief of Assessments Staff), 1975–78; High Comr, Cyprus, 1979–82; Ambassador, Greece, 1982–85. Chm., Anglo-Hellenic League, 1986–90; Vice-Pres. British Sch., Athens, 1982–. FRSA 1988. *Recreations:* photography, reading. *Address:* Pond House, Thorpe Morieux, Bury St Edmunds, Suffolk IP30 0NW. *Club:* Travellers'.

RHODES, Prof. Peter John, FBA 1987; Professor of Ancient History, University of Durham, since 1983; *b* 10 Aug. 1940; *s* of George Thomas Rhodes and Elsie Leonora Rhodes (*née* Pugh); *m* 1971, Jan Teresa Adamson. *Educ:* Queen Elizabeth's Boys' Grammar Sch., Barnet; Wadham Coll., Oxford (minor schol.; BA (1st cl. Mods, 1st cl. Greats); MA; DPhil). Harmsworth Schol., Merton Coll., Oxford, 1963–65; Craven Fellow, Oxford Univ., 1963–65; Lectr in Classics and Ancient History, 1965, Sen. Lectr, 1977, Durham Univ. Fellow, Center for Hellenic Studies, Washington, DC, 1978–79; Visiting Fellow: Wolfson Coll., Oxford, 1984; Univ. of New England, Aust., 1988; Corpus Christi Coll., Oxford, 1993; Leverhulme Res. Fellow, 1994–95. Mem., Inst. for Advanced Study, Princeton, USA, 1988–89. *Publications:* The Athenian Boule, 1972; Greek Historical Inscriptions 359–323 BC, 1972; Commentary on the Aristotelian Athenaion Politeia, 1981; (trans.) Aristotle: the Athenian Constitution, 1984; The Athenian Empire, 1985; The Greek City States: a source book, 1986; (ed) Thucydides Book II, 1988; (ed) Thucydides Book III, 1994; articles and reviews in jls. *Recreations:* music, typography, travel. *Address:* Department of Classics, University of Durham, 38 North Bailey, Durham, DH1 3EU. *T:* Durham (0191) 374 2073.

See also J. A. Rhodes.

RHODES, Philip, FRCS, FRCOG, FRACMA, FFOM; Regional Postgraduate Dean of Medical Studies, and Professor of Postgraduate Medical Education, Southampton University, 1980–87, retired; *b* 2 May 1922; *s* of Sydney Rhodes, Dore, Sheffield; *m* 1946, Mary Elizabeth Worley, Barrowden, Rutland; three *s* two *d*. *Educ:* King Edward VII Sch., Sheffield; Clare Coll., Cambridge; St Thomas's Hospital Medical School. BA(Cantab) 1943, MB, BChir(Cantab) 1946; FRCS 1953; MRCOG 1956; FRCOG 1964; FRACMA 1976; FFOM 1990. Major RAMC, 1948–50. Medical appointments held in St Thomas' Hosp., Folkestone, Harrogate, Chelsea Hosp. for Women, Queen Charlotte's Hosp., 1946–58; Consultant Obstetric Physician, St Thomas' Hosp., 1958–63; Prof. of Obstetrics and Gynæcol., St Thomas's Hosp. Med. Sch., Univ. of London, 1964–74, Dean, 1968–74; Dean, Faculty of Medicine, Univ. of Adelaide, 1975–77; Postgrad. Dean and Dir, Regional Postgrad. Inst. for Med. and Dentistry, Newcastle Univ., 1977–80. Member: SW Metropolitan Regional Hosp. Board, 1967–74; SE Thames Reg. Health Authority, 1974; GMC, 1979–89 (Educn Cttee, 1984–89). Mem. Steering Cttee of DHSS on management of NHS, 1971–72. Mem., Adv. Cttee, Nat. Inst. of Medical Hist., Australia, 1976. Chm., Educn Cttee, King Edward's Hosp. Fund for London, 1981–87; Member: UGC Working Party on Continuing Educn, 1983; Council for Postgrad. Med. Educn in England and Wales, 1984–87. Governor: Dulwich Coll., 1966–74; St Thomas' Hosp., 1969–74; Pembroke Sch., Adelaide, 1976–77. FRSA 1989. *Publications:* Fluid Balance in Obstetrics, 1960; Introduction to Gynæcology and Obstetrics, 1967; Reproductive Physiology for Medical Students, 1969; Woman: A Biological Study, 1969; The Value of Medicine, 1976; Dr John Leake's Hospital, 1978; Letters to a Young Doctor, 1983; An Outline History of Medicine, 1985; Wakerley: a village in Northamptonshire, 1994; Associate Editor, The Oxford Companion to Medicine, 1986; articles in Jl of Obstetrics and Gynæcology of the British Empire, Lancet, Brit. Med. Jl, Med. Jl of Australia. *Recreations:* reading, gardening, photography. *Address:* 1 Wakerley Court, Wakerley, Oakham, Leics LE15 8PA.

RHODES, Reginald Paul; Chairman, Southern Gas Region, 1975–83; *b* 10 April 1918; *s* of Edwin Rhodes and Dorothy Lena Molyneux; *m* 1940, Margaret Frances Fish; two *s* three *d*. *Educ:* Merchant Taylors Sch., Northwood. Joined Gas Light & Coke Co., 1937; North Thames Gas, 1948 (Dep. Chm., 1972). Deputy Chairman: Southampton Industrial Therapy Organisation, 1980–89; Solent Productivity Assoc., 1983–90; Chm., Solent Business Fund, 1983–90; Member: Wessex RHA, 1984–90; Shaw Trust, 1984–90. Mem., Co. of Pikemen, Honourable Artillery Company. FIGasE. *Recreations:* music, gardening. *Address:* 3 The Paddock, Brockenhurst, Hants SO42 7QU. *T:* Lymington (01590) 22399.

RHODES, Richard David Walton, JP; Headmaster, Rossall School, since 1987; *b* 20 April 1942; *er s* of Harry Walton Rhodes and Dorothy Rhodes (*née* Fairhurst); *m* 1966, Stephanie Heyes, 2nd *d* of Frederic William Heyes and Catherine Heyes; two *d*. *Educ:* Rossall Sch.; St John's Coll., Durham (BA 1963). Asst Master, St John's Sch., Leatherhead, 1964–75 (Founder Housemaster, Montgomery House, 1973–75); Deputy Headmaster, Arnold Sch., Blackpool, 1975–79, Headmaster, 1979–87. Member: Lancs CC Social Services Adv. Cttee, 1992–; Lancs Magistrates' Courts Cttee, 1993–. Chairman: NW Div., HMC, 1987; Northern ISIS, 1993–. Member Council: Univ. of Salford, 1987–93; Lawrence Hse Sch., Lytham St Annes, 1988–93; Trustee, Lawrence House Trust, 1994–; Gov., Terra Nova Sch., Jodrell Bank, 1989–. JP Fylde, 1978. *Recreations:* photography, sports, motoring, gardening in the Lake District. *Address:* The Hall, Rossall School, Fleetwood, Lancs FY7 8JW. *T:* Fleetwood (01253) 774201. *Club:* East India, Devonshire, Sports and Public Schools.

RHODES, Robert Elliott; QC 1989; a Recorder, since 1987; *b* 2 Aug. 1945; *s* of late Gilbert G. Rhodes, FCA and of Elly, who *m* 2nd, Leopold Brook, *qv*; *m* 1971, Georgina Caroline, *d* of J. G. Clarfelt, *qv*; two *s* one *d*. *Educ:* St Paul's School; Pembroke Coll., Oxford. MA. Called to the Bar, Inner Temple, 1968. Second Prosecuting Counsel to Inland Revenue at Central Criminal Court and Inner London Crown Courts, 1979, First Prosecuting Counsel, 1981–89. Dep. Chm., IMRO Membership Tribunal Panel, 1992–. *Recreations:* opera, reading, cricket, real tennis, fishing. *Address:* Littleton Building, 3 King's Bench Walk North, Temple, EC4Y 7HR. *T:* 0171–797 8600. *Clubs:* MCC; Epee.

RHODES, Zandra Lindsey, RDI 1977; DesRCA, FCSD; Managing Director, Zandra Rhodes (UK) Ltd and Zandra Rhodes (Shops) Ltd, since 1975; *b* 19 Sept. 1940; *d* of Albert James Rhodes and Beatrice Ellen (*née* Twigg). *Educ:* Medway Technical Sch. for Girls, Chatham; Medway Coll. of Art; Royal Coll. of Art (DesRCA 1964). FSIAD 1982. With Alexander MacIntyre, set up print factory and studio, 1965; sold designs (and converted them on to cloth) to Foale and Tuffin and Roger Nelson; formed partnership with Sylvia Ayton and began producing dresses using her own prints, 1966; opened Fulham Road Clothes Shop, designing dresses as well as prints, first in partnership, 1967–68, then (Fulham Road shop closed) alone, producing first clothes range in which she revolutionised use of prints in clothes by cutting round patterns to make shapes never before used; took collection to USA, 1969; sold to Fortnum and Mason, London, 1969, Piero de Monzi, 1971; began building up name and business in USA (known for her annual spectacular Fantasy Shows); also started designing in jersey and revolutionised its treatment with lettuce edges and seams on the outside; with Knight and Stirling founded Zandra Rhodes (UK) Ltd and Zandra Rhodes (Shops) Ltd, 1975–86; opening first shop in London, 1975; others opened in Bloomingdales NY, Marshall Field, Chicago, Seibu, Tokyo and Harrods, London, 1976; new factory premises opened in Hammersmith, London, 1984; closed Mayfair shop, 1991 to show on a more personal and individual scale in her Hammersmith showroom. Since 1976 Zandra Rhodes has tried to reach a wider public through licensing her name in UK, USA, Australia and Japan, making full use of the Zandra Rhodes textile design talent for: wallpapers and furnishing fabrics, bathmats, mens ties, sheets and bed linen, printed shawls and scarves, hosiery, teatowels, kitchen accessories and jewellery. Notable licences include: Eve Stillman Lingerie, 1977 (USA), Wamsutta sheets and pillowcases, 1976 (USA), CVP Designs interior fabrics and settings, 1977 (UK), Philip Hockley Decorative Furs, 1986 (UK) and Zandra Rhodes Saris, 1987 (India) (which she launched with 'West meets East' shows of Saris and Shalwar Chamises in Bombay and Delhi—the first Western designer to do so), Littlewoods Catalogues, 1988 (UK) for printed T-shirts and Intasia sweaters. One-man exhibitions: Oriel, Cardiff (Welsh Arts Council), 1978; Texas Gall., Houston, 1981; Otis Parsons, Los Angeles, 1981; La Jolla Museum of Contemporary Art, San Diego, 1982; ADITI Creative Power, Barbican Centre, 1982; Sch. of Art Inst., Chicago, 1982; Parsons Sch. of Design, NY, 1982; Art Museum of Santa Cruz Co., Calif, 1983; retrospective exhibition of 'Works of Art' with textiles, Museum of Art, El Paso, Texas, 1984; retrospective of Garments & Textiles (also Lead Speaker for Art to Wear exhibn), Columbus, Ohio, 1987; retrospectives for Seibu Seed Hall, Seibu, Tokyo, 1987 and 1991; water colour exhibitions: Dyansen Galls, NY, LA and New Orleans, 1989; Mint Mus., N Carolina, 1992. Work represented in major costume collections: UK: V&A; City Mus. and Art Gall., Stoke-on-Trent; Bath Mus.; Royal Pavilion Brighton Mus.; Platt Fields Costume Mus., Manchester; City Art Gall., Leeds; overseas: Metropolitan Mus., NY; Chicago Historical Soc.; Smithsonian Instn; Royal Ontario Mus.; Mus. of Applied Arts and Scis, Sydney; Nat. Mus. of Victoria, Melbourne; La Jolla Mus. of Contemp. Art. Opening speaker, Famous Women of Fashion, Smithsonian Inst., Washington, 1978. Hon. DFA Internat. Fine Arts Coll, Miami, Florida, 1986; Hon. Dr RCA, 1986; Hon. DD CNAA, 1987. Designer of the Year, English Fashion Trade UK, 1972; Emmy Award for Best Costume Designs in Romeo and Juliet on Ice, CBS TV, 1984; Woman of Distinction award, Northwood Inst., Dallas, 1986; citations and commendations from USA estabs. *Publications:* The Art of Zandra Rhodes, 1984, US edn 1985; The Zandra Rhodes Collection by Brother, 1988; *relevant publications:* in English Vogue, 1978 and 1982; Architectural Digest, 1978 and 1988; The Connoisseur, 1981; comment and illus. in numerous books and articles since 1971. *Recreations:* travelling, drawing. *Address:* (factory) 87 Richford Street, Hammersmith, W6 7HJ. *T:* (business) 0181–749 3216.

RHODES JAMES, Sir Robert (Vidal), Kt 1991; DL; Chairman, History of Parliament Trust, 1983–92; *b* 10 April 1933; *y s* of late Lieut-Col W. R. James, OBE, MC; *m* 1956, Angela Margaret Robertson, *er d* of late R. M. Robertson; four *d*. *Educ:* private schs in India; Sedbergh Sch.; Worcester Coll., Oxford. Asst Clerk, House of Commons, 1955–61; Senior Clerk, 1961–64. Fellow of All Souls Coll., Oxford, 1965–68, 1979–81; Dir, Inst. for Study of Internat. Organisation, Univ. of Sussex, 1968–73; Principal Officer, Exec. Office of Sec.-Gen. of UN, 1973–76. Kratter Prof. of European History, Stanford Univ., Calif., 1968. Consultant to UN Conf. on Human Environment, 1971–72; UK Mem., UN Sub-Commn on Prevention of Discrimination and Protection of Minorities, 1972–73. MP (C) Cambridge, Dec. 1976–1992. PPS, FCO, 1979–82; Mem., Chairmen's Panel, H of C, 1987–92. Conservative Party Liaison Officer for Higher and Further Educn, 1979–85 and 1987; Chm., Conservative Friends of Israel, 1989–. Vice-Pres., Anglo-Israel Assoc., 1990–. FRSL 1964; NATO Fellow, 1965; FRHistS 1973; Professorial Fellow, Univ. of Sussex, 1973; Fellow, Wolfson Coll., Cambridge, 1991–. DL Cambs, 1993. Hon. DLitt Westminster Coll., Fulton, Missouri, 1986. *Publications:* Lord Randolph Churchill, 1959; An Introduction to the House of Commons, 1961 (John Llewelyn Rhys Memorial Prize); Rosebery, 1963 (Royal Society Lit. Award); Gallipoli, 1965; Standardization and Production of Military Equipment in NATO, 1967; Churchill: a study in failure, 1900–39, 1970; Ambitions and Realities: British politics 1964–70, 1972; Victor Cazalet: a portrait, 1976; The British Revolution 1880–1939, vol. I, 1976, vol. II, 1977, 1 Vol. edn, 1978; Albert, Prince Consort, 1983; Anthony Eden, 1986; Bob Boothby: a portrait, 1991 (Angel Lit. Award, 1992); Henry Wellcome, 1994; *edited:* Chips: The Diaries of Sir Henry Channon, 1967; Memoirs of a Conservative: J. C. C. Davidson's Memoirs and Papers, 1969; The Czechoslovak Crisis 1968, 1969; The Complete Speeches of Sir Winston Churchill, 1897–1963, 1974; contrib. to: Suez Ten Years After, 1967; Essays From Divers Hands, 1967; Churchill: four faces and the man, 1969; International Administration, 1971; The Prime Ministers, vol. II, 1975. *Address:* The Stone House, Great Gransden, near Sandy, Beds SG19 3AF. *T:* Great Gransden (01767) 677025. *Clubs:* Carlton, Travellers', Grillion's.

RHYMES, Rev. Canon Douglas Alfred; Canon Residentiary and Librarian, Southwark Cathedral, 1962–69, Hon. Canon, 1969, Canon Emeritus since 1984; *b* 26 March 1914; *s* of Peter Alfred and Jessie Rhymes; unmarried. *Educ:* King Edward VI School, Birmingham; Birmingham Univ.; Ripon Hall Theological College, Oxford. BA (2nd Cl. Hons 1st Div.) Philosophy 1939. Asst Curate, Dovercourt, Essex, 1940–43; Chaplain to the Forces, 1943–46; Asst Curate, Romford, Essex (in charge of St George's, Romford and St Thomas', Noak Hill), 1946–49; Priest-in-charge, Ascension, Chelmsford, 1949–50; Sacrist, Southwark Cathedral, 1950–54; Vicar, All Saints, New Eltham, SE9, 1954–62; Director of Lay Training, Diocese of Southwark, 1962–68; Vicar of St Giles, Camberwell, 1968–76; Parish Priest of Woldingham, 1976–84; Lectr in Ethics, Chichester Theol Coll., 1984–92. Proctor in Convocation and Mem. of Gen. Synod, 1975–85. *Publications:* (jtly) Crisis Booklets, Christianity and Communism, 1952; (jtly) Layman's Church, 1963; No New Morality, 1964; Prayer in the Secular City, 1967; Through Prayer to Reality, 1974; (jtly) Dropping the Bomb, 1985; Time Past to Time Future, 1993. *Recreations:* theatre, conversation, country walks. *Address:* Chillington Cottage, 7 Dukes Road, Fontwell, W Sussex BN18 0SP. *T:* Eastergate (01243) 543268.

RHYS, family name of **Baron Dynevor.**

RHYS, Prof. David Garel, OBE 1989; FIMI; Head of Economics and Professor of Motor Industry Economics, Cardiff Business School, University of Wales College of Cardiff, since 1988; *b* 28 Feb. 1940; *s* of Emyr Lewys Rhys and Edith Phyllis Rhys (*née* Williams); *m* 1965, Charlotte Mavis Walters; one *s* two *d*. *Educ:* Ystalyfera Grammar Sch.; University Coll., Swansea (BA); Univ. of Birmingham (MCom). IOTA 1972. Asst Lectr, then Lectr in Econs, Univ. of Hull, 1965–70; University College, Cardiff: Lectr in Econs, 1971–77; Sen. Lectr, 1977–84; Prof. of Motor Industry Econs, 1984–88; Hd, Econs Dept, 1988;

Dir, Centre for Automotive Industry Res., Cardiff Business Sch., UWCC, 1991–. *Publications:* The Motor Industry: an economic survey, 1972; The Motor Industry in the European Community, 1989; contrib. Jl Industrial Econs. *Recreations:* walking, gardening, theatre and opera, sports' spectator. *Address:* 14 Maes Yr Awel, Radyr, Cardiff CF4 8AN. *T:* Cardiff (01222) 842714. *Club:* Royal Automobile.

RHYS JONES, Griffith; actor, writer, director and producer; *b* 16 Nov. 1953; *s* of Elwyn Rhys Jones and Gwyneth Margaret Jones; *m* 1981, Joanna Frances Harris; one *s* one *d*. *Educ:* Brentwood Sch.; Emmanuel Coll., Cambridge. BBC Radio Producer, 1976–79; *television:* Not the Nine O'Clock News (also co-writer), 1979–81; Alas Smith and Jones (also co-writer), 1982–87; Porterhouse Blue (serial), 1987; The World according to Smith and Jones, 1987; Small Doses (series of short plays) (writer, Boat People), 1989; A View of Harry Clark, 1989; Smith and Jones, 1992, 1995; Demob (drama series), 1993; Bookworm (presenter), 1994; *theatre:* Charley's Aunt, 1983; Trumpets and Raspberries, 1985; The Alchemist, 1985; Arturo Ui, 1987; Smith & Jones (also co-writer), 1989–; The Wind in the Willows, Royal Nat. Th., 1990; dir, Twelfth Night, RSC, 1991; The Revengers' Comedies, Strand, 1991; An Absolute Turkey, Globe, 1994; *films:* Morons from Outer Space, 1985; Wilt, 1989; As You Like It, 1992; Staggered, 1994; *opera:* Die Fledermaus, Royal Opera Covent Garden, 1989. Director: Talkback, Advertising and Production; Playback, 1987–; Smith Jones Brown & Cassie, 1988–. *Address:* c/o TalkBack, 33 Percy Street, W1P 9FG. *T:* 0171–631 3940.

RHYS WILLIAMS, Sir (Arthur) Gareth (Ludovic Emrys), 3rd Bt *cr* 1918, of Miskin, Parish of Llantrisant, Co. Glamorgan; Managing Director: Rexham Custom Europe, since 1994; Rexham Ltd, since 1992; *b* 9 Nov. 1961; *s* of Sir Brandon Rhys Williams, 2nd Bt, MP and of Caroline Susan, *e d* of L. A. Foster; *S* father, 1988. *Educ:* Eton; Durham Univ. (BSc Hons Eng); Insead (MBA). CEng; MIEE; MBPICS; MIMgt. Systems Analyst, STC Components, 1983–85; Lucas CAV: Optimised Prodn Technol. Analyst, 1986–87; Materials Manager, 1987–88; Man. Dir, NFI Electronics, 1990–93. *Recreations:* Territorial Army (Captain); shooting, travel, chess. *Heir:* none. *Address:* 32 Rawlings Street, SW3 2LT. *Club:* Brooks's.

RIABOUCHINSKA, Tatiana, (Mme Lichine); Ballerina of Russian Ballet; owns and operates the Lichine Ballet Academy, Beverly Hills; *b* 23 May 1916; *d* of Michael P. Riabouchinsky, Moscow (Banker), and Tatiana Riabouchinska (*d* 1935), Dancer of Moscow Imperial School of Dance; *m* 1942, David Lichine (*d* 1972); one *d*. *Educ:* Cour Fénelon, Paris. Trained first by her mother; then by Volinine (dancer of the Moscow Imperial Grand Theatre); then by Mathilde Kchesinska. First appeared as child dancer with Balieff's Chauve Souris in London, 1931; joined new Russian Ballet (de-Basil), 1932, and danced with them in nearly all countries of Western Europe, Australia and N and S America. Contribution to books on dancing by: Andre Levinson, Arnold L. Haskell, Irving Deakin, Rayner Heppenstall, Kay Ambrose, Prince Peter Lieven, Cyril W. Beaumont, Cyril Brahms, Adrian Stokes, A. V. Coton, Ninette de Valois, etc. Citizen of Honor, Beverly Hills, 1990. *Publication:* (contrib.) Garcia-Marquez, The Ballets Russes: Colonel de Basil's Ballets Russe de Monte Carlo 1932–52, 1991. *Address:* 965 Oakmont Drive, Los Angeles, CA 90049, USA; Lichine Ballet School, 405 North Foothill Road, Beverley Hills, CA 90210, USA.

RIBBANS, Prof. Geoffrey Wilfrid, MA; Kenan University Professor of Hispanic Studies, Brown University, USA, since 1978; *b* 15 April 1927; *o s* of late Wilfrid Henry Ribbans and Rose Matilda Burton; *m* 1956, Magdalena Cumming (*née* Willmann), Cologne; one *s* two *d*. *Educ:* Sir George Monoux Grammar Sch., Walthamstow; King's Coll., Univ. of London. BA Hons Spanish 1st cl., 1948; MA 1953. Asst Lectr, Queen's Univ., Belfast, 1951–52; Asst, St Salvator's Coll., Univ. of St Andrews, 1952–53; Univ. of Sheffield: Asst Lectr, 1953–55; Lectr, 1955–61; Sen. Lectr, 1961–63; Gilmour Prof. of Spanish, Univ. of Liverpool, 1963–78; First Director, Centre for Latin-American Studies, 1966–70; Dean, Faculty of Arts, 1977–78; Chm., Dept of Hispanic and Italian Studies, Brown Univ., USA, 1981–84. Andrew Mellon Vis. Prof., Univ. of Pittsburgh, 1970–71; Leverhulme Res. Fellow, 1975; NEH Univ. Fellowship, 1991; Hon. Prof., Univ. of Sheffield, 1994–; Vis. Prof., Univ. of Salamanca, 1995. Lectures: Fundación Juan March, Madrid, 1984; E. Allison Peers, Univ. of Liverpool, 1985, 1994; Norman Maccoll, Univ. of Cambridge, 1985; Fordham Cervantes, NY, 1988. Vice-Pres., Internat. Assoc. of Hispanists, 1974–80 (Pres., Local Organising Cttee, 8th Congress, Brown Univ., 1983); Pres., Anglo-Catalan Soc., 1976–78. Dir, Liverpool Playhouse, 1974–78. Editor, Bulletin of Hispanic Studies, 1964–78. Hon. Fellow, Inst. of Linguists, 1972. Corresp. Member: Real Academia de Buenas Letras, Barcelona, 1978; Hispanic Soc. of Amer., 1981. MA *ad eund.* Brown Univ., 1979. *Publications:* Catalunya i València vistes pels viatgers anglesos del segle XVIIIè, 1955, 2nd edn 1993; Niebla y Soledad: aspectos de Unamuno y Machado, 1971; ed, Soledades, Galerias, otros poemas, by Antonio Machado, 1975, 12th edn 1994; Antonio Machado (1875–1939): poetry and integrity, 1975; B. Pérez Galdós: Fortunata y Jacinta, a critical guide, 1977 (trans. Spanish 1989); (ed) Campos de Castilla, by Antonio Machado, 1989, 4th edn 1993; History and Fiction in Galdós's Narratives, 1993; numerous articles on Spanish and Catalan literature in specialised publications; *festschrift:* Hispanic Studies in Honour of Geoffrey Ribbans, 1992. *Recreations:* travel, fine art. *Address:* c/o Department of Hispanic Studies, Box 1961, Brown University, Providence, Rhode Island 02912, USA.

RICE; *see* Spring Rice, family name of Baron Monteagle of Brandon.

RICE, Dennis George, PhD; Social Security (formerly National Insurance) Commissioner, since 1979; a Child Support Commissioner, since 1993; a Recorder, since 1991; *b* 27 Nov. 1927; *s* of George Henry Rice and Ethel Emily Rice; *m* 1959, Jean Beryl Wakefield; one *s*. *Educ:* City of London Sch.; King's Coll., Cambridge (Scholar and Prizeman; 1st Cl. Classical Tripos Pt I, Law Tripos Pt II; BA 1950, LLB 1951, MA 1955); London Sch. of Econs (PhD 1956). Called to the Bar, Lincoln's Inn, 1952. Served RAF, 1946–48. Entered J. Thorn and Sons Ltd, 1952; Dir, 1955; Man. Dir, 1956; Chm. and Man. Dir, 1958–69; in practice at Chancery Bar, 1970–79. Member: Cttee of Timber Bldg Manufrs Assoc., 1967–69; Cttee of Joinery and Woodwork Employers Fedn, 1968–69. *Publications:* Rockingham Ornamental Porcelain, 1965; Illustrated Guide to Rockingham Pottery and Porcelain, 1971; Derby Porcelain: the golden years, 1750–1770, 1983; English Porcelain Animals of the Nineteenth Century, 1989; articles on company law in legal jls and on Rockingham porcelain in art magazines. *Recreations:* history of English porcelain, gardening. *Address:* c/o Office of the Social Security Commissioners, Harp House, 83 Farringdon Street, EC4A 4DH. *Club:* Reform.

RICE, Maj.-Gen. Sir Desmond (Hind Garrett), KCVO 1989 (CVO 1985); CBE 1976 (OBE 1970); Vice Adjutant General, 1978–79; *b* 1 Dec. 1924; *s* of Arthur Garrett Rice and Alice Constance (*née* Henman); *m* 1954, Denise Ann (*née* Ravenscroft); one *d*. *Educ:* Marlborough College. Commissioned into The Queen's Bays, 1944; psc 1954; 1st The Queen's Dragoon Guards, 1958; jssc 1963; First Comdg Officer, The Royal Yeomanry, 1967–69; Col GS 4 Div., 1970–73; BGS (MO) MoD, 1973–75; rcds 1976; Director of Manning (Army), 1977–78. Col, 1st The Queen's Dragoon Guards, 1980–86. Sec., Central Chancery of Orders of Knighthood, 1980–89. An Extra Gentleman Usher to the Queen, 1989–. *Recreations:* field sports, skiing, gardening. *Address:* Fairway, Malacca Farm, West Clandon, Surrey GU4 7UQ. *T:* Guildford (01483) 222677. *Club:* Cavalry and Guards.

RICE, Gordon Kenneth; His Honour Judge Rice; a Circuit Judge, since 1980; *b* 16 April 1927; *m* 1967. *Educ:* Brasenose Coll., Oxford (MA). Called to the Bar, Middle Temple, 1957. *Address:* 83 Beach Avenue, Leigh-on-Sea, Essex SS9 1HD.

RICE, Maureen; *see* Rice-Knight, M.

RICE, Noel Stephen Cracroft, MD; FRCS, FRCOphth; Consultant Surgeon, Moorfields Eye Hospital, since 1967; Dean, Institute of Ophthalmology, University of London, since 1991; *b* 26 Dec. 1931; *s* of late Raymond Arthur Cracroft Rice and Doris Ivy Rice (*née* Slater); *m* 1957, Karin Elsa Brita Linell (*d* 1992); two *s* one *d*. *Educ:* Haileybury and ISC; Clare Coll., Cambridge (MA, BChir, MD); St Bartholomew's Hosp. House appts, St Bartholomew's Hosp., 1956–57; Jun. Specialist, RAF, 1957–60 (Flt Lt); Registrar, Sen. Registrar, Moorfields Eye Hosp., 1962–65; Sen. Lectr, 1965–70, Clin. Teacher, 1970–91, Inst. of Ophthalmology. Vice-Pres., Ophthalmol Soc.; Member: Council, Coll. of Ophthalmologists; Internat. Council of Ophthalmol.; Acad. Ophth. Internat. Vis. Prof., Nat. Univ. of Singapore. St Eric's Medal, Karolinska Inst., Stockholm. Order of the Falcon (Iceland). *Publications:* contribs to sci. jls on subjects related to ophthalmology. *Recreation:* fly fishing. *Address:* 25 Wimpole Street, W1M 7AD. *T:* 0171–935 6305. *Clubs:* Oriental; Piscatorial Society.

RICE, Olwen Mary; Editor, Woman's Weekly, since 1993; *b* 2 Aug. 1960; *d* of James Rice and Mary Rice (*née* Wood); *m* 1990, Andrew Tilley. *Educ:* Hagley Park Comprehensive Sch.; London Coll. of Printing. News Reporter, Oxford Mail, 1980–84; News Editor, Fitness mag., 1984–85; Health and Beauty Editor, Chat mag., 1985–87; Asst Editor, then Dep. Editor, Best, 1987–88; Editor, Living, 1988–93. *Recreations:* swimming, reading, cycling, writing. *Address:* c/o King's Reach Tower, Stamford Street, SE1 9LS. *T:* 0171–261 6131.

RICE, Peter Anthony Morrish; stage designer; *b* 13 Sept. 1928; *s* of Cecil Morrish Rice and Ethel (*née* Blacklaw); *m* 1954, Patricia Albeck; one *s*. *Educ:* St Dunstan's Coll., Surrey; Royal Coll. of Art (ARCA 1951). Designed first professional prodn, Sex and the Seraphim, Watergate Theatre, London, 1951, followed by The Seraglio, Sadler's Wells Opera, 1952, and Arlecchino, Glyndebourne, 1954; subsequently has designed over 100 plays, operas and ballets, including: *plays:* Time Remembered, 1954; The Winter's Tale, and Much Ado About Nothing, Old Vic, 1956; Living for Pleasure, 1956; A Day in the Life of . . ., 1958; The Lord Chamberlain Regrets, and Toad of Toad Hall, 1961; The Farmer's Wife, The Italian Straw Hat, and Heartbreak House, Chichester, 1966; Flint, and Arms and the Man, 1970; Happy Birthday, 1977; Private Lives, Greenwich and West End, 1980; Present Laughter, Greenwich and West End, 1981; Cavell, and Goodbye Mr Chips, Chichester, 1982; The Sleeping Prince, Chichester and West End, 1983; Forty Years On, Chichester and West End, 1984; Thursday's Ladies, Apollo, 1987; Hay Fever, Chichester, and Re: Joyce!, Fortune, 1988; Don't Dress for Dinner, Apollo, 1990; *operas:* Count Ory, Sadler's Wells, 1962; Arabella, Royal Opera, 1964, Paris Opera, 1981, Chicago, 1984, and Covent Garden, 1986; The Thieving Magpie, and The Violins of St Jacques, Sadler's Wells, 1967; La Bohème, Scottish Opera, 1970; The Magic Flute, Ottawa, 1974; Tosca, Scottish Opera, 1980; The Secret Marriage, Buxton Fest., 1981; The Count of Luxembourg, Sadler's Wells, 1982, 1987; Death in Venice, Antwerp, and Die Fledermaus, St Louis, USA, 1983; Manon, Covent Garden, 1987; Così Fan Tutte, Ottawa, 1990, Hong Kong, 1991; Carmen, Hong Kong, 1992; Ottone, Tokyo, 1992, QEH, 1993; Madama Butterfly, Holland, 1993; L'Infedelta Delusa, Garsington, 1993; *ballets:* Romeo and Juliet, Royal Danish Ballet, 1955, and London Festival Ballet, 1985; Sinfonietta, Royal Ballet, 1966; The Four Seasons, Royal Ballet, 1974. Theatre interiors: Vaudeville Theatre, London; Grand Theatre, Blackpool; His Majesty's Theatre, Aberdeen; Minerva Studio Theatre, Chichester. *Publications:* The Clothes Children Wore, 1973; Farming, 1974; Narrow Boats, 1976. *Recreation:* ancient films. *Address:* 4 Western Terrace, W6 9TX. *T:* 0181–748 3990. *Club:* Garrick.

RICE, Peter D.; *see* Davis-Rice.

RICE, Sir Timothy (Miles Bindon), Kt 1994; writer and broadcaster; *b* 10 Nov. 1944; *s* of late Hugh Gordon Rice and of Joan Odette Rice; *m* 1974, Jane Artereta McIntosh; one *s* one *d*. *Educ:* Lancing Coll. EMI Records, 1966–68; Norrie Paramor Org., 1968–69. Lyrics for stage musicals (with music by Andrew Lloyd Webber): Joseph and the Amazing Technicolor Dreamcoat, 1968 (rev. 1973); Jesus Christ Superstar, 1970; Evita, 1976 (rev. 1978); Cricket, 1986; (with music by Stephen Oliver) Blondel, 1983; (with music by Benny Andersson and Björn Ulvaeus) Chess, 1984 (rev. 1986); (with music by Michel Berger and book by Luc Plamondon) Tycoon, 1992; (with music by Alan Menken) Beauty and the Beast, 1994; lyrics for film musical: (with music by Alan Menken) Aladdin, 1992; (with music by Elton John) The Lion King, 1994. Producer, Anything Goes, Prince Edward Theatre, 1989. Lyrics for songs, 1975–, with other composers, incl. Marvin Hamlisch, Rick Wakeman, Vangelis, Paul McCartney, Mike Batt, Francis Lai, John Barry, Freddie Mercury, Richard Kerr and Graham Gouldman. Awards include: Oscar and Golden Globe for Best Original Film Song, A Whole New World (music by Alan Menken), 1992, and for Can You Feel the Love Tonight (music by Elton John), 1994; gold and platinum records in over 20 countries, 10 Ivor Novello Awards, 2 Tony Awards and 5 Grammy Awards. Founder and Director: GRRR Books, 1978–; Pavilion Books, 1981–. TV includes: Lyrics by Tim Rice; Three More Men in a Boat; Musical Triangles (series); Tim Rice (series); radio incls: numerous quiz shows from Just a Minute and Trivia Test Match downwards; script for 15-part series on hist. of Western popular music for BBC World Service Broadcasts to China. Film début as actor in insultingly small rôle, The Survivor, 1980. Chairman: Stars Organization for Spastics, 1983–85; Shaftesbury Avenue Centenary Cttee, 1984–86; Foundn for Sport and the Arts, 1991–; Pres., Lord's Taverners, 1988–90. *Publications:* Heartaches Cricketers' Almanack, yearly, 1975–; (ed) Lord's Taverners Sticky Wicket Book, 1979; Treasures of Lord's, 1989; (with Andrew Lloyd Webber): Evita, 1978; Joseph and the Amazing Technicolor Dreamcoat, 1982; (jtly) Guinness Books of British Hit Singles and Albums and associated pubns, 1977–, 30th bk in series, 1995. *Recreations:* cricket, history of popular music. *Clubs:* Garrick, MCC (Mem., Main Cttee, 1992–94; Mem., Arts and Liby Sub-cttee, 1986–), Groucho, Dramatists', Saints and Sinners (Chm., 1990); Cricket Writers; Fonograf (Budapest).

RICE-KNIGHT, Maureen, (Maureen Rice); Editor, Options magazine, since 1991; *b* 13 Dec. 1958; *d* of Patrick Rice and Anastasia Rice (*née* McGuire); *m* 1986, David Peter Knight; one *s* one *d*. *Educ:* Gumley House Convent Grammar Sch., Isleworth; Polytechnic of Central London (BA Hons Media Studies). Magazines: Features Editor, Mizz, 1985; Dep. Editor, No 1, 1985; Editor, Mizz, 1986; Editor, 19, 1988. *Recreations:* reading, cinema. *Address:* IPC, Kings Reach Tower, Stamford Street, SE1 9LS. *T:* 0171–261 6601.

RICE-OXLEY, James Keith, CBE 1981; Chairman, Merchant Navy Training Board, since 1981; *b* 15 Aug. 1920; *o s* of late Montague Keith Rice-Oxley and Margery Hyacinth Rice-Oxley (*née* Burrell), Kensington; *m* 1949, Barbara, *yr d* of late Frederick Parsons,

Gerrards Cross; two *d. Educ:* Marlborough Coll.; Trinity Coll., Oxford. MA(Law). Served War of 1939–45: Wiltshire Regt, Royal West Kents (wounded El Alamein); GSO III, HQ 3 Corps; GSO II, HQ Land Forces, Greece (despatches). Joined Shipping Fedn, 1947, Dir, 1965–75; Dir, Internat. Shipping Fedn, 1970–80; Dir, Gen. Council of British Shipping, 1975–80. Chm., Nat. Sea Training Trust, 1965–80; Mem. Nat. Maritime Bd, 1965–80; Mem., Merchant Navy Welfare Bd, 1965–80; Internat. Shipowners' Chm. and British Shipowners' Rep. on Jt Maritime Commn of ILO, 1970–80; Chm., Shipowners' Gp at Internat. Labour (Maritime) Confs, 1969, 1970, 1975, 1976; a Vice-Pres., IMCO/ILO Maritime Conf., 1978. Chm., Maritime Studies Cttee, BTEC, 1980–87; Mem. Industrial Tribunals (England and Wales), 1981–88; General Comr of Income Tax, 1986–95. Barnardo's: Mem. Council and Exec. Cttee, 1981–; Vice-Chm. Council, 1988–89 and 1993–94; Chm., Shaftesbury Civic Soc., 1982–85; Mem. Council, King George's Fund for Sailors, 1965–82; UK Mem., Bd of Governors, World Maritime Univ., Malmö, 1983–89. *Recreations:* squash, ceramics. *Address:* Ox House, Bimport, Shaftesbury SP7 8AX. *T:* Shaftesbury (01747) 52741.

RICH, Michael Anthony; Regional Chairman, Industrial Tribunals, Southampton, since 1987; *b* 16 March 1931; *s* of Joseph and Kate Alexandra Rich; *m* 1959, Helen Kit Marston, MB, BS; one *s* one *d. Educ:* Kimbolton Sch., Hunts; Leicester Univ. (LLM). Admitted Solicitor, 1954. Army Legal Aid, 1954–56; Partner, Rich and Carr, Leicester, 1960–76; Part-time Chm., 1972, Permanent Chm., 1976, Industrial Tribunals. President: Leicester Law Soc., 1976–77; Council of Industrial Tribunal Chairmen, 1993–94. Trustee, Ulverscroft Foundn, 1972–. *Publication:* (with I. A. Edwards) Mead's Unfair Dismissal, 5th edn, 1994. *Recreations:* railway modelling, France. *Address:* 4 Hickory Drive, Harestock, Winchester, Hants SO22 6NJ.

RICH, Michael Samuel, QC 1980; **His Honour Judge Rich;** a Circuit Judge, since 1991; *b* 18 Aug. 1933; *s* of late Sidney Frank Rich, OBE and of Erna Babette; *m* 1963, Janice Sarita Benedictus; three *s* one *d. Educ:* Dulwich Coll.; Wadham Coll., Oxford (MA, 1st Class Hons PPE). Called to the Bar, Middle Temple, 1958, Bencher, 1985; a Recorder, 1986–91; authorized to undertake Official Referee's business, 1991; Deputy High Court Judge: Chancery Div., 1992–; QBD, 1993–. Mem., Lands Tribunal, 1993–. Medal of Merit, Boy Scouts Assoc., 1970. *Publication:* (jtly) Hill's Law of Town and Country Planning, 5th edn, 1968. *Address:* 18 Dulwich Village, SE21 7AL. *T:* 0181–693 1957. *Club:* Garrick.

RICH, Nigel Mervyn Sutherland, CBE 1995; Chief Executive, Trafalgar House, since 1994; *b* 30 Oct. 1945; *s* of Charles Albert Rich and Mina Mackintosh Rich; *m* 1970, Cynthia Elizabeth (*née* Davies); two *s* two *d. Educ:* Sedbergh Sch.; New Coll., Oxford (MA). FCA. Deloitte, Plender Griffiths, London, 1967–71; Deloitte, Haskins & Sells, New York, 1971–73; Jardine Matheson, 1974–94; served in varying positions in Hong Kong, Johannesburg (Rennies Consolidated Holdings) and Manila (Jardine Davies); seconded to Hongkong Land, 1983–88; Man. Dir, Jardine Matheson Holdings Ltd, 1989–94. Hon. Steward, Royal HK Jockey Club, 1994–. Liveryman, Tobacco Pipemakers and Tobacco Blenders Co.; Freeman, City of London, 1970. *Recreations:* tennis, golf, windsurfing, horseracing. *Address:* 1 Berkeley Street, W1A 1BY. *Clubs:* MCC, Hurlingham, Army and Navy; Royal and Ancient Golf.

RICHARD, family name of **Baron Richard.**

RICHARD, Baron *cr* 1990 (Life Peer), of Ammanford in the County of Dyfed; **Ivor Seward Richard;** PC 1993; QC 1971; Leader of the Opposition, House of Lords, since 1992; *b* 30 May 1932; *s* of Seward Thomas Richard, mining and electrical engineer, and Isabella Irene Richard; *m* (marr. diss.); two *s* one *d*; *m* 1989, Janet Jones; one *s. Educ:* St Michael's Sch., Bryn, Llanelly; Cheltenham Coll.; Pembroke Coll., Oxford (Wightwick Scholar; Hon Fellow, 1981). BA Oxon (Jurisprudence) 1953; MA 1970; called to Bar, Inner Temple, 1955, Bencher, 1985. Practised in chambers, London, 1955–74. UK Perm. Representative to UN, 1974–79; Mem., Commn of EEC, 1981–84; Chm., Rhodesia Conf., Geneva, 1976. Parly Candidate, S Kensington, 1959; MP (Lab) Barons Court, 1964–Feb. 1974. Delegate: Assembly, Council of Europe, 1965–68; Western European Union, 1965–68; Vice-Chm., Legal Cttee, Council of Europe, 1966–67; PPS, Sec. of State for Defence, 1966–69; Parly Under-Sec. (Army), Min. of Defence, 1969–70; Opposition Spokesman, Broadcasting, Posts and Telecommunications, 1970–71; Dep. Spokesman, Foreign Affairs, 1971–74. Chm., World Trade Centre Wales Ltd (Cardiff), 1985–. Member: Fabian Society; Society of Labour Lawyers; Inst. of Strategic Studies; Royal Inst. of Internat. Affairs. *Publications:* (jt) Europe or the Open Sea, 1971; We, the British, 1983 (USA); articles in various political jls. *Recreations:* playing piano, watching football matches, talking. *Address:* 11 South Square, Gray's Inn, WC2.

RICHARD, Sir Cliff, Kt 1995; OBE 1980; singer, actor; *b* 14 Oct. 1940; *s* of Rodger Webb and Dorothy Webb. *Educ:* Riversmead Sch., Cheshunt. Awarded 13 Gold Discs for records: Living Doll, 1959; The Young Ones, 1962; Bachelor Boy, 1962; Lucky Lips, 1963; Congratulations, 1968; Power to all Our Friends, 1973; Devil Woman, 1976; We Don't Talk Anymore, 1979; Wired for Sound, 1981; Daddy's Home, 1981; Living Doll (with The Young Ones), 1986; All I Ask of You (with Sarah Brightman), 1986; Mistletoe and Wine, 1988; also 37 Silver Discs and 2 Platinum Discs (Daddy's Home, 1981; All I Ask of You, 1986). Films: Serious Charge, 1959; Expresso Bongo, 1960; The Young Ones, 1962; Summer Holiday, 1963; Wonderful Life, 1964; Finders Keepers, 1966; Two a Penny, 1968; His Land, 1970; Take Me High, 1973. Own TV series, ATV and BBC. Stage: rep. and variety seasons; Time, Dominion, 1986–87. Top Box Office Star of GB, 1962–63 and 1963–64. *Publications:* Questions, 1970; The Way I See It, 1972; The Way I See It Now, 1975; Which One's Cliff, 1977; Happy Christmas from Cliff, 1980; You, Me and Jesus, 1983; Mine to Share, 1984; Jesus, Me and You, 1985; Single-minded, 1988; Mine Forever, 1989. *Recreations:* swimming, tennis. *Address:* c/o PO Box 46C, Esher, Surrey KT10 0RB. *T:* Esher (01372) 467752. *Club:* All England Lawn Tennis and Croquet.

RICHARDS, family name of **Baron Milverton.**

RICHARDS, Alun; *see* Richards, R. A.

RICHARDS, Archibald Banks, CA; retired; *b* 29 March 1911; *s* of late Charles Richards and Margaret Pollock Richards; *m* 1st, 1941, Edith Janet Sinclair (*d* 1987); one *s* one *d*; 2nd, 1990, Constance Mary Fleming Mason. *Educ:* Daniel Stewart's Coll., Edinburgh. Partner, A. T. Niven & Co., Chartered Accountants, Edinburgh, 1939–69, Touche Ross & Co., Chartered Accountants, 1964–78. Inst. of Chartered Accountants of Scotland: Mem., 1934; Mem. Council, 1968–73; Vice Pres., 1974–76; Pres., 1976–77. *Address:* 7 Midmar Gardens, Edinburgh EH10 6DY. *T:* 0131–447 1942.

RICHARDS, Arthur Cyril, FIA; consultant; *b* 7 April 1921; *s* of Ernest Arthur Richards and Kate Richards (*née* Cooper); *m* 1st, 1944, Joyce Bertha Brooke (marr. diss. 1974); two *s* two *d*; 2nd, 1975, Els Stoyle (*née* van der Stoel); two step *s* one step *d. Educ:* Tollington Sch., London. FIA 1949; FSVA 1962. Insurance, 1937–41. Served RAF, 1941–46. Insurance, consulting actuary, steel manufacture, investment banking, internat. property devel t, 1946–64; Advr, Samuel Montagu & Co. Ltd, 1965–67; Gp Finance Dir, Bovis Ltd, 1967–71; United Dominions Trust Ltd: Gp Finance Dir, 1971–76; Gp Man. Dir, 1976–80; Chief Exec., 1981–83; Dir, 1978–88, Chm., 1983–88, Blackwood Hodge plc. Chm., Federated Land, 1982; Director: MSL Gp Internat., 1970–81; TSB Trust Co., 1981–88; Combined Lease Finance PLC, 1985–89; Hermes Gp, 1990–. *Recreations:* sailing, windsurfing, antiques. *Address:* Caboose, Tilt Meadow, Cobham, Surrey KT11 3AJ.

RICHARDS, Bertrand; *see* Richards, E. B. B.

RICHARDS, Brian Henry, CEng, FIEE; Weapon Systems Director, GEC-Marconi Dynamics Ltd, since 1995; *b* 19 July 1938; *s* of Alfred Edward Richards and Lilian Maud Richards (*née* Bennett); *m* 1961, Jane Wilkins; one *s* one *d. Educ:* Buckhurst Hill County Grammar Sch.; St John's College, Cambridge (Mech. Sci. Tripos, 1st Class Hons 1959, BA 1960; MA 1965). GEC Electronics, later Marconi Defence Systems, 1960–87: Guided Weapons Division: develt, systems, project management appts, 1960–76; Business Develt Manager, 1977; Manager, 1978; Asst Gen. Manager and Manager, 1982; Dir, Guided Weapons, 1985; RCDS, 1986; Asst Man. Dir, 1987; Technical Dir, Hunting Engineering, 1988–90; Chief Exec., Atomic Weapons Estabt, 1990–95. *Recreations:* golf, listening to music, water colour painting, DIY, gardening. *Address:* GEC-Marconi Dynamics Ltd, Stanmore, Mddx HA7 4LY.

RICHARDS, Dr Brian Mansel, CBE 1990; Executive Chairman, Peptide Therapeutics Group plc, since 1995; *b* 19 Sept. 1932; *s* of Cyril Mansel Richards and Gwendolyn Hyde Richards; *m* 1952, Joan Lambert Breese; one *s* one *d. Educ:* Lewis Sch., Pengam, Glam; University Coll. of Wales, Aberystwyth (BSc); King's College London (PhD). British Empire Cancer Fellowship, 1955–57; Nuffield Fellowship, 1957; MRC Biophysics Research Unit, 1957–64; Reader in Biology, Univ. of London, 1964–66; Research Div., G. D. Searle & Co., 1966–86; Vice-Pres., UK Preclinical R&D, 1980–86; Chairman: British Bio-technology Ltd, 1986–89; British Bio-technology Gp, 1989–94. Hon. Prof. in Life Scis, UCW, Aberystwth, 1991–. Chm., Biotechnology Working Party, CBI, 1988; Mem., Res. and Manufg Cttee, CBI, 1988; Mem., Sci. Bd, SERC, 1987; Chairman: Biotechnology Jt Adv. Bd, SERC/DTI, 1989; Science-based Cos Cttee, London Stock Exchange, 1994; Member: Adv. Cttee for Genetic Modification (previously Manipulation), HSE, 1984; Gene Therapy Adv. Cttee, DoH, 1994–; BBSRC, 1994–; Consultant on Biotechnology, OECD, 1987; Specialist Advr, H of L Select Cttee II on Biotechnol. Regulation, 1993. *Publications:* papers in sci. jls. *Recreations:* collecting Jaguar cars, photography, deprecating ball games. *Address:* Peptide Therapeutics Group plc, 321 Cambridge Science Park, Milton Road, Cambridge CB4 4WG.

RICHARDS, Sir Brooks; *see* Richards, Sir F. B.

RICHARDS, Charles Anthony Langdon, CMG 1958; *b* 18 April 1911; *s* of T. L. Richards, Bristol, Musician; *m* 1937, Mary Edith Warren-Codrington; two *s. Educ:* Clifton Coll.; Brasenose Coll., Oxford. Appointed Colonial CS, Uganda, 1934; Major, 7th King's African Rifles, 1939–41: duties in Mauritius, 1941–46; District Officer, Uganda, 1946–50; Commissioner for Social Development, Tanganyika, 1950–53; Commissioner for Community Development, Uganda, 1953–54; Resident, Buganda, Oct. 1954–60; Minister of Local Government, Uganda, 1960–61. *Recreation:* gardening. *Address:* The Wall House, Oak Drive, Highworth, Wilts SN6 7BP.

RICHARDS, Clare Mary Joan; *see* Spottiswoode, C. M. J.

RICHARDS, David Anthony Stewart; QC 1992; *b* 9 June 1951; *s* of Kenneth Richards and Winifred Richards; *m* 1979, Gillian, *er d* of Lt-Col W. A. Taylor; one *s* twin *d. Educ:* Oundle; Trinity Coll., Cambridge (BA 1973; MA 1980). Called to the Bar, Inner Temple, 1974; Junior Counsel (Chancery), DTI, 1989–92. *Address:* Erskine Chambers, 30 Lincoln's Inn Fields, WC2A 3PF.

RICHARDS, David Gordon, CBE 1989; FCA; Non-Executive Chairman, Walker Greenbank plc, since 1990 (Director, since 1988); *b* 25 Aug. 1928; *s* of late Gordon Charles Richards and Vera Amy (*née* Barrow); *m* 1960, Stephanie, *er d* of late E. Gilbert Woodward, Metropolitan Magistrate and of Mrs Woodward; one *s* two *d. Educ:* Highgate Sch. FCA 1961. Articled to Harmood Banner & Co., 1945; served, 8th Royal Tank Regt, 1947–49; Partner: Harmood Banner & Co., 1955–74; Deloitte Haskins & Sells, 1974–84. Admitted Associate Mem. Inst. of Chartered Accountants in England and Wales, 1951 (Council, 1970–87; Vice-Pres., 1977–78; Dep. Pres., 1978–79; Centenary Pres., 1979–80; Mem., Gen. Purposes and Finance Cttee, 1977–83; Chm., Internat. Affairs Cttee, 1980–83); Mem., Cttee of London Soc. of Chartered Accountants, 1966–70, 1981–82 (Chm., 1969–70); Chm., Cons. Cttee of Accountancy Bodies, 1979–80; UK and Ireland rep. on Council, Internat. Fedn of Accountants, 1981–83. Dep. Chm., Monopolies and Mergers Commn, 1983–90; Member: Cttees of Investigation under Agricultural Marketing Act (1958), 1972–88; Council for Securities Industry, 1979–80; Panel on Take Overs and Mergers, 1979–80; Review Body on Doctors' and Dentists' Remuneration, 1984–90; Chm., Disciplinary Bd, BPsS, 1988–. Governor: Highgate Sch., 1982– (Chm. 1983–); Associated Bd of Royal Schs of Music, 1987–; Trustee: The Bob Champion Cancer Trust, 1983–94; Royal Acad. of Music Foundn, 1985–; Prince's Youth Business Trust, 1986–93. Pres., Old Cholmeleian Soc., 1988–89. Master, Worshipful Co. of Chartered Accountants in England and Wales, 1986–87. *Publications:* numerous contribs to professional press and lectures on professional topics given internationally. *Recreations:* golf, lawn tennis, sailing, shooting, silviculture, music. *Address:* Eastleach House, Eastleach, Glos GL7 3NW. *T:* Southrop (01367) 850416.

RICHARDS, Denis Edward, CMG 1981; HM Diplomatic Service, retired; Ambassador to the United Republic of Cameroon and the Republic of Equatorial Guinea, 1979–81; *b* 25 May 1923; *m* 1947, Nancy Beryl Brown; one *d* (and one *d* decd). *Educ:* Wilson's Grammar Sch., London; St Peter's Coll., Oxford. Lieut RNVR, 1941–46; Colonial Service (HMOCS), 1948–60: District Admin. and Min. of Finance, Ghana (Gold Coast); HM Diplomatic Service, 1960–81: CRO, 1960; Karachi, 1961–63; FO (News Dept), 1964–68; Brussels (NATO), 1969; Brussels (UK Negotiating Delegn), 1970–72; Counsellor, Kinshasa, 1972–74; Consul-Gen., Philadelphia, 1974–79. *Recreations:* music, watching cricket. *Address:* Tresco House, Spencer Road, Birchington, Kent CT7 9EY. *T:* Thanet (01843) 845637.

RICHARDS, Denis George, OBE 1990; author; *b* 10 Sept. 1910; *s* of late George Richards and Frances Amelia Gosland; *m* 1940, Barbara, *d* of J. H. Smethurst, Heaton, Bolton; four *d. Educ:* Owen's Sch.; Trinity Hall, Cambridge (Scholar). BA 1931 (1st Cl. in both Parts of Historical Tripos); MA 1935; Asst Master, Manchester Grammar School, 1931–39; Senior History and English Master, Bradfield Coll., 1939–41; Narrator in Air Ministry Historical Branch, writing confidential studies on various aspects of the air war, 1942–43; Sen. Narrator, 1943–47; Hon. Sqdn Ldr RAFVR, 1943–47; engaged in writing, under Air Min. auspices, an official History of the Royal Air Force in the Second World War, 1947–49; was established in Admin. Civil Service, Principal, Department of Permanent Under Secretary of State for Air, 1949–50; Principal, Morley College, 1950–65; Longman Fellow in Univ. of Sussex, 1965–68. Chm., Women's League of Health and Beauty, 1966–88; Vice-Pres., Purcell Sch. for Young Musicians, 1984–. *Publications:* An Illustrated History of Modern Europe, 1938; Modern Europe (1919–39 section for revised

edn of work by Sydney Herbert), 1940; (with J. W. Hunt) An Illustrated History of Modern Britain, 1950; (with late Hilary St G. Saunders) Royal Air Force 1939–45–an officially commissioned history in 3 volumes, 1953–54 (awarded C. P. Robertson Memorial Trophy, 1954); (with J. Evan Cruikshank) The Modern Age, 1955; Britain under the Tudors and Stuarts, 1958; Offspring of the Vic: a history of Morley College, 1958; (with Anthony Quick) Britain 1714–1851, 1961; (with J. A. Bolton) Britain and the Ancient World, 1963; (with Anthony Quick) Britain, 1851–1945, 1967; (with Anthony Quick) Twentieth Century Britain, 1968; (with A. W. Ellis) Medieval Britain, 1973; Portal of Hungerford, 1978; (with Richard Hough) The Battle of Britain: the Jubilee history, 1989; (ed) The Few and the Many, 1990; The Hardest Victory: RAF Bomber Command in the Second World War, 1994. *Recreations:* music, pictures, golf, travel in the more civilized parts of Europe, the lighter tasks in the garden. *Address:* 16 Broadlands Road, N6 4AN. *T:* 0181–340 5259. *Clubs:* Arts, Garrick, Royal Air Force, PEN.
See also W. P. Shovelton.

RICHARDS, His Honour (Edmund) Bertrand (Bamford); a Circuit Judge, 1972–86; *b* 14 Feb. 1913; *s* of Rev. Edmund Milo Richards, Llewesog Hall, Denbigh; *m* 2nd, 1966, Jane, *widow* of Edward Stephen Porter. *Educ:* Lancing Coll.; Corpus Christi Coll., Oxford. Served War, RA, 1940–46. Called to Bar, Inner Temple, 1941. Dep. Chm., Denbighshire QS, 1964–71. Hon. Recorder of Ipswich, 1975. *Address:* Melton Hall, near Woodbridge, Suffolk IP12 1PF.

RICHARDS, Sir (Francis) Brooks, KCMG 1976 (CMG 1963); DSC and Bar, 1943; *b* 18 July 1918; *s* of Francis Bartlett Richards; *m* 1941, Hazel Myfanwy, *d* of Lt-Col Stanley Price Williams, CIE; one *s* one *d*. *Educ:* Stowe School; Magdalene College, Cambridge. Served with RN, 1939–44 (Lieut-Comdr RNVR). HM Embassy: Paris, 1944–48; Athens, 1952–54; First Sec. and Head of Chancery, Political Residency, Persian Gulf, 1954–57; Assistant Private Secretary to Foreign Secretary, 1958–59; Counsellor (Information), HM Embassy, Paris, 1959–64; Head of Information Policy Dept, 1964, and of Jt Inf. Policy and Guidance Dept, FO/CRO, 1964–65; seconded to Cabinet Office, 1965–69; HM Minister, Bonn, 1969–71; HM Ambassador, Saigon, 1972–74; HM Ambassador, Greece, 1974–78; Dep. Sec., Cabinet Office, 1978–80; NI Office, 1980–81. Chm., CSM Parliamentary Consultants Ltd, 1984–. Vice-Pres., Friends of Imperial War Museum, 1991– (Chm., 1989–91); Chairman: Paintings in Hosps, 1990–; Anglo Hellenic League, 1990–93. Chevalier, Légion d'Honneur and Croix de Guerre (France), 1944. *Recreations:* collecting, gardening, travelling. *Clubs:* Travellers', Special Forces.
See also F. N. Richards.

RICHARDS, Francis Neville, CMG 1994; CVO 1991; HM Diplomatic Service; Assistant Under-Secretary of State, Foreign and Commonwealth Office, since 1995; *b* 18 Nov. 1945; *s* of Sir Francis Brooks Richards, *qv*; *m* 1971, Gillian Bruce Nevill, *d* of late I. S. Nevill, MC and of Dr L. M. B. Dawson; one *s* one *d*. *Educ:* Eton; King's Coll., Cambridge (MA). Royal Green Jackets, 1967 (invalided, 1969). FCO, 1969; Moscow, 1971; UK Delegn to MBFR negotiations, Vienna, 1973; FCO, 1976–85 (Asst Private Sec. to Sec. of State, 1981–82); Economic and Commercial Counsellor, New Delhi, 1985–88; FCO, 1988–90 (Head, S Asian Dept); High Comr, Windhoek, 1990–92; Minister, Moscow, 1992–95. *Recreations:* walking, travelling, riding. *Address:* c/o Foreign and Commonwealth Office, SW1A 2AH. *Clubs:* Travellers'; President's Estate Polo (New Delhi).

RICHARDS, Gordon Waugh; racehorse trainer, National Hunt, since 1964; *b* 7 Sept. 1930; *s* of Thomas Henry Richards and Gladys Florence Thompson; *m* 1st, Jean Charlton (decd); one *s* one *d*; 2nd, 1980, Joan Dacre Lacey, *d* of Hon. Henry Howard. *Educ:* Bath. Apprentice jockey, 1943; National Hunt jockey, 1950–63, trainer, 1964–; trained 2 Grand National winners: Lucius, 1978; Hello Dandy, 1984. Trainer of more than 100 winners in a season, 1977–78, 1990–91 and 1992–93. *Recreations:* tennis, reading. *Address:* The Old Rectory, Greystoke, Penrith, Cumbria CA11 0TJ.

RICHARDS, (Isaac) Vivian (Alexander), OBE 1994; cricketer; Captain, West Indies Cricket Team, 1985–91; *b* St Johns, Antigua, 7 March 1952; *s* of Malcolm Richards; *m* Miriam Lewis; one *s* one *d*. *Educ:* Antigua Grammar School. First class débuts, Leeward Islands, 1971, India (for WI), 1974; played for: Somerset, 1974–86; Queensland, 1976–77; Rishton, Lancs League, 1987; Glamorgan, 1990–93; played in 100th Test Match, 1988; scored 100th first class century, 1988; 100th Test Match catch, 1988; highest Test score, 291, *v* England, Oval, 1976; highest first class score, 322, *v* Warwicks, Taunton, 1985; fastest Test century *v* England, Antigua, 1986; highest number of Test runs by a West Indian batsman, 1991. Hon. DLitt Exeter, 1986. *Publications:* (with David Foot) Viv Richards (autobiog.), 1982; (with Patrick Murphy) Cricket Masterclass, 1988; (with Michael Middles) Hitting across the Line (autobiog.), 1991. *Recreations:* tennis, music, football. *Address:* c/o Nick Leigh, Kennedy Street Management, Kennedy House, 31 Stamford Street, Altrincham, Cheshire WA14 1ES. *T:* 0161–941 5151.

RICHARDS, James Alan, OBE 1979; Agent-General for Western Australia in London, 1975–78, retired; *b* 8 Oct. 1913; *s* of James Percival Richards and Alice Pearl Richards (*née* Bullock) Adelaide; *m* 1939, Mabel Joyce, *d* of R. H. Cooper, Riverton, S Austr.; three *s* one *d*. *Educ:* Unley High Sch.; Coll. of Business Admin, Univ. of Hawaii. Served War of 1939–45, 2nd AIF. Ampol Petroleum Ltd, 1946–75: Sales Man., South Australia, 1952–53; State Man., Western Australia, 1954–75. *Recreation:* bowls. *Address:* 98/7 Harman Road, Sorrento, WA 6020, Australia.

RICHARDS, Rt. Rev. John; *see* Ebbsfleet, Bishop Suffragan of.

RICHARDS, John Arthur; Under-Secretary, Department of Education and Science, 1973–77; *b* 23 June 1918; *s* of late Alderman A. J. Richards and Mrs Annie Richards, Dulwich; *m* 1946, Sheelagh, *d* of late Patrick McWalter and Katherine McWalter, Balla, Co. Mayo; two *s* one *d*. *Educ:* Brockley Sch.; King's Coll., London. BA, AKC, Dip. in Educn. Hon. Sec., King's Coll. Union Soc., 1939. Served War: Captain RA; Directorate of Personnel Selection, War Office, 1945–46. Temp. Third Sec., Foreign Office, 1946; Staff, Hackney Downs Grammar Sch., 1948; Ministry of Education: Asst Principal and Principal, 1949 (Jt Sec., Secondary Schs Examinations Council, 1956–57); Asst Sec. (also Dept of Educn and Science), 1963–73. *Publications:* occasional verse and contribs to journals. *Recreations:* journalism, writing verse. *Address:* 14 Blacksmiths Hill, Sanderstead, Surrey CR2 9AY. *T:* 0181–657 1275.

RICHARDS, Lt-Gen. Sir John (Charles Chisholm), KCB 1980; KCVO 1991; HM Marshal of the Diplomatic Corps, 1982–92; Extra Equerry to the Queen, since 1992; *b* 21 Feb. 1927; *s* of Charles C. Richards and Alice Milner; *m* 1953, Audrey Hidson; two *s* one *d*. *Educ:* Worksop Coll., Notts. Joined Royal Marines, 1945; 45 Commando, Malaya, 1950–52; Instructor, Officers' Sch., 1953–55; HMS Birmingham, 1955–56; Canadian Army Staff Coll., 1959–61; Adjt and Company Comdr, 43 Commando, 1962–63; Naval staff, 1963–64; Instructor, Staff Coll., Camberley, 1965–67; 45 Commando: 2nd in Comd, Aden, 1967; CO, 1968–69; GSO1 Plymouth Gp, 1969; CO 42 Commando, 1970–72; Chief of Staff, Brit. Def. Staff, Washington DC, UN Deleg., and Mem. Mil. Staff Cttee, 1972–74; Comdr 3rd Commando Bde, 1975–76; Commandant General, Royal Marines, 1977–81. Col Comdt, RM, 1987–88, Representative Col Comdt, 1989–90. Admiral, Texas Navy, 1983. Director: DSC Communications (Europe), 1986–92; Andrew Ltd, 1987–95. CIMgt (CBIM 1980). Freeman, City of London, 1982. *Recreations:* golf, swimming, gardening. *Address:* c/o National Westminster Bank, 36 St James's Street, SW1A 1JF. *Club:* Army and Navy.

RICHARDS, John Deacon, CBE 1978; RSA 1989 (ARSA 1974); RIBA; PPRIAS; architect; Principal, John Richards Associates, since 1986; *b* 7 May 1931; *s* of late William John Richards and Ethel Richards; *m* 1958, Margaret Brown, RIBA, ARIAS; one *s* three *d*. *Educ:* Geelong Grammar Sch., Vic.; Cranleigh Sch.; Architect. Assoc. Sch. of Arch., London (Dipl. 1954). RIBA 1955; FRIAS 1968 (PRIAS, 1983–85). RE, 1955–57. Partner, 1964–86, Chm., 1983–86, Senior Consultant, 1986–90, Robert Matthew, Johnson-Marshall and Partners. Buildings include: Stirling Univ., 1965–; Royal Commonwealth Pool, Edinburgh, 1970. Member: Royal Fine Art Commn for Scotland, 1975–89; Bd, Housing Corp., 1982–89 (Chm., Scottish Cttee, 1982–89); Bd, Scottish Homes, 1988–93 (Dep. Chm., 1989–93). Housing Assoc. Ombudsman for Scotland, 1994–. Mem., Agrément Bd, 1980–83. Trustee, Nat. Galleries of Scotland, 1986–90. Hon. DUniv Stirling, 1976. Gold Medallist, RSA, 1972. *Recreation:* country life. *Address:* Lady's Field, Whitekirk, Dunbar, East Lothian EH42 1XS. *T:* Whitekirk (01620) 870206. *Club:* Athenæum.

RICHARDS, Michael Anthony, CBiol, FIBiol 1985; MRCVS; Chief Inspector, Animals (Scientific Procedures) Act 1986 (formerly Cruelty to Animals Act (1876)), Home Office, 1982–87, retired; *b* 12 Oct. 1926; *s* of Edward Albert Richards and Clara Muriel (*née* Webb); *m* 1956, Sylvia Rosemary, *d* of Geoffrey Charles Pain, JP; two *d*. *Educ:* St Albans Coll., St George's Coll., and J. M. Estrada Coll., all in Buenos Aires; Royal Vet. Coll., London Univ. MRCVS 1953. Served Army, Intell. Corps, 1945–47. In general practice, 1953; Lectr in Vet. Medicine, Univ. of London, 1963–67; Lectr in Vet. Pathology, Univ. of Edinburgh, 1967–69; Home Office, 1969–87. *Publications:* scientific contribs to standard works and med. and vet. jls. *Recreation:* philately. *Address:* 10 Westfield Place, Forfar, Angus DD8 1HL. *T:* Forfar (01307) 461268.

RICHARDS, Maj.-Gen. Nigel William Fairbairn, OBE 1987; Chief of Combat Support, HQ Allied Command Europe Rapid Reaction Corps, since 1994; *b* 15 Aug. 1945; *s* of late Lt-Col William Fairbairn Richards and of Marjorie May Richards; *m* 1968, Christine Anne Helen Woods; two *s* one *d*. *Educ:* Eastbourne Coll.; RMA Sandhurst; Peterhouse, Cambridge (MA). Commissioned, RA, 1965; reglt duty, 1966–76, UK, Germany, NI, Cyprus, Malaya; RN Staff Coll., 1976–77; MoD, 1978–80; Comd J Anti-Tank Battery, RHA, 1980–81; Directing Staff, RMCS, 1982–83; CO 7 Para Regt, RHA, 1983–86; MoD, 1986–88; Higher Comd and Staff Course, 1988; Comdr 5 Airborne Brigade, 1989–90; RCDS 1991; Dir Army Staff Duties, MoD, 1991–93. *Recreations:* cricket, tennis, golf. *Club:* Army and Navy.

RICHARDS, Prof. Peter; Dean and Professor of Medicine, 1979–95, St Mary's Hospital Medical School (part of Imperial College of Science, Technology and Medicine, since 1988), University of London; Pro-Rector (Medicine), Imperial College, 1988–95; *b* 25 May 1936; *s* of William and Barbara Richards; *m* 1st, 1959, Anne Marie Larsen (marr. diss. 1986); one *s* three *d*; 2nd, 1987, Dr Carol Ann Seymour. *Educ:* Monkton Combe Sch.; Emmanuel Coll., Cambridge (BA 1957; MB BChir 1960; MA 1961; MD 1971); St George's Hosp. Medical Sch.; Royal Postgraduate Medical Sch. (PhD 1966); FRCP 1976. Consultant Physician, St Peter's Hosp., Chertsey and Hon. Sen. Lectr in Medicine, St Mary's Hosp. Med. Sch., 1970–73; Sen. Lectr in Medicine, St George's Hosp. Med. Sch., 1973–79. Chm., Council of Deans of UK Med. Schs and Faculties, 1994–95. Member: GMC, 1994–; Council, RCP, 1994–. *Publications:* The Medieval Leper, 1977; (ed jtly) Clinical Medicine and Therapeutics, Vol. I, 1977, Vol. II, 1979; Understanding Water, Electrolyte and Acid/Base Metabolism, 1983; Learning Medicine, 1983, 10th edn 1993; Living Medicine, 1990; scientific papers esp. concerning kidney disease and criteria for selection of medical students in Lancet, BMJ, etc. *Recreations:* walking, listening to music, Finland, social history. *Address:* St Mary's Hospital Medical School, Paddington, W2 1PG. *Club:* Garrick.

RICHARDS, Peter Graham Gordon; Stipendiary Magistrate for Staffordshire, since 1991; *b* 16 July 1939; *s* of David Gordon and Irene Florence Richards; *m* 1965, Jeanette Uncles; two *d*. *Educ:* Univ. of London (LLM 1966). Schoolmaster, 1962–65; Lectr, 1965–68; called to the Bar, Middle Temple, 1968; Midland and Oxford Circuit, 1968–91. *Recreations:* sports broadcasting, travel, theatre, astronomy. *Address:* c/o Clerk to the Justices, Baker Street, Fenton, Stoke on Trent ST4 3BX. *T:* Stoke on Trent (01782) 45353.

RICHARDS, Sir Rex (Edward), Kt 1977; DSc Oxon 1970; FRS 1959; FRSC; Chancellor, Exeter University, since 1982; *b* 28 Oct. 1922; *s* of H. W. and E. N. Richards; *m* 1948, Eva Edith Vago; two *d*. *Educ:* Colyton Grammar School, Devon; St John's College, Oxford. Senior Demy, Magdalen College, Oxford, 1946; MA; DPhil; Fellow, Lincoln College, Oxford, 1947–64, Hon. Fellow, 1968; Research Fellow, Harvard University, 1955; Dr Lee's Prof. of Chemistry, Oxford, 1964–70; Fellow, Exeter College, 1964–69; Warden, Merton Coll., Oxford, 1969–84, Hon. Fellow, 1984; Vice-Chancellor, Oxford Univ., 1977–81; Hon. Fellow, St John's Coll., Oxford, 1968; Associate Fellow, Morse Coll., Yale, 1974–79. Director: IBM-UK Ltd, 1978–83; Oxford Instruments Group, 1982–91. Chm., BPMF, 1986–93; Dir, Leverhulme Trust, 1984–93; Member: Chemical Society Council, 1957, 1987–93; Faraday Society Council, 1963; Royal Soc. Council, 1973–75; Scientific Adv. Cttee, Nat. Gall., 1978–; ABRC, 1980–83; ACARD, 1984–87; Comr, Royal Comm for the Exhibition of 1851, 1984–; Pres., Royal Soc. of Chemistry, 1990–92; Trustee: CIBA Foundn, 1978–; Nat. Heritage Memorial Fund, 1980–84; Tate Gall., 1982–88, 1991–93; Nat. Gall., 1982–88, 1989–93; Henry Moore Foundn, 1989– (Vice Chm., 1993–94; Chm., 1994–). Tilden Lectr, 1962. FRIC 1970. Hon. FRCP 1987; Hon. FBA 1990; Hon. FRAM 1991. Hon. DSc: East Anglia, 1971; Exeter, 1975; Leicester, 1978; Salford, 1979; Edinburgh, 1981; Leeds, 1984; Kent, 1987; Birmingham, 1993; London, 1994; Hon. LLD Dundee, 1977; Hon. ScD Cambridge, 1987. Centenary Fellow, Thames Polytechnic (subseq. Univ. of Greenwich), 1990. For. Associate, Académie des Sciences, France, 1995. Corday-Morgan Medal of Chemical Soc., 1954; Davy Medal, Royal Soc., 1976; Award in Theoretical Chemistry and Spectroscopy, Chem. Soc., 1977; Educn in Partnership with Industry or Commerce Award, DTI, 1982; Medal of Honour, Rheinische Friedrich-Wilhelms Univ., Bonn, 1983; Royal Medal, Royal Soc., 1986; President's Medal, Soc. of Chemical Ind., 1991. *Publications:* various contributions to scientific journals. *Recreation:* enjoying painting and sculpture. *Address:* 13 Woodstock Close, Oxford OX2 8DB. *T:* Oxford (01865) 513621.

RICHARDS, (Richard) Alun; Welsh Secretary in charge of Welsh Office Agriculture Department, 1978–81, retired; *b* 2 Jan. 1920; *s* of Sylvanus and Gwladys Richards, Llanbrynmair, Powys; *m* 1944, Ann Elonwy Mary, (Nansi), Price (decd), Morriston, Swansea; two *s*. *Educ:* Machynlleth County Sch.; Liverpool Univ. (BVSc, MRCVS, 1942). Veterinary Officer with State Vet. Service, Caernarfon and Glamorgan, 1943–57; Divl Vet. Officer, HQ Tolworth and in Warwick, 1957–65; Dep. Reg. Vet. Officer (Wales), 1965–67; seconded to NZ Govt to advise on control of Foot and Mouth disease,

1967–68; Reg. Vet. Officer, HQ Tolworth, 1968–71; Asst Chief Vet. Officer, 1971–77; Asst Sec., Welsh Dept, MAFF, 1977–78; Under-Sec., 1978. *Publications:* contrib. to vet. jls. *Recreations:* beekeeping, fishing, shooting. *Address:* Isfryn, Llandre, Aberystwyth, Dyfed SY24 5BS. *T:* Aberystwyth (01970) 828246.

See also S. P. Richards.

RICHARDS, Lt-Comdr Richard Meredyth, JP, DL; RN; Vice Lord-Lieutenant of Gwynedd, since 1985; *b* 27 Dec. 1920; *s* of late Major H. M. Richards, OBE, JP, VL and Mrs Mary Richards, MBE, MSc; *m* 1945, Pamela Watson; three *s* (one *d* decd). *Educ:* RNC, Dartmouth (Naval Cadet). Midshipman, 1939; Sub-Lt 1940; Lieut 1942; Lt-Comdr 1950; served in FAA, 1941–49; returned to gen. service, 1949; retd 1954 (to take over family estate). High Sheriff, Merioneth, 1960; DL Merioneth, 1967; JP Tal-y-Bont (Dolgellau), 1969. *Recreations:* fishing, shooting, sailing, ski-ing. *Address:* Caerynwch, Dolgellau, Gwynedd LL40 2RF. *T:* Dolgellau (01341) 422263.

RICHARDS, Roderick; MP (C) Clywd North West, since 1992; Parliamentary Under-Secretary of State, Welsh Office, since 1994; *b* 12 March 1947; *s* of Ivor George Richards and Lizzie Jane Richards (*née* Evans); *m* 1975, Elizabeth Knight; two *s* one *d*. *Educ:* Llandovery College; Univ. of Wales (BSc Econ). Short service commn, RM, 1969–71. Ministry of Defence, 1977–83; broadcaster and journalist, 1983–89; Special Adviser to Sec. of State for Wales, 1990; PPS to Minister of State, FCO, 1993–94. Mem. Welsh Affairs Select Cttee, 1992–93. Contested (C): Carmarthen, 1987; Vale of Glamorgan, May 1989. *Recreations:* Rugby, cricket, walking, games. *Address:* House of Commons, SW1A 0AA. *T:* 0171–219 6591. *Clubs:* Special Forces; Llanelli Rugby.

RICHARDS, Rt. Rev. Ronald Edwin, MA, ThD (*jd*); *b* Ballarat, Vic., 25 Oct. 1908; *s* of Edward and Margaret Elizabeth Richards, Ballarat; *m* 1937, Nancy, *d* of W. E. Lloyd Green; one *d*. *Educ:* Ballarat High Sch.; Trinity Coll., Melbourne Univ. BA 2nd Cl. Hons Phil., 1932, MA 1937; Asst Master, Ballarat C of E Gram. Sch., 1926, Malvern C of E Gram. Sch., 1927–28; deacon, 1932; priest, 1933; Curate of Rokewood, 1932–33, Priest-in-charge, 1934; Priest-in-charge, Lismore, 1934–41 and 1945–46; Chaplain AIF, 1941–45; Vicar of Warrnambool, 1946–50; Archdeacon of Ballarat, and Examining Chapl. to Bp of Ballarat, 1950–57; Vicar-Gen., 1952–57; Bishop of Bendigo, 1957–74. *Address:* Madron, 119 Dare Street, Ocean Grove, Victoria 3226, Australia. *Clubs:* Royal Automobile of Victoria (Melbourne); Barwon Heads Golf.

RICHARDS, Stephen Price; First Junior Treasury Counsel, Common Law, since 1992; *b* 8 Dec. 1950; *s* of Richard Alun Richards, *qv*; *m* 1976, Lucy Elizabeth Stubbings, MA; two *s* one *d*. *Educ:* King's Coll. Sch., Wimbledon; St John's Coll., Oxford (open schol.; BA Lit.Hum. 1972; BA Jurisprudence 1974; MA 1977). Called to the Bar, Gray's Inn, 1975 (Arden Schol. and Bacon Schol.; Bencher, 1992); Second Jun. Counsel, 1987–89, Standing Counsel, 1989–91, to Dir Gen. of Fair Trading; a Jun. Counsel to the Crown, Common Law, 1990–91; an Asst Recorder, 1992–. *Publication:* (ed jtly) Chitty on Contracts, 25th edn 1983, 26th edn 1989. *Recreation:* the Welsh hills. *Address:* 4 Raymond Buildings, Gray's Inn, WC1R 5BP. *T:* 0171–405 7211.

RICHARDS, Vivian; *see* Richards, I. V. A.

RICHARDSON, family name of **Barons Richardson** and **Richardson of Duntisbourne.**

RICHARDSON, Baron *cr* 1979 (Life Peer), of Lee in the County of Devon; **John Samuel Richardson,** 1st Bt, *cr* 1963; Kt 1960; LVO 1943; MD, FRCP; retired; President, General Medical Council, 1973–80; Hon. Consulting Physician: St Thomas' Hospital; King Edward VII's Hospital for Officers; Consultant Emeritus to the Army; Consulting Physician: Metropolitan Police, 1957–80; London Transport Board, since 1964; *b* 16 June 1910; *s* of Major John Watson Richardson, solicitor, and Elizabeth Blakeney, *d* of Sir Samuel Roberts, 1st Bt, both of Sheffield; *m* 1933, Sybil Angela Stephanie (*d* 1991), *d* of A. Ronald Trist, Stanmore; two *d*. *Educ:* Charterhouse; Trinity Coll., Cambridge (Hon. Fellow, 1979); St Thomas' Hosp. (Bristowe Medal; Hadden Prize, 1936; Perkins Fellowship, 1938). MB BChir 1936, MD 1940; MRCP 1937, FRCP 1948; FRCPE 1975. Major, RAMC (temp.), 1939; Lt-Col, RAMC (temp.), 1942. 1st asst, Med. Professorial Unit, St Thomas' Hosp., 1946; Physician to St Thomas' Hosp., 1947–75. Examiner to Univs of Cambridge, London, Manchester, NUI, RCP London and Edinburgh Conjoint Bd. President: Internat. Soc. of Internal Medicine, 1966–70 (Hon. Pres. 1970); Royal Soc. of Medicine, 1969–71 (Hon. Librarian, 1957–63; Pres., Med. Educn Sect., 1967–68); BMA, 1970–71; 2nd Congress, Assoc. Européene de Médicine Interne d'Ensemble, Bad-Godesberg, 1973 (Hon. Mem. 1974); Assoc. for the Study of Med. Educn, 1978–80 (Vice-Pres., 1974–78, Hon. Mem., 1980); Vice-President: Med. Soc. of London, 1961–63 (Hon. Fellow, 1981); Royal Coll. of Nursing, 1972–; Chairman: Jt Consultants Cttee, 1967–72; Council for Postgrad. Med. Educn in England and Wales, 1972–80; Medico-Pharmaceutical Forum, 1973–76; Armed Forces Med. Adv. Bd, MoD, 1975–80. Mem., Bd of Governors, St Thomas's Hosp., 1953–59, 1964–74. Mem. Ct, Soc. of Apothecaries, 1960–85 (Master, 1971–72). Lectures: Lettsomian, Med. Soc. of London, 1963; Scott Heron, Royal Victoria Hosp., Belfast, 1969; Maudsley, RCPsych, 1971; Wilkinson Meml, Inst. of Dental Surgeons, London Univ., 1976; Harveian Oration, RCP, 1978; Orator, Med. Soc. of London, 1981. Hon. Fellow: Swedish Soc. Med. Scis, 1970; RSocMed 1973; Heberden Soc., 1973; Osler Club of London, 1973; Hon. Mem., Assoc. of Clinical Tutors of GB, 1980; Hon. FPS, 1974; Hon. FRCPI 1975; Hon. FFCM 1977; Hon. FRCPsych 1979; Hon. FRCS 1980; Hon. FRCPSG 1980; Hon. FRCPE 1981; Hon. Fellow, UMDS. Hon. Bencher, Gray's Inn, 1974. Hon. DSc: NUI, 1975; Hull, 1981; Hon. DCL Newcastle, 1980; Hon. LLD: Nottingham, 1981, Liverpool, 1983. CStJ 1970. Baron de Lancey Law Prize, RSM, 1978; Gold Medal, BMA, 1982; Guthrie Medal, RAMC, 1982. Editor-in-Chief, British Encylopaedia of Medical Practice, 1970–74. *Publications:* The Practice of Medicine, 2nd edn 1960; Connective Tissue Disorders, 1963; Anticoagulant Prophylaxis and Treatment (jointly), 1965. *Heir* to baronetcy: none. *Address:* Windcutter, Lee, near Ilfracombe, North Devon EX34 8LW. *T:* Ilfracombe (01271) 63198.

RICHARDSON OF DUNTISBOURNE, Baron *cr* 1983 (Life Peer), of Duntisbourne in the County of Gloucestershire; **Gordon William Humphreys Richardson,** KG 1983; MBE 1944; TD 1979; PC 1976; DL; Chairman, Morgan Stanley International Inc., since 1986; Governor, Bank of England, 1973–83, Member, Court of the Bank of England, 1967–83; *b* 25 Nov. 1915; *er s* of John Robert and Nellie Richardson; *m* 1941, Margaret Alison, *er d* of Canon H. R. L. Sheppard; one *s* one *d*. *Educ:* Nottingham High School; Gonville and Caius College, Cambridge (MA, LLB). Commnd S Notts Hussars Yeomanry, 1939; Staff Coll., Camberley, 1941; served until 1946. Called to Bar, Gray's Inn, 1946 (Hon. Bencher, 1973); Mem. Bar Council, 1951–55; ceased practice at Bar, Aug. 1955. Industrial and Commercial Finance Corp. Ltd, 1955–57; Director: J. Henry Schroder & Co., 1957; Lloyds Bank Ltd, 1960–67 (Vice-Chm., 1962–66); Legal and General Assurance Soc., Ltd, 1956–70 (Vice-Chm. 1959–70); Director: Rolls Royce (1971) Ltd, 1971–73; ICI Ltd, 1972–73; Chairman: J. Henry Schroder Wagg & Co. Ltd, 1962–72; Schroders Ltd, 1966–73; Schroders Inc. (NY), 1968–73. Chm., Industrial Develt Adv. Bd, 1972–73. Mem. Company Law Amendment Committee (Jenkins Committee), 1959–62; Chm. Cttee on Turnover Taxation, 1963. Member: Court of London University, 1962–65; NEDC, 1971–73, 1980–83; Trustee, National Gallery, 1971–73, Chm., Pilgrim Trust, 1984–88. One of HM Lieutenants, City of London, 1974–; High Steward of Westminster, 1985–89; DL Glos, 1983. Deputy High Steward, Univ. of Cambridge, 1982–; Hon. Fellow: Gonville and Caius Coll., 1977; Wolfson Coll., Cambridge, 1977. Hon. LLD Cambridge, 1979; Hon. DSc: City Univ., 1976; Aston, 1979; Hon. DCL East Anglia, 1984. Benjamin Franklin Medal, RSA, 1984. *Address:* c/o Morgan Stanley UK Group, 25 Cabot Square, Canary Wharf, E14 4QA. *T:* 0171–425 8004. *Clubs:* Athenæum, Brooks's.

See also Sir John Riddell, Bt.

RICHARDSON, Anthony; *see* Richardson, H. A.

RICHARDSON, Sir Anthony (Lewis), 3rd Bt *cr* 1924; *b* 5 Aug. 1950; *s* of Sir Leslie Lewis Richardson, 2nd Bt, and of Joy Patricia, Lady Richardson, *d* of P. J. Rillstone, Johannesburg; *S* father, 1985; *m* 1985, Honor Gillian Dauney; one *s* one *d*. *Educ:* Diocesan College, Cape Town, S Africa. Stockbroker with L. Messel & Co., London, 1973–75; Insurance Broker with C. T. Bowring, London and Johannesburg, 1975–76; Stockbroker with Fergusson Bros, Hall, Stewart & Co., Johannesburg and Cape Town, 1976–78; Stockbroker with W. Greenwell & Co., London, 1979–81; with Rowe & Pitman, subseq. S. G. Warburg Securities, London, 1981– (Dir, 1986–), seconded to Potter Partners, Melbourne and Sydney, 1986–89. *Recreations:* various sports, photography. *Heir: s* William Lewis Richardson, *b* 15 Oct. 1992. *Address:* 7 Westover Road, SW18 2RE. *Clubs:* Boodle's, Hurlingham.

RICHARDSON, David; Director, London Office, International Labour Organisation, 1982–91; *b* 24 April 1928; *s* of Harold George Richardson and Madeleine Raphaële Richardson (*née* Lebret); *m* 1951, Frances Joan Pring; three *s* one *d*. *Educ:* Wimbledon Coll.; King's Coll., London (BA Hons). FIPM 1986. RAF, 1949. Unilever, 1951. Inland Revenue, 1953; Min. of Labour, 1956; Sec., Construction Industry Training Bd, 1964; Chm., Central Youth Employment Exec., 1969; Royal Coll. of Defence Studies, 1971; Under Sec., Dept of Employment, 1972; Dir, Safety and Gen. Gp, Health and Safety Exec., 1975; Dir and Sec., ACAS, 1977. Director: The Tablet, 1985–; Industrial Training Service Ltd, 1987–93. *Recreations:* music, walking, landscape gardening, ceramics. *Address:* 183 Banstead Road, Carshalton, Surrey SM5 4DP. *T:* 0181–241 4614.

RICHARDSON, Elliot Lee; Partner, Milbank, Tweed, Hadley & McCloy, Washington DC, 1980–92; *b* 20 July 1920; *s* of Dr Edward P. and Clara Lee Richardson; *m* 1952, Anne F. Hazard; two *s* one *d*. *Educ:* Harvard Coll.; Harvard Law Sch. BA 1941, LLB 1947, *cum laude*. Served with US Army, 1942–45 (Lieut): litter-bearer platoon ldr, 4th Inf. Div., Normandy Landing (Bronze Star, Purple Heart). Law clerk, 1947–49; Assoc., Ropes, Gray, Best, Coolidge and Rugg, lawyers, Boston, 1949–53 and 1955–56; Asst to Senator Saltonstall, Washington, 1953 and 1954; Asst Sec. for Legislation of Dept of Health, Educn and Welfare, 1957–59 (Actg Sec., April-July 1958); US Attorney for Massachusetts, 1959–61; Special Asst to Attorney General of US, 1961; Partner, Ropes & Gray, 1961–62 and 1963–64; Lieut Governor of Mass, 1964; Attorney General of Mass, 1966; Under Sec. of State, 1969–70; Sec. of Health, Educn and Welfare, 1970–73; Sec. of Defense, Jan.–May 1973; Attorney General of US, May-Oct. 1973, resigned; Ambassador to UK, 1975–76; Sec. of Commerce, 1976–77; Ambassador-at-large and Special Rep. of the US Pres. to the Law of the Sea Conf., 1977–80. Special Rep. of Pres. for multilateral assistance initiative for the Philippines, 1989–94; Personal Rep. of UN Sec. for monitoring electoral process in Nicaragua, 1989–90. Fellow, Woodrow Wilson Internat. Center for Scholars, 1973–74. Holds numerous hon. degrees. *Publications:* The Creative Balance, 1976; numerous articles on law, social services and govt policy. *Address:* 1100 Crest Lane, McLean, VA 22101, USA.

RICHARDSON, Sir Eric; *see* Richardson, Sir J. E.

RICHARDSON, Maj.-Gen. Frank McLean, CB 1960; DSO 1941; OBE 1945; MD; FRCPE; Director Medical Services, BAOR, 1956–61; *b* 3 March 1904; *s* of late Col Hugh Richardson, DSO, and of Elizabeth Richardson; *m* 1944, Sylvia Innes, *d* of Col S. A. Innes, DSO; two *s* one *d*. *Educ:* Glenalmond; Edinburgh Univ. MB, ChB 1926. MD 1938. FRCPE 1986. Joined RAMC, 1927; Captain 1930; Major 1936; Lt-Col 1945; Col 1949; Brig. 1956; Maj.-Gen. 1957. Honorary Surgeon to the Queen, 1957–61. Hon. Col 51 (H) Div. Dist RAMC, TA, 1963–67. *Publications:* Napoleon: Bisexual Emperor, 1972; Napoleon's Death: An Inquest, 1974; Fighting Spirit: psychological factors in war, 1978; The Public and the Bomb, 1981; Mars without Venus: a study of some homosexual Generals, 1981; (with S. MacNeill) Piobaireachd and its Interpretation, 1987. *Address:* c/o Royal Bank of Scotland, Kirkland House, SW1; 4B Barnton Avenue West, Edinburgh EH4 6DE.

RICHARDSON, George Barclay, CBE 1978; Warden, Keble College, Oxford, 1989–94 (Hon. Fellow, 1994); Pro-Vice-Chancellor, Oxford University, 1988–94; *b* 19 Sept. 1924; *s* of George and Christina Richardson; *m* 1957, Isabel Alison Chalk; two *s*. *Educ:* Aberdeen Central Secondary Sch. and other schs in Scotland; Aberdeen Univ.; Corpus Christi Coll., Oxford (Hon. Fellow, 1987). BSc Physics and Maths, 1944 (Aberdeen); MA (Oxon) PPE 1949. Admty Scientific Res. Dept, 1944; Lieut, RNVR, 1945. Intell. Officer, HQ Intell. Div. BAOR, 1946–47; Third Sec., HM Foreign Service, 1949; Student, Nuffield Coll., Oxford, 1950; Fellow, St John's Coll., Oxford, 1951–89, Hon. Fellow, 1989; University Reader in Economics, Oxford, 1969–73; Sec. to Delegates and Chief Exec., OUP, 1974–88 (Deleg., 1971–74). Economic Advr, UKAEA, 1968–74. Member: Economic Develt Cttee for Electrical Engineering Industry, 1964–73; Monopolies Commn, 1969–74; Royal Commn on Environmental Pollution, 1973–74; Council, Publishers Assoc., 1981–87. Mem., UK Delegation, CSCE Cultural Forum, 1985. Visitor, Ashmolean Mus., 1992–. Hon. DCL Oxon, 1988. *Publications:* Information and Investment, 1960, 2nd edn 1991; Economic Theory, 1964; articles in academic jls. *Address:* 33 Belsyre Court, Oxford OX2 6HU. *Club:* United Oxford & Cambridge University.

RICHARDSON, George Taylor; Chairman and Managing Director, James Richardson & Sons, Limited, Winnipeg, Canada, since 1993 (President 1966–93; Vice-President 1954); Hon. Chairman, Richardson Greenshields of Canada Ltd; *b* 22 Sept. 1924; *s* of late James Armstrong Richardson and Muriel (*née* Sprague); *m* 1948, Tannis Maree Thorlakson; two *s* one *d*. *Educ:* Grosvenor Sch. and Ravenscourt Sch. Winnipeg; Univ. of Manitoba (BComm). Joined family firm of James Richardson & Sons Ltd, 1946. Dir of cos owned by James Richardson & Sons Ltd; Director: Inco Ltd; Du Pont Canada Inc. Member: Chicago Bd of Trade; Chicago Mercantile Exchange; Winnipeg Commodity Exchange. Hon. Dir, Canada's Aviation Hall of Fame. Hon. LLD: Manitoba; Winnipeg. *Recreations:* hunting, helicopter flying. *Address:* (business) James Richardson & Sons, Limited, Richardson Building, One Lombard Place, Winnipeg, Manitoba R3B 0Y1, Canada. *T:* (904) 9345811. *Clubs:* Manitoba, St Charles (Winnipeg); Vancouver (Vancouver); Toronto (Toronto).

RICHARDSON, (Henry) Anthony; a Recorder of the Crown Court, since 1978; a Deputy Traffic Commissioner and a Deputy Licensing Authority, North Eastern Traffic Area, 1989–93; barrister; *b* 28 Dec. 1925; *er s* of late Thomas Ewan Richardson and Jessie (*née* Preston), Batley, W Yorks; *m* 1954, Georgina (*née* Lawford), *d* of Rosamond Bedford and step *d* of Gp Captain G. R. Bedford, MB, ChB, RAF retd. *Educ:* Giggleswick Sch.; Leeds Univ. (LLB 1950, LLM 1956). Called to the Bar, Lincoln's Inn, 1951; North-Eastern Circuit; Dep. Circuit Judge, 1972–78. Chm., a Police Disciplinary Appeal Tribunal, 1983. *Publications:* articles in legal periodicals. *Recreations:* walking, gardening, listening to music. *Address:* (home) Grey Thatch, Wetherby Road, Scarcroft, Leeds LS14 3BB. *T:* Leeds (0113) 289 2555; (chambers) 37 Park Square, Leeds LS1 2NZ. *T:* Leeds (0113) 243 9422.

RICHARDSON, Horace Vincent, OBE 1968; HM Diplomatic Service, retired; *b* 28 Oct. 1913; *s* of late Arthur John Alfred Richardson and late Mrs Margaret Helena Jane Richardson (*née* Hooson); *m* 1942, Margery Tebbutt; two *s* one *d* (and one *d* decd). *Educ:* Abergele Grammar Sch.; King's Coll., London (LLB). Served with Army, 1940–45. LCC, 1931–35; Supreme Court of Judicature, 1935–47; FO, 1947–48; British Vice-Consul, Shanghai, 1948–50; Washington, 1950–53; 2nd Sec., Rome, 1953–56; FO, 1956–61; Consul, Philadelphia, 1961–63; FO, 1963–66; Consul, Cairo, 1966–68; 1st Sec., Washington, 1968–70; Head of Nationality and Treaty Dept, FCO, 1970–73. Rep. HM Govt at 9th and 10th Sessions of Hague Conf. of Private Internat. Law. FRGS. *Recreations:* golf, gardening. *Address:* 34 Friern Barnet Lane, N11 3LX. *T:* 0181–368 1983. *Clubs:* MCC, Civil Service; Turf (Cairo); Highgate Golf.

RICHARDSON, Hugh; Director, Rights and Obligations, Directorate General for Personnel and Administration, European Commission, since 1991; *b* 12 May 1947; *s* of Robert Richardson and Pauline (*née* Broadhurst); *m* (separated); two *s* two *d*. *Educ:* Pembroke Coll., Oxford (BA 1969; BCL 1970). Commission of the European Communities: with Secretariat Gen., 1974–79; Directorate-Gen. for External Relns, 1979–84; Counsellor and Dep. Head, Tokyo Delegn, 1984–88; Asst to DG for External Relns, 1988–91. *Publication:* EC-Japan Relations: after adolescence, 1989. *Recreations:* sailing, ski-ing, running. *Address:* Commission of the European Communities, 200 rue de la Loi, 1049 Brussels, Belgium. *T:* (2) 2959096.

RICHARDSON, Hugh Edward, CIE 1947; OBE 1944; *b* 22 Dec. 1905; *s* of Hugh Richardson, DSO, MD, and Elizabeth (*née* McLean); *m* 1951, Huldah (*née* Walker), *widow* of Maj.-Gen. T. G. Rennie, Black Watch, killed in action 1945. *Educ:* Trinity College, Glenalmond; Keble College, Oxford (Hon. Fellow, 1981). Entered Indian Civil Service, 1930; SDO, Tamluk, Midnapore Dist, Bengal, 1932–34; entered Foreign and Political Service of Govt of India, 1934; APA Loralai, Baluchistan, 1934–35; British Trade Agent, Gyantse, and O-in-C British Mission, Lhasa, 1936–40; service in NWFP, 1940–42; 1st Sec. Indian Agency-General in China, Chungking, 1942–43; Dep. Sec. to Govt of India, EA Dept, 1944–45; British Trade Agent, Gyantse, and O-in-C, British Mission, Lhasa, 1946–47; Indian Trade Agent, Gyantse and Officer-in-charge, Indian Mission, Lhasa, 1947–50. Retd from ICS, 1950. Hon. FBA 1986. Hon. DLitt St Andrews, 1985. *Publications:* Tibet and its History, 1962; (with D. L. Snellgrove) A Cultural History of Tibet, 1968; A Corpus of Early Tibetan Inscriptions, 1985; Ceremonies of the Lhasa Year, 1993. *Recreation:* golf. *Address:* c/o Grindlay's Bank, 13 St James's Square, SW1Y 4LF. *Club:* Royal and Ancient Golf (St Andrews).

RICHARDSON, Ian William, CBE 1989; actor; *b* 7 April 1934; *s* of John Richardson and Margaret Drummond; *m* 1961, Maroussia Frank; two *s*. *Educ:* Tynecastle; Edinburgh; Univ. of Glasgow. Studied for stage at Coll. of Dramatic Art, Glasgow (James Bridie Gold Medal, 1957). FRSAMD 1971. Joined Birmingham Repertory Theatre Co. 1958 (leading parts incl. Hamlet); joined Shakespeare Meml Theatre Co. (later RSC), 1960; rôles, Stratford and Aldwych, 1960–: Arragon in Merchant of Venice; Sir Andrew Aguecheek, 1960; Malatesti in Duchess of Malfi, 1960; Oberon in A Midsummer Night's Dream, 1961; Tranio in Taming of the Shrew, 1961; the Doctor in The Representative, 1963; Edmund in King Lear, 1964; Antipholus of Ephesus in Comedy of Errors, 1964; Herald and Marat in Marat/Sade, 1964, 1965; Ithamore, The Jew of Malta, 1964; Ford, Merry Wives of Windsor, 1964, 1966, 1969; Antipholus of Syracuse in Comedy of Errors, 1965; Chorus, Henry V, 1965; Vindice, The Revengers Tragedy, 1965, 1969; Coriolanus, 1966; Bertram, All's Well That Ends Well, 1966; Malcolm, Macbeth, 1966; Cassius, Julius Caesar, 1968; Pericles, 1969; Angelo, Measure for Measure, 1970; Buckingham, Richard III, 1970; Proteus, Two Gentlemen of Verona, 1970; Prospero, The Tempest, 1970; Richard II/Bolingbroke, Richard II, 1973; Berowne, Love's Labour's Lost, 1973; Iachimo, Cymbeline, 1974; Shalimov, Summer Folk, 1974; Ford, Merry Wives of Windsor, 1975; Richard III, 1975; tours with RSC: Europe and USSR, NY, 1964; NY, 1965; USSR, 1966; Japan, 1970; NY, 1974, 1975; Tom Wrench in musical Trelawny, Sadler's Wells, 1971–72; Professor Higgins, My Fair Lady, Broadway, 1976 (Drama Desk Award, 1976); Jack Tanner, in Man and Superman, and Doctor in The Millionairess, Shaw Festival Theatre, Niagara, Ont; The Government Inspector, Old Vic, 1979; Romeo and Juliet, Old Vic, 1979; Lolita, Broadway, 1981; The Miser, Chichester, 1995. *Films:* Captain Fitzroy in The Darwin Adventure, 1971; Priest in Man of la Mancha, 1972; Montgomery in Ike—the War Years, 1978; Charlie Muffin, 1979; The Sign of Four, 1982; Hound of the Baskervilles, 1982; Brazil, 1984; Whoops Apocalypse, 1987; The Fourth Protocol, 1987; Burning Secret, 1989; The Year of the Comet, 1992; M. Butterfly, 1994; Words upon the Window Pane, 1995. *Television: plays:* Danton's Death, 1978; Churchill and the Generals, 1979; A Cotswold Death, Passing Through, 1981; Russian Night, Kisch-Kisch, Beauty and the Beast, Salad Days, 1982; Slimming Down, 1984; Star Quality, 1985; The Devil's Disciple, 1987; The Winslow Boy, 1989; An Ungentlemanly Act, 1992; *films:* Monsignor Quixote, 1985; Blunt, 1987; Rosencrantz and Guildenstern Are Dead, 1990; *serials and series:* Eyeless in Gaza, 1971; Tinker, Tailor, Soldier, Spy, 1979; Private Schulz, 1981; The Woman in White, 1982; Ramsay Macdonald, in Number 10, 1982; The Master of Ballantrae, 1984; Six Centuries of Verse, 1984; Mistral's Daughter, 1985; Nehru, in Mountbatten—the last Viceroy, 1986; Porterhouse Blue, 1987; Troubles, 1988; Twist of Fate, 1989; Under a Dark Angel's Eye, 1989; Phantom of the Opera, 1990; The Plot to Kill Hitler, 1990; The Gravy Train, 1990; House of Cards, 1990 (BAFTA Best Actor Award, 1991); The Gravy Train Goes East, 1991; To Play the King, 1993; Remember, 1994; Catherine the Great, 1994. RTS Award, 1982. *Publication:* Preface to Cymbeline (Folio Soc.), 1976. *Recreations:* music, exploring churches and castles. *Address:* c/o London Management, 2–4 Noel Street, W1V 3RB. *T:* 0171–237 9000. *Club:* Garrick.

RICHARDSON, Rt. Hon. Sir Ivor (Lloyd Morgan), Kt 1986; PC 1978; SJD; **Rt. Hon. Mr Justice Richardson;** Judge, Court of Appeal of New Zealand, since 1977; *b* 24 May 1930; *s* of W. T. Richardson; *m* 1955, Jane, *d* of I. J. Krchma; three *d*. *Educ:* Canterbury Univ. (LLB); Univ. of Mich (LLM, SJD). Partner, Macalister Bros, Invercargill, 1957–63; Crown Counsel, Crown Law Office, Wellington, 1963–66; Prof. of Law, Victoria Univ. of Wellington, 1967–73 (Dean of Law Faculty, 1968–71; Pro-Chancellor, 1979–84; Chancellor, 1984–86); Partner, Watts & Patterson, Wellington, 1973–77. Chm., Cttees of Inquiry into Inflation Accounting, 1975–76, into Solicitors Nominee Cos, 1983. Chairman: Council of Legal Educn, 1983–92; Royal Commn on Social Policy, 1986–88; Orgnl Rev. of Inland Revenue Dept, 1993–94. Hon. LLD: Canterbury, 1987; Victoria, 1989. *Publications:* books and articles on legal subjects. *Address:* 29 Duthie Street, Wellington 5, New Zealand. *T:* (4) 4769310. *Club:* Wellington (Wellington, NZ).

RICHARDSON, Hon. James Armstrong, PC (Can.); President, Jarco Ltd; Chairman, Max Bell Foundation; *b* Winnipeg, Manitoba, 28 March 1922; *s* of James Armstrong Richardson and Muriel Sprague; *m* 1949, Shirley Anne, *d* of John Rooper, Shamley Green, Surrey, England; two *s* three *d*. *Educ:* St John's-Ravenscourt, Winnipeg; Queen's Univ., Kingston, Ont. (BA). Pilot with No 10 BR Sqdn, before entering family firm of James Richardson & Sons, Ltd, Winnipeg, Oct. 1945; he was Chm. and Chief Exec. Officer of this company, but resigned to enter public life, 1968. MP (L), June 1968 (re-elected Oct. 1972, July 1974); Minister, Canadian Federal Cabinet, July 1968; Minister of Supply and Services, May 1969; Minister of Nat. Defence, 1972–76; resigned from Federal Cabinet over constitutional language issue, Oct. 1976; crossed floor of House to sit as an Independent MP, 27 June 1978. Hon. Pres., Commonwealth Games Assoc. of Canada, Inc. *Address:* 407 Bower Boulevard, Winnipeg, Manitoba R3P 0L6, Canada.
See also G. T. Richardson.

RICHARDSON, Rev. Canon James John; Priest-in-Charge of Great Brington, Whilton and Norton (Northampton), diocese of Peterborough, since 1993 and of East Haddon and Holdenby, Church and Chapel Brampton and Harlestone, since 1994; *b* 28 March 1941; *s* of late James John Richardson and of Gladys May (*née* Evans); *m* 1966, Janet Rosemary Welstand; two *s* one *d*. *Educ:* Catford Central Sch.; Hull Univ. (BA); Sheffield Univ. (DipEd); Cuddesdon Coll., Oxford; MA Leicester 1995. Assistant Master, Westfield Comp. Sch., Sheffield, 1964–66; Curate, St Peter's Collegiate Church, Wolverhampton, 1969–72; Priest i/c, All Saints, Hanley, Stoke-on-Trent, 1972–75; Rector of Nantwich, 1975–82; Vicar of Leeds, 1982–88; Exec. Dir, CCJ, 1988–92. Hon. Canon, 1982–88, Canon Emeritus, 1988–, Ripon Cathedral. Chaplain: to Earl Spencer, 1993–; to High Sheriff of Northants, 1995–96. Chm., Racial Harrassment Commn, Leeds, 1986–87; N of England Vice-Pres., UN Year of Peace, 1986–87. Member: Council, Centre for the Study of Judaism and Jewish/Christian Relations, Selly Oak Coll., 1989–94; Internat. Council of Christians and Jews Adv. Cttee, 1992–. Mem. Court, Leeds Univ., 1986–88; Chairman of Governors: Abbey Grange High Sch., Leeds, 1982–86; Leeds Grammar Sch., 1983–88; Governor: Leeds Girls' High Sch., 1982–88; Leeds Music Fest., 1982–88. FRSA 1991. *Publications:* (contrib.) Four Score Years, 1989; contrib. Yorkshire Post, 1982–90. *Recreations:* leading pilgrimages to Israel, biography—especially life and times of Rupert Brooke, deciphering Elizabethan churchwardens' accounts. *Address:* The Rectory, Great Brington, Northampton NN7 4JB. *T:* Northampton (01604) 770402.

RICHARDSON, Joanna, MA Oxon; FRSL; author; *o d* of late Frederick Richardson and late Charlotte Elsa (*née* Benjamin). *Educ:* The Downs School, Seaford; St Anne's College, Oxford. Contributions to BBC include: translated plays; interviews; numerous features for Radios 3 and 4. Mem. Council, Royal Soc. of Literature, 1961–86. Chevalier de l'Ordre des Arts et des Lettres, 1987. *Publications include:* Fanny Brawne: a biography, 1952; Théophile Gautier: his Life and Times, 1958; Edward FitzGerald, 1960; (ed) FitzGerald: Selected Works, 1962; The Pre-Eminent Victorian: a study of Tennyson, 1962; The Everlasting Spell: a study of Keats and his Friends, 1963; (ed) Essays by Divers Hands (trans. Royal Soc. Lit.), 1963; introd. to Victor Hugo: Choses Vues (The Oxford Lib. of French Classics), 1964; Edward Lear, 1965; George IV: a Portrait, 1966; Creevey and Greville, 1967; Princess Mathilde, 1969; Verlaine, 1971; Enid Starkie, 1973; (ed and trans.) Verlaine, Poems, 1974; Stendhal: a critical biography, 1974; (ed and trans.) Baudelaire, Poems, 1975; Victor Hugo, 1976; Zola, 1978; Keats and his Circle: an album of portraits, 1980; (trans.) Gautier, Mademoiselle de Maupin, 1981; The Life and Letters of John Keats, 1981; Letters from Lambeth: the correspondence of the Reynolds family with John Freeman Milward Dovaston 1808–1815, 1981; Colette, 1983; Judith Gautier, 1987 (trans. French 1989; Prix Goncourt for Biography); Portrait of a Bonaparte: the life and times of Joseph-Napoleon Primoli 1851–1927, 1987; Baudelaire, 1994; has contributed to The Times, The Times Literary Supplement, Sunday Times, Spectator, New Statesman, New York Times Book Review, The Washington Post, French Studies, French Studies Bulletin, Modern Language Review, Keats-Shelley Memorial Bulletin, etc. *Recreations:* antique-collecting, sketching. *Address:* 55 Flask Walk, NW3 1EY. *T:* 0171–435 5156.

RICHARDSON, John Charles; Managing Director, Historical Publications Ltd, since 1975; *b* 7 June 1935; *s* of Joseph and Vera Richardson; *m* 1st, 1957, Laura Caroline Bourne Webb (marr. diss. 1962); two *s*; 2nd, 1967, Elizabeth Noel Ballard (marr. diss. 1981); two *s*; 3rd, 1981, Helen Warnock English. *Educ:* Barking Abbey GS. J. Walter Thompson, 1965–72; KMP, 1974–84. Member: St Pancras BC, 1959–66; Camden BC, 1966–71. Joint Founder: GLAA, 1966; Camden Arts Centre, 1966; Chm., Bubble Theatre Co., 1968–74. Chm., Camden Hist. Soc., 1970–. *Publications:* The Local Historian's Encyclopedia, 1974; Covent Garden, 1979; Highgate: its history since the fifteenth century, 1983; Hampstead One Thousand, 1985; Islington Past, 1986; Highgate Past, 1989; Camden Town and Primrose Hill Past, 1991; London and its People, 1995; Covent Garden Past, 1995. *Recreations:* visiting the London Library, architecture. *Address:* 32 Ellington Street, N7 8PL. *T:* 0171–607 1628.

RICHARDSON, John David Benbow, CBE 1988; MC 1942, and Bar 1943; President, Northern Rent Assessment Panel, since 1979 (Vice-President, 1968–79); *b* 6 April 1919; *s* of His Honour Judge Thomas Richardson, OBE, and Winifred Ernestine (*née* Templer); *m* 1946, Kathleen Mildred (*née* Price-Turner); four *s*. *Educ:* Harrow; Clare Coll., Cambridge. Called to Bar, Middle Temple, 1947. Served War of 1939–45, as Captain in King's Dragoon Guards (wounded; MC and Bar). ADC to Governor of South Australia (Lt-Gen. Sir Willoughby Norrie, later Lord Norrie), 1946–47. Dep. Chm., Durham County Quarter Sessions, 1964–71, and Recorder, 1972–73. Mem., Police Complaints Bd, 1977–82. *Recreations:* fishing, gardening, golf. *Address:* The Old Vicarage, Nine Banks, Whitfield, near Hexham, Northumberland NE47 8DB. *T:* Hexham (01434) 345217. *Clubs:* MCC; York County Stand; Northern Counties (Newcastle upon Tyne).

RICHARDSON, Sir (John) Eric, Kt 1967; CBE 1962; PhD, DSc, BEng, CEng, FIEE, MIMechE, FBHI, FBOA, FPS; FRSA; Director, The Polytechnic of Central London, 1969–70; *b* 30 June 1905; *e surv. s* of late William and Mary Elizabeth Richardson, Birkenhead; *m* 1941, Alice May, *d* of H. M. Wilson, Hull; one *s* two *d* (and one *d* decd). *Educ:* Birkenhead Higher Elementary Sch.; Liverpool Univ. BEng 1st Cl. Hons, 1931, PhD 1933, Liverpool. Chief Lectr in Electrical Engineering, 1933–37, Head of Engineering Dept, 1937–41, Hull Municipal Technical Coll.; Principal: Oldham Municipal Technical Coll., 1942–44; Royal Technical Coll., Salford, 1944–47; Northampton Polytechnic, London, EC1, 1947–56; Dir Nat. Coll. of Horology and Instrument Technology, 1947–56; Dir of Educn, Regent Street Polytechnic, W1, 1957–69. Hon. Sec., Assoc. of Technical Insts, 1957–67, Chm., 1967–68; Pres. Assoc. of Principals of Technical Instns, 1961–62; Dep. Chm., Council for Overseas Colls of Arts, Science and Technology, 1949–62; Member: Council for Tech. Educn and Trng in Overseas Countries, 1962–73 (Chm. Technical Educn Cttee, 1971–73); and Vice-Chm. Council and Cttees, London and Home Counties Regional Adv. Council for Technol Educn, 1972–84; Chm., Adv. Cttee on Educn for Management, 1961–66; Pres. and Chm., CICRIS, 1972–89; Member: Governing Council of Nigerian Coll. of Art, Science and Technology, 1953–61; Council, Univ. Coll., Nairobi, 1961–70; Provisional Council, Univ. of East Africa, 1961–63; Governing Body, College of Aeronautics, Cranfield, 1956–59; Council of British

Horological Institute, 1951–56; Gen. Optical Council, 1959–78 (Chm., 1975–78); Assoc. of Optical Practitioners (Vice-Pres., 1983–84; Pres., 1984–); Science and Technol Cttee of CNAA, 1965–71; Electrical Engrg Bd of CNAA (Chm.); Industrial Trg Bd for Electricity Supply Industry, 1965–71; Univ. and Polytechnic Grants Cttee, Hong Kong, 1972–77; Council, RSA, 1968–78 (Chm. Exams Cttee, 1969–78, Hon. Treasurer, 1974–78); Council and Exec. Cttee, Leprosy Mission, 1970–84 (Chm., 1974–84; Vice-Pres., 1984–); Council and Exec. Cttee, City and Guilds of London Inst., 1969–80 (Chm. Policy and Overseas Cttees; Vice-Chm. Technical Educn Cttee; Jt Hon. Sec., 1970–80; Vice-Pres., 1979–82; Hon. FCGI 1981); Chm., Ealing Civic Soc., 1972–76. Chairman: Africa Evangelical Fellowship (SAGM), 1950–70; Nat. Young Life Campaign, 1949–64; Council, Inter-Varsity Fellowship of Evangelical Unions, 1966–69; Pres., Crusaders Union, 1972–86. Chm. Governors, Clarendon Sch., Abergele, 1971–75; Governor, London Bible Coll., 1968– (Chm., 1970–77; Pres., 1978–90). *Publications:* paper in IEE Jl (Instn Prize); various papers on higher technological education in UK and Nigeria. *Recreations:* gardening, photography. *Address:* 73 Delamere Road, Ealing, W5 3JP. *T:* 0181–567 1588.

RICHARDSON, John Eric, MS; FRCS; Surgeon: The London Hospital, 1949–81; The Royal Masonic Hospital, 1960–81; King Edward VII's Hospital for Officers, 1960–81; Prince of Wales Hospital, Tottenham, N15, 1958–65; former Consultant Surgeon to the Navy; *b* Loughborough, 24 February 1916; *s* of late C. G. Richardson, MD, FRCS; *m* 1st, 1943, Elisabeth Jean (*d* 1991), *d* of late Rev. John Webster; one *s* one *d*; 2nd, 1994, Bettine, *widow* of R. O. B. Long. *Educ:* Clifton College; London Hospital. MB, BS London (Hons and Distinction, Pathology), 1939; MRCS, LRCP 1939. Andrew Clarke Prize, London Hosp., 1939. Resident Appointments, London Hospital and Poplar Hospital, 1939–41; Surgeon Lieut RNVR, HMS Prince of Wales (Surgical Specialist), 1941–46; Surgical Registrar, London Hosp., 1946–47; Rockefeller Travelling Fellow, 1947–48; Research Fellow in Surgery, Harvard Univ., 1947–48; Fellow in Clinical Surgery, Massachusetts Gen. Hosp., Boston, Mass, 1947–48. Surgeon, St Andrews Hosp., Dollis Hill, 1965–73. Mem., Med. Appeal Tribunal, 1980–88. Hunterian Prof., RCS, 1953; Lettsomian Lectr, Med. Soc. of London, 1973. Pres., Med. Soc. of London, 1974–75. Examr in Surgery to Soc. of Apothecaries, London, 1959–67 and Univ. of London, 1962–63, 1965–66. Mem., Bd of Governors, London Hosp., 1964–73. *Publications:* contrib. to Lancet, BMJ and Brit. Jl of Surgery on gastro-enterology and endocrine disease. *Address:* Swallowfield Park, Swallowfield, Reading RG7 1TG. *T:* Reading (01734) 886156.

RICHARDSON, John Francis; Director and Chief Executive, National & Provincial Building Society, 1985–86; *b* 16 June 1934; *s* of Francis and Stella Richardson; *m* 1960, Jacqueline Mary Crosby; two *d*. *Educ:* Wadham College, Oxford (PPE). FCBSI. Burnley Building Society, 1959–82; Chief General Manager, 1980–82; Dep. Chief Executive, National & Provincial Building Society, 1983–85. Pres., CBSI, 1985. *Recreations:* golf, gardening, military history. *Address:* Low Gables, Spofforth Hill, Wetherby, West Yorks LS22 4SF. *Club:* Pannal Golf.

RICHARDSON, Rt. Rev. John Henry; *see* Bedford, Bishop Suffragan of.

RICHARDSON, Very Rev. John Stephen; Provost of Bradford Cathedral, since 1990; *b* 2 April 1950; *s* of James Geoffrey and Myra Richardson; *m* 1972, Elizabeth Susan Wiltshire; one *s* two *d* (and one *s* decd). *Educ:* Haslingden Grammar Sch.; Univ. of Southampton (BA Hons Theology); St John's Theological Coll., Nottingham. Deacon 1974, priest 1975; Asst Curate, St Michael's, Bramcote, 1974–77; Priest-in-Charge, Emmanuel Church, Radipole and Melcombe Regis, 1977–80; Asst Diocesan Missioner and Lay Trainer Adviser, dio. of Salisbury and Priest-in-Charge of Stinsford, Winterborne Monkton and Winterborne Came with Witcombe, 1980–83; Vicar of Christ Church, Nailsea, 1983–90; Adviser in Evangelism, dio. of Bath and Wells, 1985–90. Bishop's Selector, ABM, 1993–. Mem., General Synod, 1993–. Member: Exec. Bd, Common Purpose, 1992–; BBC North Adv. Panel, 1990–94; Bradford Breakthrough, 1992–; Council, Evangelical Alliance Management Gp, 1994–. Mem. Council, Bradford Chamber of Commerce, 1992–. Trustee: Acorn Healing Trust, 1990–; Spennithorne Hall, 1990–. Council Mem., St John's Theological Coll., Nottingham, 1988–94; Governor: Bradford Grammar Sch., 1990–; Giggleswick Sch., 1993–; Fairfax Sch., 1994–. Chaplain to High Sheriff, W Yorks, 1994–95. MInstD 1994. *Publication:* Ten Rural Churches, 1988. *Recreations:* football, cricket, North Western Municipal Bus Operators, walking, writing, broadcasting. *Address:* The Provost's House, 1 Cathedral Close, Bradford BD1 4EG. *T:* Bradford (01274) 732023, *Fax:* Bradford (01274) 722898. *Clubs:* National Liberal; Bradford (Bradford).

RICHARDSON, Rev. Kathleen Margaret; Moderator, Free Church Federal Council, since 1995; a President, Churches Together in England, since 1995; Co-ordinating Secretary, Unit for Inter-Church and Other Relationships, Methodist Church, since 1995; *b* 24 Feb. 1938; *d* of Francis and Margaret Fountain; *m* 1964, Ian David Godfrey Richardson; three *d*. *Educ:* St Helena Sch., Chesterfield; Stockwell Coll. (Cert Ed); Deaconess Coll., Ilkley; Wesley House, Cambridge. School teacher, 1958–61. Wesley Deaconess, Champness Hall, Rochdale, 1961–64; Lay Worker, Team Ministry, Stevenage, 1973–77; Minister, Denby Dale and Clayton West Circuit, 1979–87; ordained presbyter, 1980; Chm., West Yorks Dist, 1987–95. Pres., Methodist Conf., 1992–93. Hon. DLitt Bradford, 1994. *Recreations:* reading, needlework, homemaking.

RICHARDSON, Kenneth Augustus, CVO 1994; CBE 1989; JP; Secretary to the Cabinet, Bermuda, 1984–93; *b* 13 Feb. 1939; *s* of Augustus J. Richardson; *m* 1966, Brenda Joyce (*née* Smith); one *s* one *d*. *Educ:* Howard Univ., Washington DC (BSc); Manchester Polytechnic (Dip. Personnel Admin and Labour Relations). Teacher, Sandys Secondary School, Bermuda, 1964; Admin. Cadet, Colonial Sec.'s Office, 1967; Training and Recruitment Officer, Bermuda Govt, 1969; Perm. Sec., Labour and Home Affairs, 1974. MIPM 1973; MInstD 1988. JP 1984. *Recreations:* sport (soccer, tennis). *Address:* Mahogany, 19 Trimingham Hill, Paget, Bermuda; PO Box HM 1703, Hamilton HM GX, Bermuda. *T:* 236 1788.

RICHARDSON, Margaret Ann; Curator, Sir John Soane's Museum, since 1995 (Assistant Curator, 1985–95); *b* 11 Sept. 1937; *d* of late James Ballard and Edna (*née* Johnstone); *m* 1963, Anthony George Richardson; two *d*. *Educ:* Harrogate Coll.; University Coll. London (BA Hons); Courtauld Inst. of Art (Acad. Dip.). Asst Curator, 1963–68, Jt Dep. Curator, 1972–85, Drawings Collection, British Architectural Liby. Pres., Twentieth Century Soc., 1995– (Mem. Cttee, 1984–); Trustee: Save Britain's Heritage, 1975–; Lutyens Trust, 1984– (Chm., 1994–). Hon. FRIBA 1994. *Publications:* (ed) RIBA Catalogue series, vols A, B, C–F, and S, 1969–76; Edwin Lutyens, 1973; Lutyens and the Sea Captain, 1981; (jtly) Great Drawings from the RIBA, 1983; Architects of the Arts and Crafts Movement, 1983; 66 Portland Place: the London headquarters of the RIBA, 1984; (jtly) The Art of the Architect, 1984; Sketches by Lutyens, 1994. *Address:* Sir John Soane's Museum, 13 Lincoln's Inn Fields, WC2A 3BP. *T:* 0171–405 2107.

See also J. G. Ballard.

RICHARDSON, Michael Elliot; Director of Continuing Education and Secretary, Board of Continuing Education, University of Cambridge, and Fellow of Wolfson College, Cambridge, since 1990; *b* 29 Sept. 1938; *s* of late Rev. Emery Lonsdale Richardson and Margaret Ann Richardson (*née* Elliot); *m* 1968, Gillian Miles Jones; two *d*. *Educ:* Pocklington Sch., York; St John's Coll., Cambridge (MA 1967); Lincoln Theol Coll.; Univ. of Nottingham (DipAdEd 1970). FITD. Schoolmaster, Middlesborough Boys' High Sch., 1964–65; Adult Educn Tutor, Ibstock Community Coll., 1965–67; Principal, Alfreton Hall Adult Educn Centre, 1967–69; Open University, 1969–90: Dep. Regl Dir, Northern, 1969–76; Regl Dir, NW, 1976–79; Dir, Educnl Services for Cont. Educn, 1979–81; Pro-Dir, 1981–84, Dir, 1984–86, Centre for Cont. Educn; Pro-Vice Chancellor, Cont. Educn, 1985–90. Chm., Council for Educn and Training of Youth and Community Workers, 1985–90; Mem., numerous Cttees and Boards, 1980–. DUniv Open 1994. FRSA. *Publications:* Preparing to Study, 1979; Continuing Education for the Post Industrial Society, 1982; contribs to educn jls. *Recreations:* gardening, angling, walking. *Address:* University of Cambridge Board of Continuing Education, Madingley Hall, Madingley, Cambridge CB3 8AQ. *T:* Madingley (01954) 210636.

RICHARDSON, Michael John; Under Secretary, Head of School Organisation Branch, Department for Education, since 1992; *b* 17 March 1946; *s* of Philip George Richardson and Susan Rowena (*née* Pearce); *m* 1967, Celia, *d* of Rev. Canon Peter and Daphne Bradshaw; one *s* one *d*. *Educ:* Eton Coll.; St Edmund Hall, Oxford (BA Lit.Hum. 1968). Joined HM Diplomatic Service, 1968; Hong Kong, 1969–71; 3rd, later 2nd Sec., Peking, 1972–74; 1st Secretary: FCO, 1974–75; EEC, 1976; Western European Dept, FCO, 1977–78; Private Secretary to: Minister of State, 1978–79; Lord Privy Seal, 1979–80; 1st Sec., Rome, 1980–85; Asst Head, EC Dept, 1985; Head, EC Presidency Unit, FCO, 1986–87; Dept for Educn, 1987–. *Recreations:* family, reading, gardening, theatre-going. *Address:* 12 Northumberland Place, W2 5BS.

RICHARDSON, Sir Michael (John de Rougemont), Kt 1990; Vice Chairman, J. O. Hambro Magan & Co., since 1995; Consultant, Smith New Court plc, since 1995 (Chairman, 1990–94); *b* 9 April 1925; *s* of Arthur Wray Richardson and Audrey de Rougemont; *m* 1949, Octavia Mayhew; one *s* two *d*. *Educ:* Harrow; Kent Sch., Conn, USA. Captain, Irish Guards, 1943–49. Drayton Gp, 1949–52; Partner: Panmure Gordon & Co., 1952–71; Cazenove & Co., 1971–81; Man. Dir, 1981–90, Vice Chm., 1990–94, N. M. Rothschild & Sons Ltd. *Recreations:* fox hunting, sailing. *Address:* (office) 32 Queen Anne's Gate, SW1H 9AB. *Clubs:* Island Sailing, Bembridge Sailing (IoW).

RICHARDSON, Miranda; actress; *b* 3 March 1958; *d* of William Alan Richardson and Marian Georgina Townsend. *Educ:* St Wyburn, Southport, Merseyside; Southport High Sch. for Girls; Bristol Old Vic Theatre Sch. Repertory: Manchester Library Theatre, 1979–80; Derby Playhouse, Duke's Playhouse, Lancaster, Bristol Old Vic and Leicester Haymarket, 1982–83; West End début, Moving, Queen's, 1980–81; Royal Court: Edmund, 1985; A Lie of the Mind, 1987; Etta Jenks, 1990; National Theatre: The Changeling, and Mountain Language, 1988. *Television:* series include: Agony; Sorrell and Son; Blackadder II and III; Die Kinder, 1990; The True Adventures of Christopher Columbus, 1992; plays include: The Master Builder; The Demon Lover; After Pilkington; Sweet as You Are (RTS Award, 1987–88); Ball-trap on the Côte Sauvage, 1989; Old Times, 1991; *films:* Dance with a Stranger (role, Ruth Ellis) (City Limits Best Film Actress, 1985; Evening Standard Best Actress, 1985; Variety Club Most Promising Artiste, 1985); Underworld; Death of the Heart; Empire of the Sun; The Mad Monkey; Eat the Rich; Redemption, 1991; Enchanted April, 1992 (Golden Globe Award, Best Comedy Actress, 1993); Mr Wakefield's Crusade, The Bachelor, 1992; Damage (BAFTA Award, Best Supporting Actress, 1993; NY Critics Circle Award; Film Critics Circle, Best Actress 1994; Royal Variety Club of GB, Best Film Actress of 1994); The Crying Game, 1992; Century, 1993; Tom and Viv, 1994; La Nuit et Le Moment, 1994. *Recreations:* reading, walking, softball, gardening, music, junkshops, occasional art, animals. *Address:* c/o Kerry Gardner Management, 15 Kensington High Street, W8 5NP. *T:* 0171–603 1142.

RICHARDSON, Natasha Jane; actress; *b* 11 May 1963; *d* of late Tony Richardson and of Vanessa Redgrave, *qv*; *m* 1st, 1990, Robert Fox (marr. diss. 1994); 2nd, 1994, Liam Neeson. *Educ:* Lycée Française de Londres; St Paul's Girls' Sch.; Central Sch. of Speech and Drama. Season at Leeds Playhouse; A Midsummer Night's Dream, New Shakespeare Co.; Ophelia in Hamlet, Young Vic; The Seagull, Lyric Hammersmith, tour and Queen's, 1985; China, Bush Th., 1986; High Society, Leicester Haymarket and Victoria Palace, 1986; Anna Christie, Young Vic, 1990, NY, 1992 (Outer Critics Circle Award, 1993). *Films:* Every Picture Tells a Story, 1985; Gothic, 1987; A Month in the Country, 1987; Patty Hearst, 1988; Fat Man and Little Boy, 1989; The Handmaid's Tale, 1990; The Comfort of Strangers, 1990; The Favour, the Watch and the Very Big Fish, 1992; Past Midnight; Widows Peak, 1994 (Best Actress, Prague Film Fest., 1994); Nell, 1994. *Television:* In a Secret State, 1985; Ghosts, 1986; Hostages, 1992; Suddenly Last Summer, 1993; Zelda, 1993. Most Promising Newcomer Award, Plays and Players, 1986; Best Actress: Evening Standard Film Awards, 1990; London Theatre Critics, 1990; Plays and Players, 1990.

RICHARDSON, Nigel Peter Vincent; Headmaster, Perse School, Cambridge, since 1994; *b* 29 June 1948; *s* of Vincent Boys Richardson and Jean Frances (*née* Wrangles); *m* 1979, (Averon) Joy James; two *s*. *Educ:* Highgate Sch.; Trinity Hall, Cambridge (MA Hist.); Bristol Univ. (PGCE). Uppingham School: Hist. Dept, 1971–89; Sixth Form Tutor, 1977–83; Second Master, 1983–89; Headmaster, Dragon Sch., Oxford, 1989–92; Dep. Headmaster and Dir of Studies, King's Sch., Macclesfield, 1992–94. Course Dir, Summer Lang. Sch., Sweden and Bell Sch., Cambridge, 1972–82. BBC Radio 4: jt question compiler, Top of the Form, 1982–87; contrib., Thought for the Day. Gov., Greycotes Sch., Oxford, 1989–92. *Publications:* The Effective Use of Time, 1984, 2nd edn 1989; First Steps in Leadership, 1987; various histories and bibliographies for school use; contrib. TES, The Times, Conference and Common Room, etc. *Recreations:* music, writing, sport, travel. *Address:* The Perse School, Hills Road, Cambridge CB2 2QF. *T:* Cambridge (01223) 568300.

RICHARDSON, Rt Rev. Paul; *see* Wangaratta, Bishop of.

RICHARDSON, Prof. Peter Damian, FRS 1986; Professor of Engineering and Physiology, Brown University, USA, since 1984; *b* West Wickham, Kent, 22 Aug. 1935; *s* of Reginald William Merrells Richardson and late Marie Stuart Naomi (*née* Ouseley). *Educ:* Imperial College, Univ. of London (BSc (Eng) 1955; PhD 1958; DSc (Eng) 1974; ACGI 1955; DIC 1958; DSc 1983); MA Brown Univ. 1965. Demonstrator, Imperial Coll., 1955–58; Brown University: Vis. Lectr, 1958–59; Research Associate, 1959–60; Asst Prof. of Engrg, 1960–65; Associate Prof. of Engrg, 1965–68; Prof. of Engrg, 1968–84; Chair, University Faculty, 1987– (Vice-Chair, 1986–87). Sen. Vis. Fellow, Univ. of London, 1967; Prof. d'échange, Univ. of Paris, 1968; leave at Orta Doğu Teknik Univ., Ankara, 1969. FASME 1983. Humboldt-Preis, A. von Humboldt Sen. Scientist Award, 1976; Laureate in Medicine, Ernst Jung Foundn, 1987. *Publications:* numerous articles in learned jls. *Recreations:* photography, travel, country life. *Address:* Box D, Brown University, Providence, Rhode Island 02912, USA. *T:* (401) 8632687.

RICHARDSON, Robert Augustus; HM Chief Inspector of Schools, Department of Education and Science, 1968–72; *b* 2 Aug. 1912; *s* of late Ferdinand Augustus Richardson and Muriel Emma Richardson; *m* 1936, Elizabeth Gertrude Williamson; one *d*. *Educ:* Royal College of Art. Schoolmaster, 1934; Headmaster, Sidcup School of Art, 1937. Served in Royal Navy, 1941–46. Principal: Folkestone Sch. of Art, 1946; Maidstone Coll. of Art, 1948. Dept of Education and Science: HM Inspector of Schools, 1958; HM Staff Inspector, 1966. ARCA 1934. *Recreations:* theatre, music. *Address:* Amber Cottage, Sigglesthorne, Hull, North Humberside HU11 5QA. *T:* Hornsea (01964) 534596.

RICHARDSON, Lt-Gen. Sir Robert (Francis), KCB 1982; CVO 1978; CBE 1975 (OBE 1971; MBE 1965); Lieutenant of the Tower of London, 1992–95; Administrator, MacRobert Trusts, since 1985; *b* 2 March 1929; *s* of late Robert Buchan Richardson and Anne (*née* Smith); *m* 1st, 1956, Maureen Anne Robinson (*d* 1986); three *s* one *d*; 2nd, 1988, Alexandra Inglis (*née* Bomford); two step *s*. *Educ:* George Heriot's Sch., Edinburgh; RMA Sandhurst. Commnd into The Royal Scots, 1949; served in BAOR, Korea, and Middle East with 1st Bn The Royal Scots until 1960; Defence Services Staff Coll., India, 1960–61; psc 1961; GSO II MO4, MoD, 1961–64; jssc 1964; Brigade Major Aden Bde, 1967 (Despatches); GSO II ACDS (Ops), MoD, 1968–69; CO 1st Bn The Royal Scots, 1969–71; Col Gen. Staff, Staff Coll. Camberley, 1971–74; Comdr 39 Infantry Bde, Northern Ireland, 1974–75; Deputy Adjutant General, HQ BAOR, 1975–78; GOC Berlin (British Sector), 1978–80; Vice Adjutant Gen. and Dir of Army Manning, 1980–82; GOC NI, 1982–85. Col, The Royal Scots (The Royal Regt), 1980–90. *Recreations:* golf and other outdoor sports, gardening. *Address:* c/o Bank of Scotland, London Chief Office, 38 Threadneedle Street, EC2P 2EH. *Clubs:* Royal Scots (Edinburgh); Hon. Co. of Edinburgh Golfers (Muirfield).

RICHARDSON, Ruth Margaret; consultant; Ruth Richardson (NZ) Ltd, strategic and economic policy advice, since 1994; *b* 13 Dec. 1950; *d* of Ross Pearce Richardson and Rita Joan Richardson; *m* 1975, Andrew Evan Wright; one *s* one *d*. *Educ:* Canterbury Univ., NZ (LLB Hons 1971). Admitted to the Bar, 1973; Legal Adviser: Law Reform Div., Dept of Justice, 1972–75; Federated Farmers of NZ, 1975–80. MP (Nat. Party) Selwyn, NZ, 1981–94; Opposition spokesman: on Education and on Youth Issues, 1984–87; on Finance, 1987–90; Minister of Finance, 1990–93. *Recreations:* running, swimming, gardening. *Address:* RD5, Christchurch, New Zealand. *T:* (3) 3479146.

RICHARDSON, Prof. Sam Scruton, AO 1980; CBE 1965 (OBE 1960); Commissioner for Law Revision, Northern States of Nigeria, since 1987; Foundation Principal, Canberra College of Advanced Education (subsequently University of Canberra), 1969–84, Emeritus Fellow, 1984–90, Emeritus Professor, since 1990; *b* 31 Dec. 1919; *s* of Samuel and Gladys Richardson; *m* 1949, Sylvia May McNeil; two *s* one *d*. *Educ:* Magnus Sch., Newark-on-Trent; Trinity Coll., Oxford (State Scholar, 1937; BA PPE, 1940; MA 1946); Sch. of Oriental and African Studies, Univ. of London. Called to the Bar, Lincoln's Inn, 1958. Served War, 1940–46: commnd Royal Marines; Commando Bdes, Europe and Far East (despatches); demob., Major, 1946. Dist Comr, Sudan Polit. Service, 1946–54 (served in Kordofan and Darfur, 1946–53; Resident, Dar Masalit, 1953–54); HMOCS, Nigeria, 1954–67: Dist Comr, Bornu Prov., 1954–58; Comr for Local Courts in Attorney Gen.'s Chambers, N Nigeria, 1958–60; Dir, Inst. of Admin, Zaria, 1960–67; Dep. Vice-Chancellor, Ahmadu Bello Univ., Nigeria, 1962–67; Prof. of Public Admin, 1967–68, and Acting Vice-Chancellor, 1968, Univ. of Mauritius; occasional Lectr in Islamic Law, ANU, 1971–82; Vis. Prof., Ahmadu Bello Univ., Nigeria, 1986. Consultant: Aust. Law Reform Commn, 1980–; Museum of Australia, 1985–. Chm., Aust. Conf. of Principals, 1979–80; Pres., Internat. Assoc. of Schs and Insts of Admin, 1982–89; Member: Council, Inst. of Admin, Papua New Guinea, 1970–84; Immigration Adv. Council, 1971–74; Nat. Standing Control Cttee on Drugs of Dependence, 1974–84; Australian Council on Overseas Prof. Qualifications, 1975–; Adv. Council, Aust. Jt Services Staff Coll., 1977–84; Academic Adv. Council, RAN Coll., Jervis Bay, 1978–; Council, ANU, 1981–84; Exec. Cttee, Internat. Inst. of Admin. Scis, 1982–90. Mem., Bd of Management, Aust. Inst. of Sport, 1980–84. Governor, Portsmouth Polytechnic, 1989–92 (Hon. Fellow, 1984). Nat. Pres., Australia Britain Soc., 1980–84; Vice-Pres., Britain Australia Soc., 1984–. Freeman, City of London, 1989–. Hon. Fellow, Univ. of Portsmouth, 1993. Hon. LLD Ahmadu Bello, 1967; Hon. Dr Canberra, 1990. *Publications:* Notes on the Penal Code of N Nigeria, 1959, 4th edn 1987; (with T. H. Williams) The Criminal Procedure Code of N Nigeria, 1963; (with E. A. Keay) The Native and Customary Courts of Nigeria, 1965; Parity of Esteem—the Canberra College of Advanced Education 1968–78, 1979; A Saga 1961–1991: the history of International Association of Schools and Institutes of Administration, 1992; regular book revs in Canberra Times, 1970–; articles on public admin, customary law and higher educn in learned jls. *Recreations:* travel, reading, community service. *Address:* The Malt House, Wylye, Warminster, Wilts BA12 0QP. *T:* Wylye (01985) 248348. *Clubs:* United Oxford & Cambridge University; University House (ANU, Canberra).

RICHARDSON, Sir Simon Alaisdair S.; *see* Stewart-Richardson.

RICHARDSON, Maj.-Gen. Thomas Anthony, (Tony), CB 1976; MBE 1960; Secretary: British Christmas Tree Growers Association, since 1980; Christmas Tree Growers Association of Western Europe, since 1989; *b* 9 Aug. 1922; *s* of late Maj.-Gen. T. W. Richardson, Eaton Cottage, Unthank Road, Norwich, and late Mrs J. H. Boothby, Camberley; *m* 1st, 1945, Katharine Joanna Ruxton Roberts (*d* 1988), Woodland Place, Bath; one *s* one *d*; 2nd, 1991, Anthea Rachel Fry, Wimbledon. *Educ:* Wellington Coll., Berks. Technical Staff Course, psc, Fixed Wing Pilot, Rotary Wing Pilot, Parachutist. War of 1939–45: enlisted, Feb. 1941; commissioned, RA, March 1942; Essex Yeomanry (France and Germany), 1942–45; Air Observation Post, 1945–46. Tech. Staff/G Staff, 1949–52, 1954–55, 1959–60, 1963–64; Regt duty, 1942–45, 1952–54, 1957–58, 1961–62. Instr, Mil. Coll. Science, 1955–56; CO, 7th Para, RHA, 1965–67; CRA, 2 Div., 1967–69; Dir, Operational Requirements (Army), 1969–71; Dir, Army Aviation, 1971–74; Defence and Military Advr, India, 1974–77. Col Comdt, RA, 1978–83. Asst Sec., 1978–80, Sec. 1980–84, Timber Growers England and Wales Ltd; Dep. Chm., 1984–86, Chm., 1986–88, Tree Council. *Recreations:* sailing, skiing, fishing, shooting. *Address:* 12 Lauriston Road, Wimbledon, SW19 4TQ. *Club:* Army and Navy.

RICHARDSON, Thomas Legh, CMG 1991; HM Diplomatic Service; Assistant Under-Secretary of State (Western Europe), Foreign and Commonwealth Office, since 1994; *b* 6 Feb. 1941; *s* of Arthur Legh Turnour Richardson and Penelope Margaret Richardson; *m* 1979, Alexandra Frazier Wasiqullah (*née* Ratcliff). *Educ:* Westminster Sch.; Christ Church, Oxford. MA (Hist.). Joined Foreign Office, 1962; seconded to Univ. of Ghana, 1962–63; FO, 1963–65; Third Sec., Dar-Es-Salaam, 1965–66; Vice-Consul (Commercial), Milan, 1967–70; seconded to N. M. Rothschild & Sons, 1970; FCO, 1971–74; First Sec., UK Mission to UN, 1974–78; FCO, 1978–80; seconded to Central Policy Review Staff, Cabinet Office, 1980–81; Head of Chancery, Rome, 1982–86; Head of Economic Relns Dept, FCO, 1986–89; UK Dep. Perm. Rep. to UN, with personal rank of Ambassador, 1989–94. *Recreations:* reading, walking, travel, music. *Address:* c/o Foreign and Commonwealth Office, SW1A 2AH. *Club:* United Oxford & Cambridge University.

RICHARDSON, Maj.-Gen. Tony; *see* Richardson, Maj.-Gen. Thomas A.

RICHARDSON, William, CBE 1981; DL; CEng; FRINA; retired, 1983; Chairman: Vickers Shipbuilding and Engineering Ltd, 1976–83 (Managing Director, 1969–76); Vosper Thornycroft (UK) Ltd, 1978–83; Barclay Curle Ltd, 1978–83; Brook Marine Ltd, 1981–83; Member Board, British Shipbuilders (from incorporation), 1977–83, Deputy Chairman 1981–83; Director, Vickers Cockatoo Dockyard Pty Ltd, Australia, 1977–84; *b* 15 Aug. 1916; *s* of Edwin Richardson, marine engr, and Hannah (*née* Remington); *m* 1941, Beatrice Marjorie Iliffe; one *s* one *d*. *Educ:* Ocean Road Boys' Sch., Walney Is, Barrow-in-Furness; Jun. Techn. and Techn. Colls, Barrow-in-Furness (part-time). HNC (Dist.) Naval Architecture; HNC (1st Cl.) Mech. Engrg. CBIM 1981 (FBIM 1977); FInstD 1977–83. Vickers Ltd, Barrow-in-Furness: Shipbldg Apprentice, 1933–38; Techn. Dept, 1938–39; Admiralty Directorate of Aircraft Maintenance and Repair, UK and Far East, 1939–46; Vickers Ltd Barrow Shipyard: Techn. Depts, 1946–51; Asst Shipyard Manager, 1951–60; Dockside Outfitting Man., 1960–61; Dep. Shipyard Man., 1961–63; Shipyard Man., 1963–64; Dir and Gen. Man., 1964–66; Dir and Gen. Man., Vickers Ltd Naval Shipyard, Newcastle upon Tyne, 1966–68; Dep. Man. Dir, Swan Hunter & Tyne Shipbldrs Ltd, 1968–69. Director: Slingsby Sailplanes, 1969–70 (co. then incorp. into Vickers Ltd); Vickers Oceanics, 1972–77; Chm., Clark & Standfield (subsid. of Vickers Gp), 1976–83; Dir, Vosper Shiprepairers, 1978–82. Dir of Trustees, 1976–, Mem. Res. Council and Office Bearer, 1976–78, BSRA; Mem. Exec. Council, 1969–77, Chm. Management Bd, 1976–78, SRNA; Pres. Brit. Productivity Assoc., Barrow and Dist, 1969–72; Shipbldg Ind. Rep., DIQAP, 1972–82; Mem., Shipbuilding Industry Trng Bd, 1979–82; Mem., NE Coast IES, 1967–. FRINA 1970 (ARINA 1950, MRINA 1955). Liveryman, Shipwrights' Co., 1978. DL Cumbria, 1982. Queen's Silver Jubilee Medal, 1977. *Publications:* papers on various aspects of UK shipbldg industry; contribs to techn. jls. *Recreations:* sailing, small-bore shooting, golf, fishing. *Address:* Sequoia, Sunbrick Lane, Baycliff, Ulverston, Cumbria LA12 9RQ. *T:* Ulverston (01229) 869434. *Club:* National Small-Bore Rifle Association.

RICHARDSON, William Eric, CEng, FIEE, FIMgt; Chairman, South Wales Electricity Board, 1968–77; Member, Electricity Council, 1968–77; retired 1977; *b* 21 May 1915; *o s* of William Pryor and Elizabeth Jane Richardson, Hove, Sussex; *m* (she *d* 1975); one *s*; *m* 1976, Barbara Mary Leech. *Educ:* Royal Masonic Sch., Bushey. Engineer with Brighton Corp., 1934–37; Southampton Corp., 1937–39; Norwich Corp., 1939–46; Distribution Engr with Newport (Mon) Corp., 1946–48; Area Engr with S Wales Electricity Bd, 1948–57; Area Manager, 1957–65; Chief Commercial Engr, 1965–67; Dep. Chm., 1967–68. *Recreations:* sailing, golf, gardening. *Address:* 57 Allt-yr-Yn View, Newport, Gwent NP9 5DN. *T:* Newport (Gwent) (01633) 264388.

RICHARDSON-BUNBURY, Sir (Richard David) Michael, *see* Bunbury.

RICHBOROUGH, Bishop Suffragan of, since 1995; **Rt Rev. Edwin Ronald Barnes;** Episcopal Visitor for the Province of Canterbury; *b* 6 Feb. 1935; *s* of Edwin and Dorothy Barnes; *m* 1963, Jane Elizabeth (*née* Green); one *s* one *d*. *Educ:* Plymouth College; Pembroke Coll., Oxford (MA). Rector of Farncombe, Surrey, 1967–78; Vicar of Hessle, dio. York, 1978–87; Principal, St Stephen's House, Oxford, 1987–95. Proctor in Convocation, Canterbury 1975–78, York 1985–87; Mem., General Synod of C of E, 1990–95 (Mem. Standing Cttee, 1992–95). Hon. Canon of Christ Church, Oxford, 1994. *Address:* 36 James Street, Oxford OX4 1ET. *T:* Oxford (01865) 201446.

RICHES, Anne Clare, (Mrs T. C. Coltman); FSA; free-lance architectural historian, since 1989; *b* 12 April 1943; *d* of Rt Rev. Kenneth Riches, *qv* and Kathleen Mary Riches (*née* Dixon); *m* 1989, Timothy Charles Coltman. *Educ:* Headington Sch., Oxford; Edinburgh Univ. (MA 1965; Dip. Hist of Art 1966). FSA 1985. Historian, Historic Bldgs Div., GLC, 1966–78; Inspector, then Principal Inspector/Grade 7, Historic Bldgs and Monuments Directorate, Scottish Develt Dept, 1978–89. Comr, RCHM, 1991–. Society of Architectural Historians of Great Britain: Sec., 1978–83; Conf. Sec., 1978–85; Chm., 1985–88. Member: Adv. Panel, Railway Heritage Trust, 1985–; Nat. Cttee, Assoc. of Preservation Trusts, 1989–; Royal Commn on Ancient and Historical Monuments of Scotland, 1995–; Trustee, Scottish Historic Bldgs Trust, 1989–; Heritage Trust for Lincolnshire: Dir, 1990–; Chm., Archaeol. Adv. Cttee, 1991–94; Chm., Bldgs Adv. Cttee, 1992–. *Publications:* (with R. Barber) A Dictionary of Fabulous Beasts, 1972; Victorian Church Building and Restoration in Suffolk, 1982; (jtly) Building of Scotland: Glasgow, 1990; contrib. Architectl Hist. *Recreations:* gardening, hill-farming, visiting buildings. *Address:* Skellingthorpe Hall, Lincoln LN6 5UU. *T:* Lincoln (01522) 694609.

RICHES, Sir Derek (Martin Hurry), KCMG 1963 (CMG 1958); Ambassador to Lebanon, 1963–67, retired; *b* 26 July 1912; *s* of late Claud Riches and Flora Martin; *m* 1942, Helen Barkley Hayes (*d* 1989), Poughkeepsie, NY, USA; one *d*. *Educ:* University College School; University College, London. Appointed Probationer Vice-Consul, Beirut, Dec. 1934. Subsequently promoted and held various appts, Ethiopia and Cairo; Foreign Office, 1944; promoted one of HM Consuls serving in FO, 1945. Kabul, 1948 (in charge, 1948 and 1949); Consul at Jedda, 1951 (Chargé d'Affaires, 1952); Officer Grade 6, Branch A, Foreign Service and apptd Trade Comr, Khartoum, 1953. Attached to Imperial Defence College, 1955; returned to Foreign Office, 1955; Counsellor in the Foreign Office, Head of Eastern Department, 1955; British Ambassador in Libya, 1959–61; British Ambassador to the Congo, 1961–63. *Address:* 48 The Avenue, Kew Gardens, Surrey TW9 2AH.

RICHES, General Sir Ian (Hurry), KCB 1960 (CB 1959); DSO 1945; *b* 27 Sept. 1908; *s* of C. W. H. Riches; *m* 1936, Winifred Eleanor Layton; two *s*. *Educ:* Univ. Coll. Sch., London. Joined Royal Marines, 1927; Major, 1946; Lt-Colonel, 1949; Colonel, 1953; Maj.-Gen., 1957; Lt-Gen., 1959; General, 1961. Maj.-Gen., RM, Portsmouth Group, 1957–59; Commandant-General, Royal Marines, 1959–62; Regional Dir of Civil Defence, 1964–68; Representative Col Comdt, 1967–68. *T:* Winchester (01962) 854067.

RICHES, Rt. Rev. Kenneth, DD, STD; Assistant Bishop of Louisiana, USA, 1976–77; *b* 20 Sept. 1908; *s* of Capt. A. G. Riches; *m* 1942, Kathleen Mary Dixon, JP 1964; two *s* one *d*. *Educ:* Royal Gram. Sch., Colchester; Corpus Christi Coll., Cambridge. Curate of St Mary's, Portsea, 1932–35; St John's, East Dulwich, 1935–36; Chaplain and Librarian, Sidney Sussex Coll., Cambridge, 1936–42; Examining Chaplain to Bishops of Bradford and Wakefield, 1936; Editorial Sec., Cambridgeshire Syllabus, 1935; Editor, Cambridge Review, 1941–42; Rector of Bredfield with Boulge, Suffolk, and Dir of Service Ordination Candidates, 1942–45; Principal of Cuddesdon Theological Coll., Oxford, and Vicar of Cuddesdon, 1945–52; Hon. Canon of Portsmouth Cathedral, 1950–52; Bishop Suffragan of Dorchester, Archdeacon of Oxford and Canon of Christ Church, 1952–56; Bishop of Lincoln, 1956–74. Select Preacher: University of Cambridge, 1941, 1948, 1961, and 1963; University of Oxford, 1954–55. Mem. Archbishops' Commission on Training for the Ministry, 1942; Sec. of Theol. Commn on the Church of Faith and Order Movement. Visiting Lecturer the General Theological Seminary, New York, 1956 and 1962. Hon. Fellow: Sidney Sussex Coll., Cambridge, 1958; Lincoln Coll., Oxford, 1974; Corpus Christi Coll., Cambridge, 1975. Chm., Central Advisory Council for the Ministry, 1959–65. *Recreations:* gardening, antiques, and country life. *Address:* Little Dingle, Dunwich, Saxmundham, Suffolk IP17 3EA. *T:* Westleton (01728) 648316.

See also A. C. Riches.

RICHINGS, Lewis David George; *b* 22 April 1920; *s* of Lewis Vincent Richings and Jessie Helen (*née* Clements); *m* 1944, Margaret Alice Hume; three *d*. *Educ:* Battersea Grammar Sch.; Devonport High Sch.; Darlington Grammar Sch.; London Sch. of Econs and Polit. Science (part-time). Served War, Army, 1939–46: commnd 2 Lieut Inf., 1940; attached 8 DLI, 1940–41; seconded 11 KAR, 1941–45; Actg Major, 1945; various postings, UK, 1945–46. MAFF, 1937–58; attached MoD, 1958; Gen. Administrator, AWRE, 1958–65; Health and Safety Br., UKAEA, 1965–70; Sec., Nat. Radiol Protection Bd, 1970–79, Dep. Dir, 1978–80. Mem., Radiol Protection and Public Health Cttee, Nuclear Energy Agency, OECD, 1966–80 (Chm., 1972–74). FRSA. *Publications:* articles in press and jls on admin and technical matters relating to common land, rural electrification, earthquakes, and radiol protection. *Recreation:* boats. *Address:* 31 Kennedy Street, Blairgowrie, Vic 3942, Australia; 26 Three Acre Road, Newbury, Berks RG14 7AW.

RICHLER, Mordecai; author; *b* 27 Jan. 1931; *s* of late Moses Isaac Richler and Lily Rosenberg; *m* 1960, Florence Wood; three *s* two *d*. *Educ:* Sir George Williams Univ., Montreal (left without degree). Writer-in-residence, Sir George Williams Univ., 1968–69; Vis. Prof., English Dept, Carleton Univ., Ottawa, 1972–74. Edit. Bd, Book-of-the-Month Club, NY. Canada Council Senior Arts Fellowship, 1960; Guggenheim Fellowship, Creative Writing, 1961. *Publications: novels:* The Acrobats, 1954; A Choice of Enemies, 1955; Son of a Smaller Hero, 1957; The Apprenticeship of Duddy Kravitz, 1959, repr. 1972 (filmed, Golden Bear Award, Berlin Film Fest., 1974; Writers Guild of America Annual Award, 1974; Academy Award nomination, 1974); The Incomparable Atuk, 1963; Cocksure, 1968 (Governor-General's Award for Literature, 1969; Paris Review Humour Prize, 1969); St Urbain's Horseman, 1971 (Governor-General's Award for Literature, 1972); Joshua Then and Now, 1980 (filmed, 1985); Solomon Gursky Was Here, 1990 (Commonwealth Writers Prize, 1990); *non-fiction:* Oh Canada! Oh Quebec!, Lament for a Divided Country, 1992; *essays:* Hunting Tigers Under Glass, 1969; Shovelling Trouble, 1973; Home Sweet Home, 1984; Broadsides, 1991; *autobiography:* The Street, 1972; *memoir:* This Year in Jerusalem, 1994; *children's books:* Jacob Two-Two Meets the Hooded Fang, 1975; Jacob Two-Two and the Dinosaur, 1987; Jacob Two-Two's First Spy Case, 1995; *anthology:* (ed) The Best of Modern Humour, 1983; (ed) Writers on World War II, 1991; contrib. Encounter, Commentary, New York Review of Books, etc. *Recreations:* poker, snooker. *Address:* Apt 80C, 1321 Sherbrooke Street W, Montreal, Quebec H3G 1J4, Canada. *T:* (514) 2882008.

RICHMAN, Stella; television producer; *b* 9 Nov. 1922; *d* of Jacob Richman and Leoni Richman; *m* 1st, Alec Clunes; 2nd, 1953, Victor Brusa (*d* 1965); one *s* one *d*. *Educ:* Clapton County Secondary Sch. for Girls. Started TV career at ATV, running Script Dept 1960; created and produced Love Story, 1963; joined Rediffusion, 1964; Exec. Head of Series (prod The Informer); Exec. Prod., award-winning Man of Our Times, Half Hour Story and Blackmail; prod first 6 plays, Company of Five, for newly formed London Weekend Television, 1968; Man. Dir, London Weekend Internat., 1969, and Controller of Programmes, London Weekend Television, 1970–71 (first woman to sit on bd of a television co.); in partnership with David Frost formed Stella Richman Productions (first independent TVco.), 1972–78: resp. for Miss Nightingale, Jennie, Clayhanger, Bill Brand, Just William. Chm. and owner, White Elephant Club, 1960–88. FRTS 1982. *Publications:* The White Elephant Cook Books, 1973, 1979. *Recreations:* travel, reading biographies, theatre. *Address:* Garden Flat, 5 Hill Road, NW8 9QE.

RICHMOND, 10th Duke of, *cr* 1675, **AND GORDON,** 5th Duke of, *cr* 1876; **Charles Henry Gordon-Lennox;** Baron Settrington, Earl of March, 1675; Lord of Torboulton, Earl of Darnley, Duke of Lennox (Scot.) 1675; Earl of Kinrara, 1876; Duc d'Aubigny (France), 1684; Hereditary Constable of Inverness Castle; Lord-Lieutenant of West Sussex, 1990–94; *b* 19 Sept. 1929; *s* of 9th Duke of Richmond and Gordon, and Elizabeth Grace (*d* 1992), *y d* of late Rev. T. W. Hudson; *S* father, 1989; *m* 1951, Susan Monica, *o d* of late Colonel C. E. Grenville-Grey, CBE, Hall Barn, Blewbury, Berks; one *s* four *d*. *Educ:* Eton; William Temple Coll. 2nd Lieut, 60th Rifles, 1949–50. Chartered Accountant, 1956. Dir of Industrial Studies, William Temple Coll., 1964–68; Chancellor, Univ. of Sussex, 1985– (Treasurer, 1979–82). Church Commissioner, 1963–76; Mem. Gen. Synod of Church of England, formerly Church Assembly, 1960–80 (Chm., Bd for Mission and Unity, 1967–77); Mem., Central and Exec. Cttees, World Council of Churches, 1968–75; Chairman: Christian Orgn Res. and Adv. Trust, 1965–87; House of Laity, Chichester Diocesan Synod, 1976–79; Vice-Chm., Archbishop's Commn on Church and State, 1966–70; Mem., W Midlands Regional Economic Planning Council, 1965–68; Chairman: Goodwood Group of Cos, 1969–; Ajax Insurance (Holdings) Ltd, 1987–89; John Wiley and Sons Ltd, 1992– (Dir, 1984–); Dir, Radio Victory Ltd, 1982–87. Historic Houses Association: Hon. Treas., 1975–82; Chm., SE Region, 1975–78; Dep. Pres., 1982–86; President: Sussex Rural Community Council, 1973–; British Horse Soc., 1976–78; South of England Agricultural Soc., 1981–82; SE England Tourist Bd, 1990– (Vice-Pres., 1974–90); Chm., Assoc. of Internat. Dressage Event Organisers, 1987–94; Chairman: Rugby Council of Social Service, 1961–68; Dunford Coll., (YMCA), 1969–82; Dir, Country Gentlemen's Assoc. Ltd, 1975–89. Chairman: of Trustees, Sussex Heritage Trust, 1978–; Planning for Economic Prosperity in Chichester and Arun, 1984–89; Chichester Cathedral Develt Trust, 1985–91; President: Chichester Festivities, 1975–; Sussex CCC, 1991–. DL W Sussex, 1975–90. CIMgt (CBIM 1982). Hon LLD Sussex, 1986. Medal of Honour, British Equestrian Fedn, 1983. *Heir: s* Earl of March and Kinrara, *qv*. *Address:* Goodwood House, Chichester, W Sussex PO18 0PX. *T:* (office) Chichester (01243) 774107; (home) Chichester (01243) 532815.

See also Lord N. C. Gordon Lennox.

RICHMOND, Archdeacon of; *see* Good, Ven. K. R.

RICHMOND, Sir Alan (James), Kt 1969; engineering consultant, expert witness and arbitrator; *b* 12 Oct. 1919; *m* 1951, Sally Palmer (*née* Pain); one step *s* one step *d*. *Educ:* Berlin; Gland près Nyon, Switzerland; Wimbledon Tech. Coll.; Acton Tech. Coll.; Northampton Polytechnic, London. Trained and employed Engineering Industry, 1938–45; London Univ., BSc(Eng) 1945, PhD 1954; Lecturer, Battersea Polytechnic, 1946–55; Head of Engineering Dept, Welsh Coll. of Advanced Technology, 1955–58; Principal, Lanchester College of Technology, Coventry, 1959–69; Director, Lanchester Polytechnic, 1970–72; Principal, Strode Coll., Street, 1972–81; Associate Tutor, Further Education Staff Coll., Blagdon, Bristol, 1982–85. Chairman: Coventry Productivity Assoc., 1964–67; CNAA Mech./Prodn Engrg Subject Bd, 1965–68; CNAA Cttees for Sci. and Technology, 1968–72; Founder Chm., Cttee of Dirs of Polytechnics, 1970–72; Member: Home Office Deptl Cttee of Enquiry into Fire Service in GB, 1967–70; Open Univ. Planning Cttee, 1967–69; Open Univ. Council, 1969–71. FIMechE; FCIArb. Hon. DSc CNAA, 1972. *Publications:* (with W. J. Peck) Applied Thermodynamics Problems for Engineers, 1950; Problems in Heat Engines, 1957; various lectures, reviews and articles. *Recreations:* gardening, reading. *Address:* 5 The Orchard, Westfield Park South, Bath BA1 3HT. *T:* Bath (01225) 333393. *Club:* Commonwealth Trust.

RICHMOND, Rear-Adm. Andrew John, CB 1987; Chief Executive (formerly Executive Director), Royal Society for the Prevention of Cruelty to Animals, 1987–91; *b* 5 Nov. 1931; *s* of Albert George Richmond and Emily Margaret (*née* Denbee); *m* 1957, Jane Annette (*née* Ley); one *s* two *d*. *Educ:* King's School, Bruton; Nautical College, Pangbourne. Joined RN 1950; staff of C-in-C East Indies, 1953; flying training, 1955; Cyprus 847 Sqdn, 1956; HMS Victorious 824 Sqdn, 1958; staff of FO Arabian Sea, 1960; BRNC Dartmouth, 1963; Sec., FO Carriers and Amphibious Ships, 1968; Supply School, HMS Pembroke, 1970; Fleet Supply Officer, 1974; Asst Dir Naval Manpower, 1976; Sec., C-in-C Naval Home Comd, 1977; Captain, HMS Cochrane, 1979; Dir, Naval Logistic Planning, 1982; ADC 1984; ACDS (Logistics), 1985, and Chief Naval Supply and Secretariat Officer, 1986. *Recreations:* home, gardening, golf. *Address:* c/o Royal Bank of Scotland, South Street, Chichester, West Sussex PO19 1DS. *Club:* Goodwood Golf.

RICHMOND, Rt. Hon. Sir Clifford (Parris), PC 1973; KBE 1977; Kt 1972; Judge of the Court of Appeal of New Zealand, 1972–81, President, 1976–81; *b* 23 June 1914; *s* of Howard Parris Richmond, QC, and Elsie Wilhelmina (*née* MacTavish); *m* 1938, Valerie Jean Hamilton; two *s* one *d*. *Educ:* Wanganui Collegiate Sch.; Victoria and Auckland Univs. LLM (1st cl. Hons). Served War of 1939–45: 4 Field Regt 2NZEF, North Africa and Italy, 1942–45 (despatches, 1944). Partner, legal firm, Buddle Richmond & Co., Auckland, 1946–60. Judge of the Supreme Court of New Zealand, 1960–71. *Recreations:* golf, fishing. *Address:* 16 Glanville Terrace, Parnell, Auckland, New Zealand. *T:* (9) 3077104. *Club:* Northern (Auckland).

RICHMOND, Rt. Rev. Francis Henry Arthur; *see* Repton, Bishop Suffragan of.

RICHMOND, Prof. John, CBE 1993; MD, FRCP, FRCPE; FRSE; President, Royal College of Physicians of Edinburgh, 1988–91; Emeritus Professor of Medicine, University of Sheffield, since 1989; *b* 30 May 1926; *er s* of late Hugh Richmond and Janet Hyslop Brown; *m* 1951, Jenny Nicol, 2nd *d* of T. Nicol; two *s* one *d*. *Educ:* Doncaster Grammar Sch.; Univ. of Edinburgh. MB, ChB 1948 (with Distinction in Medicine); MD 1963. FRCPE 1963; FRCP 1970; FRCPS 1988; FRCPI 1990; FCPS (Pak) 1990; FRCSE 1991; Hon. FACP 1990; Hon. FFPM 1990; Hon. FRACP 1991; Hon. FCP(SoAf) 1991; Hon. FFPHM 1991. House Officer, in Edinburgh hosps and Northants, 1948–49, 1952–54; RAMC, Military Mission to Ethiopia, Captain 1st Bn King's African Rifles, N Rhodesia, 1949–50; Rural Gen. Practice, Galloway, Scotland, 1950–52; Res. Fellow, Meml Sloan Kettering Cancer Center, New York, 1958–59; Sen. Lectr, later Reader in Medicine, Univ. of Edinburgh, 1963–73; University of Sheffield: Prof. of Medicine, 1973–89; Chm., Academic Div. of Medicine, 1978–85; Hon. Dir of Cancer Res., 1983–88; Dean of Medicine and Dentistry, 1985–88. Censor, 1981–82, Sen. Vice-Pres. and Sen. Censor, 1984–85, RCP; Mem. Council, RCPE, 1987–88. Chm., MRCP (UK) Part 2 Examining Bd, 1985–89. Member: Sheffield HA, 1982–84; Clin. Standards Adv. Gp, Dept of Health, 1991–94; Bd of Advrs, London Univ., 1984–93; External Advr, Chinese Univ. of Hong Kong, 1984–. Member: Council of Management, Yorkshire Cancer Res. Campaign, 1989–93; Scottish Adv. Cttee, British Council, 1991–; Scottish Cttee, Marie Curie Meml Foundn, 1992–. High Constables of Edinburgh, 1961–70. Hon. MD Sheffield, 1994; *Publications:* contribs to books and papers in med. jls, mainly on haematology and oncology. *Address:* 15 Church Hill, Edinburgh EH10 4BG. *Club:* New (Edinburgh).

RICHMOND, Sir John (Frederick), 2nd Bt, *cr* 1929; *b* 12 Aug. 1924; *s* of Sir Frederick Henry Richmond, 1st Bt (formerly Chm. Debenham's Ltd and Harvey Nichols & Co. Ltd), and Dorothy Agnes (*d* 1982), *d* of Frances Joseph Sheppard; *S* father 1953; *m* 1965, Mrs Anne Moreen Bentley; one *d*. *Educ:* Eton; Jesus Coll., Cambridge. Lt 10th Roy. Hussars; seconded Provost Br., 1944–47. *Address:* Shimpling Park Farm, Bury St Edmunds, Suffolk IP29 4HY. *Club:* MCC.

RICHMOND, Sir Mark (Henry), Kt 1986; PhD, ScD; FRCPath; FRS 1980; Group Head of Research, Glaxo Holdings, since 1993; *b* 1 Feb. 1931; *s* of Harold Sylvester Richmond and Dorothy Plaistowe Richmond; *m* 1958, Shirley Jean Townrow; one *s* one *d* (and one *d* decd). *Educ:* Epsom College; Clare Coll., Cambridge. BA, PhD, ScD. Scientific Staff, MRC, 1958–65; Reader in Molecular Biology, Univ. of Edinburgh, 1965–68; Prof. of Bacteriology, Univ. of Bristol, 1968–81; Vice-Chancellor, and Prof. of Molecular Microbiol., Victoria Univ. of Manchester, 1981–90; Chm., SERC, 1990–94 (Mem., 1981–85). Member: Bd, PHLS, 1976–85; Fulbright Commn, 1980–84; Chairman: British Nat. Cttee for Microbiol., 1980–85; CVCP, 1987–89; Cttee on Microbiological Food Safety, 1989–91; Member: Genetic Manipulation Adv. Gp 1976–84; Adv. Cttee on Genetic Manipulation, 1984–85. Pres., Epsom Coll., 1992–. Member: IBM Academic Adv. Bd, 1984–90; Knox Fellowship Cttee, 1984–87; CIBA-Geigy Fellowship Trust, 1984–91; Jarrett Cttee for University Efficiency, 1985; Governing Body, Lister Inst., 1987–90; Council, ACU, 1988–90; Council, Royal Northern Coll. of Music, 1990–92; Educn Cttee, Royal Anniversary Trust, 1994–; Trustee: Nat. Gall., 1994–; Dyson Perrins Mus., Worcester, 1993–. *Publications:* several in microbiology and biochemistry jls. *Recreation:* hill-walking. *Address:* Glaxo Holdings plc, Lansdowne House, Berkeley Square, W1X 6BQ. *Club:* Athenæum.

RICHMOND, Prof. Peter, PhD; CPhys, FInstP; Professor, School of Information Systems, University of East Anglia, since 1986; *b* 4 March 1943; *s* of John Eric Richmond and Nellie (*née* Scholey); *m* 1967, Christine M. Jackson; one *s* one *d*. *Educ:* Whitcliffe Mount Grammar Sch., Cleckheaton; Queen Mary Coll., London (BSc, PhD); London Univ. (DSc). MRSC. ICI Res. Fellow, Univ. of Kent, 1967–69; Univ. of NSW, 1969–71; Queen Elizabeth II Res. Fellow, Inst. of Advanced Studies, ANU, 1971–73; Unilever Res., 1973–82; Hd, Process Physics, AFRC Food Res. Inst., Norwich, 1982–86; Industrial Prof., Univ. of Loughborough, 1985–88; Dir, AFRC Inst. of Food Res., Norwich Lab., 1986–92; Gen. Man., CWS Quality and Consumer Care, 1992–94; Head of Regulatory Affairs, CWS, 1994–95. Member: MAFF/DoH Adv. Cttee on novel foods and processes, 1988–94; FDF Scientific and Technical Cttee, 1992–95; FDF Res. Strategy Gp, 1993–; Council, 1995–, Gen. Merchandise Cttee, 1995–, British Retail Consortium. *Publications:* (with R. D. Bee and J. Mingins) Food Colloids, 1989; contribs to learned jls. *Recreations:* music, ideas, cooking. *Club:* Athenæum.

RICHTER, Prof. Burton; Paul Pigott Professor in the Physical Sciences, Stanford University, USA, since 1980 (Professor of Physics, since 1967), and Director, Stanford Linear Accelerator Center, since 1984 (Technical Director, 1982–84); *b* 22 March 1931; *s* of Abraham Richter and Fannie Pollack; *m* 1960, Laurose Becker; one *s* one *d*. *Educ:* Massachusetts Inst. of Technology. BS 1952, PhD (Physics) 1956. Stanford University: Research Associate, Physics, High Energy Physics Lab., 1956–60; Asst Prof., 1960–63; Associate Prof., 1963–67; full Prof., 1967. Loeb Lectr, Harvard, 1974; De Shalit Lectr, Weizmann Inst., 1975. Mem. Bd of Directors: Varian Corp., 1989–; Litel Instruments, 1990–. FAPS 1984 (Pres., 1994); Fellow, Amer. Acad. of Arts and Scis, 1990 (Mem., 1989); Mem., Nat. Acad. of Scis, 1977. E. O. Lawrence Award, 1975; Nobel Prize for Physics (jointly), 1976. *Publications:* over 300 articles in various scientific journals. *Address:* Stanford Linear Accelerator Center, PO Box 4349, Stanford University, Stanford, CA 94309, USA.

RICHTER, Sviatoslav Theofilovich; Hero of Socialist Labour, 1975; pianist; *b* Zhitomir, Ukraine, 20 March 1915; *m* Nina Dorliak. *Educ:* Moscow State Conservatoire. Gave first piano recital at age of nineteen and began to give concerts on a wide scale in 1942.

Appeared at the Royal Albert Hall and the Royal Festival Hall, London, 1961; Royal Festival Hall, 1963, 1966, 1977, 1979, 1989, 1992. FRCM 1992. Hon. DMus Oxon, 1992. Awarded Lenin Prize, and also holds the title of Peoples' Artist of the USSR; Order of Lenin, 1965; Order of October Revolution, 1991. *Recreations:* walking, ski-ing and painting. *Address:* c/o Victor Hochhauser, 4 Oak Hill Way, NW3 7LR. *T:* 0171–794 0987.

RICKARD, Dr John Hellyar; IMF Fiscal Adviser to Ministry of Finance, Republic of Moldova, since 1995; *b* 27 Jan. 1940; *s* of Peter John Rickard and Irene Eleanor (*née* Hales); *m* 1963, Christine Dorothy Hudson; one *s* two *d*. *Educ:* Ilford County High Sch.; St John's Coll., Oxford (MA 1966; DPhil 1976); Univ. of Aston in Birmingham (MSc 1969). Lectr, Univ. of Aston, 1967–70; Economist, Programmes Analysis Unit, AEA, Harwell, 1970–72; Res. Associate, and Dep. Head, Health Services Evaluation Gp, Dept of Regius Prof. of Medicine, Univ. of Oxford, 1972–74; Econ. Adviser, Dept of Health, 1974–76; Sen. Econ. Adviser: Dept of Prices and Consumer Protection, 1976–78; Central Policy Review Staff, Cabinet Office, 1978–82; HM Treasury, 1982–84; Econ. Adviser, State of Bahrain, 1984–87; Chief Economic Advr, Dept of Transport, 1987–91; Under Sec. (Econs), HM Treasury, 1991–94; Chief Econ. Advr, Dept of Transport, 1994–95. *Publications:* (with D. Aston) Macro-Economics: a critical introduction, 1970; Longer Term Issues in Transport, 1991; articles in books and learned jls. *Recreations:* sailing, music. *Address:* 24 Condray Place, Battersea, SW11 3PE. *T:* 0171–223 8359. *Club:* Civil Service Sailing Association.

RICKARD, Prof. Peter, DPhil, PhD, LittD; Drapers Professor of French, University of Cambridge, 1980–82, Emeritus since 1983; Fellow of Emmanuel College, Cambridge, 1953, Professorial Fellow, 1980, Life Fellow, since 1983; *b* 20 Sept. 1922; *yr s* of Norman Ernest Rickard and Elizabeth Jane (*née* Hosking); unmarried. *Educ:* Redruth County Grammar Sch., Cornwall; Exeter Coll., Oxford (Final Hons Mod. Langs (French and German), Cl. I, 1948; MA 1948). DPhil Oxon 1952; PhD Cantab 1952; LittD Cambridge 1982. Served War, 1st Bn Seaforth Highlanders and Intell. Corps, India, 1942–46. Heath Harrison Travelling Scholar (French), 1948; Amelia Jackson Sen. Scholar, Exeter Coll., Oxford, 1948–49; Lectr in Mod. Langs, Trinity Coll., Oxford, 1949–52; Univ. of Cambridge: Asst Lectr in French, 1952–57, Lectr, 1957–74; Reader in French Lang., 1974–80; Mem., St John's Coll., 1952–; Tutor, Emmanuel Coll., 1954–65. *Publications:* Britain in Medieval French Literature, 1956; La langue française au XVIe siècle, 1968; (ed with T. G. S. Combe) The French Language: studies presented to Lewis Charles Harmer, 1970; (ed and trans.) Fernando Pessoa, Selected Poems, 1971; A History of the French Language, 1974; Chrestomathie de la langue française au XVe siècle, 1976; (ed with T. G. S. Combe) L. C. Harmer, Uncertainties in French Grammar, 1979; The Embarrassments of Irregularity, 1981; The French Language in the 17th Century: contemporary opinion in France, 1992; articles in Romania, Trans Phil Soc., Neuphilologische Mitteilungen, Cahiers de Lexicologie, and Zeitschrift für Romanische Philologie. *Recreations:* travel, music. *Address:* Emmanuel College, Cambridge CB2 3AP. *T:* Cambridge (01223) 334223; Upper Rosevine, Portscatho, Cornwall TR2 5EW. *T:* Portscatho (01872) 580582.

RICKARDS, Dr (Richard) Barrie, CGeol, FGS; Reader in Palaeobiology, University of Cambridge, since 1990; Curator, Sedgwick Museum of Geology, since 1969; Fellow, Emmanuel College, Cambridge, since 1977; Hon. Curator, Emmanuel College Museum, since 1994; *b* 12 June 1938; *s* of Robert Rickards and Eva (*née* Sudborough); *m* 1960, Christine Townsley (marr. diss. 1991); one *s*. *Educ:* Goole Grammar Sch.; Univ. of Hull (BSc; PhD 1963; DSc 1990). MA Cantab, 1969; ScD Cantab, 1976. FGS 1960; Founder MIFM 1969; CGeol 1990. Reckitt Scholar, Univ. of Hull, 1960–63; Curator, Garwood Library, UCL, 1963; Asst in Research, Univ. of Cambridge, 1964–66; SSO, BM (Natural History), 1967; Lecturer: TCD, 1967–69; Univ. of Cambridge, 1969–90; Official Lectr, Emmanuel Coll., Cambridge, 1977–. Founder and first Sec., Pike Anglers' Club; Founding Mem., Nat. Anglers' Council; Deleg, E Reg., 1987–, Mem., Gen. Purposes Cttee, 1989–, Nat. Fedn of Anglers; Mem. Council, Waterbeach Angling Club, 1980–84; first Fishery Manager, Leland Water, 1982–83. Consultant, Shakespeare Co. (UK) Ltd, 1988–. President: Lure Fishing Soc. of GB, 1992–; Nat. Assoc. of Specialist Anglers, 1993–; Trustee, Specialist Anglers' Conservation Gp. Gov., Caldecote Co. Primary Sch., Cambs, 1994–95. Murchison Fund, Geol Soc., 1982; John Phillips Medal, Yorks Geol Soc., 1988. *Publications: angling:* (with R. Webb) Fishing for Big Pike, 1971, (sole author) 3rd edn, as Big Pike, 1986; Perch, 1974; (with R. Webb) Fishing for Big Tench, 1976, 2nd edn 1986; Pike, 1976; (with K. Whitehead) Plugs and Plug Fishing, 1976, and Spinners, Spoons and Wobbled Baits, 1977, rev. edn of both titles as A Textbook of Spinning, 1987; (with N. Fickling) Zander, 1979, 2nd edn 1990; (with K. Whitehead) Fishing Tackle, 1981; (with K. Whitehead) A Fishery of Your Own, 1984; Angling: fundamental principles, 1986; (with M. Gay) A Technical Manual of Pike Fishing, 1986; (ed) River Piking, 1987; (ed) Best of Pikelines, 1988; (with M. Gay) Pike, 1989; (with M. Bannister) The Ten Greatest Pike Anglers, 1991; (jtly) Encyclopaedia of Fishing, 1991; Success with Pike, 1992; Success with the Lure, 1993; over 400 articles on angling in newspapers and magazines; *geology:* Graptolites: writing in the rocks, 1991; (ed with D. C. Palmer) H. B. Whittington, Trilobites, 1992; upwards of 180 scientific articles and monographs in internat. jls, mostly on fossils (graptolites) and evolution. *Recreations:* angling, marathon running, angling administration (from local to national). *Address:* Emmanuel College, Cambridge CB2 3AP. *T:* Cambridge (01223) 334282.

RICKETS, Brig. Reginald Anthony Scott, (Tony); Managing Director, Irvine Development Corporation, 1981–95; *b* 13 Dec. 1929; *s* of Captain R. H. Rickets and Mrs V. C. Rickets (*née* Morgan) *m* 1952, Elizabeth Ann Serjeant; one *s* one *d*. *Educ:* St George's Coll., Weybridge; RMA Sandhurst. 2nd Lieut, RE, 1949; served with airborne, armoured and field engrs in UK, Cyrenaica, Egypt, Malaya, Borneo, Hong Kong and BAOR; special employment military forces Malaya, 1955–59; Staff Coll., Camberley, 1962; BM Engr Gp, BAOR, 1963–66; OC 67 Gurkha Indep. Field Sqn, 1966–68; DS Staff Coll., 1968–70; Comdt Gurkha Engrs/CRE Hong Kong, 1970–73; COS British Sector, Berlin, 1973–77; Col GS RSME, 1977–78; Chief Engr UKLF, 1978–81. President: Ayrshire Chamber of Industries, 1985–86; Ayrshire Chamber of Commerce and Industry, 1989–91 (Vice Pres., 1992–); Chm., Scottish Cttee, German British Chamber of Industry and Commerce, 1992–; Mem. Exec. Bd, Scottish Council (Develt and Industry), 1990–92; Director: Enterprise Ayrshire, 1990–; ASSET Enterprise Trust, 1995–; Kelvin Travel, 1995–. Dir, Ex-Services Mentally Disabled Welfare Soc., 1986–. *Recreation:* sailing. *Address:* 10 Waterside Street, Largs, Ayrshire KA30 9LN. *Club:* Royal Engineer Yacht (Commodore, 1979–81).

RICKETT, Sir Denis Hubert Fletcher, KCMG 1956 (CMG 1947); CB 1951; Director: Schroder International, 1974–79; De La Rue Co., 1974–77; Adviser, J. Henry Schroder Wagg & Co., 1974–79; *b* 27 July 1907; *s* of late Hubert Cecil Rickett, OBE, JP; *m* 1946, Ruth Pauline (MB, BS, MRCS, LRCP), *d* of late William Anderson Armstrong, JP; two *s* one *d*. *Educ:* Rugby School; Balliol College, Oxford (Schol. 1925; Jenkyns Exhibnr 1929; 1st cl. Hon. Mods 1927; 1st cl. Lit.Hum. 1929). Fellow of All Souls College, Oxford, 1929–49. Joined staff of Economic Advisory Council, 1931; Offices of War Cabinet, 1939; Principal Private Secretary to Right Honourable Oliver Lyttelton, when Minister of Production, 1943–45; Personal Assistant (for work on Atomic Energy) to Rt Hon. Sir John Anderson, when Chancellor of the Exchequer, 1945; transferred to Treasury, 1947; Principal Private Secretary to the Rt Hon. C. R. Attlee, when Prime Minister, 1950–51; Economic Minister, British Embassy, Washington, and Head of UK Treasury and Supply Delegation, 1951–54; Third Secretary, HM Treasury, 1955–60, Second Secretary, 1960–68. Vice-Pres., World Bank, 1968–74. *Recreation:* music. *Address:* 9 The Close, Salisbury, Wilts SP1 2EB. *T:* Salisbury (01722) 320125.*Clubs:* Athenæum, Brooks's.

See also W. F. S. Rickett.

RICKETT, Sir Raymond (Mildmay Wilson), Kt 1990; CBE 1984; BSc, PhD, CChem, FRSC; Chairman, Mid Kent Health Care Trust, since 1992; *b* 17 March 1927; *s* of Mildmay Louis Rickett and Winifred Georgina Rickett; *m* 1958, Naomi Nishida; one *s* two *d*. *Educ:* Faversham Grammar Sch.; Medway Coll. of Technology (BSc London); Illinois Inst. of Technology (PhD). Royal Navy, 1946–48; Medway Coll. of Technology, 1953–55; Illinois Inst. of Technology, 1955–59; Plymouth Coll. of Technology, 1959; Lectr, Liverpool Coll. of Technology, 1960–62; Senr Lectr/Principal Lectr, West Ham Coll. of Technology, 1962–64; Head of Dept, Wolverhampton Coll. of Technology, 1965–66; Vice-Principal, Sir John Cass Coll., 1967–69; Vice-Provost, City of London Polytechnic, 1969–72; Dir, Middlesex Polytechnic, 1972–91; Chm., CNAA, 1991–93. Chairman: Cttee of Dirs of Polytechnics, 1980–82 and 1986–88; UK Nat. Commn for UNESCO Educn Adv. Cttee, 1983–85; IUPC, 1988–91; Cttee for Internat. Co-operation in Higher Educn, 1988–91; UK Erasmus Students Grants Council, 1988–93; Kent Council on Addiction, 1991–; Member: Oakes Cttee, 1977–78; Higher Educn Review Group for NI, 1978–82; NAB Bd, 1981–87; Open Univ. Council, 1983–93; Council for Industry and Higher Educn, 1985–91; British Council Bd, 1988–91; Erasmus (EEC) Adv. Cttee, 1988–90. Governor, Yehudi Menuhin Live Music Now Scheme, 1977–. Member: Council, Univ. of Kent, 1991–; Corp., Canterbury Coll., 1992–; Council, Strode Park Foundn, 1992–. Officer's Cross, Order of Merit (FRG), 1988. *Publications:* Experiments in Physical Chemistry (jtly), 1962, new edn 1968; 2 chapters in The Use of the Chemical Literature, 1962, 3rd edn 1992; articles on Polytechnics in the national press and contribs to learned jls. *Recreations:* cricket, theatre-going, opera. *Address:* 1 The Barn, Pontus Farm, Knockwood Lane, Molash, near Canterbury, Kent CT4 8HW. *Club:* Athenæum.

RICKETT, William Francis Sebastian; Director of Finance (Central), Department of the Environment, since 1993; *b* 23 Feb. 1953; *s* of Sir Denis Rickett, *qv*; *m* 1979, Lucy Caroline Clark; one *s* one *d*. *Educ:* Eton; Trinity Coll., Cambridge (BA 1974). Joined Department of Energy, 1975; Private Sec. to Perm. Under Sec. of State, 1977; Principal, 1978; Private Sec. to Prime Minister, 1981–83; seconded to Kleinwort Benson Ltd, 1983–85; Asst Sec., Oil Div., Dept of Energy, 1985; Asst Sec., Electricity Privatisation, 1987; Grade 4, Electricity Div., 1989; Under Sec., 1990; Dir Gen., Energy Efficiency Office, Dept of Energy, 1990–92, DoE, 1992–93. *Recreations:* children, painting, sports. *Address:* Department of the Environment, 2 Marsham Street, SW1P 3EB. *T:* 0171–276 3000.

RICKETTS, (Anne) Theresa, (Lady Ricketts), CBE 1983; Chairman, National Association of Citizens' Advice Bureaux, 1979–84; *b* 12 April 1919; *d* of late Rt Hon. Sir (Richard) Stafford Cripps, CH, FRS, QC, and Dame Isobel Cripps, GBE; *m* 1945, Sir Robert Ricketts, Bt, *qv*; two *s* two *d*. *Educ:* Oxford University. Second Officer, WRNS, War of 1939–45. Joined Citizens' Advice Bureaux Service, 1962. Member: Electricity Consumers' Council, 1977–90; Council, Direct Mail Services Standards Board, 1983–92. *Recreations:* gardening, field botany. *Address:* Forwood House, Minchinhampton, Stroud, Glos GL6 9AB. *T:* Stroud (01453) 882160. *Club:* Commonwealth Trust.

RICKETTS, Prof. Martin John, DPhil; Professor of Economic Organisation, University of Buckingham, since 1987; *b* 10 May 1948; *s* of Leonard Alfred Ricketts and Gertrude Dorothy (*née* Elgar); *m* 1975, Diana Barbara Greenwood; one *s* one *d*. *Educ:* City of Bath Boys' Sch.; Univ. of Newcastle upon Tyne (BA Hons Econ.); Univ. of York (DPhil). Econ. Asst, Industrial Policy Gp, 1970–72; Res. Fellow, Inst. Econ. and Social Res., Univ. of York, 1975–77; University College at Buckingham, later University of Buckingham: Lectr in Econs, 1977–82; Sen. Lectr, 1982–85; Reader, 1985–87; Dean, Sch. of Accountancy, Business and Econs, 1993–; Pro-Vice-Chancellor, 1993. Economic Dir, NEDO, 1991–92. Vis. Prof., Virginia Poly. Inst. and State Univ., 1984. Trustee, Inst. of Econ. Affairs, 1992–. *Publications:* (with M. G. Webb) The Economics of Energy, 1980; The Economics of Business Enterprise: new approaches to the firm, 1987, 2nd edn 1994; papers on public finance, public choice, housing econs and econ. orgn. *Recreation:* music, student of piano and oboe. *Address:* 22 Bradfield Avenue, Buckingham MK18 1PR; School of Economics, University of Buckingham, Hunter Street, Buckingham MK18 1EG.

RICKETTS, Michael Rodney, MA; Headmaster, Sutton Valence School, 1967–80; *b* 29 Sept. 1923; *er s* of late Rt Rev. C. M. Ricketts, Bishop of Dunwich, and Dorothy Ricketts; *m* 1958, Judith Anne Caroline Corry; two *s* two *d*. *Educ:* Sherborne; Trinity Coll., Oxford. Served War of 1939–45: in 8th Army, Africa, Italy, with 60th Rifles, 1942–47. Trinity Coll., Oxford, 1947–50; Asst Master and Housemaster, Bradfield Coll., 1950–67. Dir, ISIS (Eastern England), 1980–; Nat. ISIS Management Cttee, 1981–. Member: HMC Cttee, 1976–79 (Chm., HMC/SHA Services Cttee, 1975–80); British Atlantic Cttee, 1974–, Council, 1979–; Chairman: British Atlantic Educn Cttee, 1984–87 (Mem., 1974–); Atlantic Educn Cttee, 1986–. Governor: Gresham's Sch.; Orwell Park; Vinehall. Fellow, Woodard Corp. *Recreations:* cricket, shooting, country activities. *Address:* Church Farm, Saxlingham, Holt, Norfolk NR25 7JY. *T:* Binham (01328) 830307. *Clubs:* East India, Devonshire, Sports and Public Schools, Free Foresters, Harlequins, I Zingari, MCC; Vincent's (Oxford).

RICKETTS, Sir Robert (Cornwallis Gerald St Leger), 7th Bt, *cr* 1828; retired Solicitor; *b* 8 Nov. 1917; *s* of Sir Claude Albert Frederick Ricketts, 6th Bt, and Lilian Helen Gwendoline (*d* 1955), *o d* of Arthur M. Hill, late 5th Fusiliers; *S* father 1937; *m* 1945, Anne Theresa Cripps (*see* A. T. Ricketts); two *s* two *d*. *Educ:* Haileybury; Magdalene College, Cambridge (2nd Cl. Hons in History and Law, BA 1939, MA 1943). Served War of 1939–45 (Captain, Devon Regiment); Personal Assistant to Chief of Staff, Gibraltar, 1942–45; ADC to Lieutenant-Governor of Jersey, 1945–46. Formerly Partner in Wellington and Clifford. FRSA. Hon. Citizen, Mobile, USA, 1970. *Heir: s* Robert Tristram Ricketts, *qv*. *Address:* Forwood House, Minchinhampton, Stroud, Glos GL6 9AB. *TA* and *T:* Stroud (01453) 882160.

See also G. F. P. Mason.

RICKETTS, (Robert) Tristram; Chief Executive, British Horseracing Board, since 1993; *b* 17 April 1946; *s* of Sir Robert Ricketts, Bt, *qv* and Lady Ann Theresa Ricketts, *qv*; *m* 1969, Ann Lewis; one *s* one *d*. *Educ:* Winchester Coll.; Magdalene Coll., Cambridge (BA Hons 1968; MA 1972). Admin. Officer, GLC, 1968–72; Personal Asst to Leader of GLC, 1972–73; Horserace Betting Levy Board: Asst Principal Officer, 1974–76; Dep. Sec., 1976–79; Sec., 1980–84; Chief Exec., 1984–93. *Recreations:* horseracing, theatre, cinema, making bonfires. *Address:* 47 Lancaster Avenue, SE27 9EL. *T:* 0181–670 8422. *Club:* Athenæum.

RICKETTS, Theresa; *see* Ricketts, A. T.

RICKETTS, Tristram; *see* Ricketts, R. T.

RICKFORD, Jonathan Braithwaite Keevil; Director of Corporate Strategy, British Telecommunications plc, since 1993; *b* 7 Dec. 1944; *s* of R. B. K. Rickford, MD, FRCS, FRCOG and of Dorothy Rickford (*née* Lathan); *m* 1968, Dora R. Sargant; one *s* two *d*. *Educ:* Sherborne School; Magdalen College, Oxford (BA (Jurisp.); BCL). Barrister, 1970–85; Solicitor, 1985–. Teaching Associate, Univ. of California Sch. of Law, 1968–69; Lectr in Law, LSE, 1969–72; Legal Asst, Dept of Trade, 1972–73; Senior Legal Assistant: Dept of Prices and Consumer Protection, 1974–76; Law Officers' Dept, Attorney General's Chambers, 1976–79; Dept of Trade and Industry (formerly Dept of Trade): Asst Solicitor (Company Law), 1979–82; Under Sec. (Legal), 1982–85; Solicitor, 1985–87; British Telecom: Solicitor and Chief Legal Advr, 1987–89; Dir of Govt Relns, 1989–93. FRSA 1992. *Publications:* articles in learned jls. *Recreation:* sailing. *Address:* BT Centre, 81 Newgate Street, EC1A 7AJ. *T:* 0171–356 6233. *Club:* Reform.

RICKMAN, Alan; actor. *Educ:* Latymer Upper Sch.; Chelsea Sch. of Art (DipAD); Royal Coll. of Art; RADA. *Theatre* includes: The Devil is an Ass, Measure for Measure, Birmingham, Edinburgh Fest., Nat. Theatre, European tour, 1976–77; The Tempest, Captain Swing, Love's Labour's Lost, Antony and Cleopatra, RSC, 1978–79; The Summer Party, Crucible, 1980; Commitments, Bush, 1980; The Devil Himself, Lyric Studio, 1980; Philadelphia Story, Oxford Playhouse, 1981; The Seagull, Royal Court, 1981; Brothers Karamazov, Edinburgh Fest. and USSR, 1981; The Last Elephant, Bush, 1981; Bad Language, Hampstead, 1983; The Grass Widow, 1983, The Lucky Chance, 1984, Royal Court; As You Like It, Troilus and Cressida, Les Liaisons Dangereuses, Mephisto, RSC, 1985–86; Les Liaisons Dangereuses, West End and Broadway, 1986–87; Tango at the End of Winter, Edinburgh and West End, 1991; Hamlet, Riverside Studios and Brit. Tour, 1992; *director:* Desperately Yours, NY, 1980; (asst dir) Other Worlds, Royal Ct, 1983; Live Wax, Edin. Fest., 1986; Wax Acts, West End and tour, 1992; The Winter Guest, Almeida, 1995; *films:* Die Hard, 1988; The January Man, 1989; Quigley Down Under, 1990; Truly, Madly, Deeply, 1991; Closetland, 1991; Close My Eyes, 1991; Robin Hood, Prince of Thieves, 1991; Bob Roberts, 1992; Fallen Angels (TV, USA), 1993; An Awfully Big Adventure, 1995; Sense and Sensibility, 1996; *television* includes: Thérèse Raquin, 1979; Barchester Chronicles, 1982; Pity in History, 1984; Revolutionary Witness, Spirit of Man, 1989; also radio performances. Bancroft Gold Medal, RADA, 1974; Seattle Film Fest. Best Actor, 1991; Time Out Award for Tango at the End of Winter, 1992; BAFTA Film Award for Best Supporting Actor, 1992; Evening Standard Film Award for Best Actor, 1992; Best Actor, Montreal Film Fest., 1994. *Publication:* (contrib.) Players of Shakespeare, Vol 2, 1989. *Address:* c/o ICM, Oxford House, 76 Oxford Street, W1R 1RB.

RICKMAN, Prof. Geoffrey Edwin, FBA 1989; Professor of Roman History, since 1981, and Master of the United College of St Salvator and St Leonard, since 1992, University of St Andrews; *b* 9 Oct. 1932; *s* of Charles Edwin Rickman and Ethel Ruth Mary (*née* Hill); *m* 1959, Ann Rosemary Wilson; one *s* one *d*. *Educ:* Peter Symonds' Sch., Winchester; Brasenose Coll., Oxford (MA, DipClassArchaeol, DPhil). FSA 1966. Henry Francis Pelham Student, British Sch. at Rome, 1958–59; Jun. Res. Fellow, The Queen's Coll., Oxford, 1959–62; University of St Andrews: Lectr in Ancient History, 1962–68; Sen. Lectr, 1968–81. Vis. Fellow, Brasenose Coll., Oxford, 1981; Mem., Faculty of Archaeol., History and Letters, British Sch. at Rome, 1979–87 (Chm., 1983–87). *Publications:* Roman Granaries and Storebuildings, 1971; The Corn Supply of Ancient Rome, 1980. *Recreations:* opera, swimming, walking beside the sea. *Address:* 56 Hepburn Gardens, St Andrews, Fife KY16 9DG. *T:* St Andrews (01334) 472063.

RICKS, Prof. Christopher Bruce, FBA 1975; Professor of English, Boston University, since 1986; *b* 18 Sept. 1933; *s* of James Bruce Ricks and Gabrielle Roszak; *m* 1st, 1956, Kirsten Jensen (marr. diss.); two *s* two *d*; 2nd, 1977, Judith Aronson; one *s* two *d*. *Educ:* King Alfred's Sch., Wantage; Balliol Coll., Oxford (Hon. Fellow, 1989). 2nd Lieut, Green Howards, 1952. BA 1956, BLitt 1958, MA 1960, Oxon. Andrew Bradley Jun. Res. Fellow, Balliol Coll., Oxford, 1957; Fellow of Worcester Coll., Oxford, 1958–68 (Hon. Fellow, 1990); Prof. of English, Bristol Univ., 1968–75; University of Cambridge: Prof. of English, 1975–82; King Edward VII Prof. of English Lit., 1982–86; Fellow, Christ's Coll., 1975–86 (Hon. Fellow, 1993). Visiting Professor: Berkeley and Stanford, 1965; Smith Coll., 1967; Harvard, 1971; Wesleyan, 1974; Brandeis, 1977, 1981, 1984. Lectures: Lord Northcliffe, UCL, 1972; Alexander, Univ. of Toronto, 1987; T. S. Eliot, Univ. of Kent, 1988; Clarendon, Univ. of Oxford, 1990; Clark, Trinity Coll., Cambridge, 1991. A Vice-Pres., Tennyson Soc. Co-editor, Essays in Criticism. Fellow, American Acad. of Arts and Scis, 1991. George Orwell Meml Prize, 1979; Beefeater Club Prize for Literature, 1980. *Publications:* Milton's Grand Style, 1963; (ed) The Poems of Tennyson, 1969, rev. edn 1987; Tennyson, 1972, rev. edn 1989; Keats and Embarrassment, 1974; (ed with Leonard Michaels) The State of the Language, 1980, new edn 1990; The Force of Poetry, 1984; (ed) The New Oxford Book of Victorian Verse, 1987; (ed) A. E. Housman: Collected Poems and Selected Prose, 1988; T. S. Eliot and Prejudice, 1988; (ed with William Vance) The Faber Book of America, 1992; Beckett's Dying Words, 1993. *Address:* 39 Martin Street, Cambridge, MA 02138, USA. *T:* (617) 3547887; Lasborough Cottage, Lasborough Park, near Tetbury, Glos GL8 8UF. *T:* Leighterton (01666) 890252.

RICKS, David Trulock, OBE 1981; British Council Director, France, and Cultural Counsellor, British Embassy, Paris, since 1990; *b* 28 June 1936; *s* of Percival Trulock Ricks and Annetta Helen (*née* Hood); *m* 1960, Nicole Estelle Aimée Chupeau; two *s*. *Educ:* Kilburn Grammar Sch.; Royal Acad. of Music; Merton Coll., Oxford (MA); Univ. of London Inst. of Educn; Univ. of Lille (LèsL). Teaching in Britain, 1960–67; joined British Council, 1967: Rabat, 1967–70; Univ. of Essex, 1970–71; Jaipur, 1971–74, New Delhi, 1974; Dar Es Salaam, 1974–76; Tehran, 1976–80; London, 1980–85; Rep., Italy, and Cultural Counsellor, British Embassy, Rome, 1985–90. FRSA 1989. *Publications:* (jtly) Penguin French Reader, 1967; (jtly) New Penguin French Reader, 1992. *Recreations:* music, playing the piano, ski-ing. *Address:* c/o The British Council, 10 Spring Gardens, SW1A 2BN. *T:* 0171–930 8466. *Club:* United Oxford & Cambridge University.

RICKS, Robert Neville; Legal Adviser, Department for Education (formerly Department of Education and Science), since 1990; *b* 29 June 1942; *s* of Sir John Plowman Ricks. *Educ:* Highgate Sch.; Worcester Coll., Oxford (MA). Admitted Solicitor, 1967. Entered Treasury Solicitor's Dept as Legal Asst, 1969; Sen. Legal Asst, 1973; Asst Solicitor, 1981; Prin. Asst Solicitor, 1986. *Recreations:* collecting original cartoons, wine. *Address:* 2 Eaton Terrace, Aberavon Road, E3 5AJ. *T:* 0181–981 3722.

RICKUS, Gwenneth Margaret, CBE 1981; Director of Education, London Borough of Brent, 1971–84; *b* 1925; *d* of Leonard William Ernest and Florence Rickus. *Educ:* Latymer Sch., Edmonton; King's Coll., Univ. of London. BA, PGCE. Teaching, 1948–53; Asst Sec., AAM, 1953–61; Education Administration: Mddx CC, 1961–65; London Borough of Brent, 1965–84. Cllr (Lib Dem), New Forest DC, 1991–. Co-opted Mem. Educn Cttee, Hampshire CC, 1985–. Comr for Racial Equality, 1977–80. *Recreations:* walking, reading, crafts, gardening, music, politics.

RIDD, John William Gregory; HM Diplomatic Service, retired; Regional Director, British Executive Service Overseas, since 1994; *b* 4 June 1931; *s* of William John and Lilian Gregory Cooke; adoptive *s* of Philip and Elizabeth Anne Ridd; *m* 1956, Mary Elizabeth Choat; three *s* one *d*. *Educ:* Lewis' Sch., Pengam; Wallington County Grammar Sch.; St Edmund Hall, Oxford (BA Hons 1954). National Service, 1949–51 (Army). Foreign Office, 1954; Buenos Aires, 1957–61; First Sec., Cairo, 1963–66, Prague, 1968–70, Brasilia, 1974–77; First Sec., later Counsellor, FCO, 1978–91. *Recreations:* books, distance running, allotment gardening, travel, music, singing.

RIDDELL, (John) Alistair, OBE 1988; Treasurer, British Medical Association, since 1987; *b* 11 Feb. 1930; *s* of Alexander Riddell and Mamie McFarlane MacKintosh; *m* 1956, Elizabeth Park McDonald Davidson; one *s* three *d*. *Educ:* Glasgow Acad.; Glasgow Univ. (MB ChB). FRCGP 1983. GP E Glasgow, 1956–95; Clinical Asst, Geriatrics, Lightburn Hosp., 1968–78. Member: Glasgow Local Med. Cttee, 1964–95 (Med. Sec., 1978–91); Scottish GDC, 1975–82; Gen. Med. Services Cttee, 1972– (Negotiator, 1982–87; Vice-Chm., 1985–87); Chairman: Scottish Gen. Med. Services Cttee, 1983–86; Glasgow Area Med. Cttee. Mem. Council, BMA, 1983– (Chm., Community Care Cttee, 1991–); Treas., Commonwealth Med. Assoc., 1979–. Dir, GP Finance Corp., 1975–90 (Vice-Chm., 1989–90); Dir, BMAS, 1987–. Mem., CAB Easter House, 1974–77. Mem., Bonnetmakers' Craft and Grand Antiquity Soc., Glasgow. *Publications:* contrib. BMJ and Scottish Med. Jl. *Recreations:* golf, ski-ing, sailing. *Address:* 4 Easter Drumlins, 47 Partickhill Road, Glasgow G11 5AB. *T:* 0141–337 3304; Town Head, 16 Alexandra Parade, Glasgow G31 2ES. *Club:* Royal Society of Medicine.

RIDDELL, Sir John (Charles Buchanan), 13th Bt, *cr* 1628; CVO 1990; CA; DL; Extra Equerry to HRH the Prince of Wales, since 1990; *b* 3 Jan. 1934; *o s* of Sir Walter Buchanan Riddell, 12th Bt, and Hon. Rachel Beatrice Lyttelton (*d* 1965), *y d* of 8th Viscount Cobham; *S* father 1934; *m* 1969, Hon. Sarah (LVO 1993), *o d* of Baron Richardson of Duntisbourne, *qv*; three *s*. *Educ:* Eton; Christ Church, Oxford. 2nd Lieut Rifle Bde, 1952–54. With IBRD, Washington DC, 1969–71; Associate, First Boston Corp., 1972–75; Director: First Boston (Europe) Ltd, 1975–78; UK Provident Instn, 1975–85; Northern Rock Bldg Soc., 1981–85, 1990– (Dep. Chm., 1992–); Northumbrian Water Gp, 1992–; Alpha Bank London Ltd, 1995–; Chm., Govelt Strategic Investment Trust, 1995–; Dep. Chm., Credit Suisse First Boston Ltd, 1990–95 (Dir, 1978–85). Dep Chm., IBA, 1981–85; Private Sec., 1985–90, and Treasurer, 1986–90, to TRH the Prince and Princess of Wales; Member, Prince's Council, 1985–90. Contested (C): Durham NW, Feb. 1974; Sunderland S, Oct. 1974. Mem., Bloomsbury DHA, 1982–85; Trustee, Buttle Trust, 1981–87. Chm., Northumbria Regl Cttee, NT, 1995–. FRSA 1990. DL Northumberland, 1990. *Heir: s* Walter John Buchanan Riddell, *b* 10 June 1974. *Address:* Hepple, Morpeth, Northumberland NE65 7LN. *TA:* Hepple; 49 Campden Hill Square, W8 7JR. *Clubs:* Garrick; Northern Counties (Newcastle upon Tyne).

See also R. L. Ollard, Sir J. L. Pumphrey.

RIDDELL, Norman Malcolm Marshall; Chief Executive, INVESCO Group, since 1993; *b* 30 June 1947; *s* of Malcolm Riddell and Euphemia Richardson Riddell (*née* Wight); *m* 1969, Leila Jean White; three *s*. *Educ:* George Heriot's Sch., Edinburgh. MCIBS, AIIMR. National Commercial Bank and Royal Bank of Scotland, 1965–78; Man. Dir, Britannia Investment Services, 1978–86; Chief Exec., Capital House Investment Management, 1986–93; Dir, Charterhouse Gp, 1986–89; Life Assce Hldg Corp., 1995–. *Recreations:* plate collecting, gardening, most sports (spectator), travel, music. *Address:* INVESCO, 11 Devonshire Square, EC2M 4TR; Long Bar, Little Hallingbury, Bishops Stortford, Herts CM22 7QU. *T:* Bishops Stortford (01279) 726545. *Club:* Capital.

RIDDELL, Peter John Robert; Political Columnist, since 1991 and Assistant Editor (Politics), since 1993, The Times; *b* 14 Oct. 1948; *s* of late Kenneth Robert Riddell and of Freda Riddell (*née* Young); *m* 1994, Avril Walker. *Educ:* Dulwich Coll.; Sidney Sussex Coll., Cambridge (BA Hist. and Econs 1970, MA). Joined Financial Times, 1970: Property Corresp., 1972–74; Lex Column, 1975–76; Economics Corresp., 1976–81; Political Editor, 1981–88; US Editor and Washington Bureau Chief, 1989–91; joined The Times, 1991, Political Editor, 1992–93. Regular broadcaster, Week in Westminster, Talking Politics, Radio 4, and on TV. Wincott Award for Economic and Financial Journalism, 1981; House Magazine Political Journalist of the Year, 1986. *Publications:* The Thatcher Government, 1983, rev. edn 1985; The Thatcher Decade, 1989, rev. edn as The Thatcher Era, 1991; Honest Opportunism, the rise of the career politician, 1993; contrib. chaps in books, incl. A Conservative Revolution?, 1994, and The Major Effect, 1994; contrib. to Spectator, New Statesman, Political Qly, British Journalism Rev., TLS, Jl of Lesgislative Studies. *Recreations:* watching cricket, opera, theatre. *Address:* 22 Falkland Road, NW5 2PX. *T:* 0171–267 0495. *Clubs:* Garrick, MCC.

RIDDELL-WEBSTER, John Alexander, MC 1943; farmer; Member (C) Tayside Regional Council, 1986–94; *b* 17 July 1921; *s* of Gen. Sir Thomas Riddell-Webster, GCB, DSO; *m* 1960, Ruth, *d* of late S. P. L. A. Lithgow; two *s* one *d*. *Educ:* Harrow; Pembroke Coll., Cambridge. Seaforth Highlanders (Major), 1940–46. Joined Anglo-Iranian Oil Co., 1946; served in Iran, Iraq, Bahrain, Aden; Vice-Pres. Marketing, BP Canada, 1959; Dir, Shell-Mex and BP, 1965, Man. Dir, Marketing, 1971–75; Dir, BP Oil Ltd, 1975–82 (Dep. Man. Dir, 1976–80); Dir, Public Affairs, Scotland, BP, 1979–81. Mem. Cttee, AA, 1980–90; Mem. Exec. Cttee, Scottish Council (Develt and Industry), 1981–84; Member of Council: Advertising Assoc., 1974–80; Inc. Soc. of British Advertisers, 1968–80; for Vehicle Servicing and Repair, 1972–80 (Chm., 1975); Royal Warrant Holders' Assoc. (Vice-Pres., 1979; Pres., 1980); British Road Fedn, 1971–80; Chm., Transport Action Scotland, 1982–; Pres., Oil Industries Club, 1977–78. CIMgt. *Recreations:* shooting, fishing, gardening. *Address:* Lintrose, Coupar Angus, Perthshire PH13 9JQ. *T:* Coupar Angus (01828) 627472. *Clubs:* New (Edinburgh); Royal Perth Golfing Society.

RIDDELSDELL, Dame Mildred, DCB 1972; CBE 1958; Second Permanent Secretary, Department of Health and Social Security, 1971–73; (Deputy Secretary, 1966–71); *b* 1 Dec. 1913; 2nd *d* of Rev. H. J. Riddelsdell. *Educ:* St Mary's Hall, Brighton; Bedford Coll., London. Entered Min. of Labour, 1936; Asst Sec., Min. of National Insurance, 1945; Under Secretary, 1950; On loan to United Nations, 1953–56; Secretary, National Incomes Commission, 1962–65; Ministry of Pensions and National Insurance, 1965, Social Security, 1966. Chm., CS Retirement Fellowship, 1974–77. *Recreation:* gardening. *Address:* 26A New Yatt Road, Witney, Oxon OX8 6NZ.

RIDDICK, Graham Edward Galloway; MP (C) Colne Valley, since 1987; *b* 26 Aug. 1955; *s* of John Julian Riddick and late Cecilia Margaret Riddick (*née* Ruggles-Brise); *m* 1988, Sarah Northcroft; one *s* one *d*. *Educ:* Stowe Sch., Buckingham; Univ. of Warwick (Chm., Warwick Univ. Cons. Assoc.). Sales management with Procter & Gamble, 1977–82; Coca-Cola, 1982–87. PPS to Financial Sec. to HM Treasury, 1990–92, to Sec. of State for Transport, 1992–. Vice Chm., Cons. Trade and Industry Cttee, 1990;

Secretary: Cons. Employment Cttee, 1988–90; All Party Textiles Gp, 1988–. Chm., Angola Study Gp, 1988–; Mem. Nat. Council, Freedom Assoc, 1988–; Pres., Yorks CPC, 1993–. First Cons. MP in Colne Valley for 102 years. *Recreations:* fishing, shooting, sports, bridge. *Address:* House of Commons, SW1A 0AA. *T:* 0171–219 4215. *Clubs:* Carlton; Yorkshire Cricket.

RIDDLE, Hugh Joseph, (Huseph), RP 1960; Artist; Portrait Painter; *b* 24 May 1912; *s* of late Hugh Howard Riddle and late Christine Simons Brown; *m* 1936, Joan Claudia Johnson (*d* 1994); one *s* two *d*. *Educ:* Harrow; Magdalen, Oxford; Slade School of Art; Byam Shaw School of Art and others. *Recreations:* sailing, swimming, gardening. *Address:* 18 Boulevard Verdi, Domaine du château de Tournon, Montauroux 83440, France.

RIDEOUT, Prof. Roger William; Professor of Labour Law, University College, London, since 1973; *b* 9 Jan. 1935; *s* of Sidney and Hilda Rideout; *m* 1st, 1959, Marjorie Roberts (marr. diss. 1976); one *d*; 2nd, 1977, Gillian Margaret Lynch. *Educ:* Bedford School; University Coll., London (LLB, PhD). Called to the Bar, Gray's Inn, 1964. National Service, 1958–60; 2nd Lt RAEC, Educn Officer, 1st Bn Coldstream Guards. Lecturer: Univ. of Sheffield, 1960–63; Univ. of Bristol, 1963–64. University Coll., London: Sen. Lectr, 1964–65; Reader, 1965–73; Dean of Faculty of Laws, 1975–77. ILO missions to The Gambia, 1982–83, Somalia, 1989–90, Egypt, 1992–. Dep. Chairman: Central Arbitration Cttee; Industrial Tribunals. ACAS panel arbitrator, 1981–; Vice-Pres., Industrial Law Society. Mem., Zool Soc. of London. Jt Editor, Current Legal Problems, 1975–92; Gen. Editor, Federation News, 1989–. *Publications:* The Right to Membership of a Trade Union, 1962; The Practice and Procedure of the NIRC, 1973; Trade Unions and the Law, 1973; Principles of Labour Law, 1972, 5th edn 1989. *Address:* 255 Chipstead Way, Woodmansterne, Surrey SM7 3JW. *T:* Downland (01737) 552033. *Club:* MCC.

RIDER, Stephen Henry; Main Presenter, BBC Grandstand, since 1992; *b* 28 April 1950; *s* of Alfred Charles Rider and Shirley Jeanette (*née* Walls); *m* 1985, Jane Eydmann; one *s* one *d*. *Educ:* Roan Grammar Sch., Blackheath. Local sports journalist, S London and sports presenter for London Broadcasting, 1969–76; Sports Presenter: Anglia TV, 1976–80; ITV Network, incl., World of Sport, 1980 Olympics, Midweek Sports Special, Network Golf, 1980–85; Network Presenter for BBC Sport: Main Presenter, Sportsnight, 1985–92; network golf coverage; Seoul and Barcelona Olympics, 1988 and 1992; Commonwealth Games, 1986, 1990 and 1994; main network golf presenter, 1991–; motor sport specialist; Presenter, Grandstand, 1985–. Sports Presenter of Year, TRIC, 1994. *Recreations:* golf, family. *Address:* c/o Blackburn Sachs Associates, Eastgate House, 16–19 Eastcastle Street, W1N 7PA.

RIDGE, Anthony Hubert; Director-General, International Bureau, Universal Postal Union, Bern, 1973–74 (Deputy Director-General, 1964–73); *b* 5 Oct. 1913; *s* of Timothy Leopold Ridge and Magdalen (*née* Hernig); *m* 1938, Marjory Joan Sage; three *s* one *d*. *Educ:* Christ's Hospital; Jesus College, Cambridge. Entered GPO, 1937; seconded to Min. Home Security, 1940; GPO Personnel Dept, 1944; PPS to Postmaster General, 1947; Dep. Dir, London Postal Region, 1949; Asst Sec., Overseas Mails, 1951, Personnel, 1954, Overseas Mails, 1956; Director of Clerical Mechanization and Buildings, and Member of Post Office Board, GPO, 1960–63. Mem., Postling Parish Council, 1979–87. Governor, Christ's Hosp. *Recreations:* music, languages, transport, gardening, two donkeys. *Address:* Staple, Postling, Hythe, Kent CT21 4HA. *T:* Lyminge (01303) 862315. *Clubs:* Christ's Hospital, United Oxford & Cambridge University, Cambridge Society.

RIDGE, Rupert Leander Pattle; International Director, Leonard Cheshire Foundation, since 1994; *b* 18 May 1947; *y s* of late Major Robert Vaughan Ridge and Marian Ivy Edith Ridge (*née* Pattle); *m* 1971, Mary Blanche Gibbs; two *s* two *d*. *Educ:* King's Coll., Taunton. Officer, LI, 1969–73. BAC, then British Aerospace Defence Ltd, 1973–94. Trustee, Action around Bethlehem Children with Disability, 1994–. *Recreations:* gardening, being in the country. *Address:* (office) 26–29 Maunsel Street, SW1P 2QN. *Club:* Army and Navy.

RIDGERS, John Nalton Sharpe; Deputy Chairman and Treasurer, Lloyd's Register of Shipping, 1973–78; Director: Smit International (UK) Ltd, 1974–84; *b* 10 June 1910; 4th *c* and *o s* of Sharpe Ridgers; *m* 1936, Barbara Mary, *o d* of Robert Cobb; five *d*. *Educ:* Wellington College. Entered Lloyd's, 1928; underwriting member, 1932. Member Cttee Lloyd's Underwriters' Association, 1951–61, 1964–69, Chm. 1961; Member Joint Hull Cttee, 1957–69, Dep. Chm., 1968, Chm., 1969. Mem. Cttee of Lloyd's, 1957–60, 1962–65, Dep. Chm., 1962, Chm., 1963. Director: London Trust Co. Ltd, 1963–80; Arbuthnot Insurance Services Ltd, 1974–80; Danae Investment Trust Ltd, 1975–80. *Recreations:* snooker, carpentry. *Address:* Little Watlynge, 4 Chestnut Lane, Sevenoaks, Kent TN13 3AR.

See also R. W. Acworth.

RIDGWAY, David Frederick Charles, OBE 1988; HM Diplomatic Service; Ambassador to Bolivia, since 1995; *b* 9 June 1941; *m* 1966, Dora Beatriz Siles; one *s* one *d*. Entered FO, 1960; served La Paz, Colombo and Durban, 1963–77; First Sec. (Commercial), Buenos Aires, 1980–82; FCO, 1982–84; Chargé d'Affaires *ai*, San Salvador, 1984–87; FCO, 1988–91; Dir of Trade Promotion, Madrid, 1991–95. *Address:* c/o Foreign and Commonwealth Office, SW1A 2AH.

RIDLER, Anne (Barbara); author; *b* 30 July 1912; *o d* of late H. C. Bradby, housemaster of Rugby School, and Violet Milford; *m* 1938, Vivian Ridler, *qv*; two *s* two *d*. *Educ:* Downe House School; King's College, London; and in Florence and Rome. *Publications: poems:* Poems, 1939; A Dream Observed, 1941; The Nine Bright Shiners, 1943; The Golden Bird, 1951; A Matter of Life and Death, 1959; Selected Poems (New York), 1961; Some Time After, 1972; (contrib.) Ten Oxford Poets, 1978; New and Selected Poems, 1988; Collected Poems, 1994; *plays:* Cain, 1943; The Shadow Factory, 1946; Henry Bly and other plays, 1950; The Trial of Thomas Cranmer, 1956; Who is my Neighbour?, 1963; The Jesse Tree (libretto), 1972; The King of the Golden River (libretto), 1975; The Lambton Worm (libretto), 1978; Crucifixion Cantata (libretto), 1993; *translations:* Italian opera libretti: Rosinda, 1973; Orfeo, 1975; Eritrea, 1975; Return of Ulysses, 1978; Orontea, 1979; Agrippina, 1981; Calisto, 1984; Così fan Tutte, 1986; Don Giovanni, 1990; Marriage of Figaro, 1991; Coronation of Poppea, 1992; *biography:* Olive Willis and Downe House, 1967; *criticism:* (jtly) Profitable Wonders: aspects of Traherne, 1989; A Measure of English Poetry, 1991; *edited:* Shakespeare Criticism, 1919–35; A Little Book of Modern Verse, 1941; Best Ghost Stories, 1945; Supplement to Faber Book of Modern Verse, 1951; The Image of the City and other essays by Charles Williams, 1958; Shakespeare Criticism 1935–60, 1963; Poems of James Thomson, 1963; Thomas Traherne, 1966; (with Christopher Bradby) Best Stories of Church and Clergy, 1966; Selected Poems of George Darley, 1979; Poems of William Austin, 1983; A Victorian Family Postbag, 1988. *Recreations:* music; the theatre; the cinema. *Address:* 14 Stanley Road, Oxford OX4 1QZ. *T:* Oxford (01865) 247595.

RIDLER, Vivian Hughes, CBE 1971; MA Oxon 1958 (by decree; Corpus Christi College); Printer to the University of Oxford, 1958–78; *b* 2 Oct. 1913; *s* of Bertram Hughes Ridler and Elizabeth Emmeline (*née* Best); *m* 1938, Anne Barbara Bradby (*see* A. B. Ridler); two *s* two *d*. *Educ:* Bristol Gram. Sch. Appren. E. S. & A. Robinson, Ltd, 1931–36. Works Manager University Press, Oxford, 1948; Assistant Printer, 1949–58. Pres., British Federation of Master Printers, 1968–69. Professorial Fellow, St Edmund Hall, 1966, Emeritus Fellow, 1978. *Recreations:* printing, theatre, cinema, cinematography. *Address:* 14 Stanley Road, Oxford OX4 1QZ. *T:* Oxford (01865) 247595.

RIDLEY, family name of **Viscount Ridley.**

RIDLEY, 4th Viscount, *cr* 1900; **Matthew White Ridley,** KG 1992; GCVO 1994; TD 1960; JP; DL; Baron Wensleydale, *cr* 1900; Bt 1756; Lord-Lieutenant and Custos Rotulorum of Northumberland, since 1984; Chancellor, University of Newcastle, since 1989; Lord Steward of HM Household, since 1989; *b* 29 July 1925; *e s* of 3rd Viscount Ridley; *S* father, 1964; *m* 1953, Lady Anne Lumley, 3rd *d* of 11th Earl of Scarbrough, KG, PC, GCSI, GCIE, GCVO; one *s* three *d*. *Educ:* Eton; Balliol College, Oxford. ARICS 1951. Coldstream Guards (NW Europe), 1943–46, Captain, 1946; Northumberland Hussars, 1947–64 (Lt-Col 1961, Bt Col 1964); Hon. Colonel: Northumberland Hussars Sqdn, Queen's Own Yeomanry, 1979–86; Queen's Own Yeomanry RAC TA, 1984–86; Northumbrian Univs OTC, 1986–90; Col Comdt, Yeomanry RAC TA, 1982–86. Director: Northern Rock Building Soc., 1962– (Chm., 1987–92); Tyne Tees Television, 1964–90; Barclays Bank (NE) Ltd, 1964–90; Municipal Mutual Insurance, 1982–93. Pres., British Deer Soc., 1970–73. Member: Layfield Cttee of Enquiry into Local Govt Finance, 1974–; Commonwealth War Graves Commn, 1991–. Chm., Internat. Dendrology Soc., 1988–93. Chm., N of England TA Assoc., 1980–84; Pres., TA & VRA Council, 1984–. Chm., Newcastle Univ. Develt. Trust, 1981–84; Chancellor, 1978–80, Hon. Fellow, 1980, Newcastle upon Tyne Polytechnic. Hon. FRHS 1986; Hon. FRICS 1986. JP 1957, CC 1958, CA 1963, DL 1968, Northumberland; Chm., Northumberland CC, 1967–74, Chm., new Northumberland CC, 1974–79; Pres., ACC, 1979–84. KStJ 1984; Hon. DCL Newcastle, 1989. Order of Merit, West Germany, 1974. *Heir: s* Hon. Matthew White Ridley [*b* 7 Feb. 1958; *m* 1989, Dr Anya Hurlbert, *d* of Dr Robert Hurlbert, Houston, Texas; one *s*]. *Address:* Blagdon, Seaton Burn, Newcastle upon Tyne NE13 6DD. *T:* Stannington (01670) 789236. *Clubs:* Turf, Pratt's; Northern Counties (Newcastle upon Tyne).

RIDLEY, Sir Adam (Nicholas), Kt 1985; Executive Director, Hambros Bank PLC, since 1985; *b* 14 May 1942; *s* of Jasper Maurice Alexander Ridley and Helen Cressida Ridley (*née* Bonham Carter); *m* 1981, Margaret Anne Passmore; three *s* (inc. twin *s*). *Educ:* Eton Coll.; Balliol Coll., Oxford (1st cl. hons PPE 1965); Univ. of California, Berkeley. Foreign Office, 1965, seconded to DEA, 1965–68; Harkness Fellow, Univ. of California, Berkeley, 1968–69; HM Treasury, 1970–71, seconded to CPRS, 1971–74; Economic Advr to shadow cabinet and Asst Dir, Cons. Res. Dept, 1974–79; Special Advr to Chancellor of the Exchequer, 1979–84, to Chancellor of the Duchy of Lancaster, 1985. Mem., National Lottery Charities Bd, 1994– (Dep. Chm., 1995). *Publications:* articles on regional policy, public spending, international and Eastern European economics. *Recreations:* music, pictures, travel. *Address:* c/o Hambros Bank, 41 Tower Hill, EC3N 4HA. *Club:* Garrick.

RIDLEY, Dame Betty; *see* Ridley, Dame M. B.

RIDLEY, Prof. Brian Kidd, FRS 1994; Research Professor of Physics, University of Essex, since 1991; *b* 2 March 1931; *s* of Oliver Archbold Ridley and Lillian Beatrice Ridley; *m* 1959, Sylvia Jean Nicholls; one *s* one *d*. *Educ:* Univ. of Durham (BSc 1st Cl. Hons Physics, PhD). CPhys, FInstP. Research Physicist, Mullard Research Lab., Redhill, 1956–64; Essex University: Lectr in Physics, 1964–67; Sen. Lectr, 1967–71; Reader, 1971–84; Prof., 1984–91. Dist. Vis. Prof., Cornell Univ., 1967; Vis. Prof. at univs in USA, Denmark, Sweden and Holland. *Publications:* Time, Space and Things, 1976, 3rd edn 1995; The Physical Environment, 1979; Quantum Processors in Semiconductors, 1982, 3rd edn 1993. *Recreations:* tennis, piano. *Address:* Department of Physics, University of Essex, Colchester CO4 3SQ. *T:* Colchester (01206) 872873.

RIDLEY, Edward Alexander Keane, CB 1963; Principal Assistant Solicitor, Treasury Solicitor's Department, 1956–69, retired; *b* 16 April 1904; *s* of late Major Edward Keane Ridley, Dudswell House, near Berkhamsted, Herts, and late Ethel Janet Ridley, *d* of Alexander Forbes Tweedie; unmarried. *Educ:* Wellington College; Keble College, Oxford. Admitted Solicitor, 1928. Entered Treasury Solicitor's Department, 1934. Hon. RCM 1977. *Publications:* Wind Instruments of European Art Music, 1975; Catalogue of Wind Instruments in the Museum of the Royal College of Music, 1982. *Recreation:* music. *Address:* c/o Coutts & Co., 440 Strand, WC2R 0QS.

RIDLEY, Prof. Frederick Fernand, OBE 1978; PhD; Senior Fellow, Institute of Public Administration and Management, and Professor Emeritus, University of Liverpool, since 1995 (Professor of Political Theory and Institutions, 1965–95); *b* 11 Aug. 1928; *s* of late J. and G. A. Ridley; *m* 1967, Paula Frances Cooper Ridley, *qv*; two *s* one *d*. *Educ:* The Hall, Hampstead; Highgate Sch.; LSE (BScEcon, PhD); Univs of Paris and Berlin. Lectr, Univ. of Liverpool, 1958–65. Vis. Professor: Graduate Sch. of Public Affairs, Univ. of Pittsburgh, 1968; Coll. of Europe, Bruges, 1975–83. Manpower Services Commission, Merseyside: Chm., Job Creation Prog., 1975–77; Vice-Chm., 1978–87, Chm., 1987–88, Area Manpower Bd. Member: Jt Univ. Council for Social and Public Admin, 1964– (Chm., 1972–74); Exec., Polit. Studies Assoc., 1967–75; Council, Hansard Soc., 1970–; Polit. Science Cttee, SSRC, 1972–76; Cttee, European Gp on Public Admin, 1973–92; Public and Social Admin Bd, CNAA, 1975–82; Social Studies Res. Cttee, CNAA, 1980–83 (Chm.); Academic Cttee, Assoc. Internat. de la Fonction Publique, 1988–93; Vice Pres., Rencontres Européennes des Fonctions Publiques, 1990–. Member: Exec., Merseyside Arts (RAA), 1979–84; Adv. Council, Granada Foundn, 1984–; Council, Forschungsinst. für Verwaltungswissenschaft, Speyer, 1993–; Trustee, Friends of Merseyside Museums and Galleries, 1977–85. Hon. Pres., Politics Assoc., 1976–81. Editor: Political Studies, 1969–75; Parliamentary Affairs, 1975–. *Publications:* Public Administration in France, 1964; (ed) Specialists and Generalists, 1968; Revolutionary Syndicalism in France, 1970; The Study of Government, 1975; (ed) Studies in Politics, 1975; (ed) Government and Administration in W Europe, 1979; (ed) Policies and Politics in W Europe, 1984; numerous articles on political sci. and public admin. *Address:* Riversdale House, Grassendale Park, Liverpool L19 0LR. *T:* 0151–427 1630.

RIDLEY, Gordon, OBE 1980; MA; FICE, FIHT; retired; Director of Planning and Transportation, Greater London Council, 1978–80; *b* 1 Nov. 1921; *s* of Timothy Ridley and Lallah Sarah Ridley; *m* 1952, Doreen May Browning; one *s* one *d*. *Educ:* Selwyn Coll., Cambridge (MA). FICE 1965; FIMunE 1964; FInstHE 1966. Served War, Admiralty Signals Estab., 1941–46. Engrg appts, various local authorities, 1946–55; Bridges Br., MoT, 1955–58; AEA, 1958–63; LCC, 1963–65; engrg appts, GLC, 1965–78. *Publications:* papers on engrg topics presented to learned instns. *Recreation:* words. *Address:* 26 Greenacres, Preston Park Avenue, Brighton BN1 6HR. *T:* Brighton (01273) 559951.

RIDLEY, Harold; *see* Ridley, N. H. L.

RIDLEY, Jasper Godwin; author; *b* 25 May 1920; *s* of Geoffrey Ridley and Ursula (*née* King); *m* 1949, Vera, *d* of Emil Pollak of Prague; two *s* one *d*. *Educ:* Felcourt Sch.; Sorbonne, Paris; Magdalen Coll., Oxford. Certif. of Honour, Bar Finals. Called to Bar,

Inner Temple, 1945. St Pancras Borough Council, 1945–49. Pres., Hardwicke Soc., 1954–55. Contested (Lab): Winchester, 1955; Westbury, 1959. Vice-Pres. for life, English Centre of Internat. PEN, 1985. Mem. Ct of Assts, Carpenters' Co. (Master, 1988–89, 1990–91). Has written many radio scripts on historical subjects. FRSL 1963. *Publications:* Nicholas Ridley, 1957; The Law of Carriage of Goods, 1957; Thomas Cranmer, 1962; John Knox, 1968; Lord Palmerston, 1970 (James Tait Black Meml Prize, 1970); Mary Tudor, 1973; Garibaldi, 1974; The Roundheads, 1976; Napoleon III and Eugénie, 1979; History of England, 1981; The Statesman and the Fanatic: Thomas Wolsey and Thomas More, 1982; Henry VIII, 1984; Elizabeth I, 1987; The Tudor Age, 1988; The Love Letters of Henry VIII, 1988; Maximillian and Juárez, 1993; Tito, 1994; The Carpenters' Company, 1995. *Recreations:* walking, tennis, chess. *Address:* 6 Oakdale Road, Tunbridge Wells, Kent TN4 8DS. *T:* Tunbridge Wells (01892) 522460.

RIDLEY, Michael; *see* Ridley, R. M.

RIDLEY, Michael Kershaw, CVO 1992; Clerk of the Council, Duchy of Lancaster, since 1981; *b* 7 Dec. 1937; *s* of George K. and Mary Ridley; *m* 1968, Diana Loraine McLernon; two *s*. *Educ:* Stowe; Magdalene College, Cambridge. MA. FRICS. Grosvenor Estate, Canada and USA, 1965–69, London, 1969–72; Property Manager, British & Commonwealth Shipping Co., 1972–81. A Gen. Comr of Income Tax, 1984–. Mem., Adv. Panel, Greenwich Hosp., 1978–. Mem. Court, Lancaster Univ., 1981–. *Recreation:* golf. *Address:* Duchy of Lancaster Office, 1 Lancaster Place, Strand, WC2E 7ED. *Clubs:* Brooks's, Garrick; Royal Mid-Surrey Golf.

RIDLEY, Dame (Mildred) Betty, DBE 1975; MA (Lambeth) 1958; Third Church Estates Commissioner, 1972–81; a Church Commissioner, 1959–81; *b* 10 Sept. 1909; *d* of late Rt Rev. Henry Mosley, sometime Bishop of Southwell; *m* 1929, Rev. Michael Ridley (*d* 1953), Rector of Finchley; three *s* one *d*. *Educ:* North London Collegiate School; Cheltenham Ladies' College. Member: General Synod of Church of England, 1970–81, and its Standing Cttee, 1971–81; Central Board of Finance, 1955–79; Mem., Faculty Jurisdiction Commn, 1980–83; Vice-Pres. British Council of Churches, 1954–56. Hon. DSc (SocSc) Southampton, 1993. *Recreation:* listening to music. *Address:* 6 Lions Hall, St Swithun Street, Winchester SO23 9HW. *T:* Winchester (01962) 855009. *Club:* Reform.

RIDLEY, (Nicholas) Harold (Lloyd), MD; FRCS; FRS 1986; Hon. Consultant Surgeon, Moorfields Eye Hospital, 1971 (Surgeon, 1938–71); Hon. Consultant Surgeon, Ophthalmic Department, St Thomas' Hospital, 1971 (Ophthalmic Surgeon, 1946–71); *b* 10 July 1906; *s* of late N. C. Ridley, MB (London), FRCS, Royal Navy retired, Leicester; *m* 1941, Elisabeth Jane, *d* of late H. B. Wetherill, CIE; two *s* one *d*. *Educ:* Charterhouse; Pembroke Coll., Cambridge; St Thomas' Hospital, London. MB 1931, MD 1946, Cambridge; FRCS 1932; Hon. FCOphth 1989. Originator in 1949 of intraocular implants. Late Hon. Ophthalmic Surgeon, Royal Buckinghamshire Hospital. Temp. Major, RAMC. Hon. Cons. in Ophthalmology to Min. of Defence (Army), 1964–71; Life Pres., Internat. Intraocular Implants Club, 1972; late Vice-Pres., Ophthalmological Soc. of UK; Mem. Advisory Panel, WHO, 1966–71; Hon. Mem., Oxford Ophthalmological Congress. Hon. Fellow International College of Surgeons, Chicago, 1952; Hon. FRSM 1986; Hon. Member: Peruvian Ophthalmic Society, 1957; Ophthalmological Society of Australia, 1963; Irish Ophthalmological Society; Ophthalmological Soc. of UK, 1984; Amer. Intraocular Implants Soc., 1974; European Intra-Ocular Implantlens Council, 1983; Canadian Intraocular Implant Soc. Hon. LHD Med. Univ. of SC, 1989; Hon. DSc City Univ., 1990. Galen Medal, Apothecaries' Soc., 1986; Lord Crook Gold Medal, Spectacle Makers' Co., 1987; Gullstrand Medal, Swedish Med. Soc., 1992; Gonin Medal, Internat. Council of Ophthalmol., 1994. *Publications:* Monograph on Ocular Onchocerciasis; numerous contrib. in textbooks and medical journals on intraocular implant surgery and other subjects. *Recreation:* fly-fishing. *Address:* Keeper's Cottage, Stapleford, Salisbury, Wilts SP3 4LT. *T:* Salisbury (01722) 790209. *Club:* Flyfishers'.

RIDLEY, Paula Frances Cooper, JP; DL; MA; Chair, Liverpool Housing Action Trust, since 1992; Director, Merseyside Development Corporation, since 1991; Trustee: Tate Gallery, since 1988; National Gallery, since 1995; *b* 27 Sept. 1944; *d* of Ondrej Clyne and Ellen (*née* Cooper); *m* 1967, Frederick Fernand Ridley, *qv*; two *s* one *d*. *Educ:* Kendal High Sch., Westmorland; Univ. of Liverpool. BA, MA; Lady Pres., Guild of Undergraduates, Clerk of Convocation, 1972–74, Mem., Univ. Court, 1972–, Univ. of Liverpool. Lectr in Politics and Public Admin., Liverpool Polytechnic, 1966–71; Proj. Coordinator, Regeneration Projects Ltd, 1981–84; Dir, Community Initiatives Res. Trust, 1983–90; Consultant, BAT Industries Small Businesses Ltd, 1983–95; Bd Mem., Brunswick Small Business Centre Ltd, 1984–95; Associate, CEI Consultants, 1984–88. Presenter and Assoc. Editor, Granada Action, 1989–92; Mem., IBA, 1982–88. Chm., Stocktonwood County Primary Sch., 1976–79; Member: Liverpool Heritage Bureau, 1971–88; Management Cttee, Liverpool Victoria Settlement, 1971–86 (Vice-Chm., 1977–86); Merseyside Enterprise Forum, 1986–89; Mersey Partnership, 1990–92; Granada Telethon Trust, 1988–94. Life Governor, Liverpool and Huyton Colls, 1979–94. Chm., Tate Gall., Liverpool, 1988–; Merseyside Civic Society: Hon. Sec., 1971–82; Vice-Chm., 1982–86; Chm., 1986–91. JP Liverpool, 1977. DL Merseyside, 1989. FRSA. *Address:* Riversdale House, Grassendale Park, Liverpool L19 0LR. *T:* 0151–427 1630.

RIDLEY, Philip Waller, CB 1978; CBE 1969; Deputy Secretary, Department of Industry, 1975–80; *b* 25 March 1921; *s* of Basil White Ridley and Frida (*née* Gutknecht); *m* 1942, Foye Robins; two *s* one *d*. *Educ:* Lewes County Grammar Sch.; Trinity Coll., Cambridge. Intelligence Corps, 1941–47 (Major); German Section, FO, 1948–51; Min. of Supply, 1951–55; BoT, 1955–56 and 1960–66; Atomic Energy Office, 1956–60; Counsellor (Commercial), British Embassy, Washington, 1966–70; Under-Sec., Dept of Industry, 1971–75. Dir, Avon Rubber Co., 1980–89. *Recreations:* music, gardening, ski-ing, walking. *Address:* Old Chimneys, Plumpton Green, Lewes, East Sussex BN8 4EN. *T:* Plumpton (01273) 890342.

RIDLEY, (Robert) Michael; Principal, Royal Belfast Academical Institution, since 1990; *b* 8 Jan. 1947; *s* of Maurice Roy Ridley and Jean Evelyn Lawther (*née* Carlisle); *m* 1985, Jennifer Mary Pearson; two *d*. *Educ:* Clifton Coll.; St Edmund Hall, Oxford (MA, Cert Ed). Wellington Coll., Berks, 1970–82 (Housemaster, 1975–82); Hd of English, Merchiston Castle Sch., Edinburgh, 1982–86; Headmaster, Denstone Coll., 1986–90. *Recreations:* cricket (Oxford Blue, 1968–70), golf, reading, travel. *Address:* The Royal Belfast Academical Institution College Square East, Belfast BT1 6DL. *T:* Belfast (01232) 240461. *Clubs:* East India; Vincent's (Oxford); Boat of Garten Golf (Inverness-shire).

RIDLEY, Prof. Tony Melville, CBE 1986; PhD; FEng 1992; FICE; FCIT; Rees Jeffreys Professor of Transport Engineering, Imperial College of Science, Technology and Medicine, since 1991; *b* 10 Nov. 1933; *s* of late John Edward and of Olive Ridley; *m* 1959, Jane (*née* Dickinson); two *s* one *d*. *Educ:* Durham Sch.; King's Coll. Newcastle, Univ. of Durham (BSc); Northwestern Univ., Ill (MS); Univ. of California, Berkeley (PhD); Stanford Univ., Calif (Sen. Exec. Prog.). Nuclear Power Group, 1957–62; Univ. of California, 1962–65; Chief Research Officer, Highways and Transportation, GLC, 1965–69; Director General, Tyne and Wear Passenger Transport Exec., 1969–75; Man. Dir, Hong Kong Mass Transit Rly Corp., 1975–80; Bd Mem., 1980–88, Man. Dir (Rlys), 1980–85, LTE, then LRT; Chm., 1985–88, Man. Dir, 1985–88, Chief Exec., 1988, London Underground Ltd; Man. Dir-Project, Eurotunnel, 1989–90 (Dir, 1987–90). Chm., Docklands Light Railway Ltd, 1987–88; Director: Halcrow Fox and Associates, 1980–; London Transport Internat., 1982–88. Pres., Light Rail Transit Assoc., 1974–92; Vice-Pres., CIT, 1987–90; Mem. Council, ICE, 1990– (Chm., Transport Bd, 1990–93; Vice Pres., 1992–95; Pres., 1995–Nov. 1996). Freeman, City of London, 1982. FHKIE, FITE, FIHT 1992. Highways Award, Instn of Highways and Transportn, 1988. *Publications:* articles in transport, engrg and other jls. *Recreations:* theatre, music, international affairs, rejuvenation of Britain. *Address:* University of London Centre for Transport Studies, Department of Civil Engineering, Imperial College, SW7 2BU. *T:* 0171–589 5111, *Fax:* 0171–823 7659. *Clubs:* Hong Kong, Jockey (Hong Kong).

RIDLEY, Rear-Adm. William Terence Colborne, CB 1968; OBE 1954; Admiral Superintendent/Port Admiral, Rosyth, 1966–72; Chairman, Ex-Services Mental Welfare Society, 1973–83; *b* 9 March 1915; *s* of late Capt. W. H. W. Ridley, RN and late Vera Constance (*née* Walker); *m* 1st, 1938, Barbara Allen (*d* 1989); one *s*; 2nd, 1993, Joan Elaine Norman. *Educ:* Emsworth House; RNC, Dartmouth (Robert Roxburgh Prize); RNEC, Keyham. HMS Exeter, 1936; HMS Valiant, 1939; HMS Firedrake, 1940 (despatches twice); E-in-C Dept Admty, 1941; HMS Indefatigable, 1944; Admty Fuel Experimental Stn, 1947; Seaslug Project Officer, RAE Farnborough, 1950; HMS Ark Royal, 1956; E-in-C Dept Admty, Dreadnought Project Team, 1958; CO, RNEC, 1962; Staff of C-in-C Portsmouth, 1964. Lt-Comdr 1944; Comdr 1947; Capt. 1957; Rear-Adm. 1966. *Recreations:* gardening, do-it-yourself. *Address:* 4 Hill View Road, Bath, Avon BA1 6NX. *T:* Bath (01225) 333584.

RIDLEY-THOMAS, Roger; Managing Director, Thomson Regional Newspapers Ltd, since 1989; *b* 14 July 1939; *s* of late John Montague Ridley-Thomas, MB, ChB, FRCSE, Norwich, and Christina Anne (*née* Seex); *m* 1962, Sandra Grace McBeth Young; two *s* two *d*. *Educ:* Gresham's Sch. Served Royal Norfolk Regt, 1958–60. Newspaper Publisher: Eastern Counties Newspapers, 1960–65; Thomson Regional Newspapers, 1965– (Dir, 1985–); Managing Director: Aberdeen Journals, 1980–84; Scotsman Publications, 1984–89; Director: Caledonian Offset, 1979–; Radio Forth, 1978–81; TRN Viewdata, 1978–89; Thomson Scottish Organisation, 1984–89; Northfield Newspapers, 1984–89; The Scotsman Communications, 1984–; The Scotsman Publications, 1984–; Central Publications, 1984–; Aberdeen Journals, 1980–84, 1990–; Belfast Telegraph Newspapers, 1990–; Chester Chronicle, 1990–; Newcastle Chronicle & Journal, 1990–; Western Mail & Echo, 1990–; Aberdeen Chamber of Commerce, 1981–84; Scottish Business in the Community, 1984–89; Scottish Business Achievement Award Trust, 1985–; Edinburgh Ch. of Commerce and Manufrs, 1985–88. Pres., Scottish Daily Newspaper Soc., 1983–85; Mem. Council, CBI, 1983–86; Mem., Scottish Wildlife Appeal Cttee, 1985–88. *Recreations:* vegetable growing, shooting, fishing, golf, tennis, travel. *Address:* (office) Hannay House, 39 Clarendon Road, Watford, Herts WD1 1JA; Copse Hill House, Flaunden Lane, near Bovingdon, Herts HP3 0PA. *T:* Hemel Hempstead (01442) 834052. *Clubs:* Caledonian; New (Edinburgh).

RIDSDALE, Sir Julian (Errington), Kt 1981; CBE 1977; *b* 8 June 1915; *m* 1942, Victoire Evelyn Patricia Bennett (*see* V. E. P. Ridsdale); one *d*. *Educ:* Tonbridge; Sandhurst. 2nd Lieutenant, Royal Norfolk Regiment, 1935; attached British Embassy, Tokyo, 1938–39; served War of 1939–45: Royal Norfolk Regt, Royal Scots, and Somerset Light Infantry; Asst Mil. Attaché, Japan, 1940; GSO3, Far Eastern Sect., War Office, 1941; GSO2, Joint Staff Mission, Washington, 1944–45; retired from Army with rank of Major, 1946. Contested SW Islington (C), LCC, 1949, N Paddington (C), Gen. Elec., 1951; MP (C) Harwich Div. of Essex, Feb. 1954–1992. PPS to Parly Under-Sec. of State for Colonies, 1957–58; PPS to Minister of State for Foreign Affairs, 1958–60; Parly Under-Sec. of State: for Air and Vice-President of the Air Council, 1962–64; for Defence for the Royal Air Force, Ministry of Defence, April-Oct. 1964. Chairman: British Japanese Parly Group, 1964–92; Parly Gp for Engrg Devclt, 1985–92; Vice-Chm., UN Parly Assoc., 1966–82; Mem., Select Cttee of Public Accounts, 1970–74. Leader, Parly Delegns to Japan, 1973, 1975, annually 1977–82, 1988. Member: Trilateral Commn, EEC, USA and Japan, 1973–92; North Atlantic Assembly, 1979–92 (Vice-Pres., Political Cttee, 1983–87). Dep. Chm., Internat. Triangle, USA, Japan and Europe, 1981–85. Chm., Japan Soc., London, 1976–79. British Comr Gen., British Garden Expo 90, Osaka, Japan, 1990. Master, Skinners' Co., 1970–71. Hon. Fellow UCL, 1992. Order of the Sacred Treasure, Japan, 1967, Grand Cordon, 1990. *Recreations:* tennis, chess, gardening, travelling, and sailing. *Address:* 12 The Boltons, SW10 9TD. *T:* 0171–373 6159. *Clubs:* Carlton, MCC, Hurlingham.

See also Sir P. H. Newall.

RIDSDALE, Victoire Evelyn Patricia, (Paddy), (Lady Ridsdale), DBE 1991; *b* 11 Oct. 1921; *d* of Col J. and Edith Marion Bennett; *m* 1942, Sir Julian Ridsdale, *qv*; one *d*. *Educ:* Sorbonne. Sec., DNI, 1939–42; Sec. to her husband, 1953–. Chm., Conservative MP's Wives, 1978–91. *Address:* 12 The Boltons, SW10 9TD. *T:* 0171–373 6159.

See also Sir P. H. Newall.

RIESCO ZAÑARTU, Germán; commercial entrepreneur; Chilean Ambassador to the Court of St James's, 1990–93, and non-resident Ambassador to Ireland, 1992–93; *b* 17 Aug. 1941; *s* of Ignacio Riesco and Eliana Zañartu de Riesco; *m* 1974, Jacqueline Cassel; four *s* two *d*. *Educ:* Colegio San Ignacio, Santiago; Univ. of California, Davis (agric. degree; Special Award); Univ. of California, Berkeley (Economics). MP Nuble (National Party), 1969–73; Pres., Cttee on Economy, Chamber of Deputies; Dir, Agric. Planning Office, 1976–78. Vice-Pres., Nat. Party, 1983–88; Pres., Nat. Party for No Vote, 1988; Pres., PAC-Centre Alliance Party, 1988–90. Board Mem., Fundación Chile, 1983–90. Pres., Nat. Agric. Soc., Chile, 1979–81, 1981–83. Negotiator at FAO, World Bank and other internat. orgns. *Publications:* papers on Chilean agric. and econs. *Recreations:* music, theatre, tennis, ski-ing. *Address:* 5308 Agustín Denegri, Vitacura, Santiago, Chile. *T:* (562) 2182799, 2184049. *Clubs:* Chile, De La Union, Los Leones Country (Santiago, Chile).

RIFKIN, Joshua; Founder, and Director, The Bach Ensemble, since 1978; *b* 22 April 1944; *s* of Harry H. Rifkin and Dorothy (*née* Helsh); one *d*. *Educ:* Juilliard Sch. of Music (BS 1964); Princeton Univ. (MFA 1969). Musical Consultant, later Musical Dir, Nonesuch Records, NY, 1963–75; Brandeis University: Instructor, 1970–71; Asst Prof., 1971–77; Associate Prof., 1977–82. Visiting Professor, 1973–94; NY Univ.; Harvard Univ.; Yale Univ.; Rutgers Univ.; Bard Coll.; Princeton Univ.; Stanford Univ.; King's Coll. London; Universität Basel; Ohio State Univ. Numerous concerts with Bach Ensemble in UK, Europe, US and Canada; Guest Conductor: English Chamber Orch., 1983, 1984; Scottish Chamber Orch., 1984, 1994; St Louis SO, 1985; Schola Cantorum Basiliensis, 1986, 1990; Victoria State SO, 1989; San Francisco SO, 1989; St Paul Chamber Orch., 1989; LA Chamber Orch., 1990; City of Glasgow SO, 1992; Cappella Coloniensis, Germany, 1993, 1994; Orch. Haydn/Bolzano, 1995. Numerous recordings. Fellow, Wissenschaftskolleg, Berlin, 1984–86. *Publications:* contrib. New Grove Dictionary of Music and Musicians; numerous articles in scholarly jls. *Recreations:* food, wine, cinema, theatre, computers, fiction. *Address:* c/o Clarion Seven Muses, 47 Whitehall Park, N19 3TW.

RIFKIND, Rt. Hon. Malcolm (Leslie), PC 1986; QC (Scot.) 1985; MP (C) Edinburgh, Pentlands, since Feb. 1974; Secretary of State for Foreign and Commonwealth Affairs, since 1995; *b* 21 June 1946; *yr s* of late E. Rifkind, Edinburgh; *m* 1970, Edith Amalia Rifkind (*née* Steinberg); one *s* one *d*. *Educ:* George Watson's Coll.; Edinburgh Univ. LLB, MSc. Lectured at Univ. of Rhodesia, 1967–68. Called to Scottish Bar, 1970. Contested (C) Edinburgh, Central, 1970. Opposition front-bench spokesman on Scottish Affairs, 1975–76; Parly Under Sec. of State, Scottish Office, 1979–82, FCO, 1982–83; Minister of State, FCO, 1983–86; Sec. of State for Scotland, 1986–90, for Transport, 1990–92, for Defence, 1992–95. Jt Sec., Cons. Foreign and Commonwealth Affairs Cttee, 1978; Member: Select Cttee on Europ. Secondary Legislation, 1975–76; Select Cttee on Overseas Develt, 1978–79. Hon. Pres., Scottish Young Conservatives, 1975–76. Mem., Royal Co. of Archers, Queen's Bodyguard for Scotland, 1992. *Recreations:* walking, reading, field sports. *Address:* House of Commons, SW1A 0AA. *Club:* New (Edinburgh).

RIGBY, Bryan; Director, MEDEVA plc, since 1993; Chairman, Streamline Holdings Ltd, since 1994; Vice-President, British Association for the Advancement of Science, since 1992; *b* 9 Jan. 1933; *s* of William George Rigby and Lily Rigby; *m* 1978, Marian Rosamund; one *s* one *d* of a former marriage, and one step *s* one step *d*. *Educ:* Wigan Grammar Sch.; King's Coll., London (BSc Special Chemistry, Dip. Chem. Engrg). UKAEA Industrial Gp, Capenhurst, 1955–60; Beecham Gp, London and Amsterdam, 1960–64; Laporte Industries (Holdings) Ltd, 1964–78; Dep. Dir-Gen., CBI, 1978–83; Man. Dir, UK Ops, 1984–87, UK, Ireland and Scandinavia, 1987–93, BASF Group. Mem., Social Security Adv. Cttee, 1994–. Trustee, Anglo-German Foundn, 1992–; Gov., Henley Management Coll., 1993–. *Recreations:* music, golf, gardening. *Address:* Cluny, 61 Penn Road, Beaconsfield, Bucks HP9 2LW. *T:* Beaconsfield (01494) 673206. *Club:* Reform.

RIGBY, Lt-Col Sir (Hugh) John (Macbeth), 2nd Bt, *cr* 1929; ERD and 2 clasps; Director, Executors of James Mills Ltd, retired 1977; *b* 1 Sept. 1914; *s* of Sir Hugh Mallinson Rigby, 1st Bt, and Flora (*d* 1970), *d* of Norman Macbeth; *S* father, 1944; *m* 1946, Mary Patricia Erskine Leacock (*d* 1988); four *s*. *Educ:* Rugby; Magdalene Coll., Cambridge (MA). Lt-Col RCT, retd, 1967. *Heir: s* Anthony John Rigby [*b* 3 Oct. 1946; *m* 1978, Mary, *e d* of R. G. Oliver, Park Moor Cottage, Pott Shrigley, Macclesfield; three *s* one *d*]. *Address:* 5 Park Street, Macclesfield, Cheshire SK11 6SR. *T:* Macclesfield (01625) 613959; Casa das Palmeiras, 8365 Armação de Pêra, Algarve, Portugal. *T:* (82) 312548.

RIGBY, Jean Prescott, (Mrs Jamie Hayes); mezzo-soprano; Principal, English National Opera, 1982–90; *d* of late Thomas Boulton Rigby and of Margaret Annie Rigby; *m* 1987, Jamie Hayes; three *s*. *Educ:* Birmingham and Midland Inst. Sch. of Music (ABSM 1976); Royal Acad. of Music (Dip.RAM; Hon. ARAM 1984; Hon. FRAM 1989). ARCM 1979. Début: Royal Opera House, Covent Garden, 1983; Glyndebourne Festival Opera, 1984; rôles, 1990–, include: Nicklaus, in The Tales of Hoffmann, Royal Opera; Penelope, in The Return of Ulysses, ENO; Isabella, in The Italian Girl in Algiers, Buxton; title rôle, in The Rape of Lucretia, ENO; Amastris, in Xerxes, ENO. Several TV performances. *Recreations:* British heritage, sport, cooking. *Address:* c/o John Coast, 31 Sinclair Road, W14 0NS.

RIGBY, Sir John; *see* Rigby, Sir H. J.

RIGBY, Norman Leslie; company chairman, retired; *b* 27 June 1920; *s* of Leslie Rigby and Elsie Lester Wright; *m* 1950, Mary Josephine Calderhead; two *d* (one *s* decd). *Educ:* Cowley Sch., St Helens. Served War, RAF, 1939–45, Intell. Officer to Free French Air Force. Management Trainee, Simon Engineering Group, 1946–48; Marketing Exec., Procter & Gamble Ltd, 1948–55; Marketing Dir, Macleans Ltd (Beecham Group), 1955–59; Nabisco Ltd: Marketing Dir 1959; Man. Dir 1960; Vice-Chm. 1962; Chm. 1964; Industrial Adviser, 1968–70, Co-ordinator of Industrial Advisers, HM Govt, 1969–70; Dir, Spillers Ltd, 1970–80 (Divl Man. Dir, 1977–80); Chm., Allan H. Williams Ltd and associated cos, 1981–82. *Recreations:* gardening, golf. *Address:* 38 West Common Way, Harpenden, Herts AL5 2LG. *T:* Harpenden (01582) 715448.

RIGBY, Peter William Jack, PhD; Head, Genes and Cellular Controls Group and Laboratory of Eukaryotic Molecular Genetics, MRC National Institute for Medical Research since 1986; *b* 7 July 1947; *s* of Jack and Lorna Rigby; *m* 1st, 1971, Paula Webb (marr. diss. 1983); 2nd, 1985, Julia Maidment; one *s*. *Educ:* Lower Sch., John Lyon, Harrow; Jesus Coll., Cambridge (BA, PhD). MRC Lab. of Molecular Biol., Cambridge, 1971–73; Helen Hay Whitney Foundn Fellow, Stanford Univ. Med. Sch., 1973–76; Imperial College London: Lectr, then Sen. Lectr in Biochem., 1976–83; Reader in Tumour Virology, 1983–86; Vis. Prof., 1986–. Chm., MRC Gene Therapy Co-ordinating Cttee, 1992–; Member: MRC Cell Bd, 1988–92; EMBO, 1979; Science Council, Celltech Ltd, 1982–; Scientific Adv. Bd, Somatix Therapy Corp., 1989–; Scientific Cttee, Cancer Res. Campaign, 1983–88. European Editor, Cell, 1984–. *Publications:* papers on molecular biology in sci. jls. *Recreations:* narrow boats, listening to music, sunbathing. *Address:* National Institute for Medical Research, The Ridgeway, Mill Hill, NW7 1AA. *T:* 0181–913 8533.

RIGBY, Reginald Francis, TD 1950 and Clasp 1952; Deputy Circuit Judge, 1973–77; a Recorder of the Crown Court, 1977–83; *b* Rudyard, Staffs, 22 June 1919; *s* of Reginald Rigby, FRIBA, FRICS, and Beatrice May Rigby, *d* of John Frederick Green, Woodbridge, Suffolk; *m* 1949, Joan Edwina, *d* of Samuel E. M. Simpson, Newcastle-under-Lyme, and of Dorothy C. Simpson; one *s* (and one *s* decd). *Educ:* Manchester Grammar Sch.; Victoria Univ., Manchester. Solicitor, 1947 (Hons; John Peacock and George Hadfield Prizeman, Law Society Art Prize, 1962); practised Newcastle-under-Lyme; retired as Sen. Partner, Rigby Rowley Cooper & Co., 1984. Served War: commissioned 2nd Lieut 41 Bn, Royal Tank Corps, TA, 1939; served AFV Sch.; volunteered for maritime service: Captain in RASC motor boat companies in home coastal waters, India, Burma, Malaya and its Archipelago; demob. 1946; Major, QORR, The Staffordshire Yeomanry. Mem., Market Drayton RDC, 1966–71; Chm., Woore Parish Council, 1971–79; Hon. Sec., North Staffs Forces Help Soc., 1964–84; Mem., Staffs War Pensions Cttee; Pres., Uttoxeter Flyfishing Club, 1975–77; Mem., Birdsgrove Flyfishing Club, Ashbourne. Life Mem., Clan Morrison Soc. Member, Military and Hospitaller Order of St Lazarus of Jerusalem. *Recreation:* fishing. *Address:* The Rookery, Woore, Salop CW3 9RG. *T:* Pipe Gate (01630) 647414. *Clubs:* Army and Navy, Flyfishers'.

RIGG, Dame Diana, DBE 1994 (CBE 1988); actress; Director, United British Artists, since 1982; *b* Doncaster, Yorks, 20 July 1938; *d* of Louis Rigg and Beryl Helliwell; *m* 1982, Archibald Stirling; one *d*. *Educ:* Fulneck Girls' Sch., Pudsey. Trained for the stage at Royal Academy of Dramatic Art. First appearance on stage in RADA prod. in York Festival, at Theatre Royal, York, summer, 1957 (Natella Abashwili in The Caucasian Chalk Circle); after appearing in repertory in Chesterfield and in York she joined the Royal Shakespeare Company, Stratford-upon-Avon, 1959; first appearance in London, Aldwych Theatre, 1961 (2nd Ondine, Violanta and Princess Berthe in Ondine); at same theatre, in repertory (The Devils, Becket, The Taming of the Shrew), 1961; (Madame de Tourvel, The Art of Seduction), 1962; Royal Shakespeare, Stratford-upon-Avon, Apr. 1962 (Helena in A Midsummer Night's Dream, Bianca in The Taming of the Shrew, Lady Macduff in Macbeth, Adriana in The Comedy of Errors, Cordelia in King Lear); subseq. appeared in the last production at the Aldwych, Dec. 1962, followed by Adriana in The Comedy of Errors and Monica Stettler in The Physicists, 1963. Toured the provinces, spring, 1963, in A Midsummer Night's Dream; subseq. appeared at the Royal Shakespeare, Stratford, and at the Aldwych, in Comedy of Errors, Dec. 1963; again played Cordelia in King Lear, 1964, prior to touring with both plays for the British Council, in Europe, the USSR, and the US; during this tour she first appeared in New York (State Theatre), 1964, in same plays; Viola in Twelfth Night, Stratford, June 1966; Heloise in Abelard and Heloise, Wyndham's, 1970, also at the Atkinson, New York, 1971; joined The National Theatre, 1972: in Jumpers, 'Tis Pity She's a Whore and Lady Macbeth in Macbeth, 1972; The Misanthrope, 1973, Washington and NY, 1975; Phaedra Britannica, 1975 (Plays and Players Award for Best Actress); The Guardsman, 1978; Pygmalion, Albery, 1974; Night and Day, Phoenix, 1978 (Plays and Players award, 1979); Colette, USA, 1982; Heartbreak House, Haymarket, 1983; Little Eyolf, Lyric, Hammersmith, 1985; Antony and Cleopatra, Chichester, 1985; Wildfire, Phoenix, 1986; Follies, Shaftesbury, 1987; Love Letters, San Francisco, 1990; All for Love, Almeida, 1991; Berlin Bertie, Royal Court, 1992; Medea, Almeida, 1992, transf. Wyndhams, 1993–94 (Evening Standard Drama Award), then NY, 1994 (Tony Award); *films include:* A Midsummer Night's Dream, Assassination Bureau, On Her Majesty's Secret Service, Julius Caesar, The Hospital, Theatre of Blood, A Little Night Music, The Great Muppet Caper, Evil Under the Sun (Film Actress of the Year Award, Variety Club, 1983); *TV appearances include:* Sentimental Agent, The Comedy of Errors, The Avengers, Married Alive, Diana (US series), In This House of Brede (US), Three Piece Suite, The Serpent Son, Hedda Gabler, The Marquise, Little Eyolf, King Lear, Witness of the Prosecution, Bleak House, Mother Love (BAFTA award), Unexplained Laughter, and others. Chair: Islington Fest.; MacRoberts Arts Centre; Member: Council, ABSA; BM Develt Fund. A Vice-Pres., Baby Life Support Systems (BLISS), 1984–. *Publications:* No Turn Unstoned, 1982; So to the Land, 1994. *Recreations:* reading and trying to get organized. *Address:* c/o London Management, 235 Regent Street, W1A 2JT.

RIGGE, Marianne, (Mrs Trevor Goodchild); Director, College of Health, since 1983; *b* 10 May 1948; *d* of late Dr Patrick Noel O'Mahony and of Elizabeth Nora O'Mahony (*née* Daly); *m* 1st, 1968, John Simon Rigge; two *d* (one *s* decd); 2nd, 1990, Trevor Goodchild. *Educ:* St Angela's Ursuline Convent, London; University College London (BA Hons French). PA, Consumers' Assoc., 1971–76; Res. Asst to Chm., Nat. Consumer Council, 1976–77; founder Dir, Mutual Aid Centre, 1977–83. Mem., Clinical Outcomes Gp, 1983–. Editor, Self Health, 1985–87. *Publications:* (with Michael Young) Mutual Aid in a Selfish Society, 1979; Building Societies and the Consumer, 1981; Hello, Can I Help You, 1981; Prospects for Worker Co-operatives in Europe, 1981; (with Michael Young) Revolution from Within, 1983; Annual Guide to Hospital Waiting Lists, 1984–92. *Recreations:* gardening, cooking, music. *Address:* 157 Whipps Cross Road, E11 1NP. *T:* 0181–530 4420.

RIGGS, David George; Director of Finance, Benefits Agency, since 1991; *b* 6 May 1942. *Educ:* Bury GS; Manchester Univ. (BA Econ.). With Bury CBC, 1958–68; Greater London Council, 1968–82: Finance Officer, 1968–74; Hd of Public Services Finance, 1974–76; Asst Comptroller of Finance, 1976–82; Dir of Finance, ILEA, 1982–90. *Address:* Benefits Agency, Quarry House, Quarry Hill, Leeds LS2 7UA.

RIGNEY, Howard Ernest; HM Diplomatic Service, retired; Consul-General, Lyons, 1977–82; *b* 22 June 1922; *o s* of late Wilbert Ernest and Minnie Rigney; *m* 1950, Margaret Grayling Benn; one *s*. *Educ:* Univs of Western Ontario, Toronto and Paris. BA Western Ont. 1945, MA Toronto 1947. Lectr, Univ. of British Columbia, 1946–48; grad. studies, Paris Univ., 1948–50; COI, 1953–56; CRO, 1956; Regional Information Officer, Dacca, 1957–60, Montreal, 1960–63; CRO, 1963–65; FO/CO, 1965–67; Consul (Information), Chicago, 1967–69; Dep. Consul-Gen., Chicago, 1969–71; Head of Chancery and Consul, Rangoon, 1971–73; Head of Migration and Visa Dept, FCO, 1973–77. Hon DLitt, Winston Churchill Coll., Ill, 1971. *Recreations:* opera, book-collecting, gardening, golf. *Address:* The Old Rectory, Frinstead, Sittingbourne, Kent ME9 0TQ.

RILEY, Bridget Louise, CBE 1972; Artist; *b* 24 April 1931; *d* of John Riley and late Louise (*née* Gladstone). *Educ:* Cheltenham Ladies' College; Goldsmiths' School of Art; Royal College of Art. ARCA 1955. AICA critics Prize, 1963; Stuyvesant Bursary, 1964; Ohara Mus. Prize, Tokyo, 1972; Gold Medal, Grafik Biennale, Norway, 1980. Mem., RSA. One-man shows: London, 1962, 1963, 1969, 1971 (retrospective, at Hayward Gall.), 1976, 1981, 1983, 1987, 1989, 1992 (retrospective, at Hayward Gall.), 1994 (retrospective, at Tate Gall.); New York, Los Angeles, 1965; New York, 1967, 1975, 1978, 1986, 1990; Hanover, 1970; Turin, Düsseldorf, Berne, Prague, 1971; Basle, 1975; Sydney, 1976; Tokyo, 1977, 1983, 1990; Stockholm and Zurich, 1987; touring retrospective, USA, Aust. and Japan, 1978–80. Exhibited in group shows: England, France, Israel, America, Germany, Italy. Represented Britain: Paris Biennale, 1965; Venice Biennale, 1968 (awarded Chief internat. painting prize). Public collections include: Tate Gallery, Victoria and Albert Museum, Arts Council, British Council, Museum of Modern Art, New York', Australian Nat. Gallery, Canberra, Museum of Modern Art, Pasadena, Ferens Art Gallery, Hull, Allbright Knox, Buffalo, USA, Museum of Contemporary Art, Chicago, Ulster Museum, Ireland, Stedelijk Museum, Berne Kunsthalle. Designed Colour Moves, for Ballet Rambert, 1983. Trustee, Nat. Gallery, 1981–88. Hon. DLitt: Manchester, 1976; Ulster, 1986; Oxford, 1993. *Address:* c/o Karsten Schubert Ltd, 41–42 Foley Street, W1P 7LD.

RILEY, Christopher John; Under Secretary, HM Treasury, since 1988; *b* 20 Jan. 1947; *s* of Bernard Francis Riley and Phyllis (*née* Wigley); *m* 1982, Helen Marion Mynett; two *s*. *Educ:* Ratcliffe Coll., Leicester; Wadham Coll., Oxford (MA Maths); Univ. of East Anglia (MA Econs). Economist, HM Treasury, 1969–77; Res. Fellow, Nuffield Coll., Oxford, 1977–78; Sen. Economic Advr, HM Treasury, 1978–88. *Publications:* various articles in books and learned jls. *Recreation:* music, especially choral singing. *Address:* c/o HM Treasury, Parliament Street, SW1P 3AG. *T:* 0171–270 4439.

RILEY, Major John Roland Christopher; Chairman, Channel Islands Communications (TV) Group (formerly Channel Television), since 1982; *b* 4 July 1925; *s* of Christopher John Molesworth Riley and Bridget Maisie Hanbury; *m* 1956, Penelope Ann Harrison (*d* 1978); two *d*. *Educ:* Winchester College. Commissioned Coldstream Guards, 1943; served NW Europe, Palestine, Malaya; Instructor, Army Staff Coll., 1960–62; retired 1962; Elected Deputy, States of Jersey, 1963, Senator, 1975; retired from Govt, 1981. Director: Air UK, 1963–91; Jersey Gas Co., 1970–92; Chase Bank and Trust Co. (CI), 1975–91; Fuel Supplies CI, 1976–; Servisair Jersey, 1976–; Royal Trust Asset Management (CI) Ltd, 1980–92; Royal Trust Fund Management (CI) Ltd, 1984–92. Seigneur de la Trinité. *Recreations:* horse riding (Master Jersey Drag Hunt), yachting. *Address:* Trinity Manor, Jersey, Channel Islands JE3 5DD. *T:* Jersey (01534) 861026, *Fax:* Jersey (01534) 864526. *Clubs:* Cavalry and Guards, Royal Yacht Squadron.

RILEY, Very Rev. Kenneth Joseph; Dean of Manchester, since 1993; *b* 25 June 1940; *s* of Arthur and Mary Josephine Riley; *m* 1968, Margaret; two *d*. *Educ:* Holywell GS; UCW,

Aberystwyth (BA 1961); Linacre Coll., Oxford (BA 1964; MA); Wycliffe Hall., Oxford. Ordained deacon, 1964, priest, 1965; Asst Curate, Emmanuel Ch., Fazakerley, Liverpool, 1964–66; Chaplain: Brasted Place Coll., 1966–69; Oundle Sch., 1969–74; Liverpool Univ., 1974–83; Vicar, Mossley Hill, Liverpool, 1975–83; RD, Childwall, 1982–83; Canon Treas., 1983–87, Canon Precentor, 1987–93, Liverpool Cathedral. *Publication:* Liverpool Cathedral, 1987. *Recreations:* music, drama, films. *Address:* Manchester Cathedral, Manchester M3 1SX. *T:* 0161–833 2220.

RILEY, Sir Ralph, Kt 1984; DSc; FRS 1967; Deputy Chairman, 1983–85, Secretary, 1978–85, Agricultural and Food Research Council; *b* 23 Oct. 1924; *y c* of Ralph and Clara Riley; *m* 1949, Joan Elizabeth Norrington; two *d. Educ:* Audenshaw Gram. Sch.; Univ. of Sheffield. Infantry Soldier, 1943–47; Univ. of Sheffield, 1947–52; Research worker, Plant Breeding Inst., Cambridge, 1952–78; Head of Cytogenetics Dept, 1954–72; Dir, 1971–78. National Research Council/Nuffield Foundn Lectr at Canadian Univs, 1966; Special Prof. of Botany, Univ. of Nottingham, 1970–78. Fellow of Wolfson Coll., Cambridge, 1967–92, Emeritus Fellow, 1992–. Lectures: Sir Henry Tizard Meml, 1973; Holden, Univ. of Nottingham, 1975; Woodhull, Royal Instn, 1976; Bewley, Glasshouse Crops Res. Inst., 1980; Bernal, Birkbeck Coll., 1983. Sec., Internat. Genetics Fedn, 1973–78; Board Member: Internat. Rice Res. Inst., Manila, 1974–77; Internat. Centre Agricl Res. Dry Areas, Aleppo, 1989–93; Chairman: Rothamsted Experimental Station, 1990–; Bd, British Technol. Gp Ltd, 1984–; Sci. Adv. Cttee, Prog. Rice Biotech., Rockefeller Foundn, 1985–; UGC Working Pty on Vet. Educn., 1987–89; Mem., Tech. Adv. Cttee, Consultative Gp on Internat. Agricl Res., 1993–. President: Genetical Soc., 1973–75; Sect. K, BAAS, 1979; Hon. Vice-Pres., 16th Internat. Congress of Genetics, Toronto, 1988, Pres., 17th Congress, Birmingham, 1993. For. Fellow, INSA, 1976; For. Correspondent, Acad. d'Agriculture de France, 1981; For. Associate, Nat. Acad. Scis, USA, 1982; Fellow, Indian Nat. Acad. of Agricl Sci., 1992–. Hon. FRASE, 1980. Hon. DSc: Edinburgh, 1976; Hull, 1982; Cranfield, 1985; Hon. LLD Sheffield, 1984. William Bate Hardy Prize, Cambridge Phil. Soc., 1969; Royal Medal, Royal Soc., 1981; Wolf Foundn Prize in Agriculture, 1986. *Publications:* scientific papers and articles on genetics of chromosome behaviour, plant cytogenetics and evolution and breeding of crop plants especially wheat. *Address:* 16 Gog Magog Way, Stapleford, Cambridge CB2 5BQ. *T:* Cambridge (01223) 843845, *Fax:* Cambridge (01223) 845825. *Club:* Athenæum.

RILEY, Victor; Lord Mayor of Cardiff, 1993–94; *b* 4 Oct. 1916; *s* of William Riley and Constance Evelyn Riley (*née* Cator); *m* 1944, Zoë Marion Elsie Sowden; four *d. Educ:* Hull Grammar Sch. FIHospE 1970. Electrical Apprenticeship, Hull Corp. Engineers Dept, 1932–37; Electrical Engineer: Hull Elect. Dept, 1937–40; HM Ships in Dockyards, NE Coast, 1940–44; Engr in Group of Hosps and subseq. in NHS, 1944–56; Elect. Engr, Crown Agents, Nairobi, 1956–60; Principal Asst Engr, Welsh Health Tech. Services, 1960–81, retired. Councillor, Cardiff City Council, 1976–. Mem., Whitchurch Royal British Legion. *Recreations:* gardening, Rugby, cricket. *Address:* 20 Bishops Road, Whitchurch, Cardiff CF4 1LZ. *T:* Cardiff (01222) 613850. *Club:* Cardiff Athletic.

RILEY-SMITH, Prof. Jonathan Simon Christopher, FRHistS; Dixie Professor of Ecclesiastical History, Cambridge University, and Fellow, Emmanuel College, Cambridge, since 1994; *b* 27 June 1938; *s* of late William Henry Douglas Riley-Smith and Elspeth Agnes Mary Riley-Smith (*née* Craik Henderson); *m* 1968, Marie-Louise Jeannetta, *d* of Wilfred John Sutcliffe Field; one *s* two *d. Educ:* Eton College; Trinity College, Cambridge (MA, PhD). Dept of Mediaeval History, University of St Andrews: Asst Lectr, 1964–65; Lectr, 1966–72; Faculty of History, Cambridge: Asst Lectr, 1972–75; Lectr, 1975–78; Queens' College, Cambridge: Fellow and Dir of Studies in History, 1972–78; Praelector, 1973–75; Librarian, 1973, 1977–78; Prof. of History, Univ. of London, 1978–94 (at RHC, 1978–85, at RHBNC, 1985–94); Head of Dept of History, RHC, then RHBNC, 1984–90. Chairman: Bd of Management, Inst. of Historical Res., 1988–94; Victoria County Hist. Cttee, 1989–; Pres., Soc. for the Study of the Crusades and the Latin East, 1990–95. KStJ 1969 (Librarian of Priory of Scotland, 1966–78, of Grand Priory, 1982–); KM 1971 (Officer of Merit, 1985). Prix Schlumberger, Acad. des Inscriptions et Belles-Lettres, Paris, 1988. *Publications:* The Knights of St John in Jerusalem and Cyprus, 1967; (with U. and M. C. Lyons) Ayyubids, Mamlukes and Crusaders, 1971; The Feudal Nobility and the Kingdom of Jerusalem, 1973; What were the Crusades?, 1977, 2nd edn 1992; (with L. Riley-Smith) The Crusades: idea and reality, 1981; The First Crusade and the Idea of Crusading, 1986; The Crusades: a short history, 1987 (trans. French, 1990, Italian, 1994); (ed) The Atlas of the Crusades, 1991 (trans. German 1992); articles in learned jls. *Recreation:* the past and present of own family. *Address:* Emmanuel College, Cambridge CB2 3AP. *T:* Cambridge (01223) 334200.

RIMER, Hon. Sir Colin (Percy Farquharson), Kt 1994; **Hon. Mr Justice Rimer;** a Judge of the High Court of Justice, Chancery Division, since 1994; *b* 30 Jan. 1944; *s* of Kenneth Rowland Rimer and Maria Eugenia Rimer (*née* Farquharson); *m* 1970, Penelope Ann Gibbs; two *s* one *d. Educ:* Dulwich Coll.; Trinity Hall, Cambridge (MA, LLB). Legal Assistant, Inst. of Comparative Law, Paris, 1967–68; called to the Bar, Lincoln's Inn, 1968; QC 1988; in practice, 1969–94. *Recreations:* music, photography, novels, sailing, walking. *Address:* Royal Courts of Justice, Strand, WC2A 2LL.

RIMINGTON, John David, CB 1987; Director-General, Health and Safety Executive, 1984–95; *b* 27 June 1935; *s* of John William Rimington and Mabel Dorrington; *m* 1963, Stella Rimington, *qv*; two *d. Educ:* Nottingham High Sch.; Jesus Coll., Cambridge (Cl. I Hons History, MA). Nat. Service Commn, RA, 1954–56. Joined BoT, 1959; seconded HM Treasury (work on decimal currency), 1961; Principal, Tariff Div., BoT, 1963; 1st Sec. (Economic), New Delhi, 1965; Mergers Div., DTI, 1969; Dept of Employment, 1970; Asst Sec. 1972 (Employment Policy and Manpower); Counsellor, Social and Regional Policy, UK perm. representation to EEC, Brussels, 1974; MSC, 1977–81; Under Sec. 1978; Dir, Safety Policy Div., HSE, 1981–83; Dep. Sec., 1984; Permanent Sec., 1992. CIMgt 1993. Hon. DSc Sheffield, 1995. *Publications:* articles on risk; contrib. to RIPA Jl, New Asia Review, etc. *Recreations:* walking, gardening, watching cricket. *Address:* 9 Highbury Hill, N5 1SU.

RIMINGTON, Stella; Director General, Security Service, since 1992; *b* 1935; *m* 1963, John David Rimington, *qv*; two *d. Educ:* Nottingham High Sch. for Girls; Edinburgh Univ. (MA). Security Service, 1969.

RIMMER, Prof. Frederick William, CBE 1980; MA (Cantab), BMus (Dunelm); FRCO; FRSAMD; Gardiner Professor of Music, University of Glasgow, 1966–80, now Emeritus Professor; Director of Scottish Music Archive, 1968–80; *b* 21 Feb. 1914; 2nd *s* of William Rimmer and Amy Graham McMillan, Liverpool; *m* 1941, Joan Doreen, *d* of Major Alexander Hume Graham and Beatrice Cecilia Myles; two *s* one *d. Educ:* Quarry Bank High Sch., Liverpool. FRCO (Harding Prize), 1934; BMus (Dunelm), 1939. Served War: 11th Bn, The Lancashire Fusiliers, Middle East, 1941–45 (Maj. 1944). Selwyn Coll., Cambridge (Organ Scholar), 1946–48; Sen. Lectr in Music, Homerton Coll., Cambridge, 1948–51; Cramb Lectr in Music, Univ. of Glasgow, 1951–56; Sen. Lectr, 1956–66, and Organist to the Univ., 1954–66. Henrietta Harvey Vis. Prof., Memorial Univ. of Newfoundland, 1977. A Dir of Scottish Opera, 1966–80; Chm., BBC's Scottish Music Adv. Cttee, 1972–77; Mem., Music Adv. Cttee, British Council, 1973–82, Scottish Adv. Cttee, 1979–82. Hon. Fellow, Selwyn Coll., Cambridge, 1982. Hon. DMus Durham, 1991. Special Award for services to contemp. music in Scotland, Composers' Guild of GB, 1975. *Publications:* contrib. to: A History of Scottish Music, 1973; Companion to Scottish Culture, 1981; articles on 20th century music, in: Tempo; Music Review; Organists' Review; compositions for solo organ: Five Preludes on Scottish Psalm Tunes, Pastorale and Toccata, Invenzione e Passacaglia Capricciosa, Ostinato Mesto, Fugato Giocoso, Variations on a theme of Paganini; for choir and organ: Sing we merrily; Christus natus est alleluia; O Lord, we beseech thee; O Blessed God in Trinity; Five carols of the Nativity; Magnificat and Nunc Dimittis; for solo soprano and organ: Of a Rose; Born is the Babe. *Recreations:* travel, reading and gardening. *Address:* Manor Farmhouse, 6 Mill Way, Grantchester, Cambridge CB3 9NB. *T:* Cambridge (01223) 840716.

RIMMER, Henry, (Harry), CBE 1994; Member (Lab) Liverpool City Council, 1952–53 and since 1987; Leader, Liverpool City Council, since 1990; *b* 19 May 1928; *s* of Thomas and Sarah Ellen Rimmer; *m* 1st, 1951, Doreen Taylor (marr. diss. 1978); three *s* one *d*; 2nd, 1978, Joan Conder. *Educ:* Oulton High Sch.; Liverpool Collegiate Sch. Mem., Merseyside CC, 1981–86 (Dep. Leader, 1982–86). Member: Merseyside Police Authy, 1987– (Vice-Chm., 1990–92); Bd, Merseyside Develt Corp., 1991–. Director: Wavertree Technology Park Co., 1987–; Liverpool Airport PLC, 1989–. *Recreations:* country walking, supporting Liverpool Football Club. *Address:* 21 Ash Grange, Brookside Avenue, Knotty Ash, Liverpool L14 7NE. *T:* 0151–220 6022.

RINFRET, Hon. Gabriel-Edouard, OC 1983; PC (Canada) 1949; Chief Justice of Québec, 1977–80, retired; *b* St-Jérôme, PQ, 12 May 1905; *s* of Rt Hon. Thibaudeau Rinfret, Chief Justice of Canada, and Georgine, *d* of S. J. B. Rolland; *m* 1929; two *s*; *m* 1982. *Educ:* Collège Notre-Dame, Côte des Neiges, PQ; Petit Séminaire, Montréal; Collège Ste-Marie (BA with distinction); McGill Univ., Montréal (LLM with distinction); pupil of Hon. J. L. Perron. Admitted to practice, 1928; joined law office of Campbell, McMaster, Couture, Kerry and Bruneau; partner, Campbell, Weldon, MacFarlane and Rinfret, 1945. KC 1943. Sec. or Legal Adviser to various provincial govt commns of enquiry, 1934–45. Pres., Jeunesse Libérale de Montréal, 1934; Co-founder and 1st Pres., Assoc. de la Jeunesse Libérale de la Province de Québec, 1934–35; MP (L) Outremont, 1945–49, Outremont-St Jean 1949–52, House of Commons of Canada; Postmaster General in St Laurent Cabinet. A Judge of the Court of Appeal of Québec, 1952–80. Pres. or Director: Concerts Symphoniques de Montréal; Inst. Internat. de Musique; Grands Ballets Canadiens; Dominion Drama Festival (organised Montréal Festival, 1961; Pres., W Québec Region, and Mem., Nat. Exec. Cttee, 1962–68; Canadian Drama Award, 1969); Vice Pres., Conservatoire Lassalle, 1967–. Hon. LLD, Univ. of British Columbia, 1979. *Publications:* Répertoire du théâtre canadien d'expression française, vol. 1, 1975, vol. 2, 1976, vol. 3, 1977, vol. 4, 1978; Histoire du Barreau de Montréal, 1989. *Recreations:* cabinet-work, Canadian paintings; formerly baseball, lacrosse, tennis, hockey, ski-ing. *Address:* 121 Melbourne Avenue, Town of Mount Royal, Québec, H3P 1G3, Canada.

RING, Prof. James, CBE 1983; Emeritus Professor of Physics, Imperial College of Science, Technology and Medicine, since 1984; *b* 22 Aug. 1927; *s* of James and Florence Ring; *m* 1949, Patricia, *d* of Major H. J. Smith, MBE; two *s. Educ:* Univ. of Manchester (BSc, PhD). FInstP, FRAS. Reader in Spectrometry, Univ. of Manchester, 1957; Prof. of Applied Physics, Hull Univ., 1962; Prof. of Physics, 1967, and Associate Hd of Physics Dept, 1979, Imperial Coll. of Sci. and Technol. Director: Queensgate Instruments, 1979–; Infrared Engrg, 1970–91; IC Optical Systems, 1970–. Member: IBA, 1974–81; ITC, 1991–94; Inquiry into Cable Expansion and Broadcasting Policy, 1982; Dep. Chm., Cable Authority, 1984–90. *Publications:* numerous papers and articles in learned jls. *Recreations:* stargazing, dinghy sailing. *Address:* 1 Mude Gardens, Mudeford, Dorset BH23 4AR.

RING, Sir Lindsay (Roberts), GBE 1975; JP; Chairman, Ring & Brymer (Birchs) Ltd; Lord Mayor of London for 1975–76; *b* 1 May 1914; *y s* of George Arthur Ring and Helen Rhoda Mason Ring (*née* Stedman); *m* 1940, Hazel Doris, *d* of A. Trevor Nichols, CBE; two *s* one *d. Educ:* Dulwich Coll.; Mecklenburg, Germany. Served 1939–45, Europe and Middle East, Major RASC. Underwriting Member of Lloyd's, 1964. Fellow, Hotel and Catering Inst.; Chm., Hotel and Catering Trades Benevolent Assoc., 1962–71; Member: Bd of Verge of Royal Palaces, 1977–84; Gaming Bd for GB, 1977–83; NI Develt Agency, 1977–81. Chm., City of London (Arizona) Corp., 1981–84. Chancellor, City Univ., 1975–76. Governor, Farringtons Sch. Freeman, City of London, 1935; Member, Court of Assistants: Armourers' and Brasiers' Co. (Master 1972); Chartered Secretaries' and Administrators' Co. Common Councilman, City of London (Ward of Bishopsgate), 1964–68; Alderman (Ward of Vintry), 1968–84; Sheriff, City of London, 1967–68; Governor, Hon. Irish Soc., 1980–84. HM Lieut for City of London; JP Inner London, 1964. Hon. Col, 151 (Greater London) Regt, RCT(V). Hon. Burgess, Borough of Coleraine, NI. KStJ 1976. FCIS 1976. Hon. DSc City Univ., 1976; Hon. DLitt Ulster, 1976. Comdr, Legion of Honour, 1976; Order of Rio Branca (Brazil), 1976. *Address:* Chalvedune, Wilderness Road, Chislehurst, Kent, BR7 5EY. *Club:* City Livery.

RINGADOO, Sir Veerasamy, GCMG 1986; Kt 1975; QC 1983; Officier de l'Ordre National Malgache 1969; President, Republic of Mauritius, 1992 (Governor-General and Commander-in-Chief of Mauritius, 1986–92); *b* 1920; *s* of Nagaya Ringadoo; *m* 1954, Lydie Vadamootoo; one *s* one *d. Educ:* Port Louis Grammar Sch.; LSE Eng. (LLB; Hon. Fellow, 1976). Called to Bar, 1949. Municipal Councillor, Port Louis, 1956; MLC for Moka-Flacq, 1951–67; Minister: Labour and Social Security, 1959–63; Education, 1964–67; Agriculture and Natural Resources, 1967–68; Finance, 1968–82; attended London Constitutional Conf., 1965; first MLA (Lab) for Quartier Militaire and Moka, 1967, re-elected 1976. Governor, IMF and African Develt Bank, 1970–82; Chm., Bd of Governors, African Development Bank and African Development Fund, 1977–78. Hon. DCL Mauritius, 1976; Hon. DLit Andhra, 1978; Dr *hc*: Bordeaux Univ., 1988; Bharatidasan Univ., Tiruchirapalli, 1988. Médaille de l'Assemblée Nat. Française, 1971. *Address:* Cur Antelme and Farquhar Streets, Quatre Bornes, Mauritius.

RINGEN, Prof. Stein; Professor of Sociology and Social Policy, and Fellow of Green College, University of Oxford, since 1990; *b* 5 July 1945; *s* of John Ringen and Anna Ringen (*née* Simengard). *Educ:* Univ. of Oslo (MA, dr. philos.). Broadcasting reporter, Norwegian Broadcasting Corp., 1970–71; Fellow, Internat. Peace Res. Inst., Oslo, 1971–72; Head of Secretariat, Norwegian Level of Living Study, 1972–76; Fellow, Inst. for Social Res., Oslo, 1976–78; Head of Res., Min. of Consumer Affairs and Govt Admin, Oslo, 1978–83; Prof. of Welfare Studies, Univ. of Stockholm, 1983–86; Sen. Res. Scientist, Central Bureau of Statistics, Oslo, 1986–88; Asst Dir Gen., Min. of Justice, Oslo, 1988–90. *Publication:* The Possibility of Politics, 1987. *Address:* University of Oxford, Department of Applied Social Studies and Social Research, Barnett House, Wellington Square, Oxford OX1 2ER. *T:* Oxford (01865) 270325.

RINGROSE, Prof. John Robert, FRS 1977; FRSE; Professor of Pure Mathematics, 1964–93, now Emeritus, and a Pro-Vice-Chancellor, 1983–88, University of Newcastle upon Tyne; *b* 21 Dec. 1932; *s* of Albert Frederick Ringrose and Elsie Lilian Ringrose (*née* Roberts); *m* 1956, Jean Margaret Bates; three *s. Educ:* Buckhurst Hill County High School,

Chigwell, Essex; St John's Coll., Cambridge (MA, PhD). Lecturer in Mathematics: King's Coll., Newcastle upon Tyne, 1957–61; Univ. of Cambridge (also Fellow of St John's Coll.), 1961–63; Sen. Lectr in Mathematics, Univ. of Newcastle upon Tyne, 1963–64. Pres., London Mathematical Soc., 1992–94. *Publications:* Compact Non-self-adjoint Operators, 1971; (with R. V. Kadison) Fundamentals of the Theory of Operator Algebras, 1983; mathematical papers in various research jls. *Address:* 6 Polwarth Road, Brunton Park, Newcastle upon Tyne NE3 5ND. *T:* 0191–236 3035.

RINK, Margaret Joan; *see* Suttill, Dr. M. J.

RIORDAN, Stephen Vaughan; QC 1992; a Recorder, since 1990; *b* 18 Feb. 1950; *s* of Charles Maurice Riordan and Betty Morfydd Riordan; *m* 1983, Jane Elizabeth Thomas; two *d. Educ:* Wimbledon Coll.; Univ. of Liverpool (LLB Hons). Called to the Bar, Inner Temple, 1972; Asst Recorder, 1986–90. *Recreation:* singing. *Address:* 25–27 Castle Street, Liverpool L2 4TA. *T:* 0151–236 5072.

RIPA di MEANA, Carlo; Leader, Green Party, Italy, since 1993; *b* 15 Aug. 1929; *m* 1982, Marina Punturieri. Editor, Il Lavoro (Ital. Gen. Conf. of Labour weekly newspaper), and Editor, foreign dept, Unita (Ital. Communist Party daily paper), 1950–53; rep. of Italy on UIE, Prague, 1953–56; founded jointly Nuova Generazione, 1956; left Ital. Communist Party, 1957; founded jointly Passato e Presente, 1957 (chief editor); joined Italian Socialist Party (PSI), 1958; worked in publishing until 1966; Councillor for Lombardy (PSI), 1970–74 (Chm., Constitutional Cttee); leader, PSI Group, regional council; head, international relations PSI, 1979–80; left PSI 1993; Mem., European Parlt, 1979–84; Mem. for Italy, EEC, 1985–92; Minister for Environment, Italy, 1992–93. Pres., Inst. for Internat. Economic Cooperation and Develt Problems, 1983; Sec.-Gen., Club Turati, Milan, 1967–76; Mem. Board, Scala Theatre, Milan, 1970–74; Mem. Council, Venice Biennale 1974–82 (Chm., 1974–79); founder Mem., Crocodile Club; Pres., Fernando Santi Inst.; Pres., Unitary Fedn, Italian Press abroad; Vice-Chm., Internat. Cttee for Solidarity with Afghan People. *Publications:* Un viaggio in Viet-Nam (A Voyage to Vietnam), 1956; A tribute to Raymond Roussel and his Impressions of Africa, 1965; Il governo audiovisivo (Audiovisual Government), 1973. *Recreations:* horse riding, sailing. *Address:* Camera dei Deputati, Rome, Italy.

RIPLEY, Prof. Brian David, PhD; FRSE; Professor of Applied Statistics, and Fellow of St Peter's College, University of Oxford, since 1990; *b* 29 April 1952; *s* of Eric Lewis Ripley and Sylvia May (*née* Gould); *m* 1973, Ruth Mary Appleton. *Educ:* Farnborough Grammar Sch.; Churchill Coll., Cambridge (MA, PhD). FIMS 1987; FRSE 1990. Lectr in Statistics, Imperial Coll., London, 1976–80; Reader, Univ. of London, 1980–83; Prof. of Statistics, Univ. of Strathclyde, 1983–90. Mem., Internat. Statistical Inst., 1982. Adams Prize, Univ. of Cambridge, 1987. *Publications:* Spatial Statistics, 1981; Stochastic Simulation, 1987; Statistical Inference for Spatial Processes, 1988; Modern Applied Statistics with S-Plus, 1994; Pattern Recognition and Neural Networks, 1995; numerous papers on statistics and applications in astronomy, biology, chemistry and earth sciences. *Recreation:* natural history. *Address:* 1 South Parks Road, Oxford OX1 3TG. *T:* Oxford (01865) 272861.

RIPLEY, Dillon; *see* Ripley, S. D.

RIPLEY, Sir Hugh, 4th Bt, *cr* 1880; former Director, John Walker & Sons Ltd, Scotch Whisky Distillers, retired 1981; *b* 26 May 1916; *s* of Sir Henry William Alfred Ripley, 3rd Bt, and Dorothy (*d* 1964), *e d* of late Robert William Daker Harley; *S* father 1956; *m* 1st, 1946, Dorothy Mary Dunlop Bruce-Jones (marr. diss. 1971); one *s* one *d*; 2nd, 1972, Susan, *d* of W. Parker, Leics; one *d. Educ:* Eton. Served in Africa and Italy with 1st Bn KSLI (despatches twice, American Silver Star); retired regular Major. *Publication:* Whisky for Tea, 1991. *Recreations:* golf, fishing, shooting. *Heir: s* William Hugh Ripley, *b* 13 April 1950. *Address:* 20 Abingdon Villas, W8 6BX; The Oak, Bedstone, Bucknell, Salop SY7 0BJ. *Club:* Boodle's.

RIPLEY, (Sidney) Dillon, II, Hon. KBE 1979; PhD; Secretary, Smithsonian Institution, 1964–84, now Secretary Emeritus; *b* 20 Sept. 1913; *s* of Louis Arthur Ripley and Constance Baillie (*née* Rose); *m* 1949, Mary Moncrieffe Livingston; three *d. Educ:* St Paul's Sch., Concord, NH; Yale Univ. (BA 1936); Harvard Univ. (PhD 1943). Staff, Acad. of Natural Sciences, Philadelphia, 1936–39; Volunteer Asst, Amer. Museum of Natural History, New York, 1939–40; Teaching Asst, Harvard Univ., 1941–42; Asst Curator of Birds, Smithsonian Instn, 1942; OSS, 1942–45; Lectr, Curator, Associate Prof. of Zool. and Prof. of Biol., Yale Univ., 1946–64; Dir, Peabody Museum of Nat. Hist., 1959–64. Dir, Riggs Nat. Corp., Washington, 1984. Chm. (US), E-SU, 1984. Pres., 1958–82, Pres. Emeritus, 1982–, ICBP. Benjamin Franklin Fellow, RSA, 1968. Member: Amer. Acad. of Arts and Scis, 1984; Nat. Acad. of Sci., 1968; Hon. Mem., Amer. Inst. of Architects, 1975–. Hon. MA Yale Univ., 1961; Hon DHL: Marlboro Coll., 1965; Williams Coll., 1972; Johns Hopkins, 1984; Washington Coll., 1986; Hon. DSc: George Washington Univ., 1966; Catholic Univ., 1968; Univ. of Md, 1970; Cambridge Univ., 1974; Brown Univ., 1975; Trinity Coll., 1977; Hon. LLD: Dickinson Coll., 1967; Hofstra Univ., 1968; Yale Univ., 1975; Gallaudet Coll., 1981; Harvard, 1984; Hon. DE Stevens Inst. of Technol., 1977. Order of White Elephant, Thailand, 1949; Order of the Sacred Treasure, 2nd Cl., Japan, 1982; Officer: l'Ordre des Arts et des Lettres, France, 1975; Order of Leopold, Belgium, 1981; Légion d'Honneur, France, 1985; Commander: Order of Golden Ark, Netherlands, 1976; Order of Merit, State Council of Polish People's Republic, 1979; Order of Orange-Nassau, Netherlands, 1982; Comdr's Cross, Order of the Dannebrog, Denmark, 1976; Caballero Gran Cruz, Orden del Merito Civil, Spain, 1976; Order of James Smithson, Smithsonian Instn, 1984; Padma Bhushan, India, 1986. Freedom Medal, Thailand, 1949; President's Medal of Freedom, USA, 1985; Gold Medal: New York Zool Soc., 1966; Royal Zool Soc. of Antwerp, 1970; Thomas Jefferson Award, Amer. Soc. of Interior Designers, 1974; Medal for Distinguished Achievement, Holland Soc. of New York, 1977; F. K. Hutchinson Medal, Garden Club of America, 1979; Medal of Honor, National Soc. of Daughters of Amer. Revolution, 1981; Delacour Medal, ICBP, 1982; Henry Shaw Medal, St Louis Botannical Garden, 1982; Gold Medal, Acad. of Soc. Sci., New York, 1982; Addison Emery Verrill Medal, Peabody Mus., Yale Univ., 1984; Olympia Prize, Onassis Foundn, 1984; Medal of Distinction, Barnard Coll., 1985; Cosmos Club Award, Washington, 1988; Bishop Mus. Medal, Hawaii, 1990. *Publications:* The Trail of the Money Bird, 1942 (Sweden, 1945; UK 1947); Search for the Spiny Babbler, 1952, re-issued as A Naturalist's Adventure in Nepal, 1978; A Paddling of Ducks, 1957 (UK 1959); A Synopsis of the Birds of India and Pakistan, 1961, rev. edn 1982; (ed with Lynette L. Scribner) Ornithological Books in the Yale University Library, 1961; The Land and Wildlife of Tropical Asia, 1964, rev. edns 1971 and 1974; (with H. G. Deignan and R. A. Paynter, Jr) Check-list of Birds of the World, Vol. X (continuation of work of James L. Peters), 1964; The Sacred Grove, 1969; The Paradox of the Human Condition, 1975; Rails of the World, 1977; (with Sálim Ali) Handbook of the Birds of India and Pakistan: Vol. I, 1968, rev. edn 1978; Vol. II, 1969, rev. edn 1979; Vol. III, 1969, rev. edn 1981; Vol. IV, 1970, rev. edn 1984; Vol. V, 1972, rev. edn 1987; Vol. VI, 1971; Vol. VII, 1972; Vol. VIII, 1973; Vol. IX, 1973; Vol. X, 1974; (with Sálim Ali) A Pictorial Guide to Birds of the Indian Subcontinent, 1983, rev. edn 1988. *Recreation:* watching ducks. *Address:* 2324 Massachusetts Avenue, NW, Washington, DC 20008, USA. *T:* (202) 2323131; Paddling Ponds, Litchfield, CT 06759, USA. *T:* (203) 5678208. *Clubs:* English-Speaking Union; Alliance Française, Pilgrims of the US, Knickerbocker, Century Association, Yale (New York); Cosmos, Society of Cincinnati, Alibi, Metropolitan (Washington, DC); Himalayan (New Delhi).

RIPON, Bishop of, since 1977; **Rt. Rev. David Nigel de Lorentz Young;** *b* 2 Sept. 1931; *s* of late Brig. K. de L. Young, CIE, MC and Ada Lilian Young (*née* Tollinton); *m* 1962, Rachel Melverley Lewis (*d* 1966); one *s* one *d*; *m* 1967, Jane Havill, *y d* of late L. H. and E. M. Collison; three *s. Educ:* Wellington Coll.; Balliol Coll., Oxford (MA 1st. cl. Maths). 2nd Lt RE, Sch. of Military Survey, 1950–51; Wycliffe Hall, Oxford (BD qualifying exam 1959). Res. mathematician, Plessey Co., 1955–56. Ordained deacon, 1959, priest, 1960; Curate: All Hallows, Allerton, 1959–62; St Mark's, St John's Wood, 1962–63; studied Sanskrit and Pali, SOAS, 1962–63; CMS Missionary, Sri Lanka, 1964–67; Director, Dept of Buddhist Studies, Theological Coll. of Lanka, 1965–67; Lecturer in Buddhist Studies, Manchester Univ., 1967–70; Vicar of Burwell, Cambridge, 1970–75; Lectr, Faculty of Divinity, Univ. of Cambridge, 1970–75; Archdeacon of Huntingdon, 1975–77; Vicar of Great with Little and Steeple Gidding, 1975–77; Rector of Hemingford Abbots, 1977; Hon. Canon of Ely Cathedral, 1975–77. Entered H of L, 1984. Mem., Doctrine Commn, 1978–81; Chairman: Partnership for World Mission, 1978–86; Governing Body, SPCK, 1979–88; Anglican Interfaith Consultants, 1981–91; Scargill Council, 1984–90; Leeds Educn 2000, 1990–; C of E Bd of Educn, 1994–. *Publications:* contribs to Religious Studies. *Recreations:* walking, running, tennis, sailing. *Address:* Bishop Mount, Ripon, N Yorks HG4 5DP. *Club:* Army and Navy.

RIPON, Dean of; *see* Methuen, Very Rev. J. A. R.

RIPPENGAL, Derek, CB 1982; QC 1980; Counsel to Chairman of Committees, House of Lords, since 1977; *b* 8 Sept. 1928; *s* of William Thomas Rippengal and Margaret Mary Rippengal (*née* Parry); *m* 1963, Elizabeth Melrose (*d* 1973); one *s* one *d. Educ:* Hampton Grammar Sch.; St Catharine's Coll., Cambridge (Scholar; MA). Called to Bar, Middle Temple, 1953 (Harmsworth schol.). Entered Treasury Solicitor's Office, 1958, after Chancery Bar and univ. posts; Sen. Legal Asst, 1961; Asst Treasury Solicitor, 1967; Principal Asst Treasury Solicitor, 1971; Solicitor to DTI, 1972–73; Dep. Parly Counsel, 1973–74, Parly Counsel, 1974–76, Law Commn. *Recreations:* music, fishing. *Address:* Wychwood, Bell Lane, Little Chalfont, Amersham, Bucks HP6 6PF. *Club:* Athenæum.

RIPPON, family name of **Baron Rippon of Hexham.**

RIPPON OF HEXHAM, Baron *cr* 1987 (Life Peer), of Hesleyside in the county of Northumberland; **(Aubrey) Geoffrey (Frederick) Rippon;** PC 1962; QC 1964; *b* 28 May 1924; *o s* of late A. E. S. Rippon; *m* 1946, Ann Leyland, OBE 1984, *d* of Donald Yorke, MC, Prenton, Birkenhead, Cheshire; one *s* three *d. Educ:* King's College, Taunton; Brasenose College, Oxford (Hulme Open Exhibitioner; MA), Hon. Fellow, 1972. Secretary and Librarian of the Oxford Union, 1942; Pres. Oxford University Conservative Assoc., 1942; Chm., Federation of University Conservative Associations, 1943. Called to the Bar, Middle Temple, 1948 (Robert Garraway Rice Pupillage Prizeman), Bencher, 1979. Member Surbiton Borough Council, 1945–54; Alderman, 1949–54; Mayor, 1951–52; Member: LCC (Chelsea), 1952–61 (Leader of Conserv. Party on LCC, 1957–59); President: British Section (individual members), CEMR; British Sect., European League for Economic Co-operation; London Mayors' Assoc., 1968–71; Surrey Mayors' Assoc., 1974–76; Assoc. of District Councils, 1986–; Town and Country Planning Assoc., 1988–; Inst. of Credit Management, 1992–. Chairman: Hansard Soc. Commn on Legislative Process, 1992; H of L Cttee on Scrutiny of Legislation, 1992–95. Admiral of the Manx Herring Fleet, 1971–74. Chm. Conservative National Advisory Committee on Local Government, 1957–59, Pres., 1972–74; Vice-Pres., Council of Europe's Local Government Conference, 1957 and 1958; Contested (C) Shoreditch and Finsbury, General Elections, 1950 and 1951; MP (C): Norwich South, 1955–64; Hexham, 1966–87. PPS, Min. of Housing and Local Govt, 1956–57, Min. of Defence, 1957–59; Parly Sec., Min. of Aviation, 1959–61; Jt Parly Sec., Min. of Housing and Local Govt, Oct. 1961–July 1962; Minister of Public Building and Works, 1962–64 (Cabinet, 1963–64); Chief Opposition Spokesman on housing, local govt and land, 1966–68, on defence, 1968–70; Minister of Technology (incorporating Mins of Industry, Fuel and Power, Aviation and Supply), 1970; Chancellor of the Duchy of Lancaster, 1970–72 (resp. for negotiating Britain's entry into the EEC); Sec. of State for the Environment (incorporating Mins of Trans., Housing, Land, Local Govt, Public Bldg and Works), 1972–74; Chief Opposition Spokesman on Foreign and Commonwealth Affairs, 1974–75. Chm., Parly Foreign and Commonwealth Affairs Cttee, 1979–81; Leader: Cons. Party Delegn to Council of Europe and WEU, 1967–70; Cons. Gp, European Parlt, 1977–79; Chm., Council of Ministers, EFTA, 1970–72. Chairman: Dun and Bradstreet Ltd, 1976–; Britannia Arrow Hldgs, subseq. Invesco MIM, 1977–89 (Pres., 1989–93); Brassey's Defence Publishers, 1977–; Singer & Friedlander Hldgs, 1984–87; Robert Fraser and Partners, 1985–91; Michael Page Plc, 1987–95; UniChem, 1990–; Guerisle Investment Trust, 1992–; Holland, Hannen & Cubitts, 1965–69; Dep. Chm., Drake & Gorham, 1969–70; Director: Fairey Co. Ltd, 1965–70; Bristol Aeroplane Co., 1965–69; Hotung Estates, 1974–75; Groupe Bruxelles Lambert, 1982–90; Maxwell Communications Corp., 1986–92; Acer Group Ltd, 1991–93 (Chm., 1992–93). Mem. Council (formerly Court), London Univ., 1958– (Chm., Court, 1991–94, Council (1st Chm.), 1994–); Pro-Chancellor, London Univ., 1994–. FCIArb; FRSA; Hon. Mem., Rating and Valuation Assoc. Hon. LLD London, 1989. Knight Grand Cross, Royal Order of North Star (Sweden); Grand Cross, Order of Merit (Liechtenstein). *Publications:* (co-author) Forward from Victory, 1943; The Rent Act, 1957; various pamphlets and articles on foreign affairs, local government and legal subjects. *Recreations:* watching cricket, travel. *Address:* The Old Vicarage, Broomfield, near Bridgwater, Somerset; 1 Essex Court, Temple, EC4Y 9AR; 4 Breams Buildings, EC4A 1AQ. *T:* 0171–353 4962. *Clubs:* Whites, Pratt's, MCC.

RISELEY-PRICHARD, Air Vice-Marshal Richard Augustin; Principal Medical Officer, Royal Air Force Support Command, 1980–85, retired; Member, Swindon District Health Authority, 1988–90 (Associate Member, 1990–93); *b* 19 Feb. 1925; *s* of late Dr J. A. Prichard and Elizabeth (*née* Riseley); *m* 1953, Alannah *d* of late Air Cdre C. W. Busk, CB, MC, AFC; four *d. Educ:* Beaudesert Park; Radley Coll.; Trinity Coll., Oxford (MA, BM, BCh); St Bartholomew's Hosp., London. FFCM. Commnd RAF Med. Br., 1951; pilot trng, 1951–52; served at RAF Coll., Cranwell, 1953–56; Dep. Principal Med. Officer (Flying), HQ Transport Comd and HQ RAF Germany, 1956–63; RAF Staff Coll., 1964; SMO, British Forces, Aden, 1967; Dep. Principal Med. Officer, HQ Strike Comd, 1970–73; Commanding Officer: RAF Hosp. Wegberg, Germany, 1973–76; Princess Alexandra Hosp., Wroughton, 1977–80. QHS 1980–85. Hon. Air Cdre, No 4626, RAuxAF Sqn, 1986–. Gen. Comr of Income Tax, 1987–. Dir (non-exec.) and Vice Chm., Wiltshire Ambulance Service NHS Trust, 1993–. Mem., Armed Forces Cttee, BMA, 1989–. Governor: Dauntsey's Sch., 1982– (Vice-Chm., 1985–86, Chm., 1986–); BUPA Medical Foundn, 1990–. CStJ. *Recreations:* tennis, squash, bridge, gardening. *Address:* The Little House, Allington, Devizes, Wilts SN10 3NN. *T:* Devizes (01380) 860662. *Clubs:* Royal Air Force; All England Lawn Tennis.

RISK, Douglas James; QC (Scot.) 1992; Sheriff Principal of Grampian, Highland and Islands, since 1993; *b* 23 Jan. 1941; *s* of James Risk and Isobel Katherine Taylor Risk (*née* Dow); *m* 1967, Jennifer Hood Davidson; three *s* one *d*. *Educ:* Glasgow Academy; Gonville and Caius Coll., Cambridge (BA 1963, MA 1967); Glasgow Univ. (LLB 1965). Admitted to Faculty of Advocates, 1966; Standing Junior Counsel, Scottish Education Dept, 1975; Sheriff of Lothian and Borders at Edinburgh, 1977–79; Sheriff of Grampian, Highland and Islands at Aberdeen and Stonehaven, 1979–93. Hon. Prof., Faculty of Law, Univ. of Aberdeen, 1994– (Hon. Lectr, 1981–94). *Address:* Sheriff Court House, The Castle, Inverness IV2 3EG. *T:* Inverness (01463) 230782; Sheriff Court House, Castle Street, Aberdeen AB9 1AP. *T:* Aberdeen (01224) 648316. *Club:* Royal Northern and University (Aberdeen).

RISK, Sir Thomas (Neilson), Kt 1984; FRSE; Governor of the Bank of Scotland, 1981–91; (Director, 1971; Deputy Governor, 1977–81); *b* 13 Sept. 1922; *s* of late Ralph Risk, CBE, MC, and Margaret Nelson Robertson; *m* 1949, Suzanne Eiloart; three *s* (and one *s* decd). *Educ:* Kelvinside Academy; Glasgow Univ. (BL). Flight Lieut, RAF, 1941–46; RAFVR, 1946–53. Partner, Maclay Murray & Spens, Solicitors, 1950–81; Director: Standard Life Assurance Co., 1965–88 (Chm., 1969–77); British Linen Bank, 1968–91 (Governor, 1977–86); Howden Group, 1971–87; Merchants Trust, 1973–94; MSA (Britain) Ltd, 1958–; Shell UK Ltd, 1982–92; Barclays Bank, 1983–85; Bank of Wales, 1986–91; Chm., Scottish Financial Enterprise, 1986–89. Member: Scottish Industrial Develt Bd, 1972–75; Scottish Econ. Council, 1983–91; NEDC, 1987–91. Chm., Univ. of Glasgow Trust, 1992–; Trustee, Hamilton Bequest. FRSE 1988. Hon. LLD Glasgow, 1985; Dr *hc* Edinburgh, 1990. *Address:* 10 Belford Place, Edinburgh EH4 3DH. *T:* 0131–332 9425. *Clubs:* Royal Air Force; New (Edinburgh).

RISK, William Symington, CA; Chairman, Fleming and Ferguson Ltd, 1980–87; *b* 15 Sept. 1909; *er s* of late William Risk and Agnes Hetherington Symington, Glasgow; *m* 1937, Isobel Brown McLay; one *s* one *d*. *Educ:* Glasgow Academy; Glasgow Univ.; Edinburgh Univ. (BCom). FCMA 1944, JDipMA 1969. Served War, with Admiralty, on torpedo production at RN Torpedo Factory, at Greenock and elsewhere, 1940–45. Partner, Robson, Morrow & Co., 1945–53; Managing Director: H. W. Nevill Ltd (Nevill's Bread), 1953; Aerated Bread Co. Ltd, 1956; Chm., The London Multiple Bakers' Alliance, 1958–59; Regional Dir for Southern England, British Bakeries Ltd, 1960; Industrial Consultant, Hambros Bank Ltd, 1963; Chm., Martin-Black Ltd, 1976–79. Inst. of Chartered Accountants of Scotland: Mem. Exam. Bd, 1951–55; Mem. Council, 1963–68; Pres., 1974–75; Jt Dip. in Management Accounting Services, and First Chm. of Bd, 1966; Inst. of Cost and Management Accountants: Mem. Council, 1952–70; Pres. of Inst., 1960–61; Gold Medal of Inst., for services to the Inst. and the profession, 1965. Mem. Bd of Governors, Queen Charlotte's Hosp., 1970–80. *Publications:* technical papers on Accountancy and Management subjects; papers to internat. Congress of Accountants (London, 1952, Paris, 1967). *Recreation:* reading. *Address:* Craigowrie, Strathspey Drive, Grantown on Spey, Morayshire PH26 3EY. *T:* Grantown on Spey (01479) 873001. *Clubs:* Caledonian; New (Edinburgh); Royal Scottish Automobile (Glasgow).

RISNESS, Eric John, CBE 1982; FEng 1990; FIEE; Managing Director, STC Technology Ltd, 1987–90; *b* 27 July 1927; *s* of Kristen Riisnaes and Ethel Agnes (*née* Weeks); *m* 1952, Colleen Edwina Armstrong; two *s* two *d*. *Educ:* Stratford Grammar School, London; Corpus Christi College, Cambridge (MA, PhD). RN Scientific Service, Admiralty Research Lab., 1954; Naval Staff Coll., 1959; Admiralty Underwater Weapons Estabt, 1961; RCDS 1970; Ministry of Defence: Defence Science, 1974; Underwater Research, 1975; Sting Ray Torpedo Project, 1977; Underwater Weapons Projects, 1979; Admiralty Surface Weapons Estabt, 1980; Dir of Naval Analysis, 1982; Dir-Gen., Surface Weapons Projects, 1983; Man. Dir, Admiralty Res. Estabt, Portland, 1984–87. *Recreations:* music, genealogy, golf. *Address:* 8 Orchard Road, Shalford, Guildford, Surrey GU4 8ER. *T:* Guildford (01483) 34581.

RIST, Prof. John Michael, FRSC; Professor of Classics and Philosophy, University of Toronto, since 1983; *b* 6 July 1936; *s* of Robert Ward Rist and Phoebe May (*née* Mansfield) *m* 1960, Anna Thérèse (*née* Vogler); two *s* two *d* *Educ:* Trinity Coll., Cambridge (BA 1959, MA 1963). FRSC 1976. Univ. of Toronto: firstly Lectr, finally Prof. of Classics, 1959–80; Chm., Grad. Dept of Classics, 1971–75; Regius Prof. of Classics, Aberdeen Univ., 1980–83. *Publications:* Eros and Psyche, Canada 1964; Plotinus: the road to reality, 1967; Stoic Philosophy, 1969; Epicurus: an introduction, 1972; (ed) The Stoics, USA 1978; On the Independence of Matthew and Mark, 1978; Human Value, 1982; Platonism and its Christian Heritage, 1985; The Mind of Aristotle, 1989; Augustine, 1994; contrib. classical and phil jls. *Recreations:* travel, swimming, hill-walking. *Address:* University of Toronto, 16 Hart House Circle, Toronto, Ontario M5S 1A1, Canada.

RITBLAT, John Henry, FSVA; Chairman and Managing Director, The British Land Company plc, since 1970; *b* 3 Oct. 1935; *m* 1st, 1960, Isabel Paja (*d* 1979); two *s* one *d*; 2nd, 1986, Jill Zilkha (*née* Slotover). *Educ:* Dulwich Coll.; London Univ. College of Estate Management. Articles with West End firm of Surveyors and Valuers, 1952–58. Founder Partner, Conrad Ritblat & Co., Consultant Surveyors and Valuers, 1958; Man. Dir, Union Property Holdings (London) Ltd, 1969. Comr, Crown Estate Paving Commn, 1969–. Hon. Surveyor, King George's Fund for Sailors, 1979. Member: Council, Business in the Community, 1987–; Prince of Wales' Royal Parks Tree Appeal Cttee, 1987–; British Olympic Assoc., 1979; Olympic Appeal Cttee, 1984 and 1988; Patrons of British Art, Tate Gall.; English Heritage; Royal Horticultural Soc.; Architecture Club; SPAB; Royal Acad. (Mem. Cttee); Nat. Art-Collections Fund; Life Member: Nat. Trust; Zool Soc. of London; Georgian Gp; RGS; Trollope Soc. Trustee, Zool Soc. of London Develt Trust, 1986–89. Patron, London Fedn of Boys' Clubs Centenary Appeal; Founder Sponsor, Young Explorers Trust; Sponsor: RGS, 1982–85; (sole), British Nat. Ski Championships, 1978–96; Pres., British Ski Fedn, 1994– (Vice-Pres., 1984–89). Dep. Chm. Governors, Hall Sch.; Member, Board of Governors: London Business Sch., 1990–; The Weizmann Inst., 1991–. FRGS 1982; CIMgt; Life FRSA. *Recreations:* antiquarian books and libraries, old buildings and the countryside, bees, Real tennis, golf, skiing. *Address:* 10 Cornwall Terrace, Regent's Park, NW1 4QP. *T:* 0171–486 4466. *Clubs:* Carlton, Royal Automobile, MCC, The Pilgrims, Queen's; Cresta (St Moritz).

RITCHESON, Prof. Charles Ray; University Professor of History and University Librarian Emeritus, University of Southern California, since 1991; *b* 26 Feb. 1925; *s* of Charles Frederick and Jewell Vaughn Ritcheson; *m* 1st, 1953, Shirley Spackman (marr. diss. 1964); two *s*; 2nd, 1965, Alice Luethi; four *s*. *Educ:* Univs of Harvard, Zürich, Oklahoma and Oxford. DPhil (Oxon). FRHistS. Prof. and Chm. of History, Kenyon Coll., 1953–65; Chm. and Dir, Graduate Studies, Southern Methodist Univ., 1965–70; Lovell Prof. of History, Univ. of Southern Calif., 1971–74; Cultural Attaché, US Embassy, 1974–77; University of Southern California: Lovell Distinguished Prof. of History, 1977–84; Lovell Univ. Prof., Univ. Librarian, Dean and Special Asst. to Pres., 1984–91. Chm., British Inst. of the US, 1979–81. Vice-Pres., Board of Dirs, Amer. Friends of Covent Garden, 1978–84; Exec. Vice Pres., Fund for Arts and Culture in Central and Eastern Europe, 1992–; Member: National Council for the Humanities, 1983–87 and 1988–91; US Bd of Foreign Scholarships, 1987–88; Adv. Council, Ditchley Foundn, 1977–; Adv. Council, Univ. of Buckingham (formerly UC Buckingham), 1977–. Hon. DLitt Leicester, 1976. *Publications:* British Politics and the American Revolution, 1954; Aftermath of Revolution: British policy toward the United States 1783–1795, 1969 (paperback, 1971); The American Revolution: the Anglo-American relation, 1969; (with E. Wright) A Tug of Loyalties, 1971. *Recreations:* horseback riding, swimming, opera. *Address:* 85 Boulevard Haussmann, 75008 Paris, France. *T:* 47424484. *Clubs:* Beefsteak, Brooks's; California (Los Angeles); Cosmos (Washington).

RITCHIE, family name of **Baron Ritchie of Dundee.**

RITCHIE OF DUNDEE, 5th Baron *cr* 1905; **Harold Malcolm Ritchie;** English and Drama Teacher, Bedgebury School, Kent, retired 1984; Social and Liberal Democrat (formerly Liberal) spokesman on education, House of Lords, since 1985; *b* 29 Aug. 1919; 4th *s* of 2nd Baron Ritchie of Dundee and Sarah Ruth (*d* 1950), *d* of J. L. Jennings, MP; *S* brother, 1978; *m* 1948, Anne, *d* of late Col C. G. Johnstone, MC; one *s* one *d*. *Educ:* Stowe School; Trinity College, Oxford. MA 1940. Served in Middle East, Italy and Greece, Captain KRRC, 1940–46. Assistant Headmaster, Brickwall House School, Northiam, Sussex, 1952–65; Headmaster, 1965–72. *Recreations:* gardening, drama, music. *Heir:* *s* Hon. Charles Rupert Rendall Ritchie [*b* 15 March 1958; *m* 1984, Tara Van Tuyl Koch (marr. diss. 1992)]. *Address:* House of Lords, SW1.

RITCHIE, Albert Edgar, CC 1975; Canadian Diplomat, retired Nov. 1981; *b* 20 Dec. 1916; *m*; two *s* two *d*. *Educ:* Mount Allison Univ., New Brunswick (BA 1938); Queen's College, Oxford (Rhodes Scholar, 1940; BA). Officer, Econ. Affairs Dept, UN, and Secretariat of Gen. Agreement on Tariffs and Trade, 1946–48; Counsellor, Office of Canadian High Comr, London, UK, 1948–52; Deputy Under-Secretary of State for External Affairs, Canada, 1964–66; Canadian Ambassador to USA, 1966–70; Under-Sec. of State for External Affairs, Canada, 1970–74; Special Advisor to Privy Council Office, Canada, 1974–76; Canadian Ambassador to Republic of Ireland, 1976–81. Hon. LLD: Mount Allison Univ., 1966; St Thomas Univ., 1968; Carleton Univ., 1985. *Address:* 601/2374 Carling Avenue, Ottawa, Ont K2B 7G5, Canada. *Club:* Rideau (Ottawa).

RITCHIE, Alexander James Otway; Chairman, Union Discount Co. of London plc, 1970–90; *b* 5 May 1928; *s* of Charles Henry Ritchie and Marjorie Alice Ritchie (*née* Stewart); *m* 1953, Joanna Willink Fletcher; two *s* (one *d* decd). *Educ:* Stowe; St John's Coll., Cambridge (MA). Joined Glyn, Mills and Co., 1951 (Dir, 1964); Exec. Dir, Williams & Glyn's Bank, 1970; resigned Williams & Glyn's Bank, 1977; Dep. Chm., Grindlays Bank plc, 1977–83, Chief Exec. 1980–83; Dep. Chm., Grindlays Holdings, 1978–83; Chairman: Grindlays Bank, 1984–87; ANZ Hldgs (UK), 1985–87; Dep. Chm., Italian Internat. Bank, 1989–93 (Dir, 1986–93). Director: Australian and New Zealand Banking Gp, 1984–87; European Investment Bank, 1986–93; Debenham Tewson & Chinnocks Holdings plc, 1987–93; Archdale Holdings, 1991–. Mem., London Cttee, Ottoman Bank, 1966–; Mem., Export Guarantees Adv. Council, 1977–82 (Dep. Chm., 1980–81). Dir, Bath Abbey Trust, 1991–. Chairman of Governors: Windlesham House Sch., 1986–93; Downe House Sch., 1991–. *Address:* 54 Sydney Buildings, Bath, Avon BA2 6DB.

RITCHIE, Anthony Elliot, CBE 1978; MA, BSc, MD; FRSE; Secretary and Treasurer, 1969–86, Trustee, since 1987, Carnegie Trust for the Universities of Scotland; *b* 30 March 1915; *s* of late Prof. James Ritchie; *m* 1941, Elizabeth Lambie Knox, MB, ChB, *y d* of John Knox, Dunfermline; one *s* three *d*. *Educ:* Edinburgh Academy; Aberdeen and Edinburgh Universities. MA (Aber), 1933; BSc 1936, with Hunter Memorial Prize. MB, ChB (Edin.) 1940. Carnegie Research Scholar, Physiology Dept, Edin. Univ., 1940–41; Asst Lectr 1941; Lectr 1942. Ellis Prize in Physiology, 1941; Gunning Victoria Jubilee Prize, 1943; MD (Edin.) with Gold Medal Thesis, 1945; senior lecturer grade, 1946. Lecturer in Electrotherapy, Edin. Royal Infirmary, 1943–48, 1972–; Chandos Prof. of Physiology, Univ. of St Andrews, 1948–69; Dean, Faculty of Science, 1961–66. Hon. Physiologist Gogarburn Nerve Injuries Hospital, 1941–46; Honeyman Gillespie Lecturer, 1944; Hon. Consultant in Electrotherapy, Scot. E Regional Hospital Board, 1950–69; Fellow Royal Soc. of Edinburgh, 1951 (Council RSE 1957–60, 1979–80; Secretary to Ordinary Meetings, 1960–65, Vice-President, 1965–66 and 1976–79; General Secretary, 1966–76); Scientific Adviser, Civil Defence, 1961–80; Adv. Cttee on Med. Research, Scotland, 1961–, Vice-Chm., 1967–69; Chairman: Scottish Cttee on Science Educn, 1970–78; Blood Transfusion Adv. Gp, 1970–80; Scottish Universities Entrance Bd, 1963–69; St Leonard's Sch., St Andrews, 1968–69; Mem., Council for Applied Science in Scotland, 1978–86; Mem., British Library Bd, 1973–80; Trustee, Nat. Library of Scotland. Mem., Cttee of Inquiry into Teachers' Pay. Examiner, Chartered Soc. of Physiotherapy, Pharmaceutical Soc. of Great Britain, and RCSE. RAMC (TA) commission, 1942–44. Hon. FCSP 1970; Hon. FRCPE 1986. Hon. DSc St Andrews, 1972; Hon. LLD Strathclyde, 1985. Bicentenary Medal, RSE, 1983. *Publications:* (with J. Lenman) Clinical Electromyography, 1976, 4th edn 1987; medical and scientific papers on nerve injury diagnosis and medical electronics. *Recreations:* reading, hill walking, motor cars. *Address:* 12 Ravelston Park, Edinburgh EH4 3DX. *T:* 0131–332 6560. *Clubs:* Caledonian; New (Edinburgh).

RITCHIE, David Robert; Regional Director, Government Office for the West Midlands, since 1994 (Regional Director, West Midlands Regional Office, Departments of the Environment and Transport, 1989–94); *b* 10 March 1948; *s* of late James Ritchie and of Edith Ritchie (*née* Watts); *m* 1989, Joan Gibbons. *Educ:* Manchester Grammar School; St John's College, Cambridge (BA, MA). Min. of Transport, 1970; DoE, 1970–. *Recreations:* fell-walking, cooking. *Address:* Five Ways Tower, Frederick Road, Edgbaston, Birmingham B15 1SJ. *T:* 0121–626 2570.

RITCHIE, Prof. Donald Andrew, PhD; FIBiol, CBiol; FRSE; Professor of Genetics, since 1978, and Pro-Vice-Chancellor, since 1992, University of Liverpool; *b* 9 July 1938; *s* of Andrew Ritchie and Winifred Laura (*née* Parkinson); *m* 1962, Margaret Jeanne (*née* Collister); one *s* one *d*. *Educ:* Latymer's Sch., London; Univ. of Leicester (BSc Hons Botany, 1959); RPMS, London (PhD 1964). FIBiol 1978; CBiol 1985; FRSE 1979. MRC Microbial Genetics Res. Unit, London, 1959–64; Res. Associate, Biophysics Dept, Johns Hopkins Univ., Baltimore, USA, 1964–66; Lectr, 1966–72, Sen. Lectr, 1972–78, Virology Dept, Univ. of Glasgow. Royal Soc. Leverhulme Trust Sen. Res. Fellow, 1991–92. Mem., Biotechnol. Jt Adv. Bd, DTI, 1990–95. Member: NERC, 1990–95 (Chm., Terrestrial and Freshwater Life Scis Cttee, 1991–95); Science Bd, SERC, 1989–92; Food Res. Cttee, AFRC, 1991–94. Mem. Council, Marine Biol Assoc., 1991–94. *Publications:* (with T. H. Pennington) Molecular Virology, 1971; (with K. M. Smith) Introduction to Virology, 1980; pubns on microbial and molecular genetics in learned jls. *Recreations:* painting, gardening, walking. *Address:* Department of Genetics and Microbiology, University of Liverpool, Liverpool L69 3BX. *T:* 0151–794 3624. *Club:* Athenæum (Liverpool).

RITCHIE, Rear-Adm. George Stephen, CB 1967; DSC 1942; writer; retired hydrographer; *b* 30 Oct. 1914; *s* of Sir (John) Douglas Ritchie, MC and late Margaret Stephen, OBE 1946, JP, Officer of the Order of Orange-Nassau, *d* of James Allan, Methlick, Aberdeenshire; *m* 1942, Mrs Disa Elizabeth Smith (*née* Beveridge); three *s* one *d. Educ:* RNC, Dartmouth. Joined RN Surveying Service, 1936; attached Eighth Army, 1942–43; served in HM Survey Ship Scott for invasion of Europe, 1944; comd HMS Challenger on scientific voyage round world, 1950–51; comd HM New Zealand Survey Ship Lachlan and NZ Surveying Service, 1953–56; comd HM Surveying Ship Dalrymple, Persian Gulf, 1959; comd HM Surveying Ship Vidal, West Indies and Western Europe, 1963–65; ADC to the Queen, 1965; Hydrographer of the Navy, 1966–71; Vis. Research Fellow, Southampton Univ., 1971–72; Pres., Directing Cttee, Internat. Hydrographic Bureau, Monaco, 1972–82; Founder Pres., 1972–73, Emeritus Mem., 1988–, Hydrographic Soc. Hon. Member: Canadian Hydrographic Assoc., 1981; Hydrographic Soc. of SA, 1985; Challenger Soc., 1992. Chm., Collieston Harbour Trustees, 1992–. Founder's Medal, RGS, 1972; Prix Manley-Bendall, Académie de Marine, Paris, 1977; Gold Medal, Royal Inst. of Navigation, 1978. *Publications:* Challenger, 1957; The Admiralty Chart, 1967, new edn 1995; No Day Too Long, 1992; papers on navigation and oceanography in various jls, including Developments in British Hydrography since days of Captain Cook (RSA Silver Medal, 1970). *Recreations:* conserving Collieston, boules, sea-fishing. *Address:* Sea View, Collieston, Ellon, Aberdeenshire AB41 8RS. *Clubs:* Reform; Royal Northern and University (Aberdeen); Collieston Boules; Monte Carlo (Emeritus Mem.).

RITCHIE, Ian Carl, RIBA; Principal, Ian Ritchie Architects, since 1981; Consultant, Rice Francis Ritchie, since 1987; *b* 25 May 1947; *s* of Christopher Charles Ritchie and Mabel Berenice (*née* Long); *m* 1972, Jocelyne van den Bossche; one *s*. *Educ:* Varndean, Brighton; Liverpool Sch. of Architecture; Polytechnic of Central London Sch. of Architecture (Dip. Arch. distinction). MCSD. With Foster Associates, 1972–76; in private practice in France, 1976–78; Partner, Chrysalis Architects, 1979–81; Director: Rice, Francis Ritchie, 1981–87; Lhermitte-Ritchie, 1987–90. Major works include: Ecology Gall., Nat. Hist. Mus.; B8, Stockley Park, London; Roy Square housing, Limehouse, London; Eagle Rock House, E Sussex; Culture Centre, Albert, France; roofs, Louvre Sculpture Court, Paris; roof and glass facade, Mus. Nat. de Science, Techniques et de l'Industrie, La Villette, Paris; pharmacy, Boves, France; Fluy House, Picardy, France; glass towers, Centro de Arte Reina Sofia, Madrid; Leipzig Glashalle. Royal Fine Art Comr, 1995–. Architectural Advr, Natural Hist. Mus., 1991–. External examiner, RIBA, 1986–. Vis. Prof., Vienna Technical Univ., 1994–95. Council Mem., Steel Construction Inst., 1994–. FRSA. Tableau de l'Ordre des Architectes Français, 1982; Architectural Design Silver Medal, 1982; IRITECNA (Italian state construction industry) European Prize, 1992; Eric Lyons Meml Award, for European housing, 1992; Robert Matthew Award, Commonwealth Assoc. of Architects, 1994. *Publication:* (Well) Connected Architecture, 1994. *Recreations:* art, swimming, reading, writing, film making. *Address:* 14 Garford Street, E14 9JG. *T:* 0171–515 4989.

RITCHIE, Ian Charles Stewart; Director, Highland Festival, since 1994; *b* 19 June 1953; *s* of Kenneth John Stewart Ritchie and Wanda Margaret Angela Ritchie; *m* 1977, Angela Mary (marr. diss. 1993); two *d*. *Educ:* Stowe Sch.; Royal Coll. of Music; Trinity Coll., Cambridge (MA); Guildhall Sch. of Music and Drama. General Manager, City of London Sinfonia, 1979–84; Artistic Dir, City of London Fest., 1983–84; Man. Dir, Scottish Chamber Orchestra, 1984–93; Gen. Dir, Opera North, 1993–94. Artistic Co-Dir, St Magnus Fest., Orkney, 1988–93. Adjudicator, adviser, broadcaster and commentator on musical and general artistic subjects. *Recreations:* wine, cricket, golf, tennis, ski-ing, song. *Address:* 25/7 St James Square, Edinburgh EH1 3AY. *T:* 0131–556 0077. *Club:* MCC.

RITCHIE, Ian Russell; Managing Director, London News Network, since 1994; *b* 27 Nov. 1953; *s* of Hugh Russell Ritchie and Sheelah Ritchie; *m* 1982, Jill Evelyn Middleton-Walker; two *s*. *Educ:* Leeds Grammar Sch.; Trinity Coll., Oxford (MA Jurisprudence). Called to the Bar, Middle Temple, 1976. Practised at the Bar, 1976–78; Industrial Relations Advr, EEF, 1978–80; Granada TV, 1980–88 (Head of Prodn Services, 1987–88); Dir of Resources, 1988–91, Man. Dir, 1991–93, Tyne Tees TV; Gp Dep. Chief Exec., Yorkshire Tyne Tees TV, 1992–93; Man. Dir, Nottingham Studios, Central Television, 1993–94. *Recreations:* golf, tennis, theatre, music. *Address:* Virginia Water, Surrey. *Club:* Vincent's (Oxford).

RITCHIE, James Walter, MC; Director, Inchcape & Co. Ltd, 1972–84, retired; *b* 12 Jan. 1920; *m* 1951, Penelope June (*née* Forbes); two *s* two *d*. *Educ:* Ampleforth Coll.; Clare Coll., Cambridge. Gordon Highlanders. *Recreations:* hunting, fishing, golf. *Address:* Lockeridge Down, Lockeridge, near Marlborough, Wilts SN8 4EL. *T:* Lockeridge (01672) 861244. *Clubs:* Oriental; Muthaiga Country (Nairobi).

RITCHIE, Jean Harris, (Mrs G. T. K. Boney); QC 1992; a Recorder, since 1993; *b* 6 April 1947; *d* of late Walter Weir Ritchie and of Lily (*née* Goodwin); *m* 1976, Guy Thomas Knowles Boney, *qv*; two *s*. *Educ:* King's Coll., London (LLB); McGill Univ., Montreal (LLM). Called to the Bar, Gray's Inn, 1970 (Churchill Schol., 1968); on Western Circuit. Chm., Clunis Inquiry (care in the community for patients suffering from schizophrenia), 1993–94. Mem., Supreme Ct Rule Cttee, 1993–. *Publication:* (contrib.) Safe Practice in Obstetrics and Gynaecology, ed R. V. Clements, 1994. *Recreation:* family. *Address:* 4 Paper Buildings, Temple, EC4Y 7CX. *T:* 0171–353 3366.

RITCHIE, Dr John Hindle, MBE 1985; architect; development management consultant; *b* 4 June 1937; *s* of Charles A. Ritchie; *m* 1963, Anne Leyland; two *d*. *Educ:* Royal Grammar School, Newcastle upon Tyne; Univ. of Liverpool (BArch Hons); Univ. of Sheffield (PhD Building Science). Science Research Council, 1963–66; Town Planner, Liverpool City Council, 1966–69; Rowntree Housing Trust, Univ. of Liverpool, 1969–72; R&D Architect, Cheshire County Council, 1972–74; Asst County Planner (Envmt), Merseyside CC, 1974–80; Dir of Develt, 1980–85, Chief Exec. and Mem., 1985–91, Merseyside Develt Corp. Chm., Merseyside Educn Training Enterprise Ltd, 1986–91; Member: Merseyside Tourism Bd, 1986–88; Internat. Organising Cttee, Grand Regatta Columbus '92, 1986–92; Gardners Row Business Centre, 1987–90; Merseyside Enterprise Trust, 1988–91; Instant Muscle Ltd, 1993–; Merseyside Sculptors Guild, 1993–; Wirral Community Healthcare Trust, 1993–. Major projects include: natural resource management, pollution control, land reclamation and urban conservation progs and projects, Merseyside Strategic Plan; Liverpool South docks and riverside reclamation and develt, Liverpool Internat. Garden Fest., 1984 (Civic Trust Award); Albert Dock Conservation (European Gold Medal, 1986; Civic Trust Jubilee Award, 1987). CIMgt; FRSA. *Publications:* scientific and planning papers on urban environment obsolescence and regeneration. *Address:* The Mount, Heswall, Wirral L60 4RD.

RITCHIE, Prof. J(oseph) Murdoch, PhD, DSc; FRS 1976; Eugene Higgins Professor of Pharmacology, Yale University, since 1968; *b* 10 June 1925; *s* of Alexander Farquharson Ritchie and Agnes Jane (*née* Bremner); *m* 1951, Brenda Rachel (*née* Bigland); one *s* one *d*. *Educ:* Aberdeen Central Secondary Sch.; Aberdeen Univ. (BSc Maths); UCL (BSc Physiol., PhD, DSc; Fellow 1978). MInstP. Res. in Radar, Telecommunications Res. Estabt, Malvern, 1944–46; University Coll. London: Hon. Res. Asst, Biophysics Res. Unit, 1946–49; Lectr in Physiol., 1949–51; Mem. staff, Nat. Inst. for Med. Res., Mill Hill, 1951–55; Asst Prof. of Pharmacology, 1956–57, Associate Prof., 1958–63 and Prof., 1963–68, Albert Einstein Coll. of Medicine, NY; Overseas Fellow, Churchill Coll., Cambridge, 1964–65; Chm., Dept of Pharmacol., 1968–74, Dir, Div. of Biol Scis, 1975–78, Yale Univ. Hon. MA Yale, 1968; Hon. DSc Aberdeen, 1987. *Publications:* papers on nerve and muscle physiol. and biophysics in Jl of Physiol. *Recreations:* skiing, chess. *Address:* 47 Deepwood Drive, Hamden, CT 06517, USA. *T:* (home) (203) 7770420 (office) (203) 7854567. *Club:* Yale (NYC).

RITCHIE, Kenneth Gordon, CMG 1968; HM Diplomatic Service, retired; *b* 19 Aug. 1921; *s* of Walter Ritchie, Arbroath; *m* 1951, Esme Stronsa Nash. *Educ:* Arbroath High Sch.; St Andrews Univ. (MA). Joined FO, 1944; Embassy, Ankara, 1944–47; Foreign Office, 1947–49; Khorramshahr, 1949–50; Tehran, 1950–52; Djakarta, 1952–55; Foreign Office, 1955–57; Peking, 1957–62; Santiago, 1962–64; Elisabethville, 1965–66; Dep. High Commissioner, Lusaka, 1966–67; High Commissioner, Guyana, 1967–70; Head of Perm. Under-Sec.'s Dept, FCO, 1970–73; High Comr, Malaŵi, 1973–77. *Recreations:* cinephotography, model railways. *Address:* Dalforbie, North Esk Road, Edzell, Angus DD9 7TW.

RITCHIE, Margaret Claire; JP; Headmistress of Queen Mary School, Lytham, since 1981; *b* 18 Sept. 1937; *d* of Roderick M. Ritchie, Edinburgh. *Educ:* Leeds Girls' High Sch.; Univ. of Leeds (BSc). Postgraduate Certificate in Education, Univ. of London. Asst Mistress, St Leonards Sch., St Andrews, 1960–64; Head of Science Dept, Wycombe Abbey Sch., High Wycombe, 1964–71; Headmistress, Queenswood Sch., 1972–81. JP Fylde, 1991. *Address:* Queen Mary School, Clifton Drive South, Lytham St Annes, Lancs FY8 1DS.

RITCHIE, Robert Blackwood; grazier running family sheep and cattle property, Western Victoria, since 1958; Director, Amskan Ltd, since 1986; *b* 6 April 1937; *s* of Alan Blackwood Ritchie and Margaret Louise (*née* Whitcomb); *m* 1965, Eda Natalie Sandford Beggs; two *s* one *d*. *Educ:* Geelong Grammar Sch.; Corpus Christi Coll., Cambridge (MA; Rowing Blue, 1958). Dir, Agricl Investments Australia, 1968–89 (Chm., 1968–85). Exec. Mem., Graziers Assoc. of Vic, 1968–72; Mem., National Rural Adv. Council, 1974–75; Chairman: Exotic Animal Disease Preparedness Consultative Council, 1990–; Renewable Energy Authority, Vic, 1993–. Dir-Gen., Min. for Economic Develt, Vic, 1981–83. Geelong Grammar School: Mem. Council, 1966–78 (Chm., 1973–78); Chief Exec., 1979–80 (during period between Head Masters). *Recreation:* sailing. *Address:* Blackwood, Penshurst, Vic 3289, Australia. *T:* (55) 765432. *Club:* Melbourne (Melbourne).

RITCHIE, Shirley Anne; *see* Anwyl, S. A.

RITTERMAN, Janet Elizabeth, PhD; Director, Royal College of Music, since 1993; *b* 1 Dec. 1941; *d* of Charles Eric Palmer and Laurie Helen Palmer; *m* 1970, Gerrard Peter Ritterman. *Educ:* North Sydney Girls' High Sch.; NSW State Conservatorium of Music; Univ. of Durham (BMus 1971); King's Coll. London (MMus 1977; PhD 1985). Pianist, accompanist, chamber music player; Senior Lecturer in Music: Middlesex Poly., 1975–79; Goldsmiths' Coll., Univ. of London, 1980–87; Dartington College of Arts: Head of Music, 1987–90; Dean, Academic Affairs, 1988–90; Acting Principal, 1990–91; Principal, 1991–93; Hon. Vis. Prof. of Music Educn, Univ. of Plymouth, 1993–. Chm., Assoc. Bd of Royal Schs of Music (Publishing) Ltd, 1993–. Former Mem., music educn orgns; Member: Music Panel, Arts Council, 1992–; Council, Royal Musical Assoc., 1994–; Vice-Pres., Nat. Assoc. of Youth Orchestras, 1993–. Governor, Assoc. Bd, Royal Schs of Music, 1993–. Trustee, Countess of Munster Musical Trust, 1993–. Hon. RAM 1995. *Publications:* articles in learned jls, France and UK. *Recreations:* reading, theatre-going. *Address:* Royal College of Music, Prince Consort Road, SW7 2BS. *T:* 0171–589 3643.

RITTNER, Luke Philip Hardwick; Director of Marketing and Communications, Sotheby's, Europe, since 1992; *b* 24 May 1947; *s* of late George Stephen Hardwick Rittner and of Joane (*née* Thunder); *m* 1974, Corinna Frances Edholm; one *d*. *Educ:* Blackfriars School, Laxton; City of Bath Technical Coll.; Dartington Coll. of Arts; London Acad. of Music and Dramatic Art. Asst Administrator, Bath Festival, 1968–71, Jt Administrator, 1971–74, Administrative Director, 1974–76; Founder, and Dir, Assoc. for Business Sponsorship of the Arts, 1976–83; Sec. Gen., Arts Council of GB, 1983–90. Chm., English Shakespeare Co., 1990–94. UK Cultural Dir, Expo '92, Seville; Corporate Advr on cultural sponsorship to: Eurotunnel; J. Sainsbury plc. Non-exec. Bd Mem., Carlton Television, 1991–93. Member: Adv. Council, V&A Museum, 1980–83; Music Panel, British Council, 1979–83; Drama Panel, Olivier Awards, 1992–94; Council, and Chm., F&GP Cttee, LAMDA, 1994–. Chm., London Choral Soc., 1994–. Trustee: Bath Preservation Trust, 1968–73; Theatre Royal, Bath, 1979–82; Foundn Trustee, Holburne Museum, Bath, 1981–; Governor, Urchfont Manor, Wiltshire Adult Educn Centre, 1982–83. *Recreations:* the arts, people, travel. *Address:* 29 Kelso Place, W8 5QG. *Club:* Garrick.

RIVERDALE, 2nd Baron, *cr* 1935; **Robert Arthur Balfour,** Bt 1929; DL; President, Balfour Darwins Ltd, 1969–75 (Chairman, 1961–69); *b* Sheffield, 1 Sept. 1901; *er s* of 1st Baron Riverdale, GBE; *S* father, 1957; *m* 1st, 1926, Nancy Marguerite (*d* 1928), *d* of late Rear-Adm. Mark Rundle, DSO; one *s*; 2nd, 1933, Christian Mary (*d* 1991), *er d* of late Major Rowland Hill; one *s* one *d*. *Educ:* Aysgarth; Oundle. MRINA. Served with RNVR, 1940–45, attaining rank of Lt-Comdr. Joined Arthur Balfour & Co. Ltd, 1918; Dir, 1924; Man. Dir, 1949; Chm. and Man. Dir, 1957–61; Exec. Chm., 1961–69. Director: National Provincial Bank, Main Central Bd, 1964–69 (Local Bd, 1949–69); National Westminster Bank, E Region, 1969–71; Light Trades House Ltd, 1956–65; Yorkshire Television, 1967–73. The Association of British Chambers of Commerce: Mem. Exec. Council, 1950–; Vice-Pres., 1952–54; Dep. Pres., 1954–57; Pres., 1957–58; Chm., Overseas Cttee, 1953–57. President: Nat. Fedn of Engineers' Tool Manufacturers, 1951–57 (Hon. Vice-Pres., 1957–; Representative on Gauge and Tool Adv. Council, 1946–64); Sheffield Chamber of Commerce, 1950 (Jt Hon. Sec., 1957–); Milling Cutter and Reamer Trade Assoc., 1936–54 (Vice-Pres., 1954–57); Twist Drill Traders' Assoc., 1946–55; Chm., British Council, Aust. Assoc. of British Manufacturers, 1954–57 (Vice-Chm., 1957–65; Hon. Mem., 1965–); Member: Management and Tech. Cttee, High Speed Steel Assoc., 1947–65; British Nat. Cttee of Internat. Chamber of Commerce Adv. Cttee, 1957–58; Nat. Production Adv. Cttee, 1957–58; Consultative Cttee for Industry, 1957–58; Standing Cttee, Crucible and High Speed Steel Conf., 1951–64; Western Hemisphere Exports Council (formerly Dollar Exports Council), 1957–61; Governor, Sheffield Savings Bank, 1948–58 (Patron, 1958–); Master Cutler, 1946; Trustee, Sheffield Town Trust, 1958–; Town Collector, Sheffield, 1974–; Guardian of Standard of Wrought Plate within City of Sheffield, 1948–; Belgian Consul for Sheffield area, 1945–. JP, City of Sheffield, 1950–66 (Pres., S Yorks Br. Magistrates' Assoc., 1971–); DL, S Yorks (formerly WR Yorks and City and County of York), 1959–. Pres., Derwent Fly Fishing Club. Is a Churchman and a Conservative. Chevalier of Order of the Crown, Belgium, 1956; La Médaille Civique de première classe; Officier de l'Ordre de Leopold II, 1971. *Publication:* Squeeze the Trigger Gently, 1990. *Recreations:* yachting, yacht designing, shooting, stalking, fishing. *Heir:* *s* Hon. Mark Robin Balfour, *qv*. *Address:* Ropes, Grindleford, via Sheffield S30 1HX. *T:* Hope Valley (01433) 30408. *Clubs:* Royal Cruising (Commodore, 1962–66); Sheffield (Sheffield).

RIVERINA, Bishop of, since 1993; **Rt. Rev. Bruce Quinton Clark;** *b* Brisbane, Qld, 22 May 1939; *s* of Quinton Clark; *m* 1965, Elizabeth Shufflebotham. *Educ:* Brisbane Boys Coll.; St Francis Theol Coll., Brisbane (ThL). Ordained deacon and priest, 1963; Assistant Curate: All Saints, Chermside, 1963–65; St Matthew's, Groveley, 1965–67; Vicar, St Luke's, Miles, 1967–70; Rector: St Matthew's, Gayndah, 1970–76; St Peter's, Gympie, 1976–83; St Paul's, Maryborough, 1983–89; Surfers Paradise Parish, 1989–93. Archdeacon: Wide Bay, Burnett, 1985–89; Moreton, 1989–91; Gold Coast and Hinterland, 1991–93. *Recreations:* restoring furniture, music, photography. *Address:* Bishop's Lodge, 127 Audley Street, Narrandera, NSW 2700, Australia. *T:* Narrandera (69) 591177.

RIVETT, Dr Geoffrey Christopher; Senior Principal Medical Officer, Department of Health (formerly of Health and Social Security), 1985–92; *b* 11 Aug. 1932; *s* of Frank Andrew James Rivett and Catherine Mary Rivett; *m* 1976, Elizabeth Barbara Hartman; two *s* by previous marr. *Educ:* Manchester Grammar Sch.; Brasenose Coll., Oxford (MA 1st Cl. Hons Animal Physiol.); University Coll. Hosp. (BM, BCh); FRCGP, DObst RCOG. House Officer, Radcliffe Inf., Oxford, 1957; House Phys., London Chest Hosp., 1958; RAMC, 1958–60; GP, Milton Keynes, 1960–72; DHSS, subseq. DoH, 1972–92. Liveryman: Soc. of Apothecaries, 1981–; Co. of Barbers, 1993–. ARPS 1971. *Publication:* The Development of the London Hospital System 1823–1982, 1986. *Recreations:* photography, house conversion. *Address:* Shilling Orchard, Shilling Street, Lavenham, Suffolk CO10 9RH. *T:* Lavenham (01787) 247808. *Club:* Royal Society of Medicine.

RIVETT-CARNAC, Miles James; Chairman, Baring Securities, 1993–94; *b* 7 Feb. 1933; *s* of Vice-Adm. James William Rivett-Carnac, CB, CBE, DSC (2nd *s* of 6th Bt) (*d* 1970), and Isla Nesta Rivett-Carnac (*d* 1974), *d* of Harry Officer Blackwood; *heir-pres.* to brother, Rev. Canon Sir Nicholas Rivett-Carnac, Bt, *qv*; *m* 1958, April Sally Villar; two *s* one *d*. *Educ:* Royal Naval College, Dartmouth, RN, 1950–70 (despatches 1965); Commander, 1965; US Staff Coll., 1966; Commanded HMS Dainty, 1967–68; MoD, 1968–70. Joined Barings, 1971; Dir. Baring Bros & Co., 1976; Pres., Baring Bros Inc., 1978; Managing Dir, Baring Bros & Co., 1981; Dep. Chm., Barings plc, 1988–93; Chm., Baring Asset Management, 1989–93. Chm., Tribune Investment Trust, 1985–; Director: London Stock Exchange, 1991–; Allied Lyons plc, 1992–. Chm., Hampshire Boys' Clubs, 1982–. Mem. Council, King George V Fund for Sailors, 1989. Elder Brother, Trinity House, 1992–. High Sheriff, Hants, 1995. *Recreations:* tennis, golf, shooting, philately (FRPS). *Address:* Martyr Worthy Manor, Winchester, Hants SO21 1DY. *T:* Itchen Abbas (01962) 779311. *Clubs:* White's, Naval and Military; Links, Racquet (NY).

RIVETT-CARNAC, Rev. Canon Sir (Thomas) Nicholas, 8th Bt *cr* 1836; Pastor, Ashburnham Place, Battle, since 1993; Hon. Canon of Southwark Cathedral, since 1980; *b* 3 June 1927; *s* of Vice-Admiral James William Rivett-Carnac, CB, CBE, DSC (2nd *s* of 6th Bt) (*d* 1970), and of Isla Nesta Rivett-Carnac (*d* 1974), *d* of Harry Officer Blackwood; *S* uncle, 1972; *m* 1977, Susan Marigold MacTier Copeland, *d* of late Harold and Adeline Copeland. *Educ:* Marlborough College. Scots Guards, 1945–55. Probation Service, 1957–59. Ordained, 1963; Curate: Holy Trinity, Rotherhithe, 1963–68; Holy Trinity, Brompton, 1968–72; Vicar, St Mark's, Kennington, 1972–89; Rural Dean of Lambeth, 1978–82; Pastor, Kingdom Faith Ministries, Roffey Place, Horsham, 1989–93. *Heir: b* Miles James Rivett-Carnac, *qv*. *Address:* 1 The Stable, Ashburnham Place, Battle, East Sussex TN33 9NF.

RIVETT-DRAKE, Brig. Dame Jean (Elizabeth), DBE 1964 (MBE 1947); JP; DL; Member, Hove Borough Council, 1966–84; Mayor of Hove, 1977–78; Lay Member, Press Council, 1973–78; Director, Women's Royal Army Corps, 1961–64, retd; *b* 13 July 1909; *d* of Comdr Bertram Gregory Drake and of late Dora Rivett-Drake. Served War of 1939–45 (despatches, 1946). Hon. ADC to the Queen, 1961–64. Mem., East Sussex CC, 1973–77 (Mem. Educn and Social Services Cttees, AHA). JP 1965; DL E Sussex, 1983. *Address:* 9 Kestrel Close, Hove, East Sussex BN3 6NS. *T:* Brighton (01273) 505839; c/o Barclays Bank, PO Box 358, Brighton BN1 1SF. *Club:* English-Speaking Union.

RIVLIN, Geoffrey, QC 1979; **His Honour Judge Rivlin;** a Circuit Judge, since 1989; *b* 28 Nov. 1940; *s* of late M. Allenby Rivlin and late May Rivlin; *m* 1974, Maureen Smith, violinist; two *d*. *Educ:* Bootham Sch.; Leeds Univ. (LLB). Called to the Bar, Middle Temple, 1963 (Colombos Prize, Internat. Law); Bencher, 1987. NE Circuit Junior 1967; a Recorder, 1978–89. Mem., Senate of Inns of Court and the Bar, 1976–79. Gov., St Christopher's Sch., Hampstead, 1990–. *Address:* 4 Paper Buildings, Temple, EC4Y 7EX.

RIX, family name of **Baron Rix**.

RIX, Baron *cr* 1992 (Life Peer), of Whitehall in the City of Westminster and of Hornsea in Yorkshire; **Brian Norman Roger Rix**, Kt 1986; CBE 1977; actor-manager, 1948–77; Chairman: Mencap (Royal Society for Mentally Handicapped Children and Adults), since 1988 (Secretary-General, 1980–87); Mencap City Foundation, since 1988 (Founder and Governor, since 1984); Vice Lord-Lieutenant of Greater London, since 1988; *b* 27 Jan. 1924; *s* of late Herbert and Fanny Rix; *m* 1949, Elspet Jeans Macgregor-Gray; two *s* two *d*. *Educ:* Bootham Sch., York. Stage career: joined Donald Wolfit, 1942; first West End appearance, Sebastian in Twelfth Night, St James's, 1943; White Rose Players, Harrogate, 1943–44. Served War of 1939–45, RAF and Bevin Boy. Became actor-manager, 1948; ran repertory cos at Ilkley, Bridlington and Margate, 1950; toured Reluctant Heroes and brought to Whitehall Theatre, 1950–54; Dry Rot, 1954–58; Simple Spymen, 1958–61; One For the Pot, 1961–64; Chase Me Comrade, 1964–66; went to Garrick Theatre, 1967, with repertoire of farce: Stand By Your Bedouin; Uproar in the House; Let Sleeping Wives Lie; after 6 months went over to latter, only, which ran till 1969; then followed: She's Done It Again, 1969–70; Don't Just Lie There, Say Something!, 1971–73 (filmed 1973); New Theatre, Cardiff, Robinson Crusoe, 1973; Cambridge Theatre, A Bit Between The Teeth, 1974; Fringe Benefits, Whitehall Theatre, 1976; returned to theatre 1988; Dry Rot, Lyric Theatre, 1989; dir., You'll Do For Me!, tour, 1989. Entered films, 1951: subsequently made eleven, including Reluctant Heroes, 1951, Dry Rot, 1956. BBC TV contract to present farces on TV, 1956–72; first ITV series Men of Affairs, 1973; A Roof Over My Head, BBC TV series, 1977. Presenter, Let's Go . . ., BBC TV series (first ever for people with a mental handicap), 1978–83; BBC Radio 2 series, 1978–80. Dir and Theatre Controller, Cooney-Marsh Group, 1977–80; Trustee, Theatre of Comedy, 1983–93; Arts Council: Mem., 1986–93; Chairman: Drama Panel, 1986–93; Monitoring Cttee, Arts and Disabled People, 1988–93; Indep. Develt Council for People with Mental Handicap, 1981–86; Friends of Normansfield, 1975–; Libertas, 1987–. DL Greater London, 1987. Hon. MA: Hull, 1981; Open, 1983; DUniv Essex, 1984; Hon. LLD: Manchester, 1986; Dundee, 1994; Hon. DSc Nottingham, 1987. Hon. Fellow, Humberside Coll. of Higher Educn, 1984. *Publications:* My Farce from My Elbow: an autobiography, 1975; Farce about Face (autobiog.), 1989; Tour de Farce, 1992; Life in the Farce Lane, 1995. *Recreations:* cricket, amateur radio (G2DQU; Hon. Vice-Pres., Radio Soc. of GB, 1979). *Address:* House of Lords, SW1A 0PW. *Clubs:* Garrick, Lord's Taverners (Pres. 1970), MCC; Yorkshire County Cricket.

RIX, Hon. Sir Bernard (Anthony), Kt 1993; **Hon. Mr Justice Rix;** a Judge of the High Court of Justice, Queen's Bench Division, since 1993; *b* 8 Dec. 1944; *s* of Otto Rix and Sadie Silverberg; *m* 1983, Hon. Karen Debra, *er d* of Baron Young of Graffham, *qv*; three *s* two *d* (inc. twin *s*). *Educ:* St Paul's School, London; New College, Oxford (BA: Lit.Hum. 1966, Jur. 1968; MA); Harvard Law School (Kennedy Scholar 1968; LLM 1969). Called to Bar, Inner Temple, 1970, Bencher, 1990; QC 1981; a Recorder, 1990–93. Member: Senate, Inns of Court and Bar, 1981–83; Bar Council, 1981–83. Chm., Commercial Bar Assoc., 1992–93. Dir, London Philharmonic Orchestra, 1986–. Vice-Chm., Central Council for Jewish Community Services, 1994– (author, report on youth services and orgns, 1994). Chm., British Friends of Bar-Ilan Univ., 1987–; Mem. Bd of Trustees, Bar-Ilan Univ., 1988–. *Recreations:* music, opera, Italy, formerly fencing. *Address:* Royal Courts of Justice, Strand, WC2A 2LL.

RIX, Sir John, Kt 1977; MBE 1955; DL; FEng 1979; Chairman, Seahorse International Ltd, 1986–89; Deputy Chairman, The Victorian Cruise Line Ltd, since 1987; *b* 1917; *s* of Reginald Arthur Rix; *m* 1953, Sylvia Gene Howe; two *s* one *d*. *Educ:* Southampton Univ. FRINA; FIMarE. Chm. and Chief Exec., Vosper Thornycroft (UK) Ltd, 1970–78; Chm. and Dir, Vosper PLC, 1978–85; Chairman: Vosper Shiprepairers Ltd, 1977–78; David Brown Vosper (Offshore) Ltd, 1978–85; Vosper Hovermarine Ltd, 1980–85; David Brown Gear Industries Ltd, 1980–85; Mainwork Ltd, 1980–85; Director: Vosper Private Ltd, 1966–77 and 1978–85; Charismarine Ltd, 1976–88; Southampton Cable Ltd, 1986–88; Chilworth Centre Ltd, 1986–94. Liveryman, Shipwrights' Co., 1973–. DL Hants 1985. *Recreations:* sailing, tennis, golf, walking. *Address:* Lower Baybridge House, Owslebury, Winchester, Hants SO21 1JN. *T:* Owslebury (01962) 777306. *Club:* Royal Thames Yacht.

RIX, Timothy John; Chairman, Longman Group Ltd, 1984–90 (Chief Executive, 1976–89); *b* 4 Jan. 1934; *s* of late Howard Terrell Rix and Marguerite Selman Rix; *m* 1st, 1960, Wendy Elizabeth Wright (marr. diss. 1967); one *d*; 2nd, 1967, Gillian Diana Mary Greenwood; one *s* one *d*. *Educ:* Radley Coll.; Clare Coll., Cambridge (BA); Yale Univ., USA. Sub-Lieut, RNVR, 1952–54. Mellon Fellow, Yale, 1957–58; joined Longmans, Green & Co. Ltd, subseq. Longman Gp, 1958; Overseas Educnl Publisher, 1958–61; Publishing Manager, Far East and SE Asia, 1961–63; Head of English Language Teaching Publishing, 1964–68; Divl Man. Dir, 1968–72; Jt Man. Dir, 1972–76. Director: Pearson Longman Ltd, 1979–83; Goldcrest Television, 1981–83; Yale Univ. Press, London, 1984–; ECIC (Management) Ltd, 1990–92; Blackie and Son Ltd, 1990–93; B. H. Blackwell Ltd, 1990–; Blackwell Ltd, 1993–; HEA Publishing Adv. Bd, 1993–. Chm., Book Marketing Ltd, 1990–; Sen. Consultant, Pofcher Co., 1990–. Chm., Pitman Examns Inst., 1987–90. Publishers Association: Chm., Trng Cttee, 1974–78; Chm., Book Develt Council, 1979–81; Vice-Pres., 1980–81 and 1983–84; Pres., 1981–83. Chairman: Book Trust, 1986–88; Book House Training Centre, 1986–89; British Library Centre for the Book, 1990–; Society of Bookmen, 1990–92; British Library Publishing, 1992–; Book Aid International, 1994–. Member: Exec. Cttee, NBL, 1979–86 (Dep. Chm., 1984–86); Publishers Adv. Panel, British Council, 1978– (Chm., 1994–); Arts Council Literature Panel, 1983–86; British Library Adv. Council, 1982–86; British Library Bd, 1986–; British Council Bd, 1988–; Finance Cttee, Delegacy of OUP, 1992–. Hon. Pres., Independent Publishers' Guild, 1993–. Gov., Bell Educnl Trust, 1990– (Chm. Govs, 1995–). CIMgt (CBIM 1981); FRSA 1986. *Publications:* articles on publishing in trade jls. *Recreations:* reading, landscape, wine. *Address:* Top Flat, 27 Wolseley Road, N8 8RS. *T:* 0181–341 4160. *Club:* Garrick.

RIZA, Alper Ali; QC 1991; *b* 16 March 1948; *s* of Ali Riza and Elli Liasides; *m* 1981, Vanessa Hall-Smith; two *d*. *Educ:* American Academy, Larnaca, Cyprus; English Sch., Nicosia. Called to the Bar, Gray's Inn, 1973. Pupillage, 1974–75; Turnpike Lane Law and Advice, 1975–77; Appeals Lawyer, Jt Council for Welfare of Immigrants, 1977–82; private practice, 1982–; Assistant Recorder, 1991–. *Publication:* (ed jtly) Butterworth's Immigration Law Service, 1991. *Recreations:* chess, music. *Address:* 14 Took's Court, Cursitor Street, EC4A 1LB. *T:* 0171–405 8828.

RIZK, Waheeb, CBE 1984 (OBE 1977); MA, PhD; FEng, FIMechE; Engineering Consultant, W R Associates, since 1986; *b* 11 Nov. 1921; *s* of Dr and Mrs I. Rizk; *m* 1952, Vivien Moyle, MA (Cantab); one *s* one *d* (and one *d* decd). *Educ:* Emmanuel College, Cambridge. MA, PhD. Joined English Electric Co., 1954, Chief Engineer, Gas Turbine Div., 1957, Gen. Manager, new div., combining gas turbines and industrial steam turbines, 1967; after merger with GEC became Man. Dir, GEC Gas Turbines Ltd, 1971; Chairman: GEC-Ruston Gas Turbines Ltd, 1983–86; GEC Diesels Ltd, 1983–86. Chm. of Bd, BSI, 1982–85. Pres., IMechE, 1984–85 (Mem. Council, 1978–89); Mem. Council, Fellowship of Engrg, 1982–85. Pres., Internat Council on Combustion Engines (CIMAC), 1973–77. Chm., Smallpeice Trust, 1991–. Mem. Council, Cranfield Inst. of Technology, 1985–95; Mem. Court, Brunel Univ., 1986–. Liveryman and Mem. Ct of Assistants, Worshipful Co. of Engineers. Gold Medal, CIMAC, 1983. *Publications:* technical papers to IMechE, Amer. Soc. of Mech. Engineers and CIMAC. *Recreations:* intelligent tinkering with any mechanism, photography, old motor cycles. *Address:* 231 Hillmorton Road, Rugby CV22 5BD. *T:* Rugby (01788) 565093. *Club:* Athenæum.

RIZZELLO, Michael Gaspard, OBE 1977; PPRBS; FCSD; sculptor and coin designer; *b* 2 April 1926; *s* of Arthur Rizzello and Maria Rizzello (*née* D'Angelo); *m* 1950, Sheila Semple Maguire; one *d*. *Educ:* Oratory Central Boys Sch., SW3; Royal College of Art. Military Service, 1944–48; served in India and Far East; commissioned 1945. Major Travelling Scholarship (Sculpture) and Drawing Prize, RCA, 1950. ARCA 1950; ARBS 1955, FRBS 1961, PRBS 1976–86; FCSD (FSIAD 1978). Pres., Soc. of Portrait Sculptors, 1968. Prix de Rome (Sculpture), 1951. Sir Otto Beit Medal for Sculpture, 1961. Sculptor: National Memorial to David Lloyd George, Cardiff; Official Medals for Investiture of HRH Prince of Wales, 1969, and 25th anniv., 1994; 900th Anniversary of Westminster Abbey, 1965; Churchill Centenary Trust, 1974; Sir Thomas Beecham bust, Royal Opera House, 1979, and Royal Festival Hall, 1986; sculptures at Nat. Postal Mus., 1972 and London Docklands, 1988 and 1990; bronze water feature and fountain, Hemel Hempstead, 1993. Designer and Sculptor of coinages for over 90 countries. *Recreation:* people. *Address:* Melrose Studio, 7 Melrose Road, SW18 1ND. *T:* 0181–870 8561. *Club:* Reform.

ROACH, Prof. Gary Francis, FRSE; Professor of Mathematics, University of Strathclyde, since 1979; *b* 8 Oct. 1933; *s* of John Francis Roach and Bertha Mary Ann Roach (*née* Walters); *m* 1960, Isabella Grace Willins Nicol. *Educ:* University Coll. of S Wales and Monmouthshire (BSc); Univ. of London (MSc); Univ. of Manchester (PhD, DSc). FRAS, FIMA. RAF (Educn Branch), Flying Officer, 1955–58; Research Mathematician, BP, 1958–61; Lectr, UMIST, 1961–66; Vis. Prof., Univ. of British Columbia, 1966–67; University of Strathclyde: Lectr, 1967; Sen Lectr, 1970; Reader, 1971; Prof., 1979; Dean, Faculty of Science, 1982–. Mem., Edinburgh Mathematical Soc. (Past Pres.). Hon. ScD Lodz, 1993. FRSA 1991. *Publications:* Green's Functions, 1970, 2nd edn 1982; articles in learned jls. *Recreations:* mountaineering, photography, philately, gardening, music. *Address:* 11 Menzies Avenue, Fintry, Glasgow G63 0YE. *T:* Fintry (01360) 860335.

ROADS, Dr Christopher Herbert; Associate Director (Consultancy), Research & Development Department, British Library, 1992–95; consultant in museums and audio visual archives; *b* 3 Jan. 1934; *s* of late Herbert Clifford Roads and Vera Iris Roads; *m* 1976, Charlotte Alicia Dorothy Mary Lothian; one *d*. *Educ:* Cambridge and County Sch.;

Trinity Hall, Cambridge (MA; PhD 1961). Nat. Service, 2nd Lieut, RA, Egypt, 1952–54. Adviser to WO on Disposal of Amnesty Arms, 1961–62; Imperial War Museum: Keeper of Dept of Records, 1962–70; Dep. Dir-Gen. at Main Building, Southwark, 1964–79, at Duxford, Cambridge, 1976–79, HMS Belfast, Pool of London, 1978–79; Dir, Museums & Archives Develt Associates Ltd, 1977–85; Dir, Nat. Sound Archive, 1983–92. UNESCO consultant designing major audio visual archives or museums in Philippines, Panama, Bolivia, Kuwait, Jordan and Saudi Arabia, 1976–. Founder and Dir, Cambridge Coral/Starfish Res. Gp, 1968–; Director: Nat. Discography Ltd, 1986–92; Historic Cable Ship John W. Mackay, 1986–; AVT Communications Ltd, 1988–92; Cedar Audio Ltd, 1989–92. Chm., Coral Conservation Trust, 1972–; President: Historical Breechloading Small Arms Assoc., 1973–; Internat. Film and TV Council (UNESCO Category A), 1990–92 (Pres., Archives Commn, 1970–); Vice President: World Expeditionary Assoc., 1971–; Duxford Aviation Soc., 1974–; English Eight Club, 1980–; Cambridge Univ. Rifle Assoc., 1987– (Mem. Council, 1955–87); Mem. Council, Scientific Exploration Soc., 1971–82; Sec., Nat. Archives Cttee, Internat. Assoc. of Sound Archives, 1988–92; Hon. Sec., Cambridge Univ. Long Range Rifle Club, 1979–. Trustee: HMS Belfast Trust, 1970–78; Nat. Life Stories Collection, 1986–92; NSA Wild Life Sound Trust, 1986–92. Adjt, English VIII, 1964–. Churchill Fellowship, 1970; Vis. Fellow, Centre of Internat. Studies, Univ. of Cambridge, 1983–84. FRGS. Silver Jubilee Medal, 1977. Order of Independence, 2nd cl. (Jordan), 1977. *Publications:* The British Soldier's Firearm, 1850–1864, 1964; (jtly) New Studies on the Crown of Thorns Starfish, 1970; The Story of the Gun, 1978. *Recreations:* rifle shooting, marine and submarine exploration, wind surfing, motorcycling, videography. *Address:* The White House, 90 High Street, Melbourn, near Royston, Herts SG8 6AL. *T:* Royston (01763) 260866, *Fax:* (01763) 262521; DX 12 Urbanización Bahia Dorada, 29693 Estepona, Málaga, Spain. *T:* and *Fax:* (52) 796407. *Clubs:* United Oxford & Cambridge University; Hawks (Cambridge).

ROADS, Peter George, MD; FFCM; Regional Medical Officer, South West Thames Regional Health Authority, 1973–82, retired; *b* 14 Nov. 1917; *s* of Frank George Roads and Mary Dee Hill (*née* Bury); *m* 1949, Evelyn Clara (*née* Daniel); one *s* one *d*. *Educ:* Bedford Sch.; Univ. of London (St Mary's Hosp. Med. Sch.); Hon. Society of Inner Temple. MD (London); FFCM, Royal Colls of Physicians. Served War, in China, 1944–46. MRC, Pneumoconiosis Unit, 1949–50; Dep. MOH, etc, City and Co. of Bristol, 1956–59; MOH, Principal Sch. Med. Officer and Port Med. Officer for City and Port of Portsmouth, 1959–73; Med. Referee to Portchester Crematorium, 1959–73. Mem., Central Midwives Bd, 1964–76; Adviser on Health Services, Assoc. of Municipal Corporations, 1966–74. FRSocMed; Fellow, Soc. of Public Health (formerly of Community Medicine) (Pres., 1988–89); FFPHM. Chairman: Bucks Br., Historical Assoc., 1987–93; Bucks Family History Soc., 1990–93; Bucks Management Cttee, Oxford Diocesan Council for the Deaf, 1991–93. Mem. Deanery Synod, and Church Warden, Stone Dinton and Hartwell, 1988–91. *Publications:* Care of Elderly in Portsmouth, 1970; Medical Importance of Open Air Recreation (Proc. 1st Internat. Congress on Leisure and Touring), 1966. *Recreations:* open air, walking, forestry, history, touring. *Address:* Pasture Cottage, School Lane, Dinton, near Aylesbury, Bucks HP17 8UG. *T:* Aylesbury (01296) 748504.

ROARK, Helen Wills; *b* California, 1905; *d* of Dr Clarence A. Wills (surgeon) and Catherine A. Wills; *m* 1st, 1929, Frederick Schander Moody (marr. diss. 1937); 2nd, 1939, Aidan Roark. *Educ:* Anna Head School, Berkeley, California; University of California; Phi Beta Kappa (Scholarship Society). *Publications:* three books on tennis; Mystery Book, 1939; articles in various magazines and periodicals. *Recreations:* American Lawn Tennis Championship, 1923–24–25–27–28–29 and 1931; English Lawn Tennis Championship, 1927–28–29–30–32–33–35–38; French, 1927–28–29–30; has held exhibitions of drawing and paintings at Cooling Galleries, London, 1929 (drawings); Grand Central Art Galleries, New York, 1930 (drawings), 1936 (flower paintings in oil); Berheim-Jenne Galleries, Paris, 1932 (etchings). *Clubs:* All England Lawn Tennis; Colony, West Side Lawn Tennis (New York); Burlingame Country (California).

ROB, Prof. Charles Granville, MC 1943; Professor of Surgery, Uniformed Services University of the Health Sciences, Bethesda, Maryland, since 1983; *b* 4 May 1913; *s* of Joseph William Rob, OBE, MD; *m* 1941, Mary Dorothy Elaine Beazley; two *s* two *d*. *Educ:* Oundle School; Cambridge Univ.; St Thomas's Hospital. FRCS 1939; MChir Cantab, 1941. Lt-Col RAMC Surgeon, St Thomas' Hospital, 1948; Professor of Surgery, London University, 1950–60; Professor and Chm. Dept of Surgery, Univ. of Rochester, NY, 1960–78; Prof. of Surg., E Carolina Univ., 1978–83. Formerly Surgeon and Director of the Surgical Professorial Unit, St Mary's Hospital; Consultant Vascular Surgeon to the Army. *Publications:* (ed, with Rodney Smith) Operative Surgery (8 vols), 1956–57, (14 vols), 1968–69; various surgical. *Recreations:* mountaineering, ski-ing. *Address:* Uniformed Services University of the Health Sciences, Bethesda, MD 20814, USA. *Club:* Alpine.

ROBARTS, (Anthony) Julian; Director and Chief Executive, Iveagh Trustees Ltd, since 1993; Managing Director, Coutts & Co., 1986–91; *b* 6 May 1937; *s* of late Lt-Col Anthony V. C. Robarts, DL and of Grizel Mary Robarts (Grant); *m* 1961, Edwina Beryl Hobson; two *s* one *d*. *Educ:* Eton College. National Service, 11th Hussars (PAO), 1955–57; joined Coutts & Co., 1958, Dir, 1963, Dep. Man. Dir, 1976–86; Director: Coutts Finance Co., 1967–91; F. Bolton Group, 1970–; International Fund for Institutions Inc., USA, 1983–93; Chm., Hill Martin, 1993–; Regional Dir, Nat. Westminster Bank, 1971–92. Hon. Treasurer, Union Jack Club. *Recreations:* shooting, gardening, opera. *Address:* Bromley Hall, Standon, Ware, Herts SG11 1NY. *Clubs:* Pratt's, MCC.

ROBARTS, Basil; Director, 1964–85, and Chief General Manager, 1963–75, Norwich Union Insurance Group; *b* 13 Jan. 1915; *s* of late Henry Ernest Robarts and Beatrice Katie (*née* Stevens); *m* 1941, Sheila Margaret Cooper Thwaites; one *s* one *d*. *Educ:* Gresham's Sch., Holt. Served Army, 1939–45 (Lt-Col, RA). Joined Norwich Union Life Insce Soc., 1934; Gen. Man. and Actuary, 1953. Institute of Actuaries: Fellow (FIA), 1939; Treas., 1965–67; Gen. Commissioner of Income Tax, 1958–90; Chm., British Insce Assoc., 1969–71. Trustee, Charities Official Investment Fund, 1977–85. *Recreation:* music. *Address:* 466B Unthank Road, Norwich NR4 7QJ. *T:* Norwich (01603) 51135.

ROBARTS, Julian; *see* Robarts, A. J.

ROBATHAN, Andrew Robert George; MP (C) Blaby, since 1992; *b* 17 July 1951; *s* of Robert Douglas Brice Robathan and Sheena Mary Martin (*née* Gimson); *m* 1991, Rachael Maunder. *Educ:* Merchant Taylors' Sch., Northwood; Oriel Coll., Oxford (MA). Served Coldstream Guards, 1974–89, resigned as Major; rejoined Army for Gulf War, Jan.–April 1991 (COS, POW Guard Force). Councillor, London Borough of Hammersmith and Fulham, 1990–92. Chairman: Cons. Back bench Defence Cttee, 1994–; All-Party Cycling Gp, 1994–; Vice Chm., Parly Renewable and Sustainable Energy Gp, 1992–94. *Recreations:* hill-walking, ski-ing, running, shooting, architecture, history, conservation. *Address:* House of Commons, SW1A 0AA. *T:* 0171–219 3000.

ROBB, Prof. James Christie; Professor of Physical Chemistry, 1957–84, and Head of Department of Chemistry, 1981–84, University of Birmingham; *b* 23 April 1924; *s* of James M. Robb, Rocklands, The House of Daviot, Inverurie, Aberdeenshire; *m* 1951, Joyce Irene Morley; three *d*. *Educ:* Daviot School; Inverurie Academy; Aberdeen University (BSc Hons, 1945, PhD 1948); DSc Birmingham, 1954. DSIR Senior Research Award, Aberdeen, 1948–50. ICI Fellow, Birmingham Univ., 1950–51; on Birmingham Univ. staff, 1951–84. A Guardian of Birmingham Assay Office, 1980–95. Mem. Council, Birmingham Civic Soc., 1981–93. Pres., Birmingham Rotary Club, 1982–83. *Publications:* scientific contrib. to Proc. Royal Soc., Trans. Faraday Soc., etc. *Recreations:* motoring, photography, computing. *Address:* 32 Coleshill Close, Hunt End, Redditch, Worcs B97 5UN.

ROBB, John Weddell; Chief Executive, 1990–95, and Chairman, 1994–95, Wellcome Plc (Deputy Chief Executive, 1989–90); *b* 27 April 1936; *s* of John and Isabella Robb; *m* 1965, Janet Teanby; two *s* one *d*. *Educ:* Daniel Stewart's College, Edinburgh. Beecham Group: Marketing Exec., Toiletry Div., Beecham Products, 1966; Man. Dir, Beecham (Far East), Kuala Lumpur, 1971; Vice-Pres., W. Hemisphere Div., Beecham Products, USA, 1974; Man. Dir, Food and Drink Div., Beecham Products, 1976; Group Board, 1980; Chm., Food and Drink Div., 1980; Chm., Beecham Products, 1984–85; Gp Man. Dir, 1985–88. Non-Exec. Dep. Chm., NFC, 1990–95 (Non-Exec. Dir, 1983–95); Non-Executive Director: Allied-Lyons, 1991–; De La Rue Co., 1993–. Dep. Chm., Horserace Betting Levy Bd, 1993–. *Recreations:* golf, gardening, racing. *Club:* Sunningdale.

ROBBE-GRILLET, Alain, literary consultant, writer and cinéaste; Editions de Minuit, Paris, since 1955; *b* 18 Aug. 1922; *s* of Gaston Robbe-Grillet and Yvonne Canu; *m* 1957, Catherine Rstakian. *Educ:* Lycée Buffon, Paris; Lycée St Louis, Paris; Institut National Agronomique, Paris. Engineer: Institut National de la Statistique, 1945–49; Institut des Fruits et Agrumes Coloniaux, 1949–51. *Films:* L'Immortelle, 1963; Trans-Europ-Express, 1966; L'Homme qui ment, 1968; L'Eden et après, 1970; Glissements progressifs du plaisir, 1974; Le jeu avec le feu, 1975; La belle captive, 1983; Un Bruit qui rend fou, 1995. *Publications:* Les Gommes, 1953 (The Erasers, 1966); Le Voyeur, 1955 (The Voyeur, 1959); La Jalousie, 1957 (Jealousy, 1960); Dans le labyrinthe, 1959 (In the Labyrinth, 1967); L'Année dernière à Marienbad, 1961 (Last Year in Marienbad, 1962); Instantanés, 1962 (Snapshots, and, Towards a New Novel, 1965); L'Immortelle, 1963 (The Immortal One, 1971); Pour un nouveau roman, 1964; La Maison de rendezvous, 1965 (The House of Assignation, 1968); Projet pour une révolution à New York, 1970 (Project for a Revolution in New York, 1972); Glissements progressifs du plaisir, 1974; Topologie d'une cité fantôme, 1976 (Topology of a Phantom City, 1978); La Belle captive, 1976; Souvenirs du Triangle d'or, 1978 (Recollections of the Golden Triangle, 1985); Un Régicide, 1978; Djinn, 1981; Le Miroir qui revient (autobiog.), 1985 (Ghosts in the Mirror, 1988); Angélique ou l'enchantement (autobiog.), 1988; Les Derniers jours de Corinthe, 1994. *Address:* 18 Boulevard Maillot, 92200 Neuilly-sur-Seine, France. *T:* 47223122.

ROBBINS, Prof. Frederick C., MD; Bronze Star (US Army), 1945; President, Institute of Medicine, National Academy of Sciences, Washington, DC, 1980–85; University Professor, Case Western Reserve University, 1985, Emeritus, since 1986 (Professor of Pediatrics, School of Medicine, 1950–80, Dean, 1966–80, now Emeritus); *b* 25 Aug. 1916; *s* of William J. Robbins and Christine Chapman Robbins; *m* 1948, Alice Havemeyer Northrop; two *d*. *Educ:* University of Missouri (AB); University of Missouri Medical School (BS); Harvard Medical School (MD). US Army, 1942–46; rank on discharge, Major. Various posts in the Children's Hospital, Boston, from 1940, finishing as Chief Resident in Medicine, 1948; Sen. Fellow in Virus Diseases, National Research Council, 1948–50; Research Fellow in Pediatrics, Harvard Med. Sch., 1948–50; Instr in Ped., 1950–51, Associate in Ped., 1951–52, at Harvard Medical School; Dir, Department of Pediatrics, Cleveland Metropolitan General Hospital, 1952–66. Associate, Research Div. of Infectious Diseases, the Children's Medical Center, Boston, 1950–52; Research Fellow in Ped., the Boston Lying-in Hospital, Boston, Mass, 1950–52; Asst to Children's Medical Service, Mass Gen. Hosp., Boston, 1950–52. Visiting Scientist, Donner Lab., Univ. of California, 1963–64. President: Soc. for Pediatric Research, 1961–62; Amer. Pediatric Soc., 1973–74. Member: Nat. Acad. of Sciences, 1972 (Co-Chm., Forum on Human Experimentation, 1974); Amer. Philosophical Soc., 1972; Adv. Cttee, Office of Technol. Assessment for Congress, 1973; Adv. Cttee on Med. Research, Pan American Health Organization, WHO, 1981– . First Mead Johnson Award, 1953; Nobel Prize in Physiology or Medicine, 1954; Award for Distinguished Achievement (Modern Medicine), 1963; Med. Mutual Honor Award for 1969; Abraham Flexner Award for Distinguished Service to Medical Educn, AAMC, 1987; Camille Cosby World of Children Award, Judge Baker Children's Center, 1988; NASA Public Service Award, 1989; Ohio Sci. and Technology Hall of Fame, 1992. Hon. Dr of Science: John Carroll University, 1955; Missouri, 1958; North Carolina, 1979; Tufts, 1983; Med. Coll. of Ohio, 1983; Albert Einstein Coll. of Medicine, 1984; Med. Coll. of Wisconsin, 1984; Hon. Dr of Laws, New Mexico, 1968; Hon. Dr Med. Sci., Med. Coll. of Pa, 1984. *Publications:* numerous in various jls, primarily on subject of viruses and infectious diseases. *Recreations:* music, tennis, sailing. *Address:* 2626 West Park Boulevard, Shaker Heights, OH 44120, USA; (office) CWRU School of Medicine, 10900 Euclid Avenue, Cleveland, OH 44106–4945, USA.

ROBBINS, Harold; writer; *b* 21 May 1916; *m* Grace; one *d*; *m* 1992, Jann Stapp. *Educ:* New York. Formerly sugar exporter, film publicist, film impresario, etc. *Publications:* The Dream Merchants, 1949; 79 Park Avenue, 1955; A Stone for Danny Fisher, 1955; Never Leave Me, 1956; Never Love a Stranger, 1958; Stiletto, 1960; The Carpetbaggers, 1961; Where Love Has Gone, 1964; The Adventurers, 1966; The Inheritors, 1969; The Betsy, 1971 (filmed 1978); The Pirate, 1974; The Lonely Lady, 1976; Dreams Die First, 1977; Memories of Another Day, 1979; Goodbye, Janette, 1981; Spellbinder, 1982; Descent from Xanadu, 1984; The Storyteller, 1985; The Piranhas, 1991. *Address:* c/o Simon and Schuster, 1230 6th Avenue, New York, NY 10020, USA.

ROBBINS, Jerome; Choreographer and Director; Co-Ballet Master in Chief, New York City Ballet, 1983–89 (Ballet Master, 1969–83; Associate Artistic Director, 1949–59); Founder Choreographer, Ballets: USA, 1958–61; *b* New York, 11 Oct. 1918; *s* of Harry and Lena Robbins. *Educ:* Woodrow Wilson High School, Weehawken, NJ; New York University. Studied ballet with Antony Tudor and Eugene Loring, and Modern, Spanish and oriental dance. First stage experience with Sandor-Sorel Dance Center, New York, 1937; dancer in chorus of American musicals, 1938–40; Ballet Theatre, 1940–44 (soloist 1941), London season, 1946; formed own company, Ballets: USA, 1958. Ballets performed by cos including: Amer. Ballet Theatre; Australian Ballet; Dance Theatre of Harlem; Nat. Ballet of Canada; Kirov Ballet, Royal Ballet; Paris Opera Ballet; Royal Danish Ballet. Member: NY State Council on the Arts/Dance Panel, 1973–77; Nat. Council on the Arts, 1974–80. Hon. Mem., AAIL, 1985. Hon. degrees: Ohio, 1974; CUNY, 1980; Hon. DFA New York, 1985. City of Paris Award, 1971; Handel Medallion, NYC, 1976; Kennedy Center Honoree, 1981, and many other awards. Chevalier: Order of Arts and Letters (France), 1964; Légion d'Honneur (France), 1993. *Ballets include:* (for Ballet Theater) Fancy Free, 1944; (for Concert Varieties) Interplay, 1945; (for New York City Ballet) Age of Anxiety, 1950; The Cage, 1951; Afternoon of a Faun, 1953; Fanfare, 1953; The Concert, 1956; (for American Ballet Theater) Les Noces, 1965; Dances at a Gathering, 1969; In the Night, 1970; The Goldberg Variations, 1971; Watermill, 1972; Requiem

Canticles, 1972; An Evening's Waltzes, 1973; Dybbuk (later The Dybbuk Variations, then renamed Suite of Dances), 1974; Concerto in G (later in G Major), 1975; Ma Mère l'Oye (later Mother Goose), 1975; Chansons Madécasses, 1975; The Four Seasons, 1979; Opus 19, The Dreamer, 1979; Rondo, 1981; Piano Pieces, 1981; The Gershwin Concerto, 1982; Four Chamber Works, 1982; Glass Pieces, 1983; I'm Old Fashioned, 1983; Antique Epigraphs, 1984; (for School of American Ballet) 2 and 3 Part Inventions, 1994; (with Twyla Tharp) Brahms/Handel, 1984; Eight Lines, 1985; In Memory Of, 1985; Quiet City, 1986; Piccolo Balleto, 1986; Ives, Songs, 1988; (with Mikhail Baryshnikov) A Suite of Dances, 1994; (for Ballets: USA) NY Export: Opus Jazz, 1958; Moves, 1959; (for Star Spangled Gala) Other Dances, 1976. *Musicals include:* On the Town, 1945; Billion Dollar Baby, 1946 (Donaldson award); High Button Shoes, 1947 (Donaldson and Tony awards); Miss Liberty, 1949; Call Me Madam, 1950; The King and I, 1951 (Donaldson award); Two's Company, 1952 (Donaldson award); Peter Pan, 1954; Bells Are Ringing, 1956; West Side Story, 1957 (Tony, Evening Standard, Laurel and two Academy awards); Gypsy, 1959; Fiddler on the Roof, 1964 (two Tony awards and Drama Critics' award); Jerome Robbins's Broadway, NY, 1989. Has directed and choreographed films, drama and TV (inc. Peter Pan with Mary Martin, 1955 (Emmy award)). *Address:* c/o New York City Ballet, New York State Theater, Lincoln Center, New York, NY 10023, USA.

ROBBINS, Prof. Keith Gilbert; Vice-Chancellor (formerly Principal), University of Wales (formerly St David's University College), Lampeter, since 1992; Senior Vice-Chancellor, University of Wales, since 1995; *b* 9 April 1940; *s* of Gilbert Henry John and Edith Mary Robbins; *m* 1963, Janet Carey Thomson; three *s* one *d*. *Educ:* Bristol Grammar Sch.; Magdalen and St Antony's Colls, Oxford. MA, DPhil (Oxon); DLitt (Glas.). FRSE 1991. University of York: Asst Lectr in History, 1963; Lectr in Hist., 1964; Prof. of History, 1971–79, Dean of Faculty of Arts, 1977–79, UCNW, Bangor; Prof. of Modern Hist., Glasgow Univ., 1980–91. Visiting Professor: British Columbia Univ., 1983; Univ. of Western Australia, 1995. Lectures: Enid Muir, Newcastle Univ., 1981; A. H. Dodd, UCNW, Bangor, 1984; Raleigh, British Acad., 1984; Ford, Oxford Univ., 1986–87. Winston Churchill Travelling Fellow, 1990. Pres., Historical Assoc., 1988–91; Humanities Res. Bd, British Acad., 1994–. Editor, History, 1977–86; Member: Editorial Bd, Jl of Ecclesiastical History, 1978–93. *Publications:* Munich 1938, 1968; Sir Edward Grey, 1971; The Abolition of War: The British Peace Movement 1914–1919, 1976; John Bright, 1979; The Eclipse of a Great Power: Modern Britain 1870–1975, 1983; The First World War, 1984; Nineteenth-Century Britain: integration and diversity, 1988; Appeasement, 1988; (ed) Blackwell Biographical Dictionary of British Political Life in the Twentieth Century, 1990; (ed) Protestant Evangelicalism, 1991; Churchill, 1992; History, Religion and Identity in Modern British History, 1993; Politicians, Diplomacy and War in Modern British History, 1994; articles in Historical Jl, Internat. Affairs, Jl of Contemporary Hist., Jl of Ecclesiastical Hist., Jl of Commonwealth and Imperial Hist., etc. *Recreations:* music, gardening, walking. *Address:* University of Wales, Lampeter, Dyfed SA48 7ED. *T:* Lampeter (01570) 422351.

ROBBINS, Michael; *see* Robbins, Raymond F. M.

ROBBINS, Michael; *see* Robbins, Richard M.

ROBBINS, Dr (Raymond Frank) Michael, CBE 1987; Director, Polytechnic South West (formerly Plymouth Polytechnic), 1974–89, Hon. Fellow, 1989; *b* 15 Feb. 1928; *s* of Harold and Elsie Robbins; *m* 1955, Eirian Meredith Edwards; two *d*. *Educ:* Grove Park Grammar Sch., Wrexham; UCW Aberystwyth. PhD 1954; FRIC 1962. Research Chemist, Monsanto Chemicals Ltd, 1954–55; Research Fellow, Univ. of Exeter, 1955–56; Lectr, Nottingham Coll. of Technology, 1956–59; Sen. Lectr, Hatfield Coll. of Technology, 1960–61; Head of Dept of Chem. Sciences, Hatfield Polytechnic, 1961–70; Dep. Dir, Plymouth Polytechnic, 1970–74. Chm., Sci. Prog. Adv. Gp, PCFC, 1989–92; Mem., British Accreditation Council, 1984–93. *Publications:* papers on organic chemistry in chem. jls, various reviews and articles in sci. and educnl press. *Recreations:* hill walking, creative gardening. *Address:* Lent Hill Cottage, Ashburton, Devon TQ13 7NW.

ROBBINS, (Richard) Michael, CBE 1976; *b* 7 Sept. 1915; *er s* of late Alfred Gordon Robbins and Josephine, *d* of R. L. Capell, Northampton; *m* 1939, Rose Margaret Elspeth, *er d* of late Sir Robert Reid Bannatyne, CB (*d* 1993), Lindfield, Sussex; one *s* two *d*. *Educ:* Westminster Sch. (King's Schol.); Christ Church, Oxford (Westminster Schol.; MA); Univ. of Vienna. Joined London Passenger Transport Board, 1939. War service, RE (Transportation), 1939–46: Persia and Iraq, 1941–43; GHQ, MEF, 1943–44; Major, AML (Greece), 1944–45. Rejoined London Transport, 1946; Sec. to Chm., 1947–50; Sec., London Transp. Exec., 1950–55; Sec. and Chief Public Relations Off., 1955–60; Chief Commercial and Pub. Rel. Off., 1960–65; Mem., London Transport Exec., 1965–80 (Man. Dir, Rlys, 1971–78). Chm., Transport Adv. Cttee, Transport and Road Res. Lab., 1977–81. Pres., Inst. of Transport, 1975–76 (Mem. Council, 1957–60 and 1962–64; Chm., Metrop. Sect., 1962–63; Chm., Educn and Trg Cttee, 1969–72; Vice-Pres., 1972–75); Pres., Omnibus Soc., 1965; Chairman: Middx Victoria County History Council, 1963–76; Middx Local History Council, 1958–65; Internat. Metrop. Rlys Cttee, Internat. Union of Public Transport, 1976–81; Victorian Soc., 1978–81; President: London and Middx Archæol. Soc., 1965–71 (Mem. Council, 1951–56 and 1960–65); Greater London Industrial Archæol. Soc., 1969–; Rly Students Assoc., 1967–68; St Marylebone Soc., 1971–74; Mem., Ancient Monuments Adv. Cttee, English Heritage, 1986–91. Dunhill lectr on industrial design, Australia, 1974. FSA 1957; Pres., Soc. of Antiquaries, 1987–91 (Mem. Council, 1965–67, 1970–71; Treas., 1971–87); Chm., Museum of London, 1979–90 (Governor, 1968–); Vice Chm., Greater Manchester Museum of Science and Industry, 1987–90 (Trustee, 1982–90); Trustee, London Museum, 1970–75. Hon. DLitt City Univ., 1987. *Publications:* The North London Railway, 1937; 190 in Persia, 1951; The Isle of Wight Railways, 1953; Middlesex, 1953; (ed) Middlesex Parish Churches, 1955; The Railway Age, 1962; (with T. C. Barker) History of London Transport, vol. 1, 1963, vol. 2, 1974; George and Robert Stephenson, 1966, rev. edn 1981; Points and Signals, 1967; A Public Transport Century, 1985; Joint Editor, Journal of Transport History, 1953–65; contribs to transport and historical jls. *Recreations:* exploring cities and suburbs; travelling abroad and in branch railway trains; concert-going. *Address:* 7 Courthope Villas, Wimbledon, SW19 4EH. *T:* 0181–946 7308. *Club:* Athenæum.

ROBBINS, Stephen Dennis; His Honour Judge Robbins; a Circuit Judge, since 1994; *b* 11 Jan. 1948; *s* of Lt-Col Dennis Robbins, OBE, TD and Joan Robbins (*née* Mason); *m* 1974, Amanda Smith, JP; three *d*. *Educ:* Orwell Park; Marlborough; Coll. d'Europe, Bruges (Churchill Award). Infantry, HAC, 1966–69. Called to the Bar, Gray's Inn, 1969; practised SE Circuit, 1972–94; Asst Recorder, 1983–87; Recorder, 1987–94. Former Mem. Senate, Overseas Cttee, Bar Council; Hon. Sec., London Common Law Bar Cttee; Hon. Legal Advr, Katharine Lowe Centre, Battersea, 1974–79. Pres., Mental Health Rev. Tribunals, 1994–. Chm., Disciplinary Cttee, Potato Marketing Bd. *Recreations:* collecting ephemera, shooting, swimming, walking, music. *Address:* Hillcrest Farm, Sevington, near Ashford, Kent TN24 0LJ. *T:* Ashford (01233) 502732; 1/2 The Studios, 17/19 Edge Street, Kensington Church Street, W8 7PN. *T:* 0171–727 7216.

ROBENS, family name of **Baron Robens of Woldingham.**

ROBENS OF WOLDINGHAM, Baron *cr* 1961, of Woldingham (Life Peer); **Alfred Robens,** PC 1951; President, Snamprogetti, since 1988 (Chairman, 1980–88); Chairman, Alfred Robens Associates, since 1984; a Director: Times Newspapers Holdings Ltd, 1980–83 (Times Newspapers Ltd, 1967–80); AAH, since 1971; AMI (Europe) Ltd, since 1981; Chairman, Engineering Industries Council, since 1976; *b* 18 Dec. 1910; *s* of George and Edith Robens; *m* 1937, Eva, *d* of Fred and late Elizabeth Powell. *Educ:* Manchester Secondary Sch. Official of Union of Distributive and Allied Workers, 1935–45; Manchester City Councillor, 1942–45. MP (Lab) Wansbeck Div. of Northumberland, 1945–50, and for Blyth, 1950–60. Parliamentary Private Secretary to Minister of Transport, 1945–47; Parliamentary Secretary, Ministry of Fuel and Power, 1947–51; Minister of Labour and National Service, April–Oct. 1951. Chairman: National Coal Bd, 1961–71; Vickers Ltd, 1971–79; St Regis Internat., 1976–81; MLH Consultants, 1971–81; Johnson Matthey PLC, 1971–83 (Hon. Pres., 1983–); St Regis Newspapers, Bolton, 1975–80 (Dir, 1976); a Director: Bank of England, 1966–81; St Regis Paper Co. (NY), 1976–80; Trust House Forte Ltd, 1971–86; British Fuel Co., 1967–87. Chairman: Foundation on Automation and Employment, 1962; Engrg Industries Council, 1976–80; Member: NEDC, 1962–71; Royal Commn on Trade Unions and Employers' Assocs, 1965–68. President: Advertising Assoc., 1963–68; Incorporated Soc. of British Advertisers, 1973–76; Chairman: Jt Steering Cttee for Malta, 1967; Jt Econ. Mission to Malta, 1967. Member: Council of Manchester Business School, 1964–79 (Dep. Chm., 1964–70; Chm., 1970–79); Court of Governors, LSE, 1965; Chancellor, Univ. of Surrey, 1966–77. Governor, Queen Elizabeth Training Coll. for the Disabled, 1951–80; Chairman: Bd of Govs, Guy's Hosp., 1965–74; Guy's Hosp. Medical and Dental Sch., 1974–82; Cttee on Safety and Health of people at their place of work, 1970–72; Fellow, Manchester Coll. of Science and Technology, 1965–; Hon. FRCR, 1975. Hon. DCL: Univ. of Newcastle upon Tyne, 1964; Manchester Univ., 1974; Hon. LLD: Leicester, 1966; London, 1971. Hon. MInstM, 1968; Hon. FIOB, 1974. Mackintosh Medal, Advertising Assoc., 1970; Albert Medal, RSA, 1977. *Publications:* Engineering and Economic Progress, 1965; Industry and Government, 1970; Human Engineering, 1970; Ten Year Stint, 1972; sundry articles to magazines, journals and newspapers. *Address:* House of Lords, SW1A 0PW.

ROBERG, Rabbi Meir; Headmaster, Hasmonean High School, London, since 1980; *b* 25 June 1937; *s* of late Julius and Hannchen Roberg; *m* 1961, Mirjam Nager; three *s* two *d*. *Educ:* Manchester Grammar Sch. (Gratrix Scholar); Talmudical Coll., Israel (Rabbinical Diploma); Univ. of London (BA 1st Cl. Hons 1960; DipEd 1970; MPhil 1972). Asst Teacher, 1960–62, Dep. Head, 1962–65, Yavneh Grammar Sch., London; Asst Teacher and Head of Classics, 1965–71, Dep. Head, 1971–80, Hasmonean High Sch. Lectr, Colls of Further Educn, 1962–; Headmaster, Mddx Regl Centre, 1965–73. Delegate, Internat. Religious Conf., Jerusalem, 1963 and 1980. Member: Keren Hatorah; Hendon Adass; Massoret Inst. (Chm., 1980–); Assoc. of Headteachers of Jewish Day Schs (Pres., 1991–). *Publications:* reviews for Comparative Education, Jewish Tribune, and Parent-Teacher Monthly (NY). *Recreations:* Talmudic research, mountaineering. *Address:* Hasmonean High School, Holders Hill Road, NW4 1NA.

ROBERTS, family name of **Baron Clwyd.**

ROBERTS, Prof. Adam; *see* Roberts, E. A.

ROBERTS, Albert, JP; DL; *b* 14 May 1908; *s* of Albert Roberts and Annie Roberts (*née* Ward); *m* 1932, Alice Ashton (*d* 1989); one *s* one *d*. *Educ:* Woodlesford School; Normanton and Whitwood Technical College, Yorks. Sec., Woodlesford Br., Yorks Miners Assoc., 1935–41; Safety Board, Mines Inspector, 1941–51. Mem., Rothwell UDC, 1937–52. MP (Lab) Normanton, 1951–83; Exec. Mem., British Group, Inter-Parly Union, 1955–83 (Chm., 1968–70). Exec. Mem., Yorkshire Area Heart Foundn; Vice-Pres., Yorkshire Soc. JP 1946, DL 1967, W Yorks. Order of Isabela la Católica (Spain), 1967; Diplomatic Order of Merit, Korean Republic, 1979. *Publication:* One of a Family (autobiog.), 1988. *Recreations:* cricket, bowls. *Address:* Cordoba, 14 Aberford Road, Oulton-Woodlesford, near Leeds LS26 8JR. *T:* Leeds (0113) 282 2303.

ROBERTS, Allan Deverell; Under-Secretary (Principal Assistant Solicitor), Solicitor's Office, Departments of Health and of Social Security, since 1989; *b* 14 July 1950; *s* of Irfon Roberts and Patricia Mary (*née* Allan); *m* 1991, Irene Anne Graham Reilly; two *s*. *Educ:* Eton Coll.; Magdalen Coll., Oxford (MA). Solicitor in private practice, 1974–76; Solicitor's Office, DHSS, 1976–. *Recreations:* tegestology, football, listening to music. *Address:* (office) New Court, 48 Carey Street, WC2A 2LS. *T:* 0171–962 8000.

ROBERTS, Alwyn; Pro Vice Chancellor, University of Wales, Bangor, since 1994; *b* 26 Aug. 1933; *s* of late Rev. Howell Roberts and Buddug Roberts; *m* 1960, Mair Rowlands Williams; one *s*. *Educ:* Penygroes Grammar Sch.; Univ. of Wales, Aberystwyth and Bangor (BA, LLB); Univ. of Cambridge (MA). Tutor, Westminster Coll., Cambridge, 1959; Principal, Pachhunga Meml Govt Coll., Aijal, Assam, India, 1960–67; Lectr in Social Admin, University Coll., Swansea, 1967–70; University College of North Wales, later University of Wales, Bangor: Lectr, subseq. Sen. Lectr, Dept of Social Theory and Instns, 1970–79; Dir of Extra Mural Studies, 1979–95; Vice Principal, 1985–94. BBC National Governor for Wales, 1979–86; Chm., Broadcasting Council for Wales, 1979–86 (Mem., 1974–78); Member: Welsh Fourth TV Channel Auth., 1981–86; Gwynedd CC, 1973–81 (Chm., Social Services Cttee, 1977–81); Gwynedd AHA, 1973–80; Royal Commn on Legal Services, 1976–79; Parole Bd, 1987–90. Pres., Royal National Eisteddfod of Wales, 1994– (Vice-Chm., 1987–89; Chm., 1989–92; Mem. Council, 1979–); Chm., Acen (Cyf.), 1989–; Vice Chm., Arts Council of Wales, 1994–; Mem. Bd, Cwmni Theatr Cymru, 1982–86. *Address:* Brithdir, 43 Talycae, Tregarth, Bangor, Gwynedd LL57 4AE. *T:* Bangor (01248) 600007.

ROBERTS, Air Vice-Marshal Andrew Lyle, CB 1992; CBE 1983; AFC 1969; FRAeS; military consultant; Member, Lord Chancellor's Panel of Independent Inspectors, since 1994; *b* 19 May 1938; *s* of Ronald and Norah Roberts; *m* 1962, Marcia Isabella Ward, *d* of Lt-Col C. L. C. Ward; three *d*. *Educ:* Cranbrook Sch.; RAF Coll., Cranwell. Commnd RAF, 1958; ADC to AOC No 18 Gp, 1965–66; Flight Comdr, 201 Sqdn, 1967–68 (AFC); RNSC, 1969; Personal Air Sec. to Parly Under-Sec. of State (RAF), MoD, 1970–71; i/c 236 Operational Conversion Unit, 1972–74; US Armed Forces Staff Coll., 1974; staff, SACLANT, 1975–77; i/c RAF Kinloss, 1977–79; Gp Capt. Ops, HQ Strike Command, 1980–82 (CBE); RCDS, 1983; Dir, Air Plans, MoD, 1984–86; C of S, HQ No 18 Gp, 1987–89; ACDS (Concepts), 1987–92; Hd of RAF Manpower Structure Study Team, 1992–94, retd. MIMgt. *Recreations:* cross-country and hill walking, natural history, classical music, church organ, choral singing, off-shore sailing. *Address:* c/o Midland Bank, 61 High Street, Staines, Middx TW18 4QW. *Club:* Royal Air Force.

ROBERTS, Angus Thomas; Director of Litigation and Prosecution, Post Office Solicitor's Office (formerly Principal Assistant Solicitor to General Post Office), 1965–74; *b* 28 March 1913; *s* of late Edward Roberts and late Margaret (*née* Murray); *m* 1940, Frances Monica, *d* of late Frederick and late Agnes Bertha Cane; two *s*. *Educ:* Felsted School. Admitted Solicitor, 1936. Entered Post Office Solicitor's Dept, 1939. Served in Royal Navy, 1941–46 (Lieut, RNVR). Asst Solicitor to GPO, 1951. *Recreations:* golf, fishing, gardening.

Address: 1 The Mulberries, The Inner Silk Mill, Malmesbury, Wilts SN16 9LP. *T:* Malmesbury (01666) 824981.

ROBERTS, Ann; *see* Clwyd, Ann.

ROBERTS, (Anthony) John, CBE 1991; Board Member, since 1985 and Managing Director, Group Services, since 1993, The Post Office; Chairman, Post Office Counters Ltd and Subscription Services, since 1993; *b* 26 Aug. 1944; *s* of Douglas and Margaret Roberts; *m* 1970, Diana June (*née* Lamdin); two *s*. *Educ:* Hampton Sch.; Exeter Univ. (BA Hons). Open Entrant, Administrative Class Civil Service, The Post Office, 1967; PA to Dep. Chairman and Chief Executive, 1969–71; Principal, Long Range Planning, 1971–74; Controller Personnel and Finance, North Western Postal Board, 1974–76; Principal Private Sec. to Chairman, 1976–77; Director, Chairman's Office, 1977–80; Secretary Designate, 1980–81, Sec., 1981–82; Dir, 1981–85, Man. Dir, 1985–93, Counter Services, subseq. Post Office Counters Ltd. Chm., South Thames TEC, 1989–92; Member: Govt Assessors Cttee for TECs; Adv. Cttee, SEMA Gp UK. CIMgt; FRSA 1992. Freeman, City of London, 1983; Liveryman, Gardeners' Co., 1988. *Recreations:* squash, golf, gardening, music. *Address:* The Post Office Headquarters, 148 Old Street, EC1V 9HQ. *T:* 0171–250 2273. *Clubs:* Oxshott Squash Rackets, Betchworth Park Golf.

ROBERTS, Arthur Loten, OBE 1971; Emeritus Professor, formerly Livesey Professor of Coal Gas and Fuel Industries, 1947–71, and Chairman of the Houldsworth School of Applied Science, 1956–70, University of Leeds; Pro-Vice-Chancellor, 1967–69; *b* 1 April 1906; *s* of Arthur James Roberts, Hull, and Alice Maude Loten, Hornsea, E Yorks; *m* 1941, Katherine Mary Hargrove; one *s* one *d*. *Educ:* Christ's Hospital; Univ. of Leeds. BSc 1928, PhD 1930, Assistant Lecturer, Lecturer, Senior Lecturer, Leeds Univ. Part-time mem. North-Eastern Area Gas Board, 1950–71; Mem. Gas Corp. Res. Cttee (formerly Gas Council Research Cttee), 1951–79; Hon. Sec. Advisory Research Cttee of Gas Council and University, 1947–71; Chm., former Joint Refractories Cttee of British Ceramic Research Assoc. and the Gas Corporation; Pres. British Ceramic Society, 1957–58; Member of Technology Sub-Cttee, UGC, 1960–69. FRIC, FInstF, Hon. Fellow Inst. Ceram., Hon. FInstGasE, Hon. FIChemE. *Publications:* numerous contributions to chemical, ceramic and fuel jls. *Recreations:* painting, pianoforte, garden. *Address:* Hillside, 6 King's Road, Bramhope, Leeds, W Yorks LS16 9JN. *T:* Leeds (0113) 267 4977.

ROBERTS, Barbara Haig; *see* MacGibbon, B. H.

ROBERTS, Prof. Benjamin Charles, MA Oxon; Professor of Industrial Relations, London School of Economics, University of London, 1962–84, now Emeritus; *b* 1 Aug. 1917; *s* of Walter Whitfield Roberts and Mabel Frances Roberts; *m* 1945, Veronica Lilian, *d* of George Frederick and Vera Lilian Vine-Lott; two *s*. *Educ:* LSE (Hon. Fellow, 1988); New Coll., Oxford. Research Student, Nuffield Coll., Oxford, 1948–49; Part-time Lectr, Ruskin Coll., Oxford, 1948–49; London Sch. of Economics: Lectr in Trade Union Studies, 1949–56; Reader in Industrial Relations, 1956–62; Mem. Ct of Govs, 1964–69, 1979–83. Vis. Prof: Princeton Univ., 1958; MIT 1959; Univ. of Calif., Berkeley, 1965. Assoc., Internat. Inst. of Labour Studies, Geneva, 1966; Member: Council, Inst. Manpower Studies; British-N American Cttee; Nat. Reference Tribunal of Coal Mining Industry, 1970–; Council, ACAS, 1979–86; Bruges Gp, 1990–. Editor, British Jl of Industrial Relations, 1963–89, Hon. Editor, 1990–. Pres., British Univs Industrial Relations Assoc., 1965–68; Pres., Internat. Industrial Relations Assoc., 1967–73. Consultant to EEC, 1976–79. Chm., Economists' Bookshop, 1979–87. Wincott Lecture, IEA, 1987. *Publications:* Trade Unions in the New Era, 1947; Trade Union Government and Administration in Great Britain, 1956; National Wages Policy in War and Peace, 1958; The Trades Union Congress, 1868–1921, 1958; Trade Unions in a Free Society, 1959; (ed) Industrial Relations: Contemporary Problems and Perspectives, 1962; Labour in the Tropical Territories of the Commonwealth, 1964; (ed) Manpower Planning and Employment Trends 1966; (with L. Greyfié de Bellecombe) Collective Bargaining in African Countries, 1967; (ed) Industrial Relations: Contemporary Issues, 1968; (with John Lovell) A Short History of the TUC, 1968; (with R. O. Clarke and D. J. Fatchet) Workers' Participation in Management in Britain, 1972; (with R. Loveridge and J. Gennard) Reluctant Militants: a study of industrial technicians, 1972; (with H. Okomoto and G. Lodge) Collective Bargaining and Employee Participation in Western Europe, North America and Japan, 1979; also Evidence to Royal Commn on Trade Unions, 1966, and Report to ILO on Labour and Automation: Manpower Adjustment Programmes in the United Kingdom, 1967; Industrial Relations in Europe: the imperatives of change, 1985; (with T. Kochan and N. Meltz) New Departures in Industrial Relations: developments in USA, the UK and Canada, 1988; Europe—Uniformity or Freedom?: the real EC questions, 1991. *Address:* 28 Temple Fortune Lane, NW11 7UD. *T:* 0181–458 1421. *Clubs:* Reform, Political Economy.

ROBERTS, Bernard, FRCM; concert pianist; Piano Professor, Royal College of Music, since 1962; *b* 23 July 1933; *s* of William Wright Roberts and Elsie Alberta Roberts (*née* Ingham); *m* 1st, 1955, Patricia May Russell (marr. diss. 1988); two *s*; 2nd, 1992, Caroline Velleman Ireland. *Educ:* William Hulme's Grammar Sch., Manchester; Royal Coll. of Music (ARCM 1951; FRCM 1982). Début as concert pianist, Wigmore Hall, 1957; recital, concerto and chamber music pianist, 1957–; has appeared with major British orchestras as soloist, incl. Promenade Concerts, 1979; recitals in UK and abroad, incl. master classes in major centres; has broadcast on BBC Radio 3. Member: Parikian-Fleming-Roberts Trio, 1975–84; Piano Trio with sons, 1991–. DUniv Brunel, 1989. *Recreations:* philosophy, religion, model railways. *Address:* Uwchlaw'r Coed, Llanbedr, Gwynedd LL45 2NA. *T:* Llanbedr (01341) 241532.

ROBERTS, Bertie; Director, Department of the Environment (Property Services Agency), 1971–79; *b* 4 June 1919; *y s* of late Thomas and Louisa Roberts, Blaengarw, S Wales; *m* 1st, 1946, Dr Peggy Clark; one *s*; 2nd, 1962, Catherine Matthew. *Educ:* Garw Grammar School. HM Forces, 1942–46, Captain RAOC (active service in France (Normandy), Belgium); leader of study on feasibility of using computers in Min. of Public Bldg and Works, 1958; formed and directed operational computer orgn, 1962; Comptroller of Accounts, 1963, also Dir of Computer Services, 1967; Head of Organisation and Methods, 1969; Dir of Estate Management Overseas, Dept of the Environment (with FCO), 1971; Reg. Dir, DoE (Maj.-Gen.), British Forces Germany, 1976–79. Mem., Community Health Council (Hastings Health Dist), 1982–90. *Recreations:* travel, music. *Address:* Fairmount, 41 Hollington Park Road, St Leonards on Sea, E Sussex TN38 0SE. *T:* Hastings 714177. *Club:* Rotary of St Leonard's-on-Sea.

ROBERTS, Brian Stanley; HM Diplomatic Service, retired; Head of Art History, Putney High School, since 1989; *b* 1 Feb. 1936; *s* of Stanley Victor Roberts and Flora May (*née* McInnes); *m* 1st, 1961, Phyllis Hazel Barber (marr. diss. 1976); two *s*; 2nd, 1985, Jane Catharine Chisholm; one *d*. *Educ:* Liverpool Collegiate Sch., Christ's Coll., Cambridge (MA); Courtauld Institute, London (MA). Served Royal Navy, 1955–57. Staff, Edinburgh Univ., 1960–62; Lecturer in Art History, Goldsmiths' Coll., London, 1962–69; entered FCO, 1970: First Secretary, Capetown/Pretoria, 1972; FCO, 1974; attached to Hong Kong Govt, 1977; FCO, 1980; Counsellor, Stockholm, 1983–87; Cabinet Office, 1987. Teacher, Art Hist., Cheltenham Ladies' Coll., 1988–89. *Recreations:* walking, looking at pictures. *Address:* 21 Crieff Road, SW18 2EB. *Club:* Lansdowne.

ROBERTS, Sir Bryan Clieve, KCMG 1973 (CMG 1964); QC; JP; Life Vice-President, Commonwealth Magistrates' and Judges' Association (formerly Commonwealth Magistrates' Association), 1994 (Chairman, 1979–94); *b* 22 March 1923; *s* of late Herbert Roberts, MA, and Doris Evelyn Clieve; *m* 1st, 1958, Pamela Dorothy Campbell (marr. diss.); 2nd, 1976, Brigitte Patricia Reilly-Morrison (marr. diss.); 3rd, 1985, Barbara Forter. *Educ:* Whitgift School; Magdalen Coll., Oxford (MA). Served War of 1939–45: commissioned in RA and RHA, 1941–46; active service in Normandy, Belgium, Holland and Germany, 1944–45. Called to Bar, Gray's Inn, 1950; in chambers in Temple, 1950–51; Treasury Solicitor's Dept, 1951–53. Crown Counsel, N Rhodesia, 1953–60; Dir of Public Prosecutions, N Rhodesia, 1960–61; QC (Fedn of Rhodesia and Nyasaland) 1961; Nyasaland: Solicitor-General, 1961–64; Minister of Justice, 1962–63; Mem., Legislative Council, 1961–63; Attorney-Gen. of Malawi, 1964–72; Perm. Sec. to Office of the President, Sec. to the Cabinet, and Head of Malawi Civil Service, 1965–72; Chairman: Malawi Army Council; Nat. Security and Intell. Council; Nat. Develt and Planning Council, 1966–72. Lord Chancellor's Office, 1973–82 (Under Sec., 1977–82). A Metropolitan Stipendiary Magistrate, 1982–93. JP Inner London, 1975 (Dep. Chm., South Westminster Bench, 1977–82). Officer of the Order of Menelik II of Ethiopia, 1965; Comdr, Nat. Order of Republic of Malagasy, 1969. *Address:* 3 Caroline Place, W2 4AW; Stonebarrow Lodge, Charmouth, Dorset. *Club:* Oriental.

ROBERTS, Dr Brynley Francis, CBE 1993; FSA; Librarian, National Library of Wales, 1985–94; *b* 3 Feb. 1931; *s* of Robert F. Roberts and Laura Jane Roberts (*née* Williams); *m* 1957, Rhiannon Campbell; twin *s*. *Educ:* Grammar School, Aberdare; University College of Wales, Aberystwyth (BA Hons Welsh, MA, PhD). Fellow, Univ. of Wales, 1956–57; Lectr, Sen. Lectr, Reader, Dept of Welsh, University Coll. of Wales, Aberystwyth, 1957–78; Prof. of Welsh Language and Literature, University Coll. Swansea, 1978–85. Sir John Rhys Fellow, Jesus Coll., Oxford, 1973–74. Chairman: United Theological Coll., Aberystwyth, 1977–; Gwasg Pantycelyn, Caernarfon, 1977–. Pres., Welsh Library Assoc., 1985–94; Chm., Welsh Books Council, 1989–94 (Vice-Chm., 1986–89); Mem., HEFCW, 1993–. Editor, Dictionary of Welsh Biography, 1987–. Hon. FLA 1994. *Publications:* Gwasanaeth Meir, 1961; Brut y Brenhinedd, 1971, 2nd edn 1984; Cyfranc Lludd a Llefelys, 1975; Brut Tysilio, 1980; Edward Lhuyd: the making of a scientist, 1980; Gerald of Wales, 1982; Itinerary through Wales, 1989; Studies on Middle Welsh Literature, 1992; articles in learned jls. *Recreations:* walking, music. *Address:* Hengwrt, Llanbadarn Road, Aberystwyth SY23 1HB. *T:* Aberystwyth (01970) 623577.

ROBERTS, Rear-Adm. Cedric Kenelm, CB 1970; DSO 1952; *b* 19 April 1918; *s* of F. A. Roberts; *m* 1940, Audrey, *d* of T. M. Elias; four *s*. *Educ:* King Edward's Sch., Birmingham. Joined RN as Naval Airman 2nd Cl., 1940; commnd Temp. Sub-Lt (A), RNVR, 1940; sunk in HMS Manchester, 1942, Malta Convoy; interned in Sahara; released, Nov. 1942; Personal Pilot to Vice-Adm. Sir Lumley Lyster, 1943; HMS Trumpeter, Russian Convoys, 1944; perm. commn as Lt RN, HMS Vindex, Pacific, 1945; CO 813 Sqdn, 1948; Naval Staff Coll., 1949; CO 767 Sqdn, 1950–51; CO 825 Sqdn, 1951–52: served Korean War; shot down, rescued by US Forces; lent to RAN as Dep. Dir, Air Warfare, 1953–55; CO, RNAS Eglinton, 1958–59; Chief Staff Officer: FONFT, 1959–61; FOAC, 1961–62; Capt., HMS Osprey, 1962–64; Capt., RNAS Culdrose, 1964–65; Chief Staff Officer (Ops), Far East Fleet, 1966–67; Flag Officer, Naval Flying Training, 1968–71; retired 1971; farmed in Somerset, 1971–79; emigrated to Australia, 1979. Comdr 1952; Capt. 1958; Rear-Adm. 1968. *Recreations:* sitting in the sun, drinking plonk, and watching the sheilas go by. *Address:* 11 Collins Street, Merimbula, NSW 2548, Australia. *T:* Merimbula (64) 951754.

ROBERTS, Cedric P.; *see* Prys-Roberts.

ROBERTS, Christopher William, CB 1986; Deputy Secretary, Department of Trade and Industry, since 1983; *b* 4 Nov. 1937; *s* of Frank Roberts and Evelyn Dorothy Roberts. *Educ:* Rugby Sch.; Magdalen Coll., Oxford (MA). Lectr in Classics, Pembroke Coll., Oxford, 1959–60; Asst Principal, BoT, 1960; Second Sec. (Commercial), British High Commn, New Delhi, 1962–64; Asst Private Sec. to Pres. of BoT, 1964–65; Principal, 1965; Cabinet Office, 1966–68; Private Sec. to Prime Minister, 1970–73; Asst Sec., 1972; Dept of Trade, 1973–77; Under Secretary: Dept of Prices and Consumer Protection, 1977–79; Dept of Trade, 1979–82; Chief Exec., BOTB, 1983–87. *Recreations:* travel, cricket, opera. *Clubs:* United Oxford & Cambridge University, MCC.

ROBERTS, His Honour David Ewart; a Circuit Judge, 1982–93; *b* 18 Feb. 1921; *s* of John Hobson Roberts and Dorothy Roberts. *Educ:* Abingdon Sch.; St John's Coll., Cambridge. MA, LLB. Served War, 1941–46; commnd RA (Field); service in Middle East, North Africa, Italy, Yugoslavia and Germany. Called to Bar, Middle Temple, 1948. Asst Recorder, Coventry QS, 1966–71; a Recorder of the Crown Court, 1978–82. *Recreations:* travel, photography. *Address:* 4 Greville Drive, Birmingham B15 2UU. *T:* 0121–440 3231.

ROBERTS, David Francis; Deputy Director General, Agriculture, European Commission, since 1990; *b* 28 Aug. 1941; *s* of Arthur Roberts and Mary Roberts; *m* 1974, Astrid Suhr Henriksen; two *s* one *d*. *Educ:* Priory Grammar School, Shrewsbury; Worcester College, Oxford (MA). Joined MAFF, 1964; seconded to FCO as First Sec. (Agric.), Copenhagen, 1971–74; Principal Private Sec. to Minister of Agriculture, 1975–76; seconded to HM Treasury as Head of Agric. Div., 1979–80; Under Sec., 1985, seconded to FCO as Minister (Agric.), UK Repn to the European Communities, Brussels, 1985–90. *Recreations:* sailing, squash. *Address:* Directorate-General VI, Commission of the European Communities, 120 rue de la Loi, 1049 Brussels, Belgium.

ROBERTS, (David) Gwilym (Morris), CBE 1987; FEng 1986; Chairman: Acer Group Ltd, 1987–92; Acer-ICF Ltd, 1990–92; *b* 24 July 1925; *er s* of late Edward and Edith Roberts of Crosby; *m* 1st, 1960, Rosemary Elizabeth Emily (*d* 1973), *d* of late J. E. Giles of Tavistock; one *s* one *d*; 2nd, 1978, Wendy Ann, *d* of late Dr J. K. Moore of Beckenham and Alfriston. *Educ:* Merchant Taylors' School, Crosby; Sidney Sussex College, Cambridge (Minor Scholar, MA; Hon. Fellow, 1993). FICE, FIMechE. Engineering Officer, RNVR, 1945–47; Lieut Comdr RNR, retired 1961. Asst Engineer, 1947–55, Partner, 1956–90 (Sen. Partner, 1981–90), John Taylor & Sons; principally development of water and wastewater projects, UK towns and regions, and Abu Dhabi, Bahrain, Egypt, Iraq, Kuwait, Mauritius, Qatar, Saudi Arabia and Thailand. Director: Acer Gp Ltd, 1987–92; various transportation projects in UK and abroad. Vis. Prof., Loughborough Univ., 1991–. Chairman: BGS Programme Bd, 1989–93; Football Stadia Adv. Design Council, 1990–93; 2nd Severn Crossing Technical Adjudication Panel, 1991–; Member: UK Cttee, IAWPRC, 1967–83; Bd of Control, AMBRIC (American British Consultants), 1978–92; (Construction Industry) Group of Eight, 1983–85, 1987–88; President: IPHE, 1968–69 (IPHE Silver Medal 1974; Gold Medal 1987); ICE, 1986–87 (Vice-Pres., 1983–86; Overseas Premium, 1978; Halcrow Premium, 1985; George Stephenson Medal, 1986). Council Member: Brighton Polytechnic, 1983–86; NERC, 1987–93; CIRIA, 1988–92. Member: Exec. Cttee, British Egyptian Soc., 1991–93; Nat. Cttee, British-Arab Univ.

Assoc., 1991–93. Governor: Chailey Sch., 1988–92; Roedean Sch., 1989–93. Freeman, City of London, 1977; Liveryman: Engineers' Co., 1985; Constructors' Co., 1990. Hon. FCIWEM. *Publications:* (co-author) Civil Engineering Procedure, 3rd edn 1979; Built By Oil, 1995; From Kendal's Coffee House to Great George Street, 1995; papers to Royal Soc., Arab League, ICE, IPHE. *Recreations:* tennis, golf, engineering archaeology in Middle East. *Address:* North America Farm, Hundred Acre Lane, Westmeston, Hassocks, Sussex BN6 8SH. *T:* Plumpton (01273) 890324. *Clubs:* St Stephen's Constitutional, United Oxford & Cambridge University, MCC; Piltdown Golf.

ROBERTS, Rt. Rev. (David) John; Abbot of Downside, 1974–90; *b* 31 March 1919; *s* of Albert Edward and Elizabeth Minnith Roberts. *Educ:* Downside School; Trinity Coll., Cambridge (MA). Royal Sussex Regt, Oct. 1939–Nov. 1945 (POW Germany, May 1940–April 1945). Entered monastery, Feb. 1946; ordained, 1951. House Master, Downside School, 1953–62; Novice Master, 1962–66; Prior 1966–74. Titular Abbot of St Albans, 1990. *Address:* Downside Abbey, Stratton-on-the-Fosse, Bath BA3 4RH.

ROBERTS, Maj.-Gen. David Michael, MD; FRCP, FRCPE; formerly equestrian centre proprietor; *b* 9 Sept. 1931; *s* of James Henry and Agnes Louise Roberts; *m* 1964, Angela Louise Squire; one *s* two *d*. *Educ:* Emanuel Sch., London; Royal Free Hospital School of Medicine (MB, BS). Qualified in medicine, 1954; commissioned RAMC, 1955; service in field units, BAOR, 1955–59; Hon. Registrar in Medicine, Radcliffe Infirmary, Oxford, 1960; various medical specialty appts in military hosps in UK, BAOR and Hong Kong, 1960–75; graded consultant physician, 1968; Joint Professor of Military Medicine, RAMC and RCP, London, 1975–81; Command Cons. Physician, BAOR, 1981–84; Dir of Army Medicine and Cons. Physician to the Army, 1984–88, retired. Consulting Physician, Royal Hosp., Chelsea, 1984–88; MO (Res.), MoD, 1988–90. Lectr in Tropical Medicine, Mddx Hosp. Medical Sch., 1976–81; Examiner in Tropical Medicine for RCP, 1981–88. Mem., British Soc. of Gastroenterology, 1973–90. QHP 1984–88. *Publications:* many articles on gastroenterological subjects. *Recreation:* horse trials follower.

ROBERTS, Denis Edwin, CBE 1974 (MBE 1945); Managing Director, Posts, 1977–80; *b* 6 Jan. 1917; *s* of late Edwin and Alice G. Roberts; *m* 1940, Edith (*née* Whitehead); two *s*. *Educ:* Holgate Grammar Sch., Barnsley. Served War of 1939–45, Royal Signals, France, N Africa, Italy and Austria. Entered Post Office, Barnsley, 1933; various appts, 1933–71; Dir Postal Ops, 1971–75; Sen. Dir, Postal Services, 1975–77. Mem., Industrial Tribunal, 1982–86. Chm., British Philatelic Trust, 1981–85. Liveryman, Gardeners' Co. *Address:* 302 Gilbert House, Barbican, EC2Y 8BD. *T:* 0171–638 0881. *Clubs:* City of London, City Livery.

ROBERTS, Hon. Sir Denys (Tudor Emil), KBE 1975 (CBE 1970; OBE 1960); SPMB; **Hon. Mr Justice Roberts;** Chief Justice of Negara Brunei Darussalam, since 1979; *b* 19 Jan. 1923; *s* of William David and Dorothy Elizabeth Roberts; *m* 1st, 1949, Brenda Marsh (marr. diss. 1973); one *s* one *d*; 2nd, 1985, Anna Fiona Dollar Alexander; one *s*. *Educ:* Aldenham; Wadham Coll., Oxford, 1942 and 1946–49 (MA 1948, BCL 1949; Hon. Fellow, 1984); served with Royal Artillery, 1943–46, France, Belgium, Holland, Germany, India (Captain). English Bar, 1950–53; Crown Counsel, Nyasaland, 1953–59; QC Gibraltar 1960; QC Hong Kong 1964; Attorney-General, Gibraltar, 1960–62; Solicitor-General, Hong Kong, 1962–66; Attorney-General, Hong Kong, 1966–73; Chief Secretary, Hong Kong, 1973–78; Chief Justice, Hong Kong, 1979–88; Pres., Court of Appeal, Bermuda, 1988–94. Hon. Bencher, Lincoln's Inn, 1978. SPMB (Negara Brunei Darussalam), 1984. *Publications:* Smuggler's Circuit, 1954; Beds and Roses, 1956; The Elwood Wager, 1958; The Bones of the Wajingas, 1960; How to Dispense with Lawyers, 1964. *Recreations:* cricket, walking, writing. *Address:* The Supreme Court, Bandar Seri Begawan, Brunei; PO Box 338, Paphos, Cyprus. *Clubs:* Garrick, MCC (Pres., 1989–90).

ROBERTS, Derek Franklyn, FCII, FCIB; Director and Chief Executive, Yorkshire Building Society, since 1987; Chairman, Yorkshare Ltd, since 1993; *b* 16 Oct. 1942; *s* of Frank Roberts, MBE, and May Evelyn Roberts; *m* 1969, Jacqueline (*née* Velho); two *s* one *d*. *Educ:* Park High Grammar Sch., Birkenhead; Liverpool Coll. of Commerce; Harvard Business Sch. (AMP (Grad.)). Royal Insurance Co. Ltd, 1961–72; Huddersfield Building Society: Insce Services Man., 1972; apptd to Executive, as Business Develt Man., 1975; Develt Man., 1979; on formation of Yorkshire Building Soc., 1982, apptd Asst Gen. Man. (Marketing). Dir, Bradford City Challenge Ltd, 1993–; Mem., W Yorks Rural Develt Cttee, 1992–. CIMgt. *Recreations:* golf, gardening, ski-ing, walking the dogs, keeping friendships in constant repair. *Address:* Lower Snow Lea Farm, Lamb Hall Road, Longwood, Huddersfield, West Yorks HD3 3TH. *T:* Huddersfield (01484) 659588. *Clubs:* Huddersfield Golf, Royal Liverpool Golf; Huddersfield Rugby Union FC.

ROBERTS, Sir Derek Harry, Kt 1995; CBE 1983; FRS 1980, FEng, FInstP; Provost of University College London, since 1989; *b* 28 March 1932; *s* of Harry and Alice Roberts; *m* 1958, Winifred (*née* Short); one *s* one *d*. *Educ:* Manchester Central High Sch.; Manchester Univ. (BSc). MIEE. Joined Plessey Co.'s Caswell Res. Lab., 1953; Gen. Man., Plessey Semiconductors, 1967; Dir, Allen Clark Res. Centre, 1969; Man. Dir, Plessey Microelectronics Div., 1973; Technical Dir, 1983–85, Jt Dep. Man. Dir (Technical), 1985–88, GEC. Hon. DSc: Bath, 1982; Loughborough, 1984; City, 1985; Lancaster, 1986; Manchester, 1987; Salford, Essex, London, 1988; DUniv Open, 1984. *Publications:* about 20 pubns in scientific and technical jls. *Recreations:* reading, gardening. *Address:* University College London, Gower Street, WC1E 6BT. *T:* 0171–380 7234.

ROBERTS, Prof. (Edward) Adam, FBA 1990; Montague Burton Professor of International Relations and Fellow of Balliol College, Oxford, since 1986; *b* 29 Aug. 1940; *s* of Michael Roberts and Janet Roberts (*see* Janet Adam Smith); *m* 1966, Frances P. Dunn; one *s* one *d*. *Educ:* Westminster School; Magdalen College, Oxford (BA 1962, MA 1981). Asst Editor, Peace News Ltd, 1962–65; Noel Buxton Student in Internat. Relations, LSE, 1965–68; Lectr in Internat. Relations, LSE, 1968–81; Alastair Buchan Reader in Internat. Relations, Oxford, and Professorial Fellow, St Antony's Coll., Oxford, 1981–86. Mem., Council, RIIA, 1985–91. *Publications:* (ed) The Strategy of Civilian Defence, 1967; (jtly) Czechoslovakia 1968, 1969; Nations in Arms, 1976, 2nd edn, 1986; (ed jtly) Documents on the Laws of War, 1982, 2nd edn 1989; (ed jtly) United Nations, Divided World, 1988, 2nd edn 1993; (ed jtly) Hugo Grotius and International Relations, 1990. *Recreations:* rock climbing, mountaineering, running. *Address:* Balliol College, Oxford OX1 3BJ. *T:* Oxford (01865) 277777. *Club:* Alpine.

ROBERTS, Rev. Canon Edward Eric, JP; Canon Emeritus of Southwell, since 1980; *b* 29 April 1911; *o s* of late Edward Thomas Roberts and Mrs Charlotte Roberts, Liverpool; *m* 1938, Sybil Mary (*née* Curren); two *d*. *Educ:* Univ. of Liverpool; St Augustine's Coll., Canterbury. Youth Officer: City of Oxford LEA, 1938–43; Wallasey CB, LEA, 1943–44; Training Officer, Church of England Youth Council, 1944–52; Southwell Diocesan Director: of Further Educn, 1952–61; of Educn, 1961–68. Canon, 1964; Canon Residentiary, Vice-Provost of Southwell Cathedral and Personal Chaplain to Bishop of Southwell, 1969–79; Ecumenical Officer, Diocese of Southwell, 1973–79. Sec., Nottingham Council of Churches, 1980–84. JP, City of Nottingham, 1958–. *Recreation:* photography. *Address:* 24 Manor Close, Southwell, Nottinghamshire NG25 0AP. *T:* Southwell (01636) 813246.

ROBERTS, Sir (Edward Fergus) Sidney, Kt 1978; CBE 1972; former Federal President, Australian Country Party; grazier and manager of companies; *b* 19 April 1901; *s* of late E. J. Roberts. *Educ:* Scots Coll., Sydney. Gen. Manager, Ungra, Brisbane, 1957–70; owner, Boolaroo Downs, Clermont, Qld, 1928–63. United Graziers' Assoc., Qld: Mem. Council, 1948–76; Vice-Pres., 1950–52. Aust. Road Fedn: Mem., 1954–63; Nat. Pres., 1962–63. Mem. Bd, Queensland Country Life Newspaper, 1969–77; Pres., Aust. Country Party, Qld, 1967; Chm., Federal Council, ACP, 1969–74. Knighthood awarded for distinguished service to Primary Industry, Australia. *Address:* 53 Eldernell Avenue, Hamilton, Queensland 4007, Australia. *Club:* Queensland (Brisbane).

ROBERTS, Rt. Rev. Edward James Keymer; *b* 18 April 1908; *s* of Rev. Arthur Henry Roberts; *m* 1st, 1941, Dorothy Frances (*d* 1982), *d* of Canon Edwin David Bowser, Deal; three *s* one *d*; 2nd, 1984, Diana, *widow* of Dr Christopher Grey. *Educ:* Marlborough; Corpus Christi Coll., Cambridge; Cuddesdon Theological Coll. BA 2nd class Theological Tripos, 1930; MA 1935; DD (*hc*) Cambridge, 1965. FRSCM 1977. Deacon, 1931; priest, 1932; Curate of All Saints, Margaret Street, 1931–35; Vice-Principal Cuddesdon Coll., 1935–39; Examining Chaplain to Bishop of Portsmouth and Commissary, Johannesburg, 1936–39; Vicar of St Matthew, Southsea, 1940–45; Curate-in-charge of St Bartholomew, Southsea, 1941–45; Examining Chaplain to Bishop of Portsmouth, 1942–56; Proctor in Convocation, Portsmouth, 1944–49; Commissary, Northern Rhodesia, 1946–51; Hon. Canon of Portsmouth, 1947–49; Archdeacon of Isle of Wight, Vicar of Brading, Rector of Yaverland, 1949–52; Archdeacon of Portsmouth, 1952–56; Suffragan Bishop of Malmesbury, 1956–62; Examining Chaplain to Bishop of Bristol, 1959–62; Suffragan Bishop of Kensington, 1962–64; Bishop of Ely, 1964–77. Episcopal Commissary, Portsmouth, 1984–85. Hon. Fellow, Corpus Christi Coll., Cambridge, 1964–. Select Preacher, University of Cambridge, 1966, 1978. *Recreation:* shoe cleaning. *Address:* The House on the Marsh, Quay Lane, Brading, IoW PO36 0BD. *T:* Isle of Wight (01983) 407434.

See also H. A. Roberts.

ROBERTS, Eirlys Rhiwen Cadwaladr, CBE 1977 (OBE 1971); Deputy Director, Consumers' Association (Which?), 1973–77 (Head of Research and Editorial Division, 1958–73); *b* 3 Jan. 1911; *d* of Dr Ellis James Roberts and Jane Tennant Macaulay; *m* 1941, John Cullen (marr. diss.); no *c*. *Educ:* Clapham High School; Girton College, Cambridge. BA (Hons) Classics. Sub-editor in Amalgamated Press; Military, then Political Intelligence, 1943–44 and 1944–45; Public Relations in UNRRA, Albanian Mission, 1945–47; Information Division of the Treasury, 1947–57. Chief Exec., Bureau of European Consumer Orgns, 1973–78. Mem., Royal Commn on the Press, 1974–77. Mem., Economic and Social Cttee of EEC, 1973–82 (Chm., Environment and Consumer Protection section, 1978–82); Chm., European Res. into Consumer Affairs, 1978–. *Publication:* Consumers, 1966. *Recreations:* walking, reading detective novels. *Address:* 8 Lloyd Square, WC1X 9BA. *T:* 0171–837 2492.

ROBERTS, Rt. Rev. Eric Matthias; *b* 18 Feb. 1914; *s* of Richard and Jane Roberts; *m* 1944, Nancy Jane Roberts (*née* Davies); two *s*. *Educ:* Friars Sch., Bangor; University Coll., Bangor; St Edmund Hall, Oxon (MA); St Michael's Coll., Llandaff. Curate, Penmaenmawr, 1938–40; Sub-Warden, St Michael's Coll., Llandaff, 1940–47; Vicar: Port Talbot, 1947–56; Roath, 1956–65; Archdeacon of Margam, 1965–71; Bishop of St David's, 1971–81. ChStJ 1973. *Address:* 2 Tudor Close, Westbourne Road, Penarth, South Glamorgan CF6 2BR.

ROBERTS, Sir Frank (Kenyon), GCMG 1963 (KCMG 1953; CMG 1946); GCVO 1965; Director, Hoechst (UK); Daimler-Benz (UK); Vice-President: European Atlantic Group, since 1983 (Chairman, 1970–73; President, 1973–83); Atlantic Treaty Association, since 1973 (President, 1969–73); Atlantic Council of UK (formerly British Atlantic Committee), since 1982 (President, 1968–81); *b* Buenos Aires, 27 Oct. 1907; *s* of Henry George Roberts, Preston, and Gertrude Kenyon, Blackburn; *m* 1937, Celeste Leila Beatrix (*d* 1990), *d* of late Sir Said Shoucair Pasha, Cairo, Financial Adviser to Sudan Government; no *c*. *Educ:* Bedales; Rugby; Trinity College, Cambridge (Scholar). Entered Foreign Office, 1930; served HM Embassy, Paris, 1932–35 and at HM Embassy, Cairo, 1935–37; Foreign Office, 1937–45; Chargé d'Affaires to Czechoslovak Govt, 1943; British Minister in Moscow, 1945–47; Principal Private Secretary to Secretary of State for Foreign Affairs, 1947–49; Deputy High Commr (UK) in India, 1949–51; Deputy-Under Secretary of State, Foreign Office, 1951–54; HM Ambassador to Yugoslavia, 1954–57; United Kingdom Permanent Representative on the North Atlantic Council, 1957–60; Ambassador: to the USSR, 1960–62; to the Federal Republic of Germany, 1963–68. Vice-Pres., German Chamber of Commerce in UK, 1974– (Pres., 1971–74); Mem. Governing Body, Internat. Chamber of Commerce, 1978. UK Mem., FCO Review Cttee on Overseas Representation, 1968–69. Pres., Anglo-German Assoc.; Vice-Pres., Britain-Russia Centre. Hon. LLD Manchester, 1991. Grand Cross, German Order of Merit, 1965. *Publication:* Dealing with Dictators, 1991. *Address:* 25 Kensington Court Gardens, W8 5QF. *Clubs:* Brooks's, Royal Automobile.

ROBERTS, Prof. Gareth Gwyn, FRS 1984; Vice-Chancellor, University of Sheffield, since 1991; Visiting Professor of Electronic Engineering, Department of Engineering Science and Fellow, Brasenose College, Oxford University, since 1985; *b* 16 May 1940; *s* of Edwin and Meri Roberts; *m* 1st, 1962; two *s* one *d*; 2nd, 1994, Carolyn Mary Butler; two step *d*. *Educ:* UCNW, Bangor (BSc, PhD, DSc); MA Oxon 1987. Lectr in Physics, Univ. of Wales, 1963–66; Res. Physicist, Xerox Corp., USA, 1966–68; Sen. Lectr, Reader, and Professor of Physics, NUU, 1968–76; Prof. of Applied Physics and Head, Dept of Applied Physics and Electronics, Univ. of Durham, 1976–85; Dir of Research, 1986–90, Thorn EMI plc (Chief Scientist, 1985). Chairman: Defence Scientific Adv. Council, 1993–; CVCP, 1995–. BBC/Royal Instn Christmas Lectures, 1988. Mem., UFC, 1989–. Holweck Gold Medal and Prize, Inst. of Physics, 1986. *Publications:* Insulating Films on Semiconductors, 1979; Langmuir-Blodgett Films, 1990; many publications and patents on physics of semiconductor devices and molecular electronics. *Recreations:* soccer, duplicate bridge, classical music. *Address:* The Croft, Snaithing Lane, Sheffield S10 3LF. *T:* Sheffield (0114) 282 4305.

ROBERTS, Prof. Geoffrey Frank Ingleson, CBE 1978; FEng 1978; Chairman, British Pipe Coaters Ltd, 1978–88; Professor of Gas Engineering, University of Salford, 1983–89, Professorial Fellow, 1989–91; *b* 9 May 1926; *s* of late Arthur and Laura Roberts; *m* 1949, Veronica (*d* 1993), *d* of late Captain J. Busby, Hartlepool; two *d*. *Educ:* Cathedral Sch., and High Sch. for Boys, Hereford; Leeds Univ. (BSc hons). FIChemE; FInstE. Pupil engr, Gas Light & Coke Co., and North Thames Gas Bd, 1947–50; North Thames Gas Board: Asst Engr, 1950–59; Stn Engr, Slough, 1959–61; Dept. Stn Engr, Southall Stn, 1961–66; Group Engr, Slough Group, 1966–68; Dep. Dir (Ops) Gas Council, 1968–71; Mem. for Production and Supply, Gas Council, later British Gas Corp., 1972–78; Mem. for External Affairs, British Gas Corp., 1979–81, retired. President: IGasE, 1980–81 (Hon. FIGasE); Inst. of Energy, 1983–84. *Recreations:* gardening, reading. *Address:* Ranmoor, St Nicholas Road, Middleton, Ilkley, West Yorks LS29 0AN. *T:* Ilkley (01943) 608915.

ROBERTS, Brig. Sir Geoffrey P. H.; *see* Hardy-Roberts.

ROBERTS, George Arnott; Head of Administration Department, House of Commons, 1988–91; *b* 16 April 1930; *s* of David Roberts and Doris (*née* Sykes); *m* 1956, Georgina (*née* Gower); two *s* one *d*. *Educ:* Rastrick Grammar Sch.; London Univ. (extra-mural). Min. of Labour, then Dept of Employment, 1947–74; Advisory, Conciliation and Arbitration Service, 1974–85: Sec., Central Arbitration Cttee, 1978–80; Dir of Administration, 1980–83; Dir, London Region, 1983–85; House of Commons, 1985–91: Hd of Establishment Office, 1985–88. *Recreations:* golf, gardening. *Club:* Sonning Golf.

ROBERTS, Maj.-Gen. (George) Philip (Bradley), CB 1945; DSO 1942; MC 1941; late RTR; *b* 5 Nov. 1906; *m* 1st, 1936, Désirée (*d* 1979), *d* of Major A. B. Godfray, Jersey; two *s* two *d*; 2nd, 1980, Annie Cornelia, *d* of Lt-Col F. E. W. Toussieng, Kt of Dannebrog, and *widow* of Brig. J. K. Greenwood, OBE. *Educ:* Marlborough; RMC, Sandhurst. 2nd Lieut Royal Tank Corps, 1926; served War of 1939–45 (MC, DSO and two Bars, CB, despatches thrice); Officier Légion d'Honneur; Croix de Guerre avec palmes. Adjt 6 RTR 1939; DAQMG 7th Armed Div., Bde Maj. 4th Armed Bde, GSO II 7th Armed Div., AQMG 30 Corps, CO 3 RTR 1939–41; Comd 22nd Armed Bde, Comd 26th Armed Bde, Comd 30th Armed Bde, 1941–43; Commander 11th Armoured Div., 1943–46; Comdr 7th Armoured Div., 1947–48; Dir, Royal Armoured Corps, War Office, 1948–49; retired pay, 1949. Hon. Col Kent and County of London Yeomanry Squadron, The Royal Yeomanry Regt, T&AVR, 1963–70. JP County of Kent, 1960–70. *Publication:* From the Desert to the Baltic, 1987. *Address:* Greenbank, West Street, Mayfield, E Sussex TN20 6DS; c/o Royal Bank of Scotland, Drummonds Branch, 49 Charing Cross, Admiralty Arch, SW1A 2DX. *Club:* Army and Navy.
See also Sir R. M. H. Vickers.

ROBERTS, Sir Gilbert (Howland Rookehurst), 7th Bt *cr* 1809; *b* 31 May 1934; *s* of Sir Thomas Langdon Howland Roberts, 6th Bt, CBE, and of Evelyn Margaret, *o d* of late H. Fielding-Hall; *S* father, 1979; *m* 1958, Ines, *o d* of late A. Labunski; one *s* one *d*. *Educ:* Rugby; Gonville and Caius Coll., Cambridge (BA 1957). CEng, MIMechE. *Recreation:* hang gliding. *Heir:* *s* Howland Langdon Roberts, *b* 19 Aug. 1961. *Address:* 3340 Cliff Drive, Santa Barbara, CA 93109, USA.

ROBERTS, Gillian Frances; Academic Registrar, University of London, since 1983; *b* 3 Nov. 1944; *d* of late Frank Murray and of Mabel Murray; *m* 1969, Andrew Clive Roberts. *Educ:* Sydenham High Sch.; Southampton Univ. (BA Hist., 1966). Academic Dept, London Univ., 1967–83. Mem. Local Governing Body, Bromley High Sch., 1989–. Trustee, City Parochial Foundn, 1993–. *Address:* Senate House, University of London, Malet Street, WC1E 7HU. *T:* 0171–636 8000.

ROBERTS, Prof. Gordon Carl Kenmure, PhD; Professor of Biochemistry, since 1986, Director, Leicester Biological NMR Centre, since 1986, and Centre for Mechanisms of Human Toxicity, since 1991, University of Leicester; *b* 28 May 1943; *s* of Rev. Douglas M. A. K. Roberts and Hilda (*née* Engelmann); *m* 1963, Hilary Margaret Lepper; two *s* one *d*. *Educ:* University Coll., London (BSc Hons Biochem. 1964); PhD Biochem. London 1967. Res. Chemist, Merck Sharp & Dohme Res. Labs, Rahway, NJ, 1967–69; Member scientific staff: MRC Molecular Pharmacol. Res. Unit, Dept of Pharmacol., Univ. of Cambridge, 1969–72; NIMR, 1972–86. *Publications:* NMR in Molecular Biology (with O. Jardetzky), 1981; (ed) NMR of Biological Macromolecules, 1993; numerous papers in scientific jls. *Recreation:* gardening. *Address:* Centre for Mechanisms of Human Toxicity, Hodgkin Building, University of Leicester, PO Box 138, Lancaster Road, Leicester LE1 9HN. *T:* Leicester (0116) 252 5534.

ROBERTS, Sir Gordon (James), Kt 1984; CBE 1975; JP; DL; Chairman, Oxford Regional Health Authority, 1978–90; Member, Commission for the New Towns, 1978–94 (Deputy Chairman, 1978–82); *b* 30 Jan. 1921; *s* of Archie and Lily Roberts; *m* 1944, Barbara Leach; one *s* one *d*. *Educ:* Deanshanger Sch., Northants. Chairman: Northants AHA, 1973–78; Supervisory Bd, NHS Management Adv. Service, 1982–85; NHS Computer Policy Cttee, 1981–85; RHA Chairmen, 1982–84; Member: Oxford Reg. Hosp. Bd, 1968–74; St Crispin Hosp. Management Cttee, 1965–74; Northants Exec. Council, NHS, 1954–74; E Midlands Econ. Planning Council, 1975–79; Bd, Northampton Develt Corp., 1976–85 (Dep. Chm., 1985). Contested (Lab) S Northants, 1970. Mem., Towcester RDC, 1953–56; Mem., Northants CC, 1954–77 (Leader, 1973–77). JP Northants, 1952; Chm., Towcester Bench, 1977–83. DL Northants, 1984, High Sheriff, 1989. FRSA 1985. *Publication:* (with Dr O. F. Brown) Passenham—the history of a forest village, 1975. *Recreations:* music, reading, walking, local history. *Address:* 114 Ridgmont, Deanshanger, Milton Keynes, Bucks MK19 6JG. *T:* Milton Keynes (01908) 562605.

ROBERTS, Gwilym; *see* Roberts, D. G. M.

ROBERTS, Gwilym Edffrwd, PhD; FIS; *b* 7 Aug. 1928; *s* of William and Jane Ann Roberts; *m* 1954, Mair Griffiths; no *c*. *Educ:* Brynrefail Gram. Sch.; UCW (Bangor); City Univ. BSc. Industrial Management, 1952–57; Lecturer (Polytechnic and University), 1957–66, 1970–74. MP (Lab): South Bedfordshire, 1966–70; Cannock, Feb. 1974–1983; PPS, DoI, 1976–79. Contested (Lab): Ormskirk, 1959; Conway, 1964; S Beds, 1970; Cannock and Burntwood, 1983, 1987. Business Analyst, Economic Forecasting, Market and Operational Research, 1957–. Institute of Statisticians: Vice-Pres., 1978–; Hon. Officer, 1983–84; Editor, Newsletter, 1967–78. FIMgt. Hon. Fellow, Royal Stat. Soc., 1993. *Publications:* many articles on technical, political, parliamentary and European matters. *Recreations:* cricket, table tennis. *Address:* 60 Swasedale Road, Luton, Beds LU3 2UD. *T:* Luton (01582) 573893; 8 Main Road, Brereton, Rugeley, Staffs WS15 1DT. *T:* Rugeley (01889) 583601.

ROBERTS, (Herbert) John, CMG 1965; a Director, Rural Development Corporation of Zambia, since 1980; *b* 22 Nov. 1919; *m* 1946, Margaret Pollard; three *s* one *d*. *Educ:* Holy Trinity, Weymouth; Milton, Bulawayo. Served War of 1939–45; Somaliland, Ethiopia, Burma. Elected MLC, 1954; Leader of Northern Rhodesia United Federal Party, 1959–63; Founder of National Progress Party, 1963; MP Zambia, Nat. Progress Party 1964–66, Ind. 1967–69; Min. of Labour and Mines, 1959–61; Leader of Opposition (NR), 1961–64; Leader of Opposition (Zambia), 1964–65; disbanded Nat. Progress Party, 1966. *Address:* Chanyanya Ranch, PO Box 32037, Lusaka, Zambia.

ROBERTS, Hugh Ashley, LVO 1995; FSA; Deputy Surveyor of the Queen's Works of Art, 1988–March 1996; Director of the Royal Collection and Surveyor of the Queen's Works of Art, from March 1996; *b* 20 April 1948; *s* of Rt Rev. Edward J. K. Roberts, *qv*; *m* 1975, Hon. Priscilla Jane Stephanie Low (*see* Hon. P. J. S. Roberts); two *d*. *Educ:* Winchester Coll.; Corpus Christi Coll., Cambridge (MA). FSA 1994. With Christie Manson and Woods, 1970–87 (Dir, 1978–87). Mem., Sec. of State's Adv. Gp, Historic Royal Palaces Agency, 1990–. Member: Exec. Cttee, NACF, 1988–; Arts Panel, NT, 1988–; Council, Attingham Trust, 1988–. Mem., Soc. of Dilettanti, 1991–. *Publications:* contrib. to Furniture History, Burlington Mag., Apollo, etc. *Recreation:* gardening. *Address:* Adelaide Cottage, Home Park, Windsor, Berks SL4 2JQ. *T:* Windsor (01753) 855581.

ROBERTS, Hugh Eifion Pritchard, QC 1971; DL; **His Honour Judge Eifion Roberts;** a Circuit Judge, since 1977; *b* 22 Nov. 1927; *er s* of late Rev. and Mrs E. P. Roberts, Anglesey; *m* 1958, Buddug Williams; one *s* two *d*. *Educ:* Beaumaris Grammar Sch.; University Coll. of Wales, Aberystwyth (LLB); Exeter Coll., Oxford (BCL). Called to Bar, Gray's Inn, 1953; practised as a Junior Counsel on Wales and Chester Circuit, Sept. 1953–April 1971. Dep. Chairman: Anglesey QS, 1966–71; Denbighshire QS, 1970–71; a Recorder of the Crown Court, 1972–77. Formerly Asst Parly Boundary Comr for Wales; Mem. for Wales of the Crawford Cttee on Broadcasting Coverage. DL Clwyd, 1988. *Recreation:* gardening. *Address:* Maes-y-Rhedyn, Gresford Road, Llay, Wrexham, Clwyd LL12 0NN. *T:* Wrexham (01978) 852292.

ROBERTS, Hugh Martin P.; *see* Plowden Roberts.

ROBERTS, Ian White; HM Diplomatic Service, retired; Hon. Visiting Fellow, School of Slavonic and East European Studies, University of London, 1985; *b* 29 March 1927; *s* of George Dodd Roberts and Jessie Dickson Roberts (*née* White); *m* 1956, Pamela Johnston; one *d*. *Educ:* Royal Masonic Sch., Bushey, Herts; Gonville and Caius Coll., Cambridge (MA 1st Cl. Hons Mod. Langs). Served Royal Air Force (Pilot Officer), 1948–50; postgrad. student, Cambridge (Scarbrough Award), 1950. Joined Foreign Office, 1951–: Klagenfurt, 1952; Munich, 1954; Berlin, 1955; FCO, 1957–61; Second (later First) Secretary, Budapest, 1961–63; FCO, 1963; Bujumbura, 1965; FCO, 1965–66; Buenos Aires, 1966; FCO, 1969–74; Oslo, 1974–76; FCO, 1976–84; Counsellor, 1976. *Publications:* Nicholas I and the Russian Intervention in Hungary, 1991; History of School of Slavonic and East European Studies, University of London, 1991; articles in philatelic jls. *Recreations:* music, reading, philately. *Address:* c/o Lloyds Bank, 1 Butler Place, SW1H 0PR. *Club:* Travellers'.

ROBERTS, Rt. Hon. Sir (Ieuan) Wyn (Pritchard), Kt 1990; PC 1991; MP (C) Conwy, since 1983 (Conway, 1970–83); *b* 10 July 1930; *s* of late Rev. E. P. Roberts and Margaret Ann; *m* 1956, Enid Grace Williams; three *s*. *Educ:* Harrow; University Coll., Oxford. Sub-editor, Liverpool Daily Post, 1952–54; News Asst, BBC, 1954–57; TWW Ltd: News, Special Events and Welsh Language Programmes Producer, 1957–59; Production Controller, 1959–60; Exec. Producer, 1960–68; Welsh Controller, 1964–68; Programme Exec., Harlech TV, 1969. PPS to Sec. of State for Wales, 1970–74; Opposition Front-Bench Spokesman on Welsh Affairs, 1974–79; Parly Under-Sec of State, 1979–87, Minister of State, 1987–94, Welsh Office. Vice-Pres., Assoc. of District Councils, 1975–79. Mem. of Gorsedd, Royal National Eisteddfod of Wales, 1966. Member, Court of Governors: Nat. Library of Wales; Nat. Museum of Wales; University Coll. of Wales, Aberystwyth, 1970–91. *Recreation:* gardening. *Address:* Tan y Gwalia, Conwy, Gwynedd LL32 8TY. *T:* Tyn y Groes (01492) 650371. *Clubs:* Savile; Cardiff and County (Cardiff).

ROBERTS, Ivor Anthony, CMG 1995; HM Diplomatic Service; Chargé d'Affaires, Belgrade, since 1994; *b* 24 Sept. 1946; *s* of late Leonard Moore Roberts and of Rosa Maria Roberts (*née* Fusco); *m* 1974, Elizabeth Bray Bernard Smith; two *s* one *d*. *Educ:* St Mary's Coll., Crosby; Keble Coll., Oxford (schol.; MA); FIL 1991. Entered HM Diplomatic Service, 1968; MECAS, 1969; Third, later Second Sec., Paris, 1970–73; Second, later First Sec., FCO, 1973–78; First Sec., Canberra, 1978–82; Dep. Head of News Dept, FCO, 1982–86; Head, Security Co-ordination Dept, FCO, 1986–88; Minister and Dep. Head of Mission, Madrid, 1989–93. *Recreations:* opera, ski-ing, golf, photography. *Address:* c/o Foreign and Commonwealth Office, King Charles Street, SW1A 2AH. *Clubs:* United Oxford & Cambridge University; Downhill Only (Wengen).

ROBERTS, Hon. Jane; *see* Roberts, Hon. P. J. S.

ROBERTS, Jeremy Michael Graham; QC 1982; Barrister; a Recorder of the Crown Court, since 1981; *b* 26 April 1941; *s* of late Lt-Col J. M. H. Roberts and E. D. Roberts; *m* 1964, Sally Priscilla Johnson. *Educ:* Winchester; Brasenose Coll., Oxford. BA. Called to the Bar, Inner Temple, 1965, Bencher, 1992. *Recreations:* racing, reading, theatre, opera, canals. *Address:* 9 Gough Square, EC4A 3DE. *T:* 0171–353 5371.

ROBERTS, John; *see* Roberts, A. J.

ROBERTS, Rt. Rev. John; *see* Roberts, Rt Rev. D. J.

ROBERTS, John; *see* Roberts, H. J.

ROBERTS, John Anthony; QC 1988; a Recorder of the Crown Court, since 1987; *b* Sierra Leone, 17 May 1928; *s* of late John Anthony Roberts of Brazil and Regina Roberts of Sierra Leone; *m* 1961, Eulette Valerie; one *s*. *Educ:* St Edward's RC Secondary Sch., Sierra Leone; Inns of Court Sch. of Law. FCIArb. Costs Clerk, Taylor Woodrow W Africa Ltd; Civil Servant, Sierra Leone; RAF 1952–62 (GSM Malaya), served UK, Europe, Near East, Far East, S Pacific; qualified Air Traffic Control Officer, 1962–64; qualified pilot; Civil Service, UK, 1964–69, incl. Inland Revenue; part time law student; called to the Bar, Gray's Inn, 1969; Mem., Lincoln's Inn, 1972; Head of Chambers, 1975–92; Asst Recorder, 1983–87. First person of African ancestry to be appointed QC at the English Bar; called to the Bar in: Jamaica, 1973; Sierra Leone, 1975; Trinidad and Tobago, 1978; Bahamas, 1984; St Kitts and Nevis, 1988. Judge, Supreme Cts of BVI and Anguilla, 1992–93. Bencher, Council of Legal Educn, Sierra Leone, 1990. Tutor, Inns of Ct Sch. of Law, London, 1990–92. Mem., UK Br., West Indian Ex-Servicemen's Assoc. Hon. Citizen, Atlanta, Ga, USA, 1991. *Recreations:* music, singing in a choir (Latin Mass and Gregorian Chant), flying light aircraft, playing piano, organ and guitar, reading, dancing, athletics, boxing (former sprinter and boxer, RAF).

ROBERTS, John Arthur, CEng, FIEE; Under-Secretary, Department of Energy, 1974–77; *b* 21 Dec. 1917; *s* of late John Richard and Emily Roberts; *m* 1st, 1944, Winifred Wilks Scott (*d* 1976); two *s* one *d*; 2nd, 1977, Rosetta Mabel Price. *Educ:* Liverpool Institute; Liverpool Univ. (BEng). Apprentice, Metropolitan-Vickers Electrical Co Ltd, 1939. Served War, Royal Signals, 1940–46, Major. Sen. Lectr, Applied Science, RMA, Sandhurst, 1947–49; SSO and PSO, RAE, Farnborough, 1949–59; Head, Control and Computers Section, Applications Br., Central Electricity Generating Bd, 1959–62; Project Ldr, Automatic Control, CEGB, 1962–67; DCSO, Min. of Tech. and DTI, 1967–72; Under-Sec., DTI, 1972–74. *Address:* 27 Ashcombe Court, Ilminster, Somerset TA19 0ED. *T:* Ilminster (01460) 57749.

ROBERTS, John Charles Quentin; Co-Chairman, International Advisory Board of State Library for Foreign Literature, Moscow, since 1994; Director, Britain-Russia Centre (formerly Great Britain-USSR Association), 1974–93; *b* 4 April 1933; *s* of Hubert and Emilie Roberts; *m* 1st, 1959, Dinah Webster-Williams (marr. diss.); one *s* one *d*; 2nd, 1982, Elizabeth Roberts (*née* Gough-Cooper); two step *d*. *Educ:* King's Coll., Taunton (open scholar); Merton Coll., Oxford (MA). MIL 1972. Royal Air Force CSC Interpreter, 1953; Russian Language Tutor, SSEES, Univ. of London, 1953; Shell International Petroleum Co. Ltd, 1956; Shell Co. of E Africa Ltd: Representative, Zanzibar and S Tanganyika, 1957, Kenya Highlands, 1958; PA to Man. Dir, Shell Austria AG Vienna, 1960; Pressed Steel Co. Ltd, Oxford, 1961; Asst Master, Marlborough Coll., 1963–74. Chairman: Organising Cttee for British Week in Siberia, 1978; Steering Cttee, British Month in USSR (Kiev), 1990. Member: Council, SSEES, Univ. of London, 1981–93; Internat. Adv. Bd, State Library for Foreign Literature, Moscow, 1991–93; Vice Pres.,

Assoc. of Teachers of Russian, 1984–89. Governor, Cobham Hall, 1984–88. *Publications:* translations from Russian literature; contribs to specialist jls; occasional journalism. *Recreations:* family, landscape, walking, gardening. *Address:* 52 Paultons Square, SW3 5DT. *T:* 0171–352 3882, *Fax:* 0171–352 7108; Crookedstane Rig South, by Elvanfoot, Biggar, Lanarks ML12 6TJ. *Clubs:* Athenæum, Special Forces.

ROBERTS, John Edward, CEng, FIEE, FCCA; Chief Executive, Manweb plc, since 1992; *b* 2 March 1946; *s* of Arthur and Dora Roberts; *m* 1970, Pamela Baxter; one *s* one *d. Educ:* Liverpool Univ. (BEng). FCCA 1983; CEng, FIEE 1988; DMS; CIMgt. Merseyside and North Wales Electricity Board, subseq. Manweb: Chief Accountant, 1984–90; Finance Dir, 1990–91; Man. Dir, 1991–92. *Recreations:* squash, walking, gardening. *Club:* West Cheshire Squash Rackets.

ROBERTS, John Eric, DSc (Leeds); CPhys; FInstP; Emeritus Professor of Physics, University of London, 1969; Physicist to Middlesex Hospital, W1, 1946–70; Consultant Adviser in Physics, Department of Health and Social Security, 1960–71; *b* Leeds, 1907; *e s* of late James J. Roberts, Normanton, Yorks; *m* Sarah, *o d* of late Thomas Raybould, Normanton, Yorks; two *d. Educ:* Normanton Grammar School; University of Leeds (Brown Scholar; BSc (Physics Hons) 1928; Univ. Res. Schol., 1928; PhD 1930; DSc 1944). FInstP 1938; CPhys 1985. Research Assistant in Physics, University of Leeds, 1930; Assistant Physicist, Royal Cancer Hospital, 1932; Senior Asst Physicist, Middlesex Hosp., 1937; Joel Prof. of Physics Applied to Medicine, Univ. of London, 1946–69; Regional Adviser, ME, Internat. Atomic Energy Agency, 1963–64. Pres., British Inst. of Radiology, 1951–52; Pres. Hospital Physicists Assoc., 1950–51; Editor, Physics in Medicine and Biology, 1956–60; Editor, British Jl of Radiology, 1964–67. Hon. Mem., Royal Coll. of Radiologists; Hon. FIPSM 1989. *Publications:* Nuclear War and Peace, 1956; What Must I Believe?, 1989; An Incoherence of Churches and Chapels, 1993; scientific papers in various journals. *Address:* Wood Lea, School Road, Apperley, Glos GL19 4DJ. *T:* Gloucester (01452) 780610.

ROBERTS, Air Vice-Marshal John Frederick, CB 1967; CBE 1960 (OBE 1954); *b* 24 Feb. 1913; *y s* of late W. J. Roberts, Pontardawe; *m* 1st, 1942, Mary Winifred (*d* 1968), *d* of late J. E. Newns; one *s*; 2nd, 1976, Mrs P. J. Hull, *d* of A. Stiles. *Educ:* Pontardawe Gram. Sch., Glam. Chartered Accountant, 1936. Joined RAF, 1938; service in Middle East, 1942–45 (despatches); Mem. Directing Staff, RAF Staff Coll., Bracknell, 1954–56; SASO, RAF Record Office, 1958–60; Dep. Comptroller, Allied Forces Central Europe, 1960–62; Stn Comdr RAF Uxbridge, 1963; Dir of Personal Services I, Min. of Def. (Air), 1964–65; Dir-Gen. of Ground Training (RAF), 1966–68; retd, 1968. With Deloitte & Co., Chartered Accountants, Swansea, 1969–78. *Recreations:* cricket, golf, cabinet-making. *Address:* 1 Lon Cadog, Sketty, Swansea SA2 0TS. *T:* Swansea (01792) 203763. *Clubs:* Royal Air Force, MCC; Pontardawe Golf (Pres., 1978–88).

ROBERTS, John Herbert; consultant, tax administration, since 1994; *b* 18 Aug. 1933; *s* of late John Emanuel Roberts and Hilda Mary Roberts; *m* 1965, Patricia Iris; one *s* three *d. Educ:* Canton High Sch.; London School of Economics (BScEcon Hons). Entered Civil Service by Open Competition as Inspector of Taxes, 1954; National Service, commnd RASC, 1955–57; returned to Inland Revenue, 1957; Principal Inspector, 1974; Sen. Principal Inspector, 1979; Under Secretary, 1981; Director of Operations, 1981–85; Dir, Technical Div. 2, 1985–88; Dir, Compliance and Collection Div., 1988–92; Dir of Ops (DO2), 1992–93. *Recreations:* music, walking.

ROBERTS, John Houghton; His Honour Judge John H. Roberts; a Circuit Judge, since 1993; *b* 14 Dec. 1947; *s* of John Noel Roberts and Ida Roberts, Irby, Wirral; *m* 1st, 1972, Anna Elizabeth (marr. diss. 1990), *e d* of Peter and Elizabeth Sheppard; three *s*; 2nd, 1991, Janice Mary, *er d* of Frederic and Patricia Wilkinson, Blundellsands. *Educ:* Calday Grange Grammar Sch., West Kirby; Trinity Hall, Cambridge (Schol; BA Double 1st Cl. Hons Law Tripos; MA). Lectr in Law, Liverpool Univ., 1969–71; called to the Bar, Middle Temple, 1970 (Harmsworth Major Entrance Exhibn 1968; Astbury Law Schol. 1970). Practised Northern Circuit, 1970–93. Asst Recorder, 1983; Recorder, 1988–93. *Recreations:* Rugby football, golf, cricket, music. *Address:* Crown Court, Crown Square, Manchester M3 3FL. *T:* 0161–954 1800. *Clubs:* Athenæum (Liverpool); Heswall Golf; Birkenhead Park Football; Oxton Cricket.

ROBERTS, Dr John Laing; Health Economist/Planner, Ministry of Economic Planning and Development, Mauritius, 1994–Oct. 1996; Director, Adhealth, since 1989; Consultant, World Health Organisation Office for Europe, since 1992; Hon. Senior Research Fellow, University of Manchester, since 1990; *b* 26 Dec. 1939; *s* of Charles F. Roberts and May Roberts; *m* 1st, 1963, Meriel F. Dawes (marr. diss. 1980); three *d*; 2nd, 1981, Judith Mary Hare. *Educ:* Latymer Upper School; Univ. of Birmingham. PhD, BSocSc. FHA. NHS Nat. Administrative Trainee, 1962–63; Senior Administrative Asst, United Birmingham Hosps, 1964–66; Sen. Res. Associate, Dept of Social Medicine, Univ. of Birmingham, 1966–69; Dep. Dir, Res. Div., Health Education Council, 1969–74; Operational Services Gen. Administrator, S Glamorgan AHA (T), 1974–77; Regional Gen. Administrator, W Midlands RHA, 1977–82; Regional Administrator, 1983–85, Regl Prevention Manager, 1985–89, N Western RHA; Regl Advr in Health Services, WHO Office for Europe, Copenhagen, 1990–92. *Publications:* papers on health education, health service administration, economics and health; PhD thesis, Studies of Information Systems for Health Service Resource Planning and Control. *Recreations:* swimming, hill walking. *Address:* (until Oct. 1996) c/o Ministry of Economic Planning and Development, Emmanuel Anquetil Building, Port Louis, Mauritius.

ROBERTS, John Lewis, CMG 1987; Assistant Under-Secretary of State (Equipment Collaboration), Ministry of Defence, 1985–88; *b* 21 April 1928; *s* of Thomas Hubert and Meudwen Roberts; *m* 1952, Maureen Jocelyn (*née* Moriarty); two *s. Educ:* Pontardawe Grammar Sch.; Trinity Hall, Cambridge. BA (Hons) History. Joined Min. of Civil Aviation, 1950; Private Sec. to the Parly Sec., 1953; Principal: in Railways, then in Sea Transport; branches of MoT and Civil Aviation, 1954–59; Civil Air Attaché, Bonn Embassy, 1959–62; Defence Supply Counsellor, Paris Embassy, 1966–69; Ministry of Defence: Asst Sec., Internat. Policy Div., 1971–74; Assistant Under-Secretary of State: Air MoD PE, 1974–76; Sales, 1976–77; Personnel, (Air), 1977–80; Supply and Organisation, (Air), 1980–82; Internat. and Industrial Policy, PE, 1982–85. FRSA 1988. *Recreations:* angling, sailing.

ROBERTS, Dr John Morris; Warden, Merton College, Oxford, 1984–94; a Governor of the BBC, 1988–93; *b* 14 April 1928; *s* of late Edward Henry Roberts and late Dorothy Julia Roberts, Bath, Som.; *m* 1964, Judith Cecilia Mary, *e d* of late Rev. James Armitage and Monica Armitage; one *s* two *d. Educ:* Taunton Sch.; Keble Coll., Oxford (Schol.; Hon. Fellow, 1981). National Service, 1949–50; Prize Fellow, Magdalen Coll., Oxford, 1951–53; Commonwealth Fund Fellow, Princeton and Yale, 1953–54; Merton College, Oxford: Fellow and Tutor, 1953–79 (Hon. Fellow, 1980–84, 1994–); acting Warden, 1969–70, 1977–79; Sen. Proctor, Oxford Univ., 1967–68; Vice-Chancellor and Prof., Southampton Univ., 1979–85. Mem., Inst. for Advanced Study, Princeton, 1960–61; Vis. Prof., Univ. of S Carolina, 1961; Sec. of Harmsworth Trust, 1962–68; Member: Council, European Univ. Inst., 1980–88; US/UK Educn Commn, 1981–88; Gen. Cttee, Royal Literary Fund, 1975–; Bd, British Council, 1991–. Trustee, Nat. Portrait Gall., 1984–; Rhodes Trustee, 1988–94. Editor, English Historical Review, 1967–77. Pres. Council, Taunton Sch., 1978–89. Presenter, TV series, The Triumph of the West, 1985. Hon. DLitt Southampton, 1987. Cavalier, Order of Merit (Italy), 1991. *Publications:* French Revolution Documents, 1966; Europe 1880–1945, 1967; The Mythology of the Secret Societies, 1972; The Paris Commune from the Right, 1973; Revolution and Improvement: the Western World 1775–1847, 1976; History of the World, 1976, rev. edn 1992; The French Revolution, 1978; The Triumph of the West, 1985; General Editor: Purnell's History of the 20th Century; The New Oxford History of England; The Short Oxford History of the Modern World; articles and reviews in learned jls. *Recreation:* music. *Address:* c/o Merton College, Oxford OX1 4JD. *Clubs:* Reform, Groucho.

ROBERTS, Rear-Adm. John Oliver, CB 1976; MNI; Managing Director, Demak Ltd, International Consultants, since 1983; *b* 4 April 1924; *er s* of J. V. and M. C. Roberts; *m* 1st, 1950, Lady Hermione Mary Morton Stuart (marr. diss. 1960; she *d* 1969); one *d*; 2nd, 1963, Honor Marigold Gordon Gray (marr. diss 1987); one *s* one *d*; 3rd, 1987, Sheila Violet Mary Traub (*née* Barker). *Educ:* RN Coll., Dartmouth. Served War: Midshipman, HM Ships Renown and Tartar, 1941–43; Sub-Lt, HMS Serapis, 1943–44; Lieut, 1945; Pilot Trg, 1944–46. HMS Triumph, 1947–49; RNAS, Lossiemouth, 1949–51; Flag-Lt to FOGT, 1952; Lt-Comdr, 1953; HMAS Vengeance and Sydney, 1953–54; RNVR, Southern Air Div., 1954–56; CO, No 803 Sqdn, HMS Eagle, 1957–58; Comdr, 1958; RNAS, Brawdy, 1958–60; CO, HMS St Bride's Bay, 1960–61; Naval Staff, 1962–64; Captain, 1964; CSO, Flag Officer Aircraft Carriers, 1964–66; CO, HMS Galatea, 1966–68; Naval Staff, 1968–70; CO, HMS Ark Royal, 1971–72; Rear-Adm., 1972; Flag Officer Sea Training, 1972–74; COS to C-in-C Fleet, 1974–76; Flag Officer, Naval Air Command, 1976–78. Non-exec. Dir, Aeronautical & General Instruments Ltd, 1981–82 (Head of Marketing and Sales, Defence Systems Div., 1980–81); Dir Gen., British Printing Industries Fedn, 1981–82. FRSA. *Recreations:* Rugby football, cricket, athletics, sailing, skiing. *Address:* Priory House, Blakesley, Northants. *Club:* East India, Devonshire, Sports and Public Schools.

ROBERTS, Julian; *see* Roberts, R. J.

ROBERTS, Prof. Lewis Edward John, CBE 1978; FRS 1982; Wolfson Professor of Environmental Risk Assessment, University of East Anglia, 1986–90; Emeritus Professor, since 1990; *b* 31 Jan. 1922; *s* of William Edward Roberts and Lilian Lewis Roberts; *m* 1947, Eleanor Mary Luscombe; one *s. Educ:* Swansea Grammar Sch.; Jesus Coll., Oxford (MA, DPhil). Clarendon Laboratory, Oxford, 1944; Scientific Officer, Chalk River Res. Estabt, Ont, Canada, 1946–47; AERE, Harwell, 1947, Principal Scientific Officer, 1952; Commonwealth Fund Fellow, Univ. of Calif, Berkeley, 1954–55; Dep. Head, Chemistry Div., 1966, Asst Dir, 1967, Dir, 1975–86, AERE. Mem., UKAEA, 1979–86. Pres., British Nuclear Energy Soc., 1985–87; Mem. Council and Vice Pres., Royal Instn, 1991–94. R. M. Jones Lectr, QUB, 1981; Rutherford Meml Lectr, Royal Soc., 1992. Governor, Abingdon Sch., 1978–86. *Publications:* Nuclear Power and Public Responsibility, 1984; Power Generation and the Environment, 1990; papers in qly revs and in scientific journals and IAEA pubns. *Recreations:* reading, gardening. *Address:* Penfold Wick, Chilton, Didcot OX11 0SH. *T:* Abingdon (01235) 834309.

ROBERTS, Martin Geoffrey; Head of Investigations Division, Department of Trade and Industry, since 1992; *b* 3 July 1946; *s* of Arthur and Mary Roberts; *m* 1969, Christine Muriel George; two *s. Educ:* Priory Grammar Sch., Shrewsbury; Worcester Coll., Oxford (MA). Min. of Technology, 1970; Private Sec. to Minister without Portfolio, 1973–74; seconded: to FCO, 1979–82; to DoE as Controller, Yorks and Humberside Regl Office, 1984–85; Sec., BOTB, 1985–89. *Recreation:* sailing. *Address:* Department of Trade and Industry, Ashdown House, 123 Victoria Street, SW1E 6RB.

ROBERTS, Prof. Michael, FBA 1960; Director, Institute for Social and Economic Research, Rhodes University, 1974–76; Professor of Modern History, The Queen's University, Belfast, 1954–73; Dean of the Faculty of Arts, 1957–60; *b* 21 May 1908; *s* of Arthur Roberts and Hannah Elizabeth Landless; *m* 1941, Ann McKinnon Morton; one *d. Educ:* Brighton Coll.; Worcester Coll., Oxford. Gladstone Meml Prizeman, 1931; A. M. P. Read Scholar (Oxford), 1932. Procter Vis. Fellow, Princeton Univ., USA, 1931–32; Lectr, Merton Coll., Oxford, 1932–34; Asst Lectr, Univ. of Liverpool, 1934–35; DPhil, Oxford, 1935; Prof. of Modern History, Rhodes Univ., S Africa, 1935–53. Lieut, SA Int. Corps, 1942–44. British Council Representative, Stockholm, 1944–46. Public Orator, Rhodes Univ., 1951–53; Hugh Le May Vis. Fellow, Rhodes Univ., 1960–61; Lectures: A. L. Smith, Balliol Coll., Oxford, 1962; Enid Muir Meml, Univ. of Newcastle upon Tyne, 1965; Creighton in History, Univ. of London, 1965; Stenton, Univ. of Reading, 1969; James Ford special, Oxford Univ., 1973; Wiles, QUB, 1977. Hon. Fellow, Worcester Coll., Oxford, 1966; Vis. Fellow, All Souls Coll., Oxford, 1968–69; Leverhulme Faculty Fellow in European Studies, 1973; Vis. Fellow, Pomona Coll., Claremont, Calif, 1978. Vis. Fellow, Trevelyan Coll., Univ. of Durham, 1981. MRIA 1968. For. Member: Roy. Swedish Acad. of Letters, History and Antiquities; Royal Swedish Academy of Science; Hon. Mem. Samfundet för utgivande av handskrifter rörande Skandinaviens historia. FRHistS; Fil dr (*hc*) (Stockholm), 1960; Hon. DLit QUB, 1977; Hon. DLitt Rhodes, 1988. Kungens medalj i Serafimerband (Sweden), 1981. Chevalier, Order of North Star (Sweden), 1954. *Publications:* The Whig Party, 1807–1812, 1939; (with A. E. G. Trollip) The South African Opposition, 1939–1945, 1947; Gustavus Adolphus: A History of Sweden, 1611–1632, Vol. I, 1953, Vol. II, 1958; Essays in Swedish History, 1967; The Early Vasas: A History of Sweden 1523–1611, 1968; Sweden as a Great Power 1611–1697, 1968; Sverige och Europa, 1969; Gustav Vasa, 1970; (contrib.) Studies in Diplomatic History in Memory of D. B. Horn, 1970; Gustavus Adolphus and the Rise of Sweden, 1973, 2nd edn 1992; (ed) Sweden's Age of Greatness, 1973; Macartney in Russia, 1974; The Swedish Imperial Experience 1560–1718, 1979; British Diplomacy and Swedish Politics, 1758–1773, 1980; Sverige som Stormakt, 1980; (contrib.) L'Età dei Luni, 1985; The Age of Liberty: Sweden 1719–1772, 1986; (ed and trans.) Swedish Diplomats at Cromwell's Court, 1988; From Axel Oxenstierna to Charles XII, four studies, 1991; (trans.) The Journals and Letters of Johan August Wahlberg 1838–1856, 1994; Frihetstiden, 1995; trans. from Swedish of works by Nils Ahnlund, F. G. Bengtsson, Gunnar Wennerberg (Gluntarne), Birger Sjöberg (Fridas bok), Carl Michael Bellman (Epistles and Songs, I–III), Anna Maria Lenngren; articles in New Cambridge Mod. Hist., EHR, History, Historical Jl, Past and Present, Scandia, Karolinska Förbundets Årsbok, South African Archives Yearbook, etc. *Recreation:* music. *Address:* 1 Allen Street, Grahamstown, CP 6140, South Africa. *T:* Grahamstown 24855.

ROBERTS, Rev. Michael Graham Vernon; Principal, Westcott House, Cambridge, since 1994; *b* 4 Aug. 1943; *s* of Walter Graham Southall Roberts and Pamela Middleton Roberts (*née* Abel, now Murray); *m* 1970, Susan Elizabeth (*née* Merry); one *s* two *d. Educ:* Eton Coll.; Keble Coll., Oxford (BA 1965; MA); Cuddesdon Coll.; Church Divinity Sch. of Pacific, Berkeley, Calif. (MDiv 1967). Curate, Exmouth, 1967–70; Chaplain, Clare Coll., Cambridge, 1970–74; Vicar, St Mark, Bromley, 1974–79; Tutor, Queen's Coll., Birmingham, 1979–85; Team Rector, High Wycombe, 1985–90; Vice-Principal, Westcott House, Cambridge, 1990–93. *Recreations:* Devon, Israel, reading, walking, gardening.

Address: Westcott House, Jesus Lane, Cambridge CB5 8BP. *T:* Cambridge (01223) 350074.

ROBERTS, Michèle Brigitte, (Mrs L. J. Latter); novelist and poet; *b* 20 May 1949; *d* of Reginald George Roberts and Monique Pauline Joseph (*née* Caulle); *m* 1991, Laurence James Latter. *Educ:* Somerville Coll., Oxford (MA); University Coll. London. ALA 1972. British Council Librarian, Bangkok, 1973–74; writer, 1974–; Poetry Editor: Spare Rib, 1974; City Limits, 1981–83. Vis. Fellow in Creative Writing, UEA, 1992; Research Fellow in Writing, Nottingham Trent Univ., 1995–96. *Publications: novels:* A Piece of the Night, 1978; The Visitation, 1983; The Wild Girl, 1984; The Book of Mrs Noah, 1987; In the Red Kitchen, 1990; Daughters of the House, 1992 (W. H. Smith Literary Award, 1993); Flesh and Blood, 1994; *stories:* During Mother's Absence, 1993; *poetry:* The Mirror of the Mother, 1986; Psyche and the Hurricane, 1991; All the Selves I Was, 1995; *plays:* The Journeywoman, 1988; Child-Lover, 1995; *film:* The Heavenly Twins, 1993. *Recreations:* cooking, gardening. *Address:* c/o Gillon Aitken, Aitken Stone & Wylie, 29 Fernshaw Road, SW10 0TG. *T:* 0171–351 7561.

ROBERTS, Patrick John; Director of Business and Corporate Affairs (formerly Public Affairs), Edelman Public Relations Worldwide, since 1990 (Director of European Affairs, 1989–90); *b* 21 Oct. 1942; *s* of Frank and Hilda Mary Roberts; *m* 1978, Alison Mary Taylor; one *s* one *d*. *Educ:* Rotherham Grammar Sch.; Lincoln Coll., Oxford (BA Hons Modern Langs). Foreign Office, 1965; Bangkok, 1966; FCO, 1970; First Sec., Lagos, 1971; FCO, 1974; UK Repn to EEC, Brussels, 1977; FCO, 1980; Counsellor (Inf.), Paris, 1984. *Recreations:* shooting, swimming, cooking. *Address:* Daniel J. Edelman Ltd, 28–29 Haymarket, SW1Y 4SP. *T:* 0171–344 1200.

ROBERTS, Prof. Paul Harry, PhD, ScD; FRS 1979; FRAS; Professor of Mathematics, University of California at Los Angeles, since 1986; *b* 13 Sept. 1929; *s* of Percy Harry Roberts and Ethel Frances (*née* Mann); *m* 1989, Maureen Frances (*née* Tabrett). *Educ:* Ardwyn Grammar Sch., Aberystwyth; University Coll. of Wales, Aberystwyth; Gonville and Caius Coll., Cambridge (George Green Student; BA, MA, PhD, ScD). FRAS 1955. Res. Associate, Univ. of Chicago, 1954–55; Scientific Officer, AWRE, 1955–56; ICI Fellow in Physics, 1956–59, Lectr in Phys, 1959–61, Univ. of Durham; Associate Prof. of Astronomy, Univ. of Chicago, 1961–63; Prof. of Applied Maths, Univ. of Newcastle upon Tyne, 1963–85. Fellow, Amer. Geophysical Union. Editor, Geophysical and Astrophysical Fluid Dynamics, 1976–91. *Publications:* An Introduction to Magnetohydrodynamics, 1967; contrib. to Geophys. and Astrophys. Fluid Dyn., Jl Low Temp. Phys., Astrophys. Jl, Jl Fluid Mech., Jl Phys. Soc. and Proc. and Trans Royal Soc. *Recreations:* playing bassoon, chess. *Address:* Pacific House, 6120 Cavalleri Road, Malibu, CA 90265, USA. *T:* (310) 5892521; Department of Mathematics or Institute of Geophysics and Planetary Physics UCLA, Los Angeles, CA 90095, USA. *T:* (310) 8257764; (310) 2062707.

ROBERTS, Percy Charles; Chairman and Chief Executive, Mirror Group Newspapers Ltd, 1977–80; *b* 30 July 1920; *s* of late Herbert Bramwell Roberts and Alice (*née* Lang); *m* 1st 1946, Constance Teresa Violet Butler (marr. diss. 1977); two *s*; 2nd, 1978, Pauline Moore. *Educ:* Brighton Hove and Sussex Grammar Sch. Reporter, Sussex Daily News, 1936–39. Served War of 1939–45: Sussex Yeomanry, in France and ME (Captain). Sub-Editor, Egyptian Mail, Cairo, 1946; Reporter, Mid-East Mail, Palestine, 1947; Sub-Editor: Sussex Daily News, 1948; Liverpool Daily Post, 1949; Editor, Nigerian Citizen, 1949–51; Editorial Adviser, Gen. Manager, Managing Dir, Nigerian Daily Times, 1951–60; Managing Dir, Mirror Gp Newspapers in Caribbean, 1960–62; Gen. Manager, Mirror Newspapers in Manchester, 1962–66; Dir, 1964–80, Managing Dir, 1966–80, Daily Mirror Newspapers Ltd; Vice-Chm., West of England Newspapers Ltd, 1965–69; Managing Dir, IPC Newspapers Ltd, 1968–75; Dir, Scottish Daily Record & Sunday Mail Ltd, 1969–74; Chm., Overseas Newspapers Ltd, 1969–75; Dep. Chm. and Chief Exec., Mirror Gp Newspapers Ltd, 1975–77. Dir, Reed Publishing Holdings Ltd, 1975–80; Mem., Reed Internat. UK Cttee, 1975–80. Mem., CBI Employment Policy Cttee, 1975–78. Mem. Council, CPU, 1979–83. CIMgt. *Address:* Magnolia Cottage, Bromsash, Ross-on-Wye, Herefordshire HR9 7PR. *T:* Ross-on-Wye (01989) 750706. *Clubs:* MCC, Royal Automobile; Ross Rotary (Pres., 1992–93).

ROBERTS, Maj.-Gen. Philip; *see* Roberts, Maj.-Gen. G. P. B.

ROBERTS, Philip Bedlington; a Recorder of the Crown Court, 1982–93; Consultant, Scholfield Roberts & Hill, since 1990; *b* 15 Dec. 1921; *s* of late R. J. S. Roberts, solicitor and A. M. Roberts; *m* 1944, Olive Margaret, *d* of E. R. Payne, Mugswell, Chipstead, Surrey; one *s* one *d*. *Educ:* Dawson Court, Kensington; St Matthew's Sch., Bayswater. RAFVR, 1940–46. Admitted solicitor, 1949; in private practice with Scholfield Roberts & Hill, 1950–75; part-time Chm. of Industrial Tribunals, 1966–75, 1990–94, Chm., 1975–84, Regional Chm. (Bristol), 1984–90, retd. Chairman: Nat. Insce Tribunals, 1959–75; Compensation Appeals Tribunal, 1962. Solicitor, Somerset British Legion, 1960–75. *Publications:* contribs to professional jls. *Recreation:* gardening. *Address:* Charlynch House, Spaxton, Bridgwater, Somerset TA5 1BY. *T:* Spaxton (01278) 671356. *Club:* Royal Air Force.

ROBERTS, Phyllida Katharine S.; *see* Stewart-Roberts.

ROBERTS, Hon. (Priscilla) Jane (Stephanie), (Hon. Mrs Roberts), LVO 1995 (MVO 1985); Curator of the Print Room, Royal Library, Windsor Castle, since 1975; *b* 4 Sept. 1949; *d* of Baron Aldington, *qv*; *m* 1975, Hugh Ashley Roberts, *qv*; two *d*. *Educ:* Cranborne Chase School; Westfield College, Univ. of London (BA Hons); Courtauld Inst., Univ. of London (MA). *Publications:* Holbein, 1979; Leonardo: Codex Hammer, 1981; Master Drawings in the Royal Collection, 1985; Royal Artists, 1987; (jtly) Leonardo da Vinci, 1989; A Souvenir Album of Sandby Views of Windsor, 1990; A King's Purchase: King George III and the Collection of Consul Smith, 1993; Holbein and the Court of Henry VIII, 1993; articles in Burlington Magazine, Report of Soc. of Friends of St George's. *Recreations:* singing, sewing. *Address:* Adelaide Cottage, Home Park, Windsor, Berks SL4 2JQ. *T:* Windsor (01753) 855581.

ROBERTS, Ven. Raymond Harcourt, CB 1984; Chairman, Customer Service Committee for Wales, Office of Water Services, since 1990; Hon. Chaplain of Llandaff Cathedral, since 1991; *b* 14 April 1931; *s* of Thomas Roberts and Carrie Maud Roberts. *Educ:* St Edmund Hall, Oxford (MA English); St Michael's Theol Coll., Llandaff. Nat. Service, RN, 1949–51. Deacon 1956, priest 1957, dio. of Monmouth (Curate of Bassaleg); Chaplain RNVR, 1958, RN, 1959; Destroyers and Frigates, Far East, 1959; HMS Pembroke, 1962; Dartmouth Trng Sqdn, 1963; RM Commando Course, 1965; 45 Commando, S. Arabia, 1965; RN Engrg Coll., 1967; HMS Bulwark, 1968; BRNC Dartmouth, 1970; HMS Ark Royal, 1974; Commando Trng Centre, RM, 1975; HMS Drake and HM Naval Base, Plymouth, 1979; Chaplain of the Fleet and Archdeacon for RN, 1980–84, Archdeacon Emeritus, 1985–; QHC, 1980–84; Hon. Canon, Cathedral of Holy Trinity, Gibraltar, 1980–84; Gen. Sec., Jerusalem and ME Church Assoc., 1985–89; licensed, dio. of Guildford, 1986–91. Pres., Llandaff N Div., St John Ambulance Bde, 1993–. Chaplain: Welsh Livery Guild, 1993–; to the High Sheriff of S Glam, 1993–94. Governor, Rougemont Sch., Gwent, 1993–. *Recreations:* cooking and listening to Mozart, not necessarily simultaneously. *Address:* 1 Woolmer Close, Danescourt, Llandaff, Cardiff CF5 2QY. *T:* Cardiff (01222) 564804.

ROBERTS, Richard (David Hallam); occasional supply teacher, freelance academic and writer, yachtmaster, bookbinder's mate, virtually-trained househusband, gardener, woodman, antiquarian cyclist; *b* 27 July 1931; *s* of Arthur Hallam Roberts, Barrister-at-law, sometime Attorney-General, Zanzibar, and Ruvé Constance Jessie Roberts; *m* 1960, Wendy Ewen Mount; three *s*. *Educ:* King's Sch., Canterbury; Jesus Coll., Cambridge. Commissioned into RA 6th Field Regt, 1952. Asst Master, King's Sch., Canterbury, 1956; Housemaster, 1957; Head of Modern Language Dept, 1961; Senior Housemaster, 1965; Headmaster: Wycliffe Coll., Stonehouse, 1967–80; King Edward's Sch., Witley, 1980–85. Chm., Alde and Ore Assoc., 1991–94. *Address:* Smithy Cottage, Orford, Suffolk IP12 2NW. *Club:* Orford Sailing.

ROBERTS, Rear-Adm. Richard Douglas, CB 1971; CEng; FIMechE; Rear-Admiral Engineering on staff Flag Officer Naval Air Command, 1969–72; *b* 7 Nov. 1916; *s* of Rear-Adm. E. W. Roberts and Mrs R. E. Roberts (*née* Cox); *m* 1943, Mary Norma Wright; one *s* one *d*. *Educ:* RNC Dartmouth; RNEC Keyham. Frobisher, 1934; RNEC Keyham, 1935–38 (qual. Marine Eng); HM Ships: Kent, 1938–40; Exeter, 1941; Bermuda, 1942; Mauritius, 1943–45; RNEC Manadon, 1945 (qual. Aero Eng); RNAY Donibristle, 1946 (AMIMechE); RNAS Worthy Down, 1947; RNAS Yeovilton, 1948–49; Staff of Rear-Adm. Reserve Aircraft, 1949–50; Comdr, 1950; RN Staff Coll., 1951; RNAY Fleetlands, 1952–53 (Production Man.); HMS Newfoundland, 1954–56 (Engr Officer); Engr-in-Chief's Dept, Bath, 1956–60; Captain 1960; RNAY Belfast, 1961–62 (Supt); idc, 1963 (MIMechE); Dir, Fleet Maintenance, 1964–66; Dir, Naval Officer Appts (E), 1966–68; Naval ADC to the Queen, 1968; Rear-Adm. 1969. FBIM 1982. *Recreations:* sailing (RNSA, 1936), fishing; light railways; Vice Pres., Axe Vale Conservation Soc. *Club:* Army and Navy.

ROBERTS, Dr Richard John, FRS 1995; Director of Research, New England Biolabs, since 1992; *b* 6 Sept. 1943; *s* of John Walter Roberts and Edna Wilhelmina Roberts; *m* 1st, 1965, Elizabeth Dyson; one *s* one *d*; 2nd, 1986, Jean (*née* Tagliabue); one *s* one *d*. *Educ:* Sheffield Univ. (BSc Chm. 1965; PhD 1968). Harvard University: Res. Fellow, 1969–70; Res. Associate in Biochem., 1971–72; Cold Spring Harbor Laboratory: Sen. Staff Investigator, 1972–86; Asst Dir for Research, 1986–92. Miller Prof., UC Berkeley, 1991. Mem., Editl Bd, Computer Applications in the Bioscis, 1985–; Exec. Editor, Nucleic Acids Res., 1987– (Mem. Editl Bd, 1977–); Panel Mem., NLM Study Section, Comp. Biol, 1993–. Hon. MD Uppsala, 1992; Hon. MD Bath, 1994; Hon. DSc Sheffield, 1994. (Jtly) Nobel Prize in Physiology or Medicine, 1993. *Publications:* numerous papers on restriction endonucleases, DNA methylases, computational molecular biology. *Recreations:* collecting games, croquet. *Address:* New England Biolabs, 32 Tozer Road, Beverly, MA 01915, USA. *T:* (508) 9273382.

ROBERTS, (Richard) Julian, FSA; Deputy Librarian, since 1986, and Keeper of Printed Books, since 1974, Bodleian Library, Oxford; Fellow of Wolfson College, Oxford, since 1975; *b* 18 May 1930; *s* of A. R. and K. M. Roberts; *m* 1957, Anne Ducé; one *s* one *d*. *Educ:* King Edward's Sch., Birmingham; Magdalen Coll., Oxford. ALA 1956; FSA 1983. Asst Keeper, BM, 1958–74. Vicegerent, Wolfson Coll., Oxford, 1983–85. Regents' Prof., UCLA, 1991. Pres., Bibliographical Soc., 1986–88. *Publications:* (ed) Beawty in Raggs: poems by Cardell Goodman, 1958; John Dee's Library Catalogue, 1990; contrib. to Library, Book Collector, Jl of Librarianship, etc. *Recreations:* walking, antiquarianism. *Address:* St John's Farm House, Tackley, Oxford OX5 3AT. *T:* Tackley (01869) 331249.

ROBERTS, Robert Evan, CBE 1976; National General Secretary, National Council of YMCAs, 1965–75; *b* 16 July 1912; *s* of late Robert Thomas Roberts, Llanilar, Denbighshire; *m* 1939, Rhoda, *d* of late William Driver, Burnley, Lancs; one *s* one *d*. *Educ:* Cilcain, Flintshire; Liverpool. YMCA: Asst Sec.: Central YMCA Liverpool, 1933; Hornsey (N London), 1935; Asst Div. Sec., Lancs/Cheshire, 1937; Div. Sec., NW Div. (Cumberland, Westmorland, N Lancs), 1939; Dep. Dir, YMCA Welfare Services, NW Europe, 1944–46 (despatches); Mem. 21st Army Gp, Council of Voluntary Welfare Work, 1944–46. Nat. Sec., Ireland, 1946; Sec., Personnel Dept, Nat. Council of YMCAs, London, 1948; Nat. Sec., Nat. Council of YMCAs, Wales, 1956–65; Hon. Sec/Treasurer, Assoc. of Secs of YMCAs of Gt Brit. and Ireland, 1963–65; Dep. Chm., Welsh Standing Conf. of Nat. Vol. Youth Orgs. 1963–65. Past Member: Welsh Nat. Council of Social Service; Welsh Jt Educn Cttee; Nat. Inst. of Adult Educn. Member: Nat. Council of Social Service, 1965–75; Brit. Council of Churches (and its Exec.), 1965–74; Council of Voluntary Welfare Work, 1965–75; World Council of YMCAs (and its Finance Cttee), 1965–75; Vice-Pres., Welsh Nat. Council of YMCAs, 1975; Chm., Job Creation Programme, Barrow and S Lakeland, 1976–80; Exec. Member: SE Cumbria Community Health Council, 1977–82; S Lakeland Voluntary Action, 1978–85; S Cumbria Community Health Council, 1982–92 (Vice-Chm., 1986–89); S Cumbria DHA Ethics of Research Cttee, 1983–92; Cumbria FHSA, 1990–92; CHC Observer, Cumbria FPC, 1984–90. Trustee, Framlington Trust, 1973–. Age Concern: Mem., 1976–82, Vice Chm., 1981–82, Exec. Cttee, Cumbria; Chm., S Lakeland, 1977–82; Exec. Mem. and Trustee, Kendal and Ulveston. Dist Judge, Cumbria Best Kept Village, 1977–85; Warden, Lakeland Horticultural Soc. Gardens, 1977–. Fellow, Royal Commonwealth Soc., 1974. Silver Jubilee Medal, 1977. *Recreation:* gardening. *Address:* 5 Priory Crescent, Kents Bank, Grange over Sands, Cumbria LA11 7BL. *T:* Grange over Sands (015395) 32161.

ROBERTS, Prof. Ronald John, PhD; FRCPath, FIBiol, FRCVS; FRSE; Professor of Aquatic Pathobiology and Director, Institute of Aquaculture, University of Stirling, since 1971, *b* 28 March 1941; *s* of Ronald George Roberts and Marjorie Kneale; *m* 1964, Helen, *d* of Gordon Gregor Macgregor; two *s*. *Educ:* Campbeltown Grammar Sch., Argyll; Univ. of Glasgow Vet. Sch. (PhD, BVMS). FIBiol 1984; FRCPath 1988; FRCVS 1992; FRSE 1978. Univ. of Glasgow: Asst in Microbiology, 1964–66; Lectr in Vet. Pathology, 1966–71. Consultant in Fish Diseases: Dept Agric. and Fisheries for Scotland, 1968–71; ODA, 1974–, FAO, Rome, 1978–83; World Bank, 1989. Dir, Machrihanish Marine Envmtl Res. Lab., 1991–. Mem., Cabinet Office Science Panel, 1993–94. Editor: Jl Fish Diseases, 1978–; Aquaculture Research (formerly Aquaculture and Fisheries Management), 1978–. Chm., Stirling Aquaculture, 1987–; Director: Stirling Salmon, 1987–94; Tarbert Fyne Foods, 1987–90; Stirling Aquatic Technology, 1987–90; Campbeltown and Kintyre Enterprise, 1992–. Chm., Argyll and Bute Countryside Trust, 1994–. Buckland Prof. and Medallist, 1985–86; C-Vet Award, BVA, 1989; Dalrymple-Champneys Cup and Medal, BVA, 1990. Commander, Most Noble Order of the Crown (Thailand), 1992. *Publications:* Handbook of Salmon and Trout Diseases, 1974; Fish Pathology, 1978, 2nd edn 1989; various scientific publications on histopathology of fishes. *Recreations:* arboriculture, rhododendron culture, golf, squash, admiring and conserving the Scottish natural environment, travelling in SE Asia. *Address:* 9 Alexander Drive, Bridge of Allan, Stirling FK9 4QB. *T:* Stirling (01786) 833078; Carrick Point Farm, Ardnacross Shorelands, by Campbeltown, Argyll PA28 6QP. *T:* Campbeltown (01586) 554417. *Clubs:* Farmers', Commonwealth Trust, Royal Society of Medicine; Machrihanish Golf (Kintyre).

ROBERTS, Sir Samuel, 4th Bt *cr* 1919, of Ecclesall and Queen's Tower, City of Sheffield; Chairman, Cleyfield Properties Ltd, since 1984; *b* 16 April 1948; *s* of Sir Peter Geoffrey Roberts, 3rd Bt, and of Judith Randell, *d* of late Randell G. Hempson; *S* father, 1985; *m* 1977, Georgina Ann, *yr d* of David Cory; one *s* three *d*. *Educ:* Harrow School; Sheffield Univ. (LLB); Manchester Business School. Called to the Bar, Inner Temple, 1972. Director: Wombwell Management Co. Ltd, 1974–84; Curzon Steels Ltd, 1978–84; Sterling Silverware Ltd, 1978–84; Wellman plc, 1981–84. *Heir: s* Samuel Roberts, *b* 12 Aug. 1989. *Address:* 6 Caversham Street, SW3 4AH.

ROBERTS, Sir Sidney; *see* Roberts, Sir E. F. S.

ROBERTS, Stephen Cheveley; Headmaster, Felsted School, since 1993; *b* 23 Aug. 1956; *s* of David Roberts and Elizabeth Roberts (*née* Thornborough); *m* 1985, Joanna Meryl Cunnison; two *s*. *Educ:* Mill Hill Sch.; University Coll., Oxford (BA 1978; PGCE 1979; MA 1982). Credit Analyst, Orion Bank, 1979–80; Asst Master, Christ's Hosp., Horsham, 1980–86; Oundle School: Hd of Physics, 1986–90; Housemaster, 1990–93. *Recreations:* hockey, music, reading. *Address:* Headmaster's House, Felsted School, Felsted, Dunmow, Essex CM6 3LL. *T:* Great Dunmow (01371) 820258. *Clubs:* East India; Vincent's (Oxford).

ROBERTS, Sir Stephen (James Leake), Kt 1981; Chairman, Milk Marketing Board, 1977–87; *b* 13 April 1915; *s* of Frank Roberts and Annie Leake; *m* 1940, Muriel Hobbins; two *s* two *d*. *Educ:* Wellington Grammar Sch. Farmer; founded Wrekin Farmers Ltd, 1960 (Chm., 1960–77); Shropshire delegate to NFU Council, 1962–70; Member: MMB for W Midland Region, 1966–87 (Vice-Chm., 1975–77); Food from Britain Council, 1983–87. *Recreation:* football (now spectator). *Address:* Lydebrook House, Coalmoor Road, Little Wenlock, Telford, Shropshire TF6 5AS. *T:* Telford (01952) 504569. *Club:* Farmers'.

ROBERTS, Stephen Pritchard; baritone; professional singer, since 1972; *b* 8 Feb. 1949; *s* of Edward Henry Roberts and Violet Pritchard. *Educ:* Royal College of Music (schol.). ARCM 1969; GRSM 1971. Professional Lay-Cleric, Westminster Cathedral Choir, 1972–76; now sings regularly in London, UK and Europe, with all major orchs and choral socs; has also sung in USA, Canada, Israel, Hong Kong, Singapore and S America. Mem., Vocal Faculty, Royal London Colls, 1993–. *Opera* rôles include: Count, in Marriage of Figaro; Falke, in Die Fledermaus; Ubalde, in Armide; Ramiro, in Ravel's L'Heure Espagnole; Aeneas, in Dido and Aeneas; Don Quixote, in Master Peter's Puppet Show; Mittenhofer, in Elegy for Young Lovers; *television* appearances include: Britten's War Requiem; Weill's Seven Deadly Sins; Delius' Sea Drift; Handel's Jeptha; Handel's Judas Maccabaeus; Penderecki's St Luke Passion, 1983 Proms; Walton's Belshazar's Feast, 1984 Proms; *recordings* include: Tippett's King Priam; Birtwistle's Punch and Judy; Gluck's Armide; Orff's Carmina Burana; Vaughan Williams' Five Mystical Songs, Epithalamion, Sea Symphony, Fantasia on Christmas Carols, and Hodie; Elgar's Apostles, and Caractacus; Penderecki's St Luke Passion; Fauré's Requiem; and works by J. S. Bach, C. P. E. Bach and Duruflé. *Address:* 144 Gleneagle Road, SW16 6BA. *T:* 0181–769 1512.

ROBERTS, Thomas Somerville, JP; FCIT; Chairman, Milford Haven Conservancy Board, 1976–82; *b* Ruabon, N Wales, 10 Dec. 1911; *s* of Joseph Richard Roberts, Rhosllanerchrugog and Lily Agnes (*née* Caldwell); *m* 1st, 1938, Ruth Moira Teasdale; two *s*; 2nd, 1950, Margaret Peggy Anderson, Sunderland. *Educ:* Roath Park Elem. Sch., Cardiff; Cardiff High Sch.; Balliol Coll., Oxford (Domus Exhibnr). Traffic Apprentice, LNER, 1933; Docks Manager, Middlesbrough and Hartlepool, 1949; Chief Docks Manager: Hull, 1959; S Wales, 1962; Port Dir, S Wales Ports, 1970–75. Chm., S Wales Port Employers, 1962–75; Member: Nat. Jt Council for Port Transport Industry, 1962–75; Nat. Dock Labour Bd, 1970–75; Race Relations Bd, 1968–76. Dir, Develt Corp. for Wales, 1965–80, Vice-Pres. 1979–83; Dep. Chm., Welsh Develt Agency, 1976–80. Member: Court, Univ. of Wales; Pwyllgor Tywysog Cymru (Prince of Wales' Cttee), 1977–81; Exec. Cttee, Welsh Environment Foundn, 1977–. Hon. Fellow and Life Governor, Univ. of Wales Coll. Cardiff (formerly University Coll., Cardiff and UWIST). JP City of Cardiff, 1966. *Recreation:* TV. *Address:* Marcross Lodge, 9 Ely Road, Llandaff, Cardiff CF5 2JE. *T:* Cardiff (01222) 561153.

ROBERTS, Sir William (James Denby), 3rd Bt *cr* 1909; *b* 10 Aug. 1936; *s* of Sir James Denby Roberts, 2nd Bt, OBE, and of Irene Charlotte D'Orsey, *yr d* of late William Dunn, MB, CM; *S* father, 1973. *Educ:* Rugby; Royal Agricultural Coll., Cirencester. MRAC, FRICS. Farms at Strathallan Castle. Founder, 1969, and owner 1969–81, Strathallan Aircraft Collection. *Recreations:* swimming and flying. *Heir: nephew* James Elton Denby Roberts-Buchanan, *b* 12 July 1966. *Address:* Strathallan Castle, Auchterarder, Perthshire PH3 1JZ. *T:* Auchterarder (01764) 62131.

ROBERTS, Rt. Hon. Sir Wyn; *see* Roberts, Rt Hon. Sir I. W. P.

ROBERTS-JONES, Ivor, CBE 1975; RA 1973 (ARA 1969); sculptor; Teacher of sculpture, Goldsmiths' College School of Art, 1946–68; *b* 2 Nov. 1913; *s* of William and Florence Robert-Jones; *m* 1940, Monica Florence Booth; one *d* (one *s* decd). *Educ:* Oswestry Grammar Sch.; Worksop Coll.; Goldsmiths' Coll. Art Sch.; Royal Academy Schs. Served in RA, 1939–46; active service in Arakan, Burma. One-man Exhibitions of Sculpture: Beaux Arts Gall., 1957; Oriel, Welsh Arts Council Gall., Cardiff 1978; Eisteddfod, 1983. Works purchased by: Tate Gall.; National Portrait Gall.; Arts Council of Gt Brit.; Welsh Arts Council; Beaverbrook Foundation, New Brunswick; Nat. Mus. of Wales. Public commissions: Winston Churchill, Parliament Square; Augustus John Memorial, Fordingbridge; Saint Francis, Lady Chapel, Ardleigh, Essex; Apsley Cherry Garrard, Wheathampstead; Winston Churchill, Oslo, 1975; Winston Churchill, New Orleans, 1977; Earl Attlee, Members' Lobby, House of Commons, 1979; Janus Rider (equestrian group), Harlech Castle, 1982; Rupert Brooke memorial, Rugby, 1988; Field Marshal Lord Slim, Whitehall, 1990; Field Marshal Lord Alanbrooke, Whitehall, 1993. Exhibited at: The John Moore, Leicester Galls, Royal Academy, Arts Council travelling exhibitions, Jubilee Exhibn of Modern British Sculpture, Battersea Park, 1977, etc. Work is in many private collections. Best known portraits include: Paul Claudel, Somerset Maugham, Yehudi Menuhin, The Duke of Edinburgh, Geraint Evans, Speaker George Thomas, Sir James Callaghan. Hon. LLD Wales, 1983. *Publications:* poetry published in Welsh Review, Poets of the Forties, etc. Sculpture illustr. in British Art since 1900 by John Rothenstein; British Sculptors, 1947; Architectural Review, etc. *Address:* The Bridles, Hall Lane, Shimpling, near Diss, Norfolk IP21 4UH. *T:* Diss (01379) 740204.

ROBERTS-WEST, Lt-Col George Arthur Alston-; *see* West.

ROBERTSHAW, Patrick Edward; His Honour Judge Robertshaw; a Circuit Judge, since 1994; *b* 7 July 1945; *s* of George Edward Robertshaw and May (*née* Allis); *m* 1972, Sally Christine Greenburgh (*née* Searle); two *s* two *d*. *Educ:* Hipperholme Grammar Sch.; Southampton Univ. (LLB). Called to the Bar, Inner Temple, 1968; a Recorder, 1989–94. *Publications:* contrib. to legal periodicals. *Recreations:* reading, listening to music, travel. *Address:* c/o Crown Court, Sheffield S3 8LW. *T:* Sheffield (0114) 273 7511.

ROBERTSON, family name of **Baron Robertson of Oakridge** and **Baroness Wharton.**

ROBERTSON, Hon. Lord; Ian Macdonald Robertson, TD 1946; a Senator of the College of Justice in Scotland, 1966–87; *b* 30 Oct. 1912; *s* of late James Robertson and Margaret Eva Wilson, Broughty Ferry, Angus, and Edinburgh; *m* 1938, Anna Love Glen, *d* of late Judge James Fulton Glen, Tampa, Florida, USA; one *s* two *d*. *Educ:* Merchiston Castle School; Balliol College, Oxford; Edinburgh University. BA Oxford (Mod. Greats), 1934; LLB Edinburgh 1937; Vans Dunlop Schol. in Law, Edinburgh 1937. Member Faculty of Advocates, 1939; Advocate-Depute, 1949–51; QC (Scot.), 1954; Sheriff of Ayr and Bute, 1961–66; Sheriff of Perth and Angus, 1966. Chairman: Medical Appeals Tribunal, 1957–63; Scottish Jt Council for Teachers' Salaries, 1965–81; Scottish Valuation Adv. Council, 1977–86; Member Court of Session Rules Council; UK Rep., Central Council, Internat. Union of Judges, 1974–87. Formerly, External Examiner in law subjects, Aberdeen, Glasgow, Edinburgh and St Andrews Universities; Member Committee on Conflicts of Jurisdiction affecting Children, 1958; Governor of Merchiston Castle School, 1954, Chm., 1970–; Assessor on Court of Edinburgh Univ., 1967–81. Chairman: Edinburgh Centre of Rural Economy, 1967–85; Edinburgh Centre for Tropical Veterinary Medicine. Served War of 1939–45, 8th Bn The Royal Scots (The Royal Regt); commd 1939; SO (Capt.), 44th Lowland Brigade (15th Scottish Division), Normandy and NW Europe (despatches). *Publication:* From Normandy to the Baltic, 1945. *Recreation:* golf. *Address:* 13 Moray Place, Edinburgh EH3 6DT. *T:* 0131–225 6637. *Clubs:* New, Honourable Company of Edinburgh Golfers (Captain 1970–72).

ROBERTSON OF OAKRIDGE, 2nd Baron *cr* 1961; **William Ronald Robertson;** Bt 1919; Member of the London Stock Exchange, 1973–95; *b* 8 Dec. 1930; *s* of General Lord Robertson of Oakridge, GCB, GBE, KCMG, KCVO, DSO, MC, and Edith (*d* 1982), *d* of late J. B. Macindoe; *S* father, 1974; *m* 1972, Celia Jane, *d* of William R. Elworthy; one *s*. *Educ:* Hilton Coll., Natal; Charterhouse; Staff Coll., Camberley (psc). Served The Royal Scots Greys, 1949–69. Mem. Salters' Co (Master, 1985–86). *Heir: s* Hon. William Brian Elworthy Robertson, *b* 15 Nov. 1975.

ROBERTSON, Dr Alan, CBE 1982; PhD; CChem, FRSC; Vice-President, National Waterways Museum, since 1994; *b* 15 Aug. 1920; *s* of William Arthur Robertson and Clarice Firby Robertson; *m* 1948, Dorothy Eileen Freeman; two *s* one *d*. *Educ:* Middlesbrough High Sch.; BSc London; University Coll., Durham (PhD); Balliol Coll., Oxford (PhD 1947). CChem, FRSC 1970. ICI, 1936–82: variety of posts in research and works management; served on Boards of Dyestuffs Div., Mond Div., ICI Australia and ICI USA; Dep. Chm., Organics Div., 1965–73; Chm., Plant Protection Div., 1973–75; Main Bd Dir, 1975–82 (Agricl Product Dir, Management Services Dir, and Territorial Dir, Pacific and Far East). Chm., Agricultural Genetics Co., 1983–89. Vice-Chm., British Waterways Bd, 1983–89; Chm. Council of Management, Nat. Waterways Mus. Trust, 1989–94. Dir, First Step Housing Co. Ltd, 1990–. Royal Society of Chemistry: Mem. Council, 1978–81; Chm., Environment Gp, 1978–81; Chm., Indust. Div., 1978–81; Industrial Medal, 1982. Chairman: Eur. Chemical Industry Ecology and Toxicology Centre, 1978–83; British Nutrition Foundn, 1981–83 (Mem. Council, 1983–95); Member: NEDC for Paper and Paper Bd Industry, 1964–67; Teijin Agrochemicals Bd, 1975–82; British Industrial Biol Res. Assoc. Council, 1980–82; London Bd, Halifax Bldg Soc., 1980–83; Kao Atlas Bd, 1975–82; Indust. Cttee, C of E Bd for Social Responsibility, 1980–86; Council, China Soc., 1985–; Vice-President: Heulwen Trust, 1986–; Pestalozzi Children's Village Trust, 1994– (Mem. Council, 1985–94); Mem. Court and Dep. Chm. of Council, UMIST, 1968–73; Governor, Lister Inst. of Preventive Medicine, 1985–. *Publications:* scientific papers in learned jls. *Recreations:* most sports (now non-active), gardening, industrial archaeology, biographical history, all matters oriental, children's and old people's welfare. *Address:* Woodlands, Tennyson's Lane, Haslemere, Surrey GU27 3AF. *T:* Haslemere (01428) 644196. *Club:* Oriental.

ROBERTSON, Prof. Anne Strachan, DLitt; FRSE; FSA, FSAScot; Titular Professor of Roman Archaeology, Glasgow University, 1974–75, retired; *d* of John Anderson Robertson and Margaret Purden. *Educ:* Hillhead High Sch.; Glasgow High Sch. for Girls; Glasgow Univ. (MA, DLitt); London Univ. (MA). FRSE 1975; FMA 1958; FRNS 1937; FSA 1958; FSAScot 1941. Glasgow University: Dalrymple Lectr in Archaeol., 1939; Under-Keeper, Hunterian Museum and Curator, Hunter Coin Cabinet, 1952; Reader in Roman Archaeol., Keeper of Cultural Collections and of Hunter Coin Cabinet, Hunterian Museum, 1964; Keeper of Roman Collections and of Hunter Coin Cabinet, 1974. Hon. Mem., Internat. Numismatic Commn, 1986; Hon. Life Mem., Amer. Numismatic Soc., 1995. Silver Medal, RNS, 1964; Silver Huntington Medal, Amer. Numismatic Soc., 1970. *Publications:* An Antonine Fort: Golden Hill, Duntocher, 1957; The Antonine Wall, 1960, 4th edn 1990; Sylloge of Anglo-Saxon Coins in the Hunter Coin Cabinet, 1961; Catalogue of Roman Imperial Coins in the Hunter Coin Cabinet: Vol. 1, 1962; Vol. 2, 1971; Vol. 3, 1977; Vol. 4, 1978; Vol. 5, 1982; The Roman Fort at Castledykes, 1964; Birrens (Blatobulgium), 1975; contrib. to Britannia, Numismatic Chron., Proc. Soc. of Antiquaries of Scotland. *Recreations:* reading, writing, photography, walking, gardening. *Address:* 31 Upper Glenburn Road, Bearsden, Glasgow G61 4BN. *T:* 0141–942 1136.

ROBERTSON, Bryan Charles Francis, OBE 1961; author, broadcasting and television, etc; regular contributor to The Spectator; *b* 1 April 1925; *yr s* of A. F. Robertson and Ellen Dorothy Black; unmarried. *Educ:* Battersea Grammar School. Worked and studied in France and Germany, 1947–48; Director: Heffer Gallery, Cambridge, 1949–51; Whitechapel Art Gallery, London, 1952–68. Mem. Arts Council Art Panel, 1958–61, 1980–84; Mem. Contemporary Art Soc. Cttee, 1958–73. US Embassy Grant to visit United States, 1956; Lectr on art, Royal Ballet School, 1958; Ford Foundn Grant for research for writing, 1961; British Council Lecture Tour, SE Asia and Australian State Galleries, 1960. Dir, State Univ. of NY Museum, 1970–75. Since 1953 has organized major exhibitions at Whitechapel, including Turner, Hepworth, Moore, Stubbs, John Martin, Rowlandson and Gillray, Bellotto, Mondrian, de Stäel, Nolan, Davie, Smith, Malevich, Pollock, Richards, Australian Painting, Rothko, Tobey, Vaughan, Guston, Poliakof, Caro, Medley, etc. *Publications:* Jackson Pollock, a monograph, 1960; Sidney Nolan, a monograph, 1961; (jtly) Private View, 1965; (with H. Tatlock Miller) Loudon Sainthill, 1973; Edward Burra, 1978; contribs (art criticism) to London Magazine, Art News (US), Spectator, Harpers & Queen, Twentieth Century, Listener, Cambridge Review, Museums Jl, etc. *Address:* 73 Barnsbury Street, N1 1EJ. *Club:* Athenæum.

ROBERTSON, Rev. Charles; Parish Minister, Canongate (The Kirk of Holyroodhouse), since 1978; Chaplain: to the Queen in Scotland, since 1991; to the High Constables and Guard of Honour of Holyroodhouse, since 1993; *b* 22 Oct. 1940; *s* of late Thomas Robertson and Elizabeth Halley; *m* 1965, Alison Margaret Malloch; one *s* two *d*. *Educ:* Camphill School, Paisley; Edinburgh Univ. (MA); New College, Edinburgh. Asst Minister, North Morningside, Edinburgh, 1964–65; Parish Minister, Kiltearn, Ross-shire, 1965–78. Chaplain to Lord High Comr, 1990–91. Convener, Gen. Assembly's Panel on Worship, 1995– (Sec., 1982–95); C of S rep. on Joint Liturgical Group, 1984– (Chm., 1994). Mem., Broadcasting Standards Council, 1988–91, 1992–93. Chaplain: Clan Donnachaidh Soc., 1981–; New Club, Edinburgh, 1986–; Moray House Coll. of Educn, 1986–; No 2 (City of Edinburgh) Maritime HQ Unit, RAAF, 1987–. Lectr, St Colm's Coll., 1980–94. Mem., Historic Buildings Council for Scotland, 1990–. Chm., Bd of Queensberry House

Hosp., 1989– (Mem., 1978–); Gov., St Columba's Hospice, 1986–; Trustee: Edinburgh Old Town Trust, 1987–; Church Hymnary Trust, 1987–; Pres., Church Service Soc., 1988–91. JP Edinburgh, 1980–. Sec. of cttees which compiled Hymns for a Day, 1983, Songs of God's People, 1988, Worshipping Together, 1991, Clann ag Urnaigh, 1991 and Common Order, 1994; Sec., Cttee. to revise Church Hymnary, 1995–. *Publications:* (ed) Singing the Faith, 1990; (ed) St Margaret Queen of Scotland and her Chapel, 1994; contribs to Record of the Church Service Soc. *Recreations:* Scottish and Edinburgh history and literature, hymnody, collecting Canongate miscellanea. *Address:* Manse of Canongate, Edinburgh EH8 8BR. *T:* 0131–556 3515. *Clubs:* Athenæum; New (Edinburgh).

ROBERTSON, Prof. Charles Martin; FBA 1967; Lincoln Professor of Classical Archæology and Art, University of Oxford, 1961–78; *b* 11 Sept. 1911; *s* of late Professor Donald Struan Robertson, FBA, FSA, and Petica Coursolles Jones; *m* 1st, 1942, Theodosia Cecil Spring Rice (*d* 1984); four *s* two *d*; 2nd, 1988, Louise Berge (*née* Holstein). *Educ:* Leys School, Cambridge; Trinity College, Cambridge (Hon. Fellow, 1987). BA Cambridge, 1934, MA 1947; student at British School of Archæology, Athens, 1934–36; Asst Keeper, Dept of Greek and Roman Antiquities, British Museum, 1936–48 (released for service, War of 1939–45, 1940–46); Yates Professor of Classical Art and Archæology in the Univ. of London (Univ. Coll.), 1948–61. Corresp. Mem., German Archæological Inst., 1953; Ordinary Mem., 1953; Chm., Man. Cttee, British School at Athens, 1958–68. Mem., Inst. for Advanced Study, Princeton, 1968–69. Guest Schol., J. Paul Getty Museum, Malibu, 1980 and 1988. Hon. Fellow: Lincoln Coll., Oxford, 1980; UCL, 1980. For. Hon. Mem., Archaeological Inst. of America, 1985. Hon. DLit QUB, 1978. Kenyon Medal, British Acad., 1987. *Publications:* Why Study Greek Art? (Inaugural Lecture), 1949; Greek Painting, 1959; Between Archæology and Art History (Inaugural Lecture), 1963; Crooked Connections (poems), 1970; indexes and editorial work in late Sir John Beazley's Paralipomena, 1971; For Rachel (poems), 1972; A History of Greek Art, 1975; (with Alison Frantz) The Parthenon Frieze, 1975; A Hot Bath at Bedtime (poems), 1977; The Sleeping Beauty's Prince (poem), 1977; (with John Boardman) Corpus Vasorum Antiquorum, Castle Ashby, 1978; A Shorter History of Greek Art, 1981; The Attic Black-figure and Red-figure Pottery, in Karageorghis, Excavations at Kition IV, 1981; Catalogue of Greek, Etruscan and Roman Vases in the Lady Lever Art Gallery, 1987; The Art of Vase-painting in Classical Athens, 1992; articles, notes and reviews since 1935, in British and foreign periodicals. *Address:* 7a Parker Street, Cambridge CB1 1JL. *T:* Cambridge (01223) 311913.

ROBERTSON, Charles Robert Suttie; Member, Management Committee of The Distillers Company plc, 1970–82, retired; chartered accountant; *b* 23 Nov. 1920; *s* of late David Young McLellan Robertson and Doris May Beaumont; *m* 1949, Shona MacGregor Riddel (*d* 1985), *d* of late Robert Riddel, MC, and Phyllis Mary Stewart; one *s*. *Educ:* Dollar Academy. Joined DCL group, 1949; appointed: Managing Director, Scottish Malt Distillers, 1960; Sec., DCL, 1966, Finance Director, 1967. *Recreation:* hill walking. *Address:* The Arch, Edzell, Angus DD9 7TF. *T:* Edzell (01356) 648484.

ROBERTSON, Sheriff Daphne Jean Black, WS; Sheriff of Glasgow and Strathkelvin, since 1979; *b* 31 March 1937; *d* of Rev. Robert Black Kincaid and Ann Parker Collins; *m* 1965, Donald Buchanan Robertson, *qv*. *Educ:* Hillhead High Sch.; Greenock Acad.; Edinburgh Univ. (MA); Glasgow Univ. (LLB). Admitted solicitor, 1961; WS 1977. *Address:* Sheriff Court House, Glasgow G5 9DA.

ROBERTSON, David Lars Manwaring, CVO 1990; Director, Kleinwort Benson Group plc, 1970–87; *b* 29 Jan. 1917; *m* 1939, Pamela Lauderdale Meares; three *s*. *Educ:* Rugby; University Coll., Oxford. Served Welsh Guards, 1940–45. Man. Dir, Charterhouse Finance Corp. Ltd, 1945–55; joined Kleinwort, Sons & Co. Ltd, 1955; Dir, Kleinwort, Benson Ltd, 1955–81; Chairman: MK Electric Group plc, 1975–87; Provident Mutual Life Assurance Assoc., 1973–89; Provident Mutual Managed Pensions Funds Ltd, 1974–89; Dir, Berry Bros and Rudd. JP Crowborough, 1971–87. *Recreations:* skiing, golf, fishing. *Address:* 12 Lennox Gardens Mews, SW1X 0DP. *Clubs:* Boodle's, MCC.

See also S. M. Robertson.

ROBERTSON, Donald Buchanan, QC (Scot.) 1973; Temporary Judge, Court of Session, Scotland, since 1991; *b* 29 March 1932; *s* of Donald Robertson, yachtbuilder, Sandbank, Argyll, and Jean Dunsmore Buchanan; *m* 1st, 1955, Louise Charlotte, *d* of Dr J. Linthorst-Homan; one *s* one *d*; 2nd, 1965, Daphne Jean Black Kincaid (*see* D. J. B. Robertson). *Educ:* Dunoon Grammar Sch.; Glasgow Univ. (LLB). Admitted Solicitor, 1954; Royal Air Force (National Service), 1954–56. Passed Advocate, 1960; Standing Junior to Registrar of Restrictive Practices, 1970–73. Member: Sheriff Court Rules Council, 1972–76; Royal Commn on Legal Services in Scotland, 1976–80; Legal Aid Central Cttee, 1982–85; Criminal Injuries Compensation Bd, 1986–; Chm., VAT Tribunal, 1978–85. Hon. Sheriff, Lothian and Peebles, 1982–. FSA (Scot.) 1982. *Recreations:* shooting, numismatics. *Address:* 11 Grosvenor Crescent, Edinburgh EH12 5ED. *T:* 0131–337 5544; Cranshaws Castle, By Duns, Berwickshire TD11 3SJ. *T:* Longformacus (01361) 890268. *Club:* New (Edinburgh).

ROBERTSON, Geoffrey Ronald; QC 1988; barrister; author; *b* 30 Sept. 1946; *s* of Francis Albert Robertson and Bernice Joy (*née* Beattie); *m* 1990, Kathy Lette; one *s* one *d*. *Educ:* Epping Boys' High Sch.; Univ. of Sydney (BA 1966; LLB Hons 1970); University Coll., Oxford (BCL 1972; Rhodes Schol.). Called to the Bar, Middle Temple, 1973; Supreme Court of NSW, 1977, of Antigua, 1990, of Trinidad, 1992. An Asst Recorder, 1993–. Head, Doughty Street Chambers, 1990–. Visiting Fellow: Univ. of NSW, 1977; Warwick Univ., 1980–81. Consultant on Human Rights to Attorney Gen. of Australia, 1983; Consultant (Commonwealth Secretariat) to Constitutional Convention, Seychelles, 1993. Chm., Inquiry into Press Council, 1982–83. Member: BFI Wkg Party on New Technologies, 1984; Exec. Council, ICA, 1987–; Freedom of Inf. Campaign, 1987–; Charter 88, 1988–; Justice, 1991–. Chm., BMA Cttee on Medical Inf. and Patient Privacy, 1994–. Trustee, Parents for Safe Food, 1990–. *Television:* Moderator, Hypotheticals, 1981–; writer and presenter, Tree of Liberty, 1982; Chm., The World This Week, 1987; writer and narrator, 44 Days (documentary), 1992. Editor, legal column, The Guardian, 1980–85. Freedom of Information Award, 1993. *Publications:* The Trials of Oz (play), 1973 (televised 1991); Whose Conspiracy?, 1974; Reluctant Judas, 1976; Obscenity, 1979; People Against the Press, 1983; (with A. Nicol) Media Law, 1984, 3rd edn 1992; Hypotheticals, 1986; Does Dracula have Aids?, 1987; Freedom, the Individual and the Law, 6th edn 1989, 7th edn 1993; Geoffrey Robertson's Hypotheticals, 1991; contribs to anthologies and learned jls. *Recreations:* tennis, opera, fishing. *Address:* Doughty Street Chambers, 11 Doughty Street, WC1N 2PG. *T:* 0171–404 1313.

ROBERTSON, George Islay Macneill; MP (Lab) Hamilton, since 1978; *b* 12 April 1946; *s* of George Phillip Robertson and Marion I. Robertson; *m* 1970, Sandra Wallace; two *s* one *d*. *Educ:* Dunoon Grammar Sch.; Univ. of Dundee (MA Hons 1968). Res. Asst, Tayside Study, 1968–69; Scottish Res. Officer, G&MWU, 1969–70, Scottish Organiser, 1970–78. PPS to Sec. of State for Social Services, 1979; opposition spokesman on Scottish Affairs, 1979–80, on Defence, 1980–81, on Foreign and Commonwealth Affairs, 1981–93; principal spokesman on European Affairs, 1984–93; opposition front bench spokesman on Scotland, 1993–. Chm., Scottish Council of Labour Party, 1977–78; Mem., Scottish Exec. of Lab. Party, 1973–79; Sec., Manifesto Gp of PLP, 1979–84; Chm., British-German Parly Gp, 1992–93 (Hon. Pres., 1993–). Vice Chm. Bd, British Council, 1985–94; Vice-Pres., Operation Raleigh, 1982–; Member: Bd, Scottish Develt Agency, 1975–78; Bd, Scottish Tourist Bd, 1974–76; Council, National Trust for Scotland, 1976–82 and 1983–85; Police Adv. Bd for Scotland, 1974–78; Council, British Atlantic Cttee, 1981–; Governing Body, GB/E Europe Centre, 1983–91 (Vice Chm., 1990–91); Steering Cttee, annual British-German Königswinter Conference, 1983–92; Council, RIIA, 1984–91; Steering Cttee, Atlantic Conf., 1987–; Council, GB/Russia Centre, 1986– (Vice-Chm., 1995–); Council, BESO, 1991–; Vice-Chm., Westminster Foundn for Democracy, 1992–94. Editorial Bd, European Business Jl, 1988–. Chm., Seatbelt Survivors Club, 1981–. Governor, Ditchley Foundn, 1989–. Commander's Cross, Order of Merit (Germany), 1991. *Recreations:* photography, golf. *Address:* House of Commons, SW1A 0AA. *T:* 0171–219 3000; 3 Argyle Park, Dunblane, Central Scotland FK15 9DZ.

ROBERTSON, Air Vice-Marshal Graeme Alan, CBE 1988 (OBE 1985); Assistant Chief of Defence Staff (Programmes), Ministry of Defence, since 1994; *b* 22 Feb. 1945; *s* of Ronald James Harold Robertson and Constance Rosemary (*née* Freeman); *m* 1972, Barbara Ellen (*née* Mardon); one *d*. *Educ:* Bancroft's Sch.; RAF Coll., Cranwell. BA Open Univ. Pilot: 8 Sqn, 1968–69; 6 Sqn, 1970–72; 228 OCU, 1972–73; Flight Commander: 550 TFTS, USAF, 1973–76; 56 Sqn, 1976–77; RAF Staff Coll., 1977–78; OR/Air Plans Staff, MoD, 1978–82; Commanding Officer: 92 Sqn, 1982–84; 23 Sqn, 1984–85; RAF Wattisham, 1985–87; Hon. ADC to the Queen, 1985–87; Dir of Air Staff Briefing and Co-ordination, MoD, 1987–88; RCDS, 1989; Dir of Defence Programmes, MoD, 1990–91; Dep. C-in-C, RAF Germany, 1991–93; AOC No 2 Gp, 1993–94. QCVSA 1973. *Recreations:* shooting, sailing, golf, winter sports. *Address:* c/o National Westminster Bank, Sleaford, Lincs NG34 7BJ. *Clubs:* Royal Air Force, MCC.

ROBERTSON, Hamish, CB 1992; MBE 1966; Under Secretary, Scottish Office Education Department (formerly Scottish Education Department), 1987–92; *b* 6 April 1931; *s* of James and Elizabeth Robertson, Huntly; *m* 1955, Barbara Suzanne Taylor, *d* of late Dr G. C. Taylor, Peterhead; two *s* two *d*. *Educ:* The Gordon Schs, Huntly; Aberdeen Univ. (MA); St John's Coll., Cambridge. RA, 1952–54. Joined Colonial Admin. Service; Nyasaland, 1954–64; HMOCS, Malawi, 1964–67; Scottish Office: Principal, 1967; Asst Sec., 1973. *Recreations:* country pursuits. *Address:* 14 Harviestoun Road, Dollar FK14 7HG. *T:* Dollar (01259) 742374.

ROBERTSON, (Harold) Rocke, CC (Canada) 1969; MD, CM, FRCS(C), FRCSE, FACS, FRSC; Principal and Vice-Chancellor of McGill University, 1962–70; *b* 4 Aug. 1912; *s* of Harold Bruce Robertson and Helen McGregor Rogers; *m* 1937, Beatrice Roslyn Arnold; three *s* one *d*. *Educ:* St Michael's Sch., Victoria, BC; Ecole Nouvelle, Switzerland; Brentwood College, Victoria, BC; McGill University. Montreal Gen. Hospital: rotating, 1936; pathology, 1937–38; Clin. Asst in Surg., Roy. Infirmary, Edinburgh, 1938–39; Demonstr in Anat., Middx Hosp. Med. Sch., 1939; Jun. Asst in Surg., Montreal Gen. Hosp., 1939–40; RCAMC, 1940–45; Chief of Surgery: Shaughnessy Hosp., DVA, Vancouver, 1945–59 (Prof. of Surg., Univ. of BC, 1950–59); Vancouver Gen. Hosp., 1950–59; Montreal Gen. Hosp., 1959–62 (Prof. of Surg., McGill University, 1959–62). Member: Nat. Research Coun., 1964; Science Council of Canada, 1976–82. Pres., Traffic Injury Res. Foundn, 1969–72, 1977–79; Hon. Pres., Mont St Hilaire Nature Conservation Centre, 1974–. Hon. DCL, Bishop's Univ., 1963; Hon. LLD: Manitoba, 1964; Toronto, 1964; Victoria, 1964; Glasgow, 1965; Michigan, 1967; Dartmouth, 1967; Sir George Williams, 1970; McGill, 1970; Hon. DSc: Brit. Columbia, 1964; Memorial, 1968; Jefferson Med. Coll., 1969; Dr de l'Univ., Montreal, 1965. FRSA 1963. *Publications:* article on wounds, Encyclopædia Britannica; numerous contribs to scientific journals and text books. *Recreations:* tennis, fishing, gardening, golf. *Address:* RR2, Mountain, Ontario K0E 1S0, Canada. *T:* (613) 9892967.

ROBERTSON, Iain Samuel, CA; Managing Director, Corporate and Institutional Banking Division, Royal Bank of Scotland, since 1992; *b* 27 Dec. 1945: *s* of Alfred and Kathleen Robertson; *m* 1972, Morag; two *s* two *d*. *Educ:* Jordanhill College Sch.; Glasgow Univ. (LLB). Industry and professional practice 1966–72; Civil Servant, 1972–83. Director: Scottish Development Finance, 1983–90; Locate in Scotland, 1983–86; Selective Assets Trust plc, 1988–; Chief Exec., SDA, 1987–90; Gp Finance Dir, County Natwest, 1990–92. *Recreations:* golf, reading. *Address:* Waterhouse Square, EC1N 2TH. *T:* 0171–427 8115.

ROBERTSON of Brackla, Maj.-Gen. Ian Argyll, CB 1968; MBE 1947; MA; DL; Vice-Lord-Lieutenant, Highland Region (Nairn), 1980–88; Representative in Scotland of Messrs Spink & Son, 1969–76; Chairman, Royal British Legion, Scotland, 1974–77 (Vice-Chairman, 1971–74); *b* 17 July 1913; 2nd *s* of John Argyll Robertson and Sarah Lilian Pitt Healing; *m* 1939, Marjorie Violet Isobel Duncan; two *d*. *Educ:* Winchester Coll.; Trinity Coll., Oxford. Commnd Seaforth Highlanders, 1934; Brigade Major: 152 Highland Bde, 1943; 231 Infantry Bde, 1944; GSO2, Staff College, Camberley, 1944–45; AAG, 15 Indian Corps, 1945–46; GSO1, 51 Highland Div., 1952–54; Comdg 1st Bn Seaforth Highlanders, 1954–57; Comdg Support Weapons Wing, 1957–59; Comdg 127 (East Lancs) Inf. Bde, TA, 1959–61; Nat. Defence College, Delhi, 1962–63; Comdg School of Infantry, 1963–64; Commanding 51st Highland Division, 1964–66; Director of Army Equipment Policy, Ministry of Defence, 1966–68; retd. Mem. Council, Nat. Trust for Scotland, 1972–75. DL Nairn 1973. *Recreations:* various in a minor way. *Address:* Brackla House, Nairn IV12 5QY. *T:* Cawdor (01667) 404220. *Clubs:* Army and Navy, MCC; Vincent's (Oxford).

ROBERTSON, Rear-Adm. Ian George William, CB 1974; DSC 1944; *b* 21 Oct. 1922; *s* of late W. H. Robertson, MC, and Mrs A. M. Robertson; *m* 1947, Barbara Irène Holdsworth; one *s* one *d*. *Educ:* Radley College. Joined RNVR, 1941; qual. Pilot; Sub-Lt 1943; air strike ops against enemy shipping and attacks against German battleship Tirpitz, 1944 (DSC); Lieut, RN, 1945; flying and instructional appts, 1944–53; Comdr (Air): RNAS Culdrose, 1956; HMS Albion, 1958; in comd: HMS Keppel, 1960; HMS Mohawk, 1963; RNAS Culdrose, 1965; HMS Eagle, 1970; Admiral Comdg Reserves, 1972–74; retd 1974. Comdr 1954; Captain 1963; Rear-Adm. 1972; idc 1968. Dir-Gen., Navy League, 1975–76; Scoutreach Resources Organiser, Scout Assoc., 1976–79. Pres., Craft Club, 1992–. *Recreations:* golf, sailing, fishing. *Address:* Moons Oast, Barcombe Road, Piltdown, Sussex TN22 3XG. *T:* Newick (01825) 722279. *Clubs:* Naval; Piltdown Golf.

ROBERTSON, Ian Gordon, FMA; Director, National Army Museum, since 1988; *b* 4 April 1943; *s* of Major Gordon Pentelow Robertson and Florence (*née* Alder); *m* 1968, Barbara Burton; one *d*. *Educ:* Highgate Sch.; Queen's Coll., Oxford (MA). Asst Curator, Chelmsford and Essex Mus., 1965–67; Curator, Passmore Edwards Mus., London, 1967–88. Member: Exec. Council, Area Museums Service for S Eastern England; Exec. Council, ICOM (UK); Ancient Monuments Adv. Cttee, English Heritage, 1984–90. Museums Association: Mem. Council, 1977–88; Hon. Treasurer, 1981–84; Vice Pres., 1984–86; Pres., 1986–88. Founder Pres., London Fedn of Museums and Art Galleries;

President: South Midlands Museums Fedn; Soc. for Post-Medieval Archaeology, 1982–85. Served TA, 7th Bn Mddx Regt and 4th/5th Bn Essex Regt. *Publications:* papers on museological and allied topics. *Recreations:* gardening, Essex local history. *Address:* National Army Museum, Royal Hospital Road, Chelsea, SW3 4HT. *T:* 0171–730 0717.

ROBERTSON, Ian Macdonald; *see* Robertson, Hon. Lord.

ROBERTSON, Maj.-Gen. James Alexander Rowland, CB 1958; CBE 1956 (OBE 1949; MBE 1942); DSO 1944 (Bar 1945); DL; *b* 23 March 1910; *s* of Colonel James Currie Robertson, CIE, CMG, CBE, IMS, and Catherine Rowland Jones; *m* 1st, 1949, Ann Madeline Tosswill (*d* 1949); 2nd, Joan Wills (*née* Abercromby), *widow* of R. L. Wills, CBE, MC. *Educ:* Aysgarth School; Epsom College, RMC, Sandhurst. Commissioned 2 Lieutenant IA, 1930, attached 1st KOYLI; posted 6th Gurkha Rifles, 1931; Instructor Sch. of Physical Training, 1936–37; Staff Coll., Quetta, July-Dec. 1941; Bde Major 1 (Maymyo) Bde, Jan.-June, 1942; Bde Major, 106 I Inf. Bde, 1942–44; Comdr 1/7 Gurkha Rifles, 1944–45; Comdr 48 Ind. Inf. Bde, 1945–47; GSO 1, Instr Staff Coll., Quetta, June-Nov., 1947; Comdr 1/6th Gurkha Rifles, 1947–48; GSO 1 Gurkha Planning Staff, March-June, 1948; GSO 1 Malaya comd, June-Nov. 1948; BGS 1948–49. GSO 1, War Office, 1950–52; Col GS, 1 Corps, Germany, 1952–54; Comdr 51 Indep. Bde, 1955–57; Commander 17 Gurkha Division Overseas Commonwealth Land Forces, and Maj.-Gen. Brigade of Gurkhas, 1958–61; GOC Land Forces, Middle East Command, 1961–63; Gurkha Liaison Officer, War Office, 1963–64, retd. Personnel Dir, NAAFI, 1964–69. Colonel, 6th Queen Elizabeth's Own Gurkha Rifles, 1961–69; Chm., 1968–80, Pres., 1980–87, Life Vice-Pres., 1987–, Gurkha Brigade Assoc. DL Greater London, 1977. *Recreations:* fishing, sculpture.

ROBERTSON, James Andrew Stainton, PhD; Chief Economic Adviser, Department for Education and Employment (formerly Department of Employment), since 1993; *b* 23 April 1949; *s* of James Robertson and Margaret Elodie Robertson (*née* Stainton); *m* 1979, Ann Leatherbarrow; one *s* one *d*. *Educ:* Highgate Sch.; Univ. Of Essex (BA Econs); LSE (MSc Econs, PhD). Sen. Econ. Asst and Econ. Advr, Dept of Employment, 1975–82; Econ. Advr, Dept of Energy, 1982–86; Senior Economic Adviser: DTI, 1986–89; Dept of Transport, 1989–90; Hd of Industrial and Regl Econs, DTI, 1990–93. *Publications:* contrib. various learned jls. *Recreations:* family, do-it-yourself, recreational computing. *Address:* Department for Education and Employment, Caxton House, Tothill Street, SW1H 9NF.

ROBERTSON, James Downie, RSA 1989 (ARSA 1974); RSW 1962; RGI 1979; Senior Lecturer in Fine Art (Drawing and Painting), Glasgow School of Art, since 1975; *b* 2 Nov. 1931; *s* of Thomas Robertson and Mary Welsh; *m* 1970, Ursula Orr Crawford; two step *s* one step *d*. *Educ:* Hillhead High Sch., Glasgow; Glasgow Sch. of Art. DA Glasgow. RGI 1980. Taught at Keith Grammar Sch., 1957–58; Glasgow School of Art: part time Lectr, 1959; Lectr in Drawing and Painting, 1967. Vis. Lectr, Art Schools and Univs, Scotland, England and overseas; one-man exhibitions, 1961–, UK, Ireland, Spain, USA, including: Christopher Hull Gallery, London, 1984, 1987, 1989; Jorgenson Gall., Dublin, 1995; numerous group exhibns; annual exhibns at RSA, RSW, RGI, RA; works in public collections of arts socs, art galleries (incl. RSA), corporations, banks, univs and in many private collections. Awards: RGI, 1971, 1982, 1990; RSW, 1976, 1981, 1987; RSA, 1993 (Scottish Post Office Award); Shell Exploration and Production Award, 1985. *Recreations:* drawing, painting. *Address:* Carruthmuir, by Kilbarchan, Renfrewshire PA10 2QA. *T:* Kilbarchan (01505) 613592. *Club:* Glasgow Art.

ROBERTSON, James Geddes, CMG 1961; formerly Under-Secretary, Department of the Environment, and Chairman, Northern Economic Planning Board, 1965–71, retired 1971; *b* 29 Nov. 1910; *s* of late Captain A. M. Robertson, Portsoy, Banffshire; *m* 1939, Marion Mitchell Black; one *s* one *d*. *Educ:* Fordyce Academy, Banffshire; George Watson's College, Edinburgh; Edinburgh University. Kitchener Schol., 1928–32, MA 1st cl. Hons History (Edinburgh), 1932. Entered Ministry of Labour as Third Class Officer, 1933; Principal, 1943; on exchange to Commonwealth Dept of Labour and Nat. Service, Australia, 1947–49; Asst Sec., Min of Labour, 1956; Member of Government Delegations to Governing Body and Conference of ILO, 1956–60, and Social Cttee, Council of Europe, 1953–61; Safety and Health Dept, 1961–63; Training Department, Ministry of Labour, 1963–65. Member: Industrial Tribunals Panel, 1971–73; Northern Rent Scrutiny Bd, 1973–74; Rent Assessment Panel for Scotland, 1975–81. Served War of 1939–45, RAF 1942–45. *Address:* 1/1 Wyvern Park, The Grange, Edinburgh EH9 2JY. *T:* 0131–662 4367.

ROBERTSON, Rev. Canon James Smith, OBE 1984; Canon Emeritus, Zambia, 1965; Secretary, United Society for the Propagation of the Gospel, 1973–83; a Chaplain to the Queen, 1980–87; *b* 4 Sept. 1917; *s* of Stuart Robertson and Elizabeth Mann Smith, Forfar; *m* 1950, Margaret Isabel Mina Mounsey; one *d*. *Educ:* Glasgow Univ.; Edinburgh Theol Coll.; London Univ. MA Glasgow 1938; PCE London 1953. Curate, St Salvador's, Edinburgh, 1940–45; Mission Priest, UMCA, N Rhodesia, 1945–50; St Mark's Coll., Mapanza, 1950–55; Chalimbana Trng Coll., Lusaka, 1955–65, Principal 1958–65; Head, Educn Dept, Bede Coll., Durham, 1965–68; Sec., Church Colls of Educn, Gen. Synod Bd of Educn, 1968–73; Sec., USPG, 1973–83. British Council of Churches: Chm., Conf. for World Mission, 1977–81; Vice-Pres., 1984–87. Fellow, Selly Oak Colls, Birmingham, 1993. *Publications:* contributed to: Education in South Africa, 1970; The Training of Teachers, 1972; Values and Moral Development in Higher Education, 1974; Grow or Die, 1981; A Dictionary of Religious Education, 1984; Stepping Stones, 1987. *Recreations:* music, electronics, philosophy. *Address:* Flat 8, 26 Medway Street, SW1P 2BD. *T:* 0171–222 1091.

ROBERTSON, Jean, CBE 1986; RRC 1981; Matron-in-Chief, Queen Alexandra's Royal Naval Nursing Service, 1983–86; Director of Defence Nursing Services, Ministry of Defence, and Director of Royal Naval Nursing Services, 1985–86; working voluntarily for Queen Elizabeth Foundation for the Disabled, since 1989; *b* 21 Sept. 1928; *d* of late Alexander Robertson and Jean Robertson (*née* McCartney). *Educ:* Mary Erskine's School for Girls, Edinburgh. Registered Sick Children's Nurse, 1948, General Nurse, 1951; Ward Sister, Edinburgh Sick Children's Hospital, 1953; QARNNS 1955; QHNS, 1983–86. SSStJ 1981. *Recreations:* reading, swimming, knitting, making soft toys. *Address:* 14 The Haven, Alverstoke, Hants PO12 2BD. *T:* Gosport (01705) 582301.

ROBERTSON, John David H.; *see* Home Robertson.

ROBERTSON, Sir John (Fraser), KCMG 1994; CBE 1982; consultant; Chief Ombudsman, New Zealand, 1984–94; *b* 3 Aug. 1925; *s* of Maurice Leigh Robertson and Violet Caroline Robertson (*née* Poultny); *m* 1947, Phyllis Irene Walter; two *s* one *d*. *Educ:* Univ. of Canterbury, NZ; Victoria Univ. of Wellington (DPA). FCA. Public Administration, 1946–82, incl. Sec. of Defence, 1969–79, Sec. for Justice, 1979–82; company dir and management consultant, 1982–84. Harkness Commonwealth Fund Fellow, 1961–62; RCDS 1968. Pres., Internat. Ombudsman Inst., 1992–94. *Publications:* numerous articles on public admin issues. *Recreations:* golf, bowls, bush and beach walking. *Address:* 5 Kabul Street, Khandallah, Wellington, New Zealand. *T:* (4) 4791338.

ROBERTSON, Rear Adm. John Keith, CB 1983; FIEE; *b* 16 July 1926; *s* of G. M. and J. L. Robertson; *m* 1951, Kathleen (*née* Bayntun); one *s* three *d*. *Educ:* RNC Dartmouth; Clare Coll., Cambridge (BA 1949). FIEE 1981; FBIM 1980. RNC Dartmouth, 1940–43; served, 1943–83 (Clare Coll., Cambridge, 1946–49): HM Ships Queen Elizabeth, Zest, Gabbard, Aisne and Decoy; Staff, RNC Dartmouth; Grad. Recruiting; Weapon Engr Officer, HMS Centaur; Comdr, RNEC Manadon; RCDS; Captain Technical Intell. (Navy), 1974–76; Captain Fleet Maintenance, Portsmouth, 1976–78; Dir, Naval Recruiting, 1978–79; Dir, Management and Support of Intelligence, MoD, 1980–82; ACDS (Intelligence), 1982–83. *Recreations:* hockey, tennis, golf, wood carving. *Address:* Alpina, Kingsdown, Corsham, Wilts SN13 8BJ. *Clubs:* Corkscrew (Bath); Kingsdown Golf.

ROBERTSON, John Windeler; Senior Partner, Wedd Durlacher Mordaunt, 1979–86; *b* 9 May 1934; *s* of late John Bruce Robertson and Evelyn Windeler Robertson; *m* 1st 1959, Jennifer-Ann Gourdou (marr. diss.); one *s* one *d*; 2nd 1987, Rosemary Helen Jane Banks. *Educ:* Winchester Coll. National Service, RNVR, 1953–55. Joined Wedd Jefferson & Co. (Members of Stock Exchange), 1955; Partner, 1961. Dep. Chm., Barclays de Zoete Wedd Securities Ltd (BZW), 1986–88. Dep. Chm., Stock Exchange, 1976–79 (Mem. Council, 1966–86); Dir, Securities Assoc., 1986–88. Mem., City Capital Markets' Cttee, 1981–88. Trustee, TSB Foundn, 1991–. Mem., GDBA, 1989– (Chm., 1993–). *Recreations:* golf, deer stalking, 17th and 18th century marine art. *Address:* Eckensfield Barn, Compton, near Chichester, West Sussex PO18 9NT. *T:* Compton (01705) 631239. *Club:* City of London.

ROBERTSON, Julia Ann; *see* Burdus, J. A.

ROBERTSON, Sir Lewis, Kt 1991; CBE 1969; FRSE; industrialist and administrator; Chairman, Postern Executive Group Ltd, since 1991; *b* 28 Nov. 1922; *s* of John Farquharson Robertson and Margaret Arthur; *m* 1950, Elspeth Badenoch; two *s* one *d* (and one *s* decd). *Educ:* Trinity Coll., Glenalmond. Accountancy training; RAF Intelligence. Chm., 1968–70, and Man. Dir, 1965–70, Scott & Robertson Ltd; Chief Executive, 1971–76, and Dep. Chm., 1973–76, Grampian Holdings plc; Director: Scottish and Newcastle Breweries plc, 1975–87; Whitman (International) SA (formerly IC Industries (International) SA), Geneva, 1987–90; Bank of Edinburgh Group (formerly Aristuein), 1990–94; EFM Income Trust plc, 1991–; Scottish Financial Enterprise, 1991–93; Berkeley Hotel Co., 1995–; Chairman: Girobank Scotland, 1984–90; Borthwicks (formerly Thomas Borthwick & Sons plc), 1985–89; F. J. C. Lilley, subseq. Lilley, 1986–93; Triplex Lloyd, 1987–90 (F. H. Lloyd Hldgs, 1982–87; Triplex, 1983–87); Havelock Europa plc, 1989–92; Stakis plc, 1991–95. Mem, 1975–76, Dep. Chm. and Chief Exec., Scottish Develt Agency, 1976–81. Chairman: Eastern Regional Hosp. Bd (Scotland), 1960–70; Carnegie Trust for Univs of Scotland, 1990– (Trustee, Exec. Cttee, 1963–); Member: Provincial Synod, Episcopal Church of Scotland, 1963–83 (Chm. Policy Cttee, 1974–76); (Sainsbury) Cttee of Enquiry, Pharmaceutical Industry, 1965–67; Court (Finance Convener), Univ. of Dundee, 1967–70; Monopolies and Mergers Commn, 1969–76; Arts Council of GB (and Chm., Scottish Arts Council), 1970–71; Scottish Economic Council, 1977–83; Scottish Post Office Bd, 1984–90; British Council (Chm., Scottish Adv. Cttee), 1978–87; BESO, 1995–; Council, Scottish Business School, 1978–82; Restrictive Practices Court, 1983–; Edinburgh Univ. Press Cttee, 1985–88; Bd, Friends of Royal Scottish Acad., 1986–; Chairman: Bd for Scotland, BIM, 1981–83; Scotland, Imperial Soc. of Kts Bachelor, 1994–. Mem., Adv. Bd, critical edn of Waverley novels, 1984–. Trustee, Foundn for Study of Christianity and Society, 1980–88. FRSE 1978 (Mem. Council, 1992–; Treasurer, 1994–); FRSA 1981; CIMgt (CBIM 1976). Hon. LLD Dundee, 1971; Hon. DBA Napier, 1992; DUniv Stirling, 1993. *Recreations:* work, foreign travel, computer use, music, reading, things Italian. *Address:* 32 Saxe Coburg Place, Edinburgh EH3 5BP. *T:* 0131–332 5221. *Clubs:* Athenæum; New (Edinburgh).

ROBERTSON, Commandant Dame Nancy (Margaret), DBE 1957 (CBE 1953; OBE 1946); retired as Director of Women's Royal Naval Service (Dec. 1954–April 1958); *b* 1 March 1909; *er d* of Rev. William Cowper Robertson and Jessie Katharine (*née* McGregor). *Educ:* Esdaile School, Edinburgh; Paris. Secretarial work, London and Paris, 1928–39; WRNS, 1939. *Recreations:* needlework, gardening.

ROBERTSON, Nelson; *see* Robertson, W. N.

ROBERTSON, Prof. Noel Farnie, CBE 1978; BSc Edinburgh; MA Cantab; PhD Edinburgh; FRSE; Professor of Agriculture and Rural Economy, University of Edinburgh, and Principal, East of Scotland College of Agriculture, 1969–83; *b* 24 Dec. 1923; *o s* of late James Robertson and Catherine Landles Robertson (*née* Brown); *m* 1948, Doreen Colina Gardner; two *s* two *d*. *Educ:* Trinity Academy, Edinburgh; University of Edinburgh; Trinity College, Cambridge. Plant Pathologist, West African Cacao Research Institute, 1946–48; Lecturer in Botany, University of Cambridge, 1948–59; Prof. of Botany, Univ. of Hull, 1959–69. Pres., British Mycol Soc., 1965; Trustee, Royal Botanic Garden, Edinburgh, 1986–92. Chm. of Governors, Scottish Crop Res. Inst., 1983–89 (Governor, 1973–). *Publications:* (with I. J. Fleming) Britain's First Chair of Agriculture at the University of Edinburgh 1790–1990, 1990; (with Kenneth Blaxter) From Dearth to Plenty: the second agricultural revolution 1936–1986, 1995. *Address:* Woodend, Juniper Bank, Walkerburn, Peeblesshire EH43 6DE. *T:* Walkerburn (01896) 870523. *Club:* Farmers'.

ROBERTSON, Prof. Norman Robert Ean, CBE 1991; FDSRCPSGlas; Professor of Orthodontics, 1970–92, Dean of the Dental School, 1985–92, University of Wales College of Medicine; Hon. Consulting Orthodontist, South Glamorgan Health Authority, since 1992 (Hon. Consultant in Orthodontics, 1970–92); *b* 13 March 1931; *s* of late Robert Robertson and Jean Robertson (*née* Dunbar); *m* 1954, Morag Wyllie, *d* of George McNicol, MA; three *s* two *d*. *Educ:* Hamilton Acad.; Glasgow Univ. (BDS); Manchester Univ. (MDS 1962; DDS 1989). FDSRCPSGlas 1967. Registrar, then Sen. Registrar in Orthodontics, Glasgow Dental Hosp., 1957–59; Lectr in Orthodontics, 1960–62, Sen. Lectr in Orthodontics, 1962–70, Manchester Univ. Member: GDC, 1985–94; Standing Dental Adv. Cttee, 1989–92; S Glamorgan HA, 1976–92. *Publications:* Oral Orthopaedics and Orthodontics for Cleft Lip and Palate, 1983; articles in dental and med. jls. *Recreations:* leisure painting, sailing in summertime, walking in wintertime. *Address:* 26 Heol Tyn y Cae, Rhiwbina, Cardiff CF4 6DJ. *T:* Cardiff (01222) 613439.

ROBERTSON, Patrick Allan Pearson, CMG 1956; *b* 11 Aug. 1913; *s* of A. N. McI. Robertson; *m* 1st, 1939, Penelope Margaret Gaskell (*d* 1966); one *s* two *d*; 2nd, 1975, Lady Stewart-Richardson. *Educ:* Sedbergh School; King's College, Cambridge. Cadet, Tanganyika, 1936; Asst Dist Officer, 1938; Clerk of Exec. and Legislative Councils, 1945–46; Dist Officer, 1948; Principal Asst Sec., 1949; Financial Sec., Aden, 1951; Asst Sec., Colonial Office, 1956–57; Chief Sec., Zanzibar, 1958; Civil Sec., Zanzibar, 1961–64; Deputy British Resident, Zanzibar, 1963–64; retired, 1964. Associate Member, Commonwealth Parliamentary Association. Freeman, City of London. *Recreations:* golf, tennis, fishing. *Address:* Lynedale, Longcross, Chertsey, Surrey KT16 0DP. *T:* Ottershaw (01932) 872329. *Club:* Commonwealth Trust.

See also Sir Simon Stewart-Richardson, Bt.

ROBERTSON, Raymond Scott; MP (C) Aberdeen South, since 1992; Parliamentary Under-Secretary of State, Scottish Office, since 1995; *b* 11 Dec. 1959; *s* of James and Marion Robertson. *Educ:* Glasgow Univ. (MA Hist. and Politics); Jordanhill Coll. Teacher, Hist. and Mod. Studies, Smithycroft Secondary Sch., Glasgow, 1982–83, Dumbarton Acad., 1983–89; NE Political Dir, 1989–92, Vice-Chm., 1993–95, Scottish Cons. Party. PPS to Min. of State, NI Office, 1994–95. *Address:* House of Commons, SW1A 0AA. *T:* 0171–219 3000.

ROBERTSON, (Richard) Ross, RSA, FRBS; DA; sculptor; *b* Aberdeen, 10 Sept. 1914; *s* of Rev. R. R. Robertson; *m* Kathleen May Matts; two *d. Educ:* Glasgow School of Art; Gray's School of Art, Aberdeen (DA). Lectr, Gray's Sch. of Art, 1946–79. FRBS 1963 (ARBS 1951); RSA 1977 (ARSA 1969). *Recreation:* study of art. *Address:* Creaguir, Woodlands Road, Rosemount, Blairgowrie, Perthshire PH10 7JX.

ROBERTSON, Robert, CBE 1967; JP; Member, Strathclyde Regional Council, 1974–86; *b* 15 Aug. 1909; *s* of late Rev. William Robertson, MA; *m* 1938, Jean, *d* of late James Moffatt, MA, Invermay, Broomhill, Glasgow; one *s* one *d. Educ:* Forres Academy; Royal Technical Coll., Glasgow. Civil Engr, retd 1969. Mem., Eastwood Dist Council, 1952–58; Chm., Renfrewshire Educn Cttee, 1962–73; Convener, Renfrewshire County Council, 1973–75 (Mem., 1958); Mem., Convention of Scottish Local Authorities, 1975–86. Chm., Sec. of State's Cttee on Supply and Trng of Teachers for Further Educn, 1962–78; Chm., Nat. Cttee for Inservice Trng of Teachers, 1965–78. Mem. Scottish Council for: Research in Educn, 1962–80; Commercial Admin. and Professional Educn, 1960–69; Development of Industry, 1973–75. Chm., Sch. of Further Educn for training of teachers in Scotland, 1969–83. Governor: Jordanhill Coll. of Educn, 1966–83; Watt Memorial and Reid Kerr Colls, 1966–75, 1977–86. Member: Scottish Nat. School Camps Assoc., 1975–80; Scottish Assoc. of Young Farmers' Clubs, 1975–83; Glasgow Educnl Trust, 1978–86; Hutchison Educnl Trust, 1978–86; Council, Glasgow Coll. of Bldg and Printing, 1978–86. Fellow, Educnl Inst. of Scotland (FEIS), at Stirling Univ., 1970; Hon. Warden, Co. of Renfrew, Ont., Canada, 1970. JP Renfrewshire, 1958. *Publications:* Robertson Report on: The Training of Teachers in Further Education (HMSO), 1965. *Recreations:* fishing, painting. *Address:* 24 Broadwood Park, Alloway, Ayrshire KA7 4UR. *T:* Alloway (01292) 443820; Castlehill, Maybole, Ayrshire KA19 8JT. *T:* Dunure (01292) 500337. *Club:* RNVR (Scotland).

ROBERTSON, Robert Henry; Australian diplomat, retired; President, Argentina–Australia Chamber of Commerce of Victoria, since 1993; *b* 23 Dec. 1929; *s* of James Rowland Robertson and Hester Mary (*née* Kay); *m*; 2nd, 1958, Jill Bryant Uther (marr. diss. 1982); two *s* one *d*; 3rd, 1986, Isabelle Costa de Beauregard, French Consul-Gen., Melbourne, *d* of Comte and Comtesse René Costa de Beauregard. *Educ:* Geelong Church of England Grammar Sch.; Trinity Coll., Univ. of Melbourne (LLB). Third Secretary, Australian High Commn, Karachi, 1954–56; Second Sec., Mission to UN, New York, 1958–61; First Sec., later Counsellor, Washington, 1964–67; Ambassador to Jugoslavia, Romania and Bulgaria, 1971–73; Asst Sec., Personnel Br., Dept of Foreign Affairs, Canberra, 1974–75; First Asst Sec., Western Div., 1975–76, Management and Foreign Service Div., 1976–77; Ambassador to Italy, 1977–81; Dep. High Comr in London, 1981–84; Perm. Rep. to UN in Geneva, 1984–88; Ambassador to Argentina, Uruguay and Paraguay, 1989–92. Chm., Exec. Cttee, UN High Comr for Refugees, 1987–88. *Address:* 18 Derby Street, Armadale, Vic 3143, Australia. *T:* and *Fax:* (3) 98229447. *Club:* Melbourne.

ROBERTSON, Ross; *see* Robertson, R. R.

ROBERTSON, Prof. Sir Rutherford (Ness), AC 1980; Kt 1972; CMG 1968; DSc; PhD; FRS 1961; FAA; Emeritus Professor; *b* 29 Sept. 1913; *o c* of Rev. J. Robertson, MA, and Josephine Robertson; *m* 1937, Mary Helen Bruce Rogerson; one *s. Educ:* St Andrew's Coll., NZ; Univ. of Sydney; St John's Coll., Cambridge (Hon. Fellow 1973). DSc Sydney 1961; FAA 1954. Sydney Univ. Science Res. Schol., 1934–35, Linnean Macleay Fell., 1935–36. Exhibn of 1851 Res. Schol., 1936–39; Res. at Botany Sch., Cambridge, in plant physiology, 1936–39, PhD 1939; Asst Lectr, later Lectr, Botany Sch., Univ. of Sydney, 1939–46; Sen. Res. Offr, later Chief Res. Offr, Div. of Food Preservation, CSIRO, 1946–59 (res. in plant physiol. and biochem.); Sydney University: jointly in charge of Plant Physiol. Unit, 1952–59, Hon. Res. Associate, 1954–59; Hon. Vis., Sch. of Biol. Scis, 1979–87; Visiting Prof., Univ. of Calif, Los Angeles, 1958–59; Kerney Foundn Lectr, Univ. of Calif, Berkeley, 1959; Mem. Exec., CSIRO 1959–62; Prof. of Botany, Univ. of Adelaide, 1962–69, now Emeritus; Dir, Res. Sch. of Biol Scis, ANU, 1973–78, now Emeritus Professor (Master, University House, 1969–72); Pro-Chancellor, ANU, 1984–86. Chm., Aust. Res. Grants Cttee, 1965–69; Dep. Chm., Aust. Sci. and Tech. Council, 1977–81. Pres. Linnean Soc. of NSW, 1949; Hon. Sec. Austr. Nat. Res. Council, 1951–55; President: Australian Academy of Science, 1970–74 (Sec. Biological Sciences, 1957–58); Aust. and NZ Assoc. for the Advancement of Science, 1964–66; XIII Internat. Botanical Congress, Sydney, 1981. Patron, Aust. Cttee, Cambridge Commonwealth Trust, 1993–. Corresp. Mem., Amer. Soc. of Plant Physiologists, 1953; For. Associate, US Nat. Acad. of Scis, 1962; Hon. Mem., Royal Soc. of NZ, 1971; Hon. FRSE 1983; For. Mem., Amer. Philosophical Soc., 1971; For. Hon. Mem., Amer. Acad. of Arts and Scis, 1973. Three Societies Lecture, 1988. Hon. DSc: Tasmania, 1965; Monash, 1970; ANU, 1979; Hon ScD Cambridge, 1969. Clarke Meml Medal, Royal Soc. of NSW, 1955; Farrer Meml Medal, 1963; ANZAAS Medal, 1968; Mueller Medal, 1970; Burnet Medal, 1975. *Publications:* (with G. E. Briggs, FRS, and A. B. Hope) Electrolytes and Plant Cells, 1961; Protons, Electrons, Phosphorylation and Active Transport, 1968; The Lively Membranes, 1983; various scientific papers on plant physiology and biochemistry. *Recreations:* reading, water colours. *Address:* PO Box 9, Binalong, NSW 2584, Australia. *Club:* Union (Sydney).

ROBERTSON, Brig. Sidney Park, MBE 1962; TD 1967; JP; Vice Lord-Lieutenant of Orkney, 1987–90; Director, S. & J. D. Robertson Group Ltd (Chairman, 1965–79); *b* 12 March 1914; *s* of John Davie Manson Robertson and Elizabeth Park Sinclair; *m* 1940, Elsa Miller Croy; one *s* one *d. Educ:* Kirkwall Grammar Sch.; Edinburgh Univ. (BCom 1939). MIBS 1936. Served War; commnd RA, 1940 (despatches, NW Europe, 1945). Managerial posts, Anglo-Iranian Oil Co., ME, 1946–51; Manager, Operation/Sales, Southern Div., Shell Mex and BP, 1951–54; founded Robertson firm, 1954. Chm., Orkney Hosps Bd of Management/Orkney Health Bd, 1965–79. Maj. comdg 861 (Ind.) LAA Batt., RA (Orkney and Zetland) TA, 1956–61; Lt-Col comdg Lovat Scouts, TA, 1962–65; CRA 51st Highland Div., TA, 1966–67 (Brig.); Hon. Col, 102 (Ulster and Scottish) Light Air Defence Regt, RA (TA), 1975–80; Hon. Col Comdt, RA, 1977–80; Chm., RA Council of Scotland, 1980–84; Vice Pres., Nat. Artillery Assoc., 1977–; Hon. Vice Pres., Royal British Legion, Orkney, 1975–; Hon. President: Orkney Bn, Boys' Bde, 1972–; Friends of St Magnus Cathedral, 1994; Vice-Pres., RNLI, 1985–. Pres., Villars Curling Club, 1978–80, 1986–88. DL Orkney, 1968; Hon. Sheriff, Grampian, Highlands and Islands, 1969–. Freedom of Orkney, 1990. *Recreations:* travel, hill walking, angling. *Address:* Daisybank, Kirkwall, Orkney KW15 1LX. *T:* Kirkwall (01856) 872085. *Clubs:* Army and Navy, Caledonian; New (Edinburgh).

ROBERTSON, Simon Manwaring; Deputy Chairman, Kleinwort Benson, since 1992; *b* 4 March 1941; *s* of David Lars Manwaring Robertson, *qv*; *m* 1965, Virginia Norman; one *s* two *d. Educ:* Eton. Joined Kleinwort Benson, 1963; Dir, 1977–. *Recreations:* ski-ing, golf, tennis. *Address:* Kleinwort Benson Ltd, 20 Fenchurch Street, EC3. *Club:* Boodle's.

ROBERTSON, Stanley Stewart John, CEng, FIEE; HM Chief Inspecting Officer of Railways, Health and Safety Executive, since 1993; *b* 14 July 1938; *s* of Jock Stanley Robertson and Florence Kathleen Robertson (*née* Carpenter); *m* 1961, Valerie Housley; two *s* two *d. Educ:* Liverpool Poly. (Dip. EE 1961). FIEE 1987; MCIT 1994. Student engrg apprentice, UKAEA, 1956–62; Asst Electrical Engr, CEGB, 1961–67; Elec. Engrg Manager, Shell Chemicals UK, 1967–74; Health and Safety Executive: Sen. Electrical Inspector, 1974–77; Dep. Superintending Inspector, 1977–80; Superintending Inspector, 1980–91; Dep. Chief Inspector and Regl Dir, 1991–93. Chairman: Rly Industry Adv. Cttee, HSC, 1993–; Nat. Inspection Council for Elec. Installation Contracting, 1993–95. Non-exec. Dir, NQA Ltd, 1993–. *Publications:* tech. papers on electrical safety matters. *Recreations:* listening to music, gardening. *Address:* HM Railway Inspectorate, Rose Court, 2 Southwark Bridge, SE1 9HS. *T:* 0171–717 6501.

ROBERTSON, Toby, (Sholto David Maurice Robertson), OBE 1978; director and actor, theatre, opera and television; Director, Theatr Clwyd, Mold, 1985–92; *s* of David Lambert Robertson and Felicity Douglas (*née* Tomlin); *m* 1963, Teresa Jane McCulloch (marr. diss. 1981); two *s* two *d. Educ:* Stowe; Trinity Coll., Cambridge (BA 1952, MA 1981). Formerly an actor. Dir. first prof. prodn, The Iceman Cometh, New Shakespeare, Liverpool, 1958. Dir. plays, London, Pitlochry and Richmond, Yorks, and for RSC, 1959–63. Member: Bd, Prospect Productions Ltd, 1964– (Artistic Dir, Prospect Theatre Co., 1964–79); Bd, Cambridge Theatre Co., 1970–74; Director: Old Vic Theatre, 1977–80, Old Vic Co., 1979–80; Acting Co., Kennedy Centre, Washington, 1983; Associate Dir, Circle Rep., New York, 1983–84. Drama Advr, Argo Records, 1979–; Prof. of Theatre, Brooklyn Coll., City Univ. NY, 1981–82; Hon. Prof. of Drama, 1987–90, Hon. Prof. of English, 1990–92, UCNW. Lectures: Wilson Meml, Cambridge Univ., 1974; Hamlet, Athens Univ., 1978; Rikstheatre, Stockholm, 1980; Hamlet, Gulbenkian Foundn, Lisbon, 1987. Director of over 40 prodns for *Prospect Theatre Co.*, many staged in London and Edinburgh, 1964–79, including: The Soldier's Fortune; You Never Can Tell; The Confederacy; The Importance of Being Earnest; The Square; Howard's End; The Man of Mode; Macbeth; The Tempest; The Gamecock; A Murder of No Importance; A Room with a View; No Man's Land; The Beggar's Opera; The Servant of Two Masters; Edward II; Much Ado About Nothing; Boswell's Life of Johnson; Venice Preserved; King Lear and Love's Labour's Lost (Australian tour); Alice in Wonderland; Richard III; Ivanov; The Grand Tour; Twelfth Night, Pericles and The Royal Hunt of the Sun (internat. fests, Moscow, Leningrad and Hong Kong); The Pilgrim's Progress; A Month in the Country (Chichester Fest.); directed for *Old Vic Co.*: War Music; Antony and Cleopatra; Smith of Smiths; Buster; The Lunatic, The Lover and The Poet; Romeo and Juliet; The Government Inspector; The Padlock; Ivanov; Hamlet (Elsinore, and first visit by a British co., China, 1980); directed for *Theatr Clwyd*: Medea (also Young Vic), 1986; Barnaby and the Old Boys, 1987 (also Vaudeville, 1989); Edward III (jtly adapted, attrib. William Shakespeare) (also Cambridge and Taormina Fests), 1987; Captain Carvallo, 1988, transf. Greenwich; Revenger's Tragedy, 1988; The Old Devils, 1989; Othello, 1989; The Importance of Being Earnest, 1990; Enemy of the People, 1991, transf. Lyric Hammersmith; The Cherry Orchard, 1991 (also Brighton Festival); Marching Song, 1992; Hamlet (also Nat. Tour), 1991–92; The Seagull, 1992; directed *other productions*, including: Next Time I'll Sing to You, Greenwich, 1980; Beggar's Opera, Lyric, Hammersmith, 1980; Measure for Measure, People's Arts Theatre, Peking, 1981; Pericles, NY, 1981 (Obie award, 1982); Night and Day (opening prodn), 1982 and The Taming of the Shrew, 1983, Huntingdon Theatre Co., Boston; The Tempest (opening prodn), New Cleveland Playhouse, 1983; Love's Labour's Lost, Shakespeare Workshop, 1983, Circle Rep., 1984, NYC; York Cycle of Mystery Plays, York Fest., 1984; Midsummer Night's Dream, Open Air Theatre, Regent's Park, 1985; (jt dir) Antony and Cleopatra, The Taming of the Shrew, Haymarket, 1986; Coriolanus, festivals in Spain, 1986, You Never Can Tell, Haymarket, 1988; Richard II, Folger Theatre, Washington; Trelawny of the 'Wells', Comedy, 1992; The Old Devils, Philadelphia, 1993; The Taming of the Shrew, Regent's Park, 1993; Macbeth, Tel Aviv, 1994. *Opera:* for Scottish Opera, incl.: A Midsummer Night's Dream, 1972; Hermiston, 1975; Marriage of Figaro, 1977; for Opera Co. of Philadelphia: Elisir d'Amore (with Pavarotti and winners of Pavarotti competition), Dido and Aeneas, Oedipus Rex, 1982; Faust, 1984; Wiesbaden: A Midsummer Night's Dream, 1984; NY City Opera: Barber of Seville, 1984; Wexford Opera: The Kiss, 1984. Asst Dir, Lord of the Flies (film), 1961. Dir of more than 25 television prodns, incl.: The Beggar's Opera; Richard II; Edward II. *Recreations:* painting, sailing. *Address:* 210 Brixton Road, SW9. *Club:* Garrick.

ROBERTSON, Vernon Colin, OBE 1977; self employed consultant, specialising in environmental issues in developing countries; *b* 19 July 1922; *s* of Colin John Trevelyan Robertson and Agnes Muriel Robertson (*née* Dolphin). *Educ:* Imperial Service College, Windsor; Univ. of Edinburgh (BSc Agr subs. Forestry); Univ. of Cambridge (Dip Agr 1950; MA). Joined Home Guard, 1940; enlisted RA, 1941, commissioned 1942; served 12th HAC Regt RHA, N Africa, Italy, Austria, 1942–45 (despatches 1945); with 1st Regt RHA, Italy, 1945–46 (Adjutant). Staff, Sch. of Agric., Cambridge, 1950; joined Hunting Aerosurveys Ltd, 1953, as ecologist heading new natural resources survey dept; developed this into overseas land and water resource consultancy, renamed Hunting Technical Services Ltd (Managing Director, 1959–77; after retirement continuing as Director and Consultant until 1987), development planning in Africa, Asia and Latin America. Director: Hunting Surveys and Consultants Ltd, 1962–77; Groundwater Development Consultants (International) Ltd, 1975–85; Vice-Chm. and acting Chm., Environmental Planning Commn, Internat. Union for Conservation of Nature, 1972–78; Chm., Trop. Agric. Assoc. (UK), 1981–85; Mem. Bd, Commonwealth Develt Corp., 1982–90. *Publications:* articles in learned jls. *Recreations:* natural history, esp. plants and birds, gardening, painting, photography, music, sailing. *Address:* Brickfields, Quay Lane, Kirby-le-Soken, Essex CO13 0DP. *T:* Frinton-on-Sea (01255) 674585. *Clubs:* Honourable Artillery Company, Farmers'.

ROBERTSON, Prof. William Bruce, MD, FRCPath; Professor of Histopathology, St George's Hospital Medical School, 1968–84, now Emeritus; Director of Studies, Royal College of Pathologists, 1984–92; *b* 17 Jan. 1923; *s* of late William Bruce Robertson and Jessie Robertson (*née* McLean); *m* 1948, Mary Patricia Burrows two *d. Educ:* The Academy, Forfar; Univ. of St Andrews. BSc 1944, MB ChB 1947, MD 1959; MRCPath 1963, FRCPath 1969. Junior appts, Cumberland Infirm., Carlisle, 1947–48; RAMC, E Africa, 1948–50; Registrar Pathology, Cumberland Infirm., 1950–53; Demonstr Pathology, Royal Victoria Infirm., Newcastle upon Tyne, 1953–56; Sen. Lectr Pathology, Univ. of the West Indies, Jamaica, 1956–64; Reader in Morbid Anatomy, St George's Hosp. Med. Sch., Univ. of London, 1964–68. Visiting Professor: Louisiana State Univ., New Orleans, USA, 1961–62; Katholieke Universiteit te Leuven, Belgium, 1972–73. *Publications:* scientific papers and book chapters in various med. jls and publns. *Address:* 3 Cambisgate, Church Road, Wimbledon, SW19 5AL. *T:* 0181–947 6731.

ROBERTSON, Air Cdre William Duncan, CBE 1968; Royal Air Force, retired; Senior Air Staff Officer, HQ 38 Group, Royal Air Force, 1975–77; *b* 24 June 1922; *s* of William and Helen Robertson, Aberdeen; *m* 1st, 1952, Doreen Mary (*d* 1963), *d* of late Comdr G. A. C. Sharp, DSC, RN (retd); one *s* one *d*; 2nd, 1968, Ute, *d* of late Dr R. Koenig, Wesel, West Germany; one *d*. *Educ:* Robert Gordon's Coll., Aberdeen. Sqdn Comdr, No 101 Sqdn, 1953–55, No 207 Sqdn, 1959–61. Gp Dir, RAF Staff Coll., 1962–65; Station Comdr, RAF Wildenrath, 1965–67; Dep. Dir, Administrative Plans, 1967; Dir of Ops (Plans), 1968; Dir of Ops Air Defence and Overseas, 1969–71; RCDS, 1971–72; SASO RAF Germany, 1972–74; SASO 46 Group, 1975. *Recreations:* golf, tennis. *Address:* Parkhouse Farm, Leigh, Surrey RH2 8QE. *Club:* Royal Air Force.

ROBERTSON, (William) Nelson, FCII; Group Chief Executive, General Accident plc, 1990–95; *b* 14 Dec. 1933; *s* of James Bogue and Eleanor Robertson; *m* 1964, Sheila Catherine Spence; two *d*. *Educ:* Berwick Grammar Sch.; Edinburgh Univ. (MA). FCII 1963. Served RA, 1955–57. General Accident Fire & Life Assurance Corporation Ltd, later General Accident plc, 1958–95: Asst Gen. Man. (Overseas), 1972; Gen. Man., 1980; Dir, 1984; Dep. Chief Gen. Man., 1989. Dir, Morrison Construction Gp, 1995–. *Recreations:* hill-walking, gardening. *Address:* General Accident plc, Pitheavlis, Perth PH2 0NH. *T:* Perth (01738) 621202. *Club:* Caledonian.

ROBEY, Douglas John Brett, CMG 1960; HM Diplomatic Service, retired; *b* 7 Aug. 1914; *s* of late E. J. B. and Margaret Robey; *m* 1943, Elizabeth, *d* of late Col David D. Barrett, US Army; two *s* one *d*. *Educ:* Cranleigh School; St John's College, Oxford; Ecole des Sciences Politiques, Paris. BA (History); Editor of The Cherwell. Joined HM Foreign Service, 1937. Served in China, USA, Paris, Berlin, Baghdad; Consul-Gen., Chicago, 1966–69; Ambassador and Permanent UK Representative, Council of Europe, Strasbourg, 1969–74. *Publication:* The Innovator, 1945. *Recreations:* reading, writing, and the Niebelung Ring. *Address:* Allan Down House, Rotherfield, East Sussex TN6 3RT. *T:* Rotherfield (01892) 852329. *Club:* Cercle Européen de Strasbourg (Hon. Life Pres.).

ROBIN, Dr Gordon de Quetteville; Director, 1958–82, Senior Associate, since 1982, Scott Polar Research Institute, University of Cambridge; Fellow since 1964 and Vice-Master, 1974–78, Darwin College, Cambridge; *b* Melbourne, 17 Jan. 1921; *s* of Reginald James Robin and Emily Mabel Robin; *m* 1953, Jean Margaret Fortt, Bath; two *d*. *Educ:* Wesley Coll., Melbourne; Melbourne Univ. ScD Cantab, MSc Melbourne, PhD Birmingham; FInstP. War service, RANVR: anti-submarine, 1942–44; submarine, RN, 1944–45 (Lieut). Physics Dept, Birmingham Univ.: research student, lectr, ICI Research Fellow, 1945–56; Sen. Fellow, Geophysics Dept, ANU, 1957–58. Meteorologist and Officer i/c Signy Is, South Orkneys, with Falkland Is Dependencies Survey, 1947–48; Physicist and Sen. British Mem. of Norwegian-British-Swedish Antarctic Expedn, 1949–52 (made first effective measurements of Antarctic ice thickness); further researches in Antarctic in 1959, 1967, 1969, 1974, and in Arctic, 1964, 1966, 1973; Sec., 1958–70, Pres., 1970–74, and Hon. Mem., Scientific Cttee on Antarctic Research of ICSU; Mem. Adv. Bd, Geophysical Inst., Univ. of Alaska, 1974–81. President: Antarctic Club, 1974; Arctic Club, 1986; Chm., Trans Antarctic Assoc., 1992–. Hon. DPhil Stockholm, 1978. Kongens Fortjensmedalje, Norway, 1952; Back Grant, RGS, 1953; Bruce Medal, RSE, 1953; Polar Medal, 1956; Patrons Medal, RGS, 1974; Seligman Crystal, Internat. Glaciological Soc., 1986. *Publications:* scientific reports of Norwegian-British-Swedish Antarctic Expedition (Glaciology III, 1958; Upper Winds, 1972); (ed) Annals of the IGY, Vol. 41, Glaciology, 1967; (ed and contrib.) The Climatic Record in Polar Ice Sheets, 1983; papers and articles on polar glaciology in scientific jls. *Recreations:* Mallorca, walking. *Address:* 10 Melbourne Place, Cambridge CB1 1EQ. *T:* Cambridge (01223) 358463.

ROBIN, Ian (Gibson), FRCS; retired; *b* 22 May 1909; *s* of Dr Arthur Robin, Edinburgh, and Elizabeth Parker; *m* 1939, Shelagh Marian (*d* 1978), *d* of late Colonel C. M. Croft; one *s* two *d*. *Educ:* Merchiston Castle School; Clare College, Cambridge. MA, MB, BCh Cantab 1933; LRCP 1933; FRCS 1935. Guy's Hosp.; late House Phys.; Sen. Science Schol., 1930; Treasurer's Gold Medals in Clinical Surgery and Medicine, 1933; Arthur Durham Travelling Schol., 1933; Charles Oldham Prize in Ophthalmology, 1933; Registrar and Chief Clin. Asst, ENT Dept, 1935–36; late Consulting ENT Surgeon: Royal Chest Hosp., 1939–44; Royal Northern Hosp., 1937–74; St Mary's Hosp., Paddington, 1948–74; Princess Louise (Kensington) Hosp. for Children, 1948–69; Paddington Green Children's Hosp., 1969–74; Surgeon EMS, Sector III London Area, 1939–45. Late Vice-Chm., Royal Nat. Institute for the Deaf. Member Hunterian Soc.; Council of Nat. Deaf Children's Soc.; Past Pres., Brit. Assoc. of Otolaryngologists, 1971–72; Past Pres., Laryng. Section, RSM, 1967–68; Vice-Pres., Otolog. Section, RSM, 1967–68, 1969; late Examiner for DLO of RCS of England. Lectures: Yearsley, 1968; Jobson Horne, 1969. Mem., Royal Water-Colour Soc. *Publications:* (jt) Diseases of Ear, Nose and Throat (Synopsis Series), 1957; papers in various med. treatises, jls, etc. *Recreations:* golf, gardening, sketching; formerly athletics and Rugby. *Address:* 28 The Vineries, Nizells Avenue, Hove BN3 1PY. *Clubs:* Hawks (Cambridge); Achilles (Great Britain); Hampstead Golf.

ROBINS, David Anthony; Chief Executive Officer, UBS Ltd, since 1994; *b* 2 Sept. 1949; *s* of John Anthony Robins and Ruth Wenefrede Robins (*née* Thomas); *m* 1981, Joanna Christina Botting; two *s* one *d*. *Educ:* University Coll. London (BSc Econ). Economic Analyst, Investment and Res. Dept, Commonwealth Bank, Sydney, Australia, 1973–74; Economist, Overseas Dept, Bank of England, 1976–78; Exec., Japanese Dept, James Capel, 1978–80; Chief Internat. Economist, Phillips & Drew, 1980–86; Hd of Res., UBS Phillips & Drew Ltd, Tokyo, 1986–88; Hd, Internat. Securities Dept, UBS Securities Inc., NY, 1988–90; Functional Advr, Securities and Res., Union Bank of Switzerland, Zurich, 1990–93. *Recreations:* tennis, swimming, walking, reading, theatre, music, film. *Address:* UBS Ltd, 100 Liverpool Street, EC2M 2RH. *T:* 0171–901 3667, *Fax:* 0171–901 4981.

ROBINS, John Vernon Harry; Chief Executive, Guardian Royal Exchange plc, since 1994; *b* 21 Feb. 1939; *s* of Col William Vernon Harry Robins, DSO and Charlotte Mary (*née* Grier); *m* 1962, Elizabeth Mary Banister; two *s* one *d*. *Educ:* Winchester Coll. Nat. Service, 2nd Lieut 2/10 Princess Mary's Own Gurkha Rifles, 1959–61. Man. Dir, SNS Communications Ltd, 1966–74; Chief Exec., Bally Gp (UK) Ltd, 1974–79; Group Financial Director: Fitch Lovell plc, 1979–84; Willis Faber, subseq. Willis Corroon Gp plc, 1984–94. *Recreations:* clocks, Baroque music, grand-children. *Address:* (office) Royal Exchange, EC3V 3LS. *Club:* Brooks's.

ROBINS, Group Captain Leonard Edward, CBE (mil.) 1979; AE 1958 (and 2 clasps); DL; Representative DL, Borough of Wandsworth, since 1979; Inspector, Royal Auxiliary Air Force, 1973–83; *b* 2 Nov 1921; *yr s* of late Joseph Robins, Bandmaster RM, and late Louisa Josephine (*née* Kent); *m* 1949, Jean Ethelwynne (Headteacher) (*d* 1985), *d* of late Roy and Bessie Searle, Ryde, IoW. *Educ:* Singlegate, Mitcham, Surrey; City Day Continuation School, EC. Entered Civil Service, GPO, 1936; War service RAF, UK, SEAC, Ceylon, India, 1941–46; resumed with GPO, 1946; Min. of Health, 1948; Min. of Housing and Local Govt, 1962; DoE, 1970–80, retired. Airman, No 3700 (Co. of London) Radar Reporting Unit RAuxAF, 1950; Commissioned 1953, radar branch; transf. to No 1 (Co. of Hertford) Maritime HQ Unit RAuxAF, intelligence duties, 1960; OC No 1 Maritime Headquarters Unit, RAuxAF, 1969–73; Gp Capt., Inspector RAuxAF, 1973. ADC to the Queen, 1974–83. Selected Air Force Mem., Greater London TAVRA, 1973–83 and City of London TAVRA, 1980–84. Lord Mayor of London's personal staff, 1977–78, 1980–81, 1982–83 and 1986–94. Pres., Wandsworth Victim Support Scheme, 1980–87. Trustee, Royal Foundn of Greycoat Hosp., 1983–88. Freeman, City of London, 1976. Coronation Medal, 1953; Silver Jubilee Medal, 1977. Officer of Merit with Swords, SMO Malta, 1986. DL Greater London, 1978–. FIMgt. *Recreations:* naval, military and aviation history; book hunting; kipping; speech writing. *Address:* 16 Summit Way, Upper Norwood, SE19 2PU. *T:* 0181–653 3173. *Club:* Royal Air Force.

ROBINS, Malcolm Owen, CBE 1978; Learned Societies Officer, Royal Society/British Academy, 1979–81; a Director, Science Research Council, 1972–78; *b* 25 Feb. 1918; *s* of late Owen Wilfred Robins and Amelia Ada (*née* Wheelwright); *m* 1944, Frances Mary, *d* of late William and Frances Hand; one *s* one *d*. *Educ:* King Edward's Sch., Stourbridge; The Queen's Coll., Oxford (Open Scholar in Science). MA (Oxon) 1943. On scientific staff of Royal Aircraft Establishment, 1940–57; a Div. Supt in Guided Weapons Dept, RAE, 1955–57; Asst Dir, Guided Weapons, Min. of Supply, London, 1957–58; UK Project Manager for jt UK/USA Space Research programme, and hon. Research Associate, University Coll. London, 1958–62; a Dep. Chief Scientific Officer and Head of Space Research Management Unit, Office of Minister for Science (later Dept of Educn and Science), 1962–65; Head of Astronomy, Space and Radio Div., SRC, 1965–68; a Research Planning post in Min. of Technology (later Dept of Trade and Industry), 1968–72. Vis. Prof., University Coll., London, 1974–77. FInstP 1945; FRAS 1974. *Publications:* (with Sir Harrie Massey) History of British Space Science, 1986; (with K. Proust and S. C. B. Gascoigne) The Creation of the Anglo-Australian Observatory, 1990; papers on space research in scientific jls. *Recreations:* gardening, golf. *Address:* Wychbury, Gorse Lane, Farnham, Surrey GU10 4SD. *T:* Farnham (01252) 723186.

ROBINS, Sir Ralph (Harry), Kt 1988; FEng 1988; FRAeS; Chairman, Rolls-Royce plc, since 1992; *b* 16 June 1932; *s* of Leonard Haddon and Maud Lillian Robins; *m* 1962, Patricia Maureen Grimes; two *d*. *Educ:* Imperial Coll., Univ. of London (BSc, ACGI; FIC). MIMechE; FRAeS 1990. Development Engr, Rolls-Royce, Derby, 1955–66; Exec. Vice-Pres., Rolls-Royce Inc., 1971; Man. Dir, RR Industrial & Marine Div., 1973; Commercial Dir, RR Ltd, 1978; Chm., International Aero Engines AG, 1983–84; Rolls-Royce plc: Man. Dir, 1984–89; Dep. Chm., 1989–92; Chief Exec., 1990–92. Chm., Defence Industries Council, 1986–; Dep. Pres., Soc. of British Aerospace Companies, 1987–88 (Pres., 1986–87). Mem., Council for Sci. and Technology, 1993–. *Recreations:* tennis, golf, music. *Address:* Rolls-Royce plc, 65 Buckingham Gate, SW1E 6AT.

ROBINS, Prof. Robert Henry, FBA 1986; Professor of General Linguistics, 1966–86, now Emeritus, and Dean, Faculty of Arts, 1984–86, University of London; Head of Department of Phonetics and Linguistics, School of Oriental and African Studies, University of London, 1970–85; *b* 1 July 1921; *s* of John Norman Robins, medical practitioner, and Muriel Winifred (*née* Porter); *m* 1953, Sheila Marie Fynn (*d* 1983). *Educ:* Tonbridge Sch.; New Coll., Oxford, 1940–41 and 1945–48, MA 1948; DLit London 1968. Served war, RAF Intelligence, 1942–45. Lectr in Linguistics, Sch. of Oriental and African Studies, London, 1948–55; Reader in General Linguistics, Univ. of London, 1955–65. Mem. Senate, Univ. of London, 1980–85. Research Fellow, Univ. of California, 1951; Vis. Professor: Washington, 1963; Hawaii, 1968; Minnesota, 1971; Florida, 1975; Salzburg, 1977, 1979; Leverhulme Emeritus Fellow, 1990–91. President: Societas Linguistica Europaea, 1974; CIPL, 1977– (British Rep., 1970–77); Philological Soc., 1988–92 (Hon. Sec., 1961–88). Mem., Academia Europaea, 1991. Hon. Mem., Linguistic Soc. of Amer., 1981–. *Publications:* Ancient and Mediaeval Grammatical Theory in Europe, 1951; The Yurok Language, 1958; General Linguistics: an introductory survey, 1964; A Short History of Linguistics, 1967; Diversions of Bloomsbury, 1970; Ideen- und Problemgeschichte der Sprachwissenschaft, 1973; System and Structure in Sundanese, 1983; The Byzantine Grammarians: their place in history, 1993; articles in Language, TPS, BSOAS, Lingua, Foundations of Language, Man, etc. *Recreations:* gardening, travel. *Address:* 65 Dome Hill, Caterham, Surrey CR3 6EF. *T:* Caterham (01883) 343778. *Clubs:* Athenæum, Commonwealth Trust.

ROBINS, William Edward Charles; Metropolitan Stipendiary Magistrate, 1971–89; solicitor; *b* 13 March 1924; *s* of late E. T. and late L. R. Robins; *m* 1946, Jean Elizabeth, *yr d* of Bruce and Flora Forsyth, Carlyle, Saskatchewan, Canada; one *s* one *d*. *Educ:* St Alban's Sch. Served War: commissioned as Navigator, RAF, 1943–47. Admitted as a Solicitor, 1948; joined Metropolitan Magistrates' Courts' service, 1950; Dep. Chief Clerk, 1951–60; Chief Clerk, 1960–67; Sen. Chief Clerk, Thames Petty Sessional Div., 1968–71. Sec., London Magistrates' Clerks' Assoc., 1953–60 (Chm. 1965–71). Member, Home Office working parties, on: Magistrates' Courts' Rules; Legal Aid; Motor Vehicle Licences; Fines and Maintenance Orders Enforcement, 1968–71; Member: Lord Chancellor's Sub-Cttee on Magistrates' Courts' Rules, 1969–70; Adv. Council on Misuse of Drugs, 1973–86. Fellow Commoner, Corpus Christi Coll., Cambridge, Michaelmas 1975. *Recreations:* touring off the beaten track, music, theatre.

ROBINS, Maj.-Gen. William John Pherrick, OBE 1984 (MBE 1979); CEng, FIEE; Director General, Information and Communication Services, Ministry of Defence, since 1995; *b* 28 July 1941; *s* of John Robins and Helen Hamilton (*née* Urry); *m* 1st, 1967, Anne Marie Cornu (marr. diss. 1985); one *s* one *d*; 2nd, 1993, Kathy Walsh. *Educ:* Henry Mellish Grammar Sch., Nottingham; Welbeck Coll.; RMA Sandhurst; RMC Shrivenham (BSc (Eng) London, 1966); Staff Coll., Camberley; Cranfield Inst. of Technology (MPhil (Information Systems) 1993). CEng 1991, FIEE 1992. 16 Parachute Bde, 1966–70; Special Communications, 1970–72; Germany and UK, 1972–79; CO 14 Signal Regt (Electronic Warfare), 1979–82; Mil. Asst to MGO, 1982–84; Army ADP Co-ordinator, 1984–87; Project Dir, 1987–89; Dir, CIS (Army), 1989–92; ACDS (Command, Control, Communications and Information Systems), 1992–94. Hon. Fellow, Sch. of Defence Management, Cranfield Univ., 1994. *Recreations:* cartoons, looking at pictures, running, hill walking, fussing over details. *Address:* Main Building, Ministry of Defence, Whitehall, SW1A 2HB; c/o Barclays Bank, 2 Victoria Street, SW1H 0ND. *Club:* Special Forces.

ROBINSON, family name of **Baron Martonmere.**

ROBINSON, Alastair; *see* Robinson, F. A. L.

ROBINSON, Sir Albert (Edward Phineas), Kt 1962; Director, E. Oppenheimer and Son (Pty) Ltd, since 1963; *b* 30 December 1915; *s* of late Charles Phineas Robinson (formerly MP Durban, S Africa) and of late Mabel V. Robinson; *m* 1st, 1944, Mary Judith Bertram (*née* Bertish) (*d* 1973); four *d*; 2nd, 1975, Mrs M. L. Royston-Piggot (*née* Barrett). *Educ:* Durban High School; Universities of Stellenbosch, London (LSE), Cambridge (Trinity Coll.) and Leiden; MA (Cantab). Pres., Footlights Club, Cambridge, 1936–37. Barrister, Lincoln's Inn. Served War of 1939–45, in Imperial Light Horse, Western Desert, N Africa, 1940–43. Member Johannesburg City Council, 1945–48 (Leader United Party in Council, 1946–47); MP (United Party), S African Parlt, 1947–53; became permanent resident in Rhodesia, 1953. Dep. Chm., General Mining and Finance Corp. Ltd, 1963–71; Chairman: Johannesburg Consolidated Investment Co., 1971–80; Rustenburg Platinum Mines, 1971–80; Australian Anglo American Ltd, 1980–85; Director: Anglo American Corp., Zimbabwe Ltd, 1964–86; Founders Bldg Soc., 1954–86; Rand Mines Ltd,

1965–71; Anglo American Corp. of SA Ltd, 1965–88; Johannesburg Consolidated Investment Co., 1965–85; Standard Bank Investment Corp., 1972–86; Director, in Zimbabwe and South Africa, of various Mining, Financial and Industrial Companies. Chm. Central African Airways Corp., 1957–61. Member, Monckton Commission, 1960; High Commissioner in the UK for the Federation of Rhodesia and Nyasaland, 1961–63. Chancellor, Univ. of Bophuthatswana, 1980–91. Hon. DComm Univ. of Bophuthatswana, 1990. *Recreations:* people, music and conversation. *Address:* 36 Smits Road, Dunkeld, Johannesburg 2196, South Africa. *Clubs:* Carlton; City (Capetown).

ROBINSON, Alwyn Arnold; Managing Director, Daily Mail, 1975–89; *b* 15 Nov. 1929. Mem., Press Council, 1977–87 (Jt Vice-Chm., 1982–83).

ROBINSON, Ann; *see* Robinson, M. A.

ROBINSON, Dr Ann; Director General, National Association of Pension Funds Ltd, since 1995; *b* 28 Jan. 1937; *d* of Edwin Samuel James and Dora (*née* Thorne); *m* 1961, Michael Finlay Robinson; two *s*. *Educ:* St Anne's Coll., Oxford (MA); McGill Univ. (MA, PhD). Financial journalist, Beaverbrook Newspapers, 1959–61; University Lecturer: Durham, 1962–63; Bristol, 1970–72; Bath, 1972–75; Cardiff, 1972–89 (Sen. Lectr, 1987–89); Head of Policy Unit, Inst. of Dirs, 1989–95. Member: Equal Opportunities Commn, 1980–85; Econ. and Social Cttee, EEC, 1986–93 (Chm., Industry Section, 1990–92); Welsh Arts Council, 1991–93; HEFCW, 1993–; Monopolies and Mergers Commn, 1993–. Dir, WNO, 1992–94. Member: Council, RIIA, 1991–; Bd of Academic Govs, Richmond Coll., London, 1992–; Bd of Govs, Commonwealth Inst., 1992–. Contested (C) S E Wales, EP election, 1979. *Publications:* Parliament and Public Spending, 1978; (jtly) Tax Policy Making in the United Kingdom, 1984; articles in acad. jls and chapters on public expenditure control by Parliament. *Recreations:* Alpine sports (summer and winter), gardening. *Address:* National Association of Pension Funds Ltd, 12–18 Grosvenor Gardens, SW1W 0DH. *T:* 0171–730 0585.

ROBINSON, Anne Josephine; journalist and broadcaster; *b* 26 Sept. 1944; *d* of Bernard James Robinson and Anne Josephine Robinson (*née* Wilson); *m* 1st, 1968, Charles Martin Wilson, *qv* (marr. diss. 1973); one *d*; 2nd 1980, John Penrose. *Educ:* Farnborough Hill Convent; Les Ambassadrices, Paris. Reporter: Daily Mail, 1967–68; Sunday Times, 1968–77; Daily Mirror: Women's Editor, 1979–80; Asst Editor, 1980–93; columnist, 1983–93; columnist: Today, 1993–; The Times, 1993–. Presenter, Anne Robinson Show, Radio 2, 1988–93; presenter and writer: Points of View, BBC TV, 1988–; Watchdog, BBC TV, 1993–. *Recreations:* dogs, houses, gossip, having opinions. *Address:* P. Schnabl Management, 72 Vincent Square, SW1P 2PA. *T:* 0171–630 6955. *Clubs:* Academy; Bibury Cricket (Vice-Pres.), Bibury Tennis (Pres.).

ROBINSON, Arthur Alexander; Director of Computing Centre, University of Wales College of Cardiff (formerly at University of Wales Institute of Science and Technology), 1976–91; *b* 5 Aug. 1924; *o s* of Arthur Robinson and Elizabeth (*née* Thompson); *m* 1956, Sylvia Joyce Wagstaff; two *s* one *d*. *Educ:* Epsom Coll.; Clare Coll., Cambridge (MA); Univ. of Manchester (PhD). English Electric Co. Ltd, 1944; Ferranti Ltd, 1950; Dir and Gen. Man., Univ. of London Atlas Computing Service, 1962; Dir, Univ. of London Computer Centre, 1968; Dir, National Computing Centre Ltd, 1969–74. *Publications:* papers in Proc. IEE. *Recreations:* travel, gardening. *Address:* 6 Portland Close, Penarth, S Glamorgan CF64 3DY.

ROBINSON, (Arthur) Geoffrey, CBE 1978; Chairman, Medway Ports Authority, 1978–87; *b* 22 Aug. 1917; *s* of Arthur Robinson and Frances M. Robinson; *m* 1st, 1943, Patricia MacAllister (*d* 1971); three *s* one *d*; 2nd, 1973, Hon. Mrs Treves, *d* of Rt Hon. Lord Salmon; three step *s* one step *d*. *Educ:* Lincoln Sch.; Jesus Coll., Cambridge (MA); Sch. of Oriental and African Studies, London Univ. Served War, RA, 1939–46. Solicitor, 1948; Treasury Solicitor's Dept, 1954–62; PLA, 1962–66; Man. Dir, Tees and Hartlepool Port Authority, 1966–77; Chm., English Indust. Estates Corp., 1977–83. Member: National Dock Labour Bd, 1972–77; National Ports Council, 1980–81; Chm., British Ports Assoc., 1983–85. *Publications:* Hedingham Harvest, 1977; various articles. *Recreation:* music. *Address:* 6 Archery Square, Deal, Kent CT14 7HP. *T:* Deal (01304) 379056; La Baume, Uzès, 30700 Gard, France. *T:* 66225544. *Club:* United Oxford & Cambridge University.

See also P. H. Robinson.

ROBINSON, Hon. (Arthur Napoleon) Raymond; SC; MP; Prime Minister, Trinidad and Tobago, 1986–91; Leader, National Alliance for Reconstruction, Trinidad and Tobago, 1986–92; *b* 16 Dec. 1926; *s* of late James Alexander Andrew Robinson, Headmaster, and Emily Isabella Robinson; *m* 1961, Patricia Rawlins; one *s* one *d*. *Educ:* Bishop's High Sch., Tobago; St John's Coll., Oxford (Hon. Fellow 1988). LLB (London); MA (PPE) Oxon. Called to Bar, Inner Temple; in practice, 1956–61. Treas., People's Nat. Movt (governing Party) 1956; Mem. Federal Parlt, 1958–; MHR for Tobago East, 1961–71 and 1976–80; Minister of Finance, 1961–66; Dep. Political Leader of Party, 1966; Actg Prime Minister (during his absence), April and Aug. 1967; Minister of External Affairs, Trinidad and Tobago, 1967–68; Chm., Democratic Action Congress, 1971–86; Chm., Tobago House of Assembly, 1980–86. Member: Legal Commn on US Leased Areas under 1941 Agreement, 1959; Industrial Develt Corp., 1960; Council, Univ. of West Indies, 1960–62. Consultant, Foundn for establishment of an Internat. Criminal Court, 1972–75, Exec. Dir, 1976–77. Member: UN Expert Gp on Crime and the Abuse of Power, 1979; Adv. Council, Nuclear Age Peace Foundn, 1994; Pres. and Exec. Mem., Parliamentarians for Global Action, 1995. Hon. DCL Obafemi Awolowo Univ., Nigeria. Dist. Internat. Criminal Law Award, Internat. Criminal Court Foundn, 1977; Dist. Human Develt Award, Internat. Conf. on Human Rights and Humanitarian Law, UN Affiliate, 1983; Commendation Award, and Freeman, City of a Thousand Oaks, Calif, 1987; Dist. Service Award, Calif Lutheran Univ., 1987; Individual of the Year Award, Friends of Tobago Liby Cttee, 1995. Freeman: LA, 1988; Caracas, 1990. KStJ 1992. Gran Cordon, Orden de El Libertador (Venezuela), 1990; Chief of Ile Ife (Nigeria), 1991. *Publications:* The New Frontier and the New Africa, 1961; Fiscal Reform in Trinidad and Tobago, 1966; The Path of Progress, 1967; The Teacher and Nationalism, 1967; The Mechanics of Independence, 1971; Caribbean Man, 1986; articles and addresses. *Address:* 21 Ellerslie Park, Maraval, Trinidad and Tobago; (office) Robinson Street, Scarborough, Trinidad and Tobago.

ROBINSON, Basil William, FBA 1981; retired; *b* 20 June 1912; *o c* of William Robinson and Rebecca Frances Mabel, *d* of Rev. George Gilbanks; *m* 1st, 1945, Ailsa Mary Stewart (*d* 1954); 2nd, 1958, Oriel Hermione Steel; one *s* one *d*. *Educ:* Winchester (Exhibitioner); CCC Oxford. BA 1935; MA, BLitt, 1938. Asst Keeper, Victoria and Albert Museum, 1939. Min. of Home Security, 1939–40. Served as Captain, 2nd Punjab Regt, India, Burma, Malaya, 1943–46. Deputy Keeper, V&A Museum, 1954, Keeper, Dept of Metalwork, 1966–72, Keeper Emeritus, 1972–76. Pres., Royal Asiatic Soc., 1970–73; Vice-Pres., Arms and Armour Soc., 1953; Hon. Pres., Tō-ken Soc. of Great Britain, 1967–93. FSA 1974. *Publications:* A Primer of Japanese Sword-blades, 1955; Persian Miniatures, 1957; Japanese Landscape Prints of the 19th Century, 1957; A Descriptive Catalogue of the Persian Paintings in the Bodleian Library, 1958; Kuniyoshi, 1961; The Arts of the Japanese Sword, 1961, 2nd edn, 1971; Persian Drawings, 1965; part-author, vols 2 and 3, Catalogue of Persian MSS and Miniatures in the Chester Beatty Library, 3 vols, 1958–62; Persian Miniature Painting, 1967; Persian Paintings in the India Office Library, 1976; (ed. and jt author) Islamic painting in the Keir Collection, 1976; Japanese Sword-fittings in the Baur Collection, 1980; Persian Paintings in the John Rylands Library, 1980; Kuniyoshi: the Warrior Prints, 1982 (Uchiyama Meml Prize, Japan Ukiyoe Soc.); Persian Painting and the National Epic (Hertz Lecture, British Acad.), 1983; (jtly) The Aldrich Book of Catches, 1989; Fifteenth Century Persian Painting (Kevorkian Lectures, NY Univ.), 1991; Collection Jean Pozzi, 1992; numerous booklets, articles and reviews on Persian and Japanese art. *Recreations:* catch singing (founder and Chairman, Aldrich Catch Club); cats. *Address:* 41 Redcliffe Gardens, SW10 9JH. *T:* 0171–352 1290. *Club:* Hurlingham.

ROBINSON, Bill; *see* Robinson, P. W.

ROBINSON, Brian Gordon, QFSM 1992; FIFireE; Chief Fire Officer and Chief Executive (formerly Chief Officer), London Fire Brigade, since 1991; *b* 21 April 1947; *s* of Gordon and Theodora Robinson, Colchester, Essex. FIFireE 1992. Joined London Fire Brigade, 1968; Accelerated Promotion Course, 1974, Sen. Course Dir, 1982, Fire Service Coll.; Divl Comdr, London, 1983; Asst Chief Officer, 1985; Dep. Chief Officer, 1990. *Recreation:* golf. *Address:* London Fire Brigade Headquarters, 8 Albert Embankment, SE1 7SD. *T:* 0171–587 4000.

ROBINSON, Air Vice-Marshal Brian Lewis; Senior Partner, Belmont Consultants, advising on aviation matters and business potential especially in Eastern Europe, since 1991; *b* 2 July 1936; *s* of Frederick Lewis Robinson and Ida (*née* Croft); *m* 1961, Ann Faithfull; one *s* one *d*. *Educ:* Bradford Grammar Sch. Served, 1956–76: 74 Sqn; Oxford Univ. Air Sqn; 73 Sqn; Canberra Trials and Tactical Evaluation Unit; Directorate of Flight Safety, MoD; RAF Staff Coll.; RAF Valley; 2 ATAF Germany; Canadian Forces Comd and Staff Coll., and 411 Air Reserve Sqn, Toronto; Chief Instr, 4 Flying Trg Sch., 1976–78, OC, 1978–80, RAF Valley; Internat. Mil. Staff HQ, NATO, Brussels, 1980–82; Defence and Air Attaché, Moscow, 1983–86; Dir of Orgn and Quartering, RAF, MoD, 1986–88; RAF Long-term Deployment Study, 1988; AOC Directly Administered Units, and AO Admin, HQ Strike Command, 1989–91. Editor, Flight Safety section, Air Clues, 1967–69. Mem., RAF and British Bobsleigh teams, 1967–74. *Recreations:* travel, beekeeping, aerobatic display pilot. *Address:* Cheldon House, Cheldon, Chulmleigh, Devon EX18 7JB. *T:* Chulmleigh (01769) 580117. *Club:* Royal Air Force.

See also Sir J. C. N. Wakeley, Bt.

ROBINSON, Air Vice-Marshal Bruce, CB 1968; CBE 1953; Air Officer Commanding No 24 Gp, RAF, 1965–67; retired, 1967; *b* 19 Jan. 1912; *s* of late Dr G. Burton Robinson, Cannington, Somerset; *m* 1940, Elizabeth Ann Compton, *d* of Air Commodore D. F. Lucking; one *s* one *d*. *Educ:* King's School, Bruton. Commissioned in SR of O, The Somerset Light Infty, 1931–33; Commissioned in RAF, 1933; No 16 (Army Co-op. Sqdn), 1934–37; Specialist Engineer course, 1937–39. Served War of 1939–45: Technical duties in Fighter and Bomber Commands, UK Senior Technical Staff Officer, Rhodesian Air Training Group, 1946–48; on loan to Indian Air Force (Director of Technical Services), 1951–53; Commandant, No 1 Radio School, RAF Locking, 1953–55; Sen. RAF Officer at Wright Patterson Air Force Base, Dayton, Ohio, 1958–60; Commandant No 1 Sch. of Technical Training, RAF Halton, Bucks, 1961–63. Director of RAF Aircraft Development, Min. of Aviation, 1963–65. *Recreations:* golf, painting, writing.

ROBINSON, Christopher John, CVO 1992 (LVO 1986); Organist, Director of Music, and Fellow, St John's College, Cambridge, since 1991; *b* 20 April 1936; *s* of late Prebendary John Robinson, Malvern, Worcs; *m* 1962, Shirley Ann, *d* of H. F. Churchman, Sawston, Cambs; one *s* one *d*. *Educ:* St Michael's Coll., Tenbury; Rugby; Christ Church, Oxford (BMus); MA (Oxon and Cantab). FRCO; Hon. RAM. Assistant Organist of Christ Church, Oxford, 1955–58; Assistant Organist of New College, Oxford, 1957–58; Music Master at Oundle School, 1959–62; Assistant Organist of Worcester Cathedral, 1962–63; Organist and Master of Choristers: Worcester Cathedral, 1963–74; St George's Chapel, Windsor Castle, 1975–91. Conductor: City of Birmingham Choir, 1963–; Oxford Bach Choir, 1977–; Leith Hill Musical Festival, 1977–80. Pres., RCO, 1982–84. Hon. Fellow, Univ. of Central England (formerly Birmingham Poly.), 1990. Hon. MMus Birmingham, 1987. *Recreations:* watching cricket, travel. *Address:* St John's College, Cambridge CB2 1TP. *Club:* MCC.

ROBINSON, Sir Christopher Philipse, 8th Bt *cr* 1854, of Toronto; *b* 10 Nov. 1938; *s* of Christopher Robinson, QC (*d* 1974) (*g s* of 1st Bt) and Neville Taylor (*d* 1991), *d* of Rear-Adm. Walter Rockwell Gherardi, USN; *S* kinsman, Sir John Beverley Robinson, 7th Bt, 1988; *m* 1962, Barbara Judith, *d* of late Richard Duncan; two *s* (and one *s* decd). *Heir:* *s* Peter Duncan Robinson, *b* 31 July 1967. *Address:* Kirks Ferry, 460 RR1, Chelsea, Quebec J0X 1N0, Canada.

ROBINSON, Mrs Clare; *see* Panter-Downes, M. P.

ROBINSON, Clifton Eugene Bancroft, CBE 1985 (OBE 1973); JP; a Deputy-Chairman, Commission for Racial Equality, 1977–85; *b* 5 Oct. 1926; *s* of Theodore Emanuel and Lafrance Robinson; *m* (marr. diss.); one *s* three *d*; *m* 1977, Margaret Ann Ennever. *Educ:* Kingston Technical Coll., Jamaica; Birmingham Univ.; Leicester Univ.; Lancaster Coll. of Educn. BA, DipEd. Served War, RAF, 1944–49. Teacher: Mellor Sch., Leicester, 1951–61; i/c Special Educn Unit, St Peter's Sch., Leicester, 1961–64; Dep. Headteacher, Charnwood Sch., Leicester, 1964–68; Headteacher: St Peter's Sch., Leicester, 1968–70; Uplands Sch., Leicester, 1970–77. A Vice-Pres., Internat. Friendship League; President: Leicester United Caribbean Assoc.; Roots Coll. JP Leicester, 1974. *Recreations:* music (mainly classical), walking; when there is time, gardening. *Address:* 83 Numa Court, Justin Close, Brentford, Middlesex TW8 8QF.

ROBINSON, Prof. Colin, FSS, FInstPet; Professor of Economics, University of Surrey, since 1968; Editorial Director, Institute of Economic Affairs, since 1992; *b* 7 Sept. 1932; *s* of late James Robinson and Elsie (*née* Brownhill); *m* 1st, 1957, Olga West; two *s*; 2nd, 1983, Eileen Marshall; two *s* two *d*. *Educ:* Univ. of Manchester (BA Econ). FSS 1970; FInstPet 1985. Economist, Procter and Gamble, 1957–60; Economist, subseq. Head of Economics Dept, Esso Petroleum Co., 1960–66; Econ. Advr, Natural Gas, Esso Europe, 1966–68. Mem., Monopolies and Mergers Commn, 1992–. *Publications:* Business Forecasting, 1970; (with Jon Morgan) North Sea Oil in the Future, 1978; (with Eileen Marshall) Can Coal Be Saved?, 1985; papers on energy economics in learned jls. *Recreations:* walking, music, home improvements. *Address:* Department of Economics, University of Surrey, Guildford GU2 5XH.

ROBINSON, Prof. David Antony, PhD; Vice Chancellor and President, University of South Australia, since 1992; *b* 24 July 1941; *s* of Harry Robinson and Marjorie Newcombe Robinson (*née* Patchett); *m* 1st, 1965, Marjorie Rose Collins (marr. diss. 1970); 2nd, 1976, Yvonne Ann Salter; one *s*. *Educ:* Royal Masonic Schs; University Coll., Swansea (BA, PhD 1967). University College, Swansea: Res. Asst, Dept of Sociol., 1964–67; Res. Fellow, DHSS Med. Sociol. Res. Centre, 1967–71; Lectr, then Sen. Lectr, DHSS-MRC

Addiction Res. Unit, Inst. of Psychiatry, Univ. of London, 1974–80; University of Hull: Sen. Lectr and Actg Dir, 1980–82, Dir, 1982–91, Inst. for Health Studies; Prof. of Health Studies, 1984–91; Hd of Dept, Social Policy and Professional Studies, 1985–86; Dean, Sch. of Social and Pol Scis, 1986–89; Pro Vice-Chancellor, 1989–91; Co-Dir, ESRC Addiction Res. Centre, Univs of Hull and York, 1983–88; Dir, WHO Collaborating Centre for Res. and Trng in Psycho-social and Econ. Aspects of Health, 1986–91. Member: Editl Bd, Brit. Jl of Addiction, 1978–89; Editl Adv. Bd, Sociol. of Health and Illness, 1987–90. Member: Exec. Council of Soc. for Study of Addictions, 1979–82; Exec. Cttee, Nat. Council on Alcoholism, 1979–82; Exec. Cttee, Nat. Council on Gambling, 1980–87; Health Services Res. Cttee, MRC, 1981–84; Social Affairs Cttee, ESRC, 1982–85. Member: Australian Vice Chancellors Cttee, 1992–, Dir, 1995–; Business/Higher Educn Round Table, 1992–, Dir, 1995–; Australian Higher Educn Industrial Assoc., 1992– (Mem., Exec. Cttee, 1993–). FAIM 1993. FRSA 1990. *Publications:* (jtly) Hospitals, Children and their Families, 1970; The Process of Becoming Ill, 1971; Patients, Practitioners and Medical Care: aspects of medical sociology, 1973, 2nd edn 1978; From Drinking to Alcoholism: a sociological commentary, 1976; (ed jtly) Studies in Everyday Medical Life, 1976; (with S. Henry) Self-help and Health: mutual aid for modern problems, 1977; Talking Out of Alcoholism: the self-help process of Alcoholics Anonymous, 1979; (with Y. Robinson) From Self-help to Health: a guide to self-help groups, 1979; (ed) Alcohol Problems: reviews, research and recommendations, 1979; (with P. Tether) Preventing Alcohol Problems: a guide to local action, 1986; (ed jtly) Local Action on Alcohol Problems, 1989; (ed jtly) Controlling Legal Addictions, 1989; (ed jtly) Manipulating Consumption: information, law and voluntary controls, 1990; (with A. Maynard et al) Social Care and HIV–AIDS, 1993; contrib. numerous pamphlets, book chapters and papers in learned and professional jls. *Recreations:* walking, golf, cinema. *Address:* Chancellery, University of South Australia, North Terrace, Adelaide, SA 5000, Australia. *T:* (8) 3022502.

ROBINSON, (David) Duncan; Director and Marlay Curator, Fitzwilliam Museum, Cambridge, since 1995; Professorial Fellow, Clare College, Cambridge, since 1995; *b* 27 June 1943; *s* of Tom and Ann Robinson; *m* 1967, Elizabeth Anne Sutton; one *s* two *d.* *Educ:* King Edward VI Sch., Macclesfield; Clare Coll., Cambridge (MA); Yale Univ. (Mellon Fellow, 1965–67; MA). Asst Keeper of Paintings and Drawings, 1970–76, Keeper, 1976–81, Fitzwilliam Museum, Cambridge; Fellow and Coll. Lectr, Clare Coll., Cambridge, 1975–81; Dir, Yale Center for British Art, New Haven, Conn, Chief Exec., Paul Mellon Centre for Studies in British Art, London, 1981–95; Adjunct Prof. of History of Art, and Fellow of Berkeley Coll., Yale Univ., 1981–95. Mem. Cttee of Management, and Chm., Exhibns Cttee, Kettle's Yard, Cambridge Univ., 1970–81. Member: Art Panel, Eastern Arts Assoc., 1973–81 (Chm., 1979–81); Arts Council of GB, 1981 (Mem., 1978–81, Vice-Chm., 1981, Art Panel); Assoc. of Art Mus. Dirs (USA), 1982–88; Bd of Managers, Lewis Walpole Library, Farmington Ct, USA, 1982–95; Council of Management, The William Blake Trust, 1983–95; Vis. Cttee, Dept of Paintings Conservation, Metropolitan Museum of Art, NY, 1984–94; Walpole Soc., 1983– (Mem. Council, 1985–87); Connecticut Acad. of Arts and Scis, 1991–95; Chm., Art and Artifacts Indemnity Adv. Panel (USA), 1992–94 (Mem., 1991). Member, Board of Directors: New Haven Colony Historical Soc., 1991–94; Amer. Friends of Georgian Gp, 1992–95. Gov., Yale Univ. Press, 1987–95; Trustee: Yale Univ. Press, London, 1990–95; Charleston Trust (USA), 1990–92. FRSA 1990. Organised Arts Council exhibitions: Stanley Spencer, 1975; William Nicholson, 1980. *Publications:* Companion Volume to the Kelmscott Chaucer, 1975, re-issued as Morris, Burne-Jones and the Kelmscott Chaucer, 1982; Stanley Spencer, 1979, rev. edn 1990; (with Stephen Wildman) Morris & Company in Cambridge, 1980; Town, Country, Shore & Sea: English Watercolours from van Dyck to Paul Nash, 1982; catalogues; articles and reviews in Apollo, Burlington Magazine, etc. *Address:* Fitzwilliam Museum, Cambridge CB2 1RB. *T:* Cambridge (01223) 332900. *Clubs:* Athenæum; Knickerbocker (NY); Elizabethan (New Haven).

ROBINSON, David Julien; film critic, The Times, since 1974; *b* 6 Aug. 1930; *s* of Edward Robinson and Dorothy Evelyn (*née* Overton). *Educ:* Lincoln Sch.; King's Coll., Cambridge (BA Hons). Associate Editor, Sight and Sound, and Editor, Monthly Film Bulletin, 1956–58; Programme Dir, NFT, 1959; Film Critic, Financial Times, 1959–74; Editor, Contrast, 1962–63. Vis. Prof. of Film, Westfield Coll., Univ. of London. Director: Garrett Robinson Co., 1987–88; The Davids Film Co., 1988–. Guest Dir, Edinburgh Film Fest., 1989–91. Films produced and directed: Hetty King — Performer, 1969; (Co-dir) Keeping Love Alive, 1987; (Co-dir) Sophisticated Lady, 1989. *Publications:* Hollywood in the Twenties, 1969; Buster Keaton, 1969; The Great Funnies, 1972; World Cinema, 1973, 2nd edn 1980 (US edn The History of World Cinema, 1974, 1980); Chaplin: the mirror of opinion, 1983; Chaplin: his life and art, 1985; (ed and trans.) Luis Buñuel (J. F. Aranda); (ed and trans.) Cinema in Revolution (anthology); (ed jtly) The Illustrated History of the Cinema, 1986. *Recreations:* collecting optical toys, model theatres. *Address:* 96–100 New Cavendish Street, W1M 7FA. *T:* 0171–580 4959; 1 Winifreds Dale, Cavendish Road, Bath BA1 2UD. *T:* Bath (01225) 420305.

ROBINSON, Derek, CBE 1979; Fellow of Magdalen College, Oxford, since 1969; Senior Research Officer, Oxford Institute of Economics and Statistics; *b* 9 Feb. 1932; *s* of Benjamin and Mary Robinson; *m* 1956, Jean Evelyn (*née* Lynch); one *s* one *d.* *Educ:* Barnsley Holgate Grammar Sch.; Ruskin Coll., Oxford; Lincoln Coll., Oxford. MA (Oxon), DipEcPolSci (Oxon). Civil Service, 1948–55. Sheffield Univ., 1959–60; Senior Research Officer, Oxford Inst. of Economics and Statistics, 1961–. Economic Adviser, Nat. Bd for Prices and Incomes, 1965–67; Sen. Economic Adviser, Dept of Employment and Productivity, 1968–70; Dep. Chm., Pay Bd, 1973–74; Chm., SSRC, 1975–78. Mem., British Library Bd, 1979–82. Visiting Professor: Cornell Univ., 1983; Univ. of Hawaii, 1983. Chairman: Oxfordshire Dist Manpower Cttee, 1980–83 (Oxf. and S Bucks, 1975–79); Cttee of Inquiry into the remuneration of members of local authorities, 1977; Chilterns Area Bd, Manpower Services Commn Special Programmes, 1978–79. Inter-regional Adviser on Wage Policy, ILO, 1986–88. *Publications:* Non-Wage Incomes and Prices Policy, 1966; Wage Drift, Fringe Benefits and Manpower Distribution, 1968; Workers' Negotiated Savings Plans for Capital Formation, 1970; (ed) Local Labour Markets and Wage Structures, 1970; Prices and Incomes Policy: the Austrian Experience (with H. Suppanz), 1972; Incomes Policy and Capital Sharing in Europe, 1973; (with J. Vincens) Research into Labour Market Behaviour, 1974; (with K. Mayhew *et al*) Pay Policies for the Future, 1983; Introduction to Economics, 1986; Monetarism and the Labour Market, 1986; Civil Service Pay in Africa, 1990; contributor to Bulletin of Oxford Univ. Inst. of Economics and Statistics; Industrial Relations Jl, etc. *Address:* 56 Lonsdale Road, Oxford OX2 7EP. *T:* Oxford (01865) 52276. *Club:* Reform.

ROBINSON, Derek Anthony, DPhil; Head, Physical Sciences and Engineering Group (formerly Keeper, Department of Physical Sciences, later Head of Science Group), Science Museum, London, since 1987; *b* 21 April 1942; *s* of late Charles Frederick Robinson and of Mary Margaret Robinson; *m* 1965, Susan Gibson (*d* 1991); two *s.* *Educ:* Hymers Coll., Hull; The Queen's Coll., Oxford (BA 1963; MA, DPhil 1967). Post-doctoral Res. Fellow, Dept of Chemistry, Univ. of Reading, 1967–69; Mem. scientific staff, Molecular Pharmacology Unit of MRC, Cambridge, 1969–72; Sen. Asst in Res., Dept of Haematol Medicine, Cambridge Univ. Med. Sch., 1972–74; Science Museum: Asst Keeper I, Dept of Chem., 1974–77; Dep. Keeper (formerly Asst Keeper I), Wellcome Mus. of History of Medicine, and Sec. of Adv. Council, 1977–78; Keeper, Dept of Museum Services, 1978–87. Mem., British Nat. Cttee for History of Sci., Medicine and Technology, 1987–88; Mem., CGLI, 1984–; Dir, Bd, Mus. Documentation Assoc., 1989–92. *Publications:* (contrib.) 2nd edn Acridines, ed R. M. Acheson, 1973; (contrib.) Vol. VI, The History of Technology, ed T. I. Williams, 1978; (contrib.) Cambridge General Encyclopaedia, ed D. Crystal, 1990; papers on heterocyclic chemistry, molecular pharmacol., and leukaemia chemotherapy, in Jl Chem. Soc., Brit. Jl Pharmacol., and Biochem. Trans. *Recreations:* cricket, Rugby referee, travel, walking. *Address:* 3 Broadwater Avenue, Letchworth, Herts SG6 3HE. *T:* Letchworth (01462) 686961, (office) 0171–938 8040.

ROBINSON, Dr Derek Charles, FRS 1994; Research Director, UKAEA Government Division, Fusion, since 1992; *b* 27 May 1941; *s* of Alexander Robinson and Grace Kitchen; *m* 1968, Marion Quarmby; one *d.* *Educ:* Queen Elizabeth Sch., Kirkby Lonsdale; Manchester Univ. (BSc, PhD). FInstP. AERE Harwell, 1965–68; Vis. Scientist, I. V. Kurchatov Inst. of Atomic Energy, Moscow, 1968–69; research at UKAEA Culham Lab., 1970–78; Vis. Scientist, Tokyo, Nagoya and S Australia, 1978–79; Group Leader, 1979–86, Div. Head, 1986–92, Culham Lab. Member: Jet Sci. Council, 1983–; Sci. Adv. Bd, Max Planck Inst. für Plasma Physik, 1988–; Tech. Adv. Cttee, Internat. Thermonuclear Exp. Reactor, 1991–. C. V. Boys Prize, Inst. of Physics, 1979. *Publications:* contribs to learned jls. *Recreations:* plantsman, photography, hill walking. *Address:* The Thatched Cottage, Church Street, Appleford, Abingdon, Oxon OX14 4PA. *T:* Abingdon (01235) 848500.

ROBINSON, Rt. Rev. Donald William Bradley, AO 1984; Archbishop of Sydney and Metropolitan of New South Wales, 1982–93; *b* 9 Nov. 1922; *s* of Rev. Richard Bradley Robinson and Gertrude Marston Robinson (*née* Ross); *m* 1949, Marie Elizabeth Taubman; three *s* one *d.* *Educ:* Sydney Church of England Gram. Sch.; Univ. of Sydney (BA); Queens' Coll., Cambridge (MA). Australian Army, 1941–45, Lieut Intell. Corps, 1944. Deacon 1950, Sydney; priest 1951; Curate, Manly, NSW, 1950–52; St Philip's, Sydney, 1952–53; Lecturer: Moore Coll., 1952–81 (Vice-Principal, 1959–72); Sydney Univ., 1964–81; Asst Bishop, Diocese of Sydney (Bishop in Parramatta), 1973–82. Hon. ThD Aust. Coll. of Theology, 1979. *Address:* 1 Jubilee Avenue, Pymble, NSW 2073, Australia. *T:* (2) 4493033.

ROBINSON, Duncan; *see* Robinson, David D.

ROBINSON, Eric Embleton; Director, Lancashire Polytechnic (formerly Preston Polytechnic), 1982–90; *b* 12 March 1927; *s* of Cyril Robinson and Florence Mary Embleton. *Educ:* local authority schools, Nelson and Colne, Lancs; London Univ. (MSc). Teaching, Prescot Grammar Sch., 1948, Acton Tech. Coll., 1949–56, Brunel Coll., 1956–62, Enfield Coll., 1962–70; Dep. Dir, NE London Polytechnic, 1970–73; Principal, Bradford Coll., 1973–82. Pres., Assoc. of Teachers in Tech. Instns, 1962; Exec. Mem., Nat. Union of Teachers, 1961–67; Member: Burnham Cttees, 1961–67; Nat. Council for Training and Supply of Teachers, 1964–66; Minister's Working Party on Polytechnics, 1965–66; Equal Opportunities Commn, 1976–81; CNAA, 1976–82; UNESCO Nat. Commn, 1975–78. Vice Pres., Socialist Educn Assoc., 1966–. Hon. Advr, Peking Inst. of Business, 1987–; Hon. Vis. Prof., Wolverhampton Polytechnic, 1990–. Hon. Fellow, Sheffield City Polytechnic, 1990. Hon. DEd CNAA, 1990. *Publications:* The New Polytechnics, 1968; numerous articles and papers. *Address:* 5 Millfield Road, Chorley, Lancs PR7 1RF. *T:* Chorley (01257) 415099. *Club:* Savile.

ROBINSON, (Francis) Alastair (Lavie); Group Vice-Chairman, Barclays Bank, since 1992; *b* 19 Sept. 1937; *s* of late Stephen and Patricia Robinson; *m* 1961, Lavinia Elizabeth Napier; two *d.* *Educ:* Eton. Nat Service, 4th/7th Royal Dragoon Guards, 1956–58 (2nd Lieut). Mercantile Credit: management trainee, 1959; Gen. Manager, 1971; Mem. Board, 1978; Chief Exec. Officer and Pres., Barclays American, USA, 1981; Regional Gen. Manager, Asia-Barclays International, 1984; Dir Personnel, Barclays Bank, 1987, Exec. Dir, UK Ops, 1990, Exec. Dir, Banking Div., 1991. *Recreations:* music, opera, gardening, fishing, shooting. *Address:* Barclays Bank plc, 54 Lombard Street, EC3P 3AH. *Club:* Cavalry and Guards.

ROBINSON, Prof. Francis Christopher Rowland, PhD; Professor of History of South Asia, University of London, since 1990; Head, Department of History, Royal Holloway, University of London, since 1990; *b* Southgate, 23 Nov. 1944; *s* of Leonard Robinson and Joyce (*née* King); *m* 1971, Patricia Courtenay Hughes; one *s* one *d.* *Educ:* County Grammar Sch. for Boys, Bexhill-on-Sea; Trinity Coll., Cambridge (MA, PhD). Prize Fellow, Trinity Coll., Cambridge, 1969–73; Royal Holloway College, then Royal Holloway and Bedford New College, University of London: Lectr in History, 1973–85; Reader, 1985–90; Mem., Council, 1991–; Mem., Academic Cttee, 1994–, Academic Council, 1995–, London Univ. Vis. Prof., S Asia Program, 1982 and 1986, Near East Program, 1985, Jackson Sch. of Internat. Studies, Univ. of Washington; Directeur d'Etudes Associé, Ecole des Hautes Etudes en Sciences Sociales, Paris, 1985. Mem., Council, RAS, 1990–93. Iqbal Centenary Medal (Pakistan), 1978. *Publications:* Separatism among Indian Muslims: the politics of the United Provinces' Muslims 1860–1923, 1974, 2nd edn 1993; (with F. Harcourt) Twentieth Century World History: a select bibliography, 1979; Atlas of the Islamic World since 1500, 1982; (with P. R. Brass) Indian National Congress and Indian Society 1885–1985, 1987; Varieties of South Asia Islam, 1988; (ed) Cambridge Encyclopedia of India, Pakistan, Bangladesh, Sri Lanka, 1989; (ed) Cambridge Illustrated History of the Islamic World, 1996; contrib. Modern Asian Studies, Encyclopedia of Islam, Indian Sociology, etc. *Recreations:* ball games, gardening, people, books, travel, food and wine. *Address:* Department of History, Royal Holloway, University of London, Egham, Surrey TW20 0EX. *T:* Egham (01784) 443314. *Club:* Hawks.

ROBINSON, Geoffrey; *see* Robinson, A. G.

ROBINSON, Geoffrey; MP (Lab) Coventry North-West, since March 1976; *b* 25 May 1938; *s* of Robert Norman Robinson and Dorothy Jane Robinson (*née* Skelly); *m* 1967, Marie Elena Giorgio; one *s* one *d.* *Educ:* Emanuel School; Cambridge and Yale Univs. Labour Party Research Assistant, 1965–68; Senior Executive, Industrial Reorganisation Corporation, 1968–70; Financial Controller, British Leyland, 1971–72; Managing Director, Leyland Innocenti, Milan, 1972–73; Chief Exec., Jaguar Cars, Coventry, 1973–75; Chief Exec. (unpaid), Meriden Motor Cycle Workers' Co-op, 1978–80 (Dir, 1980–82). Chm., TransTec PLC, 1986–. Dir, W Midlands Enterprise Bd, 1980–84. Opposition spokesman on science, 1982–83, on regional affairs and industry, 1983–86. *Recreations:* reading, architecture, gardens. *Address:* House of Commons, SW1A 0AA. *T:* 0171–219 3000.

ROBINSON, Dr Geoffrey Walter, FEng 1994; FIEE; FBCS; Director, IBM UK Laboratories, 1988–92 and since 1994; *b* 9 Nov. 1945; *s* of late George Robinson and Edith Margaret (*née* Wilson); *m* 1967 Edwina Jones; one *s* one *d.* *Educ:* Aireborough Grammar Sch.; Nottingham Univ. (BSc 1st Cl. Maths; PhD). IBM UK: Lab. posts, 1969–82; Manager of Scientific Centre, 1982–84; Technical Progs Advr, 1984–85;

Technical Dir, 1986–88; Chief Advr on Sci. and Technol., DTI, 1992–94. Member: Sci. Adv. Cttee, Ordnance Survey, 1986–89; CEST, 1986–92; Strategy Rev. Panel, BCS, 1988–92; SERC, 1992–94; NERC, 1992–94; PPARC, 1994–; Council, Central Lab. of the Res. Councils, 1995–. Mem., Co. of Inf. Technologists, 1988–. Gov., King Alfred's Coll., Winchester, 1993– (Hon. DTech 1992). FBCS (Dep. Pres., 1994–). FRSA. *Publications:* articles on science, technol. and society. *Recreation:* music. *Address:* Fardale, Hookwood Lane, Ampfield, Romsey, Hants SO51 9BZ. *T:* Chandler's Ford (01703) 261837. *Club:* Athenæum.

ROBINSON, Gerrard Jude; Chief Executive, Granada Group plc, since 1991; Chairman: London Weekend Television, since 1994; ITN, since 1995; BSkyB, since 1995; *b* 23 Oct. 1948; *s* of Anthony and Elizabeth Ann Robinson; *m* 1st, 1970, Maria Ann Borg (marr. diss. 1990); one *s* one *d*; 2nd, 1990, Heather Peta Leaman; one *d*. *Educ:* St Mary's Coll., Castlehead. FCMA 1991. Works Accountant, Lesney Products, 1970–1974; Financial Controller, Lex Industrial Distribution and Hire, 1974–80; Coca Cola: Finance Dir, 1980–81; Sales and Mkting Dir, 1981–83; Man. Dir, 1983–84; Man. Dir, Grand Metropolitan Contract Services, 1984–87; Chief Exec., Compass Gp plc, 1987–91. *Recreations:* golf, opera, chess, ski-ing, reading, music. *Address:* 77 Addison Road, Holland Park, W14 8EB. *T:* 0171–603 9488. *Clubs:* Roehampton; Wisley Golf.

ROBINSON, Ian, FEng; FIChemE; Chief Executive, Scottish Power plc, since 1995; *b* 3 May 1942; *s* of Thomas Mottram Robinson and Eva Iris Robinson (*née* Bird); *m* 1967, Kathleen Crawford Leay; one *s* one *d*. *Educ:* Leeds Univ. (BSc); Harvard Univ. FIChemE 1982; FEng 1994. With Kellogg International Co. Ltd, 1964–72; Managing Director: Ralph M. Parsons Co. Ltd, 1972–86; John Brown Engrgs & Constructors, 1986–92; Dir and Chm., Engrg Div., Trafalgar House plc, 1992–95. *Recreations:* golf, gardening, theatre. *Address:* Scottish Power, 1 Atlantic Quay, Glasgow G2 8SP. *T:* 0141–248 8200. *Clubs:* Royal Automobile, Les Ambassadeurs.

ROBINSON, Jancis Mary, (Mrs N. L. Lander), MW; wine writer and broadcaster; *b* 22 April 1950; *d* of Thomas Edward Robinson and Ann Sheelagh Margaret Robinson (*née* Conacher); *m* 1981, Nicholas Laurence Lander; one *s* two *d*. *Educ:* Carlisle and County High Sch. for Girls; St Anne's Coll., Oxford (MA). Editor, Wine & Spirit, 1976–80; Founder and Editor, Drinker's Digest (now Which? Wine Monthly), 1977–82; Editor, Which? Wine Guide, 1980–82; Sunday Times Wine Corresp., 1980–86; Evening Standard Wine Corresp., 1987–88; Financial Times Wine Columnist, 1989–; freelance journalism, particularly on wine, food and people, 1980–; freelance television and radio broadcasting, on various subjects, 1983–; Writer/Presenter: The Wine Programme, 1983 (Glenfiddich Trophy), 1985, 1987; Jancis Robinson Meets . . ., 1987; Matters of Taste, 1989, 1991; Vintners' Tales, 1992; Jancis Robinson's Wine Course, 1995; wine judging and lecturing, 1983–. *Publications:* The Wine Book, 1979, rev. edn 1983; The Great Wine Book, 1982 (Glenfiddich Award); Masterglass, 1983, rev. edn 1987; How to Choose and Enjoy Wine, 1984; Vines, Grapes and Wines, 1986 (André Simon Meml Prize, Wine Guild Award, Clicquot Book of the Year); Jancis Robinson's Adventures with Food and Wine, 1987; Jancis Robinson on the Demon Drink, 1988; Vintage Timecharts, 1989; (ed) The Oxford Companion to Wine, 1994 (André Simon Meml Prize, Clicquot Book of the Year); Jancis Robinson's Wine Course, 1995. *Recreations:* wine, food and words. *Address:* c/o A. P. Watt, 20 John Street, WC1N 2DR.

ROBINSON, John Armstrong, CMG 1969; HM Diplomatic Service, retired; Ambassador to Israel, 1980–81; *b* 18 Dec. 1925; *m* 1952, Marianne Berger; one *s* one *d*. HM Forces, 1944–46; Foreign Office, 1949–50; Second Secretary, Delhi, 1950–52; Foreign Office, 1952–53; Helsinki, 1953–56; Second later First Secretary, Paris, 1956–58; Foreign Office, 1958–61; First Secretary in UK Delegation to European Communities, Brussels, 1962–67; Counsellor, Foreign Office, 1967; Head of European Economic Integration Dept, FCO, 1968–70; appointed Member of team of nine officials for negotiations on British entry into the Common Market, Brussels, 1970–71; Asst Under-Sec. of State, FCO, 1971–73; Ambassador to Algeria, 1974–77; Minister, Washington, 1977–80. *Address:* La Sirgarié, St Martin Laguépie, 81170 Cordes, Tarn, France.

ROBINSON, John Harris, CEng; FIChemE; Chief Executive, Smith & Nephew, since 1990; *b* 22 Dec. 1940; *s* of Thomas and Florence Robinson; *m* 1963, Doreen Alice Gardner; one *s* one *d*. *Educ:* Woodhouse Grove Sch.; Birmingham Univ. (BSc). CEng 1968; FIChemE 1983. ICI plc, 1962–65; Fisons plc, 1965–70, PA Consulting Gp, 1970–75; Woodhouse and Rixson, 1975–79; Smith & Nephew plc: Man. Dir, Healthcare Div., 1979–82; Dir, 1982–89; Dep. Chief Exec., 1989–90. Non-Exec. Dir, Delta plc, 1993–. Mem. Council, CBI, 1991–. Mem., Adv. Bd, Birmingham Univ. Business Sch., 1993–. Gov., Hymer Coll., Hull, 1983–. CIMgt 1991. *Recreations:* golf, cricket, theatre. *Address:* 35 Marsham Court, Marsham Street, SW1P 4JY. *T:* 0171–834 6838. *Clubs:* Lansdowne; Brough Golf (E Yorks).

ROBINSON, Sir John (James Michael Laud), 11th Bt *cr* 1660; DL; Chairman, Northampton General Hospital NHS Trust, since 1994; *b* 19 Jan. 1943; *s* of Michael Frederick Laud Robinson (*d* 1971) and Elizabeth (*née* Bridge); *S* grandfather, 1975; *m* 1968, Gayle Elizabeth (*née* Keyes); two *s* one *d*. *Educ:* Eton; Trinity Coll., Dublin (MA, Economics and Political Science). Chartered Financial Analyst. Chm., St Andrews Hosp., Northampton, 1984–94. Pres., British Red Cross, Northants Br., 1982–90. DL Northants, 1984. *Heir: s* Mark Christopher Michael Villiers Robinson, *b* 23 April 1972. *Address:* Cranford Hall, Cranford, Kettering, Northants NN14 4AL.

ROBINSON, Rev. Canon Joseph, MTh, FKC; Master of the Temple since 1980; *b* 23 Feb. 1927; *er s* of Thomas and Maggie Robinson; *m* 1953, Anne Antrobus; two *s* two *d*. *Educ:* Upholland Grammar Sch., Lancs; King's Coll., London. BD (1st cl. Hons); AKC (1st cl.) 1951; MTh 1958; FKC 1973. Deacon, 1952; Priest, 1953; Curate, All Hallows, Tottenham, 1952–55; Minor Canon of St Paul's Cathedral, 1956–68; Sacrist, 1958–68; Lectr in Hebrew and Old Testament Studies, King's Coll., London, 1959–68; Canon Residentiary, Canterbury Cathedral, 1968–80, now Canon Emeritus; Librarian, 1968–73; Treasurer, 1972–80; Exam. Chaplain to Archbishop of Canterbury, 1968–80. Golden Lectr, 1963; St Antholin Lectr, 1964–67. Chaplain, Worshipful Co. of Cutlers, 1963–; Sub Chaplain, Order of St John of Jerusalem, 1965–. Hon. Bencher, Inner Temple, 1994. *Publications:* The Cambridge Bible Commentary on 1 Kings, 1972, 2 Kings, 1976; articles in: Church Quarterly Review, Expository Times, Church Times; many reviews in various jls. *Recreations:* reading, gardening. *Address:* The Master's House, The Temple, EC4Y 7BB. *T:* 0171–353 8559. *Club:* Athenæum.

ROBINSON, Kathleen Marian, (Mrs Vincent F. Sherry; Kathleen M. Sherry); FRCS, FRCOG, MD; retired; Hon. Obstetrician, and Hon. Gynæcologist, Royal Free Hospital; Hon. Obstetrician, Queen Charlotte's Hospital; *b* 25 May 1911; *d* of late James Robinson and Ruth Robinson (*née* Edmeston); *m* 1946, Vincent Francis Sherry; one *s* one *d* (and one *d* decd). *Educ:* Penrhos College, Colwyn Bay; Royal Free Hospital School of Medicine, London University. MB, BS, 1936; MRCS, LRCP 1936; MD London 1940; FRCS 1940; MRCOG 1941; FRCOG 1953. House Surgeon: Royal Free Hospital; Samaritan Hospital, Royal Marsden Hospital, Queen Charlotte's Hospital. Resident Obstetrician, Queen Charlotte's Hospital. Recognised Teacher of the London University. FRSM; FRHS. *Publications:* contributor to Queen Charlotte's Text Book of Obstetrics, also to Practical Motherhood and Parentcraft. *Recreations:* gardening, cooking, travel. *Address:* 17 Herondale Avenue, SW18 3JN. *T:* 0181–874 8588.

ROBINSON, Keith; *see* Robinson, L. K.

ROBINSON, Rt. Hon. Sir Kenneth, Kt 1983; PC 1964; Hon. DLitt; FCIT; Chairman, Arts Council of Great Britain, 1977–82; *b* Warrington, Lancs, 19 March 1911; *s* of late Clarence Robinson, MRCS, LRCP; *m* 1941, Helen Elizabeth Edwards (*d* 1993); one *d*. *Educ:* Oundle Sch. Insurance Broker at Lloyd's, 1927–40. Served War of 1939–45, RN 1941–46; Ord. Seaman, 1941; commissioned, 1942; Lieut-Comdr RNVR, 1944; served Home Fleet, Mediterranean, Far East and Pacific. Company Secretary, 1946–49. MP (Lab) St Pancras N, 1949–70; Asst Whip (unpaid), 1950–51, an Opposition Whip, 1951–54; Minister of Health, 1964–68; Minister for Planning and Land, Min. of Housing and Local Govt, 1968–69. Dir, Social Policy, 1970–72, Man. Dir (Personnel and Social Policy Div.), 1972–74, British Steel Corp.; Chm., LTE, 1975–78. Chairman: English National Opera, 1972–77; Young Concert Artists Trust, 1983–90; Carnegie Council Arts and Disabled People, 1985–87; Jt Treas., RSA, 1983–88. Trustee, Imperial War Mus., 1978–84. Hon. FRCGP; Hon. MRCP 1989; Hon. DLitt Liverpool, 1980. *Publications:* Wilkie Collins, a Biography, 1951; Policy for Mental Health, 1958; Patterns of Care, 1961; Look at Parliament, 1962. *Recreations:* looking at paintings, reading, listening to music. *Address:* 12 Grove Terrace, NW5 1PH.

ROBINSON, Kenneth Ernest, CBE 1971; MA, FRHistS; *b* 9 March 1914; *o s* of late Ernest and Isabel Robinson, Plumstead, Kent; *m* 1938, Stephanie (*d* 1994), *o d* of late William Wilson, Westminster; one *s* one *d*. *Educ:* Monoux Grammar School, Walthamstow; Hertford College, Oxford (Scholar, 1st Cl. PPE; 1st Cl. Mod. Hist.; Beit Senior Schol. in Colonial History); London School of Economics. Colonial Office, 1936; Asst Sec. 1946; resigned 1948. Fellow of Nuffield Coll. (Hon. Fellow, 1984) and Reader in Commonwealth Govt, Oxford, 1948–57; Dir, Inst. of Commonwealth Studies and Prof. of Commonwealth Affairs, Univ. of London, 1957–65 (Hon. Life Mem., 1980–); Vice-Chancellor, Univ. of Hong Kong, 1965–72; Hallsworth Res. Fellow, Univ. of Manchester, 1972–74; Dir, Commonwealth Studies Resources Survey, Univ. of London, 1974–76. Leverhulme Res. Fellow, 1952–53; Vis. Lectr, Sch. of Advanced Internat. Studies, Johns Hopkins Univ., 1954; Carnegie Travel Grant, East, Central and S Africa, 1960; Reid Lectr, Acadia Univ., 1963; Vis. Prof., Duke Univ., NC, 1963; Callander Lectr, Aberdeen, 1979. Editor, Jl of Commonwealth Political Studies, 1961–65; Special Commonwealth Award, ODM, 1965. Member: (part-time) Directing Staff, Civil Service Selection Bd, 1951–56, Assessor Panel, 1973–77; Colonial Economic Res. Cttee, 1949–62; Colonial SSRC, 1958–62; Inter-Univ. Council for Higher Educn Overseas, 1973–79; Mem. Council: Overseas Develt Inst. 1960–65; RIIA, 1962–65; Internat. African Inst., 1960–65; African Studies Assoc., UK, 1963–65, 1978–81; ACU, 1967–68; Hong Kong Management Assoc., 1965–72; Chinese Univ. of Hong Kong, 1965–72; Univ. of Cape Coast, 1972–74; Royal Commonwealth Soc., 1974–87 (Vice Pres., 1984–); Royal African Soc., 1983–89 (Pres., 1989–); Life Mem. Ct, Univ. of Hong Kong, 1972. Governor, LSE, 1959–65. Corresp. Mem., Académie des Sciences d'Outre-Mer, Paris. Hon. LLD Chinese Univ. of Hong Kong, 1969; Hon. DLitt, Univ. of Hong Kong, 1972; DUniv Open, 1978. JP Hong Kong, 1967–72. *Publications:* (with W. J. M. Mackenzie) Five Elections in Africa, 1960; (with A. F. Madden) Essays in Imperial Government presented to Margery Perham, 1963; The Dilemmas of Trusteeship, 1965; (with W. B. Hamilton & C. D. Goodwin) A Decade of the Commonwealth 1955–64 (USA), 1966. Contrib. to Africa Today (USA), 1955; Africa in the Modern World (USA), 1955; University Cooperation and Asian Development (USA), 1967; L'Europe du XIXe et du XXe Siècle, Vol. 7 (Italy), 1968; Experts in Africa, 1980; Perspectives on Imperialism and Decolonisation, 1984; papers in learned jls; *festschriften:* Imperialism, the State, and the Third World, ed M. Twaddle, 1992; Decolonisation and the International Community, 1993. *Address:* The Old Rectory, Church Westcote, Oxon OX7 6SF. *T:* Shipton under Wychwood (01993) 830586. *Clubs:* Commonwealth Trust, Lansdowne; Hong Kong.

ROBINSON, Lee Fisher, CEng; Chairman: Graesser (Contactors) Ltd, since 1979; Biotechna Ltd, since 1982; HMC Technology plc, since 1983; ABG Ltd, since 1993; Bio-Electrical Ltd, since 1993; *b* 17 July 1923; *m* 1st, 1944; three *d*; 2nd, 1976, June Edna Hopkins. *Educ:* Howard Sch.; Cardiff Tech. College. MICE; ACIArb. Royal Engrs, Sappers and Miners, IE, 1942–45. Turriff Const. Corp. Ltd, HBM (BCC), 1963; Man. Dir, Power Gas Corp. Ltd, 1964; Chief Exec. and Dep. Chm., Turriff Construction Corp., 1970–73. Director: Davy-Ashmore Ltd, 1970; Combustion Systems (NRDC), 1972– (Chm., 1978); Redwood Internat. (UK) Ltd, 1972; Altech SA, 1976–; Protech SA, 1976–; BCS Ltd, 1976–; Charterhouse Strategic Development Ltd, 1976–80 (Gp Indust. Adviser, Charterhouse Gp); Ingeco Laing SA, 1977–; RTR (Oil Sands) Alberta, 1977–; RTR Canada Ltd, 1977–; RTR SA (also Chief Exec.), 1977–; RTL SA (also Vice-Pres.), 1977–; Thalassa (North Sea) Ltd, 1980–; Marcent Natural Resources Ltd (Man. Dir), 1980–; Hydromet Mineral Co., 1983–; Solvex Corp., 1988–; Chm. and Chief Exec. Officer, Biotechna Environmental Ltd. Consultant, Internat. Management Consultants, 1972–. Chm., Warren Spring Adv. Bd, 1969–72; Mem. Adv. Council for Technology, 1968–69. *Publications:* Cost and Financing of Fertiliser Projects in India, 1967; various articles. *Recreations:* badminton, sailing. *Address:* Flat 3, Athenaeum Hall, Vale-of-Health, NW3 1AP. *Club:* Wig and Pen.

ROBINSON, (Leonard) Keith, CBE 1981; DL; management consultant, 1985–87; County Chief Executive, Hampshire County Council, 1973–85; Clerk of Lieutenancy, 1973–85; *b* 2 July 1920; *m* 1948, Susan May Tomkinson; two *s* two *d*. *Educ:* Queen Elizabeth's Grammar Sch., Blackburn; Victoria Univ. of Manchester (LLB). Solicitor. RAFVR, 1940–46 (Navigator, Sqdn-Ldr). Asst Solicitor, City and County of Bristol, 1948–55; Dep. Town Clerk, Birkenhead Co. Borough Council, 1955–66; Town Clerk, Stoke-on-Trent City Council, 1966–73. Association of County Councils: Mem., Officers Adv. Gp, 1974–83 (Chm., 1977–82); Adviser, Policy Cttee, 1975–82; Adviser, Local Govt Finance Cttee, 1976–85; Chm., Assoc. of County Chief Execs, 1975–77. Member: W Mids Econ. Planning Council, 1967–73; Keele Univ. Council, 1968–73; Central Cttee for Reclamation of Derelict Land, 1971–74; Quality Assce Council, BSI, 1973–77; Job Creation Programme Action Cttee for London and SE, 1976–77; District Manpower Cttee, 1980–83; Adv. Council for Energy Conservation, 1982–84; Local Authorities' Mutual Investment Trust, 1982–83; Hillier Arboretum Management Cttee, 1985– (Sec., 1977–85); Southern Arts, 1985–91; Exec. Cttee, Hampshire Develt Assoc., 1985–91; Asst Comr, Local Govt Boundary Commn, 1986–91. Mem. Exec. Cttee, Hampshire Gardens Trust, 1985–; Dir, Salisbury Playhouse, 1979–93; Vice-Chm., Nuffield Theatre Bd, 1985–; Trustee, New Theatre Royal (Portsmouth) Ltd, 1976–; Pres., Winchester Dramatic Soc., 1979–. DL Hants, 1985. Knight, Hon. Soc. of Knights of the Round Table, 1984–. *Publications:* contrib. local govt and legal jls. *Recreations:* fly-fishing, theatre, photography, gardening. *Address:* Bransbury Mill Cottage, Bransbury, Barton Stacey, Winchester, Hants SO21 3QJ. *Club:* MCC.

ROBINSON, Lloyd; *see* Robinson, T. L.

ROBINSON, Group Captain Marcus, CB 1956; AFC 1941 and Bar 1944; AE 1942; DL; Chairman, Robinson, Dunn & Co. Ltd and subsidiary companies, 1966–77, retired; *b* 27 May 1912; *s* of Wilson and Eileen Robinson; *m* 1st, 1941, Mrs Mary Playfair (marr. diss. 1951); 2nd, 1953, Mrs Joan E. G. O. Weatherlake (*née* Carter); one *s* one *d*. *Educ:* Rossall. Commissioned AAF, 602 Sqdn, 1934; Squadron Ldr, 1940, commanding 616 Squadron; Wing Comdr, 1942; Group Capt., 1945; re-formed 602 Squadron, 1946; Member Air Advisory Council, Air Ministry, 1952–56; Chairman Glasgow TA and AFA, 1953–56; Chairman Glasgow Rating Valuation Appeals Cttee, 1963–74 (Dep. Chm., 1958–63). A Vice-Pres., Earl Haig Fund, Scotland, 1978– (Chm., 1974–78). DL Glasgow, 1953. Silver Jubilee Medal, 1977. *Recreations:* ski-ing, sailing. *Address:* Rockfort, Helensburgh, Dunbartonshire G84 7BA. *Club:* Royal Northern and Clyde Yacht (Rhu).

ROBINSON, Mark Noel Foster; MP (C) Somerton and Frome, since 1992; Director (non-executive), Leopold Joseph & Sons Ltd, since 1991 (Director, 1988–91; Consultant, 1987); *b* 26 Dec. 1946; *s* of late John Foster Robinson, CBE, TD and Margaret Eve Hannah Paterson; *m* 1982, Vivien Radclyffe (*née* Pilkington); one *s* one *d*. *Educ:* Harrow School; Christ Church, Oxford. MA Hons Modern History. Called to the Bar, Middle Temple, 1975. Research Assistant to Patrick Cormack, 1970–71; Special Asst to US Congressman Hon. F. Bradford Morse, 1971–72; Special Asst to Chief of UN Emergency Operation in Bangladesh, 1972–73; Second Officer, Exec. Office, UN Secretary-General, 1974–77; Asst Dir, Commonwealth Secretariat, 1977–83. Contested (C) Newport West, 1987; MP (C) Newport West, 1983–87. PPS to Sec. of State for Wales, 1984–85; Parly Under Sec. of State, Welsh Office, 1985–87; PPS to Minister for Overseas Develt and to Parly Under-Sec. of State, FCO, 1992–94, to Sec. of State for Foreign and Commonwealth Affairs, 1994–. Mem., Foreign Affairs Select Cttee, 1983–84. Vice-Chm., UN Parly Gp, 1992– (Hon. Sec., 1983–85). Mem., Commonwealth Develt Corp., 1988–92. Mem. Council, Winston Churchill Meml Trust, 1993–. Fellow, Industry and Parlt Trust, 1985. Member: RUSI, 1984; RIIA, 1984. FIMgt (FBIM 1983); FRSA 1990. *Recreations:* include the countryside and fishing. *Address:* House of Commons, SW1A 0AA. *Club:* Travellers'.

ROBINSON, Mary; President of Ireland, since 1990; *b* 21 May 1944; *d* of Aubrey and Tessa Bourke; *m* 1970, Nicholas Robinson; two *s* one *d*. *Educ:* Trinity Coll. Dublin (BA; LLB 1967); Harvard Law Sch. (LLM). Called to the Bar, King's Inn, Dublin, 1967, Middle Temple, 1973 (Hon. Bencher, 1991); SC 1980. Reid Prof. of Constitutional and Criminal Law, TCD, 1969–75. Mem., Irish Senate, 1969–89 (Chm., Social Affairs Sub-Cttee, 1977–87, Chm., Legal Affairs Cttee, 1987–89, Parly Jt Cttee). Former Member: Adv. Bd, Common Market Law Review; Internat. Commn of Jurists; European Air Law Assoc. Pres., Cherish, 1973–90. Hon. Fellow, Hertford Coll., Oxford, 1993. *Address:* Aras an Uachtaráin, Phoenix Park, Dublin 8, Ireland.

ROBINSON, Air Vice-Marshal Michael Maurice Jeffries, CB 1982; *b* 11 Feb. 1927; *s* of Dr Maurice Robinson and Muriel (*née* Jeffries); *m* 1952, Drusilla Dallas Bush; one *s* two *d*. *Educ:* King's Sch., Bruton; Queen's Coll., Oxford; RAF Coll., Cranwell. psa 1961, jssc 1965. MA History, Univ. of West of England, 1994. Commnd, 1948; 45 Sqdn, Malaya, 1948–51; CFS, 1953–55; OC 100 Sqdn, 1962–64; Comd, RAF Lossiemouth, 1972–74; Asst Comdt, RAF Coll., Cranwell, 1974–77; SASO No 1 Gp, 1977–79; Dir Gen. of Organisation (RAF), 1979–82, retd. Wing Comdr 1961, Gp Captain 1970, Air Cdre 1976, Air Vice-Marshal 1980. Sec. (Welfare), RAF Benevolent Fund, 1982–87. Chm., SSAFA, Somerset, 1991–. Governor: King's Sch., Bruton, 1980–; Duke of Kent Sch. (RAF Benevolent Fund), 1982–. *Recreations:* golf, gardening, going to the opera. *Address:* Midland Bank, 1 Market Place, Wells, Somerset BA5 2RN. *Club:* Royal Air Force.

ROBINSON, (Moureen) Ann, (Mrs Peter Robinson); Chief Executive, Scope (formerly The Spastics Society), 1993–95; *d* of William and Winifred Flatley; *m* 1961, Peter Crawford Robinson. DHSS, 1969–74; Central Policy Review Staff, 1974–77; nurses and midwives pay, educn and professional matters, 1981–85; liaison with Health Authorities, NHS planning and review, 1985–86; social security operations, 1986–93; Dir of Policy and Planning, Benefits Agency, DSS, 1990–93. FRSA 1992. *Recreations:* walking, fine wine, bridge, fun tennis and badminton. *Address:* 1 Heathfield Road, Maidstone, Kent ME14 2AD; 29 Upper Berkeley Street, W1H 7PG.

ROBINSON, Ven. Neil; Archdeacon of Suffolk, 1987–94; *b* 28 Feb. 1929; *s* of James and Alice Robinson; *m* 1956, Kathlyn Williams; two *s* two *d*. *Educ:* Penistone Grammar School; Univ. of Durham (BA, DipTh). Curate of Holy Trinity Church, Hull, 1954–58; Vicar of St Thomas, South Wigston, Leicester, 1958–69; Rector and RD of Market Bosworth, Leicester, 1969–83; Residentiary Canon of Worcester Cathedral, 1983–87. *Recreation:* hill walking. *Address:* Skell Green, 32 Mallorie Park Drive, Ripon, N Yorks HG4 2QF. *T:* Ripon (01765) 603075.

ROBINSON, Sir Niall B. L.; *see* Lynch-Robinson.

ROBINSON, Oliver John; Editor, Good Housekeeping, 1947–65, Editor-in-Chief, 1965–67; *b* 7 April 1908; *s* of late W. Heath and Josephine Constance Robinson; *m* 1933, Evelyn Anne Laidler. *Educ:* Cranleigh Sch. Art Editor, Good Housekeeping, 1930; Art Editor, Nash's, 1933. Temporary commission, Queen's Royal Regt, 1941; Camouflage Development and Training Centre, 1942; Staff Officer, War Office, 1944. *Address:* 92 Charlbert Court, Eamont Street, NW8 7DA. *T:* 0171–722 0723. *Club:* Savage.

ROBINSON, Oswald Horsley, CMG 1983; OBE 1977; HM Diplomatic Service, retired; Director, RCC Pilotage Foundation, since 1985; *b* 24 Aug. 1926; *s* of Sir Edward Stanley Gotch Robinson, CBE, FSA, FBA, and Pamela, *d* of Sir Victor Horsley, CB, FRS; *m* 1954, Helena Faith, *d* of Dr F. R. Seymour; two *s* one *d*. *Educ:* Bedales Sch.; King's Coll., Cambridge. Served RE, 1943–48. Joined FO, 1951; served: Rangoon and Maymyo, 1954; FO, 1958; Mexico and Guatemala, 1961; Quito and Bogotá, 1963; FO (later FCO), 1965; Georgetown, Guyana, 1973; Bangkok, 1976; FCO, 1979–84. *Publications:* (compiled) Atlantic Spain and Portugal, 1988; (ed) Ports and Anchorages of the Antilles, 1991; (ed) North Africa, 1991; (ed) A Baltic Guide, 1992. *Recreation:* sailing. *Clubs:* Royal Cruising; Ocean Cruising.

ROBINSON, Dr Patrick William, (Bill); Director, London Economics, since 1993; *b* 6 Jan. 1943; *s* of Harold Desmond Robinson and Joyce Grover; *m* 1966, Heather Jackson; two *s* one *d*. *Educ:* Bryanston Sch.; St Edmund Hall, Oxford; DPhil Sussex 1969; MSc LSE 1971. Economic Asst, 10 Downing Street, 1969–70; Cabinet Office, 1970–71; Economic Adviser, HM Treasury, 1971–74; Head of Div., European Commn, 1974–78; Sen. Res. Fellow, London Business Sch., 1979–86; Adviser, Treasury and Civil Service Cttee, 1981–86; Dir, Inst. for Fiscal Studies, 1986–91; econ. columnist, The Independent, 1989–91; Special Advr to Chancellor of Exchequer, 1991–93. Mem., Retail Prices Index Adv. Cttee, 1988–91. Editor: Exchange Rate Outlook, LBS, 1979–86; Economic Outlook, LBS, 1980–86; IFS Green Budget, 1987–91. *Publications:* Medium Term Exchange Rate Guidelines for Business Planning, 1983; Britain's Borrowing Problem, 1993; numerous articles. *Recreations:* bassoon playing, opera, ski-ing, sailboarding. *Address:* London Economics, 91 New Cavendish Street, W1M 7FS.

ROBINSON, Peter; Director, Tootal Ltd, 1973–91; *b* 18 Jan. 1922; *s* of Harold Robinson and Jane Elizabeth Robinson; *m* Lesley Anne, step-*d* of Major J. M. May, TD; two *s* two *d*. *Educ:* Prince Henry's Sch., Otley; Leeds Coll. of Technology (Diploma in Printing). Mem., Inst. of Printing; CBIM. Management Trainee, 1940–41; flying duties, RAFVR, 1942–46; Leeds Coll. of Technol., 1946–49; Asst Manager, Robinson & Sons Ltd, Chesterfield, 1949–53; Works Dir and Man. Dir, Taylowe Ltd, 1953–62; Director: Hazell Sun, 1964; British Printing Corp., 1966–81, Man. Dir 1969–75; Chm. and Chief Exec., BPC Ltd (formerly British Printing Corp.), 1976–81. Formerly Council Mem., PIRA. *Recreations:* military history, cricket, golf. *Address:* 20 Links Road, Flackwell Heath, High Wycombe, Bucks HP10 9LY.

ROBINSON, Peter Damian, CB 1983; Deputy Secretary, Lord Chancellor's Department, 1980–86; *b* 11 July 1926; *s* of late John Robinson and Jill Clegg (*née* Easten); *m* 1st, 1956, Mary Katinka Bonner (*d* 1978), Peterborough; two *d*; 2nd, 1985, Mrs Sheila Suzanne Gibbins (*née* Guille). *Educ:* Corby Sch., Sunderland; Lincoln Coll., Oxford. MA. Royal Marine Commandos, 1944–46. Called to Bar, Middle Temple, 1951; practised common law, 1952–59; Clerk of Assize, NE Circuit, 1959–70; Administrator, NE Circuit, 1970–74; Circuit Administrator, SE Circuit, 1974–80; Dep. Clerk of the Crown in Chancery, Lord Chancellor's Dept, 1982–86. Advr on Hong Kong Judiciary, 1986. Member, Home Office Departmental Cttee on Legal Aid in Criminal Proceedings (the Widgery Cttee), 1964–66; Chm., Interdeptl Cttee on Conciliation, 1982–83. Mem., MENSA. *Recreations:* reading, the countryside, world travel. *Address:* 15 Birklands Park, St Albans AL1 1TS.

ROBINSON, Peter David; MP (DemU) Belfast East, since 1979 (resigned seat Dec. 1985 in protest against Anglo-Irish Agreement; re-elected Jan. 1986); *b* 29 Dec. 1948; *s* of David McCrea Robinson and Sheliah Robinson; *m* 1970, Iris Collins; two *s* one *d*. *Educ:* Annadale Grammar School; Castlereagh Further Education College. Gen. Secretary, Ulster Democratic Unionist Party, 1975–79, Dep. Leader, 1980–87. Mem. (DemU) Belfast E, NI Assembly, 1982–86; Member, Castlereagh Borough Council, 1977; Deputy Mayor, 1978; Mayor of Castlereagh, 1986. *Publications:* (jtly) Ulster—the facts, 1982; booklets: The North Answers Back, 1970; Capital Punishment for Capital Crime, 1978; Self Inflicted, 1981; Ulster in Peril, 1981; Savagery and Suffering, 1981; Their Cry Was "No Surrender", 1989. *Address:* 51 Gransha Road, Dundonald, Northern Ireland; 296 Albertbridge Road, Belfast BT5 4GX.

ROBINSON, Peter James, FCIS, FCIB; Group Chief Executive, Woolwich Building Society, since 1995; *b* 28 April 1941; *s* of Percival Albert Robinson and Lillian Caroline (*née* Pantling); *m* 1st, 1963 (marr. diss.); twin *s* one *d*; 2nd, 1984, Janice Helen Jones; two *d*. *Educ:* Erith Co. Grammar Sch.; City of London Poly. FCIS 1967, FCIB 1967. Woolwich Building Society: mgt trainee, 1963–68; PA to Gen. Managers, 1968–70; Ops and Mkting Manager, 1970–72; Co. Sec., 1972–75; Asst Gen. Manager (Develt), 1975–81; Gen. Manager (Ops), 1981–86; Dep. Chief Exec. and Dir, 1986–91; Man. Dir, 1991–95. Chm., Metropolitan Assoc. of Building Socs, 1992. Freeman, City of London, 1982. MInstD 1988; CIMgt 1991. *Publications:* contrib. articles to Finance Gazette, Economist, Mgt Today, various newspapers. *Recreations:* cricket, golf, gardening, dogs. *Address:* Woolwich Building Society, Corporate Headquarters, Watling Street, Bexleyheath, Kent DA6 7RR. *T:* 0181–298 5015. *Clubs:* Royal Automobile; MCC (Playing Mem.).

ROBINSON, Prof. Peter Michael; Professor of Econometrics, London School of Economics and Political Science, since 1984; *b* 20 April 1947; *s* of Maurice Allan Robinson and Brenda Margaret (*née* Ponsford); *m* 1981, Wendy Rhea Brandmark; one *d*. *Educ:* Brockenhurst Grammar Sch.; University Coll. London (BSc); London School of Economics (MSc); Australian National Univ. (PhD). Lectr, LSE, 1969–70; Asst Prof. 1973–77, Associate Prof. 1977–79, Harvard Univ.; Associate Prof., Univ. of British Columbia, 1979–80; Prof., Univ. of Surrey, 1980–84. Fellow, Econometric Soc., 1989. Co-Editor, Econometrica, 1991–. *Publications:* articles in books, and in learned jls, incl. Econometrica, Annals of Statistics. *Recreation:* walking. *Address:* Department of Economics, London School of Economics and Political Science, Houghton Street, WC2A 2AE. *T:* 0171–955 7516.

ROBINSON, Philip; Director of Finance, City of Bradford Metropolitan Council, since 1987; *b* 2 March 1949; *s* of late Clifford Robinson and of Vera Robinson; *m* 1974, Irene Langdale. *Educ:* Grange Grammar Sch., Bradford. IPFA, IRRV. Principal Accountant 1982, Asst Dir of Finance 1985, City of Bradford Metropolitan Council. *Recreations:* sport, music, theatre. *Address:* City of Bradford Metropolitan Council, Directorate of Finance, Britannia House, Hall Ings, Bradford BD1 1HX. *T:* Bradford (01274) 752700.

ROBINSON, Philip Henry; Director, CLF Municipal Bank plc, since 1993 (Chairman, Audit Committee, since 1993); *b* 4 Jan. 1926; *s* of Arthur Robinson and Frances M. Robinson; *m* 1st, 1959, Helen Wharton (marr. diss. 1979); one *s* one *d*; 2nd, 1985, Mrs A. L. D. Baring; two step *s*. *Educ:* Lincoln Sch.; Jesus Coll., Cambridge (Exhibr, MA); Sch. of Oriental and African Studies, London Univ.; NY Univ. Graduate Sch. of Business Admin. Member, Gray's Inn. Royal Navy, 1944–47; N. M. Rothschild & Sons, 1950–54; Actg Sec., British Newfoundland Corp., Montreal, 1954–56; Asst Vice-Pres., J. Henry Schroder Banking Corp., New York, 1956–61; J. Henry Schroder Wagg & Co. Ltd, 1961; Director: J. Henry Schroder Wagg & Co. Ltd, 1966–85; Siemens Ltd, 1967–86; Schroders & Chartered Ltd Hong Kong, 1971–85; Schroder International Ltd, 1973–85 (Exec. Vice-Pres., 1977–85); Standard Chartered PLC, 1986–91 (Chm., Audit Cttee, 1989–91); Chairman: Schroder Leasing Ltd, 1979–85; Sunbury Investment Co. Ltd, 1985–94; Berkertex Hldgs Ltd, 1987–88; Man. Trustee, Municipal Mutual Insurance Ltd, 1977–92 (Dep. Chm., 1992); Dir, Capital Re Corp., NY, 1993– (Chm., Audit Cttee, 1993–). Member: Nat. Coal Board, 1973–77; Estates Cttee, Canterbury Cath., 1993–. Hon. Treasurer, Nat. Council for One Parent Families, 1977–79. *Recreations:* music, tennis. *Address:* Stone Hall, Great Mongeham, Deal, Kent CT14 0HB. *Club:* Brooks's.
See also A. G. Robinson.

ROBINSON, Hon. Raymond; *see* Robinson, Hon. A. N. R.

ROBINSON, Robert Henry; writer and broadcaster; *b* 17 Dec. 1927; *o s* of Ernest Redfern Robinson and Johanna Hogan; *m* 1958, Josephine Mary Richard; one *s* two *d*. *Educ:* Raynes Park Grammar Sch.; Exeter Coll., Oxford (MA). Editor of Isis, 1950. TV columnist, Sunday Chronicle, 1952; film and theatre columnist, Sunday Graphic, and radio critic, Sunday Times, 1956; editor Atticus, Sunday Times, 1960; weekly column, Private View, Sunday Times, 1962; film critic, Sunday Telegraph, 1965. Writer and presenter of TV programmes: Picture Parade, 1959; Points of View, 1961; Divided We Stand, 1964; The Look of the Week, 1966; Reason to Believe?, The Fifties, 1969; Chm., Call My Bluff, Ask The Family, 1967; The Book Programme, Vital Statistics, 1974; Word for Word, 1978; The Book Game, 1983 and 1985; Behind The Headlines, 1989–; films for TV: Robinson's Travels - the Pioneer Trail West, 1977; B. Traven: a mystery solved, 1978; From Shepherd's Bush to Simla, 1979; Robinson Cruising, 1981; The Auden Landscape, 1982; Robinson Country, 1983, 1987, 1993; In Trust—Houses and Heritage, 1986; The Magic Rectangle, 1986; presenter of: BBC radio current affairs programme Today, 1971–74; Chm., Brain of Britain, 1973–; Chm., Stop the Week, 1974–92; Ad Lib, 1989–. Mem., Kingman Cttee on the teaching of the English Language, 1987–88. Pres., Johnson Soc. of Lichfield, 1982. Radio Personality of the Year: Radio Industries Club, 1973; Variety Club of GB, 1980. *Publications:* (ed) Poetry from Oxford, 1951;

Landscape with Dead Dons, 1956; Inside Robert Robinson (essays), 1965; (contrib.) To Nevill Coghill from Friends, 1966; The Conspiracy, 1968; The Dog Chairman, 1982; (ed) The Everyman Book of Light Verse, 1984; Bad Dreams, 1989; Prescriptions of a Pox Doctor's Clerk, 1990; Skip All That, 1995. *Address:* 16 Cheyne Row, SW3 5HL; Laurel Cottage, Buckland St Mary, Somerset TA20 3SJ. *Club:* Garrick.

ROBINSON, Prof. Roger James, FRCP; Professor of Paediatrics, United Medical and Dental Schools of Guy's and St Thomas's Hospitals (formerly Guy's Hospital Medical School), University of London, 1975–90, now Emeritus; *b* 17 May 1932; *s* of Albert Edward and Leonora Sarah Robinson; *m* 1962, Jane Hippisley Packham; two *s* one *d*. *Educ:* Poole Grammar Sch.; Balliol Coll., Oxford (Brackenbury schol.; MA, DPhil, BM, BCh). Lectr of Christ Church, Oxford, 1953; appts at Radcliffe Infirmary, Oxford, National Hosp., Queen Square, and Hammersmith Hosp., 1960–66; Visiting Fellow, Harvard, 1967; Sen. Lectr, Inst. of Child Health, Hammersmith Hosp., 1967; Cons. Paediatrician, Guy's Hosp., 1971. *Publications:* Brain and Early Behaviour: development in the fetus and infant, 1969; (jtly) Medical Care of Newborn Babies, 1972; papers on paediatrics and child neurology. *Recreations:* literature (especially poetry), theatre, walking, canoeing. *Address:* 60 Madeley Road, Ealing, W5 2LU.

ROBINSON, Prof. Ronald Edward, CBE 1970; DFC 1944; Beit Professor of the History of the British Commonwealth, and Fellow of Balliol College, Oxford University, 1971–87; Director, University of Oxford Development Records Project, 1978–87; *b* 3 Sept. 1920; *e s* of William Edward and Ada Theresa Robinson, Clapham; *m* 1948, Alice Josephine Denny; two *s* two *d*. *Educ:* Battersea Grammar Sch.; St John's Coll., Cambridge. Major Scholar in History, St John's Coll., 1939; BA 1946, PhD 1949, Cantab. F/Lt, 58 Bomber Sqn, RAF, 1942–45. Research Officer, African Studies Branch, Colonial Office, 1947–49; Lectr in History, 1953–66, Smuts Reader in History of the British Commonwealth, 1966–71, Univ. of Cambridge; Tutor 1961–66, Fellow 1949–71, St John's Coll., Cambridge; Chm., Faculty Bd of Modern Hist., Oxford, 1974–76, Vice-Chm., 1979–87. Inst. for Advanced Studies, Princeton, 1959–60. Mem., Bridges Cttee on Trng in Public Administration, 1961–62; Chm., Cambridge Confs on Problems of Developing Countries, 1961–70. UK observer, Zimbabwe election, 1980. *Publications:* Africa and the Victorians, 1961; Developing the Third World, 1971; (ed jtly) Bismarck, Europe and Africa, 1988; Railway Imperialism, 1991; articles in Cambridge History of the British Empire, Vol. III, 1959, and The New Cambridge Modern History, Vol. XI, 1963; reports on Problems of Developing Countries, 1963–71; articles and reviews in learned jls. *Recreation:* room cricket. *Address:* c/o Balliol College, Oxford. *Clubs:* Commonwealth Trust; Hawks (Cambridge); Gridiron (Oxford).

ROBINSON, Stanley Scott, MBE 1944; TD 1950; BL; SSC; Sheriff of Grampian, Highland and Islands (formerly Inverness (including Western Isles), Ross, Cromarty, Moray and Nairn), 1973–83; retired; *b* 27 March 1913; *s* of late William Scott Robinson, Engineer, and of Christina Douglas Robinson; *m* 1937, Helen Annan Hardie; three *s*. *Educ:* Boroughmuir Sch., Edinburgh; Edinburgh Univ. Admitted as solicitor, 1935; Solicitor in the Supreme Courts. Commissioned in TA, 1935. Served War: France and Belgium, 1939–40, Captain RA; France, Holland and Germany, 1944–45 (despatches twice); Major, RA, 1943; Lt-Col, 1948. Solicitor in gen. practice in Montrose, Angus, 1935–72 (except during war service). Hon. Sheriff: of Perth and Angus, 1970–72; of Inverness, 1984. Mem. Council of Law Society of Scotland, 1963–72 (Vice-Pres., 1971–72); Dean, Soc. of Solicitors of Angus, 1970–72. *Publications:* The Law of Interdict, 1987; The Law of Game and Fishing in Scotland, 1989; contribs to Stair Memorial Encyclopaedia and Jl of Law Society of Scotland. *Recreations:* golf, bowling, military history. *Address:* Flat 3, Drumallin House, Drummond Road, Inverness IV2 4NB. *T:* Inverness (01463) 233488. *Club:* Highland (Inverness).

ROBINSON, Stephen Joseph, OBE 1971; FRS 1976; FEng, FIEE; FInstP; Director, Royal Signals and Radar Establishment, Ministry of Defence, 1989–91, retired (Deputy Director, 1985–89); *b* 6 Aug. 1931; *s* of Joseph Allan Robinson and Ethel (*née* Bunting); *m* 1957, Monica Mabs Scott; one *s* one *d*. *Educ:* Sebright Sch., Wolverley; Jesus Coll., Cambridge (MA Natural Sciences). RAF, 1950–51. Mullard Res. Labs, 1954–72; MEL Div., Philips Industries (formerly MEL Equipment Co. Ltd), 1972–79; Product Dir, 1973–79; Man. Dir, Pye TVT Ltd, 1980–84. Vis. Prof., Birmingham Univ., 1990–91. Mem. Council, Royal Soc., 1982–. *Recreations:* sailing, ski-ing.

ROBINSON, Rev. Thomas Hugh, CBE 1989; Team Rector, Cleethorpes, since 1990; *b* Murree, India, 11 June 1934; *s* of Lt-Col James Arthur Robinson, OBE and Maud Loney Robinson; *m* 1959, Mary Elizabeth Doreen Clingan; two *s* one *d*. *Educ:* Bishop Foy School, Waterford; Trinity Coll., Dublin (BA 1955, MA 1971). Pres., Univ. Philosophical Soc., 1955–56. Deacon 1957, priest 1958; Curate, St Clement's, Belfast, 1957–60; Chaplain, Missions to Seamen, Mombasa, 1961–64; Rector of Youghal, Diocese of Cork, 1964–66; CF, 1966–89; DACG, 2 Armoured Div., 1977–80; Senior Chaplain: RMCS, 1980–82; Eastern Dist, 1982–84; 1st British Corps, 1984–85; BAOR, 1985–86; Dep. Chaplain Gen. to the Forces, 1986–89. QHC 1985–89. *Recreations:* travel, photography. *Address:* St Peter's Rectory, 42 Queens Parade, Cleethorpes, S Humberside DN35 0DG. *T:* Cleethorpes (01472) 693234.

ROBINSON, Thomas Lloyd, TD; Honorary President, The Dickinson Robinson Group Ltd, 1988–92 (Chairman, 1974–77, Deputy Chairman, 1968); *b* 21 Dec. 1912; *s* of late Thomas Rosser Robinson and Rebe Francis-Watkins; *m* 1939, Pamela Rosemary Foster; one *s* two *d*. *Educ:* Wycliffe Coll. Served War, 1939–45: Royal Warwickshire Regt, 61 Div., and SHAEF; Staff Coll., Camberley. Director, E. S. & A. Robinson Ltd, 1952; Jt Managing Dir, 1958; Dep. Chm., E. S. & A. Robinson (Holdings) Ltd, 1963; Director: Bristol Waterworks Co., 1978–84; Van Leer Groep, Holland, 1977–81; Legal & General Assurance Society (now Legal & General Group plc), 1970–83 (Vice-Chm., 1978–83); Chm., Legal & General South and Western Advisory Bd, 1972–84. Chm., Council of Governors, Wycliffe Coll., 1970–83, Pres., 1988–; Mem. Council, Univ. of Bristol, 1977–94, Pro-Chancellor, 1983–94. Master, Soc. of Merchant Venturers, Bristol, 1977–78. High Sheriff, Avon, 1979–80; President: Glos CCC, 1980–83; Warwicks Old County Cricketers Assoc., 1989. Hon. LLD Bristol, 1985. *Recreations:* music, golf. *Address:* Lechlade, 23 Druid Stoke Avenue, Stoke Bishop, Bristol BS9 1DB. *T:* Bristol (0117) 968 1957. *Clubs:* Army & Navy, MCC; Royal and Ancient (St Andrews); Clifton (Bristol).

ROBINSON, Victor, CEng, FIChemE; Vice-President, Fédération Européenne d'Associations Nationales d'Ingénieurs, since 1992; *b* 31 July 1925; *s* of Arthur Worsley Robinson and Nellie (*née* Halliwell); *m* 1948, Sadie Monica (*née* Grut); one *s* five *d*. *Educ:* Manchester Grammar Sch.; Cambridge Univ. (MA); Admin. Staff Coll., Henley. CEng, FIChemE 1960. Simon Carves Ltd: R&D Proj. Engrg, 1945; Technical Dir, 1961; Dir, 1964; Man. Dir Overseas Ops and Dir, Sim-Chem Ltd and subsid. cos, 1966; Man. Dir, Turriff Taylor Ltd, 1974–76; Dir, Davy Internat. Projects, 1976–85; Industrial Adviser, Dept of Trade (on secondment from Davy Corp. Ltd), 1978–81. *Recreation:* fell and alpine walking. *Address:* 15 Adams Close, Surbiton, Surrey KT5 8LB.

ROBINSON, Vivian; QC 1986; a Recorder, since 1986; *b* 29 July 1944; *s* of late William and of Ann Robinson; *m* 1975, Louise Marriner; one *s* two *d*. *Educ:* Queen Elizabeth Grammar School, Wakefield; The Leys School, Cambridge; Sidney Sussex College, Cambridge (BA). Called to the Bar, Inner Temple, 1967 (Bencher, 1991). Liveryman, and Mem., Court of Assistants, Gardeners' Co. *Address:* Queen Elizabeth Building, Temple, EC4Y 9BS. *Clubs:* Garrick, Royal Automobile, MCC.

ROBINSON, Sir Wilfred (Henry Frederick), 3rd Bt, *cr* 1908; Staff, Diocesan College School, Rondebosch, South Africa, 1950–77, Vice-Principal, 1969–77; *b* 24 Dec. 1917; *s* of Wilfred Henry Robinson (*d* 1922) (3rd *s* of 1st Bt), and Eileen (*d* 1963), *d* of Frederick St Leger, Claremont, SA; *S* uncle, Sir Joseph Benjamin Robinson, 2nd Bt, 1954; *m* 1946, Margaret Alison Kathleen, *d* of late Frank Mellish, MC, Cape Town, SA; one *s* two *d*. *Educ:* Diocesan Coll., Rondebosch; St John's Coll., Cambridge, MA 1944. Served War of 1939–45, Devonshire Regt and Parachute Regt, Major. Finance Officer, Soc. of Genealogists, 1980–92. *Heir:* *s* Peter Frank Robinson, [*b* 23 June 1949; *m* 1988, Alison Jane, *e d* of D. Bradley, Rochester, Kent; two *d*]. *Address:* 24 Ennismore Gardens, SW7 1AB.

ROBINSON, Ven. William David; Archdeacon of Blackburn, since 1986; *b* 15 March 1931; *s* of William and Margaret Robinson; *m* 1955, Carol Averil Roma Hamm; one *s* one *d*. *Educ:* Queen Elizabeth's Grammar School, Blackburn; Durham Univ. (MA, DipTh). Curate: Standish, 1958–61; Lancaster Priory (i/c St George), 1961–63; Vicar, St James, Blackburn, 1963–73; Diocesan Stewardship Adviser, Blackburn, and Priest-in-charge, St James, Shireshead, 1973–86; Hon. Canon, Blackburn Cathedral, 1975–86; Vicar of Balderstone, 1986–87. *Recreation:* fell walking. *Address:* 7 Billinge Close, Blackburn BB2 6SB. *T:* Blackburn (01254) 53442.

ROBINSON, William Good; Deputy Secretary, Department of the Civil Service, Northern Ireland, 1978–80, retired; *b* 20 May 1919; *s* of William Robinson and Elizabeth Ann (*née* Good); *m* 1947, Wilhelmina Vaughan; two *d*. *Educ:* Clones High Sch.; Queen's Univ. of Belfast (BScEcon, BA). Served War, RAF, 1941–46 (Flt Lieut, Navigator). Entered NI Civil Service, 1938; Min. of Labour and National Insurance, NI, 1946–63; Principal, Min. of Home Affairs, NI, 1963; Asst Sec., 1967; Sen. Asst Sec., NI Office, 1973. *Recreations:* do-it-yourself, reading history. *Address:* Stormochree, 47 Castlehill Road, Belfast BT4 3GN. *T:* Belfast (01232) 763646.

ROBINSON, Rt. Rev. William James; *b* 8 Sept. 1916; *s* of Thomas Albert Robinson and Harriet Mills; *m* 1946, Isobel Morton; one *s* three *d*. *Educ:* Bishop's Univ., Lennoxville, PQ. BA in Theology; DCL (*hc*) 1973. Deacon, 1939; Priest, 1940; Asst Curate in Trenton, 1939–41; Rector of: Tweed and Madoc, 1941–46, Tweed and N Addington, 1946–47; Napanee, 1948–53; St Thomas' Church, Belleville, 1953–55; St John's Church, Ottawa, 1955–62; Church of Ascension, Hamilton, 1962–67; St George's Church, Guelph, 1967–70. Canon of Christ Church Cathedral, Hamilton, 1964–68; Archdeacon of Trafalgar (Niagara Diocese), 1968–70; Bishop of Ottawa, 1970–81; retired. *Recreations:* woodworking and gardening. *Address:* 168 Inverness Crescent, Kingston, Ont K7M 6N7, Canada. *T:* (613) 5497599.

ROBINSON, William Rhys Brunel; Under Secretary, Overseas Division, Department of Employment, 1980–89; *b* 12 July 1930; *s* of late William Robinson and Elizabeth Myfanwy Robinson (*née* Owen); *m* 1988, Pamela Mary Hall. *Educ:* Chepstow Secondary Grammar Sch.; St Catherine's Soc., Oxford (MA,BLitt). Entered Min. of Labour, 1954; Asst Private Sec. to Minister, 1958–59; Principal, Min. of Labour, 1959; Asst Sec., 1966; London Sch. of Economics, 1972–73 (MSc Industrial Relations, 1973); Asst Sec., Trng Services Agency, 1973–75; Dep. Chief Exec., Employment Service Agency, 1975–77; Under-Sec. and Dir of Establishments, Dept of Employment, 1977–80. Chm., Governing Body, ILO, 1986–87. FSA 1978; FRHistS 1991. *Publications:* articles in historical jls. *Recreation:* historical research. *Address:* 7 Shere Avenue, Cheam, Surrey SM2 7JU. *T:* 0181–393 3019.

ROBLES, Marisa, FRCM; harpist; Professor of Harp, Royal College of Music, since 1971; *b* 4 May 1937; *d* of Cristobal Robles and Maria Bonilla; *m* 1985, David Bean; two *s* one *d* by previous marriage. *Educ:* Madrid National Sch.; Royal Madrid Conservatoire. Prof. of Harp, Royal Madrid Conservatoire, 1958–60. Recitals and solo appearances with major orchestras in UK, Europe, Africa, Canada, USA, South America, Japan, China and Australia. Mem., UK Harp Assoc. Recordings include concerti by Handel, Dittersdorf, Boildieu, Debussy, Rodrigo, Moreno-Buendia, solo repertoire by Beethoven, Mozart, Fauré, Hasselmans, Tournier, Guridi and others, and chamber music by Alwyn, Roussel, Britten, Ravel, Debussy and others. Hon. Royal Madrid Conservatoire 1958; Hon. RCM 1973; FRCM 1983. *Recreations:* theatre, gardening, indoor plants, family life in general. *Address:* 38 Luttrell Avenue, Putney, SW15 6PE. *T:* 0181–785 2204. *Club:* Royal Over-Seas League.

ROBLIN, Ven. Graham Henry, OBE 1983; Vicar, Bere Regis and Affpuddle with Turnerspuddle, since 1993; *b* 18 Aug. 1937; *s* of Ewart and Marjorie Roblin; *m* 1964, Penelope Ann Cumberlege; one *s* one *d*. *Educ:* Cathedral Sch., Exeter; King's Coll., Taunton; King's Coll., London (AKC). Deacon, 1962; priest, 1963; Curate of St Helier, Southwark, 1962–66; joined Army Chaplaincy Service, 1966; Dep. Asst Chaplain Gen., Hong Kong, 1979–81; Dep. Asst Chaplain Gen., 2nd Armd Div., 1981–83; Warden, RAChD Centre, Bagshot Park, 1983–86; Senior Chaplain: 1st British Corps, 1986–87; BAOR, 1987–89; Dep. Chaplain Gen. to Forces, 1989–93; Archdeacon to the Army, 1990–93, Archdeacon Emeritus, 1994–. QHC 1987–93. Mem., Gen. Synod of C of E, 1990–. *Recreation:* writing. *Address:* The Vicarage, Bere Regis, Wareham, Dorset BH20 7HQ. *T:* Bere Regis (01929) 471262.

ROBOROUGH, 3rd Baron *cr* 1938, of Maristow; **Henry Massey Lopes;** Bt 1805; *b* 2 Feb. 1940; *s* of 2nd Baron and of Helen, *o d* of Lt-Col E. A. F. Dawson; *S* father, 1992; *m* 1st, 1968, Robyn Zenda Carol (marr. diss. 1986), *e d* of John Bromwich; two *s* two *d*; 2nd, 1986, Sarah Anne Pipon, 2nd *d* of Colin Baker; two *d*. *Educ:* Eton. ARICS. Late Lt Coldstream Guards. Farmer, managing Maristow Estate, Plymouth. Racehorse owner and breeder. *Heir:* *s* Hon. Massey John Henry Lopes, *b* 22 Dec. 1969. *Address:* c/o House of Lords, SW1A 0PW. *Club:* Turf.

ROBOTHAM, Hon. Sir Lascelles (Lister), Kt 1987; Justice of Appeal, Belize, since 1992; *b* 22 Oct. 1923; *s* of Vivian Constantine Robotham and Ethline Blanche Robotham; *m* 1949, Gloria Angela Stiebel; one *s* one *d*. *Educ:* Calabar Coll., Jamaica. Called to the Bar, Lincoln's Inn, 1955, Hon. Bencher, 1988. Crown Counsel, Jamaica, 1955–58; Dep. Dir of Public Prosecutions, 1958–62; Resident Magistrate, 1962–64; Puisne Judge, 1964–76; Justice of Appeal, Jamaica, 1976–79; Justice of Appeal, Eastern Caribbean Supreme Court, 1979–84; Pres., Eastern Caribbean Court of Appeal, 1984–91; Chief Justice, Eastern Caribbean Supreme Court, 1984–91. *Recreations:* reading, gardening, cricket. *Address:* PO Box 1950, Castries, St Lucia, West Indies. *T:* (home) 28566.

ROBSON, family name of **Baroness Robson of Kiddington.**

ROBSON OF KIDDINGTON, Baroness *cr* 1974 (Life Peer), of Kiddington; **Inga-Stina Robson,** JP; Chairman, South-West Thames Regional Health Authority, 1974–82; *b* 20 Aug. 1919; *d* of Erik R. Arvidsson and Lilly A. Arvidsson (*née* Danielson); *m* 1940, Sir

Lawrence W. Robson (*d* 1982); one *s* two *d*. *Educ:* Stockholm, Sweden. Swedish Foreign Office, 1939–40; Min. of Information, 1942–43. Contested (L) Eye Div., 1955 and 1959, Gloucester City, 1964 and 1966. President: Women's Liberal Fedn, 1968–69 and 1969–70; Liberal Party Org., 1970–71; Chm., Liberal Party Environment Panel, 1971–77. Chairman: Bd of Governors, Queen Charlotte's and Chelsea Hosps, 1970–84; Midwife Teachers Training Coll.; Nat. Assoc. of Leagues of Hosp. Friends, 1985–94; Member: Bd of Governors, University Coll. Hosp., 1966–74; Council, Surrey Univ., 1974. Chm., Anglo-Swedish Soc., 1983–92. JP Oxfordshire, 1955. *Recreations:* sailing, skiing. *Address:* The Dower House, Kiddington, Woodstock, Oxon OX20 1BU.

ROBSON, Alan; General Secretary, Confederation of Shipbuilding and Engineering Unions, since 1993; *b* 24 Dec. 1941; *s* of John William Robson and Bridgit Robson; *m* 1964, Joyce Lydia. *Educ:* Ellison C of E Sch. Fitter-turner, 1958–90; Asst Gen. Sec., CSEU, 1990–93. *Recreations:* reading, supporting the arts, football. *Address:* 20 York Avenue, Jarrow, Tyne and Wear. *T:* 0191–421 6883. *Clubs:* Labour, Elmfield, Ex-Service Men's (Jarrow).

ROBSON, Brian Ewart, CB 1985; FRHistS; Deputy Under-Secretary of State (Personnel and Logistics), Ministry of Defence, 1984–86; *b* 25 July 1926; 2nd *s* of late Walter Ewart Robson; *m* 1962, Cynthia Margaret, *o d* of late William James Scott, Recife, Brazil; two *d*. *Educ:* Steyning Grammar Sch.; Varndean Sch., Brighton; The Queen's Coll., Oxford (BA Modern History). FRHistS 1995. Royal Sussex Regt and Kumaon Regt, Indian Army, 1944–47. Air Min., 1950; Asst Private Sec. to Sec. of State for Air, 1953–55; Principal, 1955; Asst Sec., 1965; Imperial Defence Coll., 1970; Ecole Nationale d'Administration, Paris, 1975; Asst Under-Sec. of State, MoD, 1976–82; Dep. Under-Sec. of State (Army), 1982–84. Mem., Central Finance Bd of C of E, 1985–. Comr, Royal Hosp., 1982–85; Chm., Soc. for Army Historical Res., 1993–; Member Council: Army Records Soc., 1984–89, 1993–; Nat. Army Museum, 1982–93; Trustee, Imperial War Museum, 1984–86. Governor: Whitelands Coll., 1988–; Roehampton Inst., 1991–. *Publications:* Swords of the British Army, 1975; The Road to Kabul: the Second Afghan War 1878–1880, 1986; Roberts in India: military papers of Lord Roberts, 1993; Fuzzy Wuzzy: the campaigns in the Eastern Sudan 1884–85, 1993; Onward and Upward: a history of Varndean 1884–1975, 1993; numerous articles on weapons and military history. *Recreations:* military history, cricket, travel. *Address:* 17 Woodlands, Hove, East Sussex BN3 6TJ. *T:* Brighton (01273) 505803. *Club:* Oxford Union.

ROBSON, David Ernest Henry, QC 1980; a Recorder of the Crown Court (NE Circuit), since 1979; *b* 1 March 1940; *s* of late Joseph Robson and of Caroline Robson. *Educ:* Robert Richardson Grammar Sch., Ryhope; Christ Church, Oxford (MA). Called to the Bar, Inner Temple, 1965 (Profumo Prize, 1963), Bencher, 1988. NE Circuit, 1965–. Artistic Dir, Royalty Studio Theatre, Sunderland, 1986–88. Pres., Herrington Burn YMCA, Sunderland 1987–. *Recreations:* acting, Italy. *Address:* Whitton Grange, Whitton, Rothbury, Northumberland NE65 7RL. *T:* Rothbury (01669) 20929. *Club:* County (Durham).

ROBSON, Prof. Elizabeth Browel; Galton Professor of Human Genetics, University College London, 1978–93; *b* 10 Nov. 1928; *d* of Thomas Robson and Isabella (*née* Stoker); *m* 1955, George MacBeth, writer (marr. diss. 1975, he *d* 1992). *Educ:* Bishop Auckland Girls' Grammar Sch.; King's Coll., Newcastle upon Tyne. BSc Dunelm; PhD London. Rockefeller Fellowship, Columbia Univ., New York City, 1954–55; external scientific staff of MRC (London Hosp. Med. Coll. and King's Coll. London), 1955–62; Member and later Asst Director, MRC Human Biochemical Genetics Unit, University Coll. London, 1962–78; Hd, Dept of Genetics and Biometry, UCL, 1978–90. Jt Editor, Annals of Human Genetics, 1978–93. *Publications:* papers on biochemical human genetics and gene mapping in scientific jls. *Address:* 44 Sheen Road, Richmond, Surrey TW9 1AW.

ROBSON, Frank Elms, OBE 1991; Senior Partner, Winckworth and Pemberton, Solicitors, Oxford and Westminster, since 1990 (Partner, 1962); Registrar: Diocese of Oxford, since 1970; Province of Canterbury, since 1982; *b* 14 Dec. 1931; *s* of Joseph A. Robson and Barbara Robson; *m* 1958, Helen (*née* Jackson) four *s* one *d*. *Educ:* King Edward VI Grammar Sch., Morpeth; Selwyn Coll., Cambridge (MA). Admitted solicitor, 1954. DCL Lambeth, 1991. *Recreations:* fell-walking, clocks, following Oxford United. *Address:* 2 Simms Close, Stanton St John, Oxford OX9 1HB. *T:* Stanton St John (01865) 351393.

ROBSON, Godfrey; Under Secretary, Industrial Expansion, Scottish Office, Glasgow, since 1993; *b* 5 Nov. 1946; *s* of late William James Robson and of Mary Finn; one *s*. *Educ:* St Joseph's Coll., Dumfries; Edinburgh Univ. (MA). Joined Scottish Office, 1970; Pvte Sec. to Parly Under-Sec. of State, 1973–74, to Minister of State, 1974; Prin. Pvte Sec. to Sec. of State for Scotland, 1979–81; Assistant Secretary: Roads and Transport, 1981–86; Local Govt Finance, 1986–89; Under Sec., 1989; Scottish Fisheries Sec., 1989–93. *Recreations:* walking, travel by other means, reading history. *Address:* 50 East Trinity Road, Edinburgh EH5 3EN. *T:* 0131–552 9519. *Club:* National Liberal.

ROBSON, Prof. Sir (James) Gordon, Kt 1982; CBE 1977; MB, ChB; FRCS; FFARCS; Professor of Anaesthetics, University of London, Royal Postgraduate Medical School and Hon. Consultant, Hammersmith Hospital, 1964–86, retired; Chairman, Advisory Committee on Distinction Awards, 1984–94; *b* Stirling, Scot., 18 March 1921; *o s* of late James Cyril Robson and Freda Elizabeth Howard; *m* 1st, 1945, Dr Martha Graham Kennedy (*d* 1975); one *s*; 2nd, 1984, Jennifer Kilpatrick. *Educ:* High Sch. of Stirling; Univ. of Glasgow. FRCS 1977. RAMC, 1945–48 (Captain). Sen. Registrar in Anaesthesia, Western Inf., Glasgow, 1948–52; First Asst, Dept of Anaesthetics, Univ. of Durham, 1952–54; Cons. Anaesth., Royal Inf., Edinburgh, 1954–56; Wellcome Res. Prof. of Anaesth., McGill Univ., Montreal, 1956–64. Consultant Advr in Anaesthetics to DHSS, 1975–84; Hon. Consultant in Anaesthetics to the Army, 1983–88. Royal College of Surgeons: Master, Hunterian Inst., 1982–88. Mem. Bd of Faculty of Anaesthetists, 1968–85 (Dean of Faculty, 1973–76); Mem. Council, 1973–81, 1982–88 (a Vice-Pres., 1977–79); Chm., Jt Cttee on Higher Trng of Anaesthetists, 1973–76; Member: AHA, Ealing, Hammersmith and Hounslow, 1974–77 (NW Met. RHB, 1971–74); Chief Scientists' Res. Cttee and Panel on Med. Res., DHSS, 1973–77; Neurosciences Bd, MRC, 1974–77; Clin. Res. Bd, MRC (Chm. Grants Cttee II), 1969–71; Mem. Council, RPMS (Vice-Chm. Academic Bd, 1973–76; Chm. 1976–80); Mem., Rock Carling Fellowship Panel, 1976–78; Vice-Chm., Jt Consultants' Cttee, 1974–79. Special Trustee, Hammersmith Hosp., 1974–77; Chm., Cttee of Management, Inst. of Basic Med. Scis, 1982–85; Hon. Sec., Conf. of Med. Royal Colls and Their Faculties, UK, 1976–82; Examiner, Primary FFARCS, 1967–73; Member: Editorial Bd (and Cons. Editor), British Jl of Anaesthesia, 1965–85; Edit. Bd, Psychopharmacology; Council, Assoc. of Anaeths of GB and Ire., 1973–84; Physiol. Soc., 1966–; Cttee of AA, 1979–91; Hon. Mem., Assoc. of Univ. Anaesths (USA), 1963–; President: Scottish Soc. of Anaesthetists, 1985–86; RSocMed, 1986–88. Royal National Life-boat Institution: Mem. Cttee of Mgt, 1988–; a Vice-Pres., 1992–; Mem., Med. and Survival Cttee, 1981– (Chm., 1988–91). Sir Arthur Sims Commonwealth Trav. Prof., 1968; Visiting Prof. to many med. centres, USA and Canada; Lectures: Wesley Bourne, McGill Univ., 1965; First Gillies Meml, Dundee, 1978; 2nd Gilmartin, Faculty of Anaesthetists, RCSI, 1986; Morrell Mackenzie, Inst. of Laryngology, 1989; (first) J. D. Robertson Meml, Edinburgh Univ., 1992. Hon. FFARACS 1968; Hon. FFARCSI 1980; Hon. FDSRCS 1979; Hon. FRCP(C) 1988; Hon. FRSM 1989; Hon. FRCPSGlas 1993. Hon. DSc: McGill, 1984; Glasgow, 1991. Joseph Clover Medal and Prize, Fac. of Anaesths, RCS, 1972; John Snow Medal, Assoc. of Anaesthetists of GB and Ireland, 1986. *Publications:* on neurophysiol., anaesthesia, pain and central nervous system mechanisms of respiration, in learned jls. *Recreations:* golf, wet fly fishing.

ROBSON, Prof. James Scott, MD; FRCP, FRCPE; Professor of Medicine, University of Edinburgh, 1977–86, now Emeritus; Consultant Physician, and Physician in charge, Medical Renal Unit, Royal Infirmary, Edinburgh, 1959–86; *b* 19 May 1921; *s* of William Scott Robson, FSA and Elizabeth Hannah Watt; *m* 1948, Mary Kynoch MacDonald, MB ChB, FRCP, *d* of late Alexander MacDonald, Perth; two *s*. *Educ:* Edinburgh Univ. (Mouat Schol.). MB ChB (Hons) 1945, MD 1946; FRCPE 1960, FRCP 1977. Captain, RAMC, India, Palestine and Egypt, 1945–48. Rockefeller Student, NY Univ., 1942–44; Rockefeller Res. Fellow, Harvard Univ., 1949–50. Edinburgh University: Sen. Lectr in Therapeutics, 1959; Reader, 1961; Reader in Medicine, 1968. Hon. Associate Prof., Harvard Univ., 1962; Merck Sharp & Dohme Vis. Prof., Australia, 1968. External examnr in medicine to several univs in UK and overseas. Mem., Biomed. Res. Cttee, SHHD, 1979–84; Chm., Sub-cttee in Medicine, Nat. Med. Consultative Cttee, 1983–85. Pres., Renal Assoc., London, 1977–80. Hon. Mem., Australasian Soc. of Nephrology. Sometime Mem. Editl Bd, and Dep. Chm., Clinical Science, 1969–73, and other med. jls. *Publications:* (ed with R. Passmore) Companion to Medical Studies, vol. 1, 1968, 3rd edn 1985; vol. 2, 1970, 2nd edn 1980; vol. 3, 1974; contribs on renal physiology and disease to med. books, symposia and jls. *Recreations:* gardening, theatre, reading, writing, contemporary art of Scotland. *Address:* 1 Grant Avenue, Edinburgh EH13 0DS. *T:* 0131–441 3508. *Clubs:* New, University Staff (Edinburgh).

ROBSON, Sir John (Adam), KCMG 1990 (CMG 1983); HM Diplomatic Service, retired; Ambassador to Norway, 1987–90; *b* 16 April 1930; *yr s* of Air Vice-Marshal Adam Henry Robson, CB, OBE, MC; *m* 1958, Maureen Molly, *er d* of E. H. S. Bullen; three *d*. *Educ:* Charterhouse; Gonville and Caius Coll., Cambridge (Major Scholar). BA 1952, MA 1955, PhD 1958. Fellow, Gonville and Caius Coll., 1954–58; Asst Lectr, University Coll. London, 1958–60. HM Foreign Service (later Diplomatic Service), 1961; Second Sec., British Embassy, Bonn, 1962–64; Second, later First, Secretary, Lima, 1964–66; First Sec., British High Commn, Madras, 1966–69; Asst Head, Latin American Dept, FCO, 1969–73; Head of Chancery, Lusaka, 1973–74; RCDS, 1975; Counsellor, Oslo, 1976–78; Head of E African Dept, FCO, and Comr for British Indian Ocean Territory, 1979–82; Ambassador to Colombia, 1982–87. Leader, UK Delegn, Conf. on Human Dimension, CSCE, 1990–91. Panel Mem., Home Office Assessment Consultancy Unit, 1992–. Chm. Mgt Cttee, Seven Springs Cheshire Home, 1992–; Mem. Ct, Kent Univ., 1990–. Royal Order of Merit (Norway), 1988. *Publications:* Wyclif and the Oxford Schools, 1961; articles in historical jls. *Recreation:* gardening. *Address:* Biggenden Oast, Paddock Wood, Tonbridge, Kent TN12 6ND. *Club:* United Oxford & Cambridge University.

ROBSON, Rev. John Phillips; Chaplain to the Queen, since 1993; Chaplain of the Queen's Chapel of the Savoy and Chaplain of the Royal Victorian Order, since 1989; *b* 22 July 1932; *s* of Thomas Herbert and Nellie Julia Robson. *Educ:* Hele's School, Exeter; Brentwood School; St Edmund Hall, Oxford (Liddon Exhibnr 1954); King's College London (AKC 1958). Deacon 1959, priest 1960; Curate, Huddersfield Parish Church, 1959–62; Asst Chaplain 1962–65, Senior Chaplain 1965–80, Christ's Hospital, Horsham; Senior Chaplain of Wellington College, Berks, 1980–89. *Recreations:* golf, cinema, theatre. *Address:* The Queen's Chapel of the Savoy, Savoy Hill, Strand, WC2R 0DA. *T:* 0171–836 7221. *Club:* Garrick.

ROBSON, Prof. Peter Neville, OBE 1983; FRS 1987; FEng 1983; Professor of Electronic and Electrical Engineering, University of Sheffield, since 1968; *b* 23 Nov. 1930; *s* of Thomas Murton and Edith Robson; *m* 1957, Anne Ross Miller Semple; one *d*. *Educ:* Cambridge Univ. (BA); PhD Sheffield. FIEE, FIEEE. Res. Engr, Metropolitan Vickers Electrical Co., Manchester, 1954–57; Lectr 1957–63, Sen. Lectr 1963–66, Sheffield Univ.; Res. Fellow, Stanford Univ., USA, 1966–67; Reader, University Coll. London, 1967–68. *Publications:* Vacuum and Solid State Electronics, 1963; numerous papers on semiconductor devices and electromagnetic theory. *Address:* Department of Electronic and Electrical Engineering, Sheffield University, Mappin Street, Sheffield S1 3JD. *T:* Sheffield (0114) 276 8555, ext. 5131.

ROBSON, Air Vice-Marshal Robert Michael, OBE 1971; sheep farmer; *b* 22 April 1935; *s* of Dr John Alexander and Edith Robson; *m* 1959, Brenda Margaret (*née* Croysdill); one *s* two *d*. *Educ:* Sherborne; RMA Sandhurst. Commissioned 1955; RAF Regt, 1958; Navigator Training, 1959; Strike Squadrons, 1965; Sqdn Comdr, RAF Coll., 1968; Defence Adviser to British High Comr, Sri Lanka, 1972; Nat. Defence Coll., 1973; CO 27 Sqdn, 1974–75; MoD staff duties, 1978; CO RAF Gatow, 1978–80; ADC to the Queen, 1979–80; RCDS 1981; Dir of Initial Officer Training, RAF Coll., 1982–84; Dir of Public Relations, RAF, 1984–87; Hd, RAF Study of Officers' Terms of Service, 1987; retired. Chairman: Turbo (UK) Ltd, 1995–; Fuel Mechanics Ltd, 1995–; Dir, Advanced Technology Industries Ltd, 1993–. Chm., Prince's Trust, Lincs, 1993–. FIMgt (FBIM 1980). *Recreations:* fly fishing, photography. *Club:* Royal Air Force.

ROBSON, Robert William, CBE 1991; Head Coach, Futebol Clube Do Porto, Portugal, since 1994; *b* 18 Feb. 1933; *s* of Philip and Lilian Robson; *m* 1955, Elsie Mary Gray; three *s*. *Educ:* Langley Park Primary Sch.; Waterhouses Secondary Mod. Sch., Co. Durham. Professional footballer: Fulham FC, 1950–56 and 1962–67; West Bromwich Albion FC, 1956–62; twenty appearances for England; Manager: Vancouver FC, 1967–68; Fulham FC, 1968–69; Ipswich Town FC, 1969–82; England Assoc. Football Team, and Nat. Coach, 1982–90; Manager, PSV Eindhoven, Netherlands, 1990–92; Head Coach, Sporting Lisbon, Portugal, 1992–93. *Publications:* Time on the Grass (autobiog.), 1982; (with Bob Harris) So Near and Yet So Far: Bobby Robson's World Cup diary, 1986; (with Bob Harris) Against The Odds, 1990. *Recreations:* golf, squash, reading, gardening. *Address:* c/o Futebol Clube Do Porto, Estadio das Antas, 4100 Porto, Portugal.

ROBSON, Stephen Arthur, PhD; Deputy Secretary, Industry and Financial Institutions, HM Treasury, since 1993; *b* 30 Sept. 1943; *s* of Arthur Cyril Robson and Lilian Marianne (*née* Peabody); *m* 1974, Meredith Hilary Lancashire; two *s*. *Educ:* Pocklington Sch.; St John's Coll., Cambridge (MA, PhD); Stanford Univ., USA (MA). Joined Civil Service (HM Treasury), 1969; Private Sec. to Chancellor of the Exchequer, 1974–76; seconded to Investors in Industry plc, 1976–78; Under Sec., Defence Policy and Material Gp, 1987–89, Public Enterprises and Privatisation Gp, 1990–93. *Recreation:* sailing. *Address:* c/o HM Treasury, Parliament Street, SW1P 3AG. *Club:* Bosham Sailing.

ROBSON, William Michael; Deputy Chairman, The Standard Bank Ltd, 1965–83 (Director, 1960–83); *b* 31 Dec. 1912; *e s* of late Col the Hon. Harold Burge Robson, TD, DL, JP, Pinewood Hill, Witley, Surrey and late Ysolt Robson (*née* Leroy-Lewis); *m* 1st, 1939, Audrey Isobel Wales (*d* 1964), *d* of late Maj. William Dick, Low Gosforth Hall, Northumberland; two *s* one *d*; 2nd, 1965, Frances Mary Wyville, *d* of late James Anderson

Ramage Dawson, Balado House, Kinross, and *widow* of Andrew Alexander Nigel Buchanan (he *d* 1960). *Educ:* Eton; New College, Oxford. Served War of 1939–45: with Grenadier Guards (Maj. 1944), England and Europe BAOR. A Vice-Chm., Victoria League for Commonwealth Friendship, 1962–65. Director: Booker McConnell Ltd, 1955–78 (Chm., Booker Pensions, 1957–78); United Rum Merchants Ltd, 1965–78; British South Africa Co., 1961–66 (Vice-Chm., Jt East & Central African Bd, 1956–63); Antony Gibbs & Sons (Insurance) Ltd, 1946–48, 1973–76; Antony Gibbs (Insurance Holdings), 1976–80; Antony Gibbs, Sage Ltd, 1976–80; Anton Underwriting Agencies Ltd, 1977–82; Chm., Standard Bank Finance & Develt Corp. Ltd, 1966–73; Deputy Chairman: The Chartered Bank, 1974–83; Standard and Chartered Banking Gp Ltd, 1974–83 (Dir, 1970–83). Mem., BNEC, Africa, 1965–71 (Dep. Chm., 1970–71). High Sheriff of Kent, 1970. Liveryman, Vintners Co., 1953. Mem. Council of The Shrievalty Assoc., 1971–76. *Club:* Brooks's.

ROCARD, Michel Louis Léon; Member (Party of European Socialists), European Parliament, since 1994; Prime Minister of France, 1988–91; *b* 23 Aug. 1930; *s* of late Yves Rocard and of Renée (*née* Favre); *m* 1st; one *s* one *d*; 2nd, 1972, Michèle Legendre; two *s*. *Educ:* Lycée Louis-le-Grand, Paris; Univ. of Paris (Nat. Sec., Association des étudiants socialistes, 1953–55); Ecole Nationale d'Administration, 1956–58. Inspecteur des Finances, 1958; Econ. and Financial Studies Service, 1962; Head of Econ. Budget Div., Forecasting Office, 1965; Sec.-Gen., Nat. Accounts Commn, 1965. Nat. Sec., Parti Socialiste Unifié, 1967–73; candidate for Presidency of France, 1969; Deputy for Yvelines, 1969–73, 1978–81, 1986–93; Minister of Planning and Regl Develt, 1981–83; Minister of Agriculture, 1983–85. Joined Parti Socialiste, 1974: Mem., Exec. Bureau, 1975–81 and 1986–88; Nat. Sec. in charge of public sector, 1975–79; First Sec., 1993–94. Mayor, Conflans-Sainte-Honorine, 1977–94. *Publications:* Le PSU et l'avenir socialiste de la France, 1969; Des militants du PSU présentés par Michel Rocard, 1971; Questions à l'Etat socialiste, 1972; Un député, pour quoi faire?, 1973; (jtly) Le Marché commun contre l'Europe, 1973; (jtly) L'Inflation au cœur, 1975; Parler vrai, 1979; A l'épreuve des faits: textes politiques 1979–85, 1986; Le coeur à l'ouvrage, 1987; Un pays comme le nôtre, 1989. *Address:* 63 rue de Varenne, 75007, Paris, France.

ROCH, Rt. Hon. Sir John (Ormond), Kt 1985; PC 1993; **Rt. Hon. Lord Justice Roch;** a Lord Justice of Appeal, since 1993; *b* 19 April 1934; *s* of Frederick Ormond Roch and Vera Elizabeth (*née* Chamberlain); *m* 1967, Anne Elizabeth Greany (*d* 1994); three *d*. *Educ:* Wrekin Coll.; Clare Coll., Cambridge (BA, LLB). Called to Bar, Gray's Inn, 1961, Bencher, 1985; QC 1976; a Recorder, 1975–85; a Judge of the High Court of Justice, QBD, 1985–93; Presiding Judge, Wales and Chester Circuit, 1986–90. *Recreations:* sailing, music. *Address:* c/o Royal Courts of Justice, Strand, WC2A 2LL. *Clubs:* Dale Yacht, Bar Yacht.

ROCH, Muriel Elizabeth Sutcliffe, BA; Headmistress, School of S Mary and S Anne, Abbots Bromley, Staffs, 1953–77; *b* 7 Sept. 1916; *d* of late Rev. Sydney John Roch, MA Cantab, Pembroke and Manchester. *Educ:* Manchester High Sch.; Bedford Coll., London; Hughes Hall, Cambridge. Teaching appointments at: Devonport High School, 1939–41; Lady Manners, Bakewell, 1941–44; Howells School, Denbigh, 1944–47; Talbot Heath, Bournemouth, 1947–53. *Recreations:* music, travel. *Address:* Northdown Cottage, Lamphey, Dyfed SA71 5PL. *T:* Lamphey (01646) 672577. *Club:* University Women's.

ROCHAT, Dr Philippe Henri Pierre; Secretary General, International Civil Aviation Organisation, since 1991; *b* 19 Oct. 1942; *m* 1967, Catherine Dupuy; two *s* one *d*. *Educ:* Gymnase de Lausanne; Lausanne Univ. (LLB 1966; LLD 1974). Journalist and reporter, Swiss Radio–TV, 1967–74; Asst to Dep. Dir, Federal Office for Civil Aviation, Bern, 1975–77; Admin. and Commercial Dir, Geneva Airport, 1977–85; International Civil Aviation Organisation Council: Alternate Rep. of Belgium, 1985–86; Rep. of Switzerland, 1986–89; Dir, Mkting and Envmt, Geneva Airport, 1989–91. *Publications:* articles, reports and lectures on civil aviation and envmt, airports' structure and mgt, challenges in civil aviation, etc. *Recreations:* ski-ing, tennis, hiking, various cultural activities. *Address:* 1000 Sherbrooke Street West, Suite 981, Montreal, Quebec H3A 2R2, Canada.

ROCHDALE, 2nd Viscount *cr* 1960; **St John Durival Kemp;** Baron 1913; *b* 15 Jan. 1938; *s* of 1st Viscount Rochdale, OBE and of Elinor Dorothea Pease, CBE, JP; *S* father, 1993; *m* 1st, 1960, Serena Jane Clark-Hall (marr. diss. 1974); two *s* two *d*; 2nd, 1976, Elizabeth Anderton. *Educ:* Eton. *Heir:* *s* Hon. Jonathan Hugo Durival Kemp [*b* 10 June 1961; *m* 1994, Mingxian Zhu]. *Address:* Rosetrees, Lingholm, Keswick, Cumbria CA12 5TZ.

ROCHDALE, Archdeacon of; *see* Dalby, Ven. J. M. M.

ROCHE, family name of **Baron Fermoy.**

ROCHE, Barbara Maureen; MP (Lab) Hornsey and Wood Green, since 1992; *b* 13 April 1954; *d* of Barnett Margolis and Hannah (*née* Lopes Dias); *m* 1977, Patrick Roche; one *d*. *Educ:* JFS Comprehensive Sch., Camden; Lady Margaret Hall, Oxford (BA). Called to the Bar, Middle Temple, 1977. *Recreations:* theatre, detective fiction. *Address:* House of Commons, SW1A 0AA. *T:* 0171–219 3000. *Club:* Wood Green Labour.

ROCHE, Sir David (O'Grady), 5th Bt *cr* 1838 of Carass, Limerick; FCA; Chairman, Roche & Co. Ltd; *b* 21 Sept. 1947; *s* of Sir Standish O'Grady Roche, 4th Bt, DSO, and of Evelyn Laura, *d* of Major William Andon; *S* father, 1977; *m* 1971, Hon. (Helen) Alexandra Briscoe Frewen, *d* of 3rd Viscount Selby; one *s* one *d* (and one *s* decd). *Educ:* Wellington Coll., Berks; Trinity Coll., Dublin. Liveryman, Worshipful Co. of Saddlers, 1970. *Heir:* *s* David Alexander O'Grady Roche, *b* 28 Jan. 1976. *Address:* Bridge House, Starbotton, Skipton, N Yorks BD23 5HY. *T:* Skipton (01756) 760863; 36 Coniger Road, SW6 3TA. *T:* 0171–736 0382. *Clubs:* Buck's; Kildare Street and University (Dublin); Royal Yacht Squadron.

ROCHE, Hon. Thomas Gabriel, QC 1955; Recorder of the City of Worcester, 1959–71; *b* 1909; *yr s* of late Baron Roche, PC. *Educ:* Rugby; Wadham Coll., Oxford. Called to the Bar, Inner Temple, 1932. Served War of 1939–45 (Lt-Col 1944, despatches). Church Commissioner, 1961–65; Member, Monopolies Commission, 1966–69. *Address:* Chadlington, Oxford. *Club:* United Oxford & Cambridge University.

ROCHESTER, 2nd Baron, of the 4th creation, *cr* 1931, of Rochester in the County of Kent; **Foster Charles Lowry Lamb,** DL; *b* 7 June 1916; *s* of 1st Baron Rochester, CMG, and Rosa Dorothea (*née* Hurst); *S* father 1955; *m* 1942, Mary Carlisle, *yr d* of T. B. Wheeler, CBE; two *s* one *d* (and one *d* decd). *Educ:* Mill Hill; Jesus College, Cambridge. MA. Served War of 1939–45: Captain 23rd Hussars; France, 1944. Joined ICI Ltd, 1946: Labour Manager, Alkali Div., 1955–63; Personnel Manager, Mond Div., 1964–72. Pro-Chancellor, Univ. of Keele, 1976–86. Chairman: Cheshire Scout Assoc., 1974–81; Governors of Chester Coll., 1974–83. DL Cheshire, 1979. DUniv Keele, 1986. *Heir:* *s* Hon. David Charles Lamb [*b* 8 Sept. 1944; *m* 1969, Jacqueline Stamp; two *s*. *Educ:* Shrewsbury Sch.; Univ. of Sussex]. *Address:* The Hollies, Hartford, Cheshire CW8 1PG. *T:* Northwich (01606) 74733. *Clubs:* Reform, MCC; Hawks (Cambridge).

ROCHESTER, Bishop of, since 1994; **Rt. Rev. Dr Michael Nazir-Ali;** *b* 19 Aug. 1949; *s* of James and Patience Nazir-Ali; *m* 1972, Valerie Cree; two *s*. *Educ:* St Paul's School and St Patrick's Coll., Karachi; Univ. of Karachi (BA 1970, Econs and Sociology); Fitzwilliam Coll. and Ridley Hall, Cambridge; St Edmund Hall, Oxford (BLitt 1974). MLitt Cantab 1976; MLitt Oxon 1981; PhD Aust. Coll. of Theol. (Univ. of NSW) with Centre for World Religions, Harvard, 1983. Assistant: Christ Church, Cambridge, 1970–72; St Ebbe's, Oxford, 1972–74; Burney Lectr in Islam, Cambridge, 1973–74; Tutorial Supervisor in Theology, Univ. of Cambridge, 1974–76; Assistant, Holy Sepulchre, Cambridge, 1974–76; Tutor, then Sen. Tutor, Karachi Theol Coll., 1976–81; Assoc. Priest, Holy Trinity Cathedral, Karachi, 1976–79; Priest-in-charge, St Andrew's, Akhtar Colony, Karachi, 1979–81; Provost of Lahore Cathedral, 1981–84; Bishop of Raiwind, Pakistan 1984–86; Asst to Archbp of Canterbury, Co-ordinator of Studies and Editor for Lambeth Conf., 1986–89; Director-in-Residence, Oxford Centre for Mission Studies, 1986–89; Gen. Sec., CMS, 1989–94; Canon Theologian, Leicester Cathedral, 1992–94. Sec., Archbp's Commn on Communion and Women in the Episcopate (Eames Commn), 1988–; Archbishops' nominee, CCBI, 1990–94; Chm., C of E Mission Theol Adv. Gp, 1992–; Member: ARCIC II, 1991–; C of E Bd of Mission, 1991–94. *Publications:* Islam: a Christian perspective, 1983; Frontiers in Muslim-Christian Encounter, 1987; Martyrs and Magistrates: toleration and trial in Islam, 1989; From Everywhere to Everywhere, 1990; Mission and Dialogue, 1995; *edited:* Working Papers for the Lambeth Conference, 1988; The Truth shall Make you Free: report of the Lambeth Conference, 1988; Trustworthy and True: Pastoral letters from the Lambeth Conference, 1988; articles and contribs to jls. *Recreations:* cricket, hockey, table tennis, reading detective fiction, humour and poetry, writing fiction and poetry. *Address:* Bishopscourt, Rochester, Kent ME1 1TS. *T:* Medway (01634) 842721.

ROCHESTER, Dean of; *see* Shotter, Very Rev. E. F.

ROCHESTER, Archdeacon of; *see* Warren, Ven. N. L.

ROCHESTER, Prof. George Dixon, FRS 1958; FInstP; Professor of Physics, University of Durham, 1955–73, now Professor Emeritus; *b* 4 Feb. 1908; *s* of Thomas and Ellen Rochester; *m* 1938, Idaline, *o d* of Rev. J. B. and Mrs Bayliffe; one *s* one *d*. *Educ:* Wallsend Secondary Sch. and Technical Inst.; Universities of Durham, Stockholm and California. BSc, MSc, PhD (Dunelm). Earl Grey Memorial Scholar, Armstrong College, Durham University, 1926–29; Earl Grey Fellow, at Stockholm Univ., 1934–35; Commonwealth Fund Fellow at California Univ., 1935–37; Manchester University: Asst Lectr, 1937–46; Lectr, 1946–49; Sen. Lectr, 1949–53; Reader, 1953–55. Scientific Adviser in Civil Defence for NW Region, 1952–55. (Jt) C. V. Boys Prizeman of the Physical Society of London, 1956; Symons Memorial Lecturer of the Royal Meteorological Soc., 1962. Member: Council CNAA, 1964–74; Council, British Assoc. for Advancement of Science, 1971–72; Council, Royal Soc., 1972–74; Chm., NE Branch, Inst. of Physics, 1972–74. Second Pro-Vice-Chancellor, Univ. of Durham, 1967–69, Pro-Vice-Chancellor, 1969–70. Hon. DSc: Newcastle upon Tyne, 1973; CNAA, 1975; Hon. Fellow, Newcastle upon Tyne Polytechnic, 1977. Methodist. *Publications:* (with J. G. Wilson) Cloud Chamber Photographs of the Cosmic Radiation, 1952; scientific papers on spectroscopy, cosmic rays, history of the strange particles, and Durham astronomy. *Recreations:* outdoor activities, history of physics and astronomy. *Address:* 18 Dryburn Road, Durham DH1 5AJ. *T:* Durham (0191) 3864796.

ROCK, Prof. Paul Elliot; Professor of Sociology, since 1986, and Director, Mannheim Centre for Study of Criminology and Criminal Justice, since 1992, London School of Economics and Political Science; *b* 4 Aug. 1943; *s* of Ashley Rock and Charlotte (*née* Dickson); *m* 1965, Barbara Ravid; two *s*. *Educ:* London School of Economics (BScSoc); Nuffield Coll., Oxford (DPhil). London School of Economics: Asst Lectr, 1967; Lectr, 1970; Sen. Lectr, 1976; Reader in Sociology, 1980; Reader in Social Institutions, 1981. Vis. Prof., Princeton Univ., 1974–75; Vis. Schol., Ministry of Solicitor Gen. of Canada, 1981–82. *Publications:* Making People Pay, 1973; Deviant Behaviour, 1973; The Making of Symbolic Interactionism, 1979; (with D. Downes) Understanding Deviance, 1982, 2nd edn 1988; A View from the Shadows, 1986; Helping Victims of Crime, 1990; The Social World of an English Crown Court, 1993. *Recreation:* stained glass. *Address:* London School of Economics and Political Science, Houghton Street, Aldwych, WC2A 2AE. *T:* 0171–955 7296.

ROCKEFELLER, David; banker; *b* New York City, 12 June 1915; *s* of John Davison Rockefeller, Jr and Abby Greene (Aldrich) Rockefeller; *m* 1940, Margaret, *d* of Francis Sims McGrath, Mount Kisco, NY; two *s* four *d*. *Educ:* Lincoln School of Columbia University's Teachers College; Harvard Coll. (BS); London School of Economics; Univ. of Chicago (PhD). Sec. to Mayor Fiorello H. LaGuardia, 1940–41; Asst Regional Dir, US Office of Defense Health and Welfare Services, 1941. Served in US Army, N Africa and France, 1942–45 (Captain). Joined Chase National Bank, NYC, 1946; Asst Manager, Foreign Dept, 1946–47; Asst Cashier, 1947–48; Second Vice-Pres., 1948–49; Vice-Pres., 1949–51; Senior Vice-Pres., 1951–55; Chase Manhattan Bank (merger of Chase Nat. Bank and Bank of Manhattan Co.): Exec. Vice Pres., 1955–57; Dir, 1955–81; Vice-Chm., 1957–61; Pres. and Chm., Exec. Cttee, 1961–69; Chm. of Bd and Chief Exec. Officer, 1969–81; Chairman: Chase Internat. Investment Corp., 1961–75; Chase Internat. Adv. Cttee, 1980–; Rockefeller Brothers Fund Inc., 1981–87; The Rockefeller Group Inc., 1983–; Rockefeller Center Properties Inc., 1985–92. Director: Internat. Exec. Service Corps (Chm., 1964–68); NY Clearing House, 1971–78; Center for Inter-American Relations (Chm. 1966–70); Overseas Develt Council; US-USSR Trade and Econ. Council, Inc.; Chairman: Americas Soc.; Council on Foreign Relations; NY Chamber of Commerce and Industry; Rockefeller Univ., 1950–75; NYC Partnership, 1979–88; US Business Cttee on Jamaica, 1980–; N America Chm., Trilateral Commn; Member: Exec. Cttee, Museum of Modern Art (Chm., 1962–72, 1987–93); Harvard Coll. Bd of Overseers, 1954–60, 1962–68; Urban Develt Corp., NY State, Business Adv. Council, 1968–72; US Adv. Cttee on Reform of Internat. Monetary System, 1973–; Sen. Adv. Gp, Bilderberg Meetings; US Exec. Cttee, Dartmouth Conf.; Bd, Inst. of Internat. Economics. Director: Downtown-Lower Manhattan Assoc., Inc. (Chm., 1958–65); Internat. House, NY, 1940–63; Morningside Heights Inc., 1947–70 (Pres., 1947–57, Chm., 1957–65); B. F. Goodrich Co., 1956—64; Equitable Life Assce Soc. of US, 1960–65. Trustee: Univ. of Chicago, 1947–62 (Life Trustee, 1966); Carnegie Endowment for Internat. Peace, 1947–60; Council of the Americas (Chm., 1965–70, 1983–92); Sleepy Hollow Restorations, 1981–. Member: American Friends of LSE; US Hon. Fellows, LSE; Founding Mem., Business Cttee for the Arts; Hon. Mem., Commn on White House Fellows, 1964–65; Hon. Chm., Japan Soc. World Brotherhood Award, Jewish Theol Seminary, 1953; Gold Medal, Nat. Inst. Social Sciences, 1967; Medal of Honor for city planning, Amer. Inst. Architects, 1968; C. Walter Nichols Award, NY Univ., 1970; Reg. Planning Assoc. Award, 1971. Hon. LLD: Columbia Univ., 1954; Bowdoin Coll., 1958; Jewish Theol Seminary, 1958; Williams Coll., 1966; Wagner Coll., 1967; Harvard, 1969; Pace Coll., 1970; St John's Univ., 1971; Middlebury, 1974; Univ. of Liberia, 1979; Rockefeller Univ., 1980; Hon. DEng: Colorado Sch. of Mines, 1974; Univ. of Notre Dame, 1987. Holds civic awards. Grand Officer, Legion of Honour, France, 1955; Order of Merit of the Republic, Italy; Order of the Southern Cross, Brazil; Order of the White Elephant and Order of the Crown, Thailand; Order of the Cedar, Lebanon; Order of the Sun, Peru; Order of Humane African Redemption, Liberia; Order of the Crown, Belgium; National Order of Ivory Coast; Grand Cordon, Order of Sacred Treasure, Japan, 1991. *Publications:* Unused Resources and Economic Waste, 1940; Creative Management in Banking, 1964. *Recreation:* sailing. *Address:* 30 Rockefeller Plaza, New York, NY 10112, USA. *Clubs:* Century, Harvard, River, Knickerbocker, Links, University, Recess (New York); New York Yacht.

See also L. S. Rockefeller.

ROCKEFELLER, James Stillman; President and Director, Indian Spring Land Co.; Vice-President and Director, Indian Rock Corp.; *b* New York, 8 June 1902; *s* of William Goodsell Rockefeller and Elsie (*née* Stillman); *m* 1925, Nancy Carnegie; two *s* two *d*. *Educ:* Yale University (BA). With Brown Bros & Co., NYC, 1924–30; joined National City Bank of New York (later First Nat. City Bank; now Citibank, NA), 1930; Asst Cashier, 1931; Asst Vice-Pres. 1933; Vice-Pres., 1940–48; Sen. Vice-Pres., 1948–52; Exec. Vice-Pres., 1952; Pres. and Director, 1952–59; Chairman, 1959–67. Rep. Greenwich (Conn.) Town Meeting, 1933–42. Served as Lieutenant-Colonel in US Army, 1942–46. Member Board of Overseers, Memorial Hospital for Cancer and Allied Diseases, NY; Trustee of Estate of William Rockefeller; Trustee American Museum of National History. *Address:* 425 Park Avenue, New York, NY 10022, USA. *Clubs:* Down Town Assoc., Union League, University (New York); Metropolitan (Washington, DC); Field, Round Hill (Greenwich, Conn).

ROCKEFELLER, Laurance Spelman, OBE (Hon.) 1971; conservationist and business executive; Director, Rockefeller Center Inc., 1936–78 (Chairman, 1953–56, 1958–66); *b* New York, 26 May 1910; *s* of John Davison Rockefeller, Jr, FRS and Abby Greene Aldrich; *m* 1934, Mary French; one *s* three *d*. *Educ:* Lincoln School of Teachers College; Princeton University (BA). War service, Lt-Comdr, USNR, 1942–45. Chairman: Citizens' Adv. Cttee on Environmental Quality, 1969–73 (Mem., 1973–79); Meml Sloan-Kettering Cancer Center, 1960–82 (Hon. Chm., 1982–); NY Zool Soc., 1970–75 (Hon. Chm., 1975–); Jackson Hole Preserve Inc.; Woodstock Resort Corp.; Director: Eastern Air Lines, 1938–60, 1977–81, Adv. Dir, 1981–87; Readers' Digest Assoc., 1973–; Pres., Palisades Interstate Park Commn, 1970–77 (Comr Emeritus, 1978–); Adv. Trustee, Rockefeller Bros Fund, 1982–85 (Chm., 1958–80; Vice-Chm., 1980–82); Charter Trustee, Princeton Univ.; Trustee: Alfred P. Sloan Foundn, 1950–82; Greenacre Foundn; Sleepy Hollow Restorations, 1975– (Chm., 1981–85); Hon. Trustee, Nat. Geog. Soc.; Life Mem., Mass Inst. of Technology; Dir, Community Blood Council of Gtr NY; Mem., Nat. Cancer Adv. Bd, 1977–79; Chairman: Outdoor Recreation Resources Review Commn, 1958–65; Hudson River Valley Commn, 1956–66; 1965 White House Conf. on Nat. Beauty; Delegate UN Conf. on Human Environment, 1972. Holds numerous awards, medals and hon. degrees. Comdr, Royal Order of the Lion, Belgium, 1950; US Medal of Freedom, 1969; Congressional Gold Medal, 1990. *Address:* Room 5600, 30 Rockefeller Plaza, New York, NY 10112, USA. *Clubs:* Boone and Crockett, River, Princeton, Lotos, University, Brook, New York Yacht, Links, Knickerbocker (New York City).

See also David Rockefeller.

ROCKHAMPTON, Bishop of, since 1981; **Rt. Rev. George Arthur Hearn;** *b* 17 Nov. 1935; *s* of Albert Frederick and Edith Maxham Hearn; *m* 1957, Adele Taylor; two *s* one *d*. *Educ:* Northcote High School; University High School; Latrobe Univ., Melbourne. BA, ThL 1965, DipRE, ThSchol Aust. Coll. of Theology; MACE. Deacon 1964, priest 1965, Diocese of Gippsland; Curate of Traralgon, 1964–66; Vicar of Omeo, 1966–69; Rector of Wonthaggi, 1969–73; Rector of Kyabram, dio. Bendigo, 1973–77; Field Officer, Dept of Christian Education, Diocese of Melbourne, 1977–79; Dir, Gen. Bd of Religious Education, 1978–81. *Recreations:* gardening, reading, golf, music. *Address:* PO Box 6158, Rockhampton Mail Centre, Qld 4702, Australia. *T:* (79) 273188.

ROCKLEY, 3rd Baron *cr* 1934; **James Hugh Cecil;** Chairman, Kleinwort Benson Group, since 1994 (Vice-Chairman, 1988–93); Director: Christies International, since 1989; FR Group, since 1990; Abbey National, since 1990; Foreign and Colonial Investment Trust, since 1991; *b* 5 April 1934; *s* of 2nd Baron Rockley, and Anne Margaret (*d* 1980), *d* of late Adm. Hon. Sir Herbert Meade-Featherstonhaugh, GCVO, CB, DSO; *S* father, 1976; *m* 1958, Lady Sarah Primrose Beatrix, *e d* of 7th Earl Cadogan, *qv*; one *s* two *d*. *Educ:* Eton; New Coll., Oxford. Wood Gundy & Co. Ltd, 1957–62; Kleinwort Benson Ltd, 1962–. Chairman: Dartford River Crossing, 1988–93; Kleinwort Develt Fund, 1991–93; Midland Expressway, 1992–93; Dir, Equity and Law, 1980–92. Mem., Design Council, 1987–93; Trustee, Nat. Portrait Gall., 1981–88. *Heir: s* Hon. Anthony Robert Cecil [*b* 29 July 1961; *m* 1988, Katherine Jane, *d* of G. A. Whalley; two *d*]. *Address:* Lytchett Heath, Poole, Dorset BH16 6AE. *T:* Lytchett Minster (01202) 622228.

ROCKLIN, David Samuel; Chairman, Norton Opax, 1973–89; *b* 15 Aug. 1931; *s* of Alfred Rocklin and Ada Rebecca Rocklin; *m* 1955, Dorothy Ann; two *s* two *d*. *Educ:* Heles School, Exeter. Managing Director, Norton Opax, 1969–73. *Recreations:* books, travel, music, painting, good food and conversation.

RODD, family name of **Baron Rennell.**

RODDA, James, (Jim), FCA; Director of Finance and Administration, House of Commons, since 1991; *b* 16 Aug. 1945; *s* of George Rodda and Ruby (*née* Thompson); *m* 1967, Angela Hopkinson; one *s* two *d*. *Educ:* Maldon Grammar Sch.; Reading Univ. (BA Hons); Leicester Univ. FCA 1971. Spicer and Pegler, 1967–71; Coopers and Lybrand, 1971–77; Thomas Cook Group, 1977–84; Lonconex Group, 1984–85; Mercantile Credit, 1985–86; London Commodity Exchange, 1986–91. *Recreations:* rambling, music. *Address:* House of Commons, SW1A 0AA. *T:* 0171–219 5460.

RODDICK, Anita Lucia, OBE 1988; Founder and Chief Executive, The Body Shop; *b* 23 Oct. 1942; *d* of Henry Perilli and Gilda de Vita; *m* 1970, Thomas Gordon Roddick; two *d*. *Educ:* Maude Allen Secondary Modern Sch. for Girls; Newton Park Coll. of Educn, Bath. 1962–76: worked in library of Internat. Herald Tribune, Paris; Teacher of History and English; worked in Women's Rights Dept, ILO, at UN, Geneva; owned and managed restaurant and hotel; opened first br. of The Body Shop, Brighton, 1976, Man. Dir, to 1994, Chief Exec., 1994. Trustee, The Body Shop Foundn, 1989–; Patron, START, 1987–. DUniv Sussex, 1988; Hon. LLD: Nottingham, 1990; New England Coll., 1991; Hon. DSc Portsmouth, 1994. Veuve Clicquot Business Woman of the Year, 1984; County NatWest Retailer of the Year, 1988; Global 500 award, UNEP, 1989; World Vision Award, 1991; Internat. Banksia Envmtl Award, 1993. *Publication:* Body and Soul, 1991. *Address:* The Body Shop International PLC, Watersmead, Littlehampton, W Sussex BN17 6LS.

RODDICK, (George) Winston; QC 1986; a Recorder, since 1987; *b* Caernarfon, 2 Oct. 1940; *s* of William and Aelwen Roddick; *m* 1966, Cennin Parry; one *s* one *d*. *Educ:* University Coll. London (LLB, LLM). Called to the Bar, Gray's Inn, 1968. Mem., Welsh Language Bd, 1988–93; Dir and Trustee, Wales Diabetes Res. Trust, 1987–95. Mem. Editl Bd, Cambridge Jl of Financial Crime, 1995–. *Recreation:* walking the countryside. *Address:* 17 Llandennis Avenue, Cyncoed, Cardiff CF2 6JD. *T:* Cardiff (01222) 759376. *Clubs:* National Liberal; Cardiff and County (Cardiff); Caernarfon Sailing.

RODDIE, Prof. Ian Campbell, CBE 1988; TD 1967; FRCPI; Head of Medical Education, 1990–94, and Deputy Medical Director, 1991–94, King Khalid National Guard Hospital, Jeddah; Dunville Professor of Physiology, Queen's University, Belfast, 1964–87, now Emeritus; *b* 1 Dec. 1928; *s* of Rev. J. R. Wesley Roddie and Mary Hill Wilson; *m* 1st, 1958, Elizabeth Ann Gillon Honeyman (decd); one *s* three *d*; 2nd, 1974, Katherine Ann O'Hara (marr. diss.); one *s* one *d*; 3rd, 1987, Janet Doreen Saville (*née* Lennon). *Educ:* Methodist Coll., Belfast; Queen's Univ., Belfast. Malcolm Exhibnr, 1951, McQuitty Schol., 1953; BSc (1st cl. Hons Physiol.), MB BCh, BAO, MD (with gold medal), DSc; MRCPI; MRIA. Major RAMC (T&AVR); OC Med. Sub-unit, QUB OTC, retd 1968. Resident MO, Royal Victoria Hosp., Belfast, 1953–54; Queen's University, Belfast: Lectr in Physiology, 1954–60; Sen. Lectr, 1961–62; Reader, 1962–64; Dep. Dean, 1975–76, Dean, 1976–81, Faculty of Medicine; Pro-Vice-Chancellor, 1983–87. Consultant Physiologist: NI Hosps Authority, 1962–72; Eastern Health Bd, NI, 1972–88. Staff Consultant, Asian Develt Bank, Manila, 1987–88. Harkness Commonwealth Fund Fellow, Univ. of Washington, Seattle, 1960–61; Visiting Professor: Univ. of NSW, 1983–84; Chinese Univ. of Hong Kong, 1988–90; Res. Fellow, Japan Soc. for Promotion of Science, Matsumoto, Japan, 1984. External Examiner: Univs of Aberdeen, Baghdad, Benghazi, Birmingham, Bristol, Glasgow, Ireland, Jeddah, Jos, Lagos, Leeds, London, Sheffield, Southampton, Zimbabwe; RCS, RCSE, RCPGlas, RCSI. Chief Reg. Sci. Advr for Home Defence, NI, 1977–88; Member: Home Defence Sci. Adv. Conf., 1977–88; Eastern Area Health and Social Services Bd, NI, 1976–81; Physiol Systems Bd, MRC, 1974–76; Med. Adv. Cttee, Cttee of Vice-Chancellors and Principals, 1976–81; GMC, 1979–81; GDC, 1979–81. President: Royal Acad. of Medicine in Ireland, 1985–88; Biol Scis Sect., Royal Acad. of Medicine in Ireland, 1964–66; Ulster Biomed. Engrg Soc., 1979–83; Chm. Cttee, Physiol Soc., 1985–88 (Mem. Cttee, 1966–69; Hon. Mem., 1989). Arris and Gale Lectr, RCS, 1962. Conway Bronze Medal, Royal Acad. of Medicine in Ireland, 1977. *Publications:* Physiology for Practitioners, 1971, 2nd edn 1975; Multiple Choice Questions in Human Physiology, 1971, 5th edn 1996; The Physiology of Disease, 1975; papers on physiology and pharmacology of vascular, sudorific and lymphatic systems. *Address:* Calle San Bernabe 3, Las Lomas del Marbella Club-Pueblo, 29600 Marbella, Málaga, Spain. *T:* (5) 2772596, *Fax:* (5) 2778641.

RODECK, Prof. Charles Henry, DSc, FRCOG, FRCPath; Professor of Obstetrics and Gynaecology, University College London Medical School (formerly University College and Middlesex School of Medicine), since 1990; *b* 23 Aug. 1944; *s* of Heinz and Charlotte Rodeck; *m* 1971, Elisabeth (*née* Rampton); one *s* one *d*. *Educ:* University College London (BSc Anatomy 1966); UCH Med. Sch. (MB BS 1969); DSc (Med) London 1991. MRCOG 1975; FRCOG 1987; FRCPath 1994. House appts to 1975; King's College Hospital Medical School: Registrar, 1975; Lectr, 1976; Sen. Lectr/Consultant, 1978; Dir, Harris Birthright Res. Centre for Fetal Medicine, 1983–86; Prof., Inst. of Obstetrics and Gynaecol., RPMS, Queen Charlotte's and Chelsea Hosp., 1986–90. Member, Council: Obst. and Gyn. Sect., RSocMed; British Assoc. of Perinatal Med.; RCOG, 1991– (Chm., Subspeciality Bd, 1989–92); Mem., Working Party on Antenatal Diagnosis, RCP, 1986–89; Chm., Steering Gp for Tissue Bank, MRC, 1989–; Mem., EEC Working Party on Chorion Villus Sampling, 1983–85. Examr, RCOG and Univs of Aberdeen, Brussels, London, Oxford, Reading, Singapore; Vis. Prof., USA Univs. Mem. or Hon. Mem., med. socs Europe and USA. Pres., Internat. Fetal Medicine and Surgery Soc., 1986. Mem., editl bds of professional jls, UK and overseas; Associate Editor, Prenatal Diagnosis, 1985–. *Publications:* (ed) Prenatal Diagnosis, 1984; (ed) Fetal Diagnosis of Genetic Defects, 1987; (ed) Fetal Medicine, 1989; (co-ed) Prenatal Diagnosis and Screening, 1992; (co-ed) Fetus and Neonate, 1993; articles on prenatal diagnosis and fetal medicine. *Recreation:* stroking the cat. *Address:* Department of Obstetrics and Gynaecology, University College London Medical School, 86–96 Chenies Mews, WC1E 6HX. *T:* 0171–380 9874. *Club:* Athenæum.

RODEN, 10th Earl of *cr* 1771 (Ire.); **Robert John Jocelyn;** Baron Newport 1743; Viscount Jocelyn 1755; Bt 1665; *b* 25 Aug. 1938; *s* of 9th Earl of Roden and Clodagh Rose (*d* 1989), *d* of Edward Robert Kennedy; *S* father, 1993; *m* 1st, 1970, Sara Cecilia (marr. diss. 1982), *d* of Brig. Andrew Dunlop; one *d*; 2nd, 1986, Ann Margareta Maria, *d* of Dr Gunnar Henning; one *s*. *Educ:* Stowe. *Heir: s* Viscount Jocelyn, *qv*. *Address:* 4 The Boltons, SW10 9TB.

RODERICK, Caerwyn Eifion; Councillor, South Glamorgan County Council, since 1980; *b* 15 July 1927; *m* 1952, Eirlys Mary Lewis; one *s* two *d*. *Educ:* Maes-y-Dderwen County Sch., Ystradgynlais; University Coll. of North Wales, Bangor. Asst Master, Caterham Sch., Surrey, 1949–52; Sen. Master, Chartesey Sch., LCC, 1952–54; Sen. Maths Master, Boys' Grammar Sch., Brecon, 1954–57; Method Study Engineer, NCB, 1957–60; Sen. Maths Master, Hartridge High Sch., Newport, Mon, 1960–69; Lecturer, Coll. of Educn, Cardiff, 1969–70. MP (Lab) Brecon and Radnor, 1970–79; PPS to Rt Hon. Michael Foot. Mem. Council: UC, Cardiff; formerly Mem. Council, RCVS. *Address:* 29 Charlotte Square, Rhiwbina, Cardiff CF4 6NE. *T:* Cardiff (01222) 628269.

RODGER OF EARLSFERRY, Baron *cr* 1992 (Life Peer), of Earlsferry in the District of North East Fife; **Alan Ferguson Rodger;** PC 1992; FBA 1991; Lord Advocate, since 1992; *b* 18 Sept. 1944; *er s* of Prof. Thomas Ferguson Rodger and Jean Margaret Smith Chalmers. *Educ:* Kelvinside Acad., Glasgow; Glasgow Univ. (MA, LLB, LLD); New Coll., Oxford (MA (by decree), DPhil; DCL). Dyke Jun. Res. Fellow, Balliol Coll., Oxford, 1969–70; Fellow, New Coll., Oxford, 1970–72; Mem., Faculty of Advocates, 1974; Clerk of Faculty, 1976–79; QC (Scot.) 1985; Advocate Depute, 1985–88, Home Advocate Depute, 1986–88; Solicitor-Gen. for Scotland, 1989–92. Member: Mental Welfare Commn for Scotland, 1981–84; UK Delegn to CCBE, 1984–89; Acad. of European Private Lawyers, 1994. Maccabaean Lectr, British Acad., 1991. FRSE 1992. Hon. Bencher, Lincoln's Inn, 1992. Hon. Mem., SPTL, 1992. *Publications:* Owners and Neighbours in Roman Law, 1972 (asst editor) Gloag and Henderson's Introduction to the Law of Scotland, 10th edn, 1995; articles mainly on Roman Law. *Recreation:* walking. *Address:* Crown Office, 25 Chambers Street, Edinburgh EH1 1LA. *T:* 0131–226 2626. *Club:* Athenæum.

RODGER, Allan George, OBE 1944; Under-Secretary, Scottish Education Department, 1959–63, retired; *b* Kirkcaldy, 7 Jan. 1902; *s* of Allan Rodger, Schoolmaster, and Annie Venters; *m* 1930, Barbara Melville Simpson; one *s* one *d*. *Educ:* Pathhead Primary School, Kirkcaldy; Kirkcaldy High School; Edinburgh University (MA (Hons) Maths, BSc, MEd, Dip Geog). Teacher, Viewforth School, Kirkcaldy, 1926–29; Lecturer, Moray House Training Coll. and Univ. Dept of Educ. (Edinburgh), 1929–35; HM Inspector of Schools, 1935–45, with special duties in regard to geography, special schools, and training colleges (seconded to special administrative duties in Education Dept, 1939–45); Asst Secretary, Scottish Educ. Dept, 1945–59. Served on Educational Commission for Govts of Uganda and Kenya, 1961. Chairman of various Govt Cttees on Scottish Educ. matters. *Publications:*

contrib. to Jl of Educational Psychology and other educational journals. *Recreations:* reading, music.

RODGER, Rt. Rev. Patrick Campbell; an Assistant Bishop, Diocese of Edinburgh, since 1986; *b* 28 Nov. 1920; *s* of Patrick Wylie and Edith Ann Rodger; *m* 1952, Margaret Menzies Menzies, MBE (*d* 1989); one *s* (and one *s* decd). *Educ:* Cargilfield; Rugby; Christ Church, Oxford (Hon. Student, 1990); Theological College, Westcott House, Cambridge; Deacon, 1949; Priest, 1950. Asst Curate, St John's Church, Edinburgh, 1949–51, and Chaplain to Anglican Students in Edinburgh, 1951–54. Study Secretary, SCM of Gt Brit. and Ire., 1955–58; Rector, St Fillan's, Kilmacolm, with St Mary's Bridge of Weir, 1958–61; Exec. Sec. for Faith and Order, World Council of Churches, 1961–66; Vice-Provost, St Mary's Cathedral, Edinburgh, 1966–67; Provost, 1967–70; Bishop of Manchester, 1970–78; Bishop of Oxford, 1978–86; Mem., House of Lords, 1974–86. Chm., Churches' Unity Commn, 1974–78; Pres., Conf. of European Churches, 1974–86. *Publications:* The Fourth World Conference on Faith and Order, Montreal (ed), 1964; Songs in a Strange Land, 1989. *Recreations:* music and walking. *Address:* 12 Warrender Park Terrace, Edinburgh EH9 1EG. *T:* 0131–229 5075. *Club:* New (Edinburgh).

RODGERS, family name of **Baron Rodgers of Quarry Bank.**

RODGERS OF QUARRY BANK, Baron *cr* 1992 (Life Peer), of Kentish Town in the London Borough of Camden; **William Thomas Rodgers,** PC 1975; Chairman, Advertising Standards Authority, since 1995; *b* 28 Oct. 1928; *s* of William Arthur and Gertrude Helen Rodgers; *m* 1955, Silvia, *d* of Hirsch Szulman; three *d. Educ:* Sudley Road Council Sch.; Quarry Bank High School, Liverpool; Magdalen College, Oxford. General Secretary, Fabian Society, 1953–60. Contested: (Lab) Bristol West, March 1957; (SDP) Stockton N, 1983; (SDP/Alliance) Milton Keynes, 1987. MP (Lab 1962–81, SDP 1981–83) Stockton-on-Tees, 1962–74, Teesside, Stockton, 1974–83; Parly Under-Sec. of State: Dept of Econ. Affairs, 1964–67, Foreign Office, 1967–68; Leader, UK delegn to Council of Europe and Assembly of WEU, 1967–68; Minister of State: BoT, 1968–69; Treasury, 1969–70; MoD, 1974–76; Sec. of State for Transport, 1976–79. Chm., Expenditure Cttee on Trade and Industry, 1971–74. Vice-Pres., SDP, 1982–87. Dir-Gen., RIBA, 1987–94. Borough Councillor, St Marylebone, 1958–62. Hon. FRIBA; Hon. FIStructE. *Publications:* Hugh Gaitskell, 1906–1963 (ed), 1964; (jt) The People into Parliament, 1966; The Politics of Change, 1982; (ed) Government and Industry, 1986; pamphlets, etc. *Address:* 43 North Road, N6 4BE. *Club:* Garrick.

RODGERS, (Andrew) Piers (Wingate); Secretary, Royal Academy of Arts, London, since 1982; *b* 24 Oct. 1944; second *s* of Sir John Rodgers, 1st Bt and of Betsy, *y d* of Francis W. Aikin-Sneath; *heir-pres.* to *b* Sir Tobias Rodgers, 2nd Bt, *qv*; *m* 1979, Marie Agathe Houette; two *s. Educ:* Eton Coll.; Merton Coll., Oxford (BA 1st Cl. Honour Mods, Prox. acc. Hertford and De Paravicini Prizes). J. Henry Schroder Wagg & Co. Ltd, London, 1967–73: Personal Asst to Chairman, 1971–73; Director, International Council on Monuments and Sites (ICOMOS), Paris, 1973–79; Consultant, UNESCO, Paris, 1979–80; Member, Technical Review Team, Aga Khan Award for Architecture, 1980, 1983; Secretary, UK Committee of ICOMOS, 1981. FRSA 1973. Mem. Bd, Warburg Inst., Univ. of London, 1993–. Mem., Court of Assts, Masons' Co., 1982–. Chevalier de l'Ordre des Arts et des Lettres (France), 1987; Chevalier de l'Ordre National du Mérite (France), 1991; Cavaliere dell'Ordine al Merito della Repubblica Italiana, 1992. *Publications:* articles on protection of cultural heritage. *Recreations:* music, Islamic art. *Address:* 18 Hertford Street, W1Y 7DB. *T:* 0171–409 3110. *Clubs:* Brooks's, Pratt's, MCC.

RODGERS, George; Library Officer, Labour Party Headquarters, 1988–90, retired; *b* 7 Nov. 1925; *s* of George and Lettitia Georgina Rodgers; *m* 1952, Joan, *d* of James Patrick and Elizabeth Graham; one *s* two *d. Educ:* St Margaret's and Holy Trinity, Liverpool; St Michael's, Sylvester, Rupert Road and Longview, Huyton. Co-operative Soc., Whiston, Lancs, 1939–43. Served War, RN, 1943–46 (War Medals, France, Germany Star). White's, Engrs, Widnes, 1946–50; with Civil Engineers: Eave's, Blackpool, 1950–53; Costain, Liverpool, 1953–54; Brit. Insulated Callender Cables, 1954–74. Sales Organiser, 1980, Circulation and Promotion Manager, 1980–87, Labour Weekly; Campaigns Officer, PLP, 1988. Mem., Huyton UDC, 1964–74 (Chm., Educn Cttee, 1969–73; Chm., Local Authority, 1973–74); Mem. Liverpool Regional Hosp. Bd, 1967–74. MP (Lab) Chorley, Feb. 1974–1979; Chm., NW Region Lab MPs, 1975–79. Contested (Lab) Pendle, 1983. *Publication:* (with Ivor Clemitson) A Life to Live: beyond full employment, 1981. *Recreations:* cycling, political history, amateur boxing (spectator). *Address:* 32 Willoughby Road, Huyton, Liverpool L14 6XB. *T:* 0151–489 1913. *Club:* Labour (Huyton).

RODGERS, Prof. Harold William, OBE 1943; FRCS 1933; Professor of Surgery, Queen's University of Belfast, 1947–73; Professor Emeritus, 1973; *b* 1 Dec. 1907; *s* of Major R. T. Rodgers; *m* 1938, Margaret Boycott; one *s* three *d. Educ:* King's College School; St Bartholomew's Hospital. St Bartholomew's Hospital: House Surgeon, Demonstrator in Anatomy, Chief Asst, Casualty Surgeon, Senior Asst Surgeon. Served War of 1939–45, RAMC, North Africa, Italy, France; Hon. Lt-Col. Prof. of Surgery and Head of Div. of Hosp. Care, Univ. of Ife, Nigeria, 1974–77, retd. Nuffield Medical Visitor to African Territories; WHO Vis. Prof. to India; Vice-Pres. Intervarsity Fellowship; Past President: Section of Surgery, RSM; British Society of Gastro-enterology; Christian Medical Fellowship; British Surgical Research Soc.; YMCA (Belfast); Past Chairman, Ct of Examiners of RCS; Pres., Hibernian CMS. District Surgeon, St John's Ambulance Brigade. Mem., RIIA, 1947–. Hon. Fellow, Polish Soc. of Surgeons, 1972. Hon. MD QUB, 1981. OStJ 1968. *Publications:* Gastroscopy, 1937; general articles in surgical and medical journals. *Recreations:* painting, travel, gardening, poetry. *Address:* 47 Fordington Road, N6 4TH.

RODGERS, Sir (John Fairlie) Tobias, 2nd Bt *cr* 1964, of Groombridge, Kent; antiquarian bookseller, publisher and journalist; *b* 2 July 1940; *s* of Sir John Rodgers, 1st Bt and Betsy (*née* Aikin-Sneath); *S* father, 1993. *Educ:* Eton; Worcester Coll., Oxford. *Recreations:* travelling, reading, bridge, tennis. *Heir: b* (Andrew) Piers (Wingate) Rodgers, *qv*. *Address:* 34 Warwick Avenue, W9 2PT. *T:* 0171–286 4376. *Clubs:* Brooks's, Garrick, Pratt's.

RODGERS, Dr Patricia Elaine Joan; Permanent Secretary, Ministry of Tourism, Commonwealth of the Bahamas, since 1995; *b* 13 July 1948; *d* of late Dr Kenneth V. A. Rodgers, OBE and Anatol C. Rodgers, MBE. *Educ:* Univ. of Aberdeen (MA Hons English, 1970); Inst. of Internat. Relations, St Augustine, Trinidad (Dip. in Internat. Relns (Hons) 1972); Inst. Univ. des Hautes Etudes Internationales, Geneva (PhD 1977). Joined Ministry of Foreign Affairs, Nassau, Bahamas, 1970; Minister-Counsellor, Washington, 1978–83; Actg High Comr to Canada, 1983–86, High Comr, 1986–88; High Comr to UK, 1988–92, also Ambassador (non-resident) to: FRG and Belgium, 1988–92, to EC and France, 1989–92; Perm. Rep. to IMO, 1991–92; Chief of Protocol, Min. of For. Affairs, 1993–95. *Publication:* Mid-Ocean Archipelagos and International Law: a study of the progressive development of international law, 1981. *Recreations:* folk painting, gourmet cooking, theatre. *Address:* Ministry of Tourism, PO Box N3701, Market Plaza, Bay Street, Nassau, Bahamas.

RODGERS, Piers; *see* Rodgers, A. P. W.

RODGERS, Sir Tobias; *see* Rodgers, Sir J.F.T.

RODNEY, family name of **Baron Rodney.**

RODNEY, 10th Baron *cr* 1782; **George Brydges Rodney;** Bt 1764; *b* 3 Jan. 1953; *o s* of 9th Baron Rodney and of Régine, *d* of Chevalier Pangaert d'Opdorp, Belgium; *S* father, 1992. *Educ:* Eton. *Heir: cousin* Nicholas Simon Harley Rodney [*b* 20 Dec. 1947; *m* 1973, Maité Bernadette Edith, *d* of Henri Pinet des Ecots]. *Address:* 38 Pembroke Road, W8 6NU.

RODRIGUES, Sir Alberto, Kt 1966; CBE 1964 (OBE 1960; MBE (mil.) 1948); ED; General Medical Practitioner, Hong Kong; Senior Unofficial Member Executive Council 1964–74; Pro-Chancellor and Chairman of Executive Council, University of Hong Kong; *b* 5 November 1911; *s* of late Luiz Gonzaga Rodrigues and late Giovanina Remedios; *m* 1940, Cynthia Maria da Silva; one *s* two *d. Educ:* St Joseph's College and University of Hong Kong. MB BS Univ. of Hong Kong, 1934; FRCPE 1988. Post graduate work, London and Lisbon, 1935–36; Medical Practitioner, 1937–40; also Medical Officer in Hong Kong Defence Force. POW, 1940–45. Medical Practitioner, 1945–50; Post graduate work, New York, 1951–52; Resident, Winnipeg Maternity Hosp. (Canada), 1952–53; General Medical Practitioner, 1953–. Member: Urban Council (Hong Kong), 1940–41; 1947–50; Legislative Council, 1953–60; Executive Council, 1960–74. Med. Superintendent, St Paul's Hospital, 1953–. Director: Jardine Strategic Hldgs (formerly Jardine Securities), 1969–; Lap Heng Co. Ltd, 1970–; HK & Shanghai Hotels Ltd, 1969–; Peak Tramways Co. Ltd, 1971–; Li & Fung Ltd, 1973; HK Commercial Broadcasting Co. Ltd, 1974–; Hong Kong and Shanghai Banking Corporation, 1974–76. Officer, Ordem de Cristo (Portugal), 1949; Chevalier, Légion d'Honneur (France), 1962; Knight Grand Cross, Order of St Sylvester (Vatican), 1966. *Recreations:* cricket, hockey, tennis, swimming, badminton. *Address:* St Paul's Hospital Annexe, Causeway Bay, Hong Kong. *T:* 760017. *Clubs:* Royal Hong Kong Jockey, Hong Kong Country, Lusitano, Recreio (all Hong Kong).

RODRÍGUEZ IGLESIAS, Gil Carlos; President, Court of Justice of European Communities, since 1994; *b* 26 May 1946; *m* 1972, Teresa Diez Gutierrez; two *d. Educ:* Oviedo Univ. (licenciado 1968); Madrid Autonomous Univ. (doctorate 1975). Internat. law asst, then Lectr, Oviedo, Freiburg, Madrid Autonomous and Madrid Complutense Univs, 1969–82; Professor: Madrid Complutense Univ., 1982–83; Granada Univ., 1983–86; Judge, EC Court of Justice, 1986–94. Encomienda de la Orden de Isabel la Católica (Spain), 1976; Cruz de Honor de la Orden de San Raimundo de Peñafort (Spain), 1986. *Publications:* El régimen juridico de los monopolios de Estado en la Comunidad Económica Europea, 1976; various articles and studies on EC law and internat. law. *Address:* Court of Justice of the European Communities, Plateau du Kirchberg, 2925, Luxembourg. *T:* 43032265 and 43032200, *Fax:* 43032777.

RODWELL, Daniel Alfred Hunter; QC 1982; **His Honour Judge Rodwell;** a Circuit Judge, since 1986; *b* 3 Jan. 1936; *s* of late Brig. R. M. Rodwell, AFC, and Nellie Barbara Rodwell (*née* D'Costa); *m* 1967, Veronica Ann Cecil; two *s* one *d. Educ:* Munro Coll., Jamaica; Worcester Coll., Oxford, 1956–59 (BA Law). National service, 1954–56; 2/Lieut 1st West Yorks, PWO, 1955; TA, 1956–67: Captain and Adjt 3 PWO, 1964–67. Called to Bar, Inner Temple, 1960. A Deputy Circuit Judge, 1977; a Recorder, 1980–86. *Recreations:* gardening, sailing. *Address:* Luton Crown Court, 7 George Street, Luton LU1 2AA. *T:* Luton (0582) 488488.

ROE, Anthony Maitland, DPhil; CChem, FRSC; Executive Secretary, Council of Science and Technology Institutes, 1987–94; *b* 13 Dec. 1929; *s* of late Percy Alex Roe and Flora Sara Roe (*née* Kisch); *m* 1958, Maureen, *d* of late William James Curtayne and of Kathleen (*née* Wigfull); two *s* one *d. Educ:* Harrow Sch.; Oriel Coll., Oxford (BA, MA, DPhil). ARIC 1955; FRSC, CChem 1976. Commnd Intell. Corps, 1955–57. Univ. of Rochester, NY, 1957–59; Sen. Chemist, Smith Kline & French Res. Inst., 1959–65; Hd of Chemistry Gp, Smith Kline & French Labs Ltd, 1965–78; Dir of Chemistry, Smith Kline & French Res. Ltd, 1978–86. Royal Society of Chemistry: Mem. Council, 1982–85, 1987–91; Vice-Pres., Perkin Div., 1986–88; Chm., Heterocyclic Gp, 1986–88; Chm., 'Chemistry in Britain' Management Cttee, 1987–91. Founder Cttee Mem., Soc. for Drug Res., 1966–77; Mem., Bd for Science, BTEC, 1985–88. *Publications:* research papers, patents and reviews in field of organic and medicinal chem. *Recreations:* listening to music, walking, good food and wine. *Address:* 10 Lodge Drive, Hatfield, Herts AL9 5HN. *T:* Hatfield (Herts) (01707) 265075.

ROE, Chang Hee; Ambassador of the Republic of Korea to the Court of St James's, since 1993; *b* 25 Feb. 1938; *m* 1963, Chung Ja Lee; one *s* one *d. Educ:* Seoul Nat. Univ., Korea (BA Econ 1960). Joined Min. of Foreign Affairs, 1960: Dir of Legal Affairs, 1968–69; First Sec., Korean Embassy, Canada, 1969–72; Private Sec. to Minister of Foreign Affairs, 1972–73; Dir, Treaties Div., 1973–75; Counsellor, Sweden, 1975–78; Dep. Dir-Gen., American Affairs Bureau, 1978–80; Dir-Gen., Treaties Bureau, 1980–82; Minister and Dep. Chief of Mission, USA, 1982–85; Ambassador to Nigeria, 1985–88; Sen. Protocol Sec. to Pres., 1988–91; Ambassador and Perm. Rep. to UN, 1991–92; Vice Minister of Foreign Affairs, 1992–93. *Recreation:* golf. *Address:* 4 Palace Gate, W8 4NF. *T:* 0171–581 0247. *Clubs:* Army and Navy, Garrick, Travellers.

ROE, Geoffrey Eric; Director-General Commercial, Ministry of Defence, since 1995; *b* 20 July 1944; *s* of Herbert William Roe and Florence Roe (*née* Gordon); *m* 1968, Elizabeth Anne Ponton; one *s* one *d. Educ:* Tottenham Grammar School. Min. of Aviation, 1963; Asst Private Sec. to Sir Ronald Melville, 1967–69; Exports and Internat. Relations Div., Min. of Technology, 1969–74; Guided Weapons Contracts Branch, 1974–76; seconded British Aerospace, 1976–78; Rocket Motor Exec., 1978–81; Asst Dir Contracts (Air), 1981–86; Dir of Contracts (Underwater Weapons), 1986–89; Head, Material Co-ord. (Naval), 1989–90; Principal Dir, Navy and Nuclear Contracts, 1990–91; Dir-Gen., Defence Contracts, MoD, 1991–95. *Recreations:* ski-ing, fell-walking, sailing, private flying. *Adddress:* Ministry of Defence, Whitehall, SW1A 2HB.

ROE, James Kenneth; Director, Jupiter Tyndall Group, since 1993; Member, Monopolies and Mergers Commission, since 1993; *b* 28 Feb. 1935; *s* of late Kenneth Alfred Roe and Zirphie Norah Roe (*née* Luke); *m* 1958, Marion Audrey Keyte (*see* M. A. Roe); one *s* two *d. Educ:* King's Sch., Bruton. National Service commn, RN, 1953–55. Joined N. M. Rothschild & Sons, 1955; Director, 1970–92. Chairman: Equity Consort Investment Trust, 1973–; China Investment Trust, 1993–; Halkin Holdings, 1993–; Dep. Chm., Kleeneze Holdings, 1985–; Director: Rothschild Trust Corp., 1970–95; Jupiter European Investment Trust, 1990–; GAM Selection Inc., 1992–; Microvitec, 1993–. FRSA; FInstD. *Recreations:* walking, reading, theatre, opera. *Address:* Petleys, Downe, Kent BR6 7JS. *Clubs:* Brooks's, MCC.

ROE, Marion Audrey; MP (C) Broxbourne, since 1983; *b* 15 July 1936; *d* of William Keyte and Grace Mary (*née* Bocking); *m* 1958, James Kenneth Roe, *qv*; one *s* two *d. Educ:* Bromley High Sch. (GPDST); Croydon High Sch. (GPDST); English Sch. of Languages, Vevey. Member: London Adv. Cttee, IBA, 1978–81; Gatwick Airport Consultative Cttee, 1979–81; SE Thames RHA, 1980–83. Member (C): Bromley Borough Council, 1975–78;

for Ilford N, GLC, 1977–86 (Cons. Dep. Chief Whip, 1978–82). Contested (C) Barking, 1979. Parly Private Secretary to: Parly Under-Secs of State for Transport, 1985; Minister of State for Transport, 1986; Sec. of State for Transport, 1987; Parly Under Sec. of State, DoE, 1987–88. Member, Select Committee: on Agriculture, 1984–85; on Social Services, 1988–89; on Procedure, 1990–92; on Sittings of the House, 1991–92; Chm., Select Cttee on Health, 1992–; Mem., H of C Admin. Cttee, 1991–; Vice Chairman: All-Party Fairs and Showgrounds Gp, 1992– (Jt Chm., 1989–92); All-Party Parly Garden Club, 1995–; Chm., All-Party Hospices Gp, 1992– (Sec., 1990–92); Chairman: Cons. Backbench Horticulture and Markets Sub-Cttee, 1989–; Cons. Backbench Social Security Cttee, 1990–; Vice-Chm., Cons. Backbench Environment Cttee, 1990–; Secretary: Cons. Backbench Horticulture Cttee, 1983–85; Cons. Backbench Party Orgn Cttee, 1985; British-Canadian Parly Gp, 1991–; Member: Exec., 1922 Cttee, 1992–; Adv. Cttee on Women's Employment, Dept of Employment, 1989–92; Substitute Mem., UK Delegn to Parly Assemblies of Council of Europe and WEU, 1989–92. Vice-Pres., Women's Nat. Cancer Control Campaign, 1985–; Patron, UK Nat. Cttee for UN Develt Fund for Women, 1985–87; Gov., Research into Ageing Trust, 1988–; Managing Trustee, Parly Contributory Pension Fund, 1990–. Fellow, Industry and Parlt Trust, 1990. Hon. MIHort, 1993. Freeman, City of London, 1993; Liveryman, Gardeners' Co., 1993–. *Recreations:* ballet, opera. *Address:* House of Commons, SW1A 0AA.

ROE, Dame Raigh (Edith), DBE 1980 (CBE 1975); JP; Director, Airlines of Western Australia, since 1981; World President, Associated Country Women of the World, 1977–80; *b* 12 Dec. 1922; *d* of Alwyn and Laura Kurts; *m* 1941, James Arthur Roe; three *s*. *Educ:* Perth Girls' Sch., Australia. Country Women's Association: State Pres., 1967–70; National Pres., 1969–71. World Ambassador, WA Council, 1978–; Hon. Ambassador, State of Louisiana, USA, 1979–. Comr, ABC, 1978–83; Nat. Dir (Aust.), Queen Elizabeth II Silver Jubilee Trust for Young Australians, 1978–. JP Western Australia, 1966. Australian of the Year, 1977; Brooch of Merit, Deutscher Landfrauenverband, Fed. Republic of Germany, 1980. *Address:* 76 Regency Drive, Crestwood, Thornlie, WA 6108, Australia. *T:* 4598765.

ROE, Air Chief Marshal Sir Rex (David), GCB 1981 (KCB 1977; CB 1974); AFC; retired 1981; *b* 1925; *m* 1948, Helen Sophie (*née* Nairn) (*d* 1981); one *s* two *d*. *Educ:* City of London Sch.; London University. Joined RAF 1943; trained in Canada; served with Metropolitan Fighter Sector, No 11 Group, 203 Sqn, 1950–51; Sch. of Maritime Reconnaissance, 1951–53; Central Flying School and Flying Training Units, 1953–55; Commanded RNZAF Central Flying School, 1956–58; RAF Staff College, 1959; Commanded No 204 Sqn, 1960–62; College of Air Warfare, 1962–64; SASO No 18 (Maritime) Gp, 1964–67; Stn Comdr RAF Syerston, 1967–69; Director of Flying Trng, 1969–71; RCDS, 1971; Deputy Controller Aircraft (C), MoD (Procurement Executive), 1972–74; SASO HQ Near East Air Force, 1974–76; AOC-in-C Training Comd, 1976–77; AOC-in-C, Support Command, 1977–78; Air Mem. for Supply and Organisation, 1978–81. *Recreations:* reading, Rugby football. *Address:* c/o Lloyds Bank, 7 Pall Mall, SW1Y 5NA. *Club:* Royal Air Force.

ROE, Rt. Rev. William Gordon; *see* Huntingdon, Bishop Suffragan of.

ROEBUCK, Roy Delville; Barrister-at-law; *b* Manchester, 25 Sept. 1929; *m* 1957, Dr Mary Ogilvy Adams; one *s*. *Educ:* various newspapers. Called to the Bar, Gray's Inn, 1974. Served RAF (National Service), 1948–50 (FEAF). Journalist, Stockport Advertiser, Northern Daily Telegraph, Yorkshire Evening News, Manchester Evening Chronicle, News Chronicle, Daily Express, Daily Mirror and Daily Herald, 1950–66; freelance, 1966–. MP (Lab) Harrow East, 1966–70; Member, Select Committee: on Estimates, 1968–70; on Parly Comr, 1968–70; PA to Rt Hon. George Wigg, Paymaster-Gen., 1966–67; Advr to Lord Wigg, Pres. of Betting Office Licensees Assoc., 1975–83. Contested (Lab): Altrincham and Sale, 1964 and Feb. 1965; Leek, Feb. 1974. Member: Islington CHC, 1988–92; Bd of Governors, Moorfields Eye Hospital, 1984–88. Fellow, Atlantic Council, 1993–. Governor, Thornhill Sch., Islington, 1986–88. *Recreations:* tennis, ski-ing, music, reading Hansard, watching Coronation Street on Mondays, Wednesdays and Fridays. *Address:* 12 Brooksby Street, N1 1HA. *T:* 0171–607 7057; Bell Yard Chambers, 116–118 Chancery Lane, WC2A 1PP. *T:* 0171–306 9292. *Club:* Royal Automobile.

ROEG, Nicolas Jack; film director; *b* 15 Aug. 1928; *s* of Jack Roeg and Gertrude Silk; *m* 1st, 1957, Susan (marr. diss.), *d* of Major F. W. Stephen, MC; four *s*; 2nd, Theresa Russell; two *s*. *Educ:* Mercers' Sch. Fellow, BFI, 1994–. Hon. DLitt Hull. Original story of Prize of Arms; Cinematographer: The Caretaker, 1963; Masque of the Red Death, 1964; Nothing But the Best, 1964; A Funny Thing Happened on the Way to the Forum, 1966; Fahrenheit 451, 1966; Far From the Madding Crowd, 1967; Petulia, 1968, etc; 2nd Unit Director and Cinematographer: Lawrence of Arabia, 1962; Judith, 1965; Co-Dir, Performance, 1968; Director: Walkabout, 1970; Don't Look Now, 1972; The Man who Fell to Earth, 1975; Bad Timing, 1979; Eureka, 1983; Insignificance, 1985; Castaway, 1986; Track 29, 1987; Aria, 1987; Sweet Bird of Youth, 1989; Witches, 1990; Cold Heaven, 1991; Heart of Darkness, 1993; Two Deaths, 1994; Exec. Producer, Without You I'm Nothing, 1989. *Address:* c/o ICM, Oxford House, 76 Oxford Street, W1R 1RB.

ROFF, Derek Michael, OBE 1972; HM Diplomatic Service, retired; Regional Director, British Executive Service Overseas, since 1993; *b* 1 Aug. 1932; *m* 1957, Diana Susette Barrow; three *s*. *Educ:* Royal Grammar Sch., Guildford; St Edmund Hall, Oxford (BA). National Service with The Cameronians (Scottish Rifles) and King's African Rifles, 1952–54. ICI Ltd, 1958–67; entered Foreign Office, 1967; Consul (Economic), Frankfurt, 1968; First Sec., UK Delegn to the European Communities, Brussels, 1970; Consul (Economic), Düsseldorf, 1973; First Sec., FCO, 1977; Counsellor, FCO, 1981–92.

ROFFEY, Harry Norman, CMG 1971; Assistant Secretary, Department of Health and Social Security, 1954–72, retired; *b* 2 March 1911; *s* of Henry Roffey and Ella Leggatt; *m* 1964, Florence Dickie; no *c*. *Educ:* Brighton Grammar Sch.; St Catharine's Coll., Cambridge (BA Hons, MA); Inst. of Education, London Univ. (Teacher's Dip.). Teaching (languages), 1935–40. Air Ministry and Foreign Office, 1940–45 (left as Wing Comdr); Min. of Health (Principal), 1946–54; Dept of Health and Social Security, 1954–72 (as Asst Sec. i/c Internat. Affairs, on the Health side). *Recreations:* travel, music, etc. *Address:* 2 Sunnyside Place, Wimbledon, SW19 4SJ. *T:* 0181–946 4991.

ROGAN, Rev. Canon John; Canon Residentiary, 1983–93, and Chancellor, 1989–93, Bristol Cathedral (Precentor, 1983–89), Canon Emeritus since 1993; Bishop's Adviser in Social Responsibility, 1983–93; *b* 20 May 1928; *s* of William and Jane Rogan; *m* 1953, Dorothy Margaret Williams; one *s* one *d*. *Educ:* Manchester Central High School; St John's Coll., Univ. of Durham. BA 1949, MA 1951; DipTheol with distinction, 1954; BPhil 1981. Education Officer, RAF, 1949–52. Asst Curate, St Michael and All Angels, Ashton-under-Lyne, 1954–57; Chaplain, Sheffield Industrial Mission, 1957–61; Secretary, Church of England Industrial Cttee, 1961–66; Asst Secretary, Board for Social Responsibility, 1962–66; Vicar of Leigh, Lancs, 1966–78; Sec., Diocesan Bd for Social Responsibility, 1967–74, Chm. 1974–78; Rural Dean of Leigh, 1971–78; Hon. Canon of Manchester, 1975–78; Provost, St Paul's Cathedral, Dundee, 1978–83. *Publication:* (ed jtly) Principles of Church Reform: Thomas Arnold, 1962. *Recreations:* Roman archaeology, walking, music. *Address:* 84 Concorde Drive, Bristol BS10 6PX.

ROGERS, Rt. Rev. Alan Francis Bright, MA; Hon. Assistant Curate, St Mary's, Twickenham, since 1985; *b* 12 Sept. 1907; *s* of Thomas and Alice Rogers, London, W9; *m* 1st, 1932, Millicent Boarder (*d* 1984); two *s*; 2nd, 1985, Barbara Gower. *Educ:* Westminster City Sch.; King's Coll., London; Leeds Univ.; Bishop's Coll., Cheshunt (Kitchener Schol., 1926–30). Curate of St Stephen's, Shepherds Bush, 1930–32; Holy Trinity, Twickenham, 1932–34; Civil Chaplain, Mauritius, 1934–49; Archdeacon of Mauritius, 1946–49; Commissary to Bishop of Mauritius, 1949–59; Vicar of Twickenham, 1949–54; Proctor in Convocation, 1951–59; Vicar of Hampstead, 1954–59; Rural Dean of Hampstead, 1955–59; Bishop of Mauritius, 1959–66; Suffragan Bishop of Fulham, 1966–70; Suffragan Bishop of Edmonton, 1970–75; Priest-in-Charge: Wappenham, 1977–80; Abthorpe with Slapton, 1977–83. An Hon. Assistant Bishop: of Peterborough, 1975–84; Dio. of London (Kensington Area), 1985–91. Chm., Archbishops' Bd of Examiners, USPG, 1972–83. MA Lambeth 1959. *Publications:* Threads of Friendship (autobiog.), 1989; Walking with God as a Friend, 1990. *Recreations:* swimming, crosswords, theatre-going, travel. *Address:* 20 River Way, Twickenham, Middx TW2 5JP. *T:* 0181–894 2031. *Club:* Royal Over-Seas League.

ROGERS, Allan Ralph, FGS; MP (Lab) Rhondda, since 1983; *b* 24 Oct. 1932; *s* of John Henry Rogers and Madeleine Rogers (*née* Smith); *m* 1955, Ceridwen James; one *s* three *d*. *Educ:* University College of Swansea (BSc Hons Geology). Geologist, UK, Canada, USA, Australia, 1956–63; Teacher, 1963–65; Tutor-organiser, WEA, 1965–70, District Sec., 1970–79. Opposition spokesman: on defence, 1987–92; on foreign affairs, 1992–. European Parliament: Mem. (Lab) SE Wales, 1979–84; Vice-Pres., 1979–82. *Recreation:* all sports. *Address:* House of Commons, SW1A 0AA. *Club:* Workmen's (Treorchy).

ROGERS, Anthony Gordon; JP; Hon. Mr Justice Rogers; Judge of the High Court, Hong Kong, since 1993; *b* 16 Feb. 1946; *s* of late Gordon Victor Rogers and of Olga Elena Rogers; *m* 1970, Barbara Ann Zimmern; one *s* two *d*. *Educ:* Beaumont Coll. Called to the Bar, Gray's Inn, 1969; practised at the Bar: London, 1970–76; Hong Kong, 1976–93; QC (Hong Kong) 1984. Chm., Hong Kong Bar Assoc., 1990, 1991. Mem., Basic Law Consultative Cttee, 1985–90. JP Hong Kong 1988. *Recreations:* rowing, tennis, golf, music, keeping the family happy. *Address:* The Supreme Court, 38 Queensway, Hong Kong. *T:* 28254532, *Fax:* 25523327. *Clubs:* Royal Automobile, Oriental; Hong Kong, Royal Hong Kong Jockey, Hong Kong Country, Shek-O, Lion Rock Rowing (Hong Kong).

ROGERS, Maj.-Gen. Anthony Peter Vernon, OBE 1985; Director of Army Legal Services, since 1994; *b* 10 July 1942; *s* of Kenneth David Rogers and Eileen (*née* Emmott); *m* 1965, Anne-Katrin Margarethe, *d* of Dr Ewald Lembke; two *d*. *Educ:* Highgate Sch.; Coll. of Law; Liverpool Univ. (LLM 1994). Admitted Solicitor, 1965. Commnd as Capt., Army Legal Services, 1968; served HQ BAOR, Command Legal Aid Section, BAOR, MoD, SHAPE, HQ UKLF, 3 and 1 Armoured Divs; Col ALS 2, MoD, 1989–92; Brig. Legal, HQ BAOR, 1992–94. Vice Pres., Internat. Soc. for Mil. Law and Law of War, 1994–; Mem., Internat. Inst. of Humanitarian Law, 1992– (Chm., Cttee for Mil. Instruction, 1993–). FRSA 1995. *Publications:* Law on the Battlefield, 1995; articles on law of war. *Recreations:* music, the arts, playing the piano (especially as accompanist), walking (preferably in mountains), cricket. *Address:* Directorate of Army Legal Services, Worthy Down, Winchester SO21 2RG. *T:* Winchester (01962) 887715.

ROGERS, General Bernard William; General, United States Army, retired; Supreme Allied Commander, Europe, 1979–87; *b* 16 July 1921; *s* of late Mr and Mrs W. H. Rogers; *m* 1944, Ann Ellen Jones; one *s* two *d*. *Educ:* Kansas State Coll.; US Mil. Acad. (BS); Oxford Univ. (Rhodes Scholar; BA, MA); US Army Comd Staff Coll., Fort Leavenworth, Kansas; US Army War Coll., Carlisle Barracks, Pa. CO 3rd Bn, 9th Inf. Regt, 2nd Inf. Div., Korea, 1952–53; Bn Comdr 1st Bn, 23rd Inf., 2nd Inf. Div., Fort Lewis, Washington, 1955–56; Comdr, 1st Battle Gp, 19th Inf., Div. COS, 24th Inf. Div., Augsburg, Germany, 1960–61; Exec. Officer to Chm., Jt Chiefs of Staff, Washington, DC, 1962–66; Asst Div. Comdr, 1st Inf. Div., Republic of Vietnam, 1966–67; Comdt of Cadets, US Mil. Acad., 1967–69; Comdg Gen., 5th Inf. Div., Fort Carson, Colo, 1969–70; Chief of Legislative Liaison, Office of Sec. to the Army, Washington, DC, 1971–72; Dep. Chief of Staff for Personnel, Dept of the Army, Washington, DC, 1972–74; Comdg Gen., US Army Forces Comd, Fort McPherson, Ga, 1974–76; Chief of Staff, US Army, Washington, DC, 1976–79. Hon. Fellow, University Coll., Oxford, 1979. Hon. LLD: Akron, 1978; Boston, 1981; Hon. DCL Oxon, 1983. *Publications:* Cedar Falls-Junction City: a Turning Point, 1974; contribs to: Foreign Affairs, RUSI, 1982; Strategic Review, NATO's Sixteen Nations, 1983; Europa Archiv, Defense, NATO Review, 1984; Europäische Wehrkunde, Rivista Militaire, 1985; The Adelphi Papers, 1986; Soldat und Technik, 1987. *Recreations:* golf, reading. *Address:* 1467 Hampton Ridge Drive, McLean, VA 22101, USA.

ROGERS, Surgeon Rear-Adm. (D) Brian Frederick, CB 1980; Director of Naval Dental Services, 1977–80; *b* 27 Feb. 1923; *s* of Frederick Reginald Rogers, MIMechE, MIMarE, and Rosa Jane Rogers; *m* 1946, Mavis Elizabeth (*née* Scott); one *s* two *d*. *Educ:* Rock Ferry High Sch.; Liverpool Univ. (LDS 1945). House Surgeon, Liverpool Dental Hosp., 1945; joined RNVR, 1946; transf. to RN, 1954; served HMS Ocean, 1954–56 and HMS Eagle, 1964–66; Fleet Dental Surg. on staff of C-in-C Fleet, 1974–77; Comd Dental Surg. to C-in-C Naval Home Comd, 1977. QHDS 1977. *Recreations:* European touring, photography, DIY. *Address:* 22 Trerieve, Downderry, Torpoint, Cornwall PL11 3LY. *T:* Downderry (01503) 250526; Montana roja, Lanzarote, Canary Islands. *T:* (28) 517150.

ROGERS, Prof. C(laude) Ambrose, FRS 1959; Astor Professor of Mathematics, University College, London, 1958–86, now Emeritus; *b* 1 Nov. 1920; *s* of late Sir Leonard Rogers, KCSI, CIE, FRS; *m* 1952, Mrs J. M. Gordon, *widow* of W. G. Gordon, and *d* of F. W. G. North; two *d*. *Educ:* Berkhamsted School; University Coll., London; Birkbeck Coll., London. BSc, PhD, DSc (London, 1941, 1949, 1952). Experimental officer, Ministry of Supply, 1940–45; lecturer and reader, University College, London, 1946–54; Prof. of Pure Mathematics, Univ. of Birmingham, 1954–58. Mem. Council, Royal Soc., 1966–68 and 1983–84; Pres., London Mathematical Soc., 1970–72; Chm., Jt Mathematical Council, 1982–84. *Publications:* Packing and Covering, 1964; Hausdorff Measures, 1970; articles in various mathematical journals. *Recreation:* string figures. *Address:* Department of Mathematics, University College, WC1E 6BT; 8 Grey Close, NW11 6QG. *T:* 0181–455 8027.

ROGERS, Ven. David Arthur; Archdeacon of Craven, 1977–86; *b* 12 March 1921; *s* of Rev. Canon Thomas Godfrey Rogers and Doris Mary Cleaver Rogers (*née* Steele); *m* 1951, Joan Malkin; one *s* three *d*. *Educ:* Saint Edward's School, Oxford (scholar); Christ's College, Cambridge (exhibitioner). BA 1947, MA 1952. War service with Green Howards and RAC, 1940–45; Christ's Coll. and Ridley Hall, Cambridge, 1945–49; Asst Curate, St George's, Stockport, 1949–53; Rector, St Peter's, Levenshulme, Manchester, 1953–59; Vicar of Sedbergh, Cautley and Garsdale, 1959–79; Rural Dean of Sedbergh and then of

Ewecross, 1959–77; Hon. Canon of Bradford Cathedral, 1967. *Address:* Borrens, Leck, via Carnforth, Lancs LA6 2JG. *T:* Kirkby Lonsdale (015242) 71616.

ROGERS, David Bryan, CB 1984; Deputy Secretary and Director General, Board of Inland Revenue, 1981–89; *b* 8 Sept. 1929; *s* of Frank Rogers and Louisa Rogers; *m* 1955, Marjory Geraldine Gilmour Horribine; one *s* two *d. Educ:* Grove Park, Wrexham; University Coll., London (BA Classics). Inspector of Taxes, 1953; Principal Inspector, 1968; Sen. Principal Inspector, 1976; Under Sec. and Dir of Operations, Bd of Inland Revenue, 1978–81. Mem. Council, UCL, 1983–93. *Recreations:* piano, organ, singing, reading.

ROGERS, Rev. Edward; General Secretary, Methodist Division of Social Responsibility (formerly Christian Citizenship Department), 1950–75; *b* 4 Jan. 1909; *s* of Capt. E. E. Rogers, Fleetwood; *m* 1st, 1937, Edith May, *o d* of A. L. Sutton, Plaistow; 2nd, 1979, Lucy Eveline Howlett. *Educ:* Baines's Poulton-Le-Fylde Grammar School; Manchester University; Hartley Methodist Coll. Kitchener Scholar, Shuttleworth Scholar, Hulme Hall, Manchester. MA (Econ. and Pol.) 1931, BD, 1933, Manchester Univ. Methodist Circuit Minister: East London Mission, Bakewell, Birmingham (Sutton Park), Southport, 1933–50. Lectures: Fernley, 1951; Ainslie, 1952; Beckly, 1957; Peake 1971. Editorial Dir, Methodist Newspaper Co., 1949–; Organising Dir, Methodist Relief Fund, 1953–75; Chairman, Inter-Church Aid and Refugee Service, British Council of Churches, 1960–64; Pres., Methodist Conf., 1960; Moderator, Free Church Federal Council, 1968 (Chm., Exec., 1974–80); Vice-Pres., British Council of Churches, 1971–74. Chairman: Standing Commn on Migration, 1964–70; Churches Cttee on Gambling Legislation, 1967–73; Exec. Council, UK Immigrants Adv. Service, 1970; Community and Race Relations Unit, 1971–75; Avec Board, 1977–89; Select Committee on Cruelty to Animals, 1963. *Publications:* First Easter, 1948; A Commentary on Communism, 1951; Programme for Peace, 1954; God's Business, 1957; That They Might Have Life, 1958; The Christian Approach to the Communist, 1959; Church Government, 1964; Living Standards, 1964; Law, Morality and Gospel, 1969; Search for Security, 1973; Plundered Planet, 1973; Money, 1976; Thinking About Human Rights, 1978; Changing Humanity: genetic engineering, 1989. *Recreations:* travel, indiscriminate reading. *Address:* 49 Fernhurst Road, Croydon, Surrey CR0 7OJ. *T:* 0181–656 1729.

ROGERS, Eric William Evan, DSc(Eng); FRAeS; Deputy Director (A), Royal Aircraft Establishment, Farnborough, Hants, 1978–85; *b* 12 April 1925; *o s* of late W. P. Rogers, Southgate, N London; *m* 1950, Dorothy Joyce Loveless; two *s* one *d. Educ:* Southgate County Grammar Sch.; Imperial Coll., London. FCGI, DIC. Aerodynamics Div., NPL, 1945–70 (Head of Hypersonic Research, 1961); Aerodynamics Dept, RAE, 1970 (Head, 1972). *Publications:* various papers on aerodynamics and on industrial aerodynamics, in ARC (R and M series), RAeS jls and elsewhere. *Recreations:* music, history. *Address:* 64 Thetford Road, New Malden, Surrey KT3 5DT. *T:* 0181–942 7452.

ROGERS, Sir Frank (Jarvis), Kt 1988; Deputy Chairman, The Telegraph (formerly Daily Telegraph) plc, since 1986 (Director, since 1985); Director, EMAP plc (formerly East Midland Allied Press), 1971–91 (Chairman, 1973–90); *b* 24 Feb. 1920; *s* of Percy Rogers and Elsie Mary (*née* Jarvis); *m* 1949, Esma Holland; two *d. Educ:* Wolstanton Grammar School. Journalist, 1937–49; Military Service, 1940–46; Gen. Man., Nigerian Daily Times, 1949–52; Manager, Argus, Melbourne, 1952–55; Man. Dir, Overseas Newspapers, 1958–60; Dir, Daily Mirror, 1960–65; Man. Dir, IPC, 1965–70. Chairman: Nat. Newspaper Steering Gp, 1970–72; Newspaper Publishers Assoc. Ltd, 1990– (Vice-Chm., 1968–69; Dir, 1971–73); European Publishers Council, 1991–. Adviser on Corporate Affairs, The Plessey Co. Ltd, 1973–81. Trustee, Reuters Founders Share Co., 1989–. Mem., British Exec. Cttee, Internat. Press Inst., 1988– (Chm., 1978–88). Mem. Council and Chm., Exec. Cttee, Industrial Soc., 1976–79; Chm. Council, Industry and Parliament Trust, 1979–81; Mem. Council, Advertising Standards Authority, 1985–90. *Recreations:* motoring, golf. *Address:* Greensleeves, Loudwater Drive, Rickmansworth, Herts WD3 4HJ.

ROGERS, (George) Stuart L.; *see* Lawson-Rogers.

ROGERS, George Theodore; retired; Under-Secretary, Department of Trade, 1974–79; *b* 26 Feb. 1919; *s* of late George James and Margaret Lilian Rogers; *m* 1944, Mary Katherine Stedman; three *s* two *d. Educ:* Portsmouth Grammar Sch.; Keble Coll., Oxford (Open Schol. in Classics). Served War, Indian Infy, Burma, 1939–45. Resumed univ. educn (PPE), 1945–48; NATO Defence Coll., 1953–54. Min. of Supply/Min. of Aviation, 1948–65; Univ. Grants Cttee, 1965–68; Min. of Technology, 1968–70; DTI, 1970–74; Under-Sec., 1973. *Recreations:* gardening, travel, aviation. *Address:* 39 Sandy Lane, Cheam, Surrey SM2 7PQ. *T:* 0181–642 6428.

ROGERS, Henry Augustus, OBE 1976 (MBE 1967); HM Diplomatic Service, retired; *b* 11 Dec. 1918; *s* of Henry Augustus Rogers and Evelyn Mary Rogers (*née* Casey); *m* 1947, Margaret May Stainsby; three *s. Educ:* The Fox Sch.; West Kensington Central Sch., London, W. With Solicitors, Wedlake Letts & Birds, Temple, prior to war. Joined RNVR, 1938; served war, 1939–45. Joined Foreign Office, 1945; Buenos Aires, 1946; Havana, 1953; Vice-Consul, Guatemala City, 1954; Vice-Consul, Los Angeles, 1958; Second Sec., Belgrade, 1961; FO, 1963; Second Sec., Kaduna, 1965; First Sec., Head of Chancery and Consul, Tegucigalpa, 1967; FCO, 1971; Consul, Luanda, Angola, 1973; Consul-Gen., Brisbane, 1976–77; FCO, 1978. Malta GC 50th Anniv. Medal, 1992. *Recreations:* reading, classical literature and modern history, art (the Impressionists), music. *Address:* 18 Carew Views, 30/36 Carew Road, Eastbourne, East Sussex BN21 2JL. *T:* Eastbourne (01323) 730915.

ROGERS, Very Rev. John; Dean of Llandaff, since 1993; *b* 1934; *s* of William Harold and Annie Mary Rogers; *m* 1972, Pamela Mary Goddard; one *s* one *d. Educ:* Jones' W Monmouth Sch., Pontypool; St David's Coll., Lampeter (BA 1955); Oriel Coll., Oxford (BA 1957; MA 1960); St Stephen's House, Oxford, 1957–59. Ordained deacon, 1959, priest, 1960; Assistant Curate: St Martin's, Roath (dio. of Llandaff), 1959–63; St Sidwell's, Lodge, with Holy Redeemer, Ruimveldt, Guyana, 1963–67; Vicar: Holy Redeemer, Ruimveldt, Guyana, 1967–69; Wismar and Lower Demerara River Missions, 1969–71; Caldicot, 1971–77; Monmouth, 1977–84; Rector, Ebbw Vale, 1984–93. Rural Dean: Monmouth, 1981–84; Blaenau Gwent, 1986–93; Canon of St Woolos Cathedral, 1988–93. *Recreations:* gardening, beer and wine making. *Address:* The Deanery, The Cathedral Green, Llandaff, Cardiff CF5 2YF. *T:* Cardiff (01222) 561545.

ROGERS, Prof. (John) Michael, DPhil; FSA; FBA 1988; Khalili Professor of Islamic Art, School of Oriental and African Studies, University of London, since 1991; *b* 25 Jan. 1935. *Educ:* Ulverston Grammar Sch.; Corpus Christi Coll., Oxford (MA, DPhil). FSA 1974. Robinson Sen. Student, Oriel Coll., Oxford, 1958–61; Tutor in Philosophy, Pembroke and Wadham Colls, Oxford, 1961–65; Asst, then Associate, Prof. of Islamic Art and Archaeol., Center for Arabic Studies, Amer. Univ. in Cairo, 1965–77; Dep. Keeper, Dept of Oriental Antiquities, BM, 1977–91. Vis. Sen. Res. Fellow, Merton Coll., Oxford, 1971–72; Slade Prof. of Fine Art, Oxford Univ., 1991–92. Pres., British Inst. of Persian Studies, 1993–. Corresp. Mem., Deutsches Archäologisches Inst., Berlin, 1988. Order of the Egyptian Republic, 2nd cl., 1969. *Publications:* The Spread of Islam, 1976; Islamic Art and Design 1500–1700, 1983; (with R. M. Ward) Süleyman the Magnificent, 1988; Mughal Painting, 1993; numerous articles on hist. and archaeol. of Islamic Turkey, Egypt, Syria, Iran and Central Asia. *Recreations:* walking, music, botany. *Address:* School of Oriental and African Studies, Thornhaugh Street, Russell Square, WC1H 0XG. *Club:* Beefsteak.

ROGERS, John Michael Thomas; QC 1979; barrister-at-law; a Recorder of the Crown Court, since 1976; *b* 13 May 1938; *s* of Harold Stuart Rogers and Sarah Joan Thomas; *m* 1971, Jennifer Ruth Platt (marr. diss. 1984); one *d. Educ:* Rydal Sch.; Birkenhead Sch.; Fitzwilliam House, Cambridge (MA, LLB). Called to Bar, Gray's Inn, 1963, Bencher 1991. Leader, Wales and Chester Circuit, 1990–92. *Recreations:* farming, gardening. *Address:* Gayla House, Ruthin, Clwyd, N Wales; 9 Gough Square, EC4A 3DE. *T:* 0171–353 5371. *Clubs:* Reform; Pragmatists; Ruthin Rugby Football.

ROGERS, Air Chief Marshal Sir John (Robson), KCB 1982; CBE 1971; FRAeS; Executive Chairman, Motor Sports Association, since 1989; Vice-Chairman, Royal Automobile Club, since 1990; *b* 11 Jan. 1928; *s* of B. R. Rogers; *m* 1955, Gytha Elspeth Campbell; two *s* two *d. Educ:* Brentwood Sch.; No 1 Radio Sch., Cranwell; Royal Air Force Coll., Cranwell. OC 56(F) Sqdn, 1960–61; Gp Captain, 1967; OC RAF Coningsby, 1967–69; Air Commodore, 1971; Dir of Operational Requirements (RAF), 1971–73; Dep. Comdt, RAF Coll., 1973–75; RCDS, 1976; Air Vice-Marshal, 1977; Dir-Gen. of Organisation, RAF, 1977–79; AOC Training Units, RAF Support Comd, 1979–81; Air Mem. for Supply and Organisation, MoD, 1981–83; Controller Aircraft, MoD PE, 1983–86, retired. Dir, First Technology Gp, 1986–93. FRAeS 1983. *Recreation:* motor racing. *Address:* c/o Lloyds Bank, 27 High Street, Colchester, Essex. *Clubs:* Royal Automobile, Royal Air Force.

ROGERS, John Willis; QC 1975; **His Honour Judge Rogers;** a Circuit Judge, since 1991; *b* 7 Nov. 1929; *s* of late Reginald John Rogers and late Joan Daisy Alexandra Rogers (*née* Willis); *m* 1952, Sheila Elizabeth Cann; one *s* one *d. Educ:* Sevenoaks Sch.; Fitzwilliam House, Cambridge (MA). Called to Bar, Lincoln's Inn, 1955 (Cholmeley Schol.); Bencher, 1984. 1st Prosecuting Counsel to Inland Revenue, SE Circuit, 1969–75; a Recorder, 1974–91. Hon. Recorder, City of Canterbury, 1985. Chm., Adv. Cttee on Conscientious Objectors, 1991–. *Recreations:* cricket, gardening, change ringing. *Address:* 3 Serjeants' Inn, Temple, EC4Y 1BQ. *T:* 0171–353 5537. *Clubs:* Garrick, MCC, Band of Brothers.

ROGERS, Malcolm Austin, DPhil; FSA; Director, Museum of Fine Arts, Boston, Mass, since 1994; *b* 3 Oct. 1948; *s* of late James Eric Rogers and Frances Anne (*née* Elsey). *Educ:* Oakham School; Magdalen College, Oxford (Open Exhibnr); Christ Church, Oxford (Senior Scholar). Violet Vaughan Morgan Prize, 1967; BA (Eng. Lang. and Lit. 1st cl.), 1969; MA 1973; DPhil 1976. National Portrait Gallery: Asst. Keeper, 1974–83; Dep. Keeper, 1983–85; Keeper, 1985–94; Dep. Dir, 1983–94. Freeman, City of London, 1992; Liveryman, Girdlers' Co., 1992. *Publications:* Dictionary of British Portraiture, 4 vols (ed jtly), 1979–81; Museums and Galleries of London, 1983, 3rd edn 1991; William Dobson, 1983; John and John Baptist Closterman: a catalogue of their works, 1983; Elizabeth II: portraits of sixty years, 1986; Camera Portraits, 1989; Montacute House, 1991; (with Sir David Piper) Companion Guide to London, 1992; (ed) The English Face, by Sir David Piper, 1992; Master Drawings from the National Portrait Gallery, 1993; articles and reviews in Burlington Magazine, Apollo, TLS. *Recreations:* food and wine, opera, travel. *Address:* 20 Charles River Square, Boston, MA 02114, USA. *T:* (617) 7425195. *Club:* Beefsteak.

ROGERS, Martin Hartley Guy; HM Diplomatic Service, retired; *b* 11 June 1925; *s* of late Rev. Canon T. Guy Rogers and Marguerite Inez Rogers; *m* 1959, Jean Beresford Chinn; one *s* three *d. Educ:* Marlborough Coll.; Jesus Coll., Cambridge. CRO, 1949; 2nd Sec., Karachi, 1951–53; CRO, 1953–56 and 1958–60; seconded to Govt of Fedn of Nigeria, 1956–57, ndc 1960–61; 1st Sec., Ottawa, 1961–62; Adviser to Jamaican Min. of External Affairs, 1963; CRO, later Commonwealth Office, 1963–68; Dep. High Comr, Bombay, 1968–71, Kaduna, 1972–75; High Comr, The Gambia, 1975–79; on loan to CSSB as Asst Dir, 1979–85. *Recreation:* bridge. *Address:* Croftside, Harrow Road East, Dorking, Surrey RH4 2AX. *T:* Dorking (01306) 883789.

ROGERS, Martin John Wyndham; Director, Farmington Institute for Christian Studies, and Associate Fellow, Manchester College, Oxford, since 1991; *b* 9 April 1931; *s* of late John Frederick Rogers and Grace Mary Rogers; *m* 1957, Jane Cook; two *s* one *d. Educ:* Oundle Sch.; Heidelberg Univ.; Trinity Hall, Cambridge (MA); MA Oxon 1995. Henry Wiggin & Co., 1953–55; Westminster School: Asst Master, 1955–60; Sen. Chemistry Master, 1960–64; Housemaster, 1964–66; Under Master and Master of the Queen's Scholars, 1967–71; Headmaster of Malvern Coll., 1971–82; Chief Master, King Edward's Sch., Birmingham, Headmaster of the Schs of King Edward VIth in Birmingham, 1982–91. Seconded as Nuffield Research Fellow (O-level Chemistry Project), 1962–64; Salter's Company Fellow, Dept of Chemical Engrg and Chemical Technology, Imperial Coll., London, 1969. Chairman: Curriculum Cttee of HMC, GSA and IAPS, 1979–86; HMC, 1987; Mem. Council, GPDST, 1991–93. Chm., European Council, Nat. Assocs of Indep. Schs, 1994–. Mem. Council, Birmingham Univ., 1985–92. Governor: Oundle Sch., 1988–; Westonbirt Sch., 1991–; Elmhurst Ballet Sch., 1991–95. *Publications:* John Dalton and the Atomic Theory, 1965; Chemistry and Energy, 1968; (Editor) Foreground Chemistry Series, 1968; Gas Syringe Experiments, 1970; (co-author) Chemistry: facts, patterns and principles, 1972. *Address:* Manchester College, Oxford OX1 3TD. *Club:* East India, Devonshire, Sports and Public Schools.

ROGERS, Maurice Arthur Thorold; Secretary, Royal Institution, 1968–73; Joint Head, Head Office Research and Development Department, ICI, 1962–72; *b* 8 June 1911; *s* of A. G. L. Rogers; *g s* of Prof. J. E. Thorold Rogers; *m* 1947, Margaret Joan (*née* Craven) one *s* two *d. Educ:* Dragon Sch.; Westminster Sch.; University Coll., London. 1st Class hons BSc (Chem.) UCL 1932, PhD (Chem.) 1934. Chemist, ICI Dyestuffs Div., 1934–45; Head of Academic Relations Dept, 1946–58; Head of Head Office Research Dept, ICI, 1958–62. *Publications:* numerous papers in: Jl of Chem. Soc.; Nature; etc. *Recreations:* climbing, gardening, china restoration, conservation of countryside. *Address:* Mount Skippet, Ramsden, Oxford OX7 3AP. *T:* Ramsden (01993) 868253.

ROGERS, Michael; *see* Rogers, J. M.

ROGERS, Nigel David; free-lance singer, conductor and teacher; Professor of Singing, Royal College of Music, since 1979; *b* 21 March 1935; *m* 1961, Frederica Bement Lord (*d* 1992); one *d; m* 1991, Sheila W. Barnes. *Educ:* Wellington Grammar Sch.; King's Coll., Cambridge (MA). Studied in Italy and Germany. Professional singer, 1961–; began singing career in Munich with group Studio der frühen Musik. Is a leading specialist in field of Baroque music, of which he has made about 70 recordings; gives concerts, recitals, lectures and master classes in many parts of world; most acclaimed role in opera as Monteverdi's Orfeo. Formed vocal ensemble Chiaroscuro, to perform vast repertory of Italian Baroque music, 1979, later extended to include Chiaroscuro Chamber Ensemble and Chiaroscuro Baroque Orch. Has lectured and taught at Schola Cantorum Basiliensis, Basle, Switzerland.

Hon. RCM 1981. *Publications:* chapter on Voice, Companion to Baroque Music (ed J. A. Sadic), 1991; articles on early Baroque performance practice in various periodicals in different countries. *Address:* Chestnut Cottage, East End, East Woodhay, near Newbury, Berks RG15 0AB. *T:* Highclere (01635) 253319, *Fax:* (01635) 255242.

ROGERS, Maj.-Gen. Norman Charles, FRCS 1949; consultant surgeon, retired; *b* 14 Oct. 1916; *s* of Wing Comdr Charles William Rogers, RAF, and Edith Minnie Rogers (*née* Weaver); *m* 1954, Pamela Marion (*née* Rose); two *s* one *d*. *Educ:* Imperial Service Coll.; St Bartholomew's Hosp. MB, BS London; MRCS, LRCP 1939. Emergency Commn, Lieut RAMC, Oct. 1939; 131 Field Amb. RAMC, Dunkirk (despatches, 1940); RMO, 4th Royal Tank Regt, N Africa, 1941–42; Italy, 1942–43 (POW); RMO 1st Black Watch, NW Europe, 1944–45 (wounded, despatches twice). Ho. Surg., St Bartholomew's Hosp., 1946–47; Registrar (Surgical) Appts, Norwich, 1948–52; Sen. Registrar Appts, Birmingham, 1952–56; granted permanent commn, RAMC, 1956; surgical appts in mil. hospitals: Chester, Dhekelia (Cyprus), Catterick, Iserlohn (BAOR), 1956–67; Command Consultant Surgeon, BAOR, 1967–69; Dir, Army Surgery, 1969–73; QHS, 1969–73. Clin. Supt, 1975–80, and Consultant, 1973–81, Accident and Emergency Dept, Guy's Hosp; Civilian Consultant Surgeon: BMH Iserlohn, 1983–86; BMH Munster, 1986. *Publications:* contribs on surgical subjects. *Address:* 29 Ponsonby Terrace, SW1P 4PZ.

ROGERS, Mrs P. E.; *see* Box, B. E.

ROGERS, Parry; see Rogers, T. G. P.

ROGERS, Paul; actor; *b* Plympton, Devon, 22 March 1917; *s* of Edwin and Dulcie Myrtle Rogers; *m* 1st, 1939, Jocelyn Wynne (marr. diss. 1955); two *s*; 2nd, 1955, Rosalind Boxall; two *d*. *Educ:* Newton Abbot Grammar School, Devon. Michael Chekhov Theatre Studio, 1936–38. First appearance on stage as Charles Dickens in Bird's Eye of Valour, Scala, 1938; Stratford-upon-Avon Shakespeare Memorial Theatre, 1939; Concert Party and Colchester Rep. Co. until 1940. Served Royal Navy, 1940–46. Colchester Rep. Co. and Arts Council Tour and London Season, Tess of the D'Urbervilles, 1946–47; Bristol Old Vic, 1947–49; London Old Vic (incl. tour S Africa and Southern Rhodesia), 1949–53; also at Edinburgh, London and in USA, 1954–57; London, 1958; tour to Moscow, Leningrad and Warsaw, 1960. Roles with Old Vic include numerous Shakespearean leads; Gloucester, in King Lear, 1989. Other parts include: Sir Claude Mulhammer in The Confidential Clerk, Edinburgh Festival and Lyric, London, 1953; Lord Claverton in The Elder Statesman, Edinburgh Fest. and Cambridge Theatre, London, 1958; Mr Fox in Mr Fox of Venice, Piccadilly, 1959; Johnny Condell in One More River, Duke of York's and Westminster, 1959; Nickles in JB, Phœnix, 1961; Reginald Kinsale in Photo Finish, Saville, 1962; The Seagull, Queen's, 1964; Season of Goodwill, Queen's, 1964; The Homecoming, Aldwych, 1965; Timon of Athens, Stratford-upon-Avon, 1965; The Government Inspector, Aldwych, 1966; Henry IV, Stratford-upon-Avon, 1966; Max in The Homecoming, New York, 1967 (Tony Award and Whitbread Anglo-American Award); Plaza Suite, Lyric, 1969; The Happy Apple, Apollo, 1970; Sleuth, St Martin's, 1970, NY, 1971 and 1974; Othello, Nat. Theatre Co., Old Vic, 1974; Heartbreak House, Nat. Theatre, 1975; The Marrying of Ann Leete, Aldwych, 1975; The Return of A. J. Raffles, Aldwych, 1975; The Zykovs, Aldwych, 1976; Volpone, The Madras House, Nat. Theatre, 1977; Eclipse, Royal Court, 1978; You Never Can Tell, Lyric, Hammersmith, 1979; The Dresser, New York, 1981, 1982; The Importance of Being Earnest, A Kind of Alaska, Nat. Theatre, 1982; The Apple Cart, Theatre Royal, Haymarket, 1986; Danger: Memory!, Hampstead, 1988; Other People's Money, Lyric, 1990. Appears in films and television. *Publication:* a Preface to Folio Soc. edition of Shakespeare's Love's Labour's Lost, 1959. *Recreations:* gardening, carpentry, books. *Address:* 9 Hillside Gardens, Highgate, N6 5SU. *T:* 0181–340 2656.

ROGERS, Rev. Percival Hallewell, MBE 1945; Headmaster, Portora Royal School, Enniskillen, 1954–73; *b* 13 Sept. 1912; *m* 1940, Annie Mary Stuart, 2nd *d* of Lt-Col James Morwood; two *s* one *d*. *Educ:* Brentwood School; St Edmund Hall, Oxford. BA Class II, Hons English, Oxford, 1935; Diploma in Education, 1936; MA 1946. Two terms of teaching, Westminster School; Master in charge of English, Haileybury, 1936; served War, 1940–45 (despatches twice, MBE): RA, Major; DAA QMG; Bishop's College, Cheshunt, 1946; ordained, 1947; Asst Chaplain and English Master, Haileybury, 1947; Chaplain and English Master, 1949; student, Internat. Acad. for Continuous Educn, Sherborne, 1973–74; Chaplain, Gresham's Sch., Holt, 1974–75; Dean, Internat. Acad. for Continuous Educn, 1975–76; Asst Priest, Trinity Episcopal Church, New Orleans, 1976–80; Dir of Ordinands, Warden of Lay Readers, Dio. of Clogher, 1982–84; Priest-in-Charge, Sandford-on-Thames, 1985–86. Life Mem., Oxford Union. *Publications:* The Needs of the Whole Man, Systematics, 1971; Editor and contrib. to A Guide to Divinity Teaching (SPCK), 1962. *Address:* 7 Eyot Place, Iffley Fields, Oxford OX4 1SA. *T:* Oxford (01865) 244976. *Club:* East India, Devonshire, Sports and Public Schools.

ROGERS, Peter Brian; Deputy Chief Executive and Director of Finance, Independent Television Commission, since 1991; *b* 8 April 1941; *s* of late William Patrick Rogers and Margaret Elizabeth Rogers; *m* 1966, Jean Mary Bailey; one *s* two *d*. *Educ:* De La Salle Grammar Sch., Liverpool; Manchester Univ. (1st Cl. Hons BAEcon; Cobden Prize); London Sch. of Econs and Pol. Science, London Univ. (MSc Econs). Tax Officer, Inland Revenue, 1959–67; Res. Associate, Manchester Univ., 1967–68; Econ. Adviser, HM Treasury, 1968–73; Sen. Econ. Adviser, Central Policy Review Staff, Cabinet Office, 1973–74; Dir of Econ. Planning, Tyne and Wear CC (on secondment from Central Govt), 1974–76; Sen. Econ. Adviser, DoE, 1976–79; Dep. Chief Exec., Housing Corp., 1979–82; Dir of Finance, IBA, 1982–90. Dir, Channel Four Television Co., 1982–92. *Recreations:* woodwork, windsurfing. *Address:* Riverhead Cottage, Kilmeston Road, Cheriton, Alresford, Hants SO24 0NJ. *T:* Bramdean (01962) 771790.

ROGERS, Peter Richard; Supreme Court Taxing Master, since 1992; *b* 2 April 1939; *s* of Denis Roynan Rogers and Lucy Gwynneth (*née* Hopwood); *m* 1966, Adrienne Winifred Haylock. *Educ:* Bristol Univ. (LLB Hons). Solicitor of the Supreme Court. Articled Clerk, then solicitor, Turner Kenneth Brown (formerly Kenneth Brown Baker Baker) (solicitors), 1961–92; Partner, 1968–92; Dep. Supreme Court Taxing Master, 1991–92. Mem., London No 13 Legal Aid Cttee, 1980–92. *Recreations:* weather, steam and other railways, environmental concerns. *Address:* Supreme Court Taxing Office, Cliffords Inn, Fetter Lane, EC4A 1DQ. *T:* 0171–936 6224. *Club:* Wig and Pen.

ROGERS, Raymond Thomas, CPhys, FInstP; Under Secretary, and Executive Director Information Management Group, Department of Health, since 1991; *b* 19 Oct. 1940; *s* of late Thomas Kenneth Rogers and of Mary Esther Rogers (*née* Walsh); *m* 1964, Carmel Anne Saunders; two *s* one *d*. *Educ:* Gunnersbury Grammar Sch.; Birmingham Univ. (BSc). CPhys, FInstP 1962. Basic Med. Physicist, London Hosp., 1962–66; Sen. Med. Physicist, Westminster Hosp., 1966–70; Department of Health and Social Security, later Department of Health: PSO, Scientific and Tech. Br., 1970; Supt Engr, then Dir 1984; Asst Sec., Health Inf. Br., 1984–91. *Publications:* contribs to scientific jls and books. *Recreations:* trekking, opera, science, peace. *Address:* One Bannisters Road, Onslow Village, Guildford, Surrey GU2 5RA. *T:* Guildford (01483) 573078.

ROGERS, Col Richard Annesley C.; *see* Coxwell-Rogers.

ROGERS, Sir Richard (George), Kt 1991; RA 1984 (ARA 1978); MArch; RIBA; architect; Chairman, Richard Rogers Architects Ltd, London, Tokyo and Berlin; Director: River CADS Ltd; River Cafe, Thames Wharf Studios, London; *b* 23 July 1933; *s* of Dada Geiringer and Nino Rogers; *m* 1961, Sue Rogers; three *s*; *m* 1973, Ruth Elias; two *s*. *Educ:* Architectural Assoc. (AA Dipl.); Yale Univ. (MArch; Fulbright, Edward D. Stone, and Yale Scholar); Royal Inst. of British Architects. Reith Lectr, 1995. Winner: of internat. competition for Centre Pompidou, 1971–77 (Internat. Union of Architects August Perret Prize for most outstanding internat. work, 1975–78); of Lloyd's internat. comp. for HQ in City of London, 1978 (FT Architecture at Work Award, 1987; Civic Trust Award, 1987; RIBA Award, 1988; PA Award for innovation in bldg design and construction, 1988). *Other major projects include:* Creek Vean House, Cornwall (RIBA Award for work of outstanding quality, 1969); Reliance Controls, Swindon, 1967 (FT Award for most outstanding indust. bldg, 1966–67); B&B factory, Como, Italy, 1972–73; HQ and Labs, Universal Oil Products, 1973–74 (BSC Award, 1975; RIBA Regional Award (Commendation), 1975); Res. Labs, PA Technology, Melbourn, Herts, 1975–83 (FT Indust. Arch. Award, 1975; RIBA Commendation, 1975); Music Res. Centre for Pierre Boulez and Min. of Cultural Affairs, IRCAM, Paris, 1977; Fleetguard Manufg and Distribn Centre, Quimper, France, 1979–81 (Premier Award for most exceptional steel structure); Inmos Microprocessor factory, Newport, S Wales, 1982 (UK Steel Design Award, 1982; FT Architecture at Work Award (Commendation), 1983); apptd by City of Florence to revitalise banks of River Arno, 1983; PA Technology, Princeton, NJ, USA, 1984; Linn hi-fi equipment, Glasgow, 1985 (Constructa-Preis, 1992); appt master plan architects for Royal Docks, London, 1986; Reuters Docklands Bldg, 1988 (RIBA Award, 1993); Billingsgate redevelt, London, 1988 (Civic Trust Award, 1989); Pumping Station, Victoria Docks, London, 1989 (Constructa-Preis, 1992); masterplanning, Potsdamer/Leipziger Platz, Berlin, 1991; airport masterplanning and extension, Marseille, 1992; office develt, Kabuchi-cho, Tokyo, 1993; Channel 4 HQ, London, 1994; European Court of Human Rights, Strasbourg, 1995. *Current projects:* masterplanning, 5th Terminal and alterations to Terminal 1, Heathrow Airport; masterplanning, King's Dock, Liverpool; HQ, Lloyd's Register of Shipping, London; HQ, Daiwa Europe, London; library, Thames Valley Univ.; law court, Bordeaux; office develt, Potsdamer Platz, Berlin; underground network, Berlin; offices and lab., Gifu, Japan. *Exhibitions:* ICA; Royal Acad.; Mus. of Modern Art, NY; Graham Foundn, Chicago; UCLA; Mus. of Mod. Art, Warsaw; Deutsches Architekturmuseum, Frankfurt; Magasins d'Usines, Centre Pompidou, Paris; Louvre Mus. of Decorative Arts, Paris; AIA San Francisco; Berlin Aedes Gall.; Venice Biennale, 1991; Nara, Japan, 1992; Meuble et Immeuble, Centre Pompidou, 1993. *Taught at:* AA, London; Cambridge Univ.; Yale, Princeton, Harvard and Cornell Univs, and Univ. of Calif, LA and Berkeley; McGill Univ., Canada; Aachen Univ., Germany; Eero Saarinem Prof. of Arch., Yale, 1985. Chairman: Bd of Trustees, Tate Gall., 1984–88; Nat. Housing Tenants Trust; Building Experiences Trust; Architecture Foundn; Vice-Chm., Arts Council of England, 1994–; Member: UN Architects Cttee; Council and Policy Cttees, RIBA, Hon. FAIA; Hon. Fellow, Royal Acad. of Art, The Hague; Hon. Dr RCA. Royal Gold Medal for Arch., 1985. Chevalier de la Légion d'Honneur, France. Subject of several television documentaries on architecture. *Publications:* Richard Rogers + Architects, 1985; A+U: Richard Rogers 1978–1988, 1988; Architecture: a modern view, 1990; (jtly) A New London, 1992; *relevant publications:* Richard Rogers, a biography, by Bryan Appleyard, 1986; Richard Rogers, by Kenneth Powell, 1994; The Architecture of Richard Rogers, by Deyan Sudjic, 1994. *Recreations:* friends, food, art, architecture, travel. *Address:* (office) Thames Wharf, Rainville Road, W6 9HA. *T:* 0171–385 1235.

ROGERS, Thomas Edward, CMG 1960; MBE 1945; HM Diplomatic Service, retired; *b* 28 Dec. 1912; *s* of T. E. Rogers, MBE and Lucy Jane Browne; *m* 1950, Eileen Mary, *d* of R. J. Speechley; no *c*. *Educ:* Bedford Sch.; Emmanuel Coll., Cambridge (Exhibnr); School of Oriental Studies, London. Apptd to Indian Civil Service, 1936, and to Indian Political Service, 1941; served in Bengal, 1937–41; in Persia and Persian Gulf, 1941–45; Political Agent, Quetta, 1947; Dep. Sec. (Cabinet Secretariat), Pakistan Govt, 1947–48. Entered Foreign Service, 1948: FO, 1948–50; Bogotá, 1950–53; jssc, 1953–54; Coun. (Comm.), Madrid, 1954–58; Coun. (Econ.), Belgrade, 1958–62; Minister (Econ.), Buenos Aires, 1963–66; Dep. UK High Comr, Canada, 1966–70, Actg High Comr, 1967–68; Ambassador to Colombia, 1970–73. Chm., Anglo-Colombian Soc., 1981–88. Great Cross of St Carlos, Colombia, 1974. *Publication:* Great Game Grand Game (memoirs), 1991. *Recreation:* travel. *Address:* Chintens, Firway, Grayshott, Hindhead, Surrey GU26 6JQ. *Club:* United Oxford & Cambridge University.

ROGERS, (Thomas Gordon) Parry, CBE 1991; Chairman, ECCTIS 2000 Ltd, since 1989; *b* 7 Aug. 1924; *s* of late Victor Francis Rogers and Ella (*née* May); *m* 1st, 1947, Pamela Mary (*née* Greene) (marr. diss. 1973); one *s* seven *d*; 2nd, 1973, Patricia Juliet (*née* Curtis); one *s* one *d*. *Educ:* West Hartlepool Grammar Sch.; St Edmund Hall, Oxford. MA; CIPM, CIMgt; FRSA; FInstD. Served RAC and RAEC, 1944–47. Procter & Gamble Ltd, 1948–54; Mars Ltd, 1954–56; Hardy Spicer Ltd, 1956–61 (Dir, 1957–61); IBM United Kingdom Ltd, 1961–74 (Dir, 1964–74); The Plessey Co. plc, 1974–86 (Dir, 1976–86); Chm., Percom Ltd, 1984–94; Director: MSL Gp Internat. Ltd, 1970–78; ICL plc, 1977–79; Hobsons Publishing plc, 1985–90; Butler Cox plc, 1985–91; Norman Broadbent Internat. Ltd, 1985–90; Ocean Group plc, 1988–94; Future Perfect (Counselling) Ltd, 1986–92; PRIMA Europe Ltd, 1987–93; BNB Resources plc, 1990–94. Chm., Plessey Pension Trust, 1978–86; Trustee, BNB Resources Pension Trust, 1991–94. Chairman: BTEC, 1986–94; SW London Coll. HEC, 1989–91; IT Skills Agency, 1984–96; Salisbury HA, 1986–90; Commn on Charitable Fundraising, NCSS, 1970–76; Member: Employment Appeal Tribunal, 1978–87; Standing Cttee on Pay Comparability, 1980–81; Nat. Steering Gp, Trng and Vocational Educn Initiative, MSC, 1983–86; CBI/BIM Panel on Mgt Educn, 1968–78; CBI Employment Policy Cttee, 1980–86; Rev. Team, Children and Young Persons Benefits, DHSS, 1984–85; Oxford Univ. Appts Cttee, 1972–87; Member Council: CRAC, 1965–94; ISCO, 1988–95; Inst. of Manpower Studies, 1970–86; Indust. Participation Assoc., 1972–86; Inst. of Dirs, 1980–95 (Chm., 1985–88; Vice Pres., 1988–95); Inst. of Personnel Management, 1954– (Pres., 1975–77); EEF, 1980–86; Econ. League, 1982–86; E Europe Trade Council, 1982–85. Governor: Ashridge Management Coll., 1985–94; Warminster Sch., 1989–; St Mary's Sch., Shaftesbury, 1991–94. Trustee, Ella Rogers Music Trust. Patron, Dorset Chamber Orch.; Freeman, City of London, 1987; Mem., Information Technologists' Co., 1987–. *Publications:* The Recruitment and Training of Graduates, 1970; contribs on management subjects to newspapers and jls. *Recreations:* birdwatching, golf, tennis, photography, listening to music. *Address:* St Edward's Chantry, Bimport, Shaftesbury, Dorset SP7 8BA. *T:* Shaftesbury (01747) 852789; 32 Romulus Court, Justin Close, Brentford, Mddx TW8 8QP. *T:* 0181–568 6060. *Clubs:* Savile; Sherborne Golf.

ROGERS, William Pierce; Partner, law firm of Rogers & Wells, since 1973 (of Royall, Koegel, Rogers and Wells, 1961–69); *b* 23 June 1913; *s* of Harrison A. and Myra Beswick Rogers; *m* 1937, Adele Langston; three *s* one *d*. *Educ:* Canton High School, Canton, New York; Colgate University; Cornell Law School. Law firm of Cadwalader, Wickersham and Taft, NY City, 1937; an Asst District Attorney in NY County, 1938; US Navy,

1942–46; Dist Attorney's Office in New York, 1946; Chief Counsel, Senate Investigating Cttee, 1947; Counsel, Senate Permanent Investigating Cttee, 1949; law firm of Dwight, Royall, Harris, Koegel and Caskey, offices in New York and Washington, 1950; Dep. Attorney-General, 1953; Attorney-General of the US, 1957–61; Secretary of State, USA, 1969–73. Holds several hon. degrees in Law, from Univs and Colls in the USA, 1956–60. Mem. Bar Assocs in the USA. US Representative: to 20th Session of UN General Assembly, 1965; on UN Ad Hoc Cttee on SW Africa, 1967; Mem., President's Commn on Law Enforcement and Administration of Justice, 1965–67. *Recreations:* golf, tennis, swimming. *Address:* Rogers & Wells, 200 Park Avenue, New York, NY 10166–0153, USA. *Clubs:* Metropolitan (Washington); Burning Tree (Bethesda); Racquet and Tennis, The Sky (NYC); Chevy Chase (Chevy Chase).

ROGERSON, Rt. Rev. Barry; *see* Bristol, Bishop of.

ROGERSON, Nicolas; Chairman, Dewe Rogerson International, since 1985; Chief Executive, Dewe Rogerson Group, since 1969 (Deputy Chairman, 1969–88); *b* 21 May 1943; *s* of Hugh and Olivia Rogerson; *m* 1972, Elizabeth, Baroness Rummel; two step *s*. *Educ:* Cheam Sch.; Winchester Coll.; Magdalene Coll., Cambridge. Staff Journalist, Investors Chronicle, 1964–65; Executive, Angel Court Consultants, 1966–68; formed Dewe Rogerson, 1969. Appeals Chm., King George's Fund for Sailors. *Recreations:* sailing, ski-ing, Real tennis, field sports, languages and European history. *Address:* (office) 3 London Wall Buildings, London Wall, EC2M 5SY. *Clubs:* City of London, Turf; Pitt (Cambridge); Racquet (New York).

ROGERSON, Philip Graham; Executive Director, British Gas plc, since 1994; *b* 1 Jan. 1945; *s* of Henry and Florence Rogerson; *m* 1968, Susan Janet Kershaw; one *s* two *d*. *Educ:* William Hulme's Grammar Sch., Manchester. Dearden, Harper, Miller & Co., Chartered Accountants, 1962–67; Hill Samuel & Co. Ltd, 1967–69; Thomas Tilling Ltd, 1969–71; Steetley Ltd, 1971–72; J. W. Chafer Ltd, 1972–78; with ICI plc, 1978–92 (General Manager, Finance, 1989–92); Man. Dir, Finance, British Gas plc, 1992–94. Non-exec. Dir, Leeds Permanent Bldg Soc., 1994–. *Recreations:* golf, tennis, theatre. *Address:* British Gas plc, Rivermill House, 152 Grosvenor Road, SW1V 3JL. *T:* 0171–821 1444.

ROGERSON, Susan, (Mrs T. S. Rogerson); *see* Darling, S.

ROGG, Lionel; organist and composer; Professor of Organ and Improvisation, Geneva Conservatoire de Musique, since 1961; *b* 1936; *m* Claudine Effront; three *s*. *Educ:* Conservatoire de Musique, Geneva (1st prize for piano and organ). Concerts or organ recitals on the five continents. Records include works by Alain, Buxtehude (complete organ works; Deutscher Schallplatten Preis, 1980), Couperin and Martin; also complete works of J. S. Bach (Grand Prix du Disque, 1970, for The Art of the Fugue). *Compositions:* Acclamations, 1964; Chorale Preludes, 1971; Partita, 1975; Variations on Psalm 91, 1983; Cantata "Geburt der Venus", 1984; Introduction, Ricerare and Toccata, 1985; Two Etudes, 1986; Monodies, 1986; Psalm 92, 1986; Piece for Clarinette, 1986; Face-à-face for two pianos, 1987; Organ Concerto, 1991. DèsL Univ. de Genève, 1989. *Publication:* Eléments de Contrepoint, 1969. *Address:* Conservatoire de Musique, Place Neuve, Geneva, Switzerland; 38A rte de Troinex, 1234 Vessy-Genève, Switzerland.

ROH, Tae Woo, Hon. GCMG 1989; President of Republic of Korea, 1988–93; *b* 4 Dec. 1932; *m* 1959, Kim-Ok-Sook; one *s* one *d*. *Educ:* Korean Military Academy; Republic of Korea War College. Commander, Capital Security, 1978, Defence Security, 1980; retd as Army General; Minister of State for Nat. Security and Foreign Affairs, 1981; Minister of Sports, and of Home Affairs, 1982; President: Seoul Olympic Organizing Cttee, 1983; Asian Games Organizing Cttee, 1983; Korean Olympic Cttee, 1984. Mem., Nat. Assembly and Pres., Ruling Democratic Justice Party, 1985. Hon. Dr George Washington Univ., 1989. Order of Nat. Security Merit (Sam Il Medal) (Korea), 1967; Grand Order of Mugunghwa (Korea), 1988; foreign decorations, incl. France, Germany, Kenya, Paraguay. *Publications:* Widaehan pot'ongsaram ui shidae (A great era of the ordinary people), 1987, trans. Japanese, 1988; Korea: A Nation Transformed, 1990. *Recreations:* tennis, swimming, golf, music, reading. *Address:* c/o Chong Wa Dae, #1 Sejongno, Chongno-gu, Seoul 110–050, Korea.

ROHMER, Eric, (Maurice Henri Joseph Schérer); French film director and writer; *b* 21 March 1920; *s* of Désiré Schérer and Jeanne Monzat; *m* 1957, Thérèse Barbet. *Educ:* Paris. Teacher, 1942–55; journalist, 1951–55. Film critic, Revue du cinéma, Arts, Temps Modernes, La Parisienne, 1949–63; Jt Founder, La Gazette du cinéma (also former Jt Editor). Dir of educnl films for French television, 1964–70. Co-Dir, Société des Films du Losange, 1964–. Films include (director and writer): Charlotte et son steak (short film), 1951; Le signe du lion, 1959; La boulangère de Monceau (short film), 1962; La collectionneuse, 1966; Ma nuit chez Maud, 1969 (prix Max Ophüls, 1970); Le genou de Claire, 1970 (prix Louis-Delluc, prix Méliès, 1971); L'amour l'après-midi, 1972; La Marquise d'O, 1976; Perceval le Gallois, 1978; Le beau mariage, 1982; Pauline à la plage, 1982; Les nuits de la pleine lune, 1984; Le rayon vert (Lion d'or, Venice Film Fest., prix de la critique internationale), 1986; L'ami de mon amie, 1988; A Winter's Tale, 1992; L'Arbre, le maire et le médiathèque, 1993. Best Dir Award, Berlin Film Fest., 1983. *Publications:* Alfred Hitchcock, 1973; Charlie Chaplin, 1973; Six contes moraux, 1974; L'organisation de l'espace dans le "Faust" de Murnau, 1977; The Taste for Beauty (essays), 1992. *Address:* Les Films du Losange, 26 avenue Pierre 1er de Serbie, 75116 Paris, France.

ROHRER, Dr Heinrich; IBM Research Division, Zurich Research Laboratory, since 1963, and IBM Fellow, since 1986; *b* 6 June 1933; *s* of Henrich and Katharina Rohrer; *m* 1961, Rose-Marie Egger; two *d*. *Educ:* Federal Inst. of Technology, ETH, Zürich (Dr. sc. nat); PhD 1960. Post-doctoral Fellow, Rutgers Univ., 1961–63; joined IBM Res. Div. as Res. Staff Mem., 1963; then various managerial posts. Vis. Scientist, Univ. of Calif. at Santa Barbara, 1974–75. Mem. Bd, Swiss Fed. Insts of Technol., 1993–. Mem., Swiss Acad. of Technical Scis, 1988; For. Associate, US Acad. of Sci., 1988; Hon. Member: Swiss Physical Soc., 1990; Swiss Assoc. of Engrs and Architects, 1991; Zurich Physical Soc., 1992. Hon. Fellow, RMS, 1988. Hon. Dr: Rutgers, 1987; Marseille, 1988; Madrid, 1988; Magnum Seal, Bologna, 1988; Tsukuba, Japan, 1994. (Jtly) King Faisal Internat. Prize for Science, 1984; Hewlett Packard Europhysics Prize, 1984; (jtly) Nobel Prize in Physics, 1986; (jtly) Cresson Medal, Franklin Inst., Philadelphia, 1987. *Recreations:* ski-ing, hiking, gardening. *Address:* IBM Research Division, Zürich Research Laboratory, 8803 Rüschlikon, Switzerland. *T:* (1) 7248111.

ROITH, Oscar, CB 1987; FEng, FIMechE; Chief Engineer and Scientist, Department of Trade and Industry, 1982–87; *b* London, 14 May 1927; *s* of late Leon Roith and Leah Roith; *m* 1950, Irene Bullock; one *d*. *Educ:* Gonville and Caius Coll., Cambridge (minor schol.; Mech. Scis Tripos; MA). FIMechE 1967; FEng 1983; Eur Ing 1988. CBIM. FRSA. Research Dept, Courtaulds, 1948; Distillers Co. Ltd: Central Engrg Dept, 1952; Engrg Manager, Hull Works, 1962; Works Manager, 1968, Works Gen. Manager, 1969, BP Chemicals, Hull; General Manager: Engrg and Technical, BP Chemicals, 1974; Engrg Dept, BP Trading, 1977; Chief Exec. (Engrg), BP Internat., 1981. Director: Trueland Ltd, 1987–; British Maritime Technology, 1987–. Mem., Yorks and Humberside Economic Planning Council, 1972–74. Comr, Royal Commn for Exhibition of 1851, 1988–. Chm., Mech. and Electrical Engrg Requirements Bd, 1981–82; Member: Mech. Engrg and Machine Tools Requirements Bd, 1977–81; (non-exec.) Res. Cttee. British Gas, 1987–; ACORD, 1982–87; ACARD, 1982–87; Process Plant EDC, NEDO, 1979–82; SERC, 1982–87; NERC, 1982–87; Bd (part-time), LRT, 1988–; Chm., Res. Adv. Gp, PCFC, 1989–92. Pres., IMechE, 1987–88 (Dep. Pres., 1985–87; Mem. Council, 1981–92; Mem., Process Engrg Gp Cttee, 1962–68); Dep. Chm. Council, Foundn for Science and Technol., 1988–; Hon. Sec., Mech. Engrg, Council of Fellowship of Engrg, 1988–91. Hon. Prof., Dept of Mgt Sci., Univ. of Stirling, 1992–; Hon. Fellow, Univ. of Brighton, 1992. Gov., Brighton Polytechnic, 1988–91. Hon. DSc West of England, 1993. *Recreations:* cricket, gardening, walking. *Address:* 20 Wraymill House, Wraymill Park, Batts Hill, Reigate, Surrey RH2 0LQ. *T:* Redhill (01737) 779633. *Club:* Athenæum.

ROITT, Prof. Ivan Maurice, FRS 1983; Emeritus Professor of Immunology, University College London, since 1992; Professor, 1968–92, and Head of Department of Immunology, 1968–92, and of Rheumatology Research, 1984–92, University College and Middlesex School of Medicine (formerly Middlesex Hospital Medical School); *b* 30 Sept. 1927; *e s* of Harry Roitt; *m* 1953, Margaret Auralie Louise, *d* of F. Haigh; three *d*. *Educ:* King Edward's Sch., Birmingham; Balliol Coll., Oxford (exhibnr; BSc 1950; MA 1953; DPhil 1953; DSc 1968). FRCPath 1973; FRCP 1995. Res. Fellow, 1953, Reader in Immunopathol., 1965–68, Middlesex Hosp. Med. Sch. Chm., WHO Cttee on Immunolog. Control of Fertility, 1976–79; Mem., Biol. Sub-Cttee, UGC. Mem., Harrow Borough Council, 1963–65; Chm., Harrow Central Lib. Assoc., 1965–67. Florey Meml Lectr, Adelaide Univ., 1982. Hon. MRCP (London). (Jtly) Van Meter Prize, Amer. Thyroid Assoc., 1957; Gairdner Foundn Award, Toronto, 1964. *Publications:* Essential Immunology, 1971, 8th edn 1994; (jtly) Immunology of Oral Diseases, 1979; (jtly) Immunology, 1985, 3rd edn 1993; (jtly) Current Opinion in Immunology (series), 1989–; (jtly) Clinical Immunology, 1991; Slide Atlas of Essential Immunology, 1992; (with Peter J. Delves) Encyclopedia of Immunology, 1992; (ed jtly) Medical Microbiology, 1993; 250 contribs to learned scientific jls. *Address:* University College London, Windeyer Building, Cleveland Street, W1P 6DB.

ROKISON, Kenneth Stuart; QC 1976; a Recorder, 1989–94; *b* 13 April 1937; *s* of late Frank Edward and late Kitty Winifred Rokison; *m* 1973, Rosalind Julia (*née* Mitchell); one *s* two *d*. *Educ:* Whitgift School, Croydon; Magdalene College, Cambridge (BA 1960). Called to the Bar, Gray's Inn, 1961, Bencher, 1985. *Recreation:* acting. *Address:* Ashcroft Farm, Gadbrook, Betchworth, Surrey RH3 7AH. *T:* Dawes Green (01306) 611244.

ROLAND, Nicholas; *see* Walmsley, Arnold Robert.

ROLF, Percy Henry; a Recorder of the Crown Court, 1978–87; Consultant, Robinson Jarvis & Rolf, Solicitors, Isle of Wight, since 1986 (Partner 1948; Senior Partner, 1964); *b* 25 Dec. 1915; *s* of Percy Algernon Rolf and Lydia Kate (*née* Arnold); *m* 1939, Cecilia Florence Cooper; one *s* one *d*. *Educ:* Sandown Grammar Sch.; London Univ. (LLB). Solicitor. Served War, RAF, 1940–46: Wing Comdr; Sen. Air Traffic Control Officer, Transport Comd, 1945–46. Member: Eastbourne Br., Hour of Revival Assoc., 1959–92 (Chm., 1987–90); Holly Soc. of America Inc., 1986–. *Publications:* The Budding of the Fig Tree, 1992; The Seed of Abraham, 1993. *Recreations:* golf, gardening. *Address:* Ashlake Water, Fishbourne, Isle of Wight PO33 4EY. *T:* Wootton Bridge (01983) 882513. *Club:* Shanklin-Sandown Golf (Hon. Pres., 1990–94).

ROLFE; *see* Neville-Rolfe.

ROLFE, Rear-Adm. Henry Cuthbert Norris, CB 1959; *b* 1908; *s* of Benedict Hugh Rolfe, MA Oxon; *m* 1931, Mary Monica Fox; one *s* two *d*. *Educ:* Pangbourne Nautical College. Joined Royal Navy, 1925. Served War of 1939–45: HMS Hermes, 1939; South-East Asia, 1944; Staff of Director of Air Warfare, Admiralty, 1947; commanded HMS Veryan Bay, 1948; service with Royal Canadian Navy, 1949; commanded: HMS Vengeance, 1952; RN Air Station, Culdrose, 1952, HMS Centaur, 1954–56; RN Air Station, Ford, 1956–57; Asst Chief of Naval Staff (Warfare) 1957–60; Regional Director, Northern Region, Commonwealth Graves Commission, 1961–64, retd. Naval ADC to the Queen, 1957; Rear-Admiral, 1957. Liveryman, Worshipful Company of Coachmakers and Coach Harnessmakers, 1962. *Address:* 43 Nuns Road, Winchester, Hants SO23 7EF.

ROLFE, Hume B.; *see* Boggis-Rolfe.

ROLFE, William David Ian, PhD; FRSE, FGS, FMA; Keeper of Geology, National Museums of Scotland, since 1986; *b* 24 Jan. 1936; *s* of late William Ambrose Rolfe and Greta Olwen Jones; *m* 1960, Julia Mary Margaret, *d* of late Capt. G. H. G. S. Rayer, OBE; two *d*. *Educ:* Royal Liberty Grammar Sch., Romford; Birmingham Univ. (BSc 1957; PhD 1960). FGS 1960; FMA 1972; FRSE 1983. Demonstrator in Geol., UC of N Staffs, 1960; Fulbright Schol., and Asst Curator, Mus. of Comparative Zool., Harvard Coll., Cambridge, Mass, 1961–62; Geol. Curator, Univ. Lectr, then Sen. Lectr in Geol., Hunterian Mus., Univ. of Glasgow, 1962–81; Dep. Dir, 1981–86. Vis. Scientist, Field Mus. of Natural Hist., Chicago, 1981. Mem., Trng Awards Cttee, NERC, 1980–83. Pres., Palaeontol Assoc., 1992–94 (Vice-Pres., 1974–76); Soc. Hist. Natural Hist., 1987. Geological Society of Glasgow: Ed., Scottish Jl of Geol., 1967–72; Pres., 1973–76; Geological Society: Editl Chm., Journal, 1973–76; Chm., Conservation Cttee, 1980–85; Murchison Fund, 1978; Tyrrell Res. Fund, 1982; Coke Medal, 1984; Pres., Edinburgh Geological Soc., 1989–91. FRSA 1985. *Publications:* (ed) Phylogeny and Evolution of Crustacea, 1963; Treatise on Invertebrate Paleontology, part R, 1969; Geological Howlers, 1980; papers on fossil phyllocarid crustaceans and palaeontol., esp. other arthropods, and hist. of 18th century natural sci. illustration. *Recreations:* visual arts, walking, swimming, music. *Address:* 4A Randolph Crescent, Edinburgh EH3 7TH. *T:* 0131–226 2094. *Clubs:* Geological; University Staff (Edinburgh).

ROLFE JOHNSON, Anthony, CBE 1992; tenor; *b* 5 Nov. 1940; *m* (marr. diss.); two *s*; *m* Elisabeth Jones Evans; one *s* two *d*. Has performed at Glyndebourne, Covent Garden, Hamburg State Opera, La Scala Milan, Royal Albert Hall, Coliseum, Queen Elizabeth Hall, Aldeburgh Festival, Royal Festival Hall, Barbican Centre, Wigmore Hall, Salzburg Festival, Metropolitan NY. Has appeared with all major British orchestras and with Chicago Symphony Orchestra, Boston Symphony Orchestra, New York Philharmonic Orchestra and others. *Current rôles include:* Ulisse, Orfeo (Monteverdi), Idomeneo, Aschenbach, Peter Grimes, Lucio Silla, Tamino. *Address:* c/o Lies Askonas Ltd, 6 Henrietta Street, WC2E 8LA.

ROLL, family name of **Baron Roll of Ipsden.**

ROLL OF IPSDEN, Baron *cr* 1977 (Life Peer), of Ipsden in the County of Oxfordshire; **Eric Roll,** KCMG 1962 (CMG 1949); CB 1956; Director of the Bank of England, 1968–77; Chancellor, University of Southampton, 1974–84; Joint Chairman, S. G. Warburg & Co. Ltd, 1983–87 (Chairman, 1974–83; Deputy Chairman, 1967–74); President: S. G. Warburg Group Plc, since 1987; *b* 1 Dec. 1907; *yr s* of Mathias and Fany Roll; *m* 1934, Winifred, *o d* of Elliott and Sophia Taylor; two *d*. *Educ:* on the Continent; Univ. of Birmingham. BCom 1928; PhD 1930; Gladstone Memorial Prize, 1928; Univ. Research Scholarship, 1929. Prof. of Economics and Commerce, Univ. Coll. of Hull,

1935–46 (leave of absence 1939–46). Special Rockefeller Foundation Fellow, USA, 1939–41. Member, later Dep. Head, British Food Mission to N America, 1941–46; UK Dep. Member and UK Exec. Officer, Combined Food Board, Washington, until 1946; Asst Sec., Ministry of Food, 1946–47; Under-Secretary, HM Treasury (Central Economic Planning Staff), 1948; Minister, UK Delegation to OEEC, 1949. Deputy Head, United Kingdom Delegation to North Atlantic Treaty Organization, Paris, 1952; Under Secretary Ministry of Agriculture, Fisheries and Food, 1953–57; Executive Dir, International Sugar Council, 1957–59; Chm., United Nations Sugar Conf., 1958; Deputy Secretary, Ministry of Agriculture, Fisheries and Food, 1959–61; Deputy Leader, UK Delegation for negotiations with the European Economic Community, 1961–63; Economic Minister and Head of UK Treasury Delegation, Washington, 1963–64, also Exec. Dir for the UK International Monetary Fund and International Bank for Reconstruction and Development; Permanent Under-Sec. of State, Dept of Economic Affairs, 1964–66. Chm., subseq. Hon. Chm., Book Development Council, 1967–. Independent Mem., NEDC, 1971–80. Director: Times Newspapers Ltd, 1967–80; Times Newspapers Holdings Ltd, 1980–83; also other Directorships; President: Mercury Securities Ltd, 1985–87 (Chm., 1974–84); Mercury Internat. Gp, 1985–87. Hon. DSc Hull, 1967; Hon. DSocSci Birmingham, 1967; Hon. LLD Southampton, 1974. Grosses Goldene Ehrenzeichen mit Stern (Austria), 1979; Comdr 1st Cl., Order of the Dannebrog (Denmark), 1981; Officier, Légion d' Honneur, 1984; Grand Cordon, Order of the Sacred Treasure (Japan), 1993. *Publications:* An Early Experiment in Industrial Organization, 1930; Spotlight on Germany, 1933; About Money, 1934; Elements of Economic Theory, 1935; Organized Labour (collaborated), 1938; The British Commonwealth at War (collaborated), 1943; A History of Economic Thought, 1954, 5th edn 1992; The Combined Food Board, 1957; The World After Keynes, 1968; The Uses and Abuses of Economics, 1978; (ed) The Mixed Economy, 1982; Crowded Hours (autobiog.), 1985; Where Did We Go Wrong, 1995; articles in Economic Jl, Economica, American Economic Review, etc. *Recreation:* reading. *Address:* D2 Albany, Piccadilly, W1V 9RG. *Club:* Brooks's.

ROLL, Rev. Sir James (William Cecil), 4th Bt, *cr* 1921; Vicar of St John's, Becontree, 1958–83, retired; *b* 1 June 1912; *s* of Sir Cecil Ernest Roll, 3rd Bt, and Mildred Kate (*d* 1926), *d* of William Wells, Snaresbrook; *S* father, 1938; unmarried. *Educ:* Chigwell School, Essex; Pembroke College, Oxford; Chichester Theological College. Deacon, 1937. Curate East Ham Parish Church, 1944–58. *Heir:* none. *Address:* 82 Leighcliff Road, Leigh on Sea, Essex SS9 1DN. *T:* Southend-on-Sea (01702) 713050.

ROLLAND, Lawrence Anderson Lyon, PPRIBA; PPRIAS; FRSE; Senior Partner, The Hurd Rolland Partnership (formerly Robert Hurd and Partners), since 1965; President of Royal Institute of British Architects, 1985–87; *b* 6 Nov. 1937; *s* of Lawrence Anderson Rolland and Winifred Anne Lyon; *m* 1960, Mairi Melville; two *s* two *d*. *Educ:* George Watson Boys' College, Edinburgh; Duncan of Jordanstone College of Art. Diploma of Art (Architecture) 1959; ARIBA 1960; FRIAS 1965 (Pres., RIAS, 1979–81); FRSE 1989. Sen. Partner, L. A. Rolland & Partners, 1959–65. Founder Mem., Scottish Construction Industry Group, 1979–81; Mem., Bldg EDC, NEDC, 1982–88. Architect for: The Queen's Hall, concert hall, Edinburgh; restoration and redesign of Bank of Scotland Head Office (original Architect, Sibbald, Reid & Crighton, 1805 and later, Bryce, 1870); much housing in Fife's royal burghs; British Golf Museum, St Andrews; General Accident Life Assurance, York. Gen. Trustee, Church of Scotland. Chm. Bd. of Govs, Duncan of Jordanstone Coll. of Art, 1993–; Mem. Court, Univ. of Dundee, 1993–94. FRSA 1988. Winner of more than 20 awards and commendations from Saltire Soc., Stone Fedn, Concrete Soc., Civic Trust, Europa Nostra, RIBA, and Times Conservation Award. *Recreations:* music, fishing, food, wine, cars. *Address:* Rossend Castle, Burntisland, Fife KY3 0DF. *T:* Burntisland (01592) 873535. *Clubs:* Reform, Arts.

ROLLINSON, Timothy John Denis; Secretary, Forestry Commission, since 1994; *b* 6 Nov. 1953; *s* of William Edward Denis Rollinson and Ida Frances Rollinson (*née* Marshall); *m* 1975, Dominique Christine Favardin; one *s* two *d*. *Educ:* Chigwell Sch.; Edinburgh Univ. (BSc Hons). MICFor 1978, FICFor 1995. Forestry Commission: District Officer: Kent, 1976–78; New Forest, 1978–81; Head of: Growth and Yield Studies, 1981–88; Land Use Planning, 1988–90; Parly and Policy Div., 1990–93. FRSA 1995. *Publications:* Thinning Control in British Woodlands, 1985; articles in forestry jls. *Recreations:* golf, tennis, swimming, food, France. *Address:* Forestry Commission, 231 Corstorphine Road, Edinburgh EH12 7AT. *T:* 0131–334 0303. *Club:* Craigmillar Park Golf (Edinburgh).

ROLLO, family name of **Lord Rollo.**

ROLLO, 13th Lord *cr* 1651; **Eric John Stapylton Rollo;** Baron Dunning, 1869; JP; *b* 3 Dec. 1915; *s* of 12th Lord and Helen Maud (*d* 1928), *o c* of Frederick Chetwynd Stapylton of Hatton Hill, Windlesham, Surrey; *S* father, 1947; *m* 1938, Suzanne Hatton; two *s* one *d*. *Educ:* Eton. Served War of 1939–45, Grenadier Guards, retiring with rank of Captain. JP Perthshire, 1962. *Heir:* *s* Master of Rollo, *qv*. *Address:* Pitcairns, Dunning, Perthshire PH2 9BX. *T:* Dunning (01764) 684202.

ROLLO, Master of; Hon. David Eric Howard Rollo; *b* 31 March 1943; *s* and *heir* of 13th Lord Rollo, *qv*; *m* 1971, Felicity Anne Christian, *o d* of Lt-Comdr J. B. Lamb; three *s*. *Educ:* Eton. Late Captain Grenadier Guards. *Address:* 20 Draycott Avenue, SW3 3AA. *Clubs:* Cavalry and Guards, Turf.

ROLO, Cyril Felix, CMG 1975; OBE 1959; HM Diplomatic Service, retired; *b* 13 Feb. 1918; *s* of late I. J. Rolo and Linda (*née* Suares); *m* 1948, Marie Luise Christine (*née* Baeurle); one *s*. *Educ:* Charterhouse; Oriel Coll., Oxford (MA). Served with Armed Forces, 1940–46 (Major): Oxf. and Bucks LI, later on Gen. Staff; Western Desert, E Africa, Italy, Austria. Joined HM Foreign (subseq. Diplomatic) Service, 1946: Allied Commn for Austria, 1947–48; 2nd Sec., Rome, 1948–50; Political Adviser's Office, Berlin, 1950–52; FO, 1952–57; 1st Sec., Vienna, 1957–62; FO (subseq. FCO), 1962–76; Counsellor, 1971. *Recreations:* travel, golf, reading. *Address:* 12 Roxburghe Mansions, 32 Kensington Court, W8 5BQ. *T:* 0171–937 4696. *Clubs:* Travellers'; Sunningdale Golf.

ROMAIN, Roderick Jessel Anidjar; Metropolitan Stipendiary Magistrate, 1972–83; *b* 2 Dec. 1916; *s* of late Artom A. Romain and Winifred (*née* Rodrigues); *m* 1947, Miriam (*d* 1991), *d* of late Semtob Sequerra; one *s* one *d*. *Educ:* Malvern Coll.; Sidney Sussex Coll., Cambridge. Called to the Bar, Middle Temple, 1939. Commissioned from HAC to 27th Field Regt, RA, 1940. Served War of 1939–45; France and Belgium, also N Africa and Italy, JAG Staff, 1943–45; JA at Neuengamme War Crimes Trial. Admitted a Solicitor, 1949, in practice as Partner, in Freke Palmer, Romain & Gassman, until 1972; recalled to Bar, 1973; a Dep. Circuit Judge, 1975–78.

ROMANES, Professor George John, CBE 1971; PhD; Professor of Anatomy, 1954–84, and Dean of Faculty of Medicine, 1979–83, Edinburgh University; Professor of Anatomy, Royal Scottish Academy, since 1983; *b* 2 Dec. 1916; *s* of George Romanes, BSc, AMICE, and Isabella Elizabeth Burn Smith; *m* 1945, Muriel Grace Adam (*d* 1992), Edinburgh; four *d*. *Educ:* Edinburgh Academy; Christ's College, Cambridge (BA, PhD); Edinburgh University (MB, ChB). Marmaduke Sheild Scholar in Human Anatomy, 1938–40; Demonstrator in Anatomy, Cambridge, 1939; Beit Memorial Fellow for Medical Research, Cambridge, 1944–46; Lectr in Neuroanatomy, Edinburgh, 1946; Prof. of Anatomy, Edinburgh, 1954. Commonwealth Fund Fell., Columbia Univ., NY, 1949–50. Chm., Bd of Management, Edinburgh Royal Infirmary, 1959–74. Mem. Anatomical Soc. of Gt Brit. and Ireland; Mem. Amer. Assoc. of Anatomists; Assoc. Mem. Amer. Neurological Assoc. FRSE 1955; FRCSE 1958. Hon. DSc Glasgow, 1983. *Publications:* (ed) Cunningham's Textbook and Manuals of Anatomy; various papers on the anatomy and development of the nervous system in Jl of Anatomy and Jl of Comparative Neurology. *Recreations:* angling and curling. *Address:* Camus na Feannag, Kishorn, Strathcarron, Ross-shire IV54 8XA. *T:* Kishorn (01520) 733273.

ROMANOW, Hon. Roy John, QC (Can.); MLA (NDP) Saskatoon–Riversdale; Premier of Saskatchewan, since 1991; *b* 1939; *s* of Mike and Tekla Romanow; *m* 1967, Eleanore Boykowich. *Educ:* Univ. of Saskatchewan (Arts and Law degrees). First elected to Saskatchewan Legislative Assembly, 1967; Dep. Premier, 1971–82; Attorney General, 1971–82; Minister of Intergovtl Affairs, 1979–82; Opposition House Leader for NDP Caucus, 1986; Leader, Saskatchewan NDP, 1987–. *Publication:* (jtly) Canada Notwithstanding, 1984. *Address:* Saskatchewan Legislative Building, Regina, Sask S45 OB3, Canada.

ROME, Alan Mackenzie, FRIBA, FSA; architect in private practice, since 1960; *b* 24 Oct. 1930; *s* of John and Evelyn Rome; *m* 1956, Mary Lilyan Barnard; one *s* one *d*. *Educ:* King's Sch., Bruton; Royal West of England Academy Sch. of Architecture (DipArch 1955). FRIBA 1971; FSA 1979. Pupil in office of Sir George Oatley, 1947–49; Nat. Service, RE, 1949–50; Asst to Stephen Dykes Bower at Westminster Abbey, 1955–60; Associate Architect with Michael Torrens and Alan Crozier Cole, 1960–64. Cathedral Architect to Deans and Chapters of Bristol and Truro; Consulting Architect to Provosts and Chapters of Leicester and St Edmundsbury; Architect for: Bath Abbey; Glastonbury Abbey; St Mary Redcliffe, Bristol; Lancing Coll. Chapel; and other churches in Devon, Somerset and Wilts. Member: Council for the Care of Churches, 1972– (Mem., Organs Adv. Cttee, 1991–); Churches Conservation Trust (formerly Redundant Churches Fund), 1980–; Cttee of Hon. Consulting Architects, Historic Churches Preservation Trust, 1990–; Bath and Wells DAC, 1978–. Occasional Lectr, Bristol Univ. *Publications:* papers and addresses on architectural subjects. *Recreations:* walking, sketching, music. *Address:* 19 High Street, Yatton, Bristol BS19 4JD; 11 Mayfair Avenue, Nailsea, Bristol BS19 2LR. *T:* Nailsea (01275) 853215.

ROMER, Mark Lemon Robert; a Metropolitan Stipendiary Magistrate since 1972; *b* 12 July 1927; *s* of late Rt Hon. Sir Charles Romer, OBE, and Hon. Lady Romer; *m* 1st, 1953, Philippa Maynard Tomson (marr. diss. 1991); one *s* two *d*; 2nd, 1991, Mary Eileen Hunt (*née* Hernaman). *Educ:* Bryanston; Trinity Hall, Cambridge (MA, LLM). Called to Bar, Lincoln's Inn, 1952; practised privately until 1958 when joined Govt Legal Service. *Recreations:* bird-watching, reading, music. *Address:* Gillings Hill, Arkesden Road, Clavering, Essex CB11 4QU. *T:* Saffron Walden (01799) 550792.

ROMNEY, 7th Earl of, *cr* 1801; **Michael Henry Marsham;** Bt 1663; Baron of Romney, 1716; Viscount Marsham, 1801; *b* 22 Nov. 1910; *s* of Lt-Col the Hon. Reginald Hastings Marsham, OBE (*d* 1922) (2nd *s* of 4th Earl) and Dora Hermione (*d* 1923), *d* of late Charles North; *S* cousin, 1975; *m* 1939, Frances Aileen, *o d* of late Lt-Col James Russell Landale, IA. *Educ:* Sherborne. Served War of 1939–45, Major RA. Pres., Marine Soc., 1990–. *Heir:* *cousin* Julian Charles Marsham [*b* 28 March 1948; *m* 1975, Catriona Ann, *d* of Lt-Col Robert Christie Stewart, *qv*; two *s* one *d*]. *Address:* Wensum Farm, West Rudham, King's Lynn, Norfolk PE31 8SZ. *T:* East Rudham (01485) 528249.

ROMSEY, Lord; Norton Louis Philip Knatchbull; *b* 8 Oct. 1947; *s* and *heir* of Baron Brabourne, *qv* and of Countess Mountbatten of Burma, *qv*; *m* 1979, Penelope Meredith Eastwood; one *s* one *d* (and one *d* decd). *Educ:* Dragon School, Oxford; Gordonstoun; University of Kent (BA Politics). *Heir:* *s* Hon. Nicholas Louis Charles Norton Knatchbull, *b* 15 May 1981. *Address:* Broadlands, Romsey, Hants SO51 9ZD. *T:* Romsey (01794) 517888.

RONALD, Edith, (Mrs Edmund Ronald); *see* Templeton, Mrs Edith.

RONALDSHAY, Earl of; Robin Lawrence Dundas; Managing Director, Musks Ltd, since 1993; Director: Redcar Race Co., since 1989; Catterick Racecourse Co., since 1988; *b* 5 March 1965; *s* and *heir* of Marquess of Zetland, *qv*. *Educ:* Harrow; Royal Agricl Coll., Cirencester. *Recreations:* tennis, golf. *Club:* Slainte Mhah.

RONAY, Egon; Founder of the Egon Ronay hotel and restaurant guides (taken over by the Automobile Association, 1985, and purchased by Leading Guides Ltd, 1992); *m* 1967, Barbara Greenslade; one *s*, and two *d* of previous marr. *Educ:* School of Piarist Order, Budapest; Univ. of Budapest (LLD); Academy of Commerce, Budapest. Dip. Restaurateurs' Guild, Budapest; FHCIMA. After univ. degree, trained in kitchens of family catering concern; continued training abroad, finishing at Dorchester Hotel, London; progressed to management within family concern of 5 restaurants, of which eventually he took charge; emigrated from Hungary, 1946; Gen. Manager, Princes Restaurant, Piccadilly, then Society Restaurant, Jermyn Street, followed by 96 Restaurant, Piccadilly; opened own restaurant, The Marquee, SW1, 1952–55; started eating-out and general food, wine and tourism weekly column in Daily Telegraph and later Sunday Telegraph, 1954–60, also eating-out guide, 1957; weekly dining out column in Evening News, 1968–74; Ed.-in-Chief, Egon Ronay Recommends (BAA Airports magazine), 1992–94. Founder and Pres., British Acad. of Gastronomes, 1983–; Mem. l'Académie des Gastronomes, France, 1979; Founding Vice Pres., Internat. Acad. of Gastronomy, 1985. Médaille de la Ville de Paris, 1983; Chevalier de l'Ordre du Mérite Agricole, 1987. *Publications:* Egon Ronay's Guide to Hotels and Restaurants, annually, 1956–85; Egon Ronay's Just A Bite, annually, 1979–85; Egon Ronay's Pub Guide, annually, 1980–85; Egon Ronay's Guide to 500 Good Restaurants in Europe's main cities, annually, 1983–85; The Unforgettable Dishes of My Life, 1989; various other tourist guides to Britain, to ski resorts in Europe, to Scandinavian hotels and restaurants and to eating places in Greece.

RONE, Ven. James; Archdeacon of Wisbech, since 1995; *b* 28 Aug. 1935; *s* of James and Bessie Rone; *m* 1st, 1956, Ivy Mylchreest (*née* Whitby) (*d* 1970); one *s* one *d*; 2nd, 1976, Mary Elizabeth (*née* Angove). *Educ:* Skerry's Coll., Liverpool; St Stephen's House, Oxford. FSCA 1971. RAMC, 1953–56. Accountant, ICI Ltd, 1957–64; Hawker Siddeley Dynamics, 1964–65; Subsidiary co. dir and Sec., Reed International, 1965–71; Gp Chief Accountant, Leigh & Sillavan, 1971–73; Finance Officer, Oxford Diocesan Bd of Finance, 1973–79. Ordained deacon 1980, priest 1981; Curate, Stony Stratford, dio. of Oxford, 1980–82; Vicar, SS Peter and Mary Magdalene, Fordham and Rector of Kennett, 1982–89; Canon Residentiary, Ely Cathedral, 1989–95. MInstD. *Recreations:* walking, Rugby (now non-playing), classical music, theatre, good food and wine. *Address:* Powcher's Hall, The College, Ely, Cambs CB7 4DL. *T:* Ely (01353) 662909.

RONSON, Gerald Maurice; Chief Executive: Heron Corporation PLC; Heron International PLC; Chairman and Chief Executive, Snax 24 Corporation Ltd; *b* 27 May 1939; *s* of Henry and Sarah Ronson; *m* 1967, Gail; four *d*. Chief Executive: Heron Corp. PLC, 1976– (Chm., 1978–93); Heron International PLC, 1983– (Chm., 1983–93).

Ambassador of Druse community on Mount Carmel. *Recreations:* yachting, shooting. *Address:* Heron House, 19 Marylebone Road, NW1 5JL. *T:* 0171–486 4477. *Club:* Royal Southern Yacht (Southampton).

ROOK, Peter Francis Grosvenor; QC 1991; a Recorder, since 1995; *b* 19 Sept. 1949; *s* of Dr Arthur James Rook and Frances Jane Elizabeth Rook (*née* Knott); *m* 1978, Susanna Marian Tewson; one *s* two *d*. *Educ:* Charterhouse; Trinity College, Cambridge (Open Exhibnr; MA Hist.); Bristol Univ. (Dip. Soc. Studies). Called to the Bar, Gray's Inn, 1973; 2nd Standing Counsel to Inland Revenue at Central Criminal Court and Inner London Courts, 1981, 1st Standing Counsel, 1989; Asst Recorder, 1990–95. *Publication:* Rook and Ward on Sexual Offences, 1990. *Recreations:* tennis, squash, cricket, theatre, growing tropical plants. *Address:* 5 King's Bench Walk, Temple, EC4Y 7DN. *T:* 0171–353 4713. *Club:* Coolhurst Lawn Tennis and Squash.

ROOKE, Daphne Marie; author; *b* 6 March 1914; *d* of Robert Pizzey and Marie Knevitt; *m* 1937, Irvin Rooke; one *d*. *Educ:* Durban, S Africa. *Publications:* A Grove of Fever Trees, 1950, repr. 1989; Mittee, 1951, repr. 1987; Ratoons, 1953, repr. 1990; The South African Twins, 1953; The Australian Twins, 1954; Wizards' Country; The New Zealand Twins, 1957; Beti, 1959; A Lover for Estelle, 1961; The Greyling, 1962; Diamond Jo, 1965; Boy on the Mountain, 1969; Double Ex!, 1970; Margaretha de la Porte, 1974; A Horse of his Own, 1976. *Recreation:* walking. *Address:* 54 Regatta Court, Oyster Row, Cambridge CB5 8NS. *T:* Cambridge (01223) 314293.

ROOKE, Sir Denis (Eric), Kt 1977; CBE 1970; BSc (Eng.); FRS 1978; FEng 1977; Chairman, British Gas plc (formerly British Gas Corporation and earlier, The Gas Council), 1976–89 (Deputy Chairman, 1972–76); Chancellor, Loughborough University of Technology, since 1989; *b* 2 April 1924; *yr s* of F. G. Rooke; *m* 1949, Elizabeth Brenda, *d* of D. D. Evans, Ystradgynlais, Brecon; one *d*. *Educ:* Westminster City Sch.; Addey and Stanhope Sch.; University Coll., London (Fellow, 1972). Served with REME, UK and India, 1944–49 (Major). Joined staff of S Eastern Gas Bd as Asst Mechanical Engr in coal-tar by-products works, 1949; Dep. Man. of works, 1954; seconded to N Thames Gas Bd, 1957, for work in UK and USA on liquefied natural gas; mem. technical team which sailed in Methane Pioneer on first voyage bringing liquefied natural gas to UK, 1959; S Eastern Gas Bd's Development Engr, 1959; Development Engr, Gas Council, 1960; Mem. for Production and Supplies, 1966–71. Chm., CNAA, 1978–83; Member: Adv. Council for R&D, 1972–77; Adv. Council for Energy Conservation, 1974–77; Offshore Energy Technology Bd, 1975–78; BNOC, 1976–82; NEDC, 1976–80; Energy Commn, 1977–79. President: IGasE, 1975; Assoc. for Science Educn, 1981; Fellowship of Engineering, 1986–91; BAAS, 1990; Inst. of Quality Assce, 1990–92. Foreign Associate, NAE, 1987. Trustee, Science Museum, 1983–; Comr, Royal Commn for Exhibn of 1851, 1984–. Hon. Sen. Fellow, RCA, 1991. Hon. DSc: Salford, 1978; Leeds, 1980; City, 1985; Durham, 1986; Cranfield Inst. of Technol., 1987; London, 1991; Loughborough Univ. of Technol., 1994; Hon. DTech CNAA, 1986; Hon. LLD Bath, 1987; Hon. DEng: Bradford, 1989; Liverpool, 1994; DUniv Surrey, 1990. KStJ 1989. Rumford Medal, Royal Soc., 1986; Prince Philip Medal, Royal Acad. of Engrg, 1992. *Publications:* papers to Instn of Gas Engrs, World Power Conf., World Petroleum Conf., etc. *Recreations:* photography, listening to music. *Address:* 23 Hardy Road, Blackheath, SE3 7NS. *Clubs:* Athenæum, English-Speaking Union.

ROOKE, Giles Hugh, TD 1963; QC 1979; **His Honour Judge Rooke;** a Circuit Judge, since 1981; Resident Judge, Canterbury, since 1995; *b* 28 Oct. 1930; *s* of late Charles Eustace Rooke, CMG, and Irene Phyllis Rooke; *m* 1968, Anne Bernadette Seymour, *d* of His Honour John Perrett; four *s* one *d*. *Educ:* Stowe; Exeter Coll., Oxford (MA). Kent Yeomanry, 1951–61, Kent and County of London Yeomanry, 1961–65 (TA), Major. Called to Bar, Lincoln's Inn, 1957; practised SE Circuit, 1957–81; a Recorder of the Crown Court, 1975–81. Hon. Recorder of Margate, 1980–. *Address:* The Law Courts, Chaucer Road, Canterbury CT1 1ZA. *T:* Canterbury (01227) 819200; St Stephen's Cottage, Bridge, Canterbury CT4 5AH. *T:* Canterbury (01227) 830298.

ROOKE, James Smith, CMG 1961; OBE 1949; Grand Decoration of Honour in Gold, of the Austrian Republic, 1981; Chief Executive, British Overseas Trade Board, 1972–75; HM Diplomatic Service, retired; now lecturer, Diplomatic Academy, Vienna; *b* 6 July 1916; *s* of Joseph Nelson Rooke and Adeline Mounser (*née* Woodgate); *m* 1938, Maria Theresa Rebrec, Vienna; one *s* two *d*. *Educ:* Workington Grammar Sch.; University College, London; Vienna Univ. Apptd to Dept of Overseas Trade, 1938. Military service, 1940–45, KRRC and AEC. Second Secretary (Commercial), British Embassy, Bogotá, 1946; UK Delegation to ITO Conf., Havana, 1947; Dep. UK Commercial Rep., Frankfurt, 1948; First Secretary (Commercial), British Embassy, Rome, 1951; Consul (Commercial), Milan, 1954; Deputy Consul-General (Commercial), New York, 1955–59; HM Counsellor (Commercial) British Embassy, Berne, 1959–63, Rome, 1963–66; Minister (Commercial), British High Commn, Canberra, 1966–68; Minister (Economic), British Embassy, Paris, 1968–72. *Recreations:* climbing, tennis, ski-ing. *Address:* Flotowgasse 26/3/1, 1190 Vienna, Austria. *Club:* East India, Devonshire, Sports and Public Schools.

ROOKE, Brig. Vera Margaret, CB 1984; CBE 1980; RRC 1973; Matron-in-Chief (Army) and Director of Army Nursing Services, 1981–84; *b* 21 Dec. 1924; *d* of late William James Rooke and Lily Amelia Rooke (*née* Cole). *Educ:* Girls' County Sch., Hove, Sussex. Addenbrooke's Hosp., Cambridge (SRN); Royal Alexandra Children's Hosp., Brighton (RSCN); St Helier Hosp., Carshalton (Midwifery). Joined Queen Alexandra's Royal Army Nursing Corps, 1951; appointments include: service in military hospitals, UK, Egypt, Malta, Singapore; Staff Officer in Work Study; Liaison Officer, QARANC, MoD, 1973–74; Assistant Director of Army Nursing Services and Matron: Military Hosp., Hong Kong, 1975; Royal Herbert Hosp. and Queen Elizabeth Military Hosp., Woolwich, 1976–78; Dep. Dir, Army Nursing Services, HQ UKLF, 1979–80. QHNS, 1981–84. Lt-Col 1972, Col 1975, Brig. 1981. *Recreations:* gardening, walking, cookery, opera. *Address:* c/o Lloyds Bank, 208 Portland Road, Hove, Sussex.

ROOKER, Jeffrey William, CEng; MP (Lab) Birmingham, Perry Barr, since Feb. 1974; *b* 5 June 1941; *m* 1972, Angela. *Educ:* Handsworth Tech. Sch.; Handsworth Tech. Coll.; Warwick Univ. (MA); Aston Univ. (BScEng). CEng, FIEE; MIMgt. Apprentice toolmaker, King's Heath Engrg Co. Ltd, Birmingham, 1957–63; student apprentice, BLMC, 1963–64; Asst to Works Manager, Geo. Salter & Co., West Bromwich, 1964–65, Assembly Manager, 1965–67; Prodn Manager, Rola Celestion Ltd, Thames Ditton and Ipswich, 1967–70; Industrial Relations and Safety Officer, Metro-Cammell, Birmingham, 1971; Lectr, Lanchester Polytechnic, Coventry, 1972–74. Opposition spokesman on social services, 1979–80, on social security, 1980–83, on treasury and economic affairs, 1983–84, on housing, 1984–87, on local government, 1987–88, on health and social services, 1990–92, on higher educn, 1992–93; Dep. Leader of the Opposition, 1994–. Mem., Public Accounts Cttee, 1989–91. Chair, Labour Campaign for Electoral Reform, 1989–. Mem. Council, Instn of Prodn Engrs, 1975–81. *Recreation:* full-time MP. *Address:* House of Commons, SW1A 0AA. *T:* (home) 0121–350 6186.

ROOLEY, Anthony; lutenist; Artistic Director: The Consort of Musicke, since 1969; Musica Oscura, since 1993; *b* 10 June 1944; *s* of Madge and Henry Rooley; *m* 1967, Carla Morris; three *d*; one *s* by Emma Kirkby, *qv*. *Educ:* Royal Acad. of Music. LRAM (Performers). Recitals in Europe, USA, Middle East, Japan, S America, New Zealand, Australia; radio and TV in UK, Europe and USA; numerous recordings, British and German. Hon. FRAM 1990. *Publications:* Penguin Book of Early Music. 1982; Performance—revealing the Orpheus within, 1990. *Recreations:* food, wine, gardening, philosophy. *Address:* 54A Leamington Road Villas, W11 1HT.

ROOME, Maj. Gen. Oliver McCrea, CBE 1973; Vice Lord-Lieutenant, Isle of Wight, 1987–95; *b* 9 March 1921; *s* of late Maj. Gen. Sir Horace Roome, KCIE, CB, CBE, MC, DL, late Royal Engineers; *m* 1947, Isobel Anstis, *d* of Rev. A. B. Jordan; two *s* one *d*. *Educ:* Wellington Coll. Commissioned in Royal Engineers, 1940. Served War: UK, Western Desert, Sicily, Italy, 1939–45. Various appts, UK, Far and Middle East, Berlin, 1946–68; IDC, 1969; Director of Army Recruiting, 1970–73; Chief, Jt Services Liaison Organisation, Bonn, 1973–76; retired. Col Comdt, RE, 1979–84. County Comr, Scouts, Isle of Wight, 1977–85. DL Isle of Wight, 1981; High Sheriff of the Isle of Wight, 1983–84. *Recreations:* sailing, youth activities. *Address:* The White Cottage, Hill Lane, Freshwater, Isle of Wight PO40 9TQ. *Clubs:* Army and Navy, Royal Ocean Racing, Royal Cruising; Royal Yacht Squadron.

ROONEY, Maureen Gowran; National Women's Officer, Amalgamated Engineering & Electrical Union, since 1990; Co-Chair, Women's National Commission, 1993–95; *b* Blantyre, Lanarks, 27 April 1947; *d* of James Cunningham and Mary Conroy Cunningham; *m* 1966, Philip Rooney; one *s* three *d*. *Educ:* Elmwood Convent, Bothwell. Hairdresser, 1963–66; machine operator, Hoover plc, 1974–90. Mem., TUC Gen. Council, 1990–; Labour Party NEC's Women's Cttee, 1989–. Vice-Pres., Nat. Childminders' Assoc., 1994–; Bd of Mgt, Adult Literacy and Basic Skills Unit, 1992–. *Recreations:* music, reading, cinema, theatre, knitting, walking. *Address:* 84 Goodhart Way, West Wickham, Bromley, Kent BR4 0EY. *Club:* Blantyre Miners Welfare.

ROONEY, Michael John, RA 1991 (ARA 1990); Lecturer in Painting, Royal Academy Schools, since 1991; *b* 5 March 1944; *s* of Elisabeth and John Rooney; *m* 1st, 1967, Patricia Anne Lavender (marr. diss. 1984); one *s* one *d*; 2nd, 1988, Alexandra Grascher, Vienna; one *s*. *Educ:* primary and secondary schools; Sutton Sch. of Art; Wimbledon Sch. of Art (NDD); Royal Coll. of Art (MA RCA, ARCA); British Sch. at Rome (Austin Abbey Award). Part-time lectr, various art colls; artist-in-residence, Towner Art Gall., Eastbourne, 1983; one man exhibns in Holland, London, Edinburgh and other UK locations; work in public collections: Sussex; Birmingham; Punta del Este, Uruguay; London. Prizes include: Calouste Gulbenkian Printmakers' Award, 1984; John Player Portrait Award, Nat. Portrait Gallery, 1985; RA Summer Exhibn Awards, 1986, 1988, 1989. *Recreation:* cooking. *Address:* The Old Sorting House, 19 Alder Road, Mortlake, SW14 8ER. *T:* 0181–876 0459. *Clubs:* Arts, Chelsea Arts.

ROONEY, Terence Henry; MP (Lab) Bradford North, since Nov. 1990; *b* 11 Nov. 1950; *s* of Eric and Frances Rooney; *m* 1969, Susanne Chapman; one *s* two *d*. *Educ:* Buttershaw Comprehensive Sch.; Bradford Coll. Formerly: commercial insurance broker; Welfare Rights Advice Worker, Bierley Community Centre. Councillor, Bradford City, 1983–90 (Dep. Leader, 1990). *Address:* c/o House of Commons, SW1A 0AA.

ROOSE-EVANS, James Humphrey; freelance theatre director and author; non-stipendiary Anglican priest; *b* 11 Nov. 1927; *s* of Jack Roose-Evans and Catharina Primrose Morgan. *Educ:* Univ. of Oxford (MA). Started career in repertory, as an actor; Artistic Dir, Maddermarket Theatre, Norwich, 1954–55 (dir. English première of The Language of Flowers, 1955); Faculty of Julliard Sch. of Music, NY, 1955–56; on staff of RADA, 1956–; founded Hampstead Theatre, 1959; Resident Dir, Belgrade Theatre, Coventry, 1961. Regularly tours USA, lecturing and leading workshops. Productions directed include: *Hampstead Theatre:* The Square, 1963; The Little Clay Cart (also adapted), 1964; Adventures in the Skin Trade, world première, The Two Character Play, world première, Letters from an Eastern Front (also adapted), 1966; An Evening with Malcolm Muggeridge (also devised), 1966; *West End:* Cider with Rosie (also adapted), Private Lives, 1963; An Ideal Husband, 1966; The Happy Apple, 1967; 84 Charing Cross Road (also adapted), 1981 (Best Dir, Drama award), NY 1982 (awards for Best Play and Best Dir); Seven Year Itch, 1986; The Best of Friends, 1988 (also prod Comédie des Champs-Elysées, Paris, 1989); Temptation, 1990; Irving (also jt author with Barry Turner), 1995; *other productions:* Venus Observed, Chichester, 1992. Author, Re: Joyce!, West End, 1991. Consultant, Theatre Mus. Founder and Chm., Bleddfa Trust-Centre for Caring and the Arts, Powys, 1974–. Columnist (Something Extra), Woman, 1986–88. Ordained priest, 1981. *Publications:* adaptation of The Little Clay Cart, by King Sudraka, 1965; Directing a Play, 1968; Experimental Theatre, 1970, 4th rev. edn, 1988; London Theatre, 1977; play version of 84 Charing Cross Road, by Helen Hanff, 1983; Inner Journey, Outer Journey, 1987 (US as The Inner Stage, 1990); (introd. and ed) Darling Ma: the letters of Joyce Grenfell, 1988; The Tale of Beatrix Potter, 1988; (with Maureen Lipman) Re:Joyce!, 1988; (introd and ed) The Time of My Life: wartime journals of Joyce Grenfell, 1989; (trans.) Obey, On the Edge of Midnight, 1989; Passages of the Soul: ritual today, 1994; Cider with Rosie (stage adaptation), 1994; *for children:* The Adventures of Odd and Elsewhere, 1971; The Secret of the Seven Bright Shiners, 1972; Odd and the Great Bear, 1973; Elsewhere and the Gathering of the Clowns, 1974; The Return of the Great Bear, 1975; The Secret of Tippity-Witchit, 1975; The Lost Treasure of Wales, 1977. *Recreations:* the Bleddfa Trust-Centre for Caring and the Arts in the Welsh Marches—otherwise work! *Address:* c/o David Higham Associates, 5–8 Lower John Street, Golden Square, W1R 3PE. *Clubs:* Athenæum, Garrick, Dramatists.

ROOT, Rev. Canon Howard Eugene; Preceptor of Malling Abbey, since 1993; *b* 13 April 1926; *s* of Howard Root and Flora Hoskins; *m* 1952, Celia (MA Lambeth), *e d* of Col R. T. Holland, CBE, DSO, MC; two *s* two *d*. *Educ:* Univ. of Southern California (BA 1945; Teaching Fellow, 1945–47); St Catherine's Coll. and Magdalen Coll., Oxford; Ripon Hall, Oxford. BA Oxon 1951; MA Oxon 1970; MA Cantab 1953. Instructor, American Univ., Cairo, 1947–49; Sen. Demy, Magdalen Coll., Oxford, and Liddon Student, 1951–53. Deacon, 1953; Priest, 1954. Curate of Trumpington, 1953; Asst Lectr in Divinity, Cambridge, 1953–57; Lectr, 1957–66; Fellow, Emmanuel Coll., Cambridge, 1954–66, Chaplain, 1954–56, Dean, 1956–66; Prof. and Hd of Dept of Theology, Univ. of Southampton, 1966–81; Dir, Anglican Centre, Rome, and Counsellor on Vatican affairs to Archbishop of Canterbury, 1981–91; St Augustine Canon, Canterbury Cathedral, 1980–91, Canon Emeritus, 1991–. Wilde Lectr, Oxford Univ., 1957–60; Senior Denyer and Johnson Scholar, Oxford, 1963–64; Bampton Lectr, Univ. of Oxford, 1972; Pope Adrian VI Chair, Univ. of Louvain, 1979; Vis. Prof., Pontificial Gregorian Univ., Rome, 1984–91. Exam. Chaplain to Bishops of Ripon, 1959–76, Southwark, 1964–81, Bristol, 1965–81, Winchester, 1971–81, and Wakefield, 1977–81; Commissary to Bishop in Jerusalem, 1976–. Official Anglican Observer at Second Vatican Council, 1963–65; Consultant, Lambeth Conf., 1968 and 1988. Chm., Archbishops' Commn on Marriage, 1968–71; Member: Academic Council, Ecumenical Inst., Jerusalem, 1966–81; Anglican-RC Preparatory Commn, 1967–68; Archbishops' Commn on Christian Doctrine, 1967–74; Anglican-Roman Catholic Internat. Commn, 1969–81. Hon. Chaplain, Winchester Cathedral, 1966–67; Canon Theologian of Winchester, 1967–80. Mem.,

BBC Central Religious Adv. Cttee, 1971–75. Jt Editor, Jl of Theol Studies, 1969–74. Corresp. Fellow, Pontifical Internat. Marian Acad., Rome, 1993–. *Recreations:* music, silence. *Club:* Brooks's.

ROOTES, family name of **Baron Rootes.**

ROOTES, 3rd Baron *cr* 1959; **Nicholas Geoffrey Rootes;** author and freelance copy-writer; *b* 12 July 1951; *s* of 2nd Baron and of Marion, *d* of Lt-Col H. R. Hayter, DSO and *widow* of Wing Comdr J. H. Slater, AFC; *S* father, 1992; *m* 1976, Dorothy Anne Burn-Forti (*née* Wood); one step *s* one step *d*. *Educ:* Harrow Sch. *Publication:* The Drinker's Companion, 1987. *Recreations:* ski-ing, fly-fishing. *Heir: cousin* William Brian Rootes [*b* 8 Nov. 1944; *m* 1969, Alicia, *y d* of Frederick Graham Roberts, OBE; two *d*]. *Address:* 2 Cedars Road, Barnes SW13 0HP. *T:* 0181–876 6965. *Club:* Ski of Great Britain.

ROOTS, Guy Robert Godfrey; QC 1989; *b* 26 Aug. 1946; *s* of William Lloyd Roots and Elizabeth Colquhoun Gow (*née* Gray); *m* 1975, Caroline (*née* Clarkson); three *s*. *Educ:* Winchester College; Brasenose College, Oxford (MA). Called to the Bar, Middle Temple, 1969; Harmsworth Scholar, 1970. Liveryman, Drapers' Co., 1972. *Publication:* (ed) Ryde on Rating, 1986. *Recreations:* sailing, fishing, ski-ing, photography, woodworking. *Address:* 2 Mitre Court Buildings, Temple, EC4Y 7BX. *T:* 0171–583 1380. *Club:* Itchenor Sailing.

ROOTS, Paul John; Director of Industrial Relations, Ford Motor Co. Ltd, 1981–86, retired; *b* 16 Oct. 1929; *s* of John Earl and Helen Roots; *m* 1951, Anna Theresa Pateman; two *s* two *d*. *Educ:* Dormers Wells Sch.; London Sch. of Economics. Cert. in Personnel Admin. CIPM; CIMgt. RN, 1947–54: service in Korean War. Personnel Officer, Brush Gp, 1955; Labour Officer, UKAEA, 1956, Labour Manager, 1959; Ford Motor Co. Ltd: Personnel Manager, Halewood, 1962; Forward Planning Manager, 1966; Labour Relations Manager, 1969; Dir of Employee Relations, 1974. Vice-Pres., IPM, 1981–83. Chairman: CBI Health and Safety Policy Cttee, 1984–; CBI Health and Safety Consultative Cttee, 1984–; Member: Council of Management, CBI Educn Foundn, 1981–; CBI Working Party on the Employment of Disabled People, 1981–; CBI Employment Policy Cttee, 1983–; CBI Council, 1984–; Engrg Industry Training Bd, 1985–. *Publications:* (jtly) Communication in Practice, 1981; (jtly) Corporate Personnel Management, 1986; Financial Incentives for Employees, 1988; articles in personnel management jls. *Recreations:* riding, theatre, music.

ROOTS, William; Chief Executive and Director of Finance, City of Westminster, since 1994; *b* 12 April 1946; *s* of William Roots and Violet (*née* Frost); *m* 1st, 1963, Norma Jane Smith; one *s* one *d*; 2nd, 1980, Susan Grace Sharratt; two *s*. *Educ:* Wandsworth Sch. Sun Life Assce Soc., 1962–64; joined GLC as trainee, 1964; Hd of Budget, 1980; London Borough of Southwark: Head of: Exchequer, 1980–81; Finance, 1982–82; Director of Finance: London Borough of Bexley, 1982–90; City of Westminster, 1990–94. Mem., CIPFA 1970. *Recreations:* sport (esp. Rugby), eating and drinking, films. *Address:* Westminster City Hall, Victoria Street, SW1E 6QP. *T:* 0171–798 2030.

ROPER; *see* Trevor-Roper.

ROPER, Brian Anthony; Vice-Chancellor and Chief Executive, University of North London, since 1994; *b* 15 Dec. 1949; *s* of Harold Herbert Albert Roper and Elizabeth Roper (*née* Rooney); *m* 1971, Margaret Patricia Jones; one *s* one *d*. *Educ:* UWIST (BSc Hons Econs 1971); Univ. of Manchester (MA Econs 1973). FSS 1988. Tutor in Econs, UWIST, 1971–72; Lectr in Econs, Teeside Poly., 1973–75; Sen. Lectr, then Principal Lectr, Leicester Poly., 1975–80; Hd, Sch. of Econs, Dean, Faculty of Social Scis and Asst Dir, Resources, Newcastle upon Tyne Poly., 1980–90; Dep. Vice Chancellor Acad. Affairs and Dep. Chief Exec., Oxford Poly., subseq. Oxford Brookes Univ., 1991–94. FIMgt 1993. *Publications:* contrib. Econ. Theory and Policy, Higher Educn Policy and Mgt. *Recreations:* Rugby Union, Italian opera, Impressionist painting, hill-walking. *Address:* University of North London, 166–220 Holloway Road, N7 8BD. *T:* 0171–753 5181. *Club:* Tynedale Rugby Football.

ROPER, Rev. Geoffrey Edward Hodgess; General Secretary, Free Church Federal Council, from April 1996; *b* 24 April 1940; *y s* of late Rev. Frederick Mabor Hodgess Roper and of Ellen Frances (*née* Brockway); *m* 1967, Janice Wakeham; one *s* one *d*. *Educ:* Christ's Hosp.; Magdalen Coll., Oxford (MA (PPE and Theol.)); Mansfield Coll., Oxford. Ordained 1965; Minister: Trinity Congregational Church, Ifield, Crawley, 1965–71; Streatham Congregational Church, 1971–78 (URC from 1972); Seaford URC, 1978–85; Christ Church, Chelmsford, 1985–95. Sec., URC Deployment Cttee, 1978–84; URC Ecumenical Officer: Sussex East, 1979–85; Essex, 1986–95. Mem., Eastbourne CHC, 1980–85 (Vice-Chm., 1983–84). British Isles Mem., Exec. Cttee, Leuenberg Doctrinal Conversations of Reformed and Lutheran Churches in Europe, 1987–94. Dir, Highway Trust, 1977–94. Chm of Cttee, Friends of Dr Williams's Library, 1991–. *Recreation:* listening. *Address:* 27 Tavistock Square, WC1H 9HH. *T:* 0171–387 8413.

See also J. F. H. Roper.

ROPER, John Charles Abercromby, CMG 1969; MC; HM Diplomatic Service, retired; *b* 8 June 1915; *s* of late Charles Roper, MD, and of Mrs Roper; *m* 1st, 1945, Valerie Armstrong-MacDonnell (marr. diss.); two *d*; 2nd, 1960, Kathryn (*d* 1984), *d* of late Edgar Bibas, New York; 3rd, 1986, Phoebe, *d* of late R. B. Foster, London and New York. *Educ:* Harrow; Universities of Cambridge and Princeton (Commonwealth Fellow). Served 1939–46, Scots Guards and Special Forces, Major (MC). HM Diplomatic Service, 1946; Athens, 1947–51; Foreign Office, 1951–54; Washington, 1954–59. Seconded to Min. of Defence and apptd Dep. Commandant (Civil) of NATO Defence College, Paris, 1960–62; Asst Sec., Cabinet Office, 1962–64; Counsellor, UK Delegn to OECD, 1964–70; Ambassador to Luxembourg, 1970–75. *Address:* Tenuta di Monteverdi, 58048 Paganico, Provincia di Grosseto, Italy. *Club:* Special Forces.

ROPER, John (Francis Hodgess); Head of Western European Union Institute for Security Studies, Paris, 1990–95; *b* 10 Sept. 1935; *e s* of late Rev. Frederick Mabor Hodgess Roper and Ellen Frances (*née* Brockway); *m* 1959, (Valerie) Hope, *er d* of late Rt Hon. L. John Edwards, PC, OBE, MP, and late Mrs D. M. Edwards; one *d*. *Educ:* William Hulme's Grammar Sch., Manchester; Reading Sch.; Magdalen Coll., Oxford; Univ. of Chicago. Nat. Service, commnd RNVR, 1954–56; studied PPE, Oxford, 1956–59 (Pres. UN Student Assoc., 1957; organised Univ. referendum on Nuclear Disarmament); Harkness Fellow, Commonwealth Fund, 1959–61; Research Fellow in Economic Statistics, Univ. of Manchester, 1961; Asst Lectr in Econs, 1962–64, Lectr 1964–70, Faculty Tutor 1968–70; RIIA, 1983–90: Editor of International Affairs, 1983–88; Head of Internat. Security Programme, 1985–88, and 1989–90; Dir of Studies, 1988–89. Contested: (Lab) High Peak (Derbys), 1964; (SDP) Worsley, 1983. MP (Lab and Co-op 1970–81, SDP 1981–83) Farnworth, 1970–83; PPS to Minister of State, DoI, 1978–79; opposition front bench spokesman on defence, 1979–81; Social Democrat Chief Whip, 1981–83. Vice-Chairman: Anglo-German Parly Gp, 1974–83; Anglo-Benelux Parly Gp, 1979–83; Chm., British-Atlantic Gp of Young Politicians, 1974–75. Council of Europe: Consultant, 1965–66; Mem., Consultative Assembly, 1973–80; Chm., Cttee on Culture and Educn, 1979–80; Mem., WEU Assembly, 1973–80; Chm., Cttee on Defence Questions and Armaments, WEU, 1977–80. Hon. Treasurer, Fabian Soc., 1976–81; Chairman: Labour Cttee for Europe, 1976–80; GB/East Europe Centre, 1987–90; Council on Christian Approaches to Defence and Disarmament, 1983–89. Research Adviser (part-time), DEA in NW, 1967–69. Director: Co-op. Wholesale Soc., 1969–74; Co-op Insurance Soc., 1973–74. Pres., Gen. Council, UNA, 1972–78; Mem. Council, Inst. for Fiscal Studies, 1975–90; Mem. Gen. Adv. Council, IBA, 1974–79. Vice-Pres., Manchester Statistical Soc., 1971–. Trustee, Hist. of Parlt Trust, 1974–84. *Publications:* Towards Regional Co-operatives, 1967; The Teaching of Economics at University Level, 1970; The Future of British Defence Policy, 1985; (ed with Karl Kaiser) British–German Defence Co-operation, 1988; (ed with Yves Boyer) Franco-British Defence Co-operation, 1988; (ed with Nicole Gnesotto) Western Europe and the Gulf, 1992; (ed with Nanette Gantz) Towards a New Partnership, 1993. *Recreations:* reading, travel. *Address:* 21 Gladstone Court, 97 Regency Street, SW1P 4AL. *T:* 0171–976 6220. *Club:* United Oxford & Cambridge University.

ROPER, Michael, CB 1992; FRHistS; Keeper of Public Records, 1988–92; *b* 19 Aug. 1932; *s* of Jack Roper and Mona Roper (*née* Nettleton); *m* 1957, Joan Barbara Earnshaw; one *s* one *d*. *Educ:* Heath Grammar Sch., Halifax; Univ. of Manchester (BA, MA; Langton Fellow). Registered Mem., Soc. of Archivists, 1987. Public Record Office: Asst Keeper, 1959–70; Principal Asst Keeper, 1970–82; Records Admin Officer, 1982–85; Dep. Keeper of Public Records, 1985–88. Lectr (part time) in Archive Studies, UCL, 1972–87, Hon. Res. Fellow, 1988–; Dist. Visitor, Univ. of BC, 1994. Sec., Adv. Council on Public Records, 1963–68; Vice-President: Soc. of Archivists, 1992– (Vice-Chm., 1983–84; Chm., 1985–86; Pres., 1989–92); British Records Soc., 1988–; RHistS, 1989–93 (Hon. Treas., 1974–80); Sec.-Gen., Internat. Council on Archives, 1988–92 (Sec. for Standardization, 1984–88; Hon. Mem., 1992); Chm., Voices from the Past, 1992–. Ext. Examr, Nat. Univ. of Ireland, 1982–86, Univ. of Liverpool, 1986–89, Univ. of London, 1988–93. Chm., Judy Segal Trust, 1990–; English Record Collections, 1994–. Hon. DLitt Bradford, 1991. *Publications:* Yorkshire Fines 1300–1314, 1965; Records of the Foreign Office 1782–1939, 1969; (with J. A. Keene) Planning, Equipping and Staffing a Document Reprographic Service, 1984; Guidelines for the Preservation of Microforms, 1986; Directory of National Standards Relating to Archives Administration and Records Management, 1986; Planning, Equipping and Staffing an Archival Preservation and Conservation Service, 1989; Geresye to Jersey: the record endures, 1991; contribs to learned jls. *Recreations:* listening to music, gardening, walking the dog. *Address:* 157B Fairfax Road, Teddington, Middx TW11 9BU. *T:* 0181–977 4642.

ROPER, Robert Burnell, CB 1978; Chief Land Registrar, 1975–83 (Deputy Chief Land Registrar, 1973–75); *b* 23 Nov. 1921; *s* of late Allen George and Winifred Roper; *m* 1948, Mary Brookes; two *s*. *Educ:* King's College Sch., Wimbledon; King's Coll., London. LLB (Hons) 1941. Called to Bar, Gray's Inn, 1948. Served War, RAF, 1942–46. Miners' Welfare Commn, 1946–48; Nat. Coal Bd, 1948–49; Treasury Solicitor's Dept, 1949–50; HM Land Registry, 1950–83. *Publications:* (Ruoff and Roper) The Law and Practice of Registered Conveyancing, 3rd edn 1972, to 6th edn 1991; Consulting Editor on Land Registration matters for Encyclopaedia of Forms and Precedents (4th edn). *Recreations:* gardening, watching sport. *Address:* 11 Dukes Road, Lindfield, Haywards Heath, West Sussex RH16 2JH.

ROPER, Prof. Warren Richard, FRS 1989; FRSNZ 1984; Professor of Chemistry, University of Auckland, New Zealand, since 1984; *b* 27 Nov. 1938; *m* 1961, Judith Delcie Catherine Miller; two *s* one *d*. *Educ:* Nelson Coll., Nelson, NZ; Univ. of Canterbury, Christchurch, NZ (MSc, PhD). FNZIC. Postdoctoral Res. Associate, Univ. of N Carolina, 1963–65; Lectr in Chemistry, Univ. of Auckland, 1966. Vis. Lectr, Univ. of Bristol, 1972; Pacific W Coast Inorganic Lectr, 1982; Brotherton Vis. Res. Prof., Univ. of Leeds, 1983; Visiting Professor: Univ. de Rennes, 1984, 1985; Stanford Univ., 1988. Mellor Lectr, NZ Inst. of Chemistry, 1985; Centenary Lectr and Medallist, RSC, 1988; Glenn T. Seaborg Lectr, Univ. of Calif., Berkeley, 1995. Fellow, Japan Soc. for Promotion of Science, 1992. RSC Award in Organometallic Chemistry, 1983; ICI Medal, NZ Inst. of Chemistry, 1984; Hector Medal, Royal Soc. of NZ, 1991; 12th Inorganic Award, Royal Australian Inst. of Chemistry, 1992. *Publications:* over 150 sci. papers in internat. jls. *Recreations:* music, espec. opera, walking. *Address:* 26 Beulah Road, Auckland 10, New Zealand. *T:* (9) 4786940.

ROPER-CURZON, family name of **Baron Teynham.**

ROPNER, David; *see* Ropner, W. G. D.

ROPNER, Sir John (Bruce Woollacott), 2nd Bt *cr* 1952; Director, Ropner PLC; *b* 16 April 1937; *s* of Sir Leonard Ropner, 1st Bt, MC, TD, and of Esmé, *y d* of late Bruce Robertson; *S* father, 1977; *m* 1st, 1961, Anne Melicent (marr. diss. 1970), *d* of late Sir Ralph Delmé-Radcliffe; two *d*; 2nd, 1970, Auriol (marr. diss. 1993), *d* of late Captain Graham Lawrie Mackeson-Sandbach, Caerllo, Llangernyw; one *s* two *d*. *Educ:* Eton; St Paul's School, USA. High Sheriff, N Yorks, 1991. *Recreation:* field sports. *Heir: s* Henry John William Ropner, *b* 24 Oct. 1981. *Address:* Thorp Perrow, Bedale, Yorks DL8 2PR. *Club:* Brooks's.

See also Viscount Knutsford.

ROPNER, John Raymond; Consultant, Ropner PLC, and other companies; *b* 8 May 1903; *s* of William Ropner; *m* 1928, Joan Redhead; two *s* one *d*. *Educ:* Harrow; Clare College, Cambridge (BAEcon 1925). Durham Heavy Bde, RA (TA), 1922–28; joined Sir R. Ropner & Co. Ltd, 1925; Ministry of War Transport, North Western Europe, 1944–45. High Sheriff of Durham, 1958. Member, Shipping Advisory Panel, 1962. Order of Oranje-Nassau, 1947. *Recreations:* gardening, fishing; formerly golf (Cambridge blue, 1925). *Address:* The Limes, Dalton, Richmond, N Yorkshire DL11 7XJ. *T:* Teesdale (01833) 21447.

ROPNER, Sir Robert Douglas, 4th Bt, *cr* 1904; *b* 1 Dec. 1921; *o s* of Sir (E. H. O.) Robert Ropner, 3rd Bt; *S* father, 1962; *m* 1943, Patricia Kathleen, *d* of W. E. Scofield, W. Malling, Kent; one *s* one *d*. *Educ:* Harrow. Formerly Captain, RA. *Heir: s* Robert Clinton Ropner, *b* 6 Feb. 1949.

ROPNER, (William Guy) David; Director, Ropner PLC, 1953–94 (Chairman, 1973–85); *b* 3 April 1924; *s* of late Sir William Guy Ropner and Lady (Margarita) Ropner; *m* 1st, 1955, Mildred Malise Hare Armitage (marr. diss. 1978); one *d* three *s*; 2nd, 1985, Hon. Mrs Charlotte M. Taddei; one *s*. *Educ:* Harrow. FICS 1953. Served War, 1942–47: 2nd Lieut RA, Essex Yeomanry; Captain 3rd Regt, RHA. Joined Sir R. Ropner and Co. Ltd, 1947; dir of various Ropner PLC gp cos, 1953–94. Member: Lloyd's, 1952–91; Gen. Cttee, Lloyd's Register of Shipping, 1961–94; Pres., Gen. Council of British Shipping, 1979–80; Chairman: Deep Sea Tramp Section, Chamber of Shipping, 1970–72; Lights Adv. Cttee, GCBS, 1978–87; Merchant Navy Welfare Bd, 1980–94; Cleveland & Durham Industrial Council, 1980–94; Dir, British Shipowners Assoc., 1954–89. Dir, Guidehouse Expansion Management, 1984–. *Recreations:* country and garden pursuits. *Address:* 1 Sunningdale Gardens, Stratford Road, W8 6PX. *Club:* St Moritz Tobogganing.

ROQUES, (David) John (Seymour); Senior Partner and Chief Executive, Touche Ross & Co., since 1990; Member, Executive Committee, Deloitte, Touche Tohmatsu

International, since 1990; *b* 14 Oct. 1938; *s* of late Frank Davy Seymour Roques and of Marjorie Mabel Hudson; *m* 1963, Elizabeth Anne Mallender; two *s* one *d*. *Educ:* St Albans Sch. Mem., Inst. of Chartered Accountants of Scotland, 1962. Touche Ross & Co.: Partner, 1967; Partner in charge, Midlands region, 1973; Partner in charge, Scottish region, 1978; Partner in charge, London office, 1984; Man. Partner, 1990. Dir (non-exec.), British Nuclear Fuels, 1990–. Mem., Financial Reporting Review Panel, 1991–94. FRSA. *Recreations:* Rugby football, racing, opera, gardening. *Address:* Stonecutter Court, 1 Stonecutter Street, EC4A 4TR. *T:* 0171–936 3000. *Clubs:* Edgbaston Golf (Edgbaston); Wasps Football (Sudbury).

RORKE, Prof. John, CBE 1979; PhD; FRSE; FIMechE; Professor of Mechanical Engineering, 1980–88, and Vice-Principal, 1984–88, Heriot-Watt University, now Professor Emeritus; *b* 2 Sept. 1923; *s* of John and Janet Rorke; *m* 1948, Jane Craig Buchanan; two *d*. *Educ:* Dumbarton Acad.; Univ. of Strathclyde (BSc, PhD). Lectr, Strathclyde Univ., 1946–51; Asst to Engrg Dir, Alexander Stephen & Sons Ltd, 1951–56; Technical Manager, subseq. Gen. Man., and Engrg Dir, Wm Denny & Bros Ltd, 1956–63; Tech. Dir, subseq. Sales Dir, Man. Dir, and Chm., Brown Bros & Co. Ltd (subsid. of Vickers Ltd), 1963–78; Man. Dir, Vickers Offshore Engrg Gp, 1978; Dir of Planning, Vickers Ltd, 1979–80. Chairman: Orkney Water Test Centre Ltd, 1987–94; Environment and Resource Technology Ltd, 1991–94. Pres., Instn of Engineers and Shipbuilders in Scotland, 1985–87. *Recreations:* golf, bridge. *Address:* 3 Barnton Park Grove, Edinburgh EH4 6HG. *T:* 0131–336 3044. *Club:* Bruntsfield Links Golfing Society (Edinburgh).

ROSCOE, (John) Gareth; Legal Adviser to the BBC, since 1989; Director, BBC Enterprises Ltd, since 1989; *b* 28 Jan. 1948; *s* of late John Roscoe and Ann (*née* Jones); *m* 1st, 1970, Helen Jane Taylor (marr. diss. 1979); one *d*; 2nd, 1980, Alexis Fayrer Brett-Holt; one *s* one *d*. *Educ:* Manchester Warehousemen and Clerks' Orphan Schools (now Cheadle Hulme Sch.); Stretford Tech. Coll.; London Sch. of Economics and Political Science (LLB). Called to the Bar, Gray's Inn, 1972; in practice, 1972–75; Legal Asst 1975–79, Sen. Legal Asst 1979, DoE; Law Officers' Dept, Attorney-General's Chambers, 1979–83; Asst Solicitor, 1983–87, Dep. Solicitor, 1987–89, DoE. Mem., Gen. Council of the Bar, 1987–90. Mem., Adv. Cttee, Centre for Communications and Information Law, UCL, 1991–. *Recreations:* music, horology. *Address:* BBC, Broadcasting House, Portland Place, W1A 1AA. *T:* 0171–765 4375, *Fax:* 0171–765 4381. *Club:* Athenæum.

ROSCOE, Sir Robert Bell, KBE 1981; FASA, ABIA, ABINZ; Director, Chase-NBA Group Ltd (Australia and New Zealand), 1969–80; Chairman: Melbourne Underground Rail Loop Authority, 1971–81; First Federation Discount Co. Ltd, 1975–84; *b* 7 August 1906; *s* of T. B. Roscoe; *m* 1931, Daphne, *d* of G. Maxwell; one *d*. *Educ:* Central Tech. Coll., Brisbane. Liquidator, Qld Nat. Bank Ltd, 1949; State Manager, Qld, 1951–54; Nat. Bank of Australasia: State Manager, Victoria, 1954–60; Chief Inspector, 1960–65; Sen. Chief Inspector, 1965–66; Asst Chief Manager, 1966–69. Director: Hoechst Australia Ltd, 1970–; All States Commercial Bills Ltd; Oceania Capital Corp. Ltd. *Address:* 833 Burwood Road, Hawthorn East, Victoria 3123, Australia. *Club:* Australian (Melbourne).

ROSE, Alan Douglas, AO 1994; President, Australian Law Reform Commission, since 1994; *b* 3 May 1944; *s* of Willfred Allen Rose and Hazel Agnes Rose (*née* Heinemann-Mirre); *m* 1966, Helen Elizabeth Haigh; two *d*. *Educ:* Univ. of Queensland (BA 1966; LLB Hons 1969); LSE, Univ. of London (LLM 1979). Barrister, Supreme Court of Queensland, 1973; Dep. Sec., Dept of Prime Minister and Cabinet, 1982–86; Sec. to Aust. Dept of Community Services, 1986–87; Associate Sec. and Sec. to Aust. Attorney-Gen. Dept, 1987–94. Affiliate, Aust. Securities Inst. *Publications:* articles in legal jls and works on public admin. *Recreations:* surfing, ski-ing, reading, travelling. *Address:* Australian Law Reform Commission, Piccadilly Tower, 133 Castlereagh Street, Sydney, NSW 2001, Australia. *T:* (6) 2577029; PO Box 3296, Manuka, ACT 2603, Australia. *T:* (2) 2846301.

ROSE, Anthea Lorrainne, (Mrs H. D. Rose); Chief Executive, Chartered Association of Certified Accountants, since 1993; *b* 2 Dec. 1946; *d* of Philip Brown and Muriel (*née* Seftor); *m* 1971, Hannan David Rose. *Educ:* St Hugh's Coll., Oxford (MA Mod. Hist.). Administrator, Open Univ., 1968–69; Personnel Officer, Beecham Pharmaceuticals, 1969–71; Administrator, Univ. of Kent, 1971–77; Chartered Association of Certified Accountants, 1977–: Under Sec., 1982–88; Dep. Chief Exec., 1988–93. FRSA 1993. *Recreations:* travel, food, wine, preparing for my retirement. *Address:* (office) 29 Lincoln's Inn Fields, WC2A 3EE. *T:* 0171–242 6855.

ROSE, (Arthur) James; Director of Inspection, Office for Standards in Education, since 1994; *m* 1960, Pauline; one *d*. *Educ:* Kesteven College; Leicester University. HM Chief Inspector for Primary Educn, DES, subseq. DFE, 1986–92; Dep. Dir of Inspection, OFSTED, 1992–94. *Address:* OFSTED, Alexandra House, 29–33 Kingsway, WC2B 6SE.

ROSE, Barry, MBE 1981; editor and publisher; Chairman, own group of companies, since 1970; *b* 17 July 1923; *s* of late William George Rose and Beatrice Mary (*née* Castle); *m* 1963, Dorothy Jean Colthrup, *d* of Lt-Col W.R. Bowden; one *d*. Editor: Justice of the Peace and Local Government Review, 1944–72; Justice of the Peace, 1972–74; Local Government Review, 1972–76; law and local govt oriented periodicals. Member: Chichester RDC, 1951–61; West Sussex CC, 1952–73 (Leader, Cons. Group, 1967–72; Alderman, 1972); Pagham Parish Council, 1952–62; Bognor Regis UDC, 1964–68; Hon. Editor, Rural District Review, 1959–63; Mem., RDCA, 1960–63, CCA 1968–72; Chm., SE Area Cons. Local Govt Adv. Cttee, 1969–73; Pres., Assoc. of Councillors, 1975–86 (Treasurer, 1960–69; Chm., Exec. Cttee, 1969–75); posts in Cons. Party, 1945–74, incl. Constituency Chm., Chichester, 1961–69; Pres., Chichester Div., Young Conservatives, 1959–69. Contested (Alternative C) Old Bexley and Sidcup, 1992. Publisher, Centre for Policy Studies, 1974–76. Sometime publisher: Parly All-Party Penal Affairs Gp; Magistrates' Assoc.; NACRO; Council for Science and Society. Liveryman, Stationers' Co., 1974. FRSA 1960. Hon. Life Mem., Justices' Clerks' Soc., 1985. *Publications:* Change of Fortune (play), 1950; Funny Business (play), 1951; England Looks at Maud, 1970; A Councillor's Work, 1971; History of the Poll Tax, 1993. *Recreations:* entertaining and being entertained. *Address:* Courtney Lodge, Sylvan Way, Bognor Regis, West Sussex PO21 2RS. *T:* Bognor Regis (01243) 829902. *Clubs:* Athenæum, Garrick, MCC, United Oxford & Cambridge University.

ROSE, Barry Michael, FRSCM; FRAM; Master of the Music, St Albans Abbey, since 1988; *b* 24 May 1934; *s* of late Stanley George Rose and Gladys Mildred Rose; *m* 1965, Elizabeth Mary Ware; one *s* two *d*. *Educ:* Sir George Monoux Grammar Sch., Walthamstow; Royal Acad. of Music (ARAM). FRSCM 1973; FRAM 1989. First Organist and Master of the Choristers, new Guildford Cathedral, 1960–74; Sub-Organist, St Paul's Cath., 1974–77; Master of the Choir, 1977–84; Master of the Choirs, The King's School, Canterbury, 1985–88. Music Adviser to Head of Religious Broadcasting, BBC, 1970–90. Hon. DMus City, 1991; MUniv Surrey, 1992. *Recreation:* collecting vintage fountain-pens. *Address:* 31 Abbey Mill Lane, St Albans, Herts AL3 4HA. *T:* and *Fax:* St Albans (01727) 851810.

ROSE, Bernard William George, OBE 1980; MusB Cantab 1938, MA Oxon, Cantab 1944, DMus Oxon 1955, FRCO; Fellow, Organist, Informator Choristarum, Magdalen College, Oxford, 1957–81, Vice-President, 1973 and 1974, Emeritus Fellow since 1981; University Lecturer in Music, 1950–81; Choragus in the University, 1958–63; *b* Little Hallingbury, Herts, 9 May 1916; *s* of William and Jessie Rose; *m* 1939, Molly Daphne, OBE, JP, DL, 5th *d* of D. G. Marshall, MBE, Cambridge; three *s*. *Educ:* Salisbury Cathedral Sch.; Royal Coll. of Music; St Catharine's Coll., Cambridge. Organ Scholar, St Catharine's, Cambridge, 1935–39; Stewart of Rannoch Scholar in Sacred Music, Cambridge, 1935–39; Organist, and Conductor of the Eaglesfield Musical Soc., The Queen's Coll., Oxford, 1939–57, Fellow, 1949. Served with 4th Co. of London Yeomanry (Sharpshooters), 1941–44, Adjutant 1942 (PoW 1943–44). Conductor, Oxford Orchestral Soc., 1971–74. Mem. Council, Royal Coll. of Organists (Pres. 1974–76). *Publications:* Catharine: an ode, 1973; various church music compositions and edns of church music; edns of Anthems of Thomas Tomkins; (ed) Early English Church Music, Vols 5, 9, 14, 27, 37 and 39; Hallische Händel Ausgabe, 'Susanna'; contrib. Proc. Royal Musical Assoc., 1955; reviews in Music and Letters, articles in Musical Times. *Recreations:* DIY, bowls. *Address:* Bampton House, Bampton, Oxford OX18 2JX. *T:* Bampton Castle (01993) 850135.

ROSE, Brian; HM Diplomatic Service, retired; *b* 26 Jan. 1930; *s* of Edwin and Emily Rose; *m* 1952, Audrey Barnes; one *d*. *Educ:* Canford Sch., Dorset. MIL 1983. Intelligence Corps, 1948–50. Min. of Food, 1950–54; CRO, 1954; Peshawar, 1955–56; Ottawa, 1958–61; Kingston, Jamaica, 1962–65; Rome, 1966; Zagreb, 1966–68; Zomba, Malawi, 1968–71; FCO, 1971–74; Düsseldorf, 1974–77; E Berlin, 1977–78; Zürich, 1978–82; Consul-Gen., Stuttgart, 1982–85; Commercial and Econ. Counsellor, Helsinki, 1985–88. *Recreations:* tennis, music. *Club:* Travellers'.

ROSE, Major Charles Frederick, CBE 1988 (MBE 1968); CEng, FICE, MCIT; independent consultant in railway engineering and safety, since 1989; *b* 9 July 1926; *s* of Charles James Rose and Ida Marguerite Chollet; *m* 1956, Huguette Primerose Lecoultre; one *s* one *d*. *Educ:* Xaverian Coll., Brighton; Royal School of Military Engineering, 1951–52 and 1957–59. Student engineer, Southern Railway Co., 1942–46; commnd RE, 1947; service with mil. railways, Palestine and Egypt, 1947–51; with a Field Sqdn in Germany, 1952–53; Engr SO, Korea, 1953–54; Instructor: Mons Officer Cadet Sch., 1954–57; Transportation Centre, Longmoor, 1959–62; OC a Field Sqdn, Germany, 1962–64; Instr, Royal Sch. of Mil. Engrg, 1964–66; Engr, RE road construction project, Thailand, 1966–68; Inspecting Officer of Railways, MoT, 1968–82; Chief Inspecting Officer of Railways, Dept of Transport, 1982–88. Chm., Anglo-French Channel Tunnel Safety Authy, 1987–89. *Recreations:* hill walking, foreign travel, music. *Address:* Hollybank, Shadyhanger, Godalming, Surrey GU7 2HR. *T:* Godalming (01483) 416429.

ROSE, Christine Brooke; *see* Brooke-Rose.

ROSE, Rt. Hon. Sir Christopher (Dudley Roger), Kt 1985; PC 1992; **Rt. Hon. Lord Justice Rose;** a Lord Justice of Appeal, since 1992; *b* 10 Feb. 1937; *s* of late Roger and Hilda Rose, Morecambe; *m* 1964, Judith, *d* of late George and Charlotte Brand, Didsbury; one *s* one *d*. *Educ:* Morecambe Grammar Sch.; Repton; Leeds Univ.; Wadham Coll., Oxford (Hon. Fellow, 1993). LLB and Hughes Prize, Leeds, 1957; 1st cl. hons BCL 1959, Eldon Scholar 1959, Oxon. Lectr in Law, Wadham Coll., Oxford, 1959–60; called to Bar, Middle Temple, 1960 (Bencher, 1983); Bigelow Teaching Fellow, Law Sch., Univ. of Chicago, 1960–61; Harmsworth Scholar, 1961; joined Northern Circuit, 1961; QC 1974; a Recorder, 1978–85; a Judge of the High Court, QBD, 1985–92; Presiding Judge, Northern Circuit, 1987–90. Chm., Criminal Justice Consultative Council, 1994–. Mem., Senate of Inns of Court and Bar, 1983–85. *Recreations:* playing the piano, listening to music, golf, travel. *Address:* Royal Courts of Justice, Strand, WC2A 2LL. *Club:* Garrick.

ROSE, Clifford; *see* Rose, F.C.

ROSE, Sir Clive (Martin), GCMG 1981 (KCMG 1976; CMG 1967); HM Diplomatic Service, retired; *b* 15 Sept. 1921; *s* of late Rt Rev. Alfred Carey Wollaston Rose and Lois Juliet (*née* Garton); *m* 1946, Elisabeth Mackenzie, *d* of late Rev. Cyril Lewis, Gilston; two *s* three *d*. *Educ:* Marlborough College; Christ Church, Oxford (MA). Rifle Bde, 1941–46 (Maj.; despatches): served in Europe, 1944–45; India, 1945; Iraq, 1945–46. CRO, 1948; Office of Deputy High Comr, Madras, 1948–49; Foreign Office, 1950–53; UK High Commn, Germany, 1953–54; British Embassy, Bonn, 1955; FO, 1956–59; 1st Sec. and HM Consul, Montevideo, 1959–62; FO, 1962–65; Commercial Counsellor, Paris, 1965–67; Imp. Defence Coll., 1968; Counsellor, British Embassy, Washington, 1969–71; Asst Under-Sec. of State, FCO, 1971–73; Head, British Delegn to Negotiations on Mutual Reduction of Forces and Armaments and Associated Measures in Central Europe, Vienna, 1973–76; Dep. Secretary, Cabinet Office, 1976–79; UK Permanent Rep. on North Atlantic Council, 1979–82. Lectr to RCDS, 1979–87 (Mem., Adv. Bd, 1985–91). Consultant, Control Risks Gp, 1983–95; Dir, Control Risks Information Services Ltd, 1986–93 (Chm., 1991–93). Pres., Emergency Planning Assoc. (formerly Assoc. of Civil Defence and Emergency Planning Officers), 1987–93; Vice-Patron, RUSI, 1993– (Chm. Council, 1983–86; Vice-Pres., 1986–93). Vice-Pres., Suffolk Preservation Soc., 1988– (Chm., 1985–88). FRSA 1982; Hon. FICD 1989. *Publications:* Campaigns Against Western Defence: NATO's adversaries and critics, 1985, 2nd edn 1986; The Soviet Propaganda Network, 1988. *Recreations:* gardening, reading Trollope, family history. *Address:* Chimney House, Lavenham, Suffolk CO10 9QT. *Club:* Army and Navy.

ROSE, David Edward; Head of Drama, Channel Four Television, 1988–90; *b* 22 Nov. 1924; *s* of Alvan Edward Rose and Gladys Frances Rose; *m* 1st, 1952, Valerie Edwards (*d* 1966); three *s* three *d*; 2nd, 1966, Sarah Reid; one *d*, and one step *s* one step *d* adopted. *Educ:* Kingswood Sch., Bath; Guildhall Sch. of Music and Drama. Repertory Theatre, 1952; Ballets Jooss, and Sadler's Wells Theatre Ballet, 1954; BBC Television, 1954–81 (in production and direction; Head of Television Training, 1969; Head of Regional Television Drama, 1971–81); Sen. Commng Editor (Fiction), Channel Four TV, 1981–88. Mem., BAFTA. Prix Italia TV Award (for film Medico), 1959; BAFTA Producer and Director's Award, (for Z Cars (prod original series)), 1963; BFI Award (for Film on Four and work of new writers and directors), 1985; Desmond Davies Award, BAFTA, 1987; Prix Roberto Rossellini (for Channel Four Television), Cannes Film Fest., 1987; Critics Circle Special Film Award, 1987; Gold Medal, RTS, 1988.

ROSE, Donald Henry Gair, LVO 1982; HM Diplomatic Service, retired; Consul-General, Jedda, 1983–86; *b* 24 Sept. 1926; *m* 1950, Sheila Munro; three *s*. HM Forces, 1944–48; Scottish Office, 1948–66; Commonwealth Office, 1966; Nairobi, 1967; Tripoli, 1971; First Sec., Cairo, 1974–77; FCO, 1977–79; High Comr, Kiribati, 1979–83. *Address:* 11 Buckstone Gardens, Edinburgh EH10 6QD.

ROSE, Eliot Joseph Benn, (Jim Rose), CBE 1979; Chairman, Penguin Books, 1973–80; Director, Pearson Longman, 1974–81; *b* 7 June 1909; *s* of late Colonel E. A. Rose, CBE, and Dula, *e d* of Eliot Lewis, JP; *m* 1946, Susan Pamela Gibson; one *s* one *d*. *Educ:* Rugby; New College, Oxford. Served War of 1939–45, RAF, Wing-Comdr. Literary Editor, The Observer, 1948–51; Director: International Press Institute, Zürich, 1951–62; Survey of Race Relations in Britain, 1963–69; Editorial Dir, Westminster Press Ltd, 1970–74. Chm., Inter-Action Trust, 1968–84; Co-founder, Runnymede Trust, 1968 (Chm.,

1980–90); Mem., Cttee of Inquiry into educn of children from ethnic minority groups, 1979–81; Special Consultant to Unicef, 1981. Trustee, Writers and Scholars Educnl Trust, 1978–. Sidney Ball Meml Lectr, Oxford, 1970. Legion of Merit (US). *Publication:* (with Nicholas Deakin) Colour and Citizenship, 1969. *Address:* 37 Pembroke Square, W8 6PE. *T:* 0171–937 3772; Rocks Farm, Groombridge, Tunbridge Wells, Kent TN3 9PG. *T:* Tunbridge Wells (01892) 864223. *Club:* Garrick.

ROSE, Dr Frank Clifford, FRCP; Director, London Neurological Centre, and Hon. Consulting Neurologist, Charing Cross Hospital, since 1991; Secretary-Treasurer General, World Federation of Neurology, since 1989; *b* 29 Aug. 1926; *s* of James and Clare Rose; *m* 1963, Angela Juliet Halsted; three *s*. *Educ:* King's Coll., London; Westminster Hosp. Med. Sch.; Univ. of California, San Francisco; Hôpital de la Salpêtrière, Paris. MB BS London; DCH; MRCS; FRCP 1971 (LRCP 1949, MRCP 1954). Medical Registrar, Westminster Hosp., 1955; Resident MO, National Hosp., Queen Square, 1957; Sen. Registrar, Dept of Neurology, St George's Hosp., 1960; Consultant Neurologist: Medical Ophthalmology Unit, St Thomas' Hosp., 1963–85; Moor House Sch. for Speech Disorders, 1965–70; Physician i/c, Dept. of Neurology, Regl Neuroscis Centre, Charing Cross Hosp., 1965–91; Dir, Academic Unit of Neuroscis, Charing Cross and Westminster Med. Sch., 1985–91; Prof. Associate, Dept of Health Scis, Brunel Univ., 1991–. PMO, Allied Dunbar (formerly Hambro Life) Assurance Co., 1970–. Mem., Wkg Pty on Stroke, RCP, 1988; Chairman: European Stroke Prevention Study, 1981–88; Res. Adv. Cttee, Assoc. for Res. in Multiple Sclerosis, 1987–91; Internat. Amyotrophic Lateral Sclerosis/Motor Neurone Disease Res. Foundn, 1987–90; Motor Neurone Disease Assoc., 1988–90 (Med. Patron, 1978–90; Scientific Advr, 1990–91); Ind. Doctors Forum, 1994–; President: Med. Soc. London, 1983–84 (Treas., 1984–89; Internat. Sec., 1995–); Assurance Med. Soc., 1983–85; Section of Neurology, RSM, 1990–91; Trustee: Migraine Trust (Chm., 1988–); The Way Ahead Appeal, 1986–91. Examr in Clinical Pharmacology and Therapeutics, Univ. of London. Lettsomian Lectr, Med. Soc. London, 1979; Guest Lectr, Scandinavian Migraine Soc., 1983. Hon. Member: Neurol Soc. of Thailand, 1992; Austrian Soc. of Neurol., 1992. Harold Wolff Award, 1981 and 1984, and Distinguished Clinician Award, 1986, Amer. Assoc. for the Study of Headache. Sen. Editor, Neuroepidemiology, 1991– (Dep. Editor, 1982–83; Editor, 1984–90); Editor: World Neurology, 1990–; Jl of Hist. of Neuroscis, 1992–; Co-editor, Headache Qly, 1991–. *Publications:* (jtly) Hypoglycaemia, 1965, 2nd edn, 1981 (Japanese trans., 1988); (jtly) Basic Neurology of Speech, 1970, 3rd edn 1983; (ed) Physiological Aspects of Clinical Neurology, 1976; (ed) Medical Ophthalmology, 1976; (ed) Motor Neurone Disease, 1977; (ed) Clinical Neuroimmunology, 1978; (ed) Paediatric Neurology, 1979; (jtly) Optic Neuritis and its Differential Diagnosis, 1979; (ed jtly) Progress in Stroke Research 1, 1979; (ed jtly) Progress in Neurological Research, 1979; (jtly) Migraine: the facts, 1979 (Spanish trans., 1981); (ed) Clinical Neuroepidemiology, 1980; (ed) Animal Models of Neurological Disorders, 1980; (ed jtly) Research Progress in Parkinson's Disease, 1981; (ed) Metabolic Disorders of the Nervous System, 1981; (ed jtly) Progress in Migraine Research 1, 1981; (jtly) Stroke: The Facts, 1981 (Dutch trans., 1982); (ed jtly) Historical Aspects of the Neurosciences, 1982; (ed jtly) Cerebral Hypoxia in the Pathogenesis of Migraine, 1982; (ed) Advances in Stroke Therapy, 1982; (ed) Advances in Migraine Research and Therapy, 1982; (ed) Research Progress in Epilepsy, 1982; (ed jtly) Immunology of Nervous System Infections, 1983; (ed) The Eye in General Disease, 1983; (ed jtly) Progress in Stroke Research 2, 1983; (ed) Research Progress in Motor Neurone Disease, 1984; (ed) Progress in Migraine Research 2, 1984; (ed) Progress in Aphasiology, 1985; (ed) Modern Approaches to the Dementias (2 vols), 1985; (ed jtly) Neuro-oncology, 1985; (ed) Migraine: clinical and research advances, 1985; Handbook of Clinical Neurology: headache, 1986; (ed) Stroke: epidemiological, therapeutic and socio-economic aspects, 1986; (jtly) Atlas of Clinical Neurology, 1986 (Japanese trans., 1989); (ed jtly) Multiple Sclerosis: diagnostic, immunological and therapeutic aspects, 1987; (ed) Advances in Headache Research, 1987; (ed) Parkinson's Disease: clinical and research advances, 1987; (ed jtly) Physiological Aspects of Clinical Neuro-ophthalmology, 1987; (jtly) Answers to Migraine, 1987; (ed jtly) Aphasia, 1988; (ed) The Management of Headache, 1988; (ed jtly) Neuromuscular Stimulation, 1989; (ed) James Parkinson, his life and times, 1989; (ed) Control of the Hypothalamic-Pituitary-Adrenal Axis, 1989; (ed) New Advances in Headache Research, 1989; (ed) Neuroscience across the Centuries, 1989; (ed jtly) Clinical Trial Methodology in Stroke, 1989; (ed jtly) Amyotrophic Lateral Sclerosis: new advances in toxicology and epidemiology, 1990; (ed) Progress in Clinical Neurologic Trials: amyotrophic lateral sclerosis, 1990; (ed) New Advances in Headache Research 2, 1991; (ed) Parkinson's Disease and the Problems of Clinical Trials, 1992; (ed) Molecular Genetics and Neurology, 1992; (ed) Advances in Clinical Neuropharmacology, 1993; (ed) ALS: from Charcot to the present and into the future, 1994; (ed) New Advances in Headache Research 3, 1994; (ed) Tropical Neurology, 1995; papers in neurological and gen. med. jls. *Recreations:* travel, reading, wine, bridge. *Address:* London Neurological Centre, 110 Harley Street, W1N 1AF. *T:* 0171–935 3546, *Fax:* 0171–935 4172. *Clubs:* Royal Society of Medicine, Savile.

ROSE, Gerald Gershon, PhD; CChem, FRSC; Director, Thornton Research Centre, Shell Research Ltd, 1975–80; *b* 4 May 1921; *m* 1945, Olive Sylvia; one *s* two *d*. *Educ:* Hendon County Grammar Sch.; Imperial Coll. of Science and Technology (BSc, ARCS, DIC, PhD). Joined Shell Group, 1944; served in refineries, Stanlow, Trinidad, Singapore and South Africa; General Manager, Shell/BP South Africa Petroleum Refineries, 1963; Manufacturing and Supply Director, Shell/BP Service Co., 1968; Manager, Teesport Refinery, 1971. *Recreations:* golf, tennis, gardening. *Address:* The Tithe Barn, Great Barrow, Chester, Cheshire CH3 7HW. *T:* Tarvin (01829) 40623.

ROSE, Graham Hunt; a Master of the Supreme Court (Queen's Bench Division), since 1992; *b* 15 July 1937; *er s* of William Edward Hunt Rose and of late Mary Musgrave Rose (*née* Kent); *m* 1962, Malvinia Ann Saunders (marr. diss. 1988); three *s*. *Educ:* Canford Sch.; University Coll., Oxford (MA). Nat. Service, RA, 1955–57: commnd 1956; active service, 1957. Called to the Bar, Inner Temple, 1961; practised at the Bar, 1961–92, Western Circuit. Jt Editor, Supreme Court Practice, 1992–. *Recreations:* most ball games, mountaineering, gardening. *Address:* Royal Courts of Justice, Strand, WC2A 2LL. *Club:* Parkstone Golf.

ROSE, Graham John; gardening correspondent, Sunday Times, since 1978; *b* 28 Jan. 1928; *s* of Herbert Trower Whitfield Rose and Grace Rose (*née* Cain); *m* 1st, 1953, Catherine Marie Louise Degrais; 2nd, 1967, Elizabeth Dorothy Goldbach (*née* Dodd). *Educ:* Dame Allan's School, Newcastle-upon-Tyne; King's College, Durham Univ. (BSc Hons); Gonville and Caius College, Cambridge. Entomologist, ICI (India), Calcutta, 1950–51; Universal Crop Protection, 1951–53; Technical Dir, Micron Sprayers, 1953–57; Consultant: Micron Sprayers, Britten Norman, SDC Pesticides, Opico (UK), 1957–68; agricultural corresp., Sunday Times, 1968–78. *Publications:* Crop Protection, 1955; Landscape with Weeds, 1980; The Low Maintenance Garden, 1983; (with Peter King) Green Words, 1986; Gardener's Almanac, 1986; The Small Garden Planner, 1987; (jtly) Gardening with Style, 1988; The Romantic Garden, 1988; Woodland and Wildflower Gardening, 1988; The Traditional Garden Book, 1989; (with Peter King) The Good Gardens Guide, (annually) 1990–; (with Peter King) The Love of Roses, 1990. *Recreations:* garden designing, building. *Address:* 58 Hugh Street, SW1V 4ER. *T:* 0171–821 9378. *Club:* Pourcairou (France).

ROSE, Prof. Harold Bertram; Visiting Professor of Finance, London Graduate School of Business Studies, since 1975 (Esmée Fairbairn Chair, 1965–75); *b* 9 Aug. 1923; *s* of late Isaac Rose and Rose Rose (*née* Barnett); *m* 1st, 1949, Valerie Frances Anne Chubb (marr. diss. 1974); three *s* one *d*; 2nd, 1974, Diana Mary Campbell Scarlett; one *s* one *d*. *Educ:* Davenant Foundn Sch.; LSE (BCom). Served with RA in Britain, India and Burma, 1942–45 (Captain). Head of Econ. Intell. Dept, Prudential Assce Co., Ltd, 1948–58; Sen. Lectr, then Reader, in Business Finance, LSE, 1958–65; Member: Council, Consumers' Assoc., 1958–63; Central Adv. Council on Primary Educn (Plowden Cttee), 1963–65; Business Studies Cttee, SSRC, 1967–68, and Univ. Grants Cttee, 1968–69; Reserve Pension Bd, 1973–75; HM Treasury Inquiry into Value of Pensions, 1980; Special Adviser to: H of C Treasury and Civil Service Cttee, 1980–81; DoI, 1980–81. Gp Economic Advr, Barclays Bank, 1975–88. Director: Economist Newspaper, 1969–71; Abbey National Building Soc., 1975–83. Mem., Retail Prices Adv. Cttee, 1985–89. Trustee, IEA, 1975– (Chm., 1995–). Gov., The Hall Sch., 1987–95. *Publications:* The Economic Background to Investment, 1959; Disclosure in Company Accounts, 1963; Management Education in the 1970's, 1970; various papers in econ. and financial jls. *Address:* 33 Dartmouth Park Avenue, NW5 1JL. *T:* 0171–485 7315. *Club:* Reform.

ROSE, Gen. Sir (Hugh) Michael, KCB 1994; CBE 1986; DSO 1995; QGM 1981; Adjutant General, since 1995; *b* 5 Jan. 1940; *s* of late Lt-Col Hugh Vincent Rose, IA and of Mrs Barbara Phoebe Masters (*née* Allcard); *m* 1968, Angela Raye Shaw; two *s*. *Educ:* Cheltenham College; St Edmund Hall, Oxford (2nd Cl. Hons PPE; Hon. Fellow, 1995); Staff College; RCDS. Commissioned Gloucestershire Regt, TAVR, 1959; RAFVR, 1962; Coldstream Guards, 1964; served Germany, Aden, Malaysia, Gulf States, Dhofar, N Ireland (despatches), Falkland Is (despatches); BM 16 Para. Bde, 1973–75; CO 22 SAS Regt, 1979–82; Comd 39 Inf. Bde, 1983–85; Comdt, Sch. of Infantry, 1987–88; DSF, 1988–89; GOC NE Dist and Comdr 2nd Inf. Div., 1989–91; Comdt, Staff Coll., 1991–93; Comdr, UK Field Army and Insp. Gen. of TA, 1993–94; Comdr, UN Protection Force, Bosnia-Hertzogovina, 1994–95; Dep. C-in-C, Land Comd, 1995. Hon. Col, Oxford OTC. Chm., Army Parachute Assoc., Cdre, Army Sailing Assoc. *Recreations:* sailing, ski-ing. *Address:* c/o Regimental HQ Coldstream Guards, Wellington Barracks, Birdcage Walk, SW1E 6HQ. *Club:* Cavalry and Guards.

ROSE, Jack, CMG 1963; MBE 1954; DFC 1942; *b* 18 Jan. 1917; *s* of late Charles Thomas Rose; *m* 1st, 1940, Margaret Valerie (*d* 1966), 2nd *d* of late Alec Stuart Budd; two *s*; 2nd, 1967, Beryl Elizabeth, 4th *d* of late A. S. Budd. *Educ:* Shooters Hill School; London University. Served RAF, 1938–46 (Wing Commander); served in fighter, fighter/bomber and rocket firing sqdns; France, 1940 and 1944; Battle of Britain; Burma, 1944–45. Joined Colonial Administrative Service, N Rhodesia, 1947; Private Secretary to Governor of Northern Rhodesia, 1950–53; seconded to Colonial Office, 1954–56; Administrative posts, Northern Rhodesia, 1956–60; Administrator, Cayman Islands (seconded), 1960–63; Assistant to Governor, British Guiana, 1963–64 (Actg Governor and Dep. Governor for periods). Member: Professional and Technical 'A' Whitley Council for Health Services, 1965–75 (Chm., 1973–75); Gen. Whitley Council for Health Services, 1973–75. Secretary: Chartered Soc. of Physiotherapy, 1965–75; Salmon and Trout Assoc., 1975–79 (Vice-Pres., 1980–). Chm., Burford Charity Trustees, 1994–. *Recreation:* writing. *Address:* The Little House, The Hill, Burford, Oxon OX18 4QY. *T:* Burford (01993) 822553.

ROSE, James; *see* Rose, A. J.

ROSE, Jeffrey David, CBE 1991; Chairman of the Royal Automobile Club, since 1981 (Deputy Chairman, 1979–81); *b* 2 July 1931; *s* of late Samuel and Daisy Rose; *m* 1958, Joyce (*née* Clompus) (separated 1990); one *s* two *d*. *Educ:* Southend High Sch.; London Sch. of Econs and Pol. Science. Nat. Service, RA, 1950–52 (Lieut). Chm., RAC Motoring Services, 1980–; Vice Chm., British Road Fedn, 1982–; Vice President: Fédn Internationale de l'Automobile, 1983–93 and 1994–; Inst. of the Motor Industry, 1992–; RAC British Motor Sports Council, 1994–; Chm., Commonwealth Motoring Conf., 1988–; Member: Management Cttee, Alliance Internationale de Tourisme, 1982–; Council, Inst. of Advanced Motorists, 1987–94; Adv. Council, Prince's Youth Business Trust, 1992–. Chm., Trustees, British Brain and Spine Foundn, 1995–; Trustee, Brooklands Mus., 1991–. FIMI 1989. Liveryman, Worshipful Co. of Coachmakers and Coach Harness Makers, 1981– (Mem. Court, 1995–). *Recreations:* walking, dining, music. *Address:* Royal Automobile Club, 89–91 Pall Mall, SW1Y 5HS; 1.2 Albany, Piccadilly, W1V 9RP. *Clubs:* Royal Automobile, Brooks's, MCC.

ROSE, Jim; *see* Rose, E. J. B.

ROSE, John Raymond; Clerk of Standing Committees, House of Commons, 1987–91; *b* 22 April 1934; *s* of late Arthur Raymond Rose and Edith Mary Rose, Minehead, Somerset; *m* 1st, 1961, Vivienne (marr. diss. 1991), *d* of late Charles Dillon Seabrooke, IoW; one *s* one *d*; 2nd, 1991, Dr Betty Webb, *d* of late Ernest Julian Webb, Statesville, NC, USA. *Educ:* Marlborough; Trinity Hall, Cambridge (Major Scholar in Classics; Law Tripos 1st Cl. Hons, Pts I and II). 2nd Lieut DCLI, Belize and Jamaica, 1953–55. Clerk's Department, House of Commons, 1958–91: Clerk of Select Cttees on Estimates (Sub-Cttee), Public Accounts, Violence in the Family, Race Relations, Abortion, European Community Secondary Legislation, Foreign Affairs, 1959–87. Vis. Kenan Prof., Meredith Coll., NC, USA, 1981. Fellow, Industry and Parlt Trust, 1987. Freeman, City of London, 1959; Liveryman, Salters' Co., 1959. *Recreations:* travel, walking, cycling, gardening, country pursuits, Scottish dancing, bridge. *Address:* 220 Hillcrest Road, Raleigh, NC 27605, USA. *T:* (919) 8283443.

ROSE, Joyce Dora Hester, CBE 1981; JP, DL; Chairman, Council and Executive, Magistrates' Association, 1990–93; *b* 14 Aug. 1929; *d* of late Abraham (Arthur) Woolf and Rebecca Woolf (*née* Simpson); *m* 1953, Cyril Rose; two *s* one *d*. *Educ:* King Alfred Sch., London; Queen's Coll., London; in N America. Chm., Watford Magistrates' Court, 1990–94 (Dep. Chm., Juvenile Panel, 1968–91, Family Proceedings (formerly Domestic) Panel, 1982– (Chm., 1979–82)); Member: Herts Magistrates' Courts Cttee, 1973–; Herts Probation Cttee, 1971–. Pres., 1979–80, Chm., 1982–83, Liberal Party; Pres. and Chm., Women's Liberal Fedn, 1972, 1973. Mem., Women's Nat. Commn, 1981–87 (Mem. Exec., 1985–87); former Mem., Nat. Exec., UK Cttee for UNICEF (Vice-Chm., 1968–70). Hon. LLD Hertfordshire, 1992. JP Herts, 1963; DL Herts, 1990. *Address:* 38 Main Avenue, Moor Park, Northwood, Middx HA6 2LQ. *T:* Northwood (01923) 821385. *Club:* National Liberal.

ROSE, Sir Julian (Day), 4th Bt *cr* 1909, of Hardwick House, and 5th Bt *cr* 1872, of Montreal; *b* 3 March 1947; 3rd and *o* surv. *s* of Sir Charles Henry Rose, 3rd Bt and of Phoebe, *d* of 2nd Baron Phillimore (*d* 1947); *S* father, 1966, and cousin, Sir Francis Cyril Rose, 4th Bt, 1979; *m* 1976, Elizabeth Goode Johnson, Columbus, Ohio, USA; one *s* one *d*. *Educ:* Stanbridge School. Actor/asst dir, Players' Theatre of New England, 1973–79; Co-founder, Inst. for Creative Develt, Antwerp, 1978–83. Co-ordinator, Organic Farming practice, Hardwick Estate, 1984–. Member: Council, Soil Assoc., 1984–; Agricl Panel,

Intermediate Technology Develt Gp, 1984–; Bd, UK Register of Organic Food Standards, Food From Britain, 1987–; BBC Rural and Agricl Affairs Adv. Cttee, 1991–; Adv. Cttee, Food and Farming, Thames Valley Univ., 1994. Agricl Correspondent, Environment Now, 1989–91. *Heir: s* Lawrence Michael Rose, *b* 6 Oct. 1986. *Address:* Hardwick House, Whitchurch-on-Thames, Oxfordshire RG8 7RB.

ROSE, Kenneth Vivian, FRSL; writer; *b* 15 Nov. 1924; *s* of Dr J. Rose, MB, ChB. *Educ:* Repton Sch.; New Coll., Oxford (scholar; MA). Served Welsh Guards, 1943–46; attached Phantom, 1945. Asst master, Eton Coll., 1948; Editorial Staff, Daily Telegraph, 1952–60; founder and writer of Albany column, Sunday Telegraph, 1961–. *Publications:* Superior Person: a portrait of Curzon and his circle in late Victorian England, 1969; The Later Cecils, 1975; William Harvey: a monograph, 1978; King George V, 1983 (Wolfson Award for History, 1983; Whitbread Award for Biography, 1983; Yorkshire Post Biography of the Year Award, 1984); Kings, Queens and Courtiers: intimate portraits of the Royal House of Windsor, 1985; (contrib.) Founders and Followers: literary lectures on the London Library, 1992; contribs to Dictionary of National Biography. *Address:* 38 Brunswick Gardens, W8 4AL. *T:* 0171–221 4783. *Clubs:* Beefsteak, Pratt's.

ROSE, Col Lewis John, OBE 1990; Vice Lord-Lieutenant of Bedfordshire, since 1991; *b* 18 Aug. 1935; *s* of Reginald George Rose and Mary Agnes Rose; *m* 1st, 1964, Aileen Beth Robertson (marr. diss. 1974); two *s*; 2nd, 1978, Gillian Mary King; one step *s* one step *d*. *Educ:* Bedford Sch.; College of Law. Served RA, 1954–56; Beds Yeomanry, later Herts & Beds Yeomanry, 1956–67. In practice as solicitor, 1962–. Comdt, Beds ACF, 1967–90; Chm., Beds TA&VR Cttee, 1991–94; Vice Chm. (Mil.), E Anglia TA&VRA, 1994–. President: Beds Small-bore Shooting Assoc., 1992–; Bedford Distict Scout Council, 1975–. DL Bedfordshire, 1981. *Recreations:* shooting, rowing (Pres., Bedford Rowing Club, 1988–91). *Address:* 11 Woodlands Close, Cople, Beds MK44 3UE. *T:* Bedford (01234) 838210. *Club:* Leander (Henley on Thames).

ROSE, Mark Willson; Agent General for British Columbia in London, 1992–95; *b* 5 March 1924; *s* of Mark C. Rose and Mildred Willson; *m* 1947, Isabel Phillips; three *d*. *Educ:* Univ. of British Columbia (BScA); Univ. of Western Washington, USA (MEd). Teacher in Okanagan, 1949; Dist Supervisor for New Westminster schools, 1958; University of British Columbia: Faculty of Educn, 1962 (Mem. Policy Council); Mem. Bd of Alumni Assoc. Exec.; Professor Emeritus 1983. Alderman, Coquitlam, 1966–67; MP (NDP) for Fraser Valley W, then Mission-Port Moody, 1968–83; Mem., standing and special cttees, incl. culture, communications, agriculture, the Constitution and alternative energy, to 1978; Chm., NDP Parly Caucus, 1979–83; MLA (NDP) for Coquitlam-Moody, British Columbia, 1983–91; Opposition House Leader, 1986–91; Mem., parly cttee to review and reform Standing Orders; Mem., Speaker's Bd of Internal Economy. Mem., Rotary Club, London. Freeman, City of London, 1993. *Recreations:* music, travel, handyman, renovations, landscaping. *Address:* c/o British Columbia House, 1 Regent Street, SW1Y 4NS. *T:* 0171–930 6857. *Clubs:* East India, Royal Over-Seas League (Hon.); University of British Columbia Faculty.

ROSE, Gen. Sir Michael; *see* Rose, Gen. Sir H. M.

ROSE, Paul (Bernard); HM Coroner, London Southern District, since 1988; *b* 26 Dec. 1935; *s* of Arthur and Norah Rose; *m* 1957, Eve Marie-Thérèse; two *s* one *d*. *Educ:* Bury Gram. Sch.; Manchester Univ.; Gray's Inn. LLB (Hons) Manch., 1956; Barrister-at-Law, 1957. Legal and Secretarial Dept, Co-op. Union Ltd, 1957–60; Lectureship, Dept of Liberal Studies, Royal Coll. of Advanced Technology, Salford, 1961–63; Barrister-at-Law, 1963–88; Asst Recorder (formerly Dep. Circuit Judge), 1974–88; Immigration Adjudicator (part-time), Hatton Cross, 1987– (Special Adjudicator, 1993–). MP (Lab) Manchester, Blackley, 1964–79; PPS to Minister of Transport, 1967–68; Opposition Front Bench Spokesman, Dept of Employment, 1970–72. Chairman: Parly Labour Home Office Group, 1968–70; Parly Labour Employment Group, 1974–79; Campaign for Democracy in Ulster, 1965–73. Delegate to Council of Europe and WEU, 1968–69; Vice-Chm., Labour Cttee for Europe, 1977–79. Mem., Campaign for Electoral Reform, 1975–. Founder Mem., SDP (Brent Area Sec., 1981–82). Chm., NW Regional Sports Council, 1966–68. Member: Coroners' Soc.; Medico-Legal Soc. AIL. *Publications:* Handbook to Industrial and Provident Societies Act, 1960; Guide to Weights and Measures Act 1963, 1965; The Manchester Martyrs, 1970; Backbencher's Dilemma, 1981; The Moonies' Unmasked, 1981; (jt) A History of the Fenian Movement in Britain, 1982; contrib. to many periodicals on political and legal topics. *Recreations:* sport, theatre, languages, travel. *Address:* Coroner's Court, Barclay Road, Croydon CR9 3NE.

ROSE, Prof. Richard, FBA 1992; Director and Professor of Public Policy, Centre for the Study of Public Policy, Strathclyde University, since 1976; *b* 9 April 1933; *o s* of Charles Imse and late Mary Conely Rose, St Louis, Mo, USA; *m* 1956, Rosemary J., *o d* of late James Kenny, Whitstable, Kent; two *s* one *d*. *Educ:* Clayton High Sch., Mo; Johns Hopkins Univ., BA (Double distinction, Phi Beta Kappa) comparative drama, 1953; London Sch. of Economics, 1953–54; Oxford University, 1957–60, DPhil (Lincoln and Nuffield Colls). Political public relations, Mississippi Valley, 1954–55; Reporter, St Louis Post-Dispatch, 1955–57; Lecturer in Govt, Univ. of Manchester, 1961–66; Prof. of Politics, Strathclyde Univ., 1966–82. Consultant Psephologist, The Times, Independent Television, Daily Telegraph, STV, UTV etc., 1964–. American SSRC Fellow, Stanford Univ., 1967; Vis. Lectr in Political Sociology, Cambridge Univ., 1967; Dir, ISSC European Summer Sch., 1973. Sec., Cttee on Political Sociology, Internat. Sociological Assoc., 1970–85; Founding Mem., European Consortium for Political Res., 1970; Member: US/UK Fulbright Commn, 1971–75; Eisenhower Fellowship Programme, 1971. Guggenheim Foundn Fellow, 1974; Visiting Scholar: Woodrow Wilson Internat. Centre, Washington DC, 1974; Brookings Inst., Washington DC, 1976; Amer. Enterprise Inst., Washington, 1980; Fiscal Affairs Dept, IMF, Washington, 1984; Vis. Prof., European Univ. Inst., Florence, 1977, 1978; Visitor, Japan Foundn, 1984; Hinkley Prof., Johns Hopkins Univ., 1987; Guest Prof., Wissenschaftsentrum, Berlin, 1988–90; Vis. Prof., Central European Univ., Prague, 1992–95. Ransone Lectr, Univ. of Alabama, 1990. Consultant Chm., NI Constitutional Convention, 1976; Mem., Home Office Working Party on Electoral Register, 1975–77. Co-Founder, British Politics Gp, 1974–; Convenor, Work Gp on UK Politics, Political Studies Assoc., 1976–88; Mem. Council, Internat. Political Science Assoc., 1976–82; Keynote Speaker, Aust. Inst. of Political Science, Canberra, 1978; Steering Cttee, World Values Study, 1995–; Technical Consultant: OECD; World Bank; Dir, ESRC (formerly SSRC) Res. Programme, Growth of Govt, 1982–86; UNDP Cons. to Pres. of Colombia, 1990; Scientific Advr, Paul Lazarsfeld Soc., Vienna, 1991–. Mem. Council, Scottish Opera Ltd, 1992–. Hon. Vice-Pres., Political Studies Assoc., UK, 1986. Editor, Jl of Public Policy, 1985–. Foreign Member: Finnish Acad. of Science and Letters, 1985; Amer. Acad. of Arts and Scis, 1994. Amex Internat. Econs Prize, 1992. Subject of prog. in Man of Action series, BBC Radio 3, 1974. *Publications:* The British General Election of 1959 (with D. E. Butler), 1960; Must Labour Lose? (with Mark Abrams), 1960; Politics in England, 1964, 5th edn 1989; (ed) Studies in British Politics, 1966, 3rd edn 1976; Influencing Voters, 1967; (ed) Policy Making in Britain, 1969; People in Politics, 1970; (ed, with M. Dogan) European Politics, 1971; Governing Without Consensus: an Irish perspective, 1971; (with T. Mackie) International Almanack of Electoral History, 1974, 3rd edn 1991; (ed) Electoral Behavior: a comparative handbook, 1974; (ed) Lessons from America, 1974; The Problem of Party Government, 1974; (ed) The Management of Urban Change in Britain and Germany, 1974; Northern Ireland: a time of choice, 1976; Managing Presidential Objectives, 1976; (ed) The Dynamics of Public Policy, 1976; (ed, with D. Kavanagh) New Trends in British Politics, 1977; (ed with J. Wiatr) Comparing Public Policies, 1977; What is Governing?: Purpose and Policy in Washington, 1978; (ed, with G. Hermet and A. Rouquié) Elections without Choice, 1978; (with B. G. Peters) Can Government Go Bankrupt?, 1978; (ed with W. B. Gwyn) Britain: progress and decline, 1980; Do Parties Make a Difference?, 1980, 2nd edn 1984; (ed) Challenge to Governance, 1980; (ed) Electoral Participation, 1980; (ed with E. Suleiman) Presidents and Prime Ministers, 1980; Understanding the United Kingdom, 1982; (with I. McAllister) United Kingdom Facts, 1982; (ed with P. Madgwick) The Territorial Dimension in United Kingdom Politics, 1982; (ed with E. Page) Fiscal Stress in Cities, 1982; Understanding Big Government, 1984; (with I. McAllister) The Nationwide Competition for Votes, 1984; Public Employment in Western Nations, 1985; (with I. McAllister) Voters Begin to Choose, 1986; (with D. Van Mechelen) Patterns of Parliamentary Legislation, 1986; (ed with R. Shiratori) The Welfare State East and West, 1986; Ministers and Ministries, 1987; (with T. Karran) Taxation by Political Inertia, 1987; The Post-Modern President: the White House meets the world, 1988, 2nd edn 1991; Ordinary People in Public Policy, 1989; (with I. McAllister) The Loyalty of Voters: a lifetime learning model, 1990; Lesson-Drawing in Public Policy: a guide to learning across time and space, 1993; (with P. L. Davies) Inheritance in Public Policy: change without choice in Britain, 1994; contribs to academic journals in Europe and America; trans. into fourteen foreign languages; broadcasts on comparative politics and public policy. *Recreations:* architecture (historical, Britain; modern, America), music, writing. *Address:* Centre for the Study of Public Policy, Livingstone Tower, Glasgow G1 1XH. *T:* 0141–552 4400, *Fax:* 0141–552 4711; Bennochy, 1 East Abercromby Street, Helensburgh, Dunbartonshire G84 7SP. *T:* Helensburgh (01436) 672164, *Fax:* Helensburgh (01436) 673125; 7430 Byron Place, St Louis Co., MO 63105, USA. *Clubs:* Reform; Cosmos (Washington DC).

ROSE, Prof. Steven Peter Russell, PhD; FIBiol; Professor of Biology and Director, Brain and Behaviour Research Group, Open University, since 1969; *b* 4 July 1938; *s* of Lionel Sydney Rose and Ruth Rose (*née* Waxman); *m* 1961, Hilary Ann Chantler; two *s*. *Educ:* Haberdashers' Aske's Sch., Hampstead; King's Coll., Cambridge (BA); Inst. of Psychiatry, Univ. of London (PhD). FIBiol 1970. Beit Meml and Guinness Res. Fellow, New Coll., Oxford, 1961–63; NIH Res. Fellow, Istituto Superiore di Sanita, Rome, 1963–64; MRC Res. Staff, Dept of Biochem., Imperial Coll., London, 1964–69. Vis. Sen. Res. Fellow, ANU, 1977; Vis. Schol., Harvard Univ., 1980; Distinguished Res. Prof., Univ. of Minn, 1992; Osher Fellow, Exploratorium, San Francisco, 1993. FRSA 1980. Anokhin Medal, Russia, 1990; Sechenov Medal, Russia, 1992; Science Book Prize, COPUS, 1993. *Publications:* The Chemistry of Life, 1966, 3rd edn 1991; (with Hilary Rose) Science and Society, 1969; The Conscious Brain, 1973; No Fire No Thunder, 1984; (jtly) Not in our Genes, 1984; The Making of Memory, 1992; numerous edited books, res. papers and scholarly articles. *Address:* Biology Department, The Open University, Milton Keynes MK7 6AA.

ROSEBERY, 7th Earl of, *cr* 1703; **Neil Archibald Primrose,** DL; Bt 1651; Viscount of Rosebery, Baron Primrose and Dalmeny, 1700; Viscount of Inverkeithing, Baron Dalmeny and Primrose, 1703; Baron Rosebery (UK), 1828; Earl of Midlothian, Viscount Mentmore, Baron Epsom, 1911; *b* 11 Feb. 1929; *o* surv. *s* of 6th Earl of Rosebery, KT, PC, DSO, MC, and Eva Isabel Marian (Eva Countess of Rosebery, DBE) (*d* 1987), *d* of 2nd Baron Aberdare; *S* father, 1974; *m* 1955, Alison Mary Deirdre, *d* of late Ronald William Reid, MS, FRCS; one *s* four *d*. *Educ:* Stowe; New Coll., Oxford. DL Midlothian, 1960. *Heir: s* Lord Dalmeny, *qv*. *Address:* Dalmeny House, South Queensferry, West Lothian EH30 9TQ.

ROSEHILL, Lord; Alexander Robert MacRae Carnegie; *b* 16 Nov. 1980; *s* and *heir* of Earl of Northesk, *qv*.

ROSEN, Charles; pianist; Professor of Music, University of Chicago; *b* New York, 5 May 1927; *s* of Irwin Rosen and Anita Gerber. *Educ:* studied piano with Mr and Mrs Moriz Rosenthal; Princeton Univ. (PhD). Début, NY, 1951. His many recordings include: first complete recording of Debussy Etudes, 1951; late keyboard works of Bach, 1969; last six Beethoven Sonatas, 1970; Schumann piano works; Diabelli Variations; also works by Liszt, Elliott Carter, Boulez, etc. Eliot Norton Prof. of Poetry, Harvard Univ., 1980; George Eastman Vis. Prof., Oxford Univ., 1987–88. Hon. MusD: Trinity Coll., Dublin, 1976; Cambridge, 1992; Hon. DMus Durham, 1980. *Publications:* The Classical Style, 1971; Schoenberg, 1976; Sonata Forms, 1980; (with H. Zerner) Romanticism and Realism: the mythology of nineteenth century art, 1984. *Recreations:* music, books. *Address:* CAMI, 160 West 57 Street, New York, NY 10024, USA. *T:* (212) 8419537.

ROSEN, Rabbi Jeremy, PhD; part-time Professor of Jewish Studies, since 1991, and President, since 1994, Faculty for Comparative Study of Religions, Wilrijk; *b* 11 Sept. 1942; *s* of Rabbi Kopul Rosen and Bella Rosen; *m* 1st, 1971, Vera Giuditta Zippel (marr. diss. 1987); two *s* two *d*; 2nd, 1988, Suzanne Kaszirer. *Educ:* Carmel Coll.; Pembroke Coll., Cambridge (MA); Mir Academy, Jerusalem. Minister, Bulawayo Hebrew Congregation, Rhodesia, 1966; Minister, Giffnock Hebrew Congregation, Scotland, 1968–71; Headmaster, 1971–84, Principal, 1983–84, Carmel Coll; Minister, Western Synagogue, subseq. (following amalgamation in 1990 with Marble Arch Synagogue) Marble Arch Western Synagogue, 1985–93. Chief Rabbi's Rep. on Inter-Faith Affairs, 1987–91. Mem. Bd, Centre Européen Juif d'Information, Brussels, 1991–. Trustee, Yakar Educn Foundn, 1990–. *Address:* 20 Bryanston Mansions, York Street, W1H 1DA; 213 Mechelsesteenweg, Antwerp 2018, Belgium.

ROSEN, Prof. Michael, CBE 1990; FRCA; FRCOG; FRCS; Consultant Anaesthetist, South Glamorgan Health Authority, since 1961; Hon. Professor, University of Wales College of Medicine, 1986–93; President, College of Anaesthetists, 1988–91 (Dean of the Faculty of Anaesthetists, Royal College of Surgeons, 1988); *b* 17 Oct. 1927; *s* of Israel Rosen and Lily Hyman; *m* 1955, Sally Cohen; two *s* one *d*. *Educ:* Dundee High Sch. (Dux, 1944); St Andrews Univ. (MB ChB 1949). FRCA (FFARCS 1957); FRCOG 1989; FRCS 1994. House appts, Bolton, Portsmouth and Bradford, 1949–52; served RAMC, 1952–54; Registrar Anaesthetist, Royal Victoria Infirmary, Newcastle upon Tyne, 1954–57; Sen. Registrar, Cardiff, 1957–60; Fellow, Case Western Reserve Univ., Ohio, 1960–61. Member: GMC, 1989–; Clinical Standards Adv. Gp, 1991–94. Mem. Bd, College (formerly Faculty) of Anaesthetists, RCS, 1978–94; Pres., Assoc. of Anaesthetists of GB and Ire, 1986–88 (Mem. Council, 1972–91; formerly Sec. and Treasurer); Founder Academician, European Acad. of Anaesthesiol., 1972 (Treas., 1985–91); Chm., Obstetric Anaesthesia Cttee, World Fedn of Socs of Anaesthesia, 1980–88; Exec. Officer and Treas., World Fedn of Socs of Anesthesiologists, 1992–. Hon. Mem., French and Australian Socs of Anaesthetists; Hon. FFARCSI 1990; Hon. Fellow, Acad. of Medicine, Malaysia, 1989. Sir Ivan Magill Gold Medal, Assoc. of Anaesthetists, 1993. *Publications:* Percutaneous Cannulation of Great Veins, 1981, 2nd edn 1992; Obstetric Anaesthesia and Analgesia: safer practice, 1982; Patient-Controlled Analgesia,

1984; Tracheal Intubation, 1985; Awareness and Pain in General Anaesthesia, 1987; Ambulatory Anaesthesia, 1991. *Recreations:* family, reading, opera. *Address:* 45 Hollybush Road, Cardiff CF2 6SZ. *T:* and *Fax:* Cardiff (01222) 753893.

ROSEN, Murray Hilary; QC 1993; *b* 26 Aug. 1953; *s* of Joseph and Mercia Rosen; *m* 1975, Lesley Samuels; one *s* three *d*. *Educ:* St Paul's Sch.; Trinity Coll., Cambridge (MA). Called to the Bar, Inner Temple, 1976; Mem., Lincoln's Inn *ad eundem*. *Recreations:* music, cricket. *Address:* 11 Stone Buildings, Lincoln's Inn, WC2A 3TG. *T:* 0171–831 6318.

ROSENBERG, Michael Anthony; Provincial Stipendiary Magistrate for South Yorkshire, since 1993; *b* 6 March 1943; *s* of late Harry Rosenberg and of Gertrude Rosenberg (*née* Silver); *m* 1969, Gillian Anne Wolff; two *s*. *Educ:* Hymers Coll., Hull; Law Soc. Joined Myer Wolff & Co., Hull, 1961: articled clerk, 1963–68; qualified as solicitor, 1969; Asst Solicitor, 1970–73; Jt Sen. Partner, 1973–93. *Recreations:* sport, gardening, music. *Address:* The Old School House, Main Road, Scalby, Gilberdyke, E Yorks HU15 2UU. *T:* (Barnsley Magistrates' Court) Barnsley (01226) 243151.

ROSENBERG, Pierre Max; President and Director, Louvre Museum, Paris, since 1994; *b* Paris, 13 April 1936; *s* of Charles Rosenberg and Gertrude (*née* Nassauer); *m* 1981, Beatrice de Rothschild. *Educ:* Lycée Charlemagne, Paris; Law Faculty, Paris (Licencé); Louvre Sch., Paris (Dip.). Chief Curator, Dept of Paintings, Louvre Mus., 1982–94. Member: Hist. of French Art Soc. (Pres., 1982–84); French Hist. of Art Cttee (Pres., 1984). *Publications:* Chardin, 1963; Peyron, 1983; Fragonard, 1987; Frères Le Nain, 1993; Poussin, 1994; exhibn catalogues. *Address:* Musée du Louvre, 34 quai du Louvre, 75058 Paris, France; 35 rue de Vaugirard, 75006 Paris, France.

ROSENBERG, Richard Morris; Chairman and Chief Executive Officer, BankAmerica Corporation and Bank of America NT&SA, since 1990; *b* 21 April 1930; *s* of Charles Rosenberg and Betty (*née* Peck); *m* 1956, Barbara C. Cohen; two *s*. *Educ:* Suffolk Univ. (BS 1956); Golden Gate Univ. (MBA 1962; LLB 1966). Served from Ensign to Lieut, USNR, 1953–59. Publicity Assistant, Crocker-Anglo Bank, San Francisco, 1959–62; Wells Fargo Bank: Banking Services Officer, 1962–65; Asst Vice Pres., 1965–68; Vice Pres., Marketing Dept, 1968; Vice Pres., Dir of Marketing, 1969; Sen. Vice Pres., Marketing and Advertising Div., 1970–75; Exec. Vice Pres., 1975–80; Vice Chm., 1980–83; Vice Chm., Crocker Nat. Corp., 1983–85; Pres., Chief Op. Officer and Dir, Seafirst Corp., 1986–87; Pres. and Chief Op. Officer, Seattle-First Nat. Bank, 1985–87; Vice Chm., BankAmerica Corp., 1987–90. Director: Airborne Express; Northrop Corp.; Pacific Telesis Corp.; Potlatch Corp.; past Chm., Mastercard Internat. Member: Bd of Dirs, Marin Ecumenical Housing Assoc.; Board of Trustees: CIT; Univ. of S Calif. Mem., State Bar of Calif. Jewish. *Recreations:* tennis, avid reader, history. *Address:* BankAmerica Corporation, 555 California Street, 40th Floor, San Francisco, CA 94104, USA. *T:* (415) 9537963. *Clubs:* Rainier (Seattle); Hillcrest (Los Angeles).

ROSENBLUM, Prof. Robert; Professor of Fine Arts, New York University, USA, since 1967; *b* 24 July 1927; *m* 1977, Jane Kaplowitz; one *s* one *d*. *Educ:* Queens Coll., Flushing, NY (BA); Yale Univ. (MA); New York Univ. (PhD); Oxford Univ. (MA). Prof. of Art and Archaeology, Princeton Univ., USA, 1956–66; Slade Prof. of Fine Art, Oxford Univ., 1971–72. Fellow, Amer. Acad. of Arts and Scis, 1984. Frank Jewett Mather Award for Art Criticism, 1981. *Publications:* Cubism and Twentieth-Century Art, 1960; Transformations in Late Eighteenth Century Art, 1967; Jean-Auguste-Dominique Ingres, 1967; Frank Stella, 1971; Modern Painting and the Northern Romantic Tradition: Friedrich to Rothko, 1975; French Painting, 1774–1830 (exhibn catalogue), 1975; Andy Warhol: Portraits of the Seventies, 1979; (with H. W. Janson) Nineteenth Century Art, 1984; The Dog in Art from Rococo to Post-Modernism, 1988; The Romantic Child from Runge to Sendak, 1988; Paintings in the Musée d'Orsay, 1989; The Jeff Koons Handbook, 1992; (with H. Geldzahler) Andy Warhol Portraits, 1993; Mel Ramos: Pop images, 1994; The Paintings of August Strindberg; The Structure of Chaos, 1995; articles in learned jls: Art Bulletin; Burlington Magazine; Jl of the Warburg and Courtauld Institutes; La Revue de l'Art, etc. *Address:* Department of Fine Arts, New York University, New York, NY 10003, USA. *T:* (212) 9988180.

ROSENBROCK, Prof. Howard Harry, DSc, FEng; FRS 1976; FIEE, FIChemE; Professor of Control Engineering, 1966–87, now Emeritus, Vice-Principal, 1977–79, University of Manchester Institute of Science and Technology, (UMIST); Science Research Council Senior Fellow, 1979–83; *b* 16 Dec. 1920; *s* of Henry Frederick Rosenbrock and Harriett Emily (*née* Gleed); *m* 1950, Cathryn June (*née* Press); one *s* two *d*. *Educ:* Slough Grammar Sch.; University Coll. London. BSc, PhD; Fellow 1978. Served War, RAFVR, 1941–46. GEC, 1947–48; Electrical Research Assoc., 1949–51; John Brown & Co., 1951–54; Constructors John Brown Ltd, 1954–62 (latterly Research Manager); ADR, Cambridge Univ., 1962–66. Mem. Council, IEE, 1966–70, Vice-Pres., 1977–78; Pres., Inst. of Measurement and Control, 1972–73; Member: Computer Bd, 1972–76; SRC Engineering Bd, 1976–78; SERC/ESRC Jt Cttee, 1981–85. Hon. FInstMC. Hon. DSc Salford, 1987. *Publications:* (with C. Storey) Computational Techniques for Chemical Engineers, 1966; (with C. Storey) Mathematics of Dynamical Systems, 1970; State-space and Multivariable Theory, 1970; Computer-aided Control System Design, 1974; (ed) Designing Human-centred Technology, 1989; Machines with a Purpose, 1990; contribs Proc. IEE, Trans IChemE, Proc. IEEE, Automatica, Internat. Jl Control, etc. *Recreations:* microscopy, photography, 17th and 18th Century literature. *Address:* Linden, Walford Road, Ross-on-Wye, Herefordshire HR9 5PQ. *T:* Ross-on-Wye (01989) 565372.

ROSENFELD, Alfred John, CB 1981; Deputy Secretary, 1979–82, and Principal Finance Officer, 1976–82, Department of Transport; *b* 27 Feb. 1922; *s* of late Ernest Rosenfeld and late Annie Jeanette Rosenfeld (*née* Samson); *m* 1955, Mary Elisabeth (*née* Prudence); two *s* one *d*. *Educ:* Leyton County High Sch. Entered Public Trustee Office, 1938. Served War, Fleet Air Arm, 1942–46. Min. of Civil Aviation, 1947 (later, Min. of Transport, and Dept of Environment); Private Sec. to Jt Parliamentary Sec., 1958–59; Asst Sec., 1967; Under-Sec., 1972. Mem., Shoreham Port Authority, 1983–92 (Dep. Chm., 1984–89; Chm., 1990–92). *Recreations:* chess, bridge, gardening. *Address:* 33 Elmfield Road, Chingford, E4 7HT. *T:* 0181–529 8160.

ROSENTHAL, Jack Morris, CBE 1994; writer; *b* 8 Sept. 1931; *s* of Samuel and Leah Rosenthal; *m* 1973, Maureen Lipman, *qv*; one *s* one *d*. *Educ:* Colne Grammar School; Sheffield Univ. (BA Eng. Lit. and Lang). *Television:* writer of over 250 productions, incl. That Was the Week That Was, 1963; 150 episodes of Coronation Street, 1961–69; The Evacuees, 1975; Bar Mitzvah Boy, 1976; Ready When You Are, Mr McGill, 1976; Spend Spend Spend, 1977; The Knowledge, 1979; P'tang Yang Kipperbang, 1982; Mrs Capper's Birthday, 1985; London's Burning, 1986; Fools on the Hill, 1986; Day to Remember, 1986; And a Nightingale Sang, 1989; Bag Lady, 1989; Sleeping Sickness, 1991; 'Bye, 'Bye, Baby, 1992; Wide-Eyed and Legless, 1993; Moving Story, 1994; *stage:* five plays, incl. Smash!, 1981; *films:* six feature films including: Lucky Star, 1980; Yentl, 1983 (co-written with Barbra Streisand); The Chain, 1985. Hon. MA Salford, 1994; Hon. LittD Manchester, 1995. BAFTA Writer's Award, 1976; RTS Writer's Award, 1976. *Publications:* (contrib.) The Television Dramatist, 1973; (anthology) First Love, 1984; numerous TV plays. *Recreations:* work, frying fish, polishing almost anything tarnished, playing the violin in enforced privacy, checking Manchester United's score, minute by minute, on teletext. *Address:* c/o William Morris Agency, 31–32 Soho Square, W1V 5DG. *T:* 0171–434 2191. *Club:* Dramatists'.

ROSENTHAL, Maureen Diane, (Mrs J. M. Rosenthal); *see* Lipman, M. D.

ROSENTHAL, Norman Leon; Exhibitions Secretary, Royal Academy of Arts, since 1977; *b* 8 Nov. 1944; *s* of Paul Rosenthal and Kate Zucker; *m* 1989, Manuela Beatriz Mena Marques, *d* of Francisco Mena and Manuela Marques de Mena, Madrid; two *d*. *Educ:* Westminster City Grammar School; University of Leicester. BA Hons History. Librarian, Thomas Agnew & Sons, 1966–68; Exhibitions Officer, Brighton Museum and Art Gallery, 1970–71; Exhibition Organiser, ICA, 1974–76; organiser of many exhibns including: Art into Society, ICA, 1974; A New Spirit in Painting, RA, 1981; Zeitgeist, West Berlin, 1982; German Art of the Twentieth Century, Royal Acad., London and Staatsgalerie, Stuttgart, 1985–86; Italian Art of the Twentieth Century, RA, 1989; Metropolis, Berlin, 1991; American Art in the Twentieth Century, Martin-Gropius Bau, Berlin, and Royal Acad., 1993. TV and radio broadcasts on contemporary art. Hon. Fellow RCA, 1987. Chevalier, l'Ordre des Arts et des Lettres, 1987; Cavaliere Ufficiale, Order of Merit (Italy), 1992; Cross, Order of Merit (Germany), 1993. *Recreations:* music, especially opera. *Address:* The Royal Academy of Arts, Burlington House, Piccadilly, W1V 0DS. *T:* 0171–439 7438.

ROSENTHAL, Thomas Gabriel; publisher, critic and broadcaster; Chairman and Managing Director, André Deutsch Ltd (joined as Joint Chairman and Joint Managing Director, 1984); *b* 16 July 1935; *o s* of late Dr Erwin I. J. Rosenthal; *m* Ann Judith Warnford-Davis; two *s*. *Educ:* Perse Sch., Cambridge; Pembroke Coll., Cambridge (Exhibnr, MA). Served RA, 1954–56, 2nd Lieut; subseq. Lieut Cambridgeshire Regt (TA). Joined Thames and Hudson Ltd, 1959; Man. Dir, Thames & Hudson Internat., 1966; joined Martin Secker & Warburg Ltd as Man. Dir, 1971; Dir, Heinemann Gp of Publishers, 1972–84; Man. Dir, William Heinemann International Ltd, 1979–84; Chairman: World's Work Ltd, 1979–84; Heinemann Zsolnay Ltd, 1979–84; William Heinemann Ltd, 1980–84; Martin Secker & Warburg Ltd, 1980–84; Kaye & Ward Ltd, 1980–84; William Heinemann, Australia and SA, 1981–82; Frew McKenzie (Antiquarian Booksellers), 1985–93; Pres., Heinemann Inc., 1981–84. Art Critic of The Listener, 1963–66. Chm., Soc. of Young Publishers, 1961–62; Member: Cambridge Univ. Appts Bd, 1967–71; Exec. Cttee, NBL, 1971–74; Trans. Panel, Arts Council, 1988–94; Cttee of Management, Amateur Dramatic Club, Cambridge (also Trustee); Council, RCA, 1982–87; exec. Council, ICA, 1987–; Trustee, Phoenix Trust. Mem. Editl Bd, Logos, 1989–93. *Publications:* Monograph on Jack B. Yeats, 1964; (with Alan Bowness) Monograph on Ivon Hitchens, 1973; (with Ursula Hoff) Monograph on Arthur Boyd, 1986; A Reader's Guide to European Art History, 1962; A Reader's Guide to Modern American Fiction, 1963; The Art of Jack B. Yeats, 1993; introdns to paperback edns of Theodore Dreiser's The Financier, The Titan and Jennie Gerhardt; articles in The Times, Guardian, TLS, London Magazine, Encounter, New Statesman, Jl of Brit. Assoc. for Amer. Studies, Studio Internat., DNB, Bookseller, Nature, etc. *Recreations:* opera, bibliomania, looking at pictures, reading other publishers' books. *Address:* c/o André Deutsch Ltd, 106 Great Russell Street, WC1B 3LJ. *T:* 0171–580 2746, *Fax:* 0171–631 3253. *Clubs:* Garrick, MCC.

ROSEVEARE, Robert William, CBE 1977; Secretary, 1967–83, and Managing Director for administrative matters, 1971–83, British Steel Corporation; *b* Mandalay, Burma, 23 Aug. 1924; *s* of late William Leonard Roseveare, MC and of Marjory C. Roseveare; *m* 1954, Patricia Elizabeth, *d* of Guy L. Thompson, FRCS, Scarborough; one *s* three *d*. *Educ:* Gresham's Sch., Holt; St John's Coll., Cambridge. Served in Fleet Air Arm, 1943–46. Entered Home Civil Service, 1949. Asst Private Sec. to Minister of Fuel and Power, 1952–54; Cabinet Office, 1958–60; British Embassy, Washington, 1960–62; Asst Sec., Ministry of Power, 1964; seconded to Organising Cttee for British Steel Corporation, 1966; left Civil Service, 1971; Dir, BSC, 1969–71; Non-exec. Dir, Community Industry Ltd, 1983–91. Mem. Exec. Cttee, Hereford Diocesan Bd of Finance, 1986–. *Recreations:* hill-walking, bird-watching, singing. *Address:* Old Pasture, Hillfield Drive, Ledbury, Herefordshire HR8 1BH. *T:* Ledbury (01531) 632913.

ROSEWARN, John; Secretary, Royal Institution of Naval Architects, since 1989; *b* 14 Jan. 1940; *s* of Ernest and Frances Beatrice Rosewarn; *m* 1963, Josephine Rita Mullis; two *s*. *Educ:* Westminster City Sch. Royal Institution of Naval Architects, 1958–: Administrator, 1958–65; Chief Clerk, 1965–75; Asst Sec., 1975–84; Sen. Asst. Sec., 1984–89. Freeman, City of London, 1976. *Recreations:* sailing, DIY, reading. *Address:* c/o Royal Institution of Naval Architects, 10 Upper Belgrave Street, SW1X 8BQ. *T:* 0171–235 4622.

ROSIER, Air Chief Marshal Sir Frederick (Ernest), GCB 1972 (KCB 1966; CB 1961); CBE 1955 (OBE 1943); DSO 1942; RAF, retired; *b* 13 Oct. 1915; *s* of E. G. Rosier; *m* 1939, Hettie Denise Blackwell; three *s* one *d*. *Educ:* Grove Park School, Wrexham. Commissioned RAF, 1935; 43 (F) Sqdn, 1936–39. Served War of 1939–45 in France, UK, Western Desert and Europe. OC Horsham St Faith, 1947; exchange duties with USAF, 1948–50; Instructor at Jt Services Staff College, 1950–52; Gp Capt. Operations at Central Fighter Establishment, 1952–54; Gp Capt. Plans at Fighter Command, 1955–56; ADC to the Queen, 1956–58; idc 1957; Director of Joint Plans, Air Ministry, 1958; Chm. Joint Planning Staff, 1959–61; AOC Air Forces Middle East, 1961–63; Senior Air Staff Officer, HQ Transport Command, 1964–66; Air Officer C-in-C, RAF, Fighter Command, 1966–68; UK Mem., Permanent Military Deputies Group, Central Treaty Organisation, Ankara, 1968–70; Dep. C-in-C, Allied Forces Central Europe, 1970–73. Air ADC to the Queen, 1972–73. Mil. Advr and Dir, British Aircraft Corp. (Preston) Ltd, 1973–77; Director i/c BAC Ltd, Saudi Arabia, 1977–80. Commander: Order of Orange Nassau, 1947; Order of Polonia Restituta, 1985. *Address:* Ty Haul, Sun Bank, Llangollen, N Wales LL20 7UH. *T:* Llangollen (01978) 861068; Flat 286, Latymer Court, Hammersmith, W6 7LD. *T:* 0181–741 0765. *Club:* Royal Air Force.

ROSIER, Rt. Rev. Stanley Bruce, AM 1987; Rector of St Oswald's, Parkside, diocese of Adelaide, 1987–94, retired; *b* 18 Nov. 1928; *s* of S. C. and A. Rosier; *m* 1954, Faith Margaret Alice Norwood; one *s* three *d*. *Educ:* Univ. of WA; Christ Church, Oxford. Asst Curate, Ecclesall, Dio. of Sheffield, 1954; Rector of: Wyalkatchem, Dio. of Perth, 1957; Kellerberrin Dio. of Perth, 1964; Auxiliary Bishop in Diocese of Perth, Western Australia, 1967–70; Bishop of Willochra, 1970–87. *Recreation:* natural history. *Address:* 5A Fowlers Road, Glenunga, SA 5064, Australia. *T:* (8) 3795213.

ROSKELL, Prof. John Smith, MA, DPhil; FBA 1968; Professor of Medieval History, University of Manchester, 1962–79, now Professor Emeritus; *b* Norden, Rochdale, 2 July 1913; *s* of John Edmund and Lucy A. Roskell; *m* 1942, Evelyn Liddle (*d* 1989); one *s* one *d*. *Educ:* Rochdale Municipal Secondary School; Accrington Grammar Sch.; University of Manchester; Balliol College, Oxford. Asst Lecturer in History, Manchester University, 1938; Lecturer, 1945; Senior Lecturer, 1950–52; Professor of Medieval History, University of Nottingham, 1952–62. President: Lancashire Parish Register Soc., 1962–84; Chetham Soc., 1972–84; Feoffee, Chetham's Hosp. and Libr., Manchester, 1963–90. Royal Navy,

1940–45; Lieut RNVR, 1942–45. *Publications:* The Knights of the Shire of the County Palatine of Lancaster (1377–1460), Chetham Society, 1937; The Commons in the Parliament of 1422, 1954; The Commons and their Speakers in English Parliaments, 1376–1523, 1965; (ed with F. Taylor) Gesta Henrici Quinti, 1975; Parliament and Politics in Late Medieval England, (3 vols), 1981–83; The Impeachment of Michael de la Pole, Earl of Suffolk, in 1386, 1984; (ed jtly) History of Parliament, The House of Commons 1386–1421, 1993. *Address:* 42 Barcheston Road, Cheadle, Cheshire SK8 1LL. *T:* 0161–428 4630.

ROSKILL, family name of **Baron Roskill.**

ROSKILL, Baron *cr* 1980 (Life Peer), of Newtown in the County of Hampshire; **Eustace Wentworth Roskill;** Kt 1962; PC 1971; DL; a Lord of Appeal in Ordinary 1980–86; *b* 6 Feb. 1911; *y s* of late John Roskill, KC and of late Sybil Mary Wentworth, *d* of Ashton Wentworth Dilke, MP; *m* 1947, Elisabeth Wallace Jackson, 3rd *d* of late Thomas Frame Jackson, Buenos Aires; one *s* two *d. Educ:* Winchester College (exhibnr; Fellow, 1981–86); Exeter Coll., Oxford (exhibnr). 1st Cl. hons, Hon. Sch. of Mod. Hist. Oxford, BA 1932; MA 1936; Harmsworth Law Schol. Middle Temple, 1932; called to Bar, Middle Temple, 1933, Bencher 1961, Reader 1978, Dep. Treasurer 1979, Treasurer 1980; Hon. Bencher of The Inner Temple, 1980. Worked at Ministries of Shipping and War Transport, 1939–45. QC 1953. Dep. Chm. Hants QS, 1951–60, Chm. 1960–71; Comr of Assize (Birmingham), 1961; Judge of the High Court of Justice, Queen's Bench Division, 1962–71; a Lord Justice of Appeal, 1971–80. Vice-Chm., Parole Bd, 1967–69; Chm., Commn on Third London Airport, 1968–70. Pres., Senate of Four Inns of Court, 1972–74; Hon. Mem., 1974; Life Mem., Canadian Bar Assoc., 1974. Chairman: Average Adjusters Assoc., 1977–78; London Internat. Arbitration Trust, 1981–88; Fraud Trials Cttee, 1983–85; Take-over Panel Appeal Cttee, 1987–93. Chairman: Horris Hill Prep. Sch. Trust, 1957–64; Barristers' Benevolent Assoc., 1960–62. Hon. Fellow, Exeter College, Oxford, 1963. Hampshire: JP 1950; DL 1972. *Recreations:* music, swimming, gardening. *Address:* Heatherfield, Newtown, Newbury, Berks RG15 9DB. *T:* Newbury (01635) 40606; New Court, Temple, EC4Y 9BE. *T:* 0171–353 8870; House of Lords, SW1A 0PW. *Club:* Reform.

ROSLING, Derek Norman, CBE 1988; FCA; Vice-Chairman, Hanson PLC, 1973–93; *b* 21 Nov. 1930; *s* of Norman and Jean Rosling; *m* (marr. diss. 1982); two *s* one *d. Educ:* Shrewsbury Sch. ACA 1955, FCA 1962. Professional practice, 1956–65; Hanson PLC, 1965–94. FRSA 1990. *Recreations:* golf, sailing, theatre. *Address:* Little Salterns, Bucklers Hard, Beaulieu, Hants SO24 7XE. *T:* Bucklers Hard (01590) 616307. *Clubs:* Roehampton; Royal Southampton Yacht; Royal Channel Island Yacht (Guernsey); Brokenhurst Manor Golf.

ROSLING, Peter Edward, CMG 1987; LVO 1972; HM Diplomatic Service, retired; *b* 17 June 1929; *s* of Peregrine Starr and Jessie Rosling; *m* 1950, Kathleen Nuell; three *s. Educ:* grammar school. Served Royal Navy, 1948–50. HM Diplomatic Service, 1946; Belgrade, Innsbruck, Cape Town, Rome (NATO Defence College), FCO; Consul-Gen., Zagreb, 1980–83; High Comr, Lesotho, 1984–88. EC Monitor, EC Monitoring Mission, Croatia, 1991. Mem. Council, British Commonwealth Ex-Services League, 1988–. *Recreations:* walking, bridge. *Address:* Southernhay, Vaughan Way, Dorking, Surrey RH4 3DR. *Club:* Commonwealth Trust.

ROSOMAN, Leonard Henry, OBE 1981; RA 1969 (ARA 1960); FSA; Tutor, Royal College of Art, 1957–78; *b* 27 Oct. 1913; *s* of Henry Rosoman; *m* 1963, Jocelyn (marr. diss. 1969), *d* of Bertie Rickards, Melbourne, Australia. *Educ:* Deacons Sch., Peterborough; Durham Univ. Teacher of Drawing and Painting, Reimann Sch. of Art, London, 1938–39; Official War Artist to Admiralty, 1943–45; Teacher: Camberwell Sch. of Art, London, 1947–48; (Mural Painting) Edinburgh Coll. of Art, 1948–56; Chelsea School of Art, 1956–57. One Man Shows: St George's Gallery, London, 1946 and 1949; Roland, Browse and Delbanco Gallery, London, 1954, 1957, 1959, 1965 and 1969; Fine Art Soc., 1974, 1978, 1983, 1990. Works bought by: HM Govt, Arts Council, British Council, York Art Gall., Contemporary Art Soc., Adelaide Art Gallery, V&A Museum, Lincoln Center, NY. Executed large mural paintings for: Festival of Britain, 1951; British Pavilion, Brussels World Fair, 1958; Harewood House, 1959; Lambeth Palace Chapel, 1988, 1992. Hon. ARCA; HRSW. *Recreation:* travelling as much as possible. *Address:* 7 Pembroke Studios, Pembroke Gardens, W8 6HX. *T:* 0171–603 3638. *Club:* Arts.

ROSPIGLIOSI, family name of **Earl of Newburgh.**

ROSS, Rt. Hon. Lord; Rt. Hon. Lord Justice-Clerk; Donald MacArthur Ross, PC 1985; a Senator of the College of Justice, Scotland, and Lord of Session, since 1977; Lord Justice-Clerk and President of the Second Division of the Court of Session, since 1985; Lord High Commissioner, General Assembly, Church of Scotland, 1990 and 1991; *b* 29 March 1927; *s* of late John Ross, solicitor, Dundee; *m* 1958, Dorothy Margaret, *d* of late William Annand, Kirriemuir; two *d. Educ:* Dundee High School; Edinburgh University. MA (Edinburgh) 1947; LLB with distinction (Edinburgh) 1951. National Service with The Black Watch (RHR), 2nd Lt, 1947–49. Territorial Service, 1949–58, Captain. Advocate, 1952; QC (Scotland) 1964; Vice-Dean, Faculty of Advocates of Scotland, 1967–73; Dean, 1973–76; Sheriff Principal of Ayr and Bute, 1972–73. Dep. Chm., Boundary Commn for Scotland, 1977–85. Member: Scottish Cttee of Council on Tribunals, 1970–76; Cttee on Privacy, 1970. Mem. Court, Heriot-Watt Univ., 1978– (Chm., 1984–90). FRSE 1988. Hon. LLD: Edinburgh, 1987; Dundee, 1991; Abertay Dundee, 1994. DUniv Heriot-Watt, 1988. *Recreations:* gardening, walking. *Address:* 33 Lauder Road, Edinburgh EH9 2JG. *T:* 0131–667 5731. *Club:* New (Edinburgh).

ROSS, Alan, CBE 1982; author, publisher and journalist; Editor of London Magazine; Managing Director, London Magazine Editions (Publishers), since 1965; *b* Calcutta, 6 May 1922; *o s* of John Brackenridge Ross, CBE and Clare, *d* of Captain Patrick Fitzpatrick, Indian Army, *m* 1949, Jennifer, *d* of Sir Geoffrey Fry, 1st and last Bt, KCB, CVO; one *s. Educ:* Haileybury; St John's College, Oxford. RN 1942–47; general service, Arctic and North Seas, 1942–44; Asst Staff Officer, Intelligence, 16th Destroyer Flotilla, 1944; on staff of Flag Officer, Western Germany, 1945, and Interpreter to British Naval Commander-in-Chief, Germany, 1946. British Council, 1947–50; on staff of The Observer 1950–71. Toured Australia as correspondent, with MCC, 1954–55, 1962–63; toured South Africa, 1956–57, 1964–65; toured West Indies, 1960, 1968. Atlantic Award for Literature (Rockefeller Foundation), 1946. FRSL 1971. *Publications:* The Derelict Day, 1947; Time Was Away, 1948, repr. 1989; The Forties, 1950; The Gulf of Pleasure, 1951; The Bandit on the Billiard Table, 1954 (revised edition South to Sardinia, 1960), repr. 1989; Something of the Sea, 1954; Australia 55, 1956, repr. 1985; Abroad (ed), 1957; Cape Summer and the Australians in England, 1957, repr. 1986; To Whom It May Concern, 1958; The Onion Man, 1959; Through the Caribbean, 1960; The Cricketer's Companion (ed), 1960; Danger on Glass Island, 1960; African Negatives, 1962; Australia 63, 1963; West Indies at Lord's, 1963, 2nd edn 1986; North from Sicily, 1965; Poems 1942–67, 1968; Tropical Ice, 1972; The Taj Express, 1973; (ed) London Magazine Stories 1–11, 1964–80; (ed) Living in London, 1974; Open Sea, 1975; (ed) Selected Poems of Lawrence Durrell, 1977; Death Valley and Other Poems, 1980; (ed) The Turf, 1982; Colours of War, 1983; Ranji, 1983; (ed) Living out of London, 1984; Blindfold Games (autobiog.), 1986; (ed) London Magazine 1961–85, 1986; The Emissary, 1986; Coastwise Lights (autobiog.), 1988; After Pusan, 1995; several trans and introductions; contrib. to various jls in England and America. *Recreations:* travel, sport (played cricket and squash for Oxford University and Royal Navy), racing. *Address:* 4 Elm Park Lane, SW3 6DB. *Clubs:* MCC; Vincent's (Oxford).

ROSS, Rev. Dr Andrew Christian; Senior Lecturer in Ecclesiastical History, University of Edinburgh, since 1966; Principal of New College and Dean of the Faculty of Divinity, 1978–84; *b* 10 May 1931; *s* of George Adams Ross and Christian Glen Walton; *m* 1953, Isabella Joyce Elder; four *s* (one *d* decd). *Educ:* Dalkeith High Sch.; Univ. of Edinburgh (MA, BD, PhD); Union Theol Seminary, New York (STM). Served Royal Air Force, Pilot Officer, then FO, 1952–54. Ordained Minister of Church of Scotland, 1958; Minister, Church of Central Africa Presbyterian (Malâwi), 1958–65; Chm., Lands Tribunal of Nyasaland, then Malâwi Govt, 1963–65; Vice-Chm., Nat. Tenders Bd of Nyasaland, then Malâwi, 1963–65. Sen. Studentship in African History, Univ. of Edinburgh, 1965–66; Mem. Court of Univ. of Edinburgh, 1971–73, Chm. Student Affairs Cttee of the Court, 1977–83. Kerr Lectr, Glasgow Univ., 1984; Coll. Lectr, Assembly's Coll., Belfast, 1985. Visiting Professor: Univ. of Witwatersrand, 1984; Dartmouth Coll., USA, 1992; Res. Fellow, Yale Univ., 1994. *Publications:* chapter in: The Zambesian Past, 1965; Religion in Africa, 1965; Witchcraft and Healing, 1969; David Livingstone and Africa, 1973; Malâwi, Past and Present, 1974; introd. and ed for micro film-prodn: Life and Work in Central Africa 1885–1914, 1969; The Records of the UMCA 1859–1914, 1971; John Philip: missions, race and politics in South Africa, 1986; A Vision Betrayed: the Jesuits in Japan and China 1542–1742, 1994; contribs to Union Qly Rev., New Left Rev., Scottish Historical Rev. *Recreation:* watching soccer. *Address:* 27 Colinton Road, Edinburgh EH10 5DR. *T:* 0131–447 5987. *Club:* University of Edinburgh Staff.

ROSS, Sir Archibald (David Manisty), KCMG 1961 (CMG 1953); HM Diplomatic Service, retired; *b* 12 Oct. 1911; *s* of late J. A. Ross, Indian Civil Service, and Dorothea, *e d* of late G. Eldon Manisty, Indian Civil Service; *m* 1939, Mary Melville, *d* of Melville Macfadyen; one *s* one *d* (and one *s* decd). *Educ:* Winchester; New College, Oxford (MA). 1st Class Hon. Mods 1932, Lit. Hum. 1934; Gaisford Greek Verse Prize, 1932; Laming Travelling Fellow, Queen's College, 1934–35. Diplomatic Service, 1936; Berlin, 1939, Stockholm, 1939–44; Foreign Office, 1944–47, Tehran, 1947–50; Counsellor, Foreign Office, 1950–53; HM Minister, Rome, 1953–56; Assistant Under Secretary of State for Foreign Affairs, 1956–60; Ambassador to Portugal, 1961–66; Ambassador to Sweden, 1966–71. Chairman: Alfa-Laval Co., 1972–82; Saab (GB), 1972–82; Scania (GB), 1972–82; Ericsson Information Systems, 1981–86. Mem. Council, RASE, 1980–85. Grand Cross, Order of the North Star, Sweden, 1981. *Address:* 17 Ennismore Gardens, SW7 1AA. *Clubs:* Travellers'; Leander.

ROSS, (Claud) Richard, CB 1973; Hon. Vice-President, European Investment Bank, since 1989 (Vice-President, and Vice-Chairman Board of Directors, 1978–89); *b* 24 March 1924; *o s* of late Claud Frederick Ross and Frances Muriel Ross, Steyning, Sussex; *m* 1954, Leslie Beatrice, *d* of late Oliver Arnell and Dr H. M. Arnell, Kitale, Kenya; two *d. Educ:* Ardingly Coll.; Hertford Coll., Oxford (Open Schol., Mod. Hist.). 1st cl. PPE, 1950; MA. Fellow of Hertford Coll., 1951–63; Lectr in Economics, Oxford Univ., 1951–52 and 1955–63; Economic Advr to HM Treasury, 1952–55; Junior Proctor, Oxford Univ., 1958–59; Bursar, Hertford Coll., 1959–63; Prof. of Economics and Dean, School of Social Studies, Univ. of East Anglia, 1963–68 (Pro-Vice-Chancellor, 1964–68); Special Consultant, OECD, Paris, 1968–71; Dep. Sec., Central Policy Review Staff, Cabinet Office, 1971–78. Adviser, Bankers' Mission to India and Pakistan, 1960; Represented HM Treasury on OECD Working Party on Policies for Economic Growth, 1961–68; Leader, British Economic Mission to Tanzania, 1965; Member: East Anglia Regional Economic Planning Council, 1966–69 (Dep. Chm., 1967–69); Jt Mission for Malta, 1967. Chm., Population Panel, 1972–73. *Publications:* Financial and Physical Problems of Development in the Gold Coast (with D. Seers), 1952; articles on economics. *Address:* 2a Oliver's Wharf, 64 Wapping High Street, E1 9PJ.

ROSS, Donald MacArthur; *see* Ross, Hon. Lord.

ROSS, Donald Nixon, FRCS; Consultant Cardiac Surgeon, National Heart Hospital and Guy's Hospital, 1963–94, now Emeritus; *b* 4 Oct. 1922; *m* 1956, Dorothy Curtis; one *d. Educ:* Boys' High Sch., Kimberley, S Africa; Univ. of Capetown (BSc, MB, ChB 1st Cl. Hons, 1946). FRCS 1949; FACC 1973; FACS 1976. Sen. Registrar in Thoracic Surgery, Bristol, 1952; Guy's Hospital: Res. Fellow, 1953; Sen. Thoracic Registrar, 1954; Cons. Thoracic Surg., 1958; Cons. Surg., National Heart Hosp., 1963, Sen. Surg., 1967; Dir, Dept of Surgery, Inst. of Cardiology, 1970. Hon. FRCSI 1984; Hon. FRCS Thailand, 1987. Hon. DSc CNAA, 1982. Clement Price Thomas Award, RCS, 1983. Order of Cedar of Lebanon, 1975; Order of Merit (1st cl.) (West Germany), 1981; Royal Order (Thailand), 1994. *Publications:* A Surgeon's Guide to Cardiac Diagnosis, 1962; (jtly) Medical and Surgical Cardiology, 1968; (jtly) Biological Tissue in Heart Valve Replacement, 1972; contrib. BMJ, Lancet, Proc. RSM, Annals Royal Coll. Surg., Amer. Jl Cardiol. *Recreations:* Arabian horse breeding, horseriding, gardening. *Address:* 35 Cumberland Terrace, Regent's Park, NW1 4HP. *T:* 0171–935 8805. *Clubs:* Garrick; Kimberley (SA).

ROSS, Duncan Alexander, CBE 1993; CEng, FIEE; Chairman, Southern Electric plc (formerly Southern Electricity Board), 1984–93, retired; *b* 25 Sept. 1928; *s* of William Duncan Ross and Mary Ross; *m* 1958, Mary Buchanan Clarke Parsons; one *s* one *d. Educ:* Dingwall Academy; Glasgow Univ. (BSc Elec. Engrg). CBIM. Various engineering posts, South of Scotland Electricity Board, 1952–57; engineering, commercial and management posts, Midlands Electricity Board, 1957–72; Area Manager, South Staffs Area, 1972–75, Chief Engineer, 1975–77; Dep. Chm., 1977–81, Chm., 1981–84, South Wales Electricity Bd. Mem., Electricity Council, 1981–90. *Recreations:* golf, ski-ing. *Address:* Winterfold, Dovers Orchard, Hoo Lane, Chipping Campden, Glos GL55 6AZ. *T:* and *Fax:* Chipping Camden (01386) 841797.

ROSS, Ernest; MP (Lab) Dundee West, since 1979; *b* Dundee, July 1942; *m*; two *s* one *d. Educ:* St John's Jun. Secondary Sch. Quality Control Engineer, Timex Ltd. Mem., MSF (formerly AUEW (TASS)). *Address:* House of Commons, SW1A 0AA.

ROSS, Prof. Graham Garland, PhD; FRS 1991; Professor of Theoretical Physics, Oxford University, since 1992; Fellow of Wadham College, Oxford, since 1983. *Educ:* Aberdeen Univ. (BSc); Durham Univ. (PhD); MA Oxon. Rutherford Atlas Res. Fellow, Pembroke Coll., Oxford, 1981–83; Lectr, 1983–90, Reader and SERC Sen. Res. Fellow in Theoretical Physics, 1990–92, Oxford Univ. *Address:* Department of Physics, 1 Keble Road, Oxford OX1 3NP. *T:* Oxford (01865) 273990; Woodcock Cottage, Lincombe Lane, Boars Hill, Oxford OX1 5DX.

ROSS, His Honour James; QC 1966; a Senior Circuit Judge, 1985–87 (a Circuit Judge (formerly a Judge of County Courts), 1971–87); *b* 22 March 1913; *s* of John Stuart Ross, FRCSE; *m* 1939, Clare Margaret (*d* 1993), *d* of Alderman Robert Cort-Cox, Stratford-on-Avon; one *d. Educ:* Glenalmond; Exeter Coll., Oxford. BA Oxon 1934. Admitted Solicitor, 1938; called to Bar, Gray's Inn, 1945. Legal Member, Mental Health Review Tribunal, Birmingham Region, 1962; Deputy Chairman, Agricultural Land Tribunal, East Midland Area, 1963; Dep. Chm. QS, Parts of Lindsey, 1968–71; Recorder of Coventry, 1968–71; Mem., Parole Bd, 1974–76. Hon. Recorder: Coventry, 1978–85; City of Birmingham, 1985–87. *Club:* Bar Yacht.

ROSS, James Alexander, MBE (mil.) 1944; MD, FRCSEd, FRCSGlas; Professor of Anatomy, King Saud University, Riyadh, 1983–84, retired; *b* 25 June 1911; *s* of James McMath Ross and Bessie Hopper Flint; *m* 1940, Catherine Elizabeth (*d* 1988), *d* of Clark Booth Curtis; one *s* one *d* (and two *d* decd). *Educ:* Merchiston Castle Sch.; Edinburgh Univ. MB ChB Ed 1934, MD Ed 1947; FRCSEd 1938, FRCSGlas 1965. Served War: RAMC, 1939–45: France, ME, Europe; then Lt-Col RAMC, RARO, 1953–55. Surgeon, Leith Hosp., 1946–61, and Royal Infirmary, Edinburgh, 1947–61; Surgeon, Eastern Gen. Hosp., 1961–76 and Edenhall Hosp., 1970–76. Hon. Sec., Royal Coll. of Surgeons of Edinburgh, 1960–68; Vice-Pres., 1971–73; Pres., RCSEd, 1973–76; Pres., Edinburgh Harveian Soc., 1977–78; Vice-Pres., Internat. Fedn of Surgical Colls, 1975–81. Hon. Cons. Surgeon to Army in Scotland, 1970–76. Lectures: McCombe, RCSE, 1977; Mason Brown Meml, RCSE, 1978; Hutchinson, Edinburgh Univ., 1979; Mitchiner Meml, RAMC, 1979; Douglas Guthrie Hist. of Medicine, RCSE, 1983. Hon. FRCSI, 1976; Hon. FRACS, 1977; Hon. FDSRCSE, 1983; Hon. Fellow: Pakistan Coll., P and S, 1976; Sri Lanka Coll. of Surgeons, 1976; Hong Kong Surgical Soc., 1976. Governor, Merchiston Castle Sch., 1964–76. Guthrie Medallist, RAMC, 1976; Farquharson Award (teaching of anatomy and surgery), RCSE, 1986. *Publications:* Memoirs of an Army Surgeon, 1948; (jtly) Manual of Surgical Anatomy, 1964; (jtly) Behaviour of the Human Ureter, in Health and Disease, 1972; The Edinburgh School of Surgery after Lister, 1978; Memoirs of an Edinburgh Surgeon, 1988. *Recreations:* walking, swimming, watching cricket. *Address:* Cluny Lodge, 10–16 Cluny Drive, Edinburgh EH10 6DP.

ROSS, Sir (James) Keith, 2nd Bt *cr* 1960; RD 1967; MS, FRCS; FRCSE; Consultant Emeritus, Southampton and Southwest Hampshire Health Authority, 1990; *b* 9 May 1927; *s* of Sir James Paterson Ross, 1st Bt, KCVO, FRCS, and Marjorie Burton Townsend (*d* 1978); *S* father, 1980; *m* 1956, Jacqueline Annella Clarke; one *s* three *d. Educ:* St Paul's School; Middlesex Hospital. MB BS 1950; MS 1965; FRCS 1956; FRCSE 1989. House Surgeon, Registrar, Sen. Registrar, Middlesex Hosp., 1950–67. Surgn Lieut, RNVR, 1952–54; Surg. Lt Comdr, RNR, retd 1972. Heller Fellowship, San Francisco, 1959; Registrar, Brompton Hosp., 1958, 1960. Consultant Thoracic Surgeon, Harefield and Central Middx Hosps, 1964–67; Consultant Surgeon, Nat. Heart Hosp., 1967–72; Consultant Cardiac Surgeon: Wessex Region, 1972–90; King Edward VII Hosp., Midhurst, 1978–92. Hunterian Prof., 1961, Mem. Council, 1986–94, RCS; Pres., Soc. of Cardiothoracic Surgeons, 1988. Hallet Prize, RCS, 1952; Bruce Medal, RCSE, 1989. *Publications:* on cardiac surgery in appropriate medical jls. *Recreations:* fly fishing, golf, painting. *Heir: s* Andrew Charles Paterson Ross, *b* 18 June 1966. *Address:* Moonhills Gate, Exbury Road, Beaulieu, Brockenhurst, Hants SO42 7YS. *T:* Beaulieu (01590) 612104. *Clubs:* Army and Navy, MCC; Royal Lymington Yacht.

ROSS, John Alexander, CBE 1993; FRAgS; President, National Farmers' Union of Scotland, since 1990; *b* 19 Feb. 1945; *m* 1967, Alison Jean Darling; two *s* one *d. Educ:* Mahaar Primary Sch., Stranraer; George Watson's Coll., Edinburgh. FRAgS 1993. National Farmers' Union of Scotland: Convener, Hill Farming Sub-cttee, 1984–90; Wigtown Area Pres., 1985–86; Convener, Livestock Cttee, 1987–90; Vice-Pres., 1986–90. Dir, Animal Diseases Res. Assoc., 1986–. Chm., Stranraer Sch. Council, 1980–89. Session Clerk, Portpatrick Parish Church, 1975–80; Elder, C of S. *Recreations:* golf, curling. *Address:* National Farmers' Union of Scotland, Rural Centre – West Mains, Ingliston, Newbridge, Midlothian EH28 8LT. *T:* 0131–335 3111. *Club:* Farmers'.

ROSS, Kenneth Alexander; Partner, Gillespie, Gifford & Brown (formerly M'Gowans), solicitors, Dumfries, since 1975; President, Law Society of Scotland, 1994–95 (Vice-President, 1993–94); *b* 21 April 1949; *s* of Alexander Cree Ross and Mary Hamilton Ross (*née* M'Lauchlan); *m* 1972, Morag Laidlaw; one *s* one *d. Educ:* Hutcheson's GS, Glasgow; Edinburgh Univ. (LLB (Hons) 1971). Pres., Edinburgh Univ. Union, 1970–71. Temp. Sheriff, 1987–. Mem. Council, Law Soc. of Scotland, 1987–. Contested (C): Kilmarnock, Feb. 1974; Galloway, Oct. 1974. *Recreations:* gardening, golf, ski-ing. *Address:* Dalton Burn, Lockerbie DG11 1DT. *T:* Carrutherstown (01387) 84243.

ROSS, Leonard Q.; *see* Rosten, L. C.

ROSS, Rear-Adm. Maurice James, CB 1962; DSC 1940; retired; *b* 31 Oct. 1908; *s* of Basil James Ross and Avis Mary (*née* Wilkinson); *m* 1946, Helen Matheson McCall; one *d. Educ:* Charterhouse. Entered Royal Navy, 1927; specialised in gunnery, 1935; Comdr, 1943; Captain, 1951; Rear-Adm., 1960. Master, Gardeners' Company, 1983. *Publications:* Ross in the Antarctic 1839–1843, 1982; Polar Pioneers: John Ross and James Clark Ross, 1994; Chippenham: an East Anglian estate village, 1995. *Address:* The School House, Chippenham, Ely, Cambs CB7 5PP. *Club:* Army and Navy.

ROSS, Michael David, FFA; Group Chief Executive, Scottish Widows' Fund and Life Assurance Society, since 1991; *b* 9 July 1946; *s* of Patrick James Forrest Ross and Emily Janet (*née* Forsyth); *m* 1973, Pamela Marquis Speakman. *Educ:* Daniel Stewart's Coll., Edinburgh. FFA 1969. Joined Scottish Widows', 1964, as Trainee Actuary; Asst Gen. Manager, 1986–88; Actuary, 1988; Gen. Manager, 1988–90; Dep. Man. Dir, 1990–91. CIMgt (CBIM 1991). *Publications:* contrib. Trans. Faculty of Actuaries. *Recreations:* golf, curling, ski-ing, gardening. *Address:* (office) 15 Dalkeith Road, Edinburgh EH16 5BU. *T:* 0131–655 6000. *Clubs:* Caledonian; Lothianburn Golf.

ROSS, Mrs Nicholas; *see* Phillpotts, M. Adelaide Eden.

ROSS, Nicholas David, (Nick Ross); broadcaster and journalist; *b* 7 Aug. 1947; *s* of late John Caryl Ross and of Joy Dorothy Ross; *m* 1985, Sarah Caplin; three *s. Educ:* Wallington County Grammar Sch.; Queen's Univ., Belfast (BA Hons Psychol). Broadcaster, BBC N Ireland, 1971–72; Radio 4: reporter, Today, World at One, 1972–75; presenter, The World Tonight, Newsdesk, 1972–74, World at One, 1982, Call Nick Ross, 1987–, Gulf News 1991; producer and dir, TV documentaries, 1979–81; presenter, BBC TV: Man Alive, Man Alive Debates, Out of Court, 1975–82; Breakfast Time, Fair Comment, Star Memories, 60 Minutes, 1982–85, Watchdog, 1985–86; Crimewatch UK, 1984–, Westminster with Nick Ross, 1994–; indep. TV incl. A Week in Politics, Ch 4, 1986–88. Member: Cttee on the Ethics of Gene Therapy, DoH, 1991–93; Gene Therapy Adv. Cttee, DoH, 1993–; Wider Working Gp on Health of the Nation, DoH, 1992–; Nat. Bd for Crime Prevention, 1993–; Victim Support Adv. Bd, 1991–; Crime Concern Adv. Bd, 1991–; COPUS, 1991– (Chm., Sci. Book Prize, 1993); President: SANE, 1990–; Healthwatch, 1990–; Vice-Pres., Patients' Assoc., 1991–; Vice-Chm., Nat. Road Safety Campaign, RoSPA, 1990–93. *Recreations:* ski-ing, scuba diving. *Address:* BBC, Broadcasting House, W1A 1AA. *T:* 0171–765 4721, *Fax:* 0171–792 9200.

ROSS, Richard; Professor of Film (formerly of Film and Television), Royal College of Art, since 1980; *b* 22 Dec. 1935; *s* of Lawrence Sebley Ross and Muriel Ross; *m* 1957, Phyllis Ellen Hamilton; one *s* one *d. Educ:* Westland High School, Hokitika, NZ; Canterbury University College, NZ. Exchange Telegraph, 1958–60; Visnews Ltd, 1960–65; BBC TV News, 1965–80. Consultant: Univ. Sains, Penang, Malaysia, 1984–; Calouste Gulbenkian Foundn, Lisbon, 1983–85. Chm., Educn Cttee, British Film Year, 1985–86. Consultant Dir, Film Educn, 1986–; Dir, Nat. Youth Film Foundn, 1988–. Fellow in Fine Arts, Trent Polytechnic, 1970–72. Fellow, RCA, 1981. *Recreations:* walking in London, eating in France, talking and drinking anywhere. *Address:* Royal College of Art, Kensington Gore, SW7 2EU; 51 Hanbury Street, E1 5JP.

ROSS, Richard; *see* Ross, C. R.

ROSS, Robert, MA, FLS; Keeper of Botany, British Museum (Natural History), 1966–77; *b* 14 Aug. 1912; *e s* of Robert Ross, Pinner, Middx; *m* 1939, Margaret Helen Steadman; one *s* three *d. Educ:* St Paul's Sch.; St John's Coll., Cambridge. Asst Keeper, British Museum (Natural History), 1936; Principal Scientific Officer, 1950; Deputy Keeper, 1962. Royal Microscopical Society: Hon. Librarian, 1947–51; Hon. Editor, 1953–71; Vice-Pres., 1959–60. Administrator of Finances, Internat. Assoc. of Plant Taxonomy, 1964–69; Sec., Gen. Cttee for Plant Nomenclature, 1964–69, Chm., 1969–81. President: British Phycological Soc., 1969–71; Quekett Microscopical Club, 1974–76; Pres., Internat. Soc. for Diatom Res., 1994– (Vice-Pres., 1992–94). *Publications:* various papers in scientific jls on botanical subjects. *Recreations:* morris dancing (Bagman, Morris Ring, 1946–50), country dancing, gardening. *Address:* The Garden House, Evesbatch, Bishop's Frome, Worcester WR6 5BD. *T:* Bosbury (01531) 640366.

See also A. F. Stevens.

ROSS, Lt-Gen. Sir Robert (Jeremy), KCB 1994 (CB 1992); OBE 1978; Commandant General Royal Marines, 1993–95; *b* 28 Nov. 1939; *s* of Gerald and Margaret Ross; *m* 1965, Sara (*née* Curtis); one *s* one *d. Educ:* Wellington Coll.; Corpus Christi Coll., Cambridge (MPhil). Entered RM, 1957; Commando and Sea Service, 1959–69; Army Staff Coll., 1970; Commando Service, 1971–78; Instr, Army Staff Coll., 1978–79; CO 40 Commando RM, 1979–81; RCDS 1982; MoD, 1984–86; Comdr 3 Commando Bde, 1986–88; Maj.-Gen. RM Trng, Reserve and Special Forces, 1988–90; Maj.-Gen. RM Commando Forces, 1990–93. Officer, Legion of Merit (USA), 1993. *Recreations:* shooting, fishing, walking. *Address:* c/o Barclays Bank, 50 Jewry Street, Winchester, Hampshire SO23 8RG. *Club:* Royal Thames Yacht.

ROSS, Sophie, (Mrs R. P. Ross); *see* Mirman, S.

ROSS, Tessa Sarah; Independents Commissioning Executive, BBC TV, since 1993; *b* 26 July 1961; *d* of E. Leonard Ross and Sharon F. Ross (*née* Kingsley), MBE; *m* 1987, Mark Scantlebury; one *s* one *d. Educ:* Somerville Coll., Oxford (BA Hons, MA Oriental Studies (Chinese)). Literary Agent, Anthony Shiel Associates, 1986–88; Script Editor, BBC Scotland, 1988–89; Hd of Develt, British Screen Finance, 1990–93. *Address:* BBC TV Centre, Wood Lane, W12. *T:* 0181–576 8536; (home) 0171–482 5830. *Club:* Groucho.

ROSS, Timothy David M.; *see* Melville-Ross.

ROSS, Victor; Chairman, Reader's Digest Association Ltd, 1978–84; *b* 1 Oct. 1919; *s* of Valentin and Eva Rosenfeld; *m* 1st, 1944, Romola Wallace; two *s*; 2nd, 1970, Hildegard Peiser. *Educ:* schs in Austria, Germany and France; London Sch. of Economics. Served in Army, 1942–45. Journalist and writer, 1945–55; joined Reader's Digest, 1955; Man. Dir and Chief Exec., 1972–81. Dir, Folio Soc., 1985–89. Pres., Assoc. of Mail Order Publishers, 1979–80, 1983–84; Mem., Data Protection Tribunal, 1985–. Mackintosh Medal for Advertising, Advertising Assoc., 1989. *Publications:* A Stranger in my Midst, 1948; Tightrope, 1952; Basic British, 1956. *Recreations:* collecting books, fishing. *Address:* Worten Mill, Great Chart, Kent TN23 3BS.

ROSS, Lt-Col Walter Hugh Malcolm, CVO 1994; OBE 1988; Comptroller, Lord Chamberlain's Office, since 1991 (Assistant Comptroller, 1987–91); *b* 27 Oct. 1943; *s* of Col Walter John Macdonald Ross, CB, OBE, MC, TD and Josephine May (*née* Cross); *m* 1969, Susie, *d* of Gen. Sir Michael Gow, *qv*; one *s* two *d. Educ:* Eton Coll.; Royal Military Acad., Sandhurst. Served in Scots Guards, 1964–87; Management Auditor, The Royal Household, 1987–89. Sec., Central Chancery of the Orders of Knighthood, 1989–91. An Extra Equerry to the Queen, 1988–. Mem., Queen's Body Guard for Scotland, Royal Company of Archers, 1981–. Freeman, City of London, 1994. *Address:* Netherhall, Bridge-of-Dee, Castle-Douglas, Kirkcudbrightshire DG7 2AA. *Clubs:* Pratt's; New (Edinburgh).

ROSS, William; MP (UU) Londonderry East, since 1983 (Londonderry, Feb. 1974–1983), resigned seat Dec. 1985 in protest against Anglo-Irish Agreement; re-elected Jan. 1986; *b* 4 Feb. 1936; *m* 1974, Christine; three *s* one *d. Recreations:* fishing, shooting. *Address:* Hillquarter, Turmeel, Dungiven, Northern Ireland BT47 4SL. *T:* Dungiven (05047) 41428. *Club:* Northern Counties (Londonderry).

ROSS, William Mackie, CBE 1987; TD 1969; DL; MD; FRCS; FRCSE; FRCR; retired; Consultant Radiotherapist, Northern Regional Health Authority, 1953–87; Lecturer in Radiotherapy, University of Newcastle upon Tyne, 1973–87; *b* 14 Dec. 1922; *s* of Harry Caithness Ross and Catherine Ross; *m* 1948, Mary Burt; one *s* two *d. Educ:* Durham and Newcastle. MB, BS 1945, MD 1953; FRCS 1956, FRCR 1960. Trainee in Radiotherapy, 1945–51; National Service, 1951–53; RAMC TA, 1953–72; Col, CO 201 Gen. Hosp., 1967–72, Hon. Col, 1977–82. President: Section of Radiology, RSM, 1978; British Inst. of Radiology, 1979; North of England Surgical Soc., 1983; Royal Coll. of Radiologists, 1983–86. Hon. FACR, 1986. DL Northumberland, 1971–74, Tyne and Wear, 1974. *Publications:* articles on cancer, its causation and treatment. *Address:* 62 Archery Rise, Durham City DH1 4LA. *T:* Durham (0191) 3869256.

ROSS GOOBEY, Alastair; Chief Executive, Hermes Pensions Management Ltd, since 1993; *b* 6 Dec. 1945; *s* of George Henry Ross Goobey and Gladys Edith (*née* Menzies); *m* 1969, Sarah Georgina Mary Stille; one *s* one *d. Educ:* Marlborough Coll.; Trinity Coll., Cambridge (BA Hons Econs). With Kleinwort Benson, 1968–72; Hume Holdings Ltd, 1972–77; Investment Manager, Pension Fund, Courtaulds Ltd, 1977–81; Dir, Geoffrey Morley & Partners Ltd, 1981–85; Special Advr to Chancellor of Exchequer, HM Treasury, 1986–87 and 1991–92; Chief Investment Strategist, James Capel & Co., 1987–93. Director: Scottish Life, 1978–86; Cheltenham and Gloucester Building Soc., 1989–91 and 1992–; TR Property Investment Trust plc, 1994–; John Wainwright & Co. Ltd, 1994–. Pres., Investment Property Forum, 1995–. Mem., Pensions Law Rev. Cttee (Goode Cttee), 1992–93. Contested (C) Leicester West, 1979. *Publications:* The Money Moguls, 1987; Bricks & Mortals, 1992, rev. edn 1993; (ed jtly) Kluwer Handbook on Pensions. *Recreations:* music, cricket, writing, broadcasting (The Board Game, Radio 4). *Address:* (office) Standon House, 21 Mansell Street, E1 8AA. *T:* 0171–702 0888. *Clubs:* Reform, MCC; Bottesford Cricket (Leics).

ROSS-MUNRO, Colin William Gordon, QC 1972; *b* 12 Feb. 1928; *s* of late William Ross-Munro and of Adela Chirgwin; *m* 1958, Janice Jill Pedrana; one step *d. Educ:* Lycée Français de Londres; Harrow Sch.; King's Coll., Cambridge. Served in Scots Guards and in Army Education Corps. Called to the Bar, Middle Temple, 1951 (Master of the Bench, 1983). *Recreations:* tennis and travel. *Address:* (home) 46 Thames Quay, Chelsea Harbour, SW10 0UY; 2 Hare Court, Temple EC4Y 7BH.

ROSS RUSSELL, Graham; Chairman, EMAP plc, 1990–94 (non-executive Director, 1970–94); Chairman: Securities Institute, since 1992; Foreign & Colonial PEP Investment Trust plc, since 1993; Tunnel Services Ltd, since 1991; *b* 3 Jan. 1933; *s* of Robert Ross Russell and Elizabeth Ross Russell (*née* Hendry); *m* 1963, Jean Margaret Symington; three *s* one *d*. *Educ:* Loretto; Trinity Hall, Cambridge (BA); Harvard Business School (MBA; Frank Knox Fellow, 1958–60). Sub Lieut, RNVR, 1951–53 (Mediterranean Fleet). Merchant banking: Morgan Grenfell & Co. and Baring Brothers, 1956–58; Philip Hill Higginson Erlanger, 1960–63; Stockbroker, Laurence Prust & Co., 1963–90, Partner, 1965; Chm., Laurence Prust & Co. Ltd, 1986–88. Chairman: Braham Miller Group, 1981–84; C. C. F. Hldgs, 1988–90; non-exec. Director: Fordath, 1971–84; Foster Braithwaite, 1988–. Dir, SIB, 1989–93; Mem. Council, Internat. Stock Exchange, subseq. London Stock Exchange, 1973–91 (Dep. Chm., 1984–88; Chairman: Pre-emption Gp, 1987–; Rev. Cttee on Initial Public Offers, 1989–90). Comr, Public Works Loan Bd, 1980–95; Chm., Domestic Promotions Cttee, British Invisible Exports Council, 1987–91. Gov., Sutton's Hosp., Charterhouse, 1988–. Pres., Trinity Hall Assoc., 1994–95. *Publications:* occasional articles in esoteric financial and fiscal jls. *Recreations:* tennis, reading. *Address:* 30 Ladbroke Square, W11 3NB. *T:* 0171–727 5017. *Clubs:* Athenæum, City of London; Hawks (Cambridge); Woodpeckers (Oxford and Cambridge).

ROSSE, 7th Earl of, *cr* 1806; **William Brendan Parsons;** Bt 1677; Baron Oxmantown 1792; Member, Advisory Council on Development Co-operation, 1984–89, and Director, Agency for Personal Service Overseas, 1986–90, Government of Ireland; *b* 21 Oct. 1936; *s* of 6th Earl of Rosse, KBE, and Anne (*d* 1992), *o d* of Lt-Col Leonard Messel, OBE; *S* father, 1979; *m* 1966, Alison Margaret, *er d* of Major J. D. Cooke-Hurle, Startforth Hall, Barnard Castle, Co. Durham; two *s* one *d*. *Educ:* Eton; Grenoble Univ.; Christ Church, Oxford. BA 1961, MA 1964. 2nd Lieut, Irish Guards, 1955–57. UN Official 1963–80, appointed successively to Accra, Cotonou, New York, Teheran, Dacca and Algiers, in posts ranging from Area Officer to Dep. Resident Rep., with specific responsibility for directing the first teams of UN volunteers (in Iran) and co-ordinating disaster relief (in Bangladesh). Director: Historic Irish Tourist Houses and Gardens Assoc., 1980–91; Lorne House Trust, 1993–; Founder, Birr Scientific and Heritage Foundn, 1985. Lord of the Manor: Towton, Womersley and Woodhall, Yorks; Newtown, Parsonstown and Roscomroe, Ireland. FRAS; Hon. FIEI. *Heir:* *s* Lord Oxmantown, *qv*. *Address:* (home) Birr Castle, Co. Offaly, Ireland. *T:* (509) 20023.

See also Earl of Snowdon.

ROSSER, Sir Melvyn (Wynne), Kt 1974; DL; FCA; Partner, Deloitte, Haskins & Sells, 1961–85; Chairman, HTV Group, 1986–91; *b* 11 Nov. 1926; *s* of late David John and of Anita Rosser; *m* 1957, Margaret; one *s* two *d*. *Educ:* Glanmor Sch., Swansea; Bishop Gore Grammar Sch., Swansea. Chartered Accountant, qual. 1949; joined staff Deloitte Plender Griffiths & Co. (later Deloitte, Haskins & Sells), Swansea, 1950; practised in Swansea, 1961–68, in Cardiff, 1968–80, in London, 1980–85, retired. Director: Develt Corp. for Wales, 1965–80; Nat. Bus Co., 1969–72; Wales and Marches Telecom. Bd, 1970–80; Welsh Regional Council, CBI, 1970–80; (non-exec.) BSC, 1972–80; (non-exec.) NCB, later British Coal, 1983–89; W Midlands and Wales Regl Bd, Nat. Westminster Bank, 1986–89. Chm., Manpower Services Cttee, Wales, 1976–88; Member: Welsh Econ. Council, 1965–68; Welsh Council, 1968–80 (Chm., 1971–80); Royal Commn on Standards of Conduct in Public Life, 1974; Prime Minister's Adv. Cttee on Outside Business Appts, 1976–83; Nat. Trng Task Force, 1989–91 (Chm., Trng Enterprise and Educn Adv. Gp for Wales, 1989–92). Pres., UCW, Aberystwyth, 1986– (Vice-Pres., 1977–86); Mem. Court, Univ. of Wales, 1987–. Mem. Gorsedd of Bards, Royal Nat. Eisteddfod of Wales. DL West Glamorgan, 1986. Hon. LLD Wales, 1987. *Recreations:* music, gardening. *Address:* Corlan, 53 Birchgrove Road, Lonlas, Swansea SA7 9JR. *T:* Swansea (01792) 812286. *Clubs:* Royal Automobile; Cardiff and County (Cardiff).

ROSSER, Prof. Rachel Mary, FRCP, FRCPsych; Professor of Psychiatry, University College London Medical School (formerly University College and Middlesex School of Medicine, London), since 1984 (Head of Department, 1984–93); *d* of late John Rosser and of Madge Rosser; *m* 1967, Vincent Challacombe Watts; one *s* one *d*. *Educ:* King's High Sch., Warwick; Newnham Coll., Cambridge (MA); St Thomas's Hosp. Med. Sch. (MB, BChir). PhD London. Res. Registrar, Dept of Medicine, Guy's Hosp., 1969–71; Registrar, Maudsley Hosp., 1971–74; Sen. Registrar, Maudsley and Hammersmith Hosps, 1974–76; Sen. Lectr 1976–82, Reader 1983–84, Charing Cross Hosp. Vis. academic posts, Green, Greyfriars and Nuffield Colls, Oxford, 1993–94. Pres., Soc. for Psychosomatic Research, 1984–86; Mem. Council, Internat. Coll. of Psychosomatic Medicine, 1993– (Treas., 1983–92). *Publications:* (jtly) Health Care Priorities, 1980; Mind Made Disease, 1981; (jtly) Quality of Life: assessment and application, 1988; sci. papers on psychotherapy, psychosomatics, disaster aftermath. *Address:* Department of Psychiatry, Middlesex Hospital, Mortimer Street, W1A 8NN. *T:* 0171–380 9475.

ROSSER, Richard Andrew, JP; General Secretary, Transport Salaried Staffs' Association, since 1989; *b* 5 Oct. 1944; *s* of Gordon William Rosser and Kathleen Mary (*née* Moon); *m* 1973, Sheena Margaret (*née* Denoon); two *s* one *d*. *Educ:* St Nicholas Grammar Sch., Northwood. BScEcon London (external degree), 1970. MCIT 1968. Clerk, London Transport, 1962–65; PA to Operating Man. (Railways), LTE, 1965–66; joined full staff of TSSA, 1966: Res. Officer, 1966–74; Asst, London Midland Div. Sec., 1974–76; Finance and Organising Officer, 1976–77; London Midland Region Div. Sec., 1977–82; Asst Gen. Sec., 1982–89. Councillor, London Bor. of Hillingdon, 1971–78 (Chm., Finance Cttee, 1974–78); contested (Lab) Croydon Central, Feb. 1974. Mem., NEC, Labour Party, 1988–. JP Middlesex, 1978. *Recreations:* walking, music, reading The Guardian, and hoping for success for Watford FC. *Address:* Transport Salaried Staffs' Association, Walkden House, 10 Melton Street, NW1 2EJ. *T:* 0171–387 2101.

ROSSI, Sir Hugh (Alexis Louis), Kt 1983; consultant in environmental law with Simmons and Simmons, solicitors; *b* 21 June 1927; *m* 1955, Philomena Elizabeth Jennings; one *s* four *d*. *Educ:* Finchley Catholic Gram. Sch.; King's Coll., Univ. of London (LLB; FKC 1986). Solicitor with Hons, 1950. Member: Hornsey Borough Coun., 1956–65; Haringey Council, 1965–68; Middlesex CC, 1961–65. MP (C) Hornsey, 1966–83, Hornsey and Wood Green, 1983–92; Govt Whip, Oct. 1970–April 1972; Europe Whip, Oct. 1971–1973; a Lord Comr, HM Treasury, 1972–74; Parly Under-Sec. of State, DoE, 1974; opposition spokesman on housing and land, 1974–79; Minister of State: NI Office, 1979–81; for Social Security and the Disabled, DHSS, 1981–83. Chm., Select Cttee on the Environment, 1983–92. Dep. Leader, UK Delegn to Council of Europe and WEU, 1972–73 (Mem., 1970–73). Consultant, Wimpey Environmental Ltd, 1993–95. Vice President: (UK), Adv. Cttee on Protection of the Seas, 1992–; Nat. Soc. for Clean Air. Chairman: UNA (UK), 1992–; Italian Hosp., London, 1988–89, Italian Hosp. Fund, 1990–; Historic Chapels Trust, 1992–. Hon. Fellow, Inst. Waste Management; Hon. FCIWEM. Knight of Holy Sepulchre, 1966; KCSG 1985. *Publications:* Guide to the Rent Act, 1974; Guide to Community Land Act, 1975; Guide to Rent (Agriculture) Act, 1976; Guide to Landlord and Tenant Act, 1987; Guide to Local Government Acts 1987 and 1988, 1988.

ROSSITER, Rt. Rev. (Anthony) Francis, OSB; Abbot President of the English Benedictine Congregation, since 1985 (Second Assistant, 1976–85); Vicar of the Abbot Primate, since 1989; *b* 26 April 1931; *s* of Leslie and Winifred Rossiter. *Educ:* St Benedict's, Ealing; Sant Anselmo, Rome (LCL). Priest, 1955; Second Master, St Benedict's School, 1960–67; Abbot of Ealing, 1967–91; Vicar for Religious, Archdiocese of Westminster, 1969–88; Pres., Conf. of Major Religious Superiors of England and Wales, 1970–74. Hon. DD St Vincent Coll., Pa, 1988. *Address:* Ealing Abbey, W5 2DY. *T:* 0181–998 2158.

ROSSLYN, 7th Earl of, *cr* 1801; **Peter St Clair-Erskine;** Bt 1666; Baron Loughborough, 1795; *b* 31 March 1958; *s* of 6th Earl of Rosslyn, and of Athenais de Mortemart, *o d* of late Duc de Vivonne; *S* father, 1977; *m* 1982, Helen, *e d* of Mr and Mrs C. R. Watters, Christ's Hospital, Sussex; two *s* two *d*. *Educ:* Eton; Bristol Univ. Metropolitan Police, 1980–94; Thames Valley Police, 1994–. Trustee, Dunimarle Museum. Dir, Ludgrove Sch. Trust. *Heir:* *s* Lord Loughborough, *qv*. *Club:* White's.

ROSSMORE, 7th Baron, *cr* 1796; **William Warner Westenra;** *b* 14 Feb. 1931; *o s* of 6th Baron and Dolores Cecil (*d* 1981), *d* of late Lieut-Col James Alban Wilson, DSO, West Burton, Yorks; *S* father, 1958; *m* 1982, Valerie Marion, *d* of Brian Tobin; one *s*. *Educ:* Eton; Trinity Coll., Cambridge (BA). 2nd Lieut, Somerset LI. Co-founder, Coolemine Therapeutic Community, Dublin. *Recreations:* drawing, painting. *Heir:* *s* Hon. Benedict William Westenra, *b* 6 March 1983. *Address:* Rossmore Park, Co. Monaghan, Eire. *T:* Monaghan 81947.

ROSSOR, Martin Neil, MD, FRCP; Consultant Neurologist, St Mary's Hospital and National Hospital For Neurology and Neurosurgery, London, since 1986; Clinical Director for Neurology, National Hospital for Neurology and Neurosurgery, since 1994; *b* 24 April 1950; *s* of Bruce and Eileen Rossor; *m* 1973, Eve Lipstein; two *s* one *d*. *Educ:* Watford Boys' Grammar Sch.; Jesus Coll., Cambridge (MA, MD); King's College Hosp. Med. Sch. (MB BChir). FRCP 1990. Clinical Scientist, MRC Neurochemical Pharmacology Unit, 1978–82; Registrar, 1982–83, Sen. Registrar, 1983–86, Nat. Hosp. for Nervous Diseases and King's Coll. Hosp.; Clinical Dir, Medical Specialities, St Mary's Hosp., 1989–92; Sen. Lectr, Inst. of Neurology, 1992–. Hon. Neurologist, St Andrew's Hosp., Northampton, 1988–. *Publications:* Unusual Dementias, 1992; papers on Alzheimer's disease and related dementias. *Recreations:* English literature, equestrian sports, sailing. *Address:* The National Hospital for Neurology and Neurosurgery, Queen Square, WC1N 3BG. *T:* 0171–837 3611. *Club:* Athenæum.

ROSSWALL, Prof. Thomas; Rector, Swedish University of Agricultural Sciences, since 1994; *b* 20 Dec. 1941; *s* of Axel Rosswall and Britta (*née* Lindroth). *Educ:* Univ. of Uppsala (BSc 1966). Asst, Dept of Biochemistry, Univ. of Uppsala, 1967–70; Res. Asst, Dept of Microbiol., Swedish Univ. of Agricl Scis, 1970–76; Programme Officer, Swedish Council for Planning and Co-ordination of Research, 1976–80; Researcher, 1980–82, Asst Prof., 1982–84, Associate Prof., 1984, Dept of Microbiol., Swedish Univ. of Agricl Research; Prof., Dept of Water and Envmtl Studies, Univ. of Linköping, 1984–92; Exec. Dir, Internat. Geosphere-Biosphere Prog., 1987–94; Prof., Stockholm Univ., 1992–94; Dir, Internat. Secretariat, System for Analysis, Res. and Trng, Washington, 1992–93. Mem., Academia Europaea, 1989; Fellow, Royal Swedish Acad. of Scis, 1989. *Publications:* edited: Systems Analysis in Northern Coniferous Forests, 1971; (jtly) IBP Tundra Biome Procs 4th International Meeting on Biological Productivity of Tundra, 1971; Modern Methods in the Study of Microbial Ecology, 1973; (jtly) Structure and Function of Tundra Ecosystems, 1975; Nitrogen Cycling in West African Ecosystems, 1980; (jtly) Terrestrial Nitrogen Cycles: processes, ecosystems strategies and management impacts, 1981; (jtly) Nitrogen Cycling in South-East Asian Wet Monsoonal Ecosystems, 1981; (jtly) The Nitrogen Cycle, 1982, (jtly) Nitrogen Cycling in Ecosystems of Latin America and the Caribbean, 1982; (jtly) Scales and Global Change: spatial and temporal variability of biospheric and geospheric processes, 1988; (jtly) Ecology of Arable Land: the role of organism in carbon and nitrogen cycling, 1989; 100 papers in scientific jls. *Address:* Office of the Rector, Swedish University of Agricultural Sciences, Box 7070, 75007 Uppsala, Sweden. *T:* (8) 671060.

ROST, Peter Lewis; energy consultant; *b* 19 Sept. 1930; *s* of Frederick Rosenstiel and Elisabeth Merz; *m* 1961, Hilary Mayo; two *s* two *d*. *Educ:* various primary schs; Aylesbury Grammar Sch. National Service, RAF, 1948–50; Birmingham Univ. (BA Hons Geog.), 1950–53. Investment Analyst and Financial Journalist with Investors Chronicle, 1953–58; firstly Investment Advisor, 1958, and then, 1962, Mem. London Stock Exchange, resigned 1977. MP (C) Derbys SE, 1970–83, Erewash, 1983–92. Secretary: Cons. Parly Trade and Industry Cttee, 1972–73; Cons. Parly Energy Cttee, 1974–77; Select Cttee on Energy, 1979–92. Treasurer, Anglo-German Parly Gp, 1974–92; Jt Chm., Alternative and Complementary Medicine Parly Gp, 1989–92. Chm., Major Energy Users' Council; Vice-Pres., Combined Heat and Power Assoc. (Hon. Life Mem.). FRGS (Mem. Council, 1980–83); Fellow, Industry and Parlt Trust, 1987; Companion, Inst. of Energy, 1992. Freeman, City of London. Grand Cross, Order of Merit, Germany, 1979. *Publications:* papers on energy. *Recreations:* tennis, ski-ing, gardening, antique map collecting. *Address:* Norcott Court, Berkhamsted, Herts HP4 1LE. *T:* Berkhamsted (01442) 866123, *Fax:* (01442) 865901.

ROSTEN, Leo C., (pseudonym: **Leonard Q. Ross);** author and social scientist; *b* 11 April 1908; *s* of Samuel C. and Ida F. Rosten; *m* 1st, 1935, Priscilla Ann Mead (decd); one *s* two *d*; 2nd, 1960, Gertrude Zimmerman. *Educ:* University of Chicago (PhD); London School of Economics (Hon. Fellow, 1975). Research Assistant, Political Science Dept, Univ. of Chicago, 1933–35; Fellow, Social Science Research Council, 1934–36; Grants from Rockefeller Foundation and Carnegie Corporation, 1938–40. Dir, Motion Picture Research Project, 1939–41. Spec. Consultant, Nat. Defense Advisory Commn, Washington, 1939; Chief, Motion Picture Div., Office of Facts and Figures, Washington, 1941–42; Dep. Dir, Office of War Information, Washington, 1942–45; Special Consultant, Sec. of War, Washington, 1945; special mission to France, Germany, England, 1945. Faculty Associate, Columbia Univ., 1953–; Lectr in Political Science, Yale Univ., 1955, New School for Social Research, NY, 1959. Ford Vis. Prof. in Pol. Sci., Univ. of California (Berkeley), USA, 1960–61. Wrote film screenplays: Sleep, My Love; The Velvet Touch; Walk East on Beacon; The Dark Corner, etc. Member: Amer. Acad. of Political and Social Science; Amer. Assoc. for Advancement of Science; Nat. Acad. of Lit. and the Arts; Authors League of America; Authors Guild of America; Educnl Policies Cttee of Nat. Educnl Assoc. Phi Beta Kappa, 1929; Freedom Foundation's Award, 1955; George Polk Meml Award, 1955; Distinguished Alumnus Award, Univ. of Chicago, 1970. Hon. DHL: Univ. of Rochester, 1973; Hebrew Union Theol Coll., 1980. *Publications:* The Education of H*y*m*a*n K*a*p*l*a*n, 1937; The Washington Correspondents, 1937; The Strangest Places, 1939; Hollywood: The Movie Colony, The Movie Makers, 1941; The Dark Corner, 1945; (ed) Guide To The Religions of America, 1957; The Return of H*y*m*a*n K*a*p*l*a*n, 1959; Captain Newman, MD, 1961;

The Story Behind the Painting, 1961; The Many Worlds of Leo Rosten; The Leo Rosten Bedside Book, 1965; A Most Private Intrigue, 1967; The Joys of Yiddish, 1968; A Trumpet for Reason, 1970; People I have Loved, Known or Admired, 1970; Rome Wasn't Burned in a Day, 1971; Leo Rosten's Treasury of Jewish Quotations, 1973; Dear "Herm", 1974; (ed) The Look Book, 1975; The 3.10 to Anywhere, 1976; O Kaplan! My Kaplan!, 1976; The Power of Positive Nonsense, 1977; Passions and Prejudices, 1978; (ed) Infinite Riches: Gems from a Lifetime of Reading, 1979; Silky!, 1979; King Silky!, 1980; Hooray for Yiddish!, 1983; Carnival of Wit, 1984; Leo Rosten's Giant Book of Laughter, 1985; The Joys of Yinglish, 1989; contrib. learned journals. *Recreations:* photography, travel. *Address:* 36 Sutton Place South, NY 10022, USA. *Clubs:* Savile, Reform, Garrick (London); Cosmos (Washington); Chaos, Round Table (New York).

ROSTOW, Prof. Eugene Victor; Sterling Professor of Law, Yale University, 1938–84, now Emeritus; Distinguished Fellow, US Institute of Peace, since 1990; *b* 25 Aug. 1913; *s* of Victor A. and Lillian H. Rostow; *m* 1933, Edna B. Greenberg; two *s* one *d*. *Educ:* Yale Coll.; King's Coll., Cambridge (LLD 1962); Yale Law Sch. Practised law, New York, 1937–38; Yale Law Faculty, 1938–; Prof. of Law, 1944–84; Dean of Law Sch., 1955–65. Dist. Vis. Res. Prof. of Law and Diplomacy, Nat. Defense Univ., Washington, 1984–90, 1992–. Asst to Asst Sec. of State Acheson, 1942–44; Asst to Exec. Sec., Econ. Commn for Europe, UN, Geneva, 1949–50; Under-Sec. of State for Political Affairs, 1966–69. Dir, Arms Control and Disarmament Agency, 1981–83. Pres., Atlantic Treaty Assoc., 1973–76. Pitt Prof., Cambridge, 1959–60; Eastman Prof., Oxford, 1970–71. Dir, American Jewish Cttee, 1972–74; Chm. Exec. Cttee, Cttee on the Present Danger (Washington), 1976–81, 1987–. Hon. LLD Boston, 1976. Dist. Civilian Service Medal, US Army, 1990. Chevalier, Legion of Honour (France), 1960; Grand Cross, Order of the Crown (Belgium), 1969. *Publications:* A National Policy for the Oil Industry, 1948; Planning for Freedom, 1959; The Sovereign Prerogative, 1962; Law, Power and the Pursuit of Peace, 1968; (ed) Is Law Dead?, 1971; Peace in the Balance, 1972; The Ideal in Law, 1978; Toward Managed Peace, 1993; contribs to legal and economic jls. *Address:* Peru, Vermont 05152, USA. *T:* (802) 8246627; 1315 4th Street SW, Washington, DC 20024, USA. *Clubs:* Century (New York); Elizabethan (New Haven); Cosmos (Washington).

See also W. W. Rostow.

ROSTOW, Walt Whitman; Professor Emeritus of Political Economy, University of Texas at Austin, Texas; *b* 7 Oct. 1916; 2nd *s* of Victor and Lillian Rostow; *m* 1947, Elspeth, *o d* of Milton J. and Harriet Vaughan Davies; one *s* one *d*. *Educ:* Yale (BA 1936; PhD 1940); Oxford (Rhodes Scholar). Social Science Research Council Fellow, 1939–40; Instructor, Columbia Univ., 1940–41; Office Strategic Services, 1941–45 (Army of the United States, 1943–45, Major; Legion of Merit; Hon. OBE); Assistant Chief Division German-Austrian Economic Affairs, Department of State, 1945–46; Harmsworth Professor American History, Oxford, 1946–47; Special Assistant to Executive Secretary, Economic Commission for Europe, 1947–49; Pitt Professor of American History, Cambridge, 1949–50; Professor of Economic History, Massachusetts Institute of Technology, 1950–61; Deputy Special Assistant to the President (USA) for National Security Affairs, Jan. 1961–Dec. 1961; Counselor and Chairman, Policy Planning Council, Department of State, 1961–66; US Mem., Inter-Amer. Cttee on Alliance for Progress, 1964–66; Special Assistant to the President, The White House, 1966–69. Chm. and Chief Exec. Officer, Austin Project, 1992–. Member: Royal Economic Society, England; American Academy of Arts and Sciences, 1957; Amer. Philos. Soc.; Massachusetts Historical Soc. Hon. LLD: Carnegie Inst. of Tech., Pittsburgh, 1962; Univ. Miami, 1965; Univ. Notre Dame, 1966; Middlebury Coll., 1967; Jacksonville Univ., 1974. Presidential Medal of Freedom, with distinction, 1969. *Publications:* The American Diplomatic Revolution, 1947; Essays on the British Economy of the Nineteenth Century, 1948; The Process of Economic Growth, 1952; (with A. D. Gayer and A. J. Schwartz) The Growth and Fluctuation of the British Economy, 1790–1850, 1953, new edn 1975; (with A. Levin and others) The Dynamics of Soviet Society, 1953; (with others) The Prospects for Communist China, 1954; (with R. W. Hatch) An American Policy in Asia, 1955; (with M. F. Millikan) A Proposal: Key to An Effective Foreign Policy, 1957; The Stages of Economic Growth, 1960, 3rd edn 1990; The United States in the World Arena, 1960; The Economics of Take-off into Sustained Growth (ed), 1963; View from the Seventh Floor, 1964; A Design for Asian Development, 1965; Politics and the Stages of Growth, 1971; The Diffusion of Power, 1972; How It All Began: origins of the modern economy, 1975; The World Economy: history and prospect, 1978; Getting from Here to There, 1978; Why the Poor Get Richer and the Rich Slow Down, 1980; Pre-Invasion Bombing Strategy: General Eisenhower's Decision of March 25, 1944, 1981; The Division of Europe after World War II: 1946, 1981; British Trade Fluctuations 1868–1896: a chronicle and a commentary, 1981; Europe after Stalin: Eisenhower's Three Decisions of March 11, 1953, 1982; Open Skies: Eisenhower's proposal of July 21, 1955, 1982; The Barbaric Counter-Revolution, 1983; Eisenhower, Kennedy and Foreign Aid, 1985; The United States and the Regional Organization of Asia and the Pacific 1965–85, 1985; Rich Countries and Poor Countries: reflections from the past, lessons for the future, 1987; Essays on a Half Century: ideas, policies and action, 1988; History, Policy and Theory: essays in interaction, 1989; Theorists of Economic Growth from David Hume to the Present, with a Perspective on the Next Century, 1990; various articles contributed to: The Economist, Economic Journal, Economic History Review, Journal of Econ. History, American Econ. Review, etc. *Address:* 1 Wild Wind Point, Austin, TX 78746, USA. *Clubs:* Elizabethan (New Haven, Conn, USA); Cosmos (Washington, DC).

See also E. V. Rostow.

ROSTROPOVICH, Mstislav, Hon. KBE 1987; 'cellist; Music Director and Conductor, National Symphony Orchestra, Washington, 1977–94; *b* 1927; *m* 1955, Galina Vishnevskaya, *qv*; two *d*. *Educ:* State Conservatoire, Moscow. Has played in many concerts in Russia and abroad from 1942; first performance of Shostakovich's 'cello concerto (dedicated to him), Edinburgh Festival, 1960. Series of concerts with London Symphony Orchestra under Gennadi Rozhdestvensky, Festival Hall, 1965 (Gold Medal); first perf. Britten's third cello suite, Aldeburgh, 1974. Pres., Evian Fest., 1987–. Mem. Union of Soviet Composers, 1950–78, 1990–. Holds over 30 honorary degrees including Hon. MusD: St Andrews, 1968; Cambridge, 1975; Harvard, 1976; Yale, 1976; Oxon, 1980. Lenin Prize, 1964; Premium Imperiale (Japan), 1992. US Presidential Medal of Freedom, 1987; Commandeur de la Légion d'Honneur (France), 1987. *Address:* c/o Jonathan Brill, CAMI, 165 West 57th Street, New York, NY 10019, USA. *T:* (212) 8419599, *Fax:* (212) 8419525.

ROTA, Anthony Bertram; Managing Director, Bertram Rota Ltd, antiquarian booksellers, since 1967; *b* 24 Feb. 1932; *s* of Cyril Bertram Rota and Florence Ellen Rota (*née* Wright); *m* 1957, Jean Mary Foster Kendall; two *s*. Entered family business, 1952. Vis. Distinguished Fellow, Univ. of Tulsa, 1988. President: Antiquarian Booksellers' Assoc., 1971–72; Internat. League of Antiquarian Booksellers, 1988–91. DeGolyer Medal, Southern Methodist Univ., 1988. *Publications:* Points at Issue, 1984; Life in a London Bookshop, 1989; The Changing Face of Antiquarian Bookselling 1950–2000 AD, 1995; articles on book-collecting and bibliography in British and American jls. *Recreations:* cinema, opera, theatre, concerts, watching cricket, walking. *Address:* 31 Long Acre, WC2E 9LT. *T:* 0171–836 0723; Oak Lodge, Beaulieu Gardens, Winchmore Hill, N21 2HR. *Clubs:* Garrick; Grolier (NY).

ROTBLAT, Prof. Joseph, CBE 1965; MA, DSc (Warsaw); PhD (Liverpool); DSc (London); FRS 1995; FInstP; Professor of Physics in the University of London, at St Bartholomew's Hospital Medical College, 1950–76, now Emeritus; Physicist to St Bartholomew's Hospital, 1950–76; President, Pugwash Conferences on Science and World Affairs, since 1988; *b* 4 Nov. 1908; *e s* of late Z. Rotblat, Warsaw. *Educ:* University of Warsaw, Poland. Research Fellow of Radiological Laboratory of Scientific Society of Warsaw, 1933–39; Asst Director of Atomic Physics Institute of Free Univ. of Poland, 1937–39; Oliver Lodge Fellow of Univ. of Liverpool, 1939–40; Lecturer and afterwards Senior Lecturer in Dept of Physics, Liverpool Univ., 1940–49; Director of Research in nuclear physics at Liverpool Univ., 1945–49; work on atomic energy at Liverpool Univ. and Los Alamos, New Mexico. Treasurer, St Bartholomew's Hosp. Med. Coll., 1974–76; Vice-Dean, Faculty of Sci., London Univ., 1974–76. Mem., Adv. Cttee on Med. Res., WHO, 1972–75; Mem., WHO Management Gp, 1984–90. Ed., Physics in Medicine and Biol., 1960–72. Sec.-Gen., Pugwash Confs on Science and World Affairs, 1957–73; Chm., British Pugwash, 1978–88. Pres., Hosp. Physicists' Assoc, 1969–70; Pres., British Inst. of Radiology, 1971–72. Mem. Governing Body of Stockholm Internat. Peace Res. Inst., 1966–71. Pres., Internat. Youth Sci. Fortnight, 1972–74. Vis. Prof. of Internat. Relations, Univ. of Edinburgh, 1975–76. Member, Polish Academy of Sciences, 1966; Hon. Foreign Member: Amer. Acad. of Arts and Sciences, 1972; Ukraine Acad. of Scis, 1994; For. Mem., Czechoslovak Acad. of Scis, 1988. Hon. Fellow, UMIST, 1985. Hon. DSc: Bradford, 1973; Liverpool, 1989; Dr *hc* Moscow, 1988. Bertrand Russell Soc. Award, 1983; Gold Medal, Czechoslovak Acad. of Sciences, 1988; Albert Einstein Peace Prize, 1992. Commander, Order of Merit (Polish People's Republic), 1987; Order of Cyril and Methodius (1st Cl.) (Bulgaria), 1988; Kt Commander's Cross, OM (FRG), 1989. *Publications:* Progress in Nuclear Physics, 1950; (with Chadwick) Radio-activity and Radioactive Substances, 1953; Atomic Energy, a Survey, 1954; Atoms and the Universe, 1956; Science and World Affairs, 1962; Aspects of Medical Physics, 1966; Pugwash, the First Ten Years, 1967; Scientists in the Quest for Peace, 1972; Nuclear Reactors: to breed or not to breed, 1977; Nuclear Energy and Nuclear Weapon Proliferation, 1979; Nuclear Radiation in Warfare, 1981; Scientists, The Arms Race and Disarmament, 1982; The Arms Race at a Time of Decision, 1984; Nuclear Strategy and World Security, 1985; World Peace and the Developing Countries, 1986; Strategic Defence and the Future of the Arms Race, 1987; Coexistence, Co-operation and Common Security, 1988; Verification of Arms Reductions, 1989; Nuclear Proliferation: technical and economic aspects, 1990; Global Problems and Common Security, 1990; Towards a Secure World in the 21st Century, 1991; Striving for Peace, Security and Development in the World, 1992; A Nuclear-Weapon-Free World: Desirable? Feasible?, 1993; A World at the Crossroads: new conflicts, new solutions, 1994; papers on nuclear physics and radiation biology in Proceedings of Royal Society, Radiation Research, Nature, etc. *Recreations:* recorded music, travel. *Address:* 8 Asmara Road, West Hampstead, NW2 3ST. *T:* 0171–435 1471. *Club:* Athenæum.

ROTH, Andrew; Political Correspondent, New Statesman, since 1984; Director, Parliamentary Profiles, since 1955; *b* NY, 23 April 1919; *s* of Emil and Bertha Roth; *m* 1949, Mathilda Anna Friederich (marr. diss. 1984); one *s* one *d*. *Educ:* City Coll. of NY (BSS); Columbia Univ. (MA); Harvard Univ. Reader, City Coll., 1939; Res. Associate, Inst. of Pacific Relations, 1940; US Naval Intell., 1941–45 (Lieut, SG); Editorial Writer, The Nation, 1945–46; Foreign Corresp., Toronto Star Weekly, 1946–50; London Corresp., France Observateur, Sekai, Singapore Standard, 1950–60; Political Corresp., Manchester Evening News, 1972–84. Ed., Westminster Confidential, 1955–. DUniv Open, 1993. *Publications:* Japan Strikes South, 1941; French Interests and Policies in the Far East, 1942; Dilemma in Japan, 1945 (UK 1946); The Business Background of MPs, 1959, 7th edn 1980; The MPs' Chart, 1967, 5th edn 1979; Enoch Powell: Tory Tribune, 1970; Can Parliament Decide . . ., 1971; Heath and the Heathmen, 1972; Lord on the Board, 1972; The Prime Ministers, Vol. II (Heath chapter), 1975; Sir Harold Wilson: Yorkshire Walter Mitty, 1977; Parliamentary Profiles: Vol. I, A–D, 1984, 3rd edn 1994; Vol. II, E–K, 1984, 2nd edn 1989; Vol. III, L–R, 1985, 2nd edn 1990; Vol. IV, S–Z, 1985, 2nd edn 1991; New MPs of '92, 1992; Mr Nice Guy and His Chums, 1993. *Recreations:* sketching, jazz-dancing. *Address:* 34 Somali Road, NW2 3RL. *T:* 0171–435 6673, 0171–222 5884, *Fax:* 0171–222 5889.

ROTH, Prof. Klaus Friedrich, FRS 1960; Emeritus Professor, University of London; Visiting Professor in Department of Mathematics, Imperial College of Science, Technology and Medicine, since 1988; *b* 29 Oct. 1925; *s* of late Dr Franz Roth and Mathilde Roth (*née* Liebrecht); *m* 1955, Melek Khairy, BSc, PhD. *Educ:* St Paul's Sch.; Peterhouse, Cambridge (Hon. Fellow, 1989); Univ. College, London (Fellow, 1979). BA (Cambridge, 1945); MSc, PhD (London, 1948, 1950). Asst Master, Gordonstoun School, 1945–46. Member of Dept of Mathematics, University College, London, 1948–66; title of Professor in the University of London conferred 1961; Prof. of Pure Maths (Theory of Numbers), Imperial College, London, 1966–88. Visiting Lecturer, 1956–57, Vis. Prof., 1965–66, at Mass Inst. of Techn., USA. Foreign Hon. Mem., Amer. Acad. of Arts and Scis, 1966. Hon. FRSE 1993. Fields Medal awarded at International Congress of Mathematicians, 1958; De Morgan Medal, London Math. Soc., 1983; Sylvester Medal, Royal Soc., 1991. *Publications:* papers in various mathematical jls. *Recreations:* chess, cinema, ballroom dancing. *Address:* Department of Mathematics, Imperial College, 180 Queen's Gate, SW7 2BZ; 24 Burnsall Street, SW3 3ST. *T:* 0171–352 1363; Colbost, 16A Drummond Road, Inverness IV2 4NB. *T:* Inverness (01463) 712595.

ROTH, Prof. Sir Martin, Kt 1972; MD; FRCP; FRCPsych; DPM; Professor of Psychiatry, University of Cambridge, 1977–85, now Emeritus; Fellow, Trinity College, Cambridge, since 1977; *b* Budapest, 6 Nov. 1917; *s* of late Samuel Simon and Regina Roth; *m* 1945, Constance Heller; three *d*. *Educ:* University of London, St Mary's Hospital. FRCP 1958. MA Cantab; MD Cantab 1984. Formerly: Senior Registrar, Maida Vale, and Maudsley Hosps; Physician, Crichton Royal Hosp., Dumfries; Director of Clinical Research, Graylingwell Hosp.; Prof. of Psychological Medicine, Univ. of Newcastle upon Tyne, 1956–77. Visiting Assistant Professor, in the Department of Psychiatry, McGill University, Montreal, 1954; Consultant, WHO Expert Cttee on Mental Health Problems of Ageing and the Aged, 1958; Member: Med. Cons. Cttee, Nuffield Provincial Hosp. Trust, 1962; Central Health Services Council, Standing Med. Adv. Cttee, Standing Mental Health Adv. Cttee, DHSS, 1966–75; Scientific Adv. Cttee, CIBA Foundn, 1970–; Syndic of Cambridge Univ. Press, 1980–87. Mayne Vis. Prof., Univ. of Queensland, 1968; Albert Sterne Vis. Prof., Univ. of Indiana, 1976; first Andrew Woods Vis. Prof., Univ. of Iowa, 1976. Adolf Meyer Lectr, Amer. Psychiatric Assoc., 1971; Linacre Lectr, St John's Coll., Cambridge, 1984. Pres., Section of Psychiatry, RSM, 1968–69; Member: MRC, 1964–68; Clinical Research Board, MRC, 1964–70; Hon. Dir, MRC Group for study of relationship between functional and organic mental disorders, 1962–68. FRCPsych (Foundn Fellow; Pres., 1971–75; Hon. Fellow, 1975); Distinguished Fellow, Amer. Psychiatric Assoc., 1972; Hon. FRCPSGlas. Corresp. Mem., Deutsche Gesellschaft für Psychiatrie und Nervenheilkunde; Hon. Mem., Société Royale de Médecine Mentale de Belgique. Hon.

Fellow: Amer. Coll. Neuropsychopharmacology; Australian and New Zealand College of Psychiatry; Canadian Psychiatric Assoc., 1972. Hon. ScD TCD, 1977; Hon. DSc Indiana, 1993. Burlingame Prize, Royal Medico Psychol Assoc., 1951; First Prize, Anna Monika Foundn, 1977; Paul Hoch Prize, Amer. Psychopathological Assoc., 1979; Gold Florin, City of Florence, 1979; Gold Medal, Soc. of Biological Psychiatry, 1980; Kesten Prize, Univ. of Southern Calif, 1983; Sandoz Prize, Internat. Assoc. of Gerontology, 1985; Gold Medal, Max-Planck Inst., 1986; Camillow Golgi Award in Neuroscience, Italian Acad. of Neuroscience, 1993. Hon. Citizen, Salamanca, Spain, 1975. Co-Editor: British Jl of Psychiatry, 1967; Psychiatric Developments, 1983–. *Publications:* (with Mayer-Gross and Slater) Clinical Psychiatry, 1954, (with Slater) rev. 3rd edn 1977 (trans. Spanish, Italian, Portuguese, Chinese); (with L. Iversen) Alzheimer's Disease and Related Disorders, 1986; (with J. Kroll) The Reality of Mental Illness, 1986; (jtly) CAMDEX: the Cambridge examination for mental disorders of the elderly, 1988; (ed jtly) Handbook of Anxiety, Vols I–V, 1988, 1990, 1992; papers on psychiatric aspects of ageing, depressive illness, anxiety states, in various psychiatric and medical journals. *Recreations:* music, literature, conversation, travel. *Address:* Trinity College, Cambridge CB2 1TQ.

ROTH, Philip; novelist; *b* 19 March 1933; *s* of Herman Roth and Bess Finkel; *m* 1990, Claire Bloom (marr. diss. 1995), *qv*. *Educ:* Bucknell Univ. (AB); Univ. of Chicago (MA). Member of Faculty: Univ. of Chicago, 1956–58; Univ. of Iowa, 1960–62; Princeton Univ., 1962–64; Univ. of Pennsylvania, 1965–78; Hunter Coll. of the City Univ. of New York, 1988–92. Hon. degrees: Bucknell, 1979; Bard Coll., 1985; Rutgers, 1987; Columbia, 1987; Hartford, 1989; Brandeis, 1991; Dartmouth, 1992; George Washington, 1993. *Publications:* Goodbye Columbus, 1959; Letting Go, 1962; When She Was Good, 1967; Portnoy's Complaint, 1969; Our Gang, 1971; The Breast, 1972; The Great American Novel, 1973; My Life as a Man, 1974; Reading Myself and Others, 1975; The Professor of Desire, 1977; The Ghost Writer, 1979; A Philip Roth Reader, 1980; Zuckerman Unbound, 1981; The Anatomy Lesson, 1983; Zuckerman Bound, 1985; The Counterlife, 1987; The Facts, 1988; Deception, 1990; Patrimony, 1991; Operation Shylock: a confession, 1993; Sabbath's theater, 1995. *Address:* c/o Wylie, Aitken & Stone, 250 W 57th Street, New York, NY 10107, USA..

ROTHERHAM, Air Vice-Marshal John Kevitt, CB 1962; CBE 1960; Director-General (Engineering), RAF, 1967–69; retired; *b* 28 Dec. 1910; *s* of Colonel Ewan Rotherham; *m* 1st, 1936, Joan Catherine Penrose (*d* 1940); one *d*; 2nd, 1941, Margot Susan Hayter. *Educ:* Uppingham; Exeter College, Oxford. Joined RAF with Univ. perm. commn, 1933; 17 (F) Sqdn, 1934; 605 (B) Sqdn, 1936; School of Aeronautical Engineering, Henlow, 1936; post-grad. course, Imperial Coll., 1938; 43 (M) Group, 1939; Kidbrooke, 1940; MAP 1941; 41 (M) Group, 1942; HQ Flying Training Comd, 1946; exchange posting with USAF, 1947; Air Ministry, 1948; Joint Services Staff Coll., 1951; No 205 Group, Middle East, 1952; Air Ministry, 1954; seconded to Pakistan Air Force, 1957; Senior Technical Staff Officer, Transport Command, RAF, 1960–63; AOC No 24 (Training) Group, Technical Training Command, RAF, 1963–65; Senior Tech. Staff Officer, Bomber Command, 1965–67. AFRAeS 1949, FRAeS 1967. *Recreation:* fishing. *Address:* Herons, Westbrook Field, Bosham, Chichester, Sussex PO18 8JP. *T:* Bosham (01243) 573346. *Clubs:* Royal Air Force; Bosham Sailing.

ROTHERHAM, Leonard, CBE 1970; DSc; FRS 1963; FEng, FIEE, SFInstE, FIM, FInstP; Hon. Professor, Bath University, since 1985 (Vice-Chancellor, 1969–76); *b* 31 Aug. 1913; *m* 1937, Nora Mary Thompson (*d* 1991); one *s* two *d*. *Educ:* Strutt School, Belper; University College, London. Physicist, Brown Firth Research Laboratories, 1935–46; Head of Metallurgy Dept, RAE Farnborough, 1946–50; Dir, R&D, UKAEA, Industrial Group, Risley, 1950–58. Mem. for Research, Central Electricity Generating Bd, 1958–69; Head of Research, Electricity Supply Industry and Electricity Council, 1965–69. Chm., Adv. Cttee for Scientific and Technical Information, 1970–74. Member: Defence Scientific Adv. Council, 1967–77 (Chm., 1974–77); Central Adv. Council for Science and Technology, 1968–70; Adv. Council for Energy Conservation, 1974–79; Adv. Council for Applied R&D, 1976–81. Governor, Imperial Coll., 1977–89. Hon. LLD Bristol, 1972; Hon. DSc Bath, 1976. Fellow UCL, 1959; FIC 1987; Hon. Fellow, Inst. of Welding, 1965; Hon. Life Mem., American Society of Mechanical Engineers, 1963; President, Instn of Metallurgists, 1964; Inst. of Metals, 1965; Member of Council, Royal Society, 1965–66. Founder Fellow, Fellowship of Engineering, 1976 (Mem. Exec Council, 1978–80). *Publications:* Creep of Metals, 1951; Research and Innovation, 1984; various scientific and technical papers; also lectures: Hatfield Memorial, 1961; Coal Science, 1961; Calvin Rice (of Amer. Soc. of Mech. Engrs), 1963; 2nd Metallurgical Engineering, Inst. of Metals, 1963. *Address:* Westhanger, Horningsham, Warminster, Wilts BA12 7LH. *Club:* Athenæum.

ROTHERMERE, 3rd Viscount *cr* 1919, of Hemsted; **Vere Harold Esmond Harmsworth;** Bt 1910; Baron 1914; Chairman: Daily Mail and General Trust plc, since 1978; Associated Newspapers Holdings Ltd, since 1970; *b* 27 Aug. 1925; *s* of 2nd Viscount Rothermere and Margaret Hunam (*d* 1991), *d* of late William Redhead; *S* father, 1978; *m* 1st, 1957, Mrs Patricia Evelyn Beverley Brooks (*d* 1992), *d* of John William Matthews, FIAS; one *s* two *d* (and one step *d*); 2nd, 1993, Maiko Joeong-shun Lee. *Educ:* Eton; Kent Sch., Conn, USA. With Anglo Canadian Paper Mills, Quebec, 1948–50; Associated Newspapers Ltd, 1951–92; launched: New Daily Mail, 1971; Mail on Sunday, 1982. Trustee, Reuters; Dir, Power Corp., Canada. Pres., Euromoney Publications plc. Pres., Commonwealth Press Union, 1983–89 (Chm., UK Section, 1976); Pres., London Press Club, 1976–81; Patron, London Sch. of Journalism, 1980–. FRSA, FIMgt. Commander: Order of Merit (Italy); Order of Lion (Finland). *Recreations:* painting, sailing, reading. *Heir:* *s* Hon. Harold Jonathan Esmond Vere Harmsworth [*b* 3 Dec. 1967; *m* 1993, Claudia, *d* of T. J. Clemence; one *s*]. *Address:* 36 rue du Sentier, Paris, France. *Clubs:* Boodle's, Beefsteak; Royal Yacht Squadron; Brook (New York City); Travellers' (Paris).
See also Lord Ogilvy.

ROTHERWICK, 2nd Baron *cr* 1939; **Herbert Robin Cayzer;** Bt 1924; *b* 5 Dec. 1912; *s* of 1st Baron Rotherwick; *S* father 1958; *m* 1952, Sarah-Jane (*d* 1978), *o d* of Sir Michael Nial Slade, 6th Bt; three *s* one *d*. *Educ:* Eton; Christ Church, Oxford (BA). Supplementary Reserve Royal Scots Greys, 1938; served War of 1939–45 with them in Middle East. Former Deputy Chairman British & Commonwealth Shipping Co. Ltd, and Director of other and associated companies. *Heir:* *s* Hon. (Herbert) Robin Cayzer, Lt Life Guards (T&AVR) [*b* 12 March 1954; *m* 1982, Sara, *o d* of R. J. McAlpine, Swettenham Hall, Cheshire; two *s* one *d*]. *Address:* Cornbury Park, Charlbury, Oxfordshire OX7 3EH. *T:* Charlbury (01608) 810311. *Club:* White's.

ROTHES, 21st Earl of, *cr* before 1457; **Ian Lionel Malcolm Leslie;** Lord Leslie 1445; Baron Ballenbreich 1457; *b* 10 May 1932; *o s* of 20th Earl of Rothes and Beryl (*d* 1994), *o d* of J. Lionel Dugdale; *S* father, 1975; *m* 1955, Marigold, *o d* of Sir David M. Evans Bevan, 1st Bt; two *s*. *Educ:* Eton. Sub-Lt RNVR, 1953. *Heir:* *s* Lord Leslie, *qv*. *Address:* Tanglewood, West Tytherley, Salisbury, Wilts SP5 1LX.

ROTHNIE, Sir Alan (Keir), KCVO 1980; CMG 1967; HM Diplomatic Service, retired; *b* 2 May 1920; *s* of late John and Dora Rothnie, Aberdeen; *m* 1953, Anne Cadogan Harris, *d* of late Euan Cadogan Harris; two *s* one *d*. *Educ:* Montrose Acad.; St Andrews University. Served RNVR, 1939–45. Entered Diplomatic Service, Nov. 1945; Foreign Office, 1945–46; 3rd Sec., HM Legation, Vienna, 1946–48; 2nd Sec., HM Embassy, Bangkok, 1949–50; FO 1951–53; 1st Sec. HM Embassy, Madrid, 1953–55; Asst Political Agent, Kuwait, 1956–58; FO, 1958–60; Middle East Centre for Arab Studies, Shemlan, 1960–62 (Chargé d'Affaires, HM Embassy, Kuwait, 1961); Commercial Counsellor: HM Embassy, Baghdad, 1963–64; HM Embassy, Moscow, 1965–68; Consul-Gen., Chicago, 1969–72; Ambassador to Saudi Arabia, 1972–76, to Switzerland, 1976–80. Chm., Newsbrief Ltd, 1985–90. Hon. LLD St Andrews, 1981. *Recreations:* rural. *Address:* Little Job's Cross, Rolvenden Layne, Kent TN17 4PP. *T:* Cranbrook (01580) 241350.

ROTHSCHILD, family name of **Baron Rothschild.**

ROTHSCHILD, 4th Baron, *cr* 1885; **Nathaniel Charles Jacob Rothschild;** Bt 1847; Chairman: St James's Place Capital plc (formerly J. Rothschild Holdings plc), since 1971; Five Arrows Ltd, since 1980; *b* 29 April 1936; *e s* of 3rd Baron Rothschild, GBE, GM, FRS and Barbara, *o d* of St John Hutchinson, KC; *S* father, 1990; *m* 1961, Serena Mary, *er d* of late Sir Philip Gordon Dunn, 2nd Bt; one *s* three *d*. *Educ:* Eton; Christ Church, Oxford. BA 1st cl. hons History. Chairman: Bd of Trustees, National Gallery, 1985–91; Nat. Heritage Meml Fund, 1992–. Pres., Inst. of Jewish Affairs, 1992–. Mem. Council, RCA, 1986– (Sen. Fellow, 1992). Hon. PhD Hebrew Univ. of Jerusalem, 1992. Hon. Fellow, City of Jerusalem, 1992. Comdr, Order of Henry the Navigator (Portugal), 1985. *Heir:* *s* Hon. Nathaniel Victor James Rothschild, *b* 12 July 1971. *Address:* 14 St James's Place, SW1A 1NP. *T:* 0171–493 8111.
See also E. Rothschild.

ROTHSCHILD, Edmund Leopold de, TD; Director, N M Rothschild & Sons Limited, since 1975 (Partner since 1946, Senior Partner, 1960–70, Chairman, 1970–75); *b* 2 Jan. 1916; *s* of late Lionel Nathan de Rothschild and Marie Louise Beer; *m* 1st, 1948, Elizabeth Edith Lentner (*d* 1980); two *s* two *d*; 2nd, 1982, Anne, JP, *widow* of J. Malcolm Harrison, OBE. *Educ:* Harrow Sch.; Trinity Coll., Cambridge. Major, RA (TA). Served France, North Africa and Italy, 1939–46 (wounded). Deputy Chairman: Brit. Newfoundland Corp. Ltd, 1963–69; Churchill Falls (Labrador) Corp. Ltd, 1966–69; Biotechna-Graesser A. P. Ltd, 1989–. Mem., Asia Cttee, BNEC, 1970–71, Chm., 1971. Trustee, Queen's Nursing Inst.; Mem. Council, Royal Nat. Pension Fund for Nurses; Pres., Res. into Ageing. Pres., Assoc. of Jewish Ex-Servicemen and Women; Vice-Pres., Council of Christians and Jews. Governor, Tech. Univ. of Nova Scotia. Hon. LLD Memorial Univ. of Newfoundland, 1961; Hon. DSc Salford, 1983. Order of the Sacred Treasure, 1st Class (Japan), 1973. *Publication:* Window on the World, 1949. *Recreations:* gardening, fishing. *Address:* New Court, St Swithin's Lane, EC4P 4DU. *T:* 0171–280 5000; Exbury House, Exbury, Southampton SO4 1AF. *Clubs:* White's, Portland.
See also L. D. de Rothschild.

ROTHSCHILD, Emma; Fellow, since 1988, and Director, Centre for History and Economics, King's College, Cambridge; *b* 16 May 1948; *d* of 3rd Baron Rothschild, GBE, GM, FRS and of Lady Rothschild, MBE (*née* Teresa Mayor); *m* 1991, Prof. Amartya Kumar Sen, *qv*. *Educ:* Somerville Coll., Oxford (MA); Massachusetts Inst. of Technology (Kennedy Schol. in Econs). Associate Professor: of Humanities, MIT, 1978–80; of Science, Technology and Society, MIT, 1979–88; Dir de Recherches Invité, Ecole des Hautes Etudes en Sciences Sociales, Paris, 1981–82. Mem., OECD Gp of Experts on Science and Technology in the New Socio-Economic Context, 1976–80; OECD Sci. Examiner, Aust., 1984–85. Member: Govg Bd, Stockholm Internat. Peace Res. Inst., 1983–93; Govg Bd, Stockholm Envmt Inst., 1989–93; Bd, Olof Palme Meml Fund (Stockholm), 1986–; Royal Commn on Environmental Pollution, 1986–94; Bd, British Council, 1993–. Mem., Bd of Dirs, Bull. of the Atomic Scientists, 1983–89. *Publications:* Paradise Lost: the Decline of the Auto-Industrial Age, 1973; articles in learned and other jls. *Address:* King's College, Cambridge CB2 1ST.

ROTHSCHILD, Sir Evelyn de, Kt 1989; Chairman, N M Rothschild & Sons Limited; *b* 29 Aug. 1931; *s* of late Anthony Gustav de Rothschild; *m* 1973, Victoria Schott; two *s* one *d*. *Educ:* Harrow; Trinity Coll., Cambridge. Chairman: Economist Newspaper, 1972–89; United Racecourses Ltd, 1977–94. Chm., British Merchant Banking and Securities Houses Assoc. (formerly Accepting Houses Cttee), 1985–89. *Recreations:* art, racing.

ROTHSCHILD, Baron Guy (Edouard Alphonse Paul) de; Officier de la Légion d'Honneur, 1959; *b* 21 May 1909; *s* of late Baron Edouard de Rothschild and late Baronne de Rothschild (*née* Germaine Halphen); *m* 1st, 1937, Baronne Alix Schey de Koromla (marriage dissolved, 1956; she *d* 1982); one *s*; 2nd, 1957, Baronne Marie-Hélène de Zuylen de Nyevelt (who *m* 1st, Comte François de Nicolay); one *s* and one step *s*. *Educ:* Lycées Condorcet et Louis le Grand, Facultés de Droit et des Lettres (Licencié en Droit). Served War of 1939–45 (Croix de Guerre). Chevalier du Mérite Agricole, 1948. Associé de MM de Rothschild Frères, 1936–67; President: Compagnie du Chemin de Fer du Nord, 1949–68; Banque Rothschild, 1968–78; Société Imétal, 1975–79. Mem., Société d'Encouragement, 1950–92. *Publications:* The Whims of Fortune (autobiog.), 1985; Mon ombre Siamoise, 1993. *Recreation:* haras et écurie de courses, golf. *Address:* 2 rue Saint-Louis-en-l'Isle, 75008 Paris, France. *Clubs:* Nouveau Cercle, Automobile Club de France.

ROTHSCHILD, Leopold David de, CBE 1985; Director, N M Rothschild & Sons Limited, since 1970 (Partner, 1956–70); *b* 12 May 1927; *yr s* of Lionel de Rothschild and Marie Louise Beer. *Educ:* Bishops Coll. Sch., Canada; Harrow; Trinity Coll., Cambridge. Director of Bank of England, 1970–83. Chairman: Anglo Venezuelan Soc., 1975–78; English Chamber Orchestra and Music Soc. Ltd, 1963; Bach Choir, 1976; Music Adv. Cttee, British Council, 1986–93; Council, RCM, 1988– (FRCM 1977). Trustee, Science Mus., 1987–; Mem. Council, Winston Churchill Meml Trust, 1990–. DUniv York, 1991. Order of Francisco de Miranda, 1st cl. (Venezuela), 1978; Gran Oficial, Order of Merit (Chile), 1993; Ordem Nacional do Cruzeiro do Sul (Brazil), 1993; Encomienda, Order of Aztec Eagle (Mexico), 1994. *Recreations:* music, walking, industrial archaeology. *Address:* New Court, St Swithin's Lane, EC4P 4DU. *T:* 0171–280 5000. *Clubs:* Brooks's; Royal Yacht Squadron.
See also E. L. de Rothschild.

ROTHSCHILD, Hon. Miriam Louisa, (Hon. Mrs Miriam Lane), CBE 1982; FRS 1985; *b* 5 Aug. 1908; *e d* of Hon. N. C. Rothschild, 2nd *s* of 1st Baron Rothschild and Rozsika de Wertheimstein; *m* 1943, Capt. George Lane, MC (marriage dissolved, 1957); one *s* three *d* (and one *s* one *d* decd). *Educ:* home. Member: Zoological and Entomological Research Coun.; Marine Biological Assoc.; Royal Entomological Soc.; Systematics Assoc.; Soc. for Promotion of Nature Reserves, etc.; Ed., Novitates Zoologica, 1938–41; Mem., Publications Cttee, Zoological Soc.; Foreign Office, 1940–42; Trustee, British Museum of Natural History, 1967–75. Mem., Amer. Acad. of Arts and Scis. Vis. Prof. in Biology, Royal Free Hosp. Romanes Lectr, Oxford, 1985. Hon. Fellow, St Hugh's Coll., Oxford. Hon. DSc: Oxford, 1968; Gothenburg, 1983; Hull, 1984; Northwestern Univ., 1986; Leicester, 1987; Open Univ., 1989. Medal, Internat. Soc. of Chemical Ecology, 1989; VMH 1990; Mendel Award, Czech Sci. Acad., 1993. Defence Medal (1940–45).

Publications: Catalogue Rothschild Collection of Fleas (British Museum): vol. I 1953, vol. II 1956, vol. III 1962,vol. IV 1966, vol. V 1971, vol. VI 1983; (with Theresa Clay) Fleas, Flukes and Cuckoos, 1952; (with Clive Farrell) The Butterfly Gardener, 1983; Dear Lord Rothschild (biog.), 1983; (with Prof. Schlein and Prof. Ito) Atlas of Insect Tissue, 1985; Animals & Man, 1986; Butterfly Cooing Like a Dove, 1990; 300 contribs to scientific jls. *Recreation:* watching butterflies. *Address:* Ashton Wold, Peterborough PE8 5LZ. *Clubs:* Queen's, Entomological.

ROTHSCHILD, Baron Robert, KCMG (Hon.) 1963; Grand Officier de l'Ordre de Leopold (Belgium); Belgian Ambassador to the Court of St James's, 1973–76; *b* 16 Dec. 1911; *s* of Bernard Rothschild and Marianne von Rynveld; one *d. Educ:* Univ. of Brussels (DrRerPol). Entered Belgian Foreign Office: Brussels, 1937; Lisbon, 1942; Chungking, China, 1944; Shanghai, 1946, Washington, USA, 1950; Paris, NATO, 1952; Brussels, 1954; Ambassador to Yugoslavia, 1958; Head of Mission, Katanga, Congo, 1960; Brussels, 1960; Ambassador to: Switzerland, 1964; France, 1966. *Publications:* La Chute de Chiang Kai-Shek, 1973 (Paris); Les Chemins de Munich, 1988 (Paris). *Recreations:* gardening, travel. *Address:* 43 Ranelagh Grove, SW1W 8PB; 1 Rue E. Dereume, Rixensart 1330, Belgium.

ROTHSTEIN, Saul; Solicitor to the Post Office, 1976–81; *b* 4 July 1920; *s* of late Simon Rothstein and late Zelda Rothstein; *m* 1949, Judith Noemi (*née* Katz); two *d. Educ:* Church Institute Sch., Bolton; Manchester Univ (LLB). Admitted solicitor, 1947. War service, RAF, 1941–46 (Flt-Lt). Entered Solicitor's Dept, General Post Office, 1949, Asst Solicitor, 1963; Director, Advisory Dept, Solicitor's Office, Post Office, 1972–76. *Recreations:* chamber music, walking, travel. *Address:* 9 Templars Crescent, Finchley, N3 3QR. *T:* 0181–346 3701.

ROTHWELL, Margaret Irene, CMG 1992; HM Diplomatic Service; Ambassador to Côte d'Ivoire, since 1990, and concurrently to the Republic of Niger and the People's Democratic Republic of Burkina; *b* 25 Aug. 1938; *d* of Harry Rothwell and Martha (*née* Goedecke). *Educ:* Southampton Grammar School for Girls; Lady Margaret Hall, Oxford (BA LitHum). Foreign Office, 1961; Third, later Second Secretary, UK Delegn to Council of Europe, Strasbourg, 1964; FO, 1966; Second Sec. (Private Sec. to Special Representative in Africa), Nairobi, 1967; Second, later First Sec., Washington, 1968; FCO, 1972; First Sec. and Head of Chancery, Helsinki, 1976; FCO, 1980; Counsellor and Hd of Trng Dept, FCO, 1981–83; Counsellor, Consul-Gen. and Head of Chancery, Jakarta, 1984–87; Overseas Inspectorate, FCO, 1987–90. *Recreations:* gardening, cooking, tennis. *Address:* c/o Foreign and Commonwealth Office, SW1A 2AH.

ROTHWELL, Sheila Gwendoline; Director, Centre for Employment Policy Studies, Henley Administrative Staff College, since 1979; *b* 22 Aug. 1935; *d* of Reginald Herbert Paine and Joyce Margaret Paine; *m* 1958, Miles Rothwell (marr. diss. 1968); one *s* one *d*; *m* 1985, Graham L. Reid. *Educ:* Wyggeston Sch., Leicester; Westfield Coll., Univ. of London (BA Hons History, 1956); LSE (MScEcon Indust. Relations, 1972). Teaching and res., London, Trinidad and Barbados, 1958–68; Res. Officer/Lectr, Indust. Relations Dept, LSE, 1969–75; Asst Sec. (Negotiations), National Union of Bank Employees, 1975–76; Asst Chief Exec., Equal Opportunities Commn, 1976–78. Res. Sec. to House of Lords Select Cttee on Anti-Discrimination Bill, 1972–73. Member: Williams Cttee on Obscenity and Film Censorship, 1978–79; ACAS Panel of Arbitrators, 1988– (ACAS Indep. Expert on Equal Pay, 1984–87); Dep. Chm., Central Arbitration Cttee, 1992–. Chm. Governors, Henley (Tertiary) Coll., 1989–94. *Publications:* Labour Turnover, 1980; (ed) Strategic Planning for Human Resources, 1991; contrib. Internat. Labour Rev., and Brit. Jl of Indust. Relations. *Recreations:* cinema, theatre, walking, dressmaking, cycling. *Address:* 4 The Gardens, Fingest, Henley, Oxon RG9 6QF.

ROUGIER, Maj.-Gen. Charles Jeremy, CB 1986; FICE; Director, Royal Horticultural Society's Garden, Rosemoor, since 1988; *b* 23 Feb. 1933; *s* of late Lt-Col and Mrs C. L. Rougier; *m* 1964, Judith Cawood Ellis; three *s* one *d. Educ:* Marlborough Coll.; Pembroke Coll., Cambridge (MA). FICE 1986. Aden, 1960; Instructor, RMA Sandhurst, 1961–62; psc 1963; MA to MGO, 1964–66; comd 11 Engineer Sqn, Commonwealth Bde, 1966–68; jssc 1968; Company Comd, RMA Sandhurst, 1969–70; Directing Staff, Staff Coll., Camberley, 1970–72; CO 21 Engineer Regt, BAOR, 1972–74; Staff of Chief of Defence Staff, 1974–77; Commandant, Royal Sch. of Military Engineering, 1977–79; RCDS 1980; COS, Headquarters Northern Ireland, 1981; Asst Chief of General Staff (Trng), 1982–83; Dir of Army Training, 1983–84; Chm., Review of Officer Training and Educn Study, 1985; Engr-in-Chief (Army), 1985–88, retd. Col Comdt, RE, 1987–92. *Recreations:* hill walking, DIY, gardening. *Address:* c/o Lloyds Bank Plc, 2 Fore Street, Torrington, Devon EX38 8HJ. *Club:* Army and Navy.

ROUGIER, Hon. Sir Richard George, Kt 1986; **Hon. Mr Justice Rougier;** Judge of the High Court of Justice, Queen's Bench Division, since 1986; *b* 12 Feb. 1932; *s* of late George Ronald Rougier, CBE, QC, and Georgette Heyer, novelist; *m* 1962, Susanna Allen Flint (*née* Whitworth); one *s. Educ:* Marlborough Coll.; Pembroke Coll., Cambridge (Exhibr, BA). Called to Bar, Inner Temple, 1956, Bencher 1979. QC 1972; a Recorder, 1973–86; Presiding Judge, Midland and Oxford Circuit, 1990–94. *Recreations:* fishing, golf, bridge. *Address:* Royal Courts of Justice, WC2A 2LL. *Clubs:* Garrick, Portland; Rye Golf.

ROULSTONE, Brig. Joan Margaret; Director, Women (Army), 1992–94; Aide-de-Camp to the Queen, 1992–95; *b* 7 Nov. 1945; *d* of Eric Laurie Frank Tyler and Jessie Tyler (*née* Louise); *m* 1971, Peter John Roulstone. *Educ:* seven schools worldwide. Commnd, WRAC, 1964; UK and BAOR, 1965–78; resigned 1978, reinstated, 1980; UK, 1980–86; Corps Recruiting and Liaison Officer, WRAC, 1986–87; Chief G1/G4 NE Dist and 2nd Inf. Div., 1988–89; Comd WRAC, UKLF, 1990–91. *Address:* c/o Barclays Bank, Priestpopple, Hexham, Northumberland NE46 1PE.

ROUND, Prof. Nicholas Grenville; Hughes Professor of Hispanic Studies, University of Sheffield, since 1994; *b* 6 June 1938; *s* of Isaac Eric Round and Laura Christabel (*née* Poole); *m* 1966, Ann Le Vin; one *d. Educ:* Boyton CP Sch., Cornwall; Launceston Coll.; Pembroke Coll., Oxford. BA (1st cl. Hons, Spanish and French) 1959; MA 1963; DPhil 1967. MITI 1990. Lecturer in Spanish, Queen's Univ. of Belfast, 1962–71, Reader, 1971–72; Warden, Alanbrooke Hall, QUB, 1970–72; Stevenson Prof. of Hispanic Studies, Glasgow Univ., 1972–94. Mem., Exec. Cttee, Strathclyde Region Labour Party, 1986–94. Officer, Order of Isabel the Catholic (Spain), 1990. *Publications:* Unamuno: Abel Sánchez: a critical guide, 1974; The Greatest Man Uncrowned: a study of the fall of Alvaro de Luna, 1986; trans., Tirso de Molina, Damned for Despair, 1986; (ed) Re-reading Unamuno, 1989; On Reasoning and Realism: three easy pieces, 1991; Libro llamado Fedrón, 1993; contribs to: Mod. Lang. Review, Bulletin Hispanic Studies, Proc. Royal Irish Academy, etc. *Recreations:* reading, music, all aspects of Cornwall. *Address:* Department of Hispanic Studies, The University, Sheffield S10 2TN. *T:* Sheffield (0114) 276 8555. *Club:* (Hon. Life Mem.) Students' Union (Belfast).

ROUNTREE, Peter Charles Robert; His Honour Judge Rountree; a Circuit Judge, since 1986; *b* 28 April 1936; *s* of late Francis Robert George Rountree and Mary Felicity Patricia Rountree (*née* Wilson); *m* 1968, Nicola Mary (*née* Norman-Butler); one *s* one step *d. Educ:* Uppingham School; St John's College, Cambridge (MA). Called to the Bar, Inner Temple, 1961; a Recorder, April–July 1986. *Recreations:* sailing, golf, tennis. *Clubs:* Boodle's, Pratt's, Royal Automobile, Royal Yacht Squadron, Royal London Yacht; New Zealand Golf.

ROUS, family name of **Earl of Stradbroke.**

ROUS, Lt-Gen. Hon. Sir William (Edward), KCB 1992; OBE 1981 (MBE 1974); Quarter Master General, Ministry of Defence, since 1994; *b* 22 Feb. 1939; *s* of 5th Earl of Stradbroke, and Pamela Catherine Mabell, *d* of Captain Hon. Edward James Kay-Shuttleworth; *m* 1970, Judith Rosemary Persse; two *s. Educ:* Harrow; Royal Military Academy, Sandhurst. Commissioned Coldstream Guards, 1959; Comd 2nd Bn Coldstream Guards, 1979–81, Comd 1st Inf. Brigade, 1983–84; Dir of Public Relations (Army), 1985–87; GOC 4th Armoured Div., BAOR, 1987–89; Comdt, Staff Coll., Camberley, 1989–91; Military Sec., MoD, 1991–94. *Address:* RHQ Coldstream Guards, Wellington Barracks, SW1E 6HQ.

ROUSE, E(dward) Clive, MBE 1946; Medieval Archæologist, retired; Specialist in Mural and Panel Paintings; Lecturer; *b* 15 October 1901; *s* of late Edward Foxwell Rouse (Stroud, Gloucestershire and Acton, Middlesex) and late Frances Sarah Rouse (*née* Sams). *Educ:* Gresham's School; St Martin's School of Art. On leaving school studied art and medieval antiquities, 1920–21; FSA London, 1937 (Mem. of Council, 1943–44); FRSA 1968. President: Royal Archæological Institute, 1969–72 (Vice-Pres., 1965); Bucks Archaeological Soc., 1969–79. Liveryman, Fishmongers' Company, 1962. Served War of 1939–45, RAFVR (Intelligence); Flight-Lt, 1941–45; MBE for special services at Central Interpretation Unit, Medmenham. Hon. MA Oxon, 1969; Hon. DLitt Sussex, 1983. *Publications:* The Old Towns of England, 1936 (twice reprinted); Discovering Wall Paintings, 1968 (reprinted); (jointly) Guide to Buckinghamshire, 1935; contributor to: The Beauty of Britain, 1935; Collins' Guide to English Parish Churches, 1958. Papers in Archæologia, Antiquaries' Journal, Archæological Journal, and publications of many County Archæological Societies. *Recreations:* reading, bird watching. *Address:* Oakfield, North Park, Gerrards Cross, Bucks SL9 8JR. *T:* Gerrards Cross (01753) 882595.

ROUSSEAU, Prof. George Sebastian, PhD; Regius Professor of English Literature, King's College, University of Aberdeen, since 1994; *b* 23 Feb. 1941; *s* of Hyman Victoire Rousseau and Esther (*née* Zacuto). *Educ:* Amherst Coll., USA (BA 1962); Princeton Univ. (MA 1964; PhD 1966). Princeton University: Osgood Fellow in English Lit., 1965–66; Woodrow Wilson Dissertation Fellow, 1966; Instructor, then Asst Prof., Harvard Univ., 1966–68; University of California, Los Angeles: Asst Prof. of English, 1968–69; Associate Prof., 1969–76; Prof., 1976–94. Fulbright Res. Prof., W Germany, 1970; Cambridge University: Hon. Fellow, Wolfson Coll., 1974–75; Overseas Fellow, 1979; Vis. Fellow Commoner, Trinity Coll., 1982; Sen. Fulbright Res. Schol., Sir Thomas Browne Inst., Netherlands, 1983; Vis. Exchange Prof., King's Coll., Cambridge, 1984; Clark Liby Prof., Univ. of Calif, 1985–86; Sen. Fellow, NEH, 1986–87; Vis. Fellow and Waynflete Lectr, Magdalen Coll., Oxford, 1993–94. Book reviewer, NY Times (Sunday), 1967–. FRSocMed 1967; FRSA 1973. *Publications:* (with M. Hope Nicolson) This Long Disease My Life: Alexander Pope and the sciences, 1968; (with N. Rudenstine) English Poetic Satire, 1969; (ed jtly) The Augustan Milieu: essays presented to Louis A. Landa, 1970; (ed jtly) Tobias Smollett: bicentennial essays presented to Lewis M. Knapp, 1971; (ed) Organic Form: the life of an idea, 1972; Goldsmith: the critical heritage, 1974; (with R. Porter) The Ferment of Knowledge: studies in the historiography of science, 1980; The Letters and Private Papers of Sir John Hill, 1981; Tobias Smollett: essays of two decades, 1982; (ed) Science and the Imagination: the Berkeley Conference, 1987; (with R. Porter) Sexual Underworlds of the Enlightenment, 1987; (with P. Rogers) The Enduring Legacy: Alexander Pope Tercentenary Essays, 1988; (with R. Porter) Exoticism in the Enlightenment, 1990; The Languages of Psyche: mind and body in enlightenment thought, 1990; Perilous Enlightenment: pre- and post-modern discourses—sexual, historical, 1991; Enlightenment Crossings: pe- and post-modern discourses—anthropological, 1991; Enlightenment Borders: pre- and post-modern discourses—medical, scientific, 1991; (jtly) Hysteria Before Freud, 1993; contrib. numerous articles to learned jls and mags. *Recreations:* chamber music, opera, ski-ing, walking, hiking. *Address:* Department of English, Taylor Building, King's College, University of Aberdeen, Aberdeen AB3 2DT. *T:* Aberdeen (01224) 272623; 1 Orchard Walk, Aberdeen AB9 2UG. *T:* Aberdeen (01224) 273681.

ROUSSEL, (Philip) Lyon, OBE 1974; Controller, Arts Division, British Council, 1979–83; retired; *b* 17 Oct. 1923; *s* of late Paul Marie Roussel and Beatrice (*née* Cuthbert; later Lady Murray); *m* 1959, Elisabeth Mary, *d* of Kenneth and Kathleen Bennett; one *s* one *d. Educ:* Hurstpierpoint Coll.; St Edmund Hall, Oxford (MA, Cert. Public and Social Admin); Chelsea Sch. of Art. Served Indian Army in Parachute Regt, 1942–46 (Major); Parachute Regt (TA), 1946–50. Sudan Political Service, 1950–55; Principal, War Office, 1955–56; Associated Newspapers, 1956–57; British Council, 1960–83: India, 1960–67 (Regional Rep., Western and Central India, 1964–67); Dir, Scholarships, 1967–71; Rep. and Cultural Attaché, British Embassy, Belgium and Luxembourg, 1971–76; Europalia-Great Britain Festival Cttee, 1973; Cultural Attaché (Counsellor), British Embassy, Washington, 1976–79. Sponsorship Consultant, National Theatre, 1983–84. Member: Fest. of India Cttee, 1981–82; British Adv. Cttee, Britain Salutes New York, 1981–83; Bd, The Hanover Band, 1984–87; Common Room, Wolfson Coll., Oxford, 1988. Hon. Organiser, Poppy Appeal, Woodstock Br., Royal British Legion, 1991–. FRGS 1981; FRSA 1979. *Recreations:* painting, looking at pictures, travel, tennis, golf and a barn in France. *Address:* 26 High Street, Woodstock, Oxford OX20 1TG. *Clubs:* Athenæum; Oxford Union; Woodstock Tennis; North Oxford Golf.

ROUSSOS, Stavros G.; Secretary General, Ministry of Foreign Affairs, Greece, 1980–82, retired; *b* 1918; *m*; two *s* one *d. Educ:* Univ. of Lyons (LèsL); Univ. of Paris (LèsL, LèsScPol, LLD). Entered Greek Diplomatic Service as Attaché, Min. of Foreign Affairs, 1946; Mem., Greek Delegn to Gen. Assembly of UN, 1948 and 1954–55; Sec. to Permanent Mission of Greece to UN in New York, 1950; Consul, Alexandria, 1955; i/c Greek Consulate General, Cairo, 1956; Counsellor, 1959; Min. of Foreign Affairs, 1959–61; Mem., Perm. Delegn of Greece to EEC, Brussels, 1962; Perm. Rep. to EEC, 1969; Dir-Gen., Econ. and Commercial Affairs, Min. of Foreign Affairs, 1972; Ambassador of Greece to UK, 1974–79; Alternate Sec. Gen., Min. of Foreign Affairs, 1979–80. Grand Comdr, Order of Phoenix; Commander: Order of Belgian Crown; Order of Merit of Egypt. *Publication:* The Status of Dodecanese Islands in International Law, 1940 (Paris). *Address:* 5 Loukianou Street, Athens 10675, Greece.

ROUT, Owen Howard, FCIB; Executive Director (UK Operations), Barclays PLC and Barclays Bank PLC, 1987–90; Chairman: Barclays Financial Services Ltd, 1988–90; Starmin plc, 1990–93 (Deputy Chairman, 1993–94); *b* 16 April 1930; *s* of Frederick Owen and Marion Rout; *m* 1954, Jean (*née* Greetham); two *d. Educ:* Grey High Sch., Port Elizabeth, SA. ACIS. Dir, Barclays Bank UK Ltd, 1977–87; Gen. Man., Barclays PLC and Barclays Bank PLC, 1982–87. Chairman: Barclays Insurance Services Co. Ltd, 1982–85; Barclays Insurance Brokers International Ltd, 1982–85; Mercantile Gp, 1989–92; Director:

Spreadeagle Insurance Co. Ltd, 1983–85; Baric Ltd, 1982–84; Albaraka Internat. Bank, 1990–93. Chartered Institute of Bankers: Mem. Council, 1985–90; Treas., 1986–90. Mem., Supervisory Bd, Banking World Magazine, 1986–90. Mem., Bd of Govs, Anglia Polytechnic Univ., 1993–. *Recreations:* watching sport—Rugby and cricket, playing golf, listening to music, gardening. *Club:* Saffron Walden Golf.

ROUTH, Donald Thomas; Under Secretary, Department of the Environment, 1978–90; *b* 22 May 1936; *s* of Thomas and Flora Routh; *m* 1961, Janet Hilda Allum. *Educ:* Leeds Modern Sch. Entered WO, Northern Comd, York, as Exec. Officer, 1954; Nat. Service, RN, 1954–56; Higher Exec. Officer, Comd Secretariat, Kenya, 1961–64; Asst Principal, Min. of Housing and Local Govt, 1964–66; Asst Private Sec. to Minister, 1966–67; Principal, 1967; on loan to Civil Service Selection Bd, 1971; Asst Sec., DoE, 1972; Under Sec., 1978; Regional Dir, West Midlands, 1978–81; Hd of Construction Industries Directorate, 1981–85; Dir of Senior Staff Management, 1985–86; Controller, The Crown Suppliers, 1986.

ROUTLEDGE, Alan, CBE 1979; *b* 12 May 1919; *s* of George and Rose Routledge, Wallasey, Cheshire; *m* 1949, Irene Hendry, Falkirk, Stirlingshire; one *s* (and one *s* decd). *Educ:* Liscard High Sch., Wallasey. Served Army, Cheshire (Earl of Chester's) Yeomanry, 1939–46. Control Commn for Germany, 1946–51; Diplomatic Wireless Service of FO (now Foreign and Commonwealth Office), 1951–79: Head, Cypher and Signals Branch, 1962; Head, Commns Planning Staff, 1973; Head, Commns Ops Dept, 1979; retired FCO, 1979. *Recreations:* English history, cricket, golf. *Address:* 15 Ilford Court, Elmbridge, Cranleigh, Surrey GU6 8TJ. *T:* Cranleigh (01483) 276669. *Clubs:* Civil Service; Old Liscardians.

ROUTLEDGE, (Katherine) Patricia, OBE 1993; actress; *b* 17 Feb. 1929; *d* of Isaac Edgar Routledge and Catherine (*née* Perry). *Educ:* Birkenhead High Sch.; Univ. of Liverpool; Bristol Old Vic Theatre Sch.; Guildhall Sch. of Music. *Theatre* appearances include: A Midsummer's Night Dream, Liverpool Playhouse, 1952; The Duenna, Westminster, 1954; musical version, The Comedy of Errors, Arts, 1956; The Love Doctor, Piccadilly, 1959; revue, Out of My Mind, Lyric, Hammersmith, 1961; Little Mary Sunshine, Comedy, 1962; Virtue in Danger, Mermaid, transf. Strand, 1963; How's the World Treating You?, Hampstead Theatre Club, 1965, New Arts, transf. Wyndham's, Comedy and Broadway, 1966; Darling of the Day, George Abbott, NY, 1967 (Antoinette Perry Award); The Caucasian Chalk Circle, The Country Wife, and The Magistrate, Chichester Fest., 1969; Cowardy Custard, Mermaid, 1972; Dandy Dick, Chichester Fest., transf. Garrick, 1973; 1600 Pennsylvania Avenue, Mark Hellinger, NY, 1976; Pirates of Penzance, NY, 1980; Noises Off, Savoy, 1981; When the Wind Blows, Whitehall, 1983; Richard III, RSC, 1984–85; Candide, Old Vic, 1988–89 (Laurence Olivier Award); Come for the Ride (one-woman show), Playhouse, 1989; The Rivals, Albery, 1994; *television* appearances include: Doris and Doreen, 1978; A Woman of No Importance, 1982; Victoria Wood As Seen on TV, 1983–86; Marjorie and Men, 1985; A Lady of Letters, 1988; Keeping Up Appearances, 1990; many radio plays. *Address:* c/o Marmont Management Ltd, Langham House, 308 Regent Street, W1R 5AL.

ROUX, Michel André; Director and Chef de Cuisine, since 1967; *b* 19 April 1941; *s* of late Henry Roux and of Germaine Triger; *m* 1984, Robyn (Margaret Joyce); one *s* two *d* by previous marr. *Educ:* Ecole Primaire, Saint Mande; Brevet de Maîtrise (Pâtisserie). Apprenticeship, Pâtisserie Loyal, Paris, 1955–57; Commis Pâtissier-Cuisinier, British Embassy, Paris, 1957–59; Commis de Cuisine with Miss Cécile de Rothschild, Paris, 1959–60; Military service, 1960–62, at Versailles and Colomb Bechar, Sahara; Chef with Miss Cécile de Rothschild, 1962–67; came to England, 1967; restaurants opened: Le Gavroche, 1967; Le Poulbot, 1969; Waterside Inn, 1972; Gavvers, 1981. Mem., UK Br., Académie Culinaire de France, 1984–. TV series, At Home with the Roux Brothers, 1988. Numerous French and British prizes and awards, including: Médaille d'Or, Cuisiniers Français, 1972; Restaurateur of the Year, Caterer & Hotelkeeper, 1985; Personnalité de l'Année, Gastronomie dans le Monde, Paris, 1985; Culinary Trophy, Assoc. of Maîtres-Pâtissiers La Saint Michel, 1986; (with Albert Roux) Men of the Year (Radar), 1989. Chevalier, National Order of Merit (France), 1987; Officer, Order of Agricultural Merit (France), 1987; Chevalier, Order of Arts and of Letters (France), 1990. *Publications:* (all with Albert Roux): New Classic Cuisine, 1983 (French edn, 1985); The Roux Brothers on Pâtisserie, 1986; At Home with the Roux Brothers, 1988; French Country Cooking, 1989; Cooking for Two, 1991; Desserts: a lifelong passion, 1994. *Recreations:* shooting, walking, skiing. *Address:* The Waterside Inn, Ferry Road, Bray, Berks SL6 2AT. *T:* Maidenhead (01628) 20691; River Cottage, Ferry Road, Bray, Berks SL6 2AT. *Club:* The Benedicts.

ROWALLAN, 4th Baron *cr* 1911; **John Polson Cameron Corbett;** Director: Heritage Circle (UK) Ltd, since 1979; Equibuild (UK) Ltd, since 1987; Rowallan Activity Centre Ltd, since 1991; Chairman, Turner-Dundas, since 1989; *b* 8 March 1947; *s* of 3rd Baron Rowallan and of his 1st wife, Eleanor Mary Boyle; *S* father, 1993; *m* 1st, 1971, Jane Green (marr. diss. 1983); one *s* one *d*; 2nd, 1984, Sandrew Bryson (marr. diss. 1994); one *s* one *d*; 3rd, 1995, Claire Dinning. *Educ:* Cothill House; Eton Coll.; RAC, Cirencester. Chartered Surveyor, 1972–; farmer, 1975–. Area Rep. Judge, BSJA, 1982–. Commentator at equestrian events. Dir of several cos, 1980–. Contested (C): Glasgow, Garscadden, Oct. 1974; Kilmarnock, 1979. *Recreations:* equestrian commentating and judging, ski-ing. *Heir:* *s* Hon. Jason William Polson Cameron Corbett, *b* 21 April 1972. *Address:* Meiklemosside, Fenwick, Ayrshire KA3 6AY. *T:* Fenwick (01560) 600769. *Club:* Lansdowne.

ROWAN, Carl Thomas; Syndicated columnist, correspondent, Chicago Sun-Times; radio and TV commentator, Post-Newsweek Broadcasting; Roving Editor, Reader's Digest; *b* 11 August 1925; *s* of Thomas D. and Johnnie B. Rowan; *m* 1950, Vivien Murphy; two *s* one *d*. *Educ:* Tennessee State University; Washburn University; Oberlin Coll., University of Minnesota. Mem. Staff of Minneapolis Tribune, 1948–61; Dept of State, 1961–63; US Ambassador to Finland, 1963–64; Director, United States Information Agency, Washington, DC, 1964–65. Hon. DLitt: Simpson Coll., 1957; Hamline Univ., 1958; Oberlin Coll., 1962; Dr of Humane Letters: Washburn Univ., 1964; Talladega Coll., 1965; St Olaf Coll., 1966; Knoxville Coll., 1966; Rhode Island Coll., 1970; Maine Univ., 1971; American Univ., 1980; Dr of Laws: Howard Univ., 1964; Alfred Univ., 1964; Temple Univ., 1964; Atlanta Univ., 1965; Allegheny Coll., 1966; Colby Coll., 1968; Clark Univ., 1971; Notre Dame, 1973; Dr of Public Admin., Morgan State Coll., 1964; Dr of Letters: Wooster Coll., 1968; Miami Univ., 1982; Drexel Inst. of Technology; Dr of Science Georgetown Med. Sch., 1982. *Publications:* South of Freedom, 1953; The Pitiful and the Proud, 1956; Go South to Sorrow, 1957; Wait Till Next Year, 1960; Between Us Blacks, 1974; Breaking Barriers, 1991. *Recreations:* tennis, golf and bowling, singing and dancing. *Address:* c/o Little, Brown & Co., 34 Beacon Street, Boston, MA 02108, USA. *Clubs:* Federal City, Indian Spring, (Washington, DC).

ROWAN, Patricia Adrienne, (Mrs Ivan Rowan); journalist; Editor, The Times Educational Supplement, since 1989; *d* of late Henry Matthew Talintyre and Gladys Talintyre; *m* 1960, Ivan Settle Harris Rowan; one *s*. *Educ:* Harrow County Grammar School for Girls. Time & Tide, 1952–56; Sunday Express, 1956–57; Daily Sketch, 1957–58; News Chronicle, 1958–60; Granada Television, 1961–62; Sunday Times, 1962–66; TES, 1972–. Hon. FRSA 1989. *Publications:* What Sort of Life?, 1980; (contrib.) Education—the Wasted Years?, 1988. *Recreations:* cookery, gardening. *Address:* The Times Educational Supplement, Admiral House, 66–68 East Smithfield, E1 9XY. *T:* 0171–782 3000. *Club:* Reform.

See also D. G. Talintyre.

ROWAN-LEGG, Allan Aubrey; President, Edcom Ltd, Canada, since 1985 (Vice President, Western Region, 1976–85); *b* 19 May 1912; *m* 1944, Daphne M. Ker; three *d*. Dir, Vice-Pres. and Gen. Sales Man., Interlake Fuel Oil Ltd, and Interlake Steel Products, 1955–57; Pres. and Dir, Superior Propane Ltd, Northern Propane Gas Co., 1957–63; Dir, Vice-Pres. and Gen. Man., Garlock of Canada Ltd, and Yale Rubber Mfg Co. of Canada Ltd, 1963–64; Regional Dir for Ont., Canadian Corp. for 1967 World Exhibn, 1964–67; Agent General for Ontario in UK and Europe, 1967–72; Man. Dir, Canada Permanent Mortgage Corp. and Canada Permanent Trust Co., 1973–75; Dir, Wedgewood Estates, 1989. Chm. and Pres., Art Gallery of Greater Victoria, BC, 1980, then ex officio, 1980–83. Dir, Internat. Probns Club, 1994–. Liveryman, Painter Stainers Co., 1969–. Freeman of City of London, 1969. Canada Centennial Medal. *Recreation:* travelling. *Address:* #9–2200 Arbutus Cove Lane 477–0017, Victoria, British Columbia V8N 6J9, Canada. *Clubs:* Union, Victoria, Harbourside Rotary (Hon. Director and Hon. Mem.; Pioneer Rotarian, 1988) (Victoria, BC).

ROWE, Prof. Adrian Harold Redfern, FDSRCS; Professor of Conservative Dentistry, University of London, at Guy's Hospital, 1971–91, now Professor Emeritus; Dean of Dental Studies, 1985–89, Dean of Dental Sch., 1989–91, and Head of Department of Conservative Dental Surgery, 1967–91, United Medical and Dental Schools of Guy's and St Thomas' Hospitals; *b* 30 Dec. 1925; *y s* of late Harold Ridges Rowe and Emma Eliza (*née* Matthews), Lymington, Hants; *m* 1951, Patricia Mary Flett; three *s*. *Educ:* King Edward VI Sch., Southampton; Guy's Hosp. Dental Sch. (BDS 1948, distinguished in Surgery, Op. Dental Surgery, Dental Surgery and Orthodontics; distinguished in Dental Anatomy, 2nd BDS, 1946); MDS London, 1965. FDSRCS 1954; MCCDRCS, 1989. Nat. Service, RADC, 1949–50. Guy's Hospital Dental School: part-time practice and teaching, 1950–63; Sen. Lectr, 1963–67; Hon. Consultant, 1966–; Univ. Reader, 1967–71; London University: Chm., Bd of Studies in Dentistry, 1980–83; Mem., Senate, 1981–83. Member: Lewisham and N Southwark DHA, 1986–90; Special HA, 1986–90. Member: Dental Sub-Cttee, UGC, 1974–83; Council, Medical Defence Union, 1977–; Specialist Adv. Cttee in Restorative Dentistry, 1979–85; Bd, Faculty in Dental Surgery, RCS, 1980–93 (Vice Dean, 1987); Faculty Advr for SE Thames reg., RCS, 1983–89; President: British Endodontic Soc., 1964 (Hon. Mem., 1974); British Soc. for Restorative Dentistry, 1978. Past examiner in dental surgery in Univs of Belfast, Birmingham, Cardiff, Colombo, Dublin, Dundee, Edinburgh, Lagos, London, Malaysia, Malta, Manchester, Nairobi, Newcastle and Singapore; Statutory Exam. of GDC; Examnr for Licence and Fellowship exams of RCS and for Fellowship of RCSI. Dir, Medical Sickness Annuity and Life Assce Soc., 1987–. Governor: UMDS of Guy's and St Thomas' Hosps, 1985–91; Eastman Dental Hosp., 1986–90. Freeman, City of London, 1990; Liveryman, Soc. of Apothecaries, 1995–. Colyer Gold Medal, Faculty in Dental Surgery, RCS, 1993. *Publications:* Companion to Dental Studies, vol. I: Book I, Anatomy, Biochemistry and Physiology, 1982; Book II, Dental Anatomy and Embryology, 1981; vol. II, Clinical Methods, Medicine, Pathology and Pharmacology, 1988; vol. III, Clinical Dentistry, 1986; contrib. to British and foreign dental jls. *Recreations:* golf, DIY, gardening. *Address:* Manor Lodge, Manor Mews, Ringwould, Deal, Kent CT14 8HT. *T:* Deal (01304) 375487.

See also O. J. T. Rowe.

ROWE, Andrew John Bernard; MP (C) Mid Kent, since 1983; *b* 11 Sept. 1935; *s* of John Douglas Rowe and Mary Katharine Storr; *m* 1st, 1960, Alison Boyd (marr. diss.); one *s*; 2nd, 1983, Sheila L. Finkle, PhD; two step *d*. *Educ:* Eton Coll.; Merton Coll., Oxford (MA). Sub Lt RNVR, 1954–56. Schoolmaster, 1959–62; Principal, Scottish Office, 1962–67; Lectr, Edinburgh Univ., 1967–74; Consultant to Voluntary Services Unit, Home Office, 1974; Dir, Community Affairs, Cons. Central Office, 1975–79; self-employed consultant and journalist, 1979–83. PPS to Minister for Trade, 1992–. Chm., Parly Panel for Personal Social Services, 1986–92. *Publications:* Democracy Renewed, 1975; pamphlets and articles incl. Somewhere to Start. *Recreations:* photography, reading, theatre. *Address:* Tudor Milgate, Milgate Park, Ashford Road, Thurnham, Maidstone ME14 4NN. *T:* Maidstone (01622) 736809.

ROWE, Bridget; Editor, The People, since 1992; *b* 16 March 1950; *d* of Peter and Myrtle Rowe; *m* James Anthony Nolan; one *s*. *Educ:* St Michael's School, Limpsfield. Editor, Look Now, 1971–76; Editor, Woman's World, 1976–81; Asst Editor, The Sun, 1981–82; Editor: Sunday Magazine, 1982–86; Woman's Own, 1986–90; TV Times, 1990–91; Sunday Mirror, 1991–92. *Recreations:* equestrian sports. *Address:* The People, 1 Canada Square, Canary Wharf, E14 5AP.

ROWE, Helen, (Mrs Brian Rowe); *see* Cresswell, H.

ROWE, Sir Jeremy, Kt 1991; CBE 1980; Deputy Chairman, Abbey National plc (formerly Abbey National Building Society), 1978–89; Chairman: Peterborough Development Corporation, 1981–88; Family Assurance Society, 1986–93; *b* 31 Oct. 1928; *s* of Charles William Dell Rowe and Alison (*née* Barford); *m* 1957, Susan Mary (*née* Johnstone); four *d*. *Educ:* Wellesley House Sch.; Uppingham Sch.; Trinity Coll., Cambridge (MA (Hons) Hist.). English-Speaking Union Scholarship to USA, 1952. Joined London Brick Co. Ltd as trainee, 1952: Personal Asst to Chm., 1954; Dir and Sales Manager, 1963–67; Man. Dir, 1967–70; Dep. Chm. and Man. Dir, 1970–79; Man. Dir, 1979–82 and Chm., 1979–84; Director: West End Bd, Sun Alliance Insce Co. Ltd, 1978–; John Maunders Group plc, 1984–; Telephone Rentals plc, 1984–89. Chm., Occupational Pensions Bd, 1987–93. *Recreations:* tennis, shooting, reading, music. *Address:* Woodside, Peasmarsh, near Rye, Sussex TN31 6YD. *Clubs:* All England Lawn Tennis, Rye Golf.

ROWE, John Jermyn, QC 1982; Barrister; a Recorder of the Crown Court, since 1978; *b* 23 March 1936; *er s* of late John Rowe and Olga Brookes Rowe; *m* 1966, Susan, *d* of Wing Comdr Walter Dring, DSO, DFC and of Sheila Mary Patricia Gerrard; two *d*. *Educ:* Manchester Grammar School; Brasenose Coll., Oxford. Served Army, 1954–56. Called to the Bar, Middle Temple, 1960, Bencher, 1985; practice on Northern Circuit; Junior, 1961; Prosecuting Counsel to the Inland Revenue, Northern Circuit, 1980–82; Leader, Northern Circuit, 1988–92. Chm. of Bar, 1993. Mem., Parole Bd, 1987–90. Reviewer of Terrorism Statutes, 1994–. Hon. Mem., Canadian Bar Assoc., 1993–. *Publication:* contrib. Bullen and Leake and Jacob on Precedents and Pleadings, 13th edn, 1991.

ROWE, Owen John Tressider, MA; retired; *b* 30 July 1922; *e s* of late Harold Ridges Rowe and Emma E. Rowe (*née* Matthews), Lymington, Hampshire; *m* 1946, Marcelle Ljufliny Hyde-Johnson (*d* 1986); one *s* one *d*. *Educ:* King Edward VI School, Southampton; Exeter College, Oxford (Scholar, MA); 1st Cl. Hons in Classical Hon. Mods, 1942. Served War of 1939–45, Lieut in Roy. Hampshire Regt, 1942–45. 1st Cl. Hons in Lit Hum, Dec. 1947; Assistant Master: Royal Grammar School, Lancaster, 1948–50; Charterhouse, 1950–60 (Head of Classical Dept); Officer Comdg Charterhouse CCF, 1954–60;

Headmaster: Giggleswick School, 1961–70; Epsom College, 1970–82; Head of Classics, St John's Sch., Leatherhead, 1982–87. Governor: Rosebery Sch., 1971–; Chinthurst Sch., Tadworth. *Recreations:* Rotary, gardening, playing the recorder. *Address:* 8 Pine Hill, Epsom KT18 7BG. *Club:* Rotary (Epsom).

See also A. H. R. Rowe.

ROWE, Rear-Adm. Patrick Barton, CBE 1990; LVO 1975; Clerk to the Worshipful Company of Leathersellers, since 1993; Deputy Master, Trinity House, since 1995; *b* 14 April 1939; *e s* of Captain G. B. Rowe, DSC, RN and Doreen Rowe (*née* Robarts), Liphook, Hants; *m* 1964, Alexandra, *e d* of Alexander Mellor, OBE; one *s* one *d*. *Educ:* Wellington College; RNC Dartmouth. MRIN. Served Far East Fleet, 1960–65; specialised in Navigation, 1966; navigation appts, 1966–70; Comd, HMS Soberton, 1970–71; Army Staff Coll., 1972; Navigation Officer, HM Yacht Britannia, 1973–75; Comd, HMS Antelope, 1977–79; Naval Staff appts, 1979–82; Comd, HMS Keren, 1983; Comd, HMS Liverpool, 1983–85; RN Presentation Team, 1985–86; Commodore, Clyde, 1986–88; RCDS 1989; Mil. Deputy, Defence Export Services, 1990–92. Elder Brother, Trinity House. FIMgt; MIPM. *Recreations:* sailing, ski-ing. *Address:* c/o Lloyds Bank, Bishop's Waltham, Southampton SO3 1GS. *Clubs:* Army and Navy; Royal Yacht Squadron.

ROWE, Prof. Peter John, PhD; Professor of Law and Head, Department of Law, Lancaster University, since 1995; *b* 5 Aug. 1947; *s* of Major Dennis Rowe and Anne (*née* Nesbitt); *m* 1970, Anne Murland, *d* of D. A. White, OBE and J. C. White; one *s* one *d*. *Educ:* Methodist Coll., Belfast; Queen's Univ. Belfast (LLB); University College London (LLM); Univ. of Liverpool (PhD). Called to the Bar, Lincoln's Inn, 1979. Appts at Anglia Poly., 1970–77 and Lancashire Poly., 1977–79; University of Liverpool, 1979–95: Prof. of Law, 1988–95; Head of Dept of Law, 1988–93. Dir of Legal Studies, Cayman Islands Law Sch., 1982–84. Chm., Ind. Tribunal Service, (pt-time) 1989–94, (full-time) 1995. Chm., UK Gp, Internat. Soc. for Mil. Law and Law of War, 1990–. *Publications:* (with S. Knapp) Evidence and Procedure in the Magistrates' Court, 1983, 3rd edn 1989; (ed with C. Whelan) Military Intervention in Democratic Societies, 1985; Defence: the legal implications, military law and the laws of war, 1987; (ed) The Gulf War 1990–91, in International and English Law, 1993; articles in learned jls. *Recreations:* sailing, hill-walking, buying at auction. *Address:* Department of Law, Lancaster University, Lancaster LA1 4YW; Bryn, Ruthin Road, Gwernymynydd, Mold, Clwyd CH7 5LQ. *T:* Mold (01352) 810309.

ROWE, Prof. Peter Noël, DSc (Eng); FEng, FIChemE; Ramsay Memorial Professor of Chemical Engineering, and Head of Department, University College London, 1965–85, now Professor Emeritus; *b* 25 Dec. 1919; *e s* of Charles Henry Rowe and Kate Winifred (*née* Storry); *m* 1952, Pauline Garmirian; two *s*. *Educ:* Preston Grammar Sch.; Manchester Coll. of Technology; Imperial Coll., London. Princ. Scientific Officer, AERE, Harwell, 1958–65. Crabtree Orator, 1980. Vis. Prof., Univ. Libre de Bruxelles, 1988, 1995. Chm., Assessment Panel, HEFCE, 1992. Non-exec. Dir, Bentham Fine Chemicals, 1985–; Consultant, SERC, 1990–. Pres., IChemE, 1981–82; Hon. Sec., Fellowship of Engrg, 1982–85. FCGI 1983. Hon. Fellow, UCL, 1993. Hon. DSc Brussels, 1978. *Publications:* scientific articles in Trans IChemE, Chem. Eng. Science, etc. *Address:* Pamber Green, Upper Basildon, Reading, Berks RG8 8PG. *T:* Upper Basildon (01491) 671382.

ROWE, Peter Whitmill, MA; Schoolteacher at Kent College, Canterbury, 1983–90, retired; *b* 12 Feb. 1928; British; *s* of Gerald Whitmill Rowe, chartered accountant, one-time General Manager of Morris Commercials Co. Ltd; *m* 1952, Bridget Ann Moyle; two *s* one *d*. *Educ:* Bishop's Stortford College; St John's College, Cambridge. BA 1950; MA (Hons) 1956. VI Form History Master, Brentwood School, Essex, 1951–54; Senior History Master, Repton School, Derbys, 1954–57; Headmaster: Bishop's Stortford Coll., Herts, 1957–70; Cranbrook Sch., Kent, 1970–81; teacher, Williston-Northampton Sch., Mass., USA, 1981–83. JP Bishop's Stortford, 1968–70, Cranbrook, 1971–81. *Recreations:* literature, music, cricket, golf.

ROWE, Richard Brian; District Judge (formerly Registrar) of the High Court (Family Division), since 1979; *b* 28 April 1933; *s* of Charles Albert Rowe and Mabel Florence Rowe; *m* 1959, Shirley Ann Symons; two *d*. *Educ:* Greenford County Grammar Sch.; King's Coll., London Univ. (LLB). National Service, RAF, 1952–54. High Court (Probate, Divorce and Admiralty Div.), 1954–66; Land Commn, 1966–69; Lord Chancellor's Office, 1969–75; Sec., High Court (Family Div.), 1975–79. *Publications:* (ed) Rayden on Divorce, 10th edn, 1967; (ed) Tristram and Coote's Probate Practice, 25th edn, 1978, to 27th edn, 1989. *Recreations:* most sports. *Address:* High Court (Family Division), Somerset House, Strand, WC2R 1LP.

ROWE, Robert Stewart, CBE 1969; Director, Leeds City Art Gallery and Temple Newsam House, 1958–83 (and also of Lotherton Hall, 1968–83); *b* 31 Dec. 1920; *s* of late James Stewart Rowe and late Mrs A. G. Gillespie; *m* 1953, Barbara Elizabeth Hamilton Baynes; one *s* two *d*. *Educ:* privately; Downing Coll., Cambridge; Richmond Sch. of Art. Asst Keeper of Art, Birmingham Museum and Art Gallery, 1950–56; Dep. Dir, Manchester City Art Galls, 1956–58. Pres., Museums Assoc., 1973–74; Member: Adv. Council, V&A Mus., 1969–74; Arts Council of GB, 1981–86; Fine Arts Adv. Cttee, British Council, 1972–84; Chm., Bar Convent Museum Trust, York, 1986–91; Trustee, Henry Moore Sculpture Trust, 1983–. Liveryman, Worshipful Co. of Goldsmiths. Hon. LittD Leeds, 1983. *Publications:* Adam Silver, 1965; articles in Burlington Magazine, Museums Jl, etc. *Recreations:* gardening, reading. *Address:* Grove Lodge, Shadwell, Leeds LS17 8LB. *T:* Leeds (0113) 265 6365.

ROWE, Dr Roy Ernest, CBE 1977; FEng 1979; consultant; Director General, Cement and Concrete Association, 1977–87; *b* 26 Jan. 1929; *s* of Ernest Walter Rowe and Louisa Rowe; *m* 1954, Lillian Anderson; one *d*. *Educ:* Taunton's Sch., Southampton; Pembroke Coll., Cambridge (MA, ScD). FICE, FIStructE, FIHE. Cement and Concrete Association, later British Cement Association: Research Engineer, 1952–57; Head, Design Research Dept, 1958–65; Dir, R&D, 1966–77. Chm., Engrg Res. Commn, SERC, 1991–93. President: IStructE, 1983–84; Comité Euro-Internat. du Béton, 1987–. Hon. Mem., Amer. Concrete Inst., 1978; For. Associate, Nat. Acad. of Engineering, USA, 1980. Hon. DEng Leeds, 1984. *Publications:* Concrete Bridge Design, 1962, 3rd impr. 1972; numerous papers in technical and professional jls. *Recreations:* fell walking, listening to music (and mutilating it on the piano). *Address:* 15 Hollesley Road, Alderton, Woodbridge, Suffolk IP12 3BX. *T:* Shottisham (01394) 411096.

ROWE-BEDDOE, David Sydney; Chairman: Welsh Development Agency, since 1993; Development Board for Rural Wales, since 1994; *b* 19 Dec. 1937; *s* of late Sydney Rowe-Beddoe and Dolan Rowe-Beddoe (*née* Evans); *m* 1st, 1964, Malinda Collison (marr. diss. 1982); three *d*; 2nd, 1984, Madeleine Harrison. *Educ:* Cathedral Sch., Llandaff; Stowe Sch.; St John's Coll., Cambridge (MA); Harvard Univ. Grad. Sch. of Business Admin (PMD). Served RN, Sub-Lt, RNVR, 1956–58, Lieut, RNR, 1958–66. Thomas de la Rue & Company, 1961–76: Chief Executive, 1971–76; Exec. Dir, De la Rue Co. plc, 1974–76; Revlon Inc., NY, 1976–81; President: Latin America and Caribbean, 1976–77; Europe, ME and Africa, 1977–81; Pres. and Chief Exec. Officer, Ges. für Trendanalysen, 1981–87; Director: Morgan Stanley-GFTA Ltd, 1983–92; Cavendish Services Ltd, 1987– (Chm., 1987–94); US Banknote Corp., 1990–; Development Securities plc, 1994–. Member: Welsh Economic Council, 1994–; Prince of Wales' Cttee, 1994–. Gov., WCMD, 1993–. Liveryman, Broderers' Co., 1993. *Recreations:* music, theatre, country pursuits. *Address:* Welsh Development Agency, Pearl House, Greyfriars Road, Cardiff CF1 3XX. *T:* Cardiff (01222) 828667. *Clubs:* Garrick, Turf; Cardiff & County; Brook (New York); Automobile (Monaco).

ROWE-HAM, Sir David (Kenneth), GBE 1986; JP; chartered accountant, since 1962; Lord Mayor of London, 1986–87; Consultant to Touche Ross & Co., 1984–93; Director of public and private companies; *b* 19 Dec. 1935; *o s* of late Kenneth Henry and of Muriel Phyllis Rowe-Ham; *m* Sandra Celia (*née* Nicholls), *widow* of Ian Glover; three *s*. *Educ:* Dragon School; Charterhouse. FCA; IIMR; FCIS. Commnd 3rd King's Own Hussars. Mem., Stock Exchange, 1964–84; Sen. Partner, Smith Keen Cutler, 1972–82. Chairman: Asset Trust plc, 1982–89; Jersey General Investment Trust Ltd, 1988–89; Olayan Europe Ltd, 1989–; Brewin Dolphin Hldgs plc, 1992–; Apta Healthcare plc, 1994–; Coral Products PLC, 1995–; Regional Dir (London), Lloyds Bank plc, 1985–91; Director: W. Canning plc, 1981–86; Savoy Theatre Ltd, 1986–; Williams Hldgs PLC, 1992–; CLS Hldgs plc, 1994–. Chm., Adv. Panel, Guinness Flight Unit Trust Managers Ltd, 1987–. Alderman, City of London, Ward of Bridge and Bridge Without, 1976–; Sheriff, City of London, 1984–85; HM Lieut, City of London, 1987–. Court Member: City Univ., 1981–86 (Chancellor, 1986–87); Worshipful Co. of Chartered Accountants in England and Wales (Master, 1985–86); Worshipful Co. of Wheelwrights; Hon. Mem., Worshipful Co. of Launderers; Mem. Ct, HAC. Gov., Royal Shakespeare Co.; Trustee, Friends of D'Oyly Carte. Pres., Black Country Mus. Develt Trust; Mem., St Bartholomew's College Council. Chm., Birmingham Municipal Bank, 1970–72; Mem., Birmingham CC, 1965–72. Chm., Political Council, Junior Carlton Club, 1977; Dep. Chm., Political Cttee, Carlton Club, 1977–79. Mem., Lord's Taverners. Governor, Christ's Hospital. JP City of London, 1976 (Chief Magistrate, 1986–87; Supp. List, 1994–). Hon. DLitt City Univ., 1986. KJStJ 1986. Commandeur de l'Ordre Mérite, France, 1984; Commander, Order of the Lion, Malaŵi, 1985; Order of the Aztec Eagle (Cl. II), Mexico, 1985; Order of King Abdul Aziz (Cl. 1), 1987; Grand Officer, Order of Wissam Alouite, Morocco, 1987; Order of Diego Losada, Caracas, Venezuela, 1987; Pedro Ernesto Medal, Rio de Janeiro, 1987. *Recreations:* theatre, shooting. *Address:* 140 Piccadilly, W1V 9FH. *Clubs:* Carlton, City Livery, Guildhall.

ROWELL, Anthony Aylett, CMG 1992; Political Adviser (Southern Africa), Racal Radio Group UK, since 1993; Director, Racal Electronics SA Ltd, since 1994; *b* 10 Jan. 1937; *s* of Geoffrey William and Violet Ella Aylett Rowell; *m* 1st, 1965, Bridget Jane Reekie (marr. diss. 1985); one *s* one *d*; 2nd, 1985, Caroline Anne Edgcumbe. *Educ:* Marlborough. With British American Tobacco, 1959–65; HM Diplomatic Service, 1966–93: 2nd Sec., Lusaka, 1968–69; 1st Secretary: FCO, 1969; Bucharest, 1970–73; FCO, 1974–78; Nicosia, 1979–80; FCO, 1981–85; Counsellor: Nairobi, 1985–90; Pretoria, 1990–93. *Recreations:* tennis, badminton, hiking, photography, fine wines. *Address:* Bracken Cottage, Cross Hands, Devauden, near Chepstow, Gwent NP6 6HW. *Club:* Muthaiga Country (Nairobi).

ROWELL, Rt. Rev. Dr (Douglas) Geoffrey; *see* Basingstoke, Bishop Suffragan of.

ROWELL, Sir John (Joseph), Kt 1980; CBE 1974; BA; Chairman, Legal Aid Commission of Queensland, 1979–90; Consultant, Neil O'Sullivan & Rowell, Solicitors, Brisbane (Senior Partner, 1968–88); *b* 15 Feb. 1916; *s* of Joseph Alfred Rowell and Mary Lilian Rowell (*née* Hooper), both born in England; *m* 1947, Mary Kathleen (*née* de Silva); three *s* two *d*. *Educ:* Brisbane Grammar School; Univ. of Queensland (BA). Served AIF, 1940–46; Captain 2/10 Fd Regt (Efficiency Medal, 1946). Admitted Solicitor, 1939; Notary Public, 1959. Pres., Queensland Law Soc. Inc., 1964–66 (Mem. Council, 1956–67); Treas., Law Council of Aust., 1961–63 (Mem. Exec., 1960–67); Mem. Bd, Faculty of Law, Univ. of Queensland, 1959–78; Chm., Legal Assistance Cttee of Queensland, 1966–79; Member: Law Reform Commn of Qld, 1967–89; Commonwealth Legal Aid Commn, 1980–85. Chairman: Qld Bulk Handling Pty Ltd; Gas Corp. of Qld Ltd, 1974–90; Qld Bd, Capita Financial Gp (formerly City Mutual Life Assce Soc. Ltd), 1986–88 (Mem. Bd, 1971–88); Concrete Constructions (Qld) Pty, until 1993; Dir of Principal Bd, Boral Ltd and Boral Resources Ltd, 1974–87; Dir, Castlemaine Tooheys Ltd, 1980–85. Former Hon. Consul of Qld for Federal Repub. of Germany, 1963–86; Dean, Consular Corps of Qld, 1978–80. Pres., Qld Br., Australia-Britain Soc., 1988–94; Vice Pres., Qld Br., ESU, 1990–93. Officer's Cross, 1st class, 1979, Comdr's Cross, Order of Merit, 1986, FRG. *Recreations:* golf, fishing, reading. *Address:* Edgecliffe, 48 Walcott Street, St Lucia, Brisbane, Qld 4067, Australia. *T:* (7) 8709070. *Clubs:* Australian (Sydney); Brisbane, United Service, Tattersall's, Queensland Turf (Brisbane).

ROWELL, John Martin, DPhil; FRS 1989; Chief Technical Officer, Conductus Inc., since 1989; *b* 27 June 1935; *s* of Frank L. and P. E. Rowell; *m* 1959, Judith A. Harte; two *s* one *d*. *Educ:* Wadham Coll., Oxford (BSc, MA; DPhil 1961). Bell Telephone Labs, 1961–84; Bell Communications Research, 1984–89. Member: Acad. of Scis, 1994; Acad. of Engrg, 1995. Fellow, Amer. Physical Soc., 1974. Fritz London Meml Low Temperature Physics Prize, 1978. *Publications:* about 100 pubns in jls. *Address:* Conductus Inc., 969 W Maude Avenue, Sunnyvale, CA 94086, USA. *T:* (408) 5239408.

ROWLAND, Rev. Prof. Christopher Charles; Dean Ireland's Professor of the Exegesis of Holy Scripture, and Fellow of Queen's College, University of Oxford, since 1991; *b* Doncaster, 21 May 1947; *s* of Eric Rowland and Frances Mary Lawson; *m* 1969, Catherine Rogers; three *s* one *d*. *Educ:* Doncaster Grammar Sch.; Christ's Coll., Cambridge; Ridley Hall, Cambridge; BA 1969, PhD 1975, Cantab. Ordained deacon, 1975, priest 1976. Lectr in Religious Studies, Univ. of Newcastle upon Tyne, 1974–79; Curate: St James', Benwell, 1975–78; All Saints', Gosforth, 1978–79; Asst Lectr in Divinity, 1983–85, Lectr in Divinity, 1985–91, Univ. of Cambridge; Fellow and Dean, Jesus Coll., Cambridge, 1979–91. *Address:* Queen's College, Oxford OX1 4AW.

ROWLAND, David; *see* Rowland, J. D.

ROWLAND, David Powys; Stipendiary Magistrate, Mid Glamorgan (formerly Merthyr Tydfil), 1961–89, retired; *b* 7 Aug. 1917; *s* of late Henry Rowland, CBE, Weston-super-Mare; *m* 1st, 1946, Joan (*d* 1958), *d* of late Group Capt. J. McCrae, MBE, Weston-super-Mare; one *s* one *d*; 2nd, 1961, Jenny (marr. diss. 1977), *d* of late Percival Lance, Swanage, and *widow* of Michael A. Forester-Bennett, Alverstoke; one *s* one *d* (and one step-*d*); 3rd, 1980, Diana, *d* of late W. H. Smith, Cannock, and *widow* of Lt-Col W. D. H. McCardie, S Staffs Regt (two step-*d*). *Educ:* Cheltenham Coll.; Oriel Coll., Oxford (BA). Lieut, Royal Welch Fusiliers, 1940–46. Called to Bar, Middle Temple, 1947. Deputy Chairman: Glamorgan QS, 1961–71; Breconshire QS, 1964–71. Mem. Nat. Adv. Council on Training of Magistrates, 1964–73. *Recreations:* fly-fishing, gardening. *Address:* Trosglwyd, Dyffryn Crawnon, Llangynidr, Crickhowell, Powys NP8 1NU. *T:* Bwlch (01874) 730635.

ROWLAND, Geoffrey Robert; QC (Guernsey) 1993; HM Solicitor-General for Guernsey, since 1992; *b* 5 Jan. 1948; *s* of Percy George Rowland and Muriel Florence (*née* Maunder); *m* 1972, Diana Janet Caryl; two *s*. *Educ:* Elizabeth Coll., Guernsey; Univ. of Southampton; Univ. of Caen. Called to the Bar, Gray's Inn, 1970; called to the Guernsey

Bar, 1971; in private practice as advocate, Guernsey, 1971–91; Sen. Partner, Collas Day and Rowland, 1984–91. Vice-Chm., Guernsey Financial Services Commn, 1988–92. Chairman: Guernsey Press Co. Ltd, 1990–92; TSB Foundn for CI, 1990–92. *Recreations:* ski-ing, reading history, international travel. *Address:* Armorica, L'Ancresse, Guernsey, CI GY3 5JR. *T:* Guernsey (01481) 47494.

ROWLAND, Air Marshal Sir James (Anthony), AC 1987; KBE 1977; DFC 1944; AFC 1953; BE; CEng, FRAeS, FIE(Aust); Governor of New South Wales, 1981–89; Chairman, Preston Group Pty, since 1991; Director: Angus & Coote Ltd, since 1989; Focus Books Ltd, since 1990; Thomson Radar Australia Corp., since 1993; *b* 1 Nov. 1922; *s* of Louis Claude Rowland and Elsie Jean Rowland; *m* 1955, Faye Alison (*née* Doughton); one *d*. *Educ:* Cranbrook Sch., Sydney; St Paul's Coll., Univ. of Sydney (BE Aero). CEng, FRAeS 1969; FIE (Aust) 1978; FTS 1988. Served War, Pilot, RAAF and RAF Bomber Comd, 1942–45. Sydney Univ., 1940–41 and 1946–47; Empire Test Pilots' Sch., Farnborough, 1949; Chief Test Pilot, RAAF R&D Unit, 1951–54; Staff Coll., 1956; Staff and unit posts, incl. OC R&D, 1957–60; RAAF Mirage Mission, Paris, 1961–64; CO No 1 Aircraft Depot, 1966; Sen. Engr SO, Ops Comd, 1968–69; RCDS, 1971; Dir Gen., Aircraft Engrg, RAAF, 1972; Air Mem. for Technical Services, 1973; Chief of Air Staff, RAAF, 1975–79. Member: Admin. Appeals Tribunal, 1979–80; Police Board of NSW, 1989–92. Chairman: NSW Air Transport Council, 1989–; Aerospace Foundn, 1992–. Consultant, OFEMA Australia, 1980. Pres., Royal Humane Soc. of NSW, 1990–. Chancellor, Univ. of Sydney, 1990–91. Hon. DEng Sydney, 1983. KStJ 1981. *Publications:* contribs to professional jls. *Recreations:* surfing, reading, golf. *Address:* 21/171 Walker Street, North Sydney, NSW 2060, Australia. *Clubs:* Royal Air Force; Australian, Royal Automobile, Union (Sydney); United Services (Brisbane); Royal Sydney Golf.

ROWLAND, (John) David; Chairman of Lloyd's, since 1993; *b* 10 Aug. 1933; *s* of Cyril Arthur Rowland and Eileen Mary Rowland; *m* 1st, 1957, Giulia Powell (marr. diss. 1991); one *s* one *d*; 2nd, 1991, Diana Louise Matthews (*née* Dickie). *Educ:* St Paul's School; Trinity College, Cambridge (MA Natural Sciences). Joined Matthews Wrightson and Co., 1956, Dir, 1965; Dir, Matthews Wrightson Holdings, 1972; Dep. Chm., 1978–81, Chm., 1981–87, Stewart Wrightson Holdings plc; Dep. Chm., Willis Faber plc, 1987–88; Chief Exec., 1988–92, Chm., 1989–92, Sedgwick Gp plc. Chm., Westminster Insurance Agencies, 1981–88; Dir, Sedgwick Lloyd's Underwriting Agencies, 1988–92. Director: Project Fullemploy, 1973–88; Fullemploy Gp Ltd, 1989–90; Non-Executive Director: Royal London Mutual Insurance Soc., 1985–86; S. G. Warburg Gp, 1992–. Mem. Council, Lloyd's, 1987–90; Mem., President's Cttee, Business in the Community, 1986–92 (Mem., City of London section, 1983–86). Vice-Pres., British Insurance and Investment Brokers' Assoc. (formerly British Insurance Brokers' Assoc.), 1980–; Member of Council: Industrial Soc., 1983–88; Contemporary Applied Arts, subseq. British Crafts Centre, 1985–92; Council of Industry and Higher Educn, 1990–92. Member: Council, Templeton Coll. (Oxford Centre for Management Studies), 1980– (Chm., 1985–92); Governing Bd, City Res. Project, 1991–92; Governor: Coll. of Insurance, 1983–85; St Paul's Schs, 1991. Hon. MA Oxford, 1993. *Recreations:* golf, running slowly. *Address:* 105 Barnsbury Street, N1 1EP. *T:* 0171–609 2041; Giffords Hall, Wickhambrook, Newmarket, Suffolk CB8 8PQ. *T:* Wickhambrook (01440) 820221. *Clubs:* MCC; Royal and Ancient Golf (St Andrews), Royal St George's (Sandwich), Royal Worlington and Newmarket Golf, Sunningdale Golf.

ROWLAND, Mark; Social Security Commissioner and Child Support Commissioner, since 1993; *b* 20 July 1953; *s* of Sqdn Leader Bernard Rowland and late Elizabeth Rowland (*née* Cuerden); *m* 1977, Eileen Cleary; two *d*. *Educ:* Ampleforth Coll.; Univ. of Warwick (LLB Hons). Called to the Bar, Gray's Inn, 1975; Welfare rights adviser, CPAG, 1975–78; private practice at the Bar, 1979–93; part-time Chm., social security, medical and disability appeal tribunals, 1988–93; Dep. Social Security Comr, 1992–93; Chm., registered homes tribunal, 1995–. Gov., Stifford Co. Primary Sch. Jt Ed., Rights Guide to Non-means-tested Benefits, 1978–91. *Publications:* The Industrial Injuries Scheme, 1983; (contrib.) Medical and Disability Appeal Tribunals: the Legislation, 1993; papers on social security law. *Recreations:* railways, military history, social history, gardening. *Address:* Office of the Social Security and Child Support Commissioners, Harp House, 83 Farringdon Street, EC4A 4DH. *T:* 0171–353 5145.

ROWLAND, His Honour Robert Todd, QC 1969; County Court Judge of Northern Ireland, 1974–90; President, Lands Tribunal for Northern Ireland, 1983–90; part-time Chairman, Value Added Tax Tribunals, 1990–94; *b* 12 Jan. 1922; *yr s* of late Lt-Col Charles Rowland and Jean Rowland; *m* 1952, Kathleen, *er d* of late H. J. Busby, Lambourn, Berks; two *s*. *Educ:* Crossley and Porter Sch., Halifax, Yorks; Ballyclare High Sch.; Queen's Univ. of Belfast (LLB 1948). Called to Bar of N Ireland, 1949; Mem., Bar Council, 1967–72. Served 2nd Punjab Regt, IA, in India, Assam, Burma, Thailand, Malaya, 1942–46. Counsel to Attorney-Gen. for N Ireland, 1966–69; Sen. Crown Prosecutor for Co. Tyrone, 1969–72; Vice-Pres., VAT Tribunal for N Ireland, 1972–74. Served on County Court Rules Cttee, 1965–72; Chairman: War Pensions Appeal Tribunal, 1962–72; Commn of Inquiry into Housing Contracts, 1978; Member: Bd of Governors, Strathearn Sch., 1969–89; Legal Adv. Cttee, Gen. Synod of Church of Ireland, 1975–89. Chancellor, dioceses of Armagh, and Down and Dromore, 1978–89. *Recreations:* fly-fishing, golf, hill-walking. *Address:* Greystones, Holmewood Drive, Kirby Fields, Kirby Muxloe, Leics LE9 2EF.

ROWLANDS, Christopher John, FCA; Chief Executive, HTV Group plc, since 1993; *b* 29 Aug. 1951; *s* of late Wilfrid John Rowlands and of Margaretta (*née* Roberts); *m* 1978, Alison Mary Kelly; twin *d*. *Educ:* Roundhay Sch., Leeds; Gonville and Caius Coll., Cambridge (MA Econ). FCA 1975. Peat Marwick Mitchell: articled clerk, 1973–75; CA, 1975; Manager, 1981; seconded as Partner, Zambia, 1981–83; Sen. Manager, London, 1983–85; Asda Group plc: Controller, business planning, Asda Stores, 1985–86; Divl Dir, Gp Finance, 1986–88; Dep. Man. Dir and Finance Dir, Asda Gp/Property Devolt and Investment cos, 1988–92; Gp Finance Dir, HTV Gp plc, 1992–93. Mem. Council, ITVA, 1993– (Chm., Engrg Policy Gp, 1993–). *Recreations:* family, theatre, church, reading, ski-ing, tennis, travel. *Address:* HTV Group plc, Culverhouse Cross, Cardiff CF5 6XJ.

ROWLANDS, David, CB 1991; Deputy Secretary, Department of Transport, since 1993; *b* 31 May 1947; *s* of George and Margaret Rowlands; *m* 1975, Louise Marjorie Brown; two *s*. *Educ:* St Mary's Coll., Crosby; St Edmund Hall, Oxford. Entered Civil Service, 1974; Private Sec. to Minister of State for Industry, 1978–80; Principal, Dept of Trade, then of Transport, 1980–84; Asst Sec., 1984–90, Under Sec., 1990–93, Dept of Transport. *Address:* Department of Transport, 76 Marsham Street, SW1P 4DR.

ROWLANDS, Edward; MP (Lab) Merthyr Tydfil and Rhymney, since 1983 (Merthyr Tydfil, April 1972–1983); *b* 23 Jan. 1940; *e s* of W. S. Rowlands; *m* 1968, Janice Williams, Kidwelly, Carmarthenshire; two *s* one *d*. *Educ:* Rhondda Grammar Sch.; Wirral Grammar Sch.; King's Coll., London. BA Hons History (London) 1962. Research Asst, History of Parliament Trust, 1963–65; Lectr in Modern History and Govt, Welsh Coll. of Adv. Technology, 1965–. MP (Lab) Cardiff North, 1966–70; Parliamentary Under-Secretary of State: Welsh Office, 1969–70, 1974–75; FCO, 1975–76; Minister of State, FCO, 1976–79; Opposition spokesman on energy, 1980–87; Mem., Select Cttee on Foreign Affairs, 1987–. Chm., History of Parliament Trust, 1993–. Member: Governing Body, Commonwealth Inst., 1980–92; Academic Council, Wilton Park, 1983–92. A Booker Prize Judge, 1984. *Publications:* various articles. *Recreations:* music, golf. *Address:* House of Commons, SW1A 0AA; 5 Park Crescent, Thomastown, Merthyr Tydfil, Mid Glamorgan. *T:* Merthyr Tydfil (01685) 384912.

ROWLANDS, Rev. Canon John Henry Lewis; Warden, St Michael and All Angels' Theological College, Llandaff, since 1988; *b* 16 Nov. 1947; *s* of William Lewis and Elizabeth Mary Rowlands; *m* 1976, Catryn Meryl Parry Edwards; one *s* two *d*. *Educ:* Queen Elizabeth Grammar Sch., Carmarthen; St David's University Coll., Lampeter (BA); Magdalene Coll., Cambridge (MA); Durham Univ. (MLitt); Wescott House, Cambridge. Ordained deacon, 1972, priest, 1973 (St David's Cathedral); Curate, Rectorial Benefice of Aberystwyth, 1972–76; Chaplain, St David's University Coll., Lampeter, 1976–79; Youth Chaplain, dio. of St David's, 1976–79; Dir, Academic Studies, St Michael's Coll., Llandaff, 1979–84, Sub-Warden, 1984–88. Lectr, Faculty of Theology, University Coll., Cardiff, later Univ. of Wales Coll. of Cardiff, then Univ. of Wales, Cardiff, 1979–, Asst Dean, 1981–83; Dean, Faculty of Theol., Univ. of Wales, 1991–95. Diocesan Dir of Ordinands, Dio. Llandaff, 1985–88; Exmng Chaplain to Archbishop of Wales, 1987–91. Hon. Canon, Llandaff Cathedral, 1990–. Pres., Diwinyddiaeth (Soc. of Theol. Grads, Univ. of Wales), 1989–92. Member: (*ex officio*) Governing Body of the Church in Wales, 1988–; Court, Univ. of Wales, 1988–94; Court, Univ. of Wales Coll. of Cardiff, 1988–; Academic Bd, Univ. of Wales, 1991–; Council, Llandaff Cathedral Sch., 1991–. Fellow, Woodard Corp., 1993. *Publications:* (ed) Essays on the Kingdom of God, 1986; Church, State and Society 1827–45, 1989. *Recreations:* beachcombing, racket games, auctioneering, antique markets, cat breeding (Siamese seal-point). *Address:* The Old Registry, Cardiff Road, Llandaff, Cardiff CF5 2DQ. *T:* Cardiff (01222) 563116.

ROWLANDS, John Kendall, FSA; Keeper, Department of Prints and Drawings, British Museum, 1981–91; *b* 18 Sept. 1931; *s* of Arthur and Margaret Rowlands; *m* 1st, 1957, Else A. H. Bachmann (marr. diss. 1981); one *s* two *d*; 2nd, 1982, Lorna Jane Lowe; one *d*. *Educ:* Chester Cathedral Choir Sch.; King's Sch., Chester; Gonville and Caius Coll., Cambridge. MA Cantab 1959; MA Oxon; FSA 1976. Asst Keeper, Dept of Art, City Mus. and Art Gall., Birmingham, 1956–60; Editor, Clarendon Press, Oxford, 1960–65; Asst Keeper, 1965–74, Dep. Keeper, 1974–81, Dept of Prints and Drawings, British Museum. Vice-Chm., Lincoln Cathedral Music Appeal, 1994–; Mem. Adv. Cttee, Collected Works of Erasmus, 1979–. *Publications:* David Cox Centenary Exhibition Catalogue, 1959; Graphic Work of Albrecht Dürer, 1971; Bosch, 1975; Rubens: drawings and sketches . . . , 1977; Urs Graf, 1977; Hercules Segers, 1979; Bosch, the Garden of Earthly Delights, 1979; German Drawings from a Private Collection, 1984; Master Drawings and Watercolours in the British Museum: from Fra Angelico to Henry Moore, 1984; The Paintings of Hans Holbein the Younger, 1985; The Age of Dürer and Holbein, 1988; Drawings by German Artists in the British Museum: 15th century, and 16th century by artists born before 1530, 1993; contribs to specialist journals, festschriften. *Recreations:* rustic pursuits, music making. *Address:* The Old Rectory, Silk Willoughby, Lincs NG34 8NY. *Club:* Beefsteak.

ROWLANDS, (John) Martin, CBE 1980; Secretary for Civil Service, Hong Kong Government, 1978–85; *b* 20 July 1925; *s* of late John Walter Rowlands and of Mary Ace Maitland (*née* Roberts); *m* 1956, Christiane Germaine Madeleine Lacheny; two *d*. *Educ:* Charterhouse; Selwyn Coll., Cambridge (MA). Military service, 1943–47 (Captain, 3rd Royal Indian Artillery Field Regt, HQ XV Indian Corps, HQ ALFSEA). HMOCS, Hong Kong Admin. Service, 1952–85: Dep. Dir of Urban Services, 1966–68; Principal Asst Colonial Sec., 1968–71; Dep. Sec. for Home Affairs, 1971–74; Dir of Immigration, 1974–78; Mem., Hong Kong Legislative Council, 1978–84. *Recreations:* travel, railways, bird-watching. *Address:* Flat 3, 15 Collingham Road, SW5 0NU. *Clubs:* Hong Kong, Royal Hong Kong Jockey.

ROWLANDS, Air Marshal Sir John (Samuel), GC 1943; KBE 1971 (OBE 1954); Consultant, Civil Aviation Administration, since 1981; *b* 23 Sept. 1915; *s* of late Samuel and Sarah Rowlands; *m* 1942, Constance Wight; two *d*. *Educ:* Hawarden School, University of Wales (BSc Hons). Joined RAFVR, 1939; permanent commission in RAF, 1945. British Defence Staff, Washington, 1961–63; Imperial Defence College, 1964; Royal Air Force College, Cranwell, 1965–68; First Director General of Training, RAF, 1968–70; AOC-in-C, RAF Maintenance comd, 1970–73; Asst Principal, Sheffield Polytechnic, 1974–80. *Recreations:* photography, tennis, motoring. *Club:* Royal Air Force.

ROWLANDS, Maldwyn Jones, OBE 1979; FLA, FRGS, FLS; Head of Library Services, British Museum (Natural History), 1965–81, retired; *b* 7 March 1918; *s* of Thomas and Elizabeth Rowlands; *m* 1941, Sybil Elizabeth Price; two *s* one *d*. *Educ:* Newtown Grammar Sch., Montgomeryshire; University Coll. London. Served in Army, 1940–46: commnd 1941 (Lieut), HQ 21 Army Gp (Staff Captain), 1944–46 (C-in-C's Cert. 1945). Asst Librarian, Science Museum Library, 1946–54; Deputy Librarian: British Museum (Natural History), 1954–63; Patent Office, 1963–65. *Recreations:* old books and bindings, Welsh history and folk-lore. *Address:* Llys Hafren, Caersws, Powys SY17 5JA.

ROWLANDS, Martin; *see* Rowlands, J. M.

ROWLANDS, Martyn Omar, FCSD, FIM; Chairman, Martyn Rowlands Design Consultants Ltd, 1960–88; retired; *b* 27 July 1923; *s* of Edward and Mildred Rowlands; *m* 1st, 1951, Ann Patricia (*d* 1974); two *s* one *d*; 2nd, 1978 (marr. diss. 1986). *Educ:* Eltham Coll.; Central Sch. of Art and Design. FCSD (FSIAD 1960); FIM (FPRI 1973). Served War, RAF, 1940–45: India and Burma. Central Sch. of Art and Design, 1946–49; Head of Indust. Design, Ekco Plastics, 1954–59; started own design consultancy, 1959. Past Pres., SIAD (now CSD). *Recreation:* photography. *Address:* Parndon Mill, Harlow, Essex CM20 2HP. *T:* Harlow (01279) 641090.

ROWLEY, Sir Charles (Robert), 7th Bt *cr* 1836; *b* 15 March 1926; *s* of Sir William Joshua Rowley, 6th Bt and Beatrice Gwendoline, *d* of Rev. Augustus George Kirby; *S* father, 1971; *m* 1952, Astrid, *d* of Sir Arthur Massey, CBE; one *s* one *d*. *Educ:* Wellington. *Heir: s* Richard Charles Rowley [*b* 14 Aug. 1959; *m* 1989, Alison, *d* of late Henry Bellingham, and of Mrs Ian Baillie; two *s*]. *Address:* 21 Tedworth Square, SW3 4DR; Naseby Hall, Northamptonshire NN6 6DP.

ROWLEY, Frederick Allan, CMG 1978; OBE 1959; MC 1945; Major (retd); HM Diplomatic Service, retired; *b* 27 July 1922; *m* 1951, Anne Crawley; one *s* three *d*. *Educ:* Haig Sch., Aldershot. Served War of 1939–45: Ranks, 8th Worcs Regt (TA), 1939–40; Emergency Commnd Officer, 5th Bn, 10th Baluch Regt (KGVO), Jacob's Rifles, Indian Army, Burma Campaign (MC), June 1941–Nov. 1948. At partition of India, granted regular commn (back-dated, 1942) in Worcestershire Regt, but retd (wounded), sub. Major. Joined HM Diplomatic Service, Nov. 1948: served (with brief periods in FO) in: Egypt; Ethiopia; Turkey; Burma; Singapore; Australia; Malaysia; FCO 1971–72; Under-Sec., N Ireland Office (on secondment), 1972–73; Counsellor, FCO, 1973–79. Joint

Services Staff College (jssc), 1959. *Recreations:* cricket, golf. *Clubs:* Boodle's, Army and Navy; MCC.

ROWLEY, Geoffrey William, CBE 1989; Town Clerk, City of London, 1982–91; *b* 9 Sept. 1926; *s* of George Frederick Rowley and Ellen Mary Rowley; *m* 1950, Violet Gertrude Templeman; one *s* one *d. Educ:* Owens School. FIPD (FIPM 1974). Served War, Royal Marines, 1944–47. Corporation of the City of London, 1947–: Head, Personnel Sect., 1965–74; Dep. Town Clerk, 1974–82. Liveryman, Basketmakers' Co. (Prime Warden, 1990–91). Hon. Fellow, City of London Poly, subseq. London Guildhall Univ., 1991. DCL *hc* City, 1989. Order of White Rose, Finland, 1969; Order of Orange Nassau, Holland, 1982; Légion d'Honneur, France, 1985. OStJ 1987. *Recreations:* sport: badminton as a player, cricket and soccer as a spectator. *Address:* 3 Wensley Avenue, Woodford Green, Essex IG8 9HE. *T:* 0181–504 6270.

ROWLEY, John Charles, CMG 1977; Director, Crown Agents Board of Management, 1980–84, retired; *b* 29 Sept. 1919; *s* of John Ernest Rowley and Edith Muriel (*née* Aldridge); *m* 1st, 1945, Pamela Hilda Godfrey (marr. diss. 1971); two *d*; 2nd, 1972, Anne Patricia Dening; one *s. Educ:* Ilford; King's College, London (LLB 1948, Upper Second Cl. Hons). Inland Revenue, 1938–40. RAF, 1940–46, pilot, Flight-Lieut; Iceland, 1944 (despatches). Inland Revenue, 1946–64; Min. of Overseas Development, 1964–79, Head, Middle East Develt Div., Beirut, Lebanon and Amman, Jordan, 1971–79; Crown Agents Regional Controller for Middle East, 1979–80. *Recreations:* choral singing, sailing. *Address:* 43 Half Moon Lane, SE24 9JX.

ROWLEY, John Vincent d'Alessio; General Manager, Bracknell New Town Development Corporation, 1955–73; *b* 12 Sept. 1907; 2nd *s* of late Ven. Hugh Rowley, Archdeacon of Kingwilliamstown, S Africa; *m* 1st, 1936, Violet Maud (*d* 1969), *d* of S. H. Day, Grahamstown, S Africa; one *s*; 2nd, 1972, Kathleen Mary Hawkesworth (*née* Pullom). *Educ:* St Andrews Coll., Grahamstown; Trinity Coll., Oxford (Rhodes Schol.). BA 1929; Oxford Univ. Rugby XV, 1929. Entered Sudan Political Service, 1930; Asst District Comr and District Comr, 1930–49; seconded Sudan Defence Force, 1940–42; Dep. Gov., Kordofan Province, 1950–52; Asst Financial Sec., 1952–53; Governor, Darfur Province, 1953–55. Chm., South Hill Park Arts Centre Trust, 1979–. *Recreations:* music, gardening, golf. *Address:* The Spring, Stanford Dingley, near Bradfield, Berks RG7 6LX. *T:* Bradfield (01734) 744270. *Club:* United Oxford & Cambridge University.

ROWLEY, Sir Joshua Francis, 7th Bt, *cr* 1786; JP; Lord-Lieutenant of Suffolk, 1978–94; *b* 31 Dec. 1920; *o s* of 6th Bt and Margery Frances Bacon (*d* 1977); *S* father, 1962; *m* 1959, Hon. Celia Ella Vere Monckton, 2nd *d* of 8th Viscount Galway; one *d. Educ:* Eton; Trinity College, Cambridge. Grenadier Guards, 1940–46. Deputy Secretary, National Trust, 1952–55. Chairman: W Suffolk CC, 1971–74; Suffolk CC, 1976–78; DL 1968, High Sheriff 1971, Vice Lord-Lieutenant, 1973–78, JP 1978, Suffolk. Hon. DCL UEA, 1991. *Address:* Holbecks, Hadleigh, Ipswich, Suffolk IP7 5PF. *T:* Hadleigh (01473) 823211. *Clubs:* Boodle's, Pratt's, MCC.

ROWLEY, Peter, MC 1944; Vice President, Leonard Cheshire Foundation, since 1993 (Chairman, 1982–90); Chairman, Cheshire Homes European Regional Council, 1990–94; *b* 12 July 1918; *s* of late Roland and Catherine Isabel Rowley; *m* 1940, Ethnea Louis Florence Mary Howard Kyan; four *d. Educ:* Wembley County Sch.; University Coll., Oxford (MA). Served War of 1939–45: Queen's Westminster Rifles, 1938–39; 14th Bn Sherwood Foresters, 1940–46; Adjt, Middle East, N Africa; Company Comdr, Italy; Bde Major 13 Bde, 1944–45; GSOII 8 Corps, 1945–46. Admitted Solicitor, Titmuss Sainer & Webb, 1950; Sen. Partner, 1981–83, retd. Member, Law Society Land Law Cttee, 1970–87. Liveryman, Distillers Co., 1975. *Address:* Underlea, 34 Radnor Cliff, Folkestone, Kent CT20 2JL. *T:* Folkestone (01303) 248689. *Club:* Royal Automobile.

ROWLEY-CONWY, family name of **Baron Langford.**

ROWLEY HILL, Sir George Alfred; *see* Hill.

ROWLING, Rt. Hon. Sir Wallace (Edward), KCMG 1983; PC 1974; President, New Zealand Institute of International Affairs, since 1990; *b* Motueka, 15 Nov. 1927; *s* of A. Rowling; *m* 1951, Glen Elna, *d* of Captain J. M. Reeves; two *s* one *d. Educ:* Nelson Coll. MA. Fulbright Schol., 1955–56. Formerly Asst Dir of Educn, NZ Army. MP (Lab) for Buller (later for Tasman), NZ, 1962–84; Minister of Finance, 1972–74; Prime Minister of NZ, 1974–75; Leader of Opposition, 1975–83. Ambassador to USA, 1985–88. Chairman: Superannuation Investment Ltd, 1992–; Tasman Electric Power Trust, 1993–; Port Nelson Ltd, 1994–; Mutual Funds Ltd, 1994–. Governor for New Zealand, IMF. Rep. NZ at annual meeting of ADB, Kuala Lumpur, 1974. Pres., Asia Pacific Socialist Orgn, 1977–83. Chairman: Mus. of NZ, 1994–; Fifeshire Foundn, 1994–; NZ Orthopaedic Trust, 1994–. Col Comdt, NZ Army Educn Corps, 1977–82. Hon. LLD Canterbury, NZ, 1987. *Recreation:* golf. *Address:* PO Box 78, Motueka, Nelson, New Zealand.

ROWLINSON, Prof. John Shipley, BSc, MA, DPhil Oxon; FRS 1970; FRSC; FEng 1976; FIChemE; Dr Lee's Professor of Physical Chemistry, Oxford University, 1974–93, now Emeritus; Fellow of Exeter College, since 1974; *b* 12 May 1926; *er s* of late Frank Rowlinson and Winifred Jones; *m* 1952, Nancy Gaskell; one *s* one *d. Educ:* Rossall School (Scholar); Trinity College, Oxford (Millard Scholar; Hon. Fellow, 1992). Research Associate, Univ. of Wisconsin, USA, 1950–51; ICI Research Fellow, Lecturer, and Senior Lecturer in Chemistry, University of Manchester, 1951–60; Prof. of Chemical Technology, London Univ. (Imperial Coll.), 1961–73. Mary Upson Prof. of Engrg, 1988, Andrew D. White Prof.-at-large, 1990–, Cornell Univ. Lectures: Liversidge, Chem. Soc., 1978; von Hofmann, Gesell. Deutscher Chem., 1980; Faraday, 1983, Lennard-Jones, 1985, RSC; Guggenheim, Reading Univ., 1986; T. W. Leland, Rice Univ., Houston, Texas, 1990; Rossini, IUPAC, 1992; Dreyfus, Dartmouth Coll., 1993; Birch, ANU, 1994. Pres., Faraday Div., Chem. Soc., 1979–81; Hon. Treas., Faraday Society, 1968–71; Vice-Pres., Royal Instn of GB, 1974–76, 1993–95; Physical Sec. and Vice-Pres., Royal Soc., 1994–. Member, Sale Borough Council, 1956–59. Hon. FCGI 1987. Hon. For. Mem., Amer. Acad. of Arts and Scis, 1994. Meldola Medal, Roy. Inst. of Chemistry, 1954; Marlow Medal, Faraday Soc., 1957; Leverhulme Medal, Royal Soc., 1993. *Publications:* Liquids and Liquid Mixtures, 1959, (jtly) 3rd edn, 1982; The Perfect Gas, 1963; Physics of Simple Liquids (joint editor), 1968; (trans. jtly) The Metric System, 1969; (jtly) Thermodynamics for Chemical Engineers, 1975; (jtly) Molecular Theory of Capillarity, 1982; (ed) J. D. van der Waals, On the Continuity of the Gaseous and Liquid States, 1988; (jtly) Record of the Royal Society 1940–1989, 1993; papers in scientific journals. *Recreation:* mountaineering. *Address:* 12 Pullens Field, Headington, Oxford OX3 0BU. *T:* Oxford (01865) 67507; Physical and Theoretical Chemistry Laboratory, South Parks Road, Oxford OX1 3QZ. *T:* Oxford (01865) 275973. *Club:* Alpine.

ROWNTREE CLIFFORD, Rev. Paul; *see* Clifford.

ROWSE, Alfred Leslie, MA, DLitt; FBA; Emeritus Fellow of All Souls College, Oxford; *b* St Austell, Cornwall, 4 Dec. 1903. *Educ:* Elementary and Grammar Schools, St Austell; Christ Church Oxford (Douglas Jerrold Scholar in English Literature). Sen. Res. Associate, Huntington Library, Calif, 1962–69. Fellow of the Royal Society of Literature; President of the English Association, 1952; Raleigh Lecturer, British Academy, 1957; Trevelyan Lecturer, Cambridge, 1958; Beatty Memorial Lecturer, McGill University, 1963. Pres., Shakespeare Club, Stratford-upon-Avon, 1970–71. Benson Medal, RSL, 1982. *Publications:* Politics and the Younger Generation, 1931; Mr Keynes and the Labour Movement, 1936; Sir Richard Grenville of the Revenge, 1937; Tudor Cornwall, 1941; Poems of a Decade, 1931–41; A Cornish Childhood, 1942; The Spirit of English History, 1943; Poems Chiefly Cornish, 1944; The English Spirit: Essays in History and Literature, 1944, rev. edn 1966; West Country Stories, 1945; The Use of History, 1946; Poems of Deliverance, 1946; The End of an Epoch, 1947; The England of Elizabeth, 1950; The English Past, 1951 (rev. edn, as Times, Persons, Places, 1965); Translation and completion of Lucien Romier's History of France, 1953; The Expansion of Elizabethan England, 1955; The Early Churchills, 1956; The Later Churchills, 1958; Poems Partly American, 1958; The Elizabethans and America, 1959; St Austell: Church, Town, Parish, 1960; All Souls and Appeasement, 1961; Ralegh and the Throckmortons, 1962; William Shakespeare: A Biography, 1963; Christopher Marlowe: A Biography, 1964; A Cornishman at Oxford, 1965; Shakespeare's Southampton: Patron of Virginia, 1965; Bosworth Field and the Wars of the Roses, 1966; Poems of Cornwall and America, 1967; Cornish Stories, 1967; A Cornish Anthology, 1968; The Cornish in America, 1969; The Elizabethan Renaissance: the Life of the Society, 1971; The Elizabethan Renaissance: The Cultural Achievement, 1972; Strange Encounter (poems), 1972; The Tower of London in the History of the Nation, 1972; Westminster Abbey in the History of the Nation, 1972; Shakespeare's Sonnets: a modern edition, 1973, rev. edn with introduction and prose versions, 1984; Shakespeare the Man, 1973, rev. edn, 1987; Simon Forman: Sex and Society in Shakespeare's Age, 1974; Windsor Castle in the History of England, 1974; (with John Betjeman) Victorian and Edwardian Cornwall, 1974; Oxford in the History of the Nation, 1975; Discoveries and Reviews, 1975; Jonathan Swift: Major Prophet, 1975; A Cornishman Abroad, 1976; Brown Buck: a Californian fantasy, 1976; Matthew Arnold: Poet and Prophet, 1976; Shakespeare the Elizabethan, 1977; Homosexuals in History: Ambivalence in society, literature and the arts, 1977; Heritage of Britain, 1977; Milton the Puritan: Portrait of a Mind, 1977; The Road to Oxford: poems, 1978; (ed) The Poems of Shakespeare's Dark Lady, 1978; The Byrons and Trevanions, 1978; The Annotated Shakespeare, 3 vols (introds to vols and plays), 1978; A Man of the Thirties, 1979; Portraits and Views, 1979; Story of Britain, 1979; (ed) A Man of Singular Virtue: Roper's Life of Sir Thomas More, 1980; Memories of Men and Women, 1980; Shakespeare's Globe, 1980; A Life: Collected Poems, 1981; Eminent Elizabethans, 1983; Shakespeare's Characters: a complete guide, 1984; Night at the Carn, and Other Stories, 1984; Prefaces to Shakespeare's Plays, 1984; Shakespeare's Self-Portrait: Passages chosen from his work, with notes, 1984; Glimpses of the Great, 1985; (ed) The Contemporary Shakespeare, 1985–87; Reflections on the Puritan Revolution, 1986; The Little Land of Cornwall, 1986; Stories from Trenarren, 1986; A Quartet of Cornish Cats, 1986; The Poet Auden, 1987; Court and Country: studies in Tudor social history, 1987; Froude the Historian, 1988; Quiller Couch: portrait of Q, 1988; Shakespeare the Man, 1988; (ed and introd.) Froude, Spanish Story of the Armada, 1988; A. L. Rowse's Cornwall, 1988; Friends and Contemporaries, 1989; Transatlantic: Later Poems, 1989; The Controversial Colensos: South Africa and New Zealand, 1989; Discovering Shakespeare, 1989; Selected Poems, 1990; Prompting the Age: Poems Early and Late, 1990; Four Caroline Portraits, 1993; (ed) The Sayings of Shakespeare, 1993; All Souls in my Time, 1993; The Regicides and the Puritan Revolution, 1995; Historians I Have Known, 1995. *Address:* Trenarren House, St Austell, Cornwall PL26 6BH. *Club:* Athenæum.

ROWSELL, Edmund Lionel P.; *see* Penning-Rowsell.

ROWSON, John Anthony; Director: Royal Insurance Holdings, since 1994; Glaxo Trustees Ltd, since 1992 (Chairman, 1994); *b* 6 May 1930; *s* of Thomas Herbert Rowson and Hilda Elizabeth Rowson; *m* 1st, 1955, Elizabeth Mary (*née* Fiddes) (marr. diss. 1980); two *s* one *d*; 2nd, 1989, Molly Lesley (*née* Newman). *Educ:* Beckenham Grammar Sch.; College of Law. Admitted Solicitor, 1959. Partner, Herbert Smith, 1960, Sen. Partner, 1988–93. Master, Solicitors' Co., and Pres., City of London Law Soc., 1992–93. FRSA 1993. *Recreations:* tennis, golf, ski-ing, music. *Address:* 7 Wilton Street, SW1X 7AF. *Clubs:* Athenæum, Royal Automobile; Hurlingham.

ROWTHORN, Prof. Robert Eric; Professor of Economics, Cambridge University, since 1991; Fellow, King's College, Cambridge, since 1991; *b* 20 Aug. 1939; *s* of Eric William Rowthorn and Eileen Rowthorn; *m* 1981, Amanda Jane Wharton; one *s* one *d. Educ:* Newport High Sch. for Boys; Jesus Coll., Oxford (BA, BPhil, MA). University of Cambridge: Res. Fellow, Churchill Coll., 1964–65; College Lectr, King's Coll., 1965–66; Asst Lectr, 1966–71; Lectr, 1971–82; Reader in Economics, 1982–91. *Publications:* International Big Business, 1971; Capitalism, Conflict and Inflation, 1980; (with J. Wells) De-industrialisation and Foreign Trade, 1987; (with N. Wayne) Northern Ireland: the political economy of conflict, 1988. *Recreations:* swimming, reading, scuba-diving. *Address:* King's College, Cambridge CB2 1ST.

ROXBEE COX, family name of **Baron Kings Norton.**

ROXBURGH, Iain Edge; Chief Executive and Town Clerk, Coventry City Council, since 1989; *b* 4 Nov. 1943; *s* of John and Irene Roxburgh; *m* 1965, Tessa Breddy; two *s. Educ:* William Hulme's Grammar Sch., Manchester; Imperial Coll., London (BSc Eng, MSc, DIC). ACGI; CEng; MICE. Civil Engineer and transport planner, 1965–80; Greater London Council: Dep. Head of Personnel Services, 1981–83; Dir of Admin, 1983–85; Dep. Sec., AMA, 1985–89. *Recreations:* photography, motor cycling, walking, ski-ing. *Address:* Council House, Earl Street, Coventry CV1 5RR. *T:* Coventry (01203) 831100; Earlsdon, Coventry.

ROXBURGH, Prof. Ian Walter; Professor of Mathematics and Astronomy, since 1987, Head of School of Mathematical Sciences, since 1984, Director, Astronomy Unit, since 1983, Queen Mary and Westfield (formerly Queen Mary) College, London; *b* 31 Aug. 1939; *s* of Walter McRonald Roxburgh and Kathleen Joyce (*née* Prescott); *m* 1960, Diana Patricia (*née* Dunn); two *s* one *d. Educ:* King Edward VII Grammar Sch., Sheffield; Univ. of Nottingham (BSc Mathematics 1st Cl. Hons); Univ. of Cambridge (PhD); Elected Res. Fellow, Churchill Coll., Cambridge, 1963; Asst Lectr, Mathematics, 1963–64, Lectr, 1964–66, KCL; Reader in Astronomy, Univ. of Sussex, 1966–67; Queen Mary College, London University: Prof. of Applied Maths, 1967–87; Hd, Dept of Applied Maths, 1978–84; Pro-Principal, 1987. Chm., Cttee of Heads of Univ. Depts of Maths and Stats, 1988–93. Contested: (L) Walthamstow W, 1970; (SDP) Ilford N, 1983. *Publications:* articles in Monthly Notices RAS, Astrophys. Jl, Astronomy and Astrophysics, Jl Geophysical Res., Phil. Trans Royal Soc., Gen. Relativity and Gravitation, Jl Physics A., Foundations of Physics, Nature, Solar Physics, Brit. Jl for the Philosophy of Science. *Recreations:* politics, economics, philosophy. *Address:* 37 Leicester Road, Wanstead, E11 2DW. *T:* 0181–989 7117.

ROXBURGH, Rt. Rev. James William; Assistant Bishop, Diocese of Liverpool, since 1991; *b* 5 July 1921; *s* of James Thomas and Margaret Roxburgh; *m* 1949, Marjorie Winifred (*née* Hipkiss); one *s* one *d. Educ:* Whitgift School; St Catharine's Coll., Cambridge

(MA); Wycliffe Hall, Oxford. Deacon 1944, priest 1945; Curate: Christ Church and Holy Trinity, Folkestone, 1944–47; Handsworth, Birmingham, 1947–50; Vicar: S Matthew, Bootle, 1950–56; Drypool, Hull, 1956–65; Barking, 1965–77; Archdeacon of Colchester, 1977–83; Bishop Suffragan, later Area Bishop of Barking, 1983–90. Canon of Chelmsford, 1972–77. Pro-Prolocutor, Convocation of Canterbury, 1977–83. Pres. Barking Rotary Club, 1976–77. Hon. Freeman, Barking and Dagenham, 1990. *Recreations:* travel, philately. *Address:* 53 Preston Road, Southport, Merseyside PR9 9EE. *T:* Southport (01704) 542927. *Club:* Commonwealth Trust.

ROXBURGH, Vice-Adm. Sir John (Charles Young), KCB 1972 (CB 1969); CBE 1967; DSO 1943; DSC 1942 (Bar, 1945); *b* 29 June 1919; *s* of Sir (Thomas) James (Young) Roxburgh, CIE; *m* 1942, Philippa, 3rd *d* of late Major C. M. Hewlett, MC; one *s* one *d.* *Educ:* RNC, Dartmouth. Naval Cadet, 1933; Midshipman, 1937; Sub-Lt 1939; Lt 1941; Lt-Comdr 1949; Comdr 1952; Capt. 1958; Rear-Adm. 1967; Vice-Adm. 1970. Served in various ships, 1937–39; joined Submarine Br., 1940; served in ops off Norway, in Bay of Biscay and Mediterranean, 1940–42; comd HM Submarines H43, United and Tapir, 1942–45 in ops in Mediterranean and off Norway; HMS Vanguard, 1948–50; comd HM Submarine Turpin, 1951–53; HMS Triumph, 1955; HMS Ark Royal, 1955–56; comd HMS Contest, 1956–58; Brit. Jt Services Mission, Wash., 1958–60; comd 3rd Submarine Sqdn and HMS Adamant, 1960–61; idc 1962; Dep. Dir of Defence Plans (Navy), MoD, 1963–65; comd HMS Eagle, 1965–67; Flag Officer: Sea Training, 1967–69; Plymouth, 1969; Submarines, and NATO Comdr Submarines, E Atlantic, 1969–72, retired 1972. Chm., Grovebell Group Ltd, 1972–75. Mem. Management Cttee, The Freedom Assoc., 1978–85. Pres., Royal Naval Benevolent Trust, 1978–84. Co. Councillor, Surrey, 1977–81. *Recreations:* golf, sailing, walking, music. *Address:* Oakdene, Wood Road, Hindhead, Surrey GU26 6PT. *T:* Hindhead (01428) 605600. *Clubs:* Army and Navy; Liphook Golf, Woking Golf.

ROXBURGHE, 10th Duke of, *cr* 1707; **Guy David Innes-Ker;** Baron Roxburghe 1600; Earl of Roxburghe, Baron Ker of Cessford and Cavertoun, 1616; Bt (NS) 1625; Viscount Broxmouth, Earl of Kelso, Marquis of Bowmont and Cessford, 1707; Earl Innes (UK), 1837; *b* 18 Nov. 1954; *s* of 9th Duke of Roxburghe, and Margaret Elisabeth (*d* 1983) (who *m* 1976, Jocelyn Olaf Hambro, *qv*), *d* of late Frederick Bradshaw McConnel; *S* father, 1974; *m* 1st, 1977, Lady Jane Meriel Grosvenor (marr. diss. 1990), *yr d* of 5th Duke of Westminster, TD; two *s* one *d*; 2nd, 1992, Virginia, *d* of David Wynn-Williams; one *d.* *Educ:* Eton; RMA Sandhurst (Sword of Honour, June 1974); Magdalene Coll., Cambridge (BA (Land Economy) 1980; MA 1984). Commnd into Royal Horse Guards/1st Dragoons, 1974; RARO 1977. Mem., Fishmongers' Co.; Freeman of City of London, 1983. *Recreations:* shooting, fishing, golf, racing, ski-ing. *Heir: s* Marquis of Bowmont, *qv*. *Address:* Floors Castle, Kelso TD5 7RW. *T:* Kelso (01573) 224288. *Clubs:* Turf, White's.

ROY, Andrew Donald; economist; *b* 28 June 1920; *er s* of late Donald Whatley Roy, FRCS, FRCOG, and late Beatrice Anne Roy (*née* Barstow); *m* 1947, Katherine Juliet Grove-White; one *s* two *d.* *Educ:* Malvern Coll.; Sidney Sussex Coll., Cambridge. Maths Trip. Pt I 1939 and Econ. Trip. Pt II 1948, Class I hons. 1939–45: served Royal Artillery, in UK, India and Burma (8 Medium Regt; Adjt, 1942–44). Cambridge Univ.: Asst Lecturer, 1949–51; Lecturer, 1951–64; Jun. Proctor, 1956–57; Sidney Sussex Coll.: Fellow, 1951–64; Tutor, 1953–56; Sen. Tutor, 1956–62; Financial Bursar, 1959–61. HM Treasury: Economic Consultant, 1962; Sen. Economic Adviser, 1964; Under-Sec. (Economics), 1969–72; Under-Sec., DTI, 1972–74, MoD, 1974–76; Chief Economic Adviser, DHSS, 1976–80. Consultant, NIESR, 1981–83. Governor, Malvern Coll., 1960–. *Publications:* British Economic Statistics (with C. F. Carter), 1954; articles in economic and statistical jls. *Address:* 15 Rusholme Road, Putney, SW15 3JX. *T:* 0181–789 3180. *Club:* United Oxford & Cambridge University.

ROY, Prof. Arthur Douglas, FRCS, FRCSE, FRCSGlas, FRCSI; FACS; Chief of Surgical Services, Ministry of Health, Sultanate of Oman, 1985–88, and Professor of Surgery, Sultan Qaboos University, 1986–88, retired; Professor Emeritus, Queen's University of Belfast, 1985; *b* 10 April 1925; *s* of Arthur Roy and Edith Mary (*née* Brown); *m* 1st, 1954, Monica Cecilia Mary Bowley; three *d*; 2nd, 1973, Patricia Irene McColl. *Educ:* Paisley Grammar Sch.; Univ. of Glasgow (MB, ChB, Commendation). RAMC, 1948–50; Surgical Registrar posts in Glasgow and Inverness, 1950–54; Sen. Surgical Registrar, Aylesbury and Oxford, 1954–57; Cons. Surgeon and Hon. Lectr, Western Infirmary, Glasgow, 1957–68; Foundn Prof. of Surgery, Univ. of Nairobi, 1968–72; Prof. of Surgery, QUB, 1973–85. Non-exec. Dir, Exeter Dist Community NHS Trust, 1991–. Mem. Council, RCSE, 1979–85; Pres., Devon and Exeter Med. Soc., 1994–95 (Vice-Pres., 1993–94). *Publications:* Lecture Notes in Surgery: tropical supplement, 1975; various papers on gastro-enterology, endocrine surgery, tropical medicine, etc. *Recreations:* sailing, gliding, gardening. *Address:* Garden House, Old Feniton Village, near Honiton, Devon EX14 0BE. *T:* Honiton (01404) 850055. *Club:* Devon and Somerset Gliding.

ROY, Ian; Assistant Under-Secretary of State, Home Office, 1963–72; *b* 2 Aug. 1912; *o s* of late John Roy and Annie Froude Marshall; *m* 1939, Betty Louise Blissett; one *s* two *d.* *Educ:* Manchester Grammar School; Peterhouse, Cambridge. Assistant Inspector of Taxes, 1935; Assistant Principal, Home Office, 1936; Private Secretary to Permanent Under-Secretary of State, 1938; to Parliamentary Under-Secretary of State, 1939–40; Asst Secretary, 1947. *Address:* Flat 47, Cholmeley Lodge, Cholmeley Park, Highgate, N6 5EN. *T:* 0181–340 3143.

ROY, Paul David; Chief Executive, Smith New Court plc, since 1995; *b* 8 May 1947; *s* of Vernon Alfred Roy and Elsie Florence Roy; *m* 1985, Susan Mary Elkies; five *s* one *d.* *Educ:* Trinity Sch., Croydon; Liverpool Univ. (BA Hons Econs). Partner: Morton Bros (Stockbrokers), 1974–77; Kemp-Gee & Co., 1977–87; Jt Man. Dir, Citicorp Scrimgeour Vickers, 1987–89; Man. Dir, Smith New Court (UK), 1989–95. *Recreations:* art, golf, tennis, fishing, watching school matches. *Address:* Smith New Court House, 20 Farringdon Road, EC1M 3NH. *Club:* City of London.

ROY, Sheila; Director, Newchurch & Co., since 1991; *b* 27 Feb. 1948; *d* of Bertie and Dorothy Atkinson; *m* 1970, Robert Neil Roy. *Educ:* BA Open Univ.; RGN; DN (London); Cert Ed Leeds Univ.; RNT. Milton Keynes Health Authority: Dir, Nursing Studies, 1983–86; Actg Chief Nursing Officer and Dir, Nursing Studies, Feb.–May 1986; Dist Nursing Advr and Dir, Nurse Educn, Hillingdon HA, 1986–88; Dir of Nursing Management and Res., NW Thames RHA, 1988–91. Special Commendation, Richard J. Puttock Award, BIM, 1986. *Recreations:* riding, tennis, sailing. *Address:* Newchurch & Co., 12 Charterhouse Square, EC1M 6AX. *T:* 0171–608 1822.

ROYCE, David Nowill; Director-General, Institute of Export, 1980–85; *b* 10 Sept. 1920; *s* of late Bernard Royce and Ida Christine (*née* Nowill); *m* 1942, Esther Sylvia Yule; two *s* one *d.* *Educ:* Reading School; Vienna University. Served HM Forces, 1940–46. Major, Intelligence Corps, 1946; Asst Principal, Foreign Office, German Section, 1948; Foreign Service, 1949; First Secretary: Athens, 1953; Saigon, 1955; Foreign Office, 1957; Head of Chancery, Caracas, 1960; Counsellor (Commercial), Bonn, 1963; Counsellor (Commercial) and Consul-Gen., Helsinki, 1967–68; Commercial Inspector, FCO, 1969–71; Dir for Co-ordination of Export Services, DTI, 1971–73; Under-Secretary: Overseas Finance and Planning Div., Dept of Trade, 1973–75; CRE 3 and Export Develt Divs, Dept of Trade, 1975–77; Export Develt Div., Dept of Trade, 1977–80. Hon. Fellow, Inst. of Export, 1985. *Publication:* Successful Exporting for Small Businesses, 1990. *Recreation:* gardening. *Address:* 5 Sprimont Place, SW3 3HT. *T:* 0171–589 9148. *Club:* Hurlingham.

ROYCE, (Roger) John; QC 1987; a Recorder, since 1986; *b* 27 Aug. 1944; *s* of J. Roger Royce and Margaret A. Royce (*née* Sibbald); *m* 1979, Gillian Wendy Adderley; two *s* one *d.* *Educ:* The Leys Sch., Cambridge; Trinity Hall, Cambridge (BA). Qualified as Solicitor, 1969; called to the Bar, Gray's Inn, 1970. Cambridge Hockey Blue, 1965, 1966; Captain Somerset Hockey, 1976; Austrian qualified ski instructor. *Recreations:* cricket, ski-ing, golf, collecting corkscrews. *Address:* Guildhall Chambers, Broad Street, Bristol BS1 2HG. *T:* Bristol (0117) 927 3366. *Clubs:* Hawks (Cambridge); St Enodoc Golf.

ROYDEN, Sir Christopher (John), 5th Bt *cr* 1905; Associate Director, Gerrard Vivian Gray Ltd, since 1988; *b* 26 Feb. 1937; *s* of Sir John Ledward Royden, 4th Bt, and Dolores Catherine (*d* 1994), *d* of late Cecil J. G. Coward; *S* father, 1976; *m* 1961, Diana Bridget, *d* of Lt-Col J. H. Goodhart, MC; two *s* one *d.* *Educ:* Winchester Coll.; Christ Church, Oxford (MA). Duncan Fox & Co. Ltd, 1960–71; Spencer Thornton & Co., 1971–88: Partner, 1974–86; Dir, 1986–88. *Recreations:* fishing, shooting, gardening. *Heir: s* John Michael Joseph Royden [*b* 17 March 1965; *m* 1989, Lucilla, *d* of J. R. Stourton; two *d*]. *Address:* Flat 2, 8 Nevern Square, SW5 9NW. *Club:* Boodle's.

ROYDS, Rev. John Caress, MA Cantab; *b* 1920; 3rd *s* of Rev. Edward Thomas Hubert Royds, BA. *Educ:* Monkton Combe School, Bath; Queens' College, Cambridge. II 1 hons History, 1947. Military service with British and Indian Armies, 1940–46. Assistant master, Bryanston School, Dorset, 1947–61, House-master, 1951–61; Headmaster: General Wingate School, Addis Ababa, 1961–65; Uppingham Sch., 1965–75. Deacon, 1974; Priest, 1975; Dir of Educn for Peterborough diocese, 1976–81; Vicar of St James's, Northampton, 1981–85; with CMS, Peshawar, Pakistan, 1985–86. *Address:* 16B Donaldson Road, Salisbury SP1 3DA.

ROYLE, family name of **Baron Fanshawe of Richmond.**

ROYLE, Rev. Canon Roger Michael; freelance broadcaster and writer, since 1979; Chaplain, Southwark Cathedral, since 1993; *b* 30 Jan. 1939; *s* of Reginald and Agnes Royle. *Educ:* St Edmund's Sch., Canterbury; King's Coll. London (AKC 2nd Class Hons). Curate, St Mary's, Portsea, Portsmouth, 1962–65; Sen. Curate, St Peter's, Morden, 1965–68; Succentor, Southwark Cathedral, 1968–71; Warden of Dorney Parish, Eton Coll. Project, 1971–74; Conduct, Eton Coll., 1974–79; Chaplain, Lord Mayor Treloar Coll., 1990–92. MA Lambeth, 1990. *Publications:* A Few Blocks from Broadway, 1987; Royle Exchange, 1989; To Have and to Hold, 1990; Picking up the Pieces, 1990; Mother Teresa: her life in pictures, 1992. *Recreations:* theatre, music, patience, cooking. *Address:* 5 Denny Street, SE11 4UX.

ROYLE, Timothy Lancelot Fanshawe, FCIM; Chairman: Control Risks Group, 1975–91; Berry Palmer & Lyle, 1984–91; Hemotex Holdings, 1991–93; *b* 24 April 1931; *s* of Sir Lancelot Carrington Royle, KBE, and Barbara Rachel Royle; *m* 1959, Margaret Jill Stedeford; two *s* one *d.* *Educ:* Harrow; Mons Mil. Acad. FInstM 1977. Commnd 15th/19th King's Royal Hussars, 1949, Inns of Court Regt, TA, 1951–63. Joined Hogg Robinson Gp, 1951; Man. Dir, 1980–81. Director: Wellmarine Reinsurance Brokers, 1976–; Imperio Reinsurance Co. (UK), 1984–94. Mem., Insce Brokers Regulatory Council. Member: Church Assembly of C of E, 1950–70; Gen. Synod of C of E, 1985–; Church Comr, 1966–83. Chairman: Lindley Educn Trust, 1970–; Christian Weekly Newspapers, 1979–. Trustee: Charinco, 1977–; Charishare, 1977–. Freeman, City of London, 1976; Member: Marketors' Co., 1977; Insurers' Co., 1979. *Recreations:* country pursuits, ski-ing. *Address:* National Westminster Bank, 11 Leadenhall Street, EC3V 1PQ. *Clubs:* Cavalry and Guards, MCC; St Moritz Tobogganing (St Moritz).

See also Baron Fanshawe of Richmond.

ROZARIO, Most Rev. Michael; *see* Dhaka, Archbishop of, (RC).

ROZENTAL, Andrés; Mexican Ambassador to the Court of St James's, since 1995; *b* 27 April 1945; *s* of Leonid Rozental and Neoma Gutman; *m* 1971, Vivian Holzer; two *d.* *Educ:* Univ. of Bordeaux (Dip. French 1962); Univ. of the Americas (BA 1965); Univ. of Pennsylvania (MA 1966). Joined Foreign Service, 1967; Alternate Perm. Rep. to OAS, Washington, 1971–74; Counsellor, London, 1974–76; Prin. Advr to the Minister, 1977–79; Dir-Gen. of Diplomatic Service, 1979; Dir-Gen. for N American Affairs, 1979–82; Ambassador: to UN, Geneva, 1982–83; to Sweden, 1983–88; Sen. Vice-Pres., Banco Nacional de México, 1988; Dep. Foreign Minister, 1988–94. Orders include: Polar Star (Sweden), 1983; Civil Merit (Spain), 1991; Order of Merit (France), 1993. *Publications:* (jtly) Paradoxes of a World in Transition, 1993; (jtly) The United Nations Today: a Mexican vision, 1994; Mexican Foreign Policy in the Modern Age, 1994. *Recreations:* swimming, sailing, hiking. *Address:* Mexican Embassy, 42 Hertford Street, W1Y 7TF. *T:* 0171–495 4024. *Clubs:* Travellers', Canning.

ROZHDESTVENSKY, Gennadi Nikolaevich; Founder, Artistic Director and Chief Conductor, State Symphony Orchestra of Ministry of Culture, Russia (New Symphony Orchestra), since 1983; Music Director, Royal Stockholm Philharmonic Orchestra, since 1991; Professor of Conducting, Moscow State Conservatoire, since 1965; *b* 4 May 1931; *m* Victoria Postnikova, concert pianist. Studied piano at Moscow Conservatoire; started conducting at 18. Conductor Bolshoi Theatre, 1956–60 (Assistant Conductor, 1951); Chief Conductor, USSR Radio and Television Symphony Orchestra, 1960–74; Principal Conductor, Bolshoi Theatre, 1965–70; Chief Conductor: Stockholm Philharmonic Orchestra, 1974–77; BBC Symphony Orchestra, 1978–81; Moscow Chamber Opera, 1974–83; Vienna Symphony Orchestra, 1981–83. Guest conductor, Europe, Israel, America, Far East, Australia. Lenin Prize, 1970; People's Artist, USSR, 1972; Order of Red Banner of Labour, 1981. *Recreation:* music. *Address:* c/o Victor Hochhauser, 4 Oak Hill Way, NW3 7LR. *T:* 0171–794 0987. *Club:* Athenæum.

RUAUX, Gillian Doreen, (Mrs W. D. Partington); Her Honour Judge Ruaux; a Circuit Judge, since 1993; *b* 25 March 1945; *d* of Charles Edward Ruaux and Denise Maud Ruaux (*née* Le Page); *m* 1968, William Derek Partington; one *d.* *Educ:* Bolton Sch.; Univ. of Manchester (LLB Hons, LLM). Called to the Bar, Gray's Inn, 1968; practised at the Bar, Manchester, 1968–93. *Recreations:* theatre, opera, horse-racing, cookery. *Address:* Bolton Combined Court Centre, Blackhorse Street, Bolton, Greater Manchester BL1 1SU. *Club:* Bolton Old Links Golf.

RUBBIA, Prof. Carlo; physicist; Senior Physicist, European Organisation for Nuclear Research, since 1993 (Director-General, 1989–93); *b* 31 March 1934; *s* of Silvio and Bice Rubbia; *m* Marisa; one *s* one *d.* *Educ:* Scuola Normale Superiore, Pisa; Univ. of Pisa (Dr 1957). Research Fellow, Columbia Univ., 1958–59; Lectr, Univ. of Rome, 1960–61; CERN, 1960– (head of team investigating fundamental particles on proton-antiproton collider); scientist, Fermi Nat. Accelerator Lab., USA, 1969–73; Higgins Prof. of Physics, Harvard Univ., 1971–88. Member: Papal Acad. of Science, 1985–; Amer. Acad. of Arts and Sciences, 1985; Accademia dei XL; Accademia dei Lincei; European Acad. of Sciences; Ateneo Veneto; Foreign Member: Royal Soc.; Soviet Acad. of Scis, 1988; US Nat. Acad. of Scis; Polish Acad. of Scis. Hon. Doctorates: Boston, Chicago, Geneva, Genoa, Northwestern, Udine, Carnegie-Mellon, Loyola, Sofia, Moscow, Chile, Padova, Madrid, Rio de Janeiro, La Plata and Oxford Universities. Gold Medal, Italian Physical Soc., 1983; Lorenzo il Magnifico Prize for Sciences, 1983; Achille de Gasperi Prize for Sciences, 1984; Nobel Prize for Physics (jtly), 1984; Leslie Prize for exceptional achievements, 1985; Castiglioni di Sicilia Prize, 1985; Carlo Capodieci Gold Medal, 1985; Jesolo d'Oro, 1986. Knight Grand Cross, Italy; Officer, Legion of Honour, France, 1989. *Publications:* papers on nuclear physics: weak force quanta (W–, W+ and Z particles, intermediate vector bosons); proton-antiproton collision; sixth quark. *Address:* CERN, 1211 Geneva 23, Switzerland.

RUBENS, Bernice Ruth; writer and director of documentary films, since 1957; *m* 1947, Rudi Nassauer; two *d. Educ:* University of Wales, Cardiff (BA, Hons English; Fellow 1982; Hon. DLitt 1991). Followed teaching profession, 1950–55. American Blue Ribbon award for documentary film, Stress, 1968. *Publications:* Set on Edge, 1960; Madame Sousatzka, 1962 (filmed, 1989); Mate in Three, 1965; The Elected Member, 1969 (Booker Prize, 1970); Sunday Best, 1971; Go Tell the Lemming, 1973; I Sent a Letter to my Love, 1975; The Ponsonby Post, 1977; A Five Year Sentence, 1978; Spring Sonata, 1979; Birds of Passage, 1981; Brothers, 1983; Mr Wakefield's Crusade, 1985 (televised, 1992); Our Father, 1987; Kingdom Come, 1990; A Solitary Grief, 1991; Mother Russia, 1992; Autobiopsy, 1993; Yesterday in the Back Lane, 1995. *Recreation:* plays piano and 'cello. *Address:* 16A Belsize Park Gardens, NW3 4LD. *T:* 0171–586 5365.

RUBERTI, Prof. Antonio, FIEEE; Professor, La Sapienza University, Rome, since 1962; Member, European Commission (formerly Commission of the European Community), 1993–95 (Vice-President, 1993); *b* Aversa, Italy, 24 Jan. 1927; *m* 1955, Luisa Andreozzi; one *s* three *d. Educ:* Naples Univ. (Laurea in electrical engrg). FIEEE 1985. La Sapienza University, Rome: Head, Engrg Faculty, 1973–76; Rector, 1976–87. Minister for Co-ordination of Scientific and Technol Research and for Research and Univs, 1987–92; MP (Italian Socialist Party), Rome-Latina-Frosinone-Viterbo, 1992. Order National de la Légion d'Honneur (France), 1982; Leonardo da Vinci Medal (Italy), 1989. *Publications:* numerous scientific works on control and system theory, essays, books and encyclopedia articles on university policy concerning research and problems of technol innovation. *Address:* Via San Calepodio 36, 00152 Roma, Italy; La Sapienza University, Department of System Science and Informatics, Via Eudossiana 18, Roma, Italy. *T:* (6) 484518, *Fax:* (6) 44585367.

RUBERY, Dr Eileen Doris; Under Secretary and Head of Health Aspects of Environmental and Food Division, Department of Health, since 1995; *b* 16 May 1943; *d* of James and Doris McDonnell; *m* 1969, Philip Huson Rubery; one *d. Educ:* Westcliff High Sch. for Girls; Sheffield Univ. Med. Sch. (MB ChB Hons); Cambridge Univ. (PhD). FRCR; MRCPath; MFPHM. Royal Infirmary, Sheffield, 1966–67; MRC Res. Fellow, Dept of Biochem., Cambridge, 1967; Meres' Sen. Student, St John's Coll., Cambridge, 1971; Addenbrooke's Hospital, Cambridge: Registrar in Radiotherapy and Oncology, 1973; Sen. Registrar, 1976; Wellcome Sen. Clinical Res. Fellow; Hon. Consultant, 1978; Sen. Res. Fellow and Dir of Med. Studies, Girton Coll., 1981; SMO (Toxicology), DHSS, 1983; Department of Health: PMO, 1988; SPMO and Hd of Med. Div., Communicable Disease and Immunisation, 1989–91; SPMO and Hd of Health Promotion, Med. Div., 1991–95. QHP, 1993–. *Publications:* (ed) Indications for Iodine Prophylaxis following a Nuclear Accident, 1990; (ed) Medicine: a degree course guide, 1974–83; papers in professional jls. *Recreations:* music, theatre, tapestry work, visiting Venice, reading Proust. *Address:* Department of Health, Skipton House, 80 London Road, SE1 6LW.

RUBERY, Reginald John; His Honour Judge Rubery; a Circuit Judge, since 1995; *b* 13 July 1937; *s* of Reginald Arthur Rubery and Phyllis Margaret (*née* Payne); *m* 1st, 1961, Diana Wilcock Holgate (marr. diss.); one *s*; 2nd, 1974, Frances Camille Murphy; one step *d. Educ:* Wadham House, Hale, Cheshire; King's Sch., Worcester. Admitted Solicitor, 1963; Partner: Whitworths, Manchester, 1966–72; Taylor Kirkman & Mainprice, 1972–78; County Court and Dist Registrar, then District Judge, 1978–95; Asst Recorder, 1987–91; a Recorder, 1991–95. Mem., Manchester City Council, 1968–71. Hon. Sec., Manchester Law Soc., 1974–78. *Recreations:* golf, swimming, gardening. *Address:* Birkby, Charnes Road, Ashley, Market Drayton, Shropshire TF9 4LQ. *Clubs:* Hale Golf; Nefyn Golf.

RUBIN, His Honour Kenneth Warnell; DL; a Circuit Judge, 1972–92; *b* 8 March 1920; *s* of late Albert Reginald Rubin and late Mary Eales Rubin; *m* 1948, Jeanne Marie Louise de Wilde (*d* 1991); one *s* two *d. Educ:* King's College Sch., Wimbledon; King's Coll., London (LLB). Served HM Forces, 1939–45. Called to Bar, Gray's Inn, 1948. DL Surrey, 1989. *Address:* Tyrrellswood, Shere Road, West Horsley, Surrey KT24 6ER. *T:* East Horsley (01483) 282848.

RUBINS, Jack, FIPA; Chairman and Chief Executive, Osprey Communications plc, 1993; *b* 4 Aug. 1931; *m* 1962, Ruth Davids; three *s. Educ:* Northern Polytechnic (Architecture). Chm. and Chief Exec., DFS Dorland Advertising, 1976–87; Chm. and Chief Exec., McCann Erickson Gp UK, 1990–91; Chm., SMS Communications, 1991–93. Chm., Hist. of Advertising Trust. *Recreations:* philately, golf. *Address:* Danehurst, 34 Northwick Circle, Harrow, Middx HA3 0EE.

RUBINSTEIN, Hilary Harold; Chairman, Hilary Rubinstein Books (Literary Agents), since 1992; *b* 24 April 1926; *s* of H. F. and Lina Rubinstein; *m* 1955, Helge Kitzinger; three *s* one *d. Educ:* Cheltenham Coll.; Merton Coll., Oxford (MA). Editorial Dir, Victor Gollancz Ltd, 1952–63; Special Features Editor, The Observer, 1963–64; Dep. Editor, The Observer Magazine, 1964–65. Partner, later Director, 1965–92, Chm. and Man. Dir, 1983–92, A. P. Watt Ltd. Mem. Council, ICA, 1976–92; Trustee, Open Coll. of the Arts, 1987–. Founder-editor, The Good Hotel Guide (published in USA as Europe's Wonderful Little Hotels and Inns), 1978–. *Publications:* The Complete Insomniac, 1974; Hotels and Inns, an Oxford anthology, 1984. *Recreations:* hotel-watching, reading in bed. *Address:* 61 Clarendon Road, W11 4JE. *T:* 0171–727 9550, *Fax:* 0171–221 5291.

See also M. B. Rubinstein.

RUBINSTEIN, Michael Bernard; Senior Partner, 1969–86, Consultant, 1986–94, Rubinstein Callingham Polden & Gale (formerly Rubinstein, Nash & Co., then Rubinstein Callingham), Solicitors; *b* 6 Nov. 1920; *s* of late H. F. Rubinstein and Lina (*née* Lowy); *m* 1955, Joy Douthwaite; two *s* two *d. Educ:* St Paul's Sch. Admitted solicitor, 1948. Served War, RE (TA), 1939, and RA; Captain 1945. Mem., Lord Chancellor's Cttee on Defamation, 1971–74. Trustee, SPNM, 1967– (Chm., 1986–94; a Vice Pres., 1994–). *Publications:* (ed and contrib.) Wicked, Wicked Libels, 1972; Rembrandt and Angels (monograph), 1982; (with Rowland Parker) The Cart-Ruts on Malta and Gozo (monograph), 1984, repr. with The People of the Temples of Malta and Gozo (monograph with Rowland Parker) as Malta's Ancient Temples and Ruts, 1988; Music to my Ear, 1985; contrib. legal and other jls. *Recreations:* faxing loose-ball letters to Editors when inspired, experiencing right hemisphere mentation, ruminating, resuming 'cello practice after 40 years, otherwise practising to get along without practising. *Address:* 1 Walkern Road, Benington, Herts SG2 7LN. *T:* Benington (01438) 869539. *Club:* Garrick.

See also H. H. Rubinstein.

RUBINSTEIN, Prof. Nicolai, FBA 1971; FRHistS; Professor of History, Westfield College, London University, 1965–78, now Emeritus; *b* 13 July 1911; *s* of Bernhard and Irene Rubinstein; *m* 1954, Ruth Kidder Olitsky. *Educ:* Univs of Berlin and Florence. LittD Florence. Lectr, UC Southampton, 1942–45; Lectr, 1945–62, Reader, 1962–65, Westfield Coll., Univ. of London. Corresp. Mem., Accad. Toscana La Colombaria, 1976; Hon. Fellow: Warburg Inst., 1985; Westfield Coll., 1986. Hon. Diploma di perfezionamento, Scuola Normale Superiore, Pisa, 1991. Serena Medal, British Acad., 1974; Premio Internazionale Galileo Galilei, 1985; Fiorino d'oro, Florence, 1990; Premio della Cultura della Presidenza del Consiglio, 1993. Hon. Citizen, Florence, 1991. *Publications:* The Government of Florence under the Medici 1434–94, 1966; (ed) Florentine Studies: politics and society in Renaissance Florence, 1968; Gen. Editor, Letters of Lorenzo de'Medici and ed vol. 3, 1977, and vol. 4, 1981; articles in Jl of Warburg and Courtauld Insts, Italian Studies, Archivio Storico Italiano, Rinascimento, etc. *Address:* 16 Gardnor Mansions, Church Row, NW3 6UR. *T:* 0171–435 6995.

RUBNER, Ben; General Secretary, Furniture, Timber and Allied Trades Union, 1976–86; *b* 30 Sept. 1921; *s* of Charles and Lily Rubner; *m* 1952, Amelia Sonia Bagnari (*d* 1980); one *s* one *d*; *m* 1986, Patricia Elder, widow. *Educ* Mansford Street Central Sch., Bethnal Green, E2. Apprentice cabinet maker, 1935; Mem. Cttee, Trade Union Br., 1937. Served war in armed forces, Royal Corps of Signals: N Africa, Italy, Sicily, 1941–46. Shop Steward, Sec., Chm. and Convenor, London Furniture Workers Shop Stewards Council, 1947–52; NUFTO: London Dist Cttee, 1954; Gen. Exec. Council, 1958; London Dist Organiser, 1959. Nat. Trade Organiser, 1963; Asst Gen. Sec., FTAT, 1973–76. British TUC: London Delegate, 1955–58; full-time Officer Deleg., 1974–77. Mem., Central Arbitration Cttee, ACAS, 1977. *Recreations:* music (opera, light and grand), chess, table tennis, swimming, Scrabble, golf. *Address:* 6 Oak Avenue, Bricket Wood, St Albans, Herts AL2 3LG. *Club:* Cambridge and Bethnal Green Old Boys.

RUBYTHON, Eric Gerald, CBE 1978; Member of Aerospace Board, British Aerospace, 1977–83, retired (Deputy Chief Executive of Aircraft Group, 1977–82); *b* 11 Feb. 1921; *s* of Reginald Rubython and Bessie Rubython; *m* 1943, Joan Ellen Mills. Joined Hawker Aircraft Ltd, 1948; Co. Sec., 1953; Exec. Dir, 1959; Dir and Gen. Man., 1960; Divl Dir and Gen. Man., Hawker Blackburn Div., 1963; Hawker Siddeley Aviation: Commercial Dir, 1965; Dir and Gen. Manager, 1970; Chm. and Man. Dir, 1977. *Recreations:* golf, gardening. *Address:* 1230 San Julian Drive, Lake San Marcos, CA 92069–4807, USA.

RUCK, Peter Frederick C.; *see* Carter-Ruck.

RUCK KEENE, John Robert, CBE 1977 (MBE 1946); TD 1950; Secretary General, Royal Society of Chemistry, 1980–81; *b* 2 Jan. 1917; *s* of late Major Robert Francis Ruck Keene, OBE, and Dorothy Mary (*née* Chester); *m* 1951, Beryl M Manistre; two *s. Educ:* Eton; Trinity Coll., Cambridge (BA 1938, MA 1955). Commissioned TA, Oxford and Bucks LI, 1939; served UK and NW Europe, 1939–45 (Major 1944, MBE 1946). First appointment with Chemical Society, 1946; General Secretary, 1947–80, when the Royal Society of Chemistry was formed by unification under Royal Charter of The Chemical Society and The Royal Institute of Chemistry, 1 June 1980. Hon. FRSC, 1982. *Address:* Chenies Cottage, 8 Copperkins Grove, Amersham, Bucks HP6 5QD. *T:* Amersham (01494) 727123.

RUCKER, Jeffrey Hamilton; His Honour Judge Rucker; a Circuit Judge, since 1988; *b* 19 Dec. 1942; *s* of late Charles Edward Sigismund Rucker and Nancy Winifred Hodgson; *m* 1965, Caroline Mary Salkeld; three *s. Educ:* St Aubyn's, Rottingdean; Charterhouse. Called to the Bar, Middle Temple, 1967; a Recorder, 1984; a Circuit Judge, assigned to SE Circuit, 1988. Mem. Council of Govs, UMDS of Guy's and St Thomas', 1991–. *Recreations:* sailing, ski-ing, music. *Address:* 36 Essex Street, WC2 3AS.

RUDD, (Anthony) Nigel (Russell); Chairman: Williams Holdings, since 1982; East Midlands Electricity, since 1994 (Director, since 1990); Pilkington plc, since 1995 (Director, since 1994); *b* 31 Dec. 1946; *m* 1969, Lesley Elizabeth (*née* Hodgkinson); two *s* one *d. Educ:* Bemrose Grammar Sch., Derby. FCA. Qualified Chartered Accountant 1968; Divl Finance Dir, London & Northern Group, 1970–73; trouble shooting rôle, London & Northern, in loss making subs. cos, 1973–75; Finance Dir, Bardolin, 1975–77; (jtly) purchased C. Price & Son (building co.), 1977; purchased London & Provincial Properties (Chm.), 1981; C. Price & Son purchased W. Williams & Sons (Holdings), now Williams Holdings, 1982; sold C. Price & Son and London & Provincial Properties, 1986; Dep. Chm., Raine Industries, 1992–94 (Non-Exec. Chm., 1986–92); Non-Exec. Chm., Pendragon PLC, 1989–; Non-Exec. Director: Rother House Finance, 1978–; Coleman Investments, 1980–; Williams Management Services, 1985–; Westminster Securities, 1987–; Gartmore Value Investment, 1989–; Gartmore, 1993–; Derby Pride, 1993–; Mithras Investment Trust, 1994–. Member: City & Industrial Liaison Council, 1988; Adv. Council, Foundn for Manufacturing and Industry, 1993–. Dir, Queen Margaret's Sch., York. *Recreations:* squash, golf, shooting, ski-ing, swimming, theatre. *Address:* c/o Williams Holdings, Pentagon House, Sir Frank Whittle Road, Derby DE21 4XA. *T:* Derby (01332) 202020.

RUDD, Norman Julian Peter Joseph; His Honour Judge Rudd; a Circuit Judge, since 1988; *b* 12 May 1943; *s* of Norman Arthur Rudd and Winifred Rudd; *m* 1968, Judith Margaret Pottinger; three *s. Educ:* Paston Sch., N Walsham, Norfolk; University Coll. London (LLB, LLM). Called to the Bar, Inner Temple, 1969; Asst Recorder, 1982–87, Head of Chambers, 1982–87; a Recorder, 1987. Chm., New Forest Commoners Trust, 1993–. *Recreations:* farming, shooting. *Address:* The Courts of Justice, London Road, Southampton SO9 5AF.

RUDD-JONES, Derek, CBE 1981; PhD; Director, Glasshouse Crops Research Institute, Littlehampton, Sussex, 1971–86; *b* 13 April 1924; 2nd *s* of late Walter Henry Jones and late Doris Mary, *er d* of H. Rudd Dawes; *m* 1948, Joan, 2nd *d* of late Edward Newhouse, Hong Kong, and Malvern, Worcs; two *s* one *d. Educ:* Whitgift; Repton; Emmanuel Coll., Cambridge. BA, MA, PhD (Cantab); FIBiol; FIHort. Agricultural Research Council, postgrad. student, Botany Sch., Univ. of Cambridge, 1945–48; Plant Pathologist, E African Agric. and Forestry Research Org., Kenya, 1949–52; Nat. Research Council, Postdoctoral Fellow, Univ. of Saskatchewan, Saskatoon, Canada, 1952–53. ICI Ltd, Akers Research Laboratory, The Frythe, Welwyn, Herts, 1953–56; Jealott's Hill Research Station, Bracknell, Berks, 1956–59; Scientific Adviser to Sec., Agricl Research Council, 1959–71; Foundn Chm., 1968–72, Managing Editor, 1986–93, British Crop Protection Council (Mem., 1968–86); Pres., Section K, BAAS, 1981–82; Mem., Scientific Cttee, RHS, 1985–; formerly Mem., Adv. Cttee on Pesticides and Other Toxic Chemicals. Vis. Fellow, Univ. of Southampton, 1975–86. Governor, Chichester (formerly W Sussex) Inst. of Higher Educn, 1980–; Trustee, Thomas Phillips Price Trust, 1988–93. *Publications:* papers in scientific journals. *Recreations:* gardening, riding, fly-fishing. *Address:* Bignor Park Cottage, near Pulborough, West Sussex RH20 1HQ. *Club:* Farmers'.

RUDDEN, Prof. Bernard (Anthony), LLD; FBA 1995; Professor of Comparative Law, University of Oxford, since 1979; Fellow of Brasenose College, Oxford, since 1979; *b* 21 Aug. 1933; *s* of John and Kathleen Rudden; *m* 1957, Nancy Campbell Painter; three *s* one *d. Educ:* City of Norwich Sch.; St John's Coll., Cambridge. LLD Cantab; DCL Oxon; PhD Wales. Solicitor. Fellow and Tutor, Oriel Coll., Oxford, 1965–79. Hon. LLD McGill, 1991. *Publications:* Soviet Insurance Law, 1966; The New River, 1985; Basic Community Cases, 1987; co-author or editor of: The Law of Mortgages, 1967; Source-Book on French Law, 1973, 3rd edn 1991; Basic Community Laws, 1980, 5th edn 1994; The Law of Property, 1982; Comparing Constitutions, 1995; contrib. periodical pubns. *Address:* Brasenose College, Oxford OX1 4AJ. *T:* Oxford (01865) 277865. *Club:* United Oxford & Cambridge University.

RUDDEN, James; Advisory Head Teacher on Secondary Reorganisation, ILEA, 1976–78, retired; President: National Association of Head Teachers, 1971; London Head Teachers Association, 1969; Metropolitan Catholic Teachers Association, 1964; *b* 11 Dec. 1911; *s* of Bernard and Mary Rudden; *m* 1937, Eileen Finlay (*d* 1992); one *s* four *d. Educ:* Carlisle Grammar Sch.; St Mary's Coll., Twickenham. BSc (Special, Geo.) (London Univ.); Teacher's Cert. (London Univ.). Asst Teacher, Carlisle, 1933–47; served War, RAF Educn Officer, 1940–45. First Head: St Cuthbert's Sec. Mod. Sch., Cleator, 1948–52; St Thomas More Sec. Mod. Sch., Tottenham, 1952–59; Bishop Thomas Grant Comprehensive Sch., Streatham, 1959–75. External Examnr for BEd, Avery Hill Coll. Chairman: London Comprehensive Head Teachers Conf., 1974–75; Southwark Diocesan Schs Commn; Governing Body of Schs Council; Adv. Council for Supply and Trng of Teachers. KSG 1969. *Publications:* numerous articles on educnl topics in educational and national press. *Recreation:* indulgence in retirement pursuits. *Address:* 5 The Gorse, Rissington Road, Bourton-on-the-Water, Glos. GL54 2EJ. *T:* Cotswold (01451) 21052.

RUDDOCK, Joan Mary; MP (Lab) Lewisham, Deptford, since 1987; *b* 28 Dec. 1943; *d* of Ken and Eileen Anthony. *Educ:* Pontypool Grammar Sch. for Girls; Imperial Coll., Univ. of London (BSc; ARCS). Worked for Shelter, national campaign for the homeless, 1968–73; Dir, Oxford Housing Aid Centre, 1973–77; Special Programmes Officer with unemployed young people, MSC, 1977–79; Organiser, CAB, Reading, 1979–86. Chairperson, CND, 1981–85, a Vice Chairperson, 1985–86. Active in politics and pressure groups, and mem. of anti-racist concerns, throughout working life. Frank Cousins' Peace Award, TGWU, 1984. *Publications:* CND Scrapbook, 1987; co-author of pubns on housing; (contrib.): The CND Story, 1983; Voices for One World, 1988. *Recreations:* music, travel, gardening. *Address:* c/o House of Commons, SW1 0AA.

RUDENSTINE, Dr Neil Leon; President, and Professor of English and American Literature and Language, Harvard University, since 1991; *b* 21 Jan. 1935; *s* of Harry Rudenstine and Mae Esperito Rudenstine; *m* 1960, Angelica Zander; one *s* two *d. Educ:* Princeton Univ. (BA 1956); New Coll., Oxford (BA 1959; MA 1963; Hon. Fellow, 1992); Harvard Univ. (PhD 1964). Instructor, English and American Lit. and Lang., Harvard Univ., 1964–66, Asst Prof. 1966–68; Princeton University: Associate Prof., English Dept, 1968–73; Dean of Students, 1968–72; Prof. of English, 1973–88; Dean of College, 1972–77; Provost, 1977–88; Exec. Vice-Pres., Andrew W. Mellon Foundn, 1988–91. *Publications:* Sidney's Poetic Development, 1967; (ed with George Rousseau) English Poetic Satire: Wyatt to Byron, 1972; In Pursuit of the PhD, 1992. *Address:* Office of the President, Massachusetts Hall, Harvard University, Cambridge, MA 02138, USA. *T:* (617) 4951502.

RUDGE, Alan Walter, CBE 1995 (OBE 1987); PhD; FRS 1992; FEng 1984; Member Main Board, since 1989, and Deputy Group Managing Director, since 1995; BT (formerly British Telecom); Chairman, Engineering and Physical Sciences Research Council, since 1994; *b* 17 Oct. 1937; *s* of Walter Thomas Rudge and Emma (*née* McFayden); *m* 1969, Jennifer Joan Minott; one *s* one *d. Educ:* Hugh Myddelton Sch.; London Polytechnic; Univ. of Birmingham (PhD ElecEng). FIEE, FIEEE. Res. Engr, Illinois Inst. of Technol. Res. Inst., 1968–71; Lectr, Electronic and Elec. Engrg Dept, Univ. of Birmingham, 1971–74; Engrg Adviser, Illinois Inst. of Technol. Res. Inst., 1974–79; Man. Dir, Era Technology Ltd, 1979–86; British Telecom: Dir, Research and Technology, 1987–89; Group Technology and Develt Dir, 1989–90; Man. Dir, Develt and Procurement, 1990–95. Non-Exec. Director and Member Board: British Maritime Technology Ltd, 1984–89; Ricardo Consulting Engrs PLC, 1985–89; BT&D Technologies Ltd, 1987–93; Telecom Securicor Cellular Radio, 1989–90; MCI (USA), 1995–. Vis. Prof., Queen Mary and Westfield Coll. (formerly QMC), Univ. of London, 1985–. Pres., AIRTO, 1986. Pres., IEE, 1993–94 (Vice Chm., 1989–91; Dep. Pres., 1991; Mem., Electronics Divl Bd, 1980–89, Chm., 1984; Faraday Medal, 1991); Chm., Learned Soc. Bd, 1989–91; Member: Systems and Electronics Bd, MoD Defence Scientific Adv. Council, 1981–87; CBI Res. and Technol. Cttee, 1980–86; ACOST, 1987–90; Council for Sci. and Technology, 1993–. Member, Council: QMW, 1991–; Royal Instn, 1992–. Freeman, City of London. Hon. DEng: Birmingham, 1991; Bradford, Portsmouth, 1994; Hon. DSc: Strathclyde, 1992; Bath, Loughborough, 1995; DUniv Surrey, 1994. *Publications:* The Handbook of Antenna Design, vol. 1 1982, vol. 2 1983; papers in sci. and tech. jls on antennas, microwaves and satellite communications. *Recreations:* sailing, cycling, reading. *Address:* April Cottage, Spring Gardens, Dorking, Surrey RH4 1EE. *T:* Dorking (01306) 881597. *Clubs:* Athenæum, Royal Ocean Racing; Royal Southampton Yacht.

RUDIN, Toni Richard Perrott; Secretary, Magistrates' Association, 1986–93; *b* 13 Oct. 1934; *s* of Richard William Rudin and Sarah Rowena Mary Rudin (*née* Perrott); *m* 1958, Heather Jean (*née* Farley); one *s* three *d. Educ:* Bootham Sch.; Millfield Sch.; RMA Sandhurst; Army Staff Coll.; Coll. of Law, Guildford. Commissioned Royal Artillery, 1954; served BAOR, Cyprus, UK; MoD, 1967–69; Battery Comdr and 2 i/c 26th Field Regt, RA, BAOR, 1969–72; MoD, 1972–75; retired, 1975. Solicitor, 1978; private practice as solicitor, 1978–80; Press and Public Relations, Law Soc., 1980–86. Pt-time Chm., Pensions Appeal Tribunals, 1994. *Recreations:* 19th century history, riding, gardening, house renovation. *Address:* Otterbank House, 60 Wedgwood Avenue, Blakelands, Milton Keynes MK14 5HX.

RUDKIN, (James) David; playwright; *b* 29 June 1936; *s* of David Jonathan Rudkin and Anne Alice Martin; *m* 1967, Alexandra Margaret Thompson; two *s* two *d. Educ:* King Edward's Sch., Birmingham; St Catherine's Coll., Oxford (MA). *Screenplays:* Testimony, 1987; December Bride, 1991; *opera libretti:* Broken Strings, 1992; (with Jonathan Harvey) Inquest of Love, 1993; *radio plays:* The Lovesong of Alfred J. Hitchcock, 1993; The Haunting of Mahler, 1994. *Publications:* plays: Afore Night Come, 1963; (trans.) Moses and Aaron, 1965; The Grace of Todd (orig. opera libretto), 1969; Cries from Casement as his Bones are Brought to Dublin, 1974; Penda's Fen (film), 1975; Burglars (for children), 1976; Ashes, 1978; (trans.) Hippolytus, 1980; The Sons of Light, 1981; The Triumph of Death, 1981; (trans.) Peer Gynt, 1983; The Saxon Shore, 1986; (trans.) When We Dead Waken, 1989; (trans.) Rosmersholm, 1990; articles, reviews etc. for Encounter, Drama, Tempo. *Recreations:* piano, geology, anthropology, languages, swimming, bridge. *Address:* c/o Casarotto Ramsay Ltd, 60–66 Wardour Street, W1V 3HP. *T:* 0171–287 4450, *Fax:* 0171–287 9128.

RUDKIN, Walter Charles, CBE 1981; Director of Economic Intelligence, 1973–81, of Economic and Logistic Intelligence, 1982, Ministry of Defence; retired; *b* 22 Sept. 1922; *e s* of Walter and Bertha Rudkin; *m* 1950, Hilda Mary Hope; two *s. Educ:* Carre's Grammar Sch., Sleaford; UC Hull. BSc (Econ) London. Served with RAF, 1942–46. Lectr, Dept of Econs and Econ. History, Univ. of Witwatersrand, 1948–52. Entered Min. of Defence, 1954; appts incl. Hong Kong, 1956–59; Junior Directing Staff, Imperial Defence Coll., 1962–64; Cabinet Office, 1968–71. *Recreation:* fishing. *Address:* 9 Speen Place, Speen, Newbury, Berks RG13 1RX. *T:* Newbury (01635) 49244. *Club:* Commonwealth Trust.

RUDLAND, Margaret Florence; Headmistress, Godolphin and Latymer School, since 1986; *b* 15 June 1945; *d* of Ernest George and Florence Hilda Rudland. *Educ:* Sweyne School, Rayleigh; Bedford College, Univ. of London (BSc); Inst. of Education (PGCE). Asst Mathematics Mistress, Godolphin and Latymer Sch., 1967–70; VSO, Ilorin, Nigeria, 1970–71; Asst Maths Mistress, Clapham County Sch., 1971–72; Asst Maths Mistress and Head of Dept, St Paul's Girls' Sch., 1972–83; Deputy Headmistress, Norwich High Sch., GPDST, 1983–85. Pres., GSA, 1996 (Chm., Educn Cttee, 1993–94). Mem. Council, Nightingale Fund, 1989–. *Recreations:* opera, cinema, travel. *Address:* The Godolphin and Latymer School, Iffley Road, Hammersmith, W6 0PG. *T:* 0181–741 1936.

RUDLOFF, Hans-Jörg; Chief Executive, MC Securities Ltd, since 1994; *b* Cologne, 1940. *Educ:* Univ. of Berne (Econs, Hons). Exec. Trainee, Credit Suisse, 1966–68; with Kidder, Peabody, International, 1969–79: Manager, Swiss operation; Man. Dir; Chm., 1978; Mem. Bd, Kidder, Peabody Inc., 1975; joined Crédit Suisse-First Boston Ltd, 1980; Dep. Chm. and Mem. Bd, 1981–88, Chief Exec., 1989–93, Chm., 1989–94, Financière Crédit Suisse-First Boston. Gen. Manager, Crédit Suisse, Zurich, 1987–90; Member, Executive Board: CS First Boston Group Inc., 1990–94; CS Holding, 1993–94. Mem. numerous bds. *Address:* MC Securities Ltd, Commercial Union Tower, One Undershaft, EC3A 8LH. *T:* 0171–337 6300.

RUDMAN, Michael Edward; theatre director and producer; Artistic Director, Sheffield Theatres (Crucible and Lyceum), 1992–94; *b* Tyler, Texas, 14 Feb. 1939; *s* of M. B. Rudman and Josephine Davis; *m* 1963, Veronica Anne Bennett (marr. diss. 1981); two *d*; *m* 1983, Felicity Kendal (marr. diss. 1994), *qv*; one *s. Educ:* St Mark's Sch., Texas; Oberlin Coll. (BA *cum laude* Govt); St Edmund Hall, Oxford (MA). Pres., OUDS, 1963–64. Asst Dir and Associate Producer, Nottingham Playhouse and Newcastle Playhouse, 1964–68; Asst Dir, RSC, 1968; Artistic Director: Traverse Theatre Club, 1970–73; Hampstead Theatre, 1973–78 (Theatre won Evening Standard Award for Special Achievement, 1978); Associate Dir, Nat. Theatre, 1979–88; Dir, Lyttelton Theatre (National), 1979–81; Dir, Chichester Festival Theatre, 1989–91. Mem., Bd of Dirs, Hampstead Theatre, 1979–89. *Plays directed* include: *Nottingham Playhouse:* Changing Gear, Measure for Measure, A Man for All Seasons, 1965; Julius Caesar, She Stoops to Conquer, Who's Afraid of Virginia Woolf, Death of a Salesman, 1966; Long Day's Journey into Night, 1967; Lily in Little India, 1968; *RSC Theatregoround:* The Fox and the Fly, 1968; *Traverse Theatre:* Curtains (transf. Open Space, 1971), Straight Up (transf. Piccadilly, 1971), A Game called Arthur (transf. Theatre Upstairs, 1971), Stand for my Father, (with Mike Wearing) A Triple Bill of David Halliwell plays, 1970; The Looneys, Pantagleize, 1971; Carravagio Buddy, Tell Charlie Thanks for the Truss, The Relapse, 1972; *Hampstead Theatre:* Ride across Lake Constance, A Nightingale in Bloomsbury Square, 1973; The Black and White Minstrels, The Show-off, The Connection, The Looneys, 1974; Alphabetical Order (transf. May Fair), 1975; Clouds, 1977; Cakewalk, Beyond a Joke, Gloo-Joo (transf. Criterion), 1978; Making it Better (transf. Criterion), 1992; *National Theatre:* For Services Rendered (televised, 1980), Death of a Salesman, 1979; Thee and Me, The Browning Version/Harlequinade, Measure for Measure, 1980; The Second Mrs Tanqueray, 1981; Brighton Beach Memoirs, The Magistrate, 1986; Six Characters in Search of an Author, Fathers and Sons, Ting Tang Mine, Waiting for Godot, 1987; *Chichester:* The Merry Wives of Windsor, Rumours, 1990; *Sheffield:* A Midsummer Night's Dream, 1992; Donkeys' Years, Jane Eyre, Hamlet, Mansfield Park, 1993; The Grapes of Wrath, 1994; *West End:* Donkeys Years, Globe, 1976; Clouds, Duke of York's, 1978; Taking Steps, Lyric, 1980; Camelot, 1982; The Winslow Boy, 1983; The Dragon's Tail, Apollo, 1985; Exclusive, Strand, 1989; *New York:* The Changing Room, 1973; Hamlet, 1976; Death of a Salesman, 1984; Measure for Measure, 1993; Have you spoken to any Jews lately?, 1995. *Address:* c/o Peter Murphy Esq., Curtis Brown Group, 162–168 Regent Street, W1R 5TA. *T:* 0171–437 9700. *Clubs:* Royal Automobile; Royal Mid-Surrey Golf.

RUDOE, Wulf, CB 1975; *b* 9 March 1916; *m* 1942, Ellen Trilling; one *s* one *d. Educ:* Central Foundation School; Peterhouse, Cambridge (Open Schol. and Research Schol.). Mathematics Tripos Pt III, 1938, Distinction. Royal Aircraft Establishment, 1939. Operational Research, RAF, 1939–45. Operational Research in Building Industry, Min. of Works, 1946–48, Principal Scientific Officer 1948; Board of Trade, Statistician 1948, Chief Statistician 1952; Dir of Statistics and Research, DHSS (formerly Min. of Health), 1966–76; Asst Sec., Price Commn, 1976–79; Adviser to Govt of Ghana, 1980–81. Fellow Inst. of Statisticians; Mem. Council, 1962–78, Hon. Treasurer, 1965–74, Vice-Pres., 1974–75 and 1976–77, Roy. Statistical Soc. *Recreations:* walking, travel, languages. *Address:* 72 North End Road, NW11 7SY. *T:* 0181–455 2890.

RUE, Dame (Elsie) Rosemary, DBE 1989 (CBE 1977); Regional General Manager, 1984–88, and Regional Medical Officer, 1973–88, Oxford Regional Health Authority; *b* 14 June 1928; *d* of Harry and Daisy Laurence; divorced; two *s. Educ:* Sydenham High Sch.; Univ. of London; Oxford Univ. Med. School. MB, BS; FRCP; DCH; FRCPsych (Hon. FRCPsych 1990); FRCGP; FRCS 1994. Gen. Practitioner, 1952–58; Public Health Service, 1958–65; Hospital Service, 1965–73; SAMO, Oxford RHB, 1971. President: Faculty of Community Medicine, 1986–89; BMA, 1990–91; Past-Pres., Medical Women's Fedn. Hon. Fellow, Green Coll., Oxford, 1985. Hon. MA Oxford, 1988. *Publications:* papers on gen. practice, women in medicine, ward design, community hosps, health services, individuals requiring security. *Address:* 2 Stanton St John, Oxford OX33 1ET.

RUFFLE, Mary, (Mrs Thomas Ruffle); *see* Dilnot, Mary.

RUGAMBWA, HE Cardinal Laurean; RC Archbishop of Dar-Es-Salaam, 1969–92, now Emeritus; *b* Bukongo, 12 July 1912; *s* of Domitian Rushubirwa and Asteria Mukaboshezi. *Educ:* Rutabo, Rubya Seminary; Katigondo Seminary; Univ. of Propaganda, Rome (DCL 1951). Priest 1943; Bishop of Rutabo, 1952–60; Cardinal 1960; Bishop of Bukoba, 1960–69. Member: Knights of Columbus; Knights of St Peter Claver. Hon. Dr of Laws: Notre Dame, 1961; St Joseph's Coll., Philadelphia, 1961; Rosary Hill Coll., Buffalo, 1965; Hon. DHL New Rochelle, 1961; Hon. Dr Civil and Canon Law, Georgetown Univ. (Jesuits), 1961; Giving of the Scroll, Catholic Univ. of America, 1961. *Address:* Archbishop's House, PO Box 167, Dar-es-Salaam, Tanzania, East Africa.

RUGBY, 3rd Baron, *cr* 1947, of Rugby, Co. Warwick; **Robert Charles Maffey;** farmer; *b* 4 May 1951; *s* of 2nd Baron Rugby and of Margaret Helen, *d* of late Harold Bindley; *S* father, 1990; *m* 1974, Anne Penelope, *yr d* of late David Hale; two *s. Educ:* Brickwall House Sch., Northiam. *Recreations:* shooting, golf, woodwork and metal work. *Heir: s*

Hon. Timothy James Howard Maffey, *b* 23 July 1975. *Address:* Grove Farm, Frankton, Rugby CV23 9QG.

RUGGE-PRICE, Sir Charles Keith Napier; *see* Price.

RUGGIERO, Renato, Hon. KCMG 1980; Director-General, World Trade Organization, since 1995; *b* Naples, 9 April 1930; *s* of Antonio Ruggiero and Lucia (*née* Rubinacci); *m* 1956, Paola Tomacelli Filomarino; two *s* one *d*. *Educ:* Univ. of Naples (degree in law 1953). Joined Italian diplomatic service; served Sao Paulo, Moscow, Washington, Belgrade and Brussels; Chef de Cabinet of Pres., 1969–73, Dir-Gen. for Regional Policies, 1973–77, EC; Foreign Ministry, Rome, 1977–80; Ambassador to EEC, 1980–84; Dir-Gen. for Econ. Affairs, 1984–85, Sec. Gen., 1985–87, Foreign Ministry; Foreign Trade Minister, 1987–91. Dir and adviser, various Italian, European and American cos, 1991–95. Cavalierato di Gran Croce (Italy), 1985; Grand Cordon, Order of the Sacred Treasure (Japan), 1991. *Recreations:* sailing, hiking. *Address:* World Trade Organization, 154 Rue de Lausanne, 1211 Geneva 21, Switzerland. *T:* (22) 7395100.

RUGGLES-BRISE, Captain Guy Edward, TD, DL; *b* 15 June 1914; *s* of late Col Sir Edward Archibald Ruggles-Brise, 1st Bt, MC, TD, DL, JP, MP, and Agatha, *e d* of J. H. Gurney, DL, JP, Keswick Hall, Norfolk; *b* and *heir pres.* of Sir John Ruggles-Brise, Bt, *qv*; *m* 1st, 1940, Elizabeth (*d* 1988), *o d* of James Knox, Smithstone House, Kilwinning, Ayrshire; three *s*; 2nd, 1994, Christine Margaret Fothergill-Spencer, *o d* of late Lieut J. A. Fothergill. *Educ:* Eton. Captain 104th (Essex Yeo.) Field Bde RHA (TA), No 7 Commando. Served War of 1939–45 (PoW). DL 1967, High Sheriff 1967, Essex. *Recreations:* field sports. *Address:* Housham Tye, Harlow, Essex CM17 0PB. *T:* Bishops Stortford (01279) 731236; Ledgowan Lodge, Achnasheen, Ross-shire IV22 2EH. *T:* Achnasheen (01445) 720245. *Club:* City of London.

RUGGLES-BRISE, Col Sir John Archibald, 2nd Bt, *cr* 1935; CB 1958; OBE (mil.) 1945; TD; JP; Lord-Lieutenant of Essex, 1958–78; Pro-Chancellor, University of Essex, 1964–79; *b* 13 June 1908; *er s* of Colonel Sir Edward Archibald Ruggles-Brise, 1st Bt, MC, TD, DL, JP, MP, and Agatha (*d* 1937), *e d* of J. H. Gurney, DL, JP, of Keswick Hall, Norfolk; *S* father, 1942. *Educ:* Eton. Served AA Comd, 1939–45 (comd 1st 450 Mixed HAA Regt, and 2nd AA Demonstration and User Trials Regt); formed and comd 599 HAA Regt, 1947. Member of Lloyd's. Pres., CLA, 1957–59 (helped promote Game Fair); Church Comr, 1959–64; Chm., Council of the Baronetage, 1958–63. Patron, Essex Agricl Soc., 1970–78. Liveryman, Spectacle Makers' Co., 1948–. DL 1945, JP 1946, Vice-Lieutenant, 1947, Co. Essex. Hon. Freeman of Chelmsford. Governor of Felsted and Chigwell Schools, 1950–75. DUniv Essex, 1980. KStJ. *Recreation:* shooting. *Heir: b* Capt. Guy Edward Ruggles-Brise, *qv*. *Address:* Spains Hall, Finchingfield, Essex CM7 4PF. *T:* Great Dunmow (01371) 810266.

RÜHE, Volker; Minister of Defence, Germany, since 1992; *b* 25 Sept. 1942; *m*; three *c*. *Educ:* Univ. of Hamburg. Mem. of Bundestag, 1976–; Gen. Sec., CDU, 1989–92. *Address:* Postfach 1328, 5300 Bonn 1, Germany.

RUHFUS, Dr Jürgen; Officer's Cross, Order of Merit, Federal Republic of Germany, 1983; Hon. KBE, 1978; Chairman, Deutsch-Englische Gesellschaft, since 1993; *b* 4 Aug. 1930; three *d*. *Educ:* Universities of Munich, Münster and Denver, USA. Joined Federal Foreign Office, Bonn, 1955; Consulate General: Geneva, 1956–57; Dakar, 1958–59; Embassy, Athens, 1960–63; Dep. Spokesman of Federal Foreign Office, 1964, Official Spokesman, 1966; Ambassador to Kenya, 1970–73; Asst Under-Secretary, Federal Foreign Office, 1973–76; Adviser on Foreign Policy and Defence Affairs to Federal Chancellor Helmut Schmidt, 1976–80; Ambassador to UK, 1980–83; Head of Political Directorate-General (dealing with Third World and other overseas countries), Federal Foreign Office, Dec. 1983–June 1984; State Sec., Federal Foreign Office, FRG, 1984–87; Ambassador to USA, 1987–92. *Recreations:* golf, tennis, skiing, shooting. *Address:* Deutsch-Englische Gesellschaft, Beethovenplatz 6, 53115 Bonn, Germany.

RUHNAU, Heinz; Chairman, Deutsche Lufthansa, 1982–91; *b* Danzig, 5 March 1929; *m* Edith Loers; three *d*. Dip. in Business Administration, 1954; Head, personal office of Chm., IG-Metall, Frankfurt; Regional Dir, IG-Metall, Hamburg, 1956–65; Mem., Supervisory Bd, Hapag Lloyd; Head of Dept of Internal Affairs and Mem., Senate of Free Hanseatic City of Hamburg, 1965–73; Mem., Exec. Bd, COOP, 1973; State Sec., Ministry of Transport, 1974–82; Mem., Supervisory Bd, Vereinigte Tanklager und Transportmittel, Hamburg and Hapag Lloyd. Chm., Assoc. of European Airlines, 1988. Federal Grand Cross of Merit, 1980, with Star, 1989, FRG. *Address:* Deutsche Lufthansa, von Gablenz Strasse 2–6, 50679 Köln, Germany.

RUIZ SOLER, Antonio, (Antonio); Cross of the Order of Isabella the Catholic, 1951; Comdr Order of Civil Merit, 1964; Spanish dancer; Director, Ballet Nacional Español; *b* Seville, 4 November 1921. Studied at the Realito Dance Academy. First stage appearance at the age of eight; subsequently toured North and South America Southern and Western Europe, and Scandinavia. First stage appearance in Great Britain, Edinburgh Festival, 1950; London début, Cambridge Theatre, 1951. Golden Medal, Fine Arts, 1952. Formed Ballet Company, 1953; début in Generalife Theatre, Granada, presenting his Ballet in Europe, S and N America. Has also appeared in many festivals in Spain. Appearances with Ballet in London: Stoll, 1954; Palace, 1956; Coliseum, 1958; Royalty, 1960; Drury Lane, 1963; Coliseum, 1975. Gala perf. in Washington to President Kennedy, Ed Sullivan Show in New York, appearances Europe, 1963. Festivals of Spain, 1964–65; Madrid Season, 1965; N Amer. tour, 1965; Ed Sullivan Show, 1965. Appears on TV. Gold Medal, Swedish Acad. of Dancing, 1963; Medal of Min. of Information and Tourism, Madrid, 1963; Golden Medal, Spanish Inst., NY, 1979. *Address:* Coslada 7, Madrid, Spain.

RULE, Brian Francis; Director General of Information Technology Systems, Ministry of Defence, 1985–94; Chairman, Emeritus Plus plc, since 1994; *s* of late Sydney John Rule and Josephine Rule, Pen-y-ffordd, near Chester; *m* 1993, Irene M. Rees, Pembs. *Educ:* Daniel Owen Sch., Mold; Loughborough Univ. of Technology (MSc). Engineer, de Havilland Aircraft Co., 1955–59; Res. Assistant, Loughborough Univ., 1963–65; Lectr, Univ. of Glasgow, 1965–67; University of Aberdeen: Lectr, 1967–70; Sen. Lectr, 1970–72; Dir of Computing, 1972–78; Dir, Honeywell Information Systems Ltd, 1978–79; Dir of Scientific Services, NERC, 1979–85. *Publications:* various papers in scientific jls. *Recreations:* motoring, antique clocks. *Address:* c/o Lloyds Bank, 14 Castle Street, Cirencester, Glos GL7 1QJ.

RULE, David Charles; Dean of Postgraduate Dental Studies (Thames Regions), British Postgraduate Medical Federation, since 1990; *b* April 1937; *s* of Cyril George Leonard Rule and Ivy Rule; *m* 1972, Linda Marion Meyer; two *d*. *Educ:* Univ. of Birmingham (BDS). FDS RCS, MCCD RCS, DOrthRCS. Qualified Dental Surgeon, 1959; RADC 1960–63; Eastman Dental Hosp., 1964, Registrar, Lectr, Sen. Registrar, Consultant, 1975. President: British Paedontic Soc., 1988–89; British Soc. of Dentistry for the Handicapped, 1980; Internat. Assoc. of Dentistry for the Handicapped, 1990–92. *Recreation:* sailing. *Address:* 7 Malmains Way, Beckenham, Kent BR2 2SA. *T:* 0181–650 1895. *Clubs:* MCC.

RULE, Margaret Helen, (Mrs A. W. Rule), CBE 1983; FSA; Consultant, Mary Rose Trust, since 1994 (Research Director, 1983–94); *b* 27 Sept. 1928; *d* of Ernest Victor and Mabel Martin; *m* 1949, Arthur Walter Rule; one *s*. *Educ:* Univ. of London. FSA 1967. Dir of Excavations, Chichester Civic Soc., 1961–79; Hon. Curator, Fishbourne Roman Palace and Museum, 1968–79; Archaeol Dir, Mary Rose Trust, 1979–82. Hon. Fellow, Portsmouth Polytechnic, 1982. Hon. DLitt Liverpool, 1984. Reginald Mitchell Medal, Stoke-on-Trent Assoc. of Engrs, 1983. *Publications:* Chichester Excavations 1, 1967; The Mary Rose, 1982; A Gallo-Roman Trading Vessel from Guernsey, 1993; Life at Sea: Tudors and Stuarts, 1994; many papers in jls in Britain and USA. *Recreations:* anything in or on the water. *Address:* Crofton, East Bracklesham Drive, Bracklesham Bay, W Sussex PO20 8JW.

RUMBELOW, Arthur Anthony; QC 1990; a Recorder, since 1988; *b* Salford, Lancs, 9 Sept. 1943; *er s* of Arthur Rumbelow and Theresa (*née* Lucketti); *m* 1971, Shelagh Lewtas; three *d*. *Educ:* Salford Grammar Sch.; Queens' Coll., Cambridge (Squire Schol.; BA 1966). Called to the Bar, Middle Temple, 1967 (Harmsworth Exhibnr, Astbury Schol.); Chm., Medical Appeal Tribunal, 1988–. Mem., Rochdale MBC, 1982–84. *Recreations:* wine, theatre, Rugby, collecting. *Address:* 28 St John Street, Manchester M3 4DJ. *T:* 0161–834 8418; 1 Serjeant's Inn, Temple, EC4Y 1NH. *T:* 0171–583 1355.

RUMBELOW, (Roger) Martin, CEng; Head of Electronics and Engineering Division, Department of Trade and Industry, since 1992; *b* 3 June 1937; *s* of Leonard Rumbelow and Phyllis (*née* Perkins); *m* 1965, Marjorie Elizabeth Glover. *Educ:* Cardiff High Sch.; Bristol Univ. (BSc); Cranfield Inst. of Technol. (MSc). CEng 1966. National Service, RAF Pilot, 1955–57. British Aircraft Corporation, 1958–74: Dep. Prodn Controller, 1967–73; Concorde Manufg Project Manager, 1973–74; DTI, 1974–: Principal, 1974–78; Asst Sec., 1978–86; Under Sec., 1987–; Services Management Div., 1987–92. *Recreations:* singing, opera, theatre, computing, amateur radio, electronics, tennis. *Address:* c/o Department of Trade and Industry, 151 Buckingham Palace Road, SW1W 9SS. *Club:* Royal Air Force.

RUMBLE, Captain John Bertram, RN (retired); Director General, Royal Over-Seas League, 1979–91; *b* 30 Oct. 1928; *s* of late Major and Mrs Rumble; *m* 1st, 1953, Jennifer Wilson (marr. diss. 1992); one *s* three *d*; 2nd, 1992, Mrs Elizabeth Villiers. *Educ:* Sherborne Sch. FBIM 1980, FIIM 1980. Special Entry Cadet into Royal Navy, 1946; HMS Magpie, 1950–51; ADC (Lieut) to Governor of Malta, 1952–53; specialised in Communications, 1954; HMS Maidstone, 1955–56; Staff, BRNC Dartmouth, 1956–57; Exchange Service with RCN, 1957–59; Signal Officer, HMS Ark Royal, 1959–61; Comdr 1962; RN sc 1963; CO HMS Torquay, 1964–65; Staff Communications Officer to C-in-C EASTLANT, 1966–67; Exec. Officer, HMS Hermes, 1967–69; Captain 1970; Staff Dir, Gen. Weapons, 1970–71; CO HMS Fearless, 1974–75; Asst Chief of Staff Communications (as Cdre), C-in-C SOUTH, 1976–77; MoD (Intelligence), 1977–79. Younger Brother, Trinity House, 1977; Member: Council, Mayfair, Piccadilly and St James's Assoc., 1979–91 (Chm., 1988–90); Jt Commonwealth Societies Council, 1980–91. Pres., Colchester Sea Cadets, 1994–. *Recreations:* shooting, sailing, fishing, gold leaf gilding. *Address:* White Horse Cottage, School Street, Stoke-by-Nayland, Suffolk CO6 4QY. *T:* Colchester (01206) 262325. *Clubs:* Farmers', Royal Navy of 1765 and 1785, Royal Over-Seas League (Hon.); Stour Sailing.

RUMBLE, Peter William, CB 1984; Chief Executive, Historic Buildings and Monuments Commission, 1983–89; Director-General, Union of European Historic Houses Associations, 1991–94; *b* 28 April 1929; *s* of Arthur Victor Rumble and Dorothy Emily (*née* Sadler); *m* 1953, Joyce Audrey Stephenson; one *s* one *d*. *Educ:* Harwich County High Sch.; Oriel Coll., Oxford (MA). Entered Civil Service, 1952; HM Inspector of Taxes, 1952; Principal, Min. of Housing and Local Govt, 1963; Asst Sec., 1972, Under Sec., 1977, DoE. Vice-Chm., Architectural Heritage Fund, 1988–; Member: Cttee, Southern Region, NT, 1990–; Churches Conservation Trust (formerly Redundant Churches Fund), 1991–. Trustee, Amer. Friends of English Heritage, 1988–94. *Recreation:* music. *Address:* 11 Hillside Road, Cheam, Surrey SM2 6ET. *T:* 0181–643 1752.

RUMBOLD, Rt. Hon. Dame Angela (Claire Rosemary), DBE 1992 (CBE 1981); PC 1991; MP (C) Mitcham and Morden (formerly Merton, Mitcham and Morden), since June 1982; a Deputy Chairman, Conservative Party, since 1992; *b* 11 Aug. 1932; *d* of late Harry Jones, FRS; *m* 1958, John Marix Rumbold; two *s* one *d*. *Educ:* Notting Hill and Ealing High Sch.; King's Coll., London. Founder Member, National Assoc. for the Welfare of Children in Hospital, and National Chairman, 1974–76. Councillor, Royal Borough of Kingston upon Thames, 1974–83; Chm., Council, Local Educn Authorities, 1979–80. Mem., Doctors and Dentists Review Body, 1979–81. Co-Chm., Women's Nat. Commn, 1986–90. Mem., Social Services Select Cttee, 1982–83; PPS to Financial Sec. to the Treasury, 1983, to Sec. of State for Transport, 1983–85; Parly Under Sec. of State, DoE, 1985–86; Minister of State, DES, 1986–90, Home Office, 1990–92. Freeman, City of London, 1988. *Recreations:* swimming, cinema, reading, ballet. *Address:* House of Commons, SW1A 0AA.

RUMBOLD, Sir Henry (John Sebastian), 11th Bt *cr* 1779; Partner, Dawson Cornwell & Co., since 1991; *b* 24 Dec. 1947; *s* of Sir Horace Anthony Claude Rumbold, 10th Bt, KCMG, KCVO, CB, and Felicity Ann Rumbold (*née* Bailey); *S* father, 1983; *m* 1978, Frances Ann (*née* Hawkes, formerly wife of Julian Berry). *Educ:* Eton College; College of William and Mary, Virginia, USA (BA). Articled Stileman, Neate and Topping, 1975–77; admitted solicitor, 1977; asst solicitor, Stileman, Neate and Topping, 1977–79; Partner, 1979–81; joined Stephenson Harwood, 1981, Partner, 1982–91. *Recreations:* riding, shooting, reading. *Heir: cousin* Charles Anton Rumbold [*b* 7 Feb. 1959; *m* 1967, Susan, *er d* of J. M. Tucker]. *Address:* 19 Hollywood Road, SW10 9HT. *T:* 0171–352 9148; Hatch House, Tisbury, Wilts SP3 6PA. *T:* Tisbury (01747) 870622. *Club:* Boodle's.

RUMBOLD, Sir Jack (Seddon), Kt 1984; QC (Zanzibar) 1963; President of the Industrial Tribunals, England and Wales, 1979–84, retired; *b* 5 March 1920; *s* of William Alexander Rumbold and Jean Lindsay Rumbold (*née* Mackay), Christchurch, NZ; *m* 1st, 1949, Helen Suzanne, *d* of Col J. B. Davis, Wanganui, NZ; two *d*; 2nd, 1970, Veronica Ellie Hurt (*née* Whigham). *Educ:* St Andrew's Coll., NZ; Canterbury Univ., NZ (LLB 1940); Brasenose Coll., Oxford (Rhodes Schol.; BCL 1948). Served Royal Navy, Lieut RNZNVR, 1941–45 (despatches). Called to Bar, Inner Temple, 1948; Crown Counsel, Kenya, 1957, Sen. Crown Counsel, 1959; Attorney General, Zanzibar, 1963; Legal Adviser, Kenya Govt, 1964–66; Academic Director, British Campus of Stanford Univ., USA, 1966–72; Chairman of Industrial Tribunals (part-time), 1968; (full-time) 1972; Regional Chairman (London South), 1977. FRSA 1985. *Recreations:* books, music; formerly cricket (Oxford Blue). *Address:* 5 Church Row, Moore Park Road, SW6 2JW; Le Mas du Vallon, Le Brulat du Castellet, Var 83330, France. *Clubs:* Garrick, MCC.

RUMFITT, Nigel John; QC 1994; a Recorder, since 1995; *b* 6 March 1950; *s* of Alan Regan Rumfitt and Dorothy Rumfitt (*née* Ackroyd); *m* 1984, Dorothy Pamela Pouncey. *Educ:* Leeds Modern Sch.; Pembroke Coll., Oxford (MA, BCL). Teaching Associate, Northwestern Univ. Sch. of Law, Chicago, 1972–73; called to the Bar, Middle Temple,

1974; Asst Recorder, 1991–95. *Recreations:* ski-ing, wind-surfing, travel, reading, Francophilia. *Address:* 9 Bedford Row, WC1R 4AZ. *T:* 0171–242 3555.

RUNACRES, Eric Arthur; *b* 22 Aug. 1916; *s* of Arthur Selwyn Runacres and Mildred May (*née* Dye); *m* 1950, Penelope Jane Elizabeth Luxmoore; one *s* one *d*. *Educ:* Dulwich College; Merton College, Oxford. 1st cl. hons Lit. Hum. 1939. Commissioned Royal Engineers, Oct. 1939; served UK, Malta, Middle East, India, 1939–46 (Major). J. & P. Coats Ltd, 1946–48. Entered HM Foreign Service, 1948; First Secretary, 1951–53. British Productivity Council, 1954–71 (Deputy Director, 1959–71, and Secretary, 1962–71); Vice-Chm., OECD, Cttee on National Productivity Centres, 1960–66; Exec. Director, Commonwealth Agricultural Bureaux, 1973–77; Consultant, Industrial Facts & Forecasting Ltd, 1978–81. *Recreations:* European thought and literature; gardening. *Address:* Gables, Radbones Hill, Over Norton, Oxon OX7 5RA. *T:* Chipping Norton (01608) 643264.

RUNCIE, family name of **Baron Runcie.**

RUNCIE, Baron *cr* 1991 (Life Peer), of Cuddesdon in the County of Oxfordshire; **Rt. Rev. and Rt. Hon. Robert Alexander Kennedy Runcie,** MC 1945; PC 1980; Royal Victorian Chain, 1991; Archbishop of Canterbury, 1980–91; Hon. Assistant Bishop of St Albans, since 1991; High Steward of the University of Cambridge, since 1991; *b* 2 Oct. 1921; *s* of Robert Dalziel Runcie and Anne Runcie; *m* 1957, Angela Rosalind, *d* of J. W. Cecil Turner; one *s* one *d*. *Educ:* Merchant Taylors', Crosby; Brasenose Coll., Oxford (Squire Minor Schol.), Hon. Fellow, 1979; Westcott House, Cambridge. BA (1st Cl. Hons, Lit. Hum.), MA Oxon, 1948; FKC 1981. Served Scots Guards, War of 1939–45 (MC). Deacon, 1950; Priest, 1951; Curate, All Saints, Gosforth, 1950–52; Chaplain, Westcott House, Cambridge, 1953–54; Vice-Principal, 1954–56; Fellow, Dean and Asst Tutor of Trinity Hall, Cambridge, 1956–60, Hon. Fellow 1975; Vicar of Cuddesdon and Principal of Cuddesdon Coll., 1960–69; Bishop of St Albans, 1970–80. Canon and Prebendary of Lincoln, 1969. Hon. Bencher, Gray's Inn, 1980. Chm., BBC and IBA Central Religious Adv. Cttee, 1973–79. Teape Lectr, St Stephen's Coll., Delhi, 1962; William Noble Lectr, Harvard, 1986. Select Preacher: Cambridge, 1957 and 1975, Oxford 1959 and 1973. Anglican Chm., Anglican-Orthodox Jt Doctrinal Commn, 1973–80. Pres., Classical Assoc., 1991–92. Freeman: St Albans, 1979; City of London, 1981; Canterbury, 1984. Hon. Fellow, Merton Coll., Oxford, 1991. Hon. DD: Oxon, 1980; Cantab, 1981; New Raday Coll., Budapest, 1987; S Carolina, 1987; St Andrews, 1989; Yale, 1989; Univ. of the South, Sewanee, 1981; Trinity Coll., Toronto, 1986; Hon. DLitt Keele, 1981; Hon. LittD Liverpool, 1983; Hon. DCL West Indies, 1984; Hon. degree Berkeley Divinity Sch., USA, 1986; Hon. DrLitt Rikkyo, Japan, 1987. Council on Christian Unity's Patron of Christian Unity Award, Yale Univ., 1986; Order of St Vladimir Class II, Russian Orthodox Church, 1975; Cross of Order of the Holy Sepulchre, Greek Orthodox Church, 1986. *Publications:* (ed) Cathedral and City: St Albans Ancient and Modern, 1978; Windows onto God, 1983; Seasons of the Spirit, 1983; One Light for One World, 1988; Authority in Crisis? an Anglican response, 1988; The Unity We Seek, 1989. *Recreations:* opera, reading history and novels, owning Berkshire pigs. *Address:* 26a Jennings Road, St Albans, Herts AL1 4PD. *T:* St Albans (01727) 848021, *Fax:* (01727) 842319. *Clubs:* Athenæum, Cavalry and Guards, MCC, Lord's Taverners.

RUNCIMAN, family name of **Viscount Runciman of Doxford.**

RUNCIMAN OF DOXFORD, 3rd Viscount, *cr* 1937; **Walter Garrison Runciman (Garry),** CBE 1987; FBA 1975; Bt 1906; Baron Runciman, 1933, of Shoreston; Chairman: Walter Runciman plc, 1976–90; Andrew Weir and Co. Ltd, since 1991; Runciman Investments Ltd, since 1990; Fellow, Trinity College, Cambridge, since 1971; *b* 10 Nov. 1934; *o s* of 2nd Viscount Runciman of Doxford, OBE, AFC, AE and Katherine Schuyler (*d* 1993), *y d* of late William R. Garrison, New York; *S* father, 1989; *m* 1963, Ruth (*see* Viscountess Runciman of Doxford); one *s* two *d*. *Educ:* Eton (Oppidan Schol.); Trinity Coll., Cambridge (Schol.; Fellow, 1959–63, 1971–). National Service, 1953–55 (2/Lt, Grenadier Guards); Harkness Fellow, 1958–60; part-time Reader in Sociology, Univ. of Sussex, 1967–69, Vis. Prof., Harvard Univ., 1970; Vis. Fellow, Nuffield Coll., Oxford, 1979–87. Lectures: Radcliffe-Brown, British Acad., 1986; Spencer, Oxford Univ., 1986; Chorley, London Univ., 1993; ESRC, 1993; T. H. Marshall, Southampton Univ., 1994. Treas., Child Poverty Action Gp, 1972–; Member: SSRC, 1974–79; Securities and Investments Board, 1986– (a Dep. Chm., 1990–). Pres., Gen. Council of British Shipping, 1986–87 (Vice-Pres., 1985–86). Chm., Royal Commn on Criminal Justice, 1991–93. Hon. Foreign Mem., Amer. Acad. of Arts and Sciences, 1986. Hon. DSc (SocScis) Edinburgh, 1992; DUniv York, 1994. *Publications:* Plato's Later Epistemology, 1962; Social Science and Political Theory, 1963, 2nd edn 1969; Relative Deprivation and Social Justice, 1966, 2nd edn 1972; Sociology in its Place, and other essays, 1970; A Critique of Max Weber's Philosophy of Social Science, 1972; A Treatise on Social Theory: vol. I, 1983, vol. II, 1989; Confessions of a Reluctant Theorist, 1989; articles in academic jls. *Heir:* *s* Hon. David Walter Runciman, *b* 1 March 1967. *Address:* c/o House of Lords, SW1A 0PW. *Club:* Brooks's.

See also Hon. Sir Steven Runciman.

RUNCIMAN OF DOXFORD, Viscountess; Ruth Runciman, OBE 1991; Chairman, Mental Health Act Commission, since 1994; *b* 9 Jan. 1936; *o d* of Joseph Hellmann and Dr Ellen Hellmann; *m* 1st, 1959, Denis Mack Smith, *qv* (marr. diss. 1962); 2nd, 1963, Viscount Runciman of Doxford, *qv*; one *s* two *d*. *Educ:* Roedean Sch., Johannesburg; Witwatersrand Univ. (BA 1956); Girton Coll., Cambridge (BA 1958). Mem., Adv. Council on Misuse of Drugs, 1974–; Council Mem., Nat. Assoc. of CAB, 1978–83; Outreach advice worker, Kensington CAB, 1988–; Dep. Chm., Prison Reform Trust, 1981–. Trustee: Prince's Trust Volunteers, 1989–94; Nat. AIDS Trust, 1989–93; Mental Health Foundn, 1990–. Dir, ENO, 1978–83. *Recreations:* tennis, gardening. *Address:* c/o Mental Health Act Commission, Maid Marian House, 56 Hounds Gate, Nottingham NG1 6BG. *T:* Nottingham (0115) 950 4040.

RUNCIMAN, Hon. Sir Steven, (Hon. Sir James Cochran Stevenson Runciman), CH 1984; Kt 1958; CLit 1987; FBA 1957; FSA 1964; MA; *b* 7 July 1903; 2nd *s* of 1st Viscount Runciman of Doxford, PC. *Educ:* Eton (King's Schol.); Trinity College, Cambridge (Schol.). Fellow of Trinity College, Cambridge, 1927–38 (Hon. Fellow 1965); Lecturer at the University of Cambridge, 1932–38; Press Attaché, British Legation, Sofia, 1940; British Embassy, Cairo, 1941; Professor of Byzantine Art and History in Univ. of Istanbul, 1942–45; Rep. Brit. Council in Greece, 1945–47. Lectures: Waynflete, Magdalen Coll., Oxford, 1953–54; Gifford, St Andrews, 1960–62; Birkbeck, Trinity Coll., Cambridge, 1966; Wiles, Queen's Univ., Belfast, 1968; Robb, Auckland, 1970; Regents', Los Angeles, California, 1971; Weir, Cincinnati, 1973. Alexander White Prof., Chicago, 1963. Mem. Advisory Council, Victoria and Albert Museum, 1957–71; Pres., British Inst. of Archæology at Ankara, 1960–75; Chairman: Anglo-Hellenic League, 1951–67; Nat. Trust for Greece, 1977–84; Councillor Emeritus, Nat. Trust for Scotland, 1985–; Trustee: British Museum, 1960–67; Scottish Nat. Museum of Antiquities, 1972–77. Hon. Vice-Pres., RHistS, 1967–; Vice-Pres., London Library, 1974; Hon. Pres., Internat. Cttee for Byzantine Studies, 1976; Pres., Friends of Mt Athos, 1992; Chm., Friends of Scottish Ballet, 1984–88. For. Mem., American Philosophical Soc.; Corresp. Mem. Real Academia de Historia, Madrid. Hon. MRIA 1979. Hon. LittD Cambridge, 1955; Hon. LLD Glasgow, 1955; Hon. DLitt: Durham, 1956; St Andrews, 1969; Oxon, 1971; Birmingham, 1973; New York, 1984; Hon. LitD London, 1966; Hon. DPhil Salonika, 1951; Hon. DD Wabash, USA, 1962; Hon. DHL Chicago, 1963; Hon. DHum Ball State Univ., 1973; Hon. PhilD Sofia, 1983. Wolfson Literary Award, 1982; David Livingstone Medal, RSGS, 1992. Knight Commander, Order of the Phœnix (Greece), 1961; Order of the Madara Horseman, 1st cl. (Bulgaria), 1993. *Publications:* The Emperor Romanus Lecapenus, 1929; The First Bulgarian Empire, 1930; Byzantine Civilization, 1933; The Medieval Manichee, 1947; A History of the Crusades, Vol. I, 1951 (illustrated edn, as The First Crusade, 1980), Vol. II, 1952, Vol. III, 1954; The Eastern Schism, 1955; The Sicilian Vespers, 1958; The White Rajahs, 1960; The Fall of Constantinople, 1453, 1965; The Great Church in Captivity, 1968; The Last Byzantine Renaissance, 1970; The Orthodox Churches and the Secular State, 1972; Byzantine Style and Civilisation, 1975; The Byzantine Theocracy, 1977; Mistra, 1980; A Traveller's Alphabet, 1991; contributions to various historical journals. *Address:* Elshieshields, Lockerbie, Dumfriesshire DG11 1LY. *Club:* Athenæum.

RUNCORN, Prof. (Stanley) Keith, FRS 1965; Sydney Chapman Professor of Physical Science, University of Alaska, since 1988; Senior Research Fellow, Imperial College of Science, Technology and Medicine, since 1989; *b* 19 November 1922; *s* of W. H. Runcorn, Southport, Lancs; unmarried. *Educ:* King George V Sch., Southport; Gonville and Caius Coll., Cambridge. ScD 1963. Radar Research and Devel. Establishment (Min. of Supply), 1943–46; Asst Lecturer, 1946–48, and Lecturer, 1948–49, in Physics, Univ. of Manchester; Asst Dir of Research in Geophysics, Cambridge Univ., 1950–55; Research Geophysicist, Univ. of California at Los Angeles, 1952 and 1953; Fellow of Gonville and Caius Coll., Cambridge, 1948–55; Prof. of Physics, Univ. of Durham (King's Coll.), 1956–63, Univ. of Newcastle upon Tyne, 1963–88 (Head, Dept of Physics, 1956–88). Visiting Scientist, Dominion Observatory, Ottawa, 1955; Visiting Professor of Geophysics: Cal. Inst. of Tech., 1957; Univ. of Miami, 1966; Pa State Univ., 1967; Florida State Univ., 1968; UCLA, 1975; Kiel Univ., 1992; Max Planck Inst., Mainz, 1994; J. Ellerton Becker Senior Visiting Fellow, Australian Academy of Science, 1963; Res. Associate, Mus. of N Arizona, 1957–72; Rutherford Memorial Lectr (Kenya, Tanzania and Uganda), 1970; du Toit Meml Lectr (S Africa), 1971; Halley Lectr, Oxford Univ., 1972–73; Hitchcock Foundn Prof., Univ. of California, Berkeley, 1981; Vis. Scholar, Sydney Univ., 1991, 1993, 1995. Mem., NERC, 1965–69. Pres., Section A (Phys. and Maths), British Assoc., 1980–81. Member: Pontifical Acad. of Sciences, 1981; Academia Europæa, 1989; Hon. Member: Royal Netherlands Acad. of Arts and Sciences, 1970; Royal Norwegian Soc. of Sci. and Letters, 1985; Royal Soc., NSW, 1993; For. Mem., Indian Nat. Acad. of Science, 1980; Corresp. Mem., Bavarian Acad. of Sci., 1990. Napier Shaw Prize, Royal Met. Soc., 1959; Charles Chree Medal and Prize, Inst. of Physics, 1969; Vetlesen Prize, 1971; John Adams Fleming Medal, Amer. Geophysical Union, 1983; Gold Medal, Royal Astronomical Soc., 1984; Wegener Medal, European Union of Geoscis, 1987. Hon. DSc: Utrecht, 1969; Ghent, 1971; Paris, 1979; Bergen, 1980. *Publications:* scientific papers. *Recreations:* usual. *Address:* Blackett Laboratory, Imperial College, SW7 2BZ. *Clubs:* Athenæum; Union (Newcastle upon Tyne).

RUNDLE, Christopher John Spencer, OBE 1983; HM Diplomatic Service; Research Counsellor, Research and Analysis Department, Foreign and Commonwealth Office, since 1991; *b* 17 Aug. 1938; *s* of Percy William and Ruth Rundle (*née* Spencer); *m* 1970, Qamar Said; one *d*. *Educ:* Cranbrook Sch.; St John's Coll., Cambridge (MA). Served HM Forces, 1957–59. Central Asian Res. Centre, 1962–63; joined Diplomatic Service, 1963; Tehran, 1967–68; Oriental Sec., Kabul, 1968–70; FCO, 1970–75; seconded to Cabinet Office, 1975–77; First Secretary: FCO, 1977–81; Tehran, 1981–84; FCO, 1985. Member Council, British Inst. of Persian Studies, 1990–. *Recreations:* sports, foreign films and literature. *Address:* c/o Foreign and Commonwealth Office, SW1A 2AH.

RUNDLE, John Louis, AM 1981; JP; Agent-General for South Australia, 1980–85; *b* 11 Jan. 1930; *s* of late J. A. Rundle; *m* Elizabeth Phillipa, *d* of John P. Little, Melbourne; one *s* one *d*. *Educ:* Rostrevor Coll. Formerly Senior Partner, J. C. Rundle & Co., and Rundle, Parsons & Partners; Former Chairman: J. C. Rundle Holdings Pty Ltd; Seacliff Investments Pty Ltd; Thevenard Hotel Pty Ltd; former Director: Commonwealth Accommodation & Catering Service Ltd; Mallen & Co. Ltd; Commercial & Domestic Finance Ltd. Former Member: Nat. Employers Ind. Council (Dep. Chm., 1979–80); Confed. of Aust. Industry (Mem. Bd, 1978–80); State Develt Council, SA; Ind. Relations Adv. Council, SA; Adv. Curriculum Bd, SA; Council, Royal AA of SA. Pres., Junior Chambers, Adelaide, 1957, SA, 1958, Australia, 1959; Vice-Pres., JCI, 1960, 1963, Exec. Vice-Pres., 1964, World Pres., 1965, Pres. Senate, 1966; Councillor, Adelaide Chamber of Commerce, 1956–57, 1961–72, Vice-Pres., 1968–70, Dep. Pres., 1970–72; Vice-Pres., Chamber of Commerce & Industry, SA, 1973–75, Dep. Pres., 1975–77, Pres. 1977–79 (Chm., Commerce Div., 1973, 1974; Chm., Ind. Matters Cttee); Exec. Mem., Aust. Chamber of Commerce, 1980. Councillor: Red Cross Soc., SA Div., 1957–63 (Chm., Junior Red Cross, 1961–62); Burnside City Council, 1962–64; President: Assoc. of Indep. Schools of SA, 1972–75; Nat. Council of Indep. Schools, 1975–77; Chm., Bd of Governors, Rostrevor Coll., 1967–77. Mem. Central Council, Royal Over-Seas League, 1988–93. Freeman, City of London, 1981. JP SA, 1956. KHS 1989. *Address:* Waggoners, Tower Road, Hindhead, Surrey GU26 6ST. *T:* Hindhead (01428) 605217. *Clubs:* East India; Stock Exchange (Pres., 1979–80), Naval Military and Air Force (Adelaide).

RUNGE, Charles David; Chief Executive, Royal Agricultural Society of England, since 1992; *b* 24 May 1944; *s* of Sir Peter Runge and Hon. Fiona Margaret Stewart (*née* Macpherson), *d* of 1st Baron Strathcarron, PC, KC; *m* 1st, 1969, Harriet (marr. diss. 1979), *d* of late John Bradshaw; one *s* one *d*; 2nd, 1981, Jil, *d* of late John Liddell, Greenock; one *d*. *Educ:* Eton; Christ Church, Oxford (MA Nat. Scis); Manchester Business Sch. Tate & Lyle: Man. Dir, Transport, 1977–79; Chief Exec., Refineries, 1979–81; Man. Dir, Agribusiness, 1983–86; Dir of Corporate Affairs, 1986–87; Chief Exec., MMB, 1988–92. *Recreations:* music, walking, fishing. *Address:* Royal Agricultural Society of England, National Agricultural Centre, Stoneleigh Park, Warwickshire CV8 2LZ. *T:* Coventry (01203) 696969; Old Stables, Savages Close, Bishop's Tachbrook, Leamington Spa, Warwickshire CV33 9RL. *T:* Leamington Spa (01926) 312448. *Clubs:* Boodle's, Royal Anglo-Belgian, Farmers'.

RUPERT'S LAND, Metropolitan of; *see* Calgary, Archbishop of.

RUPERT'S LAND, Bishop of, since 1994; **Rt Rev. Patrick Vaughan Lee,** DD; *b* 20 June 1931; *s* of William Samuel Lee and Elizabeth Miriam Struthers; *m* 1958, Mary Thornton; four *d*. *Educ:* Univ. of Manitoba (BA 1953); St John's Coll., Winnipeg (LTh 1957; DD 1978). Missioner, Interlake/Eriksdale, Manitoba, 1956–59; Rector: St Bartholomew, Winnipeg, 1959–67; St Mary la Prairie, Portage la Prairie, Manitoba, 1967–75; District Dean, Portage and Pembina Deaneries, 1970–75; Dean of Cariboo and Rector, St Paul's Cathedral, Kamloops, BC, 1975–84; Dean of Training and Educn Sec., Dio. of W Buganda, 1984–90; Exec. Archdeacon of Rupert's Land, 1990–94. *Recreations:* cross country ski-ing, cycling, woodworking, reading, stamp collecting. *Address:* (office) 935 Nesbitt Bay, Winnipeg, Manitoba R3T 1W6, Canada. *T:* (204) 4536248; (home) 28

Ramblewood, Box 19, Group 150 RR#1 Vermette, Manitoba R0G 2W0, Canada. *T:* (204) 2571570.

RUSBRIDGE, Brian John, CBE 1984; Director, Association of Exhibition Organisers, since 1992; Secretary, Local Authorities' Conditions of Service Advisory Board (and all Local Authority National Negotiating Councils), 1973–87; *b* 10 Sept. 1922; *s* of late Arthur John and Leonora Rusbridge, Appleton, Berks; *m* 1951, Joyce, *d* of late Joseph Young Elliott, Darlington; two *s. Educ:* Willowfield Sch., Eastbourne; Univ. of Oxford Dept of Social and Admin. Studies (Dip. Social Admin.). Served War of 1939–45, Lieut RNVR. Personnel Manager, Imperial Chemical Industries (Teesside), 1949; British Railways Board: Dir of Industrial Relations, 1963; Divisional Manager, London, 1970. Ed., Municipal Year Book, 1987–94; Dir, Newman Books Ltd, 1991–94. CIPD; MCIT. *Recreations:* walking, golf. *Address:* 19 Beauchamp Road, East Molesey, Surrey KT8 0PA. *T:* 0181–979 4952.

RUSBRIDGER, Alan Charles; Editor, The Guardian, since 1995; *b* 29 Dec. 1953; *s* of G. H. Rusbridger and late B. E. Rusbridger (*née* Wickham); *m* 1982, Lindsay Mackie; two *d. Educ:* Cranleigh Sch.; Magdalene Coll., Cambridge (MA). Reporter, Cambridge Evening News, 1976–79; reporter, columnist and feature writer, The Guardian, 1979–86; TV Critic, The Observer, 1986–87; Washington Corresp., London Daily News, 1987; Editor, Weekend Guardian, 1988–89; The Guardian: Features Editor, 1989–93; Dep. Editor, 1993–95. *Recreations:* music, cricket, golf. *Address:* The Guardian, 119 Farringdon Road, EC1R 3ER. *T:* 0171–278 2332, *Fax:* 0171–239 9997. *Club:* Garrick.

RUSBY, Vice-Adm. Sir Cameron, KCB 1979; LVO 1965; *b* 20 Feb. 1926; *s* of late Captain Victor Evelyn Rusby, CBE, RN, and Mrs Irene Margaret Rusby; *m* 1948, Marion Elizabeth Bell; two *d. Educ:* RNC, Dartmouth. Midshipman 1943; specialised in communications, 1950; CO HMS Ulster, 1958–59; Exec. Officer, HM Yacht Britannia, 1962–65; Dep. Dir, Naval Signals, 1965–68; CO HMS Tartar, 1968–69; Dep. ACOS (Plans and Policy), staff of Allied C-in-C Southern Europe, 1969–72; Sen. Naval Off., WI, 1972–74; Rear-Adm. 1974; ACDS (Ops), 1974–77; Vice-Adm. 1977; Flag Officer Scotland and N Ireland, 1977–79; Dep. Supreme Allied Comdr, Atlantic, 1980–82. Chief Exec., 1983–91, Legislative Advr, 1991–94, Scottish SPCA. President: World Soc. for the Protection of Animals, 1992–94 (Vice Pres., 1994–96); Scottish Council, King George's Fund for Sailors, 1988–. *Recreations:* sailing, skiing, equitation. *Address:* c/o Bank of Scotland, 70 High Street, Peebles EH45 8AQ. *Club:* New (Edinburgh).

RUSH, Ann Patricia; Director, Migraine Trust, since 1992; *b* 17 March 1948; *d* of Peter Deshaw and Hanni Adele Gray; *m* 1969, Charles Anthony Rush; one *s* one *d. Educ:* Ursuline Convent. The Observer, 1966–68; RABI, 1969–76; CR Associates, 1974–88; Ed., Migraine News, 1989–92; Dep. Dir, Migraine Trust, 1990–92. *Recreations:* family, reading, sailing. *Address:* 36 Mayfield Road, Weybridge, Surrey KT13 8XB. *Club:* New Cavendish.

RUSH, Most Rev. Francis Roberts, DD; RC Archbishop of Brisbane, 1973–91; *b* 11 Sept. 1916; *s* of T. J. Rush. *Educ:* Christian Brothers' Coll., Townsville; Mt Carmel, Charters Towers; St Columba's Coll., Springwood; Coll. de Propaganda Fide, Rome. Assistant Priest, Townsville, Mundingburra and Ingham; Parish Priest, Abergowrie and Ingham; Bishop of Rockhampton, 1960–73. *Address:* Verona Villa, 169 Seventeen Mile Rocks Road, Oxley, Brisbane, Qld 4075, Australia.

RUSHBROOKE, Prof. G(eorge) Stanley, MA, PhD; FRS 1982; FRSE; Professor of Theoretical Physics, University of Newcastle upon Tyne, 1951–80; Head of Department of Theoretical Physics, 1965–80; Deputy Head, School of Physics, 1972–80; *b* 19 January 1915; *s* of George Henry Rushbrooke and Frances Isobel Rushbrooke (*née* Wright), Willenhall, Staffs; *m* 1949, Thelma Barbara Cox (*d* 1977). *Educ:* Wolverhampton Grammar School; St John's College, Cambridge. Schol. St John's Coll., Camb., 1933–37; Research Asst, Bristol Univ., 1938–39; Senior DSIR award and Carnegie Teaching Fellowship, 1939–44, UC Dundee, Univ. of St Andrews; Lectr in Mathematical Chemistry, The Univ., Leeds, 1944–48; Sen. Lectr in Theoretical Physics, Oxford, Univ. and Lecturer in Mathematics, University Coll., Oxford, 1948–51. Leverhulme Emeritus Fellow, 1981. Visiting Prof., Dept of Chemistry, Univ. of Oregon, USA, 1962–63; Vis. Prof. of Physics and Chemistry, Rice Univ., Houston, 1967. *Publications:* Introduction to Statistical Mechanics, 1949; research papers in scientific journals. *Recreations:* hillwalking, birdwatching. *Address:* 46 Belle Vue Avenue, Newcastle upon Tyne NE3 1AH.

RUSHDIE, (Ahmed) Salman, FRSL; writer; *b* 19 June 1947; *s* of Anis Ahmed Rushdie and Negin Rushdie (*née* Butt); *m* 1976, Clarissa Luard (marr. diss. 1987); one *s*; *m* 1988, Marianne Wiggins (marr. diss. 1993). *Educ:* Cathedral Sch., Bombay; Rugby Sch.; King's Coll., Cambridge (MA (Hons) History). Hon. Prof., MIT, 1993. Arts Council Literature Bursary Award; Kurt Tucholsky Prize, Sweden, 1992; Prix Colette, Switzerland, 1993; Austrian State Prize for European Literature, 1994. *Films for TV:* The Painter and the Pest, 1985; The Riddle of Midnight, 1988. *Publications:* Grimus, 1975; Midnight's Children, 1981 (Booker Prize for Fiction, 1981; James Tait Black Meml Book Prize; E-SU Literary Award; Booker of Bookers Prize, 1993); Shame, 1983 (Prix du Meilleur Livre Etranger, 1984); The Jaguar Smile: a Nicaraguan journey, 1987; The Satanic Verses, 1988 (Whitbread Novel Award); Haroun and the Sea of Stories, 1990 (Writers' Guild Award); Imaginary Homelands (essays), 1991; The Wizard of Oz, 1992; East, West, 1994; The Moor's Last Sigh, 1995; contribs to many journals. *Address:* c/o Aitken, Stone & Wylie, 29 Fernshaw Road, SW10 0TG.

RUSHFORD, Antony Redfern, CMG 1963; consultant on constitutional, international and commonwealth law; *b* 9 Feb.; *m* 1975, June Jeffrey, *widow* of Roy Eustace Wells; one step *s* one step *d. Educ:* Taunton Sch.; Trinity Coll., Cambridge (BA 1948; LLM (LLB 1948); MA 1951). FRSA. RAFVR, 1942 (active service, 1943–47, reserve, 1947–59); Sqdn Ldr, 1946. Solicitor, 1944–57 (distinction in Law Soc. final exams, 1942); Called to the Bar, Inner Temple, 1983. Asst Solicitor, E. W. Marshall Harvey & Dalton, 1948. Home Civil Service, Colonial Office, 1949–68; joined HM Diplomatic Service, 1968; CO, later FCO, retd as Dep. Legal Advr (Asst Under-Sec. of State), 1982. Crown Counsel, Uganda, 1954; Principal Legal Adviser, British Indian Ocean Territory, 1983; Attorney-Gen., Anguilla, and St Helena, 1983; Legal Adviser for Commonwealth Sec.-Gen. to Governor-Gen. of Grenada, Mem. Interim Govt, Attorney-Gen., and JP, Grenada, 1983; consultancies: FCO (special duties), 1982; Commonwealth Sec.-Gen., St Kitts and Nevis independence, 1982–83, St Lucia treaties, 1983–85; E Caribbean courts, 1983; maritime legislation for Jamaica, Internat. Maritime Orgn, 1983 and 1985; constitutional advr, Govt of St Kitts and Nevis, and Govt of St Lucia, 1982–. Has drafted many constitutions for UK dependencies and Commonwealth countries attaining independence; presented paper on constitutional develt to meeting of Law Officers from Smaller Commonwealth Jurisdictions, IoM, 1983. UK deleg. or advr at many constitutional confs and discussions; CO Rep., Inst. of Advanced Legal Studies; participant, Symposium on Federalism, Chicago, 1962; Advr, Commonwealth Law Ministers Conf., 1973. Lectr, Overseas Legal Officers Course, 1964; Special Examnr, London Univ., 1963, 1987; a dir of studies, RIPA (Overseas Services Unit), and also associate consultant on statute law, 1982–86. Mem. Editl Bd, Inst. of Internat. Law and Econ. Develt, Washington, 1977–82. Foundn Mem. Exec. Council, Royal Commonwealth Soc. for the Blind, 1969–81, 1983– (Hon. Legal Adviser, 1984–); Hon. Sec., Services Race Club, Hong Kong, 1946–47. Member: Glyndebourne Fest. Soc., 1950–; Inst. of Advanced Motoring, 1959–73; Commonwealth Lawyers Assoc., 1982–90; Commonwealth Assoc. of Legislative Counsel, 1984–; Commonwealth Magistrates and Judges Assoc., 1986–90; Anglo-Arab Assoc., 1990–; Saudi-British Soc., 1990–. Governor, Taunton Sch., 1948–. CStJ 1989 (Hon. Legal Counsellor, 1978–; Mem., Chapter-Gen., 1983–). *Address:* 63 Pont Street, Knightsbridge, SW1X 0BD. *T:* 0171–589 6448; (chambers) 12 King's Bench Walk, Temple, EC4Y 7EL. *T:* 0171–353 5692/6. *Club:* Commonwealth Trust.

RUSHTON, Ian Lawton, FIA, FCII, FSS; Chairman, Hackney Empire Ltd, since 1994; Vice Chairman, Royal Insurance Holdings plc, 1991–93 (Group Chief Executive, 1989–91); *b* 8 Sept. 1931; *s* of Arthur John and Mabel Lilian Rushton; *m* 1st, 1956, Julia Frankland (decd); one *d.*; 2nd, 1986, Anita Spencer; one step *s* one step *d. Educ:* Rock Ferry High Sch., Birkenhead; King's Coll., London (BSc Mathematics). FIA 1959; FCII 1961. Served RAF, 1953–56 (Flt-Lieut). Royal Insurance, 1956–93: Dep. Gen. Man. (UK), 1972; Exec. Vice Pres., Royal US, 1980; Gen. Man. Royal UK, 1983; Exec. Dir and Gp Gen. Man., Royal Insurance plc, 1986. Chairman: Fire Protection Assoc., 1983–87; Assoc. of British Insurers, 1991–93; Vice Pres., Inst. of Actuaries, 1986–89. FRSA. *Recreations:* golf, gardening, theatre, music. *Address:* Flat 136, 3 Whitehall Court, SW1A 2EL.

RUSHTON, William George; actor, author, cartoonist and broadcaster; *b* 18 Aug. 1937; *s* of John and Veronica Rushton; *m* 1968, Arlene Dorgan; three *s. Educ:* Shrewsbury Sch. Founder/Editor, Private Eye, 1961. Stage début in The Bed-sitting Room, by Spike Milligan, Marlowe Theatre, Canterbury, 1961; Gulliver's Travels, Mermaid, 1971, 1979; Pass the Butler, by Eric Idle, Globe, 1982; Tales from a Long Room, Hammersmith, 1988; *films:* Nothing but the Best, 1963; Those Magnificent Men in their Flying Machines, 1964, and several others; *television* includes: That Was the Week that Was, 1962; Up Sunday, 1975–78; Celebrity Squares, 1979–80; numerous Jackanory progs; *radio* includes: I'm Sorry I Haven't a Clue, 1976–; much other broadcasting in UK and Australia. *Publications:* written and illustrated: William Rushton's Dirty Book, 1964; How to Play Football: the art of dirty play, 1968; The Day of the Grocer, 1971; The Geranium of Flüt, 1975; Superpig, 1976; Pigsticking: a joy for life, 1977; The Reluctant Euro, 1980; The Filth Amendment, 1981; W. G. Grace's Last Case, 1984; Willie Rushton's Great Moments of History, 1985; The Alternative Gardener: a compost of quips for the green-fingered, 1986; Marylebone Versus the Rest of the World, 1987; (ed) Spy Thatcher, 1987; Every Cat in the Book, 1993; illustrations for many others. *Recreations:* losing weight, gaining weight, parking. *Address:* Wallgrave Road, SW5 0RL. *Clubs:* Tatty Bogle's, Lord's Taverners, Surrey CCC.

RUSHWORTH, Dr (Frank) Derek; Headmaster, Holland Park School, London, 1971–85; *b* 15 Sept. 1920; *s* of late Frank and Elizabeth Rushworth, Huddersfield; *m* 1941, Hamidah Begum, *d* of late Justice S. Akhlaque Hussain, Lahore, and Edith (*née* Bayliss), Oxford; three *d. Educ:* Huddersfield Coll.; St Edmund Hall, Oxford (Schol.; BA 1942, MA 1946); Doctorate of Univ. of Paris (Lettres), 1947. Served 6th Rajputana Rifles, Indian Army, 1942–45 (Major); began teaching, 1947; Head of Modern Languages: Tottenham Grammar Sch., 1953; Holland Park Sch., 1958; Head of Shoreditch Sch., London, 1965. Chairman: Associated Examining Board, French Committee, 1964–74; Schools Council, 16+ Examination Feasibility Study (French), 1971–75; Pres., London Head Teachers' Assoc., 1985. Governor, Holland Park Sch., 1990–. *Publications:* Our French Neighbours, 1963, 2nd edn 1966; French text-books and language-laboratory books; articles in French Studies, Modern Languages, also educnl jls. *Recreation:* photography. *Address:* 25c Lambolle Road, NW3 4HS. *T:* 0171–794 3691.

RUSSELL; *see* Hamilton-Russell, family name of Viscount Boyne.

RUSSELL, family name of **Duke of Bedford, Earl Russell, Baron Ampthill, Baron de Clifford** and **Baron Russell of Liverpool.**

RUSSELL, 5th Earl *cr* 1861; **Conrad Sebastian Robert Russell,** FBA 1991; Viscount Amberley 1861; Professor of British History, King's College London, since 1990; *b* 15 April 1937; *s* of 3rd Earl Russell, OM, FRS and Patricia Helen, *d* of H. E. Spence; *S* half brother, 1987; *m* 1962, Elizabeth Franklyn Sanders; two *s. Educ:* Merton College, Oxford (BA 1958, MA 1962; Sir Henry Savile Fellow, 1994); MA Yale 1979. FRHistS 1971. Lectr in History, Bedford College, London, 1960–74, Reader, 1974–79; Prof. of History, Yale Univ., 1979–84; Astor Prof. of British History, UCL, 1984–90. Ford Lectr, Univ. of Oxford, 1987–88; Trevelyan Lectr, Univ. of Cambridge, 1995. Takes Liberal Democrat whip, H of L. *Publications:* The Crisis of Parliaments: English History 1509–1660, 1971; (ed) The Origins of the English Civil War, 1973; Parliaments and English Politics 1621–1629, 1979; The Causes of the English Civil War, 1990; Unrevolutionary England 1603–1642, 1990; The Fall of the British Monarchies 1637–1642, 1991; Academic Freedom, 1993; articles in jls. *Recreations:* swimming, uxoriousness, cricket. *Heir: s* Viscount Amberley, *qv. Address:* Department of History, King's College, Strand, WC2R 2LS.

RUSSELL OF LIVERPOOL, 3rd Baron *cr* 1919; **Simon Gordon Jared Russell;** *b* 30 Aug. 1952; *s* of Captain Hon. Langley Gordon Haslingden Russell, MC (*d* 1975) (*o s* of 2nd Baron), and of Kiloran Margaret, *d* of late Hon. Sir Arthur Jared Palmer Howard, KBE, CVO; *S* grandfather, 1981; *m* 1984, Dr Gilda Albano, *y d* of late Signor F. Albano and of Signora Maria Caputo-Albano; two *s* one *d. Educ:* Charterhouse; Trinity Coll., Cambridge; INSEAD, Fontainebleau, France. *Heir: s* Hon. Edward Charles Stanley Russell, *b* 2 Sept. 1985. *Address:* House of Lords, SW1A 0PW.

RUSSELL, Alan Keith; Chairman, Dresden Trust, since 1993; consultant and writer; *b* 22 Oct. 1932; *s* of late Keith Russell and Gertrude Ann Russell; *m* 1959, Philippa Margaret Stoneham; two *s* one *d. Educ:* Ardingly Coll.; Oxford Univ. BA; MA Econ and Pol Sci; DPhil. Colonial Office, ODM, FCO, 1959–69, 1972–75; CS Coll., 1969–71; Dir, Inter University Council for Higher Educn Overseas, 1980–81; sen. official, Commn of EC, 1976–79, 1981–86, 1988–89; Fellow, Lincoln Coll., Oxford and Sen. Res. Associate, Queen Elizabeth House, 1986–88; management of civic improvement, 1990–92. *Publications:* ed, The Economic and Social History of Mauritius, 1962; Liberal Landslide: the General Election of 1906, 1973; contrib. Edwardian Radicalism, 1974; The Unclosed Eye (poems), 1987; articles on commodity trade, development, and Europe. *Recreations:* German and African history, services for the mentally handicapped, conservation and town planning. *Address:* 3 Western Road, Littlehampton, W Sussex BN17 5JP.

RUSSELL, (Alastair) Muir; Secretary and Head of Department, Scottish Office Agriculture, Environment and Fisheries Department, since 1995; *b* 9 Jan. 1949; *s* of Thomas and Anne Russell; *m* 1983, Eileen Alison Mackay, *qv. Educ:* High Sch. of Glasgow; Univ. of Glasgow (BSc Nat. Phil.). Joined Scottish Office, 1970; seconded as Sec. to Scottish Development Agency, 1975–76; Asst Sec., 1981; Principal Private Sec. to Sec. of State for Scotland, 1981–83; Under Sec., 1990; seconded to Cabinet Office, 1990–92; Under Sec. (Housing), Scottish Office Envmt Dept, 1992–95; Dep. Sec., 1995; Sec., Scottish Office Agric. and Fisheries Dept, Feb.–Oct. 1995. Non-exec. Dir, Stagecoach Hldgs, 1992–95. *Recreations:*

music, food, wine. *Address:* Scottish Office Agriculture, Environment and Fisheries Department, Pentland House, 47 Robb's Loan, Edinburgh EH14 1TW. *T:* 0131–244 6021. *Club:* Commonwealth Trust.

RUSSELL, (Albert) Muir (Galloway), CBE 1989; QC (Scot.) 1965; Sheriff of Grampian, Highland and Islands (formerly Aberdeen, Kincardine and Banff) at Aberdeen and Stonehaven, 1971–91; *b* 26 Oct. 1925; *s* of Hon. Lord Russell; *m* 1954, Margaret Winifred, *o d* of T. McW Millar, FRCS(E), Edinburgh; two *s* two *d*. *Educ:* Edinburgh Academy; Wellington College; Brasenose College, Oxford. BA (Hons) Oxon, 1949; LLB (Edin.), 1951. Lieut, Scots Guards, 1944–47. Member of Faculty of Advocates, 1951–. *Recreation:* golf. *Address:* Tulloch House, Aultbea, Ross-shire IV22 2JA. *T:* Aultbea (01445) 731325. *Club:* Royal Northern (Aberdeen).

RUSSELL, Alexander William; Commissioner, since 1985, and Deputy Chairman, since 1993, HM Customs and Excise; *b* 16 Oct. 1938; *s* of late William and Elizabeth W. B. Russell (*née* Russell); *m* 1962, Elspeth Rae (*née* Robertson). *Educ:* Royal High Sch., Edinburgh; Edinburgh Univ. (MA Hons); Manitoba Univ. (MA). Assistant Principal, Scottish Development Dept, 1961–64; Private Sec. to Parliamentary Under Secretary of State, Scottish Office, 1964–65; Principal, Regional Development Div. and Scottish Development Dept, 1965–72; Principal Private Sec. to Secretary of State for Scotland, 1972–73; Asst Secretary: Scottish Development Dept, 1973–76; Civil Service Dept, 1976–79; Under-Secretary: Management and Personnel Office (formerly CSD), 1979–82; Hd of Treasury MPO Financial Management Unit, 1982–85; Dir Orgn, HM Customs and Excise, 1985–90, Dir Customs, 1990–93, HM Customs and Excise. *Address:* c/o HM Customs and Excise, New Kings Beam House, 22 Upper Ground, SE1 9PJ.

RUSSELL, Andrew Victor Manson; Executive Director, Association for Spina Bifida and Hydrocephalus, since 1991; *b* 7 Dec. 1949; *s* of Manson McCausland Russell and Margaret Ivy Russell; *m* 1974, Susan Elizabeth Aykroyd; one *s* one *d*. *Educ:* Dartington Hall; Fitzwilliam Coll., Cambridge Univ. (MA). NSMHC, 1974–85; General Manager, Eastern Div., Royal MENCAP Soc., 1985–91. *Recreations:* sailing, music. *Address:* c/o ASBAH House, 42 Park Road, Peterborough PE1 2UQ. *T:* Peterborough (01733) 555988.

RUSSELL, Anna; International Concert Comedienne; *b* 27 Dec. 1911; *d* of Col C. Russell-Brown, CB, DSO, RE, and Beatrice M. Tandy; single. *Educ:* St Felix School, Southwold; Royal College of Music, London. Folk singer, BBC, 1935–40; Canadian Broadcasting Corp. programmes, 1942–46; Radio interviewer, CBC, 1945–46; Debut, Town Hall, New York, as concert comedienne, 1948; Broadway show, Anna Russell and her Little Show, 1953; Towns of USA, Canada, Great Britain, Australia, New Zealand, the Orient and South Africa, 1948–60. Television, Radio Summer Theatre, USA; recordings, Columbia Masterworks. Resident in Australia, 1968–75. Mayfair Theatre, London, 1976. *Publications:* The Power of Being a Positive Stinker (NY); The Anna Russell Song Book; I'm Not Making This Up, You Know (autobiog.). *Recreation:* gardening. *Address:* 70 Anna Russell Way, Unionville, Ontario L3R 3X3, Canada. *Club:* Zouta International (USA, Toronto Branch, Internat. Mem.).

RUSSELL, Rt. Rev. Anthony John; *see* Dorchester, Area Bishop of.

RUSSELL, Rev. Arthur Colin, CMG 1957; ED; MA; *b* 1906; *e s* of late Arthur W. Russell, OBE, WS; *m* 1939, Elma (*d* 1967), *d* of late Douglas Strachan, Hon. RSA; three *d*. *Educ:* Harrow; Brasenose College, Oxford. Barrister-at-law, Inner Temple. Cadet, Gold Coast (now Ghana), 1929; Asst Dist Comr, 1930; Dist Comr, 1940; Judicial Adviser, 1947; Senior, 1951; Regional Officer, 1952; Permanent Sec., Min. of Education and Social Welfare, 1953; Governor's Secretary, 1954; Chief Regional Officer, Ashanti, 1955–57, retd. Trained for the Ministry, 1957–59; Ordained (Church of Scotland), 1959; Parish Minister, Aberlemno, 1959–76; retd. District Councillor, Angus District, 1977–84. *Publication:* Stained Glass Windows of Douglas Strachan, 1972, 1994. *Address:* Balgavies Lodge, by Forfar, Angus DD8 2TH. *T:* Letham (Angus) (01307) 818571.

RUSSELL, Barbara Winifred, MA; Headmistress, Berkhamsted School for Girls, 1950–71; *b* 5 Jan. 1910; *er d* of Lionel Wilfred and Elizabeth Martin Russell. *Educ:* St Oran's School, Edinburgh; Edinburgh University; Oxford University, Dept of Education. History Mistress, Brighton and Hove High School, 1932–38; Senior History Mistress, Roedean School, 1938–49. *Recreations:* reading, gardening. *Address:* 1 Beech Road, Thame, Oxon OX9 2AL. *T:* Thame (01844) 212738. *Club:* East India, Devonshire, Sports and Public Schools.

RUSSELL, Cecil Anthony Francis; Director of Intelligence, Greater London Council, 1970–76; *b* 7 June 1921; *s* of late Comdr S. F. Russell, OBE, RN retd and late Mrs M. E. Russell (*née* Sneyd-Kynnersley); *m* 1950, Editha May (*née* Birch); no *c*. *Educ:* Winchester Coll.; University Coll., Oxford (1940–41, 1945–47). Civil Service, 1949–70: Road Research Lab., 1949–50; Air Min., 1950–62; Dep. Statistical Adviser, Home Office, 1962–67; Head of Census Div., General Register Office, 1967–70. FSS. *Recreation:* ocean sailing. *Address:* Pagan Hill, Whiteleaf, Princes Risborough, Bucks HP27 0LQ. *T:* Princes Risborough (01844) 343655. *Clubs:* Cruising Association; Ocean Cruising, Royal Lymington Yacht.

RUSSELL, Sir Charles Ian, 3rd Bt, *cr* 1916; Partner, Charles Russell & Co., 1947–83; retired; Captain, RHA (despatches); *b* 13 March 1918; *s* of Captain Sir Alec Charles Russell, 2nd Bt, and Monica (who *m* 2nd, 1942, Brig. John Victor Faviell, CBE, MC; she *d* 1978), *d* of Hon. Sir Charles Russell, 1st Bt; *S* father, 1938; *m* 1947, Rosemary, *er d* of late Sir John Prestige; one *s* one *d*. *Educ:* Beaumont College; University College, Oxford. Admitted Solicitor, 1947. *Recreation:* golf. *Heir:* *s* Charles Dominic Russell [*b* 28 May 1956; *m* 1986, Sarah Jane Murray Chandor, *o d* of Anthony Chandor, Haslemere, Surrey; one *s*]. *Address:* Hidden House, Sandwich, Kent CT13 9HX; 39 Egerton Gardens, SW3 2DD. *Clubs:* Garrick, Army and Navy; Royal St George's.

RUSSELL, Christopher; *see* Russell, R. C. G.

RUSSELL, Dan Chapman; Sheriff of South Strathclyde, Dumfries and Galloway at Hamilton, since 1992; *b* 25 Dec. 1939; *s* of William Morris Russell and Isabella Ritchie Stein Scott; *m* 1969, Janet McNeil; three *d*. *Educ:* Airdrie Acad.; Glasgow Univ. (MA 1960; LLB 1963). Qualified as Solicitor, 1963; in private practice, 1963–92; Partner, Bell, Russell & Co., Solicitors, Airdrie, 1965–92; Temp. Sheriff, 1976–78 and 1985–92. Reporter, Airdrie Children's Panel, 1972–75. Mem. Council, Law Soc. of Scotland, 1975–84; Dean, Airdrie Soc. of Solicitors, 1986–88. *Recreations:* golf, bridge, walking. *Address:* Sheriff Court, Almada Street, Hamilton ML3 6AA. *T:* Hamilton (01698) 282957.

RUSSELL, Rt. Rev. David Hamilton; *see* Grahamstown, Bishop of.

RUSSELL, Sir David Sturrock W.; *see* West-Russell.

RUSSELL, Rev. David Syme, CBE 1982; MA, DD, DLitt; President, Baptist Union of Great Britain and Ireland, 1983–84 (General Secretary, 1967–82); *b* 21 Nov. 1916; second *s* of Peter Russell and Janet Marshall Syme; *m* 1943, Marion Hamilton Campbell; one *s* one *d*. *Educ:* Scottish Baptist Coll., Glasgow; Trinity Coll., Glasgow; Glasgow Univ. (MA, BD, DLitt, Hon. DD); Regent's Park Coll., Oxford Univ. (MA, MLitt; Hon. Fellow, 1995). Minister of Baptist Churches: Berwick, 1939–41; Oxford, 1943–45; Acton, 1945–53. Principal of Rawdon Coll., Leeds, and lectr in Old Testament languages and literature, 1953–64; Joint Principal of the Northern Baptist College, Manchester, 1964–67. Moderator, Free Church Federal Council, 1974–75. Pres., European Baptist Fedn, 1979–81. Mem., Central Cttee, WCC, 1968–83; Vice-Pres., BCC, 1981–84. Hon. DD McMaster, 1991. *Publications:* Between the Testaments, 1960; Two Refugees (Ezekiel and Second Isaiah), 1962; The Method and Message of Jewish Apocalyptic, 1964; The Jews from Alexander to Herod, 1976; Apocalyptic: Ancient and Modern, 1978; Daniel (The Daily Study Bible), 1981; In Journeyings Often, 1982; From Early Judaism to Early Church, 1986; The Old Testament Pseudepigrapha: patriarchs and prophets in early Judaism, 1987; Daniel: an active volcano, 1989; Poles Apart: the Gospel in creative tension, 1990; Divine Disclosure: an introduction to Jewish apocalyptic, 1992; Prophecy and the Apocalyptic Dream: protest and promise, 1994; contrib. to Encyc. Britannica, 1963. *Recreation:* woodwork. *Address:* 7 Cedar Court, Glenavon Park, Stoke Bishop, Bristol BS9 1RL. *T:* Bristol (0117) 968 1131.

RUSSELL, Prof. Donald Andrew Frank Moore, FBA 1971; Fellow, St John's College, Oxford, 1948–88, now Emeritus; Professor of Classical Literature, Oxford, 1985–88; *b* 13 Oct. 1920; *s* of Samuel Charles Russell (schoolmaster) and Laura Moore; *m* 1967, Joycelyne Gledhill Dickinson (*d* 1993). *Educ:* King's College Sch., Wimbledon; Balliol Coll., Oxford (MA 1946); DLitt Oxon 1985. Served War: Army (R Signals and Intelligence Corps), 1941–45. Craven Scholar, 1946; Lectr, Christ Church, Oxford, 1947; St John's College, Oxford: Tutor, 1948–84; Dean, 1957–64; Tutor for Admissions, 1968–72; Reader in Class. Lit., Oxford Univ., 1978–85. Paddison Vis. Prof., Univ. of N Carolina at Chapel Hill, 1985; Vis. Prof. of Classics, Stanford Univ., 1989, 1991. Co-editor, Classical Quarterly, 1965–70. *Publications:* Commentary on Longinus, On the Sublime, 1964; Ancient Literary Criticism (with M. Winterbottom), 1972; Plutarch, 1972; (with N. G. Wilson) Menander Rhetor, 1981; Criticism in Antiquity, 1981; Greek Declamation, 1984; (ed) Antonine Literature, 1990; Commentary on Dio Chrysostom, Orations, 7, 12, 36, 1992; (trans) Plutarch: selected essays and dialogues, 1993; articles and reviews in classical periodicals. *Address:* 35 Belsyre Court, Oxford OX2 6HU. *T:* Oxford (01865) 56135.

RUSSELL, Rev. Prof. Edward Augustine; Principal, Union Theological College, Belfast, 1981–87; Professor of New Testament (originally at Presbyterian College, Belfast), 1961–87, Emeritus 1987; *b* 29 Nov. 1916; *s* of William Russell and Annie (*née* Sudway); *m* 1st, 1948, Emily Frances Stevenson (*d* 1978); two *s* one *d*; 2nd, 1979, Joan Evelyn Rufli (*née* Craig). *Educ:* Royal Belfast Academical Instn; London Univ. (BA, BD, MTh); Magee UC, 1942–43; Presbyterian Coll., Belfast, 1943–44, 1945–46; New Coll., Edinburgh, 1944–45. Research at Göttingen Univ. Ordained to Ministry of Presbyterian Church in Ireland, 1948; Minister: Donacloney, 1948–53; Mountpottinger Churches, 1953–61. External Examiner, Glasgow Univ., 1968, 1972–73; extra-mural Lectr, QUB, 1972–. Vis. Prof., Southwest Univ., Memphis, 1980. Member of various clerical associations. Hon. DD Presbyterian Theol Faculty of Ireland, 1966. *Publications:* contribs to: Studia Evangelica VI, Berlin 1973; Ministry and the Church, 1977; Studia Biblica vol. II, Sheffield 1980; Studia Evangelica VII, Berlin 1982; Proc. Irish Biblical Assoc., *et al.* *Recreations:* music, golf, painting, languages, bird-watching. *Address:* 30 Glenshesk Road, Ballycastle, N Ireland BT54 6PH.

RUSSELL, Edwin John Cumming, FRBS 1978; sculptor; *b* 4 May 1939; *s* of Edwin Russell and Mary Elizabeth Russell; *m* 1964, Lorne McKean; two *d*. *Educ:* Brighton Coll. of Art and Crafts; Royal Academy Schs (CertRAS). *Works:* Crucifix, limewood, pulpit, St Paul's Cathedral, 1964; St Catherine, lead, Little Cloister, Westminster Abbey, 1966; St Michael, oak, Chapel of St Michael and St George, St Paul's Cath., 1970; Bishop Bubwith, W Front Wells Cath., 1980; sundials: Jubilee Dolphin Dial, bronze, Nat. Maritime Mus., Greenwich, 1978; 3m, Sultan Qaboos Univ., Oman, 1986; Botanical Armillery, Kew Gardens, 1987; 5m, bronze, Parliament Square, Dubai, 1988; Forecourt sculpture, Rank Xerox Internat. HQ, 1989; shopping centre sculpture: Mad Hatter's Tea Party play sculpture, granite, Warrington, 1984; Lion and Lamb, teak, Farnham, 1986; public works: Suffragette Meml, 1968; 1st Gov. of Bahamas, Sheraton Hotel, Nassau, 1968; Lewis Carroll commemorative sculpture, Alice and the White Rabbit, Guildford, 1984; Panda, marble, WWF Internat. HQ, 1988; private collections: Goodwood House; Sir Robert McAlpine & Sons Ltd; Rosehaugh Stanhope Developments; Arup Associates; Bovis; YRM International; Trafalgar House plc; Cementation International; John Laing Construction; John Mowlem & Co.; ARC; Worshipful Co. of Stationers; City of London Grammar Shool. Royal Academy Gold Medal for Sculpture, 1960. *Recreation:* philosophy. *Address:* Lethendry, Polecat Valley, Hindhead, Surrey GU26 6BE. *T:* Hindhead (01428) 605655.

RUSSELL, Eileen Alison, (Mrs A. Muir Russell); *see* Mackay, E. A.

RUSSELL, Francis Mark; Chairman, B. Elliott plc, 1975–87 (Chief Executive, 1972–83); *b* 26 July 1927; *s* of W. Sidney and Beatrice M. Russell; *m* 1950, Joan Patricia Ryan; two *s* three *d*. *Educ:* Ratcliffe Coll., Leicester; Clare Coll., Cambridge (MA). CIMgt. Palestine Police, 1946–48; Director: S. Russell & Sons Ltd, 1959; B. Elliott & Co. Ltd, 1967; Chief Executive, 1969, Dir, 1969–88, Chm., 1975–87, Goldfields Industrial Corporation; Dep. Chm., B. Elliott & Co. Ltd, 1971; Dir, Johnson & Firth Brown plc, 1982–92. *Recreations:* golf, gardening. *Address:* Armour Barn, Stockwell Lane, Meadle, Aylesbury, Bucks HP17 9UG. *T:* Princes Risborough (01844) 275861. *Clubs:* Boodle's; Denham Golf.

RUSSELL, Sir George, Kt 1992; CBE 1985; Chairman: 3i Group plc, since 1993 (Director, since 1992); Independent Television Commission, since 1991; Northern Development Company, since 1994; Non-executive Chairman, Marley Plc, since 1993 (Chairman, 1989–93; Chief Executive, 1986–92); *b* 25 Oct. 1935; *s* of William H. Russell and Frances A. Russell; *m* 1959, Dorothy Brown; three *d*. *Educ:* Gateshead Grammar Sch.; Durham Univ. (BA Hons). ICI, 1958–67 (graduate trainee, Commercial Res. Officer, Sales Rep., and Product Sales Man.); Vice President and General Manager: Welland Chemical Co. of Canada Ltd, 1968; St Clair Chemical Co. Ltd, 1968; Man. Dir, Alcan UK Ltd, 1976; Asst Man. Dir, 1977–81, Man. Dir, 1981–82, Alcan Aluminium (UK) Ltd; Man. Dir and Chief Exec., British Alcan Aluminium, 1982–86; Dep. Chm., Channel Four TV, 1987–88; Chm., ITN, 1988; Chairman: Luxfer Holdings Ltd, 1976; Alcan UK Ltd, 1978; Director: Alcan Aluminiumwerke GmbH, Frankfurt, 1977–82; Northern Rock Bldg Soc., 1985–; Alcan Aluminium Ltd, 1987–; Taylor Woodrow, 1992–. Visiting Professor, Univ. of Newcastle upon Tyne, 1978. Chm., IBA, 1989–90 (Mem., 1979–86); Member: Board, Northern Sinfonia Orchestra, 1977–80; Northern Industrial Development Board, 1977–80; Washington Development Corporation, 1978–80; Board, Civil Service Pay Research Unit, 1980–81; Megaw Inquiry into Civil Service Pay, 1981–; Widdicombe Cttee of Inquiry into Conduct of Local Authority Business, 1985. Trustee, Beamish Develt Trust, 1985–. Hon. DEng Newcastle upon Tyne, 1985; Hon. DBA Northumbria, 1992. *Recreations:* tennis, badminton, bird watching. *Address:* 3i Group plc, 91 Waterloo Road, SE1 8XP.

RUSSELL, Sir George Michael, 7th Bt, *cr* 1812; *b* 30 Sept. 1908; *s* of Sir Arthur Edward Ian Montagu Russell, 6th Bt, MBE and late Aileen Kerr, *y d* of Admiral Mark Robert Pechell; *S* father, 1964; *m* 1936, Joy Frances Bedford, *d* of late W. Mitchell, Irwin, Western Australia; two *d*. *Educ:* Radley, Berkshire, England. *Heir: half-b* Arthur Mervyn Russell, *b* 7 Feb. 1923.

See also Baron Broughshane.

RUSSELL, Gerald Francis Morris, MD, FRCP, FRCPE, FRCPsych, DPM; Professor of Psychiatry, Institute of Psychiatry, University of London, and Physician, Bethlem Royal and Maudsley Hospital, 1979–93, now Professor Emeritus; Director, Eating Disorders Unit, Hayes Grove Priory Hospital, since 1993; *b* Grammont, Belgium, 12 Jan. 1928; 2nd *s* of late Maj. Daniel George Russell, MC, and late Berthe Marie Russell (*née* De Boe); *m* 1950, Margaret Taylor, MB, ChB; three *s*. *Educ:* Collège St Jean Berchmans, Brussels; George Watson's Coll., Edinburgh (Dux); Univ. of Edinburgh (Mouat Schol. in Practice of Physic). MD (with commendation), 1957. RAMC Regimental Med. Off., Queen's Bays, 1951–53; Neurological Registrar, Northern Gen. Hosp., Edin., 1954–56; MRC Clinical Res. Fellow, 1956–58; Inst. of Psychiatry, Maudsley Hospital: 1st Asst, 1959–60; Senior Lectr, 1961–70; Dean, 1966–70; Bethlem Royal and Maudsley Hospital: Physician, 1961–70; Mem. Bd of Governors, 1966–70; Mem., Special Health Authority, 1979–90; Prof. of Psychiatry, Royal Free Hosp. Sch. of Medicine, 1971–79. Chairman: Educn Cttee, Royal Medico-Psychological Assoc., 1970 (Mem. Council, 1966–71); Sect. on Eating Disorders, World Psychiatric Assoc., 1989–; Assoc. of Univ. Teachers of Psychiatry, 1991–94; Sec. of Sect. of Psychiatry, Roy. Soc. Med., 1966–68; Mem., European Soc. for Clinical Investigation, 1968–72; Pres., Soc. for Psychosomatic Res., 1989–91. Corr. Fellow, Amer. Psychiatric Assoc., 1967–. Member Editorial Boards: British Jl of Psychiatry, 1966–71; Psychological Medicine, 1970–; Jl Neurology, Neurosurgery and Psychiatry, 1971–75; Medical Education, 1975–84; Internat. Jl of Eating Disorders, 1981–. Mem., 1942 Club, 1978–. *Publications:* contrib. to Psychiatrie der Gegenwart, vol. 3, 1975; (ed jtly with L. Hersov and contrib.) Handbook of Psychiatry, vol. 4, The Neuroses and Personality Disorders, 1984; (contrib. and ed with G. I. Szmukler, P. D. Slade, P. Harris and D. Benton) Anorexia Nervosa and Bulimic Disorders: current perspectives, 1985; (contrib.) Oxford Textbook of Medicine (ed D. J. Weatherall, J. G. G. Leddingham and D. A. Warrell), 2nd edn, 1987; articles in med. jls on psychiatry, disorders of eating, dyslexia, education and neurology. *Recreations:* roses, language, photography. *Address:* Hayes Grove Priory Hospital, Prestons Road, Hayes, Kent BR2 7AS.

RUSSELL, Graham R.; *see* Ross Russell.

RUSSELL, Ven. Harold Ian Lyle; Archdeacon of Coventry, since 1989; *b* 17 Oct. 1934; *s* of Percy Harold and Emma Rebecca Russell; *m* 1961, Barbara Lillian Dixon; two *s* one *d*. *Educ:* Epsom College; London Coll. of Divinity (BD, ALCD). Shell Petroleum Co., 1951–53; RAF, Jan. 1953; RAF Regt, Nov. 1953–1956; London Coll. of Divinity, 1956–60; ordained, 1960; Curate of Iver, Bucks, 1960–63; Curate-in-charge of St Luke's, Lodge Moor, Parish of Fulwood, Sheffield, 1963–67; Vicar: St John's, Chapeltown, Sheffield, 1967–75; St Jude's, Mapperley, Nottingham, 1975–89. *Recreations:* walking, photography, sport, gardening. *Address:* 9 Armorial Road, Coventry CV3 6GH. *T:* Coventry (01203) (home) 417750, (office) 674328. *Club:* Royal Air Force.

RUSSELL, Prof. Ian John, FRS 1989; Professor of Neurobiology, Sussex University, since 1987; *b* 19 June 1943; *s* of Philip William George Russell and Joan Lillian Russell; *m* 1968, Janice Marion Russell; one *s* one *d*. *Educ:* Chatham Technical Sch.; Queen Mary Coll., London (BSc Zoology); Univ. of British Columbia (NATO Student; MSc Zool.); Univ. of Cambridge (SRC Student; Trinity Hall Res. Student; PhD Zool.). Res. Fellowship, Magdalene Coll., Cambridge, 1969–71; SRC Res. Fellowship, Cambridge, 1969–73; Royal Soc. Exchange Fellowship, King Gustav V Res. Inst., Stockholm, 1970–71; University of Sussex: Lectr in Neurobiology, 1971–79; Reader in Neurobiology, 1979–80 and 1982–87; MRC Sen. Res. Fellow, 1980–82. *Publications:* on the neurobiology of hearing, in learned jls. *Recreations:* hockey, windsurfing, reading, music, gardening, walking. *Address:* Martins, Cuilfail, Lewes, East Sussex BN7 2BE. *T:* Lewes (01273) 472351.

RUSSELL, James Francis Buchanan, QC (NI) 1968; **His Honour Judge Russell;** County Court Judge of Northern Ireland, since 1978; Recorder of Belfast, since 1995; *b* 7 July 1924; *e s* of John Buchanan Russell and Margaret Bellingham Russell; *m* 1946, Irene McKee; two *s* one *d* (and one *d* decd). *Educ:* King's Sch., Worcester; St Andrews Univ.; Queen's Univ., Belfast (LLB). Served Royal Air Force, 1941–47. Called to Bar, NI, 1952; Crown Prosecutor: Co. Fermanagh, 1970; Co. Tyrone, 1974; Co. Londonderry, 1976. Bencher, Inn of Court, N Ireland, 1972–78 and 1988–, Treasurer, 1977. Member, Standing Advisory Commn on Human Rights, 1974–78; Chairman, Pensions Appeal Tribunal, N Ireland, 1970–. *Recreations:* golf, gardening. *Address:* 5 Grey Point, Helen's Bay, Co. Down, Northern Ireland. *T:* Helen's Bay (0247) 852249. *Clubs:* Royal Air Force; Royal Belfast Golf.

RUSSELL, Prof. James Knox, MD; ChB; FRCOG; Emeritus Professor of Obstetrics and Gynæcology, University of Newcastle upon Tyne, since 1982; Dean of Postgraduate Medicine, 1968–77; Consultant Obstetrician, Princess Mary Maternity Hospital, Newcastle upon Tyne, 1956–82, now Hon. Consultant; Consultant Gynæcologist, Royal Victoria Infirmary, Newcastle upon Tyne, 1956–82, now Hon. Consultant; *b* 5 Sept. 1919; *s* of James Russell, Aberdeen; *m* 1944, Cecilia V. Urquhart, MD, DCH, *o d* of Patrick Urquhart, MA; three *d*. *Educ:* Aberdeen Grammar School; University of Aberdeen. MB, ChB 1942, MD 1954, Aberdeen; MRCOG 1949; FRCOG 1958. Served War, 1943–46, as MO in RAF, UK and Western Europe. First Assistant to Prof. of Obstetrics and Gynæcology, Univ. of Durham, 1950; Senior Lecturer in Obstetrics and Gynæcology, Univ. of Durham, 1956; Prof., first at Durham, then at Newcastle upon Tyne, 1958–82. Hon. Obstetrician, MRC Unit on Reproduction and Growth; Examiner in Obstetrics and Gynæcology, Univs of London, Birmingham, Manchester, Belfast, Aberdeen, Liverpool, RCOG, CMB, Tripoli and Kuala Lumpur; Presiding Examiner, CMB, Newcastle upon Tyne; Consultant in human reproduction, WHO. Commonwealth Fund Fellow 1962. Visiting Professor: New York, 1974; South Africa, 1978; Kuala Lumpur, 1980, 1982; Oviedo, Spain, 1987; Graham Waite Meml Lectr, Amer. Coll. of Obstetricians and Gynaecologists, Dallas, 1982. *Publications:* Teenage Pregnancy: Medical, Social and Educational Aspects, 1982; various papers, editorials and articles on obstetrical and gynæcological subjects and medical education to learned journals, newspapers and magazines. *Recreations:* writing, gardening, curing and smoking bacon, eels, salmon, etc. *Address:* Newlands, Tranwell Woods, Morpeth, Northumberland NE61 6AG. *T:* Morpeth (01670) 515666.

RUSSELL, Jeremy Jonathan, QC 1994; *b* 18 Dec. 1950; *s* of Sidney Thomas Russell and Maud Eugenie Russell; *m* 1987, Gillian Elizabeth Giles; one *s* one *d*. *Educ:* Watford Boys' GS; City of London Poly. (BA); LSE (LLM). Lectr in Law, City of London Poly., 1973–80; called to the Bar, Middle Temple, 1975; in practice, 1977–. *Recreations:* reading, gliding, classic cars. *Address:* 4 Essex Court, Temple, EC4Y 9AJ.

RUSSELL, John, CBE 1975; Art critic, The New York Times, since 1974 (Chief Art Critic, 1982–90); *b* 1919; *o s* of Isaac James Russell and Harriet Elizabeth Atkins; *m* 1st, 1945, Alexandrine Apponyi (marr. diss., 1950); one *d*; 2nd, 1956, Vera Poliakoff (marr. diss., 1971; she *d* 1992); 3rd, 1975, Rosamond Bernier. *Educ:* St Paul's Sch.; Magdalen Coll., Oxford (MA). Hon. Attaché, Tate Gall., 1940–41; MOI, 1941–43; Naval Intell. Div., Admty, 1943–46. Regular contributor, The Sunday Times, 1945–, art critic, 1949–74. Mem. art panel, Arts Council, 1958–68. Organised Arts Council exhibns: Modigliani, 1964, Rouault, 1966 and Balthus, 1968 (all at Tate Gallery); Pop Art (with Suzi Gablik), 1969 (at the Hayward Gallery); organised Vuillard exhibn (Toronto, Chicago, San Francisco), 1971. Hon. Fellow, Royal Acad. of Arts, 1989. Frank Jewett Mather Award (College Art Assoc.), 1979; Mitchell Prize for Art Criticism, 1984. Grand Medal of Honour (Austria), 1972; Officier de l'Ordre des Arts et des Lettres, 1975; Order of Merit, Fed. Repub. of Germany, 1982; Chevalier, Légion d'Honneur, 1986. *Publications:* books include: Shakespeare's Country, 1942; British Portrait Painters, 1945; Switzerland, 1950; Logan Pearsall Smith, 1950; Erich Kleiber, 1956; Paris, 1960, new and enlarged edn, 1983; Seurat, 1965; Private View (with Bryan Robertson and Lord Snowdon), 1965; Max Ernst, 1967; Henry Moore, 1968; Ben Nicholson, 1969; Pop Art Redefined (with Suzi Gablik), 1969; The World of Matisse, 1970; Francis Bacon, 1971; Edouard Vuillard, 1971; The Meanings of Modern Art, 1981, new and enlarged edn 1990; Reading Russell, 1989; London, 1994. *Recreations:* reading, writing, Raimund (1790–1836). *Address:* 166 East 61st Street, New York, NY 10021, USA. *Clubs:* Century, Knickerbocker (New York).

See also N. T. Grimshaw.

RUSSELL, John Harry; Chairman and Chief Executive, Duport plc, 1981–86; Chairman, Blagg plc, since 1994; *b* 21 Feb. 1926; *s* of Joseph Harry Russell and Nellie Annie Russell; *m* 1951, Iris Mary Cooke; one *s* one *d*. *Educ:* Halesowen Grammar Sch. FCA; FIMgt. War Service, RN. Joseph Lucas Ltd, 1948–52; Vono Ltd (Duport Gp Co.), 1952–59; Standard Motors Ltd, 1959–61; rejoined Duport Gp, 1961: Man. Dir, Duport Foundries Ltd, 1964; Dir, Duport Parent Bd, 1966; Chm., Burman & Sons Ltd (formerly part of Duport), 1968–72; Chief Exec., Duport Engrg Div., 1972–73; Dep. Gp Man. Dir, 1973–75; Gp Man. Dir, 1975–80, Dep. Chm., 1976–81, Duport Ltd. Non-exec. Dir, Birmingham Local Bd, Barclays Bank Ltd, 1976–88. Chm., Black Country Museum Trust Ltd, 1988–. Liveryman, Worshipful Co. of Glaziers and Freeman and Citizen of London, 1976. *Recreations:* reading, music, antiques. *Address:* 442 Bromsgrove Road, Hunnington, Halesowen, West Midlands B62 0JL.

RUSSELL, Ken; film director since 1958; *b* 3 July 1927; *m* Shirley Kingdom (marr. diss. 1978); five *c*; *m* 1984, Vivian Jolly; one *s* one *d*; *m* 1992, Hetty Baines; one *s*. Merchant Navy, 1945; RAF, 1946–49. Ny Norsk Ballet, 1950; Garrick Players, 1951; free-lance photographer, 1951–57; Film Director, BBC, 1958–66; free-lance film director, 1966; *Films for TV:* Elgar; Bartok; Debussy; Henri Rousseau; Isadora Duncan; Delius; Richard Strauss; Clouds of Glory; The Planets; Vaughan Williams; ABC of British Music (Emmy award); The Mystery of Dr Martinù; The Secret Life of Arnold Bax; Classic Widows; *television serial:* Lady Chatterley, 1993; *films:* French Dressing, 1964; The Billion Dollar Brain, 1967; Women in Love, 1969; The Music Lovers, 1970; The Devils, 1971; The Boy Friend, 1971; Savage Messiah, 1972; Mahler, 1973; Tommy, 1974; Lisztomania, 1975; Valentino, 1977; Altered States, 1981; Crimes of Passion, 1985; Gothic, 1987; (jtly) Aria, 1987; Salome's Last Dance, 1988; Lair of the White Worm, 1989; The Rainbow, 1989; Whore, 1991; *opera:* The Rake's Progress, Florence, 1982; Madam Butterfly, Spoleto, 1983; La Bohème, Macerata, 1984; Faust, Vienna, 1985; Princess Ida, ENO, 1992; Salome, Bonn, 1993. Screen Writers Guild Award for TV films Elgar, Debussy, Isadora and Dante's Inferno. *Publications:* A British Picture (autobiog.), 1989; Fire Over England, 1993. *Recreations:* music, walking.

RUSSELL, Sir Mark; *see* Russell, Sir R. M.

RUSSELL, Martin Guthrie, CBE 1970; Children's Division, Home Office, later Department of Health and Social Security, 1964–74; *b* 7 May 1914; *s* of William James Russell and Bessie Gertrude Meades; *m* 1951, Moira May Eynon, *d* of Capt. Richard Threlfell; one *d*. *Educ:* Alleyn's School; Sidney Sussex Coll., Cambridge (MA). Asst Principal, Home Office, 1937; Asst Private Sec. to Lord Privy Seal, 1942; Principal, Home Office, 1942; seconded to Treasury, 1949–51 and 1952–54; Asst Sec. 1950; Estabt Officer, 1954, Dep. Chm., 1960–64, Prison Commn. In charge of Interdepartmental Social Work Gp, 1969–70. *Recreations:* gardening, enjoying retirement. *Address:* 23 Sutton Lane, Banstead, Surrey SM7 3QX. *T:* Burgh Heath (01737) 354397. *Club:* United Oxford & Cambridge University.

RUSSELL, Muir; *see* Russell, A. M. and Russell, A. M. G.

RUSSELL, Hon. Sir Patrick; *see* Russell, Hon. Sir T. P.

RUSSELL, Prof. Sir Peter (Edward Lionel Russell), Kt 1995; DLitt; FBA 1977; King Alfonso XIII Professor of Spanish Studies, Oxford, 1953–81; *b* 24 Oct. 1913; *er s* of Hugh Bernard Wheeler and late Rita Muriel (*née* Russell), Christchurch, NZ; adopted surname Russell. *Educ:* Cheltenham College; Queen's College, Oxford (DLitt 1981; Hon. Fellow, 1990). Lecturer of St John's College, 1937–53 and Queen's College, 1938–45. Enlisted, 1940; commissioned (Intelligence Corps) Dec. 1940; Temp. Lt-Col, 1945; specially employed in Caribbean, W Africa and SE Asia, 1942–46. Fellow of Queen's College, 1946–53, and Univ. Lectr in Spanish Studies, 1946–53; Fellow of Exeter Coll., 1953–81, Emeritus Fellow, 1981; Taylorian Special Lectr, Oxford, 1983; Visiting Professor: Univ. of Virginia, 1982; Univ. of Texas, 1983, 1987; Johns Hopkins Univ., 1986; Vanderbilt Univ., 1987. Member: Portuguese Academy of History, 1956; Real Academia de Buenas Letras, Barcelona, 1972; UGC Cttee on Latin-American Studies in British Univs, 1962–64. FRHistS. Premio Antonio de Nebrija, Univ. of Salamanca, 1989. Comdr, Order of Isabel the Catholic (Spain), 1989; Comdr, Order of the Infante Dom Henrique (Portugal), 1993. *Publications:* As Fontes de Fernão Lopes, 1941 (Coimbra); The English Intervention in Spain and Portugal in the Time of Edward III and Richard II, 1955; Prince Henry the Navigator, 1960; (with D. M. Rogers) Hispanic Manuscripts and Books in the Bodleian and Oxford College Libraries, 1962; (ed) Spain: a Companion to Spanish Studies, 1973, Spanish edn, 1982; Temas de la Celestina y otros estudios (del Cid al Quijote), 1978; Prince Henry the Navigator: the rise and fall of a culture hero, 1984; Traducción y traductores en la Península Ibérica 1400–1550, 1985; Cervantes, 1985; La Celestina, 1991; Portugal, Spain and the African Atlantic 1343–1490, 1995; articles and reviews in Modern Language Review, Medium Aevum, Bulletin of Hispanic Studies, etc. *Recreation:* travel. *Address:* 23 Belsyre Court, Woodstock Road, Oxford OX2 6HU. *T:* Oxford (01865) 56086. *Club:* United Oxford & Cambridge University.

RUSSELL, Most Rev. Philip Welsford Richmond; *b* 21 Oct. 1919; *s* of Leslie Richmond Russell and Clarice Louisa Russell (*née* Welsford); *m* 1945, Violet Eirene, *d* of Ven. Dr. O. J. Hogarth, sometime Archdeacon of the Cape; one *s* three *d*. *Educ:* Durban High Sch.; Rhodes Univ. College (Univ. of South Africa), BA 1948; LTh 1950. Served War of 1939–45; MBE 1943. Deacon, 1950; Priest, 1951; Curate, St Peter's, Maritzburg, 1950–54; Vicar: Greytown, 1954–57; Ladysmith, 1957–61; Kloof, 1961–66; Archdeacon of Pinetown, 1961–66; Bishop Suffragan of Capetown, 1966–70; Bishop of Port Elizabeth, 1970–74; Bishop of Natal, 1974–81; Archbishop of Cape Town and Metropolitan of Southern Africa, 1981–86. *Recreations:* caravanning, fishing. *Address:* 400 Currie Road, Durban, Natal, South Africa.

RUSSELL, Robert Christopher Hamlyn, CBE 1981; formerly Director, Hydraulics Research Station, Department of the Environment (formerly Ministry of Technology), 1965–81; *b* Singapore, 1921; *s* of late Philip Charles and Hilda Gertrude Russell; *m* 1950, Cynthia Mary Roberts; one *s* two *d. Educ:* Stowe; King's Coll., Cambridge. Asst Engineer: BTH Co., Rugby, 1944; Dunlop Rubber Co., 1946; Sen. Scientific Officer, later PSO, then SPSO, in Hydraulics Research Station, 1949–65. Visiting Prof., Univ. of Strathclyde, 1967. *Publications:* Waves and Tides, 1951; papers on civil engineering hydraulics. *Address:* 29 St Mary's Street, Wallingford, Oxfordshire OX10 0ET. *T:* Wallingford (01491) 837323.

RUSSELL, Sir (Robert) Mark, KCMG 1985 (CMG 1977); HM Diplomatic Service, retired; Chairman, Commonwealth Institute, Scotland, since 1989; *b* 3 Sept. 1929; *s* of Sir Robert E. Russell, CSI, CIE; *m* 1954, Virginia Mary Rogers; two *s* two *d. Educ:* Trinity Coll., Glenalmond; Exeter Coll., Oxford (MA). Hon. Mods cl. 2, Lit. Hum. cl. 1. Royal Artillery, 1952–54; FO, 1954–56; 3rd, later 2nd Sec., HM Legation, Budapest, 1956–58; 2nd Sec., Berne, 1958–61; FO, 1961–65; 1st Sec., 1962; 1st Sec. and Head of Chancery, Kabul, 1965–67; 1st Sec., DSAO, 1967–69; Counsellor, 1969; Dep. Head of Personnel (Ops) Dept, FCO, 1969–70; Commercial Counsellor, Bucharest, 1970–73; Counsellor, Washington, 1974–78, and Head of Chancery, 1977–78; Asst Under Sec. of State, FCO and Dep. Chief Clerk and Chief Inspector, HM Diplomatic Service, 1978–82; Ambassador to Turkey, 1983–86; Dep. Under-Sec. of State (Chief Clerk), FCO, 1986–89. Chairman: Martin Currie European Investment Trust, 1990–; Margaret Blackwood Housing Assoc., 1990–; Scottish Trust for the Physically Disabled, 1990–. Mem. Bd, British Council, 1990–. *Recreations:* travel, music. *Address:* 20 Meadow Place, Edinburgh EH9 1JR. *Clubs:* Commonwealth Trust; New (Edinburgh).

RUSSELL, Prof. Roger Wolcott; Vice Chancellor, and Professor of Psychobiology, Flinders University of South Australia, 1972–79, now Emeritus Professor (engaged in research, 1979–89); Research Psychobiologist, School of Biological Sciences, since 1990, Research Neurobiologist and Fellow of the Center for the Neurobiology of Learning and Memory, since 1991 (Lifetime Distinguished Fellow, 1994), Univesity of California at Irvine; *b* 30 Aug. 1914; *s* of Leonard Walker and Sadie Stanhope Russell, Worcester, Mass, USA; *m* 1945, Kathleen Sherman Fortescue; one *s* one *d. Educ:* Worcester (Mass, USA) Public Schools; Clark Univ. (Livermore Schol., Clark Fellow in Psychology); BA 1935, MA 1936; Peabody Coll., Vanderbilt Univ. (Payne Schol.); University of Virginia (Du Pont Research Fellow); PhD 1939; DSc Univ. of London, 1954. Instructor in Psychology: Univ. of Nebraska, 1939–41, Michigan State Coll., 1941; Research Psychologist, USAF Sch. of Aviation Medicine, 1941–42; Officer USAF, 1942–46; Asst Prof. in Psychol., Univ. of Pittsburgh, 1946–47; Assoc. Prof. of Psychol., Univ. of Pittsburgh and Res. Fellow in Neurophysiol., Western Psychiatric Inst., 1947–49; Fulbright Advanced Research Schol. and Director, Animal Research Lab., Institute of Psychiatry, Univ. of London, 1949–50; Prof. of Psychology and Head of Dept of Psychol., University Coll., London 1950–57 (on leave of absence, 1956–57); Dean of Advanced Studies, Indiana Univ., 1966–67 (Prof. and Chm. Dept of Psychology, 1959–66); Vice Chancellor, Academic Affairs, and Prof. of Psychology, Psycho-Biology and of Clinical Pharmacology and Therapeutics, Univ. of Calif., Irvine, 1967–72. Member: Australian Vice-Chancellors' Cttee, 1972–79; Bd of Dirs, Australian-American Educnl Foundn, 1972–79; Commonwealth Educnl R&D Cttee, 1974–79. Visiting Professor: Sch. of Medicine, UCLA, 1976–77, 1980–90; Dept of Psychology, Univ. of Reading, 1977; Dept of Psychology, Univ. of Stockholm, 1977. Executive Sec. of the American Psychological Assoc., 1956–59, Board of Directors, 1963–65, Pres. Div. 1, 1968–69; Mem., USPHS Adv. Cttee in Psychopharmacology, 1957–63, 1967–70, 1981–85, Member: Nat. Research Coun. (USA), 1958–61, 1963–65, 1967–71; Army Sci. Adv. Panel (USA), 1958–66; Sec.-Gen. Internat. Union of Psychological Science, 1960–66 (Vice-Pres., 1966–69; Pres., 1969–72; Mem. Exec. Cttee, 1972–80); Aust.-Amer. Educn Foundn Vis. Prof., Dept of Psychol., Univ. of Sydney, 1965–66; Vis. Erskine Fellow, Univ. of Canterbury, NZ, 1966. Member, Scientific and Professional Socs in Europe, USA, Australia. FACE 1972; FASSA 1973. Hon. DSc: Newcastle, NSW, 1978; Flinders, 1979. Bronze Star Medal (USA), 1945. Army Commendation Medal (USA), 1946. *Publications:* (ed) Frontiers in Psychology, 1964; (ed) Frontiers in physiological Psychology, 1966; (ed) Matthew Flinders: The Ifs of History, 1979; (ed) Behavioral Measures of Neurotoxicity, 1990; research papers on neurochemical bases of behaviour, experimental psycho-pathology, physiological, child and social psychology, psychopharmacology. *Recreation:* writing. *Address:* Center for the Neurobiology of Learning and Memory, University of California, Irvine, CA 92717, USA; One Cherry North, Irvine, CA 92715. *T:* (714) 6510107.

RUSSELL, (Ronald) Christopher (Gordon), FRCS; Consultant Surgeon: Middlesex Hospital, since 1975; King Edward VII Hospital, since 1985; *b* 15 May 1940; *s* of Rognvald Gordon Russell and Doris Isa Russell (*née* Troup); *m* 1965, Mary Ruth Pitcher; two *s* (and one *s* decd). *Educ:* Epsom College; Middlesex Hosp. Med. Sch. (MB BS, MS). Sen. Lectr in Surgery, St Mary's Hosp., 1973–75. Associate Editor, 1978, Co-Editor, 1986–91, British Jl of Surgery; Gen. Editor, Operative Surgery, 1986–. *Publications:* (ed) Recent Advances in Surgery, vol. XI 1982, vol. XII 1985, vol. XIII 1991; (ed jtly) Bailey & Love Textbook of Surgery, 1991–; numerous contribs to surgical and gastroenterological jls. *Recreation:* travel. *Address:* 149 Harley Street, W1N 2DE; Little Orchards, Layters Way, Gerrards Cross SL9 7QY. *T:* Gerrards Cross (01753) 882264. *Club:* Royal Society of Medicine.

RUSSELL, Rudolf Rosenfeld; a Recorder of the Crown Court, since 1980; *b* 5 Feb. 1925; *s* of Robert and Johanna Rosenfeld; *m* 1952, Eva Maria Jaray; one *s. Educ:* Bryanston Sch.; Worcester Coll., Oxford (MA). Service in RAF, 1943–46. Called to the Bar, Middle Temple, 1950. *Recreations:* walking, music, skiing. *Address:* Devereux Chambers, Devereux Court, Temple, WC2R 3JJ. *T:* 0171–353 7534.

RUSSELL, Sir Spencer (Thomas), Kt 1988; FCA; FCIS; FNZIM; Governor, Reserve Bank of New Zealand, 1984–88, retired; non-executive Chairman, National Bank of New Zealand, since 1992; *b* 5 Oct. 1923; *s* of Thomas Spencer Russell and Ann Jane Russell; *m* 1953, Ainsley Russell (*née* Coull); three *s. Educ:* Wanganui Collegiate School. Served War, NZ Division, 1942–45. Joined National Bank of New Zealand, 1946; International Manager, 1956; Asst Gen. Man., 1960; Chief London Man., 1973; Chief Exec. and Dir, 1976. *Publications:* numerous articles in professional jls. *Recreations:* golf, gardening. *Address:* 6 Challenger Street, St Heliers, Auckland 5, New Zealand. *Clubs:* Wellington; Northern (Auckland); Wellington Golf.

RUSSELL, Terence Francis; Sheriff of North Strathclyde at Kilmarnock, since 1983; *b* 12 April 1931; *s* of Robert Russell and Catherine Cusker Russell; *m* 1965, Mary Ann Kennedy; two *d. Educ:* Glasgow Univ. (BL). Qualified as Solicitor, 1955; practised in Glasgow, 1955–58 and 1963–81; Solicitor in High Court, Bombay, 1958–63. Sheriff of N Strathclyde, and of Grampian, Highland and Islands, 1981–83. *Recreations:* gardening, travel.

RUSSELL, Thomas, CMG 1980; CBE 1970 (OBE 1963); HM Overseas Civil Service, retired; Representative of the Cayman Islands in UK, since 1982; *b* 27 May 1920; *s* of late Thomas Russell, OBE, MC and Margaret Thomson Russell; *m* 1951, Andrée Irma Désfossés (*d* 1989); one *s. Educ:* Hawick High Sch.; St Andrews Univ.; Peterhouse, Cambridge. MA St Andrews; Dip. Anthrop. Cantab. War Service, Cameronians (Scottish Rifles), 1941; 5th Bn (Scottish), Parachute Regt, 1943: served in N Africa and Italy; POW, 1944; Captain 1945; OC Parachute Trng Company, 1946. Cambridge Univ., 1946–47. Colonial Admin. Service, 1948; District Comr, British Solomon Is Protectorate, 1948; Asst Sec., Western Pacific High Commn, Fiji, 1951; District Comr, British Solomon Is Protectorate, 1954–56; seconded Colonial Office, 1956–57; Admin. Officer Class A, 1956; Dep. Financial Sec., 1962; Financial Sec., 1965; Chief Sec. to W Pacific High Commn, 1970–74; Governor of the Cayman Islands, 1974–81. FRAI. *Recreations:* anthropology, archæology. *Address:* 6 Eldon Drive, Frensham Road, The Bourne, Farnham, Surrey GU10 3JE. *Clubs:* Commonwealth Trust, Caledonian.

RUSSELL, Rt. Hon. Sir (Thomas) Patrick, Kt 1980; PC 1987; **Rt. Hon. Lord Justice Russell;** a Lord Justice of Appeal, since 1987; *b* 30 July 1926; *s* of late Sidney Arthur Russell and Elsie Russell; *m* 1951, Doreen (Janie) Ireland; two *d. Educ:* Urmston Grammar Sch.; Manchester Univ. (LLB). Served in Intelligence Corps and RASC, 1945–48. Called to Bar, Middle Temple, 1949, Bencher, 1978; Prosecuting Counsel to the Post Office (Northern Circuit), 1961–70; Asst Recorder of Bolton, 1963–70; Recorder of Barrow-in-Furness, 1970–71; QC 1971; a Recorder of the Crown Court, 1972–80; Leader, 1978–80, Presiding Judge, 1983–87, Northern Circuit; a Judge of the High Court of Justice, QBD, 1980–86. Mem. Senate, Inns of Court and Bar, 1978–80. Mem., Lord Justice James Cttee on Distribution of Criminal Business, 1973–76. Pres., Manchester and Dist Medico-Legal Soc., 1978–79 (Patron, 1987); Vice-Pres., Lancs CCC, 1980. Hon. LLD Manchester, 1988. *Recreation:* cricket. *Address:* Royal Courts of Justice, WC2A 2LL.

RUSSELL, William Martin, (Willy); author since 1971; *b* 23 Aug. 1947; *s* of William and Margery Russell; *m* 1969, Ann Seagroatt; one *s* two *d. Educ:* St Katharine's Coll. of Educn, Liverpool, 1970–73 (Cert. of Educn). Ladies' Hairdresser, 1963–69; Teacher, 1973–74; Fellow in Creative Writing, Manchester Polytechnic, 1977–78. Founder Mem., and Dir, Quintet Films; Hon. Dir, Liverpool Playhouse. *Theatre:* Blind Scouse (3 short plays), 1971–72; When the Reds (adaptation), 1972; John, Paul, George, Ringo and Bert (musical), 1974; Breezeblock Park, 1975; One for the Road, 1976; Stags and Hens, 1978; Educating Rita, 1979; Blood Brothers (musical), 1983; Our Day Out (musical), 1983; Shirley Valentine, 1986; *television plays:* King of the Castle, 1972; Death of a Young, Young Man, 1972; Break In (for schools), 1974; Our Day Out, 1976; Lies (for schools), 1977; Daughters of Albion, 1978; Boy with Transistor Radio (for schools), 1979; One Summer (series), 1980; *radio play:* I Read the News Today (for schools), 1976; *screenplays:* Band on the Run, 1979 (not released); Educating Rita, 1981; Shirley Valentine, 1988; Dancing Through the Dark, 1989. Hon. MA Open Univ., 1983; Hon. DLit Liverpool, 1990. *Publications:* Breezeblock Park, 1978; One for the Road, 1980, rev. edn 1985; Educating Rita, 1981; Our Day Out, 1984; Stags and Hens, 1985; Blood Brothers, 1985 (also pubd as short non-musical version for schools, 1984); Shirley Valentine, 1989; several other plays included in general collections of plays; songs and poetry. *Recreations:* playing the guitar, composing songs, gardening, cooking. *Address:* c/o Casarotto Ramsay Ltd, 60–66 Wardour Street, W1V 3HP. *T:* 071–287 4450. *Club:* Athenæum (Liverpool).

RUSSELL-DAVIS, John Darelan, FRICS; chartered surveyor, retired; *b* 23 Dec. 1912; *s* of Edward David Darelan Davis, FRCS, and Alice Mildred (*née* Russell); *m* 1st, 1938, Barbarina Elizabeth Graham Arnould (*d* 1985); one *s* one *d*; 2nd, 1986, Gaynor, *widow* of Lt-Col A. V. Brooke-Webb, RA. *Educ:* Stowe Sch.; Germany; Coll. of Estate Management, London. FRICS 1934. Served War, HAC, 1939; commnd RA, 1940; Captain 1942; mentioned in despatches, 1945. Partner, C. P. Whiteley & Son, Chartered Surveyors, 1938; Sen. Partner, Whiteley, Ferris & Puckridge, and Kemsley, Whiteley & Ferris, City of London, 1948–72. Mem., Lands Tribunal, 1972–77. Royal Instn of Chartered Surveyors: formerly Mem. Council (twice); Chm., City branch, 1959; Hon. Treasurer, Benevolent Fund. Mem., East Grinstead UDC, 1957–60 (Vice-Chm., 1960). Formerly: Mem. Council, Wycombe Abbey Sch.; Trustee, Cordwainer and Bread Street Foundn; Mem. Court, Turners Co. (Renter-Warden, 1975). *Recreations:* gardening, Somerset and Dorset countryside. *Address:* 171 Goose Hill, Bower Hinton, Martock, Somerset TA12 6LJ. *T:* Martock (01935) 822307. *Clubs:* Army and Navy; Somerset CC.

RUSSELL VICK, Arnold Oughtred; *see* Vick.

RUSSON, David; Director General, Boston Spa (formerly Science, Technology and Industry), British Library, since 1988; *b* 12 June 1944; *s* of Thomas Charles Russon and Violet Russon (*née* Jarvis); *m* 1967, Kathleen Mary Gregory; one *s* two *d. Educ:* Wellington Grammar Sch.; University College London (BSc); Univ. of York. Various appts, Office for Scientific and Technical Information, DES, 1969–74; British Library: R & D Dept, 1974–75; Lending Div., 1975–85; Dir, Document Supply Centre, 1985–88; Mem., British Liby Bd, 1988–. Pres., Internat. Council for Scientific and Technical Information, 1995– (Vice Pres., 1992–95). FRSA; FIInfSc. *Publications:* contribs to professional jls of library and inf. science. *Recreations:* village tennis and badminton. *Address:* March House, Tollerton, York YO6 2EQ. *T:* Tollerton (01347) 838253.

RUSTON, Rt. Rev. John Harry Gerald; *see* St Helena, Bishop of.

RUTHERFORD, Prof. Andrew, CBE 1993; Vice-Chancellor, University of London, since 1994; Warden of Goldsmiths' College, 1984–92, and Professor, 1988–92, now Emeritus, University of London; *b* Helmsdale, Sutherland, 23 July 1929; *s* of Thomas Armstrong Rutherford and Christian P. Rutherford (*née* Russell); *m* 1953, Nancy Milroy Browning, MA, *d* of Dr Arthur Browning and Dr Jean G. Browning (*née* Thomson); two *s* one *d. Educ:* Helmsdale Sch.; George Watson's Boys' Coll.; Univ. of Edinburgh; Merton Coll., Oxford. MA Edinburgh Univ., First Cl. Hons Eng. Lang. and Lit., James Elliott Prize, and Vans Dunlop Schol., 1951; Carnegie Schol., 1953; BLitt Oxford, 1959. Commnd Seaforth Highlanders, serving with Somaliland Scouts, 1952–53; 11th Bn Seaforth Highlanders (TA), 1953–58. Asst Lectr in English, Univ. of Edinburgh, 1955; Lectr, 1956–64; Vis. Assoc. Prof., Univ. of Rochester (NY), 1963; University of Aberdeen: Sen. Lectr, 1964; Second Prof. of English, 1965–68; Regius (Chalmers) Prof. of Eng. Lit., 1968–84; Mem. Court, 1978–84; Dean, Faculty of Arts and Soc. Scis, 1979–82; Sen. Vice-Principal, 1982–84; Mem. Court, Univ. of London, 1990–92; Hon. Fellow, Goldsmiths' Coll., 1992. Lectures: Byron Foundn, Nottingham Univ., 1964; Chatterton, British Acad., 1965; Stevenson, Edinburgh Univ., 1967. Chairman: English Bd, CNAA, 1966–73; Literature Adv. Cttee, British Council, 1987–; Pres., Internat. Assoc. of Univ. Profs of English, 1977–80. Mem., BBC Gen. Adv. Council, 1979–84; Trustee, Learning from Experience Trust, 1986–92; Courtauld Trust, 1994–. British Council lecture tours in Europe, India and S America. Freeman, City of London, 1990; Freeman, 1990, Liveryman, 1991, Goldsmiths' Co. Hon. DLitt SUNY, 1990; DUniv Athens, 1993; Hon.

LLD Aberdeen, 1995. *Publications:* Byron: A Critical Study, 1961; (ed) Kipling's Mind and Art, 1964; (ed) Byron: The Critical Heritage, 1970; (ed) 20th Century Interpretations of A Passage to India, 1970; (ed) Kipling, A Sahibs' War and other stories, 1971; (ed) Kipling, Friendly Brook and other stories, 1971; The Literature of War, 1979, 2nd edn 1989; (ed) Early Verse by Rudyard Kipling, 1986; (ed) Kipling, Plain Tales from the Hills, 1987; (ed) Kipling, Selected Stories, 1987; (ed) Kipling, War Stories and Poems, 1990; (ed) Byron: Augustan and Romantic, 1990; (ed) The Sayings of Rudyard Kipling, 1994; articles in learned journals. *Address:* Senate House, Malet Street, WC1E 7HU. *T:* 0171–636 8000. *Clubs:* Athenæum; New (Edinburgh).

RUTHERFORD, Andrew; His Honour Judge Rutherford; a Circuit Judge, since 1995; *b* 25 March 1948; *s* of Robert Mark Rutherford and Alison Wellington (*née* Clark); *m* 1994, Lucy Elizabeth Bosworth. *Educ:* Clifton Coll.; Exeter Univ. (LLB). Called to the Bar, Middle Temple, 1970; Asst Recorder, 1990–93; Recorder, 1993–95. *Address:* c/o Lord Chancellor's Department, Western Circuit Office, Bridge House, Sion Place, Clifton, Bristol BS8 4BN. *Club:* Bath and County.

RUTHERFORD, Derek Thomas Jones, FCA; financial and management accounting consultant, since 1990; *b* 9 April 1930; *s* of late Sydney Watson Rutherford and Elsie Rutherford; *m* 1956, Kathleen Robinson; one *s* four *d*. *Educ:* Doncaster Grammar School. Practising accountant and auditor, 1955–59; Company Sec./Accountant, P. Platt & Sons, 1959–61; Retail Accountant, MacFisheries, 1961–63; Factory Management Accountant, then Company Systems Manager, T. Wall & Son (Ice Cream), 1963–70; Dir of Finance, Alfa-Laval Co., 1970–74; Group Financial Dir, Oxley Printing Group, 1974; HMSO: Chief Accountant, Publications Group, 1975–76; Dir, Management Accounting Project, 1976–77; Dir of Finance and Planning Div., 1977–83; Principal Estabt and Finance Officer, 1983–84; Comr for Admin and Finance, Forestry Commn, 1984–90. *Recreations:* reading, gardening, home computing. *Address:* 83 Caiyside, Swanston, Edinburgh EH10 7HR. *T:* 0131–445 1171. *Club:* Royal Air Force.

RUTHERFORD, (Gordon) Malcolm; Assistant Editor, Financial Times, 1977–93; *b* 21 Aug. 1939; *s* of late Gordon Brown Rutherford and Bertha Brown Rutherford; *m* 1st, 1965, Susan Tyler (marr. diss. 1969); one *d*; 2nd, 1970, Elizabeth Maitland Pelen; three *d*. *Educ:* Newcastle Royal Grammar Sch.; Balliol Coll., Oxford. Arts Editor 1962, Foreign Editor 1964, The Spectator; founded the Newsletter, Latin America, 1965; Financial Times: Diplomatic Correspondent, 1967–69; Chief German Correspondent, 1969–74; Defence Specialist, 1974–77; Chief political commentator, 1977–88; Chief theatre critic, 1990–94. Mem. of Council, Chatham House, 1994–. Founding Mem., Media Law Group, 1983; Co-Founder, West-West Agenda, 1988. *Publication:* Can We Save the Common Market?, 1981, 2nd edn 1983. *Recreations:* travel, tennis, bridge. *Address:* 89 Bedford Gardens, W8 7EQ. *T:* 0171–229 2063. *Club:* Travellers'.

RUTHERFORD, (Herman) Graham, CBE 1966; QPM 1957; DL; Chief Constable of Surrey, 1956–68; retired, 1968; *b* 3 April 1908; *m* 1940, Dorothy Weaver (*d* 1987); three *s* one *d*. *Educ:* Grammar School, Consett, County Durham. Metropolitan Police, 1929–45; Chief Constable: of Oxfordshire, 1945–54; of Lincolnshire, 1954–56. Barrister, Gray's Inn, 1941. Served Army, Allied Military Government, 1943–45, Lt-Colonel. DL Surrey, 1968. *Recreation:* sailing. *Address:* Hankley Farm, Elstead, Surrey GU8 6LJ. *T:* Elstead (01252) 702200.

See also Vice-Adm. M. G. Rutherford.

RUTHERFORD, Jessica Marianne Fernande, FSA; Head of Museums, and Director of the Royal Pavilion, Brighton, since 1992; *b* 7 Feb. 1949; *d* of Raymond Denys Rutherford and Simone Genvieve (*née* Michaud). *Educ:* Brighton and Hove High Sch.; Manchester Univ. (BA Hons Hist. of Art); Sussex Univ. (PGCE). V&A Mus., 1974; Royal Pavilion, Art Gallery and Museums, Brighton: Keeper of Decorative Art, 1974–85; Principal Keeper, Royal Pavilion, 1985–87; Asst Dir (Collections), 1987–92. Decorative Arts Society: Sec., 1975–85; Trustee, 1992–; Mem. Council, Charleston Trust, 1992–; Sec. to Trustees and Governors, Friends of Royal Pavilion, Art Gall. and Museums, 1992–. Mem. Council, Sussex Univ., 1995–. *Publications:* Art Nouveau, Art Deco and the Thirties: the furniture collections at Brighton Museum, 1983; (jtly) Art Nouveau, Art Deco and the Thirties: the ceramic, glass and metalwork collections at Brighton Museum, 1986; The Royal Pavilion: the palace of George IV, 1995; *chapters in:* James Tissot, 1984; The Crace Firm of Royal Decorators 1768–1900, 1990; Country House Lighting, 1992; articles and reviews for learned jls. *Recreations:* walking, travel, historic houses, music. *Address:* The Royal Pavilion, Brighton, E Sussex BN1 1UE. *T:* Brighton (01273) 713240.

RUTHERFORD, Malcolm; *see* Rutherford, G. M.

RUTHERFORD, Vice-Adm. Malcolm Graham, CBE 1991; Leader, Study Team, Engineering Structure in Royal Navy, since 1995; *b* Tunbridge Wells, 21 March 1941; *s* of (Herman) Graham Rutherford, *qv*; *m* 1969, Fleur Margaret Ann Smith; one *s* one *d*. *Educ:* New Coll. Sch., Oxford; Gordonstoun; London Univ. (BSc (Elec. Engrg) 1964); RNC Greenwich (Nuclear Reactor Engrg Dip. 1969). Italian Interpreter, 1968. FIEE 1986; EurIng 1989. Served HM Submarines, Thermopylae, Conqueror, Sceptre, 1967–78; ndc 1978; HMS Glamorgan, 1984; Dir, Tactical Weapons System Upholder Class Subs, 1986–88; Capt., HMS Collingwood, 1988–90; Dir, Personnel, MoD, 1990–92; Naval Sec., 1992–94; DCDS (Systems), MoD, and Chief Naval Engr Officer, 1994–95. President: RNRM Mountaineering Club, 1985–; RN Winter Sports Assoc., 1993–; Mem., Higher Management Cttee, Jt Services Everest Expedns, 1988, 1992. *Recreations:* mountaineering, ski-ing, squash, cycling, running (London and NY marathons, 1989), photography, writing. *Address:* Ministry of Defence, Main Building, Whitehall, SW1A 2HB. *Clubs:* Garrick, Alpine; Escorts Squash Rackets.

RUTHERFORD, Thomas, CBE 1982; Chairman, North Eastern Electricity Board, 1977–89, retired; *b* 4 June 1924; *s* of Thomas and Catherine Rutherford; *m* 1950, Joyce Foreman; one *s* one *d*. *Educ:* Tynemouth High Sch.; King's Coll., Durham Univ. BSc(Hons); CEng, FIEE. Engrg Trainee, subseq. Research Engr, A Reyrolle & Co. Ltd, Hebburn-on-Tyne, 1943–49; North Eastern Electricity Bd: various engrg and commercial appts, 1949–61; Personal Asst to Chm., 1961–63; Area Commercial Engr, then Area Engr, Tees Area, 1964–69; Dep. Commercial Man., 1969–70; Commercial Man., 1970–72; Chief Engr, 1972–73; Dep. Chm., 1973–75; Chm., SE Electricity Board, 1975–77. *Address:* 76 Beach Road, Tynemouth, Northumberland NE30 2QW. *T:* 0191–257 1775.

RUTHNASWAMY, Elizabeth Kuanghu, (Mrs Vincent Ruthnaswamy); *see* Han Suyin.

RUTHVEN; *see* Hore-Ruthven, family name of Earl of Gowrie.

RUTHVEN OF CANBERRA, Viscount; Patrick Leo Brer Hore-Ruthven; Operations Director, Camphor Ltd; *b* 4 Feb. 1964; *s* and *heir* of 2nd Earl of Gowrie, *qv*; *m* 1990, Julie Goldsmith; one *s*. *Heir:* *s* Hon. Heathcote Patrick Cornelius Hore-Ruthven, *b* 28 May 1990.

RUTLAND, 10th Duke of, *cr* 1703; **Charles John Robert Manners,** CBE 1962; Marquess of Granby, 1703; Earl of Rutland, 1525; Baron Manners of Haddon, 1679; Baron Roos of Belvoir, 1896; Captain Grenadier Guards; *b* 28 May 1919; *e s* of 9th Duke and Kathleen (*d* 1989), 3rd *d* of late F. J. Tennant; *S* father, 1940; *m* 1946, Anne Bairstow Cumming (marr. diss. 1956), *e d* of late Major Cumming Bell, Binham Lodge, Edgerton, Huddersfield; one *d*; *m* 1958, Frances Helen, *d* of late Charles Sweeny and Margaret, Duchess of Argyll; two *s* one *d* (and one *s* decd). *Educ:* Eton; Trinity Coll., Cambridge. Owns 18,000 acres; minerals in Leicestershire and Derbyshire; picture gallery at Belvoir Castle. Chairman: E Midlands Economic Planning Council, 1971–74; Leicestershire County Council, 1974–77. *Heir:* *s* Marquis of Granby, *qv*. *Address:* Belvoir Castle, Grantham NG32 1PD; Haddon Hall, Derby DE4 1LA.

See also Marquess of Anglesey, Earl of Wemyss.

RUTT, Rev. Cecil Richard, CBE 1973; MA; *b* 27 Aug. 1925; *s* of Cecil Rutt and Mary Hare Turner; *m* 1969, Joan Mary Ford. *Educ:* Huntingdon Grammar School; Kelham Theol. Coll.; Pembroke Coll., Cambridge. RNVR, 1943–46. Deacon, 1951; Priest, 1952. Asst Curate, St George's, Cambridge, 1951–54; Dio. of Korea, 1954; Parish Priest of Anjung, 1956–58; Warden of St Bede's House Univ. Centre, Seoul, 1959–64; Rector of St Michael's Seminary, Oryu Dong, Seoul, 1964–66; Archdeacon, West Kyonggi (Dio. Seoul), 1965–66; Asst Bishop of Taejon, 1966–68; Bishop of Taejon, 1968–74; Bishop Suffragan of St Germans, 1974–79; Hon. Canon, St Mary's Cathedral, Truro, 1974–79; Bishop of Leicester, 1979–90. Received into RC Ch, 1994, ordained priest, 1995. Associate Gen. Sec., Korean Bible Soc., 1964–74; Episcopal Sec., Council of the Church of SE Asia, 1968–74; Commissary, 1974–90; Pres., Roy. Asiatic Soc., Korea Br., 1974. Chairman: Adv. Council on Relations of Bishops and Religious Communities, 1980–90; Bishop of Truro's Adv. Gp on Services in Cornish, 1990–; Mem., Anglican/Orthodox Jt Doctrinal Discussions, 1983–89. Bard of the Gorsedd of Cornwall, Cornwhylen, 1976 (Chaplain, 1993–). Hon. Fellow, Northumbrian Univs' E Asia Centre, 1990. Hon. DLitt Confucian Univ., Seoul, 1974. Tasan Cultural Award (for writings on Korea), 1964. ChStJ 1978. Order of Civil Merit, Peony Class (Korea), 1974. *Publications:* (ed) Songgonghoe Songga (Korean Anglican Hymnal), 1961; Korean Works and Days, 1964; P'ungnyu Han'guk (in Korean), 1965; (trans.) An Anthology of Korean Sijo, 1970; The Bamboo Grove, an introduction to Korean Sijo poetry, 1971; James Scarth Gale and his History of the Korean People, 1972; Virtuous Women, three masterpieces of traditional Korean fiction, 1974; A History of Handknitting, 1987; The Book of Changes: Zhouyi (trans. of Bronze Age document), 1995; contribs on Korean classical poetry and history to Trans. Royal Asiatic Soc. (Korea Br.) and various Korean publications. *Address:* 3 Marlborough Court, Falmouth, Cornwall TR11 2QU. *T:* Falmouth (01326) 312276.

RUTTER, Prof. Arthur John; Emeritus Professor, Imperial College, University of London (Professor of Botany, 1967–79 and Head of Department of Botany and Plant Technology, 1971–79); *b* 22 Nov. 1917; *s* of late W. Arthur Rutter, CBE, FRIBA and Amy, *d* of William Dyche, BA, Cardiff; *m* 1944, Betsy Rosier Stone (*d* 1978); two *s* one *d*. *Educ:* Royal Grammar Sch., Guildford; Imperial Coll. of Science and Technology. ARCS, BSc, PhD, FIBiol. Mem., ARC team for selection of oil-seed crops and develt selective herbicides, 1940–45; Asst Lectr, Imperial Coll., 1945, Lectr 1946; Reader in Ecology, Univ. of London, 1956. Vis. Prof., Univ. of the Panjab, Pakistan, 1960–61. *Publications:* papers, mainly in Annals of Botany, Jl of Ecology, Jl of Applied Ecology on water relations of plants, forest hydrology and effects of atmospheric pollution on trees. *Recreations:* gardening, walking. *Address:* 10 Thursby Road, Woking, Surrey GU21 3NZ. *T:* Brookwood (01483) 765009.

RUTTER, Sir Frank (William Eden), KBE 1986 (CBE 1981); general medical practitioner; *b* 5 June 1918; *s* of Edgar and Nellie Rutter; *m* 1947, Mary Elizabeth Milton; six *d*. *Educ:* Welsh National Sch. of Medicine, Cardiff; Westminster Hosp. Med. Sch., London. MRCGP, MRCS, LRCP; DipObst. RAMC (Airborne Forces), 1942–46; OC 195 (Parachute) Field Ambulance, 1946. Chm., Health Cttee, Cardiff RDC, 1960–62; Member: Auckland Hosp. Bd, 1971–88 (Chm., 1974–88); Auckland Area Health Bd, 1988–89; Pres., Hosp. Bds Assoc., NZ, 1977–81 and 1983–85; Chairman, National Advisory Committee: Cancer Treatment Services, 1978–89; Organ Imaging Services, 1982–89; Life-Mem., NZ National Multiple Sclerosis Soc. Patron, South Island Airedale Terrier Club, 1989–93. CStJ 1989. Silver Jubilee Medal, 1977. *Recreations:* breeding Airedale terriers and Irish terriers, watching development of fourteen grandchildren. *Address:* 10 Staffa Street, Parnell, Auckland, New Zealand. *T:* (9) 3773070; (professional) 28 Hoteo Avenue, Papatoetoe, New Zealand. *T:* (9) 2786564.

See also J. C. Rutter.

RUTTER, His Honour John Cleverdon; a Circuit Judge, 1972–92 (a Senior Circuit Judge, 1990–92); *b* 18 Sept. 1919; 2nd *s* of late Edgar John Rutter; *m* 1951, Jill (*d* 1993), *d* of late Maxwell Duncan McIntosh; one *s* one *d*. *Educ:* Cardiff High Sch.; Univ. Coll., of SW of England, Exeter (Open Schol.); Keble Coll., Oxford. MA Oxon; LLB London. Royal Artillery, 1939–46; commnd 1941; served overseas. Called to the Bar, Lincoln's Inn, 1948; practised Wales and Chester Circuit, 1948–66, Stipendiary Magistrate for City of Cardiff, 1966–71. A Legal Member, Mental Health Review Tribunal for Wales Region, 1960–66. An Assistant Recorder of: Cardiff, 1962–66; Merthyr Tydfil, 1962–66; Swansea, 1965–66; Dep. Chm., Glamorgan QS, 1969–71. *Recreations:* golf, reading. *Address:* Law Courts, Cardiff. *T:* Cardiff (0222) 45931.

See also Sir F. W. E. Rutter.

RUTTER, John Milford; composer and conductor; *b* 24 Sept. 1945; *s* of Laurence Frederick and Joan Mary Rutter; *m* 1980, JoAnne Redden; two *s* and one step *d*. *Educ:* Highgate Sch.; Clare Coll., Cambridge (MA, MusB). Fellow and Director of Music, Clare Coll., Cambridge, 1975–79; Founder and Director, Cambridge Singers, 1981–. Hon. FGCM 1988; Hon. Fellow, Westminster Choir Coll., Princeton, 1980. *Publications:* compositions include choral pieces, anthems and carols, 1969–. *Address:* Old Laceys, St John's Street, Duxford, Cambridge CB2 4RA. *T:* Cambridge (01223) 832474, *Fax:* Cambridge (01223) 836723.

RUTTER, Sir Michael (Llewellyn), Kt 1992; CBE 1985; MD; FRCP, FRCPsych; FRS 1987; Professor of Child Psychiatry, since 1973, Hon. Director, MRC Child Psychiatry Unit, since 1984, and Director, MRC Research Centre for Social, Genetic and Developmental Psychiatry, since 1994, University of London Institute of Psychiatry; *b* 15 Aug. 1933; *s* of Llewellyn Charles Rutter and Winifred Olive Rutter; *m* 1958, Marjorie Heys; one *s* two *d*. *Educ:* Moorestown Friends' Sch., USA; Wolverhampton Grammar Sch.; Bootham Sch., York; Birmingham Univ. Med. Sch. (MB ChB 1955, MD Hons 1963). MRCS 1955; LRCP 1955, MRCP 1958, FRCP 1972; FRCPsych 1971. Training in paediatrics, neurology and internal medicine, 1955–58; Maudsley Hosp., 1958–61; Nuffield Med. Travelling Fellow, Albert Einstein Coll. of Medicine, NY, 1961–62; Mem., Sci. Staff, MRC Social Psych. Res. Unit, 1962–65; Sen. Lectr, then Reader, Univ. of London Inst. of Psych., 1966–73. Fellow, Center for Advanced Study in Behavioral Scis, Stanford, Calif, 1979–80. Lectures: Goulstonian, RCP, 1973; Salmon, NY Acad. of Medicine, 1979; Adolf Meyer, Amer. Psych. Assoc., 1985; Maudsley, RCPsych, 1986. Founding Mem., Acad. Europaea, 1988; Foreign Associate Member: Inst. of Medicine,

Nat. Acad. of Scis, USA, 1988; US Nat. Acad. of Educn, 1990; Foreign Hon. Mem., Amer. Acad. of Arts and Scis, 1989. Hon. FBPsS 1978; Hon. Fellow, Amer. Acad. of Pediatrics, 1981. Hon. DSSc Univ. of Leiden, 1985; Hon. Dr Leuven, 1990; Hon. DSc: Birmingham, 1990; Chicago, 1991; Minnesota, 1993; Hon. MD Edinburgh, 1990. Numerous awards, UK and USA. *Publications:* Children of Sick Parents, 1966; (jtly) A Neuropsychiatric Study in Childhood, 1970; (ed jtly) Education, Health and Behaviour, 1970; (ed) Infantile Autism, 1971; Maternal Deprivation Reassessed, 1972, 2nd edn 1981; (ed jtly) The Child with Delayed Speech, 1972; Helping Troubled Children, 1975; (jtly) Cycles of Disadvantage, 1976; (ed jtly) Child Psychiatry, 1977, 2nd edn as Child and Adolescent Psychiatry, 1985, 4th edn, 1994; (ed jtly) Autism, 1978; Changing Youth in a Changing Society, 1979; (jtly) Fifteen Thousand Hours: secondary schools and their effects on children, 1979; (ed) Scientific Foundations of Developmental Psychiatry, 1981; A Measure of Our Values: goals and dilemmas in the upbringing of children, 1983; (jtly) Lead Versus Health, 1983; (jtly) Juvenile Delinquency, 1983; (ed) Developmental Neuropsychiatry, 1983; (ed jtly) Stress, Coping and Development, 1983; (ed jtly) Depression and Young People, 1986; (jtly) Treatment of Autistic Children, 1987; (ed jtly) Language Development and Disorders, 1987; (jtly) Parenting Breakdown: the making and breaking of inter-generational links, 1988; (ed jtly) Assessment and Diagnosis in Child Psychopathology, 1988; (ed) Studies of Psychological Risk: the power of longitudinal data, 1988; (ed jtly) Straight and Devious Pathways from Childhood to Adulthood, 1990; (ed jtly) Biological Risk Factors for Psychosocial Disorders, 1991; (jtly) Developing Minds: challenge and continuity across the life span, 1993; (ed jtly) Development Through Life: a handbook for clinicians, 1994; (ed jtly) Stress, Risk and Resilience in Children and Adolescents: processes, mechanisms and interventions, 1994; (ed jtly) Psychosocial Disorders in Young People, 1995. *Recreations:* fell walking, tennis, wine tasting, theatre, family. *Address:* 190 Court Lane, Dulwich, SE21 7ED. *Club:* Royal Society of Medicine.

RUTTER, Air Vice-Marshal (Retd) Norman Colpoy Simpson, CB 1965; CBE 1945; idc; jssc; psa; Sen. Tech. Staff Officer, Bomber Command, 1961–65; *b* 1909; *s* of Rufus John Rutter; *m* 1936, Irene Sophia (*d* 1983), *d* of late Colonel A. M. Lloyd; one *s* one *d*. Air Cdre, 1957; Air Officer Commanding and Commandant of the Royal Air Force Technical College, Henlow, 1959–61. CEng, FIMechE; FRAeS. *Address:* 37 Meadow Road, Pinner, Mddx HA5 1EB.

RUTTER, Trevor John, CBE 1990 (OBE 1976); Assistant Director General, British Council, 1990–91, retired; *b* 26 Jan. 1934; *s* of late Alfred and Agnes Rutter; *m* 1959, Josephine Henson; one *s*. *Educ:* Monmouth Sch.; Brasenose Coll., Oxford (BA). National Service, Army, 1955–57. British Council, Indonesia, W Germany (Munich), London, 1959–66; First Secretary, Foreign Office, 1967; British Council, 1968–91: Representative: Singapore, 1968–71; Thailand, 1971–75; various appointments, London, 1975–85, including: Head, Home Div., 1980; Asst Dir Gen., 1981–85; Rep. in W Germany, 1986–90. *Address:* 8 De Vere Close, Wivenhoe, Essex CO7 9AX. *T:* Wivenhoe (01206) 822562; Niederhutstrasse 49, 53474 Bad Neuenahr-Ahrweiler, Germany.

RYAN, Prof. Alan James, FBA 1986; Professor of Politics, Princeton University, 1988–Aug. 1996; Fellow, since 1969, Warden, from Sept. 1996, New College, Oxford; *b* 9 May 1940; *s* of James William Ryan and Ivy Ryan; *m* 1971, Kathleen Alyson Lane; one *d*. *Educ:* Christ's Hospital; Balliol Coll., Oxford. Lectr in Politics, Univ. of Keele, 1963–66, Univ. of Essex, 1966–69; Lectr in Politics, 1969–78, Reader, 1978–87, Univ. of Oxford. Visiting Professor in Politics: City University of New York, 1967–68; Univs of Texas, 1972, California, 1977, the Witwatersrand, 1978; Vis. Fellow, ANU, 1974, 1979; Mellon Fellow, Inst. for Advanced Study, Princeton, 1991–92; de Carle Lectr, Univ. of Otago, 1983. Official Mem., CNAA, 1975–80. Delegate, Oxford Univ. Press, 1983–87. *Publications:* The Philosophy of John Stuart Mill, 1970, 2nd edn 1987; The Philosophy of the Social Sciences, 1970; J. S. Mill, 1975; Property and Political Theory, 1984; (ed jtly) The Blackwell Encyclopaedia of Political Thought, 1987; Property, 1987; Bertrand Russell: a political life, 1988. *Recreations:* dinghy sailing, long train journeys. *Address:* (until Sept. 1996) Department of Politics, Princeton University, Princeton, NJ 08544, USA; (from Sept. 1996) Warden's Lodgings, New College, Oxford OX1 3BN. *Club:* United Oxford & Cambridge University.

RYAN, (Christopher) Nigel (John), CBE 1977; freelance writer, Chairman, TV-am News, 1989–92 (Director, 1985–92); *b* 12 Dec. 1929; *s* of late Brig. C. E. Ryan, MC, RA; *m* 1984, Susan Anne Crewe (marr. diss.), *qv*. *Educ:* Ampleforth Coll.; Queen's Coll., Oxford (MA). Joined Reuters, London, 1954; Foreign Corresp., 1957–60; joined Independent Television News, 1961, Editor, 1968–71, Editor and Chief Executive, 1971–77; Vice-Pres., NBC News, America, 1977–80; Dir of Progs, Thames Television, 1980–82. Silver Medal, Royal Television Soc., 1970; Desmond Davis Award, 1972. *Publications:* A Hitch or Two in Afghanistan, 1983; (jtly) The Scholar and the Gypsy, 1992; trans. novels from French by Georges Simenon and others. *Address:* 28 St Petersburgh Place, W2 4LD. *T:* 0171–221 4170. *Club:* Beefsteak.

RYAN, Maj.-Gen. Denis Edgar, CB 1987; Director of Army Education, 1984–87; *b* 18 June 1928; *s* of Reginald Arthur Ryan and Amelia (*née* Smith); *m* 1955, Jean Mary Bentley; one *s* one *d*. *Educ:* Sir William Borlase School, Marlow; King's College, London (LLB). Commissioned RAEC, 1950; served BAOR, 1950–54; Instr, RMA Sandhurst, 1954–56; Adjt, Army Sch. of Educn, 1957–59; Staff Coll., 1960; served in Cyprus, Kenya and UK, 1961–67; CAES, HQ 4 Div., BAOR, 1968–70; Cabinet Office, 1970–72; TDA, Staff Coll., 1972–75; Col GS MoD, 1976–78; Chief Education Officer: HQ SE Dist, 1978–79; HQ BAOR, 1979–82; Comd, Education, UK, 1982–84. Col Comdt, RAEC, 1990–92; Dep. Col Comdt, AGC, 1992–93. *Recreations:* cricket, tennis, rugby, music, theatre. *Club:* Army and Navy.

RYAN, Sir Derek (Gerald), 4th Bt *cr* 1919, of Hintlesham, Suffolk; architect; *b* 25 March 1954; *s* of Sir Derek Gerald Ryan, 3rd Bt and of Penelope Anne Hawkings; *S* father, 1990; *m* (marr. diss.). *Educ:* Univ. of California at Berkeley (BAED 1977). Washington State Architect License #4296, 1984; NCARB Certificate #32,269, 1984. *Recreations:* skiing, guitar. *Heir: cousin* Desmond Maurice Ryan [*b* 16 Sept. 1918; *m* 1942, Margaret Catherine, *d* of A. H. Brereton; three *s*]. *Address:* 4618 South Austin Street, Seattle, WA 98118, USA. *T:* (206) 7236182.

RYAN, Gerard Charles, QC 1981; a Recorder of the Crown Court, since 1986; *b* 16 Dec. 1931; *er s* of Frederick Charles Ryan, Hove, and Louie Violet Ryan (*née* Ball); *m* 1960, Sheila Morag Clark Cameron, *qv*; two *s*. *Educ:* Clayesmore Sch.; Brighton Coll.; Pembroke Coll., Cambridge (Exhibnr; MA). Served RA, 1955–57 (Lieut). Called to the Bar, Middle Temple, 1955, Bencher, 1988; Harmsworth Scholar, 1956. Chm., Tribunal of Inquiry into Loscoe (Derbyshire) gas explosion, 1986–87. Chairman: Soc. of Sussex Downsmen, 1977–80; Murray Downland Trust, 1993–. *Publication:* (with A. O. B. Harris) Outline of the Law of Common Land, 1967. *Recreations:* conservation, growing trees and other plants, walking. *Address:* 13 Westmoreland Place, SW1V 4AA; 2 Harcourt Buildings, Temple, EC4Y 9DB. *T:* 0171–353 8415. *Club:* United Oxford & Cambridge University.

RYAN, John; Management consultant and lecturer; *b* 30 April 1940; *m* 1964, Eunice Ann Edmonds; two *s*. *Educ:* Lanark Grammar School; Glasgow University. Member, National Association of Labour Student Organisations, 1958–62; formerly Youth Organiser, Lanark City Labour Party; Member, Executive Committee, North Paddington Labour Party, 1964–66. Contested (Lab) Buckinghamshire South, 1964; MP (Lab) Uxbridge, 1966–70. Member, Fabian Society, 1961; Dir, Tribune Publications Ltd, 1969–. Mem., Inst. of Marketing; Associate Member: Market Res. Soc.; BIM. *Recreations:* golf, walking.

RYAN, Most Rev. Laurence; *see* Kildare and Leighlin, Bishop of (RC).

RYAN, Nigel; *see* Ryan, C. N. J.

RYAN, Peter James, QPM 1991; National Director of Police Training and Commandant, Police Staff College, since 1993; *b* 18 May 1944; *s* of late Lawrence Joseph Ryan and of Margaret Jane (*née* Stephenson); *m* 1985, Adrienne Margaret Butterworth; two *d*. *Educ:* Newman Coll., Preston; Univ. of Lancaster (BA Hons); Preston Poly. (DMS); Open Univ. (MSc). FIPM 1994. Lancs Constabulary, 1963–83; Metropolitan Police, 1983–84; Asst Chief Constable, N Yorks Police, 1984–88; Dep. Chief Constable, Durham Constabulary, 1988–90; Chief Constable, Norfolk, 1990–93. Sec., 1991–92, Chm., 1992–93, Personnel & Trng Cttee, ACPO. Mem., BTEC, 1985–88. Vis. Fellow, UEA Sch. of Educn, 1993–; Grad., FBI Nat. Exec. Inst., 1994. Asst Dir Gen., St John Ambulance, 1995. FIMgt 1980. OStJ 1995. *Publications:* contrib. Police Jl and similar professional jls. *Recreations:* occasional golf, riding, water-colour painting, reading. *Address:* (office) Bramshill House, Bramshill, Hook, Hants RG27 0JW. *T:* Basingstoke (01256) 602236. *Club:* Royal Air Force.

RYAN, Sheila Morag Clark, (Mrs G. C. Ryan); *see* Cameron, S. M. C.

RYAN, Prof. Terence John, DM; FRCP; Clinical Professor of Dermatology, Oxford University, since 1992; Fellow, Green College, since 1979; *b* 24 July 1932; *s* of Gerald John Ryan and Kathleen May Knight; *m* 1968, Trudie Anne Merry; one *s* one *d*. *Educ:* numerous schs including: Michael Hall (Rudolf Steiner); Brickwall Sch., Northiam; Worcester Coll., Oxford (BM, BCh 1957; DM 1977). FRCP 1975. Capt. RAMC, 1955–60: O i/c Dept of Dermatol. and ENT Surgery, Colchester Mil. Hosp.; Radcliffe Infirmary, Oxford: Hse Officer, 1958; Registrar and Sen. Registrar in Dermatol., 1962–68; Lectr and Sen. Lectr, Inst. of Dermatol., London Univ., 1967–71; Dept of Dermatol., RPMS, 1968–71; Lectr in Dermatology, Oxford Univ., 1971–92. Cons. Dermatologist, Oxon HA, 1969–. Vis. Prof., Brookes Univ., Oxford, 1991–; Adjunct Prof., Jefferson Univ., Philadelphia, 1988–. Med. Advr, St Francis Leprosy Guild. Promoter, Sine Lepra and Healthy Skin for All programmes, Internat. League of Dermatologists. Pres., Section of Dermatol., RSocMed, 1990. Mem., Internat. Cttee of Dermatol., 1987–; Pres., Internat. Soc. for Dermatol., 1994–. Hon. Mem., various foreign nat. socs of dermatol. KStJ 1984 (County Surgeon Comr, then Comdr, SJAB, Oxon). *Publications:* (contrib.) Oxford Textbook of Medicine, 3rd edn, 1995; contrib. textbooks of dermatology and numerous in field of blood supply, dermatology and internat. dermatological policy. *Recreations:* painting water-colours, flowers, piano playing, foreign travel. *Address:* Department of Dermatology, The Churchill Hospital, Headington, Oxford OX3 7LJ. *T:* Oxford (01865) 228258; Abbey Willows, Rayford Lane, Middle Barton, Chipping Norton, Oxon OX7 7DD.

RYAN, Dr Thomas Anthony, (Tony); Chairman: Executive Board, GE Capital Aviation Services Inc., since 1994; Ryanair, since 1996; *b* 2 Feb. 1936; *m*; three *s*. *Educ:* Christian Brothers Sch., Thurles, Co. Tipperary; North Western Univ., Chicago. Aer Lingus, 1956–75; GPA Gp, 1975–93. Consul for Republic of Mexico to Ireland. Mem., Bd of Govs, Nat. Gall. of Ireland. Hon. Mem., Univ. of Limerick Foundn, 1986. Hon. LLD: TCD, 1987; NUI, 1987; Limerick, 1992. *Recreations:* farming, the arts. *Address:* Le Rocamar, 10 Rue Colonel Bellando De Castro, Monte Carlo 98000, Monaco-Ville.

RYBCZYNSKI, Tadeusz Mieczyslaw, FCIB; *b* 21 May 1923; *s* of Karol Rybczynski and Helena (*née* Sawicka); *m* 1951, Helena Perucka; one *d*. *Educ:* primary and secondary schs, Lwow, Poland; LSE, Univ. of London (BCom, MScEcon). FCIB (FIB 1966). Lloyds Bank, 1949–53; Lazard Brothers & Co. Ltd, 1954–88; Dir, Lazard Securities Ltd, 1969–86; Econ. Advr, Lazard Brothers & Co. Ltd, 1973–88; Dir, Euro-Canadian Internat. Investment Management, then Sund and Wrigley & Co. Ltd, 1987–93. Vis. Professor: Univ. of Surrey, 1968–74; City Univ., 1974–. Chm., Soc. of Business Economists, 1962–75 (Fellow, 1988). Member: Monopolies and Mergers Commn, 1978–81; Council of Management and Exec. Cttee, NIESR, 1968– (also Governor); Exec. Cttee and Council, Inst. of Fiscal Studies, 1988–. Dir, European Council for Trade Promotion, 1994–95. Vice-Pres., Sect. F (Econs), BAAS, 1995–; Member: Council, REconS, 1969– (Treas., 1974–87; Vice-Pres., 1987–); Governing Body, Trade Policy Res. Centre, 1968–; Cttee, Foreign Affairs Club, 1968–85; Adv. Bd in Banking and Finance, Univ. of Aston Management Centre, 1973–82; Sci. Cttee, Centre for Monetary and Banking Studies, Univ. of Geneva, 1973–; Court, Brunel Univ., 1976–79; Trustee, Centre for Res. for Post-Communist Econs. Treas. and Mem. Cttee, Round Table, 1981–95. Hon. DSc City Univ., 1990. Harms Award, Inst. for Economic Research, Univ. of Kiel, 1983; Abramson Award, Nat. Assoc. of Business Economists, USA, 1980. *Publications:* (contrib.) Comparative Banking, ed H. W. Auburn, 1960 (3rd edn 1969); (contrib.) Long Range Planning, Paris and New York, 1967; (ed jtly and contrib.) The Economist in Business, 1967; (contrib.) Readings in International Economics, ed R. E. Caves and H. Johnson, 1968; (ed and contrib.) Value Added Tax-the UK position and the European experience, 1969; (contrib.) Money in Britain 1959–69, ed R. Croome and H. Johnson, 1970; (contrib.) Problems of Investment, ed Sir Robert Shone, 1971; (contrib.) Users of Economics, ed G. D. N. Worswick, 1972; (ed) A New Era in Competition, 1973; (ed and contrib.) The Economics of the Oil Crisis, 1976; (contrib.) Financial Management Handbook, 1977; (contrib.) The International Monetary System 1971–80, 1983; (contrib.) International Lending in a Fragile World Economy, 1983; articles in serious jls, and in academic and bank revs. *Recreations:* opera, ballet, history, international affairs, travel. *Address:* 2 Windyridge Close, Parkside Avenue, SW19 5HB. *T:* 0181–946 7363. *Club:* Reform.

RYCROFT, Prof. Michael John, PhD; Professor, International Space University, France, since 1995; *b* 15 July 1938; *s* of late John Lambert Rycroft and Molly Elizabeth Rycroft (*née* Riglen); *m* 1967, Mary Cheeseright; three *s*. *Educ:* Merchant Taylors' School, Northwood; Imperial Coll., London (BSc Hons Physics); Churchill Coll., Cambridge (PhD Met. Physics). CPhys, MInstP; CMath, FIMA; FRAS; FRMetS. Lectr, Dept of Physics, Univ. of Southampton, 1966–79; Head, Atmospheric Scis Div., NERC British Antarctic Survey, Cambridge, 1979–90; Prof. of Aerospace, 1990–94, Hd, Coll. of Aeronautics, 1990–92, Cranfield Inst. of Technol., subseq. Cranfield Univ. Vis. Prof., Dept. of Physics, Univ. of Houston, 1974–75. Mem., Internat. Acad. of Astronautics, 1986. Editor-in-Chief, Jl of Atmospheric and Terrestrial Physics, 1989–. *Publications:* (with D. Shapland) Spacelab: research in Earth orbit, 1984; (ed) Cambridge Encyclopedia of Space, 1990. *Recreations:* music, outdoor activities, wining and dining. *Address:* Bassett Mead, 35 Millington Road, Cambridge CB3 9HW. *T:* Cambridge (01223) 353839; 1 rue des Bouvreuils, 67100 Strasbourg, France. *T:* 88341206.

RYCROFT, Sir Richard Newton, 7th Bt, *cr* 1784; *b* 23 Jan. 1918; *yr s* of Sir Nelson Edward Oliver Rycroft, 6th Bt, and Ethel Sylvia (*d* 1952), *d* of late Robert Nurton, Odcombe, Yeovil; *S* father 1958; *m* 1947, Ann, *d* of late Hugh Bellingham-Smith, Alfriston, Sussex, and Mrs Harvey Robarts; two *d. Educ:* Winchester; Christ Church, Oxford (BA). Served War of 1939–45: Bedfordshire and Hertfordshire Regt, on special service work in Balkans (Major, despatches); Knight's Cross of Royal Order of Phœnix with Swords (Greece). *Heir: cousin* Richard John Rycroft, *b* 15 June 1946. *Address:* Winalls Wood House, Stuckton, Fordingbridge, Hampshire SP6 2HQ. *T:* Fordingbridge (01425) 652263.
See also Viscount FitzHarris.

RYDBECK, Olof; Comdr 1st Class, Order of the Star of the North, Sweden, 1973; Commissioner-General, United Nations Relief and Works Agency, 1979–85; *b* Djursholm, 15 April 1913; *s* of Oscar Rydbeck and Signe Olson; *m* 1940, Monica Schnell; one *s* one *d. Educ:* Univ. of Uppsala, Sweden (BA 1934, LLB 1939). Attaché, Min. for Foreign Affairs, 1939; Berlin, 1940; Ankara, 1941; Stockholm, 1942; Second Sec., 1943; Washington, 1945–50 (First Sec., 1946); Bonn, 1950; Head of Press Sect., Min. for For. Affairs, 1952; Dir Gen., Swedish Broadcasting Corp., 1955–70; Perm. Rep. to UN, 1970–76; Rep. of Sweden to Security Council, 1975–76; Special Rep. of Sec. Gen. on Western Sahara, 1976; Ambassador of Sweden to the UK, 1977–79. Chairman: Adv. Cttee on Outer Space Communications, UNESCO, 1966–70; Working Gp on Direct Broadcast Satellites, UN Cttee on Peaceful Uses of Outer Space, 1969–75; Cttee of Trustees, UN Trust Fund for S Africa, 1970–75; Prep. Cttee, World Food Conf., 1974; Second Cttee, 30th Gen. Assembly, 1975. Chairman: Assoc. of Royal Swedish Nat. Defence Coll., 1957–70; Internat. Broadcasting Inst., Rome, 1967–70; Hon. Pres., EBU, 1964– (Pres., 1961–64). Member: Central Cttee, Swedish Red Cross; Nat. Swedish Preparedness Commn for Psychol. Defence, 1954–70 (Vice Chm., 1962–70); Royal Swed. Acad. of Music, 1962–. Member Boards: Swed. Inst., 1953–55; Amer.-Swed. News Exchange, 1953–55; Swed. Tourist Traffic Assoc., 1953–55; Stockholm Philharmonic Soc., 1955–62; Swed. Central News Agency, 1967–70; Swed. Inst. of Internat. Affairs, 1967–. King's Medal, 12th size, Sweden, 1980; Medal of Serahims, Sweden, 1987; Commander 1st Class: Order of the White Rose (Finland); Order of the Falcon (Iceland); Comdr, Order of the Dannebrog (Denmark); Verdienstkreutz (FRG). *Recreations:* music, books. *Address:* 3 avenue Charles de Gaulle, 69260 Charbonnières-les-Bains, France.

RYDER, family name of **Earl of Harrowby** and of **Baron Ryder of Eaton Hastings.**

RYDER OF EATON HASTINGS, Baron *cr* 1975 (Life Peer), of Eaton Hastings, Oxfordshire; **Sydney Thomas Franklin, (Don), Ryder,** Kt 1972; Chairman, National Enterprise Board, 1975–77; *b* 16 Sept. 1916; *s* of John Ryder; *m* 1950; one *s* one *d. Educ:* Ealing. Editor, Stock Exchange Gazette, 1950–60; Jt Man. Dir, 1960–61, Sole Man. Dir, 1961–63, Kelly Iliffe Holdings, and Associated Iliffe Press Ltd; Dir, Internat. Publishing Corp., 1963–70; Man. Dir, Reed Paper Gp, 1963–68; Chm. and Chief Executive, Reed International Ltd, 1968–75; Dir, MEPC Ltd, 1972–75. Industrial Advr to the govt, 1974. Member: British Gas Corp., 1973–78; Reserve Pension Bd, 1973; Council and Bd of Fellows, BIM, 1970; Court and Council, Cranfield Inst. of Technology, 1970–74; Council, UK S Africa Trade Assoc., 1974; Nat. Materials Handling Centre (Pres., 1970–77); Council, Industrial Soc., 1971; NEDC, 1976–77. Vice-Pres., RoSPA, 1973. *Recreations:* sailing, chess. *Address:* House of Lords, SW1A 0PW.

RYDER OF WARSAW, Baroness *cr* 1979 (Life Peer), of Warsaw in Poland and of Cavendish in the County of Suffolk; **(Sue Ryder);** CMG 1976; OBE 1957; Founder and Social Worker, Sue Ryder Foundation for the Sick and Disabled of all Age Groups; *b* 3 July 1923; *d* of late Charles and Elizabeth Ryder; *m* 1959, Geoffrey Leonard Cheshire (Baron Cheshire, VC, OM, DSO, DFC) (*d* 1992); one *s* one *d. Educ:* Benenden Sch., Kent. Served War of 1939–45 with FANY and with Special Ops Executive. Co-Founder, Ryder-Cheshire Foundn; Trustee: Cheshire Foundn; World Meml Fund for Disaster Relief. Hon. LLD: Liverpool, 1973; Exeter, 1980; London, 1981; Leeds, 1984; Cambridge, 1989; Hon. DLitt Reading, 1982; Hon. DCL Kent, 1986; DU Essex, 1993. Holds Commander's Cross of Order of Polonia Restituta, Poland, 1992 (Officer's Cross, 1965); Medal of Yugoslav Flag with Gold Wreath and Diploma, 1971; Golden Order of Merit, Polish People's Republic, 1976; Order of Smile (Poland), 1980. *Publications:* Remembrance (annual leaflet of the Sue Ryder Foundation); And the Morrow is Theirs (autobiog.), 1975; Child of My Love (autobiog.), 1986. *Address:* Sue Ryder Home, Cavendish, Sudbury, Suffolk CO10 8AY.

RYDER, Edward Alexander, CB 1992; HM Chief Inspector of Nuclear Installations, Health and Safety Executive, 1985–91; Joint Chairman and Head of UK Delegation, Channel Tunnel Safety Authority, since 1992; *b* 9 Nov. 1931; *s* of Alexander Harry and Gwendoline Gladys Ryder; *m* 1956, Janet; one *s* one *d. Educ:* Cheltenham Grammar School; Bristol University (BSc). CPhys; FInstP. Flying Officer, RAF, 1953–55; Engineer, GEC Applied Electronics Labs, 1955–57; Control Engineer, Hawker Siddeley Nuclear Power Co., 1957–61; Sen. Engineer, CEGB, 1961–71; Principal Inspector, then Superintending Inspector, HM Nuclear Installations Inspectorate, 1971–80; Head of Hazardous Installations Policy Branch, 1980–85, Head of Nuclear Installations Policy Branch, 1985, HSE. Sec., Adv. Cttee on Major Hazards, 1980–85. Chairman: HSC Working Gp on Ionising Radiations, 1987–91; IAEA Nuclear Safety Standards Adv. Gp, 1988–93; Mem., Intergovtl Commn for Channel Tunnel, 1992–. *Recreation:* golf—or is it nature study. *Address:* Pinewood, Baskerville Lane, Lower Shiplake, Henley on Thames, Oxon RG9 3JY.

RYDER, Eric Charles, MA, LLB; Barrister; Professor of English Law in the University of London (University College) 1960–82, now Professor Emeritus; *b* 28 July 1915; *er s* of late Charles Henry Ryder, solicitor, Hanley, Staffs, and of Ellen Miller; *m* 1941, Nancy Winifred Roberts. *Educ:* Hanley High School; Gonville and Caius College, Cambridge (scholar). BA (Law Tripos Parts I and II, 1st Cl.), 1936; LLB (1st Cl.) 1937; MA 1940; Tapp Law Scholar, Gonville and Caius College, 1937; called to Bar, Gray's Inn, 1937; practice at Chancery Bar. Ministry of Food, 1941–44; Lecturer in Law, King's College, Newcastle upon Tyne, 1944; Dean of Faculty of Law, Univ. of Durham, 1947–60; Professor of Law, Univ. of Durham (King's College), 1953–60. Practised as conveyancing counsel, Newcastle upon Tyne, 1944–53. *Publications:* Hawkins and Ryder on the Construction of Wills, 1965; contrib. to legal periodicals. *Address:* 9 Arlington Court, Kenton Avenue, Gosforth, Newcastle upon Tyne NE3 4JR. *T:* 0191–285 1172.

RYDER, Dr Peter, CB 1994; Managing Director (Operations) (formerly Deputy Chief Executive and Director of Operations), Meteorological Office, since 1990; *b* 10 March 1942; *s* of Percival Henry Sussex Ryder and Bridget (*née* McCormack); *m* 1965, Jacqueline Doris Sylvia Rigby; two *s* one *d. Educ:* Yorebridge Grammar Sch., Askrigg; Univ. of Leeds (BSc 1963; PhD 1966). Research Asst, Physics Dept, Univ. of Leeds, 1966–67; Meteorological Office, 1967–: Asst Dir, Cloud Physics Res, 1976–82; Asst Dir, Systems Develt, 1982–84; Dep. Dir, Observational Services, 1984–88; Dep. Dir, Forecasting Services, 1988–89; Dir of Services, 1989–90. Royal Meteorological Society: Mem. Council, 1980–83; Mem., Qly Jl Editing Cttee, 1981–84. William Gaskell Meml Medal, RMetS, 1981; L. G. Groves Meml Prize for Meteorology, MoD, 1982. *Publications:* papers in learned jls on experimental atmospheric physics and meteorology. *Recreations:* gardening, walking, fishing, photography, philately. *Address:* c/o Meteorological Office, London Road, Bracknell, Berks RG12 2SZ.

RYDER, Rt. Hon. Richard (Andrew), OBE 1981; PC 1990; MP (C) Mid Norfolk, since 1983; *b* 4 Feb. 1949; *s* of Richard Stephen Ryder, JP, DL, and Margaret MacKenzie; *m* 1981, Caroline, MBE, *o d* of Sir David Stephens; one *d* (one *s* decd). *Educ:* Radley; Magdalene Coll., Cambridge. BA Hons History, 1971. Chm., Univ. Cons. Assoc. Political Secretary: to Leader of the Opposition, 1975–79; to Prime Minister, 1979–81. Partner, M. Ryder and Sons; journalist. Contested (C) Gateshead E, Feb. and Oct., 1974. Parliamentary Private Secretary: to Financial Sec. to the Treasury, 1984; to Sec. of State for Foreign and Commonwealth Affairs, 1984–86; an Asst Govt Whip, 1986–88; Parly Under-Sec. of State, MAFF, 1988–89; Econ. Sec. to HM Treasury, 1989–90; Paymaster General, 1990; Parly Sec. to HM Treasury and Govt Chief Whip, 1990–95. Chm., Cons. Foreign and Commonwealth Council, 1984–89. *Address:* House of Commons, SW1A 0AA.

RYDER, Dr Richard Hood Jack Dudley; author, campaigner; Parliamentary Consultant, Political Animal Lobby Ltd, since 1991; *b* 3 July 1940; *s* of late Major D. C. D. Ryder, JP and Vera Mary (*née* Cook); *m* 1974, Audrey Jane Smith; one *s* one *d. Educ:* Sherborne Sch.; Cambridge Univ. (MA; PhD 1993); Edinburgh Univ. (DCP); Columbia Univ., NY (Fellow). AFBPsS; FZS. Sen. Clinical Psychologist, Warneford Hosp., Oxford, 1967–84; Principal Clin. Psychologist, St James Hosp., Portsmouth, 1983–84. Chm., Oxford Div. of Clin. Psych., 1981–83; Member: Oxford Regional Adolescent Service, 1971–84; DHSS Health Adv. Service, 1977–78. Royal Society for Prevention of Cruelty to Animals: Mem. Council, 1972– (Chm., 1977–79; Vice Chm., 1990–91); Chairman: Political Cttee, 1979–80; Chm., Animal Experimentation Adv. Cttee, 1983–85; Public Relns and Campaign Cttee, 1990–91; Scientific Cttee, 1992–. Founder Mem., Gen. Election Coordinating Cttee on Animal Protection, 1978; Prog. Organiser, IFAW, 1984–88; UK Delegate, Eurogroup, 1980. Chm., Liberal Animal Welfare Gp, 1981–88; Member: Liberal Party Council, 1983–87; Liberal Party Policy Panels on defence, health, home affairs, Eur. affairs, foreign affairs, environment, 1981–88; contested (L): Buckingham, 1983; Teignbridge, 1987. Pres., Lib. Democrats Animal Protection Gp, 1989–91. Chairman: Teignbridge NSPCC, 1984–87; Teignbridge Home Start, 1987–89. Broadcaster and writer on psychological, ethical, political and animal protection subjects. FRSA 1992. *Publications:* Speciesism, 1970; Victims of Science, 1975, 2nd edn 1984; (ed) Animal Rights—a Symposium, 1979; Animal Revolution: changing attitudes to speciesism, 1989; (ed) Animal Welfare and the Environment, 1992. *Recreations:* history, opera, croquet. *Clubs:* National Liberal, Royal Over-Seas League.

RYDILL, Prof. Louis Joseph, OBE 1962; FEng 1982; RCNC; Consultant in Naval Ship Design, since 1986; Professor of Naval Architecture, University College London, 1981–85, now Emeritus Professor; *b* 16 Aug. 1922; *s* of Louis and Queenie Rydill; *m* 1949, Eva (*née* Newman); two *d. Educ:* HM Dockyard Sch., Devonport; RNEC Keyham; RNC Greenwich; Royal Corps of Naval Constructors. FRINA (Gold Medallist). Asst Constructor, 1946–52; Constructor, 1952–62, incl. Asst Prof. of Naval Architecture, RNC Greenwich, 1953–57; Chief Constructor, 1962–72, incl. Prof. of Naval Architecture, RNC Greenwich and UCL, 1967–72; Asst Dir Submarines, Constructive, 1972–74; Dep. Dir Submarines (Polaris), 1974–76; Dir of Ship Design and Engrg (formerly Warship Design), MoD, 1976–81. Hon. Res. Fellow, UCL, 1974; Vis. Prof., US Naval Acad., Annapolis, Md, 1985–86. Silver Jubilee Medal, 1977. *Publication:* (jtly) Concepts in Submarine Design, 1993. *Recreations:* literature, theatre, jazz and other music. *Address:* The Lodge, Entry Hill Drive, Bath, Avon BA2 5NJ. *T:* Bath (01225) 427888.

RYKWERT, Prof. Joseph, MA (Cantab), DrRCA; Paul Philippe Cret Professor of Architecture, University of Pennsylvania, since 1988; *b* 5 April 1926; *s* of Szymon Rykwert and Elizabeth Melup; *m* 1st, 1960 (marr. diss. 1967); 2nd, 1972, Anne-Marie Sandersley; one *s* one *d. Educ:* Charterhouse; Bartlett Sch. of Architecture; Architectural Assoc. Lectr, Hochschule für Gestaltung, Ulm, 1958; Librarian and Tutor, Royal Coll. of Art, 1961–67; Prof. of Art, Univ. of Essex, 1967–80; Lectr on Arch., 1980–85, Reader, 1985–88, Univ. of Cambridge. Fellow, Inst. for Arch. and Urban Studies, NY, 1969–71; Sen. Fellow, Council of Humanities, Princeton Univ., 1971; Visiting Professor: Institut d'Urbanisme, Univ. of Paris, 1974–76; Princeton Univ., 1977; Andrew Mellon Vis. Prof., Cooper Union, NY, 1977; Slade Prof. of Fine Art, Cambridge Univ., 1979–80; Vis. Fellow, Darwin Coll., Cambridge, 1979–80; Sen. Fellow, Center for the Advanced Studies in the Visual Arts. Nat. Gall. of Art, Washington; Visiting Professor: Univ. of Louvain, 1981–84; Univ. of Pennsylvania, 1982–88; George Lurcy Vis. Prof., Columbia, 1986. Mem., Comité Internat. des Critiques d'Architecture. Mem. Commn, Venice Biennale, 1974–78. Consultant, Min. of Urban Develt and Ecology, Republic of Mexico, 1986–88. Co-ed., RES (Anthropology and Aesthetics), 1981–. Mem., Accademia di S Luca, 1993. Hon. DSc Edinburgh, 1995. Alfred Jurzykowski Foundn Award, 1990. Chevalier des Arts et des Lettres, 1984. *Publications:* The Golden House, 1947; (ed) The Ten Books of Architecture, by L. B. Alberti (annotated edn of Leoni trans. of 1756), 1955, new translation from Latin, as On the Art of Building in Ten Books, 1988; The Idea of a Town, 1963, 3rd edn 1988; Church Building, 1966; On Adam's House in Paradise, 1972, 2nd edn 1982; (ed) Parole nel Vuoto, by A. Loos, 1972; The First Moderns, 1980; The Necessity of Artifice, 1981; (with Anne Rykwert) The Brothers Adam, 1985; contrib. Arch. Rev., Burlington Mag., Lotus. *Recreations:* rare. *Address:* University of Pennsylvania, Meyerson Hall, Philadelphia, Pa 19104–6311, USA. *Club:* Savile.

RYLAND, Timothy Richard Godfrey Fetherstonhaugh; His Honour Judge Ryland; a Circuit Judge, since 1988; *b* 13 June 1938; *s* of late Richard Desmond Fetherstonhaugh Ryland and Frances Katharine Vernon Ryland; *m* 1991, Jean Margaret Muirhead. *Educ:* St Andrew's Coll.; TCD. BA (Moderatorship), LLB. Called to Bar, Gray's Inn, 1961. Dep. Circuit Judge, 1978; a Recorder, 1983–88. *Recreations:* opera, wine. *Clubs:* Lansdowne; Kildare Street and University (Dublin).

RYLANDS, George Humphrey Wolferstan, CH 1987; CBE 1961; MA; Fellow of King's College, Cambridge; Sometime Dean, Bursar, College Lecturer, and Director of Studies; University Lecturer in English Literature (retd); *b* 23 October 1902; *s* of Thomas Kirkland Rylands. *Educ:* Eton (King's Scholar); King's Coll., Cambridge (Scholar). Chm. of Directors and Trustees of the Arts Theatre, Cambridge, 1946–82; Governor of the Old Vic, 1945–78; Chm. of Apollo Soc., 1946–72. Member: Cheltenham Coll. Council, 1946–76; Council of RADA. Directed Hamlet with Sir John Gielgud, 1945; LP Recordings of the Shakespeare canon and the English Poets, for the British Council. Hon. LittD Cambridge, 1976; Hon. DLitt Durham, 1988. *Publications:* Words and Poetry, 1928; Shakespeare the Poet (in a Companion to Shakespeare Studies), 1934; Poems, 1931; The Ages of Man, a Shakespeare Anthology, 1939; Shakespeare's Poetic Energy (British Academy Lecture, 1951); Quoth the Raven "Nevermore": an anthology, 1984; Croaked the Raven: one NO more, 1988; College Verse, 1989. *Address:* King's College, Cambridge CB2 1ST. *T:* Cambridge (01223) 350411. *Clubs:* Athenæum, Garrick.

RYLE, Evelyn Margaret; Director, Business Competitiveness, Government Office for London, since 1995; *b* 26 March 1947; *d* of Paul McConnell Cassidy and Emily Margaret Cassidy (*née* Wright); *m* 1975, Group Captain Anthony E. Ryle, OBE, AFC, RAF; one *s* one *d*. *Educ:* King's Park Sch., Glasgow; Univ. of Glasgow (MA Hons; Dip. Management Studies). Dexion-Comino Internat., 1969; commnd WRAF; Flight Lieut, accountant officer, 1973; financial systems analyst: Dexion Gp, 1975; Southern Electricity, 1976; Departments of Trade and Industry, 1977–; British Steel Corp. Finance; Commercial Relations and Exports; Consumer Affairs; Vehicles Div.; Dep. Dir, IT Services, 1987; Head, Educn and Trng Policy, 1990; seconded to Design Council as Dir-Gen., 1993. MIMgt, FRSA. *Recreations:* family, music, gardening, needlework, walking. *Address:* Government Office for London, Business Competitiveness Directorate, (until April 1996) Bridge Place, 88–89 Eccleston Square, SW1V 1PT. *T:* 0171–215 0510; (from April 1996) Riverwalk House, 157–161 Millbank, SW1P 4RT. *Club:* Royal Air Force.

RYLE, Michael Thomas; Clerk of Committees, House of Commons, 1987–89, retired; *b* 30 July 1927; *s* of Peter Johnston Ryle and Rebecca Katie (*née* Boxall); *m* 1952, Bridget Moyes; one *s* two *d*. *Educ:* Newcastle upon Tyne Royal Grammar Sch.; Merton Coll., Oxford (1st Cl. Hons PPE, 1951; MA). Served RA, 1946–48 and TA, 1950–57. Entered Clerk's Dept, House of Commons, 1951; served in various offices; Clerk of Overseas Office, 1979–83; Principal Clerk, Table Office, 1983–84; Clerk of the Journals, 1985–87; attached Nova Scotia Legislature, 1976. Member: Study of Parlt Gp, 1964– (Founding Mem.; Chm., 1975–78; Pres., 1986–94); Council, Hansard Soc., 1974–94 (Mem. and Sec., Commn on the Legislative Process, 1991–93); Council, RIPA, 1982–88; Lambeth HMC, 1960–64. Governor, St Thomas' Hosp., 1964–74. Hon. Res. Fellow, Univ. of Exeter, 1990–. *Publications:* (ed with S. Walkland) The Commons in the Seventies, 1977, 2nd edn, as The Commons Today, 1981; (contrib.) The House of Commons in the Twentieth Century, 1979; (ed with P. G. Richards) The Commons Under Scrutiny, 1988; (with J. A. G. Griffith) Parliament, 1989; contrib. to books on parly practice and procedure; articles in Pol Qly, Parly Affairs, The Table, etc. *Recreations:* cricket, golf, bridge, watching birds, caravanning. *Address:* Jasmine Cottage, Winsford, Minehead, Somerset TA24 7JE. *T:* and *Fax:* Winsford (01643) 851317.

RYMAN, John; *b* 7 Nov. 1930. *Educ:* Leighton Park; Pembroke College, Oxford. Inns of Court Regt (TA), 1948–51. Called to the Bar, Middle Temple, 1957. Harmsworth Law Scholar. MP (Lab): Blyth, Oct. 1974–1983; Blyth Valley, 1983–87. Mem. Council, Assoc. of the Clergy, 1976. *Recreation:* Horses.

RYRIE, Sir William (Sinclair), KCB 1982 (CB 1979); Vice Chairman: Barings Holding Co., since 1995; Barings Investment Bank, since 1995; Deputy Chairman, Commonwealth Development Corporation, since 1994; *b* 10 Nov. 1928; *s* of Rev. Dr Frank Ryrie and Mabel Moncrieff Ryrie (*née* Watt); *m* 1st, 1953, Dorrit Klein (marr. diss. 1969); two *s* one *d*; 2nd, 1969, Christine Gray Thomson; one *s*. *Educ:* Mount Hermon Sch., Darjeeling; Heriot's Sch., Edinburgh; Edinburgh Univ. MA 1st cl. hons History, 1951. Nat. Service, 1951–53: Lieut, Intell. Corps, Malaya, 1952–53 (despatches). Colonial Office, 1953; seconded to Uganda, 1956–58; Principal 1958; transf. to Treasury, 1963; Asst Sec., internat. monetary affairs, 1966–69; Principal Private Sec. to Chancellor of Exchequer, 1969–71; Under-Sec., Public Sector Gp, HM Treasury, 1971–75; Econ. Minister, Washington, and UK Exec. Dir, IMF and IBRD, 1975–79; 2nd Perm. Sec. (Domestic Economy Sector), HM Treasury, 1980–82; Permanent Sec., ODA, FCO, 1982–84; Exec. Vice-Pres. and Chief Exec., IFC at World Bank, 1984–93. Director: Barings plc, 1994–95; W. S. Atkins Ltd, 1994–; Ashanti Goldfields Co. Ltd, 1995–. Dir, CARE Britain, 1994–. Pres., Edinburgh Univ. Devlt Trust, 1994–. CIMgt 1992; FRSA 1993. *Publication:* First World, Third World, 1995. *Recreations:* photography, walking, music. *Address:* Hawkwood, Hawkwood Lane, Chislehurst, Kent BR7 5PW. *Club:* Reform.

S

SAATCHI, Charles; Founder and Director, Saatchi & Saatchi Co., 1970–93; Partner, M & C Saatchi Agency, since 1995; *b* 9 June 1943; *m* Kay; one *d*. *Educ:* Christ's Coll., Finchley. Associate Director, Collett Dickenson Pearce, 1966–68; Director, Cramer Saatchi, 1968–70. *Address:* (office) 35 Davies Street, W1Y 1FN. *T:* 0171–486 1100.

SAATCHI, Maurice; Chairman, M & C Saatchi Agency, since 1995; *b* 21 June 1946; *s* of Daisy and Nathan Saatchi; *m* 1984, Josephine Hart; one *s*, and one step *s*. *Educ:* London School of Economics and Political Science (1st class BSc Econ). Co-Founder of Saatchi & Saatchi Co., 1970, Chm., 1985–94. *Address:* (office) 35 Davies Street, W1Y 1FN. *T:* 0171–486 1100.
See also C. Saatchi.

SABATINI, Lawrence John; retired; Assistant Under Secretary of State, Ministry of Defence, 1972–79; *b* 5 Dec. 1919; *s* of Frederick Laurence Sabatini and Elsie May Sabatini (*née* Friggens); *m* 1947, Patricia Dyson; one *s* one *d*. *Educ:* Watford Grammar School. Joined HM Office of Works, 1938. Army service, 1940–46: commnd in RTR, 1943: service in NW Europe with 5 RTR. Asst Principal, Min. of Works, 1947; Asst Private Sec. to Minister of Works, 1948–49; Principal, 1949; Principal Private Sec. to Ministers of Defence, 1958–60; Asst Sec., MoD, 1960; Defence Counsellor, UK Delegn to NATO, on secondment to Diplomatic Service, 1963–67. *Recreations:* gardening, photography, music. *Address:* 44a Batchworth Lane, Northwood, Mddx HA6 3DT. *T:* Northwood (01923) 823249. *Club:* MCC.

SABBEN-CLARE, James Paley; Headmaster, Winchester College, since 1985; *b* 9 Sept. 1941; *s* of late Ernest Sabben-Clare and Rosamond Dorothy Mary Scott; *m* 1969, Geraldine Mary Borton, LLB; one *s* one *d*. *Educ:* Winchester College (Scholar); New College, Oxford (Scholar; 1st Class Classical Hon. Mods and Greats, 1964; MA). Asst Master, Marlborough College, 1964–68; Vis. Fellow, All Souls College, Oxford, 1967–68; Winchester College, 1968–; Head of Classics Dept, 1969–79; Second Master, 1979–85. *Publications:* Caesar and Roman Politics, 1971, 2nd edn 1981; Fables from Aesop, 1976; The Culture of Athens, 1978, 2nd edn 1980; Winchester College, 1981, 2nd edn 1988; (contrib.) Winchester: history and literature, 1992; contribs to educnl and classical jls. *Recreations:* fives, Italian opera, mountains, furniture making. *Address:* Headmaster's House, Winchester College, Winchester, Hants SO23 9NA. *T:* Winchester (01962) 854328.

SABIN, Howard Westcott; Legal Adviser to Associated Newspapers Group Ltd, 1972–84; Chairman, William Morris Rolling Mills Ltd (formerly William Morris & Son (Birmingham) Ltd), since 1985; *b* 19 Oct. 1916; *s* of late John Howard Sabin and Octavia Roads (*née* Scruby); *m* 1st, 1942, Joan Eunice Noble (marr. diss. 1959); two *s* one *d*; 2nd, 1959, Janet Eileen Baillie. *Educ:* Shrewsbury; St John's Coll., Cambridge; MA (Hons in History and Law). Lieut, RNVR, 1939–46 (despatches 1944). Called to the Bar, Middle Temple, 1946. Dep. Chm., Bedfordshire QS, 1968–72; Assistant Recorder, Portsmouth, 1966, Bournemouth, 1967. Counsel for Post Office (Midland Circuit), 1964. *Recreations:* golf, swimming, music. *Address:* 40 Wynnstay Gardens, W8 6UT. *T:* 0171–937 9247. *Club:* Hadley Wood Golf.

SABIN, Paul Robert; Chief Executive, Kent County Council, since 1986; *b* 29 March 1943; *s* of Robert Reginald and Dorothy Maude Sabin; *m* 1965, Vivien Furnival; one *s* two *d*. *Educ:* Oldbury Grammar Sch. DMS Aston Univ.; IPFA 1966; FBIM (MBIM 1967). West Bromwich CBC, 1961–69; Redditch Devlt Corp., 1969–81, Chief Finance Officer, 1975–81; City of Birmingham, 1981–86: City Treas., 1982–86; Dep. Chief Exec., 1984–86. FRSA 1988. *Recreations:* antique maps and books, music. *Address:* County Hall, Maidstone ME14 1XQ. *T:* Maidstone (01622) 694000.

SABINE, Peter Aubrey, DSc; FRSE, FRSA, FIMM; CEng, CGeol, FGS; Deputy Director (Chief Scientific Officer, Chief Geologist), British Geological Survey (formerly Institute of Geological Sciences), 1977–84; *b* 29 Dec. 1924; *s* of Bernard Robert and Edith Lucy Sabine; *m* 1946, Peggy Willis Lambert, MSc, FBCS, FRSA, FSS; one *s*. *Educ:* Brockley County Sch.; Chelsea Polytechnic; Royal Coll. of Science, London. BSc, ARCS (1st Cl. Geol.; Watts medal) 1945; PhD 1951, DSc 1970 (London). Apptd Geological Survey of Gt Britain as Geologist, 1945; Geological Museum, 1946–50; in charge Petrographical Dept, Geol Survey and Museum, 1950, Chief Petrographer, 1959; Asst Dir, S England and Wales, 1970; Chief Geochemist, 1977; Dep. Dir, 1977–84. Sec., Geol Soc. of London, 1959–66, Vice-Pres., 1966–67, 1982–84 (Lyell Fund, 1955; Sen. Fellow, 1994); International Union of Geological Sciences: Mem. Commn on Systematics of Igneous Rocks, 1969–; Mem. Commn on Systematics in Petrology, 1980– (Chm., 1984–92; Vice-Chm., 1992–); Chief UK Deleg., 1980–84; Mem. Council, 1980–92; Member Council: Geologists' Assoc., 1966–70; Mineralogical Soc., 1950–53; Instn of Mining and Metallurgy, 1976–80; Mineral Industry Res. Orgn, 1983–86; Member: DTI Chem. and Mineral Research Requirements Bd, 1973–82; Minerals, Metals Extraction and Reclamation Cttee, 1981–84; EEC Cttees on minerals and geochemistry; Cttee of Dirs of W European Geolog. Surveys, 1978–84; Chm., Sub-Cttee on geochem. and cosmochem. of British Nat. Cttee for Geology, 1977–86. Royal Institution: Visitor, 1979–82; Mem., Audit Cttee, 1987–90 (Chm., 1989–90). FMSA. *Publications:* Chemical Analysis of Igneous Rocks (with E. M. Guppy), 1956; (with D. S. Sutherland) Petrography of British Igneous Rocks, 1982; (jtly) Classification of Igneous Rocks, 1989; numerous scientific contribs in Mem. Geol. Surv., Qly Jl Geol. Soc., Mineral. Mag., Phil. Trans Roy. Soc., etc. *Recreations:* gardening, genealogy. *Address:* Lark Rise, Camp Road, Gerrards Cross, Bucks SL9 7PF. *T:* Gerrards Cross (01753) 891529. *Clubs:* Athenæum; Geological Society's.

SACHS, Hon. Sir Michael (Alexander Geddes), Kt 1993; **Hon. Mr Justice Sachs;** a Judge of the High Court of Justice, Queen's Bench Division, since 1993; *b* 8 April 1932; *s* of Dr Joseph Sachs, MB, ChB, DPH, and Mrs Ruby Mary Sachs (*née* Ross); *m* 1957, Patricia Mary (*née* Conroy); two *s* two *d*. *Educ:* Sedbergh; Manchester Univ. (LLB 1954). Admitted solicitor, 1957. Partner in Slater, Heelis & Co., Solicitors, Manchester, 1962–84. A Recorder, 1980–84; a Circuit Judge, 1984–93. Pres., Manchester Law Soc., 1978–79; Chm., Greater Manchester Legal Services Cttee, 1977–81; Member: No 7 (NW) Area, Legal Aid Cttee, 1966–80 (Chm., 1975–76); Council, Law Soc., 1979–84 (Chm., Standing Cttee on Criminal Law, 1982–84); Court, Univ. of Manchester, 1977–84. Hon. Bencher, Middle Temple, 1993; Hon. Mem., Law Soc., 1993. Hon. LLD Manchester, 1994. KSS 1980. *Address:* Royal Courts of Justice, WC2A 2LL.

SACKS, The Chief Rabbi Dr Jonathan Henry; Chief Rabbi of the United Hebrew Congregations of the British Commonwealth of Nations, since 1991; *b* 8 March 1948; *s* of Louis David Sacks and Louisa (*née* Frumkin); *m* 1970, Elaine (*née* Taylor); one *s* two *d*. *Educ:* Gonville and Caius Coll., Cambridge (MA 1972); New Coll., Oxford; PhD London, 1981. Rabbinic Ordination: Jews' Coll., London, 1976; Yeshivat Etz Hayyim, London, 1976. Lectr in Moral Philosophy, Middlesex Polytechnic, 1971–73; Jews' College, London: Lectr in Jewish Philosophy, 1973–76; Lectr on the Talmud and in Phil., 1976–82; apptd (first) Sir Immanuel (now Lord) Jakobovits Prof. of Modern Jewish Thought, 1982–; Dir, Rabbinic Faculty, 1983–90; Principal, 1984–90; Rabbi, Golders Green Synagogue, 1978–82; Minister, Marble Arch Synagogue, 1983–90. Member (Univ. of London): Bd of Phil., 1985–90; Bd of Studies in Oriental Languages and Literature, 1985–90; Bd of Studies in Theology and Religious Studies, 1986–90. Member: Theol. and Religious Studies Bd, CNAA, 1984–87; Central Religious Adv. Cttee, BBC and IBA, 1987–90. Vis. Prof. of Philosophy, Univ. of Essex, 1989–90. BBC Reith Lectr, 1990. Editor, L'Eylah: A Journal of Judaism Today, 1984–90. FKC 1993. Hon. DD Cantab, 1993; DUniv Middlesex, 1993. *Publications:* Torah Studies, 1986; (ed) Tradition and Transition: essays presented to Sir Immanuel Jakobovits, 1986; Traditional Alternatives, 1989; Tradition in an Untraditional Age, 1990; The Persistence of Faith, 1991; Argument for the Sake of Heaven, 1991; Orthodoxy Confronts Modernity, 1991; Crisis and Covenant, 1992; One People? Tradition, Modernity and Jewish Unity, 1993; Will we have Jewish grandchildren?, 1994; Faith in the Future, 1995; articles, booklets and book reviews. *Address:* Adler House, Tavistock Square, WC1H 9HN. *T:* 0171–387 1066.

SACKVILLE, family name of **Earl De la Warr.**

SACKVILLE, 6th Baron, *cr* 1876; **Lionel Bertrand Sackville-West;** *b* 30 May 1913; *s* of late Hon. Bertrand George Sackville-West, *y b* of 4th Baron and Eva Adela Mabel Inigo (*d* 1936), *d* of late Maj.-Gen. Inigo Richmond Jones, CB, CVO; *S* cousin, 1965; *m* 1st, 1953, Jacobine Napier (*d* 1971), *widow* of Captain John Hichens, RA, and *d* of J. R. Menzies-Wilson; five *d*; 2nd, 1974, Arlie, Lady de Guingand (marr. diss. 1983; she *d* 1991); 3rd, 1983, Jean, *widow* of Sir Edward Imbert-Terry, 3rd Bt. *Educ:* Winchester; Magdalen Coll., Oxford. Formerly Capt. Coldstream Gds; served War, 1939–42 (POW). Member of Lloyd's, 1949. *Heir:* *b* Hugh Rosslyn Inigo Sackville-West, MC [*b* 1 Feb. 1919; *m* 1957, Bridget Eleanor, *d* of late Capt. Robert Lionel Brooke Cunliffe, CBE, RN; two *s* three *d*]. *Address:* Knole, Sevenoaks, Kent TN15 0RP.
See also Sir M. E. S. Imbert-Terry, Bt.

SACKVILLE, Hon. Thomas Geoffrey, (Tom); MP (C) Bolton West, since 1983; Parliamentary Under Secretary of State, Department of Health, since 1992; *b* 26 Oct. 1950; 2nd *s* of 10th Earl De La Warr (*d* 1988) and of Anne Rachel, *o d* of Geoffrey Devas, MC, Hunton Court, Maidstone; *m* 1979, Catherine Theresa, *d* of Brig. James Windsor Lewis; one *s* one *d*. *Educ:* St Aubyn's, Rottingdean, Sussex; Eton Coll.; Lincoln Coll., Oxford (BA). Deltec Banking Corp., New York, 1971–74; Grindlays Bank Ltd, London, 1974–77; Internat. Bullion and Metal Brokers (London) Ltd, 1978–83. PPS to Minister of State at the Treasury, 1985, to Minister for Social Security, 1987–88; an Asst Govt Whip, 1988–90; a Lord Comr of HM Treasury (Govt Whip), 1990–92. Sec., All-Party Cttee on Drug Misuse, 1984–88. *Address:* House of Commons, SW1A 0AA. *T:* 0171–219 4050.

SACKVILLE-WEST, family name of **Baron Sackville.**

SACKWOOD, Dr Mark; Regional Medical Officer, Northern Regional Health Authority, 1973–86, retired; *b* London, 18 Jan. 1926; *s* of Philip and Frances Sackwood; *m* 1953, Anne Harper Wilson; one *s* two *d*. *Educ:* King's Coll., London; Westminster Hosp. Med. School. MB, BS, FFCM, LRCP, MRCS, DPH, DRCOG. Various hosp. appts, South of England, 1949–58; mil. service, Far East, 1951–53; subseq. admin. med. appts, Middlesbrough and Newcastle upon Tyne, incl. Dep. Sen. Admin. MO with Newcastle RHB, 1968–73. *Recreations:* walking, reading, music. *Address:* 11 The Chesters, Beaumont Park, Whitley Bay, Tyne and Wear NE25 9UA. *T:* 0191–252 7401.

SADEQUE, Shahwar; a Governor, BBC, 1990–95; *b* 31 Aug. 1942; *d* of late Ali Imam and of Akhtar Imam; *m* 1962, Pharhad Sadeque; one *s* one *d*. *Educ:* Dhaka Univ., Bangladesh (BSc (Hons) Physics); Bedford Coll., London (MPhil Physics); Kingston Poly. (MSc Inf. Technol.). MBCS 1991. Computer Programmer with Baric Services Ltd, 1969–73; Teacher, Nonsuch High Sch., Sutton, 1973–84; research in computer integrated manufacture incorporating vision systems and artificial intelligence, Kingston Univ. (formerly Poly.), 1985–92. Member: Commn for Racial Equality, 1989–93; VAT Tribunals (England and Wales), 1991–; Income and Corporation Tax Tribunals, 1992–; SCAA, 1993–; NCET, 1994–; Metropolitan Police Cttee, 1995–. Mem., Waltham Forest HAT, 1991–. Councillor, CGLI, 1995–. FRSA 1994. *Publications:* papers: Education and Ethnic Minorities, 1988; Manufacturing—towards the 21st Century, 1988; A Knowledge-Based System for Sensor Interaction and Real-Time Component Control, 1988. *Recreations:* collecting thimbles and perfume bottles, cooking Indian-style, passion for keeping up-to-date with current affairs. *Address:* 59 Cheam Road, East Ewell, Epsom, Surrey KT17 3EG. *T:* 0181–393 8485.

SADGROVE, Very Rev. Michael; Provost of Sheffield, since 1995; *b* 13 April 1950; *s* of Ralph and Doreen Sadgrove; *m* 1974, (Elizabeth) Jennifer Suddes; one *s* three *d*. *Educ:* UCS; Balliol Coll., Oxford (BA (Maths and Philosophy, Theology) 1972; MA 1975); Trinity Coll., Bristol. Ordained, deacon, 1975, priest, 1976; licensed to Rural Deanery of Cowley, 1975–77; Lectr in OT studies, 1977–82, Vice-Principal, 1980–82, Salisbury and Wells Theol College; Vicar, Alnwick, Northumberland, 1982–87; Canon Residentiary, Precentor and Vice-Provost, Coventry Cathedral, 1987–95. Bishops' Inspector of Theol Colls and Courses, 1982–. Chairman: Precentors' Conf. of England and Wales, 1991–94; Church Men in the Midlands, 1991–95. *Publications:* A Picture of Faith, 1995; contributor to: Studia Biblica, 1978; Lion Handbook of the World's Religions, 1982, 1994; Rethinking Marriage, 1993; Coventry's First Cathedral, 1994; The Care Guide, 1995; articles and reviews in theol jls. *Recreations:* music (piano, organ, singing), arts, bread-making, wine-making, walking, the north-east of England. *Address:* Provost's Lodge, 22 Hallamgate Road, Sheffield S10 5BS. *T:* (0114) 266 2373; The Cathedral, Sheffield S1 1HA. *T:* Sheffield (0114) 275 3434.

SADIE, Stanley (John), CBE 1982; writer on music; Music Critic for The Times, 1964–81, thereafter freelance; Editor: The Musical Times, 1967–87; The New Grove Dictionary of Music and Musicians, since 1970; Master Musicians series, since 1976; *b* 30 Oct. 1930; *s* of David Sadie and Deborah (*née* Simons); *m* 1st, 1953, Adèle Bloom (*d* 1978); two *s* one *d*; 2nd, 1978, Julie Anne Vertrees; one *s* one *d*. *Educ:* St Paul's Sch.; Gonville and Caius Coll., Cambridge Univ. (MA, PhD, MusB). FRCM 1994. Prof., Trinity Coll. of Music, London, 1957–65. President: Royal Musical Assoc., 1989–94 (Vice-Pres., 1985–89; Mem., 1957–); Internat. Musicological Soc., 1992– (Mem., 1955–; Directorium, 1987–92; Pres., 1992–); Member: Critics' Circle, 1963–; American Musicological Soc., 1970–; Hon. Corresp. Mem., 1994. Chm., Handel Home Trust, 1994–. Hon. RAM 1981; Hon. DLitt Leicester, 1981. FRSA 1982. Writer and broadcaster on musical subjects, *circa* 1955–; Music Consultant, Man and Music, Granada TV, 1984–89; editor of many edns of 18th-century music, *circa* 1955–; Series Editor, Man and Music, 8 vols, 1989–93. *Publications:* Handel, 1962; Mozart, 1966; Beethoven, 1967; Handel, 1968; (with Arthur Jacobs) Pan Book of Opera/The Opera Guide, 1964, new edns 1969, 1984; Handel Concertos, 1973; (ed) The New Grove Dictionary of Music and Musicians, 1980; Mozart (The New Grove Biographies), 1982; (ed) New Grove Dictionary of Musical Instruments, 1984; (with Alison Latham) The Cambridge Music Guide, 1985, US edn 1993, trans. German 1994; Mozart Symphonies, 1986; (ed with H. Wiley Hitchcock) The New Grove Dictionary of American Music, 1986; (ed) The Grove Concise Dictionary of Music, 1988, rev. edn 1994; (ed) History of Opera, 1989; (ed with H. M. Brown) Performance Practice, 1989; (ed with D. W. Krummel) Music Printing and Publishing, 1989; (ed) The New Grove Dictionary of Opera, 1992; contrib.: The Musical Times, Gramophone, Opera, Music and Letters, Musical Quarterly, Proc. Roy. Musical Assoc. *Recreations:* watching cricket, canal boating, drinking (mainly wine and coffee), bridge, reading. *Address:* 12 Lyndhurst Road, NW3 5NL. *T:* 0171–435 2482, *Fax:* 0171–435 6481.

SADLER, Anthony John; Archbishops' Appointments Secretary, since 1996; *b* 2 Oct. 1938; *s* of David James Sadler and Joan Sybil (*née* Alt); *m* 1966, Marie-José Lucas; three *d*. *Educ:* Bedford Sch.; Magdalene Coll., Cambridge (MA). Personnel Manager, Hawker Siddeley Aviation, Hatfield, 1964–75; Asst Personnel Controller, Rank Orgn, 1975–78; Employee Relns Manager, Lloyds Bank Internat., 1978–83; Dir, Gp Human Resources, Minet plc, 1983–92. Vice-Pres., Internat. IPM, 1981–83; Chm., Staff Mgt Assoc., 1989–91. Chm., Southwark Welcare Centenary Appeal Cttee, 1993–95. Chm., S London Industrial Mission, 1980–82. Church Warden, St Luke, Kew, 1976–88. CIPD (CIPM 1983). *Publication:* Human Resource Management: developing a strategic approach, 1995. *Recreations:* divided between London (theatre, classical music, gardening) and Ile de Ré, France (cycling, bird-watching, swimming). *Address:* 343 Sandycombe Road, Richmond, Surrey TW9 3NA. *T:* 0181–940 3626. *Club:* Lansdowne.

SADLER, Joan; Principal, Cheltenham Ladies' College, 1979–87; *b* 1 July 1927; *d* of Thomas Harold Sadler and Florence May Sadler. *Educ:* Cambridgeshire High Sch.; Univ. of Bristol (BA Hons (History); DipEd). Downe House, Cold Ash, Newbury, Berks: Asst History teacher, 1950–56; Head of History Dept, 1956–58; Heriots Wood School, Stanmore, Mddx: Head of History Dept, 1958–68; Sen. Mistress, 1966–68; Headmistress, Howell's School, Denbigh, 1968–79. Chairman: Boarding Schools' Assoc., 1983–85; Independent Schools' Curriculum Cttee, 1986–; Trustee: Central Bureau for Educnl Visits and Exchanges; Common Entrance Examination for Girls' Schools. MInstD 1986. Hon. Freewoman: City of London; Drapers' Co., 1979. FRSA. *Recreations:* music, theatre, travel, reading. *Address:* Locke's Cottage, Caudle Green, Cheltenham, Glos GL53 9PR.

SADLER, John Stephen, CBE 1982; Chairman, Pearl Group PLC, since 1994; *b* 6 May 1930; *s* of late Bernard and Phyllis Sadler; *m* 1952, Ella (*née* McCleery); three *s*. *Educ:* Reading Sch.; Corpus Christi Coll., Oxford (MA). Board of Trade, 1952–54; Treasury, 1954–56; Board of Trade, 1956–60; British Trade Commissioner, Lagos, Nigeria, 1960–64; Board of Trade, 1964–66. John Lewis Partnership Ltd, 1966–89: Finance Dir, 1971–87; Dep. Chm., 1984–89. Chairman: Water Res. Centre, subseq. WRC, 1989–93; West End Central London Region Bd, Sun Alliance Insurance Gp, 1991–; UK Bd, Australian Mutual Provident Soc. and London Life, 1991–; Dir, Debenham Tewson & Chinnock Hldgs plc, 1987–. Dir, IMRO, 1987–94; Chm., Authorised Conveyancing Practitioners Bd, 1991–93; Mem., Monopolies and Mergers Commn, 1973–85. Trustee, British Telecommunications Staff Superannuation Scheme, 1983–. *Publication:* report of enquiry into media promotion. *Recreations:* golf, boating. *Address:* Riverlea, The Warren, Caversham, Reading RG4 7TQ. *Clubs:* Oriental, Reading Golf.

SAFFMAN, Prof. Philip Geoffrey, FRS 1988; Theodor von Kármán Professor of Applied Mathematics and Aeronautics, California Institute of Technology, since 1995 (Professor of Applied Mathematics, 1964–95); *b* 19 March 1931; *s* of Sam Ralph Saffman and Sarah Rebecca Leviten; *m* 1954, Ruth Arion; one *s* two *d*. *Educ:* Roundhay Sch., Leeds; Trinity Coll., Cambridge (BA, MA, PhD). Prize Fellow, Trinity Coll., Cambridge, 1955–59; Asst Lectr, Applied Math., Cambridge, 1958–60; Reader in Applied Math., King's Coll. London, 1960–64. Fellow, Amer. Acad. of Arts and Scis, 1978. *Publications:* Vortex Dynamics, 1992; numerous papers in sci. jls. *Recreations:* hiking, camping. *Address:* 399 Ninita Parkway, Pasadena, CA 91106, USA.

SAGAN, Françoise, pen-name of Françoise Quoirez; authoress; *b* France, 21 June 1935; *y c* of Paul Quoirez; *m* 1958, Guy Schoeller (marr. diss. 1960); *m* 1962, Robert James Westhoff (marr. diss.); one *s*. *Educ:* convent and private school. Published first novel at age of 18. Has written some songs and collaborated in scheme for ballet Le Rendez-vous Manqué, produced Paris and London, 1958. *Publications:* (all trans. into Eng., usually French title): Bonjour Tristesse, 1954; Un Certain Sourire, 1956 (filmed, 1958); Dans un mois, dans un an, 1957 (Those Without Shadows, 1958); Aimez-vous Brahms . . . . 1959 (1960); Château en Suède (play), 1960; Les Violons, parfois . . . (play), 1961; La Robe Mauve de Valentine (play), 1963; Bonheur, impair et passe (play), 1964; Toxique . . . (tr. 1965); La Chamade, 1965 (tr. 1966) (film, 1970); Le Cheval Evanoui (play), 1966; L'Echarde, 1966; Le Garde du cœur, 1968 (tr., The Heart-Keeper, 1968); Un peu de soleil dans l'eau froide, 1969 (tr., Sunlight and Cold Water, 1971); Un piano dans l'herbe (play), 1970; Des bleus à l'âme, 1972 (tr., Scars on the Soul, 1974); Zaphorie (play), 1973; Lost Profile, 1976; Silken Eyes (short stories), 1977; The Unmade Bed, 1978; Le Chien Couchant, 1980; La femme fardée, 1981 (tr., The Painted Lady, 1982); The Still Storm, 1984; Incidental Music (short stories), 1985; Avec mon meilleur souvenir (tr. With Fondest Regards), 1986; Un sang d'aquarelle, 1987; Dear Sarah Bernhardt, 1989; (with W. Denker) The Eiffel Tower, 1989; La Laisse, 1989 (tr., The Leash); Les Faux-fuyauts, 1991 (tr., The Evasion, 1993); Oeuvres (collected works), 1993; ----- et toute ma sympathie (essays). *Address:* c/o Editions Flammarion, 26 rue Racine, 75006 Paris, France.

SAGE, Lorna; journalist and critic; Professor of English Literature, since 1994, Dean of the School of English and American Studies, 1985–88, and since 1993, University of East Anglia; *b* 13 Jan. 1943; *d* of Eric and Valma Stockton; *m* 1st, 1959, Victor Sage; one *d*; 2nd, 1979, Rupert Hodson. *Educ:* Univ. of Durham (BA 1st Cl. Hons 1964); Univ. of Birmingham (MA 1966). Asst Lectr in English Literature, Univ. of East Anglia, 1965, Lectr 1968, Sen. Lectr, 1975. Florence B. Tucker Vis. Prof., Wellesley Coll., Mass, USA, 1981. *Publications:* (ed) Peacock, Satirical Novels, 1976; Doris Lessing, 1983; Women in the House of Fiction, 1992; (ed) Flesh and the Mirror, 1994; Angela Carter, 1994; reviews in Observer, TLS, Vogue, etc. *Address:* School of English and American Studies, University of East Anglia, Norwich NR4 7TJ. *T:* Norwich (01603) 456161.

SAGE, Stephen Paul; Chief Executive, The Buying Agency, since 1993; *b* 3 June 1953; *s* of late Ivor John Sage and Kathleen Gwendoline Sage (*née* Jeffrey); *m* 1982, Anne Jennifer Mickleburgh; two *s* one *d*. *Educ:* Bristol Grammar Sch.; Peterhouse, Cambridge (BA Hons Classics 1974; MA). MCIPS 1993. John Henderson Sports, 1976–78; Crown Agents, 1978–80; Department of the Environment, 1980–93: Private Sec. to Housing Minister, 1984–85; Controller, Merseyside Task Force, 1989–93. *Recreations:* reading, music, Alfa Romeos. *Address:* The Buying Agency, Royal Liver Building, Pier Head, Liverpool L3 1PE. *T:* 0151–224 2209. *Club:* Bristol City Football.

SAID, Prof. Edward W., PhD; University Professor, Columbia University, since 1992; *b* 1935; *m* 1970, Mariam Cortas; one *s* one *d*. *Educ:* Princeton Univ.; Harvard Univ. Columbia University: Instructor in English, 1963–65; Asst Prof. of English and Comparative Literature, 1967–69; Prof., 1969–77; Parr Prof., 1977–89; Old Dominion Foundn Prof. in Humanities, 1989–92. Reith Lectr, 1993. *Publications:* Joseph Conrad and the Fiction of Autobiography, 1966; Beginnings: intention and method; Orientalism, 1978; The Question of Palestine, 1979; (ed) Literature and Society, 1980; Covering Islam, 1981; The World, the Text and the Critic, 1983; After the Last Sky, 1986; (ed jtly) Blaming the Victims, 1988; Musical Elaborations, 1991; Culture and Imperialism, 1993; The Politics of Dispossession, 1994; Representations of the Intellectual, 1994. *Address:* 508 Philosophy Hall, Columbia University, New York, NY 10027, USA.

SAINSBURY, family name of **Barons Sainsbury** and **Sainsbury of Preston Candover.**

SAINSBURY, Baron, *cr* 1962, of Drury Lane (Life Peer); **Alan John Sainsbury;** Joint President of J. Sainsbury plc, since 1967 (Chairman, 1956–67); *b* 13 Aug. 1902; *er s* of John Benjamin and Mabel Miriam Sainsbury; *m* 1st, 1925, Doreen Davan Adams (marr. diss. 1939; she *d* 1985); three *s*; 2nd, 1944, Anne Elizabeth Lewy (*d* 1988); one *d*. *Educ:* Haileybury. Joined Grocery and Provision Firm of J. Sainsbury, Ltd (founded by his grandparents), 1921. Served on many war-time consultative committees of Ministry of Food; Member Williams' Committee on Milk Distribution, 1947–48; Member: Food Research Advisory Cttee, 1960–70 (Chm., 1965–70); NEDC Cttee for the Distributive Trades, 1964–68; Exec. Cttee, PEP, 1970–76; House of Lords Select Cttee on the European Communities, 1978–81; Chm., Cttee of Inquiry into Relationship of Pharmaceutical Industry with National Health Service, 1965–67. President: Multiple Shops' Fedn, 1963–65; The Grocers' Inst., 1963–66; Internat. Assoc. of Chain Stores, 1965–68; The Royal Inst. of Public Health and Hygiene, 1965–70; Pestalozzi Children's Village Trust, 1963–; Distributive Trades Educn and Trng Council, 1975–83; a Vice-President, Assoc. of Agriculture, 1965–73; Royal Society for the Encouragement of Arts, Manufactures and Commerce, 1962–66; Mem., Court of Univ. of Essex, 1966–76; Governor, City Literary Inst., 1967–69; Chairman of Trustees: Overseas Students Adv. Bureau; Uganda Asian Relief Trust, 1972–74; Vice President: World Development Movement; Internat. Voluntary Service, 1977–81; Parly Gp for World Govt, 1982–. Liberal candidate, Sudbury Div. of Suffolk, Gen. Elections of 1929, 1931 and 1935. Joined Labour Party, 1945, SDP, 1981. Hon. Fellow, Inst. of Food Sci, and Technology. *Address:* J. Sainsbury plc, Stamford House, Stamford Street, SE1 9LL.

See also Baron Sainsbury of Preston Candover, Rt Hon. Sir T. A. D. Sainsbury.

SAINSBURY OF PRESTON CANDOVER, Baron *cr* 1989 (Life Peer), of Preston Candover in the county of Hampshire; **John Davan Sainsbury,** KG 1992; Kt 1980; President, J Sainsbury plc, since 1992 (Vice-Chairman, 1967–69; Chairman, 1969–92; Director, 1958–92); *b* 2 Nov. 1927; *e s* of Baron Sainsbury, *qv*; *m* 1963, Anya Linden, *qv*; two *s* one *d*. *Educ:* Stowe School; Worcester College, Oxford (Hon. Fellow 1982). Dir, Royal Opera House, Covent Garden, 1969–85 (Chairman, 1988–92); Chairman: Friends of Covent Garden, 1969–81; Benesh Inst. of Choreology, 1986–87; Bd of Trustees, Dulwich Picture Gall., 1994–; Govs, Royal Ballet, 1995– (Gov., 1987–); Governor: Royal Ballet Sch., 1965–76, and 1987–91; Royal Opera House Trust, 1974–84 and 1987–. Dir, The Economist, 1972–80; Jt Hon. Treas., European Movt, 1972–75; Pres., British Retail Consortium, 1993– (Mem. Council, Retail Consortium, 1975–79); Member: Nat. Cttee for Electoral Reform, 1976–85; President's Cttee, CBI, 1982–84. Vice Pres., Contemporary Arts Soc., 1984– (Hon. Sec., 1965–71; Vice Chm., 1971–74); Trustee: Nat. Gall., 1976–83; Westminster Abbey Trust, 1977–83; Tate Gall., 1982–83; Rhodes Trust, 1984–. Pres., Sparsholt Coll., Hants, 1993–. Hon. Bencher, Inner Temple, 1985. FIGD 1973; Hon. FRIBA 1993. Hon. DScEcon London, 1985; Hon. DLitt South Bank, 1992; Hon. LLD Bristol, 1993. Albert Medal, RSA, 1989. *Address:* c/o Stamford House, Stamford Street, SE1 9LL. *T:* 0171–921 6000. *Clubs:* Garrick, Beefsteak.

See also Rt Hon. Sir T. A. D. Sainsbury.

SAINSBURY OF PRESTON CANDOVER, Lady; *see* Linden, Anya.

SAINSBURY, David John; Chairman and Chief Executive, J. Sainsbury plc, since 1992 (Deputy Chairman, 1988–92); *b* 24 Oct. 1940; *s* of Sir Robert Sainsbury, *qv*; *m* 1973, Susan Carole Reid; three *d*. *Educ:* King's Coll., Cambridge (BA); Columbia Univ., NY (MBA). Joined J. Sainsbury, 1963; Finance Dir, 1973–90. Mem., Cttee of Review of the Post Office (Carter Cttee), 1975–77. Trustee, Social Democratic Party, 1982–90; Mem. Governing Body, London Business Sch., 1985– (Chm., 1991–). Vis. Fellow, Nuffield Coll., Oxford, 1987–. Hon. FEng 1994. Hon. DSc Salford, 1989. *Publications:* Government and Industry: a new partnership, 1981; (with Christopher Smallwood) Wealth Creation and Jobs, 1987.

SAINSBURY, Edward Hardwicke; TD 1945; Partner, Dawson, Hart & Co., Uckfield, 1961–92 (ceased to practice, 1993), retired; District Notary Public, Uckfield, since 1965; *b* 17 Sept. 1912; *e s* of Henry Morgan Sainsbury, and *g s* of James C. Hardwicke, a pioneer of technical and other education in S Wales; *m* 1946, Ann, 2nd *d* of late Kenneth Ellis,

Tunbridge Wells; one *s* one *d*. *Educ:* Cardiff High School; University of S Wales and Monmouth. Solicitor in private practice, 1935; commissioned (TA) 1936; Prosecuting Solicitor, Cardiff, 1938, Sen. Pros. Solicitor, 1939. Served War of 1939–45; Adjutant, 77th HAA Regt, 1940; comd 240 HAA Battery Gibraltar, 1944; demobilised Nov. 1945. Hong Kong: Asst Crown Solicitor, 1946; commissioner for revision of the laws of Hong Kong, 1947; magistrate, 1948; registrar, High Court, 1949; sen. magistrate, Kowloon, 1951; Barrister, Inner Temple, 1951; Land Officer and sen. crown counsel, Hong Kong, 1952; legal draftsman, Nigeria, 1953; Principal Legal Draftsman, Fed. of Nigeria, 1958. President, Commonwealth Parliamentary Assoc., Southern Cameroons, 1959–63. Judge, High Court of Lagos, 1960–63, and of Southern Cameroons, 1961–63; Speaker, House of Assembly, 1958–63, Chm., Public Service Commn, 1961–63, Southern Cameroons. *Publication:* (jointly) Revised Laws of Hong Kong, 1948. *Recreations:* squash (a memory), golf. *Address:* Little Gassons, Fairwarp, Uckfield, East Sussex TN22 3BG. *T:* Nutley (0182571) 2100.

SAINSBURY, Jeffrey Paul, FCA; chartered accountant; Managing Director, Exchange Registers Ltd, since 1994; Lord Mayor of Cardiff, 1991–92; *b* 27 June 1943; *s* of Capt. Walter Ronald Sainsbury and Joan Margaret Slamin; *m* 1967, Janet Elizabeth Hughes; one *s* one *d*. *Educ:* Cardiff High Sch. FCA 1966. Partner, Pannell Kerr Forster, 1969. Mem., Cardiff CC, 1969–. Member: S Glamorgan HA, 1987–91; Bd, Cardiff Bay Develt Corp., 1991–. Chairman: New Theatre, Cardiff, 1983–87; Welsh Sports Aid Foundn, 1994–; Gov., Sports Aid Foundn, 1994–; Vice-Pres., Bobath Cymru, 1993–; Mem. Bd, S Glam TEC, 1994– (Vice Chm., 1995–). *Recreations:* cooking, music, theatre, sport. *Address:* 34 Heol Iscoed, Rhiwbina, Cardiff CF4 6PA. *T:* Cardiff (01222) 624489. *Club:* Cardiff & County.

SAINSBURY, Sir Robert, Kt 1967 (for services to the arts); Joint President, J. Sainsbury plc; *b* 24 Oct. 1906; *s* of late John Benjamin Sainsbury and late Mabel Miriam (*née* Van den Bergh); *m* 1937, Lisa Ingeborg (*née* Van den Bergh; second cousin); one *s* two *d* (and one *d* decd). *Educ:* Haileybury Coll.; Pembroke Coll., Cambridge (MA; Hon. Fellow, 1983). ACA, 1930, FCA, 1935. Joined J. Sainsbury Ltd, 1930; Dir, 1934; Jt Gen. Man., 1938; Dep. Chm., 1956; Chm. 1967; Jt Pres., 1969. Formerly Mem. Art Panel of Arts Council; Member: Mngt Cttee, Courtauld Inst. of Art, Univ. of London, 1979–82; Vis. Cttee to Primitive Art Dept, Metropolitan Mus of Art, New York, until 1986; Pres., British Assoc. of Friends of Museums, 1985–. Trustee, Tate Gall., 1959–73 (Vice-Chm. 1967, Chm., 1969). Founder, with wife, Sainsbury Centre for Visual Arts, UEA, 1978. Hon. Treasurer, Inst. of Med. Social Workers, 1948–71; Governor, St Thomas' Hospital, 1939–68. Hon. FRIBA 1986. Hon. Dr RCA, 1976; Hon. LittD East Anglia, 1977; Hon. LLD Liverpool, 1988.
See also D. J. Sainsbury.

SAINSBURY, Rt. Rev. Roger Frederick; *see* Barking, Area Bishop of.

SAINSBURY, Rt. Hon. Sir Timothy (Alan Davan), Kt 1995; PC 1992; MP (C) Hove, since Nov. 1973; *b* 11 June 1932; *y s* of Baron Sainsbury, *qv*; *m* 1961, Susan Mary Mitchell; two *s* two *d*. *Educ:* Eton; Worcester Coll., Oxford (MA; Hon. Fellow 1982). Dir, J. Sainsbury, 1962–83. Chm., Council for the Unit for Retail Planning Information Ltd, 1974–79. PPS to Sec. of State for the Environment, 1979–83, to Sec. of State for Defence, 1983; a Govt Whip, 1983–87; Parly Under-Sec. of State for Defence Procurement, 1987–89; Parly Under-Sec. of State, FCO, 1989–90; Minister of State, DTI, 1990–94 (Minister for Trade, 1990–92, for Industry, 1992–94). Parly Chm., Cons. Friends of Israel, 1994–. Mem. Council, RSA, 1981–83. Hon. ARICS; Hon. FRIBA. *Address:* House of Commons, SW1A 0AA.
See also Baron Sainsbury of Preston Candover, S. A. Woodward.

SAINT, Dora Jessie, (*pen name* Miss Read); writer, since 1950; *b* 17 April 1913; *d* of Arthur Gunnis Shafe and Grace Lilian Shafe; *m* 1940, Douglas Edward John Saint; one *d*. *Educ:* Bromley County Sch.; Homerton Coll., Cambridge. Teaching in Middlesex, 1933–40; occasional teaching, 1946–63. *Publications:*Village School, 1955; Village Diary, 1957; Storm in the Village, 1958; Thrush Green, 1959; Fresh from the Country, 1960; Winter in Thrush Green, 1961; Miss Clare Remembers, 1962; Chronicles of Fairacre, 1963; Over the Gate, 1964; Market Square, 1965; Village Christmas, 1966; Fairacre Festival, 1968; News from Thrush Green, 1970; Tiggy, 1971; Emily Davis, 1971; Tyler's Row, 1972; The Christmas Mouse, 1973; Farther Afield, 1974; Battles at Thrush Green, 1975; No Holly for Miss Quinn, 1976; Village Affairs, 1977; Return to Thrush Green, 1978; The White Robin, 1979; Village Centenary, 1980; Gossip from Thrush Green, 1981; Affairs at Thrush Green, 1983; Summer at Fairacre, 1984; At Home in Thrush Green, 1985; The School at Thrush Green, 1987; The World of Thrush Green, 1988; Mrs Pringle, 1989; Friends at Thrush Green, 1990; Celebrations at Thrush Green, 1992; Farewell to Fairacre, 1993; Tales from a Village School, 1994; *for children:* Hobby Horse Cottage, 1958; Hob and the Horse-Bat, 1965; The Red Bus Series, 1965; *non-fiction:* Country Bunch (anthology), 1963; Miss Read's Country Cooking, 1969; *autobiography:* A Fortunate Grandchild, 1982; Time Remembered, 1986. *Recreations:* theatre-going, reading. *Address:* Strouds, Shefford Woodlands, Hungerford, Berks RG17 7AJ. *T:* Great Shefford (01488) 648249.

ST ALBANS, 14th Duke of, *cr* 1684; **Murray de Vere Beauclerk;** Earl of Burford, Baron of Heddington, 1676; Baron Vere of Hanworth, 1750. Hereditary Grand Falconer of England; Hereditary Registrar, Court of Chancery; Partner, Burford & Co., chartered accountants, since 1981; *b* 19 Jan. 1939; *s* of 13th Duke of St Albans, OBE and Nathalie Chatham, *d* of P. F. Walker (later Mrs Nathalie C. Eldrid, *d* 1985); *S* father, 1988; *m* 1st, 1963, Rosemary Frances Scoones (marr. diss. 1974); one *s* one *d*; 2nd, 1974, Cynthia Theresa Mary, *d* of late Lt-Col W. J. H. Howard, DSO and formerly wife of Sir Anthony Robin Maurice Hooper, 2nd Bt. *Educ:* Tonbridge. Chartered Accountant, 1962. Gov.-Gen., Royal Stuart Soc., 1989–. Pres., Beaufort Opera, 1991–. *Heir: s* Earl of Burford, *qv*. *Address:* 3 St George's Court, Gloucester Road, SW7 4QZ. *T:* 0171–589 1771. *Club:* Hurlingham.

ST ALBANS, Bishop of, since 1995; **Rt Rev. Christopher William Herbert;** *b* 7 Jan. 1944; *s* of Walter Meredith Herbert (who *m* 1950, Dorothy Margaret Curnock) and late Hilda Lucy (*née* Dibbin); *m* 1968, Janet Elizabeth Turner; two *s*. *Educ:* Monmouth School; St David's Coll., Lampeter (BA); Univ. of Bristol (PGCE); Wells Theol Coll. Asst Curate, Tupsley, Hereford, 1967–71; Asst Master, Bishop's Sch., Hereford, 1967–71; Adv in Religious Educn, 1971–76, Dir of Educn, 1976–81, Dio. of Hereford; Vicar, St Thomas on the Bourne, Farnham, Surrey, 1981–90; Archdeacon of Dorking, 1990–95. Dir, Post-ordination Training, Dio. of Guildford, 1984–90; Hon. Canon of Guildford, 1984–95. *Publications:* The New Creation, 1971; A Place to Dream, 1976; St Paul's: A Place to Dream, 1981; The Edge of Wonder, 1981; Listening to Children, 1983; On the Road, 1984; Be Thou My Vision, 1985; This Most Amazing Day, 1986; The Question of Jesus, 1987; Alive to God, 1987; Ways into Prayer, 1987; Help in your Bereavement, 1988; Prayers for Children, 1993; Pocket Prayers, 1993; The Prayer Garden, 1994; Words of Comfort, 1994. *Recreations:* walking, cycling, reading, gardening, writing unpublished novels. *Address:* Abbey Gate House, St Albans, Herts AL3 4HD. *T:* St Albans (01727) 853305.

ST ALBANS, Dean of; *see* Lewis, Very Rev. C. A.

ST ALBANS, Archdeacon of; *see* Davies, Ven. P. B.

ST ALDWYN, 3rd Earl *cr* 1915; **Michael Henry Hicks Beach;** Bt 1619; Viscount St Aldwyn 1906; Viscount Quenington 1915; *b* 7 Feb. 1950; *s* of 2nd Earl St Aldwyn, GBE, TD, PC and Diana Mary Christian Smyly (*d* 1992), *o d* of Henry C. G. Mills; *S* father, 1992; *m* 1982, Gilda Maria, *o d* of Barão Saavedra, Copacabana, Rio de Janeiro; two *d*. *Educ:* Eton; Christ Church, Oxford (MA). *Heir: b* Hon. David Seymour Hicks Beach [*b* 25 May 1955; *m* 1993, Kate, *d* of Michael Henriques]. *Address:* 17 Hale House, 34 De Vere Gardens, W8 5AQ. *T:* 0171–937 6223; Williamstrip Park, Coln St Aldwyns, Cirencester, Glos GL7 5AT.

ST ANDREWS, Earl of; George Philip Nicholas Windsor; *b* 26 June 1962; *s* of HRH the Duke of Kent and HRH the Duchess of Kent; *m* 1988, Sylvana Tomaselli; one *s* two *d*. *Educ:* Eton (King's Scholar); Downing College, Cambridge. Attached to FCO, 1987–88. Consultant, rare books. Trustee, GB-Sasakawa Foundn, 1995–. Patron, Assoc. for Internat. Cancer Res., 1995–. *Heir: s* Lord Downpatrick, *qv*. *Address:* York House, St James's Palace, SW1A 1BQ.
See under Royal Family.

ST ANDREWS AND EDINBURGH, Archbishop of, (RC), since 1985; **Most Rev. Keith Michael Patrick O'Brien;** *b* Ballycastle, Co. Antrim, 17 March 1938; *s* of late Mark Joseph O'Brien and Alice Mary (*née* Moriarty). *Educ:* schools in Ballycastle, Dumbarton and Edinburgh; Edinburgh Univ. (BSc 1959, DipEd 1966); St Andrew's Coll., Drygrange; Moray House Coll. of Education, Edinburgh. Ordained Priest, 1965; pastoral appointments: Holy Cross, Edinburgh, 1965–66; St Bride's, Cowdenbeath, 1966–71 (while Chaplain and teacher of Maths and Science, St Columba's High Sch., Cowdenbeath and Dunfermline); St Patrick's, Kilsyth, 1972–75; St Mary's, Bathgate, 1975–78. Spiritual Director, St Andrew's Coll., Drygrange, 1978–80; Rector of St Mary's Coll., Blair, Aberdeen, 1980–85. *Address:* St Bennet's, 42 Greenhill Gardens, Edinburgh EH10 4BJ. *T:* 0131–447 3337.

ST ANDREWS AND EDINBURGH, Bishop Auxiliary of, (RC); *see* Rafferty, Rt Rev. K. L.

ST ANDREWS, DUNKELD AND DUNBLANE, Bishop of, since 1995; **Rt Rev. Michael Harry George Henley,** CB 1991; *b* 16 Jan. 1938; *s* of Eric Edward Henley and Evelyn Agnes Henley (*née* Lilly); *m* 1965, Rachel Jean (*née* Allen); two *d*. *Educ:* St Marylebone Grammar Sch.; St John's Hall, London (LTh). Ordained deacon, 1961, priest, 1962; Curate, St Marylebone Parish Ch., 1961–64; Chaplain: RN, 1964–68; St Andrews Univ., 1968–72; Royal Hosp. Sch., 1972–74; RN, 1974–93 (Chaplain of the Fleet, Archdeacon for RN and Dir Gen. Naval Chaplaincy Services, 1989–93); Priest i/c, Holy Trinity, Pitlochry, 1994–95. Hon. Canon, Holy Trinity Cathedral, Gibraltar, 1989–93. QHC 1989–93. *Recreations:* golf, fishing. *Address:* Bishop's House, Fairmount Road, Perth PH2 7AP. *Clubs:* Army and Navy; Leander (Henley); Royal and Ancient Golf (St Andrews).

ST ANDREWS, DUNKELD AND DUNBLANE, Dean of; *see* Watt, Very Rev. A. I.

ST ASAPH, Bishop of; *see* Wales, Archbishop of.

ST ASAPH, Dean of; *see* Goulstone, Very Rev. T. R. K.

ST AUBYN, family name of **Baron St Levan.**

ST AUBYN, Sir (John) Arscott M.; *see* Molesworth-St Aubyn.

ST AUBYN, Major Thomas Edward, CVO 1993; DL; FRGS; Lieutenant, HM Body Guard of Honourable Corps of Gentlemen at Arms, 1990–93 (Clerk of the Cheque and Adjutant, 1986–90); *b* 13 June 1923; *s* of Hon. Lionel Michael St Aubyn, MVO, and Lady Mary St Aubyn; *m* 1953, Henrietta Mary, *d* of Sir Henry Studholme, 1st Bt; three *d*. *Educ:* Eton. Served in King's Royal Rifle Corps, 1941–62; Italian Campaign, 1944–45; Adjt 1st KRRC, 1946–48; seconded to Sudan Defence Force in rank of Bimbashi, 1948–52; leader of Tibesti Mountain Expedn in Chad, 1957; Bde Adjt Green Jackets Bde, 1960–62. Mem., HM Body Guard, 1973–. High Sheriff of Hampshire, 1979–80; DL Hampshire, 1984. FRGS 1959. *Recreations:* shooting, fishing, ski-ing, stalking. *Address:* Dairy House Farm, Ashford Hill, Thatcham, Berks RG19 8BL. *T:* Kingsclere (01635) 298493. *Club:* Army and Navy.

ST BONIFACE, Archbishop of, (RC), since 1974; **Most Rev. Antoine Hacault,** STD; *b* Bruxelles, Manitoba, 17 Jan. 1926. *Educ:* Sainte-Marie Elem. Sch., Bruxelles; St Boniface Coll. (BA 1947); St Boniface Major Seminary; Angelicum Univ., Rome (STD 1954). Priest, 1951; Prof. of Theology, St Boniface Major Seminary, 1954–64; Auxiliary Bishop of St Boniface and Titular Bishop of Media, 1964; also Rector, St Boniface College, 1967–69; Bishop Coadjutor of St Boniface, 1972. Member: Vatican Secretariat for Non-Believers, 1973–83; Vatican Secretariat for promoting Christian Unity, 1976–89; Pastoral Team, Canadian Catholic Conf. of Bishops, 1973–77 and 1983–87; Admin. Bd, St Boniface Gen. Hosp., 1981–; Gen. Bd of Canadian Council of Churches, 1986–. President: Canadian Episcopal Commn for Ecumenism, 1974–87; Inter-Church Cttee, 1982–85; Western Catholic Conf., 1988–92. *Address:* Archbishop's Residence, 151 avenue de la Cathédrale, St Boniface, Manitoba R2H 0H6, Canada. *T:* (204) 2379851.

ST CLAIR, family name of **Lord Sinclair.**

ST CLAIR, Malcolm Archibald James; *b* 16 Feb. 1927: *o s* of late Maj.-Gen. George James Paul St Clair, CB, CBE, DSO and late Charlotte Theresa Orme Little; *m* 1955, Mary-Jean Rosalie Alice, *o d* of Wing-Comdr Caryl Liddell Hargreaves, Broadwood House, Sunningdale; two *s* one *d*. *Educ:* Eton. Served with Royal Scots Greys, 1944–48. Formerly Hon. Sec. to Sir Winston Churchill. Contested (C) Bristol South-East, 1959; MP (C) Bristol South-East, 1961–63. Lt Col Comdg, Royal Gloucestershire Hussars (TA), 1967–69. High Sheriff Glos, 1972. *Address:* Long Newnton Priory, Tetbury, Glos GL8 8RR. *Club:* White's.

ST CLAIR, William Linn, FBA 1992; FRSL; author; *b* 7 Dec. 1937; *s* of late Joseph and Susan St Clair, Falkirk; two *d*. *Educ:* Edinburgh Acad.; St John's Coll., Oxford. FRSL 1973. Admiralty and MoD, 1961–66; First Sec., FCO, 1966–69; transferred to HM Treasury, 1969, Under Sec., 1990–92; Consultant to OECD, 1992–. Visiting Fellow: All Souls Coll., Oxford, 1981–82; Huntington Library, Calif., 1985; Fellow, All Souls Coll., Oxford, 1992–. Cttee, London Liby. Internat. Pres., Byron Soc. *Publications:* Lord Elgin and the Marbles, 1967, rev. edn 1983; That Greece Might Still Be Free, 1972 (Heinemann prize); Trelawny, 1978; Policy Evaluation: a guide for managers, 1988; The Godwins and the Shelleys, 1989 (Time Life prize and Macmillan silver pen); Executive Agencies: a guide to setting targets and measuring performance, 1992. *Recreations:* old books, Scottish hills. *Address:* 52 Eaton Place, SW1X 8AL. *Clubs:* Athenæum, PEN.

ST CLAIR-ERSKINE, family name of **Earl of Rosslyn.**

ST CLAIR-FORD, Sir James (Anson), 7th Bt *cr* 1793, of Ember Court, Surrey; *b* 16 March 1952; *s* of Capt. Sir Aubrey St Clair-Ford, 6th Bt, DSO, RN and of Anne, *o d* of Harold Cecil Christopherson; *S* father, 1991; *m* 1st, 1977, Jennifer Margaret (marr. diss. 1984), *yr d* of Comodore Robin Grindle, RN; 2nd, 1987, Mary Anne, *er d* of His Honour Nathaniel Robert Blaker, QC. *Educ:* Wellington; Bristol Univ. *Heir: cousin* Colin Anson St Clair-Ford [*b* 19 April 1939; *m* 1964, Gillian Mary, *er d* of Rear Adm. Peter Skelton, CB; two *d*]. *Address:* 161 Sheen Lane, SW14 8NA.

ST CYRES, Viscount; John Stafford Northcote; *b* 15 Feb. 1957; *s* and *heir* of 4th Earl of Iddesleigh, *qv*; *m* 1983, Fiona Caroline Elizabeth, *d* of P. Wakefield, Barcelona, and Mrs M. Hattrell, Burnham, Bucks; one *s* one *d*. *Educ:* Downside Sch.; RAC Cirencester. *Heir: s* Hon. Thomas Stafford Northcote, *b* 5 Aug. 1985. *Address:* Hayne Barton, Newton St Cyres, Devon EX5 5AH.

ST DAVIDS, 3rd Viscount *cr* 1918; **Colwyn Jestyn John Philipps;** Baron Strange of Knokin, 1299; Baron Hungerford, 1426; Baron de Moleyns, 1445; Bt 1621; Baron St Davids, 1908; *b* 30 Jan. 1939; *s* of 2nd Viscount St Davids and Doreen Guinness (*d* 1956), *o d* of late Captain Arthur Jowett; *S* father, 1991; *m* 1965, Augusta Victoria Correa Larrain, *d* of late Don Estanislao Correa Ugarte; two *s*. *Educ:* Haverfordwest Grammar Sch.; Sevenoaks Sch.; King's Coll., London (Cert. Advanced Musical Studies, 1989). Nat. Service, 1958–60; commnd 2nd Lt Welsh Guards. Securities Agency Ltd, 1960–65; Mem., Stock Exchange, 1965; Maguire Kingsmill and Co., 1965–68; Partner, Kemp-Gee and Co., later Scrimgeour Kemp-Gee and Co., 1971; Dir, Citicorp Scrimgeour Vickers (Securities) Ltd, 1985–88; Dir, 1989–90 and 1994–, Consultant, 1991–92, Greig Middleton & Co. Ltd. A Lord in Waiting (Govt Whip), 1992–94. Mem., Baden-Powell Fellowship, 1985–. Liveryman, Musicians' Co., 1971–. *Recreations:* music, literature, natural history. *Heir: s* Hon. Rhodri Colwyn Philipps, *b* 16 Sept. 1966. *Address:* House of Lords, SW1A 0PW. *Clubs:* Garrick, City of London.

ST DAVIDS, Bishop of; *no new appointment at time of going to press.*

ST DAVIDS, Dean of; *see* Evans, Very Rev. J. W.

ST EDMUNDSBURY, Provost of; *see* Atwell, Very Rev. J. E.

ST EDMUNDSBURY AND IPSWICH, Bishop of, since 1986; **Rt. Rev. John Dennis;** *b* 19 June 1931; *s* of late Hubert Ronald and Evelyn Dennis; *m* 1956, Dorothy Mary (*née* Hinnels); two *s*. *Educ:* Rutlish School, Merton; St Catharine's Coll., Cambridge (BA 1954; MA 1959); Cuddesdon Coll., Oxford (1954–56). RAF, 1950–51. Curate, St Bartholomew's, Armley, Leeds, 1956–60; Curate of Kettering, 1960–62; Vicar of the Isle of Dogs, 1962–71; Vicar of John Keble, Mill Hill, 1971–79; Area Dean of West Barnet, 1973–79; Prebendary of St Paul's Cathedral, 1977–79; Bishop Suffragan of Knaresborough, 1979–86; Diocesan Dir of Ordinands, Dio. Ripon, 1980–86. Episcopal Guardian of Anglican Focolarini, 1981–; Chaplain to Franciscan Third Order, 1988–94. Co-Chairman: English ARC, 1988–92; Anglican-Oriental Orthodox Dialogue, 1989–95. *Recreations:* walking, gardening, wood working. *Address:* Bishop's House, 4 Park Road, Ipswich IP1 3ST. *T:* Ipswich (01473) 252829. *Club:* Royal Air Force.

ST GEORGE, Sir George (Bligh), 9th Bt *cr* 1766 (Ire.), of Athlone, Co. Westmeath; *b* 23 Sept. 1908; *s* of Sir Theophilus John St George, 6th Bt and Florence Emma Vanderplank; *S* brother, 1989; *m* 1935, Mary Somerville, *d* of John Francis Fairby Sutcliffe; two *s* three *d*. *Educ:* Christian Bros Coll., Kimberley; Natal Univ. (BA). Natal Provincial Administration, 1929–73, last appointment Dep. Dir (Admin), Addington Hospital, Durban. *Recreations:* music, bowls. *Heir: s* John Avenel Bligh [*b* 18 March 1940; *m* 1st, 1962, Margaret Carter (marr. diss. 1979); two *d*; 2nd, 1981, Linda, *d* of Robert Perry; two *s*]. *Address:* Hatley Cottage, 28 Waterfall Gardens Village, Private Bag X01, Link Hills 3652, Natal, South Africa. *T:* (31) 7633299.

ST GERMANS, 10th Earl of, *cr* 1815; **Peregrine Nicholas Eliot;** Baron Eliot 1784; *b* 2 Jan. 1941; *o s* of 9th Earl of St Germans, and Helen Mary (*d* 1951), *d* of late Lieut-Col Charles Walter Villiers, CBE, DSO, and Lady Kathleen Villiers; *S* father, 1988; *m* 1st, 1964, Hon. Jacquetta Jean Frederika Lampson (marr. diss. 1989), *d* of 1st Baron Killearn and Jacqueline Aldine Lesley (*née* Castellani); three *s*; 2nd, 1992, Elizabeth Dorythy Williams. *Educ:* Eton. *Recreation:* mucking about. *Heir: s* Lord Eliot, *qv*. *Address:* Port Eliot, St Germans, Cornwall. *Clubs:* Pratt's; Cornish Club 1768.

ST GERMANS, Bishop Suffragan of, since 1993; **Rt. Rev. Graham Richard James;** *b* 19 Jan. 1951; *s* of Rev. Lionel Dennis James and Florence Edith May James (*née* James); *m* 1978, Julie Anne Freemantle; one *s* one *d* (and one *d* decd). *Educ:* Northampton Grammar Sch.; Univ. of Lancaster (BA 1972); Univ. of Oxford (DipTh 1974); Cuddesdon Theological Coll. Deacon 1975, priest 1976; Asst Curate, Christ the Carpenter, Peterborough, 1975–78; Priest-in-charge, later Team Vicar, Christ the King, Digswell, 1979–83; Selection Sec. and Sec. for Continuing Ministerial Educn, ACCM, 1983–85; Sen. Selection Sec., ACCM, 1985–87; Chaplain to Archbishop of Canterbury, 1987–93. Hon. Canon, St Matthew's Cathedral, Dallas, Texas, 1989–; Hon. Canon, Truro Cathedral, 1993–. Mem., Churches Commn on Inter-Faith Relations, 1993–. *Publications:* (contrib.) Say One for Me, 1992; contribs to Theology. *Recreations:* theatre, discovering secondhand bookshops. *Address:* 32 Falmouth Road, Truro, Cornwall TR1 2HX. *T:* Truro (01872) 73190.

ST HELENA, Bishop of, since 1991; **Rt Rev. John Harry Gerald Ruston,** OGS; *b* 1 Oct. 1929; *s* of late Alfred Francis Gerald Ruston and Constance Mary (*née* Symonds). *Educ:* Berkhamsted Sch.; Sidney Sussex Coll., Cambridge (BA 1952; MA 1956); Ely Theol Coll. Ordained deacon 1954, priest 1955; joined OGS, 1955; Asst Curate, St Andrew's, Leicester, 1954–57; Tutor, Cuddesdon Coll., Oxford, 1957–61; Asst Curate, All Saints, Cuddesdon, 1957–61; Asst Priest, St Francis, Sekhukhuniland, Transvaal, dio. of Pretoria, 1962–70; Principal, St Francis's Coll., Sekhukhuniland, 1967–70; Canon, Pretoria, 1968–76; Sub-Dean, Pretoria, 1970–76; Archdeacon of Bloemfontein, 1976–83; Warden, Community of St Michael and All Angels, and Chaplain, St Michael's Sch., Bloemfontein, 1976–83; consecrated Bishop, 1983; Bishop Suffragan, Pretoria, 1983–91. *Recreation:* music (composition and adaptation for 3-part singing). *Address:* Bishopsholme, PO Box 62, Island of St Helena, South Atlantic Ocean. *T:* 4471, *Fax:* 4330.

ST HELENS, 2nd Baron *cr* 1964; **Richard Francis Hughes-Young;** *b* 4 Nov. 1945; *s* of 1st Baron St Helens, MC, and Elizabeth Agnes (*d* 1956), *y d* of late Captain Richard Blakiston-Houston; *S* father, 1980; *m* 1983, Mrs Emma R. Talbot-Smith; one *s* one *d*. *Educ:* Nautical College, Pangbourne. *Heir: s* Henry Thomas Hughes-Young, *b* 7 March 1986. *Address:* Marchfield House, Binfield, Berks.

ST JOHN, family name of **Baron St John of Bletso,** and of **Viscount Bolingbroke.**

ST JOHN OF BLETSO, 21st Baron *cr* 1558; **Anthony Tudor St John;** Bt 1660; consultant to Smith New Court plc, London, since 1990; Chairman, Eurotrust International, since 1993; solicitor; *b* 16 May 1957; *s* of 20th Baron St John of Bletso, TD, and of Katharine, *d* of late A. G. von Berg; *S* father, 1978; *m* 1994, Dr Helen Westlake; one *s*. *Educ:* Diocesan College, Rondebosch, Cape; Univ. of Cape Town (BSocSc 1977, BA (Law) 1978); Univ. of S Africa (BProc 1982); London Univ. (LLM 1983). Crossbencher in House of Lords, specific interests foreign affairs, envmtl protection, sport, financial services. Treasurer, Parly Human Rights Gp; Vice Chm., Parly South Africa Gp. Trustee, Television Trust for the Envmt. *Recreations:* golf, tennis and ski-ing; bridge. *Heir: s* Hon. Oliver Beauchamp St John, *b* 11 July 1995. *Address:* c/o House of Lords, SW1A 0AA. *Clubs:* Hurlingham; Royal Cape Golf.

ST JOHN OF FAWSLEY, Baron *cr* 1987 (Life Peer), of Preston Capes in the County of Northamptonshire; **Norman Antony Francis St John-Stevas;** PC 1979; FRSL 1966; Master, Emmanuel College, Cambridge, 1991–Sept. 1996; Chairman, Royal Fine Art Commission, since 1985; author, barrister and journalist; *b* London, 18 May 1929; *o s* of late Stephen S. Stevas, civil engineer and company director, and late Kitty St John O'Connor; unmarried. *Educ:* Ratcliffe; Fitzwilliam, Cambridge (Hon. Fellow 1991); Christ Church, Oxford; Yale. Scholar, Clothworkers Exhibnr, 1946, 1947; BA (Cambridge) (1st cl. hons in law), 1950, MA 1954; President, Cambridge Union, 1950; Whitlock Prize, 1950; MA 1952, BCL 1954 (Oxon); Sec. Oxford Union, 1952; DLitt Oxon 1994; LittD Cantab, 1994. Barrister, Middle Temple, 1952; Blackstone and Harmsworth schol., 1952; Blackstone Prize, 1953. Lecturer, Southampton University, 1952–53, King's Coll., London, 1953–56, tutored in jurisprudence, Christ Church, 1953–55, and Merton, 1955–57, Oxford. Founder member, Inst. of Higher European Studies, Bolzano, 1955; PhD (Lond.) 1957; Yorke Prize, Cambridge Univ., 1957; Fellow Yale Law School, 1957; Fulbright Award, 1957; Fund for the Republic Fellow, 1958; Dr of Sc. of Law (Yale), 1960; Lecture tours of USA, 1958–68. Regents' Prof., Univ. of California at Santa Barbara, 1969; Regents' Lectr, Univ. of Calif at La Jolla, 1984. Legal Adviser to Sir Alan Herbert's Cttee on book censorship, 1954–59; joined The Economist, 1959, to edit collected works of Walter Bagehot and became legal, ecclesiastical and political correspondent. Contested (C) Dagenham, 1951 MP (C) Chelmsford, 1964–87. Mem. Shadow Cabinet, 1974–79, and Opposition Spokesman on Educn, 1975–78, Science and the Arts, 1975–79; Shadow Leader of the House, 1978–79; Parly Under-Sec. of State, DES, 1972–73; Min. of State for the Arts, DES, 1973–74; Chancellor of the Duchy of Lancaster, Leader of the House of Commons and Minister for the Arts, 1979–81. Sec., Cons. Parly Home Affairs Cttee, 1969–72; Vice-Chm., Cons. Parly N Ireland Cttee, 1972–74; Mem. Executive, Cons. Parly 1922 Cttee, 1971–72 and 1974; Vice Chm., Cons. Group for Europe, 1972–75; Member: Cons. Nat. Adv. Cttee on Policy, 1971; Fulbright Commission, 1961; Parly Select Cttee: on Race Relations and Immigration, 1970–72; on Civil List, 1971–73; on Foreign Affairs, 1983–89; Deleg., Council of Europe and WEU, 1967–71; Head, British delegn to Helsinki Cultural Forum, Budapest, 1985. Chm., New Bearings for the Re-Establishment, 1970–. Hon. Sec., Fedn of Cons. Students, 1971–73, Hon. Vice-Pres. 1973. Chm., Booker McConnell Prize, 1985. Mem. Council: RADA, 1983–88; Nat. Soc. for Dance, 1983–; Nat. Youth Theatre, 1983– (Patron, 1984–); RCA, 1985–; Mem., Pontifical Council for Culture, 1987–92; Patron, Medieval Players, 1984–89; Dir, N. M. Rothschild Trust, 1990–; Trustee: Royal Philharmonic Orch., 1985–88; Philharmonic Orch., 1988–; Royal Soc. of Painters in Watercolours, 1984; Decorative Arts Soc., 1984–. Editor The Dublin (Wiseman) Review, 1961. Vice Pres., Les Amis de Napoléon III, 1974; Mem., Académie du Second Empire, 1975. Hon. FRIBA 1990; Presidential Fellow, Aspern Inst., 1980; Hon. Fellow, St Edmund's College, Cambridge, 1985. Romanes Lectr, Oxford, 1987. DD (*hc*) Univ. of Susquehanna, Pa, 1983; DLitt (*hc*): Schiller Univ., 1985; Bristol Univ., 1988; Hon. LLD Leicester, 1991. Silver Jubilee Medal, 1977. SBStJ. Gran Ufficiale, Order of Merit (Italian Republic), 1989 (Commendatore, 1965). GCKLJ 1976 (KSLJ 1963). *Publications:* Obscenity and the Law, 1956; Walter Bagehot, 1959; Life, Death and the Law, 1961; The Right to Life, 1963; Law and Morals, 1964; The Literary Works of Walter Bagehot, vols I, II, 1966, The Historical Works, vols III, IV, 1968, The Political Works, vols V, VI, VII, and VIII, 1974, The Economic Works, vols IX, X and XI, 1970, Letters and Miscellany, vols XII, XIII, XIV and XV, 1986; The Agonising Choice, 1971; Pope John Paul II, his travels and mission, 1982; The Two Cities, 1984; contrib. to: Critical Quarterly, Modern Law Review, Criminal Law Review, Law and Contemporary Problems, Twentieth Century, Times Lit. Supp., Dublin Review. *Recreations:* reading, talking, listening (to music), travelling, walking, appearing on television, sleeping. *Address:* (until Sept. 1996) The Master's Lodge, Emmanuel College, Cambridge CB2 3AP; The Old Rectory, Preston Capes, Daventry, Northants NN11 6TE. *Clubs:* White's, Garrick, Pratt's, Arts (Hon. Mem., 1980), Grillions, The Other; Hawks (Cambridge) (Hon. Mem., 1993); Emmanuel Boat (Pres., 1993).

ST JOHN, Oliver Beauchamp, CEng, FRAeS; Chief Scientist, Civil Aviation Authority, 1978–82; *b* 22 Jan. 1922; 2nd *s* of late Harold and Ella Margaret St John; *m* 1945, Eileen (*née* Morris); three *s*. *Educ:* Monkton Combe Sch.; Queens Coll., Cambridge (MA); London Univ. (External) (BSc). Metropolitan Vickers, Manchester, 1939; Royal Aircraft Estabt, Farnborough, from 1946, on automatic control of fixed-wing aircraft and helicopters; Supt, Blind Landing Experimental Unit, RAE, Bedford, 1966; Director of Technical Research & Development, CAA, 1969–78. Queen's Commendation for Valuable Services in the Air, 1956. *Publication:* A Gallimaufry of Goffering: a history of early ironing implements, 1982. *Recreations:* mountaineering, early music, instrument making. *Address:* The Old Stables, Manor Farm Barns, East Hagbourne OX11 9ND. *T:* Didcot (01235) 818437.

ST JOHN, Maj.-Gen. Roger Ellis Tudor, CB 1965; MC 1944; *b* Hexham on Tyne, 4 Oct. 1911; *s* of late Major B. T. St John, Craigveigh, Aboyne, Aberdeenshire; *m* 1943, Rosemary Jean Douglas Vickers, Englefield Green, Surrey; one *s* three *d*. *Educ:* Wellington College; RMC Sandhurst. Joined Fifth Fusiliers, 1931; served War of 1939–45 (despatches, MC), in Hong Kong, UK and NW Europe; Bde Major 11 Armoured Div., 1944–45; GSO 2 Instructor Camberley Staff Coll., 1945–46; AA and QMG 1st Division, Tripoli, 1948–50; comd 1st Bn Royal Northumberland Fusiliers, 1953–55 (despatches), Mau Mau Rebellion; AMS Mil. Secretary's Branch, War Office, 1955–57; Comdr 11 Inf. Bde Group, BAOR, 1957–60; Asst Comdt, Camberley Staff Coll., 1960–62; Comdr, British Army Staff, Military Member, British Defence Staffs, and Military Attaché, Washington, 1963–65; President, Regular Army Commissions Board, 1965–67; retired, 1967. Colonel, Royal Northumberland Fusiliers, 1965–68. Personnel Adminr, Urwick, Orr and Partners Ltd, Management Consultants, 1967–73. *Address:* Harelaw, Gorse Hill Road, Virginia Water, Surrey GU25 4AS.

ST JOHN PARKER, Michael, MA (Cantab); Headmaster, Abingdon School, Oxfordshire, since 1975; *b* 21 July 1941; *s* of Rev. Canon J. W. Parker; *m* 1965, Annette Monica Ugle; two *s* two *d*. *Educ:* Stamford Sch.; King's Coll., Cambridge. Asst Master: Sevenoaks Sch., 1962–63; King's Sch., Canterbury, 1963–69; Winchester Coll., 1969–75; Head of History Dept, Winchester Coll., 1970–75. Schoolmaster Student, Christ Church, Oxford, 1984. Member: Council, Hansard Soc., 1972–; Marsh Cttee on Politics and Industry, 1978–79. Chm., Midland Div., HMC, 1984. Governor: St Helen's Sch., 1975–83; Christ Church Cathedral Sch.; Cokethorpe Sch. (Chm., 1990); Josca's Sch. *Publications:* The British Revolution—Social and Economic History 1750–1970, 1972; various pamphlets and articles. *Recreations:* old buildings, music, books. *Address:* Lacies Court, Abingdon, Oxfordshire. *T:* Abingdon (01235) 520163. *Clubs:* Athenæum, East India; Leander.

ST JOHN-STEVAS, family name of **Baron St John of Fawsley.**

ST JOHN WILSON, Colin Alexander; *see* Wilson.

ST JOHN'S (Newfoundland), Archbishop of (RC), since 1991; **Most Rev. James Macdonald,** DD, CSC; *b* 28 April 1925; *s* of Alexander and Mary Macdonald. *Educ:* St Joseph's Univ., 1944–45. Ordained priest, 1953. Congregation of the Holy Cross: Mission Bank, 1954–56; Dir, Holy Cross Minor Seminary, St Joseph's, NB, 1956–62; Sec., Provincial Council, 1956–63; Dir of Vocations, 1962–63; Superior, Holy Cross House of Studies, 1964–69; Asst Provincial, 1966–72; Pastor, St Michael's, Waterloo, Ont., 1969–77; Dean, Waterloo County Priests, dio. of Hamilton, 1974–77; Aux. Bishop of Hamilton, 1978–82; Bishop of Charlottetown, 1982–91. *Address:* PO Box 37, St John's, Newfoundland A1C 5H5, Canada.

ST JOHNSTON, Colin David; Managing Director, PRO NED (Promotion of Non-Executive Directors), 1989–95; *b* 6 Sept. 1934; *s* of Hal and Sheilagh St Johnston; *m* 1958, Valerie Paget; three *s* one *d. Educ:* Shrewsbury Sch.; Lincoln Coll., Oxford. Booker McConnell Ltd, 1958–70; Ocean Transport and Trading Ltd, 1970–88: Dir, 1974–88; Dep. Chief Exec., 1985–88; non-Executive Director, FMC plc, 1981–83. Mem. Council: Royal Commonwealth Society for the Blind, 1967–; Industrial Soc., 1981–; Trustee, Frances Mary Buss Foundn, 1981–; Governor: Camden Sch., 1974–; Arnold House Sch. *Recreations:* music, Real and lawn tennis. *Address:* 30 Fitzroy Road, NW1 8TY. *T:* 0171–722 5932. *Club:* MCC.

ST JOHNSTON, Sir Kerry, Kt 1988; Chairman, NM Funds Management Europe, since 1993; Executive Director, Diehl and St Johnston Ltd, since 1989; Director, Wilrig AS, Norway, since 1992 (Chairman, 1989–92); *b* 30 July 1931; *s* of George Eric St Johnston and Viola Rhona Moriarty; *m* 1st, 1960, Judith Ann Nichols; two *s* one *d*; 2nd, 1980, Charlotte Ann Taylor, *d* of late John Scott Limnell Lyon and Patricia Marjorie Hambro. *Educ:* Summer Fields, Oxford; Eton Coll.; Worcester Coll., Oxford (MA Jurisprudence). Joined Ocean Steamship Co. Ltd, 1955, Man. Dir 1963; Overseas Containers Ltd: Founder Dir, 1965; Commerical Dir, 1966; Jt Man. Dir, 1969; Dep. Chm., 1973; Pres. and Chief Exec. Officer, Private Investment Co. for Asia (PICA), SA, Singapore, 1977–82; Chm. and Chief Exec., P & O (formerly Overseas) Containers Ltd, 1982–89. Director: Royal Insurance, 1973–76; Lloyds Bank Internat. Ltd, 1983–85; P&OSNCo., 1986–89. Pres., Gen. Council of British Shipping, 1987–88. *Recreations:* trout fishing, gardening. *Address:* Flat 5, 53 Drayton Gardens, SW10 9RX. *T:* 0171–373 3947. *Club:* Boodle's.

SAINT LAURENT, Yves (Henri Donat); Chevalier de la Légion d'Honneur, 1985; couturier; *b* 1 Aug. 1936; *s* of Charles and Lucienne-Andrée (Wilbaux) Mathieu Saint Laurent. *Educ:* Lycée d'Oran. Collaborator, 1954, then successor of Christian Dior, 1957–60; Dir, Société Yves Saint Laurent, 1962–. *Exhibitions:* Metropolitan Mus. of Art, NY, 1983; Fine Arts Mus., Beijing, 1985; Musée des Arts de la Mode, Paris, 1986; House of Painters of the USSR, Moscow, 1986; Hermitage Mus., Leningrad, 1987; Art Gall. of NSW, Sydney, 1987; Sezon Mus. of Art, Tokyo, 1990. *Costume design: for theatre,* Le Mariage de Figaro, 1964; Delicate Balance, 1967; *for ballet:* Cyrano de Bergerac, 1959; Adage et Variations, 1965; Notre Dame de Paris, 1965; Scheherazade, 1973; *for films:* The Pink Panther, 1962; Belle de Jour, 1967; La Chamade, 1968; La Sirène du Mississippi (with Catherine Deneuve), 1969; L'affaire Stavisky, 1974; *stage sets and costumes:* Les Chants de Maldoror, 1962; Spectacle Zizi Jeanmaire, 1961, 1963, 1968; Revue Zizi Jeanmaire, 1970, 1972, 1977; L'Aigle à deux têtes, 1978. Neiman-Marcus Award for fashion, 1958; Oscar from Harper's Bazaar, 1966; Internat. Award, Council of Fashion Designers of America, 1982; Best Fashion Designer Oscar, 1985. *Publication:* La Vilaine Lulu, 1967. *Address:* (office) 5 avenue Marceau, 75116 Paris; (home) 55 rue de Babylone, 75007 Paris, France.

ST LEGER, family name of **Viscount Doneraile.**

ST LEVAN, 4th Baron *cr* 1887; **John Francis Arthur St Aubyn,** DSC 1942; Bt 1866; landowner and company director; Vice Lord-Lieutenant of Cornwall, 1992–94; *b* 23 Feb. 1919; *s* of 3rd Baron St Levan, and Hon. Clementina Gwendolen Catharine Nicolson (*d* 1995), *o d* of 1st Baron Carnock; *S* father, 1978; *m* 1970, Susan Mary Marcia, *d* of late Maj.-Gen. Sir John Kennedy, GCMG, KCVO, KBE, CB. *Educ:* Eton Coll.; Trinity Coll., Cambridge (BA). Served RNVR, 1940–46 (Lieut). Admitted a Solicitor, 1948. High Sheriff of Cornwall, 1974; DL Cornwall, 1977. President: Friends of Plymouth City Museums and Art Gallery, 1985–; London Cornish Assoc., 1987–; Penzance YMCA, 1987–; St Ives Soc. of Artists, 1979–; Penwith NT Assoc., 1987–; Penwith and Isles of Scilly Dist Scout Council, 1991–; Cornish Maritime Trust; Vice President: Royal Bath and West and Southern Counties Soc., 1984– (Pres., 1983); Royal Cornwall Agricl Assoc., 1980– (Pres., 1979); Minack Theatre, 1989–; Hon. Patron, Penzance Sea Cadet Corps. FRSA 1974. CStJ 1990. *Publication:* Illustrated History of St Michael's Mount, 1974. *Recreation:* sailing. *Heir: b* Hon. (Oliver) Piers St Aubyn, MC [*b* 12 July 1920; *m* 1948, Mary (*d* 1987), *e d* of late Bailey Southwell; two *s* one *d*]. *Address:* St Michael's Mount, Marazion, Cornwall TR17 0HT. *Clubs:* Brooks's; Royal Yacht Squadron.

ST OSWALD, 5th Baron *cr* 1885; **Derek Edward Anthony Winn;** DL; *b* 9 July 1919; *s* of 3rd Baron St Oswald and Eve Carew (*d* 1976), *d* of Charles Greene; *S* brother, 1984; *m* 1954, Charlotte Denise Eileen, *d* of Wilfred Haig Loyd; one *s* one *d. Educ:* Stowe. Joined 60th Rifles, KRRC, as 2nd Lieut, 1938; Parachute Regt, 1942; served N Africa (wounded). Malayan Police, 1948–51. Film Producer, 1953–67. Farm owner, Nostell Priory. President: Wakefield Parachute Regt, 1985–; Wakefield Hospice, 1985–; Wakefield Multiple Sclerosis Soc., 1985–. DL W Yorks, 1987. *Publication:* I Served Caesar, 1972. *Recreation:* shooting. *Heir: s* Hon. Charles Rowland Andrew Winn [*b* 22 July 1959; *m* 1985, Louise Alexandra, *yr d* of Stewart Scott; one *s*]. *Address:* Nostell Priory, Wakefield, Yorks WF4 1QE. *T:* Wakefield (01924) 862394; The Old Rectory, Bainton, Driffield, East Yorks YO25 9NG. *Clubs:* Lansdowne, Special Forces.

ST PAUL'S, Dean of; *see* Evans, Very Rev. T. E.

ST VINCENT, 7th Viscount (*cr* 1801); **Ronald George James Jervis;** *b* 3 May 1905; *o* surv. *s* of 6th Viscount and Marion Annie (*d* 1911), *d* of James Brown, JP, Orchard, Carluke, Scotland; *S* father, 1940; *m* 1945, Phillida, *o d* of Lt-Col R. H. Logan, Taunton; two *s* one *d. Educ:* Sherborne. JP Somerset, 1950–55. *Heir: s* Hon. Edward Robert James Jervis [*b* 12 May 1951; *m* 1977, Victoria Margaret, *o d* of Wilton J. Oldham, St Peter, Jersey; one *s* one *d*]. *Address:* Les Charrieres, St Ouen, Jersey, CI.

ST VINCENT FERRERI, Marquis of; *see* San Vincenzo Ferreri.

SAINTONGE, Rolland A. A. C. de; *see* Chaput de Saintonge.

SAINTY, Sir John Christopher, KCB 1986; Clerk of the Parliaments, 1983–90, retired; *b* 31 Dec. 1934; *s* of late Christopher Lawrence Sainty and Nancy Lee Sainty (*née* Miller); *m* 1965, (Elizabeth) Frances Sherlock; three *s. Educ:* Winchester Coll.; New Coll., Oxford (MA). FSA; FRHistS. Clerk, Parlt Office, House of Lords, 1959; seconded as Private Sec. to Leader of House and Chief Whip, House of Lords, 1963; Clerk of Journals, House of Lords, 1965; Res. Asst and Editor, Inst. of Historical Research, 1970; Reading Clerk, House of Lords, 1974. Mem., Royal Commn on Historical MSS, 1991–. Sen. Res. Fellow, Inst. of Historical Res., 1994–. *Publications:* Treasury Officials 1660–1870, 1972; Officials of the Secretaries of State 1660–1782, 1973; Officials of the Boards of Trade 1660–1870, 1974; Admiralty Officials 1660–1870, 1975; Home Office Officials, 1782–1870, 1975; Colonial Office Officials 1794–1870, 1976; (with D. Dewar) Divisions in the House of Lords: an analytical list 1685–1857, 1976; Officers of the Exchequer, 1983; A List of English Law Officers, King's Counsel and Holders of Patents of Precedence, 1987; The Judges of England 1272–1990, 1993; articles in Eng. Hist. Rev., Bull. Inst. Hist. Research. *Address:* 22 Kelso Place, W8 5QG. *T:* 0171–937 9460. *Club:* Brooks's.

SAKMANN, Prof. Bert, MD; Director, Department of Cell Physiology, Max-Planck-Institut für medizinische Forschung, Heidelberg, since 1989; Professor of Physiology, Medical Faculty, University of Heidelberg, since 1990; *b* Stuttgart, 12 June 1942; *m* 1970, Dr Christiane Wülfert; two *s* one *d. Educ:* Univ. of Tübingen; Univ. of Munich; University Hosp., Munich; Univ. of Göttingen (MD). Research Asst, Max-Plancke-Institut für Psychiatrie, Munich, 1969–70; British Council Fellow, Dept of Biophysics, UCL, 1971–73; Max-Planck-Institut für biophysikalische Chemie, University of Göttingen: Res. Asst, 1974–79; Res. Associate, Membrane Biology Gp, 1979–82; Head, Membrane Physiology Unit, 1983–85; Dir 1985–87, Prof. 1987–89, Dept of Cell Physiology. Lectures: Yale, 1982; Washington Univ., Seattle, 1986, 1990; Univ. of Miami, 1989; Liverpool Univ., 1990; Univ. of Rochester, NY, 1991. Foreign Member: Royal Soc., 1994; Nat. Acad., USA. Numerous prizes and awards; (jtly) Nobel Prize for Physiology, 1991. *Publications:* (contrib.) The Visual System: neurophysiology, biophysics and their clinical applications, 1972; (contrib.) Advances in Pharmacology and Therapeutics, 1978; (contrib. and ed with E. Neher) Single Channel Recording, 1983; (contrib.) Membrane Control of Cellular Activity, 1986; (contrib.) Calcium and Ion Channel Modulation, 1988; (contrib.) Neuromuscular Junction, 1989; numerous articles in jls incl. Annual Rev. Physiol., Jl Physiol., Nature, Proc. Nat. Acad. Scis, Pflügers Archiv., Jl Exptl Physiol., Neuron, FEBS Lett., Science, Eur. Jl Biochem., Proc. Royal Soc., Jl Cell Biol. *Recreations:* tennis, ski-ing, music, reading. *Address:* Max-Planck-Institut für medizinische Forschung, Jahnstrasse 29, 69120 Heidelberg, Germany. *T:* (6221) 486460.

SALAM, Professor Abdus, Hon. KBE 1989; Sitara-i-Pakistan, 1959; Order of Nishan-i-Imtiaz, Pakistan, 1979; PhD; FRS 1959; Professor of Theoretical Physics, 1957–93, Fellow, since 1994, Imperial College, University of London; Director, 1964–94, President, since 1994, International Centre for Theoretical Physics, Trieste; *b* 29 Jan. 1926. *Educ:* Govt Coll., Lahore, Pakistan (MA); St John's Coll., Camb. (BA, PhD). Fellow, St John's Coll., Cambridge, 1951–56 (Hon. Fellow, 1972); Professor of Mathematics, Government College, Lahore, 1951–54; Lecturer in Mathematics, University of Cambridge, 1954–56. Sci. Advr to Pres. of Pakistan, 1961–74. Has made contributions to the theory of elementary particles. Member: UN Adv. Cttee on Science and Technology, 1964–75 (Chm., 1971–72); South Commn, 1987–; Vice-Pres., IUPAP, 1972–78. Founding Mem. and Pres., Third World Acad. of Scis, 1983; (first elected) Pres., Third World Network of Scientific Orgns, 1988–; Fellow: Royal Swedish Acad. of Sciences, 1970; APS, 1993; For. Mem., USSR Acad. of Scis, 1971. Hon. DSc, universities in: Punjab (Lahore), 1957; Edinburgh, 1971; Trieste and Islamabad, 1979; Lima, Cuzco, Caracas, Wroclow, Yarmouk and Istanbul, 1980; Amritsar, Aligarh, Banaras, Chittagong, Bristol and Maiduguri, 1981; Philippines, 1982; Khartoum and Madrid, 1983; New York (City Coll.) and Nairobi, 1984; Cuyo, La Plata and Göteborg, 1985; Sofia, Glasgow, Hefei and London (City Univ.), 1986; Punjab (Chandigarh), Benin, Exeter and Colombo, 1987; Gent, 1988; Bendel State and Ghana, 1990; Warwick, Dakar and Tucaman, 1991; Lagos, S Carolina, W Indies, St Petersburg, 1992; Gulbarga and Dhaka, 1993; Hon. ScD Cambridge, 1985. Hopkins Prize, Cambridge Philosophical Soc., 1957; Adams Prize, Cambridge Univ., 1958; Maxwell Medal and Prize, IPPS, 1961; Hughes Medal, Royal Society, 1964; Atoms for Peace Award, 1968; Oppenheimer Prize and Medal, 1971; Guthrie Medal and Prize, IPPS, 1976; Matteuci Medal, Accad. Naz. di XL, Rome, 1978; John Torrence Tate Medal, Amer. Inst. of Physics, 1978; Royal Medal, Royal Society, 1978; (jtly) Nobel Prize for Physics, 1979; Einstein Medal, UNESCO, Paris, 1979; Josef Stefan Medal, Josef Stefan Inst., Ljubljana, 1980; Gold Medal for outstanding contrib. to physics, Czechoslovak Acad. of Scis, Prague, 1981; Peace Medal, Charles Univ., Prague, 1981; Lomonosov Gold Medal, USSR Acad. of Scis, 1983; Genoa Internat. Develt of People's Prize, 1988; Edinburgh Medal and Prize, 1989; Ettore Majorana Erice Science for Peace Prize, 1989; Copley Medal, Royal Soc., 1990; Cataluña Internat. Prize, Spain, 1990; Internat. Leocino d'Oro Prize, Italy, 1993. Order of Andres Bello (Venezuela), 1980; Order of Istiqlal (Jordan), 1980; Cavaliere di Gran Croce, Order of Merit (Italy), 1989. *Publications:* (ed with E. P. Wigner) Aspects of Quantum Mechanics, 1972; Ideals and Realities: selected essays, 1984, 3rd edn 1989; Science and Education in Pakistan, 1987; (with Ergin Sezgin) Supergravity in Diverse Dimensions, Vols I and II, 1988; (ed) From a Life of Physics, 1989; Unification of Funadamental Forces: the first of the 1988 Dirac Memorial Lectures, 1990; Science and Technology: challenge for the South, 1992; papers on physics of elementary particles and on scientific and educnl policies for developing countries and Pakistan; *relevant publications:* Abdus Salam, by Dr Abdul Ghani, 1982; Abdus Salam, by Jagjit Singh, 1992; Selected Papers of Abdus Salam (with commentary), 1994. *Address:* International Centre for Theoretical Physics, PO Box 586, 34100 Trieste, Italy.

SALAS, Dame Margaret Laurence, (Dame Laurie), DBE 1988; QSO 1982; *b* 8 Feb. 1922; *d* of Sir James Lawrence Hay, OBE and late Davidina Mertel (*née* Gunn); *m* 1946, Dr John Reuben Salas, FRCSE, FRACS; two *s* four *d. Educ:* Christchurch; Univ. of New Zealand (BA). Teacher, audiometrist in Med. practice. National Council of Women of NZ: legislative and parly work; Nat. Sec., 1976–80; Nat. Vice-Pres., 1982–86; Vice-Convener, Internat. Council, Women's Cttee on Develt, 1985–94; Nat. Sec., Women's Internat. League for Peace and Freedom, 1985–90; Pres., UNA, NZ, 1988–92; Vice-Pres., World Fedn of UNAs, 1993–; Member: Public Adv. Cttee, Disarmament and Arms Control, 1987–; Nat. Cons. Cttee on Disarmament (Chair, 1979–90); Adv. Cttee, External Aid and Develt, 1986–88; Standing Cttee, NZ Inst. of Internat. Affairs, 1989–; Educn Cttee, Alcoholic Liquor Adv. Council, 1976–81; Nat. Review Cttee on Social Studies, Educn Dept; Cttee, SCF, 1970–76; Nat. Commn, UN Internat. Year of the Child, 1978–80; UN Internat. Year of Peace, Aotearoa Cttee, (Vice-Chair, 1986); NZ Cttee, Council for Security, Co-operation in Asia and Pacific, 1994–. Pres., Wellington Branch, NZ Fedn of Univ. Women, 1970–72; repr. NZ, overseas meetings. Silver Jubilee Medal, 1977; NZ Commemoration Medal, 1990. *Publication:* Disarmament, 1982. *Recreations:* choral and classical music, enjoying extended family. *Address:* 2 Raumati Terrace, Khandallah, Wellington 4, New Zealand. *T:* (4) 4793415.

See also Sir David Hay, Sir Hamish Hay.

SALCEDO-BASTARDO, José Luis; writer and diplomat; *b* Carúpano, Venezuela, 15 March 1926; *s* of Joaquin Salcedo-Arocha and Catalina Salcedo-Arocha (*née* Bastardo); *m* 1968, Maria Cecilia Avila; four *s. Educ:* Central Univ. of Venezuela; Univ. of Paris; London Sch. of Economics. Teacher of social sciences, 1945; Chief Editor, Nat. Magazine of Culture, 1948–50; Asst Lectr, Central Univ., 1949; Founder Rector, Univ. of Santa Maria, Caracas, 1953; Senator for State of Sucre, 1958; Mem., Senate Foreign Relations Cttee; Ambassador to Ecuador, 1959–61; to Brazil, 1961–63; Prof. of Sociology, Central Univ., 1964; Pres., Nat. Inst. of Culture and Fine Arts, 1965–67; Vice-Pres., Supreme Electoral Council, 1970–74; Ambassador to France, 1974–76; Minister, Secretariat of the Presidency, 1976–77; Minister of State for Sci., Tech. and Culture, 1977–79; Ambassador to UK, 1984–87, to GDR, 1987–90. Member, councils and commns, S America and Europe. *Publications:* Through the Sociological World of Cecilio Acosta, 1945; In Pursuit of Glory, 1947; Vision and Revision of Bolívar, 1957; Biography of Don Egidio Montesinos, 1957; Thesis for Union, 1963; Basis for Cultural Action, 1965; Fundamental History of Venezuela, 1970; Conscience of the Present, 1971; Carabobo: nationality and history, 1972; Bolívar: a continent and its destiny, 1972 (26 edns, trans into 12 langs); The First Duty, 1973; To Make History Unpolitical, 1973; Of History and Duties, 1975; Bolívar and San Martín, 1975; A Transparent Man, 1976; Crucible of Americanism, 1979; Ideological and Literary Concordances in Bolívar, 1981; Andrés Bello: an American, 1982; Bolivarian Repetition, 1983; Andrés Eloy Blanco For the Young, 1983; Simón Bolívar, 1983; Bolívar, Ideas and People, 1994; Man and Men, 1994. *Recreation:* travelling abroad. *Address:* PO Box 2777, Caracas, Venezuela.

SALEM, Daniel Laurent Manuel; Chairman, The Condé Nast Publications Ltd, London, since 1968; *b* 29 Jan. 1925; *s* of Raphael Salem and Adriana Gentili di Giuseppe; *m* 1950, Marie-Pierre Arachtingi. *Educ:* Harvard Univ., Cambridge, Mass (BA, MA). Served Free French Forces, 1943–45. Exec. Asst, Lazard Frères & Co., New York, 1946–50; exec. positions, The Condé Nast Publications Inc., New York, 1950–60, Vice-Pres., 1965–86, Dep. Chm., 1986–92; Vice Pres., Banque Paribas, Paris, 1961–65; Chm., Condé Nast International Inc., 1971–91. Chairman: Mercury Selected Trust, 1974–; Mercury Offshore Selected Trust, 1979–; Philharmonia Trust Ltd, 1985–92. Chevalier, Legion of Honour (France), 1987; Commnendatore, Order of Merit (Italy), 1988. *Recreations:* music, bridge, chess, golf. *Address:* 3 Ennismore Gardens, SW7 1NL. *T:* 0171–584 0466. *Clubs:* White's, Portland; Harvard (New York City); Travellers (Paris).

SALES, (Donald) John; Chief Gardens Adviser, The National Trust, since 1974; *b* 1 May 1933; *s* of Frederic Donald Sales and Alice Elizabeth (*née* Burrell); *m* 1958, Lyn Thompson; three *s*. *Educ:* Westminster City Sch.; Kent Horticultural Coll.; Royal Botanic Gardens, Kew. MHort (RHS) 1957; FIHort 1984. Lectr in Horticulture, Writtle Agricl Coll., Chelmsford, 1958–70; Horticulturist (Asst to Gardens Advr), NT, 1971–74. Medal of Honour, Internat. Castles Inst., 1991; VMH, RHS, 1992. *Publications:* West Country Gardens, 1980; contrib. articles in Country Life. *Recreations:* gardening, photography, walking, music, ballet, the arts generally. *Address:* The National Trust, 33 Sheep Street, Cirencester, Glos GL7 1QW; Covertside, Perrott's Brook, Cirencester, Glos GL7 7BW. *T:* Cirencester (01285) 831537.

SALFORD, Bishop of, (RC), since 1984; **Rt. Rev. Patrick Altham Kelly;** *b* 23 Nov. 1938; *s* of John Joseph Kelly and Mary Ann Kelly (née Altham). *Educ:* St Mary's Primary School, Morecambe; Preston Catholic Coll.; English College and Gregorian Univ., Rome (STL, PhL). Curate, Lancaster Cathedral, 1964–66; Lectr in Theology, 1966–79 and Rector, 1979–84, St Mary's Coll., Oscott. *Address:* Wardley Hall, Worsley, Manchester M28 2ND.

SALINGER, Jerome David; American author; *b* New York City, 1919; *m*; one *s* one *d*. *Educ:* Manhattan public schools; Military Academy, Paris. Served with 4th Infantry Division, US Army, 1942–46 (Staff Sergeant). Travelled in Europe, 1937–38. Started writing at age of 15; first story published, 1940. *Publications:* The Catcher in the Rye, 1951; For Esme-with Love and Squalor, 1953; Franny and Zooey, 1962; Raise High the Roof Beam, Carpenters and Seymour: an Introduction, 1963. *Address:* c/o Harold Ober Associates, 425 Madison Avenue, New York, NY 10017, USA.

SALINGER, Pierre (Emil George); politician, journalist; Vice Chairman, Burson Marsteller, since 1993, International Consultant, ABC News, American Broadcasting Company, since 1993, *b* San Francisco, 14 June 1925; *s* of Herbert and Jehanne Salinger; *m* 1st; one *s* one *d* (and one *s* decd); 2nd, 1957, Nancy Brook Joy (marr. diss., 1965); 3rd, 1965, Nicole Gillmann (marr. diss. 1988), Paris, France; one *s*; 4th, 1989, Nicole Beauvillain. *Educ:* Lowell High School, San Francisco; State Coll., San Francisco; Univ of San Francisco. Served War, 1942–45, with US Navy. With San Francisco Chronicle, 1942–55; Guest Lectr, Mills Coll., Calif, 1950–55; Press Officer, Democratic Presidential Campaign (Calif), 1952; West Coast Editor, Contributing Editor, Collier's Magazine, 1955–56; Investigator, Senate Labor Rackets Cttee, 1957–59; Press Sec. to President Kennedy (when Senator), 1959–61, and to President of the United States, 1961–64; appointed to serve as a US Senator, 4 Aug. 1964–2 Jan. 1965; Roving Editor, L'Express, Paris, 1973–78; ABC News: Correspondent, Paris, 1978–79; Paris Bureau Chief, 1979–87; Chief Foreign Corresp., 1983–93; Sen. Ed., Europe, 1988–93. Vice Pres.: Continental Airlines, Continental Air Services, 1965–68. Trustee, Robert F. Kennedy Meml Foundn; Hon. Chm., Bd of Trustees, American Coll. in Paris. Mem., Legion of Honour, 1978; US Navy and Marine Corps Medal, 1946. *Publications:* articles on county jail conditions in California, 1953; A Tribute to John F. Kennedy, Encyclopedia Britannica, 1964; With Kennedy, 1966; A Tribute to Robert F. Kennedy, 1968; For the Eyes of the President Only, 1971; Je suis un Americain, 1975; La France et le Nouveau Monde, 1976; America Held Hostage—the secret negotiations, 1981; (with Leonard Gross) The Dossier, 1984; (with Robert Cameron) Above Paris, 1985; (with Leonard Gross) Mortal Games, 1988; (with Eric Laurent) La Guerre du Golfe: le dossier secret, 1990. *Address:* c/o Burson Marsteller, 1850 M Street NW, Suite 900, Washington, DC 20036, USA.

SALISBURY, 6th Marquess of, *cr* 1789; **Robert Edward Peter Cecil;** DL; Baron Cecil, 1603; Viscount Cranborne, 1604; Earl of Salisbury, 1605; Captain Grenadier Guards; High Steward of Hertford since 1972; *b* 24 Oct. 1916; *s* of 5th Marquess of Salisbury, KG, PC, FRS, and Elizabeth Vere (*d* 1982), *e d* of late Lord Richard Cavendish, PC, CB, CMG; *S* father, 1972; *m* 1945, Marjorie Olein (Mollie), *d* of late Captain Hon. Valentine Wyndham-Quin, RN; four *s* one *d* (and one *s* decd). MP (C) Bournemouth West, 1950–54. Pres., Monday Club, 1974–81. DL Dorset, 1974. *Heir:* *s* Viscount Cranborne, *qv*. *Address:* Hatfield House, Hatfield, Herts AL9 5NF.

SALISBURY, Bishop of, since 1993; **Rt. Rev. David Staffurth Stancliffe;** *b* 1 Oct. 1942; *s* of late Very Rev. Michael Staffurth Stancliffe; *m* 1965, Sarah Loveday Smith; one *s* two *d*. *Educ:* Westminster School; Trinity College, Oxford (MA); Cuddesdon Theological College. Assistant Curate, St Bartholomew's, Armley, Leeds, 1967–70; Chaplain to Clifton Coll., Bristol, 1970–77; Canon Residentiary of Portsmouth Cathedral, Diocesan Director of Ordinands and Lay Ministry Adviser, 1977–82; Provost of Portsmouth, 1982–93. Member: Gen. Synod, 1985–; Liturgical Commn, 1986– (Chm., 1993–); Cathedrals' Fabric Commn, 1991–. Pres., Council, Marlborough Coll., 1994–. DLitt Portsmouth, 1993. *Recreations:* old music, Italy. *Address:* South Canonry, 71 The Close, Salisbury, Wilts SP1 2ER. *T:* Salisbury (01722) 334031.

See also M. J. Stancliffe.

SALISBURY, Dean of; *see* Dickinson, Very Rev. H. G.

SALISBURY, John; *see* Caute, J. D.

SALISSE, John Joseph, CBE 1986; Director, Marks and Spencer, 1968–85; *b* 24 March 1926; *s* of Joseph and Anne Salisse; *m* 1949, Margaret Horsfield; one *d*. *Educ:* Portsmouth Grammar Sch. Marks and Spencer, 1944–85. Chairman: CBI Distributive Trades Survey Cttee, 1983–86; St Enoch Management Centre Ltd, 1986–; Jt London Tourism Forum, 1986–; London Enterprise Agency, 1983–88; Retail Consortium, 1986–92; Director: London Tourist Bd, 1984– (Vice-Chm., 1989–); City Shops, 1986–88; Fullemploy, 1984–86; Allied Internat. Designers, 1986–87. Jt Treas., European Movement, 1982–86; Member: CBI Council, 1984–89; Cttee, Amer. European Community Assoc., 1983–90; Nat. Employers' Liaison Cttee, 1987–92; Cttee on Commerce and Distribution, 1988–93; Council for Charitable Support, 1986–89; Inst. of Dirs; Trustee, London Educn Business Partnership, 1986–92; Dir, CECD, 1986–93 (Vice-Pres., 1989–93). Hon. Vice Pres., Magic Circle, 1975– (Hon. Sec., 1965–86); Hon. Life Mem., Acad. of Magical Arts and Scis, America, 1979–. Freeman, City of London, 1992. *Publications:* various contribs to Magic literature. *Recreations:* golf, theatre, ballet, opera, history of magic, collecting Victorian theatre programmes. *Address:* 12 Hampstead Way, NW11 7LS. *Clubs:* Savage, Magic Circle, Highgate Golf; Magic Castle (Los Angeles).

SALJE, Prof. Ekhard Karl Hermann, PhD; Professor of Mineralogy and Petrology, Cambridge University, since 1994 (Professor of Mineral Physics, 1992–94); Fellow, Darwin College, Cambridge, since 1987; *b* Hanover, Germany, 26 Oct. 1946; *s* of Gerhard Salje and Hildegard (*née* Drechsler); *m* 1980, Elisabeth Démaret; one *s* four *d*. *Educ:* Univ. of Hanover (PhD 1972); MA Cantab 1986. University of Hanover: Lectr in Physics, 1972–75; Habilitation in Crystallography, 1975; Prof. of Crystallography, 1978–86; Hd, Dept of Crystallography and Petrology, 1983–86; Mem., Senate, 1980–82; Lectr, Cambridge Univ., 1987–92. Associate Prof. of Physics, Univ. of Paris, 1981; Prof. invité in Physics, Grenoble Univ., 1990–91. Advr to British, French, German and EC scientific orgns. *Publications:* Physical Properties and Thermodynamic Behaviour of Minerals, 1987; Phase Transitions in ferroelastic and co-elastic crystals, 1991; Application of Landau Theory for the Analysis of Phase Transitions in Minerals, 1992; numerous res. papers in solid state physics, crystallography and mineralogy. *Recreations:* painting, music. *Address:* 59 Glisson Road, Cambridge CB1 2HG. *T:* Cambridge (01223) 350181.

SALLON, Christopher Robert Anthony; QC 1994; *b* 3 May 1948; *s* of Alexander and Alice Sallon; *m* 1971, Jacqueline Gould; two *s*. Called to the Bar, Gray's Inn, 1973; Asst Recorder, 1992–. Bar Council: South Eastern Circuit Rep., 1992–94; Member: Professional Conduct Cttee, 1992–93; Public Affairs Cttee, 1994–; Dir, Public Affairs, 1995–. *Recreations:* swimming, cycling, music. *Address:* Doughty Street Chambers, 11 Doughty Street, WC1N 2PG. *T:* 0171–404 1313.

SALMON, Brian Lawson, CBE 1972; Chairman, J. Lyons & Co. Ltd, 1972–77 (Director, 1961–77, Joint Managing Director, 1967–69, Deputy Chairman, 1969–71); *b* 30 June 1917; *s* of Julius Salmon; *m* 1946, Annette Wilson Mackay; two *s* one *d*. *Educ:* Grenham Hse; Malvern Coll. Chm., Cttee on Sen. Nursing Staff Structure, 1963–66. Vice-Chm., Bd of Governors, Westminster Hosp. Gp, 1963–74; Chairman: Camden and Islington AHA, 1974–77; Supply Bd Working Gp, DHSS, 1977–78. *Recreations:* theatre, ballet, food and wine. *Address:* 34 Kingston House North, Princes Gate, SW7 1LN.

SALMON, Michael John; Vice Chancellor, Anglia Polytechnic University, 1992–95; *b* 22 June 1936; *o s* of Arthur and May Salmon; *m* 1st, 1958, Angela Cookson (marr. diss. 1973); one *s*; 2nd, 1973, Daphne Bird; one *s*. *Educ:* Roundhay Sch., Leeds; Leeds Univ.; Leicester Univ. Served RAF, 1957–62; commnd 1957. Teaching posts: Letchworth Coll. of Technology, 1962–65; Leeds Coll. of Technology, 1965–68; Barking Regional Coll., 1968–71; Head of Dept, NE London Poly., 1971–77; Dep. Dir, Chelmer Inst., 1977–83; Dir, Essex Inst., 1983–89; Director: Anglia HEC, 1989–91; Anglia Poly., 1991–92. Member: CNAA, 1970–92; IBA Educn Adv. Council, 1973–81; Electricity Industry Trng Council, 1971–74; PCFC, 1989–93; CBI (Eastern Region) Council, 1990–93; Dir, Essex TEC, 1990–93. Mem. Court, Essex Univ., 1987–. Director: Proshare, 1991–93; Mid-Essex NHS Hosp. Trust, 1993–. FIMgt (FBIM 1983); FRSA 1984. *Address:* Barberries, Runsell Lane, Danbury, Essex CM3 4NY. *T:* Chelmsford (01245) 223734.

SALMON, Dame Nancy (Marion); *see* Snagge, Dame Nancy.

SALMON, Thomas David; Assistant to Speaker's Counsel, House of Commons, 1980–86; retired; *b* 1 Nov. 1916; *s* of late Rev. Thomas Salmon and Isabel Salmon (*née* Littleton), North Stoneham, Hants; *m* 1950, Morris Patricia Reyner Turner, Ilford, Essex; one *s* two *d*. *Educ:* Winchester Coll.; Christ Church, Oxford (MA). Served War of 1939–45: Captain 133 Field Regt RA (despatches). Temp. Asst Principal, Cabinet Office, 1946. Admitted Solicitor, 1949; entered Treasury Solicitor's Dept, 1951; transf. to Bd of Trade, 1966; Under-Sec. (Legal), Solicitors' Dept, Depts of Industry and Trade, 1973–80. *Recreations:* walking, study of history and languages, gardening. *Address:* Tenures, 23 Sole Farm Road, Great Bookham, Surrey KT23 3DW. *T:* Bookham (01372) 452837.

SALMON, Very Rev. Thomas Noel Desmond Cornwall; Dean of Christ Church, Dublin, 1967–88; *b* Dublin, 5 Feb. 1913; *s* of Francis Allen Cornwall Salmon, BDS, and Emma Sophia, *d* of Dr Hamilton Jolly, Clonroche, Co. Wexford; unmarried. *Educ:* privately; Trinity College, Dublin; BA 1935, MA, BD. Deacon 1937; Priest 1938. Curate Assistant: Bangor, Co. Down, 1937–40; St James' Belfast, 1940–42; Larne, Co. Antrim, 1942–44; Clerical Vicar, Christ Church Cathedral, 1944–45; Curate Assistant, Rathfarnham, Dublin, 1945–50; Incumbent: Tullow, Carrickmines, 1950–62; St Ann, Dublin, 1962–67. Asst Lectr in Divinity School, TCD, 1945–63; Examining Chaplain to Archbishop of Dublin, 1949–. *Recreations:* in younger days Rugby football (Monkstown FC Dublin) and swimming; now walking, gardening and reading. *Address:* 3 Glenageary Terrace, Lower Glenageary Road, Dun Laoghaire, Co. Dublin. *T:* 2800101.

SALMON, Col William Alexander, OBE 1956; Assistant Ecclesiastical Secretary to Lord Chancellor, 1964–77, and to Prime Minister, 1964–77, retired; *b* 16 Nov. 1910; *o s* of late Lt-Colonel W. H. B. Salmon, late IA; *m* 1939, Jean Barbara Macmillan (*d* 1982), *o d* of late J. V. Macmillan, DD, OBE (Bishop of Guildford, 1934–49); one *s* two *d*. *Educ:* Haileybury College; RMC, Sandhurst. Commissioned 2nd Lt HLI 1930; ADC to Governor of Sind, 1936–38. Served during War of 1939–45: France, 1939; Middle East, Italy, Greece, Bde Major, 1942; GSO2 HQ Aegean Force, 1943; CO, 2nd Bn Beds and Herts Regt, 1945–46. CO, 2nd Bn Royal Irish Fusiliers, 1946–47; GSO1 (Trng), HQ Scottish Command, 1947–49; Chief of Staff to Lt-Gen. Glubb Pasha, HQ Arab Legion, 1950–53; CO 1st Bn HLI, 1953–55; Col, GS (O and T Div.) SHAPE, 1957–59; AQMG (QAE2), The War Office, 1959–62; AAG (AG14), The War Office, 1962–63; retd 1963. Life Governor, Haileybury and Imperial Service Coll., 1965–. Hashemite Order of El Istiqlal (2nd Cl.), 1953. *Publication:* Churches and Royal Patronage, 1983. *Recreations:* shooting, fishing, gardening. *Address:* Balcombe Place, Balcombe, Haywards Heath, West Sussex RH17 6QJ. *Club:* Army and Navy.

SALMOND, Alexander Elliot Anderson; MP (SNP) Banff and Buchan, since 1987; Leader, Scottish National Party, since 1990; *b* 31 Dec. 1954; *s* of Robert F. F. Salmond and Mary S. Milne; *m* 1981, Moira F. McGlashan. *Educ:* Linlithgow Acad.; St Andrews

Univ. (MA Hons). Govt Econ. Service, 1980; Asst Agricl and Fisheries Economist, DAFS, 1978–80; Energy Economist, Royal Bank of Scotland plc, 1980–87. Scottish National Party: Mem. Nat. Exec., 1981–; Vice-Chair (Publicity), 1985–87; Sen. Vice-Convener (Dep. Leader) (formerly Sen. Vice-Chair), 1987–90; Nat. Convener, 1990–. SNP/Plaid Cymru parly spokesperson on energy, treasury and fishing, 1987–88, on economy, energy, environment and poll tax, 1988–. *Publications:* articles and conference papers on oil and gas economics; contribs to Scottish Government Yearbook, Fraser of Allander Economic Commentary, Petroleum Review, Opec Bulletin, etc. *Address:* House of Commons, SW1A 0AA; 17 Maiden Street, Peterhead, Aberdeenshire AB42 6EE.

SALOP, Archdeacon of; *see* Frost, Ven. G.

SALSBURY, Peter Leslie; Managing Director, Marks & Spencer plc, since 1994; *b* 20 June 1949; *s* of Joseph Leslie Salsbury and Sylvia Olive (*née* Cook); *m* 1987, Susan Elizabeth Gosling; one *s* from previous *m*. *Educ:* Bancroft Sch.; London Sch. of Econs (BSc Econ). Joined Marks & Spencer, 1970: mgt trainee in stores, 1970–73; merchandiser, Head Office, 1973–76; Merchandise Manager, 1976–82; Exec., 1982–85; Sen. Exec., 1985–86; Divisional Director: Homeware Gp, 1986–88; Ladieswear Gp, 1988–90; Dir, Personnel, 1990–93, and Store Ops, 1993–94. Non-Exec. Dir, NORWEB plc, 1992–. Pres., Inst. of Employment Studies, 1995. *Address:* Marks & Spencer plc, Michael House, 47 Baker Street, W1A 1DN. *T:* 0171–935 4422.

SALT, George, FRS 1956; ScD; Fellow of King's College, Cambridge, since 1933; Reader in Animal Ecology, University of Cambridge, 1965–71, now Emeritus; *b* Loughborough, 12 Dec. 1903; *s* of late Walter Salt and Mary Cecilia (*née* Hulme); *m* 1939, Joyce Laing, Newnham Coll. and Stockton-on-Tees; two *s*. *Educ:* Crescent Heights Collegiate Inst., Calgary; Univ. of Alberta (BSc); Harvard Univ. (SM, SD); Univ. of Cambridge (PhD, ScD). National Research Fellow, Harvard Univ., 1927–28; Entomologist, Imperial Inst. Entom, 1929–31; Royal Soc. Moseley Research Student, 1932–33; Univ. Lectr in Zoology, Cambridge, 1937–65; Dean, 1939–45, Tutor for Advanced Students, 1945–51, King's Coll., Cambridge. Visiting Prof. Univ. of California, Berkeley, 1966. On biological expedns in NW Canada and Rocky Mts, Cuba, Republic of Colombia, E Africa, Pakistan. Murchison Grant, RGS, 1951. *Publications:* The Cellular Defence Reactions of Insects, 1970; papers in scientific jls on insect parasitism and ecology. *Recreations:* mountaineering, gardening, calligraphy and palaeography. *Address:* King's College, Cambridge CB2 1ST; 21 Barton Road, Cambridge CB3 9LB. *T:* Cambridge (01223) 355450.

SALT, Rear-Adm. James Frederick Thomas George, CB 1991; Military Deputy, Defence Export Services, since 1992; *b* 19 April 1940; *s* of Lieut Comdr George Salt (lost in 1939–45 War in command HMS Triad, 1940) and Lillian Bridget Lamb; *m* 1975, Penelope Mary Walker; four *s*. *Educ:* Wellington College; RNC Dartmouth (1958–59). Served Far East, Mediterranean, South Atlantic and home waters; commanded HM Sub. Finwhale, 1969–71; 2 i/c HM Sub. Resolution (Polaris), 1973–74; Comd HM Nuclear Sub. Dreadnought, 1978–79; Comd HMS Sheffield, 1982 (sank Falklands); Comd HMS Southampton, 1983; ACOS Ops C-in-C Fleet, 1984–85; Dir, Defence Intell., 1986–87; Sen. Naval Mem., Directing Staff, RCDS, 1988–90; ACNS (Gulf War), 1990–91. Liveryman, Cordwainers' Co. *Recreations:* sailing, ski-ing, shooting. *Address:* Room 0229, Main Building, Ministry of Defence, Whitehall, SW1A 2HB.

SALT, Sir Patrick (Macdonnell), 7th Bt *cr* 1869, of Saltaire, Yorkshire; *b* 25 Sept. 1932; *s* of Sir John Salt, 4th Bt and Stella Houlton Jackson (*d* 1974); *S* brother, 1991; *m* 1976, Ann Elizabeth Mary Kilham Roberts, *widow* of Denys Kilham Roberts, OBE. *Educ:* Summer Fields, Oxford; Stowe Sch. Dir, Cassidy Davis Members Agency Ltd, 1983–92. *Recreation:* fishing. *Heir: cousin* Daniel Alexander Salt [*b* 15 Aug. 1943; *m* 1968, Merchide, *d* of Dr Ahmad Emami; two *d*]. *Address:* Hillwatering Farmhouse, Langham, Bury St Edmunds, Suffolk IP31 3ED. *T:* Walsham-le-Willows (01359) 259367. *Club:* City University.

SALT, Sir (Thomas) Michael (John), 4th Bt, *cr* 1899; *b* 7 Nov. 1946; *s* of Lt-Col Sir Thomas Henry Salt, 3rd Bt, and Meriel Sophia Wilmot, *d* of late Capt. Berkeley C. W. Williams and Hon. Mrs Williams, Herringston, Dorchester; *S* father 1965; *m* 1971, Caroline, *er d* of Henry Hildyard; two *d*. *Educ:* Eton. *Heir: b* Anthony William David Salt [*b* 5 Feb. 1950; *m* 1978, Olivia Anne, *yr d* of Martin Morgan Hudson; two *s*]. *Recreations:* cricket, shooting. *Address:* Shillingstone House, Shillingstone, Dorset DT11 0QR. *Club:* Boodle's.

SALTER, Harry Charles, CMG 1983; DFC 1945; Director, Financing of Community Budget, European Economic Community, 1973–82, retired; *b* 29 July 1918; *er s* of late Harry Arnold Salter and Irene Beatrice Salter; *m* 1st, 1946, Anne Hooper (marr. diss. 1980); one *d*; 2nd, 1983, Mrs Janet Watford. *Educ:* St Albans Sch. Entered Ministry of Health, 1936. Served War, Royal Artillery, 1939–46 (despatches, DFC). Asst Sec., Min. of Health, 1963; Under-Sec., DHSS, 1971–73. *Recreations:* living, golf, bridge, antique dealing, cooking. *Address:* 5 Clos des Acacias, 1150 Brussels, Belgium. *T:* (2) 7703671.

SALTER, Ian George; a Deputy Chairman, The Stock Exchange, since 1990; *b* Hobart, Tasmania, 7 March 1943; *s* of Desmond and Diane Salter. *Educ:* Hutchins Sch., Hobart, Tasmania. AASA. Member: Hobart Stock Exchange, 1965–69; Stock Exchange, London, 1970–; Principal, Strauss Turnbull, now Société Générale Strauss Turnbull (Investment Advisers Ltd), 1978–. Mem., Stock Exchange Council, 1980–. DTI Inspector, 1984–87. *Recreations:* opera, travel, gardening. *Address:* (office) Société Générale Strauss Turnbull, Exchange House, Primrose Street, Broadgate, EC2A 2DD. *T:* 0171–638 5699.

SALTER, Richard Stanley; QC 1995; *b* 2 Oct. 1951; *s* of late Stanley James Salter and Betty Maud (*née* Topsom); *m* 1991, Shona Virginia Playfair (*née* Cannon). *Educ:* Harrow County Sch. for Boys; Balliol Coll., Oxford (MA); Inns of Court Sch. of Law. Called to the Bar, Inner Temple, 1975, Bencher, 1991; pupil to Sir Henry Brooke, 1975–76; in practice at Commercial Bar, 1976–. Mem., Council of Legal Educn, 1990–. Chm., Bd of Examnrs for Bar Vocational Course, 1992–93. *Publications:* (contrib.) Banks, Liability and Risk, 1991, 2nd edn 1995; (contrib.) Banks and Remedies, 1992; Guarantee and Indemnity, Halsbury's Laws of England, Vol. 20, 4th edn 1993. *Recreations:* books, music, theatre, cricket. *Address:* 3 Gray's Inn Place, Gray's Inn, WC1R 5EA. *T:* 0171–831 8441. *Clubs:* Savile; Shoscombe Village Cricket.

SALTHOUSE, Edward Charles, PhD; CEng, FIEE; Master of University College, Durham University, since 1979; *b* 27 Dec. 1935; *s* of Edward Salthouse, MBE, and Mrs Salthouse (*née* Boyd); *m* 1961, Denise Kathleen Margot Reid; two *s*. *Educ:* Campbell Coll., Belfast; Queen's University of Belfast (BSc, PhD). Lecturer in Electrical Engrg, Univ. of Bristol, 1962–67; University of Durham: Reader in Elec. Engrg Science, 1967–79; Chairman, Board of Studies in Engrg Science, 1976–79; Dean, Faculty of Science, 1982–85; First Chm., School of Applied Science and Engrg, 1985–87; Pro-Vice-Chancellor, 1985–88. *Publications:* papers on electrical insulation in Proc. IEE and other appropriate jls. *Recreations:* travel by train, photography. *Address:* The Master's House, The Castle, Durham DH1 3RL. *T:* Durham (0191) 3743800; Shieldaig, Hume, Kelso.

SALTHOUSE, Leonard; Assistant Under Secretary of State, Ministry of Defence, 1977–87; *b* 15 April 1927; *s* of late Edward Keith Salthouse and Dorothy Annie (*née* Clark); *m* 1950, Kathleen May (*née* Spittle); one *s* one *d*. *Educ:* Queen Elizabeth Grammar Sch., Atherstone, Warwickshire; University Coll. London (BScEcon). Home Civil Service: Asst Principal, Min. of Fuel and Power, 1950–55; Principal, Air Min., then Min. of Defence, 1955–66; Asst Sec., 1966–77. *Recreations:* gardening, music. *Address:* Highfield, 115 Cross Oak Road, Berkhamsted, Herts HP4 3HZ. *T:* Berkhamsted (01442) 877809.

SALTON, Prof. Milton Robert James, FRS 1979; Professor and Chairman of Microbiology, New York University School of Medicine, since 1964; *b* 29 April 1921; *s* of Robert Alexander Salton and Stella Salton; *m* 1951, Joy Marriott; two *s*. *Educ:* Univ. of Sydney (BSc Agr. 1945); Univ. of Cambridge (PhD 1951, ScD 1967). Beit Meml Res. Fellow, Univ. of Cambridge, 1950–52; Merck Internat. Fellow, Univ. of California, Berkeley, 1952–53; Reader, Univ. of Manchester, 1956–61; Prof. of Microbiology, Univ. of NSW, Australia, 1962–64. Hon. Mem., British Soc. for Antimicrobial Chemotherapy, 1983. Docteur en Médecine, Dhc, Université de Liège, 1967. *Publications:* Microbial Cell Walls, 1960; The Bacterial Cell Wall, 1964; Immunochemistry of Enzymes and their Antibodies, 1978; β-Lactam Antibiotics, 1981; (ed jtly) Antibiotic Inhibition of Bacterial Cell Surface Assembly and Function, 1988. *Address:* Department of Microbiology, New York University School of Medicine, 550 First Avenue, New York, NY 10016, USA. *Club:* United Oxford & Cambridge University.

SALTOUN, Lady (20th in line) *cr* 1445, of Abernethy; **Flora Marjory Fraser;** Chief of Clan Fraser; *b* 18 Oct. 1930; *d* of 19th Lord Saltoun, MC, and Dorothy (*d* 1985), *e d* of Sir Charles Welby, 5th Bt; *S* father, 1979; *m* 1956, Captain Alexander Ramsay of Mar, Grenadier Guards retd, *o s* of late Adm. Hon. Sir Alexander Ramsay, GCVO, KCB, DSO, and The Lady Patricia Ramsay, CI, VA, CD; three *d*. *Heiress: d* Hon. Katharine Ingrid Mary Isabel Fraser [*b* 11 Oct. 1957; *m* 1980, Captain Mark Malise Nicolson, Irish Guards; one *s* two *d*]. *Address:* Cairnbulg Castle, Fraserburgh, Aberdeenshire AB43 5TN.

SALUSBURY-TRELAWNY, Sir J. B.; *see* Trelawny.

SALVADOR PINHEIRO, João de Deus; *see* Pinheiro.

SALVIDGE, Paul; Under Secretary, Posts Division, Department of Trade and Industry, since 1994; *b* 22 Aug. 1946; *s* of Herbert Stephen and Winifred Alice Elisabeth Salvidge; *m* 1972, Heather Margaret (*née* Johnson); one *d*. *Educ:* Cardiff High School; Birmingham Univ. (LLB). Ministry of Power, 1967; Dept of Trade and Industry, 1972; Asst Secretary, 1982; Under Sec., Telecommunications and Posts Div., 1989–94. *Address:* Department of Trade and Industry, 151 Buckingham Palace Road, SW1W 9SS.

SAMARAKOON, Hon. Neville Dunbar Mirahawatte; Chief Justice, Democratic Socialist Republic of Sri Lanka, 1977–84; *b* 22 Oct. 1919; *s* of Alfred Charles Warnabarana Wickremasinghe Samarakoon and Rajapaksa Wasala Mudiyanselage Chandrawati Mirahawatte Kumarihamy; *m* 1949, Mary Patricia Mulholland; one *s* two *d*. *Educ:* Trinity Coll., Kandy; University Coll., Colombo; Law Coll., Colombo. Enrolled as Advocate, 1945; Crown Counsel, Attorney-General's Dept, 1948–51; reverted to Private Bar, 1951; QC 1968. Member: Bar Council, 1964–77; Disciplinary Bd for Lawyers 1971–74, 1976, 1977. Chairman: Judicial Service Commn, 1978–84; Council of Legal Educn.

SAMARANCH, Juan Antonio; Marqués de Samaranch, 1991; President, International Olympic Committee, since 1980 (Member, since 1966); *b* 17 July 1920; *s* of Francisco Samaranch and Juana Torello; *m* 1955, Maria Teresa Salisachs Rowe; one *s* one *d*. *Educ:* Instituto Superior Estudios de Empresas, Barcelona; German College; Higher Inst. of Business Studies, Barcelona. Industrialist, Bank Consultant; Pres., Barcelona Diputacion, 1973–77; Ambassador to USSR and to People's Republic of Mongolia, 1977–80. Mem., Spanish Olympic Cttee, 1954 (Pres., 1967–70); Nat. Deleg. for Physical Educn and Sport. Holds numerous decorations. *Publications:* Deporte 2000, 1967; Olympic Message, 1980. *Recreation:* philately. *Address:* Junqueras 18, 08003 Barcelona, Spain. *T:* (3) 2683288; International Olympic Committee, Château de Vidy, 1007 Lausanne, Switzerland. *T:* (21) 253271.

SAMBLES, Prof. John Roy, PhD; FInstP; Professor of Physics, Exeter University, since 1991; *b* 14 Oct. 1945; *s* of Charles Henry Sambles and Georgina (*née* Deeble); *m* 1966, Sandra Elizabeth Sloman; two *s* one *d*. *Educ:* Callington Grammar Sch., Cornwall; Imperial Coll., London Univ. (BSc 1st Cl. Hons Physics 1967; ARCS; PhD 1970; DIC). FInstP 1988. Res. Fellow, Imperial Coll., London, 1970–72; Exeter University: Lectr in Physics, 1972–85; Sen. Lectr, 1985–88; Reader, 1988–91. *Publications:* numerous papers in learned scientific jls, incl. works on liquid crystals, melting, electron microscopy, resistivity of thin samples, molecular electronics and surface plasmons. *Recreations:* writing poetry, local Methodist preacher. *Address:* Department of Physics, University of Exeter, Exeter, Devon EX4 4QL. *T:* Exeter (01392) 264103; Shirley House, Copplestone, Crediton, Devon EX17 5NS. *T:* Crediton (01363) 84356.

SAMBROOK, Gordon Hartley, CBE 1986; Chairman, Iron Trades Employers' Insurance Association, and Iron Trades Insurance Co. Ltd (formerly Iron Trades Mutual Insurance Co.), since 1984; *b* 9 Jan. 1930; *m* 1956, Patricia Joan Mary Havard; one *s*. *Educ:* Sheffield Univ. (BA(Hons), DipEd). Graduate Apprentice, Utd Steel, 1954; United Steel Cos, 1954–68; British Steel Corporation: General Manager, Rotherham, 1972; Dir, Tinplate Gp, 1973–75; Man. Dir, Personnel, 1975–77; Man. Dir, Commercial, 1977–80; Dir, 1978–90; Chief Exec., 1980–89, Chm., 1980–90, BSC General Steels, later General Steels. Director: Allied Steel & Wire Ltd, 1981–87; United Merchant Bar PLC, 1985–90; United Engineering Steels Ltd, 1986–92; Tuscaloosa Steel Corp., 1985–91. Chm. of Council, Steel Construction Inst., 1990–94.

SAMBROOK, Prof. Joseph Frank, PhD; FRS 1985; Director, Peter MacCallum Cancer Institute, Melbourne, since 1995; *b* 1 March 1939; *s* of Thomas Sambrook and Ethel Gertrude (*née* Lightfoot); *m* 1st, 1960, Thelma McGrady (marr. diss. 1984); two *s* one *d*; 2nd, 1986, Mary-Jane Gething; one *d*. *Educ:* Liverpool Univ. (BSc 1962); Australian Nat. Univ. (PhD 1965). Res. Fellow, John Curtin Sch. of Med. Res., ANU, 1965–66; Postdoctoral Fellow, MRC Lab. of Molecular Biol., 1966–67; Jun. Fellow, Salk Inst. for Biol Studies, 1967–69; Sen. Staff Investigator, 1969–77, Asst Dir, 1977–85, Cold Spring Harbor Lab.; Prof. and Chm., Dept of Biochemistry, Southwestern Medical Center, Dallas, 1985–91; Dir, McDermott Center for Human Growth and Develt, Southwestern Med. Sch., Dallas, 1991–94. *Publications:* contribs to learned jls. *Recreation:* music. *Address:* Peter MacCallum Cancer Institute, St Andrews Place, East Melbourne, Vic 3002, Australia. *T:* (3) 96561513, *Fax:* (3) 96561411; 70 Fitzgibbon Street, Parkville, Vic 3052, Australia.

SAMPLES, Reginald McCartney, CMG 1971; DSO 1942; OBE 1963; HM Diplomatic Service, retired; *b* 11 Aug. 1918; *o s* of late William and Jessie Samples; *m* 1947, Elsie Roberts Hide; two *s* one step *d*. *Educ:* Rhyl Grammar Sch.; Liverpool Univ. (BCom). Served, 1940–46; RNVR (Air Branch); torpedo action with 825 Sqn against German ships Scharnhorst, Gneisenau and Prinz Eugen in English Channel (wounded, DSO); Lieut (A). Central Office of Information (Economic Editor, Overseas Newspapers), 1947–48. CRO (Brit. Inf. Services, India), 1948; Economic Information Officer, Bombay, 1948–52; Editor-in-Chief, BIS, New Delhi, 1952; Dep.-Dir, BIS, New Delhi, 1952–56; Dir, BIS, Pakistan (Karachi), 1956–59; Dir, BIS, Canada (Ottawa), 1959–65, OBE;

Counsellor (Information) to Brit. High Comr, India, and Dir, BIS, India (New Delhi), 1965–68; Asst Under-Sec. of State, Commonwealth Office, 1968; Head of British Govt Office, and Sen. British Trade Comr, Toronto, 1969; Consul-Gen., Toronto, 1974–78. Asst Dir, Royal Ontario Museum, 1978–83. *Recreations:* watching tennis, ballet. *Address:* Apartment 1105, 44 Jackes Avenue, Toronto, Ontario M4T 1E5, Canada. *Clubs:* Naval; Queens (Toronto).

SAMPSON, Anthony (Terrell Seward); writer and journalist; *b* 3 Aug. 1926; *s* of Michael Sampson and Phyllis, *d* of Sir Albert Seward, FRS; *m* 1965, Sally, *d* of Dr P. G. Bentlif, Jersey, and of Mrs G. Denison-Smith, Islip, Oxon; one *s* one *d*. *Educ:* Westminster School; Christ Church, Oxford. Served with Royal Navy, 1944–47; Sub-Lieut, RNVR, 1946. Editor of Drum Magazine, Johannesburg, 1951–55; Editorial staff of The Observer, 1955–66; Associate Prof., Univ. of Vincennes, Paris, 1968–70; Chief American Corresp., The Observer, 1973–74. Contributing Editor, Newsweek, 1977–; Editorial Conslt, The Brandt Commn, 1978–79; Editor, The Sampson Letter, 1984–86. Presenter and narrator: The Midas Touch (BBC2), 1990; The Two-Edged Sword (BBC2), 1991. Chm., Soc. of Authors, 1992–94. Trustee, Scott Trust (Guardian/Observer), 1993–. *Publications:* Drum, a Venture into the New Africa, 1956; The Treason Cage, 1958; Commonsense about Africa, 1960; (with S. Pienaar) South Africa: two views of Separate Development 1960; Anatomy of Britain, 1962; Anatomy of Britain Today, 1965; Macmillan: a study in ambiguity, 1967; The New Europeans, 1968; The New Anatomy of Britain, 1971; The Sovereign State: the secret history of ITT, 1973; The Seven Sisters, 1975 (Prix International de la Presse, Nice, 1976); The Arms Bazaar, 1977; The Money Lenders, 1981; The Changing Anatomy of Britain, 1982; Empires of the Sky, 1984; (with Sally Sampson) The Oxford Book of Ages, 1985; Black and Gold: tycoons, revolutionaries and apartheid, 1987; The Midas Touch, 1989; The Essential Anatomy of Britain, 1992; Company Man, 1995. *Recreations:* vertical gardening, opera. *Address:* 27 Ladbroke Grove, W11 3AY. *T:* 0171–727 4188, *Fax:* 0171–221 5738; Quarry Garden, Wardour, Tisbury, Wilts SP3 6HR. *T:* Tisbury (01747) 870407. *Clubs:* Beefsteak, Groucho, Academy.

SAMPSON, Sir Colin, Kt 1993; CBE 1988; QPM 1978; DL; HM Chief Inspector of Constabulary for Scotland, 1991–93; *b* 26 May 1929; *s* of James and Nellie Sampson; *m* 1953, Kathleen Stones; two *s*. *Educ:* Stanley Sch., Wakefield; Univ. of Leeds (Criminology). Joined Police Force, 1949; served mainly in the CID (incl. training of detectives), at Dewsbury, Skipton, Doncaster, Goole, Wakefield, Huddersfield, Rotherham, Barnsley; Comdt, Home Office Detective Trng Sch., Wakefield, 1971–72; Asst Chief Constable, West Yorks, 1973; Dep. Chief Constable, Notts, 1976; Chief Constable, W Yorks, 1983–89; HM Inspector of Constabulary, 1989–90 (for NE England, 1990). President: Leeds Gilbert and Sullivan Soc., 1974; W Yorks County Scout Council, 1993; Wakefield Br., NSPCC, 1995. Vice Pres., Yorkshire Soc., 1983. Mem. Court, Univ. of Leeds, 1993–. OStJ 1988 (Chm. Council for S and W Yorks, 1989). DL West Yorks, 1994. DUniv Bradford, 1988; Hon. LLD Leeds, 1990. *Recreations:* choral music, walking, gardening. *Address:* Kid Royd House, Shepley, near Huddersfield, W Yorks HD8 8EA.

SAMSOVA, Galina; producer; a Principal Dancer, Birmingham Royal Ballet (formerly Sadler's Wells Royal Ballet), since 1980; Teacher with the company in the Royal Ballet and Royal Ballet School; Artistic Director, Scottish Ballet, since 1991; *b* Stalingrad, 1937; *d* of a Byelorussian; *m* 1st, Alexander Ursuliak; 2nd, André Prokovsky. *Educ:* the Ballet Sch., Kiev (pupil of N. Verekundova). Joined Kiev Ballet, 1956 and became a soloist; Canadian Ballet, 1961; created chief rôle in Cendrillon, Paris 1963 (Gold Medal for best danseuse of Paris Festival). Ballerina, Festival Ballet, 1964–73; headed the group of André Prokovsky, The New London Ballet, (disbanded in 1977, revived for 3 new productions, The Theatre Royal, York, 1979); has danced principal rôles in Sleeping Beauty, Nutcracker, Giselle, Swan Lake, Anna Karenina, and other classical ballets; danced in Europe, Far East and USA. Produced: Sequence from Paquita, Sadler's Wells, 1980; (with Peter Wright) Swan Lake, Sadler's Wells, 1983, Covent Garden, 1991; Giselle, London City Ballet, 1986; Les Sylphides, Birmingham Royal Ballet, 1992; Sleeping Beauty, Scottish Ballet, 1994; Swan Lake, Scottish Ballet, 1995. *Address:* Scottish Ballet, 261 West Princes Street, Glasgow G4 9EE.

SAMUEL, family name of **Viscounts Bearsted** and **Samuel.**

SAMUEL, 3rd Viscount *cr* 1937, of Mount Carmel and of Toxteth, Liverpool; **David Herbert Samuel;** Sherman Professor of Physical Chemistry, Weizmann Institute of Science, Rehovot, Israel, 1967–87, Emeritus Professor of Physical Chemistry since 1987; *b* 8 July 1922; *s* of 2nd Viscount Samuel, CMG, and Hadassah (*d* 1986), *d* of Judah Goor (Grasovsky); *S* father, 1978; *m* 1st, 1950, Esther Berelowitz; one *d*; 2nd, 1960, Rinna Dafni (*née* Grossman); one *d*; 3rd, 1980, Veronika Engelhardt Grimm. *Educ:* Balliol Coll., Oxford (MA 1948); Hebrew Univ. (PhD 1953). Served War of 1939–45 (despatches); Captain RA, in India, Burma and Sumatra. Weizmann Institute of Science, Rehovot, Israel: Member of Staff, 1949–, of Isotope Dept, 1949–86, of Dept of Neurobiology, 1986–; Dir, Center for Neurosciences and Behavioural Research, 1978–87; Head, Chemistry Gp, Science Teaching Dept, 1967–83; Dean, Faculty of Chemistry, 1971–73; Chm., Bd of Studies in Chemistry, Feinberg Grad. Sch., 1968–74. Post-doctoral Fellow, Chem. Dept, UCL, 1956; Res. Fellow, Chem. Dept, Harvard Univ., 1957–58; Res. Fellow, Lab. of Chemical Biodynamics (Lawrence Radiation Lab.), Univ. of California, Berkeley, 1965–66; Vis. Prof., Sch. of Molecular Scis, Univ. of Warwick, 1967; Royal Soc. Vis. Prof., MRC Neuroimmunology Unit, Zoology Dept, UCL, 1974–75; Vis. Prof., Pharmacol. Dept, Yale Sch. of Medicine, 1983–84; McLaughlin Prof., Sch. of Medicine, McMaster Univ., 1984. Member: Adv. Bd, Bat-Sheva de Rothschild Foundn for Advancement of Science in Israel, 1970–83; Bd, US-Israel Educnl (Fulbright) Foundn, 1969–74 (Chm., 1974–75); Bd, Israel Center for Scientific and Technol Information, 1970–74; Scientific Adv. Cttee and Bd of Trustees of Israel Center for Psychobiol., 1973–; Acad. Adv. Cttee, Everyman's (Open) Univ., 1976–83, Bd of Govs, Bezalel Acad. of Arts and Design, 1977–; Council, Israel Chemical Soc., 1977–83; Internat. Brain Res. Org. (IBRO), 1977–; Israel Exec. Cttee, America-Israel Cultural Foundn, 1978–89 (Chm., 1986–89); Bd of Governors, Tel Aviv Museum, 1980–; Cttee on Teaching of Chemistry, IUPAC, 1981–89; Anglo-Israel Assoc., 1985–; British Israel Arts Foundn, 1986–; Textile Inst., 1987–94; Bd of Trustees, Menninger Foundn, USA, 1988–; Soc. of Manufacturing Engrs, 1989–; Fibre Soc., 1990–94. Pres., Shenkar Coll. of Textile Technology and Fashion, 1987–94. Former Member, Editorial Board: Jl of Labelled Compounds & Radiopharmaceuticals; Alzheimer Disease and Associated Disorders; Brain Behaviour and Immunity. *Publications:* more than 300 papers, reviews and parts of collective volumes on isotopes, physical chemistry, reaction mechanisms, neurochemistry, psychopharmacology, animal behavior, education and the history and teaching of science. *Heir: b* Hon. Dan Judah Samuel [*b* 25 March 1925; *m* 1st, 1957, Nonni (Esther) (marr. diss. 1977), *d* of late Max Gordon, Johannesburg; one *s* two *d*; 2nd, 1981, Heather, *d* of Angus and Elsa Cumming, Haywards Heath; one *s* one *d*]. *Address:* Weizmann Institute of Science, Rehovot 76100, Israel. *T:* (office) (3) 6417235, *Fax:* 6426371; (home) (8) 468123.

SAMUEL, Adrian Christopher Ian, CMG 1959; CVO 1963; *b* 20 Aug. 1915; *s* of late George Christopher Samuel and Alma Richards; *m* 1942, Sheila, *er d* of late J. C. Barrett, Killiney, Co. Dublin; three *s* one *d*. *Educ:* Rugby Sch.; St John's Coll., Oxford. Entered HM Consular Service, 1938; served at Beirut, Tunis and Trieste. Served War, 1940–44, in Royal Air Force. Returned to HM Foreign Service and served at HM Embassies in Ankara, Cairo and Damascus; First Secretary, 1947; Counsellor, 1956; Principal Private Secretary to the Secretary of State for Foreign Affairs, Oct. 1959–63; Minister at HM Embassy, Madrid, 1963–65; resigned 1965. Director: British Chemical Engrg Contractors Assoc., 1966–69; British Agrochemicals Assoc., 1972–78; Dir-Gen., Groupement Internat. des Assocs Nats de Fabricants de Pesticides (GIFAP), 1978–79. *Publication:* An Astonishing Fellow: a life of Sir Robert Wilson, KMT, MP, 1986. *Recreations:* golf, shooting and reading. *Address:* The Laundry House, Handcross, near Haywards Heath, West Sussex RH17 6HQ. *T:* Handcross (01444) 400717. *Club:* Garrick.

SAMUEL, Gillian Patricia; Press Secretary and Chief of Information, Ministry of Defence, since 1992; *b* 19 Oct. 1945; *d* of Harry Martin Samuel and Kathleen Joyce Samuel (*née* Drake). *Educ:* Edmonton Co. Grammar Sch.; Exeter Univ. (BA Hons Hist.). Current Affairs Gp, BBC TV, 1968–70; Plessey Co., 1970–72; Department of: Nat. Savings, 1972–75; Industry, later DTI, 1975–87; Dir of Information, Dept of Transport, 1987–92. *Recreations:* walking, keep fit. *Address:* Ministry of Defence, Whitehall, SW1A 2HB.

SAMUEL, Sir John (Michael Glen), 5th Bt, *cr* 1898; *b* 25 Jan. 1944; *o s* of Sir John Oliver Cecil Samuel, 4th Bt, and of Charlotte Mary, *d* of late R. H. Hoyt, Calgary, Canada; *S* father, 1962; *m* 1st, 1966, Antoinette Sandra, *d* of late Captain Antony Hewitt, RE, 2nd SAS Regt, and of Mrs K. A. H. Casson, Frith Farm, Wolverton, Hants; two *s*; 2nd, 1982, Mrs Elizabeth Ann Molinari, *y d* of late Major R. G. Curry, Bournemouth, Dorset. *Educ:* Radley; London Univ. Director: Enfield Automotive, 1967–70; Advanced Vehicle Systems Ltd, 1971–78; Chairman: Electric Auto Corp. (USA), 1978–83; Whisper Electric Car A/S, Denmark, 1984–88; Clean Air Transport Holdings Ltd, 1992–94. *Recreation:* motor racing. *Heir: s* Anthony John Fulton Samuel, *b* 13 Oct. 1972.

SAMUEL, Richard Christopher, CMG 1983; CVO 1983; HM Diplomatic Service, retired; Ambassador to Latvia, 1991–93; *b* Edinburgh, 8 Aug. 1933; *m* 1986, Frances Draper; one *s* one *d*. *Educ:* Durham Sch.; St John's Coll., Cambridge (BA). Royal Navy, 1952–54. FO, 1957–58; Warsaw, 1958–59; Rome, 1960–63; FO, 1963; Private Sec. to Parly Under-Sec. of State, 1965–68; Hong Kong, 1968–69; 1st Sec. and Head of Chancery: Singapore, 1969–71; Peking, 1971–73; Counsellor, Washington, 1973–76; Head of Far Eastern Dept, FCO, 1976–79; Counsellor (Commercial), Moscow, 1980–82; Minister and Dep. High Comr, New Delhi, 1982–85; Under-Sec. for Asia and the Oceans, ODA, FCO, 1986–88; on loan to Inter-Amer. Develt Bank, Washington, as Exec. Dir for Belgium, Denmark, Finland, Germany, Italy, Netherlands, Norway, Sweden and UK, 1988–91. Hd of Resident Mission in Moldova, CSCE, 1994. *Address:* 41 Northumberland Place, W2 5AS. *T:* 0171–229 8357.

SAMUELS; *see* Turner-Samuels.

SAMUELS, John Edward Anthony; QC 1981; a Deputy High Court Judge, since 1981; a Recorder, since 1985; *b* 15 Aug. 1940; *s* of late Albert Edward Samuels, solicitor, Reigate, Surrey; *m* 1967, Maxine (*née* Robertson), JP; two *s*. *Educ:* Charterhouse; Perugia; Queens' Coll., Cambridge (MA). Commnd, Queen's Royal Regt (TA), 1959; Lieut, Queen's Royal Surrey Regt (TA), 1961–67. Chairman, Cambridge Univ. United Nations Assoc., 1962. Called to Bar, Lincoln's Inn, 1964 (Mansfield Schol., 1963; Bencher, 1990); South Eastern Circuit; Member: Senate of the Inns of Court and the Bar, 1983–86; Bar Council, 1992–; Council of Legal Educn, 1983–90. Asst Parly Boundary Comr, 1992–. Co-opted Mem., ILEA Education Cttee, 1964–67; Jt Chm., ILEA Disciplinary Tribunals, 1977–87; Alternate Chm., Burnham Cttee, 1981–87. Member: Richmond, Twickenham and Roehampton HA, 1982–85; Kingston and Richmond Family Practitioner Cttee, 1982–86; Chm., Jt Regulations Cttee, Inns' Council and Bar Council, 1987–90. Trustee, Richmond Parish Lands Charity, 1986– (Chairman: Educn Cttee, 1987–89; Property Cttee, 1987–). *Publications:* Action Pack: counsel's guide to chambers' administration, 1986, 2nd edn 1988; contributor to Halsbury's Laws of England, 4th edn. *Recreations:* conservation, restoration, serendipity. *Address:* 22 Old Buildings, Lincoln's Inn, WC2A 3UJ. *T:* 0171–831 0222.

SAMUELS, Prof. Michael Louis, FRSE; Professor of English Language, University of Glasgow, 1959–89; *b* 1920; *s* of late Harry Samuels, OBE, MA, barrister-at-law, and Céline Samuels (*née* Aronowitz), London; *m* 1950, Hilary, *d* of late Julius and Ruth Samuel, Glasgow; one *d*. *Educ:* St Paul's School; Balliol College, Oxford. Domus Exhibitioner in Classics, Balliol College, Oxford, 1938–40 and 1945–47; MA 1947 (First Class Hons English Lang. and Lit.). Worked for Air Ministry (Maintenance Command), 1940–45. Research Fellow, University of Birmingham, 1947–48; Assistant in English Language, University of Edinburgh, 1948–49; Lecturer in English Language, Univ. of Edinburgh, 1949–59. Chm., Scottish Studentships Selection Cttee, 1975–88. FRSE 1989. *Publications:* Linguistic Evolution, 1972; (ed jtly) A Linguistic Atlas of Late Medieval English, 1987; (jtly) Middle English Dialectology, 1989; (with J. J. Smith) The English of Chaucer, 1989; contribs to: Approaches to English Historical Linguistics, 1969; So Meny people Longages and Tonges (presented to A. McIntosh), 1981; Middle English Studies (presented to N. Davis), 1983; Proc. 4th Internat. Conf. on English Historical Linguistics, 1985; Explanation and Linguistic Change, 1987; A Companion to Piers Plowman, 1988; articles and reviews in linguistic and literary jls. *Address:* 4 Queen's Gate, Dowanhill, Glasgow G12 9DN. *T:* 0141–334 4999.

SAMUELSON, Sir (Bernard) Michael (Francis), 5th Bt *cr* 1884; *b* 17 Jan. 1917; *s* of Sir Francis Henry Bernard Samuelson, 4th Bt, and Margaret Kendall (*d* 1980), *d* of H. Kendall Barnes; *S* father, 1981; *m* 1952, Janet Amy, *yr d* of Lt-Comdr L. G. Elkington, RN retd, Chelsea; two *s* two *d*. *Educ:* Eton. Served War of 1939–45 with RA and Leicestershire Regt (despatches). *Heir: s* James Francis Samuelson [*b* 20 Dec. 1956; *m* 1987, Caroline Anne Woodley; two *d*]. *Address:* Hollingwood, Stunts Green, Herstmonceux, East Sussex BN27 4QG.

SAMUELSON, Prof. Paul A.; Institute Professor, Massachusetts Institute of Technology, 1966–86, now Emeritus; Long-Term Credit Bank of Japan Visiting Professor of Political Economy, Center for Japan—US Business and Economic Studies, New York University, since 1987; *b* Gary, Indiana, 15 May 1915; *m* 1st, 1938, Marion Crawford (*d* 1978); four *s* (inc. triplets) two *d*; 2nd, 1981, Risha Claypool. *Educ:* Univs of Chicago (BA) and Harvard (MA, PhD). SSRC Predoctoral Fellow, 1935–37; Soc. of Fellows, Harvard, 1937–40; Guggenheim Fellow, 1948–49; Ford Faculty Research Fellow, 1958–59; Hoyt Vis. Fellow, Calhoun Coll., Yale, 1962; Carnegie Foundn Reflective Year, 1965–66. MIT: Asst Prof. of Econs, 1940; Assoc. Prof. of Econs, 1944; Staff Mem., Radiation Lab., 1944–45; Prof. of Econs, 1947; Prof. of Internat. Economic Relations (part-time), Fletcher Sch. of Law and Diplomacy, 1945. Consultant: to Nat. Resources Planning Bd, 1941–43; to Rand Corp., 1948–75; to US Treasury, 1945–52, 1961–74; to Johnson Task Force on Sustained Prosperity, 1964; to Council of Econ. Advisers, 1960–68; to Federal Reserve Bd, 1965–; to Congressional Budget Office, 1974–. Economic Adviser to Senator, Candidate and President-elect John F. Kennedy, informal adviser to President Kennedy. Member: War Prodn Bd and Office of War Mobilization and Reconstruction, 1945; Bureau of the Budget, 1952; Adv. Bd of Nat Commn on Money and Credit, 1958–60;

Research Adv. Panel to President's Nat. Goals Commn, 1959–60; Research Adv. Bd Cttee for Econ. Develt, 1960; Nat. Task Force on Econ. Educn, 1960–61; Sen. Advr, Brookings Panel on Econ. Activity. Contrib. Editor and Columnist, Newsweek, 1966–81. Vernon F. Taylor Vis. Dist. Prof., Trinity Univ., Texas, 1989. Lectures: Stamp Meml, London, 1961; Wicksell, Stockholm, 1962; Franklin, Detroit, 1962; Gerhard Colm Meml, NYC, 1971; Davidson, Univ. of New Hampshire, 1971; 12th John von Neumann, Univ. of Wisconsin, 1971; J. Willard Gibbs, Amer. Mathematical Soc., 1974; 1st Sulzbacher, Columbia Law Sch., 1974; John Diebold, Harvard Univ., 1976; Alice Bourneauf, Boston Coll., 1981; Horowitz, Jerusalem and Tel Aviv, 1984; Marschak Meml, UCLA, 1984; Olin, Univ. of Virginia Law Sch., 1989; Joseph W. Martin Commemorative, Stonehill Coll., 1990; Lionel Robbins Meml, Claremont Coll., 1991. Corresp. Fellow, British Acad., 1960; Fellow: Amer. Philosoph. Soc.; Econometric Soc. (Mem. Council; Vice-Pres. 1950; Pres. 1951); Member: Amer. Acad. Arts and Sciences; Amer. Econ. Assoc. (Pres. 1961; Hon. Fellow, 1965); Phi Beta Kappa; Commn on Social Sciences (NSF), 1967–70; Internat. Econ. Assoc. (Pres. 1965–68; Hon. Pres. 1968–); Nat. Acad. of Sciences, 1970–; Omicron Delta Epsilon, Bd of Trustees (Internat. Honor Soc. in Econ.). Hon. Fellow: LSE; Peruvian Sch. of Economics, 1980. Hon. LLD: Chicago, 1961; Oberlin, 1961; Boston Coll., 1964; Indiana, 1966; Michigan, 1967; Claremont Grad. Sch., 1970; New Hampshire, 1971; Seton Hall, 1971; Keio, Tokyo, 1971; Harvard, 1972; Gustavas Adolphus Coll., 1974; Univ. of Southern Calif, 1975; Univ. of Rochester, 1976; Univ. of Pennsylvania, 1976; Emmanuel Coll., 1977; Stonehill Coll., 1978; Widener, 1982; Hon. DLitt: Ripon Coll., 1962; Northern Michigan Univ., 1973; Valparaiso Univ., 1987; Columbia Univ., 1988; Hon DSc: E Anglia, 1966; Massachusetts, 1972; Rhode Is., 1972; City Univ. of London, 1980; Tufts Univ., 1988; Hon. LHD Williams Coll., 1971; D*hc* Université Catholique de Louvain, 1976; Catholic Univ. at Riva Aguero Inst., Lima, 1980; Universidad Nacional de Educación a Distancia, Madrid, 1989; Universidad Politénica de Valencia, 1991; DUniv New Univ. of Lisbon, 1985. David A. Wells Prize, Harvard, 1941; John Bates Clark Medal, Amer. Econ. Assoc., 1947; Medal of Honor, Univ. of Evansville, 1970; Nobel Prize in Econ. Science, 1970; Albert Einstein Commemorative Award, 1971; Alumni Medal, Chicago Univ., 1983; Britannica Award, 1989; Medal and Hon. Mem., Club of Economics and Management, Valencia, Spain, 1990; Gold Scanno Prize in Economy, Naples, Italy, 1990. *Publications:* Foundations of Economic Analysis, 1947, enlarged edn 1982; Economics, 1948, (with Paul A. Samuelson and William D. Nordhaus) 12th edn, 1985, 15th edn 1994 (trans. 40 langs, 1948); (jtly) Linear Programming and Economic Analysis, 1958 (trans. French, Japanese); Readings in Economics, 1955; The Collected Scientific Papers of Paul A. Samuelson (ed J. E. Stiglitz), vols I and II, 1966, vol. III (ed R. C. Merton), 1972, vol. IV (ed H. Nagatani and K. Crowley), 1977, vol. V (ed K. Crowley), 1986; co-author, other books in field, papers in various jls, etc. *Recreation:* tennis. *Address:* Department of Economics, Massachusetts Institute of Technology E52–383, Cambridge, MA 02139, USA. *T:* (617) 2533368, *Fax:* (617) 2530560. *Club:* Belmont Hill (Mass).

SAMUELSON, Sir Sydney Wylie, Kt 1995; CBE 1978; first British Film Commissioner, since 1991; President, Samuelson Group PLC, since 1990 (Chairman, 1966–90); *b* 7 Dec. 1925; 2nd *s* of G. B. and Marjorie Samuelson; *m* 1949, Doris (*née* Magen); three *s*. *Educ:* Irene Avenue Council Sch., Lancing, Sussex. Served RAF, 1943–47. From age 14, career devoted to various aspects of British film industry: cinema projectionist, 1939–42; Asst Film Editor, 1943; Asst Film Cameraman, Cameraman and Dir of Documentary Films, 1947–59; founded company to service film, TV and, later, audio-visual prodn organisations, supplying cameras and other technical equipment, with purchase of first camera, 1954; continued filming as technician on locations throughout world until 1959, when activities concentrated on expanding his company. Permanent Trustee, 1973– and Chm. Bd of Management, 1976–, BAFTA (Vice-Chm. Film, 1971–73, Chm. of Council, 1973–76; Mem., Business Bd, 1994–; Fellow, 1993); Chm., BAFTA—Shell UK Venture Cttee, 1988–91; Member: Exec. Cttee, Cinema and Television Veterans (Pres., 1980–81); Council and Exec. Cttee, Cinema and TV Benevolent Fund, 1969–92 (Trustee, 1982–89; Pres., 1983–86); Brit. Soc. of Cinematographers (Governor, 1969–79; 1st Vice-Pres., 1976–77; award for Outstanding Contribution to Film Industry, 1967); Associate Mem., Amer. Soc. of Cinematographers; Hon. Mem., ACTT, 1990. Hon. Technical Adviser, Royal Naval Film Corp.; Hon. Fellow, Brit. Kinematograph Sound and TV Soc., 1970; Hon. Mem., Guild of British Camera Technicians (Trustee, 1993). Pres., UK Friends of Akim (Israel Assoc. for Mentally Handicapped); Vice Pres., Muscular Dystrophy Assoc. of GB; Founder Mem., Charity Projects; Mem. Bd, Young Persons Concert Foundn. Freeman, City of London, 1987. Michael Balcon Award, BAFTA, 1985; Award of Merit, Guild of Film Prodn Execs, 1986. *Recreations:* collecting recorded film music, vintage motoring, veteran jogging (finished 13,006th London Marathon 1982). *Address:* 31 West Heath Avenue, NW11 7QJ. *T:* 0181–458 4982, *Fax:* 0181–458 1957; British Film Commission, 70 Baker Street, W1M 1DJ. *T:* 0171–224 5000, *Fax:* 0171–224 1013.

SAMUELSSON, Prof. Bengt Ingemar; Professor of Medical and Physiological Chemistry, Karolinska Institutet, Stockholm, since 1972; Chairman, Nobel Foundation, Stockholm, since 1993; *b* Halmstad, Sweden, 21 May 1934; *s* of Anders and Stina Samuelsson; *m* 1958, Inga Karin Bergstein; one *s* two *d*. *Educ:* Karolinska Institutet (DMedSci 1960, MD 1961). Res. Fellow, Harvard Univ., 1961–62; Asst Prof. of Med. Chemistry, Karolinska Inst, 1961–66; Prof., Royal Vet. Coll., Stockholm, 1967–72; Chm., Dept of Chemistry, 1973–83, Dean of Med. Faculty, 1978–83, Karolinska Inst, Stockholm. Vis. Prof., Harvard, 1976; T. Y. Shen Vis. Prof. in Med. Chem., MIT, 1977; Walker-Ames Prof., Washington Univ., 1987. Lectures include: Shirley Johnson Meml, Philadelphia, 1977; Sixth Annual Marrs McLean, Houston, 1978; Harvey, NY, 1979; Lane Medical, Stanford Univ., 1981; Eighth Annual Sci. in Med., Univ. of Washington, 1981; Arthur C. Corcoran Meml, Cleveland, Ohio, 1981; Kober, Assoc. of Amer. Physicians, 1982; Brown-Razor, Rice Univ., Houston, 1984; Solomon A. Berson Meml, Mount Sinai Sch. of Medicine, NY, 1984; Angelo Minich, Venice, 1988; Hans Neurath, Univ. of Washington, 1990; Dunham, Harvard Med. Sch., 1990; First Fogarty Internat., NIH, 1992. Member: Nobel Assembly, Karolinska Inst., 1972– (Chm., 1990); Nobel Cttee for Physiol. or Medicine, 1984–89 (Chm., 1987–89); Swedish Govt Res. Adv. Bd, 1985–88; Nat. Commn on Health Policy, 1987–90. Member: Royal Swedish Acad. of Scis, 1981–; Mediterranean Acad., Catania, 1982–; US Nat. Acad. of Scis, 1984; French Acad. of Scis, 1989; Royal Soc., 1990; Royal Nat. Acad. of Medicine, Spain, 1991; Hon. Prof., Bethune Univ. of Med. Scis, China, 1986; Hon. Member: Amer. Soc. of Biological Chemists, 1976; Assoc. of American Physicians, 1982; Swedish Med. Assoc., 1982; Italian Pharmacological Soc., 1985; Acad. Nac. de Medicina de Buenos Aires, 1986; Internat. Soc. of Haematology, 1986; Spanish Soc. of Allergology and Clinical Immunology, 1989; Foreign Hon. Member: Amer. Acad. of Arts and Scis, 1982–; Internat. Acad. of Science, ICSD; Founding Mem., Academia Europaea, 1988. Hon. DSc: Chicago, 1978; Illinois, 1983; DUniv: Rio de Janeiro, 1986; Buenos Aires, 1986; Complutense, Madrid, 1991; Milan, 1993; Louisiana State, 1993. Nobel Prize in Physiology or Medicine (jtly), 1982; numerous awards and prizes. *Publications:* papers on biochemistry of prostaglandins, thromboxanes and leukotrienes. *Address:* Karolinska Institutet, 17177 Stockholm, Sweden. *T:* (8) 7287600.

SAMWORTH, David Chetwode, CBE 1985; DL; Chairman, Samworth Brothers Ltd (formerly Gorran Foods Ltd), since 1984 (Director since 1981); *b* 25 June 1935; *s* of Frank and Phyllis Samworth; *m* 1969, Rosemary Grace Cadell; one *s* three *d*. *Educ:* Uppingham Sch. Chm., Pork Farms Ltd, 1968–81; Director: Northern Foods Ltd, 1978–81; Imperial Gp, 1983–85; (non-exec.) Thorntons plc, 1988–94. Chm., Meat and Livestock Commn, 1980–84. Member: Leicester No 3 HMC, 1970–74; Trent RHA, 1974–78, 1980–84. DL Leics, 1984. *Recreations:* tennis, hunting. *Address:* PO Box 9, Melton Mowbray, Leics LE13 0XH.

SAN VINCENZO FERRERI, 8th Marquis of, **Alfio Testaferrata Ghâxaq** (Marquis Testaferrata); *b* 1911; *s* of Daniel Testaferrata Bonici Ghâxaq and Agnese (*d* 1941), *d* of Baroncino Nicola Galea di San Marciano; *S* father, 1945. *Educ:* Stonyhurst College, Blackburn; University Coll., Oxford. Member: Cttee of Privileges of Maltese Nobility, 1948–65; Royal Numismatic Society, 1962–85; Société suisse de Numismatique, 1962–85. Hereditary Knight of the Holy Roman Empire; Patrician of Rome, Messina, and Citta di Castello. *Address:* 29 Villegaignon Street, Mdina, Malta, GC. *T:* 674139. *Club:* Casino Maltese (Valletta).

SANBERK, Özdem; Turkish Ambassador to the Court of St James's, since 1995; *b* 1938; *m* Sumru Sanberk; one *d*. *Educ:* Faculty of Law, Univ. of Istanbul. Joined Turkish Ministry of Foreign Affairs, 1963; Dep. Perm. Deleg. to OECD, Paris, and to UNESCO, Paris, 1980–85; Dep. Dir-Gen. for Bilateral Economic Affairs, Min. of Foreign Affairs; Advr for external relations to Prime Minister, 1985–87; Ambassador and Perm Deleg. to EC, 1987; Under-Sec., Min. of Foreign Affairs, 1991. Numerous foreign orders. *Address:* Turkish Embassy, 43 Belgrave Square, SW1X 8PA. *T:* 0171–393 0202. *Club:* Cavalry and Guards.

SANCTUARY, Gerald Philip; Secretary, National Union of Journalists Provident Fund, 1984–95; *b* 22 Nov. 1930; *s* of late John Cyril Tabor Sanctuary, MD and Maisie Toppin Sanctuary (*née* Brooks); *m* 1956, Rosemary Patricia L'Estrange, Dublin; three *s* two *d*. *Educ:* Bryanston Sch.; Law Soc.'s Sch. of Law. National Service Pilot, 1953–55; Asst Solicitor, Kingston, 1955–56; Partner in Hasties, Solicitors, Lincoln's Inn Fields, 1957–62; Field Sec., Nat. Marriage Guidance Council, 1963–65, Nat. Secretary 1965–69; Exec. Dir, Sex Information and Educn Council of US, 1969–71; Sec., Professional and Public Relations, The Law Soc., 1971–78; Exec. Dir, Internat. Bar Assoc., 1978–79; Legal Adviser and Regional and Local Affairs Dir, Mencap, 1979–84. Hon. Treas., GAPAN, 1986–. Editor, Law Soc. series, It's Your Law, 1973–79. Regular broadcaster on radio. *Publications:* Marriage Under Stress, 1968; Divorce — and After, 1970, 2nd edn 1976; Before You See a Solicitor, 1973, 2nd edn 1983; After I'm Gone—what will happen to my Handicapped Child?, 1984, 2nd edn 1991; contrib., Moral Implications of Marriage Counselling, 1971; Vie Affective et Sexuelle, 1972; Loss Prevention Manual, 1978; The English Legal Heritage, 1979; booklets: Fishpool Street—St Albans, 1984; Tudor St Albans; St Albans and the Wars of the Roses, 1985; The Romans in St Albans, 1986; The Monastery at St Albans, 1987; Shakespeare's Globe Theatre, 1992; Abbey Theatre, St Albans, 1993. *Recreations:* amateur drama, organising murder mystery weekends. *Address:* 6 Mercers Row, St Albans, Herts AL1 2QS. *T:* St Albans (01727) 842666.

SANDARS, Christopher Thomas; Assistant Under-Secretary of State (Export Policy and Finance), Ministry of Defence, since 1990; *b* 6 March 1942; *s* of late Vice-Adm. Sir Thomas Sandars, KBE, CB and Lady Sandars; *m* 1966, Elizabeth Anne Yielder; three *s* one *d*. *Educ:* Oundle Sch.; Corpus Christi Coll., Cambridge (Foundation Schol.). Joined MoD, 1964; Asst Private Sec. to Minister of State, 1967–69; Central Policy Review Staff, Cabinet Office, 1971–74; Private Sec. to Minister of State, 1975–77; Hd, General Finance Div. 1, 1977–80; Hd, Defence Secretariat 13, 1980–84; RCDS, 1985; Hd, Secretariat 9 (Air), 1986–90. *Recreations:* tennis, badminton, painting, gardening, theatre. *Address:* Ministry of Defence, Main Building, Whitehall, SW1A 2HB.

SANDARS, Nancy Katharine, FBA 1984; FSA; archaeologist; *b* 29 June 1914; *d* of Edward Carew Sandars and Gertrude Annie Sandars (*née* Phipps). *Educ:* at home; Wychwood School, Oxford; Inst. of Archaeology, Univ. of London (Diploma 1949); St Hugh's College, Oxford (BLitt 1957). Archaeological research and travel in Europe, 1949–69; British School at Athens, 1954–55; Elizabeth Wordsworth Studentship, St Hugh's College, Oxford, 1958–61; travelled in Middle East, 1957, 1958, 1962, 1966; conferences, lectures (Prague, Sofia, McGill Univ.); excavations in British Isles and Greece. *Publications:* Bronze Age Cultures in France, 1957; The Epic of Gilgamesh, an English version, 1960; Prehistoric Art in Europe, 1967, rev. edn 1985; Poems of Heaven and Hell from Ancient Mesopotamia, 1971; The Sea-Peoples: warriors of the ancient Mediterranean, 1978. *Recreations:* walking, translating, looking at pictures. *Address:* The Manor House, Little Tew, Oxford OX7 4JF. *Club:* University Women's.

SANDARS, Prof. Patrick George Henry; Professor of Experimental Physics, since 1978, and Head of Atomic and Laser Physics, since 1990, Oxford University; *b* 29 March 1935; *s* of late P. R. and A. C. Sandars; *m* 1959, P. B. Hall; two *s*. *Educ:* Wellington Coll.; Balliol Coll., Oxford (MA, DPhil). Weir Junior Research Fellow, University Coll., and ICI Research Fellow, Clarendon Laboratory, Oxford, 1960–63; Tutorial Fellow, Balliol Coll., and Univ. Lectr, Oxford Univ., 1964–72; Reader in Physics, Oxford Univ., 1972–77; Head of Clarendon Lab., 1987–90. Junior Proctor, Oxford Univ., 1971–72. *Address:* 3 Hawkswell Gardens, Oxford OX2 7EX. *T:* Oxford (01865) 58535.

SANDBANK, Charles Peter, FEng; Deputy Director of Engineering, BBC, 1985–91; Broadcasting Technology Adviser, Department of Trade and Industry, since 1993; Director, Snell and Wilcox Ltd, since 1993; *b* 14 Aug. 1931; *s* of Gustav and Clare Sandbank; *m* 1955, Audrey Celia; one *s* two *d*. *Educ:* Bromley Grammar Sch.; London Univ. (BSc, DIC). FEng 1983; FIEE, FInstP. Prodn Engr, 1953–55, Develt Engr, 1955–60, Brimar Valve Co.; Develt Section Head, STC Transistor Div., 1960–64; Head of Electron Devices Lab., 1964–68, Manager, Communication Systems Div., 1968–78, Standard Telecommunication Laboratories; Head of BBC Research Dept, 1978–84; Asst Dir of Engrg, 1984–85, Asst to Dir of Engrg, 1991–93, BBC. Mem. Council: IEE, 1978–81, 1989–92 (Chairman: Electronics Divisional Bd, 1979–80; London Centre, 1991–92); Royal TV Soc., 1983–86, 1989–92; Chairman: EBU New Systems and Services Cttee, 1984–89; EBU High Definition TV Cttee, 1981–84; EUREKA High Definition Television Project Adv. Bd, 1988–; Jt Technical Cttee, EBU/Eur. Telecommunications Standards Inst., 1990–93; DTI Cttee for Enhanced Definition TV, 1990–; Bureau mem., EBU Tech. Cttee, 1989–93. Ext. Examr, London Univ., 1982–89. Royal Acad. of Engrg Vis. Prof. of Information Systems Design, Univ. of Bradford, 1995–. Chm., Internal Cttee of Inquiry into Legionnaires Disease Outbreak at Broadcasting House, London, 1988. Liveryman, Scientific Instrument Makers' Co., 1988–. Fellow, SMPTE, 1989; FBKSTS 1991; FRTS; FRSA. DUniv Surrey, 1994. *Publications:* Optical Fibre Communication Systems, 1980; Digital Television, 1990; papers and patents (about 200) on semiconductor devices, integrated circuits, solid-state bulk effects, compound semiconductors, microwaves, electron-phonon interactions, navigational aids, electro-optics and broadcasting technology. *Recreations:* boatbuilding, sailing, film-making, music, garden-watching. *Address:* Grailands, Beech Road, Reigate, Surrey RH2 9NA. *T:* (office) 0171–215 1825.

SANDBERG, Sir Michael (Graham Ruddock), Kt 1986; CBE 1982 (OBE 1977); Chairman: The Hongkong and Shanghai Banking Corporation, 1977–86; The British Bank of the Middle East, 1980–86; *b* 31 May 1927; *s* of Gerald Arthur Clifford Sandberg and Ethel Marion Sandberg; *m* 1954, Carmel Mary Roseleen Donnelly; two *s* two *d*. *Educ:* St Edward's Sch., Oxford. 6th Lancers (Indian Army) and First King's Dragoon Guards, 1945. Joined The Hongkong and Shanghai Banking Corp., 1949. Mem. Exec. Council, Hong Kong, 1978–86. Steward, Royal Hong Kong Jockey Club, 1972–86, Chm., 1981–86; Treasurer, Univ. of Hong Kong, 1977–86. FCIB (FIB 1977; Vice Pres. 1984–87); FRSA 1983. Freeman, City of London; Liveryman, Co. of Clockmakers. Hon. LLD: Hong Kong, 1984; Pepperdine, 1986. *Recreations:* horse racing, bridge, cricket, horology. *Address:* 54A Hyde Park Gate, SW7 5EB; Domaine de la Haute Germaine, Ste Marguerite, Le Broc, Alpes Maritimes, France. *Clubs:* Cavalry and Guards, Portland, White's, MCC, Surrey CCC (Pres. 1988).

SANDELL, Terence, (Terry), OBE 1991; Director, Visiting Arts Office of Great Britain and Northern Ireland, since 1994; *b* 8 Sept. 1948; *s* of James William Sandell and Helen Elizabeth McCombie; *m* 1984, Kate Ling; two *s*. *Educ:* Watford Grammar Sch. for Boys; Univ. of Nottingham (BA Hons); Univ. of Edinburgh; City Univ. (MA). VSO, Berber, N Sudan, 1970–72. Joined British Council, 1974: Asst Rep. Dir, Omdurman Centre, Sudan, 1974–78; Regional Officer, Soviet Union and Mongolia, London, 1978–81; 1st Sec. (Cultural), British Embassy, Moscow, 1981–83; Asst Rep., Vienna, 1983–86, Rep. 1986–89; Projects Manager, Soviet Union, London, 1989; Dir, Soviet Union/CIS, and Cultural Counsellor, British Embassy, Moscow, 1989–92; attachment to Dept of Arts Policy and Management, City Univ., 1992–93; Consultant, Arts Policy Develt, British Council, 1993–94. Special Lectr, Dept of Slavonic Studies, Univ. of Nottingham, 1993–. Mem. Bd of Trustees, State Liby for Foreign Lit., Moscow, 1991–92. *Publication:* (with Sadig Rashid) Non-Formal Education and Development in the Sudan, 1980. *Recreations:* walking, literature, theatre, travel. *Address:* 15 Mount Street, W1Y 5RA.

SANDELSON, Neville Devonshire; Barrister-at-Law; public affairs and business consultant; Deputy Chairman, Westminster and Overseas Trade Services Ltd, since 1985; Co-Founder, 1988, President, since 1990, The Radical Society (Co-Chairman, 1988–90); Executive Director, Profundis Ltd, since 1989; *b* Leeds, 27 Nov. 1923; *s* of late David I. Sandelson, OBE, and Dora Sandelson, (*née* Lightman); *m* 1959, Nana Karlinski, Neuilly sur Seine, France; one *s* two *d*. *Educ:* Westminster School; Trinity College, Cambridge; MA. Called to Bar, Inner Temple, 1946; for some years director of local newspaper and book publishing cos and producer of TV documentary programmes until resuming practice at Bar, 1964. Dep. Circuit Judge and Asst Recorder, 1977–85. Mem. London County Council, 1952–58. Travelled extensively in USA, Middle East, Asia and Europe. Contested (Lab): Ashford (Kent) 1950, 1951 and 1955; Beckenham (by-election) 1957; Rushcliffe 1959; Heston & Isleworth 1966; SW Leicester (by-election) 1967; Chichester 1970; (SDP) Hayes and Harlington, 1983. MP (Lab 1971–81, SDP 1981–83) Hayes and Harlington, June 1971–83; Founder Mem., SDP, 1981, resigned 1987. Parly spokesman on NI, 1981–82, and on the arts, 1982–83; Vice-Chm., All-Party Productivity Gp; Sec., All-Party Theatre Gp; Jt Sec., British-Greek Parly Gp; Sec., British Gibraltar Parly Gp; Vice-Chm., Afghanistan Parly Support Cttee. Promoted, as a Private Mem's Bill, the Matrimonial Proceedings (Polygamous Marriages) Act, 1972. Member: Council, Nat. Cttee for Electoral Reform, 1977–88 (resigned); Nat. Council of European Movement, 1985–; Exec. Cttee, Wider Share Ownership Council, 1979–92; founder Mem., Manifesto Gp, 1975–80 (Hon. Treas.). Mem. Ct, Brunel Univ., 1975–81. *Address:* Yorkshire House, 8 Maddox Street, W1R 9PN. *T:* 0171–408 1152. *Club:* Reform.

SANDER, Audrey Olga Helen; Her Honour Judge Sander; a Circuit Judge, since 1995; *b* 10 Nov. 1936; *d* of Ernest Sander and Marian Sander; *m* 1963, Adrian Gale; one *s* two *d*. *Educ:* St Paul's Girls' Sch.; Somerville Coll., Oxford (MA Jurisprudence). Called to the Bar, Gray's Inn, 1960; in practice at the Bar, 1960–77; Editl Asst, Legal Action Gp, 1978–83; admitted solicitor, 1986; practised as solicitor, 1986–95 (at Gill Akaster, 1989–95); Asst Recorder, 1990–94; Recorder, 1994–95. *Address:* Truro Combined Court Centre, Edward Street, Truro, Cornwall TR1 2PB.

SANDERLING, Kurt; conductor; *b* 19 Sept. 1912; *m* 1st, 1941, Nina Bobath; one *s*; 2nd, 1963, Barbara Wagner; twin *s*. *Educ:* privately. Conductor: Leningrad Philharmonic Orch., 1941–60; East Berlin Symphony Orch., 1960–95. Guest conductor of many orchs in Europe and N America. *Address:* Am Iderfenngraben 47, 13156 Berlin, Germany.

SANDERS, Cyril Woods, CB 1959; Lord of the Manor of Kavenham-Stoke-Wereham and Wretton in Norfolk; *b* 21 Feb. 1912; *er s* of Cyril Sturgis Sanders and Dorothy (*née* Woods); *m* 1944, Kate Emily Boyes, *qv*; one *s* three *d*. *Educ:* St Paul's Sch.; Queen's Coll., Oxford. BA Oxon 1934, Lit. Hum. Joined General Post Office as Assistant Principal, 1934; transferred to Board of Trade, 1935; retired from Dept of Trade and Industry (formerly Bd of Trade) as Under-Secretary, 1972. *Recreations:* walking, sailing, painting. *Address:* 41 Smith Street, Chelsea, SW3 4EP. *T:* 0171–352 8053; Giles Point, Winchelsea, Sussex TN36 4AA. *T:* Rye (01797) 226431; Canower, Cashel, Connemara, Eire. *Club:* Ski Club of Gt Britain.

SANDERS, Donald Neil, AO 1994; CB 1983; Director: Lend Lease Corp. Ltd, since 1992; MLC Life Ltd, since 1992; Queensland Investment Corp., since 1992; Australian Chamber Orchestra Ltd, since 1993; Chairman, H-G Ventures Ltd, since 1995; *b* Sydney, 21 June 1927; *s* of L. G. and R. M. Sanders; *m* 1952, Betty Elaine, *d* of W. B. and E. M. Constance; four *s* one *d*. *Educ:* Wollongong High Sch.; Univ. of Sydney (BEc). Commonwealth Bank of Australia, 1943–60; Australian Treasury, 1956; Bank of England, 1960; Reserve Bank of Australia, 1960–87: Supt, Credit Policy Div., Banking Dept, 1964–66; Dep. Manager: Banking Dept, 1966–67; Res. Dept, 1967–70; Aust. Embassy, Washington DC, 1968; Chief Manager: Securities Markets Dept, 1970–72; Banking and Finance Dept, 1972–74; Adviser and Chief Manager, Banking and Finance Dept, 1974–75; Dep. Governor and Dep. Chm., 1975–87; Commonwealth Bank of Australia: Chief Exec., 1987–92; Man. Dir, 1991–92; Man. Dir, Commonwealth Banking Corp., 1987–91. *Address:* Somerset, Taralga Road, via Goulburn, NSW 2580, Australia.

SANDERS, Prof. Ed Parish, FBA 1989; Arts and Sciences Professor of Religion, Duke University, since 1990; *b* 18 April 1937; *s* of Mildred Sanders (*née* Parish) and Eula Thomas Sanders; *m* 1963, Becky Jill Hall (marr. diss. 1978); one *d*. *Educ:* Texas Wesleyan College (BA); Southern Methodist Univ. (BD); Union Theological Seminary, NY (ThD). Asst Prof. of Religious Studies, McMaster Univ., 1966–70, Associate Prof., 1970–74, Prof., 1974–88; Dean Ireland's Prof. of Exegesis of Holy Scripture, Oxford Univ., 1984–89. Visiting Professor: Jewish Theol. Seminary, 1980; Chair of Judeo-Christian Studies, Tulane Univ., 1980; Walter G. Mason Dist. Vis. Prof., Coll. of William and Mary in Virginia, 1981; Vis. Fellow Commoner, Trinity Coll., Cambridge, 1982. Donnellan Lectr, TCD, 1982. *Publications:* The Tendencies of the Synoptic Tradition, 1969; Paul and Palestinian Judaism, 1977, 2nd edn 1981; (ed) Jewish and Christian Self-Definition, vol. I, The Shaping of Christianity in the Second and Third Centuries, 1980, vol. II, Aspects of Judaism in the Graeco-Roman Period, 1981, vol. III, Self-Definition in the Graeco-Roman World, 1982; Paul, The Law and the Jewish People, 1983; Jesus and Judaism, 1985, 3rd edn 1987; (ed) Jesus, The Gospels and the Church, 1987; (with Margaret Davies) Studying the Synoptic Gospels, 1989; Jewish Law from Jesus to the Mishnah, 1990; Paul, 1991; Judaism: practice and belief 63 BCE to 66 BCE, 1992; The Historical Figure of Jesus, 1993; articles in NT Studies, Jl of Biblical Literature, Harvard Theol. Review, Jewish Quarterly Review. *Address:* Department of Religion, Duke University, Durham, NC 27706, USA.

SANDERS, Dr Jeremy Keith Morris, FRS 1995; Reader in Chemistry and Assistant Head, Department of Chemistry, Cambridge University, since 1992; Fellow of Selwyn College, Cambridge, since 1976; *b* 3 May 1948; *s* of Sidney Sanders and Sylvia (*née* Rutman); *m* 1972, Louise Elliott; one *s* one *d*. *Educ:* Imperial Coll., London (BSc, ARCS Chem. 1969); PhD 1972, MA 1974, Cantab. FRSC, CChem. Junior Res. Fellow, Christ's Coll., Cambridge, 1972; NATO/EMBO Fellow, Stanford Univ., 1972–73; Demonstrator, 1973–78, Lectr in Chemistry, 1978–92, Cambridge Univ. Meldola Medal, 1975; Hickinbottom Award, 1981; Pfizer Award, 1984, 1988; Josef Loschmidt Prize, 1994. *Publications:* (with B. K. Hunter) Modern NMR Spectroscopy, 1987, 2nd edn 1993; contribs to chem. and biochem. jls. *Recreations:* family, cooking, music, walking. *Address:* University Chemical Laboratory, Lensfield Road, Cambridge CB2 1EW. *T:* Cambridge (01223) 336411.

SANDERS, Rear-Adm. Jeremy Thomas, CB 1994; OBE 1982; Commander British Forces, Gibraltar, 1992–94; *b* 23 Nov. 1942; *s* of late Thomas Sanders and Paulene (*née* Woodfield-Smith); *m* 1966, Judith Rosemary Jones; two *d*. *Educ:* Norwood Sch., Exeter; Pangbourne Coll. BRNC, Dartmouth, 1960; appts include: Lieut i/c HMS Chilcompton and Kellington, 1968–69; long communications course, HMS Mercury, 1970; Lt Comdr on staff of Flag Officer, Submarines, 1974–76; Comdr i/c HMS Salisbury, 1977–78; ndc 1979; SO Ops to Flag Officer, 1st Flotilla, 1981–83; Capt., 8th Frigate Sqdn and i/c HMS Andromeda, 1985–87; Dir, Maritime Tactical Sch., 1987–89; Chief Naval Signal Officer, 1989–90; Dir, Naval Warfare, 1990–92. *Recreations:* walking, gardening, sport, food and wine, arts. *Clubs:* Naval, MCC.

SANDERS, John Derek, OBE 1994; Director of Music, Cheltenham Ladies' College, since 1968; Organist and Master of the Choristers, Gloucester Cathedral, 1967–94; *b* 26 Nov. 1933; *s* of Alderman J. T. Sanders, JP, CA and Mrs E. M. Sanders (*née* Trivett); *m* 1967, Janet Ann Dawson; one *s* one *d*. *Educ:* Felsted Sch., Essex; Royal Coll. of Music; Gonville and Caius Coll., Cambridge. ARCM 1952; FRCO 1955; MusB 1956; MA 1958. Dir of Music, King's Sch., Gloucester, and Asst Organist, Gloucester Cathedral, 1958–63; Organist and Master of the Choristers, Chester Cathedral, 1964–67. Conductor: Gloucestershire Symphony Orchestra, 1967–94; Gloucester Choral Soc., 1967–94. Conductor of Three Choirs Festival, triennially, 1968–94. Pres., Cathedral Organists' Assoc., 1990–92; Mem. Council, RCO, 1979–94. Liveryman, Co. of Musicians, 1987. Freeman, City of London, 1986. DMus Lambeth, 1990. Hon. FRSCM 1991. *Publications:* Festival Te Deum, 1962; Soliloquy for Organ, 1977; Toccata for Organ, 1979; Te Deum Laudamus, 1985; Jubilate Deo, 1986; Two Prayers, 1988; A Canticle of Joy, 1991; The Reproaches, 1993; St Mark Passion, 1993. *Recreations:* gastronomy, travelling. *Address:* Ridge Cottage, Upton Bishop, Ross-on-Wye, Herefordshire HR9 7UD. *T:* Ross-on-Wye (01989) 780482.

SANDERS, John Leslie Yorath; HM Diplomatic Service, retired; *b* 5 May 1929; *s* of late Reginald Yorath Sanders and Gladys Elizabeth Sanders (*née* Blything); *m* 1953, Brigit Mary Lucine Altounyan; one *s* two *d*. *Educ:* Dulwich Coll. Prep. Sch.; Cranleigh School. Higher Dip. in Furniture Prodn and Design, London Coll. of Furniture, 1982. Nat. Service in HM Forces (RA), 1948–50; entered HM Foreign Service, 1950; FO, 1950–52; MECAS, Lebanon, 1953; Damascus, 1954–55; Bahrain, 1955–56; Vice-Consul, Basra, 1956–60; Oriental Sec., Rabat, 1960–63; FO, 1964–67; 1st Sec., Beirut, 1968–70; 1st Sec. and Head of Chancery, Mexico City, 1970–73; Counsellor, Khartoum, 1973–75; Counsellor, Beirut, 1975–76; Dir of Res., FCO, 1976–78; Ambassador to Panama, 1978–80. *Recreations:* sailing, music. *Address:* 122 Bay View Road, Northam, Bideford, N Devon EX39 1BJ.

SANDERS, Sir John Reynolds M.; *see* Mayhew-Sanders, Sir J. R.

SANDERS, Kate Emily Tyrrell, (Mrs C. W. Sanders); *see* Boyes, K. E. T.

SANDERS, Nicholas John, PhD; Head of Teachers Branch, Department for Education and Employment (formerly Department for Education), since 1993; *b* 14 Sept. 1946; *s* of Ivor and Mollie Sanders; *m* 1971, Alison Ruth Carter; one *s* one *d*. *Educ:* King Edward's Sch., Birmingham; Magdalene Coll., Cambridge (MA, PhD). Joined DES, subseq. Dept for Educn, 1971; Principal Private Sec. to Sec. of State, 1974–75; Private Sec. to Prime Minister, 1978–81; Prin. Finance Officer, 1989–93. *Address:* Department for Education and Employment, Sanctuary Buildings, Great Smith Street, SW1P 3BT. *T:* 0171–925 5000.

SANDERS, Peter Basil, CBE 1993; Chief Executive, Commission for Racial Equality, 1988–93 (Director, 1977–88); *b* 9 June 1938; *s* of Basil Alfred Horace Sanders and Ellen May Sanders (*née* Cockrell); *m* 1st, 1961, Janet Valerie (*née* Child) (marr. diss. 1984); two *s* one *d*; 2nd, 1988, Anita Jackson. *Educ:* Queen Elizabeth's Grammar Sch., Barnet; Wadham Coll., Oxford (MA, DPhil). Administrative Officer, Basutoland, 1961–66; Research in Oxford for DPhil, 1966–70; Officer, Min. of Defence, 1971–73; Race Relations Bd: Principal Conciliation Officer, 1973–74; Dep. Chief Officer, 1974–77. *Publications:* Lithoko: Sotho Praise-Poems (ed jtly and trans. with an Introd. and Notes), 1974; Moshoeshoe, Chief of the Sotho, 1975; The Simple Annals: the history of an Essex and East End family, 1989. *Address:* The Old Post Office, High Street, Widdington, Saffron Walden, Essex CB11 3SG. *T:* Saffron Walden (01799) 540273.

SANDERS, Raymond Adrian; Social Security Commissioner, since 1986; a Child Support Commissioner, since 1993; *b* 13 May 1932; *s* of Leslie Harry Sanders and Beatrice Sanders; *m* 1st, 1961, Anna Margaret Burton (marr. diss.); one *s*; 2nd, 1985, Virginia Varnell Dunn; three *d*. *Educ:* Auckland Univ. (LLB); London School of Economics (LLB). Barrister and Solicitor, New Zealand, 1956–66; Partner in Jackson, Russell and Co., Barristers and Solicitors, Auckland, NZ, 1962–66; part-time Lectr 1960–66 and Examiner 1961–66, Auckland Univ.; Solicitor, Allen and Overy, London, 1967–71; practising barrister, 1971–73; DHSS, 1973–74, 1975–84; Law Officers' Dept, 1974–75. Legal Advr to Warnock Inquiry (Human Fertilisation and Embryology), 1982–84; Regional Chm., Social Security and Medical Appeal Tribunals, 1984–86. *Publications:* Credit Management (jtly) 1966; Building Contracts and Practice, 1967. *Recreations:* theatre, music, cycling, tennis. *Address:* Office of the Social Security Commissioners, Harp House, 83 Farringdon Street, EC4A 4BL. *T:* 0171–353 5578.

SANDERS, Sir Robert (Tait), KBE 1980; CMG 1974; HMOCS; Secretary to the Cabinet, Government of Fiji, 1970–79; Treaties Adviser, Government of Fiji, 1985–87; *b* 2 Feb. 1925; *s* of late A. S. W. Sanders and Charlotte McCulloch; *m* 1951, Barbara, *d* of G. Sutcliffe; two *s* (and one *s* decd). *Educ:* Canmore Public Sch., Dunfermline; Dunfermline High Sch.; Fettes Coll., Edinburgh; Cambridge Univ. (Major Open Classical Schol., Pembroke Coll., 1943; John Stewart of Rannoch Schol. in Latin and Greek, 1947; 1st cl. Hons, Pts I and II of Classical Tripos); London Sch. of Economics, 1949–50; SOAS, 1949–50. Served War, 1943–46: Lieut, 1st Bn the Royal Scots, India and Malaya. Sir Arthur Thomson Travelling Schol., 1948; Sir William Browne Medal for Latin Epigram,

1948; MA (Cantab) 1951. Joined HM Overseas Civil Service, Fiji, as Dist Officer, 1950; Sec. to Govt of Tonga, 1956–58; Sec., Coconut Commn of Enquiry, 1963; MLC, Fiji, 1963–64; Sec. for Natural Resources, 1965–67; Actg Sec. Fijian Affairs, and Actg Chm. Native Lands and Fisheries Commn, 1967; MEC, Fiji, 1967; Sec. to Chief Minister and to Council of Ministers, 1967; apptd Sec. to Cabinet, 1970, also Sec. for Foreign Affairs, 1970–74, Sec. for Home Affairs, 1972–74 and Sec. for Information, 1975–76. Mem., Internat. Cttee, Stirling Univ., 1991–93. Fiji Independence Medal, 1970. *Publications:* Interlude in Fiji, 1963; Fiji Treaty List, 1987; articles in Corona, jl of HMOCS. *Recreations:* languages, travel, golf, music, hill-walking. *Address:* 6 Park Manor, Crieff PH7 4LJ. *Club:* Royal Scots (Edinburgh).

SANDERS, Roger Benedict; His Honour Judge Sanders; a Circuit Judge, since 1987; a Recorder of the Crown Court, since 1986; *b* 1 Oct. 1940; *s* of late Maurice and of Lilian Sanders; *m* 1969, Susan Brenner (marr. diss. 1992); two *s* (one *d* decd). *Educ:* Highgate School. Co-founder, Inner Temple Debating Soc., 1961, Chm. 1962. Called to the Bar, Inner Temple, 1965; South Eastern Circuit. Metropolitan Stipendiary Magistrate, 1980–87. A Chm., Inner London Juvenile Courts, 1980–87; Chm., Legal Cttee, Inner London Juvenile Panel, 1983–86; First Chm., No 1 (London S) Regional Duty Solicitor Cttee, 1984–85; Inner London Magistrates' Training Panel, 1983–87; Pres., Mental Health Review Tribunal, 1990–. Chairman, Walker School Assoc. (Southgate), 1976, 1977; Schools' Debating Assoc. Judge, 1976–; Mem., Haringey Schools Liaison Group, 1979. Hon. Fellow, Univ. of E London, 1993. *Address:* Harrow Crown Court, Hailsham Drive, Harrow, Middx HA1 4TU. *T:* 0181–424 2294.

SANDERS, Ronald; international affairs and business consultant; international relations consultant to Prime Minister of Antigua and Barbuda, with ambassadorial rank, since 1994; Director: Swiss American National Bank, Antigua, since 1990; Guyana Telephone and Telegraph Co., since 1991; Consultant on International Relations to Atlantic Tele Network, USA, since 1989; *b* Guyana, 26 Jan. 1948; *m* 1975, Susan Indrani (*née* Ramphal). *Educ:* Sacred Heart RC Sch., Guyana; Westminster Sch., London; Boston Univ., USA; Sussex Univ. Gen. Man., Guyana Broadcasting Service, 1973–76; Communication Cons. to Pres., Caribbean Develt Bank, Barbados, 1977; UNDP and CFTC Cons. to Govt of Antigua, 1977–81; Advr to For. Minister of Antigua and Barbuda, 1981–82; Dep. Perm. Rep. to UN, 1982–83; High Comr for Antigua and Barbuda in UK, 1984–87; Ambassador to UNESCO and EEC, 1983–87, to FRG, 1986–87. Vis. Fellow, Oxford Univ., 1988–89. Advr to Govt of Antigua and Barbuda, 1989–91. Member: Inter-Govtl Council, Internat. Prog. for Develt of Communications, UNESCO, 1983–87; Exec. Bd, UNESCO, 1985–87; RIIA, 1987–; Internat. Inst. of Communications, 1984–. *Publications:* Broadcasting in Guyana, 1977; Antigua and Barbuda: transition, trial, triumph, 1984; (ed) Inseparable Humanity—an anthology of reflections of Shridath Ramphal, Commonwealth Secretary-General, 1988; several contribs to internat. jls on communication, Antarctica, also political commentaries. *Recreations:* reading, cinema. *Address:* 24 Chelmsford Square, NW10 3AR. *Clubs:* Royal Automobile, St James's.

SANDERS, Prof. Roy, FRCS; consultant plastic surgeon, since 1974; Consultant, since 1974 at: Mount Vernon Centre for Plastic Surgery; Royal National Orthopaedic Hospital; Luton and Dunstable Hospital; Humana Hospital; Bishops Wood Hospital, Northwood; *b* 20 Aug. 1937; *s* of Leslie John Sanders and Marguerite Alice (*née* Knight); *m* 1st, 1961, Ann Ruth Costar (marr. diss.); two *s* one *d*; 2nd, 1984, Fleur Annette Chandler, Baroness von Balajthy. *Educ:* Hertford Grammar Sch.; Charing Cross Hosp. Med. Sch. (BSc Hons Anatomy, MB, BS). LRCP 1962; FRCS 1967. Various hosp. appts; Sen. Lectr in Plastic Surgery, London Univ. and Hon. Cons. Plastic Surgeon, Mt Vernon Centre for Plastic Surgery, 1972–74; Cons. Plastic Surgeon, St Andrew's Hosp., Billericay and St Bart's Hosp., 1974–76; Hon. Sen. Lectr, London Univ., 1976–93; Hd, Service Dept, Plastic Maxilo-Facial and Oral Surgery, Mt Vernon Hosp., 1986–; Vis. Prof., UCL, 1993–. Sec., Brit. Assoc. Aesthetic Plastic Surgeons, 1984–87; Pres., Brit. Assoc. Plastic Surgeons, 1993 (Sec., 1987–90). *Publications:* scientific pubns in med. jls and textbooks. *Recreations:* equestrian pursuits, watercolour, painting, books. *Address:* 82 Portland Place, W1N 3DH. *T:* 0171–580 3541; 77 Harley Street, W1N 1DE. *T:* 0171–935 7417; Upper Rye Farm, Moreton-in-Marsh, Glos GL56 9AB. *T:* Moreton-in-Marsh (01608) 650542. *Clubs:* Athenæum, Honourable Artillery Company, Royal Society of Medicine.

SANDERS, William George, CB 1991; CEng, FRINA; RCNC; consultant; Head of Royal Corps of Naval Constructors, 1986–91; Director General, Submarines, Ministry of Defence (PE), 1985–91; *b* 22 Jan. 1936; *s* of George and Alice Irene Sanders; *m* 1956, Marina Charlotte Burford; two *s* one *d*. *Educ:* Public Secondary Sch., Plymouth; Devonport Dockyard Tech. Coll.; RN Coll., Greenwich. Asst Constructor, Ship Dept, Admiralty, 1961–68; FNCO Western Fleet, 1968–70; Constructor, Ship Dept, MoD (Navy), 1970–77; Principal Naval Overseer, Scotland, 1977–79; Marconi Space and Defence Systems, 1979–81; Project Manager, Type 23, 1981–83; DG Future Material Projects (Naval), MoD (PE), 1983–85. *Recreations:* golf, painting, gardening. *Address:* 11 Chestnut Grange, Park Lane, Corsham, Wilts SN13 9XR. *T:* Corsham (01249) 701558.

SANDERSON, family name of **Baron Sanderson of Bowden.**

SANDERSON OF AYOT, 2nd Baron *cr* 1960, title disclaimed by the heir, Dr Alan Lindsay Sanderson, 1971.

SANDERSON OF BOWDEN, Baron *cr* 1985 (Life Peer), of Melrose in the District of Ettrick and Lauderdale; **Charles Russell Sanderson,** Kt 1981; DL; Chairman, Scottish Conservative Party, 1990–93; *b* 30 April 1933; *s* of Charles Plummer Sanderson and Martha Evelyn Gardiner; *m* 1958, Frances Elizabeth Macaulay; one *s* two *d* (and one *s* decd). *Educ:* St Mary's Sch., Melrose; Trinity Coll., Glenalmond; Scottish Coll. of Textiles, Galashiels; Bradford Coll. (now Bradford Univ.). Commnd Royal Signals, 1952; served: 51 (Highland) Inf. Div. Signal Regt TA, 1953–56, KOSB TA, 1956–58. Partner, Chas P. Sanderson, Wool and Yarn Merchants, Melrose, 1958–87; Chairman: Edinburgh Financial Trust (formerly Yorkshire & Lancashire Investment Trust), 1983–87; Shires Investment Trust, 1984–87; Hawick Cashmere Co., 1991–; Scottish Mortgage & Trust, 1993– (Mem. Bd, 1991–); Scottish Pride plc, 1994–; Director: Clydesdale Bank, 1986–87, and 1994–; United Auctions, 1992–; Edinburgh Woollen Mills, 1993–; Watson & Philip, 1993–; Morrison Construction Group, 1995–. Minister of State, Scottish Office, 1987–90. Chairman, Roxburgh, Selkirk and Peebles Cons. and Unionist Assoc., 1970–73; Scottish Cons. Unionist Association: Chm. Central and Southern Area, 1974–75; Vice-Pres. 1975–77; Pres. 1977–79; Vice-Chm. Nat. Union of Cons Assocs, 1979–81 (Mem. Exec. Cttee, 1975–); Chm. Exec. Cttee, Nat. Union of Cons. Assocs, 1981–86; Member: Cons. Party Policy Cttee, 1979–86; Standing Adv. Cttee of Parly Candidates, 1979–86 (Vice-Chm. with responsibility for Europe, 1980–81). Deacon, Galashiels Manufrs Corp., 1976; Chm., Eildon Housing Assoc., 1978–82. Mem. Court, Napier Univ., 1994–; Governor, St Mary's Sch., Melrose, 1977–87; Chm. Council, Trinity Coll., Glenalmond, 1982–. Comr, Gen. Assembly of Ch. of Scotland, 1972. DL Roxburgh, Ettrick and Lauderdale, 1990. *Recreations:* golf, amateur operatics (Past Pres., Producer and Mem. Melrose Amateur Operatic Soc.). *Address:* Becketts Field, Bowden, Melrose, Roxburgh TD6 0ST. *T:* St Boswell's (01835) 822736. *Clubs:* Caledonian; Hon. Co. of Edinburgh Golfers (Muirfield).

SANDERSON, Bryan Kaye; Managing Director, British Petroleum, since 1992; Chief Executive Officer, BP Chemicals, since 1990; *b* 14 Oct. 1940; *s* of Eric and Anne Sanderson; *m* 1966, Sirkka Kärki; one *s* one *d*. *Educ:* Dame Allan's Sch., Newcastle upon Tyne; LSE (BSc Econ.); Dip. Business Studies, IMEDE Lausanne, 1973. VSO Peru, 1962–64; British Petroleum, 1964; Sen. BP rep., SE Asia and China, 1984–87; Chief Exec. Officer, BP Nutrition, 1987–90. Non-exec. Dir, British Steel, 1994–. Vice Pres., Chemical Industries Assoc., 1995–. *Recreations:* reading, golf, walking, gardening. *Address:* British Petroleum, Britannic House, 1 Finsbury Circus, EC2M 7BA. *T:* 0171–496 4748. *Club:* Hampstead Golf.

SANDERSON, Charles Denis; HM Diplomatic Service, retired; Fellow, since 1985, and Bursar, since 1992, St Peter's College, Oxford (Domestic Bursar, 1985–92); *b* 18 Dec. 1934; *s* of Norman and Elsie Sanderson; *m* 1960, Mary Joyce Gillow; one *s* two *d*. *Educ:* Bishopshalt Sch., Hillingdon, Mddx; Pembroke Coll., Oxford (MA). National Service, 1953–55; Oxford, 1955–58; British Petroleum Co. Ltd, 1958–64; Second, later First Secretary, Commonwealth Relations Office, 1964–67; First Sec., Kingston, and concurrently, Haiti, 1967–70; Acting Consul, Port au Prince, 1969; First Sec., Head of Chancery and Consul, Panama, 1970–73; First Sec., FCO, 1973–75; Consul (Commercial), British Trade Development Office, New York, 1975–77; Dep. Consul General and Director Industrial Development, New York, 1977–79; Counsellor, Caracas, 1979–84; Hd, W Indian and Atlantic Dept, FCO, 1984–85. *Address:* Gilletts Farm, Asthall Leigh, Oxford OX8 5PX. *T:* Asthall Leigh (01993) 878455. *Club:* Commonwealth Trust.

SANDERSON, Eric Fenton; Chief Executive, British Linen Bank Group Ltd, since 1989; *b* 14 Oct. 1951; *s* of Francis Kirton Sanderson and Margarita Shand (*née* Fenton); *m* 1975, Patricia Ann Shaw; three *d*. *Educ:* Morgan Acad., Dundee; Univ. of Dundee (LLB); Harvard Business Sch. (AMP). MCIBS 1991. Touche Ross & Co., CA, 1973–76; CA 1976; British Linen Bank Group Ltd, 1976–: Corporate Finance Div., 1976–84; Dir, British Linen Bank and Head, Corporate Finance Div., 1984–89. Non-Executive Director: Airtours plc; English and Overseas Properties plc; Melville Street Investments plc; United Artists Communications (Scotland) Ltd. *Recreations:* tennis, photography, gardening. *Address:* British Linen Bank Group Ltd, 4 Melville Street, Edinburgh EH3 7NZ. *T:* 0131–243 8301. *Club:* New (Edinburgh).

SANDERSON, Sir Frank (Linton), 3rd Bt *cr* 1920, of Malling Deanery, South Malling, Sussex; *b* 21 Nov. 1933; *s* of Sir Bryan Sanderson, 2nd Bt and Annette Laskowska (*d* 1967); *S* father, 1992; *m* 1961, Margaret Ann, *o d* of late John Cleveland Maxwell, New York, USA; two *s* three *d* (incl. twin *d*). *Educ:* Stowe; Univ. of Salamanca. RNVR, 1950–65. J. H. Minet & Co. Ltd, 1956–93 (Dir, 1985); Dir, Knott Hotels Co. of London, 1965–75; Dir and Chm., Humber Fertilisers plc, 1972–88. Underwriting Mem. of Lloyd's, 1957–88. Mem., Chichester Dio. Synod, 1980–93. Master, Worshipful Co. of Curriers, 1993–94. *Heir:* *s* David Frank Sanderson [*b* 26 Feb. 1962; *m* 1990, Fiona Jane Ure]. *Address:* Grandturzel Farm, Burwash, East Sussex TN19 7DE. *Clubs:* Naval, City of London, Farmers'.

SANDERSON, George Rutherford, CBE 1978; British Council Representative, Spain, and Cultural Attaché, British Embassy, Madrid, 1976–79; *b* 23 Nov. 1919; *er s* of late George Sanderson and Edith Mary Sanderson, Blyth, Northumberland; *m* 1947, Jean Cecilia, *d* of late James C. McDougall, Chesterfield, Derbyshire; two *s*. *Educ:* Blyth Grammar Sch.; Univ. of London (BA 1st Cl. Hons French and Italian). War Service, 1940–46: RA, Malta and Egypt (Major). British Council, 1949–79: Actg Dir, Anglo Argentine Cultural Inst., La Plata, Argentina, 1949; Dir, Tucuman, Argentina, 1950–52; Asst Rep., Santiago, Chile, 1952–58; Dep. Area Officer, Oxford, 1958–62; Reg. Dir, and Dir Anglo Argentine Cultural Assoc., Rosario, Argentina, 1962–66; Asst Rep., Buenos Aires, 1966–69; Reg. Dir, and Dir Anglo Brazilian Cultural Soc., São Paulo, Brazil, 1969–72; Dir, Drama and Music Dept, and Dep. Controller, Arts Div., 1973; Educnl Attaché, British Embassy, Washington, 1973–76; Administering Officer, The Kennedy Scholarships and Knox Fellowships, ACU, 1979–82. *Recreations:* art, reading. *Address:* Leafield House, Holton, Oxford OX33 1PZ. *T:* Wheatley (01865) 872526. *Club:* Athenæum.

SANDERSON, Dr Michael David; Chief Executive, Engineering Training Authority, since 1995; *b* 7 June 1943; *s* of Arthur Joseph Sanderson and Betty (*née* Potter); *m* 1967, Mariana Welly Madinaveitia; one *s* one *d*. *Educ:* Strode's Sch., Egham; Univ. of Reading (BSc Hons Chem. 1964); Univ. of Leeds (PhD 1968). With Wilkinson Sword: Research Scientist, 1968–71; Technical Manager, 1971–73; Technical Dir, 1973–79; Internat. Marketing Dir, 1979–82; Engrg Dir, AMF Legg, 1982–84; with Lansing Bagnall: Export Dir, 1984–87; Gp Dir, UK Market, 1987–89; Jt Man. Dir, Lansing Linde, 1989–90; Man. Dir, AWD Bedford, 1990–91; Chief Exec., BSI, 1991–93; Chief Exec., Nat. Assoc. of Goldsmiths and Sec. Gen., Internat. Confedn of Jewellers, Precious Metal and Gemstone Dealers, 1994–95. Dep. Nat. Chm., Inst. Materials Management, 1991–93; Member Council: Inst. of Materials, 1993–; Inst. of Logistics, 1988–94. Mem., Editorial Bd, TQM Magazine, 1993–. Freeman, Clockmakers' Co., 1994–. *Publications:* contribs to learned jls on surface chemistry, thin surface films, materials management, quality and general management topics. *Recreation:* books. *Address:* 31 Murray Mews, NW1 9RH. *T:* 0171–284 3155, *Fax:* 0171–267 9453. *Clubs:* Athenæum, Wig and Pen.

SANDERSON, Rev. Peter Oliver; Vicar of All Saints' Episcopal Church, Storm Lake, Iowa, since 1991; *b* 26 Jan. 1929; *s* of Harold and Doris Sanderson; *m* 1956, Doreen Gibson; one *s* one *d* (and one *s* decd). *Educ:* St Chad's College, Durham Univ. (BA, DipTh). Asst Curate, Houghton-le-Spring, Durham Diocese, 1954–59; Rector, Linstead and St Thomas Ye Vale, Jamaica, 1959–63; Chaplain, RAF, 1963–67; Vicar, Winksley-cum-Grantley and Aldfield-with-Studley, Ripon, 1967–74; Vicar, St Aidan, Leeds, 1974–84; Provost of St Paul's Cathedral, Dundee, 1984–91. *Recreations:* gardening, music, reading. *Address:* 805 Meadow Lane, Storm Lake, IA 50588, USA.

SANDERSON, Very Rev. Roy; *see* Sanderson, Very Rev. W. R.

SANDERSON, Roy, OBE 1983; National Secretary, Federation of Professional Associations Section, Amalgamated Engineering and Electrical Union, 1992–93; *b* 15 Feb. 1931; *s* of George and Lillian Sanderson; *m* 1951, Jean (*née* Booth); two *s* (and one *s* decd). *Educ:* Carfield Sch., Sheffield. Electrical, Electronic Telecommunication & Plumbing Union: Convenor, Lucas Aerospace, Hemel Hempstead, 1952–67; Asst Educn Officer, 1967–69; Nat. Officer, 1969–87; Nat. Sec., Electrical and Engrg Staff Assoc., 1987–92. Non-exec. Dir, UKAEA, 1987–. Member: Armed Forces Pay Review Body, 1987–93; Economic and Social Cttee, EU, 1990–; Industrial Tribunals, 1992–95; Employment Appeal Tribunal, 1995–. *Recreations:* golf, snooker; supporter of Watford Football Club. *Address:* 162 Belswains Lane, Hemel Hempstead HP3 9XA. *T:* Hemel Hempstead (01442) 242033. *Club:* Shendish (Hemel Hempstead).

SANDERSON, Very Rev. (William) Roy; Parish Minister at Stenton and Whittingehame, 1963–73; Extra Chaplain to the Queen in Scotland, since 1977 (Chaplain, 1965–77); *b* 23 Sept. 1907; *er s* of late Arthur Watson Sanderson, Leith, and late Ethel Catherine Watson, Dundee; *m* 1941, Annie Muriel Easton, Glasgow; three *s* two *d*. *Educ:*

Cargilfield Sch.; Fettes Coll.; Oriel Coll., Oxford; Edinburgh University. BA 1929, MA 1933, Oxon. Ordained, 1933. Asst Minister, St Giles' Cath., Edin., 1932–34; Minister: at St Andrew's, Lochgelly, 1935–39; at the Barony of Glasgow, 1939–63. Moderator: Glasgow Presbytery, 1958; Haddington and Dunbar Presbytery, 1972–74; Convener of Assembly Cttees: on Religious Instruction of Youth, 1950–55; on Deaconesses, 1956–61; Panel of Doctrine, 1960–65; on Gen. Administration, 1967–72. Convener of Business Cttee and Leader of General Assembly of the Church of Scotland, 1965–66, 1968–72. Moderator of Gen. Assembly of the Church of Scotland, May 1967–May 1968. Chm., BBC Scottish Religious Advisory Committee, 1961–71; Member Central Religious Advisory Cttee of BBC and ITA, 1961–71. Governor, Fettes Coll., Edinburgh, 1967–76. Hon. DD Glasgow, 1959. *Publication:* Responsibility (Moderatorial address), 1967. *Recreations:* cooking, reading. *Address:* 1a York Road, North Berwick, East Lothian EH39 4LS. *T:* North Berwick (01620) 892780.

SANDFORD, 2nd Baron, *cr* 1945, of Banbury; **Rev. John Cyril Edmondson,** DSC 1942; Conservative Peer in House of Lords, since 1959; *b* 22 Dec. 1920; *e s* of 1st Baron Sandford; *S* father, 1959; *m* 1947, Catharine Mary Hunt; two *s* two *d*. *Educ:* Eton Coll.; Royal Naval Coll., Dartmouth; Westcott House, Cambridge. Served War of 1939–45: Mediterranean Fleet, 1940–41; Home Fleet, 1942; Normandy Landings, 1944 (wounded); Mediterranean Fleet, HMS Saumarez, 1946 (wounded). Staff of RN Coll., Dartmouth, 1947–49; HMS Vengeance, 1950; HMS Cleopatra, 1951–52; Staff Commander-in-Chief Far East, 1953–55; Commander of Home Fleet Flagship, HMS Tyne, 1956; retired 1956. Ordained in Church of England, 1958; Parish of St Nicholas, Harpenden, 1958–63; Exec. Chaplain to Bishop of St Albans, 1965–68. Opposition Whip, House of Lords, 1966–70; Parly Sec., Min. of Housing and Local Govt, June–Oct. 1970; Parliamentary Under-Secretary of State: DoE, 1970–73; DES, 1973–74. Dir, Ecclesiastical Insce Office, 1977–89. Chairman: Cttee to review the condition and future of National Parks in England and Wales, 1971; Standing Conf. of London and SE Regl Planning Authorities, 1981–89. A Church Comr, 1982–89. Chairman: Hertfordshire Council of Social Service, 1969–70; Church Army, 1969–70; Community Task Force, 1975–82; Redundant Churches Cttee, 1982–88; Founder Chm., Pilgrims Assoc., 1982–88; Mem., Adv. Council on Penal Reform, 1968–70. President: Anglo-Swiss Soc., 1974–84; Council for Environmental Educn, 1974–84; Assoc. of District Councils, 1980–86; Offa's Dyke Assoc., 1980–84; Countrywide Holidays Assoc., 1982–86; Vice-Pres., YHA, 1979–90. Founder Trustee, WaterAid, 1981 (Council Mem., 1984; Vice Pres., 1991). Founder, Sandford Award for Heritage Educn, 1978; inaugurated Heritage Educn Trust, 1982. Hon. Fellow, Inst. of Landscape Architects, 1971. *Heir: s* Hon. James John Mowbray Edmondson [*b* 1 July 1949; *m* 1st, 1973, Ellen Sarah, *d* of Jack Shapiro, Toronto; one *d*; 2nd, 1986, Linda, *d* of Mr and Mrs Wheeler, Nova Scotia; one *s*]. *Address:* 27 Ashley Gardens, Ambrosden Avenue, Westminster, SW1P 1QD. *T:* 0171–834 5722. *Clubs:* Ski Club of Gt Britain, Camping and Caravan, Caravan, Stroke, Castaways.

SANDFORD, Arthur, DL; Chief Executive, Manchester City Council, since 1992; *b* 12 May 1941; *s* of Arthur and Lilian Sandford; *m* 1963, Kathleen Entwistle; two *d*. *Educ:* Queen Elizabeth's Grammar Sch., Blackburn; University Coll., London (LLB Hons (Upper 2nd Class)). Preston County Borough Council: Articled Clerk to Town Clerk, 1962–65; Asst Solicitor, 1965–66; Sen. Asst Solicitor, 1966–68; Asst Solicitor, Hants CC, 1969–70; Nottinghamshire County Council: Second Asst Clerk, 1970–72; First Asst Clerk, 1972–74; Dep. Dir of Admin, 1973–75; Dir of Admin, 1975–77; Dep. Clerk and County Sec., 1977–78; Clerk and Chief Exec., 1978–89; Chief Exec., Football League, 1990–92. DL Notts, 1990. *Recreations:* watching sport, gardening. *Address:* Fairford House, 66 Loughborough Road, Bunny, Nottingham NG11 6QD. *T:* Nottingham (0115) 921 2440; 7 Mersey Meadows, Manchester M20 8GB. *T:* 0161–446 2574. *Club:* Royal Over-Seas League.

SANDFORD, Prof. Cedric Thomas; Professor of Political Economy, University of Bath, 1965–87, now Professor Emeritus; Director of Bath University Centre for Fiscal Studies, 1974–86; *b* 21 Nov. 1924; *s* of Thomas Sandford and Louisa (*née* Hodge); *m* 1945, Evelyn Belch (*d* 1982); one *s* one *d*; *m* 1984, Christina Privett; one *d*. *Educ:* Manchester Univ. (BAEcon 1948, MAEcon 1949); London Univ. (BA History (external) 1955). Undergraduate, Manchester Univ., 1942–43 and 1946–48; RAF, 1943–46 (Pilot). Graduate Research Schol., Univ. of Manchester, 1948–49; Lectr, Burnley Municipal Coll., 1949–60; Sen. Lectr, subseq. Head of General and Social Studies Dept, Bristol Coll. of Science and Technology, 1960–65; Head of Sch. of Humanities and Social Sciences, Univ. of Bath, 1965–68, 1971–74, 1977–79. Visiting Prof., Univ. of Delaware, USA, 1969; Visiting Fellow: ANU, 1981, 1985; Univ. of Melbourne, 1990; Univ. of Newcastle, NSW, 1994. Mem., Meade Cttee on Reform of Direct Tax System, 1975–78; Consultant: Fiscal Div., OECD, 1976–79, 1985–87; Irish Commn on Taxation, 1982–85; World Bank, 1986; UN 1986; IMF 1989, 1992; Nat. Audit Office, 1992–93. Partner, Fiscal Publications, 1989–. *Publications:* Taxing Inheritance and Capital Gains (Hobart Paper 32, IEA), 1965, 2nd edn 1967; Economics of Public Finance, 1969, 4th edn 1992; Realistic Tax Reform, 1971; Taxing Personal Wealth, 1971; (sen. editor and jt author) Case Studies in Economics (3 vols), 1971, 2nd edn 1977; National Economic Planning, 1972, 2nd edn 1976; Hidden Costs of Taxation, 1973; (jtly) An Accessions Tax, 1973; (jtly) An Annual Wealth Tax, 1975; Social Economics, 1977; (jtly) Grants or Loans?, 1980; (jtly) The Costs and Benefits of VAT, 1981; The Economic Framework, 1982; (jtly) Tax Policy-Making in the United Kingdom, 1983; (jtly) The Irish Wealth Tax: a study in economics and politics, 1985; Taxing Wealth in New Zealand, 1987; (jtly) Administrative and Compliance Costs of Taxation, 1989; (jtly) The Compliance Costs of Business Taxes in New Zealand, 1992; Successful Tax Reform: lessons from an analysis of tax reform in six countries, 1993; (jtly) Key Issues in Tax Reform, 1993; (jtly) More Key Issues in Tax Reform, 1995; (jtly) Tax Compliance Costs: measurement and policy, 1995; numerous articles in wide range of learned jls. *Recreations:* fishing, gardening, busking. *Address:* Old Coach House, Fersfield, Perrymead, Bath BA2 5AR. *T:* Bath (01225) 832683.

SANDFORD, Herbert Henry, OBE 1963; DFM 1942; Member for Chelsea, ILEA, 1986–90; Chief Whip, minority party, 1986–90; opposition spokesman: Staff Committee, 1986–90; General Purposes Committee, 1986–90; *b* 19 Nov. 1916; *s* of Herbert Charles Sandford and Grace Ellen (*née* Onley); *m* 1st, 1938, Irene Lucy (*née* Porter) (marr. diss. 1944); 2nd, 1948, Jessie Irene (*née* Gray). *Educ:* Minchendon Secondary Sch., Southgate. Served War, Pathfinder Sqdns, RAF, 1939–45. Elected to St Marylebone Metrop. Bor. Council, 1953; Chm., Works Cttee. City of Westminster: Councillor, Lords Ward, 1964–68; Alderman, 1968–78; Dep. Leader of Council, 1975–76; Chairman: Traffic Cttee, 1964–67; Highways and Traffic Cttee, 1967–68; Highways Cttee, 1971–72 (Vice-Chm., 1969–71); Highways and Works Cttee, 1972–75; special sub-cttee of Highways and Town Planning Cttees on redevelt of Piccadilly Circus, 1972–76; Member: Policy Cttee, 1972–74; Town Planning Cttee, 1971–76; Road Safety Cttee, 1972–74; Road Safety Adv. Cttee, 1974–76; Co-ord. Cttee, 1974–75; Housing Management Cttee, 1975–77; London Transport Passenger Cttee, 1974–76. Greater London Council: Mem. for St Marylebone, 1976–86; Dep. Chm., 1985–86; Chm., Central Area Planning Cttee, 1977–81; Member: Public Services Safety Cttee, 1977–81; Covent Garden Cttee, 1977–81; Thames Water Regional Land Drainage Cttee, 1978–82; Leading Opposition Mem., Technical Services Cttee, 1983–86; Dep. Spokesman, Finance Cttee, 1983–86. Opposition Spokesman, Staff and Gen. Cttee, 1982–86, Opposition Chief Whip, 1986–90, ILEA. Chm., Grove End Housing Assoc., Ltd, 1986– (Dir, 1976–). Chairman: St Marylebone Sea Cadet Corps, 1953; St Marylebone Boy Scouts Assoc., 1958–64. Treasurer, Wiltons Music Hall Trust, 1982–. Governor: St John's Hosp. for Skin Diseases, 1973–76; London Inst., 1986–90; Chm. Bd of Governors, Abercorn Place Sch., 1992–. *Recreations:* golf, bridge, Yoga. *Address:* 5 Elmfield House, Carlton Hill, NW8 9XB. *T:* 0171–624 9694. *Clubs:* Royal Air Force, Pathfinder.

SANDFORD, Jeremy; writer, journalist, musician; *s* of late Christopher Sandford, owner/director of the Golden Cockerel Press, and of Lettice Sandford, wood engraver, craft worker; *m* 1st, 1956, Nell Dunn (marr. diss. 1986); three *s*; 2nd, 1988, Philippa Finnis. *Educ:* Eton; Oxford. Dir, The Cyrenians; Exec., Gypsy Council; Sponsor: Shelter; The Simon Community. Editor, Romano Drom (gypsy newspaper); author/researcher, documentaries for radio and television. Screen Writers' Guild of Gt Britain Award, 1967, 1971; Prix Italia prize for TV drama, 1968; Critics Award for TV drama, 1971. *Publications:* Synthetic Fun, 1967; Cathy Come Home, 1967; Whelks and Chromium, 1968; Edna the Inebriate Woman, 1971; Down and Out in Britain, 1971; In Search of the Magic Mushrooms, 1972; Gypsies, 1973; Tomorrow's People, 1974; Prostitutes, 1975; Smiling David, 1975; Figures and Landscapes, 1991; Hey Days in Hay, 1992; contribs to Guardian, Sunday Times, etc. *Recreations:* painting, music, travel, mountain exploration, riding, wandering, windsurfing, wondering, festivals, getting to know people. *Address:* Hatfield Court, Hatfield, Leominster, Herefordshire HR6 0SD. *Club:* Chelsea Arts.

SANDFORD, Kenneth Leslie, CMG 1974; retired barrister; *b* 14 Aug. 1915; *s* of Albert Edgar Sandford and Barbara Ivy (*née* Hill); *m* 1946, Airini Ethel Scott Sergel; one *s* one *d* (and one *d* decd). *Educ:* King's Coll., Auckland, NZ; Auckland University Coll. LLB 1938. Served War: 34 Bn (NZ), rank of Captain, 1940–45. Barrister and Solicitor, 1939–72; Crown Solicitor (Hamilton), 1950–72; Chm., Accident Compensation Commn (NZ), 1972–80. *Publications:* Dead Reckoning, 1955; Dead Secret, 1957; Mark of the Lion, 1962. *Recreation:* cricket (Pres. NZ Cricket Council, 1971–73). *Address:* 1523 Kawakawa Bay, RD5 Papakura, New Zealand.

SANDFORD, Rear-Adm. Sefton Ronald, CB 1976; *b* 23 July 1925; *s* of Col H. R. Sandford and Mrs Faye Sandford (*née* Renouf); *m* 1st, 1950, Mary Ann Prins (*d* 1972); one *s*; 2nd, 1972, Jennifer Rachel Newell; two *d*. *Educ:* St Aubyns, Rottingdean, 1934–38; Royal Naval Coll., Dartmouth, 1939–42. Served War: went to sea, July 1942; commanded HMMTB 2017, Lieut, 1946–47; ADC to Comdr British Forces, Hong Kong (Lt-Gen. Sir Terence Airey), 1952–53; commanded HMS Teazer (rank Comdr), 1958; Staff of Imperial Defence Coll., 1963–65; comd HMS Protector, Captain, 1965–67; Naval Attaché, Moscow, 1968–70; comd HMS Devonshire, 1971–73; ADC to the Queen, 1974; Flag Officer, Gibraltar, 1974–76. A Younger Brother of Trinity House, 1968. *Recreations:* cricket, sailing, fishing, photography. *Address:* St Christophe, 47400 Villeton, France. *T:* 53790852. *Clubs:* Marylebone Cricket (MCC); Royal Yacht Squadron (Cowes).

SANDFORD SMITH, Richard Henry, FCIS; Chairman, Eastern Gas Region (formerly Eastern Gas Board), 1970–73; *b* 29 March 1909; *s* of late Dr H. Sandford Smith; *m* 1936, Dorothy Hewitt, *y d* of late Rev. J. F. Hewitt; one *s*. *Educ:* Haileybury Coll. London Stock Exchange, 1926. Qualified as Chartered Secretary and awarded Sir Ernest Clarke Prize, 1932. Joined Gas Light & Coke Co., 1932; Sec., SE Gas Corp. Ltd, 1939–49; Sec., SE Gas Bd, 1949–56 (Dep. Chm., 1956–69). *Recreations:* theatre, gardening. *Address:* 60 The Marlowes, St John's Wood Park, NW8 6NA. *Club:* Savile.

SANDHURST, 5th Baron, *cr* 1871; **(John Edward) Terence Mansfield,** DFC 1944; *b* 4 Sept. 1920; *er s* of 4th Baron Sandhurst, OBE, and Morley Victoria (*née* Upcher; *d* 1961); *S* father 1964; *m* 1947, Janet Mary, *er d* of late John Edward Lloyd, NY, USA; one *s* one *d*. *Educ:* Harrow. Served RAFVR, 1939–46: Bomber Command (as Navigator and Bombing Leader): 149 Sqdn, 1941; 419 (RCAF) Sqdn, 1942; 12 Sqdn, 1943–45. 1946–55: Metropolitan Special Constabulary 'C' Div., Sergeant, 1949–52; long service medal, 1955. Hon. ADC to Lieutenant-Governor of Jersey, 1969–74. *Recreation:* golf. *Heir: s* Hon. Guy Rhys John Mansfield, *qv*. *Educ:* Harrow, Oriel Coll., Oxford (MA). Called to Bar, Middle Temple, 1972]. *Address:* La Volière, Les Ruisseaux, St Brelade, Jersey JE3 8DD. *Clubs:* Royal Air Force, MCC; United (Jersey).

See also Earl of Macclesfield.

SANDIFORD, Rt. Hon. (Lloyd) Erskine, PC 1989; JP; MP St Michael South, since 1971; Prime Minister of Barbados, 1987–94; *b* 24 March 1937; *s* of Cyril and Eunice Sandiford; *m* 1963, Angelita P. Ricketts; one *s* two *d*. *Educ:* Coleridge/Parry Sec. Sch.; Harrison Coll.; Univ. of WI, Jamaica (BA Hons English); Univ. of Manchester (MAEcon). Assistant Master: Modern High Sch., Barbados, 1956–57; Kingston Coll., Jamaica, 1960–61; Asst Master, 1963–64, Sen. Graduate Master, 1964–66, Harrison Coll., Barbados; part-time Tutor and Lectr, Univ. of the WI, Barbados, 1963–65; Asst Tutor, Barbados Community Coll., 1976–86. Democratic Labour Party, Barbados: Mem., 1964–; Asst Sec., 1966–67; Gen. Sec., 1967–68; (first) Vice-Pres., 1972–74; Pres., 1974–75; Vice-Pres., 1975–76; Founder, Acad. of Politics. Member: Senate, 1967–71; House of Assembly, 1971–; Personal Asst to the Prime Minister, 1966–67; Minister: of Educn, 1967–71; of Educn, Youth Affairs, Community Develt and Sport, 1971–75; of Health and Welfare, 1975–76; Dep. Leader of Opposition, 1978–86; Dep. Prime Minister and Minister of Educn and Culture, 1986–87; Minister: for Civil Service, 1987–94; of Finance and Economic Affairs, 1987–93; of Economic Affairs, 1993–94; of Tourism and Internat. Transport, 1994. Order of the Liberator (Venezuela), 1987. *Publications:* Books of Speeches 1987–1994; *poems:* Ode to the Environment; When She Leaves You; (contrib.) Business, Government and Society, ed Monya Anyadike-Danes. *Address:* Hillvista, Porters, St James, Barbados, West Indies.

SANDILANDS, family name of **Baron Torphichen.**

SANDISON, Alexander, (Alec), FCCA; Director of Finance and Administration, The Prince's Trust and Royal Jubilee Trusts, since 1992; *b* 24 May 1943; *s* of late Alexander Sandison and Mary Roscoe; *m* 1st, 1968, Janet Firmager (marr. diss.); 2nd, 1977, Merralyn Martin (*née* Hill) (marr. diss.); two *s*; *m* 1994, Susan Dixon. *Educ:* Cambs High Sch.; Trinity Sch. of John Whitgift, Croydon. FCCA 1975 (ACCA 1970). Commercial Union Assce Co., 1962–63; John Mowlem PLC, 1964–71 (Gp Financial Accountant, 1970–71); Chief Accountant: and Co. Sec., J. E. Freeman & Co., 1972–73; Wings Ltd, 1973–78; Divl Financial Dir, Doulton Glass Inds, 1978–80; Sec. for Finance and Corporate Controller, RICS, 1980–90; Chief Exec., Surveyors Holdings Ltd, 1985–89; Chm., Imaginor Systems Ltd, 1989–90; Dir, Cruse-Bereavement Care, 1990–91. Consultant: The 'Who Cares?' Trust; Civic Trust. Mem. Charities Gp, Chartered Assoc. of Certified Accountants. *Publications:* People to People: course notes, 1985; Watton-at-Stone Village Guide, 1989; contribs, incl. brainteasers and poetry, to learned jls. *Recreations:* voluntary social work; reading, writing; avoiding involvement with and conversations about, sport. *Address:* 38 Grange Rise, Codicote, Hitchin, Herts SG4 8YR. *T:* (0860) 373121.

SANDLE, Prof. Michael Leonard, RA 1989 (ARA 1982); DFA; sculptor; Professor at the Akademie der Bildenden Künste, Karlsruhe, Germany, since 1980; *b* 18 May 1936; *s* of Charles Edward Sandle and Dorothy Gwendoline Gladys (*née* Vernon); *m* 1971, Cynthia Dora Koppel (marriage annulled 1974); *m* 1988, Demelza Spargo; one *s*. *Educ:* Douglas High Sch., IOM; Douglas Sch. of Art and Technol.; Slade Sch. of Fine Art (DFA 1959). FRBS 1994. Studied painting and printmaking, Slade Sch. of Fine Art, 1956–59; changed to sculpture, 1962; various teaching posts in Britain, 1961–70, including Lectr, Coventry Coll. of Art, 1964–68; resident in Canada, 1970–73; Vis. Prof., Univ. of Calgary, Alberta, 1970–71; Vis. Associate Prof., Univ. of Victoria, BC, 1972–73; Lectr in Sculpture, Fachhochschule für Gestaltung, Pforzheim, W Germany, 1973–77, Prof., 1977–80. Has participated in exhibns in GB and internationally, 1957–, including: V Biennale, Paris, 1966; Documenta IV, Kassel, W Germany, 1968 and Documenta VI, 1977. Work in public collections, including: Arts Council of GB, Tate Gall.; Australian Nat. Gall., Canberra; Met. Mus., NY; Stzüki Mus., Lodz; Nat. Gall., Warsaw; Wilhelm Lehmbruck Mus., Duisburg, W Germany. Designed Malta Siege Bell Meml, Valetta, 1992. Nobutaka Shikanai Special Prize, Utsukushi-Ga-Hara Open-Air Mus., Japan, 1986; Henry Hering Meml Medal, Nat. Sculpture Soc. of Amer., 1995. *Address:* Schloss Scheibenhardt, 7500 Karlsruhe, Germany. *T:* (721) 868633.

SANDLER, Prof. Merton, MD; FRCP, FRCPath, FRCPsych; Professor of Chemical Pathology, Royal Postgraduate Medical School, Institute of Obstetrics and Gynaecology, University of London, 1973–91, Professor Emeritus, since 1991; Consultant Chemical Pathologist, Queen Charlotte's Maternity Hospital, 1958–91; *b* 28 March 1926; *s* of late Frank Sandler and Edith (*née* Stein), Salford, Lancs; *m* 1961, Lorna Rosemary, *d* of late Ian Michael and Sally Grenby, Colindale, London; two *s* two *d*. *Educ:* Manchester Grammar Sch.; Manchester Univ. (MB ChB 1949; MD 1962). FRCPath 1970 (MRCPath 1963); FRCP 1974 (MRCP 1955); FRCPsych 1986. Jun. Specialist in Pathology, RAMC (Captain), 1951–53. Research Fellow in Clin. Path., Brompton Hosp., 1953–54; Lectr in Chem. Path., Royal Free Hosp. Sch. of Med., 1955–58. Visiting Professor: Univ. of New Mexico, 1983; Chicago Med. Sch., 1984; Univ. of S Fla, 1988. Recognized Teacher in Chem. Path., 1960–91; extensive examining experience for various Brit. and for. univs and Royal Colls; Mem. Standing Adv. Cttee, Bd of Studies in Path., Univ. of London, 1972–76 (also Mem. Chem. Path. Sub-Cttee, 1973–); Chm., Academic Bd, 1972–73, Bd of Management, 1975–84, Inst. of Obst. and Gyn.; Governor: Brit. Postgrad. Med. Fedn, 1976–78; Queen Charlotte's Hosp. for Women, 1978–84; Council Mem. and Meetings Sec., Assoc. of Clin. Pathologists, 1959–70; Mem. Council, Collegium Internat. Neuro-Psycho-pharmacologicum, 1982–90. Various offices in: RSM, incl. Hon. Librarian, 1977–93, and Pres. Section of Med. Exper. Med. and Therapeutics, 1979–80; Brit. Assoc. for Psychopharm., incl. Pres., 1980–82 (Hon. Mem., 1993); British Assoc. for Postnatal Illness (Pres., 1980–); office in many other learned socs and grant-giving bodies, incl. Med. Adv. Councils of Migraine Trust, 1975–80 (Chm., Scientific Adv. Cttee, 1985–91; Trustee, 1987–91), Schizophrenia Assoc. of GB, 1975–78, Parkinson's Disease Soc., 1981–, Chm. of Trustees, Nat. Soc. for Res. into Mental Health, 1983–. Chm. and Sec., Biol Council Symposium on Drug Action, 1979; Sec., Mem. Bd of Management and Chm. Awards Subcttee, Biological Council, 1983–91; Member, Executive Committee: Marcé Soc., 1983–86; Med. Council on Alcoholism, 1987–90; Sec. and Mem. Council, Harveian Soc. of London, 1979–89 (Vice Pres., 1990; Pres., 1991–92); Mem. Council of Management and Patron, Helping Hand Orgn, 1981–87. Organiser or Brit. rep. on org. cttees of many nat. and internat. meetings incl. Internat. Chm., 6th Internat. Catecholamine Congress, 1987. For. Corresp. Mem., Amer. Coll. of Neuropsychopharm., 1975; Hon. Member: Indian Acad. of Neuroscis, 1982; Hungarian Pharmacological Soc., 1985. Jt Editor: British Jl of Pharmacology, 1974–80; Clinical Science, 1975–77; Jl of Neural Transmission, 1979–82; Jt Editor-in-Chief, Jl of Psychiatric Research, 1982–93, and present or past Mem. Editorial Bds of 17 other sci. jls; eponymous lectures to various learned socs incl. 1st Cumings Meml, 1976, James E. Beall II Meml, 1980, Biol Council Lecture and Medal, 1984; F. B. Smith Meml, 1995; provision of Nat. Monoamine Ref. Laboratory Service, 1976–91. Dr *hc* Semmelweis Univ. of Medicine, Budapest, 1992. Anna Monika Internat. Prize (jtly), for Res. on Biol Aspects of Depression, 1973; Gold Medal, Brit. Migraine Assoc., 1974; Senator Dr Franz Burda Internat. Prize for Res. on Parkinson's Disease, 1988; Arnold Friedman Distinguished Clinician Researcher Award, 1991. *Publications:* Mental Illness in Pregnancy and the Puerperium, 1978; The Psychopharmacology of Aggression, 1979; Enzyme Inhibitors as Drugs, 1980; Amniotic Fluid and its Clinical Significance, 1980; The Psychopharmacology of Alcohol, 1980; The Psychopathology of Anticonvulsants, 1981; Nervous Laughter, 1990; Parkinson's Disease, 1993; *jointly:* The Adrenal Cortex, 1961; The Thyroid Gland, 1967; Advances in Pharmacology, 1968; Monoamine Oxidases, 1972; Serotonin—New Vistas, 1974; Sexual Behaviour: Pharmacology and Biochemistry, 1975; Trace Amines and the Brain, 1976; Phenolsulphotransferase in Mental Health Research, 1981; Tetrahydroisoquinolines and β-Carbolines, 1982; Progress towards a Male Contraceptive, 1982; Neurobiology of the Trace Amines, 1984; Psychopharmacology and Food, 1985; Neurotransmitter Interactions, 1986; Progress in Catecholamine Research, 1988; Design of Enzyme Inhibitors as Drugs, Vol. 1, 1989, Vol. 2, 1994; Migraine: a spectrum of ideas, 1990; 5-Hydroxytryptamine in Psychiatry, 1991; Monoamine Oxidase: basic and clinical aspects, 1993; Genetic Research in Psychiatry, 1992; numerous research pubns on aspects of biologically-active monoamine metabolism. *Recreations:* reading, listening to music, travel. *Address:* 12 Model Cottages, SW14 7PH. *T:* 0181–878 1790, *Fax:* 0181–878 7408. *Club:* Athenæum.

SANDON, Viscount; Dudley Adrian Conroy Ryder; chartered surveyor; *b* 18 March 1951; *s* and *heir* of Earl of Harrowby, *qv*; *m* 1977, Sarah Nichola Hobhouse Payne (*d* 1994), *d* of Captain Anthony Payne; three *s* one *d*. *Educ:* Eton; Univ. of Newcastle upon Tyne; Magdalene Coll., Cambridge (MA). FRICS. Exec. Dir, Compton Street Securities Ltd, 1988–. Governor, John Archer Sch., Wandsworth, 1986–88. Pres., Staffordshire Soc., 1995–. *Recreations:* shooting, fell walking, music, study of fine art and architecture. *Heir: s* Hon. Dudley Anthony Hugo Coventry Ryder, *b* 5 Sept. 1981. *Address:* Sandon Estate Office, Sandon, Stafford ST18 0DA.

SANDS, Roger Blakemore; Clerk of Public Bills, House of Commons, since 1994; *b* 6 May 1942; *s* of late Thomas Blakemore Sands and Edith Malyon (Betty) Sands (*née* Waldram); *m* 1966, Jennifer Ann Cattell; two *d*. *Educ:* University Coll. Sch., Hampstead; Oriel Coll., Oxford (scholar; MA LitHum). A Clerk, House of Commons, 1965–; Sec. to H of C Commn and Clerk to H of C (Services) Cttee, 1985–87; Clerk of Overseas Office, 1987–91; Clerk of Select Cttees and Registrar of Members' Interests, 1991–94. Sec., History of Parlt Trust, 1974–80; Chm, Study of Parlt Group, 1993–. *Publications:* (ed) Official Guide to the Houses of Parliament, 13th edn, 1977; articles and reviews in parly jls. *Recreations:* gardening, listening to music, occasional golf. *Address:* House of Commons, SW1A 0AA. *T:* 0171–219 3255.

SANDS SMITH, David; UK Permanent Representative to Food and Agriculture Organisation, United Nations, since 1993; *b* 19 April 1943; *s* of late Arthur S. Smith and Eileen Annie Smith; *m* 1966, Veronica Harris; one *s* one *d*. *Educ:* Brighton Coll. of Technology, Dept of Technical Co-operation, 1963–71; 2nd Sec., British High Commn, Kuala Lumpur, 1971–75; Overseas Development Administration: Principal: European Community Dept, 1975–80; Zimbabwe Desk, 1980–85; Asst Head, 1985–88, Head, 1988–90, European Community Dept; Head, British Develt Div. in Eastern Africa, 1990–93. *Recreation:* running. *Address:* Foreign and Commonwealth Office (Rome), King Charles Street, SW1A 2AH.

SANDWICH, 11th Earl of, *cr* 1660; **John Edward Hollister Montagu;** Viscount Hinchingbrooke and Baron Montagu, 1660; freelance journalist and researcher; *b* 11 April 1943; *er s* of (Alexander) Victor (Edward Panlet) Montagu; *S* to disclaimed Earldom of father, 1995; *m* 1968, Caroline, *o d* of Canon P. E. C. Hayman, Beaminster, Dorset; two *s* one *d*. *Educ:* Eton; Trinity College, Cambridge. Inf. Officer, 1974–85, Res. Officer, 1985–86, Christian Aid; Editor, Save the Children Fund, 1987–92; Consultant, CARE Britain, 1987–93. Trustee, TSW Telethon Trust, 1987–91; Managing Trustee, St Francis Sch., Dorset, 1987–92. *Publications:* The Book of the World, 1971; Prospects for Africa's Children, 1990; Children at Crisis Point, 1992. *Heir: s* Viscount Hinchingbrooke, *qv*. *Address:* 35 Battersea Church Road, SW11 3LY.

SANDYS, 7th Baron, *cr* 1802; **Richard Michael Oliver Hill;** DL; Captain of the Yeomen of the Guard (Deputy Government Chief Whip, House of Lords), 1979–82; Landowner; *b* 21 July 1931; *o s* of late Lt-Col the Lord Sandys and Cynthia Mary (*d* 1990), *o d* of late Col F. R. T. T. Gascoigne, DSO; *S* father, 1961; *m* 1961, Patricia Simpson Hall, *d* of late Captain Lionel Hall, MC. *Educ:* Royal Naval College, Dartmouth. Lieutenant in The Royal Scots Greys, 1950–55. A Lord in Waiting, 1974; an Opposition Whip, H of L, 1974–79. FRGS. DL Worcestershire, 1968. *Heir:* Marquess of Downshire, *qv*. *Address:* Ombersley Court, Droitwich, Worcestershire WR9 0HH. *T:* Worcester (01905) 620220. *Club:* Cavalry and Guards.

SANDYS, Julian George Winston; QC 1983; *b* 19 Sept. 1936; *s* of Baron Duncan-Sandys, CH, PC; *m* 1970, Elisabeth Jane, *o d* of late John Besley Martin, CBE; three *s* one *d*. *Educ:* Eton; Salem; Trinity Coll., Melbourne. 2nd Lt, 4th Hussars, 1955; Captain, QRIH (AER), 1964. Called to the Bar, Inner Temple, 1959. Member: Midland Circuit, 1960–76; Western Circuit, 1982–; Gray's Inn, 1970–. Contested (C) Ashfield, Notts, 1959. *Recreations:* flying, computers.

SANÉ, Pierre Gabriel; Secretary General, Amnesty International, since 1992; *b* 7 May 1948; *s* of Nicolas Sané and Therese Carvalho; *m* 1981, Ndeye Sow; one *s* one *d*. *Educ:* LSE (MSc in Public Admin and Public Policy); Ecole Supérieure de Commerce, Bordeaux (MBA); Carleton Univ., Canada (doctoral studies in pol scis). Regl Dir, Internat. Develt Research Centre, Ottawa, Canada, 1978–92. *Address:* (office) 1 Easton Street, WC1X 8DJ.

SANER, Robert Morton; *see* Morton-Saner.

SANGER, Frederick, OM 1986; CH 1981; CBE 1963; PhD; FRS 1954; on staff of Medical Research Council, 1951–83; *b* 13 Aug. 1918; *s* of Frederick Sanger, MD, and Cicely Sanger; *m* 1940, M. Joan Howe; two *s* one *d*. *Educ:* Bryanston; St John's College, Cambridge. BA 1939; PhD 1943. From 1940, research in Biochemistry at Cambridge University; Beit Memorial Fellowship for Medical Research, 1944–51; at MRC Lab. of Molecular Biol., Cambridge, 1961–83; Fellowship at King's College, Cambridge, 1954. (Hon. Fellow 1983). For. Hon. Mem., Amer. Acad. of Arts and Sciences, 1958; Hon. Mem. Amer. Society of Biological Chemists, 1961; Foreign Assoc., Nat. Acad. of Sciences, 1967. Hon. DSc: Leicester, 1968; Oxon, 1970; Strasbourg, 1970; Cambridge, 1983. Corday-Morgan Medal and Prize, Chem. Soc., 1951; Nobel Prize for Chemistry, 1958, (jointly) 1980; Alfred Benzon Prize, 1966; Royal Medal, Royal Soc., 1969; Sir Frederick Gowland Hopkins Meml Medal, 1971; Gairdner Foundation Annual Award, 1971, 1979; William Bate Hardy Prize, Cambridge Philosophical Soc., 1976; Hanbury Meml Medal, 1976; Copley Medal, Royal Soc., 1977; Horwitz Prize, Albert Lasker Award, 1979; Biochem. Analysis Prize, German Soc. Clin. Chem., 1980; Gold Medal, RSM, 1983. *Publications:* papers on Chemistry of Insulin and Nucleic Acid Structure in Biochemical and other journals. *Address:* Far Leys, Fen Lane, Swaffham Bulbeck, Cambridge CB5 0NJ.

SANGER, Dr Ruth Ann, (Mrs R. R. Race), FRS 1972; Director, Medical Research Council Blood Group Unit, 1973–83 (Member of Scientific Staff, 1946–83); *b* 6 June 1918; *yr d* of late Rev. Hubert Sanger and late Katharine M. R. Sanger (*née* Cameron), Urunga, NSW; *m* 1956, Robert Russell Race, CBE, FRS (*d* 1984); no *c*. *Educ:* Abbotsleigh, Sydney; Sydney and London Univs. BSc Sydney 1939, PhD London 1948. Scientific Staff of Red Cross Blood Transfusion Service, Sydney, 1940–46. Hon. Member: Sociedad de Hematologia del Instituto Mexicano del Seguro Social; Deutsche Gesellschaft für Bluttransfusion; Toronto Antibody Club; Norwegian Soc. of Immunohaematology; Internat. Soc. of Blood Transfusion; Genetical Soc. Hon. MD Helsinki, 1990. Landsteiner Meml Award, USA, 1957, Philip Levine Award, USA, 1970, and Gairdner Foundn Award, Canada, 1972; Oliver Meml Award for Blood Transfusion, British Red Cross, 1973. *Publications:* (with R. R. Race) Blood Groups in Man, 1950, 6th edn, 1975; many papers in genetical and med. jls. *Address:* 22 Vicarage Road, East Sheen, SW14 8RU. *T:* 0181–876 1508.

SANGSTER, Robert Edmund; *b* 23 May 1936; *o c* of late Mr Vernon Sangster and of Mrs Sangster. *Educ:* Repton Coll. Chairman: Vernons Orgn, 1980–88; Sangster Gp, 1988–. Owner of: The Minstrel (won Derby, 1977); Alleged (won Prix de l'Arc de Triomphe, 1977, 1978); Jaazeiro (won Irish Derby, 1978); Detroit (won Prix de l'Arc de Triomphe, 1980); Beldale Ball (won Melbourne Cup, 1980); Kings Lake (won Irish 2,000 Guineas, 1981); Our Paddy Boy (won Australian Jockey Club Cup, 1981); Golden Fleece (won Derby, 1982); Assert (won Irish Sweeps Derby, and French Derby, 1982); Lomond (won 2,000 Guineas, 1983); Caerleon (won French Derby, 1983); El Gran Señor (won 2,000 Guineas, Irish Sweeps Derby, 1984); Sadler's Wells (won Irish 2,000 Guineas, 1984); Gildoran (won Ascot Gold Cup, 1984, 1985, Goodwood Cup, 1984); Law Society (won Irish Derby, 1985); Committed (won Prix de l'Abbaye de Longchamp, Champion European Sprinter, Royal Heroine Champion Grass Mare, USA, 1984); Marooned (won Sydney Cup, 1986); Prince of Birds (won Irish 2,000 Guineas, 1988); Rodrigo de Triano (won 2,000 Guineas and Irish 2,000 Guineas, 1992); Las Meninas (won 1,000 Guineas, 1994); Riverina Charm (Champion, Australia); Kostroma (Champion, USA); Royal Heroine (Champion, USA). Leading winning race-horse owner, 1977, 1978, 1982, 1983 and 1984 seasons; owner of 679 Stakes winners, 1977–. *Recreation:* golf. *Address:* The Nunnery, Douglas, Isle of Man. *T:* Douglas (01624) 623351. *Club:* Jockey.

SANKEY, Guy Richard; QC 1991; a Recorder, since 1992; *b* 2 April 1944; *s* of Graham and Joan Sankey; *m* 1969, Pauline Mace Lamotte; three *d*. *Educ:* Marlborough College; New College, Oxford (MA). Called to the Bar, Inner Temple, 1966. Junior Counsel to the Crown, Common Law, 1987–91. *Recreations:* golf, ski-ing, tennis. *Address:* 1 Temple Gardens, Temple, EC4Y 9BB. *Club:* Denham Golf.

SANKEY, John Anthony, CMG 1983; Secretary General, Society of London Art Dealers, since 1991; *b* 8 June 1930; *m* 1958, Gwendoline Putman; two *s* two *d*. *Educ:* Cardinal Vaughan Sch., Kensington; Peterhouse, Cambridge (Classical Tripos Parts 1 and 2, Class 1; MA). 1st (Singapore) Regt, RA (2nd Lieut), 1952. Colonial Office, 1953–61; UK Mission to United Nations, 1961–64; Foreign Office, 1964–68; Guyana, 1968–71;

Singapore, 1971–73; NATO Defence Coll., Rome, 1973; Malta, 1973; The Hague, 1975–79 (Gov., British Sch. in the Netherlands); FCO, 1979–82; High Comr, Tanzania, 1982–85; UK Perm. Rep. to UN Office, Geneva, 1985–90. Leader, British Govt Delegn to Internat. Red Cross Conf., 1986. Director: Internat. Art and Antiques Loss Register Ltd, 1993–; Council for the Prevention of Art Theft, 1994–. Sir Evelyn Wrench Lectr, ESU, 1990. Editor, Soc. of London Art Dealers Yearbook, 1991–. *Publications:* (contrib.) The United Kingdom—the United Nations, 1990; articles on Victorian sculpture and art dealing. *Recreations:* nineteenth century sculpture. *Address:* 108 Lancaster Gate, W2 3NW.

SANKEY, Vernon Louis; Chief Executive, Reckitt & Colman plc, since 1992; *b* 9 May 1949; *s* of late Edward Sankey and Marguerite Elizabeth Louise (*née* van Maurik); *m* 1976, Elizabeth Knights; three *s* one *d*. *Educ:* Harrow School; Oriel Coll., Oxford (MA Mod. Langs). Joined Reckitt & Colman, 1971: General Manager, Denmark, 1978–80; PA to Chm. and Chief Exec., 1980–81; Man. Dir, France, 1981–85; Man. Dir, Colman's of Norwich, 1985–89; Chm. and Chief Exec. Officer, Reckitt & Colman Inc., USA, 1989–92. Non-exec. Dir, Pearson, 1993–. CIMgt 1992; FInstD 1995. *Recreations:* various, including golf, tennis, theatre-going. *Address:* c/o Reckitt & Colman plc, One Burlington Lane, Chiswick W4 2RW. *Club:* Leander (Henley).

SANTER, Jacques; President, European Commission, since 1995; Prime Minister of Luxembourg, 1984–94; *b* 18 May 1937; *m* Danièle Binot; two *s*. *Educ:* Athénée de Luxembourg; Paris Univ.; Strasbourg Univ.; Inst. d'Etudes Politiques, Paris. DenD. Advocate, Luxembourg Court of Appeal, 1961–65; Attaché, Office of Minister of Labour and Social Security, 1963–65; Govt Attaché, 1965–66; Christian Socialist Party: Parly Sec., 1966–72; Sec.-Gen., 1972–74; Pres., 1974–82; Sec. of State for Cultural and Social Affairs, 1972–74; Mem., Chamber of Deputies, 1974–79; MEP, 1975–79 (a Vice-Pres., 1975–77); Minister of Finance, Labour and Social Security, Luxembourg, 1979–84; Pres. of Govt, Minister of State and Minister of Finance, 1984–89; Minister for Cultural Affairs, 1989–94. *Address:* 200 rue de la Loi, 1049 Brussels, Belgium.

SANTER, Rt. Rev. Mark; *see* Birmingham, Bishop of.

SAOUMA, Edouard; Director-General of the Food and Agriculture Organization of the United Nations, Rome, 1976–93; agricultural engineer and international official; *b* Beirut, Lebanon, 6 Nov. 1926; *m* Inés Forero; one *s* two *d*. *Educ:* St Joseph's University Sch. of Engineering, Beirut; École Nat. Supérieure d'Agronomie, Montpellier, France. Director: Tel Amara Agric. Sch., 1952–53; Nat. Centre for Farm Mechanization, 1954–55; Sec. Gen., Nat. Fedn of Lebanese Agronomists, 1955; Dir-Gen., Nat. Inst. for Agricl Res., 1957–62; Mem. Gov. Bd, Nat. Grains Office, 1960–62; Minister of Agric., Fisheries and Forestry, 1970. Food and Agric. Organization of UN: Dep. Regional Rep. for Asia and Far East, 1962–65; Dir, Land and Water Develt Div., 1965–75; Dir-Gen., 1976, re-elected 1981, 1987. Hon. Prof. of Agronomy, Agricl Univ. of Beijing, China. Said Akl Prize, Lebanon; Chevalier du Mérite Agricole, France; Grand Cross: Order of the Cedar, Lebanon; Ordre National du Chad; Ordre Nat. du Ghana; Ordre National de Haute Volta; Mérito Agrícola of Spain; Orden Nacional al Mérito, Colombia; Kt Comdr, Order of Merit, Greece; Order of Agricl Merit, Colombia; Gran Oficial, Orden de Vasco Nuñez de Balboa, Panamá; Orden al Mérito Agrícola, Peru; Order of Merit, Egypt; Order of Merit, Mauritania; Grand Officier: Ordre de la République, Tunisia; Ordre National, Madagascar; Ordre de Commandeur, Ouissan Alouite, Morocco. Dr (*hc*): Univ. of Bologna, Italy; Agric. Univ. La Molina, Peru; Univ. of Seoul, Republic of Korea; Univ. of Uruguay; Univ. of Jakarta, Indonesia; Univ. of Warsaw; Univ. of Los Baños, Philippines; Punjab Agricultural Univ., India; Faisalabad Agricultural Univ., Pakistan; Univ. of Agricl Scis of Gödöllö, Hungary; Univ. Nacional Autónoma, Nicaragua; Univ. of Florence, Italy; Univ. of Gembloux, Belgium; Univ. of Prague, Czechoslovakia; Catholic Univ. of America; Univ. of Bologna, Italy; Agricl Inst., Mongolia. Accademico Corrispondente, Accademià Nazionale di Agricultura, Bologna, Italy. *Publications:* technical publications on agriculture. *Address:* POB H0210, Baabda, Lebanon.

SAPHIR, Nicholas Peter George; Director, Albert Fisher Group PLC, since 1993; *b* 30 Nov. 1944; *s* of Emanuel Saphir and Ann (*née* Belikoff); *m* 1971, Ena Bodin; one *s*. *Educ:* City of London Sch.; Manchester Univ. (LLB Hons). Called to the Bar, Lincoln's Inn, 1967. Chm., Hunter Saphir, 1987–; Non-Exec. Dir, Dairy Crest Ltd, 1987–93. Chairman: CCAHC, 1980–83; Food From Britain, 1983–87, Mem., Food and Drink EDC, 1984–87; Chm., British Israel Chamber of Commerce, 1991–94. *Recreations:* farming, carriage driving. *Address:* Albert Fisher Group, C Sefton Park, Bells Hill, Stoke Poges, Bucks SL2 4HS. *T:* Slough (01753) 677877. *Club:* Farmers.

SAPIN, Michel Marie; Member, Monetary Policy Council, Bank of France, since 1994; *b* 9 April 1952; *m* 1982, Yolande Millan; three *s*. *Educ:* Ecole Normale Supérieure de la rue d'Ulm (MA Hist., post-grad. degree Geog.); Institut d'Etudes Politiques de Paris; Ecole Nationale d'Administration. Joined Socialist Party, 1975; Député: Indre dist, 1981–86; Hauts-de-Seine dist, 1986–91; National Assembly: Sec., 1983–84; Vice-Chm., 1984–86; Vice-Chm., Socialist Gp, 1987–88; Pres., Law Commn, 1988–91; Minister-Delegate of Justice, 1991–92; Minister of the Economy and Finance, 1992–93; Regl Cllr, Ile de France, 1992–94; City Cllr, Nanterre, 1989–94. *Address:* (office) 9/11 rue de Valois, 75001 Paris, France.

SAPPER, Alan Louis Geoffrey; Founder and Chief Executive, Interconnect AV, since 1991; General Secretary, Association of Cinematograph, Television and Allied Technicians, 1969–91; *b* 18 March 1931; *y s* of late Max and Kate Sapper; *m* 1959, Helen Rubens; one *s* one *d*. *Educ:* Upper Latymer Sch.; Univ. of London. Botanist, Royal Botanic Gardens, Kew, 1948–58; Asst Gen. Sec., 1958–64, Dep. Gen. Sec., 1967–69, Assoc. of Cinematograph, Television and Allied Technicians; Gen. Sec., Writers' Guild of Great Britain, 1964–67. Mem. General Council, Trades Union Congress, 1970–84 (Chm., 1982). President: Confedn of Entertainment Unions, 1970–91; Internat. Fedn of Audio-Visual Workers, 1974–94; Sec., Fedn of Film Unions, 1968–91; Treas., Fedn of Broadcasting Unions, 1968–91; Member: British Copyright Council, 1964–74; British Screen Adv. Council, 1985–. Governor: BFI, 1974–94; Nat. Film School, 1980–95; Hammersmith Hosp., 1965–72; Ealing Coll. of Higher Educn, 1976–78. Chm., League for Democracy in Greece, 1970–. *Publications:* articles, short stories; stage plays, On Licence, Kith and Kin; TV play, The Return, 1961. *Recreations:* taxonomic botany, hill walking, politics and human nature. *Address:* 3 Boston Gardens, Chiswick, W4 2QJ. *T:* 0181–742 8313.

SAREI, Sir Alexis Holyweek, Kt 1987; CBE 1981; PhD; Papua New Guinea Permanent Representative to the United Nations, and Ambassador to the United States of America, 1983–86; *b* 25 March 1934; *s* of late Joseph Nambong and Joanna Mota; *m* 1972, Claire Dionne; three *s* three *d* (all adopted). *Educ:* PNG Primary to Tertiary, 1949–66; Rome Univ., 1968–71 (PhD Canon Law). RC Priest, 1966–72; Secretary to Chief Minister, PNG, 1972–73; District Comr, 1973–75; Advisor to Bougainville people, 1975–76; Premier of North Solomons Provincial Govt, 1976–80; High Comr in UK, 1980–83. PNG Independence Medal 1977; CBE for work in Provincial Govt, pioneering work in the system in PNG. Successor to his uncle, Gregory Moah, as Chief of Clan, Petisuun. *Publication:* The Practice of Marriage Among the Solos, Buka Island, 1974. *Recreations:* music, sketching, golf, swimming, sports. *Address:* 8039 Adoree Street, Downey, Calif 90242, USA.

SARELL, Captain Richard Iwan Alexander, DSO 1939; RN retd; *b* 22 Feb. 1909; *s* of late Philip Charles Sarell; *m* 1961, Mrs Ann Morgan (*née* Keenlyside). *Educ:* Royal Naval Coll., Dartmouth. Entered RNC Dartmouth, 1922; Comdr 1943; Capt. 1948; specialised in Gunnery, 1934; DSO for action against enemy submarines while in command of HMS Broke, 1939; despatches, 1943. Naval Attaché, Moscow and Helsinki, 1949–51; student Imperial Defence Coll., 1952; Defence Research Policy Staff, 1954; retd 1957. *Recreation:* fishing. *Address:* 43 Rivermead Court, Ranelagh Gardens, SW6 3RX.

SARELL, Sir Roderick (Francis Gisbert), KCMG 1968 (CMG 1958); KCVO 1971; HM Diplomatic Service, retired; *b* 23 Jan. 1913; *y s* of late Philip Charles Sarell, HM Consular Service and of Ethel Ida Rebecca, *d* of late John Dewar Campbell; *m* 1946, Pamela Muriel (*d* 1994), *d* of late Vivian Francis Crowther-Smith; three *s*. *Educ:* Ashdown House, Sussex; Radley; Magdalen College, Oxford. HM Consular Service, 1936; Vice-Consul, Persia, 1937; Italian East Africa, 1939; Iraq, 1940; 2nd Secretary, Addis Ababa, 1942; 1st Secretary, HM Foreign Service, 1946; Rome, Bucharest, 1946; Foreign Office, 1949; Acting Counsellor, 1952; Counsellor and Consul-General, Rangoon, 1953; Consul-General, Algiers, 1956–59; Head of Southern Dept, Foreign Office, 1959–61, General Dept, 1961–63; Ambassador: to Libya, 1964–69; to Turkey, 1969–73. Coronation medal, 1953. *Recreations:* swimming, building, walking. *Address:* The Litten, Hampstead Norreys, Thatcham, Berks RG18 0TD. *T:* Hermitage (01635) 201274. *Clubs:* Oriental, Royal Over-Seas League; Leander.

SARGAN, Prof. John Denis, FBA 1981; Emeritus Professor, London School of Economics and Political Science, since 1984 (Tooke Professor of Economic Science and Statistics, 1982–84; Professor of Econometrics, 1964–84); *b* 23 Aug. 1924; *s* of H. and G. A. Sargan; *m* 1953, Phyllis Mary Millard; two *s* one *d*. *Educ:* Doncaster Grammar Sch.; St John's Coll., Cambridge. Asst. Lectr, Lectr and Reader, Leeds Univ., 1948–63; Reader, 1963–64, Hon. Fellow, 1991, LSE. Fellow, Amer. Acad. of Arts and Scis, 1987. Dr *hc* Univ. Carlos III, Madrid, 1993. *Address:* 49 Dukes Avenue, Theydon Bois, Essex CM16 7HQ.

SARGANT, Sir (Henry) Edmund, Kt 1969; President of the Law Society, 1968–69; Partner in Radcliffes and Co., 1930–71, and Senior Partner for twenty years; *b* 24 May 1906; *s* of Rt Hon. Sir Charles Henry Sargant, Lord Justice of Appeal, and Amelia Julia Sargant, RRC; *m* 1st, 1930, Mary Kathleen Lemmey (*d* 1979); one *s*; 2nd, 1981, Evelyn Noel (*née* Arnold-Wallinger). *Educ:* Rugby School; Trinity College, Cambridge (MA). 3rd Cl. Hons Solicitors' final examination; admitted 1930. Served War of 1939–45 in RAF, Provost and Security Branch; (W Africa; Middle East; Acting Wing Comdr). Member, Council, Law Society, 1951–75; Chm., Disciplinary Cttee of Architects Registration Council, 1964, 1965, 1966. Master, Worshipful Co. of Merchant Taylors, 1954. *Address:* 902 Keyes House, Dolphin Square, SW1V 3NB. *Club:* United Oxford & Cambridge University.

See also Rt Hon. Lord Justice Nourse.

SARGANT, Naomi Ellen, (Lady McIntosh of Haringey); writer and consultant; *b* 10 Dec. 1933; *d* of late Tom Sargant, OBE, and of Marie Cerny (*née* Hlouskova); *m* 1st, 1954, Peter Joseph Kelly; one *s*; 2nd, 1962, Andrew Robert McIntosh (now Baron McIntosh of Haringey, *qv*); two *s*. *Educ:* Friends' Sch., Saffron Walden, Essex; Bedford Coll., London (BA Hons Sociology). Social Surveys (Gallup Poll) Ltd, 1955–67; Sen. Lectr in Market Res., Enfield Coll. of Technol., 1967–69; Open University: Sen. Lectr in Res. Methods, 1970–75; Reader in Survey Research, 1975–78; Head, Survey Res. Dept, Inst. of Educnl Technol., 1972–81; Pro Vice-Chancellor (Student Affairs), 1974–78; Prof. of Applied Social Research, 1978–81; Sen. Commng Editor for Educnl Programming, Channel 4, 1981–89. Vis. Prof. in Higher Educn (part-time), Univ. of Mass, Amherst, 1974–75; Vis. Prof., Open Univ. Quality Support Centre, 1995–. Councillor, and Chm. Children's Cttee, London Bor. of Haringey, 1964–68; Vice-Chm., London Boroughs Trng Cttee (Social Services), 1966–68. Chm., National Gas Consumers' Council, 1977–80. Pres., Nat. Soc. for Clean Air, 1981–83. Member: Council and Exec. Cttee, Social Work Adv. Service, 1966–68; Local Govt Trng Bd, 1967–68; Energy Commn, 1978–79; Commn on Energy and the Environment, 1978–81; Nat. Consumer Council, 1978–81; Adv. Council for Adult and Continuing Educn, 1977–83; Council, Bedford Coll., Univ. of London, 1977–83; Council, Polytechnic of the South Bank, 1982–86; Exec. Cttee, Nat. Inst. of Adult and Continuing Educn, 1986–89, 1992–; Gov., Haringey Coll., 1984–87; Pro-Chancellor, Univ. of E London HEC, 1992–94 (Vice-Chm., Poly. of E London HEC, 1989–92); Gov., NE London Poly., 1987–89; Acting Chief Exec., Open Poly., 1990. Vice Chm., Film, TV and Video Panel, Arts Council of GB, 1986–90; Vice-Chair, NCVO, 1992–. Trustee: Nat. Extension Coll., 1975–; Charities Aid Foundn, 1992–. Mem. RTS, 1982–. Pres., Highgate Horticultural Soc., 1990. FRSA 1991. Hon. Fellow RCA, 1988. *Publications:* A Degree of Difference, 1976 (New York 1977); (with A. Woodley) The Door Stood Open, 1980; Learning and 'Leisure', 1991; Learning for a Purpose, 1993. *Recreation:* gardening. *Address:* 27 Hurst Avenue, N6 5TX. *T:* 0181–340 1496, *Fax:* 0181–348 4641.

SARGEANT, Frank Charles Douglas, CMG 1972; HM Diplomatic Service, retired 1977; *b* 7 Nov. 1917; *s* of late John Sargeant and Anna Sargeant; *m* 1946, Joan Adene Bickerton; one *s* one *d*. *Educ:* Lincoln; St Catharine's Coll., Cambridge. MA Cantab, Natural Sciences. Cadbury Bros. Ltd, 1939. Served War: Army, 1939–46; Lt-Col, Royal Signals. Imperial Chemical Industries Ltd, 1947–48. HM Diplomatic Service: Curacao, 1948; The Hague, 1951; Kuwait, 1954; Foreign Office, 1957 (First Sec. 1958); First Sec., Head of Chancery and Consul, Mogadishu, 1959; First Sec. (Commercial) Stockholm, 1962–66; First Sec., Head of Chancery, Colombo, and Consul for the Maldive Islands, 1967; Counsellor, 1968; Consul-General, Lubumbashi, 1968–70; Dep. High Comr, Dacca, 1970–71; Sen. Officers' War Course, RN Coll., Greenwich, 1971–72; Consul Gen., Lyons, 1972–77 (Doyen of the Consular Corps). *Recreations:* shooting, fishing.

SARGEANT, Rt. Rev. Frank Pilkington; head of the Archbishop of Canterbury's staff (with title of Bishop at Lambeth), since 1994; *b* 12 Sept. 1932; *s* of John Stanley and Grace Sargeant; *m* 1958, Sally Jeanette McDermott; three *s* two *d*. *Educ:* Boston Grammar School; Durham Univ., St John's Coll. and Cranmer Hall (BA, Dip Theol); Nottingham Univ. (Diploma in Adult Education). National Service Commission, RA (20th Field Regt), 1955–57. Assistant Curate: Gainsborough Parish Church, 1958–62; Grimsby Parish Church, and Priest-in-Charge of St Martin's, Grimsby, 1962–67; Vicar of North Hykeham and Rector of South Hykeham, 1967–73; Residentiary Canon, Bradford Cathedral, 1973–77; Archdeacon of Bradford, 1977–84; Bishop Suffragan of Stockport, 1984–94. *Address:* Lambeth Palace, SE1 7JU. *T:* 0171–928 8282, *Fax:* 0171–261 9836.

SARGEAUNT, Henry Anthony, CB 1961; OBE 1949; Scientific Consultant, United Nations, New York, 1968–69; *b* 11 June 1907; *o s* of Lt-Col Henry Sargeaunt and Norah Ierne Carden; *m* 1939, Winifred Doris Parkinson; two *s* one *d*. *Educ:* Clifton Coll.; University Coll., Reading (London Univ.); Cambridge Univ. Rhodes Research Grant, 1939–42; served with HM Forces, 1944–46: France, 1944; Staff Capt. with 21 Army Group, 1944; Supt Operational Research Group (ORG) (W&E), Min. of Supply, 1946;

Supt, Army ORG, 1947–50; Dep. Scientific Adviser, 1950–52, Scientific Adviser, to Army Council, 1952–55; Asst Scientific Adviser to Supreme Allied Commander in Europe, Sept. 1955–57; Dep. Science Adviser, NATO, 1958–59; re-apptd Scientific Adviser to Army Council, 1959; Dep. Chief Scientist (B), War Office, 1960–62; Chief Scientific Adviser, Home Office, 1962–67. *Recreations:* yachting, horse-racing, bird-watching. *Address:* 7 Bond Close, Sway, Lymington, Hants SO41 6DR. *T:* Lymington (01590) 683112.

SARGENT, Dick; *see* Sargent, J. R.

SARGENT, Prof. John Reid, PhD; FRSE; FIBiol; Director, Natural Environment Research Council Unit of Aquatic Biochemistry, University of Stirling, since 1986; Professor of Biological Science, since 1986, and Head, School of Natural Sciences, 1989–93, University of Stirling; *b* 12 Oct. 1936; *s* of Alex and Annie Sargent; *m* 1961, Elizabeth Jean Buchan; two *d. Educ:* Buckie High Sch.; Robert Gordon's Coll., Aberdeen; Aberdeen Univ. (BSc 1st Cl. Hons, PhD). FIBiol 1983; FRSE 1986. Res. Fellow, Middlesex Hosp. Med. Sch., 1961–64; Lectr, Biochem. Dept, Univ. of Aberdeen, 1964–69; PSO, then SPSO, then Dir, NERC Inst. of Marine Biochem., 1970–85; Head of Dept of Biol Science, Univ. of Stirling, 1985–89. Bond Gold Medal, Amer. Oil Chemists' Soc., 1971. *Publications:* numerous research pubns in biochem. and marine biol., esp. on marine lipids and polyunsaturated fatty acids. *Recreations:* hill-walking, ski-ing, golf. *Address:* School of Natural Sciences, University of Stirling, Stirling FK9 4LA. *T:* Stirling (01786) 473171.

SARGENT, John Richard, (Dick); *b* 22 March 1925; *s* of John Philip Sargent and Ruth (*née* Taunton) *m* 1st, 1949, Anne Elizabeth Haigh (marr. diss. 1980); one *s* two *d*; 2nd, 1980, Hester Mary Campbell. *Educ:* Dragon Sch., Oxford; Rugby Sch.; Christ Church, Oxford (MA). Fellow and Lectr in Econs, Worcester Coll., Oxford, 1951–62; Econ. Consultant, HM Treasury and DEA, 1963–65; Prof. of Econs, Univ. of Warwick, 1965–73 (Pro-Vice-Chancellor, 1971–72), Hon. Prof., 1974–81. Vis. Prof. of Econs, LSE, 1981–82; Gp Economic Adviser, Midland Bank Ltd, 1974–84; Houblon-Norman Res. Fellow, Bank of England, 1984–85. Member: Doctors and Dentists Rev. Body, 1972–75; Armed Forces Pay Rev. Body, 1972–86; Channel Tunnel Adv. Gp, 1974–75; SSRC, 1980–85; Pharmacists Review Panel, 1986–; Pres., Société Universitaire Européenne de Recherches Financières, 1985–88. Editor, Midland Bank Rev., 1974–84. *Publications:* British Transport Policy, 1958; (ed with R. C. O. Matthews) Contemporary Problems of Economic Policy, 1983; articles in various economic jls, and in vols of conf. papers etc. *Recreation:* work. *Address:* Trentham House, Fulbrook, Burford, Oxon OX18 4BL. *T:* Burford (0199382) 3525. *Club:* Reform.

SARGENT, Prof. Roger William Herbert, FEng 1976; Courtaulds Professor of Chemical Engineering, Imperial College, 1966–92, now Emeritus; Senior Research Fellow, Imperial College, since 1992; *b* 14 Oct. 1926; *s* of Herbert Alfred Sargent and May Elizabeth (*née* Gill); *m* 1951, Shirley Jane Levesque (*née* Spooner); two *s. Educ:* Bedford Sch.; Imperial Coll., London (FIC 1994). BSc, ACGI, PhD, DScEng, DIC; FIChemE, FIMA. Design Engineer, Société l'Air Liquide, Paris, 1951–58; Imperial College: Sen. Lectr, 1958–62; Prof. of Chem. Engrg, 1962–66; Dean, City and Guilds Coll., 1973–76; Head of Dept of Chem. Engrg and Chem. Technology, 1975–88; Dir of Interdisciplinary Res. Centre in Process Systems Engrg, 1989–92. Member: Engrg and Technol. Adv. Cttee, British Council, 1976–89 (Chm., 1984–89); Technol. Subcttee, UGC, 1984–88. Pres., Instn of Chem. Engrs, 1973–74; For. Associate, US Nat. Acad. of Engrg, 1993. FRSA 1988. Hon. FCGI 1977. D*hc* Institut Nat. Polytechnique de Lorraine, 1987; Hon. DSc Edinburgh, 1993. *Publications:* contribs to: Trans Instn Chem. Engrs, Computers and Chemical Engrg, Jl of Optimization Theory and Applications, SIAM Jl of Optimization, Mathematical Programming, Internat. Jl of Control, etc. *Address:* Mulberry Cottage, 291A Sheen Road, Richmond, Surrey TW10 5AW. *T:* 0181–876 9623.

SARGENT, Prof. Wallace Leslie William, FRS 1981; Ira S. Bowen Professor of Astronomy, California Institute of Technology, since 1981; *b* 15 Feb. 1935; *s* of Leslie William Sargent and Eleanor (*née* Dennis); *m* 1964, Anneila Isabel Cassells, PhD; two *d. Educ:* Scunthorpe Tech. High Sch. (first pupil to go to univ., 1953); Manchester Univ. (BSc Hons, MSc, PhD). Research Fellow in Astronomy, California Inst. of Tech., 1959–62; Sen. Research Fellow, Royal Greenwich Observatory, 1962–64; Asst Prof. of Physics, Univ. of California, San Diego, 1964–66; Asst Prof. of Astronomy, Calif Inst. Tech., 1966–68, Associate Prof., 1968–71, Professor, 1971–81; Executive Officer for Astronomy, 1975–81. George Darwin Lectr, RAS, 1987; Thomas Gold Lectr, Cornell Univ., 1995. Fellow, American Acad. of Arts and Sciences, 1977. Warner Prize, American Astronomical Soc., 1968; Dannie Heineman Prize, 1991; Bruce Gold Medal, Astronomical Soc. of the Pacific, 1994. *Publications:* many papers in learned jls. *Recreations:* reading, gardening, mountain walking, watching sports. *Address:* Astronomy Dept 105–24, California Institute of Technology, Pasadena, CA 91125, USA. *T:* (818) 3564055; 400 South Berkeley Avenue, Pasadena, CA 91107, USA. *T:* (818) 7956345. *Club:* Athenæum (Pasadena).

SARGESON, Prof. Alan McLeod, FRS 1983; Professor of Inorganic Chemistry, Australian National University, since 1978; *b* 13 Oct. 1930; *s* of late H. L. Sargeson; *m* 1959, Marietta, *d* of F. Anders; two *s* two *d. Educ:* Maitland Boys' High Sch.; Sydney Univ. (BSc, PhD, DipEd). FRACI; FAA. Lectr, Chem. Dept, Univ. of Adelaide, 1956–57; Res. Fellow, John Curtin Sch. of Med. Research, ANU, 1958, Fellow 1960; Sen. Fellow, then Professorial Fellow, 1969–78, Res. Sch. of Chemistry, ANU. DSc *hc* Sydney, 1990. *Address:* Research School of Chemistry, Australian National University, Canberra, ACT 0200, Australia.

SARGINSON, Edward William; retired from Civil Service, 1976; with Confederation of British Industry until 1982; *b* 22 May 1919; *s* of Frederick William and Edith Sarginson; *m* 1944, Olive Pescod; one *s* one *d. Educ:* Barrow-in-Furness Grammar School. Entered Civil Service, War Office, 1936; served Infantry, 1939–46; Principal, Min. of Supply, 1955; Asst Sec., Min. of Aviation, 1965; Asst Under Sec. of State, MoD (PE), 1972–76. Voluntary work: with Childline, 1987–89; with Victim Support, 1990–91. *Recreations:* gardening, bowls. *Address:* 41 Kendall Avenue South, Sanderstead, Surrey CR2 0QR. *T:* 0181–660 4476.

SARK, Seigneur of; *see* Beaumont, J. M.

SAROOP, Narindar, CBE 1982; Adviser: Cancer Relief Macmillan Fund, 1992–95; National Grid plc, 1993; *b* 14 Aug. 1929; *e s* of Chaudhri Ram Saroop, Ismaila, Rohtak, India and late Shyam Devi; *m* 1st, 1952, Ravi Gill (marr. diss. 1967), *o surv. c* of the Sardar and Sardarni of Premgarh, India; two *d* (one *s* decd); 2nd 1969, Stephanie Denise, *yr d* of Alexander and Cynthia Amie Cronopulo, Zakynthos, Greece. *Educ:* Aitchison Coll. for Punjab Chiefs, Lahore; Indian Military Acad., Dehra Dun. Served as regular officer, 2nd Royal Lancers (Gardner's Horse) and Queen Victoria's Own The Poona Horse; retired, 1954. Management Trainee, Yule Catto, 1954; senior executive and Dir of subsidiaries of various multinationals, to 1976; Hon. Administrator, Oxfam Relief Project, 1964; Director: Devi Grays Insurance Ltd, 1981–84; Capital Plant International Ltd, 1982–86. Advr, Develt, Clarkson Puckle Gp, 1976–87; Advr, Banque Belge, 1987–91. Mem., BBC Adv. Council on Asian Programmes, 1977–81. Pres., Indian Welfare Soc., 1983–92. Member Council: Freedom Assoc., 1978–86; Internat. Social Services, 1981–91; Inst. of Directors, 1983–93; Founder Mem., Tory Asians for Representation Gp, 1984–85; Mem. Adv. Council, Efficiency in Local Govt, 1984. Contested (C) Greenwich, 1979 (first Asian Tory Parliamentary candidate this century); Founder and 1st Chm., UK Anglo Asian Cons. Soc., 1976–79, 1985–86; Vice Chm., Cons. Party Internat. Office, 1990–92. Councillor, Kensington and Chelsea, 1974–82; initiated Borough Community Relations Cttee (Chm., 1975–77, 1980–82); Chm., Working Party on Employment, 1978; Founder and Chm., Durbar Club, 1981–. *Publications:* In Defence of Freedom (jtly), 1978; A Squire of Hindoostan, 1983. *Recreations:* keeping fools, boredom and socialism at bay. *Address:* 25 de Vere Gardens, W8 5AN. *Clubs:* Beefsteak, Cavalry and Guards, Pratt's; Imperial Delhi Gymkhana; Royal Bombay Yacht, Royal Calcutta Golf.

SARRAUTE, Nathalie; writer; *b* Ivanowo, Russia, 18 July 1900; *d* of Ilya Tcherniak and Pauline Chatounowski; *m* 1925, Raymond Sarraute; three *d. Educ:* Sorbonne; Ecole de Droit de Paris; Oxford. Dr *hc* TCD, 1976; Univ. of Kent at Canterbury, 1980; Oxford Univ., 1991. Grand Prix National, 1982. *Publications:* Tropismes, 1939 (trans. Tropisms, 1964); Portrait d'un inconnu, 1948 (Portrait of a Man Unknown, 1959); Martereau, 1953 (trans. 1964); L'Ere du soupçon, 1956 (The Age of Suspicion, 1964); Le Planétarium, 1959 (The Planetarium, 1962); Les Fruits d'or, 1963 (The Golden Fruits, 1965) (Prix international de Littérature, 1964); Entre la vie et la mort, 1968 (Between Life and Death, 1969); Vous les entendez?, 1972 (Do You Hear Them?, 1973); "disent les imbéciles", 1976 ("fools say", 1977); L'usage de la parole, 1980 (The Use of Speech, 1983); Enfance, 1983 (Childhood, 1984) (Prix Grinzane Cavour, 1984); Tu ne t'aimes pas, 1989 (You Don't Love Yourself, 1990); *plays:* Le Silence, Le Mensonge, 1967 (Silence and The Lie, 1969); Isma, 1970 (Izzum, 1975); C'est beau, 1973 (It is Beautiful, 1978); Elle est là, 1978 (It is There, 1980); Collected Plays, 1981; Pour un oui ou pour un non, 1982; *essays:* Paul Valéry et l'enfant d'éléphant, Flaubert le précurseur, 1986; *Address:* 12 avenue Pierre I de Serbie, 75116 Paris, France. *T:* 47205828.

SARUM, Archdeacon of; *see* Hopkinson, Ven. B. J.

SASKATCHEWAN, Bishop of, since 1993; **Rt. Rev. Anthony John Burton;** *b* 11 Aug. 1959; *s* of Peter Michael Burton and Rachel Harragin Wood Greaves; *m* 1989, Anna Kristine Erickson. *Educ:* Trinity Coll., Toronto Univ. (BA (Hons) 1982); King's Coll., Dalhousie Univ.; Wycliffe Hall, Oxford (BA, MA). Ordained deacon, 1987, priest, 1988; Curate, St John the Baptist, N Sydney, Nova Scotia, 1987–88; Rector, Trinity Church, Sydney Mines, 1988–91; Rector and Canon Residentiary, Cathedral Church of St Alban the Martyr, Saskatchewan, 1991–93; Dean of Saskatchewan, 1991–94. Hon. DD King's Coll., Halifax, 1994. *Publications:* (contrib.) Anglican Essentials: reclaiming faith in the Anglican Church of Canada, 1995; contrib. to Machray Rev. *Recreations:* walking, tyrannizing the clergy. *Address:* Synod Office, Box 1088, Prince Albert, Sask S6V 5S6, Canada. *T:* (306) 7632455, *Fax:* (306) 7645172.

SASKATOON, Bishop of, since 1993; **Rt. Rev. Thomas Oliver Morgan;** *b* 20 Jan. 1941; *s* of Charles Edwin Morgan and Amy Amelia (*née* Hoyes); *m* 1963, Lillian Marie (*née* Textor); two *s* one *d. Educ:* Univ. of Saskatchewan (BA 1962); King's College, London (BD 1965); Tyndale Hall, Bristol (GOE 1966), Curate, Church of the Saviour, Blackburn, Lancs, 1966–69; Rector: Porcupine Plain, Sask, Canada, 1969–73; Kinistino, 1973–77; Shellbrook, 1977–83; Archdeacon of Indian Missions, Saskatchewan, 1983–85; Bishop of Saskatchewan, 1985–93. Hon. DD, Coll. of Emmanuel and St Chad, Saskatoon, 1986. *Address:* PO Box 1965, Saskatoon, SK S7K 3S5, Canada.

SATCHELL, Edward William John, CEng, FIEE, RCNC; Director of Engineering (Ships), 1973–76; *b* 23 Sept. 1916; *s* of Horsey John Robert Satchell and Ethel Satchell (*née* Chandler); *m* 1941, Stella Grace Cook; one *d. Educ:* Esplanade House Sch., Southsea; Royal Dockyard Sch., Portsmouth; RNC, Greenwich. Electrical Apprentice, Portsmouth Dockyard, 1932; Probationary Asst Electrical Engr, 1936; Asst Electrical Engr, 1939; Electrical Engr, 1943; Suptg Electrical Engr, 1955. Served with British Naval Mission in USA, 1951–53. Warship Electrical Supt, Scotland, 1958–61; Dep. Admty Repair Manager, Malta, 1961–64; Dep. Elec. Engrg Manager, Devonport, 1964–66; Asst Dir of Electrical Engineering, 1966; Dep. Dir of Elec. Engrg, 1970; Head of RN Engrng Service, 1973–75; Dep. Head, RCNC (L), 1975–76; retired 1976. *Recreations:* reading, gardening, bird watching. *Address:* 6 Badminton Gardens, Bath BA1 2XS. *T:* Bath (01225) 426974.

SATOW, Rear-Adm. Derek Graham, CB 1977; *b* 13 June 1923; *y s* of late Graham F. H. Satow, OBE, and Evelyn M. Satow (*née* Moore); *m* 1944, Patricia E. A. Penaliggon; two *d. Educ:* Oakley Hall Sch.; Haileybury Coll.; Royal Naval Engineering Coll. CEng, FIMechE, FIMarE. HMS Ceylon, 1945–46; RNC, Greenwich, 1946–48; HMS Duke of York, 1948–49; RAE Farnborough, 1949–51; HMS Newcastle, 1951–53 (despatches, 1953); Naval Ordnance and Weapons Dept, Admiralty, 1953–59; Dir of Engineering, RNEC, 1959–62; HMS Tiger, 1962–64; Asst and Dep. Dir of Marine Engineering, MoD, 1964–67; IDC, 1968; Captain, RNEC, 1969–71; Dir, Naval Officer Appointments (Eng), MoD, 1971–73; Chief Staff Officer, Technical, later Engineering, to C-in-C Fleet, 1974–76; Dep. Dir-Gen., Ships, MoD, 1976–79; Chief Naval Engr Officer, 1977–79. Comdr, 1955; Captain, 1964; Rear-Adm., 1973.

SATTERTHWAITE, Rt. Rev. John Richard, CMG 1991; Bishop of Gibraltar in Europe, 1980–93; an Assistant Bishop, diocese of Carlisle, since 1994; *b* 17 Nov. 1925; *s* of William and Clara Elisabeth Satterthwaite. *Educ:* Millom Grammar Sch.; Leeds Univ. (BA); Coll. of the Resurrection, Mirfield. History Master, St Luke's Sch., Haifa, 1946–48; Curate: St Barnabas, Carlisle, 1950–53; St Aidan, Carlisle, 1953–54; St Michael Paternoster Royal, London, 1955–59, Curate-in-Charge, 1959–65; Guild Vicar, St Dunstan-in-the-West, City of London, 1959–70. Gen. Sec., Church of England Council on Foreign Relations, 1959–70 (Asst Gen. Sec., 1955–59); Gen. Sec., Archbp's Commn on Roman Catholic Relations, 1965–70; Bishop Suffragan of Fulham, 1970; Bishop of Gibraltar, 1970; known as Bishop of Fulham and Gibraltar until creation of new diocese, 1980. Hon. Canon of Canterbury, 1963–71; ChStJ 1972 (Asst ChStJ 1963); Hon. Canon of Utrecht, Old Catholic Church of the Netherlands, 1969. Holds decoration from various foreign churches. *Recreations:* fell walking, music. *Address:* 25 Spencer House, St Paul's Square, Carlisle, Cumbria CA1 1DG. *T:* Carlisle (01228) 594055. *Club:* Athenæum.

SAUGMAN, Per Gotfred, Hon. OBE 1990; Knight of the Order of Dannebrog; Chairman, Blackwell Scientific Publications Ltd, Oxford, 1972–92 (Managing Director, 1954–87); *b* 26 June 1925; *s* of Emanuel A. G. Saugman and Esther (*née* Lehmann); *m* 1950, Patricia (*née* Fulford); two *s* one *d* (and one *s* decd). *Educ:* Gentofte Grammar Sch.; Commercial Coll., Copenhagen. Bookselling and publishing training in Denmark, Switzerland and England, 1941–49; Sales Manager, Blackwell Scientific Publications Ltd, 1952; Director, University Bookshops (Oxford) Ltd, 1963–92; Mem. Board, B. H. Blackwell Ltd, 1964–92; Chairman: William George's Sons Ltd, Bristol, 1965–92; Oxford Illustrators Ltd, 1968–; Blackwell North America, Inc., 1975–92; Ejnar Munksgaard Publishers Ltd, Copenhagen, 1967–92; Kooyker Boekhandel Leiden, 1973–92; Oxford Shutter Co. Ltd, 1994–. Member Council: International Publishers' Assoc., 1976–79;

Publishers' Assoc. of GB and Ireland, 1977–82; President, Internat. Group of Scientific, Technical and Medical Publishers, 1977–79. Chairman: Oxford Round Table, 1953–55; Sunningwell Sch. of Art, 1972–; Hon. Mem., British Ecological Soc., 1960–; Governor: Oxford Polytechnic, 1972–85; Dragon Sch., Oxford, 1975–; Headington Sch., Oxford, 1988–. Fellow, St Cross Coll., Oxford, 1978; Hon. MA Oxford, 1978; Hon. Fellow, Green Coll., Oxford, 1981. Chevalier, Order of Icelandic Falcon, 1984. *Publications:* From the First Fifty Years, 1989; The Way I Think it Was, 1992; The Way it Was, 1994. *Recreations:* reading, art—English watercolours, golf. *Address:* Sunningwood House, Lincombe Lane, Boars Hill, Oxford OX1 5DZ. *T:* Oxford (01865) 735503. *Clubs:* Athenæum, Royal Automobile; Frilford Golf (Oxford).

SAUL, Prof. (Samuel) Berrick, CBE 1992; PhD; Executive Chairman, Universities and Colleges Admissions Service, since 1993; Vice Chancellor, University of York, 1979–93; *b* 20 Oct. 1924; *s* of Ernest Saul and Maud Eaton; *m* 1953, Sheila Stenton; one *s* one *d*. *Educ:* West Bromwich Grammar Sch.; Birmingham Univ. (BCom 1949, PhD 1953). National Service, 1944–47 (Lieut Sherwood Foresters). Lectr in Econ. History, Liverpool Univ., 1951–63; Edinburgh University: Prof. of Econ. History, 1963–78; Dean, Faculty of Social Sciences, 1970–75; Vice Principal, 1975–77; Actg Principal, 1978. Rockefeller Fellow, Univ. of Calif (Berkeley), and Columbia Univ., 1959; Ford Fellow, Stanford Univ., 1969–70. Vis. Prof., Harvard Univ., 1973. Chairman: Central Council for Educn and Trng in Social Work, 1986–93; Standing Conf. on Univ. Entrance, 1986–93; Vice-Chm., Commonwealth Scholarship Commn, 1993–. Hon. LLD York, Toronto, 1981; Hon. Dr *hc* Edinburgh, 1986; DUniv York, 1994. *Publications:* Studies in British Overseas Trade 1870–1914, 1960; The Myth of the Great Depression, 1969; Technological Change: the US and Britain in the 19th Century, 1970; (with A. S. Milward) The Economic Development of Continental Europe 1780–1870, 1973; (with A. S. Milward) The Development of the Economies of Continental Europe 1850–1914, 1977. *Recreations:* fell walking, travel, music. *Address:* 39 Drome Road, Copmanthorpe, York YO2 3TG. *T:* York (01904) 701011.

SAULL, Rear-Adm. (Keith) Michael, CB 1982; FCIT; Chairman, New Zealand Ports Authority, 1984–88; *b* 24 Aug. 1927; *s* of Harold Vincent Saull and Margaret Saull; *m* 1952, Linfield Mabel (*née* Barnsdale); two *s* one *d*. *Educ:* Altrincham Grammar Sch.; HMS Conway. Royal Navy, 1945–50; transferred to Royal New Zealand Navy, 1951; commanded HMNZ Ships: Kaniere, Taranaki, Canterbury, 1956–71; Naval Attaché, Washington DC, 1972–75; RCDS 1976; Commodore, Auckland, 1978; Chief of Naval Staff, RNZN, 1980–83. Vice Patron, Royal NZ Coastguard Fedn, 1987–. *Recreations:* golf, fishing, sailing.

SAULTER, Paul Reginald; management consultant, since 1986; Managing Director, Heritage of Industry (formerly Cornwall of Mine) Ltd, since 1989; Administrator, St Paul's, Knightsbridge, since 1987; *b* 27 Aug. 1935; *s* of Alfred Walter Saulter and Mabel Elizabeth Oliver. *Educ:* Truro Sch.; University Coll., Oxford. MA. Admin. Asst, Nat. Council of Social Service, 1960–63; Sen. Asst and Principal, CEGB, 1963–65; Dep. Head, Overseas Div., BEAMA, 1965–69; Dir, Internat. Affairs, ABCC, 1969–73; Sec.-Gen., British Chamber of Commerce in France, 1973–81; Chief Executive: Manchester Chamber of Commerce and Industry, 1981–85; Assoc. of Exhibn Organisers, 1985–86. Exhibn Advr, London Chamber of Commerce, 1986–88. Secretary: For. Trade Working Gp, ORGALIME, 1967–69; Council of British Chambers of Commerce in Continental Europe, 1977–80; Mem., Export Promotion Cttee, CBI, 1983–86. Member: RHS; Trevithick Soc., 1986–. *Recreations:* walking, music, theatre, researching Cornish mining history. *Address:* 24 Pembridge Crescent, W11 3DS. *T:* 0171–229 2616.

SAUMAREZ, family name of **Baron de Saumarez.**

SAUMAREZ SMITH, Dr Charles Robert; Director, National Portrait Gallery, since 1994; *b* 28 May 1954; *s* of late William Hanbury Saumarez Smith, OBE and of Alice Elizabeth Harness Saumarez Smith (*née* Raven); *m* 1979, Romilly Le Quesne Savage; two *s*. *Educ:* Marlborough Coll.; King's Coll., Cambridge (BA 1st cl.History of Art 1976; MA 1978); Henry Fellow, Harvard, 1977; Warburg Inst. (PhD 1986). Christie's Res. Fellow in Applied Arts, Christ's Coll., Cambridge, 1979–82; Asst Keeper with resp. for V&A/RCA MA course in history of design, 1982–90, Head of Res., 1990–94, V & A. Vis. Fellow, Yale Center for British Art, 1983; Benno Forman Fellow, Winterthur Mus., 1988; South Square Fellow, RCA, 1990. Member, Executive Committee: Design History Soc., 1985–89; Soc. of Architectural Historians, 1987–90; Assoc. of Art Historians, 1990–94; London Library, 1992–. Trustee: Soane Monuments Trust, 1988–; Charleston, 1993–. Hon. Fellow, RCA, 1991. *Publications:* The Building of Castle Howard, 1990 (Alice Davis Hitchcock Medallion); Eighteenth Century Decoration, 1993. *Address:* National Portrait Gallery, St Martin's Place, WC2H 0HE. *T:* 0171–306 0055.

SAUNDERS, Albert Edward, CMG 1975; OBE 1970; HM Diplomatic Service, retired; Ambassador to the United Republic of Cameroon and the Republic of Equatorial Guinea, 1975–79; *b* 5 June 1919; *s* of late Albert Edward and Marie Marguerite Saunders; *m* 1945, Dorothea Charlotte Mary Whittle (*d* 1985); one *s* one *d*. *Educ:* yes. Westminster Bank Ltd, 1937. Royal Navy, 1942–45: last appt, Asst Chief Port Security Officer, Middle East. Apptd to British Embassy, Cairo, 1938 and 1945; Asst Information Officer, Tripoli, 1949; Asst Admin. Officer, Athens, 1951; Middle East Centre for Arabic Studies, 1952; Third Sec., Office of UK Trade Comr, Khartoum, 1953; Third Sec. (Information), Beirut, 1954; POMEF, Cyprus, 1956; FO, 1957; Second Sec. (Oriental), Baghdad, 1958; FO, 1959; Vice-Consul, Casablanca, 1963; Second Sec. (Oriental), Rabat, 1963; Consul, Jerusalem, 1964; First Sec., FO, 1967; Chancery, Baghdad, 1968; Head of Chancery and Consul, Rabat, 1969; Counsellor and Consul General in charge British Embassy, Dubai, 1972; Chargé d'Affaires, Abu Dhabi, 1972 and 1973; RN War Coll., Greenwich, 1974, sowc, 1975. *Recreation:* iconoclasm (20th Century). *Address:* 3 Deanhill Road, SW14 7DQ.

SAUNDERS, Andrew Downing; President, Royal Archaeological Institute, since 1993; Chairman, International Fortress Council; *b* 22 Sept. 1931; *s* of Lionel Edward Saunders; *m* 1st, 1961, Hilary Jean (*née* Aikman) (marr. diss. 1980); two *s* one *d*; 2nd, 1985, Gillian Ruth Hutchinson; one *d*. *Educ:* Magdalen Coll. Sch., Oxford; Magdalen Coll., Oxford (MA). FSA, FRHistS, FSAScot, MIFA. Joined Ancient Monuments Inspectorate, 1954; Inspector of Ancient Monuments for England, 1964; Chief Inspector of Ancient Monuments and Historic Buildings, DoE, subseq. English Heritage, 1973–89. Vice-Pres., Hendon and Dist Archaeol Soc.; Member: Adv. Cttee on Historic Wrecks; Scientific Council, Europa Nostra/Internat. Castles Inst. Chm., Fortress Study Gp. Editor, Fortress: the Castles and Fortifications Qly, 1989–. *Publications:* ed jtly and contrib., Ancient Monuments and their Interpretation, 1977; Fortress Britain, 1989; Devon and Cornwall, 1991, excavation reports on various Roman and Medieval sites and monuments, papers on castles and artillery fortification in various archæological and historical jls; guidebooks to ancient monuments. *Recreations:* opera, sailing, Staffordshire Bull Terriers. *Address:* 30 The Plantation, Blackheath, SE3 0AB. *T:* 0181–318 2073. *Club:* Athenæum.

SAUNDERS, Basil; public relations consultant; Director, Charles Barker Traverse-Healy (formerly Traverse-Healy & Regester Ltd), 1984–90; *b* 12 Aug. 1925; *s* of late Comdr J. E. Saunders, RN and Marjorie Saunders; *m* 1957, Betty Smith; two *s* four *d*. *Educ:* Merchant Taylors'; Wadham Coll., Oxford (MA). FIPR. Sub-Lt, RNVR, 1944–46. Assistant d'Anglais, Collège de Tarascon, 1950–51; Writer, General Electric Co. (USA), 1952–53; PRO, BIM, 1954–57; Public Relations Exec., Pritchard, Wood and Partners, 1957–63; Head of Public Relations Services, Wellcome Foundn Ltd, 1963–78; Dir-Gen., Aslib, 1978–80; Public Relations Officer, Arts Council, 1981. Consultant, Traverse-Healy Ltd, 1981–84. *Publications:* Crackle of Thorns (verse), 1968; (jtly) Bluff Your Way in PR, 1991; short stories in magazines and on radio; backpagers in Manchester Guardian; reviews, articles, etc. *Recreation:* throwing things away. *Address:* 18 Dartmouth Park Avenue, NW5 1JN. *T:* 0171–485 4672. *Club:* Savile.

SAUNDERS, Christopher John, MA; Headmaster, Lancing College, since 1993; *b* 7 May 1940; *s* of R. H. Saunders and G. S. Saunders (*née* Harris); *m* 1973, Cynthia Elizabeth Stiles; one *s* one *d*. *Educ:* Lancing Coll.; Fitzwilliam Coll., Cambridge (MA); PGCE Wadham Coll., Oxford. Assistant Master, Bradfield College, 1964–80 (Housemaster, 1972–80); Headmaster, Eastbourne Coll., 1981–93. Mem. Council, FA. *Recreations:* music, theatre, gardening, soccer (Oxford Blue 1963), cricket (Oxford Blue 1964), people. *Address:* Lancing College, Lancing, Sussex BN15 0RW. *Clubs:* MCC; Hawks (Cambridge).

SAUNDERS, Christopher Thomas, CMG 1953; Hon. Fellow, Sussex European Research Centre and Science Policy Research Unit, University of Sussex, since 1973; *b* 5 Nov. 1907; *s* of Thomas Beckenn Avening Saunders, clergyman, and Mary Theodora Slater; *m* 1947, Cornelia Jacomijntje Gielstra; one *s*. *Educ:* Craig School, Windermere; St Edward's School; Christ Church, Oxford. BA 1929; MA 1932; University of Liverpool: Social Survey of Merseyside, 1930–33; University of Manchester: Economic Research Dept, 1933–35; Joint Committee of Cotton Trade Organisations, Manchester, 1935–40; Cotton Control, 1940–44; Combined Production and Resources Board, Washington, 1944–45; Min. of Labour, 1945–47; Central Statistical Office, 1947–57; Dir, Nat. Inst. of Econ. and Social Research, 1957–64; Economist, UN Econ. Commn for Europe, 1965–72. *Publications:* Red Oxford (with M. P. Ashley), 1929; Social Survey of Merseyside (collaborated in), 1934; Seasonal Variations in Employment, 1936; From Free Trade to Integration?, 1975; Winners and Losers, 1977; Engineering in Britain, West Germany and France, 1978; (with D. Marsden) Pay Inequalities in the European Community, 1981; (ed) The Political Economy of New and Old Industrial Countries, 1981; (ed jtly) Europe's Industries, 1983; (ed) 11 volumes in East-West European Economic Interaction Workshop Papers, 1977–91; articles in Economic Jl, Jl of Royal Statistical Soc., The Manchester School. *Recreations:* walking and other forms of travel; painting. *Address:* 73 Wick Hall, Furze Hill, Hove BN3 1NG. *Club:* Reform.

SAUNDERS, Dame Cicely (Mary Strode), OM 1989; DBE 1980 (OBE 1967); FRCP, FRCS; Chairman, St Christopher's Hospice, since 1985 (Medical Director, 1967–85); *b* 22 June 1918; *d* of Gordon Saunders and Mary Christian Knight; *m* 1980, Prof. Marian Bohusz-Szyszko (*d* 1995), *s* of Antoni Bohusz-Szyszko, Wilno, Poland. *Educ:* Roedean Sch.; St Anne's Coll., Oxford; St Thomas's Hosp. Med. Sch.; Nightingale Sch. of Nursing. SRN 1944; MB, BS, 1957; MA 1960 (BA (war degree) 1945). FRCP 1974 (MRCP 1968); FRCN 1981; FRCS 1986. Founded St Christopher's Hospice, 1967 (St Christopher's has been a Registered Charity since 1961 and was opened as a Hospice in 1967). Mem., MRC, 1976–79; Dep. Chm., Attendance Allowance Bd, 1979–85. Hon. Consultant, St Thomas' Hosp., 1985. AIMSW 1947. Hon. FRCPsych 1988; Hon. Fellow: Sheffield City Polytechnic, 1983; Newnham Coll., Cambridge, 1986; Guy's and St Thomas' Med. Schs (UMDS), 1993. Hon. DSc: Yale, 1969; London, 1983; Glasgow, 1990; Durham, 1995; Dr of Medicine, Lambeth, 1977; Hon. MD Belfast, 1984; DUniv Open, 1978; Hon. LLD: Columbia, NY, 1979; Leicester, 1983; DHL Jewish Theological Seminary of America, 1982; DU Essex, 1983; Hon. DCL: Canterbury, 1984; Cambridge, 1986; Oxford, 1986; Hon. Dr Med. TCD, 1988. Gold Medal, Soc. of Apothecaries of London, 1979; Gold Medal, BMA, 1987; Templeton Foundation Prize, 1981. *Publications:* Care of the Dying, 1960, 2nd edn 1977; (ed) The Management of Terminal Disease, 1978, 3rd edn 1993; (ed jtly) Hospice: the living idea, 1981; Living with Dying, 1983, 2nd edn 1989; (ed) St Christopher's in Celebration, 1988; Beyond the Horizon, 1990; (ed) Hospice and Palliative Care, 1990; various papers on terminal care. *Recreation:* home. *Address:* St Christopher's Hospice, 51–59 Lawrie Park Road, Sydenham, SE26 6DZ. *T:* 0181–778 9252.

SAUNDERS, Air Vice-Marshal David John, CBE 1986; FIMechE; FRAeS; Air Officer Engineering and Supply, since 1993; *b* 12 June 1943; *s* of John Saunders and Nina Saunders (*née* Mabberley); *m* 1966, Elizabeth Jane Cairns; one *s* one *d*. *Educ:* Commonweal Grammar Sch.; RAF College; Cranfield Inst. of Technology. BSc, MSc; CEng, FRAeS 1993. Joined RAF 1961; management appts, 1966–85; Station Comdr, RAF Sealand, 1983; Command Mechanical Engineer, HQ RAF Germany, 1986; Dir of Engineering Policy (RAF), MoD, 1989–91; ACDS (Logistics), 1991–93; Hd of RAF Mobility Study, 1993. Mem. Council, RAeS. *Recreations:* hill walking, cross country ski-ing, team sports. *Address:* HQ Strike Command, RAF High Wycombe, Bucks HP14 4UE. *Club:* Royal Air Force.

SAUNDERS, David Martin St George; HM Diplomatic Service, retired; *b* 23 July 1930; *s* of late Hilary St George Saunders and Helen (*née* Foley); *m* 1960, Patricia, *d* of James Methold, CBE; one *s* one *d*. *Educ:* Marlborough Coll.; RMA Sandhurst; Staff Coll., Quetta, Pakistan. Commnd Welsh Guards, 1950; Staff Captain Egypt, 1954–56; Asst Adjt, RMA Sandhurst, 1956–58; Adjt 1st Bn Welsh Guards, 1958–60; GSO III War Office, 1960–62; sc 1962–63; Company Comdr 1st Bn Welsh Guards, 1964; GSO II British Defence Liaison Staff, Canberra, 1965–67; Guards Depot, Pirbright, 1967–68; joined Foreign Service, 1968; Consul (Economic), Johannesburg, 1970–73; First Secretary: FCO, 1973–74; Dakar, 1974–76; FCO, 1976–77; Pretoria, 1977–79; The Hague, 1979–83; Counsellor, FCO, 1983–90. *Recreations:* military history, tennis, skiing, shooting, cinema, wines of Burgundy. *Address:* 18 Garfield Road, SW11 5PN

SAUNDERS, David William, CB 1989; Second Parliamentary Counsel, since 1994; *b* 4 Nov. 1936; *s* of William Ernest Saunders and Lilian Grace (*née* Ward); *m* 1963, Margaret Susan Rose Bartholomew. *Educ:* Hornchurch Grammar Sch.; Worcester Coll., Oxford (MA). Admitted solicitor, 1964. Joined Office of Parly Counsel, 1970; Dep. Parly Counsel, 1978–80; Parly Counsel, 1980–94; with Law Commn, 1972–74, 1986–87. *Recreations:* flying, golf, bridge. *Address:* 104A Belgrave Road, SW1V 2BJ. *T:* 0171–834 4403. *Club:* United Oxford & Cambridge University.

SAUNDERS, Prof. Derek William, CBE 1986; Professor of Polymer Physics and Engineering, Cranfield Institute of Technology, 1967–87, retired 1988, Emeritus Professor, since 1989; Director, Science and Engineering Research Council/Department of Industry Teaching Company Scheme, 1981–88; *b* 4 Dec. 1925; *s* of Alfred and Elizabeth Hannah Saunders; *m* 1949, Mahalah Harrison; three *s* two *d*. *Educ:* Morley Grammar Sch.; Imperial Coll., Univ. of London. PhD, ARCS, FInstP, FIM, CEng, CPhys. Building Res. Stn, Garston, 1945–47; British Rubber Producers Res. Assoc., 1947–51; Royal Instn, 1951–54; British Rayon Res. Assoc., 1954–60; Cranfield Inst. of Technology: Sen. Lectr 1960, subseq. Reader; Head of Materials Dept, 1969–81; Pro-Vice-Chancellor, 1973–76. Chm. Council, Plastics Inst., 1973–75; Chm. Council, 1975–76, Pres., 1983–85 and 1990–91,

Plastics and Rubber Inst.; Vice-Pres., Inst. of Materials, 1992–94. Mem. Harpur Trust (Bedford Charity), 1968–88. Hon. DTech CNAA, 1990. *Publications:* chapters in several books on polymeric materials; sci. papers in various learned jls. *Address:* 98 Topcliffe Road, Thirsk, N Yorks YO7 1RY. *T:* Thirsk (01845) 523344.

SAUNDERS, Ernest Walter, MA; President, Stambridge Management (formerly Associates), since 1992; *b* 21 Oct. 1935; *m* 1963, Carole Ann Stephings; two *s* one *d. Educ:* Emmanuel Coll., Cambridge (MA). Man. Dir, Beecham Products Internat., and Dir, Beecham Products, 1966–73; Chm., European Div., Great Universal Stores, 1973–77; Pres., Nestlé Nutrition SA, and Mem. Worldwide Management Cttee, Nestlé SA, Vevey, Switzerland, 1977–81; Chm., Beechnut Corp., USA, 1977–81; Chief Exec., 1981–87, Chm., 1986–87, Arthur Guinness & Sons plc, later Guinness PLC; Chairman: Arthur Guinness Son & Co. (Great Britain), 1982–87; Guinness Brewing Worldwide, 1982–87. Dir, Brewers' Soc., 1983. Dir, Queens Park Rangers Football & Athletic Club, 1983. *Recreations:* skiing, tennis, football.

SAUNDERS, James; playwright; *b* Islington, 8 Jan. 1925; *s* of Walter Percival Saunders and Dorcas Geraldine (*née* Warren); *m* 1951, Audrey Cross; *s* two *d. Educ:* Wembley County Sch.; Southampton Univ. *Plays:* Moonshine, 1955; Alas, Poor Fred, The Ark, 1959; Committal, Barnstable, Return to a City, 1960; A Slight Accident, 1961; Double Double, 1962; Next Time I'll Sing to You (Evening Standard Drama Award), The Pedagogue, Who Was Hilary Maconochie?, 1963; A Scent of Flowers, Neighbours, 1964; Triangle, Opus, 1965; A Man's Best Friend, The Borage Pigeon Affair, 1969; After Liverpool, 1970; Games, Savoury Meringue, 1971; Hans Kohlhaas, 1972; Bye Bye Blues, 1973; The Island, 1975; Bodies, 1977; Birdsong, 1979; Fall, 1981; Emperor Waltz, 1983; Scandella, 1985; Menocchio, 1985 (BBC Radio Play Award, 1986); Making it Better, 1992; Retreat, 1995; *stage adaptations:* The Italian Girl, 1968; The Travails of Sancho Panza, 1969; A Journey to London, 1973; Player Piano, 1978; Random Moments in a May Garden, 1980; The Girl in Melanie Klein, 1980; *television:* Watch Me I'm a Bird, 1964; Bloomers, 1979 (series); television adaptations of works by D. H. Lawrence, Henry James, H. E. Bates and R. F. Delderfield; *screenplays:* Sailor's Return; The Captain's Doll. Arts Council of GB Drama Bursary, 1960; Writers' Guild TV Adaptation Award, 1966; Arts Council Major Bursary, 1984. *Address:* c/o Casarotto Ramsay Ltd, 60–66 Wardour Street, W1V 3HP.

SAUNDERS, Sir John (Anthony Holt), Kt 1972; CBE 1970; DSO 1945; MC 1944; formerly Chairman and Chief Manager, Hongkong and Shanghai Banking Corporation, 1962–72; *b* 29 July 1917; *m* 1942, Enid Mary Durant Cassidy; two *d. Educ:* Bromsgrove Sch. War Service, 1940–45; OCTU Sandhurst (Belt of Honour); N Africa, Sicily and Italy. Lived in Hong Kong 1950–72; MEC Hong Kong Govt, 1966–72. Chm. of Stewards, Royal Hong Kong Jockey Club, 1967–72.

SAUNDERS, John Henry Boulton; QC 1991; a Recorder, since 1990; *b* 15 March 1949; *s* of Kathleen Mary Saunders and Henry G. B. Saunders; *m* 1975, Susan Mary Chick; one *s* two *d. Educ:* Uppingham School; Magdalen College, Oxford (BA). Called to the Bar, Gray's Inn, 1972. *Recreations:* music, sailing. *Address:* 4 Fountain Court, Steelhouse Lane, Birmingham B4 6DR. *T:* 0121–236 3476.

SAUNDERS, Prof. Kenneth Barrett, MD; FRCP; Professor of Medicine, St George's Hospital Medical School, since 1980; *b* 16 March 1936; *s* of Harold N. Saunders and Winifred F. Saunders (*née* Gadge); *m* 1961, Philippa Mary Harrison; one *s* one *d. Educ:* Kingswood Sch., Bath; Trinity Hall, Cambridge (MA 1966; MD 1966); St Thomas's Hosp. Med. Sch. FRCP 1978. Sen. Lectr, then Reader in Medicine, Middx Hosp. Med. Sch., 1972–80; Dean, Fac. of Medicine, London Univ., 1990–94. Mem., GMC, 1992–. *Publications:* Clinical Physiology of the Lung, 1977; various papers on respiratory science and medicine. *Recreations:* English and classical literature (especially Homer), squash rackets, tennis, golf. *Address:* 77 Lee Road, Blackheath, SE3 9EN. *T:* 0181–852 8138. *Clubs:* Royal Automobile, Academy; Hampstead Cricket; Royal Blackheath Golf.

SAUNDERS, Kenneth Herbert; Chief Architect, Commission for the New Towns, 1976–82, retired; *b* 5 April 1915; *s* of William James Saunders and Anne Elizabeth Baker; *m* 1940, Kathleen Bettye Fortune (*d* 1981); one *s* one *d. Educ:* elementary sch., Worthing; Sch. of Art, Worthing; Brighton Coll. of Art. ARIBA 1940. Served War: RA Iraq and Persia; OCTU Bengal Sappers and Miners, India and Burma; Major RE ALFSEA, SORE II, 1940 (mentioned in despatches). Articled pupil, 1933; Dept of Architecture, Bor. of Worthing, 1936; City Architect's Dept, Portsmouth, 1937–39, 1946–49; Crawley Develt Corporation: Architect, 1949; Sen. Architect, 1952; Asst Chief Architect, 1958; Commission for New Towns: Asst Chief Architect, 1962; Exec. Architect, 1965; Manager (Crawley), 1978–80. *Recreations:* architecture, buildings. *Address:* Longthorpe, 22 Goffs Park Road, Crawley, West Sussex RH11 8AY. *T:* Crawley (01293) 521334.

SAUNDERS, Michael Lawrence, CB 1990; HM Procurator General, Treasury Solicitor and Queen's Proctor, since 1995; *b* 13 April 1944; *s* of Samuel Reuben Saunders and Doris Saunders; *m* 1970, Anna Stobo; one *s* one *d. Educ:* Clifton College; Birmingham University (LLB Hons); Jesus College, Cambridge (LLB Hons). Called to the Bar, Gray's Inn, 1971. Third Sec., Hague Conf. on Private Internat. Law (Permt Bureau), 1966–68; Second Sec., 1968–72; Senior Legal Assistant: DTI, 1972–73; Treasury Solicitor's Dept (Energy Branch), 1973–76; Law Officers' Dept, 1976–79; Asst Treasury Solicitor (Cabinet Office European Secretariat Asst Legal Adviser), 1979–83; Asst Legal Sec., 1983–86, Legal Sec., 1986–89, Law Officers' Dept; Solicitor to HM Customs and Excise, 1989–92; Legal Advr to Home Office and NI Office, 1992–95. *Publications:* contribs to jls on internat. law. *Address:* Queen Anne's Chambers, 28 Broadway, SW1H 9JS.

SAUNDERS, Sir Peter, Kt 1982; Chairman and Managing Director: Peter Saunders Ltd; Peter Saunders Group Ltd; Director: West End Theatre Managers Ltd; Theatre Investment Fund Ltd; Theatre Investment Finance Ltd; *b* 23 Nov. 1911; *s* of Ernest and Aletta Saunders; *m* 1st, 1959, Ann Stewart (*d* 1976); no *c*; 2nd, 1979, Catherine Baylis (*née* Imperiali dei Principi di Francavilla) (Katie Boyle); no *c. Educ:* Oundle Sch.; Lausanne. Film cameraman, film director, journalist and press agent; served War of 1939–45 (Captain); started in theatrical production, 1947; has presented over 100 plays incl. The Mousetrap, which has run since 1952 (became world's longest ever run, Dec. 1971); other West End productions include: Fly Away Peter; The Perfect Woman; Breach of Marriage; My Mother Said; The Hollow; Witness for the Prosecution; The Manor of Northstead; Spider's Web; The Water Gipsies; The Bride and the Bachelor; Subway in the Sky; Verdict; The Trial of Mary Dugan; The Unexpected Guest; A Day in the Life Of; And Suddenly it's Spring; Go Back For Murder; You Prove It; Fit To Print; Rule of Three; Alfie; The Reluctant Peer; Hostile Witness; Every Other Evening; Return Ticket; Arsenic and Old Lace; Justice Is A Woman; As You Like It; Oh Clarence!; On A Foggy Day; The Jockey Club Stakes; Move Over Mrs Markham; Lover; Cockie; Double Edge; A Murder is Announced; The Family Reunion; Cards On The Table; in 1971 acquired Volcano Productions Ltd., whose productions include No Sex Please, We're British; The Mating Game; Lloyd George Knew My Father; At The End Of The Day; Touch Of Spring; Betzi; operated repertory at Royal Artillery Theatre, Woolwich, 1951, and at Prince of Wales Theatre, Cardiff, 1956; in 1958, took over a long lease of the Ambassadors Theatre; bought the Duchess Theatre, 1961, and sold it in 1968; acquired a long lease of the St Martin's Theatre, 1968; bought the Vaudeville Theatre, 1969, and sold it in 1983; bought the Duke of York's Theatre, 1976 and sold it in 1979 to Capital Radio on condition that it remained a live theatre in perpetuity; has produced more than 1500 programmes for Radio Luxembourg; an original Dir, Yorkshire Television; Mem. consortium awarded London Gen. Radio Station by IBA, which became Capital Radio, 1973. Vice-President: Actors' Benevolent Fund, 1972–; Royal General Theatrical Fund Assoc., 1985–; Mem. Bd, SOLT (formerly Mem. Exec. Council, SWET), 1954– (Pres. 1961–62 and 1967–69, Vice Pres., 1988–93); Mem. Council, Theatrical Management Assoc., 1958–64; Pres., Stage Golfing Soc., 1963; Pres., Stage Cricket Club, 1956–65. Life Mem., Dogs Home Battersea Assoc., 1988. Governor, Christ's Hosp. Silver Heart award, Variety Club of GB, 1955. *Publications:* The Mousetrap Man (autobiog.), 1972; Scales of Justice (play), 1978. *Recreations:* cricket, chess, bridge, photography, music of George Gershwin, telephoning, collecting wills. *Address:* Monkswell, Canons Close, The Bishops Avenue, N2 0BH. *Clubs:* MCC; Highgate Golf.

SAUNDERS, Peter Gordon; Partner, Advanced Press Training, since 1991; *b* 1 July 1940; *s* of Gordon and Winifred Saunders; *m* 1964, Teresa Geraldine Metcalf; two *d. Educ:* Newport High Sch. for Boys, Gwent; London Sch. of Econs and Pol Science (BScEcon 1961). Reporter, Gloucestershire Echo, 1961–63; Sports Reporter, Sunderland Echo, 1963–64; Sub-Editor: Yorkshire Post, 1964; The Birmingham Post, 1964–69; Lectr in Journalism, Cardiff Coll. of Commerce, 1969–70; The Birmingham Post, 1971–90: successively Dep. Chief Sub-Editor, Chief Sub-Editor, Asst Editor, Exec. Editor; Editor, 1986–90. *Recreations:* Rugby Union, reading, rhythm and blues, golf. *Address:* Well Cottage, West Street, Kingham, Oxon OX7 6YG. *T:* Kingham (01608) 659010.

SAUNDERS, Raymond; Secretary, British Museum (Natural History), 1976–87; *b* 24 July 1933; *s* of late Herbert Charles Saunders and Doris May (*née* Kirkham-Jones); *m* 1959, Shirley Marion (*née* Stringer); two *s. Educ:* Poole Grammar Sch. WO, 1950; Air Min., 1956; Min. of Land and Natural Resources, 1966; Land Commn, 1967; Treasury, 1968; CSD, 1969. *Recreations:* reading biographies, gardening, sport (now as spectator). *Address:* The Old World Tea Gardens, High Street, Godshill, Isle of Wight PO38 3HZ.

SAUNDERS, Richard, FRICS; Partnership Director, Christ's Hospital, since 1993; *b* 4 July 1937; *s* of late Edward E. Saunders and Betty Saunders; *m* 1st, 1961, Suzannah Rhodes-Cooke (marr. diss.); one *s*; 2nd, 1970, Alison Fiddes. *Educ:* St Edmund's Sch., Hindhead; Uppingham. FRICS 1965. National Service, commnd The Life Guards, 1958–60. Jun. Partner, Richard Ellis, Chartered Surveyors, 1966–69; formed Richard Saunders & Partners, 1969; Baker Harris Saunders, 1977; Chm., Baker Harris Saunders Group, 1986–92; Director: Herring Baker Harris, 1992–93; (non-exec.) Herring Baker Harris Gp, 1992–93. Chm., City Br., RICS, 1979–80; Pres., Associated Owners of City Properties, 1985–87; Member: Council, British Property Fedn, 1974–90 (Hon. Treas., 1974–85); Bd, Gen. Practice Finance Corp., 1984–89. Chairman: Barbican Residential Cttee, 1979–81; Barbican Centre Cttee, 1983–86; Metropolitan Public Gardens Assoc., 1984–90; Governor: Bridewell Royal Hosp. and King Edward's Sch., Witley, 1976–93; St Edmund's Sch., Hindhead, 1979–93 (Chm., 1979–87); (also Almoner), Christ's Hosp., 1980–93; Royal Star and Garter Home, 1984–. Mem., Court of Common Council, Corp. of London, 1975–; Deputy for Ward of Candlewick, 1983–; Liveryman: Clothworkers Co., 1960– (Warden, 1989); Co. of Chartered Surveyors, 1979–93; Church Warden, St Lawrence Jewry-by-Guildhall, 1984–; Sheriff, City of London, 1987–88. *Recreations:* instant gardening, music, golf, tennis. *Address:* 13 Caroline Place, W2 4AW. *T:* 0171–600 5052; The Old Rectory, Bagendon, Cirencester, Glos GL7 7DU. *Clubs:* City Livery, MCC.

SAUNDERS, Prof. Wilfred Leonard, CBE 1982; FLA; Director, University of Sheffield Postgraduate School of Librarianship and Information Science, 1963–82, now Professor Emeritus; *b* 18 April 1920; *s* of Leonard and Annie Saunders; *m* 1946, Joan Mary Rider, *er d* of late Major W. E. Rider; two *s. Educ:* King Edward's Grammar Sch. for Boys, Camp Hill, Birmingham; Fitzwilliam House, Univ. of Cambridge (MA). FLA 1952. Served War: France, 1940; N Africa, 1942–43; Italy, 1943–46; Captain Royal Signals. Library Asst, Birmingham Reference Library, 1936–39; Dep. Lib., Inst. of Bankers, 1948–49; Lib., Univ. of Birmingham Inst. of Educn, 1949–56; Dep. Lib., Univ. of Sheffield, 1956–63; 12 months' secondment to UNESCO as Expert in Educnl Documentation, Uganda, 1962; Univ. of Sheffield: Prof. of Librarianship and Inf. Science, 1968; Dean, Faculty of Educnl Studies, 1974–77. Visiting Professor: Pittsburgh Univ. Grad. Sch. of Library and Inf. Sciences, 1968; UCLA, 1985; Commonwealth Vis. Fellow, Australia, 1969; (1st) Elsie O. and Philip Sang Internat. Lectr, Rosary Grad. Sch. of Library Science, USA, 1974. UK Rep., Internat. Fedn for Documentation/Training of Documentalists Cttee, 1966–70; Hon. Consultant, E Africa Sch. of Librarianship, Makerere Univ., 1967–73; overseas consultancy and adv. missions. Mem. Council, Library Assoc., 1979–83 (Pres. 1980); Member: Council, ASLIB, 1965–71, 1972–78; British Council, 1970– (Mem., Libraries Adv. Panel, 1970–87, Chm. 1975–81); Bd of Librarianship, CNAA, 1966–79; Library Adv. Council (England), 1970–73; Adv. Cttee, British Library Ref. Div., 1975–80; *ad hoc* Cttee on Educn and Trng (Gen. Inf. Prog.), UNESCO, 1978–85; Adv. Cttee, British Library R&D Dept, 1980–88; British Library Adv. Council, 1981–84; Adv. Council on Public Records, 1986–91; Chairman: Jt Consultative Cttee of Library Assoc., Aslib, SCONUL, Soc. of Archivists and IInfSc, 1980–81; Library and Information Services Council (formerly Library Adv. Council for Eng.), 1981–84. Hon. FIInfSc 1977; Hon. FCP 1983. Hon. LittD Sheffield, 1989. *Publications:* (ed) The Provision and Use of Library and Documentation Services, 1966; (ed) Librarianship in Britain Today, 1967; (with H. Schur and Lisbeth J. Pargeter) Education and Training for Scientific and Technological Library and Information Work, 1968; (ed) University and Research Library Studies, 1968; (with W. J. Hutchins and Lisbeth J. Pargeter) The Language Barrier: a study in depth of the place of foreign language materials in the research activity of an academic community, 1971; (ed) British Librarianship Today, 1977; (with E. M. Broome) The Library and Information Services of the British Council, 1977; Guidelines for Curriculum Development in Information Studies, 1978; Professional Education for Library and Information Work in the Socialist Republic of Macedonia, 1982; Post-graduate Training for Information Specialists (Venezuela), 1984; An Evaluation of Education for Librarianship in New Zealand, 1987; Towards a Unified Professional Organization for Library and Information Science and Services, 1989; Dunkirk Diary of a Very Young Soldier (autobiog.), 1989; jl articles and res. reports. *Recreations:* gardening, walking, listening to music, book collecting. *Address:* 15 Princess Drive, Sawston, Cambridge CB2 4DL.

SAUNDERS WATSON, Comdr (Leslie) Michael (Macdonald), CBE 1993; RN (retired); DL; Chairman: British Library Board, 1990–93; Kettering General Hospital NHS Trust, since 1993; *b* 9 Oct. 1934; *s* of Captain L. S. Saunders, DSO, RN (retd), and Elizabeth Saunders (*née* Culme-Seymour); *m* 1958, Georgina Elizabeth Laetitia, *d* of Adm. Sir William Davis, GCB, DSO; two *s* one *d. Educ:* Eton; BRNC, Dartmouth. Joined Royal Navy, 1951; specialised in Communications (Jackson Everett Prize); Comdr 1969; retired, 1971, on succession to Rockingham Castle Estate. Pres., Historic Houses Assoc., 1982–88 (Dep. Pres., 1978–82; Chm., Tax and Parly Cttee, 1975–82); Chairman:

Northamptonshire Assoc. Youth Clubs, 1977–91; Heritage Educn Year, 1977; Corby Community Adv. Gp, 1979–86; Ironstone Royalty Owners Assoc., 1979–91; Nat. Curriculum History Wkg Gp, 1988–90; Heritage Educn Trust, 1988–; Modern Records Centre Adv. Cttee, Warwick Univ.; Friends of British Library, 1994–; Vice-Chm., Northamptonshire Small Industries Cttee, 1974–79; Member: British Heritage Cttee, BTA, 1978–88; Northamptonshire Enterprise Agency, 1986–90; Country Landowners' Association: Member: Taxation Cttee, 1975–90; Exec. Cttee, 1977–82, 1987–; Legal and Land Use Cttee, 1982–87; F and GP Cttee, 1994–; Chm., Northamptonshire Branch, 1981–84. Director: Lamport Hall Preservation Trust, 1978–91; English Sinfonia, 1981–. Trustee: Royal Botanic Gdns, Kew, 1983–91 (Chm., Bldgs and Design Cttee, 1985–91); Nat. Heritage Meml Fund, 1987–. Chm., Governors Lodge Park Comprehensive Sch., 1977–82; Trustee, Oakham Sch., 1975–77. FRSA 1986. High Sheriff, 1978–79, DL 1979–, Northamptonshire. Hon. DLitt Warwick, 1991. *Recreations:* sailing, music, gardening. *Address:* Rockingham Castle, Market Harborough, Leicestershire LE16 8TH. *T:* Rockingham (01536) 770240/770326. *Club:* Brooks's (Manager, 1994–).

SAUVAGNARGUES, Jean Victor; Commander, Légion d'Honneur, Croix de Guerre avec palme (1939–45); Hon. GCMG 1976; Commander of the National Order of Merit; French Ambassador; former Foreign Minister; *b* Paris, 2 April 1915; *s* of Edmond Sauvagnargues and Alice Caplan; *m* 1948, Lise Marie L'Evesque; two *s* two *d*. *Educ:* Higher Normal Sch.; Dip., Political Science Sch.; Univ. (German) (Agrégé). Attaché, Embassy, Bucharest, 1941. Served War with Free French Forces, 1943 (Army, June 1944–May 1945). Cabinet of: the High Commn, Beirut, 1943; M Massigli, 1944; Gen. de Gaulle, 1945–46; Specialist on German questions, Quai d'Orsay, 1947–55; Cabinet of M Pinay, 1955. In negotiations about the Saar, Jan.–June 1956; Ambassador to Ethiopia, 1956–60; Director, African and Middle-Eastern Affairs, Min. of Foreign Affairs, 1960–62; Ambassador to: Tunisia, 1962–70; the Federal Republic of Germany, Bonn, 1970–74; Minister for Foreign Affairs, France, 1974–76; Ambassadeur de France, 1976; Ambassador to UK, 1977–81. *Address:* 14 avenue Pierre 1er de Serbie, 75116 Paris, France.

SAUZIER, Sir (André) Guy, Kt 1973; CBE 1959; ED; retired General Overseas Representative of Mauritius Chamber of Agriculture, 1959–79; Minister Plenipotentiary, Mauritius Mission to EEC, 1972–79; *b* 20 Oct. 1910; *s* of J. Adrien Sauzier, Mauritius; *m* 1936, Thérèse, *d* of Henri Mallac; six *s* two *d*. *Educ:* Royal Coll., Mauritius. Served War of 1939–45; late Major, Mauritius TF. A nominated Member of the Legislative Council, Mauritius, 1949–57; Member, Mauritius Political Delegn to the UK, 1955; Minister of Works and Communications, 1957–59. Represented Mauritius at the Coronation, 1953. *Address:* 15 Marloes Road, W8 6LQ.

SAVA, George, (George Alexis Milkomanovich Milkomane); Author and Consulting Surgeon; *b* 15 Oct. 1903; *s* of Col Ivan Alexandrovitch and Countess Maria Ignatiev; *nephew* of Prince Alexander Milkomanovich Milkomane; *m* 1939, Jannette Hollingdale; two *s* two *d*; one *s* by Melanie Lowy. *Educ:* Public Schools in Bulgaria and Russia. Entered Russian Imperial Naval Academy in 1913; after the Revolution studied in various medical schools, Univ. of Paris, Florence, Rome, Munich, Berlin and Bonn; domiciled in this country since 1932; further medical education at Manchester, Glasgow and Edinburgh; naturalised British subject in 1938; Research scholarships in medicine and surgery, University of Rome, Libero Docente (Professorship) of Univ. of Rome, 1954. Grand Chev. of the Crown of Bulgaria; Commendatore dell' Ordine al Merito Della Repubblica Italiana, 1961. *Publications: autobiog. medical:* The Healing Knife, 1937; Beauty from the Surgeon's Knife, 1938; A Surgeon's Destiny, 1939; Donkey's Serenade, 1940; Twice the Clock Round, 1941; A Ring at the Door, 1941; Surgeon's Symphony, 1944; They come by Appointment, 1946; The Knife Heals Again, 1948; The Way of a Surgeon, 1949; Strange Cases, 1950; A Doctor's Odyssey, 1951; Patients' Progress, 1952; A Surgeon Remembers, 1953; Surgeon Under Capricorn, 1954; The Lure of Surgery, 1955; A Surgeon at Large, 1957; Surgery and Crime, 1957; All this and Surgery too, 1958; Surgery Holds the Door, 1960; A Surgeon in Rome, 1961; A Surgeon in California, 1962; Appointments in Rome, 1963; A Surgeon in New Zealand, 1964; A Surgeon in Cyprus, 1965; A Surgeon in Australia, 1966; Sex, Surgery, People, 1967; The Gates of Heaven are Narrow, 1968; Bitter-Sweet Surgery, 1969; One Russian's Story, 1970; A Stranger in Harley Street, 1970; A Surgeon and his Knife, 1978; Living with your Psoriasis (essays), 1978; *political and historical books:* Rasputin Speaks, 1941; Valley of Forgotten People, 1942; The Chetniks, 1943; School for War, 1943; They Stayed in London, 1943; Russia Triumphant, 1944; A Tale of Ten Cities, 1944; War Without Guns, 1944; Caught by Revolution, 1952; *novels:* Land Fit for Heroes, 1945; Link of Two Hearts, 1945; Gissy, 1946; Call it Life, 1946; Boy in Samarkand, 1950; Flight from the Palace, 1953; Pursuit in the Desert, 1955; The Emperor Story, 1959; Punishment Deferred, 1966, Man Without Label, 1967; Alias Dr Holtzman, 1968; City of Cain, 1969, The Imperfect Surgeon, 1969; Nothing Sacred, 1970; Of Guilt Possessed, 1970; A Skeleton for My Mate, 1971; The Beloved Nemesis, 1971; On the Wings of Angels, 1972; The Sins of Andrea, 1972; Tell Your Grief Softly, 1972; Cocaine for Breakfast, 1973; Return from the Valley, 1973; Sheilah of Buckleigh Manor, 1974; Every Sweet Hath Its Sour, 1974; The Way of the Healing Knife, 1976; Mary Mary Quite Contrary, 1977; Crusader's Clinic, 1977; Pretty Polly, 1977; No Man is Perfect, 1978; A Stranger in his Skull, 1979; Secret Surgeon, 1979; Crimson Eclipse, 1980; Innocence on Trial, 1981; The Price of Prejudice, 1982; The Killer Microbes, 1982; Betrayal in Style, 1983; Double Identity, 1984; A Smile Through Tears, 1985; Bill of Indictment, 1986; Rose By Any Other Name, 1987; The Roses Bloom Again, 1988; also wrote numerous novels as George Borodin. *Recreations:* tennis, golf, riding, aviation. *Address:* c/o A. P. Watt Ltd, 20 John Street, WC1N 2DL.

SAVAGE, Sir Ernest (Walter), Kt 1979; FCA; company director, retired; *b* 24 Aug. 1912; *s* of Walter Edwin Savage and Constance Mary Sutton; *m* 1938, Dorothy Winifred Nicholls; one *s* one *d*. *Educ:* Brisbane Grammar School; Scots Coll., Warwick, Qld. In public practice as chartered accountant, 1940–76; retd as Sen. Partner of Coopers & Lybrand, Queensland. Chairman, Bank of Queensland, 1960–84; Director of several other public companies, retired. Institute of Chartered Accountants in Australia: Mem. Queensland State Council, 1951–74 (Chm. three years); Nat. Council, 1961–73; Aust. Pres., 1968–70; elected Life Member, 1978. Hon. Consul for Norway at Brisbane, 1950–76. Chairman: Queensland Govt Cttee of Review of Business Regulations, 1985–86; Public Sector Review Cttee, 1987. Member: Bd of Governors, Cromwell Univ. Coll., 1950–77 (Chm. 1958–67); Faculty of Commerce and Economics, Univ. of Queensland, 1960–67; Bd of Advanced Education, 1978–82 (Finance Cttee, 1974–83); Salvation Army Adv Bd, 1981–92. Trustee, Leukaemia Foundn, 1983–; Chm., Geriatric Medical Foundn, 1986–. Knight 1st class, Order of St Olav (Norway), 1966. *Recreation:* brick and concrete work. *Address:* Forest Place, R42/35b Blunder Road, Durack, Qld 4077, Australia. *T:* (7) 33722669. *Clubs:* Queensland, Brisbane (Brisbane).

SAVAGE, Francis Joseph, LVO 1986; OBE 1989; HM Diplomatic Service; Governor of Montserrat, since 1993; *b* Preston, Lancs, 8 Feb. 1943; *s* of Francis Fitzgerald Savage and late Mona May Savage (*née* Parsons); *m* 1966, Veronica Mary McAleenan; two *s*. *Educ:* Holy Cross Convent, Broadstairs; St Stephen's Sch., Welling, Kent; NW Kent Coll., Dartford. Joined FO, 1961; served in: Cairo, 1967–70; Washington, 1971–73; Vice-Consul, Aden, 1973–74; FCO, 1974–78; Vice-Consul, then Consul (Commercial), Düsseldorf, 1978–82; Consul, Peking, 1982–86; First Sec. (Consular), Lagos, and Consul for Benin, 1987–90; First Sec., FCO, 1990–93; Counsellor, 1993. Member: Catenian Assoc., 1991–; Montserrat Nat. Trust; Montserrat Cricket Assoc. *Recreations:* cricket, travel, golf, meeting people. *Address:* c/o Foreign and Commonwealth Office, SW1A 2AH; Government House, Montserrat, West Indies. *Clubs:* Royal Over-Seas League, Commonwealth Trust; Kent CC; Peking Cricket.

SAVAGE, Thomas Hixon, CBE 1990; Chairman, North American Trust Co.; *b* Belfast, 21 Nov. 1928; *s* of Thomas Hixon Savage and Martha Foy Turkington; *m* 1st, 1950, Annie Gloria Ethel Gilmore (marr. diss. 1975); one *s* two *d*; 2nd, 1976, Evelyn Phyllis Chapman. *Educ:* Belfast High Sch.; Indian Army Officers' Trng Coll.; Univ. of Toronto Dept of Extension (Indust. Management). Chm., ITT Canada, 1990–93; Chm., Abbey Life Insurance Co., Canada; formerly Chief Industrial Engineer: Union Carbide; Dunlop Canada; W. J. Gage Co.; Hallmark Greeting Cards; Electric Reduction Co.; Director: Acklands; Samuel Manu-Tech; Mem. Adv. Bd, Andersen Consulting. Former Mem., Policy Cttee, Business Council on Nat. Issues; Business Co-Chm., Canadian Labour Market & Productivity Center, 1990. Dir, Nat. Retinitis Pigmentosa Eye Res. Foundn, Canada; Chairman: Bd of Govs, West Park Hosp., 1991–94; Adv. Bd, Canadian Inst. of Management, 1971 (Life Mem.); Adv. Bd, Boys' and Girls' Clubs of Canada; NI Partnership in Canada. *Recreation:* golf. *Address:* c/o Hixon-Savage and Associates, 41 Abilene Drive, Islington, Ont M9A 2N1, Canada. *Clubs:* Ontario (Toronto); Lambton Golf and Country (Islington).

SAVAGE, (Thomas) William, CMG 1993; HM Diplomatic Service, retired; Counsellor, Foreign and Commonwealth Office, 1984–93; *b* Knockloughrim, Co. Derry, 21 Nov. 1937; *s* of late Hugh Murray Savage and of Anna Mary Savage (*née* Whyte); *m* 1966, Gloria Jean Matthews; three *d*. *Educ:* Sullivan Upper Sch., Holywood, Co. Down; Queen's Univ., Belfast (BA (Hons), DipEd); LSE. Vice-Pres. and Sec., 1961–64, Pres., 1964–66, Nat. Union of Students; journalist, ITN, 1967; joined Diplomatic Service, 1968; Dar es Salaam, 1970–73; First Sec., FCO, 1973; Counsellor, on loan to Cabinet Office, 1981. *Recreations:* amateur drama, golf, topiary. *Club:* Tanganyika Golfing Society.

SAVAGE, Wendy Diane, FRCOG; Senior Lecturer in Obstetrics and Gynaecology, Royal London Hospital Medical College, since 1977; *b* 12 April 1935; *d* of William George Edwards and Anne (*née* Smith); *m* 1960, Miguel Babatunde Richard Savage (marr. diss. 1973); two *s* two *d*. *Educ:* Croydon High School for Girls; Girton Coll., Cambridge (BA); London Hosp. Med. Coll. (MB BCh); FRCOG 1985 (MRCOG 1971). Res. Fellow, Harvard Univ., 1963–64; MO, Nigeria, 1964–67; Registrar: Surgery and Obst. and Gynaec., Kenya, 1967–69; Obst. and Gynaec., Royal Free Hosp., 1969–71; venereology, abortion work, family planning, Islington, 1971–73; Specialist in obst. and gynaec., family planning and venereology, Gisborne, NZ 1973–76; Lectr, London Hosp., 1976–77. Hon. Vis. Prof., Middx Univ., 1991–Oct. 1996. Contract as Hon. Cons. suspended for alleged incompetence, April 1985 — reinstated by unanimous vote of DHA after exoneration by HM61/112 Enquiry, July 1986. Mem., GMC, 1989–94, 1995–. *Publications:* Hysterectomy, 1982; (with Fran Reader) Coping with Caesarean Section and other difficult births, 1983; A Savage Enquiry — who controls childbirth?, 1986; (jtly) Caesarean Birth in Britain, 1993; papers on abortion, sexually transmitted disease, ultrasound, sex in pregnancy, cervical cytology, medical education. *Recreations:* playing piano duets, reading. *Address:* 19 Vincent Terrace, N1. *T:* 0171–837 7635.

SAVAGE, William; *see* Savage, T. W.

SAVARESE, Signora Fernando; *see* Elvin, Violetta.

SAVERNAKE, Viscount; Thomas James Brudenell-Bruce; *b* 11 Feb. 1982; *s* and *heir* of Earl of Cardigan, *qv*.

SAVILE, family name of **Earl of Mexborough.**

SAVILE, 3rd Baron, *cr* 1888; **George Halifax Lumley-Savile;** DL; JP; *b* 24 Jan. 1919; *s* of 2nd Baron and Esme Grace Virginia (*d* 1958), *d* of J. Wolton; *S* father, 1931. *Educ:* Eton. Served in 1939–45 War in Duke of Wellington's Regiment, and attached Lincolnshire Regiment during the Burma Campaigns. DL W Yorks, 1954. Is Patron of two livings. Owns about 18,000 acres. JP Borough of Dewsbury, 1955. CStJ 1982. *Recreations:* music and shooting. *Heir:* *b* Hon. Henry Leoline Thornhill Lumley-Savile [*b* 2 Oct. 1923; *m* 1st, 1946, Presiley June (marr. diss. 1951), *o d* of Major G. H. E. Inchbald, Halebourne House, Chobham, Surrey; one *s*; 2nd, 1961, Caroline Jeffie (*d* 1970), *o d* of Peter Clive, California, USA, and Elizabeth Clive, 58 Queens' Gate, SW7; 3rd, 1972, Margaret, *widow* of Peter Bruce; three *s* (triplets). Served War of 1939–45, in Grenadier Guards, Italy (wounded)]. *Address:* Gryce Hall, Shelley, Huddersfield HD8 8LP. *T:* Huddersfield (01484) 602774; Walshaw, Hebden Bridge, Yorks HX7 7AX. *T:* Hebden Bridge (01422) 842275. *Clubs:* Brooks's, Sloane.

SAVILE, Sir James (Wilson Vincent), Kt 1990; OBE 1971; TV and radio personality; *b* 31 Oct. 1926. *Educ:* St Anne's, Leeds. Presenter: Radio One Weekly Show, 1969–89; Independent Radio weekly show, 1989–; television: Jim'll Fix It, making dreams come true, No 1 in the ratings every year, 1975–94; Mind How You Go, road safety show; Top of the Pops. Man of many parts but best known as a voluntary helper at Leeds Infirmary, Broadmoor Hospital, and Stoke Mandeville where he raised twelve million pounds to rebuild the National Spinal Injuries Centre. Fellow of Cybernetics, Reading Univ., 1990. Hon. LLD Leeds, 1986. Hon. KCSG (Holy See), 1982; Bronze and Gold medals, SMO, St John of Jerusalem. *Publications:* As It Happens (autobiog.), 1975; Love is an Uphill Thing (autobiog.), 1975; God'll Fix It, 1978. *Recreations:* running, cycling, wrestling. *Address:* National Spinal Injuries Centre, Stoke Mandeville Hospital, Aylesbury, Bucks HP21 8AL. *T:* Aylesbury (01296) 395353. *Club:* Athenæum.

SAVILL, David Malcolm, QC 1969; **His Honour Judge Savill;** a Senior Circuit Judge and Resident Judge, Leeds Combined Court Centre, since 1991 (a Circuit Judge, 1984–91); *b* 18 Sept. 1930; *s* of late Lionel and of Lisbeth Savill; *m* 1955, Mary Arnott (*née* Eadie), JP, *d* of late Lady Hinchcliffe and step *d* of late Hon. Sir (George) Raymond Hinchcliffe; one *s* two *d*. *Educ:* Marlborough Coll.; Clare Coll., Cambridge. 2nd Lieut Grenadier Guards, 1949–50. BA (Hons) Cambridge, 1953. Called to the Bar, Middle Temple, 1954 (Bencher, 1977); Mem., Senate of Inns of Court and the Bar, 1976, 1980–83. A Recorder, 1972–84 (Hon. Recorder, Leeds, 1993); Chancellor: diocese of Bradford, 1976–; diocese of Ripon, 1987–92; Leader, NE Circuit, 1980–83. Chairman: Adv. Cttee on Conscientious Objectors, 1978–91; W Yorks Criminal Justice Liaison Cttee, 1992–. *Recreations:* cricket, golf, gardening. *Address:* The Crown Court, Oxford Place, Leeds LS1 3BG. *Club:* MCC.

SAVILL, Colonel Kenneth Edward, CVO 1976; DSO 1945; DL; Member, HM Bodyguard of Hon. Corps of Gentlemen at Arms, 1955–76 (Lieutenant, 1973–76; Standard Bearer, 1972–73); *b* 8 August 1906; *o s* of Walter Savill, Chilton Manor, Alresford and May, *d* of Major Charles Marriott; *m* 1935, Jacqueline (*d* 1980), *o d* of Brig. John Salusbury Hughes, MC; two *d* (and one *d* decd). *Educ:* Winchester College; RMC Sandhurst.

Commissioned, 12th Royal Lancers, 1926; 1st King's Dragoon Guards, 1936; The Queen's Bays, 1947. Served War of 1939–45, France, 1939–40; N Africa and Italy, 1943–45; Col 1950; retd 1953. High Sheriff of Hampshire, 1961; DL Hampshire, 1965. Col, 1st The Queen's Dragoon Guards, 1964–68. *Address:* Chilton Manor, Alresford, Hants SO24 9TX. *T:* Preston Candover (01256) 389246. *Club:* Cavalry and Guards.

SAVILL, Rosalind Joy, FSA; Director, The Wallace Collection, since 1992; *b* 12 May 1951; *d* of Dr Guy Savill and Lorna (*née* Williams); one *d*. *Educ:* Wycombe Abbey Sch.; Châtelard Sch., sur-Montreux; Univ. of Leeds (BA Hons 1972); Study Centre, London (Dip in Fine and Decorative Arts 1973). Ceramics Dept, V&A Mus., 1973–74; The Wallace Collection: Museum Asst, 1974–78; Asst to Dir, 1978–92. Guest Scholar, J. Paul Getty Mus., 1985. Mem. Council, Attingham Trust, 1980–92. Chm., French Porcelain Soc., 1988–94. FSA 1990; FRSA 1990. Nat. Art Collections Award for Scholarship, 1990. *Publications:* The Wallace Collection Catalogue of Sèvres Porcelain, 3 vols, 1988; (contrib.) Treasure Houses of Britain, 1985; Boughton House, 1992; Versailles: tables royales, 1993; articles in Apollo, Burlington Mag., Antologia di Belle Arti, J. Paul Getty Mus. Jl, Ars Ceramica, Antique Collector. *Recreations:* music, birds, wildlife, gardens. *Address:* The Wallace Collection, Hertford House, Manchester Square, W1M 6BN. *T:* 0171–935 0687.

SAVILLE, Clive Howard; Grade 3, Department for Education and Employment (formerly Department of Education and Science, then Department for Education), since 1987; *b* 7 July 1943; *s* of Rev. Frank Saville and Gracie (*née* Mackie); *m* 1967, Camille Kathleen, *yr d* of late Edmund St C. Burke and Camille (*née* Andrea). *Educ:* Bishop Gore Grammar Sch., Swansea; University Coll., Swansea (BA). Asst Principal, DES, 1965; Private Sec. to Minister for the Arts, 1968–70; Principal, DES, 1970; UGC, 1973–75; Cabinet Office, 1975; Principal Private Sec. to Lord Pres. of the Council and Leader of House of Commons, 1975–77; Asst Sec., DES, 1977. Vis. Associate, Center for Studies in Higher Educn, Univ. of California, Berkeley, 1987. FRSA 1991. *Address:* Department for Education and Employment, Sanctuary Buildings, Great Smith Street, SW1P 3BT. *T:* 0171–925 5000.

SAVILLE, Prof. John; Emeritus Professor of Economic and Social History, University of Hull; *b* 2 April 1916; *o s* of Orestes Stamatopoulos, Volos, Greece, and Edith Vessey (name changed by deed poll to that of step-father, 1937); *m* 1943, Constance Betty Saunders; three *s* one *d*. *Educ:* Royal Liberty Sch.; London Sch. of Economics. 1st Cl. Hons BSc (Econ) 1937. Served War, RA, 1940–46; Chief Scientific Adviser's Div., Min. of Works, 1946–47; Univ. of Hull, 1947–82, Prof. of Economic and Social History, 1972–82. Leverhulme Emeritus Fellow, 1984–86. Mem., British Communist Party, 1934–56; Chm., Oral Hist. Soc., 1976–87; Vice-Chm., and then Chm., Soc. for Study of Labour Hist., 1974–82; Mem. Exec. Cttee and Founder-Mem., Council for Academic Freedom and Democracy, 1971–81, Chm. 1982–89; Chm., Economic and Social Hist. Cttee, SSRC, 1977–79. Trustee, Michael Lipman Trust, 1977–93. Vice-Chm., Friends of the Brynmor Jones Library, Hull Univ., 1988–. *Publications:* Ernest Jones, Chartist, 1952; Rural Depopulation in England and Wales 1851–1951, 1957; 1848, The British State and the Chartist Movement, 1987; The Labour Movement in Britain: a commentary, 1988; The Politics of Continuity: British Foreign Policy and the Labour Government 1945–46, 1993; numerous articles; Co-Editor: (with E. P. Thompson) Reasoner and New Reasoner, 1956–59; (with Asa Briggs) Essays in Labour History, 1960, 1971, 1977; (with Ralph Miliband) Socialist Register (annual, 1964–90); (with Joyce M. Bellamy) Dictionary of Labour Biography, 1972–. *Recreations:* working for socialism, looking at churches. *Address:* 152 Westbourne Avenue, Hull HU5 3HZ. *T:* Hull (01482) 43425.

SAVILLE, Rt. Hon. Sir Mark (Oliver), Kt 1985; PC 1994; **Rt. Hon. Lord Justice Saville;** a Lord Justice of Appeal, since 1994; *b* 20 March 1936; *s* of Kenneth Vivian Saville and Olivia Sarah Frances Gray; *m* 1961, Jill Gray; two *s*. *Educ:* St Paul's Primary Sch., Hastings; Rye Grammar Sch.; Brasenose Coll., Oxford (BA, BCL). Nat. Service, 2nd Lieut Royal Sussex Regt, 1954–56; Oxford Univ., 1956–60 (Vinerian Schol. 1960); called to Bar, Middle Temple, 1962 (Bencher, 1983); QC 1975; Judge of the High Court, QBD, 1985–93. *Recreations:* sailing, flying. *Address:* Royal Courts of Justice, Strand, WC2A 2LL.

SAVORY, Hubert Newman, MA, DPhil Oxon; FSA; Keeper of Archæology, National Museum of Wales, Cardiff, 1956–76; *b* 7 Aug. 1911; *s* of William Charles Newman Savory and Alice Amelia (*née* Minns); *m* 1949, Priscilla Valerie Thirkell; four *s* two *d*. *Educ:* Magdalen College Sch., Oxford; St Edmund Hall, Oxford Univ. BA Oxon 1934 (Lit. Hum. 1st Cl.); DPhil Oxon 1937; Randall MacIver Student in Iberian Archæology, 1936–38. Assistant, 1938, Asst Keeper, 1939, Dept of Archæology, National Museum of Wales. Chm., Royal Commn on Ancient Monuments (Wales), 1979–83 (Mem., 1970–83); Mem., Ancient Monuments Board for Wales, 1957–84; Pres., Cambrian Archæological Assoc., 1975–76; Chm., Glamorgan Gwent Archæological Trust, 1975–84. Conducted excavations of various Welsh megaliths, round barrows, hill-forts, etc. Served War of 1939–45, in Army, 1940–45. *Publications:* Spain and Portugal: The Prehistory of the Iberian Peninsula, 1968; Guide Catalogues of the Early Iron Age Collections, 1976, and the Bronze Age Collections, 1980, National Museum of Wales; (ed) Glamorgan County History, vol. II, 1984; contrib. to: Celtic Art in Ancient Europe, 1976; Hillforts, 1976; Settlement and Society in Wales, 1989; Proc. of Prehistoric Soc.; Archæologia Cambrensis, etc. *Recreations:* walking, gardening, genealogy. *Address:* 31 Lady Mary Road, Cardiff CF2 5NT. *T:* Cardiff (01222) 753106.

SAVOURS, Dale Norman C.; *see* Campbell-Savours.

SAWARD, Rev. Canon Michael John; Treasurer and Canon Residentiary of St Paul's Cathedral, since 1991; *b* 14 May 1932; *s* of late Donald and Lily Saward; *m* 1956, Jackie, *d* of late Col John Atkinson, DSO, OBE, and Eileen Atkinson, MBE; one *s* three *d*. *Educ:* Eltham Coll.; Bristol Univ. (BA Theology). 2nd Lieut, RA, 1950–52, RWAFF (Nat. Service). Deacon 1956, priest 1957; curacies in Croydon, 1956–59, and Edgware, 1959–64; Sec., Liverpool Council of Churches, 1965–67; C of E Radio and Television Officer, 1967–72; Vicar: St Matthew, Fulham, 1972–78; Ealing, 1978–91; Prebendary of St Paul's Cathedral, 1985–91. Mem., General Synod, 1975–95 (Mem., House of Clergy Standing Cttee, 1981–86); a Church Comr, 1978–93 (Member: Redundant Churches Cttee, 1978–81; Houses Cttee, 1981–88; Bd of Govs, 1986–93; Pastoral Cttee, 1988–93); Chairman: C of E Pensions Measure Revision Cttee, 1987–88; Care of Cathedrals (Supplementary Provisions) Measure Revision Cttee, 1992–93; Member: Lambeth Conf., Preparatory Cttee, 1967–68; Archbishops' Council on Evangelism, 1975–78; C of E Evangelical Council, 1976–93; Nat. Partners in Mission Wkg Party, 1979–81; Dioceses Commn, 1981–89; Cttee, CPAS, 1992–. Sec., Gen. Synod Broadcasting Commn, 1970–73. Trustee: Church Urban Fund, 1989–90; Christian Evidence Soc., 1992–. Mem. Council, Trinity Theol Coll., 1974–78; Gov., St Paul's Cathedral Choir Sch., 1991–. Journalist, broadcaster, lectr, reviewer. Winston Churchill Travelling Fellowship, 1984. Freeman, City of London, 1993–. Words Editor, Hymns for Today's Church, 1974–82. Prizewinner: Southern TV Hymn for Britain competition, 1966; BBC-TV Songs of Praise new hymn competition, 1985. *Publications:* Leisure, 1963 (Norwegian edn 1971); Christian Youth Groups, 1965; Cracking the God-Code, 1974, 3rd edn 1989 (Chinese and Swedish edns 1976); And So To Bed?, 1975; God's Friends, 1978; All Change, 1983; Evangelicals on the Move, 1987. *Recreations:* reading (esp. military history), music, cricket, travel, food and drink, writing hymns. *Address:* 6 Amen Court, EC4M 7BU. *T:* 0171–248 8572. *Clubs:* Athenæum, Nikaean.

SAWDY, Peter Bryan; Director: Griffin International Ltd, since 1988; Yule Catto PLC, since 1990; Lazard Birla Indian Investment Fund plc, since 1994; *b* 17 Sept. 1931; *s* of Alfred Eustace Leon Sawdy and Beatrice Sawdy; *m* 1st, 1955, Anne Stonor (marr. diss. 1989; she *d* 1995); two *d*; 2nd, 1989, Judith Mary Bowen. *Educ:* Ampleforth Coll.; Regent St Polytechnic; LSE. Trainee, Brooke Bond Ltd, 1952; Chm., Brooke Bond Ceylon Ltd, 1962–65; Director: Brooke Bond Ltd, 1965–68; Brooke Bond Liebig Ltd, 1968–75; Brooke Bond Group: Man. Dir, 1975–77; Gp Chief Exec., 1977–81; Dep. Chm. and Gp Chief Exec., 1981–85. Chm., Costain Gp, 1990–93. *Recreations:* golf, opera, collecting modern first editions. *Address:* 13 Clarendon Street, SW1V 2EN. *Clubs:* Naval and Military; Royal Ashdown Golf (Forest Row), Royal Mid-Surrey Golf (Richmond).

SAWERS, David Richard Hall; writer; *b* 23 April 1931; *s* of late Edward and Madeline Sawers; unmarried. *Educ:* Westminster Sch.; Christ Church, Oxford (MA). Research Asst to Prof. J. Jewkes, Oxford Univ., 1954–58; Journalist, The Economist, 1959–64; Vis. Fellow, Princeton Univ., 1964–65; Econ. Adviser, Min. of Aviation and of Technology, 1966–68; Sen. Econ. Adviser, Min. of Technology, Aviation Supply, and DTI, 1968–72; Under-Sec., Depts of Industry, Trade and Prices and Consumer Protection, 1972–76; Under-Sec., Depts of Environment and Transport, 1976–83; Principal Res. Fellow, Technical Change Centre, 1984–86. *Publications:* (with John Jewkes and Richard Stillerman) The Sources of Invention, 1958; (with Ronald Miller) The Technical Development of Modern Aviation, 1968; Competition in the Air, 1987; Should the Taxpayer Support the Arts, 1993; articles in daily press and journals. *Recreations:* listening to music, looking at pictures, gardening. *Address:* 10 Seaview Avenue, Angmering-on-Sea, Littlehampton BN16 1PP. *T:* Worthing (01903) 785571.

SAWERS, Robert John; HM Diplomatic Service; Counsellor, Washington, from July 1996; *b* 26 July 1955; *s* of Colin Simon Hawkesley Sawers and Daphne Anne Sawers; *m* 1981, Avril Helen Shelley Lamb; two *s* one *d*. *Educ:* Beechen Cliff Sch., Bath; Univ. of Nottingham (BSc Hons Physics and Philosophy). FCO 1977; served Sana'a, 1980; Damascus, 1982; FCO, 1984; Private Sec. to Minister of State, FCO, 1986; Pretoria/Cape Town, 1988; Head, European Community Dept (Presidency), 1991; Principal Private Sec. to Sec. of State for Foreign and Commonwealth Affairs, 1993–95; Career Develt Attachment, Harvard Univ., 1995–96. *Recreations:* mountaineering, tennis. *Address:* c/o Foreign and Commonwealth Office, SW1A 2AH. *T:* 0171–270 3000.

SAWKO, Prof. Felicjan, DSc; Professor of Civil Engineering and Head of Department at the Sultan Qaboos University, Oman, since 1986; *b* 17 May 1937; *s* of Czeslaw Sawko and Franciszka (*née* Nawrot); *m* 1960, Genowefa Stefania (*née* Bak); four *s* one *d*. *Educ:* Leeds Univ. (BSc Civil Engrg, 1958; MSc 1960; DSc 1973). Engr, Rendel Palmer & Tritton, London, 1959–62; Lectr, 1962–67, Reader, 1967, Leeds University; Prof. of Civil Engrg, Liverpool Univ., 1967–86. Henry Adams Award, IStructE, 1980. *Publications:* (ed) Developments in Prestressed Concrete, Vols 1 and 2, 1968; (with Cope and Tickell) Numerical Methods for Civil Engineers, 1981; some 70 papers on computer methods and structural masonry. *Recreations:* travel, bridge, numismatics. *Address:* 9 Harthill Road, Liverpool L18 6HU. *T:* 0151–724 2726; PO Box 32483, Al-Khod, Oman.

SAWYER, Anthony Charles; Director Outfield, and Commissioner, HM Customs and Excise, since 1991; *b* 3 Aug. 1939; *s* of Charles Bertram and Elizabeth Sawyer; *m* 1962, Kathleen Josephine McGill; two *s* one *d*. *Educ:* Surrey; Munster, W Germany. Nat. Service, RA, 1960. Underwriter, Northern Assurance Group, 1962; Customs and Excise, 1964–: Collector, Edinburgh, 1984; Dep. Dir, Outfield, 1988. *Recreations:* sport, theatre, music. *Address:* HM Customs and Excise, New King's Beam House, 22 Upper Ground, SE1 9PJ. *T:* 0171–865 5017. *Clubs:* National Liberal; Royal Scots (Edinburgh).

SAWYER, John Stanley, MA; FRS 1962; Director of Research, Meteorological Office, 1965–76; *b* 19 June 1916; *s* of late Arthur Stanley Sawyer and Emily Florence Sawyer (*née* Frost); *m* 1951, Betty Vera Beeching (*née* Tooke), *widow*; one *d*. *Educ:* Latymer Upper Sch., Hammersmith; Jesus Coll., Cambridge. Entered Meteorological Office, 1937. Mem., NERC, 1975–81. Pres., Commn for Atmospheric Sciences, World Meteorological Organisation, 1968–73 (IMO Prize, 1973); Pres., Royal Meteorological Soc., 1963–65 (Hugh Robert Mill Medal 1956, Buchan Prize 1962, Symons Medal 1971). *Publications:* Ways of the Weather, 1958; scientific papers largely in Quart. Jl Roy. Met. Soc. *Address:* 16 Tanfield Park, Wickham, Hants PO17 5NP. *T:* Wickham (01329) 833409.

SAXBEE, Rt. Rev. John Charles; *see* Ludlow, Bishop Suffragan of.

SAXON, Prof. David Harold, DPhil, DSc; CPhys, FInstP; FRSE; Kelvin Professor of Physics, University of Glasgow, since 1990; *b* 27 Oct. 1945; *s* of Rev. Canon Eric Saxon and Ruth (*née* Higginbottom); *m* 1968, Margaret Flitcroft; one *s* one *d*. *Educ:* Manchester Grammar Sch.; Balliol Coll., Oxford (MA, DSc); Jesus Coll., Oxford (DPhil). CPhys 1985; FInstP 1985; FRSE 1993. Jun. Res. Fellow, Jesus Coll., Oxford, 1968–70; Res. Officer, Nuclear Physics Dept, Oxford, 1969–70; Res. Associate, Columbia Univ., NY, 1970–73; Rutherford Appleton Laboratory, Oxford: Res. Associate, 1974–75; SSO, 1975–76; PSO, 1976–89; Grade 6, 1989–90. Member, SERC Committees: Particle Physics Experiment Selection Panel, 1989–92; Particle Physics, 1991–94 (Chm., 1992–94); Nuclear Physics Bd, 1992–93; Particles, Space & Astronomy Bd, 1993–94. Chairman: PPARC Particle Physics Cttee, 1994–; 27th Internat. Conf. on High Energy Physics, 1994. Member: CERN Scientific Policy Cttee, Geneva, 1993–; Physics Res. Cttee, Deutsches Elektronen Synchrotron, Hamburg, 1993–. *Recreation:* staying close to home. *Address:* Department of Physics and Astronomy, University of Glasgow, Glasgow G12 8QQ. *T:* 0141–330 4673.

SAXON, David Stephen, PhD; Hon. Chairman of the Corporation, Massachusetts Institute of Technology, since 1990 (Chairman, 1983–90); *b* 8 Feb. 1920; *s* of Ivan Saxon and Rebecca Moss; *m* 1940, Shirley Goodman; six *d*. *Educ:* Massachusetts Institute of Technology (BS 1941; PhD 1944). Massachusetts Institute of Technology: Res. physicist, Radiation Lab., 1943–46; Philips Labs, 1946–47. Univ. of California at Los Angeles: Mem. of Faculty, 1947–75; Prof. of Physics, 1958–75; Chm. of Dept, 1963–66; Dean of Physical Sciences, 1966–68; Vice-Chancellor, 1968–75; Provost, Univ. of California, 1974–75, Pres., 1975–83. Guggenheim Fellow, 1956–57 and 1961–62; Fulbright grant, 1961–62. Vis. Prof., Univ. of Paris, Orsay, France, 1961–62; Vis. scientist, Centre d'Etudes Nucléaires, France, 1968–69; Vis. Research Fellow, Merton Coll., Oxford, 1981; consultant to research organisations, 1948–. Special research into theoretical physics: nuclear physics, quantum mechanics, electromagnetic theory and scattering theory. Dir, Eastman Kodak Co., 1983–90. Fellow: Amer. Phys. Soc.; Amer. Acad. of Arts and Scis; Member: Amer. Assoc. Physics Teachers; Amer. Inst. Physics; Amer. Assoc. for the Advancement of Science; Technical Adv. Council for Ford Motor Co., 1979–; Corp. of MIT, 1977–; Dir, Houghton Mifflin Co., 1984–90. Recipient of several honorary degrees. Member: Phi Beta Kappa; Sigma Pi Sigma; Sigma Xi. Royal Order of the Northern Star

(Nordstjärnan), 1979. *Publications:* Elementary Quantum Mechanics, 1968; The Nuclear Independent Particle Model (with A. E. S. Green and T. Sawada), 1968; Discontinuities in Wave Guides (with Julian Schwinger), 1968; Physics for the Liberal Arts Student (with William B. Fretter), 1971. *Address:* University of California, Los Angeles, Department of Physics, Knudsen Hall Room 2130J, 405 Hilgard Avenue, Los Angeles, CA 90024-1547, USA.

SAXTON, Robert Louis Alfred, DMus; Head of Composition, Guildhall School of Music and Drama, since 1990; *b* 8 Oct. 1953; *s* of Jean Augusta Saxton (*née* Infield) and Ian Sanders Saxton. *Educ:* Bryanston Sch.; St Catharine's Coll., Cambridge (MA); Worcester Coll., Oxford (BMus; DMus 1992). FGSM 1987. Lectr, Bristol Univ., 1984–85; Fulbright Arts award, 1985; Vis. Fellow, Princeton Univ., 1986. Finalist, BBC Young Composers' Comp., 1973; First Prize, Gaudeamus Music Fest., Holland, 1975; early works at ISCM Fest., Bonn, 1977, Royan Fest., 1977; later works, majority recorded, include: The Ring of Eternity, 1983; Concerto for Orchestra, 1984; The Circles of Light, 1985; The Child of Light (carol), 1985; The Sentinel of the Rainbow, 1984; Viola Concerto, 1986; Night Dance, 1986–87; I Will Awake the Dawn, 1987; In the Beginning, 1987; Elijah's Violin, 1988; Chacony, 1988; Music to celebrate the Resurrection of Christ, 1988; Violin Concerto, Leeds Fest., 1990; Caritas (opera with libretto by Arnold Wesker), 1990–91; Paraphrase on Mozart's Idomeneo, 1991; At the Round Earth's Imagined Corners (anthem), 1992; 'Cello Concerto, 1992; Psalm—a song of ascents, 1992; O Sing unto the Lord a new song (anthem), 1993; Fantazia, 1993; Canticum Luminis, 1994; A Yardstick to the Stars, 1994; Ring, Time, 1994; works commissioned by: Fires of London, London Sinfonietta, BBC, LSO, ECO, Aldeburgh Fest., Cheltenham Fest., Opera North, LPO, RPO, City of London Fest./St Paul's Cathedral, Leeds Fest. *Publications:* all compositions; contribs TLS, Musical Times, etc. *Recreations:* reading, theatre, cinema, studying mathematics, watching cricket. *Address:* c/o Chester Music, 8–9 Frith Street, W1V 5TZ. *T:* 0171–434 0066.

SAY, Rt. Rev. Richard David, KCVO 1988; DD (Lambeth) 1961; an Assistant Bishop, diocese of Canterbury, since 1988; *b* 4 Oct. 1914; *s* of Commander Richard Say, OBE, RNVR, and Kathleen Mary (*née* Wildy); *m* 1943, Irene Frances (OBE 1980, JP 1960), *e d* of Seaburne and Frances Rayner, Exeter; one *s* two *d* (and one *s* decd). *Educ:* University Coll. Sch.; Christ's College, Cambridge (MA); Ridley Hall, Cambridge. Ordained deacon, 1939; priest, 1940. Curate of Croydon Parish Church, 1939–43; Curate of St Martin-in-the-Fields, London, 1943–50; Asst Sec. Church of England Youth Council, 1942–44; Gen. Sec., 1944–47; Gen. Sec. British Council of Churches, 1947–55; Church of England delegate to World Council of Churches, 1948, 1954 and 1961. Select Preacher, University of Cambridge, 1954 and University of Oxford, 1963; Rector of Bishop's Hatfield, 1955–61; Hon. Canon of St Albans, 1957–61; Bishop of Rochester, 1961–88; High Almoner to HM the Queen, 1970–88. Domestic Chaplain to Marquess of Salisbury and Chaplain of Welfield Hospital, 1955–61; Hon. Chaplain of The Pilgrims, 1968–. Entered House of Lords, 1969. Chaplain and Sub-Prelate, Order of St John, 1961. Mem., Court of Ecclesiastical Causes Reserved, 1984–93. Dep. Pro-Chancellor, 1977–83, Pro-Chancellor, 1983–93, Kent Univ.; Governor, University Coll. Sch., 1980–88. A Vice-Pres., UNA of GB, 1986–; Pres., Friends of Kent Churches, 1988–. Chm., Age Concern, England, 1986–89 (Vice Pres., 1990–94; Patron, 1994–). Freeman of City of London, 1953; Hon. Freeman: of Tonbridge and Malling, 1987; of Rochester upon Medway, 1988. Hon. Member: Smeatonian Soc., 1977; Instn of Royal Engineers, 1987. Hon. DCL Kent, 1987. *Recreations:* walking, travel. *Address:* 23 Chequers Park, Wye, Ashford, Kent TN25 5BB. *T:* Wye (01233) 812720. *Club:* United Oxford & Cambridge University.

SAYCE, Roy Beavan, FRICS, FAAV; MRAC; Director, RPS Group (formerly Rural Planning Services) PLC, Didcot, 1980–88; *b* 19 July 1920; *s* of Roger Sayce, BScAgric, NDA, and Lilian Irene Sayce; *m* 1949, Barbara Sarah (*née* Leverton) (marr. diss. 1990); two *s*. *Educ:* Culford, Royal Agricultural Coll. (MRAC; Silver Medal 1948). FRICS 1949; FAAV 1978. Univ. of London, 1938–40. Served War, Intell., RAFVR, 1940–46. Agricultural Land Service: Asst Land Comr, Chelmsford, 1949–50; Sen. Asst Land Comr, Norwich, 1950–63; Divl Land Comr, Oxford, 1963–71; Reg. Surveyor, Land Service, Agric. Develt and Adv. Service, Bristol, 1971–76; Chief Surveyor, Land Service, Agric. Develt and Adv. Service, MAFF, 1977–80. Royal Instn of Chartered Surveyors: Mem., Gen. and Divl Councils, 1970–80; Divl Pres., Land Agency and Agric. Div., 1973–74. Chm., Farm Buildings Information Centre, 1980–85. Governor, Royal Agric. Coll., Cirencester, 1975–88. Hon. Mem., CAAV, 1978. *Publications:* Farm Buildings, 1966; (contrib.) Walmsley's Rural Estate Management, 1969; The History of the Royal Agricultural College, 1992; contrib. professional jls. *Recreations:* golf, historical writing. *Address:* 13 Haywards Close, Wantage, Oxon OX12 7AT. *T:* Wantage (01235) 766704. *Clubs:* Farmers', Civil Service.

SAYE AND SELE, 21st Baron *cr* 1447 and 1603; **Nathaniel Thomas Allen Fiennes;** DL; *b* 22 September 1920; *s* of Ivo Murray Twisleton-Wykeham-Fiennes, 20th Baron Saye and Sele, OBE, MC, and Hersey Cecilia Hester, *d* of late Captain Sir Thomas Dacres Butler, KCVO; *S* father, 1968; *m* 1958, Mariette Helena, *d* of Maj.-Gen. Sir Guy Salisbury-Jones, GCVO, CMG, CBE, MC; three *s* one *d* (and one *s* decd). *Educ:* Eton; New College, Oxford. Served with Rifle Brigade, 1941–49 (despatches twice). Chartered Surveyor. Partner in firm of Laws and Fiennes. Regl Dir, Lloyds Bank, 1982–90. Trustee, Ernest Cook Trust, 1960–95 (Chm. Trustees, 1965–92). DL Oxfordshire, 1979. Fellow, Winchester Coll., 1967–83. *Heir: s* Hon. Richard Ingel Fiennes, *b* 19 August 1959. *Address:* Broughton Castle, Banbury, Oxon OX15 5EB. *T:* Banbury (01295) 262624.

See also Very Rev. Hon. O. W. Fiennes.

SAYEED, Dr (Abulfatah) Akram, OBE 1976; FRCPE; MRCGP; General Medical Practitioner in Leicester, since 1963; Hon. Adviser in UK to Ministry of Health, Government of Bangladesh, since 1991; Chairman, Overseas Doctors' Association in UK, 1993–Sept. 1996; *b* Bangladesh, 23 Nov. 1935; *s* of late Mokhles Ahmed, school teacher; registered British; *m* 1959, Hosne-ara Ali, *d* of M. S. Ali; two *s* one *d*. *Educ:* St Joseph's Sch., Khulna; Dacca Univ. MB, BS 1958. FRSM 1981; FODA 1985; FRIPHH 1991; FRSH 1991; FCPS (Bangladesh) 1991. Editor, Dacca Med. Coll. Jl and Magazines, 1957–58; Lit. Sec., Students Union. Went to USA, 1960; resident in Britain from 1961. Mem. Staff, Leicester Royal Infirmary, 1964–89; Member: Leics Local Medical Cttee, 1977–; Leics Family Practitioner Cttee, 1982–87; Leics Med. Adv. and Audit Gp. Member: DHSS Working Party on Asian Health Gp, 1979; DHSS Adv. Council on Violence Against NHS Staff, 1986–89; Home Office Statutory Adv. Council on Community and Race Relations, 1983–88; Health Care Planning Team, Leics HA, 1984–86; Policy Planning (formerly Unit Management) Team, Leics Central Unit, 1986–; Gen. Optical Council. British Medical Association: Mem., 1979–; Mem. Gen. Med. Services Cttee, 1993–; Pres., Leics Div., 1993–94; Fellow, 1995. Co-founder, Nat. Fedn of Pakistani Assocs in GB, 1963; Adviser, NCCI, 1965–68; Founder Member: Leicester Council for Community Relations, 1965; British-Bangladesh Soc.; Member: Community Relations Commn, 1968–77; E Midlands Adv. Cttee, CRE, 1978–; Regl Inner City Task Force, 1991–; Stop Rickets Campaign (Chm., Leicester Campaign); Central Exec. Council, Bangladesh Med. Assoc. in UK; Hon. Med. Advr in UK, Min. of Health, Govt of Bangladesh; Chm., Standing Conf. of Asian Orgns in UK, 1973–77 (Vice-Chm., 1970–73; Pres., 1977–90); Hon. Sec., Inst. of Transcultural Health Care, 1985–93; Pres., Pakistan Assoc., Leics, 1965–71. Mem., BBC Asian Programme Adv. Cttee, 1972–77. Special interest in problems of Asians; initiated study of problems of second generation Asians (CRE report Between Two Cultures); Overseas Doctors' Association: Founder Chm., 1975, Sponsor Chm., 1975; Gen. Sec., 1975–77; Vice-Pres., 1979–84; Vice-Chm., 1984–90; Chm., Annual Reps Meeting, 1990–93; Fellow, 1985; Mem. Editl Bd, ODA News Review, 1986–; Associate Mem., MJA. Attended First World Conf. on Muslim Educn, Mecca, 1977; has done much work with disaster funds, etc. *Publications:* (ed jtly) Asian Who's Who, 1975–76, 8th edn 1992–93; contribs on socio-med. aspects of Asians in Britain to various jls. *Recreations:* gardening, reading, stamp collecting. *Address:* Ramna, 2 Mickleton Drive, Leicester LE5 6GD. *T:* Leicester (0116) 241 6703. *Club:* Royal Over-Seas League.

SAYEED, Jonathan; Chairman, Ranelagh Ltd, since 1992; *b* 20 March 1948; *m* 1980, Nicola Anne Parkes Power; two *s*. *Educ:* Woolverstone Hall; Britannia Royal Naval Coll., Dartmouth; Royal Naval Engrg Coll., Manadon. MP (C) Bristol E, 1983–92; contested (C) Bristol E, 1992. PPS to Paymaster General and Minister of State for NI, 1991–92. Vice-Chm., 1987–91, Chm., 1991–92, Cons. Backbench Shipping and Shipbuilding Cttee; Dep. Chm., All Party Maritime Group, 1987–92; Member: Environment Select Cttee, 1987–92; Defence Select Cttee, 1988–91. Pres., Bristol E Cons. Assoc., 1995–. Pres., Bristol West Indian Cricket Club, 1986. *Recreations:* golf, riding, classical music, architecture. *Address:* 1 Love Lane, EC2V 7JJ.

SAYER, Guy Mowbray, CBE 1978; JP; retired banker; *b* 18 June 1924; *yr s* of late Geoffrey Robley and Winifred Lily Sayer; *m* 1951, Marie Anne Sophie, *o d* of late Henri-Marie and Elisabeth Mertens; one *s* two *d*. *Educ:* Mill Mead Prep. Sch.; Shrewsbury School. FIB 1971. Royal Navy, 1942–46. Joined Hongkong & Shanghai Banking Corp., 1946; Gen. Man. 1969; Exec. Dir 1970; Dep. Chm. 1971; Chm., 1972–77. Treas., Hong Kong Univ., 1972–77. Mem., Exchange Fund Adv. Cttee, Hong Kong, 1971–77. MLC, 1973–74, MEC, 1974–77, Hong Kong. JP Hong Kong, 1971. Governor, Suttons Hosp. in Charterhouse. Hon. LLD Hong Kong, 1978. *Recreations:* golf, walking. *Address:* 5 Pembroke Gardens, W8 6HS. *T:* 0171–602 4578. *Clubs:* Oriental, MCC; Royal Wimbledon Golf; West Sussex Golf; Hong Kong, Shek O Country (Hong Kong).

SAYER, John Raymond Keer, MA; Director, E. C. Tempus Project: Developing Schools for Democracy in Europe, Oxford University, since 1991; Vice-Chairman, GTC (England and Wales), since 1994 (Hon. Secretary, 1990–94); Co-Director, European School of Educational Management, since 1991; *b* 8 Aug. 1931; *s* of Arthur and Hilda Sayer; *m* 1955, Ilserose (*née* Heyd); one *s* one *d*. *Educ:* Maidstone Grammar Sch.; Brasenose Coll., Oxford (Open Scholar; MA). FBIM 1979. Taught languages, 1955–63; Dep. Head, Nailsea Sch., Somerset, 1963–67; Headmaster, Minehead Sch., Somerset, 1967–73; Principal, Banbury Sch., 1973–84; Vis. Fellow, Univ. of London Inst. of Educn, 1985–92 (Dir, Educn Management Unit, 1987–90). Chairman: Reform of Assessment at Sixteen-Plus, 1972–75; PUBANSCO publishing gp, 1975–; Chm., External Relations Cttee, Headmasters' Assoc., 1974–77; Secondary Heads Association: Mem. Exec., 1978–86; Press and Publications Officer, 1978–79, 1982–84; Pres., 1979–80. Chm., Jt Council of Heads, 1981; Member: Exec., UCCA, 1975–84; Schools Panel, CBI, 1975–82; Heads Panel, TUC, 1975–80; National Adv. Council on Educn for Industry and Commerce, 1974–77; Adv. Cttee on Supply and Educn of Teachers, 1982–85. Trustee and Mem. Exec., Education 2000, 1983–89 (Hon. Sec., 1987–89); Mem. Exec., Schools Curriculum Award, 1986–91. *Publications:* (ed) The School as a Centre of Enquiry, 1975; (ed) Staffing our Secondary Schools, 1980; (ed) Teacher Training and Special Educational Needs, 1985; What Future for Secondary Schools?, 1985; Secondary schools for All?, 1987, 2nd edn 1994; (ed) Management and the Psychology of Schooling, 1988; Schools and External Relations, 1989; Managing Schools, 1989; Towards the General Teaching Council, 1989; The Future Governance of Education, 1993; Developing Schools for Democracy in Europe, 1995; frequent contribs on educnl topics to learned jls and symposia. *Recreation:* postal history. *Address:* 8 Northmoor Road, Oxford OX2 6UP. *T:* Oxford (01865) 56932.

SAYERS, Prof. Bruce McArthur, PhD, DScEng; FEng 1990; FIEE; Professor Emeritus of Computing Applied to Medicine, and Senior Research Fellow, Imperial College of Science, Technology and Medicine, since 1993; *b* 6 Feb. 1928; *s* of John William McArthur Sayers and Mabel Florence Sayers (*née* Howe); *m* 1951, R Woolls Humphery. *Educ:* Melbourne Boys' High School; Univ. of Melbourne (MSc); Imperial College, Univ. of London (PhD, DIC, DScEng). Biophysicist, Baker Med. Research Inst. and Clinical Research Unit, Alfred Hosp., Melbourne, 1949–54; Imperial College, London: Research Asst, 1955–56; Philips Elec. Ltd Research Fellow, 1957; Lectr, 1958; Senior Lectr, 1963; Reader, 1965; Prof. of Electrical Engrg Applied to Medicine, 1968–84; Head of Dept of Electrical Engrg, 1979–84; Prof. of Computing Applied to Medicine and Head of Dept of Computing, 1984–89; Kobler Prof. of the Management of IT, and Dir, Centre for Cognitive Systems, 1990–93; Dean, City and Guilds Coll., 1984–88, and 1991–93. Pres., Section of Measurement in Medicine, Royal Soc. of Medicine, 1971–72; Hon. Consultant, Royal Throat, Nose and Ear Hosp., 1974–93; UK rep., Bio-engineering Working Group, EEC Cttee for Med. Res., 1976–80; Temp. Adviser, WHO, 1970–76, 1981–87 and 1995–; Member: WHO Adv. Cttee for Health Res., 1988–94 (Vice Chm., 1990–92); Engrg Adv. Cttee, Science Mus., 1987–93. Consultant: Data Laboratories, 1968–80; Data Beta, 1981–93; Advent Eurofund, 1981–89; Shinan Investment Services SA, Switzerland, 1984–87; Advent Capital Ltd, 1985–89; Neuroscience Ltd, 1985–90; Transatlantic Capital (Biosciences) Fund, 1985–; Director: Imperial Software Technology Ltd, 1984–90; Imperial Information Technology Ltd, 1986–90. Former Visiting Prof., Univs of Melbourne, Rio de Janeiro, McGill, Toronto. Travelling Lectr: Nuffield Foundn-Nat. Research Council, Canada, 1971; Inst. of Electron. and Radio Engrs, Australia, 1976. Member: (PC nominee), Academic Adv. Council, 1988–, Council, 1994–, Buckingham Univ.; Internat. Academic Cttee on Energy Studies, Ecole Polytechnique Fédérale de Lausanne, 1989–; Scientific Council, Internat. Center of Biocybernetics, Warsaw, 1993–. FCGI 1983 (Pres., City and Guilds Coll. Assoc., 1995–96). Hon. Fellow, British Cybernetics Soc., 1986. Hon. Foreign Mem., Medico-Chirurgical Soc. of Bologna, 1965; Hon. Member, Eta Kappa Nu (USA), 1980. Freeman of the City of London, 1986; Liveryman, Scientific Instrument Makers' Co., 1986. *Publications:* papers, mainly on biomedical signals and control systems, epidemiology, cardiology and audiology. *Recreations:* restoring an old property in France, music. *Address:* 40 Queen's Gate, SW7 5HR. *T:* 0171–581 3690; La Payrastrié, 81360 Montredon-Labessonnié, France. *T:* 63751018. *Club:* Athenæum.

SAYERS, (Matthew Herbert) Patrick, OBE 1945; MD; FRCPath; Major-General, Army Medical Services (retired); formerly Consulting Pathologist, Employment Medical Advisory Service, Department of Employment and Health and Safety Executive, 1967–75; Hon. Physician to HM The Queen, 1965–67; Director of Army Pathology and Consulting Pathologist to the Army, 1964–67; *b* 17 Jan. 1908; *s* of late Herbert John Ireland Sayers, Musician, and late Julia Alice Sayers (*née* Tabb); *m* 1935, Moira, *d* of Robert Dougall; two *s* one *d*. *Educ:* St Joseph's Coll., SE19; Whitgift School; St Thomas's Hospital, London.

MRCS, LRCP 1932; MB, BS London 1933; MD London 1961; FCPath 1964. Commissioned Lieutenant RAMC, 1935; served India and Far East, 1936–46 (despatches, 1946): Asst Dir of Pathology, HQ 14th Army, 1943–44; Dep. Dir of Pathology, Allied Land Forces, SE Asia, 1945. Asst Dir-Gen., War Office, 1948; OC The David Bruce Laboratories, 1949–52 and 1955–61; Asst Dir of Pathology, Middle East Land Forces, 1953–55; Editor, Journal RAMC, 1955–61; Dep. Dir of Pathology, Far East Land Forces, 1961–64. Mem., Johnson Socs of London and Lichfield. CStJ 1968. *Publications:* contribs (jtly) to scientific jls on scrub typhus, immunology and industrial medicine. *Recreations:* gardening, music, cricket, field sports. *Address:* High Trees, Walmer, Kent CT14 7LP. *T:* Deal (01304) 363526. *Clubs:* Army and Navy; MCC.

See also J. C. O. R. Hopkinson.

SAYERS, Michael Patrick; QC 1988; a Recorder of the Crown Court, since 1986; *b* 28 March 1940; *s* of Major Herbert James Michael Sayers, RA (killed on active service, 1943) and late Joan Sheilah de Courcy Holroyd (*née* Stephenson); *m* 1976, Mrs Moussie Brougham (*née* Hallstrom); one *s* one *d*, and one step *s*. *Educ:* Harrow School; Fitzwilliam College, Cambridge (Evelyn Rothschild Scholar; MA). Called to the Bar, Inner Temple, 1970, Bencher, 1994; South Eastern Circuit; Junior, Central Criminal Court Bar Mess, 1975–78; Supplementary Prosecuting Counsel to the Crown, Central Criminal Court, 1977–88. Chm., Harrow Assoc., 1992–. *Recreations:* shooting, stalking, theatre, Sweden. *Address:* 2 Harcourt Buildings, Temple, EC4Y 9DB. *T:* 0171–353 2112; 1 Pembroke Villas, W8 6PG. *T:* 0171–937 6033. *Clubs:* Garrick, Pratt's; Queen's, Swinley Forest Golf.

SAYNOR, John, CMG 1992; JP; Secretary and Director-General, Commonwealth War Graves Commission, 1989–92; *b* 28 Sept. 1930; *s* of Charles Herbert Saynor and Emily Saynor (*née* Mundie); *m* 1954, Jennifer Ann Nelson; two *s*. *Educ:* Doncaster Grammar Sch. Commnd RASC, 1949–51. Post Office, 1951–69; Dept for National Savings, 1969–74; Commonwealth War Graves Commn, 1974–92. Chm., High Wycombe YMCA, 1992–. JP Berks, 1983. *Recreations:* gardening, golf, bridge. *Address:* 12 The Meadows, Flackwell Heath, High Wycombe, Bucks HP10 9LX. *T:* Bourne End (01628) 523459.

SCADDING, John Guyett, MD (London), FRCP; Emeritus Professor of Medicine in the University of London; Hon. Consulting Physician, Brompton and Hammersmith Hospitals; *b* 30 August 1907; *e s* of John William Scadding and Jessima Alice Guyett; *m* 1940, Mabel Pennington; one *s* two *d*. *Educ:* Mercers' School; Middlesex Hospital Medical School, University of London. MRCS, LRCP, 1929; MB, BS (London), 1930. Resident appts, Middx Hosp., Connaught Hosp., Walthamstow, and Brompton Hosp., 1930–35; MRCP 1932; MD (London, Univ. gold medal), 1932; First Asst, Dept of Med., Brit. Postgrad. Med. Sch., 1935; FRCP 1941; RAMC 1940–45 (Lt-Col, O i/c Med. Div.); Phys., Hammersmith Hosp., Royal Postgrad. Med. Sch., 1946–72; Physician, Brompton Hosp., 1939–72; Inst. of Diseases of the Chest: Dean, 1946–60; Dir of Studies, 1950–62; Prof. of Medicine, 1962–72; Hon. Cons. in Diseases of the Chest to the Army, 1953–72 (Guthrie Medal, 1973). Visiting Professor: Univ. Oklahoma, 1963; Stanford Univ. and Univ. Colorado, 1965; McMaster Univ., 1973; Univ. Manitoba, 1974; Univ. Chicago, 1976; Dalhousie Univ., 1977. Mem. Central Health Services Council, and Standing Medical Advisory Cttee, 1954–66; Mem. Clinical Research Board, 1960–65. Royal College of Physicians: Bradshaw Lectr, 1949; Mitchell Lectr, 1960; Tudor Edwards Lectr, 1970; Lumleian Lectr, 1973; Councillor, 1949–52; Censor, 1968–70; Second Vice-Pres., 1971–72; Moxon Medal, 1975; Lettsomian Lectr, Med. Soc. of London, 1955. Editor, Thorax, 1946–59. President: British Tuberculosis Assoc., 1959–61; Section of Medicine, RSM, 1969–71; Thoracic Soc., 1971–72. Fellow, RPMS, 1993. Dr *hc* Reims, 1978. *Publications:* Sarcoidosis, 1967, 2nd edn 1985; contributions to textbooks and articles, mainly on respiratory diseases, in medical journals. *Recreations:* music, pottering about. *Address:* 18 Seagrave Road, Beaconsfield, Bucks HP9 1SU. *T:* Beaconsfield (01494) 676033. *Club:* Athenæum.

SCALES, Prof. John Tracey, OBE 1986; FRCS, LRCP; CIMechE; Hon. Director, 1988–93 and Director, Pressure Sore Prevention, since 1994, RAFT Institute of Plastic Surgery (formerly Department of Research in Plastic Surgery), Regional Plastic and Oral Surgery Centre, Mount Vernon Hospital; Professor of Biomedical Engineering, Institute of Orthopaedics, University of London, 1974–87, now Emeritus; *b* 2 July 1920; *s* of late W. L. Scales and E. M. Scales (*née* Tracey); *m* 1945, Cecilia May (*d* 1992), *d* of late A. W. Sparrow; two *d*. *Educ:* Haberdashers' Aske's Sch., Hampstead; King's Coll., London; Charing Cross Hosp. Med. Sch. MRCS, LRCP 1944; Hon. FRCS 1969. CIMechE 1966. Captain RAMC, 1945–47. Casualty Officer and Resident Anaesthetist, Charing Cross Hosp., 1944; Royal National Orthopaedic Hosp., Stanmore: House Surgeon, 1944–45 and 1947–49; MO i/c Plastics Res. Unit, 1949–50; Hon. Registrar, 1950–52; Hon. Sen Registrar, 1952–57; Lectr i/c Plastics Res. Unit, Inst. of Orth., Stanmore, 1951–52; Sen. Lectr i/c Plastics Res. Unit (re-named Dept. of Biomechanics and Surg. Materials, 1956; re-named Dept of Biomed. Engrg, 1968), Inst. of Orth., Univ. of London, 1952–68; Consultant in Orthopaedic Prosthetics, 1958–68, in Biomedical Engrg, 1968–87, Royal Nat. Orthopaedic Hosp., Stanmore and London (Hon. Consultant); Reader in Biomed. Engrg, Dept of Biomed. Engrg, Inst. of Orth., Univ. of London, 1968–74; Consultant in Biomed. Engrg, Mt Vernon Hosp., Northwood, 1969–85; Consultant, Royal Orthopaedic Hosp., Birmingham, 1978–87. Chairman: BSI Cttee on Orthopaedic Joint-replacements, 1981–91; ISO Cttee on Bone and Joint Replacements; Member: IMechE Engrg in Medicine Gp, 1966–91 (Founder Mem.); Adv. Panel on Med. Engrg, National Fund for Res. into Crippling Diseases (Chm., 1981–85); British Orth. Res. Soc., 1962–; Biol Engrg Soc., 1960– (Founder Mem.); Eur. Soc. of Biomaterials, 1974– (Founder Mem.); Hon. Member: Eur. Soc. of Biomechanics, 1976– (Former Pres., Founder Mem.); British Assoc. of Plastic Surgeons, 1993–. Ext. Examiner, Univ. of Surrey, 1969–84, and other univs. FRSocMed 1950; Companion Fellow, British Orth. Assoc., 1959; FBES 1994. Thomas Henry Green Prize in Surgery, Charing Cross Hosp. Med. Sch., 1943; Robert Danis Prize, Internat. Soc. of Surgery, Brussels, 1969; James Berrie Prize, RCS, 1973; Clemson Univ. Award, USA, 1974; S. G. Brown Award, Royal Soc., 1974; A. A. Griffith Silver Medal, Materials Science Club, 1980; Jackson Burrows Medal, Royal Nat. Orthopaedic Hosp., Stanmore, 1985; Don Julius Groen Prize, IMechE, 1988. Kentucky Colonel, 1986. Member Editorial Board: Engineering in Medicine; Clinical Materials, 1986–; Wounds, 1989–. *Publications: chapters in:* Modern Trends in Surgical Materials, ed Gillis, 1958; Aspects of Medical Physics, ed Rotblat, 1966; Surgical Dressings and Wound Healing, ed Harkiss, 1971; (and ed jtly) Bed Sore Biomechanics, 1976; Surgical Dressings in the Hospital Environment, ed Turner and Brain, 1976; Treatment of Burns, ed Donati, Burke and Bertelli, 1976; Scientific Foundations of Orthopaedics and Traumatology, ed Owen, Goodfellow and Bullough, 1980; also jt author of chapters in med. books; contrib. Proc. RSM, Proc. IMechE, Proc. Physiol Soc., BMJ, Jl of Bone and Jt Surg., Lancet, Nature, and other med. and scientific jls; contrib. conf. and symposia reports. *Recreations:* walking dogs, Goss china. *Address:* Fairbanks, Riverview Road, Pangbourne, Berks RG8 7AU. *T:* Pangbourne (01734) 843568.

SCALES, Prunella, (Prunella Margaret Rumney West), CBE 1992; actress; *d* of John Richardson Illingworth and Catherine Scales; *m* 1963, Timothy Lancaster West, *qv*; two *s*. *Educ:* Moira House, Eastbourne; Old Vic Theatre School, London; Herbert Berghof Studio, New York (with Uta Hagen). Repertory in Huddersfield, Salisbury, Oxford, Bristol Old Vic, etc; seasons at Stratford-on-Avon and Chichester Festival Theatre; plays on London stage include: The Promise, 1967; Hay Fever, 1968; It's a Two-Foot-Six-Inches-Above-The-Ground-World, 1970; The Wolf, 1975; Breezeblock Park, 1978; Make and Break, 1980; An Evening with Queen Victoria, 1980; The Merchant of Venice, 1981; Quartermaine's Terms, 1981; Big in Brazil, 1984; When We Are Married, 1986; Single Spies (double bill), 1988; The School for Scandal, 1990; Long Day's Journey into Night, 1991; Mother Tongue, 1992; regional theatre: Happy Days, Leeds, 1993; The Matchmaker, Chichester, 1993; *television:* Fawlty Towers (series), 1975, 1978; Grand Duo, The Merry Wives of Windsor, 1982; Mapp and Lucia (series), 1985–86; Absurd Person Singular, 1985; The Index Has Gone Fishing, What the Butler Saw, 1987; After Henry (series), 1988, 1990; The Rector's Wife, Fair Game, 1994; Signs and Wonders, 1995; frequent broadcasts, readings, poetry recitals and fringe productions. Has directed plays at Bristol Old Vic, Arts Theatre, Cambridge, Billingham Forum, Almost Free Theatre, London, Nottingham Playhouse, Palace Theatre, Watford, W Yorks Playhouse, Leeds, Nat. Theatre of WA, Perth, and taught at several drama schools. *Recreation:* growing vegetables. *Address:* c/o Jeremy Conway, 18–21 Jermyn Street, SW1Y 6HP. *Club:* BBC.

SCALIA, Antonin; Associate Justice, United States Supreme Court, since 1986; *b* 11 March 1936; *s* of S. Eugene Scalia and Catherine Louise (*née* Panaro); *m* 1960, Maureen McCarthy; five *s* four *d*. *Educ:* Georgetown Univ. (AB 1957); Fribourg Univ., Switzerland; Harvard (LLB 1960; Sheldon Fellow, 1960–61). Admitted to Ohio Bar, 1962, to Virginia Bar, 1970. Associate, Jones, Day, Cockley & Reavis, Cleveland, 1961–67; Associate Prof., 1967–70, Prof., 1970–74, Univ. of Virginia Law Sch.; Gen. Counsel, Office of Telecommunications, Exec. Office of Pres., 1971–72; Chm., Admin. Conf. US, Washington, 1972–74; Asst Attorney Gen., US Office of Legal Counsel, Justice Dept, 1974–77; Prof., Law Sch., Chicago Univ., 1977–82; Judge, US Court Appeals (DC Circuit), 1982–86. American Bar Association: Mem. Council, 1974–77, Chm., 1981–82, Section Admin. Law; Chm., Conf. Section, 1982–83. Jt Editor, Regulation Magazine, 1979–82. *Address:* US Supreme Court, 1 First Street NE, Washington, DC 20543, USA.

SCANLAN, Dorothy, (Mrs Charles Denis Scanlan); *see* Quick, Dorothy.

SCANLAN, Prof. John Oliver, PhD, DSc; FIEEE, FIEE, FIMA, FIEI; Professor of Electronic Engineering, University College Dublin, since 1973; President, Royal Irish Academy, since 1993; *b* 20 Sept. 1937; *s* of John and Hannah Scanlan; *m* 1961, Ann Weadock. *Educ:* University Coll. Dublin (BE, ME); Leeds Univ. (PhD); NUI (DSc). FIMA 1971; FIEE 1972; FIEEE 1976; FIEI 1980. Lectr, 1963–68, Prof. of Electronic Engrg, 1968–73, Univ. of Leeds. Dir, Telecom Eireann, 1984–. MRIA 1977 (Sec., 1981–89). Editor, Internat. Jl of Circuit Theory and Applications, 1973–. *Publications:* Analysis and Synthesis of Tunnel Diode Circuits, 1966; Circuit Theory, vol. I, 1970, (with R. Levy) vol. II, 1973; numerous contribs to learned jls. *Recreations:* golf, music. *Address:* Department of Electronic and Electrical Engineering, University College Dublin, Dublin 4, Ireland. *T:* 2693244.

SCANLON, family name of **Baron Scanlon.**

SCANLON, Baron *cr* 1979 (Life Peer), of Davyhulme in the County of Greater Manchester; **Hugh Parr Scanlon;** President, Amalgamated Union of Engineering Workers, 1968–78; Member, British Gas Corporation, 1976–82; *b* 26 Oct. 1913; *m* 1943, Nora; two *d*. *Educ:* Stretford Elem. Sch.; NCLC. Apprentice, Instrument Maker, Shop Steward-Convener, AEI, Trafford Park; Divisional Organiser, AEU, Manchester, 1947–63; Member: Exec. Council, AEU, London, 1963–67; TUC Gen. Council, 1968–78; TUC Econ. Cttee, 1968–78. Member: NEDC, 1971–; Metrication Bd, 1973–78; NEB, 1977–79; Govt Cttee of Inquiry into Teaching of Maths in Primary and Secondary Schs in England and Wales, 1978–; Chm., Engineering Industry Training Bd, 1975–82. Vice-Pres., Internat. Metalworkers' Fedn, 1969–78; Pres., European Metal Workers' Fedn, 1974–78. Hon. DCL Kent, 1988. *Recreations:* golf, swimming, gardening. *Address:* 23 Seven Stones Drive, Broadstairs, Kent. *Club:* Eltham Warren Golf.

SCANNELL, Vernon, FRSL; free-lance author, poet and broadcaster, since 1962; *b* 23 Jan. 1922. *Educ:* elementary schools; Leeds Univ. Served with Gordon Highlanders (51st Highland Div.), ME and Normandy, 1940–45; Leeds Univ. (reading Eng. Lit.), 1946–47; various jobs incl. professional boxer, 1945–46, English Master at Hazelwood Prep. Sch., 1955–62. Southern Arts Assoc. Writing Fellowship, 1975–76; Vis. Poet, Shrewsbury Sch., 1978–79; Res. Poet, King's Sch. Canterbury, Michaelmas Term 1979. FRSL 1960. Granted a civil list pension, 1981, for services to literature. *Publications: novels:* The Fight, 1953; The Wound and the Scar, 1953; The Big Chance, 1960; The Face of the Enemy, 1961; The Shadowed Place, 1961; The Dividing Night, 1962; The Big Time, 1965; The Dangerous Ones (for children), 1970; A Lonely Game (for younger readers), 1979; Ring of Truth, 1983; *poetry:* The Masks of Love, 1960 (Heinemann Award, 1960); A Sense of Danger, 1962; Walking Wounded: poems 1962–65, 1968; Epithets of War: poems 1965–69, 1969; Mastering the Craft (Poets Today Series) (for children), 1970; (with J. Silkin) Pergamon Poets, No 8, 1970; Selected Poems, 1971; The Winter Man: new poems, 1973; The Apple Raid and other poems (for children), 1974 (Cholmondeley Poetry Prize, 1974); The Loving Game, 1975 (also in paperback); New and Collected Poems 1950–80, 1980; Winterlude and other poems, 1982; Funeral Games and other poems, 1987; The Clever Potato (for children), 1988; Soldiering On: poems of military life, 1989; Love Shouts and Whispers (for children), 1990; A Time for Fires, 1991; Travelling Light (for children), 1991; Collected Poems 1950–93, 1994; *edited:* (with Ted Hughes and Patricia Beer) New Poems: a PEN anthology, 1962; Sporting Literature: an anthology, 1987; *criticism:* Not Without Glory: poets of World War II, 1976; How to Enjoy Poetry, 1982; How to Enjoy Novels, 1984; *autobiography:* The Tiger and the Rose, 1971; A Proper Gentleman, 1977; Argument of Kings, 1987; Drums of Morning, 1992. *Recreations:* listening to radio (mainly music), drink, boxing (as a spectator), films, reading, learning French, loathing Tories. *Address:* 51 North Street, Otley, W Yorks LS21 1AH. *T:* Otley (01943) 467176.

SCARASCIA-MUGNOZZA, Carlo; Hon. President: International Centre for Advanced Mediterranean Agronomic Studies, Paris, since 1988 (President, 1983–87); Council of State, Italy (Member, 1977–90); President, Accademia Nazionale di Danza, Rome, since 1968; *b* Rome, 19 Jan. 1920. Mem., Italian Chamber of Deputies, for Lecce-Brindisi-Taranto, 1953; Vice-Pres., Christian Democrat Parly Gp, 1958–62; Leader, Italian Delegn to UNESCO, 1962; Secretary of State: for Educn, 1962–63; for Justice, June 1963–Dec. 1963; Mem., European Parliament, 1961–72, Chm., Political Cttee, 1969–72; a Vice-Pres., EEC, 1972–77. Mem., Accademia Agricoltura di Francia. *Address:* Via Timavo 32, 00195 Rome, Italy. *T:* (6) 3508842; International Centre for Advanced Mediterranean Agronomic Studies, 11 rue Newton, 75116 Paris, France; Accademia Nazionale di Danza, Largo Arrigo VII 5, 00153 Rome.

SCARBROUGH, 12th Earl of, *cr* 1690; **Richard Aldred Lumley;** Viscount Lumley (Ire.), 1628; Baron Lumley, 1681; Viscount Lumley, 1690; Vice Lord-Lieutenant of South Yorkshire, since 1990; *b* 5 Dec. 1932; *o s* of 11th Earl of Scarbrough, KG, PC, GCSI, GCIE, GCVO, and Katharine Isobel, Dowager Countess of Scarbrough, DCVO (*d* 1979), *d* of late R. F. McEwen; *S* father, 1969; *m* 1970, Lady Elizabeth Ramsay, *d* of Earl of Dalhousie, *qv*; two *s* one *d*. *Educ:* Eton; Magdalen College, Oxford. 2nd Lt 11th Hussars, 1951–52; formerly Lt Queen's Own Yorkshire Dragoons. ADC to Governor and C-in-C, Cyprus, 1956. Hon. Col, 1st Bn The Yorkshire Volunteers, 1975–88. President: Northern Area, Royal British Legion, 1984–93; York Georgian Soc., 1985–92; Northern Assoc. of Building Socs (formerly Yorkshire and North Western Assoc. of Building Socs), 1985–95. Mem., Royal Commn on Historical MSS, 1994–. Hon. RIBA, Yorks Region. DL S Yorks, 1974. *Heir: s* Viscount Lumley, *qv*. *Address:* Sandbeck Park, Maltby, Rotherham, S Yorks S66 8PF. *T:* Doncaster (01302) 742210. *Clubs:* White's, Pratt's; Jockey (Newmarket).

See also Lady Grimthorpe.

SCARD, Dennis Leslie; General Secretary, Musicians' Union, since 1990; *b* 8 May 1943; *s* of Charles Leslie Scard and Doris Annie (*née* Farmer); *m* (marr. diss); two *s*; partner, Linda Perry. *Educ:* Lascelles Co. Secondary Sch.; Trinity Coll. of Music, London. Professional horn player, 1962–85, performed with leading symphony and chamber orchestras. Part-time instrumental teacher, London Borough of Hillingdon, 1974–85. Musicians' Union: Chm., Central London Br., 1972–85; Mem., Exec. Cttee, 1979–85; full-time Official, Birmingham, 1985–90. *Recreations:* music, home wine making, walking, theatre. *Address:* (office) 60/62 Clapham Road, SW9 0JJ. *T:* 0171–582 5566.

SCARFE, Gerald, RDI 1989; artist; *b* 1 June 1936; *m* Jane Asher, *qv*; two *s* one *d*. *Educ:* scattered (due to chronic asthma as a child). Punch, 1960; Private Eye, 1961; Daily Mail, 1966; Sunday Times, 1967; cover artist to illustrator, Time Magazine, 1967; animation and film directing for BBC, 1969–. Has taken part in exhibitions: Grosvenor Gall., 1969 and 1970; Pavillon d'Humour, Montreal, 1967 and 1971; Expo '70, Osaka, 1970. One-man exhibitions of sculptures and lithographs: Waddell Gall., New York, 1968 and 1970; Grosvenor Gall., 1969; Vincent Price Gall., Chicago, 1969; National Portrait Gall., 1971; retrospective exhibn, Royal Festival Hall, 1983; Langton Gall., 1986; Chris Beetles Gall., 1989. Animated film for BBC, Long Drawn Out Trip, 1973 (prizewinner, Zagreb); Dir, Scarfe by Scarfe, BBC (BAFTA Award, 1987); Designer and Dir, animated sequences in film, The Wall, 1982; designer: Who's A Lucky Boy?, Royal Exchange, Manchester, 1984; Orpheus in the Underworld, ENO, 1985; Born Again, Chichester, 1990; The Magic Flute, Los Angeles, 1993; An Absolute Turkey, Globe, 1994. *Publications:* Gerald Scarfe's People, 1966; Indecent Exposure (ltd edn), 1973; Expletive Deleted: the life and times of Richard Nixon (ltd edn), 1974; Gerald Scarfe, 1982; Father Kissmass and Mother Claws, 1985; Scarfe by Scarfe (autobiog), 1986 (televised, 1987); Scarfe's Seven Deadly Sins, 1988; Scarfe's Line of Attack, 1988; Scarfeland: a lost world of fabulous beasts and monsters, 1989; Scarfe on Stage, 1992; Scarfeface, 1993. *Recreations:* drawing, painting and sculpting. *Address:* c/o ICM, Oxford House, 76 Oxford Street, W1N 0AX.

SCARFE, Jane; *see* Asher, J.

SCARGILL, Arthur; President, National Union of Mineworkers, since 1981; *b* 11 Jan. 1938; *o c* of Harold and Alice Scargill; *m* 1961, Anne, *d* of Elliott Harper; one *d*. *Educ:* Worsbrough Dale School; White Cross Secondary School; Leeds Univ. Miner, Woolley Colliery, 1953; Mem., NUM branch cttee, 1960; Woolley branch deleg. to Yorks NUM Council, 1964; Mem., Nat. Exec., 1972, Pres., 1973, Yorks NUM. Mem., TUC Gen. Council, 1986–88. Member: Young Communists' League, 1955–62; Co-op Party, 1963; Labour Party, 1966; CND. *Address:* National Union of Mineworkers, Holly Street, Sheffield S1 2GT.

SCARLETT, family name of **Baron Abinger.**

SCARLETT, His Honour James Harvey Anglin; a Circuit Judge, 1974–89; *b* 27 Jan. 1924; *s* of Lt-Col James Alexander Scarlett, DSO, RA, and Muriel Scarlett, *d* of Walter Blease; unmarried. *Educ:* Shrewsbury Sch.; Christ Church, Oxford (MA). Barrister-at-law. Served War, Royal Artillery (Lieut), 1943–47. Called to the Bar, Inner Temple, 1950. A Recorder of the Crown Court, 1972–74. Malayan Civil Service, 1955–58. *Recreation:* fell walking. *Address:* Chilmington Green, Great Chart, near Ashford, Kent TN23 3DP. *Clubs:* Athenæum; Athenæum (Liverpool); Border County (Carlisle).

SCARMAN, family name of **Baron Scarman.**

SCARMAN, Baron *cr* 1977 (Life Peer), of Quatt in the county of Salop; **Leslie George Scarman,** PC 1973; Kt 1961; OBE 1944; a Lord of Appeal in Ordinary, 1977–86; *b* 29 July 1911; *s* of late George Charles and Ida Irene Scarman; *m* 1947, Ruth Clement Wright; one *s*. *Educ:* Radley College; Brasenose College, Oxford. Classical Scholar, Radley, 1925; Open Classical Scholar, Brasenose Coll., 1930; Hon. Mods 1st cl., 1932; Lit. Hum. 1st cl., 1934; Harmsworth Law Scholar, Middle Temple, 1936, Barrister, 1936; QC 1957. A Judge of the High Court of Justice, Probate, Divorce, and Admiralty Div., later Family Div., 1961–73; a Lord Justice of Appeal, 1973–77. Chairman: Law Commn, 1965–73; Council of Legal Educn, 1973–76; President: Constitutional Reform Centre, 1984–; Citizen Action Compensation Campaign, 1988–. Chm., Univ. of London Court, 1970–86 (Dep. Chm., 1966–70); Chancellor, Univ. of Warwick, 1977–89. Vice-Chm., Statute Law Cttee, 1967–72. Pres., Senate of Inns of Court and Bar, 1976–79. Mem. Arts Council, 1968–70, 1972–73; Vice-Chm., ENO, 1976–81. Pres., RIPA, 1981–89. Hon. Fellow: Brasenose College, Oxford, 1966; Imperial Coll., Univ. of London, 1975; UCL, 1985; LSE, 1985; Leeds, 1987; Brunel, 1988. Hon. LLD: Exeter, 1965; Glasgow, 1969; London, 1971; Keele, 1972; Freiburg, 1973; Warwick, 1974; Bristol, 1976; Manchester, 1977; Kent, 1981; Wales, 1985; QUB, 1990; Dundee, 1990; Hon. DCL: City, 1980; Oxon, 1982. RAFVR, 1940–45; Chm., Malcolm Clubs, RAF. Order of Battle Merit (Russia), 1945. *Publications:* Pattern of Law Reform, 1967; English Law—The New Dimension, 1975. *Recreations:* gardening, walking. *Address:* House of Lords, SW1A 0PW. *Club:* Royal Air Force.

SCARSDALE, 3rd Viscount *cr* 1911; **Francis John Nathaniel Curzon;** Bt (Scotland) 1636, (England) 1641; Baron Scarsdale 1761; late Captain, Scots Guards; *b* 28 July 1924; *o s* of late Hon. Francis Nathaniel Curzon, 3rd *s* of 4th Baron Scarsdale, and late Winifred Phyllis (*née* Combe); *S* cousin, 1977; *m* 1st, 1948, Solange (marr. diss. 1967, she *d* 1974), *yr d* of late Oscar Hanse, Mont-sur-Marchienne, Belgium; two *s* one *d*; 2nd, 1968, Helene Gladys Frances, *o d* of late Maj. William Ferguson Thomson, Kinellar, Aberdeenshire; two *s*. *Educ:* Eton. *Recreations:* racing, shooting, piping, photography. *Heir: s* Hon. Peter Ghislain Nathaniel Curzon [*b* 6 March 1949; *m* 1983, Mrs Karen Osborne; one *d*]. *Address:* Kedleston Hall, Derby DE22 5JH. *T:* Derby (01332) 840386. *Club:* County (Derby).

SCATCHARD, Vice-Adm. John Percival, CB 1963; DSC 1941; first Bar, 1944; second Bar, 1945; *b* 5 Sept. 1910; *s* of Dr James P. Scatchard, MB, BS, Tadcaster, Yorks; *m* 1943, Edith Margaret Niven; one *d*. *Educ:* Aysgarth School, Yorkshire; RNC Dartmouth. Joined RN, 1924; served War of 1939–45, in HMS Kashmir-Garth and Termagent; Captain (D) Portsmouth, 1951–52; Captain 5th Destroyer Squadron, 1957–58; Director Naval Equipment, Admiralty, 1959–60; Commandant, Joint Services Staff College, Latimer, Bucks, 1960–62; Flag Officer, Second-in-Command, Far East Fleet, 1962–64; retd list, 1964. *Recreation:* gardening. *Address:* Reachfar, Warsash, near Southampton, Hants SO31 9FZ.

SCHAFFTER, Ernest Merill James; Secretary, Royal Aeronautical Society, 1973–82 (Deputy Secretary, 1970–73); Director, Engineering Sciences Data Unit Ltd, 1975–82; *b* 1922; *er s* of late Dr Charles Merill Schaffter and of Bertha Grace Brownrigg, of the CMS in Isfahan, Iran; *m* 1951, Barbara Joy, *o c* of Alfred Bennett Wallis and Hilda Frances Hammond; three *d*. *Educ:* Trent Coll., Nottinghamshire; King's Coll., Cambridge. BA 1950, MA 1955. Served War: RAF, as Pilot with Coastal and Transport Command, Flt Lt, 1941–46. De Havilland Aircraft Co., Hatfield, as Aerodynamicist and Engr, 1950–54; Marshall's Flying Sch., Cambridge, as Engr, 1954–60; Marshall of Cambridge (Eng) Ltd, as Personal Asst to Chief Designer and later as Design Office Manager, 1960–70. Freeman, GAPAN, 1978. FRAeS, AFAIAA, AFCASI, FIMgt. *Address:* 43 Speldhurst Road, W4 1BX. *T:* 0181–995 0708. *Clubs:* Royal Air Force, Les Ambassadeurs.

SCHALLER, George Beals; Director for Science, Wildlife Conservation Society, New York, since 1966; *b* 26 May 1933; *m* 1957 Kay Morgan; two *s*. *Educ:* Univ. of Alaska (BA, BS 1955); Univ. of Wisconsin (PhD 1962). Fellow, Center for Advanced Study in the Behavioral Sciences, Stanford Univ., 1962–63; Res. Associate, Johns Hopkins Univ., 1963–66; Wildlife Conservation (formerly NY Zoological) Soc., 1966–. *Publications:* The Mountain Gorilla, 1963; The Year of the Gorilla, 1964; The Deer and the Tiger, 1967; The Serengeti Lion, 1972; Serengeti: a kingdom of predators, 1972; Golden Shadows, Flying Hooves, 1973; Mountain Monarchs: wild sheep and goats of the Himalaya, 1977; Stones of Silence, 1980; (with Chinese co-authors) The Giant Pandas of Wolong, 1985; The Last Panda, 1993. *Recreations:* watching wildlife, photography. *Address:* Wildlife Conservation Society, 185th Street and Southern Boulevard, Bronx, NY 10460, USA.

SCHALLY, Dr Andrew Victor; Chief of Endocrine, Polypeptide and Cancer Institute, since 1962 and Senior Medical Investigator, since 1973, Veterans Administration Medical Center, New Orleans; Professor of Medicine, since 1967, and Head, Section of Experimental Medicine, since 1978, Tulane University School of Medicine, New Orleans (Associate Professor, 1962–67); *b* Wilno, Poland, 30 Nov. 1926; US Citizen (formerly Canadian Citizen); *s* of Casimir and Maria Schally; *m* 1st, 1956, Margaret White (marr. diss.); one *s* one *d*; 2nd, 1976, Ana Maria Comaru. *Educ:* Bridge of Allan, Scotland (Higher Learning Cert.); London (studied chemistry); McGill Univ., Montreal, Canada (BSc Biochem., 1955; PhD Biochem., 1957). Res. Assistant: Dept of Biochem., Nat. Inst. for Med. Res., MRC, Mill Hill, 1949–52; Endocrine Unit, Allan Meml Inst. for Psych., McGill Univ., Montreal, 1952–57; Baylor University Coll. of Medicine, Texas Med. Center: Res. Associate, Dept of Physiol., 1957–60; Asst Prof. of Physiol., Dept of Physiol., and Asst Prof. of Biochem., Dept of Biochem., 1960–62. Member: Endocrine Soc., USA; AAAS; Soc. of Biol Chemists; Amer. Physiol Soc.; Soc. for Experimental Biol. and Med.; Internat. Soc. for Res. in Biol. of Reprodn; Internat. Brain Res. Org.; Nat. Acad. of Medicine, Mexico; Nat. Acad. of Medicine, Brazil; Nat. Acad. of Medicine, Venezuela; Nat. Acad. of Scis (US); Hungarian Acad. of Scis; Acad. of Scis, Russia, 1991. Hon. Member: Internat. Family Planning Res. Assoc., Inc.; Chilean Endocrine Soc.; Mexican Soc. of Nutrition and Endocrinol.; Acad. of Med. Sciences of Cataluna and Baleares; Endocrine Soc. of Madrid; Polish Soc. of Internal Med.; Endocrine Soc. of Ecuador; Endocrine Soc. of Peru. Dr *hc* State Univ. of Rio de Janeiro, 1977; Rosario, Argentina, 1979; Univ. Peruana Cayetano Heredia, Lima, 1979; Univ. Nat. de San Marcos, Lima, 1979; MD *hc* Tulane, 1978; Cadiz, 1979; Univ. Villareal-Lima, 1979; Copernicus Med. Acad., Cracow, 1979; Chile, 1979; Buenos Aires, 1980; Salamanca, 1981; Complutense Univ., Madrid, 1984; Pécs Univ., 1986; Hon. DSc McGill, 1979; Hon. Dr Université René Descartes, Paris, 1987; Hon. Dr rer. nat. Regensburg Univ., 1992. Nobel Prize in Physiology or Medicine, 1977. Veterans Administration: William S. Middleton Award, 1970; Exceptional Service Award and Medal, 1978. Van Meter Prize, Amer. Thyroid Assoc., 1969; Ayerst-Squibb Award, US Endocrine Soc., 1970; Charles Mickle Award, Faculty of Med., Univ. of Toronto, 1974; Gairdner Foundn Internat. Award, Toronto, 1974; Edward T. Tyler Award, 1975; Borden Award, Assoc. of Amer. Med. Colls, 1975; Albert Lasker Basic Med. Res. Award, 1975; Spanish Pharmaceutical Soc., 1977; Laude Award, 1978; Heath Meml Award from M. D. Anderson Tumour Inst., 1989. Member Editorial Board: Proc. of Society for Experimental Biology and Medicine, 1973–; Life Sciences, 1980–; Peptides, 1980–; The Prostate, 1985–; Internat. Jl of Fertility, 1987–. *Publications:* (compiled and ed with William Locke) The Hypothalamus and Pituitary in Health and Disease, 1972; over 1800 other pubns (papers, revs, books, abstracts). *Address:* Quadrant F, 7th Floor Veterans Administration Medical Center, 1601 Perdido Street, New Orleans, LA 70146, USA. *T:* (504) 5895230.

SCHAPERA, Prof. Isaac, MA (Cape Town) 1925; PhD (London) 1929; DSc (London) 1939; FBA 1958; FRSSAf 1934; Emeritus Professor, University of London (London School of Economics), 1969; *b* Garies, South Africa, 23 June 1905; 3rd *s* of late Herman and Rose Schapera. *Educ:* S African Coll. Sch., Cape Town; Universities of Cape Town and London. Prof. of Social Anthropology, Univ. of Cape Town, 1935–50; Prof. of Anthropology, Univ. of London (LSE), 1950–69, now Emeritus; Hon. Fellow, 1974. Many anthropological field expeditions to Bechuanaland Protectorate, 1929–50. Chairman Association of Social Anthropologists of the British Commonwealth, 1954–57; President, Royal Anthropological Inst., 1961–63. Hon. DLitt: Cape Town, 1975; Botswana, 1985; Hon. LLD Witwatersrand, 1979. *Publications:* The Khoisan Peoples of South Africa, 1930; A Handbook of Tswana Law and Custom, 1938; Married Life in an African Tribe, 1940; Native Land Tenure in the Bechuanaland Protectorate, 1943; Migrant Labour and Tribal Life, 1948; The Ethnic Composition of Tswana Tribes, 1952; The Tswana, 1953; Government and Politics in Tribal Societies, 1956; Praise Poems of Tswana Chiefs, 1965; Tribal Innovators, 1970; Rainmaking Rites of Tswana Tribes, 1971; Kinship Terminology in Jane Austen's Novels, 1977; Editor: Western Civilization and the Natives of South Africa, 1934; The Bantu-speaking Tribes of South Africa, 1937; David Livingstone's Journals and Letters, 1841–56 (6 vols), 1959–63; David Livingstone: South African Papers 1849–1853, 1974; contrib. to many learned journals. *Address:* 457 White House, Albany Street, NW1 3UP.

SCHAPIRO, Isabel Margaret; *see* Madariaga, I. M. de.

SCHAPIRO, Meyer; University Professor, Columbia University, 1965–73, now Emeritus Professor; *b* Shavly, Lithuania, 23 Sept. 1904; *s* of Nathan Menahem Schapiro and Fege Edelman; *m* 1928, Dr Lillian Milgram; one *s* one *d*. *Educ:* Boys' High Sch., Brooklyn; Columbia University. PhD Columbia, 1929. Columbia University: Lectr, Dept of Art History and Archæology, 1928; Asst Prof., 1936; Assoc. Prof., 1948; Prof., 1952; University Prof., 1965. Visiting Lecturer: Institute of Fine Arts, NY University, 1931–36; New School for Social Research, NY, 1938–50; Vis. Prof.: Univ. of London, 1947, 1957; Univ. of Jerusalem, 1961; Messenger Lectr, Cornell Univ., 1960; Patten Lectr, Indiana Univ., 1961; Charles Eliot Norton Prof., Harvard Univ., 1966–67; Slade Prof. of Fine Art, Oxford Univ., 1968; Vis. Lectr, Collège de France, 1974. Guggenheim Fellow, 1939, 1943; Fellow: Amer. Acad. of Arts and Sciences, 1952; Inst. for Advanced Study in Behavioral Sciences, Palo Alto, 1962–63; Amer. Philosophical Soc., 1969; Mediaeval Acad., 1970; Amer. Inst. of Arts and Letters, 1976; Corresponding FBA, 1990. Hon. degrees: Columbia Univ.; Harvard Univ.; Yale Univ.; Jewish Theological Seminary, NY; New Sch. for Social Research; Univ. of Hartford. Bd of Editors: Jl of History of Ideas;

Semiotica; Dissent. Award for Distinction, Amer. Council of Learned Socs, 1960; Mitchell Prize, 1979; Aby M. Warburg Prize, Hamburg, 1985. *Publications:* The Romanesque Sculpture of Moissac, 1931; Van Gogh, 1950; Cézanne, 1952; The Parma Ildefonsus, 1964; Words and Pictures, 1973; Selected Papers, vol. I, Romanesque Art, 1976, vol. II, Modern Art, 1978; vol. III, Late Antique, Early Christian and Medieval Art, 1980; Style, Artiste et Société, 1983; articles in collective books and in Art Bulletin, Gazette des Beaux-Arts, Jl Warburg and Courtauld Insts, Jl History of Ideas, Jl Architectural Historians, Kritische Berichte, Amer. Jl Sociology, Partisan Review, Encounter, etc. *Address:* 279 West 4th Street, New York, NY 10014, USA.

SCHARPING, Rudolf; Member, Bundestag, since 1994; Chairman, Social Democratic Party of Germany, and Leader of the Opposition, since 1994; Chairman, Social Democratic Party of Europe, since 1994; *b* Niederelbert, Westerwald, 2 Dec. 1947. *Educ:* Univ. of Bonn. State Chm. and Nat. Dep. Chm., Jusos (Young Socialists), 1966; joined SPD, 1966; Rhineland-Palatinate: Mem., State Parlt, 1975–94; Leader, SPD, 1985–91; Leader of Opposition, 1987–91; Minister-Pres., 1991–94. *Address:* Office of the Chairman, Social Democratic Party of Germany, Ollenhauerstrasse 1, 53113 Bonn, Germany.

SCHÄUBLE, Dr Wolfgang, Grosskreuz des Verdienstordens der Bundesrepublik Deutschland, 1990; Chairman, CDU/CSU Parliamentary Group, Germany, since 1991; *b* 18 Sept. 1942; *s* of Karl Schäuble and Gertrud (*née* Göhring); *m* 1969, Ingeborg Hensle; one *s* three *d.* *Educ:* Univ. of Freiburg; Univ. of Hamburg (Dr jur 1971). Tax Revenue Dept, State of Baden-Württemberg, 1971–72; Mem., Bundestag, 1972–; solicitor, 1978–84; Parly Sec., CDU/CSU, 1981–84; Federal Minister and Head of Federal Chancellery, 1984–89; Federal Minister of the Interior, 1989–91. Chairman: CDU Cttee on Sports, 1976–84; Working Gp, European Border Regions, 1979–82. *Publication:* Der Vertrag, 1991. *Recreation:* classical music. *Address:* Görresstrasse 15, 53113 Bonn, Germany.

SCHAUFUSS, Peter; ballet dancer, producer, choreographer; Director, Royal Danish Ballet, Copenhagen, since 1994; *b* 26 April 1950; *s* of Frank Schaufuss and Mona Vangsaae, former solo dancers with Royal Danish Ballet. *Educ:* Royal Danish Ballet School. Apprentice, Royal Danish Ballet, 1965; soloist, Nat. Ballet of Canada, 1967–68; Royal Danish Ballet, 1969–70; Principal, London Festival Ballet, 1970–74; NY City Ballet, 1974–77; Principal, National Ballet of Canada, 1977–83; Artistic Dir, London Fest. Ballet, later English Nat. Ballet, 1984–90; Dir of Ballet, Deutsche Oper, Berlin, 1990–93. Guest appearances in Austria, Canada, Denmark, France, Germany, Greece, Israel, Italy, Japan, Norway, S America, Turkey, UK, USA, USSR; Presenter, Dancer, BBC, 1984; numerous TV appearances. Roles created for him in: Phantom of the Opera; Orpheus; Verdi Variations; The Steadfast Tin Soldier; Rhapsodie Espagnole. Produced ballets: La Sylphide (London Fest. Ballet, Stuttgart Ballet, Roland Petit's Ballet de Marseille, Deutsche Oper Berlin, Teatro Comunale, Florence, Vienna State Opera, Opernhaus Zurich, Teatro dell' Opera di Roma, Hessisches Staatstheater, Wiesbaden, Ballet du Rhin, Royal Danish Ballet); Napoli (Nat. Ballet of Canada, Teatro San Carlo, English Nat. Ballet); Folktale (Deutsche Oper Berlin); Dances from Napoli (London Fest. Ballet); Bournonville (Aterballetto); The Nutcracker (London Fest. Ballet, Deutsche Oper, Berlin); Giselle, Tchaikovsky Trilogy (Deutsche Oper, Berlin). Solo award, 2nd Internat. Ballet Competition, Moscow, 1973; Star of the Year, Munich Abendzeitung, 1978; Evening Standard and SWET ballet award, 1979; Manchester Evening News theatre award, 1986; Berlin Co. award, Berlinerzeitung, 1991; Edinburgh Festival Critics' Prize, 1991. Knight of the Dannebrog (Denmark), 1988. *Recreation:* boxing. *Address:* c/o Papoutsis Representation Ltd, 18 Sundial Avenue, SE25 4BX.

SCHAWLOW, Prof. Arthur Leonard, PhD; J. G. Jackson—C. J. Wood Professor of Physics, Stanford University, 1961–91, now Professor Emeritus; *b* Mt Vernon, New York, 5 May 1921; *s* of Arthur Schawlow and Helen Schawlow (*née* Mason); *m* 1951, Aurelia Keith Townes; one *s* two *d.* *Educ:* Univ. of Toronto, Canada. BA 1941, MA 1942, PhD 1949. Postdoctoral Fellow and Research Associate, Columbia Univ., 1949–51; Research Physicist, Bell Telephone Laboratories, 1951–61; Visiting Assoc. Prof., Columbia Univ., 1960. Hon. MRIA 1991. Hon. DSc: Ghent, 1968; Bradford, 1970; Alabama, 1984; TCD, 1986; Hon. LLD, Toronto, 1970; Hon. DTech Lund, 1988; Hon. DSL Victoria Univ., Toronto, 1993. Ballantine Medal, Franklin Inst., 1962; Liebmann Prize, Inst. of Electrical and Electronic Engrs, 1963; Thomas Young Medal and Prize (GB), 1963; California Scientist of the Year, 1973; Ives Medal, Optical Soc. of America, 1975; Marconi Internat. Fellowship, 1977; (jtly) Nobel Prize in Physics, 1981; Arthur L. Schawlow Medal, Laser Inst. of America, 1982; US Nat. Medal of Science, 1991; Arata Award, High Temperature Soc. of Japan, 1994. *Publications:* (with C. H. Townes) Microwave Spectroscopy, 1955; many contribs to learned journals. *Recreation:* jazz music. *Address:* Department of Physics, Stanford University, Stanford, CA 94305–4060, USA. *T:* (415) 7234356.

SCHEEL, Walter; Grand Cross First Class of Order of Merit of Federal Republic of Germany; President of the Federal Republic of Germany, 1974–79; *b* 8 July 1919; *m* 1969, Dr Mildred Wirtz (*d* 1985); one *s* two *d,* and one *s* of previous *m;* *m* 1988, Barbara Wiese. *Educ:* Reform Gymnasium, Solingen. Served in German Air Force, War of 1939–45. Mem. of Bundestag, 1953–74; Federal Minister for Economic Co-operation, 1961–Oct. 1966, Vice-President of Bundestag, 1967–69; Vice-Chancellor and Foreign Minister, 1969–74. Mem., Landtag North Rhine Westphalia, 1950–54; Mem. European Parlt, 1958–61 (Vice-Chm., Liberal Gp; Chm., Cttee on Co-operation with Developing Countries). Free Democratic Party: Mem., 1946; Mem. Exec. Cttee for North Rhine/ Westphalia, 1953–74; Mem. Federal Exec., 1956–74; Chm., 1968–74; Hon. Pres., 1979. Holds numerous hon. degrees and foreign decorations. *Publications:* Konturen einer neuen Welt, 1965; Formeln deutscher Politik, 1968; Warum Mitbestimmung und wie—eine Diskussion, 1970; Reden und Interviews, 1969–79; Vom Recht des anderen, 1977; Die Zukunft der Freiheit, 1979; Wen schmerzt noch Deutschlands Teilung?, 1986. *Address:* Flemingstrasse 107, 81925 München, Germany.

SCHEELE, Nicholas Vernon; Chairman and Chief Executive, Jaguar Cars, since 1992; *b* 3 Jan. 1944; *s* of Werner James Scheele and Norah Edith Scheele (*née* Gough); *m* 1967, Rosamund Ann Jacobs; two *s* one *d.* *Educ:* Durham Univ. (BA). Purchasing, Supply, Procurement, Ford of Britain, 1966–78; Ford of US: Purchasing, Supply, Procurement Management, 1978–83; Dir, Supply Policy and Planning, 1983–85; Dir, Body and Chassis Parts Purchasing, 1985–88; Pres., Ford of Mexico, 1988–91; Vice-Chm., Jaguar Cars, Jan.–April 1992. *Recreations:* reading, classical music, tennis, squash. *Address:* Jaguar Cars, Browns Lane, Coventry CV5 9DR. *T:* Coventry (01203) 402121. *Clubs:* Royal Automobile; Catawba Island (Great Lakes).

SCHEMBRI, His Honour Carmelo; Chief Justice of Malta and President of the Constitutional Court, Court of Appeal and Court of Criminal Appeal, 1981–87; *b* 2 Sept. 1922; *s* of Joseph Schembri and Lucia (*née* Tabone Adami); *m* 1949, Helen (*née* Holland); six *s* five *d.* *Educ:* The Lyceum, Malta; Royal Univ. of Malta (LLD 1946). Called to the Bar, 1947; elected Mem., Malta Legislative Assembly (Nationalist Party), 1950; Dep. Speaker and Chm., Cttees until dissolution of Assembly, 1951; returned to Parliament in General Election, 1951 and re-elected Dep. Speaker and Chm. Cttees; Minister of Educn, 1952–53; Asst Crown Counsel and Officer i/c Inland Revenue Dept, Gozo, 1954–62; Magistrate: for Gozo, 1962–68; Malta, 1968–78; Judge of Superior Courts, 1978–81. Coronation Medal 1953. *Recreations:* football, woodwork, collecting match boxes. *Address:* 2 Holland Court, Bisazza Street, Sliema, Malta.

SCHERER, Prof. Jacques, DèsL; Professor, University of Paris-III, 1979–95, now Emeritus; *b* 24 Feb. 1912; *s* of Maurice Scherer and Madeleine Franck; *m* 1965, Colette Bié. *Educ:* Ecole Normale Supérieure; Sorbonne Univ., Paris (Agrégé des Lettres, Docteur ès Lettres). Prof. of French Literature, Univ. of Nancy, 1946–54; Prof. of French Literature and Theatre, Sorbonne Univ., 1954–73; Marshal Foch Prof. of French Literature and Fellow of All Souls Coll., Univ. of Oxford, 1973–79. *Publications:* L'expression littéraire dans l'œuvre de Mallarmé, 1947; La dramaturgie classique en France, 1950; La dramaturgie de Beaumarchais, 1954; Le 'Livre' de Mallarmé, 1957 (new edn 1977); Structures de Tartuffe, 1966; Sur le Dom Juan de Molière, 1967; Le cardinal et l'orang-outang, essai sur Diderot, 1972; Théâtre du XVIIe siècle, 1975, vols I and II (ed jtly), 1987; Grammaire de Mallarmé, 1977; Racine et/ou la cérémonie, 1982; Le théâtre de Corneille, 1984; Dramaturgies d'Œdipe, 1987; Le théâtre en Afrique noire francophone, 1992; Dramaturgies de vrai-faux, 1994. *Address:* 11 rue de la Colonie, 75013 Paris, France.

SCHERER, Paul Joseph; Chairman, Transworld Publishers Ltd, since 1995 (Managing Director, 1982–95); *b* 28 Dec. 1933; *s* of François Joseph Scherer and Florence (*née* Haywood); *m* 1959, Mary Fieldus; one *s* three *d.* *Educ:* Stonyhurst Coll. National Service, commnd BUFFS (Royal E Kent Regt), 1952–54. Bailey Bros & Swinfen, 1954–56; Jun. Editor, G. Bell & Sons, 1956–58; Sales Man., Penguin Books, 1958–63; Gp Sales Dir, Paul Hamlyn, 1963–68; William Collins Sons & Co.: Man. Dir, Internat. Div., 1968–77; Pres., Collins & World USA, 1974–75; Man. Dir, Mills & Boon, 1977–82; Sen. Vice Pres., Bantam Doubleday Dell Publishing Gp Inc., 1990–; Director: (non-exec.) Bloomsbury Publishing plc, 1993–; Book Tokens Ltd, 1995–. Member Board: Book Develt Council, 1971–74; Book Marketing Council, 1977–84 (Chm., 1982–84); Mem. Council, Publishers Assoc., 1982–84 and 1989–94 (Pres., 1991–93); Pres., Book Trade Benevolent Soc., 1995–. Founding Chm., Unicorn Sch., Kew, 1970–73. Gov., Worth Sch., 1993–. *Recreation:* laughing at my own jokes. *Address:* Flat 6, 62 Queen's Gate, SW7 5JP. *T:* 0171–581 9831. *Clubs:* Savile, Arts, Hurlingham.

SCHERMERS, Prof. Dr Henry Gerhard; Professor of Law, University of Leiden, since 1978; *b* 27 Sept. 1928; *s* of Petrus Schermers and Amelia M. Gooszen; *m* 1957, Hotsche A. C. Tans; one *s* two *d.* *Educ:* Leiden Univ. (LLM 1953; LLD 1957). Ministry of Foreign Affairs: Internat. Orgns Dept, 1953–56; Asst Legal Advr, 1956–63; University of Amsterdam: Lectr in Internat. Law, 1963–65; Prof. of Law, 1965–78. Visiting Professor: Ann Arbor, Michigan, 1968; Louisiana, 1981; QMC, 1988. Mem., Eur. Commn of Human Rights, 1981–. Corresp. Fellow, British Acad., 1990; Mem., Inst. de Droit Internat., 1989. Chief Editor, Common Market Law Review, 1978–93. Dr (*hc*): Edinburgh, 1993; Osnabrück, 1994. Kt of Netherlands Lion, 1984; Comdr, Order of Oranje Nassau, 1993; Officer, Crown of Belgium, 1962. *Publications:* International Institutional Law, 1972, 3rd edn 1995; Judicial Protection in the European Communities, 1976, 5th edn 1991; numerous articles in Common Market Law Review and professional jls. *Recreations:* hiking, ski-ing, carpentry. *Address:* Herengracht 15, 2312 LA Leiden, Netherlands. *T:* (71) 124294.

SCHIEMANN, Rt Hon. Sir Konrad Hermann Theodor, Kt 1986; PC 1995; **Rt Hon. Lord Justice Schiemann;** a Lord Justice of Appeal, since 1995; *b* 15 Sept. 1937; *s* of Helmuth and Beate Schiemann; *m* 1965, Elisabeth Hanna Eleonore Holroyd-Reece; one *d.* *Educ:* King Edward's Sch., Birmingham; Pembroke Coll., Cambridge (Schol.; MA, LLB). Served Lancs Fusiliers, 1956–58 (commnd, 1957). Called to Bar, Inner Temple, 1962 (Bencher, 1985); Junior Counsel to the Crown, Common Law, 1978–80; QC 1980; a Recorder of the Crown Court, 1985–86; a Justice of the High Court, QBD, 1986–95. Chairman of panel conducting Examinations in Public of: North-East Hants and Mid Hants Structure Plans, 1979; Merseyside Structure Plan, 1980; Oxfordshire Structure Plan, 1984. Mem., Parole Bd, 1990–92 (Vice-Chm., 1991–92). Trustee, St John's, Smith Square, 1990– (Chm., 1994–). Gov., English Nat. Ballet, 1995–. *Recreations:* music, reading. *Address:* c/o Royal Courts of Justice, Strand, WC2A 2LL.

SCHIFF, András; concert pianist; *b* 21 Dec. 1953; *s* of Odon Schiff and Klara Schiff (*née* Csengeri). *Educ:* Franz Liszt Academy of Music, Budapest; with Prof. Pal Kadosa, Ferenc Rados and Gyorgy Kurtag; private study with George Malcolm. Artistic Dir, September Chamber Music Fest., Mondsee, Austria, 1989–. Regular orch. engagements include: NY Philharmonic, Chicago Symphony, Vienna Phil., Concertgebouw, Orch. de Paris, London Phil., London Symph., Royal Phil., Israel Phil., Philadelphia, Washington Nat. Symph.; major festival performances include: Salzburg, Edinburgh, Aldeburgh, Tanglewood. Recordings include: extensive Bach repertoire (Grammy Award for recording of English Suites, 1990); all Mozart Piano Sonatas; all Mozart Piano Concertos; Lieder records with Peter Schreier. Prizewinner, Tchaikovsky competition, Moscow, 1974 and Leeds comp., 1975; Liszt Prize, 1977; Premio, Accademia Chigiana, Siena, 1987; Wiener Flotenuhr, 1989; Bartok Prize, 1991; Instrumentalist of the Year, Internat. Classical Music Awards, 1993. *Recreations:* literature, languages, soccer. *Address:* c/o Harrison Operations Ltd, The Orchard, Market Street, Charlbury, Oxon OX7 3PJ.

SCHILD, Geoffrey Christopher, CBE 1993; PhD; DSc; FRCPath; FIBiol; Director, National Institute for Biological Standards and Control, since 1985; *b* 28 Nov. 1935; *s* of Christopher and Georgina Schild; *m* 1961, Tora Madland; two *s* one *d.* *Educ:* High Storrs Sch., Sheffield; Univ. of Reading (BSc Hons 1954; DSc 1993); Univ. of Sheffield (PhD 1963). FIBiol 1978; FRCPath 1993. Hon. MRCP 1995. Res. Fellow 1961–63, Lectr in Virology 1963–67, Univ. of Sheffield; National Institute for Medical Research: Mem., Scientific Staff of MRC, 1967–75; Dir, World Influenza Centre, 1970–75; Hd, Div. of Virology, Nat. Inst. for Biol Standards, 1975–85; Dir, MRC Directed Prog. of AIDS Res., 1987–. Chm., WHO Steering Cttee on Biomed. Res. on AIDS, 1987–90; Mem., WHO Scientific Adv. Gp on Vaccine Devel t, 1991–. Freeman, City of London, 1989. *Publications:* Influenza, the Virus and the Disease, 1975, 2nd edn 1985; some 300 original res. papers on virology in learned jls. *Recreations:* hill walking, music, ornithology. *Address:* National Institute for Biological Standards and Control, Blanche Lane, South Mimms, Potters Bar, Hertfordshire EN6 3QG. *T:* Potters Bar (01707) 654753.

SCHILLING, Prof. Richard Selwyn Francis, CBE 1975; MD (London); DSc (London); FRCP; FFPHM; FFOM; DPH; Professor of Occupational Health, London School of Hygiene and Tropical Medicine, University of London, 1960–76, now Emeritus, Hon. Fellow 1979; Director, TUC Centenary Institute of Occupational Health, 1968–76; *b* 9 Jan. 1911; *s* of late George Schilling and of Florence Louise Schilling, Kessingland, Suffolk; *m* 1937, Heather Maude Elinor Norman; one *s* two *d.* *Educ:* Epsom College; St Thomas' Hospital. Obstetric house physician, St Thomas' Hosp., 1935; house physician, Addenbrooke's Hosp., Cambridge, 1936; Asst Industrial MO, ICI (metals) Ltd, Birmingham, 1937; Medical Inspector of Factories, 1939–42. Served War of 1939–45, Captain RAMC, France and Belgium, 1939–40. Sec. Industrial Health Research Board of Med. Research Council, 1942–46; Nuffield Fellow in Industrial Health, 1946–47; Reader in Occupational Health, Univ. of Manchester, 1947–56; WHO Consultant, 1956–69.

Lectures: Milroy, RCP, 1956; Mackenzie, BMA, 1956; Cantor, RSA, 1963; C.-E. A. Winslow, Yale Univ., 1963; Ernestine Henry, RCP, 1970. Former Vice-Pres., Perm. Commn, Internat. Assoc. Occupational Health. Former President: Assoc. of Industrial Medical Officers; British Occupational Hygiene Soc.; Occup. Med. Sect. of Roy. Soc. Med. Member: Committee of Inquiry into Trawler Safety, 1968; Royal Commn on Civil Liability and Compensation for Personal Injury, 1973–78. Hon. Mem., Amer. Occupational Med. Assoc., 1986. Hon. FRSM 1976; Hon. DIH, Soc. of Apothecaries, 1988; Hon. FFOM, RCPI, 1990; Hon. Fellow, UMDS, 1994. *Publications:* (ed) Modern Trends in Occupational Health, 1960; (ed) Occupational Health Practice, 1973, 2nd edn 1980; original papers on Byssinosis (respiratory disease of textile workers) and other subjects in occupational health in BMJ, Lancet, Brit. Jl of Industrial Medicine, and foreign journals. *Recreation:* fishing. *Address:* 11c Prior Bolton Street, N1 2NX. *T:* 0171–359 1627.

SCHLESINGER, Arthur (Meier), Jr; writer; educator; Schweitzer Professor of the Humanities, City University of New York, 1966–95; *b* Columbus, Ohio, 15 Oct. 1917; *s* of late Arthur Meier and of Elizabeth Bancroft Schlesinger; *m* 1st, 1940, Marian Cannon (marr. diss. 1970); two *s* two *d*; 2nd, 1971, Alexandra Emmet; one *s*. *Educ:* Phillips Exeter Acad. AB (Harvard), 1938; Henry Fellow, Peterhouse, Cambridge, 1938–39. Soc. of Fellows, Harvard, 1939–42; US Office of War Information, 1942–43; US Office of Strategic Services, 1943–45; US Army, 1945. Mem. Adlai Stevenson Campaign Staff, 1952, 1956. Professor of History, Harvard University, 1954–61 (Associate, 1946–54); Special Assistant to President Kennedy, 1961–63. Film Reviewer: Show, 1962–65; Vogue (US), 1966–70; Saturday Review, 1977–80; Amer. Heritage, 1981. Member of Jury, Cannes Film Festival, 1964. Holds 26 honorary doctorates, incl. DLitt Oxford, 1987. Mem. of numerous Socs and Instns; Pres., Amer. Inst. of Arts and Letters, 1981–84; Chancellor, Amer. Acad., 1985–88. Pulitzer Prize: History, 1946; Biography, 1966; Nat. Book Award for Biog., 1966 (for A Thousand Days: John F. Kennedy in the White House), 1979 (for Robert Kennedy and His Times); Amer. Inst. of Arts and Letters, Gold Medal for History, 1967. Commander, Order of Orange-Nassau (Netherlands), 1987. *Publications:* Orestes A. Brownson: a Pilgrim's Progress, 1939; The Age of Jackson, 1945; The Vital Center, 1949, (in UK) The Politics of Freedom, 1950; The General and the President (with R. H. Rovere), 1951; (co-editor) Harvard Guide to American History, 1954; The Age of Roosevelt: I: The Crisis of the Old Order, 1957; II: The Coming of the New Deal, 1958; III: The Politics of Upheaval, 1960; Kennedy or Nixon, 1960; The Politics of Hope, 1963; (ed with Morton White) Paths of American Thought, 1963; A Thousand Days: John F. Kennedy in the White House, 1965; The Bitter Heritage: Vietnam and American Democracy 1941–1966, 1967; The Crisis of Confidence: ideas, power & violence in America, 1969; (ed with F. L. Israel) History of American Presidential Elections, 1971; The Imperial Presidency, 1973; (ed) History of US Political Parties, 1973; Robert Kennedy and His Times, 1978; The Cycles of American History, 1986; The Disuniting of America, 1991; articles to magazines and newspapers. *Recreations:* theatre, movies, tennis. *Address:* (office) Box 540, 33 W 42nd Street, New York, NY 10036, USA. *T:* (212) 6422060; 455 E 51st Street, New York, NY 10022, USA. *Clubs:* Century (New York), Federal City (Washington).

SCHLESINGER, John Richard, CBE 1970; film director; *b* 16 Feb. 1926; *s* of late Bernard Schlesinger, OBE, MD, FRCP and Winifred Henrietta (*née* Regensburg). *Educ:* Uppingham; Balliol Coll., Oxford (BA; Hon. Fellow 1981). Associate Dir, Nat. Theatre, 1973–88. Mem., Theatre Dirs' Guild of GB, 1983–. Directed: *films:* for Monitor and Tonight (BBC TV), 1958–60; Terminus, for British Transport Films, 1960 (Golden Lion Award, Venice Film Fest., 1961); A Kind of Loving, 1961 (Golden Bear Award, Berlin Film Festival, 1962); Billy Liar, 1962–63; Darling, 1964–65 (NY Critics Award); Far from the Madding Crowd, 1966–67; Midnight Cowboy, 1968–69 (Soc. of TV and Film Acad. Award for Best Dir; Dir's Guild of America Award; American Oscar); Sunday, Bloody Sunday, 1971 (Soc. of TV and Film Acad. Award for Best Dir; David di Donatello Award); contrib. Visions of Eight, 1973; Day of the Locust, 1975; Marathon Man, 1976; Yanks, 1978 (New Evening Standard Award, 1980); Honky Tonk Freeway, 1980; The Falcon and the Snowman, 1984; The Believers, 1987; Madame Sousatzka, 1988 (screenplay with Ruth Prawer Jhabvala); Pacific Heights, 1991; The Innocent, 1994; *television:* Separate Tables, 1982; An Englishman Abroad, 1983 (BAFTA Award, Broadcasting Press Guild Award, Barcelona Film Fest. Award and Nat. Bd of Review Award, 1984); A Question of Attribution, 1991 (BAFTA Award); Cold Comfort Farm, 1995; *plays:* No, Why, for RSC, 1964; Timon of Athens, and Days in the Trees, for RSC, 1964–66; I and Albert, Piccadilly, 1972; Heartbreak House, 1975, Julius Caesar, 1977, and True West, 1981, for Nat. Theatre; *opera:* Les Contes d'Hoffmann, 1980 (SWET Award, 1981), and Der Rosenkavalier, 1984, for Covent Garden; Un Ballo in Maschera, for Salzburg Fest., 1989. David di Donatello Special Award, 1980; Shakespeare Prize, FVS Foundn of Hamburg, 1981. *Recreations:* gardening, travel, music, antiques. *Address:* c/o Duncan Heath, ICM, 76 Oxford Street, W1R 1RB.

SCHMIDHUBER, Peter Michael; Member, Commission of the European Communities, 1987–94; lawyer; *b* 15 Dec. 1931; *s* of Jakob Schmidhuber and Anna (*née* Mandlmayr); *m* 1960, Elisabeth Schweigart; one *d*. *Educ:* Univ. of Munich (MA Econs 1955). Qualified as lawyer, 1960. Member: Bundestag, 1965–69 and 1972–78; Bundesrat, Bavarian Parliament, 1978–87 (Bavarian Minister of State for Federal Affairs). Mem., CSU. *Address:* Bodenseestrasse 21, 81241 Munich, Germany.

SCHMIDT, Benno Charles, Jr; President and Chief Executive, The Edison Project, since 1992; *b* 20 March 1942; *s* of Benno Charles Schmidt and Martha Chastain; *m* 1980, Helen Cutting Whitney; one *s* two *d*. *Educ:* Yale Univ. (BA 1963; LLB 1966). Mem., DC Bar, 1968; Law Clerk to Chief Justice Earl Warren, 1966–67; Special Asst Atty Gen., Office of Legal Counsel, US Dept of Justice, Washington, 1967–69; Harlan Fiske Stone Prof. of Constitutional Law, Columbia Univ., 1969–86, Dean of Law School, 1984–86; Professor of Law, and President, Yale Univ., 1986–92. Hon. Bencher, Gray's Inn, 1988. Hon. degrees: LLD Princeton, 1986; DLitt Johns Hopkins, 1987; LLD Harvard, 1987. Hon. AM, 1989. *Publications:* Freedom of the Press Versus Public Access, 1974; (with A. M. Bickel) The Judiciary and Responsible Government 1910–1921, 1985. *Address:* 333 Main Street, Knoxville, TN 37902, USA. *T:* (615) 5953000.

SCHMIDT, Helmut H. W.; Chancellor, Federal Republic of Germany, 1974–82; Member of Bundestag, Federal Republic of Germany, 1953–61, and 1965–87; Publisher, Die Zeit, since 1983; *b* 23 Dec. 1918; *s* of Gustav Lentfält Schmidt and Ludovica Schmidt; *m* 1942, Hannelore Glaser; one *d*. *Educ:* Univ. of Hamburg. Diplom-Volkswirt, 1948. Manager of Transport Administration, State of Hamburg, 1949–53; Social Democratic Party: Member, 1946–; Chm., Parly Gp, 1967–69; Vice-Chm. of Party, 1968–84; Senator (Minister) for Domestic Affairs in Hamburg, 1961–65; Minister of Defence, 1969–72; Minister of Finance and Economics, 1972; Minister of Finance, 1972–74. Hon LLD: Newberry Coll., S Carolina, 1973; Johns Hopkins Univ., 1976; Cambridge, 1976; Hon. DCL Oxford, 1979; Hon. Doctorate: Harvard, 1979; Sorbonne, 1981.; Georgetown, 1986. Athinai Prize for Man and Mankind, Onassis Foundn, Greece, 1986. *Publications:* Defence or Retaliation, 1962; Beiträge, 1967; Balance of Power, 1971; Auf dem Fundament des Godesberger Programms, 1973; Bundestagsreden, 1975; Kontinuität und Konzentration, 1975; Als Christ in der politischen Entscheidung, 1976; (with Willy Brandt) Deutschland 1976—Zwei Sozialdemokraten im Gespräch, 1976; Der Kurs heisst Frieden, 1979; Freiheit verantworten, 1980; Pflicht zur Menschlichkeit, 1981; A Grand Strategy for the West, 1985; Menschen und Mächte, 1987 (trans. as Men and Powers, 1989); Die Deutschen und ihre Nachbarn, 1990; Handeln fur Deutschland, 1993; Das Jahr der Entscheidung, 1994. *Recreations:* sailing, chess, playing the organ. *Address:* c/o Deutscher Bundestag, Görresstrasse 15, Bundeshaus, 53113 Bonn, Germany.

SCHNEIDER, Rt. Hon. Sir Lancelot Raymond A.; *see* Adams-Schneider.

SCHNEIDER, Dr William George, OC 1977; FRS 1962; FRSC 1951; Research Consultant, National Research Council of Canada, Ottawa, since 1980 (President, 1967–80); *b* Wolseley, Saskatchewan, 1 June 1915; *s* of Michael Schneider and Phillipina Schneider (*née* Kraushaar); *m* 1940, Jean Frances Purves; two *d*. *Educ:* University of Saskatchewan; McGill University; Harvard University. BSc 1937, MSc 1939, University of Saskatchewan; PhD (in physical chem.), 1941, McGill Univ. Research physicist at Woods Hole Oceanographic Inst., Woods Hole, Mass, USA, 1943–46 (US Navy Certificate of Merit, 1946). Joined Nat. Research Council, Division of Pure Chemistry, Ottawa, 1946; Vice-President (Scientific), 1965–67. Pres., Internat. Union of Pure and Applied Chemistry, 1983–85. Chemical Inst. of Canada Medal, 1961, Montreal Medal, 1973; Henry Marshall Tory Medal, RSC, 1969. Hon. DSc: York, 1966; Memorial, 1968; Saskatchewan, 1969; Moncton, 1969; McMaster, 1969; Laval, 1969; New Brunswick, 1970; Montreal, 1970; McGill, 1970; Acadia, 1976; Regina, 1976; Ottawa, 1978; Hon. LLD: Alberta, 1968; Laurentian, 1968. *Publications:* (with J. A. Pople and H. J. Bernstein) High Resolution Nuclear Magnetic Resonance, 1959; scientific papers in chemistry and physics research jls. *Recreations:* tennis, ski-ing. *Address:* #2–65 Whitemarl Drive, Ottawa, Ontario K1L 8J9, Canada. *T:* (613) 7489742.

SCHNITTKE, Alfred; composer; *b* Engels, Saratov Region, 24 Nov. 1934; *s* of Harry Schnittke and Maria Vogel; *m* 1st, 1956, Galina Koltsina (marr. diss. 1958); 2nd, 1961, Irina Katayeva; one *s*. *Educ:* Moscow Conservatory. Teacher of instrumentation, polyphony and composition, Moscow Conservatory, 1961–71. Member: USSR Composers' Union, Film Makers' Union; W Berlin Acad. of Fine Arts; Royal Swedish Music Acad.; Corresp. Mem., Bavarian Acad. of Fine Arts; Hon. Mem., Hamburg Acad. of Fine Arts. State Prize, RSFSR, 1986. Compositions include: 8 symphonies, 4 violin concertos, 5 concerti grossi, 2 concertos for viola and orchestra, 2 concertos for 'cello and orchestra; Peer Gynt (ballet); Life with an Idiot (opera); choral music, chamber music, film and theatre music. *Publications:* musicological articles. *Address:* ul. Dmitrija Uljanowa d. 4, korp. 2, kw. 155, 117 333 Moscow, Russia. *T:* 1374817; Magdalenenstrasse 62, 2000 Hamburg 13, Germany. *T:* (40) 446391.

SCHOFIELD, Prof. Andrew Noel, MA, PhD (Cantab); FRS 1992; FEng 1986; FICE; Professor of Engineering, Cambridge University, since 1974; Fellow of Churchill College, Cambridge, 1963–66 and since 1974; *b* 1 Nov. 1930; *s* of late Rev. John Noel Schofield and of Winifred Jane Mary (*née* Eyles); *m* 1961, Margaret Eileen Green; two *s* two *d*. *Educ:* Mill Hill Sch.; Christ's Coll., Cambridge. John Winbolt Prize, 1954. Asst Engr, in Malawi, with Scott Wilson Kirkpatrick and Partners, 1951. Cambridge Univ.: Demonstrator, 1955, Lectr, 1959, Dept of Engrg. Research Fellow, California Inst. of Technology, 1963–64. Univ. of Manchester Inst. of Science and Technology: Prof. of Civil Engrg, 1968; Head of Dept of Civil and Structural Engrg, 1973. Chairman: Andrew N. Schofield & Associates Ltd, 1984–; Centrifuge Instrumentation and Equipment (formerly Cambridge Equipment) Ltd, 1987–. Rankine Lecture, ICE British Geotechnical Soc., 1980. Chm., Tech. Cttee on Centrifuge Testing, Int. Soc. for Soil Mech. and Foundn Engrg, 1982–85. James Alfred Ewing Medal, ICE, 1993. US Army Award, Civilian Service 1979. *Publications:* (with C. P. Wroth) Critical State Soil Mechanics, 1968; (ed with W. H. Craig and R. G. James and contrib.) Centrifuges in Soil Mechanics, 1988; (ed with J. R. Gronow and R. K. Jain and contrib.) Land Disposal of Hazardous Waste, 1988; papers on soil mechanics and civil engrg. *Address:* 9 Little St Mary's Lane, Cambridge CB2 1RR. *T:* Cambridge (01223) 314536.

SCHOFIELD, Bertram, CBE 1959; MA, PhD, LittD; Keeper of Manuscripts and Egerton Librarian, British Museum, 1956–61; *b* 13 June 1896; *m* 1928, Edith (*d* 1981), *d* of Arthur William and Edith Emily Thomas; one *s* two *d*. *Educ:* University Sch., Southport; University of Liverpool (Charles Beard and University Fellow); Sorbonne, Ecole des Chartes and Ecole des Hautes Etudes, Paris; Emmanuel College, Cambridge (Open Research Student). Served European War, with Roy. Wilts Yeomanry, 1917–19. Asst Keeper, Dept of MSS, British Museum, 1922; Deputy-Keeper, 1947; Keeper, 1956. Seconded to Min. of Economic Warfare, 1940–42, and for special duties with Inter-Services Intelligence and Combined Ops, HQ, 1942–44. Member: Bd of Studies in Palæography, University of London; Committee of Inst. of Historical Research, 1951–61; Council of Royal Historical Society, 1956–59; Canterbury and York Society; Vice-Pres. British Records Assoc., 1956–61; Governor: North London Collegiate School and Camden High Sch. for Girls, 1955–64. *Publications:* Muchelney Memoranda (Somerset Record Soc.), 1927; (with A. J. Collins) Legal and Manorial Formularies, 1933; The Knyvett Letters, 1949; contrib. to Musical Quarterly, Music Review, Music and Letters. British Museum Quarterly, Studies presented to Sir Hilary Jenkinson, 1957; Musik in Geschichte und Gegenwart, etc. *Recreations:* gardening and music. *Address:* 4 Farm Close, Kidlington, Oxford OX5 2BE. *T:* Kidlington (018675) 374110.

SCHOFIELD, Grace Florence; Regional Nursing Officer to the South West Thames Regional Health Authority, 1974–82, retired; *b* 24 Feb. 1925; *d* of Percy and Matilda Schofield. *Educ:* Mayfield Sch., Putney; University College Hosp. (SRN, SCM); Univ. of London (Dip. in Nursing); Royal College of Nursing (Dip. in Nursing Admin. (Hosp.)). Asst Matron, Guy's Hosp., 1960–61; Dep. Matron, Hammersmith Hosp., 1962–66, Matron, Mount Vernon Hosp. Northwood, and Harefield Hosp., Harefield, 1966–69; Chief Nursing Officer, University Coll. Hosp., 1969–73. *Address:* 42 Briarwood Road, Stoneleigh, Epsom, Surrey KT17 2LY.

SCHOFIELD, Kenneth Douglas; Executive Director, European Golf Tour, Professional Golfers' Association, since 1975; *b* 3 Feb. 1946; *s* of late Douglas Joseph and Jessie Schofield (*née* Gray); *m* 1968, Evelyn May Sharp; two *d*. *Educ:* Auchterarder High Sch. Associate, Savings Bank Inst., 1966. Joined Trustee Savings Bank, Perth, 1962: Br. Manager, Dunblane, 1969–71; George Simms Public Relations Co., 1971–74; Sec., PGA European Tour, 1975. Order of Merit, Royal Spanish Golf Fedn, 1993. *Publication:* Pro Golf: the official PGA European Tour Media Guide, 1972–1975. *Recreations:* golf, cricket, soccer, walking. *Address:* Riding Cottage, 2 The Riding, Woodham, Woking, Surrey GU21 5TA. *T:* Woking (01483) 714984; (office) Bracknell (01344) 842881. *Clubs:* Caledonian; Wentworth Golf; Crieff Golf; Auchterarder Golf.

SCHOFIELD, Dr Malcolm; Reader in Ancient Philosophy, University of Cambridge, since 1989; Fellow, St John's College, Cambridge, since 1972; *b* 19 April 1942; *er s* of Harry Schofield and Ethel Schofield (*née* Greenwood); *m* 1970, Elizabeth Milburn; one *s*. *Educ:* St Albans Sch.; St John's Coll., Cambridge; Balliol Coll., Oxford. Asst Prof. of Classics, Cornell Univ., 1967–69; Dyson Res. Fellow in Greek Culture, Balliol Coll.,

Oxford, 1970–72; Cambridge University: Lectr in Classics, 1972–89; Mem., Gen. Bd, 1991–94; Chm. Council, Sch. of Arts and Humanities, 1993–94; St John's College: Dean, 1979–82; Tutor, 1982–89; Pres., 1991–95. Editor, Phronesis, 1987–92. Hon. Sec., Classical Assoc., 1989–. Hon. Citizen, Rhodes, 1992. *Publications:* (ed jtly) Articles on Aristotle, 4 vols, 1975–79; (ed jtly) Doubt and Dogmatism, 1980; An Essay on Anaxagoras, 1980; (ed with M. Nussbaum) Language and Logos, 1982; (ed jtly) Science and Speculation, 1982; (with G. S. Kirk and J. E. Raven) The Presocratic Philosophers, 2nd edn, 1983; (ed with G. Striker) The Norms of Nature, 1986; The Stoic Idea of the City, 1991; (ed with A. Laks) Justice and Generosity, 1995. *Address:* St John's College, Cambridge CB2 1TP. *T:* Cambridge (01223) 338644.

SCHOFIELD, Neill; Director, Training, Infrastructure and Employers Division, Training, Enterprise and Education Directorate, Department for Education and Employment (formerly Department of Employment), since 1994; *b* 2 Aug. 1946; *m* 1969, Carol; two *d.* *Educ:* Univ. of Leeds (BA Econs 1967); QMC, Univ. of London (MSc 1975). DoE, 1970–78; Dept of Energy, 1978–82; Department of Employment, later Department for Education and Employment, 1982–: Dir, Business and Enterprise, 1990–92, Quality Assurance, 1992–93. *Recreations:* walking, theatre, family. *Address:* (office) Moorfoot, Sheffield S1 4PQ. *T:* Sheffield (0114) 259 3948.

SCHOFIELD, Dr Roger Snowden, FRHistS; FBA 1988; FSS; Senior Research Associate, Cambridge Group for the History of Population and Social Structure, Economic and Social Research Council, since 1994 (Director, 1974–94); Hon. Reader in Historical Demography, University of Cambridge, since 1991; Fellow of Clare College, Cambridge, since 1969; *b* 26 Aug. 1937; *s* of Ronald Snowden Schofield and Muriel Grace Braime; *m* 1961, Elizabeth Mary Cunliffe; one *d.* *Educ:* Leighton Park Sch., Reading; Clare Coll., Cambridge (BA (History); PhD 1963). FRHistS 1970; FSS 1987. Vis. Prof., Div. of Humanities and Social Scis, CIT, 1992–94. Member: Computing Cttee, SSRC, 1970–75; Stats Cttee, SSRC, 1974–78; Software Provision Cttee, UK Computer Bd, 1977–79. Mem., Population Investigation Cttee, 1976– (Treas., 1987–); British Society for Population Studies: Mem., Council, 1979–87; Treas., 1981–85; Pres., 1985–87. *Publications:* (with E. A. Wrigley) The Population History of England 1541–1871: a reconstruction, 1981, repr. with introd. essay, 1993; (ed with John Walter) Famine, Disease, and the Social Order in Early Modern Society, 1989; contrib. to Population Studies, Jl of Interdisciplinary Hist., Jl of Family Hist. *Address:* Clare College, Cambridge CB2 1TL. *T:* Cambridge (01223) 333267.

SCHOLAR, Michael Charles, CB 1991; Permanent Secretary, Welsh Office, since 1993; *b* 3 Jan. 1942; *s* of Richard Herbert Scholar and Mary Blodwen Scholar; *m* 1964, Angela Mary (*née* Sweet); three *s* (one *d* decd). *Educ:* St Olave's Grammar School, Bermondsey; St John's College, Cambridge (PhD, MA); Univ. of California at Berkeley. ARCO. Loeb Fellow, Harvard Univ., 1967; Asst Lectr, Leicester Univ., 1968; Fellow, St John's College, Cambridge, 1969–70; HM Treasury, 1969; Private Sec. to Chief Sec., 1974–76; Barclays Bank International, 1979–81; Private Sec. to Prime Minister, 1981–83; Under Secretary, HM Treasury, 1983–87, Dep. Sec., 1987–93. *Address:* Welsh Office, Cathays Park, Cardiff CF1 3NQ. *T:* Cardiff (01222) 823289.

SCHOLES, Alwyn Denton; Senior Puisne Judge, Hong Kong, 1970–71 (Acting Chief Justice, 1970); *b* 16 Dec. 1910; *s* of Denton Scholes and Mrs Scholes (*née* Birch); *m* 1939, Juliet Angela Ierne Pyne; one *s* four *d.* *Educ:* Cheltenham College; Selwyn College, Cambridge. Legal Tripos Parts I and II, Cantab, 1932, 1933; MA 1933. Called to the Bar, 1934; practised at the Bar in London and on Midland Circuit, 1934–38; apptd District Magistrate, Gold Coast, 1938; Acting Crown Counsel and Solicitor General, Gold Coast, 1941; apptd Magistrate, Hong Kong, 1948; First Magistrate: Kowloon, 1949; Hong Kong, 1949. Appointed District Judge, Hong Kong, 1953, Puisne Judge, Hong Kong, 1958. Comr, Supreme Ct of State of Brunei, 1964–67, 1968–71. Pres. or Mem., Hong Kong Full Ct of Appeal, on occasions, 1949–71. Member: Sidmouth Parochial Church Council, 1972–82; Ottery Deanery Synod, 1973–82. Governor, St Nicholas Sch., Sidmouth, 1984–89. *Recreations:* walking, gardening. *Address:* West Hayes, Convent Road, Sidmouth, Devon EX10 8RL. *Club:* Commonwealth Trust.

SCHOLES, Hon. Gordon Glen Denton, AO 1993; MHR for Corio (Victoria), Australia, 1967–93; *b* 7 June 1931; *s* of Glen Scholes and Mary Scholes; *m* 1957, Della Kathleen Robinson; two *d.* *Educ:* various schs. Loco-engine driver, Victorian Railways, 1949–67. Councillor, Geelong City, 1965–67; Pres., Geelong Trades Hall Council, 1965–66. House of Representatives: Chm. cttees, 1973–75; Speaker, 1975–76; Shadow Minister for Defence, 1977–83; Minister for Defence, 1983–84; Minister for Territories, 1984–87. Amateur Boxing Champion (Heavyweight), Vic, 1949. *Recreations:* golf, reading. *Address:* 20 Stephen Street, Newtown, Vic 3220, Australia.

SCHOLES, Hubert, CB 1977; a Commissioner of Customs and Excise, 1978–81; *b* 22 March 1921; *s* of late Hubert Scholes and Lucy (*née* Carter); *m* 1949, Patricia Caldwell; one *s.* *Educ:* Shrewsbury Sch.; Balliol Coll., Oxford. Served RA, 1940–45. Asst Principal, Min. of Fuel and Power, 1946; Principal, 1950; Ministry of Housing and Local Govt, 1956–57; Principal Private Sec. to Minister of Power, 1959–62; Asst Sec., 1962; Under-Sec., Min. of Power, subseq. Min. of Technol., DTI and Dept of Industry, 1968–78. Specialist Advr to H of C Employment Cttee, 1981–82. *Address:* 5A Lancaster Avenue, Farnham, Surrey GU9 8JY. *T:* Farnham (01252) 723992.

SCHOLES, Mary Elizabeth, (Mrs A. I. M. Haggart), OBE 1983; SRN; Chief Area Nursing Officer, Tayside Health Board, 1973–83; *b* 8 April 1924; *d* of late John Neville Carpenter Scholes and Margaret Elizabeth (*née* Hines); *m* 1983, Most Rev. Alastair Iain Macdonald Haggart, *qv.* *Educ:* Wyggeston Grammar Sch. for Girls, Leicester; Leicester Royal Infirmary and Children's Hosp. (SRN 1946); Guy's Hosp., London (CMB Pt I Cert. 1947); Royal Coll. of Nursing, London (Nursing Admin (Hosp.) Cert. 1962). Leicester Royal Infirmary and Children's Hospital: Staff Nurse, 1947–48; Night Sister, 1948–50; Ward Sister, 1950–56; Night Supt, 1956–58; Asst Matron, 1958–61; Asst Matron, Memorial/Brook Gen. Hosp., London, 1962–64; Matron, Dundee Royal Infirm. and Matron Designate, Ninewells Hosp., Dundee, 1964–68; Chief Nursing Officer, Bd of Management for Dundee Gen. Hosps and Bd of Man. for Ninewells and Associated Hosps, 1968–73. Pres., Scottish Assoc. of Nurse Administrators, 1973–77. Member: Scottish Bd, Royal Coll. of Nursing, 1965–70; Gen. Nursing Council for Scotland, 1966–70, 1979–; Standing Nursing and Midwifery Cttee, Scotland, 1971–74 (Vice-Chm., 1973–74); UK Central Council for Nursing, Midwifery and Health Visiting, 1980–84; Management Cttee, State Hosp., Carstairs, 1983–92; Scottish Hosp. Endowments Res. Trust, 1986–; Chm., Scottish National Bd for Nursing, Midwifery and Health Visiting, 1980–84. *Recreations:* travel, music. *Address:* 19 Eglinton Crescent, Edinburgh EH12 5BY. *Club:* Royal Over-Seas League.

SCHOLES, Rodney James; QC 1987; a Recorder, since 1986; *b* 26 Sept. 1945; *s* of late Henry Scholes and of Margaret Bower; *m* 1977, Katherin Elizabeth (*née* Keogh); three *s.* *Educ:* Wade Deacon Grammar Sch., Widnes; St Catherine's Coll., Oxford (scholar) (BA; BCL). Lincoln's Inn: Hardwicke Schol., 1964; Mansfield Schol., 1967; called to the Bar, 1968. Mem., Northern Circuit, 1968–. *Recreations:* watching Rugby League football, dog walking. *Address:* 25 Byrom Street, Manchester M3 4PF. *T:* 0161–834 5238; 61 Fleet Street, EC4Y 1JU. *T:* 0171–353 4363.

SCHOLEY, Sir David (Gerald), Kt 1987; CBE 1976; Chairman, S. G. Warburg Group plc (formerly Mercury International Group), since 1984; a Director, Bank of England, since 1981; *b* 28 June 1935; *s* of Dudley and Lois Scholey; *m* 1960, Alexandra Beatrix, *d* of Hon. George and Fiorenza Drew, Canada; one *s* one *d.* *Educ:* Wellington Coll., Berks; Christ Church, Oxford. Nat Service, RAC, 9th Queen's Royal Lancers, 1953–55; 3/4 CLY (Sharpshooters); Metropolitan Special Constabulary (Thames Div.). Thompson Graham & Co. (Lloyd's brokers), 1956–58; Dale & Co. (Insce brokers), Canada, 1958–59; Guinness Mahon & Co. Ltd, 1959–64; joined S. G. Warburg & Co. Ltd, 1964, Dir 1967, Dep. Chm., 1977, Jt Chm., 1980–87; Director: Mercury Securities plc, 1969 (Chm., 1984–86); Orion Insurance Co. Ltd, 1963–87; Stewart Wrightson Holdings Ltd, 1972–81; Union Discount Co. of London, Ltd, 1976–81; British Telecom plc, 1985–94; Chubb Corp., 1991–; General Electric Co., 1992–95; London First, 1993. Mem., Export Guarantees Adv. Council, 1970–75 (Dep. Chm. 1974–75); Chairman: Construction Exports Adv. Bd, 1975–78; UK Council, INSEAD (Mem. Bd, 1992–); Member: Inst. Internat. d'Etudes Bancaires, 1976–94 (Pres., 1988); Cttee on Finance for Industry, NEDO, 1980–87; Industry and Commerce Gp, SCF, 1989–95; President's Cttee, BITC, 1988–91; Ford Foundn Adv. Gp on UN Financing, 1992–93. Gov., BBC, 1994–95. Trustee: Glyndebourne Arts Trust, 1989–; Nat. Portrait Gallery, 1992–. Hon. Treasurer, IISS, 1984–91. Governor: Wellington Coll., 1977–89; NIESR, 1984–; LSE, 1993. FRSA. Hon. DLitt London Guildhall, 1993. *Address:* (office) 1 Finsbury Avenue, EC2M 2PA.

SCHOLEY, Sir Robert, Kt 1987; CBE 1982; FEng 1990; Chairman, British Steel plc (formerly British Steel Corporation), 1986–92; *b* 8 Oct. 1921; *s* of Harold and Eveline Scholey; *m* 1946, Joan Methley; two *d.* *Educ:* King Edward VII Sch. and Sheffield Univ. Associateship in Mech Engrg. United Steel Companies, 1947–68; British Steel Corporation, 1968–92: Dir and Chief Executive, 1973–86; Dep. Chm., 1976–86. Dir, Eurotunnel Bd, 1987–94. Mem., HEFCE, 1992–95. Pres., Eurofer, 1985–90. Chm., Internat. Iron and Steel Inst., 1989–90; Pres., Inst. of Metals, 1989–90. Hon. DEng Sheffield, 1987. *Recreations:* outdoor life, history.

SCHOLTENS, Sir James (Henry), KCVO 1977 (CVO 1963); Director, Office of Government Ceremonial and Hospitality, Department of the Prime Minister and Cabinet, Canberra, 1973–80, retired; Extra Gentleman Usher to the Queen, since 1981; *b* 12 June 1920; *s* of late Theo F. J. Scholtens and late Grace M. E. (*née* Nolan); *m* 1945, Mary Maguire, Brisbane; one *s* five *d.* *Educ:* St Patrick's Marist Brothers' Coll., Sale, Vic. Served War, RAAF, 1943–45. Joined Aust. Public Service, 1935; PMG's Dept, Melbourne, 1935; Dept of Commerce, Melb., 1938; transf. to Dept of Commerce, Canberra, 1941; Dept of Prime Minister, Canberra: Accountant, 1949; Ceremonial Officer, 1954; Asst Sec., Ceremonial and Hospitality Br., 1967. Dir of visits to Australia by the Sovereign and Members of the Royal Family, Heads of State, Monarchs and Presidents, and by Heads of Govt and Ministers of State. *Address:* 74 Boldrewood Street, Turner, Canberra, ACT 2601, Australia. *T:* (6) 2486639. *Clubs:* Canberra, Southern Cross (Canberra); Royal Automobile of Australia (Sydney).

SCHOLZ, Prof. Dr Rupert; Professor of Public Law, Institut für Politik und öffentliches Recht, University of Munich, since 1981; *b* 23 May 1937; *s* of Ernst and Gisela Scholz (*née* Merdas); *m* 1971, Dr Helga Scholz-Hoppe. *Educ:* Abitur, Berlin; studied law and economics, Berlin and Heidelberg; Dr Jur., Univ. of Munich. Prof., Univ. of Munich, taught in Munich, Berlin, Regensburg, Augsburg; Public Law Chair, Berlin and Munich, 1978. Senator of Justice, Land Berlin, 1981; Acting Senator for Federal Affairs; Mem., Bundesrat, 1982; Mem., N Atlantic Assembly, 1982; Senator for Federal Affairs, Land Berlin, 1983; MHR, Berlin, and Senator for Justice and Federal Affairs, 1985; Federal Minister of Defence, FRG, 1988–89; Mem., German Bundestag, 1990–. *Publications:* numerous papers in jurisp., German policy, foreign policy, economic policy. *Address:* Institut für Politik und öffentliches Recht, Universität München, Ludwigstrasse 28, 8000 München, Germany.

SCHOPPER, Prof. Herwig Franz; Professor of Physics, University of Hamburg, 1973–89, now Emeritus; *b* 28 Feb. 1928; *s* of Franz Schopper and Margarete Hartmann; *m* 1949, Dora Klara Ingeborg (*née* Stieler); one *s* one *d.* *Educ:* Univ. of Hamburg. Dip. Phys. 1949, Dr rer nat 1951. Asst Prof. and Univ. Lectr, Univ. of Erlangen, 1954–57; Prof., Univ. of Mainz, 1957–60; Prof., Univ. of Karlsruhe and Dir of Inst. for Nuclear Physics, 1961–73; Chm., Scientific Council, Kerforschungszentrum, Karlsruhe, 1967–69; Chm., Deutsches Elektronen Synchrotron particle physics Lab., Hamburg, 1973–80; European Organisation for Nuclear Research (CERN): Res. Associate, 1966–67; Head, Dept of particle physics and Mem., Directorate for experimental prog., 1970–73; Chm., Intersecting Storage Ring Cttee, 1973–76; Mem., Sci. Policy Cttee, 1979–80; Dir-Gen., 1981–88. Chm., Assoc. of German Nat. Research Centres, 1978–80; Mem., Scientific Council, IN2P3, Paris. President: German Physical Soc., 1992–94; European Physical Soc., 1995–. Member: Akad. der Wissenschaften Leopoldina, Halle; Joachim Jungius Gesellschaft, Hamburg; Sudetendeutsche Akad. der Wissenschaft, 1979; Acad. Scientiarium et Artium, Vienna, 1993; MAE 1992; Corresp. Mem., Bavarian Acad. of Scis, 1981. Dr *hc*: Univ. of Erlangen, 1982; Univ. of Moscow, 1989; Univ. of Geneva, 1989; Univ. of London, 1989. Physics Award, Göttinger Akad. der Wissenschaft, 1957; Carus Medal, Akad. Leopoldina, 1958; Ritter von Gerstner Medal, 1978; Sudetendeutscher Kulturpreis, 1984; Golden Plate Award, Amer. Acad. of Achievement, 1984; Gold Medal, Weizmann Inst., 1987; Wilhelm Exner Medal, Gewerbeverein, Austria, 1991; Purkyne Meml Medal, Czech Acad. of Scis. Grosses Bundesverdienstkreuz (FRG), 1989. *Publications:* Weak Interactions and Nuclear Beta Decay, 1966; Matter—Antimatter, 1989; papers on elementary particle physics, high energy accelerators, relation of science and society. *Recreations:* music, gardening. *Address:* c/o CERN, 1211 Geneva 23, Switzerland. *T:* (22) 7675350.

SCHOUVALOFF, Alexander, MA; Chairman, Theatre Design Trust, since 1993; *b* 4 May 1934; *s* of Paul Schouvaloff (professional name Paul Sheriff) and Anna Schouvaloff (*née* Raevsky); *m* 1st, Gillian Baker; one *s*; 2nd, 1971, Daria Chorley (*née* de Mérindol). *Educ:* Harrow Sch.; Jesus Coll., Oxford (MA). Asst Director, Edinburgh Festival, 1965–67; Dir, North West Arts Assoc., 1967–74; Curator, Theatre Mus., V & A Mus., 1974–89; Director: Rochdale Festival, 1971; Chester Festival, 1973. Sec. Gen., Société Internat. des Bibliothèques et des Musées des Arts du Spectacle, 1980–90; Cttee Mem. for Dance Collection, NY Public Liby for Performing Arts, 1993–. Trustee, London Archives of the Dance, 1976–. BBC Radio plays: Summer of the Bullshine Boys, 1981; No Saleable Value, 1982. Cross of Polonia Restituta, 1971. *Publications:* Place for the Arts, 1971; Summer of the Bullshine Boys, 1979; (with Victor Borovsky) Stravinsky on Stage, 1982; (with April FitzLyon) A Month in the Country, 1983; Thyssen-Bornemisza Collection: catalogue of set and costume designs, 1987; (with Catherine Haill) The Theatre Museum, 1987; Theatre on Paper, 1990; Léon Bakst: The Theatre Art, 1991. *Recreation:* swimming. *Address:* 10 Avondale Park Gardens, W11 4PR. *T:* 0171–727 7543. *Club:* Garrick.

SCHRAM, Prof. Stuart Reynolds; Professor of Politics (with reference to China) in the University of London, School of Oriental and African Studies, 1968–89, now Emeritus;

Research Associate, Harvard University, since 1989; *b* Excelsior, Minn, 27 Feb. 1924; *s* of Warren R. Schram and Nada Stedman Schram; *m* 1972, Marie-Annick Lancelot; one *s*. *Educ:* West High Sch., Minneapolis, Minn; Univ. of Minnesota (BA, 1944); Columbia Univ. (PhD 1954). Dir, Soviet and Chinese Section, Centre d'Etude des Relations Internationales, Fondation Nationale des Sciences Politiques, Paris, 1954–67; Head, Contemporary China Inst., SOAS, 1968–72. *Publications:* Protestantism and Politics in France, 1954; The Political Thought of Mao Tse-Tung, 1963, rev. edn 1969; Le marxisme et l'Asie 1853–1964, 1965, rev. and enl. English edn 1969; Mao Tse-tung, 1966; Mao Zedong: a preliminary re-assessment, 1983; Ideology and Policy in China since the Third Plenum, 1978–84, 1984; (ed) The Scope of State Power in China, 1985; (ed) Foundations and Limits of State Power in China, 1987; The Thought of Mao Tse-tung, 1989; (ed) Mao's Road to Power: Revolutionary Writings 1912–1949, vol. I 1992, vol. II 1994, vol. III 1995. *Recreations:* concert- and theatre-going, walking in the country, fishing. *Address:* John King Fairbank Center for East Asian Research, Harvard University, 1737 Cambridge Street, Cambridge, MA 02138, USA.

SCHRAMEK, Sir Eric (Emil) von; *see* von Schramek.

SCHREIBER, family name of **Baron Marlesford.**

SCHREYER, Rt Hon. Edward Richard, CC (Canada) 1979; CMM 1979; CD 1979; PC 1984; High Commissioner for Canada in Australia, and concurrently Ambassador to Vanuatu, 1984–88; *b* Beausejour, Man., 21 Dec. 1935; *s* of John and Elizabeth Schreyer, a pioneer family of the district; *m* 1960, Lily, *d* of Jacob Schulz, MP; two *s* two *d*. *Educ:* Beausejour, Manitoba; United Coll., Winnipeg; St John's Coll., Winnipeg, Univ. of Manitoba (BA, BEd, MA). While at university served as 2nd Lieut, COTC, Royal Canadian Armored Corps, 1954–55. Member, Legislative Assembly of Manitoba, 1958; re-elected, 1959 and 1962; MP: for Springfield, 1965; for Selkirk, 1968; chosen as Leader of New Democratic Party in Manitoba, 1969, and resigned seat in House of Commons; MLA for Rossmere and Premier of Manitoba, 1969–77; Minister of: Dominion-Provincial Relns, 1969–77; Hydro, 1971–77; Finance, 1972–74; re-elected MLA, 1977; Governor-Gen. and C-in-C of Canada, 1979–84. Prof. of Political Science and Internat. Relns, St John's Coll., Univ. of Manitoba, 1962–65. Distinguished Vis. Prof., Univ. of Winnipeg, 1989–90; Vis. Prof., Simon Fraser Univ., Vancouver, 1991; Distinguished Fellow, Inst. for Integrated Energy Systems, Univ. of Victoria, 1992–94; Univ. of BC, 1995–. Director: Perfect Pacific Investments, 1989–; China International Trade and Investment Corp., Canada, 1991–; Saskatchewan Energy Conservation and Develt Authy, 1993–; Alternate Fuel Systems Inc. (Calgary), 1994–; Cephalon Oil & Gas Resource Corp. (Calgary), 1994–. Chm., Canadian Shield Foundn, 1984–; Member: Internat. Assoc. of Energy Economists; CPA; IPU. Hon. LLD: Manitoba, 1979; Mount Allison, 1983; McGill, 1984; Simon Fraser, 1984; Lakehead, 1985; Hon. Dr Sci. Sociale Ottawa, 1980. *Recreations:* reading, golf, sculpting, woodworking. *Address:* 401–250 Wellington Crescent, Winnipeg, Man R3M 0B3, Canada. *T:* (204) 9897580, *Fax:* (204) 9897581. *Clubs:* Rideau (Ottawa); York, Upper Canada (Toronto).

SCHRIEFFER, Prof. John Robert, PhD; University Professor, Florida State University, and Chief Scientist, National High Magnetic Field Laboratory, since 1992; *b* Oak Park, Ill, 31 May 1931; *s* of John Henry Schrieffer and Louise Anderson; *m* 1960, Anne Grete Thomsen; one *s* two *d*. *Educ:* MIT(BS); Univ. of Illinois (MS, PhD). Nat. Sci. Foundn Fellow, Univ. of Birmingham, and Niels Bohr Inst. for Theoretical Physics, Copenhagen, 1957–58; Asst Prof., Univ. of Chicago, 1957–59; Asst Prof., Univ. of Illinois, 1959–60, Associate Prof., 1960–62; Univ. of Pennsylvania: Mem. Faculty, 1962–79; Mary Amanda Wood Prof. of Physics, 1964–79; University of California, Santa Barbara: Prof. of Physics, 1980–91; Chancellor's Prof., 1984–91; Dir, Inst. for Theoretical Physics, 1984–89. Guggenheim Fellow, Copenhagen, 1967. Member: Nat. Acad. Scis; Amer. Acad. of Arts and Scis; Amer. Philos. Soc.; Amer. Phys Soc. (Vice-Pres., 1994); Danish Royal Acad. Sci.; Acad. of Sci. of USSR, 1989. Hon. ScD: Technische Hochschule, Munich, 1968; Univ. of Geneva, 1968; Univ. of Pennsylvania, 1973; Illinois Univ., 1974; Univ. of Cincinnati, 1977; Hon. DSc Tel-Aviv Univ., 1987. Buckley Prize, Amer. Phys Soc., 1968; Comstock Prize, Nat. Acad. Scis, 1968; (jtly) Nobel Prize for Physics, 1972; John Ericsson Medal, Amer. Soc. of Swedish Engineers, 1976; Nat. Medal of Science, USA, 1985. *Publications:* Theory of Superconductivity, 1964; articles on solid state physics and chemistry. *Recreations:* painting, gardening, wood working. *Address:* NHMFL/FSU, 1800 E Paul Dirac Drive, Tallahassee, FL 32306–3016, USA.

SCHUBERT, Sir Sydney, Kt 1985; Chief Executive, Daikyo Group Australia, since 1988; Co-ordinator General and Permanent Head, 1982–88, Director General, 1987–88, Premier's Department, Government of Queensland, Australia; *b* 22 March 1928; *s* of Wilhelm F. Schubert and Mary A. Price; *m* 1961, Maureen Kistle; two *d*. *Educ:* Univ. of Queensland; Univ. of Durham. Queensland Government: Civil Engr, 1950; Dep. Chief Engr, Main Roads Dept, 1965–69; Chief Engr Dept., 1969–72; Dep. Co-ordinator General, 1972–76. Director: Jupiters, 1988–92 (Dep. Chm., 1990–92); Coffey Internat., 1990–; APN Hldgs, 1992–; Victoria Hotels Pty Ltd (Christchurch), 1990–; Premier Hotels Pty Ltd (Christchurch), 1990–; Christchurch Casinos Pty Ltd, 1992–. Chancellor, Bond Univ., 1987–89. Mem., Gt Barrier Reef Marine Park Authy, 1978–88; Deputy Chairman: Brisbane Exposition and S Bank Redevelt Authy, 1984–88; Qld Cultural Centre Trust, 1986–88. Member: Bd of Management, Graduate Sch. of Management, Univ. of Queensland, 1985–88; Exec. Council, Australia Japan Assoc. Qld, 1988–90. Eisenhower Fellow, Aust., 1972. FIE(Aust); FAIM; Hon. Fellow, Aust. Instn of Engrs. *Recreation:* golf. *Address:* 15 Apex Street, Clayfield, Brisbane, Qld 4011, Australia. *Clubs:* Queensland, Royal Queensland Golf.

SCHULTZ, Rt. Rev. Bruce Allan; *see* Grafton, NSW, Bishop of.

SCHULTZ, Prof. Theodore W., PhD; Charles L. Hutchinson Distinguished Service Professor of Economics, University of Chicago, since 1952; *b* 30 April 1902; *s* of Henry E. Schultz and Anna Elizabeth Weiss; *m* Esther Florence Werth; one *s* two *d*. *Educ:* South Dakota State Coll. (BS); Univ. of Wisconsin (MS, PhD). Iowa State College: Faculty of Economics, 1930–43; Head, Dept of Economics and Sociology, 1934–43; University of Chicago: Prof. of Economics, from 1943; Chairman, Dept of Economics, 1946–61. Hon. LLD: Grinnell Coll. 1949, Michigan State 1962; Illinois 1968; Wisconsin 1968; Catholic Univ. of Chile 1979; Dijon 1981; N Carolina State Univ. 1984. Francis A. Walker Medal, Amer. Econ. Assoc., 1972; Leonard Elmhirst Medal, Internat. Agricl Econ. Assoc., 1976; Nobel Prize for Economic Science, 1979. *Publications:* Redirecting Farm Policy, 1943; Agriculture in an Unstable Economy, 1945; The Economic Organization of Agriculture, 1953; The Economic Value of Education, 1963; Transforming Traditional Agriculture, 1964; Economic Growth and Agriculture, 1968; Investment in Human Capital: role of education and research, 1971; Human Resources: policy issues and research opportunities, 1972; (ed) Distortions of Agricultural Incentives, 1978; Investing in People: the economics of population quality, 1981; Restoring Economic Equilibrium: human capital in the modernizing economy, 1990; The Economics of Being Poor, 1993; Origins of Increasing Returns, 1993. *Address:* 5620 South Kimbark Avenue, Chicago, IL 60637, USA. *T:* (312) 4936083.

SCHUMANN, Maurice; Hon. GCMG 1972; Chevalier de la Légion d'Honneur; Compagnon de la Libération; Croix de Guerre (1939–45); Senator from the Department of the Nord, since 1974; Vice-President of the Senate, 1977–92; Member, Académie Française, since 1974; writer and broadcaster; *b* Paris, 10 April 1911; *s* of Julien Schumann and Thérèse Michel; *m* 1944, Lucie Daniel; three *d*. *Educ:* Lycées of Janson-de-Sailly and Henry IV; Faculty of Letters, Univ. of Paris (Licencié ès Lettres). Attached to l'Agence Havas in London and later Paris, 1935–39; Chief Official Broadcaster, BBC French Service, 1940–44; Liaison Officer with Allied Expeditionary Forces at end of war; Mem. Provisional Consultative Assembly, Nov. 1944–July 1945; Deputy for Nord, 1945–67 and 1968–73; Mem. Constituent Assemblies, Oct. 1945–May 1946 and June–Nov. 1946. Chm., Popular Republican Movement (MRP); Deputy of this group, 1945–73 (Pres., 1945–49; Hon. Pres., 1949–); Dep. Minister for Foreign Affairs, 1951–54; Pres., For. Affairs Cttee of Nat. Assembly, 1959; Minister of State (Prime Minister's Office), April–May 1962; Minister of State, in charge of scientific res. and atomic and spacial questions, 1967–68; Minister of State for Social Affairs, 1968–69; Minister for Foreign Affairs, 1969–73. Chm., Commn on Cultural Affairs, 1986–. Has been Pres. of various organisations, incl. Internat. Movement for Atlantic Union, 1966–. Associate Prof., Faculté Catholique de Lille, 1975–. Pres., Assoc. des Ecrivains catholiques, 1980–. Mem. Editl Bd, Le Revue des Deux Mondes, 1984–. Hon. LLD: Cantab, 1972; St Andrews, 1974; Hon. Dr Oxon, 1972. *Publications:* Le Germanisme en marche, 1938; Mussolini, 1939; Les problèmes Ukrainiens et la paix européenne, 1939; Honneur et Patrie, 1945; Le vrai malaise des intellectuels de gauche, 1957; La Mort née de leur propre vie: essai sur Péguy, Simone Weil et Gandhi, 1974; Un Certain 18 Juin, 1980 (Prix Aujourd'hui); Qui a tué le duc d'Enghien?, 1984; Une grande Imprudence, 1986; *novels:* Le Rendezvous avec quelqu'un, 1962; Les Flots roulant au loin, 1973; La Communication, 1974; Angoisse et Certitude, 1978 (Grand Prix de Littérature Catholique); Le Concerto en Ut Majeur, 1982; La victoire et la nuit, 1989; Bergson où le retour de Dieu, 1995; chapters in: Mazarin, 1960; Talleyrand, 1962; Clemenceau, 1974; many articles etc (under pseudonym of André Sidobre) to L'Aube (Paris daily), Le Temps présent and La Vie catholique, etc. *Address:* 53 avenue du Maréchal-Lyautey, Paris 16e, France.

SCHUSTER, Sir (Felix) James (Moncrieff), 3rd Bt, *cr* 1906; OBE 1955; TD; Senior Partner, Sheppards and Chase, 1970–75, retired; *b* 8 January 1913; *o s* of Sir Victor Schuster, 2nd Bt, and Lucy, *d* of W. B. Skene, Pitlour-Halyards, Fife; *S* father, 1962; *m* 1937, Ragna (*d* 1995), *er d* of late Direktor Sundø, Copenhagen; two *d*. *Educ:* Winchester. Served War of 1939–45, with The Rifle Brigade (Middle East and Combined Operations). Lt-Col comdg London Rifle Brigade. Rangers (RB), TA, 1952; Bt-Colonel, 1955. Hon. Col, 5th Bn Royal Green Jackets, 1970–75. *Heir:* none. *Address:* Piltdown Cottage, Piltdown, Uckfield, East Sussex TN22 3XB. *T:* Newick (01825) 722916. *Clubs:* Naval and Military, Lansdowne.

SCHUSTER, Sir James; *see* Schuster, Sir F. J. M.

SCHUSTER, Rt. Rev. James Leo; Assistant Bishop of George, since 1980; *b* 18 July 1912; *s* of Rev. Harold Vernon Schuster and Elsie Jane (*née* Roberton); *m* 1951, Ilse Henriette Emmy Gottschalk; three *s* two *d* (and one *s* decd). *Educ:* Lancing; Keble Coll., Oxford. Deacon, 1937; Priest, 1938; Asst Missioner, Clare Coll. Mission, Rotherhithe, 1937–38; Chaplain St Stephen's House, Oxford, 1938–40; CF (EC), 1940–46; wounded, 1942; despatches, 1943. Chaplain, St Stephen's House, Oxford, 1946–49; Principal St Bede's Coll., Umtata, 1949–56; Bishop of St John's, 1956–79; Archdeacon of Riversdale, 1980–86; Rector of Swellendam, 1980–87. *Address:* PO Box 285, 19 Aanhuizen Street, Swellendam 6740, South Africa.

SCHWARTZ, Melvin, PhD; Associate Director for High Energy and Nuclear Physics, Brookhaven National Laboratory, Upton, New York, since 1991; *b* 2 Nov. 1932; *s* of Harry Schwartz and Hannah Schwartz (*née* Shulman); *m* 1953, Marilyn Fenster; one *s* two *d*. *Educ:* Columbia College, NY (AB 1953); Columbia Univ., NY (PhD 1958). Associate Physicist, Brookhaven Nat. Lab., 1956–58; Asst Prof., Associate Prof. and Prof. of Physics, Columbia Univ., 1958–66; Prof. of Physics, 1966–83, Consulting Prof., 1983–, Stanford Univ. Chm., 1970–, Chief Exec. Officer, 1970–91, Digital Pathways Inc. Mem., Nat. Acad. of Scis, 1975. Hughes Prize, 1964; (jtly) Nobel Prize in Physics, 1988. *Publication:* Principles of Electrodynamics, 1972. *Recreations:* ski-ing, photography, woodworking. *Address:* 61 South Howells Point Road, Bellport, New York, NY 11713, USA. *T:* (office) (516) 2827711.

SCHWARZ-BART, André; French writer; *b* Metz, Lorraine, France, 23 May 1928; 2nd *s* of parents from Poland; *m* 1961, Simone Schwarz-Bart; two *c*. *Educ:* self-educated; Trades Sch., Sillac; Sorbonne. Joined French Resistance at 15. Has worked in factories as a fitter and in Les Halles, Paris, while writing; has travelled to Israel, Africa and to the West Indies. *Publications:* Le Dernier des Justes, 1959 (Prix Goncourt, 1959; Eng. trans., 1960); (with Simone Schwarz-Bart) Un plat de porc aux bananes vertes, 1967 (Jerusalem Prize, 1967); La Mulâtresse Solitude, 1972 (Eng. trans., A Woman Named Solitude, 1973). *Address:* c/o Editions du Seuil, 27 rue Jacob, 75261 Paris Cedex 06, France.

SCHWARZKOPF, Dame Elisabeth, DBE 1992; soprano; *b* 9 Dec. 1915; *o d* of Gymnasialdirektor Friedrich Schwarzkopf and Elisabeth (*née* Fröhlich); *m* Walter Legge (*d* 1979). *Educ:* High School for Music, Berlin; studied with Maria Ivogün-Raucheisen, Austrian concert singer. Sang at Vienna State Opera, Royal Opera House, Covent Garden, La Scala, Milan, 1948–64, Metropolitan Opera, NY, San Francisco Opera; Inauguration, Bayreuther Fest. after the war. Film, Der Rosenkavalier, 1961. Hon. Member: Royal Swedish Acad. for Arts and Sciences; Accad. S Cecilia, Roma; RAM; Corres. Mem., Bayerischer Akad. der Künste. MusD (*hc*) Cambridge, 1976; Hon. Dr Amer. Univ. Washington, DC, 1982; Hon. DMus Glasgow, 1990. Lilli Lehmann Medal, Salzburg, 1950; first Premio Orfeo d'oro, Mantua; Lily Pons Medal, Paris; Hugo Wolf Verein Medal, Vienna, 1973; Premio Viotti, Vercelli, 1991; UNESCO Mozart Medal, Paris, 1991. Grosse Verdienstkreuz, Germany, 1974; Order of Merit for Sci. and the Arts (Germany), 1983; 1st class Order of Dannebrog, Denmark. *Publication:* (ed) On and Off the Record: a memoire of Walter Legge, 1982. *Recreations:* music, theatre, gardening, ski-ing, mountain walking.

SCHWARZKOPF, Gen. H. Norman, Hon. KCB 1991; Commander, Allied Forces, Gulf War, Jan.–Feb. 1991; Commander in Chief, US Central Command, MacDill Air Force Base, Florida, 1988–91; *b* 22 Aug. 1934; *s* of Herbert Norman Schwarzkopf and Ruth (*née* Bowman); *m* 1968, Brenda Holsinger; one *s* two *d*. *Educ:* Bordentown Mil. Inst.; Valley Forge Mil. Acad. (football schol.); US Mil. Acad., West Point; Univ. of S Calif (MME 1964). Commnd 2nd Lieut. Inf. and airborne trng, Fort Benning, Ga; 101st Airborne Div., Fort Campbell, Ky; Teacher, Mil. Acad., West Point, 1964 and 1966–68; Task-Force Advr, S Vietnamese Airborne Div., 1965; Comdr, 1st Bn, 6th Inf., 198th Inf. Bde, Americal Div., 1969–73; Dep. Comdr, 172nd Inf. Bde, Fort Richardson, Alaska, 1974–76; Comdr, 1st Bde, 9th Inf. Div., Fort Lewis, Wash, 1976–78; Dep. Dir of Plans, US Pacific Comd, Camp Smith, Hawaii, 1978–80; Asst Div. Comdr, 8th Mechanized Inf. Div., W Germany, 1980–82; Dir, Military-Personnel Management, Office of Dep. Chief of Staff for Personnel Management, Office of Dep. Chief of Staff for Personnel,

Washington, DC, 1982–83; Comdr, 24th Mechanized Inf. Div., Fort Stewart, Ga, 1983–85; Comdr, US Ground Forces and Dep. Comdr, Jt Task Force, Grenada op. Oct. 1983; Asst Dep. Chief of Staff, Army Ops, Washington DC, 1985–86; Comdr, I Corps, Fort Lewis, Wash, 1986–87; Dep. Chief for Ops and Plans, Washington, DC, 1987–88. DSM with oak leaf cluster; DFC; Silver Star with 2 oak leaf clusters; Bronze Star with 3 oak leaf clusters; Purple Heart with oak leaf cluster; Congressional Gold Medal, 1991. *Publication:* (with Peter Petre) It Doesn't Take a Hero (autobiog.), 1992. *Address:* c/o Marvin Josephson, International Creative Management, 40 West 57th Street, New York, NY 10019, USA.

SCHWEITZER, Louis; Chairman and Chief Executive Officer, Renault, since 1992; *b* Geneva, 8 July 1942; *s* of late Pierre-Paul Schweitzer; *m* 1972, Agnès Schmitz; two *d*. *Educ:* Institut d'Etudes Politiques, Paris; Faculté de Droit, Paris; Ecole Nationale d'Administration, Paris. Inspectorate of Finance, 1970–74; special assignment, later Dep. Dir, Min. of Budget, 1974–81; Chief of Staff: to Minister of Budget, 1981–83; of Industry and Research, 1983; to Prime Minister, 1984–86; Régie Renault: Vice-Pres. for Finance and Planning, 1986–90; Chief Finance Officer, 1988–90; Exec. Vice-Pres., 1989–90; Pres. and Chief Operating Officer, 1990–92. Prof., Inst. d'Etudes Politiques de Paris, 1982–86. Director: Inst. Pasteur, 1988–; Pechiney, 1989–; Inst Français des Relations Internats, 1989–; Réunion Musées Nationaux, 1990–; Fondation de l'Ecole Polytechnique, 1992–; Renault Véhicules Industriels, 1992–; BNP, 1993–; Roussel-Uclaf, 1994–. Mem., Légion d'Honneur (France), 1988; Officier, Ordre National du Mérite (France), 1992. *Address:* Renault SA, 34 quai du Point du Jour, 92109 Boulogne, Billancourt cedex, France.

SCHWEITZER, Prof. Miguel; Minister for Foreign Affairs, Chile, 1983; *b* 22 July 1940; *s* of Miguel Schweitzer and Cora Walters; *m* 1964, Maria Luisa Fernándes; two *s* one *d*. *Educ:* The Grange School, Santiago (preparatory and secondary schooling); Law School, Univ. of Chile (law degree). Doctorate in Penal Law, Rome, 1964–65; Professor of Penal Law: Law Sch., Univ. of Chile, 1966; High Sch. of Carabineros (Police), 1968, 1970 and from 1974; Director, Dept of Penal Sciences, Univ. of Chile, 1974–76; Chile's Alternate Representative with the Chilean Delegn to UN, 1975, 1976, 1978; Ambassador on special missions, 1975–80; Chilean Delegate to OAS, 1976–78; Ambassador to the Court of St James's, 1980–83. *Publications:* El Error de Derecho en Materia Penal (Chile), 1964; Sull elemento soggettivo nel reato di bancarotta del l'imprenditore (Rome), 1965; Prospectus for a Course on the Special Part of Penal Law (USA), 1969. *Recreations:* music, reading, golf, tennis, Rugby. *Address:* Floor 15, Miraflores 178, Santiago, Chile. *Clubs:* Temple Golf; Prince of Wales Country (Santiago).

SCIAMA, Prof. Dennis William, PhD; FRS 1983; Professor of Astrophysics, International School of Advanced Studies, Trieste, since 1983; Consultant, International Centre for Theoretical Physics, Trieste, since 1983; *b* 18 Nov. 1926; *s* of Abraham and Nelly Sciama; *m* 1959, Lidia Dina; two *d*. *Educ:* Malvern Coll.; Trinity Coll., Cambridge (MA, PhD). Fellow, Trinity Coll., Cambridge, 1952–56; Mem., Inst. for Advanced Study, Princeton, 1954–55; Agassiz Fellow, Harvard Univ., 1955–56; Res. Associate, KCL, 1958–60; Lectr in Maths, 1961–70, and Fellow of Peterhouse, 1963–70, Cambridge Univ.; Sen. Res. Fellow, 1970–85, Emeritus Fellow, 1985–, All Souls Coll., Oxford; Extraordinary Fellow, Churchill Coll., Cambridge, 1986–94. Vis. Prof., Cornell Univ., 1960–61; Luce Prof., Mount Holyoke Coll., 1977–78; Prof. of Physics, Univ. of Texas at Austin, 1978–83. Foreign Member: Amer. Philosophical Soc., 1981; Amer. Acad. of Arts and Scis, 1982; Accademia Nazionale dei Lincei, 1984. Guthrie Medal, Inst. of Physics, 1991. *Publications:* The Unity of the Universe, 1959; The Physical Foundations of General Relativity, 1969; Modern Cosmology, 1971, 2nd edn 1975; Modern Cosmology and the Dark Matter Problem, 1993; contribs to physics and astronomy jls. *Address:* 7 Park Town, Oxford OX2 6SN. *T:* Oxford (01865) 59441.

SCICLUNA, Martin Leonard Andrew; Financial Counsellor, UK Delegation to NATO, since 1993; *b* 16 Nov. 1935; *s* of Richard Hugh Scicluna and Victoria Mary (*née* Amato-Gauci); *m* 1st, 1960, Anna Judith Brennand (marr. diss. 1988); one *s*; 2nd, 1989, Loraine Jean Birnie; two step *d*. *Educ:* St Edward's Coll., Cottonera, Malta; RMA, Sandhurst. Royal Malta Artillery, 1953–65 (commnd 1955); transferred to RA, 1965–74 (Army Staff Coll., 1965). Joined Civil Service, MoD, 1974; Principal: Naval Personnel Div., 1974–76; Naval and Army Defence Secretariats, 1976–80; Asst Sec., 1980; Hd, Air Force Logistics Secretariat, 1980–83; Dep. Chief, Public Relns, 1983–85; Hd, Gen. Staff Secretariat, 1985–89; RCDS, 1989; Hd, Manpower Resources and Progs, 1990–91; Hd, Resources and Progs (Management Planning), 1991; Asst Under Sec. of State (Adjt Gen.), MoD, 1992; on secondment to FCO, 1993–. Chm. of Comrs, Duke of York's Royal Mil. Coll., Kent, 1992–; formerly Comr, Royal Hosp., Chelsea. Commissioner: Queen Victoria Sch., Dunblane, 1992–; Welbeck Coll., Notts, 1992–. Chm., of Trustees, Army Welfare Fund, 1992–; Trustee: Nat. Army Mus., 1992–; Army Benevolent Fund, 1992–. *Recreations:* painting, theatre, watching sport, other sedentary pursuits. *Address:* c/o Barclays Bank plc, 212 Regent's Street, W1A 4BP; Dar San Martin, Qrendi, Malta.

SCLATER, Prof. John George, PhD; FRS 1982; Professor, Scripps Institution of Oceanography, University of California at San Diego, since 1991; *b* 17 June 1940; *s* of John George Sclater and Margaret Bennett Glen; *m* 1st, 1968, Fredrica Rose Felcyn; two *s*; 2nd, 1985, Paula Ann Edwards (marr. diss. 1985); 3rd, 1992, Naila Gloria Cortez. *Educ:* Carlekemp Priory School; Stonyhurst College; Edinburgh Univ. (BSc); Cambridge Univ. (PhD 1966). Research Scientist, Scripps Instn of Oceanography, 1965; Massachusetts Institute of Technology: Associate Prof., 1972; Professor, 1977; Dir, Jt Prog. in Oceanography and Oceanographic Engrg with Woods Hole Oceanographic Instn, 1981; Prof., Dept of Geol Scis, and Associate Dir, Inst. for Geophysics, 1983–91, Shell Dist. Prof., 1983–88, Univ. of Texas at Austin. Fellow Geological Soc. of America; Fellow Amer. Geophysical Union; Mem., US Nat. Acad. of Scis, 1989. Rosenstiel Award in Oceanography, Rosenstiel Sch., Univ. of Miami, 1979; Bucher Medal, Amer. Geophysical Union, 1985. *Recreations:* running, swimming, golf. *Address:* Scripps Institution of Oceanography, La Jolla, CA 92093–0215, USA.

SCLATER, John Richard; Chairman, Hill Samuel Bank Ltd, since 1992 (Director, since 1990; Vice-Chairman, 1990–92); *b* 14 July 1940; *s* of Arthur William Sclater and Alice Sclater (*née* Collett); *m* 1st, 1967, Nicola Mary Gloria Cropper (marr. diss.); one *s* (one *d* decd); 2nd, 1985, Grizel Elizabeth Catherine Dawson. *Educ:* Charterhouse; Gonville and Caius Coll., Cambridge (schol., 1st Cl. Hons History Tripos, BA, MA); Commonwealth Fellow, 1962–64; Yale Univ. (MA 1963); Harvard Univ. (MBA 1968). Glyn, Mills & Co., 1964–70; Dir, Williams, Glyn & Co., 1970–76; Man. Dir, Nordic Bank, 1976–85 (Chm., 1985); Dir, 1985–87, Jt Dep. Chm., 1987, Guinness Peat Gp PLC; Dir and Dep. Chm., 1985–87, Chm., 1987, Guinness Mahon & Co. Ltd; Pres., Equitable Life Assurance Soc., 1994– (Dir, 1985–); Chairman: Foreign and Colonial Investment Trust PLC, 1985– (Dir, 1981–); Foreign & Colonial Enterprise Trust PLC, 1986–; Foreign & Colonial Ventures Ltd, 1989–; Berisford plc, 1990– (Dir, 1986–); Foreign & Colonial Private Equity Trust PLC, 1994–; Pountney Hill Hldgs, 1989–; Deputy Chairman: Yamaichi International (Europe) Ltd, 1985–; Union (formerly Union Discount Co. of London) plc, 1986– (Dir, 1981–); Director: James Cropper PLC, 1972–; Holker Estates Co. Ltd, 1974–; Grosvenor Estate Hldgs, 1989–; Fuel Tech (Europe), 1990–; Delian Lloyd's Investment Trust plc, 1993–; Member, London Bd of Halifax Building Soc., 1983–90. Mem., City Taxation Cttee, 1973–76. Chm., Assoc. of Consortium Banks, 1980–82. Mem., City Adv. Gp, CBI, 1988–. Trustee, Grosvenor Estate, 1973–; Mem. Council, Duchy of Lancaster, 1987–. Governor: Internat. Students House, 1976–; Brambletye Sch. Trust, 1976–. Freeman, City of London, 1992; Liveryman, Goldsmiths' Co., 1992–. *Recreations:* country pursuits. *Address:* Sutton Hall, Barcombe, near Lewes, Sussex BN8 5EB. *T:* Barcombe (01273) 400450. *Clubs:* Brooks's, Pratt's; University Pitt (Cambridge).

SCLATER-BOOTH, family name of **Baron Basing.**

SCOBIE, Kenneth Charles, CA; Chairman: Lovells Confectionery Ltd, since 1991; Allied Leisure, since 1994; *b* 29 July 1938; *s* of Charles Scobie and Shena (*née* Melrose); *m* 1973, Adela Jane Hollebone; one *s* one *d*. *Educ:* Daniel Stewart's Coll., Edinburgh; Edinburgh Univ. CA 1961. Romanes-Munro, CA, 1956–61; BMC (Scotland) Ltd, 1961–63; Rolls-Royce Ltd, 1963–66; Robson Morrow & Co., 1966–70; Black & Decker, 1971–72; Vavasseur South Africa Ltd, 1972–76; H. C. Sleigh Ltd, 1979–83; Blackwood Hodge plc, 1984–90; Dep. Chm. and Chief Exec., Brent Walker Group, 1991–93; Chm., William Hill Group, 1992–93; Dep. Chm., Addis, 1993–94; Dir, Postern Exec. Gp., 1991–. Non-exec. Director, Albrighton plc., 1990–93; Gartmore Venture Capital. CIMgt (CBIM 1987). *Recreations:* sport, Bridge. *Address:* Path Hill House, Path Hill, Goring Heath, Oxon RG8 7RE. *T:* Reading (01734) 842417. *Clubs:* London Scottish Rugby; Huntercombe Golf.

SCOBLE, (Arthur William) John; Chairman, Economic Planning Board, South West Region (Bristol), 1965–71, retired; *er s* of Arthur Scoble; *m* 1935, Constance Aveline (*d* 1995), *d* of Samuel Robbins; three *d*. Min. of Nat. Insce, 1945–50; jssc 1950; Min. of Works, 1951–59; UN, Buenos Aires, 1960–61; Min. of Works, 1962–64; Dept of Economic Affairs, 1965–70; Dept of the Environment, 1970–71, 1972–73. Chm., Agricl Housing Adv. Cttee, 1977–81. Dir, Bath Preservation Trust, 1973–74. Regional Advisor, Employment Fellowship, 1975–79. Clerk to Bathampton Council, 1980–86. *Address:* 4 Somerset Road, Southsea, Hants PO5 2NL. *T:* Portsmouth (01705) 750508.

SCOBLE, Christopher Lawrence; Assistant Under-Secretary of State, Police Department, Home Office, since 1994; *b* 21 Nov. 1943; *s* of Victor Arthur Oliphant Scoble and Mabel Crouch; *m* 1972, Rosemary Hunter; one *s* one *d*. *Educ:* Kent Coll., Canterbury; Corpus Christi Coll., Oxford. Asst Principal, Home Office, 1965; Private Sec. to Minister of State, Welsh Office, 1969–70; Home Office: Principal, 1970; Sec. to Adv. Council on the Penal System, 1976–78; Asst Sec., 1978; Asst Under-Sec. of State, Broadcasting and Miscellaneous Dept, 1988–91, Establishment Dept, 1991–94. Vice-Chm., Media Policy Cttee, Council of Europe, 1985–87. CS (Nuffield and Leverhulme) Travelling Fellowship, 1987–88. *Address:* Home Office, 50 Queen Anne's Gate, SW1H 9AT. *T:* 0171–273 2435.

SCOFIELD, (David) Paul, CBE 1956; actor; *b* 21 Jan. 1922; *s* of Edward H. and M. Scofield; *m* 1943, Joy Parker (actress); one *s* one *d*. *Educ:* Varndean Sch. for Boys, Brighton. Theatre training, Croydon Repertory, 1939; London Mask Theatre School, 1940. Shakespeare with ENSA, 1940–41; Birmingham Repertory Theatre, 1942; CEMA Factory tours, 1942–43; Whitehall Theatre, 1943; Birmingham Repertory, 1943–44–45; Stratford-upon-Avon, 1946–47–48. Mem., Royal Shakespeare Directorate, 1966–68. Associate Dir, Nat. Theatre, 1970–71. London theatres: Arts, 1946; Phoenix, 1947; Adventure Story, and The Seagull, St James's, 1949; Ring Round the Moon, Globe, 1950; Much Ado About Nothing, Phœnix, 1952; The River Line, Edin. Fest., Lyric (Hammersmith), Strand, 1952; John Gielgud's Company, 1952–53: Richard II, The Way of the World, Venice Preserved, etc; A Question of Fact, Piccadilly, 1953–54; Time Remembered, Lyric, Hammersmith, New Theatre, 1954–55; Hamlet, Moscow, 1955; Paul Scofield-Peter Brook Season, Phœnix Theatre, 1956; Hamlet, The Power and the Glory, Family Reunion; A Dead Secret, Piccadilly Theatre, 1957; Expresso Bongo, Saville Theatre, 1958; The Complaisant Lover, Globe Theatre, 1959; A Man For All Seasons, Globe Theatre, 1960, New York, 1961–62; Coriolanus and Love's Labour's Lost, at Shakespeare Festival Season, Stratford, Ont., 1961; King Lear: Stratford-on-Avon, Aldwych Theatre, 1962–63, Europe and US, 1964; Timon of Athens, Stratford-on-Avon, 1965; The Government Inspector, also Staircase, Aldwych, 1966; Macbeth, Stratford-on-Avon, 1967, Russia, Finland, 1967, Aldwych, 1968; The Hotel in Amsterdam, Royal Court, 1968; Uncle Vanya, Royal Court, 1970; Savages, Royal Court and Comedy, 1973; The Tempest, Wyndhams, 1975; Dimetos, Comedy, 1976; The Family, Royal Exchange, Manchester, and Haymarket, 1978; I am Not Rappaport, Apollo, 1986–87; Exclusive, Strand, 1989; Heartbreak House, Haymarket, 1992; *National Theatre:* The Captain of Kopenick, The Rules of the Game, 1971; Volpone, The Madras House, 1977; Amadeus, 1979; Othello, 1980; Don Quixote, A Midsummer Night's Dream, 1982. *Films:* The Train, 1964; A Man for All Seasons, 1966 (from the play); Bartleby, King Lear, 1971; Scorpio, 1973; A Delicate Balance, 1974; Nineteen Nineteen, 1985; When the Whales Came, 1989; Henry V, 1989; Hamlet, 1991; Utz, 1992; Quiz Show, 1995; *TV films:* Anna Karenina, 1985; The Attic, 1988; *TV serial:* Martin Chuzzlewit, 1994. Hon. LLD Glasgow, 1968; Hon. DLit Kent, 1973; Hon. DLitt Sussex, 1985. Shakespeare prize, Hamburg, 1972. *Relevant publication:* Paul Scofield, by J. C. Trewin, 1956. *Address:* The Gables, Balcombe, W Sussex RH17 6ND. *T:* Balcombe (01444) 811378. *Club:* Athenæum.

SCOON, Sir Paul, GCMG 1979; GCVO 1985; OBE 1970; Governor General of Grenada, 1978–92; *b* 4 July 1935; *m* 1970, Esmai Monica McNeilly (*née* Lumsden); two step *s* one step *d*. *Educ:* St John's Anglican Sch., Grenada; Grenada Boys' Secondary Sch.; Inst. of Education, Leeds; Toronto Univ. BA, MEd. Teacher, Grenada Boys' Secondary Sch., 1953–67. Chief Educn Officer, 1967–68, Permanent Sec., 1969, Secretary to the Cabinet, 1970–72, Grenada; Dep. Director, Commonwealth Foundn, 1973–78. Governor, Centre for Internat. Briefing, Farnham Castle, 1973–78; Vice-Pres., Civil Service Assoc., Grenada, 1968; Co-founder and former Pres., Assoc. of Masters and Mistresses, Grenada. *Recreations:* reading, tennis. *Address:* PO Box 180, St George's, Grenada. *T:* (440) 2180.

SCOPES, Sir Leonard Arthur, KCVO 1961; CMG 1957; OBE 1946; *b* 19 March 1912; *s* of late Arthur Edward Scopes and Jessie Russell Hendry; *m* 1938, Brunhilde Slater Rolfe; two *s* two *d*. *Educ:* St Dunstan's College; Gonville and Caius College, Cambridge (MA). Joined HM Consular Service, 1933; Vice-Consul: Antwerp, 1933, Saigon, 1935; Canton, 1937; Acting Consul, Surabaya, 1941; Vice-Consul, Lourenço Marques, 1942; Consul, Skoplje and Ljubljana, 1945; Commercial Secretary, Bogota, 1947; Assistant in United Nations (Economic and Social) Department of Foreign Office, 1950; Counsellor, Djakarta, 1952; Foreign Service Inspector, 1954; HM Ambassador to Nepal, 1957–62; HM Ambassador to Paraguay, 1962–67; Mem., UN Jt Inspection Unit, Geneva, 1968–71. *Recreation:* retirement. *Address:* 2 Whaddon Hall Mews, Milton Keynes, Bucks MK17 0NA.

SCORER, Philip Segar; Consultant solicitor, Burton & Co., Lincoln, since 1991 (Partner, 1952–91); *b* 11 March 1916; *s* of late Eric W. Scorer and Maud Scorer (*née* Segar); *m* 1950, Monica Smith; one *s* three *d*. *Educ:* Repton. Admitted Solicitor, 1938; London County Council Legal Dept, 1938–40. Served War, Army (Royal Signals: War Office, SHAEF and BAS, Paris), 1940–46. Solicitors' Dept, New Scotland Yard, 1947–51; Clerk of the Peace, City of Lincoln, 1952–71; Under-Sheriff of Lincolnshire, 1954–, of Humberside,

1974–; a Recorder, 1976–83. Pres., Under Sheriffs Assoc., 1978–84. *Address:* (office) Stonebow, Lincoln LN2 1DA. *T:* Lincoln (01522) 523215. *Club:* National Liberal.

SCORSESE, Martin; American film director; *b* 17 Nov. 1942; *s* of Charles Scorsese and Catherine (*née* Cappa); *m* 1st, 1965, Laraine Marie Brennan (marr. diss.); one *d*; 2nd, Julia Cameron (marr. diss.); one *d*; 3rd, 1979, Isabella Rossellini (marr. diss. 1983); 4th, 1985, Barbara DeFina. *Educ:* Univ. of New York (BS 1964; MA 1966). Faculty Asst, 1963–66, Lectr, 1968–70, Dept of Film, Univ. of New York; dir and writer of documentaries. *Films* include: Who's That Knocking At My Door? (also writer), 1968; Mean Streets (also co-writer), 1973; Alice Doesn't Live Here Any More, 1974; Taxi Driver, 1976; New York, New York, 1977; The Last Waltz (also actor), 1978; Raging Bull, 1980; After Hours, 1985 (Best Dir Award, Cannes Film Fest., 1986); The Color of Money, 1986; acted in 'Round Midnight, 1986; The Last Temptation of Christ, 1988; Goodfellas, 1990; Cape Fear, 1992; The Age of Innocence, 1993; producer: Mad Dog and Glory, 1993; Naked in New York, 1994. *Address:* c/o CAA, 9830 Wilshire Boulevard, Los Angeles, CA 90212, USA.

SCOTFORD, Garth Barrie, OBE 1994; QFSM 1982; County Manager, Berkshire County Council, since 1993; *b* 28 Oct. 1943; *s* of Albert Edward Scotford and Louisa Emily Jane Scotford (*née* Leach); *m* 1964, Gillian Avril Patricia Constable; one *s* two *d*. *Educ:* Reading Grammar Sch. Joined Fire Service, 1961: served in Reading, Liverpool, Hants and Gtr Manchester; Chief Fire Officer, Berks, 1984–93, retd. FIFireE 1977 (Pres., 1985). *Recreations:* opera, bridge, American football. *Address:* 1 Park Avenue, Wokingham, Berks RG40 2AJ. *T:* Wokingham (01734) 780359.

See also J. E. Scotford.

SCOTFORD, John Edward, CBE 1993; Treasurer, Hampshire County Council, since 1983; *b* 15 Aug. 1939; *s* of Albert and Louisa Scotford; *m* 1962, Marjorie Clare Wells; one *s*. *Educ:* Reading Grammar Sch. IPFA. Reading County Borough Council, 1955–62; Coventry County Borough Council, 1962–65; Hampshire CC, 1965–; Dep. County Treasurer, 1977–83. Public Works Loan Comr, 1992–. Freeman, City of London. *Address:* Hampshire County Council, The Castle, Winchester SO23 8UJ.

SCOTHERN, Mark Francis; Director, Crisis (formerly Crisis at Christmas), since 1991; *b* 2 July 1960; *s* of late Norman Scothern and of Joan Scothern. *Educ:* Austin Friars Sch., Carlisle. Co-ordinator, Thamesdown Housing Link, 1984–88; Policy Officer, CHAR (Housing Campaign for Single People), 1988–91. *Recreations:* film, contemporary music, food, biographies, sleep. *Address:* Crisis, 7 Whitechapel Road, E1 1DU. *T:* 0171–377 0489.

SCOTHORNE, Prof. Raymond John, BSc, MD Leeds; MD Chicago; FRSE; FRCSGlas; Regius Professor of Anatomy, University of Glasgow, 1972–90, now Emeritus; *b* 1920; *s* of late John and Lavinia Scothorne; *m* 1948, Audrey, *o d* of late Rev. Selwyn and Winifred Gillott; one *s* two *d*. *Educ:* Royal Grammar School, Newcastle upon Tyne; Universities of Leeds and Chicago, BSc (Hons) 1st cl. (Leeds), 1941; MD (Chicago), Rockefeller Student, 1941–43; MB (Hons) 1st cl. (Leeds), 1944; MD (with Distinction) (Leeds), 1951. Demonstrator and Lecturer in Anatomy, 1944–50, Univ. of Leeds; Sen. Lecturer in Anatomy, 1950–60, Univ. of Glasgow; Prof., Univ. of Newcastle upon Tyne, 1960–72. Hon. Sec., Anat. Soc. of Great Britain and Ireland, 1967–71, Pres., 1971–73; Hon. Fellow, British Assoc. of Clinical Anatomists (Pres., 1986–88); Mem., Med. Sub-Cttee, UGC, 1967–76. Hon. Mem., Assoc. des Anatomistes. Struthers Prize and Gold Medal in Anatomy, Univ. of Glasgow, 1957. Anatomical Editor, Companion to Medical Studies; Editor, Clinical Anatomy, 1987–. *Publications:* chapter on Peripheral Nervous System in Hamilton's Textbook of Anatomy, 2nd edn, 1975; chapters on Early Development, on Tissue and Organ Growth, on Skin and on the Nervous System in Companion to Medical Studies, 3rd edn, 1985; chapter on Development and Structure of Liver in Pathology of Liver, 1979, 3rd edn 1994; chapter on Respiratory System in Cunningham's Textbook, 12th edn, 1981; chapter on Development of Spinal Cord and Vertebral Column in Surgery of the Spine, 1992; papers on embryology, histology and tissue transplantation. *Address:* Southernknowe, Linlithgow, West Lothian EH49 6BQ. *T:* Linlithgow (01506) 842463.

SCOTLAND, Miss Patricia Janet; QC 1991. *Educ:* London Univ. (LLB). Called to the Bar, Middle Temple, 1977; Mem., Antigua Bar. Former Mem., Commn for Racial Equality; Mem., Millennium Commn, 1994–. *Address:* 1 Gray's Inn Square, WC1R 5AG. *T:* 0171–404 3000, *Fax:* 0171–404 9942.

SCOTT, family name of **Earl of Eldon.**

SCOTT; *see* Hepburne-Scott, family name of Lord Polwarth.

SCOTT; *see* Maxwell Scott and Maxwell-Scott.

SCOTT; *see* Montagu Douglas Scott, family name of Duke of Buccleuch.

SCOTT, Alan James, CVO 1986; CBE 1982; Governor, Cayman Islands, 1987–92; *b* 14 Jan. 1934; *er s* of Rev. Harold James Scott and Mary Phyllis Barbara Scott; *m* 1st, 1958, Mary Elizabeth Ireland (*d* 1969); one *s* two *d*; 2nd, 1971, Joan Hall; one step *s* two step *d*. *Educ:* King's Sch., Ely; Selwyn Coll., Cambridge Univ. Suffolk Regt, Italy and Germany, 1952–54. HMOCS, 1958–87: Fiji: Dist Officer, 1958; Estabts Officer, 1960; Registry of Univ. of S Pacific, 1968; Controller, Organisation and Estabts, 1969; Hong Kong: Asst Financial Sec., 1971; Prin. Asst Financial Sec., 1972; Sec. for CS, 1973; MLC, 1976–85; Sec. for Housing, and Chm. Hong Kong Housing Authy, 1977; Sec. for Information, 1980; Sec. for Transport, 1982; Dep. Chief Sec., 1985–87. President: Fiji AAA, 1964–69; Hong Kong AAA, 1978–87. *Recreations:* boule, golf, dilatory travel, writing.

SCOTT, Prof. Alastair Ian, FRS 1978; FRSE 1981; Davidson Professor of Chemistry and Biochemistry, Texas A & M University, since 1981; *b* 10 April 1928; *s* of William Scott and Nell Florence (*née* Newton); *m* 1950, Elizabeth Wilson (*née* Walters); one *s* one *d*. *Educ:* Glasgow Univ. (BSc, PhD, DSc). Postdoctoral Fellow, Ohio State Univ., 1952–53; Technical Officer, ICI (Nobel Div.), 1953–54; Postdoctoral Fellow, London and Glasgow Univs, 1954–57; Lectr, Glasgow Univ., 1957–62, Professor: Univ. of British Columbia, 1962–65; Univ. of Sussex, 1965–68; Yale Univ., 1968–77; Texas A&M Univ., 1977–80; Edinburgh Univ., 1980–83 (Forbes Prof., 1980–81). Lectures: Karl Folkers, Wisconsin Univ., 1964; Burger, Virginia Univ., 1975; Benjamin Rush, Pennsylvania Univ., 1975; 5 colls, Mass, 1977; Andrews, NSW Univ., 1979; Dreyfus, Indiana Univ., 1983; Centenary, RSC, 1994; Gottlieb Meml, Univ. of Illinois, 1995; Bakerian, Royal Soc., 1996. FAAAS 1988. Hon. Mem., Pharmaceutical Soc. of Japan, 1985. Hon. MA Yale, 1968; Hon. DSc: Coimbra, 1990; Paris, 1992. Corday-Morgan Medallist, Chemical Soc., 1964; Ernest Guenther Medallist, 1976, Cope Scholar Award, 1992, Amer. Chem. Soc.; Res. Achievement Award, Amer. Soc. of Pharmacognosy, 1993. *Publications:* Interpretation of Ultraviolet Spectra of Natural Products, 1964; (with T. K. Devon) Handbook of Naturally Occurring Compounds, 1972; numerous pubns in learned jls. *Recreations:* music, gardening. *Address:* Department of Chemistry, Texas A & M University, College Station, TX 77843–3255, USA. *T:* (409) 8453243. *Club:* Athenæum.

SCOTT, Andrew John, CEng; FMA; Head, National Railway Museum, since 1994; *b* 3 June 1949; *s* of Cyril John Scott and Gertrude Ethel (*née* Miller); *m* 1972, Margaret Anne Benyon, JP, BA. *Educ:* Bablake Sch., Coventry; Univ. of Newcastle upon Tyne (BSc Civil Engrg 1970; MSc Mining Engrg 1971). CEng, MICE 1976. AMA 1987, FMA 1993. Practising civil engr, 1972–84; Actg Dir, W Yorks Transport Mus., 1984–86; Keeper of Technol., Bradford City Museums, 1986–87; Dir, London Transport Mus., 1988–94. Mem., North Eastern Locomotive Preservation Gp, 1967– (Cttee Mem., 1972–84); Council Member: Assoc. of Indep. Museums, 1991–; Internat. Assoc. of Transport Museums, 1992–; Vice-Chm., Assoc. of British Transport and Engrg Museums, 1992–; Mem., F and GP Cttee, S Eastern Museums Service, 1992–94; Chm., London Museums Consultative Cttee, 1992–94. Director: FNRM Enterprises Ltd, 1994–; York Visitor and Conf. Bureau Ltd, 1995–. Trustee, Friends of London Tspt Mus., 1994–; Exec. Mem., Friends of Nat. Rlwy Mus., 1994–; Pres., London Underground Railway Soc., 1995–96. *Publications:* North Eastern Renaissance, 1991; contrib. to railway and museological jls and books. *Recreations:* travel, railways, ecclesiastical architecture. *Address:* National Railway Museum, Leeman Road, York YO2 4XJ. *T:* York (01904) 621261; 10A Moreton Avenue, Harpenden, Herts AL5 2ET.

SCOTT, Anthony Douglas, TD 1972; chartered accountant in public practice; *b* 6 Nov. 1933; *o s* of Douglas Ernest and Mary Gladys Scott; *m* 1962, Irene Robson; one *s* one *d*. *Educ:* Gateshead Central Technical Secondary Sch. Articled to Middleton & Middleton, also J. Stanley Armstrong, Chartered Accountants, Newcastle upon Tyne, 1952–57; National Service, WO Selection Bd, 1957–59; Accountant with Commercial Plastics Ltd, 1959; joined ICI Ltd (Agricl Div), 1961; seconded by ICI to Hargreaves Fertilisers Ltd, as Chief Accountant, 1966; ICI Ltd (Nobel Div.) as Asst Chief Acct, 1970; seconded by ICI to MoD as Dir-Gen. Internal Audit, 1972–74. Dir of Consumer Credit, Office of Fair Trading, 1974–80. Chief Exec. and Dir, CoSIRA, 1981–88. Chm., Teesside Soc. of Chartered Accts, 1969–70; Mem. Cttee, London Chartered Accountants, 1974–79. Chm., Jt Working Party on Students' Societies (ICAE&W), 1979–80. *Publications:* Accountants Digests on Consumer Credit Act 1974, 1980; Accountants Digest on Estate Agents Act 1979, 1982. *Recreations:* antiquary, walking, gardening; TA, 1959–91. *Address:* 2 Oakfield Road, Harpenden, Herts AL5 2NE. *T:* Harpenden (01582) 763067.

SCOTT, Sir Anthony (Percy), 3rd Bt *cr* 1913; Chairman and Managing Director, L. M. (Moneybrokers) Ltd, 1986–95; *b* 1 May 1937; *s* of Sir Douglas Winchester Scott, 2nd Bt, and of Elizabeth Joyce, *d* of W. N. C. Grant; *S* father, 1984; *m* 1962, Caroline Theresa Anne, *er d* of Edward Bacon; two *s* one *d*. *Educ:* Harrow; Christ Church, Oxford. Barrister, Inner Temple, 1960. *Recreation:* racing. *Heir:* *s* Henry Douglas Edward Scott, *b* 26 March 1964. *Address:* Longbarrow, Goodworth Clatford, Andover, Hants, SP11 7SE.

SCOTT, Brough; *see* Scott, J. B.

SCOTT, Dame Catherine Margaret Mary; *see* Scott, Dame M.

SCOTT, Sir (Charles) Peter, KBE 1978 (OBE 1948); CMG 1964; HM Diplomatic Service, retired; Member, Council of Anglo-Norse Society, since 1978; *b* 30 Dec. 1917; *er s* of late Rev. John Joseph Scott and late Dorothea Scott (*née* Senior); *m* 1954, Rachael, *yr d* of C. W. Lloyd Jones, CIE; one *s* two *d*. *Educ:* Weymouth Coll.; Pembroke Coll., Cambridge. Indian Civil Service: Probationer, 1939; appointed to Madras Presidency, 1940; Asst Private Sec. to Viceroy, 1946–47. Entered HM Diplomatic Service, 1947, Second Sec., Tokyo, 1948; First Sec., 1949; Foreign Office, 1950; Private Sec. to Gen. Lord Ismay at NATO, Paris, 1952; First Sec., Vienna, 1954; First Sec. at British Information Services, NY, 1956; Counsellor and Consul-General, Washington, 1959; Student at IDC, 1962; Head of UK Mission to European Office of the United Nations, Geneva, 1963; Minister at HM Embassy, Rome, 1966–69; Temp. Vis. Fellow at Centre for Contemporary European Studies, Univ. of Sussex, 1969–70; Asst Under-Sec. of State, FCO, 1970–75; Ambassador to Norway, 1975–77. Private Sec., 1978–79, Treasurer, 1979–81, to HRH Prince Michael of Kent. *Recreations:* walking, and such as offer. *Address:* Bisley Farmhouse, Irstead, near Norwich, Norfolk NR12 8XT. *T:* Horning (01692) 630413. *Clubs:* United Oxford & Cambridge University; Norfolk (Norwich).

SCOTT, Charles Thomas, FCA; Chairman, Cordiant plc, since 1995; *b* 22 Feb. 1949. FCA 1979. Binder Hamlyn, 1967–72; ITEL Internat. Corp., 1972–77; IMS Internat. Inc., 1978–89; Saatchi & Saatchi Co. plc, later Cordiant plc, 1990–: Chief Exec., 1993–95. *Recreations:* golf, tennis, sport in general. *Address:* Cordiant plc, 83/89 Whitfield Street, W1A 4XA. *T:* 0171–436 4000.

SCOTT, Prof. Clive, DPhil; FBA 1994; Professor of European Literature, University of East Anglia, since 1991; *b* 13 Nov. 1943; *s* of Jesse Scott and Nesta Vera Scott (*née* Morton); *m* 1st, 1965, Elizabeth Anne (*née* Drabble) (marr. diss.); one *s* one *d*; 2nd, 1984, Marie-Noëlle Guillot; two *s*. *Educ:* St John's Coll., Oxford (MA, MPhil, DPhil). University of East Anglia: Asst Lectr, 1967–70; Lectr, 1970–88; Reader, 1988–91. *Publications:* French Verse-Art: a study, 1980; Anthologie Eluard, 1983; A Question of Syllables: essays in nineteenth-century French verse, 1986; The Riches of Rhyme: studies in French verse, 1988; Vers Libre: the emergence of free verse in France 1886–1914, 1990; Reading the Rhythm: the poetics of French free verse 1910–1930, 1993. *Address:* School of Modern Languages and European Studies, University of East Anglia, University Plain, Norwich NR4 7TJ. *T:* Norwich (01603) 56161.

SCOTT, Rt. Rev. Colin John Fraser; *see* Hulme, Bishop Suffragan of.

SCOTT, Prof. Dana Stewart, FBA 1976; Hillman University Professor of Computer Science and Mathematical Logic, Carnegie Mellon University, since 1981; *b* Berkeley, Calif, 11 Oct. 1932; *m* 1959, Irene Schreier; one *d*. *Educ:* Univ. of Calif, Berkeley (BA); Princeton Univ. (PhD). Instructor, Univ. of Chicago, 1958–60; Asst Prof., Univ. of Calif, Berkeley, 1960–63; Associate Prof. and Prof., Stanford Univ., 1963–69; Prof., Princeton, 1969–72; Prof. of Mathematical Logic, Oxford Univ., 1972–81. Visiting Prof., Amsterdam, 1968–69; Guggenheim Fellow, 1978–79. Mem., US Nat. Acad. of Scis, 1988. *Publications:* papers on logic and mathematics in technical jls. *Address:* School of Computer Science, Carnegie Mellon University, 5000 Forbes Avenue, Pittsburgh, PA 15213-3890, USA.

SCOTT, Sir David; *see* Scott, Sir W. D. S.

SCOTT, David; *b* 6 Sept. 1916; *er s* of late Sir Basil Scott and late Gertrude, MBE, 2nd *d* of Henry Villiers Stuart of Dromana, MP; *m* 1951, Hester Mary, MA, *y d* of late Gilbert Ogilvy of Winton and Pencaitland; one *s* three *d*. *Educ:* Stowe; New College, Oxford (MA). War Service 1939–45: Argyll and Sutherland Highlanders (SR), Reconnaissance Corps and Highland Light Infantry; T/Capt., 1941; Asst to Political Adviser for Khuzistan, Iran, 1944; Actg Vice Consul, Ahwaz, 1944–45. Clerk, House of Commons, 1946; Deputy Principal Clerk, 1962; Clerk of Standing Cttees, 1966–70; Clerk of Select Cttees, 1970–73; Clerk of Private Bills, an Examiner of Petitions for Private Bills and Taxing Officer, House of Commons, 1974–77; retired 1977. Mem., Cttee on Canons, General Synod, Scottish Episcopal Church, 1983–91. *Recreation:* fishing. *Address:* 6a Stafford House, Maida Avenue, W2 1TE. *T:* 0171–723 8398; Glenaros, Aros, Isle of Mull PA72 6JP. *T:* Aros (01680) 300337.

SCOTT, Ven. David; Archdeacon of Stow, 1975–89; Chaplain to the Queen, 1983–94; *b* 19 June 1924; *m*; two *c*. *Educ:* Trinity Hall, Cambridge (BA 1950, MA 1954); Cuddesdon Theological College. Deacon 1952, priest 1953, dio. Portsmouth; Curate of St Mark, Portsea, 1952–58; Asst Chaplain, Univ. of London, 1958–59; PC, Old Brumby, 1959–66; Vicar of Boston, Lincs, 1966–75; Rural Dean of Holland East, 1971–75; Surrogate, 1972–75; Vicar of Hackthorn with Cold Hanworth, 1975–89; Priest-in-Charge of North and South Carlton, 1978–89; Canon and Prebendary of Lincoln Cathedral, 1971–89. Mem. Gen. Synod, 1978–80, 1983–85, 1985–89. *Address:* 4 Honing Drive, Southwell, Notts NG25 0LB. *T:* Southwell (01636) 813900.

SCOTT, Sir David (Aubrey), GCMG 1979 (KCMG 1974; CMG 1966); HM Diplomatic Service, retired 1979; *b* 3 Aug. 1919; *s* of late Hugh Sumner Scott and Barbara E. Scott, JP; *m* 1941, Vera Kathleen, *d* of late Major G. H. Ibbitson, MBE, RA; two *s* one *d*. *Educ:* Charterhouse; Birmingham University (Mining Engrg). Served War of 1939–45, Royal Artillery, 1939–47; Chief Radar Adviser, British Military Mission to Egyptian Army, 1945–47, Major. Appointed to CRO, 1948; Asst Private Secretary to Secretary of State, 1949; Cape Town/Pretoria, 1951–53; Cabinet Office, 1954–56; Malta Round Table Conf., 1955; Secretary-General, Malaya and Caribbean Constitutional Confs, 1956; Singapore, 1956–58; Monckton Commn, 1960; Dep. High Comr, Fedn of Rhodesia and Nyasaland, 1961–63; Imperial Defence College, 1964; Dep. High Comr, India, 1965–67; British High Comr to Uganda, and Ambassador (non-resident) to Rwanda, 1967–70; Asst Under-Sec. of State, FCO, 1970–72; British High Comr to New Zealand, and Governor, Pitcairn Is., 1973–75; HM Ambassador to Republic of S Africa, 1976–79. Chairman: Ellerman Lines plc, 1982–83; Nuclear Resources Ltd, 1984–88; Director: Barclays Bank International Ltd, 1979–85; Mitchell Cotts plc, 1980–86; Delta Metal Overseas Ltd, 1980–83; Bradbury Wilkinson plc, 1984–86; Consultant, Thomas De La Rue & Co. Ltd, 1986–88. Pres., Uganda Soc. for Disabled Children, 1984–; Vice-Pres., UK South Africa Trade Assoc., 1980–85. Mem., Manchester Olympic Bid Cttee, 1989–93. Gov., Sadler's Wells Trust, 1984–89. Trustee, John Ellerman Foundn, 1979–. Freeman, City of London, 1982; Liveryman, Shipwrights' Co., 1983. *Publications:* Ambassador in Black and White, 1981; contrib. DNB. *Recreations:* music, birdwatching. *Address:* Wayside, Moushill Lane, Milford, Surrey GU8 5BQ. *T:* Godalming (01483) 421935. *Club:* Royal Over-Seas League (Chm., 1981–86; Vice-Pres., 1986–).
See also Sir R. D. H. Scott, Sir J. B. Unwin.

SCOTT, David Gidley; Registrar of the High Court in Bankruptcy, since 1984; *b* 3 Jan. 1924; *s* of late Bernard Wardlaw Habershon Scott, FRIBA and Florence May Scott; *m* 1948, Elinor Anne, *d* of late Major Alan Garthwaite, DSO, MC, and Mrs Garthwaite; two *s* two *d*. *Educ:* Sutton Valence School (scholarship); St John's College, Cambridge (exhibnr, MA, LLM). Army service, 1942–47, Royal Engineers; Assault RE European theatre, 1944–45 (wounded); Acting Major, Palestine. Called to the Bar, Lincoln's Inn, 1951; practised Chancery Bar, 1951–84. *Recreations:* sailing, choral singing. *Address:* 45 Benslow Lane, Hitchin, Herts SG4 9RE. *T:* Hitchin (01462) 434391. *Clubs:* Bar Yacht, Parkstone Yacht.

SCOTT, Donald; *see* Scott, W. D.

SCOTT, Douglas Andrew Montagu-Douglas-, OBE 1994; Chief Executive and Director, Cancer Relief Macmillan Fund, 1987–95; *b* 21 June 1930; *s* of late Col C. A. Montagu-Douglas-Scott, DSO and Lady Victoria Haig, *d* of Field Marshal 1st Earl Haig, KT, GCB, OM, GCVO, KCIE; *m* 1st, 1954, Bridget George (marr. diss. 1976), *d* of Air Vice-Marshal Sir Robert George, KCMG, KCVO, KBE, CB, MC; two *d* (one *s* decd); 2nd, 1977, Daphne Shortt, *d* of Dr Cyril Shortt, Winchcombe. *Educ:* Eton; RMA, Sandhurst. Commnd Irish Guards, 1950. ADC to Gov. of S Australia, 1953–55; Tubemakers of Australia, 1955–63; TI Group, 1963–83: Dir, Accles & Pollock Ltd, 1966–76; Man. Dir, TI Chesterfield Ltd, 1976–81; Dir, TI Gp Overseas Ops, 1981–83; Recruitment Consultant, PE Internat. plc, 1984–87. *Recreations:* painting, shooting, gardening, opera. *Address:* Halford House, Shipston-on-Stour, Warwicks CV36 5BS. *T:* Stratford-upon-Avon (01789) 740068. *Clubs:* White's, Pratt's, MCC.

SCOTT, Prof. Douglas Frederick Schumacher; Professor of German in the University of Durham (late Durham Colleges), 1958–75, now Emeritus Professor; *b* Newcastle under Lyme, Staffs, 17 Sept. 1910; *o s* of Frederick Scott and Magdalena (*née* Gronbach); *m* 1942, Margaret (*d* 1972), *o d* of late Owen Gray Ellis, Beaumaris, Anglesey, and Helen (*née* Gibbs); two *d*. *Educ:* Queen Mary's Grammar School, Walsall, Staffs; Dillmann-Realgymnasium Stuttgart, Germany; University of Tübingen, Göttingen (Dr phil.); University College, London (MA). Part-time Assistant, German Dept, University Coll., London, 1935–37; Lecturer in charge German Dept, Huddersfield Technical Coll., 1937–38; Lecturer in German, King's Coll., Newcastle, 1938–46; released for service with Friends' Ambulance Unit, 1940–46; Lecturer in German, King's Coll., London, 1946–49; Reader and Head of Dept of German, The Durham Colls, 1949–58. *Publications:* Some English Correspondents of Goethe, 1949; W. v. Humboldt and the Idea of a University, 1960; Luke Howard: his correspondence with Goethe and his continental journey of 1816, 1976; articles and reviews on German lit. and Anglo-German literary relations in various English and German journals. *Recreations:* music, travel. *Address:* 6 Fieldhouse Terrace, Durham DH1 4NA. *T:* Durham (0191) 3864518.

SCOTT, Douglas Keith, (Doug Scott), CBE 1994; *b* Nottingham, 29 May 1941; *s* of George Douglas Scott and Edith Joyce Scott; *m* 1962, Janice Elaine Brook (marr. diss. 1988); one *s* two *d*; *m* 1993, Sharavati, (Sharv), Prabhu; one *s*. *Educ:* Cottesmore Secondary Modern Sch.; Mundella Grammar Sch., Nottingham; Loughborough Teachers' Trng Coll. (Teaching Certificate). Began climbing age of 12, British crag climbing, and most weekends thereafter; visited the Alps age of 17 and every year thereafter; first ascent, Tarso Teiroko, Tibest Mts, Sahara, 1965; first ascents, Cilo Dag Mts, SE Turkey, 1966; first ascent, S face Koh-i-Bandaka (6837 m), Hindu Kush, Afghanistan, 1967; first British ascent, Salathé Wall, El Capitain, Yosemite, 1971; 1972: Spring, Mem., European Mt Everest Expedn to SW face; Summer, first ascent, E Pillar of Mt Asgard, Baffin Island Expedn; Autumn, Mem., British Mt Everest Expedn to SW face; first ascent, Changabang (6864 m), 1974; first ascent, SE spur, Pic Lenin (7189 m), 1974; reached summit of Mt Everest, via SW face, with Dougal Haston, as Members, British Everest Expedn, 24th Sept. 1975 (first Britons on summit); first Alpine ascent of S face, Mt McKinley (6226 m), via new route, British Direct, with Dougal Haston, 1976; first ascent, East Face Direct, Mt Kenya, 1976; first ascent, Ogre (7330 m), Karakoram Mountains, 1977; first ascent, N Ridge route, Kangchenjunga (8593 m), without oxygen, 1979; first ascent, N Summit, Kussum Kangguru, 1979; first ascent, N Face, Nuptse, 1979; Alpine style, Kangchungtse (7640 m), 1980; first ascent Shivling E Pillar, 13-day Alpine Style push, 1981; Chamlang (7366 m) North Face to Central Summit, with Rheinhold Messner, 1981; first ascent, Pungpa Ri (7445 m), 1982; first ascent Shishapangma South Face (8046 m), 1982; first ascent, Lobsang Spire (Karakoram), and ascent Broad Peak (8047 m), 1983; Mt Baruntse (7143 m), first ascent, East Summit Mt Chamlang (7287 m), and traverse over unclimbed central summit Chamlang, Makalu SE Ridge, Alpine Style, to within 100 m of summit, 1984; first Alpine style ascent, Diran (7260 m), 1985; first ascent of rock climbs in S India, 1986; first ascent of rock climbs, Wadi Rum, Jordan, 1987; Mt Jitchu Drake (Bhutan) (6793 m), South face first ascent of peak, Alpine style, 1988; first ascent, Indian Arete Latok III, 1990; first ascent, Hanging Glacier Peak South (6294 m), via South Ridge, 1991; first British ascent of Chimtarga (5482 m), Fanskiye Mountains, Tadzhikistan, 1992. Pres., Alpine Climbing Gp, 1976–82; Vice-Pres., British Mountaineering Council, 1993. A vegetarian, 1978–. Hon. MA: Nottingham, 1991; Loughborough, 1993. *Publications:* Big Wall Climbing, 1974; (with Alex MacIntyre) Shishapangma, Tibet, 1984; Himalayan Climber, 1992; contrib. to Alpine Jl, Amer. Alpine Jl, Mountain Magazine and Himal Magazine. *Recreations:* rock climbing, photography, organic gardening. *Address:* Chapel House, Low Cotehill, Carlisle CA4 0EL. *T:* Carlisle (01228) 562358. *Clubs:* Alpine (Vice-Pres., 1991–93); Alpine Climbing Group; Nottingham Climbers'.

SCOTT, Edward McM.; *see* McMillan-Scott.

SCOTT, Most Rev. Edward Walter, CC 1978; Archbishop, and Primate of All Canada, 1971–86; *b* Edmonton, Alberta, 30 April 1919; *s* of Tom Walter Scott and Kathleen Frances Ford; *m* 1942, Isabel Florence Brannan; one *s* three *d*. *Educ:* Univ. of British Columbia; Anglican Theological Coll. of BC. Vicar of St Peter's, Seal Cove, 1943–45; SCM Secretary, Univ. of Manitoba, 1945–59; Staff of St John's Coll., Winnipeg, 1947–48; Rector: St John the Baptist, Fort Garry, 1949–55; St Jude's, Winnipeg, 1955–60; Dir, Diocesan Council for Social Service, Diocese of Rupert's Land, and Priest Dir of Indian Work, 1960–64; Associate Sec., Council for Social Service, Anglican Church of Canada, 1964–66; Bishop of Kootenay, 1966–71. Moderator of Executive and Central Cttees, WCC, 1975–83; Pres., Canadian Council of Churches, 1985. Mem. Commonwealth Eminent Persons Gp on South Africa, Dec. 1985–June 1986. DD Lambeth, 1986; Hon. DD: Anglican Theol Coll., BC, 1966; Trinity Coll., Toronto, 1971; Wycliffe Coll., Toronto, 1971; Huron Coll., Ont., 1973; United Theol Coll., Montreal, 1971; Renison Coll., Waterloo; Coll. of Emmanuel & St Chad, Saskatoon, 1979; Univ. of Victoria Coll., Toronto, 1986; Queen's Univ., Kingston, 1987; Hon. DCL St John's Coll., Winnipeg, 1971; Hon. STD: Dio. Theol Coll., Montreal, 1973; Thorneloe Coll., Ont., 1974; Hon. LLD York, 1987. Human Relations Award, Canadian CCJ, 1987. *Recreation:* carpentry. *Address:* 29 Hawthorn Avenue, Toronto, Ont M4W 2Z1, Canada.

SCOTT, Elinor Mary, (Mrs D. J. Scott); *see* Goodman, E. M.

SCOTT, Esme, (Lady Scott), CBE 1985; WS; Chair, Volunteer Centre UK, since 1993; *b* 7 Jan. 1932; *d* of David Burnett, SSC and Jane Burnett (*née* Thornton); *m* 1st, 1956, Ian Macfarlane Walker, WS (*d* 1988); one *s*; 2nd, 1990, Sir Kenneth Scott, *qv*; one step *s* one step *d*. *Educ:* St George's School for Girls, Edinburgh; Univ. of Edinburgh (MA, LLB). NP; Mem., Law Soc. of Scotland; Vice-Pres., Inst. of Trading Standards Admin. Lectr in Legal Studies, Queen Margaret College, Edinburgh, 1977–83. Voluntary worker, Citizens' Advice Bureau, 1960–85; Chm., Scottish Assoc. of CABx, 1986–88. Comr, Equal Opportunities Commn, 1986–90. Chm., Scottish Consumer Council, 1980–85; Vice-Chm., Nat. Consumer Council, 1984–87; Chm., Volunteer Development Scotland, 1989–92; Member: Expert Cttee, Multiple Surveys and Valuations (Scotland), 1982–84; Working Party on Procedure for Judicial Review of Admin. Action, 1983–84; Cttee on Conveyancing, 1984; Scottish Cttee, Council on Tribunals, 1986–92; Social Security Adv. Cttee, 1990–; Direct Mail Services Standards Bd, 1990–95; Privacy Adv. Cttee, Common Services Agency, 1990–; SIB, 1991–93; Monopolies and Mergers Commn, 1992–95; Exec. Cttee, NCVO, 1993–. Member: Court, Edinburgh Univ., 1989–92; Council, St George's Sch. for Girls, 1989–. FRSA. *Recreation:* crosswords. *Address:* 13 Clinton Road, Edinburgh EH9 2AW. *T:* 0131–447 5191. *Club:* New (Edinburgh).

SCOTT, Finlay McMillan, TD 1984; Chief Executive and Registrar, General Medical Council, since 1994; *b* 25 May 1947; *s* of Finlay McMillan Scott and Anne Cameron Robertson Coutts Scott; *m* 1969, Eileen Frances Marshall; one *s* one *d*. *Educ:* Greenock High Sch.; Open Univ. (BA Hons); Durham Univ. (MSc). Department of Education and Science, subseq. Department for Education, 1975–94: Head of Pensions Br. and Controller, Darlington, 1983–86; Head of Inf. Systems Br., 1986–90; on secondment: to UFC, 1990–93; to PCFC, 1992–93; to HEFCE, 1992–94; Under Sec., 1990–94. Lt-Col, RAOC, 1989–93, RLC, 1993–95, TA. Mem., NIHEC, 1993–. *Recreations:* squash, tennis, Dartmoor letter-boxing, hill walking. *Address:* General Medical Council, 178–202 Great Portland Street, W1N 6JE. *T:* 0171–915 3564.

SCOTT, Dr Graham Alexander; Consultant in Public Health Medicine, Borders Health Board, 1990–93; *b* 26 Nov. 1927; *s* of Alexander Scott and Jessie Scott; *m* 1951, Helena Patricia Margaret Cavanagh; two *s* one *d*. *Educ:* Daniel Stewart's Coll., Edinburgh; Edinburgh Univ. (MB, ChB). FRCPE, FFCM, DPH. RAAMC, 1951–56 (Dep. Asst Dir, Army Health, 1st Commonwealth Div., Korea, 1953–54). Sen. Asst MO, Stirling CC, 1957–62, Dep. County MO, 1962–65; Scottish Home and Health Department: MO, 1965–68; SMO, 1968–74; PMO, 1974–75; Dep. CMO, 1975–89. QHP 1987–90. *Recreations:* gardening, walking. *Address:* Parkcroft House, Earlston, Berwickshire TD4 6AD.

SCOTT, Hardiman; *see* Scott, P. H.

SCOTT, Sir Ian Dixon, KCMG 1962 (CMG 1959); KCVO 1965; CIE 1947; *b* Inverness, 6 March 1909; *s* of Thomas Henderson Scott, OBE, MICE, and Mary Agnes Dixon, Selkirk; *m* 1937, Hon. Anna Drusilla Lindsay, *d* of 1st Baron Lindsay of Birker, CBE, LLD; one *s* four *d*. *Educ:* Queen's Royal College, Trinidad; Balliol College, Oxford (MA); London School of Economics. Entered Indian Civil Service, 1932; Indian Political Service, 1935; Assistant Director of Intelligence, Peshawar, 1941; Principal, Islamia College, Peshawar, 1943; Deputy Private Secretary to the Viceroy of India, 1945–47. Dep. Dir of Personnel, John Lewis & Co. Ltd, 1948–50. Appointed to Foreign Service, 1950; First Secretary, Foreign Office, 1950–51; British Legation, Helsinki, 1952; British Embassy, Beirut, 1954; Counsellor, 1956; Chargé d'Affaires, 1956, 1957, 1958; idc 1959; Consul-General, then Ambassador to the Congo, 1960–61; Ambassador to Sudan, 1961–65, to Norway, 1965–68. Chm., Clarksons Holidays Ltd, 1972–73 (Dir, 1969–73). Chm., Suffolk AHA, 1973–77; Member: Council, Dr Barnardo's, 1970–84 (Chm., 1972–78; elected Vice-Pres., 1984–); Bd of Governors, Felixstowe Coll., 1971–84 (Chm., 1972–78); Chm., Indian Civil Service (retd) Assoc., 1977–. *Publication:* Tumbled House, 1969. *Recreation:* sailing. *Address:* Ash House, Alde Lane, Aldeburgh, Suffolk IP15 5DZ.

SCOTT, Prof. Ian Richard, PhD; Barber Professor of Law, University of Birmingham, since 1978; *b* 8 Jan. 1940; *s* of Ernest and Edith Scott; *m* 1971, Ecce Cole; two *d*. *Educ:* Geelong Coll.; Queen's Coll., Univ. of Melbourne (LLB); King's Coll., Univ. of London (PhD). Barrister and Solicitor, Supreme Court of Victoria. Dir, Inst. of Judicial Admin, 1975–82. Exec. Dir, Victoria Law Foundn, 1982–84; Dean, Faculty of Law, Univ. of Birmingham, 1985–94. Mem., Lord Chancellor's Civil Justice Review Body, 1985–88; Chm., N Yorks Magistrates' Courts Inquiry, 1989. Hon. Bencher, Gray's Inn, 1988. Fellow, Aust. Inst. of Judicial Admin, 1990. *Recreation:* law. *Address:* Faculty of Law, University of Birmingham, Birmingham B15 2TT. *T:* 0121–414 6291.

SCOTT, Jack Hardiman; *see* Scott, (Peter) Hardiman.

SCOTT, Prof. James, FRCP; Professor and Chairman of Medicine, Royal Postgraduate Medical School, since 1992; Director of Medicine, since 1994, and Chief of Service Medical Cardiology, Hammersmith Hospitals NHS Trst; *b* 13 Sept. 1946; *s* of Robert Bentham Scott and Iris Olive Scott (*née* Hill); *m* 1976, Diane Marylin Lowe; two *s* one *d.* *Educ:* London Univ. (BSc 1968); London Hosp. Med. Coll. (MB, BS 1971; MSc Biochem. 1978). MRCP 1974, FRCP 1986. House Officer: London Hosp., 1971–72; Hereford Co. Hosp., 1972; Sen. House Officer, Midland Centre for Neurosurgery and Neurol., and Queen Elizabeth Hosp., Birmingham, 1972–73; Registrar in Medicine: General Hosp., Birmingham, 1973–74; Acad. Dept of Medicine, Royal Free Hosp., 1975–76; MRC Res. Fellow and Hon. Sen. Registrar, RPMS and Hammersmith Hosp., 1977–80; European Molecular Biol. Fellow, Dept of Biochem., Univ. of Calif, San Francisco, 1980–83; MRC Clinical Scientist and Hon. Consultant Physician, MRC Clinical Res. Centre and Northwick Park Hosp., 1983–91; Hon. Consultant Physician, Hammersmith Hosp., 1992–; Hon. Dir, MRC Molecular Medicine Gp, 1992–. Member: RCP Res. Cttee, 1988–91; Assoc. of Physicians of GB and Ireland, 1987; European Molecular Biol. Orgn, 1993–. Lectures include: Humphrey Davy Rolleston, RCP, 1989; Pfizer, Clin. Res. Inst., Montreal; Guest, Japan Atherosclerosis Soc., 1992. Graham Bull Prize, RCP, 1989; Squibb Bristol Myers Award for Cardiovascular Res., 1993. *Publications:* numerous on molecular medicine, molecular genetics, atherosclerosis, RNA modification, RNA editing and gene expression. *Recreations:* family and friends, the twentieth century novel, British Impressionists and modern painting, long distance running, swimming. *Address:* Department of Medicine, Royal Postgraduate Medical School, Hammersmith Hospital, Du Cane Road, W12 0NN.

SCOTT, Prof. James Alexander, CBE 1986; Regional Medical Officer, Trent Regional Health Authority, 1973–88, retired; Special Professor of Health Care Planning, Nottingham University, since 1974; Professor Associate in Health Service Planning, Department of Community Medicine, Sheffield University, since 1988; *b* 3 July 1931; *s* of Thomas Scott, MA Oxon and Margaret L. Scott; *m* 1957, Margaret Olive Slinger, BA, SRN; one *s* two *d.* *Educ:* Doncaster Grammar Sch.; Trinity Coll., Dublin Univ. BA 1953; MB, BCh, BAO 1955; MA, MD 1965; FFCM 1974; FRCP 1985. Pathologist, Sir Patrick Dun's Hosp., Dublin, 1957–59; Registrar in Clinical Pathology, United Sheffield Hosps, 1959–61; Trainee, later Asst and Principal Asst Sen. MO, Sheffield RHB, 1961–70; Sen. Lectr in Community Medicine, Nottingham Univ., 1967–71; Sen. Admin. MO, Sheffield RHB, 1971–73. Chm., English Regional MOs Gp, 1978–80; Pres., Hospital Cttee, EEC, 1980–86. Member: Health Services Res. Cttee, MRC, 1986–88; Nat. Cttee for Review of Blood Transfusion Service, 1986–87; Chm., Med. Adv. Cttee, Family Health Services Appeal Unit, 1992–94. Treas., Fac. of Community Medicine, RCP, 1984–86. Chm., Bd of Govs, Mid-Trent Coll. of Nursing and Midwifery, 1989–. Masur Fellow, Nuffield Provincial Hospitals Trust, 1983. QHP, 1980–83. Hon. LLD Sheffield, 1983. *Publications:* contrib. Lancet. *Recreation:* stamp collecting. *Address:* 5 Slayleigh Lane, Sheffield S10 3RE. *T:* Sheffield (0114) 230 2238; La Gardelle, 24260 Le Bugue, Dordogne, France.

SCOTT, James Alexander, OBE 1987; FCA; Partner, Binder Hamlyn, Chartered Accountants, since 1969; *b* 30 April 1940; *s* of Douglas McPherson Scott and Mabel Mary (*née* Skepper); *m* 1965, Annette Goslett; three *s* two *d.* *Educ:* Uppingham Sch.; Magdalene Coll., Cambridge (Schol.; MA); London Business Sch. (MSc). Joined Binder Hamlyn, 1961; Man. Partner, London Region, 1980–88; Nat. Man. Partner, 1988–89. Director: Frederick Leyland & Co., 1992–; Schroder Exempt Property Unit Trust, 1994–. Mem., Agricl Wages Bd for England and Wales, 1971–86; Sec., Review Bd for Govt Contracts, 1969–; Member: NHS Pharmacists Remuneration Review Panel, 1982; Restrictive Practices Court, 1993–. DTI Inspector, Atlantic Computers plc, 1990. *Recreations:* walking, golf, tennis, ski-ing. *Address:* Southbrook, Shrubbs Hill, Chobham, Surrey GU24 8ST. *Clubs:* Berkshire Golf; St Enodoc Golf.

SCOTT, James Archibald, CB 1988; LVO 1961; FRSE; Non-executive Director, Scottish Power plc, since 1992; *b* 5 March 1932; *s* of late James Scott, MBE, and Agnes Bone Howie; *m* 1957, Elizabeth Agnes Joyce Buchan-Hepburn; three *s* one *d.* *Educ:* Dollar Acad.; Queen's Univ. of Ont.; Univ. of St Andrews (MA Hons). FRSE 1993. RAF aircrew, 1954–56. Asst Principal, CRO, 1956; served in New Delhi, 1958–62, and UK Mission to UN, New York, 1962–65; transf. to Scottish Office, 1965; Private Sec. to Sec. of State for Scotland, 1969–71; Asst Sec., Scottish Office, 1971; Under-Sec., Scottish Economic Planning Dept, later Industry Dept for Scotland, 1976–84; Sec., Scottish Educn Dept, 1984–87; Sec., Industry Dept for Scotland, 1987–90; Chief Exec., SDA, 1990–91; Exec. Dir, Scottish Financial Enterprise, 1991–94. Non-exec. Dir, Dumyat Investment Trust plc, 1995. Fellow, SCOTVEC, 1990. *Recreations:* music, golf. *Address:* 38 Queen's Crescent, Edinburgh EH9 2BA. *T:* 0131–667 8417.

SCOTT, Sir James (Jervoise), 3rd Bt *cr* 1962, of Rotherfield Park, Alton, Hants; farmer and landowner; *b* 12 Oct. 1952; *e s* of Lt-Col Sir James Walter Scott, 2nd Bt, and of Anne Constantia (*née* Austin); *S* father, 1993; *m* 1982, Judy Evelyn, *d* of Brian Trafford and Hon. Mrs Trafford; one *s* one *d.* *Educ:* Eton; Trinity Coll., Cambridge (MA). Agricultural journalist, 1977–88. *Recreation:* shooting. *Heir:* *s* Arthur Jervoise Trafford Scott, *b* 2 Feb. 1984. *Address:* Estate Office, Rotherfield Park, East Tisted, Alton, Hampshire GU34 3QL. *T:* Alton (01420) 588207. *Clubs:* White's, Travellers.

SCOTT, James Steel; Professor of Obstetrics and Gynæcology, 1961–89, and Dean of Faculty of Medicine, 1986–89, University of Leeds, now Professor Emeritus; *b* 18 April 1924; *s* of late Dr Angus M. Scott and late Margaret Scott; *m* 1958, Olive Sharpe; two *s.* *Educ:* Glasgow Academy; University of Glasgow. MB, ChB 1946, MD 1959; FRCSEd 1959; FRCOG 1962 (MRCOG 1953); FRCS (*ad eund*) 1986. Service in RAMC, 1947–49. Liverpool University: Obstetric Tutor, 1954; Lecturer, 1958; Senior Lecturer, 1960. *Publications:* contrib. to New Engl. Jl of Medicine, Lancet, BMJ, Jl of Obst. and Gynæc. of Brit. Empire, Amer. Jl of Obstetrics and Gynæcology, etc. *Recreations:* skiing, biography. *Address:* Byards Lodge, Boroughbridge Road, Knaresborough, N Yorks HG5 0LT.

SCOTT, Jean Grant; Headmistress, South Hampstead High School, since 1993; *b* 7 Oct. 1940; *d* of Dr Duncan W. D. MacLaren and Etta M. MacLaren (*née* Speirs); *m* 1964, John Scott (*d* 1979); two *s.* *Educ:* George Watson's Ladies' Coll., Edinburgh; Wellington Sch., Ayr; Univ. of Glasgow (BSc Hons Zool.); Univ. of London Inst of Educn (PGCE). Research Biologist: Glaxo Labs Ltd, 1962–65; ICI, Alderley Edge, 1966–67; part-time Lectr in Biol., Newcastle-under-Lyme Coll. of FE, 1969–70; Teacher of Biology: (part-time) Dr Challoner's High Sch., 1970–76; Northgate Grammar Sch., Ipswich, 1976–77; Hd of Biol. and Sen. Mistress, Ipswich High Sch. (GPDST), 1977–86; Headmistress, St George's Sch. for Girls, Edinburgh, 1986–93. *Recreations:* concerts, theatre, film, swimming, ski-ing, loch fishing, travel abroad. *Address:* South Hampstead High School, 3 Maresfield Gardens, NW3 5SS. *T:* 0171–435 2899.

SCOTT, Sir John; *see* Scott, Sir P. J. and Scott, Sir W. J.

SCOTT, (John) Brough; Editorial Director, Racing Post, since 1988; Chief Presenter, Channel 4 Racing, since 1985; Chief Sports Writer, Sunday Telegraph, since 1995; *b* 12 Dec. 1942; *s* of Mason Hogarth Scott and Irene Florence Scott, Broadway, Worcs; *m* 1973, Susan Eleanor MacInnes; two *s* two *d.* *Educ:* Radley College; Corpus Christi, Oxford (BA History). Amateur, then professional, Nat. Hunt jockey, 1962–71 (100 winners, incl. Imperial Cup and Mandarin Chase). ITV presenter, sports programmes and documentaries, 1971–; chief racing presenter, ITV, 1979–85; Evening Standard sports correspondent, 1972–74; sports journalist: Sunday Times, 1974–90, 1993–94; The Independent on Sunday, 1990–92. Vice-Pres., Jockeys' Assoc., 1969–71; Trustee: Injured Jockeys Fund; Professional Riders' Insurance Scheme; Racing Welfare. Lord Derby Award, 1978 (racing journalist of the year); Clive Graham Trophy, 1982; Sports Journalist of the Year, 1983; Sports Feature Writer of the Year, 1985, 1991, 1992. *Publications:* World of Flat Racing, 1983; On and Off the Rails, 1984; Front Runners, 1991; Up Front—Willie Carson, 1994. *Recreation:* making bonfires. *Address:* 120 Coombe Lane, Raynes Park, SW20 0BA. *T:* 0181–879 3377.

SCOTT, Rev. Prof. John Fraser, AO 1990; Vice-Chancellor, La Trobe University, Melbourne, 1977–90; Associate Priest, St George's, Malvern, since 1992; *b* 10 Oct. 1928; *s* of Douglas Fraser Scott and Cecilia Louise Scott; *m* 1956, Dorothea Elizabeth Paton Scott; one *s* three *d.* *Educ:* Bristol Grammar Sch.; Trinity Coll., Cambridge (MA); Melbourne Coll. of Divinity (BD 1994). FIS. Research Asst, Univ. of Sheffield, 1950–53; Asst, Univ. of Aberdeen, 1953–55; Lectr in Biometry, Univ. of Oxford, 1955–65; University of Sussex: Reader in Statistics, 1965–67; Prof. of Applied Statistics, 1967–77; Pro-Vice-Chancellor, 1971–77. Adv. Prof., E China Normal Univ., 1988. Visiting Consultant in Statistics: Nigeria, 1961, 1965; Sweden, 1969; Kuwait, 1973, 1976; Iraq, 1973; Malaysia, 1976. Reader, Church of England, 1971–77; Examining Chaplain to Bp of Chichester, 1974–77; Diocesan Lay Reader, Anglican Dio. of Melbourne, 1977–90; ordained deacon, then priest, 1990; Asst Curate, St George's, E Ivanhoe, 1990–91. Chairman: Jt Cttee on Univ. Statistics, 1978–86; Cttee of Review of Student Finances, 1983; Aust. Univs Industrial Assoc., 1986–; AVCC, 1986–88 (Dep. Chm., 1986, Chm., Wkg Party on Attrition, 1981–86); Council for Chaplains in Tertiary Instns, 1990–94; Member: Grad. Careers Council of Aust., 1980–86; Council, 1986–, Exec. Cttee, 1986–88, ACU; ABC Victorian State Adv. Cttee, 1978–81; Ethics Cttee, Victorian State Dept of Health, 1990–; Pres., Victorian State Libraries Bd, 1990. Editor, Applied Statistics, 1971–76; Mem., Editl Bd, The Statistician, 1987–. DUniv La Trobe, 1990. *Publications:* The Comparability of Grade Standards in Mathematics, 1975; Report of Committee of Review of Student Finances, 1983; papers in JRSS, Lancet, BMJ, Chemistry and Industry, Statistician, etc. *Recreations:* wine, women and song; canals. *Address:* 1/18 Riversdale Road, Hawthorn, Victoria 3122, Australia. *T:* (3) 98191862. *Club:* Melbourne.

SCOTT, John Gavin, FRCO; Organist and Director of Music, St Paul's Cathedral, since 1990; *b* 18 June 1956; *s* of Douglas Gavin Scott and Hetty Scott (*née* Murphy); *m* 1979, Carolyn Jane Lumsden; one *s* one *d.* *Educ:* Queen Elizabeth Grammar Sch., Wakefield; St John's Coll., Cambridge (MA, MusB). Asst Organist, Wakefield Cath., 1970–74; Organ Scholar, St John's Coll., Cambridge, 1974–78; Assistant Organist: Southwark Cath., 1978–85; St Paul's Cath., 1978–85; Sub-Organist, St Paul's Cath., 1985–90. Prof., Royal Acad. of Music, 1988–91. Asst Conductor and Accompanist, Bach Choir, 1978–91. Hon. RAM 1990. First Prizewinner: Manchester Internat. Organ Fest., 1978; Leipzig Internat. J. S. Bach Competition, 1984. *Recreations:* reading, travel, ecclesiastical architecture. *Address:* 5 Amen Court, EC4M 7BU. *T:* 0171–248 6868.

SCOTT, John Hamilton; Lord-Lieutenant for Shetland, since 1994; farming in Bressay and Noss; *b* 30 Nov. 1936; *s* of Dr Thomas Gilbert Scott and Elizabeth M. B. Scott; *m* 1965, Wendy Ronald; one *s* one *d.* *Educ:* Bryanston; Cambridge Univ.; Guy's Hosp., London. Shepherd, Scrabster, Caithness, 1961–64. Chm., Woolgrowers of Shetland Ltd, 1981–. Pres., Shetland NFU, 1976; Chairman: Shetland Crofting, Farming and Wildlife Adv. Gp, 1984–95; Shetland Arts Trust, 1993–; Member: Nature Conservancy Council Cttee for Scotland, 1984–91; NE Regl Bd, Nature Conservancy Council for Scotland, 1991–92, Scottish Natural Heritage, 1992–. *Recreations:* mountain climbing, Up-Helly-Aa, music. *Address:* Gardie House, Bressay, Shetland ZE2 9EL. *T:* Bressay (01595) 820281. *Club:* Alpine.

SCOTT, John James, PhD; Associate, Save & Prosper Group, since 1985; *b* 4 Sept. 1924; *s* of late Col John Creagh Scott, DSO, OBE and Mary Elizabeth Marjory (*née* Murray of Polmaise); *m* 1st, Katherine Mary (*née* Bruce); twin *d*; 2nd, Heather Marguerite (*née* Douglas Brown); 3rd, June Rose (*née* Mackie); twin *s.* *Educ:* Radley (Schol.); Corpus Christi Coll., Cambridge (Schol.); National Inst. for Medical Research, London. War Service, Captain, Argyll and Sutherland Highlanders, 1944–47. BA 1st cl. hons Nat. Sci. Tripos, Pts I and II, 1950, MA 1953, Cantab; PhD London 1954. Senior Lectr in Chem. Pathology, St Mary's Hosp., 1955–61; Mem. Editorial Bd, Biochem. Jl, 1956–61; Mem. Cttee of Biochem. Soc., 1961; Vis. Scientist, Nat. Insts of Health, Bethesda, Md, 1961. Entered Diplomatic Service, 1961; Office of Comr Gen. for SE Asia, Singapore, 1962; Office of Political Adviser to C-in-C, Singapore, 1963; FO, 1966; Counsellor, Rio de Janeiro and Brasilia, 1971; seconded to NI Office as Asst Sec., Stormont, 1974–76; Asst Under-Sec., FCO, 1978–80; Asst Managing Dir, later Commercial Dir, Industrial Engines (Sales) Ltd, Elbar Group, 1980; Man. Dir, Dudmass Ltd, 1983–93. Francis Bacon Prize, Cambridge, 1950. *Publications:* papers in Biochem. Jl, Proc. Royal Soc. and other learned jls. *Recreations:* botany, photography, music. *Address:* The Cottage, South Rauceby, Sleaford, Lincs NG34 8QG. *T:* Sleaford (01529) 488254. *Clubs:* Carlton, Institute of Directors; Leander (Henley-on-Thames); Hawks (Cambridge); Ski Club of GB.

SCOTT, Sir Kenneth (Bertram Adam), KCVO 1990; CMG 1980; Deputy Private Secretary to the Queen, 1990–96; *b* 23 Jan. 1931; *s* of late Adam Scott, OBE, and Lena Kaye; *m* 1st, 1966, Gabrielle Justine (*d* 1977), *d* of R. W. Smart, Christchurch, New Zealand; one *s* one *d*; 2nd, 1990, Esme Walker (*see* Esme Scott); one step *s.* *Educ:* George Watson's Coll., Edinburgh; Edinburgh Univ. MA Hons 1952. Foreign Office, 1954; Third Sec., Moscow 1956; Second Sec., (Commercial), Bonn, 1958; FO, 1961; First Sec., Washington, 1964; Head of Chancery and Consul, Vientiane, 1968; Counsellor and Head of Chancery, Moscow, 1971; Sen. Officers' War Course, RNC, Greenwich, 1973; Dep. Head, Personnel Ops Dept, FCO, 1973; Counsellor and Head of Chancery, Washington, 1975; Head of E European and Soviet Dept, FCO, 1977; Minister and Dep. UK Perm. Rep. to NATO, 1979–82; Ambassador to Yugoslavia, 1982–85; Asst Private Sec. to the Queen, 1985–90. *Address:* (until March 1996) 25a Friary Court, St James's Palace, SW1A 1BJ. *T:* 0171–839 6579; 13 Clinton Road, Edinburgh EH9 2AW. *Clubs:* Royal Over-Seas League; New (Edinburgh).

SCOTT, Kenneth Farish, MC 1943 and Bar, 1944; FEng 1979, FICE; Senior Partner, 1977–84, Senior Consultant, 1984–87, Sir Alexander Gibb & Partners; *b* 21 Dec. 1918; *s* of Norman James Stewart and Ethel May Scott; *m* 1945, Elizabeth Mary Barrowcliff; one *s* one *d.* *Educ:* Stockton Grammar School; Constantine Tech. Coll. Served Royal Engineers, 1939–46. Joined Sir Alexander Gibb & Partners, 1946; Resident Engineer, Hydro-Electric Works, Scotland, 1946–52; Chief Rep., NZ, 1952–55, Scotland, 1955–59; Partner 1959, Senior Partner 1977; responsible for design and supervision of construction of major water resource develt projects, incl. Latiyan Dam, 1959–67, Lar Dam 1968–82, Greater Tehran Water Supply, 1959–82; major maritime works incl. modernisation Devonport Dockyard, 1970–80; internat. airports at Tripoli, 1966–70, Bahrain, 1970–72.

Pres., Soc. des Ingénieurs et Scientifiques de France (British Section), 1975; Vice-Pres., ICE, 1985–87. Chm., Assoc. of Consulting Engineers, 1976. Hon. Mem., Instn of RE, 1982. *Publications:* papers to ICE and International Congress of Large Dams. *Recreations:* sailing, golf, wood working. *Address:* Forest House, Brookside Road, Brockenhurst, Hants SO42 7SS. *T:* Lymington (01590) 623531. *Clubs:* Special Forces, Royal Over-Seas League; RE Yacht, Royal Southampton Yacht.

SCOTT, Malcolm Charles Norman; QC (Scot.) 1991; *b* 8 Sept. 1951; *s* of James Raymond Scott and Marjorie Stewart Simpson. *Educ:* Trinity Coll., Glenalmond; Gonville and Caius Coll., Cambridge (BA 1972); Glasgow Univ. (LLB 1975). Advocate 1978. Dir, Mid Wynd International Investment Trust plc, 1990–. *Recreations:* fishing, ski-ing, hill walking. *Address:* 72 Northumberland Street, Edinburgh EH3 6JG. *Club:* New (Edinburgh).

SCOTT, Dame Margaret, (Dame Catherine Margaret Mary Denton), DBE 1981 (OBE 1977); Founding Director of the Australian Ballet School, 1964–90, retired; *b* 26 April 1922; *d* of John and Marjorie Douglas-Scott; *m* 1953, Prof. Derek Ashworth Denton, FAA, FRACP; two *s*. *Educ:* Parktown Convent, Johannesburg, S Africa. Sadler's Wells Ballet, London, 1940–43; Principal: Ballet Rambert, London and Australia, 1944–49; National Ballet, Australia, 1949–50; Ballet Rambert, and John Cranko Group, London, 1951–53; private ballet teaching, Australia, 1953–61; planned and prepared the founding of the Aust. Ballet Sch., 1962–64. Hon. Life Mem., Australian Ballet Foundn, 1988. Hon. LLD Melbourne, 1989. *Recreations:* music, theatre, garden. *Address:* 816 Orrong Road, Toorak, Melbourne, Vic 3142, Australia. *T:* (3) 98272640. *Club:* Alexandra (Melbourne).

SCOTT, Maurice FitzGerald, FBA 1990; Official Fellow in Economics, Nuffield College, Oxford, 1968–92, now Emeritus Fellow; *b* 6 Dec. 1924; *s* of Colonel G. C. Scott, OBE and H. M. G. Scott; *m* 1953, Eleanor Warren (*née* Dawson) (*d* 1989); three *d*. *Educ:* Wadham Coll., Oxford (MA); Nuffield Coll., Oxford (BLitt). Served RE, 1943–46. OEEC, Paris, 1949–51; Paymaster-General's Office (Lord Cherwell), 1951–53; Cabinet Office, 1953–54; NIESR, London, 1954–57; Tutor in Economics and Student of Christ Church, Oxford, 1957–68; NEDO, London, 1962–63; OECD, Paris, 1967–68. *Publications:* A Study of U.K. Imports, 1963; (with I. M. D. Little and T. Scitovsky) Industry and Trade in Some Developing Countries, 1970; (with J. D. MacArthur and D. M. G. Newbery) Project Appraisal in Practice, 1976; (with R. A. Laslett) Can We get back to Full Employment?, 1978; (with W. M. Corden and I. M. D. Little) The Case against General Import Restrictions, 1980; A New View of Economic Growth, 1989. *Recreation:* walking. *Address:* 11 Blandford Avenue, Oxford OX2 8EA. *T:* Oxford (01865) 59115. *Club:* Political Economy (Oxford).

SCOTT, Sir Michael, KCVO 1979 (MVO 1961); CMG 1977; HM Diplomatic Service, retired; *b* 19 May 1923; *yr s* of late John Scott and Kathleen Scott; *m* 1st, 1944, Vivienne Sylvia Vincent-Barwood; three *s*; 2nd, 1971, Jennifer Slawikowski (*née* Cameron Smith), *widow* of Dr George J. M. Slawikowski. *Educ:* Dame Allan's School; Durham Univ. War Service: Durham Light Infantry, 1941; 1st Gurkha Rifles, 1943–47. Joined Colonial Office, 1949; CRO, 1957; First Secretary, Karachi, 1958–59; Deputy High Commissioner, Peshawar, 1959–62; Counsellor and Director, British Information Services in India, New Delhi, 1963–65; Head of E and Central Africa Dept, FCO, 1965–68; Dep. High Comr, British High Commn, Nicosia, 1968–72; RCDS, 1973; Ambassador to Nepal, 1974–77; High Comr in Malaŵi, 1977–79; High Comr in Bangladesh, 1980–81. Sec.-Gen., Royal Commonwealth Soc., 1983–88. Dir, Tiger Mountain Gp (Nepal and India), 1984–93. Mem., Governing Council, ODI, 1983–93; Trustee, Internat. Agricl Trng Programme, 1988–. Dep. Chm., Drive for Youth Programme, 1987–93. *Address:* 87A Cornwall Gardens, SW7 4AY. *T:* 0171–589 6794. *Club:* Oriental.

SCOTT, Maj.-Gen. Michael Ian Eldon, CBE 1987; DSO 1982; Military Secretary, since 1995; *b* 3 March 1941; *s* of Col Eric Scott and Rose-Anne Scott; *m* 1968, Veronica Daniell; one *s* one *d*. *Educ:* Bradfield Coll. Commnd Scots Guards, 1960; Regtl service in UK, E Africa, N Ireland, BAOR; Staff Coll., Camberley, 1974; 2nd MA to CGS, 1975; COS Task Force Delta, 1979; Armed Forces Staff Coll., USA, 1981; CO, 2nd Bn Scots Guards, London, Falklands War and Cyprus, 1981–84; Comd 8th Inf. Bde, N Ireland, 1984–86; RCDS 1987; Dep. Mil. Sec., 1988; GOC Scotland and Gov., Edinburgh Castle, 1993–95. *Recreations:* travel, visual arts, outdoor pursuits. *Club:* Pratt's.

SCOTT, Michael John; broadcaster; *b* 8 Dec. 1932; *s* of Tony and Pam Scott; *m* 1956, Sylvia Hudson; one *d*. *Educ:* Latymer Upper Sch., Hammersmith; Clayesmore, Iwerne Minster, Dorset. National Service, RAOC, 1951–53. Stagehand with Festival Ballet, and film extra, 1954; TV production trainee, Rank Organization, 1955; Granada TV: joined as floormanager, 1956; Programme Director, 1957; Producer/Performer, daily magazine programme, 1963–65; Presenter, Cinema, 1965–68; Executive Producer, local programmes, 1968–73; World in Action interviewer, and producer/performer of other programmes, 1974–75; Executive Producer and Reporter, Nuts and Bolts of the Economy, 1975–78; Dep. Programme Controller, 1978–79; Prog. Controller, 1979–87; returned to active broadcasting, via live daily programme The Time . . . The Place, 1987–93. Director: Channel 4 Television Co., 1984–87; Granada TV, 1978–87. *Recreations:* watching the box, jogging, a 1932 Lagonda, a garden. *Address:* Flat 1, 39 Gloucester Walk, W8 4HY. *T:* 0171–937 3962.

SCOTT, Rt. Hon. Sir Nicholas (Paul), KBE 1995 (MBE 1964); PC 1989; JP; MP (C) Chelsea, since Oct. 1974; *b* 5 Aug. 1933; *e s* of late Percival John Scott; *m* 1st, 1964, Elizabeth Robinson (marr. diss. 1976); one *s* two *d*; 2nd, 1979, Hon. Mrs Cecilia Anne Tapsell, *d* of 9th Baron Hawke; one *s* one *d*. *Educ:* Clapham College. Served Holborn Borough Coun., 1956–59 and 1962–65; contested (C) SW Islington, 1959 and 1964; MP (C) Paddington S, 1966–Feb. 1974; PPS to: Chancellor of the Exchequer, Rt Hon. Iain Macleod, 1970; Home Sec., Rt. Hon. Robert Carr, 1972–74; Parly Under-Sec. of State, Dept of Employment, 1974; Opposition spokesman on housing, 1974–75; Parly Under Sec. of State, 1981–86, Minister of State, 1986–87, Northern Ireland Office; Minister of State, DHSS, then DSS, 1987–94. Mem., 1922 Exec. Cttee, 1978–81; Dir, London Office, European Cons. Gp in European Parlt, 1974. Nat. Chm., Young Conservatives, 1963 (Vice-Pres., 1988–89); Chm., Conservative Parly Employment Cttee, 1979–81 (Vice-Chm., 1967–72). Chairman: Westminster Community Relations Council, 1967–72; Paddington Churches Housing Assoc., 1970–76; British Atlantic Gp Younger Politicians, 1970–73; Nat. Pres., Tory Reform Gp. Dep. Chm., British Caribbean Assoc.; Mem. Council, Community Service Volunteers; Governor, British Inst. of Human Rights; Dep. Chm., Youthaid, 1977–79. Mem., Cttee, MCC, 1972–75. Churchwarden, St Margaret's, Westminster, 1971–73. Man. Dir, E. Allom & Co., 1968–70; Chm., Creative Consultants Ltd, 1969–79; Director: A. S. Kerswill Ltd, 1970–81; Eastbourne Printers Ltd, 1970–81; Juniper Studios Ltd, 1970–81; Midhurst White Holdings Ltd, 1977–78; Bonusbond Hldgs Ltd, 1980–81; Bonusplan Ltd, 1977–81; Cleveland Offshore Fund Inc., 1970–81; Throgmorton Securities Ltd, 1970–74; Ede & Townsend, 1977–80; Learplan Ltd, 1978–81; Consultant: Campbell-Johnson Ltd, 1970–76; Roulston & Co. Inc., 1970–78; Lombard North Central Ltd, 1971–74; Clevebourne Investments Ltd, 1974–76; Claremont Textiles Ltd, 1974–76; Procter & Gamble Ltd, 1974–78; Hill & Knowlton (UK) Ltd, 1981; VSO, 1974–76; Council, Bank Staff Assocs, 1968–77. Freeman, City of London, 1979; Liveryman, GAPAN, 1988–. JP London, 1961. *Recreations:* cricket, tennis, golf, flying. *Address:* House of Commons, SW1A 0AA. *Clubs:* Pratt's, Garrick, MCC.

SCOTT, Norman Bruce St Clair, CMG 1994; Director, United Nations Secretariat, retired; Professor, Graduate Institute of International Studies, Geneva; Consultant, International Monetary Fund; *b* 13 April 1933; *s* of John Reid Scott and Isobel Carmichael-Brown; *m* 1955, Mirjana Matejovic; one *s* one *d*. *Educ:* Glasgow Univ. (MA 1954); Univ. of Belgrade; Univ. of Geneva; Coatbridge Acad. UN Economic Commission for Europe: Sen. Economist, Res. Div., 1966–73; Dir, Technol. Div., 1974–83; Dir, Trade Div., 1983–93; Sen. Dir, Secretariat, retd 1993. Pres., Centre for Res. on Internat. Instns, Geneva, 1986–. *Publications:* numerous essays on comparative economic systems and policies in collective works; contrib. economic and technical jls. *Recreations:* amateur theatre, angling, antique map collecting. *Address:* 2 avenue de Warens, 1203 Geneva, Switzerland. *T:* (22) 3448664; Glower, Birsay, Orkney KW17 2ND. *Clubs:* Athenæum, Oriental.

SCOTT, Sir Oliver (Christopher Anderson), 3rd Bt, of Yews, Westmorland, *cr* 1909; Radiobiologist, Richard Dimbleby Cancer Research Department, St Thomas' Hospital, 1982–88; Radiobiologist, 1954–66, Director, 1966–69, British Empire Cancer Campaign Research Unit in Radiobiology; *b* 6 November 1922; *s* of Sir Samuel H. Scott, 2nd Bt and Nancy Lilian (*née* Anderson); *S* father 1960; *m* 1951, Phoebe Ann Tolhurst; one *s* two *d*. *Educ:* Charterhouse; King's College, Cambridge. Clinical training at St Thomas' Hosp., 1943–46; MRCS, LRCP, 1946; MB, BCh, Cambridge, 1946; MD Cambridge, 1976; Surgeon-Lieutenant RNVR, 1947–49. Dir, Provincial Insurance Co., 1955–64. Hon. Consultant, Inst. of Cancer Res., Sutton, 1974–82. Pres., Section of Oncology, RSM, 1987–88. Mem. Council, Cancer Res. Campaign, 1978–91. High Sheriff of Westmorland, 1966. *Publications:* contributions to scientific books and journals. *Recreations:* music, walking. *Heir:* *s* Christopher James Scott, [*b* 16 Jan. 1955; *m* 1988, Emma, *o d* of Michael Boxhall; two *s* one *d*]. *Address:* 31 Kensington Square, W8 5HH. *T:* 0171–937 8556. *Club:* Brooks's.

SCOTT, Oliver Lester Schreiner; Emeritus Consultant: Skin Department, Charing Cross Hospital, since 1985 (Physician-in-Charge, 1956–84); South West Metropolitan Regional Hospital Board, since 1985 (Consultant Dermatologist, 1951–84); *b* London, 16 June 1919; *s* of Ralph Lester Scott, FRCSE, and Ursula Hester Schreiner; *m* 1943, Katherine Ogle Branfoot (*d* 1987); two *d*. *Educ:* Diocesan College, Cape Town; Trinity College, Cambridge; St Thomas's Hospital, London. MRCS, LRCP 1942; MA, MB, BChir, (Cantab) 1943; MRCP (London) 1944. FRCP 1964. Med. Specialist, RAF Med. Branch, 1943–46 (Sqn Leader). Consultant, Medical Insurance Agency, 1976–93; Hon. Consultant: Dispensaire Française, 1960–86; King Edward VII Hosp. for Officers, London, 1975–84. Hon. Treas., RSocMed, 1978–82 (Pres., Dermatology Section, 1977–78); Vice-Pres., Royal Medical Foundn of Epsom Coll. (Hon. Treas., 1978–93); Hon. Mem., British Assoc. of Dermatologists (Pres., 1982–83). Chevalier, l'Ordre National du Mérite, France. *Publications:* section on skin disorders in Clinical Genetics, ed A. Sorsby; medical articles in Lancet, British Journal of Dermatology, etc. *Recreations:* fishing, gardening. *Address:* South Lodge, 7 South Side, Wimbledon Common, SW19 4TL. *T:* 0181–946 6662.

SCOTT, Paul Henderson, CMG 1974; writer; HM Diplomatic Service, retired 1980; *b* 7 Nov. 1920; *s* of Alan Scott and Catherine Scott (*née* Henderson), Edinburgh; *m* 1953, Beatrice Celia Sharpe; one *s* one *d*. *Educ:* Royal High School, Edinburgh; Edinburgh University (MA, MLitt). HM Forces, 1941–47 (Major RA). Foreign Office, 1947–53; First Secretary, Warsaw, 1953–55; First Secretary, La Paz, 1955–59; Foreign Office, 1959–62; Counsellor, Havana, 1962–64; Canadian National Defence College, 1964–65; British Deputy Commissioner General for Montreal Exhibition, 1965–67; Counsellor and Consul-General, Vienna, 1968–71; Head of British Govt Office, 1971, Consul-Gen., 1974–75, Montreal; Research Associate, IISS, 1975–76; Asst Under Sec., FO (negotiator on behalf of EEC Presidency for negotiations with USSR, Poland and East Germany), 1977; Minister and Consul-General, Milan, 1977–80. Chairman: Adv. Council for the Arts in Scotland, 1981–; Steering Cttee for a Scottish Nat. Theatre, 1988–; Mem., Constitutional Steering Cttee, which drew up A Claim of Right for Scotland, published 1988; Dep. Chm., Saltire Soc., 1981–; Member: Council, Nat. Trust for Scotland, 1981–87; Assoc. for Scottish Literary Studies, 1981–; Scots Language Soc., 1981–91; Cockburn Assoc., 1982–85; Council, Edinburgh Internat. Fest., 1984–87; Chm., Friends of Dictionary of Older Scottish Tongue, 1984–; President: Andrew Fletcher Soc., 1988–; Scottish Centre, PEN Internat., 1992–. Mem., NEC, SNP, 1989–; SNP spokesman on educn and the arts, 1991–; Vice-Pres., SNP, 1992–; contested (SNP) Eastwood, 1992. Convener, Scottish Centre for Econ. and Social Res., 1990–. Rector, Dundee Univ., 1989–92. Grosse Goldene Ehrenzeichen, Austria, 1969. *Publications:* 1707: The Union of Scotland and England, 1979; (ed with A. C. Davis) The Age of MacDiarmid, 1980; Walter Scott and Scotland, 1981; (ed) Walter Scott's Letters of Malachi Malagrowther, 1981; (ed) Andrew Fletcher's United and Separate Parliaments, 1982; John Galt, 1985; In Bed with an Elephant, 1985; (ed with George Bruce) A Scottish Postbag, 1986; The Thinking Nation, 1989; Towards Independence, 1991; Andrew Fletcher and the Treaty of Union, 1992; Scotland in Europe: a dialogue with a sceptical friend, 1992; (ed) Scotland: a concise cultural history, 1993; Defoe in Edinburgh and Other Papers, 1994; articles and book reviews esp. in Economist, Scotsman and other periodicals. *Recreations:* ski-ing, sailing. *Address:* 33 Drumsheugh Gardens, Edinburgh EH3 7RN. *T:* 0131–225 1038. *Clubs:* New, Scottish Arts (Edinburgh).

SCOTT, Sir Peter; *see* Scott, Sir C. P.

SCOTT, Peter Denys John, QC 1978; *b* 19 April 1935; *s* of John Ernest Dudley Scott and Joan G. Steinberg. *Educ:* Monroe High Sch., Rochester, NY, USA; Balliol Coll., Oxford (MA). Second Lieut, RHA, Lieut (TA), National Service, 1955. Called to the Bar, Middle Temple (Harmsworth Scholar), 1960, Bencher, 1984; Standing Counsel: to Dir, Gen. of Fair Trading, 1973–78; to Dept of Employment, 1974–78. Member: Home Sec's Cttee on Prison Disciplinary System, 1984; Interception of Communications Tribunal, 1986–; Lord Chancellor's Adv. Cttee on Legal Educn and Conduct, 1991–94; Chm., Appeal Bd, Inst. of Actuaries, 1995. Vice-Chm., Senate of the Inns of Court and the Bar, 1985–86; Chm., General Council of the Bar, 1987; Mem., Senate and Bar Council, 1981–87; Chm., London Common Law Bar Assoc., 1983–85. Chm., N Kensington Amenity Trust, 1981–85. *Recreations:* gardening, theatre. *Address:* 4 Eldon Road, W8 5PU. *T:* 0171–937 3301.

SCOTT, (Peter) Hardiman, OBE 1989; Chief Assistant to Director General BBC, 1975–80; *b* King's Lynn, 2 April 1920; named Jack Hardiman Scott at birth; *s* of Thomas Hardiman Scott and Dorothy Constance Smith; *m* 1st, 1942, Sheilah Stewart Roberts (marr. diss.); two *s*; 2nd, Patricia Mary (Sue) Windle. *Educ:* Grammar Sch.; privately. Northampton Chronicle and Echo series, 1939; then various provincial newspapers; Associated Press, and finally Hants and Sussex News, when began freelance broadcasting, 1948. Joined BBC; Asst News Editor Midland Region, 1950; gen. reporting staff, London, 1954; various foreign assignments, incl. Suez war; BBC's first Polit. Corresp., 1960; subseq.

first Polit. Editor until 1975. Member: Study Gp on Future of Broadcasting in Zimbabwe, 1980; Broadcasting Complaints Commn, 1981–89. Pres., Suffolk Poetry Soc., 1979–. *Publications:* Secret Sussex, 1949; (ed) How Shall I Vote?, 1976; Many a Summer, 1991; *poems:* Adam and Eve and Us, 1946; When the Words are Gone, 1972; Part of Silence, 1984; (ed) Selected Poems of Sir Thomas Wyatt, 1996; *novels:* Within the Centre, 1946; The Lonely River, 1950; Text for Murder, 1951; Operation 10, 1982; No Exit, 1984; Deadly Nature, 1985; (with Becky Allan) Bait of Lies, 1986; contribs to: TV and Elections, 1977; BBC Guide to Parliament, 1979; Politics and the Media, 1980. *Recreations:* poetry, paintings, listening to music, conservation, East Anglia. *Address:* 4 Butchers Lane, Boxford, Sudbury, Suffolk CO10 5DZ. *T:* Boxford (Suffolk) (01787) 210320.

SCOTT, Sir (Philip) John, KBE 1987; FRCP; FRACP; FRSNZ; Professor of Medicine, University of Auckland, since 1975; *b* 26 June 1931; *s* of Horace McD. Scott and Doris A. Scott (*née* Ruddock); *m* 1956, Elizabeth Jane MacMillan; one *s* three *d. Educ:* Univ. of Otago (BMedSci; MB, ChB); Univ. of Birmingham (MD). Qual. in medicine, Dunedin, 1955; hosp. and gen. practice experience, Auckland, 1956–58; postgrad. trng, RPMS, London, 1959–60; Queen Elizabeth Hosp. and Univ. of Birmingham, 1960–62; Med. Res. Fellowships, Auckland, 1962–68; Sen. Lectr, Univ. of Otago, based on Auckland Hosp., 1969–72; University of Auckland: Sen. Lectr, 1970–72; Associate Prof., 1973–75; Hd, Dept of Medicine, the Univ.'s Sch. of Medicine, 1979–87. Res. interests in lipoprotein metabolism, arterial disease, human nutrition, med. econs and educn, professional ethics. *Publications:* (first author/co-author) articles in sci./med. jls and in press, on aspects of coronary artery disease, atherosclerosis, lipoprotein metabolism, human nutrition, ethical issues. *Recreations:* music, pottery, gardening. *Address:* 64 Temple Street, Meadowbank, Auckland 5, New Zealand. *T:* (9) 5215384.

SCOTT, Sheriff Richard John Dinwoodie; Sheriff of Lothian and Borders at Edinburgh, since 1986; *b* 28 May 1939; *s* of late Prof. Richard Scott and Mary Ellen Maclachlan; *m* 1969, Josephine Moretta Blake; two *d. Educ:* Edinburgh Academy; Univ. of Edinburgh (MA, LLB) (Vans Dunlop Schol. in Evidence and Pleading, 1963). Lektor in English, British Centre, Sweden, 1960–61; Tutor, Faculty of Law, Univ. of Edinburgh, 1964–72; admitted to Faculty of Advocates, 1965; Standing Jun. Counsel to Min. of Defence (Air) in Scotland, 1968–77. Sheriff of Grampian, Highland and Islands, at Aberdeen and Stonehaven, 1977–86. Hon. Lectr, Univ. of Aberdeen, 1980–86. *Publications:* various articles in legal jls. *Address:* Sheriff Court House, 27 Chambers Street, Edinburgh EH1 1LB.

SCOTT, Rt. Hon. Sir Richard (Rashleigh Folliott), Kt 1983; PC 1991; Vice-Chancellor of the Supreme Court, since 1994; *b* 2 Oct. 1934; *s* of Lt-Col C. W. F. Scott, 2/9th Gurkha Rifles and Katharine Scott (*née* Rashleigh); *m* 1959, Rima Elisa, *d* of Salvador Ripoll and Blanca Korsi de Ripoll, Panama City; two *s* two *d. Educ:* Michaelhouse Coll., Natal; Univ. of Cape Town (BA); Trinity Coll., Cambridge (BA, LLB). Bigelow Fellow, Univ. of Chicago, 1958–59. Called to Bar, Inner Temple, 1959, Bencher, 1981. QC 1975; Attorney Gen., 1980–83, Vice-Chancellor, 1987–91, Duchy and County Palatine of Lancaster; Judge of the High Court of Justice, Chancery Div., 1983–91; a Lord Justice of Appeal, 1991–94. Inquiry into arms to Iraq, 1992–95. Chm. of the Bar, 1982–83 (Vice-Chm., 1981–82). Hon. Member: Amer. Bar Assoc., 1983; Canadian Bar Assoc., 1983. *Recreations:* hunting, tennis, bridge; formerly Rugby (Cambridge Blue, 1957). *Address:* Royal Courts of Justice, Strand, WC2A 2LL. *Clubs:* Hawks (Cambridge); Vanderbilt Racquet.

SCOTT, Ridley; film director; *b* S Shields, 30 Nov. 1937. *Educ:* Royal Coll. of Art. *Films include:* The Duellists, 1976; Alien, 1978; Blade Runner, 1980; Someone to Watch over Me, 1987; Thelma and Louise, 1991; 1492: Conquest of Paradise, 1992; White Squall, 1995. *Address:* Scott Free, 42–44 Beak Street, W1R 3DA. *T:* 0171–437 7426.

SCOTT, Robert, CBE 1976; Director, Polytechnic, Wolverhampton, 1969–77, retired; *b* 7 July 1913; 2nd *s* of H. Scott, Westhoughton, Bolton; *m* 1940, Dorothy M. Howell, Westhoughton; one *s* one *d. Educ:* Hindley and Abram Grammar Sch., Lancs; Univ. of Liverpool; St John's Coll., Cambridge (Wrangler; MA). BSc 1st cl. hons 1934, DipEd 1937, Liverpool; BA Cantab, 1936; FIMA. Asst Master, Newton-le-Willows Grammar Sch., 1937–41; Army and WO Staff, 1941–46; Scientific Civil Service at RMCS Shrivenham, 1946–54; Vice-Principal, Bolton Techn. Coll., 1954–57; Principal, Wolverhampton and Staffs Coll. of Technology, 1958–69. *Recreations:* motoring, reading. *Address:* 25 Market Road, Battle, E Sussex TN33 0XA. *T:* Battle (01424) 774328.

SCOTT, Robert Avisson; Group Chief Executive, General Accident plc, since 1996; *b* 6 Jan. 1942; *s* of Robert Milligan Scott and Phyllis Winifred Scott; *m* 1979, Joanne Rose Adams; two *d. Educ:* Scots Coll., Wellington, NZ. Associate: Australian Ins. Inst.; Ins. Inst. NZ. South British Insurance Co. Ltd, later NZI Corp. Ltd, then General Accident plc, 1959–: Asst Gen. Manager, NZ, 1981–83; Australia: Asst Gen. Manager, 1983–85; Gen. Manager, 1985–87; Chief Gen. Manager, 1987–90; Dep. Gen. Manager, UK, 1990–91, Gen. Manager, 1991–94; Dep. Chief Exec., 1994–96. *Recreations:* sporting interests, walking, do it yourself. *Address:* General Accident plc, Pitheavlis, Perth PH2 0NH. *T:* Perth (01738) 621202.

SCOTT, Sir Robert (David Hillyer), Kt 1994; DL; arts and sports administrator; Special Projects Director, Apollo Leisure Group, since 1994; Chairman: Manchester Commonwealth Games Bid Committee, since 1993; Piccadilly Radio, since 1993; *b* 22 Jan. 1944; *s* of Sir David (Aubrey) Scott, *qv*; *m* 1972; two *s* one *d. Educ:* Haileybury; Merton Coll., Oxford. Actor, 1966–67; Administrator: 69 Theatre Co., Manchester, 1968–74; Royal Exchange Theatre Trust, 1974–77; Man. Dir, Manchester Theatres Ltd, 1978–; Chm., Manchester Olympic Bid Cttee, 1985–93. Mem., Central Manchester Develt Corp., 1988–. Chairman: Cornerhouse Manchester, 1984–; Granada Foundn, 1993–; Director: Royal Exchange Theatre, 1976–94; Hallé Concerts Soc., 1989–94; Mem. Cttee, Whitworth Art Gall., 1989–. DL Greater Manchester, 1988. Hon. RNCM 1990. Hon Fellow: Manchester Poly., 1987; UMIST, 1989. Hon. MA: Manchester, 1988; Salford, 1991. Officier de l'Ordre des Arts et des Lettres (France), 1991. *Publication:* The Biggest Room in the World, 1976. *Recreations:* food, travel, talking, sport, theatre. *Address:* 81 Fountain Street, Manchester M2 2EE. *T:* 0161–228 2000.

SCOTT, Col Robert Edmond Gabriel, MBE 1959; MC 1953; Director General, Engineering Industries Association, 1981–82; *b* 3 Aug. 1920; *s* of Edmond James and Lilian Kate Scott; *m* 1942, Anna Maria Larkin; two *s. Educ:* Roan, Greenwich. Commissioned into Durham Light Inf., 1942; regimental service with this regt in Western Desert, Italy, Korea and Rhine Army, 1942–52; Staff duties, MoD and Eastern Comd, 1952–56; service with W African Frontier Force, 1956–60; comd inf. batt., Home Service, 1960–66; seconded to Diplomatic Service, as Defence Adviser, Lagos, 1966–70; Dep. Comd, W. Midland Dist, 1970–72; retired, 1972. Engineering Industries Association: Export Sec. and Dep. Dir, 1973–77; Dir, 1977–81. *Recreations:* rough shooting, country pursuits, philately. *Address:* Zaria, 22 Crail Close, Wokingham, Berks RG11 2PZ. *T:* Wokingham (01734) 776595.

SCOTT, Robin; *see* Scutt, R. H.

SCOTT, Prof. Roger Davidson, PhD; CPhys, FInstP; FRSE; Director, Scottish Universities Research and Reactor Centre, since 1991; Titular Professor, University of Glasgow, since 1994; *b* 17 Dec. 1941; *s* of Alexander N. Scott and Jessie H. Scott (*née* Davidson); *m* 1965, Marion S. McCluckie; two *s* one *d. Educ:* Anderson Inst., Lerwick; Univ. of Edinburgh (BSc 1st Cl. Hons Physics; PhD Nuclear Physics). University Demonstrator, Univ. of Edinburgh, 1965–68; Lectr, 1968–88, Depute Dir, 1988–91, Scottish Univs Res. and Reactor Centre. FRSE 1995. *Publications:* articles on nuclear physics and envmtl radioactivity; contribs to learned jls. *Recreations:* watching football, walking wife and dogs, home maintenance. *Address:* Scottish Universities Research and Reactor Centre, East Kilbride, Glasgow G75 0QF. *T:* East Kilbride (01355) 223332; 4 Inch Keith, East Kilbride, Glasgow G74 2JZ. *T:* (01355) 229536.

SCOTT, Roger Martin; His Honour Judge Scott; a Circuit Judge, since 1993; *b* 8 Sept. 1944; *s* of Hermann Albert and Sarah Margaret Scott; *m* 1966, Diana Elizabeth Clark; two *s* one *d. Educ:* Mill Hill Sch.; St Andrews Univ. (LLB). Called to the Bar, Lincoln's Inn, 1968. *Recreations:* golf, cricket, walking, theatre. *Address:* North Eastern Circuit Administrator's Office, West Riding House, Albion Street, Leeds LS1 5AA. *T:* Leeds (0113) 244 1841. *Club:* Yorkshire County Cricket (Leeds).

SCOTT, Ronald, OBE 1981; musician; *b* 28 Jan. 1927. *Educ:* Jews' Infant Sch., Aldgate, E1; Benthal Road Elementary Sch., N16; Central Foundation Sch., Cowper St, E1. Musician (Tenor Saxophone), 1943–. Opened Ronnie Scott's Club, 1959 (Director, with Pete King); opened second Ronnie Scott's Club, Birmingham, 1991. *Publication:* (with Michael Hennessey) Some of My Best Friends are Blues, 1979; *relevant publication:* Let's Join Hands and Contact the Living (biography), by John Fordham, 1989. *Recreation:* motor sport. *Address:* 47 Frith Street, W1V 5TE. *T:* 0171–439 0747. *Club:* just his own.

SCOTT, Prof. Thomas Frederick McNair, MA Cantab, MD Cantab, MRCS; FRCP; Associate Director of Ambulatory Pediatrics, 1983–85, retired, now Emeritus Professor of Paediatrics, Hahnemann University (Professor of Paediatrics, 1974, Co-ordinator of Ambulatory Care Teaching, 1974–75, and Co-Director of Ambulatory Paediatrics, 1975–83, Hahnemann Medical College and Hospital); Senior Physician, The Children's Hospital of Philadelphia, 1940–69, now Physician Emeritus; *b* 18 June 1901; *e s* of Robert Frederick McNair Scott, MB, ChB (Edin.), and Alice Nystrom; *m* 1936, Mary Dwight Baker, PhD (Radcliffe), *o d* of late Clarence Dwight Baker, Wisconsin, USA; one *s* one *d. Educ:* Cheltenham College; Caius College, Cambridge (Scholar). Natural Science Tripos Pt I Class I, Part II (Physiology) Class II; Junior University Entrance Scholarship to St George's Hospital, 1924; Brackenbury Prize in Medicine, 1926; Qualified conjoint board, 1927; MRCP 1928; FRCP 1953; MD (Cantab) 1938; Casualty Officer, House Surgeon, House Physn, Resident Obst. Asst, Medical Registrar, at St George's Hospital, 1927–29; House Physician Queens Hospital for Children, 1930; Research Fellow of Medicine, Harvard University, Mass, USA, 1930–31; Instructor in Pædiatrics Johns Hopkins University, Baltimore, Md, USA, 1931–34; Assistant Resident Physician at Hospital of Rockefeller Institute for Medical Research, New York, USA, working on Virus diseases, 1934–36; Assistant Physician i/c of Children's Out-patients, Lecturer in Children's Diseases, at St George's Hospital, SW1, Assistant Physician at Queens Hospital for Children, E2, 1936–38; Prof. of Pediatrics, Temple Univ. Med. Sch., Philadelphia, 1938–40; Research Prof. of Pediatrics, Univ. of Pennsylvania, 1940–66, Prof. of Paediatrics, 1966–69, now Emeritus. Dist. Service Award, The Children's Hosp. of Philadelphia, 1977; Corp. medal, Hahnemann Med. Coll., 1978; Alumni Award, Children's Hosp. Alumni Orgn, 1989. Elected Faculty Mem., Medical Students' Honor Soc. (AOA), 1981. *Publications:* Papers on Cytology and Blood diseases, Lead poisoning in children, Virus diseases of the central nervous system, Herpes simplex infections, Common exanthemata, History of measles and herpes. *Address:* 2 Franklin Town Boulevard 1605, Philadelphia, PA 19103, USA.

SCOTT, Dame Thora; *see* Hird, Dame T.

SCOTT, Sir (Walter) John, 5th Bt *cr* 1907, of Beauclerc, Bywell St Andrew, Northumberland; farmer, *b* 24 Feb. 1948; *s* of Sir Walter Scott, 4th Bt and Diana Mary (*d* 1985), *d* of J. R. Owen; *m* 1st, 1969, Lowell Patria (marr. diss. 1971), *d* of late Pat Vaughan Goddard, Auckland, NZ; one *d*; 2nd, 1977, Mary Gavin, *d* of Alexander Fairly Anderson, Gartocharn, Dunbartonshire; one *s* one *d. Recreations:* field sports. *Heir: s* Walter Samuel Scott, *b* 6 Dec. 1984. *Address:* Newhouse Farm, Chalvington, East Sussex BN27 3TB. *T:* Eastbourne (01323) 811233.

SCOTT, William Clifford Munro, MD; Consulting Psychiatrist, Montreal Children's Hospital, and Montreal General Hospital; *b* 11 March 1903; *o s* of late Rev. Robert Smyth Scott and late Katherine Munro Hopper; *m* 1934, Emmy Luise (marr. diss.), *er d* of late Hugo Böcking; two *s*; *m* 1970, Evelyn Freeman Fitch. *Educ:* Parkdale Collegiate, Toronto; University of Toronto. BSc (Med.), MD (Tor.), DPM (London), LMSSA. James H. Richardson Fellow, Department of Anat., 1922–24; Lectr in Anat. and Physiol., Margaret Eaton Sch. of Phys. Educ., Toronto, 1923–25; Post-Grad. Educ. in Psychiatry: Johns Hopkins Med. Sch., 1928–29; Boston Psychopathic Hosp., Harvard Univ. Med. Sch., 1929–30; Commonwealth Fund Fellow, Dept of Psychiatry, Harvard Univ., 1930–33; studied at Nat. Hosp., Queen Sq., London, 1931–32, and at Inst of Psycho-Analysis, London, 1931–33. Staff positions Maudsley Hosp., 1933–35, Cassel Hosp., 1935–38; private practice, 1938–. EMS Psychiatrist, Min. of Health, London, Sheffield and S Wales, 1939–46; Psychiatric Cons. to St Dunstan's, 1945. Mem. Cttee of Management, Inst. of Psychiatry (Univ. of London), 1951–53; Med. Dir London Clinic of Psycho-Analysis, 1947–53; Senior Psychotherapist, Bethlem Royal Hosp. and Maudsley Hosp., 1948–54; Teacher Inst. of Psychiatry (Univ. of London), 1948–54; Associate Professor in charge of Training in Psycho-Analysis, Department of Psychiatry, McGill University, Montreal, 1954–59; Post-Grad. Teacher (Psychiatry and Psycho-Analysis), 1945–. Chm. Psychotherapy and Social Psychiatry Section, Roy. Medico Psychological Assoc., 1952–54; Pres. Brit. Psycho-Analytical Soc., 1953–54; Mem. Bd Dirs, Inst. of Psycho-Analysis, 1947–54 (Chm. 1954); Director of Canadian Inst. of Psycho-Analysis, 1965–67. FRCPsych; FBPsS; ex-Chm. Med. Sect. and Mem. Council, Brit. Psychological Soc.; ex-Mem Cttee Sect. Psychiatry; Roy. Soc. Med.; Amer. Psychiatric Assoc.; Vice-Pres., Psychiatric Sect., BMA, 1952 and 1955; ex-Asst Ed. Internat. Jl Psycho-Analysis; ex-Asst Ed., Brit. Jl Med. Psychology. Mem., Montreal AAA. *Publications:* chiefly in Brit. Jl of Med. Psychol. and Internat. Jl of Psycho-Analysis. *Recreations:* people and books. *Address:* 488 Mount Pleasant, Westmount, Quebec H3Y 3H3, Canada.

SCOTT, Rear-Adm. Sir (William) David (Stewart), KBE 1977; CB 1974; *b* 5 April 1921; *y s* of Brig. H. St G. Scott, CB, DSO and Ida Christabel Trower Scott (*née* Hogg); *m* 1952, Pamela Dorothy Whitlock; one *s* two *d. Educ:* Tonbridge. Naval Cadet, 1938; comd HM Submarines: Umbra, 1944; Vulpine, Satyr, 1945; Andrew, 1953; Thermopylae, 1955; comd HM Ships: Gateshead, 1951; Surprise, 1960; Adamant, 1963; Fife, 1969; Trng Comdr, BRNC, Dartmouth, 1956; Fleet Ops Officer, Home Fleet, 1958; US Naval War Coll., 1962; Dep. Dir of Defence Plans, Navy, 1965; Chief of British Navy Staff, Washington, UK Rep. to SACLANT, and Naval Attaché to USA, 1971–73; Deputy Controller, Polaris, 1973–76; Chief Polaris Executive, 1976–80; Comdr 1956; Captain

1962; Rear-Adm. 1971. FInstD 1979. *Address:* c/o Lloyds Bank, Pall Mall Branch, 8–10 Waterloo Place, SW1Y 4BE.

SCOTT, (William) Donald, CBE 1968; MA (Oxon); BSc (Yale); *b* 22 May 1903; *s* of late Reverend William Scott and Sara Jane (*née* Platt); *m* 1928, Muriel Barbara, *d* of late Louis F. Rothschild, NYC; two *s* one *d*. *Educ:* Taunton Sch., Taunton; Univ. College, Oxford (open scholar); Yale University, USA (Henry P. Davison Scholar). Hercules Powder Co., USA and Rotterdam, 1926–28; British Paint & Lacquer Co., Cowley, Oxford, 1928–35; ICI Ltd: Nobel Div., 1935–41; Dyestuffs Div., 1941–43; Southern Sales Region, Dep. Regional Manager, 1943–45; Regional Manager, 1945–51; Billingham Div., Jt Man. Dir, 1951–55; Main Board Director, 1954–65. Director, 1952–60, and Chairman, 1956–60, Scottish Agricultural Industries Ltd; Chm., Home Grown Cereals Authority, 1965–68; Director: Canadian Industries Ltd, 1957–62; Glaxo Group Ltd, 1965–68; Laporte Industries Ltd, 1965–68. Mem., Western Hemisphere Exports Council, 1961–64. FRSA 1968. *Recreations:* cricket, golf. *Address:* 42 Cumberland Terrace, Regent's Park, NW1 4HP.

SCOTT, Rev. W(illiam) G.; *see* Gardiner-Scott.

SCOTT, William Wootton, CB 1990; Under Secretary, Industry Department for Scotland, 1985–90; *b* 20 May 1930; *s* of Dr Archibald C. Scott and Barbara R. Scott; *m* 1958, Margaret Chandler, SRN; three *s* one *d*. *Educ:* Kilmarnock Academy; Dollar Academy; Glasgow Univ. (MA, 1st Cl. Hons History). National Service in Royal Artillery, 1952–54. Assistant Principal, 1954, Principal, 1958, Min. of Transport and Civil Aviation; Principal Private Sec. to Minister of Transport, 1965–66; Asst Sec., 1966; Regional Controller (Housing and Planning), Northern Regional Office of DoE, 1971–74; joined Scottish Development Dept, 1974, Under Sec., 1978. *Publications:* occasional historical notes. *Recreations:* historical research, music, gardening, reading. *Address:* Whitethorn, Hardgate, Castle Douglas, Kirkcudbrightshire DG7 3LD. *T:* Haugh-of-Urr (01556) 660200. *Club:* Commonwealth Trust.

SCOTT-BARRETT, Lt-Gen. Sir David (William), KBE 1976 (MBE 1956); MC 1945; GOC Scotland and Governor of Edinburgh Castle, 1976–79; Chairman, Army Cadet Force Association, since 1982; *b* 16 Dec. 1922; 2nd *s* of late Brig. Rev. H. Scott-Barrett, CB, CBE; *m* 1st, 1948, Marie Elise (*d* 1985), *d* of late Norman Morris; three *s*; 2nd, 1992, Judith, *widow* of Major John Waring. *Educ:* Westminster School. Commnd Scots Guards, 1942; served NW Europe, 3rd Armd Bn Scots Guards; GSO3 Gds Div., 1948; Co. Comdr 2nd Bn Malaya, 1951; GSO2, 1st Div., 1955; DS Camberley, 1961; Comdt Gds Depot, 1963; GSO1, 4th Div. BAOR, 1965; comd 6 Inf. Bde BAOR, 1967; idc 1970; GOC Eastern District, 1971–73; GOC Berlin, 1973–75. Col Comdt, Scottish Div., 1976–79; Hon. Col, 205 (Scottish) Gen. Hosp., RAMC, TAVR, 1981–88. *Address:* 36 The Mansion, Albury Park, Guildford GU5 9BB. *Club:* Cavalry and Guards.

SCOTT-BOWDEN, Maj.-Gen. Logan, CBE 1972 (OBE 1964); DSO 1944; MC 1944 and Bar 1946; *b* 21 Feb. 1920; *s* of late Lt-Col Jonathan Scott-Bowden, OBE, TD, and Mary Scott-Bowden (*née* Logan); *m* 1950, Helen Jocelyn, *d* of late Major Sir Francis Caradoc Rose Price, 5th Bt, and late Marjorie Lady Price; three *s* three *d*. *Educ:* Malvern Coll.; RMA Woolwich. Commissioned Royal Engineers, 1939; served in War of 1939–45: Norway, 1940; Adjt, 53rd (Welsh) Div. RE, 1941; Liaison Duties in Canada and USA, 1942; Normandy Beach Reconnaissance Team (Major), 1943; OC 17 Fd Co RE, NW Europe, 1944; psc 1945; Singapore, Burma (Bde Maj. 98 Indian Inf. Bde), Palestine, Libya, 1946–51; Korea, 1953; jssc 1956; Arabia, 1958–60 (Lt-Col 1959); CRE 1st Div., BAOR, 1960; Head, UK Land Forces Planning Staff, 1963; Asst Dir, Def. Plans MoD (Col), 1964; Comd Trg Bde RE (Brig.), 1966; Nat. Defence Coll. (India), 1969; Comd Ulster Defence Regiment, 1970–71; Head of British Defence Liaison Staff, India, 1971–74, retd 1974. Col Comdt RE, 1975–80. *Recreations:* riding, ski-ing, travel.

SCOTT-ELLIOT, Aydua Helen, CVO 1970 (MVO 1958); FSA; retired 1970; *b* 11 Dec. 1909; *d* of late Lewis Alexander Scott-Elliot and of Princess Eydua Odescalchi. *Educ:* St Paul's Girls' School and abroad. Temp. Asst Civilian Officer, Admty, 1941–46; Keeper of Prints and Drawings, Royal Library, Windsor Castle, 1946–69. *Publications:* articles in Burlington Magazine, Apollo, Papers of the Bibliographical Soc. of America, etc. *Address:* Shaldon, Mayfield, East Sussex TN20 6BW. *Club:* University Women's.

SCOTT ELLIOT, Major-General James, CB 1954; CBE 1945 (OBE 1940); DSO 1943, Bar 1944; HM Lieutenant of the County of Dumfries, 1962–67; *b* 6 Nov. 1902; *s* of late Lt-Col W. Scott Elliot, DSO and Marie Theresa Scott Elliot (*née* Lyon); *m* 1st, 1932, Cecil Margaret Du Buisson; one *s* two *d*; 2nd, 1971, Mrs Fay Courtauld. *Educ:* Wellington College; Sandhurst. 2nd Lieut KOSB, 1923; Capt. Argyll and Sutherland Highlanders, 1936; psc 1937–38; Major, 1940; served in Egypt, China, India, Malta, Palestine. War of 1939–45: France, N Africa, Sicily, Italy; Temp. Lt-Col 1941; Temp. Brig. 1944; despatches, 1945; Germany, 1946–47; War Office, 1948–49; Maj.-Gen., 1954; GOC 51st (Highland) Division and Highland Dist, 1952–56; retd, 1956. Colonel King's Own Scottish Borderers, 1954–61. Mem. (Ind.) for Caerlaverock, Dumfriesshire CC, 1958–67. President: Dumfries and Galloway Natural History and Antiquarian Soc., 1962–65; Soc. of Antiquaries of Scotland, 1965–67; Brit. Soc. of Dowsers, 1966–75. *Publication:* Dowsing One Man's Way, 1977. *Address:* 14 King Street, Emsworth, Hants PO10 7AZ. *T:* Emsworth (01243) 372401.

SCOTT-ELLIS, family name of **Baron Howard de Walden.**

SCOTT-JAMES, Anne Eleanor, (Lady Lancaster); author and journalist; *b* 5 April 1913; *d* of R. A. Scott-James and Violet Brooks; *m* 2nd, 1944, Macdonald Hastings (*d* 1982); one *s* one *d*; 3rd, 1967, Sir Osbert Lancaster, CBE (*d* 1986). *Educ:* St Paul's Girls' Sch.; Somerville Coll., Oxford (Class. Schol.). Editorial staff of Vogue, 1934–41; Woman's Editor, Picture Post, 1941–45; Editor, Harper's Bazaar, 1945–51; Woman's Editor, Sunday Express, 1953–57; Woman's Adviser to Beaverbrook Newspapers, 1959–60; Columnist, Daily Mail, 1960–68; freelance journalist, broadcasting, TV, 1968–. Member: Council, RCA, 1948–51, 1954–56; Council, RHS, 1978–82. *Publications:* In the Mink, 1952; Down to Earth, 1971; Sissinghurst: The Making of a Garden, 1975; (with Osbert Lancaster) The Pleasure Garden, 1977; The Cottage Garden, 1981; (with Christopher Lloyd) Glyndebourne—the Gardens, 1983; The Language of the Garden: a personal anthology, 1984; (introd.) Our Village, by Mary Russell Mitford, 1987; The Best Plants for your Garden, 1988; (with Ray Desmond) The British Museum Book of Flowers, 1989; Gardening Letters to My Daughter, 1990; Sketches from a Life (autobiog.), 1993. *Recreations:* reading, gardening, travelling looking at churches and flowers. *Address:* 78 Cheyne Court, Royal Hospital Road, SW3 5TT.

See also M. M. Hastings.

SCOTT-JOYNT, Rt Rev. Michael Charles; *see* Winchester, Bishop of.

SCOTT-MALDEN, (Charles) Peter, CB 1966; retired civil servant; *b* 29 June 1918; *e s* of late Gilbert Scott Scott-Malden and Phyllis Dorothy Scott-Malden (*née* Wilkinson); *m* 1941, Jean Honor Chamberlain Silver, *yr d* of late Lt-Col J. P. Silver, CBE, DSO, RAMC; two *s* two *d*. *Educ:* Winchester Coll. (Schol.); King's College, Cambridge (major Scholar). Entered Ministry of Transport, 1939. War of 1939–45; RAMC 1940–41; Glider Pilot Regiment, 1942–45. Min. of Transport (later DoE): Asst Sec., 1949; Under-Sec., 1959; Dep. Sec., 1968, retired, 1976. Member: Transport Tribunal, 1978–88; Management Cttee, Hanover Housing Assoc., 1978–93; Nat. Exec. Cttee, Abbeyfield Soc., 1983–90. *Recreations:* music, golf, walking the South West Way. *Address:* 18A Tower Road, Tadworth, Surrey KT20 5QY. *T:* Tadworth (01737) 812326.

SCOTT-MALDEN, Air Vice-Marshal (Francis) David (Stephen), DSO 1942; DFC 1941; RAF (Retd); *b* 26 Dec. 1919; *s* of late Gilbert Scott Scott-Malden and Phyllis Dorothy Wilkinson; *m* 1955, Anne Elizabeth Watson; two *s* two *d*. *Educ:* Winchester Coll. (Scholar; Goddard Scholar, 1938); King's Coll., Cambridge (Scholar, Sir William Browne Medal for Greek Verse, 1939). Joined Cambridge University Air Squadron, Nov. 1938; called up into RAFVR as Pilot Officer, Oct 1939; flying on operations, 1940–42, as Pilot Officer, Flight Lt, Squadron Leader, and Wing Comdr (DFC and Bar, DSO, Norwegian War Cross; Commander, Order of Orange Nassau, 1945). Visited International Youth Assembly at Washington, DC, as rep. of English Universities, and toured USA as member of United Nations delegation, Sept.-Nov. 1942. RAF Selection Board (Dep. Pres.), 1946; on staff of RAF College, 1946–48; Central Fighter Establishment, 1948; RAF Staff Coll., Bracknell, 1951; psa; RAF Flying Coll., 1954–55; pfc; Jt Planning Staff, Min. of Defence, 1955–57; Group Capt. 1958; Imperial Defence College, 1957–59; idc. Dep. Dir Plans, Air Ministry, 1959–61; Air Cdre 1962; Air Vice-Marshal, 1965. Department of Transport, 1966–78. *Recreations:* shooting, fishing, sailing. *Address:* Roughwood, 1 White House Gardens, Upgate, Poringland, Norwich, Norfolk NR14 7RU. *T:* Framingham Earl (01508) 494779.

SCOTT-MALDEN, Peter; *see* Scott-Malden, C. P.

SCOTT-MONCRIEFF, William; Under-Secretary for Finance (Health), Department of Health and Social Security, 1977–82; *b* 22 Aug. 1922; *s* of Major R. Scott-Moncrieff and Mrs R. Scott-Moncrieff; *m* 1950, Dora Rosemary Knollys; two *d*. *Educ:* Trinity Coll., Glenalmond; Emmanuel Coll., Cambridge (BA Mech. Sciences). Served RE, 1941–65 (Lt-Col); DHSS (formerly Min. of Social Security), 1965–82. *Recreation:* fishing. *Address:* Combe Cottage, Chiddingfold, Surrey GU8 4XL. *T:* Wormley (01428) 682937.

SCOTT-SMITH, Catharine Mary, MA Cantab; Principal of Beechlawn Tutorial College, Oxford, 1966–71, retired; *b* 4 April 1912; *d* of Edward Montagu Scott-Smith and Catharine Lorance (*née* Garland). *Educ:* Wycombe Abbey School, Bucks; Girton College, Cambridge. Classics Mistress: St Katharine's School, Wantage, 1933–37; Godolphin School, Salisbury 1937–41; Classics Mistress and house-mistress, Headington School, Oxford, 1941–47, Second Mistress, 1946–47; Classics Mistress and house-mistress, Wycombe Abbey School, Bucks, 1947–55, Second Mistress, 1951–54; Headmistress of Westonbirt School, Tetbury, Gloucestershire, 1955–64. Member Council: Berkhamsted School for Girls; Berkhamsted School; Mem. Exec. Cttee, GBGSA, 1975–78. Pres., Wycombe Abbey School Seniors, 1974–79. *Address:* 62 Lower Waites Lane, Fairlight, Hastings, East Sussex TN35 4DD. *T:* Hastings (01424) 813071. *Club:* University Women's.

SCOTT WHYTE, Stuart; *see* Whyte, J. S. S.

SCOTT WRIGHT, Prof. Margaret, PhD; Dean, 1979–84, and Professor, 1979–86, now Emeritus, Faculty of Nursing, University of Calgary; *b* 10 Sept. 1923; *d* of Ebenezer Wright and Margaret Greig Masson. *Educ:* Wallington County Grammar Sch.; Univ. of Edinburgh; St George's and Queen Charlotte's Hosps, London. MA Hons Hist., PhD and Dipl. Med. Services Admin, Edinburgh; SRN and SCM. Research Asst, Unilever Ltd, 1947–50; Student Nurse, St George's Hosp., 1950–53; Student Midwife, Queen Charlotte's Hosp. and E Sussex CC, 1954–55; Staff Nurse and Sister, St George's Hosp., London, 1955–57; Boots Research Fellow in Nursing, Dept of Social Medicine, Univ. of Edinburgh, 1957–61; Rockefeller Fellow, USA, 1961–62; Deputy Matron, St George's Hosp., 1962–64; Matron, Middlesex Hosp., 1965–68; Dir, Dept of Nursing Studies, Univ. of Edinburgh, 1968–71; Prof. of Nursing Studies, Univ. of Edinburgh, 1972–76; Dir and Prof. of Sch. of Nursing, Dalhousie Univ., Nova Scotia, 1976–79. Second Vice-Pres., Internat. Council of Nurses, 1973–77. Margaret Scott Wright Annual Lecture in Nursing Research established in Faculty of Nursing, Univ. of Alberta, 1984. Silver Jubilee Medal, 1977. *Publications:* Experimental Nurse Training at Glasgow Royal Infirmary, 1963; Student Nurses in Scotland, 1968. *Recreations:* walking, music, reading, travel. *Address:* 3 Osborne Court, Norwich NR2 2NN.

SCOULLER, (John) Alan; independent consultant; Head of Industrial Relations, Midland Bank Group, 1975–88; Visiting Professor in Industrial Relations, Kingston University (formerly Kingston Polytechnic), since 1988; Senior Visiting Fellow, City University Business School, since 1989; *b* 23 Sept. 1929; *e s* of late Charles James Scouller and Mary Helena Scouller; *m* 1954, Angela Geneste Ambrose; two *s* five *d*. *Educ:* John Fisher Sch., Purley. Army service, Queen's Own Royal W Kent Regt, 1948–58 (Captain). Joined Unilever as management trainee, 1958; Personnel Man., Wall's Ice Cream, 1959–62; Domestos, 1963–66; Holpak, 1966–68; Commercial Plastics and Holpak, 1968–69; left Unilever to join Commn on Industrial Relations, 1969; Dir of Industrial Relations until 1973, full-time Comr, 1973–74. Member: Employment Appeal Tribunal, 1976–; Educn Bd, RC Dio. of Westminster, 1990–. FIPD. *Recreations:* studying employment law, walking, listening to music, looking after grandchildren. *Address:* Shortlands, 32 Sollershott West, Letchworth, Herts SG6 3PX. *T:* Letchworth (01462) 682781.

SCOURFIELD, Edward Grismond Beaumont D.; *see* Davies-Scourfield.

SCOURSE, Rear-Adm. Frederick Peter, MBE 1972; CEng, FIEE; Director-General, Surface Ships, since 1994; *b* 23 June 1944; *s* of Frederick David John Scourse and late Margaret Elaine Scourse; *m* 1967, Nicolette Jean Somerville West; one *s*. *Educ:* Wells Cathedral Sch.; RN Coll., Dartmouth; Churchill Coll., Cambridge (MA Mech Sci, Elect. Sci). Served HM Ships: Dido, 1963–64; Warspite, 1969–72; Renown, 1974–77; MoD (PE), 1979–82; NDC, 1982–83; MoD (PE), 1983–89; Dir-Gen., Surface Weapons (Navy), 1989–94. *Recreations:* fly fishing, snorkelling, singing, wine. *Address:* Director-General Surface Ships, Ministry of Defence, Foxhill, Bath BA1 5AB. *Club:* Naval.

SCOWCROFT, Gen. Brent, Hon. KBE 1993; President, Forum for International Policy, since 1993; *b* 19 March 1925; *s* of James Scowcroft and Lucile (*née* Ballantyne); *m* 1951, Marian (Jackie) Horner; one *d*. *Educ:* Ogden City Schs; US Mil. Acad.; Columbia Univ. (MA 1953; PhD 1967); Lafayette Coll.; Georgetown Univ. Joined Army 1943; qualified pilot 1948; Prof. of Russian History, US Mil. Acad., 1953–57; service in Washington, Yugoslavia, Colorado, Western Hemisphere Region; with Jt Chiefs of Staff, 1970; MA to President, 1972–73; Dep. Asst, 1973–75, and Asst 1975–77 and 1989–93, to successive Presidents, for Nat. Security Affairs; retired from mil. service, 1975; Dir, Council on Foreign Relations, 1983–89; served on major US cttees, commns and bds, 1977–89. Vice-Chm., Kissinger Associates, 1982–89. Chm., CSIS/Pacific Forum, 1993–. Mem. Bd of Visitors, USAF Acad., 1993–. US Medal of Freedom, 1991; numerous Service medals and awards. *Recreation:* ski-ing. *Address:* Forum for International Policy, 1750 K Street NW, Suite 800, Washington, DC 20006, USA. *T:* (202) 4294299, *Fax:* (202) 4294298; 6114 Wynnwood Road, Bethesda, MD 20816, USA. *T:* (301) 2291928.

SCOWEN, Sir Eric (Frank), Kt 1973; MD, DSc; FRCP, FRCS, FRCPE, FRCPath, FRPharmS, FRCGP; Director, Medical Professorial Unit, 1955–75; Physician to St Bartholomew's Hospital, 1946–75; Professor of Medicine, University of London, 1961–75 (Reader in Medicine, 1938–61); *b* 22 April 1910; *s* of late Frank Edward Scowen and Eleanor Betsy (*née* Barnes) (*d* 1969). *Educ:* City of London School; St Bartholomew's Hospital Medical College. MD 1935, DSc 1962, MA 1988, London. FRCP 1941; FRCS 1960; FRCPE 1965; FRCPath 1965; FRPharmS 1984; FRCGP 1989. St Bartholomew's Hospital: House Physician, 1931, Second Assistant, 1933, to Medical Professorial Unit; Baly Research Fell. in Clin. Med., 1933; First Asst to Med. Professorial Unit, 1935; Asst Dir of Med. Prof. Unit, and Asst Phys, 1937; Rockefeller Research Fell. to Columbia Univ., New York, 1937. Chairman: Council, Imperial Cancer Research Fund, 1967–82 (Vice-Pres., 1982); Cttee on Safety of Drugs, 1969– (Mem., 1963); British Pharmacopœia Commission, 1963–69; Cttee on Safety of Medicines, 1970–80; Cttee on the Review of Medicines, 1975–78; Poisons Bd (Home Office), 1976–83. Chm. Council, Sch. of Pharmacy, Univ. of London, 1979–88 (Hon. Fellow, 1986). Hon. LLD Nottingham, 1979. *Publications:* various in medical and scientific journals. *Address:* Flat 77, 6/9 Charterhouse Square, EC1M 6EX. *T:* 0171–251 3212. *Club:* Athenæum.

SCRAFTON, Douglas; HM Diplomatic Service; Ambassador to Republic of Yemen, since 1995; *b* 14 July; *s* of late Douglas Scrafton and of Irene Hilda Kirk (formerly Scrafton, *née* Hammett); *m* 1975, Carolyn Patricia Collison; one *s* one *d*. Joined FCO, 1967; Mem., UK Delegn (later UK Perm. Repn) to EC, 1970–73; Kampala, 1973–74; Mbabane, 1975–77; FCO, 1977–80; Jedda, 1980–82; British Liaison Office, Riyadh, 1982–84; Cairo, 1984–85; FCO, 1985–87; on loan to Cabinet Office, 1987–88; Ottawa, 1989–92; FCO, 1992–94. *Recreations:* photography, reading, gardening. *Address:* c/o Foreign and Commonwealth Office, King Charles Street, SW1A 2AH.

SCRASE-DICKINS, Mark Frederick Hakon, CMG 1991; HM Diplomatic Service, retired; *b* 31 May 1936; *s* of late Alwyne Rory Macnamara Scrase-Dickins and Ingeborg Oscara Frederika Scrase-Dickins; *m* 1969, Martina Viviane Bayley; one *s* one *d* (and one *d* decd). *Educ:* Eton Coll.; RMA, Sandhurst. Commnd Rifle Bde (later Royal Green Jackets), 1956; Malaya, 1956–57 (despatches); ADC to GOC Ghana Army, 1958–59; ADC to Chief of Imperial Gen. Staff, 1959–60; SE Asia, 1962–65; Army Staff Coll., 1967; Hong Kong, 1968–70; transferred to FCO, 1973; Vientiane, 1975; Muscat, 1976; Counsellor: Jakarta, 1983; Riyadh, 1990. *Recreation:* field sports. *Address:* Coolhurst Grange, Horsham, West Sussex RH13 6LE. *T:* Horsham (01403) 252416. *Clubs:* Buck's, Special Forces.

SCREECH, Rev. Prof. Michael Andrew, FBA 1981; FRSL; Extraordinary Fellow, Wolfson College, Oxford, since 1993; Senior Research Fellow, All Souls College, Oxford, 1984–93, now Fellow Emeritus; *b* 2 May 1926; 3rd *s* of Richard John Screech, MM and Nellie Screech (*née* Maunder); *m* 1956, Anne (*née* Reeve); three *s*. *Educ:* Sutton High Sch., Plymouth; University Coll. London (BA (1st cl. Hons) 1950; Fellow, 1982); University of Montpellier, France; Oxford Ministry Course. DLitt Birmingham, 1959; DLit London, 1982; DLitt Oxon 1990. Other Rank, Intelligence Corps (mainly Far East), 1944–48. Asst, UCL, 1950–51; Birmingham Univ.: Lectr, 1951–58; Sen. Lectr., 1959–61; UCL: Reader, 1961–66; Personal Chair of French, 1966–71; Fielden Prof. of French Language and Lit., London Univ., 1971–84. Ordained deacon, 1993, priest, 1994; Asst Curate (NSM), St Giles with St Philip, and St James with St Margaret, Oxford, 1993–. Visiting Professor: Univ. of Western Ontario, 1964–65; Univ. of New York, Albany, 1968–69; Johnson Prof., Inst. for Research in the Humanities, Madison, Wisconsin, 1978–79; Vis. Fellow, All Souls, Oxford, 1981; Edmund Campion Lectr, Regina, 1985; Wiley Vis. Prof., N Carolina, 1986; Professeur, Collège de France, 1989; Prof. Associé, Paris IV (Sorbonne), 1990; Leverhulme Emeritus Fellow, 1995–. Member: Cttee, Warburg Inst., 1970–84; Comité d'Humanisme et Renaissance, 1971–; Comité de parrainage des Classiques de l'Humanisme, 1988–; Corresp. Mem., Société Historique de Genève, 1988. Hon. DLitt Exeter, 1993. Chevalier dans l'Ordre National du Mérite, 1983; Médaille de la Ville de Tours, 1984; Chevalier, Légion d'Honneur, 1992. *Publications:* The Rabelaisian Marriage, 1958, rev. edn trans. French, 1992; L'Evangélisme de Rabelais, 1959, rev. edn trans. English, 1992; Tiers Livre de Pantagruel, 1964; Les épistres et évangiles de Lefèvre d'Etaples, 1964; (with John Jollife) Les Regrets et autres oeuvres poëtiques (Du Bellay), 1966; Marot évangélique, 1967; (with R. M. Calder) Gargantua, 1970; La Pantagrueline Prognostication, 1975; Rabelais, 1980, rev. edn trans. French, 1992; Ecstasy and the Praise of Folly, 1981, rev. edn trans. French, 1991; Montaigne and Melancholy, 1983, rev. edn trans. French, 1992; (with Anne Screech) Erasmus' Annotations on the New Testament: The Gospels, 1986, Acts, Romans, I and I Corinthians, 1990, Galatians—Revelation, 1993; (ed trans.) Montaigne, An Apology for Raymond Sebond, 1987; (with Stephen Rawles *et al.*) A New Rabelais Bibliography: editions before 1626, 1987; (ed trans.) The Essays of Montaigne, 1991, Some Renaissance Studies, ed. M. Heath, 1992; Clément Marot: a Renaissance poet and the challenge of the Gospel, 1993; *edited reprints:* Le Nouveau Testament de Lefèvre d'Etaples, 1970; F. de Billon: Le Fort inexpugnable de l'Honneur du Sexe Femenin, 1970; Opuscules d'Amour par Héroët et autres divins poëtes, 1970; Amyot: Les œuvres morales et meslées de Plutarque, 1971; Warden Mocket of All Souls: Doctrina et Politia Ecclesiae Anglicanae 1616 and 1617, 1995; articles on Renaissance, Reformation, and the history of the classical and Christian tradition in: Bibliothèque d'Humanisme et Renaissance, Etudes rabelaisiennes, Jl of Warburg Inst., etc; contribs to several collective volumes. *Recreation:* walking. *Address:* 5 Swanston-field, Whitchurch-on-Thames RG8 7HP. *T:* Pangbourne (01734) 842513. *Club:* Athenæum.

SCRIMSHAW, Frank Herbert; *b* 25 Dec. 1917; *s* of late John Leonard Scrimshaw and Jessie Scrimshaw (*née* Sewell), Lincoln; *m* 1950, Joan Olive, *d* of Leslie Stephen Paskall, Felixstowe; one *s*. *Educ:* The City Sch., Lincoln; University Coll., Nottingham. BSc London. Joined Scientific Civil Service, 1939; various posts at RAE, Farnborough, and Blind Landing Experimental Unit, RAF Martlesham Heath, 1939–58; Dir of Scientific Research (Electronics), Min. of Aviation, 1959–61; RRE, Malvern: Head of Guided Weapons Group, 1961–65; Head of Mil. and Civil Systems Dept, 1965–67; Dir Gen., Electronics R&D, Min. of Technology, later MoD, 1967–72; Dep. Dir, RAE, Farnborough, 1972–78, retired. *Address:* 53 Feoffees Road, Somersham, near Huntingdon, Cambs PE17 3JQ. *T:* Ramsey (Cambs) (01487) 840143.

SCRIVEN, Rt Rev. Henry William; *see* Gibraltar in Europe, Suffragan Bishop of.

SCRIVEN, Pamela; QC 1992; *b* 5 April 1948; *d* of Maurice Scriven and Evelyn Scriven (*née* Stickney); *m* 1973; two *s*. *Educ:* University College London (LLB Hons). Called to the Bar, Inner Temple, 1970 (Bencher, 1995); Asst Recorder, 1993–. Member: Family Law Bar Assoc. Cttee, 1991–; Race Relations Cttee, 1992–, Professional Conduct Cttee, 1995–, Bar Council; Council for Family Proceedings, 1993–. *Recreations:* theatre, travel. *Address:* 1 King's Bench Walk, Temple, EC4Y 7DB. *T:* 0171–583 6266.

SCRIVEN, Wilton Maxwell, AO 1983; Member, Casino Supervisory Authority, since 1987; Director, Rib Loc International Ltd, since 1986; *b* 10 Dec. 1924; *m* 1948, Marjorie Reta Shaw; two *s* two *d*. *Educ:* Univ. of Adelaide. BSc; FIEAust. Flying Officer RAAF; served with RAF Sqdn 622 Mildenhall, 1943–45. Engr, PMG's Dept, 1946–64; Regional Dir, Dept of Trade, 1965–66; Chm., Australian Industrial Research and Develt Grants Bd, 1967–68; Dir of Industrial Develt, S Australian Govt, 1969–76; Agent General for S Australia in London, 1977–80; Dir Gen., S Aust. Dept of Premier and Cabinet, 1980–83; Dir Gen., Dept of Lands, SA, 1983–84. Mem. Bd, Investigator Sci. and Technol. Centre, 1992–. *Recreations:* tennis, golf, flute. *Address:* 7 Knightsbridge Road, Leabrook, SA 5068, Australia. *Clubs:* Adelaide Rotary; Mount Osmond Golf.

SCRIVENER, Anthony Frank Bertram, QC 1975; a Recorder of the Crown Court, since 1976; *b* 31 July 1935; *s* of late Frank Bertram Scrivener and of Edna Scrivener; *m* 1964, Irén Becze (marr. diss.); one *s* one *d*; *m* 1993, Ying Hui Tan. *Educ:* Kent Coll., Canterbury; University Coll. London (LLB). Called to Bar, Gray's Inn, 1958 (Holt Scholar); Bencher, Lincoln's Inn, 1985. Lectr in Law, Ghana, 1959–61; practice as Junior, 1961–75. Chm., Gen. Council of Bar, 1991 (Vice-Chm., 1990). *Recreations:* tennis, chess, cricket, car racing, taking the dog for a walk. *Address:* 2–3 Gray's Inn Square, WC1R 5JH.

SCRIVENER, Christiane, Officier de la Légion d'Honneur, 1978; Member, Commission of the European Communities, 1989–95; *b* 1 Sept. 1925; *m* 1944, Pierre Scrivener; one *s* decd. *Educ:* Lycée de Grenoble; Faculté de lettres et de droit de Paris. Dip. Psychol.; Dip. Harvard Business Sch. Directeur Général: l'Assoc. pour l'organisation des Stages en France, 1958–69; l'Assoc. pour l'organisation des missions de coopération technique, 1961–69; l'Agence pour la coopération technique industrielle et économique, 1969–76; Sec. d'Etat à la Consommation, 1976–78; Pres., la Commission chargée d'étudier les problèmes éthiques de la publicité, 1978; Sec. Gen. Adj. du parti républicain, 1978–79; Mem., Parlement européen (UDF), 1979–89; Mem., Conseil d'admin des Assurances Générales de France, 1986–89. Alumni Achievement Award (Harvard Business Sch.), 1976. Officier, Polonia Restituta, 1968; Médaille d'Or du Mérite Européen, 1990. *Publications:* L'Europe, une bataille pour l'avenir, 1984; (pour les enfants) L'histoire du Petit Troll, 1986. *Recreations:* ski-ing, tennis, classical music. *Address:* 21 avenue Robert-Schumann, 92100 Boulogne-Billancourt, France.

SCRIVENER, Ronald Stratford, CMG 1965; HM Diplomatic Service, retired; *b* 29 Dec. 1919; *s* of Sir Patrick Scrivener, KCMG; *m* 1st, 1947, Elizabeth Drake-Brockman (marr. diss., 1952); 2nd, 1962, Mary Alice Olga Sofia Jane Hohler, *d* of late Squadron-Leader Robert Charlton Lane; two step-*s* two step-*d*. *Educ:* Westminster School; St Catharine's College, Cambridge. Served with Royal Air Force Volunteer Reserve, 1940–45. Appointed HM Diplomatic Service, Dec. 1945. Served in Berlin, Buenos Aires, Vienna, Caracas, Berne, Bangkok; Ambassador to: Panama, 1969–70; Czechoslovakia, 1971–74; Asst Under-Sec. of State, FCO, 1974–76. Mem. Council, Franco-British Soc., 1978–. Freeman of City of London, 1984; Liveryman, Scriveners' Co., 1984–. *Publications:* Economic Handbook to the Soviet Union, 1986; Market Survey of Spain, 1987. *Recreations:* travel, fishing. *Address:* 38 Lysia Street, SW6 6NG. *T:* 0171–385 3013. *Clubs:* White's, Pratt's, Beefsteak.

SCRIVENOR, Sir Thomas (Vaisey), Kt 1960; CMG 1956; *b* 28 Aug. 1908; *e s* of late John Brooke Scrivenor, ISO, formerly Dir of Geological Survey, Malaya; *m* 1934, Mary Elizabeth Neatby; one *s* three *d*. *Educ:* King's School, Canterbury; Oriel College, Oxford (MA). Temp. Assistant Principal, Colonial Office, 1930–33; Assistant District Officer, Tanganyika, 1934–37; Assistant District Commissioner, Palestine, 1937–43; Assistant Lt-Governor, Malta, 1943–44; Principal, Colonial Office, 1944–46; Principal Asst Sec., Palestine, 1946–48; Civil Service Comr, Nigeria, 1948–53; Deputy High Commissioner for Basutoland, the Bechuanaland Protectorate, and Swaziland, 1953–60. Sec. to Exec. Council of Commonwealth Agric. Bureaux, 1961–73. *Address:* Vine Cottage, Minster Lovell, Oxon OX8 5RN. *T:* Witney (01993) 775620.

SCRIVER, Prof. Charles Robert, OC 1986; FRS 1991; FRSC 1973; Alva Professor of Human Genetics, since 1994, Professor of Pediatrics, Faculty of Medicine, and Professor of Biology, Faculty of Science, since 1969, McGill University, Montreal; *b* 7 Nov. 1930; *s* of Walter DeMoulpied Scriver and Jessie Marion (*née* Boyd); *m* 1956, Esther-Katherine Peirce; two *s* two *d*. *Educ:* McGill Univ., Montreal (BA *cum laude* 1951, MD, CM *cum laude* 1955). Intern, Royal Victoria Hosp., Montreal, 1955–56; Resident: Royal Victoria and Montreal Children's Hosps, 1956–57; Children's Med. Center, Boston, 1957–58; McLaughlin Travelling Fellow, UCL, 1958–60; Chief Resident in Pediatrics, Montreal Children's Hosp., 1960–61; Asst, Associate Prof., Pediatrics, 1961–69, Markle Schol., 1962–67, McGill Univ. Rutherford Lectr, RSCan, 1983. Associate, MRC, 1968–; Dir, MRC Gp (Med. Genetics), 1982–; Associate Dir, Can. Genetic Diseases Networks (Centers of Excellence), 1989–. President: Can. Soc. Clinical Investigation, 1974–75; Soc. Pediatric Res., 1975–76, Amer. Soc. Human Genetics, 1986–87; Amer. Pediatric Soc., 1994–95. FAAAS 1992; Member: Amer. Soc. Clinical Investigation; Assoc. Amer. Physicians; Hon. Member: Brit. Paediatric Assoc.; Soc. Française de Pédiatrie. Wood Gold Medal, McGill Univ., 1955; Mead Johnson Award, 1968, Borden Award 1973, Amer. Acad. Pediatrics; Borden Award, Nutrition Soc. Can., 1969; Allan Award, Amer. Soc. Human Genetics, 1978; G. Malcolm Brown Award, Can. Soc. Clin. Invest., 1979; Gairdner Internat. Award, Gairdner Foundn, 1979; McLaughlin Medal, RSC, 1981; Ross Award, Can. Pediatric Soc., 1990; Award of Excellence, Genetic Soc. of Canada, 1992. *Publications:* (jtly) Amino Acid Metabolism and its Disorders, 1973; (Sen. editor) Metabolic Basis of Inherited Disease, 1986, 7th edn as Metabolic and Molecular Basis of Inherited Disease; numerous res. pubns. *Recreations:* history, music, photography, literature. *Address:* McGill University—Montreal Children's Hospital Research Institute, 2300 Tupper Street, Montreal, PQ H3H 1P3, Canada. *T:* (514) 9344418, *Fax:* (514) 9344329; 232 Strathearn N, Montreal, PQ H4X 1Y2, Canada. *T:* (514) 4860742.

SCROGGIE, Alan Ure Reith, CBE 1973 (OBE 1961); QPM 1968; one of HM's Inspectors of Constabulary 1963–75; *b* 1912; *s* of late Col W. R. J. Scroggie, CIE, IMS, Callander, Perthshire; *m* 1940, Shiela Catherine, *d* of late Finlay Mackenzie, Elgin, Morayshire; two *s*. *Educ:* Cargilfield Preparatory Sch.; Fettes Coll.; Edinburgh Univ. (BL). Joined Edinburgh City Police, 1930; Asst Chief Constable of Bucks, 1947–53; Chief Constable of Northumberland, 1953–63. OStJ 1955. *Recreations:* golf, fishing, gardening. *Address:* Fowler's Cottage, Abercrombie, by St Monans, Anstruther, Fife KY10 2DE. *Clubs:* Royal and Ancient (St Andrews); Golf House (Elie).

SCROGGS, Cedric Annesley; Chief Executive, Fisons plc, 1992–93; *b* 2 Jan. 1941; *s* of Richard B. H. Scroggs and Vera Wesley Shutte (*née* Coombs); *m* 1964, Patricia Mary Sutherland Ogg; two *s* one *d*. *Educ:* Reading Sch.; St John's Coll., Oxford (Sir Thos White Scholar; BA 1962). Marketing posts: AEI-Hotpoint Ltd, 1962–67; General Foods Ltd, 1967–73; Cadbury Ltd, 1973–76 (Mkting Dir, 1974–76); Mkting Dir, Leyland Cars, 1976–78; Fisons plc: Man. Dir, Scientific Equipment Div., 1979–81; Dir and Div. Chm., 1981; Non-executive Director: Caradon plc, 1988–89; Y. J. Lovell (Holdings) plc, 1990; Hillingdon Hosp. NHS Trust, 1991–92; Genus Ltd, 1994. President: BEAMA, 1991–92; MMB, 1991; CBI Nat. Mfg Council, 1992–94. Vis. Fellow, Nuffield Coll., Oxford, 1993. *Recreations:* boating, golf, diving. *Address:* Sotwell Priory, Wallingford, Oxon OX10 0RH. *Clubs:* Royal Automobile; Leander (Henley); Goring and Streatley Golf (Oxon).

SCRUBY, Ven. Ronald Victor, MA; Archdeacon of Portsmouth, 1977–85, now Emeritus; *b* 23 Dec. 1919; 6th *s* of late Thomas Henry Scruby and late Florence Jane

Scruby, Norwood Green, Southall, Middx; *m* 1955, Sylvia Tremayne Miles (*d* 1995), *e d* of late Rear-Adm. Roderic B. T. Miles, Trotton, Sussex; two *s* one *d*. *Educ:* Southall Technical Coll.; Trinity Hall, Cambridge. Engineering Apprentice, London Transport, 1936–39. Royal Engineers, 1939–45; Capt. 1943. Trinity Hall, Cambridge, 1945–48; Cuddesdon Coll., Oxford, 1948–50. Asst Curate, Rogate, Sussex, 1950–53; Chaplain, King Edward VII Hosp., Midhurst, 1950–53; Chaplain, Saunders-Roe, Osborne, E Cowes, 1953–58; Vicar of Eastney, Portsmouth, 1958–65; Rural Dean of Portsmouth, 1960–65; Archdeacon of the Isle of Wight, 1965–77. *Address:* The Dower House, Rogate, Petersfield, Hants GU31 5EG. *T:* Rogate (01730) 821325.

SCRUTON, Prof. Roger Vernon; Professor of Philosophy, Boston University, Massachussetts, since 1992; *b* 27 Feb. 1944; *s* of John Scruton and Beryl C. Haynes; *m* 1973, Danielle Laffitte (marr. diss.). *Educ:* Jesus Coll., Cambridge (MA, PhD). Called to the Bar, Inner Temple, 1978. Res. Fellow, Peterhouse, 1969–71; Lectr in Philosophy, Birkbeck Coll., London, 1971–79, Reader, 1979–85, Prof. of Aesthetics, 1985–92. Founder and Dir, The Claridge Press, 1987–. Editor, Salisbury Review, 1982–. *Publications:* Art and Imagination, 1974, 2nd edn 1982; The Aesthetics of Architecture, 1979; The Meaning of Conservatism, 1980; From Descartes to Wittgenstein, 1981; Fortnight's Anger (novel), 1981; The Politics of Culture, 1981; Kant, 1982; A Dictionary of Political Thought, 1982; The Aesthetic Understanding, 1983; (with Baroness Cox) Peace Studies: A Critical Survey, 1984; Thinkers of the New Left, 1985; (jtly) Education and Indoctrination, 1985; Sexual Desire, 1986; Spinoza, 1986; A Land held Hostage, 1987; Untimely Tracts, 1987; The Philosopher on Dover Beach (essays), 1990; Francesca (novel), 1991; A Dove Descending and Other Stories, 1991; (ed) Conservative Texts: an anthology, 1992; Xanthippic Dialogues (novel), 1993; Modern Philosophy, 1994; The Classical Vernacular, 1994; contribs to The Times, Guardian, etc. *Recreations:* music, architecture, literature. *Address:* University Professors' Program, 745 Commonwealth Avenue, Boston, MA 02215, USA. *Club:* Athenæum.

SCRYMGEOUR, family name of **Earl of Dundee.**

SCRYMGEOUR, Lord; Henry David; *b* 20 June 1982; *s* and *heir* of 12th Earl of Dundee, *qv*.

SCUDAMORE, Peter Michael, MBE 1990; National Hunt jockey, 1979–93; Director, Chasing Promotions, since 1989; *b* 13 June 1958; *s* of Michael and Mary Scudamore; *m* 1980, Marilyn Linda Kington; two *s*. *Educ:* Belmont Abbey, Hereford. Champion Jockey, 1981–82 and annually, 1986–93; rode for British Jump Jockeys; winners in Australia, Belgium, Germany, New Zealand, Norway; John Player Amateur Flat Race, Galway; Leading Jockey, Ritz Club Charity Trophy, Cheltenham Festival, 1986; leading jockey, Cheltenham, 1986, 1987; set new record for number of winners ridden in career, 1989, for number in one season (221), 1989; rode 1,500th winner, 1992; record 1,678 wins on retirement. Racing journalist, Daily Mail, 1993–; Commentator for Nat. Hunt racing, Grandstand, BBC TV, 1993–. *Publications:* (with Alan Lee) A Share of Success: the Scudamore Family, 1983; Scu: the autobiography of a champion, 1993. *Recreations:* cricket, music, watching sport. *Fax:* Guiting Power (01451) 850569.

SCULLARD, Geoffrey Layton, OBE 1971; HM Diplomatic Service, retired; Head of Accommodation and Services Department, Foreign and Commonwealth Office, 1978–80; *b* 5 July 1922; *s* of late William Harold Scullard and late Eleanor Mary Scullard (*née* Tomkin); *m* 1945, Catherine Margaret Pinington; three *d*. *Educ:* St Olave's Grammar Sch. Joined Foreign Office, 1939. Served War (RAF Signals), 1942–46. Diplomatic service at: Stockholm, Washington, Baghdad, Los Angeles, Moscow. *Recreations:* fishing, golf. *Address:* 2 Albury Heights, 8 Albury Road, Guildford, Surrey GU1 2BT. *T:* Guildford (01483) 39915. *Clubs:* Civil Service; Bramley Golf.

SCULLY, Prof. Crispian Michael, FDSRCPSG; FFDRCSI; FDSRCS; Dean and Director of Studies, since 1994, and Clinical Director, since 1995, Eastman Dental Institute, University of London; Professor of Oral Medicine, Pathology and Microbiology, University of London, since 1993; *b* 24 May 1945; *s* of Patrick and Rosaleen Scully; *m* Zoitsa Boucoumani; one *d*. *Educ:* Univ. of London (BSc, BDS, PhD); Univ. of Glasgow; Univ. of Bristol (MD, MDS). MRCS; LRCP; LDS RCS; FRCPath. MRC Research Fellow, Guy's Hosp., 1975–78; Lectr, 1979–81, Sen. Lectr, 1981–82, Univ. of Glasgow; Prof. of Stomatology, Univ. of Bristol, 1982–93. Hon. Consultant, Inst. of Dental Surgery, subseq. Eastman Dental Inst., London Univ., 1993–. Consultant Adviser in Dental Research, DHSS, 1986–. Member: GDC, 1984–94; Adv. Council for Misuse of Drugs, 1985–89; Chm., Central Examining Bd for Dental Hygienists, 1989–94; Member: Medicines Control Agency Cttee on Dental and Surgical Materials, 1990–93; Standing Dental Adv. Cttee, 1992–. *Publications:* Medical Problems in Dentistry, 1982, 3rd edn 1993; (jtly) Multiple Choice Questions in Dentistry, 1985; Handbook for Hospital Dental Surgeons, 1985; (jtly) Slide Interpretation in Oral Disease, 1986; Dental Surgery Assistants' Handbook, 1988; Colour Atlas of Stomatology, 1988, 2nd edn 1995; Colour Aids to Oral Medicine, 1988, 2nd edn 1992; The Dental Patient, 1988; The Mouth and Perioral Tissues, 1989; Patient Care: a dental surgeon's guide, 1989; (jtly) Occupational Hazards in Dentistry, 1990; (jtly) Clinic Virology in Oral Medicine and Dentistry, 1992; (jtly) Medicine and Surgery for Denistry, 1993; (jtly) Colour Atlas of Oral Diseases in Children and Adolescents, 1993; (jtly) Colour Atlas of Oral Pathology, 1995; contribs to learned jls. *Recreations:* music, ski-ing. *Address:* Eastman Dental Institute, 256 Gray's Inn Road, WC1X 8LD. *T:* 0171–915 1038.

SCURR, Dr Cyril Frederick, CBE 1980; LVO 1952; FRCS, FRCA; Hon. Consulting Anaesthetist, Westminster Hospital, since 1985 (Consultant Anaesthetist, 1949–85); Hon. Anaesthetist, Hospital of SS John and Elizabeth, 1952–94, now Emeritus; *b* 14 July 1920; *s* of Cyril Albert Scurr and Mabel Rose Scurr; *m* 1947, Isabel Jean Spiller; three *s* one *d*. *Educ:* King's Coll., London; Westminster Hosp. MB, BS. Served War of 1939–45: RAMC, 1942–47, Major, Specialist Anaesthetist. Faculty of Anaesthetists: Mem. Bd, 1961–77; Dean, 1970–73; Mem. Council, RCS, 1970–73; Pres., Assoc. of Anaesthetists of GB and Ireland, 1976–78; Mem. Health Services Bd, 1977–80; Chm., Scientific Programme, World Congress of Anaesthetists, London, 1968; Pres., 1978–79, Hon. Mem., 1988, Anaesthetics Section, RSocMed; Mem. Adv. Cttee on Distinction Awards, 1973–84; Vice-Chm., Jt Consultants Cttee, 1979–81; past Member: Cttee, Competence to Practise; Standing Med. Adv. Cttee, DHSS. Mem. d'Honneur, Société Française d'Anesthésie et de Réanimation, 1978; Academician, European Acad. of Anaesthesiology, 1978. Frederick Hewitt Lectr, RCS, 1971; Magill Centenary Oration, RCS, 1988. Dudley Buxton Prize, RCS, 1977; Gold Medal, Faculty of Anaesthetists, 1983; John Snow Medal, Assoc. of Anaesthetists of GB and Ireland, 1984. Hon. FFARCSI 1977. *Publications:* Scientific Foundations of Anaesthesia, 1970, 4th edn 1990; (jtly) Drug Mechanisms in Anaesthesia, 1987, 2nd edn 1993. *Recreations:* photography, gardening. *Address:* 16 Grange Avenue, Totteridge Common, N20 8AD. *T:* 0181–445 7188.

SCUSE, Dennis George, MBE 1957; TD 1946; Managing Director, Dennis Scuse Ltd, PR Consultants in Radio and TV, 1976–87; *b* 19 May 1921; *yr s* of late Charles H. and Katherine Scuse; *m* 1948, Joyce Evelyn, *yr d* of late Frank and Frances Burt; one *s*. *Educ:* Park Sch., Ilford; Mercers' Sch., London. Joined Martins Bank, 1937. TA (RA), 1938; mobilised, Sept. 1939. Served War, commissioned 78th (HyAA) Regt, RA, 1940. Air Defence of Gt Britain, 1940–41; Command Entertainment Officer, Ceylon Army Comd, 1942; subseq. 65th (HyAA) Regt, in MELF and CMF, 1943–44; joined Army Broadcasting Service, CMF: commanded stations in Bari, Rome and Athens, 1945–46; demobilised, Sept. 1946. Joined Overseas Div. BBC and seconded to War Office for Forces Broadcasting Service in Benghasi and Canal Zone; Chief Programme Officer, 1947–48; Asst Dir, British Forces Network, Germany, 1949–50; Dir, 1950–57. Introduced "Two-Way Family Favourites", 1952–57; Sen. Planning Asst, BBC-TV, 1958–59; Chief Asst (Light Entertainment), BBC-TV, 1960; Chief Asst (TV), BBC New York Office, Sept. 1960; BBC Rep. in USA, July 1962; Gen. Manager, BBC-TV Enterprises, 1963–72, and BBC Radio Enterprises, 1968–72. Trident Management Ltd, 1972; Man. Dir, Trident Internat. TV Enterprises Ltd, 1972–76. Consultant, Hanson Trust, 1984–89. *Publications:* numerous articles on broadcasting, television programme exports, etc. *Recreations:* journalism, watching television. *Address:* 2 York House, Courtlands, Sheen Road, Richmond, Surrey TW10 5BD. *T:* 0181–948 4737. *Club:* Royal Greenjackets.

SCUTT, Robin Hugh, CBE 1976; television producer; Member: International Committee, Monte Carlo Television Festival, since 1989; Programme Advisory Committee, London Weekend Television, 1990–94; *b* Sandgate, Kent, 24 Oct. 1920; *s* of late Rev. A. O. Scutt, MA and Freda M. Scutt (*née* Palmer); *m* 1st, 1943, Judy Watson (marr. diss. 1960); two *s*; 2nd, 1961, Patricia A. M. Smith. *Educ:* Fonthill; Bryanston; Jesus Coll., Cambridge (MA Mod. Lang.). Served Intell. Corps, 1941–42 (invalided out). BBC Eur. Service (French Section), 1942; BBC TV Outside Broadcasts Producer, 1955; BBC Paris Rep., 1958; Gen. Man., Trans Europe Television, 1962; rejoined BBC TV Outside Broadcasts, 1963; Asst Head of BBC TV Presentation (BBC1), 1966; Controller: BBC Radio 1 and 2, 1967–68; BBC 2, 1969–74; Development TV, 1974–77; Dep. Man. Dir, BBC TV, 1977–80; Dir, LWT, 1981–90; Dir of Production, NVC Arts, 1991–94. Chm., New Technologies Working Party, Broadcast Res. Unit, BFI, 1981–83. TV Producer for National Video Corp.: Tales of Hoffmann, Peter Grimes, La Bohème, Fanciulla del West, Manon Lescaut, Die Fledermaus, Der Rosenkavalier, Nutcracker and Don Carlo, Covent Gdn, 1981–85; Ernani, Il Trittico, I Lombardi, Andrea Chenier, Aida, Madame Butterfly and Nabucco, La Scala, 1982–86; Otello, Turandot, Madame Butterfly, Tosca, Il Trovatore and Attila, Verona, 1982–85; Don Quixote, and ABT at the Met, and at San Francisco, Amer. Ballet Theatre, 1983–85; Natasha (Natalia Makarova), and Carols for Christmas, 1985; Napoli and La Sylphide, Royal Theatre Copenhagen, 1986–88; Boris Godunov, and The Golden Age, Bolshoi Theatre, 1987; Cinderella, 1987, Diaghilev Tribute, 1990, Paris Opera Ballet; Le Corsaire, 1989, Swan Lake, 1990, The Stone Flower, 1991, Coppelia, 1993, Kirov Ballet, St Petersburg; Life for the Tsar, and Mlada, Bolshoi Theatre, 1992; La Traviata, La Fenice, Venice, 1992; Maid of Orleans, Bolshoi Th., 1993; Billboards, Joffrey Ballet, NY, 1993; Holy Russia at Christmas, 1994. FRTS 1978 (Gold Medallist, 1980); FRSA 1984. Officier de la Légion d'Honneur (France), 1983; Officier de l'Ordre du Mérite Culturel (Monaco), 1991. *Recreations:* music, theatre, gardening. *Address:* The Abbey Cottage, Cockfield, Suffolk IP30 0LY. *Club:* Garrick.

SEABORG, Glenn Theodore; University Professor of Chemistry, University of California, Berkeley, since 1971; *b* 19 April 1912; *s* of Herman Theodore and Selma Erickson Seaborg; *m* 1942, Helen Lucille Griggs; four *s* two *d*. *Educ:* Univ. of Calif, Los Angeles (BA); Univ. of Calif, Berkeley (PhD). University of California, Berkeley: Res. Associate (with Prof. Gilbert N. Lewis), Coll. of Chem., 1937–39; Instr, Dept of Chem., 1939–41, Asst Prof., 1941–45, Prof., 1945–71; Chancellor, 1958–61; Lawrence Berkeley Laboratory: Associate Dir, 1954–61, and 1972–; Dir, Nuclear Chem. Div., 1946–58, and 1972–75, Dir, Lawrence Hall of Science, 1982–; Head, Plutonium Chem. Metall. Lab., Univ. of Chicago, 1942–46; Chm., US Atomic Energy Commn, 1961–71. Member, US Delegns to: 3rd (Chm.) and 4th (Chm. and Pres.) UN Internat. Confs on Peaceful Uses of Atomic Energy, Geneva, 1964 and 1971; 5–15th annual Gen. Confs of Internat. Atomic Energy Agency, 1961–71; USSR, for signing of Memorandum on Cooperation in the Field of Utilization of Atomic Energy for Peaceful Purposes (Chm.), 1963; USSR, for signing of Limited Test Ban Treaty, 1963. Member: Nat. Council on Marine Resources and Engineering Development, 1966–71; Nat. Aeronautics and Space Council, 1961–71; Fed. Council for Science and Tech., 1961–71; Pres.'s Cttee on Manpower, 1964–69; Fed. Radiation Council, 1961–69; Nat. Sci. Bd, Nat. Sci. Foundn, 1960–61; Pres.'s Science Adv. Cttee, 1959–61; 1st Gen. Adv. Cttee, US Atomic Energy Commn, 1946–50; Commn on the Humanities, 1962–65; Scientific Adv. Bd, Robert A. Welch Foundn, 1957–; Bd of Dirs, Nat. Educnl TV and Radio Centre, 1958–64, 1967–70; Bd of Dirs, World Future Soc., 1969–; Nat. Programming Council for Public TV, 1970–72; Bd of Governors, Amer.-Swedish Hist. Foundn, 1972–; Steering Cttee, Chem. Educn Material Study (Chm.), 1959–74; Nat. Cttee on America's Goals and Resources, Nat. Planning Assoc., 1962–64; Electoral Coll. Hall of Fame for Great Americans, 1969–; California Inventors' Hall of Fame, 1983–; Council on Foreign Relations, 1965–; Bd of Trustees: Pacific Science Centre Foundn, 1962–; Science Service, 1965– (Pres., 1966–); Amer.-Scandinavian Foundn, 1968–; Educnl Broadcasting Corp., 1970–73; Amer. Assoc. for the Advancement of Science (Pres. 1972, Chm. 1973); Amer. Chem. Soc. (Pres., 1976); Chm. Bd, Swedish Council of America, 1978–. Mem. and Hon. Mem., Fellow and Hon. Fellow, numerous scientific and professional socs and instns, Argentina, German Dem. Republic., German Fed. Republic, Japan, Poland, Spain, Sweden, UK, USA, USSR; Foreign Mem., Royal Society, 1985; Hon. FRSC 1982. Holds 50 hon. doctorates from univs and colls. Named one of America's 10 Outstanding Young Men, 1947. Awards (1947–) include: Nobel Prize for Chemistry (jtly), 1951; Perkin Medal (Amer. Sect. Soc. Chem. Ind.), 1957; USAEC Enrico Fermi Award, 1959; Priestley Meml Award, 1960; Franklin Medal (Franklin Inst. of Philadelphia), 1963; Award in Pure Chem., 1947, Charles Lathrop Parsons Award, (Amer. Chem. Soc.), 1964; Chem. Pioneer Award, 1968, Gold Medal Award, (Am. Inst. of Chemists), 1973; Arches of Science Award (Pacific Science Centre, Seattle), 1968; John R. Kuebler Award, Alpha Chi Sigma, 1978; Priestley Medal, Amer. Chem. Soc., 1979; Henry DeWolf Smyth Award, Amer. Nuclear Soc., 1982; Actinide Award, 1984; Great Swedish Heritage Award, 1984. Officer, French Legion of Honour, 1973. Co-discoverer of: nuclear energy source isotopes Pu-239 and U-233; elements (1940–74): 94, plutonium; 95, americium; 96, curium; 97, berkelium; 98, californium; 99, einsteinium; 100, fermium; 101, mendelevium; 102, nobelium; element 106. *Publications:* (jtly) The Chemistry of the Actinide Elements, 1958, 2nd edn 1986; The Transuranium Elements (Silliman Lectures), 1958; (jtly) Elements of the Universe, 1958; Man-made Transuranium Elements, 1963; (jtly) Education and the Atom, 1964; (jtly) The Nuclear Properties of the Heavy Elements, 1964; (jtly) Oppenheimer, 1969; (jtly) Man and Atom, 1971; Nuclear Milestones, 1972; (ed) Transuranium Elements—Products of Modern Alchemy, 1978; Kennedy, Khrushchev and the Test Ban, 1981; (jtly) Nuclear Chemistry, 1982; Stemming the Tide: arms control Johnson years, 1987; contrib. numerous papers on nuclear chem. and nuclear physics, transuranium elements, high energy nuclear reactions and educn in Physical Rev., Jl Amer. Chm. Soc., Annual Rev. of Nuclear Science, etc. *Recreations:* golf, reading, hiking. *Address:* (business) Lawrence Berkeley Laboratory, University of California, Berkeley, CA 94720, USA; (home) 1154 Glen Road, Lafayette, CA 94549, USA. *Clubs:* Faculty (Univ. Calif, Berkeley); Commonwealth Club of California, Bohemian (San Francisco); Chemists (NY); Cosmos, University (Washington).

SEABROOK, Air Vice-Marshal Geoffrey Leonard, CB 1965; *b* 25 Aug. 1909; *s* of late Robert Leonard Seabrook; *m* 1949, Beryl Mary (*née* Hughes); one *s* one *d*. *Educ:* King's Sch., Canterbury. Commissioned in RAF (Accountant Branch), 1933; served in: Middle East, 1935–43; Bomber Command, 1943–45; Transport Command, 1945–47; Iraq, 1947–49; Signals Command, 1949–51; Air Ministry Organisation and Methods, 1951–53; Home Command Group Captain Organisation, 1953–56; Far East Air Force, 1957–59; idc 1960; Director of Personnel, Air Ministry, 1961–63; Air Officer Administration, HQ, RAF Tech. Trg Comd, 1963–66; retired June 1966. Air Cdre 1961; Air Vice-Marshal, 1964. Head of Secretarial Branch, Royal Air Force, 1963–66. FCA 1957 (Associate, 1932). *Recreations:* sailing, golf. *Address:* Long Pightle, Piltdown, Uckfield, E Sussex TN22 3XB. *T:* Newick (01825) 722322. *Clubs:* Royal Air Force; Piltdown Golf.

SEABROOK, Graeme; Managing Director, Dairy Farm International, since 1993; *b* 1 May 1939; *s* of Norman and Amy Winifred Seabrook; *m* 1967, Lorraine Ellen Ludlow; one *s* one *d*. G. J. Coles & Co. (later Coles Myer), Australia, 1955; Chief Gen. Manager, G. J. Coles, 1982; acquisition of Myer, 1985; Man. Dir, Discount Stores Group, 1985; Jt Man. Dir, Coles Myer, 1987, resigned 1988; joined Dairy Farm International, Hong Kong and seconded to Kwik Save Group, 1988: Man. Dir, 1988–93, Chief Exec., 1989–93, non-exec. Dir, 1993–. *Recreations:* tennis, photography. *Address:* Dairy Farm International Holdings Ltd, 33F Windsor House, Causeway Bay, Hong Kong.

SEABROOK, Robert John; QC 1983; a Recorder, since 1985; *b* 6 Oct. 1941; *s* of Alan Thomas Pertwee Seabrook, MBE and late Mary Seabrook (*née* Parker); *m* 1965, Liv Karin Djupvik, Bergen, Norway; two *s* one *d*. *Educ:* St George's Coll., Salisbury, Southern Rhodesia; University Coll., London (LLB). Called to the Bar, Middle Temple, 1964, Bencher, 1990. Leader, SE Circuit, 1989–92; Chm., Bar Council, 1994. Member: Brighton Fest. Cttee, 1976–86; Court, Univ. of Sussex, 1988–93. Gov., Brighton Coll., 1993–. Liveryman, Curriers' Co., 1972–. *Recreations:* travel, listening to music, wine. *Address:* (chambers) 1 Crown Office Row, Temple, EC4Y 7HH. *T:* 0171–797 7500. *Club:* Les Six.

SEABROOKE, George Alfred; consultant in education and training; Director, The Polytechnic, Wolverhampton, 1977–85; *b* 8 Dec. 1923; *s* of late John Arthur Seabrooke and Elsie Seabrooke; *m* 1945, Evelyn Sargent; two *s*. *Educ:* Keighley Boys' Grammar Sch.; Bradford Technical Coll.; Stoke-on-Trent Tech. Coll.; King's Coll., London Univ. FBIM 1978. National Service, 1946–48. Post Office Engrg Dept, 1940–50; Estate Duty Office, Comrs of Inland Revenue, 1950–56; SW London Coll. of Commerce, 1956–60; Trent Polytechnic, Nottingham (and precursor Colls), 1960–73; Dep. Dir, NE London Polytechnic, 1974–77. *Publications:* Air Law, 1964; contrib. learned jls. *Recreations:* music, cricket, rugby. *Address:* 6 John Trundle Court, Barbican, EC2Y 8DJ.

SEAFIELD, 13th Earl of, *cr* 1701; **Ian Derek Francis Ogilvie-Grant;** Viscount Seafield, Baron Ogilvy of Cullen, 1698; Viscount Reidhaven, Baron Ogilvy of Deskford and Cullen, 1701; *b* 20 March 1939; *s* of Countess of Seafield (12th in line), and Derek Studley-Herbert (who assumed by deed poll, 1939, the additional surnames of Ogilvie-Grant; he *d* 1960); *S* mother, 1969; *m* 1st, 1960, Mary Dawn Mackenzie (marr. diss., 1971), *er d* of Henry Illingworth; two *s*; 2nd, 1971, Leila, *d* of Mahmoud Refaat, Cairo. *Educ:* Eton. *Recreations:* shooting, fishing, tennis. *Heir:* *s* Viscount Reidhaven, *qv*. *Address:* Old Cullen, Cullen, Banffshire AB56 2XW. *T:* Cullen (01542) 840221. *Club:* White's.

SEAGA, Rt. Hon. Edward Philip George, PC 1982; MP for Western Kingston, since 1962; Leader of the Jamaica Labour Party, since 1974; *b* 28 May 1930; *s* of late Philip Seaga and of Erna (*née* Maxwell); *m* 1965, Marie Elizabeth (*née* Constantine) (Miss Jamaica, 1964); two *s* one *d*. *Educ:* Wolmers Boys' Sch., Kingston, Jamaica; Harvard Univ., USA (BA Social Science, 1952). Did field research in connection with Inst. of Social and Econ. Res., University Coll. of the West Indies (now Univ. of the WI), Jamaica, on develt of the child, and revival spirit cults, by living in rural villages and urban slums; proposed estabt of Unesco Internat. Fund for Promotion of Culture, 1971, and is founding mem. of its Administrative Council. Nominated to Upper House (Legislative Council), 1959 (youngest mem. in its history); Asst Sec., Jamaica Labour Party, 1960–62, Sec., 1962; Minister of Develt and Social Welfare, 1962–67; Minister of Finance and Planning, 1967–72, and 1980–89; Leader of Opposition, 1974–80; Prime Minister, 1980–89. Director: Consulting Services Ltd, to 1979; Capital Finance Co. Ltd, to 1979. Hon. LLD Miami, 1981. Grand Collar, and Golden Mercury Internat. Award, Venezuela, 1981; Gold Key Award, Avenue of the Americas, NYC, 1981; Grand Cross, Order of Merit of Fed. Rep. of Germany, 1982. Religion Anglican. *Publications:* The Development of the Child; Revival Spirit Cults. *Recreations:* classical music, reading, shooting, hockey, football, cricket, tennis, swimming. *Address:* Vale Royal, Kingston, Jamaica. *Clubs:* Kingston Cricket, Jamaica Gun (Jamaica).

SEAGER, family name of **Baron Leighton of Saint Mellons.**

SEAGER, Major Ronald Frank, RA, retired; Executive Director, RSPCA, 1971–78 (Secretary, 1966–71); Advisory Director, International Society for Protection of Animals; *b* 27 May 1918; *s* of Frank Seager and Lilias K. (*née* Parr); *m* 1941, Josephine, *d* of Rev. R. M. Chadwick; one *s* one *d*. *Educ:* St Albans School. Royal Artillery (HAC), 1939; commnd, 1941; Italy, 1944–45; seconded Royal Pakistan Artillery, 1949–50; served Korean War, 1953–54; Perm. Pres. Courts Martial, Eastern Command, 1960–63. Joined RSPCA, 1963. *Recreations:* golf, gardening. *Address:* 4 Thornbank Court, Long Street, Sherborne, Dorset DT9 3BS. *T:* Sherborne (01935) 816223.

SEAGER BERRY, Thomas Henry; Master of the Supreme Court Taxing Office, since 1991; *b* 29 Jan. 1940; *s* of Thomas Geoffrey Seager Berry, CBE and Ann Josephine Seager Berry. *Educ:* Shrewsbury Sch. Admitted solicitor, 1964; Sherwood & Co., 1964–69 (Partner, 1966–69); Partner, Boodle Hatfield, 1969–91. Pres., London Solicitors Litigation Assoc., 1982–84; Mem. Cttee, Media Soc., 1985–91; Mem. Council, Feathers Clubs Assoc., 1986–. Liveryman, Merchant Taylors' Co., 1967. *Publication:* Longman's Litigation Practice, 1988. *Recreations:* tennis, gardening, wine-tasting, walking. *Address:* Supreme Court Taxing Office, Clifford's Inn, Fetter Lane, EC4A 1DQ. *T:* 0171–936 6505. *Clubs:* Hurlingham, MCC.

SEAGROATT, Conrad; Hon. Mr Justice Seagroatt; a Judge of the High Court of Hong Kong, since 1995; a Recorder of the Crown Court, since 1980; *s* of late E. G. Seagroatt, Solicitor of the Supreme Court and Immigration Appeals Adjudicator, and of Gray's Inn, and of Barbara C. Seagroatt; *m* Cornelia Mary Anne Verdegaal; five *d*. *Educ:* Solihull Sch., Warwicks; Pembroke Coll., Oxford (MA Hons Modern History). Admitted Solicitor of the Supreme Court, 1967; called to the Bar, Gray's Inn, 1970, Bencher, 1991; QC 1983. Member, Senate of the Inns of Court and the Bar, 1980–83; Criminal Injuries Compensation Bd, 1986–94. *Recreations:* running, fairweather ski-ing, hockey. *Address:* Supreme Court, Hong Kong. *Club:* Western (Glasgow)

SEAL, Dr Barry Herbert; Member (Lab) Yorkshire West, European Parliament, since 1979; *b* 28 Oct. 1937; *s* of Herbert Seal and Rose Anne Seal; *m* 1963, Frances Catherine Wilkinson; one *s* one *d*. *Educ:* Heath Grammar Sch., Halifax; Univ. of Bradford (MSc, PhD); European Business Sch., Fontainebleau. CEng. Served RAF, 1955–58. Trained as Chem. Engr, ICI Ltd, 1958–64; Div. Chem. Engr, Murex Ltd, 1964–68; Sen. Engr, BOC Internat., 1968–71; Principal Lectr in Systems, Huddersfield Polytechnic, 1971–79; consultant on microprocessors. Parly Candidate (Lab), Harrogate, 1974; Leader, Bradford Met. Dist Council Labour Gp, 1976–79. European Parliament: Leader, British Lab. Gp, 1988–89; Chm., Econ., Monetary and Industrial Policy Cttee, 1984–87. *Publications:* papers on computer and microprocessor applications. *Recreations:* walking, reading, films, sailing, flying. *Address:* (office) City Hall, Bradford, West Yorks BD1 1HY. *T:* Bradford (01274) 752091; (home) Brookfields Farm, Wyke, Bradford, West Yorks BD12 9LU.

SEAL, Richard Godfrey, FRCO; FRSCM; Organist of Salisbury Cathedral, since 1968; *b* 4 Dec. 1935; *s* of William Godfrey Seal and Shelagh Seal (*née* Bagshaw); *m* 1975, Dr Sarah Helen Hamilton; two *s*. *Educ:* New Coll. Choir Sch., Oxford; Cranleigh Sch., Surrey; Christ's Coll., Cambridge (MA). FRCO 1958; FRSCM 1987. Assistant Organist: Kingsway Hall, London, 1957–58; St Bartholomews the Great, London, 1960–61; Chichester Cathedral (and Dir of Music, Prebendal Sch.) Sussex, 1961–68. DMus Lambeth, 1992. *Address:* 5 The Close, Salisbury, Wilts SP1 2EF. *T:* Salisbury (01722) 336828. *Club:* Crudgemens (Godalming).

SEALE, Douglas (Robert); producer, actor and director (stage); *b* 28 Oct. 1913; *s* of Robert Henry Seale and Margaret Seale (*née* Law). *Educ:* Rutlish. Studied for stage at Royal Academy of Dramatic Art and became an actor. First appeared as Starling in The Drums Begin, Embassy, 1934; subseq. in Repertory. Served in Army, 1940–46, commissioned in Royal Signals. Joined Shakespeare Memorial Theatre Company, Stratford-on-Avon season's 1946 and 1947. From 1948 produced at Birmingham Repertory Theatre, at The Bedford, Camden Town (under Donald Wolfit), and again at Birmingham where he became Director of Productions, 1950. Later Productions include: Figaro and Fidelio, Sadler's Wells; Shaw's Caesar and Cleopatra at Birmingham Rep. Theatre, 1956 (later presented at Théâtre Sarah Bernhardt, Paris, and Old Vic). Season 1957: The Tempest, at Univ. of BC, Vancouver; King John, Stratford-on-Avon; Richard III, Old Vic; Trilogy of Henry VI, Old Vic; Season 1958; The World of the Wonderful Dark, for first Vancouver Festival; King Lear, Old Vic; Much Ado about Nothing, Stratford-on-Avon. Old Vic productions as Associate Director, 1958: Julius Caesar; Macbeth; 1959: Molière's Tartuffe; Pinero's The Magistrate; Dryden-Davenant-Purcell version of Shakespeare's The Tempest; St Joan; She Stoops to Conquer, 1960, Landscape with Figures, by Cecil Beaton, Dublin Festival, 1960: King John, Festival Theatre, Stratford, Ontario, 1960; Director of tours in Russia and Poland for Old Vic Theatre Co., 1961: prod. The Importance of Being Earnest, New York, 1962; The Comedy of Errors, Henry V, Stratford, Connecticut, 1963; Regent's Prof., Univ. of Calif. at Santa Barbara, Jan.-June 1965; Artistic Director, Center Stage, Baltimore, Maryland, USA, 1965–67; directed and acted, Meadowbrook Theater, Rochester, Mich, 1968; co-producing Director, Goodman Theater, Chicago, 1969–72 (productions incl.: Soldiers, Marching Song, Heartbreak House (Jefferson award), The Tempest, Twelfth Night, own musical adaptation of Lady Audley's Secret); directed and acted in Lady Audley's Secret, Washington and New York, 1972; Giovani, in Pirandello's Henry IV, New York, 1973; directed: King Lear, Marin Shakespeare Festival, San Francisco; Doll's House and Look Back in Anger, Cleveland, Getting Married, New Haven, 1973; Sorin in The Seagull, Seattle; Artistic Dir, Philadelphia Drama Guild, 1974–80; The Last Few Days of Willie Callendar, Philadelphia, 1979; Summer, Philadelphia, 1980; directed at Shaw Festival, Ont.: Too True to be Good, 1974; Caesar and Cleopatra, 1975; Lady Audley's Secret, 1978; Director: The Winslow Boy, NY, 1980, and tour; The Dresser, Witness for the Prosecution, Miami, 1982; acted in: Frankenstein, NY, 1980; The Dresser, NY, 1981; Noises Off, 1983; acted in *films:* Amadeus, 1983; Heaven Help Us, 1984; Haunted by her Past, 1987; Ernest Saves Christmas, 1988; Triplicity, 1989; I'm No Angel, 1990; Mr Destiny, 1990; Rescue Down Under (voice of Koala Bear), 1991; Aladdin (voice of Sultan), 1992; For Love or Money, 1992; acted in, *TV:* Lucy Arnaz Show (series), 1985; Amazing Stories, 1985; Rags to Riches (series, 1987). Hon. DFA Washington Coll., Md, 1967. Mensa Annual Achievement Award, 1979. *Address:* Apt 14c, One University Place, New York, NY 10003, USA.

SEALE, Sir John Henry, 5th Bt, *cr* 1838; RIBA; *b* 3 March 1921; *s* of 4th Bt; *S* father, 1964; *m* 1953, Ray Josephine, *d* of Robert Gordon Charters, MC, Christchurch, New Zealand; one *s* one *d*. *Educ:* Eton; Christ Church, Oxford. Served War of 1939–45: Royal Artillery, North Africa and Italy; Captain, 1945. ARIBA 1951. *Heir:* *s* John Robert Charters Seale, *b* 17 Aug. 1954. *Address:* Slade, Kingsbridge, Devon TQ7 4BL. *T:* Kingsbridge (01548) 550226.

SEALES, Peter Clinton; Chairman, PSL Associates; *s* of James Seales, Solicitor, and Angela Seales; *m* Bernadette Rogers; one *d*. Called to the Bar, King's Inns, 1953. Group Marketing Dir, Raleigh Industries Ltd, 1962–74; Dir, E Midlands Electricity Board, 1972–74; Man. Dir, Potterton International, and Chm. overseas subsidiaries in France, Belgium, Germany, Holland and Japan, 1974–76; International Marketing Dir, Ever Ready Holdings, 1977. Chief Executive: Sea Fish Industry Authority, 1982–83; Operation Raleigh, 1984–85; Consultant to Saatchi & Saatchi Compton, 1984; Group Marketing Dir, Wassen Internat. Ltd, 1986–92; Consultant, Gazzoni 1907 SpA, 1995– (Dir for Internat. Develts, 1992–95); Dir, Jephson Housing Assoc. Gp, 1994–. Hon. Council Mem., Operation Innervator, 1987–. Mem., Finance Cttee, Warwicks BRCS, 1994–. FInstD 1972. *Recreations:* sailing, music. *Clubs:* Wig and Pen; Real Tennis (Leamington Spa).

SEALY, Austin Llewellyn; High Commissioner for Barbados in the United Kingdom, and Ambassador to Israel, 1993–94; *b* 17 Sept. 1939; *s* of Kenneth Llewellyn Sealy and Gerdsene Elaine Sealy (*née* Crawford); *m* 1964, Rita Anita Pilgrim; three *s*. *Educ:* St Mary's Boys' Sch., Barbados; Harrison Coll., Barbados. Banker, 1958–93: Sen. Mgt Official with Barclays Bank PLC in Caribbean. Pres., Nat. Olympic Cttee of Barbados, 1982–; Hon. Treas., Commonwealth Games Fedn, 1986–; Member: IOC, 1994–; Exec. Council, Assoc. of Nat. Olympic Cttees, 1995–. Silver Crown of Merit (Barbados), 1985. *Recreations:* cricket, tennis, golf. *Address:* Crestview, 35 Highgate Gardens, St Michael, Barbados. *T:* 4272256.

SEALY, Prof. Leonard Sedgwick, PhD; S. J. Berwin Professor of Corporate Law, University of Cambridge, since 1991; Fellow, Gonville and Caius College, Cambridge, since 1959; *b* 22 July 1930; *s* of Alfred Desmond Sealy and Mary Louise Sealy, Hamilton, NZ; *m* 1960, Beryl Mary Edwards; one *s* two *d*. *Educ:* Stratford High Sch.; Auckland Univ. (MA, LLM); Gonville and Caius Coll., Cambridge (PhD). Barrister and solicitor, NZ, 1953; in practice at NZ Bar, 1953–55 and 1958–59. Faculty of Law, University of Cambridge: Asst Lectr, 1959–61; Lectr, 1961–91; Tutor, 1961–70, Sen. Tutor, 1970–75, Gonville and Caius Coll. *Publications:* Cases and Materials in Company Law, 1971, 5th edn 1992; Company Law and Commercial Reality, 1984; (with D. Milman) Guide to the 1986 Insolvency Legislation, 1987, 4th edn as Guide to the Insolvency Legislation, 1994; (with R. Hooley) Cases and Materials in Commercial Law, 1994; (ed with A. G. Guest *et al.*) Benjamin's Sale of Goods, 1974, 4th edn 1992; (General Editor): British Company Law and Practice, 1989; International Corporate Procedures, 1992. *Address:* Gonville and Caius College, Cambridge CB2 1TA. *T:* Cambridge (01223) 332471.

SEAMAN, Christopher; international conductor; Music Director, Naples Philharmonic Orchestra, Florida, since 1993; Conductor-in-Residence, Baltimore Symphony Orchestra, since 1987; *b* 7 March 1942; *s* of late Albert Edward Seaman and Ethel Margery Seaman (*née* Chambers). *Educ:* Canterbury Cathedral Choir Sch.; The King's Sch., Canterbury; King's Coll., Cambridge. MA, double first cl. Hons in Music; ARCM, ARCO. Principal Timpanist, London Philharmonic Orch., 1964–68 (Mem., LPO Bd of Dirs, 1965–68); Asst Conductor, 1968–70, Principal Conductor, 1971–77, BBC Scottish Symphony Orchestra; Princ. Conductor and Artistic Dir, Northern Sinfonia Orch., 1974–79; Principal Guest Conductor, Utrecht Symphony Orch., 1979–83; Principal Conductor, BBC Robert Mayer concerts, 1978–87; also works widely as a guest conductor, and appears in America, Holland, France, Germany, Belgium, Italy, Norway, Spain, Portugal, Czechoslovakia, Israel, Hong Kong, Japan, Australia, New Zealand and all parts of UK. FGSM 1972. *Recreations:* people, reading, walking, theology. *Address:* 25 Westfield Drive, Glasgow G52 2SG.

SEAMAN, Gilbert Frederick, AO 1981; CMG 1967; Chairman, State Bank of South Australia, 1963–83; Deputy Chairman, Electricity Trust of SA, 1970–84; Trustee, Savings Bank of SA, 1973–81; *b* 7 Sept. 1912; *s* of Eli S. Seaman, McLaren Vale, South Australia; *m* 1935, Avenal Essie Fong; one *s* one *d*. *Educ:* University of Adelaide. BEc, Associate of University of Adelaide, 1935, High School Teacher, Port Pirie and Unley, 1932–35; South Australian Public Service, 1936–41; Seconded to Commonwealth of Australia as Assistant Director of Manpower for SA, 1941–46; Economist, SA Treasury, 1946–60; Under Treasurer for SA, 1960–72. *Address:* 27 William Street, Hawthorn, SA 5062, Australia. *T:* (8) 2714271.
See also Sir K. D. Seaman.

SEAMAN, Sir Keith (Douglas), KCVO 1981; OBE 1976; Governor of South Australia, 1977–82; *b* 11 June 1920; *s* of late E. S. and E. M. Seaman; *m* 1946, Joan, *d* of F. Birbeck; one *s* one *d*. *Educ:* Unley High Sch.; Univ. of Adelaide (BA, LLB); Flinders Univ. (MA, DipHum). South Australian Public Service, 1937–54; RAAF Overseas HQ, London, 1941–45, Flt-Lieut. Entered Methodist Ministry, 1954: Renmark, 1954–58; Adelaide Central Methodist Mission, 1958–77 (Supt, 1971–77). Sec., Christian Television Assoc. of S Australia, 1959–73; Mem. Executive, World Assoc. of Christian Broadcasting, 1963–70; Director, 5KA, 5AU and 5RM Broadcasting Companies, 1960–77; Chm., 5KA, 5AU and 5RM, 1971–77. Mem., Australian Govt Social Welfare Commn, 1973–76. KStJ 1978. *Recreations:* reading, gardening. *Address:* Victor Harbor, SA 5211, Australia.
See also G. F. Seaman.

SEAMMEN, Diana Jill; Assistant Under-Secretary of State, Programmes, Ministry of Defence, since 1994; *b* 24 March 1948. *Educ:* Univ. of Sussex. HM Treasury, 1969–89; Dir, VAT Control, and a Comr, HM Customs and Excise, 1989–91; Asst Under-Sec. of State, Air, 1992, Finance, 1993, MoD (PE). *Address:* Ministry of Defence, Main Building, Whitehall, SW1A 2HB.

SEARBY, Philip James, CBE 1981; Secretary and Authority Finance Officer, UK Atomic Energy Authority, 1976–84; *b* 20 Sept. 1924; *s* of Leonard James and Lillian Mary Searby; *m* 1955, Mary Brent Dudley; two *s*. *Educ:* Bedford Sch.; Wadham Coll., Oxford (MA). Entered Civil Service, Min. of Nat. Insurance, 1949; Prime Minister's Statistical Branch, 1951; Private Sec. to Paymaster Gen. (Lord Cherwell), 1952; Principal, Atomic Energy Office, 1954. Joined UK Atomic Energy Authority, 1956; Dep. Gen. Sec., Harwell, 1959; Principal Economics and Programmes Officer, 1965; Authority Finance and Programmes Officer, 1971. St Albans Diocesan Reader, 1950. *Recreations:* reading, committee work. *Address:* 5 Borodale, Kirkwick Avenue, Harpenden, Herts AL5 2QW. *T:* Harpenden (01582) 760837.

SEARBY, Richard Henry; QC (Aust.) 1971; Deputy Chairman, Times Newspapers Holdings Ltd, since 1981; *b* 23 July 1931; *s* of late Henry and Mary Searby; *m* 1962, Caroline (*née* McAdam); three *s*. *Educ:* Geelong Grammar Sch., Corio, Vic; Corpus Christi Coll., Oxford Univ. (MA Hons). Called to Bar, Inner Temple, London, 1956; admitted Barrister and Solicitor, Victoria, Aust., 1956; called to Victorian Bar, 1957; Associate to late Rt Hon. Sir Owen Dixon, Chief Justice of Aust., 1956–59; commenced practice, Victorian Bar, 1959; Independent Lectr in Law relating to Executors and Trustees, Univ. of Melbourne, 1961–72. Director: Equity Trustees Executors & Agency Co. Ltd, 1975– (Chm., 1980–); CRA Ltd, 1977–; Shell Australia Ltd, 1977–; News Corp. Ltd, 1977–92 (Chm., 1981–91; Dep. Chm., 1991–92); News Ltd, 1977–92 (Chm., 1981–92); News International plc, 1980–92 (Chm., 1981–89); South China Morning Post Ltd, 1986–92 (Chm., 1987–92); Reuters Founders Share Co. Ltd, 1987–93; BRL Hardy Ltd, 1992–; Amrad Corp. Ltd, 1992–; Tandem Australian Ltd, 1992–. Member Council: Nat. Library of Australia, 1992–; Council, Mus. of Victoria, 1993–. Pres., Aust. Inst. of Internat. Affairs, 1993–. Chm., Geelong Grammar Sch., 1983–89. *Publication:* (jtly) report on Conciliation and Arbitration Act, 1981. *Recreations:* reading, music, tennis, fishing. *Address:* 126 Kooyong Road, Armadale, Vic 3143, Australia. *T:* (3) 8225095. *Clubs:* Melbourne, Australian (Melbourne).

SEARLE, Ronald William Fordham, RDI 1988; AGI; artist; *b* Cambridge, 3 March 1920; *m* 1st, Kaye Webb (marr. diss. 1967); one *s* one *d*; 2nd, 1967, Monica Koenig. *Educ:* Cambridge School of Art. Served with 287 Field Co. RE, 1939–46; captured by the Japanese at fall of Singapore, 1942; Prisoner of War in Siam and Malaya, 1942–45; Dept of Psychological Warfare, Allied Force HQ Port Said Ops, 1956. Creator of the schoolgirls of St Trinian's, 1941 (abandoned them in 1953); Cartoonist to Tribune, 1949–51; to Sunday Express, 1950–51; Special Feature artist, News Chronicle, 1951–53; Weekly Cartoonist, News Chronicle, 1954; Punch Theatre artist, 1949–62; Contributor: New Yorker and New York Times, 1966–; Le Monde, 1995–. Designer of commemorative medals for: the French Mint, 1974–; British Art Medal Soc., 1983–. *One Man Exhibitions include:* Leicester Galls, 1948, 1950, 1954, 1957; New York, 1959, 1963, 1969, 1976; Galerie La Pochade, Paris, 1966, 1967, 1968, 1969, 1971; Galerie Gurlitt, Munich, 1967, 1968, 1969, 1970, 1971, 1973, 1976; Grosvenor Gall., London, 1968; Bibliothèque Nat., Paris, 1973; Galerie Carmen Casse, Paris, 1975, 1976, 1977; Staatliche Mus., Berlin, 1976; Rizzoli Gall., NY, Gal. Bartsch & Chariau, Munich, 1981; Cooper-Hewitt Museum, NY, 1984; Neue Galerie Wien, 1985, 1988; Imperial War Museum, BM, 1986; Fitzwilliam Museum, Cambridge, 1987; Mus. of Fine Arts, San Francisco, 1987–88; Heineman Galls, NY, 1994; Wilhelm-Busch Mus., Hanover, 1995. *Works in permanent collections:* V&A, BM, Imperial War Museum, Tate Gall.; Bibliothèque Nat., Paris; Wilhelm-Busch Museum, Hanover; Staatlische Mus., Berlin-Dahlem; Cooper-Hewitt Museum, NY; Univ. of Texas, Austin; Mus. of Fine Arts, San Francisco. *Films based on the characters of St Trinian's:* The Belles of St Trinian's, 1954; Blue Murder at St Trinian's, 1957; The Pure Hell of St Trinian's, 1960; The Great St Trinian's Train Robbery, 1966; The Wildcats of St Trinian's, 1980. *Films designed:* John Gilpin, 1951; On the Twelfth Day, 1954 (Acad. Award Nomination); Energetically Yours (USA), 1957; Germany, 1960 (for Suddeutschen RTV); The King's Breakfast, 1962; Those Magnificent Men in their Flying Machines (Animation Sequence), 1965; Monte Carlo or Bust (Animation Sequence), 1969; Scrooge (Animation Sequence), 1970; Dick Deadeye, 1975. *Publications:* Forty Drawings, 1946; Le Nouveau Ballet Anglais, 1947; Hurrah for St Trinian's!, 1948; The Female Approach, 1949; Back to the Slaughterhouse, 1951; John Gilpin, 1952; Souls in Torment, 1953; Rake's Progress, 1955; Merry England, etc, 1956; A Christmas Carol, 1961; Which Way Did He Go?, 1961; Searle in the Sixties, 1964; From Frozen North to Filthy Lucre, 1964; Pardong M'sieur, 1965; Searle's Cats, 1967; The Square Egg, 1968; Take one Toad, 1968; Baron Munchausen, 1960; Hello—where did all the people go?, 1969; Hommage à Toulouse-Lautrec, 1969; Secret Sketchbook, 1970; The Addict, 1971; More Cats, 1975; Drawings from Gilbert and Sullivan, 1975; The Zoodiac, 1977; Ronald Searle (Monograph), 1978; The King of Beasts, 1980; The Big Fat Cat Book, 1982; Illustrated Winespeak, 1983; Ronald Searle in Perspective (monograph), 1984; Ronald Searle's Golden Oldies 1941–61, 1985; To the Kwai—and Back, 1986; Something in the Cellar, 1986; Ah Yes, I Remember It Well . . ., 1987; Ronald Searle's Non-Sexist Dictionary, 1988; Slightly Foxed—but still desirable, 1989; Carnet de Croquis: le plaisir du trait, 1992; The Curse of St Trinian's, 1993; Marquis de Sade meets Goody Two-Shoes, 1994; *in collaboration:* (with D. B. Wyndham Lewis) The Terror of St Trinian's, 1952; (with Geoffrey Willans) Down with Skool, 1953; How to be Topp, 1954; Whizz for Atomms, 1956; The Compleet Molesworth, 1958; The Dog's Ear Book, 1958; Back in the Jug Agane, 1959; (with Kaye Webb) Paris Sketchbook, 1950 and 1957; Looking at London, 1953; The St Trinian's Story, 1959; Refugees 1960, 1960; (with Alex Atkinson) The Big City, 1958; USA for Beginners, 1959; Russia for Beginners, 1960; Escape from the Amazon!, 1964; (with A. Andrews & B. Richardson) Those Magnificent Men in their Flying Machines, 1965; (with Heinz Huber) Haven't We Met Before Somewhere?, 1966; (with Kildare Dobbs) The Great Fur Opera, 1970; (with Irwin Shaw) Paris! Paris!, 1977; Ronald Searle: a biography, by Russell Davies, 1990. *Address:* c/o Tessa Sayle Agency, 11 Jubilee Place, SW3 3TE. *T:* 0171–823 3883. *Club:* Garrick.

SEARS, Hon. Raymond Arthur William; Hon. Mr Justice Sears; Judge of the Supreme Court of Hong Kong, since 1986; Commissioner of the Supreme Court of Brunei Darussalam, since 1987; *b* 10 March 1933; *s* of William Arthur and Lillian Sears; *m* 1960 (marr. diss. 1981); one *s* one *d*. *Educ:* Epsom Coll.; Jesus Coll., Cambridge. BA 1956. Lieut RA (TA) Airborne, 1953. Called to Bar, Gray's Inn, 1957. QC 1975; Recorder of the Crown Court, 1977–86. Vice-Chm., Judges' Forum, Internat. Bar Assoc., 1993. *Recreations:* watching horse-racing; music. *Address:* Supreme Court, Hong Kong. *Clubs:* Royal Automobile; Hong Kong, Royal Hong Kong Jockey.

SEATON, Colin Robert; Chairman: Medical Appeal Tribunals, since 1989; Disability Appeal Tribunals, since 1992; Barrister-at-Law; *b* 21 Nov. 1928; 2nd *s* of late Arthur William Robert Seaton and Helen Amelia Seaton (*née* Stone); *m* 1952, Betty (*née* Gosling); two *s*. *Educ:* Wallington County Grammar Sch. for Boys; Worcester Coll., Oxford. BA 1953; MA 1956. Royal Air Force, 1947–49. Called to Bar, Inner Temple, 1956 (Profumo Prize, 1953, 1954); Schoolmaster for LCC, 1953–57; Solicitor's Dept, Ministries of Health and Housing and Local Govt, also Dept of the Environment, 1957–71; Sec. (Master) of Nat. Industrial Relations Court, 1971–74; Under Sec., Lord Chancellor's Dept, 1974–88; Circuit Administrator: Northern Circuit, 1974–82; SE Circuit, 1982–83; Head, Legislation Gp, 1983–88. Sec., Lord Chancellor's Law Reform Cttee, 1983–88; Sec. to Univ. Comrs, 1988–94. *Publication:* Aspects of the National Health Service Acts, 1966. *Recreations:* photography, reading. *Address:* Tree Tops, The Drive, Coulsdon, Surrey CR5 2BL. *T:* 0181–668 5538. *Club:* Civil Service.
See also M. J. Seaton.

SEATON, Prof. Michael John, FRS 1967; Professor of Physics, Department of Physics and Astronomy, University College London, 1963–88, now Emeritus; Senior Fellow, Science and Engineering Research Council, 1984–88; *b* 16 Jan. 1923; *s* of late Arthur William Robert Seaton and Helen Amelia Seaton; *m* 1st, 1943, Olive May (*d* 1959), *d* of Charles Edward Singleton; one *s* one *d*; 2nd, 1960, Joy Clarice, *d* of Harry Albert Balchin; one *s*. *Educ:* Wallington Co. Sch., Surrey; University Coll., London (Fellow, 1972). BSc 1948, PhD 1951, London. Dept of Physics, UCL: Asst Lectr, 1950; Lectr, 1953; Reader, 1959; Prof., 1963. Chargé de Recherche, Institut d'Astrophysique, Paris, 1954–55; Univ. of Colorado, 1961; Fellow-Adjoint, Jt Inst. for Laboratory Astrophysics (Nat. Inst. of Standards and Technology and Univ. of Colorado), Boulder, Colo, 1964–. Hon. Mem., Amer. Astronomical Soc., 1983; For. Associate, Amer. Nat. Acad. of Scis, 1986. Pres., RAS, 1979–81, Gold Medal, 1983; Guthrie Medal and Prize, Inst. of Physics, 1984; Hughes Medal, Royal Soc., 1992. Dr *hc* Observatoire de Paris, 1976; Hon. DSc QUB, 1982. *Publications:* papers on atomic physics and astrophysics in various jls. *Address:* 51 Hall Drive, Sydenham, SE26 6XL. *T:* 0181–778 7121.
See also C. R. Seaton.

SEAWARD, Colin Hugh, CBE 1987; HM Diplomatic Service, retired; *b* 16 Sept. 1926; *s* of late Sydney W. Seaward and Molly W. Seaward; *m* 1st, 1949, Jean Bugler (decd); three *s* one *d*; 2nd, 1973, Judith Margaret Hinkley; two *d*. *Educ:* RNC, Dartmouth. Served Royal Navy, 1944–65. Joined HM Diplomatic Service, 1965; served: Accra, 1965; Bathurst (Banjul), 1966; FO, 1968; Rio de Janeiro, 1971; Prague, 1972; FCO, 1973; RNC, Greenwich (sowc), 1976; Counsellor (Econ. and Comm.), Islamabad, 1977–80; Consul-General, Rio de Janeiro, 1980–86, retd; re-employed in FCO, 1987–91. Sec., Anglo-Brazilian Soc., 1992–95 (Hon. Sec., 1986–91). Freeman, City of London, 1987. *Address:* Brasted House, Brasted, Westerham, Kent TN16 1JA.

SEBAG-MONTEFIORE, Harold Henry; Barrister-at-law; Deputy Circuit Judge, 1973–83; *b* 5 Dec. 1924; *e s* of late John Sebag-Montefiore and Violet, *o c* of late James Henry Solomon; *m* 1968, Harriet, *o d* of Benjamin Harrison Paley, New York; one *d*. *Educ:* Stowe; Lower Canada Coll., Montreal; Pembroke Coll., Cambridge (MA). Served War of 1939–45, RAF. Called to Bar, Lincoln's Inn, 1951. Mem., Disciplinary Tribunal, Bar Council. Contested (C) North Paddington, Gen. Elec., 1959; Chm., Conservative Parly Candidates Assoc., 1960–64. Member: LCC, 1955–65 (last Alderman, Co. of London, 1961–65); GLC, for Cities of London and Westminster, 1964–73, First Chm., GLC Arts and Recreation Cttee, 1968–73; Sports Council, 1972–74. Pres., Anglo-Jewish Assoc., 1966–71; Jt Pres., Barkingside Jewish Youth Centre, 1988–94; Mem. Council, Anglo-Netherlands Soc., 1988–. Freeman, City of London, and Liveryman, Spectacle Makers' Co. Trustee: Royal Nat. Theatre Foundn; Internat. Festival of Youth Orchestras; Whitechapel Art Gall.; Touro National Heritage, RI; Mem., Cttee of Honour: RAH Centenary; "Fanfare for Europe"; William and Mary Tercentenary; Centenary of Montefiore Hosp., NY. Rode winner of Bar Point-to-Point, 1957 and 1959. Chevalier, Légion d'Honneur, 1973. *Publications:* obituaries; book reviews and articles on Polo under *nom-de-plume* of "Marco II". *Recreations:* theatre, travel, collecting conductors' batons. *Clubs:* Carlton, Garrick, Hurlingham, Pegasus (Pres., 1979).

SEBASTIAN, Timothy; freelance writer and journalist; *b* 13 March 1952; *s* of Peter Sebastian and Pegitha Saunders; *m* 1977, Diane Buscombe; one *s* two *d*. *Educ:* Westminster School; New College, Oxford. BA (Hons) Mod. Lang. BBC Eastern Europe correspondent, 1979–82; BBC TV News: Europe correspondent, 1982–84; Moscow correspondent, 1984–85; Washington correspondent, 1986–89. TV journalist of the year, RTS, 1982; Richard Dimbleby Award, BAFTA, 1982. *Publications:* Nice Promises, 1985; I Spy in Russia, 1986; *novels:* The Spy in Question, 1988; Spy Shadow, 1989; Saviour's Gate, 1990; Exit Berlin, 1992; Last Rights, 1993; Special Relations, 1994; War Dance, 1995.

SEBRIGHT, Sir Peter Giles Vivian, 15th Bt *cr* 1626, of Besford, Worcs; *b* 2 Aug. 1953; *s* of Sir Hugo Giles Edmund Sebright, 14th Bt and of Deirdre Ann, *d* of late Major Vivian Lionel Slingsby Bethell; *S* father, 1985; *m* 1st, 1977, Regina Maria (marr. diss.), *d* of Francis Steven Clarebrough, Melbourne; one *s*; 2nd, Madeleine; one *s*. *Heir: s* Rufus Hugo Giles Sebright, *b* 31 July 1978.

SECCOMBE, family name of **Baroness Seccombe.**

SECCOMBE, Baroness *cr* 1991 (Life Peer), of Kineton in the County of Warwickshire; **Joan Anna Dalziel Seccombe,** DBE 1984; JP; Vice-Chairman, with special responsibility for women, Conservative Party, since 1987; Chairman, National Union of Conservative and Unionist Associations, 1987–88 (Vice-Chairman, 1984–87; Member of Executive, since 1975); *b* 3 May 1930; *d* of Robert John Owen and Olive Barlow Owen; *m* 1950, Henry Lawrence Seccombe; two *s*. *Educ:* St Martin's Sch., Solihull. Member: Heart of England Tourist Bd, 1977–81 (Chm., Marketing Sub-Cttee, 1979–81); Women's Nat. Commn., 1984–90; Chairman: Lord Chancellor's Adv. Cttee, 1975–93; W Midlands Area Cons. Women's Cttee, 1975–78; Cons. Women's Nat. Cttee, 1981–84; Cons. Party Social Affairs Forum, 1985–87; Dep. Chm., W Midlands Area Cons. Council, 1979–81. Mem., W Midlands CC, 1979–81 (Chm., Trading Standards Cttee, 1979–81). Governor, Nuffield Hosps, 1988–. JP Solihull, 1968 (Chm., 1981–84). *Recreations:* golf, ski-ing. *Address:* Trethias, Norton Grange, Little Kineton, Warwicks CV35 0DP. *T:* Kineton (01926) 640562. *Club:* St Enedoc Golf (Pres., 1992–).
See also Hon. Sir J. A. D. Owen.

SECCOMBE, Hugh Digorie, CBE 1976; Chairman, Seccombe Marshall & Campion Ltd, 1962–77; *b* 3 June 1917; *s* of Lawrence Henry Seccombe, CBE and Norah (*née* Wood); *m* 1947, Eirene Rosemary Banister, *d* of Richard Whittow and Eirene, and *widow* of Lieut P. C. McC. Banister, DSC, RN; one *s* one *d*. *Educ:* Stowe; Sidney Sussex Coll., Cambridge (BA 1938, MA 1942). RNVR, 1939–50; retd, Lt-Comdr. Joined Seccombe Marshall & Campion, 1938; Dir, 1947. Chm., YWCA Central Club, 1971–86. Fellow, Inst. of Bankers, 1964. *Recreations:* gardening, fishing. *Address:* Brook End, Gosden Common, Bramley, Guildford, Surrey GU5 0AE. *T:* Guildford (01483) 893296; Benmore Lodge, Isle of Mull, Argyllshire PA71 6HU. *T:* Aros (01680) 300351.

SECCOMBE, Sir (William) Vernon (Stephen), Kt 1988; JP; Chairman, Plymouth Hospitals NHS Trust, since 1993; former electrical contractor; *b* 14 Jan. 1928; *s* of Stephen Seccombe and Edith Violet (*née* Smith); *m* 1950, Margaret Vera Profit; four *s*. *Educ:* Saltash Grammar Sch.; Plymouth and Devonport Tech. Coll. Mem., E Cornwall Water Bd, 1960–74 (Vice-Chm., 1963–66; Chm., 1966–69); Chairman: Cornwall and Isles of Scilly DHA, late AHA, 1981–82; S Western RHA, 1983–90; Plymouth HA, 1990–93; Dep. Comr, 1970–79, Comr, 1979–82, Western Area Traffic Comrs. Member: Saltash BC, 1953–74 (Chairman: Works Cttee, 1956–62; Finance and Estabs Cttee, 1963–74; Mayor, 1962–63); Caradon DC, 1973–79 (Vice-Chm., 1973–76; Chm., 1976–78). Governor, Saltash Comprehensive Sch., 1970–81 (Chm., 1974–78). JP SE Cornwall, 1970. *Recreations:* industrial and local archaeology, genealogy, good wine, military music. *Address:* Derriford Hospital, Derriford Road, Plymouth PL6 8DH.

SECKER-WALKER, Prof. Lorna Margaret, PhD; Professor of Cancer Cytogenetics, Royal Free Hospital School of Medicine, since 1993; *b* 17 Nov. 1933; *d* of late William Elmer Lea and Margaret Violet Lea (*née* Rees); *m* 1957, David Secker-Walker; one *s* three *d*. *Educ:* numerous schs; St Anne's Coll., Oxford (BA 1955; MA 1959); Inst. of Orthopaedics, London Univ. (PhD 1961). MRCPath 1985. Res. Fellow, MRC Unit for bone seeking isotopes, Oxford, 1955–56; Post-grad. Scholarship, Louvain Univ., Belgium, 1956–57; Royal Marsden Hospital, 1967–84; Non-clinical Lectr in cytogenetics of leukaemia; Gordon Jacobs, MRC and Leukaemia Res. Fund Fellowships; Royal Free Hospital School of Medicine: Lectr, 1984–85; Sen. Lectr, 1985–93. Member Editorial Board: Acta Haematological, 1988–; Cancer Genetics; Cytogenetics, 1987–; Leukemia, 1994–. Chm., UK Cancer Cytogenetics Gp, 1988–; Dir, Leukaemia Res. Fund Leukaemia Cytogenetics Gp and UK Cancer Cytogenetics Gp karyotype database in Acute Lymphoblastic Leukaemia, 1992–; Mem. Fac., European Sch. of Haematol., 1986–. Advr to MRC on cytogenetics of leukaemia, 1985–. Member: Brit. Soc. Haematol., 1975; Internat. Soc. Hematol., 1976; British Assoc. of Cancer Res., 1976; Genetical Soc., 1976; RSocMed, 1984; Assoc. of Clin. Cytogeneticists, 1984; Amer. Soc. Hematol., 1994; European Haematol. Assoc., 1994; European Soc. Human Genetics, 1994. *Publications:* chapters in: Postgraduate Haematology, 1989; Haematological Oncology, 1994; numerous papers on cytogenetics and genetics of leukaemia. *Recreations:* theatre, opera, travel, jigsaw puzzles. *Address:* Royal Free Hospital School of Medicine, Cytogenetics Laboratory, Department of Haematology, Pond Street, NW3 2QG. *T:* 0171–830 2298.

SECOMBE, Sir Harry (Donald), Kt 1981; CBE 1963; actor, comedian and singer; *b* 8 Sept. 1921; *m* 1948, Myra Joan Atherton, Swansea; two *s* two *d*. *Educ:* Dynevor School, Swansea. Served with Royal Artillery, 1939–46. Windmill Theatre, 1947–48; General Variety since 1948. Appearances include: at London Palladium, 1956, 1958, 1959, 1961, 1966; in Roy. Command Perfs, 1951, 1955, 1957, 1958, 1963, 1966, 1969, 1975, 1978, 1987; (musical) Pickwick, Saville, 1963, Chichester Fest., Sadler's Wells, and nat. tour, 1993; (musical) The Four Musketeers, Drury Lane, 1967; The Plumber's Progress, Prince of Wales, 1975. Radio: Goon Show, 1949–60, and special performance of Goon Show for 50th Anniversary of BBC, 1972. Television: BBC, ITV, CBS (New York), Yorkshire TV, 1950–; Presenter: Highway, Tyne Tees TV, 1983–93; Sunday Morning with Secombe, STV, 1994. Films: Davy, for Ealing Films, 1957; Jetstorm, 1959; Bed-Sitting Room, 1968; Mr Bumble in Oliver!, 1968; Bjornsen in Song of Norway, 1969; Rhubarb, 1969; Doctor in Trouble, 1970; The Magnificent Seven Deadly Sins, 1971; Sunstruck, 1972. Has made recordings for HMV, 1953–54, Philips Records, 1955–80, Celebrity Records, 1980–; Telstar, and Word Records, 1987. FRSA 1971. Hon. DMus Wales, 1986. *Publications:* Twice Brightly, 1974; Goon for Lunch, 1975; Katy and the Nurgla, 1978; Welsh Fargo, 1981; Goon Abroad, 1982; The Harry Secombe Diet Book, 1983; Harry Secombe's Highway, 1984; The Highway Companion, 1987; Arias and Raspberries (autobiog.), 1989; The Nurgla's Magic Tear, 1990. *Recreations:* film photography, literature, travel, golf, cricket. *Address:* 46 St James's Place, SW1A 1NS. *T:* 0171–629 2768. *Clubs:* Savage, Royal Automobile, Lord's Taverners, Variety Club of Great Britain, St James's (Founder Mem.).

SECONDÉ, Sir Reginald (Louis), KCMG 1981 (CMG 1972); CVO 1968 (MVO 1957); HM Diplomatic Service, retired; Ambassador to Venezuela, 1979–82; *b* 28 July 1922; *s* of late Lt-Col Emile Charles Secondé and Doreen Secondé (*née* Sutherland); *m* 1951, Catherine Penelope, *d* of late Thomas Ralph Sneyd-Kynnersley, OBE, MC and late Alice Sneyd-Kynnersley; one *s* two *d*. *Educ:* Beaumont; King's Coll., Cambridge. Served, 1941–47, in Coldstream Guards: N Africa and Italy (despatches); Major. Entered Diplomatic Service, 1949; UK Delegn to the UN, New York, 1951–55; British Embassy: Lisbon, 1955–57; Cambodia, 1957–59; FO, 1959–62; British Embassy, Warsaw, 1962–64; First Secretary and later Political Counsellor, Rio de Janeiro, 1964–69; Head of S European Dept, FCO, 1969–72; Royal Coll. of Defence Studies, 1972–73; Ambassador to Chile, 1973–76, to Romania, 1977–79. *Address:* Gosfield Hall, Apt 14, Gosfield, Halstead, Essex CO9 1SF. *T:* Halstead (01787) 477191. *Club:* Cavalry and Guards.

SECRETAN, Lance Hilary Kenyon; consultant, lecturer, journalist, author and entrepreneur, since 1981; Founder and President, The Thaler Corporation Inc., since 1972; President, Thaler Resources Ltd, since 1981; *b* 1 Aug. 1939; *s* of late Kenyon and Marie-Therese Secretan; *m* 1st, 1961, Gloria Christina (marr. diss. 1990); two *d* (and one *d* decd); 2nd, 1993, Patricia Edith Sheppard. *Educ:* Los Cocos, Argentina; Italia Conti, London; St Peters, Bournemouth; Univ. of Waterloo, Canada; Univ. of Southern California (MA in International Relations, *cum laude*); LSE (PhD in International Relations). Sales Manager, J. J. Little and Ives, Toronto, 1959; Analyst, Toronto Stock Exchange, 1960; Sales Manager, Office Overload Co. Ltd, 1960–67; Man. Dir, Manpower Ltd Gp of Cos, UK, Ireland, Middle East and Africa, 1967–81. Prof. of Entrepreneurship, McMaster Univ., 1981–82; Vis. Prof., York Univ., Toronto, 1983–84; Special Goodwill Ambassador for Canadian Assoc., UNEP, 1989–93. FIEC 1969; FRSA 1981. *Publications:* How to be an Effective Secretary, 1972; From Guns to Butter, 1983; Managerial Moxie, 1985, rev. edn 1992; The State of Small Business in Ontario, 1986; The Masterclass, 1988; The Way of the Tiger, 1989; The Personal Masterclass, 1991; Living the Moment, 1992. *Recreations:* life, music, ski-ing, Mother Earth. *Address:* RR2, Alton, Ontario, L0N 1A0, Canada; 38 Chester Terrace, Regent's Park, NW1 4ND. *Clubs:* Mensa, White Elephant; University (Toronto).

SEDAT, Elizabeth Helen, (Mrs J. W. Sedat); *see* Blackburn, E. H.

SEDCOLE, Cecil Frazer, FCA; a Vice Chairman, Unilever PLC, 1982–85; *b* 15 March 1927; *s* of late William John Sedcole and Georgina Irene Kathleen Bluett (*née* Moffatt); *m* 1962, Jennifer Bennett Riggall; one *s* one *d*. *Educ:* Uppingham Sch., Rutland. FCA 1952; CBIM 1982. Joined Unilever Group of Cos, 1952: Dir, Birds Eye Foods, 1960–66; Vice-Chairman: Langnese-Iglo, Germany, 1966–67; Frozen Products Gp, Rotterdam, 1967–71; Dir, Unilever PLC and Unilever NV, 1974–85; Chm., UAC International, 1976–79; Mem., 1971–75, Chm., 1979–85, Overseas Cttee, Unilever; Dir, Tate & Lyle, 1982–90; Dep. Chm., Reed International, 1985–87. Mem., BOTB, 1982–86; Mem. Bd, Commonwealth Devlt Corp., 1984–88. Trustee, Leverhulme Trust, 1982–. Governor: Bedales Sch., 1983–90; Queen Elizabeth's Foundn for Disabled People, 1993–. *Recreation:* golf. *Address:* Beeches, Tyrrell's Wood, Leatherhead, Surrey KT22 8QH. *Club:* Royal Air Force.

SEDDON, Richard Harding, PhD; RWS 1976 (ARWS 1972); ARCA; artist and writer; President, Royal Watercolour Society, since 1995; *b* 1 May 1915; *s* of Cyril Harding Seddon; *m* 1946, Audrey Madeline Wareham. *Educ:* King Edward VII School; Roy. Coll. of Art; Univ. of Reading (PhD 1946). Demonstrator in Fine Art, Univ. of Reading, 1944; Extra-Mural Staff Tutor in Fine Art, Univ. of Birmingham, 1947; Director, Sheffield City Art Galleries, 1948–63; Curator, Ruskin Collection, 1948–63; Dir of Art History and Liberal Studies, Sch. of Design and Furniture, Buckinghamshire Coll. of Higher Educn, 1963–80. Hon. Advisory Panel, Hereford Art Galls, 1948; Arts Council Selection Bd (Art Students Exhib.), 1947; Pres. Ludlow Art Soc., 1947–67; Hon. Member: Sheffield Soc. of Artists; Oxford Folk Art Soc.; Sheffield Photographic Soc.; Mem., Oxford Bureau for Artists in War-time, 1940; Chm. Selection Cttee, Nottingham Artists Exhibition, 1953; Guest Speaker Educational Centres Association Annual Conference, 1951; West Riding Artists Exhibition Selection Committee, 1956; Northern Young Artists Exhibition Selection Committee, 1958; Member Sheffield Univ. Court; Sheffield Diocesan Advisory Cttee, 1948. Exhibitor at: RA; NEAC; RI; RBA; Internat. Artists; Architectural Assoc.; RIBA; National Gallery (War Artists) 1943; Leicester Galleries; Redfern Galleries. Official acquisitions: V. & A. Museum, 1939; Pilgrim Trust, 1942; Imperial War Museum (War Artists), 1943, 1956 (ten paintings); Graves Gall., Sheffield, 1943 and 1956; Atkinson Gall., Southport, 1953; Reading Art Gall., 1956; Leeds Education Cttee Collection, 1956. Extra Mural and Univ. Extension lectr on art to Univs of Oxford, Birmingham, London and Sheffield, 1948–; initiated Sheffield Conference on Nation's Art Treasures, 1958; FMA, 1951–74; Mem. Yorkshire Fed. Museums and Art Galls, 1948 (Committee 1952 and 1957, President, 1954–55, Vice-President, 1955–56); Secretary Yorks Museums Regional Fact Finding Committee, 1959; National Art Collections Fund Rep. for Yorks, 1954–63; Judge for Wakefield Art Galls Open Art Competition, 1984. Hon. Adviser to Co. of Cutlers in Hallamshire, 1950–64; Dep. Chm., Sheffield Design Council for Gold, Silver and Jewelry Trades, 1960; Mem. BBC '51 Soc., 1960; Mem. Govg Council, Design and Res. Centre, 1960; Mem. Art Adv. Cttee Yorks Area Scheme for Museums and Art Galleries, 1963; Art Critic: Birmingham Post, 1963–71; Yorkshire Post, 1974–92; Jl Fedn of British Artists, 1975–83; Mem. Recognised Panel of London Univ. Extension Lectrs, 1964; Mem. Council and Hon. Treasurer, 1976, Trustee, 1983–86, RWS; Hon. Treas., Artists' League of GB, 1984–86. Hon. Mem., Mark Twain Soc., USA, 1976. War Service with RAOC Field Park, France, 1940 (King's Badge); facilities by War Office Order to make war drawings in Maginot Line, 1940. *Publications:* The Technical Methods of Paul Nash (Memorial Vol.), 1949; The Artist's Vision, 1949; The Academic Technique of Oil Painting, 1960; A Hand Uplifted (war memoirs), 1962; Art Collecting for Amateurs, 1964; (ed) Dictionary of Art Terms, 1981; The Artist's Studio Book, 1983; articles on fine art for Jl of Aesthetics (USA), Burlington Magazine, Apollo, The Studio, The Connoisseur, Arch. Review, The Artist, The Antique Collector and daily press; lectures on art in England and abroad; criticisms; book reviews; broadcasts. *Recreation:* gardening. *Address:* 6 Arlesey Close, Putney, SW15 2EX. *T:* 0181–788 5899.

SEDGEMORE, Brian Charles John; MP (Lab) Hackney South and Shoreditch, since 1983; *b* 17 March 1937; *s* of Charles John Sedgemore, fisherman; *m* 1964 (marr. diss.); one *s*. *Educ:* Newtown Primary Sch.; Heles Sch.; Oxford Univ. (MA). Diploma in public and social administration. Called to Bar, Middle Temple, 1966. RAF, 1956–58; Oxford, 1958–62. Administrative Class, Civil Service, Min. of Housing and Local Govt, 1962–66 (Private Sec. to R. J. Mellish, MP, then junior Minister of Housing, 1964–66). Practising barrister, 1966–74. MP (Lab) Luton West, Feb. 1974–1979; PPS to Tony Benn, MP, 1977–78. Researcher, Granada TV, 1980–83. *Publications:* The How and Why of Socialism, 1977; Mr Secretary of State (fiction), 1979; The Secret Constitution, 1980; Power Failure (fiction), 1985; Big Bang 2000, 1986; Pitiless Pursuit (fiction), 1994; Insider's Guide to Parliament, 1995; one time contributor to Britain's top satirical magazine. *Recreation:* sleeping on the grass. *Address:* 71 Riverside Close, Hackney, E5 9SR; House of Commons, SW1A 0AA.

SEDGMAN, Francis Arthur, AM 1980; Lawn Tennis Champion: Australia, 1949, 1950; USA, 1951, 1952; Wimbledon, 1952; Italy, 1952; Asia, 1952; Professional Tennis Player since 1953; *b* Victoria, Australia, 29 Oct. 1927; *m* 1952, Jean Margaret Spence; four *d*. *Educ:* Box Hill High School, Vic, Australia. First played in the Australian Davis Cup team, 1949; also played in winning Australian Davis Cup team, 1950, 1951, 1952. With John Bromwich, won Wimbledon doubles title, 1948; with Kenneth McGregor, won the Australian, French, Wimbledon and American doubles titles in the same year (1951), the only pair ever to do so; with Kenneth McGregor also won Australian, French and Wimbledon doubles titles, 1952; with Doris Hart, won French, Wimbledon and US mixed doubles titles, 1952. Last male player to win three titles at Wimbledon in one year,

1952. Director of many private companies. USA Hall of Fame, 1987; Australian Hall of Fame, 1988. *Publication:* Winning Tennis, 1955. *Recreations:* golfing, racing. *Address:* 19 Bolton Avenue, Hampton, Victoria 3188, Australia. *T:* (3) 5986341. *Clubs:* All England Tennis and Croquet, Queen's; Melbourne Cricket (Melbourne); Kooyong Tennis; Grace Park Tennis; Victoria Amateur Turf, Victoria Racing; Royal Melbourne Golf, Carbine (Melbourne); Mornington Racing (Mem. Cttee).

SEDGWICK, (Ian) Peter; Vice-Chairman, Schroders, since 1995; *b* 13 Oct. 1935; *m* 1956, Verna Mary Churchward; one *s* one *d.* National Westminster Bank, 1952–59; Ottoman Bank, 1959–69; J. Henry Schroder Wagg & Co., 1982–89; Schroder Investment Management, 1985–; Schroders, 1987–; Dir, Equitable Life Assurance Soc. *Recreation:* golf. *Address:* Burrows Dene, Tilford Road, Farnham, Surrey GU9 8JA.

SEDGWICK, Nina, (Mrs A. R. M. Sedgwick); *see* Milkina, N.

SEDGWICK, Peter; *see* Sedgwick, I. P.

SEDGWICK, Peter Norman; Head of Education, Training and Employment Group, HM Treasury, since 1994; *b* 4 Dec. 1943; *s* of Norman Victor Sedgwick and Lorna Clara (*née* Burton); *m* 1984, Catherine Jane, *d* of Mr and Mrs B. D. T. Saunders; two *s* two *d.* *Educ:* Westminster Cathedral Choir Sch.; Downside; Lincoln Coll., Oxford (MA PPE, BPhilEcon). HM Treasury: Economic Asst, 1969; Economic Adviser, 1971; Sen. Economic Adviser, 1977; Under Sec., 1984; Hd of Internat. Finance Gp, 1990–94. Chm. 1979–84, Mem. Develt Cttee 1984–, London Symphony Chorus. *Recreation:* singing. *Address:* c/o HM Treasury, Parliament Street, SW1P 3AG.

SEDLEY, David Neil, PhD; FBA 1994; Reader in Ancient Philosophy, University of Cambridge, since 1989; Fellow, Christ's College, Cambridge, since 1976; *b* 30 May 1947; *s* of William Sedley and Rachel Sedley (*née* Seifert); *m* 1973, Beverley Anne Dobbs; two *s* one *d.* *Educ:* Westminster Sch.; Trinity Coll., Oxford (BA Lit. Hum. 1969; MA 1973); University Coll. London (PhD 1974). Dyson Jun. Res. Fellow in Greek Culture, Balliol Coll., Oxford, 1973–75; University of Cambridge: Asst Lectr in Classics, 1975–78; Lectr, 1978–89. Editor, Classical Qly, 1986–92. *Publications:* (with A. A. Long) The Hellenistic Philosophers, 2 vols, 1987; articles in classical and philosophical jls and collaborative vols. *Recreation:* vegetable growing. *Address:* Christ's College, Cambridge CB2 3BU. *T:* Cambridge (01223) 334910; 97 Hills Road, Cambridge CB2 1PG. *T:* Cambridge (01223) 368845.

See also Hon. Sir S. J. Sedley.

SEDLEY, Hon. Sir Stephen (John), Kt 1992; **Hon. Mr Justice Sedley;** a Judge of the High Court of Justice, Queen's Bench Division, since 1992; *b* 9 Oct. 1939; *s* of William and Rachel Sedley; *m* 1968, Ann Tate (separated); one *s* two *d.* *Educ:* Mill Hill Sch. (entrance schol.); Queens' Coll., Cambridge (open schol./exhibnr; BA Hons 1961). Freelance writer, interpreter, musician, translator, 1961–64; called to the Bar, Inner Temple, 1964, Bencher, 1989; QC 1983; Pres., Nat. Reference Tribunals for the Coalmining Industry, 1983–88. Chm., Sex Discrimination Cttee, Bar Council, 1992–. Vis. Professorial Fellow, Warwick Univ., 1981; Vis. Fellow, Osgoode Hall Law Sch., Canada, 1987; Distinguished Visitor, Hong Kong Univ., 1992; Hon. Professor: Univ. of Wales, Cardiff, 1993–; Univ. of Warwick, 1994–. Paul Sieghart Meml Lect., 1995. A Dir, Public Law Project, 1989–93; Hon. Vice-Pres., Administrative Law Bar Assoc., 1992–. Mem., Internat. Commn on Mercenaries, Angola, 1976. Sec., Haldane Soc., 1964–69. FRSA 1991. *Publications:* (trans.) From Burgos Jail, by Marcos Ana and Vidal de Nicolas, 1964; (ed) Seeds of Love (anthology), 1967; Whose Child? (report of inquiry into death of Tyra Henry), 1987; (ed) A Spark in the Ashes: writings of John Warr, 1992; contributed: Orwell: inside the myth, 1984; Civil Liberty, 1984; Police, the Constitution and the Community, 1986; Challenging Decisions, 1986; Public Interest Law, 1987; Civil Liberties in Conflict, 1988; Law in East and West, 1988; Citizenship, 1991; contrib. DNB: Missing Persons; London Review of Books, Public Law, Modern Law Review, Jl of Law and Soc., Civil Justice Qly, Law Qly Review, Industrial Law Jl. *Recreations:* carpentry, music, cycling, walking, changing the world. *Address:* c/o Royal Courts of Justice, Strand, WC2A 2LL.

See also D. N. Sedley.

SEDOV, Leonid I.; 6 Orders of Lenin, Hero of Socialist Labour, USSR; Professor, Moscow University, since 1937; Chief of Department of Hydrodynamics, since 1941; Member, Russian Academy of Sciences; *b* 14 Nov. 1907; *m* 1931, Galya Tolstova; one *s* one *d.* *Educ:* Moscow University. Chief Engineer, Associate Chief lab., N.E. Zhukovsky Aerohydrodynamic Inst., Moscow, 1930–47; Vice-President, International Astronautical Federation, 1962–80 (Pres., 1959–61); Internat. Astronautical Acad., 1980–. Hon. Member: American Academy of Arts and Sciences; Internat. Astronautical Acad.; Serbian Academy, Belgrade; Tech. Academy, Finland; For. Associate, Acad. of Sciences, Paris; Academia Leopoldina. Hon. doctorates from many foreign universities. Medal of Obert; State Prize; Chaplygin Prize; Lomonosov Prize; Lyapunov Medal; Guggenheim Award; Van Allen Award. Commandeur de la Légion d'Honneur (France). *Publications:* Theory of Plane Flow of Liquids, 1939; Plane Problems of Hydrodynamics and Aerodynamics, 1950, 1966, 1980; Similarity and Dimensional Methods in Mechanics, 1944, 1951, 1953, 1957, 1960, 1965, 1967, 1977; Introduction into the Mechanics of Continua, 1962; Mechanics of Continuous Media, 2 vols, 1970, 1973, 1976, 1983–84; Thoughts about Science and Scientists, 1980; (with A. G. Tsypkin) Fundamentals of Electromagnetical and Gravitational Macroscopic Theories, 1989; numerous articles. *Address:* Moscow University, Zone I, kv 84 Leninskie Gory, Moscow 119899, Russia.

SEEAR, family name of **Baroness Seear.**

SEEAR, Baroness *cr* 1971 (Life Peer), of Paddington; **Beatrice Nancy Seear,** PC 1985; formerly Reader in Personnel Management, University of London, The London School of Economics, retired 1978, Hon. Fellow, 1980; Deputy Leader, Liberal Democrats (formerly Social & Liberal Democrats), House of Lords, since 1988 (Liberal Leader, 1984–88); *b* 7 Aug. 1913; *d* of late Herbert Charles Seear and Beatrice Maud Catchpole. *Educ:* Croydon High Sch.; Newnham Coll., Cambridge (Hon. Fellow, 1983); London Sch. of Economics and Political Science. BA (Cambridge Hist. Tripos). Personnel Officer, C. & J. Clark Ltd, shoe manufacturers, 1936–46; seconded as Mem. (pt-time), staff of Production Efficiency Bd at Min. of Aircraft Production, 1943–45; Teacher at London School of Economics, 1946–78. Vis. Prof. of Personnel Management, City Univ., 1980–87. Member: Hansard Soc. Commn on Electoral Reform, 1975–76; Top Salaries Review Body, 1971–84. Chm., Council, Morley Coll. President: BSI, 1974–77; Women's Liberal Fedn, 1974; Fawcett Soc., 1970–85; Inst. of Personnel Management, 1977–79; Carers Nat. Assoc. Mem. Council, Industrial Soc., 1972–84. Hon. LLD: Leeds, 1979; Exeter, 1989; Hon. DLit Bath, 1982. *Publications:* (with P. Jephcott and J. H. Smith) Married Women Working, 1962; (with V. Roberts and J. Brock) A Career for Women in Industry?, 1964; Industrial Social Services, 1964; The Position of Women in Industry, 1967; The Re-Entry of Women into Employment, 1971. *Recreations:* travel, gardening. *Address:* 189b Kennington Road, SE11 6ST. *T:* 0171–587 0205. *Clubs:* Commonwealth Trust, National Liberal.

SEED, John Junior, CEng, FIEE; Chief Executive, South Western Electricity plc, since 1992; *b* 25 Oct. 1938; *s* of John Seed and Elizabeth (*née* Earley); *m* 1961, Maureen Syder; two *d.* *Educ:* City of Norwich Grammar Sch.; Norwich City Coll. CEng 1972; FIEE 1986. Eastern Electricity: Dist Manager, Bury St Edmunds, 1976–80; Area Manager, Suffolk, 1980–82; Dir of Engrg, 1982–86; Dep. Chm., S Western Electricity Bd, 1986–90; Man. Dir, S Western Electricity plc, 1990–92. CIMgt (FBIM 1980). *Recreations:* golf, walking, bridge. *Address:* (office) 800 Park Avenue, Aztec West, Almondsbury, Bristol BS12 4SE. *T:* Almondsbury (01454) 201101.

SEEL, Derek, FDSRCS; FRCS; FRCA; Dental Postgraduate Dean, University of Bristol, since 1986; *b* 2 April 1932; *s* of William Alfred and Olive Seel; *m* 1960, Gillian Henderson. *Educ:* Stockport Sch.; Manchester Univ. Inst. of Dental Surgery (BDS). MOrthRCS; FRCS 1994; FRCA 1995. General dental practice, 1956–62; orthodontic trainee, 1962–68; Lectr in Orthodontics, Bristol Univ., 1967–69; Consultant Orthodontist, Univ. of Wales Coll. of Medicine, 1969–; Consultant in Orthodontics, Welsh RHA, 1969–94. Dean, Faculty of Dental Surgery, RCS, 1990–92. Hon. DGDP 1994. *Recreations:* music, ski-ing, photography. *Address:* 20 Blenheim Road, Bristol BS6 7JP. *T:* Bristol (0117) 973 6635.

SEELY, family name of **Baron Mottistone.**

SEELY, Sir Nigel (Edward), 5th Bt *cr* 1896; Dorland International; *b* 28 July 1923; *s* of Sir Victor Basil John Seely, 4th Bt and of Sybil Helen, *d* of late Sills Clifford Gibbons; *S* father, 1980; *m* 1949, Loraine, *d* of late W. W. Lindley-Travis; three *d*; *m* 1984, Trudi Pacter, *d* of Sydney Pacter. *Educ:* Stowe. *Heir: half-b* Victor Ronald Seely [*b* 1 Aug. 1941; *m* 1972, Annette Bruce, *d* of Lt-Col J. A. D. McEwen; one *s* one *d*]. *Address:* 3 Craven Hill Mews, W2 3DY. *Clubs:* Buck's; Royal Solent.

SEENEY, Leslie Elon Sidney, OBE 1978; Director General (formerly General Secretary), National Chamber of Trade, 1971–87; *b* 19 Jan. 1922; *s* of Sidney Leonard and Daisy Seeney, Forest Hill; *m* 1947, Marjory Doreen Greenwood, Spalding; one *s.* *Educ:* St Matthews, Camberwell. RAFVR, 1941–46 (Flt Lt, Pilot). Man. Dir, family manufrg business (clothing), 1946–63, with other interests in insce and advertising. Mem., West Lewisham Chamber of Commerce, 1951, subseq. Sec. and Chm.; Delegate to Nat. Chamber of Trade, 1960; joined NCT staff, 1966. Mem., Home Office Standing Cttee on Crime Prevention, 1971–87. Council Member: (founding) Retail Consortium, 1971–87; Assoc. for Prevention of Theft from Shops, 1976–87. Fellow, Soc. of Assoc. Executives, 1970. *Publications:* various articles. *Recreations:* genealogy, travel, photography. *Address:* 16 Barn Close, Southcote, Reading, Berks RG30 3EE. *T:* Reading (01734) 575478.

SEENEY, Noel Conway; Commissioner of Stamp Duties, Queensland, 1975–86; *b* 7 April 1926; *s* of Percy Matthew Mark Seeney and Wilhelmina Augusta Zanow; *m* 1949, Valrae Muriel Uhlmann; two *d.* *Educ:* Teachers' Coll., Brisbane; Univ. of Queensland (BCom). Assoc. Accountancy, Assoc. Coll. of Preceptors, London. Teacher, 1944; Dep. Principal, Secondary Sch., 1960; Principal 1964; Official Sec., Office of Agent-General for Qld in London, 1969; Agent-General for Qld in London, 1973. *Recreations:* golf, tennis. *Address:* 20 Nawarra Street, Indooroopilly, Qld 4068, Australia. *Clubs:* United Service (Brisbane); Indooroopilly Golf.

SEETO, Sir (James Hip) Ling, Kt 1988; MBE 1975; Managing Director, Lingana Pty Ltd, Port Moresby, Papua New Guinea, since 1965; Director and part owner, Kwila Insurance Co., Port Moresby, since 1978; *b* 19 June 1933; *s* of Yeeying Seeto and Kamfoung Mack; *m* 1960, Anna Choiha Peng; two *s.* *Educ:* Rabaul Public Sch., PNG; Mowbray House Sch., Sydney, Australia; Trinity Grammar Sch., Sydney. Pings Co., Rabaul, PNG, 1954–58; Shell Co., Rabaul, 1958–62; Rabaul Metal Industries, Rabaul, 1962–64. Former Board Member: Nat. Investment and Develt Authy, PNG; PNG Develt Bank; Harbors Board; Water Resources Bd of PNG; Salvation Army Adv. Bd, PNG. A Youth Leader, Rabaul Methodist Ch., 1954–60. Silver Jubilee Medal, 1977; PNG Independence Medal, 1986. *Recreations:* golf, swimming, gardening, cooking. *Address:* PO Box 1756, Boroko, National Capital District, Papua New Guinea. *T:* (office) 254966, (home) 211873. *Clubs:* Cathay (Port Moresby) (Patron); Port Moresby Golf.

SEEYAVE, Sir René (Sow Choung), Kt 1985; CBE 1979; Group Chairman, Happy World Ltd, since 1986 (Group Managing Director, 1968–86); *b* 15 March 1935; *s* of late Antoine Seeyave, CBE and Lam Tung Ying; *m* 1961, Thérèse How Hong; one *s* four *d.* *Educ:* Royal College, Port Louis, Mauritius. Chm., Happy World Foods (formerly Mauritius Farms) Ltd, 1974–. Chm., Electricity Adv. Cttee, 1972–76. Vice Chairman: Mauritius Employers' Fedn, 1972; Mauritius Broadcasting Corp., 1980–81. Director: Mauritius Development Investment Trust Ltd, 1968–; Swan Insurance Co. Ltd, 1969–; Mauritius Marine Authority, 1980–. Vice-Chm. Council, Univ. of Mauritius, 1985–87. Hon. Pres., Heen Foh Soc., 1991–. *Address:* Happy World Ltd, Level 8, Happy World House, 37 Sir William Newton Street, Port Louis, Mauritius. *T:* 2086886, *Fax:* 2086699. *Clubs:* Mauritius Gymkhana, Port Louis City.

SEFTON, family name of **Baron Sefton of Garston.**

SEFTON OF GARSTON, Baron *cr* 1978 (Life Peer), of Garston in the County of Merseyside; **William Henry Sefton;** Chairman, North West Economic Planning Council, 1975–89; Vice-Chairman and Board Member, Warrington and Runcorn Development Corporation, 1981–85 (Chairman, 1974–81, Board Member, 1964–81, Runcorn Development Corporation); *b* 5 Aug. 1915; *s* of George and Emma Sefton; *m* 1940, Phyllis Kerr. *Educ:* Duncombe Road Sch., Liverpool. Joined Liverpool CC, 1953, Leader 1964; Chm. and Leader, Merseyside CC, 1974–77, Opposition Leader, 1977–79. Joined Runcorn Develt Corp., 1964, Dep. Chm. 1967. Member: New Towns Commn, 1978–85; SSRC, 1978. *Recreations:* gardening, woodwork. *Address:* House of Lords, SW1A 0PW.

SEGAL, Prof. Erich; Adjunct Professor of Classics, Yale University, 1981–88; Hon. Research Fellow, Classics, University College London, since 1982; Supernumerary Fellow, Wolfson College, Oxford, since 1985; *b* 16 June 1937; *s* of Samuel M. Segal, PhD, DHL and Cynthia Shapiro Segal; *m* 1975, Karen James; two *d* (one *s* decd). *Educ:* Harvard (Boylston Prize 1957, Bowdoin Prize 1959; AB 1958, AM 1959, PhD 1965). Teaching Fellow, Harvard, 1959–64; Lectr in Classics, Yale, 1964, Asst Prof., 1965–68, Associate Prof., 1968–73; Vis. Prof. in Classics: Munich, 1973; Princeton, 1974–75; Tel Aviv, 1976–77; Vis. Prof. in Comp. Lit., Dartmouth, 1976–78; Vis. Fellow, Wolfson Coll., Oxford, 1979–80, Mem. Common Room, 1984–. Member: Acad. of Literary Studies, USA, 1981; Nat. Adv. Council, 1970–72, Exec. Cttee, 1971–72, Peace Corps, USA (Presidential Commendation for Service to Peace Corps, 1971). Lectures: Amer. Philological Assoc., 1971, 1972; Amer. Comparative Lit. Assoc., 1971; German Classical Assoc., 1974; Boston Psychoanalytic Inst., 1974; Istituto Nazionale del Dramma Antico, Sicily, 1975; Brit. Classical Assoc., 1977; William Kelley Prentice Meml, Princeton, 1981; Inaugural Andrea Rosenthal Meml, Brown Univ., 1992. Author and narrator, The Ancient Games, 1972; TV commentator, ABC–TV, US, radio commentator in French, RTL Paris, Olympic Games, 1972 and 1976. Screenplays include: The Beatles' Yellow

Submarine, 1968; The Games, 1969; Love Story, 1970 (Golden Globe Award, 1970); Oliver's Story, 1978; Man, Woman and Child, 1983. Mem., Authors Guild. (With Mother Teresa and Peter Ustinov) Premio San Valentin di Terni, 1989. *Publications:* Roman Laughter: the comedy of Plautus, 1968, rev. edn 1987; (ed) Euripides: a collection of critical essays, 1968; (ed and trans.) Plautus: Three Comedies, 1969, rev. edn 1985; (ed) Oxford Readings in Greek Tragedy, 1983; (ed with Fergus Millar) Caesar Augustus: seven aspects, 1984; (ed) Plato's Dialogues, 1985; Oxford Readings in Aristophanes, 1995; *novels:* Love Story, 1970; Fairy Tale (for children), 1973; Oliver's Story, 1977; Man, Woman and Child, 1980; The Class, 1985 (Prix Deauville, France, and Premio Bancarella Selezione, Italy, 1986); Doctors, 1988; Acts of Faith, 1992; Prizes, 1995; articles and reviews in Amer. Jl of Philology, Classical World, Harvard Studies in Classical Philology, Classical Review, Greek, Roman and Byzantine Studies, TLS, New York Times Book Review, New Republic, The Independent, Washington Post. *Recreations:* swimming, athletics. *Address:* Wolfson College, Oxford OX2 6UD. *T:* Oxford (01865) 274100. *Clubs:* Athenæum; Harvard, Yale (New York).

SEGAL, Prof. Graeme Bryce, DPhil; FRS 1982; Lowndean Professor of Astronomy and Geometry, and Fellow of St John's College, Cambridge University, since 1990; *b* 21 Dec. 1941; *s* of Reuben Segal and Iza Joan Harris; *m* 1962, Desley Rae Cheetham (marr. diss. 1972). *Educ:* Sydney Grammar School; Univ. of Sydney (BSc 1962); Univ. of Cambridge; Univ. of Oxford (MA, DPhil 1967). Oxford University: Junior Res. Fellow, Worcester Coll., 1964–66; Junior Lectr in Mathematics, 1965–66; Fellow, St Catherine's Coll., 1966–90; Reader in Maths, 1978–89; Prof. of Maths, 1989–90. Mem., Inst. for Advanced Study, Princeton, 1969–70. Editor, Topology, 1970–90. *Publications:* (with A. Pressley) Loop Groups, 1986; articles in learned jls. *Address:* 16 Champneys Walk, Cambridge CB3 9AW. *T:* Cambridge (01223) 64263.

SEGAL, Prof. Judah Benzion, MC 1942; FBA 1968; Professor of Semitic Languages in the University of London, School of Oriental and African Studies, 1961–79, now Emeritus; *b* 21 June 1912; *s* of Prof. Moses H. Segal and Hannah Leah Segal; *m* 1946, Leah (*née* Seidemann); two *d.* *Educ:* Magdalen College School, Oxford; St Catharine's College, Cambridge. Jarrett Schol., 1932; John Stewart of Rannoch Schol., in Hebrew, 1933; 1st Cl. Oriental Langs Tripos, 1935; Tyrwhitt Schol. and Mason Prizeman, 1936; BA (Cambridge), 1935; MA 1938. Colours, Cambridge Univ. Boxing Club, 1935, 1936. Mansel Research Exhibitioner, St John's Coll., Oxford, 1936–39; James Mew Schol., 1937; DPhil (Oxon.), 1939. Deputy Assistant Director, Public Security, Sudan Government, 1939–41; served War of 1939–45, GHQ, MEF, 1942–44, Captain; Education Officer, British Military Administration, Tripolitania, 1945–46. Head of Dept of Near and Middle East, Sch. of Oriental and African Studies, 1961–68 (Hon. Fellow 1983); Visiting Lectr, Ain Shams Univ., Cairo, 1979; Res. Fellow, Hebrew Univ., Jerusalem, 1980; Leverhulme Emeritus Fellowship, S India, 1981. Principal, Leo Baeck Coll., 1982–85, Pres., 1985–. Mem., Council of Christians and Jews; President: North Western Reform Synagogue; British Assoc. for Jewish Studies, 1980; Vice-Pres., Reform Synagogues of GB, 1985–91. Freedom, City of Urfa, Turkey, 1973. *Publications:* The Diacritical Point and the Accents in Syriac, 1953; The Hebrew Passover, 1963; Edessa, 1970; Aramaic Texts From North Saqqara, 1983; A History of the Jews of Cochin, 1993; articles in learned periodicals. *Recreations:* walking, meditation. *Address:* 17 Hillersdon Avenue, Edgware, Mddx HA8 7SG. *T:* 0181–958 4993.

SEGAL, Michael John; District Judge (formerly Registrar), Principal Registry, Family Division, since 1985; *b* 20 Sept. 1937; *s* of Abraham Charles Segal and Iris Muriel (*née* Parsons); *m* 1963, Barbara Gina Fluxman; one *d.* *Educ:* Strode's Sch., Egham. Called to the Bar, Middle Temple, 1962. Practised at Bar, Midland and Oxford Circuit, 1962–84. Mem., Civil and Family Cttee, Judicial Studies Bd, 1990–94. Editor, Family Div. section, Butterworth's Cost Service, 1987–; Jt Editor, Supreme Court Practice, 1991–94. *Recreations:* reading, listening to music. *Address:* 28 Grange Road, N6 4AP. *T:* 0181–348 0680. *Club:* Athenæum.

SEGALL, Anne Celia, (Mrs D. H. Evans); Economics Correspondent, Daily Telegraph, since 1985; *b* 20 April 1948; *d* of John Segall and Marsha (*née* Greenberg); *m* 1973, David Howard Evans, *qv*; two *s.* *Educ:* St Paul's Girls' Sch.; St Hilda's Coll., Oxford (BA Hons PPE 1969); LSE. Econs, then Banking corresp., Investors' Chronicle, 1971–76; Banking correspondent: The Economist, 1976–80; Daily Telegraph, 1981–85. Wincott Award for Financial Journalism, 1975. *Recreations:* swimming, reading, theatre. *Address:* 24 Pembroke Gardens, W8 6HU. *T:* (office) 0171–538 5000. *Clubs:* Roehampton; Riviera Golf (France).

SEIFERT, Robin (also known as **Richard**); JP; FRIBA; Principal R. Seifert and Partners, Architects, since 1934; *b* 25 Nov. 1910; *s* of William Seifert; *m* 1939, Josephine Jeanette Harding; two *s* one *d.* *Educ:* Central Foundation Sch., City of London; University College, London (DipArch), Fellow, 1971. Commenced architectural practice, 1934. Corps of Royal Engineers, 1940–44; Indian Army, 1944–46; Hon. Lt-Col, 1946; Certif. for Meritorious Services Home Forces, 1943. Returned to private practice, 1948. Designed: ICI Laboratories, Dyestuffs Div., Blackley, Manchester; The Times Newspapers building, Printing House Square; Centre Point, St Giles Circus; Drapers Gardens, Nat. West. Bank Tower, City; The Royal Garden Hotel, Kensington; Tolworth Towers, Surbiton; Guiness Mahon Bank, Gracechurch Street; HQ of ICT, Putney; Kellogg House, Baker Street; Dunlop House, King Street, St James's; BSC Res. Labs, Middlesbrough; Britannia Hotel; Park Tower Hotel; London Heathrow Hotel; Sobell Sports Centre; ATV Centre, Birmingham; Central Television Complex, Nottingham; International Press Centre; Metropolitan Police HQ, Putney; Wembley Conference Centre; Princess Grace Hospital, Marylebone Road; Princess Margaret Hospital, Windsor; Churchill Hospital, Harrow; BUPA Hospital, Bushey; The Pirate Castle, Camden; British Rail HQ Offices, Euston Station. RIBA Architectural Exhibition (depicting 50 years of practice), Heinz Gall., 1984. Member: MoT Road Safety Council, 1969 (now disbanded); Home Office Cttee of Management, Housing Assoc. for Discharged Offenders; (part-time) British Waterways Bd, 1971–74; Council, RIBA, 1971–74. FRSA 1976. Liveryman, Glaziers' Co. City of London. JP Barnet, 1969. *Recreations:* chess, violin. *Address:* Eleventrees, Milespit Hill, Mill Hill, NW7 2RS. *T:* 0181–959 3397. *Clubs:* Army and Navy, City Livery, Arts.

SEIGNORET, Sir Clarence (Henry Augustus), GCB 1985; OBE 1966; Award of Honour, Dominica, 1993; President of the Commonwealth of Dominica, 1983–93; *b* 25 Feb. 1919; *s* of Clarence Augustus Seignoret and Violet Elizabeth (*née* Riviere); *m* 1950; two *s.* *Educ:* Dominica Grammar Sch.; Balliol Coll., Oxford. Civil Servant, 1936–77: Permanent Sec., 1956–67; Sec. to Cabinet, Hd of Civil Service, 1967–77; Administrator's Dep., Governor's Dep., Actg Pres. on six occasions, 1966–83. Exec. Sec., Dominica Assoc. of Industry and Commerce, 1980–83. Pres., Internat. Develt and Management Ltd, 1994–. Mem., Girl Guide Council of Dominica. Patron: Community Hostels Inc.; Nat. Develt Foundn of Dominica; Dominica Special Olympics. Kt Comdr Grand Cross of Grace, Order of Imperial Russian Order of St John of Jerusalem Ecumenical (Kt of Malta), 1992. Collar of Order of the Liberator (Simon Bolivar), Venezuela, 1987. *Recreations:* agriculture, horticulture. *Address:* 24 Cork Street, Roseau, Commonwealth of Dominica, West Indies. *T:* (office) 4498777; (home) 4482108. *Club:* Lions Club of Dominica (Hon. Mem.).

SEIPP, Walter, Dr jur; Chairman, Supervisory Board, Commerzbank AG, since 1991; *b* 13 Dec. 1925. *Educ:* Univ. of Frankfurt (Law studies); final legal examination and doctorate in Law, 1950–53. Military Service, 1943–45. Deutsche Bank AG, 1951–74: Exec. Vice Pres., 1970–74; Vice Chm., UBS–DB Corp., New York, 1972–74; Westdeutsche Landesbank Girozentrale, 1974–81: Mem. Bd, 1974–81, and Dep. Chm. of the Bd, 1977–81; Chm., Bd of Man. Dirs, Commerzbank AG, 1981–91; Member, Supervisory Board: Linde AG, 1983–; Hochtief AG, 1986–; MAN AG, 1986–; Thyssen AG, 1986–; Deutsche Shell AG, 1989–; Parker Hannifin Corp., Cleveland, 1992–; Parker Hannifin GmbH, Köln, 1993–. Pres., Internat. Monetary Conf., 1987–88. *Publications:* multiple. *Address:* Neue Mainzer Strasse 32–36, 60005 Frankfurt/Main, Germany. *T:* (69) 13620.

SEITZ, Raymond George Hardenbergh; a Senior Managing Director, Lehman Brothers, since 1995; *b* Hawaii, 8 Dec. 1940; *s* of Maj.-Gen. John Francis Regis Seitz and Helen Johnson Hardenbergh; two *s* one *d*; *m* 1985, Caroline Richardson. *Educ:* Yale University (BA History 1963). Joined Foreign Service, Dept of State, 1966; served Montreal, Nairobi, Bukavu, Zaire, 1966–72; Staff Officer, later Director, Secretariat Staff, Washington, Special Asst to Dir Gen., Foreign Service, 1972–75; Political Officer, London, 1975–79; Dep. Exec. Sec., Washington, 1979–81; Senior Dep. Asst Sec., Public Affairs, Washington, 1981–82; Exec. Asst to Secretary George P. Shultz, Washington, 1982–84; Minister and Dep. Chief of Mission, US Embassy, London, 1984–89; Asst Sec. for European and Canadian Affairs, State Dept, Washington, 1989–91; Ambassador to UK, 1991–94. Kt Comdr's Cross (Germany), 1991. *Address:* Lehman Brothers International (Europe), One Broadgate, EC2M 7HA.

SEKERS, David Nicholas Oliver, OBE 1986; FMA; Regional Director of National Trust, Southern Region, since 1989; *b* 29 Sept. 1943; *s* of Sir Nicholas Sekers, MBE and Lady Sekers; *m* 1965, Simone, *er d* of Moran Caplat, *qv*; one *d.* *Educ:* Eton: Worcester College, Oxford (BA). West Cumberland Silk Mills, 1965–73, Dir, 1968–73; Dir, Gladstone Pottery Museum (Museum of the Year 1976), 1973–78; Museum Dir, Quarry Bank Mill (Museum of the Year 1984), 1978–89. Mem., Crafts Council, 1984–86; Chm., Assoc. of Independent Museums, 1987–89. *Publications:* (booklet) Role of Museum Trustees, 1987; other booklets on Staffordshire pottery and the Potteries; articles for museum jls. *Recreations:* fishing, fell-walking. *Address:* c/o National Trust, Polesden Lacey, Dorking, Surrey RH5 6BD. *T:* Bookham (01372) 453401. *Club:* Garrick.

SELBORNE, 4th Earl of, *cr* 1882; **John Roundell Palmer,** KBE 1987; FRS 1991; DL; Baron Selborne, 1872; Viscount Wolmer, 1882; Chairman, Joint Nature Conservation Committee, since 1991; *b* 24 March 1940; *er s* of William Matthew, Viscount Wolmer (killed on active service, 1942), and of Priscilla (who *m* 1948, Hon. Peter Legh, later 4th Baron Newton), *d* of late Captain John Egerton-Warburton; *S* grandfather, 1971; *m* 1969, Joanna Van Antwerp, PhD, *yr d* of Evan Maitland James, *qv*; three *s* one *d.* *Educ:* Eton; Christ Church, Oxford (MA). Chm., AFRC, 1983–90 (Mem., 1975–90; Vice-Chm., 1980–83); Vice-Chm., Apple and Pear Develt Council, 1969–73; Mem., Hops Mkting Bd, 1972–82 (Chm., 1978–82); Pres., British Crop Protection Council, 1977–80; Chm., SE Regl Panel, MAFF, 1979–83. Member: Royal Commn on Environmental Pollution, 1993–; Govt Panel on Sustainable Develt, 1994–. Chairman: H of L Select Cttee on Sci. and Technol., 1993–; Sub-Cttee D (Agric. and Food), H of L Select Cttee on European Communities, 1991–93. Director: Agricl Mortgage Corp., 1990– (Chm., 1995–); Lloyds Bank, 1994–. President: South of England Agric. Soc., 1984; RASE, 1988; Royal Bath & West Agricl Soc., 1995; Vice-Pres., Foundn for Sci. and Technol., 1994–. Trustee, Royal Botanic Gardens, Kew, 1993–. Treas., Bridewell Royal Hosp. (King Edward's Sch., Witley), 1972–83. Mem., Hampshire County Council, 1967–74. FIBiol 1984; FRAgS 1986. Master, Mercers' Co., 1989–90. JP Hants 1971–78; DL Hants 1982. Hon. LLD Bristol, 1989; Hon. DSc Cranfield, 1991. *Heir: s* Viscount Wolmer, *qv*. *Address:* Temple Manor, Selborne, Alton, Hants GU34 3LR. *T:* Bordon (01420) 473646. *Club:* Brooks's.

SELBY, 4th Viscount, *cr* 1905; **Michael Guy John Gully;** *b* 15 Aug. 1942; *s* of 3rd Viscount and of Veronica, *er d* of late J. George and of Mrs Briscoe-George; *S* father, 1959; *m* 1965, Mary Theresa, *d* of late Capt. Thomas Powell, London, SW7; one *s* one *d.* *Heir: s* Hon. Edward Thomas William Gully [*b* 21 Sept. 1967; *m* 1992, Charlotte, *yr d* of Rolph Brege].

SELBY, Bishop Suffragan of, since 1991; **Rt. Rev. Humphrey Vincent Taylor;** *b* 5 March 1938; *s* of late Maurice Humphrey Taylor and of Mary Patricia Stuart Taylor (*née* Wood), now Pearson; *m* 1965, Anne Katharine Dart; two *d.* *Educ:* Harrow School; Pembroke College, Cambridge (MA); London University (MA). Nat. Service Officer, RAF, 1956–58; Cambridge 1958–61; College of the Resurrection, Mirfield, 1961–63; Curate in London, 1963–66; Rector of Lilongwe, Malaŵi, 1967–71; Chaplain, Bishop Grosseteste Coll., Lincoln, 1971–74; Sec. for Chaplaincies in Higher Education, Gen. Synod Bd of Education, 1974–80; Mission Programmes Sec., USPG, 1980–84; Sec., USPG, 1984–91. Hon. Canon of Bristol Cathedral, 1986–91; Provincial Canon of Southern Africa, 1989–. Moderator, Conf. for World Mission, BCC, 1987–90. *Recreations:* music, gardening. *Address:* 10 Precentor's Court, York YO1 2EJ. *T:* York (01904) 656492.

SELBY, Rt. Rev. Peter Stephen Maurice, PhD; William Leech Professorial Fellow in Applied Christian Theology, University of Durham, since 1992; Hon. Assistant Bishop, dioceses of Durham and Newcastle, since 1992; *b* 7 Dec. 1941. *Educ:* Merchant Taylors' School; St John's Coll., Oxford (BA 1964, MA 1967); Bishops' Coll., Cheshunt. PhD (London) 1975. Asst Curate, Queensbury, 1966–68; Assoc. Director of Training, Southwark, 1969–73; Asst Curate, Limpsfield with Titsey, 1969–77; Vice-Principal, Southwark Ordination Course, 1970–72; Asst Missioner, Dio. Southwark, 1973–77; Canon Residentiary, Newcastle Cathedral, 1977–84; Diocesan Missioner, Dio. Newcastle, 1977–84; Suffragan Bishop of Kingston-upon-Thames, 1984–92. *Publications:* Look for the Living, 1976; Liberating God, 1983; Belonging, 1991; Rescue, 1995. *Address:* Department of Theology, University of Durham, Abbey House, Palace Green, Durham DH1 3RS.

SELBY, Ralph Walford, CMG 1961; HM Diplomatic Service, retired; *b* 20 March 1915; *e s* of late Sir Walford Selby, KCMG, CB, CVO; *m* 1947, Julianna Snell (*d* 1994); three *d.* *Educ:* Eton; Christ Church, Oxford. Entered HM Diplomatic Service, Sept. 1938; served in Foreign Office until Oct. 1939. Enlisted in Army and served with Grenadier Guards, March 1940–Feb. 1945, when returned to Foreign Office; seconded to Treasury for service in India as First Secretary in Office of High Commissioner for UK, Sept. 1947; transferred to The Hague, 1950; returned to FO, 1953–56; transf. to Tokyo as Counsellor, 1956, to Copenhagen in 1958, to Djakarta in 1961, to Warsaw in 1964; Chargé d'Affaires in 1952, 1958, 1959, 1960, 1961, 1962, 1964, 1965, 1969, 1970; Consul-Gen., Boston, 1966–69; Minister, British Embassy, Rome, 1969–72; Ambassador to Norway, 1972–75. *Recreations:* beagling, sail cruising, hill walking. *Address:* Mengeham House, Mengham Lane, Hayling Island, Hants PO11 9JX. *Clubs:* MCC; Royal Yacht Squadron (Cowes).

SELBY WRIGHT, Very Rev. Ronald (William Vernon); *see* Wright.

SELDON, Arthur, CBE 1983; economist and writer; a Founder President, Institute of Economic Affairs, since 1990; Founder Editor, Economic Affairs, since 1980; *b* 29 May 1916; *m* Audrey Marjorie, *d* of Wilfred Willett and Eileen Willett (*née* Stenhouse) three *s*. *Educ:* Dempsey St Elementary Sch., Stepney; Raine's Foundation Sch. (State Scholar); LSE. BCom 1937 (1st cl. hons). Army service in Africa and Italy, 1942–45. Editor, Store, 1946–49; economist in industry, 1949–1959; Editorial Dir, Inst. of Economic Affairs, 1957–88; Chm., Liberal Party Cttee on the Aged, 1948–49; Mem., BMA Cttee on Health Financing, 1968–70; Adviser, Australian Cabinet Cttee on Welfare, 1968; Vice-Pres., Mont Pélerin Soc., 1980–86; Founder Trustee, Social Affairs Unit, 1980. Member of advisory board: Jl of Post-Misesian Economics (Washington), 1983–; Inst für Bildungs- und Forschungspolitik (Cologne), 1983–; Libertariansk Allianse (Oslo), 1983–; Ludwig von Mises Institut (Brussels), 1983–. Hon. DSocSc Francisco Marroguin, Guatemala, 1995. *Publications:* Pensions in a Free Society, 1957; (with Lord Harris of High Cross) Advertising in a Free Society, 1959; Pensions for Prosperity, 1960; Everyman's Dictionary of Economics (with F. G. Pennance), 1965, 2nd edn 1976; After the NHS, 1968; The Great Pensions Swindle, 1970; Charge, 1977; (with Lord Harris of High Cross) Over-ruled on Welfare 1963–78, 1979; Corrigible Capitalism, Incorrigible Socialism, 1980; Wither the Welfare State, 1981; Socialism Explained, 1983 (US edn as Socialism: the grand delusion, 1986); (ed) The New Right Enlightenment, 1985; The Riddle of the Voucher, 1986; (with Lord Harris of High Cross) Welfare Without the State, 1987; Capitalism, 1990 (Fisher Prize, 1991); The State is Rolling Back, 1994; (contrib.) Democracy and Public Choice: essays in honour of Gordon Tullock, ed C. K. Rowley, 1987. *Recreations:* writing, cricket, opera, parties for non-conformists. *Address:* The Thatched Cottage, Godden Green, Sevenoaks, Kent TN15 0HR. *T:* Sevenoaks (01732) 761499.

SELF, Hugh Michael, QC 1973; a Recorder, 1975–93; *b* 19 March 1921; *s* of Sir (Albert) Henry Self, KCB, KCMG, KBE; *m* 1950, Penelope Ann, *d* of late John Drinkwater, poet and dramatist and Daisy (*née* Kennedy), violinist; two *d*. *Educ:* Lancing Coll.; Worcester Coll., Oxford (BA). Royal Navy, 1942–46, Lieut RNVR 1946. Called to Bar, Lincoln's Inn, 1951, Bencher, 1980. *Recreations:* golf, walking in England, literature. *Address:* 59 Maresfield Gardens, Hampstead, NW3 5TE. *T:* 0171–435 8311. *Club:* Savile.
See also Prof. P. J. O. Self.

SELF, Prof. Peter John Otter; Emeritus Professor of Public Administration, University of London; Visiting Fellow, Australian National University, since 1984; *b* 7 June 1919; *s* of Sir (Albert) Henry Self, KCB, KCMG, KBE; *m* 1st, 1950, Diana Mary Pitt (marr. diss.); 2nd, 1959, Elaine Rosenbloom Adams (marr. diss.); two *s*; 3rd, 1981, Sandra Guerita Gough (*née* Moiseiwitsch). *Educ:* Lancing Coll.; Balliol Coll., Oxford (MA). Editorial staff of The Economist, 1944–62; Extra-mural Lectr, London Univ., 1944–49; Lectr in Public Administration, LSE, 1948–61; Reader in Political Science, LSE, 1961–63; Prof. of Public Admin, Univ. of London, 1963–82; Sen. Res. Fellow, ANU, 1982–84. Dir of Studies (Administration), Civil Service Dept, 1969–70. Chm., Australian Govt Inquiry into Local Govt Finance, 1984–85. Mem. Exec. and Coun., 1954, Vice-Chm. Exec., 1955, Chm. Exec., 1961–69, Chm. Council, 1979–82, Town and Country Planning Assoc.; Mem., SE Regional Economic Planning Coun., 1966–79. Hon. Mem., RTPI. *Publications:* Regionalism, 1949; Cities in Flood: The Problems of Urban Growth, 1957; (with H. Storing) The State and the Farmer, 1962; Administrative Theories and Politics, 1972; Econocrats and the Policy Process, 1976; Planning the Urban Region, 1982; Political Theories of Modern Government, 1985; Government by the Market?, 1993; numerous articles on administration, politics and planning. *Recreations:* walking, golf, story-telling. *Address:* 7 Hobbs Street, O'Connor, ACT 2601, Australia. *T:* (62) 477383. *Club:* Reform.
See also H. M. Self.

SELIGMAN, Madron; *see* Seligman, R. M.

SELIGMAN, Sir Peter (Wendel), Kt 1978; CBE 1969; BA; FIMechE; *b* 16 Jan. 1913; *s* of late Dr Richard Joseph Simon Seligman and of Hilda Mary Seligman; *m* 1937, Elizabeth Lavinia Mary Wheatley; two *s* four *d*. *Educ:* King's Coll. Sch., Wimbledon; Harrow Sch.; Kantonschule, Zürich; Caius Coll., Cambridge. Joined APV Co. Ltd, as Asst to Man. Dir, 1936; appointed Dir, 1939; Man. Dir, 1947; Dep. Chm., 1961; Chm., APV Holdings Ltd, 1966–77. Director: St Regis International Ltd, 1973–83 (Vice-Chm., 1981–83); EIBIS International Ltd, 1980–90; Bell Bryant Pty Ltd, 1976–80; St Regis ACI Pty Ltd, 1980–84. Mem., Engineering Industries Council, 1975–77. Chm., Nat. Ski Fedn of GB, 1977–81. *Recreations:* travelling, carpentry, boating. *Address:* King's Lea, King's Saltern Road, Lymington, Hants SO41 3QF. *T:* Lymington (01590) 676569. *Clubs:* South Africa; Royal Lymington Yacht; Hawks (Cambridge); Ski of Great Britain (Invitation Life Mem.); Kandahar Ski (Chm., 1972–77; Hon. Mem.).
See also R. M. Seligman.

SELIGMAN, (Richard) Madron, CBE 1994; *b* 10 Nov. 1918; 4th *s* of late Dr Richard Seligman, FCGI, FIM, and Hilda Mary (*née* MacDowell); *m* 1947, Nancy-Joan, *d* of Julian Marks; three *s* one *d*. *Educ:* Rokeby Sch., Wimbledon; Harrow Sch.; Balliol Coll., Oxford (BA (Hons) PPE; MA). Oxford Univ. ski team, 1938–39; President, Oxford Union, 1940. Served war, 6th Armoured Divisional Signals, N Africa and Italy, 1941–46, Major 1945. Chm., Incinerator Company, Eaton Socon, 1960–88. MEP (C) Sussex W, 1979–94. Vice Pres., European Energy Foundn, 1982–94. *Recreations:* tennis, ski-ing, gardening, piano, sailing. *Address:* Micklepage House, Nuthurst, near Horsham, Sussex RH13 6RG. *T:* Horsham (01403) 891533 or 891259. *Clubs:* Royal Thames Yacht, Royal Institute of International Affairs, MCC.
See also Sir Peter Seligman.

SELKIRK, Earldom of; *succession not determined at time of going to press.*

SELL, Anthony Lawrence; Chief Executive, British Tourist Authority, since 1993; *b* 19 April 1943; *s* of late Richard Geoffrey Sell and Zena Warren Sell (*née* Goddard); *m* 1975, Susan Constance; two *s* one *d*. *Educ:* Berkhamsted; Christ's Coll., Cambridge (Open Schol., MA); Univ. of Wisconsin (Fulbright Schol.); London Business Sch. (MSc). ICI Organics Div., 1965–67; Booz Allen & Hamilton Internat., 1969–73; Internat. Investment Corp. for Yugoslavia, 1973–74; Foseco Internat. Exports, 1974–78; Man. Dir, Kemwell, 1978–82; Commercial Dir, Metalchem Internat., 1982–86; Exec. Dir, Boosey & Hawkes, 1986–89; Pres.-Dir-Gen., Buffet Crampon, 1986–88; Man. Dir, Continental Europe, Thomas Cook Gp, 1989–93 (Pres., Chm., Mem., Thomas Cook subsidiaries, France, Switzerland, Netherlands, Italy, Sweden, Czechoslovakia). Mem., London Tourist Bd, 1993–. Gov., Warwick Sch., 1983–85. FRSA; MInstD. *Recreations:* music, the clarinet, occasional golf. *Address:* British Tourist Authority, Thames Tower, Black's Road, W6 9EL. *T:* 0181–563 3031.

SELLARS, John Ernest, CBE 1994; CEng; CMath; FIMA, FRSA; MRAeS; Chief Executive, Business and Technology (formerly Business and Technician) Education Council, 1983–94; *b* 5 Feb. 1936; *s* of late Ernest Buttle Sellars and of Edna Grace Sellars; *m* 1958, Dorothy Beatrice (*née* Morrison); three *d*. *Educ:* Wintringham Grammar Sch., Grimsby; Manchester Univ. (BSc, MSc). Research Engineer, English Electric (GW) Ltd, 1958–61; Lectr, Royal College of Advanced Technology (now Univ. of Salford), 1961–67; Head of Mathematics, Lanchester College of Technology, Coventry, 1967–71; Head of Computer Science, Lanchester Polytechnic, Coventry/Rugby, 1971–74; Chief Officer, Business Educn Council, 1974–83. Member: Bd, Nat. Adv. Body for Public Sector Higher Educn, 1982–88; BBC School Broadcasting Council for UK, 1982–87; City Technology Colls Trust, 1989–94; Engrg and Technol. Adv. Cttee, British Council, 1990–; Engrg Council, 1994– (Mem., Standing Cttee for Engrg Profession, 1994–). Mem. Exec. Cttee, RoSPA, 1994–. Governor, London Guildhall Univ., 1994–. FInstD. Hon. FCP 1989. DUniv Sheffield Hallam. *Publications:* papers on mathematics, computer science and business educn. *Recreation:* walking. *Address:* 306 Cassiobury Drive, Watford WD1 3AW. *Club:* Reform.

SELLERS, Basil Alfred; Chairman and Chief Executive, Gestetner Holdings, 1987–93; *b* 19 June 1935; *s* of William Alfred Sellers and Irene Ethel Sellers (*née* Freemantle); *m* 2nd, 1980, Gillian Clare Heinrich; two *s* one *d* from previous marr. *Educ:* King's College, Adelaide, SA. Clerk, State Bank of SA, 1952; Clerk, Cutten & Harvey, Adelaide, 1954–69 (Investment Advr, 1969); owner, Devon Homes, SA, 1970; bought Ralph Symonds Ltd, 1975 (Man. Dir). *Recreations:* cricket, art, music. *Address:* 22 Chester Street, Belgravia, SW1X 7BL. *T:* 0171–245 9694. *Clubs:* Cricketers'; University (Australia).

SELLERS, Geoffrey Bernard; CB 1991; Parliamentary Counsel, since 1987; *b* 5 June 1947; *s* of late Bernard Whittaker Sellers and Elsie (*née* Coop); *m* 1971, Susan Margaret Faulconbridge (*d* 1995); two *s* two *d*. *Educ:* Manchester Grammar Sch. (Scholar); Magdalen Coll., Oxford (Mackinnon Scholar; BCL 1st Cl. Hons; MA). Called to the Bar, Gray's Inn, 1971 (Macaskie Scholar). Legal Assistant: Law Commn, 1971; Commn on Industrial Relations, 1971–74; joined Office of Parly Counsel, 1974; with Law Commn, 1982–85, and 1991–93. *Address:* 36 Whitehall, SW1A 2AY. *Club:* Royal Automobile.

SELLERS, Philip Edward; Chairman, Pegasus Group, since 1992; *b* 20 March 1937; *s* of George Edward and Helen Sellers; *m* 1962, Brenda Anne Bell; two *s*. *Educ:* Ernest Bailey Grammar School, Matlock; CIPFA. Local Govt, 1953–72; Controller of Audit, British Gas Corp., 1972–76; Finance Dir, North Thames Gas, 1976–80; Dir of Finance and Planning, British Rail Board, 1980–84; Board Mem. for Corporate Finance and Planning, Post Office, 1984–89. Mem., Postel Property Cttee, 1992–94; non-exec. Dir, Postel Investment Management, 1994–95; Trustee, Post Office Pension Funds, 1985–. Non-Executive Chairman: CSL Group, 1989–93; Inner City Enterprises, 1992–; non-exec. Dir, Etam Gp, 1991–; Chm., CFM Ltd, 1989–. UK rep., IFAC Public Sector Cttee, 1987–90; Philip Sellers Communications and Consultancy, 1989–. Mem., NCC Impact Adv. Bd, 1989–. Pres., CIPFA, 1985–86; Chm., Nationalised Industries Finance Panel, 1986–89; Mem., Audit Cttee, DTI, 1994–. Non-exec. Dir, London Festival Orch., 1994–. *Recreations:* tennis, ski-ing. *Address:* Yarrimba, 31 Howards Thicket, Gerrards Cross, Bucks SL9 7NT. *T:* Gerrards Cross (01753) 884669.

SELLERS, Robert Firth, ScD; FRSE; MRCVS; consultant on foreign animal diseases; *b* 9 June 1924; *s* of Frederick Sellers and Janet Walkinshaw Shiels; *m* 1951, Margaret Peterkin; one *s* one *d*. *Educ:* Christ's Hospital; Gonville and Caius Coll., Cambridge (MA, ScD); Royal (Dick) School of Veterinary Studies, Edinburgh (PhD, BSc). FIBiol. Served War, Royal Artillery, 1943–46. Research Institute (Animal Virus Diseases), Pirbright, 1953–58; Wellcome Research Laboratories, Beckenham, 1958–62; Instituto Venezolano de Investigaciones Cientificas, Venezuela, 1962–64; Animal Virus Research Institute, Pirbright, 1964–84, Dep. Dir, 1964–79, Dir, 1979–84; Consultant, Foreign Animal Disease Unit, Agriculture, Canada, 1985–88. J. T. Edwards Meml Medal, 1976. *Publications:* papers on animal viruses in scientific jls. *Recreation:* archaeology. *Address:* 4 Pewley Way, Guildford, Surrey GU1 3PY.

SELLIER, Robert Hugh, FICE; Chief Executive, Y. J. Lovell, since 1991; *b* 15 Nov. 1933; *s* of Major Philip Joseph Sellier and Lorna Geraldine Sellier (*née* Luxton); *m* 1st, 1963, Cynthia Ann Dwelly (*d* 1985); one *d*; 2nd, 1987, Gillian Dalley (*née* Clark). *Educ:* St Joseph's Coll., Oxford; King's Coll., Durham Univ. (BScCivEng). FIHT. Man. Dir, New Ideal Homes, 1972–74; Dep. Man. Dir, Cementation International, 1974–79; Man. Dir, Cementation Construction, 1979–83; Chm., Cementation Gp of Companies, 1983–86; Gp Man. Dir, George Wimpey, 1986–91. Non-Exec. Dir, Welsh Water, 1993–. *Recreations:* ski-ing, shooting, scuba, flying. *Address:* Archers, Summersales Hill, London Road, Crowborough, East Sussex TN6 1UT. *T:* Crowborough (01892) 663413.

SELLORS, Patrick John Holmes, LVO 1990; FRCS; Surgeon-Oculist to the Queen, since 1980; Ophthalmic Surgeon, King Edward VIIth Hospital for Officers, since 1975; *b* 11 Feb. 1934; *s* of Sir Thomas Holmes Sellors, DM, MCh, FRCP, FRCS; *m* 1961, Gillian Gratton Swallow; two *s* one *d*. *Educ:* Rugby Sch.; Oriel Coll., Oxford; Middlesex Hosp. Med. School. MA Oxon; BM, BCh Oxon 1958; FRCS 1965. Registrar, Moorfields Eye Hosp., 1962–65; recognised teacher in Ophthalmology, St George's Hosp., 1966; Ophthalmic Surgeon: St George's Hosp., 1965–82 (Hon., 1983); Croydon Eye Unit, 1970–94; Surgeon-Oculist to HM Household, 1974–80; Hon. Consultant Ophthalmic Surgeon, St Luke's Hosp. for the Clergy, 1983–. Sec. to Ophthalmic Soc. of UK, 1970–72; Examr for Diploma of Ophthalmology, 1974–77; Pres., Ophthalmology Section, RSocMed, 1992–94; Vice-Pres., Coll. of Ophthalmologists, 1992– (Mem. Council, 1988–); Member, Council: Faculty of Ophthalmologists, 1977–88; Med. Defence Union, 1977–; Gen. Optical Council, 1978–. Dep. Master, Oxford Congress, 1991. *Publications:* (jtly) Outline in Ophthalmology, 1985; articles in BMJ and Trans OSUK. *Recreations:* gardening, golf. *Address:* 149 Harley Street, W1N 2DE. *T:* 0171–935 4444.

SELLS, Oliver Matthew; QC 1995; a Recorder of the Crown Court, since 1991; *b* 29 Sept. 1950; *s* of late Sir David Perronet Sells and Beryl Cecilia Sells (*née* Charrington); *m* 1986, Lucinda Jane, *d* of late Gerard William Mackworth-Young and Lady Eve Mackworth-Young; one *s* one *d*. *Educ:* St Peter's, Seaford; Wellington Coll.; Coll. of Law, London. Mem., Hon. Soc. of Inner Temple, 1969–; called to the Bar, Inner Temple, 1972; SE Circuit, 1974–; Supplementary Counsel to the Crown, 1981–86. Member: Gen. Council of the Bar, 1977–80 and 1986–91; Commonwealth Law Assoc.; Hon. Mem., Amer. Bar Assoc.; Dir, Music for Charity. *Recreations:* shooting, cricket, fishing. *Address:* 5 Paper Buildings, Temple, EC4Y 7HB. *T:* 0171–583 6117. *Clubs:* Boodle's, MCC; Norfolk (Norwich).

SELLY, Susan, (Mrs Clifford Selly); *see* Strange, S.

SELSDON, 3rd Baron, *cr* 1932, of Croydon; **Malcolm McEacharn Mitchell-Thomson;** Bt 1900; banker; *b* 27 Oct. 1937; *s* of 2nd Baron Selsdon (3rd Bt, *cr* 1900), DSC; *S* father, 1963; *m* 1965, Patricia Anne, *d* of Donald Smith; one *s*. *Educ:* Winchester College. Sub-Lieut, RNVR. Deleg. to Council of Europe and WEU, 1972–78. C. T. Bowring Gp, 1972–76; Midland Bank Group, 1976–90: EEC Advr, 1979–85; Public Finance Advr, 1985–90. Dir of various companies. Chm., Committee for Middle East Trade (COMET), 1979–86; Member: BOTB, 1983–86; E European Trade Council, 1985–87. Pres., British Exporters Assoc., 1990–. Chm., Greater London and SE Regional Council for Sport and Recreation, 1977–83. *Recreations:* rackets, squash, tennis, lawn tennis, ski-ing, sailing. *Heir:* *s* Hon. Callum Malcolm McEacharn Mitchell-Thomson, *b* 7 Nov. 1969. *Address:* c/o House of Lords, SW1A 0PW. *Club:* MCC.

SELWOOD, Maj.-Gen. David Henry Deering; His Honour Judge Selwood; a Circuit Judge, since 1992; *b* 27 June 1934; *s* of Comdr George Deering Selwood, RN, and Enid Marguerite Selwood (*née* Rowlinson); *m* 1973, Barbara Dorothea (*née* Hütter); three *s* one *d*. *Educ:* Kelly Coll., Tavistock; University College of the South-West; Law Society's School of Law. Articled to G. C. Aldhouse, Esq., Plymouth, 1952–57; admitted Solicitor 1957; National Service, RASC 2/Lieut, 1957–59; private practice, Plymouth, 1959–61; TA 4 Devons, Lieut, 1959–61; commnd Army Legal Services Staff List, 1961; service on legal staffs, MoD, Headquarters: BAOR, MELF, FARELF, UKLF, Land Forces Cyprus, 1961–85; Brig., Legal, HQ BAOR, 1986–90; Dir of Army Legal Services, MoD, 1990–92; Asst Recorder, SE Circuit, 1980, Recorder, 1985–92. Hon. Advocate, US Court of Military Appeals, 1972–. *Publication:* (jtly) Criminal Law and Psychiatry, 1987. *Address:* c/o Barclays Bank, PO Box 1353, Salisbury, Wilts SP1 2YH. *Club:* Army and Navy.

SELWYN, John Sidney Augustus, OBE 1962 (MBE 1939); HM Diplomatic Service, retired; *b* 17 Oct. 1908; *s* of Rev. A. L. H. Selwyn; *m* 1932, Cicely Georgina Armour (marr. diss.); one *s* one *d* (and one *d* decd); *m* 1952, Janette Bruce Mullin (*d* 1968); one *s*; *m* 1971, Sonja Fischer; one *d*. *Educ:* St Lawrence College, Ramsgate; Royal Military Coll., Sandhurst. Entered the Indian Police, 1928. Served in NWF Campaigns, 1930, 1937 and 1941. Major, 12th Frontier Force Regt, active service in Burma, 1942–46, Allied Control Commission, Germany, 1946–48. Entered Diplomatic Service, 1948. Served in Bucharest, Lisbon, London, Lima, Santos, Beirut; Consul-General: Berlin, 1963; Strasbourg, 1964–68; Vice-Consul, Calais, 1969–73. *Recreation:* walking. *Address:* Erlaufstrasse 35/2/6, 2344 Maria Enzersdorf-Südstadt, Austria. *Club:* Civil Service.

SEMKEN, John Douglas, CB 1980; MC 1944; Legal Adviser to the Home Office, 1977–83; *b* 9 Jan. 1921; *s* of Wm R. Semken and Mrs B. R. Semken (*née* Craymer); *m* 1952, Edna Margaret, *yr d* of T. R. Poole; three *s*. *Educ:* St Albans Sch.; Pembroke Coll., Oxford (MA, BCL). Solicitor's articled clerk, 1938–39. Commnd in Sherwood Rangers Yeo., 1940; 1st Lieut 1941, Captain 1942, Major 1944; 8th Armd Bde, N Africa, 1942–43; Normandy beaches to Germany, 1944. Called to Bar, Lincoln's Inn, 1949; practised at Chancery Bar, 1949–54; joined Legal Adviser's Br., Home Office, 1954; Mem., Criminal Law Revision Cttee, 1980–83. Silver Star Medal (USA), 1944. *Address:* 2 The Ridgeway, Mill Hill, NW7 1RS. *T:* 0181–346 3092. *Club:* Lawrenny Yacht.

SEMMENCE, Dr Adrian Murdoch, CB 1986; Civil Service Medical Adviser, 1979–86, retired; Medical Officer, Health Control Unit, Heathrow Airport, since 1993; Consultant, Cabinet Office (Office of the Minister for the Civil Service), since 1986; *b* 5 April 1926; *e s* of late Adrian George Semmence, MA, and Henrietta Scorgie Semmence (*née* Murdoch), MA; *m* 1949, Joan, *o d* of Hugh Wood and Bobbie (*née* Weatherill); four *s* one *d*. *Educ:* Robert Gordon's Coll.; Univ. of Aberdeen (MB, ChB 1953; MD 1957); Univ. of London (MSc 1972); DObstRCOG, FRCGP, DIH, FFOM. Served War, Pilot FAA 1943–44, RN 1944–47, Observer Trng, in mine-sweeping and Destroyer flotillas in Mediterranean and Channel (able seaman torpedoman). General Practitioner, E Yorks, Berks and Oxon, 1954–76; Upjohn Fellow, Univ. of Edinburgh, 1967; Nuffield Travelling Fellow, 1969–70; Unit of Clinical Epidemiology, Univ. of Oxford, 1970–76; Principal MO, CSD, 1976–79. FRSM (Pres. Sect. of Occupational Med., 1985–86). *Recreations:* pottering, rumination. *Address:* Stone Cottage, 13 High Street, Steventon, Abingdon OX13 6RZ. *T:* Abingdon (01235) 831527. *Clubs:* Royal Society of Medicine; Frilford Heath Golf (Abingdon).

SEMMENS, Victor William; Chairman and Partner, Eversheds Solicitors; *b* 10 Oct. 1941; *s* of Ronald William Semmens and Cecile Maude Semmens; *m* 1964, Valerie Elizabeth Norton; two *s*. *Educ:* Blundell's. Qualified Solicitor, 1964; Partner, Wells & Hurd, subseq. Eversheds, Nottingham, 1968–. *Recreations:* golf, tennis, ski-ing. *Address:* 14 Fletcher Gate, Nottingham NG1 2FX. *T:* Nottingham (0115) 950 6201. *Club:* Combined Services (Notts).

SEMPER, Very Rev. Colin (Douglas); Canon of Westminster, since 1987; *b* 5 Feb. 1938; *s* of William Frederick and Dorothy Anne Semper; *m* 1962, Janet Louise Greaves; two *s*. *Educ:* Lincoln School; Keble College, Oxford (BA); Westcott House, Cambridge. Curate of Holy Trinity with St Mary, Guildford, 1963–66; Recruitment and Selection Sec., ACCM, 1966–69; Head of Religious Programmes, BBC Radio, and Deputy Head of Religious Broadcasting, BBC, 1969–82; Provost of Coventry Cathedral, 1982–87. *Recreations:* travel, reading modern novels, canals. *Address:* 8 Little Cloister, Westminster Abbey, SW1P 3PL.

SEMPILL, family name of **Baron Sempill.**

SEMPILL, 21st Baron *cr* 1489; **James William Stuart Whitemore Sempill;** Director, Special Projects, Scottish & Newcastle, since 1995 (Trade Marketing Director, 1993–95); *b* 25 Feb 1949; *s* of Lady Sempill (20th in line), and Lt-Col Stuart Whitemore Chant-Sempill (*d* 1991); *S* mother, 1995; *m* 1977, Josephine Ann Edith, *e d* of J. Norman Rees, Johannesburg; one *s* one *d*. *Educ:* The Oratory School; St Clare's Hall, Oxford (BA Hons History, 1971); Hertford Coll., Oxford. Gallaher Ltd, 1972–80; PA to Man. Dir, Sentinel Engineering Pty Ltd, Johannesburg, 1980–81; Manager, TWS Public Relations Company, Johannesburg, 1981–83; investment manager, Alan Clarke and Partners, 1982–83; Marketing Manager, S African Breweries, 1983; Account Director: Bates Wells (Pty), 1986; Partnership in Advertising, Johannesburg, 1988–90; Client Service Dir, Ogilvy & Mather, Cape Town, 1990–92. *Heir: s* Master of Sempill, *qv*. *Clubs:* Vincent's, Carlton (Oxford); Edinburgh Academicals Football.

SEMPILL, Master of; Hon. Francis Henry William Forbes Sempill; *b* 4 Jan. 1979; *s* and *heir* of Baron Sempill, *qv*. *Educ:* Merchiston Castle Sch., Edinburgh.

SEMPLE, Prof. Andrew Best, CBE 1966; VRD 1953; QHP 1962; Professor of Community and Environmental Health (formerly of Public Health), University of Liverpool, 1953–77, now Professor Emeritus; *b* 3 May 1912; *m* 1941, Jean (*née* Sweet); one *d*. *Educ:* Allan Glen's School, Glasgow; Glasgow Univ. MB, ChB 1934, MD 1947, DPH 1936, Glasgow. FFCM 1972. Various hospital appointments, 1934–38; Asst MOH and Deputy Medical Superintendent, Infectious Diseases Hosp., Portsmouth, 1938–39; Asst MOH and Asst School Medical Officer, Blackburn, 1939–47 (interrupted by War Service); Senior Asst MOH, Manchester, 1947–48; Deputy MOH, City and Port of Liverpool, 1948–53, MOH and Principal Sch. Med. Officer, 1953–74; Area MO (teaching), Liverpool AHA, 1974–77. Served War of 1939–46; Surgeon Commander, RNVR; Naval MOH, Western Approaches, Malta and Central Mediterranean. Chm. Council and Hon. Treasurer, RSH, 1963. *Publications:* various regarding infectious disease, port health, hygiene, etc. *Address:* Kelvin, 433 Woolton Road, Gateacre, Liverpool L25 4SY. *T:* 0151–428 2081.

SEMPLE, Andrew Greenlees; Consultant, Samuel Montagu Ltd, since 1993; *b* 16 Jan. 1934; *s* of late William Hugh Semple and Madeline, *d* of late E. H. Wood, Malvern, Worcs; *m* 1961, Janet Elizabeth Whates (*d* 1993); one *s* one *d*. *Educ:* Winchester Coll.; St John's Coll., Cambridge (MA). Entered Min. of Transport and Civil Aviation, 1957; Private Sec. to Permanent Sec., 1960–62; Principal, 1962; Asst Sec., 1970; Private Sec. to successive Secs of State for the Environment, 1972–74; Under Sec., DoE, 1976; Principal Finance Officer, PSA, DoE, 1980–83; Sec., Water Authorities Assoc., 1983–87; Man. Dir, Anglian Water Authority, 1987–89; Gp Man. Dir, 1989–90, Vice-Chm., 1990–92, Anglian Water plc. Mem., Bd, Eureau, 1983–92. Chm., Huntingdonshire Enterprise Agency, 1990–. Gov., Huntingdonshire Regl Coll., 1992–. Hon. Mem., IWO (AWO, 1988). FCIWEM 1994. *Recreations:* reading, gardens, watching cricket. *Address:* 83 Burbage Road, SE24 9HB. *T:* 0171–274 6550; 3 Church Lane, Covington, Cambs PE18 0RT. *T:* Huntingdon (01480) 860497. *Club:* Surrey CC.

SEMPLE, John Laughlin, CB 1993; Permanent Secretary, Department of Finance and Personnel for Northern Ireland, since 1988; *b* 10 Aug. 1940; *s* of late James E. Semple and of Violet E. G. Semple; *m* 1970, Maureen Anne Kerr; two *s* one *d*. *Educ:* Campbell Coll., Belfast; Corpus Christi Coll., Cambridge (MA). BScEcon London. Joined Home CS as Asst Principal, Min. of Aviation, 1961; transf. to NI CS, 1962; Asst Principal, Mins of Health and Local Govt, Finance, and Health and Social Services, 1962–65; Dep. Principal, Min. of Health and Social Services, 1965; Principal: Min. of Finance, 1968; Min. of Community Relations, 1970–72; Asst Sec. (Planning), Min. of Develt, 1972; Asst Sec. (Housing), DoE, 1977–79; Under Sec. (Housing), DoE for N Ireland, 1979–83; Under Sec., Dept of Finance and Personnel for NI, 1983–88. *Recreations:* golf, tennis, gardening.

SEMPLE, Prof. Stephen John Greenhill, MD, FRCP; Professor of Medicine, and Head, Department of Medicine, University College and Middlesex School of Medicine, University College London, 1987–91, now Emeritus Professor; *b* 4 Aug. 1926; *s* of late John Edward Stewart and Janet Semple; *m* 1961, Penelope Ann, *y d* of Sir Geoffrey Aldington, KBE, CMG; three *s*. *Educ:* Westminster; London Univ. MB, BS, 1950, MD 1952, FRCP 1968. Research Asst, St Thomas' Hosp. Med. Sch., 1952; Jun. Med. Specialist, RAMC, Malaya, 1953–55; Instr, Med. Sch., Univ. of Pennsylvania, USA, 1957–59; St Thomas' Hosp. Medical Sch.: Lectr, 1959; Sen. Lectr, 1961; Reader, 1965; Prof. in Medicine, 1969; Prof. of Medicine, The Middlesex Hosp. Medical Sch., 1970–87. *Publications:* Disorders of Respiration, 1972; articles in: Lancet, Jl Physiol. (London), Jl Applied Physiol. *Recreations:* tennis, music. *Address:* White Lodge, 3 Claremont Park Road, Esher, Surrey KT10 9LT. *T:* Esher (01372) 465057. *Club:* Queen's.

SEN, Prof. Amartya Kumar, FBA 1977; Professor of Economics and Philosophy, since 1987 and Lamont University Professor, since 1988, Harvard University; *b* 3 Nov. 1933; *s* of late Dr Ashutosh Sen, Dhaka, and of Amita Sen, Santiniketan, India; *m* 1st, 1960, Nabaneeta Dev (marr. diss. 1975); two *d*; 2nd, 1978, Eva Colorni (*d* 1985); one *s* one *d*; 3rd, 1991, Emma Rothschild, *qv*. *Educ:* Calcutta Univ.; Cambridge Univ. MA, PhD. Prof. of Economics, Jadavpur Univ., Calcutta, 1956–58; Trinity Coll., Cambridge: Prize Fellow, 1957–61; Staff Fellow, 1961–63; Hon. Fellow, 1991; Professor of Economics: Delhi Univ., 1963–71 (Chm., Dept of Economics, 1966–68, Hon. Prof., 1971–); LSE, 1971–77; Oxford Univ., 1977–80; Fellow, Nuffield College, Oxford, 1977–80 (Associate Mem., 1980–89); Drummond Prof. of Political Economy, and Fellow, All Souls Coll., Oxford, 1980–88. Hon. Dir, Agricultural Economics Research Centre, Delhi, 1966–68 and 1969–71. Res. Advr, World Inst. for Develt Econ. Res., Helsinki, Finland, 1985–93. Vis. Professor: MIT, 1960–61; Univ. of Calif at Berkeley, 1964–65; Harvard Univ., 1968–69; Andrew D. White Professor-at-large, Cornell Univ., 1978–84. Chm., UN Expert Gp Meeting on Role of Advanced Skill and Technology, New York, 1967. President: Develt Studies Assoc., 1980–82; Econometric Soc., 1984 (Fellow 1968–, Vice-Pres. 1982–83); Internat. Economic Assoc., 1986–89; Indian Econ. Assoc., 1989; Amer. Econ. Assoc., 1994; Soc. for Social Choice and Welfare, 1993–94; Vice-Pres., Royal Economic Soc., 1988– (Mem. Council, 1977–87); Trustee, Inst. for Advanced Study, Princeton, 1987–. Foreign Hon. Mem., Amer. Acad. of Arts and Sciences, 1981; Hon. Mem., Amer. Econ. Assoc., 1981. Hon. Fellow: Inst. of Social Studies, The Hague, 1982; LSE, 1984; IDS, Sussex Univ., 1984. Hon. DLitt: Saskatchewan, 1980; Visva-Bharati Univ., 1983; Georgetown, 1989; Jadavpur, Kalyani, 1990; Williams Coll., City of London Poly., 1991; New Sch. for Social Res., NY, Calcutta, 1992; Syracuse, 1994; Hon. DHumLit, Oberlin Coll., 1993; Hon. DSc Bath, 1984; DU Essex, 1984; Dr *hc*: Caen, 1987; Bologna, 1988; Univ. Catholique de Louvain, 1989; Athens Univ. of Econs and Business, 1991; Valencia, Zurich, 1994; Hon. LLD: Tulane, 1990; Queen's Univ., Kingston, Ont., 1993. Agnelli Internat. Prize, 1990; Alan Shawn Feinstein World Hunger Award, 1990. *Publications:* Choice of Techniques, 1960, 3rd edn 1968; Growth Economics, 1970; Collective Choice and Social Welfare, 1971; On Economic Inequality, 1973; Employment, Technology and Development, 1975; Poverty and Famines: an essay on entitlement and deprivation, 1981; (ed with Bernard Williams) Utilitarianism and Beyond, 1982; Choice, Welfare and Measurement, 1982; Resources, Values and Development, 1984; Commodities and Capabilities, 1985; On Ethics and Economics, 1987; The Standard of Living, 1987; (with Jean Drèze) Hunger and Public Action, 1989; (ed with Jean Drèze) The Political Economy of Hunger, 3 vols, 1990–91; Inequality Re-examined, 1992; articles in various jls in economics, philosophy, political science, decision theory, demography and law. *Address:* Harvard University, Cambridge, MA 02138, USA. *T:* (617) 4951871.

SEN, Emma; *see* Rothschild, Emma.

SENDAK, Maurice Bernard; writer and illustrator of children's books; theatrical designer; Artistic Director, The Night Kitchen, national children's theater; *b* 10 June 1928; *yr s* of Philip Sendak and Sarah (*née* Schindler). *Educ:* Lafayette High School, Brooklyn; Art Students' League, NY. Worked part-time at All American Comics; window display work with Timely Service, 1946–48, F. A. O. Schwartz, 1948–50; illustrated over 50 books by other writers, 1951–. Retrospective one-man exhibitions: Sch. of Visual Arts, NY, 1964; Ashmolean, Oxford, 1975; Amer. Cultural Center, Paris, 1978. *Stage designs:* The Magic Flute, Houston, 1980; The Cunning Little Vixen, NY, 1981; The Love of Three Oranges, Glyndebourne, 1982, Where the Wild Things Are, NT, 1984; L'enfant et les sortilèges, L'Heure espagnole, Glyndebourne, 1987. Hon. RDI 1986. *Publications:* Kenny's Window, 1956; Very Far Away, 1957; The Sign on Rosie's Door, 1960; Nutshell Library set, 1962; Where the Wild Things Are, 1963 (Amer. Liby Assoc. Caldecott Medal, 1964; opera, by Oliver Knussen, Glyndebourne, 1984); Higglety Pigglety Pop!, 1967; Hector Protector, 1967; In the Night Kitchen, 1971; (with Charlotte Zolotow) Rabbit and the Lovely Present, 1971; Pictures, 1972; Maxfield Parrish Poster Book, 1974; (with Matthelo Margolis) Some Swell Pup, 1976; Charlotte and the White Horse, 1977; (ed) Disney Poster Book, 1977; Seven Little Monsters, 1977; (with Doris Orgel) Sarah's Room, 1977; Very Far Away, 1978; Outside Over There, 1981; (with Frank Corsaro) The Love for Three Oranges, 1984; (with Ralph Manheim) Nutcracker, 1984; Dear Mili, 1988; Caldecott and Company (essays), 1989; We are all in the Dumps with Jack and Guy, 1993. *Address:* c/o HarperCollins, 10 East 53rd Street, New York, NY 10022, USA.

SENDALL, Bernard Charles, CBE 1952; Deputy Director-General, Independent Broadcasting Authority (formerly Independent Television Authority), 1955–77; *b* 30 April 1913; *s* of late William Sendall, Malvern, Worcestershire; *m* 1963, Barbara Mary, *d* of late Ambrose Coviello, DCM, FRAM; one step *s*. *Educ:* Magdalen College, Oxford; Harvard University. Entered Civil Service in the Admiralty, 1935; Principal Private Secretary to Minister of Information 1941–45; Controller (Home), Central Office of Information,

1946–49; Controller, Festival of Britain Office, 1949–51; Assistant Secretary, Admiralty, 1951–55. *Publication:* Independent Television in Britain, vol. I, 1982, vol. II, 1983. *Address:* 144 Montagu Mansions, York Street, W1H 1LA.

SENIOR, (Alan) Gordon, CBE 1981; CEng, FICE, FIStructE; Managing Partner, Gordon Senior Associates, Engineering and Management Consultants, since 1980; *b* 1 Jan. 1928; *s* of late Oscar Senior and Helen Senior (*née* Cooper); *m* 1st, 1955, Sheila Lockyer (marr. diss. 1961); 2nd, 1968, Lawmary Mitchell (marr. diss. 1978); one *s*. *Educ:* Normanton Grammar School; Leeds Univ. (BSc 1948, MSc 1949). J. B. Edwards (Whyteleafe) Ltd, 1949–51; Oscar Faber & Partners, Consulting Engineers, 1951–54; W. S. Atkins & Partners, Consulting Engineers, 1954–80: Technical Dir, 1967; Man. Dir of Atkins Research and Development, 1972; Director, W. S. Atkins & Partners, 1976. Chairman: Surface Engineering and Inspection Ltd, 1983–86; Masta Corp. Ltd, 1987–91; Aptech Ltd, 1988–89; Director: Ansen Offshore Consultants Ltd and McMillan Sloan & Partners, 1981–84; Armstrong Technology Services Ltd, 1986. Member, Navy Dept Advisory Cttee on Structural Steels, 1967–71. Science and Engineering Research Council: Mem., Engineering Bd, 1974–78; Chm., Transport and Civil Engineering Cttee, 1974–78; Chm., Marine Technology Management Cttee, 1980–83. Department of Trade and Industry: Mem., Ship and Marine Technology Requirements Bd, and Chm., Marine Technology Cttee, 1976–81; Mem., Maritime Technology Cttee, 1981–86; Chm., Adv. Cttee on Resources from the Sea, 1983–86. Member: Dept of Energy Programme Cttee, Offshore Energy Technology Bd, 1978–85; HSE Offshore Safety and Tech. Bd, 1985–92. Chm., Greenwich Forum, 1991–; Vice-Pres. and Chm. of Council, Soc. for Underwater Technology, 1979–81. *Publications:* (co-author) Brittle Fracture of Steel Structures, 1970; papers on welding, fatigue, brittle fracture, design of steel structures, computer aided design and manufacture, and future developments offshore and in the oceans. *Recreations:* food and wine, travel, ski-ing. *Address:* 3 Briar Patch, Charterhouse, Godalming, Surrey GU7 2JB. *T:* Godalming (01483) 417781. *Club:* Athenæum.

SENIOR, Gordon; *see* Senior, A. G.

SENIOR, Olive Edith, JP, MPhil, SRN; Regional Nursing Officer, Trent Regional Health Authority, 1973–86; Fellow, Nottingham University, 1988; *b* 26 April 1934; *d* of Harold and Doris Senior, Mansfield, Notts. *Educ:* Harlow Wood Orthopaedic Hosp., 1949–52; St George's Hosp., Hyde Park Corner, 1952–56; City Hosp., Nottingham (Pt I, CMB 1956); Nottingham Univ. (HV Cert. 1957, MPhil 1978). Health Visitor, Notts CC, 1958–60; St George's Hosp., London (Ward Sister), 1960–63; S Africa, June-Dec. 1963; Forest Gate Hosp., London (SCM), 1964; St Mary's Hosp., Portsmouth (Asst Matron/Night Supt), 1964–66; NE Metropolitan Regional Hosp. Bd (Management Services), 1966–71; Chief Nursing Officer, Nottingham and Dist. Hosp. Management Cttee, 1971–73. Secretary of State Fellow, 1973. JP Nottingham Guildhall, 1973. *Publications:* An Analysis of Nurse Staffing Levels in Hospitals in the Trent Region (1977 Data), 1978; Dependency and Establishments, 1979; contrib. to Nursing Times (Determining Nursing Establishments). *Address:* 94 Oak Tree Lane, Mansfield, Notts NG18 3HL. *Club:* Nottingham University (Nottingham).

SENNITT, John Stuart; His Honour Judge Sennitt; a Circuit Judge, since 1994; *s* of late Stuart Osland Sennitt and Nora Kathleen Sennitt; *m* 1966, Janet Ann Freeman; one *s* two *d*. *Educ:* Culford Sch., Bury St Edmunds; St Catharine's Coll., Cambridge (MA, LLB). Admitted Solicitor, 1961; Partner, Wild, Hewitson & Shaw, Cambridge, 1963–83; County Court Registrar, then Dist Judge, 1983–94; Asst Recorder, 1988–92; a Recorder, 1992–94. *Address:* c/o South Eastern Circuit Office, New Cavendish House, 18 Maltravers Street, WC2R 3EU.

SENSI, His Eminence Cardinal (Giuseppe M.); *b* 27 May 1907. Ordained, 1929; Sec. of Apostolic Nunciature in Roumania, 1934–38; Secretary and Auditor of Apostolic Nunciature in Switzerland, 1938–46; Councillor of Apostolic Nunciature in Belgium, 1946–47; Chargé d'Affaires of the Holy See in Prague, 1948–49; Councillor in the Secretariat of State of His Holiness, 1949–53; Permanent Observer of the Holy See at UNESCO in Paris, 1953–55; apptd Nuncio Apostolic to Costa Rica, May 1955, and consecrated Titular Archbishop of Sardi, July 1955; Apostolic Delegate to Jerusalem, 1957; Apostolic Nuncio to Ireland, 1962–67; Apostolic Nuncio to Portugal, 1967–76; Cardinal, 1976. Chevalier, Grand Cross SMO Malta, 1959; Grand Cross, Santi Maurizio e Lazzaro, 1975; Grand Cross, Ordre Militaire du Christ (Portugal), 1976; Grand Cross, Ordre Equestre du St Sepolcre de Gerusalemme, 1978. Hon. Mem., Accademia Cosentina, 1976. *Address:* Piazza S Calisto 16, 00153 Rome, Italy. *T:* (6) 6987265/6987388/5897827.

SEPÚLVEDA, Bernardo, Hon. GCMG 1985; Ambassador of Mexico to the Court of St James's, 1989–93; *b* 14 Dec. 1941; *s* of Bernardo Sepúlveda and Margarita Amor; *m* 1970, Ana Yturbe; three *s*. *Educ:* Univ. of Mexico (Law Degree *magna cum laude*, 1964); Queens' Coll., Cambridge (LLB 1966; Hon. Fellow, 1990). Prof. of Internat. Law, El Colegio de México, 1967–81; Dep. Dir Gen. for Legal Affairs to Secretary of the Presidency, 1968–70; Asst Sec. for Internat. Affairs, Min. of the Treasury, 1976–80; Principal Advisor on Internat. Affairs to the Minister of Planning and Budget, 1981; Ambassador to USA, 1982; Minister of Foreign Relations, Mexico, 1982–88. Dr *hc* Univ. of San Diego, Calif, 1982; Univ. of Leningrad, 1987. Principe de Asturias Prize, Spain, 1984; Simón Bolívar Prize, UNESCO, 1985. Grand Cross, Order of: Civil Merit (Spain), 1979; Isabel the Catholic (Spain), 1983; Southern Cross (Brazil), 1983; Boyacá (Colombia), 1984; Merit (FRG), 1984; Liberator San Martín (Argentina), 1984; Vasco Núñez de Balboa (Panama), 1984; Manuel Amador Geurrero (Panama), 1985; Christ (Portugal), 1985; Crown (Belgium), 1985; Quetzal (Guatemala), 1986; Prince Henry the Navigator (Portugal), 1986; Sun (Peru), 1987; Rio Branco (Brazil), 1988; Grand Officier, Nat. Order of Legion of Honour (France), 1985; also orders and decorations from Korea, Venezuela, Poland, Yugoslavia, Greece, Japan, Egypt and Jamaica. *Publications:* The United Nations: dilemma at 25, 1970; Foreign Investment in Mexico, 1973; Transnational Corporations in Mexico, 1974; articles on internat. law in prof. jls. *Recreations:* reading, music. *Address:* c/o Mexican Embassy, 42 Hertford Street, W1Y 7TF. *Clubs:* Brooks's, Travellers'.

SERAFÍN, David; *see* Michael, I. D. L.

SERBY, John Edward, CB 1958; CBE 1951; FRAeS; Consultant; *b* 15 March 1902; *m* 1933, Clarice Lilian (*née* Hawes); one *d*. *Educ:* Haberdashers' Aske's School; Emmanuel College, Cambridge (BA). Junior Scientific Officer, Admiralty, 1927–30; Scientific Officer, RAE, 1930–38; Headquarters, MAP, 1938–50; Deputy Director, Royal Aircraft Establishment, Farnborough, 1950–54; Dir-Gen. of Guided Weapons, Min. of Aviation, 1954–61. Dep. Controller Guided Weapons, Ministry of Aviation, 1961–63. *Recreation:* gardening. *Address:* Overwey, Bishopsmead, Farnham, Surrey GU9 0HQ. *T:* Farnham (01252) 713526.

SERGEANT, Sir Patrick (John Rushton), Kt 1984; City Editor, Daily Mail, 1960–84; Founder, 1969, and Chairman, 1985–92, Euromoney Publications (Managing Director, 1969–85); *b* 17 March 1924; *s* of George and Rene Sergeant; *m* 1952, Gillian Anne Wilks, Cape Town; two *d*. *Educ:* Beaumont Coll. Served as Lieut, RNVR, 1945. Asst City Editor, News Chronicle, 1948; Dep. City Editor, Daily Mail, 1953. Director: Associated Newspapers Group, 1971–83; Daily Mail General Trust, 1983–; (non-exec.) Euromoney Publications, 1992–. Domus Fellow, St Catherine's Coll., Oxford, 1988. Freeman, City of London, 1987. Wincott Award, Financial Journalist of the Year, 1979. *Publications:* Another Road to Samarkand, 1955; Money Matters, 1967; Inflation Fighters Handbook, 1976. *Recreations:* skiing, tennis, swimming, talking. *Address:* One The Grove, Highgate Village, N6 6JU. *T:* 0181–340 1245. *Clubs:* Royal Automobile, Annabel's; All England Lawn Tennis and Croquet.

SERIES, Sir Emile; *see* Seriès, Sir J. M. E.

SERIES, Sir (Joseph Michel) Emile, Kt 1978; CBE 1974; FCIS, FAIA, FSCA, FREconS, FInstD, FRSA; Chairman and General Manager, Flacq United Estates Ltd and WEAL Group (West East Ltd), since 1968; *b* 29 Sept. 1918; *s* of late Emile Seriès and Julie (*née* Langlois); *m* 1942, Rose-Aimée Jullienne; two *s* two *d*. *Educ:* Royal Coll., Mauritius; London Univ. MCom Delhi Commercial Univ., 1967. FIMgt; FCCS 1958. Accounts Dept, General Electric Supply Co. of Mauritius Ltd, 1936–52 (final position, Chief Acct); Chief Acct and Econ. Adviser, Union Flacq Sugar Estate Ltd and Flacq United Estates Ltd, 1952–61; Manager, Union Flacq Sugar Estate Ltd, 1961–68. Chairman: Rogers & Co. Ltd; Alcohol & Molasses Co. Ltd; Compagnie Mauricienne de Commerce Ltd. Director: Maur. Commercial Bank Ltd; Anglo-Maur. Assurance Society Ltd, and other cos in Mauritius. Past President: Maur. Chamber of Agriculture; Maur. Sugar Industry Research Inst. Member: Maur. Sugar Producers' Assoc.; Maur. Sugar Syndicate; Amer. Management Assoc., New York; National Assoc. of Accts, New York. Chevalier de l'Ordre National du Mérite (France), 1978; Chevalier de la Légion d'Honneur, 1988. *Recreations:* sailing, shooting, photography, classical music, horse racing. *Address:* Flacq United Estates Ltd, Union Flacq, Mauritius. *T:* 532583 and 535535. *Clubs:* Dodo, Mauritius Turf, Le Morne Anglers', Grand'Baie Yacht (Mauritius).

SERJEANT, Graham Roger, CMG 1981; MD; FRCP; Director, Medical Research Council Laboratories, Jamaica, since 1974; *b* 26 Oct. 1938; *s* of Ewart Egbert and Violet Elizabeth Serjeant; *m* 1965, Beryl Elizabeth, *d* of late Ivor Edward King, CB, CBE. *Educ:* Sibford Sch., Banbury; Bootham Sch., York; Clare Coll., Cambridge (BA 1960, MA 1965); London Hosp. Med. Sch.; Makerere Coll., Kampala. MB BChir 1963, MD 1971, Cantab; MRCP 1966, FRCP 1977. House Physician: London Hosp., 1963–64; Royal United Hosp., Bath, 1965–66; RPMS, 1966; Med. Registrar, University Hosp. of WI, 1966–67; Wellcome Res. Fellow, Dept of Medicine, Univ. of WI, 1967–71; Medical Research Council: Mem., Scientific Staff, Abnormal Haemoglobin Unit, Cambridge, 1971–72; Epidemiology Res. Unit, Jamaica, 1972–74. Hon. Prof. Faculty of Medicine, Univ. of WI, 1981. *Publications:* The Clinical Features of Sickle Cell Disease, 1974; Sickle Cell Disease, 1985, 2nd edn 1992; numerous papers on the nat. hist. of sickle cell disease, in med. jls. *Recreation:* squash. *Address:* Medical Research Council Laboratories, University of the West Indies, Mona, Kingston 7, Jamaica, WI. *T:* 9272471, 9272984. *Club:* Liguanea (Kingston).

SERJEANT, William Ronald, FRHistS; County Archivist, Suffolk, 1974–82, retired; Vice-President, Society of Archivists, since 1988 (President, 1982–88); Hon. Archivist to the Lords de Saumarez and Tollemache; *b* 5 March 1921; *s* of Frederick William and Louisa (*née* Wood); *m* 1961, Ruth Kneale (*née* Bridson); one *s*. *Educ:* Univ. of Manchester (BA Hons History); Univ. of Liverpool (Dip. Archive Admin. and Study of Records). Archivist/Librarian: Univ. of Sheffield, Sheffield City Library, Liverpool Record Office, 1952–56; Librarian/Archivist, Manx Nat. Library and Archives, Dep. Dir, Manx Mus. and Nat. Trust, 1957–62; County Archivist, Notts, 1962–70; Jt County Bor. and County Archivist, Ipswich and E Suffolk, 1970–74. Member: Lord Chancellor's Adv. Council on Public Records, 1982–88; Suffolk Heraldry Soc., 1982–; Member, Executive Committee: Suffolk Local History Council, 1970–; Ipswich Film Soc., 1974–; Council Member: Suffolk Inst. of Archeology and History, 1970–90; Suffolk Records Soc., 1970–; British Records Soc., 1974–; Ipswich Building Preservation Trust, 1988–; British Assoc. for Local History, 1994– (Chm., 1988–91; Hon. Sec., Publications Cttee, 1988–); Trustee, Leiston Long Shop Museum, 1983–. Editor: Jl of the Manx Museum, 1957–62; The Suffolk Review, 1970–82; The Blazon (Suffolk Heraldry Soc.), 1984–88. *Publications:* The History of Tuxford Grammar School, 1969; (ed) Index to the Probate Records of the Court of the Archdeacon of Suffolk 1444–1700, 1979–80; (ed) Index to the Probate Records of the Court of the Archdeacon of Sudbury 1354–1700, 1984; articles in county and other local history periodicals. *Recreations:* walking, participation in local historical and heraldic studies and activities, theatre and cinema going; any gaps filled by reading novels. *Address:* 51 Derwent Road, Ipswich, Suffolk IP3 0QR. *T:* Ipswich (01473) 728997.

SERMON, Thomas Richard, FCIS; Chief Executive, Shandwick International, since 1990; *b* 25 Feb. 1947; *s* of Eric Thomas Sermon and Marjorie Hilda (*née* Parsons); *m* 1970, Rosemary Diane, *yr d* of Thomas Smith; one *s* one *d*. *Educ:* Nottingham High Sch. FCIS 1972. Crest Hotels, 1969–74; Good Relations Gp, 1974–79; Shandwick Consultants, 1979–90; Man. Dir, Shandwick Consulting Gp, 1987–88; Chief Exec., Shandwick Europe, 1988–90; public relns advr, Goldman Sachs Internat., 1992–; Director: Wrightson Wood Associates, 1994–; One Step Beyond, 1995–; Mem., PPP, 1993–. Mem., Nat. Adv. Council on Employment of People with Disabilities, 1994–. Mem. Council, C & G, 1993–. Vice-Pres., RADAR, 1987–; Mem. Exec. Cttee, London Fedn of Clubs for Young People, 1994– (Hon. Treas., 1995–). *Address:* Friars Well, Aynho, Banbury, Oxon OX17 3BG. *T:* Croughton (01869) 810284. *Clubs:* City of London, City Livery.

SEROTA, family name of **Baroness Serota.**

SEROTA, Baroness, *cr* 1967 (Life Peer), of Hampstead in Greater London; **Beatrice Serota,** DBE 1992; JP; a Deputy Speaker, House of Lords, since 1985; *b* 15 Oct. 1919; *m* 1942, Stanley Serota, BSc (Eng), FICE; one *s* one *d*. *Educ:* John Howard School; London School of Economics (BSc (Econ); Hon. Fellow, 1976). Member: Hampstead Borough Council, 1945–49; LCC for Brixton, 1954–65 (Chm., Children's Cttee, 1958–65); GLC for Lambeth, 1964–67 (Chief Whip). Baroness in Waiting, 1968–69; Minister of State (Health), Dept of Health and Social Security, 1969–70; Prin. Dep. Chm. of Cttees, and Chm., European Communities Select Cttee, H of L, 1986–92. Founder Chm., Commn for Local Admin, 1974–82; Member: Adv. Council in Child Care, and Central Training Council in Child Care, 1958–68; Adv. Council on Treatment of Offenders, 1960–64; Longford Cttee on "Crime—A Challenge to us all", 1964; Royal Commn on Penal System, 1964–66; Latey Cttee on Age of Majority, 1965–67; Adv. Council on Penal System, 1966–68, 1974–79 (Chm., 1976–79); Seebohm Cttee on Organization of Local Authority Personal Social Services, 1966–68; Community Relations Commn, 1970–76; BBC Complaints Commn, 1975–77; Governor, BBC, 1977–82. JP Inner London (West Central Division). Peerage conferred for services to children. Hon. DLitt Loughborough, 1983. *Recreations:* needlepoint, gardening, collecting shells. *Address:* The Coach House, 15 Lyndhurst Terrace, NW3 5QA.

See also N. A. Serota.

SEROTA, Daniel; QC 1989; a Recorder, since 1989; *b* 27 Sept. 1945; *s* of Louis and N'eema Serota; *m* 1970; two *d*. *Educ:* Carmel Coll.; Jesus Coll., Oxford (MA). Called to the Bar, Lincoln's Inn, 1969. *Address:* 3 King's Bench Walk North, Temple, EC4Y 7HR. *T:* 0171–797 8600.

SEROTA, Nicholas Andrew; Director of the Tate Gallery, since 1988; *b* 27 April 1946; *s* of Stanley Serota and Beatrice Serota (*see* Baroness Serota); *m* 1973, Angela Mary Beveridge (marr. diss. 1995); two *d. Educ:* Haberdashers' Aske's Sch., Hampstead and Elstree; Christ's Coll., Cambridge (BA); Courtauld Inst. of Art, London (MA). Regional Art Officer and Exhibn Organiser, Arts Council of GB, 1970–73; Dir, Museum of Modern Art, Oxford, 1973–76; Dir, Whitechapel Art Gallery, 1976–88. Chm., Visual Arts Adv. Cttee, British Council, 1992– (Mem., 1976–); Trustee: Public Art Develt Trust, 1983–87; Architecture Foundn, 1991–. Hon. Fellow, QMC 1988; Hon. FRIBA 1992. Hon. DLitt: City, 1990; Plymouth, 1993; Keele, 1994; Hon. Dr Arts City of London Polytechnic, 1990. *Address:* Tate Gallery, Millbank, SW1P 4RG. *T:* 0171–887 8000.

SERPELL, Sir David Radford, KCB 1968 (CB 1962); CMG 1952; OBE 1944; FCIT; Member, British Railways Board, 1974–82; *b* 10 Nov. 1911; 2nd *s* of Charles Robert and Elsie Leila Serpell, Plymouth; *m* 1st, Ann Dooley (marr. diss.); three *s*; 2nd, Doris Farr. *Educ:* Plymouth Coll.; Exeter Coll., Oxford (Hon. Fellow, 1992); Univ. of Toulouse (DèsL); Syracuse University, USA; Fletcher School of Law and Diplomacy, USA. (Fell.) Imp. Economic Cttee, 1937–39; Min. of Food, 1939–42; Min. of Fuel and Power, 1942–45; Under-Sec., HM Treasury, 1954–60; Dep. Sec., MoT, 1960–63; Second Sec., BoT, 1963–66; Second Permanent Sec., 1966–68; Second Sec., Treasury, 1968; Permanent Secretary: MoT, 1968–70; DoE, 1970–72. Private Sec. to Parly Sec., Ministry of Food, 1941–42; Principal Private Sec. to Minister of Fuel and Power, 1942–45. Chairman: Nature Conservancy Council, 1973–77; Ordnance Survey Review Cttee, 1978–79; Cttee on the Review of Railway Finances, 1982; Member: NERC, 1973–76; Council, National Trust, 1973–77. *Recreations:* walking, golf. *Address:* 25 Crossparks, Dartmouth, Devon TQ6 9HP. *T:* Dartmouth (01803) 832073. *Club:* United Oxford & Cambridge University.

SERVAN-SCHREIBER, Prof. Jean-Jacques; engineer, author, politician; Professor of Strategic Thinking and Chairman, International Committee, Carnegie-Mellon University, since 1985; *b* Paris, 13 Feb. 1924; *s* of late Emile Servan-Schreiber, journalist, and Denise Bresard; *m*; four *s. Educ:* Ecole Polytechnique, Paris. Served as US-trained fighter pilot, Free French Air Force, World War II. Diplomatic Editor of Le Monde, 1948–53; Founder and Editor of weekly news-magazine, L'Express, 1953–73. Deputy for Lorraine, French National Assembly, 1970–78; Minister of Reforms, June 1974. Pres., Region of Lorraine, 1975–78. Pres., Radical Party, 1971–79; Chm., World Center for Computer Literacy, Paris, 1981–85. Chm., Internat. Cttee, Carnegie-Mellon Univ., Pittsburgh, USA, 1986–. Holds military cross for valour, with bar. *Publications:* Lieutenant en Algérie, 1957 (Lieutenant in Algeria); Le Défi américain, 1967 (The American Challenge); Le Manifeste Radical, 1970 (The Radical Alternative); Le Défi mondial, 1980 (The World Challenge); Les Fossoyeurs, 1993 (The Gravediggers). *Address:* 825 Morewood Avenue (#M), Pittsburgh, PA 15213, USA.

SERVICE, Alastair Stanley Douglas, CBE 1995; writer, publisher and campaigner; Chairman, Wiltshire and Bath District Health Authority, since 1994; *b* 8 May 1933; *s* of late Douglas William Service and Evelyn Caroline (*née* Sharp); *m* 1st, 1959, Louisa Anne (*née* Hemming), *qv* (marr. diss. 1984); one *s* one *d*; 2nd, 1992, Zandria Madeleine Pauncefort. *Educ:* Westminster Sch.; Queen's Coll., Oxford. Midshipman, RNR, 1952–54. Director: McKinlay, Watson and Co. Ltd, Brazil, USA and London, 1959–64 (export finance); Seeley, Service and Co. Ltd (publishers), 1965–79; Municipal Journal Ltd, 1970–78. Hon. Parly Officer: Abortion Law Reform Assoc., organising passage of Abortion Act, 1964–67; Divorce Law Reform Union, organising passage of Divorce Reform Act, 1967–69; Chm., Birth Control Campaign, organising passage of NHS (Family Planning) Amendment Act, 1972, and NHS Reorganisation Act, 1973 (made vasectomy and contraception available free from NHS); involved in other parly campaigns, incl.: Town and Country Amenities Act, 1974; Children's Act, 1975; Public Lending Right for Authors; One-Parent Families. Family Planning Association: Chm., 1975–80; Gen. Sec., 1980–89; Vice-Chm., Health Educn Council, 1979–87; Dep. Chm. (Sec. of State appointee), Health Educn Authy, 1987–89. Chairman: Wilts and Bath Health Commn, 1992–; Wessex RHA, 1993–94. (Dir, 1990–94; Vice-Chm., 1992–93). Member: Nat. Cttee, Population Concern, 1973– (Chm., 1975–79); Nat. Cttee, Victorian Soc., 1976– (Chm., Publications Cttee, 1982–89); Hon. Sec., Action for River Kennet, 1990–. *Publications:* A Birth Control Plan for Britain (with Dr John Dunwoody and Dr Tom Stuttaford), 1972; The Benefits of Birth Control—Aberdeen's Experience, 1973; Edwardian Architecture and its Origins, 1975; Edwardian Architecture, 1977; The Architects of London from 1066 to Present Day, 1979; London 1900, 1979; (with Jean Bradbery) Megaliths of Europe, 1979; Lost Worlds, 1981; Edwardian Interiors, 1982; series editor, The Buildings of Britain, 1981–84, and author, Anglo-Saxon and Norman Buildings vol., 1982; Victorian and Edwardian Hampstead, 1989; The Standing Stones of Europe, 1993; articles in Arch. Rev., Guardian, etc. *Recreations:* looking at buildings (old, new and megalithic), opera (esp. Verdi and Bellini), cycling et al. *Address:* Swan House, Avebury, Wilts SN8 1RA. *Club:* Garrick.

SERVICE, Louisa Anne, JP; Joint Chairman: The Hemming Group (formerly The Municipal Group) of Companies, since 1976; Hemming Publishing Ltd, since 1987; *d* of late Henry Harold Hemming, OBE, MC, and Alice Louisa Weaver, OBE; *m* 1959, Alastair Stanley Douglas Service, *qv* (marr. diss. 1984); one *s* one *d. Educ:* private and state schs, Canada, USA and Britain; Ecole des Sciences Politiques, Paris; St Hilda's Coll., Oxford (BA and MA, PPE). Export Dir, Ladybird Appliances Ltd, 1957–59; Municipal Journal Ltd and associated cos: Financial Dir, 1966; Dep. Chm., 1974; Chm., Merchant Printers Ltd, 1975–80; Dir, Brintex Ltd, 1965–; Dir, Glass's Information Services Ltd, 1971, Dep. Chm. 1976–81, Chm., 1982–. Member: Dept of Trade Consumer Credit Act Appeals Panel, 1981–; Cttee of Magistrates, 1985–88; FIMBRA Appeals Panel, 1988–92; Cttee, Solicitors Complaints Bureau, 1992–93. JP Inner London Juvenile Courts, 1969; Chm., Hackney Youth Court, 1975–82, Westminster Juvenile Ct, 1982–88, Hammersmith and Fulham Juvenile Court, 1988–94, Camden Youth and Family Proceedings Ct, 1994–; JP Inner London (5) PSD, 1980–; Chairman: Exec. Cttee, Inner London Juvenile Courts, 1977–79; Inner London Juvenile Liaison Cttee, 1986–88 (Mem., 1980–86); Member: working party on re-org. of London Juvenile Courts, 1975; Inner London Family Proceedings Courts, 1991–; Inner London Youth Courts, 1992–; Inner London Magistrates' Cts Cttee, 1995–; Vice-Chm., Paddington Probation Hostel, 1976–86. Corres. mem., SDP Policy Gp on Citizens' Rights, 1982–89. Chm. Council, Mayer-Lismann Opera Workshop, 1976–91; Hon. Sec., Women's India Assoc. of UK, 1967–74. Dir, Arts Club Ltd, 1981–84; Mem. Management Council: Friends of Covent Garden, 1982–94; Haydn-Mozart Soc., 1988–93; Chm., Youth & Music, 1990– (Dir, 1988–90); Mem., E-SU Music Cttee, 1984–91. *Publications:* articles on a variety of subjects. *Recreations:* travel, and attractive and witty people including my family. *Address:* c/o Hemming Publishing Ltd, 32 Vauxhall Bridge Road, SW1V 2SS. *T:* 0171–973 6404.

See also J. H. Hemming.

SESHADRI, Prof. Conjeevaram Srirangachari, PhD; FRS 1988; Dean, School of Mathematics, SPIC Science Foundation, since 1989; *b* 29 Feb. 1932; *s* of C. Srirangachari and Chudamani; *m* 1962, Sundari; two *s. Educ:* Loyola College, Madras (BA Hons Maths Madras Univ. 1953); PhD Bombay Univ. 1958. Tata Institute of Fundamental Research: Student, 1953; Reader, 1961; Professor, 1963; Senior Professor, 1975–84; Sen. Prof., Inst. of Math. Scis, India, 1984–89. *Publications:* Fibres Vectorials sur les courtes algébriques, Asterisque, 96, 1982; Introduction to the Theory of Standard Monomials, 1985. *Recreation:* south Indian classical music. *Address:* School of Mathematics, SPIC Science Foundation, East Coast Chambers, IV Floor, 92 G. N. Chetty Road, T Nagar, Madras 600 017, India. *T:* (44) 8284232, 8284251; (home) (44) 4914534.

SESSFORD, Rt. Rev. George Minshull; Bishop of Moray, Ross and Caithness, 1970–93; *b* Aintree, Lancs, 7 Nov. 1928; *o s* of Charles Walter Sessford and Eliza Annie (*née* Minshull); *m* 1st, 1952, Norah (*d* 1985), *y d* of David Henry Hughes and Ellen (*née* Whitely); three *d*; 2nd, 1987, Joan Gwendoline Myra Black, *widow* of Rev. C. W. Black. *Educ:* Warbreck Primary Sch.; Oulton High and Liverpool Collegiate Schs; St Andrews Univ. (MA). Curate, St Mary's Cathedral, Glasgow, 1953; Chaplain, Glasgow Univ., 1955; Priest-in-Charge, Cumbernauld New Town, 1958; Rector, Forres, Moray, 1966. *Recreations:* Lanchester motor cars, donkey breeding, sailing. *Address:* Caladh No Sith, 33 Mellon Charles, Aultbea, Wester Ross IV22 2JL. *T:* Aultbea (01445) 731303.

SESSIONS, John, (John Marshall); actor, writer; *b* 11 Jan. 1953; *s* of John Marshall and Esmé Richardson. *Educ:* Univ. of Wales (MA). Plays and one-man shows, 1982–85; *television:* Spitting Image, 1986; Porterhouse Blue, 1987; A Day in Summer, 1988; Whose Line is it, Anyway?, 1988; Single Voices, 1990; Life with Eliza, 1992; The Soldier's Tale, 1993; A Tour of the Western Isles, 1993; Citizen Locke, 1994; one-man shows: New Year Show, 1988; On the Spot, 1989; Tall Tales, 1991; Likely Stories, 1994; *theatre:* The Life of Napoleon, Albery, 1987; The Common Pursuit, Phoenix, 1988; The American Napoleon, Phoenix, 1989; Die Fledermaus, Royal Opera House, 1990; Travelling Tales, Haymarket, 1991; Tartuffe, Playhouse, 1991; My Night with Reg, Royal Court, 1994; *films:* Princess Caraboo, 1994; In the Bleak Midwinter, 1995. *Recreation:* dinner parties. *Address:* c/o Markham & Froggatt, 4 Windmill Street, W1P 1HF. *T:* 0171–636 4412. *Club:* Groucho.

SESSIONS, John Lionel; His Honour Judge Sessions; a Circuit Judge, since 1992; Judge Advocate of the Fleet, since 1995; *b* 8 Jan. 1941; *s* of Geoffrey and Anita Sessions; *m* 1967, Patrizia Corinna Sanminiatelli; one *s* two *d. Educ:* King Edward's Sch., Birmingham; BRNC, Dartmouth. Joined RN, 1959; served in HM Ships incl. Venus, Roebuck, Protector, Agincourt and Leopard; Naval interpreter in Italian, 1966; Comdr, 1976; retd 1981. Called to the Bar, Middle Temple, 1972; in practice (Common Law), 1981–92; Recorder, 1989–92. Mem., Assoc. of Italian-Speaking Jurists. *Publication:* Naval Interpreters, 1972 (Italian edn). *Recreation:* sailing. *Address:* 2 Harcourt Buildings, Temple, EC4Y 9DB. *Clubs:* Anchorites; Bar Yacht; Royal London Yacht (Cowes).

SETCHELL, Marcus Edward, FRCSE, FRCS, FRCOG; Surgeon-Gynaecologist to the Queen, since 1990; Head of Department of Obstetrics and Gynaecology, St Bartholomew's Hospital, since 1984; *b* 4 Oct. 1943; *s* of late Eric Hedley Setchell and Barbara Mary (*née* Whitworth); *m* 1973, Dr Sarah French; two *s* two *d. Educ:* Felsted Sch.; Gonville and Caius Coll., Cambridge; St Bartholomew's Hosp. MA, MB BChir. Consultant Obstetrician and Gynaecologist, Bart's and Homerton Hosps, 1975–; Hon. Consultant Gynaecologist: King Edward VII Hosp. for Officers, 1982–; St Luke's Hosp. for Clergy, 1983–. Convener, Scientific Meetings, 1989–92, Mem. Council, 1994–, RCOG; Mem., Council, 1990–94, Pres., Section of Obstetrics and Gynaecology, 1994–95, RSocMed. *Publications:* (with R. J. Lilford) Multiple Choice Questions in Obstetrics and Gynaecology, 1985, 2nd edn 1991; Ten Teachers in Obstetrics and Gynaecology, 1990; (with E. E. Philipp) Scientific Foundations of Obstetrics and Gynaecology, 1991. *Recreations:* tennis, ski-ing, gardening, walking. *Address:* 149 Harley Street, W1N 2DE. *T:* 0171–935 4444. *Clubs:* Royal Society of Medicine, St Albans Medical; David Lloyd Tennis.

SETON, Sir Iain (Bruce), 13th Bt *cr* 1663 (NS), of Abercorn; *b* 27 Aug. 1942; *s* of Sir (Christopher) Bruce Seton, 12th Bt and of Joyce Vivien, *d* of late O. G. Barnard; *S* father, 1988; *m* 1963, Margaret Ann, *d* of Walter Charles Faulkner; one *s* one *d. Educ:* Colchester and Chadacre. Farming until 1972; mining, 1972–. *Heir: s* Laurence Bruce Seton [*b* 1 July 1968; *m* 1990, Rachel, *d* of Jeffery Woods]. *Address:* Bellavista, PO Box 253, Bridgetown, WA 6255, Australia. *T:* (97) 611349.

SETON, Sir James (Christall), 12th Bt *cr* 1683 (NS), of Pitmedden, Aberdeenshire; *b* 21 Jan. 1913; *s* of Christall Dougal Seton (*d* 1969), *g s* of Sir William Coote Seton, 7th Bt, and Sara Johnson Moore (*d* 1958); *S* kinsman, Sir Robert James Seton, 11th Bt, 1993; *m* 1939, Evelyn, *d* of Ray Hafer. Served US Army, 1943–46 (Corp.). Freemason (Patron, Eastern Star Chapter, 1961). *Recreations:* formerly golf, now hand weaving, calligraphy. *Heir: nephew* Charles Wallace Seton [*b* 25 Aug. 1948; *m* 1974, Rebecca, *d* of Robert Lawry]. *Address:* Otterbein Home, 585 North State Route 741, Lebanon, OH 45036–9551, USA.

SETON, Lady, (Julia), OBE 1989; VMH; (Julia Clements, professionally); author, speaker, international floral art judge; flower arrangement judge for RHS and National Association of Flower Arrangement Societies; *d* of late Frank Clements; *m* 1962, Sir Alexander Hay Seton, 10th Bt, of Abercorn (*d* 1963); no *c. Educ:* Isle of Wight; Zwicker College, Belgium. Organised and conducted first Judges' School in England at Royal Horticultural Society Halls; has since conducted many other courses for judges all over Europe. VMH, RHS, 1974. *Publications:* Fun with Flowers; Fun without Flowers; 101 Ideas for Flower Arrangement; Party Pieces; Flower Arranging for All Occasions; Flower Arrangements in Stately Homes; Julia Clements' Gift Book of Flower Arranging; Flowers in Praise; The Art of Arranging a Flower, etc; My Life with Flowers, 1993. *Address:* 122 Swan Court, SW3 5RU. *T:* 0171–352 9039. *Clubs:* Women's Press, Royal Anglo-Belgian.

SETSHOGO, Boithoko Moonwa; Managing Director, Merchandising Associates Pty Ltd; Chairman, Via Afrika Pty Ltd; *b* Serowe, 16 June 1941; *m* 1971, Jennifer Tlalane; two *d. Educ:* Moeng Coll.; Univ. of Botswana, Lesotho and Swaziland (BA). District Officer, Kanye, 1969–70; First Sec., High Commn, London, 1970–72; Clerk to the Cabinet, 1972–73; Under-Sec., Min. of Commerce and Industry, 1973–75; High Comr of Botswana in London, 1975–78; Dir of Inf. and Broadcasting, 1978–80. Director: Aeriel Services (Botswana) Pty; Maungo Consultancy Services Pty. *Address:* (office) PO Box 73, Gaborone, Botswana.

SETTRINGTON, Lord; Charles Henry Gordon-Lennox; *b* 20 Dec. 1944; *s* and *heir* of Earl of March and Kinrara, *qv*.

SEVER, (Eric) John; *b* 1 April 1943; *s* of Eric and Clara Sever. *Educ:* Sparkhill Commercial School. Travel Executive with tour operator, 1970–77. MP (Lab) Birmingham, Ladywood, Aug. 1977–1983; PPS to the Solicitor General, 1978–79. Contested (Lab) Meriden, 1983. *Recreations:* theatre, cinema, reading.

SEVERIN, Prof. Dorothy Virginia Sherman, PhD; FSA; Gilmour Professor of Spanish, University of Liverpool, since 1982; *b* 24 March 1942; *d* of Wilbur B. and Virginia L. Sherman; marr. diss.; one *d. Educ:* Harvard Univ. AB 1963; AM 1964; PhD 1967. FSA

1989. Teaching Fellow and Tutor, Harvard Univ., 1964–66; Vis. Lectr, Univ. of W Indies, 1967–68; Asst Prof., Vassar Coll., 1968; Lectr, Westfield Coll., London Univ., 1969–82; Pro-Vice-Chancellor, Univ. of Liverpool, 1989–92. Member: NI Higher Educn Council, 1993–; Res. Panel, British Acad. Humanities Res. Council, 1994–96. Vis. Associate Prof., Harvard Univ., 1982; Visiting Professor: Columbia Univ., 1985; Yale Univ., 1985. Editor, Bulletin of Hispanic Studies, 1982–. *Publications:* (ed) de Rojas, La Celestina, 1969, 15th edn 1988; Memory in La Celestina, 1970; (ed) Diego de San Pedro, La pasión trobada, 1973; (ed) La Lengua de Erasmo romançada por muy elegante estilo, 1975; The Cancionero de Martínez de Burgos, 1976; (ed with K. Whinnom) Diego de San Pedro, Poesía (Obras completas III), 1979; (ed with Angus MacKay) Cosas sacadas de la Historia del rey Juan el Segundo, 1982; (ed) Celestina, trans. James Mabbe (Eng./Spanish text), 1987; (ed) Celestina (Spanish edn), 1987; Tragicomedy and Novelistic Discourse in Celestina, 1989; Cancionero de Oñate-Castañeda, 1990; Admyte: The Paris Cancioneros, 1993 (PN2 with M. Garcia, PN13 with F. Maguire); The Colombina (LB3) and Egerton (SV2) Cancioneros, 1995; Witchcraft in Celestina, 1995; contribs to learned jls incl. Hispanic Rev., Romance Philology, Medium Aevum, MLR and THES. *Address:* Department of Hispanic Studies, The University, PO Box 147, Liverpool L69 3BX. *T:* 0151–794 2773.

SEVERIN, (Giles) Timothy; author, traveller and historian; *b* 25 Sept. 1940; *s* of Maurice Watkins and Inge Severin; *m* 1966, Dorothy Virginia Sherman (marr. diss. 1979); one *d*. *Educ:* Tonbridge School; Keble Coll., Oxford. MA, BLitt. Commonwealth Fellow, USA, 1964–66. Expeditions: led motorcycle team along Marco Polo route, 1961; R Mississippi by canoe and launch, 1965; Brendan Voyage from W Ireland to N America, 1977; Sindbad Voyage from Oman to China, 1980–81; Jason Voyage from Iolkos to Colchis, 1984; Ulysses Voyage from Troy to Ithaca, 1985; first Crusade route by horse to Jerusalem, 1987–88; travels by horse in Mongolia, 1990; N Pacific voyage by bamboo sailing raft, 1993. Founders Medal, RGS; Livingstone Medal, RSGS; Sykes Medal, RSAA. *Publications:* Tracking Marco Polo, 1964; Explorers of the Mississippi, 1967; The Golden Antilles, 1970; The African Adventure, 1973; Vanishing Primitive Man, 1973; The Oriental Adventure, 1976; The Brendan Voyage, 1978; The Sindbad Voyage, 1982; The Jason Voyage, 1985; The Ulysses Voyage, 1987; Crusader, 1989; In Search of Genghis Khan, 1991; The China Voyage, 1994. *Address:* Timoleague, Co. Cork, Eire. *T:* Bandon (23) 46233. *Club:* United Oxford & Cambridge University.

SEVERN, David; *see* Unwin, David Storr.

SEVERN, Prof. Roy Thomas, CBE 1992; FEng 1981; FICE; Professor of Civil Engineering, Bristol University, 1968–95, now Emeritus; *b* 6 Sept. 1929; *s* of Ernest Severn and Muriel Woollatt; *m* 1957, Hilary Irene Saxton; two *d*. *Educ:* Deacons School, Peterborough; Imperial College (DSc). Lectr, Imperial College, 1949–54; Royal Engineers (Survey), 1954–56; Bristol University: Lectr, 1956–65; Reader, 1965–68; Dean of Faculty of Engrg, 1970–73 and 1991–94; Pro-Vice Chancellor, 1981–84. Pres., ICE, 1991. *Publications:* (ed) Engineering Structures: developments in the twentieth century, 1983; contribs to Procs of ICE, Jl Earthquake Eng. and Structural Dynamics. *Recreations:* sailing, gardening, cricket. *Address:* 49 Gloucester Road, Rudgeway, Bristol BS12 2SF. *T:* Thornbury (01454) 412027.

SEVERNE, Air Vice-Marshal Sir John (de Milt), KCVO 1988 (LVO 1961); OBE 1968; AFC 1955; DL; Extra Equerry to the Queen, since 1984; *b* 15 Aug. 1925; *s* of late Dr A. de M. Severne, Wateringbury, Kent; *m* 1951, Katharine Veronica, *d* of late Captain V. E. Kemball, RN (Retd); three *d*. *Educ:* Marlborough. Joined RAF, 1944; Equerry to Duke of Edinburgh, 1958–61; Stn Comdr, RAF Kinloss, 1971–72; RCDS 1973; Comdt, Central Flying School, RAF, 1974–76; Air Cdre Flying Training, HQ RAF Support Comd, 1976–78; Comdr, Southern Maritime Air Region, 1978–80, retd; recalled as Captain of the Queen's Flight, 1982–89. ADC to The Queen, 1972–73. Hon. Air Cdre, No 3 (Co. of Devon) Maritime HQ Unit, RAuxAF, 1990–. President: SW Area, RAFA, 1981–95; Queen's Flight Assoc., 1990–; CFS Assoc., 1993–. Won King's Cup Air Race, British Air Racing Champion, 1960. Pres., RAF Equitation Assoc., 1976–79; Chm., Combined Services Equitation Assoc., 1977–79. DL Somerset, 1991. *Address:* c/o National Westminster Bank, 9 York Buildings, Cornhill, Bridgwater, Som TA6 3BA.

SEWARD, Guy William, QC 1982; IRRV; *b* 10 June 1916; *s* of late William Guy Seward and Maud Peacock; *m* 1946, Peggy Dearman. *Educ:* Stationers' Sch. Called to the Bar, Inner Temple, 1956. FRVA 1948. Chairman: Medical Service Cttee, 1977–81; Examination in Public, Devon Structure Plan, 1980; E Herts Health Authority, 1982–90; Member: Mid-Herts HMC, 1966–70; Napsbury HMC, 1970–74 (Chm., 1972–74); Bd of Governors, UCH, 1970–74; Herts AHA, 1974–82 (Vice Chm., 1980–82); Herts FPC, 1974–82; Council, Rating and Valuation Assoc., 1983. Freeman, City of London, 1949. *Publications:* (jtly) Enforcement of Planning Control, 1956; (jtly) Local Government Act, 1958; Howard Roberts Law of Town and Country Planning, 1963; (jtly) Rent Act, 1965; (jtly) Land Commission Act, 1967; (jtly) Leasehold Reform, 1967. *Recreations:* travel, gardening. *Address:* Stocking Lane Cottage, Ayot St Lawrence, Welwyn, Herts AL6 9BW. *Club:* Garrick.

SEWARD, Margaret Helen Elizabeth, CBE 1994; President, General Dental Council, since 1994; *b* 5 Aug. 1935; *d* of Dr Eric Oldershaw and Gwen Oldershaw; adopted, 1938, by John Hutton Mitchell and Marion Findlay Mitchell; *m* 1962, Prof. Gordon Seward, CBE; one *s* one *d*. *Educ:* Latymer Sch., Edmonton; London Hosp. Med. Coll. Dental Sch. (BDS Hons 1959; MDS 1970). FDSRCS 1962; MCCDRCS 1989. Dental practice: Highlands Hosp., 1962–64; Cheshunt Community Clinic, 1969–75; Royal London Hosp., 1980–94. Sen. Res. Fellow, BPMF, Univ. of London, 1975–77. Member: GDC, 1976–; Bd, Faculty of Dental Surgery, RCS, 1980–94 (Vice-Dean, 1990). President: Section of Odontology, RSM, 1991; BDA, 1993–94. Editor: Brit. Dental Jl, 1979–92; Internat. Dental Jl, 1990–95. Dir, Teamwork Project, DoH, 1991–95. Chm., Communication Cttee, FDI, 1984–89. Hon. Pres., Women in Dentistry, 1989–92; Hon. Member: Amer. Dental Assoc., 1992; Amer. Coll. of Dentists, 1994. Chm. Govs, Latymer Sch., 1984–94. Hon. FDSRCSE. Hon. DDSc Newcastle; Hon DDS Birmingham. *Publications:* Disturbances Associated with the Eruption of the Primary Dentition, 1969; Provision of Dental Care by Women Dentists in England and Wales, 1975, 2nd survey 1985; numerous articles in learned jls, UK and internationally. *Recreations:* cooking, entertaining, house-work! *Address:* 37 Wimpole Street, W1M 8DQ. *T:* 0171–486 2171. *Clubs:* Royal Society of Medicine; No 1 Yacht.

SEWARD, William Richard, RCNC; General Manager, HM Dockyard, Portsmouth, 1975–79, retired; *b* 7 Feb. 1922; *s* of William and Gertrude Seward, Portsmouth; *m* 1946, Mary Deas Ritchie; one *d*. *Educ:* Portsmouth Dockyard Techn. Coll.; RNC Greenwich; Royal Corps of Naval Constructors. Asst Constructor, HM Dockyard, Rosyth, 1945–47; Constructor, Naval Construction Dept, Admty, 1947–58; Admty Constructor Overseer, Birkenhead, 1958–63; Chief Constructor, MoD (N), 1963–70; Prodn Man., HM Dockyard, Chatham, 1970–73, Gen. Manager, 1973–75. *Recreations:* reading, music, caravanning, hill walking. *Club:* Civil Service.

SEWELL, Thomas Robert McKie; HM Diplomatic Service, retired; international grains consultant; *b* 18 Aug. 1921; *s* of late O. B. Fane Sewell and late Frances M. Sewell (*née* Sharp); *m* 1955, Jennifer Mary Sandeman; one *d* (and one *d* decd). *Educ:* Eastbourne Coll.; Trinity Coll., Oxford (Schol., Heath Harrison Prize, MA); Lausanne and Stockholm Univs (Schol.). HM Forces, 1940–45 (despatches); Major. Entered Foreign Service, 1949; Second Sec., Moscow, 1950–52; FO, 1952–55; First Sec., 1954; Madrid, 1955–59; Lima, 1959–61; Chargé d'Affaires, 1960; FO, 1961–63; Counsellor and Head of Chancery, Moscow, 1964–66; Diplomatic Service Rep. at IDC, 1966; Head of Associated States, West Indies and Swaziland Depts, Commonwealth Office, 1967–68; Head of N American and Caribbean Dept, FCO, 1968–70; Asst Sec., MAFF, 1970–81; UK Rep. to Internat. Wheat Council, 1972–81. Chm., World Grain Conf., Brussels, 1990. Contested (C) Greater Manchester Central, Europ. Parly elecn, 1984. Vis. Fellow, Hubert H. Humphrey Inst. of Public Affairs and Dept of Agricl and Applied Econs, Univ. of Minnesota, 1985. *Publications:* (with John de Courcy Ling) Famine and Surplus, 1985; The World Grain Trade, 1992. *Recreations:* ski-ing, inland waterways cruising. *Address:* c/o Barclays Bank, 22–25 Northumberland Avenue, WC2N 5BH. *Clubs:* Farmers', Airborne.

SEWELL, Maj.-Gen. Timothy Patrick T.; *see* Toyne Sewell.

SEYCHELLES, Bishop of, since 1979; **Rt Rev. French Kitchener Chang-Him;** Archbishop of the Indian Ocean, 1984–95; *m* 1975, Susan Talma; twin *d*. *Educ:* Lichfield Theolog. Coll.; St Augustine's Coll., Canterbury; Trinity Coll., Univ. of Toronto (LTh 1975). Deacon, Sheffield, 1962; priest, Seychelles,1963; Curate of Goole, 1962–63; Rector of Praslin, Seychelles, 1963–66 and 1969–71; Asst Priest, St Leonard's, Norwood, Sheffield, 1967–68; Vicar General, Seychelles, 1972–73; Rector, S Mahé Parish, 1973–74; Archdeacon of Seychelles, 1973–79; Priest-in-charge, St Paul's Cathedral, Mahé, 1977–79; Dean, Province of the Indian Ocean, 1983–84. DD (*hc*) Trinity Coll., Toronto, 1991. *Address:* Box 44, Victoria, Mahé, Seychelles. *T:* 224242, *Fax:* 224296.

SEYMOUR, family name of **Marquess of Hertford** and **Duke of Somerset.**

SEYMOUR, Lord; Sebastian Edward Seymour; *b* 3 Feb. 1982; *s* and *heir* of 19th Duke of Somerset, *qv*.

SEYMOUR, David; Principal Assistant Legal Adviser (Grade 3), Home Office, since 1994; *b* 24 Jan. 1951; *s* of Graham Seymour and late Betty (*née* Watson); *m* 1972, Elisabeth Huitson; one *s* two *d*. *Educ:* Trinity Sch., Croydon; Queen's Coll., Oxford (Open Exhibn; BA Jurisprudence 1972; MA 1977); Fitzwilliam Coll., Cambridge (LLB 1974). Law clerk, Rosenfeld, Meyer & Susman (Attorneys), Beverly Hills, Calif, 1972–73; called to the Bar, Gray's Inn (Holt Schol.), 1975; pupillage, 1975–76; Legal Advr's Br., Home Office, 1976–. Vis. Lectr in European Human Rights Law, Univ. of Conn Sch. of Law, 1986. *Recreations:* hockey, squash, walking. *Address:* Home Office, 50 Queen Anne's Gate, SW1H 9AT. *T:* 0171–273 3000. *Clubs:* United Oxford & Cambridge University, MCC.

SEYMOUR, Dr Francis, FFPHM; Director of Clinical and Scientific Services (formerly Regional Medical Officer), North West Thames Regional Health Authority, 1982–89; *b* 29 June 1928; *s* of Francis Reginald and Drusilla Seymour; *m* 1953, Ivy Esther; two *d*. *Educ:* Wallasey Grammar School; Liverpool University. MB ChB 1951; DPH 1955; MFCM 1972. Dep. MOH, N Bucks, 1955–58; MOH, Mid Bucks Districts, 1958–62; Div. MO, Runcorn and Mid Cheshire, 1962–70; Dep. County MO, Herts, 1970–74; Area MO, Herts AHA, 1974–82. *Recreations:* walking, sailing, theatre. *Address:* The Fennings, Back Ends, Chipping Campden, Glos GL55 6AU. *T:* Evesham (01386) 840483.

SEYMOUR, Julian Roger; Director, Lady Thatcher's Private Office, since 1991; *b* 19 March 1945; *s* of Evelyn Roger Seymour and Rosemary Evelyn Seymour (*née* Flower); *m* 1984, Diana Elizabeth Griffith; one *s* one *d*. *Educ:* Eton. Director: Collett, Dickinson, Pearce Ltd, 1969–79; Robert Fox Ltd, 1980–85; Dir, Corporate Finance, Lowe Gp PLC, 1985–91. Non-executive Director: Chime Communications PLC, 1990–; Taiwan Investment Trust PLC, 1994–. Comr, English Heritage, 1992–. *Recreations:* gardening, shooting. *Address:* 35 Chesham Place, SW1X 8HB.

SEYMOUR, Lynn, CBE 1976; Ballerina; Artistic Director, Ballet of the Bavarian State Opera, Munich, 1979–80; *b* Wainwright, Alberta, 8 March 1939; *d* of E. V. Springbett; *m* 1st, 1963, Colin Jones, photo-journalist (marr. diss.); 2nd, 1974, Philip Pace; three *s*; 3rd, 1983, Vanya Hackel (marr. diss.). *Educ:* Vancouver; Sadler's Wells Ballet School. Joined Sadler's Wells Ballet Company, 1957; Deutsche Oper, Berlin, 1966. *Roles created:* Adolescent, in The Burrow, Royal Opera House, 1958; Bride, in Le Baiser de la Fée, 1960; Girl, in The Invitation, 1960; Young Girl, in Les Deux Pigeons, 1961; Principal, in Symphony, 1963; Principal, in Images of Love, 1964; Juliet, in Romeo and Juliet, 1964; Albertine, BBC TV, 1966; Concerto, 1966; Anastasia, 1966; Flowers, 1972; Side Show, 1972; A Month in the Country, 1976; Five Brahms Waltzes in the manner of Isadora Duncan, 1976; mother, in Fourth Symphony, 1977; Mary Vetsera, in Mayerling, 1978; Take Five, 1978. *Other appearances include:* Danses Concertantes; Solitaire; La Fête Etrange; Sleeping Beauty; Swan Lake; Giselle (title-role); Cinderella; Das Lied von der Erde; The Four Seasons; Voluntaries; Manon, Sleeping Beauty, Dances at a Gathering, The Concert, Pillar of Fire, Romeo and Juliet (Tudor, Nureyev and Cranko), Las Hermañas, Moor's Pavane, Auriole, Apollon, Le Corsaire, Flower Festival, La Sylphide (Sylph and Madge), A Simple Man, Onegin. *Choreography for:* Rashomon, for Royal Ballet Touring Co., 1976; The Court of Love, for SWRB, 1977; Intimate Letters, 1978 and Mac and Polly, for Commonwealth Dance Gala, 1979; Boreas, and Tattoo, for Bavarian State Opera Ballet, 1980; Wolfi, for Ballet Rambert, 1987; Bastet, for SWRB, 1988. A Time to Dance (film), 1986. *Publication:* Lynn: leaps and boundaries (autobiog.), 1984.

SEYMOUR, Commander Sir Michael Culme-, 5th Bt, *cr* 1809; Royal Navy (retired); *b* 26 April 1909; *o s* of Vice-Admiral Sir M. Culme-Seymour, 4th Bt, and Florence Agnes Louisa (*d* 1956), *y d* of late A. L. Nugent; *S* father, 1925; *m* 1948, Lady (Mary) Faith Nesbitt (*d* 1983), *er d* of 9th Earl of Sandwich; one step-*d* (adopted) (two *s* decd). Succeeded Rev. Wentworth Watson to the Rockingham Castle estates, 1925, and transferred them to his nephew, Cmdr L. M. M. Saunders Watson, RN, 1967; is a farmer and a landowner. ADC to Governor-General of Canada, 1933–35; served War of 1939–45 (despatches); served Imperial Defence College, 1946–47; retired from RN 1947. JP Northants, 1949; Mem. Northants CC 1948–55; DL Northants, 1958–71; High Sheriff of Northants, 1966. Bledisloe Gold Medal for Landowners, 1972. *Heir to baronetcy:* cousin Michael Patrick Culme-Seymour [*b* 28 April 1962; *m* 1986, Karin Fleig; two *s*]. *Address:* Wytherston, Powerstock, Bridport, Dorset DT6 3TQ. *T:* Powerstock (01308) 485211. *Club:* Brooks's.

SEYMOUR, Richard William; QC 1991; a Recorder, since 1995; *b* 4 May 1950; *e s* of Albert Percy and Vera Maud Seymour; *m* 1971, Clare Veronica, BSS, MSc, *d* of Stanley Victor Peskett, *qv*; one *s* one *d*. *Educ:* Brentwood Sch.; Royal Belfast Academical Instn; Christ's Coll., Cambridge (schol.; BA 1971; MA 1975). Holker Jun. Exhibn, 1970, Holker Sen. Schol., 1972, Gray's Inn; called to the Bar, Gray's Inn, 1972. Asst Recorder, 1991–95. *Publications:* (ed jtly) Kemp and Kemp, The Quantum of Damages, 4th edn 1975; legal chapters in: Willis and Willis, Practice and Procedure for the Quantity Surveyor, 8th edn 1980; Willis and George, The Architect in Practice, 6th edn 1981. *Recreations:* archaeology, walking, foreign travel. *Address:* 4 Raymond Buildings, Gray's Inn, WC1R 5BP. *T:* 0171–405 7211.

SEYS-LLEWELLYN, His Honour John Desmond; a Circuit Judge (formerly a County Court Judge), 1971–85; *b* 3 May 1912; *s* of Charles Ernest Llewellyn, FAI and Hannah Margretta Llewellyn, of Cardiff; *m* 1st, 1939, Elaine (*d* 1984), *d* of H. Leonard Porcher, solicitor, and Mrs Hilda Porcher, JP, of Pontypridd; three *s*; 2nd, 1986, Mrs Joan Banfield James, *d* of R. H. Cumming, JP, of Plymouth. *Educ:* Cardiff High School; Jesus College, Oxford; Exhibitioner, MA. Joined Inner Temple, 1936. War Service, RTR, 1940–46 (Captain). Called to the Bar, Inner Temple, in absentia OAS, 1945; Profumo Prizeman, 1947; practised on Wales and Chester Circuit, 1947–71; Local Insurance Appeal Tribunal, 1958–71; Dep. Chm., Cheshire QS, 1968–71; joined Gray's Inn, *ad eundem*, same day as youngest son, 1967. Contested Chester Constituency (L), 1955 and 1956. *Recreations:* languages, travel, archaeology, art galleries, music, swimming, English Setter. *Address:* Little Chetwyn, Green Pastures, Gresford, Clwyd LL12 8RT. *T:* Gresford (01978) 856818. *Club:* Athenæum (Liverpool).

SHACKLE, Prof. Christopher, PhD; FBA 1990; Professor of Modern Languages of South Asia, University of London, since 1985; *b* 4 March 1942; *s* of late Francis Mark Shackle and Diana Margaret Shackle (*née* Harrington, subseq. Thomas); *m* 1st, 1964, Emma Margaret Richmond (marr. diss.); one *s* two *d*; 2nd, 1988, Shahrukh Husain; one *s* one *d*. *Educ:* Haileybury and ISC; Merton College, Oxford (BA 1963); St Antony's College, Oxford (DipSocAnthrop 1965; BLitt 1966); PhD London, 1972. School of Oriental and African Studies, University of London: Fellow in Indian Studies, 1966; Lectr in Urdu and Panjabi, 1969; Reader in Modern Languages of South Asia, 1979. *Publications:* Teach Yourself Punjabi, 1972; (with D. J. Matthews) An Anthology of Classical Urdu Love Lyrics, 1972; The Siraiki Language of Central Pakistan, 1976; Catalogue of the Panjabi and Sindhi Manuscripts in the India Office Library, 1977; A Guru Nanak Glossary, 1981; An Introduction to the Sacred Language of the Sikhs, 1983; The Sikhs, 1984; (with D. J. Matthews and S. Husain) Urdu Literature, 1985; (with R. Snell) Hindi and Urdu since 1800, 1990; (with Z. Moir) Ismaili Hymns from South Asia, 1992; (with R. Snell) The Indian Narrative, 1992; numerous articles. *Address:* Department of South Asia, School of Oriental and African Studies. Thornhaugh Street, Russell Square, WC1H 0XG. *T:* 0171–637 2388.

SHACKLETON, Keith Hope; artist and naturalist; President, Society of Wildlife Artists, 1978–83; Chairman, Artists League of Great Britain; *b* 16 Jan. 1923; *s* of W. S. Shackleton; *m* 1951, Jacqueline Tate; two *s* one *d*. *Educ:* Oundle. Served RAF, 1941–46. Civil Pilot and Dir, Shackleton Aviation Ltd, 1948–63; natural history programmes for television, 1964–68; joined naturalist team aboard MS Lindblad Explorer, 1969. Pres., Royal Soc. of Marine Artists, 1973–78. Member: RGS; Zool Soc. of London; NZ Antarctic Soc. Hon. LLD Birmingham, 1983. *Publications:* Tidelines, 1951; Wake, 1953; Wild Animals in Britain, 1959; Ship in the Wilderness, 1986; Wildlife and Wilderness, 1986; illustrations for books. *Recreations:* small Boat Sailing, exploration field work. *Address:* Woodley Wood Farm, Woodleigh, Devon TQ7 4DR. *Club:* Itchenor Sailing.

SHACKLETON, Prof. Nicholas John, PhD; FRS 1985; Director, Institute for Quaternary Research, Department of Earth Sciences, University of Cambridge, since 1995 (Director, Sub-Department of Quaternary Research, 1988–95); Fellow of Clare Hall, since 1980; *b* 23 June 1937; *s* of Prof. Robert Millner Shackleton, *qv*; *m* 1986, Vivien Law. *Educ:* Cranbrook Sch.; Clare Coll., Cambridge (BA, PhD); ScD Cantab 1984. Cambridge University: Senior Asst in Research, 1965–72, Asst Dir of Res., 1972–87, Reader, 1987–91, Prof., 1991–, sub-dept of Quaternary Res.; Research Fellow, Clare Hall, 1974–80, Official Fellow, 1980–. Sen. Vis. Res. Fellow, Lamont Doherty Geol Observatory of Columbia Univ., 1974–75. Founding Mem., Academia Europaea, 1988. Carus Medal, Deutsche Akad. der Naturforscher Leopoldina, 1985; Sheppard Medal, SEPM, 1985; Lyell Medal, Geol Soc. of London, 1987; Huntsman Award, Bedford Inst. of Oceanography, Canada, 1991; Crafoord Prize, 1995. *Publications:* numerous articles on marine geology, geological history of climate, etc; articles in New Grove Dictionary of Music and Musicians. *Recreations:* clarinet playing, researching history of clarinet, Thai food. *Address:* 12 Tenison Avenue, Cambridge CB1 2DY. *T:* Cambridge (01223) 311938.

SHACKLETON, Prof. Robert Millner, BSc, PhD; FRS 1971; Hon. Senior Research Fellow, Open University, since 1977; Professor of Geology, University of Leeds, 1962–75, now Emeritus; Director, Research Institute of African Geology, University of Leeds, 1966–75; *b* 30 Dec. 1909; *m* 1st, 1934, Gwen Isabel Harland; one *s* two *d*; 2nd, 1949, Judith Wyndham Jeffreys (marr. diss. 1978); one *s* one *d*; 3rd, 1984, Peigi Wallace. *Educ:* Sidcot School; University of Liverpool. BSc (Hons) 1931, PhD 1934, Liverpool; Beit Fellow, Imperial College, 1932–34; Chief Geologist to Whitehall Explorations Ltd in Fiji, 1935–36; on teaching staff, Imperial College, 1936–40 and 1945–48; Geologist, Mining and Geological Dept, Kenya, 1940–45; Herdman Professor of Geology, University of Liverpool, 1948–62. Royal Society Leverhulme Vis. Prof., Haile Sellassie I Univ., 1970–71; Trevelyan Coll. Fellow, Durham Univ., 1984–85. Vice-Pres., Geolog. Soc. of London, 1966. Hon. FGS. Murchison Medal, 1970. *Publications:* Mining and Geological Dept of Kenya Reports 10, 11, 12; papers in geological journals, etc. *Address:* The Croft Barn, Church Street, East Hendred, Oxon OX12 8LA. *T:* Abingdon (01235) 834802.

See also N. J. Shackleton.

SHACKLETON BAILEY, D. R.; *see* Bailey.

SHACKLOCK, Constance, OBE 1971; LRAM 1940; FRAM 1953; International Opera and Concert Singer; Professor, Royal Academy of Music, 1968–84; *b* 16 April 1913; *e d* of Randolph and Hilda Shacklock, Nottingham; *m* 1947, Eric Mitchell (*d* 1965). *Educ:* Huntingdon Street Secondary School, Nottingham; RAM. Principal mezzo-soprano, Covent Garden, 1946–56. Outstanding roles: Carmen, Amneris (Aida), Octavian (Der Rosenkavalier), Brangaene (Tristan und Isolde). Guest artist: Wagner Society, Holland, 1949; Berlin State Opera, 1951; Edinburgh Festival, 1954; Berlin Festival, 1956; Teatro Colon, Buenos Aires, 1956; Bolshoi Theatre, Moscow, 1957; Kirov Theatre, Leningrad, 1957; Elizabethan Theatre Trust, Sydney, 1958; Liège Opera, 1960; London production of The Sound of Music, 1961–66. President: English Singers and Speakers, 1978–79; Royal Acad. of Music, 1979–80; Royal Borough of Kingston Arts Fest., 1988–. DUniv Kingston, 1993. *Recreations:* gardening, reading, tapestry. *Address:* East Dorincourt, Kingston Vale, SW15 3RN.

SHAFER, Prof. Byron Edwin; Andrew W. Mellon Professor of American Government, Oxford, since 1985; Professorial Fellow, Nuffield College, Oxford, since 1985; *b* 8 Jan. 1947; *s* of Byron Henry Shafer and Doris Marguerite (*née* Von Bergen); *m* 1981, Wanda K. Green; one *s*. *Educ:* Yale Univ. (BA Magna Cum Laude, Deptl Hons in Pol. Sci. with Excep. Dist. 1968); Univ. of California at Berkeley (PhD Pol. Sci. 1979). Resident Scholar, Russell Sage Foundn, USA, 1977–84; Associate Prof. of Pol. Sci., Florida State Univ., 1984–85. Hon. MA Oxford, 1985. E. E. Schattschneider Prize, 1980, Franklin L. Burdette Prize, 1990, Amer. Pol. Sci. Assoc. *Publications:* Presidential Politics: readings on nominations and elections, 1980; Quiet Revolution: the struggle for the Democratic Party and the shaping of post-reform politics, 1983; Bifurcated Politics: evolution and reform in the National Party Convention, 1988; Is America Different?: a new look at American exceptionalism, 1991; The End of Realignment?: interpreting American electoral eras, 1991; articles in learned jls. *Recreations:* furniture restoration, gardening, travel. *Address:* Nuffield College, Oxford OX1 1NF. *T:* Oxford (01865) 278509; Briar Post, Stratford Road, Drayton, near Banbury OX15 6EG. *T:* Banbury (01295) 730289.

SHAFFER, Anna; *see* Wintour, A.

SHAFFER, Elinor Sophia, PhD; FBA 1995; Reader in English and Comparative Literature, University of East Anglia, since 1977; *b* 6 April 1935; *d* of Vernon Cecil Stoneman and Helene Dorothy Stoneman (*née* Nieschlag); *m* 1964, Brian M. Shaffer; two *s*. *Educ:* Chicago Univ. (BA 1954); St Hilda's Coll., Oxford (BA 1958; MA 1962); PhD Columbia Univ., NY, 1966; MA Cantab 1968. Fellow, Columbia Univ., 1961–63; Instr, 1963–64, Asst Prof., 1964–65, Dept of English, Univ. of Calif, Berkeley; Res. Fellow, Clare Hall, Cambridge, 1968–71; Lectr, UEA, 1971–77. Visiting Professor: Brown Univ., 1983–84; Zurich Univ., 1986; Stanford Univ., 1988; Vis. Lectr, Free Univ., Berlin, 1979; Study Fellow, ACLS, 1971; Leverhulme Fellowship, 1976; Research Fellow: Humanities Research Centre, ANU, 1982; Univ. of Calif, 1991; Dist. Fellow, Eur. Humanities Res. Centre, Oxford, 1995–; Vis. Fellow, All Souls Coll., Oxford, 1996. Editor, Comparative Criticism, 1979–. *Publications:* Kubla Khan and the Fall of Jerusalem: the mythological school in Biblical criticism and secular literature 1770–1880, 1975; Erewhons of the Eye: Samuel Butler as painter, photographer and art critic, 1988; Coleridge's Literary Theory, 1996; (ed) Coleridge's Writings: On Criticism, vol. I, 1996; *chapters in:* The Coleridge Connection, 1990; Romanticism and the Sciences, 1990; Aesthetic Illusion: theoretical and historical approaches, 1990; Reflecting Senses: perception and appearance in literature, culture and the arts, 1994; Milton, the Metaphysicals and the Romantics, 1994; Apocalypse Theory and the Ends of the World, 1995; many lectures, reviews and contribs to learned jls. *Recreations:* theatre, travelling, photography, wine. *Address:* 9 Cranmer Road, Cambridge CB3 9BL. *T:* Cambridge (01223) 357406.

SHAFFER, Peter Levin, CBE 1987; FRSL; playwright; *b* 15 May 1926; *s* of Jack Shaffer and Reka Shaffer (*née* Fredman). *Educ:* St Paul's School, London; Trinity College, Cambridge. Literary Critic, Truth, 1956–57; Music Critic, Time and Tide, 1961–62. Cameron Mackintosh Vis. Prof. of Contemporary Theatre, and Fellow, St Catherine's Coll., Oxford Univ., 1994. Hamburg Shakespeare Prize, 1989; William Inge Award for Distinguished Achievement in the American Theatre, 1992. *Stage Plays:* Five Finger Exercise, prod. Comedy, London, 1958–60, and Music Box Theatre, NY, 1960–61 (Evening Standard Drama Award, 1958; NY Drama Critics Circle Award (best foreign play), 1959–60); (double bill) The Private Ear (filmed 1966) and The Public Eye, produced, Globe, London, 1962, Morosco Theater, New York 1963 (filmed 1972); The Merry Roosters Panto (with Joan Littlewood and Theatre Workshop) prod. Wyndham's Theatre, Christmas, 1963; The Royal Hunt of the Sun, Nat. Theatre, Chichester Festival, 1964, The Old Vic, and Queen's Theatres, 1964–67, NY, 1965–66 (filmed 1969); Black Comedy, Nat. Theatre, Chichester Fest., 1965, The Old Vic and Queen's Theatres, 1965–67; as double bill with White Lies, NY, 1967, Shaw, 1976; The White Liars, Lyric, 1968; The Battle of Shrivings, Lyric, 1970; Equus, Nat. Theatre, 1973–74, Plymouth Theatre, NY, 1976, Albery Theatre, 1976–77 (NY Drama Critics' and Antoinette Perry Awards) (filmed 1977); Amadeus, Nat. Theatre, 1979 (Evening Standard Drama Award, Plays and Players Award, London Theatre Critics Award), Broadhurst Theatre, NY, 1980 (Antoinette Perry Award, Drama Desk Award), Her Majesty's, 1981 (filmed 1984, Acad. Award, Golden Globe Award, Los Angeles Film Critics Assoc. Award, Premi David di Donatello, 1985); Yonadab, Nat. Theatre, 1985; Lettice and Lovage, Globe, 1987, Barrymore Theatre, NY, 1990 (Evening Standard Drama Award for Best Comedy, 1988); The Gift of the Gorgon, Barbican, 1992, transf. Wyndhams, 1993. Plays produced on television and sound include: The Salt Land (ITV), 1955; Balance of Terror (BBC TV), 1957, Whom Do I Have the Honour of Addressing? (radio), 1989, etc. *Recreations:* music, architecture. *Address:* c/o McNaughton-Lowe Representation, 200 Fulham Road, SW10. *Club:* Garrick.

SHAFTESBURY, 10th Earl of, *cr* 1672; **Anthony Ashley-Cooper;** Bt 1622; Baron Ashley 1661; Baron Cooper of Paulet, 1672; Director, PKL Group, since 1989; *b* 22 May 1938; *o s* of Major Lord Ashley (*d* 1947; *e s* of 9th Earl of Shaftesbury, KP, PC, GCVO, CBE) and of Françoise Soulier; *S* grandfather, 1961; *m* 1st, 1966, Bianca Maria (marr. diss. 1976), *o d* of late Gino de Paolis; 2nd, 1976, Christina Eva, *o d* of Ambassador Nils Montan; two *s*. *Educ:* Eton; Christchurch, Oxford. Chm., London Philharmonic Orchestra Council, 1966–80. Vice-Pres., British Butterfly Conservation Soc., 1992–. Hon. Pres., Shaftesbury Soc., 1961. (Jtly) Nat. Duke of Cornwall's Award for Forestry and Conservation, Royal Forestry Soc., 1992. Hon. Citizen, South Carolina, USA, 1967. Patron of seven livings. *Recreations:* mountains, music, ecology. *Heir: s* Lord Ashley, *qv*. *Address:* St Giles, Wimborne, Dorset BH21 5NH. *T:* Cranborne (01725) 517312. *Clubs:* Pratt's, Turf.

SHAGARI, Alhaji Shehu Usman Aliyu; President of Nigeria and Commander-in-Chief of the Armed Forces, 1979–83; *b* April 1925; *s* of Magaji Aliyu; *m* 1946; three *s* three *d*. *Educ:* Middle Sch., Sokoto; Barewa Coll., Kaduna; Teacher Trg Coll., Zaria. Teacher of science, Sokoto Middle Sch., 1945–50; Headmaster, Argungu Sen. Primary Sch., 1951–52; Sen. Visiting Teacher, Sokoto Prov., 1953–58. Entered politics as Mem. Federal Parl., 1954–58; Parly Sec. to Prime Minister, 1958–59; Federal Minister: Economic Develt, 1959–60; Establishments, 1960–62; Internal Affairs, 1962–65; Works, 1965–66; Sec., Sokoto Prov. Educl Develt Fund, 1966–68; State Comr for Educn, Sokoto Province, 1968–70; Fed. Comr for Econ. Develt and Reconstruction, 1970–71; for Finance, 1971–75. Mem., Constituent Assembly, Oct. 1977–; Mem., Nat. Party of Nigeria. *Publications:* (poetry) Wakar Nijeriya, 1948; Dun Fodia, 1978; (collected speeches) My Vision of Nigeria, 1981. *Recreations:* Hausa poetry, reading, farming, indoor games.

SHAKER, Mohamed Ibrahim, PhD; Order of the Arab Republic of Egypt (Second Grade), 1976; Order of Merit (Egypt) (First Grade), 1983; Ambassador of the Arab Republic of Egypt to the Court of St James's, since 1988; *b* 16 Oct. 1933; *s* of Mahmoud Shaker and Zeinab Wasef; *m* 1960, Mona El Kony; one *s* one *d*. *Educ:* Cairo Univ. (Lic. en Droit); Inst. of Internat. Studies, Geneva (PhD). Representative of Dir-Gen. of IAEA to UN, New York, 1982–83; Amb. and Dep. Perm. Rep. of Egypt to UN, New York, 1984–86; Amb. to Austria, 1986–88; Hd of Dept of W Europe, Min. of For. Affairs, Cairo, 1988. President: Third Review Conf. of the Parties to the Treaty on Non-Proliferation of Nuclear Weapons, Geneva, 1985; UN Conf. for the Promotion of Internat. Co-operation in the Peaceful Uses of Nuclear Energy, Geneva, 1987; Member: UN Sec. General's Adv. Bd on Disarmament, 1993– (Chm., 1995–); Core Gp of Prog. for Promotion of Non-Proliferation of Nuclear Weapons, 1987–. *Publications:* The Nuclear Non-Proliferation Treaty: origin and implementation 1959–1979, 1980; several articles. *Recreations:* tennis, music. *Address:* Egyptian Embassy, 75 South Audley Street, W1Y 5FF. *Clubs:* Royal Automobile, Queen's (Hon. Member); Guizera Sporting (Cairo).

SHAKERLEY, Sir Geoffrey (Adam), 6th Bt *cr* 1838; Managing Director, Photographic Records Ltd, since 1970; *b* 9 Dec. 1932; *s* of Sir Cyril Holland Shakerley, 5th Bt, and

Elizabeth Averil (MBE 1955; *d* 1990), *d* of late Edward Gwynne Eardley-Wilmot; *S* father, 1970; *m* 1st, 1962, Virginia Elizabeth (*d* 1968), *d* of W. E. Maskell; two *s*; 2nd, 1972, Lady Elizabeth Georgiana, *d* of late Viscount Anson and Princess Georg of Denmark; one *d*. *Educ:* Harrow; Trinity College, Oxford. *Publications:* Henry Moore Sculptures in Landscape, 1978; The English Dog at Home, 1986. *Heir: s* Nicholas Simon Adam Shakerley, *b* 20 Dec. 1963. *Address:* 57 Artesian Road, W2 5DB.

SHAKESPEARE, John William Richmond, CMG 1985; LVO 1968; HM Diplomatic Service, retired; *b* 11 June 1930; *s* of late Dr W. G. Shakespeare; *m* 1955, Lalage Ann, *d* of late S. P. B. Mais; three *s* one *d*. *Educ:* Winchester; Trinity Coll., Oxford (Scholar, MA). 2nd Lieut Irish Guards, 1949–50. Lectr in English, Ecole Normale Supérieure, Paris, 1953–54; on editorial staff, Times Educational Supplement, 1955–56 and Times, 1956–59; entered Diplomatic Service, 1959; Private Sec. to Ambassador in Paris, 1959–61; FO, 1961–63; 1st Sec., Phnom-Penh, 1963–64; 1st Sec., Office of Polit. Adviser to C-in-C Far East, Singapore, 1964–66; Dir of British Information Service in Brazil, 1966–69; FCO, 1969–73; Counsellor and Consul-Gen., Buenos Aires, 1973–75; Chargé d'Affaires, Buenos Aires, 1976–77; Head of Mexico and Caribbean Dept, FCO, 1977–79; Counsellor, Lisbon, 1979–83; Ambassador to Peru, 1983–87, to Kingdom of Morocco, 1987–90. Officer, Order of Southern Cross (Brazil), 1968. *Recreations:* tennis, sailing, bicycling, gardening, music (light), poetry. *Address:* 10 South End Row, Kensington, W8 5BZ. *Club:* Garrick.

See also N. W. R. Shakespeare.

SHAKESPEARE, Nicholas William Richmond; author and journalist; *b* 3 March 1957; *s* of J. W. R. Shakespeare, *qv*. *Educ:* Dragon Sch., Oxford; Winchester Coll.; Magdalene Coll., Cambridge (MA English). BBC TV, 1980–84; Dep. Arts and Literary Editor, The Times, 1985–87; Literary Editor: London Daily News, 1987–88; Daily Telegraph, 1988–91; Sunday Telegraph, 1989–91; film critic, Illustrated London News, 1989. Work for TV includes: writer and narrator: The Evelyn Waugh Trilogy; Mario Vargas Llosa (Omnibus); Iquitos; For the Sake of the Children; presenter, Cover to Cover. *Publications:* The Men who would be King, 1984; Londoners, 1986; The Vision of Elena Silves, 1989 (Somerset Maugham Prize, 1990); The High Flyer, 1993. *Recreations:* travelling, drawing. *Address:* 5 Bassett Road, W10 6LA. *Clubs:* Beefsteak, Groucho.

SHAKESPEARE, Sir William (Geoffrey), 2nd Bt *cr* 1942; Medical Adviser to Buckinghamshire Adoption Panel, since 1987; General Practitioner, Aylesbury, 1968–87; Hospital Practitioner, Mental Subnormality, Manor House Hospital, Aylesbury, since 1972; *b* 12 Oct. 1927; *s* of Rt Hon. Sir Geoffrey Hithersay Shakespeare, 1st Bt, and Aimée Constance (*d* 1950), *d* of Walter Loveridge; *S* father, 1980; *m* 1964, Susan Mary, *d* of A. D. Raffel, Colombo, Ceylon; two *s*. *Educ:* Radley; Clare Coll., Cambridge (BA Hons Nat. Scis, MA 1957); St George's Hospital. MB BChir Camb. 1958; DCH Eng. 1961. Boston Children's Hosp., USA, 1963–64; Paediatric Registrar, Stoke Mandeville Hosp., 1964–66. Mem., Snowdon Working Party, Integration of Handicapped, 1974–76. Vice-President: Physically Handicapped & Able-Bodied, 1977–; Restricted Growth Assoc. (formerly Assoc. for Res. into Restricted Growth), 1982–. Member BMA. Trustee, Shakespeare Globe Trust, 1992–. *Heir: s* Thomas William Shakespeare, *b* 11 May 1966. *Address:* Manor Cottage, Stoke Mandeville, Bucks HP22 5XA. *Clubs:* MCC; Leander.

SHALIKASHVILI, Gen. John Malchase David; US Army General; Chairman, Joint Chiefs of Staff, USA, since 1993; *b* Poland, 27 June 1936; *s* of Dimitri Shalikashvili and Maria Shalilkashvili (*née* Ruediger); *m* 1st, 1963, Gunhild Bartsch (*d* 1965); 2nd, 1966, Joan Zimpelman; one *s*. *Educ:* Bradley Univ. (BS Mech Eng 1958); George Washington Univ. (MS Internat. Affairs 1970); Officer Candidate Sch. Commissioned Artillery, 1959; served USA, Germany, Vietnam, Korea, Italy; Office of DCSOPS, 1981–84 and 1986–87; Asst Div. Comdr, 1st Armd Div., 1984–86; Commanding Gen., 9th Inf. Div., 1987–89; Dep. C-in-C, US Army Europe and 7th Army, 1989–91; Asst to Chm., Jt Chiefs of Staff, 1991–92; Supreme Allied Comdr, Europe, and C-in-C, US European Command, 1992–93. *Address:* Chairman, Joint Chiefs of Staff, Washington, DC 20318–0001, USA.

SHAMS-UD DOHA, Aminur Rahman; Minister for Foreign Affairs, Government of the People's Republic of Bangladesh, 1982–84; Publisher and Editor-in-Chief: Dialogue Publications Ltd, Dhaka; Dialogue, international English weekly, since 1988; *b* 1929; *m*; two *s*; *m* 1981, Wajiha Moukaddem. *Educ:* Calcutta and Dacca Univs (BSc Hons; BA). Commnd 2nd Lieut, Pakistan Artillery, 1952; Sch. of Artillery and Guided Missiles, Ft Sill, Okla, USA, 1957–58; Gen. Staff Coll., Quetta, 1962; GS Inf. Bde HQ, 1963; RMCS, Shrivenham, 1964–65; Sen. Instr, Gunnery, 1965; GS GHQ, 1965–66, retired. Editor and Publisher, Inter-Wing, Rawalpindi, 1968–71; Gen. Sec., Awami League, Rawalpindi, 1969–71, and Mem. Working Cttee; Ambassador of Bangladesh to: Yugoslavia and Roumania, 1972–74; Iran and Turkey, 1974–77; High Comr for Bangladesh in UK, 1977–82; Minister for Information, Bangladesh, March-June 1982. Member and Leader of Bangladesh delegns to numerous internat., Islamic and Commonwealth meetings. Associate Mem., Inst. of Strategic Studies, London. C-in-C's Commendation, 1964; several military awards and decorations. Order of the Lance and Flag, Cl. 1 (Yugoslavia); Order of Diplomatic Service, Gwanha Medal (S Korea). *Publications:* Arab-Israeli War, 1967; The Emergence of South Asia's First Nation State; Aryans on the Indus (MS); In the Shadow of the Eagle and the Bear (MS). *Recreations:* sport (selected for London Olympics, 1948), writing, gardening. *Address:* Farm View, Indira Road, Tejgaon, Dhaka 15, Bangladesh; Dialogue Publications Ltd, 19 Kazi Nazrul Islam Avenue, Dhaka 15. *Clubs:* English-Speaking Union; Golf (Dhaka).

SHAND, Major Bruce Middleton Hope, MC 1940, and Bar 1942; Vice Lord-Lieutenant, East Sussex, 1974–92; *b* 22 Jan. 1917; *s* of late P. Morton Shand; *m* 1946, Rosalind Maud, *d* of 3rd Baron Ashcombe; one *s* two *d*. *Educ:* Rugby; RMC, Sandhurst. 2nd Lieut 12th Royal Lancers, 1937; Major 1942; wounded and PoW 1942; retd 1947. Exon, Queen's Body Guard of the Yeomen of the Guard, 1971, Ensign, 1978–85, Adjutant and Clerk of the Cheque, 1985–87. Joint or Acting Master, Southdown Fox Hounds, 1956–75. DL Sussex, 1962. *Publication:* Previous Engagements, 1991. *Recreations:* hunting, gardening. *Address:* The Laines, Plumpton, near Lewes, East Sussex BN7 3AJ. *T:* Plumpton (01273) 890248. *Club:* Cavalry and Guards.

See also Lady Howe.

SHAND, Rt. Rev. David Hubert Warner; Assistant Bishop and Bishop in Geelong, Diocese of Melbourne, Archbishop's Provincial Assistant, 1985–88; *b* 6 April 1921; *s* of late Rev. Canon Rupert Warner Shand and Madeleine Ethel Warner Shand; *m* 1946, Muriel Jean Horwood Bennett; one *s* three *d*. *Educ:* The Southport Sch., Queensland; St Francis' Theological Coll., Brisbane (ThL, 2nd Cl. Hons); Univ. of Queensland (BA, 2nd Cl. Hons). Served War, AIF, 1941–45: Lieut, 1942. St Francis' Coll., Brisbane, 1946–48. Deacon, 1948; Priest, 1949; Asst Curate, Lutwyche. Served in Parishes: Moorooka, Inglewood, Nambour, Ipswich; Org. Sec., Home Mission Fund, 1960–63; Rural Dean of Ipswich, 1963–66; Dio. of Brisbane: Chaplain CMF, 1950–57; Vicar, Christ Church, South Yarra, 1966–69; St Andrew's, Brighton, 1969–73; Rural Dean of St Kilda, 1972–73; Dio. of Melbourne: consecrated Bishop, St Paul's Cathedral, Melbourne, Nov. 1973; Bishop of St Arnaud, 1973–76 (when diocese amalgamated with that of Bendigo); Vicar of St Stephen's, Mt Waverley, 1976–78; Bishop of the Southern Region, 1978–85. Chm., Gen. Bd of Religious Educn, 1974–84. *Recreation:* carpentry. *Address:* 40 Volitans Avenue, Mount Eliza, Vic 3930, Australia.

SHAND, John Alexander Ogilvie; His Honour Judge Shand; a Circuit Judge, since 1988; *b* 6 Nov. 1942; *s* of late Alexander Shand and Marguerite Marie Shand; *m* 1st, 1965, Patricia Margaret (*née* Toynbee) (marr. diss.); two *s* one *d*; 2nd, 1990, Valerie Jean (*née* Bond). *Educ:* Nottingham High Sch.; Queens' Coll., Cambridge (MA, LLB; Chancellor's Medal for Law 1965). Called to the Bar, Middle Temple, 1965 (Harmsworth Scholarship); practised on Midland and Oxford Circuit (Birmingham), 1965–71 and 1973–81 (Dep. Circuit Judge, 1979); a Recorder, 1981–88. Chm. of Industrial Tribunals (Birmingham Reg.), 1981–88. Fellow and Tutor, Queens' Coll., Cambridge, 1971–73. Chancellor: Dio. Southwell, 1981–; Dio. Lichfield, 1989–. *Publications:* (with P. G. Stein) Legal Values in Western Society, 1974; contrib. various articles in Cambridge Law Jl. *Address:* c/o Courts Administrator's Office, Kemley House, 2 Victoria Road, Stafford ST16 2AE.

SHANKAR, Pandit Ravi; Presidential Padma Vibhushan Award, 1980; musician and composer; MP (Member of Rajya Sabha) since 1986; *b* 7 April 1920; *m* 1989, Sukanya Rajan; one *s* two *d*. Studied with brother Uday Shankar in Paris, 1930, with Ustad Allaudin Khan in Maihar, 1938–. Music Dir, All-India Radio, 1949–56; music and choreography for ASIAD 82 (Asian Games, New Delhi, 1982). Fellow, Sangeet Natak Akademi, 1977 (President's Award, 1962); Member, Nat. Acad. for Recording Arts and Sciences, 1966. Over 50 recordings, including recordings with Yehudi Menuhin, Jean-Pierre Rampal, Philip Glass, and others. Has received hon. doctorates in letters and arts from California, 1968; Colgate, NY, 1972; Rabindra Bharati, Calcutta; Benares Hindu Univ.; New England Conservatory of Music; Univ. of Delhi; Univ. of Calcutta, Deshikottam Award, 1982. *Compositions:* Indian ragas; music for ballet, and films incl. Gandhi, 1983; Concertos for sitar and orch., No 1, 1971, No 2, 1981; Ghanashyam—A Broken Branch, 1989. *Publication:* My Music My Life, 1968. *Recreations:* films, people, music, theatre. *Address:* c/o Tennant Artists, Unit 2, 39 Tadema Road, SW10 0PY; Ravi Shankar Institute of Performing Arts, New Delhi.

SHANKS, Duncan Faichney, RSA 1990 (ARSA 1972); RGI 1982; RSW 1987; artist; *b* 30 Aug. 1937; *s* of Duncan Faichney Shanks and Elizabeth Clark; *m* 1966, Una Brown Gordon. *Educ:* Glasgow School of Art; DA (Post Diploma) 1960. Travelling scholarship to Italy, 1961; part-time teacher, Glasgow Sch. of Art, 1963–79; full-time artist, 1979–. *Recreations:* classical and contemporary music.

SHANKS, Ian Alexander, PhD; FRS 1984; FEng 1992; Divisional Science Advisor, Research and Engineering Division, Unilever Research, since 1994; *b* 22 June 1948; *s* of Alexander and Isabella Affleck (*née* Beaton); *m* 1971, Janice Smillie Coulter; one *d*. *Educ:* Dumbarton Acad.; Glasgow Univ. (BSc); Glasgow Coll. of Technology (PhD); CEng, MIEE 1983, FIEE 1990. Projects Manager, Scottish Colorfoto Labs, 1970–72; Research Student, Portsmouth Polytechnic, 1972–73 (liquid crystal displays); RSRE, Malvern, 1973–82 (displays and L-B films); Unilever Research, 1982, Principal Scientist, 1984–86 (electronic biosensors); Chief Scientist, THORN EMI plc, 1986–94. Vis. Prof. of Electrical and Electronic Engrg, Univ. of Glasgow, 1985–. Chm., Inter-Agency Cttee for Marine Sci. and Technol., 1991–93; Member: Opto-electronics Cttee, Rank Prize Funds, 1985–; Science Consultative Gp, BBC, 1989–91; ABRC, 1990–93. A Vice-Pres. and Mem. Council, Royal Soc., 1989–91. Paterson Medal and Prize, Inst. of Physics, 1984; Best Paper Award, Soc. for Inf. Display, 1983. *Publications:* numerous sci. and tech. papers; numerous patents. *Recreations:* music, horology. *Address:* Kings Close, 11 Main Road, Biddenham, Bedford MK40 4BB.

SHANNON, 9th Earl of, *cr* 1756; **Richard Bentinck Boyle;** Viscount Boyle, Baron of Castle-Martyr, 1756; Baron Carleton (GB), 1786; late Captain Irish Guards; Director of companies; *b* 23 Oct. 1924; *o s* of 8th Earl of Shannon; *S* father, 1963; *m* 1st, 1947, Catherine Irene Helen (marr. diss. 1955), *d* of the Marquis Demetrio Imperiali di Francavilla; 2nd, 1957, Susan Margaret (marr. diss. 1979), *d* of late J. P. R. Hogg; one *s* two *d*; 3rd, 1994, Almine, *d* of late Rocco Catorsia de Villiers, Cape Town. *Educ:* Eton College. A Dep. Speaker and Dep. Chm. of Cttees, House of Lords, 1968–78; Chm., British-Armenian All-Party Parly Gp. Dir, Cttee of Dirs of Res. Assocs, 1969–85; Sec. and Treas., Fedn of Eur. Indust. Co-operative Res. Orgns, 1971–86; President: Architectural Metalwork Assoc., 1966–74; Kent Br., BIM, 1970–87; Vice-President: Aslib, 1974; British Hydromechanics Res. Assoc., 1975–87; Foundn for Sci. and Tech. (Chm., 1977–83); IWA. Hon. Pres., Foundn for the Educn of the Underachieving and Dyslexic. FRSA, FIMgt, FBHI. *Heir: s* Viscount Boyle, *qv*. *Address:* Pimm's Cottage, Man's Hill, Burghfield Common, Berks RG7 3BD. *Club:* White's.

SHANNON, David William Francis, PhD; Chief Scientist (Agriculture and Horticulture), Ministry of Agriculture, Fisheries and Food, since 1986; *b* 16 Aug. 1941; *s* of late William Francis Shannon and Elizabeth (*née* Gibson); *m* 1967, Rosamond (*née* Bond); one *s* one *d*. *Educ:* Wallace High Sch., Lisburn, NI; Queen's Univ., Belfast (BAgr, PhD); DMS Napier Coll., Edinburgh, 1976. Poultry Res. Centre, ARC, Edinburgh, 1967; study leave; Dept of Animal Science, Univ. of Alberta, Edmonton, 1973–74; Hd of Nutrition Sect., Poultry Res. Centre, AFRC, 1977, Dir, 1978. Mem., AFRC, 1986–94; Pres., UK Br., World's Poultry Science Assoc., 1986–90. Chm., Exec. Council, CAB Internat., 1988–91. *Publications:* contribs to learned jls on poultry science and animal nutrition. *Recreations:* golf, bridge. *Address:* Ministry of Agriculture, Fisheries and Food, Nobel House, 17 Smith Square, SW1P 3HX. *T:* 0171–238 5526.

SHAPCOTT, Sidney Edward, CEng, FIEE, FInstP; Director-General, Airborne Weapons and Electronic Systems, Ministry of Defence, 1976–80; *b* 20 June 1920; *s* of late Percy Thomas and Beatrice Shapcott; *m* 1943, Betty Jean Richens; two *s* one *d*. *Educ:* Hele's School, Exeter; King's College, London. BSc. Joined Air Defence Experimental Establishment, 1941; various appointments in Min. of Supply and Min. of Aviation, 1941–62; DCSO, 1963; Dir of Projects, ESRO, 1963–65; Min. of Defence, Navy Dept, 1965–75; CSO, 1968; Dep. Dir, Admiralty Surface Weapons Establishment, 1968–72; Dir, Underwater Weapon Projects, Admiralty Underwater Weapons Establishment, Portland, 1972–75. Defence Engrng Consultant, 1981–85. *Address:* 23 Upper Churston Rise, Seaton, Devon EX12 2HD. *T:* Seaton (01297) 21545.

SHAPER, Prof. (Andrew) Gerald, FRCP; FRCPath; FFPHM; Professor of Clinical Epidemiology and Head of Department of Public Health and Primary Care, Royal Free Hospital School of Medicine, University of London, 1975–92, now Professor Emeritus; *b* 9 Aug. 1927; *s* of Jack and Molly Shaper; *m* 1952, Lorna June Clarke; one *s*. *Educ:* Univ. of Cape Town (MB ChB); DTM&H with Milne Medal (Liverpool). Ho. Phys./Surg., Harare, 1952; SHO, Trop. Diseases Unit, Sefton Gen. Hosp., Liverpool, and Res. Asst, Liverpool Sch. of Trop. Med., 1953–54; Registrar: Clatterbridge Gen. Hosp., 1954–55; Hammersmith Hosp. and Post Grad. Med. Sch., 1955–56; Lectr, Sen. Lectr, Reader in Medicine and Prof. of Cardiovascular Disease, Makerere Univ. Med. Sch., Kampala, 1957–69; Mem. Sci. Staff, MRC Social Medicine Unit, LSHTM, 1970–75; Hon. Cons. Phys. (Cardiology), UCH, 1975–87; Hon. Consultant in Community Medicine, subseq. Public Health Medicine, Hampstead HA, 1975–92. RCP Milroy Lectr, 1972; Pickering

Lectr, British Hypertension Soc., 1993. Chm., Jt Wkg Party of RCP and Brit. Cardiac Soc. on Prevention of Coronary Heart Disease, 1976; Member: DHSS Cttee on Med. Aspects of Water Quality, 1978–84; DHSS Cttee on Med. Aspects of Food Policy, 1979–83; Chairman: MRC Health Services Res. Panel, 1981–86; Heads of Academic Depts of Public Health (formerly Community) Medicine, 1987–90; Member: WHO Expert Adv. Panel on Cardiovascular Disease, 1975–; DHSS Central Health Monitoring Unit Steering Gp, 1989–91. Elected Mem., Commonwealth Caribbean MRC, 1986–. Alwyn Smith Prize Medal, FPHM, 1991. *Publications:* (ed) Medicine in a Tropical Environment, 1972; (ed) Cardiovascular Disease in the Tropics, 1974; Coronary Heart Disease: risks and reasons, 1988. *Recreations:* walking, second-hand/antiquarian books, theatre. *Address:* 8 Wentworth Hall, The Ridgeway, Mill Hill, NW7 1RJ. *T:* 0181–959 8742.

SHAPIRO, Dr Harold Tafler; President of Princeton University, since 1988; *b* Montreal, 1936; *m* Vivian; four *d. Educ:* McGill Univ. (Lieut Governor's Medal; BA 1956); Graduate Sch., Princeton (PhD Econ 1964). University of Michigan: Asst Prof. of Economics, 1964; Associate Prof., 1967; Prof., 1970–88; Vice-Pres. for Acad. Affairs and Chm., Cttee on Budget Admin, 1977; President, 1980–88; Prof. of Economics and Public Affairs, Princeton, 1988–. Director: Dow Chemical Co.; Nat. Bureau of Economic Research; Member: Conference Board Inc.; Bretton Woods Cttee; Govt-Univ.-Industry Res. Round-table; Inst. of Medicine, Nat. Acad. of Scis; Council of Advrs to Pres. Bush on Sci. and Technology, 1990–92. Mem., Amer. Philosophical Soc.; Fellow, Amer. Acad. of Arts and Scis. Trustee: Alfred P. Sloan Foundn; Univs Res. Assoc. *Address:* Princeton University, Princeton, NJ 08544, USA.

SHAPLAND, Maj.-Gen. Peter Charles, CB 1977; MBE 1960; MA; Senior Planning Inspector, Department of the Environment, 1980–93; *b* 14 July 1923; *s* of late F. C. Shapland, Merton Park, Surrey; *m* 1954, Joyce Barbara Shapland (*née* Peradon); two *s. Educ:* Rutlish Sch., Merton Park; St Catharine's Coll., Cambridge. Served War: commissioned Royal Engineers, 1944; QVO Madras Sappers and Miners, Indian Army, 1944–47. Served United Kingdom, Middle East (Canal Zone) and Cyprus, 1948–63. Attended Staff Coll., 1952; jssc, 1960. Lt-Col, 1965; comd in Aden, 1965–67; Brig., Dec. 1968; comd 30 Engineer Bde. Attended Royal Coll. of Defence Studies, 1971. Dep. Comdr and Chief of Staff, HQ SE Dist, 1972–74; Maj.-Gen. 1974; Dir, Volunteers Territorials and Cadets, MoD (Army), 1974–78, retired. Hon. Col, 73 Engineer Regt, TA, 1979–89; Col Comdt, RE, 1981–86. Chm., Combined Cadet Forces Assoc., 1982–; Pres., Instn of Royal Engrs, 1982–87. Mem., Worshipful Co. of Painter-Stainers, 1983–. *Publications:* contribs to Royal Engineers' Jl. *Recreations:* sailing, swimming. *Address:* c/o Royal Bank of Scotland, Drummonds London Branch, 49 Charing Cross, Admiralty Arch, SW1A 2DX. *Clubs:* Royal Ocean Racing; Royal Engineer Yacht (Chatham).

SHAPLAND, Sir William (Arthur), Kt 1982; Trustee, Bernard Sunley Charitable Foundation; *b* 20 Oct. 1912; *s* of late Arthur Frederick Shapland and of Alice Maud (*née* Jackson); *m* 1943; Madeline Annie (*née* Amiss); two *d. Educ:* Tollington Sch., Muswell Hill. Incorporated Accountant, 1936; Chartered Accountant, 1946. Allan Charlesworth & Co, Chartered Accountants, London, Cambridge and Rangoon, 1929–55; Blackwood Hodge, 1955–83 (Chm., 1965–83). Waynflete Fellow, Magdalen Coll., Oxford, 1981–; Hon. Fellow, St Catherine's College, Oxford, 1982. Hon. FRCS 1978. Past Master, Paviors' Co. KStJ 1987 (OStJ 1981). Hon. DSc Buckingham, 1983; Hon. DLitt Leicester, 1985. *Recreations:* golf, gardening, travel. *Address:* 44 Beech Drive, N2 9NY. *T:* 0181–883 5073.

SHARIF, Mohammad Nawaz; Member, and Leader of the Opposition, National Assembly of Pakistan; *b* 25 Dec. 1949; *m* Kalsoom Nawaz Sharif; two *s* two *d. Educ:* St Anthony Sch., Lahore; Government Coll., Lahore; University Law Coll., Lahore. Finance Minister, Govt of Punjab, 1981–85; Chief Minister, Punjab, 1985–90; Prime Minister of Pakistan, 1990–93. *Recreations:* sports, especially cricket. *Address:* 180-H, Model Town, Lahore, Pakistan. *T:* 5835000.

SHARKEY, Colum John, CMG 1984; MBE 1973; HM Diplomatic Service, retired; *b* 9 June 1931; *s* of late Andrew Sharkey and late Sarah Josephine Sharkey (*née* Whelan); *m* 1962, Olivia Anne (*née* Brassil); two *s* one *d.* Commonwealth Relations Office, 1954; served in New Delhi, 1955, Calcutta, 1956–58; Second Secretary: Dacca, 1959–61; Melbourne, 1962–66; Montevideo, 1967–68 (joined HM Diplomatic Service, 1968); First Sec. and Consul, Asuncion, 1969; First Sec., Montevideo, 1971; seconded to Dept of Trade, 1972–74; Consul, Vancouver, 1974–78; Consul-Gen., Bilbao, 1978–81; Ambassador to Honduras, 1981–84 and non-resident Ambassador to El Salvador, 1982–84; Head of British Interests Section, Buenos Aires, 1984–87; Ambassador to Bolivia, 1987–89, to Uruguay, 1989–91, retd, then re-engaged as Personnel Assessor, FCO, 1991–93. *Recreations:* tennis, adjusting pictures, golf. *Address:* c/o Foreign and Commonwealth Office, King Charles Street, SW1A 2AH.

SHARLAND, (Edward) John; HM Diplomatic Service, retired; High Commissioner, the Seychelles, 1992–95; *b* 25 Dec. 1937; *s* of late William Rex Sharland and Phyllis Eileen Sharland (*née* Pitts); *m* 1970, Susan Mary Rodway Millard; four *d. Educ:* Monmouth Sch.; Jesus Coll., Oxford. BA Hons History; MA. FO, 1961–62; Bangkok, 1962–67; Far Eastern Dept, FCO, 1967–69; Dep. Perm. Rep. to UNIDO and Dep. Resident Rep. to IAEA, Vienna, 1969–72; Bangkok, 1972–75; Montevideo, 1976–79; Cultural Relations Dept, FCO, 1979–82; Consul-Gen., Perth, 1982–87; Consul-Gen., Cleveland, 1987–89; High Comr, PNG, 1989–91. *Recreations:* tennis, bridge, stamp collecting. *Address:* 21 Maidstone Road, Lenham, Kent ME17 2QH. *Club:* Royal Bangkok Sports.

SHARMA, Dr Shanker Dayal; President of India, since 1992; *b* 19 Aug. 1918. *Educ:* Lucknow Univ.; Cambridge Univ.; Lincoln's Inn. MA, LLM, PhD. Lawyer, 1942–; Mem., All India Congress Cttee, 1950–; Pres., Bhopal State Congress Cttee, 1950–52; Chief Minister, Bhopal, 1952–56; Minister, Madhya Pradesh Govt, 1956–67; Gen. Sec., Indian Nat. Congress, 1968–72; Pres., All India Congress Cttee, 1972–74; Mem., Lokh Sabha, 1971–77; Minister of Communications, 1974–77; former Governor, Andhra Pradesh, 1985, Punjab, 1985–86; suspended from Congress Party (I), 1986; Vice Pres. of India, 1987–92. Editor in Chief, Light and Learning, Ilm-au-Noor; Editor, Lucknow Law Jl. Hon. DPA London; Hon. LLD: Vikram and Bhopal Univs; Cantab, 1993. *Publication:* Congress Approach to International Affairs. *Address:* Rashtrapati Bhavan, New Delhi 110004, India.

SHARMA, Usha Kumari, (Mrs V. K. Sharma); *see* Prashar, U. K.

SHARMAN, Maj.-Gen. Alan George, CEng, FIMechE; Director General Land Systems, Ministry of Defence (Procurement Executive), since 1995; *b* 14 May 1942; *s* of late Major Frederick Sharman and Margaret (*née* Watkins); *m* 1st, 1967, Caroline Anne Lister; one *d*; 2nd, 1977, Juanita Jane Lawson; one *s* one *d. Educ:* Hutton Grammar Sch.; Welbeck Coll.; RMC, Sandhurst; Army Staff Coll. Commnd REME, 1962; served Aden and Oman, 1963; EME The Life Guards, Singapore, 1967–68; Comd AMF(L) Workshop, 1978–79; Mil. Sec's Dept, MoD, 1979–80; Comdr Maintenance, 1 (Br) Corps Troops, 1984; Col. EME 7, 1985–87; Project Manager, Logistic Vehicles, MoD (PE), 1987–89; Prog. Dir, Tank Systems, MoD (PE), 1991–95. Chm., Auto. Div., IMechE, 1996. *Recreations:* sailing, photography, family. *Address:* c/o Drummonds, 49 Charing Cross, SW1A 2DX. *Club:* Royal Air Force Yacht.

SHARMAN, Colin Morven, OBE 1979; FCA; Chairman and Senior Partner, KPMG, since 1994; *b* 19 Feb. 1943; *s* of Col Terence John Sharman and Audrey Emmiline Sharman (*née* Newman); *m* 1966, Angela M. Timmins; one *s* one *d. Educ:* Bishops Wordsworth Sch., Salisbury. FCA 1977. Qualified as Chartered Accountant with Woolgar Hennel & Co., 1965; joined Peat Marwick Mitchell, later KPMG Peat Marwick, then KPMG, 1966; Manager, Frankfurt office, 1970–72; The Hague, 1972–81 (Partner 1973, Partner i/c, 1975); London, 1981–; Sen. Partner (Nat. Mkting and Industry Gps), 1987–90; Sen. Mgt Consultancy Partner, 1989–91; Sen. Regl Partner (London and SE), 1990–93. Liveryman, Co. of Gunmakers, 1992. *Recreations:* shooting, sailing, opera, wine and food. *Address:* KPMG, 8 Salisbury Square, EC4Y 8BB. *T:* 0171–311 1000. *Clubs:* Carlton; Bembridge Sailing.

SHARMAN, Evelyn Janet, (Jane); Director of Conservation, English Heritage, since 1991; *b* 5 July 1943; *d* of Kenneth Blair Austin Dobson and Evelyn Barbara Dobson (*née* Phillips); *m* 1972, John Matthew Reid Sharman; two *s. Educ:* St Andrews Univ. (MA 1st Cl. Hons Mod. and Med. History); Bryn Mawr Coll., USA. Asst Principal, MPBW then DoE, 1968–72; Principal, DoE, 1972–85 (incl. secondment to Cabinet Office and Royal Commn on Envmtl Pollution); English Heritage: Head, Ancient Monuments Div., 1985–89; Actg Dir of Conservation, 1989–91. Sec., Historic Buildings Council, 1981–84. *Recreations:* reading, walking, travelling. *Address:* 51 Foyle Road, SE3 7RQ. *T:* 0181–858 7341.

SHARMAN, Peter William, CBE 1984; Director, 1974–95 and Chief General Manager, 1975–84, Norwich Union Insurance Group; *b* 1 June 1924; *s* of William Charles Sharman and Olive Mabel (*née* Burl); *m* 1946, Eileen Barbara Crix; one *s* two *d. Educ:* Northgate Grammar Sch., Ipswich; Edinburgh Univ. MA 1950; FIA 1956. War service as Pilot, RAF. Joined Norwich Union Insce Gp, 1950; Gen. Man. and Actuary, 1969. Chairman: Life Offices' Assoc., 1977–78; British Insurance Assoc., 1982–83. *Recreations:* tennis, badminton, golf. *Address:* 28B Eaton Road, Norwich NR4 6PZ. *T:* Norwich (01603) 451230.

SHARP, Sir Adrian, 4th Bt *cr* 1922, of Warden Court, Maidstone, Kent; *b* 17 Sept. 1951; *s* of Sir Edward Herbert Sharp, 3rd Bt and of Beryl Kathleen, *d* of Leonard Simmons-Green; *S* father, 1986; *m* 1st, 1976, Hazel Patricia Bothwell (marr. diss. 1986), *o d* of James Trevor Wallace; 2nd, 1994, Denise, *o d* of Percy Edward Roberts; one *s. Heir: s* Hayden Sean Sharp, *b* 27 Aug. 1994. *Address:* 91 Pentz Drive, Flamingovlei, Tableview, Cape Town, South Africa.

SHARP, His Honour Alastair George, MBE 1945; QC 1961; DL; a Circuit Judge (formerly Judge of County Courts), 1962–84; Liaison Judge, Durham County Magistrates Courts, 1972–84; *b* 25 May 1911; *s* of late Alexander Sharp, Advocate in Aberdeen, and of late Mrs Isabella Sharp, OBE; *m* 1940, Daphne Sybil, *d* of late Maj. Harold Smithers, RGA, and late Mrs Connor; one *s* two *d. Educ:* Aberdeen Grammar School; Fettes; Clare College, Cambridge (Archdeacon Johnson Exhibitioner in Classics). BA 1933, 1st Class Hons Classical Tripos Part II, Aegrotat Part I. Boxed Cambridge Univ., 1931–32; Cambridge Union Debating Team in America, 1933. On staff of Bonar Law College, Ashridge, 1934–35; Barrister, Middle Temple, 1935; Harmsworth Law Scholar; North Eastern Circuit, 1936. Dep. Chm. of Agricultural Land Tribunal, Northern Area, 1958–62; Asst Recorder of Huddersfield, 1958–60; Recorder of Rotherham, 1960–62; Dep. Chm., N Riding Yorks QS, 1959–65; Dep. Chm., 1965–70, Chm., 1970–71, Durham QS. Chm., Washington New Town Licensed Premises Cttee, 1966–78; Jt Pres., Council of Circuit Judges, 1979. Commissioned, The Gordon Highlanders, Feb. 1939; served War of 1939–45: Staff Coll., 1943; 2nd Bn The London Scottish, 1943; Gen. Staff, War Office, 1944–45, Temp. Major. Governor, Sherburn Hosp. Charity, 1972–81. Mem. Board, Faculty of Law, Durham Univ., 1976–84. DL Co. Durham, 1973. *Recreations:* golf, gardening, music, hill walking, fishing. *Address:* High Point, Western Hill, Durham DH1 4RG; The Old Kennels, Tomintoul, Banffshire AB37 9EN. *Clubs:* Durham County; Brancepeth Castle Golf.

See also Baron Mackie of Benshie, Sir R. L. Sharp.

SHARP, Christopher; *see* Sharp, J. C.

SHARP, Derek Joseph; British Council Representative, Italy, 1981–85, retired; *b* 12 June 1925; *s* of Joseph Frank Sharp and Sylvia May (*née* Allen); *m* 1957, Hilda Francesca Cernigoj; two *s. Educ:* Preston Grammar School; Queen's Coll., Oxford; MA, DipEd. Lectr, British Inst., Milan, 1956–58; British Council, 1958; served Indonesia, Bristol, Bangkok, Addis Ababa, Pretoria and London, 1958–77; Controller, Africa and Middle East Div., 1977–81. Mem., British Cttee for Preservation of Venice (Venice in Peril Fund), 1989–. *Address:* 3 Hartley Close, Bickley, Kent BR1 2TP.

SHARP, Sir George, Kt 1976; OBE 1969; JP; DL; Managing Trustee, Municipal Mutual Insurance Co. Ltd, 1979–91; Chairman, Glenrothes Development Corporation, 1978–86 (Vice-Chairman, 1973–78); *b* 8 April 1919; *s* of Angus Sharp and Mary S. McNee; *m* 1948, Elsie May Rodger, *o d* of David Porter Rodger and Williamina S. Young; one *s. Educ:* Thornton Public Sch.; Buckhaven High Sch. Engine driver, 1962; PRO, 1962–69. Fife County Council: Mem., 1945–75; Chm., Water and Drainage Cttee, 1955–61; Chm., Finance Cttee, 1961–72; Convener, 1972–75; Convener, Fife Regional Council, 1974–78. President: Assoc. of County Councils, 1972–74; Convention of Scottish Local Authorities, 1975–78. Chairman: Kirkcaldy Dist Council, 1958–75; Fife and Kinross Water Bd, 1967–75; Forth River Purification Bd, 1955–67 and 1975–78; Scottish River Purification Adv. Cttee, 1967–75; Scottish Tourist Consultative Council, 1979–83. Vice-Chairman: Forth Road Bridge Cttee, 1972–78; Tay Road Bridge Cttee, 1992–. Member: Scottish Water Adv. Cttee, 1962–69; Cttee of Enquiry into Salmon and Trout Fishing, 1963; Potato Marketing Bd, 1965–71; Scottish Valuation Adv. Cttee, 1972; Cttee of Enquiry into Local Govt Finance, 1974–76; Scottish Develt Agency, 1975–80; Royal Commn on Legal Services in Scotland, 1978–80; Econ. and Soc. Cttee, EEC, 1982–86. Director: Grampian Television, 1975–89; National Girobank Scotland, 1985–90. JP Fife, 1975; DL Fife, 1978. *Recreations:* golf, gardening. *Address:* Strathlea, 56 Station Road, Thornton, Fife KY1 4AY. *T:* Glenrothes (01592) 774347.

SHARP, Lt-Col Granville Maynard, MA (Cantab); *b* 5 Jan. 1906; *s* of Walter Sharp, Cleckheaton, Yorks; *m* 1935, Margaret, *d* of Dr J. H. Vincent, Wembley Hill; two *d. Educ:* Cleckheaton Grammar School; Ashville College, Harrogate; St John's College, Cambridge, MA (Hons) (Economics). Lecturer in Economics at West Riding Technical Institutes, 1929–34; Chairman, Spenborough Housing and Town Planning Committee, 1935–39; Hon. Secretary, Spen Valley Divisional Labour Party, 1936–39; Battery Capt. 68 Anti-Tank Regt RA, 1939–42; Staff Capt. and DAQMG Belfast Area, 1942–43; Senior British Staff Officer, Economics Section, Allied Control Commission, Italy, 1943–44; Chief Economics and Supply Officer, Military Govt, Austria, 1944–45. MP (Lab) for Spen Valley Div. of West Riding of Yorks, 1945–50; PPS Min. of Civil Aviation,

1946; Chairman, Select Cttee of Estimates Sub-Cttee, 1946–48; Parliamentary Private Sec. to Minister of Works, 1947–50. Keymer Parish Councillor, 1969–83 (Vice-Chm., 1976–80); CC E Sussex, 1970–74; CC W Sussex, 1973–85 (Chm., Rts of Way Cttee, 1974–83); Member: Cuckfield RDC, 1971–74; Mid-Sussex DC, 1973–76. *Recreations:* swimming, singing, scything, Sussex Downs; attempting to preserve the local rural environment by every practical means, from collecting litter and clearing Rights of Way to chivvying authority (Queen Mother's Tidy Britain Award Certificate, 1989). *Address:* 31 Wilmington Close, Hassocks, West Sussex BN6 8QB. *T:* Hassocks (01273) 842294.

SHARP, (James) Christopher, CBE 1993; solicitor; Managing Director, Northern Rock Building Society, since 1985; *b* 24 Dec. 1939; *s* of late Stanley Sharp and Annie (*née* Owrid); *m* 1963, Mary Bromfield; one *s* two *d*. *Educ:* Stockport Grammar Sch.; Pembroke Coll., Oxford (MA). FCIB (FCBSI 1989). Salop CC, 1963–68; G. H. Morgan and Co., Solicitors, Shrewsbury, 1968–70; Northern Rock Building Soc., 1970–. CIMgt (CBIM 1989). *Recreations:* reading, resting, walking. *Address:* Northern Rock House, Gosforth, Newcastle upon Tyne, NE3 4PL. *T:* 0191–285 7191. *Club:* Northern Counties (Newcastle upon Tyne).

SHARP, Dr John, OBE 1994; Headmaster of Rossall School, 1973–87; *b* 18 Dec. 1927; *o s* of late Alfred and May Sharp, North Ives, Oxenhope, Keighley; *m* 1950, Jean Prosser; one *s* two *d*. *Educ:* Boys' Grammar Sch., Keighley; Brasenose Coll., Oxford (MA, MSc, DPhil). RAF Educn Br., 1950–52; research at Oxford, 1952–54; Marlborough College: Asst Master, 1954–56; Senior Chemistry Master, 1956–62; Senior Science Master, 1959–62; Headmaster, Christ Coll., Brecon, 1962–72. Co-opted Mem., Oxford and Cambridge Schools Examn Bd, 1966–74; Selected Mem., Breconshire Educn Cttee, 1966–72; Co-opted Mem., Lancs Educn Cttee, 1974–81; Divisional Chm., HMC, SW 1971 and NW 1977–78; Chm., HMC Acad. Policy Sub-Cttee, 1982–85. Chm., Independent Schs' Jt Council Accreditation and Consultancy Service, 1987–93; Governor: City Technology Coll., Kingshurst, Solihull, 1989–; Christ Coll., Brecon, 1992– (Chm., 1993–). *Publications:* contrib. Anal. Chim. Acta. *Recreations:* fishing, photography, roses and shrubs. *Address:* Woodend Cottage, St Michael's, Tenbury Wells, Worcs WR15 8TG. *Club:* East India.

SHARP, J(ohn) M(ichael) Cartwright; Secretary of Law Commission, 1968–78; *b* 11 Aug. 1918; *s* of W. H. Cartwright Sharp, KC, and Dorothy (*née* Shelton). *Educ:* Rossall Sch.; Lincoln Coll., Oxford. Royal Artillery, 1940–46. Called to Bar, Middle Temple, 1947. Lord Chancellor's Office, 1951–65; Legal Sec. to Law Officers, 1965; Asst Solicitor, Law Commn, 1966. *Recreations:* travel, reading. *Address:* 4 Down, The Quadrangle, Morden College, Blackheath SE2 0PW. *T:* 0181–305 1278. *Club:* Reform.

SHARP, Sir Kenneth (Johnston), Kt 1984; TD 1960; Partner, Baker, Tilly & Co. (formerly Howard, Tilly), Chartered Accountants, 1983–89; *b* 29 Dec. 1926; *s* of Johnston Sharp and late Ann Sharp (*née* Routledge); *m* 1955, Barbara Maud Keating; one *s*. *Educ:* Shrewsbury Sch.; St John's Coll., Cambridge (MA). ACA 1955, FCA 1960. Partner, Armstrong, Watson & Co., Chartered Accountants, 1955–75; Head, Govt Accountancy Service and Accountancy Advr to DoI, 1975–83. Indian Army, 1945–48; TA, 251st (Westmorland and Cumberland Yeo.) Field Regt RA, 1948–62; 2nd-in-Comd, 1959–62. Inst. of Chartered Accountants: Mem. Council, 1966–83; Vice-Pres., 1972–73; Dep. Pres., 1973–74; Pres., 1974–75. Master, Co. of Chartered Accountants in England and Wales, 1979–80. Mem., Governing Body, Shrewsbury Sch., 1976–. JP Carlisle, 1957–73. *Publications:* The Family Business and the Companies Act 1967, 1967; articles in professional accountancy press. *Recreation:* gardening. *Address:* Holly Tree House, Kelliwith, Feock, Truro, Cornwall TR3 6QZ. *Club:* United Oxford & Cambridge University.

SHARP, Leslie, QPM 1986; Chief Constable of Strathclyde Police, since 1991; *b* 14 May 1936; *s* of George James Sharp and Lily Mabel (*née* Moys); *m* 1st, 1956, Maureen (*née* Tyson) (decd); two *d*; 2nd, 1985, Audrey (*née* Sidwell); two *d*. *Educ:* University Coll. London (LLB). MRC, 1952–54; Nat. Service, Mddx Regt, 1954–56; Metropolitan Police, 1956–80; Asst Chief Constable, 1980–83, Dep. Chief Constable, 1983–88, W Midlands Police; Chief Constable, Cumbria Constab., 1988–91. FIMgt (FBIM 1986); FRSA 1992. *Recreations:* angling, cricket umpire, watercolour painting, gardening. *Address:* Police Headquarters, 173 Pitt Street, Glasgow G2 4JS.

SHARP, Michael Cartwright; *see* Sharp, J. M. C.

SHARP, Sir Milton Reginald, 3rd Bt, *cr* 1920; Capt. REME, TA; *b* 21 Nov. 1909; *s* of Sir Milton Sharp, 2nd Bt, and Gertrude (*d* 1940), *d* of John Earl, of London; *S* father, 1941; *m* 1951, Marie-Louise de Vignon, Paris. *Educ:* Shrewsbury; Trinity Hall, Cambridge. *Heir: cousin* Samuel Christopher Reginald Sharp [*b* 25 April 1936; *m* 1st, 1958, Sheila Moody (marr. diss. 1967); 2nd, 1969, Anna Rossi].

SHARP, Hon. Mitchell William, OC 1983; PC (Can.) 1963; Personal adviser to the Prime Minister of Canada, since 1993; *b* 11 May 1911; *s* of Thomas Sharp and Elizabeth (*née* Little); *m* 1938, Daisy Boyd (decd); one *s*; *m* 1976, Jeannette Dugal. *Educ:* University of Manitoba; London School of Economics. Statistician, Sanford Evans Statistical Service, 1926–36; Economist, James Richardson & Sons Ltd, 1937–42; Officer, Canadian Dept of Finance, Ottawa, 1942–51; Director Economic Policy Division, 1947–51; Associate Deputy Minister, Canadian Dept Trade and Commerce, 1951–57; Dep. Minister, 1957–58; Minister, 1963–65; elected to Canadian House of Commons, 1963; Minister of Finance, 1965–68; Sec. of State for External Affairs, 1968–74; Pres., Privy Council, 1974–76; Govt Leader in House of Commons, 1974–76; resigned from Parliament, 1978. Comr, Northern Pipeline Agency, 1978–88; Policy Associate, Strategicon Inc., Ottawa, 1988–93. Vice-Pres., Brazilian Traction, Light & Power Co., Toronto, 1958–62. Hon. LLD: Univ. of Manitoba, 1965; Univ. of Western Ontario, 1977; Carleton Univ., 1994; Hon. DrSocSci Ottawa, 1970. *Recreations:* music, walking. *Address:* 33 Monkland Avenue, Ottawa, Ontario K1S 1Y8, Canada. *T:* (613) 2388668.

SHARP, Prof. Phillip Allen, PhD; Salvador E. Luria Professor, since 1992 and Head, Department of Biology, since 1991, Center for Cancer Research, Massachusetts Institute of Technology; *b* 6 June 1944; *s* of Joseph W. Sharp and Katherin (*née* Colvin); *m* 1964, Ann Christine Holcombe; three *d*. *Educ:* Union Coll., Barbourville, Ky (BA 1966); Univ. of Illinois (PhD 1969). NIH Postdoctoral Fellow, CIT, 1969–71; Sen. Res. Investigator, Cold Spring Harbor Lab., NY, 1972–74; Massachusetts Institute of Technology: Associate Prof., 1974–79; Prof. of Biol., 1979–86; Class of '41 Prof., 1986–87; John D. MacArthur Prof., 1987–92; Associate Dir, 1982–85, Dir, 1985–91, Center for Cancer Res. Biogen, Inc.: Co-founder and Mem., Scientific and Director Bds, 1978–; Chm., Scientific Bd, 1987–. Member, Editorial Board: Cell, 1974–95; Jl Virol., 1974–86; Molecular and Cellular Biol., 1974–85. Nobel Prize in Physiology or Medicine, 1993. *Publications:* numerous scientific articles in jls and other pubns. *Recreations:* reading, fishing at summer house in Maine. *Address:* Center for Cancer Research, Room E17–529, Massachusetts Institute of Technology, 40 Ames Street, Cambridge, MA 02139–4307, USA. *T:* (617) 2536421.

SHARP, Sir Richard (Lyall), KCVO 1982; CB 1977; Ceremonial Officer, Management and Personnel Office (formerly Civil Service Department), 1977–82; *b* 27 March 1915; *s* of late Alexander Sharp, Advocate, Aberdeen, and late Mrs Isabella Sharp, OBE; *m* 1950, Jean Helen, *er d* of late Sir James Crombie, KCB, KBE, CMG; two *s* two *d* (and one *d* decd). *Educ:* Fettes Coll.; Aberdeen Univ.; Clare Coll., Cambridge. MA with 1st Class Hons Classics, Aberdeen 1937; BA with 1st Class in Classical Tripos pt II, Cambridge 1939. Served Royal Northumberland Fusiliers, 1939–46 (POW, Singapore and Siam, 1942–45). Principal, HM Treasury, 1946; Private Sec. to Chancellor of Exchequer, 1948–50 and to Minister of State for Economic Affairs, 1950; UK Treasury and Supply Delegn, Washington, 1952–56; Asst Sec., 1954; IDC, 1961; Under-Secretary: Nat. Bd for Prices and Incomes, 1966–68; HM Treasury, 1968–77. *Recreations:* playing the viola, viticulture, gardening. *Address:* Home Farm House, Briston, Melton Constable, Norfolk NR24 2HN. *T:* Melton Constable (01263) 860445.

See also Baron Mackie of Benshie, A. G. Sharp.

SHARP, Robert Charles, CMG 1971; Director of Public Works, Tasmania, 1949–71; *b* 20 Sept. 1907; *s* of Robert George Sharp and Gertrude Coral (*née* Bellette); *m* 1st, 1935, Margaret Fairbrass Andrewartha (*d* 1975); one *d*; 2nd, 1978, Marie, widow of Alan C. Wharton, St Albans, Herts. *Educ:* Univ. of Tasmania. BE 1929. Bridge Engr, Public Works, 1935. Enlisted RAE (Major): comd 2/4 Aust. Field Sqdn RAE, 1942; 1 Aust. Port Mtce Co. RAE, 1943; HQ Docks Ops Gp, 1944. Chief Engr, Public Works, 1946; State Co-ordinator of Works, 1949–71. *Address:* The Coach House, Wickwood Court, Sandpit Lane, St Albans, Herts AL1 4BP; 594 Sandy Bay Road, Hobart, Tasmania 7005, Australia. *Club:* Athenæum.

SHARP, Robin John Alfred, CB 1993; Director, Global Environment, Department of the Environment, 1994–95; *b* 30 July 1935; *s* of Robert Arthur Sharp and Yona Maud (*née* Brazier); *m* 1963, Anne Elizabeth Davison. *Educ:* Brentwood Sch.; Brasenose Coll., Oxford (MA); Wesley House, Cambridge (BA). Methodist Minister, West Mersea, 1960–62; Theol Colls Sec., SCM, 1962–65; Minister, Paddington, 1965–66. Principal, Min. of Housing and Local Govt and DoE, 1966–72; Asst Sec., 1972; Special Advr to Chancellor of Duchy of Lancaster, Cabinet Office, 1972; Department of the Environment: Road Safety Div., 1972–75; Housing Div., 1975–81; Under Sec., 1981; Public Housing and Right to Buy, 1981–86; Local Govt, 1986–91; Dir of Rural Affairs, 1991–94. *Publications:* (jtly) Preparing for the Ministry of the 1970's, 1964; (jtly) Worship in a United Church, 1964. *Recreations:* bird-watching, walking, concert-going, travel. *Address:* 30 Windermere Avenue, NW6 6LN. *T:* 0181–969 0381.

SHARP, Thomas, (Tom), CBE 1987; retired; General Manager, Names' Interests, Lloyd's of London, 1987–91; *b* 19 June 1931; *s* of late William Douglas Sharp and Margaret Sharp (*née* Tout); *m* 1962, Margaret Lucy Hailstone; two *d*. *Educ:* Brown Sch., Toronto; Abbotsholme Sch., Derbs; Jesus Coll., Oxford. BoT and DTI (with short interval HM Treasury), 1954–73; Counsellor (Commercial), British Embassy, Washington, 1973–76; Dept of Trade, 1976–79; Dept of Industry, 1979–83; DTI, 1983–87. Member (Lib Dem): Surrey CC, 1989– (Chm., Social Services Cttee, 1993–95); Guildford BC, 1991–. *Address:* 96 London Road, Guildford, Surrey GU1 1TH. *T:* Guildford (01483) 572669.

SHARP, William Johnstone, CB 1983; Controller and Chief Executive, Her Majesty's Stationery Office and Queen's Printer of Acts of Parliament, 1981–86; *b* 30 May 1926; *s* of Frederick Matthew and Gladys Evelyn Sharp; *m* 1952, Joan Alice Clark, MBE, *d* of Arnold and Violet Clark. *Educ:* Queen Elizabeth Grammar Sch., Hexham; Emmanuel Coll., Cambridge (MA). Army Service, Reconnaissance Corps, Durham LI and Staff, 1944–48. Entered Min. of Transport, 1949; Private Sec. to Perm. Sec., 1951–53; Principal, Min. of Civil Aviation, 1953; Asst Sec., Min. of Transport, 1962; Under-Sec., DoE, 1970; Controller of Supplies, PSA, 1976–80. FRSA 1984. Hon. Life Member: Nat. State Printing Assoc. (USA), 1987; Internat. Govt Printers Assoc., 1988. *Recreation:* the Turf. *Address:* 43 Friars Quay, Norwich NR3 1ES. *T:* Norwich (01603) 624258.

SHARPE, Brian Sidney; Consultant, financial and marketing presentation, since 1985; *b* 12 Feb. 1927; *s* of S. H. Sharpe and Norah Sharpe; *m* 1967, Susan Lillywhite; two *s*. *Educ:* Haberdashers' Aske's Sch., Hampstead; Guildhall Sch. of Music and Drama. Royal Fusiliers (att. Forces Broadcasting Service), 1945–48; BBC: Announcer, Midland Region, 1955; Television Presentation, 1956; Producer, African Service, External Services, 1957; Senior Producer: Overseas Talks and Features, 1965; The Financial World Tonight, Radio 4, 1974; Money Programme, Sept-Dec. 1979; on secondment as Exec. Dir, City Communications Centre, 1976–79; Director: Charles Barker Lyons, 1980–85; Charles Barker City, 1983–85. Town Councillor (Lib Dem), 1986–, Town Mayor, 1991–92, Godalming; Bor. Councillor (Lib Dem), Waverley, 1987–. *Publications:* How Money Works (with A. Wilson), 1975; several articles on corporate and other forms of communication. *Recreations:* offshore fishing, music. *Address:* 26 Hallam Road, Godalming, Surrey GU7 3HW. *T:* Godalming (01483) 421551.

SHARPE, David Thomas, OBE 1986; FRCS; Consultant Plastic Surgeon, St Luke's Hospital, Bradford, Bradford Royal Infirmary, Royal Halifax Infirmary and Huddersfield Royal Infirmary, since 1985; Director, Plastic Surgery and Burns Research Unit, University of Bradford, since 1986; Chairman and Managing Director: Plastech Research and Design Ltd, since 1984; Leeds Central Helicopters Ltd, since 1993; *b* 14 Jan. 1946; *s* of Albert Edward Sharpe and Grace Emily Sharpe; *m* 1971, Patricia Lilian Meredith; one *s* two *d*. *Educ:* Grammar School for Boys, Gravesend; Downing Coll., Cambridge (MA); Clin. Med. Sch., Oxford (MB BChir); FRCS 1975. Ho. Surg., Radcliffe Inf., Oxford, 1970–71; Senior House Officer: Plastic Surgery, Churchill Hosp., Oxford, 1971–72; Accident Service, Radcliffe Inf., 1972; Pathology, Radcliffe Inf., 1972–73; Gen. Surgery, Royal United Hosp., Bath, 1973–75; Plastic Surgery, Welsh Plastic Surgery Unit, Chepstow, 1976; Registrar, Plastic Surgery: Chepstow, 1976–78; Canniesburn Hosp., Glasgow, 1978–80; Sen. Registrar, Plastic Surgery, Leeds and Bradford, 1980–84; Visiting Consultant Plastic Surgeon: Yorkshire Clinic, Bradford, 1985–; BUPA Hosp., Elland, W Yorks, 1985–; Cromwell Hosp., London, 1985–. Inventor and designer of med. equipment and surgical instruments and devices; exhibitor, Design Council, London, 1987. British Design Award, 1988; Prince of Wales Award for Innovation and Production, 1988. *Publications:* chapters, leading articles and papers on plastic surgery topics, major burn disaster management, tissue expansion and breast reconstruction. *Recreations:* painting, shooting, flying. *Address:* Hazelbrae, Calverley, Leeds LS28 5QQ. *T:* Leeds (0113) 257 0027.

SHARPE, Hon. Sir John (Henry), Kt 1977; CBE 1972; JP; *b* 8 Nov. 1921; *s* of Harry Sharpe; *m* 1948, Eileen Margaret, *d* of George Morrow, BC, Canada; one *s* one *d*. *Educ:* Warwick Acad., Warwick, Bermuda; Mount Allison Commercial Coll., Sackville, New Brunswick. Served War of 1939–45: Pilot Officer, with Bomber Comd, NW Europe, RCAF, attached RAF. Chm., Purvis Ltd (Importers), Bermuda. MP Warwick W, Bermuda, 1963–93; Minister of Finance, 1968–75; Dep. Leader of Govt, 1971–75; Premier of Bermuda, 1975–77, resigned; Minister: of Transport, May-Dec. 1980; of Marine and Air Services, 1980–82; of Home Affairs, 1982–88; of Legislative and Delegated Affairs, 1988–90; of Labour and Home Affairs, 1990–92; of Delegated and Legislative Affairs, 1990–93. Formerly Member several Parliamentary Select Cttees, and of Bd of Educn, Bermuda; also Dep. Chm., Central Planning Authority and Defence Bd. Delegate to Constitutional Conf., London, 1966. Mem., War Veterans Assoc., Bermuda; Warden,

Anglican Church. Hon. Life Vice Pres., Bermuda FA. *Address:* Uplands, Harbour Road, Warwick West, Bermuda; PO Box WK 223, Warwick WKBX, Bermuda.

SHARPE, John Herbert S.; *see* Subak-Sharpe.

SHARPE, Peter Samuel, QPM 1994; Chief Constable of Hertfordshire, since 1994; *b* 21 Nov. 1944; *s* of Arthur Samuel Sharpe and May Elizabeth Sharpe (*née* Eade); *m* 1985, Julia Anne Richens; one *s*. *Educ:* Varndean Grammar Sch., Brighton. Sussex Police: constable, Brighton Borough Police, 1963, rising to rank of Chief Superintendent, 1988–89; Mem. staff, Police Staff Coll., Bramshill, 1983–84; Surrey Police: Asst Chief Constable, 1989–91; Dep. Chief Constable, 1991–94. *Recreations:* cricket, golf. *Address:* Hertfordshire Police Headquarters, Stanborough Road, Welwyn Garden City, Herts AL8 6XF. *Club:* XL.

SHARPE, Thomas Anthony Edward; QC 1994; *b* 21 Dec. 1949; *e s* of late James Sharpe, MC, Maxwelltown, Dumfriesshire and of Lydia de Gegg, Donauworth, Germany; *m* 1st, 1974, Sheena M. Carmichael (marr. diss. 1987), *o d* of Lord Carmichael of Kelvingrove, *qv* and of Catherine McIntosh Carmichael, *qv*; one *s* one *d*; 2nd, 1988, Phillis M. Rogers, *y d* of late W. P. Rogers; one *s* one *d*. *Educ:* Trinity Hall, Cambridge (MA). Called to the Bar, Lincoln's Inn, 1976; Fellow in Law, Wolfson and Nuffield Coll., Oxford, 1979–88; in practice at the Bar, 1987–. Exec. Dir (part-time), Inst. for Fiscal Studies, 1981–87. *Publications:* monographs and articles in law jls on competition law, utility regulation and EC law. *Recreations:* opera, children. *Address:* 1 Essex Court, Temple, EC4Y 9AR. *T:* 0171–583 2000, *Fax:* 0171–583 0118. *Club:* Reform.

SHARPE, Thomas Ridley; novelist; *b* 30 March 1928; *s* of Rev. George Coverdale Sharpe and Grace Egerton Sharpe; *m* 1969, Nancy Anne Looper; three *d*. *Educ:* Lancing College; Pembroke Coll., Cambridge (MA). National service, Royal Marines, 1946–48. Social worker 1952, teacher 1952–56, photographer 1956–61, in S Africa; Lecturer in History, Cambridge Coll. of Arts and Technology, 1963–71; full time novelist, 1971–. *Publications:* Riotous Assembly, 1971; Indecent Exposure, 1973; Porterhouse Blue, 1974 (televised, 1987); Blott on the Landscape, 1975 (televised, 1985); Wilt, 1976 (filmed, 1989); The Great Pursuit, 1977; The Throwback, 1978; The Wilt Alternative, 1979; Ancestral Vices, 1980; Vintage Stuff, 1982; Wilt on High, 1984. *Recreations:* gardening, photography. *Address:* 38 Tunwells Lane, Great Shelford, Cambridge CB2 5LJ.

SHARPE, William, OBE 1967; HM Diplomatic Service, retired; Overseas Relations Adviser, Potato Marketing Board, 1979–89; *b* 9 Dec. 1923; *s* of late William Joseph Sharpe and of Phoebe Irene (*née* Standen); *m* 1959, Marie-Antoinette Rodesch; one *s*. *Educ:* High Sch., Chichester; London Univ. BA (Hons), MA, BSc Econ (Hons). Served RAF, 1943–47. Joined Foreign (subseq. Diplomatic) Service, 1947; Foreign Office 1947–52; Cologne and Bonn, 1952–54; Leopoldville, 1954–57; UK Mission to UN, New York, 1957–61; Foreign Office, 1961–66; Milan, 1966–70; FCO, 1971–72; Kuwait, 1972–75; Consul-Gen., Berlin, 1975–78. *Recreations:* reading, music, walking. *Address:* 15 Regis Avenue, Aldwick Bay, Bognor Regis, Sussex PO21 4HQ.

SHARPE, Prof. William Forsyth; Professor of Finance, Stanford University, since 1993 (Timken Professor of Finance, 1970–89); *b* 16 June 1934; *s* of Russell Thornley Sharpe and Evelyn Jillson Maloy; *m* 1st, 1954, Roberta Ruth Brandon; one *s* one *d*; 2nd, 1986, Kathryn Peck. *Educ:* UCLA (AB 1955; MA 1956; PhD 1961). Economist, Rand Corp., 1957–61; University of Washington: Asst Prof. of Economics, 1961–63; Associate Prof., 1963–67; Prof., 1967–68; Prof., Univ. of California, Irvine, 1968–70. Pres., William F. Sharpe Associates, 1986–92. Graham and Dodd Award, 1972, 1973, 1986, 1988, Nicholas Molodovsky Award, 1989, Financial Analysts Fedn; (jtly) Nobel Prize in Economics, 1990. *Publications:* Economics of Computers, 1969; Portfolio Theory and Capital Markets, 1970; Investments, 1978, 4th edn 1989; Fundamentals of Investments, 1989. *Recreations:* sailing, opera, music. *Address:* Graduate School of Business, Stanford University, Stanford, CA 94305-5015, USA. *T:* (415) 7251876.

SHARPLES, family name of **Baroness Sharples.**

SHARPLES, Baroness *cr* 1973 (Life Peer); **Pamela Sharples;** Director, TVS, 1981–90 and 1991–93; *b* 11 Feb. 1923; *o d* of late Lt-Comdr K. W. Newall and of Violet (who *m* 2nd, Lord Claud Hamilton, GCVO, CMG, DSO); *m* 1st, 1946, Major R. C. Sharples, MC, Welsh Guards (later Sir Richard Sharples, KCMG, OBE, MC, assassinated 1973); two *s* two *d*; 2nd, 1977, Patrick D. de Laszlo (*d* 1980); 3rd, 1983, Robert Douglas Swan. *Educ:* Southover Manor, Lewes; Florence. WAAF, 1941–46. Mem., Review Body on Armed Forces Pay, 1979–81. *Recreations:* gardening, fishing, tennis, golf. *Address:* 60 Westminster Gardens, SW1P 4JG. *T:* 0171–821 1875; Well Cottage, Higher Coombe, Shaftesbury, Dorset SP7 9LR. *T:* Shaftesbury (01747) 852971.
See also Hon. C. J. Sharples.

SHARPLES, Hon. Christopher John; Chairman, GNI Ltd, since 1994; *b* 24 May 1947; *s* of Sir Richard Sharples, KCMG, OBE, MC and of Baroness Sharples, *qv*; *m* 1975, Sharon Joanne Sweeny, *d* of late Robert Sweeny, DFC and Joanne Sweeny; one *s* two *d*. MSI 1992. VSO, India, 1965–66; C. Czarnikow Ltd (commodity brokers), 1968–72; Co-founder and Dir, Inter-Commodities Ltd, 1972– (renamed GNI Ltd, 1984); Director: GNI Holdings Ltd, 1984–; GNI Wallace Ltd, 1986–; Founder Dir and Chm., ICV Ltd, 1981–; Founder Dir and Chm., Intercom Data Systems, 1982–90; Chm., GH Asset Management Ltd, 1991–94; Dir, Gerrard Vivian Gray, 1994–. Member: Adv. Panel to SIB, 1986–87; City Panel on Takeovers and Mergers, 1991–; Association of Futures Brokers and Dealers, 1987–92: Chairman: Rules Cttee, 1987–91; F and GP Cttee, 1987–91; Chm., Securities and Futures Authority, 1991–95 (Chairman: Exec. Cttee, 1991–95; Capital Rules Cttee, 1991–95; Finance Cttee, 1991–95). International Petroleum Exchange: Dir, 1981–87; Dep. Chm., 1986–; Mem., Public Relns Cttee, 1981–; Member: Public Relns Cttee, London Commodity Exchange, 1983–; Clearing Cttee, LIFFE, 1982–; Taxation Cttee, British Fedn of Commodity Assocs, 1985–; London Markets Adv. Gp on Regulation, 1986–. *Recreations:* sailing, tennis, shooting, flying. *Address:* (office) Cannon Bridge, 25 Dowgate Hill, EC4R 2GN. *Clubs:* White's; Royal Yacht Squadron; Royal Bermuda Yacht.

SHARPLES, Florence Elizabeth; Executive Director, Young Women's Christian Association of Great Britain, 1987–93 (National General Secretary, 1978–87); *b* 27 May 1931; *d* of late Flying Officer Albert Sharples, RAFVR, and Kathleen (*née* Evans). *Educ:* Alice Ottley Sch., Worcester; Homerton Coll., Cambridge (Teachers' Cert.); King's Coll., London (Cert. Prof. in Religious Knowledge). Head of Religious Education: Bruton Sch. for Girls, Somerset, 1953–57; Loughton High Sch., Essex, 1957–60; Housemistress, Headington Sch., Oxford, 1960–66; Headmistress, Ancaster House, Bexhill, Sussex, 1966–78. Former Mem., New Philharmonia Chorus. *Recreation:* the theatre.

SHARPLEY, Ven. Roger Ernest Dion; Archdeacon of Hackney and Vicar of Guild Church of St Andrew, Holborn, 1981–92; *b* 19 Dec. 1928; *s* of Frederick Charles and Doris Irene Sharpley; unmarried. *Educ:* Dulwich College; Christ Church, Oxford (MA); St Stephen's House, Oxford. Deacon, 1954; Priest, 1955; Curate of St Columba, Southwick, 1954–60; Vicar of All Saints', Middlesbrough, 1960–81; Curate-in-charge, St Hilda with St Peter, Middlesbrough, 1964–72; RD of Middlesbrough, 1970–81; Canon and Prebendary of York Minster, 1974–81; Priest-in-charge, St Aidan, Middlesbrough, 1979–81. *Recreations:* hill and country walking. *Address:* 2 Hill Meadows, High Shincliffe, Durham DH1 2PE. *T:* Durham (0191) 3861908.

SHATTOCK, David John, CBE 1995; QPM 1985; Chief Constable, Avon and Somerset Constabulary, since 1989; *b* 25 Jan. 1936; *s* of Herbert John Shattock and Lucy Margaret Shattock; *m* 1973, Freda Thums; three *s*. *Educ:* Sir Richard Huish's Sch., Taunton. Joined as Constable, final post Asst Chief Constable, Somerset and Bath, later Avon and Somerset Constabulary, 1956–82; Deputy Chief Constable: Wilts Constab., 1983–85; Dyfed-Powys Police, 1985–86; Chief Constable, Dyfed-Powys Police, 1986–89. OStJ 1989. *Recreations:* racket sports, particularly badminton, antique restoration, keeping fit, horse riding. *Address:* PO Box 37, Portishead BS20 8QJ. *T:* Pill (01275) 818181. *Club:* Bristol Shakespeare (Bristol).

SHATTOCK, Sir Gordon, Kt 1985; Vice-Chairman, Veterinary Drug Co. PLC, since 1990 (Director, since 1982); Divisional Bursar, Western Division, Woodard Schools, since 1988; *b* 12 May 1928; *s* of Frederick Thomas and Rose May Irene Shattock; *m* 1952, Jeanne Mary Watkins (*d* 1984); one *s* one *d*; *m* 1988, Mrs Wendy Sale. *Educ:* Hele's Sch., Exeter; Royal Veterinary Coll., London. MRCVS. Senior Partner, St David's Vet. Hosp., Exeter, 1954–84. Mem., Exeter HA, 1987–93. Fellow of Woodard Corp., 1973–88; Executive Member: Animal Health Trust, 1978–; GBA, 1986–89; Mem. of Council, Guide Dogs for the Blind, 1985–; Chairman: Grenville Coll., 1982–88; Exeter Cathedral Music Foundn Trust, 1987–. FRSocMed 1987; FRSA 1990. Hon. FRVC 1994; Hon. Mem., BVA, 1989. Farriers' Company: Liveryman, 1978–; Mem. Ct of Assistants, 1986–; Master, 1992. *Publications:* contrib. to Jl Small Animal Practice; papers to British Veterinary Assoc. *Recreation:* gardening. *Address:* Lea House, Bishopsteignton, near Teignmouth, Devon TQ14 9TP.

SHAUGHNESSY, family name of **Baron Shaughnessy.**

SHAUGHNESSY, 3rd Baron, *cr* 1916, of Montreal; **William Graham Shaughnessy,** CD 1955; Director, Arbor Memorial Services Inc., Toronto, since 1972; *b* 28 March 1922; *s* of 2nd Baron and Marion (*d* 1936), *d* of late R. K. Graham, Montreal; *S* father, 1938; *m* 1944, Mary Whitley, *o d* of late John Whitley, Copthorne House, Letchworth; one *s* two *d* (and one *s* decd). *Educ:* Bishop's Coll. Sch. and Bishop's Univ., Lennoxville, Canada; BA 1941; MSc Columbia Univ., NY, 1947. Dir, Canada-UK Chamber of Commerce, 1981–. Member: Jt Cttee on Statutory Instruments, H of L, 1984–; Delegated Powers Scrutiny Cttee, H of L, 1992–. Trustee: The Last Post Fund Inc., Canada; Canada Meml Foundn (UK). Major (retd), Canadian Grenadier Guards; served NW Europe in World War II (despatches). *Heir: s* Hon. Michael James Shaughnessy, *b* 12 Nov. 1946. *Address:* House of Lords, SW1A 0PW. *Clubs:* Cavalry and Guards; University (Montreal).

SHAVE, Alan William, CVO 1994; OBE 1991; HM Diplomatic Service, retired; Governor, Anguilla, 1992–95; *b* 3 Nov. 1936; *s* of late William Alfred Shave and of Emily Shave; *m* 1961, Lidia Donoso Bertolotto; one *s* one *d*. *Educ:* George Green's Grammar sch., Poplar. Cert., Nat. Council of Journalists. Journalist, E London Advertiser, 1953–57; Nat. Service, RAF, 1957–59; Journalist: Greenock Telegraph, 1960; Bristol Evening World, 1961; Asst Information Officer, COI, 1961; joined CRO, 1961; Salisbury, Rhodesia, 1961–62; Dar es Salaam, 1962–64; Sydney, 1964–66; La Paz, 1966–70; FCO, 1970–72; Santiago, 1972–76; Consul (Commercial): Barcelona, 1977–81; Milan, 1981–84; First Sec., FCO, 1984–88; Dep. Hd of Mission and Consul, La Paz, 1988–92. *Recreations:* cycle racing, ornithology, travel. *Address:* c/o Foreign and Commonwealth Office, King Charles Street, SW1A 2AH.

SHAVE, Kenneth George, CEng, FIMechE; Member, London Transport Executive, 1967–73, retired; *b* 25 June 1908; *s* of George Shave and Frances Larkin; *m* 1935, Doris May Stone, one *s* one *d*. *Educ.* St Paul's School. Apprenticed London General Omnibus Company, 1925, Rolling Stock Engineer, East Surrey Traction Company, 1930; London Transport: Asst Divisional Engineer, 1935; Divisional Engineer, 1948; Rolling Stock Engineer, 1956; Chief Mechanical Engineer, 1965. CStJ 1971 (OStJ 1963). *Recreations:* golf, bridge, gardening. *Address:* 5 St Katherine's Road, Henley on Thames, Oxon RG9 1PJ. *T:* Henley (01491) 57 3379.

SHAW, family name of **Barons Craigmyle** and **Shaw of Northstead.**

SHAW OF NORTHSTEAD, Baron *cr* 1994 (Life Peer), of Liversedge in the County of West Yorkshire; **Michael Norman Shaw;** Kt 1982; JP; DL; *b* 9 Oct. 1920; *e s* of late Norman Shaw; *m* 1951, Joan Mary Louise, *o d* of Sir Alfred L. Mowat, 2nd Bt; three *s*. *Educ:* Sedbergh. Chartered Accountant. MP (L and C) Brighouse and Spenborough, March 1960–Oct. 1964; MP (C) Scarborough and Whitby, 1966–74, Scarborough, 1974–92. PPS to Minister of Labour, 1962–63, to Sec. of State, Dept of Trade and Industry, 1970–72, to Chancellor of the Duchy of Lancaster, 1973. Mem., UK Delegn to European Parlt, 1974–79. FCA. JP Dewsbury, 1953; DL W Yorks, 1977. *Address:* Duxbury Hall, Liversedge, W Yorkshire WF15 7NR. *T:* Heckmondwike (01924) 402270. *Club:* Carlton.

SHAW, Angela Brigid L.; *see* Lansbury, A. B.

SHAW, Maj.-Gen. Anthony John, CB 1988; CBE 1985; Director General, Army Medical Services, 1988–90, retired; *b* 13 July 1930; *s* of late Lt Col W. A. Shaw, MC and Mrs E. Shaw (*née* Malley); *m* 1961, Gillian Shaw (*née* Best); one *s* one *d*. *Educ:* Epsom College; Clare College, Cambridge (MA; MB BChir); Westminster Hosp. MRCS; LRCP 1954; D(Obst)RCOG 1956; DTM&H 1961; FFCM 1983; FRCP 1989. Casualty Officer, Westminster Hosp.; House Surgeon and Obst. House Officer, Kingston Hosp., 1955–56; Commissioned Lieut RAMC, 1956; Staff College, 1963; served in UK, Malta, Berlin, BAOR, MoD, Malaya, Nepal, Penang, Cameron Highlands; CO Field Ambulance, 1969–70; Chief Instructor, RAMC Training Centre, 1970–72; Nat. Defence Coll., 1973; ADGMS, MoD, 1973–76; CO Cambridge Mil. Hosp., 1977–79; Comdr Med. 2 Armd Div., BAOR, 1979–81; Comdr Med. SE Dist., 1981; Dir of Med. Supply, MoD, 1981–83; DDGAMS, 1983–84; Dir, Army Community and Occupational Medicine, 1983–87; Comdr Medical Servs, UKLF, 1984–87. QHP 1983–90. Member: BMA; Board of Faculty of Community Medicine, 1983–87. Fellow, Med. Soc. of London, 1988. CStJ 1989. *Recreations:* sailing, skiing, gardening, music, military history. *Club:* Lansdowne.

SHAW, Antony Michael Ninian; QC 1994; *b* 4 Oct. 1948; *s* of Harold Anthony Shaw and Edith Beatrice Sandbach (*née* Holmes); *m* 1983, Louise Göta Faugust; one *s* two *d*. *Educ:* King's Sch., Canterbury; Trinity Coll., Oxford (Schol.; BA Juris. 1969). Researcher in Law, Bedford Coll., London, 1972–74; called to the Bar, Middle Temple, 1975. Major cases: Guinness; Eagle Trust; Polly Peck; BCCI. Vice Chm., Fees and Legal Aid Cttee, Gen. Council of the Bar, 1995. *Publications:* contrib. Halsbury's Laws of England, 1977; (ed jtly) Archbold: Criminal Pleading, Evidence and Practice, 1991–; contrib. various law jls. *Recreations:* history, most literature. *Address:* 4 Brick Court, Temple, EC4Y 9AD. *T:* 0171–797 7766.

SHAW, Sir Barry; *see* Shaw, Sir C. B.

SHAW, Prof. Bernard Leslie, FRS 1978; Professor of Chemistry, University of Leeds, 1971–94; *b* Springhead, Yorks, 28 March 1930; *s* of Thomas Shaw and Vera Shaw (*née* Dale); *m* 1951, Mary Elizabeth Neild; two *s* (and one *s* decd). *Educ:* Hulme Grammar Sch., Oldham; Univ. of Manchester (BSc, PhD). Sen. DSIR Fellow, Torry Research Station, Aberdeen, 1953–55; Scientific Officer, CDEE, Porton, 1955–56; Technical Officer, ICI Ltd, Akers Research Labs, Welwyn, 1956–61; Lectr, Reader, and Prof., Univ. of Leeds, 1962–. Visiting Professor: Univ. of Western Ontario, 1969; Carnegie Mellon Univ., 1969; ANU, 1983; Univ. of Auckland, 1986; Univ. of Strasbourg, 1993. Liversidge Lectr, 1987–88, Ludwig Mond Lectr, 1992–93, Sir Edward Frankland Prize Lectr, 1996, RSC. Member: Royal Soc. Cttees; Royal Chem. Soc. Cttees; SERC (formerly SRC) Chem. Cttee, 1975–78, 1981–84 (and Inorganic Panel, 1977–78, Co-operative Grants Panel, 1982–84); Tilden Lectr and Prizewinner, 1975; Chem. Soc. Medal and Prize for Transition Metal Chem., 1975. *Publications:* Transition Metal Hydrides, 1967; (with N. Tucker) Organotransition Metal Chemistry, and Related Aspects of Homogeneous Catalysis, 1973; numerous original papers and reviews in chem. jls. *Recreations:* squash, tennis, pottery, music, walking, gardening. *Address:* School of Chemistry, The University of Leeds, Leeds LS2 9JT. *T:* Leeds (0113) 233 6401.

SHAW, Sir Brian (Piers), Kt 1986; Chairman: Port of London Authority, since 1993 (Member of the Authority, since 1987); Automobile Association, since 1995 (Committee Member, since 1988; Treasurer, 1990–93; Vice-Chairman, 1992–95); *b* 21 March 1933; *s* of late Percy Augustus Shaw and late Olive Shaw (*née* Hart); *m* 1962, Penelope Reece; three *s*. *Educ:* Wrekin Coll.; Corpus Christi Coll., Cambridge (MA). National Service (2nd Lieut, Cheshire Regt), 1951–53. Called to Bar, Gray's Inn, 1957, Bencher, 1992. Joined Pacific Steam Navigation Co., Liverpool, 1957; Company Secretary, 1960; Company Sec., Royal Mail Lines, London, 1961; Dir, Royal Mail Lines, 1968; Furness Withy & Co.: Manager, 1969; Dir, 1973; Man. Dir, 1977–87; Chm., 1979–90; Chairman: Shaw Savill & Albion Co., 1973; ANZ Grindlays Bank, 1987–95; Director: Overseas Containers Ltd, 1972–80; Nat. Bank of NZ, 1973–77 (London Board, 1977–80; Chm., London Adv. Cttee, 1980–84); New Zealand Line, 1974–79; Grindlays Bank, 1977–85; Orient Overseas (Holdings), 1980–91; ANZ Holdings (UK), 1985–87; Enterprise Oil, 1986–; Walter Runciman, 1988–90; Andrew Weir, 1991–. Mem., Gen. Cttee, Lloyd's Register of Shipping, 1974–; Chairman: Internat Chamber of Shipping, 1987–92; Council of European and Japanese Nat. Shipowners' Assocs (CENSA), 1979–84; Pres., Gen. Council of British Shipping, 1985–86. Pres., New Zealand Soc., 1979–80; Chm., Cook Soc., 1995. Prime Warden, Shipwrights' Co., 1993–94; Freeman, Watermen and Lightermen's Co., 1994; Elder Brother, Trinity House, 1989–. *Recreations:* golf, music, theatre, cricket. *Address:* The Coach House, Biddestone, Wilts SN14 7DQ. *T:* Corsham (01249) 713112. *Clubs:* Brooks's, MCC; Denham Golf.

SHAW, Sir (Charles) Barry, Kt 1980; CB 1974; QC 1964; DL; Director of Public Prosecutions for Northern Ireland, 1972–89; *b* 12 April 1923; *s* of late Ernest Hunter Shaw and Sarah Gertrude Shaw, Mayfield, Balmoral, Belfast; *m* 1964, Jane (*née* Phillips). *Educ:* Inchmarlo House, Belfast; Pannal Ash Coll., Harrogate; The Queen's Univ. of Belfast (LLB). Served War: commissioned RA, 97 A/Tk Regt RA, 15th (Scottish) Div., 1942–46. Called to Bar of Northern Ireland, 1948, Bencher 1968; called to Bar, Middle Temple, 1970, Hon. Bencher, 1986. DL Co. Down, 1990. *Address:* c/o Royal Courts of Justice, Belfast, Northern Ireland BT1 3NX.

SHAW, Prof. C(harles) Thurstan, CBE 1972; FBA 1991; Professor of Archaeology, University of Ibadan, 1963–74; *b* 27 June 1914; 2nd *s* of late Rev. John Herbert Shaw and Grace Irene (*née* Woollatt); *m* Gilian Ione Maud (*d* 1992), *e d* of late Edward John Penberthy Magor and Gilian Sarah (*née* Westmacott); two *s* three *d*. *Educ:* Blundell's Sch.; Sidney Sussex Coll., Cambridge; Univ. of London Inst. of Education. 1st cl. hons Arch. and Anthrop. Tripos 1936, MA, PhD Cantab; DipEd London. FRAI 1938; FSA 1947. Curator, Anthropology Museum, Achimota Coll., Gold Coast, 1937–45; Cambs Educn Cttee, 1945–51; Cambridge Inst. of Educn, 1951–63; Dir of Studies, Archaeol. and Anthrop., Magdalene Coll., Cambridge, 1976–79. Vis. Fellow, Clare Hall, Cambridge, 1973; Vis. Prof., Northwestern Univ., USA, 1969; Vis. Res. Prof., Ahmadu Bello Univ., 1975–78; Visiting Lecturer: Harvard, 1975; Yale, 1979; Calgary, 1980; Hans Wolff Meml Lectr, Indiana Univ., 1984. Founder and Editor: W African Archaeological Newsletter, 1964–70; W African Jl of Archaeology, 1971–75. Mem. Perm. Council, Internat. Union of Pre- and Proto-historic Sciences, 1965–74; Vice-Pres., Panafrican Congress on Prehistory and Study of Quaternary, 1966–77; Dir, and Mem. Exec. Cttee, World Archaeol Congress, 1986–89. Founder, and Chm., Icknield Way Assoc., 1984–89, Pres., 1989–; Pres., Prehistoric Soc., 1986–90. Mem. Council, Univ. of Ibadan, 1969–71. Hon. DSc: Univ. of Nigeria, 1982; Ibadan, 1989. Amaury Talbot Prize, Royal Anthrop. Inst., 1970 and 1978; Gold Medal, Soc. of Antiquaries, 1990. Onuna-Ekwulu Ora of Igbo-Ukwu, 1972; Onyofuonka of Igboland, 1989; Onuna Ekwulu Nri, 1989; Olokun-Ayala of Ife, 1991. *Publications:* Excavation at Dawu, 1961; Archaeology and Nigeria, 1964; (with J. Vanderburg) Bibliography of Nigerian Archaeology, 1969; (ed) Nigerian Prehistory and Archaeology, 1969; Igbo-Ukwu: an account of archaeological discoveries in eastern Nigeria, 2 vols, 1970; Discovering Nigeria's Past, 1975; Why 'Darkest' Africa?, 1975; Unearthing Igbo-Ukwu, 1977; Ancient People and Places: Nigeria, 1978; (with S. G. H. Daniels) Excavations at Iwo Eleru, Ondo State, Nigeria, 1988; (with K. D. Aiyedun) Prehistoric Settlement and Subsistence in the Kaduna Valley, Nigeria, 1989; (ed jtly) The Archaeology of Africa, 1993; numerous articles on African archaeology and prehistory in jls. *Recreations:* walking, music, calligraphy. *Address:* 26 Kingsdale Court, Peacocks, Great Shelford, Cambridge CB2 5AT. *T:* Cambridge (01223) 842283. *Clubs:* Athenæum; Explorers' (New York).

SHAW, Prof. Charles Timothy, CEng; Professor of Mining, since 1980, and Dean, since 1991, Royal School of Mines (Head of Department of Mineral Resources Engineering, 1980–85); *b* 4 Oct. 1934; *s* of Charles John and Constance Olive Shaw (*née* Scotton); *m* 1962, Tuulike Raili Linari-Linholm; one *s* two *d*. *Educ:* Univ. of Witwatersrand (BSc(Mining) 1956); McGill Univ. (MSc(Applied) (Mineral Exploration) 1959). Mine Manager's, Mine Overseer's and Mine Surveyor's Certs of SA; Chartered Engineer. Johannesburg Consolidated Investment Co. Ltd (JCI): numerous positions at various levels, 1960–67; Head of Computer Div., 1967–70; Manager, 1970–72 (as such an appointed dir of 14 cos incl. Consolidated Murchison Ltd and Alternate Dir of 9 cos); Consulting Engr, Consolidated Murchison Ltd, Randfontein Estates Gold Mining Co. (Wits.) Ltd and Shangani Mining Corp. (Zimbabwe), 1972–74; Consulting Engr and Alternate Dir, Rustenburg Platinum Mines Ltd, 1974–76; Chief Consulting Engr and Alternate Dir, Johannesburg Consolidated Investment Co. Ltd, also Man. Dir, Western Areas Gold Mining Co. Ltd, 1976–77; Associate Prof., Virginia Polytechnic Inst. and State Univ., 1977–80. Rep. for JCI on Technical Adv. Cttee of SA Chamber of Mines, 1974–77; Alternate Mem. for Gold Producers Cttee, 1976–77. Sec. Gen., Soc. of Mining Professors, 1990–; Member Council: InstnMM, 1981–88; IMinE, 1989– (Pres., S Counties Br., 1988–89). *Publications:* (with J. R. Lucas) The Coal Industry: Industry Guides for Accountants, Auditors and Financial Executives, 1980; papers both in technical literature and in house at Johannesburg Consolidated Investment Co. Ltd. *Recreations:* golf, mining history. *Address:* Department of Mineral Resources Engineering, Royal School of Mines, SW7 2BP. *T:* 0171–589 5111.

SHAW, Colin Don, CBE 1993; writer and lecturer; Director, Broadcasting Standards Council, since 1988; *b* 2 Nov. 1928; *s* of late Rupert M. Shaw and Enid F. Shaw (*née* Smith); *m* 1955, Elizabeth Ann, *d* of late Paul Bowker; one *s* two *d*. *Educ:* Liverpool Coll.; St Peter's Hall, Oxford (MA). Called to the Bar, Inner Temple, 1960. Nat. Service, RAF, 1947–49. Joined BBC as Radio Drama Producer, North Region, 1953; Asst, BBC Secretariat, 1957–59; Asst Head of Programme Contracts Dept, 1959–60; Sen. Asst, BBC Secretariat, 1960–63; special duties in connection with recruitment for BBC2, 1963; Asst Head of Programmes, BBC North Region, 1963–66; various posts in TV Programme Planning, ending as Head of Group, 1966–69; Secretary to the BBC, 1969–72, Chief Secretary, 1972–76; Dir of Television, IBA, 1977–83; Dir, Programme Planning Secretariat, ITCA, 1983–87. Vis. Fellow, Europ. Inst. for the Media, Düsseldorf, 1985–; Vis. Lectr, Annenberg Sch. of Communications, Univ. of Pa, 1988. Member: Arts Council of GB, 1978–80 (Chairman: Arts Council Research Adv. Gp, 1978–80; Housing the Arts Cttee, 1979–80; Touring Cttee, 1980); Home Office Working Party on Fear of Crime, 1990. Trustee, Internat. Inst. of Communications, 1983–89; Governor, E-SU of the Commonwealth, 1976–83; Chm., Bd of Governors, Hampden House Sch., 1972–77. FRTS 1987; FRSA 1978. *Publications:* several radio plays and a stage-play for children. *Recreations:* going to the theatre, reading. *Address:* Lesters, Little Ickford, Aylesbury, Bucks HP18 9HS. *T:* Ickford (018447) 339225. *Club:* Reform.

SHAW, David; Executive Director, International Badminton Federation, since 1992; *b* 19 Oct. 1936; *s* of Thomas Young Boyd Shaw and Elizabeth Shaw; *m* 1961, Margaret Esmé Bagnall; one *s* one *d*. *Educ:* Univ. of Birmingham (BA (Hons) Geography); Univ. of Sussex (Adv. Dip. Educnl Technology). Education Officer in Royal Air Force, final rank Sqn Ldr, 1960–76; Training Adviser to North Western Provincial Councils, 1976–78; Gen. Sec., British Amateur Athletic Bd, 1978–81; Gen. Sec., ITCA, then Dir, Indep. Television Assoc., 1981–92. Represented Great Britain in Athletics (3000 metres steeplechase), 1958; British Universities Cross-Country Champion, 1959. *Recreations:* reading, hill-climbing, sketching. *Address:* (business) 4 Manor Park, Mackenzie Way, Cheltenham, Glos GL51 9TX. *Club:* Royal Air Force.

SHAW, Prof. David Aitken, CBE 1989; FRCP, FRCPE; Professor of Clinical Neurology, University of Newcastle upon Tyne, 1976–89, now Emeritus; *b* 11 April 1924; *s* of John James McIntosh Shaw and Mina Draper; *m* 1960, Jill Parry; one *s* two *d*. *Educ:* Edinburgh Academy; Edinburgh Univ. MB ChB (Edin) 1951; FRCPE 1968; FRCP (Lond.) 1976. Served as Lieut RNVR, 1943–46. Hospital appts, Edinburgh Royal Infirmary, 1951–57; Lectr, Inst. of Neurology, Univ. of London, 1957–64; Mayo Foundation Fellow, 1962–63; University of Newcastle upon Tyne: Sen. Lectr, 1964–76; Public Orator, 1976–79; Dean of Medicine, 1981–89. Mem., GMC, 1979–94. Hon. FCST 1988. *Publications:* (with N. E. F. Cartlidge) Head Injury, 1981; chapters in books and scientific articles in medical jls. *Recreations:* golf and fishing. *Address:* The Coach House, 82 Moor Road North, Newcastle upon Tyne NE3 1AB. *T:* Newcastle upon Tyne (0191) 2852029. *Club:* Athenæum.

SHAW, David Lawrence; MP (C) Dover, since 1987; chartered accountant; Founder and Managing Director, Sabrelance Ltd; *b* 14 Nov. 1950; *m* 1986, Dr Lesley Brown; one *s* one *d*. *Educ:* King's Sch., Wimbledon; City of London Polytechnic. FCA 1974. Coopers & Lybrand, 1971–79; County Bank, 1979–83. Director: Hoskyns Brewery PLC; The Adscene Group PLC; Palladian Estates PLC. Mem., Royal Borough of Kingston upon Thames Council, 1974–78. Contested (C) Leigh, 1979. Chm., Bow Gp, 1983–84 (Founder, Transatlantic Conf., 1982); Jt Chm., All Party Cttee on Dolphins, 1989–; Mem., Social Security Cttee, 1991–; Vice Chm., Cons. Backbench Smaller Businesses Cttee, 1990– (Sec., 1987–90); Sec., Cons. Backbench Finance Cttee, 1990–. Vice-Chm., Kingston and Malden Cons. Assoc., 1979–86. *Address:* House of Commons, SW1A 0AA.

SHAW, Maj.-Gen. Dennis, CB 1991; CBE 1983 (OBE 1978); FIMechE; Director General Electrical and Mechanical Engineering (Army), 1988–91; *b* 11 May 1936; *s* of Nathan Shaw and Frances Ellen (*née* Cookson); *m* 1955, Barbara Tate; two *d*. *Educ:* Humberstone Foundn Sch.; Scunthorpe Grammar Sch.; Royal Military Coll. of Science. BScEng 1st Cl. Hons, London. Commd into REME, 1956; served in Cyprus, 1957–58, and with 3 Commando Bde, Far East, 1963–66; sc Shrivenham and Camberley, 1967–68; Staff of High Commn, Ottawa, 1969–70; comd 1 Corps Troops Workshop, W Germany, 1971–72; Dep. Asst Adjt Gen., MoD, 1972–74; NDC Latimer, 1974–75; comd Commando Logistic Regt, RM, 1975–78; Instr, Ghana Armed Forces Staff Coll., Accra, 1978–80; ACOS in Comd HQ, 1981–83; served Logistic Executive (Army), 1983; RCDS 1984; ACOS, HQ UKLF, 1985–87. Col Comdt, REME, 1991–. Dir, Greig Fester Group Services Ltd, 1994– (Gp Advr, 1992–). Liveryman, Turners' Co., 1990. Freeman, City of London, 1990. *Recreations:* golf, motoring. *Address:* c/o Royal Bank of Scotland, Laurie House, Victoria Road, Farnborough, Hants GU14 7NR. *Club:* Army and Navy.

SHAW, Dr Dennis Frederick, CBE 1974; Fellow, 1957, Professorial Fellow, 1977, Emeritus Fellow, 1992, Keble College, Oxford; Keeper of Scientific Books, Bodleian Library, Oxford, 1975–91; *b* 20 April 1924; 2nd *s* of Albert Shaw and Lily (*née* Hill), Teddington; *m* 1949, Joan Irene, *er d* of Sidney and Maud Chandler; one *s* three *d*. *Educ:* Harrow County Sch.; Christ Church, Oxford. BA 1945, MA 1950, DPhil 1950. FInstP 1971, CPhys; FZS. Jun. Sci. Officer, MAP, 1944–46; Res. Officer in Physics, Clarendon Lab., Oxford, 1950–57, Sen. Res. Officer 1957–64; Univ. Lectr in Physics, Oxford, 1964–75. Vis. Prof. of Physics and Brown Foundn Fellow, Univ. of the South, Tennessee, 1974. Hon. Mem., Internat. Assoc. of Technol Univ. Libraries, 1992 (Sec., 1983–85; Pres., 1986–90); International Federation of Library Associations: Chm., Cttee for Sci. and Technol. Libys, 1987–91 (Mem., 1985–87); Finance Officer, Special Libraries Div., 1991–93; Mem., Press Cttee, ICSU, 1991–. Mem., Oxford City Council, 1963–67; Chm., Oxford City Civil Emergency Cttee, 1966–67; Member: Home Office Sci. Adv. Council, 1966–78; Home Defence Sci. Adv. Cttee, 1978–; Hebdomadal Council, 1980–89; Chairman: Oxford Univ. Delegacy for Educnl Studies, 1969–73; Home Office Police Equipment Cttee, 1969–70; Home Office Police Sci. Develt Cttee, 1971–74. Member: Amer. Phys. Soc., 1957; NY Acad. of Scis, 1981. Almoner, Christ's Hosp., 1980–. *Publications:* An Introduction to Electronics, 1962, 2nd edn 1970; A Review of Oxford University Science Libraries, 1977, 2nd edn 1981; (ed) Information Sources in Physics, 1985, 3rd edn 1994; papers in sci. jls. *Recreations:* riding, gardening, enjoying music. *Address:* Keble College, Oxford OX1 3PG. *T:* Oxford (01865) 272727. *Club:* United Oxford & Cambridge University.

SHAW, Rev. Douglas William David; Professor of Divinity, 1979–91, and Principal, St Mary's College, 1986–92, University of St Andrews; *b* 25 June 1928; *s* of William David Shaw and Nansie Smart. *Educ:* Edinburgh Acad.; Loretto; Ashbury Coll., Ottawa; Univs of Cambridge and Edinburgh. MA (Cantab), BD (Edin.), LLB (Edin.). WS. Practised law as Partner of Davidson and Syme, WS, Edinburgh, 1953–57. Ordained Minister of Church of Scotland, 1960; Asst Minister, St George's West Church, Edinburgh, 1960–63; Official Observer of World Alliance of Reformed Churches at Second Vatican Council, Rome, 1962. University of Edinburgh: Dean, Faculty of Divinity, and Principal, New College, 1974–78; Lectr in Divinity, 1963–79; Dean, Faculty of Divinity, Univ. of St Andrews, 1983–86. Croall Lectr, New Coll., Edinburgh, 1983; Alexander Robertson Lectr, Univ. of Glasgow, 1991–92. Hon. DD Glasgow, 1991. *Publications:* Who is God? 1968, 2nd edn

1970; The Dissuaders, 1978; trans. from German: F. Heyer: The Catholic Church from 1648 to 1870, 1969; (ed) In Divers Manners—a St Mary's Miscellany, 1990; Dimensions—Literary and Theological, 1992; various articles in theological jls. *Recreations:* squash (Scottish Amateur Champion, 1950–51–52), golf. *Address:* 40 North Street, St Andrews, Fife KY16 9JU. *T:* St Andrews (01334) 477254. *Clubs:* New (Edinburgh); Royal and Ancient (St Andrews); Luffness New; Edinburgh Sports.

SHAW, Very Rev. Duncan, JP; PhD; Minister Emeritus of the parish of Craigentinny, Edinburgh; *b* 27 Jan. 1925; *s* of Neil Shaw (Mac Gille Chainnich), master carpenter, and Mary Thompson Borthwick; *m* 1st, 1955, Ilse (*d* 1989), *d* of Robert Peiter and Luise Else Mattig, Dusseldorf; one *s* two *d*; 2nd, 1991, Prof. Anna Libera Irma Domitilla, DrPhil, *d* of Prof. Luigi Dallapiccola and Dr Laura Coen Luzzatto, Florence. *Educ:* Univ. of Edinburgh (PhD). Served REME, TA(WR), 1943–47 (Warrant Officer, cl. I 1946). Minister of parish: of St Margaret, Dumbiedykes, Edinburgh, 1951–59, of Craigentinny, Edinburgh, 1959–95. Scottish Rep. of Aktion Zühnezeichen, Berlin, 1966–71; Chm. of Bd, St Andrew Press, 1967–74; Editorial Dir, Edina Press, Edinburgh, 1974–; Chm., IMS Trust and Instant Muscle (Scotland) plc, 1988–92; Dir, Instant Muscle plc, London, 1988–. Dir, Centre for Theological Exploration Inc. USA, 1989–. Trustee: Nat. Museum of Antiquities of Scotland, 1974–85; Edinburgh Old Town Charitable Trust, 1989–; Founder and Chm. of Council, Scottish Soc. for Reformation History, 1980–. University of Edinburgh: Sec. of Gen. Council, 1965–93; Sen. Hume Brown Prizeman for Scottish History, 1965; Visiting Fellow, Inst. for Advanced Studies in the Humanities, 1975; part-time Lectr in Theological German, Faculty of Divinity, 1975–81; Sec., Gen. Council Trust, 1982–90; Dr *hc* 1990. Guest Prof., Lancaster Theolog. Seminary and Vis. Lectr, Princeton Theolog. Seminary, USA, 1967; Hastie Lectr in Divinity, Univ. of Glasgow, 1968–71; Visiting Lecturer: Univ. of Munich, 1980; Univ. of Heidelberg, 1983; McGill Univ., Montreal, 1984; Univ. of Mainz, 1991. Member of Advisory Commitee: Christian Peace Conf., Prague, 1960–68; Conf. of European Churches, 1970–86 (acted as Gen. Sec., 1971). Hon. Mem., United Church of Berlin Brandenburg, 1969; Mem. of Cons. Cttee, Selly Oak Colls, Birmingham, 1976–87; Moderator, Presbytery of Edinburgh, 1978; Moderator, Gen. Assembly of Church of Scotland, 1987–88. Freeman, City of London, 1990; Liveryman, Scriveners' Co., 1990. JP 1974; Chm., City of Edinburgh Justices Cttee, 1984–87. KStJ 1983 (Mem., Chapter Gen., 1984–93, Chancellor of Scotland, 1986–92, Order of St John). ThDr *hc* Comenius Faculty of Theology, Charles Univ., Prague, 1969. Patriarchal Cross of Romanian Orthodox Church, 1978; Bundesverdienstkreuz, 1st cl., 1980; Com. al Merito Melitense (SMO Malta), 1987; Order of St Sergius, second class, Russian Orthodox Church, 1987. *Publications:* The General Assemblies of the Church of Scotland 1560–1600: their Origins and Development, 1964; (contrib. and ed) Reformation and Revolution: Essays presented to Principal Emeritus Hugh Watt, 1967; Inauguration of Ministers in Scotland 1560–1600, 1968; (contrib. and ed) John Knox: A Quartercentenary Reappraisal, 1975; Knox and Mary, Queen of Scots; (contrib. foreword and supervised translation) Zwingli's Thought: New Perspectives (by G. W. Locher), 1981; (contrib. and ed with I. B. Cowan) The Renaissance and Reformation in Scotland: Essays in Honour of Gordon Donaldson, 1983; A Voice in the Wilderness, 1995; contribs to learned jls, particularly to Records of Scottish Church History Soc. *Address:* 4 Sydney Terrace, Edinburgh EH7 6SL. *T:* 0131–669 1089; 12 Castelnau Gardens, Arundel Terrace, SW13 9DU. *T:* 0181–746 3087. *Club:* Highland (Inverness).

SHAW, Elizabeth Angela; Executive Director and Secretary, Charity Commission, since 1991; *b* 5 June 1946; *d* of John Edward Comben and Irene (*née* Thomson); *m* 1st, 1970, Graham Shaw (marr. diss. 1985); two *s* one *d*; 2nd, 1993, Adrian Carter. *Educ:* Sydenham High School. Executive Officer: Home Office, 1965–68; FCO, 1968–70; DSS, 1970–72; Department of Health and Social Security: HEO (Develt), 1972–77; Principal, 1977–84; Asst Sec., 1984–87; Dir of Finance, Planning and Marketing, Civil Service Coll., 1987–90; Head of Staff Develt, DoH, 1990–91. *Recreations:* music, literature, walking, swimming, family. *Address:* Charity Commission, St Alban's House, 57/60 Haymarket, SW1Y 4QX. *T:* 0171–210 4414.

SHAW, (Francis) Michael; Managing Director, 1985–93, Executive Vice Chairman, 1993–94, Britannia Building Society; *b* 12 Aug. 1936; *s* of Joseph Stanley Shaw and Irene Shaw (*née* Weldrake); *m* 1960, Margaret Elinor Russum; two *d*. *Educ:* Rotherham Grammar Sch. Qualified as chartered accountant, 1957. National Service, RAF, 1958–60; Peat Marwick Mitchell & Co., Sheffield, 1960–61; Company Sec. and Accountant, John Speed & Co., 1961–67; Chief Accountant, Eastern Counties Building Soc., 1967–74; Britannia Building Society: Chief Accountant, 1974–77; Gen. Manager, 1977–83; Chief Gen. Manager, 1983–85. Chm., BSA, 1992–93; Pres., N Staffs Chamber of Commerce, 1993–95. *Recreations:* golf, foreign travel, photography. *Club:* Leek Golf.

SHAW, Dr Gavin Brown, CBE 1981; FRCP, FRCPE, FRCPGlas; Consultant Physician, Southern General Hospital, Glasgow, 1956–84, Hon. Consultant, since 1984; *b* 24 May 1919; *s* of Gavin Shaw and Christian Douglas Cormack; *m* 1943, Margaret Mabon Henderson (*d* 1990); two *d* (one *s* decd). *Educ:* Glasgow Academy; Glasgow Univ., 1936–42 (BSc, MB ChB). President, Students' Representative Council, 1940–41. House Phys. to Sir J. W. McNee, 1942; Temporary Surg.-Lieut, RNVR, 1942–45; Asst Phys., Southern Gen. Hosp., Glasgow, 1948–56. Actg post-Grad. Dean., Glasgow Univ., 1983–84. Royal College of Physicians and Surgeons of Glasgow: Hon. Sec., 1957–65; Visitor, 1977–78; Pres., 1978–80. Mem., West Regional Hosp. Bd, 1971–74; Chairman: Greater Glasgow Med. Adv. Cttee, 1973–76; Jt Cttee for Higher Med. Trng, 1979–83; Specialty Adviser in Medicine, W of Scotland Post-Graduate Cttee, 1971–83. Mem., GMC, 1982–89. Hon. FACP 1979; Hon. FRCPI 1979; Hon. FRCPsych 1980; Hon. FRCGP 1980. *Publications:* (ed jtly) Cardiac Resuscitation and Pacing, 1964; occasional contributor to BMJ, Brit. Heart Jl, Lancet, Practitioner, Amer. Heart Jl, Scottish Med. Jl. *Recreations:* walking, gardening, bird watching and one-time sailor, listening to music, painting, reading. *Address:* 4 Horseshoe Road, Bearsden, Glasgow G61 2ST. *T:* 0141–942 4553. *Club:* Royal Scottish Automobile.

SHAW, Rev. Canon Geoffrey Norman; Hon. Canon Emeritus of Christ Church Cathedral, Oxford, since 1989 (Hon. Canon, 1985–89); *b* 15 April 1926; *s* of Samuel Norman Shaw and Maud Shaw; *m* 1948, Cynthia Brown; one *s* two *d*. *Educ:* Holgate Grammar Sch., Barnsley; Jesus Coll., Oxford (MA); Wycliffe Hall, Oxford. Asst Curate, St Mary, Rushden, 1951–54; Vicar of St Paul, Woking, 1954–62; Rector of St Leonards-on-Sea, Sussex, 1962–68; Asst Master, Ecclesfield Grammar Sch., Sheffield, 1968–69; Head of Religious Educn and Classics, Silverdale Sch., Sheffield, 1969–72; Vice-Principal, Oak Hill Theol Coll., Southgate, 1972–79; Principal, Wycliffe Hall, Oxford, 1979–89. *Recreations:* bird watching, walking, golf, music. *Address:* 15A West Street, Kingham, Oxon OX7 6YF. *T:* Kingham (01608) 658006.

SHAW, Geoffrey Peter; QC 1991; *b* 19 April 1944; *s* of late James Adamson Shaw and Hilda Gargett Shaw (*née* Edwards); *m* 1985, Susan Cochrane. *Educ:* Worksop College, Notts; Worcester College, Oxford (BA, BCL). Teaching Fellow, Univ. of Chicago Law Sch., 1966; Arden Scholar of Gray's Inn, 1967; called to the Bar, Gray's Inn, 1968. *Recreations:* walking, travel, gardening. *Address:* 1 Brick Court, Temple, EC4Y 9BY. *T:* 0171–353 8845.

SHAW, Sir (George) Neville B.; *see* Bowman-Shaw.

SHAW, Sir Giles; *see* Shaw, Sir J. G. D.

SHAW, Sir John Calman, Kt 1995; CBE 1989; CA; FRSE; Director (non-executive), since 1990, and Deputy Governor, since 1991, Bank of Scotland; *b* 10 July 1932; *m* 1960, Shirley Botterill; three *d*. *Educ:* Strathallan Sch.; Edinburgh Univ. BL; FCMA, MBCS, JDipMA. Qualified Chartered Accountant, 1955. National Service, RAF, 1955–57. Partner in Graham, Smart & Annan (later Deloitte, Haskins & Sells), 1960, Sen. Edinburgh Partner, 1980–87. Pres., Inst. of Chartered Accountants of Scotland, 1983–84. Johnstone Smith Prof. of Accountancy (pt-time appt), 1977–82, Vis. Prof., 1986–, Glasgow Univ. Chairman: Scottish American Investment Trust, 1991– (Dir, 1986–); US Smaller Cos Investment Trust, 1991–; Scottish Financial Enterprise, 1995– (Exec. Dir, 1986–90); Director: Scottish Metropolitan Property plc; Scottish Mortgage and Trust PLC, 1982–; Templeton Emerging Markets Investment Trust plc, 1994–; Templeton Latin America Investment Trust plc, 1994–. Member: Scottish Industrial Develt Adv. Bd, 1987–; Bd, Scottish Enterprise, 1990–; Financial Reporting Council, 1990–; UFC, 1991–93; HEFCE, 1992–94; Chm., SHEFC, 1992–. Chm., David Hume Inst., 1995–. Dep. Chm., Edinburgh Fest. Soc., 1991–. Receiver General, The Priory of Scotland of Most Venerable Order of St John, 1992; KStJ. *Publications:* (ed) Bogie on Group Accounts (3rd edn), 1973; The Audit Report, 1980; (jtly) Information Disclosure and the Multinational Corporation, 1984; numerous articles in Accountant's Magazine and Accounting and Business Research and Accountancy, etc. *Recreations:* opera, theatre, walking. *Address:* Bank of Scotland Executive Office, The Mound, Edinburgh EH1 1YZ. *T:* 0131–243 5511. *Clubs:* Caledonian; New (Edinburgh); Western (Glasgow).

SHAW, John Campbell; Managing Director, East Kilbride Development Corporation, since 1990; *b* 2 Aug. 1949; *s* of late John C. B. Shaw and of May B. Shaw; *m* 1974, Sheila Kerr Thomson; two *d*. *Educ:* Grosvenor High Sch., Belfast; QUB (BSc Hons in Urban Geography); Heriot-Watt Univ. (MSc in Town & Country Planning). Lanarkshire CC, 1973–75; Motherwell DC, 1975–78; East Kilbride Development Corporation, 1978–: Head of Planning, 1982; Tech. Dir, 1986; Bd Mem., Lanarkshire Develt Agency, 1991–. *Recreation:* sport. *Address:* East Kilbride Development Corporation, Atholl House, East Kilbride G74 1LU. *T:* East Kilbride (013552) 41111, *Fax:* East Kilbride (013552) 42224; 7 Maidens, Stewartfield, East Kilbride G74 4RS. *T:* East Kilbride (013552) 65145.

SHAW, John Frederick; Director of Corporate Affairs, National Health Service Management Executive, since 1993; *b* 7 Dec. 1936; *s* of James Herbert and Barbara Shaw; *m* 1964, Ann Rodden; two *s* one *d*. *Educ:* Loretto Sch., Musselburgh; Worcester Coll., Oxford (MA). National Service, 2/Lieut KOYLI, 1955–57. Church Comrs, 1960–62; Industrial Christian Fellowship, 1962–63; HQ Staff, VSO, 1963–73; Principal (Direct Entry), DHSS, 1973, Asst Sec. 1978; Under Sec., DHSS, then DoH, 1987–93. Chm., REACH, 1988–92. *Recreations:* church activities, singing, gardening. *Address:* NHS Executive, Quarry House, Quarry Hill, Leeds LS2 7UE. *T:* (0113) 254 5673.

SHAW, Sir (John) Giles (Dunkerley), Kt 1987; MP (C) Pudsey since Feb. 1974; *b* 16 Nov. 1931; *y s* of Hugh D. Shaw; *m* 1962, Dione Patricia Crosthwaite Ellison; one *s* two *d*. *Educ:* Sedbergh Sch.; St. John's Coll., Cambridge (MA). President of the Union, Cambridge, 1954. Joined Rowntree & Co. Ltd, 1955. Served on Flaxton RDC, 1957–64. Marketing Dir, Confectionery Div., Rowntree Mackintosh Ltd, 1970–74. Contested (C) Kingston upon Hull West, 1966. Parliamentary Under-Secretary of State: NI Office, 1979–81; DoE, 1981–83; Dept of Energy, 1983–84; Minister of State: Home Office, 1984–86; DTI, 1986–87. Mem., House of Commons Select Cttee on Nationalised Industries, 1976–79; Chm., Select Cttee on Sci. and Technol., 1992–; Member: Speaker's Panel of Chairmen, 1988–; H of C Privileges Cttee, 1994–; Intelligence and Security Cttee, 1994–; Vice-Chm., Cons. Prices and Consumer Affairs Cttee, 1976–78; Joint-Sec., All Party Wool Textile Group, 1978–79; Treasurer, 1922 Cttee, 1988–. *Recreations:* ornithology, fishing. *Address:* 83 Town Street, Horsforth, Leeds LS18 5BP; House of Commons, SW1A 0AA.

SHAW, John Michael, MC 1940; QC 1967; Barrister-at-Law; Regional Chairman of Industrial Tribunals, 1972–84; *b* 14 Nov. 1914; *yr s* of late M. J. Shaw (killed in action, 1916); *m* 1940, Margaret L. *yr d* of Robert T. D. Stoneham, CBE; two *s* two *d*. *Educ:* Rugby; Worcester Coll., Oxford. Called to the Bar, Gray's Inn, 1937. Served War of 1939–45 (Major): commissioned Royal Fusiliers, 1940. *Recreation:* gardening. *Address:* South Knighton House, South Knighton, near Newton Abbot, Devon TQ12 6NP.

SHAW, Sir John Michael Robert B.; *see* Best-Shaw.

SHAW, Dr Mark Robert; Keeper of Natural History, National Museums of Scotland (formerly Royal Scottish Museum), since 1983; *b* 11 May 1945; *s* of William Shaw and Mabel Courtenay Shaw (*née* Bower); *m* 1970, Francesca Dennis Wilkinson; two *d*. *Educ:* Dartington Hall Sch.; Oriel Coll., Oxford (BA 1968; MA, DPhil 1972). Res. Assistant, Manchester Univ., 1973–76; Univ. Res. Fellow, Reading Univ., 1977–80; Asst Keeper, Dept of Natural History, Royal Scottish Museum, 1980–83. *Publications:* contribs to chemical jls and (mainly on parasitic wasps) entomological jls. *Recreations:* field entomology, family life, gardening. *Address:* 48 St Alban's Road, Edinburgh EH9 2LU. *T:* 0131–667 0577. *Club:* University of Edinburgh Staff (Edinburgh).

SHAW, Group Captain Mary Michal, RRC 1981; Director and Matron-in-Chief, Princess Mary's Royal Air Force Nursing Service, and Deputy Director, Defence Nursing Services (Operations and Plans), 1985–88; *b* 7 April 1933; *d* of Ven. Archdeacon Thorndike Shaw and Violet Rosario Shaw. *Educ:* Wokingham Grammar School for Girls. SRN 1955, Royal Berkshire Hosp., Reading; SCM 1957, Central Middlesex Hosp., London and Battle Hosp., Reading; PMRAFNS, 1963–88; QHNS, 1985–88. OStJ 1974. *Recreations:* gardening, home crafts. *Address:* 33 Whiting Street, Bury St Edmunds, Suffolk IP33 1NP. *T:* Bury St Edmunds (01284) 705836.

SHAW, Max S.; *see* Stuart-Shaw.

SHAW, Michael; *see* Shaw, F. M.

SHAW, Michael Hewitt, CMG 1990; HM Diplomatic Service, retired; *b* 5 Jan. 1935; *s* of late Donald Shaw and of Marion (*née* Hewitt); *m* 1963, Elizabeth Rance; three *d* (and one *d* decd). *Educ:* Sedbergh; Clare College, Cambridge (MA); UCL (MA 1992). HM Forces, 1953. HMOCS Tanganyika, 1959–62; joined Diplomatic Service, 1963; served The Hague, FCO and Vientiane, 1964–68; First Sec., FCO, 1968–72, Valletta, 1972–76, FCO, 1976–82, Brussels, 1982–84; Counsellor, Brussels, 1984–86, FCO, 1986–95. *Recreations:* cricket, theatre, travel, historical research. *Address:* The Close, Marley Common, Haslemere, Surrey GU27 3PT. *Clubs:* Army and Navy, MCC.

SHAW, Sir Neil (McGowan), Kt 1994; Chairman: Tate & Lyle PLC, London, since 1986 (Director, since 1975; Chief Executive, 1986–92); Tate & Lyle Holdings, since 1981; Tate

& Lyle Industries, since 1981; Tunnel Refineries, since 1982 (Director, since 1981); Vice-Chairman: Redpath Industries, since 1981 (Director, since 1972); A. E. Staley Manufacturing Co., since 1988; *b* 31 May 1929; *s* of late Harold LeRoy Shaw and Fabiola Marie Shaw; *m* 1952, Audrey Robinson (marr. diss.); two *s* three *d*; *m* 1985, Elizabeth Fern Mudge-Massey. *Educ:* Knowlton High Sch.; Lower Canada Coll., Canada. Trust Officer, Crown Trust Co., Montreal, 1947–54; Merchandising Manager, Canada & Dominion Sugar Co. (later Redpath Industries Ltd), Montreal, 1954–66; Vice Pres., Canada & Dominion Sugar Co., Toronto, 1967–72; Pres., Redpath Industries Ltd, 1972–80; Gp Man. Dir, Tate & Lyle PLC, 1980–86. Director: Americare Corp., 1980–; Alcantara, 1983–; Canadian Imperial Bank of Commerce (Toronto), 1986–; United Biscuits (Hldgs), 1988–. Director, World Sugar Res. Orgn, 1982–; Gov., World Food and Agro Forum, 1988–. Chairman: Business in the Community, 1991–94; Assoc. of Lloyd's Members, 1992–94. Gov., Montreal Gen. Hosp. *Recreations:* sailing, skiing, golfing. *Address:* Tate & Lyle plc, Sugar Quay, Lower Thames Street, EC3R 6DQ. *Clubs:* Brooks's; Wentworth Golf; Toronto (Toronto).

SHAW, Sir Neville B.; *see* Bowman-Shaw.

SHAW, Nicholas Glencairn B.; *see* Byam Shaw.

SHAW, Peter Alan; Director of Services (personnel, analytical and information systems services), Department for Education, since 1994; *b* 31 May 1949; *s* of late Frank Shaw and of Ursula Lister Shaw (*née* Dyson); *m* 1975, Frances Willcox; two *s* one *d*. *Educ:* Bridlington Sch.; Durham Univ. (BSc Geography); Bradford Univ. (MSc Traffic Eng. and Planning); Regent Coll., Univ. of British Columbia (Master in Christian Studies). FIHT. Department of Education and Science, subseq. Department for Education, 1972–: Private Sec. to Perm. Sec., 1975–76; Principal Private Sec. to Sec. of State, 1979–81; Asst Sec., 1981–91; on loan to HM Treasury, 1985–86; Press Sec. to DES Sec. of State, 1988–89; Grade 3, 1991–; on loan to Depts of the Envmt and Transport as Regl Dir, Northern Reg., 1991–93; Dir of Estabts and Personnel, 1993–94. Anglican lay Reader, 1972–, dio. of Guildford. *Recreations:* walking, travelling. *Address:* Department for Education, Sanctuary Buildings, Great Smith Street, SW1P 3BT. *T:* 0171–925 5000.

SHAW, Captain Peter Jack, CBE 1990; RN (retd); General Secretary, British Group Inter-Parliamentary Union, 1979–90; Consultant to President, Interparliamentary Council, 1991–93; *b* Geelong, Australia, 27 Oct. 1924; *s* of late Jack and Betty Shaw; *m* 1951, Pauline, *e d* of Sir Frank Madge, 2nd Bt, and Lady (Doris) Madge, East Grinstead; one *s* one *d*. *Educ:* Watford Grammar School; RNC Dartmouth; RN Staff Coll. Greenwich; NATO Defence Coll., Paris. FIL 1957. War service in HM Ships Kenya, Resolution, Quadrant, Kelvin, incl. Malta and Russian Convoys and Normandy invasion; comd HM Ships Venus, Carron, Vigilant, 1958–61; Staff, C-in-C Portsmouth and MoD, 1961–65; SHAPE, Paris and Mons, 1966–68; Comdr, RN Coll. Greenwich, 1968–70; Defence and Naval Attaché, The Hague, 1971–73; Captain of Port and Queen's Harbourmaster, Plymouth, 1973–76; Captain of Port, Chatham, 1976–79. MBIM. *Recreations:* international relations, foreign languages, domestic pursuits. *Address:* Woodside, Rogate, Petersfield, Hants GU31 5DJ. *T:* Rogate (01730) 821 344.

SHAW, Richard John Gildroy; Chairman, since 1992, and Chief Executive, since 1979, Lowndes Lambert Group Holdings; Chairman and Chief Executive, Lowndes Lambert Group, since 1979; *b* 7 June 1936; *s* of Edward Philip Shaw and Mary Elizabeth Shaw (*née* Tanner); *m* 1973, Yvonne Kathleen Maskell; one *s*. *Educ:* Dragon Sch.; Eton. J. H. Minet & Co., 1957–66; H. J. Symons & Co., 1967–70; Dep. Chm., C. E. Heath & Co. (Insce Broking Ltd), 1970–79; Chm. and Managing Dir, C. E. Heath (Internat.), 1970–79; Chm., C. E. Heath (Latin America), 1970–79; Dep. Chm., Lowndes Lambert Gp Hldgs, 1979–92; Dir, Hill Samuel Gp, 1979–88. *Recreations:* golf, yachting, reading, cricket. *Address:* Lowndes Lambert Group, Lowndes Lambert House, Friary Court, Crutched Friars, EC3N 2NP. *T:* 0171–560 3000; 18 Phillimore Gardens, W8 7QE. *T:* 0171–937 2942. *Clubs:* Carlton, City of London, Portland, Clermont, St James's, Royal Thames Yacht; Lloyd's Golf, Lloyds Yacht, Sunningdale Golf.

SHAW, Prof. Richard Wright; Vice-Chancellor and Principal, University of Paisley, since 1992 (Principal, Paisley College, 1987–92); *b* 22 Sept. 1941; *s* of late George Beeley Shaw and Bella Shaw; *m* 1965, Susan Angela Birchley; two *s*. *Educ:* Lancaster Royal Grammar Sch.; Sidney Sussex Coll., Cambridge (MA). Leeds University: Asst Lectr in Management, 1964–66; Lectr in Econs, 1966–69; Stirling University: Lectr in Econs, 1969–75; Sen. Lectr, 1975–84; Head of Dept of Econs, 1982–84; Paisley College: Head, Dept of Econs and Management and Prof., 1984–86; Vice Principal, 1986–87. *Publications:* (with C. J. Sutton) Industry and Competition, 1976; articles in Jl Industrial Econs, Scottish Jl Pol Econ., Managerial and Decision Econs. *Recreations:* walking, listening to music. *Address:* University of Paisley, High Street, Paisley PA1 2BE. *T:* 0141–848 3671.

SHAW, Sir Robert, 7th Bt *cr* 1821; Design Engineer, Shaw Consulting; *b* Nairobi, Kenya, 31 Jan. 1925; *s* of Sir Robert de Vere Shaw, 6th Bt, MC, and Joan (*d* 1967), *d* of Thomas Cross; *S* father, 1969; *m* 1954, Jocelyn, *d* of late Andrew McGuffie, Swaziland; two *d*. *Educ:* Harrow; Univs of Oklahoma and Missouri, USA. RN, 1943–47 (Lieut RN retd). BS Civil Eng. Oklahoma, 1962; MS Civil Eng. Missouri, 1964; Professional Engineer, Alberta; Mem., Assoc., of Prof. Engrs, Geologists and Geophysicists of Alberta. *Recreation:* sailing. *Heir:* *n* Charles de Vere Shaw [*b* 1 March 1957; *m* 1985, Sonia, *e d* of Thomas Geoffrey Eden; one *s* one *d*]. *Address:* 234 40th Avenue SW, Calgary, Alberta T2S 0X3, Canada.

SHAW, Dr Robert Macdonald, CB 1968; Deputy Chief Medical Officer, Department of Health and Social Security (formerly Ministry of Health), 1965–77; *b* 16 Sept. 1912; *s* of late Peter Macdonald and late Ellen Shaw; *m* 1941, Grace Helen Stringfellow; two *s* one *d*. *Educ:* Mill Hill School; Victoria Univ. of Manchester. Miscellaneous hospital appointments, etc, 1936–39. Emergency Commission, RAMC, 1939–45. Asst County MOH, Essex, 1945–48; Department of Health and Social Security (formerly Ministry of Health), 1948–77. QHP 1971–74. *Address:* The Lodge, Tor Bryan, Ingatestone, Essex CM4 9HN.

SHAW, Sir Roy, Kt 1979; writer and theatre critic; Secretary General of the Arts Council of Great Britain, 1975–83; *b* 8 July 1918; *s* of Frederick and Elsie Shaw; *m* 1946, Gwenyth Baron; five *s* two *d*. *Educ:* Firth Park Grammar School, Sheffield; Manchester Univ. BA(Hons). Newspaper printing department 'copy-holder', 1937; newspaper publicity, 1938; Library Asst, Sheffield City Library, 1939; Cataloguer, Manchester Univ. Library, 1945; Organizing Tutor, WEA, 1946; Adult Educn Lectr, Leeds Univ., 1947; Warden, Leeds Univ. Adult Educn Centre, Bradford, 1959; Professor and Dir of Adult Educn, Keele Univ., 1962. Vis. Prof., Centre for Arts, City Univ., London, 1977–83. Consultant, Cheshire Sch. of Dance and Drama, 1989–93. Theatre critic, The Tablet, 1992–. Hon. DLitt: City, 1978; Southampton, 1984; DUniv Open, 1981. *Publications:* The Arts and the people, 1987; (ed) The Spread of Sponsorship, 1993; contrib. chapters to: Trends in English Adult Education, 1959; The Committed Church, 1966; Your Sunday Paper, 1967; over 170 articles and book chapters on cultural policy, adult education and the mass media. *Recreations:* reading, theatre, opera, films, concerts and art galleries, swimming, watching the best of television—and sometimes, for clinical reasons, the worst. *Address:* 48 Farrer Road, N8 8LB. *T:* 0181–348 1857. *Club:* Arts.

SHAW, Roy Edwin, OBE 1991; Council Member, London Borough of Camden, since 1964; *b* 21 July 1925; *s* of Edwin Victor and Edith Lily Shaw. Hampstead Borough Council, 1956–62; St Pancras Borough, 1962–65; Camden Borough Council: Chm., Planning Cttee, 1967–68; Chm., Finance Cttee, 1971–74; Chief Whip and Dep. Leader, 1965–73; Leader, 1975–82; Dep. Leader, 1990–94. Vice-Chm., AMA, 1979–83; Dep. Chm. and Leader of Labour Party, London Boroughs Assoc. Part-time Mem., London Electricity Bd, 1977–83; Member: Transport Users Consultative Cttee for London, 1974–80; Adv. Cttee on Local Govt Audit, 1979–82; Audit Commn, 1983–91; Consult. Council on Local Govt Finances, 1978–84. *Recreations:* listening to music; entertaining attractive women. *Address:* Town Hall, Euston Road, NW1 2RU. *T:* 0171–278 4444.

SHAW, Sir Run Run, Kt 1977; CBE 1974; Founder and Chairman, Shaw Organisation, since 1963; Founder and Chairman, Shaw Foundation, since 1973; *b* 14 Oct. 1907; *m* 1932, Lily Wong Mee Chun (decd); two *s* two *d*. Left China for Singapore and began making films and operating cinemas, 1927; left Singapore for Hong Kong and built Shaw Movietown, making and distributing films, 1959. Pres., Hong Kong Red Cross Soc., 1972–. Chairman: Hong Kong Arts Festival, 1974–88; Bd of Governors, Hong Kong Arts Centre, 1978–88; Television Broadcasts Ltd, 1980–. Chinese University of Hong Kong: Mem. Council, 1977–92; Chm., Bd of Trustees, United Coll., 1983–92; Founder, Shaw Coll., 1986. Hong Kong Advr appointed by Govt of People's Republic of China, 1992. Hon. LLD: Hong Kong Univ., 1980; Pepperdine, 1992; Hon. Dr Soc. Scis: Chinese Univ. of Hong Kong, 1981; Univ. of E Asia, Macau, 1985; Hon. DLitt: Sussex, 1987; Hong Kong Baptist Coll., 1990; Hon. DSc City Poly., Hong Kong, 1988; Hon. DHL SUNY at Stony Brook, 1989; Hon. DCL Oxford, 1992; Hon. DBA Hong Kong Poly., 1991. Queen's Badge, Red Cross, 1982; Montblanc de la Culture Award, 1993. Comdr, Order of the Crown of Belgium, 1989; Chevalier, Légion d'Honneur (France), 1991. *Recreations:* shadow-boxing, golf. *Address:* Shaw House, Lot 220 Clear Water Bay Road, Kowloon, Hong Kong. *T:* 7198371.

SHAW, Thurstan; *see* Shaw, C. T.

SHAW, Prof. William V., MD; Professor of Biochemistry, University of Leicester, since 1974; *b* Philadelphia, Pennsylvania, 13 May 1933. *Educ:* Williams Coll., Williamstown, Mass (BA Chemistry 1955); Columbia Univ., New York (MD 1959). Diplomate: Amer. Bd of Med. Examrs, 1960; Amer. Bd of Internal Med., 1968 (Examiner, 1970). Appts, Presbyterian Hosp., New York, Nat. Heart Inst., Bethesda, Maryland, and Columbia Univ., New York, until 1966; Asst Prof. of Medicine, Columbia Univ., New York, 1966–68; University of Miami School of Medicine, Miami, Florida: Associate Prof. of Medicine and Biochemistry, 1968–73; Chief, Infectious Diseases, 1971–74; Prof. of Medicine, 1973–74. Vis. Scientist, MRC Lab. of Molecular Biology, Cambridge, Eng., 1972–74. Member: MRC Cell Biology and Disorders Bd, 1976–80 (Bd Chm. and Mem. Council, 1978–80); Science Council, Celltech Ltd, 1980–89 (Chm., 1983–89); Lister Inst. Sci. Adv. Council, 1981–85; AFRC, 1990–94. Member: Amer. Soc. for Clinical Investigation, 1971; Infectious Disease Soc. of Amer., 1969; Amer. Soc. of Biol Chemists; Biochem. Soc. (UK); Amer. Soc. for Microbiology; Soc. for Gen. Microbiology (UK). *Publications:* contribs to professional works and jls in microbial biochemistry and molecular enzymology. *Address:* Department of Biochemistry, University of Leicester, University Road, Leicester LE1 7RH. *T:* Leicester (0116) 252 3470, *Fax:* (0116) 252 3369.

SHAW-STEWART, Sir Houston (Mark), 11th Bt *cr* 1667; MC 1950; TD; Vice Lord-Lieutenant, Strathclyde Region (Eastwood, Renfrew and Inverclyde Districts), 1980–95; *b* 24 April 1931; *s* of Sir Guy Shaw-Stewart, 9th Bt, MC, and Diana (*d* 1931), *d* of late George Bulteel; *S* brother, 1980; *m* 1982, Lucinda Victoria, *yr d* of Alexander Fletcher, Old Vicarage, Wighill, near Tadcaster; one *s*. *Educ:* Eton. Joined Coldstream Guards, 1949; served as 2/Lt Royal Ulster Rifles, Korea, 1950 (MC); joined Ayrshire Yeomanry, 1952; retired, 1969; Hon. Col A (Ayrshire Yeomanry) Sqdn, Queen's Own Yeomanry RAC, TA, 1984–87. Member of the Royal Company of Archers, Queen's Body Guard for Scotland. Joint Master, Lanark and Renfrewshire Foxhounds, 1974–79. DL Renfrewshire, 1970. *Recreations:* hunting, shooting and racing. *Heir:* *s* Ludovic Houston Shaw Stewart *b* 12 Nov. 1986. *Address:* Ardgowan, Inverkip, Renfrewshire PA16 0DW. *T:* Wemyss Bay (01475) 521226. *Clubs:* White's, Turf, Pratt's.

SHAWCROSS, family name of **Baron Shawcross.**

SHAWCROSS, Baron, *cr* 1959 (Life Peer), of Friston; **Hartley William Shawcross,** PC 1946; GBE 1974; Kt 1945; QC 1939; Special Adviser, Morgan Guaranty Trust of New York, 1965–94 (Chairman, International Advisory Council, 1967–74); Director, Hawker Siddeley Group, 1968–82; Director, The Observer, 1981–93; *b* 4 Feb. 1902; *s* of John Shawcross, MA, and Hilda Shawcross; *m* 1st, 1924, Rosita Alberta Shyvers (*d* 1943); 2nd, 1944, Joan Winifred Mather (*d* 1974); two *s* one *d*. *Educ:* Dulwich Coll.; abroad. Certificate of Honour for 1st place in Bar Final; called to Bar, Gray's Inn, 1925 (Bencher, 1939); practised on Northern Circuit. Sen. Law Lectr, Liverpool Univ., 1927–34. Chm., Enemy Aliens Tribunal, 1939–40; left practice at Bar for War Service, 1940; Chief Prosecutor for UK before Internat. Military Tribunal at Nuremberg. Asst Chm. of E Sussex QS, 1941; Recorder of Salford, 1941–45; Dep. Regional Comr, South-Eastern Region, 1941; Regional Comr, North-Western Region, 1942–45; Recorder of Kingston-upon-Thames, 1946–61; retired from practice at Bar, 1958. MP (Lab) St Helens, 1945–58; Attorney-General, 1945–51; Pres., BoT, April-Oct. 1951. A Principal Deleg. for UK to Assemblies of UN, 1945–49; a UK Mem., Permanent Court of Arbitration at The Hague, 1950–67. Independent Chm., Kent District Coal Mining Board, 1940–45; Chairman: Catering Wages Commn, 1943–45; Bar Council, 1952–57; Royal Commn on the Press, 1961–62; MRC, 1961–65; Internat. Law Section of British Inst. of Internat. and Comparative Law; Justice (British Br. of Internat. Commn of Jurists), 1956–72; Panel on Take-overs and Mergers, 1969–80; Press Council, 1974–78; ICC Commn on Unethical Practices, 1976. President: Rainer Foundn (formerly London Police Court Mission), 1951–71; British Hotels and Restaurants Assoc., 1959–71. Member: Home Secretary's Adv. Council on Treatment of Offenders, 1944–45; Council, Internat. Law Assoc., 1958–74; Exec. Cttee, Internat. Commn of Jurists, 1959. Hon. Member: Bar Council; Amer. and New York Bar Assoc.; Fellow, Amer. Bar Foundn. Director: Shell Transport and Trading Co., 1961–72; EMI Ltd, 1965–81; Rank-Hovis-McDougall Ltd, 1965–79; Caffyns Motors Ltd, 1965–; Morgan et Cie International SA, 1966–77; Morgan et Cie SA, 1967–90; Times Newspapers Ltd, 1967–74; Upjohn & Co Ltd, 1967–76 (Chm.); Birmingham Small Arms Co. Ltd, 1968–73 (Chm., 1971–73); European Enterprises Development Co. SA, 1970–78 (Chm., 1973–78); Chairman: Dominion Lincoln Assurance Co. Ltd, 1969–76; Thames Television Ltd, 1969–74; London and Continental Bankers, 1974–80; Chm. Bd of Governors, Dulwich Coll.; Member: Court, London Univ., 1958–74; Council and Exec. Cttee, Sussex Univ., 1959– (Pro-Chancellor, 1960–65; Chancellor, 1965–85); Council, Eastbourne Coll., 1965–70. Hon. FRCS 1981; Hon. FRCOG 1978. Hon. Degrees from Universities of Bristol, Columbia, Hull, Lehigh, Liverpool, London, Loughborough, Massachusetts (Ann Arbor), Michigan, Sussex. JP

Sussex, 1941–68. Chm., Soc. of Sussex Downsmen, 1962–75. Knight Grand Cross, Imperial Iranian Order of Homayoon, 1st Cl., 1974. *Publication:* Life Sentence: the memoirs of Hartley Shawcross, 1995. *Recreation:* sailing. *Address:* Friston Place, Sussex BN20 0AH; The Anchorage, St Mawes, Cornwall TR2 5DR. *Clubs:* Pratt's, Garrick; Travellers' (Paris); Royal Cornwall Yacht (Falmouth); Royal Yacht Squadron (Cowes); New York Yacht (US).

See also Hon. O. Polizzi, Hon. W. H. H. Shawcross.

SHAWCROSS, Roger Michael; His Honour Judge Shawcross; a Circuit Judge, since 1993; *b* 27 March 1941; *s* of Michael and Friedel Shawcross; *m* 1969, Sarah Broom; one *s* one *d. Educ:* Radley Coll.; Christ Church, Oxford (MA). Called to the Bar, Gray's Inn, 1967; a Recorder, 1985–93. *Recreations:* playing tennis, following most other sports, history, literature, music (especially piano playing), cinema, travel, admiring my wife's gardening skills.

SHAWCROSS, Hon. Mrs William; *see* Polizzi, Hon. Olga.

SHAWCROSS, Hon. William (Hartley Hume); writer and broadcaster; *b* 28 May 1946; *s* of Baron Shawcross, *qv*; *m* 1st, 1971, Marina Sarah Warner, *qv*; one *s*; 2nd, 1981, Michal Levin; one *d*; 3rd, 1993, Hon. Olga Polizzi, *qv. Educ:* Eton; University Coll., Oxford. Writer for Sunday Times, New Statesman, Washington Post, Spectator. Chm., Article 19, Internat. Centre on Censorship. *Publications:* Dubcek, 1970; Crime and Compromise, 1974; Sideshow: Kissinger, Nixon and the destruction of Cambodia, 1979; The Quality of Mercy: Cambodia, holocaust and modern memory, 1984; The Shah's Last Ride, 1989; Kowtow: a plea on behalf of Hong Kong, 1989; Murdoch, 1992; Cambodia's New Deal, 1994. *Recreations:* walking, sailing. *Address:* Friston Place, East Dean, E Sussex BN20 0AH. *T:* 0171–289 8089. *Clubs:* Academy; St Mawes Sailing.

SHAWE-TAYLOR, Desmond (Christopher), CBE 1965; music critic and journalist; *b* 29 May 1907; *s* of Frank Shawe-Taylor and Agnes Ussher. *Educ:* Shrewsbury Sch.; Oriel Coll., Oxford. Literary and occasional musical criticism, New Statesman, etc until 1939. Served War of 1939–45 with the Royal Artillery. Music Critic, New Statesman, 1945–58; Guest Music Critic, New Yorker, 1973–74; Chief Music Critic, The Sunday Times, 1958–83, thereafter frequent contributor on music and gramophone records. *Publications:* Covent Garden, 1948; (with Edward Sackville-West, later Lord Sackville), The Record Guide (with supplements and revisions, 1951–56). *Recreations:* travel, croquet, gramophone. *Address:* Long Crichel House, Wimborne, Dorset BH21 5JU. *T:* Tarrant Hinton (01258) 830250. *Clubs:* Brooks's, Groucho.

SHEA, Michael Sinclair MacAuslan, CVO 1987 (LVO 1985); PhD; *b* 10 May 1938; *s* of late James Michael Shea and of Mary Dalrymple Davidson MacAuslan, North Berwick; *m* 1968, Mona Grec Stensen, Oslo; two *d. Educ:* Gordonstoun Sch.; Edinburgh Univ. (MA, PhD Econs). FO, 1963; Inst. of African Studies, Accra, Ghana, 1963; FO, 1964; Third, later Second Sec., CRO, 1965; Second, later First Sec. (Econ.), Bonn, 1966; seconded to Cabinet Office, 1969; FO, 1971; Head of Chancery, Bucharest, 1973; Dep. Dir Gen., Brit. Inf. Services, New York, 1976; Press Sec. to the Queen, 1978–87. Dir of Public Affairs, Hanson PLC, 1987–92 (Political Consultant, 1992–); Chairman: MacInnes Younger, 1992–; Connoisseurs Scotland, 1992–; China Gateway, 1994–; non-executive Director: Caledonian Newspaper Publishing, 1993–; P & A Gp. Director: Murray International Trust, 1992–; Murray Income Trust, 1992–; Murray Smaller Markets Trust, 1992–. Vis. Prof., Strathclyde Univ. Grad. Business Sch., 1991–. Trustee, Nat. Galls of Scotland, 1992–. Mem. Court, Edinburgh Univ., 1992–; Gov., Gordonstoun Sch., 1988–. Vice-Chm., Foundn for Skin Res. *Publications:* Britain's Offshore Islands, 1981; Maritime England, 1981; Tomorrow's Men, 1982; Influence: how to make the system work for you, 1988; Leadership Rules, 1990; Personal Impact: the art of good communication, 1993; Spin Doctor, 1995; (as Michael Sinclair): Sonntag, 1971; Folio Forty-One, 1972; The Dollar Covenant, 1974; A Long Time Sleeping, 1976; The Master Players, 1978; (with David Frost): The Mid-Atlantic Companion, 1986; The Rich Tide, 1986; Spin Doctor, 1995. *Recreations:* writing, sailing. *Address:* c/o 1 St Colme Street, Edinburgh EH3 6AA. *Clubs:* Garrick; New (Edinburgh).

SHEARER, Rt. Hon. Hugh Lawson, OJ 1990; PC 1969; President, Bustamante Industrial Trade Union, Jamaica, since 1977; *b* 18 May 1923. *Educ:* St Simons Coll., Jamaica. Journalist on weekly newspaper, Jamaica Worker, 1941–44, subseq. Editor. Apptd Asst Gen. Sec., Bustamante Industrial TU, 1947, Island Supervisor, 1953–67, Vice-Pres., 1960–79 (on leave of absence, 1967–72). Mem. Kingston and St Andrew Corp. Council, 1947; MHR for West Kingston, 1955–59; MLC, later Senator, 1962–67; Leader of Govt Business in Senate, 1962–67; MP SE Clarendon, 1967–93; Prime Minister of Jamaica, 1967–72; Minister of Defence and of External Affairs, 1967–72; Leader of the Opposition, 1972–74; Dep. Prime Minister, and Minister of For. Affairs and For. Trade, 1980–89; Leader, Jamaica Labour Party, 1967–74. Chm., Jt Trade Unions Res. Develt Centre, 1992; Pres., Jamaica Confedn of Trade Unions, 1994. Hon. Dr of Laws: Howard Univ., Washington, DC, 1968; Univ. of WI, Jamaica, 1994. *Address:* Bustamante Industrial Trade Union, 98–100 Duke Street, Kingston, Jamaica.

SHEARER, Rt. Hon. Ian Hamilton; *see* Avonside, Rt Hon. Lord.

SHEARER, Janet Sutherland; *see* Avonside, Lady.

SHEARER, Very Rev. John, (Jack), OBE 1994; Dean of Belfast, since 1985; *b* 30 Dec. 1926; *s* of William and Isabelle Shearer; *m* 1956, Morag Williamson; one *s* one *d. Educ:* Trinity College, Dublin. BA (Respondent) 1948; MA, BD 1953. Ordained, 1950; Rector of Ballynahinch, Co. Down, 1958; Rector of Seagoe, Co. Armagh, 1964. *Publication:* Stewardship Step by Step, 1961. *Recreation:* computing. *Address:* The Deanery, 5 Deramore Drive, Belfast BT9 5JQ. *T:* Belfast (01232) 660980.

SHEARER, Magnus MacDonald; JP; Lord-Lieutenant of Shetland, 1982–94; Managing Director, J. & M. Shearer Ltd (Est. 1919), 1960–85; *b* 27 Feb. 1924; *s* of late Lt-Col Magnus Shearer, OBE, TD, JP, and Flora MacDonald Stephen; *m* 1949, Martha Nicolson Henderson, *d* of late Captain John Henderson, DSM, and late Martha Nicolson; one *s. Educ:* Anderson Educational Institute, Shetland; George Watson's Coll., Edinburgh. Served RN in Atlantic, Mediterranean and Far East, 1942–46. 2nd Lieut, RA (TA), 1949; Captain, TARO, 1959. Hon. Consul: for Sweden in Shetland and Orkney, 1958–94; for Federal Republic of Germany in Shetland, 1972–87. Mem., Lerwick Harbour Trust, 1960–75 (Chm., 1967–72); Hon. Sec., RNLI Lerwick Branch, 1968–92; Mem. Lerwick Town Council, 1963–69; JP 1969, DL 1973, Shetland. Knight 1st Class, Royal Order of Vasa (Sweden), 1969; Officer 1st Class, Order of Merit (Federal Republic of Germany), 1983; Officer 1st Class, Order of Polar Star (Sweden), 1983. *Recreations:* reading, bird watching and ships. *Address:* Birka, Cruester, Bressay, Shetland ZE2 9EL. *T:* Bressay (01595) 820363.

SHEARER, Moira, (Lady Kennedy); writer; *b* Dunfermline, Fife, 17 Jan. 1926; *d* of Harold King; *m* 1950, Sir Ludovic Kennedy, *qv*; one *s* three *d. Educ:* Dunfermline High School; Ndola, N Rhodesia; Bearsden Acad., Scotland. Professional training: Mayfair Sch.; Nicolas Legat Studio. Début with International Ballet, 1941; joined Sadler's Wells Ballet, 1942, during following ten years danced all major classic roles and full repertoire of revivals and new ballets; first ballerina rôle in Sleeping Beauty, Royal Opera House, Covent Gdn, 1946; created rôle of Cinderella, 1948; Carmen, with Roland Petit, Théâtre Marigny, 1950; George Balanchine's Ballet Imperial, Covent Garden, 1950; Titania in Old Vic production of A Midsummer Night's Dream (Edin. Festival, 1954, and tour of US and Canada); American tours with Sadler's Wells Ballet, 1949, 1950–51. Toured as Sally Bowles in I am a Camera, 1955; joined Bristol Old Vic, 1955; Major Barbara, Old Vic, 1956; Man of Distinction, Edin. Fest., 1957; Madame Ranevskaya in The Cherry Orchard, Royal Lyceum, Edin., 1977; Judith Bliss in Hay Fever, Royal Lyceum, 1978; Elizabeth Lowry, in A Simple Man (Gillian Lynne's ballet for L. S. Lowry's centenary), BBC TV, 1987; Juliana Bolderean in The Aspern Papers, Citizens Th., Glasgow, 1994. Recorded: Thomas Hardy's Tess of the D'Urbervilles, 1977; Muriel Spark's The Ballad of Peckham Rye, BBC Radio 4, 1982; Dame Ninette de Valois' short stories, Acad. of Sound and Vision, 1990. Member: Scottish Arts Council, 1971–73; BBC Gen. Adv. Council, 1970–77; Dir, Border TV, 1977–82. Toured US, lecturing on history of ballet and Sergei Diaghilev, 1973; regular lecturing in England and Wales. Lectured and gave recitals on three world cruises, Queen Elizabeth II. Poetry and prose recitals, Edinburgh Festivals, 1974 and 1975; now in regular performance with Ludovic Kennedy, and harpist Gillian Tingay. *Films:* Ballerina in The Red Shoes (première, 1948); Tales of Hoffmann, 1950; Story of Three Loves, 1952; The Man Who Loved Redheads, 1954; Peeping Tom, 1960; Black Tights, 1961. Regular book reviewer for Daily and Sunday Telegraphs. *Publication:* Balletmaster: a dancer's view of George Balanchine, 1986 (USA 1987).

SHEARLOCK, Very Rev. David John; Dean and Rector of St Mary's Cathedral, Truro, since 1982; *b* 1 July 1932; *s* of Arthur John Shearlock and Honora Frances Hawkins; *m* 1959, Jean Margaret Marr; one *s* one *d. Educ:* Univ. of Birmingham (BA); Westcott House, Cambridge. Assistant Curate: Guisborough, Yorks, 1957–60; Christchurch Priory, Hants, 1960–64; Vicar: Kingsclere, 1964–71; Romsey Abbey, 1971–82; Diocesan Director of Ordinands (Winchester), 1977–82; Hon. Canon of Winchester, 1978–82. FRSA 1991; FRGS 1992. *Publication:* The Practice of Preaching, 1990. *Recreations:* model railways, music, walking the Cornish coastal footpath. *Address:* The Deanery, Lemon Street, Truro, Cornwall TR1 2PE. *T:* Truro (01872) 72661.

SHEARMAN, Rt. Rev. Donald Norman, OBE 1978; *b* 6 Feb. 1926; *s* of late S. F. Shearman, Sydney; *m* 1952, Stuart Fay, *d* of late Chap. F. H. Bashford; three *s* three *d. Educ:* Fort St and Orange High Schools; St John's Theological College, Morpeth, NSW. Served War of 1939–45: air crew, 1944–46. Theological College, 1948–50. Deacon, 1950; Priest, 1951. Curate: of Dubbo, 1950–52; of Forbes, and Warden of St John's Hostel, 1953–56; Rector of Coonabarabran, 1957–59; Director of Promotion and Adult Christian Education 1959–62; Canon, All Saints Cathedral, Bathurst, 1962; Archdeacon of Mildura and Rector of St. Margaret's, 1963; Bishop of Rockhampton, 1963–71; Chairman, Australian Board of Missions, Sydney, 1971–73; Bishop of Grafton, 1973–85; Asst Bishop, dio. of Brisbane, 1989–91. ChStJ 1989. *Address:* 123 Turner Street, Scarborough, Qld 4020, Australia.

SHEARMAN, Prof. John Kinder Gowran, PhD; FBA 1976; Adams University Professor, Harvard University, since 1994; *b* 24 June 1931; *s* of Brig. C. E. G. Shearman; *m* 1957, Jane Dalrymple Smith; one *s* three *d; m* 1983, Deirdre Roskill. *Educ:* St Edmund's, Hindhead; Felsted; Courtauld Inst., London Univ.; BA, PhD 1957. Lectr, Courtauld Inst., 1957–67; Research Fellow, Inst. for Advanced Study, Princeton, 1964; Reader, Courtauld Inst., 1967–74, Prof. of the History of Art, 1974–79 (Dep. Dir, 1974–78); Prof., Dept of Art and Archaeology, Princeton Univ., 1979–87 (Chm., 1979–85); Prof. of Fine Arts, Harvard Univ., 1987–94 (Chm. of Dept, 1990–93). Member: Accademia del Disegno, Florence, 1979; Amer. Acad. of Arts and Scis, 1993. Serena Medal, British Acad., 1979. *Publications:* Andrea del Sarto, 1965; Mannerism, 1967, 8th edn 1990; Raphael's Cartoons, 1972; Catalogue of the Early Italian Paintings in the Collection of HM the Queen, 1983; Funzione e Illusione, 1983; Only Connect . . ., 1992; contribs to British, French, German, American jls. *Recreations:* sailing, music. *Address:* 3 Clement Circle, Cambridge, MA 02138, USA. *Club:* Bembridge Sailing.

SHEBBEARE, Thomas Andrew, (Tom); Director: The Prince's Trust and The Royal Jubilee Trusts, since 1988; The Prince's Youth Business Trust, since 1995; *b* 25 Jan. 1952; *s* of late Robert Austin Shebbeare and of Frances Dare Graham; *m* 1976, Cynthia Jane Cottrell; one *s* one *d. Educ:* Malvern Coll.; Univ. of Exeter (BA Politics). World University Service (UK), 1973–75; Gen. Sec., British Youth Council, 1975–80; Administrator, Council of Europe, 1980–85; Exec. Dir, European Youth Foundn, 1985–88. Dir, Inst. for Citizenship Studies, 1991–. *Recreations:* family, cooking, food and drink. *Address:* (office) 8 Bedford Row, WC1R 4BA. *T:* 0171–430 0524.

SHEDDEN, Alfred Charles; Senior Partner, McGrigor Donald, solicitors, since 1993; *b* 30 June 1944; *s* of Alfred Henry Shedden and Jane Murray Shedden; *m* 1st, 1968, Rosalyn Terris; one *s*; 2nd, 1978, Irene McIntyre; one *d. Educ:* Aberdeen Univ. (MA, LLB). Mem., Law Soc. of Scotland. McGrigor Donald: apprentice, 1967; Partner, 1971; Managing Partner, 1985. Non-Executive Director: Standard Life Assurance Co., 1992–; Scottish Financial Enterprise, 1988–. Chm., Legal Resources Gp, 1990–. *Recreations:* Scottish art, football spectator. *Address:* Pacific House, 70 Wellington Street, Glasgow G2 6SB. *T:* 0141–248 6677.

SHEDDEN, Rev. John; QHC 1994; Principal Chaplain, Church of Scotland and Free Churches, Royal Air Force, since 1994; *b* 23 June 1943; *s* of Robert Blair Arnott Shedden and Grace Roberts (*née* Henderson); *m* 1965, Jeannie Lillian Gilling; one *s* one *d. Educ:* Johnstone High Sch.; Univ. of St Andrews (BD Hons; Dip. in Pastoral and Social Studies). Asst Minister, Paisley Abbey, 1970–72; ordained 1971; Parish Minister, Thornhill, Dumfries, 1972–75; Social Welfare Officer, Salisbury, Rhodesia, 1975–76; Chaplain, RN, 1977–84; Minister, St Mark's, Moose Jaw, Sask., 1984–86; Chaplian, RAF, 1986–. *Recreations:* hill-walking, D-I-Y, reading, radio. *Address:* 8 Millwell Park, Innerleithen, Peebles EH44 6JF; 36 Nicolson Close, Innsworth, Gloucester GL3 1DN. *Club:* Royal Air Force.

SHEEHAN, Albert Vincent; Sheriff of Tayside, Central and Fife, since 1983; *b* 23 Aug. 1936; *s* of Richard Greig Sheehan and May Moffat; *m* 1965, Edna Georgina Scott Hastings; two *d. Educ:* Bo'ness Acad.; Edinburgh Univ. (MA 1957; LLB 1959). Admitted as Solicitor, 1959. 2nd Lieut, 1st Bn The Royal Scots (The Royal Regt), 1960; Captain, Directorate of Army Legal Services, 1961. Depute Procurator Fiscal, Hamilton, 1961–71; Sen. Depute Procurator Fiscal, Glasgow, 1971–74; Depute Crown Agent for Scotland, 1974–79; Asst Solicitor, Scottish Law Commn, 1979–81; Sheriff of Lothian and Borders, 1981–83. Leverhulme Fellow, 1971. *Publications:* Criminal Procedure in Scotland and France, 1975; Criminal Procedure, 1990. *Recreations:* naval history, travel, legal history. *Address:* Sheriff's Chambers, Sheriff Court House, Falkirk FK1 4AR.

SHEEHY, Sir Patrick, Kt 1991; Chairman, B.A.T Industries, 1982–95; *b* 2 Sept. 1930; *s* of Sir John Francis Sheehy, CSI and Jean Newton Simpson; *m* 1964, Jill Patricia Tindall; one *s* one *d. Educ:* Australia; Ampleforth Coll., Yorks. Served Irish Guards, 1948–50; rank on leaving 2nd Lieut. Joined British-American Tobacco Co., 1950, first appt in Nigeria;

Ghana, 1951; Reg. Sales Manager, Nigeria, 1953; Ethiopian Tobacco Monopoly, 1954; Marketing Dir, Jamaica, 1957; Barbados, 1961; Marketing Advr, London, 1962; Gen. Man., Holland, 1967; Mem., Gp Bd, 1970; Mem., Chm.'s Policy Cttee, and Chm., Tobacco Div. Bd, 1975; Dep. Chm., 1976–81, Vice-Chm., 1981–82, B.A.T Industries; Chm., British-American Tobacco Co., 1976–82. Chairman: B.A.T Financial Services, 1985–90; BATUS Holdings Inc., 1986–93; S London Business Initiative, 1986–; Director: BATUS Inc., 1979–82; Eagle Star Hldgs, 1984–87; BP, 1984–; The Spectator (1828) Ltd, 1988–; Cluff Resources, 1992–; Asda Property Hldgs, 1994–. Chm., Inquiry into Police Responsibilities and Rewards, 1992–93. Member: Action Cttee for Europe, 1985–; Council of Internat. Advrs, Swiss Bank Corp., 1985–; European Round Table, 1986–; Council, RIIA. *Recreations:* golf, ski-ing, reading. *Address:* c/o B.A.T Industries plc, Windsor House, 50 Victoria Street, SWlH 0NL. *T:* 0171–222 7979.

SHEEHY, Terence Joseph; Editor, Catholic Herald, 1983–88; *b* 12 May 1918; 2nd *s* of Michael Sheehy and Mary (*née* O'Sullivan); *m* 1955, Margaret Patricia Barry, *y d* of Dr T. St John Barry; one *s* three *d.* *Educ:* by Jesuits in London and Dublin. Editorial staff, Irish Catholic, Dublin, 1942–46; publisher and Editor, Irish Cinema Quarterly, Editor, Irish Hotelier, and Editor, Irish Licensing World, 1946–50; Gen. Manager and Dir, Ron Harris (Ireland), film distributors, 1950–52; Bord Fáilte Éireann (Irish Tourist Board): Asst Gen. Manager, N America, 1952–56; Gen. Manager (Britain), and Dir of Publicity, 1956–82; Editor, Irish Observer, 1982. Chm., Banstead CVS, 1990–. Allied Irish Banks' Irish Post Community Award, 1977. Knight Cross, Order of Polonia Restituta (Poland), 1989. *Publications:* Ireland in Colour, 1975; Ireland, 1978; Ireland and Her People, 1980; Journey through Ireland, 1986; An Irish Moment, 1989. *Recreations:* reading, writing, conversation. *Address:* Ballinona, 7 Tower Road, Tadworth, Surrey KT20 5QY. *T:* Tadworth (01737) 814241.

SHEEN, Sir Barry (Cross), Kt 1978; a Judge of the High Court of Justice, Queen's Bench Division (Admiralty Court), 1978–93; *b* 31 Aug. 1918; 2nd *s* of late Ronald Sheen, FCA, St John's Wood; *m* 1st, 1946, Diane (*d* 1986), *d* of late C. L. Donne, MD; three *s*; 2nd, 1988, Helen Ursula, *widow* of Philip Spink; two step *d.* *Educ:* Haileybury College, Hill School (USA); Trinity Hall, Cambridge (MA). Served in RNVR, 1939–46; Commanding Officer, HMS Kilkenzie, 1943–45. Called to Bar, Middle Temple, 1947, Master of the Bench, 1971, Reader, 1990; Member Bar Council, 1959–63; QC 1966. Junior Counsel to Admiralty, 1961–66; a Recorder of the Crown Court, 1972–78. On Panel of Wreck Comrs (Eng.) under Merchant Shipping Acts, 1966–78; Mem., Panel of Lloyd's Arbitrators in Salvage Cases, 1966–78, Appeal Arbitrator, 1977–78. Presided over Inquiry into Zeebrugge ferry disaster, 1987; Vice-Pres., British Maritime Law Assoc., 1979–93. Life Governor, Haileybury (Pres., Haileybury Soc., 1982); Hon. Mem., Assoc. of Average Adjusters, 1979– (Chm., 1986). Liveryman, Shipwrights' Co. Younger Brother, Trinity House, 1993–. Hon. FNI 1993. *Recreations:* golf, travel, carpentry. *Address:* 107 Rivermead Court, Ranelagh Gardens, SW6 3SB. *T:* 0171–731 7275. *Clubs:* Hurlingham; Royal Wimbledon Golf.

SHEERIN, John Declan; His Honour Judge Sheerin; a Circuit Judge, since 1982; *b* 29 Nov. 1932; *s* of late John Patrick Sheerin and Agnes Mary Sheerin; *m* 1958, Helen Suzanne (*née* LeRoux); two *s* two *d.* *Educ:* Wimbledon Coll.; London Sch. of Econs and Polit Science (LLB 1954). Served RAF, 1958–60 (Flying Officer). Admitted solicitor, 1957; Partner, Greene & Greene, 1962–82; a Recorder of the Crown Court, 1979–82. Resident Judge, Cambridge. *Recreation:* golf. *Address:* c/o Crown Court, Downing Street, Cambridge CB2 3DS. *Club:* Flempton Golf.

SHEERMAN, Barry John; MP (Lab and Co-op) Huddersfield, since 1983 (Huddersfield East, 1979–83); *b* 17 Aug. 1940; *s* of late Albert William Sheerman and Florence Sheerman (*née* Pike); *m* 1965 Pamela Elizabeth (*née* Brenchley); one *s* three *d.* *Educ:* Hampton Grammar Sch.; Kingston Technical Coll.; LSE. BSc (Economics) Hons; MSc Hons. Lectr, Univ. Coll. of Swansea, 1966–79. An opposition front bench spokesman on: employment, dealing with training, small business and tourism, 1983–88; home affairs, dealing with police, prisons, crime prevention, drugs, civil defence and fire service, 1988–92; disabled people's rights, 1992–94. Mem., Public Accounts Cttee, 1981–83; Chairman: Parly Adv. Council on Transport Safety, 1981–83; Labour Campaign for Criminal Justice, 1989–92; Co-Chm., Parly Manufg Industry Gp; Vice-Chm., Parly Univ. Gp. Chm., Internat. Cttee for Andean Aid, 1989–. FRSA; FRGS 1989. *Publications:* (jtly) Harold Laski: a life on the Left, 1993; pamphlets on education and training, tourism, and justice. *Address:* House of Commons, SW1A 0AA.

SHEFFIELD, 8th Baron; *see under* Stanley of Alderley, 8th Baron.

SHEFFIELD, Bishop of, since 1980; **Rt. Rev. David Ramsay Lunn;** *b* 1930. *Educ:* King's College, Cambridge (BA 1953, MA 1957); Cuddesdon College, Oxford. Deacon 1955, priest 1956, Newcastle upon Tyne; Curate of Sugley, 1955–59; N Gosforth, 1959–63; Chaplain, Lincoln Theological College, 1963–66; Sub-Warden, 1966–70; Vicar of St George, Cullercoats, 1970–75, Rector, 1975–80; Rural Dean of Tynemouth, 1975–80. *Address:* Bishopscroft, Snaithing Lane, Sheffield, S Yorks S10 3LG.

SHEFFIELD, Provost of; *see* Sadgrove, Very Rev. Michael.

SHEFFIELD, Archdeacon of; *see* Lowe, Ven. S. R.

SHEFFIELD, John Julian Lionel George; Chairman, Portals Holdings PLC, since 1979 (Director, since 1969); *b* 28 Aug. 1938; *s* of John Vincent Sheffield, *qv*; *m* 1961, Carolyn Alexander Abel Smith; three *s* one *d.* *Educ:* Eton Coll.; Christ's Coll., Cambridge. Joined Portals Ltd, 1962. Director: Norcros, 1974– (Chm., 1989–93); Guardian Royal Exchange, 1981– (Dep. Chm., 1988–); Tex Hldgs, 1985–; North Foreland Lodge, 1987–; Newbury Racecourse, 1988–. Mem., Economic and Commercial Cttee, EEF, 1974–90. Mem. Council, St John's Sch., Leatherhead, 1966–. Trustee, Winchester Cathedral Trust, 1984–. Chm., Bd of Govs, N Foreland Lodge, 1992–. *Recreations:* outdoor sports, collecting. *Address:* Laverstoke Mill House, Whitchurch, Hants RG28 7NR. *T:* Basingstoke (01256) 892360. *Clubs:* White's, MCC.

SHEFFIELD, John Vincent, CBE 1984; Chairman, Norcros Ltd, 1956–81; *b* 11 Nov. 1913; *y s* of Sir Berkeley Sheffield, 6th Bt; *m* 1st, 1936, Anne (*d* 1969), *d* of Sir Lionel Faudel-Phillips, 3rd Bt; one *s* three *d*; 2nd, 1971, Mrs France Crosthwaite, *d* of Brig.-Gen. Goland Clarke, CMG, DSO. *Educ:* Eton; Magdalene College, Cambridge (MA). Private Secretary to Minister of Works, 1943–44; Chairman: Portals Ltd, 1968–78; Atlantic Assets Trust Ltd, 1972–83. Chm., BEC, 1980–83; Vice-Chm., BTEC, 1983. High Sheriff of Lincolnshire, 1944–45. *Address:* New Barn House, Laverstoke, Whitchurch, Hants RG28 7PF. *T:* Whitchurch (Hants) (01256) 893187. *Club:* White's.

See also *J. J. L. G. Sheffield.*

SHEFFIELD, Sir Reginald (Adrian Berkeley), 8th Bt *cr* 1755; DL; Managing Director, Normanby Estate Co. Ltd, and other companies; Member of Lloyd's, since 1977; *b* 9 May 1946; *s* of Edmund Charles Reginald Sheffield, JP, DL (*d* 1977) and of Nancie Miriel Denise, *d* of Edward Roland Soames; *S* uncle, 1977; *m* 1st, 1969, Annabel Lucy Veronica (marr. diss.), *d* of late T. A. Jones; two *d*; 2nd, 1977, Victoria Penelope, *d* of late R. C. Walker, DFC; one *s* two *d.* *Educ:* Eton. Member of Stock Exchange, 1973–75. Vice-Chm., S Humberside Business Advice Centre Ltd, 1984–. Pres., S Humberside CPRE, 1985–; Member: Cttee, Lincs and S Humberside Br., CLA, 1987–; Taxation Cttee, CLA, 1989–95; Central Transport Consultative Cttee (NE Reg.), 1988–94; Rail Users Consultative Cttee for NE England, 1994–. Mem. (C) for Ermine Ward, Humberside County Council, 1985–93. Pres., Scunthorpe United Football Club, 1982–94. Pres., Scunthorpe and Dist, Victim Support Scheme, 1989–. DL Humberside, 1985. *Heir:* *s* Robert Charles Berkeley Sheffield, *b* 1 Sept. 1984. *Address:* Estate Office, Normanby, Scunthorpe, S Humberside DN15 9HS. *T:* Scunthorpe (01724) 720618. *Clubs:* White's; Lincolnshire (Sleaford).

SHEFTON, Prof. Brian Benjamin, FBA 1985; FSA 1980; Professor of Greek Art and Archaeology, University of Newcastle upon Tyne, 1979–84, now Emeritus; *b* 11 Aug. 1919; *yr s* of late Prof. I. Scheftelowitz (Cologne, Germany, until 1933 and Oxford) and Frieda (*née* Kohn); *m* 1960, Jutta Ebel of Alingsås, Sweden; one *d.* *Educ:* Apostelngymnasium, Cologne; St Lawrence Coll., Ramsgate; Magdalen Coll. Sch., Oxford; Oriel Coll., Oxford (Open Scholar, 1938; Hon. Mods Greek and Latin Lit. 1940; Lit Hum 1947, Class I). War service, HM Forces (change of name), 1940–45. Sch. Student, British Sch. at Athens, 1947; Derby Scholar, Oxford, 1948; Bishop Fraser Scholar, Oriel Coll., Oxford, 1949, in Aegean to 1950; excavated at Old Smyrna; Lectr in Classics, University Coll., Exeter, 1950–55; Lectr in Greek Archaeology and Ancient History, 1955, Sen. Lectr, 1960, Reader, 1974–79, King's Coll., Univ. of Durham (later Univ. of Newcastle upon Tyne). Established and directed Univ.'s Greek Museum (renamed Shefton Mus. of Greek Art and Archaeology, 1994), 1956–84, Hon. Advr, 1985–; Trustee, Oriental Mus., Durham Univ., 1989–93. Vis. Res. Fellow, Merton Coll., Oxford, 1969; British Acad. Vis. Scholar to Albania, 1973; Munro Lectr, Edinburgh Univ., 1974; British Acad. European Exchange Fellow, Marburg Univ., 1975; German Academic Exchange Fellow, Marburg and Cologne, 1976; Leverhulme Res. Fellow, 1977; Webster Meml Lectr, Stanford Univ., 1981; Vis. Prof. of Classical Archaeology, Vienna Univ. (winter), 1981–82; British Council Vis. Scholar to Soviet Union, 1982, to Spain, 1985; Jackson Knight Meml Lectr, Exeter Univ., 1983; Leverhulme Emeritus Fellow, 1984–86; Balsdon Sen. Fellow, British Sch. at Rome, 1985; Vis. Scholar, J. Paul Getty Museum, 1987; British Acad. Exchange Fellow, Jerusalem, 1993; Bulgaria, 1996. Mem., German Archaeological Inst., 1961; Foreign Mem., Inst. of Etruscan and Italic Studies, Florence, 1990. Hon. Dr.phil Cologne, 1989. Aylwin Cotton Award, 1977. *Publications:* History of Greek Vase Painting (with P. Arias and M. Hirmer), 1962; Die rhodischen Bronzekannen, 1979; chapters in: Perachora II, 1962; Phoenizier im Westen, 1982; The Eye of Greece, 1982; Das Kleinaspergle, 1988; Kotinos, 1992; Cultural Transformations and Interactions in Eastern Europe, 1993; The Archaeology of Greek Colonization, 1994; Social Complexity and the Development of Towns in Iberia, 1995; Italy in Europe: economic relations 700BC–AD50, 1995; articles in British and foreign periodicals. *Recreations:* music, travel. *Address:* 24 Holly Avenue, Newcastle upon Tyne NE2 2PY. *T:* 0191–281 4184.

SHEGOG, Rev. Eric Marshall; Director of Communications, Church of England, since 1990; *b* 23 July 1937; *s* of George Marshall Shegog and Helen (*née* Whitefoot); *m* 1961, Anne Thomas; two *s* one *d.* *Educ:* Leigh Grammar School; College of St Mark and St John; Whitelands College; Lichfield Theol College; City Univ. (MA). CertEd London; DipTh London. Asst Master, Holy Trinity Primary Sch., Wimbledon, 1960–64; Asst Curate, All Saints, Benhilton, 1965–68; Asst Youth Adviser, Dio. of Southwark, 1968–70; Vicar, St Michael and All Angels, Abbey Wood, 1970–75; Town Centre Chaplain, Sunderland, 1976–83; Head of Religious Broadcasting, IBA, 1984–90. Chairman: BBC Adv. Cttee for NE, 1980–83; Age Concern, Sunderland, 1980–83; Dir, World Assoc. for Christian Communication, 1990–93 (Vice-Chm., Eur. Region, 1990–93). FRSA 1992. *Publications:* (jtly) Religious Television: controversies and conclusions, 1990; (jtly) Religious Broadcasting in the 90s, 1991; (contrib.) Elvy, Opportunities and Limitations in Religious Broadcasting, 1991; (contrib.) The Communication of Values, 1993. *Recreations:* gardening, opera, jogging. *Address:* 3 The Pleasance, Harpenden, Herts AL5 3NA. *T:* Harpenden (01582) 460406.

SHEHADIE, Sir Nicholas (Michael), AC 1990; Kt 1976; OBE 1971; Managing Director, Nicholas Shehadie Pty Ltd, since 1959; *b* 15 Nov. 1926; *s* of Michael and Hannah Shehadie; *m* 1957, Dr Marie Roslyn Bashir, AO; one *s* two *d.* *Educ:* Sydney. Elected Alderman, City of Sydney, Dec. 1962; Dep. Lord Mayor, Sept. 1969–73; Lord Mayor of Sydney, Sept. 1973–75. Chm., Special Broadcasting Services. Rugby Union career: Captained NSW and Australia; played 30 Internationals and 6 overseas tours; Mem., Barbarians'. Chm., Sydney Cricket Ground, 1990–. *Recreations:* Rugby, surfing, horse racing, bowls. *Address:* 118 Old Canterbury Road, Lewisham, Sydney, NSW 2090, Australia. *Clubs:* Randwick Rugby, Tattersall's (Sydney).

SHEIKHOLESLAMI, Prof. Ali Reza, PhD; Soudavar Professor of Persian Studies, Oxford University, since 1990; Fellow, Wadham College, Oxford, since 1990; *b* 21 July 1941; *s* of Ali Soltani Sheikholeslami and Shah-Zadeh Mansouri; *m* 1989, Shirin Khoshnevis. *Educ:* Columbia Univ., NY (BA); Northwestern Univ. (MA); UCLA (PhD). Asst Prof. of Pol Sci., Univ. of Washington, Seattle, 1975–85; Res. Fellow, Harvard Univ., 1987–88; Iranian Fellow, St Antony's Coll., Oxford, 1988–90. *Publications:* Political Economy of Saudi Arabia, 1984; articles on 19th and 20th Century Persia in jls and book chapters. *Recreations:* reading, travelling. *Address:* Wadham College, Oxford OX1 3TN. *T:* Oxford (01865) 278200, 278223.

SHEIL, Hon. Sir John (Joseph), Kt 1989; **Hon. Mr Justice Sheil;** a Judge of the High Court of Northern Ireland, since 1989; *b* 19 June 1938; *y s* of late Hon. Mr Justice (Charles Leo) Sheil and Elizabeth Josephine Sheil (*née* Cassidy); *m* 1979, Brenda Margaret Hale Patterson, *o d* of late Rev. Forde Patterson and Elizabeth Patterson (*née* Irwin); one *s.* *Educ:* Clongowes Wood Coll.; Queen's Univ. Belfast (LLB); Trinity Coll., Dublin (MA). Called to Bar: NI, 1964 (Bencher 1988), QC 1975; Gray's Inn, 1974; Ireland, 1976. Chairman: Mental Health Rev. Tribunal, 1985–87; Fair Employment Appeals Bd, 1986–89; Mem., Standing Adv. Commn on Human Rights, 1981–83. Senator, QUB, 1987–. *Recreations:* golf, travel. *Address:* Royal Courts of Justice, Belfast BT1 3JY.

SHELBURNE, Earl of; Charles Maurice Petty-Fitzmaurice, DL; *b* 21 Feb. 1941; *s* and *heir* of 8th Marquess of Lansdowne, *qv*; *m* 1st, 1965, Lady Frances Eliot, *o d* of 9th Earl of St Germans; two *s* two *d*; 2nd, 1987, Fiona Merritt, *d* of Lady Davies and Donald Merritt. *Educ:* Eton. Page of Honour to The Queen, 1956–57. Served with Kenya Regt, 1960–61; with Wiltshire Yeomanry (TA), amalgamated with Royal Yeomanry Regt, 1963–73. Pres., Wiltshire Playing Fields Assoc., 1965–74; Wiltshire County Councillor, 1970–85; Mem., South West Economic Planning Council, 1972–77; Chairman: Working Committee Population & Settlement Pattern (SWEPC), 1972–77; North Wiltshire DC, 1973–76; Mem., Calne and Chippenham RDC, 1964–73. Mem., Historic Bldgs and Monuments Commn, 1983–89; Pres., HHA, 1988–93 (Dep. Pres., 1986–88). Mem., Prince's Council, 1990–; President: Wiltshire Assocs Boys Clubs and Youth Clubs, 1976–; North-West Wiltshire District Scout Council, 1977–88; N Wilts Cons. Assoc., 1986–. Contested (C) Coventry North East, 1979. DL Wilts, 1990. *Heir:* *s* Viscount Calne and

Calstone, *qv*. *Address:* Bowood House, Calne, Wiltshire SN11 0LZ. *T:* Calne (01249) 813343. *Clubs:* Turf, Brooks's.

SHELDON, Bernard, CB 1981; *b* 14 June 1924; *s* of Gerald Walter Sheldon and Doris Sheldon (*née* Hopkins); *m* 1951, Dorothy Kirkland; one *s* two *d*. *Educ:* Hurstpierpoint Coll. (Scholar). War service, N Atlantic and Pacific, 1943–46 (Lieut RNVR). Called to the Bar, Middle Temple, 1949. Joined Colonial Legal Service, 1951; Federal Counsel and Dep. Public Prosecutor, Fedn of Malaya, 1951–59; Legal Adviser: Pahang, 1953; Kedah and Perlis, 1955–59; War Office, 1959–67; MoD, 1967–87, retired 1987. Badlishah Decoration for Loyalty, Kedah, 1958. *Recreation:* chess. *Address:* c/o Lloyds Bank, 64 High Street, Epsom, Surrey KT19 8AT.

SHELDON, Hon. Sir Gervase; *see* Sheldon, Hon. Sir J. G. K.

SHELDON, Harold; District Councillor; *b* 22 June 1918; *s* of Charles Edwin Sheldon and Lily Sheldon (*née* Taylor); *m* 1941, Bessie Sheldon (*née* Barratt); two *s* one *d*. HM Forces, 1939–45 (Sgt; wounded D Day landings). Local Government: elected Batley Borough Council, 1953; Mayor of Batley, 1962–63; W Yorkshire County Council, 1973–86 (Chm., 1976–77); re-elected 1977, 1981; Mem., Kirklees MDC, 1987– (Mayor, 1994–95). Chairman: Batley Sports Develt Council, 1965–; Kirklees Dist Sports Council, 1974–; Mem., Yorks and Humberside Council for Sport and Recreation, 1977–86 and 1991–; President: Batley Boys' Club (Founder Mem.), 1975–; Batley CAB, 1987–; Batley Sports for the Disabled Assoc., 1987–. *Address:* 5 Norfolk Avenue, Carlton Grange, Batley, West Yorkshire WF17 7AR. *T:* Batley (01924) 473619.

SHELDON, John Denby; General Secretary, National Union of Civil and Public Servants, since 1993 (Deputy General Secretary, 1988–93); *b* 31 Jan. 1941; *s* of Frank and Doreen Sheldon; *m* 1976; two *s*. *Educ:* Wingate County Primary and West Leeds High School. Oxford Univ. Diploma in Social Studies. Post Office Engineer, 1957–68; student, Ruskin Coll., 1968–70; full time Trade Union Official, Instn of Professional Civil Servants, 1970–72; Civil Service Union: National Officer, 1972–78; Deputy Gen. Sec., 1978–82; Gen. Sec., 1982–88. *Recreations:* cricket; Rugby League as spectator; family. *Address:* 2 Wincroft Road, Reading, Berks RG4 7HH. *T:* Reading (01734) 477810.

SHELDON, Sir (John) Gervase (Kensington), Kt 1978; a Judge of the High Court, Family Division, 1978–88; an Additional Judge of the High Court, 1988–93; *b* 4 Oct. 1913; *s* of John Henry Sheldon, MD, DPH, and Eleanor Gladys Sheldon, MB, BS; *m* 1st, 1940, Patricia Mary Mardon; one *s*; 2nd, 1960, Janet Marguerite Seager; two *s* one *d*. *Educ:* Winchester Coll.; Trinity Coll., Cambridge (MA; 1st Cl. Hons Law). Barrister-at-Law, called Lincoln's Inn, 1939 (Cert. of Honour, Cholmeley Schol.), Bencher, 1978. Served RA (TA), 1939–45 (despatches twice): Egypt, N Africa, Italy; Major, RA, 1943. A Circuit Judge (formerly a County Court Judge), 1968–78; Presiding Judge, Western Circuit, 1980–84. *Recreation:* family and home. *Address:* Hopton, Churt, Surrey GU10 2LD. *T:* Frensham (01252) 792035. *Clubs:* United Oxford & Cambridge University, MCC.

SHELDON, Mark Hebberton; Consultant, Linklaters & Paines, Solicitors, since 1994; President of The Law Society, 1992–93; *b* 6 Feb. 1931; *s* of late George Hebberton Sheldon and Marie Sheldon (*née* Hazlitt); *m* 1971, Catherine Ashworth; one *s* one *d*. *Educ:* Wycliffe Coll.; Corpus Christi Coll., Oxford (BA Jurisprudence (Hons), MA; Hon. Fellow, 1995). National Service, 1949–50, TA, 1950–54, Royal Signals (Lieut). Linklaters & Paines: articled clerk, 1953–56; Asst Solicitor, 1957–59; Partner, 1959–93, Sen. Partner, 1988–91, Jt Sen. Partner, 1991–93. Resident Partner, New York, 1972–74. Mem. Council 1978–, Treas. 1981–86, Vice-Pres., 1991–92, Law Soc.; Mem. Court 1975–, Master 1987–88, City of London Solicitors' Co.; Pres., City of London Law Soc., 1987–88. Hon. Bencher, Inner Temple, 1993. Nominated Mem., Council of Corp. of Lloyd's, 1989–90; Member: Financial Reporting Council, 1990–; Cadbury Cttee on Financial Aspects of Corporate Governance, 1991–95; Financial Law Panel, 1993–; Sen. Salaries Rev. Body, 1994–; Panel of Conciliators, Internat. Centre for Investment Disputes, 1995–; Adv. Panel, Inst. for Socio-Legal Studies, Univ. of Oxford, 1995–. Hon. Member: Canadian Bar Assoc., 1993–; SPTL, 1993–. Trustee, Oxford Inst. of Legal Practice, 1993–. Chm., Corpus Assoc., 1983–89. *Recreations:* music, English water-colours, wine, swimming. *Address:* 5 St Albans Grove, W8 5PN. *T:* 0171–937 3120, *Fax:* 0171–938 4771. *Clubs:* Travellers', City of London.

SHELDON, Rt. Hon. Robert (Edward), PC 1977; MP (Lab) Ashton-under-Lyne, since 1964; *b* 13 Sept. 1923; *m* 1st, 1945, Eileen Shamash (*d* 1969); one *s* one *d*; 2nd 1971, Mary Shield. *Educ:* Elementary and Grammar Schools; Engineering Apprenticeship; Technical Colleges in Stockport, Burnley and Salford; WhSch 1944. Engineering diplomas; external graduate, London University. Contested Withington, Manchester, 1959; Chm., Labour Parly Economic Affairs and Finance Group, 1967–68; Opposition Front Bench Spokesman on Civil Service and Machinery of Govt, also on Treasury matters, 1970–74; Minister of State, CSD, March-Oct. 1974; Minister of State, HM Treasury, Oct. 1974–June 1975; Financial Sec. to the Treasury, 1975–79; Opposition front bench spokesman on Treasury matters, 1981–83; Chm., Public Accounts Cttee, 1983– (Mem., 1965–70, 1975–79); Member: Public Expenditure Cttee (Chm. Gen. Sub-Cttee), 1972–74; Select Cttee on Treasury and Civil Service, 1979–81 (Chm., Sub-Cttee); Fulton Cttee on the Civil Service, 1966–68. Chm., NW Gp of Labour MPs, 1970–74. *Address:* 27 Darley Avenue, Manchester M20 8ZD; 2 Ryder Street, SW1.

SHELFORD, Cornelius William, DL; retired; *b* 6 July 1908; *s* of William Heard Shelford and Maud Ethel Shelford, Horncastle, Sharpthorne, Sussex, and Singapore; *m* 1934, Helen Beatrice Hilda Schuster; one *s* two *d*. *Educ:* private tutor and Trinity College, Cambridge. Chartered Accountant, 1934; Partner, Rowley Pemberton & Co., 1940 (retd 1960); Chm., Mills & Allen Ltd, 1964 (retd 1969); Chm., London County Freehold & Leasehold Properties Ltd, 1964 (retd 1970). East Sussex CC, 1952 (CA, 1957; Chm., 1964–67; Chm., Finance Cttee, 1970–74); High Sheriff of Sussex, 1954; DL Sussex, 1968–. Governor and Mem. Management Cttee, Chailey Heritage Craft Schs and Hosp., for 30 years (Jt Founder, League of Friends); Pestalozzi Children's Village Trust: Mem. Council, 1974–; Vice-Chm., 1975–83; Chm., 1983–85. *Recreations:* travelling, walking, gardening. *Address:* Heasmans, Chailey Green, near Lewes, E Sussex BN8 4DA. *T:* Newick (01825) 722530. *Club:* Carlton.

SHELLARD, Maj.-Gen. Michael Francis Linton, CBE 1989; General Manager, Regular Forces Employment Association, since 1994; *b* 19 Aug. 1937; *s* of Norman Shellard and Stella (*née* Linton); *m* 1960, Jean Mary Yates; one *s* one *d*. *Educ:* Queen's Coll., Taunton; RMA, Sandhurst. Commnd, RA, 1957; Staff Coll., Camberley, 1969; NDC, Latimer, 1974; GSO1 MO4, MoD, 1975–76; CO 22 AD Regt, 1977–79; Col, 1983; Brig., 1985; Comd 1st Artillery Bde and Dortmund Garrison, 1985–88; Comdr Artillery, 1st British Corps, 1990–92. Dir, NATO Area, Short Brothers plc, 1992–94. Col Comdt, RA, 1993–; Hon. Col 22nd Regt, RA, 1993–. Chairman: RA Historical Affairs Cttee; RA Historical Trust. Gov., Queen's Coll., Taunton, 1989–. *Recreations:* golf, bird watching, gardening. *Address:* c/o Midland Bank, High Street, Amesbury, Wilts SP4 7DN.

SHELLEY, Alan John; Senior Partner, Knight, Frank & Rutley, 1983–92; *b* 7 Aug. 1931; *s* of Stanley and Ivy Shelley; *m* 1958, Josephine (*née* Flood); one *s* one *d*. *Educ:* People's College, Nottingham. FRICS. Senior Partner, Knight, Frank & Rutley (Nigeria), 1965. General Commissioner of Income Tax, 1984–. Chairman: W Africa Cttee, 1985–; Mansfield Settlement, 1992–. Mem. Ct of Governors, Royal Shakespeare Theatre, 1990–. *Recreations:* theatre, squash. *Address:* 54 Bathurst Mews, W2 2SB. *T:* 0171–262 1991; Thatch Farm, Glaston, Rutland, Leics LE15 9BX. *T:* Uppingham (01572) 282396. *Clubs:* Oriental, MCC.

SHELLEY, Howard Gordon; concert pianist and conductor; Principal Guest Conductor, London Mozart Players, since 1992 (Associate Conductor, 1990–92); *b* 9 March 1950; *s* of Frederick Gordon Shelley and Katharine Anne Taylor; *m* 1975, Hilary Mary Pauline Macnamara; one *s*, and one step *s*. *Educ:* Highgate Sch.; Royal College of Music (ARCM Hons 1966; Foundn Schol. 1967–71); Boise Schol. 1971–72; ARCO 1967. Studied with Vera Yelverton, Harold Craxton, Kendall Taylor, Lamar Crowson and Ilona Kabos. Recital début, Wigmore Hall, 1971; televised Henry Wood Prom début, 1972; conducting début, London Symphony Orch., Barbican, 1985. Internat. solo career extending over five continents; performed world's first complete exposition of solo piano works of Rachmaninov, Wigmore Hall, 1983. Discography includes: Rachmaninov solo works (8 vols), Rachmaninov two-piano works, Rachmaninov Complete Piano Concertos, Mozart and Mendelssohn Piano Concertos (conductor/soloist), Chopin, Schumann recitals, Schubert recital on fortepiano, piano concertos of Alwyn, Gershwin, Tippett, Vaughan Williams, Howard Ferguson and Peter Dickinson. 2 piano partnership with Hilary Macnamara, 1976–. Chappell Gold Medal and Peter Morrison Prize, 1968, Dannreuther Concerto Prize, 1971, RCM; Silver Medal, Co. of Musicians, 1971. *Address:* c/o Intermusica, 16 Duncan Terrace, N1 8BZ. *T:* 071–278 5455.

SHELLEY, James Edward, CBE 1991; Secretary to Church Commissioners, 1985–92; *b* 1932; *s* of Vice-Adm. Richard Shelley and Eve Cecil; *m* 1956, Judy Grubb; two *s* two *d*. *Educ:* Eton; University College, Oxford (MA). Joined Church Commissioners' staff, 1954; Under Secretary General, 1976–81; Assets Secretary, 1981–85. Dir, Save & Prosper, 1987–94. *Recreations:* country pursuits. *Address:* Mays Farm House, Ramsdell, Tadley, Hants RG26 5RE. *T:* Basingstoke (01256) 850770. *Club:* Naval and Military.

SHELLEY, Sir John (Richard), 11th Bt *cr* 1611; (professionally Dr J. R. Shelley); general medical practitioner; Partner, Drs Shelley, Doddington and Ayres, Health Centre, South Molton, Devon; *b* 18 Jan. 1943; *s* of John Shelley (*d* 1974), and of Dorothy, *d* of Arthur Irvine Ingram; *S* grandfather, 1976; *m* 1965, Clare, *d* of Claud Bicknell, *qv*; two *d*. *Educ:* King's Sch., Bruton; Trinity Coll., Cambridge (BA 1964, MA 1967); St Mary's Hosp., London Univ. MB, BChir 1967; DObstRCOG 1969; MRCGP 1978. Partner in Drs Harris, Barkworth, Savile, Shelley and Gurney, Eastbourne, Sx, 1969–74; Partnership, Health Centre, S Molton, 1974–. Member: Exeter Diocesan Synod for South Molton Deanery, 1976–79; BMA; CLA; NFU. *Heir: b* Thomas Henry Shelley [*b* 3 Feb. 1945; *m* 1970, Katherine Mary Holton; three *d*]. *Address:* Health Centre, 9–10 East Street, South Molton, Devon EX36 3BZ; Shobrooke Park, Crediton, Devon EX17 1DG. *T:* South Molton (01769) 573101.

SHELTON, Shirley Megan, (Mrs W. T. Shelton); Editor, Home & Freezer Digest, 1988–90; *b* 8 March 1934; *d* of Lt-Col T. F. Goodwin; *m* 1960, William Timothy Shelton; one *s* two *d*. *Educ:* various schs. Home Editor 1970–75, Assistant Editor, 1975–78, Editor, 1978–82, Woman and Home magazine. *Address:* 59 Croftdown Road, NW5 1EL. *T:* 0171–485 4936.

SHELTON, Sir William (Jeremy Masefield), Kt 1989; MA Oxon; *b* 30 Oct. 1929; *s* of late Lt-Col R. C. M. Shelton, MBE, St Saviour's, Guernsey, and Mrs R. E. P. Shelton (*née* Coode), London Place, Oxford; *m* 1960, Anne Patricia, *o d* of John Arthur Warder, CBE; one *s* one *d*. *Educ:* Radley Coll.; Tabor Academy, Marion, Mass; Worcester Coll., Oxford; Univ. of Texas, Austin, Texas. Colman, Prentis & Varley Ltd, 1952–55; Corpa, Caracas, Venezuela, 1955–60; Managing Director: CPV (Colombiana) Ltd, Bogota, Colombia, 1960–64; CPV (International) Ltd, 1967–74 (Dir, 1964); Grosvenor Advertising Ltd, 1969–74 (Dir, 1964); Chairman: Fletcher, Shelton, Delaney & Reynolds Ltd, 1974–81; GGK London Ltd, 1984–86; non-executive Chairman: MacFalane & Associates; Ocean Dusk Travel, 1993–; Car Park Advertising, 1994–; Consultant, Gilchrists, solicitors. Member for Wandsworth, GLC, 1967–70; Chief Whip, on ILEA, 1968–70. MP (C) Clapham, 1970–74, Streatham, 1974–92; contested (C) Streatham, 1992. PPS to Minister of Posts and Telecommunications, 1972–74; PPS to Rt Hon. Margaret Thatcher, MP, 1975; Parly Under-Sec. of State, DES, 1981–83. Mem., Council of Europe and WEU, 1987–92. *Recreations:* golf, reading, painting. *Address:* The Manor House, Long Crendon, Bucks HP18 9AN. *T:* Long Crendon (01844) 208748. *Club:* Carlton.

SHENFIELD, Dame Barbara (Estelle), DBE 1986; Chairman, Women's Royal Voluntary Service, 1981–88 (Vice Chairman, 1976–81); *d* of George and Jane Farrow, Bearwood, Staffs; *m* 1st, Flt-Lt Gwilym Ivor Lewis, RAF (killed in action); one *s*; 2nd, Arthur A. Shenfield (*d* 1990); one *s*. *Educ:* Langley High Sch., Worcs; Univ. of Birmingham (Hons Social and Political Science). Lectr in Soc. Studies, Univ. of Birmingham, 1945–56; Lectr, Dept of Econs and Soc. Studies, Bedford Coll., London Univ., 1959–65; Academic Dir, UC at Buckingham, 1972–73. Visiting Professor: Michigan State Univ., 1960; Temple Univ., Philadelphia, 1974; Distinguished Vis. Prof., Rockford Coll., Ill, 1969–71, 1974. Consultant, US Dept of Labor, 1964; Dir, PEP Study of Co. Bds' Soc. Responsibilities, 1965–68. Member: UK Govt Cttee on Local Taxation, 1965–66; UK Govt Cttee on Abuse of Welfare Services, 1971–73; Govt Review Team on Social Security, 1984–85. Chairman: Nat Exec., Nat. Old People's Welfare Council (now Age Concern), 1971–73; Friends of the Imperial War Mus., 1991–. Dir, Mont Pelerin Soc., 1988–. Trustee, Social Affairs Unit, 1990–. DUniv Buckingham, 1987. *Publications:* Social Policies for Old Age, 1957; The Social Responsibilities of Company Boards, 1971; The Organisation of a Voluntary Service, 1972; Myths of Social Policy, 1975; monographs and articles on gerontological and other social subjects. *Recreations:* gardening, music, viticulture. *Address:* 22 Lower Sloane Street, SW1W 8BJ. *T:* 0171–730 5810.

SHEPARD, Giles Richard Carless, CBE 1994; Managing Director, Savoy Hotel plc, 1979–94; *b* 1 April 1937; *er s* of Richard S. H. Shepard, MC, TD; *m* 1966, Peter Carolyn Fern Keighley; one *s* one *d*. *Educ:* Heatherdown, Ascot; Eton (King's Scholar); Harvard Business School (PMD 1967). Commissioned Coldstream Guards, 1955–60. Director: Charrington & Co., 1960–64; H. P. Bulmer & Co., 1964–70; Managing Director: Findlater Mackie, Todd, 1967–70; Westminster & Country Properties, 1970–76; Director: Dorchester Hotel, 1972–76; Savoy Hotel, 1976–79; Guinness Mahon & Co. Ltd, 1994–; Longshot Ltd, 1994–; Chm., Searcy Tansley & Co. Ltd, 1995–. Director: Kleinwort Develt Fund, 1990–; London First, 1993–. Mem., Adv. Council for the Royal Parks, 1993–; Hon. Catering Advr to the Army, 1994–. Mem. Council, Union Jack Club, 1980–. Chm., City and Guilds of London Art Sch. Mem., Court of Assistants, Fishmongers' Co. (Prime Warden, 1987–88); High Sheriff of Greater London, 1986–87. Governor, Gresham's School, Holt, 1980–. *Recreations:* gardening, shooting, embroidery. *Address:*

Wallop House, Nether Wallop, near Stockbridge, Hants SO20 8HE. *Clubs:* White's, Pratt's, Beefsteak.

SHEPHARD, Rt Hon. Gillian (Patricia); PC 1992; MP (C) South West Norfolk, since 1987; Secretary of State for Education and Employment (formerly for Education), since 1994; *b* 22 Jan. 1940; *d* of Reginald and Bertha Watts; *m* 1975, Thomas Shephard; two step *s. Educ:* North Walsham High Sch. for Girls; St Hilda's Coll., Oxford (MA Mod. Langs; Hon. Fellow, 1991). Educn Officer and Schools Inspector, 1963–75; Lectr, Cambridge Univ. Extra-Mural Bd, 1965–87. Councillor, Norfolk CC, 1977–89 (Chm. of Social Services Cttee, 1978–83, of Educn Cttee, 1983–85); Chairman: W Norfolk and Wisbech HA, 1981–85; Norwich HA, 1985–87; Co-Chm., Women's Nat. Commn, 1990–91. PPS to Economic Sec. to the Treasury, 1988–89; Parly Under Sec. of State, DSS, 1989–90; Minister of State, HM Treasury, 1990–92; Sec. of State for Employment, 1992–93; Minister of Agric., Fisheries and Food, 1993–94. Dep. Chm., Conservative Party, 1991–92. *Recreations:* music, gardening, France. *Address:* House of Commons, SW1A 0AA. *T:* (constituency office) Downham Market (01366) 385072.

SHEPHARD, Air Cdre Harold Montague, CBE 1974 (OBE 1959); Provost Marshal (RAF) and Director of Security, 1971–74, retired; *b* 15 Aug. 1918; *s* of late Rev. Leonard B. Shephard; *m* 1939, Margaret Isobel (*née* Girdlestone); one *s* one *d. Educ:* St John's, Leatherhead. Metropolitan Police (CID), 1937–41. Served War, RAF, 1941; commissioned for Provost duties, 1943. Seconded Public Safety Br., CCG, 1945; Wing Comdr, SIB, BAFO, 1947–50; OC, RAF Police Sch., 1951–52; DAPM, Hong Kong; PMI, Air Ministry; Command Provost Marshal, Cyprus; OC, 4 RAF Police District; PM4, Air Ministry; Comdt, RAF Police Depot, Debden, 1963–64; CPM, FEAF, 1964–67; Comdt, Police Depot, 1967–69; Comd Provost and Security Officer, RAF Germany, 1969–71; Air Cdre, 1971. MBIM. *Recreations:* watching all sports, reading, writing to newspapers. *Address:* 6 Bennetts Mews, Tenterden, Kent TN30 6JN. *Club:* Royal Air Force.

SHEPHEARD, Major-General Joseph Kenneth, CB 1962; DSO 1943, and Bar, 1945; OBE 1949; *b* 15 Nov. 1908; *s* of late J. D. Shepheard, Poole and Bournemouth; *m* 1939, Maureen, *d* of late Capt. R. McG. Bowen-Colthurst, Oak Grove, County Cork; three *d. Educ:* Monmouth School; RMA Woolwich; Christ's Coll., Cambridge (BA Hons). Commissioned RE, 1928; served in India with King George V's Own Bengal Sappers and Miners, 1933–38; served in France with BEF as Adjt 4 Div. RE, 1939–40; Staff College, Camberley, 1940; Bde Major 161 (Essex) Inf. Bde in UK, Sierra Leone and Western Desert, 1940–41; Bde Major 18 Indian Inf. Bde in Iraq, 1941; GSO1 4 Indian Div. in N Africa and Italy, 1942–44; Comd 6 Assault Regt RE, Normandy to Baltic, 1944–46; JSSC, Latimer, Bucks, 1947; GSO1, FarELF, 1948–49; Staff Officer to Dir of Operations, Malaya, 1950; Comd 27 Fd Enrg Regt and CRE 6 Armd Div., 1951–53; Defence Research Policy Staff, 1953–56; Imperial Defence Coll., 1957; CCRE 1 (Br.) Corps in Germany, 1958–60; Chief of Staff, Northern Comd, 1960–62; Chief Engineer, Northern Army Group and BAOR, 1962–64. Col Comdt, RE, 1967–72. Gen. Sec., The Officers' Assoc., 1966–74. *Address:* Comfrey Cottage, Fields Farm Lane, Layer-de-la-Haye, Colchester, Essex CO2 0JN.

SHEPHEARD, Sir Peter (Faulkner), Kt 1980; CBE 1972; PPRIBA, MRTPI, PPILA; architect, town planner and landscape architect in private practice since 1948 (Shepheard, Epstein & Hunter); Professor of Architecture and Environmental Design, Graduate School of Fine Arts, University of Pennsylvania, since 1971; *b* 11 Nov. 1913; *s* of Thomas Faulkner Shepheard, FRIBA, Liverpool; *m* 1943, Mary Bailey; one *s* one *d. Educ:* Birkenhead Sch.; Liverpool Sch. of Architecture. BArch. (1st Cl. Hons) Liverpool, 1936; Univ. Grad. Scholar in Civic Design, 1936–37. Asst to Derek Bridgwater, 1937–40; Min. of Supply, Royal Ordnance Factories, 1940–43; Min. of Town and Country Planning: technical officer, first on Greater London Plan (Sir Patrick Abercrombie's staff), later on research and master plan for Stevenage New Town, 1943–47. Dep. Chief Architect and Planner, Stevenage Develt Corp., 1947–48. Vis. Prof., Landscape Architecture, 1959 and 1962–71, and Dean of Fine Arts, 1971–79, Univ. of Pennsylvania. Member: Nat. Parks Commn, 1966–68; Countryside Commn, 1968–71; Royal Fine Art Commn, 1968–71. Artistic Advr, Commonwealth War Graves Commn, 1977–. Works include: housing and schools for GLC and other authorities; Landscape of part of Festival of Britain South Bank Exhibition, London, 1951; Master plan and buildings for University of Lancaster; work for the Universities of Keele, Liverpool, Oxford, and Ghana, and for Winchester College; gardens in England and USA. President: RIBA, 1969–71; Architectural Association, 1954–55; Inst. of Landscape Architects, 1965–66. Master, Art Workers' Guild, 1984. RIBA Distinction in Town Planning, 1956. Hon. FRAIC; Hon. FAIA. *Publications:* Modern Gardens, 1953; Gardens, 1969; various articles, lectures and broadcasts on architecture and landscape; drawings and illustrations of architecture and other things; illustr. A Book of Ducks, and Woodland Birds (King Penguins). *Recreations:* music and poetry; drawing, gardening and the study of natural history. *Address:* 21 Well Road, NW3 1LH. *T:* 0171–435 3019. *Club:* Athenæum.

SHEPHERD, family name of **Baron Shepherd.**

SHEPHERD, 2nd Baron, *cr* 1946, of Spalding; **Malcolm Newton Shepherd,** PC 1965; Chairman, Chequepoint International, since 1989; *b* 27 Sept. 1918; *s* of 1st Baron Shepherd, PC, and Ada Newton (*d* 1975); *S* father, 1954; *m* 1941, Allison Wilson Redmond; two *s. Educ:* Lower Sch. of John Lyon; Friends' Sch., Saffron Walden. War of 1939–45: commissioned RASC, 1941; served in Desert, N Africa, Sicily, Italy. Deputy Opposition Chief Whip, House of Lords, 1960. Member Parly Labour Party Exec., 1964; Deputy Speaker, House of Lords, subseq. Opposition Chief Whip, 1964; Captain of the Hon. Corps of Gentlemen-at-Arms and Government Chief Whip, House of Lords, 1964–67; Minister of State, FCO, 1967–70; Deputy Leader of the House of Lords, 1968–70; Opposition Dep. Leader, House of Lords, 1970–74; Lord Privy Seal and Leader, House of Lords, 1974–76, resigned. Dep. Chm., Sterling Gp of Cos, 1976–86. First Chm., CS Pay Res. Unit Bd, 1978–81; Chairman: MRC, 1978–82; Packaging Council, 1978–82; Nat. Bus Co., 1979–84; President: Centre Européen de l'Enterprise Publique, 1985–; Inst. of Road Transport Engrs, 1987–. *Recreation:* golf. *Heir: s* Hon. Graeme George Shepherd, *b* 6 January 1949. *Address:* 29 Kennington Palace Court, Sancroft Street, SE11 5UL. *T:* 0171–582 6772.

SHEPHERD, Alan Arthur, CBE 1984; PhD; FEng 1986; FInstP; Director, Ferranti plc, 1981–94; *b* 6 Sept. 1927; *s* of Arthur and Hannah Shepherd; *m* 1953, Edith Hudson; two *d. Educ:* Univ. of Manchester (BSc, MSc, PhD). Lectr, Physics Dept, Univ. of Keele, 1950–54; Ferranti Ltd: Chief Engineer, Electronic Components Div., 1954–67; Gen. Manager, Instrument Dept, 1967–70; Gen. Manager, Electronic Components Div., 1970–78; Man. Dir, Ferranti Electronics, 1978–87; Dep. Man. Dir, Ops, Ferranti, then Ferranti Internat. Signal plc, 1987–89; Chm., Ferranti California Group of Cos, 1978–87. Hon. Fellow, UMIST, 1988. J. J. Thomson Medal, IEE, 1985. *Publication:* The Physics of Semiconductors, 1957. *Recreations:* golf, swimming, photography. *Address:* 6 Southern Crescent, Bramhall, Cheshire SK7 3AH. *T:* 0161–439 2824. *Club:* St James's (Manchester).

SHEPHERD, Archie; HM Diplomatic Service, retired; Counsellor and Head of Migration and Visa Department, Foreign and Commonwealth Office, 1977–80; *b* 2 Nov. 1922; *s* of William Shepherd and Edith (*née* Browning); *m* 1959, Dorothy Annette Walker; one *s. Educ:* Torquay Grammar Sch. Prison Commission, 1939; served War, RAF, 1942–46. Foreign Office, 1949; Asst Political Agent and Vice Consul, Muscat, 1951–53; FO, 1954–55; Second Sec., UK Delegn to United Nations, Geneva, 1956–57; HM Consul: Warsaw, 1958–60; Rabat, 1960–62; FO, 1963–67; Consul, Cape Town, 1968–72; First Sec. (Commercial), Beirut, 1973–75. *Recreations:* tennis, gardening. *Address:* 9 Oaks Way, Kenley, Surrey CR2 5DT. *T:* 0181–660 1299. *Clubs:* Civil Service, Commonwealth Trust.

SHEPHERD, Rear-Adm. Charles William Haimes, CB 1972; CBE 1968 (OBE 1958); *b* 10 Dec. 1917; *s* of William Henry Haimes Shepherd and Florence (*née* Hayter); *m* 1940, Myra Betty Joan Major (*d* 1988); one *s. Educ:* Public Central Sch., Plymouth; HMS Fisgard and RNC Greenwich. Entered RN as Artificer Apprentice, 1933; specialised Engrg Officer, 1940; served War of 1939–45 in HMS: Repulse; Hero; Royal Sovereign; Gambia (RNZN); Staff of C-in-C Pacific (Sydney); R&D, Guided Weapons, 1946–49 and 1954–58 incl. Flotilla Eng Officer 3rd Trng Flotilla (HMS Crispin), 1949–51; Sen. Officers War Course, 1961–62; Tech. Dir, UK Polaris Weapon System, 1962–68; Dir Project Teams (Submarines), and Dep. Asst Controller (Polaris), MoD (Navy), 1968–71; Dep. Controller (Polaris), MoD, 1971–73. Sub-Lt 1940; Lieut 1941; Lt-Comdr 1949; Comdr 1952; Captain 1960; Rear-Adm. 1970; retired 1974. Past Pres., Plymouth Albion RFC. *Address:* 5 Underhill Road, Stoke, Plymouth PL3 4BP. *T:* Plymouth (01752) 556888. *Club:* Royal Plymouth Corinthian Yacht.

SHEPHERD, Colin; MP (C) Hereford, since Oct. 1974; *b* 13 Jan. 1938; *s* of late T. C. R. Shepherd, MBE; *m* 1966, Louise, *d* of late Lt-Col E. A. M. Cleveland, MC; three *s. Educ:* Oundle; Caius Coll., Cambridge; McGill Univ., Montreal. RCN, 1959–63. Dir, Haigh Engineering Co. Ltd, 1963–. PPS to Sec. of State for Wales, 1987–90. Jt Sec., Cons. Parly Agr. Fish. and Food Cttee, 1975–79, Vice-Chm., 1979–87, 1991–92; Member: Select Cttee on H of C Services, 1979–92; Select Cttee on H of C Finance and Services, 1993–; Sec., Cons. Parly Hort. Sub-Cttee, 1976–87; Chairman: Library Sub-Cttee, 1983–91; Catering Cttee, 1991–. Chm., UK Br., CPA, 1991– (Mem. Exec. Cttee, 1986–; Treas., 1991–93, Chm., 1993–, Internat. Exec. Cttee). Council Mem., RCVS, 1983–; Governor, Commonwealth Inst., 1989–. Fellow, Industry and Parlt Trust, 1985. *Address:* House of Commons, SW1A 0AA; Manor House, Ganarew, near Monmouth, Gwent NP5 3SU. *T:* Symonds Yat (01600) 890220. *Club:* Naval.

SHEPHERD, David; *see* Shepherd, R. D.

SHEPHERD, George Anthony, CMG 1986; HM Diplomatic Service, retired; *b* 8 Sept. 1931; *m* 1961, Sarah Eirlys Adamson; one *s* two *d. Educ:* Blundell's School; RMA Sandhurst. Served 4th Royal Tank Regt, in Egypt and BAOR, 1951–57; Trucial Oman Scouts, 1957–59; 2nd RTR, 1959–60; Durham Univ., 1960–61; Federal Regular Army, Aden, 1961–64; 2nd RTR, 1965; Asst Defence Adviser, British High Commission, Lagos, 1967–69; retd as Major RTR, 1969. 1st Secretary, FCO, Bahrain, Dubai and Islamabad, 1969–82; Counsellor, British High Commn, New Delhi, 1982–86; FCO, 1986. Life Member, Fauna Preservation Soc., 1964; Mem., Anglo Yemeni Soc., 1993–. *Publications:* Arabian Adventure, 1961; Flight of the Unicorns, 1964. *Recreations:* walking, bird watching, poetry. *Address:* c/o Foreign and Commonwealth Office, SW1A 2AH. *Club:* Army and Navy.

SHEPHERD, James Rodney; Under-Secretary, Department of Trade and Industry (formerly Department of Industry), 1980–89, retired; *b* 27 Nov. 1935; *s* of Richard James Shepherd and Winifred Mary Shepherd. *Educ:* Blundell's; Magdalen Coll., Oxford (PPE; Diploma in Statistics). National Inst. of Economic and Social Res., 1960–64; Consultant to OECD, 1964; HM Treasury, 1965–80 (Under-Sec., 1975–80). *Publications:* articles in technical jls.

SHEPHERD, John Alan, CMG 1989; HM Diplomatic Service; Minister, Bonn, since 1991; *b* 27 April 1943; *s* of William (Mathieson) Shepherd and (Elsie) Rae Shepherd; *m* 1969, Jessica Mary Nichols; one *d. Educ:* Charterhouse; Selwyn Coll., Cambridge (MA); Stanford Univ., Calif (MA). Merchant Navy, 1961; HM Diplomatic Service, 1965–: CO, 1965–66; MECAS, Lebanon, 1966–68; 3rd Sec., Amman, 1968–70; 2nd Sec., Rome, 1970–73; 1st Secretary: FCO, 1973–76; The Hague, 1977–80; First Sec., 1980–82, Counsellor and Hd of Chancery, 1982–84, Office of UK Rep. to EEC , Brussels; Head of European Community Dept (External), FCO, 1985–87; Ambassador to Bahrain, 1988–91. *Recreations:* hills, birds, tennis, squash. *Club:* United Oxford & Cambridge University.

SHEPHERD, John Dodson, CBE 1979; Regional Administrator, Yorkshire Regional Health Authority, 1977–82, retired; *b* 24 Dec. 1920; *s* of Norman and Elizabeth Ellen Shepherd; *m* 1948, Marjorie Nettleton; one *s* two *d. Educ:* Barrow Grammar School. RAF, 1940–46: N Africa, Italy, Middle East, 1943–46. Asst Sec., Oxford RHB, 1956–58; Dep. Sec., Newcastle upon Tyne HMC, 1958–62; Sec., East Cumberland HMC, 1962–67; Sec., Liverpool RHB, 1967–73; Reg. Administrator, Mersey RHA, 1973–77. Pres., Inst. of Health Service Administrators, 1974–75 (Mem. Council, 1969–78). Trustee, Leonard Cheshire Foundn, 1989–95. *Recreations:* golf, music. *Address:* 14 Leconfield Garth, Follifoot, Harrogate HG3 1NF. *T:* Harrogate (01423) 870520. *Clubs:* Harrogate Golf, Harrogate Rotary (Pres., 1990–91).

SHEPHERD, Sir Peter (Malcolm), Kt 1976; CBE 1967; DL; FCIOB; CIMgt; Director: Shepherd Building Group Ltd (Chairman, 1958–86); Shepherd Construction Ltd, since 1940 (Chairman, 1958–88); *b* 18 Oct. 1916; *s* of Alderman Frederick Welton Shepherd and Mrs Martha Eleanor Shepherd; *m* 1940, Patricia Mary Welton; four *s. Educ:* Nunthorpe and Rossall Schs. Chairman: Wool, Jute and Flax ITB, 1964–74; Jt Cttee, Textile ITBs, 1966–74; Construction ITB, 1973–76; Mem. Council, CBI, 1976–89. Chartered Inst. of Building: Pres., 1964–65; Member: Nat. Council, 1956–87; Professional Practice Bd, 1963– (Chm. 1963–75; Vice-Chm., 1975–88); Mem., Bd of Bldg Educn, 1957–75 (Chm. 1965–68). British Inst. of Management: Mem., Nat. Council, 1965–71; Mem., Bd of Fellows, 1969–73; Founder Chm., Yorks and N Lincs Adv. Bd, 1969–71. Mem., President's Consult. Cttee, Building Employers Confedn (formerly Nat. Fedn of Building Trades Employers), 1956–89; Mem. Council, Fedn of Civil Eng Contractors, 1952–60; Founder Mem., Technician Education Council, 1973–79. Chm., York and N Yorks Scanner Trust, 1979–. Mem., Co. of Merchant Adventurers of City of York (Governor, 1984–85). Mem. Court, York Univ., 1976–; Governor, St Peter's Sch., York, 1970–92. DL N Yorks, 1981. FCIOB (Hon. Fellow, 1987); Hon. Fellow, Leeds Metropolitan Univ. (formerly Leeds Poly.), 1987. Hon. DSc Heriot-Watt, 1979; DUniv York, 1981. *Recreation:* sailing. *Address:* Galtres House, Rawcliffe Lane, York YO3 6NP. *T:* York (01904) 624250. *Club:* Yorkshire (York).

SHEPHERD, Richard Charles Scrimgeour; MP (C) Aldridge-Brownhills, since 1979; *b* 6 Dec. 1942; *s* of late Alfred Reginald Shepherd and of Davida Sophia Wallace. *Educ:* LSE; Johns Hopkins Univ. (Sch. of Advanced Internat. Studies). Director: Shepherd Foods (London) Ltd, 1970–; Partridges of Sloane Street Ltd, 1972–. Mem., SE Econ. Planning

Council, 1970–74. Underwriting Mem. of Lloyds, 1974–94. Mem., Treasury and Civil Service Select Cttee, 1979–83; Secretary: Cons. Parly Industry Cttee, 1980–81; Cons. Parly European Cttee, 1980–81. Backbencher of the Year, Spectator, 1987; Special Award, Council for Freedom of Information, 1988. *Recreations:* book collecting; searching for the Home Service on the wireless. *Address:* House of Commons, SW1A 0AA. *Clubs:* Carlton, Beefsteak, Chelsea Arts.

SHEPHERD, (Richard) David, OBE 1980; artist; *b* 25 April 1931; *s* of Raymond Oxley Shepherd and Margaret Joyce Shepherd (*née* Williamson); *m* 1957, Avril Shirley Gaywood; four *d*. *Educ:* Stowe. Art trng under Robin Goodwin, 1950–53; started career as aviation artist (Founder Mem., Soc. of Aviation Artists). Exhibited, RA, 1956; began painting African wild life, 1960. First London one-man show, 1962; painted 15 ft reredos of Christ for army garrison church, Bordon, 1964; 2nd London exhibn, 1965; Johannesburg exhibns, 1966 and 1969; exhibn, Tryon Gall., London, 1978. Painted: HE Dr Kaunda, President of Zambia, 1967; HM the Queen Mother for King's Regt, 1969; HE Sheikh Zaid of Abu Dhabi, 1970; 3rd London exhibn, 1971. Auctioned 5 wildlife paintings in USA and raised sufficient to purchase Bell Jet Ranger helicopter to combat game poaching in Zambia, 1971; painted Tiger Fire, for Operation Tiger, 1973; presented with 1896 steam locomotive by Pres. of Zambia (its return to Britain subject of BBC TV documentary, Last Train to Mulobezi); purchased 2 main line steam locomotives from BR, 1967 (92203 Black Prince, 75209 The Green Knight); Founder Chm., E Somerset Railway. BBC made 50-minute colour life documentary, The Man Who Loves Giants, 1970; series, In Search of Wildlife, in which he is shown tracking down and painting endangered species, Thames TV, 1988. Established The David Shepherd Conservation Foundn, 1984. Mem. of Honour, World Wildlife Fund, 1979. FRGS 1989; FRSA 1986. Hon. DFA, Pratt Inst., New York, for services to wildlife conservation, 1971; Hon. DSc Hatfield Polytechnic, 1990. Order of the Golden Ark, Netherlands, for services to wildlife conservation (Zambia, Operation Tiger, etc), 1973. *Publications:* Artist in Africa, 1967; (autobiog.) The Man who Loves Giants, 1975; Paintings of Africa and India, 1978; A Brush with Steam, 1983; David Shepherd: the man and his paintings, 1985; An Artist in Conversation, 1992; David Shepherd: my painting life, 1995. *Recreations:* driving steam engines, raising money for wildlife. *Address:* Winkworth Farm, Hascombe, Godalming, Surrey GU8 4JW. *T:* Hascombe (01483) 208220.

SHEPHERD, Rt. Rev. Ronald Francis; Bishop of British Columbia, 1985–92; *b* 15 July 1926; *s* of Herbert George Shepherd and Muriel Shepherd (*née* Grant); *m* 1952, Ann Alayne Dundas, *d* of Rt Hon. R. S. Dundas; four *s* two *d*. *Educ:* Univ. of British Columbia (BA Hons 1948); King's Coll., London (AKC 1952). Fellow, Coll. of Preachers, Washington, DC, 1972. Curate, St Stephen's, Rochester Row, London SW, 1952–57; Rector: St Paul's, Glanford, Ont, 1957–59; All Saints, Winnipeg, 1959–65; Dean and Rector: All Saints Cathedral, Edmonton, 1965–69; Christ Church Cathedral, Montreal, 1970–83; Rector, St Matthias, Victoria, 1983–84. Hon. DDiv. St John's Coll., Winnipeg, 1988. *Recreations:* reading, gardening, walking. *Address:* Easter Hill, 110 Ensilwood, Salt Spring Island, BC V8K 1N1, Canada. *T:* (604) 5371399. *Club:* Union of British Columbia (Victoria).

SHEPHERD, William Stanley; *b* 1918; *s* of W. D. Shepherd; *m* 1942, Betty, *d* of late T. F. Howard, MP for Islington South, 1931–35; two *s*. Served in Army, War of 1939–45. A managing director of businesses which he has established; MP (C) for Cheadle Division of Cheshire, 1950–66 (Bucklow Division of Cheshire, 1945–50); Member of the Select Committee on Estimates; Joint Hon. Sec. Conservative Parliamentary Committee in Trade and Industry, 1945–51. Joined SDP, 1982. Hon. Mem., Valuers Institution. FREconS. *Address:* (office) 77 George Street, W1H 5PL. *T:* 0171–935 0753; (home) 33 Queens Grove, St John's Wood, NW8. *T:* 0171–722 7526. *Club:* Savile.

SHEPHERDSON, Prof. John Cedric, ScD; FBA 1990; FIMA; H. O. Wills Professor of Mathematics, Bristol University, 1977–91, now Emeritus; *b* 7 June 1926; *s* of Arnold Shepherdson and Elsie (*née* Aspinall); *m* 1957, Margaret Smith; one *s* two *d*. *Educ:* Manchester Grammar Sch.; Trinity Coll., Cambridge (BA, MA, ScD). Asst Experimental Officer, Aerodynamics and Maths Div., NPL, 1946; Bristol University: Asst Lectr in Maths, 1946–49; Lectr, 1949–55; Reader, 1955–63; Prof. of Pure Maths, 1964–77. Mem., Inst. for Advanced Study, Princeton, 1953–54; Vis. Associate Prof., 1958–59, Vis. Prof., 1966–67, Univ. of Calif at Berkeley; Vis. Prof., Monash Univ., 1971, 1986, 1991, 1992, 1994; Vis. Scientist, IBM Res. Labs, Yorktown Heights, NY, 1973, 1975, 1979; Guest, Technische Hochschule, Zürich, 1988. *Publications:* papers in mathematical, logical and computer sci. jls. *Recreations:* walking, ski-ing, board-sailing, occasional climbing. *Address:* Oakhurst, North Road, Leigh Woods, Bristol BS8 3PN. *T:* Bristol (0117) 973 5410. *Clubs:* Fell & Rock Climbing (Lake District); Bristol Corinthian Yacht.

SHEPLEY, Christopher John; Chief Planning Inspector and Chief Executive, Planning Inspectorate Agency, Department of the Environment and Welsh Office, since 1994; *b* 27 Dec. 1944; *s* of George Frederick Shepley and Florence Mildred Shepley (*née* Jepson); *m* 1967, Jennifer Webber (marr. diss. 1992); one *s* one *d*. *Educ:* Stockport Grammar Sch.; LSE (BA Hons Geography); Univ. of Manchester (DipTP). MRTPI. Manchester City Council, 1966–73; Greater Manchester County Council, 1973–85 (Dep. County Planning Officer, 1984–85); Plymouth City Council: City Planning Officer, 1985–92; Dir of Develt, 1992–94. Pres., RTPI, 1989. Hon. Vis. Prof., Univ. of Manchester Dept of Planning and Landscape, 1990–94. FRSA. *Publications:* The Grotton Papers, 1979; (contrib.) Plymouth: a maritime city in transition, 1990; articles in planning and local govt jls. *Recreations:* music, watching sport, travel, walking. *Address:* Planning Inspectorate, Tollgate House, Houlton Street, Bristol BS2 9DJ. *T:* Bristol (0117) 987 8963. *Club:* Manchester United Football.

SHEPPARD OF DIDGEMERE, Baron *cr* 1994 (Life Peer), of Roydon in the County of Essex; **Allen John George Sheppard;** Kt 1990; Chairman, Grand Metropolitan plc, 1987–96 (Chief Executive, 1986–93); *b* 25 Dec. 1932; *s* of John Baggott Sheppard and Lily Marjorie Sheppard (*née* Palmer); *m* 1st, 1959, Peggy Damaris (*née* Jones) (marr. diss. 1980); 2nd, 1980, Mary (*née* Stewart). *Educ:* Ilford County School; London School of Economics (BSc Econ). FCMA, FCIS, ATII. Ford of Britain and Ford of Europe, 1958–68; Rootes/Chrysler, 1968–71; British Leyland, 1971–75; Grand Metropolitan, 1975–96. Non. Exec. Dir, later Chm., UBM Group, 1981–85; Chm., Mallinson-Denny Group, 1985–87. Chairman: McBride Ltd, 1993–; Group Development Capital Trust PLC, 1994–; Deputy Chairman: Meyer Internat., 1992–94 (Non-exec. Dir, 1989–94); Brightreasons Group PLC, 1994–; part time Mem., BR Board, 1985–90; Dir, Bowater, 1993–. Chairman: Adv. Bd, British American Chamber of Commerce, 1991–94; BITC, 1994– (Dep. Chm., 1989–94); Dep. Chm., Internat. Business Leaders Forum, 1990–; Member: Nat. Trng Task Force, 1989–92; NEDC, 1990–92. Chairman: Bd of Trustees, Prince's Youth Business Trust, 1990–94; Adv. Bd, Prince of Wales' Trusts, 1995–; Mem., Princess Royal's Industry Cttee, Animal Health Trust, 1992–. Chm., London First, 1992–; Co-Chair, London Pride Partnership; Trustee, London Meml Trust. Mem., Bd of Management, Conservative Party, 1993–. Governor, LSE, 1989– (Chm., Campaign Cttee, 1993–). CIMgt (CBIM 1982; Gold Medal, 1994); FRSA. Hon. FCGI 1993; Hon. Fellow, London Business Sch., 1993. Hon. Dr: Internat. Management Centre, 1989; South Bank Univ., 1994; Brunel, 1994. *Publications:* Your Business Matters, 1958; articles in professional jls. *Recreations:* gardens, reading, red setter dogs. *Address:* c/o House of Lords, SW1A 0PW.

SHEPPARD, Rt. Rev. David Stuart; *see* Liverpool, Bishop of.

SHEPPARD, Francis Henry Wollaston; General Editor, Survey of London, 1954–82, retired; *b* 10 Sept. 1921; *s* of late Leslie Alfred Sheppard; *m* 1st, 1949, Pamela Gordon Davies (*d* 1954); one *s* one *d*; 2nd, 1957, Elizabeth Fleur Lees; one *d*. *Educ:* Bradfield; King's Coll., Cambridge (MA); PhD London. FRHistS. Asst Archivist, West Sussex CC, Chichester, 1947–48; Asst Keeper, London Museum, 1948–53. Mayor of Henley on Thames, 1970–71; Pres., Henley Symphony Orchestra, 1973–76. Visiting Fellow, Leicester Univ., 1977–78; Alice Davis Hitchcock Medallion of Soc. of Architectural Historians of Gt Britain, 1964. *Publications:* Local Government in St Marylebone 1688–1835, 1958; London 1808–1870: The Infernal Wen, 1971; Brakspear's Brewery, Henley on Thames, 1779–1979, 1979; The Treasury of London's Past, 1991; (ed) Survey of London, Vols XXVI–XLI, 1956–83. *Recreation:* music. *Address:* 10 Albion Place, West Street, Henley on Thames, Oxon RG9 2DT. *T:* Henley on Thames (01491) 574658.

SHEPPARD, Maurice Raymond, RWS; painter; President, Royal Society of Painters in Water-Colours, 1984–87; *b* 25 Feb. 1947; *s* of late Wilfred Ernest Sheppard and of Florence Hilda (*née* Morris). *Educ:* Loughborough; Kingston upon Thames (Dip AD Hons 1970); Royal College of Art (MA 1973). ARWS 1974, RWS 1977, Vice-Pres., 1978–83, Trustee, 1983–95. One man exhibitions: New Grafton Gallery, 1979; Christopher Wood Gall., 1989; inaugural exhibn of L'Institut Europ. de l'Aquarelle, Brussels, 1986; works in: Royal Library, Windsor; BM; Contemporary Art Soc. for Wales; V&A; Nat. Museum of Wales; Beecroft Museum and Art Gallery, Southend; Birmingham City Mus. and Art Gallery; watercolour: The Golden Valley (for film, Shadowlands, 1993). British Instn Award, 1971; David Murray Landscape Award, 1972; Geoffrey Crawshay Meml Travelling Schol., Univ. of Wales, 1973. *Publications:* articles and essays in jls and catalogues; *relevant publication:* Maurice Sheppard, RWS, by Felicity Owen (Old Watercolour Society Club, vol. 59, 1984). *Recreations:* cycling, a small garden, the pursuit of quiet. *Address:* Mole Bridge Cottage, 14 Apsley Street, Rusthall Common, Tunbridge Wells, Kent TN4 8NU. *T:* Tunbridge Wells (01892) 513405.

SHEPPARD, Prof. Norman, FRS 1967; Professor of Chemical Sciences, University of East Anglia, Norwich, 1964–86, now Emeritus; *b* 16 May 1921; *s* of Walter Sheppard and Anne Clarges Sheppard (*née* Finding); *m* 1949, Kathleen Margery McLean; two *s* one *d* (and one *s* decd). *Educ:* Hymers Coll., Hull; St Catharine's Coll., Cambridge. BA Cantab 1st cl. hons 1943; PhD and MA Cantab 1947. Vis. Asst Prof., Pennsylvania State Univ., 1947–48; Ramsay Memorial Fellow, 1948–49; Senior 1851 Exhibn, 1949–51; Fellow of Trinity Coll., Cambridge and Asst Dir of Research in Spectroscopy, Cambridge Univ., 1955–64. *Publications:* scientific papers on spectroscopy and surface chemistry in Proc. Roy. Soc., Faraday Trans., Jl Chem. Soc., Spectrochimica Acta, etc. *Recreations:* architecture, classical music, philosophy of science, walking. *Address:* 5 Hornor Close, Norwich NR2 2LY. *T:* Norwich (01603) 453052.

SHEPPARD, Maj.-Gen. Peter John, CB 1995; CBE 1991 (OBE 1982); Director General Logistic Policy (Army), Ministry of Defence, since 1993; *b* 15 Aug. 1942; *s* of Kenneth Wescombe Sheppard and Margaret Sheppard; *m* 1964, Sheila Elizabeth Bell; one *s* one *d*. *Educ:* Welbeck Coll.; RMA Sandhurst; RMCS (BScEng 1st Class Hons London Univ.). Commnd Royal Engineers, 1962; Staff Coll., 1974 (psc); British Embassy, Washington, 1975; OC 29 Field Sqn, 1977 (despatches 1978); GSO1 Mil. Ops, MoD, 1980; CO 35 Engineer Regt, 1982; ACOS, HQ 1st (BR) Corps, 1984; Comdr Corps RE, 1st (BR) Corps, 1986; Dir, Army Plans and Programmes, MoD, 1989; COS HQ BAOR, 1991. *Publications:* contribs to RE Jl, NATO's 16 Nations. *Recreations:* golf, philately, travel. *Address:* c/o Lloyds Bank, 3 Allendale Place, Tynemouth, Tyne and Wear NE30 4RA. *Club:* Army and Navy.

SHEPPERD, Sir Alfred (Joseph), Kt 1989; Chairman and Chief Executive: Wellcome plc, 1986–90; The Wellcome Foundation Ltd, 1977–90; Chairman, Burroughs Wellcome Co., 1986–90; *b* 19 June 1925; *s* of Alfred Charles Shepperd and Mary Ann Williams; *m* 1950, Gabrielle Marie Yvette Bouloux; two *d*. *Educ:* Archbishop Tenison's Sch.; University Coll., London (BSc Econ; Fellow, 1986). Rank Organisation, 1949; Selincourt & Sons Ltd, 1963; Chamberlain Group, 1965; Managing Director, Keyser Ullmann Industries Ltd, 1967; Dir, Keyser Ullmann Ltd, 1967; Financial Dir, Laporte Industries Ltd, 1971, Wellcome Foundation Ltd, 1972; Director: Anglia Maltings (Holdings) Ltd, 1972–; Mercury Asset Management Group (formerly Holdings) Ltd, 1987–; Isoscelles plc, 1991–93; Oxford Instruments plc, 1991–95; National Transcommunications Ltd, 1992–; Dep. Chm., Zoo Ops Ltd, 1988–91. Mem., ACOST, 1989–93. Member: Adv. Bd, British-Amer. Chamber of Commerce, 1988–; Governing Body, Internat. Chamber of Commerce UK, 1988–. Mem., Adv. Panel, Common Law Inst. of Intellectual Property, 1986–; Governor: NIESR, 1981–; Royal Agricl Soc. of England, 1977–90. Chm., Barts NHS Trust, 1991–93. Commendatore della Repubblica, Italy, 1983; Encomienda al Merito de Sanidad, Spain, 1988; Comdr, Order of Leopold II, Belgium, 1989. *Address:* Courtmead, 6 Guildown Avenue, Guildford, Surrey GU2 5HB. *Club:* Oriental.

SHEPPERSON, Prof. George Albert, CBE 1989; William Robertson Professor of Commonwealth and American History, University of Edinburgh, 1963–86, now Emeritus; *b* 7 Jan. 1922; *s* of late Albert Edward Shepperson and Bertha Agnes (*née* Jennings); *m* 1952, Joyce Irene (*née* Cooper); one *d*. *Educ:* King's Sch., Peterborough; St John's Coll., Cambridge (Schol.; 1st Class Hons: English Tripos, Pt I, 1942; Historical Tripos, Pt II, 1947); 1st Cl. CertEd (Cantab), 1948. Served War, commnd Northamptonshire Regt, seconded to KAR, 1942–46. Edinburgh University: Lectr in Imperial and American History, 1948, Sen. Lectr, 1960, Reader, 1961; Dean of Faculty of Arts, 1974–77. Visiting Professor: Roosevelt and Chicago Univs, 1959; Makerere Coll., Uganda, 1962; Dalhousie Univ., 1968–69; Rhode Is Coll., 1984; Vis. Scholar, W. E. B. DuBois Inst. for Afro-American Res., Harvard Univ., 1986–87; Lectures: Herskovits Meml, Northwestern Univ., 1966 and 1972; Livingstone Centenary, RGS, 1973; Soc. of the Cincinnati, State of Virginia, 1976; Sarah Tryphena Phillips, in Amer. Lit. and Hist., British Acad., 1979; Rhodes Commem., Rhodes Univ., 1981; Alan Graham Meml, Queen's Univ., Belfast, 1992. Chairman: British Assoc. for American Studies, 1971–74; Mungo Park Bicentenary Cttee, 1971; David Livingstone Documentation Project, 1973–89; Commonwealth Inst., Scotland, 1973–89; Mem., Marshall Aid Commemoration Commn, 1976–88. FEIS 1990. DUniv: York, 1987; Edinburgh, 1991. Jt Editor, Oxford Studies in African Affairs, 1969–85. *Publications:* Independent African: John Chilembwe, 1958, 5th edn 1987; David Livingstone and the Rovuma, 1964; many articles and chapters in learned jls, collaborative vols and encycs. *Recreations:* reading, music. *Address:* 15 Farleigh Fields, Orton Wistow, Peterborough PE2 6YB. *T:* Peterborough (01733) 238772.

SHER, Antony; actor, writer; *b* 14 June 1949; *s* of Emmanuel and Margery Sher. *Educ:* Sea Point Boys' Junior and High Schools, Cape Town; Webber-Douglas Acad. of Dramatic Art, London, 1969–71. Repertory seasons at Liverpool Everyman, Nottingham Playhouse and Royal Lyceum, Edinburgh; John, Paul, George, Ringo and Bert; Teeth and Smiles;

Goose-Pimples; Torch Song Trilogy, Albery, 1985; National Theatre: True West; The Trial, The Resistable Rise of Arturo Ui, 1991; Uncle Vanya, 1992; Royal Shakespeare Co.: Associate Artist, 1982–; Richard III, Merchant of Venice, Twelfth Night, King Lear, The Revenger's Tragedy, Molière, Tartuffe, Hello and Goodbye, Maydays, Red Noses, Singer, Tamburlaine the Great, Travesties; Titus Andronicus, Johannesburg and RNT, 1995; *films:* Shadey, 1986; Mark Gertler; *television series:* The History Man, 1982; The Land of Dreams, 1990; *television film:* Genghis Cohn, 1994. Best Actor Awards: Drama Magazine, 1984; Laurence Olivier, 1985; London Standard, 1985. *Publications:* Year of the King, 1985; Middlepost (novel), 1988; Characters (paintings and drawings), 1989; Changing Step (TV filmscript), 1989; The Indoor Boy (novel), 1991; Cheap Lives (novel), 1995. *Address:* c/o Hope and Lyne, 108 Leonard Street, EC2A 4RH. *T:* 0171–739 6200.

SHER, Samuel Julius; QC 1981; a Recorder, since 1987; *b* 22 Oct. 1941; *s* of Philip and Isa Phyllis Sher; *m* 1965, Sandra Maris; one *s* two *d. Educ:* Athlone High Sch., Johannesburg; Univ. of the Witwatersrand (BComm, LLB); New Coll., Oxford (BCL). Called to the Bar, Inner Temple, 1968, Bencher, 1988. *Recreation:* tennis. *Address:* 12 Constable Close, NW11 6TY. *T:* 0181–455 2753.

See also V. H. Sher.

SHER, Victor Herman, (Harold), CA (SA); Chief Executive, Amalgamated Metal Corporation Plc, since 1992 (Group Managing Director, 1988–92); *b* 13 Jan. 1947; *s* of Philip Sher and Isa Phyllis Sher; *m* 1979, Molly Sher; one *s* three *d. Educ:* King Edward VII Sch., Johannesburg; Univ. of the Witwatersrand, Johannesburg (BComm). Chartered Accountant, Fuller, Jenks Beechcroft, 1972–73; Amalgamated Metal Corporation: Taxation Manager, 1973; Finance Manager, 1977; Dir of Corporate Finance, 1978; Dir of Corporate Treasury, 1981; Finance Dir, 1983; Finance and Trading Dir, 1986. Chm. of Trustees, Amalgamated Metal Corp. Pension Scheme, 1983– (Trustee, 1978). *Recreation:* tennis. *Address:* 42 Southway, Hampstead Garden Suburb, NW11 6SA. *T:* 0181–455 6160.

See also S. J. Sher.

SHERBORNE, Area Bishop of; Rt. Rev. John Dudley Galtrey Kirkham; appointed Bishop Suffragan of Sherborne, 1976; Canon and Prebendary of Salisbury Cathedral, since 1977; Bishop to the Forces, since 1992; *b* 20 Sept. 1935; *s* of late Rev. Canon Charles Dudley Kirkham and Doreen Betty Galtrey; *m* 1986, Mrs Hester Gregory. *Educ:* Lancing Coll.; Trinity Coll., Cambridge (BA 1959, MA 1963). Commnd, Royal Hampshire Regt, seconded to 23 (K) Bn, King's African Rifles, 1954–56. Trinity Coll., Cambridge, 1956–59; Westcott House, 1960–62; Curate, St Mary-le-Tower, Ipswich, 1962–65; Chaplain to Bishop of Norwich, 1965–69; Priest in Charge, Rockland St Mary w. Hellington, 1967–69; Chaplain to Bishop of New Guinea, 1969; Asst Priest, St Martin-in-the-Fields and St Margaret's, Westminster, 1970–72; Domestic Chaplain to Archbishop of Canterbury, 1972–76; Canterbury Diocesan Director of Ordinands, 1972–76. Archbishop of Canterbury's Advr to HMC, 1990–92. Commissary to Bp of Polynesia and Archbp of PNG. ChStJ 1991; Chaplain to the Guild of the Nineteen Lubricators. Croix d'Argent de Saint-Rombaut, 1973. *Recreations:* running, cross-country ski-ing. *Address:* Little Bailie, Sturminster Marshall, Wimborne, Dorset BH21 4AD. *Clubs:* Army and Navy, Kandahar.

SHERBORNE, Archdeacon of; *see* Wheatley, Ven. P. C.

SHERBORNE, Montague; QC 1993; *b* 2 Dec. 1930; *s* of Abraham and Rose Sherborne; *m* 1963, Josephine Valerie Jay; two *s* one *d. Educ:* East Ham Grammar Sch.; New Coll., Oxford (BA Hons PPE); London Univ. (PGCE). Teaching, E London, 1954–58; called to the Bar, Middle Temple, 1960 (Harmsworth Schol.). *Recreations:* bridge, Chinese food, singing, amateur dramatics. *Address:* 3 Raymond Buildings, Gray's Inn, WC1R 5BH. *T:* 0171–831 3833.

SHERBOURNE, Stephen Ashley, CBE 1988; Managing Director, Lowe Bell Consultants, since 1992; Chairman, Lowe Bell Political, since 1994; *b* 15 Oct. 1945; *s* of late Jack and of Blanche Sherbourne. *Educ:* Burnage Grammar Sch., Manchester; St Edmund Hall, Oxford (BA PPE). Hill Samuel, 1968–70; Conservative Research Dept, 1970–75: Head of Economic Section, 1973–74; Asst Dir, 1974–75; Head of Rt Hon. Edward Heath's Office, 1975–76; Gallaher, 1978–82; Special Adviser to Rt Hon. Patrick Jenkin, (then) Sec. of State for Industry, 1982–83; Political Sec. to the Prime Minister, 1983–88; Sen. Corporate Communications Consultant, Lowe Bell Communications, 1988–92. *Recreations:* cinema, tennis, music. *Club:* Reform.

SHERBROOKE, Archbishop of, (RC), since 1968; **Most Rev. Jean-Marie Fortier;** *b* 1 July 1920. *Educ:* Laval University, Quebec. Bishop Auxiliary, La Pocatière, PQ, 1961–65; Bishop of Gaspé, PQ, 1965–68. Elected Pres., Canadian Catholic Conference, 1973–75. Prés. de l'Assemblée des Evêques du Québec, 1984–89. *Publication:* contrib. to Dictionnaire d'Histoire et de Géographie. *Address:* 130 rue de la Cathédrale, Sherbrooke, PQ J1H 4M1, Canada. *T:* (819) 5639934.

SHERFIELD, 1st Baron, *cr* 1964; **Roger Mellor Makins,** GCB 1960 (KCB 1953); GCMG 1955 (KCMG 1949; CMG 1944); FRS 1986; DL; Chancellor of Reading University, 1970–92, Chancellor Emeritus, since 1992; *b* 3 Feb. 1904; *e s* of late Brigadier-General Sir Ernest Makins, KBE, CB, DSO; *m* 1934, Alice (*d* 1985), *e d* of late Hon. Dwight F. Davis; two *s* four *d. Educ:* Winchester; Christ Church, Oxford. First Class Honours in History, 1925; Fellow of All Souls College, 1925–39 and 1957–; called to Bar, Inner Temple, 1927; Foreign Office, 1928; served Washington, 1931–34, Oslo, 1934; Foreign Office, 1934; Assistant Adviser on League of Nations Affairs, 1937; Sec. Intergovernmental Cttee on Refugees from Germany, 1938–39; Adviser on League of Nations Affairs, 1939; Acting First Secretary, 1939; Acting Counsellor, 1940; Adviser to British Delegation, International Labour Conference, New York, 1941; served on Staff of Resident Minister in West Africa, 1942; Counsellor, 1942; Asst to Resident Minister at Allied Force Headquarters, Mediterranean, 1943–44; Minister at British Embassy, Washington, 1945–47; UK rep. on United Nations Interim Commission for Food and Agriculture, 1945; Asst Under-Sec. of State, FO, 1947–48, Dep. Under-Sec. of State, 1948–52; British Ambassador to the United States, 1953–56; Joint Permanent Secretary of the Treasury, 1956–59; Chm., UKAEA, 1960–64. Chairman: Hill, Samuel Group, 1966–70; Finance for Industry Ltd, 1973–74; Finance Corp. for Industry Ltd, 1973–74; Industrial & Commercial Finance Corp., 1964–74; Estate Duties Investment Trust, 1966–73; Ship Mortgage Finance Co., 1966–74; Technical Develt Capital, 1966–74; A. C. Cossor, 1968–82; Raytheon Europe Internat. Co., 1970–82; Wells Fargo Ltd, 1972–84, and other companies; Director: Times Publishing Co., 1964–67; Badger Ltd, 1981–83; Mem., Wells Fargo Bank Adv. Council, 1973– (Chm., 1974–86). Pres., BSI, 1970–73. Pres., Parly and Scientific Cttee, 1969–73; Chm., H of L Select Cttee on Science and Technology, 1984–87. Vice-Chm., The Ditchley Foundn, 1965–74 (Chm., 1962–65); Pres., Centre for Internat. Briefing, 1972–85; Mem., Foundn for Science and Technology, 1990–. Chm., Governing Body and Fellow of Imperial Coll. of Science and Technology, 1962–74. Fellow, Winchester College, 1962–79 (Warden, 1974–79). Chairman: Marshall Aid Commemoration Commn, 1965–73; Lindemann Trust Fellowship Cttee, 1973–83; Mem. of Council, Royal Albert Hall, 1959–87; Trustee, The Times Trust, 1968–73. DL Hants, 1978. Attlee Foundn Lectr, 1986. Hon. Student, Christ Church, Oxford, 1973; Hon. FICE 1964; Hon. DCL Oxford; Hon. DLitt Reading; Hon. LLD: Sheffield; London; Hon. DL North Carolina; and other American universities and colleges. Benjamin Franklin Medal, RSA, 1982. *Publications:* (ed) Economic and Social Consequences of Nuclear Energy, 1972; Lord Penney (Royal Soc. biographical memoir), 1994; lectures and articles on science policy. *Recreations:* gardening, travel. *Heir: s* Hon. Christopher James Makins [*b* 23 July 1942; *m* 1976, Wendy Cortesi]. *Address:* 81 Onslow Square, SW7 3LT; Ham Farm House, Ramsdell, Tadley, Hants RG26 5SD. *Clubs:* Boodle's, Pratt's, MCC.

See also Baron Milford, Viscount Norwich.

SHERGOLD, Harold Taplin, CMG 1963; OBE 1958 (MBE 1945); served in Foreign and Commonwealth Office (formerly Foreign Office), 1954–80; *b* 5 Dec. 1915; *s* of late Ernest Henry Shergold; *m* 1949, Bevis Anael, *d* of late William Bernard Reid; no *c. Educ:* Peter Symonds' School, Winchester; St Edmund Hall, Oxford; Corpus Christi Coll., Cambridge. Asst Master, Cheltenham Grammar Sch., 1937–40. Joined Hampshire Regt, 1940; transferred to Intelligence Corps, 1941; served in Middle East and Italy, 1941–46 (despatches). Joined Foreign Office, 1947; served in Germany, 1947–54. Chm., 1983–90, Pres., 1990–, Richmond, Twickenham & Dist Br., Guide Dogs for the Blind Assoc. *Address:* 1 Ancaster Court, Queens Road, Richmond, Surrey TW10 6JJ. *T:* 0181–948 2048.

SHERIDAN, Cecil Majella, CMG 1961; company director, since 1984; *b* 9 Dec. 1911; *s* of late J. P. Sheridan, Liverpool, and Mrs Sheridan (*née* Myerscough), Preston, Lancs; *m* 1949, Monica, *d* of H. F. Ereaut, MBE, Jersey, CI; two *s* one *d. Educ:* Ampleforth College, York. Admitted Solicitor, England, 1934; called to Bar, Innner Temple, 1952. Practised as solicitor in Liverpool (Messrs Yates, Sheridan & Co.), 1934–40. Served in RAFVR, General Duties Pilot, 1940–46; resigned with hon. rank of Squadron Leader. Joined Colonial Legal Service, 1946; Crown Counsel and Dep. Public Prosecutor, Malayan Union, 1946–48; Legal Adviser, Malay States of Pahang, Kelantan, Trengganu and Selangor and Settlement of Penang, 1948–55; Legal Draftsman, Fedn of Malaya, 1955–57; Solicitor-General, Fedn of Malaya, 1957–59; Attorney-General, Fedn of Malaya, 1959–63; Attorney-General, Malaysia, retd. Mem. (Fedn of Malaya) Inter-Governmental Cttees for Borneo Territories and Singapore, 1962–63. Chm. Traffic Comrs, E Midland Traffic Area, 1965–81, Dep. Chm., 1981–82. Pres., British Assoc. of Malaysia, 1964–65. Chm., Malaysia Housing Soc., 1964–65. Associate Mem., Commonwealth Parly Assoc. (UK Branch). Hon. PMN (Malaysia), 1963. *Address:* Roselea Cottage, 65 Main Street, Queniborough, Leicester LE7 3DB.

SHERIDAN, Christopher Julian; Deputy Chairman, since 1988, and Chief Executive, since 1984, Samuel Montagu & Co.; *b* 18 Feb. 1943; *s* of late Mark Sheridan and of Olive Maud Sheridan (*née* Hobbs); *m* 1972, Diane Virginia (*née* Wadey); one *d. Educ:* Berkhamsted School. Joined Samuel Montagu & Co., 1962; Dir, 1974; Managing Dir, 1981. *Recreations:* theatre, tennis, ski-ing. *Address:* 10 Lower Thames Street, EC3R 6AE. *T:* 0171–260 9594. *Club:* Buck's.

SHERIDAN, Prof. Lionel Astor, PhD, LLD; Professor of Law, University College, Cardiff, 1971–88 (Acting Principal, 1980 and 1987); retired; *b* 21 July 1927; *s* of Stanley Frederick and Anne Agnes Sheridan; *m* 1948, Margaret Helen (*née* Béghin); one *s* (one *d* decd). *Educ:* Whitgift Sch., Croydon; University College London (LLB 1947; LLD 1969); Queen's Univ., Belfast (PhD 1953). Called to the Bar, Lincoln's Inn, 1948. Part-time Lectr, Univ. of Nottingham, 1949; Lectr, QUB, 1949–56; Prof. of Law, Univ. of Singapore (formerly Univ. of Malaya in Singapore), 1956–63; Prof. of Comparative Law, QUB, 1963–71. Hon. LLD Univ. of Singapore, 1963. *Publications:* Fraud in Equity, 1957; Constitutional Protection, 1963; Rights in Security, 1974; *jointly:* The Cy-près Doctrine, 1959; Constitution of Malaysia, 1961, 4th edn 1987; Malaya, Singapore, The Borneo Territories, 1961; Equity, 1969, 3rd edn 1987; Survey of the Land Law of Northern Ireland, 1971; The Modern Law of Charities, 1971, 4th edn 1992; The Law of Trusts, 10th edn 1974, 12th edn 1993; The Comparative Law of Trusts in the Commonwealth and the Irish Republic, 1976; Digest of the English Law of Trusts, 1979; papers in jls. *Recreations:* reading, theatre-going. *Address:* Cherry Trees, Broadway Green, St Nicholas, Vale of Glam CF5 6SR. *T:* Peterston-super-Ely (01446) 760403. *Club:* Athenæum.

SHERIDAN, Peter, QC 1977; *b* 29 May 1927; *s* of Hugo and Marie Sheridan. *Educ:* eight schools; Lincoln Coll., Oxford Univ. BA Hons, 1950. Called to the Bar, Middle Temple, 1955, Bencher, 1988. *Recreations:* motor cars, archery. *Address:* 11 Stone Buildings, Lincoln's Inn, WC2A 3TG. *T:* 0171–831 6381; 17 Brompton Square, SW3. *T:* 0171–584 7250; Pile Oak Lodge, Donhead St Andrew, Wilts. *T:* Donhead (01747) 828484.

SHERIDAN, Roderick Gerald, OBE 1978; MVO 1968; HM Diplomatic Service, retired; Consul-General, Barcelona and Andorra, 1977–80; *b* 24 Jan. 1921; *s* of late Sir Joseph Sheridan; *m* 1942, Lois Mary (*née* Greene); one *s* one *d. Educ:* Downside Sch.; Pembroke Coll., Cambridge. Served War, Coldstream Guards, N Africa and Italy, 1940–46. HM Overseas Colonial Service: Zanzibar and Cyprus, 1946–60; retd as District Comr, Nicosia; HM Diplomatic Service, 1960–: First Sec., Cyprus, 1960–63; Foreign Office, 1964–66; First Sec., Brasilia, 1966–69; FO, 1969–70; Head of Chancery, Oslo, 1970–73; Consul, Algeciras, 1973–77. Hon. Vice-Consul, Menorca, 1983–93. *Recreations:* tennis, golf, skiing.

SHERLOCK, Dr Alexander, CBE 1989; medical practitioner; *b* 14 Feb. 1922; *s* of Thomas Sherlock, MM, and Evelyn M. Sherlock (*née* Alexander); *m* 1st, 1945, Clarice C. Scarff; one *s* two *d*; 2nd, 1976, Eileen Hall; one step *d. Educ:* Magdalen College Sch., Oxford; Stowmarket Grammar Sch.; London Hospital. MB BS (Hons) 1945. Ho. Phys., Ho. Surg., London Hosp.; RAF, 1946–48; Medical Practitioner, Felixstowe, and Consultant/Adviser to many organisations in matters of occupational health, safety and welfare. Called to the Bar, Gray's Inn, 1961. Member: Felixstowe UDC, 1960–74; E Suffolk CC, 1966–74; Suffolk CC, 1974–79 (Chairman, Fire and Public Protection Cttee, 1977–79). MEP (C) SW Essex, 1979–89; former Mem. of Envmt Cttee (Eur. Democratic (C) Leader) and Develt Cttee; spokesman on Envmt, Health and Consumer Protection, 1979–89. Vice-President: Inst. of Trading Officers, 1981–; Assoc. of Envmtl Health Officers, 1981–; Soc. of Dist Councils, 1981–. FRSA. OStJ 1974. *Recreation:* gardening. *Address:* 58 Orwell Road, Felixstowe IP11 7PS. *T:* Felixstowe (01394) 284503. *Club:* Royal Air Force.

SHERLOCK, David Christopher, FCSD; Senior Inspector, Art, Design and Performing Arts, Further Education Funding Council for England, since 1993; *b* 6 Nov. 1943; *s* of Frank Ernest Sherlock and Emily Edna (*née* Johnson); *m* 1st, 1970, Jean Earl; 2nd, 1976, Cynthia Mary (*née* Hood); one *s* one *d. Educ:* Rutlish Sch., Merton, Newcastle upon Tyne; College of Art and Industrial Design, Univ. of Nottingham (BA, MPhil). Nottingham Coll. of Art, 1966–70; Trent Polytechnic, 1970–74; Dep. Dir, Nat. College of Art and Design, Dublin, 1975–80; Principal, Winchester Sch. of Art, 1980–87; Exec. Chm., Hampshire Consortium for Art, Design and Architecture, 1985–87; Head of Central Saint Martin's Coll. of Art and Design and Asst Rector, London Inst., 1988–91; Dir of Develt, RCA, 1991–93. FRSA. *Recreations:* sailing, mountain biking, opera, advising developing countries on design, cooking, good wine. *Address:* Further Education Funding Council, Cheylesmore House, Quinton Road, Coventry CV1 2WT; Woodside, Park Road, Winchester, Hampshire SO22 6AA. *T:* Winchester (01962) 854661. *Club:* Royal Southern Yacht (Hamble).

SHERLOCK, (Edward) Barry (Orton), CBE 1991; Chairman, Life Assurance and Unit Trust Regulatory Organisation, since 1986; *b* 10 Feb. 1932; *s* of Victor Edward and Irene Octavia Sherlock; *m* 1955, Lucy Trerice Willey; two *d*. *Educ:* Merchant Taylors' School; Pembroke College, Cambridge (MA 1st cl. Hons Maths). FIA. Joined Equitable Life Assurance Society, 1956; qualified actuary, 1958; Asst Actuary, 1962; Asst Gen. Manager, 1968; Gen. Manager and Actuary, 1972–91; Dir, 1972–94. Director: USS Ltd, 1978– (Dep. Chm., 1993–); M & G Group, 1994–; Medical Defence Union Ltd, 1994–. Institute of Actuaries: Hon. Sec., 1978–80; Vice-Pres., 1981–84. Chairman: Life Offices' Assoc., 1985; Life Insurance Council, Assoc. of British Insurers, 1985–86. Trustee, Harvest Help, 1993–. Liveryman, Co. of Actuaries. *Recreations:* music, gardening. *Address:* 63 Sunnyfield, Mill Hill, NW7 4RE. *T:* 0181–959 5193. *Club:* Actuaries'.

SHERLOCK, Sir Philip (Manderson), KBE 1967 (CBE 1953); Vice President, Caribbean Resources Development Foundation Inc., since 1983; *b* Jamaica, 25 Feb. 1902; *s* of Rev. Terence Sherlock, Methodist Minister, and Adina Sherlock; *m* 1942, Grace Marjorye Verity; two *s* one *d*. *Educ:* Calabar High Sch., Jamaica. Headmaster, Wolmer's Boys' Sch., Jamaica, 1933–38; Sec., Inst. of Jamaica, 1939–44; Educn Officer, Jamaica Welfare, 1944–47; Dir, Extra-Mural Dept, University Coll. of West Indies, 1947–60, also Vice-Principal, University Coll. of W Indies, 1952–62; Pro-Vice-Chancellor, Univ. of West Indies, 1962, Vice-Chancellor, 1963–69; Sec.-Gen., Assoc. of Caribbean Univs & Res. Insts, 1969–79; Sec., Assoc. of Caribbean Univs Foundn, 1979–83. Hon. LLD: Leeds, 1959; Carleton, 1967; St Andrews, 1968; Hon. DCL New Brunswick, 1966; Hon. DLitt: Acadia, 1966; Miami, 1971; Univ. of WI, 1972; Florida, 1975. Order of Andres Bello with collar (Venezuela), 1978. *Publications:* Anansi the Spider Man, 1956; (with John Parry) Short History of the West Indies, 1956, 4th edn 1987; Caribbean Citizen, 1957; West Indian Story, 1960; Three Finger Jack, 1961; Jamaica, A Junior History, 1966; West Indian Folk Tales, 1966; West Indies, 1966; Land and People of the West Indies, 1967; Belize, a Junior History, 1969; The Iguana's Tail, 1969; West Indian Nations, 1973; Ears and Tails and Common Sense, 1974; Shout for Freedom, 1976; Norman Manley, a biography, 1980; Keeping Company with Jamaica, 1984; educational books and articles. *Recreations:* reading, writing, cooking. *Address:* Caribbean Resources Development Foundation Inc., PO Box 248074, Coral Gables, FL 33124, USA. *Club:* National Liberal.

SHERLOCK, Prof. Dame Sheila (Patricia Violet), DBE 1978; MD; FRCP; FRCPEd; Professor of Medicine, University of London, at the Royal Free Hospital School of Medicine, since 1959; *b* 31 March 1918; *d* of late Samuel Philip Sherlock and Violet Mary Catherine Beckett; *m* 1951, David Geraint James, *qv*; two *d*. *Educ:* Folkestone County Sch.; Edinburgh Univ. Ettles Scholar, 1941; Beit Memorial Research Fellow, 1942–47; Rockefeller Fellow, Yale University, USA, 1948. Physician and Lecturer in Medicine, Postgraduate Medical School of London, 1948–59. RCP Lectures: Bradshaw, 1961; Rolleston, 1968; Lumleian, 1978; Harveian, 1985. RCP: Councillor, 1964–68; Censor, 1970–72; Senior Censor and Vice-Pres., 1976–77. Mem. Senate, Univ. of London, 1976–81. Hon. Member: Gastro-enterological Societies of America, 1963, Australasia, 1965, Mexico, 1968, Czechoslovakia, 1968, Yugoslavia, 1981, Sweden, 1983; Assoc. of Amer. Physicians, 1973; Assoc. of Alimentary Surgeons, 1973; Alpha Omega Alpha Assoc., 1992. Hon. FACP; Hon. FRCPC; Hon. FRACP 1984; Hon. FRCPI; Hon. FRCPS 1986; Hon. FRCS 1989. Hon. DSc: City Univ. of NY, 1977; Yale Univ., USA, 1983; Edinburgh, 1985; London, 1989; Cambridge, 1995; Hon. MD: Lisbon, 1981; Oslo, 1981; Leuven, 1984; Barcelona, 1991; Mainz, 1991; TCD, 1992; Valloldalid, 1994; Wisconsin, 1995; Hon. LLD Aberdeen, 1982. William Cullen Prize, 1962 (shared); Jimenez-Diaz Prize, 1980; Thannhauser Prize, 1980; Fothergill Gold Medal, Med. Soc. of London, 1983; Gold Medal, BMA, 1985. *Publications:* Diseases of the Liver and Biliary System, 1955, 9th edn 1992; papers on liver structure and function in various medical journals, since 1943. *Recreations:* cricket, travel. *Address:* 41 York Terrace East, NW1 4PT. *T:* 0171–486 4560, 0171–431 4589.

SHERMAN, Sir Alfred, Kt 1983; journalist; public affairs advisor in private practice; co-founder, Centre for Policy Studies, 1974 (Director of Studies until 1984); *b* 10 Nov. 1919; *m* 1958, Zahava (*d* 1993), *d* of Dr Gideon Levin; one *s*. Served in International Brigade, Spanish Civil War, 1937–38; war of 1939–45 in field security and occupied enemy territory administration. Mem., economic adv. staff of Israeli Govt, in 1950s; leader writer, Jewish Chronicle; various appts with Daily Telegraph, 1965–86, as leader writer 1977–86. Vis. Fellow, LSE, 1983–85. Broadcaster. Councillor, RBK&C, 1971–78. *Publications:* Local Government Reorganisation and Industry, 1970; Councils, Councillors and Public Relations, 1973; Local Government Reorganization and the Salary Bill, 1974; (with D. Mallam) Waste in Wandsworth, 1976; Crisis Calls for a Minister for Denationalization, 1980; The Scott Report, 1981; (introd.) The Grenada Documents, ed Brian Crozier, 1987; (contrib.) Revisionism, 1961; Communism and Arab Nationalism: a reappraisal; Capitalism and Liberty; Our Complacent Satirists; Political Violence in Britain; contribs to newspapers and periodicals. *Address:* 14 Malvern Court, Onslow Square, SW7 3HU. *T:* 0171–581 4075. *Cables:* SHERMANIA LONDON SW7. *Club:* Reform.

SHERMAN, Sir Louis, (Sir Lou Sherman), Kt 1975; OBE 1967; JP; Chairman, Housing Corporation, 1977–80; Deputy Chairman, Harlow Development Corporation. Initiated Lea Valley Regional Park Authority. Mayor of Hackney, 1961. JP Inner London Area. *Recreations:* politics, reading, talking. *Club:* Reform.

SHERRARD, Michael David, QC 1968; Director, Middle Temple Advocacy; a Recorder of the Crown Court, 1974–93; *b* 23 June 1928; *er s* of late Morris and Ethel Sherrard; *m* 1952, Shirley (C. B. Piper, writer), *d* of late Maurice and Lucy Bagrit; two *s*. *Educ:* King's Coll., London. LLB 1949. Called to Bar, Middle Temple, 1949 (Bencher 1977; Treas., 1996); Mem., Inner Temple, 1980; Mem. Senate, 1977–80. Mem., SE Circuit, 1950. Mem., Winn Cttee on Personal Injury Litigation, 1966; Mem. Council and Exec. Cttee, Justice, British Section, Internat. Commn of Jurists, 1974–; Dept of Trade Inspector, London Capital Group, 1975–77; Chm., Normansfield Hosp. Inquiry, 1977–78; Comr for trial of local govt election petitions (under Representation of the People Act 1949), 1978–80. Mem., Bar Assoc. of NYC, 1986–. FRSA 1991. *Recreations:* oil painting, oriental art, listening to opera. *Address:* Middle Temple Treasury, Middle Temple Lane, EC4Y 9AT. *T:* 0171–353 4634; 26 Eton Avenue, Hampstead, NW3 3HL. *T:* 0171–431 0713.

SHERRATT, Prof. David John, PhD; FRS 1992; FRSE; Iveagh Professor of Microbiology, and Fellow, Linacre College, Oxford, since 1994; *b* 14 June 1945; *m* 1968, Susan Bates (marr. diss. 1992); one *s* two *d*. *Educ:* Manchester Univ. (BSc 1st Cl. Biochem. 1966); Edinburgh Univ. (PhD Molecular Biol. 1969). FRSE 1984. Post-doctoral Fellow, Univ. of California, 1969–71; Lectr in Microbial Genetics, Univ. of Sussex, 1971–80; Prof. of Genetics, Inst. of Genetics, Glasgow Univ., 1980–93. Mem., EMBO, 1983–. *Publications:* scientific papers and reviews; editor of several jls. *Recreations:* variety of outdoor pursuits. *Address:* Linacre College, Oxford OX1 3JA.

SHERRIN, Ned, (Edward George Sherrin); film, theatre and television producer, presenter, director and writer; *b* Low Ham, Som, 18 Feb. 1931; *s* of late T. A. Sherrin and D. F. Sherrin (*née* Drewett). *Educ:* Sexey's Sch., Bruton; Exeter Coll., Oxford; Gray's Inn. Producer: ATV, Birmingham, 1955–57; BBC TV, 1957–66 (prod. and dir. That Was The Week That Was). Produced films: The Virgin Soldiers (with Leslie Gilliat) 1968; Every Home Should Have One, 1969; (with Terry Glinwood) Up Pompeii, 1971; Up the Chastity Belt, 1971; Girl Stroke Boy, 1971; Rentadick, 1971; Up the Front, 1972; The National Health, 1972; acted in film: Orlando, 1993; TV plays (with Caryl Brahms) include: Little Beggars; Benbow was his Name; Take a Sapphire; The Great Inimitable Mr Dickens; Feydeau Farces; plays (with Caryl Brahms): No Bed for Bacon; Cindy-Ella or I Gotta Shoe, 1962–63; The Spoils, 1968; Nicholas Nickleby, 1969; Sing a Rude Song, 1970; Fish out of Water, 1971; Liberty Ranch, 1972; Nickleby and Me, 1975; Beecham, 1980; The Mitford Girls, 1981; Oh, Kay! (new book with Tony Geiss), 1984; directed: Come Spy with Me, Whitehall, 1967; (and appeared in) Side by Side by Sondheim, Mermaid, 1976, NY 1977; Only in America (with D. Yakir), Roundhouse, 1980; Noël, Goodspeed, USA, 1981; Mr & Mrs Nobody, Garrick, 1986; Jeffrey Bernard is Unwell, Apollo, 1989; Same Old Moon, Nuffield, Southampton, 1990; Bookends, Apollo, 1990; Our Song, Apollo, 1992; A Passionate Woman, Comedy, 1994; directed and co-adapted: The Ratepayers' Iolanthe, QEH, 1984 (Olivier Award); The Metropolitan Mikado, QEH, 1985; Small Expectations, QEH, 1986; dir, The Sloane Ranger Revue, Duchess, 1985; scripted (with A. Beaton) Ziegfeld, London Palladium, 1988. TV appearances include: Song by Song, BBC and Yorkshire TV series; Quiz of the Week, BBC; The Rather Reassuring Programme, ITV; We Interrupt this Week, PBS, NY; Friday Night Saturday Morning, BBC-2; Countdown, Channel 4; radio appearances: Midweek (host), Medium Dry Sherrin, Extra Dry Sherrin, And So to Ned; Loose Ends; Counterpoint. Governor, BFI, 1980–84. Guild of TV Producers and Directors' Awards; Ivor Novello Award, 1966. *Publications:* (with Caryl Brahms) Cindy-Ella or I Gotta Shoe, 1962; Rappell 1910, 1964; Benbow was his Name, 1967; Ooh la! la! (short stories), 1973; After You Mr Feydeau, 1975; A Small Thing—Like an Earthquake (memoirs), 1983; (with Caryl Brahms) Song by Song, 1984; Cutting Edge, 1984; (with Neil Shand) 1956 and all that, 1984; (with Caryl Brahms) Too Dirty for the Windmill, 1986; Loose Neds, 1990; Theatrical Anecdotes, 1991; Ned Sherrin in his Anecdotage, 1993; (ed) The Oxford Dictionary of Humorous Quotations, 1995; many songs. *Address:* c/o Casarotto Ramsay Ltd, 60–66 Wardour Street, W1V 3HP. *T:* 0171–287 4450.

SHERRINGTON, Prof. David, PhD; FRS 1994; CPhys, FInstP; Wykeham Professor of Physics, University of Oxford, since 1989; Fellow, New College, Oxford, since 1989; *b* 29 Oct. 1941; *s* of James Arthur Sherrington and Elfreda (*née* Cameron); *m* 1966, Margaret Gee-Clough; one *s* one *d*. *Educ:* St Mary's Coll.; Univ. of Manchester (BSc 1st Cl. Hons Physics, 1962; PhD Theoretical Physics, 1966). FInstP 1974; CPhys. Asst Lectr in Theoretical Physics, 1964–67, Lectr, 1967–69, Univ. of Manchester; Asst Res. Physicist, UCSD, 1967–69; Imperial College, University of London: Lectr in Theor. Solid State Phys, 1969–74; Reader in Theor. Solid State Phys, 1974–83; Prof. of Phys, 1983–89; Cadre Supérieur, Inst Laue Langevin, Grenoble, France, 1977–79. Fellow, Amer. Physical Soc., 1985. Editor, Advances in Physics, 1984–; Hon. Editor, Jl of Physics A: Mathematical and General, 1989. Hon. MA Oxford, 1989. *Publications:* (ed jtly) Phase Transitions in Soft Condensed Matter, 1990; (ed jtly) Spontaneous Formation of Space-Time Structures and Criticality, 1991; (ed jtly) Phase Transitions and Relaxation in Systems with Competing Energy Scales, 1993; (ed jtly) Physics of Biomaterials: fluctuations, self-assembly and evolution, 1995; papers in learned jls. *Recreations:* wine tasting, travel, theatre, ski-ing. *Address:* 53 Cumnor Hill, Oxford OX2 9EY.

SHERRINGTON, Air Vice-Marshal Terence Brian, OBE 1984; Air Officer Administration, HQ Strike Command, since 1994; Head of RAF Administrative Branch, since 1992; *b* 30 Sept. 1942; *s* of Thomas and Edna Sherrington; *m* 1969, Anne Everall; one *s* one *d*. *Educ.* Ottershaw Sch.; Westminster Technical Coll. Commnd RAF, 1963; served Aden, Sharjah, Germany and UK, 1963–78; RAF Staff College, 1979; MoD, 1980–81; OC Admin Wing, RAF Leuchars, 1981–83; OC, RAF Hereford, 1983–85; RCDS, 1986; Sen. Officer Admin, HQ 11 Gp, 1987–88; Dir of Personnel (Ground), MoD, 1988–91; AOA and AOC Support Units, RAF Support Comnd, 1992–93. FIMgt; MHCIMA. *Recreations:* windsurfing, fishing, golf, Rugby. *Address:* c/o Lloyds Bank, Shipston-on-Stour, Warwicks CV36 4AJ. *Club:* Royal Air Force.

SHERRY, Prof. Norman, FRSL 1985; writer; Mitchell Distinguished Professor of Literature, Trinity University, San Antonio, Texas, 1983–91; *b* 6 July 1935; *m* 1960, Sylvia Brunt. *Educ:* Univ. of Durham (BA Eng Lit); Univ. of Singapore (PhD). Lectr, Univ. of Singapore, 1961–66; Lectr and Sen. Lectr, Univ. of Liverpool, 1966–70; Prof. of English, Univ. of Lancaster, 1970–82. Fellow, Humanities Research Center, N Carolina, 1982; Guggenheim Fellow, 1989–90. *Publications:* Conrad's Eastern World, 1966; The Novels of Jane Austen, 1966; Charlotte and Emily Bronte, 1969; Conrad's Western World, 1971; Conrad and his World, 1972; (ed) Conrad: the Critical Heritage, 1973; (ed) An Outpost of Progress and Heart of Darkness, 1973; (ed) Lord Jim, 1974; (ed) Nostromo, 1974; (ed) The Secret Agent, 1974; (ed) The Nigger of Narcissus, Typhoon, Falk and Other Stories, 1975; (ed) Joseph Conrad: a commemoration, 1976; The Life of Graham Greene, vol. I, 1904–1939, 1989, vol. II, 1939–1955, 1994 (Edgar Allan Poe Award, Britannica Book of the Year, 1990); contribs to Review of English Studies, Notes & Queries, Modern Language Review, TLS, Observer, The Daily Telegraph, The Guardian, The Independent, Sunday Times, New York Times. *Recreations:* reading, writing, jogging, body building. *Address:* Trinity University, 715 Stadium Drive, San Antonio, TX 78212, USA.

SHERRY, Mrs Vincent; *see* Robinson, Kathleen M.

SHERSBY, Sir (Julian) Michael, Kt 1995; MP (C) Uxbridge, since Dec. 1972; *b* Ickenham, 17 Feb. 1933; *s* of William Henry and Elinor Shersby; *m* 1958, Barbara Joan, *d* of John Henry Barrow; one *s* one *d*. *Educ:* John Lyon Sch., Harrow-on-the-Hill. Mem., Paddington Borough Council, 1959–64; Mem., Westminster City Council, 1964–71; Deputy Lord Mayor of Westminster, 1967–68. Chm., Uxbridge Div. Young Conservatives, 1951–52; Conservative and Unionist Party Organisation, 1952–58; Sec., Assoc. of Specialised Film Producers, 1958–62; Dir, British Industrial Film Assoc., 1962–66; Dir, 1966–77, Dir-Gen., 1977–88, Sugar Bureau (formerly British Sugar Bureau); Sec., UK Sugar Industry Assoc., 1978–88, Parly Advr, 1988–; Treas., World Sugar Res. Orgn, 1982–. PPS to Minister of Aerospace and Shipping, DTI, 1974; Member: Speaker's Panel of Chairmen, 1983–; Public Accounts Cttee, 1983–. Parly Advr to Police Fedn, 1989–; promoted Private Member's Bills: Town and Country Amenities Act, 1974; Parks Regulation (Amendment) Act, 1974; Stock Exchange (Completion of Bargains) Act, 1976; Gaming (Amendment) Act, 1980; Copyright Act (1956) Amendment Act, 1982; British Nationality (Falkland Islands) Act, 1983; Firearms (Amendment) Act, 1994. Jt Sec., 1977–80, Vice-Pres., 1980–83, Parly and Scientific Cttee. Chm., Falkland Is Gp, 1982–, Mem. Exec. Cttee, UK Br., 1988–, CPA. Pres., London Green Belt Council, 1989–. Mem. Court, Brunel Univ., 1975–; Pres., Abbeyfield Uxbridge Soc., 1975–. FIPR 1994. DUniv Brunel, 1994. *Recreations:* theatre, fishing, travel. *Address:* House of Commons, SW1A 0AA. *T:* 0171–219 5023; Bay Lodge, 36 Harefield Road,

Uxbridge, Middx UB8 1PH. *T:* Uxbridge (01895) 239465. *Clubs:* Carlton; Conservative (Uxbridge).

SHERSTON-BAKER, Sir Robert (George Humphrey), 7th Bt *cr* 1796, of Dunstable House, Richmond, Surrey; *b* 3 April 1951; *o s* of Sir Humphrey Sherston-Baker, 6th Bt and of Margaret Alice (*m* 2nd, Sir Ronald Leach, *qv*), *o d* of Henry William Binns; *S* father, 1990; *m* 1991, Vanessa, *y d* of C. E. A. Baird; one *s* one *d*. *Heir: s* David Arbuthnot George Sherston-Baker, *b* 24 Nov. 1992. *Address:* Deal House, Stour Street, Canterbury, Kent CT1 2NZ.

SHERVAL, Rear-Adm. David Robert, CB 1989; CEng; FIMechE; FIMarE; Chief Surveyor and Deputy General Manager, The Salvage Association, since 1990; *b* 4 July 1933; *s* of William Robert Sherval and Florence Margaret Sherval (*née* Luke); *m* 1961, Patricia Ann Phillips; one *s* one *d*. *Educ:* Portsmouth Southern Grammar School. Artificer Apprentice, 1950; BRNC Dartmouth, 1951; Training: at sea, HM Ships Devonshire, Forth and Glasgow, 1951–52 and 1955; RNEC, 1952–53, 1956; served: HM Ships Eagle, Tiger, Hampshire, HM Dockyard Gibraltar and HMY Britannia, 1957–68; BRNC, 1968–70; HMS Juno, 1970–72; NDC, 1972–73; Naval Plans, MoD, 1973–75; Staff of FO Sea Training, 1975–76; Naval Op. Requirements, MoD, 1976–77; NATO Defence Coll., Rome, 1979; ACOS (Intell.) to SACLANT, 1979–82; Fleet Marine Engineer Officer, 1982–84; Dir, Naval Logistic Planning, 1984–85; CSO (Engrg) to C-in-C Fleet, 1985–87; Dir Gen. Ship Refitting, 1987–89. *Recreation:* music.

SHERWOOD, Bishop Suffragan of, since 1989; **Rt. Rev. Alan Wyndham Morgan;** *b* 22 June 1940; *s* of A. W. Morgan; *m* 1965, Margaret Patricia, *d* of W. O. Williams; one *s* one *d*. *Educ:* Boys' Grammar School, Gowerton; St David's Coll., Lampeter (BA 1962); St Michael's Coll., Llandaff. Deacon 1964, priest 1965; Assistant Curate: Llangyfelach with Morriston, 1964–69; Cockett, 1969–72; St Mark with St Barnabas, Coventry, 1972–73; Team Vicar, St Barnabas, Coventry East, 1973–77; Bishop's Officer for Social Responsibility, Diocese of Coventry, 1978–83; Archdeacon of Coventry, 1983–89. Mem., Gen. Synod, 1980–89. President: Nottingham Help the Homeless Assoc. Ltd, 1989; Notts Assoc. of Voluntary Orgns, 1991; Vice-Pres., NCVO, 1989– (Chm., 1986–89); Chairman: Dio. of Southwell Ministry Gp, 1990; Additional Needs and Equal Opportunities Gp; Wkg Pty on The Family, Bd of Social Responsibility, 1992–95; Dir, Greater Nottingham TEC, 1991. *Address:* Sherwood House, High Oakham Road, Mansfield, Notts NG18 5AJ.

SHERWOOD, James Blair; Founder and President, Sea Containers Group, Bermuda and London, since 1965; Chairman, Orient-Express Hotels, since 1987; *b* 8 Aug. 1933; *s* of William Earl Sherwood and Florence Balph Sherwood; *m* 1977, Shirley Angela Masser Cross; two step *s*. *Educ:* Yale Univ. (BA Economics 1955). Lieut US Naval Reserve, Far East service, afloat and ashore, 1955–58. Manager, French Ports, later Asst General Freight Traffic Manager, United States Lines Co., Le Havre and NY, 1959–62; Gen. Manager, Container Transport Internat. Inc., NY and Paris, 1963–64. In partnership with Mark Birley, established Harry's Bar Club in London, 1979. Restored, and brought into regular service, the Venice Simplon-Orient-Express, 1982. Trustee, Solomon R. Guggenheim Foundn, 1989–. *Publication:* James Sherwood's Discriminating Guide to London, 1975, 2nd edn 1977. *Recreations:* sailing, tennis, skiing. *Address:* Hinton Manor, Hinton Waldrist, Oxon SN7 8SA. *T:* Oxford (01865) 820260. *Clubs:* Hurlingham, Pilgrims.

SHERWOOD, (Peter) Louis (Michael); Chairman, HTV Group, since 1991; *b* 27 Oct. 1941; *s* of Peter Louis Sherwood and Mervyn Sherwood (*née* de Toll); *m* 1970, Nicole Dina; one *s* two *d*. *Educ:* New Coll., Oxford (BA 1963; MA 1966); Stanford Univ. (MBA 1965). Morgan Grenfell & Co., Corporate Finance Officer, 1965–68; Asst to Chm., Fine Fare (Supermarkets), 1968–69; Man. Dir, Melias (Fine Fare subsid.), 1969–72; Dir, Anglo-Continental Investment & Finance Co., 1972–79; Sen. Vice-Pres. for Development, Grand Union Co., USA, 1979–85; Pres., Great Atlantic & Pacific Tea Co., USA, 1985–88; Chm. and Chief Exec., Gateway Foodmarkets, 1988–89. *Recreations:* mountain walking, collecting fine wine. *Address:* 10 College Road, Clifton, Bristol BS8 3HZ. *Club:* Lansdowne.

SHERWOOD, (Robert) Antony (Frank), CMG 1981; Assistant Director-General, British Council, 1977–81, retired; *b* 29 May 1923; *s* of Frank Henry Sherwood and Mollie Sherwood (*née* Moore); *m* 1953, Margaret Elizabeth Simpson; two *s* two *d*. *Educ:* Christ's Hospital; St John's Coll., Oxford (BA 1949, MA 1953). War service, RAF, 1942–46. Apptd to British Council, 1949; served in Turkey, Nigeria (twice), Syria, Uganda, Somalia and at HQ. Help the Aged: Vice-Chm., Internat. Cttee, 1982–88, Chm., 1988–92; Trustee, 1988–94; Mem. Council and Exec. Cttee, HelpAge Internat., 1983–93; Hon. PRO, Surrey Voluntary Service Council, 1982–88. Vice-Chm., Management Cttee, Guildford Inst. of Univ. of Surrey, 1993– (Chm., Finance Cttee, 1988–93). *Publication:* (ed) Directory of Statutory and Voluntary Health, Social and Welfare Services in Surrey, 1987. *Recreations:* travel, genealogy and family history, reading. *Address:* 18 Rivermount Gardens, Guildford, Surrey GU2 5DN. *T:* Guildford (01483) 38277.

SHERWOOD, Prof. Thomas, FRCP, FRCR; Clinical Dean, University of Cambridge, since 1984 (Professor of Radiology, 1978–94); Fellow of Girton College, Cambridge, since 1982; *b* 25 Sept. 1934; *m* 1961, Margaret Gooch; two *s* one *d*. *Educ:* Frensham Heights Sch.; Guy's Hospital, London. MA; DCH. Consultant Radiologist, Hammersmith Hospital and St Peter's Hospitals, 1969–77. Chm. Govs, Frensham Heights Sch., 1996–. *Publications:* Uroradiology, 1980; Roads to Radiology, 1983; Blow the Wind Southerly, 1988; papers in medical and radiological jls, 1964–. *Recreations:* music, reading and writing. *Address:* Clinical School, Addenbrooke's Hospital, Hills Road, Cambridge CB2 2SP. *T:* Cambridge (01223) 336733; 19 Clarendon Street, Cambridge CB1 1JU.

SHESTOPAL, Dawn Angela, (Mrs N. J. Shestopal); *see* Freedman, D. A.

SHETH, Pranlal, CBE 1994; Director, Reed Executive plc, 1990–93; Member, Independent Television Commission, 1991–95; *b* 20 Dec. 1924; *s* of Purashotam Virji Sheth and Sakarben Sheth; *m* 1951, Indumati Sheth; one *s* one *d*. Called to the Bar, Lincoln's Inn, 1962. Journalist, Kenya, 1943–52; Chm., Nyanza Farmers' Cooperative Soc., 1954–60; Mem., Central Agriculture Bd, Kenya, 1963–66; Chm., Asian Hosp. Authority, 1964–66; Mem., Economic Planning and Develt Council, Kenya, 1964–66. Group Sec., 1971, Legal Advr and Dir, 1985–88, Abbey Life Gp of Cos; Legal Dir, Hartford Europe Gp of Cos, 1977–86; Director: Abbey Life Assurance Co. Ltd, 1977–89; Ambassador Life Assce Co. Ltd, 1980–88; Abbey Life Assurance (Ireland), 1981–85; Gp Sec., ITT cos in UK, 1983–86. Dir, Round House Arts Centre, 1986–90; Member: BBC Consultative Gp on Industry and Business Affairs, 1986–89; BBC Asian Progs Adv. Cttee, 1986–89; IBA, 1990. Founder, and Chief Editor, Gujarat Samachar Weekly, 1972–73; Mem., N Metropolitan Conciliation Cttee, Race Relations Bd, 1973–77; a Dep. Chm., CRE, 1977–80; Vice Pres., UKIAS, 1986–93. Trustee: Project Fullemploy (Charitable Trust), 1977–89; Assoc. of Asian Women, 1979–; Runnymede Trust, 1987–; Urban Trust, 1987–; Windsor Fellowship, 1988–; Womankind Worldwide Trust, 1989–; One World Broadcasting Trust, 1991–; Gujarati Literary Acad., 1992–; Vice-Patron, UK Assoc., Internat. Year of the Child, 1978–80; Patron, Internat. Centre for Child Studies. Dir, Shelter, 1987–91; Hon. Legal Advr and Mem. Exec. Cttee, Nat. Assoc. of Victim Support Schemes, 1988–95. FInstD 1977; FIMgt (FBIM 1980). Mem., Bd of Dirs, Univ. (formerly Poly.) of N London, 1979–. Mem. Editorial Adv. Panel, Equal Opportunities Review, 1984. *Address:* 70 Howberry Road, Edgware, Mddx HA8 6SY. *Clubs:* Royal Over-Seas League, Commonwealth Trust.

SHEUMACK, Rt. Rev. Colin Davies; Bishop of Gippsland, 1987–94; *b* 9 Feb. 1929; *s* of Joseph Sheumack and Gwladys (*née* Davies); *m* 1951, Ena Beryl Dickson (*d* 1994); one *s* three *d*. *Educ:* Tingha Central and Inverell High School; Moore Theological Coll. (ThL 2nd cl. Hons). Deacon 1952, priest 1953, Canberra Goulburn; Rector: Kemeruka, 1954–59; Kyabram, Vic., 1959–67; Archdeacon of Bendigo, 1967–83; Vicar General, 1968–83; Dean of Bathurst, 1983–87. *Recreations:* gardening, fishing. *Address:* 12 Nijorie Close, Kincumber, NSW 2251, Australia. *T:* (43) 683860. *Club:* Royal Automobile of Victoria (Melbourne).

SHEVARDNADZE, Eduard Amvrosiyevich; Chairman, Georgian State Council, since 1992; Founder, Movement for Democratic Reform, 1991; *b* Georgia, 25 Jan. 1928; christened Georgi, 1992, but continues to be known as Eduard. *Educ:* Pedagogical Institute, Kutaisi. Mem., CPSU, 1948–91; Sec., Komsomol Cttee in Kutaisi, 1952–56, of Georgia, 1956–61; 1st Sec., Regional Party Cttee, Mtsheta, 1961–63, Tbilisi, 1963–64; Minister of Internal Affairs, Georgia, 1964–72; 1st Sec., Republican Party Cttee, Georgia, 1972–85; Mem., Politburo, 1985–91; Minister of Foreign Affairs, USSR, 1985–90, 1991. Order of Lenin (five times); Hero of Socialist Labour (twice); Order of Red Banner of Labour. *Publication:* The Future Belongs to Freedom, 1991.

SHEWRY, Prof. Peter Robert, CBiol, FIBiol; Head of Long Ashton Research Station (Institute of Arable Crops Research) and Professor of Agricultural Sciences, University of Bristol, since 1989; *b* 19 March 1948; *s* of Robert Thomas Shewry and Mary Helen Shewry; *m* 1969, Rosemary Willsdon; one *s* one *d*. *Educ:* Bristol Univ. (BSc, PhD, DSc). Postdoctoral Res. Fellow, Westfield Coll., Univ. of London, 1972; Rothamsted Experimental Station: Res. Scientist, 1974; Head of Biochem. Dept, 1986. *Publications:* (ed with Steven Gutteridge) Plant Protein Engineering, 1992; (ed) Barley: genetics, biochemistry, molecular biology and biotechnology, 1992; (ed with A. K. Stobart) Seed Storage Compounds, 1993; numerous papers in sci. jls on plant genetics, biochem. and molecular biol. *Address:* Long Ashton Research Station, Long Ashton, Bristol BS18 9AF. *T:* Long Ashton (01275) 392181.

SHIACH, Allan George; film writer and producer; Chairman: Macallan-Glenlivet plc, since 1980; Rafford Films Ltd, since 1983; *b* Elgin; *er s* of late Gordon Leslie Shiach, WS and Lucy Sybil (*née* De Freitas); *m* 1966, Kathleen Swarbreck; two *s* one *d*. *Educ:* Gordonstoun Sch.; L'Ecole des Roches; McGill Univ. (BA). Writer of TV and radio drama, 1965–72; screenwriter and co-writer of films, including: Don't Look Now, 1975; Joseph Andrews, 1977; Martin's Day, 1980; D.A.R.Y.L., 1984; Castaway, 1985; A Shadow on the Sun, 1987; The Witches, 1989; Cold Heaven, 1990; Two Deaths, 1994; also Exec. Producer, Cold Heaven, Two Deaths, and Shallow Grave, 1994. Dir, Scottish Television plc, 1993–. Mem., BBC Broadcasting Council (Scotland), 1987–90; Chairman: Writers' Guild of GB, 1989 and 1990; Scottish Film Council, 1991–; Scottish Film Prodn Fund, 1992–; Governor, BFI, 1993–. Mem., Amer. Acad. of Motion Picture Arts & Scis, 1991–. Mem. Council, Scotch Whisky Assoc., 1983–. Liveryman, Distillers' Co., 1989–. *Recreations:* writing, cooking, tennis. *Address:* Rafford Films Ltd, 1 Hereford Square, SW7 4TT. *T:* 0171–370 2694, *Fax:* 0171–373 4044. *Club:* Savile.

SHIACH, Sheriff Gordon Iain Wilson; Sheriff of Lothian and Borders, at Edinburgh, since 1984; *b* 15 Oct. 1935; *o s* of late Dr John Crawford Shiach, FDS, QHDS, and of Florence Bygott Wilson; *m* 1962, Margaret Grant Smith; two *d*. *Educ:* Lathallan Sch.; Gordonstoun Sch.; Edinburgh Univ. (MA, LLB); Open Univ. (BA Hons). Admitted to Faculty of Advocates, 1960; practised as Advocate, 1960–72; Tutor, Dept of Evidence and Pleading, Univ. of Edinburgh, 1963–66; Clerk to Rules Council of Court of Session, 1963–72; Standing Jun. Counsel in Scotland to Post Office, 1969–72; Sheriff of: Fife and Kinross, later Tayside, Central and Fife, at Dunfermline, 1972–79; Lothian and Borders at Linlithgow, 1979–84; Hon. Sheriff at Elgin, 1986–. Member: Council, Sheriffs' Assoc., 1989– (Pres., 1994–); Bd, Lothian Family Conciliation Service, 1989–93; Standing Cttee on Criminal Procedure, 1989–93; Parole Bd for Scotland, 1990–; Council, Faculty of Advocates, 1993–; Shrieval Training Gp, 1994–; Review Gp on Social Work Nat. Standards for Throughcare, 1994–. Chm., The Scottish Soc., 1992–93. *Recreations:* walking, swimming, music, art, theatre, film. *Address:* Sheriff's Chambers, Sheriff Court House, 27 Chambers Street, Edinburgh EH1 1LB. *T:* 0131–225 2525. *Club:* New (Edinburgh).

SHIELD, Leslie, TD; DL; a Recorder of the Crown Court, 1980–91; *b* 8 May 1916; *s* of Tom Shield and Annie Maud Shield; *m* 1941, Doris Leather; one *s*. *Educ:* Cowley Sch., St Helens; Univ. of Liverpool (LLB 1936, LLM 1938). Qualified solicitor, 1939, admitted 1945. Served War, 1939–46: commnd 5th Bn Prince of Wales' Volunteers (S Lancs) Regt; demob., Major. Entered into gen. practice as solicitor, 1946. DL Merseyside, 1976. *Recreations:* gardening (particular interest, orchids), music. *Address:* 185 Higher Lane, Rainford, St Helens, Merseyside WA11 8NF. *T:* Rainford (01744) 882708.

SHIELDS, Elizabeth Lois; Chairman, Ryedale Housing Association, since 1990; *b* 27 Feb. 1928; *d* of Thomas Henry Teare and Dorothy Emma Elizabeth Roberts-Lawrence; *m* 1961, David Cathro Shields. *Educ:* Whyteleafe Girls' Grammar School; UCL (BA Hons Classics); Avery Hill College of Education (Cert Ed); MA York 1988. Asst Teacher, St Philomena's Sch., Carshalton, 1954–59; Head of Department: Jersey Coll. for Girls, 1959–61; Whyteleafe Girls' Grammar Sch., 1961–62; Trowbridge Girls' High Sch., 1962–64; St Swithun's, Winchester, 1964–65; Queen Ethelburga's, Harrogate, 1967–69; Malton Sch., N Yorks, 1976–86; Univ. of York (on secondment), 1985–86 (Medieval Studies). Mem., Ryedale DC, 1980– (Chm., 1989–90; Chm., Community Services Cttee). Contested (L) Howden, 1979, Ryedale, 1983, 1992; MP (L) Ryedale, May 1986–87. Lib Dem spokesman on envmt, Yorks and Humberside Reg., 1989–; Chm., Yorks and Humberside Lib Dem Candidates' Assoc., 1988–. Chm., Ryedale Housing Assoc., 1990–91; President: Ryedale Motor Neurone Disease Assoc., 1990–; Ryedale Cats' Protection League, 1991–. *Recreations:* gardening, music, theatre. *Address:* Firby Hall, Kirkham Abbey, Westow, York YO6 7LH. *T:* Whitwell-on-the-Hill (01653) 618474. *Clubs:* National Liberal; Ryedale House.

SHIELDS, John Sinclair; *b* 4 Feb. 1903; *s* of Rev. W. H. Shields and Margaret Louisa (*née* Sinclair); *m* 1st, 1924, Norah Fane Smith; three *d*; 2nd, 1963, Mrs Noreen Moultrie, *widow* of Comdr John Moultrie. *Educ:* Charterhouse; Lincoln Coll., Oxford (MA). Headmaster: Wem Grammar School, 1934–47; Queen Mary's School, Basingstoke, 1947–56; Headmaster, Peter Symonds' School, Winchester, 1957–63; Vice-Pres. Classical Assoc., 1958; Mem., Broadcasting Cttee, 1960. *Recreations:* golf, gardening. *Address:* Rodmore Farm Cottage, Kings Stag, Sturminster Newton, Dorest DT10 2BE. *T:* Bishops Caundle (01963) 23018.

SHIELDS, (Leslie) Stuart, QC 1970; a Recorder of the Crown Court, 1972–91; *b* 15 May 1919; *m* 1st, 1941, Maureen Margaret McKinstry (*d* 1989); two *s* two *d* (and one *s* decd); 2nd, 1990, Barbara Diana Lloyd. *Educ:* St Paul's School; Corpus Christi College, Oxford. Paid Local Serjeant, Oxford and Buckinghamshire Light Infantry, 1945–47. Called to the Bar, Middle Temple, 1948; Bencher, 1977. Member: Criminal Injuries Compensation Bd, 1981–92; Independent Review Body for Coal Industry, 1985–90. *Recreations:* music, travel. *Address:* Devereux Chambers, Devereux Court, Temple, WC2R 3JJ.

SHIELDS, Michael; *see* Shields, R. M. C.

SHIELDS, Sir Neil (Stanley), Kt 1964; MC 1946; management consultant and company director; Chairman, Commission for the New Towns, 1982–95 (Chairman designate, 1981–82); *b* 7 September 1919; *o s* of late Archie Shields and Mrs Hannah Shields; *m* 1970, Gloria Dawn Wilson. Member of Honourable Artillery Company 1939–. Served in Royal Artillery, 1939–46; commnd 1940; Major 1943. Chairman: Anglo Continental Investment & Finance Co., 1965–74; Standard Catalogue Co., 1976–84; Holcombe Hldgs, 1978–84; Trianco Redfyre, 1979–84; Director: Chesham Amalgamations & Investments, 1964–84; Continental Bankers Agents, 1965–74; Central and Sheerwood, 1969–84; Newton Chambers & Co., 1972–84; Paxall Engineering, 1976–79. London Transport (formerly London Regional Transport): Mem. Bd, 1986–93; Chm., 1988–89, Dep. Chm., 1989–93; Chm., Property Bd, 1986–95. Prospective candidate (C) North St Pancras 1947 and contested by-election 1949. Chairman: Camden Conservative Cttee, 1965–67; Hampstead Conservative Assoc., 1954–65 (Vice-Chm., 1951–54); Hon. Treas. 1965–67; National Union of Conservative and Unionist Assocs: Chm. of London Area, 1961–63 (Vice-Chm., 1959–61); Mem. of National Executive, 1955–59, 1961–67, 1968–69; Hampstead Borough Council: Mem. 1947–65; Deputy Leader, 1952–61; Chm. of Works Cttee, 1951–55; Chm. of Finance Cttee, 1955–59. Mem. Council, Aims of Industry, 1976–. Governor, Bedford Coll., London Univ., 1983–85. Freeman, City of London, 1993. Hon. MRICS 1993. *Recreations:* reading, music, wining and dining. *Address:* 12 London House, Avenue Road, NW8 7PX. *Clubs:* Carlton, HAC.

SHIELDS, Sir Robert, Kt 1990; DL; MD, FRCS, FRCSE, FRCPS; Professor of Surgery, University of Liverpool, since 1969; Consultant Surgeon, Royal Liverpool Hospital and Broadgreen Hospital, since 1969; President, Royal College of Surgeons of Edinburgh, since 1994; *b* 8 Nov. 1930; *o s* of late Robert Alexander Shields and Isobel Dougall Shields; *m* 1957, Grace Marianne Swinburn; one *s* two *d*. *Educ:* John Neilson Institution, Paisley; Univ. of Glasgow. MB, ChB 1953 (Asher-Asher Medal and MacLeod Medal); MD (Hons and Bellahouston Medal) 1965; FRCSE 1959; FRCS 1966; FRCPS 1993. House appts, Western Infirmary, Glasgow, 1953–54; RAMC, Captain attached 1 Bn Argyll and Sutherland Highlanders, 1954–56; RAMC (TA), Major (Surg. Specialist) attached 7 Bn A and SH, 1956–61. Hall Fellow, Univ. of Glasgow, 1957–58; Mayo Foundn Fellow, 1959–60; Lectr in Surgery, Univ. of Glasgow, 1960–63; Sen. Lectr and Reader in Surgery, Welsh Nat. Sch. of Medicine, 1963–69; Dean, Faculty of Medicine, Univ. of Liverpool, 1982–85. Mem., GMC, 1982–94. Royal College of Surgeons: Mem., Ct of Examrs, 1980–86; Mem. Bd, Hunterian Inst., 1986–94; Zachary Cope Lectr, 1992; Vice Chm., Royal Liverpool Univ. Hosp. Trust, 1992–95 (non-exec. Trustee, 1991–); Member: Liverpool AHA (T) (Chm., Area/Univ. Liaison Cttee), 1974–78; Mersey RHA, 1982–85 (Vice-Chm., 1985; Regl Advr, 1986–94); Liverpool Med. Instn (Vice-Pres., 1983–84; Pres., 1988–89); Council, RCSE, 1985–; MRC, 1987–91 (Member: Cell Bd, 1974–77; Strategy Cttee, 1987–91); Exec. Cttee, Council of Military Educn Cttees of Univs of UK, 1990–94. Member: Surgical Research Soc. (Hon. Sec. 1972–76 and Pres. 1983–85); British Soc. of Gastroenterology (Mem. Council, 1984–86; Pres., 1990–91); N of England Gastroent. Soc. (Pres., 1981–83); Internat. Surgical Gp; James IV Assoc. of Surgeons, 1986– (Dir, 1991–; Pres., 1994–); Assoc. of Surgs of GB and Ire. (Mem. Council 1966–69; Pres., 1986–87); Chm., Med. Adv. Cttee, British Liver Trust (formerly British Liver Foundn), 1991–94; Vice-Chm., Brit. Jl of Surgery Soc., 1989–95. Member: Panel of Assesssors, Nat. Health and Med. Res. Council of Commonwealth and Australia, 1983–; List of Assessors for Cancer Grants, Anti-Cancer Council of Vic, Australia, 1986–. Chm., Merseyside, Lancashire and Cheshire Council on Alcoholism, 1992–94. Marjorie Budd Prof., Univ. of Bristol, 1983; Wilson Wang Vis. Prof., Chinese Univ. of Hong Kong, 1990; Wellcome Prof., Coll. of Medicine of S Africa, 1991. Former Visiting Prof., Univs of Toronto, Virginia, Witwatersrand, Rochester (NY), Hong Kong, Calif, Yale, and Examiner in Surgery, Univs of Glasgow, Edinburgh, Dundee, Leicester, Sheffield, Cambridge, Lagos, Amman, Riyadh, Malta; Dist. Lectr, Alpha Omega Alpha Assoc., 1994. Mem. Bd of Advrs in Surgery, London Univ., 1983–. Member: Editorial Board: Gut, 1969–76; Brit. Jl of Surgery, 1970–85, 1989–95; Internat. Editl Bd, Current Practice in Surgery, 1989–. Hon. Col Liverpool Univ. OTC, 1994–. DL Merseyside, 1991. Hon. FACS 1990; Hon. FCSSA 1991; Hon. Fellow. Amer. Surgical Assoc., 1993; Hong Kong Coll. of Surgeons, 1995; Hon. Mem., Indian Assoc. of Surgeons, 1993. Hon. DSc Wales, 1990. Moynihan Medal, Assoc. of Surgs of GB and Ire., 1966. *Publications:* (ed jtly): Surgical Emergencies II, 1979; Textbook of Surgery, 1983; Gastrointestinal Emergencies, 1992; contribs to medical and surgical jls relating to surgery and gastroenterology. *Recreations:* sailing and walking. *Address:* 81 Meols Drive, West Kirby, Wirral L48 5DF. *T:* 0151–632 3588. *Club:* Army and Navy.

SHIELDS, (Robert) Michael (Coverdale); Chief Executive, Trafford Park Development Corporation, since 1987; *b* 23 Jan. 1943; *s* of Thomas and Dorothy Shields; *m* 1965, Dorothy Jean Dennison; two *s* one *d*. *Educ:* Durham Johnston Grammar Tech. Sch.; Durham Univ. (BSc Hons); Newcastle Univ. (DipTP). MRTPI. Planning Departments: Newcastle upon Tyne, 1964–65; Durham CC, 1965–69; Nottingham, 1969–73; Dep. Dir of Planning, Leeds City Council, 1973–78; City Tech. Services Officer and Dep. Chief Exec., Salford City Council, 1978–83; Chief Exec., Trafford BC, 1983–87. Director: Salford Phoenix Initiative Ltd; Trafford Business Educn Partnership Ltd; Manchester Business Link; Salford Univ. Business Services Ltd. Dep. Chm of Govs, UC, Salford, Gov., Altrincham Grammar Sch.; Pro Vice Chancellor and Dep. Chair Council, Salford Univ. *Recreations:* family, school and college Governor, books. *Address:* Trafford Park Development Corporation, Wharfside, Trafford Wharf Road, Trafford Park, Manchester M17 1EX. *T:* 0161–848 8000. *Club:* St James's (Manchester).

SHIELDS, Stuart; *see* Shields, L. S.

SHIELL, James Wyllie, BSc, FICE; chartered civil engineer, retired; *b* 20 Aug. 1912; *yr s* of late George Douglas Shiell, farmer, Rennieston, Jedburgh and Janet Gladstone Wyllie; *m* 1941, Maureen Cameron Macpherson Hunter, *d* of late Thomas Hunter, Leeds; two *s*. *Educ:* Jedburgh Grammar and Kelso High Schools; Edinburgh Univ. Municipal Engrg posts in Edinburgh, Southampton, Sunderland and Leeds, 1934–39; Sen. Engr on Staff of J. D. & D. M. Watson, Consulting Engrs, Westminster, 1939–43 and 1945–47; Civil Engr on wartime service with Admty, 1943–45; Sen. Engr, Min. of Agriculture, 1947–49; Engrg Inspector, Dept of Health for Scotland, 1949–62; Dep. Chief Engr, Scottish Development Dept, 1962–68; Under Sec. and Chief Engr, Scottish Development Dept, 1968–75. Hon. FCIWEM. *Recreations:* walking with friends, listening to radio and tapes. *Address:* 25 Mortonhall Road, Edinburgh EH9 2HS. *T:* 0131–667 8528.

SHIERLAW, Norman Craig; Senior Partner, N. C. Shierlaw & Associates (Stock and Sharebrokers), since 1968; *b* 17 Aug. 1921; *s* of Howard Alison Shierlaw and Margaret Bruce; *m* 1944, Patricia Yates; two *d*. *Educ:* Pulteney Grammar Sch., Adelaide; St Peter's Coll., Adelaide; Univ. of Adelaide (BE). Assoc. Mem. Australian Inst. Mining and Metallurgy; FSASM; Mining Manager's Certificate. War Service, AIF, 1941–45 (War Service medals). Mining Engr with North Broken Hill Ltd, 1949–58; Sharebroker's Clerk, 1959–60; Partner, F. W. Porter & Co. (Sharebrokers), 1960–68. Director: Australian Development Ltd, 1959–; Poseidon Ltd, 1968–77; North Flinders Mines Ltd, 1969–77; Nobelex NL, 1974–. FAIM 1971. *Recreations:* golf, tennis. *Clubs:* Royal Automobile (Sydney); Naval, Military and Air Force, Stock Exchange, Kooyonga Golf (Adelaide); West Australian (Perth).

SHIFFNER, Sir Henry David, 8th Bt, *cr* 1818; Company Director; *b* 2 Feb. 1930; *s* of Major Sir Henry Shiffner, 7th Bt, and Margaret Mary (*d* 1987), *er d* of late Sir Ernest Gowers, GCB, GBE; *S* father, 1941; *m* 1st, 1949, Dorothy Jackson (marr. diss. 1956); one *d* (and one *d* decd); 2nd, 1957, Beryl (marr. diss. 1970), *d* of George Milburn, Saltdean, Sussex; one *d*; 3rd, 1970, Joaquina Ramos Lopez. *Educ:* Rugby; Trinity Hall, Cambridge. *Heir: cousin* George Frederick Shiffner [*b* 3 August 1936; *m* 1961, Dorothea Helena Cynthia, *d* of late T. H. McLean; one *s* one *d*]. *Address:* PO Box 90, St Helier, Jersey, CI. *Club:* Royal Automobile.

SHIFFNER, Rear-Adm. John Robert, CB 1995; Director General Fleet Support (Equipment and Systems), Ministry of Defence, 1993–95; *b* 30 Aug. 1941; *s* of late Captain John Scarlett Shiffner, RN and Margaret Harriet Shiffner (*née* Tullis); *m* 1969, Rosemary Tilly; two *s* one *d*. *Educ:* Sedbergh Sch.; BRNC Dartmouth; RNEC Manadon; RNC Greenwich (BSc). CEng, FIMarE. Joined RN, 1959; served in HM Ships Centaur, Glamorgan, Andromeda, Zulu; Staff Marine Engineer Officer, CBNS Washington, 1980; RCDS 1983; MoD Procurement Executive: Project Manager, Type 42 Destroyer/Aircraft Carrier, 1984–86; Dir, Mechanical Engineering, 1987–88; Captain, Britannia RNC, Dartmouth, 1989–91; ADC to the Queen, 1989–91; COS to C-in-C Naval Home Comd, 1991–93. MInstD. *Recreations:* golf, shooting, ski-ing, garden taming. *Address:* c/o Lloyds Bank, 2 Spithead, Dartmouth, Devon TQ6 9PU. *Club:* Naval and Military.

SHIGEHARA, Kumiharu; Head, Economics Department, Organisation for Economic Co-operation and Development, since 1992; *b* 5 Feb. 1939; *s* of Seizaburo Shigehara and Rutsu (*née* Tanabe); *m* 1965, Akiko Yoshizawa; one *s* one *d*. *Educ:* Law Sch., Univ. of Tokyo (Hozumi Hon. Award, 1960). Joined Bank of Japan, 1962; joined OECD, 1970: Principal Administrator, 1971–72; Hd, Monetary Div., 1972–74; Councillor on policy planning, and Associate Advr on Internat. Finance, Bank of Japan, 1974–80; Dep. Dir, Gen. Econs Br., OECD, 1980–82; Manager of Res., Inst. for Monetary and Econ. Studies, Bank of Japan, 1982–87, Dep. Dir, 1987; Dir, Gen. Econs Br., OECD, 1987–89; Dir, Inst. for Monetary and Econ. Studies, Bank of Japan, 1989–92. *Publications:* The Rôle of Monetary Policy in Demand Management (with Niels Thygesen), 1975; Stable Economic Growth and Monetary Policy, 1991; New Trends in Monetary Theory and Policy, 1992. *Recreations:* tennis, golf. *Address:* c/o Organisation for Economic Co-operation and Development, 2 rue André Pascal, 75116 Paris, France. *T:* 45248710. *Club:* Akiyama Country (Japan).

SHILLINGFORD, Arden; *see* Shillingford, R. A. C.

SHILLINGFORD, Prof. John Parsons, CBE 1988; MD (Harvard and London), FRCP, FACP; FACC; Sir John McMichael Professor of Cardiovascular Medicine, Royal Postgraduate Medical School, London University, 1976–79, now Emeritus Professor (Director, Cardiovascular Research Unit, and Professor of Angiocardiology, 1966–76); Consultant Medical Director, British Heart Foundation, 1981–86; *b* 15 April 1914; *s* of Victor Shillingford and Ethel Eugenie Parsons; *m* 1947, Doris Margaret Franklin; two *s* one *d*. *Educ:* Bishops Stortford; Harvard Univ.; London Hosp. Med. Sch. Rockefeller Student, Harvard Med. Sch., 1939–42; House appts, Presbyterian Hosp., New York, and London Hosp., 1943–45; Med. First Asst, London Hosp., 1945–52; Sen. Lectr Royal Postgrad. Med. Sch., 1958–62. Pres., Sect. Experimental Med., Royal Soc. Med., 1968; Sec., Brit. Cardiac Soc., 1963–70; Chm. Org. Cttee, Sixth World Congress Cardiology, 1970; Lumleian Lectr, RCP, 1972. Member: Assoc. Physicians Gt Brit.; Med. Res. Soc.; Med. Soc. London; Royal Soc. Med.; Comité Recherche Médicale, EEC; various cttees, Brit. Heart Foundn. Hon. Mem.: Hellenic Cardiac Soc.; Cardiac Soc. of Yugoslavia; Polish Cardiac Soc.; Cardiological Soc. of India; French Cardiac Soc.; Corr. Mem., Australian Cardiac Soc.; Fellow, Amer. Coll. of Cardiology; Hon. FACP, Editor, Cardiovascular Research. Visiting Prof., Australian Heart Foundn, 1965; lectured extensively in Europe, USA, S America, Africa, Middle East. James Berry Prize, RCS. *Publications:* numerous scientific papers, mainly on heart disease and coronary thrombosis. *Recreation:* sailing. *Address:* 5 Chester Close, Queens Ride, Barnes, SW13 0JE. *T:* 0181–789 3629. *Club:* Hurlingham.

SHILLINGFORD, (Romeo) Arden (Coleridge), MBE 1977; Permanent Secretary, Ministry of Legal Affairs, Commonwealth of Dominica, since 1992; *b* 11 Feb. 1936; *s* of Stafford Shillingford and Ophelia Thomas, step *d* of Hosford Samuel O'Brien and *d* of Clarita (*née* Hunt), Roseau, Dominica; *m* 1st, Evelyn Blanche Hart; one *s* one *d*; 2nd, Maudline Joan Green; three *s*. *Educ:* Wesley High Sch., Roseau Boys' Sch., Dominica; grammar school; School of Law. Member, Hon. Soc. Inner Temple. Joined Dominican Civil Service, 1957, after brief period as solicitor's clerk; junior clerk, various Govt Depts, Dominica, 1957–59; Clerk of Court, then Chief Clerk, Magistrates' Office, 1960–61; joined staff, Eastern Caribbean Commn, London, on secondment from Dominican CS, 1965; served variously as Migrants' Welfare Officer, Students' Officer, Asst Trade Sec. and PA to Comr, 1968–71; Admin. Asst, Consular and Protocol Affairs, 1973–78 (actg Comr, several occasions, 1975–78); High Comr in UK, 1978–85 (concurrently non-resident Ambassador to France, Spain, Belgium, W Germany and EEC, Brussels, and Perm. Rep. to UNESCO); Perm. Sec., Min. of Community Develt and Social Affairs, Dominica, 1985–92. Mem., Bd of Trustees, Dominica Conservation Assoc., 1989–92. Past Member, numerous cttees and *ad hoc* bodies for West Indian Immigrant Welfare and Education; Dep. Chm., Bd of Governors, W Indian Students' Centre, 1970–75, Chm., 1976–79; Member, West India Cttee (Vice-Pres. 1979–). Liaison Officer, Victoria League for Commonwealth Friendship; Founder-Mem. and Vice-Chm., Jaycees (Dominica Jun. Chamber of Commerce); Mem., Nat. Scouts Council Assoc. *Recreations:* cricket, collecting authentic folk music, swimming. *Address:* Ministry of Legal Affairs, Government Headquarters, Roseau, Commonwealth of Dominica, W Indies.

SHILLINGTON, Sir (Robert Edward) Graham, Kt 1972; CBE 1970 (OBE 1959; MBE 1951); DL; Chief Constable, Royal Ulster Constabulary, 1970–73; *b* 2 April 1911; *s* of Major D. Graham Shillington, DL, MP, and Mrs Louisa Shillington (*née* Collen); *m* 1935, Mary E. R. Bulloch (*d* 1977), Holywood, Co. Down; two *s* one *d*. *Educ:* Sedbergh Sch., Yorks; Clare Coll., Cambridge. Royal Ulster Constabulary: Officer Cadet, 1933; 3rd Class District Inspector, 1934; 2nd Class District Inspector, 1936; 1st Class District Inspector, 1944; County Inspector, 1953; Commissioner, Belfast, 1961; Deputy Inspector General (Deputy Chief Constable), 1969–70. Chm., Belfast Voluntary Welfare Soc.,

1976–81. DL Co. Down, 1975. King's Coronation Medal, 1937; Queen's Coronation Medal, 1953; Police Long Service and Good Conduct Medal, 1955; RUC Service Medal, 1985. *Recreations:* golf, gardening. *Address:* Ardeevin, 184 Bangor Road, Holywood, Co. Down BT18 0BY. *T:* Holywood (01232) 423471. *Clubs:* Royal Over-Seas League; Royal Belfast Golf.

SHILLITO, Charles Henry; Under-Secretary, Ministry of Agriculture, Fisheries and Food, 1974–82; *b* 8 Jan. 1922; *s* of Charles Cawthorne and Florence Shillito; *m* 1947, Elizabeth Jean (*née* Bull); two *d*. *Educ:* Hugh Bell Sch., Middlesbrough. Clerk, Min. of Agriculture and Fisheries, 1938; War Service, Lieut RNVR, 1941–46; Principal, MAFF, 1957; Asst Sec. 1966; Section Head, Nat. Econ. Develt Office, 1966–69 (on secondment). Hon. ARCVS 1986; Hon. Mem., BVA, 1989. *Recreations:* gardening, nautical pursuits. *Address:* 62 Downs Road, Coulsdon, Surrey CR5 1AB. *T:* Downland (01737) 553392.

SHILTON, Peter, OBE 1991 (MBE 1986); footballer; *b* 19 Sept. 1949. *Educ:* King Richard III Sch., Leicester. Goalkeeper; started playing, 1964, for Leicester City; scored a goal, 1967; Stoke City, 1974; Nottingham Forest, 1977; Southampton, 1982; Derby County, 1987; Plymouth Argyle, 1992–95 (player-manager); first played for England, 1970; 125 England caps (record); final appearance, World Cup, 1990. PFA Footballer of the Year, 1978.

SHIMMON, Ross Michael, FLA; Chief Executive, Library Association, since 1992; *b* 10 Jan. 1942; *s* of John Ross Shimmon and Eileen Margaret Shimmon; *m* 1967, Patricia, *d* of Ronald George Hayward, *qv*; one *s* two *d*. *Educ:* St John's Coll., Southsea; Poly. of North London; Coll. of Librarianship, Wales. FLA 1972. Liby Assistant, Portsmouth City Libraries, 1960; Asst Librarian, 1962, Area Librarian, Havant, 1964, Hants County Liby; Lectr, Southampton Coll. of Technol., 1964; Librarian (Tech. Assistant), London Bor. of Bexley, 1966; Professional Assistant to Library Advisers, DES, 1968; Lectr, Coll. of Librarianship, Wales, 1970; Services Librarian, Preston Poly., 1975; Head, Liby Studies Dept, Admin. Coll. of PNG, 1979; Sec. for Manpower and Educn, 1984, Dir, Professional Practice, 1988, Library Assoc. Member: Adv. Council, 1992–, Adv. Cttee, 1994–, British Library; BookAid Internat. Council, 1994–. Pres., Eur. Bureau of Liby, Inf. and Documentation Assocs, 1992–. Hon. Mem. PNG Liby Assoc., 1983. *Publications:* Reader in Library Management, 1976; conf. papers and contribs to liby jls. *Recreations:* cricket, photography, railways (prototype and model). *Address:* The Library Association, 7 Ridgmount Street, WC1E 7AE; 7 Nobel Court, Faversham, Kent ME13 7SD.

SHINGLES, Godfrey Stephen, (Geoff), CBE 1987; CEng, FIEE; FBCS; Chairman: VideoLogic Group PLC, since 1995; Digital Equipment Co. Ltd, 1991–94; Vice President, Digital Equipment Corporation, 1981–92; *b* 9 April 1939; *s* of Sidney and Winifred Shingles; *m* 1963, Jaqueline Margaret Crouch (marr. diss.); two *s*. *Educ:* Paston Sch., N Walsham; Leeds Univ. (BSc). Member Council: Education 2000; ABSA. FInstD. Freeman, City of London; Liveryman, Co. of Inf. Technologists. *Recreations:* sailing, squash, Rugby, ballet, ski-ing. *Address:* VideoLogic Group PLC, Home Park Estate, Kings Langley, Herts WD4 8LZ.

SHINNIE, Prof. Peter Lewis; Professor of Archæology, in the University of Calgary, 1970–80, now Emeritus; *b* 1915; *s* of late Andrew James Shinnie, OBE; *m* 1st, 1940, Margaret Blanche Elizabeth Cloake (*d* 1995); two *s* one *d*; 2nd, Ama Nantwi. *Educ:* Westminster Sch.; Christ Church, Oxford. Served War with RAF, 1939–45. Temp. Asst Keeper, Ashmolean Museum, 1945; Asst Commissioner for Archæology, Sudan Government, 1946; Commissioner for Archæology, Sudan Govt, 1948; Director of Antiquities, Uganda, 1956; Prof. of Archæology: Univ. of Ghana, 1958–66; Univ. of Khartoum, 1966–70. FSA. Hon. LLD Calgary, 1983. *Publications:* Excavation at Soba, 1955; Medieval Nubia, 1954; Ghazali: A Monastery in Northern Sudan, 1960; Meroe-Civilization of the Sudan, 1967; The African Iron Age, 1971; Debeira West, 1978; (with R. J. Bradley) The Capital of Kush, 1980; (ed with R. Haaland) African Iron Working: ancient and traditional, 1985; (with F. J. Kense) Archaeology in Gonja: excavations at Daboya, 1989; Early Asante, 1995; articles in Journal of Egyptian Archæology, Sudan Notes and Records, Kush. *Recreations:* reading, photography, travelling in Greece. *Address:* Department of Archæology, University of Calgary, Calgary, T2N 1N4 Canada. *T:* (403) 2205227.

SHIRLEY, family name of **Earl Ferrers.**

SHIRLEY, David Andrew; a Special Commissioner of Income Tax, since 1988; *b* 23 Nov. 1926; *er s* of Rev. Canon F. J. Shirley, DD (Oxon), FSA, and Dorothy, *d* of John Howard, Aberfeldy; *m* 1st, 1955, Dorothy Evelyn Finn (*d* 1969); 2nd, 1973, (Alysia) Rosemary (*d* 1993), *d* of Col Gerald Trimmer-Thompson, Cayton Park, Wargrave. *Educ:* Winchester Coll.; New Coll., Oxford (2nd Cl. Jurisprudence). 2nd Lieut Black Watch, 1946; ADC to Gov. of NW Frontier Province, 1947–48; Captain Black Watch (TA). Called to the Bar, Lincoln's Inn (Cholmeley Schol.), 1951; (*ad eundem*) Inner Temple, 1964; Bencher, Lincoln's Inn, 1978. Part-time Chm., VAT Tribunal, 1978–. *Recreations:* hunting, ski-ing, silviculture. *Address:* Litmore Shaw, Ibstone, High Wycombe, Bucks HP14 3XX. *T:* Turville Heath (01491) 638204.

SHIRLEY, Philip Hammond; retired; *b* 4 Oct. 1912; *s* of Frank Shillito Shirley and Annie Lucy (*née* Hammond); *m* 1st, 1936, Marie Edna Walsh (*d* 1972); one *s* one *d*; 2nd, 1973, Norma Jones. *Educ:* Sydney Church of England Grammar School (Shore). Qualified in Australia as Chartered Accountant, 1934; with Peat Marwick Mitchell & Co., Chartered Accountants, London, 1937–49; with Unilever from 1951; Dep. Chief Accountant, 1951–52; Chief Accountant, 1952–58; Chm. Batchelors Foods Ltd 1958–61; Mem. BTC (Oct. 1961–Nov. 1962); Mem. BR Bd, 1962–67 (Vice-Chm. Bd, 1964–67); Dep. Chm., Cunard Steamship Co., 1968–71; Chief Commissioner of Public Transport, NSW, 1972–75. *Recreation:* bowls. *Address:* 11, 25 Belmont Avenue, Wollstonecraft, NSW 2065, Australia.

SHIRLEY, Mrs Stephanie; *see* Shirley, Mrs V. S.

SHIRLEY, Mrs (Vera) Stephanie, (Steve), OBE 1980; CEng; FBCS; Life President, FI Group PLC (formerly F International Group); *b* 16 Sept. 1933; *d* of late Arnold Buchthal and Mrs Margaret Brook (formerly Buchthal, *née* Schick); name changed to Brook on naturalisation, 1951; *m* 1959, Derek George Millington Shirley; one *s*. *Educ:* Sir John Cass Coll., London. BSc (Spec.) London 1956. CIMgt (CBIM 1984); FBCS 1971; CEng 1990. PO Res. Stn, Dollis Hill, 1951–59; CDL (subsid. of ICL), 1959–62; F International Group, later FI Group, and its associated cos, 1962–93 (Founder Dir and sometime Chm.); Director: AEA Technology, 1992–; Tandem Computers Inc., 1992–. Member: Computer, Systems and Electronics Requirements Bd, 1979–81; Electronics and Avionics Requirements Bd, 1981–83; Open Tech, MSC, 1983–86; Council, Industrial Soc., 1984–90; NCVQ, 1986–89. Pres., British Computer Soc., 1989–90. Consulting Editor on information processing, J. Wiley & Sons, 1978–87. Member: Council, Duke of Edinburgh's Seventh Commonwealth Study Conf., 1991–92; British–N American Cttee, 1992–. Chm., Women of Influence, 1993. Trustee, Help The Aged, 1987–90; Patron, Disablement Income Gp, 1989–; Founder, Kingwood Trust, 1993. Master, Information Technologists' Co., 1992 (Liveryman, 1992); Freeman, City of London, 1987. FRSA 1985. Hon. FCGI 1989. Hon. Fellow: Manchester Metropolitan Univ. (formerly Poly.), 1989; Staffordshire Univ. (formerly Poly.), 1991; Sheffield Hallam Univ., 1992. Hon. DSc: Buckingham, 1991; Aston, 1993; Nottingham Trent, 1994; Hon. DTech: Loughborough, 1991; Kingston, 1995; DUniv Leeds Metropolitan, 1993; Hon. DLitt de Montfort, 1993; Hon. DBA West of England, 1995. Recognition of Information Technology Achievement Award, 1985; BIM Gold Medal, 1991. US Nat. Women's Hall of Fame, 1995. *Publications:* articles in prof. jls, reviews, proc. of confs, and papers. *Recreation:* sleep. *Address:* 47 Thames House, Phyllis Court Drive, Henley-on-Thames, Oxon RG9 2NA. *T:* Henley-on-Thames (01491) 574995. *Club:* Phyllis Court (Henley-on-Thames).

SHIRLEY-QUIRK, John Stanton, CBE 1975; bass-baritone singer; Member, Voice Faculty, Peabody Conservatory, Baltimore, since 1991; *b* 28 Aug. 1931; *s* of Joseph Stanley and Amelia Shirley-Quirk; *m* 1st, 1955, Patricia Hastie (*d* 1981); one *s* one *d*; 2nd, 1981, Sara V. Watkins; one *s* two *d*. *Educ:* Holt School, Liverpool; Liverpool University. Violin Scholarship, 1945; read Chemistry, Liverpool Univ., 1948–53; BSc (Hons), 1952; Dipl. in Educn 1953; became professional singer, 1961. Officer in Education Br., RAF, 1953–57. Asst Lectr in Chemistry, Acton Technical Coll., 1957–61; Lay-clerk in St Paul's Cathedral, 1961–62. First Appearance Glyndebourne Opera in Elegy for Young Lovers, 1961; subseq. 1962, 1963. Sang in first performance of Curlew River, 1964, The Burning Fiery Furnace, 1966, The Prodigal Son, 1968, Owen Wingrave, 1970, Death in Venice, 1973, Confessions of a Justified Sinner, 1976, The Ice Break, 1977. Has sung world wide. First American tour, 1966; Australian tour, 1967; first appearance Metropolitan Opera, NY, 1974. Has made numerous recordings: operas, songs, cantatas, etc. Mem. Court, Brunel Univ., 1977–. Hon. RAM 1972; Hon. DMus Liverpool, 1976; DUniv Brunel, 1981. Liverpool Univ. Chem. Soc. Medal, 1965; Sir Charles Santley Meml Gift, Worshipful Co. of Musicians, 1969. *Recreations:* trees, canals, clocks. *Address:* 6062 Red Clover Lane, Clarksville, MD 21029–1272, USA.

SHIRRAS, Rev. Edward Scott; Vicar, Christ Church, Winchester, since 1992; *b* 23 April 1937; *s* of Edward Shirras and Alice Emma Shirras (*née* Morten); *m* 1962, Pamela Susan Mackenzie; two *s* two *d*. *Educ:* Sevenoaks School; St Andrews Univ. (BSc); Union Coll., Schenectady, NY, USA; Clifton Theolog. Coll., Bristol. Curate: Christ Church, Surbiton Hill, 1963–66; Jesmond Parish Church, Newcastle upon Tyne, 1966–68; Church Pastoral Aid Society: Youth Sec., 1968–71; Publications Sec., 1971–74; Asst Gen. Sec., 1974–75; Vicar of Christ Church, Roxeth, dio. London, 1975–85; Area Dean of Harrow, 1982–85; Archdeacon of Northolt, 1985–92. *Recreations:* transport photography (Scottish), Aberdeen FC. *Address:* Christ Church Vicarage, Sleepers Hill, Winchester, Hants SO22 4ND. *T:* Winchester (01962) 862414.

SHIVAS, Mark; Head of Films, BBC Television, since 1993; *b* 24 April 1938; *s* of James Dallas Shivas and Winifred Alice Lighton (*née* Bristow). *Educ:* Whitgift School; Merton College, Oxford (MA Law). Asst Editor, Movie Magazine, 1962–64; freelance journalist; joined Granada TV, 1964, Director-Producer, 1965–68; Producer of Drama, 1969–88, Head of Drama, 1988–93, BBC TV; Creative Dir, Southern Pictures, 1979–81. Productions include: The Six Wives of Henry VIII (BAFTA awards, Prix Italia), The Evacuees (BAFTA and Emmy awards), Casanova, The Glittering Prizes, Rogue Male, Professional Foul (BAFTA award), Telford's Change, On Giant's Shoulders (Emmy award); for Channel 4: The Price, What if it's Raining?, The Storyteller (Emmy award); feature films include: Moonlighting, 1982; A Private Function, 1984; The Witches, 1988; Truly, Madly, Deeply, 1991; Enchanted April, 1991; The Snapper, 1993; Priest, 1995. *Publications:* articles in art jls. *Recreations:* Italy, gardens, swimming, cycling, moviegoing. *Address:* BBC TV, Wood Lane, W12 7TS. *T:* 0181–743 8000.

SHOCK, Sir Maurice, Kt 1988; Rector, Lincoln College, Oxford, 1987–94; *b* 15 April 1926; *o s* of Alfred and Ellen Shock; *m* 1947, Dorothy Donald; one *s* three *d*. *Educ:* King Edward's Sch., Birmingham; Balliol Coll., Oxford (MA); St Antony's Coll., Oxford. Served Intell. Corps, 1945–48. Lectr in Politics, Christ Church and Trinity Coll., Oxford, 1955–56; Fellow and Praelector in Politics, University Coll., Oxford, 1956–77, Hon. Fellow, 1986; Estates Bursar, 1959–74; Vice-Chancellor, Leicester Univ., 1977–87. Sen. Treasurer, Oxford Union Soc., 1954–72 (Trustee, 1988–); Member: Franks Commn of Inquiry into the University of Oxford, 1964–66; Hebdomadal Council, Oxford Univ., 1969–75; Chairman: Univ. Authorities Panel, 1980–85; CVCP, 1985–87. Vis. Prof. of Govt, Pomona Coll., 1961–62, 1968–69. Member: ESRC, 1981–85; GMC, 1989–; a Governing Trustee, 1980–, Chm., 1988–, Nuffield Provincial Hosps Trust. Hon. Vice-Pres., Political Studies Assoc., 1989. Hon. FRCP 1989. Hon. LLD Leicester, 1987. *Publications:* The Liberal Tradition; articles on politics and recent history. *Recreations:* gardening, theatre. *Address:* 4 Cunliffe Close, Oxford OX2 7BL.

SHOENBERG, Prof. David, MBE 1944; FRS 1953; Professor of Physics, Cambridge University and Head of Low Temperature Physics Group, Cavendish Laboratory, 1973–78, now Emeritus; Life Fellow of Gonville and Caius College; *b* 4 Jan. 1911; *s* of Isaac and Esther Shoenberg; *m* 1940, Catherine Félicitée Fischmann; one *s* two *d*. *Educ:* Latymer Upper School, W6; Trinity College, Cambridge (Scholar). PhD 1935; Exhibition of 1851 Senior Student, 1936–39; Research in low temperature physics, 1932–, in charge of Royal Soc. Mond Laboratory, 1947–73; Univ. Lectr in Physics, 1944–52; Univ. Reader in Physics, 1952–73; UNESCO Adviser on Low Temperature Physics, NPL of India, 1953–54. Mellon Prof., Univ. of Pittsburgh, 1962; Gauss Prof., Univ. of Göttingen, 1964; Visiting Professor: Univ. of Maryland, 1968; Univ. of Toronto, 1974; Univ. of Waterloo, 1977; Lectures: Guthrie, 1961; Rutherford Meml, India and Sri Lanka, 1980; Krishnan Meml, New Delhi, 1988. Hon. Foreign Mem., Amer. Acad. of Arts and Sciences, 1982. Dr (*hc*) Univ. of Lausanne, 1973. Fritz London Award for Low Temperature Physics, 1964; Hughes Medal, Royal Soc., 1995. *Publications:* Superconductivity, 1938, revised edn, 1952; Magnetism, 1949; Magnetic Oscillations in Metals, 1984; (ed jtly) Kapitza in Cambridge and Moscow, 1990; scientific papers on low temperature physics and magnetism. *Address:* 2 Long Road, Cambridge CB2 2PS; Cavendish Laboratory, Madingley Road, Cambridge CB3 0HE. *T:* Cambridge (01223) 337389.

SHONE, Rev. John Terence; Team Vicar, Cullercoats Team, Marden St Hilda, Diocese of Newcastle, since 1989; *b* 15 May 1935; *s* of late Arthur Shone and E. B. Shone; *m* 1st, 1958, Ursula Ruth Buss (marr. diss.); three *s*; 2nd, 1987, Annette Simmons, *d* of William Caterer and late Ada Caterer. *Educ:* St Dunstan's College; Selwyn Coll., Cambridge (BA 1958, MA 1962); Lincoln Theological Coll.; Newcastle Univ. (MA 1992). Deacon 1960, priest 1961, London; Curate, St Pancras Parish Church, 1960–62; Chaplain, St Andrew's Cathedral, Aberdeen, 1962–65; Chaplain to Anglican Students, Aberdeen, 1962–68; Lectr, Aberdeen Coll. of Education, 1965–68; Exam. Chaplain to Bishop of Aberdeen, 1966–68; Vicar, St Andrew and St Luke, Grimsby, 1968–69; Rector, St Saviour, Bridge of Allan, 1969–86; Chaplain, Stirling Univ., 1969–80; Priest i/c, St John's, Alloa, 1977–85, and St James', Dollar, 1981–86; Canon, St Ninian's Cathedral, Perth, 1980–82; Dean, United Dio. of St Andrews, Dunkeld and Dunblane, 1982–89; Diocesan R & D Officer, 1986–89. *Address:* St Hilda's Vicarage, Preston Gate, Marden, North Shields NE29 9QB. *T:* 0191–257 6595.

SHOOTER, Prof. Eric Manvers, FRS 1988; Professor of Neurobiology, Stanford University, since 1975; *b* 18 April 1924; *s* of Fred and Pattie Shooter; *m* 1949, Elaine Staley Arnold; one *d.* *Educ:* Gonville and Caius Coll., Cambridge (BA 1945; MA 1950; PhD 1950; ScD 1986); DSc London 1964. Senior Scientist, Brewing Industry Research Foundn, 1950–53; Lectr in Biochem., University Coll. London, 1953–63; Stanford University: Associate Prof. of Genetics, 1963–68; Prof. of Genetics and Prof. of Biochem., 1968–75; Prof. and Chm. of Neurobiol., 1975–87. Macy Faculty Scholar, Univ. of Geneva, 1974–75. Foreign Assoc., Inst. of Medicine, Nat. Acad. of Scis, USA, 1989; Fellow, American Acad. of Arts and Scis, 1993. Wakeman Award, 1988. *Publications:* (associate editor) Annual Review of Neuroscience, vols 6–15, 1983–93; numerous papers in sci jls. *Address:* Department of Neurobiology, Stanford University School of Medicine, Stanford, CA 94305–5401, USA. *T:* (415) 7236638.

SHOOTER, Prof. Reginald Arthur, CBE 1980; Emeritus Professor of Medical Microbiology, London University, since 1981; *b* 1916; *s* of Rev. A. E. Shooter, TD and M. K. Shooter; *m* 1946, Jean Wallace, MB, ChB; one *s* three *d.* *Educ:* Mill Hill Sch.; Caius Coll., Cambridge; St Bartholomew's Hosp. BA 1937; MB, BChir 1940; MRCS, LRCP 1940; MA 1941; MD 1945; MRCP 1961; FRCP 1968; FRCS 1977; FRCPath 1963 (Vice-Pres., 1971–74). After various Hosp. appts became Surgeon Lieut, RNVR. Appointments at St Bartholomew's Hospital from 1946; Rockefeller Travelling Fellow in Medicine, 1950–51; Reader in Bacteriology, 1953–61, Prof. of Medical Microbiology, 1961–81, Univ. of London; Bacteriologist to St Bartholomew's Hosp., 1961–81 and Dean, Medical Coll., 1972–81. Member: City and E London AHA (T), 1974–81; Gloucester HA, 1981–85; Chm., Regional Computing Policy Steering Gp, SW RHA, 1983–85. Mem., Public Health Lab. Service Bd, 1970–82; Chm., Dangerous Pathogens Adv. Gp, 1975–81. Mem., Scientific Adv. Council, Stress Foundn, 1981–90. Governor: St Bartholomew's Hosp., 1972–74; Queen Mary Coll., 1972–81; Trustee: Mitchell City of London Trust, 1958–82; Jenner Trust, 1989–. Mem. Court, City Univ., 1972–81. Pybus Medal, N of England Surg. Soc., 1979. Asst Editor, British Jl of Exp. Pathology, 1953–58; Hon. Editor, RSocMed, 1960–65. *Publications:* books, and articles in medical journals. *Recreations:* archaeology, gardening, fishing. *Address:* Eastlea, Back Edge Lane, The Edge, Stroud, Glos GL6 6PE. *T:* Painswick (01452) 812408.

SHORE, David Teignmouth, OBE 1982; FEng 1979; Director (Technical), APV PLC, 1984–88; *b* 15 Nov. 1928; *e s* of Geoffrey and Cecilia Mary Shore; *m* 1950, Pamela Goodge; one *s* two *d.* *Educ:* Tiffin Boys' Sch., Kingston; Imperial Coll., London (MSc(Eng)). FIMechE 1967; FIChemE 1970; FIFST 1970; FCGI 1979. Engrg apprenticeship, 1944–47; Thermal Engr, Foster Wheeler Ltd, 1953–54; APV Co. Ltd: Research Engr, 1950–52; Process Devel Engr, 1954–65; Research Dir, 1965–77; Man. Dir, 1977–82; Chm., 1982–84; Divisional Dir, APV Holdings PLC, 1982–84. Chm., British Food Manufg Industries Res. Assoc., 1984–87; Chm. Engrg Bd, 1985–89 and Mem. Council, 1985–89, SERC; Member: Bd of Advisers in Chemical Engrg, Univ. of London, 1983–; Bd of Food Studies, Univ. of Reading, 1984–93; Jt Delegacy for Food Res. Inst., Reading, 1985–; Council, Univ. of Reading, 1987–93. *Publications:* technical articles on rheology, heat transfer and food process engrg in learned jls. *Recreations:* walking, astronomy, wine-making. *Address:* Hembury, Garratts Lane, Banstead, Surrey SM7 2EA. *T:* Burgh Heath (01737) 53721.

SHORE, Dr Elizabeth Catherine, CB 1980; Associate Dean of Postgraduate Medical Education, North Thames Region, since 1993; Hon. Senior Lecturer, Charing Cross and Westminster Medical School, since 1993; *b* 1927; *d* of Edward Murray Wrong and Rosalind Grace Smith; *m* 1948, Rt Hon. Peter David Shore, *qv*; one *s* two *d* (and one *s* decd). *Educ:* Newnham Coll., Cambridge; St Bartholomew's Hospital. MRCP, FRCP; MRCS, FFCM, DRCOG. Joined Medical Civil Service, 1962; Dep. Chief Medical Officer, DHSS, 1977–85. Dean of Postgrad. Medicine, NW Thames Reg., 1985–93. Mem., GMC, 1989–94 (Member: Standards Cttee, 1989–91; Professional Conduct Cttee, 1991–93; Educnl Cttee, 1992–93; Prelim. Proceeding Cttee, 1993). Pres., Med. Women's Fedn, 1990–92 (Chm., Careers Cttee, 1989–); Chair, BMA Career Progress Cttee, 1994–. Mem. Council, PSI, 1992–. Trustee, Child Accident Prevention Trust, 1985–91 (Chm., Council and Professional Cttee, 1985–90). Editor, Medical Women, 1992–. *Recreations:* reading, cookery, swimming in rough seas. *Address:* 23 Dryburgh Road, SW15 1BN.

SHORE, Jack; President, Royal Cambrian Academy of Art, 1977–83; *b* 17 July 1922; *s* of Frank and Maggie Shore; *m* 1970, Olive Brenda Williams; one *s* one *d.* *Educ:* Accrington and Manchester Schools of Art. Lectr, Blackpool School of Art, 1945–60; Head, Chester Sch. of Art, 1960–81. Paintings in public and private collections, including USA. RCamA 1962 (ARCamA 1961). Jubilee Medal, 1977. *Recreations:* gardening, enjoyment of music. *Address:* 11 St George's Crescent, Queens Park, Chester CH4 7AR. *T:* Chester (01244) 675017.

SHORE, Rt. Hon. Peter (David), PC 1967; MP (Lab) Bethnal Green and Stepney, since 1983 (Stepney, 1964–74; Stepney and Poplar, 1974–83); *b* 20 May 1924; *m* 1948, Elizabeth Catherine Wrong (*see* E. C. Shore); one *s* two *d* (and one *s* decd). *Educ:* Quarry Bank Grammar Sch., Liverpool; King's Coll., Cambridge. Political economist. Joined Labour Party, 1948; Head of Research Dept, Labour Party, 1959–64. Member of Fabian Society. Contested (Lab) St Ives, Cornwall, 1950, Halifax, 1959. PPS to the Prime Minister, 1965–66; Jt Parly Sec.: Min. of Technology, 1966–67; Dept of Economic Affairs, 1967; Sec. of State for Economic Affairs, 1967–69; Minister without Portfolio, 1969–70; Dep. Leader of House of Commons, 1969–70; Opposition Spokesman on Europe, 1971–74; Sec. of State for Trade, 1974–76; Sec. of State for the Environment, 1976–79; Opposition Spokesman on Foreign Affairs, 1979–80, on Treasury and Economic Affairs, 1980–83; Opposition Spokesman on Trade and Industry, 1983–84; Shadow Leader of the House of Commons, 1984–87. Member: Select Cttee on Foreign Affairs, 1987–; Cttee on Standards in Public Life, 1994. *Publications:* Entitled to Know, 1966; Leading the Left, 1993. *Recreation:* swimming. *Address:* House of Commons, SW1A 0AA; 23 Dryburgh Road, SW15.

SHORROCK, John Michael; QC 1988; a Recorder of the Crown Court, since 1982; *b* 25 May 1943; *s* of late James Godby Shorrock and of Mary Patricia Shorrock (*née* Lings); *m* 1971, Marianne (*née* Mills); two *d.* *Educ:* Clifton College, Bristol; Pembroke College, Cambridge. MA. Called to the Bar, Inner Temple, 1966; practising on Northern Circuit, 1966–: Junior, 1968; Sec., Exec. Cttee, 1981–85. *Recreations:* walking, gardening, opera, theatre, cinema. *Address:* 45 Hardman Street, Manchester M3 3HA. *T:* 0161–832 3791.

SHORT, family name of **Baron Glenamara.**

SHORT, Bernard David, CBE 1995; Head of Further Education Support Unit, Department for Education, since 1993; *b* 9 June 1935; *s* of late Bernard Charles and of Ethel Florence Short; *m* 1960, Susan Yvonne Taylor; two *s* one *d.* *Educ:* St Edmund Hall, Oxford (MA). Served The Royal Scots, 1953–56 (commnd 1954). Taught at Ingiliz Erkek Lisesi, Istanbul, Turkey, 1960–63; Lectr, Univ. of Kyushu, Japan, 1963–65; Asst Lectr, Garretts Green Technical Coll., Birmingham, 1966–67; Lectr, Bournville Coll. of Further Educn, Birmingham, 1967–71; Sen. Lectr, Henley Coll. of Further Educn, Coventry, 1971–73; Head, Dept of Gen. Studies, Bournville Coll., Birmingham, 1973–76; HM Inspectorate of Schools, 1976–93: Inspector, 1976; Staff Inspector, 1984; Chief Inspector, Further Education, 1986. FRSA 1991. *Publications:* A Guide to Stress in English, 1967; Humour, 1970. *Recreations:* music, gardening, boats.

SHORT, Clare; MP (Lab) Birmingham Ladywood, since 1983; *b* 15 Feb. 1946; *d* of Frank and Joan Short; *m* 1981, Alexander Ward Lyon (*d* 1993), sometime MP for York. *Educ:* Keele Univ.; Leeds Univ. (BA Hons Political Sci.). Home Office, 1970–75; Dir, All Faiths for One Race, Birmingham, 1976–78; Dir, Youth Aid and the Unemployment Unit, 1979–83. Chm., All Party Parly Gp on Race Relations, 1985–86; Mem., Home Affairs Select Cttee, 1983–85; front bench spokesperson on employment, 1985–88, on social security, 1989–91, on envmtl protection, 1993, on women, 1993, Mem., Labour Party NEC, 1988–. *Publications:* Talking Blues: a study of young West Indians' views of policing, 1978; Handbook of Immigration Law, 1978; Dear Clare . . . this is what women think about Page 3, 1991. *Recreations:* family and friends, swimming. *Address:* House of Commons, SW1A 0AA. *T:* 0171–219 3000.

SHORT, Prof. David Somerset, MD, FRCP, FRCPE; Clinical Professor in Medicine, University of Aberdeen, 1983, now Emeritus; Hon. Consultant Physician, Aberdeen Royal Infirmary, since 1983 (Consultant Physician, 1960–83); *b* 6 Aug. 1918; *s* of Latimer James Short, MD, DPH, Bristol, and Mabel Annie Wood, SRN, Nottingham; *m* 1948, Joan Anne McLay, BSc, MB, ChB, Cardiff; one *s* four *d.* *Educ:* Bristol Grammar Sch.; Cambridge Univ.; Bristol Royal Hospitals. MD 1948; PhD 1957; FRCP 1964; FRCPE 1966. Served with RAMC, 1944–47; Registrar, Southmead Hosp., Bristol, 1947–49; Sen. Registrar, National Heart Hosp. and London Hosp., 1950–54; Lecturer in Medicine, Middlesex Hosp., 1955–59. Physician to the Queen in Scotland, 1977–83. *Publications:* Medicine as a Vocation, 1978, 2nd edn 1987; contribs to medical journals, mainly on cardiovascular and pulmonary diseases. *Recreations:* touring, music. *Address:* 48 Victoria Street, Aberdeen, Scotland AB9 2PL. *T:* Aberdeen (01224) 645853.

SHORT, Rt. Rev. Hedley Vicars Roycraft; retired 1985; *b* 24 Jan. 1914; *s* of Hedley Vicars Short and Martha Hallam Parke; *m* 1953, Elizabeth Frances Louise Shirley; one *s* four *d.* *Educ:* Trinity College, Univ. of Toronto (BA, LTh, BD). Deacon, 1943, priest, 1944, Assistant Curate St Michael and All Angels, Toronto; Junior Chaplain, Coventry Cathedral, England, 1946–47; Lecturer, Trinity Coll., Toronto, 1947–51; Dean of Residence, 1949–51; Rector, Cochrane, Ont, 1951–56; Rector, St Barnabas, St Catharines, Ont, 1956–63; Canon, Christ's Church Cathedral, Hamilton, Ont, 1962; Dean of Saskatchewan, 1963–70; Archdeacon of Prince Albert, 1966–70; Bishop of Saskatchewan, 1970–85. Member of General Synod, 1955–83; Examining Chaplain successively to Bishops of Moosonee, Niagara and Saskatchewan. Mem., Northern Devel Adv. Council, Province of Saskatchewan, 1987–88. Pres. Council, Coll. of Emmanuel and St Chad, Saskatoon, 1974–80; Chm., Natonum Community Coll., Prince Albert, 1974–76; Chancellor, 1975–80, Hon. Fellow, 1980, Univ. of Emmanuel Coll. Hon. DD: Trinity Coll., Toronto, 1964; Emmanuel Coll., Saskatoon, 1983. *Publication:* (contrib.) Eucharistic Dimensions, 1977. *Recreations:* music, sketching, reading. *Address:* 355 19th Street W, Prince Albert, Saskatchewan S6V 4C8, Canada.

SHORT, Rt. Rev. Kenneth Herbert, AO 1988; Dean of Sydney (St Andrew's Cathedral), 1989–92; *b* 6 July 1927; *s* of Cecil Charles Short and Joyce Ellen Begbie; *m* 1950, Gloria Noelle Funnell; one *s* two *d.* *Educ:* Moore Theological Coll. (ThL and Moore Coll. Dipl.). Commissioned AIF, 1946; with BCOF, 1946–48; theological training, 1949–52; ordained Anglican Ministry, 1952; Minister in Charge, Provisional Parish of Pittwater, 1952–54; with CMS in Tanzania, E Africa, 1955–64; Chaplain, Tabora 1955, Mwanza 1955–59; founding Principal, Msalato Bible School, 1961–64; Gen. Secretary, CMS NSW Branch, 1964–71, including Sec. for S America. Canon of St Andrew's Cathedral, Sydney, 1970–75; Exam. Chaplain to Archbishop of Sydney, 1971–82; Rector of St Michael's, Vaucluse, 1971–75; Archdeacon of Wollongong and Camden, 1975–79; Chaplain General (CE), Australian Army, 1979–81; Bishop in Wollongong, Dio. of Sydney, 1975–82; Anglican Bishop to Aust. Defence Force (Army, Navy and Air Force), 1979–89; Bishop of Parramatta, Dio. of Sydney, 1982–89. ChStJ 1989. *Publications:* Guidance, 1969; (contrib.) Evangelism and Preaching in Secular Australia, 1989. *Recreations:* rock fishing, reading, walking, wood turning. *Address:* 16 Chapman Street, Kiama, NSW 2533, Australia. *T:* (42) 321261.

SHORT, Nigel David; professional chess player; *b* 1 June 1965; *s* of David Malcolm Short and Jean Short (*née* Gaskill); *m* 1987, Rhea Argyro, *d* of Nikolaos Karageorgiou; one *d.* *Educ:* Bolton Sch. British chess champion: 1979 (equal first), 1984, 1987, 1991; internat. master 1980; grandmaster 1984; world championship candidate, 1985–93 (finalist, 1992, defeating Anatoly Karpov in semi-final). Resigned from FIDE, 1993 and formed Professional Chess Assoc. (with Gary Kasparov), 1993. *Recreation:* guitar.

SHORT, Sir Noel (Edward Vivian), Kt 1977; MBE 1951; MC 1945; Speaker's Secretary, House of Commons, 1970–82; *b* 19 Jan. 1916; *s* of late Vivian A. Short, CIE, Indian Police, and late Annie W. Short; *m* 1st, 1949, Diana Hester Morison (*d* 1951); one *s*; 2nd, 1957, Karin Margarete Anders; one *s* one *d.* *Educ:* Radley College; RMA Sandhurst. Commissioned Indian Army, 1936; joined 6th Gurkha Rifles, 1937. Active service: NW Frontier of India, 1937, 1940–41; Assam and Burma, 1942, 1944–45; New Guinea, 1943–44; Malaysia, 1950–51, 1952–53, 1956–57. Staff College, 1946–47; jssc, 1953; Comdr, 63 Gurkha Bde, Malaysia, 1960–61; Comdr, 51 Infty Bde, Tidworth, 1962–63. Principal, Home Office, 1964–70. Col, 6th Queen Elizabeth's Own Gurkha Rifles, 1978–83.

SHORT, Peter, BA; IPFA; Managing Director, Greater Manchester Buses South Ltd, since 1993; *b* 21 June 1945; *s* of Christopher John Grewcock Short and Isabella Short; *m* 1967, Eileen Short (*née* Makin); one *s* one *d.* *Educ:* South Shields Grammar Sch.; Univ. of Exeter (2nd Cl. Hons, Div. 1, Modern Economic History). IPFA (1st place Final, 1970). Local Govt Accountant with Manchester City Council, 1967–73; Leeds City Council, 1973–78; Dir of Finance, South Tyneside MDC, 1978–83; City Treas., Manchester CC, 1983–89; Dep. Chief Exec. and Dir of Finance, Greater Manchester Buses Ltd, 1989–93. *Recreations:* reading, walking, caravanning, avoiding household maintenance, planning to walk the Pennine Way. *Address:* 2 Netherwood Road, Northenden, Manchester M22 4BQ.

SHORT, Mrs Renee; *m*; two *d.* *Educ:* Nottingham County Grammar Sch.; Manchester Univ. Freelance journalist. Member: Herts County Council, 1952–67; Watford RDC, 1952–64; West Herts Group Hosp. Management Cttee; former Chm. Shrodell's Hosp., Watford. Governor: Watford Coll. of Technology; Watford Grammar Sch. Contested (Lab) St Albans, 1955, Watford, 1959. MP (Lab) Wolverhampton NE, 1964–87; TGWU sponsored Member of Parliament. Member: Delegation to Council of Europe, 1964–68; Estimates Cttee, 1964–69; Expenditure Cttee, 1970–79 (Chm., Social Services and Employment Sub-Cttee); Chairman: Select Cttee for Social Services, 1979–87; Parly and Scientific Cttee, 1982–85 (Vice-Pres., 1986–); Associate Mem., Parly IT Cttee, 1987–. Vice-Chm., Parly East-West Trade Gp, 1968–87; Chairman: British-GDR Parly Gp, 1972–87; British-Soviet Parly Gp 1984–87 (Sec., 1972–84); Pres., British-Romanian Friendship Assoc. Mem., Nat. Exec. Cttee of Labour Party, 1970–81, 1983–88. Member: MRC, 1988–; Research in Patients Cttee, RCP, 1988–; IVF Cttee, BMA, 1988–; AIDS

Study Gp, Inst. of Medical Ethics, 1989–; Special Hosps Services Authority, 1991–. National President: Nursery Schools Assoc., 1970–80; Campaign for Nursery Educn, 1970–83; Pres., Action for the Newborn, 1988–; Vice-President: Women's Nat. Cancer Control Campaign; Health Visitors' Assoc. Mem., Roundhouse Theatre Council; Chm., Theatres' Advisory Council, 1974–80. Hon. Fellow, Wolverhampton Polytechnic, 1987; Hon. FRCPsych 1988; Hon. MRCP 1989. *Publication:* The Care of Long Term Prisoners, 1979. *Address:* 70 Westminster Gardens, Marsham Street, SW1P 4JG. *T:* 0171–828 6110.

SHORT, Roger Guy, MVO 1971; HM Diplomatic Service; Ambassador to Bulgaria, since 1994; *b* 9 Dec. 1944; *s* of Harold Short and Alice Ames Short (*née* Fox); *m* 1971, Sally Victoria Taylor; one *s* two *d. Educ:* Malvern; University Coll., Oxford (schol.; BA Lit.Hum.; MA). Served FCO and Ankara, 1967–78; Consul (Commercial), Rio de Janeiro, 1978–80; Head of Chancery, Ankara, 1981–84; Counsellor and Dep. Head of Permanent Under-Sec. of State's Dept, FCO, 1984–86; Head of Chancery and Consul-Gen., Oslo, 1986–90; Head of Personnel Services Dept, FCO, 1990–94. *Recreations:* music, classical studies, languages, wine. *Address:* c/o Foreign and Commonwealth Office, SW1A 2AH.

SHORT, Prof. Roger Valentine, FRCOG; FRS 1974; FRSE; FRCVS; FAA; Professor of Reproductive Biology, Monash University, Australia, since 1982; *b* 31 July 1930; *s* of F. A. and M. C. Short, Weybridge; *m* 1st, 1958, Dr Mary Bowen Wilson (marr. diss. 1981); one *s* three *d*; 2nd, 1982, Dr Marilyn Bernice Renfree; two *d. Educ:* Sherborne Sch.; Univs of Bristol (BVSc, MRCVS), Wisconsin (MSc) and Cambridge (PhD, ScD). FRSE 1974; FRCVS 1976; FAA 1984; FRCOG 1991. Mem., ARC Unit of Reproductive Physiology and Biochemistry, Cambridge, 1956–72; Fellow, Magdalene Coll., Cambridge, 1962–72; Lectr, then Reader, Dept of Veterinary Clinical Studies, Cambridge, 1961–72; Dir, MRC Unit of Reproductive Biology, Edinburgh, 1972–82. Hon. Prof., Univ. of Edinburgh, 1976–82. Chm., Bd of Dirs, Family Health Internat., NC, USA, 1984–90. Hon. DSc Guelph, 1988. *Publications:* (ed, with C. R. Austin) Reproduction in Mammals, vols 1–8, 1972–80, 2nd edn vols 1–5, 1982–86; (ed, with D. T. Baird) Contraceptives of the Future, 1976; contrib. Jl Endocrinology, Jl Reproduction and Fertility, Jl Zoology, Lancet, Nature. *Recreations:* gardening, wildlife, history of biology. *Address:* Department of Physiology, Monash University, Melbourne, Victoria 3168, Australia.

SHORTIS, Maj.-Gen. Colin Terry, CB 1988; CBE 1980 (OBE 1977; MBE 1974); General Officer Commanding North West District, 1986–89; *b* 18 Jan. 1934; *s* of late Tom Richardson Shortis and Marna Evelyn Shortis (*née* Kenworthy); *m* 1957, Sylvia Mary, *o d* of H. C. A. Jenkinson; two *s* two *d. Educ:* Bedford School. Enlisted Army 1951; 2nd Lieut Royal Fusiliers, 1953; transf. to Dorset Regt, 1955; served Hong Kong, Korea, Suez Canal Zone, Sudan, BAOR, Aden, Singapore and British Guiana, 1953–63; Instructor, Sch. of Infantry, 1964–65; Staff Coll., 1966; Co. Comdr, 1st Devonshire and Dorset, 1967–73; served Malta, NI, Belize, Cyprus, BAOR, CO 1974–77; Directing Staff, Staff Coll., 1977; Comdr, 8 Infantry Brigade, 1978–80; RCDS 1981; Comdr, British Mil. Adv. and Training Team, Zimbabwe, 1982–83; Dir of Infantry, 1983–86. Col Comdt, The Prince of Wales Div., 1983–88; Col, Devonshire and Dorset Regt, 1984–90. *Recreation:* sailing. *Address:* c/o Barclays Bank, 137 Brompton Road, SW3 1QF. *Club:* Army and Navy.

SHORTRIDGE, Jon Deacon; Grade 3, Welsh Office, since 1992; *b* 10 April 1947; *s* of late Eric Creber Deacon Shortridge and Audrey Joan Shortridge (*née* Hunt); *m* 1972, Diana Jean Gordon; one *s* one *d. Educ:* Chichester High Sch.; St Edmund Hall, Oxford (MA); Edinburgh Univ. (MSc). Min. of Housing, then Countryside Commn, subseq. DoE, 1969–75; Shropshire County Planning Dept, 1975–84; Principal, Welsh Office, 1984–88, Pvte Sec. to Sec. of State for Wales, 1987–88; Asst Sec., Welsh Office, 1988–92. *Recreations:* sailing, tennis, walking, rowing, reading. *Address:* Welsh Office, Crown Buildings, Cathays Park, Cardiff CF1 3NQ. *T:* Cardiff (01222) 823060.

SHOTTER, Very Rev. Edward Frank; Dean of Rochester, since 1989; *b* 29 June 1933; *s* of late Frank Edward Shotter and Minnetta Shotter (*née* Gaskill); *m* 1978, Jane Edgcumbe; two *s* one *d. Educ:* Humberstone Foundation School, Clee; Durham Univ. School of Architecture; St David's Coll., Lampeter, Univ. of Wales (BA 1958); St Stephen's House, Oxford. Deacon 1960, priest 1961; Curate of St Peter, Plymouth, 1960–62; Intercollegiate Sec., SCM, London, 1962–66; Director of Studies, London Medical Group, 1966–89; Director, Inst. of Medical Ethics, 1974–89 (Amulree Fellow, 1991–); Chaplain to Univ. of London, 1969–89; Prebendary of St Paul's Cathedral, 1977–89. Leverhulme Sen. Educnl Fellowship, 1976–79. Chairman: Cttee on Welfare of Czechoslovak Med. Students in Britain, 1968–69; Educn Sub-Cttee, Faculty of History and Phil. of Medicine, Apothecaries Soc., 1976–81; Church, Commerce and Industry Project, 1991–; Member: SCM Trust Assoc. Exec., 1965–79; Univ. Chaplains' Cttee, C of E Bd of Educn, 1968–70; Archbishop of Canterbury's Counsellors on Foreign Relations, 1971–82; BCC East/West Relations Adv. Cttee, 1971–81; Liberal Party Foreign Affairs Panel (Chm. East Europe Sub-Cttee), 1974–81; St Christopher's Hospice Educn Cttee, 1982–89; Wking Party on ethics of med. involvement in torture, 1989–91; Chm., IME working party on ethics of prolonging life and assisting death, 1991–. Chm., Medway Enterprise Agency, 1993–; Dir, Firmstart Medway Ltd, 1991–. C of E rep. on Churches Council of Health and Healing, 1975–76. Chm., Governing Body, King's School, Rochester, 1989–; Pres., St Bartholomew's Hosp., Rochester, 1989–. Founder, Jl of Medical Ethics, 1975. FRSocMed 1976. Patriarchal Cross, Romanian Orthodox Church, 1975. *Publications:* (ed) Matters of Life and Death, 1970; (with K. M. Boyd and B. Callaghan, SJ) Life Before Birth, 1986. *Recreations:* hill walking, restoring country houses and their gardens. *Address:* The Deanery, Rochester, Kent ME1 1TG. *T:* Medway (01634) 844023; Northseat of Auchedly, Tarves, Aberdeenshire AB4 0NB. *Club:* Reform.

SHOTTON, Prof. Edward; Professor of Pharmaceutics, University of London, 1956–77, now Emeritus; *b* 15 July 1910; *s* of Ernest Richard and Maud Shotton; *m* 1943, Mary Constance Louise Marchant; one *d. Educ:* Smethwick (Junior) Technical School; Birkbeck College, University of London. Pharmaceutical Chemist (PhC), 1933; BSc (London), 1939; PhD (London), 1955; Hon. ACT (Birmingham), 1961. FRIC 1949. Pharmaceutical research and development work at Burroughs, Wellcome & Co., Dartford, 1939–48. Sen. Lecturer in Pharmaceutics, Univ. of London, 1948–56. Chairman, British Pharmaceutical Conference, 1966. *Publications:* (with K. Ridgway) Physical Pharmaceutics, 1974; research papers, mainly in Jl of Pharmacy and Pharmacology. *Recreations:* gardening, cricket, fly-fishing. *Address:* 2 Raglan House, Kilfillan Gardens, Berkhamsted, Herts HP4 3LU. *T:* Berkhamsted (01442) 866402. *Club:* Athenæum.

SHOTTON, Dr Keith Crawford, CEng, FIEE; CPhys, FInstP; Head of Management and Technology Services Division, Department of Trade and Industry, since 1994; *b* 11 Sept. 1943; *s* of William Crawford Shotton and Mary Margaret Shotton (*née* Smith); *m* 1969, Maria Elizabeth Gonszor; two *d. Educ:* Newcastle upon Tyne Royal Grammar Sch.; Trinity Coll., Cambridge (Schol.; MA, PhD). CPhys, FInstP 1982; CEng, FIEE 1988. Post-doctoral Fellow (laser physics and spectroscopy), NRCC, 1969–71; National Physical Laboratory: mem. team measuring speed of light, 1971–77; Head, Ultrasonics Metrology Unit, 1977–80; Head, Marketing and Inf. Services, 1980–84; DCSO, Supt, Div. of Radiation Sci. and Acoustics, 1984–87; Department of Trade and Industry: Dir, Radio Technology, Radio Communications Div., 1987–90; Hd, IT Div., 1990–92; Hd, Inf. and Manufg Technols Div., 1992–93; Hd, Technol. Progs and Services Div., 1993–94. *Publications:* papers in sci. jls, principally in spectroscopy, laser physics, ultrasonics and instrumentation. *Recreations:* fell walking, sailing, motor cars, food. *Address:* Department of Trade and Industry, 151 Buckingham Palace Road, SW1W 9SS. *T:* 0171–215 1239.

SHOVELTON, Prof. David Scott, FDSRCS; Professor of Conservative Dentistry, University of Birmingham, 1964–89, Professor Emeritus, since 1990; Honorary Consultant in Conservative Dentistry, Central Birmingham Health Authority, since 1989; *b* 12 Sept. 1925; *s* of Leslie Shovelton, LDSRCS, and Marion de Winton (*née* Scott); *m* 1949, Pearl Holland; two *s. Educ:* The Downs Sch., Colwall; King's Sch., Worcester; Univ. of Birmingham (BSc, LDS, BDS). House Surg., Birmingham Dental Hosp., 1951; gen. dental practice, Evesham, Worcs, 1951; Dental Officer, RAF, 1951–53; Birmingham University: Lectr in Operative Dental Surg., 1953–60; Sen. Lectr, 1960–64; Dir, 1974–78, Dep. Dir, 1982–84, Dental Sch.; Consultant Dental Surgeon, Utd Birmingham Hosps, subseq. Central Birmingham HA, 1960–89. Vis. Asst Prof. of Clin. Dentistry, Univ. of Alabama, 1959–60. Hon. Cons. Dental Surg., Birmingham Reg. Hosp. Bd, 1962–74. Pres., British Soc. for Restorative Dentistry, 1970–71 (Vice-Pres., 1968–70 and 1971–72). Consultant, Commn on Dental Practice, Fédn Dentaire Internat., 1972–79; Consultant Adviser in Restorative Dentistry, DHSS, 1983–89. Member: Gen. Dental Council, 1974–89; Birmingham Area Health Authority (Teaching), 1973–79; Cttee of Management, Sch. for Dental Therapists, 1977–80; Jt Cttee for Higher Trng in Dentistry, 1979–84 (Chm., Specialist Adv. Cttee in Restorative Dentistry, 1979–84); Standing Dental Adv. Cttee, 1982–88; Bd, Faculty of Dental Surgery, RCS, 1983–91; Jt Dental Cttee of MRC, Health Depts and SERC, 1984–87; Cttee of Enquiry into unnecessary dental treatment, 1984–85. Ext. Examnr in dental subjects, univs and colls, 1968–94. *Publications:* Inlays, Crowns and Bridges (jtly), 1963, 5th edn 1993 (trans. Portuguese 1991); articles in med. and dental jls, 1957–. *Recreations:* music, learning about wine, gardening, caravanning. *Address:* 86 Broad Oaks Road, Solihull, West Midlands B91 1HZ. *T:* 0121–705 3026. *Club:* Royal Air Force.

SHOVELTON, (Walter) Patrick, CB 1976; CMG 1972; FCIT; Vice-Chairman, Maersk Co., since 1987 (Director, 1985); Adviser, Maersk Air Ltd, since 1995 (Director, 1993–95); *b* 18 Aug. 1919; *s* of late S. T. Shovelton, CBE, and May Catherine (*née* Kelly), cousin of Patrick and Willie Pearse, Irish patriots; *m* 1st, 1942, Marjorie Lucy Joan Manners (marr. diss. 1967); one *d*; 2nd, Helena Richards, 3rd *d* of D. G. Richards, *qv. Educ:* Charterhouse; Keble Coll., Oxford (scholar of both). Rep. Oxford Univ. at Eton Fives. Served in RA and RHA, 1940–46; DAAG, War Office, 1945–46. Entered Administrative Civil Service as Asst Principal, Min. of War Transport, 1946; Principal 1947; Admin. Staff College, 1951; Private Sec. to Secretary of State for Co-ordination of Transport, Fuel and Power, 1951–53; Asst Sec., Road Transport, 1957; transferred to Min. of Aviation, 1959; IDC, 1962; Under Secretary, 1966; transferred to Min. of Technology, 1966, and to DTI, 1970; Mem., UK Negotiating Team for entry into EEC, 1970–72; Deputy Secretary: DTI, 1972–74; Dept of Prices and Consumer Protection, 1974–76; Dept of Trade, 1976–78; Dir-Gen., Gen. Council of British Shipping, 1978–85; Dir, British Airports Authy, 1982–85. Chm., Birmingham Executive, later European, Airways, 1988–93. Led UK Negotiating Team for Bermuda 2, 1977. William and Mary Tercentenary Trust: Chairman: Maritime Cttee, 1985–89; Finance and Sponsorship Cttee, 1988–89. Council, CIT, 1982–85; Advr, Inquiries into EEC Maritime Transport Policy H of L, 1985–86, into Merchant Shipping, H of C, 1986–88. Brancker Lectr (civil aviation), 1979; Grout Lectr (shipping), 1985. Founder and Chm., Friends of Tunbridge Wells and Rusthall Commons, 1991–. Officer, Order of Orange-Nassau (Netherlands), 1989. *Recreations:* competitive golf, reading, opera. *Address:* 63 London Road, Tunbridge Wells, Kent TN1 1DT. *T:* Tunbridge Wells (01892) 527885. *Clubs:* Brooks's; Jesters; Royal Ashdown Forest Golf, Rye Golf, Hampstead Golf, Seniors Golf.

SHOWALTER, Prof. Elaine, PhD; Professor of English and Avalon Foundation Professor of Humanities, Princeton University, since 1984; *b* 21 Jan. 1941; *d* of Paul Cottler and Violet Rottenberg; *m* 1963, English Showalter; one *s* one *d. Educ:* Bryn Mawr Coll. (BA 1962); Univ. of California, Davis (PhD 1970). Departments of English: Douglass Coll., 1966–78; Rutgers Univ., 1966–84. *Publications:* A Literature of Their Own, 1977; The Female Malady, 1985; Sexual Anarchy, 1990; Sister's Choice: tradition and change in American women's writing, 1991. *Address:* 119 Snowden Lane, Princeton, NJ 08540, USA. *T:* (609) 9240832. *Club:* Princeton (NY).

SHRAPNEL, Norman; Parliamentary Correspondent of the Guardian, 1958–75; *b* 5 Oct. 1912; *yr s* of Arthur Edward Scrope Shrapnel and Rosa Brosy; *m* 1940, Mary Lilian Myfanwy Edwards; two *s. Educ:* King's School, Grantham. Various weekly, evening and morning newspapers from 1930; Manchester Guardian (later the Guardian) from 1947, as reporter, theatre critic and reviewer; contributor to various journals. Political Writer of the Year Award (the Political Companion), 1969. *Publications:* A View of the Thames, 1977; The Performers: politics as theatre, 1978; The Seventies, 1980. *Recreations:* walking, music. *Address:* 27A Shooters Hill Road, Blackheath, SE3 7AS. *T:* 0181–858 7123.

SHREEVE, Ven. David Herbert; Archdeacon of Bradford, since 1984; *b* 18 Jan. 1934; *s* of Hubert Ernest and Ivy Eleanor Shreeve; *m* 1957, Barbara (*née* Fogden); one *s* one *d. Educ:* Southfield School, Oxford; St Peter's Coll., Oxford (MA); Ridley Hall, Cambridge. Asst Curate, St Andrew's Church, Plymouth, 1959–64; Vicar: St Anne's, Bermondsey, 1964–71; St Luke's, Eccleshill, 1971–84; RD of Calverley, 1978–84. Mem., Gen. Synod and Proctor in Convocation, 1977–90, 1993–; Mem., Dioceses Commn, 1988–. Hon. Canon of Bradford Cathedral, 1983–84. *Recreations:* walking, camping, jogging, photography. *Address:* Rowan House, 11 The Rowans, Baildon, Shipley, W Yorks BD17 5DB. *T:* Bradford (01274) 583735.

SHRESTHA, Surya Prasad; Ambassador of Nepal to the Court of St James's, since 1992; *b* 1 March 1937; *s* of late L. P. Shrestha and Mrs G. K. Shrestha; *m* 1958, Ginni Baba Shrestha; two *s* two *d. Educ:* Tribhuvan Univ. (MA Pol Sci.); LSE (Dip. Econs and Social Admin). Joined HM Govt service, Nepal, 1958; Section Officer, Parlt Secretariat and Min. of Develt, 1958–63; Under Secretary: Min. of Home and Panchayat, 1963–65; Election Commn, 1965–66; Jt Zonal Comr, 1970–74, Zonal Comr, 1974–78, Bagmati Zone; Actg Sec., Home and Panchayat Min., 1978–79; Sec. of Industry and Commerce, 1979–83; Jt Mem., Nat. Planning Commn, 1983–85; Chief Election Comr, 1985–92. Prabal Gorkha Dakshin Bahu, III Cl. (Nepal), 1966, Prasiddha, II Cl., 1976; Trishakti Patta, Vikhyat, III Cl. (Nepal), 1973, Suvikhyat, II Cl., 1991. *Recreations:* reading, gardening. *Address:* Royal Nepalese Embassy, 12A Kensington Palace Gardens, W8 4QU. *T:* 0171–229 1594.

SHREWSBURY, Bishop Suffragan of, since 1994; **Rt. Rev. David Marrison Hallatt;** *b* 15 July 1937; *s* of John Vincent Hallatt and Edith Elliott Hallatt; *m* 1967, Margaret Smitton; two *s. Educ:* Birkenhead School; Southampton Univ. (BA Hons Geography 1959); St Catherine's Coll., Oxford (BA Theology 1962; MA 1966). Curate, St Andrew's, Maghull, Liverpool, 1963–67; Vicar, All Saints, Totley, dio. Sheffield, 1967–75; Team

Rector, St James & Emmanuel, Didsbury, Manchester, 1975–89; Archdeacon of Halifax, 1989–94. *Recreations:* walking, birdwatching, music, crosswords. *Address:* Athlone House, 68 London Road, Shrewsbury SY2 6PG. *T:* Shrewsbury (01743) 235867, *Fax:* (01743) 243296.

SHREWSBURY, Bishop of, (RC), since 1980; **Rt. Rev. Joseph Gray,** DCL; *b* 20 Oct. 1919; *s* of Terence Gray and Mary Gray (*née* Alwill). *Educ:* Patrick's Coll., Cavan, Eire; St Mary's Seminary, Oscott, Birmingham; Dunboyne House, St Patrick's Coll., Maynooth, Eire; Pontifical Univ. of St Thomas Aquinas, Rome. Priest, 1943; Asst Priest, Sacred Heart, Aston, Birmingham, 1943–48; Dunboyne House, 1948–50 (Licentiate in Canon Law, 1950); Sec. to Archbp of Birmingham, 1950–55. Diocesan Chancellor, Birmingham, 1951–69; Pontifical Univ., 1959–60 (Doctorate in Canon Law, 1960); Vicar-Gen., Birmingham, 1960–69; Parish Priest, St Michael's, Birmingham, 1955–69. Papal Chamberlain, 1960; Domestic Prelate, 1966. Episcopal Ordination, Cathedral of Christ the King, Liverpool, Feb. 1969; Titular Bishop of Mercia and Auxiliary Bishop of Liverpool, 1969–80. Pres., Liturgy Commn of Bishops' Conf. of England and Wales, 1976–84; Chm., Commn for Religious Life, 1984–. *Recreations:* music, reading, travel. *Address:* Bishop's House, Eleanor Road, Birkenhead L43 7QW. *T:* 0151–653 3600.

SHREWSBURY AND WATERFORD, 22nd Earl of, *cr* 1442 and 1446; **Charles Henry John Benedict Crofton Chetwynd Chetwynd-Talbot;** DL; Baron Talbot, 1733; 7th Earl Talbot, Viscount Ingestre, 1784; Premier Earl on the Rolls of England and Ireland, Hereditary Great Seneschal or Lord High Steward of Ireland; Lord of Dungarvan; director and consultant; *b* 18 Dec. 1952; *s* of 21st Earl of Shrewsbury and Waterford, and of Nadine, *yr d* of late Brig.-Gen. C. R. Crofton, CBE; *S* father, 1980; *m* 1974, Deborah, *o d* of Noel Hutchinson; two *s* one *d. Educ:* Harrow. Director: Britannia Building Soc., 1984–92 (Dep. Chm., 1987–89; Jt Dep. Chm., 1989–92); Richmount Enterprise Zone Managers, 1988–94. Member, Executive Committee: Staffs Assoc. of Boys Clubs, 1981–; Staffs Br., Game Conservancy Trust, 1988–. Pres., Staffordshire Soc., 1989–91; Vice-Pres., Midland & West Assoc. of Building Socs, 1984–92; Pres., BSA, 1993–. Chm., Firearms Consultative Cttee, 1994–. Chancellor, Univ. of Wolverhampton, 1993–. Patron: St Giles Hospice, Lichfield, 1988–; Staffs Br., BRCS, 1989–92. Hon. President: Shropshire Bldg Preservation Trust, 1984–; Lord Roberts Wkshops and SSAFA (Wolverhampton Br.), 1987–; Staffs Small Bore Rifle Assoc., 1988–; Hon. Vice-Pres., Rugeley Rugby FC. Hon. Pres., Shropshire Hospice, 1983–88. Patron of 11 livings. DL Stafford, 1994. Hon. LLD Wolverhampton, 1994. *Recreations:* racing, shooting, fishing. *Heir: s* Viscount Ingestre, *qv. Address:* Wanfield Hall, Kingstone, Uttoxeter, Staffs ST14 8QT.

SHRIMPLIN, John Steven; consultant, since 1994; UK Representative, European Space Policy Committee, since 1994; *b* 9 May 1934; *s* of late John Reginald Shrimplin and of Kathleen Mary (*née* Stevens); *m* 1957, Hazel Baughen; two *s. Educ:* Royal Grammar Sch., Colchester; King's Coll., London (BSc Maths). Joined RAE, Farnborough, 1956; Defence Operational Analysis Estabt, 1966; JSSC, 1970; Weapons Dept, RAE, 1971; Defence R&D Staff, British Embassy, Washington, 1972; Asst Dir, Future Systems, Air Systems Controllerate, MoD PE, 1974; Asst Chief Scientist, RAF, 1978; Head of Weapons Dept, RAE, 1983; Dep. Hd, British Defence Staff, and Minister/Counsellor, Defence Equipment, British Embassy, Washington, DC, 1985–88; Dir, Defence Science (Studies), MoD, 1988–91; Dep. Dir Gen. and Dir, Space Technol., BNSC, 1991–94. FRAeS 1993. *Recreations:* travel, camping, walking. *Address:* c/o National Westminster Bank, 2 Alexandra Road, Farnborough, Hants GU14 6BZ.

SHRIMSLEY, Bernard; journalist; Associate Editor, Daily Express, since 1986; *b* 13 Jan. 1931; *er s* of John and Alice Shrimsley, London; *m* 1952, Norma Jessie Alexandra, *d* of Albert and Maude Porter, Southport; one *d. Educ:* Kilburn Grammar School, Northampton. Press Association, 1947; Southport Guardian, 1948; RAF, 1949–51; Daily Mirror, 1953; Sunday Express, 1958; Northern Editor, Daily Mirror, 1963; Editor, Daily Post, Liverpool, 1968–69; Editor, The Sun, 1972–75; Editor, News of the World, and Dir, News Group Newspapers Ltd, 1975–80; Editor designate (subseq. Editor), The Mail on Sunday, and Dir (subseq. Vice-Chm.), The Mail on Sunday Ltd, 1980–82; Asst Editor, Daily Express, 1983–86. Mem., Press Council, 1989–90 (Jt Vice-Chm., 1990); Mem., Defence, Press and Broadcasting Cttee, 1989–93. Mem. judging panel, British Press Awards, 1988–95. *Publications:* The Candidates, 1968; Lion Rampant, 1984 (US Book of the Month Choice). *Address:* Daily Express, Ludgate House, 245 Blackfriars Road, SE1 9UX. *T:* 0171–928 8000. *Club:* Garrick.

SHRIVER, (Robert) Sargent; Partner, 1971–86, Lawyer Of Counsel, Fried, Frank, Harris, Shriver & Jacobson, since 1986; Chairman, Special Olympics International, since 1990 (President, 1984–90); *b* Westminster, Md, 9 Nov. 1915; *s* of Robert Sargent and Hilda Shriver; *m* 1953, Eunice Mary Kennedy; four *s* one *d. Educ:* parochial schools, Baltimore; Canterbury School, New Milford, Conn.; Yale College; Yale University. BA (*cum laude*) 1938; LLB 1941; LLD 1964. Apprentice Seaman, USNR, 1940; Ensign, 1941. Served War of 1941–45: Atlantic and Pacific Ocean Areas aboard battleships and submarines; Lt-Comdr, USNR. Admitted to: New York Bar, 1941; Illinois Bar, (retd) 1959; US Supreme Court, 1966; District of Columbia Bar, 1971. With legal firm of Winthrop, Stimson, Putnam & Roberts, NYC, 1940–41; Asst Editor, Newsweek, 1945–46; associated with Joseph P. Kennedy Enterprises, 1946–48; Asst Gen. Man., Merchandise Mart, 1948–61; President: Chicago Bd of Educn, 1955–60; Catholic Interracial Council of Chicago, 1954–59; Dir, Peace Corps, Washington, 1961–66; Dir, Office of Economic Opportunity and Special Asst to Pres. Johnson, 1964–68; US Ambassador to France, 1968–70. Vice-Presidential candidate (Democrat), Nov. 1972. Democrat; Roman Catholic. *Address:* Suite 500, 1350 New York Avenue NW, Washington, DC 20005, USA.

SHRUBSOLE, Alison Cheveley, CBE 1982; Principal, Homerton College, Cambridge, 1971–85; Fellow of Hughes Hall, Cambridge, 1974; *b* 7 April 1925; *d* of Rev. Stanley and Mrs Margaret Shrubsole. *Educ:* Milton Mount Coll.; Royal Holloway Coll.; Inst. of Education. BA Hons London; MA Cantab; Postgraduate Cert. in Educn. FCP. Teaching in schools in South London, 1946–50; Lectr and Sen. Lectr, Stockwell Coll., 1950–57; Principal: Machakos Training Coll., Kenya, 1957–62; Philippa Fawcett Coll., London SW16, 1963–71. DUniv. Open, 1985. *Recreations:* music, architecture, travel, mountaineering, gardening, cooking. *Address:* 4 Chancellor House, Mount Ephraim, Tunbridge Wells, Kent TN4 8BT; Cortijo Abulagar, Rubite, Granada, Spain.

SHUCKBURGH, Sir Rupert (Charles Gerald), 13th Bt *cr* 1660, of Shuckburgh, Warwickshire; *b* 12 Feb. 1949; *s* of Sir Charles Gerald Stewkley Shuckburgh, 12th Bt, TD and Nancy Diana Mary, OBE (*d* 1984), *o d* of late Captain Rupert Lubbock, RN; *S* father, 1988; *m* 1st, 1976, Judith (marr. diss. 1987), *d* of W. G. Mackaness; two *s*; 2nd, 1987, Margaret Ida, *d* of late W. Evans. *Heir: s* James Rupert Charles Shuckburgh, *b* 4 Jan. 1978. *Address:* Shuckburgh Hall, Daventry, Northants NN11 6DT. *Club:* Farmers'.

SHUFFREY, Ralph Frederick Dendy, CB 1983; CVO 1981; Deputy Under-Secretary of State and Principal Establishment Officer, Home Office, 1980–84; *b* 9 Dec. 1925; *s* of late Frederick Arthur Shuffrey, MC and Mary Shuffrey (*née* Dendy) *m* 1953, Sheila, *d* of late Brig. John Lingham, CB, DSO, MC, and Juliet Judd; one *s* one *d. Educ:* Shrewsbury; Balliol Coll., Oxford. Served Army, 1944–47 (Captain). Entered Home Office, 1951; Private Sec. to Parly Under-Sec. of State, 1956–57; Private Sec. to Home Sec., 1965–66; Asst Sec., 1966–72; Asst Under-Sec. of State, 1972–80. Chairman: The Cranstoun Projects Ltd, 1988–; Fire Service Res. and Trng Trust, 1989–. Hon. Sec., Soc. for Individual Freedom, 1985–89. *Address:* Flat D, Campden House, 29 Sheffield Terrace, W8 7ND. *Club:* Reform.

SHULL, Prof. Clifford Glenwood, PhD; Professor of Physics, Massachusetts Institute of Technology, 1955–86, now Emeritus Professor; *b* 23 Sept 1915; *s* of David H. and Daisy B. Shull; *m* 1941, Martha-Nuel Summer; three *s. Educ:* Carnegie Inst. of Technology (BS 1937); New York Univ. (PhD 1941). Research Physicist: The Texas Co., 1941–46; Oak Ridge Nat. Lab., 1946–55. Buckley Prize, Amer. Phys. Soc., 1956; Humboldt Sen. US Scientist Award, 1980; Aminoff Prize, Royal Swedish Acad. of Scis, 1993; (jtly) Nobel Prize for Physics, 1994. *Publications:* numerous scientific articles. *Address:* 4 Wingate Road, Lexington, MA 02173, USA. *T:* (617) 8628627.

SHULMAN, Alexandra; Editor, British Vogue, since 1992; *b* 13 Nov. 1957; *d* of Milton Shulman, *qv* and Drusilla Beyfus, *qv*; *m* 1994, Paul, *s* of late Rev. Dr Robert W. Spike, NY; one *s. Educ:* St Paul's Girls' Sch.; Sussex Univ. (BA Social Anthropology). Tatler: Commissioning Editor, 1982–84; Features Editor, 1984–87; Sunday Telegraph: Editor, Women's Page, 1987; Dep. Editor, 7 Days Mag., 1987–88; Features Editor, Vogue, 1988–90; Editor, GQ, 1990–92. *Address:* Condé Nast Publications, Vogue House, Hanover Square, W1R 0AD. *T:* 0171–499 9080.

SHULMAN, Drusilla Norman; *see* Beyfus, Drusilla N.

SHULMAN, Milton; writer, journalist, critic; *b* Toronto; *s* of late Samuel Shulman, merchant, and of Ethel Shulman; *m* 1956, Drusilla Beyfus, *qv*; one *s* two *d. Educ:* Univ. of Toronto (BA); Osgoode Hall, Toronto. Barrister, Toronto, 1937–40. Armoured Corps and Intelligence, Canadian Army, 1940–46 (despatches, Normandy, 1945); Major. Film critic, Evening Standard and Sunday Express, 1948–58; book critic, Sunday Express, 1957–58; theatre critic, Evening Standard, 1953–91; TV critic, Evening Standard, 1964–73; columnist, social and political affairs, Daily Express, 1973–75; film critic, Vogue Magazine, 1975–87; columnist, art affairs, Evening Standard, 1991–. Executive producer and producer, Granada TV, 1958–62; Asst Controller of Programmes, Rediffusion TV, 1962–64. Mem., Adv. Council, British Theatre Museum, 1981–83. Regular panel mem., Stop the Week, BBC Radio 4. IPC Award, Critic of the Year, 1966. *Publications:* Defeat in the West, 1948; How To Be a Celebrity, 1950; The Ravenous Eye, 1973; The Least Worst Television in the World, 1973; *children's books:* Preep, 1964; Preep in Paris, 1967; Preep and The Queen, 1970; *novel:* Kill Three, 1967; *novel and film story:* (with Herbert Kretzmer) Every Home Should Have One, 1970. *Recreations:* modern art, history, tennis. *Address:* 51 Eaton Square, SW1W 9BE. *T:* 0171–235 7162. *Clubs:* Garrick, Hurlingham.

See also Marquis of Normanby, A. Shulman.

SHULTZ, George Pratt; Secretary of State, United States of America, 1982–89; Distinguished Fellow, Hoover Institution, since 1989; *b* New York City, 13 Dec. 1920; *s* of Birl E. Shultz and Margaret Pratt; *m* 1946, Helena Maria O'Brien; two *s* three *d. Educ:* Princeton Univ., 1942 (BA Econ); Massachusetts Inst. of Technology, 1949 (PhD Industrial Econ). Served War, US Marine Corps, Pacific, 1942; Major, 1945. Faculty, MIT, 1949–57; Sen. staff economist, President's Council of Economic Advisers, 1955–56 (on leave, MIT); Univ. of Chicago, Graduate Sch. of Business: Prof. of Industrial Relations, 1957–68; Dean, 1962–69; Prof. of Management and Public Policy, Stanford Univ., Graduate Sch. of Business, 1974. Secretary of Labor, 1969–July 1, 1970; Dir, Office of Management and Budget, 1970–72; Secretary of the Treasury, 1972–74; Exec. Vice-Pres., Bechtel Corp., 1974–75, Pres. 1975–77; Vice-Chm., Bechtel Corp., 1977–81 (Dir); Pres., Bechtel Group Inc., San Francisco, 1981–82. Chairman: President's Economic Policy Adv. Bd, 1981–82; Internat. Council, J. P. Morgan, 1989–; Adv. Council, Inst. of Internat. Studies, 1989–. Director: General Motors Corp., 1981–82, 1989–91; Boeing Corp., 1989–93; Bechtel Gp Inc., 1989–; Tandem Computers Inc., 1989–92; Chevron Corp., 1989–93; Gulfstream Aerospace Corp., 1992–; AirTouch Communications, 1994–; Mem., GM Corporate Adv. Council. Chm., State of California Gov's Econ. Policy Adv. Bd. Hon. Dr of Laws: Notre Dame Univ., 1969; Loyola Univ., 1972; Pennsylvania, 1973; Rochester, 1973; Princeton, 1973; Carnegie-Mellon Univ., 1975. *Publications:* Pressures on Wage Decisions, 1951; The Dynamics of a Labor Market (with C. A. Myers), 1951; Labor Problems: cases and readings (with J. R. Coleman), 1953; Management Organization and the Computer (with T. L. Whisler), 1960; Strategies for the Displaced Worker (with Arnold R. Weber), 1966; Guidelines, Informal Controls, and the Market Place (with Rober Z. Aliber), 1966; Workers and Wages in the Urban Labor Market (with Albert Rees), 1970; Leaders and Followers in an Age of Ambiguity, 1975; Economic Policy Beyond the Headlines (with Kenneth W. Dam), 1977; Turmoil and Triumph: my years as Secretary of State, 1993. *Recreations:* golf, tennis. *Address:* Hoover Institution, Stanford University, Stanford, CA 94305–6010, USA.

SHURMAN, Laurence Paul Lyons; Banking Ombudsman, since 1989; *b* 25 Nov. 1930; *s* of Joseph and Sarah Shurman; *m* 1963, Mary Seamans (*née* McMullan); two *s* one *d. Educ:* Newcastle upon Tyne Royal Grammar Sch.; Magdalen Coll., Oxford (MA). Solicitor. Articles, John H. Sinton & Co., Newcastle, 1954–57; Assistant Solicitor: Haswell Croft, Newcastle, 1957–58; Hall Brydon, London, 1958–60; Kaufman & Siegal, London, 1960–61; Partner: Shurman & Bindman, Solicitors, London, 1961–64; Shurman & Co., London, 1964–67; Kingsley Napley, London, 1967–89 (Managing Partner, 1975–89). Legal Mem., Mental Health Review Tribunal, 1976–94; Mem. Council, Justice, 1973–. Lectures: Gilbart, 1990; Ernest Sykes Meml, 1991. Pres., City of Westminster Law Soc., 1980–81; Chm., British and Irish Ombudsman Assoc., 1993–. Governor: Channing Sch., 1985– (Vice-Chm., 1988–); Newcastle upon Tyne Royal Grammar Sch., 1991–. *Publications:* The Practical Skills of the Solicitor, 1981, 2nd edn 1985; contributor on Mental Health Tribunals in Vol. 26 of Atkin's Encyc. of Court Forms, 2nd edn 1985. *Recreations:* reading, fell walking, swimming, jogging, law reform. *Address:* Office of the Banking Ombudsman, 70 Gray's Inn Road, WC1X 8NB. *T:* 0171–404 9944. *Club:* Leander (Henley).

SHUTE, Prof. Charles Cameron Donald, MD; Professor of Histology, Cambridge University, 1969–84, now Emeritus; Life Fellow of Christ's College, Cambridge, 1957; *b* 23 May 1917; *s* of late Cameron Deane Shute; *m* 1st, 1947, Patricia Cameron (*d* 1952), *d* of F. H. Doran; 2nd, 1954, Lydia May (Wendy) (*née* Harwood) (marr diss. 1980); one *s* three *d*; 3rd, 1980, Rosemary Gay Robins. *Educ:* Eton; King's Coll., Cambridge; Middlesex Hosp., London. MA, MB, BChir Cambridge, 1945; MD Cambridge 1958. Resident posts at Middlesex Hosp., 1945–47; RAMC (otologist), 1947–49; Demonstrator and Lectr in Anatomy, London Hosp. Med. Coll., 1951; Univ. Demonstrator and Lectr, Cambridge, 1952–69; Univ. Reader in Neuroanatomy, Cambridge, 1969. *Publications:* The McCollough Effect, 1979; (with R. G. Robins) The Rhind Mathematical Papyrus, 1987; papers in biological and Egyptological jls. *Recreation:* Egyptology. *Address:* 400 Princeton Way NE, Atlanta, GA 30307, USA. *T:* (404) 6339452.

SHUTLER, (Ronald) Rex (Barry), CB 1992; FRICS; FAAV; Vice President, Leasehold Valuation Tribunal and Rent Assessment Panel, since 1994; *b* 27 June 1933; *s* of Ronald Edgar Coggin Shutler and Helena Emily Shutler (*née* Lawes); *m* 1958, Patricia Elizabeth Longman; two *s*. *Educ:* Hardye's, Dorchester. Articled pupil and assistant, chartered surveyors, Dorchester, 1952–59; joined Valuation Office (Inland Revenue), 1959; District Valuer, Hereford and Worcester, 1970; Superintending Valuer, Wales, 1976; Dep. Chief Valuer, 1984–88; Chief Valuer, then Chief Exec., Valuation Office Agency, 1988–94. FRICS 1972; FAAV 1962; Hon. FSVA. *Recreations:* golf, country pursuits, gardening. *Address:* Newlands House, 37–40 Berners Street, W1P 4BP. *T:* 0171–580 2000. *Clubs:* Hereford Golf, Chartridge Park Golf.

SHUTTLE, Penelope (Diane); writer and poet; *b* 12 May 1947; *d* of Jack Frederick Shuttle and Joan Shepherdess Lipscombe; *m* Peter Redgrove, *qv*; one *d*. *Educ:* Staines Grammar Sch.; Matthew Arnold County Secondary Sch., Mddx. Radio plays: The Girl who Lost her Glove, 1975 (Jt 3rd Prize Winner, Radio Times Drama Bursaries Comp., 1974); The Dauntless Girl, 1978. Poetry recorded for Poetry Room, Harvard Univ. Arts Council Awards, 1969, 1972 and 1985; Greenwood Poetry Prize, 1972; E. C. Gregory Award for Poetry, 1974. *Publications: novels:* An Excusable Vengeance, 1967; All the Usual Hours of Sleeping, 1969; Wailing Monkey Embracing a Tree, 1974; Rainsplitter in the Zodiac Garden, 1976; Mirror of the Giant, 1979; *poetry:* Nostalgia Neurosis, 1968; Midwinter Mandala, 1973; Photographs of Persephone, 1973; Autumn Piano, 1973; Songbook of the Snow, 1973; Webs on Fire, 1977; The Orchard Upstairs, 1981; The Child-Stealer, 1983; The Lion from Rio, 1986; Adventures with my Horse, 1988; Taxing the Rain, 1992; *with Peter Redgrove:* The Hermaphrodite Album (poems), 1973; The Terrors of Dr Treviles (novel), 1974; The Wise Wound (psychology), 1978, rev. edn 1986; Alchemy for Women, 1995. *Recreations:* listening to music, Hatha Yoga, walking, reading, feline contemplation. *Address:* c/o David Higham Associates Ltd, 5–8 Lower John Street, Golden Square, W1R 4HA.

SHUTTLEWORTH, 5th Baron *cr* 1902, of Gawthorpe; **Charles Geoffrey Nicholas Kay-Shuttleworth;** Bt 1850; DL; Chairman, National & Provincial Building Society, since 1994 (Director, since 1983; Deputy Chairman, 1983–94); Chairman, Rural Development Commission, since 1990; *b* 2 Aug. 1948; *s* of 4th Baron Shuttleworth, MC, and Anne Elizabeth (*d* 1991), *er d* of late Col Geoffrey Phillips, CBE, DSO; *S* father, 1975; *m* 1975, Mrs Ann Mary Barclay, *d* of James Whatman, MC; three *s*. *Educ:* Eton. Partner, Burton, Barnes & Vigers, Chartered Surveyors, 1977–; Director: Burnley Bldg Soc., 1978–82 (Vice-Chm., 1982); Rank Foundn, 1993–. Chairman: Lancs Small Industries Cttee, COSIRA, 1978–83; Lancs Youth Clubs Assoc., 1980–86, Pres., 1986–; Member: Skelmersdale Develt Corp., 1982–85; NW Regional Cttee, National Trust, 1980–89 (Vice Chm., 1983–89); Council, CBI, 1993–. President: Royal Lancashire Agricl Soc., 1985–86; Assoc. of Lancastrians in London, 1986–87. Mem. Council, Lancaster Univ., 1990–93; Governor, Giggleswick Sch., 1981– (Chm., 1984–). FRICS. DL Lancs, 1986. *Heir: s* Hon. Thomas Edward Kay-Shuttleworth, *b* 29 Sept. 1976. *Address:* 14 Sloane Avenue, SW3 3JE; Leck Hall, Carnforth, Lancs LA6 2JF. *Clubs:* Brooks's, MCC.

SIAGURU, Sir Anthony (Michael), KBE 1990; Partner, Blake Dawson Waldron, 1987–90 and since 1995; *b* 4 Nov. 1946; *s* of Khaisir Petrus Siaguru and Kandambi Maria Krakemoine; *m* 1972, Wilhelmina Isikini; three *s*. *Educ:* Univ. of Papua New Guinea (Law); Harvard Univ. (Public Admin). Entered Foreign Service as Cadet Diplomat, 1972; apptd Permanent Sec., Foreign Affairs and Trade on PNG's Independence, 1975; MP, 1982; Minister for: Public Service, 1982–84; Youth and Develt, 1985; Dep. Sec.-Gen. (Pol) of the Commonwealth, 1990–95. Fulbright Scholar, 1980. *Publications:* (contrib.) Ethics in Government, 1983; (contrib.) The Red Orchestra, 1987. *Recreations:* gardening, tennis, fishing. *Address:* PO Box 5917, Boroko, NCD, Papua New Guinea. *Clubs:* Reform; Papua (Port Moresby, PNG).

SIBBETT, Prof. Wilson, PhD; FInstP; FRSE; Professor of Natural Philosophy, since 1985 and Director of Research, School of Physics and Astronomy, since 1994, University of St Andrews; *b* 15 March 1948; *s* of John Sibbett and Margaret (*née* McLeister); *m* 1979, Barbara Anne Brown; three *d*. *Educ:* Ballymena Tech. Coll.; Queen's Univ., Belfast (BSc 1st Cl. Hons Physics); Imperial Coll., London (PhD Laser Physics 1973). FInstP 1986. Blackett Laboratory, Imperial College, London: Postdoctoral Res. Asst, 1973–77; Lectr in Physics, 1977–84; Reader, 1984–85; University of St Andrews: Head, Physics Dept, 1985–88; Chm., Physics and Astronomy Dept, 1988–94. FRSE 1988. Hubert Schardin Gold Medal for Res. in Ultrafast Lasers and Diagnostics, 1978; C. V. Boys Prize and Medal for Exptl Physics, Inst. of Physics, 1993. *Publications:* numerous on laser physics and related diagnostic techniques in internat. scientific jls. *Recreations:* golf, gardening, DIY. *Address:* School of Physics and Astronomy, University of St Andrews, North Haugh, St Andrews, Fife KY16 9SS. *T:* St Andrews (01334) 463100.

SIBERRY, John William Morgan; Under-Secretary, Welsh Office, 1964–73, retired; Secretary to Local Government Staff Commission for Wales, and NHS Staff Commission for Wales, 1973–75; *b* 26 Feb. 1913; *s* of late John William and Martha (*née* Morgan) Siberry; *m* 1949, Florence Jane Davies (*d* 1995); one *s* one *d*. *Educ:* Porth County School, Rhondda; Univ. Coll. Cardiff. Entered Civil Service as Asst Principal, Unemployment Assistance Board (later Nat. Assistance Board), 1935; Principal, 1941; Asst Sec., 1947; transferred to Min. of Housing and Local Govt as Under-Sec., 1963; Welsh Secretary, Welsh Office and Office for Wales of the Ministry of Housing and Local Government, 1963–64. Chm., Working Party on Fourth Television Service in Wales, 1975. *Recreation:* golf. *Address:* Northgates, 59 Pwllmelin Road, Llandaff, Cardiff CF5 2NG. *T:* Cardiff (01222) 564666. *Club:* Cardiff and County.
See also W. R. Siberry.

SIBERRY, William Richard; QC 1989; *b* 11 Dec. 1950; *s* of John William Morgan Siberry, *qv*; *m* 1976, Julia Christine Lancaster. *Educ:* King's Coll., Taunton; Pembroke Coll., Cambridge (MA, LLB). Fellow, Pembroke Coll., Cambridge, 1973–75. Called to the Bar, Middle Temple, 1974. *Recreations:* music, gardening, walking, photography, North West Highlands of Scotland. *Address:* Essex Court Chambers, 24 Lincoln's Inn Fields, WC2A 3ED. *T:* 0171–813 8000.

SIBLEY, Antoinette, CBE 1973; Prima Ballerina, The Royal Ballet, Covent Garden; President, Royal Academy of Dancing, since 1991 (Vice-President, 1989–91); *b* 27 Feb. 1939; *d* of Edward G. Sibley and Winifred M. Sibley (*née* Smith); *m* 1964, M. G. Somes, CBE (marr. diss. 1973; he *d* 1994); *m* 1974, Panton Corbett; one *s* one *d*. *Educ:* Arts Educational Sch. and Royal Ballet Sch. 1st performance on stage as Student with Royal Ballet at Covent Garden, a swan, Jan. 1956; joined company, July 1956; has appeared with the company or as guest artist in most opera houses worldwide. Leading role in: Swan Lake, Sleeping Beauty, Giselle, Coppelia, Cinderella, The Nutcracker, La Fille Mal Gardée, Romeo and Juliet, Harlequin in April, Les Rendezvous, Jabez and the Devil (created the role of Mary), La Fête Etrange, The Rakes Progress, Hamlet, Ballet Imperial, Two Pigeons, La Bayadère, Symphonic Variations, Scènes de Ballet, Lilac Garden, Daphnis and Chloe, Pas de Quatre (Dolin's), Konservatoriett, A Month in the Country, The Dream (created Titania), Laurentia, Good Humoured Ladies, Aristocrat in Mam'zelle Angot, Façade, Song of the Earth, Monotones (created role), Jazz Calendar (created Friday's Child), Enigma Variations (created Dorabella), Thais (created pas de deux), Anastasia (created Kshessinska), Afternoon of a Faun, Triad (created the Girl), Pavanne, Manon (created title role), Soupirs (created pas de deux), L'invitation au voyage (created), Impromptu (created pas de deux), Varii Capricci (created La Capricciosa), Fleeting Figures. *Film:* The Turning Point, 1978. *Relevant publications:* Classical Ballet—the Flow of Movement, by Tamara Karsavina, 1962; Sibley and Dowell, by Nicholas Dromgoole and Leslie Spatt, 1976; Antoinette Sibley, 1981, photographs with text by Mary Clarke; Reflections of a Ballerina, by Barbara Newman, 1986. *Recreations:* doing nothing; opera and books. *Address:* c/o Royal Academy of Dancing, 36 Battersea Square, SW11 3LT.

SIBSON, Prof. Robin, PhD; Vice-Chancellor, University of Kent at Canterbury, since 1994; *b* 4 May 1944; *o s* of late Robert Sibson and Florence Elizabeth Sibson (*née* Worth); *m* 1975, Heather Gail Gulliver; two *s*. *Educ:* Sutton County Grammar Sch.; King's Coll., Cambridge (Schol., Sen. Schol., Prizeman; Wrangler, Maths Tripos Pt II, 1965; Dist. Maths Tripos Part III, 1966; BA 1966; A. M. P. Read Schol., 1966; Smith's Prize, 1968; MA, PhD 1970). CStat 1993. Fellow, King's Coll., 1968–76, Lectr in Math. Stats, 1971–76, Univ. of Cambridge; University of Bath: Prof. of Stats, 1976–94; Head, Sch. of maths, 1979–82; Sci. Area Chm., 1984–87; Pro-Vice-Chancellor, 1989–94. Member: Stats Cttee, 1980–92, Res. Resources and Methods Cttee, 1982–85, SSRC, then ESRC; Stats Panel, 1980–85 (Chm., 1983–85), Maths Cttee, 1982–85, Science-based Archaeol. Cttee, 1982–85, Science Bd, 1986–89, SERC; Commonwealth Scholarship Adv. Panel, 1976–86; Wildfowl Trust Sci. Adv. Cttee, 1979–83; Scientific Sec., Bernoulli Soc. for Math. Stats and Probability, 1985–87. *Publications:* (with N. Jardine) Mathematical Taxonomy, 1971; papers in learned jls. *Recreation:* natural history. *Address:* The Registry, The University, Canterbury, Kent CT2 7NZ. *T:* Canterbury (01227) 764000.

SIDDALL, Sir Norman, Kt 1983; CBE 1975; DL; FEng; Member of the National Coal Board, 1971–83, Deputy Chairman 1973–82, Chairman 1982–83; *b* 4 May 1918; *s* of late Frederick and Mabel Siddall; *m* 1943, Pauline, *d* of late John Alexander and Edith Arthur; two *s* one *d*. *Educ:* King Edward VII School, Sheffield; Sheffield Univ. (BEng). National Coal Board: Production Manager, No 5 Area, East Midlands Div., 1951–56; General Manager, No 5 Area, East Midlands Div., 1956–57; General Manager, No 1 Area, East Midlands Div., 1957–66; Chief Mining Engineer, 1966–67; Dir Gen. of Production, 1967–71. Former Mem., Midland Cos Institn of Engrs (Silver Medal, 1951; Past Pres.). Chartered Engineer; FIMinE; CBIM. DL Notts, 1987. Hon. DSc Nottingham, 1982. National Association of Colliery Managers: Silver Medal, 1955; Bronze Medal, 1960; Coal Science Lecture Medal, 1972; CGLI Insignia Award in Technology (*hc*), 1978; Instn Medal, IME, 1982; Krupinski Medal, 1982. *Publications:* articles in professional journals. *Address:* Brentwood, High Oakham Road, Mansfield, Notts NG18 5AJ.

SIDDELEY, family name of **Baron Kenilworth.**

SIDDELEY, Randle; *see* Kenilworth, 4th Baron.

SIDDIQI, Prof. Obaid, Padma Bhushan 1984; FRS 1984; FIASc 1968; FNA 1977; Professor of Molecular Biology, Tata Institute of Fundamental Research, Bombay, since 1972; Director, National Centre for Biological Sciences, Bangalore, since 1992; *b* 7 Jan. 1932; *s* of M. A. Qadeer Siddiqi and Umme Kulsum; *m* 1955, Asiya Siddiqi; two *s* two *d*. *Educ:* Univ. of Aligarh (MSc); Univ. of Glasgow (PhD). Lecturer, Aligarh Univ., 1954–57; Indian Agricl Res. Inst., 1957–58; Dept of Genetics, Glasgow Univ., 1958–61; Cold Spring Harbor Lab., NY, 1961; Univ. of Pennsylvania, 1961–62; joined Tata Inst. of Fundamental Research as Fellow, 1962. Vis. Associate, Yale Univ., 1966; Vis. Prof., MIT, 1970–71; CIT Gosney Fellow, 1971–72; Sherman Fairchild Distinguished Scholar, 1981–82; Fellow, Third World Acad. of Sciences, Trieste, 1986. Hon. DSc Aligarh, 1984. *Publications:* (co-ed) Development and Neurobiology of Drosophila, 1981; several papers in learned jls on genetics and neurobiology. *Recreations:* music, tennis, photography. *Address:* Molecular Biology Unit, Tata Institute of Fundamental Research, Homi Bhabha Road, Bombay 400 005, India. *T:* (office) (22) 2152971, (22) 2152979, (residence) (22) 2152140. *Club:* Bombay Gymkhana.

SIDDLE, Prof. Kenneth, PhD; Professor of Molecular Endocrinology, University of Cambridge, since 1990; Fellow, Churchill College, Cambridge, since 1982; *b* 30 March 1947; *s* of Fred and Vera Siddle; *m* 1971, Yvonne Marie Kennedy (marr. diss. 1994); one *s*. *Educ:* Morecambe Grammar Sch.; Downing Coll., Cambridge (BA 1969). MA, PhD 1973. Lectr, Dept Medical Biochemistry, Welsh Nat. Sch. Med., Cardiff, 1971–78; Meres Sen. Student for Med. Research, St John's Coll., Cambridge, 1978–81; Wellcome Lectr, Dept Clinical Biochem., Univ. of Cambridge, 1981–90. Vis. Scientist, Joslin Diabetes Center and Harvard Med. Sch., 1989–90. Hon. Treas., Cambridge Univ. CC, 1990–. Chm. Editl Bd, Biochemical Jl, 1995–. *Publications:* articles in biochem. jls. *Recreations:* mountaineering (especially Munro bagging), cricket, bird watching, vegetable gardening. *Address:* 26 Fairhaven Close, Lode, Cambridge CB5 9HG. *T:* Cambridge (01223) 811302. *Club:* Lancashire County Cricket.

SIDDLE, Oliver Richard, CB 1995; OBE 1983; General Manager, Enterprises Group, and Assistant Director-General, British Council, since 1992; *b* 11 March 1936; *s* of George Siddle and Grace (*née* Hatfield); *m* 1964, Kathleen Barbara Dods; one *s* one *d*. *Educ:* Hymers Coll., Hull; Queen's Coll., Oxford (BA 2nd Cl. Hons Mod. Hist. 1959). Joined British Council, 1961: Budget Dept, 1961–63; Poland, 1963–65; Argentina, 1965–68; Nigeria, 1968–70; Mgt Trng, Heriot-Watt Univ., 1970–71; Staff Trng Dept, 1971–74; Dir, Budget Dept, 1974–76; Representative: Peru, 1976–80; Hong Kong, 1980–85; Malaysia, 1985–87; Gen. Manager, Direct Teaching, 1987–92. FRSA 1982. *Recreations:* hill-walking, gardening, drawing. *Address:* c/o British Council, 10 Spring Gardens, SW1A 2BN; 21 Bannister Close, Oxford OX4 1SH. *T:* Oxford (01865) 251875.

SIDDONS, Arthur Harold Makins, MChir Cantab; FRCS; FRCP; Hon. Consulting Surgeon, St George's Hospital; *b* 17 Jan. 1911; *s* of late A. W. Siddons, Housemaster, Harrow School; *m* 1st, 1939, Joan Richardson Anderson (*née* McConnell) (*d* 1949); one *s* one *d*; 2nd, 1956, Eleanor Mary Oliver (*née* Hunter) (*d* 1970); 3rd, 1971, Margaret Christine Beardmore (*née* Smith). *Educ:* Harrow; Jesus College, Cambridge; St George's Hospital. MB, BCh Cantab 1935. Surgeon, St George's Hospital, 1941; Consultant General and Thoracic Surgeon, St George's Hosp. and others, 1948–76. Served RAF Medical Branch, 1942–46. Member of Court of Examiners, Royal College of Surgeons of England, 1958–63. *Publications:* Cardiac Pacemakers, 1967; sections on lung surgery in various textbooks. *Recreations:* travel, gardens, birds. *Address:* Robin Hey, Tilford Road, Farnham, Surrey GU9 8HX. *T:* Farnham (01252) 715667.

SIDEBOTTOM, Edward John; a Chief Inspector, Department of Education and Science, 1973–80 (Divisional Inspector, 1969–73); *b* 1918; *s* of late Ernest Sidebottom, Wylam, Northumberland; *m* 1949, Brenda Millicent, *d* of late Alec H. Sadler, Wandsworth. *Educ:* Queen Elizabeth Grammar School, Hexham; Hatfield College, Durham (BSc). Entered Iraq Government education service, 1939; lecturer, Leavesden Green Emergency Training College, 1946; County Youth Organiser for Hampshire, 1947; HM Inspector of Schools, 1949–80. Sec. to Albemarle Cttee on the Youth Service in England and Wales, 1958–59;

seconded as first Principal, Nat. Coll. for the Training of Youth Leaders, 1960–64. Chm., Jt Working Gp on Training for Staff Working with Mentally Handicapped People, 1981–83. *Address:* 3 Queen's Court, Marlborough Road, West Cliff, Bournemouth, Dorset BH4 8DB.

SIDELL, Ron Daniel; architect; Sidell Gibson Partnership (private practice), since 1970; *b* 20 April 1941; *s* of Daniel Sidell and Dorothy Eady; *m* Sally Hodgson; one *d.* *Educ:* Canterbury Coll. of Architecture; York Univ. Winner: Grand Buildings Trafalgar Square Internat. Competition, 1986; City of Winchester Central Redevelt Proposal Comp., 1989. *Recreations:* just about most things. *Address:* Fitzroy Yard, Fitzroy Road, Primrose Hill, NW1 8TF. *T:* 0171–722 5009.

SIDEY, Air Marshal Sir Ernest (Shaw), KBE 1972; CB 1965; MD, ChB, FFCM, DPH; Director-General, Chest, Heart and Stroke Association, 1974–85; *b* 2 Jan. 1913; *s* of Thomas Sidey, Alyth, Perthshire; *m* 1946, Doreen Florence, *y d* of late Cecil Ronald Lurring, Dalkey, Ireland; one *d* (and one *d* decd). *Educ:* Morgan Acad., Dundee; St Andrews Univ. Commissioned in RAF, 1937. Served in Burma Campaign during War of 1939–45. Recent appts include: Chief, Med. Adv. Staff, Allied Air Forces Central Europe, 1957–59; PMO: Flying Trg Comd, 1961–63; Middle East Comd, 1963–65; Transport Command, 1965–66; DDGMS, RAF, 1966–68. PMO, Strike Command, 1968–70; Dir-Gen., RAF Med. Services, 1971–74; QHS 1966–74. Governor, Royal Star and Garter Home, 1974–86. *Recreations:* racing, golf, bridge. *Address:* Callums, Tugwood Common, Cookham Dean, Berks SL6 9TU. *T:* Marlow (01628) 483006. *Club:* Royal Air Force.

SIDEY, Thomas Kay Stuart, CMG 1968; Founder Patron, Wickliffe Press Ltd, since 1993 (Managing Director, 1961–83; Executive Chairman, 1983–93); Barrister and Solicitor, NZ, since 1932; *b* 8 Oct. 1908; *s* of Sir Thomas Kay Sidey; *m* 1933, Beryl, *d* of Harvey Richardson Thomas, Wellington, NZ; one *s* one *d.* *Educ:* Otago Boys' High School; Univ. of Otago (LLM; Hon LLD, 1978). Served War of 1939–45 (despatches): 2nd NZEF; 4 years, Middle East and Italy, rank of Major. Dunedin City Council, 1947–50, 1953–65, 1968–83; Dep. Mayor, 1956–59, 1968–77; Mayor, 1959–65. Mem., Univ. of Otago Council, 1947–83, Pro-Chancellor, 1959–70, Chancellor, 1970–76. Past President: Dunedin Chamber of Commerce; Automobile Assoc., Otago; Trusteebank Otago; NZ Library Assoc.; Otago Old People's Welfare Council; Otago Boys' High Sch. Old Boys' Soc. *Recreations:* fishing, boating, ski-ing. *Address:* 16 Tolcarne Avenue, Dunedin, New Zealand. *T:* (3) 4775694. *Club:* Dunedin (Dunedin, NZ).

SIDMOUTH, 7th Viscount *cr* 1805; **John Tonge Anthony Pellew Addington;** *b* 3 Oct. 1914; *s* of 6th Viscount Sidmouth and of Gladys Mary Dever (*d* 1983), *d* of late Thomas Francis Hughes; *S* father, 1976; *m* 1st, 1940, Barbara Mary (*d* 1989), *d* of Bernard Rochford, OBE; one *s* five *d* (and one *s* decd); 2nd, 1993, Mrs Thérèse Pollen. *Educ:* Downside School (Scholar); Brasenose Coll., Oxford (Scholar). Colonial Service, E Africa, 1938–54. Mem. Council and Chm. Glasshouse Cttee, Nat. Farmers Union, 1962–69; Member: Agricultural Research Council, 1964–74; Central Council for Agricultural Cooperation, 1970–73. Mem., Select Cttee on European Communities, 1984–87. Pres., Nat. Council on Inland Transport, 1978–84. Trustee, John Innes Foundation, 1974–89. Chm. of Governing Body, Glasshouse Crops Research Inst., 1981–84. Knight of Malta, 1962. *Recreation:* gardening. *Heir: s* Hon. Jeremy Francis Addington [*b* 29 July 1947; *m* 1st, 1970, Grete Henningsen; one *s* one *d*; 2nd, 1986, Una Coogan; one *s* one *d*]. *Address:* 12 Brock Street, Bath, Avon BA1 2LW. *T:* Bath (01225) 301946.

SIDNEY, family name of **Viscount De L'Isle.**

SIDWELL, Martindale, FRAM; FRCO; Organist and Choirmaster, Hampstead Parish Church, 1945–92; Organist and Director of Music, St Clement Danes (Central Church of the RAF), 1957–92; Conductor: Martindale Sidwell Choir, since 1956; St Clement Danes Chorale and Martindale Sidwell Sinfonia, since 1983; *b* 23 Feb. 1916; *s* of John William Sidwell, Little Packington, Warwicks, and Mary Martindale, Liverpool; *m* 1944, Barbara Anne (*née* Hill) (pianist, harpsichordist and Prof. of Piano and Harpsichord, Royal Coll. of Music, under the name Barbara Hill); two *s.* *Educ:* Wells Cathedral Sch., Somerset; Royal Academy of Music. Sub-Organist, Wells Cathedral, 1932. Served War of 1939–45, Royal Engineers. Organist, Holy Trinity Church, Leamington Spa, and Director of Music, Warwick School, 1943, also at same time Conductor of Royal Leamington Spa Bach Choir; Conductor, Hampstead Choral Soc., 1946–81; Founder 1967, and Director and Conductor, 1967–81, London Bach Orch.; Conductor, St Clement's Orch., 1983–87. Prof., RSCM, 1958–66; Prof. of Organ, RAM, 1963–84. Mem. Council, RCO, 1966–. Harriet Cohen International Bach Medal, 1967. Frequent broadcasts as Conductor and as Organ Recitalist, 1944–. *Address:* 1 Frognal Gardens, Hampstead, NW3 6UY. *T:* 0171–435 9210. *Clubs:* Savage, Wig and Pen.

SIE, Sir Banja T.; *see* Tejan-Sie.

SIEFF, family name of **Baron Sieff of Brimpton.**

SIEFF OF BRIMPTON, Baron *cr* 1980 (Life Peer), of Brimpton in the Royal County of Berkshire; **Marcus Joseph Sieff;** Kt 1971; OBE 1944; Chairman, First International Bank of Israel Financial Trust Ltd, 1983–94. *Educ:* Manchester Grammar School; St Paul's; Corpus Christi College, Cambridge (MA), Hon. Fellow, 1975. Served War 1939–45, Royal Artillery. Joined Marks and Spencer Ltd, 1935; Dir, 1954; Asst Man. Dir, 1963; Vice-Chm., 1965; Jt Man. Dir, 1967–83; Dep. Chm., 1971; Chm., 1972–84; Pres., 1984–85; Hon. Pres., 1985–. Non-exec. Chm., The Independent, 1986–93; non-exec. Director: Wickes PLC, 1986–93; Sock Shop Internat. plc, 1987–89. Mem., BNEC, 1965–71 (Chm., Export Cttee for Israel, 1965–68). Hon. President: Anglo-Israel Chamber of Commerce, 1975–; Joint Israel Appeal, 1984–. Chancellor, Weizmann Inst. of Sci. Vice Pres., Policy Studies Institute (formerly PEP) Exec., 1975–. Trustee, Nat. Portrait Gallery, 1986–93. Hon. FRCS 1984. Hon. LLD: St Andrews, 1983; Leicester, 1988; Hon. Dr Babson Coll., Mass, 1984; Hon. DLitt Reading; DUniv Stirling, 1986; Hon. DPhil: Tel Aviv, 1991; Hebrew, 1992. Hambro Award, Businessman of the Year, 1977; Aims National Free Enterprise Award, 1978; B'nai B'rith Internat. gold medallion for humanitarianism, 1982; Retailer of the Year Award, National Retail Merchants' Assoc., USA, 1982; BIM Gold Medal, 1983. *Publications:* Don't Ask the Price (autobiog.), 1987; Marcus Sieff on Management, 1990.

See also Hon. D. D. Sieff.

SIEFF, Hon. David Daniel; Director, Marks and Spencer plc, since 1972; *b* 22 March 1939; *s* of Baron Sieff of Brimpton, *qv*, and late Rosalie Cottage; *m* 1962, Jennifer Walton; two *s.* *Educ:* Repton. Joined Marks & Spencer, 1957; Alternate Director, 1968; Full Director, 1972. Non-exec. Chm., First Internat. Bank of Israel (UK) Ltd, 1994–; Dir, UK-Japan 2000 Gp, 1995–. Chairman, North Metropolitan Conciliation Cttee of Race Relations Board, 1969–71; Vice-Chm., Inst. of Race Relations, 1971–72; part-time Member, National Freight Corp., 1972–78; Member: Policy Studies Inst. (formerly PEP), 1976–84; Bd, Business in the Community; Council, Industrial Soc., 1975–90. Governor: Weizmann Inst. of Science, Rehovot, Israel, 1978– (Chm. Exec. Cttee, UK Foundn, 1984–); Shenkar Coll. of Textile Technology (Israel), 1980–; Hon. Pres., British ORT, 1983–. Trustee, Glyndebourne Arts Trust, 1971–. Pres., Racehorse Owners Assoc., 1975–78; Chairman: Racing Welfare Charities, 1988–; Nat. Lottery Charities Bd, 1994–; Member: Jockey Club, 1977–; Bd, Newbury Racecourse, 1988–; Horserace Totalisator Bd, 1991–. FRSA 1989. *Address:* Michael House, 47 Baker Street, W1A 1DN. *T:* 0171–935 4422. *Club:* White's.

SIEGBAHN, Prof. Kai Manne Börje; Professor of Physics, University of Uppsala, 1954–84; *b* 20 April 1918; *s* of Manne Siegbahn and Karin Siegbahn (*née* Högbom); *m* 1944, Anna-Brita (*née* Rhedin); three *s.* *Educ:* Univ. of Uppsala (BSc 1939; Licentiate of Philosophy 1942); Univ. of Stockholm (Dr of Philosophy 1944). Research Associate, Nobel Inst. of Physics, 1942–51; Prof. of Physics, Royal Inst. of Technology, Stockholm, 1951–54. Founder, and Editor 1957–, Internat. Jl of Nuclear Instruments and Methods in Physics Res. Member: Roy. Swedish Acad. of Sci.; Roy. Swedish Acad. of Engrg Scis; Roy. Soc. of Sci.; Roy. Acad. of Arts and Sci. of Uppsala; Roy. Physiographical Soc. of Lund; Societas Scientiarum Fennica; Norwegian Acad. of Sci.; Roy. Norwegian Soc. of Scis and Letters; Nat. Acad. of Sciences; Pontifical Acad. of Sci.; European Acad. of Arts, Scis and Humanities. Hon. Mem. Amer. Acad. of Arts and Scis; Membre de Comité des Poids et Mesures, Paris; Pres., IUPAP, 1981–84. Dr of Science, *hc:* Durham, 1972; Basel, 1980; Liège, 1980; Upsala Coll., East Orange, NJ, 1982; Sussex, 1983. Lindblom Prize, 1945; Björkén Prize, 1955, 1977; Celsius Medal, 1962; Sixten Heyman Award, 1971; Harrison Howe Award, 1973; Maurice F. Hasler Award, 1975; Charles Frederick Chandler Medal, 1976; Torbern Bergman Medal, 1979; (jtly) Nobel Prize for Physics, 1981; Pittsburgh Award of Spectroscopy, 1982; Röntgen Medal, 1985; Fiuggi Award, 1986; Humboldt Award, 1986; Premio Castiglione Di Sicilia, 1990. *Publications:* Beta- and Gamma-Ray Spectroscopy, 1955; Alpha-, Beta- and Gamma-Ray Spectroscopy, 1965; ESCA—Atomic, Molecular and Solid State Structure Studied by Means of Electron Spectroscopy, 1967; ESCA Applied to Free Molecules, 1969; Some Current Problems in Electron Spectroscopy, 1983; around 400 scientific papers. *Recreations:* tennis, skiing and music. *Address:* Institute of Physics, University of Uppsala, Box 530, 751 21 Uppsala, Sweden. *T:* (18) 146963.

SIEGERT, Air Vice-Marshal Cyril Laurence, CB 1979; CBE 1975; MVO 1954; DFC 1944; AFC 1954; *b* 14 March 1923; *s* of Lawrence Siegert and Julia Ann Siegert; *m* 1948, Shirley Berenice Dick; two *s* two *d.* *Educ:* Fairlie High School; St Kevin's Coll., Oamaru; Victoria Univ. of Wellington. Joined RNZAF, 1942; served in UK with Nos 299 and 190 Sqdns; on loan to BOAC, 1945–47; Berlin airlift, 1949; NZ, 1952–54; NZ Defence Staff, Washington, 1954–56; RAF Staff Coll., 1957; NZ, 1958–62; Comdt, RNZAF's Command and Staff Sch., 1962; RAF Coll. of Air Warfare, 1963; Singapore, 1963–65; CO, No 3 Battlefield Support Sqdn and RNZAF Transport Wing, 1965–69; AOC RNZAF Ops Group, 1969–70; IDC 1970; RNZAF Air Staff, 1971; Chief of Staff, ANZUK Joint Force HQ, Singapore, 1971–73; Dep. Chief of Defence Staff (Policy), 1973–76; Chief of Air Staff, RNZAF, 1976–79. Gen. Manager, Marine Air Systems, 1980–84; Mem., Air Services Licensing Authority, 1980–87. *Recreations:* fishing, tramping, gardening. *Address:* 46 Wyndrum Avenue, Lower Hutt, New Zealand. *Clubs:* United Services (Wellington); Wellington Racing.

SIEPMANN, Mary Aline, (Mary Wesley), CBE 1995; writer; *b* 24 June 1912; *d* of Col Harold Mynors Farmar, CMG, DSO and Violet Hyacinth (*née* Dalby); *m* 1st, 1937, 2nd Baron Swinfen (marr. diss. 1945); two *s*; 2nd, 1952, Eric Siepmann (*d* 1970); one *s.* *Educ:* at home (governesses); LSE (Hon. Fellow). DUniv Open, 1993; Hon. DLitt Exeter, 1993. *Publications:* Speaking Terms (for children), 1968; The Sixth Seal (for children), 1968; Haphazard House (for children), 1983; Jumping the Queue, 1983; The Camomile Lawn, 1984; Harnessing Peacocks, 1985; The Vacillations of Poppy Carew, 1986; Not That Sort of Girl, 1987; Second Fiddle, 1988; A Sensible Life, 1990; A Dubious Legacy, 1993; An Imaginative Experience, 1994. *Recreation:* reading. *Address:* c/o Transworld Publishers, 61–63 Uxbridge Road, W5 5SA.

SIGMON, Robert Leland; lawyer; *b* Roanoke, Va, 3 April 1929; *s* of Ottis Leland Sigmon and Aubrey Virginia (*née* Bishop); *m* 1st, 1963, Marianne Rita Gellner (marr. diss.); 2nd, 1992, Jean Mary Anderson. *Educ:* Univ. of Virginia; Sorbonne; London Sch. of Economics. BA, DrJur. Member of the Bar: US Supreme Court; Court of Appeals, Second and District of Columbia Circuits; Virginia; District of Columbia. Vice-Pres., Pilgrims Soc. of GB, 1993– (Chm., Exec. Cttee, 1977–93); Founder Member: Associates of the Victoria and Albert Museum, 1976 (Dir, 1976–87); Amer. and Internat. Friends of V&A Mus. (Trustee, 1985–). Mem., Council of Management, British Inst. of Internat. and Comparative Law, 1982–. Trustee: American Sch. in London, 1977–91; Magna Carta Trust, 1984–94; Vice-Chm., Mid-Atlantic Club of London, 1977–; Vice-Pres., European-Atlantic Gp, 1978–94; Member: Exec. Cttee, Amer. Soc. in London, 1969– (Chm. 1974); Amer. Soc. of Internat. Law; Selden Soc.; Guild of St Bride's Church, Fleet Street; Ends of the Earth; Gov., E-SU, 1984–90. Chevalier du Tastevin. *Publications:* contribs to legal periodicals. *Recreations:* collecting antiquarian books, oenology. *Address:* 2 Plowden Buildings, Middle Temple, EC4Y 9AS. *T:* 0171–583 4851. *Club:* Reform.

SIGURDSSON, Niels P.; Ministry of Foreign Affairs, Iceland, since 1990; *b* Reykjavik, 10 Feb. 1926; *s* of Sigurdur B. Sigurdsson and Karitas Einarsdóttir; *m* 1953, Olafia Rafnsdóttir; two *s* one *d.* *Educ:* Univ. of Iceland (Law). Joined Diplomatic Service 1952; First Sec., Paris Embassy, 1956–60; Dep. Permanent Rep. to NATO and OECD, 1957–60; Dir, Internat. Policy Div., Min. of Foreign Affairs, Reykjavik, 1961–67; Delegate to UN Gen. Assembly, 1965; Ambassador and Permanent Rep. of Iceland to N Atlantic Council, 1967–71. Ambassador: to Belgium and EEC, 1968–71; to UK, 1971–76; to Fed. Republic of Germany, 1976–78; Ministry of Foreign Affairs, Reykjavik, 1979–84; Ambassador to Norway, 1985–89. *Recreations:* swimming, riding. *Address:* Sólheimar 15, 104 Reykjavík, Iceland.

SIKORA, Prof. Karol, FRCP, FRCR; Professor of Clinical Oncology, Royal Postgraduate Medical School, Hammersmith Hospital, since 1986; Deputy Director (Clinical Research), Imperial Cancer Research Fund, since 1995; *b* 17 June 1948; *s* of Witold Karol Sikora and Thomasina Sikora; *m* 1974, Alison Mary Rice; one *s* two *d.* *Educ:* Dulwich Coll.; Corpus Christi Coll., Cambridge (MA, MB, BChir, PhD); Middlesex Hospital. Middlesex Hosp., 1972; Hammersmith Hosp., 1973; MRC Clinical Fellow, Lab. for Molecular Biol., Cambridge, 1974–77; Clinical Fellow, Stanford Univ., 1978–79; Dir, Ludwig Inst. for Cancer Research, Cambridge, 1980–86. *Publications:* Monoclonal Antibodies, 1984; Interferon, 1985; Cancer: a student guide, 1988; Treatment of Cancer, 1990; Fight Cancer, 1990; Genes and Cancer, 1990; contrib. Gene Therapy. *Recreations:* boating, travelling. *Address:* Department of Clinical Oncology, Hammersmith Hospital, W12 0HS. *T:* 0181–740 3060. *Clubs:* Athenæum, Polish Hearth.

SILBER, Stephen Robert; QC 1987; a Recorder, since 1987; a Law Commissioner for England and Wales, since 1994; *b* 26 March 1944; *s* of late J. J. Silber and of Marguerite Silber; *m* 1982, Lucinda, *d* of Lt-Col David St John Edwards, retd; one *s* one *d.* *Educ:* William Ellis Sch.; University Coll. London; Trinity Coll., Cambridge. Called to Bar, Gray's Inn, 1968. Bencher, 1994. Mem., Criminal Law Cttee, Judicial Studies Bd, 1994–. *Recreations:* photography, walking, music, watching sport, theatre. *Address:* Law Commission, Conquest House, 37/38 John Street, WC1N 2BQ. *T:* 0171–453 1219.

SILBERSTON, Prof. (Zangwill) Aubrey, CBE 1987; Professor of Economics, University of London, at Imperial College of Science and Technology, 1978–87, now Emeritus, and Head of Department of Social and Economic Studies, 1981–87; Senior Research Fellow, Management School, Imperial College, since 1987; *b* 26 Jan. 1922; *s* of Louis and Polly Silberston; *m* 1st, 1945, Dorothy Marion Nicholls (marr. diss.); one *s* (one *d* decd); 2nd, 1985, Michèle Ledić. *Educ:* Hackney Downs Sch., London; Jesus Coll., Cambridge. MA (Cantab); MA (Oxon). Courtaulds Ltd, 1946–50; Kenward Res. Fellow in Industrial Admin, St Catharine's Coll., Cambridge, 1950–53; University Lectr in Economics, Cambridge, 1953–71; Fellow, 1958–71, Dir of Studies in Econs, 1965–71, St John's Coll., Cambridge; Chm., Faculty Bd of Econs and Politics, Cambridge, 1966–70; Official Fellow in Econs, 1971–78, and Dean, 1972–78, Nuffield Coll., Oxford. Rockefeller Fellow, Univ. of Calif, Berkeley, 1959–60; Visiting Professor: Queensland Univ., 1977; Univ. of the South, Sewanee, 1984. Member: Monopolies Commn, 1965–68; Board of British Steel Corp., 1967–76; Departmental Cttee on Patent System, 1967–70; Econs Cttee, SSRC, 1969–73; Royal Commn on the Press, 1974–77; Restrictive Practices Ct, 1986–92; Royal Commn on Environmental Pollution, 1986–; Biotechnol. Adv. Commn, Stockholm Envmt Inst., 1993–. Dir, Brussels Office, London Economics, 1992–; Economic Adviser, CBI, 1972–74; Specialist Advr, Eur. Communities Cttee, H of L, 1993; Chm., Assoc. of Learned Societies in the Social Sciences, 1985–87; President: Section F, British Assoc., 1987; Confedn of European Economic Assocs, 1988–90 (Vice-Pres., 1990–92); Vice-Pres., REconS, 1992– (Sec.-Gen., 1979–92). *Publications:* Education and Training for Industrial Management, 1955; (with G. Maxcy) The Motor Industry, 1959; (jtly) Economies of Large-scale Production in British Industry, 1965; (jtly) The Patent System, 1967; (with C. T. Taylor) The Economic Impact of the Patent System, 1973; (ed) Industrial Management: East and West, 1973; (with A. Cockerill) The Steel Industry, 1974; (jtly) Microeconomic Efficiency and Macroeconomic Performance, 1983; The Multi-Fibre Arrangement and the UK Economy, 1984; (jtly) British Manufacturing Investment Overseas, 1985; The Economic Importance of Patents, 1987; (ed) Technology and Economic Progress, 1989; Patent Policy: is the pharmaceutical industry a special case?, 1989; The Future of the Multi-Fibre Arrangement, 1989; (ed with Gianna Boero) Environmental Economics, 1995; (with C. Raymond) The Changing Industrial Map of Europe, 1995; (jtly) Beyond the Multifibre Arrangement, 1995; articles in Econ. Jl, Bulletin of Oxford Inst. of Statistics, Oxford Economic Papers, Jl of Royal Statistical Society. *Recreations:* music, ballet. *Address:* 53 Prince's Gate, SW7 2PG. *T:* 0171–589 5111. *Club:* Travellers'.

SILK, Rt. Rev. David; *see* Silk, Rt Rev. R. D.

SILK, Dennis Raoul Whitehall, CBE 1995; MA; Warden of Radley College, 1968–91; Chairman, Test and County Cricket Board, since 1994; *b* 8 Oct. 1931; 2nd *s* of late Rev. Dr Claude Whitehall Silk and Mrs Louise Silk; *m* 1963, Diana Merilyn, 2nd *d* of W. F. Milton, Pitminster, Somerset; two *s* two *d*. *Educ:* Christ's Hosp.; Sidney Sussex Coll., Cambridge (Exhibr). MA (History) Cantab. Asst Master, Marlborough Coll., 1955–68 (Housemaster, 1957–68). JP Abingdon, 1972–89. *Publications:* Cricket for Schools, 1964; Attacking Cricket, 1965. *Recreations:* antiquarian, literary, sporting (Blues in cricket (Capt. Cambridge Univ. CC, 1955) and Rugby football). *Address:* Sturts Barn, Huntham Lane, Stoke St Gregory, Taunton, Somerset TA3 6EG. *T:* North Curry (01823) 490348. *Clubs:* East India, Devonshire, Sports and Public Schools, MCC (Pres., 1992–94); Hawks (Cambridge).

SILK, Rt. Rev. (Robert) David; *see* Ballarat, Bishop of.

SILK, Robert K.; *see* Kilroy-Silk.

SILKE, William James; Justice of Appeal, Supreme Court of Hong Kong, 1981–94; Vice-President, Court of Appeal, 1987–94; *b* 21 Sept. 1929; *s* of William Joseph Silke and Gertrude (*née* Delany). *Educ:* Dominican Convent, Wicklow; Xavier Sch., Donnybrook; King's Inns, Dublin. Called to Irish Bar (South Eastern Circuit, Leinster Bar), 1955; Magistrate, North Borneo/Malaysia, 1959; Registrar, High Court in Borneo (Sabah-Sarawak), 1965; Puisne Judge, 1966; retired under compensation scheme during Malaysianisation, 1969; Hong Kong: Magistrate, 1969; President, Tenancy Tribunal, 1971; Acting Asst Registrar, High Court, 1972; President, Lands Tribunal, 1974; Judge, District Court, 1975; Judicial Commissioner, State of Brunei, 1978–91; Judge of the High Court, 1979. *Recreations:* horse racing/breeding, music, travel. *Address:* 16 Seabank Court, Marine Parade, Sandycove, Co. Dublin. *T:* 2808739. *Clubs:* Royal Over-Seas League; Stephen's Green (Dublin); Royal Sabah Turf (Sabah, Malaysia); Hong Kong, Royal Hong Kong Jockey (Hong Kong).

SILKIN, 2nd Baron, *cr* 1950, of Dulwich [disclaimed his peerage for life, 1972]; *see under* Silkin, Arthur.

SILKIN, Arthur; Lecturer in Public Administration, Civil Service College, Sunningdale, 1971–76, on secondment from Department of Employment; retired 1976; *b* 20 Oct. 1916; *e s* of 1st Baron Silkin, PC, CH; *S* father, 1972, as 2nd Baron Silkin, but disclaimed his peerage for life; *m* 1969, Audrey Bennett. *Educ:* Dulwich College; Peterhouse, Cambridge. BA 1938; Diploma in Govt Administration, 1959; Dip. in Hist. of Art, London Univ., 1990. Served 1940–45, Royal Air Force (A and SD Branch), Pilot Officer, 1941, subsequently Flying Officer. Entered Ministry of Labour and National Service, 1939; formerly 2nd Secretary, British Embassy, Paris. First Secretary: High Commissioner's Office, Calcutta, 1960–61; British Embassy, Dakar, May 1962–Mar. 1964; British Embassy, Kinshasa, 1964–66. *Publications:* contrib. to Public Administration, Political Qly. *Address:* Cuzco, 33 Woodnook Road, SW16 6TZ. *T:* 0181–677 8733.

SILKIN, Jon, FRSL 1986; poet; *b* 2 Dec. 1930; *s* of Dora Rubenstein and late Joseph Silkin, solicitor; three *s* one *d* (one *s* decd); *m* Lorna Tracy (American writer and co-editor of Stand). *Educ:* Wycliffe Coll.; Dulwich Coll.; Univ. of Leeds. BA Hons Eng. Lit. 1962. Journalist, 1947; Nat. Service, teaching in Educn Corps, Army; subseq. six years as manual labourer, London and two years teaching English to foreign students. Founded magazine Stand, 1952. Several poetry-reading tours, USA; Vis. Lectr, Denison Univ., Ohio; taught at Writers' Workshop, Univ. of Iowa, 1968–69 and 1991; Visiting Writer: for Australian Council for the Arts, 1974; College of Idaho, Caldwell, 1978; Mishkenot Sha'ananim, Jerusalem, 1980; Bingham Vis. Poet, Univ. of Louisville, 1981; Elliston Poet-in-Residence, Univ. of Cincinnati, 1983; Distinguished Writer in Residence, The Amer. Univ., 1989; Residency, Dumfries and Galloway Arts, 1990; Lectr in English and Amer. Literature, Tsukuba Univ., Japan, 1991–. C. Day Lewis Fellowship, 1976–77. Vis. Speaker, World Congress of Poets: Korea, 1979; Madrid, 1982; Corfu, 1985; Florence, 1986. *Publications:* The Peaceable Kingdom, 1954, reprint 1976; The Two Freedoms, 1958; The Re-ordering of the Stones, 1961; Nature with Man, 1965 (Geoffrey Faber Meml Prize, 1966); (with Murphy and Tarn) Penguin Modern Poets 7, 1965; Poems New and Selected, 1966; Killhope Wheel, 1971; Amana Grass, 1971; Out of Battle: the poetry of the Great War, 1972, revd edn 1995; (ed) Poetry of the Committed Individual, 1973; The Principle of Water, 1974; The Little Time-keeper, 1976; (ed) Penguin Book of First World War Poetry, 1979; (ed with Peter Redgrove) New Poetry, 1979; The Psalms with Their Spoils, 1980; Selected Poems, 1980, rev. and enl. edn 1988; (ed jtly) Stand One, 1984; Gurney (verse play), 1985; (ed) Wilfred Owen: the Collected Poems, 1985; The Ship's Pasture (poems), 1986; (with Jon Glover) The Penguin Book of First World War Prose, 1989; The Lens-breakers, 1992; Selected Poems, 1994; (ed) The War Poems of Wilfred Owen, 1994. *Recreation:* travelling. *Address:* 13 Queens Terrace, Newcastle upon Tyne NE2 2PJ. *T:* 0191–281 2614.

SILLARS, James; management consultant; Assistant to Secretary-General, Arab-British Chamber of Commerce, since 1993; *b* Ayr, 4 Oct. 1937; *s* of Matthew Sillars; *m* 1st, 1957; one *s* one *d*; 2nd, 1981, Mrs Margo MacDonald, *qv*. *Educ:* Newton Park Sch., Ayr; Ayr Academy. Former official, Fire Brigades Union; Past Member Ayr Town Council and Ayr County Council Educn Cttee; Mem., T&GWU. Head of Organization and Social Services Dept, Scottish TUC, 1968–70. Full-time Labour Party agent, 1964 and 1966 elections. Contested (SNP): Linlithgow, 1987; Glasgow, Govan, 1992. MP: (Lab) South Ayrshire, March 1970–1976, (SLP) 1976–79; (SNP) Glasgow, Govan, Nov. 1988–1992. Among the founders of the Scottish Labour Party, Jan. 1976. Man. Dir, Scoted Ltd, 1980–83. Especially interested in education, social services, industrial relations, development policies. *Publications:* Scotland—the Case for Optimism, 1986; Labour Party pamphlets on Scottish Nationalism; Tribune Gp pamphlet on Democracy within the Labour Party. *Recreations:* reading, camping, tennis, swimming. *Address:* 97 Grange Loan, Edinburgh EH9 2ED.

SILLARS, Margo; *see* MacDonald, M.

SILLERY, William Moore; Headmaster, Belfast Royal Academy, since 1980; *b* 14 March 1941; *s* of William and Adeline Sillery; *m* 1963, Elizabeth Margaret Dunwoody; two *d*. *Educ:* Methodist Coll., Belfast; St Catharine's Coll., Cambridge. Head of Modern Languages, Belfast Royal Academy, 1968, Vice-Principal 1974, Deputy Headmaster 1976. Educnl Advr, Ulster Television, 1985–94. Chm., Ministerial Working Party on Modern Langs in NI Curriculum, 1991; Member: NI Cttee, UFC, 1989–93; Belfast Educn and Liby Bd, 1994–. *Recreations:* golf, bridge. *Address:* Ardmore, 15 Saintfield Road, Belfast BT8 4AE. *T:* Belfast (01232) 645260. *Clubs:* East India; Belvoir Park (Belfast).

SILLITOE, Alan; writer since 1948; *b* 4 March 1928; *s* of Christopher Sillitoe and Sabina (*née* Burton); *m* 1959, Ruth Fainlight; one *s* one *d*. *Educ:* various elementary schools in Nottingham. Raleigh Bicycle Factory, 1942; air traffic control asst, 1945–46; wireless operator, RAF, 1946–49. Lived in France and Spain, 1952–58. Vis. Prof. of English, De Montfort Univ., 1994–. FRGS; Hon. Fellow, Manchester Polytechnic, 1977. Hon. DLitt: Nottingham Poly., 1990; Nottingham Univ., 1994. *Publications: novels:* Saturday Night and Sunday Morning, 1958 (Authors' Club Award for best first novel of 1958; filmed, 1960, play, 1964); The General, 1960 (filmed 1967 as Counterpoint); Key to the Door, 1961; The Death of William Posters, 1965; A Tree on Fire, 1967; A Start in Life, 1970; Travels in Nihilon, 1971; Raw Material, 1972; The Flame of Life, 1974; The Widower's Son, 1976; The Storyteller, 1979; Her Victory, 1982; The Lost Flying Boat, 1983; Down from the Hill, 1984; Life Goes On, 1985; Out of the Whirlpool, 1987; The Open Door, 1989; Last Loves, 1990; Leonard's War: a love story, 1991; Snowstop, 1993; *stories:* The Loneliness of the Long Distance Runner, 1959 (Hawthornden Prize; filmed, 1962); The Ragman's Daughter, 1963 (filmed, 1972); Guzman, Go Home, 1968; Men, Women and Children, 1973; The Second Chance, 1981; The Far Side of the Street, 1988; Collected Stories, 1995; *poetry:* The Rats and Other Poems, 1960; A Falling Out of Love, 1964; Love in the Environs of Voronezh, 1968; Storm and Other Poems, 1974; Snow on the North Side of Lucifer, 1979; Sun before Departure, 1984; Tides and Stone Walls, 1986; Collected Poems, 1993; *for children:* The City Adventures of Marmalade Jim, 1967; Big John and the Stars, 1977; The Incredible Fencing Fleas, 1978; Marmalade Jim at the Farm, 1980; Marmalade Jim and the Fox, 1985; *travel:* Road to Volgograd, 1964; (with Fay Godwin) The Saxon Shore Way, 1983; (with David Sillitoe) Nottinghamshire, 1987; Leading the Blind, 1995; *plays:* (with Ruth Fainlight) All Citizens are Soldiers, 1969; Three Plays, 1978; *essays:* Mountains and Caverns, 1975; *autobiography:* Life Without Armour, 1994; *miscellaneous:* Every Day of the Week, 1987. *Recreations:* travel, shortwave wireless telegraphy listening. *Club:* Savage.

SILLITOE, Leslie Richard, OBE 1977; JP; General Secretary, Ceramic and Allied Trades Union, 1975–80, now Life Member; *b* 30 Aug. 1915; *s* of Leonard Richard Sillitoe and Ellen (*née* Sutton); *m* 1939, Lucy (*née* Goulding); two *d*. *Educ:* St George's and St Giles' Sch., Newcastle, Staffs; Stoke-on-Trent School of Art; WEA, N Staffs Technical Coll. Modeller and mouldmaker on leaving school. Served War, Royal Artillery, sen. non-commnd officer, 1939–46. Ceramic and Allied Trades Union: General President, 1961–63; Organiser, 1963; Asst Gen. Sec., 1967. Dep. Chm., Ceramics, Glass and Mineral Products Industry Trng Bd, 1977–82; Chm., Nat. Jt Council for Ceramic Industry, 1975–81. Member: Industrial Tribunals, 1971–84; VAT Tribunals, 1973–91. Chm., N Staffs Manpower Services Cttee, 1975–83; Life Mem., N Staffs Trades Council (Pres., 1963–81); Member: N Staffs Tourist Assoc.; N Staffs Medical Inst.; Staffordshire Soc.; Pottery & Glass Benevolent Inst. (Vice-Pres., 1980–); N Staffs Community Health Council, 1975–85; Staffordshire War Pensions Cttee, 1980–; Council, Univ. of Keele, 1976–85, 1989– (Mem. Court, 1989–); BBC Local Radio Council, 1978–81; Wetley Moor Jt Cttee, 1989–; Mem. Bd of Management, and Custodian Trustee, N Staffs Trustee Savings Bank; Vice-President: N Staffs District WEA, 1976–86; Muscular Dystrophy N Staffs Gp, 1978–; Pres., Staffordshire Lads and Dads Assoc., 1981–82, Vice-Pres. 1982–; Sec. and Treas., Ceramic Ind. Welfare Soc., 1971–81. Mem., Staffs Develt Assoc., 1977–81. Mem., Magistrates' Assoc.; Gideons Internat. Mem., Stoke-on-Trent District Council, 1953–83, 1986– (Vice-Chm., Museums Cttee); Lord Mayor, Stoke-on-Trent, 1981–82, Dep. Lord Mayor 1982–83. Governor: St Peters High Sch., Penkhull, 1975–; Cauldon Coll. of Further Educn, Stoke-on-Trent, 1976–; Thistley Hough High Sch., Penkhull, 1982–86. Mem., W Midland TAVRA, 1979–83; Chairman: Friends of the Staffordshire Regt (N Staffs), 1982–; N Staffs Normandy Veterans' Assoc., 1986–. Gov., Stoke Harpfield Primary Sch., 1982–. Pres., Longton Rotary Club, 1987–88. Former Member: Boy Scouts; St John's Ambulance Brigade. Territorial Efficient Service Medal, 1944. JP Stoke-on-Trent 1963–. Freeman, City of Stoke-on-Trent, 1993. *Publication:* foreword to The History of the Potters Union, 1977. *Recreations:* walking, photography, swimming, history. *Address:* 19 Sillitoe Place, Penkhull, Stoke-on-Trent ST4 5DQ. *T:* Stoke-on-Trent (01782) 47866.

SILLS, Beverly, (Mrs P. B. Greenough); former Director, New York City Opera; former leading soprano, New York City Opera and Metropolitan Opera; *b* 25 May 1929; *d* of late Morris Silverman and of Sonia Bahn; *m* 1956, Peter B. Greenough; one *s* one *d*. *Educ:* Professional Children's Sch., NYC; privately. Vocal studies with Estelle Liebling, piano with Paulo Gallico. Operatic debut, Philadelphia Civic Opera, 1947; San Francisco Opera, 1953; New York City Opera, 1955; Vienna State Opera, 1967; Teatro Colon, Buenos Aires, 1968; La Scala, Milan, 1969; Teatro San Carlo, Naples, 1970; Royal Opera, Covent Garden, London, 1970; Deutsche Oper, W Berlin, 1971; NY Metropolitan Opera, 1975, etc. Repeated appearances as soloist with major US symphony orchestras; English orchestral debut with London Symphony Orch., London, 1971; Paris debut, orchestral concert, Salle Pleyel, 1971. Repertoire includes title roles of Norma, Manon, Lucia di Lammermoor, Maria Stuarda, Daughter of Regiment, Anna Bolena, Traviata, Lucrezia Borgia, Thais, Louise, Cleopatra in Giulio Cesare, Elizabeth in Roberto

Devereux, Tales of Hoffmann, Elvira in Puritani, Rosina in Barber of Seville, Norina in Don Pasquale, Pamira in Siege of Corinth; created title role, La Loca, San Diego Opera, 1979. Subject of BBC-TV's Profile in Music (Nat. Acad. of TV Arts and Sciences Emmy Award, 1975); other TV includes: Sills and Burnett at the Met, 1976; Hostess/Commentator for Young People's Concerts, NY Philharmonic, 1977; Moderator/Hostess, Lifestyles with Beverly Sills, 1976, 1977 (Emmy 1978). Hon. DMus: Temple Univ., 1972; New York Univ., 1973; New England Conservatory, 1973; Harvard Univ., 1974. Woman of the Year, Hasty Pudding Club, Harvard, 1974; Handel Medallion, NYC; US Presidential Medal of Freedom. *Publications:* Bubbles: a self-portrait, 1976; (autobiog. with Lawrence Linderman) Beverly. *Recreations:* fishing, bridge. *Address:* c/o Edgar Vincent-Patrick Farrell Associates, 157 West 57 Street, New York City, NY 10019, USA. *T:* (212) 5417666, *Fax:* (212) 5417767.

SILSOE, 2nd Baron *cr* 1963; **David Malcolm Trustram Eve,** Bt 1943; QC 1972; Barrister, Inner Temple, since 1955; *b* 2 May 1930; *er* twin *s* of 1st Baron Silsoe, GBE, MC, TD, QC, and Marguerite (*d* 1945), *d* of late Sir Augustus Meredith Nanton, Winnipeg; *S* father, 1976; *m* 1963, Bridget Min, *d* of Sir Rupert Hart-Davis, *qv*; one *s* one *d*. *Educ:* Winchester; Christ Church, Oxford (MA); Columbia Univ., New York. 2nd Lt, Royal Welch Fusiliers, 1949–50; Lieut, Queen Victoria's Rifles (TA), 1950–53. Bar Auditor, Inner Temple, 1965–70; Bencher, 1970. *Recreations:* music, singing. *Heir:* *s* Hon. Simon Rupert Trustram Eve, *b* 17 April 1966. *Address:* Neals Farm, Wyfold, Reading, Berks RG4 9JB. *Club:* Ski of Great Britain.

SILUNGWE, Hon. Annel Musenga; Hon. Mr Justice Silungwe; Judge, Court of Appeal, Seychelles, since 1992; *b* 10 Jan. 1936; *s* of late Solo Musenga Silungwe and Janet Nakafunda Silungwe; *m* 1960, Abigail Nanyangwe; two *s* four *d*. *Educ:* Council of Legal Educn; Univ. of Zambia (LLM 1977). Called to the Bar, Inner Temple, 1966; State Counsel, Zambia, 1974; Judge of the High Court, Zambia, 1971–75; Minister of Legal Affairs and Attorney-General, 1973–75; Chief Justice of Zambia, 1975–92. Award of Merit, Rotary Internat. Dist 9210, 1989. *Publications:* contrib. learned jls. *Recreations:* music, photography, reading, golf, tennis, cycling, swimming. *Address:* PO Box 50777, Lusaka, Zambia. *T:* 223559, 223557, *Fax:* 223559.

SILVER, Clinton Vita, CBE 1993; Chairman, British Fashion Council, since 1994; Deputy Chairman, 1991–94, and Managing Director, 1990–94, Marks & Spencer plc; *b* 26 Sept. 1929; *s* of Sidney (Mick) Silver and Mina Silver (*née* Gabriel); *m* 1973, Patricia Ann (Jill) Vernon; one *s* one *d*. *Educ:* Upton House Sch.; Southampton Univ. (BSc Econ). Nat. Service, 1950–52. Joined Marks & Spencer, 1952; Alternate Dir, 1974; Dir, 1978. Director: Hillsdown Hldgs, 1994–; Pentland, 1994–; Tommy Hilfiger Corp., 1994–. Vice-Pres., British Overseas Trade Gp for Israel; Exec., British/Israel Chamber of Commerce; Chm., Jewish Assoc. for Business Ethics, 1995. Mem., Bd, Youth and Music; Vice-Chm., Bd of Caldicott Sch.; Southampton Univ. Develt Trust; Chm., Israel/Diaspora Trust. CIMgt 1993; CompTI 1994. *Recreations:* gardening, music, art. *Address:* (office) 47 Baker Street, W1A 1DN.

SILVER, Prof. Ian Adair; Professor of Comparative Pathology, University of Bristol, 1970–93, Emeritus Professor of Pathology, since 1993; Adjunct Professor of Neurology, University of Pennsylvania, since 1977; *b* 28 Dec. 1927; *s* of Captain George James Silver and Nora Adair Silver; *m* 1950, Dr Marian Scrase (*d* 1994), *d* of Dr F. J. Scrase; two *s* two *d*. *Educ:* Rugby School; Corpus Christi Coll., Cambridge (BA, MA); Royal Veterinary Coll. MRCVS 1952, FRCVS 1990. University of Cambridge: Univ. Demonstrator, Zoology, 1952–57; Univ. Lectr, Anatomy, 1957–70; Official Fellow and Coll. Lectr, Churchill Coll., 1965–70; Sen. Tutor for Advanced Students, Churchill Coll., 1966–70; University of Bristol: Hd, Dept of Path., later Path. and Microbiol., 1982–93; Dean, Faculty of Medicine, 1987–90; Chairman, Southmead Health Services NHS Trust, Bristol, 1992–Nov. 1996. Vis. Fellow, Weitzmann Inst., Rehovot, 1963; Vis. Prof., Louisiana Tech Univ., 1973; Royal Soc. Vis. Prof., Fed. Univ. of Rio de Janeiro, 1977. Mem., SERC Biol. Scis Cttee, 1975–80; President: Internat. Soc. for O_2 Transport to Tissue, 1976 and 1986; RCVS, 1985–86 and 1987 (Sen. Vice-Pres., 1986–87 and 1987–88). RAgS Silver Medal, 1952; Sir Frederick Hobday Meml Medal, British Equine Vet. Assoc., 1982; Dalrymple-Champneys Medal, BVA, 1984. *Publications:* Editor of scientific books, 1971–; numerous articles in scientific jls. *Recreations:* farming, exploring, fishing, DIY. *Address:* Department of Anatomy, School of Veterinary Science, University of Bristol, Southwell Street, Bristol BS2 8EJ. *T:* Bristol (0117) 928 8362.

SILVER, Prof. Peter Hele S.; *see* Spencer-Silver.

SILVER, Prof. Robert Simpson, CBE 1967; FRSE; FIMechE; FInstP; James Watt Professor of Mechanical Engineering, University of Glasgow, 1967–79; *b* Montrose, Angus, 13 March 1913; *s* of Alexander Clark Silver and Isabella Simpson; *m* 1937, Jean McIntyre Bruce (*d* 1988), *er d* of Alexander and Elizabeth Bruce (*née* Livingstone); two *s*. *Educ:* Montrose Academy; University of Glasgow. MA, 1932; BSc (1st Class Hons Nat. Phil) 1934; PhD 1938; DSc 1945. Research Physicist, ICI (Explosives), 1936–39; Head of Research, G. & J. Weir Ltd, 1939–46; Asst Director, Gas Research Board, 1947–48; Director of Research, Federated Founderies Ltd, 1948–54; Chief Designer, John Brown Land Boilers Ltd, 1954–56; Chief of Development and Research, G. & J. Weir Ltd, 1956–62 (Director 1958–); Prof. of Mech. Engrng, Heriot-Watt Coll. (now Univ.), 1962–66. FInstP 1942; MIMechE 1953; FRSE 1963. Hon. DSc Strathclyde, 1984. Foreign Associate, Nat. Acad. of Engineering, USA, 1979. Unesco Prize for Science, 1968. *Publications:* An Introduction to Thermodynamics, 1971; The Bruce, Robert I King of Scots (play), 1986, revd edn as The Hert o Scotland, 1994; Conflict and Contexts: poems of the quarter-century 1930–1955, 1992; papers on physics and engineering, with special emphasis on thermo-dynamics, desalination, combustion, phase-change, and heat transfer; also on philosophy of science and education. *Recreations:* fishing, music, theatre, Scottish history and affairs. *Address:* 5 Panmure Street, Montrose, Angus DD10 8EZ. *T:* Montrose (01674) 77793.

SILVERLEAF, Alexander, CB 1980; FEng; FRINA; FICE; FCIT; Co-ordinator, International Transport Group (INTRA), since 1981; *b* 29 Oct. 1920; *m* 1950, Helen Marion Scott; two *d*. *Educ:* Kilburn Grammar Sch., London; Glasgow Univ. (BSc 1941). Wm Denny and Bros Ltd, Shipbuilders, Dumbarton, 1937–51: Student apprentice, 1937–41; Head, Design Office, 1947–51; National Physical Laboratory, 1951–71: Superintendent, Ship Div., 1962–67; Dep. Dir, 1966–71; Dir, Transport and Road Res. Lab., 1971–80. Chm., UK Council for Computing Develt, 1981–86. Hon. FIHT. *Publications:* papers in Trans. Royal Instn Naval Architects and other technical jls. *Address:* 64 Fairfax Road, Teddington, Mddx TW11 9BZ. *T:* 0181–977 6261. *Club:* Athenæum.

SILVERMAN, Prof. Hugh Richard, ARIBA; Professor of Architecture and Head of Welsh School of Architecture, since 1986; *b* 23 Sept. 1940; *m* 1963, Kay Sønderskov-Madsen; two *d*. *Educ:* Edinburgh Univ. (MSc Soc. Sci). Lectr, then Sen. Lectr, Univ. of Bristol, 1971–82. Partner, Alec French Partnership, Architects, Bristol, 1984–86. Built project, 1 Bridewell St, Bristol, 1985 (RIBA Regl Award). Member: Bldg Sub-Cttee, SERC, 1983–85; Architecture Bd, CNAA, 1981–84; Board, Cardiff Bay Develt Corp., 1990–. FRSA 1989. *Address:* Bute Building, King Edward VII Avenue, Cardiff CF1 3AP. *T:* Cardiff (01222) 874431.

SILVERMAN, Julius; Barrister-at-law; *b* Leeds, 8 Dec. 1905; *s* of Nathan Silverman; *m* 1959, Eva Price. *Educ:* Central High School, Leeds (Matriculated). Entered Gray's Inn as student in 1928; called to Bar, 1931; joined Midland Circuit, 1933, practised in Birmingham. Birmingham City Councillor, 1934–45. Contested Moseley Division, 1935. MP (Lab) Birmingham, Erdington, 1945–55 and 1974–83, Birmingham, Aston, 1955–74. Apptd Chm., by Birmingham City Council, of Handsworth Inquiry (into disturbances in Handsworth), 1985 (report published by Council, 1986). Chm., India League, 1971–. Freeman, City of Birmingham, 1982. Hon. Fellow, City of Birmingham Polytechnic, 1987. Padma Bhushan (India), 1990. *Publication:* (contrib.) Centenary History of the Indian National Congress, 1986. *Address:* c/o 50 Ramsay Road, Oxford OX3 8AY.

SILVERSTONE, Judith Anne; *see* Hunt, J. A.

SILVESTER, Frederick John; Chairman and Managing Director, Advocacy Partnership Ltd, since 1987; *b* 20 Sept. 1933; *s* of William Thomas Silvester and Kathleen Gertrude (*née* Jones); *m* 1971, Victoria Ann, *d* of James Harold and Mary Lloyd Davies; two *d*. *Educ:* Sir George Monoux Grammar Sch.; Sidney Sussex Coll., Cambridge. Called to the Bar, Gray's Inn, 1957. Teacher, Wolstanton Grammar School, 1955–57; Political Education Officer, Conservative Political Centre, 1957–60. Member, Walthamstow Borough Council, 1961–64; Chairman, Walthamstow West Conservative Association, 1961–64. Contested (C) Manchester, Withington, 1987. MP (C): Walthamstow West, Sept. 1967–70; Manchester, Withington, Feb. 1974–1987. An Opposition Whip, 1974–76; PPS to Sec. of State for Employment, 1979–81, to Sec. of State for NI, 1981–83. Member: Public Accounts Cttee, 1983–87; Procedure Cttee, 1983–87; Exec., 1922 Cttee, 1985–87; Vice-Chm., Cons. Employment Cttee, 1976–79. Sen. Associate Dir, J. Walter Thompson, 1970–88. *Address:* 27 King Edward Walk, SE1 7PR.

SIM, Andrew Fraser; Solicitor to British Railways Board, since 1993; *b* 27 Nov. 1948; *s* of Donald Fraser Sim and Pamela Jean Sim; *m* 1975, Antonia Rolfe Tweedie Aitken; two *s* one *d*. *Educ:* Haileybury Coll., Herts; City of London Poly. (BA Business Law). Admitted Solicitor. British Railways Board: Asst Solicitor, 1975; Head of Litigation, 1982; Dep. Solicitor, 1986. *Recreation:* the countryside. *Address:* Macmillan House, Paddington Station, W2 1YG. *T:* 0171–922 6668.

SIMCOX, Richard Alfred, CBE 1975 (MBE 1956); Hon. Member of the British Council; *b* 29 March 1915; *s* of Alfred William and Alice Simcox; *m* 1951, Patricia Elisabeth Gutteridge; one *s* two *d*. *Educ:* Gonville and Caius Coll., Cambridge. BA Class. Tripos. Served with N Staffs Regt, 1939–43; British Council from 1943: Rep. in Jordan, 1957–60; in Libya, 1960; in Jordan (again), 1960; Cultural Attaché, British Embassy, Cairo, 1968–71; British Council Representative, Iran, 1971–75. Governor, Gabbitas-Thring Educnl Trust. *Recreations:* gardening, philately. *Address:* Little Brockhurst, Lye Green Road, Chesham, Bucks HP5 3NH. *T:* Chesham (01494) 783797.

SIMEON, Sir John Edmund Barrington, 7th Bt, *cr* 1815; Civil Servant in Department of Social Welfare, Provincial Government, British Columbia, retired 1975; lately in Real Estate business; *b* 1 March 1911; *s* of Sir John Walter Barrington Simeon, 6th Bt, and Adelaide Emily (*d* 1934), *e d* of late Col Hon. E. A. Holmes-à-Court; *S* father 1957; *m* 1937, Anne Robina Mary Dean; one *s* two *d*. *Educ:* Eton; Christ Church, Oxford. Motor business, 1931–39. Served with RAF, 1939–43; invalided, rank of Flight Lt, 1943. Civil Servant, Ministry of Agriculture, 1943–51. Took up residence in Vancouver, Canada, 1951. *Recreations:* sailing, painting. *Heir:* *s* Richard Edmund Barrington Simeon, PhD Yale; Professor of Political Science and Law, Toronto Univ. [*b* 2 March 1943; *m* 1st, 1966, Agnes Joan (marr. diss. 1989), *d* of George Frederick Weld; one *s* one *d*; 2nd, 1993, Maryetta Cheney]. *Address:* c/o Jerome & Co., Solicitors, 98 High Street, Newport, Isle of Wight PO30 1BD; 987 Wavertree Road, N Vancouver, BC V7R 1S6, Canada.

SIMEON, John Power Barrington, OBE 1978; HM Diplomatic Service, retired; *b* 15 Nov. 1929; *o s* of late Cornwall Barrington Simeon and Ellaline Margery Mary (*née* Le Poer Power, Clonmel, Co. Tipperary); *m* 1970, Carina Renate Elisabeth Schüller; one *s*. *Educ:* Beaumont Coll.; RMA, Sandhurst. Commnd 2nd Lieut Royal Corps of Signals, 1949; Lieut 1951; resigned, 1952. Ferrous and non-ferrous metal broker, London and Europe, 1953–57; Rank Organisation: served in Germany, Thailand, Singapore, India, ME, N Africa, Hong Kong and London, 1957–65; entered HM Diplomatic Service, 1965; First Sec. (Commercial): Colombo, 1967; Bonn, 1968–70; First Sec., and sometime Actg High Comr, Port of Spain, 1970–73; FCO, 1973–75; Dep. High Comr and Head of Post, Ibadan, Nigeria, 1975–79. Counsellor, 1978; HM Consul-General: Berlin, 1979–81; Hamburg, 1981–84. *Recreations:* travel, photography, reading, music. *Address:* 4 Cliff Road, Dovercourt, Harwich, Essex CO12 3PP. *T:* Harwich (01255) 552820.

SIMEONE, Reginald Nicola, CBE 1985; FRMetS; Adviser to the Chairman, Nuclear Electric plc, since 1990; *b* 12 July 1927; *s* of late Nicola Francisco Simeone, FCIS, and Phyllis Simeone (*née* Iles); *m* 1954, Josephine Frances Hope; two *s*. *Educ:* Raynes Park Grammar Sch.; St John's Coll., Cambridge (Schol.; MA). FRMetS 1993. Instr Lieut, Royal Navy, 1947–50; Admiralty: Asst Principal, 1950–55; Principal, 1955–59; UKAEA: Finance Br., 1959–61; Economics and Programmes Br., 1961–65; Chief Personnel Officer, AWRE, 1965–69; Principal Estabts Officer, 1970–76; Authority Personnel Officer, 1976–84; Comptroller of Finance and Administration, 1984–86; Bd Mem., 1987–88; Advr to the Chm., 1988–90. Chm., Atomic Energy Constabulary Police Cttee, 1986–90; Exec. Vice Pres., European Atomic Energy Soc., 1987–90. *Recreations:* travel, theatre, opera. *Address:* 31 Portsmouth Avenue, Thames Ditton, Surrey KT7 0RU. *Club:* United Oxford & Cambridge University.

SIMEONS, Charles Fitzmaurice Creighton, DL; MA; Consultant: Environmental Control, Market and Behavioural Studies, Health and Safety at Work, Electronic Information Technology, Communications with Government, technical programmes for conferences and annual events in internat. chemical control, London and Washington; Director, Action Learning Trust, 1978–82; *b* 22 Sept. 1921; *s* of Charles Albert Simeons and Vera Hildegarde Simeons; *m* 1st, 1945, Rosemary (*née* Tabrum) (*d* 1991); one *s* one *d*; 2nd, 1991, Constance Anne Dowson (*née* Restell). *Educ:* Oundle; Queens' Coll., Cambridge. Royal Artillery with 8th Indian Div., 1942–45, HQ RA E African Comd and Northern Comd (Major). Man. Dir, supplier to photographic industry, 1957–70. MP (C) Luton, 1970–Feb. 1974. Chm., Luton Cons. Assoc., 1960–63. President: Luton, Dunstable and District Chamber of Commerce, 1967–68; Rotary Club of Luton, 1960; District Gov., Rotary International, 1967–68; Mem., Rotary Club of Holt, 1992; Advisor, Eastern Area, Prince's Youth Business Trust, 1994–; Chm. of cttees raising funds for disabled and cancer research and for National Children's Homes; Member: Nat. Appeals Cttee, Cancer Res. Campaign, 1977–78; Children in Danger Campaign, 1985–. Chm., Adv. Cttee, Rotary Internat. Bd on Environmental Research and Resources, 1973–74; Vice Pres., Nat. Industrial Material Recovery Assoc., 1972–77; Member: Internat. Cttee, Water Pollution Control Federation, Washington, DC, 1974–77; Customer Consultative Cttee, Anglian Water, 1984–89, Thames Water, 1986–89; Anglian Customer Services Cttee,

Water Services, 1990–; Council, Smaller Business Assoc., 1974–76; ABCC Small Firms Panel; Chm., Central Govt Cttee, Union of Independent Cos. Founder Chm., Friends of Pensthorpe Waterfowl Trust, 1993– (Founder Patron of Trust, 1990). Hon. Mem., Inst. of Water Pollution Control, 1973. Liveryman: Worshipful Co. of Feltmakers (Master, 1987–88); Guild of Freemen of City of London; Mem., Co. of Water Conservators, 1991. FIIM; FRSA. Hon. FIWEM. Pres., Old Oundelian Club, 1976–77; Hon. Sec., 8th Indian Clover Club, 1984–. JP Luton, 1959–74; DL Beds, 1987. *Publications:* Energy Research in Western Europe, 1976; Coal: its role in tomorrow's technology, 1978; Water as a Source of Energy, 1980; A Review of Chemical Response Data Bases in Europe and the United States, 1985; Studies on Incidents Involving Chemicals on Board Ship, in Port, and at Sea in Europe and the United States, 1985; Data Bases capable of response to Chemical Incidents Worldwide, 1986. *Recreations:* watching football, cricket, gardening. *Address:* Mill Leet, High Street, Cley-next-the-Sea, Norfolk NR25 7RR. *T:* Sheringham (01263) 740772. *Club:* City Livery.

SIMHA, Maj.-Gen. Bharat Kesher; Tri Sakti Patta, 1st Class; Gorkha Dakchhina Bahu, 1st Class; Nepal Kirtimaya Shreepad, 3rd Class; Ambassador of Nepal to the Court of St James's, 1988–92, concurrently accredited to Finland, Iceland, Sweden, Norway and Denmark; *b* 15 Aug. 1934; *s* of Lt-Gen. Dharma Bahadur Simha and Chaitanya Rajya Laxmi Simha; *m* 1955, Teeka Rajya Laxmi Rana; three *s*. *Educ:* Durbar High Sch., Kathmandu; Col Brown's Cambridge Sch., Dehradun; Indian Mil. Acad., Dehradun (grad. 1954). Commnd into Royal Nepalese Army, 1952; appts as Adjt, Co. Comdr, ADC to C-in-C, 1954–55; various courses in England, 1956; attached BAOR, 1956; Instr, Sch. of Inf., 1957–59; GSO 3 Directorate of Mil. Ops and Staff Duties, also ADC to C-in-C, 1960; Mem., Nepal–China Jt Boundary Commn, 1960–63; sc Camberley, 1964 (grad.); Resident Mil. Attaché, UK, with accreditation to France, W Germany, Belgium, Netherlands, Sweden, 1964–67; Dir of Mil. Intelligence, 1967–68; Para Overall Comdr, 1968–70; Dir of Res. and Planning, 1970; Asst Dir of Mil. Ops and Staff Duties, 1971; Dir of Mil. Trng, 1972–73; Officiating Dir of Mil. Ops and Staff Duties, 1974; Master-Gen. of Ordnance, 1975; Comdr, No 4 Bde, 1975–77; Dir, Mil. Ops, Staff Duties, Res. and Planning, 1978–80; Adjt-Gen., 1980; QMG, 1982–83; CGS, 1983–85 (retired); ADC Gen. to King of Nepal, 1986. Mem. Exec. Cttee, Pashupati Area Develt Trust, 1987–. Army Long Service Medal. Comdr OM (France), 1966; OM (Jugoslavia), 1974; Grand Cross: Order of the Lion of Finland, 1989; Order of the Dannebrog (Denmark), 1989. *Recreations:* hunting, jogging, squash, tennis, trekking. *Address:* Dharma Ashram, CHHA 3/150 Kaldhara, Kathmandu 3, Nepal. *T:* 412270. *Clubs:* Travellers', Royal Automobile; Tribhuwan Army Officers (Kathmandu).

SIMINOVITCH, Dr Louis, CC 1989 (OC 1980); PhD, FRS 1980; FRSC 1965; Director, Samuel Lunenfeld Research Institute of Mount Sinai Hospital (formerly Mount Sinai Hospital Research Institute), University of Toronto, 1983–94, now Director Emeritus; *b* Montreal, PQ, 1 May 1920; *s* of Nathan Siminovitch and Goldie Watchman; *m* 1944, Elinore, *d* of late Harry Faierman; three *d*. *Educ:* McGill Univ. (BSc 1941, PhD 1944; Arts and Sci. schol. 1939, Sir William McDonald schol. 1940, Anne Molson prize in Chem. 1941). With NRC at Ottawa and Chalk River, Ont., 1944–47; NRC Studentship and Fellowship, 1942–44; with Centre Nat. de la Recherche Scientifique, Paris, 1949–53; Nat. Cancer Inst. Canadian Fellowships, 1953–55; Connaught Med. Res. Labs, Univ. of Toronto, 1953–56. Head of Div. of Biolog. Research, Ontario Cancer Inst., Toronto, 1963–69; Chm., Dept of Med. Cell Biology, Univ. of Toronto, 1969–72; Chm., Dept of Med. Genetics, 1972–79, Univ. Prof., 1976–85, Toronto Univ. Founding Mem. and Pres., Editorial Bd, Science Forum, 1966–79; Pres., Canadian Cell Biology Soc., 1967. Member: Bd of Dirs, Nat. Cancer Inst. of Canada, 1975–85 (Pres., 1982–84); Nat. Bd of Dirs, Canadian Cancer Soc., 1981–84; Bd, Ontario Cancer Treatment and Res. Foundn, 1979–94; Scientific Adv. Cttee, Connaught Res. Inst., 1980–84; Alfred P. Sloan, Jr, Selection Cttee, General Motors Cancer Res. Foundn, 1980–81, 1983–84; Health Res. and Develt Council of Ont, 1983–86. Chairman, Scientific Advisory Committee: Loeb Inst. for Med. Res., Ottawa, 1988–; Rotman Res. Inst., Toronto, 1988–; Ontario Cancer Treatment and Res. Foundn, 1985–; Member, Scientific Advisory Committee: Montreal Neurol Inst., 1992–; Med. Discoveries Fund, Ontario, 1994–; Mem. Bd, Baycrest Centre for the Aged, Toronto, 1992–. Ed., Jl of Molecular and Cellular Biology, 1980–90; Member Editorial Board: Jl Cancer Surveys (London), 1980–89; Somatic Cell and Molecular Genetics, 1984–. Hon. DSc: Meml Univ., Newfoundland, 1978; McMaster Univ., 1978; Hon. Dr: Univ. of Montreal, 1990; McGill Univ., Montreal, 1990; Univ. of Western Ont, London, 1990; Univ. of Toronto, 1995. Flavelle Gold Medal, RSC, 1978; Univ. of Toronto Alumni Assoc. Award, 1978; Izaak Walton Killam Meml Prize, 1981; Gairdner Foundn Wightman Award, 1981; Medal of Achievement Award, Institut de Recherches Cliniques de Montreal, 1985; Environmental Mutagen Society Award, Baltimore, Maryland, 1986; R. P. Taylor Award, Canadian Cancer Soc., Nat. Cancer Inst., 1986; Distinguished Service Award, Canadian Soc. for Clinical Investigation, 1990; Toronto Biotechnol. Initiative Community Service Award, 1991. Silver Jubilee Medal, 1977; Gov.-Gen.'s Commemorative Medal for 125th Anniversary of Canadian Confedn, 1992. Has specialised in the study of bacterial and somatic cell genetics. *Publications:* many contribs to scientific and learned journals. *Address:* c/o Samuel Lunenfeld Research Institute of Mount Sinai Hospital, 600 University Avenue, Toronto, Ont M5G 1X5, Canada; 106 Wembley Road, Toronto. Ont., Canada.

SIMKINS, Charles Anthony Goodall, CB 1968; CBE 1963; *b* 2 March 1912; *s* of Charles Wyckens Simkins; *m* 1938, Sylvia, *d* of Thomas Hartley, Silchester, Hants; two *s* one *d*. *Educ:* Marlborough; New Coll., Oxford (1st Class Hons Mod. Hist.). Barrister, Lincoln's Inn, 1936; served 1939–45 as Captain, Rifle Bde (POW); attached War Office (later MoD), 1945–71. *Publication:* (with Sir Harry Hinsley) British Intelligence in the Second World War: vol. IV, security and counter-intelligence, 1990. *Address:* The Cottage, 94 Broad Street, near Guildford, Surrey GU3 3BE. *T:* Guildford (01483) 572456. *Clubs:* Naval and Military, MCC; Woking Golf.

SIMMERS, Graeme Maxwell, OBE 1982; Chairman, Scottish Sports Council, since 1992; *b* 2 May 1935; *s* of W. Maxwell Simmers and Gwen Simmers; *m* 1965, Jennifer Roxburgh; two *s* two *d*. *Educ:* Glasgow Acad.; Loretto Sch. CA 1959. National Service, commnd Royal Marines, 1959–61. Sen. Partner, S. Easton Simmers & Co., 1960–86; Dir, Scottish Highland Hotels Gp, 1962–92 (Chm., 1972–92). Mem., Scottish Tourist Bd, 1979–86; British Hospitality Association (formerly British Hotels & Restaurants Association): Chm., Bd of Management, 1987–88; Mem. Nat. Exec., 1991–. Dir, Stirling Royal Infirm. NHS Trust, 1993–. Governor: Loretto Sch., 1968– (Chm., 1992–); Queen's Coll., Glasgow, 1989–93. Treasurer and Elder, Killearn Kirk. *Address:* Kincaple, Boquhan, Balfron, Glasgow G63 0RW. *Clubs:* All England Lawn Tennis; Royal and Ancient Golf (Chm., Championship Cttee, 1988–91); Prestwick Golf.

SIMMONDS, John Andrew; Registrar in Bankruptcy, High Court of Justice, since 1993; *b* 8 March 1939; *s* of Frank Andrew Simmonds and Eugenie Marie Alexandra (*née* Longyear); *m* 1968, Maire Clare Kelly; one *s*. *Educ:* Holloway Grammar Sch. Admitted solicitor, 1968; Partner, Stafford Clark & Co., 1971–93. Mem., Insolvency Practitioners Tribunal, 1987–. *Publication:* Statutory Demands: use and abuse, 1992. *Recreations:* shooting, fishing, working dogs. *Address:* Parkhill Road, NW3. *Club:* Royal Automobile.

SIMMONDS, Rt. Hon. Dr Kennedy Alphonse, PC 1984; Prime Minister, Federation of St Christopher (St Kitts) and Nevis, since 1983; *b* 12 April 1936; *s* of Bronte Clarke and Arthur Simmonds; *m* 1976, Mary Camella (*née* Matthew); three *s* two *d*. *Educ:* St Kitts and Nevis Grammar School; Leeward Islands Scholar, 1954; Univ. of West Indies (studies in Medicine), 1955–62. Senior Bench Chemist, Sugar Assoc. Res. Lab., St Kitts, 1955; Internship, Kingston Public Hosp., 1963; medical practice, St Kitts, Anguilla and Nevis, 1964–66; postgrad. studies, Princess Margaret Hosp., Bahamas, 1966; Resident in Anaesthesiology, Pittsburgh, 1968–69; medical practice, St Kitts, 1969–80; Premier of St Christopher (St Kitts) and Nevis, 1980–83. Foundn Mem., People's Action Movement Opposition Party, 1965, Pres., People's Action Movement, 1976. Fellow, Amer. Coll. of Anaesthesiology, 1970. *Recreations:* tennis, cricket, football, video taping. *Address:* PO Box 186, Government Headquarters, Basseterre, St Kitts, West Indies. *T:* 2103.

SIMMONDS, Posy; freelance illustrator/cartoonist, since 1969; *b* 9 Aug. 1945; *d* of Reginald A. C. Simmonds and Betty Cahusac; *m* 1974, Richard Hollis. *Educ:* Queen Anne's Sch., Caversham; L'Ecole des Beaux Arts, Paris; Central Sch. of Art and Design, London (BA Art and Design). Cartoonist: The Guardian, 1977–87, 1988–90, 1992–; The Spectator, 1988–90. Exhibitions: The Cartoon Gall. (formerly the Workshop), 1974, 1976, 1979, 1981, 1982, 1984; Mus. of Modern Art, Oxford, 1981; Manor House Mus. & Art Gall., Ilkley, 1985. TV documentary, Tresoddit for Easter, 1991. Hon. DArt Plymouth, 1993. Cartoonist of the Year: Granada TV/What The Papers Say, 1980; British Press Awards, 1981. *Publications:* Bear Book, 1969; Mrs Weber's Diary, 1979; True Love, 1981; Pick of Posy, 1982; (illustrator) Daisy Ashford, The Young Visiters, 1984; Very Posy, 1985; Fred, 1987; Pure Posy, 1987; Lulu and the Flying Babies, 1988; The Chocolate Wedding, 1990; (illustrator) Hilaire Belloc, Matilda, who told such Dreadful Lies, 1991; Mustn't Grumble, 1993; Bouncing Buffalo, 1994; F-Freezing ABC, 1995. *Address:* c/o Peters, Fraser & Dunlop, 5th Floor, The Chambers, Chelsea Harbour, Lots Road, SW10 0XF. *T:* 0171–376 7676.

See also R. J. Simmonds.

SIMMONDS, Richard James; consultant surveyor and industrialist; farmer of free range poultry and breeder of Jersey cattle; Chairman, Countryside Commission, since 1995; *b* 2 Aug. 1944; *s* of Reginald A. C. Simmonds and Betty Cahusac; *m* 1967, Mary (*née* Stewart); one *s* two *d*. *Educ:* Trinity Coll., Glenalmond. Councillor, Berkshire CC (Chm. of Environment, Property, Transport, and Development Cttees), 1973–79. National Vice-Chm. of Young Conservatives, 1973–75; Founding Vice-Chm. of Young European Democrats, 1974; Personal Asst to Rt Hon. Edward Heath, 1973–75; MEP (C) Midlands W, 1979–84, Wight and Hampshire E, 1984–94; PPS to Sir James Scott-Hopkins, Leader of European Democratic Gp, European Parlt, 1979–82; Cons. spokesman on youth and educn, European Parlt, 1982–84, on budget control, 1984–87; Whip, 1987–89; Chief Whip, 1992–94. Mem., Agric., Fisheries, Food and Rural Develt Cttee, 1992–94. Fellow of Parly & Industry Trust. Founding Pres., Mounted Games Assoc. of GB, 1984–. Liveryman, Gunmakers' Co., 1989. Chm. of Governors, Berkshire Coll. of Agriculture, 1979–92. *Publications:* The Common Agricultural Policy—a sad misnomer, 1979; An A to Z of Myths and Misunderstandings of the European Community, 1981, 3rd edn 1993; European Parliamentary report on farm animal welfare, 1985, 1987, 1990. *Recreations:* resisting bureaucracy, getting things done. *Address:* Woodlands Farm, Cookham Dean, Berkshire SL6 9PJ. *Clubs:* Carlton, United & Cecil, Ancient Britons, Tamworth.

See also Posy Simmonds.

SIMMONS, Alan Gerald; His Honour Judge Simmons; a Circuit Judge, since 1990; *b* 7 Sept. 1936; *s* of late Maurice Simmons and Sophie Simmons (*née* Lasserson); *m* 1961, Mia, *d* of late Emanuel and Lisa Rosenstein; one *s* one *d*. *Educ:* Bedford Modern Sch.; Quintin Sch. RAF, 1956–58. Director: Aslon Labs; Record Productions (Surrey); Ashcourt. Called to the Bar, Gray's Inn, 1968; SE Circuit; Assistant Recorder, 1985; Recorder, 1989. Mem., Mental Health Rev. Tribunal, 1993–. Member: Board of Deputies of British Jews, 1982–88; Council, United Synagogue, 1979–93. *Recreations:* music, reading, fencing.

SIMMONS, Fr Eric, CR; Prior of St Michael's Priory, Burleigh Street, London, since 1993; *b* 1930. *Educ:* Univ. of Leeds. BA (Phil) 1951. Coll. of the Resurrection, Mirfield, 1951; deacon, 1953, priest, 1954; Curate of St Luke, Chesterton, 1953–57; Chaplain, University Coll. of N Staffordshire, 1957–61; licensed to officiate: Dio. Wakefield, 1963–65 and 1967–; Dio. Ripon, 1965–67; Warden and Prior of Hostel of the Resurrection, Leeds, 1966–67; subseq. Novice Guardian, CR, looking after young Community members; Superior, Community of the Resurrection, Mirfield, Yorks, 1974–87; permission to officiate, Dio. London; the Community is an Anglican foundation engaged in evangelism and teaching work, based in Yorkshire but with work in Southern Africa. *Address:* St Michael's Priory, 14 Burleigh Street, WC2E 7PX.

SIMMONS, Guy Lintorn, MVO 1961; HM Diplomatic Service, retired; *b* 27 Feb. 1925; *s* of late Captain Geoffrey Larpent Simmons, RN and Frances Gladys Simmons (*née* Wright); *m* 1951, Sheila Jacob; three *d*. *Educ:* Bradfield Coll.; Oriel Coll., Oxford. RAF, 1943–46; CRO, 1949; 2nd Sec., British High Commn: Lahore, 1950; Dacca, 1952; CRO, 1954–58 and 1964–66; 1st Sec.: Bombay, 1958; New Delhi, 1961; Commercial Counsellor: New Delhi, 1966–68; Cairo, 1968–71; Head of Trade Policy Dept, FCO, 1971–73; Diplomatic Service Inspectorate, 1973–76; Commercial Counsellor, Copenhagen, 1976–79; Consul-General: Karachi, 1979–82; Montreal, 1982–84; FCO, 1984–90. Chm., Crouch End Open Space, 1992–94. *Recreations:* the arts, travel, country pursuits. *Address:* c/o Bank of Scotland, Threadneedle Street, EC2P 2EH. *Club:* Sind (Karachi).

SIMMONS, Jack; Professor of History, University of Leicester, 1947–75, now Professor Emeritus; Pro-Vice-Chancellor, 1960–63; Public Orator, 1965–68; *b* 30 Aug. 1915; *o c* of Seymour Francis Simmons and Katharine Lillias, *d* of Thomas Finch, MB, Babbacombe, Devon. *Educ:* Westminster Sch.; Christ Church, Oxford. Beit Lectr in the History of the British Empire, Oxford Univ., 1943–47. FSA. Mem., Adv. Council, Science Museum, 1969–84; Chm., Nat. Railway Museum Cttee, York, 1981–84; Leicestershire Archæological and Historical Society: Hon. Editor, 1948–61; Pres. 1966–77. Chm., Leicester Local Broadcasting Council, 1967–70. Hon. Fellow, Nat. Railway Mus., York, 1992. Jt Editor, The Journal of Transport History, 1953–73. Editor: A Visual History of Modern Britain; Classical County Histories. *Publications:* African Discovery: An Anthology of Exploration (edited with Margery Perham), 1942; Southey, 1945; Edition of Southey's Letters from England, 1951; Journeys in England: an Anthology, 1951; Parish and Empire, 1952; Livingstone and Africa, 1955; New University, 1958; The Railways of Britain, 1961, 3rd edn, 1986; Transport, 1962; Britain and the World, 1965; St Pancras Station, 1968; Transport Museums, 1970; A Devon Anthology, 1971; (ed) Memoirs of a Station Master, 1973; Leicester Past and Present (2 vols), 1974; (ed) Rail 150: The Stockton and Darlington Railway and What Followed, 1975; The Railway in England and Wales 1830–1914, 1978; A Selective Guide to England, 1979; Dandy Cart to Diesel: the National Railway Museum, 1981; (ed) F. R. Conder, The Men who Built Railways, 1983; Image of the Train, pt 1 1985, pt 2 1993; The Railway in Town and Country 1830–1914, 1986; The Victorian Railway, 1991; Railways: an Anthology, 1991; The Express Train and

Other Railway Studies, 1994. *Address:* Flat 6, 36 Victoria Park Road, Leicester LE2 1XB. *Club:* United Oxford & Cambridge University.

SIMMONS, Jean; film actress; *b* London, 31 Jan. 1929; *m* 1950, Stewart Granger (marr. diss. 1960; he *d* 1993); one *d*; *m* 1960, Richard Brooks (marr. diss. 1977; he *d* 1992); one *d*. *Educ:* Orange Hill Sch.; Aida Foster School of Dancing. First film appearance in Give Us the Moon, 1942; minor parts in Cæsar and Cleopatra, The Way to the Stars, etc., 1942–44; since then has appeared in numerous British films, including: Great Expectations, Black Narcissus, Hungry Hill, Uncle Silas, Hamlet (Best Actress Award, Venice Film Festival, 1950), So Long at the Fair, The Blue Lagoon, Trio, Adam and Evalyn, Clouded Yellow; The Grass is Greener, 1960; Life at the Top, 1965; Say Hello to Yesterday, 1971; began American film career, 1950; American films include: Androcles and the Lion, Young Bess, The Actress, Desirée, Footsteps in the Fog, Guys and Dolls, This Could be the Night, Spartacus, Elmer Gantry, All the Way Home; Divorce, American Style, 1967; The Happy Ending, 1970; The Thorn Birds, 1982 (Emmy award, 1983); television includes: Down at the Hydro, 1982. Musical: A Little Night Music, Adelphi, 1975. Outstanding Film Achievement Award, Italy, 1989. Comdr, Order of Arts and Letters (France), 1990. *Address:* c/o A. Morgan Maree, Jr & Assoc., Inc., 4727 Wilshire Boulevard, Suite 600, Los Angeles, CA 90010–3875, USA.

SIMMONS, John Barry Eves, OBE 1987; VMH 1987; Curator, Royal Botanic Gardens, Kew, 1972–95; *b* 30 May 1937; *s* of Alfred John and Gladys Enid Simmons; *m* 1958, Valerie Lilian Dugan; two *s* one *d*. *Educ:* Harrow County Grammar Sch.; Herts Coll. of Agric. and Hort.; Regent Street Polytechnic; Sch. of Horticulture, Kew. MHort, FIHort; FIBiol, CBiol. Royal Botanic Gardens, Kew: Supervisor, Tropical Propagation Unit, 1961–64; Asst Curator, Temperate Section, 1964–68; Deputy Curator, 1968–72. Chm., Nat. Council for Conservation of Plants and Gardens, 1994– (Mem. Council, 1985–; Vice-Chm., 1991–94; Pres., Norfolk Gp, 1993–); Member: RHS Award and Judging Cttees, 1969–; Longwood Gardens (Pennsylvania) Visiting Cttee, 1984–91; Westonbirt Arboretum Consultative Cttee, 1986–; Chm., Bedgebury Pinetum Consultative Cttee, 1992–; Trustee, Stanley Smith (UK) Horticultural Trust, 1994–. Pres., Inst. of Horticulture, 1987–88. Gov., Writtle Agricl Coll., 1990–93. *Publications:* The Life of Plants, 1974, 2nd edn 1990; (series editor) Kew Gardening Guides, 1987–; (gen. editor) Kew Gardens Book of Indoor Plants, 1988; ed and contrib. to learned jls. *Recreations:* photography, walking, gardening (own garden!).

SIMMONS, Marion Adèle; QC 1994; *b* 11 April 1949; *d* of late Sidney Simmons and of Bella Simmons (*née* Byer). *Educ:* Hendon County Grammar Sch.; Queen Mary Coll., Univ. of London (LLB Hons, LLM). Called to the Bar, Gray's Inn, 1970 (Bencher, 1993); Asst Recorder, 1990–. *Address:* 3/4 South Square, Gray's Inn, WC1R 5HP. *T:* 0171–696 9900.

SIMMONS, Air Marshal Sir Michael (George), KCB 1989 (CB 1988); AFC 1976; Secretary, Council of Justice for Animals and Humane Slaughter Association, since 1992; *b* 8 May 1937; *s* of George and Thelma Simmons; *m* 1964, Jean Aliwell; two *d*. *Educ:* Shrewsbury Sch.; RAF Coll., Cranwell. Commissioned 1958; No 6 Squadron, Cyprus, 1959–61; ADC to AOC-in-C FTC, 1961–64; No 39 Sqdn, Malta, 1964–66; No 13 Sqdn, Malta, 1966–67; No 51 Sqdn, Wyton, 1967–69; RN Staff Coll., 1970; MoD, 1971–72; OC No XV Sqdn, Germany, 1973–76; MoD, 1976–79; OC RAF Cottesmore, 1980–82; MoD, 1982–84; SASO, HQ Strike Comd, 1984–85; AOC No 1 Gp, RAF, 1985–87; ACAS, 1987–89; Dep. Controller Aircraft, MoD, 1989–92. ADC to the Queen, 1980–81. Council, RAF Benevolent Fund, 1994–. Chm. Bd of Govs, Duke of Kent Sch., 1994–. *Recreations:* clock repairing, gardening, golf. *Address:* c/o Royal Bank of Scotland, Drummonds Branch, 49 Charing Cross, Admiralty Arch, SW1A 2DX. *Club:* Royal Air Force.

SIMMONS, Peter Patrick; High Commissioner for Barbados in the United Kingdom, since 1995; *b* 13 April 1942; *s* of late Kenneth G. Simmons and of Sybil Louise Simmons; *m* 1968, Rosalind Cecelia Hinds; one *s* one *d*. *Educ:* London Sch. of Journalism (Diploma); New York State Univ. (BA); Univ. of WI, St Augustine (Cert. Govt Admin). Sub-Editor, Barbados Advocate, 1961–73; Min. of Foreign Affairs, London, NY, Bridgetown, 1963–76; Asst Registrar, Univ. of WI, Cave Hill Campus, 1976–79; Dep. Perm. Rep. and Chargé d'Affaires, Barbados Mission to UN, 1979–82; Chief Develt Planner (Agric.), Min. of Finance and Planning, 1982–84; Dir of Communications, Barbados, 1984–86; Political Specialist, US Embassy, Bridgetown, 1986–91; Chm., SBG Develt Corp., 1991–94. ITV documentary: The Red Legs of Barbados, 1986. *Publications:* Red Legs: class and colour contradictions in Barbados, 1976; (with Sir Garfield Sobers) The Changing Face of Cricket, 1995. *Recreations:* reading, public affairs, cricket, cooking, walking. *Address:* High Commission for Barbados, 1 Great Russell Street, WC1B 3JY. *T:* 0171–631 4975; Iverta, Boyle Farm, Burtenshaw Road, Thames Ditton, Surrey KT7 0TP. *T:* 0181–398 1873.

SIMMONS, Prof. Robert Malcolm, FRS 1995; Professor of Biophysics, King's College London, since 1983; *b* 23 Jan. 1938; *s* of Stanley Laurence Simmons and Marjorie Amys; *m* 1967, Mary Ann (Anna) Ross; one *s* one *d*. *Educ:* King's College London (BSc Physics 1960); Royal Institution (PhD London 1965); University College London (MSc Physiol. 1967). Department of Physiology, University College London: Sharpey Scholar, 1967–70; Lectr, 1970–79; MRC Res. Fellow, 1979–81; King's College London: MRC Cell Biophysics Unit, 1981–83; Associate Dir, 1983–91; Head of Dept of Biophysics, 1983–88; Head of Div. of Biomolecular Scis, 1988–91; Hon. Dir, MRC Muscle and Cell Motility Unit, 1991–. *Publications:* (ed) Muscular Contraction, 1992; contribs on physiol. and biophys to learned jls. *Recreations:* music, fishing. *Address:* Randall Institute, King's College London, 26–29 Drury Lane, WC2B 5RL. *Club:* Athenæum.

SIMMONS, Sir Stanley (Clifford), Kt 1993; FRCS, FRCOG; Consultant Obstetrician and Gynaecologist, Windsor, 1965–92; *b* 28 July 1927; *s* of Lewis Alfred and Ann Simmons; *m* 1956, Ann Wine; one *s* three *d*. *Educ:* Hurstpierpoint Coll.; St Mary's Hosp., London Univ. (MB BS 1951). FRCS 1957, FRCOG 1971. National Service, Royal West African Frontier Force, 1953–55. Resident MO, Queen Charlotte's Hosp. and Chelsea Hosp. for Women, 1955–56; Registrar, St Mary's Hosp. Paddington, 1957–59; Sen. Registrar, St Thomas' Hosp., 1960–64. Member: GMC, 1975–84; Council, RCOG, 1971–72, 1973–78, 1982– (Vice-Pres., 1986; Sen. Vice-Pres., 1987; Pres., 1990–93); Council, RCS (co-opted), 1984–86; President: Hosp. Consultants and Specialists Assoc., 1972; Windsor Med. Soc., 1983; Section of Obst. and Gyn., RSocMed, 1985. Hon. FRCSE 1994; Hon. FRACOG 1992; Hon. FACOG 1993; Hon. Fellow, Inst. of Gynaecologists, RCPI, 1993. *Publications:* (jtly) General Surgery in Gynaecological Practice, 1974; contribs to med. jls. *Recreations:* flying, sailing, golf, ski-ing, painting. *Address:* Coach House, Kennel Avenue, Ascot, Berks SL5 7PB. *T:* Ascot (01344) 23184. *Clubs:* Royal Society of Medicine, Royal Ocean Racing; Wentworth.

SIMMS, Neville Ian, CEng, FICE, FCIOB; Group Chief Executive, since 1992, and Deputy Chairman, since 1994, Tarmac plc; *b* 11 Sept. 1944; *s* of late Arthur Neville Simms and of Anne Davidson Simms (*née* McCulloch). *Educ:* Queen Elizabeth's GS, Crediton; Univ. of Newcastle upon Tyne (BSc 1st cl. Hons 1966); Univ. of Glasgow (MEng 1971). CEng 1970; FICE 1995; FCIOB 1995. Structural Engr, Ove Arup and Partners, 1966–69; joined Tarmac plc as Sect. Engr, Roads Div., Tarmac Civil Engrg, 1970; Jt Man. Dir, Tarmac Internat., 1983–85; Man. Dir, Tarmac Regl Construction, 1985–88; Chief Exec., Tarmac Construction Ltd, 1988–92. Dir, Bank of England, 1995–; non-exec. Dir, Courtaulds, 1994–; Dir, Private Finance Panel Ltd. MInstD 1995; CIMgt 1992; FRSA 1992. *Address:* Hilton Hall, Hilton Lane, Essington, Wolverhampton WV11 2BQ. *T:* Wolverhampton (01902) 307407.

SIMON, family name of **Viscount Simon,** of **Baron Simon of Glaisdale** and of **Baron Simon of Wythenshawe.**

SIMON, 3rd Viscount *cr* 1940; **Jan David Simon;** *b* 20 July 1940; *o s* of 2nd Viscount Simon, CMG and of James Christie, *d* of William Stanley Hunt; *S* father, 1993; *m* 1969, Mary Elizabeth, *d* of late John Joseph Burns, Sydney, NSW; one *d*. *Educ:* Westminster; Sch. of Navigation, Univ. of Southampton; Sydney Tech. Coll. *Heir:* none. *Address:* House of Lords, SW1A 0PW.

SIMON OF GLAISDALE, Baron *cr* 1971 (Life Peer), of Glaisdale, Yorks; **Jocelyn Edward Salis Simon,** PC 1961; Kt 1959; DL; a Lord of Appeal in Ordinary, 1971–77; *b* 15 Jan. 1911; *s* of Frank Cecil and Claire Evelyn Simon, 51 Belsize Pk, NW3; *m* 1st, 1934, Gwendolen Helen (*d* 1937), *d* of E. J. Evans; 2nd, 1948, Fay Elizabeth Leicester, JP, *d* of Brig. H. G. A. Pearson; three *s*. *Educ:* Gresham's School, Holt; Trinity Hall, Cambridge (Exhibitioner). Called to Bar, Middle Temple, 1934 (Blackstone Prizeman). Served War of 1939–45; commissioned RTR, 1939; comd Spec. Service Sqn, RAC, Madagascar, 1942; Burma Campaign, 1944; Lieut-Col. 1945. Resumed practice at Bar, 1946; KC 1951. MP (C) Middlesbrough West, 1951–62; Mem. of the Royal Commission on the Law relating to Mental Illness and Mental Deficiency, 1954–57. Jt Parly Under-Sec. of State, Home Office, 1957–58; Financial Sec. to the Treasury, 1958–59; Solicitor-General, 1959–62. President, Probate, Divorce and Admiralty Div. of the High Court of Justice, 1962–71. Elder Brother, Trinity House, 1975. Hon. Fellow, Trinity Hall, Cambridge, 1963. DL NR (now North) Yorks, 1973. Hon. Dr en Droit Laval, 1961; Hon. LLD Cambridge, 1994. *Publications:* Change is Our Ally, 1954 (part); Rule of Law, 1955 (part); The Church and the Law of Nullity, 1955 (part). *Address:* c/o House of Lords, SW1A 0PW.

See also Hon. P. C. H. Simon.

SIMON OF WYTHENSHAWE, 2nd Baron, *cr* 1947, of Didsbury; **Roger Simon;** *b* 16 Oct. 1913; *S* father, 1960 (but does not use the title and wishes to be known as Roger Simon); *m* 1951 (Anthea) Daphne May; one *s* one *d*. *Educ:* Gresham's School; Gonville and Caius College, Cambridge. *Heir:* *s* Hon. Matthew Simon, *b* 10 April 1955. *Address:* Oakhill, Chester Avenue, Richmond, Surrey TW10 6NP.

See also B. Simon.

SIMON, Prof. Brian; Emeritus Professor of Education, University of Leicester; *b* 26 March 1915; *yr s* of 1st Baron Simon of Wythenshawe and Shena D. Potter; *m* 1941, Joan Home Peel; two *s*. *Educ:* Gresham's Sch., Holt; Schloss Schule, Salem; Trinity Coll., Cambridge; Inst. of Educn, Univ. of London. MA. Pres., Nat. Union of Students, 1939–40; Royal Corps of Signals, GHQ Liaison Regt (Phantom), 1940–45; teaching Manchester and Salford schs, 1945–50; Univ. of Leicester: Lectr in Educn, 1950–64; Reader, 1964–66; Professor, 1966–80; Dir, Sch. of Educn, 1968–70, 1974–77. Chairman: History of Educn Soc., 1976–79; Internat. Standing Conf. for Hist. of Educn, 1979–82; President: British Educn Res. Assoc., 1977–78; Council for Educational Advance, 1991–. Mem., Nat. Acad. of Educn, USA, 1992–. Editor, Forum (for discussion of new trends in educn), 1958–90; Jt Editor, Students Library of Education, 1966–77. Dr *hc* Cath. Univ. of Leuven, 1980. DUniv Open Univ., 1981. *Publications:* A Student's View of the Universities, 1943; Intelligence Testing and the Comprehensive School, 1953; The Common Secondary School, 1955; (ed) New Trends in English Education, 1957; (ed) Psychology in the Soviet Union, 1957; Studies in the History of Education 1780–1870, 1960; (ed, with Joan Simon) Educational Psychology in the USSR, 1963; (ed) The Challenge of Marxism, 1963; (ed) Non-streaming in the Junior School, 1964; Education and the Labour Movement 1870–1920, 1965; (ed) Education in Leicestershire 1540–1940, 1968; (with D. Rubinstein) The Evolution of the Comprehensive School 1926–66, 1969 (revised edn 1973); (with Caroline Benn) Half-Way There: Report on the British Comprehensive School Reform, 1970 (revised edn 1972); Intelligence, Psychology and Education, 1971 (revised edn 1978); (ed) The Radical Tradition in Education in Britain, 1972; The Politics of Educational Reform 1920–1940, 1974; (ed with Ian Bradley) The Victorian Public School, 1975; (with Maurice Galton) Inside the Primary Classroom, 1980; Progress and Performance in the Primary Classroom, 1980; (ed with William Taylor) Education in the Eighties, the central issues, 1981; (ed with John Willcocks) Research and Practice in the Primary Classroom, 1981; Does Education Matter?, 1985; (ed with Detlef Müller and Fritz Ringer) The Rise of the Modern Educational System, 1987; Bending the Rules: the Baker "reform" of education, 1988; (ed) The Search for Enlightenment: the working class and adult education in the twentieth century, 1989; Education and the Social Order 1940–1990, 1991; What Future for Education?, 1992; (ed with Clyde Chitty) Education Answers Back, 1993; (with Clyde Chitty) SOS Save Our Schools, 1993; The State and Educational Change: essays in the history of education and pedagogy, 1994. *Address:* 11 Pendene Road, Leicester LE2 3DQ. *T:* Leicester (0116) 270 5176.

SIMON, Claude (Henri Eugène); French writer and vine grower; *b* Madagascar, 10 Oct. 1913; *s* of Antoine Simon and Suzanne (*née* Denamiel); *m* 1978, Réa Karavas. *Educ:* Collège Stanislas, Paris. Jury Mem., Prix Médicis, 1968–70. Nobel Prize for Literature, 1985. *Publications:* Le tricheur, 1945; La corde raide, 1947; Gulliver, 1952; Le sacre du printemps, 1954; Le vent, 1957; L'herbe, 1958 (trans. The Grass, 1961); La route des Flandres (Prix de l'Express), 1960 (trans. The Flanders Road, 1962); Le palace, 1962 (trans. 1964); Histoire (Prix Médicis), 1967 (trans. 1969); La bataille de Pharsale, 1969 (trans. The Battle of Pharsalus, 1971); Orion aveugle, 1970; Les corps conducteurs, 1971 (trans. Conducting Bodies, 1975); Triptyque, 1973 (trans. 1977); Leçon de choses, 1975; Les Géorgiques, 1981 (trans. 1985); L'Acacia, 1989; articles in journals. *Address:* c/o Editions de Minuit, 7 rue Bernard-Palissy, 75006 Paris, France.

SIMON, Sir David Alec Gwyn, Kt 1995; CBE 1991; Chairman, The British Petroleum Co. plc, since 1995; a Director, Bank of England, since 1995; *b* 24 July 1939; *s* of late Roger Albert Damas Jules Simon and of Barbara (*née* Hudd); *m* 1st, 1964, Hanne (*née* Mohn) (marr. diss. 1987); two *s*; 2nd, 1992, Sarah (*née* Roderick Smith). *Educ:* Christ's Hospital; Gonville and Caius College, Cambridge (MA Hons); MBA INSEAD. Joined BP 1961; Man. Dir, 1986–95; Dep. Chm., 1990–95; Gp Chief Exec., 1992–95. Non-exec. Dir, Grand Metropolitan plc, 1989–; Member: Adv. Bd, Deutsche Bank, 1991–; Internat. Adv. Council, Allianz AG Holding, 1993–. Member: International Council and UK Adv. Bd, INSEAD, 1985–; President's Cttee, CBI, 1992–; European Round Table, 1993–; EU Competitiveness Adv. Gp, 1995–. Mem., Sports Council, 1988–92, 1994–. Hon. DSc(Econ) Hull, 1990. *Recreations:* golf, books, music. *Address:* c/o The British Petroleum Co. plc, Britannic House, 1 Finsbury Circus, EC2M 7BA. *T:* 0171–496 4000. *Clubs:* Brooks's, Groucho; Highgate Golf, Hunstanton Golf.

SIMON, Prof. Herbert A(lexander), PhD; Richard King Mellon University Professor of Computer Science and Psychology, Carnegie-Mellon University, since 1967; *b* 15 June 1916; *s* of Arthur Simon and Edna Merkel Simon; *m* 1937, Dorothea Pye; one *s* two *d*. *Educ:* University of Chicago (BA, PhD). Staff member, Internat. City Managers' Assoc., 1936–39; Study Director, Bureau of Public Admin., Univ. of California (Berkeley), 1939–42; Asst Prof. to Professor, Illinois Inst. of Technology, 1942–49 (Head, Dept of Pol. and Social Sci., 1946–49); Professor of Administration, Carnegie-Mellon Univ., 1949–67 (Associate Dean, Graduate Sch. of Industrial Admin., 1957–73). Mem., Nat. Acad. of Scis, 1967 (Mem. Council, 1978–81, 1983–86). Hon. degrees: DSc: Case Inst. of Technol., 1963; Yale, 1963; Marquette, 1981; Columbia, 1983; Gustavus Adolphus, 1985; Duquesne, 1988; Illinois Inst. of Technol., 1988; Michigan Inst. of Technol., 1988; Carnegie Mellon, 1990; LLD: Chicago, 1964; McGill, 1970; Michigan, 1978; Pittsburgh, 1979; Univ. Paul-Valéry, 1984; Harvard, 1990; FilDr, Lund, 1968; DrEconSci, Erasmus (Rotterdam), 1973; DrPolitSci, Pavia, 1988; DPsych Rome, 1993. Hon. Professor: Tianjin Univ., 1980; Beijing Univ., 1986; Hon. Res. Fellow, Inst. of Psych., Chinese Acad. of Sciences, 1985. Nobel Prize in Economics, 1978; Dist. Sci. Contrib. Award, Amer. Psych. Assoc., 1969; Turing Award, Assoc. for Computing Machinery, 1975; James Madison Award, Amer. Political Science Assoc., 1984; National Medal of Science, 1986; John Von Neumann Theory Prize, Operations Res. Soc. of Amer. and Inst. of Management Sci., 1988; Gold Medal Award in Psychol Sci., Amer. Psychol. Foundn, 1988; Lifetime Contribn to Psychology, Amer. Psychol. Assoc., 1993; Award for Res. Excellence, IJCAI, 1995. *Publications:* Administrative Behavior, 1947, 3rd edn 1976; Models of Man, 1957; (with J. G. March) Organizations, 1958; The New Science of Management Decision, 1960, rev. edn 1977; The Sciences of the Artificial, 1969, 2nd edn 1981; (with A. Newell) Human Problem Solving, 1972; Models of Discovery, 1977; (with Y. Ijiri) Skew Distributions and the Sizes of Business Firms, 1977; Models of Thought, vol. 1, 1979, vol. 2, 1989; Models of Bounded Rationality (2 vols), 1982; Reason in Human Affairs, 1983; (with K. A. Ericsson) Protocol Analysis, 1984; (with P. Langley *et al*) Scientific Discovery, 1987; Models of my Life, 1991; other books, and articles in sci. jls. *Recreations:* walking, piano, painting. *Address:* Department of Psychology, Carnegie-Mellon University, Pittsburgh, PA 15213, USA. *T:* (412) 2682787. *Clubs:* University (Pittsburgh); Cosmos (Washington).

SIMON, Neil; playwright; *b* NYC, 4 July 1927; *s* of Irving and Mamie Simon; *m* 1st, 1953, Joan Baim (decd); 2nd, 1973, Marsha Mason; 3rd, 1987, Diane Lander. *Educ:* De Witt Clinton High Sch.; entered Army Air Force Reserve training programme as an engineering student at New York University; discharged with rank of corporal, 1946. Went to New York Offices of Warner Brothers Pictures to work in mail room. Hon. LHD Hofstra Univ., 1981; Dr *hc* Williams Coll., 1984. *Screenplays include:* After The Fox (produced 1966); Barefoot in the Park, 1967; The Odd Couple, 1968; The Out-of-Towners, 1970; Plaza Suite, 1971; The Last of the Red Hot Lovers, 1972; The Heartbreak Kid, 1973; The Prisoner of 2nd Avenue, 1975; The Sunshine Boys, 1975; Murder by Death, 1976; The Goodbye Girl, 1977; The Cheap Detective, 1978; California Suite, 1978; Chapter Two, 1979; Seems Like Old Times, 1980; Only When I Laugh, 1981; I Ought To Be In Pictures, 1982; Max Dugan Returns, 1983; adapt. Lonely Guy, 1984; The Slugger's Wife, 1984; Brighton Beach Memoirs, 1986; Biloxi Blues, 1988; The Marrying Man, 1991; Broadway Bound (TV film), 1992; Lost in Yonkers, 1993; other films based on his stage plays: Come Blow Your Horn, 1963; Sweet Charity, 1969; The Star-Spangled Girl, 1971. *Plays produced:* Come Blow Your Horn, 1961 (publ. 1961); (jtly) Little Me, 1962 (publ. 1979), rev. version 1982, West End 1984; Barefoot in the Park, 1963 (publ. 1964); The Odd Couple, 1965 (publ. 1966); (jtly) Sweet Charity, 1966 (publ. 1966); The Star-Spangled Girl, 1966 (publ. 1967); Plaza Suite, 1968 (publ. 1969); (jtly) Promises, Promises, 1968 (publ. 1970); Last of the Red Hot Lovers, 1969 (publ. 1970), Criterion, 1979; The Gingerbread Lady, 1970 (publ. 1971); The Prisoner of Second Avenue, 1971 (publ. 1972); The Sunshine Boys, 1972 (publ. 1973); The Good Doctor, 1973 (publ. 1974); God's Favorite, 1974 (publ. 1975); California Suite, 1976 (publ. 1977); Chapter Two, 1977 (publ. 1979); (jtly) They're Playing Our Song, 1979 (publ. 1980); I Ought To Be In Pictures, 1980 (publ. 1981); Fools, 1981 (publ. 1982); Brighton Beach Memoirs, 1983 (publ. 1984), NT, 1986, West End, 1987; Biloxi Blues, 1985 (Tony Award for Best Play, 1985) (publ. 1986); The Odd Couple (female version), 1985 (publ. 1992); Broadway Bound, 1986 (publ. 1988); Rumors, 1988 (publ. 1990), Chichester, 1990; Lost in Yonkers, 1991 (Pulitzer Prize, Tony Award for Best Play, 1991) (publ. 1992), West End, 1992; Jake's Women, 1992 (publ. 1994); (jtly) The Goodbye Girl, 1993; Laughter on the 23rd Floor, 1993 (publ. 1995); London Suite, 1995. *Address:* c/o G. DaSilva, 10100 Santa Monica Boulevard, Los Angeles, CA 90067–4008, USA.

SIMON, Hon. Peregrine Charles Hugo, FLS; QC 1991; *b* 20 June 1950; *s* of Lord Simon of Glaisdale, *qv*, and Fay Elizabeth Leicester, *d* of Brig. Guy Pearson; *m* 1980, Francesca Fortescue Hitchins, *d* of Major Tom Fortescue Hitchins; two *s* two *d*. *Educ:* Westminster School; Trinity Hall, Cambridge (MA). Called to the Bar, Middle Temple, 1973. Mem. Council, Zool Soc., 1992– (Vice-Pres., 1995–). *Address:* Brick Court Chambers, 15/19 Devereux Court, WC2R 3JJ. *T:* 0171–583 0777.

SIMON, Robin John Hughes; Editor, Apollo, since 1990; *b* 23 July 1947; *s* of Most Rev. (William) Glyn (Hughes) Simon, sometime Archbishop of Wales, and Sarah Sheila Ellen (*née* Roberts); *m* 1st, 1971, Jette Margaret Brooke (marr. diss.); one *s* one *d*; 2nd, 1979, Joanna Christine Ross; one *d*. *Educ:* Cardiff High Sch.; Univ. of Exeter (BA Hons English); Courtauld Inst. of Art (MA Hist. European Art). Lectr in Hist. of Art and English, Univ. of Nottingham, 1972–78; Historic Bldgs Rep., NT, 1979–80; Dir, Inst. European Studies, London, 1980–90. Vis. Lectr in Hist. of Art, Univ. of Warwick, 1978; Vis. Prof. in Hist. of Art and Architecture, Westminster Coll., Fulton, Mo, 1989. Arts Corresp., 1987–90, Art Critic, 1990–, Daily Mail; columnist, Tatler, 1994–. Delmas Foundn Fellow, Venice, 1978. Member: Council, Walpole Soc., 1991–; Adv. Council, Paul Mellon Centre for Studies in British Art, 1993–; Exec. Cttee, Assoc. of Art Historians, 1993–; Cttee, Courtauld Assoc. of Former Students, 1992–; Patron, Lord Leighton Centenary Trust, 1994–. *Publications:* (with Alastair Smart) The Art of Cricket, 1983; The Portrait in Britain and America, 1987; (ed) Buckingham Palace: a complete guide, 1993; articles in Apollo, Burlington Mag., TLS, Papers of Brit. Sch. at Rome, Spectator, Tatler, Opera Now, Country Life, etc. *Recreations:* cricket (Captain, Poor Fred's XI), music. *Address:* c/o Apollo, 29 Chesham Place, SW1X 8HB. *T:* 0171–235 1676. *Clubs:* Athenæum, Academy.

SIMON, Roger; *see* Simon of Wythenshawe barony.

SIMON, Prof. Ulrich Ernst, DD; Professor of Christian Literature, 1972–80, Dean, 1978–80, King's College, London; *b* 21 Sept. 1913; *s* of James and Anna Simon; *m* 1949, Joan Edith Raynor Westlake; two *s* one *d*. *Educ:* Grunewald Gymnasium, Berlin; King's Coll., London. BD, MTh, DD, FKC. Ordained in Church of England, 1938; Univ. Lectr, 1945; Reader, 1960. *Publications:* Theology of Crisis, 1948; Theology of Salvation, 1953; Heaven in the Christian Tradition, 1958; The Ascent to Heaven, 1961; The End is not Yet, 1964; Theology Observed, 1966; A Theology of Auschwitz, 1967 (paperback 1978); The Trial of Man, 1973; Story and Faith, 1975; Sitting in Judgment, 1978; Atonement, 1987; Pity and Terror, 1989. *Recreations:* gardening, chamber music, walking. *Address:* 22 Collingwood Avenue, N10 3ED. *T:* 0181–883 4852.

SIMON, William Edward; Chairman, William E. Simon & Sons, Inc., with offices in New Jersey, Los Angeles and Hong Kong; *b* 27 Nov. 1927; *s* of Charles Simon and Eleanor Kearns; *m* 1950, Carol Girard; two *s* five *d*. *Educ:* Newark Academy, NJ; Lafayette Coll. (BA). Joined Union Securities, NYC 1952, Asst Vice-Pres. and Manager of firm's Municipal Trading Dept, 1955–57; Vice Pres., Weeden & Co., 1957–64; Sen. Partner and Mem. Exec. Cttee, Salomon Brothers, NYC, 1964–72. Dep. Sec., US Treasury Dept, and Administrator, Federal Energy Office, 1973–74; Secretary of the Treasury, May 1974–Jan. 1977. Sen. Cons., Booz Allen & Hamilton Inc., 1977–79; Sen. Advr, Blyth Eastman Dillon & Co. Inc., 1977–80; Dep. Chm., Olayan Investments Co. Estabt, 1980; Chairman: Crescent Diversified Ltd, 1980; Wesray Corp., 1981–86, now Emeritus; Wesray Capital Corp., 1984–86; Co-Chairman: WSPG International Inc., 1987–92; WSPG Partners, LP, 1990–92. Director: Pompano Park Realty, Inc.; East Hampton Beach Preservation Soc., Sheridan Arts Foundn; Univ. of Limerick Foundn; Hoover Instn; Sequoia Inst. Member: President's Cttee on the Arts and Humanities; Atlantic Council of US; Boys Harbor Catholic Big Brothers; Citizens Against Govt Waste; Citizens Network for Foreign Affairs; Covenant House; Gerald R. Ford Foundn; Internat. Foundn for Educn and Self-Help; Kissinger Assoc.; Nat. Football Hall of Fame; World Cup 1994 Organizing Cttee; Mem. Exec. Bd, US Olympic Cttee (former Pres.); Chm., Bd of Trustees, US Olympic Foundn. Pres., John M. Olin Foundn, 1977–; Trustee: Lafayette Coll.; Univ. of Rochester; Boston Univ.; Hudson Inst.; Hillsdale Coll.; John M. Templeton Foundn; Adelphi Univ. Hon. Dr of Laws: Lafayette Coll., 1973; Pepperdine Univ., 1975; Manhattanville Coll., 1978; Washington, Boston, 1980; Washington Coll., Rider Coll., Seton Hall, Fairleigh Dickenson, 1984; Rutgers, Rochester, 1985; Hon. DCL Jacksonville Univ., 1976; Hon. PhD Tel Aviv, 1976; Hon. Scriptural Degree, Israel Torah Res. Inst., 1976; Hon. DSc New England Coll., 1977; Dr of Humanics, Springfield, 1986; Hon. Dr of Econs Hanyang Univ., Seoul, Korea, 1988. Numerous honours and awards. *Publications:* A Time for Truth, 1978; A Time for Action, 1980. *Address:* William E. Simon & Sons Inc., 310 South Street, PO Box 1913, Morristown, NJ 07962–1913, USA; Nomis Hill, Sand Spring Road, New Vernon, NJ 07976, USA. *Clubs:* Sunningdale Golf; Links, Brook, Bond, Municipal Bond, Explorers, Pilgrims of US, New York Yacht, New York Athletic (New York, NY); Maidstone (East Hampton, NY); Alfalfa (Washington, DC); Balboa Bay, Commonwealth, Bel-Air Country (Calif); Morris County Golf (Convent Station, NJ); Rolling Rock (Pa); Country (Colo); Waialae Country, Oahu Country, Maui Country (Hawaii); Gulf Stream Golf (Fla); Lyford Cay (Bahamas).

SIMONDS-GOODING, Anthony James Joseph; Chairman, SP Lintas, since 1994; *b* 10 Sept. 1937; *s* of Major and Mrs Hamilton Simonds-Gooding; *m* 1st, 1961, Fiona (*née* Menzies) (marr. diss. 1982); four *s* two *d*; 2nd, 1982, Marjorie Anne, *d* of late William and Wendy Pennock; one step *s*. *Educ:* Ampleforth Coll.; BRNC, Dartmouth. Served RN, 1953–59; Unilever, 1960–73; Marketing Dir, subseq. Man. Dir (UK), finally Gp Man. Dir, Whitbread & Co. plc, 1973–85; Saatchi plc, 1985–87 (Chm. and Chief Exec. of all communication and advertising cos worldwide); Chief Exec., British Satellite Broadcasting, 1987–90. Director: Aqueduct Enterprises, 1992–94; Robinson and Sons, Chesterfield, 1993–; Lilliput Group, 1993–94; Community Hosps Gp plc, 1995–. Chm., D&AD, 1992–94; Director: ICA, 1992–94; Cancer Relief Macmillan Fund, 1992–; Brixton Prison Bd, 1994–. *Recreations:* family, opera, sport, travel, art. *Address:* c/o SP Lintas, 84 Eccleston Square, SW1V 1PX. *Clubs:* Hurlingham, Queen's.

SIMONET, Henri François; Commander, Order of Leopold, 1974; Member, Belgian Parliament, 1966–92; *b* Brussels, 10 May 1931; *m* 1960, Marie-Louise Angenent; one *s* one *d*. *Educ:* Univ. Libre de Bruxelles (DenD, DèsSc); Columbia Univ., USA. Assistant, Univ. Libre de Bruxelles, 1956–58, now Prof.; Financial Adv., Inst. Nat. d'Etudes pour le Développement du Bas-Congo, 1958–59; Legal Adv., Commn of Brussels Stock Exchange, 1956–60; Dep. Dir, Office of Econ. Programming, 1961; Director of Cabinet: of Min. of Econ. Affairs and Power, 1961–65; of Dep. Prime Minister responsible for co-ordination of Econ. Policy, 1965; Minister of Econ. Affairs, 1972; Vice-Pres., Commn of the European Communities, 1973–77; Foreign Minister, Belgium, 1977–80; Sec. of State, Brussels Regional Economy, 1977–79. Mayor of Anderlecht, 1966–84. Commander, Légion d'Honneur (France), 1985. *Publications:* various books and articles on economics, financial and political topics. *Address:* 34 avenue Franklin Roosevelt, 1050 Brussels, Belgium.

SIMONET, Sir (Louis Marcel) Pierre, Kt 1985; CBE 1980 (OBE 1972); Director and Proprietor, Pharmacie Simonet, since 1955 (founded by father, 1926); *b* 6 March 1934; *s* of Marcel Simonet and Marguerite Simonet. *Educ:* Collège du St Esprit up to Higher School Certificate. Town Council of Curepipe: Mem., 1960; Vice-Chm., 1962; Chm., 1964; 1st Mem. for Curepipe, Legislative Assembly, 1976. Judge Assessor, Permt Arbitration Tribunal, 1984. Dir, Central Electricity Bd, 1972. Chm., Central Housing Authority, 1986–88. Mem., Ex-servicemen's Assoc., 1977; Pres., Widows and Orphans Pension Fund, 1978; Past Pres., Lions Club of Curepipe; Chm., Centre Culturel d'Expression Française (Founder Mem., 1960). Pres., Soc. of St Vincent de Paul. Testimonial, Royal Humane Soc. for life saving, 1962; Chevalier de l'Ordre National du Mérite (France), 1980. *Address:* Queen Mary Avenue, Floreal, Mauritius. *T:* (office) 6763532, (residence) 6865240. *Club:* Mauritius Racing.

SIMONS, (Alfred) Murray, CMG 1983; HM Diplomatic Service, retired; Head of UK Delegation to Negotiations on Mutual Reduction of Armed Forces and Armaments and Associated Measures in Central Europe, at Vienna, 1982–85, with personal rank of Ambassador; *b* 9 Aug. 1927; *s* of late Louis Simons and of Fay Simons; *m* 1975, Patricia Jill, *d* of late David and May Barclay, Westbury on Trym, Bristol; two *s*. *Educ:* City of London Sch.; Magdalen Coll., Oxford (MA). FO, 1951; 3rd Sec., Moscow, 1952–55; FO, 1955–56; Columbia Univ., 1956; 2nd Sec., Bogota, 1957; 1st Sec., Office of Comr-Gen. for SE Asia, Singapore, 1958–61; FO, 1961–64; 1st Sec., British High Commn, New Delhi, 1964–68; FCO, 1968–71; Counsellor, 1969; British Embassy, Washington, 1971–75; Head of SE Asia Dept, FCO, 1975–79; Consul General, Montreal, 1980–82. Mem., International Institute of Strategic Studies. Pres., John Carpenter Club, 1992–93. Freeman, City of London, 1990. *Recreations:* tennis, theatre. *Address:* 128 Longland Drive, Totteridge, N20 8HL. *T:* 0181–446 3163.

SIMONS, Prof. John Philip, PhD, ScD; FRS 1989; CChem, FRSC; Dr Lee's Professor of Chemistry, Oxford University, since 1993; Fellow of Exeter College, Oxford, since 1993; *b* 20 April 1934; *s* of Mark Isaac Simons and Rose (*née* Pepper); *m* 1st, 1956, Althea Mary (*née* Screaton) (*d* 1989); three *s*; 2nd, 1992, Elizabeth Ann Corps. *Educ:* Haberdashers' Aske's Hampstead Sch.; Sidney Sussex Coll., Cambridge (BA; PhD 1958; ScD 1975). CChem, FRSC 1975. Chemistry Department, University of Birmingham: ICI Fellow, 1959; Lectr, 1961; Reader in Photochemistry, 1977; Prof. of Photochem., 1979; Prof. of Physical Chemistry, Univ. of Nottingham, 1981–93. Vice Pres., and Hon. Sec., 1981–93, Pres., 1993–95, Faraday Div., RSC. Tilden Lectr, RSC, 1983. Member: Chemistry Cttee, 1983–85, Laser Facility Cttee, 1983–87, SERC; Comité de Direction, CNRS Lab. de Photophysique Moleculaire, Orsay, 1985–90; specially promoted scientific programme panel, NATO, 1985–88. Adv. Councillor, Ramsay Meml Fellowship Trust, 1991–. Member Editorial Boards: Molecular Physics, 1980–; Chemical Physics Letters, 1982–; Jl

Chem. Soc. Faraday Trans, 1990–; Chemical Physics, 1994–. Chemical Dynamics Award, RSC, 1994. *Publications:* Photochemistry and Spectroscopy, 1970; research papers in learned jls of molecular/chemical physics, *eg* Jl Chem. Soc. Faraday Trans, Molecular Physics, and Chem. Phys. Lett. *Recreations:* writing and reading verse. *Address:* Physical and Theoretical Chemistry Laboratory, South Parks Road, Oxford OX1 3QZ. *T:* Oxford (01865) 275402.

SIMPLE, Peter; *see* Wharton, Michael B.

SIMPSON, Alan, MA, DPhil Oxon, LHD, LLD; President and Professor of History, Vassar College, Poughkeepsie, NY, 1964–77; *b* Gateshead, Durham, England, 23 July 1912; *s* of George Hardwick Simpson and Isabella Simpson (*née* Graham); *m* 1938, Mary McQueen McEldowney, Chicago Heights, Ill; one *s* two *d. Educ:* Worcester Coll., Oxford (BA); Merton Coll., Oxford (MA, DPhil); Harvard Univ. (Commonwealth Fellow). Served War of 1939–45, RA, Major. Sen. Lectr in Modern British History and American History, Univ. of St Andrews, and Lectr in Constitutional Law, Law Sch., University Coll., Dundee, 1938–46; Asst Prof. of History, Univ. of Chicago, 1946–54; Associate Prof., 1954–59; Thomas E. Donnelley Prof. of History and Dean of the College, Univ. of Chicago, 1959–64. Member Board of Trustees: Colonial Williamsburg; Salve Regina Coll., Newport; Old Dartmouth Hist. Soc.; Mem., Amer. Antiquarian Soc.; Former Member: Council of the Inst. of Early Amer. History and Culture, Williamsburg, Va, 1957–60; Midwest Conf. of British Historians (Co-Founder, 1954; Sec., 1954–61); Commn on Academic Affairs and Bd of Dirs, Amer. Council on Educn; Commn on Liberal Learning, Assoc. of Amer. Colls; Hudson River Valley Commn. *Publications:* (Co-Editor) The People Shall Judge: Readings in the Formation of American Policy, 1949; Puritanism in Old and New England, 1955; The Wealth of the Gentry, 1540–1660: East Anglian Studies, 1961; (co-ed with Mary Simpson): Diary of King Philip's War by Benjamin Church, 1975; (with Mary Simpson) I Too Am Here: selections from the letters of Jane Welsh Carlyle, 1977; (with Mary Simpson) Jean Webster, Storyteller, 1984; The Mysteries of the "Frenchman's Map" of Williamsburg, Virginia, 1984. *Address:* Yellow Gate Farm, Little Compton, RI 02837, USA. *Club:* Century (New York).

SIMPSON, Alan; author and scriptwriter since 1951 (in collaboration with Ray Galton, *qv*); *b* 27 Nov. 1929; *s* of Francis and Lilian Simpson; *m* 1958, Kathleen Phillips (*d* 1978). *Educ:* Mitcham Grammar Sch. *Television:* Hancock's Half Hour, 1954–61 (adaptation and trans., Fleksnes, Scandinavian TV, film and stage); Comedy Playhouse, 1962–63; Steptoe and Son, 1962–74 (US TV Version, Sanford and Son, Dutch TV, Stiefbeen And Zoon, Scandinavian TV, Albert Och Herbert); Galton-Simpson Comedy, 1969; Clochemerle, 1971; Casanova '74, 1974; Dawson's Weekly, 1975; The Galton and Simpson Playhouse, 1976–77; *films:* The Rebel, 1960; The Bargee, 1963; The Wrong Arm of the Law, 1963; The Spy with a Cold Nose, 1966; Loot, 1969; Steptoe and Son, 1971; Steptoe and Son Ride Again, 1973; Den Siste Fleksnes (Scandinavia), 1974; Skraphandlarne (Scandinavia), 1975; *theatre:* Way Out in Piccadilly, 1966; The Wind in the Sassafras Trees, 1968; Albert och Herbert (Sweden), 1981; Fleksnes (Norway), 1983; Mordet pa Skölgatan 15 (Sweden), 1984. Awards: Scriptwriters of the Year, 1959 (Guild of TV Producers and Directors); Best TV Comedy Series (Steptoe and Son, 1962, 1963, 1964, 1965 (Screenwriters Guild)); John Logie Baird Award (for outstanding contribution to Television), 1964; Best Comedy Series (Stiefbeen And Zoon, Dutch TV), 1966; Best Comedy Screenplay (Steptoe and Son, Screenwriters Guild), 1972. *Publications:* (jointly with Ray Galton, *qv*): Hancock, 1961; Steptoe and Son, 1963; The Reunion and Other Plays, 1966; Hancock Scripts, 1974; The Best of Hancock, 1986. *Recreations:* Hampton FC (Pres.), gourmet travelling, guest speaking. *Address:* c/o Tessa Le Bars Management, 54 Birchwood Road, Petts Wood, Kent BR5 1NZ. *T:* Orpington (01689) 837084.

SIMPSON, Alan; His Honour Judge Simpson; a Circuit Judge, since 1985; *b* 17 April 1937; *s* of William Henry Simpson and Gladys Simpson; *m* 1965, Maureen O'Shea; one *s* one *d. Educ:* Leeds Grammar Sch.; Corpus Christi Coll., Oxford (MA). Called to the Bar, Inner Temple, 1962, a Recorder, 1975–85. Prosecuting Counsel to DHSS, North Eastern Circuit, 1977–85. Admin. Steward, BBB of C, 1994. *Recreations:* music, books, sport (especially cricket and boxing). *Address:* c/o Sheffield Crown Court, Castle Street, Sheffield S1 1QN. *T:* Sheffield (0114) 273 7511.

SIMPSON, Alan John; MP (Lab) Nottingham South, since 1992; *b* 20 Sept. 1948; *s* of Reginald James and Marjorie Simpson; *m* (separated); one *d* two *s. Educ:* Bootle Grammar Sch.; Nottingham Poly. (BSc Econ). Asst Gen. Sec., Nottingham Council of Voluntary Service, 1970–72; Develt Officer, Home Office Pilot Programme (Non Custodial Treatment of Offenders), 1972–74; Community Worker, Nottingham Areas Project, 1974–78; Res. and Inf. Officer, Nottingham Racial Equality Council, 1979–92. Cllr, Notts CC, 1985–93. Member: CND; Shelter; Oxfam. *Publications:* (contrib.) Issues in Community Education, 1980; Stacking the Decks: a study of race and council housing, 1981; (contrib.) The Right to a Home, 1984; Cuckoos in the Nest—Task Forces and urban policy, 1988; Against a Rising Tide—racism, Europe and 1992, 1991; Beyond the Famished Road—new policies for common security, 1994. *Recreations:* tennis, football (lifelong supporter, Everton FC), vegetarian cooking, eclectic interest in music and reading. *Address:* 222A Bluebell Hill Road, St Anns, Nottingham NG3 3EA. *T:* Nottingham (0115) 950 3769.

SIMPSON, Sir Alfred (Henry), Kt 1985; Chief Justice of Kenya, 1982–85; *b* 29 Oct. 1914; *s* of John Robertson Simpson, Dundee; *m* 1941, Hilda Corson Rodgers; one *d. Educ:* Grove Academy; St Andrews University; Edinburgh University. MA St Andrews, 1935; LLB Edinburgh, 1938 and Solicitor. Served in RASC, 1940–46, Middle East and Italy; Military Mission to the Italian Army and Allied Commission, Austria. Legal Officer, BMA, Cyrenaica, 1946–48. Member of the Faculty of Advocates, 1952. Crown Counsel, Singapore, 1948–56; Legal Draftsman, Gold Coast, 1956; Solicitor-General, Ghana, 1957, then Puisne Judge, Supreme Court, 1957–61; Puisne Judge, Combined Judiciary of Sarawak, North Borneo and Brunei, 1962; Senior Puisne Judge, Fedn of Malaysia High Court in Borneo, 1964; Reader, Faculty of Law, ANU, Canberra, 1965; Barrister-at-Law, NSW, 1967; Puisne Judge, High Court of Kenya, 1967–82. *Publication:* (with others) The Laws of Singapore, revised edn, 1955. *Recreation:* golf. *Address:* 23 Downes Place, Hughes, ACT 2605, Australia. *Clubs:* Commonwealth Trust, Royal Over-Seas League; Royal Canberra Golf.

SIMPSON, Alfred Moxon, AC 1978; CMG 1959; Chairman, SA Telecasters Ltd, 1964–92 (Director, 1962–92); *b* 17 Nov. 1910; *s* of late A. A. Simpson, CMG, CBE; *m* 1938, Elizabeth Robson Cleland; one *s. Educ:* St Peter's College; University of Adelaide, (BSc). Associate (Commerce) of Univ. of Adelaide, 1940. Chm., Simpson Holdings Ltd, 1939–83. Pres. Adelaide Chamber of Commerce, 1950–52; Sen. Vice-Pres. Associated Chambers of Commerce of Aust., 1953–55; Pres. SA Chamber of Manufrs, 1956–58; Pres. Associated Chambers of Manufrs of Aust., 1957–58. Director: Bank of Adelaide, 1952–79; Elder Smith Goldsbrough Mort Ltd, 1954–81; Adelaide Steamship Co. Ltd, 1960–83; QBE Insurance Group Ltd, 1975–83 (Local Dir, 1935). Mem. Hulme Cttee on Rates of Depreciation, 1956; Report on employment security of overseas officers in Papua-New Guinea, 1972, adopted by govt, 1973. Mem. Council, Flinders Univ., 1965–76. *Recreations:* carpentry, lawnmowing. *Address:* 31 Heatherbank Terrace, Stonyfell, SA 5066, Australia. *T:* (8) 311285. *Clubs:* Adelaide, Naval, Military and Airforce, Mt Lofty Ski (Adelaide).

SIMPSON, Prof. (Alfred William) Brian, DCL; FBA 1983; JP; Charles F. and Edith J. Clyne Professor of Law, University of Michigan, since 1987; Professor of Law, University of Kent, 1973–85, now Emeritus; *b* 17 Aug. 1931; *s* of Rev. Canon Bernard W. Simpson and Mary E. Simpson; *m* 1st, 1954, Kathleen Anne Seston (marr. diss. 1968); one *s* one *d*; 2nd, 1969, Caroline Elizabeth Ann Brown; one *s* two *d. Educ:* Oakham Sch., Rutland; The Queen's Coll., Oxford (MA 1958, DCL 1976). Nat. Service with RWAFF, 1950–51. Junior Research Fellow, St Edmund Hall, Oxford, 1954–55; Fellow and Tutor, Lincoln Coll., Oxford, 1955–73; Dean: Faculty of Law, Univ. of Ghana, 1968–69; Faculty of Social Sciences, Univ. of Kent, 1975–78; Prof. of Law, Univ. of Chicago, 1984–86. Called to the Bar, Gray's Inn, 1994. Visiting Professor: Dalhousie Univ., 1964; Univ. of Chicago, 1979, 1980, 1982, 1984; Univ. of Michigan, 1985; Goodhart Prof. of Legal Sci., Univ. of Cambridge, 1993–94. Hon. Dep. District Attorney, Denver City, 1982. Member, Deptl Cttee on Obscenity and Film Censorship, 1977–79. Fellow, Amer. Acad. of Arts and Scis, 1993. JP Canterbury and St Augustine's, 1968–. Hon. Fellow, Lincoln Coll., Oxford, 1995. Hon. DLitt Ghana, 1993. *Publications:* Introduction to the History of the Land Law, 1961, new edn as A History of the Land Law, 1986; (ed) Oxford Essays in Jurisprudence, 2nd Series, 1973; A History of the Common Law of Contract, 1975; Pornography and Politics, 1983; Cannibalism and the Common Law, 1984; (ed) A Biographical Dictionary of the Common Law, 1984; Legal Theory and Legal History: essays on the common law, 1987; Invitation to Law, 1988; In the Highest Degree Odious: detention without trial in wartime Britain, 1992; Leading Cases in the Common Law, 1995; articles in legal jls. *Recreations:* sailing, flying. *Address:* University of Michigan Law School, Hutchins Hall, Ann Arbor, MI 48109–1215, USA. *T:* (313) 7630413; 36 High Street, Wingham, Canterbury, Kent CT3 1AB. *T:* Canterbury (01227) 720979.

SIMPSON, Anthony Maurice Herbert, TD 1973; Member, Inspectorate-General of Services, European Commission, since 1994; *b* 28 Oct. 1935; *y s* of late Lt-Col Maurice Rowton Simpson, OBE, TD, DL and Mrs Renée Claire Simpson; *m* 1961, Penelope Gillian, *d* of late Howard Dixon Spackman; one *s* two *d. Educ:* Rugby; Magdalene College, Cambridge. BA 1959, LLM (LLB 1961), MA 1963. Leics and Derbys (PAO) Yeomanry, 1956–59; TA 1956–74, Major 1968. Called to Bar, Inner Temple, 1961; practised Midland and Oxford Circuit, 1961–75; Mem., Legal Service of European Commn, Brussels, 1975–79; MEP (C) Northamptonshire, 1979–94; contested (C) Northamptonshire and Blaby, Eur. Parly elecns, 1994; Quaestor of the European Parlt, 1979–87, and 1989–94; EDG spokesman on develt and co-operation, 1987–89. Contested (C) West Leicester, Feb. and Oct. 1974. Common Market Law Editor, Current Law, 1965–72. *Recreations:* walking, travelling. *Address:* Bassets, Great Glen, Leicestershire LE8 9GQ. *T:* Great Glen (0116) 259 2386; Avenue Michel-Ange 57, 1040 Brussels, Belgium. *T:* (2) 7364219.

SIMPSON, Athol John Dundas, OBE 1976; Director of North American Operations, Crown Agents for Oversea Governments and Administrations, since 1985; *b* 4 May 1932; *s* of John Simpson and Helen Murray Simpson (*née* Cubie); *m* 1956, Ricki Ellen Carter; one *s* two *d. Educ:* Reigate Grammar Sch. Joined Crown Agents, 1950; served, Royal Air Force, 1951–53; Crown Agents' Representative in E Africa, 1965–69; seconded as Managing Director, Millbank Technical Services (Iran) Ltd, 1973–77; returned to Bd appt as Dir of Marketing and Development with Crown Agents, Nov. 1977; Dir, Crown Agents, 1978–85. *Recreations:* Rugby football, golf, reading. *Address:* 66 Archel Road, West Kensington, W14 9QP. *T:* 0171–381 0759. *Clubs:* Travellers'; International (Washington, DC).

SIMPSON, Prof. Brian; *see* Simpson, Prof. A. W. B.

SIMPSON, Brian, Member (Lab) Cheshire East, European Parliament, since 1989; *b* Leigh, Lancs, 6 Feb. 1953; *s* of late John Hartley Simpson and of Freda Simpson; *m* 1975, Linda Jane Gwynn; one *s* two *d. Educ:* Golborne Comprehensive Sch., Wigan; W Midlands Coll. of Educn, Walsall (Cert Ed). Teacher, City of Liverpool, 1974–89. Councillor: Merseyside CC, 1981–85; Warrington Bor. Council, 1987–91. *Recreations:* Rugby League, cricket, British and European history, steam railways. *Address:* Gilbert Wakefield House, 67 Bewsey Street, Warrington WA2 7JQ. *T:* Warrington (01925) 654074. *Club:* Golborne Sports and Social (Wigan).

SIMPSON, Air Vice-Marshal Charles Ednam; Director (Scotland), Royal Air Force Benevolent Fund, 1989–94; *b* 24 Sept. 1929; *s* of Charles and Margaret Simpson; *m* 1955, Margaret Riddell; two *s* one *d. Educ:* Stirling and Falkirk High Schools; Univ. of Glasgow (MB ChB); University of London (MSc). FFOM 1986; MFCM. British Defence Staff, Washington DC, 1975; Dep. Dir, Aviation Medicine, RAF, 1978; CO, RAF Hosp., Wegberg, 1981; CO, Princess Alexandra Hosp., Wroughton, 1982; Dir of Health and Research, RAF, 1984; Asst Surgeon General (Envtl Medicine and Res.), 1985; PMO HQ RAF Strike Comd, 1986–89; QHS 1985–89. HM Comr, Queen Victoria Sch., Dunblane, 1990–. *Recreations:* golf, birdwatching. *Address:* Am Bruach, Fore Road, Kippen, Stirling FK8 3DT. *T:* Kippen (01786) 870281. *Club:* Royal Air Force.

SIMPSON, Commander Cortlandt James Woore, CBE 1956; DSC 1945; retired 1961; *b* 2 Sept. 1911; *s* of late Rear-Admiral C. H. Simpson, CBE, and Edith Octavia (*née* Busby); *m* 1st, Lettice Mary Johnstone; 2nd, Ann Margaret Cubitt; 3rd, Joan Mary Watson; one *d*; 4th, Vanessa Ann Stainton (*née* Heald). *Educ:* St Ronans, Worthing; RN College, Dartmouth; London Univ. (BSc Engineering, Hons). Joined RN (Dartmouth), 1925; Lieut, 1934. Served War of 1939–45 in Home and Mediterranean Fleets; Commander, 1948. Summer expeditions to Greenland, 1950, 1951, Leader of British North Greenland Expedition, 1952–54. Polar Medal, 1954; Royal Geographical Society, Founder's Medal, 1955. *Publication:* North Ice, 1957. *Recreations:* mountaineering, sailing, walking. *Address:* Lower Lambie, Luxborough, Watchet, Somerset TA23 0SJ. *Club:* Alpine.

SIMPSON, David; Metropolitan Stipendiary Magistrate, since 1993 (Chairman, Youth Courts); *b* 29 July 1947; *s* of Albert Edward Simpson and Lily Simpson; *m* 1975, Jane Richards; one *s. Educ:* N Cestrian GS, Altrincham; Worthing High Sch. for Boys; King's Coll., London (LLM 1987). Admitted a solicitor, 1974. British Bank of ME, 1966–67; Court Clerk, Magistrates' Court: Worthing, 1967–74; Mansfield, 1975–76; Dep. Clerk, 1976–82, Clerk, 1982–93, to the Justices, Uxbridge. Vice-Pres., Assoc. of Magisterial Officers, 1981–82; Member: Sentencing Cttee, Justice, 1987–89; Council, Justices' Clerks' Soc., 1987–93; Magisterial Cttee, Judicial Studies Bd, 1990–93. *Recreations:* gardening, golf, reading, railways. *Address:* Inner London Magistrates' Courts Service, 65 Romney Street, SW1P 3RD.

SIMPSON, David Rae Fisher; Economist, Standard Life Assurance Co., since 1988; *b* 29 Nov. 1936; *s* of late David Ebenezer Simpson and of Roberta Muriel Wilson; *m* 1980, Barbara Dianne Goalen, *d* of N. and Mrs G. Inglis, Edinburgh; one *s* (and one step *s* one step *d*). *Educ:* Skerry's Coll.; Edinburgh and Harvard Univs. MA 1st cl. hons Econs Edinburgh; PhD Econs Harvard. Instr in Econs, Harvard Univ., 1963–64; Assoc. Statistician, UN Hdqtrs, NY, 1964–65; Res. Officer, Econ. Res. Inst., Dublin, 1965–67;

Lectr in Polit. Economy, UCL, 1967–69; Sen. Lectr in Econs, Univ. of Stirling, 1969–74; University of Strathclyde: Prof. and Dir, Fraser of Allander Inst., 1975–80, Res. Prof., 1980–85; Prof., Dept of Economics, 1985–88. Contested (SNP) Berwick and E Lothian Division, 1970 and Feb. 1974. *Publications:* Problems of Input-Output Tables and Analysis, 1966; General Equilibrium Analysis, 1975; The Political Economy of Growth, 1983; The Challenge of New Technology, 1987; The End of Macro Economics?, 1994; articles in Econometrica, Rev. Econs and Statistics, Scientific American. *Recreations:* swimming, reading. *Address:* 30 Craiglockhart Dell Road, Edinburgh EH14 1JP.

SIMPSON, David Richard Salisbury, OBE 1989; Founder and Director, International Agency on Tobacco and Health, since 1991; *b* 1 Oct. 1945; *s* of late Richard Salisbury Simpson and of Joan Margaret Simpson (*née* Braund). *Educ:* Merchiston Castle School, Edinburgh. ACA 1969; FCA 1979 (but resigned from Institute, 1981). Teacher at Cadet College, Hasan Abdal, West Pakistan, 1963–64 (VSO). Peat, Marwick, Mitchell & Co., Chartered Accountants, 1964–72; Scottish Director, Shelter, Campaign for the Homeless, 1972–74; Director: Amnesty International (British Section), 1974–79; ASH, 1979–90. Sundry journalism, broadcasting and public lectures. Consultant, Internat. Union Against Cancer Special Project on Smoking and Cancer, 1980–. Trustee, Pier Arts Centre, Stromness, 1994–. Hon. MFPHM 1991. *Publications:* contribs to national newspapers and magazines. *Recreations:* friends, reading, music, hill-walking, Orkney. *Address:* 109 Gloucester Place, W1H 3PH. *T:* 0171–935 3519.

SIMPSON, Lt-Col (Retd) David Sackville Bruce, CBE 1990; Chief Executive, Civil Service Catering Organisation, 1981–91, retired; *b* 18 March 1930; *s* of Henry and Violet Simpson; *m* 1956, Margaret Elizabeth Goslin; two *s* three *d*. *Educ:* Brockley Grammar Sch.; Westminster Technical Coll. FHCIMA. Regular Officer, Army Catering Corps (retd in rank of Lt-Col), 1950–75; Principal Education Catering Organiser, Inner London Education Authority, 1975–81. *Recreations:* golf, squash. *Address:* 1 Tavistock Road, Fleet, Hants GU13 8EH. *T:* Fleet (01252) 625795.

SIMPSON, Dennis Charles; business consultant and lecturer; Managing Director, Axtel (UK) Ltd, 1986–88; *b* 24 Oct. 1931; *s* of late Arthur and Helen Simpson; *m* 1st, 1964, Margery Bruce Anderson (marr. diss.); three *s* one *d*; 2nd, 1983, Susan Gaynor Conway-Williams. *Educ:* Manchester Univ. (BA). FInstPS. 2nd Lieut Royal Signals, 1952–54; commercial appts, Philips Electrical Industries, 1956–63; Group Purchasing Manager, STC Ltd, 1963–66; Gp Purchasing Controller, Rank Organisation, 1966–69; Gen. Man., Cam Gears (S Wales) Ltd, 1969–72; Industrial Dir for Wales, Dept of Industry, 1972–75; Industrial Dir for Wales, Welsh Office, 1975–76; Business Agent, Welsh Develt Agency, 1983–85. Chairman: Spencer Harris Ltd, 1976–81; Grainger Hydraulics Ltd, 1976–81; Wellfield Engineering, 1976–81; Director: Beechwood Holdings, 1976–81; Gower Technology Ltd, 1983–87; Video Interactive Systems Ltd, 1983–87; Gower Alarms Ltd, 1985–87; Video Interactive Teaching Aids Ltd, 1985–87. *Recreations:* golf, bridge, reading war histories.

SIMPSON, Edward Alexander, CB 1993; Director, Northern Ireland Court Service, 1987–95; *b* 25 Dec. 1935; *s* of late Robert Simpson and Eva (*née* Graham); *m* 1960, Audrey Gordon; two *s*. *Educ:* Regent House Sch., Newtownards; Queen's Univ., Belfast (BSc Econ). Joined Ministry of Finance, 1953; various posts in Mins of Health and Local Govt and DoE, 1956–77; Asst Sec., Transportation and the Fire Service, 1977–81; Belfast Develt Officer, 1981–87. *Recreations:* golf, walking, wine. *Address:* 28 Londonderry Avenue, Comber, Newtownards BT23 5ES.

SIMPSON, Edward Hugh, CB 1976; FSS 1947; Visiting Research Fellow, University of Warwick, since 1993; Deputy Secretary, Department of Education and Science, 1973–82, retired; *b* 10 Dec. 1922; *o s* of Hugh and Mary Simpson, of Brookfield, Ballymena, Co. Antrim; *m* 1947, Rebecca, *er d* of Sam and Elizabeth Gibson, Ernevale, Kesh, Co. Fermanagh; one *s* one *d*. *Educ:* Coleraine Academical Institution; Queen's Univ., Belfast (BSc (1st cl. Hons Mathematics), 1942); Mathematical Statistics res., Christ's Coll., Cambridge (Scholar), 1945–47. Foreign Office, Bletchley Park, 1942–45; Min. of Education, 1947–50 and 1952–56; HM Treasury, 1950–52; Commonwealth Fund Fellow, USA, 1956–57; Private Sec. to Lord President of Council and Lord Privy Seal, 1957–60; Dep. Dir, Commonwealth Educn Liaison Unit, 1960–62; Sec., Commonwealth Educn Conf., New Delhi, 1962; Asst Sec., DES, 1962–68; Under-Sec., Civil Service Dept, 1968–71, DES, 1971–73. Sen. Hon. Res. Fellow, Birmingham Univ., 1983–88. Chairman: Nat. Assessment Panel, Schools Curriculum Award, 1983–; Educn Grants Adv. Service, 1987–; Gov. and Chm., Professional Cttee, Bishop Grosseteste Coll., Lincoln, 1984–; Trustee, Educn 2000, 1987–. Consultant: Educn Management Information Exchange, 1986–89; Dixons plc, 1987–. FRSA 1991. Hon. LLD Hull, 1992. *Publications:* articles in statistical and educn journals. *Address:* 40 Frays Avenue, West Drayton, Mddx UB7 7AG. *T:* West Drayton (01895) 443417. *Club:* Athenæum.

SIMPSON, Esther Eleanor, MD, FRCP, FFPHM, DPH, DCH; former Senior Principal Medical Officer, Department of Education and Science, and Department of Health and Social Security, retired 1979; *b* 28 May 1919. *Educ:* Kendal High Sch.; London Univ. Medical Officer, London County Council, then to Province of Natal Centre, Inst. of Child Health; joined Medical Br., Min. of Education, 1961. Hon. FCSLT (Hon. FCST 1984). *Recreations:* music, reading, walking. *Address:* 19 Belsize Lane, NW3 5AG. *T:* 0171–794 5623.

SIMPSON, Ffreebairn Liddon, CMG 1967; General Manager, Central Water Authority, Mauritius, 1976–78; *b* 11 July 1916; *s* of late James Liddon Simpson and Dorothy (*née* Blyth); *m* 1947, Dorina Laura Magda, MBE (*née* Ilieva) (*d* 1991); one *s*. *Educ:* Westminster School; Trinity College, Cambridge. HM Diplomatic/Foreign Service, 1939–48; HM Treasury, 1948–50; Administrative Officer, Gold Coast, 1950–55; Dep. Colonial Sec., Mauritius, 1955; Perm. Secretary: Min. of Works and Internal Communications, 1961; Premier's Office, 1966; Sec. to the Cabinet, Mauritius, 1967–76. *Recreations:* reading, theatre, family history research. *Club:* United Oxford & Cambridge University.

SIMPSON, George, FCCA; FIMI; FCIT; Chief Executive, Lucas Industries plc, since 1994; *b* 2 July 1942; *s* of William Simpson and Elizabeth Simpson; *m* 1964, Eva Chalmers; one *s* one *d*. *Educ:* Morgan Acad., Dundee; Dundee Inst. of Technology. ACIS. Sen. Accountant, Gas Industry, Scotland, 1962–69; Central Audit Man., BLMC, 1969–73; Financial Controller, Leyland Truck and Bus Div., 1973–76; Dir of Accounting, Leyland Cars, 1976–78; Finance and Systems Dir, Leyland Trucks, 1978–80; Managing Director: Coventry Climax Ltd, 1980–83; Freight Rover Ltd, 1983–86 ; Chief Exec. Officer, Leyland DAF, 1986–88; Man. Dir, 1989–91, Chm., 1991–94, and Chief Exec., 1991–92, Rover Gp; Dep. Chief Exec., BAe, 1992–94 (Dir, 1990–94); Chairman: Ballast Nedam Construction Ltd, 1992–94; Arlington Securities, 1993–94. Mem. Supervisory Bd and non-exec. Director: Pilkington plc, 1992–; Northern Venture Capital, 1992–; Pro Share, 1992–; ICI plc, 1995–. Mem., Exec. Cttee, SMMT, 1986– (Vice Pres., 1986–95, Pres., 1995–96, Council). *Recreations:* golf, squash and Rugby (now spectating). *Address:* Lucas Industries plc, Stratford Road, Shirley, Solihull, West Midlands B90 4LA. *Clubs:* Royal Birkdale Golf; Leamington and County Golf, Wisley Golf, Alyth Golf, Kenilworth RFC.

SIMPSON, Gordon Russell, DSO 1944 and Bar 1945; LVO 1979; TD; stockbroker; Partner, Bell, Cowan & Co. (now Brewin Dolphin Bell Lawrie Ltd), 1938–82; *b* 2 Jan. 1917; *s* of A. Russell Simpson, WS; *m* 1943, Marion Elizabeth King (*d* 1976); two *s*. *Educ:* Rugby School. Served with 2nd Lothians and Border Horse, 1939–46 (comd 1944–46). Chm., Edinburgh Stock Exchange, 1961–63; Chm., Scottish Stock Exchange, 1965–66; Pres., Council of Associated Stock Exchanges, 1971–73; Dep. Chm., Stock Exchange, 1973–78. Chm., General Accident Fire & Life Assurance Corporation Ltd, 1979–87 (Dir, 1967–87). Ensign, Queen's Body Guard for Scotland (Royal Company of Archers). Mem. Court, Stirling Univ., 1980–88; Comr, Queen Victoria Sch., 1982–92. DL Stirling and Falkirk Dists (Central Region), 1981–92. *Recreations:* music, ski-ing, archery. *Address:* c/o Brewin Dolphin Bell Lawrie Ltd, Erskine House, 7 Drumsheugh Gardens, Edinburgh EH3 7QH. *Club:* New (Edinburgh).

SIMPSON, Ian; artist and writer; East Regional Organizer, Visual Arts Course Leader, The Open College of the Arts, since 1992; *b* 12 Nov. 1933; *s* of Herbert William and Elsie Simpson; *m* 1st, 1958, Joan (*née* Charlton) (marr. diss. 1982); two *s* one *d*; 2nd, 1982, Birgitta Willcocks (*née* Brädde). *Educ:* Bede Grammar Sch., Sunderland; Sunderland Coll. of Art; Royal Coll. of Art. ARCA 1958. Freelance artist and illustrator, 1958–63; Hornsey Coll. of Art: Lectr, 1963–66; Head, Dept of Visual Research, 1966–69; Head, Dept of Co-ordinated Studies, 1969–72; Principal, 1972–86, Head, 1986–88, St Martin's Sch. of Art; Asst Rector, London Inst., 1986–88. Exhibited various exhibns, Britain, USA, etc; one-man exhibn, Cambridge, 1975, Durham, 1977, Blandford, 1985, Chappel, Colchester, 1994. Mem. Council, CNAA, 1974–80 (Chm., Fine Art Bd, 1976–81). Pres., Nat. Soc. for Art Educn, 1976. Consultant, Leisure Study Group Ltd, 1986–87. FSAE 1976; FRSA 1983. *Publications:* Eyeline, 1968; Drawing: seeing and observation, 1973; Picture Making, 1973; Guide to Painting and Composition, 1979; Painters Progress, 1983; Encyclopedia of Drawing Techniques, 1987; The Challenge of Landscape Painting, 1990; The New Guide to Illustration, 1990; Anatomy of Humans, 1991; Collins Complete Painting Course, 1993; Collins Complete Drawing Course, 1994. *Television Programmes:* Eyeline (10 programmes), 1968, 1969; Picture Making (10 programmes), 1973, 1976; Reading the Signs (5 programmes), 1977–78. *Recreations:* reading, music. *Address:* Motts Farm House, Chilton Street, Clare, Sudbury, Suffolk CO10 8QS.

SIMPSON, Ian Christopher; Sheriff of South Strathclyde, Dumfries and Galloway at Airdrie, since 1991 (Floating Sheriff, 1988–91); *b* 5 July 1949; *s* of David F. Simpson and J. O. S. Simpson (M. S. Dickie); *m* 1973, Anne Strang; two *s*. *Educ:* Glenalmond; Edinburgh Univ. (LLB). Admitted Faculty of Advocates, 1974. *Recreations:* golf, dog-walking. *Address:* 30 Cluny Drive, Edinburgh EH10 6DP. *T:* 0131–447 3363. *Clubs:* Royal and Ancient (St Andrews); Dunbar Golf.

SIMPSON, Very Rev. James Alexander; Moderator of the General Assembly of the Church of Scotland, 1994–95; Minister of Dornoch Cathedral, since 1976; Chaplain to the Queen in Scotland, since 1992; *b* 9 March 1934; *s* of Robert and Marion Simpson; *m* 1960, Helen Gray McCorquodale; three *s* two *d*. *Educ:* Glasgow Univ. (BSc Hons 1955; BD 1958); Union Seminary, New York (STM 1959); Aberdeen Univ. (DD). Minister: Grahamston Church, Falkirk, 1960–66; St John's Renfield Church, Glasgow, 1966–76. *Publications:* There is a Time To, 1971; Marriage Questions Today, 1975; Doubts Are Not Enough, 1982; Holy Wit, 1986, 3rd edn 1991; Laughter Lines, 1988, 2nd edn 1991; The Master Mind, 1989; History of Dornoch Cathedral, 1989; More Holy Wit, 1990; Keywords of Faith, 1992; Royal Dornoch Golf Club (a pictorial history), 1992; All about Christmas, 1994. *Recreation:* golf. *Address:* Cathedral Manse, Dornoch IV25 3HN. *T:* Dornoch (01862) 810296. *Club:* Royal Dornoch Golf (Captain, 1993).

SIMPSON, John Andrew; Chief Editor, Oxford English Dictionary, since 1993; Fellow of Kellogg College (formerly Rewley House), Oxford, since 1991; *b* 13 Oct. 1953; *s* of Robert Morris Simpson and Joan Margaret (*née* Sersale); *m* 1976, Hilary Croxford; two *d*. *Educ:* Dean Close Sch., Cheltenham; Univ. of York (BA Hons English Literature); Univ. of Reading (MA Medieval Studies). Editorial Asst, Supplement to OED, 1976–79; Editor, Concise Oxford Dictionary of Proverbs, 1979–81; Sen. Editor, Supplement to OED, 1981–84; Editor (New Words), OED, 1984–86; Co-editor, OED, 1986–93. Mem., Faculty of English, Univ. of Oxford, 1993–. Editl Consultant, Australian National Dictionary, 1986–88. Vis. Asst Prof., Dept of English, Univ. of Waterloo, Ont, Canada, 1985. Mem., Philolog. Soc., 1994–. *Publications:* (ed) Concise Oxford Dictionary of Proverbs, 1982, 2nd edn 1992; (contrib.) Oxford English, 1986; (contrib.) Words, 1989; (ed with Edmund Weiner) Oxford English Dictionary, 2nd edn 1989; (contrib.) Wörterbücher: ein internationales Handbuch zur Lexikographie, 1990; (ed with John Ayto) Oxford Dictionary of Modern Slang, 1992; (ed with Edmund Weiner) OED Additions series, vols 1 and 2, 1993; articles in Medium Aevum, English Today, and other lexicographical and linguistic periodicals. *Recreations:* cricket, computing. *Address:* Chestnut Lodge, St Mary's Close, Wheatley, Oxford OX33 1YP. *T:* Oxford (01865) 267728.

SIMPSON, Very Rev. John Arthur; Dean of Canterbury, since 1986; *b* 7 June 1933; *s* of Arthur Simpson and Mary Esther Simpson; *m* 1968, Ruth Marian (*née* Dibbens); one *s* two *d*. *Educ:* Cathays High School, Cardiff; Keble Coll., Oxford (BA, 2nd cl. Mod. History 1956, MA 1960); Clifton Theological Coll. Deacon 1958, priest 1959; Curate: Leyton, 1958–59; Christ Church, Orpington, 1959–62; Tutor, Oak Hill Coll., Southgate N14, 1962–72; Vicar of Ridge, Herts, 1972–79; Director of Ordinands and Post-Ordination Training, Diocese of St Albans, 1975–81; Hon. Canon of St Albans Cathedral, 1977–79; Residentiary Canon, St Albans, and Priest-in-charge of Ridge, 1979–81; Archdeacon of Canterbury and Canon Res. of Canterbury Cathedral, 1981–86. Dir, Ecclesiastical Insurance Group (formerly Ecclesiastical Insurance Office), 1983. Chm. Govs, King's Sch., Canterbury, 1986–. Hon. DD Kent, 1994. *Recreations:* travel, theatre, opera. *Address:* The Deanery, Canterbury, Kent CT1 2EP. *T:* Canterbury (01227) 762862. *Club:* Athenæum.

SIMPSON, John (Cody Fidler-), CBE 1991; Foreign Affairs Editor, BBC, since 1988; Associate Editor, The Spectator, since 1991; *b* 9 Aug. 1944; *s* of Roy Simpson Fidler-Simpson and Joyce Leila Vivienne Cody; *m* 1965, Diane Jean Petteys (marr. diss. 1995), El Cajon, California; two *d*; partner, Adèle Krüger. *Educ:* St Paul's School; Magdalene Coll., Cambridge (MA). FRGS 1990. Reporter, BBC Radio News, 1970; BBC correspondent, Dublin, 1972; Common Market correspondent (based in Brussels), 1975; Southern Africa correspondent (based in Johannesburg), 1977; Diplomatic correspondent, BBC Television News, 1978; BBC Political Editor, 1980; Presenter and Correspondent, BBC-TV News, 1981; Diplomatic Editor, BBC-TV, 1982–88. Hon. DLitt De Montfort, 1995. *Publications:* (ed jtly) The Best of Granta, 1966; The Disappeared: voices from a secret war, 1985; Behind Iranian Lines, 1988; Despatches from the Barricades, 1990; From the House of War: Baghdad and the Gulf, 1991; The Darkness Crumbles: the death of Communism, 1992; In the Forests of the Night: drug-running and terrorism in Peru, 1993; (ed) The Oxford Book of Exile, 1995; (jtly) Lifting the Veil: life in revolutionary Iran, 1995; *novels:* Moscow Requiem, 1981; A Fine And Private Place, 1983. *Recreations:* collecting obscure books, travelling to obscure places, and returning to Suffolk. *Address:* BBC Television Centre, Wood Lane, W12 7RJ. *T:* 0181–743 8000. *Clubs:* Athenæum, Chelsea Arts.

SIMPSON, John Ernest Peter, FRCS; Medical Adviser, London Implementation Group, since 1993; *b* 30 Jan. 1942; *s* of John and Alice Bewick Simpson; *m* 1964, Valerie Joan Lamb (marr. diss. 1987); one *s* one *d*. *Educ:* Jesus Coll., Oxford (MA, BM BCh); St Thomas's Hosp. Med. Sch. (Schol.). MFPHM. Surgical training, St Thomas' and Northwich Park Hosps, 1966–78; Lectr, Community Medicine, St Thomas' Hosp., 1974–75; Tutor, King's Fund Coll., 1975–78; Management, Planning Policy and Internat. Divs, DHSS, 1978–88; Regl MO, Mersey RHA, 1988–93. *Publications:* Going Home (from hospital) (ed jtly), 1981; articles on day case surgery and organisation of surgical and other clinical services. *Recreations:* golf, music. *Address:* 31 Hillbrow, Richmond Hill, Richmond on Thames TW10 6PH. *T:* 0181–940 0935. *Clubs:* Hurlingham, Royal Society of Medicine.

SIMPSON, John Liddle, CMG 1958; TD 1950; QC 1980; *b* 9 Oct. 1912; *s* of late James Simpson; *m* 1st, 1939, Nellie Lavender Mussett (*d* 1944); 2nd, 1959, Ursula Vaughan Washington (*nee* Rigby). *Educ:* George Watson's Coll.; Edinburgh Univ. (MA, DLitt). Barrister, Middle Temple, 1937. Served War of 1939–45; GSO1, 1945. Principal, Control Office for Germany and Austria, 1946; Senior legal assistant, FO (German Section), 1948; transferred to Foreign (now Diplomatic) Service and promoted Counsellor, 1954; Legal Counsellor, FO, 1954–59 and 1961–68; Legal Adviser, United Kingdom Mission to the United Nations, New York, 1959–61; Dep. Legal Adviser, 1968–71, Second Legal Adviser (Dep. Under-Sec. of State), 1971–72, FCO; returned to practice at the Bar, 1973; elected alternate Pres. of Arbitral Tribunals, Internat. Telecommunications Satellite Org., 1974 and 1976. Mem., Dubai/Sharjah Boundary Court of Arbitration, 1978–81; Chm., UNESCO Appeals Bd, 1980–85. Freeman, City of London, 1976. *Publications:* Germany and the North Atlantic Community: A Legal Survey (with M. E. Bathurst), 1956; International Arbitration; Law and Practice (with Hazel Fox), 1959; articles and notes in legal journals. *Address:* 137a Ashley Gardens, Thirleby Road, SW1P 1HN. *T:* 0171–834 4814; 5 Paper Buildings, Temple, EC4Y 7HB. *T:* 0171–583 9275.

SIMPSON, Keith Taylor; His Honour Judge Keith Simpson; a Circuit Judge, since 1990; *b* 8 May 1934; *m* 1961, Dorothy Preece; two *s* one *d*. *Educ:* privately; Jesus Coll., Oxford (MA). Called to the Bar, Middle Temple, 1958; joined SE Circuit; general Common Law practice. *Recreations:* walking, gardening, tennis, fishing, reading, opera. *Address:* c/o South Eastern Circuit Office, New Cavendish House, 18 Maltravers Street, WC2R 3EU.

SIMPSON, Kenneth John, CMG 1961; HM Diplomatic Service, retired; *b* 5 Feb. 1914; *s* of Bernard and Ann Simpson, Millhouses, Sheffield; *m* 1939, Harriet (Shan) Hughes; three *s*. *Educ:* Downing College, Cambridge. Entered HM Foreign (now Diplomatic) Service, 1937; lastly Consul-Gen., Hanoi and Stuttgart, Inspector, Diplomatic Service and Counsellor, FCO. *Address:* 33 The Westerings, Tye Green, Cressing, Braintree, Essex CU17 8HQ. *T:* Braintree (01376) 321565.

SIMPSON, Malcolm Carter; Director of Finance, Leeds City Council, 1978–82, retired; *b* 15 June 1929; *s* of Arthur and Rhoda Simpson; *m* 1st, 1952, Doreen Patricia Wooler; two *d*; 2nd, 1980, Andrea Gillian Blythe. *Educ:* Stanningley Council Sch. DPA; CIPFA. Employed by Leeds CC for whole of working life, 1943–82: Asst Dir of Finance, 1968; Dep. Dir of Finance, 1973. Board Member: Yorks Water Authority, 1983–88; S Yorks Residuary Body, 1985–89. *Recreations:* golf, bridge. *Address:* Swiss Cottage, 44 Millbeck Green, Collingham Bridge, Leeds LS22 5AJ. *T:* Collingham Bridge (01937) 573917.

SIMPSON, Rear-Adm. Michael Frank, CB 1985; CEng, FIMechE; FRAeS; Chairman, Aircraft Engineering Division, Hunting Aviation Ltd, since 1994; *b* 27 Sept. 1928; *s* of Robert Michael Simpson and Florence Mabel Simpson; *m* 1973, Sandra MacDonald (*née* Clift); two *s* one *d*. *Educ:* King Edward VI Sch., Bath; RN Engrg Coll., Manadon. CEng, FIMechE 1983; FRAeS 1983. Joined RN, 1944; qual. as Air Engr Officer, 1956; served in FAA Sqdns, cruisers and carriers; served with US Navy on exchange, 1961–66; Air Engr Officer, HMS Ark Royal, 1970–72; MoD appts, 1972–78; Supt, RN Aircraft Yard, Fleetlands, 1978–80; Cdre, RN Barracks, Portsmouth, 1981–83; Dir Gen. Aircraft (Naval), 1983–85; Dir and Gen. Man., 1985–88, Man. Dir, 1988–94, Field, later Hunting, Airmotive Ltd; Chm., Somet Ltd, 1988. Mem. Council and Dir, SBAC, 1995–. Chairman: RN/RM Children's Home Management Cttee, 1980–83; RN Athletics Assoc., 1981–83. Mem. Court, Cranfield Inst. of Technology, 1983–86. *Publications:* articles on helicopter engrg in Jl of Naval Engrg; symposium paper on helicopter environmental design, 1975. *Recreations:* sailing, ski-ing, shooting, making things, military history, swimming. *Address:* Keppel, Blackhills, Esher, Surrey KT10 9JW. *Clubs:* Army and Navy; Royal Naval Sailing Association (Captain, Portsmouth Br., 1981–83); Royal Navy Ski.

SIMPSON, Morag; *see* Macdonald, M.

SIMPSON, Oliver, CB 1977; MA, PhD, FInstP; Chief Scientist, Deputy Under-Secretary of State, Home Office, 1974–83; *b* 28 Oct. 1924; *y s* of late Sir George C. Simpson, KCB, FRS, and Dorothy (*née* Stephen); *m* 1946, Joan (*d* 1993), *d* of late Walter and Maud Morgan; one *s* (and one *s* decd). *Educ:* Highgate Sch.; Trinity Coll., Cambridge. War Service: Admiralty Research Laboratory, Teddington, on submarine detection, 1944–46. Research Scholar, 1946–49, Fellow of Trinity Coll., Cambridge, 1949–53; Asst Prof. of Physics, Univ. of Michigan, USA, 1949–52; Imperial Chemical Industries Fellow in Dept. of Theoretical Chemistry, Cambridge, 1952–53; joined Services Electronics Research Laboratory, Admty, 1953, Head of Solid State Physics, 1956–63; Supt, Basic Physics Div., Nat. Physical Laboratory, 1964–66; Dep. Dir, Nat. Physical Laboratory, 1966–69; Under-Sec., Cabinet Office, 1969–74. *Publications:* articles in scientific jls on infra-red detectors, semiconductors, fluorescence and standards of measurement. *Address:* 4 Highbury Road, Wimbledon, SW19 7PR. *T:* 0181–946 3871. *Club:* Athenæum.

SIMPSON, Peter Robert; His Honour Judge P. R. Simpson; a Circuit Judge, since 1989; Second Judge, Mayor's and City of London Court, since 1994; *b* 9 Feb. 1936; *o s* of late Surg. Capt. (D) Donald Lee Simpson, RN and of Margaret Olive (*née* Lathan); *m* 1st, 1968, Mary Elizabeth (marr. diss. 1994), *d* of late Thomas Kirton and Frances Florence Cecilia Kirton; two *s*; 2nd, 1995, Megan Elizabeth, *o d* of late Kenneth John Dodd and Melva Dodd. *Educ:* St John's Coll., Southsea, Hants. Admitted Solicitor, 1960; called to the Bar, Inner Temple, 1970, *ad eundem* Lincoln's Inn, 1972. Practised on S Eastern Circuit, then at Chancery Bar, mainly in property and conveyancing matters; a Recorder, 1987–89. *Recreations:* playing chess, reading legal and political biographies, listening to music, dining out. *Address:* Mayor's and City of London Court, 32 Threadneedle Street, EC2R 8AY; 12 New Square, Lincoln's Inn, WC2A 3SW; Erskine House, 1 Old Fold Close, Hadley Green, Barnet, Herts EN5 4QL. *Club:* Guildhall.

SIMPSON, Ven. Rennie, LVO 1974; MA Lambeth 1970; Archdeacon of Macclesfield, 1978–85, Emeritus since 1986; Rector of Gawsworth, 1978–85; Chaplain to the Queen, 1982–90; *b* 13 Jan. 1920; *o s* of late Doctor Taylor Simpson and late May Simpson, Rishton; *m* 1949, Margaret, *er d* of late Herbert Hardy and Olive Hardy, South Kirkby; one *s* one *d*. *Educ:* Blackburn Tech. Coll.; Kelham Theol College. Curate of S Elmsall, Yorks, 1945–49; Succentor of Blackburn Cath., 1949–52; Sacrist and Minor Canon of St Paul's Cath., 1952–58, Hon. Minor Canon, 1958–, Jun. Cardinal, 1954–55, Sen. Cardinal, 1955–58; Vicar of John Keble Church, Mill Hill, 1958–63; Precentor, 1963–74, Acting Sacrist, 1973–74, Westminster Abbey; Canon Residentiary, 1974–78, Vice-Dean, 1975–78, Chester Cathedral. Chaplain, RNVR, 1953–55; Dep. Chaplain, Gt Ormond St Hosp., 1954–58; Asst Chaplain, 1956–64, Officiating Chaplain, 1964–, Sub-Prelate, 1973–, Order of St John of Jerusalem; Deputy Priest to the Queen, 1956–67; Priest-in-Ordinary to the Queen, 1967–74. Life Governor, Imperial Cancer Research Fund, 1963. Liveryman of Waxchandlers' Co. and Freeman of City of London, 1955; Hon. Chaplain, Worshipful Soc. of Apothecaries of London, 1984–85. Jt Hon. Treas., Corp. Sons of the Clergy, 1967–74; Governor: King's School, Chester, 1974–78; King's Sch., Macclesfield, 1979–85. *Recreations:* football, cricket, theatre. *Address:* 18 Roseberry Green, North Stainley, Ripon, N Yorks HG4 3HZ.

SIMPSON, Rt. Hon. Dr Robert, PC (N Ireland) 1970; *b* 3 July 1923; *er s* of Samuel and Agnes Simpson, Craigbilly, Ballymena; *m* 1954, Dorothy Isobel, 2nd *d* of Dr Robert Strawbridge, MA, DD, and Anne Strawbridge; two *s* one *d*. *Educ:* Ballymena Academy; Queen's University, Belfast. MB, BCh, BAO, 1946; Founder Mem., RCGP; LRCPI (Occupational Medicine), 1980. House Surgeon, Belfast City Hosp., 1947; Resident Anaesthetist, Royal Infirmary, Leicester, 1948; GP, Ballymena, Co. Antrim, 1949–; Medical Correspondent: Belfast Telegraph, Irish Times (Dublin), Evening News (Edinburgh) and Leicester Mercury; Medical Representative, NI, Europ Assistance; Medical Officer, Flexibox Ltd, Ballymena, Northern Dairies Ltd. Founder Chm., Ballymena Round Table, 1951. NI Deleg. to CPA Conf. in NZ and Australia, 1965. Minister of Community Relations, N Ireland, 1969–71; MP (U) Mid-Antrim, Parlt of N Ireland, 1953–72. Vice-Pres., Co. Antrim Agricl Assoc., 1960–; Vice-Pres., Ballymena Musical Fest. Assoc., 1989–. *Publications:* contribs to newspapers and magazines on medical, country and travel subjects. *Recreations:* gardening, trees and the countryside. *Address:* Random Cottage, Craigbilly, Ballymena, Co. Antrim BT42 4HL. *T:* Ballymena (01266) 653105. *Club:* Royal Over-Seas League.

SIMPSON, Robert Brian; Chief Executive, The Press Association Ltd, since 1990; *b* 12 Sept. 1944; *s* of Harold and Clara Simpson; *m* 1966, Vivienne Jones; three *s*. *Educ:* Liverpool Inst.; University Coll. London (BA 1966). Asst to Marketing Dir, Holt, Rinehart & Winston (Publishers) Ltd, 1966–68; Asst Develt Manager, later Develt Manager, and Dep. Hd of Inf. Services, Consumers' Assoc., 1968–73; Marketing Manager, Universal News Services Ltd, 1973–74; Marketing Dir, later Man. Dir, University Microfilms Internat. Ltd. 1974–79; Marketing and Develt Manager, later Commercial Manager, Press Assoc., 1979–86; Chief Exec., Universal News Services Ltd, 1986–90; Chm. and Chief Exec., PNA Ltd, 1989–90. Chairman: Two-Ten Communications Ltd, 1990–; Tellex Monitors Ltd, 1990–; PA Data Design Ltd, 1990–; PA Sport Ltd, 1993–; PA News Ltd, 1994–; Dir, Canada NewsWire, 1986–. *Recreations:* music, walking, reading, gardening. *Address:* The Press Association Ltd, PA News Centre, 292 Vauxhall Bridge Road, SW1V 1AE. *T:* 0171–963 7000.

SIMPSON, Robert Watson, (Robin); Director, Brewers and Licensed Retailers Association (formerly Brewers' Society), since 1993; *b* 14 June 1940; *s* of Robert Simpson and Susan Simpson (*née* Rolland). *Educ:* Perth Academy; University of St Andrews (BSc Hons). Board of Trade (Patent Office), 1962; Dept of Trade (Aviation), 1973; Dept of Industry (Indust. Develt Unit), 1976; Dept of Trade (Shipping), 1979; Department of Trade and Industry: (Management Services and Manpower), 1982; Under Sec., and NE Regl Dir, 1986; Head, Business Task Force Div. (incl. Envmt Unit), 1990–92; Head, Steel, Metals and Minerals Div., 1992. *Recreations:* history, commemorative pottery, bridge.

SIMPSON, Robert Wilfred Levick, DMus; composer; BBC Music Producer, 1951–80; *b* Leamington, Warwickshire, 2 March 1921; *s* of Robert Warren Simpson (British) and Helena Hendrika Govaars (Dutch); *m* 1946, Bessie Fraser (*d* 1981); *m* 1982, Angela Musgrave. *Educ:* Westminster City Sch.; studied with Herbert Howells. DMus (Dunelm) 1952. Holder of: Carl Nielsen Gold Medal (Denmark), 1956; Medal of Honor of Bruckner Soc. of America, 1962. Mem., British Astronomical Assoc.; FRAS. *Compositions:* Symphonies: No 1, 1951 (recorded); No 2, 1956 (recorded); No 3, 1962 (recorded); No 4, 1972 (recorded); No 5, 1972; Nos 6 and 7, 1977 (recorded); No 8, 1981; No 9, 1986 (recorded); No 10, 1988 (recorded); No 11, 1990; Concertos: Piano, 1967; Flute, 1989; Cello, 1991; String Quartets: No 1, 1952 (recorded); No 2, 1953 (recorded); No 3, 1954 (recorded); No 4, 1973 (recorded); No 5, 1974 (recorded); No 6, 1975 (recorded); No 7, 1977 (recorded); No 8, 1979 (recorded); No 9, 1982 (recorded); No 10 (For Peace), 1983 (recorded); No 11, 1984 (recorded); No 12, 1987 (recorded); No 13, 1989; No 14, 1990; No 15, 1991; Piano Sonata, 1946; Variations and Finale on a Theme of Haydn, for piano, 1948; Variations and Finale on a Theme of Beethoven for piano, 1990; Allegro Deciso, for string orchestra (from String Quartet No 3); Canzona for Brass, 1958 (recorded); Variations and Fugue for recorder and string quartet, 1959; Incidental Music to Ibsen's The Pretenders, 1965; Trio for clarinet, cello and piano, 1967; Quintet for clarinet, and strings, 1968 (recorded); Energy, Symphonic Study for brass band (test piece for 1971 World Championship) (recorded); Incidental Music to Milton's Samson Agonistes, 1974; *Media morte in vita sumus* (Motet for choir, brass, and timpani), 1975; Quartet for horn, violin, cello and piano, 1976; Volcano, for brass band, 1979 (test piece for Nat. Championship, 1979) (recorded); Sonata for two pianos, 1980; Quintet for double basses, clarinet and bass clarinet, 1981 (also for string trio, clarinet and bass clarinet); The Four Temperaments, for brass band, 1982 (recorded); Variations on a theme of Carl Nielsen, for orchestra, 1983; Trio for horn, violin and piano, 1984; Sonata for violin and piano, 1984; Eppur si muove, for organ, 1985; Introduction and Allegro on a bass by Max Reger, for brass band, 1986 (recorded); Tempi, for a cappella choir, 1987; String Quintet, 1987 (recorded); String Trio (Prelude and Fugue), 1987; Quintet for Brass, 1989; Vortex, for brass band, 1989 (recorded); Variations and Fugue on a theme of Bach, for string orch., 1991; String Quintet No 2, 1994. *Publications:* Carl Nielsen, Symphonist, 1952, rev. edn 1977; The Essence of Bruckner, 1966, rev. edn 1992; The Proms and Natural Justice, 1981; numerous articles in various jls and three BBC booklets (Bruckner and the Symphony, Sibelius and Nielsen, and The Beethoven Symphonies); contrib. to: Encycl. Brit.; Musik in Geschichte und Gegenwart; (ed) The Symphony (Pelican), 1966. *Recreation:* astronomy. *Address:* Síocháin, Killelton, near Camp, Tralee, Co. Kerry, Eire. *T:* Tralee (66) 30213.

SIMPSON, Robin; *see* Simpson, Robert W.

SIMPSON, Robin Muschamp Garry; QC 1971; *b* 19 June 1927; *s* of Ronald Maitland Simpson, actor and Lila Maravan Simpson (*née* Muschamp); *m* 1st, 1956, Avril Carolyn Harrisson; one *s* one *d*; 2nd, 1968, Mary Faith Laughton-Scott; one *s* one *d*. *Educ:* Charterhouse; Peterhouse, Cambridge (MA). Called to Bar, Middle Temple, 1951, Bencher, 1979; SE Circuit; former Mem., Surrey and S London Sessions; a Recorder of the Crown Court, 1976–86. Mem., CCC Bar Mess. Appeal Steward, British Boxing Bd of Control. *Recreations:* real tennis, sailing. *Address:* 116 Station Road, Barnes, SW13 0NB. *T:* 0181–878 9898. *Clubs:* Garrick, MCC; Aldeburgh Yacht.

SIMPSON, Roderick Alexander C.; *see* Cordy-Simpson.

SIMPSON, William George; Librarian and College Archivist, Trinity College Dublin, since 1994; *b* 27 June 1945; *s* of William Anion Simpson and Sarah Jane Simpson; *m* 1968, Margaret Lilian Pollard; two *d*. *Educ:* Liverpool Inst.; Univ. of Liverpool (BA 1st class Hons); MA Dublin. ALA. Gilroy Scholar in Semitic Languages, Univ. of Aberdeen, 1968; Asst Librarian, Univ. of Durham, 1969–73; Asst Librarian, Sub-Librarian and Senior Sub-Librarian, John Rylands Univ. Library of Manchester, 1973–85; University Librarian: Surrey, 1985–90; London, 1990–94. Chairman: Guildford Inst., 1987–90; Amer. Studies Library Gp, 1992–94; Mem., Humanities and Social Scis Adv. Cttee, 1991–92, London Adv. Cttee, 1992–94, British Library; Dir, Consortium of University Res. Libraries, 1992–. Dir, IRIS, 1994–; Member: An Chomhairle Leabharlanna, 1995–; COLICO, 1995–; Nat. Preservation Adv. Cttee, 1994–. FRAS 1994; FRSA 1988. *Publications:* Libraries, Languages and the Interpretation of the Past, 1988; articles in learned jls. *Recreations:* astronomy, genealogy, languages, travel. *Address:* Trinity College Library, College Street, Dublin 2, Ireland. *T:* (1) 7021665; Cranhurst, Station Road, Farncombe, Godalming, Surrey GU7 3NF.

SIMPSON, Sir William (James), Kt 1984; Chairman, Health and Safety Commission, 1974–83; *b* Falkirk, 20 May 1920; *s* of William Simpson and Margaret Nimmo; *m* 1942, Catherine McEwan Nicol; one *s*. *Educ:* Victoria Sch. and Falkirk Techn. Sch., Falkirk. Served War of 1939–45, Argyll and Sutherland Highlanders (Sgt). Apprenticed to moulding trade, 1935; returned to foundry, 1946. Mem. Nat. Exec. Council, Amalgamated Union of Foundry Workers, 1955–67; Gen. Sec., AUEW (Foundry Section), 1967–75. Chm. of Labour Party, 1972–73; Member: Race Relations Board; Ct of Inquiry into Flixborough explosion, 1974; Chm., Adv. Cttee on Asbestos, 1976–79. *Publication:* Labour: The Unions and the Party, 1973.

SIMPSON-JONES, Peter Trevor, CBE 1971; Président d'Honneur, Société Française des Industries Lucas, since 1980 (Président-Directeur Général, 1957–80); *b* 20 March 1914; *s* of Frederick Henry Jones and Constance Agnès Simpson; *m* 1948, Marie-Lucy Sylvain; one *s* one *d*. *Educ:* Royal Navy School. British Chamber of Commerce, France: Vice-Pres., 1967–68 and 1970–72; Pres., 1968–70. Mem., RNSA, 1955–. Chevalier de la Légion d'Honneur, 1948, Officier 1973. *Recreation:* yachting. *Address:* 11 rue Max Blondat, 92 Boulogne-sur-Seine, France. *T:* 48250120. *Clubs:* Special Forces; Polo (Paris).

SIMPSON-ORLEBAR, Sir Michael (Keith Orlebar), KCMG 1991 (CMG 1982); HM Diplomatic Service, retired; Director-General, The Hispanic and Luso Brazilian Council (Canning House), since 1992; *b* 5 Feb. 1932; *s* of late Aubrey Orlebar Simpson, Royal Artillery and Laura Violet, *d* of Captain Frederick Keith-Jones; *m* 1964, Rosita Duarte Triana; two *s* one *d*. *Educ:* Eton; Christ Church, Oxford (MA). 2nd Lieut, KRRC, 1950–51. Joined Foreign Service, 1954; 3rd Sec., Tehran, 1955–57; FO, 1957–62; Private Sec. to Parly Under-Sec. of State, 1960–62; 1st Sec. (Commercial) and Consul, Bogotá, 1962–65; seconded to Urwick, Orr and Partners Ltd, 1966; FO, 1966–68; 1st Sec., Paris, 1969–72; Counsellor (Commercial), Tehran, 1972–76; Head of UN Dept, FCO, 1977–80; Minister, HM Embassy, Rome, 1980–83; Head of British Interests Section, Tehran, 1983–85; Ambassador to Portugal, 1986–89; Ambassador to Mexico, 1989–92. Dir, Murray Emerging Economies Trust plc, 1994–. Chm., British Mexican Soc., 1992–95. Order of the Aztec Eagle, 1st Cl. (Mexico), 1994. *Recreations:* gardening, fishing. *Address:* Canning House, 2 Belgrave Square, SW1X 8PJ. *T:* 0171–235 2303.

SIMS, Prof. Andrew Charles Petter, MD; FRCPsych, FRCPE; Professor of Psychiatry, since 1979, Chairman, Division of Psychiatry and Behavioural Sciences in Relation to Medicine, since 1994, University of Leeds; *b* 5 Nov. 1938; *s* of late Dr Charles Henry Sims and of Dr Norah Winifred Kennan Sims (*née* Petter); *m* 1964, Ruth Marie Harvey; two *s* two *d*. *Educ:* Monkton Combe Sch.; Emmanuel Coll., Cambridge (MA; MD 1973); Westminster Hosp. DObstRCOG; FRCPsych 1979; FRCPE 1993. House Surgeon, Westminster Hosp., 1963–64; Registrar in Psychiatry, Manchester Royal Infirmary, 1966–69; Consultant Psychiatrist, All Saints Hosp., Birmingham, 1971–76; Sen. Lectr, Univ. of Birmingham, 1976–79; Head of Dept of Psychiatry, Univ. of Leeds, 1980–83, 1986–89. Royal College of Psychiatrists: Sub-Dean, 1984–87; Dean, 1987–90; Pres., 1990–93; Dir, Continuing Professional Develt, 1993–. Chairman: Confidential Inquiry into Homicides and Suicides by Mentally Ill People, 1993–; Schizophrenia Cttee, Clinical Standards Adv. Gp, DoH, 1994–. Hon. FCPS(Pak) 1994. MD Lambeth, 1995. *Publications:* Neurosis in Society, 1983; Psychiatry (Concise Medical Textbooks), 5th edn (with Sir William Trethowan), 1983, 6th edn (with D. Owens), 1993; (with W. I. Hume) Lecture Notes in Behavioural Sciences, 1984; Symptoms in the Mind: introduction to descriptive psychopathology, 1988 (Italian edn 1993), 2nd edn 1995; (with R. P. Snaith) Anxiety in Clinical Practice, 1988 (German edn 1993); (ed) Advances in Psychiatric Treatment, 1994; Speech and Language Disorders in Psychiatry, 1995. *Recreations:* gardening, music, theatre, walking. *Address:* Gledholt, Oakwood Grove, Leeds LS8 2PA. *T:* Leeds (0113) 243 3144. *Clubs:* Christian Medical Fellowship, Royal Society of Medicine. *Club:* Athenæum.

SIMS, Prof. Geoffrey Donald, OBE 1971; FEng 1980; Vice-Chancellor, University of Sheffield, 1974–90; *b* 13 Dec. 1926; *s* of Albert Edward Hope Sims and Jessie Elizabeth Sims; *m* 1949, Pamela Audrey Richings; one *s* two *d*. *Educ:* Wembley County Grammar School; Imperial College of Science and Technology, London. Research physicist, GEC, 1948–54; Sen. Scientific Officer, UKAEA, 1954–56; Lecturer/Senior Lecturer, University College, London, 1956–63; University of Southampton: Prof. and Head of Dept of Electronics, 1963–74; Dean, Faculty of Engrg, 1967–70; Senior Dep. Vice-Chancellor, 1970–72. Member: Council, British Association for the Advancement of Science, 1965–69 (Chm., Sheffield Area Council, 1974–); EDC for Electronics Industry, 1966–75; Adv. Cttee for Scientific and Technical Information, 1969–74; CNAA Electrical Engineering Bd, 1970–73; Planning Cttee for British Library, 1971–73 (Chm., British Library R&D Adv. Cttee, 1975–81); Adv. Council, Science Museum, 1972–84; British Nat. Cttee for Physics, 1972–78; Royal Soc. Cttee on Sci. Information, 1972–81; Electronics Res. Council, 1973–74; Annan Cttee on Future of Broadcasting, 1974–77; Naval Educn Adv. Cttee, 1974–79; Trent RHA, 1975–84; British Council Engrg and Tech. Adv. Cttee, 1976–84 (Chm.); Interim Action Cttee on British Film Industry, 1977–81; EEC Adv. Cttee on Scientific and Technical Trng, 1977–81; Univs Council for Adult and Continuing Educn, 1978–84 (Chm., 1980–84); CNAA, 1979–83; Liaison Cttee on Highly Qualified Technol Manpower, 1979–82; Council, Nat. Inst. of Adult Educn, 1980–84; SRC, later SERC Engrg Bd, 1980–84; Inter Univ. and Polytechnic Council, 1981–91 (IUC and Exec. Cttee, 1974–81; Vice-Chm., IUPC, 1985–91); Cttee for Internat. Co-operation in Higher Educn, 1981–94 (Vice-Chm., 1985–91); EEC Adv. Cttee on Programme Management, 1981–84; BBC Engrg Adv. Cttee, 1981–90 (Chm.); Council, Fellowship of Engrg, 1986–88; Museums and Galleries Commn, 1983–88; Hong Kong City Polytechnic Sub-cttee, 1984–86, Hong Kong Univ. of Sci. and Technol. Sub-cttee, 1987–91, UPGC, Hong Kong; Mem. of Council and Hon. Dep. Treas., ACU, 1984–90; Chm., Council for Commonwealth Educn, 1991–. UK rep. on Perm. Cttee of Conf. of European Rectors, 1981–84; *ad personem* rep. on Perm. Cttee and Bureau of Conf. of European Rectors, 1984–94; rep. on Liaison Cttee, Rectors' Confs of EEC Mem. States, 1985–90 (Pres., 1987–89). Chairman of Governors: Southampton College of Technology, 1967–69; Southampton Sch. of Navigation, 1972–74; Sheffield High Sch., 1978–85; Fellow, Midland Chapter, Woodard Schools, 1977–; Custos, Worksop Coll., 1984–92. Trustee, Church Burgesses Trust, Sheffield, 1984–, Capital, 1988–89. FIEE 1963; FCGI 1980. Hon. Fellow, Sheffield City Polytechnic, 1990. Hon. DSc Southampton, 1979; Hon. ScD Allegheny Coll., Penn, USA, 1989; Hon. DSc (Eng) QUB, 1990; Hon. LLD: Dundee, 1987; Sheffield, 1991. Symons Medal, ACU, 1991. Founder Mem., 1966, Reviews Editor, 1969–, Chm., 1987–, Jl of Materials Science Bd. *Publications:* Microwave Tubes and Semiconductor Devices (with I. M. Stephenson), 1963; Variational Techniques in Electromagnetism (trans.), 1965; numerous papers on microwaves, electronics and education in learned jls. *Recreations:* golf, travel, music. *Address:* North Leigh, 53 Sandygate Park Road, Sheffield S10 5TX. *Club:* Athenæum.

SIMS, Monica Louie, OBE 1971; MA, LRAM, LGSM; Director of Production, Children's Film and Television Foundation, since 1985; *d* of late Albert Charles Sims and Eva Elizabeth Preen, both of Gloucester. *Educ:* Girls' High School, Gloucester; St Hugh's College, Oxford. Tutor in Literature and Drama, Dept of Adult Educn, Hull Univ., 1947–50; Educn Tutor, Nat. Fedn of Women's Institutes, 1950–53; BBC Sound Talks Producer, 1953–55; BBC Television Producer, 1955–64; Editor of Woman's Hour, BBC, 1964–67; Head of Children's Programmes, BBC TV, 1967–78; Controller, BBC Radio 4, 1978–83; Dir of Programmes, BBC Radio, 1983–84. Vice-Pres., British Bd of Film Classification, 1985–; Chm., Careers Adv. Bd, Univ. of Bristol, 1991–. *Address:* 97 Gloucester Terrace, W2 3HB.

SIMS, Roger Edward, JP; MP (C) Chislehurst since Feb. 1974; *b* 27 Jan. 1930; *s* of late Herbert William Sims and Annie Amy Savidge; *m* 1957, Angela Mathews; two *s* one *d*. *Educ:* City Boys' Grammar Sch., Leicester; St Olave's Grammar Sch., London. MCInstM. National Service, 1948–50. Coutts & Co., 1950–51; Campbell Booker Carter Ltd, 1953–62; Dodwell & Co. Ltd, 1962–90; Dir, Inchcape International Ltd, 1981–90. Contested (C) Shoreditch and Finsbury, 1966 and 1970; PPS to Home Sec., 1979–83. Mem., Nat. Commn of Inquiry into the Prevention of Child Abuse, 1995–. Mem., GMC, 1989–. Mem., Central Exec. Cttee, NSPCC, 1980–93. Mem. Chislehurst and Sidcup UDC, 1956–62; JP Bromley, 1960–72 (Dep. Chm. 1970–72); Chm., Juvenile Panel, 1971–72. *Recreations:* swimming; music, especially singing (Mem. Royal Choral Soc. from 1950). *Address:* House of Commons, SW1A 0AA. *Clubs:* Bromley Conservative (Bromley); Chislehurst British Legion.

SIMS-WILLIAMS, Prof. Nicholas John, PhD; FBA 1988; Professor of Iranian and Central Asian Studies, School of Oriental and African Studies, University of London, since 1994; *b* 11 April 1949; *s* of late Rev. M. V. S. Sims-Williams; *m* 1972, Ursula Mary Judith, *d* of late Prof. Hugh Seton-Watson, CBE, FBA; two *d*. *Educ:* Trinity Hall, Cambridge (BA, MA; PhD 1978). Res. Fellow, Gonville and Caius Coll., Cambridge, 1975–76; Lectr in Iranian Langs, 1976–89, Reader in Iranian Studies, 1989–94, SOAS, Univ. of London. Corresp. Mem., Austrian Acad. of Scis, 1990. *Publications:* The Christian Sogdian manuscript C2, 1985 (Prix Ghirshman, Inst. de France, 1988); Sogdian and other Iranian Inscriptions of the Upper Indus, vol. I, 1989, vol. II, 1992; (with James Hamilton) Documents turco-sogdiens du IXe–Xe siècle de Touen-houang, 1990; Partita, 1993; contrib. on Iranian and Central Asian langs and culture to learned jls. *Recreation:* music. *Address:* 11 Park Parade, Cambridge CB5 8AL. *T:* Cambridge (01223) 368903.

SIMSON, Michael Ronald Fraser, OBE 1966; Secretary of the National Corporation for the Care of Old People, 1948–73; *b* 9 Oct. 1913; *er s* of Ronald Stuart Fraser Simson and Ethel Alice Henderson; *m* 1939, Elizabeth Joan Wilkinson; one *s*. *Educ:* Winchester Coll.; Christ Church, Oxford. OUAFC 1936 and 1937. Asst Master, West Downs Sch., 1938–40; RNVR, 1941–46; Asst Sec., Nat. Fedn of Housing Socs, 1946–48. Member: Min. of Labour Cttee on Employment of Older Men and Women, 1953–55; Cttee on Local Authority and Allied Personal Social Services (Seebohm Cttee), 1966–68; Supplementary Benefits Commn, 1967–76; Adv. Cttee on Rent Rebates and Rent Allowances, 1973–75, resigned 1975; Personal Social Services Council, 1973–78. *Recreations:* gardening, interested in all forms of sport. *Address:* Summerhill, Kingsdon, Somerton, Somerset TA11 7JU. *T:* Ilchester (01935) 840858.

SINATRA, Francis Albert, (Frank); singer, actor, film producer, publisher; *b* Hoboken, New Jersey, USA, 12 Dec. 1915; *s* of late Natalie and Martin Sinatra; *m* 1st, 1939, Nancy Barbato (marr. diss.); one *s* two *d*; 2nd 1951, Ava Gardner (marr. diss.); 3rd, 1966, Mia Farrow (marr. diss.); 4th, 1976, Barbara Marx. *Educ:* Demarest High School, New Jersey. Started in radio, 1936; then became band singer with orchestras. First appearance in films, 1943. *Films include:* From Here to Eternity (Oscar for best supporting actor, 1953), Anchors Aweigh, On the Town, The Tender Trap, High Society, Guys and Dolls, The Man with the Golden Arm, Johnny Concho, The Joker is Wild, Kings Go Forth, Some Came Running, A Hole in the Head, Ocean's 11, The Devil at Four O'Clock, Sergeants Three, Manchurian Candidate, Come Blow Your Horn, Four for Texas, Robin and the Seven Hoods, None But the Brave, Marriage on the Rocks, Von Ryan's Express, Assault on a Queen, The Naked Runner, Tony Rome, The Detective, Lady in Cement, Dirty Dingus Magee, The First Deadly Sin, Cannonball Run II. Owner music publishing companies, etc. Jean Hersholt Humanitarian Award, 1971. *Publications:* composed numerous popular songs. *Address:* Scoop Marketing, 3701 Wilshire Boulevard, Los Angeles, CA 90010, USA.

SINCLAIR, family name of **Earl of Caithness, Viscount Thurso,** and **Baron Sinclair of Cleeve.**

SINCLAIR, 17th Lord, *cr* 1449 (Scotland); **Charles Murray Kennedy St Clair,** CVO 1990 (LVO 1953); Major, late Coldstream Guards; Extra Equerry to Queen Elizabeth the Queen Mother since 1953; Lord-Lieutenant, Dumfries and Galloway Region (District of Stewartry), 1982–89 (Vice-Lord-Lieutenant, 1977–82); Member Queen's Body Guard for Scotland (Royal Company of Archers); *b* 21 June 1914; *o s* of 16th Lord Sinclair, MVO, and Violet (*d* 1953), *d* of Col J. Murray Kennedy, MVO; *S* father, 1957; *m* 1968, Anne Lettice, *yr d* of Sir Richard Cotterell, 5th Bt, CBE; one *s* two *d*. *Educ:* Eton; Magdalene Coll., Cambridge. Served War of 1939–45, Palestine, 1939 (wounded, despatches). Retired as Major Coldstream Guards, 1947. Portcullis Pursuivant of Arms, 1949–57; York Herald, 1957–68, retired. A Representative Peer for Scotland, 1959–63. DL Kirkcudbrightshire, 1969. *Heir:* *s* Master of Sinclair, *qv*. *Address:* Knocknalling, St John's Town of Dalry, Castle Douglas, Kirkcudbrightshire, Scotland DG7 3ST. *T:* Dalry (01644) 430221. *Club:* New (Edinburgh).

SINCLAIR, Master of; Hon. Matthew Murray Kennedy St Clair; *b* 9 Dec. 1968; *s* and *heir* of 17th Lord Sinclair, *qv*.

SINCLAIR OF CLEEVE, 3rd Baron *cr* 1957, of Cleeve, Somerset; **John Lawrence Robert Sinclair;** Teaching Support Staff Governor at an Inner London comprehensive school, since 1985; *b* 6 Jan. 1953; *s* of 2nd Baron Sinclair of Cleeve, OBE, and of Patricia, *d* of late Major Lawrence Hellyer; *S* father, 1985. *Educ:* Winchester College; Manchester Univ. *Recreations:* motor cycling, mime, music.

SINCLAIR, Alexander Riddell; HM Diplomatic Service, retired; *b* 28 Aug. 1917; *s* of Henry W. Sinclair and Mary Turner; *m* 1948, Alice Evelyn Nottingham; three *d*. *Educ:*

Greenock High School. DipCAM. Inland Revenue, 1935–37; Admty, 1938–47 (Comdr RNVR, 1945–46); 2nd Sec., HM Embassy, Moscow, 1947–48; Vice-Consul: Detroit, 1949; Mosul, 1950; FO, 1952; 1st Secretary, HM Embassy: Saigon, 1953–56; Amman, 1957–58; FO, 1959; 1st Sec. (Cultural), Budapest, 1962; FO, 1964; 1st Secretary (Information): Beirut, 1967–70; Rome, 1970–71; Consul-Gen., Genoa, 1972–76; FCO Library, 1977–85. Silver Jubilee Medal, 1977. *Publications:* literary articles in learned jls. *Recreations:* reading, book browsing, walking. *Address:* 2 Ruthven Place, St Andrews, Fife KY16 8SJ. *Club:* Civil Service.

SINCLAIR, Andrew Annandale; author; Managing Director, Timon Films, since 1967; *b* 21 Jan. 1935; *m* 1960, Marianne, *d* of Mr and Mrs Arsène Alexandre; *m* 1972, Miranda, *o d* of Mr and Hon. Mrs George Seymour; two *s*; *m* 1984, Sonia Lady Melchett (*see* S. E. Sinclair), *d* of Dr and Mrs Roland Graham. *Educ:* Eton Coll.; Trinity Coll., Cambridge (BA, PhD); Harvard. Ensign, Coldstream Guards, 1953–55. Harkness Fellow of the Commonwealth Fund, 1959–61; Dir of Historical Studies, Churchill Coll., Cambridge, 1961–63; Fellow of American Council of Learned Societies, 1963–64; Lectr in American History, University Coll., London, 1965–67. Dir/Writer Mem., ACTT. FRSL 1973; Fellow Soc. of American Historians, 1974. Somerset Maugham Literary Prize, 1966. *Film:* (dir) Under Milk Wood, 1971. *Publications:* The Breaking of Bumbo, 1958; My Friend Judas, 1959; The Project, 1960; Prohibition, 1962; The Hallelujah Bum, 1963; The Available Man: Warren E. Harding, 1964; The Better Half, 1964; The Raker, 1965; Concise History of the United States, 1966; Albion Triptych: Gog, 1967, Magog, 1972, King Ludd, 1988; The Greek Anthology, 1967; Adventures in the Skin Trade, 1968; The Last of the Best, 1969; Guevara, 1970; Dylan Thomas: poet of his people, 1975; The Surrey Cat, 1976; The Savage, 1977; Jack: the biography of Jack London, 1977; A Patriot for Hire, 1978; John Ford, 1979; The Facts in the Case of E. A. Poe, 1979; Corsair, 1981; The Other Victoria, 1981; Sir Walter Raleigh and the Age of Discovery, 1984; Beau Bumbo, 1985; The Red and the Blue, 1986; Spiegel, 1987; War Like a Wasp, 1989; (ed) The War Decade, an anthology of the 1940s, 1989; The Need to Give, 1990; The Far Corners of the Earth, 1991; The Naked Savage, 1991; The Strength of the Hills, 1992; The Sword and the Grail, 1993; Francis Bacon: his life and violent times, 1993; In Love and Anger, 1994; Arts and Cultures: the history of the fifty years of the Arts Council of Great Britain, 1995. *Recreations:* old cities, old movies. *Address:* 16 Tite Street, SW3 4HZ.

SINCLAIR, Carolyn Elizabeth Cunningham, (Mrs S. J. Bowen); Assistant Under-Secretary of State, Home Office, since 1992; *b* 13 July 1944; *d* of John Archibald Sinclair and Grace Margaret Stuart Sinclair (*née* Cunningham); *m* 1979, Stephen John Bowen. *Educ:* Laurel Bank Sch., Glasgow; Brown Univ., RI; Edinburgh Univ. (MA Hist.); Univ. of E Africa (Leverhulme Schol.; MA Pol Sci.). Joined FCO, 1968; Vienna, 1970–73; Private Sec. to Minister of State, 1977–78; transferred to HM Treasury, 1979; Prime Minister's Policy Unit, 1988–92. *Recreations:* gardening, listening to music, reading, seeing friends. *Address:* Home Office, 50 Queen Anne's Gate, SW1H 9AT. *Club:* Royal Automobile.

SINCLAIR, Charles James Francis; Group Chief Executive, Daily Mail and General Trust PLC, since 1988; *b* 4 April 1948; *s* of Sir George (Evelyn) Sinclair, *qv*; *m* 1974, Nicola Bayliss; two *s*. *Educ:* Winchester Coll.; Magdalen Coll., Oxford (BA). ACA 1974. VSO, Zambia, 1966–67. Dearden Farrow, CA, 1970; joined Associated Newspapers Holdings, 1975; Asst Man. Dir and Mem. Main Bd, 1986; Man. Dir, 1988 (Associated Newspapers Holdings became the wholly-owned operating subsid. of Daily Mail and General Trust, 1988); Director: Whittle Communications, Tennessee, 1985–; Euromoney Publications PLC, 1985–; Schroders plc, 1990–; Westcountry Television Ltd, 1991–; Reuters Holdings plc, 1994–. Chm. of Trustees, Minack Theatre Trust, Porthcurno, Cornwall, 1985–;. *Recreations:* opera, fishing, ski-ing. *Address:* Northcliffe House, 2 Derry Street, Kensington, W8 5TT. *Clubs:* Athenæum; Vincent's (Oxford).

SINCLAIR, Sir Clive (Marles), Kt 1983; Chairman, Sinclair Research Ltd, since 1979; *b* 30 July 1940; *s* of George William Carter Sinclair and Thora Edith Ella (*née* Marles); *m* 1962, Ann (*née* Trevor Briscoe) (marr. diss. 1985); two *s* one *d*. *Educ:* Boxgrove Prep. Sch., Guildford; Highgate; Reading; St George's Coll., Weybridge. Editor, Bernards Publishers Ltd, 1958–61; Chairman: Sinclair Radionics Ltd, 1962–79; Sinclair Browne Ltd, 1981–85; Cambridge Computer Ltd, 1986–90; Dir, Shaye Communications Ltd, 1986–91. Vis. Fellow, Robinson Coll., Cambridge, 1982–85; Vis. Prof., Dept of Elec. Engrg, Imperial Coll. of Science, Technol. and Medicine, London, 1984–92 (Hon. Fellow, 1984). Chm., British Mensa, 1980–. Hon. Fellow UMIST, 1984. Hon. DSc: Bath, 1983; Warwick, 1983; Heriot-Watt, 1983. Mullard Award, Royal Soc., 1984. *Publications:* Practical Transistor Receivers, 1959; British Semiconductor Survey, 1963. *Recreations:* music, poetry, mathematics, science, poker. *Address:* 18 Shepherd House, 5 Shepherd Street, W1Y 7LD. *T:* 0171–408 0199, (office) 0171–636 4488. *Club:* Chelsea Arts.

SINCLAIR of Freswick, Maj.-Gen. David Boyd A.; *see* Alexander-Sinclair.

SINCLAIR, Prof. David Cecil; Emeritus Professor, University of Western Australia; *b* 28 Aug. 1915; *s* of Norman James Sinclair and Annie Smart Sinclair; *m* 1945, Grace Elizabeth Simondson, Melbourne, Vic.; one *s* one *d*. *Educ:* Merchiston Castle Sch.; St Andrews University. MB, ChB (Commendation) St Andrews, 1937; MD (Hons and Rutherford Gold Medal) St Andrews, 1947; MA Oxon, 1948; DSc Western Australia, 1965. Served in RAMC, 1940–46: AMF, 1943–45; Head of Physiology Sect., Aust. Chem. Warfare Research and Experimental Stn, 1943–44; Dep. Chief Supt, Aust. Field Experimental Stn, 1944–45. Sen. Res. Off., Dept of Human Anatomy, Oxford, 1946–49; Univ. Demonstrator in Anatomy, Oxford, 1949–56; Lectr in Anatomy, Pembroke Coll., Oxford, 1950–56; Lectr in Anatomy, Ruskin Sch. of Fine Art, 1950–56; first Prof. of Anatomy, Univ. of W Australia, 1957–64, Dean of Med. Sch., 1964; Regius Prof. of Anatomy, Univ. of Aberdeen, 1965–75; Dir of Postgrad. Med. Educn, Queen Elizabeth II Med. Centre, WA, 1975–80. FRCSE 1966. Life Governor, Aust. Postgrad. Fedn in Medicine, 1983. *Publications:* Medical Students and Medical Sciences, 1955; An Introduction to Functional Anatomy, 1957 (5th edn 1975); A Student's Guide to Anatomy, 1961; Cutaneous Sensation, 1967, Japanese edn 1969; Human Growth after Birth, 1969 (5th edn 1989); Muscles and Fascia (section in Cunningham's Anatomy), 11th edn, 1972, 12th edn, 1981; Basic Medical Education, 1972; The Nerves of the Skin (section in Physiology and Pathophysiology of the Skin, ed Jarrett), 1973; Growth, section in Textbook of Human Anatomy (ed Hamilton), 1976; Mechanisms of Cutaneous Sensation, 1981; Not a Proper Doctor (autobiog.), 1989; Outside the Dissecting Room, 1989; papers on chemical warfare, neurological anatomy, experimental psychology, and medical education; Editor, Jl of Anatomy, 1970–73. *Recreations:* reading, writing, photography, chess problems. *Address:* Flat 3, Netherby, Netherby Road, Cults, Aberdeen AB1 9HL.

SINCLAIR, Maj.-Gen. George Brian, CB 1983; CBE 1975; Engineer-in-Chief (Army), 1980–83; *b* 21 July 1928; *s* of Thomas S. Sinclair and Blanche Sinclair; *m* 1953, Edna Margaret Richardson; two *s* one *d*. *Educ:* Christ's College, Finchley; RMA Sandhurst. Commissioned, Royal Engineers, 1948; served UK, BAOR, Korea, and Christmas Island, 1948–66; Directing Staff, Staff College, Camberley, 1967–69; CRE, Near East, 1970–71; Col GS, HQ 1st British Corps, 1972–74; Nat. Defence Coll., India, 1975; Commandant Royal School of Military Engineering, 1976–77; BGS, Military Operations, MoD, 1978–80. Col Comdt, RE, 1983–91; Hon. Col, Engineer and Transport Staff Corps, 1988–93. Vice Pres., Red R (formerly Register of Engrs for Disaster Relief), 1985–; Trustee: Imperial War Mus., 1990–; RE Museum Foundn, 1993–. Mem. Council, Friends of Rochester Cathedral, 1984–95 (Chm. Council, 1988–91). Governor, King's Sch., Rochester, 1984–. *Recreations:* hill walking, running, bird watching and discussion. *Address:* 6 Prospect Row, Brompton, Gillingham, Kent ME7 5AL. *T:* Medway (01634) 842364. *Club:* Army and Navy (Chm., 1995–).

SINCLAIR, Sir George (Evelyn), Kt 1960; CMG 1956; OBE 1950; *b* Cornwall, 6 November 1912; 2nd *s* of late F. Sinclair, Chynance, St Buryan, Cornwall; *m* 1st, 1941, Katharine Jane Burdekin (*d* 1971); one *s* three *d*; 2nd, 1972, Mary Violet, *widow* of George Lester Sawday, Saxmundham, Suffolk. *Educ:* Abingdon School; Pembroke College, Oxford (MA; Hon. Fellow, 1986). Entered Colonial Administrative Service, 1936; appointed to Gold Coast Administration; Asst District Comr, 1937. Military service, 1940–43. District Commissioner, Gold Coast, 1943; seconded to Colonial Office, 1943–45; Sec. to Commn on Higher Education in West Africa, 1943–45; returned to Gold Coast, 1945; Senior Assistant Colonial Secretary, 1947; Principal Assistant Secretary, 1950; Regional Officer, Trans-Volta Togoland Region, 1952; Deputy Governor, Cyprus, 1955–60; retired, 1961. MP (C) Dorking, Surrey, Oct. 1964–1979. Member, Parly Select Committees on: Procedure, 1965–66; Race Relations, 1969–70; Overseas Aid, 1969–70; Race Relations and Immigration, 1970–74; Members Interests, 1975; Abortion Act (Amendment) Bill; Joint Secretary: Cons. Parly Commonwealth Affairs Cttee, 1966–68; Cons. Parly Educn Cttee, 1974–79, Vice-Chm., 1974; Member: Intermediate Technology Develt Gp (Vice-Pres., 1966–79; Dir, 1979–82); Nat. Exec. Cttee, UNA (UK Branch), 1968–70; Council, Overseas Services Resettlement Bureau; Council of PDSA, 1964–70; Council, Christian Aid, 1973–78; Steering Cttee, UN/FPA World Conf. of Parliamentarians on population and develt, 1978–79; Vice-Chm., Family Planning Assoc., 1979–81; Consultant: UN Fund for Population Affairs, 1979–82; IPPF, 1979–83; special advr to Global Cttee on Population and Develt, 1982–88. Trustee: Runnymede Trust, 1969–75; Human Rights Trust, 1971–74; Physically Handicapped and Able Bodied (Foundn Trustee), 1973–81; Wyndham Place Trust. Mem., Wimbledon Borough Council, 1962–65. Member, Board of Governors: Abingdon Sch., 1970–87 (Chm., 1971–79); Felixstowe Coll., 1980–87; Campion Sch., Athens, 1983–94; Chm., Assoc. of Governing Bodies of Independent Schools, 1979–84 (Mem., 1973–); Member: Direct Grant Jt Cttee, 1974–80; Indep. Schools Jt Council, 1979–84 (Chm. 1980–83, Dep. Chm., 1984); Council, Oxford Soc., 1982–93. Chm. Planning Office, 1988 Internat. Conf. of Spiritual and Parly Leaders on Human Survival, 1986–88. *Recreations:* golf, fishing. *Address:* Carlton Rookery, Saxmundham, Suffolk IP17 2NN; South Minack, Porthcurno, Cornwall TR19 6JU. *Clubs:* Athenæum, Commonwealth Trust; Aldeburgh Golf; Aldeburgh Yacht.

See also C. J. F. Sinclair.

SINCLAIR, Hon. Ian David, OC 1979; QC (Can.) 1961; Member, Senate of Canada, 1983–88; *b* Winnipeg, 27 Dec. 1913; *s* of late John David Sinclair and late Lillian Sinclair; *m* 1942, Ruth Beatrice, *d* of Robert Parsons Drennan, Winnipeg; two *s* two *d*. *Educ:* public schs, Winnipeg; Univ. of Manitoba (BA Econs 1937); Manitoba Law School (LLB 1941). Barrister, Guy Chappell & Co., Winnipeg, 1937–41; Lectr in Torts, Univ. of Manitoba, 1942–43; joined Canadian Pacific Law Dept as Asst Solicitor, Winnipeg, 1942; Solicitor, Montreal, 1946; Asst to General Counsel, 1951; General Solicitor, 1953; Vice-Pres. and Gen. Counsel, 1960; Vice-Pres., Law, 1960; Canadian Pacific Railway Co.: Vice-Pres., Dir and Mem. Exec. Cttee, 1961; Pres., 1966; Chief Exec. Officer, 1969; Chm. and Chief Exec. Officer: Canadian Pacific Ltd, 1972–81; Canadian Pacific Enterprises Ltd, 1972–82 (Chm., 1982–84); Director: Canadian Investment Fund, Ltd, 1972–89; Canadian Marconi Co., 1967–; Union Carbide Canada Ltd, 1968–; Public Dir, Investment Dealers Assoc. of Canada, 1984–88; Public Gov., Car Investors Protection Fund, 1990–; Mem., Internat. Adv. Cttee, Chase Manhattan Bank, N America, 1973–87; Trustee, Alliance Global Fund, 1987–. Hon. LLD Manitoba, 1967; Hon. DBA Laval, 1981; Hon. DCL Acadia, 1982. Mem., Canadian Business Hall of Fame. *Address:* 1 University Avenue, Suite 1400, Toronto, Ont M5J 2P1, Canada. *Club:* Toronto (Toronto).

SINCLAIR, Rt. Hon. Ian (McCahon), PC 1977; MHR for New England, NSW, since 1963; Leader, National Party of Australia, 1984–89 (Deputy Leader, 1971–84); *b* 10 June 1929; *s* of George McCahon Sinclair and Gertrude Hazel Sinclair; *m* 1st, 1956, Margaret Tarrant (*d* 1967); one *s* two *d*; 2nd, 1970, Rosemary Fenton; one *s*. *Educ:* Knox Grammar Sch., Wahroonga, NSW; Sydney Univ. BA, LLB. Grazier. Mem. Legislative Council, NSW, 1961–63; Minister for: Social Services, 1965–68; Trade and Industry (Minister Assisting Minister), 1966–71; Shipping and Transport, 1968–71; Primary Industry, 1971–72; Leader of House for Opposition, 1974–75; Country Party spokesman for Defence, Foreign Affairs, Law and Agriculture, 1973; Opposition spokesman on primary industry, 1974–75; Leader of House, 1975–79; Minister for: Agriculture and N Territory, Nov.–Dec. 1975; Primary Industry, 1975–79; Special Trade Representations, 1980; Communications, 1980–82; Defence, 1982–83; Leader of the House for the Opposition, 1983–89; Shadow Minister: Defence, 1983–87; Trade and Resources, 1987–89; of State, Jan.–May 1994. Member Committee: House of Reps Standing Orders, 1974–79, 1980–82, 1983–84; Privileges, 1980–82; Legal and Constitutional Affairs, 1990–; Jt Foreign Affairs, Defence and Trade, 1990–; Nat. Crime Authority, 1990–; Mem., Jt Standing Cttee on Migration Regulations, 1990–; Jt Cttee on Corps and Securities; Parly Code of Conduct Working Gp. *Address:* Parliament House, Canberra, ACT 2600, Australia. *T:* (6) 2774064, *Fax:* (6) 2774972. *Clubs:* Australian, American, Union (Sydney); Tamworth; Killara Golf.

SINCLAIR, Sir Ian (McTaggart), KCMG 1977 (CMG 1972); QC 1979; Barrister-at-Law; Visiting Professor of International Law, King's College, London, 1989–93; *b* 14 Jan. 1926; *s* of late John Sinclair, company director; *m* 1954, Barbara Elizabeth (*née* Lenton); two *s* one *d*. *Educ:* Merchiston Castle Sch. (Scholar); King's Coll., Cambridge; BA 1948, LLB 1949 (1st cl. hons). Served Intelligence Corps, 1944–47. Called to the Bar, Middle Temple, 1952; Bencher, 1980. Asst Legal Adviser, Foreign Office, 1950–56; Legal Adviser, HM Embassy, Bonn, 1957–60; Asst Legal Adviser, FO, 1960–64; Legal Adviser, UK Mission to the UN, New York, and HM Embassy, Washington, 1964–67; Foreign and Commonwealth Office: Legal Counsellor, 1967–71; Dep. Legal Advr, 1971–72; Second Legal Advr, 1973–75; Legal Advr, 1976–84. Has been Legal Adviser to UK delegn at numerous internat. confs, incl. Geneva Conf. on Korea and Indo-China, 1954, and Brussels negotiations for UK entry into the EEC, 1961–63; Dep. Chm., UK delegn to Law of Treaties Conf., Vienna, 1968–69; Legal Adviser to UK delegn on negotiations for UK entry into EEC, 1970–72; Member: Bureau of European Cttee on Legal Co-operation, Council of Europe, 1979–81; Panel of Conciliators, Annex to Vienna Convention on Law of Treaties, 1981–; Internat. Law Commn, 1981–86; Panel of Arbitrators, Internat. Centre for Settlement of Investment Disputes, 1988–; Panel of Legal Experts under INTELSAT Convention, 1990–; Perm. Ct of Arbitration, 1992–. Mem., Committee of Management: British Inst. of Internat. and Comparative Law, 1976–; Inst. of Advanced Legal Studies, 1980–84. Associate Mem., Inst de Droit Internat., 1983, elected Mem., 1987; Hon. Mem., Amer. Soc. of Internat. Law, 1987. *Publications:* Vienna Convention on the Law of Treaties, 1973, 2nd edn 1984; International Law Commission, 1987; articles in British Yearbook of International Law, International and Comparative Law Qly and other legal jls. *Recreations:* golf, fishing, watching sea-birds. *Address:* Lassington, Chithurst, Petersfield, Hants GU31 5EU. *T:* Midhurst (01730) 815370; 10B South Park Road, Wimbledon, SW19 8ST. *T:* 0181–543 1843; (chambers) 2 Hare Court, Temple, EC4Y 7BH. *T:* 0171–583 1770. *Club:* Athenæum.

SINCLAIR, Isabel Lillias, (Mrs J. G. MacDonald), QC (Scotland) 1964; Sheriff of Lothian and Borders (formerly Roxburgh, Berwick, and Selkirk), 1968–79, now Honorary Sheriff; Honorary Sheriff of Bute; *d* of William Sinclair, Glasgow, and Isabella (*née* Thomson), Glasgow; *m* 1938, J. Gordon MacDonald (decd), BL, Solicitor, Glasgow. *Educ:* Shawlands Academy; Glasgow Univ. MA 1932; BL 1946. Worked as a newspaper-woman from 1932. Admitted to Faculty of Advocates, Edinburgh, 1949. Sheriff-Substitute of Lanarkshire at Airdrie, 1966–68. *Address:* 30 Ravelston Garden, Edinburgh EH4 3LE. *T:* 0131–337 9797. *Club:* Royal Scottish Automobile (Glasgow).

SINCLAIR, Prof. John McHardy; Professor of Modern English Language, University of Birmingham, since 1965; *b* 14 June 1933; *s* of late George Ferguson Sinclair and Isabella (*née* Palmer); *m* 1956, Margaret Myfanwy Lloyd; two *s* one *d*. *Educ:* George Heriot's Sch., Edinburgh; Edinburgh Univ. (MA). Served Royal Air Force (Flt-Lt), 1955–58. Lectr, Edinburgh Univ., 1959–65. Adjunct Prof., Shanghai Jiao Tong Univ., 1986–. *Publications:* A Course in Spoken English—Grammar, 1972; (with R. M. Coulthard) Towards an Analysis of Discourse, 1975, 2nd edn 1978; (with D. C. Brazil) Teacher Talk, 1982; Corpus, Concordance, Collocation, 1991; Editor in Chief, Cobuild: Collin's Cobuild English Language Dictionary, 1987; Collins Cobuild English Grammar, 1990. *Recreation:* printing. *Address:* School of English, The University, Edgbaston, Birmingham B15 2TT. *T:* 0121–414 5688.

SINCLAIR, Air Vice-Marshal Sir Laurence (Frank), GC 1941; KCB 1957 (CB 1946); CBE 1943; DSO 1940 (and Bar, 1943); *b* 13 June 1908; *m* 1941, Valerie (*d* 1990), *d* of Lt-Col Joseph Dalton White; one *s* one *d*. *Educ:* Imperial Service Coll.; RAF Coll. Cranwell. Comd No 110 Sqdn in 1940; Comd RAF Watton, 1941; Comd Tactical Light Bomber Force in North Africa and Italy, 1943–44; ADC to King George VI, 1943–44; subsequently Sen. Air Staff Officer, Balkan Air Force; Imperial Defence Coll., 1947; commanded No 2 Light Bomber Group (Germany), 1948–49; Assistant Commandant RAF Staff College, 1949–50; Commandant, Royal Air Force College Cranwell, 1950–52; Commandant, School of Land/Air Warfare, 1952–53; Asst Chief of the Air Staff (Operations), 1953–55; Comdr British Forces, Arabian Peninsula, 1955–57; Commandant Joint Services Staff College, 1958–60, retired from RAF. Controller of Ground Services, Min. of Aviation, 1960–61; Controller, Nat. Air Traffic Control Services, Min. of Aviation, and MoD, 1962–66. Legion of Merit (American), 1943; Legion of Honour, 1944; Partisan Star (Yugoslavia). *Address:* The Old Prebendal House, Shipton-under-Wychwood, Oxford OX7 6BQ.

SINCLAIR, Rt. Rev. Maurice Walter; *see* Northern Argentina, Bishop of.

SINCLAIR, Michael; *see* Shea, M. S. MacA.

SINCLAIR, Sir Patrick (Robert Richard), 10th Bt *cr* 1704 (NS), of Dunbeath, Caithness-shire; barrister; *b* 21 May 1936; s of Alexander Robert Sinclair (Robin) (*d* 1972) (*b* of 8th Bt) and Vera Mabel (*d* 1981), *d* of late Walter Stephings Baxendale; *S* cousin, 1990; *m* 1974, Susan Catherine Beresford Davies, *e d* of Geoffrey Clive Davies, OBE; one *s* one *d*. *Educ:* Winchester; Oriel Coll., Oxford. Nat. Service, RNVR, 1954–56 (Actg Sub-Lieut). Called to the Bar, Lincoln's Inn, 1961, Bencher, 1994; in practice at Chancery Bar. *Recreations:* sailing, tennis. *Heir:* *s* William Robert Francis Sinclair, *b* 27 March 1979. *Address:* 5 New Square, Lincoln's Inn, WC2A 3RJ. *T:* 0171–404 0404. *Club:* Pin Mill Sailing (Suffolk).

SINCLAIR, Rear-Adm. Peter Ross, AC 1992 (AO (mil.) 1986); Governor of New South Wales, since 1990; farmer, Flagship Poll Hereford Stud; *b* 16 Nov. 1934; *s* of late G. P. Sinclair; *m* 1957, Shirley, *d* of J. A. McLellan; one *s* two *d*. *Educ:* North Sydney Boys' High Sch.; Royal Aust. Naval Coll.; Royal Coll. of Defence Studies. jssc. Joined RAN 1948; served HM Australian ships Australia, Tobruk, Vengeance, Arunta, Swan, Sydney, Vendetta, Vampire, Penguin, HMS Maidstone, HMS Jutland; CO HMAS Duchess, 1970–72; CO HMAS Hobart, 1974–77; Dir, Naval Plans, 1979–80; Dir-Gen., Mil. Staff Branch, Strategic and Internat. Policy Div., Defence Dept, 1980–82; Chief of Staff, 1983–84; First Comdt, Aust. Defence Force Acad., 1984–86; Maritime Comdr Australia, 1986–90 and Dep. Chief of Naval Staff, 1989. Hon. FIEAust 1994; CPEng 1994. DUniv Sydney, 1992. KStJ 1991. *Recreations:* painting, sketching, whittling, reading, cricket, golf, tennis. *Address:* Government House, Sydney, NSW 2000, Australia.

SINCLAIR, Sir Ronald Ormiston, KBE 1963; Kt 1956; President, Court of Appeal: for the Bahamas and for Bermuda, 1965–70; for British Honduras, 1968–70; Chairman, Industrial Tribunals (England and Wales), 1966–69; *b* 2 May 1903; *yr s* of Rev. W. A. Sinclair, Auckland, NZ; *m* 1935, Ellen Isabel Entrican; two *s*. *Educ:* New Plymouth Boys' High School, NZ; Auckland University College, NZ; Balliol College, Oxford. Barrister and Solicitor of Supreme Court of New Zealand, 1924; LLM (NZ) (Hons) 1925; Administrative Service, Nigeria, 1931; Magistrate, Nigeria, 1936; Resident Magistrate, Northern Rhodesia, 1938; Barrister-at-Law, Middle Temple, 1939; Puisne Judge, Tanganyika, 1946; Chief Justice, Nyasaland, 1953–55; Vice-President, East African Court of Appeal, 1956–57, Pres., 1962–64; Chief Justice of Kenya, 1957–62. *Address:* 158 Victoria Avenue, Remuera, Auckland, New Zealand.

SINCLAIR, Sonia Elizabeth, (Mrs A. A. Sinclair); Board Member, Royal Court Theatre, since 1974; *b* 6 Sept. 1928; *d* of Col R. H. Graham; *m* 1st, 1947, Hon. Julian Mond, later 3rd Baron Melchett (*d* 1973); one *s* two *d*; 2nd, 1984, Dr Andrew Annandale Sinclair, *qv*. *Educ:* Royal School, Bath. Board Member: NSPCC, 1960–70; Nat. Theatre, then RNT, 1984–94. JP Marylebone, 1962–72. *Publications:* Tell Me, Honestly, 1964; Someone is Missing, 1987; Passionate Quests, 1991. *Recreations:* reading, walking, swimming, foreign travel. *Address:* 16 Tite Street, SW3 4HZ. *T:* 0171–352 7645.

See also Baron Melchett.

SINCLAIR-LOCKHART, Sir Simon (John Edward Francis), 15th Bt *cr* 1636 (NS); *b* 22 July 1941; *s* of Sir Muir Edward Sinclair-Lockhart, 14th Bt, and of Olga Ann, *d* of late Claude Victor White-Parsons, Hawkes Bay, NZ; *S* father, 1985; *m* 1973, Felicity Edith, *d* of late I. L. C. Stewart, NZ; twin *s* one *d*. *Heir:* *er* twin *s* Robert Muir Sinclair-Lockhart, *b* 12 Sept. 1973. *Address:* 13 Franklin Terrace, Havelock North, Hawke's Bay, New Zealand.

SINCLAIR-STEVENSON, Christopher Terence; Consultant, Sinclair-Stevenson, since 1995; *b* 27 June 1939; *s* of George and late Gloria Sinclair-Stevenson; *m* 1965, Deborah Susan (*née* Walker-Smith). *Educ:* Eton Coll.; St John's Coll., Cambridge (MA). Joined Hamish Hamilton Ltd, 1961, Dir, 1970, Man. Dir, 1974–89; Man. Dir, Sinclair-Stevenson Ltd, 1989–92; Publisher, Sinclair-Stevenson, and Editor-in-Chief, Reed Consumer Books, 1992–95. *Publications:* The Gordon Highlanders, 1968; Inglorious Rebellion, 1971; The Life of a Regiment, 1974; Blood Royal, 1979; That Sweet Enemy, 1987. *Recreations:* music, travel, food, the written word. *Address:* 3 South Terrace, SW7 2TB. *T:* 0171–584 8087.

SINDALL, Adrian John, CMG 1993; HM Diplomatic Service; Ambassador to Syria, since 1994; *b* 5 Oct. 1937; *s* of Stephen Sindall and Clare Mallet; *m* 1st, 1958; one *s* one *d*; 2nd, 1978, Jill Margaret Cowley. *Educ:* Battersea Grammar Sch. FO, 1956–58; ME Centre for Arab Studies, 1958–60; Third Sec. (Commercial), Baghdad, 1960–62; Second Sec., British Embassy, Rabat, 1962–67; First Secretary: FCO, 1967–70; Beirut, 1970–72; First Sec. and Head of Chancery, British Embassy, Lima, 1972–76; FCO, 1976–79; Counsellor, Head of Chancery and Consul-Gen., Amman, 1979–82; Hd of S America Dept, FCO, 1982–85; Consul-Gen., Sydney, 1985–88; ME Marketing Dir, Defence Export Services Orgn, MoD, on secondment, 1988–91; High Comr, Brunei, 1991–94. SPMB (Negara Brunei Darussalam), 1992. *Address:* c/o Foreign and Commonwealth Office, SW1A 2AH.

SINDELL, Marion Harwood; Chief Executive, Equal Opportunities Commission, 1979–85; *b* 23 June 1925; *d* of Arthur Barrett Sindell and Ethel Maude Sindell. *Educ:* Lincoln Girls' High Sch.; St Hilda's Coll., Oxford (MA). Solicitor. Deputy Town Clerk: Workington, 1959–64; Nuneaton, 1964–66; Town Clerk, Goole, 1966–74; Chief Exec., Boothferry Bor. Council, 1974–79. *Address:* The Granary, Skelton, Penrith, Cumbria.

SINDEN, Donald Alfred, CBE 1979; actor; *b* 9 Oct. 1923; *s* of Alfred Edward Sinden and Mabel Agnes (*née* Fuller), Sussex; *m* 1948, Diana, *d* of Daniel and Muriel Mahony; two *s*. First appearance on stage, 1942, in Charles F. Smith's Co., Mobile Entertainments Southern Area; Leicester Repertory Co., 1945; Memorial Theatre Co., Stratford upon Avon, 1946 and 1947; Old Vic and Bristol Old Vic, 1948; The Heiress, Haymarket, 1949–50; Bristol Old Vic, 1950; Red Letter Day, Garrick, 1951. Under contract to Rank Organisation, 1952–60, appearing in 23 films including The Cruel Sea, Doctor in the House, etc. Returned to theatre, appearing in Odd Man In, St Martin's, 1957; Peter Pan, Scala, 1960; Guilty Party, St Martin's, 1961; Royal Shakespeare Co., playing Richard Plantagenet in Henry VI (The Wars of the Roses), Price in Eh!, etc, 1963 and 1964; British Council tour of S America in Dear Liar and Happy Days, 1965; There's a Girl in my Soup, Globe, 1966; Lord Foppington in The Relapse, RSC, Aldwych, 1967; Not Now Darling, Strand, 1968; RSC, Stratford, 1969 and Aldwych, 1970 playing Malvolio; Henry VIII; Sir Harcourt Courtly in London Assurance, revived at New Theatre, 1972, tour of the USA, 1974 (Drama Desk Award); In Praise of Love, Duchess, 1973; Stockmann in An Enemy of the People, Chichester, 1975; Habeas Corpus, USA, 1975; Benedick in Much Ado About Nothing, King Lear, RSC, Stratford, 1976, Aldwych, 1977 (Variety Club of GB Stage Actor of 1976; Evening Standard Drama Award, Best Actor, 1977); Shut Your Eyes and Think of England, Apollo, 1977; Othello, RSC, Stratford, 1979, Aldwych, 1980; Present Laughter, Vaudeville, 1981; Uncle Vanya, Haymarket, 1982; The School for Scandal, Haymarket and Duke of York's (Eur. tour, 1984), 1983; Ariadne auf Naxos, Coliseum, 1983 and 1992; Two Into One, Shaftesbury, 1984; The Scarlet Pimpernel, Chichester transf. to Her Majesty's, 1985; Major Barbara, Chichester, 1988; Over My Dead Body, Savoy, 1989; Oscar Wilde, Playhouse, 1990; Out of Order, Shaftesbury, 1990, nat. tour, 1990–91, Australia, 1992–93; Venus Observed, Chichester, 1992; She Stoops to Conquer, Queen's, 1993; Hamlet, Gielgud, 1994; dir, The Importance of Being Earnest, Royalty, 1987; *television series include:* Our Man from St Marks; Two's Company; Discovering English Churches; Never the Twain; has appeared in many films. Assoc. Artist, RSC, 1967–. Member: Council, British Actors Equity Assoc., 1966–77 (Trustee, 1988–); Council, RSA, 1972; Adv. Council, V&A Museum, 1973–80; Arts Council Drama Panel, 1973–77; Leicestershire Educn Arts Cttee, 1974–; BBC Archives Adv. Cttee, 1975–78; London Acad. of Music and Dramatic Art Council, 1976–; Kent and E Sussex Reg. Cttee, National Trust, 1978–82; Arts Council of GB, 1982–86; Chairman: British Theatre Museum Assoc., 1971–77; Theatre Museum Adv. Council, 1973–80; President: Fedn of Playgoers Socs, 1968–93; Royal Theatrical Fund, 1983–; Vice-Pres., London Appreciation Soc., 1960–. FRSA 1966. *Publications:* A Touch of the Memoirs (autobiog.), 1982; Laughter in the Second Act (autobiog.), 1985; (ed) The Everyman Book of Theatrical Anecdotes, 1987; The English Country Church, 1988. *Recreations:* theatrical history, architecture, ecclesiology, genealogy, serendipity, London. *Address:* 60 Temple Fortune Lane, NW11 7UE; Rats Castle, Isle of Oxney, Kent TN30 7HX. *Clubs:* Garrick (Trustee, 1980–), Beefsteak, MCC.

SINGER, Alfred Ernst; Chairman, London American Growth Trust PLC; *b* 15 Nov. 1924; *s* of late Dr Robert Singer and Mrs Charlotte Singer; *m* 1st, 1951, Gwendoline Doris Barnett (*d* 1985); one *s* one *d*; 2nd, 1988, Christine Annette McCarron (*née* Evans). *Educ:* Halesowen Grammar Sch. Served War of 1939–45: Army, 1943–47. Subseq. professional and exec. posts with: Callingham, Brown & Co, Bunzl Pulp & Paper Ltd, David Brown Tractors Ltd; Rank Xerox Ltd, 1963–70 (Dir, 1967); Tesco Stores (Holdings) Ltd, 1970–73 (Dep. Managing Dir); Man. Dir (Giro), PO Corp., 1973–76; Chairman: PO Staff Superannuation Fund, 1977–79; Cannon Assurance Ltd, 1980–86. Chairman: Long Range Planning Soc., 1970–73; Council, Assoc. of Certified Accountants, 1972–81 (Vice-Pres., 1979–80); Member: Cttee for Industrial Technologies, DTI, 1972–76; National Economic Develt Council: Chm., Electronic Computers Sector Working Party; Member: Electronics EDC; Food and Drink Manufacturing Industry EDC, 1976–77. Governor, Centre for Environmental Studies, 1977–85 (Chm., 1981–85). *Address:* York Cottage, Lower Chedworth, Cheltenham, Glos GL54 5AN. *T:* Fossebridge (01285) 720523. *Clubs:* Athenæum, MCC.

SINGER, Aubrey Edward, CBE 1984; Managing Director, White City Films, since 1984; *b* 21 Jan. 1927; *s* of Louis Henry Singer and late Elizabeth (*née* Walton); *m* 1949, Cynthia Hilda Adams; one *s* two *d* (and one *d* decd). *Educ:* Giggleswick; Bradford Grammar School. Joined film industry, 1944; directed various films teaching armed forces to shoot; worked extensively in Africa, 1946–48; worked on children's films in Austria, 1948–49; joined BBC TV Outside Broadcasts, 1949; TV Producer Scotland, 1951; BBC New York Office, 1953; returned to London as Producer, 1956; produced many scientific programmes; Asst Head of Outside Broadcasts, 1959; Head of Science and Features, 1961; Head of Features Gp, BBC TV, 1967; Controller, BBC 2, 1974–78; Man. Dir, BBC Radio, 1978–82; Dep. Dir-Gen., and Man. Dir, Television, BBC, 1982–84. Chm., Soc. of Film and Television Arts, 1971–73. President: TV and Radio Industries Club, 1984–85; Nat. Mus. of Photography, Film and TV, 1984–. FRTS 1978 (a Vice-Pres., 1982–88); FRAS; FRSA. Hon. DLitt Bradford, 1984. *Publication:* The Lion and the Dragon, 1992. *Recreations:* walking, talking, archery. *Address:* 79 Sutton Court Road, Chiswick, W4 3EQ. *T:* 0181–994 6795. *Club:* Savile.

SINGER, Sir Hans (Wolfgang), Kt 1994; PhD; Professorial Fellow, Institute of Development Studies, University of Sussex, since 1969, Emeritus Professor, since 1980; *b* 29 Nov. 1910; *s* of Heinrich and Antonia Singer; *m* 1934, Ilse Lina Plaut; one *s* (and one *s* decd). *Educ:* Univ. of Bonn (Econ. Dip. 1931); King's Coll., Cambridge (PhD 1936). Pilgrim Trust Unemployment Enquiry, 1936–38; Manchester Univ., 1938–44; Min. of Town and Country Planning, 1945–46; Glasgow Univ., 1946–47; with United Nations Secretariat, 1947–69: Dir, Econ. Div., UNIDO, 1967–69. Hon. Fellow, Inst. of Social

Studies, The Hague, 1978. Hon. DLitt: Sussex, 1990; Santa Fe, Argentina, 1989; Glasgow, 1994; Lisbon, 1994. *Publications:* numerous books including: (jtly) Men Without Work, 1938; International Development, Growth and Change, 1964; (with J. Ansari) Rich and Poor Countries, 1977 (trans. Portuguese, 1979, Spanish, 1982), 4th edn 1988; (jtly) Food Aid: the challenge and the opportunity, 1987; (ed jtly) New World Order Series, 12 vols, 1987–92; (with S. Roy) Economic Progress and Prospects in the Third World: lessons of development experience since 1945, 1993; also articles in learned jls. *Recreations:* walking, music, chess. *Address:* Institute of Development Studies, University of Sussex, Brighton, E Sussex BN1 9RE; 18 The Vale, Ovingdean, Brighton, E Sussex BN2 7AB. *T:* Brighton (01273) 303567.

SINGER, Harold Samuel; His Honour Judge Singer; a Circuit Judge, since 1984; *b* 17 July 1935; *s* of Ellis and Minnie Singer; *m* 1966, Adèle Berenice Emanuel; one *s* two *d*. *Educ:* Salford Grammar School; Fitzwilliam House, Cambridge (MA). Called to the Bar, Gray's Inn, 1957; a Recorder, 1981–84. *Recreations:* music, painting, books, photography.

SINGER, Harry Bruce, OBE 1995; TD 1955; DL; FCA; Senior Partner, Singer & Partners, Chartered Accountants, 1968–87; *b* 21 June 1921; *er s* of Geoffrey and Agnes Singer; *m* 1945, Betty Alison Brittan (*d* 1993); one *s*. *Educ:* Cathedral Sch., Hereford. FCA 1960 (Mem., 1953). Served War: commnd 99th (London Welsh) HAA Regt, RA, 1941; served in UK and NW Europe; Instr, Sch. of AA Artillery, 1945; joined 281 (Glam Yeomanry) Field Regt, RA (TA), 1947; in comd, 1959–62. Pres., S Wales Soc. of Chartered Accountants, 1970–71; Inst. of Chartered Accountants in England and Wales: Mem. Council, 1973–85; Vice Pres., 1979–80; Dep. Pres., 1980–81; Pres., 1981–82. Hon. Treasurer, SSAFA, 1990–; Trustee, Yeomanry Benevolent Fund, 1995–. Liveryman, Worshipful Co. of Chartered Accountants, 1978–89; Freeman, City of London, 1978. Vice Chm. Wales, TA&VRA, 1984–87. DL Mid Glamorgan, 1985. *Recreations:* golf, foreign travel, Rugby football (originally as player). *Address:* 8 Windsor House, Castle Court, Cardiff CF1 1DG. *Clubs:* Army and Navy; Cardiff and County, Cardiff Golf (Cardiff).

SINGER, Hon Sir (Jan) Peter, Kt 1993; **Hon. Mr Justice Singer;** a Judge of the High Court of Justice, Family Division, since 1993; *b* 10 Sept. 1944; *s* of late Dr Hanus Kurt Singer and of Anita Singer; *m* 1970, Julia Mary Caney; one *s* one *d*. *Educ:* King Edward's School, Birmingham; Selwyn College, Cambridge. Called to the Bar, Inner Temple, 1967, Bencher, 1993; QC 1987; a Recorder, 1987–93. Chm., Family Law Bar Assoc., 1990–92 (Sec., 1980–83, Treasurer, 1983–90); Member: Matrimonial Causes Rule Cttee, 1981–85; Senate of Inns of Court and Bar, 1983–86; Law Soc. Legal Aid Cttee, 1984–89; Gen. Council of the Bar, 1990–92. Vice-Pres., European Chapter, Internat. Acad. of Matrimonial Lawyers, 1992–93. *Publication:* (ed jtly) Rayden on Divorce, 14th edn, 1983. *Recreations:* gardening, walking, travel. *Address:* Royal Courts of Justice, Strand, WC2A 2LL.

SINGER, Norbert, CBE 1990; PhD, FRSC; Vice Chancellor, University of Greenwich, 1992–93 (Director, Thames Polytechnic, 1978–92); *b* 3 May 1931; *s* of late Salomon Singer and late Mina Korn; *m* Brenda Margaret Walter, *e d* of Richard and Gladys Walter, Tunbridge Wells, Kent. *Educ:* Highbury County School; Queen Mary Coll., London. BSc, PhD, CChem, FRSC. Research Chemist and Project Leader, Morgan Crucible Co. Ltd, 1954–57; Lecturer, Senior Lectr, Principal Lectr and Dep. Head of Department, Dept of Chemistry, Northern Polytechnic, 1958–70; Head of Dept of Life Sciences 1971–74, Professor of Life Sciences 1972–74, Polytechnic of Central London; Asst Director, then Dep. Director, Polytechnic of North London, 1974–78. Council for National Academic Awards: Mem., 1982–88; Chm., Reviews Co-ordination Sub-Cttee, 1984–87; Vice Chm., Cttee for Academic and Institutional Policy, 1985–87; Mem., Accreditation Cttee, 1987–89; Chm., Cttee for CATs, 1990–93. Mem., MSC Nat. Steering Gp, TVEI, 1984–88 (Mem., Quality and Standards Gp, 1987–89). Chairman: Bexley HA, 1993–94; Oxleas (formerly Bexley Community Health) NHS Trust, 1994–. Fellow, QMW, 1993. Hon. DSc Greenwich, 1993. *Publications:* research papers in electrochemistry, theoretical chemistry and surface chemistry in scientific jls. *Recreations:* walking, reading. *Address:* Croft Lodge, Bayhall Road, Tunbridge Wells, Kent TN2 4TP. *T:* Tunbridge Wells (01892) 523821.

SINGER, Hon. Sir Peter; *see* Singer, Hon. Sir J. P.

SINGER, Philip Francis; QC 1994; a Recorder, since 1989; *b* 1 Dec. 1940; *s* of late Abraham Singer and of Sylvia (*née* Hyman); *m* 1978, Heather Angela Cutt. *Educ:* Bedford Modern Sch.; Bishop's Stortford Coll.; St John's Coll., Cambridge (MA, LLM). Called to the Bar, Inner Temple, 1964. *Address:* 2 Pump Court, Temple, EC4Y 7AH. *T:* 0171–353 5597.

SINGER, Susan Honor; Headmistress, Guildford High School, since 1991; *b* 23 Feb. 1942; *d* of late Brig. John James McCully, DSO and of Honor Goad (*née* Ward, now Mrs E. B. Elliott); *m* 1964, Christopher Ronald Morgan Singer; one *s* two *d*. *Educ:* St Mary's, Calne; Open Univ. (BA); Garnett Coll. (PGCE). Set up and ran pre-school playgroup, E Sheen, 1968–74; St Paul's Girls' School: maths teacher, 1980–91; Head of Middle School, 1988–91; Head of Maths, 1990–91. *Recreations:* sailing 1907 gaff cutter, reading, theatre, concerts, ski-ing. *Address:* Guildford High School, London Road, Guildford, Surrey GU1 1SJ. *T:* Guildford (01483) 61440; 39 East Sheen Avenue, SW14 8AR. *T:* 0181–876 4031.

SINGH, Dinesh; Minister without portfolio, India, since 1995; Member (Congress (I)) Rajya Sabha, Haryana, since 1993; *b* 19 July 1925; *s* of Raja Avadhesh Singh and Rani Lakshmi Kumari; *m* 1944, Neelima Kumari; six *d*. *Educ:* Doon Sch., Dehradun; Colvin Coll., Lucknow; Univ. of Lucknow. Member of Parliament: Lok Sabha, 1957–77; Rajya Sabha, 1977–82; Lok Sabha, 1984–91. Ministry of External Affairs: Dep. Minister, 1962–66; Minister of State, 1966–67; Minister of: Commerce, 1967–69; Ext. Affairs, 1969–70 and 1993–95; Industrial Develt and Internal Trade, 1970–71; Water Resources, Feb.–June 1988; Commerce, 1988–89. Leader Indian delegation to: The Economic and Social Council, 1963 and 1967; UNCTAD II, 1969 (Pres., 1968–72); UN Gen. Assembly, 1969, 1993. *Publications:* Towards New Horizons, 1971; India and the Changing Asian Scene, 1973; articles in magazines and nat. newspapers. *Recreations:* photography, wild life. *Address:* 1 Thyagaraja Marg, New Delhi 110011, India. *T:* (11) 3011766/3792945. *Clubs:* Delhi Gymkhana, Delhi Golf (New Delhi); Cricket of India (Bombay).

SINGH, Khushwant; Padma Bhushan, 1974; Member of Parliament, India, since 1980; Barrister-at-Law; *b* Feb. 1915; *m* Kaval (*née* Malik); one *s* one *d*. *Educ:* Univ. of London (LLB); called to Bar. Practising Lawyer, High Court, Lahore, 1939–47; Min. of External Affairs, of India; PRO Ottawa and London, 1947–51; UNESCO, 1954–56. Visiting Lectr: Oxford (Spalding Trust); USA: Rochester, Princeton, Hawaii, Swarthmore; led Indian Delegn to Writers' Conf., Manila, Philippines, 1965; Guest Speaker at Montreal 'Expo 67'. Has written for many nat. dailies and foreign jls: New York Times; Observer and New Statesman (London); Harper's (USA); Evergreen Review (USA); London Magazine. Editor, The Illustrated Weekly of India, Bombay, 1969–78; Chief Editor, New Delhi, 1979–80; increased circulation of Illustrated Weekly of India from 80,000 to 410,000 in 9 yrs; Editor-in-chief, The Hindustan Times and Contour, New Delhi, 1980–83. *Broadcasting and Television:* All India Radio, BBC, CBC; LP recordings. Awards include: from Punjab Govt: 5,000 rupees and Robe of Honour, for contrib. to Sikh literature; Mohan Singh Award: 1,500 rupees for trans. of Sikh hymns, etc. *Publications: Sikh History and Religion:* The Sikhs, 1953; A History of the Sikhs: vol. i, 1469–1839, 1964; vol. ii, 1839–1964, 1967; Ranjit Singh, Maharajah of the Punjab, 1780–1839, 1963; Fall of the Kingdom of the Punjab; Sikhs Today; (ed) Sunset of the Sikh Empire, by Dr Sita Ram Kohli (posthumous); Hymns of Nanak The Guru. *Fiction:* The Mark of Vishnu and other stories, 1951; Train to Pakistan, 1956; I Shall Not Hear the Nightingales, 1961; *stories:* The Voice of God and other stories; Black Jasmine and other stories; A Bride for the Sahib and other stories. (*Co-author*): Sacred Writing of the Sikhs; (with Arun Joshi) Shri Ram: a biog., 1969; (with Satindra Singh) Ghadr Rebellion; (with Suneet Veer Singh) Homage to Guru Gobind Singh; *miscellaneous:* Love and Friendship (editor of anthology); Khushwant Singh's India—collection of articles (ed Rahul Singh); Shri Ram—a biography; Delhi—a Profile, 1982; The Sikhs, 1984; (with Kuldip Nayar) Punjab Tragedy, 1984; *translations:* Umrao Jan Ada, Courtesan of Lucknow, by Mohammed Ruswa (with M. A. Husaini); The Skeleton (by Amrita Pritam); Land of the Five Rivers; I Take This Woman, by Rajinder Singh Bedi; Iqbal's Dialogue with Allah (Shikwah and Jawab-e-Shikwah); We Indians. *Recreation:* bird watching. *Address:* 49E Sujan Singh Park, New Delhi 110003, India. *T:* (11) 690159. *Clubs:* Authors'; Imperial Gymkhana (New Delhi); Bombay Gymkhana (Bombay 1).

SINGH, Laleshwar Kumar Narayan; High Commissioner for Guyana in London, since 1993; also non-resident Ambassador to The Netherlands, France and Russia, since 1993; *b* 2 April 1941; *m* 1972, Latchmin Ramrattan; two *d*. *Educ:* Windsor Forest Govt Sch., Guyana; Indian Educn Trust Coll., Guyana; Univ. of London (ext. student; Intermediate Exam. in Laws); Court Clerk Trng Course. Left Guyana, 1961 to work and study in England; worked with BR and as Despatch Clerk, Olney Amsden Ltd; Inner London Magistrates' Courts Service, 1971–93: work in magistrates' courts and Admin Office, Principal Chief Clerk's Office; Personnel Officer, 1988–89. *Address:* Guyana High Commission, 3 Palace Court, Bayswater Road, W2 4LP. *T:* 0171–229 7684.

SINGH, Margaret Stella; Chair, Association of District Councils, since 1993; *b* 10 Aug. 1945; *d* of Edward Richard Jones and Stella Jones; *m* (marr. diss.); one *s* one *d*. Working in and for local govt, 1962–; Mem. (Lab) Reading BC, 1976–. *Recreations:* reading, walking the dogs, listening to people. *Address:* 34 Knights Way, Emmer Green, Reading RG4 8RH. *T:* Reading (01734) 462620.

SINGH, Mota; QC 1978; **His Honour Judge Mota Singh;** a Circuit Judge, since 1982; *b* 26 July 1930; *s* of Dalip Singh and Harnam Kaur; *m* 1950, Swaran Kaur; two *s* one *d*. *Educ:* Duke of Gloucester Sch., Nairobi, Kenya; Hon. Soc. of Lincoln's Inn. Called to the Bar, 1956. Left school, 1947; Solicitor's Clerk, Nairobi, 1948–54; Lincoln's Inn, London, 1954–56; Advocate, High Court of Kenya, 1957–65; Alderman, City of Nairobi, 1958–63; Vice-Chm., Kenya Justice; Sec., Law Soc. of Kenya, 1963–64. A Deputy Circuit Judge, 1976–82; a Recorder of the Crown Court, 1979–82. Member: London Rent Assessment Panel, 1965–67; Race Relations Bd, 1968–77. Hon. LLD Guru Nanak Dev Univ., Amritsar, 1981. *Recreations:* reading; formerly cricket (represented Kenya). *Address:* Cedarwood, 3 Somerset Road, Wimbledon SW19 5JU. *T:* 0181–947 2271.

SINGH, Vishwanath Pratap; Prime Minister of India, 1989–90; *b* 25 June 1931; *s* of Raja Bahadur Ram Gopal Singh; *m* 1955, Sita Kumari; two *s*. *Educ:* Poona Univ.; Allahabad Univ. (Vice-Pres., Students Union; LLB); Udip Pratap College, Varanasi (Pres., Students Union). Participated in Bhoodan Movement, 1957, and donated farm, Pasna, Allahabad; Mem. Exec., Allahabad Univ., 1969–71; founded Gopal Vidyalaya, Intermediate Coll., Koraon, Allahabad. Uttar Pradesh appointments: MLA, 1969–71 and 1981–83; Whip, Congress Legislature Party, 1970–71; MLC, 1980–81; Chief Minister, 1980–82; Pres., UP Congress Cttee, 1984. Mem., Lok Sabha, 1971–77, 1980, 1988–89 and 1989–94; Mem., Rajya Sabha, 1983–88; Union Dep. Minister (Commerce), 1974–76; Union Minister of State (Commerce), 1976–77; Union Minister (Commerce), 1983 (also i/c Dept of Supply); Union Finance Minister, 1984–87; Defence Minister, Jan.–April 1987. Founded Jan Morcha, 1987; Pres., Janata Dal, 1988; Convenor, Nat. Front, 1988. *Address:* c/o Office of the Prime Minister, South Block, New Delhi 110011, India.

SINGHANIA, Sir Padampat, Kt 1943; President of the JK Organisation, India; *b* 1905; *s* of late Lala Kamlapat Singhania; *m* Srimati Anusiya Devi; four *s* one *d*. *Educ:* Home. A pioneer of Cotton, Rayon, Nylon, Jute, Woollen Textiles, Sugar, Aluminium, Steel and Engineering, Plastic, Strawboard, Paper, Chemicals, Oil Industries, Shipping, Cement, Tyres and Tubes, Dry Cell Batteries, Banking; Patron, large number of social, educational, political, and literary institutions. Founder of the Merchants' Chamber of UP: ex-Pres. of Federation of Indian Chambers of Commerce and Industry; ex-Pres., Employers' Assoc. of Northern India; Member 1st Indian Parliament, 1947–52, and many government and semi-govt bodies; formerly Chairman, Board of Governors, IIT Kanpur. Dr of Letters, Kanpur Univ., 1968. *Recreations:* riding, music, buildings, and studies. *Address:* Kamla Tower, Kanpur 208001, India. *TA:* Laljuggi, Kanpur. *T:* 69854, 51147 and 62988. *Telex* KP215.

SINGHVI, Dr Laxmi Mall; High Commissioner for India in the United Kingdom, since 1991; Senior Advocate, Supreme Court of India, since 1967 (Advocate, 1951–67); *b* 9 Nov. 1931; *s* of D. M. Singhvi and Akal Kaur Singhvi; *m* 1957, Kamla Singhvi; one *s* one *d*. *Educ:* Allahabad Univ. (BA); Rajasthan Univ. (LLB); Harvard Univ. Law Sch. (LLM); Cornell Univ. Law Sch. (SJD). MP, Independent, Lok Sabha, 1962–67; Senior Standing Counsel, State of UP, Union of India, 1967–71; Advocate-Gen., 1972–77. Dep. Leader, Indian Parly Delegn to CPA, 1964, Leader Parly Delegn, 1966; Chm. and Founder, Inst. of Constitutional and Parly Studies, 1964–. Chairman: Indian Fedn of Unesco Assocs, 1974–; World Colloquium on Legal Aid, 1975; State Bar Council, 1975–77; Indian Nat. Cttee for Abolition of Death Penalty, 1977–; Nat. Sch. of Drama, 1978–82; Supreme Court Law Reforms Cttee, 1981–82; Asian Conf. on Approaches to Human Rights, 1985; Govt of India Cttee on Revitalisation of Rural Local Self-Govt, 1986–87; Govt of India Task Force on Child Labour; Govt of India Cttee on Brain Death and Organ Transplantation, 1991; Founder Chm., 1972, Hon. Patron, 1983, Commonwealth Legal Educn Assoc.; Founder-Pres., Indian Centre for Human Rights Educn and Research, 1980; Pres., World Congress on Human Rights, 1990; Member: UN Human Rights Sub-Commn, Geneva, 1978–82 (Vice-Chm.); Nat. Commn for Unesco; Govt of India Expert Cttee on Legal Aid, 1971–73; Commn on Inf. and Broadcasting, 1964–68; Internat. Forum on Freedoms and Rights of Man, Paris, 1985–. President: Supreme Court Bar Assoc., 1977, 1978, 1980, 1982; Supreme Court Bar Trust, 1981–; Nat. Legal Aid Assoc., 1970–; Indian Centre for Independence of Judges and Lawyers, 1979–; UN Special Rapporteur on Independence of Judges and Lawyers, 1979–; Hon. Mem. and Adv. Panelist, Comparative Const. Law Project and Bicentennial of Amer. Constitution, Amer. Council of Learned Socs, 1986–88. Trustee and Mem. Jury, G. D. Birla Award on Humanism. Life Trustee and Pres., India Internat. Centre; Pres. Emeritus, Authors Guild of India (Pres., 1986–90). Hon. Tagore Law Prof., 1975–; Visiting Professor and Fellow: Univ. of Leicester, 1991–; Univ. of Hull, 1994–. Rede Lectr, Univ. of Cambridge, 1993. Hon. Bencher, Middle Temple, 1987. Hon. LLD: Jabalpur, 1983; Banaras Hindu, 1984;

Tamil, Tamilnadu, 1991; Buckingham, 1993; N London, 1993; Osmania, 1994; De Montfort, 1994. Hon. Nyayavacaspati, Gurukul, 1968. *Publications:* Horizons of Freedom, 1969; (ed) Law and Poverty, 1970; Indian Federalism, 1974; Legal Aid, 1985; Law Day, 1985; Independence of Justice, 1985; Jain Declaration on Nature, 1990; Freedom on Trial, 1991; The Evening Sun (poems), 1991; A Third International Covenant for the Prevention of Ecocide, 1991. *Recreations:* theatre, poetry, chess, gardening, classical Indian dance appreciation, archaeology. *Address:* Indian High Commission, India House, Aldwych WC2B 4NA. *Club:* Athenæum.

SINGLETON, Barry Neill; QC 1989; *b* 12 April 1946; *s* of late Clifford and Moyna Singleton; *m* 1971, Anne Mary Potter; one *s* two *d*. *Educ:* Downside Sch.; Gonville and Caius Coll., Cambridge (MA). Called to the Bar, Gray's Inn, 1968. *Address:* 1 King's Bench Walk, Temple, EC4Y 7DB. *T:* 0171–583 6266, *Fax:* 0171–583 2068.

SINGLETON, Norman, CB 1966; retired civil servant; *b* 21 March 1913; *s* of Charles and Alice Singleton, Bolton, Lancs; *m* 1936, Cicely Margaret Lucas, Claverdon, Warwick; one *s* two *d*. *Educ:* Bolton School; Emmanuel College, Cambridge. Min. of Labour, 1935; Under-Secretary: Civil Service Pay Research Unit, 1956–60; Min. of Labour (now Dept of Employment), 1960–69; Sec., 1969–72, Dep. Chm., 1973–74, Commn on Industrial Relns; Dep. Chm., Central Arbitration Cttee, 1976–85; Arbitrator and Mediator, ACAS, 1976–87. *Publication:* Industrial Relations Procedures, 1976. *Address:* 34 Willoughby Road, Hampstead, NW3 1RU. *T:* 0171–435 1504.
See also E. A. Woods.

SINGLETON, Roger; Senior Director, Barnardo's, since 1984; *b* 6 Nov. 1942; *s* of late Malcolm and Ethel Singleton, Nether Edge, Sheffield; *m* 1966, Ann Hasler; two *d*. *Educ:* City Grammar Sch., Sheffield; Durham Univ. (MA); Bath Univ. (MSc); London Univ. (DipSocStud); Leeds (Cert. Ed.). Appts in care and educn of deprived and delinquent young people, 1961–71; professional adviser to Children's Regional Planning Cttee, 1971–74; Dep. Dir, Dr Barnardo's, 1974–84. Chm., Nat. Council of Voluntary Child Care Organisations, 1990–92; Member: Central Council for Educn and Training in Social Work, 1984–86; Council, Nat. Children's Bureau, 1982–84; Council, Nat. Youth Bureau, 1986–91. Company Dir. CIMgt (FBIM 1982); FRSA 1991. *Publications:* contribs to professional jls. *Recreations:* home and garden. *Address:* Littleacres, Blackmore End, near Braintree, Essex CM7 4DT. *T:* Great Dunmow (01371) 850918; Barnardo's, Tanners Lane, Barkingside, Ilford, Essex IG6 1QG. *T:* 0181–550 8822. *Club:* Reform.

SINGLETON, Valerie, OBE 1994; television broadcaster, travel writer; with BBC, 1962–93; *b* 9 April 1937; *d* of Wing Comdr Denis G. Singleton, OBE and late Eileen Singleton, LRAM. *Educ:* Arts Educational Sch. (3 times Drama Cup); RADA (schol.). Bromley Rep.; commercial voice-overs; TV advertising magazines; joined BBC as announcer, 1962; presenter: Blue Peter, 1962–71; Blue Peter Special Assignments, covering capital cities, islands, famous houses, 1972–75, and Rivers Niagra and Yukon, 1980; Val Meets the VIPs, 1972–75; Nationwide, 1972–78; Tonight, and Tonight in Town, 1978–79; Echoes of Holocaust, documentary, BBC 2, Midweek, Radio 4, 1980; The Money Programme, BBC 2, 1980–88; Radio 4 PM, 1981–93; numerous other radio and TV progs; corporate videos, business confs. Work for British Wildlife Appeal and Dr Barnardo's. *Recreations:* sailing, ski-ing, water ski-ing, photography, exploring London, travelling anywhere, riding, pottering in museums and antique shops. *Address:* c/o Arlington Enterprises, 1-3 Charlotte Street, W1P 1HD. *Clubs:* Hurlingham; Hayling Island Sailing.

SINGLETON, William Brian, CBE 1974; FRCVS; retired; Director, Animal Health Trust, 1977–88; *b* 23 Feb. 1923; *s* of William Max Singleton and Blanche May Singleton; *m* 1947, Hilda Stott; two *s* one *d* (and one *s* decd). *Educ:* Queen Elizabeth Grammar Sch., Darlington; Royal (Dick) Sch. of Vet. Medicine, Edinburgh. Vis. Prof. Surgery, Ontario Vet. Coll., Guelph, Canada, 1973–74; Hon. Vet. Advr to Jockey Club, 1977–88. Member: Govt Cttee of Inquiry into Future Role of Veterinary Profession in GB (Chm., Sir Michael Swann), 1971–75; UGC Wkg Pty on Vet. Educn into the 21st Century (Chm., Sir Ralph Riley, FRS), 1987–89. President: British Small Animal Vet. Assoc., 1960–61; RCVS, 1969–70; World Small Animal Vet. Assoc., 1975–77. Hon. Diplomate, Amer. Coll. of Vet. Surgeons, 1973; Hon. DVM & S Edinburgh, 1993. Dalrymple-Champneys Award, 1987. *Publications:* (ed jtly) Canine Medicine and Therapeutics, 1979; chapter in International Encyclopaedia of Veterinary Medicine, 1966; chapters in Animal Nursing Part II, 1966; numerous papers in veterinary and comparative pathology jls. *Recreations:* gardening, sailing, bird watching, horse riding. *Address:* Vine Cottage, Morston Road, Blakeney, Holt, Norfolk NR25 7BE. *T:* Cley (01263) 740246. *Club:* Farmers'.

SINHA, 4th Baron *cr* 1919, of Raipur; **Susanta Prasanna Sinha;** *b* 1953; *s* of 3rd Baron and of Madhabi, *d* of late Monoranjan Chatterjee; *S* father, 1989; *m* 1972, Patricia Orchard; one *d* (and one *s* one *d* decd). *Address:* 7 Lord Sinha Road, Calcutta, India.

SINNATT, Maj.-Gen. Martin Henry, CB 1984; Senior Executive and Secretary, Kennel Club, 1984–93, retired; *b* 28 Jan. 1928; *s* of Dr O. S. Sinnatt and Mrs M. H. Sinnatt (*née* Randall); *m* 1957, Susan Rosemary Clarke; four *d*. *Educ:* Hitchin Grammar School; Hertford College, Oxford (1 Year Army Short Course); RMA Sandhurst. Commissioned RTR, 1948; served Germany, Korea, UK, Hong Kong, 1948–58; psc 1959; Aden, 1959–62; Germany and UK, 1962–64; MA to C-in-C AFNE, Norway, 1964–66; jssc 1967; Germany and UK, 1967–69; CO 4 RTR, BAOR, 1969–71; Nat. Defence Coll., 1971–72; Comdr RAC, 1 (BR) Corps, BAOR, 1972–74; Dir Operational Requirements MoD, 1974–77; rcds 1978; Dir, Combat Development (Army), 1979–81; Chief of Staff to Live Oak, SHAPE, 1982–84; completed service, 1984. *Recreations:* medieval history, gardening and swimming; also, when time and finances permit, skiing and golf. *Address:* Meadowside Farmhouse, Tulls Lane, Standford, Bordon, Hants GU35 8RB.

SINNOTT, John Brian; Chief Executive, Leicestershire County Council and Clerk of Lieutenancy, since 1994; *b* 11 March 1949; *s* of William John Sinnott and Mary Josephine Sinnott (*née* Foley); *m* 1970, Helen Mary Turner; two *s* two *d*. *Educ:* St Mary's Coll., Crosby; Univ. of Liverpool (MA, Dip. Public Admin). Liverpool CC, 1970–74; PA to Chm. and Leader of Council, Head of Leader's office, Merseyside CC, 1974–86; Management Consultant, Coopers and Lybrand Associates, 1986–87; Leicestershire County Council: Asst, then Sen. Asst, County Clerk, 1987–90; Asst Chief Exec., 1990–92; Dir, Corporate Management, 1992–94. Dir, Leics TEC, 1994–. *Publications:* papers in local govt jls. *Recreations:* sport, cricket literature, history of rock music. *Address:* County Hall, Glenfield, Leicester LE3 8RA. *T:* Leicester (0116) 265 6000; 24 Gullet Lane, Kirby Muxloe, Leics LE9 2BL. *T:* Leicester (0116) 239 3192. *Club:* Everton Football.

SINOPOLI, Giuseppe; Italian conductor and composer; Chief Conductor, Dresden Staatskapelle, since 1992; *b* Venice, 2 Nov. 1946; *s* of Giovanni and Maria Sinopoli; *m* 1979, Silvia; two *s*. *Educ:* Benedetto Marcello Conservatoire, Venice; Univ. of Padua Med. Sch. (Doctor's degree in medicine as surgeon and psychiatrist); studied conducting with Swarowsky, Vienna, 1972. Founded Bruno Maderna Ensemble, Venice, 1975; début: Macbeth, Berlin Opera, 1979; Attila, Vienna State Opera, 1980; Manon Lescaut, Covent Garden, 1983; with NY Philharmonic Orchestra, 1983; Tosca, Metropolitan, NY, 1985; Tannhäuser, Bayreuther Festspiele, 1985; Elektra, La Scala, 1994. Musical Director: Philharmonia Orch., London, 1987–94 (Prin. Conductor, 1983–87); Fest. Taormina Arte, 1990–; has conducted Boston Symphony, Chicago Symphony, Berliner Philharmoniker, Weiner Philharmoniker, Israel Philharmonic, Filarmonica della Scala. *Compositions* include: Numquid et unum; Klavierkonzert; Kammerkonzert; Tombeau d'Amour No 1, 2, 3 for Orch.; Souvenir à la Mémoire; Requiem Hashirim; Lou Salome (opera). *Recreations:* reading, studying archaeology (at University of Rome), collecting antique objects. *Address:* c/o Hannelore Tschöpe Künstlersekretariat, Feilitzschstrasse 1, 8000 München 40, Germany. *T:* (89) 339422, *Fax:* (89) 339377.

SIRS, William, JP; General Secretary, Iron and Steel Trades Confederation, 1975–85, retired; *b* 6 Jan. 1920; *s* of Frederick Sirs and Margaret (*née* Powell); *m* 1941, Joan (*née* Clark); one *s* one *d*. *Educ:* Middleton St Johns, Hartlepool; WEA. Steel Industry, 1937–63; Iron and Steel Trades Confedn: Organiser, 1963; Divisional Officer, Manchester, 1970; Asst Gen. Sec., 1973. Member: Iron and Steel Industry Trng Bd, 1973; TUC Gen. Council, 1975–85; Trade Union Steel Industry Cons. Cttee, 1973– (Chm., 1975–) and Jt Accident Prevention Adv. Cttee, 1973; Employment Appeal Tribunal, 1976–; Jt Sec., Jt Industrial Council for Slag Industry, 1973; Exec. Mem., Paul Finet Foundn, European Coal and Steel Community, 1974; Hon. Sec. (British Section), Internat. Metalworkers Fedn, 1975. Mem., Management Cttee, BSC (Industry) Ltd, 1975–. Pres., Northern Home Counties Productivity Assoc., 1985–; Mem. RIIA, 1973. Mem. Council, Winston Churchill Meml Trust, 1985–90. Director (formerly Governor), Oaklands Coll., Herts, 1991–. JP Hartlepool, Co. Durham, later Knutsford, Cheshire, then Herts, 1963. Freeman, City of London, 1984. *Publication:* Hard Labour (autobiog.), 1985. *Recreations:* sailing, squash, swimming, running. *Address:* Hatfield, Hertfordshire.

SISSON, Charles Hubert, CH 1993; writer; *b* 22 April 1914; *s* of late Richard Percy Sisson and Ellen Minnie Sisson (*née* Worlock); *m* 1937, Nora Gilbertson; two *d*. *Educ:* University of Bristol, and in France and Germany. Entered Ministry of Labour as Assistant Principal, 1936; HM Forces, in the ranks, mainly in India, 1942–45; Simon Senior Research Fellow, 1956–57; Dir of Establishments, Min. of Labour, 1962–68; Dir of Occupational Safety and Health, Dept of Employment, 1972. FRSL 1975. Hon. DLitt Bristol, 1980. Jt Editor, PN Review, 1976–84. *Publications:* An Asiatic Romance, 1953; The Spirit of British Administration, 1959; Christopher Homm, 1965; Art and Action, 1965; Essays, 1967; English Poetry 1900–1950, 1971, rev. edn 1981; The Case of Walter Bagehot, 1972; (ed) The English Sermon, Vol. II 1650–1750, 1976; David Hume, 1976; (ed) Selected Poems of Jonathan Swift, 1977; The Avoidance of Literature, 1978; (ed) Autobiographical and Other Papers of Philip Mairet, 1981; Anglican Essays, 1983; (ed) Selected Poems of Christina Rossetti, 1984; On the Look-out (autobiog.), 1989; In Two Minds, 1990; (ed) Jeremy Taylor: selected writings, 1990; English Perspectives, 1992; Is There a Church of England?, 1993; (ed) Edgar Allan Poe: Poems and Essays on Poetry, 1995; *poetry:* The London Zoo, 1961; Numbers, 1965; The Discarnation, 1967; Metamorphoses, 1968; In the Trojan Ditch, 1974; The Corridor, 1975; Anchises, 1976; Exactions, 1980; Selected Poems, 1981; Collected Poems, 1984; God Bless Karl Marx!, 1987; Antidotes, 1991; What and Who, 1994; *translations:* Versions and Perversions of Heine, 1955; Catullus, 1966; The Poetic Art: a translation of the Ars Poetica of Horace, 1975; The Poem on Nature, 1976; Some Tales of La Fontaine, 1979; The Divine Comedy, 1980; The Song of Roland, 1983; Les Regrets of Joachim du Bellay, 1983; The Aeneid of Virgil, 1986; Britannicus, Phaedra, Athaliah, of Racine, 1987. *Address:* Moorfield Cottage, The Hill, Langport, Somerset TA10 9PU. *T:* Langport (01458) 250845.

SISSON, Rosemary Anne; writer since 1929; *b* 13 Oct. 1923; *d* of Prof. C. J. Sisson, MA, DèsL and Vera Kathleen (*née* Ginn). *Educ:* Cheltenham Ladies' Coll.; University Coll., London (BA Hons English); Newnham Coll., Cambridge (MLit). Served War, Royal Observer Corps, 1943–45. Instr in English, Univ. of Wisconsin, 1949; Lecturer in English: UCL, 1950–53; Univ. of Birmingham, 1953–54; Dramatic Critic, Stratford-upon-Avon Herald, 1954–57; after prodn of first play, The Queen and the Welshman, became full-time writer, 1957. Co-Chm., Writers Guild of GB, 1979 and 1980; Member: Dramatists' Club; BAFTA. Laurel Award, for service to writers, 1985; Prince Michael of Kent Award, for services to SSAFA, 1987. *Plays:* The Queen and the Welshman, 1957; Fear Came to Supper, 1958; The Splendid Outcasts, 1959; The Royal Captivity, 1960; Bitter Sanctuary, 1963; Ghost on Tiptoe (with Robert Morley), 1974; The Dark Horse, 1978. Contributed to *TV series:* Catherine of Aragon, in The Six Wives of Henry VIII; The Marriage Game, in Elizabeth R; Upstairs, Downstairs; A Town Like Alice; The Young Indiana Jones Chronicles; *TV scripts:* Irish RM; Seal Morning; The Manions of America; The Bretts (creator of series). *Film scripts* include: Ride a Wild Pony; Escape from the Dark; Candleshoe; Watcher in the Woods; The Black Cauldron (full-length animation film) (all for Walt Disney); The Wind in the Willows (animation film), 1983 (also TV series, 1984). *Other scripts:* Heart of a Nation (Son-et-Lumière), Horse Guards Parade, 1983; Dawn to Dusk, Royal Tournament, 1984; Joy to the World, Royal Albert Hall, 1988, 1989, 1991. *Publications: children's books:* The Adventures of Ambrose, 1951; The Young Shakespeare, 1959; The Young Jane Austen, 1962; The Young Shaftesbury, 1964; *novels:* The Exciseman, 1972; The Killer of Horseman's Flats, 1973; The Stratford Story, 1975; Escape from the Dark, 1976; The Queen and the Welshman, 1979; The Manions of America, 1982; Bury Love Deep, 1985; Beneath the Visiting Moon, 1986; The Bretts, 1987; *poetry:* Rosemary for Remembrance, 1995. *Recreations:* travel, walking, riding, writing poetry. *Address:* 167 New King's Road, Parson's Green, SW6 4SN.

SISSONS, Prof. John Gerald Patrick, MD; FRCP; Professor of Medicine, University of Cambridge, and Fellow of Darwin College, since 1988; *b* 28 June 1945; *s* of Gerald William Sissons and Georgina Margaret Cockin; *m* 1971, Jennifer Ann Scovell (marr. diss. 1987); two *d*. *Educ:* Felstead Sch.; St Mary's Hosp. Med. Sch. MB London, MD. Hosp. appts, St Mary's, St George's and Hammersmith Hosps, 1968–71; Registrar and Lectr, Dept of Medicine, RPMS, 1972–77; NIH Research Fellow and Asst Mem., Res. Inst. of Scripps Clinic, California, 1977–80; Wellcome Sen. Lectr, Depts of Medicine and Virology, RPMS, 1980–86; Prof. of Infectious Diseases, RPMS, 1987. *Publications:* papers on immunology and pathogenesis of virus infections. *Recreation:* travel. *Address:* Department of Medicine, University of Cambridge Clinical School, Hills Road, Cambridge CB2 2QQ. *T:* Cambridge (01223) 336849.

SISSONS, Peter George; presenter, BBC TV 9 o'clock news, since 1994; *b* 17 July 1942; *s* of late George Robert Percival Sissons and Elsie Emma Evans; *m* 1965, Sylvia Bennett; two *s* one *d*. *Educ:* Liverpool Inst. High Sch. for Boys; University College Oxford (MA PPE). Independent Television News: graduate trainee, 1964; general reporter, 1967; industrial corresp., 1970; indust. editor, 1972–78; presenter, News at One, 1978–82; presenter: Channel Four News, 1982–89; BBC TV 6 o'clock news, 1989–93; Chm., BBC TV Question Time, 1989–93. Broadcasting Press Guild Award, 1984; RTS Judges' Award, 1988. *Recreations:* relaxing, supporting Liverpool FC. *Address:* BBC Television Centre, Wood Lane, W12 7RJ. *T:* 0181–743 8000.

SISSONS, (Thomas) Michael (Beswick); Chairman, The Peters Fraser and Dunlop Group Ltd, since 1988 (Managing Director, 1988–94); *b* 13 Oct. 1934; *s* of Captain T. E. B. Sissons (killed in action, 1940) and late Marjorie (*née* Shepherd); *m* 1st, 1960, Nicola

Ann Fowler (marr. diss. 1974); one *s* one *d*; 2nd, 1974, Ilze Kadegis (marr. diss. 1992); two *d*; 3rd, 1992, Serena Palmer. *Educ:* Winchester Coll.; Exeter Coll., Oxford (BA 1958, MA 1964). National Service, 2nd Lieut 13/18 Royal Hussars, 1953–55. Lectr in History, Tulane Univ., New Orleans, USA, 1958–59; freelance writer and journalist, 1958–59; joined A.D. Peters, Literary Agent, 1959; Dir, 1965, Chm. and Man. Dir, 1973–88, A. D. Peters & Co. Ltd. Pres., Assoc. of Authors' Agents, 1978–81; Dir, London Broadcasting Co., 1973–75; Mem. Council, Consumers Assoc., 1974–77. Mem. Bd, BFSS, 1994–. *Publication:* (ed with Philip French) Age of Austerity, 1963, repr. 1986. *Recreations:* riding, gardening, cricket, music. *Address:* The White House, Broadleaze Farm, Westcot Lane, Sparsholt, Wantage, Oxon OX12 9PZ. *T:* Childrey (01235) 751215, *Fax:* (01235) 751561. *Clubs:* Groucho, MCC (Mem. Cttee, 1984–87, 1993–; Chm., Arts and Liby Sub-Cttee, 1985–93).

SITWELL, Peter Sacheverell W.; *see* Wilmot-Sitwell.

SITWELL, Sir (Sacheverell) Reresby, 7th Bt *cr* 1808, of Renishaw; DL; *b* 15 April 1927; *s* of Sir Sacheverell Sitwell, 6th Bt, CH and Georgia Louise (*d* 1980), *d* of Arthur Doble; *S* father, 1988; *m* 1952, Penelope, *yr d* of late Col Hon. Donald Alexander Forbes, DSO, MVO; one *d*. *Educ:* Eton College; King's Coll., Cambridge (schol.). Served Grenadier Guards, 1945–48, mainly as Lieut, 2nd Bn, BAOR. Advertising and PR executive, 1948–63; operated vending machines and wholesale wine business, 1963–73. Took over Renishaw and family estates from late uncle, Sir Osbert, 1965. High Sheriff of Derbyshire, 1983; DL Derbyshire 1984. Freedom of City of London, 1984. *Publications:* (with John Julius Norwich and A. Costa) Mount Athos, 1964; Hortus Sitwellianus (epilogue), 1984. *Recreations:* art and architecture, music, travel, photography, racing. *Heir: b* Francis Trajan Sacheverell Sitwell [*b* 17 Sept. 1935; *m* 1966, Susanna Carolyn, *d* of Sir Ronald Hibbert Cross, 1st Bt, KCMG, KCVO, PC; two *s* one *d*]. *Address:* Renishaw Hall, near Sheffield S31 9WB; 4 Southwick Place, W2 2TN. *T:* 0171–262 3939. *Clubs:* White's, Brooks's, Pratt's, Society of Dilettanti; Pitt (Cambridge).

SIU, Gordon Kwing-Chue; JP; Secretary for Economic Services, Hong Kong, since 1993; *b* 29 Nov. 1945; *s* of Siu Wood-chuen and Chan Shuk-ming; *m* (marr. diss.); two *s*. *Educ:* Birmingham Univ. (MSocSci). Joined Hong Kong Civil Service, 1966; Sec.-Gen., Office of Members of Exec. and Legislative Councils, 1985; Postmaster Gen., 1988; Comr for Transport, 1989; Dir, New Airport Projects Co-ordination Office, 1992. *Recreations:* golf, music. *Address:* Economic Services Branch, Central Government Offices, Lower Albert Road, Hong Kong. *T:* 28102405. *Clubs:* Royal Hong Kong Golf, Royal Hong Kong Jockey.

SIZER, Prof. John, CBE 1989; DLitt; Chief Executive and Member, Scottish Higher Education Funding Council, since 1992; Professor of Financial Management, Loughborough University of Technology, since 1970 (on leave of absence); *b* 14 Sept. 1938; *s* of Mary and John Robert Sizer; *m* 1965, Valerie Davies; three *s*. *Educ:* Grimsby Coll. of Technology; Univ. of Nottingham (BA); DLitt Loughborough, 1989. FCMA. Teaching Fellow, later Lectr, Univ. of Edinburgh, 1965; Sen. Lectr, London Graduate Sch. of Business Studies, 1968; Loughborough University of Technology: Founding Head of Dept of Management Studies, 1971–84; Dean of Sch. of Human and Environmental Studies, 1973–76; Sen. Pro Vice-Chancellor, 1980–82; Dir, Business Sch., 1991–92. Chm., Directing Group, OECD/CERI Programme on Institutional Management in Higher Educn, 1980–84; Mem., UGC, 1984–89 (Chm., Business and Management Studies Sub-Cttee, 1984–89); Advr on Business and Management Studies, and Mem., NI Cttee, UFC, 1989–93; Member: Council, CIMA, 1981–88 (Chairman: Internat. Cttee, 1982–86; Finance Cttee, 1986–88); Nat. Forum for Management Educn and Develt, 1989– (Chm., Finance and Resourcing Cttee, 1989–; Mem., Exec. Cttee, 1989–); Sci. and Engrg Base Co-ordinating Cttee, 1993–; Chm., Soc. for Res. into Higher Educn, 1992–93. Mem., Public Sector and Not-for-Profit Cttee, Accounting Standards Bd, 1994–. FIMgt; FRSA. *Publications:* An Insight into Management Accounting, 1969, 1979, 1989; Case Studies in Management Accounting, 1974; Perspectives in Management Accounting, 1981; (ed jtly) Resources and Higher Education, 1983; (jtly) A Casebook of British Management Accounting, vol. 1, 1984, vol. 2, 1985; Institutional Responses to Financial Reductions in the University Sector, 1987; numerous articles in accounting, higher educn and management jls. *Recreations:* table tennis, walking. *Address:* SHEFC, Donaldson House, 97 Haymarket Terrace, Edinburgh EH12 5HD. *T:* 0131–313 6500.

SKARBEK, Marjorie Shiona, (Countess Skarbek); *see* Wallace, M. S.

SKEAT, Theodore Cressy, BA; Keeper of Manuscripts and Egerton Librarian, British Museum, 1961–72; *b* 15 Feb. 1907; *s* of Walter William Skeat, MA; *m* 1942, Olive Martin (*d* 1992); one *s*. *Educ:* Whitgift School, Croydon; Christ's College, Cambridge. Student at British School of Archaeology, Athens, 1929–31; Asst Keeper, Dept of Manuscripts, British Museum, 1931; Deputy Keeper, 1948. FBA, 1963–80. *Publications:* (with H. I. Bell) Fragments of an Unknown Gospel, 1935; (with H. J. M. Milne) Scribes and Correctors of the Codex Sinaiticus, 1938; The Reigns of the Ptolemies, 1954; Papyri from Panopolis, 1964; Catalogue of Greek Papyri in the British Museum, vol. VII, 1974; (with C. H. Roberts) The Birth of the Codex, 1983; The Reign of Augustus in Egypt, 1993; articles in papyrological journals. *Address:* 12 Berkeley Court, 31/33 Gordon Road, W5 2AE. *T:* 0181–998 9174.

SKEATES, Basil George; Director, Ashdown Gallery, 1985–94; Under Secretary, Department of the Environment, 1980–85; *b* 19 May 1929; *s* of George William Skeates and Florence Rachel Skeates; *m* 1957, Irene Margaret (*née* Hughes); four *s*. *Educ:* Hampton Grammar Sch. RIBA 1955. Mil. Service with RE, W Africa, 1947–49. Architect with LCC schs and special works, 1949–61; Principal Architect: NE Metrop. Reg. Hosp. Bd, 1961–64; MPBW, 1964–71; Superintending Architect, CSD, 1971–73; Asst Dir, Architectural Services, PSA, 1973–75; Dir of Works, PO Services, 1975–80; Dir of Def. Services II, DoE, 1980–85. *Publications:* articles in prof. and technical jls. *Recreation:* designing and making things.

SKEET, Muriel Harvey; Health Services adviser and consultant, World Health Organisation Headquarters and other international agencies and organisations, since 1978; *b* 12 July 1926; *y d* of late Col F. W. C. Harvey-Skeet, Suffolk. *Educ:* privately; Endsleigh House; Middlesex Hosp. SRN, MRSH; FRCN. Gen. Nursing Trg at Middx Hosp., 1946–49; also London Sch. of Hygiene and Tropical Med.; Ward Sister and Admin. Sister, Middx Hosp., 1949–60; Field Work Organiser, Opl Res. Unit, Nuffield Provincial Hosps Trust, 1961–64; Res. Org., Dan Mason Nursing Res. Cttee of Nat. Florence Nightingale Memorial Cttee of Gt Britain and N Ire., 1965–70; Chief Nursing Officer and Nursing Advr, BRCS, and St John of Jerusalem and BRCS Jt Cttee, 1970–78. WHO Res. Consultant, SE Asia, 1970; European Deleg. and First Chm. of Bd of Commonwealth Nurses' Fed., 1971. Leverhulme Fellowship, 1974–75. Member: Hosp. and Med. Services Cttee, 1970; Ex-Services War Disabled Help Cttee, 1970; British Commonwealth Nurses War Memorial Fund Cttee and Council, 1970; Council of Management of Nat. Florence Nightingale Memorial Cttee, 1970; Council of Queen's Inst. of District Nursing, 1970; Royal Coll. of Nursing and Nat. Council of Nurses; RSM, 1980. Fellow RCN, 1977. *Publications:* Waiting in Outpatient Departments (Nuffield Provincial Hospitals Trust), 1965; Marriage and Nursing (Dan Mason NRC), 1968; Home from Hospital (Dan Mason NRC), 1970; Home Nursing, 1975; Manual: Disaster Relief Work, 1977; Back to Our Basic Skills, 1977; Health needs Help, 1977; (jtly) Health Auxiliaries in the Health Team, 1978; Self Care for the People of Developing Countries, 1979; Discharge Procedures, 1980; Notes on Nursing 1860 and 1980, 1980; Emergency Procedures and First Aid for Nurses, 1981; The Third Age, 1982; Providing Continuing Care for Elderly People, 1983; First Aid for Developing Countries, 1983; Protecting the Health of the Elderly, 1983; Know Your Own Body, 1987; Add Life to Years, 1989; Tropical Health: concise notes, 1989; Better Opportunities for Disabled People, 1989; various articles in professional jls. *Recreations:* music, opera, painting, reading. *Address:* c/o Coutts & Co., 16 Cavendish Square, W1A 1EE. *Clubs:* Royal Society of Medicine, Sloane.

SKEET, Sir Trevor (Herbert Harry), Kt 1986; MP (C) Bedfordshire North, since 1983 (Bedford, 1970–83); barrister, writer and consultant; *b* 28 Jan. 1918; British; *m* 1st, 1958, Elizabeth Margaret Gilling (*d* 1973); two *s*; 2nd, 1985, Mrs Valerie Anita Edwina Benson. *Educ:* King's College, Auckland; University of New Zealand, Auckland (LLB). Served War of 1939–45, with NZ Engineers (sergeant); 2nd Lieut, NZ Anti-Aircraft (Heavy); Sub-Lieutenant, NZ Roy. Naval Volunteer Reserve; demobilised, 1945. Formerly Barrister and Solicitor of Supreme Court of New Zealand; Barrister, Inner Temple, 1947. Has considerable experience in public speaking. Formerly associated with Commonwealth and Empire Industries Assoc.; Mem. Council, Royal Commonwealth Soc., 1952–55, and 1956–69. Contested (C): Stoke Newington and Hackney, North, Gen. Election, 1951; Llanelly Div. of Carmarthenshire, Gen. Election, 1955; MP (C) Willesden East, 1959–64. Mem., Select Cttee on Science and Technol., 1993–; Vice-Chairman: Cons. Party Power Cttee, 1959–64; Energy Cttee, 1974–77; Chairman: Oil Sub-Cttee, 1959–64; Cons. Party Trade Cttee, 1971–74; Cons. Party Middle East Cttee (Foreign and Commonwealth Affairs), 1973–78; Secretary: All-Party Cttee on Airships, 1971–78; All-Party Gp on Minerals, 1971– (Co-Chm., 1979–); Vice-Pres., Steering Cttee, Parly and Scientific Cttee, 1988–91 (Mem., 1982–; Sec., 1983–85; Chm., 1985–88); Vice-Chm., British-Japanese and British-Brazilian Gps; Sec., British-Nigerian Gp. Mem., Econ. Cttee, Machine Tool Trades Association for several years; Member Technical Legislation Cttee, CBI. *Publications:* contrib. to numerous journals including New Commonwealth and Mining World, on oil, atomic energy, metals, commodities, finance, and Imperial and Commonwealth development. *Address:* (home) The Gables, Milton Ernest, Bedfordshire MK44 1RS. *T:* Oakley (01234) 822307. *Clubs:* Army and Navy, Commonwealth Trust.

SKEFFINGTON, family name of **Viscount Massereene and Ferrard.**

SKEGGS, Sir Clifford (George), Kt 1987; JP; FNZIM; Chairman and Chief Executive, Skeggs Group; Director of various public and private companies; Mayor, Dunedin City, 1978–89; *b* 19 March 1931; *s* of George Henry Skeggs and Beatrice Hannah (*née* Heathcote); *m* 1952, Marie Eleanor Ledgerwood; three *s*. *Educ:* Southland Technical Coll., New Zealand. Mem., 1968–80, Chm., 1973–77, Otago Harbour Bd. City Councillor, Dunedin, 1972–77. Mem. Council, Univ. of Otago, 1981–89. FNZIM 1985; Mem., Inst. of Dirs, 1984. JP Dunedin, 1978. OStJ 1987. *Publications:* contrib. fishing and general business publications. *Recreations:* yachting, golf, flying, power boating, squash, keen follower of Rugby. *Address:* Skeggs Group, Box 5657, Dunedin, New Zealand. *Club:* Dunedin (Dunedin).

SKEHEL, John James, PhD; FRS 1984; Director: National Institute for Medical Research, since 1987; World Influenza Centre, since 1975; *b* 27 Feb. 1941; *s* of Joseph and Ann Josephine Skehel; *m* 1962, Anita Varley; two *s*. *Educ:* St Mary's Coll., Blackburn; University College of Wales, Aberystwyth (BSc); UMIST (PhD). Post-doctoral Fellow, Marischal Coll., Aberdeen, 1965–68; Fellow, Helen Hay Whitney Foundn, 1968–71; Nat. Inst. for Med. Res.: Mem., Scientific Staff, 1971–; Head of Div. of Virology, 1984–87. Leeuwenhoek Lecture, Royal Soc., 1990. Hon. Prof., Liverpool Polytechnic Sch. of Nat. Sci., 1990. Hon. DSc CNAA, 1990. Wilhelm Feldberg prize, 1986; Robert Koch prize, 1987; Prix Louis Jeantet de Médecine, 1988. *Publications:* scientific articles in various jls. *Address:* 49 Homewood Road, St Albans, Herts AL1 4BG. *T:* St Albans (01727) 860603.

SKELMERSDALE, 7th Baron *cr* 1828; **Roger Bootle-Wilbraham;** consultant in politics and parliamentary affairs; Director, Broadleigh Nurseries Ltd, since 1991 (Managing Director, 1973–81); *b* 2 April 1945; *o s* of 6th Baron Skelmersdale, DSO, MC, and Ann (*d* 1974), *d* of late Percy Cuthbert Quilter; *S* father, 1973; *m* 1972, Christine Joan, *o d* of Roy Morgan; one *s* one *d*. *Educ:* Eton; Lord Wandsworth Coll., Basingstoke; Somerset Farm Institute; Hadlow Coll. VSO (Zambia), 1969–71; Proprietor, Broadleigh Gardens, 1972; Vice-Chm., Co En Co, 1979–81. A Lord in Waiting (Govt Whip), 1981–86; Parly Under-Sec. of State, DoE, 1986–87; Parly Under-Sec. of State, DHSS, 1987–88, Dept of Social Security, 1988–89, NI Office, 1989–90; Dep. Chm. of cttees, HoL, 1991–. President: Somerset Trust for Nature Conservation, 1980–; British Naturalists Assoc., 1980–. Chm., Stroke Assoc., 1993–. Gov., Castle Sch., Taunton, 1993–. *Recreations:* gardening, reading, bridge playing. *Heir: s* Hon. Andrew Bootle-Wilbraham, *b* 9 Aug. 1977. *Address:* c/o House of Lords, SW1A 0PW.

SKELTON, Rt. Rev. Kenneth John Fraser, CBE 1972; an Assistant Bishop, Dioceses of Sheffield and Derby; *b* 16 May 1918; *s* of Henry Edmund and Kate Elizabeth Skelton; *m* 1945, Phyllis Barbara, *y d* of James Emerton; two *s* one *d*. *Educ:* Dulwich Coll.; Corpus Christi Coll., Cambridge; Wells Theological Coll. 1st Cl. Class. Tripos, Pt 1, 1939; 1st Cl. Theol. Tripos, Pt 1, 1940; BA 1940, MA 1944. Deacon, 1941; Priest, 1942; Curate: Normanton-by-Derby, 1941–43; Bakewell, 1943–45; Bolsover, 1945–46; Tutor, Wells Theol Coll., and Priest-Vicar, Wells Cathedral, 1946–50; Vicar of Howe Bridge, Atherton, 1950–55; Rector, Walton-on-the-Hill, Liverpool, 1955–62; Exam. Chap. to Bp of Liverpool, 1957–62; Bishop of Matabeleland, 1962–70; Asst Bishop, Dio. Durham, Rural Dean of Wearmouth and Rector of Bishopwearmouth, 1970–75; Bishop of Lichfield, 1975–84. Select Preacher, Cambridge Univ., 1971, 1973. *Publications:* Bishop in Smith's Rhodesia, 1985; The Overseas Bishoprics' Fund 1941–1991, 1991. *Recreation:* music. *Address:* 65 Crescent Road, Sheffield S7 1HN. *T:* Sheffield (0114) 255 1260.

SKELTON, Robert William, OBE 1989; Keeper, Indian Department, Victoria and Albert Museum, 1978–88; *b* 11 June 1929; *s* of John William Skelton and Victoria (*née* Wright); *m* 1954, Frances Aird; three *s*. *Educ:* Tiffin Boys' Sch., Kingston-upon-Thames. Joined Indian Section of Victoria and Albert Museum, 1950; Asst Keeper, 1960; Dep. Keeper, 1972; Nuffield Travelling Fellow in India, 1962. Mem. Council: Royal Asiatic Soc., 1970–73, 1975–78, 1988–92; Soc. for S Asian Studies, 1984–; Trustee: Asia House Trust (London), 1977–; Indian Nat. Trust for Art and Cultural Heritage, UK, 1991–. *Publications:* Indian Miniatures from the XVth to XIXth Centuries, 1961; Rajasthani Temple Hangings of the Krishna Cult, 1973; (jtly) Islamic Painting and Arts of the Book, 1976; (jtly) Indian Painting, 1978; (jtly) Arts of Bengal, 1979; (jtly) The Indian Heritage, 1982; (jtly) Islamic Art in the Keir Collection, 1988; various contribs to art periodicals and conf. proc., 1956–. *Recreations:* chamber music, walking. *Address:* 10 Spencer Road, South Croydon CR2 7EH. *T:* and *Fax:* 0181–688 7187.

SKELTON, Prof. Robin, FRSL; author; Professor of English, 1966–91, and Founder Chairman of Department of Creative Writing, 1973–76, University of Victoria, British Columbia; *b* 12 Oct. 1925; *o s* of Cyril Frederick William and Eliza Skelton; *m* 1957, Sylvia Mary Jarrett; one *s* two *d*. *Educ:* Pocklington Grammar Sch., 1936–43; Christ's Coll., Cambridge, 1943–44; Univ. of Leeds, 1947–51. BA 1950, MA 1951. Served RAF, 1944–47. Asst Lectr in English, Univ. of Manchester, 1951; Lectr, 1954. Managing Dir, The Lotus Press, 1950–52; Examiner for NUJMB, 1954–58; Chm. of Examrs in English, 'O' Level, 1958–60; Co-founder and Chm., Peterloo Gp, Manchester, 1957–60; Founding Mem. and Hon. Sec., Manchester Inst. of Contemporary Arts, 1960–63; Centenary Lectr at Univ. of Massachusetts, 1962–63; Gen. Editor, OUP edn of Works of J. M. Synge, 1962–68; Associate Prof. of English, Univ. of Victoria, BC, 1963–66. Visiting Prof., Univ. of Michigan, Ann Arbor, 1967; Dir, Creative Writing Programme, Univ. of Victoria, 1967–73; Founder and co-Editor, Malahat Review, 1967–71, Editor 1972–83. Mem. Bd of Dirs, Art Gall. of Greater Victoria, BC, 1968–69, 1970–73; Dir, Pharos Press, 1972–; Editor, Sono Nis Press, 1976–83. Founder Member: Victoria Soc. of Limners, 1972–; Hawthorne Soc. of Arts and Letters, 1993 (Hon. Sec., 1993–). FRSL 1966. Chm., Writers' Union of Canada, 1982 (first Vice-Chm., 1981). *Publications: poetry* Patmos and Other Poems, 1955; Third Day Lucky, 1958; Two Ballads of the Muse, 1960; Begging the Dialect, 1960; The Dark Window, 1962; A Valedictory Poem, 1963; An Irish Gathering, 1964; A Ballad of Billy Barker, 1965; Inscriptions, 1967; Because of This, 1968; The Hold of Our Hands, 1968; Selected Poems, 1947–67, 1968; An Irish Album, 1969; Georges Zuk, Selected Verse, 1969; Answers, 1969; The Hunting Dark, 1971; Two Hundred Poems from the Greek Anthology, 1971; A Different Mountain, 1971; A Private Speech, 1971; Remembering Synge, 1971; Three for Herself, 1972; Musebook, 1972; Country Songs, 1973; Timelight, 1974; Georges Zuk: The Underwear of the Unicorn, 1975; Callsigns, 1976; Because of Love, 1977; Landmarks, 1979; Collected Shorter Poems 1947–1977, 1981; Limits, 1981; De Nihilo, 1982; Zuk, 1982; Wordsong, 1983; Distances, 1985; The Collected Longer Poems 1947–1977, 1985; Openings, 1988; Words for Witches, 1990; Popping Fuchsias, 1992; A Formal Music, 1993; Islands, 1993; Briefly Singing, 1994; I Am Me, 1994; Wrestling the Angel, 1994; A Way of Walking, 1994; The Edge of Time, 1995; *prose:* John Ruskin: The Final Years, 1955; The Poetic Pattern, 1956; Cavalier Poets, 1960; Poetry (in Teach Yourself series), 1963; The Writings of J. M. Synge, 1971; J. M. Synge and His World, 1971; The Practice of Poetry, 1971; J. M. Synge (Irish Writers series), 1972; The Poet's Calling, 1975; Poetic Truth, 1978; Spellcraft, 1978; They Call It The Cariboo, 1980; Talismanic Magic, 1985; The Memoirs of a Literary Blockhead (autobiog.), 1988; Portrait of My Father, 1989; (with Jean Kozocari) A Gathering of Ghosts, 1989; Celtic Contraries, 1990; The Magical Practice of Talismans, 1991; *fiction:* The Man who sang in his Sleep, 1984; The Parrot who Could, 1987; Telling the Tale, 1987; The Fires of the Kindred, 1987; Hanky Panky, 1990; Higgledy Piggledy, 1992; *drama:* The Paper Cage, 1982; *edited texts:* J. M. Synge: Translations, 1961; J. M. Synge, Four Plays and the Aran Islands, 1962; J. M. Synge, Collected Poems, 1962; Edward Thomas, Selected Poems, 1962; Selected Poems of Byron, 1965; David Gascoyne, Collected Poems, 1965; J. M. Synge, Riders to the Sea, 1969; David Gascoyne, Collected Verse Translations (with Alan Clodd), 1970; J. M. Synge, Translations of Petrarch, 1971; Jack B. Yeats, Collected Plays, 1971; (also trans.) George Faludy: selected poems, 1985; (also trans.) George Faludy: corpses brats and cricket music, 1987; The Selected Writings of Jack B. Yeats, 1991; (also trans.) Georg Trakl, Dark Seasons: a selection of poems translated from the German, 1994; *anthologies:* Leeds University Poetry, 1949, 1950; Viewpoint, 1962; Six Irish Poets, 1962; Poetry of the Thirties, 1964; Five Poets of the Pacific Northwest, 1964; Poetry of the Forties, 1968; The Cavalier Poets, 1970; Six Poets of British Columbia, 1980; Earth, Air, Fire and Water (with Margaret Blackwood), 1990; *symposia:* The World of W. B. Yeats (with Ann Saddlemyer), 1965; Irish Renaissance (with David R. Clark), 1965; Herbert Read: a memorial symposium, 1970. *Recreations:* book collecting, art collecting, making collages, stone carving, philately. *Address:* 1255 Victoria Avenue, Victoria, BC V8S 4P3, Canada. *T:* (604) 592–7032.

SKEMP, Terence Rowland Frazer, CB 1973; QC 1984; Barrister-at-Law; *b* 14 Feb. 1915; *s* of Frank Whittingham Skemp and Dorothy Frazer; *m* 1939, Dorothy Norman Pringle; one *s* two *d*. *Educ:* Charterhouse; Christ Church, Oxford. Called to Bar, Gray's Inn, 1938. Served War, Army, 1939–46. Entered Parliamentary Counsel Office, 1946; Parliamentary Counsel, 1964; Second Parly Counsel, 1973–80; Counsel to the Speaker, 1980–85. *Address:* 997 Finchley Road, NW11 7HB.

SKEMPTON, Prof. Alec Westley, DSc London 1949; FRS 1961; FEng; FICE; Professor of Civil Engineering in the University of London (Imperial College), 1957–81, now Emeritus; Senior Research Fellow, Imperial College, since 1981; *b* 4 June 1914; *o c* of late A. W. Skempton, Northampton, and Beatrice Edridge Payne; *m* 1940, Mary (*d* 1993), *d* of E. R. Wood, Brighouse, Yorks; two *d*. *Educ:* Northampton Grammar School; Imperial College, University of London (Goldsmiths' Bursar). Building Research Station, 1936–46; University Reader in Soil Mechanics, Imperial College, 1946–54; Professor of Soil Mechanics, Imperial College, 1955–57. Vice-Pres., 1974–76 (Member Council, 1949–54), Institute Civil Engineers; Pres., Internat. Soc. Soil Mechanics and Foundn Eng, 1957–61; Chm. Jt Cttee on Soils, Min. of Supply and Road Research Bd, 1954–59; Mem., Cathedrals Advisory Cttee, 1964–70; Mem., NERC, 1973–76; President: Newcomen Soc., 1977–79; Smeatonian Soc., 1981. Hitchcock Foundn Prof., Univ. of Calif, Berkeley, 1978; Lectures: Copenhagen, Paris, Harvard, Univ. of Illinois, Oslo, Stockholm, Madrid, Florence, Sydney, Quebec, Mexico City, Tokyo, Berkeley; Special Lectr, Architectural Assoc., 1948–57; Vis. Lectr Cambridge Univ. School of Architecture, 1962–66; Consultant to Binnie & Partners, John Mowlem & Co., etc. For. Associate, Nat. Acad. of Engineering, USA, 1976. Hon. MRIA, 1990. Hon. DSc: Durham, 1968; Aston, 1980; Chalmers, 1982. Ewing Medal, 1968; Lyell Medal, 1972; Dickinson Medal, 1974; Karl Terzaghi Award, 1981; IStructE Gold Medal, 1981. Silver Jubilee Medal, 1977. *Publications:* Early Printed Reports in the Institution of Civil Engineers, 1977; (with C. Hadfield) William Jessop, Engineer, 1979; John Smeaton, FRS, 1981; Selected Papers on Soil Mechanics, 1984; British Civil Engineering Literature (1640–1840), 1987; numerous contribs on soil mechanics, engineering geology and history of construction. *Address:* Imperial College, SW7 2AZ. *T:* 0171–589 5111; 16 The Boltons, SW10 9SU. *T:* 0171–370 3457. *Clubs:* Athenæum, Hurlingham.

SKENE, (Karen) Prudence Patricia, (Mrs B. H. Wray); Director, The Arts Foundation, since 1993; Member, Arts Council, and Chairman Arts Council Dance Panel, since 1992; *b* 9 Jan. 1944; *d* of Robert Worboys Skene and Phyllis Monica Skene (*née* Langley); *m* 1986, Brian Henry Wray; one step *s* one step *d*. *Educ:* Francis Holland Sch., London. Dep. Administrator, The Round House, Chalk Farm, 1973–75; Ballet Rambert: Administrator, 1975–78; Admin. Dir, 1978–84; Exec. Dir, 1984–86; Exec. Producer, English Shakespeare Co., 1987–90 and 1992. Vice-Pres., 1985–89, Pres., 1991–92, Theatrical Management Assoc.; Chm., Dancers Resettlement Trust and Vice-Chm., Dancers Resettlement Fund, 1988–92. FRSA. *Recreations:* travel, food, the performing arts. *Address:* 8 Prior Park Buildings, Bath BA2 4NP.

SKERMAN, Ronald Sidney, CBE 1974; Deputy Chairman, Prudential Corporation plc, 1985–87 (Director, 1980–87; Group Chief Actuary, 1979); *b* 1 June 1914; *s* of S. H. Skerman; *m* 1939, Gladys Mary Fosdike; no *c*. *Educ:* Hertford Grammar School. BA Open Univ., 1989. FIA. Actuarial Trainee with Prudential Assurance Co., 1932; Chief Actuary, 1968–79. Pres., Inst. Actuaries, 1970–72; Chm., Life Offices Assoc., 1973–74; Chm., British Insurers European Cttee, 1972–82; Mem., Royal Commn on Civil Liability, 1973–78. Gold Medal, Inst. of Actuaries, 1980. *Publications:* contrib. Jl Inst. Actuaries. *Recreations:* walking, travel, music. *Address:* 1 Rookes, Little Walden Road, Saffron Walden, Essex CB10 2EP. *T:* Saffron Walden (01799) 513158.

SKEWIS, (William) Iain, PhD; consultant; Director: Event Co. Ltd, since 1993; Development Consultancy Ltd; *b* 1 May 1936; *s* of John Jamieson and Margaret Middlemass Skewis; *m* 1963, Jessie Frame Weir; two *s* one *d*. *Educ:* Hamilton Academy; Univ. of Glasgow (BSc, PhD). MCIT 1970; FTS 1987. British Rail, 1961–63; Transport Holding Co., 1963–66; Highlands and Islands Development Bd, 1966–72; Yorkshire and Humberside Development Assoc., 1973–77; Chief Exec., Develt Bd for Rural Wales, 1977–90. Chm., Regl Studies Assoc., 1990–93. *Recreation:* soccer. *Address:* Rock House, The Square, Montgomery, Powys SY15 6PA. *T:* Montgomery (01686) 668276.

SKIDELSKY, family name of **Baron Skidelsky.**

SKIDELSKY, Baron *cr* 1991 (Life Peer), of Tilton in the County of East Sussex; **Robert Jacob Alexander Skidelsky,** DPhil; FRSL; FRHistS; FBA 1994; Professor of Political Economy, Warwick University, since 1990; *b* 25 April 1939; *s* of late Boris Skidelsky and Galia Sapelkin; *m* 1970, Augusta Mary Clarissa Hope; two *s* one *d*. *Educ:* Brighton Coll.; Jesus Coll., Oxford (BA and MA Mod. Hist.; DPhil). FRHistS 1973; FRSL 1978. Res. Fellow: Nuffield Coll., Oxford, 1965–68; British Acad., 1968–70; Associate Prof. of History, Sch. of Advanced Internat. Studies, Johns Hopkins Univ., Washington, DC, 1970–76; Head, Dept of History, Philosophy and Eur. Studies, Polytechnic of N London, 1976–78; Prof. of Internat. Studies, Warwick Univ., 1978–90. Dir, 1989–91, Chm., 1991–, Social Market Foundn; Mem., Policy Cttee, SDP, 1988–90. Chairman: Charleston Trust, 1987–92; Hands Off Reading Campaign, 1994–. Member: Adv. Council on Public Records, 1988–93; Schools Examinations and Assessment Council, 1992–93. *Publications:* Politicians and the Slump, 1967; English Progressive Schools, 1969; Oswald Mosley, 1975, 2nd edn 1980; (ed) The End of the Keynesian Era, 1977; (ed, with Michael Holroyd) William Gerhardie's God's Fifth Column, 1981; John Maynard Keynes, vol. 1 1883–1920, Hopes Betrayed, 1983, vol. 2 1921–1937, The Economist as Saviour (Wolfson History Award, British Acad.), 1992; (ed) Thatcherism, 1988; Interests and Obsessions, 1993; The World After Communism, 1995. *Recreations:* opera, ballet, cinema, tennis, table tennis. *Address:* Tilton House, Firle, East Sussex BN8 6LL. *T:* Ripe (01323) 811570.

SKILBECK, Diana Margaret; Headmistress, The Queen's School, Chester, since 1989; *b* 14 Nov. 1942; *d* of late William Allen Skilbeck and Elsie Almond Skilbeck. *Educ:* Wirral County Grammar School for Girls, Cheshire; Furzedown Coll., London (Teacher's Cert.); BA Hons London (External). Assistant Teacher: Mendell Primary Sch., 1964–67; Gayton Primary Sch., 1967–69; Wirral County Grammar Sch., 1969–74; Head of Geography, Wirral County Grammar Sch., 1974–78; Dep. Headmistress, West Kirby Grammar Sch., 1978–83; Headmistress, Sheffield High School, GPDST, 1983–89. *Recreations:* inland waterways, walking, singing, squash, skating, reading, industrial archaeology. *Address:* The Queen's School, City Walls Road, Chester CH1 2NN.

SKILBECK, Prof. Malcolm; Deputy Director (Education), Directorate (formerly Division) of Education, Employment, Labour and Social Affairs, Organisation for Economic Co-operation and Development, Paris, since 1991; *b* 22 Sept. 1932; *s* of Charles Harrison Skilbeck and Elsie Muriel Nash Skilbeck; *m* Helen Connell. *Educ:* Univ. of Sydney (BA); Acad. DipEd London, PhD London; MA Illinois. Secondary school teacher and adult educn teacher, 1958–63; Lectr. Univ. of Bristol, 1963–71; Prof., New Univ. of Ulster, 1971–75; Dir, Australian Curriculum Develt Centre, 1975–81; Dir of Studies, Schs Council for Curriculum and Exams for England and Wales, 1981–83; Prof. of Education, Univ. of London, 1981–85; Prof. and Vice-Chancellor, Deakin Univ., Australia, 1986–91. Consultancies for Unesco, British Council, OECD, etc, intermittently, 1967–; active in voluntary organizations concerned with educn for internat. understanding, eg, Chm., World Educn Fellowship, 1981–85. *Publications:* John Dewey, 1970; (jtly) Classroom and Culture, 1976; (jtly) Inservice Education and Training, 1977; A Core Curriculum for the Common School 1982; (ed) Evaluating the Curriculum in the Eighties, 1984; School Based Curriculum Development, 1984; Readings in School-Based Curriculum Development, 1984; Curriculum Reform, 1990; The Vocational Quest, 1994; numerous contribs to jls, project reports, etc. *Recreations:* gardening, travelling, walking, reading. *Address:* OECD, 2 rue André-Pascal, 75775 Paris, France.

SKILLINGTON, William Patrick Denny, CB 1964; a Deputy Secretary, Department of the Environment (formerly Ministry of Public Building and Works), 1966–73; Housing Commissioner, for Clay Cross UDC, 1973–74; *b* 13 Feb. 1913; *s* of late S. J. Skillington, Leicester; *m* 1941, Dorin Kahn, Sydney, Australia; two *d*. *Educ:* Malvern College; Exeter College, Oxford. BA 1935, MA 1939, Oxford. Articled to Clerk of Leicestershire CC, 1936–39. Commissioned in R Welch Fusiliers (SR), 1933; served War of 1939–45 (despatches); regimental officer in France and Belgium, and on staff in Sicily, Italy and Greece; AA and QMG; Lt-Col. Entered Min. of Works as Principal, 1946; Asst Sec., 1952; Under-Sec. (Dir of Establishments), Min. of Public Building and Works, 1956–64; Asst Under-Sec. of State, Home Office, 1964–66. *Address:* 95a S Mark's Road, Henley-on-Thames, Oxon RG9 1LP. *T:* Henley (01491) 573756. *Clubs:* United Oxford & Cambridge University; Phyllis Court (Henley).

SKINGSLEY, Air Chief Marshal Sir Anthony (Gerald), GBE 1992; KCB 1986 (CB 1983); Deputy Commander-in-Chief, Allied Forces Central Europe, 1989–92, retired; *b* 19 Oct. 1933; *s* of Edward Roberts Skingsley; *m* 1957, Lilwen; two *s* one *d*. *Educ:* St Bartholomew's, Newbury; Cambridge Univ. (BA, MA). Commissioned RAFVR 1954, RAF 1955; several flying appointments, then Flt Comdr 13 Sqdn, 1961–62; OC Ops Sqdn, RAF Akrotiri, 1962–63; RAF Staff Coll., Bracknell, 1964; OC 45 Sqdn, RAF Tengah, Singapore, 1965–67; jssc Latimer, 1968; RAF Project Officer for Tornado in MoD, 1968–71; OC 214 Sqdn, RAF Marham, 1972–74; Station Comdr, RAF Laarbruch, Germany, 1974–76; Hon. ADC to the Queen, 1976–78; Asst Chief of Staff, Offensive Ops, HQ 2nd ATAF, 1977; RCDS 1978; Director of Air Staff Plans, MoD, 1978–80; Asst Chief of Staff, Plans and Policy, SHAPE, 1980–83; Comdt, RAF Staff Coll., Bracknell, 1983–84; ACAS, 1985–86; Air Mem. for Personnel, 1986–87; C-in-C RAF Germany, and Comdr, Second ATAF, 1987–89. Mem., Allgemeine Rheinlaendische Industrie Gesellschaft, 1975. Pres., RAFA, Luxembourg, 1992–; Vice Pres., Forces Help Soc. and Lord Roberts Workshops, 1993–; Mem. Adv. Council, Atlantic Council, 1993–. *Recreations:* travel, off-shore sailing, music, golf. *Address:* c/o National Westminster Bank, 43 Swan Street, West Malling, Kent ME19 6LE. *Club:* Royal Air Force.

SKINNER, Prof. Andrew Stewart, FBA 1993; FSA(Scot); FRSE; Vice-Principal, since 1991, Adam Smith Professor of Political Economy, since 1994 (Daniel Jack Professor, 1985–94), University of Glasgow; *b* 11 Jan. 1935; *s* of late Andrew Paterson Skinner and Isabella Bateman (*nee* Stewart); *m* 1966, Margaret Mary Dorothy Robertson. *Educ:* Glasgow Univ. (MA 1958; BLitt 1960). FRSE 1988; FSA(Scot) 1992. Tutor and Asst

Lectr, QUB, 1959–62; Lectr, Queen's Coll., Dundee, Univ. of St Andrews, 1962–64; University of Glasgow: Lectr, 1964–70; Sen. Lectr, 1970–75; Reader, 1975–77; Prof., 1977–85; Dean, Faculty of Social Scis, 1980–83; Clerk of Senate, 1983–90. FRSA 1991. *Publications:* (ed) Sir James Steuart: principles of political economy, 1966; (ed with R. H. Campbell and W. B. Todd) Adam Smith: The Wealth of Nations, 1976; A System of Social Science: papers relating to Adam Smith, 1979; (with R. H. Campbell) Adam Smith: a short biography, 1982; (ed with P. Jones) Adam Smith Reviewed, 1992. *Recreation:* gardening. *Address:* Department of Political Economy, The University, Glasgow G12 8RT. *T:* 0141–330 4657; Glen House, Cardross, Dunbartonshire G82 5ES. *T:* Cardross (01389) 841603. *Club:* University (Glasgow).

SKINNER, Angus Mackinnon Cumming; Chief Inspector of Social Work Services for Scotland, Scottish Office, since 1992; *b* 4 Jan. 1950; *s* of Dr Theodore Skinner, OBE and Morag Mackinnon Skinner; *m* 1977, Kate (*née* Brewer); one *s* two *d*. *Educ:* Univ. of Edinburgh (BSc 1971); London Univ. (CQSW 1973); Strathclyde Univ. (MBA 1988). Social Worker, Cheshire and Kent, 1971–75; Social Work Manager, Lothian, 1975–87; Depute Dir, Borders, 1987–91; Chief Social Work Advr, Scottish Office, 1991–92. Gov., Nat. Inst. of Social Work, 1992–. *Publication:* Another Kind of Home, 1992. *Recreations:* family, friends, learning. *Address:* Social Work Services Inspectorate, James Craig Walk, Edinburgh EH1 3BA. *T:* 0131–244 5414; 37 Hadfast Road, Cousland, Midlothian EH22 2NZ. *T:* 0131–663 6151.

SKINNER, David; Chief Executive, Co-operative Wholesale Society Ltd, since 1992; *b* 27 Oct. 1931; *s* of late David Skinner and Mary (*née* Davidson); *m* 1956, Elizabeth Vera Harben (marr. diss. 1976); one *s* one *d*. *Educ:* Gateshead Grammar Sch.; Nottingham Univ. (BSc). Nat. Service, RNVR, 1953–55. Management trainee, Yorkshire Imperial Metals, 1955–57; Productivity Services Manager, Distillers' Co., 1957–60; Management Consultant, 1960–68; Food Divl Manager, Scottish CWS, 1969–73; Co-operative Wholesale Society Ltd: Non Food Controller, 1974–83; Retail Controller and Dep. Chief Exec. (Retail & Services), 1983–92. *Recreations:* family-cooking, watching Liverpool FC win. *Address:* Co-operative Wholesale Society Ltd, PO Box 53, New Century House, Corporation Street, Manchester M60 4ES. *T:* 0161–834 1212.

SKINNER, Dennis Edward; MP (Lab) Bolsover since 1970; Miner at Glapwell Colliery; *b* 11 Feb. 1932; good working-class mining stock; *m* 1960; one *s* two *d*. *Educ:* Tupton Hall Grammar Sch.; Ruskin Coll., Oxford. Miner, 1949–70. Mem., Nat. Exec. Cttee of Labour Party, 1978–92; Vice-Chm., Labour Party, 1987–88, Chm., 1988–89; Pres., Derbyshire Miners (NUM), 1966–70; Pres., NE Derbs Constituency Labour Party, 1968–71; Derbyshire CC, 1964–70; Clay Cross UDC, 1960–70. *Recreations:* tennis, cycling, walking. *Address:* House of Commons, SW1A 0AA; 86 Thanet Street, Clay Cross, Chesterfield, Derbyshire. *T:* Chesterfield (01246) 863429. *Clubs:* Miners' Welfares in Derbyshire; Bestwood Working Men's.

SKINNER, James John; QC; Social Security Commissioner, since 1986; a Child Support Commissioner, since 1993; *b* 24 July 1923; *o s* of late William Skinner, Solicitor, Clonmel, Ireland; *m* 1950, Regina Brigitte Reiss; three *s* two *d*. *Educ:* Clongowes Wood Coll.; Trinity Coll., Dublin; King's Inns, Dublin. Called to Irish Bar, 1946; joined Leinster Circuit; called to English Bar, Gray's Inn, 1950; called to Bar of Northern Rhodesia, 1951; QC (Northern Rhodesia) 1964; MP (UNIP) Lusaka East, 1964–68; Minister of Justice, 1964–65; Attorney-General, 1965–69 (in addition, Minister of Legal Affairs, 1967–68); Chief Justice of Zambia, March-Sept. 1969; Chief Justice of Malaŵi, 1970–85. Grand Comdr, Order of Menelik II of Ethiopia, 1965. *Recreation:* reading. *Address:* Office of the Social Security Commissioners, 83 Farringdon Street, EC4A 4DH. *T:* 0171–353 5145. *Club:* Commonwealth Trust.

SKINNER, Joyce Eva, CBE 1975; retired; *b* 5 Sept. 1920; *d* of Matthew and Ruth Eva Skinner. *Educ:* Christ's Hosp.; Girls' High Sch., Lincoln; Somerville Coll., Oxford. BA 1941, MA 1945. Bridlington Girls' High Sch., 1942–45; Perse Girls' Sch., 1946–50; Keswick Sch., 1950–52; Homerton Coll., Cambridge, 1952–64; Vis. Prof., Queen's Coll., NY, 1955–56; Principal, Bishop Grosseteste Coll., Lincoln, 1964–74; Dir, Cambridge Inst. of Educn, 1974–80; Academic Sec., Universities' Council for Educn of Teachers, 1979–84. Fellow: Hughes Hall, Cambridge, 1974–85; Worcester Coll. of Higher Educn, 1985. Hon. FCP 1971. Hon. DEd CNAA, 1989. *Recreations:* walking, reading, conversation. *Address:* 26 Rasen Lane, Lincoln LN1 3EY. *T:* Lincoln (01522) 529483.

SKINNER, Sir Keith; *see* Skinner, Sir T. K. H.

SKINNER, Peter William; Member (Lab) Kent West, European Parliament, since 1994; *b* 1 June 1959; *s* of William James Skinner and Jean Theresa Skinner; *m* 1990, Julie Doreen; one *d*, and one step *s* one step *d*. *Educ:* Bradford Univ. (BSc); Warwick Univ. (Post Grad. Cert. in Industl Relns); Greenwich Univ. (PGCE 1992). Industrial Relations Officer, 1982; Trades Union Organiser, 1984; Course Dir for HNC in Business and Finance, North West Kent Coll. of Technol., 1989–94. Mem., Social Affairs Cttee, EP. *Address:* 99 Kent Road, Dartford, Kent DA1 2AJ. *T:* Dartford (01322) 281500.

SKINNER, Prof. Quentin Robert Duthie, FBA 1981; Professor of Political Science, University of Cambridge, since 1978; Fellow of Christ's College, Cambridge, since 1962; *b* 26 Nov. 1940; 2nd *s* of late Alexander Skinner, CBE, and Winifred Skinner (*née* Duthie), MA; *m* 2nd, 1979, Susan Deborah Thorpe James, MA, PhD; one *s* one *d*. *Educ:* Bedford Sch.; Gonville and Caius Coll., Cambridge (BA 1962, MA 1965). Cambridge University: Lectr in History, 1967–78; Chm., Faculty of Hist., 1993–95. Visiting Fellow: Research Sch. of Social Science, ANU, 1970, 1994; Humanities Res. Centre, ANU, 1989, 1994; Institute for Advanced Study, Princeton: Mem., School of Historical Studies, 1974–75; longer-term Mem., School of Social Science, 1976–79; Gauss Seminars, Princeton Univ., 1980; Directeur d'Etudes Associé, Ecole des Hautes Etudes, 1987; Professeur Associé, Université Paris X, 1991; Cardinal Mercier Vis. Prof., Univ. of Leuven, 1992. Carlyle Vis. Lectr, Univ. of Oxford, 1980–81; Avalon Vis. Lectr, Northwestern Univ., 1995; Lectures: Messenger, Cornell Univ., 1983; Tanner, Harvard Univ., 1984; James Ford, Univ. of Oxford, 1985; Raleigh, British Acad., 1986; Hart, Oxford Univ., 1988; Prothero, RHistS, 1989; Dawes Hicks, British Acad., 1990; F. W. Bateson Meml, Oxford Univ., 1994; Eliot, Kent Univ., 1995. Mem., Council, British Acad., 1987–90. Foreign Hon. Mem., Amer. Acad. of Arts and Sciences, 1986. Fellow, Academia Europaea, 1989. Hon. LittD: Chicago, 1992; East Anglia, 1992. *Publications:* (ed jtly and contrib.) Philosophy, Politics and Society, Series 4, 1972; The Foundations of Modern Political Thought, Vol. 1, The Renaissance, 1978; Vol. 2, The Age of Reformation, 1978 (Wolfson Prize, 1979); Machiavelli, 1981; (ed jtly and contrib.) Philosophy in History, 1984; (ed and contrib.) The Return of Grand Theory in the Human Sciences, 1985; (ed jtly and contrib.) The Cambridge History of Renaissance Philosophy, 1988; Meaning and Context: Quentin Skinner and his critics, ed J. H. Tully, 1988; (ed and introd) Machiavelli: The Prince, 1988; (ed jtly and contrib.) Machiavelli and Republicanism, 1990; (ed jtly and contrib.) Political Discourse in Early-modern Britain, 1992; Reason and Rhetoric in the Philosophy of Hobbes, 1995; (ed jtly) Milton and Republicanism, 1995. *Address:* c/o Christ's College, Cambridge CB2 3BU. *T:* Cambridge (01223) 334974.

SKINNER, Samuel Knox; General Chairman, Republican National Committee, USA, since 1992; *b* 10 June 1938; *m* 1989, Mary Jacobs; two *s* one *d*. *Educ:* Univ. of Illinois (BSc); DePaul Univ. Law School. Served as Lieut and Tank Platoon Leader, US Army, 1960–61. IBM Corp., 1961–68; Illinois Northern District: Office of US Attorney, 1968–75; US Attorney, 1975–77; Partner, Sidley & Austin, 1977–89; President's Cabinet as Sec. of Transportation, 1989–91; Chief of Staff to President of USA, 1991–92. Campaigned for Republican Party Presidential nominations, 1964, 1980, 1988. *Address:* Republican National Committee, 310 First Street SE, Washington, DC 20003, USA.

SKINNER, Sir (Thomas) Keith (Hewitt), 4th Bt *cr* 1912; Director, Reed International, 1980–90; Chairman and Chief Executive, Reed Publishing and Reed Regional Publishing, 1982–90, and other companies; *b* 6 Dec. 1927; *s* of Sir (Thomas) Gordon Skinner, 3rd Bt, and Mollie Barbara (*d* 1965), *d* of Herbert William Girling; *S* father, 1972; *m* 1959, Jill, *d* of Cedric Ivor Tuckett; two *s*. *Educ:* Charterhouse. Managing Director, Thomas Skinner & Co. (Publishers) Ltd, 1952–60; also Director, Iliffe & Co. Ltd, 1958–65; Director, Iliffe-NTP Ltd; Chairman: Industrial Trade Fairs Holdings Ltd, 1977–; Business Press Internat., 1970–84. *Recreations:* publishing, shooting, fishing, gardening, golf. *Heir:* *s* Thomas James Hewitt Skinner, *b* 11 Sept. 1962. *Address:* Wood Farm, Reydon, near Southwold, Suffolk IP18 6SL. *Clubs:* Royal Automobile; Aldeburgh Golf.

SKINNER, Thomas Monier, CMG 1958; MBE; MA Oxon; *b* 2 Feb. 1913; *s* of late Lt-Col and Mrs T. B. Skinner; *m* 1st, 1935, Margaret Adeline (*née* Pope) (*d* 1969); two *s*; 2nd, 1981, Elizabeth Jane Hardie, *d* of late Mr and Mrs P. L. Hardie. *Educ:* Cheltenham Coll.; Lincoln Coll., Oxford. Asst District Officer (Cadet), Tanganyika, 1935; Asst District Officer, 1937; District Officer, 1947; Senior Asst Secretary, East Africa High Commission, 1952; Director of Establishments (Kenya), 1955–62, retired 1962. Member, Civil Service Commission, East Caribbean Territories, 1962–63; Chairman, Nyasaland Local Civil Service Commission, 1963; Salaries Commissioner, Basutoland, The Bechuanaland Protectorate and Swaziland, 1964. Reports on Localisation of Civil Service, Gilbert and Ellice Islands Colony and of British National Service, New Hebrides, 1968. Chairman: Bear Securities, 1962–73; Exeter Trust, 1973–79; Edinburgh Mortgage Corp., 1988–92; Dir, Business Mortgages Trust, 1979–87. *Recreation:* fishing. *Address:* 2 Parsonage Street, Bradninch, near Exeter, Devon EX5 4NW. *Club:* Army and Navy.

SKIPPER, David John; Director: Westminster Centre for Education, Independent Schools Joint Council, since 1991; Secondary Post Graduate Certificate of Education Course by Distance Learning, South Bank University (formerly Polytechnic), since 1991; *b* 14 April 1931; *s* of late Herbert G. and Edna Skipper; *m* 1955, Brenda Ann Williams; three *s* one *d*. *Educ:* Watford Grammar Sch.; Brasenose Coll., Oxford (2nd Cl. Hons Nat. Science (Chemistry)). Royal Air Force (Short Service Commn) (Education), 1954–57; Assistant Master: Radley Coll., 1957–63; Rugby Sch., 1963–69; Headmaster: Ellesmere Coll., Shropshire, 1969–81; Merchant Taylors' Sch., Northwood, 1982–91. Chairman: ISJC Special Educnl Needs, 1983–91; Soc. of Schoolmasters, 1985–. *Recreations:* golf, walking, drawing, music. *Address:* Dolton's Farm, Newport Road, Woburn MK17 9HX. *T:* Woburn (01525) 290093.

SKIPWITH, Sir Patrick Alexander d'Estoteville, 12th Bt, *cr* 1622; consultant editor and translator (trading as GeoEdit), since 1986; *b* 1 Sept. 1938; *o s* of Grey d'Estoteville Townsend Skipwith (killed in action, 1942), Flying Officer, RAFVR, and Sofka (*d* 1994), *d* of late Prince Peter Dolgorouky; *S* grandfather, 1950; *m* 1st, 1964, Gillian Patricia (marr. diss. 1970), *d* of late Charles F. Harwood; one *s* one *d*; 2nd, 1972, Ashkhain (separated 1986), *d* of late Bedros Atikian, Calgary, Alta. *Educ:* Harrow; Dublin (MA); London (DIC, PhD). With Ocean Mining Inc., in Tasmania, 1966–67, Malaysia, 1967–69, W Africa, 1969–70; with Min. of Petroleum and Mineral Resources, Saudi Arabia, 1970–71 and 1972–73. Editor, Bureau de Recherches Géologiques et Minières, Jiddah, 1973–86; Man. Dir, Immel Publishing Ltd, 1988–89. *Heir:* *s* Alexander Sebastian Grey d'Estoteville Skipwith, *b* 9 April 1969. *Address:* 76 rue de Pont-aux-Moines, 45450 Donnery, France. *Club:* Chelsea Arts.

SKITT, Baden Henry, BEM 1969; QPM 1990; Assistant Commissioner, Metropolitan Police, since 1994; *b* 5 Dec. 1941; *s* of Frederick Albert Skitt and Laura Kathleen (*née* Oakley). *Educ:* Rugeley Grammar Sch., Staffs; St Paul's Coll., Cheltenham (Dip of PE; CertEd). Schoolmaster, Sir Wilfrid Martineau Sch., Birmingham, 1963–67; Constable to Supt, Birmingham City, later W Midlands, Police, 1967–82; Chief Supt, 1982–84, Comdr, 1984–86, Metropolitan Police; Dep. Chief Constable, Northants, 1986–90; Chief Constable, Herts, 1990–94. Chm., Personnel and Training Cttee, 1993–, Vice Chm., Internat. Affairs Adv. Cttee, 1993–, ACPO. Dir, Police Extended Interviews, 1995– (Co-Dir, 1993–95). Member: Police Adv. Bd, 1993–; Police Trng Council, 1993–; Police Advr, Police Negotiating Bd, 1994–. Dir, Educnl Broadcasting Services Trust. *Publications:* (jtly) In Service Training: a new approach, 1974; (jtly) Education 2000, 1984; contrib. to learned jls. *Recreations:* the history and travelling of inland waterways, Rugby football, music. *Address:* New Scotland Yard, Broadway, SW1H 0BG. *Club:* Chief Constables'.

SKYNNER, (Augustus Charles) Robin, FRCPsych; consultant psychiatrist in private practice; writer; *b* 16 Aug. 1922; *e s* of Reginald C. A. Skynner and Mary F. Skynner (*née* Johns); *m* 1st, 1948, Geraldine Annella (*née* Foley) (marr. diss. 1959); 2nd, 1959, Prudence Mary (*née* Fawcett) (*d* 1987); one *s* one *d*. *Educ:* St Austell County Sch.; Blundell's Sch. MB BS London; DPM; FRCPsych 1978. War service, 1940–46, RAF, as pilot, Flight-Lieut. Med. training at University Coll. and Hosp., London, 1947–52 (Trotter Medal in Clinical Surgery); postgrad. at Inst. Psych. and Maudsley Hosp.; consultant psychiatric posts, 1959–, incl. Physician-in-Charge, Dept of Psych., Queen Elizabeth Hosp. for Children, 1965–70; Sen. Tutor in Psychotherapy, Inst. of Psych. and Hon. Consultant, Maudsley Hosp., 1971–82, Founder Mem., RCPsych, 1971; Jt Founder: Inst. of Group Analysis, 1969; Inst. of Family Therapy, 1977 (Chm., 1977–79); Mem. Council, Tavistock Inst. of Med. Psychology, 1988–92. FRSA. *Publications:* One Flesh, Separate Persons, 1976; (with John Cleese) Families and How to Survive Them, 1983; Explorations with Families, 1987; Institutes and How to Survive Them, 1989; (with John Cleese) Life and How to Survive It, 1993. *Recreation:* wind-surfing. *Address:* 88 Montagu Mansions, W1H 1LF. *T:* 0171–935 3103. *Club:* Royal Society of Medicine.

SKYRME, Sir (William) Thomas (Charles), KCVO 1974; CB 1966; CBE 1953; TD 1949; JP, DL; Chairman, Broadcasting Complaints Commission, 1985–87 (Member, 1981–87); Secretary of Commissions, 1948–77; Vice-President, Magistrates' Association of England and Wales, since 1981 (Member of Council, since 1974; Deputy Chairman, 1977–79; Chairman, 1979–81); *b* 20 March 1913; *s* of Charles G. Skyrme, Hereford, and of Katherine (*née* Smith), Maryland, USA; *m* 1st, 1938, Hon. Barbara Suzanne Lyle (marr. diss. 1953), *yr d* of 1st Baron Lyle of Westbourne; one *s* two *d*; 2nd, 1957, Mary, *d* of Dr R. C. Leaning. *Educ:* Rugby School; New College, Oxford (MA); Universities of Dresden and Paris. Called to the Bar, Inner Temple, 1935, Bencher 1988. Practised in London and on Western Circuit. Served War of 1939–45 in Royal Artillery in Middle East, North Africa and Italy (wounded twice). Lt-Col. Secretary to the Lord Chancellor, 1944. Governor and Member of Committee of Management of Queen Mary's Hosp., London, 1938–48. Mem., Magistrates' Courts Rule Cttee, 1950–66; Chm., Interdepartmental

Working Party on Legal Proceedings against Justices and Clerks, 1960; Mem., Interdepartmental Cttee on Magistrates Courts in London, 1961; Life Vice-Pres., Commonwealth Magistrates' and Judges' Assoc. (formerly Commonwealth Magistrates' Assoc.), 1979 (Founder, and first Pres., 1970–79); Chm., Commonwealth Magistrates' Confs, London, 1970, Bermuda, 1972, Nairobi, 1973, Kuala Lumpur, 1975, Tonga, 1976, Jamaica, 1977, Oxford, 1979; Vice-Chm., Adv. Cttee on Training of Magistrates, 1974–80. Hon. Life Mem., Justices' Clerks' Soc., 1979–. A General Comr of Income Tax, 1977–88; Mem., Top Salaries Review Body, 1981–90; Chm., Judicial Salaries Cttee, 1983–90. Chm., Batsford Foundn, 1983–. Freeman of City of London, 1970; HM Lieut for City of London, 1977–. DL Glos 1983. FRGS. JP (Oxfordshire), 1948, (London), 1952, (Gloucestershire), 1976. *Publications:* The Changing Image of the Magistracy, 1979; History of the Justices of the Peace, 1990; contribs to legal jls. *Recreations:* ski-ing, travel, rifle shooting (captained Oxford University, 1934). *Address:* Elm Barns, Blockley, Gloucestershire GL56 9BB; Casa Larissa, Klosters, Switzerland. *Clubs:* Army and Navy; Hurlingham.
See also Sir J. G. Waterlow, Bt.

SLABAS, Prof. Antoni Ryszard, DPhil; Professor of Plant Sciences, since 1990, and Director of Research, Department of Biological Sciences, since 1994, University of Durham; *b* 30 July 1948; *s* of Franciszek Slabas and Wiera Ruban; *m* 1st, 1978, Liza Duncan Hohenschutz (marr. diss. 1983); 2nd, 1989, Diana Susan Chase. *Educ:* Bishop Thomas Grant Sch.; QMC, Univ. of London (BSc); St Edmund Hall, Oxford (DPhil). Postdoctoral Fellow: Univ. of Sheffield, 1974–75; UCL, 1975–77; Unilever Research Laboratory, Sharnbrook, Bedford: Mem., Basic Studies Unit, 1977–80; Gp Leader, Lipid Enzymology, 1980–85; Section Manager, Protein Chem., 1985–86; Plant Molecular Biol. Prog. Leader, 1986–87; Sen. Molecular Biologist, 1988; Section Manager, Cell Scis, 1989–90. Mem., EC Seeds of Tomorrow Scientific Steering Cttee, 1990–; Agricultural and Food Research Council: Member: Engrg Bd, 1992–94; Plants and Envmt Res. Cttee, 1992–94; Wkg Gp, Protein Sci., 1992; Bd of Metabolic Regulation, 1992–94. Member: Cttee, Biochem. Soc. Lipid Gp, 1984–88; Technol. Foresight Prog., OST Health and Life Scis Panel, 1994–; Management Cttee, Agricl Systems Directorate, 1994; Governing Body, Scottish Crops Res. Inst., 1995–. Member, Editorial Board: Biochem. Jl, 1989–; Plant Molecular Biol., 1991–. *Publications:* various in area of plant and microbial lipid biochem., enzymology and gene cloning; contrib. Eur. Jl Biochem., Biochim. Biophys. Acta, Biochem. Jl, etc. *Recreations:* book collecting, classical music, walking, feeding swans by hand. *Address:* Department of Biological Sciences, University of Durham, South Road, Durham DH1 3LE. *T:* Durham (0191) 3743352.

SLABBERT, Dr Frederik Van Zyl; *b* 2 March 1940; *s* of Petrus Johannes and Barbara Zacharia Slabbert; *m* 1965, Marié Jordaan (marr. diss. 1983); one *s* one *d. Educ:* Univ. of Stellenbosch. BA, BA (Hons), MA 1964, DPhil 1967. Lectr in Sociology, Stellenbosch Univ., 1964–68; Senior Lecturer: Rhodes Univ., 1969; Stellenbosch Univ., 1970–71; Cape Town Univ., 1972–73; Prof. of Sociology, Univ. of the Witwatersrand, 1973–74. MP (Progressive Federal Party) Claremont, 1974–86; Leader, Official Opposition, S African Parlt, 1979–86. Founder and Dir, Inst. for a Democratic Alternative for South Africa, 1987. Vis. Prof., Univ. of the Witwatersrand Business Sch., 1988–. *Publications:* South African Society: its central perspectives, 1972; (jtly) South Africa's Options: strategies for sharing power, 1979; The Last White Parliament (autobiog.), 1986; contributions to: Change in Contemporary South Africa, 1975; Explorations in Social Theory, 1976; various SPROCAS (Study Project of a Christian in an Apartheid Society) publications. *Recreations:* jogging, swimming, squash, chess. *Address:* Business School, University of the Witwatersrand, Ptve Bag 3, Johannesburg, Wits 2050, South Africa.

SLACK, Dr Charles Roger, FRS 1989; FRSNZ 1983; Senior Scientist, New Zealand Institute for Crop and Food Research Ltd; *b* 22 April 1937; *s* of Albert Oram Slack and Eva (*née* Simister); *m* 1963, Pamela Mary Shaw; one *s* one *d. Educ:* Audenshaw Grammar Sch., Lancs; Sch. of Agriculture, Univ. of Nottingham (BSc; PhD 1962). Biochemist, David North Plant Res. Centre, CSR Co. Ltd, Brisbane, Australia, 1962–70; Leader, Biochemistry Group, 1970–84, Leader, Crop Physiology Group and Dep. Dir, Plant Physiol. Div., 1984–89, DSIR, NZ; Sen. Scientist, Crop Res. Div., DSIR, NZ, subseq. NZ Inst. for Crop and Food Res. Ltd, 1989–. Charles F. Kettering Award for Photosynthesis Res., Amer. Soc. of Plant Physiologists, 1980; Rank Prize for Nutrition, 1981. *Publications:* scientific pubns, mainly on aspects of photosynthesis and plant lipid synthesis. *Recreations:* hiking, trout fishing, gardening. *Address:* New Zealand Institute for Crop and Food Research Ltd, Private Bag 11030, Palmerston North, New Zealand. *T:* (6) 3568019, ext. 7580.

SLACK, His Honour George Granville; a Circuit Judge (formerly a County Court Judge), 1966–81; *b* 11 July 1906; *s* of George Edwin and Amy Beatrice Slack; *m* 1st, 1935, Ella Kathleen (*d* 1957), *d* of Henry Alexander Eason; one *d*; 2nd, 1958, Vera Gertrude, *d* of Reginald Ackland Spencer; one *s* one *d. Educ:* Accrington Grammar School; London University. BA (Hons History) 1926; LLB 1929; LLM 1932. Called to Bar, Gray's Inn, 1929. Served RAFVR, 1943–46. Judge of Croydon County Court, 1969–75, of Willesden County Court, 1976–81. Contested (L): Twickenham, 1945; Dewsbury, 1950; Chairman: London Liberal Party, 1947–48, 1950–53; Liberal Party Organisation, 1956–57. Sec., Acton Baptist Church, 1954–77. Chm., West Gp Housing Soc. Ltd (West Haven), 1961–94. *Publications:* Slack on War Damage, 1941; Liabilities (War Time Adjustment) Act, 1941; Liability for National Service, 1942. *Address:* 10 Baronsmede, Ealing, W5 4LT. *T:* 0181–567 8164. *Club:* National Liberal.

SLACK, John Kenneth Edward, TD 1964; **His Honour Judge John Slack;** a Circuit Judge, since 1977; *b* 23 Dec. 1930; *o s* of late Ernest Edward Slack, formerly Chief Clerk Westminster County Court, and late Beatrice Mary Slack (*née* Shorten), Broadstairs; *m* 1959, Patricia Helen, MA Cantab, *o d* of late William Keith Metcalfe, Southport; two *s. Educ:* University College Sch., Hampstead; St John's Coll., Cambridge (MA). Captain, RAEC, 1950. Admitted Solicitor, 1957; Partner, Freeborough Slack & Co., 1958–76; Mem. No 1 (later No 14) Legal Aid Area, 1966–69; Deputy Registrar, County Courts, 1969–72; a Recorder of the Crown Court, 1972–77; Pres., Wireless Telegraphy Appeals Tribunal, 1974–77. Captain Club Cricket Conf., 1962–66; Captain Bucks County Cricket Club, 1967–69 (Minor County Champions 1969); Active Vice-Pres., Club Cricket Conf., 1969–77, Pres., 1978. Chm. Council, University Coll. Sch., 1980–87 (Mem., 1974–90). *Recreations:* cricket (Cambridge Blue 1954), golf. *Address:* c/o Crown Court, Aylesbury, Bucks HP20 1XF. *Clubs:* Hawks (Cambridge); Beaconsfield Golf.

SLACK, Dr Paul Alexander, FBA 1990; FRHistS; Reader in Modern History, University of Oxford, since 1990; Fellow and Tutor, Exeter College, Oxford, since 1973; *b* 23 Jan. 1943; *s* of Isaac Slack and Helen (*née* Firth); *m* 1965, Diana Gillian Manby; two *d. Educ:* Bradford Grammar Sch.; St John's Coll., Oxford (Casberd Exhibnr and Schol.; 1st cl. Hons Mod. Hist. 1964; MA; DPhil 1972). FRHistS 1972. A. M. P. Read Schol., Oxford Univ., and Harmsworth Sen. Schol., Merton Coll., Oxford, 1965–66; Jun. Res. Fellow, Balliol Coll., Oxford, 1966–69; Lectr in Hist., York Univ., 1969–72; Oxford University: Sub-Rector, 1983, Sen. Tutor, 1984–86 and 1991–92, Exeter Coll.; Jun. Proctor, 1986–87; Mem., Hebdomadal Council, 1987–; Chm., Gen. Bd of Faculties, 1995–. Vis. Prof., Univ. of S Carolina, 1980; Vis. Res. Associate, Rikkyo Univ., Tokyo, 1988. Ford's Lectr in British History, Oxford, 1994–95. Member: Internat. Commn for Hist. of Towns, 1976–; Humanities Res. Bd, 1994–95. Pres., Soc. for Social Hist. of Medicine, 1991; Mem. Council, RHistS, 1984–87. Editor, Past and Present, 1985–94. *Publications:* (ed with Peter Clark) Crisis and Order in English Towns 1500–1700, 1972; (ed) Poverty in Early Stuart Salisbury, 1975; (with P. Clark) English Towns in Transition 1500–1700, 1976 (Japanese edn 1989); (ed) Rebellion, Popular Protest and the Social Order in Early Modern England, 1984; The Impact of Plague in Tudor and Stuart England, 1985; Poverty and Policy in Tudor and Stuart England, 1988; The English Poor Law 1531–1782, 1990; (ed with T. Ranger) Epidemics and Ideas, 1992; (ed jtly) Public Duty and Private Conscience in Seventeenth-Century England, 1993; contribs to learned jls. *Recreations:* opera, fell-walking. *Address:* Exeter College, Oxford OX1 3DP. *T:* Oxford (01865) 279600.

SLACK, Timothy Willatt, LVO 1995; MA; Principal, St Catharine's Foundation at Cumberland Lodge, 1985–95; *b* 18 April 1928; *yr s* of late Cecil Moorhouse Slack, MC, and Dora Willatt, Beverley, Yorks; *m* 1957, Katharine (*d* 1993), 2nd *d* of late Walter Norman Hughes, MA, and of Jean Sorsbie, Chepstow, Mon.; one *s* three *d. Educ:* Winchester Coll.; New Coll., Oxford. Hons. PPE, 1951. Asst, Lycée de Rennes, France, 1951; Asst master, the Salem School, Baden, Germany, 1952; Assistant master, Repton School, 1953–59; Headmaster of Kambawsa College, Taunggyi, Shan State, Burma, 1959–62; Headmaster, Bedales Sch., 1962–74. Chairman, Society of Headmasters of Independent Schools, 1968–70. Dep. Dir, 1975–77, Dir, 1977–83, Wiston House FCO Conf. Centre (incorp. Wilton Park Confs), Steyning; Headmaster, Hellenic Coll. of London, 1983–84. Kurt Hahn Meml Lectr, 1982. Dir, Nat. Tenants Resource Centre, 1993–. Chm. Governors, The Royal Sch., Windsor Great Park, 1988–95. Chm., Round Table Moot, 1994–. Contested (L): Petersfield, Feb. and Oct. 1974; Enfield, Southgate, Dec. 1984; (L/Alliance) Fareham, 1987. *Address:* Hamlet House, Hambledon, Hampshire PO7 4RY.
See also Sir W. W. Slack.

SLACK, Sir William (Willatt), KCVO 1990; MA, MCh, BM, FRCS; Consultant Surgeon, Middlesex Hospital, 1962–91, now Emeritus Surgeon; Senior Lecturer in Surgery, 1962–91, and Dean, 1983–87, Middlesex Hospital Medical School; Dean, Faculty of Clinical Sciences, University College and Middlesex School of Medicine, University College London, 1987–91; also Surgeon: Hospital of St John and St Elizabeth, 1970–88; King Edward VII Hospital for Officers, 1975–91; *b* 22 Feb. 1925; *s* of late Cecil Moorhouse Slack, MC, and Dora Slack (*née* Willatt); *m* 1951, Joan, 4th *d* of late Lt-Col Talbot H. Wheelwright, OBE; two *s* two *d. Educ:* Winchester Coll.; New Coll., Oxford; Middlesex Hosp. Med. Sch. Ho. Surg., Surgical Registrar and Sen. Surgical Registrar, Mddx Hosp., 1950–59; Jun. Registrar, St Bartholomew's Hosp., 1953; Fulbright Scholar, R. & E. Hosp., Univ. of Illinois, Chicago, 1959. Surgeon to the Queen, 1975–83; Serjeant Surgeon to the Queen, 1983–90. Hon. Fellow, UCL, 1987. Master, Barbers' Co., 1991–92. *Publications:* various surgical articles in med. jls and textbooks. *Recreations:* skiing, gardening; Oxford blue for Association football, 1946. *Address:* Hillside Cottage, Tower Hill, Stawell, near Bridgwater, Somerset TA7 9AJ. *T:* Bridgwater (01278) 722719.
See also T. W. Slack.

SLADE, Adrian Carnegie, CBE 1988; Co-founder and Director, Longslade (Media Training) Ltd, since 1991; *b* 25 May 1936; *y s* of late George Penkivil Slade, KC and Mary Albinia Alice Slade; *m* 1960, Susan Elizabeth Forsyth; one *s* one *d. Educ:* Eton Coll.; Trinity Coll., Cambridge (BA Law). Pres., Cambridge Footlights, 1959. Writer, J. Walter Thompson, 1959–64; S. H. Benson, 1964–71, Dir, 1970–71; Co-Founder and Managing Director: Slade Monico Bluff Ltd, 1971–75; Slade Bluff & Bigg Ltd, 1975–86; Slade Hamilton Fenech Ltd, 1986–91. Dir, Orange Tree Th., Richmond, 1986– (Chm., 1991–); Trustee, One plus One, 1987– (Chm., 1990–). Mem. (L) Richmond, GLC, 1981–86 (Leader, L/SDP Alliance Gp, 1982–86). Contested: (L) Putney, 1966, Feb. and Oct. 1974; (L/SDP Alliance) Wimbledon, 1987. Advertising and Pubns Advr to Liberal Party, gen. elections, 1966, 1970, Feb. and Oct. 1974, 1979; Pres., Liberal Party, 1987–88; Jt Pres., 1988, Vice-Pres., 1988–89, Liberal Democrats. *Recreations:* music, theatre, films, piano playing, photography. *Address:* 28 St Leonard's Road, SW14 7LX. *T:* 0181–876 8712.
See also Rt Hon. Sir C. J. Slade, J. P. Slade.

SLADE, Sir Benjamin Julian Alfred, 7th Bt *cr* 1831; Chairman, Shirlstar Container Transport Ltd, since 1973, and director of subsidiary companies; *b* 22 May 1946; *s* of Sir Michael Slade, 6th Bt and Angela (*d* 1959), *d* of Captain Orlando Chichester; *S* father, 1962; *m* 1977, Pauline Carol (marr. diss. 1991), *er d* of Major Claude Myburgh. *Educ:* Millfield Sch. Chm., Pyman Bell (Holding) Ltd. Mem., Worshipful Co. of Ironmongers. Freeman, City of London, 1979. *Recreations:* racing, polo, bridge. *Heir:* none. *Address:* Maunsel, North Newton, Bridgwater, Somerset TA7 0BU. *T:* Bridgwater (01278) 663413; Shirlstar House, 37 St John's Road, Uxbridge, Middx UB8 2UR. *T:* Uxbridge (01895) 272929, *Fax:* (01895) 234283. *Clubs:* Turf; Old Somerset Dining (Taunton).

SLADE, Brian John, FInstPS; Director General of Defence Contracts, Ministry of Defence, 1986–91; *b* 28 April 1931; *s* of late Albert Edward Victor Slade and Florence Elizabeth (*née* Eveleigh); *m* 1955, Grace, *d* of late W. McK. Murray and Mary Murray, Ayr; one *s* one *d. Educ:* Portsmouth Northern Grammar School; London University. Joined Min. of Supply, 1951; Private Sec. to Permanent Sec., Min. of Aviation, 1962–64; Head of Industrial Personnel Branch, Min. of Technology, 1968–73; Principal Dir of Contracts, Air, MoD, 1982–86. Mem. Synod, Methodist Church, London SW, 1981–90. *Recreations:* cricket, downs walking. *Address:* Doonbank, 16 Greenway, Great Bookham, Surrey KT23 3PA. *T:* Bookham (01372) 454359.

SLADE, Rt. Hon. Sir Christopher John, Kt 1975; PC 1982; a Lord Justice of Appeal, 1982–91; *b* 2 June 1927; *e s* of late George Penkivil Slade, KC, and Mary Albinia Alice Slade; *m* 1958, Jane Gwenllian Armstrong Buckley; one *e s* three *d. Educ:* Eton (Scholar); New Coll., Oxford (Scholar). Eldon Law Scholar, 1950. Called to Bar, Inner Temple, 1951; joined Lincoln's Inn *ad eundem*, 1954, Bencher, 1973 (Treas., 1994). In practice at Chancery Bar, 1951–75; QC 1965; Attorney General, Duchy of Lancaster and Attorney and Serjeant Within the County Palatine of Lancaster, 1972–75; a Judge of the High Ct, Chancery Division, 1975–82; a Judge of Restrictive Practices Ct, 1980–82, Pres., 1981–82. Member: Gen. Council of the Bar, 1958–62, 1965–69; Senate of Four Inns of Court, 1966–69; Lord Chancellor's Legal Educn Cttee, 1969–71. Master, Ironmongers' Co., 1973. *Address:* 12 Harley Gardens, SW10 9SW. *Club:* Garrick.
See also A. C. Slade, J. P. Slade.

SLADE, Elizabeth Ann; QC 1992; *b* 12 May 1949; *d* of late Dr Charles Slade and of Henriette Slade; *m* 1975; two *d. Educ:* Wycombe Abbey Sch.; Lady Margaret Hall, Oxford (Exhibnr, MA). Called to the Bar, Inner Temple, 1972, Bencher, 1990, Master of Staff, 1994–. Chm., Employment Law Bar Assoc., 1995–May 1996. *Publication:* Tolley's Employment Handbook, 1978, (ed jtly) 7th edn 1991. *Recreations:* walking, family activities, theatre, swimming. *Address:* 11 King's Bench Walk, Temple, EC4Y 7EQ.

SLADE, Julian Penkivil; author and composer since 1951; *b* 28 May 1930; *s* of G. P. Slade, KC. *Educ:* Eton College; Trinity College, Cambridge (BA). Went to Bristol Old Vic Theatre School, 1951; wrote incidental music for Bristol Old Vic production of Two Gentlemen of Verona, 1952; joined Bristol Old Vic Co. as musical director, 1952; wrote and composed Christmas in King St (with Dorothy Reynolds and James Cairncross) Bristol, 1952; composed music for Sheridan's The Duenna, Bristol, 1953; transferred to Westminster Theatre, London, 1954; wrote and composed The Merry Gentleman (with Dorothy Reynolds), Bristol, 1953; composed incidental music for The Merchant of Venice (1953 Stratford season); wrote musical version of The Comedy of Errors for TV, 1954, and for Arts Theatre, London, 1956, revd version for 400th anniv. of first perf. at Gray's Inn, 1994; wrote (with Dorothy Reynolds) Salad Days, Bristol, Vaudeville, 1954, Duke of York's, 1976, Bristol Old Vic, 1994 (adaptation for Yorks TV, 1983, and for 40th birthday recording, BBC, 1994); Free as Air, Savoy, London, 1957; Hooray for Daisy!, Bristol, 1959, Lyric, Hammersmith, 1960; Follow that Girl, Vaudeville, London, 1960; Wildest Dreams, 1960; Vanity Fair (with Alan Pryce-Jones and Robin Miller), Queen's Theatre, London, 1962; Nutmeg and Ginger, Cheltenham, 1963, revived Orange Tree Theatre, Richmond, 1991; Sixty Thousand Nights (with George Rowell), Bristol, 1966; The Pursuit of Love, Bristol, 1967; composed music for songs in: As You Like It, Bristol, 1970; A Midsummer Night's Dream and Much Ado About Nothing, Regent's Park, 1970; adapted A. A. Milne's Winnie The Pooh, Phoenix Theatre, 1970, 1975; (music and lyrics with Aubrey Woods and George Rowell) Trelawny (based on Pinero's Trelawny of the Wells), Bristol, then London West End, 1972; Out of Bounds (book, music and lyrics, based on Pinero's The Schoolmistress), 1973. Composed incidental music for Nancy Mitford's Love in a Cold Climate, Thames TV, 1980; (with Veronica Flint-Shipman and Kit Harvey) musical adaptation of J. M. Barrie's Dear Brutus, 1985; (with Gyles Brandreth) Now We Are Sixty (musical play based on works of A. A. Milne), Arts Theatre, Cambridge, 1986; (with Elizabeth Seal) concert performances of own songs, Easy to Sing, 1986–87; played and sang, gala concert to launch Questfest, Buxton Opera House Festival of Musicals, 1992. Played and sang for solo record album of own songs, Looking for a Piano, 1981; played for vocal album, Salad Days, 1982. Gold Badge of Merit, British Acad. of Songwriters, Composers and Authors, 1987. *Publications:* Nibble the Squirrel (children's book), 1946; music of: The Duenna, 1954; Salad Days, 1954; Free as Air, 1957; Follow That Girl, 1967; Trelawny, 1974; The Merry Gentleman, 1985. *Recreations:* drawing, going to theatres and cinemas, listening to music. *Address:* 86 Beaufort Street (Ground Floor/Basement), SW3 6BU. *T:* 0171–376 4480.

See also A. C. Slade, Rt Hon. Sir C. J. Slade.

SLADE, Laurie George; Insurance Ombudsman, since 1994; *b* Nairobi, 12 Feb. 1944; *yr s* of Humphrey Slade and Constance Laing Gordon. *Educ:* Duke of York's Sch., Nairobi; Magdalen Coll., Oxford (MA); London Univ. Inst. of Educn (PGCE). FCIArb 1994. Called to the Bar, Lincoln's Inn, 1966. Worked in professional theatre and TV, Kenya and UK, to 1970; stage management, acting; wrote play Out of Africa (after Karen Blixen); teaching, 1972–75; Advocate, Kenya High Court, to 1981; Legal Advr, CIArb and Dep. Registrar, London Court of Internat. Arbitration, 1982–88; Dep. Insurance Ombudsman, 1988–94. Voluntary bereavement counsellor, Hounslow Social Services, 1988–94; pt-time practice, counselling and psychotherapy, 1991–. Mem., British and Irish Ombudsman Assoc. *Publications:* professional papers and contribs to learned jls. *Recreations:* theatre, painting (2 solo exhibns in Kenya, 1974, 1979). *Address:* Insurance Ombudsman Bureau, City Gate One, 135 Park Street, SE1 9EA. *T:* 0171–928 4488.

SLADE, Leslie William, JP; Agent General for Western Australia in London, 1978–82; *b* 17 July 1915; *s* of Leonard Barrington Slade and Gwendoline (*née* Fraser); *m* 1942, Marion Joan, *d* of V. J. Devitt, Perth, WA; one *d* decd. *Educ:* Scotch Coll., Melbourne, Australia. Accountant, Myer Emporium Ltd, Melbourne, 1933–39; served RAN (Lieut-Comdr), 1939–46; Proprietor of import/export business, Perth, WA, 1947–61; Export Consultant, W Australian Govt, Perth, 1962–68; Official Rep., Govt of W Australia for Far East, Tokyo, 1968–78. Freedom of City of London, 1978. JP WA, 1978. *Recreations:* golf, cricket, fishing, sailing. *Address:* Unit 8, Kyamala, 19 Broome Street, Mosman Park, WA 6012, Australia. *Clubs:* Weld, West Australian Cricket Association, Royal Perth Yacht, Nedlands Golf (Perth); Tokyo (Tokyo).

SLADE, Patrick Buxton M.; *see* Mitford-Slade.

SLADEN, Teresa; Secretary of the Victorian Society, 1987–93; *b* 16 Sept. 1939; *d* of Robert John Fawcett and Anne (*née* Fairlie Clarke); *m* 1961, David Sladen; one *s* two *d*. *Educ:* Birkbeck Coll., London Univ. (BA Hons Hist. of Art/Italian); Courtauld Inst. (MA Medieval Art and Architecture, 1978). Royal Commn on Historical Monuments, 1978–79; part-time lectr and freelance researcher, 1980–82; Architectural Advr, Victorian Soc., 1983–87. *Publication:* contrib. jl of Garden History. *Recreations:* drawing, 19th century stained glass and painted decoration, reading 19th century novels.

SLANE, Viscount; Alexander Burton Conyngham; *b* 30 Jan. 1975; *s* and *heir* of Earl of Mount Charles, *qv*.

SLANEY, Prof. Sir Geoffrey, KBE 1984; FRCS; Barling Professor, Head of Department of Surgery, Queen Elizabeth Hospital, Birmingham University, 1971–86, now Emeritus; Hon. Consultant Surgeon: United Birmingham Hospitals and Regional Hospital Board, since 1959; Royal Prince Alfred Hospital, Sydney, since 1981; President, Royal College of Surgeons of England, 1982–86; Hon. Consulting Surgeon Emeritus, City of London and Hackney Health Authority, since 1983; *b* 19 Sept. 1922; *er s* of Richard and Gladys Lois Slaney; *m* 1956, Josephine Mary Davy; one *s* two *d*. *Educ:* Brewood Grammar Sch.; Univs of Birmingham, London and Illinois, USA. MB, ChB (Birmingham) 1947, FRCS 1953, MS (Ill) 1956, ChM (Birmingham) 1961; Hon. FRCSI 1983; Hon. FRACS 1983; Hon. FCSSL 1984; Hon. FACS 1985; Hon. FCSSA 1986; Hon. FRCSCan 1986; Hon. FRCA (Hon. FFARCS 1987). Ho. Surg. and Surgical Registrar, Gen. Hosp. Birmingham, 1947–48. Captain RAMC, 1948–50. Surgical Registrar, Coventry, London and Hackney Hosps, 1950–53; Surgical Registrar, Lectr in Surgery and Surgical Research Fellow, Queen Elizabeth Hosp., Birmingham, 1953–59; Hunterian Prof., RCS, 1961–62; Prof. of Surgery, Univ. of Birmingham, 1966–87. Member: London Adv. Group to Sec. of State, DHSS, 1980–81; Ministerial Adv. Gp on Med. Manpower, 1985–86; Res. Liaison Gp, DHSS, 1979–85; Midlands Med. Appeals Tribunal, 1964–94. Former External Examr in Surgery to Univs of: Newcastle upon Tyne, London, Cambridge, Oxford, Liverpool, Nat. Univ. of Ireland, Lagos, Zimbabwe, and Licentiate Cttee, Hong Kong; Advisor in Surgery, Univs of Bristol and London. Lectures: Richardson Meml, Massachusetts Gen. Hosp., Boston, USA, 1975; Pybus Meml, Newcastle, 1978; Simpson Smith Meml, London, 1979; Legg Meml, KCH, London, 1982; Chesledon, St Thomas' Hosp., London, 1983; Miles Meml, London, 1983; Berrill Meml, Coventry, 1984; Sandblom, Lund, Sweden, 1984; Sir John Frazer Meml, Edinburgh, 1984; Tung Wah Inaugural, Tung Wah Hosp., Hong Kong, 1986; Sir Ernest Finch Meml, Sheffield, 1986; Hunterian Oration, RCS, 1987; Budd Meml, Bristol, 1987; Annual Guest Lecture, Chicago Surgical Soc., 1987; Barney Brooks Meml, Vanderbilt Univ., Tennessee, 1987; Rutherford-Morison, Newcastle, 1987; Walter C. Mackenzie, Edmonton, 1988; Francis C. Moore, Boston, 1988; Joseph C. Finneran, Indianapolis, 1988; Annual Oration, Osler Club, 1988; Qvist Meml, Royal Free Hosp., 1988; Duke Sesquicentennial, NC, 1988; Telford Meml, Manchester, 1989; (first) Bryan Brooke, Ileostomy Assoc., 1990. Visiting Professor: Durban, Cape Town, Witwatersrand, 1970; Sir Logan Campbell and RACS, NZ, 1977; Univ. of Calif and Cedars-Sinai Hosp., LA, 1978; Pearce Gould, Middlesex Hosp., 1980; McIlrath Guest, Sydney, 1981; G. B. Ong, Univ. of Hong Kong, 1983 (Ong Inaugural Lecture); Foundn Culpepper Prof., Univ. of California, 1984; Madras Med. Coll., and Univ. of Istanbul, 1986; Univ. of Alberta, Edmonton, 1988; Harvard, 1988; Uniformed Services Univ., Bethesda, 1988; Duke Univ., 1988; Wernicke-Marks-Elk, Univ. of Zimbabwe, 1989. Mem. Council, RCS, 1975–87; Member: Moynihan Chirurgical Club (Pres., 1986–87); James IV Assoc. of Surgeons (Pres., 1985–86); Internat. Surgical Gp (Pres., 1985–86); Surgical Research Soc.; Internat. Soc. of Cardio-Vascular Surgeons; Vascular Surgical Soc., GB (Pres., 1974–75); Chm., Assoc. of Profs of Surgery of GB and Ireland, 1979–82. Mem. Council, Univ. of Zimbabwe, 1973–82. Fellow: RSM; Assoc. of Surgeons GB and Ire. (Mem. Council, 1966–76, Treasurer, 1970–76); Assoc. Clinical Anatomists; Amer. Surgical Assoc. Hon. Life Member: Los Angeles Surgical Soc.; Chicago Surgical Soc.; Warren H. Cole Surgical Soc.; William H. Scott Surgical Soc.; Hon. Member: Grey Turner Surgical Club; Assoc. of Surgeons of India. Hon. Freeman, Barbers' Co. Jacksonian Prize and Medal, RCS, 1959; Pybus Meml Medal, NE Surgical Soc., 1978; Miles Medal, Royal Marsden Hosp., 1983; Vanderbilt Univ. Medal, 1987; Brooke Medal, Ileostomy Assoc. of GB and Ireland, 1990. Mem. Editl Bd, British Jl of Surgery, 1970–84; Co-Chief Editor, Jl of Cardio-Vascular Surgery, 1988–92. *Publications:* Metabolic Derangements in Gastrointestinal Surgery (with B. N. Brooke), 1967 (USA); (jtly) Cancer of the Large Bowel, 1991; numerous contribs to med. and surg. jls. *Recreations:* fishing and family. *Address:* 23 Aston Bury, Edgbaston, Birmingham B15 3QB. *T:* 0121–454 0261.

SLATCHER, William Kenneth, CMG 1983; CVO 1975; HM Diplomatic Service, retired; High Commissioner in Guyana and non-resident Ambassador to Suriname, 1982–85; *b* 12 April 1926; *s* of John William and Ada Slatcher; *m* 1948, Erica Marjorie Konigs; one *s* one *d*. *Educ:* St John's Coll., Oxford. Royal Artillery, 1950–57; HM Diplomatic Service, 1958: Peking, 1959–60; Tokyo, 1961–63; Paris, 1965–68; New Delhi, 1968–71; Tokyo, 1974–77; Consul-Gen., Osaka, 1977–80; Head of Consular Dept, FCO, 1980–82. *Recreations:* travelling, oriental art and history, reading. *Address:* Jardin aux Fontaines, 9 rue Nazareth, 34090 Montpellier, France. *Club:* Commonwealth Trust.

SLATER, Bill; *see* Slater, W. J.

SLATER, Dr David Homfray; Chief Inspector, HM Inspectorate of Pollution, since 1991; *b* 16 Oct. 1940; *m* 1964, Edith Mildred Price; four *d*. *Educ:* University College of Wales Aberystwyth (BSc, PhD). CChem, FRIC, FIChemE, CEng, FInstE. Research Associate, Ohio State Univ., 1966–69; Sen. Res. Fellow, Dept of Chemistry, Univ. of Southampton, 1969–70; Lectr in Combustion, Dept of Chem. Engineering and Chem. Technology, Imperial College London, 1970–75; Cremer and Warner: Sen. Scientist, 1975; Partner, 1979–81; Founding Dir, Technica, 1981–91. Hon. Prof. of Life Sciences, Univ. of Wales, Aberystwyth, 1991. *Publications:* numerous contribs to sci. jls and conference procs. *Recreations:* music, photography, fishing. *Address:* HM Inspectorate of Pollution, Romney House, 43 Marsham Street, SW1P 3PY. *T:* 0171–276 8080. *Club:* Athenæum.

SLATER, Duncan, CMG 1982; HM Diplomatic Service, retired; British High Commissioner in Kuala Lumpur, 1992–94; *b* 15 July 1934; *m* 1972, Candida Coralie Anne Wheatley; one *s* two *d*. Joined FO, 1958; Asst Polit. Agent, Abu Dhabi, 1962–66; First Secretary: Islamabad, 1966; New Delhi, 1966–68; Head of Chancery, Aden, 1968–69; FO, 1969; Special Asst to Sir William Luce, 1970–71; First Sec., UK Representation to EEC, Brussels, 1973–75; UK Resident Rep. to IAEA and UK Perm. Rep. to UNIDO, Vienna, 1975–78; on staff of Government House, Salisbury, Dec. 1979–April 1980; Counsellor and Head of Chancery, Lagos, 1978–81; Ambassador to Oman, 1981–86; Asst Under Sec. of State, FCO, 1986–92. *Recreations:* walking, sailing, skiing, studying Islamic art. *Address:* c/o Foreign and Commonwealth Office, SW1A 2AH.

SLATER, Prof. Edward Charles, ScD; FRS 1975; Professor of Physiological Chemistry, University of Amsterdam, The Netherlands, 1955–85; Hon. Professor, University of Southampton, since 1985; *b* 16 Jan. 1917; *s* of Edward Brunton Slater and Violet Podmore; *m* 1940, Marion Winifred Hutley; one *d*. *Educ:* Melbourne Univ. (BSc, MSc); Cambridge Univ. (PhD, ScD). Biochemist, Australian Inst. of Anatomy, Canberra, Aust., 1939–46; Research Fellow, Molteno Inst., Univ. of Cambridge, UK, 1946–55. Pres., Internat. Union of Biochem., 1988–91. Member: Royal Netherlands Acad. of Science and Letters, 1964; Hollandsche Maatschappij van Wetenschappen, 1970; Hon. Member: Amer. Soc. of Biological Chemists, 1971; Japanese Biochemical Soc., 1973; The Biochemical Soc., 1987; Nederlandse Vereniging voor Biochemie, 1989; For. Mem., Royal Swedish Acad. of Sciences, 1975; Hon. For. Mem., Académie Royal de Méd., Belgium, 1982; Corresponding Member: Acad. Nacional de Ciencas Exactas, Fisicasy Naturales, Argentina, 1973; Australian Acad. of Science, 1985. Hon. DSc Southampton, 1993. Kt, Order of the Netherlands Lion, 1984. *Publications:* Biochimica et Biophysica Acta: story of a biochemical journal, 1986; about 450 contribs to learned jls. *Recreations:* yachting, skiing. *Address:* 9 Oaklands, Lymington, Hants SO41 3TH. *T:* (home) Lymington (01590) 679455, (work) Southampton (01703) 554347.

SLATER, Gordon Charles Henry, CMG 1964; CBE 1956; Director, Branch Office in London of International Labour Office, 1964–70; Under-Secretary, Ministry of Labour, in the Overseas Department, 1960–64, retired; *b* 14 Dec. 1903; *s* of Matthew and Florence Slater; *m* 1928, Doris Primrose Hammond; one *s* one *d*. Entered Ministry of Labour, 1928, as Third Class Officer; Assistant Secretary, Organisation and Establishments, 1945, Disabled Persons Branch, 1949; Secretary of National Advisory Council on Employment of Disabled Persons, 1949–56; Sec. of Piercy Committee on Rehabilitation of Disabled, 1953–56; Under-Sec., Ministry of Labour, 1958. Member Governing Body, ILO, 1961–64; UK Govt delegate, IL Conf., 1961–64. Mem. Berkshire CC, 1970–81, Vice-Chm., 1977–79. *Address:* White House, Altwood Road, Maidenhead, Berks SL6 4PZ. *T:* Maidenhead (01628) 27463.

SLATER, James Derrick, FCA; Chairman, Salar Properties Ltd, since 1983; *b* 13 March 1929; *o s* of Hubert and Jessica Slater; *m* 1965, Helen Wyndham Goodwyn; two *s* two *d*. *Educ:* Preston Manor County Sch. Accountant and then Gen. Man. to a gp of metal finishing cos, 1953–55; Sec., Park Royal Vehicles Ltd, 1955–58; Dep. Sales Dir, Leyland Motor Corp. Ltd, 1963; Chm., Slater Walker Securities Ltd, 1964–75; Dir, BLMC, 1969–75. FCA 1963 (ACA 1953). *Publications:* Return to Go, 1977; The Zulu Principle, 1992; Investment Made Easy, 1994; Pep Up Your Wealth, 1994; *for children:* Goldenrod, 1978; A. Mazing Monsters, 1979; Grasshopper and the Unwise Owl, 1979; The Boy Who Saved Earth, 1979. *Recreations:* chess, bridge, salmon fishing, table tennis. *Address:* 67 Victoria Road, Kensington, W8 5RH.

SLATER, John Christopher Nash; QC 1987; a Recorder, since 1990; *b* 14 June 1946; *er s* of Lt-Col Leonard Slater, *qv*; *m* 1971, Jane Schapiro; two *s* one *d*. *Educ:* Sedbergh School; University College, Oxford (MA Hon. Classical Mods 1966 and Jurisprudence 1968).

Called to the Bar, Middle Temple, 1969 (Harmsworth Scholar). Assistant Recorder, 1987–90. *Publications:* Concise College Texts: Cases and Statutes, Criminal Law, 1972, 2nd edn (jtly) 1981. *Recreations:* golf, acting, travel. *Address:* 16 Stormont Road, N6 4NL. *T:* 0181–348 2725. *Clubs:* Hampstead Golf; Hampstead Cricket.

SLATER, Adm. Sir John Cunningham Kirkwood, (Sir Jock), GCB 1992 (KCB 1988); LVO 1971; First Sea Lord and Chief of Naval Staff, and First and Principal Naval Aide-de-Camp to the Queen, since 1995; *b* 27 March 1938; *s* of late Dr James K. Slater, OBE, MD, FRCPE and M. C. B. Slater (*née* Bramwell); *m* 1972, Ann Frances, *d* of late Mr and Mrs W. P. Scott of Orkney; two *s*. *Educ:* Edinburgh Academy; Sedbergh. BRNC Dartmouth, 1956–58; served HM Ships Troubridge, Yaxham, HM Yacht Britannia, Cassandra, 1959–64; Comd HMS Soberton, 1965; specialised in navigation, HMS Dryad, 1965–66; HM Ships Victorious and Scarborough (Dartmouth Training Sqdn), 1966–68; Equerry to HM the Queen, 1968–71; Comdr 1971; Comd, HMS Jupiter, 1972–73; Directorate of Naval Ops, MoD, 1973–75; Captain 1976; Comd, HMS Kent, 1976–77; RCDS 1978; Asst Dir of Naval Warfare, MoD, 1979–81; Comd, HMS Illustrious, 1982–83; Captain, Sch. of Maritime Ops and Comd, HMS Dryad, 1983–85; Rear Adm. 1985; ACDS (Policy and Nuclear), 1985–87; Vice-Adm., 1987; Flag Officer, Scotland and NI, and NATO Comdr Northern sub area Eastern Atlantic, Comdr Nore sub area Channel and Naval Base Comdr, Rosyth, 1987–89; Chief of Fleet Support (Mem., Admiralty Bd), 1989–91; Adm. 1991; C-in-C, Fleet, Allied C-in-C, Channel, and Eastern Atlantic, 1991–92; VCDS, 1993–95. Vice Chm., RUSI, 1993–95; Mem., Bd of Management, BNSC, 1986–87. Mem., Nat. Youth Orchestra of GB, 1955. Younger Brother, Trinity Hse, 1978. Freeman, City of London, 1989; Liveryman, Shipwrights' Co., 1991. *Recreations:* outdoor. *Address:* c/o Royal Bank of Scotland, 142/144 Princes Street, Edinburgh EH2 4EQ. *Club:* Army and Navy.
See also P. J. B. Slater.

SLATER, John Fell, CMG 1972; Assistant Secretary, HM Treasury, 1968–83; *b* 3 July 1924; *s* of J. Alan Slater, FRIBA, and Friede R. Slater (*née* Flight); *m* 1951, Susan Baron; two *s* two *d* (and one *d* decd). *Educ:* Abinger Hill Preparatory Sch.; Leighton Park Sch.; New Coll., Oxford (BA). *Recreations:* gardening, photography. *Address:* 20 Upham Park Road, W4 1PG. *T:* 0181–995 8299.

SLATER, Kenneth Frederick, FEng 1985; FIEE; engineering and defence consultant; *b* 31 July 1925; *s* of Charles Frederick and Emily Gertrude Slater; *m* 1965, Marjorie Gladys Beadsworth, Northampton. *Educ:* Hull Grammar Sch.; Manchester Univ. BSc Tech (Hons). Admiralty Signal Estab. Extension, 1943–46; RRE, 1949–63; UK Mem., NATO Air Defence Planning Team, 1964; Supt, Radar Div., RRE, 1965–68; Asst Dir of Electronics R&D, Min. of Technology, 1968–70, Dir, 1970–71; Head of various groups, RRE, 1971–76; Dep. Dir, RSRE, 1976–78; Dir, Admiralty Surface Weapons Estab., 1978–84; Dir of Engrg, Marconi Underwater Systems Ltd, 1984–88. *Publications:* specialist contribs on Radar to Encyclopaedia Britannica and Encyclopaedic Dictionary of Physics; technical articles. *Recreations:* photography, music. *Address:* Valinor, Blackheath Way, West Malvern WR14 4DR. *T:* Malvern (01684) 567641.

SLATER, Leonard, CBE 1976; JP; DL; *b* 23 July 1908; *s* of S. M. Slater, Oldham, and Heysham, Lancs; *m* 1943, Olga Patricia George (*d* 1983); two *s*. *Educ:* Hulme Grammar School, Oldham; St Catharine's College, Cambridge (MA). British Guiana Exped. 1929; Research at Cambridge, 1930–32; MA 1932. Lecturer in Geography, Univ. of Rangoon, 1932–37; Geography Master, Repton School, 1937. Served War, 1940–45; RE (Survey) in UK, India and SE Asia; Lieut-Col, 1944 and Hon. Lieut-Col, 1946. Univ. of Durham: Geography Dept, Lectr, 1939; Reader, 1948; Pro-Vice-Chancellor, 1969–73; Master, University Coll., Durham, 1953–73. Mem. Peterlee Develt Corp., 1956–63; Chairman: Durham Hosp. Management Cttee, 1961–73; Durham AHA, 1973–77; Mem., Newcastle Regional Hosp. Bd, 1965–69 and 1971–74. JP 1961, DL 1978, Durham. *Publications:* articles in geographical periodicals. *Recreations:* formerly travel, tennis, golf. *Address:* Beddell House, Sherburn Hospital, Durham DH1 2SE.
See also J. C. N. Slater.

SLATER, Prof. Peter James Bramwell, FRSE; Kennedy Professor of Natural History, since 1984, and Head of School of Biological and Medical Sciences, since 1992, University of St Andrews; *b* 26 Dec. 1942; *s* of Dr James Kirkwood Slater, OBE and Margaret Claire Byrom Slater (*née* Bramwell); *m* 1968, Elisabeth Priscilla Vernon Smith; two *s*. *Educ:* Edinburgh Academy; Glenalmond; Univ. of Edinburgh (BSc 1964; PhD 1968; DSc 1983). FIBiol 1986; FRSE 1991. Shaw Macfie Lang Fellow, 1964–66, Demonstrator in Zoology, 1966–68, Univ. of Edinburgh; Lectr in Biology, Univ. of Sussex, 1968–84. Chm., Heads of Univ. Biol Scis, 1994–. Hon. Sec., Assoc. for Study of Animal Behaviour, 1973–78, Hon. Pres., 1986–89. European Editor, Animal Behaviour, 1979–82; Editor: Advances in the Study of Behavior, 1989– (Associate Editor, 1982–88); Science Progress, 1983–89. *Publications:* Sex Hormones and Behaviour, 1978; (ed with T. R. Halliday) Animal Behaviour, 1983; An Introduction to Ethology, 1985; (ed) Collins Encyclopaedia of Animal Behaviour, 1986; numerous articles in learned jls. *Recreations:* ornithology, writing, listening to music. *Address:* School of Biological and Medical Sciences, University of St Andrews, Fife KY16 9TS. *T:* St Andrews (01334) 463500.
See also Sir J. C. K. Slater.

SLATER, Richard Mercer Keene, CMG 1962; *b* 27 May 1915; *s* of late Samuel Henry Slater, CMG, CIE; *m* 1939, Barbara Janet Murdoch; four *s*. *Educ:* Eton; Magdalene Coll., Cambridge. Indian Civil Service (Punjab Commission), 1939–47; joined HM Diplomatic Service, 1947; served in Karachi (on secondment to Commonwealth Relations Office), Lima, Moscow, Rangoon and Foreign Office; Ambassador to Cuba, 1966–70; High Comr in Uganda and Ambassador to Rwanda, 1970–72; Asst Under-Sec. of State, FCO, 1973. Adviser to Commercial Union Assurance Co., 1973–81. Chm., Hampshire Br., CPRE, 1974–85. *Address:* 5 High Street, Odiham, Hook, Hants RG29 1LE.

SLATER, William Bell, CBE 1982; VRD 1959; FCIT; Chairman, The Mersey Docks & Harbour Co., 1987–93; Managing Director, The Cunard Steam-Ship Co. plc, 1974–85 (Director, 1971–85 and 1986–88); Director, Trafalgar House plc, 1975–88; *b* 7 Jan. 1925; *s* of William Bell and Mamie Slater; *m* 1950, Jean Mary Kiernan; two *s*. *Educ:* Lancaster Royal Grammar Sch. FCIT 1970. National Service, RM, 1943–47 (Captain, 3rd Commando Bde); RM Reserve, 1949–63 (Lt-Col and CO Merseyside Unit; Hon. Col, 1986–91). Trainee, Thos & Jno Brocklebank Ltd, 1947, Dir 1966–85, also Chm.; Ops Dir, 1968, Dep. Man. Dir, 1969, Man. Dir, 1971–72, Chm. 1972–85, Cunard Brocklebank Ltd. Director: Atlantic Container Line Ltd, 1968–85 (Chm., 1977–78 and 1982–83); Associated Container Transportation (Australia) Ltd, 1974–85 (Chm., 1982–85); Associated Container Transportation Ltd, 1974–85 (Chm., 1982–85); The Mersey Docks & Harbour Co., 1980– (Dep. Chm., 1985–87). External Dir, British Internat. Freight Assoc., 1989–94. Vice-Pres., CIT, 1984–87; Pres., Inst. of Freight Forwarders Ltd, 1987–88. Gen. Comr of Income Tax, 1987–. Order of El Istiqlal (2nd Cl.), Jordan, 1972. *Recreations:* Rugby and cricket (formerly Senior Club player). *Address:* Gayton Court, 419 Woodham Lane, Woodham, Addlestone, Surrey KT15 3PP. *T:* Byfleet (01932) 349389. *Club:* Naval.

SLATER, William John, (Bill Slater), OBE 1982; President, British Amateur Gymnastics Association, since 1989; Director of National Services, Sports Council, 1984–89; *b* 29 April 1927; *s* of John Rothwell Slater and Ethel May Slater; *m* 1952, Marion Warr; two *s* two *d*. *Educ:* Clitheroe Royal Grammar Sch.; Carnegie Coll. of Physical Educn (Dip. in Phys. Educn); Univ. of Birmingham (BSc). FPEA 1984. Dep. Dir, Crystal Palace Nat. Sports Centre, 1963–64; Dir of Phys. Educn, Univ. of Liverpool, 1964–70 (Warden, McNair Hall, 1966–69); Dir of Phys. Educn, Univ. of Birmingham, 1970–83. Member: Central Adv. Council for Educn (Newsom Cttee), 1961–63; Cttee of Enquiry into Association Football (Chester Cttee), 1966–68; Sports Council, 1974–83; Nat. Olympic Cttee, 1990–. Chairman: Cttee of Advrs, Sports Aid Foundn, 1978–; West Midlands Council for Sport and Recreation, 1979–83. Hon. Advisor, Foundn for Sport and the Arts, 1991–. Wolverhampton Wanderers Football Club, 1952–62; rep. England in Association Football, 1951–60; Olympic Games, Helsinki, 1952; World Cup (Assoc. Football), Sweden, 1958. Hon. MSc Birmingham, 1990. Footballer of the Year, 1960. *Recreations:* games and sports of all kinds. *Address:* 10 Inglis Road, Ealing, W5 3RN. *T:* 0181–992 7349.

SLATTERY, Dr David Antony Douglas, MBE (mil.) 1958; Chief Medical Officer, Rolls-Royce plc, 1973–92; Dean, Faculty of Occupational Medicine, Royal College of Physicians, 1988–91 (Vice-Dean, 1986–88); *b* 28 Jan. 1930; *s* of Rear-Adm. Sir Matthew Slattery, KBE, CB and Mica Mary Slattery (*née* Swain); *m* 1st, 1954, Mary Winifred Miller; two *s* two *d*; 2nd, 1974, Claire Louise McGuinness; one *s*. *Educ:* Ampleforth Coll.; St Thomas' Hosp., London. MB BS; FFOM RCPI 1977; FFOM RCP 1981; FRCP 1986. Capt., RAMC, 1954–58. MO, E Midlands Gas Bd, 1959–69; Manager, Health and Safety, BSC, Rotherham, 1969–73. Special Lectr, Dept of Community Health, Nottingham Univ., 1978–93; Vis. Prof., Dept of Public Health, Univ. of Liverpool, 1992–. Consultant Advr in occupational medicine, RAF, 1987–; Advr on occupational health policy, Mersey RHA, 1992–94. Dir, Occupational Health Service, Aintree Hosps NHS Trust, 1993–94. Member: Standing Med. Adv. Cttee, DHSS, 1988–91; Adv. Bd, CS Occupational Health Service, 1988–91. Industrial Health Advr, Derbys Br., BRCS, 1976–93. *Publications:* papers on occupational medicine and the employment of the disabled. *Recreations:* history, fishing, people. *Address:* 99 South Quay, Wapping Dock, Liverpool L3 4BW. *T:* 0151–707 2022. *Club:* Royal Society of Medicine.

SLATYER, Prof. Ralph Owen, AC 1993 (AO 1982); FRS 1975; Distinguished Scholar in Residence, Australian National University, since 1992; *b* 16 April 1929; *s* of Thomas Henry and Jean Slatyer; *m* 1953, June Helen Wade; one *s* two *d*. *Educ:* Univ. of Western Australia (DSc (Agric.). CSIRO Res. Scientist, subseq. Chief Res. Scientist, 1951–67; Prof., Inst. of Advanced Studies, 1967–89, Dir, Res. Sch. of Biol Scis, 1984–89, ANU; Chief Scientist, Dept of Prime Minister and Cabinet, Australia, 1989–92; Mem. and Exec. Officer, Prime Minister's Science Council, 1989–92. Aust. Amb. to UNESCO, 1978–81. Member: Australian Res. Grants Cttee, 1969–72; Nat. Capital Planning Cttee, 1973–76; Aust. Nat. Commn for UNESCO, 1975–78 (Chm., 1976–78); Policy Adv. Council and Bd of Management, Aust. Centre for Internat. Agricl Research, 1981–85; President: Ecol Soc. of Austr., 1969–71; UNESCO Man and the Biosphere Programme, 1977–81; UNESCO World Heritage Cttee, 1981–83; ICSU Sci. Cttee on Problems of the Environment, 1982–85; ANZAAS, 1983; Chairman: Aust. Biol. Resources Study, 1981–84; Australian Science and Technology Council, 1982–87; Co-ordination Cttee on Sci. and Technol., 1989–92; Dep. Chm., Nat. Greenhouse Adv. Cttee, 1989–93. FAA 1967; Fellow, Aust. Acad. of Technol Scis and Engrg, 1992. Hon. DSc: Univ. of WA, 1983; Duke Univ., 1986; Univ. of Qld, 1992. Edgeworth David Medal, 1960; Austr. Medal of Agric. Sci., 1968; ANZAAS Medal, 1991. For. Associate, US Nat. Acad. of Sciences, 1976; Hon. For. Mem., Amer. Acad. of Arts and Scis, 1981. *Publications:* (with I. C. McIlroy) Practical Microclimatology, 1961; Plant-Water Relationships, 1967; (ed with R. A. Perry) Arid Lands of Australia, 1969; (ed jtly) Photosynthesis and Photorespiration, 1971; (ed) Plant Response to Climatic Factors, 1974; papers in learned jls. *Recreation:* bushwalking. *Address:* 54 Musgrave Street, Yarralumla, ACT 2600, Australia.

SLAUGHTER, Audrey Cecelia, (Mrs C. V. Wintour); writer and freelance journalist; *d* of Frederick George Smith and Ethel Louise Smith; *m* 1st, 1950, W. A. Slaughter (marr. diss.); one *s* one *d*; 2nd, 1979, Charles Vere Wintour, *qv*. *Educ:* Chislehurst High Sch., Stand Grammar Sch., Manchester. Editor, Honey magazine, 1960; founded Petticoat magazine, 1964; columnist, Evening News, 1968; joined National Magazine Co., to edit Vanity Fair, 1969; founded and funded own magazine, Over 21, 1970; after sale to Morgan Grampian, 1972, remained as Dir and Editor until 1979; Associate Editor, Sunday Times, 1979; with husband founded Sunday Express colour magazine, 1981; Founder Editor, Working Woman magazine, 1984–86; Lifestyle Editor, The Independent, 1986–87. *Publications:* Every Man Should Have One (with Margaret Goodman), 1969; Getting Through . . ., 1981; Working Woman's Handbook, 1986; Your Brilliant Career, 1987; Private View (novel), 1990; Blooming (novel), 1992; Unknown Country (novel), 1994. *Recreations:* classical music, theatre, painting. *Address:* 60 East Hatch, Tisbury, Wilts SP3 6PH. *T:* Tisbury (01747) 870880.

SLAUGHTER, Frank Gill, MC; MD, FACS; novelist (self-employed); physician and surgeon (retd); *b* Washington, USA, 25 Feb. 1908; *s* of Stephen Lucius Slaughter and Sallie Nicholson Gill; *m* 1933, Jane Mundy; two *s*. *Educ:* Duke Univ. (AB); Johns Hopkins (MD). Served War, 1942–46 (MC): Major to Lt-Col, US Army Med. Corps. Intern, asst resident, and resident surgeon, Jefferson Hosp., Roanoke, Va, 1930–34; practice, specializing in surgery, Jacksonville, Fla, 1934–42; retired, 1946; Lectr, W. Colston Leigh, Inc., NY City, 1947–49. Res. Diplomate, Amer. Bd of Surgery. Mem., Sons of Amer. Revolution. Presbyterian (Elder). Hon. DHL Jacksonville Univ., 1978. *Publications:* That None Should Die, 1941; Spencer Brade, MD, 1942; Air Surgeon, 1943; Battle Surgeon, 1944; A Touch of Glory, 1945; In a Dark Garden, 1946; The New Science of Surgery, 1946; The Golden Isle, 1947; Sangaree, 1948; Medicine for Moderns, 1948; Divine Mistress, 1949; The Stubborn Heart, 1950; Immortal Magyar, 1950; Fort Everglades, 1951; The Road to Bithynia, 1951; East Side General, 1952; The Galileans, 1953; Storm Haven, 1953; The Song of Ruth, 1954; Apalachee Gold, 1954; The Healer, 1955; Flight from Natchez, 1955; The Scarlet Cord, 1956; The Warrior, 1956; Sword and Scalpel, 1957; The Mapmaker, 1957; Daybreak, 1958; The Thorn of Arimathea, 1958; The Crown and the Cross, 1959; Lorena, 1959; The Land and the Promise, 1960; Pilgrims in Paradise, 1960; Epidemic, 1961; The Curse of Jezebel, 1961; David: Warrior and King, 1962; Tomorrow's Miracle, 1962; Devil's Harvest, 1963; Upon This Rock, 1963; A Savage Place, 1964; The Purple Quest, 1965; Constantine: The Miracle of the Flaming Cross, 1965; Surgeon, USA, 1966; God's Warrior, 1967; Doctor's Wives, 1967; The Sins of Herod, 1968; Surgeon's Choice, 1969; Countdown, 1970; Code Five, 1971; Convention, MD, 1972; Life blood, 1974; Stonewall Brigade, 1975; Plague Ship, 1977; Devil's Gamble, 1978; The Passionate Rebel, 1979; Gospel Fever, 1980; Doctor's Daughters, 1981; Doctors At Risk, 1983; No Greater Love, 1985; Transplant, 1987. *Recreations:* boating, hiking, reading. *Address:* 5051 Yacht Club Road, Jacksonville, FL 32210, USA. *T:* (904) 3897677. *Club:* Timuquana Country (Jacksonville, Fla).

SLAUGHTER, Giles David, MA; Headmaster, University College School, since 1983; *b* 11 July 1937; *s* of Gerald Slaughter and Enid Lillian Slaughter (*née* Crane); *m* 1965, Gillian

Rothwell Shepherd; three *d*. *Educ:* Royal Masonic School; King's College, Cambridge. MA. Pierrepont School, Frensham, 1961–65; Campbell College, Belfast, 1965–68; Stockport Grammar School, 1968–70; Housemaster, Ormiston House, Campbell Coll., 1970–73; Headmaster, Solihull School, 1973–82. Governor: Godolphin and Latymer Sch., 1988–; Cobham Hall, 1989–; Aldwickbury Sch., 1974–; King's Coll. Sch., Wimbledon, 1995–. JP Solihull, 1977–82. FRSA 1985. *Recreations:* gardening, cricket, golf, theatre. *Address:* 5 Redington Road, Hampstead, NW3 7QX. *Club:* East India, Devonshire, Sports and Public Schools.

SLEDGE, Ven. Richard Kitson; Archdeacon of Huntingdon, since 1978; Rector of Hemingford Abbots, 1978–89; *b* 13 April 1930; *s* of Sydney Kitson and Mary Sylvia Sledge; *m* 1958, Patricia Henley (*née* Sear); one *s* two *d* (and one *s* decd). *Educ:* Epsom College; Peterhouse, Cambridge (MA). Curate of Emmanuel, Plymouth, 1954–57; Curate-in-charge of St Stephen's, Exeter, 1957–63; Rector of Dronfield, 1963–78. *Address:* The Rectory, Hemingford Abbots, Huntingdon, Cambs PE18 9AN. *T:* St Ives (01480) 380284.

SLEE, Very Rev. Colin Bruce; Provost of Southwark, since 1994; *b* 10 Nov. 1945; *s* of Herbert Samuel Slee and Miriam Clara May Slee; *m* 1971, Edith Tryon; one *s* two *d*, and one foster *s*. *Educ:* Ealing Grammar Sch.; King's Coll., London (BD, AKC); St Augustine's Coll., Canterbury. Ordained deacon, 1970, priest, 1971; Curate, St Francis, Heartsease, 1970–73; Curate, Great St Mary's, Cambridge, and Chaplain, Girton Coll., Cambridge, 1973–76; Chaplain and Tutor, KCL, 1976–82; Sub-Dean and Canon Residentiary, St Alban's Abbey, 1982–94. *Recreations:* rowing (purple, London Univ., 1967, 1968), gardening, bee keeping. *Address:* Southwark Cathedral, Montague Close, SE1 9DA. *T:* 0171–407 3708; Provost's Lodging, 51 Bankside, SE1 9JE. *T:* 0171–928 6414, *Fax:* 0171–357 7389.

SLEEMAN, His Honour (Stuart) Colin; a Circuit Judge, 1976–86; *s* of Stuart Bertram Sleeman and Phyllis Grace (*née* Pitt); *m* 1944, Margaret Emily, *d* of late William Joseph Farmer; two *s* one *d*. *Educ:* Clifton Coll.; Merton Coll., Oxford (BA 1936, MA 1963). Called to the Bar, Gray's Inn, 1938; Bencher, 1974. World War II: Admin. Officer, Prize Dept, Min. of Economic Warfare, 1939–40; Lt-Col 16th-5th Lancers; Staff Captain: RAC Wing, Combined Trng Centre, 1941; 6th Armoured Div., 1942; Adjt, RAC Range, Minehead, 1942–44; Asst Judge Advocate Gen., HQ Allied Land Forces, SE Asia, 1945. London Corresp., Scottish Law Rev., 1949–54; a Recorder, 1975–76. *Publications:* The Trial of Gozawa Sadaichi and Nine Others, 1948; (with S. C. Silkin) The 'Double Tenth' Trial, 1950. *Recreations:* travel, genealogy. *Address:* West Walls, Cotmandene, Dorking, Surrey RH4 2BL. *T:* Dorking (01306) 883616.
See also S. P. Sleeman.

SLEEMAN, Stuart Philip; His Honour Judge Sleeman; a Circuit Judge, since 1993; *s* of His Honour (Stuart) Colin Sleeman, *qv*; *m* 1973, Elisabeth Nina Brann; one *s* two *d*. *Educ:* Cranleigh Sch.; Merton Coll., Oxford (BA Jurisprudence 1969; MA 1972). Called to the Bar, Gray's Inn, 1970; a Recorder, 1986–93. Chm., Old Cranleighan Soc., 1984–; Gov., Cranleigh Sch., 1989–. *Recreations:* Oxford occasional hockey (Surrey umpire), music, history (in particular the Reformation). *Address:* 5 Essex Court, EC4Y 9AH.

SLEEP, Wayne; dancer, actor, choreographer; *b* Plymouth, 17 July 1948. *Educ:* Hartlepool; Royal Ballet Sch. (Leverhulme Scholar). Graduated into Royal Ballet, 1966; Soloist, 1970; Principal, 1973; roles in: Giselle; Dancers at a Gathering; The Nutcracker; Romeo and Juliet; The Grand Tour; Elite Syncopations; Swan Lake; The Four Seasons; Les Patineurs; Petroushka (title role); Cinderella; The Dream; Pineapple Poll; Mam'zelle Angot; 4th Symphony; La Fille mal gardée; A Month in the Country; A Good Night's Sleep (gala); Coppelia, English Nat. Ballet, 1994; chor., with Robert North, David & Goliath; also roles in operas, A Midsummer Night's Dream and Aida; roles created for him by Sir Frederick Ashton, Dame Ninette de Valois, Sir Kenneth MacMillan, Rudolf Nureyev, John Neumeier, Joe Layton and many others. *Theatre:* Ariel in The Tempest, New Shakespeare Co.; title role in Pinocchio, Birmingham Rep.; genie in Aladdin, Palladium; soldier in The Soldier's Tale, QEH, 1980 and 1981; Truffaldino in The Servant of Two Masters; chor. and played lead in The Point, Mermaid; Mr Mistoffelees in Cats, New London, 1981; co-starred in Song and Dance, Palace, 1982, Shaftesbury, 1990 (video, 1984); Cabaret, Strand, 1986; chor. Savoy Suite, 1993. Formed own company, DASH, 1980: Chichester Fest., 1980, national tour and Sadler's Wells, 1982, Apollo Victoria and national tour, Christmas season, Dominion, 1983; danced in and jtly choreographed Bits and Pieces, Dominion, 1989. *Films:* The Virgin Soldiers; The First Great Train Robbery; The Tales of Beatrix Potter, 1971. Chor. films and television, inc. Adam's Rib, and appeared in many television progs inc. Dizzy Feet and series, The Hot Shoe Show, 1983, 1984; Tony Lumpkin in She Stoops to Conquer, radio. Show Business Personality of the Year, 1983. *Publication:* Variations on Wayne Sleep, 1983. *Recreation:* entertaining. *Address:* c/o London Management, 235 Regent Street, W1R 7AG. *Clubs:* YMCA, Zanzibar.

SLEIGHT, Prof. Peter, MD (Cantab), DM (Oxon), FRCP; FACC; Field-Marshal Alexander Professor of Cardiovascular Medicine in the University of Oxford, and Fellow of Exeter College, Oxford, 1973–94, now Emeritus Professor and Fellow; *b* 27 June 1929; *s* of William and Mary Sleight, Boston Spa, Yorks; *m* 1953, Gillian France; two *s*. *Educ:* Leeds Grammar Sch.; Gonville and Caius Coll., Cambridge; St Bartholomew's Hosp., London. Ho. Phys. and Ho. Surg., Med. and Surg. Professorial Units, Bart's, 1953; Sen. Registrar, St George's Hosp., London, 1959–64; Bissinger Fellow, Cardiovascular Research Unit, Univ. of California, San Francisco, 1961–63; MRC Scientific Officer, Depts of Physiology and Medicine, Univ. of Oxford, 1964–66; Consultant Physician, Radcliffe Infirmary, Oxford, 1966–73; Visiting Prof., Univ. of Sydney (Warren McDonald Sen. Overseas Fellow of Aust. Heart Foundn), 1972–73; Hon. Prof. of Medicine, Federal Univ. of Pernambuco, 1975. Civil Consultant in Medicine, RAF, 1985–. Vice Pres., ASH, 1994– (Chm., 1982–93); President: British Hypertension Soc., 1993–; World Hypertension League, 1995–; Member Council: Internat. Soc. of Hypertension, 1978–86; European Soc. of Cardiology, 1983–88. Mem. Editorial Bd, British Heart Jl, 1976–83; Editor, Jl of Cardiovascular Res., 1983–92. Young Investigators Award, Amer. Coll. of Cardiology, 1963; Evian Prize, 1988; Merck Sharp and Dohme Award, Internat. Soc. of Hypertension, 1990. *Films:* Control of Circulation; History of Hypertension (Medal, BMA Scientific Film Competition, 1981). *Publications:* Modern Trends in Cardiology, 1976; (ed) Arterial Baroreceptors and Hypertension, 1981; Hypertension, 1982; (ed) Scientific Foundations of Cardiology, 1983; (with D. Eckberg) Human arterial baro reflexes in Health and Disease, 1992; contribs on nervous control of the circulation, hypertension and treatment of myocardial infarction in: Circulation Research; Jl Physiol; Lancet (Chm., Internat. Studies of Infarct Survival). *Recreations:* sailing, golf, travel. *Address:* Wayside, 32 Crown Road, Wheatley, Oxon OX33 1UL. *Club:* Royal Air Force.

SLEIGHT, Sir Richard, 4th Bt *cr* 1920, of Weelsby Hall, Clee; *b* 27 May 1946; *s* of Sir John Frederick Sleight, 3rd Bt and of Jacqueline Margaret, *o d* of late Maj. H. R. Carter, Brisbane, Queensland; *S* father, 1990; *m* 1978, Marie-Thérèse, *o d* of O. M. Stepan, Bromley, Kent; two *s*. *Heir:* *s* James Alexander Sleight, *b* 5 Jan. 1981. *Address:* c/o National Westminster Bank, 22 George Street, Richmond, Surrey TW9 1JW.

SLEVIN, Brian Francis Patrick, CMG 1975; OBE 1973; QPM 1968; CPM 1965; *b* 13 Aug. 1926; *s* of late Thomas and Helen Slevin; *m* 1972, Constance Gay (*d* 1991), *e d* of late Major Ronald Moody and of Amy Moody; one *s*. *Educ:* Blackrock Coll., Ireland. Palestine Police, 1946–48; Royal Hong Kong Police, 1949–79; Directing Staff, Overseas Police Courses, Metropolitan Police Coll., Hendon, London, 1955–57; Director, Special Branch, 1966–69; Sen. Asst Comr of Police, Comdg Kowloon Dist, 1969–70; Dir, Criminal Investigation Dept, 1971; Dep. Comr of Police, 1971, Comr of Police, 1974–79, Hong Kong; retired 1979. *Recreations:* walking, golf, reading, painting. *Address:* Lantau Lodge, 152 Coonanbarra Road, Wahroonga, Sydney, NSW 2076, Australia. *T:* (2) 4896671. *Clubs:* East India, Royal Automobile; Hong Kong, Royal Hong Kong Golf, Royal Hong Kong Jockey (Hong Kong).

SLEVIN, Maurice Louis, MD; FRCP; Consultant Physician, Medical Oncology Department, St Bartholomew's and Homerton Hospitals, since 1982; *b* 2 July 1949; *s* of David Slevin and Nita (*née* Rosenbaum); *m* 1st, 1975, Cherry Jacobsohn (marr. diss. 1987); two *d*; 2nd, 1993, Nicola Jane Harris. *Educ:* Univ. of Cape Town (MB ChB 1973; MD 1984). MRCP 1978, FRCP 1989. Registrar in General Medicine, Groote Schuur Hosp., Cape Town, 1977–78; Registrar in Med. Oncology, St Bartholomew's Hosp., 1978–80, Sen. Registrar, 1980–82. Chm. and Trustee, BACUP, 1987–. *Publications:* Randomised Trials in Cancer, 1986; Metastases, 1988; Challenging Cancer: from chaos to control, 1991; numerous pubns on clinical oncology, clinical pharmacology and psychosocial oncology. *Address:* Medical Oncology Department, St Bartholomew's Hospital, West Smithfield, EC1A 7BE. *T:* 0171–606 6662; 134 Harley Street, W1N 1DJ. *T:* 0171–224 0685.

SLIGO, 11th Marquess of, *cr* 1800; **Jeremy Ulick Browne;** Baron Mount Eagle 1760; Viscount Westport 1768; Earl of Altamont 1771; Earl of Clanricarde 1543 and 1800; Baron Mounteagle (UK) 1806; *b* 4 June 1939; *s* of 10th Marquess of Sligo and of José Gauche; *S* father, 1991; *m* 1961, Jennifer June, *d* of Major Derek Cooper, Dunlewey, Co. Donegal, and Mrs C. Heber Percy, Pophleys, Radnage; five *d*. *Educ:* St Columba's College, Eire; Royal Agricultural College, Cirencester. *Heir:* cousin Sebastian Ulick Browne, *b* 27 May 1964. *Address:* Westport House, Co. Mayo, Eire.

SLIM, family name of **Viscount Slim.**

SLIM, 2nd Viscount *cr* 1960, of Yarralumla and Bishopston; **John Douglas Slim,** OBE 1973; DL; Chairman, 1976–91, and non-executive Deputy Chairman, since 1991, Peek plc (formerly Peek Holdings); Director, Trailfinders Ltd, since 1984, and a number of other companies; *b* 20 July 1927; *s* of Field Marshal the 1st Viscount Slim, KG, GCB, GCMG, GCVO, GBE, DSO, MC, and Aileen (*d* 1993), *d* of Rev. J. A. Robertson, MA, Edinburgh; *S* father, 1970; *m* 1958, Elisabeth, *d* of Arthur Rawdon Spinney, CBE; two *s* one *d*. *Educ:* Prince of Wales Royal Indian Military College, Dehra Dun. Indian Army, 6 Gurkha Rifles, 1945–48; Argyll and Sutherland Highlanders, 1948; SAS, 1952; Staff Coll., Camberley, 1961; Brigade Major, HQ Highland Infantry Bde (TA), 1962–64; JSSC 1964; Lt-Col 1967; Comdr, 22 Special Air Service Regt, 1967–70; GSO1 (Special Forces) HQ UK Land Forces, 1970–72; retired 1972. President, Burma Star Association, 1971–. Vice-Pres., Britain-Australia Soc., 1988– (Chm., 1978–84); Vice-Chm., Arab-British Chamber of Commerce and Industry, 1977–. Master, Clothworkers' Co., 1995–96. FRGS 1983. DL Greater London, 1988. *Heir:* *s* Hon. Mark William Rawdon Slim [*b* 13 Feb. 1960; *m* 1992, Harriet Laura, *yr d* of Jonathan Harrison; one *s*]. *Address:* House of Lords, Westminster, SW1A 0PW. *Clubs:* White's, Special Forces.

SLINGER, Edward; His Honour Judge Slinger; a Circuit Judge, since 1995; *b* 2 Feb. 1938; *s* of Thomas Slinger and Rhoda (*née* Bradshaw); *m* 1965, Rosalind Margaret Jewitt; two *s* two *d*. *Educ:* Accrington Grammar Sch.; Balliol Coll., Oxford (Dist. Law Mods 1956; BA 1958). Admitted solicitor (with Hons), 1961; Partner, Ramsbottom & Co., Solicitors, Blackburn, 1964–95; Dep. Registrar, 1982–88; Asst Recorder, 1988–92; Recorder, 1992–95. Pres., Blackburn Incorporated Law Assoc., 1986; Mem., Immigration Law Sub-cttee, Law Soc., 1990–95. Lancashire County Cricket Club: Captain, 2nd XI, 1967–75; Mem. Cttee, 1969–; Vice-Chm., 1985–95; Trustee, 1978–. Dep. Chm., Discipline Cttee, TCCB, 1990–. Governor: Samlesbury C of E Sch., Lancs, 1986–; Westholme Sch., Blackburn, 1985–. *Recreation:* cricket. *Address:* c/o Court Administrator's Office, 10 Winckley Square. Preston, Lancs PR1 3JJ. *T:* Preston (01772) 821451. *Club:* MCC.

SLINGER, William, CBE 1991; *b* 27 Oct. 1917; *yr s* of late William Slinger and Maud Slinger, Newcastle, Co. Down; *m* 1944, Muriel, *o d* of late R. J. Johnston, Belfast; three *d*. *Educ:* Methodist Coll., Belfast; Queen's Univ., Belfast (BComSc). Entered Northern Ireland Civil Service, 1937; Private Secretary: to Minister of Labour, 1942–43 and 1945–46; to Minister of Public Security, 1944; Sec. to Nat. Arbitration Tribunal (NI), 1946–48; Principal, Min. of Labour and Nat. Insurance, Industrial Relations Div., 1954–60; Asst Sec. and Head of Industrial Relations Div., 1961–69; Sec., Dept of Community Relations, 1969–75; Dep. Sec., Dept of Educn for NI, 1975–77. CIMgt. *Recreations:* gardening, walking. *Address:* Cairnfield, Circular Road, Belfast BT4 2GD. *T:* Belfast (01232) 768240. *Clubs:* Ulster Reform (Belfast); Civil Service (N Ireland).

SLIPMAN, Sue, OBE 1994; Director, London TEC Council, since 1995; *b* 3 Aug. 1949; *d* of Marks Slipman and Doris Barham; one *s*. *Educ:* Stockwell Manor Comprehensive School; Univ. of Wales (BA Hons 1st Class English; Post Graduate Cert Ed); Univs of Leeds and London. Sec. and Nat. Pres., Nat. Union of Students, 1975–78; Mem., Adv. Council for Adult and Continuing Educn, 1978–79; Area Officer, Nat. Union of Public Employees, 1979–85; Dir, Nat. Council for One Parent Families, 1985–95. Contested (SDP/Alliance) Hayes and Harlington, 1987. Mem. Exec., NCCL, 1974–75, Vice-Chair, British Youth Council, 1977–78; Chair: Women for Social Democracy, 1983–86; Advice Guidance and Counselling Lead Body, 1992–; Member: Exec. and Chair of Training, 300 Group, 1985–86; Exec., London Voluntary Service Council, 1986–; Women's Issues Wkg Gp, Dept of Employment, 1992–94. Dir, London East TEC, 1990–; Trustee, Full Employment UK, 1990–; Dir, Social Market Foundn, 1992–. *Publications:* chapter in The Re-Birth of Britain, 1983; Helping Ourselves to Power: a handbook for women on the skills of public life, 1986. *Address:* London TEC Council, 13th Floor, Westminster Tower, 3 Albert Embankment, SE1 7SX.

SLIVE, Prof. Seymour; Gleason Professor of Fine Arts at Harvard University, 1973–91, Emeritus since 1991; Director, Fogg Art Museum, 1975–82, sometime Elizabeth and John Moors Cabot Director of Harvard Art Museums; *b* Chicago, 15 Sept. 1920; *s* of Daniel Slive and Sonia (*née* Rapoport); *m* 1946, Zoya Gregorovna Sandomirsky; one *s* two *d*. *Educ:* Univ. of Chicago. BA 1943; PhD 1952. Served US Navy, Lieut, CO Small Craft, 1943–46. Instructor in Art History, Oberlin Coll., 1950–51; Asst Prof. and Chm. of Art Dept, Pomona Coll., 1952–54; Asst Prof. 1954–57, Assoc. Prof. 1957–61, Prof., 1961–73, Chm. of Dept 1968–71, Fine Arts, Harvard Univ.; Exchange Prof., Univ. of Leningrad, 1961. Ryerson Lectr, Yale, 1962. Slade Prof. of Fine Art, Univ. of Oxford, 1972–73. Trustee, Solomon R. Guggenheim Foundn, 1978–. FAAAS 1964; Corresp. FBA 1995. For. Mem., Netherlands Soc. of Sciences, 1971. Hon. MA Harvard, 1958; Hon. MA Oxford, 1972. Officer, Order of Orange Nassau, 1962. *Publications:* Rembrandt and His

Critics: 1630–1730, 1953; Drawings of Rembrandt, 1965; (with J. Rosenberg and E. H. ter Kuile) Dutch Art and Architecture: 1600–1800, 1965, 2nd edn, 1978; Frans Hals, 3 vols, 1970–74; Jacob van Ruisdael, 1981; Frans Hals, 1989; Dutch Painting: 1600–1800, 1995; contribs to learned jls. *Address:* 1 Walker Street Place, Cambridge, MA 02138, USA.

SLOAN, Sir Andrew (Kirkpatrick), Kt 1991; QPM 1983; Chief Constable of Strathclyde, 1985–91; *b* 27 Feb. 1931; *s* of Andrew Kirkpatrick Sloan and Amelia Sarah (*née* Vernon), Kirkcudbright; *m* 1953, Agnes Sofie Storvik, Trondheim, Norway; three *d. Educ:* Kirkcudbright Acad.; Dumfries Acad.; Open Univ. (BA). Joined RN as boy seaman, 1947; served at home and abroad in cruisers and submarines, and worked in industry in Norway, 1947–55; joined W Riding Constab., 1955; apptd to CID, 1963; Det. Sgt, Barnsley, 1964; Det. Insp., Reg. Crime Squad, Leeds, 1966; Det. Chief Insp., Goole and Pontefract, 1969; Det. Supt, Reg. Crime Squad, Wakefield, 1970; Chief Supt, Toller Lane Div., Bradford, 1975; Asst Chief Constable, Operations, Lincolnshire Police, 1976–79; National Co-ordinator, Regional Crime Squads of England and Wales, 1979–81; Dep. Chief Constable, Lincs, 1981–83; Chief Constable, Beds, 1983–85. Pres., ACPO (Scotland), 1987–88. *Recreations:* reading, travel, walking, conversation. *Address:* c/o Royal Bank of Scotland, 151 High Street, Dumfries DG1 2RA.

SLOAN, Norman Alexander; QC (Scot.) 1953; Legal Adviser, British Shipbuilders, 1978–81; *b* 27 Jan. 1914; *s* of George Scott Sloan and Margaret Hutcheson Smith; *m* 1st, 1944, Peggy Perry (*d* 1982); two *s* one *d*; 2nd, 1983, Norma Olsen (*d* 1985); 3rd, 1988, Beryl Maureen Hogg, Dublin. *Educ:* Glasgow Academy; Glasgow University (BL). Solicitor, 1935; Admitted to Faculty of Advocates, 1939; Served in RNVR 1940–46. Lecturer in Industrial Law, Edinburgh University, 1946–51; Standing Counsel to Department of Health for Scotland, 1946–51; Advocate-Depute, 1951–53. Director: The Shipbuilding Employers' Federation, 1955–68; Shipbuilders and Repairers Nat. Assoc., 1968–72; Swan Hunter Group Ltd, 1973–77; Swan Hunter Shipbuilders Ltd, 1973–78. *Recreations:* golf, gardening. *Address:* Timbers, 1 Mapleleaf, Coldwaltham, Pulborough, West Sussex RH20 1LN.

SLOANE, Ian Christopher; HM Diplomatic Service; Ambassador to Mongolia, since 1994; *b* 28 Jan. 1938; *s* of Albert Henry Sloane and Ivy Rose (*née* Dennis); *m* 1968, June Barton; two *s. Educ:* Lewes Co. Grammar Sch. for Boys; DMS Poly. of Central London 1971. Joined FO, 1956; RAF, 1957–59; FO, 1959–60; MECAS, 1960–61; Vice-Consul: Khartoum, 1961–64; Algiers, 1964–66; Saigon, 1967; 2nd Secretary: Dacca, 1967; Lahore, 1967–70; FCO, 1970–73; UK Disarmament Delegn, Geneva, 1973–74; 1st Sec., Hd of Chancery and Consul, Seoul, 1974–77; 1st Sec. (Econ.), Bonn, 1978–82; W European Dept, FCO, 1983–85; Cultural Attaché, Moscow, 1985; 1st Sec. (Commercial), Ankara, 1986–88; Overseas Estate Dept, FCO, 1989–90; Counsellor and Dep. Consul-Gen, New York, 1990–93. *Recreations:* tennis, bridge, collecting antique maps, travelling. *Address:* c/o Foreign and Commonwealth Office, King Charles Street, SW1A 2AH.

SLOANE, Peter James, PhD; Jaffrey Professor of Political Economy, University of Aberdeen, since 1984; *b* 6 Aug. 1942; *s* of John Joseph Sloane and Elizabeth (*née* Clarke); *m* 1969, Avril Mary Urquhart; one *s. Educ:* Cheadle Hulme Sch.; Univ. of Sheffield (BAEcon Hons 1964); Univ. of Strathclyde (PhD 1966). Asst Lectr in Pol. Econ., Univ. of Aberdeen, 1966–67, Lectr in Pol. Econ., 1967–69; Lectr in Indust. Econs, Univ. of Nottingham, 1969–75; Economic Adviser, Unit for Manpower Studies, Dept of Employment (on secondment), 1973–74; Prof. of Econs and Management, Paisley Coll., 1975–84. Vis. Prof. (Commonwealth Fellow), Faculty of Business, McMaster Univ., Canada, 1978. Member: ESRC (formerly SSRC), 1979–85; Mergers Cttee, SHEFC, 1994–; Council, Scottish Economic Soc., 1983–. Sec., REconS Conf. of Heads of Univ. Depts of Econs, 1990–. *Publications:* (with B. Chiplin) Sex Discrimination in the Labour Market, 1976; (ed) Women and Low Pay, 1980; (with H. C. Jain) Equal Employment Issues, 1981; (with B. Chiplin) Tackling Discrimination, 1982; (with D. Carline *et al*) Labour Economics, 1985; monographs on changing patterns of working hours, discrimination and on sport in the market; articles in learned jls, incl. Econ. Jl, Economica, Econs Letters, Applied Econs, Bull. Econ. Res., Oxford Bull. of Econ. Stats, Scottish Jl of Pol. Econ., British Jl of Indust. Relations, and Managerial and Decision Econs. *Recreation:* sport. *Address:* Hillcrest, 45 Friarsfield Road, Cults, Aberdeen AB1 9LB. *T:* Aberdeen (01224) 869412. *Clubs:* Commonwealth Trust; Aboyne Golf.

SLOGGETT, Jolyon Edward, OBE 1995; CEng, FIMarE, FRINA, FICS; Secretary, Institute of Marine Engineers, since 1986; *b* 30 May 1933; *s* of Edward Cornelius Sloggett and Lena May (*née* Norton); *m* 1970, Patricia Marjorie Iverson Ward; two *d. Educ:* John Lyon Sch.; Univ. of Glasgow (BSc). CDipAF. William Denny & Brothers Ltd, Leven Shipyard, Dumbarton, 1951–57 and 1959–60. Served, Royal Navy, TA Sub Lieut (E), RNVR, 1957–58; Houlder Brothers & Co. Ltd, 1960–78, Director, 1972–78; Man. Dir, Offshore, British Shipbuilders Corp., 1978–81; Dir, Vickers Shipbuilding Group, 1979–80; Chm., Vickers Offshore (Projects & Development) Ltd, 1979–81; Consultant to Marine and Offshore Industries, 1981–86. Liveryman, Shipwrights' Co. *Publication:* Shipping Finance, 1984. *Recreations:* sailing, gardening, woodwork. *Address:* Annington House, Steyning, West Sussex BN44 3WA. *T:* Steyning (01903) 812259.

SLOMAN, Sir Albert (Edward), Kt 1987; CBE 1980; DPhil; Vice-Chancellor of University of Essex, 1962–1987; *b* Launceston, Cornwall, 14 Feb. 1921; *y s* of Albert Sloman; *m* 1948, Marie Bernadette, *d* of Leo Bergeron, Cognac, France; three *d. Educ:* Launceston Coll., Cornwall; Wadham Coll., Oxford (Pope Exhibitioner, 1939; Hon. Fellow, 1982). BA Mediæval and Mod. Langs, 1941; MA (Oxon and Dublin); DPhil (Oxon). Served War of 1939–45 (despatches): night-fighter pilot with 219 and 68 squadrons; Flight-Lieut. Lecturer in Spanish, Univ. of California, Berkeley, USA, 1946–47; Reader in Spanish, in charge of Spanish studies, Univ. of Dublin, 1947–53; Fellow TCD, 1950–53; Gilmour Professor of Spanish, University of Liverpool, 1953–62; Dean, Faculty of Arts, 1961–62. Editor of Bulletin of Hispanic Studies, 1953–62. Reith Lecturer, 1963. Chairman: Dept of Education, subseq. British Acad., Studentship Cttee, 1965–87; Cttee of Vice-Chancellors and Principals of UK Univs, 1981–83 (Vice-Chm., 1979–81); Overseas Research Students Fees Support Scheme, 1980–87; Univs' Council for Adult and Continuing Educn, 1984–86; Inter-Univ. and Polytechnic Council, 1985–88; Cttee for Internat. Co-operation in Higher Educn, 1985–88; Selection Cttee of Commonwealth Scholarship Commn, 1986–; Internat. Bd, United World Colls, 1988–92 (Mem., 1985–92); Bd, Univ. of London Inst. of Latin American Studies, 1990–92; Member: Council of Europe Cttee for Higher Educn and Research, 1963–72; Inter-Univ. Council for Higher Educn Overseas, 1964–81; Conf. of European Rectors and Vice-Chancellors, 1965–85 (Pres., 1969–74); Admin. Bd, Internat. Assoc. of Univs, 1965–75 (Vice-Pres., 1970–75); Economic and Social Cttee, EEC, 1973–82; Council, ACU, 1981–87 (Vice-Chm., 1985–87); Commonwealth Scholarship Commn, 1984–; Bd, British Council, 1985–88. Chm. Bd of Governors, Centre for Inf. on Lang. Teaching and Res., 1979–87; Member: Bd of Governors, Guyana Univ., 1966–92; Cttee of Management, British Inst. in Paris, 1982–. Pres., Penzance Library, 1990–. Director: Isys Ltd, 1987–; Close Brothers Business Expansion Secure Share Account cos, 1992–. Hon. Doctorate: Nice, 1974; Essex, 1988; Liverpool, 1989. *Publications:* The Sources of Calderón's El Principe constante, 1950; The Dramatic Craftsmanship of Calderón, 1958; A University in the Making, 1964; articles and reviews in Modern Language Review, Bulletin of Hispanic Studies, Hispanic Review, Romance Philology and other journals. *Recreation:* travel. *Address:* 19 Inglis Road, Colchester CO3 3HU. *Club:* Savile.

SLOMAN, Mrs (Margaret) Barbara; Under Secretary, Management and Personnel Office (formerly Civil Service Department), 1975–84, retired; *b* 29 June 1925; *d* of Charles and Margaret Pilkington-Rogers; *m* 1950, Peter Sloman, *qv*; one *s* one *d. Educ:* Cheltenham Ladies' Coll.; Girton Coll., Cambridge. BA Hons Classics. FIMgt. Asst Principal, Treasury, 1947, Principal 1954–65; Asst Sec., DES, 1965–69; Asst Sec., Civil Service Dept, 1970–75. *Address:* 11 Lowther Road, SW13 9NX. *T:* 0181–748 2196.

SLOMAN, Peter; retired; Education Officer, Association of Metropolitan Authorities, 1974–79; *b* Oct. 1919; *s* of H. N. P. and Mary Sloman (*née* Trinder); *m* 1950, Barbara (*see* M. B. Sloman); one *s* one *d. Educ:* Winchester Coll.; New Coll., Oxford (BA, MA 1945). War Service (RA), 1939–46; TA, 1951–61. Home Civil Service, 1946–74: Under-Secretary, 1968; Min. (later Dept) of Education; Treasury; Ministries of Defence, Land and Natural Resources, Housing and Local Govt; IDC 1960. Principal Admin. Officer: Newham, 1980–83; Surrey, 1985; Principal Administrator, ACC, 1983–88. *Address:* 11 Lowther Road, SW13 9NX. *T:* 0181–748 2196.

SLOSS; *see* Butler-Sloss.

SLOT, Peter Maurice Joseph; His Honour Judge Slot; a Circuit Judge, since 1980; *b* 3 Dec. 1932; *s* of Joseph and Marie Slot; *m* 1962, Mary Eiluned Lewis; two *s* three *d. Educ:* Bradfield Coll.; St John's Coll., Oxford (MA). Called to Bar, Inner Temple, 1957. A Recorder of the Crown Court, 1974–80. *Recreations:* golf, madrigals, argument. *Address:* The Red House, Betchworth, Surrey RH3 7DR. *T:* Betchworth (0173784) 2010. *Club:* Walton Heath Golf.

SLYNN OF HADLEY, Baron *cr* 1992 (Life Peer), of Eggington in the County of Bedfordshire; **Gordon Slynn;** Kt 1976; PC 1992; a Lord of Appeal in Ordinary, since 1992; *b* 17 Feb. 1930; *er s* of John and Edith Slynn; *m* 1962, Odile Marie Henriette Boutin. *Educ:* Sandbach Sch.; Goldsmiths' Coll., Univ. of London (BA; Hon. Fellow, 1993); Trinity Coll., Cambridge (Sen. Schol.; Sub-Lector, 1956–61; MA, LLM). Called to Bar, Gray's Inn, 1956, Bencher, 1970, Treas., 1988. Junior Counsel: Min. of Labour, 1967–68; to the Treasury (Common Law), 1968–74; QC 1974; Leading Counsel to the Treasury, 1974–76. Recorder of Hereford, 1971; a Recorder, and Hon. Recorder of Hereford, 1972–76; a Judge of the High Ct of Justice, QBD, 1976–81; an Advocate Gen., 1981–88, a Judge, 1988–92, Court of Justice of EC, Luxembourg. Pres., Employment Appeal Tribunal, 1978–81. Lecturer in Air Law, LSE, 1958–61; Visiting Professor in Law: Univ. of Durham, 1981–88; Cornell, 1983; KCL, 1985–90; Univ. of Technol., Sydney, 1990–; Nat. Univ. of India, Bangalore, 1992–; Lectures: Irvine, Cornell, 1984; Leon Ladner, Univ. of BC, 1987; Tanner, 1993, Romanes, 1994, Oxford Univ. Chief Steward of Hereford, 1978–. Chm., Exec. Council, Internat. Law Assoc., 1988– (Vice-Chm., 1986–88); Hon. Vice-Pres., Union Internat. des Avocats, 1976– (Vice-Pres., 1973–76). Fellow, Internat. Soc. of Barristers, USA; Mem., American Law Inst.; Hon. Member: Canadian Bar Assoc.; Georgia Trial Lawyers' Assoc.; SPTL. Governor: Internat. Students' Trust, 1979–85, and 1992– (Fellow, 1986–); Sadler's Wells Theatre, 1988–; Chm. Ct of Governors, Mill Hill Sch., 1989–95; Visitor, Mansfield Coll., Oxford, 1995. Trustee, America-European Community Assoc. Trust, 1989–91. President: Bentham Club, 1992; Holdsworth Club, 1993. Master, Broderers' Co., 1994–95. FKC 1995; Hon. Fellow: UC at Buckingham, 1982; St Andrews Coll., Univ. of Sydney, 1991; Liverpool Poly., 1992; Amer. Coll. of Trial Lawyers, 1992. Hon. LLD: Birmingham, 1983; Buckingham, 1983; Exeter, 1985; Univ. of Technol., Sydney, 1991; Bristol Poly. (CNAA), 1992; Sussex, 1992; Stetson, 1993; Staffordshire, 1994; Pace, NY, 1995; Hon. DCL: Durham, 1989; City 1994; Hon. Dr Juris Saarlandes, 1994; DUniv Univ. del Museo Social Argentino, 1994. Hon. Decanus Legis, Mercer Univ., Ga, USA, 1986; Cordell Hull Medal, Samford Univ., Ala, USA, 1993. Chevalier du Tastevin; Commandeur, Confrérie de St Cunibert; Commandeur d'Honneur, Commanderie du Bon Temps du Médoc et des Graves; Chevalier d'Honneur, Confrérie des Comtes de Nice et de Provence. *Publications:* (contrib.) Halsbury's Laws of England, 4th edn; Hamlyn Lectures, 1992; lectures published in legal jls. *Address:* House of Lords, SW1A 0PW. *Clubs:* Athenæum, Beefsteak, Garrick.

SMAILES, George Mason; retired barrister; *b* 23 Jan. 1916; *s* of late Thomas and Kate Smailes; *m* 1939, Evelyn Mabel Jones; one *s* two *d. Educ:* The Leys Sch., Cambridge; Leeds Univ. (LLB); Metropolitan Police College. Solicitor's articled clerk, 1933–37; Station Inspector, Metropolitan Police, 1937–47; served RAF, 1944–45. Called to Bar, Gray's Inn, 1946; practised on North-Eastern Circuit, 1947–67; acted as Deputy County Court Judge and Deputy and Asst Recorder of various boroughs, 1961–68. Part-time legal member of tribunals: Mental Health Review, 1960–67; National Insurance, Local, 1962–65; Medical Appeal (Industrial Injuries), 1965–67; Industrial, 1966–67; Regional Chm. of Industrial Tribunals, Leeds, 1967–82. Associate, Wellington Dist Law Soc. (NZ). *Recreations:* listening to music, gardening. *Clubs:* Leeds (Leeds); Masterton (Masterton).

SMALE, John Gray; Chairman: Executive Committee of Board of Directors, Procter & Gamble Co., since 1990; Board, General Motors Corporation, since 1992; *b* 1 Aug. 1927; *s* of Peter John Smale and Vera Gladys (*née* Gray); *m* 1950, Phyllis Anne Weaver; two *s* two *d. Educ:* Miami Univ., Oxford, Ohio (BS 1949). Procter & Gamble Company: Pres., 1974–81; Pres. and Chief Exec., 1981–86; Chm. Bd and Chief Exec., 1986–90. Hon. LLD: Kenyon Coll., 1974; Miami, 1979; Xavier, 1986; Hon. DSc DePauw, 1983; Hon. DCL St Augustine's Coll., 1985. *Address:* Procter & Gamble Co., PO Box 599, Cincinnati, OH 45201–0599, USA. *T:* (513) 9831100. *Clubs:* Queen City, Commercial, Cincinnati Country (Cincinnati).

SMALL, (Charles) John; development consultant, 1985–94; economist; *b* Chengdu, Sichuan, China, 19 Dec. 1919; *s* of Rev. and Mrs Walter Small; *m* 1946, Jean McNeel; four *d. Educ:* Ontario Agricultural Coll. (BSA); Univ. of Toronto (BA). LLD *hc* Univ. of Guelph, 1975. Royal Canadian Navy service, 1941–46, in N Atlantic, Mediterranean, Normandy and Australia. Mem., Dept of Trade and Commerce, 1949–55; serving in The Hague as Commercial Sec. (Agriculture), 1950–55; Dept of External Affairs, 1955–84; Chinese studies at Univ. of Toronto, 1956–57; seconded to Dept of Trade and Commerce, and apptd Canadian Govt Trade Comr, Hong Kong, 1958–61; Ottawa, 1961–63; Counsellor, Canadian High Commn, Karachi, 1963–65; Perm. Rep. of Canada to OECD, Paris, concurrently Canadian observer, Council of Europe, Strasbourg, 1965–69; Amb. to Pakistan, 1969–72, concurrently Amb. to Afghanistan; Amb. to People's Repub. of China, 1972–76, concurrently to Socialist Repub. of Viet-Nam, 1975–76; Dep. Sec.-Gen. of the Commonwealth, 1978–83; High Comr to Malaysia and concurrently to Brunei, 1983–84. Administrator, Code of Conduct concerning employment practices of Canadian cos operating in South Africa, 1986–90. Chm., Presbyterian World Service and Develt Cttee, 1989–91. Patron, Ex Terra Foundn (Canada/China Dinosaur Project), 1987–. Member: CIIA; Agricl Inst. of Canada; Royal Commonwealth Society, Ottawa. *Recreations:* tennis, golf, swimming.

SMALL, David Purvis, CMG 1988; MBE 1966; HM Diplomatic Service, retired; High Commissioner to Guyana and non-resident Ambassador to Suriname, 1987–90; *b* 17 Oct. 1930; *s* of Joseph Small and Ann (*née* Purvis); *m* 1957, Patricia Kennedy; three *s*. *Educ:* Our Lady's High Sch., Motherwell. National Service, RAF Transport Comd, 1949–51. Metropolitan Vickers, 1951–53; Clerical Officer, Admiralty, Bath, 1953–55; Exec. Officer, HM Dockyard, Rosyth, 1955–58 and Singapore, 1958–60; Admiralty, London, 1960–61; CRO, 1961; Chief Clerk, Madras, 1962–64; Second Sec., Ibadan, 1964–68; Second, later First Sec. and Head of Chancery, Quito, 1968–73; FCO, 1973–76; Head of Chancery, Dacca, 1976–80; First Sec. (Commercial), Stockholm, 1980–82; Counsellor (Economic and Commercial), Copenhagen, 1982–87. *Recreations:* golf, soccer. *Address:* Ashbank, Strachur, Argyll PA27 8BX. *T:* Strachur (01369) 860282. *Club:* Cowal Golf.

SMALL, John; *see* Small, C. J.

SMALL, Prof. John Rankin, CBE 1991; Professor of Accountancy and Finance, Heriot-Watt University, since 1967; *b* 28 Feb. 1933; *s* of David and Annie Small; *m* 1957, Catherine Wood; one *s* two *d*. *Educ:* Harris Academy, Dundee; Dundee Sch. of Econs. BScEcon London; FCCA, FCMA, JDipMA. Dunlop Rubber Co., 1956–60; Lectr, Univ. of Edinburgh, 1960–64; Sen. Lectr, Univ. of Glasgow, 1964–67; Heriot-Watt University: Dean of Faculty of Econ. and Social Studies, 1972–74; Vice-Principal, 1974–78, 1987–90; Dep. Principal, 1990–94. Director: Edinburgh Instruments Ltd, 1976–; Orkney Water Test Centre, Ltd, 1987–; Edinburgh Business School Ltd, 1988–; Environment and Resource Technology Ltd, 1991–; Petroleum Science and Technology Ltd, 1992–; Mem. Bd, Scottish Homes, 1993–. Chm., Nat. Appeal Panel for Entry to Pharmaceutical Lists (Scotland), 1987–. Trustee, Nat. Library of Scotland, 1991–. Pres., Assoc. of Certified Accountants, 1982 (Mem. Council, 1971–); Member: Educn Cttee, Internat. Fedn of Accountants, 1978–85 (Chm., 1978–82); Commn for Local Authority Accounts in Scotland, 1982–92 (Chm., 1983–92); Chm., Inst. of Offshore Engrg, 1988–90 and 1994–. *Publications:* (jtly) Introduction to Managerial Economics, 1966; (contrib.) Business and Accounting in Europe, 1973; (jtly) Acccounting, 1991; articles in accounting and financial jls on accounting and financial management. *Recreation:* golf. *Address:* 39 Caiystane Terrace, Edinburgh EH10 6ST. *T:* 0131–445 2638. *Club:* New (Edinburgh).

SMALL, Dr Ramsay George; Chief Administrative Medical Officer, Tayside Health Board, 1986–89; *b* 5 Feb. 1930; *s* of Robert Small and Ann Ramsay; *m* 1951, Aileen Masterton; four *s*. *Educ:* Harris Academy, Dundee; Univ. of St Andrews (MB ChB); FFCM; FRCPE; DPH. Asst Medical Officer of Health, Ayr CC, 1958–61; Sen. Asst/PMO, City of Dundee, 1961–74; Community Medicine Specialist, Tayside Health Bd, 1974–86. Convener, Scottish Affairs Cttee, Faculty of Community Medicine, 1983–86. Pres., Baptist Union of Scotland, 1972–73. *Recreations:* music, bird watching, mediaeval ecclesiastical buildings. *Address:* 46 Monifieth Road, Broughty Ferry, Dundee DD5 2RX. *T:* Dundee (01382) 778408.

SMALLBONE, Graham; Headmaster, Oakham School, 1985–Aug. 1996; *b* 5 April 1934; *s* of Dr E. G. Smallbone and Jane Mann; *m* 1959, Dorothea Ruth Löw; two *s* two *d*. *Educ:* Uppingham School (music scholar); Worcester College, Oxford (Hadow Scholar; MA; Pres., Oxford Univ. Music Club, 1957). ARCO, ARCM. 2nd Lieut, RA, 1952–54. Asst Master, Oundle Sch., 1958–61; Director of Music: Dean Close Sch., 1961–66; Marlborough Coll., 1967–71; Precentor and Director of Music, Eton, 1971–85. Pres., Music Masters' Assoc., 1975; Warden, Music in Educn Section, ISM, 1977; Pres., International Cello Centre, 1985. Conductor: Cheltenham Chamber Orch., 1963–66; N Wilts Orch., 1966–71; Windsor and Eton Choral Soc., 1971–85. Chm., Peterborough Cathedral Fabric Adv. Cttee, 1990–. FRSA. *Recreations:* music, golf, photography. *Address:* Deanscroft, Oakham School, Station Road, Oakham, Rutland LE15 6QY. *T:* Oakham (01572) 722179. *Club:* East India.

SMALLEY, Very Rev. Stephen Stewart; Dean of Chester since 1987; *b* 11 May 1931; *s* of Arthur Thomas Smalley and May Elizabeth Selina Smalley; *m* 1974, Susan Jane Paterson; one *s* one *d*. *Educ:* Jesus Coll., Cambridge (MA, PhD); Eden Theological Seminary, USA (BD). Assistant Curate, St Paul's, Portman Square, London, 1958–60; Chaplain of Peterhouse, Cambridge, 1960–63; Lectr and Sen. Lectr in Religious Studies, Univ. of Ibadan, Nigeria, 1963–69; Lectr in New Testament, Univ. of Manchester, 1970–77, Sen. Lectr, 1977 (also Warden of St Anselm Hall, 1972–77); Canon Residentiary and Precentor of Coventry Cathedral, 1977–86, Vice-Provost, 1986. Mem., C of E Doctrine Commn, 1981–86. Mem., Studiorum Novi Testamenti Soc., 1965–. Manson Meml Lectr, Univ. of Manchester, 1986. *Publications:* Building for Worship, 1967; Heaven and Hell (Ibadan), 1968; The Spirit's Power (Achimota), 1972; ed, Christ and Spirit in the New Testament, 1973; John: Evangelist and Interpreter, 1978, USA 1984; 1, 2, 3 John, 1984; Thunder and Love, 1994; numerous articles in learned jls, incl. New Testament Studies, Novum Testamentum, Jl of Biblical Lit. *Recreations:* literature, music, drama, travel. *Address:* The Deanery, 7 Abbey Street, Chester CH1 2JF. *T:* Chester (01244) 351380; Hadrians, Bourton-on-the-Hill, Moreton-in-Marsh, Gloucestershire GL56 9AE. *T:* Blockley (01386) 700564. *Clubs:* City, Business (Chester).

SMALLMAN, Barry Granger, CMG 1976; CVO 1972; HM Diplomatic Service, retired; Founder, Granger Consultancies, 1984; *b* 22 Feb. 1924; *s* of late C. Stanley Smallman, CBE, ARCM, and Ruby Marian Granger; *m* 1952, Sheila Knight; two *s* one *d*. *Educ:* St Paul's School; Trinity College, Cambridge (Major Scholar, MA). Served War of 1939–45, Intelligence Corps, Australia 1944–46. Joined Colonial Office, 1947; Assistant Private Secretary to Secretary of State, 1951–52; Principal, 1953; attached to United Kingdom Delegation to United Nations, New York, 1956–57, 1958, 1961, 1962; seconded to Government of Western Nigeria, Senior Assistant Secretary, Governor's Office, Ibadan, 1959–60; transferred to CRO, 1961; British Deputy High Comr in Sierra Leone, 1963–64; British Dep. High Comr in NZ, 1964–67; Imp. Defence Coll., 1968; FCO, 1969–71; Counsellor and Consul-Gen., British Embassy, Bangkok, 1971–74; British High Comr to Bangladesh, 1975–78; Resident Diplomatic Service Chm., Civil Service Selection Bd, 1978–81; High Comr to Jamaica and non-resident Ambassador to Haiti, 1982–84. Mem. Governing Council: SPCK, 1984– (Vice Chm., 1993–); Leprosy Mission, 1985–; St Lawrence Coll., Ramsgate, 1984–; Benenden Sch., 1985–92 (Chm., 1986–92). *Recreations:* tennis, golf, making and listening to music, light verse, bird watching. *Address:* Beacon Shaw, Benenden, Kent TN17 4BU. *T:* Cranbrook (01580) 240625.

SMALLMAN, David Leslie, LVO 1990; HM Diplomatic Service; Governor and Commander-in-Chief, St Helena and dependencies, since 1995; *b* 29 April 1940; *s* of Leslie Alfred Smallman and Millicent Jean Smallman (*née* Burton); *m* 1st, 1967 (marr. diss.); one *s*; 2nd, 1979, Sandra Jill (*née* Browne); one step *s* one step *d*. *Educ:* St Clement Danes; Kingston upon Hull Univ.; London Business Sch. MIEx, MIM. RAFVR/RAF, 1958–60. Nat. Assistance Bd, 1961–66; Colonial, later Foreign and Commonwealth, Office, 1966–72; served Rawalpindi, Islamabad, Nicosia; attached DTI, 1973; Singapore, 1973–77; FCO, 1977; served Aden and Rangoon, 1981–87; Head of Royal Matters, FCO, 1987–90; Dep. High Comr, Port of Spain, 1990–94. *Recreations:* riding, walking, tennis, cricket, water-sports. *Address:* c/o Foreign and Commonwealth Office, King Charles Street, SW1A 2AH. *Clubs:* MCC; Queen's Park Cricket, Trinidad Union (Trinidad).

SMALLMAN, Prof. Raymond Edward, CBE 1992; FRS 1986; FEng 1991; Feeney Professor of Metallurgy and Materials Science, University of Birmingham, since 1969; *b* 4 Aug. 1929; *s* of David Smallman and Edith French; *m* 1952, Joan Doreen Faulkner; one *s* one *d*. *Educ:* Rugeley Grammar Sch.; Univ. of Birmingham (BSc, PhD, DSc). FIM 1964. AERE Harwell, 1953–58; University of Birmingham: Lectr in Dept of Physical Metallurgy, 1958, Sen Lectr, 1963; Prof. of Phys. Metall., 1964; Head of Dept of Phys. Metall. and Sci. of Materials, 1969–81, of Metallurgy and Materials, 1981–88; Dean of Faculty of Sci. and Eng., 1984–85, of Faculty of Eng., 1985–87; Pro-Vice-Chancellor and Vice-Principal, 1987–92. Visiting Professor: Pennsylvania, 1961; Stanford, 1962; NSW, 1974; UCLA Berkeley, 1978; Cape Town, 1982; Hon. Prof., Univ. of Hong Kong, 1990–. Van Horn Dist. Lectr, Case Western Reserve Univ., 1978; Edwin Liddiard Lectr, Inst. of Metals, 1991. IUC Consultant, Hong Kong, 1979. Member: Inter-Services Cttee, MoD, 1965; Metals and Materials Cttee, SRC, 1968–71; Materials Adv. Cttee, MoD, 1971; Cttee, Engrg Profs Conf., 1985; Materials Commn, 1988–91, Council, 1992–94, SERC. President: Birmingham Metallurgical Assoc., 1972–73; Fedn of European Materials Socs, 1994–96 (Vice-Pres., 1992–94); Vice-Pres., Metals Soc., 1980–84 (Chm., Metals Sci Cttee, 1974–84); Member: Council, Inst. of Materials (Vice Pres., 1995–; Chm., Internat. Affairs Cttee, 1993–); Lunar Soc., 1991–; Steering Cttee, Industry '96, W Midlands Festival of Industry and Enterprise, 1993–. Advr, ACU, 1985–91. Warden, Birmingham Assay Office, 1994– (Guardian, 1992–94). Dir, Univ. Hosps Birmingham NHS Trust, 1995–. Gov., Tettenhall Coll., 1982–. Hon. DSc: Wales, 1990; Univ. of Novi Sad, Yugoslavia, 1990. Sir George Beilby Gold Medal, Inst. of Metals and Chem. Soc., 1969; Rosenhain Medal, Inst. Metals, 1972; Elegant Work Prize, Metals Soc., 1979; Platinum Medal, Inst. of Metals, 1989. *Publications:* Modern Physical Metallurgy, 1962, 4th edn 1985; (jtly) Modern Metallography, 1966; (jtly) Structure of Metal and Alloys, 1969; (jtly) Defect Analysis in Electron Microscopy, 1975; (jtly) Metals and Materials: science, processing and applications, 1994; sci. papers on relationship of microstructure of materials to their properties in learned jls. *Recreations:* writing, travel, friendly golf, bridge. *Address:* 59 Woodthorne Road South, Tettenhall, Wolverhampton WV6 8SN. *T:* Wolverhampton (01902) 752545. *Clubs:* Athenæum; South Staffordshire Golf.

SMALLRIDGE, Peter William, CBE 1995; Director of Social Services, Kent County Council, since 1991; *b* 8 Aug. 1943; *s* of William Smallridge and Eileen (*née* Wilson); *m* 1965, Margaret Collis; two *s* one *d*. *Educ:* Sutton High Sch.; Chichester High Sch.; North-Western Polytechnic (CSW 1965); LSE (Dip. Mental Health 1970). Sen. Mental Health Social Worker, W Sussex CC, 1965–71; Area Officer, W Sussex Social Services, 1971–73; Sen. Lectr, Croydon Coll., 1973–75; Divl Manager, Social Services, Norfolk CC, 1975–82; Dep. Dir, 1982–83, Dir, 1983–91, Social Services, Warwicks CC. Pres., Assoc. of Dirs of Social Services, 1992–93. *Recreations:* reading, walking, golf, travel. *Address:* Maltmans Hill Barn, Maltmans Hill, Smarden, Kent TN27 8RD.

SMALLWOOD, Anne Hunter, CMG 1976; Commissioner, Board of Inland Revenue, 1973–81; *b* 20 June 1922; *d* of Martin Wilkinson McNicol and Elizabeth Straiton Harper; *m* 1972, Peter Basil Smallwood (*d* 1977). *Educ:* High Sch. for Girls, Glasgow; Glasgow Univ. Entered Inland Revenue, 1943; Min. of Land and Natural Resources, 1964–66; Min. of Housing and Local Govt, 1966; Under-Sec., Inland Revenue, 1971–73. *Address:* 83 Lyncombe Hill, Bath BA2 4PJ. *Club:* United Oxford & Cambridge University.
See also G. P. McNicol.

SMALLWOOD, Air Chief Marshal Sir Denis (Graham), GBE 1975 (CBE 1961; MBE 1951); KCB 1969 (CB 1966); DSO 1944; DFC 1942; idc; jssc; psc; aws; FRSA; FRAeS; Military Adviser to British Aerospace, 1977–83; *b* 13 Aug. 1918; *s* of Frederick William Smallwood, Moseley, Birmingham; *m* 1940, Frances Jeanne (*d* 1992), *d* of Walter Needham; one *s* one *d*. *Educ:* King Edward VI School, Birmingham. Joined Royal Air Force, 1938; Asst Adjt and Flying Instructor No 605 (County of Warwick) Sqdn, RAuxAF, 1938–39; served War of 1939–45, Fighter Command, as a fighter pilot in Nos 247 and 87 Hurricane Sqns, 1940–42, and Spitfire Wing Leader, 1943–44. Asst. Sec., COS Cttee, 1946–49; Directing Staff, JSSC, 1950–52; OC RAF Biggin Hill, 1953–55; Directing Staff, IDC, 1956; Group Captain, 1957; commanded RAF Guided Missiles Station, Lincs, 1959–61; AOC and Commandant, RAF Coll. of Air Warfare, Manby, 1961–62; ACAS (Ops), 1962–65; AOC No 3 Gp, RAF Bomber Comd, 1965–67; SASO, Bomber Comd, 1967–68; Dep. C-in-C, Strike Comd, 1968–69; AOC-in-C, NEAF, Comdr, British Forces Near East, and Administrator, Sovereign Base Area, Cyprus, 1969–70; Vice-Chief of the Air Staff, 1970–74; C-in-C, RAF Strike Command, 1974–76, and C-in-C, UK Air Forces, 1975–76. ADC to the Queen, 1959–64. Life Vice-Pres., Air League, 1984 (Pres., 1981–84, Chm., 1978–81). Freeman, City of London, 1976; Liveryman, Guild of Air Pilots and Navigators, 1975. *Recreations:* shooting, gun dog training, walking, swimming, gardening. *Address:* The Flint House, Owlswick, Bucks HP27 9RH. *Clubs:* Royal Air Force, Les Ambassadeurs.

SMALLWOOD, John Frank Monton, CBE 1991; a Church Commissioner, since 1966 (Member, Board of Governors, and Member, General Purposes Committee, since 1968); *b* 12 April 1926; *s* of late Frank Theodore and Edith Smallwood; *m* 1952, Jean Margaret Lovell; one *s* two *d*. *Educ:* City of London Sch.; Peterhouse, Cambridge, 1948–51 (MA Classics). Served RAF, 1944–48 (Japanese translation and interrogation). Joined Bank of England, 1951; Private Sec. to Governors, 1959–62; Adviser, 1967; Auditor, 1969; Dep. Chief Accountant, 1974–79. Member: Church Assembly/General Synod, 1965– (Standing Cttee, 1971–); numerous *ad hoc* Cttees, etc, over years, incl. Wkg Party on State Aid for Churches in use, 1971–; Central Bd of Finance, 1965– (Dep. Vice-Chm. 1972–82); Pensions Bd, 1985–, Anglican Consultative Council, 1975–87 (Trinidad, 1976, Lambeth Conf., 1978, Canada, 1979, Newcastle, 1981, Singapore, 1987). A Trustee: City Parochial Foundn, 1969– (Vice-Chm., 1977–81; Chm., 1981–92); Trust for London, 1986– (Chm., 1986–92); Overseas Bishoprics Fund, 1977– (Chm., 1992–); Lambeth Palace Library, 1978–. Member: Southwark Dio. Bd of Finance, 1962– (Chm. 1975–); Southwark Ordination Course Council, 1960–74 and 1980–94 (Vice-Chm., 1980–94); Corp. of Church House Council, 1986–; Churches' Main Cttee, 1987–; BCC 1987–90. Lee Abbey Council, 1969–74; Lay Reader, 1983–. *Recreations:* church finances (incl. various financial pamphlets), family, music, cathedrals, old churches, historic houses, gardens. *Address:* Downsview, 32 Brockham Lane, Brockham, Betchworth, Surrey RH3 7EL. *T:* Betchworth (01737) 842032.

SMART, (Alexander Basil) Peter, CMG 1990; HM Diplomatic Service, retired; *b* 19 Feb. 1932; *s* of late Henry Prescott Smart and Mary Gertrude Todd; *m* 1955, Joan Mary Cumming; three *s* (incl. twin *s*). *Educ:* Ryhope Grammar Sch., Co. Durham. Commnd RAEC, 1951; Supervising Officer, Educn, Gibraltar Comd, 1951–52; entered HM Foreign (later Diplomatic) Service, 1953; Vice Consul, Duala, 1955; Polit. Office, ME Forces, Cyprus, 1956; 2nd Sec. (Information), Seoul, 1959; News Dept, FO, 1964; Head of Chancery, Rangoon, 1968; FCO, 1971; Head of Communications Technical Services Dept, 1975; Counsellor, 1977–82, and Dep. High Comr, 1981–82, Canberra; Counsellor and Head of Chancery, Prague, 1983–86; High Comr, Seychelles, 1986–89; Ambassador to Fiji, and High Comr (non-resident) to Republic of Nauru and to Tuvalu, 1989–92. FRSA. *Recreations:* wild nature, the arts: looking and listening. *Address:* 715 Willoughby House, Barbican, EC2Y 8BN.

SMART, Andrew, CB 1981; defence consultant, retired 1991; Director, Royal Signals and Radar Establishment, Malvern, 1978–84; *b* 12 Feb. 1924; *s* of late Mr and Mrs William S. Smart; *m* 1949, Pamela Kathleen Stephens; two *s* two *d. Educ:* Denny; High Sch. of Stirling; Glasgow Univ. MA 1944. TRE Malvern, 1943; Science 2 Air Min., 1950–53; Guided Weapons Gp, RRE, Malvern, 1953–70 (Head, 1968–70); Dep. Dir (Scientific B), DOAE, 1970; RAE, Farnborough: Head of Weapons Res. Gp, 1972; Head of Weapons Dept, 1973; Dep. Dir (W), 1974–77. *Recreations:* gardening, caravanning. *Address:* Hill Orchard, Shelsley Drive, Colwall, Malvern, Worcs WR13 6PS. *T:* Colwall (01684) 40664.

SMART, Prof. (Arthur David) Gerald, CBE 1991; FRTPI; Emeritus Professor of Urban Planning, University of London, since 1984; Professor of Urban Planning at University College London, 1975–84 and part-time, 1984–87 (Head of Bartlett School of Architecture and Planning, University College London, 1975–80); *b* 19 March 1925; *s* of Dr A. H. J. Smart and A. O. M. Smart (*née* Evans); *m* 1955, Anne Patience Smart (*née* Baxter); two *d. Educ:* Rugby Sch.; King's Coll., Cambridge; Regent St Polytechnic. MA, DipTP; ARICS, FRSA. Served in The Rifle Brigade, 1943–47 (Captain). Appts in local govt (planning), London, NE England, E Midlands, 1950–63; County Planning Officer, Hants CC, 1963–75; Member: Planning Adv. Gp, 1964–65, Cttee on Public Participation in Planning, 1968–69, Min. of Housing and Local Govt; Planning and Transportation Res. Adv. Council, DoE, 1975–79; Working Party on alternative uses of Historic Buildings, Historic Bldgs Council and BTA, 1979–81; Council, TCPA, 1983–89; Council, RSPB, 1985–90; Governing Body, British Assoc. for Central and East Europe (formerly GB/E Europe Centre), 1985–; Council, Solent Protection Soc., 1986–; House Builders' Fedn Commn on Inner Cities, 1986–87; occasional Chm., Structure Plans Exams in Public for DoE; Consultant, Countryside Commn, 1989–90. Chm., Milford-on-Sea Parish Council, 1989–93 (Councillor, 1987–). *Publications:* articles, conf. papers, in books, professional and other jls, booklets and reports. *Recreations:* sailing, ornithology, music, walking. *Address:* 10 Harewood Green, Keyhaven, Lymington, Hants SO41 0TZ. *T:* Lymington (01590) 645475. *Clubs:* Royal Lymington Yacht, Keyhaven Yacht (Lymington).

SMART, Edwin; *see* Smart, L. E.

SMART, Professor Sir George (Algernon), Kt 1978; MD, FRCP; Director, British Postgraduate Medical Federation, 1971–78, retired; *b* 16 Dec. 1913; *er s* of A. Smart, Alnwick, Northumb; *m* 1939, Monica Helen Carrick; two *s* one *d. Educ:* Uppingham; Durham Univ., BSc 1935, MB, BS 1937. MD 1939 (Durham); MRCP 1940, FRCP 1952. Commonwealth Fund Fellow, 1948–49. Lectr in Med., Univ. of Bristol, 1946–50; Reader in Medicine, Univ. of Durham, 1950–56; Prof. of Medicine, Univ. of Durham, 1956–68, Univ. of Newcastle upon Tyne, 1968–71 (Post-graduate Sub-Dean, 1962–68, Dean of Medicine, 1968–71). Censor, 1965–67, Senior Censor and Senior Vice-Pres., 1972–73, RCP. Chairman: Review Bd for Overseas Qualified Practitioners, GMC, 1979–82; Cttee of Management, and Med. and Survival Cttee, RNLI, 1979–83. Hon. Fellow, Coll. of Physicians and Surgeons, Pakistan, 1976. *Publications:* contrib. to Price's Textbook of Medicine, and Progress in Clinical Medicine (Daley and Miller); (ed) Metabolic Disturbances in Clinical Medicine, 1958; (co-author) Fundamentals of Clinical Endocrinology, 1969, 2nd edn 1974. *Recreation:* photography. *Address:* Taffrail, Crede Lane, Old Bosham, Chichester, Sussex PO18 8NX.

SMART, Gerald; *see* Smart, A. D. G.

SMART, Jack; *see* Smart, R. J.

SMART, Sir Jack, Kt 1982; CBE 1976; JP; DL; Chairman, Wakefield District Health Authority, 1982–88; *b* 25 April 1920; *s* of James and Emily Smart; *m* 1941, Ethel King; one *d. Educ:* Altofts Colliery Sch. Miner, 1934–59; Branch Sec., Glasshoughton Colliery, NUM, 1949–59; Mem., Castleford Municipal Borough Council, 1949–74; Mayor of Castleford, 1962–63; Mem., Wakefield Metropolitan Dist Council, 1973–, Leader, 1973–86. Chm., Assoc. of Metropolitan Authorities, 1977–78, 1980–84; Leader of the Opposition Group, AMA, 1978–80. Chm., Wakefield AHA, 1977–81; Mem., Layfield Cttee of Enquiry into Local Govt Finance, 1974–76. Pres., Yorkshire Soc. (1980), 1988–. Hon. Fellow, Bretton Coll., 1983. Hon. Freeman, City of Wakefield, 1985. JP Castleford, 1960; DL West Yorks, 1987. FRSA. *Recreations:* golf, music. *Address:* Churchside, Weetworth, Pontefract Road, Castleford, West Yorks WF10 4QA. *T:* Castleford (01977) 554880.

SMART, (Louis) Edwin, JD; Chairman and Chief Executive Officer, Trans World Corporation, 1978–87; Chairman of Executive Committee, Hilton International Co., since 1986 (Chairman of Board, 1978–86); *b* Columbus, Ohio, 17 Nov. 1923; *s* of Louis Edwin Smart and Esther Guthery; *m* 1st, 1944, Virginia Alice Knouff (marr. diss. 1958); one *s* one *d*; 2nd, 1964, Jeanie Alberta Milone; one *s. Educ:* Harvard Coll. (AB *magna cum laude* 1947); Harvard Law Sch. (JD *magna cum laude* 1949). Served to Lieut, USNR, 1943–46. Admitted to NY Bar, 1950; Associate, Hughes, Hubbard & Ewing, NYC, 1949–56; Partner, Hughes, Hubbard & Reed, NYC, 1957–64; Pres., Bendix Internat. and Dir, Bendix Corp. and foreign subsids, 1964–67; Trans World Airlines Inc.: Sen. Vice Pres., External Affairs, 1967–71, Corp. Affairs, 1971–75; Vice Chm. 1976; Chief Exec. Officer, 1977–78; Chm. of Bd, 1977–85; also Dir, Mem. Exec., and Mem. Finance Cttee. Chairman: Canteen Corp., 1973–; Spartan Food Systems Inc., 1979–; Director: Sonat Inc.; The Continental Corp.; NY Stock Exchange; Trustee, Cttee for Econ. Develt, 1977–. Member: Conf. Bd, 1977–; Amer. Bar Assoc.; NY County Lawyers Assoc.; Phi Beta Kappa; Sigma Alpha Epsilon. *Address:* 535 E 86th Street, New York, NY 10028, USA; Coakley Bay, Christiansted, St Croix 00820, Virgin Islands. *Clubs:* Economic of New York, Presidents, Marco Polo, Sky (NYC); St Croix Yacht.

SMART, Ninian; *see* Smart, R. N.

SMART, Peter; *see* Smart, A. B. P.

SMART, (Raymond) Jack, DL; formerly Managing Director, Bus and Truck Group, British Leyland, retired; *b* 1 Aug. 1917; *s* of Frank Smart and Emily Rose Smart; *m* 1942, Jessie Alice Tyrrell; one *s* one *d. Educ:* Redhill Technical Coll. (HNC). Apprentice Prodn Engr, Lanston Monotype Corp., 1933–38; Aeronautical Inspection Directorate, Air Min., 1939–40; Rotol Airscrews/Dowty Rotol, 1940–59: successively Chief Inspector, Prodn Controller, Works Manager; Man. Dir, British Light Steel Pressings (subsidiary of Rootes Motors Ltd), 1960–65; British Leyland (formerly BM Corp.): Man. Dir, Truck Div., 1966–72; Gp Manufg Dir, 1972–76; Gp Exec. Dir and Dep. Man. Dir, 1976–79; Man. Dir, Aveling Barford Holdings Ltd, 1979–80; non-exec. Dir, Marshall Sons & Co. Ltd, 1981–84. DL W Yorks, 1987. *Recreations:* Rugby Union, gardening. *Address:* 17 Whitecroft Park, Northfield Road, Nailsworth, Glos GL6 0NS. *T:* Nailsworth (01453) 835634.

SMART, Reginald Piers Alexander de B.; *see* de Bernière-Smart.

SMART, Prof. (Roderick) Ninian; J. F. Rowny Professor of Religious Studies, University of California, Santa Barbara, since 1988 (Professor, since 1976); Professor Emeritus, University of Lancaster, since 1989 (Professor of Religious Studies, 1967–82; Hon. Professor, 1982–89); *b* 6 May 1927; *s* of late Prof. W. M. Smart, FRSE, and Isabel (*née* Carswell); *m* 1954, Libushka Clementina Baruffaldi; one *s* two *d. Educ:* Glasgow Academy; The Queen's College, Oxford. Army service with Intelligence Corps, 1945–48, 2nd Lt, Captain, 1947; overseas service in Ceylon. Oxford: Mods (shortened), Class II, 1949; Lit. Hum. Class I, 1951; BPhil 1954. Asst Lecturer in Philosophy, Univ. Coll. of Wales, Aberystwyth, 1952–55, Lecturer, 1955; Vis. Lecturer in Philosophy, Yale Univ., 1955–56; Lecturer in History and Philosophy of Religion, Univ. of London, King's College, 1956–61; H. G. Wood Professor of Theology, University of Birmingham, 1961–66. Pro-Vice-Chancellor, Univ. of Lancaster, 1969–72. Lectures: Banaras Hindu Univ., Summer, 1960; Teape, Univ. Delhi, 1964; Gifford, Univ. of Edinburgh, 1979–80; Visiting Professor: Univ. Wisconsin, 1965; Princeton and Otago, 1971; Queensland, 1980 and 1985; Univ. of Cape Town, 1982; Harvard, 1983; Hong Kong, 1989. President: Inst. of Religion and Theology, 1980–85 (first Gen. Sec., 1973–77); British Assoc. History of Religions, 1981–85; Amer. Soc. for Study of Religion, 1984–87. Hon. LHD Loyola, 1968; Hon. DLitt: Glasgow, 1984; Kelaniya, Sri Lanka, 1991; DUniv Stirling, 1986. *Publications:* Reasons and Faiths, 1958; A Dialogue of Religions, 1960; Historical Selections in the Philosophy of Religion, 1962; Philosophers and Religious Truth, 1964; Doctrine and Argument in Indian Philosophy, 1964, 2nd edn 1991; The Teacher and Christian Belief, 1966; The Yogi and the Devotee, 1968; Secular Education and the Logic of Religion, 1968; The Religious Experience of Mankind, 1969, 4th edn as The Religious Experience, 1991; Philosophy of Religion, 1970; The Concept of Worship, 1972; The Phenomenon of Religion, 1973; The Science of Religion and the Sociology of Knowledge, 1973; Mao, 1974; A Companion to the Long Search, 1977; The Phenomenon of Christianity, 1979; Beyond Ideology, 1982; (with R. Hecht) Sacred Texts of the World, 1982; Worldviews, 1983; (with Swami Purnananda) Prophet of a New Hindu Age, 1985; Concept and Empathy, 1986; Religion and the Western Mind, 1986; World Religions, 1989; (with S. Konstantine) A Christian Systematic Theology in World Context, 1991; Buddhism and Christianity: rivals and allies, 1993; The Religions of the West, 1993; Choosing a Faith, 1995; contrib. to Mind, Philosophy, Philosophical Quarterly, Review of Metaphysics, Religion, Religious Studies. *Recreations:* cricket, tennis, poetry. *Address:* Department of Religious Studies, University of Lancaster, Bailrigg, Lancaster LA1 4YG; Department of Religious Studies, University of California at Santa Barbara, CA 93106, USA. *Club:* Athenæum.

SMART, William Norman H.; *see* Hunter Smart.

SMEALL, James Leathley, MA, JP; Principal, Saint Luke's College, Exeter, 1945–72; *b* 16 June 1907; *s* of late William Francis Smeall, MB, BCh (Edin.), and late Ethel Mary Leathley; *m* 1936, Joan Rachel Harris (*d* 1984); one *d. Educ:* Sorbonne; Queens' College, Cambridge (Scholar). Class I English Tripos, Class II Division 1 Anthropological and Archæological Tripos; Assistant Master, Merchiston, 1929–30; Staff, Royal Naval College, Dartmouth, 1930–34; Housemaster, Bradfield College, 1934–36; Head of the English Department, Epsom College, 1936–39; Headmaster, Chesterfield Grammar School, 1939–45; Commissioned RAFVR, 1941–44. Mayor of Exeter, 1965–66; President: Exeter Civic Soc., 1980–87; Exeter and Dist Br., E-SU, 1983–88. Hon. LLD Exeter, 1988. *Publication:* English Satire, Parody and Burlesque, 1952. *Recreations:* gardening and travel. *Address:* Follett Orchard, Topsham, Exeter EX3 0JP. *T:* Topsham (01392) 873892.

SMEDLEY, Hon. Sir (Frank) Brian, Kt 1995; **Hon. Mr Justice Smedley;** a Judge of the High Court, Queen's Bench Division, since 1995; *b* 28 Nov. 1934. *Educ:* West Bridgford Grammar Sch.; London Univ. LLB Hons, 1957. Called to the Bar, Gray's Inn, 1960; Midland Circuit; a Recorder, 1972; QC 1977; a Circuit Judge, 1987–95; Sen. Judge, Sovereign Base Areas, Cyprus, 1991–95 (Dep. Sen. Judge, 1989–91). Mem., Senate of the Inns of Court and the Bar, 1973–77. Freeman, City of London, 1990. *Recreations:* travel, music. *Address:* Royal Courts of Justice, Strand, WC2A 2LL. *Club:* Garrick.

SMEDLEY, George; *see* Smedley, R. R. G. B.

SMEDLEY, Sir Harold, KCMG 1978 (CMG 1965); MBE 1946; HM Diplomatic Service, retired; *b* 19 June 1920; *s* of late Dr R. D. Smedley, MA, MD, DPH, Worthing; *m* 1950, Beryl Mary Harley Brown, Wellington, New Zealand; two *s* two *d. Educ:* Aldenham School; Pembroke College, Cambridge. Served War of 1939–45, Royal Marines. Entered Dominions Office (later Commonwealth Relations Office), 1946; Private Secretary to Permanent Under-Secretary of State, 1947–48; British High Commissioner's Office: Wellington, NZ, 1948–50; Salisbury, Southern Rhodesia, 1951–53; Principal Private Sec. to Sec. of State for Commonwealth Relations, 1954–57; Counsellor, British High Comr's Office: Calcutta, 1957; New Delhi, 1958–60; British High Comr in Ghana, 1964–67; Ambassador to Laos, 1967–70; Asst Under-Sec. of State, FCO, 1970–72; Sec. Gen., Commn on Rhodesian opinion, 1971–72; High Comr in Sri Lanka, and Ambassador to Republic of Maldives, 1972–75; High Comr in NZ and concurrently Governor of Pitcairn Island, 1976–80; High Comr in Western Samoa (non-resident), 1977–80. Chm., London Bd, Bank of NZ, 1983–89. Vice Chm., Victoria League, 1981–90. Pres., Hakluyt Soc., 1987–92. Mem., W Sussex CC, 1989–93. Pres., W Sussex Assoc. for the Blind, 1991–. *Address:* 11A Beehive Lane, Ferring, Sussex BN12 5NN. *Clubs:* United Oxford & Cambridge University, Commonwealth Trust.

SMEDLEY, (Roscoe Relph) George (Boleyne); Barrister; Counsellor, HM Diplomatic Service, retired; *b* 3 Sept. 1919; *o s* of late Charles Boleyne Smedley and Aimie Blaine Smedley (*née* Relph); *m* 1st, 1947, Muriel Hallaway Murray (*d* 1975), *o d* of late Arthur Stanley Murray; one *s*; 2nd, 1979, Margaret Gerrard Gourlay (*d* 1991), *o c* of late Augustus Thorburn Hallaway and *widow* of Dr John Stewart Gourlay; 3rd, 1993, Marjorie Drummond (*d* 1994), *d* of late John Leonard Haslam and *widow* of David Drummond. *Educ:* King's Sch., Ely; King's Coll., London (LLB). Called to Bar, Inner Temple. Artists Rifles TA; commnd S Lancs Regt, 1940; Indian Army, 1942–46 (Captain); Foreign Office, 1937 and 1946; Foreign Service (subseq. Diplomatic Service): Rangoon, 1947; Maymyo, 1950; Brussels, 1952; Baghdad, 1954; FO, 1958; Beirut, 1963; Kuwait, 1965; FCO, 1969; Consul-Gen., Lubumbashi, 1972–74; British Mil. Govt, Berlin, 1974–76; FCO 1976; Head of Nationality and Treaty Dept, 1977–79. Part-time appointments (since retirement): Legal Mem., Mental Health Review Tribunal; Chm., Rent Assessment Cttee; Adjudicator under Immigration Act 1971; Inspector, Planning Inspectorate, Depts of the Environment and Transport; Dep. Traffic Comr for N Eastern Traffic Area; Mem., No 2 Dip. Service Appeal Bd. Churchwarden; Mem., diocesan and deanery synods. *Address:* Garden House, Whorlton, Barnard Castle, Co. Durham DL12 8XQ. *T:* Teesdale (01833) 627381. *Clubs:* Royal Automobile, Royal Over-Seas League.

SMEDLEY, Susan M.; *see* Marsden, S.

SMEE, Clive Harrod; Chief Economic Adviser to Department of Health, since 1988 (to Department of Health and Social Security, 1984–88 and to Department of Social Security, 1988–89); *b* 29 April 1942; *s* of Victor Woolley Smee and Leila Olive Smee (*née* Harrod); *m* 1975, Denise Eileen Sell; one *s* two *d. Educ:* Royal Grammar Sch., Guildford; LSE (BSc

Econ); Indiana Univ. (MBA); Inst. of Commonwealth Studies, Oxford. British Council, Nigeria, 1966–68; Economic Advr, ODM, 1969–75; Sen. Economic Advr, DHSS, 1975–82; Nuffield and Leverhulme Travelling Fellow, USA and Canada, 1978–79; Advr, Central Policy Review Staff, 1982–83; Sen. Economic Advr, HM Treasury, 1983–84. Consultant: NZ Treasury, 1988; NZ Dept of Health, 1991. Chm., OECD Social Policy Working Party, 1987–90. Vis. Prof. of Econs, Univ. of Surrey, 1995–. *Publications:* articles on economics in learned jls. *Recreations:* running, gardening; Anna, David and Elizabeth. *Address:* c/o Department of Health, Skipton House, 80 London Road SE1 6LW. *T:* 0171–972 5220.

SMEE, John Charles O.; *see* Odling-Smee.

SMETHAM, Andrew James, MA; Headmaster, The Purbeck School, Wareham, Dorset, since 1985; *b* 22 Feb. 1937; *s* of Arthur James Smetham and Eunice (*née* Jones); *m* 1964, Sandra Mary (*née* Owen); two *s*. *Educ:* Vaynor and Penderyn Grammar Sch., Cefn Coed, Breconshire; King's Coll., Univ. of London (BA (Hons German) 1959, DipEd 1964, MA (Educn) 1968). Assistant Master: Wandsworth Sch., 1960–66; Sedgehill Sch., 1966–70; Dep. Headmaster, Holloway Sch., 1970–74; Headmaster, Wandsworth Sch., 1974–84. *Recreations:* music, walking. *Address:* The Water Barn, East Burton, Wareham, Dorset BH20 6HE. *T:* Bindon Abbey (01929) 463727.

SMETHURST, (John) Michael; Deputy Chief Executive (formerly Director-General), British Library, London, 1991–April 1996; *b* 25 April 1934; *s* of Albert Smethurst and Nelly Smethurst (*née* Kitchin); *m* 1960, Mary Clayworth; one *s* one *d*. *Educ:* William Hulme's Grammar School, Manchester; Manchester Univ. (BA). ALA. Librarian: Bede Coll., Durham Univ., 1964–66; Inst. of Educn, Newcastle upon Tyne, 1966–69; Dep. Librarian, Univ. of Glasgow, 1969–72; Univ. Librarian, Univ. of Aberdeen, 1972–86; British Library: Dir-Gen., Humanities and Social Sciences, 1986–91; Mem. Bd, 1986–April 1996; Mem., Lending Div. Adv. Cttee, 1976–80; Mem., Adv. Council, 1982–86 (Chm., Bibliog. Services Adv. Cttee, 1983–86). Hon. Res. Fellow, UCL, 1987–. Trustee, Nat. Library of Scotland, 1976–86; Chairman: Library and Inf. Services Cttee (Scotland), 1982–86; SCONUL, 1984–86, 1989–90 (Vice-Chm., 1983–84, 1988; Mem. Council, 1977–80, 1983–92); Consortium of Eur. Res. Libraries, 1992–; Member: British Council Libraries Adv. Cttee, 1983–92; Bd, Res. Libraries Gp, USA, 1992–. President: Scottish Liby Assoc., 1983; LIBER, 1989–95. *Publications:* papers and articles in professional jls. *Recreations:* music, art, travel, gardening. *Address:* Romney, 72 Grove Road, Tring, Herts HP23 5PB. *Club:* Athenæum.

SMETHURST, Richard Good, MA; Provost, Worcester College, Oxford, since 1991; *b* 17 Jan. 1941; *s* of Thomas Good Smethurst and Madeleine Nora Foulkes; *m* 1964, Dorothy Joan (*née* Mitchenall); two *s* two *d*. *Educ:* Liverpool Coll.; Worcester Coll., Oxford; Nuffield Coll., Oxford. Webb Medley Jun. Schol. 1962; BA 1st Cl. 1963; MA Oxon. Research Fellow: St Edmund Hall, Oxford, 1964–65; Inst. for Commonwealth Studies, Oxford, 1965–66 (Consultant, UN/FAO World Food Program); University of Oxford: Fellow and Tutor in Economics, St Edmund Hall, 1966–67; Fellow and Tutor in Economics, Worcester Coll., and Univ. Lectr in Economics, 1967–76; Dir, Dept for External Studies, and Professorial Fellow, Worcester Coll., 1976–89; Supernumerary Fellow, Worcester Coll., and Chm., Gen. Bd of Faculties, 1989–91. Economic Adviser, HM Treasury, 1969–71; Policy Adviser, Prime Minister's Policy Unit, 1975–76. Dir, IMRO, 1987–. Member: Adv. Council for Adult and Continuing Educn, DES, 1977–83; Monopolies and Mergers Commn, 1978–89 (Dep. Chm., 1986–89); UGC/NAB Continuing Educn Standing Cttee, 1984–88; Acad. Consultative Cttee, Open Univ., 1986–; Adv. Bd, Music at Oxford, 1988–; Chm., Unit for Develt of Adult Continuing Educn, 1991–92. Trustee, Eur. Community Baroque Orch., 1986–. Mem. Council, Templeton Coll., Oxford (Oxford Management Centre), 1982–; Life Governor, Liverpool Coll., 1968. Foundn Hon. Fellow, Kellogg House, Oxford, 1990; Hon. Fellow, St Edmund Hall, Oxford, 1991. *Publications:* Impact of Food Aid on Donor Countries (with G. R. Allen), 1967; contribs to New Thinking About Welfare, 1969; Economic System in the UK, 1977, 2nd edn 1979; New Directions in Adult and Continuing Education, 1979; Continuing Education in Universities and Polytechnics, 1982; contrib. Jl of Development Studies, Oxford Rev. of Educn, Studies in Adult Education. *Recreation:* good food. *Address:* The Provost's Lodgings, Worcester College, Oxford OX1 2HB. *T:* Oxford (01865) 278362.

SMETTEM, Colin William; Chairman, North Eastern Region, British Gas Corporation, 1973–76; *b* 1 June 1916; *s* of William Home Smettem and Agnes Grace; *m* 1945, Sylvia Elisabeth (*née* Alcock); two *s* two *d*. Solicitor (Hons) 1938. Asst Solicitor, Scarborough Corp., 1938. Served War, RA, 1939–45: UK, India, Assam; started 14th Army Trng Sch., 1943; GII at Tactical Trng Centre, India Command, 1944. Asst Town Clerk, Wallasey, 1948; Solicitor, North Western Gas Bd, 1950; Commercial Manager, North Western Gas Bd, 1961, and Mem. Bd, 1965–68; Dep. Chm., Eastern Gas Bd, 1968. Mem., Law Soc. *Address:* The Rookery, Tinwell, via Stamford, Lincs PE9 3UJ. *T:* Stamford (01780) 53168.

SMIETON, Dame Mary Guillan, DBE 1949; MA Oxon; Permanent Secretary, Ministry of Education, 1959–63, retired; *b* 5 Dec. 1902; *d* of John Guillan Smieton, late librarian and bursar Westminster Coll., Cambridge, and of Maria Judith Toop. *Educ:* Perse Sch., Cambridge; Wimbledon High Sch.; Bedford Coll., London (1 year) (Hon. Fellow, 1971); Lady Margaret Hall. Assistant Keeper, Public Record Office, 1925–28; Ministry of Labour and National Service, 1928–46; on loan to Home Office as General Secretary, Women's Voluntary Services, 1938–40, and to UN as Director of Personnel, 1946–48; Deputy Secretary, Ministry of Labour and National Service, 1955–59 (Under-Secretary, 1946–55). UK representative, Unesco Executive Board, 1962–68. Trustee, British Museum, 1963–73; Chm., Bedford Coll. Council, 1964–70. Member: Advisory Council on Public Records, 1965–73; Standing Commn on Museums and Galleries, 1970–73; Vice Pres., Museums Assoc., 1974–77. Hon. Fellow, Lady Margaret Hall, Oxford, 1959. *Address:* 14 St George's Road, St Margaret's on Thames, Middlesex TW1 1QR. *T:* 0181–892 9279. *Club:* United Oxford & Cambridge University.

SMILEY, Lt-Col Sir John (Philip), 4th Bt *cr* 1903, of Drumalis, Larne, Co. Antrim and Gallowhill, Paisley, Co. Renfrew; *b* 24 Feb. 1934; *s* of Sir Hugh Houston Smiley, 3rd Bt and of Nancy Elizabeth Louise Hardy (*née* Beaton); *S* father, 1990; *m* 1963, Davina Elizabeth, *d* of late Denis Charles Griffiths; two *s* one *d*. *Educ:* Eton Coll.; RMA Sandhurst. Commnd Grenadier Guards, 1954; ADC to Governor of Bermuda, 1961–62; Regimental Adjt, 1970–73; served in Cyprus, BAOR, Hong Kong; Lt-Col, 1981; retired 1986. Russell Reynolds Associates, 1986–89. Governor, Oundle Sch., 1987–. Mem., Ct of Assts, Worshipful Co. of Grocers, 1987– (Master, 1992–93). *Recreations:* gardening, travel. *Heir:* *s* Christopher Hugh Charles Smiley, *b* 7 Feb. 1968. *Address:* Cornerway House, Chobham, Woking, Surrey GU24 8SW. *T:* Chobham (01276) 858992. *Club:* Army and Navy.

SMILEY, Prof. Timothy John, PhD; FBA 1984; Knightbridge Professor of Philosophy, University of Cambridge, since 1980; Fellow of Clare College, Cambridge, since 1955; *b* 13 Nov. 1930; *s* of Prof. M. T. Smiley and Mrs T. M. Smiley (*née* Browne); *m* 1955, Benita Mary Bentley; four *d*. *Educ:* Ardwyn Grammar Sch., Aberystwyth; Ampleforth Coll.; Fribourg Univ.; Clare Coll., Cambridge (BA 1952, Math. Tripos; MA, PhD 1956). Holt Scholarship, Gray's Inn, 1954; called to the Bar, 1956. Pilot Officer, RAFVR, 1954. Scientific Officer, Air Min., 1955–56; Clare Coll., Cambridge: Res. Fellow, 1955–59; Asst Tutor, 1959–65; Sen. Tutor, 1966–69; Asst Lectr in Phil., Cambridge Univ., 1957–62, Lectr, 1962–79. Vis. Professor: Cornell Univ., 1964; Univ. of Virginia, 1972; Yale Univ., 1975; Univ. of Notre Dame, 1986; Yale Univ., 1990. Sec. for Postgrad. Studies, British Acad., 1992–; Mem., Humanities Res. Bd, 1994–. *Publications:* (with D. J. Shoesmith) Multiple-conclusion Logic, 1978; articles in phil and math. jls. *Recreation:* orienteering. *Address:* Clare College, Cambridge CB2 1TL. *T:* Cambridge (01223) 352152.

SMILLIE, William John Jones; Managing Director: Gatehouse Records, since 1992; Gatehouse Publishing, since 1992; Company Secretary, Diamondport Ltd, since 1993; *b* 18 Feb. 1940; *s* of late John Smillie and Emily Mary Caroline (*née* Jones). *Educ:* Lauriston Sch., Falkirk; Territorial Sch., Stirling; Stirling High Sch. Scottish hotel family background; trained in all hotel depts in Scotland and Paris, with extensive kitchen work; progressed to management with Edward R. Barnett & Co. Ltd, industrial caterers (now taken over by Grand Metropolitan Gp), resp. for 50 outlets throughout Scotland, England and Wales (Asst Gen. Man., 1964–67); joined House of Commons Catering Dept as Personnel Manager, 1967: Personnel Manager and Asst to Catering Manager, 1970; Gen. Man., 1971; Head, 1980–91. Dir, Miller Morelle Interior Designs, 1992–. Member: British Inst. of Cleaning Science, 1976–; Hine Soc., 1979–; FHCIMA 1979; Fellow, Cookery and Food Assoc., 1967; Founder Mem., Wine Guild of UK, 1984–; Mem., Restaurateurs Assoc. of GB, 1983–; Hon. Member: Assoc. Culinaire Française, 1972; Conseil Culinaire Française de Grande Bretagne, en Reconnaissance des Services Rendus à l'Art Culinaire, 1987. Vice Pres., British Epilepsy Assoc., 1981–; Member: League Against Cruel Sports, 1983–; Musicians' Union, 1992–. *Publications:* articles for catering trade papers. *Recreations:* theatre, ballet, music, piano, motoring, boating, disc-jockey, travel, gourmandise, intervals at the opera, jazz music. *Address:* The Gatehouse, 90 Wimbledon Parkside, SW19 5LT. *T:* 0181–780 9350, *Fax:* 0171–823 8905. *Clubs:* Mortons; Preston Cross Country; Jaguar Drivers (Luton).

SMITH; *see* Abel Smith and Abel-Smith.

SMITH; *see* Boys Smith and Boys-Smith.

SMITH; *see* Darwall Smith.

SMITH; *see* Delacourt-Smith.

SMITH; *see* Dixon-Smith, family name of Baron Dixon-Smith.

SMITH; *see* Gordon-Smith.

SMITH; *see* Hamilton-Smith, family name of Baron Colwyn.

SMITH; *see* Hugh Smith.

SMITH; *see* Llewellyn Smith and Llewellyn-Smith.

SMITH; *see* Mackenzie Smith and McKenzie Smith.

SMITH; *see* Nowell-Smith.

SMITH; *see* Spencer Smith and Spencer-Smith.

SMITH; *see* Stewart-Smith.

SMITH; *see* Stuart-Smith.

SMITH; *see* Wenban-Smith.

SMITH, family name of **Viscount Hambleden, Barons Bicester, Kirkhill** and **Smith** and **Baroness Smith of Gilmorehill.**

SMITH, Baron *cr* 1978 (Life Peer), of Marlow in the County of Buckinghamshire; **Rodney Smith,** KBE 1975; MS, FRCS; Hon. Consulting Surgeon: St George's Hospital London, 1978; Royal Prince Alfred Hospital, Sydney, NSW; Wimbledon Hospital; Examiner in Surgery, University of London; External Examiner in Surgery, Universities of Cambridge, Birmingham and Hong Kong; former Advisor in Surgery to Department of Health and Social Security; Hon. Consultant in Surgery to the Army, 1972, Emeritus Consultant, 1980; *b* 10 May 1914; *o s* of Dr Edwin Smith and Edith Catherine (*née* Dyer); *m* 1st, 1938, Mary Rodwell (marr. diss. 1971); three *s* one *d*; 2nd, 1971, Susan Fry. *Educ:* Westminster Sch.; London Univ. (St Thomas's Hospital). MB, BS London, MRCS, LRCP 1937; FRCS 1939; MS London 1941. Surgical Registrar, Middlesex Hospital, 1939–41; Surgeon RAMC, 1941–45; appointed Surgeon, St George's Hospital 1946. Royal College of Surgeons: Hunterian Professor, 1947 and 1952; Arris and Gale Lecturer, 1959; Jacksonian Prizewinner, 1951; Penrose May Tutor in Surgery, 1957–63; Dean, Inst. of Basic Medical Sciences, 1966–71; Mem., Ct of Examiners, 1963–69, Chm. Feb.-July 1969; Mem. Council, 1965–78; Pres., 1973–77; Mem. Ct of Patrons; Hunterian Orator, 1975. President: Brit. Assoc. Surg. Oncologists; Harveian Soc., 1965; Pancreatic Soc., GB and Ire., 1976; Roy. Soc. Med., 1978–80; London Med. Orchestra. Chairman: ASCAB; Conf. of Med. Roy. Coll. UK, 1976–78; Armed Forces Med. Adv. Bd, 1980–84. Member: Council, Brit. Empire Cancer Campaign; Exec., Internat. Fedn Surg. Colls. Trustee, Wolfson Foundn; Governor, Motability. Vis. Lectr to S Africa Assoc. of Surgeons, 1957; McIlrath Guest Prof. in Surgery, Royal Prince Alfred Hosp., Sydney, NSW, 1966; Vis. Prof., Surg. Unit, Univ. of Illinois, Chicago, 1978; Visiting Professor of Surgery: Jackson Univ., Miss, 1979; Johns Hopkins Hosp., Baltimore, 1979; Flint Univ., Mich, 1979. Lectures: First Datuk Abdul Majid Ismail Oration and Gold Medal, Malaysian Assoc. of Surgeons, 1972; Robert Whitmarsh Oration, Providence, 1972; Cheselden, St Thomas's Hosp., 1975; Philip Mitchiner, 1976; Balfour, Toronto, 1976; Colles, RCSI, 1976; Faltin (and Medal), Helsinki, 1976; Bradshaw, RCP, 1977; Sir Robert Bradlaw, Faculty of Dental Surgery, RCS, 1978; Sir Ernest Finch Meml, Sheffield, 1978; Telford Meml, Manchester, 1978; Annual Oration Med. Soc. of London, 1978; Sir William MacEwen Meml, Glasgow, 1978; Eisenberg, Boston, 1978; Judd, Minneapolis, 1979; first Samuel Jason Mixter, New England Surgical Soc., 1985. Hon. Member: Soc. of Grad. Surgeons of LA County Hosp., 1965; Finnish Surgical Soc., 1976; Surgical Res. Soc., 1976; Surgical Soc. of Phoenix, Arizona; Soc. Surg. Alimentary Tract; Hellenic Surg. Soc.; Kentucky Surg. Soc., 1979; Internat. Biliary Assoc., 1977. Hon. Fellow: Amer. Assoc. Surg.; Assoc. Clin. Anat.; Surgical Res. Soc., 1977; Assoc. of Surgeons of France, 1979; Philadelphia Acad. of Surg., 1979; Acad. de Chirurgie de Paris, 1981; Hon. FRACS 1957; Hon. FRCSEd 1975; Hon. FACS 1975; Hon. FRCSCan 1976; Hon. FRCSI 1976; Hon. FRCS S Africa 1976; Hon. FDS; Hon. FRSocMed 1981; Hon. FRCSGlas 1982. Hon. DSc: Exeter, 1974; Leeds, 1976; Hon. MD Zürich Univ., 1979. Biennial Prize, Internat. Soc. of Surgery, 1975; Gimbernat Surg. Prize, Surg. Soc. of Barcelona, 1980; Gold Medal, BMA, 1982. Hon. Freeman, Worshipful Co. of Barbers. *Publications:* Acute Intestinal Obstruction, 1947; Surgery of Pancreatic Neoplasms, 1951; Progress in Clinical Surgery, 1953, 1961, 1969; (ed with C. G. Rob) Operative Surgery (8 Vols) 1956–57 (14 Vols)

1968–69; Surgery of the Gallbladder and Bile Ducts, 1965; Clinical Surgery (Vols 1–14), 1965–67; papers in learned journals on pancreatic surgery, general abdominal surgery, intestinal obstruction. *Recreations:* music, painting, cricket, golf, bridge. *Address:* 135 Harley Street, W1N 1DJ. *T:* 0171–935 1714. *Club:* MCC.

SMITH OF GILMOREHILL, Baroness *cr* 1995 (Life Peer), of Gilmorehill in the City of Glasgow; **Elizabeth Margaret Smith;** *b* 4 June 1940; *d* of Frederick William Moncrieff Bennett and Elizabeth Waters Irvine Shanks; *m* 1967, Rt Hon. John Smith, PC, QC (Scot.), MP (*d* 1994); three *d*. *Educ:* Hutchesons' Girls' Grammar Sch.; Univ. of Glasgow (MA, DipEd). Admin. Asst, 1962–64, Scottish Sec., 1982–88, Great Britain-USSR Assoc.; teacher of French, 1964–68. Mem., Press Complaints Commn, 1995–. *Recreations:* family, cinema, music, theatre, travel. *Address:* House of Lords, SW1A 0PW.

SMITH, Prof. Adam Neil, MD; FRCSE, FRCPE; retired consultant surgeon; *b* 27 June 1926; *s* of William Blackwood Smith and Janet Elder Robertson; *m* 1953, Sibyl Mary Veitch Johnstone; one *s* three *d*. *Educ:* Lanark Grammar Sch.; Univ. of Glasgow (MB ChB 1948; MD Hons 1959). FRCSE 1956; FRCPE 1988; FRSE 1982; FIBiol 1991. Hall Fellow, Univ. of Glasgow, 1949–50; Faulds Fellow, 1950–51; MRC Clinical Research Fellow, 1951–54; Lectr in Surgery, Univ. of Glasgow, 1954–58; St Mark's Hosp., 1958; Sen. Lectr, 1959–63, Reader in Surgery, 1963–91, Univ. of Edinburgh. James IV and Commonwealth Travelling Fellow, 1963. Royal College of Surgeons of Edinburgh: Wade Prof. of Surgical Studies, 1986–; Vice-Pres., 1991–94. Mem. Council, Assoc. of Coloproctology, 1991–94; Pres., Pelvic Floor Soc., 1989–92; Mem., James IV Surgical Assoc. Formerly Ext. Examr, Glasgow, Dundee, Newcastle, overseas. Chm., Sci. Adv. Body, and Trustee, Melville Trust for Cancer Research. *Publications:* Scientific Foundations of Gastroenterology, 1980; (contrib.) Nutrition in the Prevention of Disease, 1989; (contrib.) Clinical Measurements in Coloproctology, 1991; (contrib.) The Large Intestine, 1991; (contrib.) Coloproctology and the Pelvic Floor, 1992; (contrib.) Colorectal Physiology: Faecal Incontinence, 1994; papers in surgical, gastroenterological and cancer jls. *Recreations:* golf, art. *Address:* 2 Ravelston House Park, Edinburgh EH4 3LU. *T:* 0131–332 4077. *Clubs:* Scottish Arts, Monks of St Giles (Edinburgh).

SMITH, Alan; mining engineer; *b* 19 Jan. 1930; *s* of John Smith and Alice (*née* Williams); *m* 1958, Adele Marguerite (*née* Buckle) (marr. diss. 1986); two *s* two *d*. *Educ:* Rossall; St Catherine's Soc., Oxford. BSc Leeds 1957. MIMinE 1958. NCB, 1957–64; Principal Sci. Officer, Min. of Power, 1964; Sci. Counsellor, HM Embassy, Paris, 1965–70; Cabinet Secretariat, 1970–71; DTI, 1971–73; Dept of Industry, 1973–74; Sci. and Technol. Counsellor, HM Embassy, Washington, 1975–77; Head of Sci. and Technol. Div., OECD, 1977–80; DTI Research Gp, 1980–84. Exec. Sec., Newcomen Soc., 1988–92. De Laune Lectr, Apothecaries' Soc., 1980. *Publications:* learned articles on steam engines. *Recreation:* engineering history. *Address:* 63 Abbey House, Abbey Road, NW8 9BX.

SMITH, Sir Alan, Kt 1982; CBE 1976; DFC 1941, and Bar 1942; DL; President, Dawson International plc, since 1982; *b* 14 March 1917; *s* of Alfred and Lilian Smith; *m* 1st, 1943, Margaret Stewart Todd (*d* 1971); three *s* two *d*; 2nd, 1977, Alice Elizabeth Moncur. *Educ:* Bede College, Sunderland. Self employed, 1931–36; Unilever Ltd, 1937–39; RAF, 1939–45; Man. Dir, Todd & Duncan Ltd, 1946–60; Chm. and Chief Exec., Dawson International, 1960–82. DL Kinross, 1967. *Recreations:* sailing, swimming. *Address:* Ardgairney House, Cleish, by Kinross, Scotland KY13 7LG. *T:* Cleish Hills (01577) 850265. *Club:* Lansdowne.

SMITH, Alan Christopher; Chief Executive, Test and County Cricket Board, since 1987; *b* 25 Oct. 1936; *s* of Herbert Sidney and Elsie Smith; *m* 1963, Anne Elizabeth Boddy; one *s* one *d*. *Educ:* King Edward's Sch., Birmingham; Brasenose Coll., Oxford (BA). Played cricket: Oxford Univ. CC, 1958–60 (Captain, 1959 and 1960); Warwicks CCC, 1958–74 (Captain, 1968–74); rep. England in six Test Matches, Australia and NZ, 1962–63. Gen. Sec., Warwicks CCC, 1976–86; England overseas cricket tours: Asst Manager, Australia, 1974–75; Manager: West Indies, 1981; Fiji, NZ and Pakistan, 1984. Mem., England Cricket Selection Cttee, 1969–73, 1982–86. Director: Royds Advertising and Marketing, 1971–86; Aston Villa Football Club plc, 1972–78. *Recreations:* both football codes, golf, bridge, motoring. *Address:* (office) TCCB, Lord's Ground, NW8 8QZ. *T:* 0171–286 4405; The Old Farmhouse, Wyck Rissington, Gloucestershire GL54 2PN. *T:* Cotswold (01451) 820509. *Clubs:* MCC, I Zingari; Vincent's (Oxford).

SMITH, Alan Frederick; Group Managing Director, Anglian Water PLC, since 1990; *b* 21 July 1944; *s* of Frederick Herbert Smith and Winifred Alice Bella (*née* Farthing); *m* 1966, Judith Mary Forshaw (marr. diss. 1991); one *s* one *d*. *Educ:* Gosfield Sch., Essex. CIPFA. Trainee, Colchester BC, 1961–66; Ipswich County Borough Council: Sen. Accountant, 1966–72; Asst Treas., 1972–74; Principal Accountant, Anglian Water Authy, 1974–75; Asst Dir of Finance, Southern Water Authy, 1975–80; Dir of Finance, Anglian Water Authy, 1980–89; Dep. Man. Dir and Dir of Finance, Anglian Water PLC, 1989–90. *Recreations:* walking, photography. *Address:* Anglian House, Ambury Road, Huntingdon, Cambs PE18 6NZ.

SMITH, Alan Guy E.; *see* Elliot-Smith.

SMITH, Alan Keith Patrick; Director, Colefax & Fowler, since 1993; *b* 17 March 1941; *s* of Ernest and Mary Smith; *m* 1st, 1968, Veronica Soskin (marr. diss.); one *s* one *d*; 2nd, 1983, Joan Peregrine; two *s*. *Educ:* St Michael's Coll., Leeds; Edinburgh Univ. (MA). Marks & Spencer, 1964–93, Dir, 1978–93; Chief Exec., Kingfisher, 1993–95. *Recreations:* family, wine collecting, walking, cooking. *Address:* Colefax & Fowler, 39 Brook Street, W1Y 2JE. *T:* 0171–493 2231. *Clubs:* Brooks's, MCC.

SMITH, Alan Oliver, QPM 1986; DL; Chief Constable of Derbyshire, 1985–90; *b* 9 Sept. 1929; *s* of Thomas Allen and Lily Oliver; *m* 1950, Jane (*née* Elliott); one *d*. *Educ:* elementary schools, Birmingham; Guiseley and Bradford Tech. Coll.; courses at Police Staff Coll., 1964, 1973, 1979. Constable to Supt, Bradford City Police, 1952–74; Supt and Chief Supt, W Yorks Metropolitan Police, 1974–79; Comdt, Bishopgarth Detective Training Sch., 1977–79; Asst Chief Constable, W Yorks, 1979–83; Dep. Chief Constable, Derbyshire Constabulary, 1983–84 (Acting Chief Constable, June 1984–Dec. 1985). Vice-President: Derbys Assoc. of Boys' Clubs, 1988–93; Wirksworth Br., Royal British Legion, 1988–; Derby and Dist Br., RSPCA, 1988–93; Chm., Ashbourne and Dovedale Br., Children's Soc., 1991–93. Formerly Mem., NE Consultative Cttee, Commn for Racial Equality; Mem., Professional Adv. Cttee, NSPCC, 1980–91; Mem., St John Council for Derbyshire, 1986– (formerly Hon. County Dir, St John Ambulance, S and W Yorks). DL Derbyshire, 1992. OStJ 1988. *Recreations:* landscape artist (various exhibns; works in permt collections, Calderdale Authy, Leeds City Council, Bradford Univ.). *Address:* c/o Constabulary HQ, Butterley Hall, Ripley, Derbyshire DE5 3RS.

SMITH, Alastair Macleod M.; *see* Macleod-Smith.

SMITH, Sir Alex; *see* Smith, Sir Alexander M.

SMITH, Alexander; Member (Lab) Scotland South, European Parliament, since 1989; *b* Kilwinning, 2 Dec. 1943. *Educ:* Irvine Royal Acad. Former gardener. Chm., 1983–87, Trade Union Liaison Officer, 1986–88, Cunninghame S CLP; former Chm., Irvine and District Trades Council. Member: TGWU (Mem., Regl, Public Service and Political Cttees); Scottish CND; Anti-Apartheid Movement; Amnesty Internat.; Latin American Solidarity Campaign. *Address:* Damside, Ayr KA8 8ER.

SMITH, Prof. Alexander Crampton, (Alex. Crampton Smith); Nuffield Professor of Anaesthetics, Oxford University, and Fellow of Pembroke College, Oxford, 1965–79; now Emeritus Professor; *b* 15 June 1917; *s* of William and Mary Elizabeth Crampton Smith; *m* 1953, Marjorie (*née* Mason); three *s*; two *d* by a former marriage. *Educ:* Inverness Royal Acad.; Edinburgh University. Edinburgh Univ., 1935–41. Served War of 1939–45 (Croix de Guerre, despatches), RNVR, 1942–46. Consultant Anaesthetist, United Oxford Hospitals, 1951; Clinical Lectr in Anaesthetics, Oxford Univ., 1961. FFARCS 1953; MA Oxon 1961. Civilian Consultant Anaesthetist to Royal Navy, 1968. Mem. Bd, Faculty of Anaesthetists, 1965–80. Mem. Trustees, Nuffield Medical Benefaction, 1973–92. *Publications:* Clinical Practice and Physiology of Artificial Respiration (with J. M. K. Spalding), 1963; contribs to anaesthetic, medical and physiological jls. *Recreations:* sailing, fishing. *Address:* 10 Horwood Close, Headington, Oxford OX3 7RF. *T:* Oxford (01865) 69593.

SMITH, Sir Alexander Mair, (Sir Alex), Kt 1975; Director of various companies; *b* 15 Oct. 1922; *s* of late John S. and Anne M. Smith; *m* 1st, 1944, Muriel (*née* Harris) (*d* 1950); one *d*; 2nd, 1956, Doris Neil (*née* Patrick) (*d* 1980); one *d* (and one *d* decd); 3rd, 1984, Jennifer Lewis (*née* Pearce); two step *s*. *Educ:* Univ. of Aberdeen. MA (Maths and Nat. Phil.), PhD, FInstP. Physicist, UKAEA, 1952–56; Head of Advanced Research, Rolls Royce Ltd, 1956–67; Dir and Chief Scientist, Rolls Royce & Associates Ltd, 1967–69; Dir, Manchester Polytechnic, 1969–81. Chairman: Cttee of Dirs of Polytechnics, 1974–76; Schools Council, 1975–78; Member: UGC, 1974–76; BBC Gen. Adv. Council, 1978–81; Council, RSA, 1979–84; Vice-Pres., CGLI, 1981–91; Patron, Educnl Inst. of Design, Craft and Technology, 1977–83. *Publications:* papers in learned jls. *Recreation:* golf. *Address:* Flat 2, 6 Hall Road, Wilmslow, Cheshire SK9 5BW. *T:* Wilmslow (01625) 522011.

SMITH, Alistair; *see* Smith, E. A.

SMITH, Alwyn; *see* Smith, Ernest A.

SMITH, Andreas W.; *see* Whittam Smith.

SMITH, Andrew Charles; QC 1990; *b* 31 Dec. 1947; *s* of Charles George Smith and Winifrid Smith; *m* 1986, Indu Nathoo; one *s* two *d*. *Educ:* Wyggeston Grammar Sch. for Boys, Leicester; Wadham Coll., Oxford (BA). Called to Bar, Middle Temple, 1974. *Address:* Fountain Court, Temple, EC4Y 9DH. *T:* 0171–583 3335.

SMITH, Andrew David; MP (Lab) Oxford East, since 1987; *b* 1 Feb. 1951; *m*; one step *s*. *Educ:* Reading Grammar Sch.; St John's Coll., Oxford. Joined Labour Party, 1973. Mem., Oxford City Council, 1976–87 (Chairman: Recreation Cttee, 1980–83; Planning Cttee, 1984–87). Opposition spokesman on higher and continuing educn, 1988–92, on Treasury and Economic Affairs, 1992–94; Shadow Chief Sec. to HM Treasury, 1994–. Contested (Lab) Oxford E, 1983. Chm., Bd, Oxford Brookes Univ. (formerly Oxford Poly.), 1987–93. *Address:* 4 Flaxfield Road, Blackbird Leys, Oxford OX4 5QD; House of Commons, SW1A 0AA.

SMITH, Anne; QC (Scot) 1993; *b* 16 March 1955; *d* of John Mather and Jessica Douglas; *m* 1979, David Alexander Smith, WS; one *s* one *d*. *Educ:* Jordanhill Coll., Glasgow; Lower Peover C of E Primary Sch.; Moss Hey Sch.; Cheadle Girls' Grammar Sch.; Edinburgh Univ. (LLB Hons). Apprenticeship with Shepherd & Wedderburn WS, 1977–79; pupil of James McGhie, 1979–80; admitted Faculty of Advocates, 1980. *Recreations:* being with children, music (piano, flute), aerobics, ski-ing, swimming, gardening, walking. *Address:* Advocates' Library, Parliament House, Edinburgh EH1 1RF. *T:* 0131–226 5071.

SMITH, Annette Dionne K.; *see* Karmiloff-Smith.

SMITH, Lt-Gen. Sir Anthony Arthur D.; *see* Denison-Smith.

SMITH, Anthony David, CBE 1987; President, Magdalen College, Oxford, since 1988; *b* 14 March 1938; *s* of Henry and Esther Smith. *Educ:* Brasenose Coll., Oxford (BA; Hon. Fellow, 1994). BBC TV Current Affairs Producer, 1960–71; Fellow, St Antony's Coll., Oxford, 1971–76; Director, BFI, 1979–88 (Fellow 1988). Bd Mem., Channel Four Television Co., 1980–84. Chm., Writers and Scholars Educnl Trust, 1989– (Mem., 1982–); Member: Arts Council, 1990–94; Acton Soc. Trust, 1978–; Trustee, Cambodia Trust, 1990–. *Publications:* The Shadow in the Cave: the broadcaster, the audience and the state, 1973, 2nd edn 1976; British Broadcasting, 1974; The British Press since the War, 1976; Subsidies and the Press in Europe, 1977; The Politics of Information, 1978; Television and Political Life, 1979; The Newspaper: an international history, 1979; Newspapers and Democracy, 1980; Goodbye Gutenberg—the newspaper revolution of the 1980's, 1980; The Geopolitics of Information, 1980; The Age of the Behemoths, 1991; From Books to Bytes, 1993; The Oxford Illustrated History of Television, 1995. *Address:* Magdalen College, Oxford OX1 4AU. *T:* Oxford (01865) 276000; Albany, Piccadilly, W1V 9RP. *Club:* Grillions.

SMITH, Prof. (Anthony) David, DPhil; Professor and Head of the Department of Pharmacology, University of Oxford, since 1984; Hon. Director, MRC Anatomical Neuropharmacology Unit, Oxford, since 1985; Fellow, Lady Margaret Hall, Oxford, since 1984; *b* 16 Sept. 1938; *s* of Rev. William Beddard Smith and Evelyn Smith; *m* 1st, 1962, Wendy Diana Lee (marr. diss. 1974); one *s* one *d*; 2nd, 1975, Dr Ingegerd Östman; one *s*. *Educ:* Kingswood Sch., Bath; Christ Church, Oxford (Bostock Exhibnr; BA 1963, MA 1966, DPhil 1966). Royal Soc. Stothert Res. Fellow, Oxford, 1966–70; Res. Lectr, Christ Church, Oxford, 1966–71; Wellcome Res. Fellow, Oxford, 1970–71; Univ. Lectr in Pharmacology and Student of Christ Church, 1971–84. Member: Gen. Bd of the Faculties, Oxford, 1980–84; Neurosciences Bd, MRC, 1983–88; Physiol Soc.; Pharmacol Soc. Dir of Pubns, IBRO, 1977–; Editor: Methods in the Neurosciences (IBRO Handbook Series), 1981–; Neuroscience, 1976–; Mem., editorial bds of various scientific jls. Dr *hc* Szeged Univ., 1993. (Seventh) Gaddum Meml Prize, British Pharmacol Soc., 1979. *Publications:* (ed) Handbook of Physiology, Section 7 Vol. 6, 1974; (ed) Commentaries in the Neurosciences, 1980; articles on neuropharmacology in jls. *Recreations:* music, travel. *Address:* University Department of Pharmacology, Mansfield Road, Oxford OX1 3QT. *T:* Oxford (01865) 271883.

SMITH, Anthony (John Francis); writer, broadcaster; *b* 30 March 1926; 2nd *s* of late Hubert Smith (formerly Chief Agent, National Trust) and Diana Watkin; *m* 1st, 1956, Barbara Dorothy Newman (marr. diss. 1983); one *s* two *d*; 2nd, 1984, Margaret Ann Holloway; one *s*. *Educ:* Dragon School, Oxford; Blundell's School, Devon; Balliol College, Oxford. MA Oxon., 1951. Served with RAF, 1944–48. Oxford University, 1948–51. Manchester Guardian, 1953 and 1956–57; Drum, Africa, 1954–55; Science Correspondent, Daily Telegraph, 1957–63. Founded British Balloon and Airship Club, 1965 (Pres., 1970–). Scientific Fellow of Zoological Society. Glaxo Award for Science Writers, 1977; Cherry Kearton Medal and Award, RGS, 1978. TV series include: Balloon Safari, Balloons over the Alps, Great Zoos of the World, Great Parks of the World, Wilderness; radio series include: A Sideways Look, 1977–89; High Street Africa Revisited, 1983–84; Truth to Tell, 1990–93. *Publications:* Blind White Fish in Persia, 1953, repr. 1990; Sea Never Dry, 1958; High Street Africa, 1961; Throw Out Two Hands, 1963; The Body, 1968, new edn 1985; The Seasons, 1970; The Dangerous Sort, 1970; Mato Grosso, 1971; Beside the Seaside, 1972; Good Beach Guide, 1973; The Human Pedigree, 1975; Animals on View, 1977; Wilderness, 1978; A Persian Quarter Century, 1979; A Sideways Look, 1983; The Mind, 1984; Smith & Son, 1984; Which Animal Are You?, 1988; The Great Rift, 1988; Explorers of the Amazon, 1990; Swaps, 1992; The Free Life, 1994. *Recreations:* travel, lighter-than-air flying. *Address:* 10 Aldbourne Road, W12 0LN. *T:* 0181–248 9589; St Aidan's, Bamburgh, Northumberland NE69 7BJ. *T:* Bamburgh (01668) 214253.

SMITH, Ven. (Anthony) Michael P.; *see* Percival Smith.

SMITH, Anthony Patrick; Chief Executive, English National Board for Nursing, Midwifery and Health Visiting, since 1990; *b* 7 Aug. 1939; *s* of Edward Smith and Gladys Smith (*née* Green); *m* 1965, Barbara Marie Johnson; one *d.* *Educ:* Latymer Sch.; Open Univ. (BA Hons); Polytechnic of Central London (MA). RGN, RMN, RNT (Florence Nightingale Scholar, 1971). Asst Dir, Nurse Education, St Bartholomew's Hosp., 1969–75; Dir, Nurse Education, Southampton, 1975–81. *Recreations:* countryside pursuits, Staffordshire portrait figures. *Address:* English National Board for Nursing, Midwifery and Health Visiting, Victory House, 170 Tottenham Court Road, W1P 0HA. *T:* 0171–388 3131.

SMITH, Anthony Thomas; QC 1977; a Recorder of the Crown Court, since 1977; *b* 21 June 1935; *s* of Sydney Ernest Smith and Winston Victoria Smith; *m* 1959, Letitia Ann Wheldon Griffith; one *s* two *d.* *Educ:* Northampton, Stafford, and Hinckley Grammar Schs; King's Coll., Cambridge (Exhibnr; MA). Called to the Bar, Inner Temple, 1958, Bencher, 1985. Flying Officer, RAF, 1958–60. Founder and Chm., Birmingham Free Representation Scheme. *Recreations:* music, reading, the countryside. *Address:* Berkeley Chambers, 321 Stratford Road, Shirley, Solihull, West Midlands B90 3BL. *T:* 0121–733 6925.

SMITH, Antony Francis; HM Diplomatic Service; Deputy Head of Mission, Lisbon, since 1994; *b* 6 May 1942; *s* of Robert Smith and Barbara (*née* Cunningham); *m* 1963, Marion Frances Hickman; two *d.* *Educ:* De La Salle Coll., Manchester. Joined FO, 1960; Cambodia, 1963–64; Vice Consul, Luanda, Angola, 1964–68; Warsaw, 1968–70; Persian lang. studies, SOAS, 1970–71; Tehran, 1971–74; FCO, 1975; First Sec., Accra, 1976–78; UK Delegn, OECD, Paris, 1979–83; Lisbon, 1983–85; Counsellor, FCO, 1985–90; Consul Gen. and Counsellor, Washington, 1990–94. Official, Order of Infante Dom Henriques (Portugal), 1985. *Recreation:* Ski-ing. *Address:* c/o Foreign and Commonwealth Office, King Charles Street, SW1A 2AH; 62 Elm Park Gardens, Park Walk, SW10 0AP. *Club:* Gremio Literario (Lisbon).

SMITH, Arnold Terence, MBE 1963; HM Diplomatic Service, retired; *b* 7 Oct. 1922; *s* of Thomas Smith and Minnie Louisa (*née* Mole); *m* 1st, 1944, Mary James (*d* 1983), Preston, Yorks; one *s* one *d*; 2nd, 1985, Brenda Day (*née* Edwards), Edmonton; one step *s.* *Educ:* Christ Church, Dover; Coll. of Technol., Dover. Enlisted HM Forces, Army, 1939; served War, 1939–45; released, 1947. Joined CRO, 1948; Attaché, Karachi, 1952–56; Second Sec., Madras, 1956–60; CRO, 1960–61; First Sec., Kuala Lumpur, 1961–65; Consul, Oslo, 1965–69; FCO, 1969–73; Head of Chancery, Mbabane, 1973–77; Head of Admin, Nairobi, 1977–78; Counsellor and Consul-Gen., Lagos, Nigeria, 1978–80. *Recreations:* hiking, gardening, golf, swimming. *Address:* Flowers Cottage, Streetly End, West Wickham, Cambridgeshire CB1 6RP. *T:* Cambridge (01223) 891247.

SMITH, Ven. Arthur Cyril, VRD 1955; MA; Archdeacon of Lincoln, 1960–76, now Archdeacon Emeritus; Rector of Algarkirk, 1960–76, now Canon Emeritus; *b* 26 Jan. 1909; *s* of late Arthur Smith and of Margaret Ryde, Manchester; *m* 1940, Patricia Marion Greenwood, *d* of late Lt Col Ranolt Nelson Greenwood, MC, and Beatrice Marion, *d* of late Rev. Llewellyn L. Montford Bebb, DD; two *s* two *d.* *Educ:* St John's College, Winnipeg, Canada; Sheffield University; Westcott House, Cambridge. Curate of: Keighley, 1934–36; Bishop's Hatfield, 1936–40. Chaplain RNVR, 1940; HMS Hawkins, 1940–41; 13th Destroyer Flotilla Gibraltar, 1941–43; HMS Eaglet, 1943–44; Senior Chaplain, Liverpool 1945–46. Rector, South Ormsby Group of Parishes, 1946–60; Rural Dean, Hill North, 1955; Canon and Prebendary of Centum Solidorum, 1960. Member: Standing Cttee, House of Clergy, Church Assembly, 1966–70; General Synod, 1970–76; Inspections Cttee, Adv. Council for Churches Ministry, 1967. Church Comr, 1968. Dir, Ecclesiastical Insurance Office Ltd. *Publications:* The South Ormsby Experiment, 1960; Deaneries: Dead or Alive, 1963; Team and Group Ministry, 1965; contributor to: Mission and Communication, 1963; The Caring Church, 1964; Theology. *Address:* 28 London Court, London Road, Headington, Oxford OX3 7SL. *T:* Oxford (01865) 744788. *Club:* Army and Navy.

SMITH, Prof. Barry Edward, PhD; Head of Nitrogen Fixation Laboratory, John Innes Centre (formerly AFRC) Institute of Plant Science Research, at Sussex University, since 1987; *b* 15 Nov. 1939; *s* of late Ernest Smith and Agnes Mary Smith (*née* DeFraine); *m* 1963, Pamela Heather Pullen; one *s* one *d.* *Educ:* Dr Challoner's Grammar Sch., Amersham; Royal Melbourne Tech. Coll., Australia; Hatfield Tech. Coll.; Univ. of Exeter (BSc); Univ. of East Anglia (PhD). Lab. technician, ICIANZ, 1956–59; ICI, 1959–60; res. appts, Univ. of Washington, Seattle, 1966–68, Univ. of Oxford, 1968–69; ARC, subseq. AFRC, Unit of Nitrogen Fixation, 1969–87; Asst Dir, 1986–87. Vis. Prof., Univ. of Essex, 1988–; Hon. Professorial Fellow, Univ. of Sussex, 1989. *Publications:* numerous articles in sci. jls and chapters in books on excited state chem. and on nitrogen fixation. *Address:* Nitrogen Fixation Laboratory, John Innes Centre, Colney Lane, Norwich NR4 7UH. *T:* Norwich (01603) 452571.

SMITH, Beverley; *see* Smith, Jenkyn B.

SMITH, Brian; *see* Smith, Eric B.

SMITH, Dr Brian; *see* Smith, Dr N. B.

SMITH, Brian, CMG 1993; OBE 1975; HM Diplomatic Service, retired; High Commissioner to Trinidad and Tobago, 1991–94; *b* 15 Sept. 1935; *s* of Charles Francis Smith and Grace Amelia (*née* Pope); *m* 1955, Joan Patricia Rivers; one *s* two *d.* *Educ:* Hull Grammar School; BSc Open Univ. 1994. Foreign Office, 1952; HM Forces, 1954–57; Bahrain, 1957; Doha, 1959; Vice-Consul, Luxembourg, 1960, Casablanca, 1962; Tehran, 1964; Berne, 1967; FCO, 1969; Kampala, 1973; Tehran, 1975; FCO, 1977; New York, 1979; Counsellor (Commercial), Bonn, 1982; Overseas Inspector, FCO, 1986; High Comr, Botswana, 1989. *Recreations:* riding, photography, music, handicrafts. *Address:* Bancroft, Castle Walk, Wadhurst, E Sussex TN5 6YA.

SMITH, Brian, IPFA; Chief Executive, Stoke City Council, since 1992; *b* 16 May 1947; *s* of Albert Frederick and Gladys Smith; *m* 1972, Susan Jane Lund; two *s.* *Educ:* Bristol Univ. (BA Hons). Graduate trainee accountant, Derbyshire CC, 1968; Accountancy Asst, Berkshire CC, 1972; Group Technical Officer, South Yorkshire CC, 1974; Asst County Treasurer, Dorset CC, 1976; Sen. Asst County Treasurer, Avon CC, 1979; Dep. County Treasurer, 1981, County Treasurer, 1983, Staffordshire CC. Hon. Sec., Soc. of County Treasurers, 1990–92. *Publications:* various articles in local govt finance jls. *Recreations:* music, gardening, travel. *T:* (office) Stoke (01782) 404600; (home) Stafford (01785) 660085.

SMITH, Rt. Rev. Brian Arthur; *see* Tonbridge, Bishop Suffragan of.

SMITH, Ven. Brian John; Archdeacon of Wilts, since 1980; Team Vicar, Redhorn team, Salisbury, since 1990; *b* 21 Sept. 1933; *s* of Stanley and Doris Jessie Smith; *m* 1965, Jean Margaret, *d* of Frank and Beryl Hanning; one *s* two *d.* *Educ:* St Marylebone Grammar School; Mill Hill School; St John's Coll., Durham; Salisbury Theological Coll. Army, 1952–55; professional photographer, 1956–62. Ordained, 1965; Curate of All Saints', Whitstable, 1965–69; Vicar of Woodford, Wilsford and Durnford, and Religious Drama Adviser to Diocese of Salisbury, 1969–76; Vicar of Mere, West Knoyle and Maiden Bradley, 1976–80; RD of Heytesbury, 1977–80; Vicar of Bishop's Cannings, All Cannings and Etchilhampton, 1980–83; Non-residentiary Canon, Salisbury Cath., 1980–. Member: Gen. Synod of C of E, 1985–90; Council of RADIUS (Religious Drama Soc. of GB), 1971–76; various cttees, Diocese of Salisbury, 1969–; Chm., Diocesan Christian Stewardship Cttee, 1983–91. Author of a number of plays. *Publication:* contrib. to Religious Drama. *Recreations:* drama, photography, canals. *Address:* The Vicarage, 57 The Street, Chirton, Devizes, Wilts SN10 3QS. *T:* Devizes (01380) 840271.

SMITH, Brian Percival, CEng, FIProdE; CIMgt; independent business consultant; *b* 3 Oct. 1919; *s* of Percival Smith and Hilda Judge; *m* 1942, Phoebe (Tina) Ginno; one *s.* *Educ:* Erith, Woolwich; London Univ. (BSc). Apprentice, 1936–41, Manager, 1941–46, Royal Ordnance Factories; Gen. Manager, Cumbrian Tool Co., 1946–49; PA Management Consultants: Consultant, 1949–59; Dir, R&D, 1959–66; Man. Dir, 1966–72; Chm. of Bd, 1972–76. Mem., CAA, 1981–84. Mem., Adv. Bd, LEK Partnership, 1987–92. Mem., Design Council, 1975–80; Vice-Pres., Royal Soc. of Arts, 1976–80. Prof. of Design Management, RCA, 1977–81. Member Council: BIM, 1972–74; Instn of Prod. Engrs, 1972– (Pres., 1973–74). *Publications:* Leadership in Management, 1968; Bureaucracy in Management, 1969; Management Style, 1973; Going into Europe, Why and How, 1975; The Morality and Management of Design, 1977. *Recreations:* painting, writing, listening to music. *Address:* 4 Cliff Road, Eastbourne, East Sussex BN20 7RU. *T:* Eastbourne (01323) 731870.

SMITH, Brian Stanley, FSA, FRHistS; Secretary, Royal Commission on Historical Manuscripts, 1982–92; *b* 15 May 1932; *s* of late Ernest Stanley Smith and Dorothy (*née* Palmer); *m* 1963, Alison Margaret Hemming; two *d.* *Educ:* Bloxham; Keble College, Oxford (Holroyd Scholar). MA 1957. FSA 1972, FRHistS 1980. Assistant Archivist, Worcestershire, 1956–58, Essex, 1958–60, Gloucestershire, 1961–68; County Archivist, Gloucestershire, 1968–79; Asst Sec., Royal Commn on Historical Manuscripts, 1980–81. Heritage consultancy, St Helena, 1993. Part-time Editor, Victoria County History of Gloucestershire, 1968–70; Editor, 1971–79, Pres., 1986–87, Bristol and Gloucestershire Archaeological Soc. Chm., Soc. of Archivists, 1979–80. Lay Mem., Gloucester Diocesan Synod, 1972–76. FRSA 1991. *Publications:* History of Malvern, 1964, 2nd edn 1978; (with Elizabeth Ralph) History of Bristol and Gloucestershire, 1972, 3rd edn 1995; The Cotswolds, 1976, 2nd edn 1992; History of Bloxham School, 1978; articles in learned jls on local history and archives. *Recreations:* mountaineering, gardening. *Address:* Bryn Farm, Vowchurch Common, Hereford HR2 0RL.

SMITH, Maj.-Gen. Sir Brian W.; *see* Wyldbore-Smith.

SMITH, Brian William, AO 1988; PhD, FIEAust, Vice-Chancellor and Professor, University of Western Sydney, 1989–94; *b* 21 June 1938; *s* of William Lyle Smith and Grace Ellen Smith; *m* 1961, Josephine Peden; two *d* (one *s* decd). *Educ:* Univ. of Melbourne (BEng); Univ. of Cambridge (PhD). Australian Paper Manufacturers Ltd, 1964–70; Consolidated Electronic Industries Ltd, 1971–73; Head, School of Electrical Engineering, 1973–77, Dean, Faculty of Engineering, 1977–79, Dir, 1979–89, Royal Melbourne Inst. of Technology. FAIM. *Recreations:* golf, model railway. *Address:* 60 Faraday Street, Carlton, Vic 3053, Australia. *Clubs:* Greenacres Golf, Melbourne Cricket.

SMITH, Dr Bruce Gordon, OBE 1992; FIEE; Chairman, Economic and Social Research Council, since 1994; Chairman, Smith System Engineering Ltd, since 1987 (Managing Director, 1971–87); *b* 4 Oct. 1939; *s* of William Francis Smith and Georgina Lucy May Smith (*née* Tompkins); *m* 1964, Rosemary Jane Martineau; two *s* two *d.* *Educ:* Dulwich Coll.; Christ Church, Oxford (BA 1st cl. Hons Physics 1961; DPhil 1964; MA 1968). FIEE 1978 (MIEE 1971). Res. Associate, Univ. of Chicago, 1964–65; mem., tech. staff, Bellcomm Inc., 1965–68; Prin. Engr, Decca Radar Ltd, 1968–71. Domus Fellow, St Catherine's Coll., Oxford, 1991–. Dir, Industrial Technology Securities Ltd, 1985–. Member: Plenary Bd, RAE, 1987–91; BNSC Earth Observation Prog. Bd, 1986–; Exec. Cttee, Parly Space Cttee, 1989–; Chm., UK Industrial Space Cttee, 1992–94. Chm., Eur. Assoc. of Remote Sensing Cos, 1987–91 (Treas., British Assoc., 1985–95); Pres., Assoc. of Indep. Res. and Technol. Orgns, 1991–93; UK Deleg. and Pres., Eur. Assoc. of Contract Res. Orgns, 1995–; Mem. Council, Soc. of British Aerospace Cos, 1992–94. Vice-Chm., Surrey Br., Prince's Youth Business Trust, 1991–. *Recreations:* mountain walking, dinghy sailing, cycling, music. *Address:* 11 Oxdowne Close, Cobham, Surrey KT11 2SZ. *T:* Leatherhead (01372) 843526.

SMITH, Bryan Crossley, CBE 1982; CEng, FIGasE; Member for Marketing, British Gas Corporation, 1977–82; Chairman: C.S.E. (Wendover) Ltd, Business Consultants, since 1981; Sports & Fitness Assessment Ltd, since 1985; Turbine Power Ltd (formerly Power Generation), since 1988; *b* 28 Feb. 1925; *s* of Frank Riley Smith and Fanny Smith; *m* 1948, Patricia Mabbott; one *s* one *d.* *Educ:* Hipperholme Grammar Sch.; Bradford Technical Coll. CEng, FIGasE 1944. Articled pupil to John Corrigan, 1941; Operating Engr, Humphreys & Glasgow, 1944; Works Engr, Middlesbrough Corp. Gas Dept, 1948; N Eastern Gas Board: Asst Works Manager, Huddersfield, 1952; Engr and Man., Dewsbury, 1956; Group Sales Man., Wakefield, 1961; Conversion Man., 1966; Dep. Commercial Man., 1968; Chief Service Man., Gas Council, 1970; Service Dir, British Gas Corp., 1973. Senior Vice-Pres., IGasE, 1980–81. Chm., The Wendover Soc., 1985–. *Recreations:* golf, gardening. *Address:* Heron Path House, Wendover, Aylesbury, Bucks HP22 6NN. *T:* Wendover (01296) 622742.

SMITH, Catharine Mary S.; *see* Scott-Smith.

SMITH, Sheriff Charles; Sheriff of Tayside, Central and Fife at Cupar and Dundee, since 1991; *b* 15 Aug. 1930; *s* of late Charles Smith and Mary Allan Hunter or Smith; *m* 1959, Janet Elizabeth Hurst; one *s* one *d.* *Educ:* Kinnoull Primary Sch.; Perth Academy; St Andrews University. MA, LLB. Solicitor 1956. Practised as principal with Campbell Brooke and Myles, Perth, 1961–82; Interim Depute Procurator Fiscal, 1975–82; Temporary Sheriff, 1977–82; Sheriff (floating appointment): of Glasgow and Strathkelvin, 1982–86; of Tayside, Central and Fife at Perth, 1986–91. Tutor, 1979–82, Hon. Tutor, 1982–86, Dept of Law, Dundee Univ. Member Council: Law Soc. of Scotland, 1977–82

(Convener, various cttees); Sheriffs' Assoc., 1987–90. Mem., Perth Town Council, 1966–68. *Recreations:* tennis, golf, croquet. *Address:* c/o Sheriff Court, County Buildings, St Catherine Street, Cupar, Fife KY15 4LX. *T:* Cupar (01334) 652121. *Club:* Kinnoull Lawn Tennis.

SMITH, Sir Charles B.; *see* Bracewell-Smith.

SMITH, Charles M.; *see* Miller Smith.

SMITH, Charles Robert S.; *see* Saumarez Smith.

SMITH, (Charles) Russell, CBE 1984; Chairman, Allied Textile Companies PLC, 1983–91 (Chief Executive, 1963–86); Director, Lloyds Bank plc, since 1985 (Regional Chairman, Yorkshire and Humberside, 1984–91; Regional Director, 1973–91); *b* 19 Aug. 1925; *m* 1951, Jean Rita Thomas; one *s* three *d. Educ:* Rastrick Grammar Sch., Brighouse, W Yorks. Served War, RNVR, 1943–46 (commnd). Armitage and Norton, Chartered Accountants, Huddersfield, 1941–50; Dir, subseq. Man. Dir, R. Beanland and Co. Ltd, 1950–63. Director: Yorkshire Bank PLC, 1978–84; Lloyds Bank UK Management Ltd, 1984–85; Lloyds & Scottish PLC, 1985–86; Lloyds Abbey Life PLC (formerly Abbey Life Gp), 1988–; Lloyds Merchant Bank (Hldgs) Ltd, 1989–93; Heywood Williams Gp, 1990–. Pres., British Textile Confedn, 1982 and 1983; Chm., Wakefield Diocesan Bd of Finance, 1974–90; Mem., Yorks and Humberside Regional Develt Bd, 1975–79. *Recreations:* too few. *Address:* Tabara, 12 Wheatcroft Avenue, Scarborough, North Yorks YO11 3BN. *T:* Scarborough (01723) 376266.

SMITH, Prof. (Christopher) Colin; Professor of Spanish, University of Cambridge, 1975–90; *b* 17 Sept. 1927; *s* of Alfred Edward Smith and Dorothy May Berry; *m* 1954, Ruth Margaret Barnes; three *d* (one *s* decd). *Educ:* Varndean Grammar Sch., Brighton; St Catharine's Coll., Cambridge (MA, PhD; LittD). BA 1st cl. hons 1950. Dept of Spanish, Univ. of Leeds: Asst Lectr 1953; Lectr 1956; Sen. Lectr 1964; Sub-Dean of Arts, etc, 1963–67; Cambridge Univ.: Univ. Lectr in Spanish, 1968; Fellow, St Catharine's Coll., 1968–, Professorial Fellow, 1975–90, Tutor 1970; Chm. Faculty of Mod. and Med. Langs, 1973. Hon. Vice-Consul of Spain, Cambridge, 1983–. Corresp. Mem., Royal Spanish Acad. of the Language, 1993. Comendador de número de la Orden de Isabel la Católica (Spain), 1988. General Editor, Modern Language Review, 1976–81 (Hispanic Editor, 1974–81). *Publications:* Spanish Ballads, 1964; (ed) Poema de mio Cid, 1972 (Spanish edn 1976); Collins' Spanish-English, English-Spanish Dictionary, 1971 (Spanish edn 1972), 3rd edn 1992; Estudios cidianos, 1977; (with A. L. F. Rivet) Place-names of Roman Britain, 1979; The Making of the Poema de mio Cid, 1983 (Spanish edn 1985); Christians and Moors in Spain, vol. I, 1988, vol. II, 1989; contrib. Bull. Hispanic Studies, Mod. Lang. Rev., Bull. Hispanique, etc. *Recreations:* theatre, opera, natural history (especially entomology), archaeology. *Address:* 56 Girton Road, Cambridge CB3 0LL. *T:* Cambridge (01223) 276214.

SMITH, Rev. Christopher Hughes; Supernumerary Methodist Minister; President, National Christian Education Council, since 1995; President of the Methodist Conference, 1985–86; *b* 30 Nov. 1929; *s* of Rev. Bernard Hughes Smith and Dorothy Lucy Smith; *m* 1956, Margaret Jean Smith; three *s* and one foster *s. Educ:* Bolton School; Emmanuel College and Wesley House, Cambridge. MA Cantab. Intercollegiate Sec., SCM, 1955–58; ordained at Methodist Conf., Newcastle upon Tyne, 1958; Leicester South Methodist Circuit, 1958–65; Birmingham South-West Methodist Circuit, 1965–74; Chm., Birmingham Methodist Dist, 1974–87; Lancaster Methodist Circuit, 1987–88; Gen. Sec., Div. of Educn and Youth, Methodist Ch, 1988–95. Hon. Fellow, Selly Oak Colls, 1992. Hon. MA Birmingham, 1985. *Publications:* Music of the Heart—Methodist Spirituality, 1991; contribs to Methodist Recorder, Epworth Review. *Recreations:* gardening, music, books, walking. *Address:* c/o Methodist Conference Office, 25 Marylebone Road, NW1 5JR.

SMITH, Christopher Robert, PhD; MP (Lab) Islington South and Finsbury, since 1983; *b* 24 July 1951; *s* of Colin Smith and Gladys (*née* Luscombe). *Educ:* Cassiobury Primary Sch., Watford; George Watson's Coll., Edinburgh; Pembroke Coll., Cambridge Univ. (BA 1st Cl. Hons 1972, PhD 1979); Harvard Univ., Mass (Kennedy Scholar, 1975–76). Develt Sec., Shaftesbury Soc. Housing Assoc., 1977–80; Develt Co-ordinator, Soc. for Co-operative Dwellings, 1980–83. Councillor, London Bor. of Islington, 1978–83 (Chief Whip, 1978–79; Chm., Housing Cttee, 1981–83). Opposition spokesman on treasury and economic affairs, 1987–92; principal opposition spokesman on environmental protection, 1992–94, on Nat. Heritage, 1994–. Chairman: Tribune Gp of MPs, 1988–89 (Sec., 1985–88); Labour Campaign for Criminal Justice, 1985–88; Bd, Tribune Newspaper, 1990–93; Bd, New Century Magazine, 1993–; Mem. Exec., Fabian Soc., 1990–. Pres., Cambridge Union, 1972; Vice-Chm., Young Fabian Gp, 1974–75; Chm., Charing Cross Br., ASTMS, 1980–83; Member: Exec., NCCL, 1986–88; Bd, Shelter, 1986–92; Exec. Cttee, Nat. Trust, 1995–. Governor, Sadler's Wells Theatre, 1987–; Trustee, John Muir Trust, 1991–. *Recreations:* mountaineering, literature, theatre, music. *Address:* House of Commons, SW1A 0AA. *T:* 0171–219 5119.

SMITH, Sir Christopher Sydney Winwood, 5th Bt, *cr* 1809; *b* 20 Sept. 1906; *s* of Sir William Sydney Winwood Smith, 4th Bt, and Caroline, *o d* of James Harris, County Cork; *S* father 1953; *m* 1932, Phyllis Berenice, *y d* of late Thomas Robert O'Grady, Grafton, New South Wales, and County Waterford, Ireland; six *s* three *d* (and one *s* decd). *Heir: s* Robert Sydney Winwood Smith [*b* 1939; *m* 1971, Roslyn Nellie, *e d* of late James Keith McKensie; one *s* one *d*]. *Address:* Junction Road, via Grafton, New South Wales 2460, Australia.

SMITH, Claude C.; *see* Croxton-Smith.

SMITH, Clifford Bertram Bruce H.; *see* Heathcote-Smith.

SMITH, Colin; *see* Smith, Christopher C.

SMITH, Colin; Secretary-General, International Association Against Painful Experiments on Animals, since 1969; *b* 4 July 1941; *s* of Henry E. Smith and A. E. Smith. *Educ:* Upton House Sch., London. Asst Sec., National Anti-Vivisection Soc., 1962–71, Gen. Sec., 1971–81, Internat. Exec. Dir, 1981–86; Dir, American Fund for Alternatives to Animal Res., 1977–92. Mem., Hon. Nederlandse Laureat van de Arbeid, 1981. Editor, Animals' Defender and Anti-Vivisection News, 1967–72, 1982–86. *Publications:* Progress without Pain, 1973; Animal Experiments: steps towards reform, 1975; Moral and Social Aspects of Vivisection, 1981; International Charter for Health and Humane Research, 1989; numerous contribs to med. and scientific jls on the anti-vivisection case. *Recreations:* music, theatre, travel. *Address:* 29 College Place, St Albans, Herts AL3 4PU.

SMITH, Colin Deverell; Group Chief Executive, Argyll Group, since 1993; *b* 21 May 1947; *m* 1971, Kathy Morgan; two *s. Educ:* All Saints Sch., Bloxham, Banbury; Liverpool Univ. (BCom 1969). FCA 1973. Qualified with Arthur Andersen, Manchester; Argyll Foods: Gp Financial Controller and Co. Sec., 1979–83; Argyll Gp: Gp Financial Controller and Co. Sec., 1983–84; Dir, 1984–; Finance Dir, 1989. *Recreations:* theatre, walking, Rugby, interesting vehicles. *Address:* Safeway House, 6 Millington Road, Hayes, Middx UB3 4AY. *T:* 0181–848 8744.

SMITH, Prof. Colin John; Professor of Oral Pathology, since 1973, and Dean of Dental Studies, School of Clinical Dentistry, 1978–84 and since 1988, University of Sheffield; *b* 7 June 1938; *s* of Rowland William John Smith and Doris Emily Smith; *m* 1962, Mary Margaret Kathrine MacMahon; three *d. Educ:* Purley County Grammar Sch. for Boys; Royal Dental Hosp. Sch. of Dental Surgery, Univ. of London (BDS Hons, PhD). LDSRCS, FRCPath. House Surgeon, Royal Dental Hosp., 1961–62; MRC Scientific Asst, 1962–63, Prophit Cancer Res. Student, 1964–68, Dept of Dental Sci., RCS; Wellcome Travelling Res. Fellow, Dept of Oral Path., Royal Dental Coll., Copenhagen, 1968–69; Nuffield Dental Res. Fellow, Dept of Morbid Anatomy, RPMS, 1969–71; Sen. Lectr and Res. Fellow, Dept of Oral Medicine and Path., Guy's Hosp. Dental Sch., 1971–72. Charles Tomes Lectr, RCS, 1987. Hon. Mem., Hungarian Dental Assoc., 1991. Colgate Prize, British Div., Internat. Assoc. for Dental Res., 1964. *Publications:* Oral Cancer: epidemiology, etiology and pathology, 1990; chapters in books and contribs to professional jls. *Recreations:* lawn tennis, walking, gardening, listening to classical music. *Address:* Department of Oral Pathology, School of Clinical Dentistry, The University, Claremont Crescent, Sheffield S10 2TA; 1 Dale Mill, The Dale, Hathersage, Derbyshire S30 1AQ. *T:* Hope Valley (01433) 650938. *Club:* Royal Society of Medicine.

SMITH, Colin Milner; QC 1985; **His Honour Judge Milner Smith;** a Circuit Judge, since 1991; *b* 2 Nov. 1936; *s* of Alan Milner Smith and late Vera Ivy Smith; *m* 1979, Moira Soraya, *d* of Reginald Braybrooke; one *s* one *d. Educ:* Tonbridge; Brasenose College, Oxford (MA); Univ. of Chicago (JD). Called to the Bar, Gray's Inn, 1962; a Recorder, 1987–91. *Publication:* (jtly) The Law of Betting, Gaming and Lotteries, 1987. *Recreations:* cricket, skiing, reading. *Address:* 3 Gray's Inn Place, Gray's Inn, WC1R 5DU. *T:* 0171–831 8441. *Club:* MCC.

SMITH, Colin Roderick, CVO 1984; CBE 1995; QPM 1987; HM Inspector of Constabulary, since 1991; *s* of Humphrey and Marie Smith; *m* 1961, Patricia Joan Coppin. *Educ:* Dorking County and Bexhill Grammar Schools; Univ. of Birmingham (BSocSc, Hons Social Admin.); rcds 1981. Royal Army Service Corps (Lieut), 18 Co. (Amph), 1959–62; East Sussex Constabulary, later Sussex Police, from Constable to Chief Supt, 1962–77; Asst Chief Constable, Thames Valley Police, 1977–82; Dep. Asst Comr, Metropolitan Police, 1982–85 (incl. founder, Royalty and Diplomatic Protection Dept); Chief Constable, Thames Valley Police, 1985–91. *Recreation:* horse riding. *Address:* Office of Her Majesty's Inspector of Constabulary, Bridge House, Sion Place, Clifton Down, Bristol BS8 4XA. *T:* Bristol (0117) 973 6400. *Club:* Royal Automobile.

SMITH, Sir Colin S.; *see* Stansfield Smith.

SMITH, Sir Cyril, Kt 1988; MBE 1966; DL; Managing Director, Smith Springs (Rochdale) Ltd, 1963–87; *b* 28 June 1928; unmarried. *Educ:* Rochdale Grammar Sch. for Boys. Civil Service, 1944–45; Wages Clerk, 1945–48; Liberal Party Agent, Stockport, 1948–50; Labour Party Agent, Ashton-under-Lyne, 1950–53, Heywood and Royton 1953–55; rejoined Liberal Party, 1967; MP Rochdale, Oct. 1972–1992 (L, 1972–88, Lib Dem, 1988–92); Liberal Chief Whip, 1975–76. Newsagent (own account), 1955–58; Production Controller, Spring Manufacturing, 1958–63; founded Smith Springs (Rochdale) Ltd, 1963. Director: Ratcliffe Springs, 1987–90; Robert Riley Springs; Safe Buy UK. Councillor, 1952–66, Alderman, 1966–74, Mayor, 1966–67, Co. Borough of Rochdale (Chm., Education Cttee, 1966–72); Councillor, Rochdale Metropolitan DC, 1973–75. A Dep. Pro-Chancellor, Lancaster Univ., 1978–86. Freeman, Borough of Rochdale, 1992. DL Greater Manchester, 1991. Hon. LLD Lancaster, 1993. OStJ 1976. *Publications:* Big Cyril (autobiog.), 1977; Industrial Participation, 1977. *Recreations:* music (listener), reading, charitable work, local government. *Address:* 14 Emma Street, Rochdale, Lancs OL12 6QW. *T:* Rochdale (01706) 48840.

SMITH, Cyril Stanley, CBE 1985; MSc, PhD; Secretary to Economic and Social Research Council (formerly Social Science Research Council), 1975–85; *b* 21 July 1925; *s* of Walter and Beatrice May Smith; *m* 1968, Eileen Cameron; two *d* (by first marr.). *Educ:* Plaistow Municipal Secondary Sch.; London Sch. of Economics. HM Forces, Dorset Regt, 1943–47. Univ. of Birmingham, 1950–51; Univ. of Sheffield, 1951–52; Dulwich Coll. Mission, 1952–56; Nat. Coal Board, 1956–61; Univ. of Manchester, 1961–71; Civil Service Coll., 1971–75. Man. Dir, ReStrat, 1985–90. Visiting Prof., Univ. of Virginia, 1965; Academic Visitor, Nuffield Coll., Oxford, 1980–81, 1985–86; Senior Res. Fellow, Wissenschaftszentrum Berlin für Sozialforschung, 1987. British Nat. Expert, European Poverty Prog., 1977–82. Mem., Sec. of State's Cttee on Inequalities in Health, DHSS, 1977–80. Chm., British Sociological Assoc., 1972–74; Pres., Sociol. Sect., British Assoc., 1979. *Publications:* Adolescence, 1968; (sen. author) The Wincroft Youth Project, 1972; (ed jtly) Society and Leisure in Britain, 1973; numerous articles on youth, leisure and developments in social science. *Address:* Cornwall House, Cornwall Gardens, SW7 4AE.

SMITH, Prof. David; *see* Smith, Prof. A. D.

SMITH, Prof. David; *see* Smith, Prof. N. J. D.

SMITH, David, PhD; FInstPet; consultant; formerly Chairman and Managing Director, Esso Chemical Ltd; *b* 18 July 1927; *s* of Walter and Annie Smith; *m* 1951, Nancy Elizabeth (*née* Hawley); two *s* three *d. Educ:* Burton Grammar School; Univ. of Sheffield. BSc, PhD. Lectr in Fuel Technology and Chemical Engineering, Univ. of Sheffield, 1951–55; Esso Research Ltd, 1955–65; Dir, Products Research Div., Esso Research and Engineering, USA, 1966–68; Marketing Dir and Man. Dir, Esso Chemical Ltd, 1968–71; Vice-Pres., Essochem Europe Inc., Brussels, 1971–73; Vice-Pres., Exxon Chemical Inc., USA, 1973–78. *Recreation:* golf. *Address:* Meadowlands, Stockbridge Road, Winchester, Hants SO22 5JH. *T:* Winchester (01962) 864880. *Clubs:* MCC; Royal Winchester Golf.

SMITH, Prof. David, FRS 1988; CPhys, FInstP; Department of Biomedical Engineering and Medical Physics, University of Keele, since 1995; *b* 26 Nov. 1935; *s* of J. and F. L. Smith. *Educ:* Keele Univ. (BA 1959); DSc 1975, PhD 1962, Birmingham Univ. FInstP 1973. Res. Fellow, 1962, Prof. of Chemical Physics, 1964–90, Birmingham Univ.; Prof. of Physics, Institut für Ionenphysik der Universität Innsbruck, Austria, 1991–95. Hon. DSc Keele, 1990. *Publications:* numerous res. pubns and review articles in physics, chemistry and astrophysics, for learned jls incl. British Inst. of Physics jls and Amer. Inst. of Physics jls. *Recreations:* classical music, sport. *Address:* 9 The Elms, Porthill, Newcastle-under-Lyme, Staffs ST5 8RP; Department of Biomedical Engineering and Medical Physics, University of Keele, Thornburrow Drive, Hartshill, Stoke-on-Trent, Staffs ST4 7QB.

SMITH, David Arthur, QC 1982; **His Honour Judge David Smith;** a Circuit Judge, since 1986; *b* 7 May 1938; *s* of late Arthur Heber Smith and Marjorie Edith Pounds Smith; *m* 1967, Clementine Smith, JP (*née* Urquhart); two *s. Educ:* Lancing College; Merton Coll., Oxford (MA Hons Jurisprudence). Called to Bar, Middle Temple, 1962; Official Principal of Archdeaconry of Hackney, 1973–; a Recorder, 1978–86. Mem., Parole Bd, 1989–94. Wine Treasurer, Western Circuit, 1980–86. *Publications:* John Evelyn's Manuscript on Bees from Elysium Britannicum, 1966; (jtly) Bibliography of British Bee

Books, 1979; (with David Frimston) Beekeeping and the Law—Swarms and Neighbours, 1993. *Recreations:* acting (Mem., Old Stagers, 1982–), bees (Sec. of Internat. Bee Research Assoc., 1963–), books, canals, Rossini. *Address:* The Law Courts, Bristol BS1 1DA.

SMITH, David Arthur George, JP; Headmaster of Bradford Grammar School, since 1974; *b* 17 Dec. 1934; *o s* of Stanley George and Winifred Smith, Bath, Somerset; *m* 1957, Jennifer, *e d* of John and Rhoda Anning, Launceston, Cornwall; one *s* two *d*. *Educ:* City of Bath Boys' Sch.; Balliol Coll., Oxford. MA, Dip. Ed (Oxon). Assistant Master, Manchester Grammar Sch., 1957–62; Head of History, Rossall School, 1963–70; Headmaster, The King's School, Peterborough, 1970–74. Chm., HMC, 1988. JP West Yorks, 1975. *Publications:* (with John Thorn and Roger Lockyer) A History of England, 1961; Left and Right in Twentieth Century Europe, 1970; Russia of the Tsars, 1971. *Recreations:* writing, walking. *Address:* Bradford Grammar School, Bradford, West Yorks BD9 4JP. *T:* Bradford (01274) 545461. *Club:* Bradford Athenæum (Bradford).

SMITH, David Buchanan, FSAScot; Sheriff of North Strathclyde at Kilmarnock, since 1975; *b* 31 Oct. 1936; *s* of William Adam Smith and Irene Mary Calderwood Hogarth; *m* 1961, Hazel Mary Sinclair; one *s* one *d* (and one *s* decd). *Educ:* Paisley Grammar Sch.; Glasgow Univ. (MA); Edinburgh Univ. (LLB). Advocate, 1961; Standing Junior Counsel to Scottish Educn Dept, 1968–75. Tutor, Faculty of Law, Univ. of Edinburgh, 1964–72. Treas., Sheriffs' Assoc., 1979–89 (archivist, 1989–); Trustee, The Scottish Curling Museum Trust, 1980–. *Publications:* Curling: an illustrated history, 1981; The Roaring Game: memories of Scottish curling, 1985; George Washington Wilson in Ayrshire, 1991; contrib. The Laws of Scotland: Stair Memorial Encyclopedia, vol. 6; articles in Scots Law Times, Juridical Rev., Jl of Law Soc. of Scotland, Scottish Book Collector, The Medal, and newspapers. *Recreations:* history of the law and institutions of Scotland, curling, collecting curliana, music, architecture. *Address:* 72 South Beach, Troon, Ayrshire KA10 6EG. *T:* Troon (01292) 312130; Sheriff's Chambers, Sheriff Court House, Kilmarnock KA1 1ED. *T:* Kilmarnock (01563) 520211.

SMITH, David C.; *see* Calvert-Smith.

SMITH, Sir David (Cecil), Kt 1986; FRS 1975; FRSE; Principal and Vice-Chancellor, University of Edinburgh, 1987–93; President, Wolfson College, Oxford, since 1994; *b* 21 May 1930; *s* of William John Smith and Elva Emily Smith; *m* 1965, Lesley Margaret Mollison Mutch; two *s* one *d*. *Educ:* Colston's Sch., Bristol; St Paul's Sch., London; Queen's Coll., Oxford (Browne Schol., MA, DPhil). Christopher Welch Res. Schol., Oxford, 1951–54; Swedish Inst. Schol., Uppsala Univ., 1951–52; Browne Res. Fellow, Queen's Coll., Oxford, 1956–59; Harkness Fellow, Univ. Calif, Berkeley, 1959–60; Oxford University: Univ. Lectr, Dept Agric., 1960–74; Mem., Linacre Coll., 1962–64, Hon. Fellow, 1988; Royal Soc. Res. Fellow, 1964–71, Tutorial Fellow and Tutor for Admissions, 1971–74, Hon. Fellow, 1987, Wadham Coll.; Melville Wills Prof. of Botany, 1974–80, and Dir of Biological Studies, 1977–79, Bristol Univ.; Sibthorpian Prof. of Rural Economy, and Fellow of St John's Coll., Oxford Univ., 1980–87. Vis. Prof., UCLA, 1968. Chairman: NERC Aquatic Life Scis Cttee, 1978–81; Subject Area Rev. Cttee in Biol. Sci., London Univ., 1982–86; Member: NERC Terrestrial Life Scis Cttee, 1975–78; AFRC (formerly ARC), 1982–88 (Mem. Plants and Soils Cttee, 1976–86 (Chm., 1983–86)); Consultative Bd, JCO for Res. in Agric. and Food, 1981–83; SERC Science Board, 1983–85 (Chm., SERC Biol Scis Cttee, 1981–83); Co-ordinating Cttee on Marine Sci. and Technology, 1987–91; ABRC, 1989–90. President: British Lichen Soc., 1972–74; British Mycological Soc., 1980; Soc. for Experimental Biol., 1983–85 (Vice-Pres., 1981–83); Internat. Soc. Endocytobiology, 1981–89; Royal Society: a Vice-Pres., 1978–80, 1983–87; Biological Sec., 1983–87. Bidder Lecture, Soc. for Experimental Biology, 1985; Sir Joseph Banks Lectures, Australian bicentennial, 1988; L. F. Power Meml Lecture, James Cook Univ., 1988. Editor and Trustee, New Phytologist, 1965–. FRSE 1988. Hon. DSc: Liverpool, Exeter, 1986; Hull, 1987; Aberdeen, 1990; Napier, Heriot-Watt, 1993; Hon. LLD: Pennsylvania, 1990; Queen's Univ., Ontario, 1991; Dr *hc* Edinburgh, 1994. Linnean Medal, Linnean Soc., 1989. Commendatore dell'Ordine al Merito della Repubblica Italiana, 1991. *Publications:* (with A. Douglas) The Biology of Symbiosis, 1987; various articles on symbiosis, in New Phytol., Proc. Royal Soc., Biol. Rev., etc. *Address:* Wolfson College, Oxford OX2 6UD; The Steading, Balquhidder, Perthshire FK19 8NY. *Clubs:* Farmers'; New (Edinburgh).

SMITH, David Douglas R.; *see* Rae Smith.

SMITH, David Dury H.; *see* Hindley-Smith.

SMITH, David Grahame G.; *see* Grahame-Smith.

SMITH, Air Marshal Sir David H.; *see* Harcourt-Smith.

SMITH, David Henry; Economics Editor, since 1989, News Review Editor, since 1995, The Sunday Times; *b* 3 April 1954; *s* of Charles Henry Smith and Elizabeth Mary Smith (*née* Williams), Walsall; *m* 1980, Jane Howells, Tenby; two *s* two *d*. *Educ:* West Bromwich Grammar Sch.; UC Cardiff (BSc Econ 1st cl. hons; Tassie Medallion, 1975); Worcester Coll., Oxford; Birkbeck Coll., London (MSc Econ). Economic report writer, Lloyds Bank, 1976–77; economist, Henley Centre for Forecasting, 1977–79; economics and business writer, Now! magazine, 1979–81; Asst Editor, Financial Weekly, 1981–84; Economics Corresp., The Times, 1984–89. *Publications:* The Rise and Fall of Monetarism, 1987; Mrs Thatcher's Economics, 1988; North and South, 1989, 2nd edn 1994; From Boom to Bust, 1992, 2nd edn 1993; Mrs Thatcher's Economics: her legacy, 1992; UK Current Economic Policy, 1994. *Recreations:* squash, golf, occasional cricket, music. *Address:* 1 Pennington Street, E1 9XW. *T:* 0171–782 5750. *Club:* St James' Squash.

SMITH, Sir David (Iser), KCVO 1990 (CVO 1977); AO 1986; BA; Director: FAI Life Insurance Society Ltd, since 1991; FAI Life Ltd, since 1991; Official Secretary to the Governor-General of Australia, 1973–90; Secretary of the Order of Australia, 1975–90; *b* 9 Aug. 1933; *s* of late W. M. Smith; *m* 1955, June F., *d* of M. A. W. Forestier; three *s*. *Educ:* Scotch Coll., Melbourne; Melbourne Univ.; Australian National Univ., Canberra (BA). Commnd CMF, Melb. Univ. Regt, 1956. Entered Aust. Public Service, 1954; Dept of Customs and Excise, Melb., 1954–57; Trng Officer, Dept of the Interior, Canberra, 1957–58; Private Sec. to Minister for the Interior and Minister for Works, 1958–63; Exec. Asst to Sec., Dept of the Interior, 1963–66; Exec. Officer (Govt), Dept of the Interior, 1966–69; Sen. Adviser, Govt Br., Prime Minister's Dept, 1969–71; Sec., Federal Exec. Council, 1971–73; Asst Sec., Govt Br., Dept of the Prime Minister and Cabinet, 1972–73. Attached to The Queen's Household, Buckingham Palace, June–July 1975. Vis. Fellow in Pol Sci., Res. Sch. of Social Scis, ANU, 1991–92. Dir, Nat. Heart Foundn of Aust., 1991–. Vice-Pres., Scout Assoc. of Australia, 1991– (Dist Comr, Capital Hill Dist, 1971–74). KStJ 1991 (CStJ 1974). *Recreations:* music, reading. *Address:* 1/36 Shackleton Circuit, Mawson, ACT 2607, Australia. *T:* (6) 2865094. *Club:* Commonwealth (Canberra).

SMITH, Rt. Rev. David James; *see* Bradford, Bishop of.

SMITH, David John Harry, PhD; FRSC; Director, Research and Development, since 1994 and Board Member, since 1995, Whatman; *b* 5 Aug. 1941; *s* of Harry Nelson Smith and Mabel Freda Smith (*née* Stanford); *m* 1963, Dorothy Patricia Evans; one *s* one *d*. *Educ:* Univ. of Aston (BSc Chem. 1963); Univ of Western Ontario (PhD Organic Chem. 1967). FRSC 1982. Univ. Lectr, Chem. Dept, Univ. of Leicester, 1969–80; Res. Dir, Biosynth AG, Zürich, 1978–82; joined BP, 1980; Vice-Pres., R&D, BP America, 1987; Head, BP Gp Res. and Engrg, 1992. Member: Strategic Allocations Cttee, Nat. Sci. and Engrg Council, Canada, 1993–; Technology Foresight Steering Cttee, 1994–; EPSRC, 1994–. *Publications:* numerous scientific papers and patents. *Recreations:* educating palate, golf. *Address:* Whatman House, St Leonard's Road, 20/20 Maidstone, Kent ME16 0LS. *T:* Maidstone (01622) 676670.

SMITH, David John Leslie, PhD; CEng, FRAeS; Director of Group Services, Defence Research Agency, 1991–94; *b* 8 Oct. 1938; *s* of Gertrude Mary and late Arthur George Smith; *m* 1962, Wendy Lavinia (*née* Smith); two *d*. *Educ:* Cinderford Tech. Coll.; N Glos Tech. Coll.; Coll. of Aeronautics (MSc); Univ. of London; rcds. Mech. Engrg Apprentice, Rotol Ltd, 1954–59; Nat. Gas Turbine Estabt, Min. of Aviation, 1961, Head of Turbomachinery Dept, 1973; RCDS 1979; Ministry of Defence (PE): Dir, Aircraft Mech. and Elect. Equipment, Controllerate of Aircraft, 1980–81; Head of Aero. Dept, RAE, 1981–84; Dep. Dir (Marine Technology), 1984–85, Dep. Dir (Planning), 1986–87, ARE; Hd, Defence Res. Study Team, MoD, 1988; Asst Under-Sec. of State (Civilian Management) (Specialists), MoD, 1988–91. *Publications:* contribs to learned jls on gas turbine technology and fluid mechanics. *Recreation:* garden, including exhibiting flowers. *Address:* Michaelchurch Court, St Owens Cross, Hereford, Herefordshire HR2 8LD.

SMITH, Very Rev. David MacIntyre Bell Armour; Minister at Logie Kirk, Stirling, 1965–89; Moderator of the General Assembly of the Church of Scotland, 1985–86; *b* 5 April 1923; *s* of Frederick Smith and Matilda Shearer; *m* 1960, Mary Kulvear Cumming; three *s*. *Educ:* Monkton Combe School; Peebles High School; St Andrews Univ. (MA 1947, BD 1950; Cook and Macfarlan Scholar). Served as Pilot, RAF, 1942–45. Warrender Church, Edinburgh, 1951–60; Old Partick Parish, Glasgow, 1960–65. Member: Stirlingshire Education Cttee, 1969–79; Central Region Educn Cttee, 1986–94; Chm., Church of Scotland Bd of Education, 1979–83. DUniv Stirling, 1983. *Recreations:* gardening, philately. *Address:* 28 Millar Place, Stirling FK8 1XD. *T:* Stirling (01786) 475085.

SMITH, David S.; *see* Sands Smith.

SMITH, Delia, OBE 1995; cookery writer and broadcaster; *m* Michael Wynn Jones. Several BBC TV series; cookery writer, Evening Standard, later the Standard, 1972–85; columnist, Radio Times. Is a Roman Catholic. *Publications:* How to Cheat at Cooking, 1973; Country Fare, 1973; Recipes from Country Inns and Restaurants, 1973; Family Fare, book 1, 1973, book 2, 1974; Evening Standard Cook Book, 1974; Country recipes from "Look East", 1975; More Country Recipes from "Look East", 1976; Frugal Food, 1976; Book of Cakes, 1977; Recipes from "Look East", 1977; Food for our Times, 1978; Cookery Course, part 1, 1978, part 2, 1979, part 3, 1981, The Complete Cookery Course, 1982; A Feast for Lent, 1983; A Feast for Advent, 1983; One is Fun, 1985; (ed) Food Aid Cookery Book, 1986; A Journey into God, 1988; Delia Smith's Christmas, 1990; Delia Smith's Summer Collection, 1993. *Address:* c/o BBC Books, Woodlands, 80 Wood Lane, W12 0TT.

SMITH, Denis M.; *see* Mack Smith.

SMITH, Derek; Chief Executive, King's Healthcare NHS Trust, since 1990; *b* 26 Sept. 1948; *s* of Arthur Edmund Smith and Hazel Smith (*née* Proudlove); *m* 1970, Carol Anne Susan Cunio; one *s* one *d*. *Educ:* Univ. of Wales (BSc Hons Econs); Univ. of Strathclyde (Postgrad. Dip. in Russian Lang.). Gen. Manager, Frenchay Hosp., 1982–87, Dist Gen. Manager, S Beds HA, 1987–90. *Recreations:* squash rackets, music, sailing. *Address:* c/o King's College Hospital, Denmark Hill, SE5 9RS. *T.* 0171–346 3161.

SMITH, Derek B.; *see* Bryce-Smith.

SMITH, Derek Cyril; Under-Secretary, Export Credits Guarantee Department, 1974–87, retired; *b* 29 Jan. 1927; *s* of Albert Cyril and Edith Mary Elizabeth Smith; *m* 1st, 1949, Ursula Kulich (marr. diss. 1967); two *d*; 2nd, 1967, Nina Munday; one *s*. *Educ:* Pinner Grammar Sch.; St Catherine's Soc., Oxford. BA Mod. History 1951. Asst Principal, Min. of Materials, 1952–55; BoT, 1955–57: Asst Private Sec., Minister of State; Private Sec., Parly Sec.; Principal, ECGD, 1958–67; Asst Sec., BoT and DTI, 1967–72: Sec. to Lord Cromer's Survey of Capital Projects Contracting Overseas; Asst Sec., ECGD, 1972–74. *Recreations:* walking, reading, model-building.

SMITH, Derek Edward H.; *see* Hill-Smith.

SMITH, Derek Frank; Chairman, Sevenoaks Area National Trust Association, since 1992; *b* 11 Feb. 1929; *s* of late Frank H. and Rose V. Smith; *m* 1954, Anne Carpenter; one *s* one *d*. *Educ:* Chatham House Sch., Ramsgate. Served RAF, 1947–49. Colonial Office, 1949–66: Sec., Develt and Welfare Org. in WI, 1956–58; transf. to Min. of Overseas Develt, 1966; Financial Adviser, British Develt Div. in the Caribbean, 1966–68; Principal, India Sect., ODA, 1968–72; Asst Sec., 1972; Head of Southern African Develt Div., 1972–75; Establishment Officer, 1976–78, Head of UN Dept B, 1978–79, ODA; Alternate Exec. Dir of the World Bank, and Counsellor (Overseas Develt), Washington, 1979–84. Consultant: ODA, 1985; World Bank, 1986–87. *Address:* 3 The Close, Montreal Park, Sevenoaks, Kent TN13 2HE. *T:* Sevenoaks (01732) 452534.

SMITH, Desmond; *see* Smith, S. D.

SMITH, Donald Charles; a Master of the Supreme Court of Judicature (Chancery Division), 1969–73; *b* 23 Jan. 1910; *o s* of Charles Frederic Smith and Cecilia Anastasia Smith (*née* Toomey); *m* 1941, Joan Rowsell, twin *d* of Richard Norman Rowsell Blaker, MC. *Educ:* Stonyhurst College. Articled, Peacock & Goddard, Gray's Inn, 1927–31; admitted Solicitor, 1932; Solicitor with Thorold, Brodie & Bonham-Carter, Westminster, 1931–34; Legal Staff of Public Trustee Office, 1934–39; joined Chancery Registrars' Office, 1939; Chancery Registrar, 1952; Chief Registrar, 1963; first Chancery Registrar to be appointed a Master. Pres., Stonyhurst Assoc., 1969. Served in RNVR, Fleet Air Arm, 1943–46; Lieut, 1944–46. *Publications:* (Revising Editor) Atkin's Encyclopaedia of Court Forms, 1st edn, (Advisory Editor) 2nd edn; contribs to Law Jl. *Recreations:* cricket, walking, theatre, philately. *Address:* Reading Hall, Denham, Eye, Suffolk IP21 5DR. *T:* Eye (01379) 870500.

SMITH, Ven. Donald John; Archdeacon of Sudbury, 1984–91, Emeritus, since 1991; Hon. Canon of St Edmundsbury and Ipswich, 1973–91, Emeritus, since 1991; *b* 10 April 1926; *m* 1948, Violet Olive Goss; two *s* (one *d* decd). *Educ:* Clifton Theological Coll. Asst Curate: Edgware, 1953–56; St Margaret's, Ipswich, 1956–58; Vicar of St Mary, Hornsey Rise, Islington, 1958–62; Rector of Whitton, Ipswich, 1962–75; Rector of Redgrave cum Botesdale with The Rickinghalls, 1975–79; Archdeacon of Suffolk, 1975–84. HCF 1964. *Publications:* A Confirmation Course, 1974; (ed) Tourism and the Use of Church Buildings, 1983; Covenanting for Disunity, 1981; Thank you Lord for Alison, 1987; Straightforward and Simple: a guide for churchwardens, 1989. *Recreations:* driving, foreign travel, chess, collecting Meerschaum and antiques, drama, reading, photography, gardening, caravanning, good food, dining out, pastoral reorganisation, redundant churches. *Address:* St Peter's Cottage, Stretton-on-Fosse, Moreton-in-Marsh, Glos GL56 9SE. *T:* Moreton-in-Marsh (01608) 662790.

SMITH, Donald MacKeen; Agent General of Nova Scotia, in London, 1980–91; *b* 26 Nov. 1923; *s* of Leonard Vernard and Lena Smith (*née* MacKeen); *m* 1949, Helen Elizabeth (*d* 1987), *d* of late Lt-Col David Guildford; three *d. Educ:* Halifax Public Schs; King's College Sch.; Dalhousie Univ., Nova Scotia. Served Canadian Armored Corps, 1942–45; 18th Armored Car Regt, 1944–45. J. E. Morse and Co. Ltd, Halifax: salesman, 1946; Vice-Pres., Director, 1951; Pres., 1956–. Pres., Tea Council of Canada, 1975–78; Vice-Pres. and Dir, Tea and Coffee Assoc. of Canada, 1960–78. Member, Executive Council of Nova Scotia, 1960–69; MLA Nova Scotia (Halifax Citadel), 1960–70; Minister of Mines, Minister in Charge of Liquor Control Act, 1960–69. *Recreations:* swimming, sailing, fishing, walking. *Address:* PO Box 442, Station M, Halifax, Nova Scotia B3J 2P8, Canada; 1 Park Place, 1049 South Park Street, Halifax, NS B3H 2W5, Canada. *Clubs:* Royal Automobile; Saraguay; Halifax; Royal Nova Scotia Yacht Squadron.

SMITH, Douglas; *see* Smith, I. D.

SMITH, Sir Douglas (Boucher), KCB 1992 (CB 1982); Chairman, Advisory, Conciliation and Arbitration Service, 1987–93; *b* 9 June 1932; *m* 1956, Mary Barbara Tarran. *Educ:* Leeds Modern Sch.; Leeds Univ. Entered Ministry of Labour, 1953; successively: Private Sec. to Minister of Labour, 1967–68; to First Sec. of State and Sec. of State for Employment and Productivity, 1968–70; to Sec. of State for Employment, 1970–71; Chief Conciliation Officer, 1971–74, Under Secretary: Dept of Employment, 1974–77; Cabinet Office, 1977–79; Dep. Sec., Dept of Employment, 1979–87. *Address:* 17 Dundas Close, Bracknell, Berkshire RG12 7BX. *T:* Bracknell (01344) 54573. *Club:* Athenæum.

SMITH, Ven. Douglas Leslie B.; *see* Bartles-Smith.

SMITH, Drew; *see* Smith, F. D.

SMITH, Sir Dudley (Gordon), Kt 1983; DL; MP (C) Warwick and Leamington, since 1968 (Brentford and Chiswick, 1959–66); *b* 14 Nov. 1926; *o s* of late Hugh William and Florence Elizabeth Smith, Cambridge; 1st marr. diss.; one *s* two *d*; *m* 2nd, 1976, Catherine Amos, *o d* of late Mr and Mrs Thomas Amos, Liverpool. *Educ:* Chichester High Sch., Sussex. Worked for various provincial and national newspapers, as journalist and senior executive, 1943–66; Asst News Editor, Sunday Express, 1953–59. Vice-Chm. Southgate Conservative Assoc., 1958–59; CC Middlesex, 1958–65; Chief Whip of Majority Group, 1961–63. A Divl Dir, Beecham Group, 1966–70; Management Consultant, 1974–. Contested (C) Camberwell-Peckham, General Election, 1955. PPS to Sec. for Tech. Co-operation, 1963–64; an Opposition Whip, 1964–66; an Opposition Spokesman on Employment and Productivity, 1969–70; Parliamentary Under-Secretary of State: Dept of Employment, 1970–74; (Army) MoD, 1974. Vice Chm., Parly Select Cttee on Race Relations and Immigration, 1974–79. UK delegate to Council of Europe and WEU, 1979– (Sec.-Gen., European Democratic Group, 1983–; Chm., WEU Defence Cttee, 1989–93; Pres., WEU Assembly, 1993–); a Founder Mem., CSCE Assembly, 1992. Promoted Town and Country Planning (Amendment) Act, 1977, as a private member. Governor, Mill Hill Sch., 1958–89; Chm., United & Cecil Club, 1975–80. Freeman, City of London; Liveryman, Horners' Co. DL Warwickshire, 1988. Order of the Horseman of Madara, 1st cl. (Bulgaria), 1994; Comdr, Order of Isabella la Católica (Spain), 1994. *Publications:* Harold Wilson: A Critical Biography, 1964; etc. *Recreations:* books, travel, music, wild life and wilderness preservation. *Address:* Church Farm, Weston-under-Wetherley, near Leamington Spa, Warwicks CV33 9BY. *T:* Marton (01926) 632352.

SMITH, Dugal N.; *see* Nisbet-Smith.

SMITH, Dr (Edward) Alistair, CBE 1982; Director—North America, University of Aberdeen International Office, since 1989; *b* 16 Jan. 1939; *s* of Archibald Smith and Jean Milne Johnston. *Educ:* Aberdeen Grammar Sch.; Univ. of Aberdeen (MA, PhD); Univ. of Uppsala, Sweden. Lectr, Univ. of Aberdeen, 1963–88. Dir, Univ. of Aberdeen Develt Trust, 1982–90; Mem., Grampian Health Bd, 1983–91. Pres., Scottish Conservative and Unionist Assoc., 1979–81; Dep. Chm., Scottish Conservative Party, 1981–85. Member: Exec., Aberdeen and NE Council on Disability; Exec., Grampian ASH; Scottish Cttee, 1989–91, NE Scotland Regl Bd, 1991–92, NCC; SCOTVEC, 1989–92. *Publications:* (with R. E. H. Mellor) Europe: a geographical survey of the Continent, 1979; articles on Scandinavia, Europe and Scotland. *Recreations:* travel, photography, music. *Address:* 68A Beaconsfield Place, Aberdeen AB2 4AJ. *T:* Aberdeen (01224) 642932.

SMITH, Eileen S.; *see* Stamers-Smith.

SMITH, Emma; author; *b* 21 Aug. 1923; *m* 1951, Richard Stewart-Jones (*d* 1957); one *s* one *d. Publications:* Maidens' Trip, 1948 (awarded John Llewellyn Rhys Memorial Prize, 1948); The Far Cry, 1949 (awarded James Tait Black Memorial Prize, 1949); Emily, 1959; Out of Hand, 1963; Emily's Voyage, 1966; No Way of Telling, 1972; The Opportunity of a Lifetime, 1978. *Address:* c/o Curtis Brown, 28–29 Haymarket, SW1Y 4SP.

SMITH, (Eric) Brian, PhD, DSc; FRSC; Vice-Chancellor, University of Wales, Cardiff (formerly Principal, University of Wales College of Cardiff), since 1993; *b* 10 Oct. 1933; *s* of Eric Smith and Dilys Olwen (*née* Hughes); *m* 1st, 1957, Margaret Barr (marr. diss. 1978); two *s* one *d*; 2nd, 1983, Regina Arvidson Ball; two step *d. Educ:* Alun Grammar Sch., Mold; Wirral Grammar Sch.; Univ. of Liverpool (BSc; PhD 1957); MA Oxon 1960, DSc Oxon 1988. FRSC 1981. Res. Associate, Univ. of Calif, Berkeley, 1957–59; Oxford University: ICI Fellow, 1959–60; Lectr in Physical Chemistry, 1960–88; Member: Gen. Bd of Faculties, 1980–87 (Chm., 1985–87); Hebdomadal Council, 1985–93; St Catherine's College: Fellow, 1960–88; Vice-Master, 1984–85; Master, 1988–93; Welsh Supernumerary Fellow, Jesus Coll., 1994–95. Vis. Prof., Univ. of Calif, Riverside, 1967; Vis. Lectr, Stanford Univ., 1983, 1984 and 1985; Priestley Lectr, RSC, 1986. Chm., Thermodynamics and Statistical Mechanics Section, RSC, 1979–83; Mem., Southern Regional Council for Further Educn, 1965–76. Pott's Medal, Univ. of Liverpool, 1969. *Publications:* (jtly) Virial Coefficients of Pure Gases and Mixtures, 1969, 2nd edn 1980; Basic Chemical Thermodynamics, 1973, 4th edn 1990; (jtly) Intermolecular Forces: origin and determination, 1981; (jtly) Forces between Molecules, 1986; papers in scientific jls. *Recreation:* mountaineering. *Address:* University of Wales, Cardiff, PO Box 920, Cardiff CFI 3XP. *Clubs:* Alpine; Gorphwysfa.

SMITH, Eric John R.; *see* Radley-Smith.

SMITH, Eric Norman, CMG 1976; HM Diplomatic Service, retired; British High Commissioner in The Gambia, 1979–81; *b* 28 Jan. 1922; *s* of late Arthur Sidney David Smith; *m* 1955, Mary Gillian Horrocks. *Educ:* Colfe's Sch., London. Served War, Royal Corps of Signals, 1941–46. Foreign Office, 1947–53; HM Embassy, Cairo, 1953–55; UK Delegn to the UN, New York, 1955–57; FO, 1957–60; HM Embassy, Tehran, 1960–64; FO, 1964–68; British Information Services, New York, 1968–71; FCO, 1971–75; Singapore, 1975–79. *Recreations:* music, photography. *Address:* Troodos, Castle Lane, Budleigh Salterton, Devon EX9 7AN.

SMITH, Prof. (Ernest) Alwyn, CBE 1986; PhD; Professor of Epidemiology and Social Oncology, University of Manchester, 1979–90; Chairman, Lancaster Health Authority, 1991–94; *b* 9 Nov. 1925; *s* of Ernest Smith and Constance Barbara Smith; *m* 1950, Doreen Preston; one *s* one *d. Educ:* Queen Mary's Sch., Walsall; Birmingham Univ. MB, PhD; FRCP 1970; FRCGP 1973; FFCM 1974. Served War, RM, 1943–46. Res. Fellow in Social Medicine, Birmingham Univ., 1952–55; WHO Vis. Lectr, Univ. of Malaya, 1956–58; Lectr, Univ. of St. Andrews, 1959–61; Sen. Lectr. Univ. of Edinburgh, 1961–66; First Dir, Social Paediatric Res. Gp, Glasgow, 1966–67; Prof. of Community Medicine, Univ. of Manchester, 1967–79. Pres., FCM, 1981–86. *Publications:* Genetics in Medicine, 1966; The Science of Social Medicine, 1968; (ed) Cancer Control, 1979; (ed) Recent Advances in Community Medicine, 1982; papers on epidemiological subjects in Lancet, British Jl of Epidemiol., etc. *Recreations:* music, bird watching, sailing. *Address:* Plum Tree Cottage, Arnside, Cumbria, via Carnforth LA5 0AH. *T:* Arnside (01524) 761976.

SMITH, Maj.-Gen. Sir (Francis) Brian W.; *see* Wyldbore-Smith.

SMITH, Sir Francis Graham-, Kt 1986; FRS 1970; Langworthy Professor of Physics, Manchester University, 1987–90, now Emeritus (Professor of Radio Astronomy, 1964–74 and 1981–87); Director, Nuffield Radio Astronomy Laboratories, 1981–88; Astronomer Royal, 1982–90; *b* 25 April 1923; *s* of Claud Henry and Cicely Winifred Smith; *m* 1945, Dorothy Elizabeth (*née* Palmer); three *s* one *d. Educ:* Epsom Coll.; Rossall Sch.; Downing Coll., Cambridge. Nat. Sci. Tripos, Downing Coll., 1941–43 and 1946–47; PhD Cantab 1952. Telecommunications Research Estab., Malvern, 1943–46; Cavendish Lab., 1947–64; 1851 Exhibr 1951–52; Warren Research Fellow of Royal Soc., 1959–64; Fellow of Downing Coll., 1953–64, Hon. Fellow 1970; Dir-Designate, 1974–75, Dir, 1976–81, Royal Greenwich Observatory. Vis. Prof. of Astronomy, Univ. of Sussex, 1975. Sec., Royal Astronomical Soc., 1964–71, Pres., 1975–77. Mem. Council and Physical Sec., 1988–94, Vice-Pres., 1990–94, Royal Soc. For. Associate, RSSAf, 1988. Hon. DSc: QUB, 1986; Keele, 1987; Birmingham, 1989; TCD, 1990; Nottingham, 1990; Manchester, 1993. Royal Medal, Royal Soc., 1987; Glazebrook Medal, Inst. of Physics, 1991. *Publications:* Radio Astronomy, 1960; (with J. H. Thomson) Optics, 1971; Pulsars, 1977; (with Sir Bernard Lovell) Pathways to the Universe, 1988; (with A. G. Lyne) Pulsar Astronomy, 1990; papers in Monthly Notices of RAS, Nature and other scientific jls. *Recreations:* beekeeping, walking. *Address:* Nuffield Radio Astronomy Laboratories, Jodrell Bank, Macclesfield, Cheshire SK11 9DL; Old School House, Henbury, Macclesfield, Cheshire SK11 9PH.

SMITH, Rev. Francis Taylor; Minister of St Paul's Parish Church, Dunfermline, since 1964; *b* 22 Jan. 1933; *s* of James William Smith and Jeannie Moir Catto Cockburn; *m* 1957, Jean Millar Wallace; three *s* one *d. Educ:* Aberdeen Grammar Sch.; Aberdeen Univ. (MA); Christ's Coll., Aberdeen (Licence to Preach). Student Assistant: Queen's Cross Church, Aberdeen, 1954–56; North Church, Aberdeen, 1956–57; Sen. Asst, Govan Old Church, Glasgow, 1957–58; Parish Minister, Aberlour, Banffshire, 1958–64. Chaplain: Dunfermline and West Fife Hosp., 1964–93; Dunfermline Maternity Hosp., 1988–93; Moderator of Presbytery, 1973–74, 1995–96. Councillor, Banff CC, 1964; Chairman: West Fife Local Health Council, 1975–84; Queen Margaret Hosp. NHS Trust, Dunfermline, 1994–; Vice Chm., Cttee on Ethical Med. Res., Fife Health Bd; Vice-Pres., Assoc. of Scottish Local Health Councils, 1978–79, Pres., 1980, 1981; Crown Lay Nominee, General Medical Council, 1979–89. Chm., Fife Marriage Counselling Service, 1984–85. Governor, Aberlour Orphanage, 1964. *Recreations:* work, music, fishing, reading. *Address:* St Paul's Manse, 6 Park Avenue, Dunfermline, Fife KY12 7HX. *T:* Dunfermline (01383) 721124.

SMITH, Prof. Frank Thomas, FRS 1984; Goldsmid Professor of Applied Mathematics in the University of London, at University College London, since 1984; *b* 24 Feb. 1948; *s* of Leslie Maxwell Smith and Catherine Matilda Smith; *m* 1972, Valerie Sheila (*née* Hearn); three *d. Educ:* Bournemouth Grammar Sch.; Jesus Coll., Oxford (BA; DPhil); University College London. Research Fellow in Theoretical Aerodynamics Unit, Southampton, 1972–73; Lectr in Maths Dept, Imperial Coll., London, 1973–78; Vis. Scientist, Applied Mathematics Dept, Univ. of Western Ontario, Canada, 1978–79; Reader in Maths Dept, 1979–83, Prof. in Maths, 1983–84, Imperial Coll., London. *Publications:* on applied mathematics, fluid mechanics, computing and natural sciences, in jls. *Recreations:* the family, reading, music, sport. *Address:* Mathematics Department, University College, Gower Street, WC1E 6BT. *T:* 0171–387 7050.

SMITH, Frank William G.; *see* Glaves-Smith.

SMITH, (Fraser) Drew; senior adviser on food strategy, London Docklands Development Corporation; *b* 30 March 1950; *s* of Frank and Beatrice Smith; *m* 1988, Susan Maloney; one *s* one *d. Educ:* Westminster School. Worked on Student magazine, 1967; IPC magazines, 1969–72; Westminster Press Newspapers, 1972–81. Editor, Good Food Guide, 1982–88; launched: Good Food Directory, 1985; Budget Good Food Guide, 1986–88; Head of Media Develt, Dir's Office, Consumers' Assoc., 1988–90. Director: Taste Publishing; Food Factory; West India Co. Columnist, Guardian, 1982–; creator, TV Food File, Channel 4. Chm., Guild of Food Writers, 1990. Trustee, Jane Grigson Liby. Restaurant Writer of the Year, 1981, 1988. *Publications:* Modern Cooking, 1990; Food Watch, 1994; Baby Food Watch, 1995; Food Watch 2, 1995. *Recreations:* walking, music, cooking, people. *Address:* Kins Cottage, Foxley Manor, Foxley, Wilts SN16 0JJ.

SMITH, Prof. Frederick Viggers; Professor of Psychology, University of Durham, 1950–77, now Emeritus; *b* Hamilton, New South Wales, 24 Jan. 1912; *s* of Frederick Thomas Smith and Agnes (*née* Viggers); unmarried. *Educ:* Newcastle (NSW) High School; Sydney and London Universities. BA 1938, MA 1941, Lithgow Schol., Sydney; PhD London 1948. FBPsS, 1950 (Pres., British Psychological Society, 1959–60). Research Office, Dept of Educ., NSW, 1936; Lecturer in Psychology, The Teachers' Coll., Sydney, 1938; Lectr, Birkbeck Coll., Univ. of London, 1946; Lectr, Univ. of Aberdeen, 1948. Visiting Prof., Cornell Univ., USA, 1957, Christchurch and Wellington Univs, NZ, 1960. Consultant, Council of Europe Sub-Cttee on Crime Problems, 1973; Unesco Consultant, Univ. of Riyadh, 1973. Hon. Research Associate, Univ. of Newcastle, NSW, 1980. *Publications:* The Child's Point of View (Sydney), 1946 (under pseudonym Victor Southward); Explanation of Human Behaviour (London), 1951, 1960; Attachment of the Young: Imprinting and Other Developments, 1969; Purpose in Animal Behaviour, 1971; papers to psychological and philosophical jls. *Recreations:* mountain walking, swimming, photography, music, golf. *Address:* 58 Harbourside Haven, Shoal Bay, Port Stephens, NSW 2315, Australia.

SMITH, Sir Geoffrey J.; *see* Johnson Smith.

SMITH, Geoffrey M.; *see* Maitland Smith.

SMITH, George Iain D.; *see* Duncan Smith.

SMITH, (George) Neil, CMG 1987; HM Diplomatic Service, retired; Ambassador to Finland, 1989–95; *b* 12 July 1936; *s* of George Smith and Ena (*née* Hill); *m* 1956, Elvi Vappu Hämäläinen; one *s* one *d*. *Educ:* King Edward VII Sch., Sheffield. Joined HM Foreign (subseq. Diplomatic) Service, 1953; served RAF, 1954–56; Foreign Office, 1957; Rangoon, 1958–61; 2nd Sec., Berne, 1961–65; Diplomatic Service Administration, 1965–66; 1st Sec., CO, 1966–68; British Mil. Govt, Berlin, 1969–73; FCO, 1973–77; Counsellor (Commercial), Helsinki, 1977–80; Consul-Gen., Zürich and Principality of Liechtenstein, 1980–85; Head of Trade Relations and Export Dept, FCO, 1985–87; RCDS, 1988. *Recreations:* music, golf. *Address:* c/o Foreign and Commonwealth Office, SW1A 2AH. *Club:* Travellers'.

SMITH, Prof. Gerald Stanton; Professor of Russian, University of Oxford, and Fellow of New College, since 1986; *b* 17 April 1938; *s* of Thomas Arthur Smith and Ruth Annie Stanton; *m* 1st, 1961, Frances Wetherill (marr. diss. 1981); one *s* one *d;* 2nd, 1982, Barbara Heldt; one step *s* one step *d*. *Educ:* Stretford Grammar Sch.; Sch. of Slavonic and E European Studies, Univ. of London (BA 1964; PhD 1977). Lectr in Russian, Univ. of Nottingham, 1964–71, Univ. of Birmingham, 1971–79; Univ. Research Fellow, Univ. of Liverpool, 1980–82. Visiting Professor: Indiana Univ., 1984; Univ. of California, Berkeley, 1984; Private Scholar, Social Scis and Humanities Res. Council, Canada, 1985; John Simon Guggenheim Meml Fellow, 1986. *Publications:* (ed) Alexander Galich, Songs and Poems, 1983; Songs to Seven Strings, 1984; Russian Inside and Out, 1989; (ed) D. S. Mirsky, Uncollected Writings on Russian Literature, 1989; Contemporary Russian Poetry: a bilingual anthology, 1993; D. S. Mirsky: Letters to P. P. Suvchinskii, 1995; papers in learned jls. *Recreation:* jazz music. *Address:* Taylor Institution, The University, Oxford OX1 3NA. *T:* Oxford (01865) 270476.

SMITH, Gerard Thomas C.; *see* Corley Smith.

SMITH, Sir Gilbert; *see* Smith, Sir T. G.

SMITH, Godfrey, FRSL; writer; *b* 12 May 1926; *s* of Reginald Montague Smith and Ada May Smith (*née* Damen); *m* 1951, Mary, *d* of Jakub Schoenfeld, formerly of Vienna; three *d*. *Educ:* Surbiton County Sch.; Eggar's Grammar Sch.; Worcester Coll., Oxford (MA; Pres. of Oxford Union Soc. 1950). RAF, 1944–47. Joined Sunday Times as PA to Lord Kemsley, 1951; News Editor, 1956; Asst Editor, 1959; Editor, Magazine, 1965–72, Associate Editor, 1972–91; Editor, Weekly Review, 1972–79; columnist, 1979–; Director, 1968–81. Regent's Lectr, Univ. of California, 1970. *Publications: novels:* The Flaw in the Crystal, 1954; The Friends, 1957; The Business of Loving, 1961 (Book Society Choice); The Network, 1965; Caviare, 1976; *non-fiction:* The English Companion, 1984; The English Season, 1987; The English Reader, 1988; *anthologies:* The Best of Nat Gubbins, 1978; A World of Love, 1982; Beyond the Tingle Quotient, 1982; How it Was in the War, 1989; Take the Ball and Run, 1991. *Recreation:* chums. *Address:* Village Farmhouse, Charlton, Malmesbury, Wilts SN16 9DL. *T:* Malmesbury (01666) 822479; 10 Kensington Park Mews, W11 2EY. *T:* 0171–727 4155. *Clubs:* Garrick, Savile, MCC; Leander.

SMITH, Gordon E.; *see* Etherington-Smith.

SMITH, Gordon Edward C.; *see* Connell-Smith.

SMITH, Graham William, CBE 1990; HM Chief Inspector of Probation, since 1992; *b* 15 Aug. 1939; *s* of William George Smith and Edith May Smith; *m* 1958, Jeanne Lilian Ann Goodyear; two *s* one *d*. *Educ:* Univ. of Durham; Univ. of Newcastle upon Tyne (CQSW 1965). Durham: Probation Officer, 1965–69; Sen. Probation Officer, 1969–73; Inner London Probation Service: Asst Chief Probation Officer, 1973–79; Dep. Chief Probation Officer, 1979–80; Chief Probation Officer, 1980–92. Lectr and Examr for Home Office Probation Course, 1972–78; Vis. Prof., UN Asia and FE Inst., Tokyo, 1982. Member: Home Sec.'s Adv. Bd on Restricted Patients, 1986–92; Lord Chancellor's Adv. Cttee on Legal Educn and Conduct, 1991–. Chm., Assoc. of Chief Probation Officers, 1988. Gov., Nat. Inst. of Social Work, 1992–. Freeman, City of London, 1974. Margaret Mead Award, Internat. Assoc. of Residential and Community Alternatives, LA, 1990. *Recreations:* sport, gardening, theatre, grandchildren. *Address:* The Cottage, Swanley Village Road, Swanley Village, Kent BR8 7NG. *T:* Swanley (01322) 665427.

SMITH, Prof. Hamilton Othanel; Professor of Molecular Biology and Genetics, Johns Hopkins University School of Medicine, Maryland, USA, since 1981; *b* 23 Aug. 1931; *s* of Bunnie Othanel Smith and Tommie Harkey Smith; *m* 1957, Elizabeth Anne Bolton; four *s* one *d*. *Educ:* Univ. of Illinois; Univ. of California (AB); Johns Hopkins Univ. Sch. of Medicine (MD). Research Associate, Dept of Human Genetics, Univ. of Michigan, 1964–67; Asst Prof. of Microbiology, 1967–69, Associate Prof. of Microbiology, 1969–73, Prof. of Microbiology, 1973–81, Johns Hopkins Univ. Sch. of Medicine. During sabbatical leave in Zürich, worked in collaboration with Prof. Dr M. L. Birnstiel, Inst. für Molekularbiologie II der Univ. Zürich, 1975–76; Vis. Prof., Inst. of Molecular Pathol., Vienna, 1990–91. Nobel Prize in Medicine (jtly), 1978. *Publications:* A restriction enzyme from *Hemophilus influenzae:* I. Purification and general properties (with K. W. Wilcox), in Jl Mol. Biol. *51*, 379, 1970; A restriction enzyme from *Hemophilus influenzae:* II. Base sequence of the recognition site (with T. J. Kelly), in Jl Mol. Biol. *51*, 393, 1970. *Recreations:* piano, classical music. *Address:* Department of Molecular Biology and Genetics, Johns Hopkins University School of Medicine, 725 N Wolfe Street, Baltimore, MD 21205, USA. *T:* (410) 9553650.

SMITH, Prof. Harry, CBE 1993; PhD, DSc; FRCPath; FRS 1979; CIBiol; Professor and Head, Department of Microbiology, University of Birmingham, 1965–88, now Emeritus Professor; *b* 7 Aug. 1921; *s* of Harry and Annie Smith; *m* 1947, Janet Mary Holmes; one *s* one *d*. *Educ:* Northampton Grammar Sch.; University Coll. (of London) at Nottingham. BPharm, BScChem (1st Cl. Hons), PhD, DSc London. Analyst, Boots Pure Drug Co., Nottingham, 1942–45; Asst Lectr, then Lectr, Dept of Chemistry, UCL at Nottingham, 1945–47; Microbiological Research Establishment, Porton: Sen. Scientific Officer, 1947; Principal Sci. Officer, 1951; Sen. Prin. Sci. Officer (Research Merit), 1956; Dep. Chief Sci. Officer (Res. Merit), 1964. Visiting Professor: Dept of Bacteriology, Univ. of Calif, Berkeley, USA, 1964, UCLA, 1972; (summer) Dept of Microbiol., Univ. of Washington, Seattle, USA, 1977, Univ. of Michigan, Ann Arbor, 1981, TCD, 1991. Society for General Microbiology: Mem. Council, 1960–64; Meetings Sec., 1964–68; Treas., 1968–75; Pres., 1975–78; Hon. Mem., 1986; Treas., Fedn of Europ. Microbiol Socs, 1975–82; Pres. and Chm., Organising Cttee, 14th (1986) Internat. Congress of Microbiology, Manchester. Member: Adv. Cttee on Dangerous Pathogens, 1985–88; PHLS Bd, 1985–89; Council, Royal Soc., 1989–91; Assessor, AFRC, 1990–94. Lectures: Amer. Soc. for Microbiol., 1984; Australian Soc. for Microbiol., 1985; Fred Griffith, 1989, Jubilee (50 yrs), 1995, Soc. for Gen. Microbiol.; Leeuvenhoek, Royal Soc., 1991. Hon. MRCP 1986; Hon. ARCVS 1993. Hon. DSc Leicester, 1992. Bledisloe Vet. Award, RASE, 1992; Stuart Mudd Award, Internat. Union of Microbiol. Socs, 1994. *Publications:* over 300 papers in jls and books, mainly on mechanisms of microbial (bacterial, viral and fungal) pathogenicity. *Recreation:* interest in farming. *Address:* The Medical School, University of Birmingham, Birmingham B15 2TT. *T:* 0121–414 6920. *Club:* Athenæum.

SMITH, Harvey; *see* Smith, R. H.

SMITH, Hedworth Cunningham, CBE 1972; Chairman: Medical Appeal Tribunals, England and Scotland, 1973–84; Pensions Appeal Tribunals, England, 1973–85; Judge of the Supreme Court of the Bahama Islands, 1965–72, retired; *b* 12 May 1912; *s* of James Smith and Elizabeth (*née* Brown); unmarried. *Educ:* George Watson's Coll., Edinburgh; Edinburgh University. MA 1933; LLB 1936. Solicitor, Scotland, 1937–40; Barrister-at-Law, Gray's Inn, London, 1950. Served War of 1939–45: commnd 1940; Staff Officer, GHQ India Command, 1943–46 (Major). District Magistrate, 1946, Senior District Magistrate, 1950, Gold Coast; Judge of Supreme Court of Ghana, 1957; retd from Ghana Govt service, 1961; Legal Adviser, Unilever Ltd Gp of Cos in Ghana, 1962–64. *Recreation:* golf. *Address:* The Old (Police) House, Main Street, Aberlady, E Lothian. *T:* Aberlady (01875) 870420. *Clubs:* East India, Devonshire, Sports and Public Schools; Kilspindie Golf.

SMITH, Helen Sylvester, MA; Headmistress, Perse School for Girls, Cambridge, since 1989; *b* 7 Jan. 1942; *d* of late S. J. Smith and of K. R. Smith. *Educ:* King Edward VI High Sch. for Girls, Birmingham; St Hilda's College, Oxford (BA 1963, MA 1967 Maths); Hughes Hall, Cambridge (PGCE 1964). Cheltenham Ladies' College, 1964–69; International School of Brussels, 1969–71; Perse Sch. for Girls, 1971– (Dep. Head, 1979–82, 1988–89). FRSA. *Recreations:* music, gardening. *Address:* 6A Cavendish Avenue, Cambridge CB1 4US. *T:* Cambridge (01223) 249200.

SMITH, Prof. Henry Sidney, FBA 1985; Edwards Professor of Egyptology, 1970–86, Head of Department of Egyptology, 1970–88, University College London, now Professor Emeritus; *b* 14 June 1928; *s* of Prof. Sidney Smith, FBA, and of Mary, *d* of H. W. Parker; *m* 1961, Hazel Flory Leeper (*d* 1991). *Educ:* Merchant Taylors' Sch., Northwood; Christ's Coll., Cambridge (MA); DLit London, 1987. Lectr in Egyptology, Univ. of Cambridge, 1954–63; Budge Fellow in Egyptology, Christ's Coll., Cambridge, 1955–63; Reader in Egyptian Archaeology, University Coll. London, 1963–70. Field Dir for Egypt Exploration Soc. in Nubia, 1961, 1964–65, and at Saqqara and Memphis, Egypt, 1970–88. *Publications:* Preliminary Reports of the Egypt Exploration Society's Nubian Survey, 1962; A Visit to Ancient Egypt, 1974; The Fortress of Buhen: the inscriptions, 1976; The Fortress of Buhen: the archaeological report, 1979; (with W. J. Tait) Saqqara Demotic Papyri I, 1983; (with D. G. Jeffreys) The Anubieion at Saqqara, Vol. I, 1988; articles in Kush, Jl of Egyptian Arch., Orientalia, Rev. d'Egyptologie, Bull. Inst. Français d'Arch. Or., Z für Äg. Sprache und Altertümskunde, etc. *Address:* Ailwyn House, Upwood, Huntingdon, Cambs PE17 1QE.

SMITH, Sir Howard (Frank Trayton), GCMG 1981 (KCMG 1976; CMG 1966); HM Diplomatic Service, retired; *b* 15 Oct. 1919; *m* 1st, 1943, Winifred Mary Cropper (*d* 1982); one *d*; 2nd, 1983, Mary Penney. *Educ:* Sidney Sussex Coll., Cambridge. Employed in FO, 1939; apptd Foreign Service, 1946. Served Oslo; transf. Washington, 2nd Sec. (Inf.) 1950; 1st Sec., Dec. 1950; 1st Sec. and Consul, Caracas, 1953; FO, 1956; Counsellor: Moscow, 1961–63; Foreign Office, 1964–68; Ambassador to Czechoslovakia, 1968–71; UK Rep. in NI, 1971–72; Dep. Sec., Cabinet Office, on secondment, 1972–75; Ambassador in Moscow, 1976–78. *Club:* Travellers'.
See also R. M. J. Lyne.

SMITH, Maj.-Gen. Hugh M.; *see* Macdonald-Smith.

SMITH, Iain-Mór L.; *see* Lindsay-Smith.

SMITH, Ian Douglas, GCLM 1979; ID 1970; MP (Cons. Alliance, formerly Republican Front), Zimbabwe, 1980–88; *b* 8 April 1919; *m* Janet Watt (*d* 1994); two *s* one *d*. *Educ:* Selukwe Sch.; Chaplin Sch., Gwelo, S Rhodesia (now Zimbabwe); Rhodes Univ., Grahamstown, S Africa. Served War of 1939–45 in 237 (Rhodesia) Sqdn and 130 Sqdn, RAF. Farmer. Member: Southern Rhodesia Legislative Assembly, 1948–53; Parliament of Fedn of Rhodesia & Nyasaland, 1953–61; former Chief Whip (United Federal Party), 1958; resigned from United Federal Party, 1961; Foundn Mem. and Vice-Pres., Republican Front (formerly Rhodesian Front), 1962, President, 1964–87; Dep. Prime Minister and Minister of the Treasury, S Rhodesia, 1962–64; Prime Minister of Rhodesia, 1964–79; delivered Rhodesia's Unilateral Declaration of Independence, Nov. 1965; Minister Without Portfolio in Bishop Muzorewa's Govt, 1979; Mem., Transitional Exec. Council to prepare for transfer of power in Rhodesia, 1978–79. *Address:* Gwenoro Farm, Shurugwi, Zimbabwe; Box 8198, Causeway, Harare, Zimbabwe. *Clubs:* Harare, Harare Sports (Zimbabwe).

SMITH, Ian K; *see* Knight Smith.

SMITH, Prof. Ian William Murison, PhD; FRS 1995; CChem, FRSC; Mason Professor of Chemistry, University of Birmingham, since 1991; *b* 15 June 1937; *s* of William Murison Smith and Margaret Moir Smith; *m* 1961, Susan Morrish; two *s* two *d*. *Educ:* Giggleswick Sch.; Christ's Coll., Cambridge (BA, MA, PhD). Cambridge University: ICI Res. Fellow, 1964–65; Demonstrator, 1966–71, Lectr, 1971–85, in Physical Chem.; Christ's College: Res. Fellow, 1963–66, Fellow, 1966–85; Tutor, 1968–77; Dir of Studies, 1972–85; University of Birmingham: Prof. of Chemistry, 1985–; Head, Sch. of Chem., 1989–93. Tilden Medal, RSC; Special RSC Award for reaction kinetics; Polanyi Medal. *Publications:* Kinetics and Dynamics of Elementary Gas Reactions, 1980; (ed) Physical Chemistry of Fast Reactions: reaction dynamics, 1980; (ed) Modern Gas Kinetics, 1987; numerous contribs to learned jls. *Recreations:* occasional golf, even more occasional tennis, theatre, walking, gardening under instruction. *Address:* School of Chemistry, The University, Birmingham B15 2TT; 21 St Bernard's Road, Olton, Solihull, West Midlands B92 7AU.

SMITH, Ivor Otterbein, CMG 1963; OBE 1952; retired as Chairman of Public Service and Police Service Commissions and Member of Judicial Service Commission, British Guiana (1961–66); *b* Georgetown, British Guiana, 13 Dec. 1907; *s* of late Bryce Otterbein Smith and Florette Maud Smith (*née* Chapman); *m* 1936, Leila Muriel Fowler; one *s* two *d*. *Educ:* Queen's Coll., British Guiana; Pitman's Commercial Coll., London. Joined Brit. Guiana CS, as Clerical Asst, Treas., 1925; Sec. Commissioners of Currency, 1933; Asst Dist. Comr, 1941; Private Sec. to Gov., 1943; Dist Comr, 1945; Comr, Cayman Is, 1946–52; Dep. Comr of Local Govt, Brit. Guiana, 1953; Governor's Sec., and Clerk Exec. Coun., 1956; Dep. Chief Sec., 1960; Acted as Chief Sec. on several occasions and was Officer Administering the Govt, Sept.-Oct. 1960. Served with S Caribbean Force, 1941–43; Major, Staff Officer, Brit. Guiana Garrison. Hon. Col, British Guiana Volunteer Force, 1962–66. Chm., Nat. Sports Council, 1962–66. *Recreations:* reading; interested in sports of all kinds; rep. Brit. Guiana at Association and Rugby football, cricket, hockey. *Address:* Suite No 603, 1180 Pinetree Way, Coquitlam, BC V6B 7L2, Canada.

SMITH, Prof. Ivor Ramsay, FEng 1988; Professor of Electrical Power Engineering, Loughborough University of Technology, since 1974; *b* 8 Oct. 1929; *s* of Howard Smith and Elsie Emily Smith; *m* 1962, Pamela Mary Voake; three *s*. *Educ:* Univ. of Bristol (BSc, PhD, DSc), CEng, FIEE 1974. Design and Develt Engr, GEC, Birmingham, 1956–59; Lectr, Sen. Lectr, Reader, Univ. of Birmingham, 1959–74; Loughborough University of Technology: Hd, Dept of Electronic and Electrical Engrg, 1980–90; Dean of Engrg, 1983–86; Pro-Vice-Chancellor, 1987–91. Director: Loughborough Consultants Ltd,

1980–; E Midlands Regl Technology Network, 1989–. *Publications:* about 200 technical papers and articles on range of power engrg topics, incl. the efficient computation of power supply systems and the prodn and processing of large pulses of energy. *Recreations:* gardening, walking, reading. *Address:* Department of Electronic and Electrical Engineering, Loughborough University of Technology, Loughborough, Leics LE11 3TU. *T:* Loughborough (01509) 222821.

SMITH, Jack, ARCA 1952; artist; *b* 18 June 1928; *s* of John Edward and Laura Smith; *m* 1956, Susan Craigie Halkett. *Educ:* Sheffield College of Art; St Martin's School of Art; Royal College of Art. Exhibitions: Whitechapel Art Gallery, 1959, 1971; Beaux Arts Gallery, 1952–58; Matthiesen Gallery, 1960, 1963; Catherine Viviano Gallery, New York, 1958, 1961; Pittsburgh International, 1955, 1957, 1964; Grosvenor Gallery, 1965; Marlborough Gallery, 1968; Konsthallen, Gothenburg, Sweden, 1968; Hull Univ., 1969; Bear Lane Gallery, Oxford, 1970; Whitechapel Gall., 1970; Redfern Gall., 1973 and 1976; Serpentine Gall., 1978; Fischer Fine Art, London, 1981, 1983; British Painting, Museo Municipal, Madrid, 1983; Flowers East Gall., London, 1990, 1991, 1992, 1994. Designer, sets and costumes: Carmen Arcadiae Mechanicae Perpetuum, Ballet Rambert, 1986; Pursuit, Royal Ballet, 1987. Guggenheim Award (Nat.), 1960. Work in permanent collections: Tate Gallery; Arts Council of Great Britain; Contemporary Art Society; British Council. *Address:* 29 Seafield Road, Hove, Sussex BN3 2TP. *T:* Brighton (01273) 738312.

SMITH, Jack Stanley, CMG 1970; Professor, and Chairman, Graduate School of Business Administration, University of Melbourne, 1973–77, retired; *b* 13 July 1916; *s* of C. P. T. Smith, Avoca, Victoria; *m* 1940, Nancy, *d* of J. C. Beckley, Melbourne; one *s* two *d*. *Educ:* Ballarat Grammar Sch.; Melbourne Univ. Construction Engineer, Australasian Petroleum Co., 1938–41. Served in Australian Imperial Forces, 1942–45, Lieut. Project Engineer, Melbourne & Metropolitan Bd of Works, 1946–48. P.A. Management Consultants, UK and Australia, 1949–72, Managing Dir, 1964–72. Hon. LLD Melbourne, 1987. *Recreations:* golf, tennis. *Address:* 15 Glyndebourne Avenue, Toorak, Victoria 3142, Australia. *T:* (3) 98224581. *Clubs:* Melbourne (Melbourne); Lawn Tennis Association of Victoria, Metropolitan Golf (Vic.).

SMITH, James Aikman, TD; Sheriff of Lothian and Borders (formerly the Lothians and Peebles) at Edinburgh, 1968–76; Hon. Sheriff, 1976; *b* 13 June 1914; *s* of Rev. W. J. Smith, DD; *m* 1947, Ann, *d* of Norman A. Millar, FRICS, Glasgow; three *d*. *Educ:* Glasgow Academy; The Queen's Coll., Oxford; Edinburgh Univ. BA (Oxford) 1936; LLB (Edinburgh) 1939; Mem. of Faculty of Advocates, 1939. Served War of 1939–45 (despatches): Royal Artillery, 1939–46; Lt-Col 1944. Sheriff-Substitute: of Renfrew and Argyll, 1948–52; of Roxburgh, Berwick and Selkirk, 1952–57; of Aberdeen, Kincardine and Banff, 1957–68. Pres., Sheriffs-Substitute Assoc., 1969; Pres., Sheriffs' Assoc., 1971–72. Member Departmental Cttee on Probation Service, 1959–62. Chm., Edinburgh and E of Scotland Br., English-Speaking Union, 1971. Bronze Star (US), 1945. *Publications:* occasional articles in legal journals. *Address:* 16 Murrayfield Avenue, Edinburgh EH12 6AX. *Club:* New (Edinburgh).

SMITH, James Andrew Buchan, CBE 1959; DSc; FRSE 1952; retired as Director of the Hannah Dairy Research Institute, Ayr, Scotland, 1951–70 (Acting Director, 1948–51); *b* 26 May 1906; *yr s* of late Dr James Fleming Smith, JP, MB, CM, Whithorn, Wigtownshire; *m* 1933, Elizabeth Marion, *d* of James Kerr, Wallasey, Cheshire; four *d*. *Educ:* Leamington College, Warwicks; Univ. of Birmingham. PhD (Birmingham) 1929; DSc (London) 1940. Graduate Research Asst: at UCL, 1929–30; at Imperial College, London, 1930–32; Lectr in Biochemistry, Univ. of Liverpool, 1932–36; Biochemist, Hannah Dairy Research Inst., 1936–46; Lectr in Biochemistry, Univ. of Glasgow, 1946–47. President: Society of Dairy Technology, 1951–52; Nutrition Society, 1968–71; Treasurer, Internat. Union of Nutritional Sciences, 1969–75. Hon. LLD Glasgow, 1972. *Publications:* scientific papers in Biochemical Jl, Jl of Dairy Research, Proc. Nutrition Soc., etc. *Recreation:* gardening. *Address:* Flaxton House, 1 St Leonard's Road, Ayr KA7 2PR. *T:* Ayr (01292) 264865. *Club:* Farmers'.

SMITH, James Archibald Bruce, CBE 1981; British Council Representative, Indonesia, 1978–83; *b* 12 Sept. 1929; *s* of James Thom Smith and Anna Tyrie; *m* 1957, Anne Elizabeth Whittle; three *d*. *Educ:* Forfar Acad.; Edinburgh Univ. (MA 1952); Sch. of Econs, Dundee (BScEcon 1953); Jesus Coll., Cambridge. RAF, 1953–55. HMOCS, Dist Officer, Kenya, 1956–62; British Council, 1962–83: Asst, Edinburgh, 1962–65; Asst Rep., Tanzania, 1965–66; Reg. Dir, Kumasi, Ghana, 1966–69; Rep., Sierra Leone, 1969–72; seconded to ODM, 1973–75; Dir, Personnel Dept, 1975–77; Controller, Personnel and Staff Recruitment Div., 1977–78. *Recreations:* Angusiana, reading, walking, collecting. *Address:* Calluna, West Hemming Street, Letham, Angus DD8 2PU. *T:* Forfar (01307) 818212.

SMITH, James Cadzow, CBE 1989; DRC; FEng 1988; FIMechE, FIEE, FIMarE; FRSE 1981; Chairman, Eastern Group (formerly Eastern Electricity) plc, 1990–95 (Chief Executive, 1990–93); *b* 28 Nov. 1927; *s* of James Smith and Margaret Ann Cadzow; *m* 1954, Moira Barrie Hogg; one *s* one *d*. *Educ:* Bellvue Secondary Sch.; Heriot-Watt Coll.; Strathclyde Univ. Engineer Officer, Mercantile Marine, 1948–53; engineering and managerial appts in fossil and nuclear power generation with SSEB and CEGB, 1953–73; Director of Engineering, N Ireland Electricity Service, 1973–74; Deputy Chairman and Chief Executive, 1975–77; Chairman: E Midlands Electricity Bd, 1977–82; Eastern Electricity Bd, 1982–90. Vis. Prof., Strathclyde Univ., 1981–. Pres., IEE, 1989–90. Freeman, City of London, 1984; Liveryman, 1984, Mem. Ct of Assistants, 1991–, Engineers' Co. Hon. LLD Strathclyde, 1988. *Recreations:* music, drama, mountaineering. *Address:* N. M. Rothschild & Sons Ltd, New Court, St Swithin's Lane, EC4P 4DU.

SMITH, Dr James Cuthbert, FRS 1993; Head, Division of Developmental Biology, National Institute for Medical Research, since 1991; *b* 31 Dec. 1954; *s* of Leslie Cuthbert Smith and Freda Sarah (*née* Wragg); *m* 1979, Fiona Mary Watt; one *s*. *Educ:* Latymer Upper Sch.; Christ's Coll., Cambridge (BA 1976; MA 1979); London Univ. (PhD 1979). NATO Postdoctoral Fellow, Sidney Farber Cancer Inst. and Harvard Med. Sch., 1979–81; ICRF Postdoctoral Fellow, 1981–84; Mem., Scientific Staff, NIMR, 1984–. Chm., British Soc. for Development Biol., 1994–; Mem., EMBO, 1992–. Howard Hughes Internat. Res. Scholar, 1993–. Scientific Medal, Zool Soc. of London, 1989; Otto Mangold Prize, Ges. für Entwicklungsbiologie, 1991; EMBO Medal, 1993. *Publications:* (ed jtly) The Molecular Basis of Positional Signalling, 1989; scientific articles in various jls. *Recreations:* squash, cycling, riding, music, conversation, reading biographies. *Address:* Laboratory of Developmental Biology, National Institute for Medical Research, The Ridgeway, NW7 1AA. *T:* 0181–913 8524.

SMITH, James Ian, CB 1974; Member, Panel of Chairmen, Civil Service Selection Board, since 1984; *b* 22 April 1924; *s* of late James Smith, Ballater, Aberdeenshire, and of Agnes Michie; *m* 1947, Pearl Myra Fraser; one *s*. *Educ:* Alderman Newton's Sch., Leicester; St Andrews Univ. Served War of 1939–45: India and Burma; RA (attached Indian Mountain Artillery), Lieut, 1943–46. Entered Dept of Agriculture for Scotland, 1949; Private Sec. to Parly Under-Sec. of State, Scottish Office, 1953; Dept of Agriculture for Scotland: Principal, 1953; Asst Sec., 1959; Asst Sec., Scottish Development Dept, 1965–67; Under-Sec., Dept of Agriculture and Fisheries for Scotland, 1967–72; Sec., Dept of Agriculture and Fisheries for Scotland, 1972–84. Mem., ARC, 1967–72, 1983–84; Mem., Potato Marketing Bd, 1985–87. Mem., St Andrews Links Trust, 1985–90 (Chm., 1989–90). *Recreation:* golf. *Address:* 7 Hillpark Loan, Edinburgh EH4 7ST. *T:* 0131–336 4652.

SMITH, Janet (B.) A.; *see* Adam Smith.

SMITH, Hon. Dame Janet (Hilary), (Dame Janet Mathieson), DBE 1992; **Hon. Mrs Justice Smith;** a Judge of the High Court of Justice, Queen's Bench Division, since 1992; a Judge of the Employment Appeal Tribunal, since 1994; Presiding Judge, North Eastern Circuit, since 1995; *b* 29 Nov. 1940; *d* of Alexander Roe and Margaret Holt; *m* 1st, 1959, Edward Stuart Smith; two *s* one *d*; 2nd, 1984, Robin Edward Alexander Mathieson. *Educ:* Bolton School. Called to the Bar, Lincoln's Inn, 1972, Bencher, 1992; QC 1986; a Recorder, 1988–92. Mem., Criminal Injuries Compensation Bd, 1988–92. *Recreations:* gardening, music. *Address:* Royal Courts of Justice, Strand, WC2A 2LL.

SMITH, Prof. (Jenkyn) Beverley, FRHistS; Sir John Williams Professor of Welsh History, University of Wales, Aberystwyth, since 1986; Commissioner since 1984, Chairman since 1991, Royal Commission on Ancient and Historical Monuments for Wales; *b* 27 Sept. 1931; *s* of Cecil Nelson Smith and Hannah Jane (*née* Jenkins); *m* 1970, Llinos Olwen Wyn Vaughan; two *s*. *Educ:* Gowerton Grammar Sch.; UCW, Aberystwyth (BA, MA). FRHistS 1967. National Service, 1954–56. Researcher, Bd of Celtic Studies, Univ. of Wales, 1956–58; Asst Keeper, Dept of MSS and Records, Nat. Library of Wales, 1958–60; Lectr 1960–67, Sen. Lectr 1967–78, Reader 1978–86, Dept of Welsh History, UCW. Sir John Rhys Vis. Fellow, Univ. of Oxford, 1978–79. Member: Court and Council, Nat. Library of Wales, 1974–84; Bd of Celtic Studies, Univ. of Wales, 1965–91 (Sec., History and Law Cttee, 1979–85, Chm 1985–91). Jt Editor, Bulletin of Bd of Celtic Studies, 1972–91. *Publications:* Llywelyn ap Gruffudd, Tywysog Cymru, 1986; (ed) Medieval Welsh Society, Selected Essayss by T. Jones Pierce, 1972; (ed with G. H. Jenkins) Politics and Society in Wales 1840–1922, 1988; articles in English Hist. Review, Welsh Hist. Review, Bulletin Bd of Celtic Studies and other jls. *Recreations:* walking, Welsh terriers. *Address:* Department of Welsh History, University of Wales, Aberystwyth, Dyfed SY23 3DY.

SMITH, Jennifer A.; Principal, Harrogate Ladies' College, 1993–95; *b* 11 March 1950; *d* of Geoffrey and Elsie Bird; *m* 1974, Michael Smith; one *d*. *Educ:* Leeds Univ. (BSc Hons Physics, PGCE); Open Univ. (BA); Liverpool Univ. (MEd). Asst teacher, Physics, 1973–83, Head of Physics, 1983–85, St Richard Gwyn High Sch., Clwyd; Sen. Project Tutor, Science and Electronics, Bodelwyddau TVEI Centre, 1985–88; Dep. Head Teacher, West Kirby Grammar Sch. for Girls, 1988–93. *Recreations:* ski-ing, climbing, music, theatre, electronics.

SMITH, Jeremy Fox Eric; DL; Chairman, Smith St Aubyn (Holdings) plc, 1973–86, retired; *b* 17 Nov. 1928; *s* of late Captain E. C. E. Smith, MC, and B. H. Smith (*née* Williams); *m* 1953, Julia Mary Rona, *d* of Sir Walter Burrell, 8th Bt, CBE, TD; two *s* two *d*. *Educ:* Eton; New College, Oxford. Chairman, Transparent Paper Ltd, 1965–76. Chairman, London Discount Market Assoc., 1978–80. DL 1988, High Sheriff, 1992–93, West Sussex. *Recreations:* hunting, shooting, stalking, skiing. *Address:* The Old Rectory, Slaugham, Haywards Heath, W Sussex RH17 6AG. *T:* Handcross (01444) 400341. *Clubs:* Beefsteak; Leander (Henley on Thames).

See also Duchess of Grafton, Sir J. L. E. Smith, Earl of Verulam.

SMITH, Jeremy James Russell; Chief Executive, London Borough of Camden, since 1990; *b* 12 June 1947; *s* of Horace James Smith and Joan Alistair Russell. *Educ:* Peterhouse, Cambridge (BA Law 1968). Called to the Bar, Lincoln's Inn, 1969; Barrister, 1971–78; Sen. Legal Adviser, Brent Community Law Centre, 1978–83; Legal Services Liaison Officer, GLC, 1983–86; Clerk and Legal Advr, ILEA, 1986–89; Dir of Law and Admin, London Borough of Camden, 1989–90. *Recreations:* history, current affairs, music, rambling. *Address:* London Borough of Camden, Town Hall, Judd Street, WC1H 9JE. *T:* 0171–860 5686.

SMITH, Jock; *see* Smith, John M. M.

SMITH, Dr John, OBE 1945; TD 1950; Deputy Chief Medical Officer, Scottish Home and Health Department, 1963–75, retired; *b* 13 July 1913; *e s* of late John Smith, DL, JP, Glasgow and Symington, and Agnes Smith; *m* 1942, Elizabeth Fleming (*d* 1981), twin *d* of late A. F. Wylie, Giffnock; three *s* one *d* (and one *s* decd). *Educ:* High Sch., Glasgow; Sedbergh Sch.; Christ's Coll., Cambridge; Glasgow Univ. BA 1935; MA 1943; MB, BChir Cantab 1938; MB, ChB Glasgow 1938; MRCPG 1965; FRCPG 1967; FRCPE 1969; FFPHM (FFCM 1972). TA (RA from 1935, RAMC from 1940); War Service, 1939–46; ADMS Second Army, DDMS (Ops and Plans) 21 Army Group (despatches); OC 155 (Lowland) Fd Amb., 1950–53; ADMS 52 (Lowland) Div., 1953–56; Hon. Col 52 Div. Medical Service, 1961–67. House appts Glasgow Victoria and Western Infirmaries; joined Dept of Health for Scotland, 1947; Medical Supt, Glasgow Victoria Hosps, 1955–58; rejoined Dept of Health for Scotland, 1958; specialised in hospital planning. QHP 1971–74. Officier, Ordre de Leopold I (Belgium), 1947. *Publications:* articles on medical administration and hospital services in various medical jls. *Recreations:* rifle shooting (shot in Scottish and TA representative teams), hill walking, reading. *Address:* 5/10 Oswald Road, Edinburgh EH9 2HE. *T:* 0131–667 5617. *Clubs:* Naval and Military; New (Edinburgh).

See also Sir R. C. Smith.

SMITH, Sir John (Alfred), Kt 1994; QPM 1986; Deputy Commisssioner of the Metropolitan Police, 1991–95; *b* 21 Sept. 1938; *s* of Ruth Alice and Alfred Joseph Smith; *m* 1960, Joan Maria Smith; one *s* one *d*. *Educ:* St Olave's and St Saviour's Grammar School. Irish Guards, 1959–62. Metropolitan Police, 1962; Head, Scotland Yard drugs squad, 1979; Commander 'P' (Bromley–Lewisham) Dist., 1980; Dep. Chief Constable, Surrey Constabulary, 1981; Metropolitan Police: Dep. Asst Comr, 1984; Inspectorate and Force Reorganisation Team, 1985; Asst Comr, 1987–90; Management Support Dept, 1987–89; Specialist Ops Dept, 1989–90; Inspector of Constabulary for SE England, 1990–91. Pres., ACPO, 1993–94. *Recreations:* gardening, sport spectating, horse riding, walking. *Club:* Crystal Palace Football.

SMITH, Sir John (Cyril), Kt 1993; CBE 1983; QC 1979; FBA 1973; Professor of Law in the University of Nottingham 1958–87, now Emeritus, and Head of Department of Law 1956–74, and 1977–86; *b* 15 Jan. 1922; 2nd *s* of Bernard and Madeline Smith; *m* 1957, Shirley Ann Walters; two *s* one *d*. *Educ:* St Mary's Grammar Sch., Darlington; Downing Coll., Cambridge (Hon. Fellow, 1977). Served Royal Artillery, 1942–47 (Captain). BA 1949, LLB 1950, MA 1954, LLD 1975 Cantab. Called to Bar, Lincoln's Inn, 1950; Hon. Bencher, 1977; Hon. Mem., Midland and Oxford Circuit Bar Mess. Nottingham University: Assistant Lecturer in Law, 1950–52; Lecturer, 1952–56; Reader, 1956–57; Pro-Vice-Chancellor, 1973–77; Hon. Pres. of Convocation, 1978–87. Arthur Goodhart Vis. Prof. in Legal Science, Cambridge, 1989–90. Commonwealth Fund Fellow, Harvard Law Sch., 1952–53. Member: Criminal Law Revision Cttee, 1977– (co-opted, 1960–66 (theft reference) and 1970–77); Policy Adv. Cttee, 1975–85. Pres., Soc. of Public Teachers of Law, 1979–80. Hon. LLD: Sheffield, 1984; Nottingham, 1989; Villanova, 1993; De

Montfort, 1995. *Publications:* (with J. A. C. Thomas) A Casebook on Contract, 1957, 9th edn 1992; (with Brian Hogan) Criminal Law, 1965, 7th edn 1992; Law of Theft, 1968, 7th edn 1993; Criminal Law, Cases and Materials, 1975, 5th edn 1993; (with I. H. Dennis and E. J. Griew) Codification of the Criminal Law, 1985; Justification and Excuse in the Criminal Law (Hamlyn Lectures), 1989; Contract, 1989, 2nd edn 1993; Criminal Evidence, 1995. *Recreations:* walking, gardening. *Address:* 445 Derby Road, Lenton, Nottingham NG7 2EB. *T:* Nottingham (0115) 978 2323.

SMITH, John Derek, MA, PhD; FRS 1976; Member of Scientific Staff, Medical Research Council, Laboratory of Molecular Biology, Cambridge, 1962–88; *b* 8 Dec. 1924; *s* of Richard Ernest Smith and Winifred Strickland Smith (*née* Davis); *m* 1955, Ruth Irwin Aney (marr. diss. 1968). *Educ:* King James's Grammar Sch., Knaresborough; Clare Coll., Cambridge. Mem., Scientific Staff, Agricl Research Council Virus Research Unit, Cambridge, 1945–59; Research Fellow, Clare Coll., 1949–52; with Institut Pasteur, Paris, 1952–53; Rockefeller Foundn Fellow, Univ. of California, Berkeley, 1955–57; California Institute of Technology: Sen. Research Fellow, 1959–62; Sherman Fairchild Scholar, 1974–75. *Publications:* numerous papers in scientific jls on biochemistry and molecular biology. *Recreation:* travel. *Address:* 12 Stansgate Avenue, Cambridge CB2 2QZ. *T:* Cambridge (01223) 247841.

SMITH, Air Vice-Marshal John Edward, CB 1979; CBE 1972; AFC 1957; Air Officer Administration, Headquarters Strike Command, 1977–81; retired; *b* 8 June 1924; *m* 1944, Roseanne Margurite (*née* Eriksson); four *s* two *d* (and one *s* decd). *Educ:* Tonbridge Sch. Served in Far East, ME, USA and Germany as well as UK Stations since joining the Service in Nov. 1941. *Recreations:* sailing, travel. *Address:* 1 Butlers Grove, Great Linford, Bucks MK14 5DT. *Club:* Royal Air Force.

SMITH, Rear-Adm. John Edward D.; *see* Dyer-Smith.

SMITH, (John) Edward (McKenzie) L.; *see* Lucie-Smith.

SMITH, John Frederick; Lord Mayor of Cardiff, 1990–91; *b* 28 Sept. 1934; *s* of Charles Frederick Smith and Teresa Smith (*née* O'Brian); *m* 1962, Irene Rice (*d* 1982); one *s*. *Educ:* St Cuthbert's Jun. Sch.; St Illtyd's Grammar Sch.; Gwent Inst. of Higher Educn, 1981–82 (Dip. Trade Union Studies); University Coll., Cardiff, 1982–85 (BScEcon). Engrg apprenticeship, Edward Curran Engrg, 1951–56; Merchant Navy Engr, Blue Funnel and Andrew Weir, 1956–62; Steel Industry, GKN S Wales, 1964–81; Housing Officer, Adamsdown Housing Assoc. Ltd, 1985–. Member: Cardiff CC, 1972– (Chairman: Housing and Public Works Cttee, 1973–75; Land Cttee, 1987–90; Dep. Lord Mayor, 1988–89); S Glamorgan CC, 1973–81. AMIH 1990. JP Cardiff, 1977–87. *Recreations:* music, spectator of Cardiff RFC and Wales RU, Shakespeare, cooking. *Address:* 128 Corporation Road, Grangetown, Cardiff CF1 7AX. *T:* Cardiff (01222) 345176.

SMITH, John Herbert, CBE 1977; FCA, IPFA, CIGasE; Deputy Chairman and Chief Executive, British Gas Corporation, 1976–83; *b* 30 April 1918; *s* of Thomas Arthur Smith and Pattie Lord; *m* 1945, Phyllis Mary Baxter; two *s* three *d*. *Educ:* Salt High Sch., Shipley, Yorks. Articled Clerk, Bradford and Otley, 1934–39. Served War: RAMC, 1940–46. Dep. Clerk and Chief Financial Officer, Littleborough, Lancs, 1946–49; West Midlands Gas Bd, 1949–61 (various posts, finishing as Asst Chief Accountant); Chief Accountant, Southern Gas Bd, 1961–65; Director of Finance and Administration, East Midlands Gas Bd, 1965–68; Mem. (full-time), East Midlands Gas Bd, 1968 (Dep. Chm., 1968–72); Mem. for Finance, Gas Council, June-Dec. 1972; Mem. for Finance, British Gas Corp., 1973–76. Chm., Nationalised Industries Finance Panel, 1978–83. Chairman: Moracrest Investments, 1977–85; United Property Unit Trust (formerly Industrial and Commercial Property Unit Trust), 1986–89 (Mem., 1983–89, Chm., 1986–89, Management Cttee); Member, Management Committee: Pension Funds Property Unit Trust, 1975–89 (Dep. Chm., 1984–89); Lazard American Exempt Fund, 1976–91; British American Property Unit Trust, 1982–93. Member: Council, Inst. of Chartered Accountants, 1977–81, Trilateral Commn, 1976–85. FRSA 1985. *Recreations:* music, piano playing, walking. *Address:* 81 Albany, Manor Road, East Cliff, Bournemouth, Dorset BH1 3EJ. *T:* Bournemouth (01202) 298157.

SMITH, John Hilary, CBE 1970 (OBE 1964); Procurator, 1990–94, and Fellow, 1991–94, University College, Oxford; *b* 20 March 1928; 2nd *s* of late P. R. Smith, OBE and Edith Prince; *m* 1964, Mary Sylvester Head; two *s* one *d*. *Educ:* Cardinal Vaughan Sch., London; University Coll. London (Fellow, 1987); University Coll., Oxford. BA Hons London 1948; MA Oxon 1991. Mil. service, 1948–50, commnd Queen's Own Royal W Kent Regt. Cadet, Northern Nigerian Administration, 1951; Supervisor, Admin. Service Trng, 1960; Dep. Sec. to Premier, 1963; Dir Staff, Develt Centre, 1964; Perm. Sec., Min. of Finance, Benue Plateau State, 1968; Vis. Lectr, Duke Univ., 1970; Financial Sec., British Solomon Is, 1970; Governor of Gilbert and Ellice Islands, 1973–76, of Gilbert Islands, 1976–78; Sec., Imperial Coll., and Clerk to the Govs, 1979–89 (Fellow, 1992). Public Orator, Univ. of London, 1991–94. Dir, Fleming Ventures, 1985–. Mem. Council, Scout Assoc., 1980– (Chm., Cttee of Council, 1984–88); Pres., Pacific Is Soc. of UK and Ireland, 1981–85. Governor: St Mary's Coll., Strawberry Hill, 1980–88; Cardinal Vaughan School, 1982–88; Heythrop Coll., 1986–93; Member, Board of Management: LSHTM, 1989– (Treas., 1993–); St Mary's Sch., Shaftesbury, 1993– (Chm. Govs, 1994–). *Publications:* How to Write Letters that get Results, 1965; Colonial Cadet in Nigeria, 1968; articles in S Atlantic Quarterly, Administration, Jl of Overseas Administration, Nigeria. *Recreations:* walking, writing, music. *Address:* Pound House, Dulverton, Som TA22 9HP. *Clubs:* Athenæum, Commonwealth Trust.

SMITH, Sir John Jonah W.; *see* Walker-Smith.

SMITH, Sir John Kenneth N.; *see* Newson-Smith.

SMITH, Sir John (Lindsay Eric), Kt 1988; CH 1994; CBE 1975; *b* 3 April 1923; *s* of Captain E. C. E. Smith, MC, LLD; *m* 1952, Christian, *d* of late Col U. E. C. Carnegy of Lour, DSO, MC; two *s* two *d* (and one *d* decd). *Educ:* Eton (Fellow, 1974–89); New Coll., Oxford (MA; Hon. Fellow, 1979). Served Fleet Air Arm 1942–46 (Lieut RNVR). MP (C) Cities of London and Westminster, Nov. 1965–1970; Mem., Public Accounts Cttee, 1968–69. National Trust: Mem., Historic Bldgs Cttee, 1952–61; Mem. Exec. Cttee, 1961–85; Mem. Council, 1961–; Dep. Chm., 1980–85. Member: Standing Commission on Museums and Galleries, 1958–66; Inland Waterways Redevelopment Cttee, 1959–62; Historic Buildings Council, 1971–78; Redundant Churches Fund, 1972–74; Nat. Heritage Memorial Fund, 1980–82. Director: Coutts & Co., 1950–93; Financial Times Ltd, 1959–68; Rolls Royce Ltd, 1955–75; Dep. Governor, Royal Exchange Assurance, 1961–66. Founder, Manifold and Landmark Charitable Trusts. High Steward of Maidenhead, 1966–75. Freeman of Windsor and Maidenhead, 1975. FSA; Hon. FRIBA 1973; Hon. FRIAS 1983. JP Berks, 1964; DL 1978, Lord-Lieut, 1975–78, Berks. Hon. LLD: Exeter, 1989; Portsmouth, 1994. *Address:* Shottesbrooke Park, Maidenhead, Berks SL6 3SW; 1 Smith Square, SW1P 3PA. *Clubs:* Pratt's, Beefsteak, Brooks's; Tristan da Cunha Golf.

See also Duchess of Grafton, J. F. E. Smith, Hon. A. N. W. Soames.

SMITH, John M.; *see* Maynard Smith, J.

SMITH, John Mitchell Melvin, (Jock), WS; Partner, Masson & Glennie, Solicitors, Peterhead, 1957; retired; *b* 5 July 1930; *s* of John Mitchell Smith and Barbara Edda Smith or Glennie; *m* 1958, Elisabeth Marion Slight; two *s* one *d*. *Educ:* Fettes College; Edinburgh Univ. (BL). Pres., Law Soc. of Scotland, 1987–88. *Recreations:* golf, theatre. *Address:* 1 Winton Terrace, Edinburgh EH10 7AP. *Clubs:* New (Edinburgh); Bruntsfield Golf; Club of Deir, Peterhead Burns.

SMITH, John P.; *see* Smith, J. W. P.

SMITH, Sir John Rathborne V.; *see* Vassar-Smith.

SMITH, John Roger B.; *see* Bickford Smith.

SMITH, John William Patrick, (John P. Smith); Chief Executive, Gwent Image Partnership, since 1992; *b* 17 March 1951; *s* of John Henry Smith and Margaret Mary (*née* Collins); *m* 1971, Kathleen Mulvaney; two *s* one *d*. *Educ:* Penarth County Sch.; Gwent Coll. of Higher Educn (Dip. in Indust. Relations and Trade Union Studies); UCW Cardiff (BSc (Econ) Hons). Building worker, 1966–68; RAF, 1967–71; joiner, 1971–76; mature student, 1976–83; University Tutor, 1983–85; Sen. Lectr in Business Studies, 1985–89. MP (Lab) Vale of Glamorgan, May 1989–1992; contested (Lab) Vale of Glamorgan, 1992. PPS to Dep. Leader of the Opposition, 1989–92; Mem., Select Cttee on Welsh Affairs, 1990–92. *Recreations:* reading, boating, camping. *Address:* Barry, S Glam. *T:* Barry (01446) 740028. *Club:* Sea View Labour (Barry).

SMITH, Jonathan A.; *see* Ashley-Smith.

SMITH, Jonathan Simon Christopher R.; *see* Riley-Smith.

SMITH, Prof. Joseph Victor, FRS 1978; Louis Block Professor of Physical Sciences, since 1977, and Co-ordinator of Scientific Programs, since 1992 (Executive Director, 1988–91), Consortium for Advanced Radiation Sources, University of Chicago (Professor of Mineralogy and Crystallography, 1960–76); *b* 30 July 1928; *s* of Henry Victor Smith and Edith (*née* Robinson); *m* 1951, Brenda Florence Wallis; two *d*. *Educ:* Cambridge Univ. (MA, PhD). Fellow, Carnegie Instn of Washington, 1951–54; Demonstrator in Mineralogy and Petrology, Cambridge Univ., 1954–56; Asst then Associate Prof., Pennsylvania State Univ., 1956–60. Editor, Power Diffraction File, 1959–69. Visiting Prof., California Inst. of Technology, 1965; Consultant: Union Carbide Corp., 1956–85; UOP, 1985–. Member, US Nat. Acad. of Scis, 1986. Murchison Medal, 1980; Roebling Medal, 1982. *Publications:* Feldspar Minerals, Vols 1 and 2, 1975, 2nd edn 1987; Geometrical and Structural Crystallography, 1982; numerous articles on crystallography, inorganic chemistry, mineralogy, petrology and planetology. *Recreations:* music, art. *Address:* Department of the Geophysical Sciences, University of Chicago, 5734 S Ellis Avenue, Chicago, IL 60637, USA. *T:* (312) 7028110.

SMITH, Sir Joseph (William Grenville), Kt 1991; MD; FRCP; FRCPath; FFPHM; FIBiol; Director, Public Health Laboratory Service, 1985–92; *b* 14 Nov. 1930; *s* of Douglas Ralph and Hannah Letitia Margaret Smith; *m* 1954, Nira Jean (*née* Davies); one *s*. *Educ:* Cathays High School, Cardiff; Welsh Nat. Sch. of Medicine (MD 1966); Dip. Bact., London Univ.; FRCPath 1975; FFPHM (FFCM 1976); FRCP 1987. FIBiol 1978. Sen. Lectr, Dept of Bacteriology and Immunology, LSHTM, 1960–65; Consultant Clinical Bacteriologist, Radcliffe Infirmary, Oxford, 1965–69; Gen. Practitioner, Islington, 1970–71; Consultant Epidemiologist, Dep. Dir, Epidemiological Res. Lab., PHLS, 1971–76; Dir, Nat. Inst. for Biological Standards and Control, 1976–85. Consultant on immunisation to British Army, 1985–. Member: Cttee on Safety of Medicines, 1978–86 (Chm., Biol Sub-Cttee, 1981–86); Jt Cttee on Vaccination and Immunisation, 1976–93; British Pharmacopoea Commn, 1976–85, MRC, 1989–92; Council, RCPath, 1988–90; Chairman: Cttee on Vaccination and Immunization Procedures, MRC, 1976–93; Simian Virus Cttee, MRC, 1982–93; Tropical Medicine Res. Bd, MRC, 1989–90; Expert Adv. Gp on Immunization, WHO Eur. Reg., 1993–. Mem., Ct of Govs and Bd of Management, LSHTM, 1994–. *Publications:* (with E. B. Adams and D. R. Laurence) Tetanus, 1969; papers on tetanus, immunization, and epidemiology of infections in scientific and med. jls. *Recreation:* the arts. *Address:* c/o Public Health Laboratory Service Board, 61 Colindale Avenue, NW9 5DF.

SMITH, Hon. Kenneth George, OJ 1973; Justice of Appeal, Bahamas, 1985–90, retired; *b* 25 July 1920; *s* of Franklin C. Smith; *m* 1942, Hyacinth Whitfield Connell; two *d*. *Educ:* Primary schs; Cornwall Coll., Jamaica; Inns of Court Sch. of Law, London. Barrister-at-Law, Lincoln's Inn. Asst Clerk of Courts, 1940–48; Dep. Clerk of Courts, 1948–53; Clerk of Courts, 1953–56; Crown Counsel, 1956–62; Asst Attorney-Gen., 1962–65; Supreme Court Judge, 1965–70; Judge of Appeal, Jamaica, 1970–73; Chief Justice of Jamaica, 1973–85. *Recreations:* swimming, gardening. *Address:* 5 Wagner Avenue, Kingston 8, Jamaica.

SMITH, Kenneth Graeme Stewart, CMG 1958; JP; retired as Civil Secretary, The Gambia, West Africa, 1962; *b* 26 July 1918; 3rd *s* of late Prof. H. A. Smith, DCL; unmarried. *Educ:* Bradfield; Magdalen College, Oxford. Cadet, Colonial Administrative Service, Tanganyika, 1940; appointments in Colonial Service, 1945–62. JP Dorset, 1967. *Address:* The Old House, Newland, Sherborne, Dorset DT9 3AQ. *T:* Sherborne (01935) 812754.

SMITH, Kingsley Ward; Chief Executive, Durham County Council, since 1988; Clerk to the Lieutenancy, since 1990; *b* 24 Oct. 1946; *s* of Peter and Doris Evelyn Smith; *m* 1968, Kathy Rutherford; two *s*. *Educ:* Blue Coat Secondary Sch., Walsall, Staffs; Dame Allan's Boys' Sch., Newcastle upon Tyne. IPFA 1970. Trainee Accountant, Gateshead CBC, 1964–67; Durham County Council: Accountant, subseq. Sen. Accountant, 1967–76; Chief Internal Auditor, 1976–79; Sen. Asst County Treasurer, 1979–81; Dep. County Treasurer, 1981–84; County Treasurer, 1984–88. Director: Durham TEC, 1990–; Durham Agency Against Crime, 1990–. Chairman: E Durham Task Force, 1990–; Prince's Trust Cttee for Cleveland and Durham, 1992–; Advr, Northern Develt Co., 1986–. *Recreations:* golfing, fishing, caravanning, walking his labrador (Sam). *Address:* County Hall, Durham DH1 5UF.

SMITH, Laura; *see* Duncan, A. L. A.

SMITH, Lawrence Delpré; Senior Puisne Judge of the Supreme Court of Sarawak, North Borneo and Brunei, 1951–64, retired; *b* 29 October 1905; *m*; one *s* three *d*. *Educ:* Christ's Hospital; Hertford College, Oxford; Gray's Inn. Colonial Administrative Service, 1929; Colonial Legal Service, 1934; Tanganyika, 1929; Palestine, 1946; Gambia, 1948. *Address:* 34 The Avenue, Muswell Hill, N10 2QL. *T:* 0181–883 7198.

SMITH, Lawrence Edward; yachting consultant, since 1971; *b* 19 Feb. 1956; *s* of Harold and Jean Smith; *m* 1991, Penny Jane Smith (*née* Haydock); one *s* one *d*. *Educ:* Bury Grammar Sch. America's Cup: Skipper, British challenger, Lionheart, 1980, Victory, 1983. Winning skipper: Fastnet Race, 1985; Admiral's Cup, 1989. Whitbread Round the World Race: Skipper, Rothmans, 1990 (4th), Intrum Justitia, 1994 (2nd). Skipper, UK crew, Soling class, Olympic Games, 1988, 1992 (Bronze medal). *Publications:* Dinghy Helming, 1985; Dinghy Tuning, 1986; Yacht Tuning, 1987; Science of Speed, 1994. *Recreations:* golf, tennis. *Address:* 2 Carlton Crescent, Southampton SO15 2EY. *T:* Sway (01590) 683707.

SMITH, Lawrence Joseph, OBE 1976; Assistant General Secretary, Transport and General Workers Union, 1985–88; two *d.* Served in HM Forces, 1941–47; joined London Transport, 1947; District Officer, TGWU, 1961, London District Secretary, 1965, National Officer, 1966, National Secretary, Passenger Services Group, 1971, Exec. Officer, 1979–85. Part-time Mem., London Transport Bd, 1983–. Mem., TUC Gen. Council, 1979–88. *Recreations:* gardening, football. *Address:* c/o Transport House, Smith Square, SW1P 3JB. *T:* 0171–828 7788.

SMITH, Lawrence Roger Hines, FSA; Keeper of Japanese Antiquities, British Museum, since 1987; *b* 19 Feb. 1941; *s* of Frank Ernest Smith and Eva Lilian Smith (*née* Hines); *m* 1st, 1965, Louise Geraldine Gallini (marr. diss. 1986); one *s* five *d*; 2nd, 1993, Louise Elaine Woodroff; one *d. Educ:* Collyer's Grammar Sch., Horsham; Queens' Coll., Cambridge (BA). British Museum: Asst Keeper, Dept of Manuscripts, 1962; Dept of Oriental Antiquities, 1965; Dep. Keeper, 1976; Keeper, 1977. British Acad. Exchange Fellow, Nihon Gakujutsu Shinkōkai, Kyoto, 1974–75. Academic adviser, Great Japan Exhibn, RA, 1981–82, and contrib. to catalogue. Uchiyama Prize, Ukiyoe Soc. of Japan, 1986. *Publications:* Netsuke: the miniature sculpture of Japan (with R. Barker), 1976; Flowers in Art from East and West (with P. Hulton), 1979; Japanese Prints: 300 years of albums and books (with J. Hillier), 1980; Japanese Decorative Arts 1600–1900 (with V. Harris), 1982; The Japanese Print since 1900, 1983; Contemporary Japanese Prints, 1985; (ed) Ukiyoe: images of unknown Japan, 1988; (ed) Japanese Art: masterpieces in the British Museum, 1990; Nihonga: traditional Japanese painting, 1991; Japanese Prints, 1912–1989: woodblocks and stencils, 1994; contribs to BM multi-cultural catalogues; articles and reviews in learned jls. *Recreations:* walking, sailing, bellringing, music, wine. *Address:* 45 Lyme Farm Road, Lee, SE12 8JQ. *T:* 0181–852 4789.

SMITH, Leslie Charles, OBE 1968; Founder Director, Eastway Zinc Alloy Co. Ltd, 1965–82; *b* 6 March 1918; *s* of Edward A. Smith and Elizabeth Smith; *m* 1948, Nancy Smith; two *s* one *d. Educ:* Enfield Central School. Export Buyer, 1938–40; Lieut, RNVR, 1940–46. Founder Dir, Lesney Products, 1947, Jt Man. Dir 1947–73, Man. Dir 1973–80; Chief Exec. Officer, 1980–81, Vice-Chm., 1981–82. FInstM; FIMgt (FBIM 1976); FInstD 1979. *Recreations:* ski-ing, sailing, golf. *Address:* White Timbers, 9a Broad Walk, N21 3DA. *T:* 0181–886 1656. *Clubs:* Naval; Royal Thames Yacht, Royal Motor Yacht, Parkstone Yacht, Poole Harbour Yacht; Parkstone Golf, Hadley Wood Golf.

SMITH, Sir Leslie (Edward George), Kt 1977; Director, The BOC Group plc (formerly The British Oxygen Co. Ltd), 1966–92 (Chairman, 1972–85); *b* 15 April 1919; *m* 1st, 1943, Lorna Bell Pickworth; two *d*; 2nd, 1964, Cynthia Barbara Holmes; one *s* one *d. Educ:* Christ's Hospital, Horsham, Sussex. Served War, Army (Royal Artillery, Royal Fusiliers), 1940–46. Variety of activities, 1946–55. Joined British Oxygen as Accountant, 1956, Group Man. Dir, 1969–72, Group Chm. and Chief Exec., 1972–79, Chm., 1979–85. Dir, British Gas plc (formerly British Gas Corp.), 1982–90. Mem., Exec. Cttee, King Edward VII Hospital for Officers, 1978–88. FCA. *Recreations:* unremarkable. *Address:* Forston Farm, Dorchester, Dorset DT2 7AB.

SMITH, Prof. Lewis Lauchlan, PhD; Director, Toxicology Unit, since 1991, and Institute for Environment and Health, since 1993, Medical Research Council; *b* 21 Aug. 1947; *s* of Lewis Smith and Margaret (*née* Wilson); *m* 1972, Susan Lisbeth Baynes; one *s* two *d. Educ:* Hatfield Poly. (BSc, PhD). MRCPath 1990. ICI Central Toxicology Laboratory: Res. Scientist, 1971–80; Sen. Scientist, 1980–85; Hd, Biochem. Toxicology Sect., 1985–91. *Publications:* numerous in res. jls on mechanisms of toxicity and cellular biochem. *Recreations:* golf, eating, dieting. *Address:* Medical Research Council Toxicology Unit, Hodgkin Building, University of Leicester, PO Box 138, Lancaster Road, Leicester LE1 9HN. *T:* Leicester (0116) 252 5601.

SMITH, Llewellyn Thomas; MP (Lab) Blaenau Gwent, since 1992; *b* 16 April 1944; *m*; two *s* one *d. Educ:* Cardiff University. Formerly with Pilkington Glass, George Wimpey and Workers' Educational Assoc. MEP (Lab) SE Wales, 1984–94. Mem., CND. *Address:* c/o House of Commons, SW1A 0AA; The Mount, Uplands, Tynewydd, Newbridge, Gwent NP1 4RH.

SMITH, Lloyd Barnaby; HM Diplomatic Service; Counsellor, Foreign and Commonwealth Office, since 1993; *b* 21 July 1945; *s* of Arthur and Zena Smith; *m* 1st, 1972, Nicola Mary Whitehead (marr. diss.); 2nd, 1983, Elizabeth Mary Sumner; one *s* one *d. Educ:* Merchant Taylors' Sch., Moor Park; Brasenose Coll., Oxford (MA). Joined Diplomatic Service, 1968; Third, later Second Sec., Bangkok, 1970–74; First Secretary: FCO, 1974–77; Paris, 1977–78; Head of Chancery, Dublin, 1978–81; Ecole Nat. d'Admin, Paris, 1981–82; First Sec., then Counsellor, UK Repn to EEC, Brussels, 1982–86; Counsellor, Bangkok, 1987–90. Dir, Know How Fund for Eastern Europe, 1990–92. *Recreation:* sailing. *Address:* c/o Foreign and Commonwealth Office, SW1A 2AH. *Club:* Upper Thames Sailing.

SMITH, Prof. Lorraine Nancy, PhD; Professor of Nursing, University of Glasgow, since 1990; *b* 29 June 1949; *d* of Geoffrey Leonard Millington and Ida May (*née* Attfield); *m* 1975, Christopher Murray Smith; one *s* one *d. Educ:* Univ. of Ottawa (BScN); Univ. of Manchester (MEd, PhD). Staff Nurse, Ottawa, 1971–73; Team Leader, Montreal, 1973–76; Sister, Withington Hosp., Manchester, 1976–77; Lectr, Dept of Nursing Studies, Univ. of Manchester, 1977–90. Member: Clin. Standards Adv. Gp (UK); Scottish Adv. Council on Alcohol; Turning Point (Scotland). *Publications:* articles in Advanced Jl of Nursing, Alcohol and Alcoholism, Nursing Educn Today, Nursing Times. *Recreations:* ski-ing, sailing, reading, bridge. *Address:* Department of Nursing and Midwifery, University of Glasgow, 68 Oakfield Avenue, Glasgow G12 8LS. *T:* 0141–330 5498. *Club:* S Caernarvonshire Yacht (Abersoch, N Wales).

SMITH, Dame Maggie, (Dame Margaret Natalie Cross), DBE 1990 (CBE 1970); actress; Director, United British Artists, since 1982; *b* 28 Dec. 1934; *d* of Nathaniel Smith and Margaret Little (*née* Hutton); *m* 1st, 1967, Robert Stephens (*see* Sir Robert Stephens) (marr. diss. 1975); two *s*; 2nd, 1975, Beverley Cross, *qv. Educ:* Oxford High School for Girls. Studied at Oxford Playhouse School under Isabel van Beers. First appearance, June 1952, as Viola in OUDS Twelfth Night; 1st New York appearance, Ethel Barrymore Theatre, June 1956, as comedienne in New Faces. Played in Share My Lettuce, Lyric, Hammersmith, 1957; The Stepmother, St Martin's, 1958. Old Vic Co., 1959–60 season: The Double Dealer; As You Like It; Richard II; The Merry Wives of Windsor; What Every Woman Knows; Rhinoceros, Strand, 1960; Strip the Willow, Cambridge, 1960; The Rehearsal, Globe, 1961; The Private Ear and The Public Eye (Evening Standard Drama Award, best actress of 1962), Globe, 1962; Mary, Mary, Queen's, 1963 (Variety Club of Gt Britain, best actress of the year); The Country Wife, Chichester, 1969; Design for Living, LA, 1971; Private Lives, Queen's, 1972, Globe, 1973, NY, 1975 (Variety Club of GB Stage Actress Award, 1972); Peter Pan, Coliseum, 1973; Snap, Vaudeville, 1974; Night and Day, Phoenix, 1979; Virginia, Haymarket, 1981 (Standard Best Actress Award, 1982); The Way of the World, Chichester and Haymarket, 1984 (Standard Best Actress Award, 1985); Interpreters, Queen's, 1985; Lettice and Lovage, Globe, 1987, NY, 1990 (Tony Award, best leading actress, 1990); The Importance of Being Earnest, Aldwych, 1993; Three Tall Women, Wyndham's, 1994; *at National Theatre:* The Recruiting Officer, 1963; Othello, The Master Builder, Hay Fever, 1964; Much Ado About Nothing, Miss Julie, 1965; A Bond Honoured, 1966; The Beaux' Stratagem, 1970 (also USA); Hedda Gabler, 1970 (Evening Standard Best Actress award); War Plays, 1985; Coming in to Land, 1986; *at Festival Theatre, Stratford, Ontario:* 1976: Antony and Cleopatra, The Way of the World, Measure for Measure, The Three Sisters; 1977: Midsummer Night's Dream, Richard III, The Guardsman, As You Like It, Hay Fever; 1978: As You Like It, Macbeth, Private Lives; 1980: Virginia; Much Ado About Nothing. *Films:* The VIP's, 1963; The Pumpkin Eater, 1964; Young Cassidy, 1965; Othello, 1966; The Honey Pot, 1967; Hot Millions, 1968 (Variety Club of GB Award); The Prime of Miss Jean Brodie, 1968 (Oscar; SFTA award); Oh! What a Lovely War, 1968; Love and Pain (and the Whole Damned Thing), 1973; Travels with my Aunt, 1973; Murder by Death, 1976; California Suite, 1977 (Oscar); Death on the Nile, 1978; Quartet, 1981; Clash of the Titans, 1981; Evil Under the Sun, 1982; The Missionary, 1982; A Private Function, 1984 (BAFTA award, Best Actress, 1985); The Loves of Lily, 1985; A Room with a View, 1986 (Variety Club of GB Award; BAFTA award, Best Actress, 1986); The Lonely Passion of Judith Hearn, 1989 (Evening Standard British Films Award, 1988, and Best Film Actress BAFTA Award, 1988); Hook, 1992; Sister Act, 1992; The Secret Garden, 1993; Sister Act II, 1994; *television:* Talking Heads: Bed Among the Lentils, 1989 (RTS Award); Memento Mori, 1992; Suddenly Last Summer, 1993. Hon. DLitt St Andrews, 1971. Shakespeare Prize, 1991. *Recreation:* reading. *Address:* c/o Write on Cue, Third Floor, 15 New Row, WC2N 4LA. *T:* 0171–379 4915.

SMITH, Malcolm Andrew F.; *see* Ferguson-Smith.

SMITH, Dame Margôt, DBE 1974; *b* 5 Sept. 1918; *d* of Leonard Graham Brown, MC, FRCS, and Margaret Jane Menzies; *m* 1st, 1938, Bertram Aykroyd (marr. diss. 1947; he *d* 1983), *y s* of Sir Frederic Aykroyd, Bt; one *s* one *d*; 2nd, 1947, Roy Smith, MC, TD (*d* 1983); one *s. Educ:* Westonbirt. Chm., Nat. Conservative Women's Adv. Cttee, 1969–72; Chm., Nat. Union of Conservative and Unionist Assocs, 1973–74. Mem., NSPCC Central Exec. Cttee, 1969–86. *Address:* Howden Lodge, Spennithorne, Leyburn, N Yorks DL8 5PR. *T:* Wensleydale (01969) 23621.

See also Sir James Aykroyd, Bt.

SMITH, Maurice George, OBE 1988; retired; Under-Secretary, Ministry of Overseas Development, 1968–76; *b* 4 Sept. 1915; *s* of Alfred Graham and Laura Maria Smith; *m* 1940, Eva Margaret Vanstone; two *s. Educ:* Sir Walter St John's School, Battersea. Examiner, Estate Duty Office, 1939. Flt Lieut RAF, 1942–46. Asst Principal, Min. of Civil Aviation, 1947; Principal, 1948; transferred to Colonial Office, 1950; seconded Commonwealth Office, 1954–55; Asst Secretary, Colonial Office, 1959; transferred to Dept of Technical Co-operation, 1961; Min. of Overseas Development, 1964; Under-Sec. and Principal Finance Officer, ODM, 1968. Chairman, Knights' Assoc. of Christian Youth Clubs, Lambeth, 1970– (Hon. Sec., 1950–70). *Recreations:* voluntary work in youth service, travel. *Address:* 52 Woodfield Avenue, SW16 1LG. *T:* 0181–769 5356.

SMITH, Melvin Kenneth; actor, writer, director; *b* 3 Dec. 1952; *s* of Kenneth and Vera Smith; *m* 1988, Pamela Gay-Rees. *Educ:* Latymer Upper Sch., Hammersmith; New Coll., Oxford. Asst Dir, Royal Court Th., 1973; freelance Dir, Bristol Old Vic, 1973, Liverpool Everyman, 1974, Bush Th., 1975; Associate Director: Crucible Th., Sheffield, 1975–78; Young Vic, 1978–79; Actor/writer, TV series, Not The Nine O'Clock News, Alas Smith and Jones, 1979–81; Smith & Jones, 1982–87 and 1992; appeared in Small Doses (series of short plays), 1989. Films: The Tall Guy, 1989 (Dir); Wilt, 1989. Director: Talkback Prodns, 1982–; Playback Training Films, 1987–; Smith Jones Brown and Cassie Commercials, Ltd, 1988–. *Publications:* Not the book, 1981; Not the Nine O'Clock News Diary, 1982; Alas Smith and Jones Coffee Table Book, 1987; Janet Lives with Mel and Griff, 1988. *Club:* Groucho.

SMITH, Most Rev. Michael; *see* Meath, Bishop of, (RC).

SMITH, Prof. Michael, FRS 1986; FRSC 1981; Peter Wall Distinguished Professor of Biotechnology, since 1994, and Director, Biotechnology Laboratory, since 1987, University of British Columbia; *b* 26 April 1932; *s* of Rowland Smith and Mary Agnes Smith; *m* 1960, Helen Wood Smith; two *s* one *d. Educ:* Arnold Sch., Blackpool, England; Manchester Univ. (BSc Chemistry, PhD). Post-doctoral fellowship, Brit. Columbia Res. Council, 1956–60; Res. Associate, Inst. for Enzyme Res., Univ. of Wisconsin, 1960–61; Hd, Chemistry Sect., Vancouver Lab., Fisheries Res. Bd of Canada, 1961–66; University of British Columbia: Associate Prof., 1966–70, Prof., 1970–93, Dept of Biochem.; Univ. Prof., 1993–. Career Investigator, MRC of Canada, 1966–. Nobel Prize for Chemistry (jtly), 1993. *Recreations:* ski-ing, hiking, sailing. *Address:* University of British Columbia, Biotechnology Laboratory, Room 237 Wesbrook Building, 6174 University Boulevard, Vancouver, BC V6T 1Z3, Canada. *Clubs:* Faculty (Univ. of British Columbia); Royal Vancouver Yacht.

SMITH, Michael Edward C.; *see* Carleton-Smith.

SMITH, Michael Gerard A.; *see* Austin-Smith.

SMITH, Michael John W.; *see* Winkworth-Smith.

SMITH, Michael K.; *see* Kinchin Smith.

SMITH, Neil; *see* Smith, G. N.

SMITH, Prof. Neilson Voyne; Professor of Linguistics, University College London, since 1982; *b* 21 June 1939; *s* of Voyne Smith and Lilian Freda Smith (*née* Rose); *m* 1966, Saraswati Keskar; two *s. Educ:* Trinity College, Cambridge (BA 1961, MA 1964); UCL (PhD 1964). Lectr in W African Languages, SOAS, 1964–70; Harkness Fellow, MIT and UCLA, 1966–68; Lectr in Linguistics and W African Languages, SOAS, 1970–72; University College London: Reader in Linguistics, 1972–81; Hd, Dept of Phonetics and Linguistics, 1983–90; Vice-Dean, 1992. Pres., Assoc. of Heads and Profs of Linguistics, 1993–94. Chm., Linguistics Assoc., 1980–86. *Publications:* An Outline Grammar of Nupe, 1967; The Acquisition of Phonology, 1973; (with Deirdre Wilson) Modern Linguistics, 1979; (ed) Mutual Knowledge, 1982; Speculative Linguistics, 1983; The Twitter Machine, 1989; (jtly) The Mind of a Savant, 1995; articles in learned jls. *Recreations:* music, walking, travel, playing with children. *Address:* 32 Long Buftlers, Harpenden, Herts AL5 1JE; Department of Phonetics and Linguistics, University College London, Gower Street, WC1E 6BT. *T:* 0171–380 7173.

SMITH, Nigel Christopher S.; *see* Starmer-Smith.

SMITH, Dr (Norman) Brian, CBE 1980; Chairman, BAA plc, since 1991; *b* 10 Sept. 1928; *s* of late Vincent and Louise Smith; *m* 1955, Phyllis Crossley; one *s* one *d* (and one *s* decd). *Educ:* Sir John Deane's Grammar Sch., Northwich; Manchester Univ. (PhD Phys. Chemistry, 1954). FTI 1981. Joined ICI Ltd, Terylene Council, 1954; Fibres Division: Textile Develt Dir, 1969; Dep. Chm., 1972; Chm., 1975–78; ICI Main Bd, 1978–85; Director: Fiber Industries Inc., 1972–83; Canadian Industries Ltd, 1981–85; Territorial Dir for the Americas, and Chm., ICI Americas Inc., 1981–85 (Dir, 1980–85); Non-Exec. Dir, Carrington Viyella Ltd, 1979–81. Chairman: Metal Box plc, subseq. MB Group, 1986–89 (Dep. Chm., 1985–86); Lister & Co., 1991–94 (Dir, 1985–94; Dep. Chm., 1990–91); Hydron Ltd, 1994–; Director: Davy Corp., 1986–91; Cable & Wireless, 1988–95; Yorkshire Chemicals, 1990–91; Mercury Communications, 1990–93; Berisford, 1990–. Pres., British Textile Confedn, 1977–79; Chairman: Man-Made Fibres Producers Cttee, 1976–78; EDC for Wool Textile Industry, 1979–81; Priorities Bd for R&D in Agric. and Food, 1987–92; Heatherwood and Wexham Park Hosps Trust, 1991–; Mem., BOTB, 1980–81, 1983–87 (Chm., N American Adv. Group, 1983–87). Chm., Standing Conf. on Schools' Sci. and Technology, 1992–. Dir, Oxford Dio. Bd of Finance, 1990–. CIMgt (CBIM 1985); FCIM. Freeman, City of London, 1986; Liveryman, Glovers' Co., 1986. Hon. DBA Buckingham, 1990. *Recreations:* sailing, tennis, gardening. *Club:* Brooks's.

SMITH, Norman Jack, MA, MPhil; FInstPet; Managing Director, Smith Rea Energy Associates Ltd, since 1981; *b* 14 April 1936; *s* of late Maurice Leslie and Ellen Dorothy Smith; *m* 1967, Valerie Ann, *o d* of late A. E. Frost; one *s* one *d*. *Educ:* Grammar Sch., Henley-on-Thames; Oriel Coll., Oxford (MA); City Univ. (MPhil). FInstPet 1978. Dexion Ltd, 1957; Vickers Ltd, 1960; Baring Brothers & Co. Ltd, 1969; seconded as Industrial Director, 1977, Dir-Gen., 1978–80, Offshore Supplies Office, Dept of Energy; Chairman: British Underwater Engineering Ltd, 1980–83; Mentor Engineering Consultants, 1987–92; Director: Smith Rea Energy Analysts, 1985–; Smith Rea Energy Aberdeen, 1990–; Gas Transmission, 1989–95. Mem., Offshore Energy Technology Bd, 1978–80. Mem. Norwegian Petroleum Soc. Fellow, Soc. of Business Economists; FInstD. *Publications:* sundry articles in economic and oil industry jls. *Recreations:* walking, swimming, photography, history. *Address:* c/o Smith Rea Energy Associates Ltd, Hunstead House, Nickle, Chartham, Canterbury, Kent CT4 7PL. *T:* Canterbury (01227) 738822. *Club:* United Oxford & Cambridge University.

SMITH, Prof. (Norman John) David; Head of Department of Dental Radiology, King's College School of Medicine and Dentistry (formerly King's College Hospital Dental School), since 1972, and Professor of Dental Radiology, University of London, since 1978; *b* 2 Feb. 1931; *s* of late Norman S. Smith; *m* 1st, 1954, Regina Eileen Lugg (marr. diss.); one *s*; 2nd, 1983, Mary Christine Pocock; one *d*. *Educ:* King's Coll. Sch., Wimbledon; King's Coll., London; KCH Dental Sch. (BDS 1963; MPhil 1969); Royal Free Hosp. Sch. of Medicine (MSc 1966). Apprenticed to Pacific Steam Navigation Co., 1948–51; Officer Service, Royal Mail Lines, 1952–58 (Master Mariner, 1957); part-time posts at KCH Dental Sch., Guy's Hosp. Dental Sch. and in gen. dental practice, 1966–69; Sen. Lectr in Dental Surg., KCH Dental Sch., 1969–72; Reader in Dental Radiol., Univ. of London, 1973. Civil Consultant to RAF, 1990–. Member: Southwark Bor. Council, 1974–78; GLC for Norwood, 1977–86 (Leader of Opposition, ILEA, 1979–86); Thames Water Authority, 1977–83; SE Thames RHA, 1978–86; Council, Open Univ., 1978–81, 1982–91; Court, Univ. of London, 1982–87; Governor, Bethlem Royal and Maudsley Hosps, 1980–82; Mem., Bethlem Royal and Maudsley SHA, 1982–86. Vis. Prof. and lectr worldwide. Liveryman, Hon. Co. of Master Mariners. DUniv Open, 1993. Sir Charlton Briscoe Res. Prize, KCH Med. Sch., 1969. *Publications:* Simple Navigation by the Sun, 1974; Dental Radiography, 1980; articles in dental jls. *Recreations:* sailing, nature photography. *Address:* c/o King's College School of Medicine and Dentistry, Caldecot Road, SE5 9RW. *T:* 0171–737 4000, ext. 2503. *Club:* National Liberal.

SMITH, Paul Brierley, CBE 1994; RDI 1991; fashion designer; Chairman, Paul Smith Ltd; *b* 5 July 1946; *s* of Harold and Marjorie Smith. *Educ:* Beeston Fields Grammar Sch. Manager, Nottingham boutique, 1966; opened own shop, 1970 (part-time), 1974 (full time); consultant to Wool Secretariat, 1976; has shops in London, Nottingham, NY, Paris, Hong Kong, Singapore, Japan; exporter to numerous other countries; retains Nottingham design room. Hon. MDes, Nottingham Trent, 1991. *Address:* Paul Smith Ltd, 40–44 Floral Street, WC2E 9DG. *T:* 0171–836 7828. *Club:* Royal Automobile.

SMITH, Prof. Paul Julian, PhD; Professor of Spanish and Head of Department of Spanish and Portuguese, Cambridge University, since 1991; Fellow, Trinity Hall, Cambridge, since 1991; *b* 11 Nov. 1956; *s* of Albert Charles Smith and Margaret (*née* Tovey). *Educ:* Cambridge Univ. (BA 1980; MA 1982; PhD 1984). Res. Fellow, Trinity Hall, Cambridge, 1983–84; Lectr, QMC, London Univ., 1984–88; Reader, QMW, 1989–91. Hon. Vice-Consul, Spain, 1991. *Publications:* Quevedo on Parnassus, 1987; Writing in the Margin: Spanish literature of the Golden Age, 1988; The Body Hispanic: gender and sexuality in Spanish and Spanish American literature, 1989; A Critical Guide to El Buscon, 1991; Representing the Other: race, text and gender in Spanish and Spanish American narrative, 1992; Laws of Desire: questions of homosexuality in Spanish writing and film, 1992; Desire Unlimited: the cinema of Pedro Almodóvar, 1994. *Address:* Faculty of Modern and Medieval Languages, University of Cambridge, Sidgwick Avenue, Cambridge CB3 9DA. *T:* Cambridge (01223) 335005.

SMITH, Peter, FSA; Secretary, Royal Commission on Ancient Monuments in Wales, 1973–91, retired; *b* 15 June 1926; *s* of late L. W. Smith, HMI, and Mrs H. Smith (*née* Halsted); *m* 1954, Joyce Evelyn, *d* of late J. W. Abbott and of Alice Abbott (*née* Lloyd); two *s* one *d*. *Educ:* Peter Symonds' Sch., Winchester; Oriel Coll. and Lincoln Coll. (Open Scholar), Oxford (BA, Hons Mod. Hist. 1947); Hammersmith Sch. of Building (Inter ARIBA 1950). Royal Commission on Ancient Monuments in Wales: Jun. Investigator, 1949; Sen. Investigator, 1954; Investigator in Charge of Nat. Monuments Record, 1963. President: Cambrian Archaeological Assoc., 1979; Vernacular Architecture Gp, 1983–86. Hon. DLitt Wales, 1991. G. T. Clark Prize, 1969; Alice Davis Hitchcock Medallion, Soc. of Architectural Historians of GB, 1978. *Publications:* Houses of the Welsh Countryside, 1975, contribs to Agrarian History of England; periodical literature on historic domestic architecture. *Recreations:* reading, drawing, learning Welsh. *Address:* Tŷ-coch, Lluest, Llanbadarn Fawr, Aberystwyth, Dyfed SY23 3AU. *T:* Aberystwyth (01970) 623556.

SMITH, Peter Alan, FCA; Chairman, Coopers & Lybrand, since 1994; *b* 5 Aug. 1946; *s* of Dudley Vaughan Smith and Beatrice Ellen (*née* Sketcher); *m* 1971, Cherry Blandford; two *s*. *Educ:* Mill Hill Sch.; Univ. of Southampton (BSc); Wharton Sch., Univ. of Pennsylvania (AMP). FCA 1970. Coopers & Lybrand, 1967–. Hon. Treas., UK Housing Trust, 1979–83. Mem., Finance Cttee, Nat. Trust, 1991–. Vice Pres., Beaconsfield Cons. Assoc., 1986–95. Liveryman, Chartered Accountants' Co., 1993–. FRSA 1993. *Publication:* Housing Association Accounts and Their Audit, 1980. *Recreations:* golf, gardens. *Address:* The Old Vicarage, Hughenden, High Wycombe, Bucks HP14 4LA. *T:* High Wycombe (01494) 530364. *Clubs:* Carlton; Beaconsfield Golf.

SMITH, Peter Alexander Charles, OBE 1981; Chairman: Securicor Group plc, 1974–95; Security Services plc, 1974–95; *b* 18 Aug. 1920; *s* of Alexander Alfred Smith and Gwendoline Mary (*née* Beer); *m* 1945, Marjorie May Humphrey (*d* 1988); one *s*. *Educ:* St Paul's Sch., London. Admitted solicitor, 1948. Served RA, 1941–46: Captain; Adjt, 17th Medium Regt. Partner, Hextall, Erskine & Co., 1953–79. Chairman: British Security Industry Assoc. Ltd, 1977–81; Metal Closures Gp plc, 1983–87 (Dir, 1972, Dep. Chm., 1981). Mem. Council, Royal Warrant Holders Assoc., 1976–, Vice-Pres., 1981–82, Pres., 1982–83. Vice-Pres., Forest Philharmonic Symphony Orch., 1991–. CIMgt; FRSA. *Recreations:* golf, music, photography. *Address:* c/o Sutton Park House, 15 Carshalton Road, Sutton, Surrey SM1 4LE. *Club:* British Racing Drivers (Hon. Life Mem.).

SMITH, Peter Anthony; General Secretary, Association of Teachers and Lecturers (formerly Assistant Masters and Mistresses Association), since 1988; *b* 25 June 1940; *s* of Charles George and Margaret Patricia Smith; *m* 1961, Anne Elizabeth; one *s* one *d*. *Educ.* Haberdashers' Aske's Boys' Sch., Hatcham; Brasenose Coll., Oxford (MA). Graduate trainee, Midland Bank, 1961–63; teacher: LCC, 1963–66; Whitgift Foundn, 1966–74; Asst Sec., 1974–82, Dep. Gen. Sec., 1982–88, Asst Masters and Mistresses Assoc. Mem., Equal Opportunities Commn, 1994–. FRSA 1991. *Recreations:* cooking, listening to music, living in France. *Address:* 19 Woodstock Road, Croydon CR0 1JS. *T:* 0181–686 6726. *Clubs:* Wig and Pen, National Liberal.

SMITH, Peter Bruce; Head Master, Bradfield College, since 1985; *b* 18 March 1944; *s* of Alexander D. Smith and Grace Smith; *m* 1968, Diana Margaret Morgan; two *d*. *Educ:* Magdalen College School, Oxford; Lincoln College, Oxford (Old Members Scholar; MA). Asst Master, Rugby Sch., 1967–85 (Head of Hist. Dept, 1973–77, Housemaster of School Field, 1977–85). Mem. Governing Body, Downe House Sch., 1985–89. Captain Oxfordshire County Cricket Club, 1971–77 (Minor Counties Champions, 1974). *Recreations:* antiquarian, sporting, literary. *Address:* Headmaster's House, Bradfield College, Bradfield, Reading RG7 6AR. *Club:* Vincent's (Oxford).

SMITH, Peter Claudius G.; *see* Gautier-Smith.

SMITH, Rt Rev. Peter David; *see* East Anglia, Bishop of (RC).

SMITH, Prof. Peter George; Professor of Tropical Epidemiology, since 1989, and Head of Department of Epidemiology and Population Sciences, since 1990, London School of Hygiene and Tropical Medicine; *b* 3 May 1942; *s* of George Henry Smith and Lily Smith (*née* Phillips); *m* 1985, Jill Margaret Routledge; one *s*, and one step *s* one step *d*. *Educ:* City Univ. (BSc Applied Maths 1st Class 1963; DSc Med. Stats 1983). Statistical Res. Unit, MRC, 1965–67; Clinical and Population Cytogenetics Unit, MRC, 1967–69; Makerere Univ. Med. Sch., Uganda, 1970–71; WHO Internat. Agency for Res. on Cancer, Uganda, 1971–72; Cancer Epidemiology and Clinical Trials Unit, 1972–79; Dept of Epidemiology, Harvard Sch. of Public Health, 1975; LSH&TM, 1979–. WHO Tropical Diseases Res. Prog., Geneva, 1987–88; Mem., WHO and MRC Cttees. Hon. MFPHM, 1991. *Publications:* (ed with R. H. Morrow) Methods for field trials of interventions against tropical diseases, 1991; numerous contribs to med. res. literature. *Recreations:* gardening, walking, cycling. *Address:* Department of Epidemiology and Population Sciences, London School of Hygiene and Tropical Medicine, Keppel Street, WC1E 7HT. *T:* 0171–927 2246.

SMITH, Dr Peter Graham, CB 1988; Director General Guided Weapons and Electronics, Ministry of Defence (Procurement Executive), 1982–88; *b* 12 June 1929; *s* of James A. and Florence L. Smith; *m* 1952, Doreen Millicent (*née* Wyatt); two *d*. *Educ:* Wellington Grammar Sch., Shropshire; Birmingham Univ. (BSc, PhD). Radar Res. Estab., 1953–75: seconded to British Defence Staff, Washington, 1966–68; Supt, Airborne Defensive Radar Div., 1970–75; Dir Defence Science 8, MoD, 1975–78; Dir Surveillance and Instrument Projs, MoD (PE), 1978–82. *Recreations:* gardening, reading, modelling. *Address:* c/o Lloyd's Bank, High Street, Harpenden AL5 2TA.

SMITH, Peter J.; *see* Jefferson Smith.

SMITH, Peter John, IPFA; public sector consultant; Chairman, Gateshead Healthcare NHS Trust, since 1992; *b* 31 Dec. 1936; *s* of Frank and Sarah Ann Smith; *m* 1959, Marie Louise Smith; one *s* one *d*. *Educ:* Rastrick Grammar Sch., Brighouse, W Yorkshire. Trainee Accountant, Huddersfield CBC, 1953–59; Accountancy Asst, Bradford CBC, 1959–61; Asst Chief Accountant, Chester CBC, 1961–63; Computer Manager, Keighley BC, 1963–66; Asst City Treasurer, Gloucester CBC, 1966–69; Dep. Borough Treasurer, Gateshead CBC, 1969–73; Asst County Treasurer, Tyne and Wear CC, 1973–74, Dep. County Treasurer, 1974–80, County Treasurer, 1980–86. Gen. Manager, Tyne and Wear Residuary Body, 1985–88. Treasurer: NE Regional Airport Jt Cttee, 1980–86; Northumbria Police Authority, 1980–86; Northumbria Probation and After Care Cttee, 1980–86; Mem., Tyne and Wear Passenger Transport Exec. Bd, 1981–86. Director: N American Property Unit Trust, 1982–93; Northern Investors Co., 1983–86; Westgate Trust, 1990–92. *Recreations:* fell walking, jogging. *Address:* 6 Oak Terrace, Holmside, Edmondsley, Co. Durham DH7 6ET. *T:* Durham (0191) 3719773.

SMITH, Peter John, CBE 1995; HM Diplomatic Service; Ambassador to the Republic of Madagascar and concurrently Ambassador, non-resident, to the Islamic Republic of the Comoros, since 1993; *b* 15 May 1942; *s* of John S. Smith and Irene (*née* Waple); *m* 1964, Suzanne Pauline Duffin; one *s* one *d*. *Educ:* St Dunstan's Coll., London. Joined FO, 1962; Vietnamese lang. student, then 3rd Sec., Saigon, 1964–67; Commercial Attaché, Paris, 1968–69; Commercial Publicity Officer, British Information Services, NY, 1970–73; FCO, 1973–76; 1st Sec., Commercial, Mexico City, 1976–80; Dep. High Comr, Port Louis, Mauritius, 1981–84; FCO, 1984–86; Deputy Consul General: Montreal, 1987–88; Toronto (also Dir, Trade and Investment), 1988–92; RCDS 1992. *Recreations:* golf, cricket, chess, bridge, Woody Allen films. *Address:* c/o Foreign and Commonwealth Office, King Charles Street, SW1A 2AH. *Clubs:* MCC; Golf du Rova (Madagascar).

SMITH, Peter Lincoln Chivers, FRCS; Consultant Cardiothoracic Surgeon, Hammersmith Hospital and Ealing Hospital, since 1987; *b* 20 Sept. 1948; *s* of Alfred Stanley Chivers Smith and Cynthia Enid (*née* Anstee); *m* 1976, Susan Margaret Evans; one *s* two *d*. *Educ:* St Bartholomew's Hosp., Univ. of London (MB, BS 1975). MRCP 1978; FRCS 1980. General surgical trng, St Bartholomew's Hosp., 1976–79; cardiothoracic surgical trng, St Bartholomew's, Royal Brompton, Middlesex, Harefield and Hammersmith Hosps, 1979–86. Hunterian Prof., RCS, 1986–87. *Publications:* (jtly) The Brain and Cardiac Surgery, 1993; numerous scientific pubns on cardiac and thoracic surgical topics. *Recreations:* music, travelling. *Address:* 63 Connaught Gardens, N10 3LG. *T:* 0181–444 9491. *Club:* Royal Society of Medicine.

SMITH, Peter Vivian Henworth, CB 1989; Government Legal Adviser, and Legal Adviser, Broadcasting Standards Council, since 1989; *b* 5 Dec. 1928; *s* of Vivian and Dorothea Smith; *m* 1955, Mary Marjorie, *d* of Frank John Willsher and Sybil Marjorie Willsher; five *d*. *Educ:* Clacton County High Sch.; Brasenose Coll., Oxford (MA, BCL). Called to the Bar, Lincoln's Inn, 1953. HM Overseas Civil Service: Resident Magistrate, Nyasaland, 1955–63; Registrar, High Court, Nyasaland, 1963–64; Sen. Resident Magistrate, Malaŵi, 1964–69; Puisne Judge, Malaŵi, 1969–70; HM Customs and Excise: Legal Asst, 1970–72; Sen. Legal Asst, 1972–76; Asst Solicitor, 1976–82; Prin. Asst Solicitor, 1982–85; Solicitor, 1986–89. Legal Advr, Bldg Socs Commn, 1990–92. *Recreations:*

classical music, walking, bridge, Macintosh computers. *Address:* Likabula, 14 St Albans Road, Clacton-on-Sea CO15 6BA. *T:* Clacton-on-Sea (01255) 422053.

SMITH, Peter William; His Honour Judge Peter Smith; a Circuit Judge, since 1994; *b* 31 Dec. 1945; *s* of late William and Bessie Smith; *m* 1970, Vanessa Mary (*née* Wildash); one *s*. *Educ:* Arnold Sch., Blackpool; Downing Coll., Cambridge (MA). Called to the Bar, Middle Temple, 1969. Practised (as William Smith) on Northern Circuit; a Dep. Judge Advocate, 1983–84; a Recorder, 1991–94. Mem., Mental Health Review Tribunal, 1993–. *Recreations:* weekends in the Lake District, motorcycling. *Address:* c/o Courts of Justice, Crown Square, Manchester M3 3FL.

SMITH, Peter Winston; QC 1992; an Assistant Recorder, since 1994; *b* 1 May 1952; *s* of George Arthur Smith and Iris Muriel Smith; *m* 1980, Diane Dalgleish; one *s* two *d*. *Educ:* Selwyn Coll., Cambridge (BA 1974; MA 1976); Coll. of Law. Called to the Bar, Lincoln's Inn, 1975. Lectr, Manchester Univ., 1977–83; practice on Northern Circuit, 1979–. *Recreations:* Titanic Historical Society, reading military history, football. *Address:* 40 King Street, Manchester M2 6BA. *T:* 0161–832 9082.

SMITH, Philip; Deputy Director Warship Design (Electrical), Ministry of Defence (Navy), 1969–73, retired; *b* 19 May 1913; *m* 1940, Joan Mary Harker; one *s* one *d*. *Educ:* Bishop Wordsworth's Sch., Salisbury; Bristol Univ. BSc (First Cl. Hons). Graduate Trainee Apprentice, BTH Co., 1934–37; Outside Construction Engrg, BTH Co., 1937–38; Central Electricity Bd, 1938–39; Admty (Electrical Engrg Dept) (now MoD Navy), 1939–73; past service at Chatham Dockyard and Dockyard Dept, HQ; Electrical Engrg Design Divs; Head of Electrical Dept, Admty Engrg Laboratory, West Drayton. CEng, FIEE, FIMechE; RCNC. *Recreations:* horticulture, golf, oil painting. *Address:* Myrfield, Summer Lane, Combe Down, Bath BA2 7EU. *T:* Combe Down (01225) 833408. *Club:* Bath Golf.

SMITH, Philip George, CBE 1973; Director, Metal Market & Exchange Co. Ltd, 1954–92 (Chairman, 1967–84); Adviser, Triland Metals Ltd, since 1984; *b* 10 Sept. 1911. *Educ:* St Lawrence Coll., Ramsgate; Royal School of Mines, London. ARSM, BSc (Eng). Director: Bassett Smith & Co. Ltd, 1946–75; Bardyke Chemicals Ltd, 1968–90; (non-exec.), Comfin (Commodity & Finance) Co. Ltd, 1978–82. Mem. Cttee, London Metal Exchange, 1949–64 (Chm. 1954–64). Adviser to Dept of Trade and Industry, 1958–86; part-time Mem., Sugar Bd, 1967–76. *Address:* 67B Camlet Way, Hadley Wood, Barnet EN4 0NL.

SMITH, Rt Rev. Raymond George; Bishop of Liverpool, NSW, and an Assistant Bishop of Sydney, since 1993; *b* 7 March 1936; *s* of Gordon William Smith and Alice Mary (*née* Brett); *m* 1960, Shirley Jeanette Gilmore; three *s*. *Educ:* Australian Coll. of Theology (ThSchol); Univ. of New England (BA, Dip Cont. Educn, MEd). Parish priest, dio. of Armidale, 1959–76; Dir of Christian Educn and Archdeacon, Armidale, 1977–86; Dir of Extension Ministries, Trinity Episcopal Sch. for Ministry, Ambridge, Pa, USA, 1986–90; Rector of Wanniassa, 1990–93, and Archdeacon of S Canberra, 1991–93, dio. of Canberra and Goulburn. *Publication:* People Caring for People, 1990. *Recreations:* swimming, cycling, photography, stamp collecting, Australian history. *Address:* Level 1, St Andrews House, Sydney Square. Sydney, NSW 2000, Australia.

SMITH, (Raymond) Gordon (Antony) E.; *see* Etherington-Smith.

SMITH, Sir Raymond (Horace), KBE 1967 (CBE 1960); Chairman of Hawker Siddeley and other British companies in Venezuela; Consultant to Rolls-Royce Ltd; *b* 1917; *s* of Horace P. Smith and Mabelle (*née* Osborne-Couzens); *m* 1943, Dorothy, *d* of Robert Cheney Hart. *Educ:* Salesian College, London; Barcelona University. Served War of 1939–45, with British Security Co-ordination, NY, and with Intelligence Corps, in France, India, Burma, Malaya, Indonesia. Civil Attaché British Embassy, Caracas, 1941; Negotiator, sale of British owned railway cos to Venezuelan Govt and other S American govts, 1946–50; Rep., London Reinsurers in Venezuela, 1954–60; Consultant: Cammell Laird; Mirrlees; British Aerospace, 1952–82; Provincial Insurance Co. Ltd; Director: Daily Journal; Anglo-Venezuelan Cultural Inst., 1946–80; British Venezuelan Chamber of Commerce, 1956–86 (Hon. Pres., 1987); Pres. British Commonwealth Assoc. of Venezuela, 1955–57. Companion of Royal Aeronautical Society. Knight Grand Cross, St Lazarus of Jerusalem; Venezuelan Air Force Cross. *Recreations:* tennis, water ski-ing, winter sports (Cresta Run and ski-ing). *Address:* Quinta San Antonio, Calle El Samancito, Avenida El Saman, Caracas Country Club, Caracas 1062, Venezuela; Carlton Lodge, 37 Lowndes Street, SW1. *Clubs:* White's, Naval and Military; Caracas Country, Jockey (Caracas); St Moritz Tobogganing (Switzerland).

SMITH, Richard; *see* Smith, W. R.

SMITH, Richard Henry S.; *see* Sandford Smith.

SMITH, Richard James Crosbie W.; *see* Wilmot-Smith.

SMITH, Richard John; Australian Ambassador to the Philippines, since 1994; *b* 14 Dec. 1934; *s* of C. A. Smith and T. A. O'Halloran; *m* 1958, Janet Campbell; two *s* two *d*. *Educ:* Sydney High Sch.; Sydney Univ. (BA, LLB Hons I 1958). Teacher, London, 1958–59; Solicitor, NSW, 1959–61; Foreign Affairs Trainee, 1961; First Sec., Australian Embassy, Washington, 1967–70; Dep. Perm. Rep., Australian Mission to UN, Geneva, 1972–74; Asst Sec., Internat. Legal Branch, 1974–75; Ambassador to Israel, 1975–77; First Assistant Secretary: Legal & Treaties Div., 1977–81; Management & Foreign Service Div., 1981–83; Actg Dep. Sec., Dept of Foreign Affairs, 1983–85; Ambassador to Thailand, 1985–88; Dep. Sec., Dept of Foreign Affairs and Trade, Canberra, 1988–90; High Comr for Australia in the UK, 1991–94. *Recreations:* walking, reading, travel. *Address:* Australian Embassy, PO Box 1274, Makati, Manila, The Philippines. *Fax:* (2) 8173603.

SMITH, Prof. Richard Lyttleton, PhD; Professor of Statistical Studies, Cambridge University, since 1994; *b* 31 March 1953; *s* of Stanley Lyttleton Smith and Hilary Margaret (*née* James). *Educ:* Jesus Coll., Univ. of Oxford (BA Maths 1975; MA 1985); Cornell Univ., USA (PhD Ops Res. 1979). Lectr in Stats, Imperial Coll., London, 1979–85; Professor of Statistics: Univ. of Surrey, 1985–90; Univ. of N Carolina, 1991–94. Guy Medal in Silver, Royal Statistical Soc., 1991. *Publications:* (jtly) Statistical Analysis of Reliability Data, 1991; contrib. to Jl Roy. Statistical Soc., Proc. Royal Soc., Biometrika, Annals of Stats, etc. *Recreations:* cross-country and road running, chess, bridge, music. *Address:* 8 George Nuttall Close, Cambridge CB4 1YE. *T:* Cambridge (01223) 426480.

SMITH, Richard Maybury H.; *see* Hastie-Smith.

SMITH, Dr Richard Michael, FRHistS; FBA 1991; Director, Cambridge Group for the History of Population and Social Structure, since 1994; Fellow, Downing College, Cambridge, since 1994; *b* 3 Jan. 1946; *s* of Louis Gordon Smith and Elsie Fanny (*née* Ward); *m* 1971, Margaret Anne McFadden. *Educ:* Earls Colne Grammar Sch.; University Coll. London (BA Hons); St Catharine's Coll., Cambridge (MA 1977; PhD 1974). Lectr in Population Studies, Plymouth Poly., 1973–74; Cambridge University: Asst Lectr in Histl Geography, 1974–76; Sen. Res. Officer, 1976–81, Asst Dir, 1981–83, Cambridge Gp for the Hist. of Population and Social Structure; Fellow, 1977–83, Tutor, 1979–83, Fitzwilliam Coll.; Oxford University: Univ. Lectr in Histl Demography, 1983–89; Fellow, All Souls Coll., 1983–94; Reader in Hist. of Medicine and Dir, Wellcome Unit for Hist. of Medicine, 1990–94. Mem. Council, British Soc. for Population Studies, 1987–91. Ed., Social Hist. of Medicine, 1986–92. *Publications:* (ed jtly) Bastardy and its Comparative History, 1980; (ed) Land, Kinship and Lifecycle, 1984; (ed jtly) The World We Have Gained: histories of population and social structure, 1986; (ed jtly) Life, Death and the Elderly: historical perspectives, 1991; contribs to Annales ESC, Jl of Family Hist., Trans RHistS, Ageing and Society, Law and Hist. Rev., Population and Develt Rev. *Recreations:* listening to music, walking in Norfolk. *Address:* Cambridge Group for the History of Population and Social Structure, 27 Trumpington Street, Cambridge CB2 1QA. *T:* Cambridge (01223) 333181.

SMITH, Sir Richard P.; *see* Prince-Smith, Sir (William) Richard.

SMITH, Richard Philip Morley R.; *see* Reay-Smith.

SMITH, Prof. R(ichard) Selby, OBE 1981; MA (Oxon), MA (Harvard); Professor of Education and Head of Department of Education, University of Tasmania, 1973–79, now Professor Emeritus; *b* 1914; *s* of Selby Smith, Hall Place, Barming, Maidstone, Kent, and Annie Rachel Smith (*née* Rawlins); *m* 1940, Rachel Hebe Philippa Pease, Rounton, Northallerton, Yorks; two *s*. *Educ:* Rugby Sch.; Magdalen Coll., Oxford; Harvard Univ. Asst Master, Milton Acad., Milton, Mass, USA, 1938–39; House Tutor and Sixth Form Master, Sedbergh Sch., 1939–40; War of 1939–45: Royal Navy, 1940–46; final rank of Lt-Comdr, RNVR. Administrative Asst, Kent Education Cttee, 1946–48; Asst Education Officer, Kent, 1948–50; Dep. Chief Education Officer, Warwickshire, 1950–53; Principal, Scotch Coll., Melbourne, 1953–64; Foundation Prof. of Educn, Monash Univ., 1964, Dean of Faculty of Educn, 1965–71; Principal, Tasmanian Coll. of Advanced Education, 1971–73. Chairman: Victorian Univs and Schools Examinations Bd, 1967–71; State Planning and Finance Cttee, Australian Schools Commn, 1974–77, 1980–83; Vice-Pres., Australian Council for Educnl Research, 1976–79. Hon. LLD Monash, 1989. *Publications:* Towards an Australian Philosophy of Education, 1965; (ed jtly) Fundamental Issues in Australian Education, 1971; The Education Policy Process in Tasmania, 1980; Australian Independent Schools: yesterday, today and tomorrow, 1983. *Recreations:* fishing, gardening, sailing, riding and ornithology. *Address:* Apt 234, Derwent Waters Residential Club, Cadbury Road, Claremont, Tas 7011, Australia.

SMITH, Richard Sydney William; Editor, British Medical Journal, and Chief Executive, BMJ Publishing Group, since 1991; Professor of Medical Journalism, University of Nottingham, since 1993; *b* 11 March 1952; *s* of Sydney Smith and Hazel Smith (*née* Kirk); *m* 1977, Linda Jean Arnott; two *s* one *d*. *Educ:* Roan Grammar Sch., London; Edinburgh Univ. (BSc 1973; MB ChB 1976); Stanford Univ. (MSc in Management 1990). MFPHM 1992; FRCPE 1992; MRCP 1993. Hosp. jobs in Scotland and New Zealand, 1976–79; Asst Editor, 1979, Sen. Asst Editor, 1984, BMJ. BBC Breakfast Time doctor, 1983–87. Fellow, Acad. of Gen. Educn, Karnataka, India, 1993. *Publications:* Alcohol Problems, 1982; Prison Health Care, 1984; The Good Health Kit, 1987; Unemployment and Health, 1987; articles in learned jls. *Recreations:* jazz, cycling, running, wine, talking first and thinking second. *Address:* British Medical Journal, BMA House, Tavistock Square, WC1H 9JR.

SMITH, Robert Carr, CBE 1989; PhD; Vice-Chancellor, Kingston University, since 1992 (Director, Kingston Polytechnic, 1982–92); *b* 19 Nov. 1935; *s* of Edward Albert Smith and Olive Winifred Smith; *m* 1960, Rosalie Mary (*née* Spencer); one *s* one *d*. *Educ:* Queen Elizabeth's School, Barnet; Southampton Univ. (BSc); London Univ. (PhD). Research Asst, Guy's Hosp. Med. Sch., 1957–61; Lectr, Senior Lectr, Reader, Prof. of Electronics, Southampton Univ., 1961–82. Seconded to DoE, 1973–74. Chairman: Engineering Profs' Conf., 1980–82; Polytechnics and Colls Employers' Forum, 1988–90; Vice-Chm., Cttee of Dirs of Polytechnics, 1988–89; Member: Design Council, 1983–88; Council for Industry and Higher Educn, 1985–; Council, Inst. for Manpower Studies, 1987–; PCFC, 1988–93; TEC for Kingston, Merton and Wandsworth, 1989–; Higher Educn Statistics Agency, 1993–; Univs and Colls Employers' Assoc., 1994–. *Publications:* research papers on radiation physics, laser physics, new technology. *Recreations:* visual arts, collecting. *Address:* Maybury Cottage, Raleigh Drive, Claygate, Esher, Surrey KT10 9DE. *T:* Esher (01372) 463352.

SMITH, Sir Robert (Courtney), Kt 1987; CBE 1980; FRSE; MA, CA; Chairman, Alliance and Second Alliance Trust, since 1984; *b* 10 Sept. 1927; 4th *s* of late John Smith, DL, JP, and Agnes Smith, Glasgow and Symington; *m* 1954, Moira Rose, *d* of late Wilfred H. Macdougall, CA, Glasgow; one *s* two *d* (and one *s* decd). *Educ:* Kelvinside Academy, Glasgow; Sedbergh Sch.; Trinity Coll., Cambridge. BA 1950, MA 1957. Served, Royal Marines, 1945–47, and RMFVR, 1951–57; Hon. Col, RM Reserves Scotland, 1992–. Partner, Arthur Young McClelland Moores & Co., Chartered Accountants, 1957–78. Director: Standard Life Assurance, 1975–94 (Chm., 1982–88); Sidlaw Gp, 1977– (Chm., 1980–88); Wm Collins, 1978–89 (Vice-Chm., 1979–89); Volvo Truck and Bus (formerly Trucks (GB)), 1979–; Edinburgh Investment Trust, 1983–; British Alcan Aluminium, 1983–; Bank of Scotland, 1985–. Mem., Scottish Industrial Develt Adv. Bd, 1972–88 (Chm., 1981–88); Pres., Business Archives Council of Scotland; Chancellor's Assessor, Glasgow Univ., 1984–. Mem., Horserace Betting Levy Bd, 1977–82; Deacon Convener, Trades House of Glasgow, 1976–78; Dir, Merchants House of Glasgow, 1991–. Mem. Council, Inst. of Chartered Accountants of Scotland, 1974–79. Trustee, Carnegie Trust for Univs of Scotland. FRSE 1988. Hon. LLD: Glasgow, 1978; Aberdeen, 1991. OStJ. *Recreations:* racing, gardening. *Address:* North Lodge, Dunkeld, Perthshire PH8 0AZ. *T:* Dunkeld (01350) 727574; (professional) 64 Reform Street, Dundee DD1 1TJ. *Clubs:* East India; Western (Glasgow); Hawks (Cambridge).

See also John Smith.

SMITH, Robert Haldane, CA; FCIBS; Chairman and Chief Executive, Morgan Grenfell Development Capital Ltd, since 1989; President, Institute of Chartered Accountants of Scotland, April 1996–97 (Vice-President, 1994–April 1996); *b* 8 Aug. 1944; *s* of Robert Haldane Smith and Jean Smith (*née* Adams); *m* 1969, Alison Marjorie Bell; two *d*. *Educ:* Allan Glen's Sch., Glasgow. CA 1968; FCIBS 1993. With ICFC, 1968–82; Gen. Manager, Corporate Finance Div., Royal Bank of Scotland plc and Man. Dir, Nat. Commercial & Glyns Ltd, 1983–85; Man. Dir, Charterhouse Develt Capital Ltd and Exec. Dir, Charterhouse Bank Ltd, 1985–89. Director: Morgan Grenfell & Co. Ltd; Morgan Grenfell (Scotland) Ltd; Morgan Grenfell Gp Mgt Cttee; MFI Furniture Gp plc; Dep. Chm., Bristow Helicopter Gp Ltd. Chm., Bd of Trustees, Nat. Museums of Scotland, 1993–; Mem., Museums and Galls Commn, 1986–. Pres., British Assoc. of Friends of Museums. *Publication:* (jtly) Managing Your Company's Finances, 1981. *Recreations:* listed buildings and conservation, public speaking. *Address:* Morgan Grenfell Development Capital Ltd, 35 St Andrew Square, Edinburgh EH2 2AD. *T:* 0131–557 8600.

SMITH, (Robert) Harvey; show jumper, farmer; *b* 29 Dec. 1938; *m* 1st, Irene Shuttleworth (marr. diss. 1986); two *s*; 2nd, 1987, Susan Dye. First major win with Farmer's Boy. Leading Show Jumper of the Year; other major wins include: King George V Cup, Royal

Internat. Horse Show, 1958; has won the John Player Trophy 7 times, King George V Gold Cup once, and the British Jumping Derby 4 times; Grand Prix and Prix des Nations wins in UK, Ireland, Europe and USA; took part in Olympic Games, 1968 and 1972; best-known mounts: Farmer's Boy, Mattie Brown, Olympic Star, O'Malley, Salvador, Harvester. BBC TV Commentator, Los Angeles Olympics, 1984. *Publications:* Show Jumping with Harvey Smith, 1979; Bedside Jumping, 1985.

SMITH, Prof. Robert Henry Tufrey; Executive Director, Australian Education Office, Washington, since 1994; *b* 22 May 1935; *s* of late Robert Davidson Smith and Gladys Smith (*née* Tufrey); *m* 1959, Elisabeth Jones; one *s* one *d*. *Educ:* Farrer Memorial Agricultural High Sch., Tamworth, NSW; Univ. of New England, NSW (BA, 1st Cl. Hons Geography); Northwestern Univ. (MA); ANU (PhD). Lectr in Geography, Univ. of Melbourne, 1961–62; University of Wisconsin: Asst Prof. of Geography, 1962–64; Associate Prof., 1964–67; Prof., 1967–70; Chm., African Studies Programme, 1968–69 (on leave, 1964–66: Associate Res. Fellow, Nigerian Inst. for Social and Econ. Res., and Hon. Vis. Lectr in Geography, Univ. of Ibadan, 1964–65; Vis. Fellow, Dept of Geography, Univ. of Sydney, 1965–66); Prof. of Geography and Head of Dept, Queen's Univ., Kingston, Ontario, 1970–72; Prof. of Geography, Monash Univ., 1972–75 (Chm. of Dept, 1973–75; Associate Dean, Faculty of Arts, 1974–75); University of British Columbia: Prof. of Geography, 1975–85; Head of Dept, 1975–80; Associate Vice-Pres., Academic, 1979–83; Vice-Pres., Academic, 1983–85; Pres. *pro tem*, March–Nov. 1985; Vice-Chancellor, Univ. of WA, 1985–89; Chm., Nat. Bd of Employment, Educn and Trng, Aust., 1989–90; Vice-Chancellor, Univ. of New England, Australia, 1990–93. *Address:* Australian Education Office, 1601 Massachusetts Avenue NW, Washington, DC 20036, USA. *T:* (202) 3328285, *Fax:* (202) 3328304.

SMITH, Sir Robert Hill, 3rd Bt *cr* 1945, of Crowmallie, Co. Aberdeen; *b* 15 April 1958; *s* of Sir (William) Gordon Smith, 2nd Bt, VRD, and of Diana (*née* Goodchild); *S* father, 1983. *Educ:* Merchant Taylors' School; Aberdeen Univ. *Heir: b* Charles Gordon Smith, *b* 21 April 1959. *Address:* 5 Elmfield Avenue, Aberdeen AB2 3NU.

SMITH, Robert Lee; Under Secretary, Pupils and Parents Branch, Department for Education and Employment (formerly Department for Education), since 1994; *b* 9 Feb. 1952; *s* of John Joseph Smith and Joan Margaret Smith; *m* 1986, Susan Elizabeth Armfield; one *s* one *d*. *Educ:* St Dunstan's Coll., Catford; Magdalene Coll., Cambridge (MA Eng. Lit.). Entered Civil Service as Administrative Trainee, 1974; Principal Private Sec. to Sec. of State for Educn and Science, 1985–87. *Recreations:* folk dancing and music. *Address:* Department for Education and Employment, Sanctuary Buildings, Great Smith Street, SW1P 3BT. *T:* 0171–925 5510.

SMITH, Robin Anthony, TD 1978; DL; Senior Partner, Dibb Lupton Broomhead, solicitors, since 1993 (Managing Partner, 1988–93); *b* 15 Feb. 1943; *s* of late Tom Sumerfield Smith and of Mary Smith; *m* 1967, Jennifer Elizabeth Roslington; one *s* one *d*. *Educ:* St Michael's Coll.; Manchester Univ. (LLB). Solicitor, admitted 1966; Dibb Lupton & Co., 1966–. Mem. Council, Law Society, 1982–91; Pres., Leeds Law Soc., 1993–94. Gov., Stonyhurst Coll., 1989–. Commnd 5th Bn LI, TA, 1966; retired 1985, Lt-Col. DL W Yorks, 1991. *Recreations:* tennis, golf. *Address:* Dibb Lupton Broomhead, 117 The Headrow, Leeds LS1 5JX. *Clubs:* Army and Navy; Leeds; Alwoodley Golf.

SMITH, Rt. Rev. Robin Jonathan Norman; *see* Hertford, Bishop Suffragan of.

SMITH, Prof. Roderick Arthur, PhD; CEng; FIMechE; FIM; Professor of Mechanical and Process Engineering, since 1988, and Head of Department, since 1992, University of Sheffield; *b* 26 Dec. 1947; *s* of Eric and Gladys Mary Smith; *m* 1975, Yayoi Yamanoi. *Educ:* Hulme Grammar Sch., Oldham; St John's Coll., Oxford (BA, MA); Queens' Coll., Cambridge (MA; PhD 1975). CEng 1976; FIMechE 1991; FIM 1992. Queens' College, Cambridge: Godfrey Mitchell Res. Fellow, 1975–78; Official Fellow, College Lectr and Dir of Studies, 1978–88; Asst Lectr, Engrg Dept, Cambridge Univ., 1977–80, Lectr, 1980–88; Sheffield University: Chm., Advanced Rlwy Res. Centre, 1993–; Warden, Stephenson Hall, 1992–. Consultant to: British Steel plc, 1986–89; BR, 1992– (Mem. Bd, Res. and Tech. Cttee, 1992–). *Publications:* Thirty Years of Fatigue Crack Growth, 1986; Innovative Teaching in Engineering, 1991; Engineering for Crowd Safety, 1993; ed books; papers and articles on mech. engrg, design, manufacture, engrg educn and crowd engrg. *Recreations:* mountaineering, reading, history, Japan: its people and technology; conversation, wine. *Address:* Department of Mechanical and Process Engineering, University of Sheffield, Sir Frederick Mappin Building, Mappin Street, Sheffield S1 3JD. *T:* Sheffield (0114) 282 5522. *Clubs:* Royal Over-Seas League; Fell and Rock (Lake District).

SMITH, Rodger H.; *see* Hayward Smith.

SMITH, Roger Bonham; Chairman and Chief Executive Officer, General Motors, 1981–90 (Member, Board of Directors, since 1974); *b* Columbus, Ohio, 12 July 1925. *Educ:* Detroit University Sch.; Univ. of Michigan (BBA, MBA). Served US Navy, 1944–46. General Motors: Sen. Clerk, subseq. Director, general accounting, Detroit Central Office, 1949–58; Dir, financial analysis sect., NY Central Office, 1960, later Asst Treas.; transf. to Detroit as Gen. Asst Comptroller, then Gen. Asst Treas., 1968; Treasurer, 1970; Vice-Pres. i/c Financial Staff, 1971, also Mem. Admin Cttee, 1971–90; Vice-Pres. and Gp Exec. i/c Nonautomotive and Defense Gp, 1972; Exec. Vice-Pres., Mem. Bd of Dirs and Mem. Finance Cttee, 1974, also Mem. Exec. Cttee, 1974–90; Vice-Chm. Finance Cttee, 1975–80, Chm., 1981–90. Conceived GM Cancer Res. Awards, 1978 (Trustee); Member: Business Council, 1981–; Soc. of Automotive Engrs, 1978–. Hon. degrees from several univs. Hon. Dr DePauw, 1979; Hon. Dr Albion Coll., 1982. *Address:* General Motors Corporation, 31 Judson Street, Pontiac, MI 48342-2230, USA; (home) Bloomfield Hills, MI 48304. *Clubs:* Economic, Detroit, Detroit Athletic (Detroit); Links (NY).

SMITH, Roger John; Chairman: Central Industrial Holdings Ltd, since 1992; European Motor Holdings PLC, since 1994; *b* 20 April 1939; *s* of Horace W. Smith and Marjorie E. Pummery; *m* 1962, Margaret R. Campbell; one *s* two *d*. *Educ:* Bedford School. Nat. Service, Subaltern, RCT, 1958–60. Dir, Family Group business, incl. Lea Heating Merchants (later part of Tricentrol), 1960–70; Man. Dir, Commercial Div., 1971–75, Dir, Special Projects, 1976–78, Tricentrol International; Dir, Group Co-ordination, Tricentrol, 1978–81; Man. Dir, Commercial Div., 1981–83; Dep. Chm., Tricentrol plc, 1983–88. Chm. and Chief Exec., Trimoco plc, 1987–92. Director: Combined Technologies Corp. plc; Brengreen Hldgs plc, and other cos. Pres., Retail Motor Industry Fedn, 1991–93. Sloan Fellow, Stanford Univ., 1976. Chm. of Finance, Lord's Taverners. Liveryman, Coach and Harnessmakers' Co. *Recreations:* Methodist church activities, sailing, shooting, tennis, reading. *Address:* Gilvers, Markyate, Herts AL3 8AD. *T:* Luton (01582) 840536. *Club:* Royal Thames Yacht.

SMITH, Sir Roland, Kt 1991; a Director, Bank of England, since 1991; Professor Emeritus of Management Science, University of Manchester; *b* 1 Oct. 1928; *s* of late Joshua Smith and of Mrs Hannah Smith; *m* 1954, Joan (*née* Shaw); no *c*. *Educ:* Univs of Birmingham and Manchester. BA, MSc, PhD (Econ). Flying Officer, RAF, 1953. Asst Dir, Footwear Manufacturers' Fedn, 1955; Lectr in Econs, Univ. of Liverpool, 1960; Dir, Univ. of Liverpool Business Sch., 1963; Prof. of Marketing, 1966–88, Hon. Vis. Prof., and Chancellor, 1996–, UMIST. Non-Exec. Chm., Senior Engineering Ltd, 1973–92; Chairman: Temple Bar Investment Trust Ltd, 1980–; House of Fraser, 1981–86 (Dep. Chm., 1980–81); Readicut International, 1984– (Dep. Chm., 1982–84); Hepworth plc, 1986–; Phoenix Properties and Finance, 1986–87; Kingston Oil & Gas, 1987–91; British Aerospace, 1987–91; P & P plc, 1988–; Manchester United Plc, 1991–; Dir-Consultant to a number of public companies. *Recreation:* walking.

SMITH, Roland Hedley, CMG 1994; HM Diplomatic Service; Assistant Under-Secretary of State (International Security), Foreign and Commonwealth Office, since 1995; *b* 11 April 1943; *s* of Alan Hedley Smith and Elizabeth Louise Smith; *m* 1971, Katherine Jane Lawrence; two *d*. *Educ:* King Edward VII School, Sheffield; Keble College, Oxford (BA 1st cl. hons 1965, MA 1981). Third Sec., Foreign Office, 1967; Second Sec., Moscow, 1969; Second, later First Sec., UK Delegn to NATO, Brussels, 1971; First Sec., FCO, 1974; First Sec. and Cultural Attaché, Moscow, 1978; FCO, 1980; attached to Internat. Inst. for Strategic Studies, 1983; Political Advr and Hd of Chancery, British Mil. Govt, Berlin, 1984–88; Dep. Hd, Sci., Energy and Nuclear Dept, FCO, 1988–90; Hd of Non-Proliferation and Defence Dept, FCO, 1990–92; Minister and Dep. Perm. Rep., UK Delegn to NATO, Brussels, 1992–95. *Publication:* Soviet Policy Towards West Germany, 1985. *Recreations:* music, esp. choral singing, football (Sheffield United), trams. *Address:* c/o Foreign and Commonwealth Office, SW1A 2AH. *Club:* Commonwealth Trust.

SMITH, Prof. Roland Ralph Redfern, DPhil; Lincoln Professor of Classical Archaeology and Art, University of Oxford, since 1995; *b* 30 Jan. 1954; *s* of Rupert and Elinor Smith; *m* 1989, Ingrid Gaitet. *Educ:* Fettes Coll., Edinburgh; Pembroke Coll., Oxford (BA 1977; MPhil 1979); Magdalen Coll., Oxford (DPhil 1983). Fellow, Magdalen Coll., Oxford, 1981–86; Asst Prof. of Classical Archaeology, 1986–90, Associate Prof., 1990–95, Inst. of Fine Arts, NY Univ. Harkness Fellow, Princeton, 1983–85; Alexander von Humboldt Fellow, Munich, 1991–92. Dir, Excavations at Aphrodisias, Caria, 1991–. *Publications:* Hellenistic Royal Portraits, 1988; Hellenistic Sculpture, 1991; The Monument of C. Julius Zoilos, 1993; contrib. learned jls. *Address:* Ashmolean Museum, Oxford OX1 2PH.

SMITH, Ron, CBE 1973; Member, British Steel Corporation, 1967–77 (Managing Director (Personnel and Social Policy), 1967–72); formed British Steel Corporation (Industry) Ltd and was first Chairman, 1974–77; *b* 15 July 1915; *s* of Henry Sidney Smith and Bertha Clara (*née* Barnwell); *m* 1940, Daisy Hope (*d* 1974), *d* of Herbert Leggatt Nicholson; one *d*. *Educ:* Workers' Education Association. Post Office Messenger, 1929; Postman, 1934; Postal and Telegraph Officer, 1951; Treasurer, Union of Post Office Workers, 1953; Gen. Sec., Union of Post Office Workers, 1957–66. General Council, TUC, 1957–66; Civil Service National Whitley Council, 1957–66; Exec. Cttee, Postal, Telegraph and Telephone International, 1957–66; Vice-Chairman, Post Office Dept, Whitley Council, 1959–66. Member: Cttee on Grants to Students, 1958–60; Development Areas, Treasury Advisory Cttee, 1959–60; Cttee on Company Law, 1960–62; National Economic Development Council, 1962–66; Court of Enquiry into Ford Motor Co. Dispute, 1963; Cttee of Enquiry into Pay, etc, of London Transport Bus Staff, 1963–64; Organising Cttee for Nat. Steel Corp., 1966; (part-time) Associated British Ports Hldgs plc (formerly BTDB), 1978–86. President, Postal, Telegraph and Telephone Internat., 1966. Director, BOAC, 1964–70. *Recreations:* photography, golf. *Address:* 3 Beech Grove, Epsom, Surrey KT18 5UD. *Club:* Tyrrells Wood Golf.

SMITH, Ronald Alfred D.; *see* Dingwall-Smith.

SMITH, Ronald Good; Sheriff of North Strathclyde, since 1984; *b* 24 July 1933; *s* of Adam Smith and Selina Spence Smith; *m* 1962, Joan Robertson Beharrie; two *s*. *Educ:* Glasgow University (BL 1962). Private practice to 1984. *Recreations:* philately, photography, gardening, reading. *Address:* 29 Broomcliff, 30 Castleton Drive, Newton Mearns, Glasgow G77 5LG. *T:* 0141–639 3904.

SMITH, Rosemary Ann, (Mrs G. F. Smith); Headmistress, Wimbledon High School, GPDST, 1982–92; *b* 10 Feb. 1932; *d* of late Harold Edward Wincott, CBE, editor of the Investors Chronicle, and of Joyce Mary Wincott; *m* 1954, Rev. Canon Graham Francis Smith; two *s* two *d*. *Educ:* Brighton and Hove High School, GPDST; Westfield College, Univ. of London (BA Hons); London Univ. Inst. of Education (post grad. Cert. in Education). Assistant Teacher: Central Foundation Girls' School, 1964–69; Rosa Bassett Girls' School, 1970–77; Furzedown Secondary School, 1977–80; Deputy Head, Rowan High School, 1980–82. Mem. Council, GPDST, 1993–. *Recreations:* theatre, gardening, reading, walking. *Address:* The Haven, 9 High Street, Syresham, Brackley, Northants NN13 5HL. *T:* Syresham (01280) 850421.

SMITH, Air Marshal Sir Roy David A.; *see* Austen-Smith.

SMITH, Lt-Gen. Rupert Anthony, DSO 1991; OBE; QGM 1978; Commander, United Nations Protection Force Bosnia-Hertzegovina, since 1995; *b* 13 Dec. 1943. Parachute Regt, 1964; Dep. Comdt, Staff Coll., Camberley, 1989–90; Comdr, 1st Armoured Div., BAOR, 1990–92; ACDS (Ops), 1992–94. Lt Col, 1980; Col, 1985; Brig., 1986; Maj.-Gen., 1990; Lt-Gen., 1995. *Address:* c/o The Parachute Regiment, Aldershot, Hants GU11 2BU.

SMITH, Russell; *see* Smith, C. R.

SMITH, Sidney William; retired; Regional Administrator, East Anglian Regional Health Authority, 1975–83; *b* 17 May 1920; *s* of late Sidney John and Harriet May Smith; *m* 1943, Doreen Kelly; one *s* one *d*. *Educ:* Wirral Grammar Sch., Cheshire. FHSM; ACIS. Served RAF, 1940–46. Asst Sec., Bury Infirmary, 1939–48; Dep. Group Sec.: Mansfield Hosp. Management Cttee, 1948–61; Wolverhampton Hosp. Management Cttee, 1961–63; Group Sec., Wakefield Hosp. Management Cttee, 1963–73; Area Administrator, Wakefield Area Health Authority, 1973–75. Member: Management Side, Ancillary Staff, Whitley Council, 1969–83 (Chm., 1982–83); Cttee, Assoc. of Chief Administrators of Health Authorities, 1974–84 (Chm., 1974–76); Health Services Panel, Inst. of Chartered Secretaries and Administrators, 1978–84, 1986–95 (Chm., 1978–83); Council, Soc. of Family Practitioner Cttees, 1989–90; Vice Chm., Cambs FPC, 1985–90; Chm., Pharmaceutical Services Panel, Cambs FHSA, 1991–. Dir, Sketchley Hosp. Services Ltd, 1983–84. Freeman, City of London, 1985; Liveryman, Chartered Secretaries' and Administrators' Co., 1985–. *Recreations:* gardening, Rugby Union football. *Address:* 77 Gough Way, Cambridge CB3 9LN. *T:* Cambridge (01223) 362307.

SMITH, Prof. (Stanley) Desmond, FRS 1976; FRSE 1972; Professor of Physics and Head of Department of Physics, Heriot-Watt University, Edinburgh, since 1970 (Dean of the Faculty of Science, 1981–84); *b* 3 March 1931; *s* of Henry George Stanley Smith and Sarah Emily Ruth Smith; *m* 1956, Gillian Anne Parish; one *s* one *d*. *Educ:* Cotham Grammar Sch., Bristol; Bristol Univ. (BSc, DSc); Reading Univ. (PhD). SSO, RAE, Farnborough, 1956–58; Research Asst, Dept of Meteorology, Imperial Coll., London, 1958–59; Lectr, then Reader, Univ. of Reading, 1960–70. Chm., Edinburgh Instruments Ltd, 1971–. Member: ACARD, 1985–87; Defence Scientific Adv. Council, 1985–91;

Astronomy, Space & Radio Bd, Engrg Bd, SERC, 1985–88; ACOST, 1987–88. Principal Investigator, Scottish Collaborative Initiative in Optoelectronic Scis, 1991–. Mem. Council, Inst. of Physics, 1984–87. C. V. Boys Prizeman, Inst. of Physics, 1976; Educn in Partnership with Industry or Commerce Prize, DTI, 1982; Technical or Business Innovation in Electronics Prize, Electronics Weekly, 1986; James Scott Prize, RSE, 1987. *Publications:* Infra-red Physics, 1966; numerous papers on semi-conductor and laser physics, satellite meteorology, nonlinear optics and optical computing. *Recreations:* tennis, skiing, mountaineering, golf, raising the temperature. *Address:* Tree Tops, 29D Gillespie Road, Colinton, Edinburgh EH13 0NW. *T:* 0131–441 7225; (office) 0131–451 3021, *Fax:* 0131–449 5542.

SMITH, Stanley Frank, MA; CEng, FIMechE, FCIT; Vice-President (Technology), Urban Transport Development Company, Kingston, Ontario, 1985–86, retired; *b* 15 Dec. 1924; *s* of Frederick and Edith Maria Smith; *m* 1st, 1946, Margaret (*née* Garrett) (*d* 1984); two *s* three *d*; 2nd, 1987, Catherine Cooke Murphy. *Educ:* Purley Sch.; Hertford Coll., Oxford (MA). Served War, RAF Pilot, 1943–46. Oxford Univ., 1946–49. Rolls-Royce Ltd, 1949–65 (Chief Research Engineer, 1963); British Railways, 1965–71 (Dir of Engineering Research, 1965; Dir of Research, 1966); joined London Transport, 1971: Dir-Gen. of Research and Develt, 1971–72; Chief Mech. Engr, 1972–81, retired; Gen. Manager, Res. Develt, Urban Transport Development Co., 1981–85. *Recreations:* tennis, windsurfing, cycling, walking, ski-ing, sailing. *Address:* Rural Route 1, Bath, Ontario K0H 1G0, Canada. *T:* (613) 3527429.

SMITH, Prof. Stephen Kevin, MD; Professor of Obstetrics and Gynaecology, University of Cambridge Clinical School, Rosie Maternity Hospital, Cambridge, since 1988; Fellow, Fitzwilliam College, Cambridge, since 1991; *b* 8 March 1951; *s* of Albert and Drusilla Smith; *m* 1978, Catriona Maclean Hobkirk Smith; one *s* two *d*. *Educ:* Birkenhead Sch.; Westminster Med. Sch., Univ. of London (MB BS 1974; MD 1982); MRCOG 1979. Lecturer: Univ. of Edinburgh, 1979–82; Univ. of Sheffield, 1982–85; Cons. Gynaecologist, MRC Reproductive Biology Unit, Edinburgh, 1985–88. *Publications:* numerous contribs to sci. and med. pubns on the subject of Reproductive Medicine. *Recreations:* cricket, football, music, natural history, politics. *Address:* 14 Hertford Street, Cambridge CB4 3AG. *T:* Cambridge (01223) 467169.

SMITH, Maj.-Gen. Stephen Robert C.; *see* Carr-Smith.

SMITH, Stewart Ranson, CBE 1986; Consultant, International Relations, Complutense University of Madrid, since 1993; *b* 16 Feb. 1931; *s* of John Smith and Elizabeth Smith; *m* 1960, Lee Tjam Mui, (Amy), Singapore. *Educ:* Bedlington Grammar Sch., Northumberland; Nottingham Univ. (BA, MA); Yale Univ., USA (MA). British Council: Asst Rep., Singapore, 1957–59; Reg. Officer, Overseas A, 1959–61; Dir, Curitiba, Brazil, 1961–65; Asst Rep., Sri Lanka, 1965–69; Planning Officer, London, 1969–70; seconded Min. of Overseas Develt, 1970–73; Rep., Kenya, 1973–76; Controller, Overseas B, 1976–80; Rep., Spain, 1980–87; Controller, Higher Educn Div., 1987–89; Controller, Europe Div., 1989–90. Chm., Consortium for Madrid Capital City of Culture 1992, 1990–92. Cross, Order of Isabella la Católica (Spain). *Recreations:* music, cricket. *Address:* Flat 1, Cumberland House, Clifton Gardens, W9 1DX. *Club:* Athenæum.

SMITH, Stuart Brian, FMA; Chief Executive, Trevithick Trust, since 1993; Director, Ironbridge Gorge Museum, 1983–92; *b* 19 Aug. 1944; *s* of Jack Fearnly Smith and Edith Dorothy Turner; *m* 1969, Jacqueline Slater; two *s* one *d*. *Educ:* Rochdale Grammar Sch.; Univ. of Surrey (BSc); Univ. of Manchester (MSc). Curator of Technology, Sunderland Museum, 1968–72; Curator of Technology, 1972, Dep. Dir, 1977–83, Ironbridge Gorge Museum. Hon. Lectr, Univ. of Birmingham, 1981–; Vis. Lectr, Camborne Sch. of Mines, 1995–. Vice Pres., Assoc. for Industrial Archaeology, 1992– (Asst Sec., 1975–92); Sec., Internat. Cttee for Conservation of Industrial Heritage, 1986–. Mem., Royal Commn on Ancient and Historical Monuments in Wales, 1991–; Mem., Industrial Archaeology Panel, English Heritage, 1993–. Pres., Midlands Fedn of Museums and Galls, 1991–92 (Vice-Pres. 1989); Mem. Cttee, Icomos UK, 1987–. Mem. Council, Trevithick Soc., 1993–. Freedom of City of London, 1984. *Publications:* A View from the Ironbridge, 1979; articles in learned jls. *Recreations:* gardening, collecting. *Address:* Chygarth, 5 Beacon Terrace, Camborne, Cornwall TR14 7BU. *T:* and *Fax:* Camborne (01209) 612142.

SMITH, Rt Rev. Stuart Meldrum; Assistant Bishop, Diocese of Adelaide, since 1992; *b* 8 June 1928; *s* of late F. R. and O. E. Smith; *m* 1957, Margaret, *d* of J. L. F. and D. M. Sando; three *s* two *d*. *Educ:* Univ. of Adelaide (BA Hons English); St Michael's House (Scholar in Theol., Hons, ACT). Ordained 1953; Asst Curate, Glenelg, 1954–56; Mission Chaplain, Meadows, 1956–57; Domestic Chaplain, Bishop of Adelaide, and Precentor, St Peter's Cathedral, 1957–58; Priest-in-charge, Kilburn, 1958–61; Editor, Adelaide Church Guardian, 1959–61 and 1965–76; Rector: Clare, 1961–65; Coromandel Valley (with Blackwood, Eden and Belair), 1965–69; Belair, 1969–72; Unley, 1972–84; Canon of Adelaide, 1974–84; Archdeacon: of Sturt, 1976–84; of Adelaide, 1984–92; Dir of Home Mission and Evangelism, 1984–92. Examng Chaplain, 1970–; Visiting Lecturer: St Barnabas Coll., 1966–81; St Michael's House, 1975–77. Hon. Chaplain, Walford CEGGS, 1973–75. Mem., Gen. Synod and Gen. Synod Standing Cttee. Chm., Council of Govs, Pulteney Grammar Sch. *Recreations:* walking, reading, gardening. *Address:* Anglican Church Office, 44 Currie Street, Adelaide 5000, Australia. *T:* 2312402; 4B Eleventh Avenue, St Peters, SA 5069, Australia. *T:* 3625847.

SMITH, Sir (Thomas) Gilbert, 4th Bt, *cr* 1897; Area Manager; *b* 2 July 1937; *er s* of Sir Thomas Turner Smith, 3rd Bt, and Agnes, *o d* of Bernard Page, Wellington, New Zealand; *S* father, 1961; *m* 1962, Patricia Christine Cooper; two *s* one *d*. *Educ:* Huntley Sch.; Nelson Coll. *Recreation:* skiing. *Heir: s* Andrew Thomas Smith, *b* 17 Oct. 1965.

SMITH, Rt. Rev. Timothy D.; *see* Dudley-Smith.

SMITH, Timothy John; MP (C) Beaconsfield, since May 1982; *b* 5 Oct. 1947; *s* of late Captain Norman Wesley Smith, CBE and Nancy Phyllis Smith; *m* 1980, Jennifer Jane Scott-Hopkins, *d* of Sir James Scott-Hopkins; two *s*. *Educ:* Harrow Sch.; St Peter's Coll., Oxford (MA). FCA. Articled with Gibson, Harris & Turnbull, 1969; Audit Sen., Peat, Marwick, Mitchell & Co., 1971; Company Sec., Coubro & Scrutton (Hldgs) Ltd, 1973. Sec., Parly and Law Cttee, ICA, 1979–82. Pres., Oxford Univ. Conservative Assoc., 1968; Chm., Coningsby Club, 1977–78. MP (C) Ashfield, April 1977–1979; PPS to Chief Sec. HM Treasury, 1983, to Sec. of State for Home Dept, 1983–85; a Vice Chm. and Treas., Conservative Party, 1992–94; Parly Under-Sec. of State, NI Office, 1994. Member: Public Accts Cttee, 1987–92, 1995–; Select Cttee on NI, 1994–; Vice-Chm., Cons. Finance Cttee, 1987–92. Dir, Gartmore Value Investments PLC, 1991–93. Mem. Council, ICA, 1992–94. *Recreations:* theatre, gardening. *Address:* House of Commons, SW1A 0AA. *T:* 0171–219 3000.

SMITH, Timothy Peter P.; *see* Pigott-Smith.

SMITH, Prof. Trevor Arthur, FRHistS; Vice-Chancellor, and Hon. Professor, University of Ulster, since 1991; *b* 14 June 1937; *e s* of late Arthur and of Vera Smith, London E5; *m* 1st, 1960, Brenda Eustace (marr. diss. 1973); two *s*; 2nd, 1979, Julia Bullock; one *d*. *Educ:* LSE (BSc Econ 1958). Schoolteacher, LCC, 1958–59; temp. Asst Lectr, Exeter Univ., 1959–60; Research Officer, Acton Soc. Trust, 1960–62; Lectr in Politics, Hull Univ., 1962–67; Queen Mary College, later Queen Mary & Westfield College, London: Lectr and Sen. Lectr in Political Studies, 1967–83; Prof., Political Studies, 1983–91; Head of Dept, 1972–85; Dean of Social Studies, 1979–82; Pro-Principal, 1985–87; Sen. Pro-Principal, 1987–89; Sen. Vice-Prin., 1989–91; Mem., Senate, London Univ., 1987–91. Vis. Associate Prof., California State Univ., LA, 1969. Director: Job Ownership Ltd, 1978–85; New Society Ltd, 1986–88; Statesman & Nation Publishing Co. Ltd, 1988–90 (Chm. 1990); G. Duckworth & Co., 1990–; Government and Opposition, 1995–. Mem., Tower Hamlets DHA, 1987–91. Vice-Pres., Political Studies Assoc. of UK, 1989–91, 1993– (Chm., 1988–89; Pres., 1991–93); Dep. Pres., Inst. of Citizenship Studies, 1992–; Mem., Admin. Bd, Internat. Assoc. of Univs, 1995–; Vice-Pres., Patients' Assoc., 1988–. Mem., Liberal Party Exec., 1958–59; contested (L) Lewisham W, 1959. Mem., Unservile State Gp, 1987–92. Trustee: Joseph Rowntree Reform (formerly Social Service) Trust, 1975– (Chm., 1987–); Acton Soc. Trust, 1975–87; Employment Inst., 1987–92; Pres., Belfast Civic Trust, 1995–. Vice-Chm. Govs, Princess Alexandra and Newham Coll. of Nursing and Midwifery, 1990–91; Governor: Sir John Cass and Redcoats Sch., 1979–84; Univ. of Haifa, 1985–91; Bell Educnl Trust, 1988–93. Mem., Willesden Area Synod, 1985–88. Hon. Mem. Senate, Fachhochschule Augsberg, 1994. CIMgt (CBIM 1992). Hon. LLD: Dublin, 1992; Hull, 1993. *Publications:* (with M. Argyle) Training Managers, 1962; (with A. M. Rees) Town Councillors, 1964; Town and County Hall, 1966; Anti-Politics: consensus and reform, 1972; contrib.: Big Business and the State: changing relations in Western Europe, ed R. Vernon, 1974; Politics, Planning and Public Policy in Britain, France and Italy, ed Hayward and Watson, 1975; The Political Science and British Politics, ed Hayward and Watson, 1986; (with A. Young) The Fixers, 1995; author of 28 other articles and papers, and of various book reviews and broadcasts. *Recreation:* water colour painting. *Address:* University of Ulster, University House, Coleraine, Co. Londonderry, N Ireland BT52 1SA. *T:* Coleraine (01265) 44141. *Club:* Reform.

SMITH, Vernon Olivier; Senior Partner, Smith & Smith (Barbados), Solicitors/Attorneys-at-Law, since 1989 (Partner, 1974–86); *b* 25 June 1930; *s* of Cecil Gladstone Smith and Lilian Angelique Smith; *m* (marr. diss.); one *s* one *d*. *Educ:* Univ. of West Indies; BA London; qual. Solicitor, 1974. Classics Master, Harrison Coll., Barbados, 1953–54; Sen. Classics Master, Excelsior Coll., Jamaica, 1954–57; LCC Educn Authy, 1957–62; Sen. English Master, Ikwere-Etche Grammar Sch., E Nigeria, 1963–65; Berks Co. Educn Authy, 1965–68; Sen. Classics Master, Combermere Sch., Barbados, 1968–72; High Comr for Barbados in UK, 1986–89. *Recreations:* tennis, cricket. *Address:* Veronda, Browne's Gap, Hastings, Christ Church, Barbados.

SMITH, Adm. Sir Victor (Alfred Trumper), AC 1975; KBE 1969 (CBE 1963); CB 1968; DSC 1941; Chairman, Australian Chiefs of Staff Committee, 1970–75; Military Adviser to SEATO, 1970–74; *b* 9 May 1913; *s* of George Smith; *m* 1944, Nanette Suzanne Harrison; three *s*. *Educ:* Royal Australian Naval College. Sub-Lieut, 1935; Lieut, 1936; Lieut-Commander, 1944; Commander, 1947; Captain, 1953; Rear-Admiral, 1963; Vice-Admiral, 1968; Chief of Naval Staff and First Naval Member, Austr. Commonwealth Naval Bd, 1968–70; Admiral, 1970. *Recreation:* walking. *Address:* Fishburn Street, Red Hill, ACT 2603, Australia. *T:* (62) 2958942.

SMITH, Walter Purvis, CB 1982; OBE 1960 (MBE 1945); Director General, Ordnance Survey, 1977–85, retired; *b* 8 March 1920; *s* of John William Smith and Margaret Jane (*née* Purvis); *m* 1946, Bettie Cox; one *s* one *d*. *Educ:* Wellfield Grammar Sch., Co. Durham; St Edmund Hall, Oxford (MA). FRICS 1951. Commnd RE (Survey), 1940; served War, UK and Europe, 1940–46; CO 135 Survey Engr Regt (TA), 1957–60. Directorate of Colonial (later Overseas) Surveys: served in Ghana, Tanzania, Malaŵi, 1946–50; Gen. Man., Air Survey Co. of Rhodesia Ltd, 1950–54; Fairey Surveys Ltd, 1954–75 (Man. Dir, 1969–75); Adviser: Surveying and Mapping, UN, NY, 1975–77; Ordnance Survey Review Cttee, 1978–79. Mem., Field Mission, Argentine-Chile Frontier Case, 1965. 15th British Commonwealth Lectr, RAeS, 1968. Dir, Sys Scan (UK) Ltd, 1985–90. President: Photogrammetric Soc., 1972–73; European Council of Heads of National Mapping Agencies, 1982–84; Eur. Orgn for Photogrammetic Res., 1984–85; Guild of Surveyors, 1985–88; Chm., National Cttee for Photogrammetry and Remote Sensing, 1985–88; Dep. Chm., Govt Cttee of Enquiry into Handling of Geographical Information, 1985–87; Mem., Gen. Council, RICS, 1967–70 (Chm., Land Survey Cttee, 1963–64). Patron's Medal, RGS, 1985. *Publications:* papers and technical jls. *Recreations:* music, walking, woodworking. *Address:* 15 Forest Gardens, Lyndhurst, Hants SO43 7AF. *T:* Lyndhurst (01703) 282566.

SMITH, (Walter) Richard; Regional Chairman of Industrial Tribunals, 1976–92; *b* 12 Oct. 1926; *s* of Walter Richard and Ivy Millicent Smith; *m* 1959, Jean Monica Law; one *s* one *d*. *Educ:* Bromsgrove Sch.; Birmingham Univ. (LLB). Called to the Bar, Gray's Inn, 1954. A Chairman of Industrial Tribunals, 1971. *Address:* The Old Bakery, Broadwell, Moreton-in-Marsh, Glos GL56 0TW. *T:* Cotswold (01451) 30130.

SMITH, Wilbur Addison; author; *b* 1933; *m*; two *s* one *d*. *Educ:* Michaelhouse, Natal; Rhodes Univ. (BCom). Business executive, 1954–58; factory owner, 1958–64; full-time author, 1964–. *Publications:* When the Lion Feeds, 1964; Dark of the Sun, 1965; Sound of Thunder, 1966; Shout at the Devil, 1968; Gold Mine, 1970; Diamond Hunters, 1971; The Sunbird, 1972; Eagle in the Sky, 1974; Eye of the Tiger, 1975; Cry Wolf, 1976; Sparrow Falls, 1977; Hungry as the Sea, 1978; Wild Justice, 1979; A Falcon Flies, 1980; Men of Men, 1981; The Angels Weep, 1982; The Leopard hunts in Darkness, 1984; The Burning Shore, 1985; Power of the Sword, 1986; Rage, 1987; A Time to Die, 1989; Golden Fox, 1990; Elephant Song, 1991; River God, 1993; The Seventh Scroll, 1995. *Recreations:* fly fishing, big game angling. *Address:* c/o Charles Pick Consultancy, Flat 3, 3 Bryanston Place, W1H 7FN.

SMITH, Sir William Antony John R.; *see* Reardon Smith.

SMITH, William Austin N.; *see* Nimmo Smith.

SMITH, William Frederick Bottrill, CBE 1964; Accountant and Comptroller General of Inland Revenue, 1958–68; Principal, Uganda Resettlement Board, 1972–74; *b* 29 Oct. 1903; *s* of late Arthur and Harriet Frances Smith; *m* 1926, Edyth Kilbourne (*d* 1970). *Educ:* Newton's, Leicester. Entered the Inland Revenue Dept, Civil Service, 1934. President, Inland Revenue Staff Federation, 1945–47. Vice-Pres., CS Fedn Drama Socs. Church Warden, Holy Trinity Church, Las Palmas. *Address:* 17 Bridge Avenue Mansions, Bridge Avenue, Hammersmith, W6 9JB. *T:* 0181–748 3194.

SMITH, William Jeffrey, CB 1976; Under-Secretary, Northern Ireland Office, 1972–76; *b* 14 Oct. 1916; 2nd *s* of Frederick Smith, Sheffield, and Ellen Hickinson, Ringinglow, Derbyshire; *m* 1942, Marie Hughes; one *s* one *d*. *Educ:* King Edward VII Sch., Sheffield; University Coll., Oxford (Schol.) (MA). Employed by Calico Printers' Assoc., Manchester, 1938–40 and in 1946. Served War, Army: enlisted Sept. 1939, embodied, 1940; RA and York and Lancaster Regt (Captain), 1940–46. Dominions Office (subseq. CRO), 1946; Principal, 1948; Office of UK High Commissioner in South Africa, 1953–56; Asst Sec.,

1959; sundry internat. confs; Dept of Technical Co-operation, 1961–64; Min. of Overseas Development, 1964–70; Overseas Develt Admin., 1970–72; UK Rep. to UNESCO, 1969–72. Sec. to Widgery Tribunal on loss of life in Londonderry, 1972; Northern Ireland Office, 1972. *Recreations:* theatre, scrambling up mountains, walking, bell ringing. *Address:* Lime Tree Cottage, Norris Lane, Chaddleworth, Newbury, Berks RG20 7DZ. *T:* Chaddleworth (01488) 638610.

SMITH, William McGregor, OBE 1970; HM Inspector of Constabulary for Scotland, 1970–75, retired; *b* 14 April 1910; *s* of John Smith, Milngavie and Agnes Smith (*née* Haldane); *m* 1939, Alice Mary Ewen, Montrose; one *s* one *d*. *Educ:* Bearsden Academy and Glasgow University (MA 1930). Joined City of Glasgow Police, 1933; Deputy Commandant, Scottish Police College, 1951; Chief Constable of Aberdeen, 1963. *Recreations:* golf, bridge. *Address:* Sherwood, 2 Cherry Tree Park, Balerno, Midlothian EH14 5AQ. *Clubs:* Luffness New Golf, Baberton Golf.

SMITH, William Peter; *see* Smith, P. W.

SMITH, Sir William Reginald V.; *see* Verdon-Smith.

SMITH-CAMERON, Rev. Canon Ivor Gill; Chaplain to the Queen, since 1995; *b* 12 Nov. 1929; *s* of James Smith-Cameron and Noreen Smith-Cameron (*née* Crocker). *Educ:* Madras Christian Coll., India (MA Eng. Lang. and Lit.); Coll. of Resurrection, Mirfield, Yorks. Ordained deacon, 1954; priest, 1955; Curate, St George's, Rumboldswyke, Chichester, 1954–58; Chaplain, London Univ., 1958–72; Canon Residentiary and Diocesan Missioner, Dio. Southwark, 1972–92; Asst Curate, All Saints, Battersea, 1992–94; retd 1994; Canon Residentiary Emeritus, 1994. *Publication:* Pilgrimage: an exploration into God, 1982. *Recreations:* cooking, reading, walking. *Address:* 100 Prince of Wales Drive, SW11 4BD. *T:* 0171–622 3809.

SMITH-DODSWORTH, Sir John (Christopher), 8th Bt, *cr* 1784; *b* 4 March 1935; *s* of Sir Claude Smith-Dodsworth, 7th Bt, and Cyrilla Marie Louise von Sobbe, (*d* 1984), 3rd *d* of William Ernest Taylor, Linnet Lane, Liverpool; *S* father, 1940; *m* 1st, 1961, Margaret Anne (*née* Jones) (marr. diss. 1971); one *s* one *d*; 2nd, 1972, Margaret Theresa (*née* Grey), Auckland, NZ; one *s*. *Educ:* Ampleforth Coll., Yorks. Now resident in Coromandel, New Zealand. *Heir: s* David John Smith-Dodsworth, *b* 23 Oct. 1963.

SMITH-GORDON, Sir (Lionel) Eldred (Peter), 5th Bt *cr* 1838; engaged in book publishing, since 1960; *b* 7 May 1935; *s* of Sir Lionel Eldred Pottinger Smith-Gordon, 4th Bt, and Eileen Laura (*d* 1979), *d* of late Captain H. G. Adams-Connor, CVO; *S* father, 1976; *m* 1962, Sandra Rosamund Ann, *d* of late Wing Commander Walter Farley, DFC and of Mrs Dennis Poore; one *s* one *d*. *Educ:* Eton College; Trinity College, Oxford. Chm., Smith-Gordon and Co. Ltd; Director: Consolidated Holdings (Gresham) Ltd; Dietetic Consultants Ltd. *Heir: s* Lionel George Eldred Smith-Gordon [*b* 1 July 1964; *m* 1993, Kumi, *d* of Masashi Suzuki, Japan]. *Address:* 13 Shalcomb Street, SW10 0HZ. *T:* 0171–352 8506.

SMITH-MARRIOTT, Sir Hugh Cavendish, 11th Bt *cr* 1774, of Sydling St Nicholas, Dorset; Public Relations and Marketing Executive Director; Director, H.S.M. Marketing Ltd, Bristol, since 1988; *b* 22 March 1925; *s* of Sir Ralph George Cavendish Smith-Marriott,10th Bt and Phyllis Elizabeth (*d* 1932), *d* of Richard Kemp; *S* father, 1987; *m* 1953, Pauline Anne (*d* 1985), *d* of F. F. Holt; one *d*. *Educ:* Bristol Cathedral School. Man. Dir, Drawing Office Co., 1956; Group Marketing Executive, Bryan Brothers Group, 1976. *Recreations:* hockey (county level), cricket, painting, theatre. *Heir: b* Peter Francis Smith-Marriott [*b* 14 Feb. 1927; *m* 1961, Jean Graham Martin, *d* of James Sorley Ritchie; five *s* (including twin *s*)]. *Address:* 26 Shipley Road, Westbury-on-Trym, Bristol BS9 3HS. *T:* Bristol (0117) 950 2915. *Clubs:* MCC; Gloucestershire CC (Mem. Management Cttee), Durham CC, Bristol Savages, Bristol RF.

SMITHERS, Professor Geoffrey Victor; Professor of English Language, University of Durham, 1960–74, now Emeritus; *b* 5 May 1909; *s* of William Henry and Agnes Madeline Smithers; *m* 1953, Jean Buglass Hay McDonald; three *s* one *d*. *Educ:* Durban High School; Natal University College; Hertford College, Oxford. Rhodes Schol. for Natal, 1930; 1st Cl. in Final Hon. School of English, Oxford, 1933. Asst Lecturer: King's Coll., London, 1936; University Coll., London, 1938; Lectr in English Language, 1940, Senior Lecturer in English Language, 1950, Reader in Medieval English, 1954, Univ. of Oxford, and professorial Fellow of Merton Coll., 1954. *Publications:* 2nd edn of C. Brown's Religious Lyrics of the Fourteenth Century, 1952; Kyng Alisaunder, Vol. I 1952, Vol. II 1957; (with J. A. W. Bennett and N. Davis) Early Middle English Verse and Prose, 1966 (rev. edn 1974); Havelok, 1987; contribs to vols in honour of M. Schlauch, G. N. Garmonsway, D. Meritt, A. McIntosh and N. Davis; papers in Med. Æv., English and Germanic Studies, Archivum Linguisticum, Rev. Eng. Studies, Shakespeare Survey, Durham Univ. Jl, Neuphilologische Mitteilungen, Notes and Queries. *Recreation:* music. *Address:* 6 Manor Close, Shincliffe, Durham DH1 2NS. *T:* Durham (0191) 3861094.

SMITHERS, Sir Peter (Henry Berry Otway), Kt 1970; VRD with clasp; DPhil Oxon; Lt-Comdr RNR, retired; *b* 9 Dec. 1913; *o s* of late Lt-Col H. O. Smithers, JP, Hants, and Ethel Berry; *m* 1943, Dojean, *d* of late T. M. Sayman, St Louis, Mo; two *d*. *Educ:* Hawtrey's; Harrow Sch.; Magdalen Coll., Oxford. Demyship in History, 1931; 1st cl. Hons Modern History, 1934. Called to Bar, Inner Temple, 1936; joined Lincoln's Inn, 1937. Commn, London Div. RNVR, 1939; British Staff, Paris, 1940; Naval Intelligence Div., Admiralty; Asst Naval Attaché, British Embassy, Washington; Actg Naval Attaché, Mexico, Central Amer. Republics and Panama. RD Councillor, Winchester, 1946–49. MP (C) Winchester Div. of Hampshire, 1950–64; PPS to Minister of State for Colonies, 1952–56 and to Sec. of State for Colonies, 1956–59; Deleg., Consultative Assembly of Council of Europe, 1952–56 and 1960; UK Deleg. to UN Gen. Assembly, 1960–62; Parly Under-Sec. of State, FO, 1962–64; Sec.-Gen., Council of Europe, 1964–69, Senior Research Fellow, UN Inst. for Trng and Research, 1969–72; General Rapporteur, European Conf. of Parliamentarians and Scientists, 1970–77. Chairman: British-Mexican Soc., 1952–55; Conservative Overseas Bureau, 1956–59; Vice-Chm., Conservative Parly Foreign Affairs Cttee, 1958–62; Vice-Pres., European Assembly of Local Authorities, 1959–62. 22 one-man photographic exhibitions in museums and institutions in England, USA, France and Italy. Master, Turners' Co., 1955; Liveryman, Goldsmiths' Co. Dr of Law *hc* Zürich, 1969. Marzotto Prize, Marzotto Foundn, Italy, 1969; Alexander von Humboldt Gold Medal, 1969; Medal of Honour, Parly Assembly, Council of Europe, 1984; Gold Medal (for photography), RHS, 1981, 1983, 1990, 1991, 1992, Gold Medal and Grenfell Medal, 1985, Veitch Meml Gold Medal, 1993. Hon. Citizen, Commune of Vico Morcote, Switzerland, 1995. Chevalier de la Légion d'Honneur; Orden Mexicana del Aguila Azteca. *Publication:* Life of Joseph Addison, 1954, 2nd edn, 1966. *Recreation:* gardening. *Address:* 6921 Vico Morcote, Switzerland. *Clubs:* Carlton; The Everglades.

SMITHIES, Frederick Albert; General Secretary, National Association of Schoolmasters and Union of Women Teachers, 1983–90; *b* 12 May 1929; *s* of Frederick Albert and Lilian Smithies; *m* 1960, Olga Margaret Yates. *Educ:* St Mary's Coll., Blackburn, Lancs; St Mary's Coll., Twickenham, Mddx. Schoolteacher: Accrington, Lancs, 1948–60; Northampton, 1960–76. NAS/UWT (before 1975, NAS): Nat. Executive Member, 1966–76; Chm. of Education Cttee, 1972–76; Vice-President, 1976; Asst Gen. Secretary, 1976–81; Dep. Gen. Secretary, 1981–82; Gen. Sec. Designate, 1982–83. Member: Exec. Bd, European Trade Union Cttee for Educn, 1982–93; TUC Gen. Council, 1983–89; Exec. Bd, Internat. Fedn of Free Teachers' Unions, 1985–93 (Hon. Treas., 1989–93). *Recreations:* reading, music, theatre, fell-walking. *Address:* High Street, Guilsborough, Northampton NN6 8PY.

SMITHIES, His Honour Kenneth (Charles Lester); a Circuit Judge, 1975–90; *b* 15 Aug. 1927; *s* of late Harold King Smithies and Kathleen Margaret (*née* Walsh); *m* 1950, Joan Winifred (*née* Ellis) (*d* 1983); one *s* two *d*. *Educ:* City of London Sch. (Corporation Scholar); University College London (LLB). Volunteered 60th Rifles, 1945, later commnd in Royal Artillery, in India; demobilised, 1948. Called to Bar, Gray's Inn, 1955. *Recreations:* music, bridge, chess, pedantry. *Address:* 23 Moorhead Court, Channel Way, Ocean Village, Southampton SO14 3GQ. *T:* Southampton (01703) 223469.

SMITHSON, Rt. Rev. Alan; *see* Jarrow, Bishop Suffragan of.

SMITHSON, Peter Denham; architect in private practice since 1950; *b* 18 Sept. 1923; *s* of William Blenkiron Smithson and Elizabeth Smithson; *m* 1949, Alison Margaret (*née* Gill) (*d* 1993); one *s* two *d*. *Educ:* The Grammar School, Stockton-on-Tees; King's College, Univ. of Durham. Served War of 1939–45: Queen Victoria's Own Madras Sappers and Miners, India and Burma, 1942–45. Asst in Schools Div. LCC, 1949–50; subseq. in private practice with wife. Banister Fletcher Prof. of Architecture, UCL, 1976–77; Vis. Prof. of Architecture: Bath Univ., 1978–90; Univ. of Delft, 1982–83; Univ. of Munich, 1984–85; Univ. of Barcelona, 1985–86. *Buildings:* Hunstanton School, 1950–54; The Economist Building, St James's, 1959–64, Porch 1983; Robin Hood Gardens, Tower Hamlets, 1963–72; Garden Bldg, St Hilda's Coll., Oxford, 1968–70; Ramp at Ansty, Wilts, 1987; for Bath University: Second Arts Bldg, 1978–81; Amenity Bldg, 1979–80, 1984; Arts Barn, 1980–90; Architecture and Building Engrg, 1982–88; Porch, Ansty Plum, Wilts, 1992; *furniture:* for Tecta, Germany (with A. Smithson), 1982–; Exhibitions for Tecta, Köln and Berlin, 1993. *Publications:* (all with A. Smithson) Uppercase 3, 1960; The Heroic Period of Modern Architecture, 1965, rev. edn 1981; Urban Structuring Studies of Alison and Peter Smithson, 1967; Team 10 Primer, 1968; The Euston Arch, 1968; Ordinariness and Light, 1970; Without Rhetoric, 1973; Bath: Walks Within the Walls, 1980; The Shift, 1982; AS in DS, 1983; The 1930s, 1985; Upper Lawn, 1986; Italian Thoughts, 1993; Changing the Art of Inhabitation, 1994; theoretical work on town structuring in ILAUD Year Book, Spazio e Società and other periodicals; *relevant publications:* synopsis of professional life in Arch. Assoc.'s Arena, Feb. 1966; selective bibliography in The Shift, 1982; A.+P. Smithson, 1991. *Address:* Cato Lodge, 24 Gilston Road, SW10 9SR. *T:* 0171–373 7423.

SMOUT, Prof. (Thomas) Christopher, CBE 1994; PhD; FBA 1988; FRSE 1975; FSAScot; Director, St John's House Centre for Advanced Historical Studies, University of St Andrews, since 1992; Historiographer to the Queen in Scotland, since 1993; *b* 19 Dec. 1933; *s* of Sir Arthur and Lady (Hilda) Smout; *m* 1959, Anne-Marie Schøning; one *s* one *d*. *Educ:* The Leys Sch., Cambridge; Clare Coll., Cambridge (MA; PhD 1960). FSAScot 1991. Dept of Economic History, Edinburgh University: Asst Lectr, 1959; Lectr, 1962; Reader, 1964; Prof. of Econ. History, 1970; Prof. of Scottish History, Univ. of St Andrews, 1980–91. Visiting Professor: Strathclyde Univ., 1991–; Dundee Univ., 1993–. Dep. Chm., Scottish Natural Heritage, 1992–; Member: Cttee for Scotland, Nature Conservancy Council, 1986–91; Bd, NCC (Scotland), 1991–92; Royal Commn on Ancient and Historic Monuments of Scotland, 1987–; Bd of Trustees, Nat. Museums of Scotland, 1991–95. FRSA 1991. Hon. Fellow, TCD, 1995. Hon. DSSc QUB, 1995. *Publications:* Scottish Trade on the Eve of Union, 1963; A History of the Scottish People, 1969; (with I. Levitt) The State of the Scottish Working Class in 1843, 1979; A Century of the Scottish People, 1986; (with S. Wood) Scottish Voices, 1990. *Recreations:* birdwatching, butterflies, ferns. *Address:* Chesterhill, Shore Road, Anstruther, Fife KY10 3DZ. *T:* Anstruther (01333) 310330.

SMYTH, Desmond; *see* Smyth, J.D.

SMYTH, (James) Robert Staples; His Honour Judge Robert Smyth; a Circuit Judge, since 1986; *b* 11 July 1926; *s* of late Major Robert Smyth, Gaybrook, Co. Westmeath, and Mabel Anne Georgiana (*née* MacGeough-Bond) *m* 1971, Fenella Joan Mowat; one *s*. *Educ:* St Columba's, Dublin; Merton Coll., Oxford (BA 1948, MA). Served RAF, 1944–46. Called to Bar, Inner Temple, 1949. Resident Magistrate, Northern Rhodesia, 1951–55; a Dep. Circuit Judge, 1974; Stipendiary Magistrate, W Midlands, 1978–86; a Recorder, 1983–86. Dep. Chairman, Agricultural Land Tribunal, 1974. *Recreations:* shooting, fishing, English literature. *Address:* Leys, Shelsley Beauchamp, Worcs WR6 6RB.

SMYTH, Prof. John Fletcher, MD; FRCPE, FRCP, FRCSE; Professor of Medical Oncology, University of Edinburgh, since 1979; Hon. Director, Imperial Cancer Research Fund Medical Oncology Unit, Edinburgh, since 1980; *b* 26 Oct. 1945; *s* of Henry James Robert Smyth and Doreen Stanger (*née* Fletcher); *m* 1973, Catherine Ellis; two *d*. *Educ:* Bryanston Sch.; Trinity Coll., Cambridge (BA 1967; MA 1971); St Bartholomew's Hosp. (MB BChir 1970); MD Cantab 1976; MSc London 1975. FRCPE 1981; MRCP 1973, FRCP 1983; FRCSE 1994. House Officer posts: St Bartholomew's Hosp. and RPMS, London, 1970–72; Asst Lectr, Dept of Med. Oncology, St Bartholomew's Hosp., 1972–73; CRC Res. Fellowship, Inst. Cancer Res., 1973–75; MRC Travelling Fellowship, Nat. Cancer Inst., USA, 1975–76; Sen. Lectr, Inst. Cancer Res., 1976–79. Honorary Consultant Physician: Royal Marsden Hosp. and Brompton Hosp., 1977–79; Lothian Health Bd, 1979–; Vis. Prof. of Medicine and Associate Dir for Med. Res., Univ. of Chicago, 1979. Member of Council: EORTC, 1990–; UICC, 1990–94; Pres., European Soc. of Med. Oncology, 1991–93; Treas., Fedn of European Cancer Socs, 1992–. *Publications:* Basic Principles of Cancer Chemotherapy, 1980; The Management of Lung Cancer, 1984; contrib. various med. and scientific jls on cancer medicine, pharmacology, clinical and exptl cancer therapeutics. *Recreations:* flying and singing (sometimes simultaneously). *Address:* 18 Inverleith Avenue South, Edinburgh EH3 5QA. *T:* 0131–552 3775. *Club:* Athenæum.

SMYTH, John Jackson; QC 1979; barrister-at-law; Director of Zambesi Ministries, Zimbabwe, since 1986; *b* 27 June 1941; *e s* of Col Edward Hugh Jackson Smyth, FRCSEd, and late Ursula Helen Lucie (*née* Ross) *m* 1968, Josephine Anne, *er d* of late Walter Leggott and Miriam Moss Leggott, Manor Farm, Burtoft, Lincs; one *s* three *d*. *Educ:* Strathcona Sch., Calgary, Alberta; St Lawrence Coll.; Trinity Hall, Cambridge. MA, LLB (Cantab). Called to Bar, Inner Temple (Major Schol.), 1965. A Recorder, 1978–84. *Publications:* Discovering Christianity Today, 1985; Following Christ Today, 1987; Jabulani Bible Reading Notes, 1990–92. *Recreations:* skiing, sailing, trout fishing, real tennis. *Address:* 2 Crown Office Row, Temple, EC4Y 7HJ; PO Box CH 210, Chisipite, Harare, Zimbabwe.

SMYTH, (Joseph) Desmond, FCA; Managing Director, Ulster Television, since 1983; *b* 20 April 1950; *s* of Andrew and Annie Elizabeth Smyth; *m* 1975, Irene Janette (*née* Dale); one *s* one *d*. *Educ:* Limavady Grammar School; Queen's University, Belfast. BSc (Jt Hons Pure Maths and Statistics). Accountancy articles, Coopers and Lybrand, 1971–75; Ulster

Television: Chief Accountant, 1975–76; Financial Controller and Company Secretary, 1976–83. Pres., NI Chamber of Commerce and Industry, 1991–92. Chm., NI Region, Prince's Youth Business Trust, 1991–. FRTS. *Recreations:* fishing, gardening. *Address:* Ulster Television plc, Havelock House, Ormeau Road, Belfast BT7 1EB.

SMYTH, Rev. Martin; *see* Smyth, Rev. W. M.

SMYTH, Reginald; cartoonist (as Reginald Smythe); contracted to Mirror Publications, since 1955; *b* 10 July 1917; *s* of Richard Oliver Smyth and Florence Pearce; *m* 1949, Vera Toyne. *Educ:* Galleys Field Sch., Hartlepool, Cleveland. Served Army, Royal Northumberland Fusiliers, 1936–45. Civil Service, 1945–55. Creator, Andy Capp daily comic strip, 1956–. Best Brit. Cartoon Strip Awards, 1961–65; Premio Cartoon Award, Lucca, 1969; Best Cartoonist Award, Genoa, 1973; Best Strip Cartoon, USA Cartoonist Assoc., 1974; Italian Strip Award, Derthona, 1978. *Publications:* annual World of Andy Capp book, 1957–; annual Andy Capp books (USA), 1968–. *Address:* 96 Caledonian Road, Hartlepool, Cleveland TS25 5LB.

SMYTH, Robert Staples; *see* Smyth, J. R. S.

SMYTH, Sir Thomas Weyland Bowyer-, 15th Bt *cr* 1661; *b* 25 June 1960; *s* of Captain Sir Philip Weyland Bowyer-Smyth, 14th Bt, RN, and of Veronica Mary, *d* of Captain C. W. Bower, DSC, RN; *S* father, 1978. *Heir: kinsman* John Jeremy Windham [*b* 22 Nov. 1948; *m* 1976, Rachel Mary Finney; one *s* two *d*].

SMYTH, Dr Sir Timothy (John), 2nd Bt *cr* 1956, of Teignmouth, Co. Devon; Chief Executive Officer, Hunter Area Health Service, since 1992; *b* 16 April 1953; *s* of Julian Smyth (*d* 1974) and of Phyllis, *d* of John Francis Cannon; *S* grandfather, Brig. Rt Hon. Sir John Smyth, 1st Bt, VC, MC, 1983; *m* 1981, Bernadette Mary, *d* of Leo Askew; two *s* two *d*. *Educ:* Univ. of New South Wales. MB, BS 1977; LLB 1987; MBA (AGSM) 1985; FRACMA 1985. Resident Medical Officer, 1977–79; Medical Administrator, Prince Henry Hosp., Prince of Wales Hosp. Gp, Sydney, 1980–86; Chief Exec. Officer, Sydney Health Service, 1986–88; Gen. Man., St George Hosp., Sydney, 1988–91. *Heir: s* Brendan Julian Smyth, *b* 4 Oct. 1981. *Address:* Hunter Area Health Service, Locked Bag No 1, New Lambton, NSW 2305, Australia.

SMYTH, Rev. (William) Martin; MP (UU) Belfast South, since March 1982 (resigned seat Dec. 1985 in protest against Anglo-Irish Agreement; re-elected Jan. 1986); *b* 15 June 1931; *s* of James Smyth, JP, and Minnie Kane; *m* 1957, Kathleen Jean Johnston, BA; two *d* (and one *d* decd). *Educ:* Methodist Coll., Belfast; Magee University Coll., Londonderry; Trinity Coll., Dublin (BA 1953, BD 1961); Assembly's Coll., Belfast. Assistant Minister, Lowe Memorial, Finaghy, 1953–57; Raffrey Presbyterian Church, Crossgar, 1957–63; Alexandra Presbyterian Church, Belfast, 1963–82. Member, Northern Ireland Convention, 1975; Mem. (UU) Belfast S, NI Assembly, 1982–86 (Chm., Health and Social Services Cttee, 1983–84; Chm., Finance and Personnel Cttee, 1984–86). Chm. of Executive 1974–76, Vice-Pres. 1974–, Ulster Unionist Council. Member: Select Cttee for Social Services, 1983–90; Select Cttee on Health, 1990–. Vice-Chm., Parly Cttee for Soviet Jewry, 1983–; Member Executive: UK Branch, IPU, 1985–92, 1995–; CPA, 1986–. Governor, Belfast City Mission. Grand Master, Grand Orange Lodge of Ireland, 1972–; Grand Master of World Orange Council, 1974–82, Pres., 1985–88; Hon. Past Grand Master, Canada, and Hon. Deputy Grand Master, USA, NZ, NSW, of Orange Order. *Publications:* (ed) Faith for Today, 1961; pamphlets: Why Presbyterian?, 1963; Till Death Us Do Part, 1965; In Defence of Ulster, 1970; The Battle for Northern Ireland, 1972; A Federated People, 1988; occasional papers, and articles in Christian Irishman, Evangelical Quarterly, Biblical Theology. *Recreations:* reading, photography; former Rugby player (capped for Magee University College). *Address:* 117 Cregagh Road, Belfast BT6 0LA. *T:* Belfast (01232) 457009.

SMYTHE, Clifford Anthony, (Tony); consultant; Director, Medical Action for Global Security (formerly Medical Campaign against Nuclear Weapons), 1989–92; *b* 2 Aug. 1938; *s* of Clifford John and Florence May Smythe; *m*; four *d*. *Educ:* University College School. Conscientious Objector, 1958; General Secretary, War Resisters' International, 1959–64, Treasurer, 1982–86; Council Member, Internat. Confederation for Disarmament and Peace, 1963–71; Gen. Sec., Nat. Council for Civil Liberties, 1966–72; Field Dir, American Civil Liberties Union, 1973; Dir, Mind (Nat. Assoc. for Mental Health), 1973–81. Board Member: Volunteer Centre, 1977–81; Retired Execs Clearing Hse (REACH), 1978–90; Member: Nat. Adv. Council on Employment of Disabled People, 1975–81; Nat. Develt Council for Mentally Handicapped People, 1981; (co-opted), Mddx Area Probation Cttee, 1984–90. Chairman: Campaign for Homeless Single People, 1982–84; National Peace Council, 1982–86; Nat. Assoc. of Voluntary Hostels, 1990–92; Director: Assoc. of Community Health Councils for England and Wales, 1983–86; SHAC, 1986–88. *Publications:* Conscription: a World Survey, 1968; (with D. Madgwick) The Invasion of Privacy, 1974. *Address:* 136 Stapleton Hall Road, N4 4QB.

SMYTHE, Patricia Rosemary K.; *see* Koechlin-Smythe.

SMYTHE, Captain Quentin George Murray, VC 1942; Officer Instructor, Department of Defence, South Africa, 1970–81, retired; *b* 6 Aug. 1916; *s* of Edric Murray Smythe and *g s* of 1st Administrator of Natal (Hon. Charles Smythe, Methven Castle, Perthshire, Scotland); *m* 1945, Dale Griffiths (marr. diss. 1970), Capetown; three *s* one *d*; *m* 1970, Margaret Joan Shatwell (*d* 1980); *m* 1984, Patricia Stamper. *Educ:* Estcourt High Sch. Went through Abyssinian Campaign with Regt, Natal Carabineers; Sgt at Alem Hanza, Egypt (VC). *Recreations:* bowls, fishing, shooting. *Address:* 76 Agulhas, 3 Topham Road, Doonside 4126, Natal, Republic of South Africa.

SMYTHE, Reginald; *see* Smyth, R.

SMYTHE, Tony; *see* Smythe, C. A.

SNAGGE, John Derrick Mordaunt, OBE 1944; *b* 1904; 2nd *s* of late Judge Sir Mordaunt Snagge; *m* 1st, 1936, Eileen Mary (*d* 1979), *e d* of late H. P. Joscelyne; 2nd, 1983, Joan Mary (*d* 1992), *e d* of late William Wilson. *Educ:* Winchester College; Pembroke College, Oxford. Assistant Station Director BBC, Stoke-on-Trent, 1924; Announcer London (Savoy Hill), 1928; Assistant Outside Broadcast Department 1933; Commentator Oxford and Cambridge Boat Race, 1931–80; Assistant Director Outside Broadcasts, 1939; Presentation Director BBC, 1939–45; Head of Presentation (Home Service), 1945–57; Head of Presentation (Sound) BBC, 1957–63; Special Duties, BBC, 1963–65. Retired from BBC 1965. Chairman of the Lord's Taverners, 1956, 1960, 1961; President, 1952, 1964; Secretary, 1965–67; Trustee, 1970–76. *Publication:* (with Michael Barsley) Those Vintage Years of Radio, 1972. *Recreation:* fishing. *Address:* Delgaty, Village Road, Dorney, near Windsor, Berks SL4 6QJ. *T:* Burnham (01628) 661303. *Clubs:* MCC, Leander, Lord's Taverners, Sportsman's.

SNAGGE, Dame Nancy (Marion), DBE 1955 (OBE 1945); *b* 2 May 1906; *d* of late Henry Thomas Salmon; *m* 1962, Thomas Geoffrey Mordaunt Snagge, DSC (*d* 1984), *e s* of late His Hon. Sir Mordaunt Snagge. *Educ:* Notting Hill, High Sch. Joined the WAAF on its inception, March 1939; served as a commnd officer in the WAAF and WRAF from Sept. 1939. ADC to King George VI, 1950–52; ADC to the Queen, 1952–56; Director Women's Royal Air Force, 1950–56, retired as Air Commandant. *Address:* 5 Headbourne Worthy House, Winchester, Hants SO23 7JG. *T:* Winchester (01962) 882489.

SNAITH, George Robert, FRINA; Partner, Pi-Sigma Technology and Systems Advisers, since 1990; *b* 9 July 1930; *s* of late Robert and Clara Snaith; *m* 1953, Verna Patricia (*née* Codling); one *s* one *d*. *Educ:* University of Durham. BSc Applied Science (Naval Architecture), 1952. A. Kari & Co., Consulting Naval Architects, Newcastle, 1952–57; Northern Aluminium Co. Ltd, Banbury, 1957–59; Burness, Corlett & Partners, Consulting Naval Architects, Basingstoke, 1959–64; British Ship Research Association, 1964–77, Dir of Research, 1976–77; British Shipbuilders: Dir of Research, 1977–81; Technol. and Systems Adviser (formerly Production Systems Adviser), 1981–85; Consultant, Computervision Ltd, 1985–90. Vis. Prof., Dept of Marine Technology (formerly Naval Architecture and Shipbldg), Univ. of Newcastle upon Tyne, 1980–. FNECInst 1992. Member: Council, RINA, 1977–; Ship and Marine Technol. Requirements Bd, Dept of Industry, 1978–81; Bd, National Maritime Inst., 1978–82. *Recreations:* ships and shipbuilding, technology, reading, literature and discussion. *Address:* 10 Fieldhouse Close, Hepscott, Morpeth, Northumberland NE61 6LU. *T:* Morpeth (01670) 515319.

SNAPE, Peter Charles; MP (Lab) West Bromwich East since Feb. 1974; *b* 12 Feb. 1942; *s* of Thomas and Kathleen Snape; *m* 1963, Winifred Grimshaw (marr. diss. 1980); two *d*. *Educ:* St Joseph's RC Sch., Stockport; St Winifred's Sch., Stockport. Railway signalman, 1957–61; regular soldier, RE & RCT, 1961–67; goods guard, 1967–70; clerical officer BR, 1970–74. Mem., Council of Europe and WEU, May–Nov. 1975. An Asst Govt Whip, 1975–77; a Lord Comr, HM Treasury, 1977–79; opposition spokesman for Defence, 1979–82, for Home Affairs, 1982–83, for Transport, 1983–92. Mem., Bredbury and Romiley UDC, 1971–74 (Chm., Finance Cttee). *Address:* Hildercroft, 281 Highfield Road, Hall Green, Birmingham B28 0BU.

SNAPE, Royden Eric; a Recorder of the Crown Court, 1979–92; *b* 20 April 1922; *s* of John Robert and Gwladys Constance Snape; *m* 1949, Unity Frances Money; one *s* one *d*. *Educ:* Bromsgrove Sch. Served War, Royal Regt of Artillery (Field), 1940–46; Adjt, 80th Field Regt, 1945. Admitted Solicitor, 1949; a Deputy Circuit Judge, 1975. Chairman: Med. Appeal Tribunal, 1985–94; Disability Appeal Tribunal, 1992–94. Governor, St John's Sch., Porthcawl, 1971–88 (Chm., 1971–72). *Recreations:* golf, Rugby Union football, cricket, swimming. *Address:* West Winds, Love Lane, Llanblethian, Cowbridge, South Glamorgan, Wales CF7 7JQ. *T:* Cowbridge (01446) 772362. *Clubs:* Royal Porthcawl Golf; Cardiff Athletic; Glamorgan CCC.

SNAPE, Thomas Peter, OBE 1988; General Secretary, Secondary Heads Association and Headmasters' Conference, 1983–88; *b* 4 June 1925; *s* of Charles Snape and Jane Elizabeth Middleton; *m* 1951, Anne Christina McColl; three *d* (one *s* decd). *Educ:* Cockburn High Sch., Leeds; Exeter Coll., Oxford (MA). PCE London Univ. Asst Master, grammar and comprehensive schs, 1950–60; Headmaster: Settle High Sch., Yorks, 1960–64; King Edward VI Grammar Sch., Totnes, 1964–66; King Edward VI Comprehensive Sch., Totnes, 1966–83; Warden, Totnes Community Coll., 1971–83. Leverhulme Res. Fellow, USA, 1970. Member: Consultative Cttee, Assessment of Performance Unit, 1975–84; Teacher Educn Accreditation Council, 1984–86. Chm., Leechwell Press, 1989–92. Chm. of Govs, St Dunstan's Abbey, Plymouth, 1993–. FRSA 1989. JP Devon, 1975, Inner London 1983. *Publications:* Ten Sites in Totnes, 1990; chapters in edited works; sections of Open University readers; contrib. learned jls. *Address:* 10 Chalcot Square, NW1 8YB. *Club:* East India.

SNEATH, Prof. Peter Henry Andrews, MD; FRS 1995; Professor of Clinical Microbiology, Leicester University, 1975–89; *b* 17 Nov. 1923; *s* of Rev. Alec Andrews Sneath and Elizabeth Maud Adcock; *m* 1953, Joan Sylvia Thompson; one *s* two *d*. *Educ:* Wycliffe Coll., Stonehouse, Glos; King's Coll., Cambridge (BA 1944; MB BChir 1948, MD 1959); King's Coll. Hosp.; London Sch. of Hygiene and Trop. Med. (Dip. Bact. 1953). MRCS, LRCP 1947. RAMC, Captain and Temp. Major, 1950–52. Mem., Sci. Staff, MRC, 1953–75 and Dir, Microbial Systematics Res. Unit, 1964–75; Hon. Consultant Microbiologist, Leics HA, 1975–89. Hon. mem., microbiol. and bacteriol. socs, UK, France, USA. Hon. DSc Ghent, 1969. *Publications:* (with R. R. Sokal) Principles of Numerical Taxonomy, 1963; Planets and Life, 1970; (with R. R. Sokal) Numerical Taxonomy, 1973; papers in learned jls on microbiology and computing. *Recreations:* reading, gardening, music. *Address:* Sunnyfield, 15 Southmeads Road, Leicester LE2 2LR. *T:* Leicester (0116) 271 2206; Department of Microbiology and Immunology, The University, Leicester LE1 7RH. *T:* Leicester (0116) 252 2951.

SNEDDEN, David King, CA; Chairman, Trinity International Holdings, since 1994 (Chief Executive and Managing Director, 1982–93; Deputy Chairman, 1993–94); Chairman, Liverpool Daily Post and Echo, since 1985; *b* 23 Feb. 1933; *s* of David King Snedden and Isabella (*née* Martin); *m* 1958; two *s* one *d*. *Educ:* Daniel Stewart's College, Edinburgh. CA 1956. Flying Officer, RAF, 1956–57. Investment Adviser, Guinness Mahon, 1958–59; Chief Accountant, Scotsman Publications Ltd, Thomson British Publications Ltd, Thomson Scottish Associates Ltd, 1959–64; Commercial Controller, The Scotsman Publications Ltd, 1964–66; Managing Director: Belfast Telegraph Newspapers Ltd, 1967–70 (Director, 1979–82); The Scotsman Publications Ltd, 1970–78 (Director, 1970–82). Thomson Regional Newspapers Ltd: Dir, 1974–82; Gp Asst Man. Dir, 1979–80; Jt Man. Dir, 1980–82. Chm., Norcross Holdings, 1994–; Director: Radio Forth Ltd, 1973–77; BSkyB; Scottish Council Research Inst. Ltd, 1975–77; The Press Association Ltd, 1984–94 (Vice-Chm., 1988; Chm., 1989–94); Reuters Holdings PLC, 1988–94. Pres., Scottish Daily Newspaper Soc., 1975–78; Member: Press Council, 1976–80; Council, Newspaper Soc., 1983–94; Regional Council, CBI, NI, 1968–70. *Recreations:* golf, hill walking, fishing. *Address:* Apartment 223, The Colonnades, Albert Dock Village, Liverpool L3 4AA. *Clubs:* Caledonian; Bruntsfield Links Golfing Society; Scarista (Isle of Harris).

SNEDDON, Hutchison Burt, CBE 1983 (OBE 1968); JP; Lord-Lieutenant of Lanarkshire, Strathclyde Region (Districts of Monklands, Motherwell, Hamilton, East Kilbride and Clydesdale), since 1992; former Scottish Divisional Director, Nationwide Anglia Building Society (formerly Nationwide Building Society); *b* 17 April 1929; *s* of Robert and Catherine Sneddon; *m* 1960, Elizabeth Jardine; one *s* two *d*. *Educ:* Wishaw High School. Chm., Cumbernauld Develt Corp., 1979–83; Regl Sales Manager (Special Projects), Scottish Gas, 1983–88; Dir, National Bldg Agency, 1973–82; Vice-Chm., Scottish National Housing and Town Planning Council, 1965–71; Member: Bd, Housing Corp., 1977–83; Consultative Cttee, Scottish Develt Agency, 1979–83; Scottish Adv. Commn on Housing Rents, 1973–74; Anderson Cttee on Commercial Rating, 1972–74; Western Regional Hosp. Bd, 1968–70; Scottish Tourist Bd, 1969–83; Chm., Burns Heritage Trail, 1971–83; Sen. Vice Pres., 1988–89, Pres., 1989–90, World Fedn of Burns Clubs (Jun. Vice Pres., 1987–88). Dep. Pres., Convention of Scottish Local Authorities, 1974–76; Chairman: Gas Higher Managers Assoc., Scotland, 1984–88; Gas Higher Managers Assoc., GB, 1987–88. Motherwell and Wishaw Burgh Council: Councillor, 1958–77; Bailie, 1960–64; Chm., Housing Cttee, 1960–71; Chm., Policy and Resources Cttee, 1974–77;

Leader, 1960–77; Chm., Motherwell DC, 1974–77; Provost, Burgh of Motherwell and Wishaw, 1971–75. Gov., Erskine Hosp., 1993–. Hon. Pres., Royal Marines, Lanarks, 1993–. JP Motherwell District, 1974 (Mem. JP Adv. Cttee); DL Motherwell, Hamilton, Monklands, E Kilbride and Clydesdale Districts, 1989. Gold Medal of Schweinfurt, Bavaria, 1977 (Internat. Relations). *Recreations:* football (watching), philately. *Address:* 36 Shand Street, Wishaw, Lanarks ML2 8HN.

SNEDDON, Prof. Ian Naismith, OBE 1969; MA Cantab, DSc Glasgow; FRS 1983; FRSE; CMath, FIMA; FRSA; Member of the Polish Academy of Sciences; Emeritus Professor of Mathematics, University of Glasgow, 1985; *b* 8 Dec. 1919; *o s* of Naismith Sneddon and Mary Ann Cameron; *m* 1943, Mary Campbell Macgregor; two *s* one *d*. *Educ:* Hyndland School, Glasgow; The University of Glasgow; Trinity College, Cambridge (Senior Scholar, 1941). Scientific Officer, Ministry of Supply, 1942–45; Research Worker, H. H. Wills Physical Lab., Univ. of Bristol, 1945–46; Lecturer in Natural Philosophy, Univ. of Glasgow, 1946–50; Professor of Mathematics in University Coll. of N Staffordshire, 1950–56 (Senior Tutor of the College, 1954–56); Simson Prof. of Mathematics, Univ. of Glasgow, 1956–85 (Dean of Faculty of Science, 1970–72, Senate Assessor on Univ. Court, 1973–77); Visiting Professor: Duke Univ., North Carolina, 1959 and 1960; Michigan State Univ., 1967; Univ. of California, Berkeley, 1979; La Trobe Univ., 1984; Strathclyde Univ., 1985–91; Georgia Inst of Technol., 1986; Adjunct Prof., North Carolina State Univ., 1965–72; Visiting Lecturer: Univ. of Palermo, 1953 and 1980; Serbian Acad. of Sciences, 1958; Univ. of Warsaw, 1959, 1973, 1975; Canadian Mathematical Congress, 1961; Polish Acad. of Sciences, 1962; US Midwest Mechanics Research Seminar, 1963 and 1981; Univ. of Zagreb, 1964; Univ. of Calgary, 1968; Indiana Univ., 1970–80; Kuwait Univ., 1972; CISM, Udine, 1972, 1974; Britton Lectr, McMaster Univ., 1979; Huber Lectr, Polish Acad. of Sciences, 1980. NSF Distinguished Vis. Scientist, State Univ., New York, 1969. Member: various govt scientific cttees, 1950–80; Adv. Council on Scientific Research and Tech. Development, Min. of Supply, 1953–56, Min. of Defence, 1965–68; Univs Science and Technology Bd (SRC), 1965–69; Adv. Council of Scottish Opera, 1972–92 (Vice-Chm., 1979–92); Bd of Scottish Nat. Orch., 1976–83; Bd of Citizens Theatre, Glasgow, 1975– (Vice-Chm.); BBC Central Music Adv. Cttee, 1978–85; Chm., BBC Scottish Music Adv. Cttee, 1978–85; Mem. Council, Scottish Soc. of Composers, 1981–83; Vice-Pres., RSE, 1966–69 and 1979–82. Pres., Scottish-Polish Cultural Assoc., 1970–84. Kelvin Medal, Univ. of Glasgow, 1948; Makdougall-Brisbane Prize, RSE, 1956–58; Soc. of Engrg Sci. Medal, 1979. Mem., Order of Long-Leaf Pine, USA, 1964; Hon. Fellow, Soc. of Engng Sci., USA, 1977; Foreign Mem., Acad. of Scis, Turin. Hon. DSc: Warsaw, 1973; Heriot-Watt, 1982; Hull, 1983; Strathclyde, 1994. Comdr's Cross, Order of Polonia Restituta, 1969; Comdr, Order of Merit (Poland), 1979; Medal of Cultural Merit, Poland, 1983. *Publications:* (with N. F. Mott) Wave Mechanics and Its Applications, 1948; Fourier Transforms, 1951; Special Functions of Mathematical Physics and Chemistry, 1956; The Elements of Partial Differential Equations, 1956; Introduction to the Mathematics of Biology and Medicine (with J. G. Defares), 1960; Fourier Series, 1961; Zagadnienie Szczelin w Teorii Sprezystasci, 1962; Mixed Boundary Value Problems in Potential Theory, 1966; Crack Problems in the Mathematical Theory of Elasticity (with M. Lowengrub), 1969; An Introduction to the Use of Integral Transforms, 1972; Metoda Transformacji Calkowych w Mieszanych Zogadnieniach Brzegowych, 1974; The Linear Theory of Thermoelasticity, 1974; (ed) Encyclopedic Dictionary of Mathematics for Engineers, 1976; (with G. Eason, W. Nowacki and Z. Olesiak) Integral Transform Methods in Elasticity, 1977; (with E. L. Ince) The Solution of Ordinary Differential Equations, 1987; articles in Handbuch der Physik, 1956–58; scientific papers on quantum theory of nuclei, theory of elasticity, and boundary value problems in jls. *Recreations:* music, painting and photography. *Address:* 19 Crown Terrace, Glasgow G12 9ES. *T:* 0141–339 4114. *Club:* Glasgow Art.

SNEDDON, Robert, CMG 1976; MBE 1945; HM Diplomatic Service, retired; *b* 8 June 1920; *m* 1945, Kathleen Margaret Smith; two *d*. *Educ:* Dalziel High Sch., Motherwell; Kettering Grammar Sch.; University Coll., Nottingham. HM Forces, 1940–46: 8th Army, ME and Italy, 1942–45; 30 Corps, Germany (Major), 1945–46. Joined Foreign (subseq. Diplomatic) Service, 1946; 3rd Sec., Warsaw, 1946; 2nd Sec., Stockholm, 1950; FO, 1954; 1st Sec., Oslo, 1956; 1st Sec., Berlin, 1961; FO, 1963; Counsellor, Bonn, 1969; FCO, 1971, retired 1977. *Recreations:* golf, music. *Address:* Windrose, Church Road, Horsell, Woking, Surrey GU21 4QS. *T:* Woking (01483) 765745. *Club:* Westhill Golf.

SNELGROVE, Rt. Rev. Donald George, TD 1972; Bishop Suffragan of Hull, 1981–94; *b* 21 April 1925; *s* of William Henry Snelgrove and Beatrice Snelgrove (*née* Upshell); *m* 1949, Sylvia May Lowe; one *s* one *d*. *Educ:* Queens' Coll. and Ridley Hall, Cambridge (MA). Served War, commn (Exec. Br.) RNVR, 1943–46. Cambridge, 1946–50; ordained, 1950; Curate: St Thomas, Oakwood, 1950–53; St Anselm's, Hatch End, Dio. London, 1953–56; Vicar of: Dronfield with Unstone, Dio. Derby, 1956–62; Hessle, Dio. York, 1963–70; Archdeacon of the East Riding, 1970–81. Rural Dean of Hull, 1966–70; Canon of York, 1969–81. Director: Central Bd of Finance, 1975–; Ecclesiastical Insurance Gp, 1978–94; Church Schools Co., 1981–; Allchurches, 1992–. Chaplain T&AVR, 1960–73. *Recreation:* travel. *Address:* Kingston House, 8 Park View, Barton on Humber DN18 6AX. *T:* Barton on Humber (01652) 634484.

SNELL, Rt. Rev. George Boyd, DD, PhD; *b* Toronto, Ontario, 17 June 1907; *s* of John George Snell and Minnie Alice Boyd; *m* 1934, Esther Mary. *Educ:* Trinity College, Toronto. BA 1929, MA 1930, PhD 1937, DD 1948. Deacon, Toronto, 1931; Priest, Niagara (for Tor.), 1932; Curate of St Michael and All Angels, Tor., 1931–39; Rector, 1940–48; Private Chaplain to Bp of Tor., 1945–48; Rector of Pro-Cathedral, Calgary, and Dean of Calgary, 1948–51; Exam. Chaplain to Bp of Calgary, 1948–51; Rector of St Clem. Eglinton, Tor., 1951–56; Archdeacon of Toronto, 1953–56; Exam. Chaplain to Bp of Toronto, 1953–55. Consecrated Bp Suffragan of Toronto, 1956; elected Bp-Coadjutor of Toronto, 1959; Bishop of Toronto, 1966–72. Hon. DD: Wycliffe Coll., Toronto, 1959; Huron Coll., Ontario, 1968. *Address:* 1210 Glen Road, Mississauga, Ont. L5H 3K8, Canada. *Club:* National (Toronto).

SNELL, Dr George Davis; geneticist; *b* Bradford, Mass, 19 Dec. 1903; *s* of Cullen Bryant and Katharine Davis Snell; *m* 1937, Rhoda Carson; three *s*. *Educ:* Dartmouth Coll. (BS 1926); Harvard Univ. (MS 1928; ScD 1930). Instr in Zoology, Dartmouth Coll., 1929–30, Brown Univ., 1930–31; Res. Fellow, Texas Univ., 1931–33; Asst Prof., Washington Univ., St Louis, 1933–34; Jackson Laboratory: Res. Associate, 1935–56; Sen. Staff Scientist, 1957–73, now Emeritus. Guggenheim Fellow, Texas Univ., 1953–54. Mem., Allergy and Immunology Study Sect., NIH, 1958–62. Member: Amer. Acad. of Arts and Scis; Nat. Acad. of Scis; French Acad. of Scis (foreign associate); Amer. Philosophical Soc., 1982; Hon. Member: British Transplantation Soc.; British Soc. for Immunology, 1983. Hon. MD Charles Univ., Prague, 1967; Hon. DSc: Dartmouth, 1974; Gustavus Adolphus Coll., 1981; Bates Coll., 1981; Ohio State Univ., 1984; Hon. LLD: Univ. of Maine, 1981; Colby Coll., 1982. Bertner Foundn Award, 1962; Gregor Mendel Medal, Czechoslovak Acad. of Scis, 1967; Gairdner Foundn Award, 1976; Prize in Medicine, Wolf Foundn, 1978; (jt) Nobel Prize for Physiology or Medicine, 1980. *Publications:* (ed) The Biology of the Laboratory Mouse, 1941; (jtly) Histocompatibility, 1976; Search for a Rational Ethic, 1988; contribs to learned jls. *Address:* The Jackson Laboratory, Bar Harbor, ME 04609, USA; 21 Atlantic Avenue, Bar Harbor, ME 04609, USA.

SNELL, John Nicholas B.; *see* Blashford-Snell.

SNELL, Maeve, (Mrs Gordon Snell); *see* Binchy, M.

SNELL, Philip D.; Member (Lab), Tyne and Wear County Council, 1974–86, Chairman, General Services Committee, 1981–86; *b* 14 Oct. 1915; *s* of Alfred William Snell and Jane Herdman; *m* 1939, Selina Waite; two *d*. *Educ:* Causey Road Council Sch., Gateshead. Miner, Marley Hill Colliery, Gateshead, 1929–57; Industrial Relations Advr, NCB, 1957–61; Education and Welfare Officer: Durham CC, 1961–73; Gateshead MDC, 1973. Chm., Tyne and Wear CC, 1980–81. Trustee, Whickham Glebe Sports Club. *Recreation:* enjoying Northern Federation Brewery Beer. *Address:* School House, Marley Hill, Whickham, Gateshead, Tyne and Wear NE11 9RQ. *T:* 0191–488 7006. *Club:* Sunniside Social (Gateshead).

SNELLGROVE, Anthony; *see* Snellgrove, J. A.

SNELLGROVE, David Llewellyn, LittD, PhD; FBA 1969; Professor of Tibetan in the University of London, 1974–82, now Emeritus Professor (Reader, 1960–74, Lecturer, 1950–60); Founder Director of Institute of Tibetan Studies, Tring, 1966–82; *b* Portsmouth, 29 June 1920; *s* of Lt-Comdr Clifford Snellgrove, RN, and Eleanor Maud Snellgrove. *Educ:* Christ's Hospital, Horsham; Southampton Univ.; Queens' Coll., Cambridge. Served War of 1939–45: commissioned in Infantry, 1942; Intell. Officer in India until 1946. Then started seriously on oriental studies at Cambridge, 1946, cont. Rome, 1949–50. BA Cantab 1949, MA Cantab 1953; PhD London 1954; LittD Cantab 1969. Made expedns to India and the Himalayas, 1953–54, 1956, 1960, 1964, 1967, 1974–75, 1978–80, 1982, continued with regular travel in Indonesia, 1987–; founded with Mr Hugh E. Richardson an Inst. of Tibetan Studies, 1966. Apptd Consultant to Vatican in new Secretariat for non-Christian Religions, 1967. Many professional visits abroad, mainly to W Europe and USA. *Publications:* Buddhist Himalaya, 1957; The Hevajra Tantra, 1959; Himalayan Pilgrimage, 1961, 2nd edn 1981; Four Lamas of Dolpo, 1967; The Nine Ways of Bon, 1967, repr. 1980; (with H. E. Richardson) A Cultural History of Tibet, 1968, 2nd edn 1980; (with T. Skorupski) The Cultural Heritage of Ladakh, vol. I, 1977, vol. II, 1980; (ed) The Image of the Buddha, 1978; Indo-Tibetan Buddhism, 1987; articles in Arts Asiatiques (Paris), Bulletin of the Secretariat for non-Christian Religions (Rome), etc. *Address:* Via Matteo Gay 26/7, 10066 Torre Pellice, Italy.

SNELLGROVE, (John) Anthony; HM Diplomatic Service, retired; Secretary, British Brush Manufacturers' Association, 1977–89; *b* 29 Jan. 1922; *s* of late John Snellgrove and Anne Mary Priscilla (*née* Brown); *m* 1956, Rose Jeanne Marie Suzanne (*née* Paris); two *d*. *Educ:* Wimbledon Coll.; Stonyhurst Coll.; Peterhouse, Cambridge (1940–41 and 1945–48; BA and MA). Served War, Royal Navy, latterly as temp. actg Lieut, RNVR, 1941–45. Asst Principal, Colonial Office, 1948–49; joined Foreign Service, Oct. 1949; 2nd Sec., Prague, 1950–51; FO (Econ. Relations Dept), 1951–53; HM Vice-Consul, Tamsui (Formosa), 1953–56; 1st Sec., 1954; FO (SE Asia Dept and UN (E&S) Dept), 1956–59; 1st Sec., Bangkok, 1959–62; 1st Sec. and Consul, Mogadishu (Somali Republic), 1962–63; FO (Arabian and European Econ. Org. Depts), 1963–66; 1st Sec., Holy See, 1967–71; Counsellor, 1971; Dep. Sec.-Gen. (Economic), CENTO, 1971–73; Counsellor and Head of Chancery, Carácas, 1973–75, retired, 1977. *Recreations:* music, bridge. *Address:* 13 Chantry Hurst, Woodcote, Epsom, Surrey KT18 7BN.

SNELLING, Sir Arthur (Wendell), KCMG 1960 (CMG 1954); KCVO 1962; HM Diplomatic Service, retired; *b* 7 May 1914; *s* of Arthur and Ellen Snelling; *m* 1939, Frieda, *d* of late Lt-Col F. C. Barnes; one *s*. *Educ:* Ackworth Sch., Yorks; University Coll., London (BSc Econ.). Study Gp Sec., Royal Inst. of Internat. Affairs, 1934–36; Dominions Office, 1936; Private Sec. to Parl. Under Sec., 1939; Joint Sec. to UK Delegn to Internat. Monetary Conference, Bretton Woods, USA, 1944; accompanied Lord Keynes on missions to USA and Canada, 1943 and 1944; Dep. High Comr for UK in New Zealand, 1947–50, in S Africa, 1953–55; Assistant Under-Secretary of State, Commonwealth Relations Office, 1956–59; British High Comr in Ghana, 1959–61; Dep. Under-Sec. of State, FCO (formerly CRO), 1961–69; Ambassador to South Africa, 1970–73. Dir, Gordon and Gotch Holdings Ltd, 1973–81. Fellow, UCL, 1970; Mem., College Council, UCL, 1976–86. Vice-Pres., UK-S Africa Trade Assoc., 1974–80; Mem., Ciskei Commn, 1978–80. *Address:* 19 Albany Park Road, Kingston-upon-Thames, Surrey KT2 5SW. *T:* 0181–549 4160. *Club:* Reform.

SNODGRASS, Prof. Anthony McElrea, FSA; FBA 1979; Laurence Professor of Classical Archaeology, University of Cambridge, since 1976; Fellow of Clare College, Cambridge, since 1977; *b* 7 July 1934; *s* of William McElrea Snodgrass, MC (Major, RAMC), and Kathleen Mabel (*née* Owen); *m* 1st, 1959, Ann Elizabeth Vaughan (marr. diss.); three *d*; 2nd, 1983, Annemarie Künzl; one *s*. *Educ:* Marlborough Coll.; Worcester Coll., Oxford (BA 1959, MA, DPhil 1963). FSA 1978. Served with RAF in Iraq, 1953–55 (National Service). Student of the British School, Athens, 1959–60; University of Edinburgh: Lectr in Classical Archaeology, 1961; Reader, 1969; Prof., 1975. Sather Classical Prof., Univ. of California, Berkeley, 1984–85. Myres Meml Lectr, Oxford, 1981. British Academy: Vice-Pres., 1990–92; Mem., Humanities Res. Bd, 1994–. Corresp. Mem., German Archaeol. Inst., 1977. *Publications:* Early Greek Armour and Weapons, 1964; Arms and Armour of the Greeks, 1967; The Dark Age of Greece, 1971; Archaic Greece, 1980; Narration and Allusion in Early Greek Art, 1982; An Archaeology of Greece, 1987; contrib. Jl of Hellenic Studies, Proc. of Prehistoric Soc., Gnomon, etc. *Recreations:* mountaineering, skiing. *Address:* Museum of Classical Archaeology, Sidgwick Avenue, Cambridge CB3 9DA. *T:* Cambridge (01223) 335155. *Clubs:* Alpine, Alpine Ski.

See also J. M. O. Snodgrass.

SNODGRASS, John Michael Owen, CMG 1981; HM Diplomatic Service, retired; *b* 12 Aug. 1928; *e s* of Major W. M. Snodgrass, MC, RAMC; *m* 1957, Jennifer James; three *s*. *Educ:* Marlborough Coll.; Trinity Hall, Cambridge (MA, Maths and Moral Scis). Diplomatic Service: 3rd Sec., Rome, 1953–56; FO, 1956–60; 1st Sec., Beirut, 1960–63; S Africa, 1964–67; FCO, 1967–70; Consul-Gen., Jerusalem, 1970–74; Counsellor, South Africa, 1974–77; Hd of South Pacific Dept, FCO, 1977–80; Ambassador: to Zaire, 1980–83 (also to Burundi, Rwanda and Congo); to Bulgaria, 1983–86. CStJ 1975. *Recreations:* ski-ing, tennis, travel. *Address:* The Barn House, North Warnborough, Basingstoke, Hants RG25 1ET. *T:* Basingstoke (01256) 702816.

See also A. McE. Snodgrass.

SNOW, Adrian John, MA, MEd; Development Officer, Tennis and Rackets Association, since 1994; *b* 20 March 1939; *e s* of Edward Percy John Snow and Marjory Ellen Nicholls; *m* 1963, Alessina Teresa Kilkelly (marr. diss. 1994); one *s* one *d*. *Educ:* Hurstpierpoint Coll.; Trinity Coll., Dublin (BA, MA, HDipEd); Reading Univ. (MEd). Asst Master, The New Beacon, Sevenoaks, 1958–59; RAF Pilot Officer, 1963; Assistant Master: King's Sch., Sherborne, 1964; High Sch., Dublin, 1964–65 (part-time); Brighton Coll., 1965–66; The Oratory School: Head of Econ. and Pol Studies, 1966–73; Head of Hist., 1967–73; Housemaster, 1967–73; acting Headmaster, Sept. 1972–Mar. 1973; Headmaster, 1973–88.

Warden, Oratory Sch. Assoc., 1989–93; Director: Oratory Construction Ltd, 1988–93; Oratory Trading Ltd, 1990–93. Governor: Prior Park Coll., 1981–87 (Mem., Action Cttee, 1980–81); Moreton Hall Prep. Sch., 1984–93; St Mary's Sch., Ascot, 1986–94; St Edward's Sch. and Highlands Sch., Reading, 1987– (Chm., 1990–). Member: Berks Cttee, Prince's Trust, 1989–93 (Vice-Chm., 1990–91); RYA; Tennis Cttee, Tennis and Rackets Assoc., 1990– (Chm., Court Develt Cttee, 1992–). Pres., Old Oratorian CC, 1994–; Hon. Treas., Friends of Hardwick Tennis Court, 1990–. *Recreations:* athletics (univ. colour), cricket, hockey (Jun. Internat. trialist), Real Tennis, Rugby (Combined Univs).

SNOW, Antony Edmund, MIPA, FIPR; Chairman, Hill and Knowlton, Europe, Middle East and Africa, Ltd, since 1994; *b* 5 Dec. 1932; 2nd *s* of Thomas Maitland Snow, *qv*; *m* 1961, Caroline Wilson; one *s* two *d. Educ:* Sherborne Sch.; New College, Oxford. National Service, commnd in 10th Royal Hussars, 1952–53; Royal Wiltshire Yeomanry, TA, 1953–63. W. S. Crawford, 1958; joined Charles Barker & Sons, 1961: Dep. Chm., 1975; Dir, 1983–; Chm. and Chief Exec., 1983–87; Chief Exec. and Dep. Chm., 1991–92, Chm., 1992–94, Hill and Knowlton (UK). Non-exec. Dir, Hogg Gp (formerly Hogg Robinson & Gardner Mountain), 1988–. Vice-Pres., Market Planning, Steuben Glass, 1976; Dep. Dir, Corning Museum of Glass, 1976 (Trustee, 1983–); Dir, Rockwell Museum, 1979. Member: Cttee of Management, Courtauld Institute of Art, 1984–89; Exec. Cttee, Nat. Art-Collections Fund, 1985–; Ancient Monuments Cttee, English Heritage, 1988–91; Design Council, 1989–94. Trustee, Monteverdi Choir, 1988–. Council, RCA. *Recreation:* English watercolours. *Address:* 16 Rumbold Road, SW6 2JA. *Clubs:* Cavalry and Guards, City of London.

See also Thomas Snow.

SNOW, Jonathan George, (Jon Snow); television journalist; Presenter, Channel Four News, since 1989; *b* 28 Sept. 1947; *s* of late Rt Rev. George Snow and Joan Snow; partner, Madeleine Colvin; two *d. Educ:* St Edward's School, Oxford; Liverpool Univ. (no degree; sent down following political disturbances, 1970). VSO, Uganda, 1967–68; Co-ordinator, New Horizon Youth Centre, Covent Garden, 1970–73 (Chm., 1986–); Journalist, Independent Radio News, LBC, 1973–76; Independent Television News: Reporter, 1976–83; Washington Correspondent, 1983–86; Diplomatic Editor, 1986–89; main presenter, Election '92, ITV. Mem., NUJ. Vis. Prof., Broadcast Journalism, Nottingham Trent Univ., 1992–. Chairman: Prison Reform Trust, 1992–; Media Trust, 1995–; Trustee, Noel Buxton Trust, 1992–. Hon. DLitt Nottingham Trent, 1994. Monte Carlo Golden Nymph Award, for Eritrea Air Attack reporting, 1979; TV Reporter of the Year, for Afghanistan, Iran and Iraq reporting, RTS, 1980; Valiant for Truth Award, for El Salvador reporting, 1982; Internat. Award, for El Salvador reporting, RTS, 1982; Home News Award, for Kegworth Air Crash reporting, RTS, 1989. *Publication:* Atlas of Today, 1987. *Address:* Channel Four News, ITN, 200 Gray's Inn Road, WC1X 8HB. *T:* 0171–430 4237.

SNOW, Rear-Adm. Kenneth Arthur, CB 1987; Receiver-General and Chapter Clerk, Westminster Abbey, since 1987; *b* 14 April 1934; *s* of Arthur Chandos Pole Snow and Evelyn (*née* Joyce); *m* 1956, Pamela Elizabeth Terry (*née* Sorrell); one *s* two *d. Educ:* St Andrews College, Grahamstown; South African Nautical College. Joined RN, 1952; commanded HMS Kirkliston, 1962; qualified navigation specialist, 1963; commanded: HMS Llandaff, 1970; HMS Arethusa, 1979; HMS Hermes, 1983; Dep. Asst Chief of Staff (Ops), SACEUR, 1984–87, retired. FNI 1992. *Recreations:* gardening, painting. *Address:* 2 The Cloister, Westminster Abbey, SW1P 3PA. *Club:* Army and Navy.

See also Rear-Adm. R. E. Snow.

SNOW, Peter John; television presenter, reporter and author; *b* Dublin, 20 April 1938; *s* of Brig. John F. Snow, CBE and Peggy Mary Pringle; *m* 1st, 1964, Alison Carter (marr. diss. 1975); one *s* one *d*; 2nd, 1976, Ann Macmillan; one *s* two *d. Educ:* Wellington College; Balliol College, Oxford (BA Hons Greats 1962). 2nd Lieut, Somerset Light Infantry, 1956–58, served Plymouth and Warminster. Independent Television News: newscaster amd reporter, 1962–66; diplomatic and defence corresp., 1966–79; events covered include: Cyprus, 1964; Vietnam, Laos, Malaysia, 1968–70; China, 1972; Mideast war, 1973; Nigerian civil war, 1969; Oman, 1975; Rhodesia, 1965–79; Britain and EEC, 1970–73; co-presenter, Gen. Elections, Feb. and Oct. 1974, 1979; BBC: presenter, Newsnight, 1979–; events covered or reported include: Zimbabwe independence, 1980; Falklands war, 1982; S Africa, 1986; co-presenter, Gen. Elections, 1983, 1987 and 1992, US elections. *Publications:* (jtly) Leila's Hijack War, 1970; Hussein: a biography, 1972. *Recreations:* sailing, ski-ing, model railways, photography. *Address:* c/o BBC TV Centre, Wood Lane, W12 7RJ. *T:* 0181–576 7306.

SNOW, Philip Albert, OBE 1985 (MBE 1979); JP; MA; FRSA; FRAI; author; *b* 7 Aug. 1915; *s* of William Edward Snow, FRCO and Ada Sophia Robinson; *m* 1940, Anne Harris; one *d. Educ:* Newton's Sch., Leicester; Christ's Coll., Cambridge (MA Hons). FRAI 1952. HM Colonial Administrative Service: Provincial Comr, Magistrate and Asst Colonial Sec., Fiji and Western Pacific, 1937–52; ADC to Governor and C-in-C, Fiji, 1939; Dep. Sheriff, Fiji, 1940–52; Official Mem., Legislative Council, Fiji, 1951; Fiji Govt Liaison Officer, US and NZ Forces, 1942–44. Bursar, Rugby Sch., 1952–76. Mem., Jt Cttee, Governing Bodies of Schools' Assoc., 1958–65. President: Public Schs Bursars' Assoc., 1962–65; The Worthing Soc., 1983–; Vice-Pres., Fiji Soc., 1944–52. Founder, Suva Cricket Assoc., Nadi Cricket Assoc. and six other dist cricket assocs, 1939–49; founder, Fiji Cricket Assoc., 1946, Vice-Patron, 1952–; Captain, Fiji Cricket Team, NZ first-class tour, 1948; Liaison Officer/Manager, first Fiji Cricket Team in England, 1979. International Cricket Conference: Perm. Rep. of Fiji, 1965–90; Mem., first Cricket World Cup Cttee, 1971–75; first Chm., Associate Member Countries, 1982–87; Perm. Rep. of Fiji, Internat. Cricket Council, 1990–94. Organiser, Rugby Sch. 400th anniv. celebrations, 1967; designer, Fiji Govt stamps for centenary of Fiji cricket, 1974. Broadcasts on Fiji radio, BBC and in NZ, 1948–. Literary Executor and Executor of Lord Snow. JP Warwicks, 1967–76, and W Sussex, 1976–. FRSA 1984. Foreign Specialist Award, USA Govt, 1964. *Publications:* Air Raids Precautions Services, Lautoka, 1943; Cricket in the Fiji Islands, 1949; Report on the Visit of Three Bursars to the United States of America and Canada in 1964, 1965; Best Stories of the South Seas, 1967; Bibliography of Fiji, Tonga and Rotuma, vol. 1, 1969; (with Stefanie Waine) The People from the Horizon: an illustrated history of the Europeans among the South Sea Islanders, 1979; Stranger and Brother: a portrait of C. P. Snow, 1982; contrib. TLS, Sunday Times, Daily Telegraph, The Times, Jls of RAI, RGS, Fiji Museum, Pacific History and Polynesian Soc., Jl de la Société des Océanistes, Amer. Anthropologist, Wisden's Almanack, Barclays World of Cricket, Dictionary of Nat. Biog; numerous reviews of, and introductions to, Pacific and general books. *Recreations:* taming robins; formerly cricket (Capt., Leics 2nd XI, 1936–38, Leics, 1946, Cambridge Crusaders, Googlies, MCC (Capt., 1955–65), Authors, Fiji first-class), chess (half-Blue), table-tennis (half-Blue and Cambs), deck-tennis, tennis. *Address:* Gables, Station Road, Angmering, West Sussex BN16 4HY. *T:* Rustington (01903) 773594. *Clubs:* MCC (Hon. Life Mem. for services to internat. cricket, 1970), Stragglers of Asia (Hon. Life Mem.); De Flamingos (Hon. Mem.) (Holland); Mastermind; Hawks (Cambridge).

SNOW, Surg. Rear-Adm. Ronald Edward, CB 1991; LVO 1972; OBE 1977; Surgeon Rear Admiral (Operational Medical Services), 1989–91; *b* 17 May 1933; *s* of Arthur Chandos Pole Snow (formerly Soppitt) and Evelyn Dorothea Snow (*née* Joyce); *m* 1959, Valerie Melian French; two *d. Educ:* St Andrew's Coll., Grahamstown, S Africa; Trinity Coll., Dublin (MA, MB, BCh, BAO); MFOM, DA, LMCC. HMS Victorious, 1966; HMS Dolphin, 1967; HMY Britannia, 1970; MoD, 1973 and 1977; Inst. of Naval Medicine, 1975 and 1984; Staff of Surg. Rear Adm. (Naval Hosps), 1980; Staff of C-in-C Fleet, 1982; Asst Surg. Gen. (Service Hosps), 1985; Surg. Rear Adm. (Support Med. Services), 1987. QHP 1984–91. OStJ 1986. *Recreations:* National Hunt racing, cruising. *Clubs:* Army and Navy; Royal Naval Sailing Association (Portsmouth).

See also Rear-Adm. K. A. Snow.

SNOW, Thomas; Director, Oxford University Careers Service (formerly Secretary, Oxford University Appointments Committee), since 1970; Fellow, New College, Oxford, since 1973; *b* 16 June 1929; *e s* of Thomas Maitland Snow, *qv*; *m* 1961, Elena Tidmarsh; two *s* one *d. Educ:* Winchester Coll. (Fellow, 1985); New Coll., Oxford. Joined Crittall Manufacturing Co. Ltd as Management Trainee, 1952; Dir 1966; Director: Crittall Hope Ltd, Darlington Simpson Rolling Mills, Minex Metals Ltd, 1968. Mem. Standing Cttee, Assoc. of Graduate Careers Adv. Services, 1973–77, 1985–89. Held various positions in local govt; Marriage Counsellor, 1964–70; Chairman: Relate—Oxfordshire (formerly Oxford Marriage Guidance Council), 1974–90; Cttee of Management, Oxford Univ. Counselling Service, 1992–. JP 1964–69. *Address:* 157 Woodstock Road, Oxford OX2 7NA.

See also A. E. Snow.

SNOW, Thomas Maitland, CMG 1934; *b* 21 May 1890; *s* of Thomas Snow, Cleve, Exeter, and Edith Banbury; *m* 1st, 1927, Phyllis Annette Malcolmson; three *s*; 2nd, 1949, Sylvia, *d* of W. Delmar, Buda-Pest. *Educ:* Winchester; New Coll., Oxford. 1st Secretary, HM Diplomatic Service, 1923; Counsellor, 1930; Minister: to Cuba, 1935–37; to Finland, 1937–40; to Colombia, 1941–44 (Ambassador, 1944–45); to Switzerland, 1946–49. Retired, 1950. *Recreation:* metaphysics. *Address:* Chemin des Vuarennes 35, 1820 Montreux, Switzerland.

See also A. E. Snow, Thomas Snow.

SNOWDEN, Rt. Rev. John Samuel Philip; Bishop of Cariboo, 1974–91. *Educ:* Anglican Theological Coll., Vancouver (LTh 1951); Univ. of British Columbia (BA 1956). Deacon 1951, priest 1952; Curate: Kaslo-Kokanee, 1951–53; Oak Bay, 1953–57; Nanaimo, 1957–60; Incumbent of St Timothy, Vancouver, 1960–64; Priest Pastoral, Christ Church Cathedral, Vancouver, 1964–66; Rector of St Timothy, Edmonton, 1966–71; Dean and Rector of St Paul's Cathedral, Kamloops, 1971–74. Domestic Chaplain to Bishop of Cariboo, 1971–73.

SNOWDON, 1st Earl of, *cr* 1961; **Antony Charles Robert Armstrong-Jones,** GCVO 1969; RDI 1978; FCSD; Viscount Linley, 1961; Photographer, Telegraph Magazine, since 1990; Constable of Caernarfon Castle since 1963; Provost, Royal College of Art, since 1995; *b* 7 March 1930; *s* of Ronald Owen Lloyd Armstrong-Jones, MBE, QC, DL (*d* 1966), and Anne (*d* 1992), *o d* of Lt-Col Leonard Messel, OBE (later Countess of Rosse); *m* 1st, 1960, HRH The Princess Margaret (marr. diss. 1978); one *s* one *d*; 2nd, 1978, Lucy Lindsay-Hogg, *d* of Donald Davies; one *d. Educ:* Eton; Jesus Coll., Cambridge (coxed winning Univ. crew, 1950). Joined Staff of Council of Industrial Design, 1961, continued on a consultative basis, 1962–87, also an Editorial Adviser of Design Magazine, 1961–87; an Artistic Adviser to the Sunday Times and Sunday Times Publications Ltd, 1962–90. Designed: Snowdon Aviary, London Zoo, 1965; Chairmobile, 1972. Mem. Council, National Fund for Research for Crippling Diseases; Mem., Prince of Wales Adv. Cttee on Disability; Patron, Circle of Guide Dog Owners; Chm., Working Party on Integrating the Disabled (Report 1976); Pres. for England, Cttee, International Year for Disabled People, 1981. Founder, Snowdon Award for Disabled Students, 1980. Hon. Fellow: Institute of British Photographers; Royal Photographic Soc.; Manchester College of Art and Design; Hon. Member: North Wales Society of Architects; South Wales Institute of Architects; Royal Welsh Yacht Club; Patron: Welsh Nat. Rowing Club; Metropolitan Union of YMCAs; British Water Ski Federation. President: Contemp. Art Society for Wales; Civic Trust for Wales; Welsh Theatre Company; Mem. Council, English Stage Co., 1978–82. Senior Fellow, RCA, 1986. FRSA. Dr *hc* Bradford, 1989; Hon. LLD Bath, 1989; Hon. DLitt Portsmouth, 1994. Silver Progress Medal, RPS, 1985. *Television films:* Don't Count the Candles, 1968 (2 Hollywood Emmy Awards; St George Prize, Venice; awards at Prague and Barcelona film festivals); Love of a Kind, 1969; Born to be Small, 1971 (Chicago Hugo Award); Happy being Happy, 1973; Mary Kingsley, 1975; Burke and Wills, 1975; Peter, Tina and Steve, 1977; Snowdon on Camera, BBC (presenter), 1981. *Exhibitions include:* Photocall, London, 1958; Assignments, Cologne, London, Brussels, USA, 1972, Japan, Canada, Denmark, Holland, 1975, Australia, 1976, France, 1977; Serendipity, Brighton, Bradford, 1989, Bath, 1990. *Publications:* London, 1958; Malta (in collaboration), 1958; Private View (in collaboration), 1965; A View of Venice, 1972; Assignments, 1972; Inchcape Review, 1977; (jtly) Pride of the Shires, 1979; Personal View, 1979; Sittings, 1983; Israel: a first view, 1986; (with Viscount Tonypandy) My Wales, 1986; Stills 1983–1987, 1987; Public Appearances 1987–1991, 1991. *Heir: s* Viscount Linley, *qv. Address:* 22 Launceston Place, W8 5RL. *Clubs:* Buck's, United Oxford & Cambridge University; Leander (Henley-on-Thames); Hawks (Cambridge).

See also under Royal Family, and Earl of Rosse.

SNOWLING, (George) Christopher (Edward); Legal Member, Mental Health Review Tribunal, since 1992; *b* 12 Aug. 1934; *s* of George Edward Snowling and Winifred Beryl (*née* Cave); *m* 1961, Flora Skells; one *s* one *d. Educ:* The Mercers' Sch.; Fitzwilliam House, Cambridge (MA). Admitted Solicitor, 1961; various local govt posts, 1958–71; Law Society: Legal Aid Admin, 1971–78; Secretary: Educn and Trng, 1978–85, Professional Purposes, 1985–86; Dir, Legal Aid, 1986–89; Hd of Quality Control and Professional Standards, Durnford Ford, solicitors, 1989–92. Mem., Cuckfield UDC, 1971–74; Mem. (C) Mid Sussex District Council, 1973–: Chm., 1981–82, 1986–87, 1987–88; Chm., Policy and Resources Cttee, 1988–91; Leader majority gp, 1991–; Mem. Council, Assoc. of Dist Councils, 1990–. Member: Mid Downs CHC, 1988–; Crawley & Horsham Med. Ethics Cttee, 1990–. FIMgt (FBIM 1988). *Recreations:* local government, painting. *Address:* Eldon Lodge, Pondcroft Road, Lindfield, West Sussex RH16 2HQ. *T:* Lindfield (01444) 482172.

SNOWMAN, (Michael) Nicholas; Chief Executive, South Bank Centre, London, since 1992 (General Director (Arts), 1986–92); *b* 18 March 1944; *s* of Kenneth Snowman and late Sallie Snowman (*née* Moghi-Levkine); *m* 1983, Margo Michelle Rouard; one *s. Educ:* Hall Sch. and Highgate Sch., London; Magdalene Coll., Cambridge (BA Hons Eng. Lit.). Asst to Hd of Music Staff, Glyndebourne Fest., 1967–69; Co-Founder and Gen. Man., London Sinfonietta, 1968–72; Administrator, Music Th. Ensemble, 1968–71; Artistic Dir, IRCAM, Centre d'Art et de Culture Georges Pompidou, 1972–86. Co-Founder, 1975, Artistic Advr, 1975–92, Bd Mem., 1992–, Ensemble InterContemporain; Mem. Music Cttee, Venice Biennale, 1979–86; Artistic Dir, Projects in 1980 (Stravinsky), 1981 (Webern), 1983 (Boulez), Fest. d'Automne de Paris; Programme Consultant, Cité de la Musique, La Villette, Paris, 1991. Mem. British Sect., Franco-British Council, 1995. Officier de l'Ordre des Arts et des Lettres (France), 1990 (Chevalier, 1985); Order of

Cultural Merit (Poland), 1990; Chevalier, l'Ordre National du Mérite (France), 1995. *Publications:* (co-ed) The Best of Granta, 1967; (series ed.) The Contemporary Composers, 1982–; papers and articles on music, cultural policy. *Recreations:* films, eating, spy novels. *Address:* South Bank Centre, Royal Festival Hall, SE1 8XX. *T:* 0171–921 0608. *Club:* Garrick.

SNYDER, Prof. Allan Whitenack, FRS 1990; FAA; FTS; Professor of Optical Physics and Visual Sciences, and Head of Optical Sciences Centre, Australian National University, since 1987; *b* 23 Nov. 1940; *s* of Edward H. Snyder, philanthropist, and Zelda (*née* Cotton), Broadway actress and psychodramatherapist. *Educ:* Central High Sch., Phil. (AB); Pennsylvania State Univ. (BS); MIT (SM); Harvard Univ. (MS); University Coll. London (PhD); DSc London. Greenland Ice Cap Communications Project, 1961; Gen. Telecom. and Elec. Res. Lab., 1963–67; Cons. to Brit. PO and Standard Telecom. Lab., 1968–70; Nat. Sci. Foundn Fellow, Yale Univ., 1970–71; Sen. Res. Fellow, Sen. Fellow, Professorial Fellow, ANU, 1971–79; John Simon Guggenheim Fellow, Yale Univ. Med. Sch., 1977–78; Hd, Dept of Applied Maths, Inst. for Advanced Studies, ANU, 1980–83; Royal Soc. Quest Res. Fellow, Cambridge Univ., 1987. Associate Editor, Jl of Optical Soc. of America, 1981–83. Fellow, Optical Soc. of Amer., 1980; Foundn Fellow, Nat. Vision Res. Inst. of Aust., 1983. Research Medal, Royal Soc. Vic., 1974; Edgeworth David Medal, Royal Soc. NSW, 1974; Thomas Rankin Lyle Medal, Aust. Acad. of Sci., 1985; Stuart Sutherland Meml Medal, Aust. Acad. of Technological Sci. and Engrg, 1990. *Publications:* Photoreceptor Optics, 1975; Optical Waveguide Theory, 1983; Optical Waveguide Sciences, 1983; articles on the visual system of animals and on the physics of light propagation in internat sci. jls. *Recreations:* art, culture, language and thought. *Address:* Optical Sciences Centre, Institute of Advanced Studies, Australian National University, Canberra, ACT 2601, Australia. *T:* (6) 2492626, *Fax* (6) 2495184.

SOAME, Sir Charles (John) Buckworth-Herne-, 12th Bt *cr* 1697; *b* 28 May 1932; *s* of Sir Charles Burnett Buckworth-Herne-Soame, 11th Bt, and Elsie May (*d* 1972), *d* of Walter Alfred Lloyd; *S* father, 1977; *m* 1958, Eileen Margaret Mary, *d* of Leonard Minton; one *s*. *Heir:* *s* Richard John Buckworth-Herne-Soame, *b* 17 Aug. 1970. *Address:* Sheen Cottage, Coalbrookdale, Telford, Salop TF8 7EQ.

SOAMES, Lady; Mary Soames, DBE 1980 (MBE (mil.) 1945); Member of Council, since 1978, and Chairman of Trustees, since 1991, Winston Churchill Memorial Trust; Chairman, Royal National Theatre Board, 1989–95; *b* 15 Sept. 1922; *y d* of late Rt Hon. Sir Winston Churchill, KG, OM, CH, FRS, and late Baroness Spencer-Churchill, GBE; *m* 1947, Captain Christopher Soames, Coldstream Guards, later Baron Soames, PC, GCMG, GCVO, CH, CBE (*d* 1987); three *s* two *d*. *Educ:* privately. Served War: Red Cross and WVS, 1939–41; ATS, 1941–46, with mixed anti-aircraft batteries in UK and Europe (Jun. Comdr). Accompanied father on various journeys; campaigned with husband through six elections whilst he was Conservative MP for Bedford, 1950–66; accompanied husband to Paris where he was Ambassador, 1968–72, and to Brussels where he was first British Vice Pres. of Eur. Commn, 1973–76; accompanied husband when he was appointed last British Governor of Southern Rhodesia, Dec. 1979–April 1980. Chm., UK Assoc. for Internat. Year of the Child, 1979. Governor, Harrow Sch., 1980–95. Hon. Freewoman, Skinners' Co., 1994. JP E Sussex, 1960–74. Hon. Fellow, Churchill Coll., Cambridge, 1983. Hon DLitt Sussex, 1989. *Publications:* Clementine Churchill by Her Daughter Mary Soames, 1979 (a Wolfson Prize for History, and Yorkshire Post Prize for Best First Work, 1979); A Churchill Family Album—A Personal Anthology Selected by Mary Soames, 1982; The Profligate Duke: George Spencer-Churchill 5th Duke of Marlborough and his Duchess, 1987; Winston Churchill: his Life as a Painter: a Memoir by his Daughter Mary Soames, 1990. *Recreations:* reading, sight-seeing, gardening. *Club:* Grillions.

See also Earl Peel, Hon. A. N. W. Soames.

SOAMES, Hon. (Arthur) Nicholas (Winston); MP (C) Crawley, since 1983; Minister of State for the Armed Forces, Ministry of Defence, since 1994, *b* 12 Feb. 1948; *s* of Baron Soames, PC, GCMG, GCVO, CH, CBE and of Lady Soames, *qv*; *m* 1st, 1981, Catherine Weatherall (marr. diss. 1990); one *s*; 2nd, 1993, Serena, *d* of Sir John L. E. Smith, *qv*. *Educ:* Eton. Served 11th Hussars (PAO), 1967–70 (2nd Lieut); Equerry to the Prince of Wales, 1970–72; Asst Dir, Sedgwick Group, 1976–82. PPS to Minister of State for Employment, 1984–85, to Sec. of State, DoE, 1987–89, to Sec. of State, DTI, 1989–90; Parly Sec., MAFF, 1992–94. *Recreation:* country pursuits. *Address:* House of Commons, SW1A 0AA. *T:* 0171–219 3000. *Clubs:* White's, Turf.

SOANE, Leslie James, OBE 1985; CEng, MICE; FCIT, FIMgt; FRSA; Member of Board and Director, Railway Heritage Trust, since 1985; *b* 15 Jan. 1926; *s* of Arthur Edward Soane and Florence May Herring; *m* 1950, Joan Edith Mayo; one *s* one *d*. *Educ:* Watford Central Sch.; London Univ. Civil Engineer posts: London Midland Region, 1948–55; Eastern Region, 1955–62; LMR, 1962–71; Chief Civil Engr, Western Region, 1971–75; Dep. Gen. Manager, WR, 1975–77; Gen. Manager, Scottish Region, 1977–83; Man. Dir (Reorganisation), BRB, 1983–85. Lt-Col, then Col, Engr and Transport Staff Corps, RE (TA), 1985–. *Recreations:* theatre, reading, golf. *Address:* St Michael's Croft, Woodcock Hill, Berkhamsted, Herts HP4 3PJ. *T:* Berkhamsted (01442) 875831.

SOARES, Dr Mário Alberto Nobre Lopes; President of Portugal, since 1986; *b* 7 Dec. 1924; *s* of João Lopes Soares and Elisa Nobre Soares; *m* 1949, Maria Barroso Soares; one *s* one *d*. *Educ:* Univ. of Lisbon (BA 1951; JD 1957); Faculty of Law, Faculty of History and Philosophy, Sorbonne. LèsL, LenD. Leader, United Democratic Youth Movement and Mem., Central Cttee, 1946–48; Mem. Exec., Social Democratic Action, 1952–60; Democratic Opposition candidate, Lisbon, legis. elections, 1965, 1969; deported to São Tomé, March-Nov. 1968; Rep., Internat. League of Human Rights; imprisoned 12 times; exile, Paris, 1970–74; Founder, Portuguese Socialist Party, 1973, Sec. Gen., 1973–86, elected to Legis. Assembly as Mem. (Socialist Party) for Lisbon, 1974; Minister of Foreign Affairs, 1974–75; Minister without Portfolio, 1975; Deputy, Constituent Assembly, 1975, Legis. Assembly, 1976; Mem., Council of State; Prime Minister of Portugal 3 times, 1976–85. Joseph Lemaire Prize, 1975; Internat. Prize of Human Rights, 1977; Robert Schuman Prize, 1987; numerous hon. degrees, decorations and orders. *Publications:* As ideias político-sociais de Teófilo Braga, 1950; Escritos Políticos, 1969; Le Portugal Baillonné, 1972; Destruir o Sistema, Construir uma Vida Nova, 1973; Caminho Difícil, do Salazarismo ao Caetanismo, 1973; Escritos do Exílio, 1975; (with Willy Brandt and Bruno Kreisky) Liberdade para Portugal, 1975; Portugal, quelle Révolution?, 1976; O Futuro será o Socialismo Democrático, 1979; Resposta Socialista para o Mundo em Crise, 1983; Persistir, 1983; A Arvore e a Floresta, 1985; Intervenções: Vol. I, 1987; Vol. II, 1988; Vol. III, 1989; Vol. IV, 1990; Vol. V, 1991; Vol. VI, 1992; Vols VII and VIII, 1994; Moderador e Árbitro, 1995. *Recreations:* bibliophile; collector of contemporary Portuguese paintings. *Address:* Presidência da República, Palácio de Belém, 1300 Lisboa, Portugal; Rua Dr João Soares, 2-3°, 1600 Lisboa, Portugal.

SOBER, Phillip, FCA; European Regional Director, Horwath International, 1990–94; *b* 1 April 1931; *s* of Abraham and Sandra Sober; *m* 1957, Vivien Louise Oppenheimer; two *d* (and one *d* decd). *Educ:* Haberdashers' Aske's. Qual. as Chartered Accountant, 1953; FCA 1963. Stoy Hayward, Chartered Accountants: Partner, 1958; Internat. Partner, 1975–90; Sen. Partner, 1985–90. Crown Estate Comr, 1983–94. Director: Transatlantic Holdings, 1983–; Capital and Counties, 1993–; Capital Shopping Centres, 1994–. Mem. Council, UK Central Council for Nursing, Midwifery and Health Visiting, 1980–83. Pres., Norwood Child Care, 1990–94. Trustee, Royal Opera House Trust, 1985–91. Gov., London Inst. Higher Educn Corp., 1994–. *Publications:* articles in prof. press on various subjects but primarily on property co. accounting. *Recreations:* interested in all the arts, partic. music; golf main sporting activity. *Address:* 10 Longwood Drive, Roehampton, SW15 5DL. *T:* 0181–789 0437; Amberley Place, Amberley, West Sussex BN18 9NG. *Clubs:* Savile, Royal Automobile, Hurlingham, Roehampton.

SOBERS, Sir Garfield (St Auburn), (Sir Garry Sobers), Kt 1975; cricketer; *b* Bridgetown, Barbados, 28 July 1936; *m* 1969, Prudence Kirby; two *s* one *d*. *Educ:* Bay Street Sch., Barbados. First major match, 1953, for Barbados; played in 93 Test Matches for West Indies, 39 as Captain, 1953–74 (made world record Test Match score, Kingston, 1958); captained West Indies and Barbados teams, 1965–74; Captain of Nottinghamshire CCC, 1968–74. On retirement from Test cricket held the following world records in Test Matches: 365 not out; 26 centuries; 235 wickets; 110 catches. *Publications:* Cricket Advance, 1965; Cricket Crusader, 1966; King Cricket, 1967; (with J. S. Barker) Cricket in the Sun, 1967; Bonaventure and the Flashing Blade, 1967; (with Brian Scovell) Sobers: Twenty Years At The Top (autobiog.), 1988; (with P. P. Simmons) The Changing Face of Cricket, 1995; *relevant publication:* Sir Gary: a biography by Trevor Bailey, 1976.

SOBHI, Mohamed Ibrahim; Order of Merit, 1st Class, Egypt, 1974; Director General, International Bureau of Universal Postal Union, Berne, 1975–84, retired; *b* Alexandria, 28 March 1925; *s* of Gen. Ibrahim Sobhi and Mrs Zenab Affifi; *m* 1950, Laila Ahmed Sobhi; two *s* one *d*. *Educ:* Cairo Univ. (BE 1949). Construction of roads and airports, Engr Corps, 1950; Technical Sec., Communications Commn, Permanent Council for Develt and National Prodn, Cairo, 1954; Fellow, Vanderbilt Univ., Nashville, Tenn (studying transport and communications services in USA), 1955–56; Tech. Dir, Office of Minister of Communications for Posts, Railways and Coordination between means of transp. and communications, Cairo, 1956–61; Dir-Gen., Sea Transp. Authority (remaining Mem. Tech. Cttees, Postal Org.), 1961–64; Under Sec. of State for Communications and Mem. Bd, Postal Org., Cairo, 1964–68; Chm. Bd, Postal Org., and Sec.-Gen., African Postal Union, Cairo, 1968–74. Universal Postal Union: attended Congress, Ottawa, 1957; attended Cons. Council for Postal Studies session, Brussels, 1958; Head of Egyptian Delegn, Tokyo and Lausanne Congresses, and sessions of CCPS (set up by Tokyo Congress), 1969–74; Dir, Exec. Bureau i/c Egyptian projects in Africa, incl. construction of Hôtel de l'Amitié, Bamako, Mali, and roads, Republic of Mali, 1963–74; as Director-General of UPU, acted as Sec.-Gen. of the Congress, Exec. Council, and Cons. Council for Postal Studies; acted as intermediary between UPU and Restricted Unions, UN and internat. orgns; visited member countries and attended many meetings and congresses, inc. those of Restricted Unions, in all continents. Chm., Communications Cttee, Nat. Dem. Party of Egypt, 1985; Mem., Nat. Council of Production and Econ. Affairs of Egypt, 1985. Mem., Acad. of Scientific Res., 1990. Heinrich von Stephan Medal (Germany), 1979; Order of Postal Merit (Gran Placa) (Spain), 1979. *Recreations:* croquet, philately, music. *Address:* 4 Sheik Zakaria El-Ansary Street, Heliopolis, Cairo, Egypt.

SODANO, His Eminence Cardinal Angelo, STD, JCD; Secretary of State to His Holiness the Pope, since 1990; *b* Asti, Italy, 23 Nov. 1927; *s* of Giovanni Sodano and Delfina (*née* Brignolo). *Educ:* Seminario di Asti; Pontifical Università Gregoriana (STD); Pontifical Università Lateranense (JCD). Ordained priest, 1950; Titular Archbishop, 1978; Apostolic Nuncio, Chile, 1978–88; Sec., Council for Public Affairs of Church, later Section for Relns of Holy See with States, 1988–90. Several hon. distinctions. *Address:* Secretariat of State, 00120 Vatican City State.

SODOR AND MAN, Bishop of, since 1989; **Rt. Rev. Noël Debroy Jones**, CB 1986; Episcopal Visitor, diocese of Carlisle, since 1994; *b* 25 Dec. 1932; *s* of Brinley and Gwendoline Jones; *m* 1969, Joyce Barbara Leelavathy Arulanandam; one *s* one *d*. *Educ:* Haberdasher's West Monmouth, 1955–59; Vicar of Kano, N Nigeria, 1960–62; Chaplain, RN, 1962; GSM Brunei 1962, Borneo 1963; RM Commando Course prior to service in Aden with 42 Cdo, 1967; GSM S Arabia, 1967; Mid Service Clergy Course at St George's House, Windsor Castle, 1974; Staff Chaplain, MoD, 1974–77; Chaplain of the Fleet and Archdeacon for the Royal Navy, 1984–89. QHC 1983–89. *Recreations:* squash, swimming, music, family; formerly Rugby. *Address:* Bishop's House, Quarterbridge Road, Douglas, Isle of Man IM2 3RF. *Clubs:* Army and Navy; Sion College.

SOEHARTO, General, Hon. GCB 1974; President of Indonesia, since 1968; *b* 8 June 1921; *s* of Kertosudiro and Sukirah; *m* 1947, Siti Hartinah; three *s* three *d*. *Educ:* Elementary Sch., Puluhan Village; Junior High Sch., Wonogiri and Yogyakarta; Senior High Sch., Semarang. Military Basic Training Course and Non Commissioned Officers' Sch., 1940; Asst Police Chief, Yogyakarta (Japanese Police Unit Keibuho), 1941; Platoon Leader, Volunteer Corps, Wates, 1943; Co. Comdrs Sch., 1944; Mem., People's Security Army during Physical Revolution's counter insurgency ops against Indonesian Communist Party, 1945–50; crushed rebellion of Andi Aziz, Ujung Pandang, 1950; ops against Moslem rebels, Central Java, 1951–59; Comdg Gen., Liberation of W Irian (Western New Guinea), 1962; ops against Indonesian Communist Party, 1965; took measures to control the country, 1966; Acting President, 1967–68. Holds numerous decorations. *Address:* Office of the President, Jakarta, Indonesia.

SOFER, Mrs Anne Hallowell; Chief Education Officer, London Borough of Tower Hamlets, since 1989; *b* 19 April 1937; *d* of Geoffrey Crowther (later Baron Crowther) and Margaret Worth; *m* 1958, Jonathan Sofer; two *s* one *d*. *Educ:* St Paul's Sch.; Swarthmore Coll., USA; Somerville Coll., Oxford (MA); DipEd London. Secretary, National Assoc. of Governors and Managers, 1972–75; Additional Member, ILEA Education Cttee, 1974–77; Chairman, ILEA Schools Sub-Cttee, 1978–81; Mem. (SDP), GLC/ILEA for St Pancras N, Oct. 1981–86 (by-election) (Labour, 1977–81). Dir, Channel Four Television Co. Ltd, 1981–83; Columnist, The Times, 1983–87. Mem., SDP Nat. Cttee, 1982–. Contested Hampstead and Highgate (SDP) 1983, (SDP/Alliance) 1987. Trustee, Nuffield Foundn, 1990–. *Publication:* (with Tyrrell Burgess) The School Governors and Managers Handbook and Training Guide, 1978. *Address:* 46 Regent's Park Road, NW1 7SX. *T:* 0171–722 8970.

SOLANKI, Ramniklal Chhaganlal; author; Editor: Garavi Gujarat, newsweekly, since 1968; Asian Trader, trade journal, with controlled circulation in English, Gujarati and Urdu, since 1985; GGII, since 1990; Correspondent, Janmabhoomi Group, Bombay, since 1968; *b* 12 July 1931; *s* of Chhaganlal Kalidas and Mrs Ichchhaben Solanki, Surat, Gujarat, India; *m* 1955, Mrs Parvatiben, *d* of Makanji Dullabhji Chavda, Nani Pethan, India; two *s* two *d*. *Educ:* Irish Presbyterian Mission Sch., Surat (Matriculation Gold Medal, 1949); MTB Coll., Gujarat Univ. (BA(Econ)); Sarvajanik Law Coll., Surat, Gujarat (LLB). Pres., Rander Student Union, 1950–54; Sec., Surat Dist Students' Assoc., 1954–55. Sub-Editor, Nutan Bharat and Lok Vani, Surat, 1954–56; freelance columnist for several newspapers, while serving State Govt in India, 1956–63; London correspondent, Gujarat

Mitra Surat, 1964–68; European Correspondent, Janmabhoomi Gp of Newspapers, 1968–; Managing Director: Garavi Gujarat Publications Ltd and Garavi Gujarat Property Ltd (columnist of thought of the week on Indian philosophy, Garavi Gujarat, newsweekly); Asian Trade Publications Ltd. Member: Guild of British Newspaper Editors, 1976–; Asian Adv. Cttee, BBC, 1976–80; Nat. Centre for Ind. Language Trng Steering Gp, 1976–; Exec. Cttee, Gujarati Arya Kshtriya Maha Sabha UK, 1979–84; Exec. Cttee, Gujarati Arya Assoc., 1974–84 (Vice-Pres., 1980–81, 1982–83); CPU, 1964–; Foreign Press Assoc., 1984–; Parly Press Gallery, House of Commons; Sec., Indian Journalists Assoc. of Europe, 1978–79. Trustee, Gandhi Bapu Meml Trust, 1993–. Best Reporter of the Year in Gujarati, 1970. *Publications:* contrib. many articles. *Recreations:* reading, writing. *Address:* 74 Harrowdene Road, N Wembley, Mddx HA0 2JF. *T:* 0181–902 2879; (office): Garavi Gujarat House, 1/2 Silex Street, SE1 0DW. *T:* 0171–928 1234; *Telex:* 8955335 Gujrat G; *Fax:* 0171–261 0055.

SOLER, Antonio R.; *see* Ruiz Soler, A.

SOLESBURY, William Booth; research management consultant, since 1995; *b* 10 April 1940; *s* of William and Hannah Solesbury; *m* 1966, Felicity Andrew; one *s* two *d.* *Educ:* Hertford Grammar Sch.; Univ. of Cambridge (BA Hons Geography); Univ. of Liverpool (MCD Town Planning). London County Council, 1961–65; London Borough of Camden, 1965–66; City of Munich, 1966–67; Min. of Housing, 1967–72; NATO Res. Fellow, Univ. of California, Berkeley, 1973; Dept of Environment, 1974–89; Sec., ESRC, 1990–95. Gwilym Gibbon Res. Fellow, Nuffield Coll., Oxford, 1989–90. *Publications:* Policy in Urban Planning, 1974; articles in Public Administration, Policy and Politics. *Recreations:* home life, films, reading, travel. *Address:* 1 Oulby Road, SW6 3NE. *T:* 0171–736 2155.

SOLESBY, Tessa Audrey Hilda, CMG 1986; HM Diplomatic Service, retired; Leader, UK Delegation to Conference on Disarmament, Geneva (with personal rank of Ambassador), 1987–92; *b* 5 April 1932; *d* of Charles Solesby and Hilda Solesby (*née* Willis). *Educ:* Clifton High School; St Hugh's College, Oxford. MA; Hon. Fellow, 1988. Min. of Labour and Nat. Service, 1954–55; joined Diplomatic Service, 1956; FO, 1956; Manila, 1957–59; Lisbon, 1959–62; FO, 1962–64; First Sec., UK Mission to UN, Geneva, 1964–68; FO, 1968–70; First Sec., UK Mission to UN, NY, 1970–72; FCO, 1972–75, Counsellor, 1975; on secondment to NATO Internat. Staff, Brussels, 1975–78; Counsellor, East Berlin, 1978–81; temp. Minister, UK Mission to UN, NY, 1981–82; Head of Central African Dept, FCO, 1982–86; Minister, Pretoria, 1986–87. *Recreations:* hill-walking, music. *Address:* c/o Foreign and Commonwealth Office, SW1A 2AH.

SOLEY, Clive Stafford; MP (Lab) Hammersmith, since 1983 (Hammersmith North, 1979–83); *b* 7 May 1939. *Educ:* Downshall Sec. Modern School; Newbattle Abbey Coll.; Strathclyde Univ. (BA Hons); Southampton Univ. (Dip. in Applied Social Studies). Various appointments; Probation Officer, 1970–75; Senior Probation Officer, 1975–79. Chm., Alcohol Educn Centre, 1977–83. Opposition front bench spokesman on N Ireland, 1981–84, on Home Affairs, 1984–87, on Housing, 1987–92. Mem., Select Cttee on NI, 1994–; Chm., All Party Gp on Parenting, 1994–. *Address:* House of Commons, SW1A 0AA.

SOLLEY, Stephen Malcolm; QC 1989; a Recorder, since 1989; *b* 5 Nov. 1946; *s* of late Leslie Solley, sometime MP, and José Solley; *m* 1971, Helen Olivia Cox; four *s.* *Educ:* University College London (LLB 1968). Called to the Bar, Inner Temple, 1969. The Recorder, South Eastern Circuit, 1984–87. *Recreations:* jazz, opera, classic cars, wine, football, cooking. *Address:* Cloisters, Temple, EC4Y 7AA. *T:* 0171–583 0303. *Club:* Les Six.

SOLOMON, His Honour (Alan) Peter; a Circuit Judge, 1973–86; *b* 6 July 1923; *s* of late Jacob Ovid Solomon, Manchester; *m* 1st, 1954; one *d;* 2nd, 1973; one *d;* 3rd, 1981, Susan Jennifer Hunter. *Educ:* Mill Hill Sch.; Lincoln College, Oxford; MA. Served War 1942–46, Fleet Air Arm, Petty Officer Airman. Called to Bar, Inner Temple, 1949; practised South-Eastern circuit. *Publications: poetry:* The Lunatic, Balance, in Keats Prize Poems, 1973. *Recreations:* the turf, travel, poetry, burgundy.

SOLOMON, Sir David (Arnold), Kt 1973; MBE 1944; *b* 13 Nov. 1907; *s* of Richard Solomon and Sarah Annie Solomon (*née* Simpson); *m* 1935, Marjorie Miles (*d* 1990); two *s* one *d.* *Educ:* Leys Sch., Cambridge; Liverpool Univ. Qualified a Solicitor, 1933; became Mem. Liverpool Stock Exchange, 1935. Served War of 1939–45, RAF (MBE). Practised as a Stockbroker until retirement, March 1969. Chairman: Liverpool RHB, 1968–73; Community Health Council, SE Cumbria, 1973–76. *Recreation:* music. *Address:* Green Lane End, Spittal, Fangfoss, York YO4 5QR.

SOLOMON, David Joseph; Senior Partner, D. J. Freeman, solicitors, since 1992; *b* 31 Dec. 1930; *s* of Sydney and Rosie Harriet Solomon; *m* 1959, Hazel Boam; one *s* two *d.* *Educ:* Torquay Grammar Sch.; Univ. of Manchester (LLB). Admitted as Solicitor, 1955. Partner, Nabarro Nathanson, 1961–1968; Head of Property Dept, 1976–90, Chief Exec., 1990–93, D. J. Freeman. Pres., Highgate Literary and Scientific Instn, 1993–. Member: Architecture Club; Oriental Ceramic Soc. *Recreations:* Chinese ceramics, music, architecture, modern art, wine. *Address:* Russell House, 9 South Grove, Highgate, N6 6BS. *T:* 0181–341 6151; Longecourt les Culetre, 21230 Arnay le Duc, Côte d'Or, France. *T:* 80900555. *Club:* Athenæum.

SOLOMON, Sir Harry, Kt 1991; Chairman, 1987–93, Director, since 1993, Hillsdown Holdings (Joint Chairman, 1984–87); *b* 20 March 1937; *s* of Jacob and Belle Solomon; *m* 1962, Judith Diana Manuel; one *s* two *d.* *Educ:* St Albans School; Law Society School of Law. Qualified solicitor, 1960; in private practice, 1960–75; Managing Dir, Hillsdown Holdings, 1975–84. Chm., Harveys Holdings, 1994–; Director: Charterhouse European Holding, 1993–; Frogmore Estates, 1993–; Princedale Gp, 1993–; Maple Leaf Foods Inc., 1993–. Pres., Help Medicine, RCP, 1990–; Trustee, CORDA, 1990–. Hon. FRCP 1992. *Recreations:* jogging, tennis, theatre, collector of historical autographed letters. *Address:* 3 Coach House Yard, Hampstead High Street, NW3 1QB.

SOLOMON, Jonathan Hilali Moïse; Member, Court of Directors, since 1987, and Director, Corporate Business Development, since 1989, Cable and Wireless PLC; Director: International Digital Communications, Japan, since 1987; Tele 2, Nahodka and Sakhalin Telecom, since 1991; *b* 3 March 1939; *s* of Samuel and Moselle Solomon; *m* 1966, Hester McFarland; one *s.* *Educ:* Clifton College; King's College, Cambridge. BA Hons, MA. Research worker, Supervisor and Tutor, Cambridge and London Univs, 1960–63, 1965. Entered Home Civil Service, 1963; Asst Private Sec. to Pres. of Board of Trade, 1966–67; Principal, Companies Div., BoT, transferred to DTI, 1970; to Treasury, 1972; Asst Sec., Dept of Prices and Consumer Protection, 1974; returned to Dept of Industry, Electronics Divs, 1977–80; Under-Sec., Telecomns (formerly Posts and Telecomns) Div., DoI, 1980–84; Under Sec., Quality and Educn Div., DTI, 1984–85; Cable and Wireless: Dir of Special Projects, 1985–87; Dir, Corporate Strategy, 1987–89. Head UK Delegn, ITU Plenipotentiary Conf., Nairobi, 1982. Member Editorial Board: Telecommunications Policy, 1984–; Utilities Policy, 1990–. *Publications:* contribs to journals such as Platon, Contemporary Review, New Outlook, Frontier, Tablet, Telecommunications Policy. *Recreations:* sport, futurology, writing. *Address:* 12 Kidderpore Gardens, NW3 7SR. *T:* 0171–794 6230. *Clubs:* English-Speaking Union, Royal Automobile.

SOLOMON, Rabbi Dr Norman; Director, Centre for Study of Judaism and Jewish/Christian Relations, Selly Oak Colleges, Birmingham, 1989–94; *b* Cardiff, 31 May 1933; *s* of late Phillip Solomon and Esther Solomon (*née* Lewis); *m* 1955, Devora, (Doris), Strauss; three *s* one *d.* *Educ:* Cardiff High Sch.; St John's Coll., Cambridge (BA 1954); Univ. of Manchester (PhD 1966). London Univ (BMus 1958); ARCM 1956. Rabbi: Whitefield Synagogue, Manchester, 1961–66; Greenbank Drive Synagogue, Liverpool, 1966–74; Hampstead Synagogue, 1974–83; Central Synagogue, Birmingham, 1994; Lectr in Judaism, Selly Oak Colls, 1983–89. Vis. Lectr, Oxford Centre for Postgraduate Hebrew Studies, 1985–; Koerner Vis. Fellow, Oxford Centre for Hebrew and Jewish Studies, 1994–95. Adviser, Internat. CCJ, 1988–; Specialist Adviser, CNAA, 1989–92. Vice-Chm., World Congress of Faiths, 1992–; President: Birmingham Inter-Faiths Council, 1984–85; British Assoc. for Jewish Studies, 1994. FBIS 1986. 15th Annual Sir Sigmund Sternberg Award, CCJ, 1993. Editor, Jewish Christian Relations, 1985–91. *Publications:* Judaism and World Religion, 1991; The Analytic Movement, 1993; articles in learned jls. *Recreations:* distance running, playing chamber music. *Address:* 50 Estria Road, Edgbaston, Birmingham B15 2LQ. *T:* 0121–440 5315. *Club:* Royal Over-Seas League.

SOLOMON, Peter; *see* Solomon, A. P.

SOLOMONS, Anthony Nathan, FCA; Chairman: Singer & Friedlander Ltd, since 1976 (Chief Executive, 1973–90); Singer & Friedlander Group plc, since 1987; Anglo Leasing Plc, since 1993; Director: Bullough Ltd, since 1983; Burford Group Plc, since 1994; *b* 26 Jan. 1930; *s* of Leslie Emanuel Solomons and Susie Schneiders; *m* 1957, Jean Golding; two *d.* Qual. as chartered accountant, 1953; FCA 1963. National Service, 1953–54: commnd Dorset Regt. Accountant, Kennedy & Fox Oldfield & Co., 1955; Asst Accountant, then Chief Accountant, Lobitos Oilfields Ltd, 1955–58; Singer & Friedlander 1958–: successively Exec. Dir, Man. Dir, and Jt Chief Exec. Chm., People's Phone. Mem., Educnl Assets Bd, 1988–. *Address:* 21 New Street, EC2M 4HR. *T:* 0171–623 3000. *Club:* Carlton.

SOLOW, Prof. Robert Merton; Professor of Economics, Massachusetts Institute of Technology, since 1949; *b* 23 Aug. 1924; *s* of Milton H. Solow and Hannah Solow (*née* Sarney); *m* 1945, Barbara Lewis; two *s* one *d.* *Educ:* New York City schools; Harvard College (BA 1947); Harvard University (MA 1949, PhD 1951). Served US forces, 1942–45 (Bronze Star, 1944). Joined MIT Faculty as Asst Prof. of Statistics, 1949, Inst. Prof. of Economics, 1974–. Senior Economist, Council of Economic Advisers, 1961–62. Eastman Prof. and Fellow of Balliol Coll., Oxford, 1968–69; Overseas Fellow, Churchill Coll., Cambridge, 1984, 1991. President: Econometric Soc., 1965; Amer. Econ. Assoc., 1976; Member: Amer. Acad. of Arts and Scis, 1963; Nat. Acad. of Sciences, USA, 1972; Accademia dei Lincei, 1984; Corr. Mem., British Acad., 1975; Mem., Amer. Philosophical Soc., 1974–. Hon. degrees: Chicago, 1967; Brown, 1972; Williams, 1974; Paris I, 1975; Warwick, 1976; Lehigh, 1977; Geneva, Wesleyan, 1982; Tulane, 1983; Yale, 1986; Bryant, 1987; Massachusetts at Boston, Boston Coll., 1989; Colgate, Dartmouth, Helsinki, 1990; New York at Albany, 1991; Harvard, Glasgow, Chile, 1992. Nobel Prize for Economics, 1987. *Publications:* Linear Programming and Economic Analysis (with P. Samuelson and R. Dorfman), 1958; Capital Theory and the Rate of Return, 1964; The Sources of Unemployment in the US, 1964; Growth Theory: an exposition, 1970; The Labor Market as a Social Institution, 1990; articles in learned jls. *Recreation:* sailing. *Address:* 528 Lewis Wharf, Boston, MA 02110, USA. *T:* (617) 2274436.

SOLTI, Sir Georg, KBE 1971 (CBE (Hon.) 1968); Artistic Director, Salzburg Easter Festival, 1992 and 1993; Music Director, Chicago Symphony Orchestra, 1969–91, Music Director Laureate, since 1991; Principal Conductor and Artistic Director, London Philharmonic Orchestra, 1979–83, then Conductor Emeritus; *b* Budapest, 21 Oct. 1912; adopted British nationality, 1972; *m* 1st, 1946, Hedwig Oeschli; 2nd, 1967, Anne Valerie Pitts; two *d.* *Educ:* High School of Music, Budapest. Studied with Kodály, Bartók, and Dohnányi. Conductor and pianist, State Opera, Budapest, 1930–39; first prize, as pianist, Concours Internationale, Geneva, 1942; Musical Director, Bavarian State Opera, 1946–52; Musical Director, Frankfurt Opera, and Permanent Conductor, Museums Concerts, Frankfurt, 1952–61; Musical Director: Covent Garden Opera Co., 1961–71 (Music Director Laureate, Royal Opera, 1992); Orchestre de Paris, 1972–75. Guest Conductor: Berlin, Salzburg, Vienna, Munich, Paris, London (first conducted London Philharmonic Orchestra, 1947; Covent Garden début, 1959), Glyndebourne Festival, Edinburgh Festival, Bayreuth Festival, San Francisco, New York, Los Angeles, Chicago, etc. Has made numerous recordings (many of which have received international awards or prizes, incl. Grand Prix Mondiale du Disque (14 times), and 31 Grammy Awards (incl. special Trustees Grammy Award for recording of The Ring Cycle), Nat. Acad. of Recorded Arts and Scis). Hon. FRCM, 1980; Hon. Prof., Baden-Württemberg, 1985. Hon. Fellow, Jesus Coll., Oxford, 1990. Hon. DMus: Leeds, 1971; Oxon, 1972; Yale Univ., 1974; Harvard, 1979; Furman, 1983; Surrey, 1983; London, 1986; Hon. Dr DePaul, 1975. Médaille de Vermeil, Ville de Paris, 1985; Loyola-Mellon Humanities Award, 1987; Medal of Merit, City of Chicago, 1987; Gold Medal, Royal Philharmonic Soc., 1989; Frankfurt Music Prize, 1992; Kennedy Center Award, 1993; Hans Richter Medal, Vienna Philharmonic Orch., 1993; Von Bülow Medal, Berlin Philharmonic Orch., 1993. Kt Commander's Cross, OM (FRG), 1987; Order of the Flag (Hungarian People's Republic), 1987; Commander, Order of Leopold (Belgium), 1993; Middle Cross, Order of Merit with Star (Republic of Hungary), 1993; Grosses Verdienstskreuz mit Stern und Schulterband (Germany), 1993; Ordem Militar de Santiago de Espada (Portugal), 1994; Comdr, Order of Arts and Letters (France), 1995. *Address:* Chalet Haut Pré, Villars s. Ollon, 1884, Switzerland. *Club:* Athenæum.

SOLYMAR, Prof. Laszlo, FRS 1995; PhD; Professor of Applied Electromagnetism, University of Oxford, since 1992; Professorial Fellow of Hertford College, Oxford, since 1986; *b* 1930; *s* of Pál and Aranka Solymar; *m* 1955, Marianne Klopfer; two *d.* *Educ:* Technical University, Budapest (Hungarian equivalents of BSc and PhD in Engineering). Lectr, Technical Univ., Budapest, 1952–53; Research Engineer, Res. Inst. for Telecommunications, Budapest, 1953–56; Res. Engineer, Standard Telecom Labs, Harlow, 1956–65; Oxford University: Fellow in Engineering, Brasenose Coll., 1966–86; Lectr, 1971–86, Donald Pollock Reader in Engrg Sci., 1986–92. Visiting Professor: Ecole Normale Supérieure, Paris, 1965–66; Tech. Univ. of Denmark, 1972–73; Univ. Osnabrück, 1987; Tech. Univ., Berlin, 1990; Univ. Autónoma, Madrid, 1993; Tech. Univ., Budapest, 1994. Consultant: Tech. Univ. of Denmark, 1973–76; Thomson-CSF, Orsay, 1984; British Telecom, 1986–88; GEC Wembley, 1986–88; Pilkington Technol. Centre, 1989–90. Faraday Medal, IEE, 1992. Anaxagoras, Archimedes, Hypatia (radio plays with John Wain), 1991. *Publications:* Lectures on the Electrical Properties of Materials (with D. Walsh), 1970, 5th edn 1993; Superconductive Tunnelling and Applications, 1972; (ed) A Review of the Principles of Electrical and Electronic Engineering, 1974; Lectures on Electromagnetic Theory, 1976, 2nd edn 1984; (with D. J. Cooke) Volume Holography and Volume Gratings, 1981; Lectures on Fourier Series, 1988; articles. *Recreations:* history, languages, chess, swimming, ski-ing. *Address:* Department of Engineering Science, University of Oxford OX1 3PJ. *T:* Oxford (01865) 273110.

SOLZHENITSYN, Alexander Isayevitch; author; Hon. Fellow, Hoover Institution on War, Revolution and Peace, 1975; *b* 11 Dec. 1918; *m*; three *s*. *Educ:* Univ. of Rostov (degree in maths and physics); Moscow Inst. of History, Philosophy and Literature (correspondence course). Joined Army, 1941; grad. from Artillery School, 1942; in comd artillery battery and served at front until 1945 (twice decorated); sentenced to eight years' imprisonment, 1945, released, 1953; exile in Siberia, 1953–56; officially rehabilitated, 1957; taught and wrote in Ryazan and Moscow; expelled from Soviet Union, 1974; Soviet citizenship restored, 1990. Member Union of Soviet writers, 1962, expelled 1969; Member Amer. Acad. of Arts and Sciences, 1969. Awarded Nobel Prize for Literature, 1970; Templeton Prize for Progress in Religion, 1983; Russian State Literature Prize, 1990. *Publications:* One Day in the Life of Ivan Denisovich, 1962, new edn 1991, filmed 1971; An Incident at Krechetovka Station, and Matryona's House (publ. US as We Never Make Mistakes, 1969), 1963; For the Good of the Cause, 1964; The First Circle, 1968; Cancer Ward, part 1, 1968, part 2, 1969 (Prix du Meilleur Livre Etranger, Paris); Stories and Prose Poems, 1970; August 1914, 1972; One Word of Truth: the Nobel speech on literature, 1972; The Gulag Archipelago: an experiment in literary investigation, vol. 1, 1973, vol. 2, 1974, vol. 3, 1976 (first Russian edn, 1989); The Oak and the Calf (autobiog.), 1975; Lenin in Zurich, 1975; Prussian Nights (poem), 1977; The Red Wheel: August 1914, 1983 (revd edn of 1972 publication); October 1916, 1985; How to Reconstruct Russia, 1991; *plays:* trilogy: The Love Girl and the Innocent, 1969, Victory Celebrations, Prisoners, 1983. *Address:* c/o Harper & Row Inc., 10 East 53rd Street, New York, NY 10022, USA.

SOMARE, Rt Hon. Sir Michael (Thomas), GCMG 1990; CH 1978; PC 1977; MP; *b* 9 April 1936; *m* 1965, Veronica Somare; three *s* two *d*. *Educ:* Sogeri Secondary Sch.; Admin. Coll. Teaching, 1956–62; Asst Area Educn Officer, Madang, 1962–63; Broadcasts Officer, Dept of Information and Extension Services, Wewack, 1963–66; Journalism, 1966–68. Member for E Sepik Region (Nat. Parl.), PNG House of Assembly, 1968–; Parly Leader, Pangu Pati, 1968–; First Chief Minister, 1972–75; first Prime Minister, 1975–80, 1982–85; Leader of Opposition in House of Assembly, 1980–82; Minister for Foreign Affairs, 1988–94. Dep. Chm., Exec. Council, 1972–73, Chm., 1973–75. Mem., Second Select Cttee on Constitutional Develt, 1968–72; Mem. Adv. Cttee, Australian Broadcasting Commission. *Address:* House of Assembly, Port Moresby, Papua New Guinea; (home) Karan, Murik Lakes, East Sepik, Papua New Guinea.

SOMERLEYTON, 3rd Baron *cr* 1916; **Savile William Francis Crossley,** KCVO 1994; DL; Bt 1863; farmer; Master of the Horse, since 1991; *b* 17 Sept. 1928; *er s* of 2nd Baron Somerleyton, MC; *S* father, 1959; *m* 1963, Belinda Maris Loyd, *d* of late Vivian Loyd and of Mrs Gerald Critchley; one *s* four *d*. *Educ:* Eton Coll. Captain Coldstream Guards, 1948; retired, 1956. Royal Agricultural Coll., Cirencester, 1958–59; farming, 1959–. A Lord in Waiting to the Queen, 1978–91. Dir, Essex & Suffolk Water plc, 1994–. DL Suffolk, 1964. *Heir: s* Hon. Hugh Francis Savile Crossley, *b* 27 Sept. 1971. *Address:* Somerleyton Hall, Lowestoft, Suffolk NR32 5QQ. *T:* Lowestoft (01502) 730308. *Club:* White's.

SOMERS, 9th Baron *cr* 1784; **Philip Sebastian Somers Cocks;** Bt 1772; *b* 4 Jan. 1948; *o s* of John Sebastian Somers Cocks, CVO, CBE (*d* 1964), and of Marjorie Olive (*née* Weller); *S* cousin, 1995. *Educ:* abroad; Elston Hall, Newark; Craig-y-Parc, Cardiff. *Recreations:* opera, music generally, foreign travel. *Heir: cousin* Alan Bromley Cocks [*b* 1930; *m* 1955, Pamela Fay, *d* of A. H. Gourlay, Christchurch, NZ; one *s* three *d*]. *Address:* 19 Kempson Road, SW6 4PX.
See also A. G. Somers Cocks.

SOMERS, Rt Hon. Sir Edward (Jonathan), Kt 1989; PC 1981; Judge of the Court of Appeal, New Zealand, 1981–90; *b* 9 Sept. 1928; *s* of Ewart Somers and Muriel Ann Crossley; *m* 1953, Mollie Louise Morison; one *s* two *d*. *Educ:* Christ's Coll., Christchurch; Canterbury University Coll., Christchurch, NZ (BA, LLB). Practised as barrister and solicitor, 1952–71; practised as barrister, 1971; QC (NZ) 1973; Judge of Supreme Court of New Zealand, 1974. LLD *hc* Univ. of Canterbury, 1992. *Recreation:* gardening. *Address:* Waverley, Kaiapoi, RD2, New Zealand. *T:* (3) 3277094. *Club:* Christchurch (New Zealand).

SOMERS COCKS, Anna Gwenllian, (Mrs Anna Allemandi), FSA; Editor, 1990–94, Chairman, since 1995, The Art Newspaper; *b* 18 April 1950; *d* of John Sebastian Somers Cocks, CVO, CBE and Marjorie Olive Weller; *m* 1st, 1971, Martin Walker (marr. diss.); 2nd, 1978, John Hardy (marr. diss.); one *s* one *d*; 3rd, 1991, Umberto Allemandi. *Educ:* abroad; Convent of the Sacred Heart, Woldingham; St Anne's College, Oxford (MA); Courtauld Inst., Univ. of London (MA). Asst Keeper, Dept of Metal Work, 1973–85, Dept of Ceramics, 1985–87, Victoria and Albert Museum; Ed., Apollo Magazine, 1987–90. FRSA. *Publications:* The Victoria and Albert Museum: the making of the collection, 1980; (ed and jt author) Princely Magnificence: court jewels of the Renaissance, 1980; (with C. Truman) Renaissance Jewels, Gold Boxes and Objets de Vertu in the Thyssen Collection, 1985. *Recreations:* ski-ing, entertaining, travelling, walking. *Address:* c/o Umberto Allemandi & Co., via Mancini 8, Turin 10131, Italy. *Club:* Reform.
See also Baron Somers.

SOMERSCALES, Thomas Lawrence, CBE 1970; General Secretary, Joint Committee of the Order of St John of Jerusalem and the British Red Cross Society, 1960–78; *b* 1 July 1913; *s* of Wilfred Somerscales; *m* 1941, Ann Teresa, *d* of Robert Victor Kearney; three *s* one *d*. *Educ:* Riley High Sch., Hull. FCA 1939. KStJ 1978. Finance Sec., Jt Cttee, OStJ and BRCS, 1953–60. Mem., Adv. Council, ITA, 1964–67. *Address:* The Dormer House, The Rookery, Alveston, Stratford-upon-Avon CV31 1QP.

SOMERSET, family name of **Duke of Beaufort** and of **Baron Raglan.**

SOMERSET, 19th Duke of, *cr* 1547; **John Michael Edward Seymour,** DL; FRICS; Baron Seymour 1547; Bt 1611; *b* 30 Dec. 1952; *s* of 18th Duke of Somerset and of Gwendoline Collette (Jane), 2nd *d* of Major J. C. C. Thomas; *S* father, 1984; *m* 1978, Judith-Rose, *d* of J. F. C. Hull, *qv*; two *s* two *d*. *Educ:* Eton. DL Wilts, 1993. *Heir: s* Lord Seymour, *qv*. *Address:* c/o House of Lords, SW1A 0PW.

SOMERSET, David Henry Fitzroy, FCIB; Fellow and Financial Adviser, Peterhouse, Cambridge, since 1988; *b* 19 June 1930; *s* of late Brig. Hon. Nigel Somerset, CBE, DSO, MC and Phyllis Marion Offley (*née* Irwin); *m* 1955, Ruth Ivy, *d* of late W. R. Wildbur; one *s* one *d*. *Educ:* Wellington Coll.; Peterhouse, Cambridge (MA). Entered Bank of England, 1952; Personal Asst to Managing Director, International Monetary Fund, Washington DC, 1959–62; Private Secretary to Governor of Bank of England, 1962–63; Asst Chief Cashier, 1968–69; Asst Chief of Establishments, 1969–73; Dep. Chief Cashier, 1973–80; Chief of Banking Dept and Chief Cashier, 1980–88. Dir, Yamaichi Bank (UK) PLC, 1988–95; Chm., London Adv. Bd, Bank Julius Baer, 1991–. Comr, English Heritage, 1988–91. Mem. Council, Friends of Peterhouse, 1982–; Chm., Old Wellingtonian Soc., 1988–; Gov., Wellington Coll., 1989–. *Recreations:* gardening, racing, shooting. *Address:* White Wickets, Boars Head, Crowborough, Sussex TN6 3HE. *T:* Crowborough (01892) 661111, *Fax:* (01892) 667281. *Club:* Boodle's.

SOMERSET, Sir Henry Beaufort, Kt 1966; CBE 1961; *b* 21 May 1906; *s* of Henry St John Somerset; *m* 1930, Patricia Agnes Strickland; two *d*. *Educ:* St Peter's Coll., Adelaide; Trinity Coll., University of Melbourne; MSc 1928. Director: Humes Ltd, 1957–82 (Chm., 1961–82); Goliath Cement Hldgs Ltd, 1947–82 (Chm., 1967–82); Associated Pulp & Paper Mills Ltd, 1937–81 (Man. Dir, 1948–70; Dep. Chm., 1970–81); Electrolytic Zinc Co. of Australasia Ltd, 1953–78; Perpetual Exors Trustees Ltd, 1971–81 (Chm., 1973–81); Tioxide Australia Pty Ltd, 1949–82 (Chm., 1953–76); Central Norseman Gold Corp. Ltd, 1977–82. Chancellor, University of Tasmania, 1964–72; Member: Council, Australasian Inst. of Mining and Metallurgy, 1956–82 (President, 1958 and 1966); Exec., CSIRO, 1965–74; Council, Nat. Museum of Victoria, 1968–77; Pres., Australian Mineral Foundn, 1972–83. FRACI; FTS. Hon. DSc Tasmania, 1973. *Clubs:* Melbourne, Australian (Melbourne).

SOMERSET FRY, (Peter George Robin) Plantagenet; author and journalist, since 1955; *b* 3 Jan. 1931; *s* of late Comdr Peter K. Ll. Fry, OBE, RN, and Ruth Emily (*née* Marriott), LRAM; *m* 1st, 1958, Daphne Diana Elizabeth Caroline Yorke (*d* 1961); 2nd, 1961, Hon. Mrs Leri Butler (marr. diss. 1973, she *d* 1985); 3rd, 1974, Pamela Fiona Ileene (author: Horses, 1981; A Soldier in Wellington's Army, 1987), *d* of late Col H. M. Whitcombe, MBE. *Educ:* Lancing; St Thomas's Hosp. Med. Sch., London; St Catherine's Coll., Oxford (Sec. Oxford Union, Hilary 1956). Mem. editorial staff: Atomics and Nuclear Energy, 1957–58; The Tatler and Bystander, 1958; public relations, 1960–64; Information Officer: Incorp. Assoc. of Architects and Surveyors, 1965–67; MPBW, 1967–70; Head of Inf. Services, COSIRA, 1970–74; Editor of Books, HM Stationery Office, 1975–80. Gen. Editor, Macmillan History in Pictures Series, 1977–80. Vis. Scholar, 1980–84, Sen. Mem., 1984–, Observer Mem., Governing Body, 1992–, Wolfson Coll., Cambridge. Mem. Council, East Anglian Writers, 1977–82; Co-founder, Congress of Indep. Archaeologists, 1985; Founder and Hon. Secretary: Little Bardfield Village Community Trust, 1971–74; Daphne Somerset Fry Meml Trust for Kidney Disease Res., 1961–; Burgh Soc., 1978–80. FRSA 1966. *Publications:* Mysteries of History, 1957; The Cankered Rose, 1959; Rulers of Britain, 1967, 3rd edn 1973; They Made History, 1970, 2nd edn 1973; The World of Antiques, 1970, 4th edn 1972; Antique Furniture, 1971, 2nd edn 1972; Constantinople, 1970; The Wonderful Story of the Jews, 1970; Children's History of the World, 1972, 12th edn 1995; Answer Book of History, 1972, 2nd edn 1973; Zebra Book of Famous Men, 1972; Zebra Book of Famous Women, 1972; Collecting Inexpensive Antiques, 1973, 5th edn 1980; Zebra Book of Castles, 1974; Great Caesar, 1974; British Mediaeval Castles, 1974; 1000 Great Lives, 1975, 8th edn 1984; Questions, 1976; 2,000 Years of British Life, 1976; Chequers: the country home of Britain's Prime Ministers, 1977 (official history); 3,000 Questions and Answers, 1977, 12th edn 1984; Boudicca, 1978; David & Charles Book of Castles, 1980, 2nd edn 1990; Fountains Abbey (official souvenir guide), 1980; Beautiful Britain, 1981; (with Fiona Somerset Fry) History of Scotland, 1982, 4th edn 1995; Revolt Against Rome, 1982; Great Cathedrals, 1982; (ed) Longman Pocket History Dictionary, 1983; Roman Britain: history and sites, 1984; Battle Abbey and the Battle of Hastings (official souvenir guide), 1984, 2nd edn 1990; 3,000 More Questions and Answers, 1984; Antiques, 1985, 2nd edn 1992; Rievaulx Abbey (official souvenir guide), 1986; Children's Illustrated Dictionary, 1987; (with Fiona Somerset Fry) History of Ireland, 1988, 4th edn 1995; 1000 Great People Through the Ages, 1989; Kings & Queens of England & Scotland, 1990, 6th edn 1995; The Tower of London, 1990; Handbook of Antique Furniture, 1992; The Dorling Kindersley History of the World, 1994, 2nd edn 1994. *Recreations:* studying 18th Century French furniture, Roman history, visiting British, Irish and European castles. *Address:* Wood Cottage, Wattisfield, via Diss, Suffolk IP22 1NE. *T:* Stanton (01359) 251324.

SOMERSET JONES, Eric, QC 1978; a Recorder of the Crown Court, since 1975; *s* of late Daniel and Florence Somerset Jones; *m* 1966, Brenda Marion, *yr d* of late Hedley Shimmin and Doris (*née* Beacroft) two *d*. *Educ:* Birkenhead Institute; Lincoln College, Oxford. MA Oxon. RAF, 1944–47. Called to Bar, Middle Temple, 1952, Bencher, 1988; Mem., Northern Circuit. Member: Lord Chancellor's County Courts Rule Cttee, 1975–78; Gen. Council of the Bar, 1990–94. *Address:* (home) Southmead, Mill Lane, Willaston, Wirral, Cheshire L64 1RL. *T:* 0151–327 5138; 12 Marryat Square, SW6 6UA. *T:* 0171–381 5360; (chambers) Goldsmith Building, Temple, EC4Y 7BL. *T:* 0171–353 7881. *Club:* Royal Chester Rowing (Chester).

SOMERTON, Viscount; James Shaun Christian Welbore Ellis Agar; *b* 7 Sept. 1982; *s* and *heir* of 6th Earl of Normanton, *qv*.

SOMERVILLE, Prof. Christopher Roland, PhD; FRS 1991; Director, Department of Plant Biology, Carnegie Institution of Washington, USA and Professor of Biology, Stanford University, since 1994; *b* 11 Oct. 1947; *s* of Hubert Roland Somerville and Teresa Marie (*née* Bond); *m* 1976, Shauna Christine Phimester. *Educ:* Univ. of Alberta, Canada (PhD, BS). Asst Prof. of Genetics, Univ. of Alberta, Canada, 1980–82; Associate Prof. of Botany and Genetics, Michigan State Univ., Mich, 1982–86; Prof. of Botany and Genetics, Michigan State Univ., 1982–93. *Publications:* numerous research articles on genetics, physiology and biochemistry of plants. *Recreation:* sailing. *Address:* 5 Valley Oak, Portola Valley, CA 94305, USA; Carnegie Institution of Washington, 290 Panama Street, Stanford, CA 94305, USA. *T:* (415) 3251521.

SOMERVILLE, David, CB 1971; Under-Secretary, Department of Health and Social Security, 1968–77; *b* 27 Feb. 1917; *e s* of late Rev. David Somerville and Euphemia Somerville; *m* 1950, Patricia Amy Johnston; two *s* two *d*. *Educ:* George Watson's Coll.; Fettes Coll.; Edinburgh Univ.; Christ Church, Oxford. Served with Army, 1940–45; Major, Royal Artillery. Entered Civil Service as Asst Principal, Ministry of Health, 1946; Under-Secretary, Min. of Health, 1963–67. *Recreations:* golf, gardening, adult education. *Address:* 5 Glebe Road, Dorking, Surrey RH4 3DS. *T:* Dorking (01306) 885102.

SOMERVILLE, Jane, MD; FRCP; Consultant Physician: Royal Brompton & National Heart Hospital (formerly National Heart Hospital), since 1974; Cardiac Department, Grown-Up Congenital Heart Disease Clinic, St Bartholomew's Hospital, since 1988; *b* 24 Jan. 1933; *d* of Joseph Bertram Platnauer and Pearl Ashton; *m* 1957, Dr Walter Somerville, *qv*; three *s* one *d*. *Educ:* Queen's Coll., London; Guy's Hosp., London Univ. MB, BS (Treasurer's Gold Medal for Clin. Surg.) 1955; MD 1966. MRCS 1955; FRCP 1973 (LRCP 1955, MRCP 1957). FACC 1972. Med. Registrar, Guy's Hosp., 1956–58; Registrar, Nat. Heart Hosp., 1958–59; First Asst to Dr Paul Wood, 1959–63, Sen. Lectr 1964–74, Inst. of Cardiol.; Hon. Cons. Phys., Nat. Heart Hosp., 1967–74, Hosp. for Sick Children, Gt Ormond St, 1968–88. Lectr in Cardiovascular Disease, Turin Univ., 1973. Vis. Prof. and Guest Lectr, Europe, ME, USA, Mexico, S America, USSR, China; St Cyres Lectr, Imperial Coll., London, 1976; 6th Mahboubian Lectr, NY, 1981; World Congress Gold Medal Lectr, Bombay, 1982; Edgar Mannheimer, Hamburg, 1987; John Keith, Montreal, 1988; Tudor Edwards, RCP, 1991. Chm., Staff Cttee, 1988–89, Jt Adv. Cttee, 1989–90, Nat. Heart Hosp.; Chm., Cardiol. Cttee, Royal Brompton & Nat. Heart Hosp., 1990–. Sci. Sec., World Congress, Paed. Cardiol., 1980; Advr on congenital heart disease, Sec. of State's Hon. Med. Adv. Panel on driving and disorders of cardiovascular system, 1986–. Member: Assoc. Europ. Pæd. Cardiol.; British Cardiac Soc. (Mem., Paediatric Cardiol. Services Sub-cttee, 1987–); RSocMed; Harveian Soc.; French Cardiac

Soc.; 300 Gp; Sci. Council, Monaco Cardiothoracic Centre. Hon. Member: Argentine Pæd. Soc.; Chilean Cardiac Soc.; Argentine Soc. of Cardiol.; Brazilian Cardiac Soc.; Argentine Cardiac Soc. Founding Fellow, Europ. Soc. of Cardiol. Mem. Council, Stonham Housing Assoc. Governor: Queen's Coll., London; Nat. Heart and Chest Hosps, 1977–82, 1984–90. Woman of the Year, 1968. *Publications:* numerous contribs to med. lit. on heart disease in children, adolescents and adults, congenital heart disease and results of cardiac surgery; chapters in Paul Wood's Diseases of Heart and Circulation (3rd edn), Oxford Textbook of Medicine, and Perspectives in Pediatric Cardiology, Vols I and II. *Recreations:* collecting antiques, pictures, porcelain soldiers; chess, roof gardening, orchid culture. *Address:* 30 York House, Upper Montagu Street, W1H 1FR. *T:* 0171–262 2144; 0171–351 8200, *Fax:* 0171–351 8201.

SOMERVILLE, John Arthur Fownes, CB 1977; CBE 1964; DL; an Under-Secretary, Government Communications Headquarters, 1969–78; *b* 5 Dec. 1917; *s* of late Admiral of the Fleet Sir James Fownes Somerville, GCB, GBE, DSO; *m* 1945, Julia Elizabeth Payne; one *s* two *d*. *Educ:* RNC Dartmouth. Lieut-Comdr 1945; retd 1950. Govt Communications Headquarters, 1950–78. DL Somerset, 1985. *Recreation:* walking. *Address:* The Old Rectory, Dinder, Wells, Som BA5 3PL. *T:* Wells (01749) 674900. *Club:* Army and Navy.

SOMERVILLE, Brig. Sir (John) Nicholas, Kt 1985; CBE 1975; self employed consultant, personnel selection, since 1984; *b* 16 Jan. 1924; *s* of Brig. Desmond Henry Sykes Somerville and Moira Burke Somerville; *m* 1951, Jenifer Dorothea Nash; one *s* two *d*. *Educ:* Winchester College. Commissioned, The South Wales Borderers, 24th Regt, 1943; served: France and Germany, D-day—VE day, 1944–45 (despatches 1945); BAOR, War Office, FARELF, Aden, 1967–68 (despatches 1968); Directing Staff, JSSC, 1967–69; Comdt, Junior Div., Staff Coll., 1969–72; Dir of Army Recruiting, 1973–75; retired, 1978. Managing Director, Saladin Security Ltd, 1981–84; voluntary consultant responsible for designing Cons. Party Parly selection board procedure, 1980–. *Recreations:* sailing, gardening, house designing. *Address:* Deptford Cottage, Greywell, near Basingstoke, Hants RG25 1BS. *T:* Odiham (01256) 702796.

SOMERVILLE, Very Rev. Dr John Spenser, ONZ 1991; CMG 1978; MC 1945; Master, Knox College, Dunedin, 1963–78, retired; *b* 7 July 1910; *s* of James Cleland Hall Somerville and Grace Isabella (*née* Isherwood); *m* 1951, Janet Christina Macky (*d* 1988); four *s*. *Educ:* Univ. of Otago (MA 1934); Theol Hall, Knox Coll., Dunedin. Ordained Tapanui, 1938; Chaplain, 2 NZEF, 1942–45; Minister, St Andrews, Wellington, 1947–63. Moderator, Gen. Assembly of Presbyterian Church of NZ, 1960. Mem. Council, 1969–85, Chancellor, 1976–82, Univ. of Otago. Pres., Otago Early Settlers' Assoc., 1979–91. Hon. DD St Andrews, 1969; Hon. LLD Otago, 1979. *Publication:* Jack in the Pulpit (autobiog.), 1987. *Recreations:* cricket, bowls, reading, gardening. *Address:* 19 Constitution Street, Dunedin 9001, New Zealand. *T:* (3) 4779876. *Clubs:* Dunedin, University (Dunedin).

SOMERVILLE, Brig. Sir Nicholas; *see* Somerville, Sir J. N.

SOMERVILLE, Sir Quentin Charles Somerville A.; *see* Agnew-Somerville.

SOMERVILLE, Most Rev. Thomas David; Archbishop of New Westminster and Metropolitan of Ecclesiastical Province of British Columbia, 1975–80, retired; Anglican Chaplain, Vancouver School of Theology, 1981–84; *b* 11 Nov. 1915; *s* of Thomas Alexander Somerville and Martha Stephenson Scott; *m* 1985, Frances Best. *Educ:* King George High Sch., Vancouver; Univ. of British Columbia (BA 1937); Anglican Theological Coll. of BC (LTh 1939, BD 1951). Deacon, 1939; priest, 1940; Incumbent of: Princeton, 1940–44; Sardis with Rosedale, 1944–49; Curate of St James, Vancouver, 1949–52, Rector, 1952–60; Chapter Canon, Dio. of New Westminster, 1957; Dean of Residence, Anglican Theological Coll. of BC, 1960–65; Gen. Sec., Gen. Bd of Religious Education, Anglican Church of Canada, 1965–66; Director of Planning and Research, Anglican Church of Canada, 1966–69; Coadjutor Bishop of New Westminster, 1969–71; Bishop of New Westminster, 1971. Hon. DD: Anglican Theol. Coll. of BC, 1969; Vancouver Sch. of Theology, 1981. *Recreations:* music, botany. *Address:* 3485 Capilano Road, North Vancouver, BC V7R 4H9, Canada.

SOMERVILLE, Walter, CBE 1979; MD, FRCP; Hon. Physician to Department of Cardiology, Middlesex Hospital, since 1979 (Physician, 1954–79); to Cardiac Surgical Unit, Harefield Hospital, 1952–78; Lecturer in Cardiology, Middlesex Hospital Medical School, 1954–79; Consultant in Cardiology: to Royal Hospital Chelsea, 1963–79; to the Army, 1963–79, Hon. Consultant, 1980–85, Emeritus Consultant, 1985; Hon. Civil Consultant in Cardiology: to Royal Air Force, since 1963; to Association of Naval Officers, since 1960; to King Edward VII Convalescent Home for Officers, Osborne, since 1970; *b* 2 Oct. 1913; *s* of late Patrick and Catherine Somerville, Dublin; *m* 1957, Jane Platnauer (*see* Jane Somerville); three *s* one *d*. *Educ:* Belvedere Coll., Dublin; University College, Dublin. House appts, Mater Hosp., Dublin, 1937; out-patients Assistant, Brompton Hosp. and Chelsea Chest Clinic, 1938–39. Served in War 1939–45; attached: Canadian Dept of Defense, 1942; US Army, 1943; Lt-Col RAMC 1944. Fellow in Med., Mass General Hosp., Boston, 1946; Registrar, British Postgraduate Med. School, Hammersmith, 1947; studied in Paris, Stockholm and Univ. of Michigan, 1948; Fellow in Medicine, Peter Bent Brigham Hosp. Boston and Harvard Med. Sch., 1949; Med. Registrar, Nat. Heart Hosp. and Inst. of Cardiology, 1951; Sen. Med. Registrar, Middlesex Hosp., 1951–54. Vis. Prof., Cleveland Clinic, Cleveland, Ohio, 1980. Lectures: Carey Coombs, Bristol Univ., 1977; St Cyres, Nat. Heart Hosp., 1978; William Stokes, Irish Cardiac Soc., Belfast, 1983. Editor, British Heart Journal, 1973–80; Editorial Board: American Heart Journal, 1975–; Revista Portuguesa de cardiologia, 1982–. Mem., Med. Adv. Gp, Brewers' Soc., 1988–92. Pres., British Cardiac Soc., 1976–80; former Pres., British Acad. of Forensic Sciences; Mem., Assoc. of Physicians of Great Britain and Ireland and other socs; Corr. Member: Colombian Soc. of Cardiology; Chilean Soc. of Cardiology; Fellow, Amer. Coll. of Cardiology. Trustee, British Assoc. of Performing Arts Medicine, 1986–. Purkyne Medal, Czechoslovakian Cardiac Soc., 1981. Officer, Legion of Merit, USA, 1945. *Publications:* (ed) Paul Wood's Diseases of the Heart and Circulation (3rd edn), 1968; various articles on cardiovascular subjects in British, continental European and American journals. *Address:* 149 Harley Street, W1N 1HG. *T:* 0171–935 4444; 30 York House, Upper Montagu Street, W1H 1FR. *T:* 0171–262 2144.

SOMJEE, Shamoon; Stipendiary Magistrate, since 1991; *b* 13 Nov. 1943; *s* of Rahim Somjee, former Sessions Judge, Pakistan, and Khairunissah Somjee; *m* 1970, Isabel Fonfria Fernandez; one *s*. *Educ:* St. Lawrence's Sch., Karachi, Univ. of Karachi (BA 1963; LLB 1965). Called to the Bar, Lincoln's Inn, 1967. Mem., editl team, Halsbury's Statutes of England, and Annotated Legislation Service, Butterworths, 1967–68; Magistrates' Clerk, Inner London, 1968–91: Dep. Chief Clerk: Bow Street, 1968–75; Juvenile Courts, 1976–77; Horseferry Road, 1977–80; Chief Clerk: Wells Street, 1980–84; Old Street, 1984–90; Horseferry Road, 1990–91; Sen. Chief Clerk, S Westminster PSD, 1990–91. Chm., London Magistrates' Clerks Assoc., 1985–87. Member: Home Office Working Party on Magistrates' Courts, 1983–87; Home Office sub-group on Procedure at Substantive Hearings, 1990–91 and Appeals, Warrants and Forms, 1991. *Recreations:* cricket, music, reading. *Address:* Feltham Magistrates' Court, Hanworth Road, Feltham, Middx TW13 5AG. *T:* 0181–890 4811.

SOMMARUGA, Cornelio; President, International Committee of the Red Cross, since 1987; *b* 29 Dec. 1932; *s* of Carlo Sommaruga and Anna-Maria Valagussa; *m* 1957, Ornella Marzorati; two *s* four *d*. *Educ:* Rome; Paris; Univ. of Zürich (LLD). Bank trainee, Zürich, 1957–59; joined Diplomatic Service, 1960: Attaché, Swiss Embassy, The Hague, 1961; Sec., Bonn, 1962–64; Rome, 1965–68; Dep. Hd of Delegn to EFTA, GATT and UNCTAD, Geneva, 1969–73; Asst Sec. Gen., EFTA, 1973–75; Minister plenipotentiary, Div. of Commerce, Fed. Dept of Public Economy, Berne, 1976; Amb., 1977; Delegate, Fed. Council for Trade Agreements, 1980–84; State Sec. for External Econ. Affairs, 1984–86. Hon. Dr: (Political Affairs) Fribourg, 1985; (Internat. Relns) Minho, Braga (Portugal), 1990; (Medicine) Bologna, 1991; Univ. of Nice-Sophia Antipolis, France, 1992; (Law) Seoul Nat. Univ., 1992. *Publications:* La posizione costituzionale del Capo dello Stato nelle Costituzioni francese ed italiana da dopoguerra, 1957; numerous articles in jls and periodicals. *Address:* International Committee of the Red Cross, 19 avenue de la Paix, 1202 Geneva, Switzerland. *T:* (22) 7346001.

SONDES, 5th Earl *cr* 1880; **Henry George Herbert Milles-Lade;** Baron Sondes, 1760; Viscount Throwley, 1880; *b* 1 May 1940; *o s* of 4th Earl Sondes, and Pamela (*d* 1967), *d* of Col H. McDougall; *S* father, 1970; *m* 1st, 1968, Primrose Creswell (marr. diss. 1969), *d* of late Lawrence Stopford Llewellyn Cotter; 2nd, 1976, Sissy Fürstin zu Salm-Reifferscheidt-Raitz (marr. diss. 1981); 3rd, 1981, Sharon McCluskey (marr. diss. 1984); 4th, 1986, Phyllis Kane Schmertz. *Educ:* Eton; La Rosey. Vice Chm., Gillingham FC, 1985–. *Recreations:* shooting, skiing, the Turf. *Address:* Stringman's Farm, Faversham, Kent ME13 0LA. *T:* Canterbury (01227) 730336. *Club:* Brooks's.

SONDHEIM, Stephen Joshua; composer-lyricist; *b* 22 March 1930; *s* of Herbert Sondheim and Janet (*née* Fox). *Educ:* Williams Coll. (BA 1950). Lyrics: West Side Story, 1957; Gypsy, 1959; Do I Hear a Waltz?, 1965; (additional lyrics) Candide, 1973; music and lyrics: A Funny Thing Happened on the Way to the Forum, 1962; Anyone Can Whistle, 1964; Company, 1970; Follies, 1971; A Little Night Music, 1973 (filmed, 1976); The Frogs, 1974; Pacific Overtures, 1976; Sweeney Todd, 1979; Merrily We Roll Along, 1981; Sunday in the Park with George, 1984 (Pulitzer Prize, 1985); Into The Woods, 1987; Assassins, 1991; Passion, 1994; incidental music: Girls of Summer, 1956; Invitation to a March, 1961; Twigs, 1971; film scores: Stavisky, 1974; Reds, 1981; Dick Tracy, 1990; co-author, The Last of Sheila (film), 1973; songs for Evening Primrose (TV), 1966; anthologies: Side By Side By Sondheim, 1976; Marry Me A Little, 1981; You're Gonna Love Tomorrow, 1983; Putting It Together, 1992. Vis. Prof. of Drama, and Fellow of St Catherine's Coll., Oxford, Jan.–June 1990. Mem. Council, Dramatists Guild, 1963 (Pres., 1973–81); Mem., AAIL, 1983. Hon. Doctorate, Williams Coll., 1971. Tony Awards and New York Drama Critics' Circle Award for Into the Woods, Sweeney Todd, A Little Night Music, Follies, Company, and Passion; London Evening Standard Best Musical Award for Into the Woods; New York Drama Critics' Circle Award for Pacific Overtures and Sunday in the Park with George; London Evening Standard Best Musical Award, 1987, and SWET Laurence Olivier Award, 1988, for Follies. *Publications:* (book and vocal score): West Side Story, 1958; Gypsy, 1960; A Funny Thing Happened on the Way to the Forum, 1963; Anyone Can Whistle, 1965; Do I Hear a Waltz?, 1966; Company, 1971; Follies, 1972; A Little Night Music, 1974; Pacific Overtures, 1977; Sweeney Todd, 1979; Sunday in the Park with George, 1986. *Address:* c/o Flora Roberts, 157 West 57th Street, New York, NY 10019, USA.

SONDHEIMER, Professor Ernst Helmut, MA, ScD; Professor Emeritus of Mathematics, University of London; *b* 8 Sept. 1923; *er s* of late Max and Ida Sondheimer; *m* 1950, Janet Harrington Matthews, PhD; one *s* one *d*. *Educ:* University College School; Trinity Coll., Cambridge. Smith's Prize, 1947; Fellow of Trinity Coll., 1948–52; Research Fellow, H. H. Wills Physical Lab., University of Bristol, 1948–49; Research Associate, Massachusetts Inst. of Technology, 1949–50; London University: Lecturer in Mathematics, Imperial College of Science and Technology, 1951–54; Reader in Applied Mathematics, Queen Mary Coll., 1954–60; Prof. of Mathematics, Westfield Coll., 1960–82. Vis. Research Asst Prof. of Physics, Univ. of Illinois, USA, 1958–59; Vis. Prof. of Theoretical Physics, University of Cologne, 1967. FKC 1985; Fellow, Queen Mary and Westfield Coll., London, 1989. Editor, Alpine Journal, 1986–91. *Publications:* (with S. Doniach) Green's Functions for Solid State Physicists, 1974; (with A. Rogerson) Numbers and Infinity, 1981; papers on the electron theory of metals. *Recreations:* mountains, photography, books, growing alpines. *Address:* 51 Cholmeley Crescent, Highgate, N6 5EX. *T:* 0181–340 6607. *Clubs:* Alpine, Arts.

SONDHI, Ranjit; Senior Lecturer, Westhill College, Birmingham, since 1985; Deputy Chairman, Commission for Racial Equality, since 1993 (Member, 1991–93); *b* 22 Oct. 1950; *s* of Prem Lal Sondhi and Kanta Sondhi; *m* 1979, Anita Kumari Bhalla; one *s* one *d*. *Educ:* Bedford Sch.; Univ. of Birmingham (BSc Hons Physics). Handsworth Action Centre, Birmingham, 1972–76; Dir, Asian Resource Centre, Birmingham, 1976–85. Freelance lectr and researcher, 1975–. Member: IBA, 1987–90; Radio Authority, 1991–94; Chairman: Jt Council of Welfare for Immigrants, West Midlands, 1987–90; Refugee Employment, Trng and Educn Forum, 1990–93; Member: Digbeth Trust, 1986–90; Prince's Youth Business Trust, Birmingham, 1986–91; Royal Jubilee and Prince's Trust, Birmingham, 1986–88; Admin. Council, Prince's Trust, 1986–88; Council for Educn and Trng in Youth and Community Work, 1987–90; Ethnic Minorities Adv. Cttee, Judicial Studies Bd, 1991–; John Feeney Charitable Trust, 1991–; Trustee, Nat. Primary Centre, 1993–. Dir, Birmingham TEC, 1990–93. FRSA 1988. *Publications:* (jtly) Race in the Provincial Press, 1977; Divided Families, 1987; contribs to: Ethnicity and Social Work, 1982; Community Work and Racism, 1982; Minorities: community and identity, 1983; Analysing Inter-cultural Communication, 1987; Community Work in the Nineties, 1994. *Recreations:* Indian classical music, yoga, cooking, reading, travel, family activities. *Address:* 89 Hamstead Hall Avenue, Handsworth Wood, Birmingham B20 1JU. *T:* 0121–357 1216.

SONTAG, Susan; writer; *b* 16 Jan. 1933; one *s*. *Educ:* Univ. of Chicago (BA 1952); Harvard Univ. (MA 1955). MacArthur Foundn Fellow, 1990–95. Member: American Acad.-Inst. of Arts and Letters, 1979; Amer. Acad. of Arts and Scis, 1993; Pres., PEN Amer. Center, 1987–89. Officier de l'Ordre des Arts et des Lettres (France), 1984. *Films:* Duet for Cannibals, 1969; Brother Carl, 1971; Promised Lands, 1974; Unguided Tour, 1983. *Publications: novels:* The Benefactor, 1963; Death Kit, 1967; The Volcano Lover, 1992; *stories:* I, etcetera, 1978; The Way We Live Now, 1991; *essays:* Against Interpretation, 1966; Styles of Radical Will, 1969; On Photography, 1977; Illness as Metaphor, 1978; Under the Sign of Saturn, 1980; AIDS and its Metaphors, 1989; *filmscripts:* Duet for Cannibals, 1970; Brother Carl, 1974; *play:* Alice in Bed, 1993. *Address:* c/o Wylie, Aitken & Stone, 250 West 57th Street, Suite 2114, New York, NY 10107, USA.

SOPER, family name of **Baron Soper.**

SOPER, Baron, *cr* 1965 (Life Peer); **Rev. Donald Oliver Soper,** MA Cantab; PhD (London); Methodist Minister; President of the Methodist Conference, 1953,

Superintendent West London Mission, Kingsway Hall, 1936–78; *b* 31 Jan. 1903; *s* of late Ernest and Caroline Soper; *m* 1929, Marie Dean (*d* 1994), *d* of late Arthur Dean, Norbury; four *d*. *Educ:* Aske's School, Hatcham; St Catharine's College, Cambridge (Hon. Fellow, 1966); Wesley House, Cambridge; London School of Economics, London University. Minister, South London Mission, 1926–29; Central London Mission, 1929–36. Chm., Shelter, 1974–78. President, League against Cruel Sports. Life FTCL 1995. Hon. DD Cambridge, 1988. Peace Award, World Methodist Council, 1981. *Publications:* Christianity and its Critics; Popular Fallacies about the Christian Faith; Will Christianity Work?; Practical Christianity To-day; Questions and Answers in Ceylon; All His Grace (Methodist Lent Book for 1957); It is hard to work for God; The Advocacy of the Gospel; Tower Hill 12.30; Aflame with Faith; Christian Politics; Calling for Action, 1984. *Recreations:* music, open air speaking. *Address:* 19 Thayer Street, W1M 5LJ.

SOPER, Rt. Rev. (Andrew) Laurence, OSB; STD; Abbot of Ealing, since 1991; *b* 17 Sept. 1943; *s* of Alan and Anne Soper. *Educ:* St Benedict's Sch., Ealing; Blackfriars, Oxford; Sant Anselmo, Rome (STD); Strawberry Hill (PGCE). Banking until 1964; entered Novitiate at Ealing, 1964; St Benedict's School: Teacher, 1973–83; Bursar, 1975–91; Prior, 1984–91; Asst Chaplain, Harrow Sch., 1981–91. Substitute Prison Chaplain, 1988–. Mem. Council, Union of Monastic Superiors, 1994–. Episcopal Vicar for Religions for Western Area, 1995–. FRSA. *Publications:* (ed with Rev. Peter Elliott) Thoughts of Jesus Christ, 1970; articles and thesis on T. H. Green and 19th century English theology. *Recreations:* pastoral activities, reading, hill walking. *Address:* Ealing Abbey, W5 2DY. *T:* 0181–998 2158.

SOPWITH, Sir Charles (Ronald), Kt 1966; Second Counsel to Chairman of Committees, House of Lords, 1974–82; *b* 12 Nov. 1905; *s* of Alfred Sopwith, S Shields, Co. Durham; *m* 1946, Ivy Violet (*d* 1968), *d* of Frederick Leonard Yeates, Gidea Park, Essex. *Educ:* S Shields High School. Chartered Accountant, 1928; Solicitor, 1938. Assistant Director, Press Censorship, 1943–45; Assistant Solicitor, 1952–56, Principal Asst Solicitor, 1956–61, Solicitor, 1963–70, Board of Inland Revenue; Public Trustee, 1961–63; Deputy Sec., Cabinet Office, 1970–72. Hon. FRAM, 1984. *Recreations:* music, reading history. *Address:* Kilfillan House, Graemesdyke Road, Berkhamsted, Herts HP4 3LZ. *Club:* Reform.

SORABJI, Prof. Richard Rustom Kharsedji, FBA 1989; Professor of Ancient Philosphy, King's College London, since 1981; Director, Institute of Classical Studies, London, since 1991; *b* 8 Nov. 1934; *s* of Richard Kaikushru Sorabji and late Mary Katherine (*née* Monkhouse); *m* 1958, Margaret Anne Catherine Taster; one *s* two *d*. *Educ:* Dragon Sch.; Charterhouse; Pembroke Coll., Oxford (BA Greats; MA; BPhil). CS Commn in Russian Lang. Cornell University: joined Sage Sch. of Philosophy, 1962; Associate Prof., 1968; Sen. Res. Fellow, Soc. of Humanities, 1979; King's College, London, 1970–: Designer and Dir, King's Coll. Centre for Philosophical Studies, 1989–91; FKC 1990. Chm., Bd of Philosophical Studies, London Univ., 1979–82. Sen. Fellow, Council of Humanities, Princeton Univ., 1985. Mem., Sen. Common Room, Wolfson Coll., Oxford, 1991–, Pembroke Coll., Oxford, 1992–. Lectures: Read-Tuckwell, Bristol, 1985; Simon, Toronto, 1990; Gray, Cambridge, 1991; Townsend, Cornell, 1991–92; Gaisford, Oxford, 1993; Webster, Stanford, 1994; Donnellan, Dublin, 1995. Pres., Aristotelian Soc., 1985–86. Founder and organiser of internat. project for translating the Ancient Commentators on Aristotle, 1985–. *Publications:* Aristotle on Memory, 1973; (ed jtly) Articles on Aristotle, 4 vols, 1975–79; Necessity, Cause and Blame, 1980; Time, Creation and the Continuum, 1983; (ed) Philoponus and the Rejection of Aristotelian Science, 1987; (ed) The Ancient Commentators on Aristotle, first 23 of 60 vols, 1987–; Matter, Space and Motion, 1988 (Choice Award for Outstanding Academic Book, 1989–90); (ed) Aristotle Transformed, 1990; Animal Minds and Human Morals: the origins of the western debate, 1993. *Recreations:* architecture, archaeology, occasional verses. *Address:* Department of Philosophy, King's College, Strand, WC2R 2LS. *T:* 0171–873 2231.

SORBIE, Prof. Kenneth Stuart, DPhil; Professor of Petroleum Engineering, Heriot-Watt University, since 1992; *b* Prestwick, 15 Jan. 1950; *s* of late Kenneth Sorbie and of Lucy (*née* Ferguson); *m* 1976, Prof. Sheila Riddell; two *d*. *Educ:* Strathclyde Univ. (BSc 1st cl. Hons, 1972); Sussex Univ. (DPhil 1975). Res. Fellow, Cambridge Univ., 1975–76; teaching and lecturing, 1976–80; Group leader, oil res. and enhanced oil recovery, AEE Winfrith, 1980–88; Lectr, 1988–90, Reader, 1990–92, Heriot-Watt Univ. Mem., Soc. of Petroleum Engrs, 1985. *Publications:* Polymer Improved Oil Recovery, 1991; over 120 technical papers on petroleum-related research. *Recreations:* listening to and collecting classical music, particularly Renaissance masses and lute music, guitar and chamber music; hill walking, running, weight training—but also fond of good food and wine, alas! *Address:* Department of Petroleum Engineering, Heriot-Watt University, Edinburgh EH14 4AS. *T:* 0131–451 3139, *Fax:* 0131–451 3127; 23 Morningside Park, Edinburgh EH10 5HD. *T:* 0131–447 2894.

SORENSEN, (Kenneth) Eric (Correll); Chief Executive, London Docklands Development Corporation, since 1991; *b* 15 Oct. 1942; *m* Susan; two *s* one *d*. *Educ:* Bedford Sch.; Keele Univ. (BA(Hons) Econs and History). Voluntary work, India; joined DoE, 1967; Private Sec. to Sec. of State for Envmt, 1977; Chm., NW Regl Bd and NW Regl Dir, Depts of the Envmt and Transport, 1980–81; Dir, Merseyside Task Force, DoE, 1981–84; Dir, Inner Cities Directorate, DoE, 1984–87; Head of Urban Policy Unit, Cabinet Office, 1987–88; Dir of Personnel Management and Trng, Depts of Envmt and Transport, 1988–90; Dep. Sec., Housing and Construction Comd, DoE, 1990–91. Civil Service Comr (part-time), 1992–. *Address:* London Docklands Development Corporation, Thames Quay, 191 Marsh Wall, E14 9TJ.

SORINJ, Dr L. T.; *see* Tončić-Sorinj.

SOROKOS, Lt-Gen. John A., Greek Gold Medal for Gallantry (3 times); Greek Military Cross (twice); Medal for Distinguished Services (3 times); Silver and Gold Cross (with swords) of Order of George I; Comdr, Order of George I and Order of Phoenix; Military Medal of Merit (1st Class); Ambassador of Greece to the United States of America, 1972–74; *b* 1917; *s* of A. and P. Sorokos; *m* 1954, Pia Madaros; one *s*. *Educ:* Mil. Acad. of Greece; Staff and Nat. Defence Colls, Greece; British Staff Coll., Camberley; US Mil. Schools. Company Comdr: in Second World War in Greece, 1940–41; in El Alamein Campaign, N Africa, 1942–43; Div. Staff Officer and Bn Comdr, 1947–49; served as Staff Officer: in Mil. Units in Army HQ and Armed Forces HQ, 1952–63; in NATO Allied Forces Southern Europe, 1957–59; Instructor, Nat. Defence Coll., Greece, 1963–64; Regt Comdr, 1965; Mil. Attaché to Greek Embassies in Washington and Ottawa, 1966–68; Div. Comdr, 1968–69; Dep. Comdr, Greek Armed Forces, 1969; Ambassador to UK, 1969–72. Officer, Legion of Merit (US). *Recreations:* horses, boating, fishing. *Address:* Mimnermou 2, Athens 106 74, Greece.

SORRELL, Alec Albert; Director of Statistics, Department of the Environment, 1981–82, retired; *b* 20 July 1925; *s* of Albert Edward Sorrell and Jessie (*née* Morris); *m* 1962, Eileen Joan Orchard; one *s*. *Educ:* George Gascoigne Sch., Walthamstow; SW Essex Technical College. BSc (Econ). Statistical Officer, MAP, 1945; Board of Trade: Asst Statistician, 1950; Statistician, 1954; Chief Statistician, 1966; Chief Statistician: Min. of Technology, 1969; Dept of Trade and Industry, 1970; Central Statistical Office, 1971; Asst Dir, Central Statistical Office, Cabinet Office, 1972–78; Principal Dir of Statistics, Depts of the Environment and Transport, 1978–81. *Publications:* various articles in trade, professional and learned jls. *Recreations:* walking, reading, music, gardening. *Address:* Ranelagh, Stewarts Road, Week St Mary, Holsworthy, Devon EX22 6XA. *T:* Week St Mary (01288) 341436.

SORRELL, John William, FCSD; Chairman, Newell & Sorrell, since 1983; Chairman, Design Council, since 1994; *b* 28 Feb. 1945; *s* of late John William Sorrell and Elizabeth Jane Sorrell (*née* Taylor); *m* 1974, Frances Mary Newell; two *s* one *d*. *Educ:* Hornsey Coll. of Art (NDD 1964). Designer, Maine Wolff & Partners, 1964; Partner, Goodwin Sorrell, 1964–71; Design Manager, Wolff Olins, 1971–76; Founder, Newell & Sorrell, 1976. A Vice-Pres., CSD, 1989–92; Chm., Design Business Assoc., 1990–92. Member: BR Architecture and Design Panel, 1991–93; RSA Design Adv. Gp, 1991–93. Gov., Design Dimension, 1991–93. *Recreations:* arboriculture, Arsenal, art. *Address:* Newell & Sorrell Ltd, 4 Utopia Village, Chalcot Road, NW1 8LH. *T:* 0171–722 1113. *Club:* Groucho.

SORRELL, Martin Stuart; Group Chief Executive, WPP Group, since 1986; *b* 14 Feb. 1945; *s* of late Jack and of Sally Sorrell; *m* 1971, Sandra Carol Ann Finestone; three *s*. *Educ:* Haberdashers' Aske's School; Christ's College, Cambridge (MA); Harvard Graduate School of Business (MBA 1968). Consultant, Glendinning Associates, Conn, 1968–69; Vice-Pres., Mark McCormack Orgn, London, 1970–74; Dir, James Gulliver Associates, 1975–77; Gp Financial Dir, Saatchi & Saatchi, 1977–86. Dir, Storehouse plc, 1994–. Member: Adv. Bd, IESE, Spain, 1989–; Adv. Bd, Judge Inst. for Management Studies, Cambridge, 1990–. Gov., London Business Sch., 1990–. Trustee: Cambridge Foundn, 1990–; Princess Royal Trust for Carers, 1993–. *Recreations:* ski-ing, cricket (annual fathers' match). *Address:* WPP Group, 27 Farm Street, W1X 6RD. *T:* 0171–408 2204. *Clubs:* Reform; Harvard (NY).

SORRIE, George Strath, CB 1993; Medical Adviser and Director, Civil Service Occupational Health Service, 1987–93; *b* 19 May 1933; *s* of Alexander James Sorrie and Florence Edith Sorrie (*née* Strath); *m* 1959, Gabrielle Ann Baird; three *d*. *Educ:* Woodside Sch., Aberdeen; Robert Gordon's Coll., Aberdeen; Univ. of Aberdeen (MB ChB); Univs of London and Dundee. FFOM, DPH, DIH. Medical Branch, RAF, 1958–61; Lectr in Epidemiology, London Sch. of Hygiene and Tropical Medicine, 1965–67; GP, Rhynie, Aberdeenshire, 1967–72; Health and Safety Exec., 1972, Dep. Dir of Med. Services, 1980–87. *Address:* 30 Irvine Crescent, St Andrews, Fife KY16 8LG. *T:* St Andrews (01334) 474510.

SOUHAMI, Mark; Deputy Chairman, Dixons Group, since 1992 (Group Managing Director, 1986–92); Chairman, British Retail Consortium, since 1995; *b* 25 Sept. 1935; *s* of John Souhami and Freda Souhami (*née* Harris); *m* 1964, Margaret Austin; two *d*. *Educ:* St Marylebone Grammar School. Lieut RA, 1954–56; early career in City and timber industry; joined Dixons 1970: Group Marketing Dir, 1970; Man. Dir, 1973; Group Board, 1978. Mem. Econ. Affairs Cttee, CBI, 1978–94 (Mem. Council, 1978–91). Mem., Metropolitan Police Cttee, 1995–. Trustee, Photographers' Gall., 1978–90. CIMgt; FCIM. Founder Mem., of Marketors' Co., 1975. *Recreations:* gardening, fishing, shooting. *Address:* Brewham House, Brewham, Somerset BA10 0JG. *Clubs:* Savile, Royal Automobile, Naval and Military.

See also R. L. Souhami.

SOUHAMI, Prof. Robert Leon, MD; FRCP, FRCR; Kathleen Ferrier Professor of Clinical Oncology, University College London Medical School (formerly University College and Middlesex School of Medicine), since 1987; *b* 26 April 1938; *s* of John Souhami and Freda Harris; *m* 1966. *Educ:* St Marylebone Grammar Sch.; University Coll. Hosp. Med. Sch. (BSc, MB BS). MD 1975; FRCP 1979; FRCR 1992. Registrar, UCH, 1966–69; Hon. Lectr, St Mary's Hosp. Med. Sch., 1969–71; Sen. Registrar, UCH, 1971–73; Consultant Physician, Poole Gen. Hosp., 1973–75; Consultant Physician and Sen. Lectr, UCH, 1975–87; Hon. Consultant Physician, Whittington Hosp. and Royal Nat. Orthopaedic Hosp., 1976–. Chairman: Cancer Therapy Cttee, MRC, 1987–93; Assoc. of Cancer Physicians, 1989–92; Protocol Review Cttee, EORTC, 1994–; Mem., Science Council, Celltech, 1992–. Fellow, UCL, 1990. *Publications:* Tutorials in Differential Diagnosis, 1974, 3rd edn 1992; Cancer and its Management, 1986, 2nd edn 1994; Textbook of Medicine, 1990, 2nd edn 1994; articles on aspects of cancer medicine.

See also M. Souhami.

SOULAS, Alain; Chief Executive, Arjo Wiggins Appleton, since 1992; *b* 3 May 1943; *s* of Raymond Soulas and Denise Noyer; *m* Simone Gallian; two *d*. *Educ:* Stanford Univ. (MSc 1967); Ingénieur du Génie Maritime, Paris, 1966. Cerci, 1969–74; Cellulose du Pin, 1975–81; Socar, 1981–82; Chief Exec., Condat, 1983–85; Chief Exec., Paper Div., Saint Gobain and Chm., Cellulose du Pin, 1985–92. French National Order of Merit. *Recreations:* opera, theatre. *Address:* 23G Lennox Gardens, SW1X 0DE. *T:* 0171–584 4554. *Club:* Racing Club de France (Paris).

SOULBURY, 2nd Viscount *cr* 1954, of Soulbury; **James Herwald Ramsbotham;** Baron 1941; *b* 21 March 1915; *s* of 1st Viscount Soulbury, PC, GCMG, GCVO, OBE, MC, and Doris Violet (*d* 1954), *d* of late S. de Stein; *S* father, 1971; *m* 1949, Anthea Margaret (*d* 1950), *d* of late David Wilton. *Educ:* Eton; Magdalen College, Oxford. *Heir:* *b* Hon. Sir Peter Edward Ramsbotham, *qv*.

SOULSBY, family name of **Baron Soulsby of Swaffham Prior.**

SOULSBY OF SWAFFHAM PRIOR, Baron *cr* 1990 (Life Peer), of Swaffham Prior in the County of Cambridgeshire; **Ernest Jackson Lawson Soulsby;** Professor of Animal Pathology, University of Cambridge, 1978–93, now Emeritus; Fellow, Wolfson College, Cambridge, 1978–93; *b* 23 June 1926; *s* of William George Lawson Soulsby and Agnes Soulsby; *m* 1st, 1950, Margaret Macdonald; one *s* one *d*; 2nd, 1962, Georgina Elizabeth Annette Williams. *Educ:* Queen Elizabeth Grammar Sch., Penrith; Univ. of Edinburgh. MRCVS; DVSM; PhD; MA (Cantab). Veterinary Officer, City of Edinburgh, 1949–52; Lectr in Clinical Parasitology, Univ. of Bristol, 1952–54; Univ. Lectr in Animal Pathology, Univ. of Cambridge, 1954–63; Prof. of Parasitology, Univ. of Pennsylvania, 1964–78. Ian McMaster Fellow, CSIRO, 1958; Sen. Vis. Fellow, EEC, Poland, 1961; WHO Vis. Worker, USSR, 1962; UN Special Fund Expert, IAEA, Vienna and Zemun, Yugoslavia, 1964; Ford Foundn Visiting Prof., Univ. of Ibadan, 1964; Richard Merton Guest Prof., Justus Liebig Univ., 1974–75; Vis. Prof. Univ. of Qld, 1992. Lectures: Hume Meml, Univ. Fedn Animal Welfare, 1985; Wooldridge Meml, BVA, 1986; Sir Frederick Hobday Meml, British Equine Vet. Assoc., 1986; Richard Turk Meml, Texas A & M Univ., 1991; Harben, RIPH&H, 1991; Stoll Meml, NJ, 1995. Member: AFRC, 1984–89 (Chm., Animal Res. Grants Bd, 1986–89); Vet. Adv. Cttee, Horserace Betting Levy Bd, 1984– (Chm., 1985–); EEC Adv. Cttee on Vet. Trng, 1981–86; Animal Procedure Cttee, Home Office, 1986–95. Royal College of Veterinary Surgeons: Mem. Council, 1978–; Jun. Vice-Pres., 1983; Pres., 1984; Sen. Vice-Pres., 1985. President: World Assoc. Adv. Vet. Parasit., 1963–67 (Hon. Mem., 1985); Helminthol. Soc., Washington, 1970–71 (Hon. Mem., 1990); Cambridge Soc. for Comp. Medicine, 1984–85; Vet. Res. Club, 1985–86; Comp. Medicine Section, RSocMed, 1993–95. Council Mem., Amer. Soc. Parasitologists,

1974–78. Corresponding Member: German Parasitology Soc.; Acad. Royale de Médecine de Belgique; Hon. Member: Mexican Parasitology Soc.; Argentinian Parasitological Soc.; BVA; British Soc. for Parasitology; Expert Advisor and Consultant, and Member, Scientific Groups: various internat. agencies and govts. Hon. AM 1972, Hon. DSc 1984, Univ. of Pennsylvania; Hon. DVMS Edinburgh, 1991; Hon. DVM León, 1993; Hon. DSc Univ. of Peradeniya, Sri Lanka, 1994. R. N. Chaudhury Gold Medal, Calcutta Sch. of Tropical Med., Calcutta, 1976; Behring-Bilharz Prize, Cairo, 1977; Ludwig-Schunk Prize, Justus-Liebig Universität, Giessen, 1979; Diploma and Medal, XXI World Vet. Congress, Moscow, 1979; Distinguished Parasitologist Award, Amer. Assoc. of Vet. Parasitologists, 1987; Friedrich Mussenmeier Medal, Humboldt Univ., 1990; World Assoc. for Advancement of Vet. Parasitology/Pfizer Excellence in Teaching Award, 1993. *Publications:* Textbook of Veterinary Clinical Parasitology, 1965; Biology of Parasites, 1966; Reaction of the Host to Parasitism, 1968; Helminths, Arthropods and Protozoa of Domesticated Animals, 6th edn 1968, 7th edn 1982; Immunity to Animal Parasites, 1972; Parasitic Zoonoses, 1974; Pathophysiology of Parasitic Infections, 1976; Epidemiology and Control of Nematodiasis in Cattle, 1981; Immunology, Immunopathology and Immunoprophylaxis of Parasitic Infections, Vols I, II, III & IV, 1986; articles in jls of parasitology, immunology and pathology. *Recreations:* travel, gardening, photography. *Address:* House of Lords, SW1A 0PW. *Clubs:* Farmers', United Oxford & Cambridge University.

SOUNDY, Andrew John; Senior Partner, Ashurst Morris Crisp (Solicitors), since 1992; *b* 29 March 1940; *s* of Harold Cecil Soundy and Adele Monica Templeton (*née* Westley); *m* 1963, Jill Marion Steiner; one *s* two *d*. *Educ:* Boxgrove Sch.; Shrewsbury Sch.; Trinity Coll., Cambridge (BA, MA). Ashurst Morris Crisp: articled clerk, 1963–66; qualified as solicitor, 1966; Partner, 1969. Non-Exec. Dir, EWFact plc, 1994–. FRSA 1993. *Recreations:* pedigree cattle breeding, opera, tennis. *Address:* Bartletts Farm, Mattingley, Basingstoke, Hants RG27 8JU. *T:* Reading (01734) 326279. *Club:* Cavalry and Guards.

SOUROZH, Metropolitan of; *see* Anthony, Archbishop.

SOUTAR, Air Marshal Sir Charles (John Williamson), KBE 1978 (MBE 1958); Director-General, Medical Services (RAF), 1978–81; *b* 12 June 1920; *s* of Charles Alexander Soutar and Mary Helen (*née* Watson); *m* 1944, Joy Dorée Upton; one *s* two *d*. *Educ:* Brentwood Sch.; London Hosp. MB, BS, LMSSA, FFCM, DPH, DIH. Commissioned RAF, 1946. Various appts, then PMO, Middle East Command, 1967–68; Dep. Dir, Med. Organisation, RAF, 1968–70; OC, PMRAF Hosp., Halton, 1970–73; Comdt, RAF Inst. of Aviation Medicine, 1973–75; PMO, Strike Command, 1975–78. QHS 1974–81. CStJ 1972. *Recreations:* sport, gardening, ornithology, music. *Address:* Oak Cottage, High Street, Aldeburgh, Suffolk IP15 5AU. *T:* Aldeburgh (01728) 452201. *Club:* Royal Air Force.

SOUTER, family name of **Baron Audley.**

SOUTER, David Hackett; Associate Justice of the Supreme Court of the United States, since 1990; *b* 17 Sept. 1939. *Educ:* Harvard Univ. (LLB); Oxford Univ. (Rhodes Scholar; MA). Admitted to NH Bar; Associate, Orr & Reno, Concord, NH, 1966–68; Asst Attorney-Gen., 1968–71, Dep. Attorney-Gen., 1976, Attorney-Gen., 1976–78, New Hampshire; Associate Justice: NH Superior Court, 1978–83; NH Supreme Court, 1983–90. *Address:* Supreme Court Building, 1 First Street NE, Washington, DC 20543, USA.

SOUTH, Sir Arthur, Kt 1974; JP; Partner, Norwich Fur Company, since 1947; *b* 29 Oct. 1914; *s* of Arthur and Violet South, Norwich; *m* 1st, 1937, May Adamson (marr. diss. 1976); two *s*; 2nd, 1976, Mary June (*d* 1982), *widow* of Robert Edward Carter, JP, DL. *Educ:* City of Norwich Sch. RAF and MAP, 1941–46. Mem., Norwich, Lowestoft, Gt Yarmouth Hosp. Management Cttee, 1948–74 (Vice-Chm., 1954–66, Chm., 1966–74); Chairman: Norfolk Area Health Authority, 1974–78; E Anglian RHA, 1978–87; Mem., E Anglia Regional Hosp. Bd, 1969–74. Member: Assoc. of Educn Cttees, 1963–74; Assoc. of Municipal Corporations, 1965–74; E Anglia Econ. Planning Council, 1966–80; E Anglia Rent Assessment Panel, 1967–74; E Anglia Adv. Cttee to BBC, 1970–74; Univ. of E Anglia Council, 1964–80 (Life Mem., Court, 1964); Chairman: E Anglia Roads to Prosperity, 1987–; Norfolk Energy Forum, 1988–. Norwich: City Councillor, 1935–41 and 1946–61; Alderman, 1961–74; Sheriff, 1953–54; Lord Mayor, 1956–57, Dep. Lord Mayor, 1959–60; JP 1949; Dep. Leader, Norwich City Council, 1959–60; Chm., Labour Party Gp and Leader Norwich City Council, 1960–78. Norwich City Football Club: Vice-Pres., 1957–66; Dir, 1966–73; Chm., 1973–85; Member: FA Council, 1981–86; Football League: Mem., Management Cttee, 1981–85; Life Vice-Pres., 1985. Hon. DCL East Anglia, 1989. *Recreations:* football, bowls, cricket. *Address:* 23 Hall Lane, Drayton, Norfolk NR8 6DR. *T:* Drayton (01603) 868907. *Clubs:* MCC; Mitre Bowls, Norfolk Cricket, Norwich City Football.

SOUTH, William Lawrence, CBE 1988; FIEE; management consultant, since 1991; *b* 3 May 1933; *s* of Laurence and Anne South; *m* 1960, Lesley (*née* Donaldson); one *s* two *d*. *Educ:* Purley County Grammar Sch. FIEE 1992. RAF, 1951–55 (Pilot, 511 and 220 Sqdns). Director: Pye of Cambridge, 1977–81; Philips Electronics, 1982–94; Origin Holdings, 1990–92; Greenwich Healthcare NHS Trust, 1995–. Member: NPL Supervisory Bd, 1988–; ITAB, 1988–93; SERC Engrg Bd, 1992–94. Freeman, City of London, 1991; Liveryman, Co. of Information Technologists, 1992–. *Recreations:* sailing, music. *Address:* 22 Meadowbank, Blackheath SE3 9XD. *T:* 0181–852 3831. *Clubs:* Blackheath Football; Chichester Yacht.

SOUTHALL, Kenneth Charles; Under-Secretary, Inland Revenue, 1975–82; *b* 3 Aug. 1922; *s* of Arthur and Margarette Jane Southall; *m* 1947, Audrey Kathleen Skeels; one *s*. *Educ:* Queen Elizabeth's Grammar Sch., Hartlebury, Worcs. Inland Revenue, 1939; RAF, 1942–46; Administrative Staff College, 1962. *Address:* The Green, Brill, Bucks HP18 9RU.

SOUTHAM, Gordon Ronald, BSc; AInstP; Headmaster, Ashville College, 1958–77; *b* 20 March 1918; *s* of late G. H. Southam, Brackley; *m* 1948, Joan, *d* of late W. Thompson; one *d*. *Educ:* Magdalen College School, Brackley; Westminster College, and King's College, London. BSc (Gen. Hons) 1938, BSc (Special Physics) 1st Class Hons 1939. Teacher's diploma, 1947, AInstP 1947. Served Royal Air Force, 1940–46: Bomber Comd, 1940–43; Staff Officer in HQ, ACSEA, 1943–46 (Sqdn Ldr). Senior Physics Master, Culford School, 1947–49; Lecturer, Royal Military Academy, Sandhurst, 1950–52; Head of Department of Science, Royal Military Academy, Sandhurst, 1953–57. *Recreations:* motoring, electronics; formerly Rugby football, athletics. *Address:* Culford, 20 Oak Tree Drive, Bedale, N Yorks DL8 1UL.

SOUTHAMPTON, 6th Baron *cr* 1780; **Charles James FitzRoy;** *b* 12 Aug. 1928; *o s* of Charles FitzRoy (5th Baron, disclaimed peerage for life, 1964) and Margaret (*d* 1931), *d* of Rev. Preb. Herbert Mackworth Drake; *S* father, 1989; *m* 1951, Pamela Anne, *d* of Edward Percy Henniker; one *s* one *d* (and one *s* decd). *Educ:* Stowe. Master: Easton Harriers, 1968–71; Blaikney Foxhounds, 1971–72. *Recreations:* shooting, fishing, golf. *Heir: s* Hon. Edward Charles FitzRoy [*b* 8 July 1955; *m* 1978, Rachel Caroline Vincent, 2nd *d* of Peter John Curnow Millett; one *s* three *d*]. *Address:* Stone Cross, Stone Lane, Chagford, Newton Abbot, Devon TQ13 8JU.

SOUTHAMPTON, Bishop Suffragan of, since 1989; **Rt. Rev. John Freeman Perry;** *b* 15 June 1935; *s* of Richard and Elsie Perry; *m* 1959, Gay Valerie Brown; three *s* two *d*. *Educ:* Mill Hill School; London College of Divinity (ALCD). LTh St John's Coll., Nottingham, 1974; MPhil Westminster Coll., Oxford, 1986. Assistant Curate: Christ Church, Woking, 1959–62; Christ Church, Chorleywood, 1962–63; Vicar, St Andrew's, Chorleywood, 1963–77; RD of Rickmansworth, 1972–77; Warden, Lee Abbey, Lynton, Devon, 1977–89; RD of Shirwell, 1980–84. Hon. Canon, Winchester Cathedral, 1989–. *Publication:* Christian Leadership, 1983. *Recreations:* a large family, jogging and walking, sport, travel, classical music. *Address:* Ham House, The Crescent, Romsey, Hants SO51 7NG. *T:* Romsey (01794) 516005.

SOUTHAN, Robert Joseph; His Honour Judge Southan; a Circuit Judge, since 1986; *b* 13 July 1928; *s* of late Thomas Southan and of Kathleen Southan; *m* 1960, Elizabeth Andreas Evatt, *qv*; one *d* (one *s* decd). *Educ:* Rugby; St Edmund Hall, Oxford (MA); University Coll., London (LLM). Called to the Bar, Inner Temple, 1953; called to the Bar of NSW, 1976; a Recorder, 1983–86. *Recreations:* theatre, opera, sailing, ski-ing, squash, tennis. *Address:* c/o Harrow Crown Court, Hailsham Drive, Harrow HA1 4TU. *T:* 0181–424 2294. *Clubs:* Royal Corinthian Yacht, Bar Yacht; Cumberland Lawn Tennis.

SOUTHBY, Sir John (Richard Bilbe), 3rd Bt *cr* 1937, of Burford, Co. Oxford; General Manager (formerly District Manager), East Midlands Electricity, Milton Keynes, since 1991; *b* 2 April 1948; *s* of Sir Archibald Richard Charles Southby, 2nd Bt, OBE and Olive Marion (*d* 1991), *d* of late Sir Thomas Bilbe-Robinson; *S* father, 1988; *m* 1971, Victoria Jane, *d* of John Wilfred Sturrock; two *s* one *d*. *Educ:* Peterhouse, Marandellas, Rhodesia; Loughborough Univ. of Technology (BSc Elec. Eng). CEng, MIEE. East Midlands Electricity Board: Graduate Trainee, 1971; Asst Engineer 1973, O & M Engineer 1976, Shepshed, Leics; Senior Asst Engineer 1979, O & M Engineer 1981, Boston, Lincs; District Engineer, Grantham, 1986. *Recreations:* ski-ing, gardening, tennis, music, DIY. *Heir: s* Peter John Southby [*b* 20 Aug. 1973; *m* 1995, Katherine Margaret, *d* of Dr R. N. Priestland]. *Address:* Lomagundi, High Street, Nash, Bucks MK17 0EP. *Club:* Rotary (Milton Keynes).

SOUTHEND, Archdeacon of; *see* Jennings, Ven. D. W. M.

SOUTHERN, Michael William; Adviser to HE the Minister of Health, Kingdom of Saudi Arabia, 1978, now retired; Regional Administrator, South West Thames Regional Health Authority, 1973–77; *b* 22 June 1918; *s* of William Southern and Ida Frances Southern; *m* 1945, Nancy Russell Golsworthy; three *d*. *Educ:* Tiffin Boys' Sch., Kingston-upon-Thames; London Univ. (DPA); Open Univ. (BA Humanities). Surrey CC Public Health Dept, 1934–39 and 1945–48; served with RAMC (NCO), 1939–45: Technician in No 1 Malaria Field Lab., 1940–41; POW Germany, 1941–44; Planning Officer and later Sec. of SW Metropolitan Regional Hosp. Bd, 1948–73. Royal British Legion: Chairman: Surrey Council, 1985–88; Richard Sharples Court, Sutton, 1988–93; Duke of Connaught Meml Br., 1993–. *Recreations:* music, travel, philately. *Address:* 14 Poole Road, West Ewell, Epsom, Surrey KT19 9RY. *T:* 0181–393 5096.

SOUTHERN, Sir Richard (William), Kt 1974; FBA 1960; FRSL 1973; President of St John's College, Oxford, 1969–81, Honorary Fellow, 1981; *b* 8 Feb. 1912; 2nd *s* of Matthew Henry Southern, Newcastle upon Tyne; *m* 1944, Sheila (*née* Cobley), *widow* of Sqdn Ldr C. Crichton-Miller; two *s*. *Educ:* Royal Grammar Sch., Newcastle upon Tyne; Balliol College, Oxford (Domus Exhibnr). 1st Class Hons Modern History, 1932. Junior Research Fellow, Exeter College, Oxford, 1933–37 (Hon. Fellow, 1991); studied in Paris, 1933–34 and Munich, 1935; Fellow and Tutor, Balliol Coll., Oxford, 1937–61 (Hon. Fellow 1966). Served Oxford and Bucks LI, 1940; 2nd Lt Durham LI 1941; 155th Regt RAC, 1942; Captain 1943; Major 1944; Political Intelligence Dept, Foreign Office, 1943–45. Junior Proctor, Oxford Univ., 1948–49; Birkbeck Lectr in Ecclesiastical History, Trinity College, Cambridge, 1959–60; Chichele Prof. of Modern History, Oxford, 1961–69; President: Royal Historical Soc., 1968–72; Selden Soc., 1973–76. Lectures: Raleigh, British Academy, 1962; David Murray, Glasgow Univ., 1963; Gifford, Glasgow Univ., 1970–72; G. M. Trevelyan, Cambridge Univ., 1980–81. Corresponding Fellow: Medieval Academy of America, 1965; Monumenta Germaniae Historica, 1982; For. Hon. Mem., Amer. Acad. of Arts and Scis, 1972. Hon. Fellow, Sidney Sussex Coll., Cambridge, 1971; Hon. DLitt: Glasgow, 1964; Durham, 1969; Cantab, 1971; Bristol, 1974; Newcastle, 1977; Warwick, 1978; St Anselm's Coll., 1981; Columbia, 1982; Univ. of the South, 1985; Hon. LLD Harvard, 1977. Balzan Prize, Fondazione Internazionale Balzan, Milan, 1987. *Publications:* The Making of the Middle Ages, 1953 (numerous foreign translations); (ed) Eadmer's Vita Anselmi, 1963; St Anselm and his Biographer, 1963; Western Views of Islam in the Middle Ages, 1962; (ed with F. S. Schmitt) Memorials of St Anselm, 1969; Medieval Humanism and other studies, 1970 (RSL award 1970); Western Society and the Church in the Middle Ages, 1970; Robert Grosseteste, 1986; St Anselm: a portrait in a landscape, 1990; Scholastic Humanism and the Unification of Europe, vol 1, 1995; articles in English Historical Review, Medieval and Renaissance Studies, etc. *Address:* 40 St John Street, Oxford OX1 2LH.

SOUTHERN, Sir Robert, Kt 1970; CBE 1953; General Secretary, Co-operative Union Ltd, 1948–72; *b* 17 March 1907; *s* of Job Southern and Margaret (*née* Tonge); *m* 1933, Lena Chapman; one *s* one *d*. *Educ:* Stand Grammar Sch.; Co-operative Coll.; Manchester University. Co-operative Wholesale Soc., Bank Dept, 1925–29; Co-operative Union Ltd, 1929. *Publication:* Handbook to the Industrial and Provident Societies' Act, 1938. *Address:* 22 Glebelands Road, Prestwich, Manchester M25 5NE. *T:* 0161–773 2699.

SOUTHERTON, Thomas Henry, BSc (Eng); CEng, MIEE; Senior Director, Data Processing, Post Office, 1975–78, retired; *b* 1 July 1917; *s* of C. H. Southerton, Birmingham; *m* 1st, 1945, Marjorie Elizabeth Sheen (*d* 1979); one *s*; 2nd, 1981, Joyce Try. *Educ:* Bemrose Sch., Derby; Northampton Coll., London (BSc(Eng)). PO Apprentice, Derby, 1933–36; Engineering Workman, Derby and Nottingham, 1936–40; Inspector, Engineer-in-Chief's Office, 1940–45; Engineer, 1945–50; Sen. Exec. Engr, 1950–53; Factory Manager, PO Provinces, 1953–56; Dep. Controller, Factories Dept, 1956–64; Controller, Factories Dept, 1964–67; Dir, Telecommunications Management Services, 1967–73; Sen. Dir Telecommunications Personnel, 1973–75. Mem., Industrial Tribunals, 1978–86. *Recreations:* art, architecture, music.

SOUTHESK, Earl of; David Charles Carnegie; *b* 3 March 1961; *s* and *heir* of 3rd Duke of Fife, *qv*; held courtesy title Earl of Macduff until 1992; *m* 1987, Caroline, *d* of Martin Bunting, *qv*; three *s*. *Educ:* Eton; Pembroke Coll., Cambridge (BA Law 1982; MA 1986); Royal Agricultural College, Cirencester; Edinburgh Univ. (MBA 1990). Cazenove & Co., 1982–85; Bell Lawrie & Co., 1988–89; trainee chartered accountant, Reeves & Neylan. *Heir: s* Lord Carnegie, *qv*.

SOUTHEY, Sir Robert (John), Kt 1976; AO 1993; CMG 1970; Federal President, Liberal Party of Australia, 1970–75; Chairman, National Council, Australian Ballet, 1991–95 (Chairman, Australian Ballet, 1980–90); *b* 20 March 1922; *s* of Allen Hope

Southey and Ethel Thorpe McComas, MBE; *m* 1st, 1946, Valerie Janet Cotton (*d* 1977), *y d* of late Hon. Sir Francis Grenville Clarke, KBE, MLC; five *s*; 2nd, 1982, Marigold Merlyn Baillieu, *yr d* of late Sidney and Dame Merlyn Myer, DBE, and *widow* of Ross Shelmerdine, CMG, OBE. *Educ:* Geelong Grammar Sch.; Magdalen Coll., Oxford (MA). Coldstream Guards, 1941–46 (Captain 1944, served N Africa, Italy). BA, 1st cl. PPE Oxon, 1948. Wm Haughton & Co. Ltd: Dir 1953; Man. Dir, 1959–75; Chm. 1968–80; Chm., General Accident Insurance Co. Australia Ltd, later NZI Insurance Australia Ltd, 1987–92; Director: ICL Australia Pty Ltd, 1961–72, 1977–90; BP Australia Holdings Ltd, 1962–91; Kinnears Ltd, 1975–84; National Westminster Finance Australia Ltd, 1983–85; Nat West Australia Bank Ltd, 1985–87; Kawasaki (Australia) Pty Ltd, 1986–; Chairman: McArthur Shipping (Vic.) Pty Ltd, 1974–81; Australian Adv. Council, General Accident Assurance Corp. PLC, 1978–89. Mem. Executive, Liberal Party, 1966–82; Victorian State Pres., Liberal Party, 1966–70; Chm. of Council, Geelong Grammar Sch., 1966–72; Pres., Geelong Grammar Foundn, 1975–88; Chm. Australian Adv. Cttee, Nuffield Foundn, 1970–81; Mem., Rhodes Scholarship Selection Cttee, Victoria, 1973–76. *Publication:* (with C. J. Puplick) Liberal Thinking, 1980. *Recreations:* fishing, music. *Address:* 16 Horsburgh Grove, Armadale, Vic 3143, Australia. *Clubs:* Cavalry and Guards, MCC; Melbourne (Melbourne); Vincent's (Oxford); Leander.

SOUTHGATE, Sir Colin (Grieve), Kt 1992; Chairman: THORN EMI plc, since 1989 (Director, since 1984); PowerGen, since 1993 (Director, since 1990); Director, Bank of England, since 1991; *b* 24 July 1938; *s* of Cyril Alfred and Edith Isabelle Southgate; *m* 1962, Sally Patricia Mead; two *s* two *d*. *Educ:* City of London Sch. ICT, later ICL, 1960–70; formed Software Sciences, 1970; apptd Chief Exec., BOC Computer Services Div. on sale of Software Sciences to BOC, 1980–82; Chief Exec., THORN EMI Information Technology, 1983; Non-executive Director: Lucas, 1987–92; Prudential Corp., 1989–92; Dir, South Bank Bd, 1990–92. Member: Industry and Commerce Gp, Save the Children Fund, 1991–94; Business Council for Sustainable Develt, 1994–; Vice Patron, Home Farm Develt Trust, 1991– (Trustee, 1988–91). Gov., Wellington Coll., 1989–92; Mem. Court of Govs, Henley, the Management Coll., 1991–. *Recreation:* gardening. *Address:* THORN EMI plc, 4 Tenterden Street, Hanover Square, W1A 2AY. *T:* 0171–355 4848.

SOUTHGATE, Air Vice-Marshal Harry Charles, CB 1976; CBE 1973 (MBE 1950); Director General of Engineering and Supply Policy and Planning, Ministry of Defence (Air), 1973–76, retired; *b* 30 Oct. 1921; *s* of George Harry Southgate and Lily Maud (*née* Clarke); *m* 1945, Violet Louise Davies (*d* 1991); one *s*. *Educ:* St Saviour's Sch., Walthamstow. Entered RAF, 1941; India, 1942–45; HQ 90 Gp, 1946–50; RAF Stafford, 1950–52; Air Min., 1952–53; transf. to Equipment Br., 1953; RAF Tangmere, 1953–55; Singapore, 1955–57; psc 1957; Air Min., 1958–60; jssc 1961; Dirg Staff, RAF Staff Coll., Bracknell, 1961–64; CO 35 MU RAF Heywood, 1965–66; SESO, RAF Germany, 1967–68; idc 1969; Dir Supply Management, MoD Air, 1970–73. Chm., Ripon Arts, 1989–; Patron, Yorkshire Air Mus., 1990–. *Recreations:* travel, golf, painting, bird-watching. *Address:* The Rushings, Winksley, near Ripon, North Yorkshire HG4 3NR. *T:* Kirkby Malzeard (01765658) 582. *Club:* Royal Air Force.

SOUTHGATE, Very Rev. John Eliot; Dean of York, 1984–94, now Dean Emeritus; *b* 2 Sept. 1926; *m* 1958, Patricia Mary Plumb; two *s* one *d*. *Educ:* City of Norwich Sch.; Durham Univ. BA 1953, DipTh 1955. Ordained 1955; Vicar of Plumstead, 1962; Rector of Old Charlton, 1966; Dean of Greenwich, 1968; York Diocesan Sec. for Mission and Evangelism, 1972–81, and Vicar of Harome, 1972–77; Archdeacon of Cleveland, 1974–84. A Church Comr, 1987–94. Chm., Assoc. of English Cathedrals, 1990–94. DUniv York, 1989. *Recreations:* music, sailing, Egyptology. *Address:* 39 Churchfields, Hethersett, Norwich NR9 3PH. *Clubs:* Royal Over-Seas League, Commonwealth Trust.

SOUTHGATE, Malcolm John; Deputy Managing Director, European Passenger Services Ltd, since 1990; *b* 11 Nov. 1933; *s* of Harold Edwin Southgate and Mary (*née* Kelleher), *m* 1959, Anne Margaret Yeoman; two *s*. *Educ.* Royal Grammar Sch., Colchester; Corpus Christi Coll., Cambridge (BA). British Railways: Divl Manager, S Eastern Div., 1972; Chief Operating Manager, 1975, Dep. Gen. Man., 1977, Southern Region; Dir of Ops, 1980, Dir of Policy Unit, 1983, BRB; Gen. Man., LMR, 1983; Dir, Channel Tunnel, BRB, 1986. *Recreations:* Rugby, education administration, transport affairs. *Address:* 4 Langdale Rise, Maidstone, Kent ME16 0EU. *T:* Maidstone (01622) 753792.

SOUTHGATE, Robert; Member, Arts Council, since 1993; *b* 20 Jan. 1934; *s* of Robert Bevis Southgate and Ann Southgate (*née* Boyes); *m* 1957, Elizabeth Benson; four *s*. *Educ:* Morecambe Grammar Sch. Work on national newspapers, 1954–64; Dep. Northern Editor, The Sun, 1964–68; Reporter and Presenter, ITN, 1969–78; Presenter, Thames TV, 1978–80; Controller, News and Current Affairs: TVS, 1980–84; Central TV, 1984–92; non-executive Director: Meridian TV; Central Broadcasting (former Dep. Man. Dir and Man. Dir). Chairman: W Midlands Regl Arts Bd, 1992–; City of Birmingham Touring Opera, 1992–; Mem., Adv. Bd, Birmingham Royal Ballet. *Publication:* Inside Broadcasting, 1995. *Recreations:* Lyric Theatre, travel, food, wine. *Address:* The Old Rectory, Shrawley, Worcester WR6 6TN. *T:* Worcester (01905) 620145.

SOUTHGATE, Sir William (David), Kt 1995; conductor, composer and arranger; *b* Waipukurau, NZ, 4 Aug. 1941; *s* of Alfred John Southgate and Phyllis (*née* Maden); *m* 1967, (Alison) Rosemary Martin, *d* of (Alexander James) Lloyd Martin. *Educ:* Otago Boys High Sch.; Otago Univ. (MA Hons First Cl.; BMus Hons First Cl.); Guildhall Sch. of Music and Drama. Worked in UK with variety of musical orgns incl. Phoenix Opera Co., RSC and BBC TV, 1969–74; worked in NZ, 1974–; Musical Dir, then Principal Guest Conductor, Christchurch Symphony Orch., 1986–; Guest Conductor, NZ Symphony Orch., 1974–, and all main NZ orchs and opera cos; Musical Advr to Royal NZ Ballet, 1976–93; Musical Dir, Wellington Youth Orch., 1978–90. Has conducted orchs in Europe, NZ and Australia, incl. Essen Philharmonic, Hallé, Royal Scottish Nat. and Sydney, Melbourne, Queensland, Adelaide, Tasmanian and W Australian Symphony Orchs. Arts and music progs on TV and radio in NZ. Hon. DMus Otago, 1994. Kirk-Burnnand and Brown Citation, Composers' Assoc. of NZ, 1993. *Recreations:* sports of all kinds (Otago University Blue), dining with friends, gardening. *Address:* Box 10229, The Terrace, Wellington, New Zealand.

SOUTHWARD, Sir Leonard (Bingley), (Sir Len), Kt 1986; OBE 1978; Founder (with Lady Southward) of Southward Museum Trust Inc., Paraparaumu, New Zealand, 1972; *b* 20 Sept. 1905; *s* of Philip Edmund Southward and Elizabeth Sarah Southward; *m* 2nd, 1954, Vera Thelma Bellamore; two *s* of former marriage. *Educ:* Te Aro Sch., Wellington, NZ. Started motorcycle repair business, 1926; changed to car repairs, 1935; started prodn engrg and manufacture of steel tubing, 1939; Governing Dir, Southward Engrg Co. Ltd, 1957–. The Southward Museum, which was opened to the public in 1979, contains one of the largest and most varied privately owned collection of veteran and vintage cars in the Southern Hemisphere. *Recreations:* veteran and vintage cars, rallies, etc; formerly speed boat racing, Australasia (first man in region to travel at over 100 mph on water). *Address:* Main Road North, Paraparaumu, New Zealand. *T:* (4) 2984627.

SOUTHWARD, Dr Nigel Ralph, CVO 1995 (LVO 1985); Apothecary to the Queen, Apothecary to the Household and to the Households of Princess Margaret Countess of Snowdon, Princess Alice Duchess of Gloucester and the Duke and Duchess of Gloucester, since 1975, and of Queen Elizabeth the Queen Mother, since 1986; *b* 8 Feb. 1941; *s* of Sir Ralph Southward, *qv*; *m* 1965, Annette, *d* of J. H. Hoffmann; one *s* two *d*. *Educ:* Rugby Sch.; Trinity Hall, Cambridge; Middlesex Hosp. Med. Sch. MA, MB, BChir, 1965; MRCP 1969. Ho. Surg., Mddx Hosp., 1965; Ho. Phys., Royal Berkshire Hosp., Reading, 1966; Ho. Phys., Central Mddx Hosp., 1966; Casualty MO, Mddx Hosp., 1967; Vis. MO, King Edward VII Hosp. for Officers, 1972–. *Recreations:* sailing, golf, ski-ing. *Address:* 9 Devonshire Place, W1N 1PB. *T:* 0171–935 8425; Drokesfield, Bucklers Hard, Beaulieu, Hants SO42 7XE. *Clubs:* Royal Yacht Squadron, Royal Cruising.

SOUTHWARD, Sir Ralph, KCVO 1975; Apothecary to the Household of Queen Elizabeth the Queen Mother, 1966–86, to the Household of HRH the Duke of Gloucester, 1966–75, to HM Household, 1964–74, to HM the Queen, 1972–74; *b* 2 Jan. 1908; *s* of Henry Stalker Southward; *m* 1935, Evelyn, *d* of J. G. Tassell; four *s*. *Educ:* High School of Glasgow; Glasgow Univ. MB, ChB (Glasgow) 1930; MRCP 1939; FRCP 1970. Western Infirmary, and Royal Hospital for Sick Children, Glasgow; Postgraduate Medical School, Hammersmith, London. Served War of 1939–45: Medical Officer, 215 Field Ambulance, North Africa, 1940–41; Medical Specialist, Egypt, India and Ceylon, and Lieut-Colonel in charge Medical Division, 1942–43; Colonel Comdg Combined General Hospital, 1944–45. Hon. Freeman, Worshipful Soc. of Apothecaries of London, 1975. *Recreations:* trout and salmon fishing, golf, travel. *Address:* 9 Devonshire Place, W1N 1PB. *T:* 0171–935 7969; Amerden Priory, Amerden Lane, Taplow, Maidenhead, Berks SL6 0EE. *T:* Maidenhead (01628) 23525.

See also N. R. Southward.

SOUTHWARK, Archbishop and Metropolitan of, (RC), since 1977; **Most Rev. Michael George Bowen;** *b* 23 April 1930; *s* of late Major C. L. J. Bowen and Lady Makins (who *m* 1945, Sir Paul Makins, Bt, *qv*). *Educ:* Downside; Trinity Coll., Cambridge; Gregorian Univ., Rome. Army, 1948–49, 2nd Lieut Irish Guards; Wine Trade, 1951–52; English Coll., Rome, 1952–59; ordained 1958; Curate at Earlsfield and at Walworth, South London, 1959–63; taught theology, Beda Coll., Rome, 1963–66; Chancellor of Diocese of Arundel and Brighton, 1966–70; Coadjutor Bishop with right of succession to See of Arundel and Brighton, 1970–71; Bishop of Arundel and Brighton, 1971–77. *Recreations:* golf, tennis. *Address:* Archbishop's House, St George's Road, SE1 6HX. *T:* 0171–928 2495.

SOUTHWARK , Bishop of, since 1991; **Rt. Rev. Robert Kerr Williamson, (Roy);** *b* 18 Dec. 1932; *s* of James and Elizabeth Williamson; *m* 1956, Anne Boyd Smith; three *s* two *d*. *Educ:* Elmgrove School, Belfast; Oak Hill College, London. London City Missionary, 1955–61; Oak Hill Coll., 1961–63; Asst Curate, Crowborough Parish Church, 1963–66; Vicar: St Paul, Hyson Green, Nottingham, 1966–71; St Ann w. Emmanuel, Nottingham, 1971–76; St Michael and All Angels, Bramcote, 1976–79; Archdeacon of Nottingham, 1978–84; Bishop of Bradford, 1984–91. Chm., Central Religious Adv. Cttee to BBC and ITA, 1993–; Co-Chm., Inter-Faith Network for the UK, 1994–. *Recreations:* walking, bird watching, reading, music. *Address:* Bishop's House, 38 Tooting Bec Gardens, SW16 1QZ.

SOUTHWARK, Auxiliary Bishops in, (RC); *see* Henderson, Rt Rev. C. J.; Jukes, Rt Rev. J.; Tripp, Rt Rev. H. G.

SOUTHWARK, Provost of; *see* Slee, Very Rev. C. B.

SOUTHWARK, Archdeacon of; *see* Bartles-Smith, Ven. D. L.

SOUTHWELL, family name of **Viscount Southwell.**

SOUTHWELL, 7th Viscount, *cr* 1776; **Pyers Anthony Joseph Southwell;** Bt 1662; Baron Southwell, 1717; International Management and Marketing Consultant; *b* 14 Sept. 1930; *s* of Hon. Francis Joseph Southwell (2nd *s* of 5th Viscount) and Agnes Mary Annette Southwell (*née* Clifford); *S* uncle, 1960; *m* 1955, Barbara Jacqueline Raynes; two *s*. *Educ:* Beaumont Coll., Old Windsor, Berks; Royal Military Academy, Sandhurst. Commissioned into 8th King's Royal Irish Hussars, 1951; resigned commission, 1955. *Recreation:* golf. *Heir: s* Hon. Richard Andrew Pyers Southwell, *b* 15 June 1956. *Clubs:* Army and Navy, MCC.

SOUTHWELL, Bishop of, since 1988; **Rt. Rev. Patrick Burnet Harris;** *b* 30 Sept. 1934; *s* of Edward James Burnet Harris and Astrid Kendall; *m* 1968, Valerie Margaret Pilbrow; two *s* one *d*. *Educ:* St Albans School; Keble Coll., Oxford (MA). Asst Curate, St Ebbe's, Oxford, 1960–63; Missionary with S American Missionary Soc., 1963–73; Archdeacon of Salta, Argentina, 1969–73; Diocesan Bishop of Northern Argentina, 1973–80; Rector of Kirkheaton and Asst Bishop, Dio. Wakefield, 1981–85; Sec., Partnership for World Mission, 1986–88; Asst Bishop, Dio. Oxford, 1986–88. *Recreations:* ornithology, S American Indian culture, music, harvesting. *Address:* Bishop's Manor, Southwell, Notts NG25 0JR. *Club:* Commonwealth Trust.

SOUTHWELL, Provost of; *see* Leaning, Very Rev. D.

SOUTHWELL, Richard Charles; QC 1977; Judge of the Courts of Appeal of Jersey and Guernsey; Deputy High Court Judge; Recorder; *s* of late Sir Philip Southwell, CBE, MC and Mary Burnett; *m* Belinda Mary, *d* of late Col F. H. Pownall, MC; two *s* one *d*. Dep. Pres., Lloyd's Appeal Tribunal. *Address:* 1 Hare Court, Temple, EC4Y 7BE. *T:* 0171–353 3171, *Fax:* 0171–583 9127.

SOUTHWELL, Ven. Roy; Archdeacon of Northolt, 1970–80, Archdeacon Emeritus, since 1980; Warden of the Community of All Hallows, Ditchingham, Norfolk, 1983–89; *b* 3 Dec. 1914; *s* of William Thomas and Lilian Southwell; *m* 1948, Nancy Elizabeth Lindsay Sharp; two *d*. *Educ:* Sudbury Grammar Sch.; King's Coll., London (AKC 1942). Curate: St Michael's, Wigan, 1942–44; St John the Divine, Kennington, 1944–48; Vicar of Ixworth, 1948–51; Vicar of St John's, Bury St Edmunds, 1951–56; Rector of Bucklesham with Brightwell and Foxhall, 1956–59; Asst Director of Religious Education, Diocese of St Edmundsbury and Ipswich, 1956–58, Director, 1959–67. Hon. Canon of St Edmundsbury, 1959–68; Vicar of Hendon, 1968–71. *Recreations:* reading, singing and watching TV. *Address:* 397 Sprowston Road, Norwich NR3 4HY. *T:* Norwich (01603) 405977.

SOUTHWOOD, Prof. David John, PhD; Professor, since 1986, and Head of Physics Department, since 1994, Imperial College, London University; *b* 30 June 1945; *s* of H. H. J. Southwood and H. M. Southwood; *m* 1967, Susan Elizabeth Fricker; two *s* one *d*. *Educ:* Torquay Boys' Grammar Sch.; Queen Mary Coll., London (BA); Imperial Coll., London (PhD, DIC). UCLA 1970; Lectr, Imperial Coll., London, 1971–86. Vis. Prof., UCLA, 1976. Mem., SERC Boards, 1989–94; Chairman: Commn D, COSPAR, 1986–92; Space Sci. Adv. Cttee, ESA, 1990–93; Sci. Prog. Cttee, ESA, 1993–96. Fellow, Amer. Geophys. Union (James B. Macelwane Award, 1981); Corresp. Mem., Internat. Acad. of Astronautics. *Publications:* numerous contribs in solar terrestrial physics and planetary science to learned jls. *Recreations:* reading, theatre, cinema. *Address:* Blackett Laboratory, Imperial College, SW7 2BZ. *T:* 0171–594 7500.

SOUTHWOOD, Captain Horace Gerald, CBE 1966; DSC 1941; Royal Navy; Managing Director, Silley, Cox & Co. Ltd, Falmouth Docks, 1974–78; Chairman, Falmouth Group, 1976–78; *b* 19 April 1912; *s* of late Horace George Southwood; *m* 1936, Ruby Edith Hayes; two *s* one *d*. *Educ:* HMS Fisgard, RN Coll., Greenwich. Joined RN, 1927; HMS Resolution, Medit. Stn, 1932–34; HMS Barham, 1934–35; RN Coll., Greenwich, 1935–36; HMS Royal Oak, Home Fleet, 1936–38; specialised in Submarines, 1938; HMS Lucia, 1938–39. HM Submarine, Regent, 1939–41, China and Medit. (despatches, 1941; DSC); HMS Medway, Medit., 1941–42; HM Submarine, Amphion (first of Class), 1943–45. HMS Dolphin, 1946–48; HMS Vengeance, 1948–49; Comdr, 1948; HMS Glory, 1949–51; HMS Forth, 1951–52; Admty, Whitehall, 1952–54; HM Dockyard, Portsmouth (Dep. Man.), 1954–58; jssc, 1958–59; Capt., 1958. Chief Engr, Singapore, 1959–62; Sen. Officers' War Course, 1962; Manager, Engrg Dept, HM Dockyard, Portsmouth, 1963–67; Gen. Manager, HM Dockyard, Devonport, 1967–72, retd. Management Consultant, Productivity and Management Services Ltd, 1972–74. CEng, FIMechE. *Recreations:* sailing, fishing, golf, caravanning. *Address:* Dolphin Cottage, Riverside, Newton Ferrers, Devon PL8 1AA. *T:* Plymouth (01752) 872401. *Clubs:* Royal Western Yacht (Plymouth); Yealm Yacht (Newton Ferrers).

SOUTHWOOD, Prof. Sir (Thomas) Richard (Edmund), Kt 1984; DL; FRS 1977; Professor of Zoology, University of Oxford and Fellow of Merton College, Oxford, since 1979 (Linacre Professor of Zoology, 1979–93); Pro Vice-Chancellor, University of Oxford, 1987–89 and since 1993 (Vice-Chancellor, 1989–93); Director, Glaxo Wellcome (formerly Glaxo Holdings) plc, since 1992; *b* 20 June 1931; *s* of late Edmund W. Southwood and A. Mary, *d* of Archdeacon T. R. Regg, and *g s* of W. E. W. Southwood; *m* 1955, Alison Langley, *d* of late A. L. Harden, Harpenden, Herts; two *s*. *Educ:* Gravesend Grammar Sch.; Imperial Coll., London. BSc, ARCS 1952; PhD London 1955; DSc London 1963; MA Oxon 1979; DSc Oxon 1987. FIBiol 1968; Hon. FRCP 1991. ARC Research Schol., Rothamsted Experimental Station, 1952–55; Res. Asst and Lecturer, Zoology Dept, Imperial Coll., London, 1955–64; Vis. Prof., Dept. of Entomology, University of California, Berkeley, 1964–65; Reader in Insect Ecology, University of London, 1964–67; Prof. of Zoology and Applied Entomology, London Univ., Head of Dept of Zoology and Applied Entomol., and Dir of Field Station, Imperial Coll., 1967–79; Dean, Royal Coll. of Science, 1971–72; Chm., Division of Life Sciences, Imperial Coll., 1974–77. A. D. White Prof.-at-Large, Cornell Univ., 1985–91. Member: ARC Adv. Cttee on Plants and Soils, 1970–72; ARC Res. Grants Bd, 1972–78; JCO Arable and Forage Crops Bd, 1972–79; NERC Terrestrial Life Sciences (formerly Nature Conservancy) Grants Cttee, 1971–76 (Chm., 1972–76); Council, St George's House, Windsor, 1974–80; Adv. Bd Research Councils, 1977–80; Trop. Medicine Panel, Wellcome Trust, 1977–79; Chairman: Royal Commn on Envmtl Pollution, 1981–86 (Mem., 1974–86); Management Cttee, Royal Soc., Royal Swedish Acad. and Norwegian Acad. Surface Water Acidification Prog., 1984–90; NRPB, 1985–94 (Mem., 1980–); Dept of Health and MAFF Working Party on Bovine Spongiform Encephalopathy, 1988–89; UGC Working Party on Biology in Univs, 1988–89; co-Chm., UK Round Table on Sustainable Develt, 1995–. Vice-Pres., Royal Soc., 1982–84; President: British Ecological Soc., 1976–78 (Hon. Treas., 1960–64 and 1967–68; Hon. Mem., 1988); Royal Entomological Soc., 1983 (Vice-Pres., 1963–64); Hon. Vice-President: Inst. of Envmtl Health Offices, 1984–; Game Conservancy, 1986–. Governor, Glasshouse Crops Research Inst., 1969–81; Trustee: British Museum (Natural History), 1974–83 (Chm., 1980–83); East Malling Trust, 1984–; Rhodes Trust, 1986–; Lawes Trust, 1987– (Chm., 1991–); Rank Prize Funds Trust, 1993–; Delegate, OUP, 1980–94; Mem., Hebdomadal Council, 1981–94. Lectures: Spencer, Univ. of British Columbia, 1978; Bawden, British Crop Protection Conf., 1979; Le Conte, Georgia, 1989; F. E. Williams, RCP, 1990; Crookshank, RCR, 1993; Croonian, Royal Soc., 1995. Member: Academia Europaea, 1989; Pontifical Acad. of Scis, 1992; Foreign Member: Amer. Acad. of Arts and Sciences, 1981; Norwegian Acad. of Sci. and Letters, 1987; US Nat. Acad. of Science, 1988; Hon. Mem., Ecol Soc. of America, 1986. Fellow, Eton Coll., 1993; Hon. Fellow: Imperial Coll., 1984; Entomological Soc. of Amer., 1986. Hon. DSc: Griffith, 1983; McGill, 1988; Warwick, 1989; Liverpool, 1992; Durham, 1994; Sussex, 1994; Victoria, 1994; Hon. LLD: London, 1991; Oxford Brookes, 1993; Bristol, 1994; Fil. Doc. *hc* Lund, 1986; Hon. ScD E Anglia, 1987. Scientific Medal, Zool. Soc., London, 1969; Linnean Medal, Linnean Soc. of London, 1988. DL Oxfordshire, 1993. Cavaliere Ufficale, Order of Merit, Republic of Italy, 1991; Ordem de Merito (cl. II), Republic of Portugal, 1993. *Publications:* (with D. Leston) Land and Water Bugs of the British Isles, 1959; Life of the Wayside and Woodland, 1963; Ecological Methods, 1966, 2nd edn 1978; (jtly) Insects on Plants, 1984; (ed with B. J. Juniper) Insects and the Plant Surface, 1986; (ed with R. R. Jones) Radiation and Health: the biological effects of low-level exposure to ionizing radiation, 1987; (ed jtly) The Treatment and Handling of Wastes, 1992; many papers in entomological and ecological jls. *Recreations:* natural history, reading, travel, conversation. *Address:* Merton College, Oxford OX1 4JD. *Clubs:* Athenæum, United Oxford & Cambridge University.

See also W. F. W. Southwood.

SOUTHWOOD, William Frederick Walter, MD; MChir; FRCS; Consultant Surgeon, Bath Health District, 1966–90; *b* 8 June 1925; *s* of late Stuart W. Southwood, MC, and of Mildred M. Southwood, and *g s* of W. E. W. Southwood; *m* 1965, Margaret Carleton Holderness, *d* of late Sir Ernest Holderness, Bt, CBE, and Lady Holderness; two *s*. *Educ:* Charterhouse; Trinity Coll., Cambridge (MA 1951, MD 1964, MChir 1956); Guy's Hosp. FRCS 1954. Captain, RAMC, 1949–51. Surg. Registrar, West London Hosp. and St Mark's Hosp. for Diseases of the Rectum, 1954–60; Sen. Surg. Registrar, Royal Infirmary, Bristol, 1960–66. Hunterian Prof., RCS, 1961. Vis. Prof. of Surgery, Univ. of Cape Town, 1987. Chm., Professional and Linguistic Assessment Bd, 1984–87 (Mem., 1976–87; Vice-Chm., 1983–84). Member: Court of Assts, Worshipful Soc. of Apothecaries of London, 1975– (Chm., Exams Cttee, 1981–85; Jun. Warden, 1984–85; Sen. Warden, 1985–86; Master, 1986–87); Cttee, Non-Univ. Medical Licencing Bodies, 1979–90. Examr in Anatomy and Surgery to GNC, 1957–72. *Publications:* articles in surgical jls. *Recreations:* fishing, snooker. *Address:* 1 Aldwick Avenue, Bognor Regis, W Sussex PO21 3AQ. *T:* Bognor Regis (01243) 823073. *Club:* East India.

SOUTHWORTH, Sir Frederick, Kt 1965; QC; Chief Justice, Malawi, 1964–70, retired 1970; *b* Blackburn, Lancashire, 9 May 1910; *s* of late Harper Southworth, Blackburn, Lancs; *m* 1942, Margaret, *d* of James Rice, Monaghan, Ireland; three *d*. *Educ:* Queen Elizabeth's Grammar Sch., Blackburn; Exeter Coll., Oxford. Called to the Bar, Gray's Inn, 1936. War of 1939–45; commissioned 1939; served with South Lancashire Regiment and Lancashire Fusiliers, and with Department of the Judge Advocate General in India, 1939–46; Hon. Colonel, Crown Counsel, Palestine, 1946–47; Crown Counsel, Tanganyika, 1947–51; Attorney-General, Bahamas, 1951–55; QC Bahamas, 1952; Acting Governor, July-Aug. 1952; Acting Chief Justice, July-Oct. 1954; Puisne Judge, Nyasaland, 1955–64; Acting Governor-General, Malawi, 1964 and 1965. *Publications:* Specimen Charges, in use in the courts of Tanzania, Zanzibar, Kenya and Uganda; The Southworth Commission Report: an inquiry into allegations made by the international press against the Nyasaland Police, 1960. *Address:* 40 Waverley Lane, Farnham, Surrey GU9 8BJ.

SOUTHWORTH, Jean May, QC 1973; a Recorder of the Crown Court, 1972–93; *b* 20 April 1926; *o c* of late Edgar and Jane Southworth, Clitheroe. *Educ:* Queen Ethelburga's Sch., Harrogate; St Anne's Coll., Oxford (MA). Served in WRNS, 1944–45. Called to Bar, Gray's Inn, 1954; Bencher, 1980. Standing Counsel to Dept of Trade and Industry for Central Criminal Court and Inner London Sessions, 1969–73. Chm., Police Discipline Appeals Tribunal, 1990–. Fellow, Woodard Corporation (Northern Div.), 1974–90. *Recreations:* music, tapestry. *Address:* 21 Caroline Place, W2 4AN.

SOUYAVE, Sir (Louis) Georges, Kt 1971; District Judge, Hong Kong, 1980–89; *b* 29 May 1926; *m* 1953, Mona de Chermont; two *s* four *d*. *Educ:* St Louis Coll., Seychelles; Gray's Inn, London. Barrister-at-Law, Gray's Inn, 1949. In private practice, Seychelles, 1949–56; Asst Attorney-Gen., Seychelles, 1956–62; Supreme Court, Seychelles: Additional Judge, 1962–64; Puisne Judge, 1964–70; Chief Justice, 1970–76; New Hebrides: Resident Judge of the High Court (British jurisdiction) and British Judge of the Supreme Ct of the Condominium, 1976–80. *Recreations:* walking, swimming. *Address:* 1 Flinders Court, Mount Ommaney, Brisbane, Qld 4074, Australia.

SOUZAY, Gérard, (*né* Gérard Marcel Tisserand), Chevalier, Légion d'Honneur; Chevalier de l'Ordre des Arts et Lettres; French baritone; *b* 8 Dec. 1921. *Educ:* Paris Conservatoire Musique. World Première, Stravinsky's Canticum Sacrum, Venice Festival, 1956; Bach B Minor Mass at Salzburg Festival; Pelléas et Mélisande, Rome Opera, Opera Comique, 1962, Scala, Milan, 1973; Don Giovanni, Paris Opera, 1963; second tour of Australia and New Zealand, 1964. Also tours in US, South America, Japan, Africa, Europe. Annual Lieder recitals, Salzburg Festival. Has made recordings; Grand Prix du Disque, for Ravel Recital, etc. *Recreations:* tennis, painting. *Address:* 26 rue Freycinet, 75116 Paris, France.

SOWARD, Prof. Andrew Michael, FRS 1991; Professor of Applied Mathematics, University of Exeter, since 1996; *b* 20 Oct. 1943; *s* of Arthur Layton Soward and Sybil Jessica Lilian Soward (*née* Greathurst); *m* 1968, Elaine Celia McCaully; one *s* one *d*. *Educ:* St Edward's Sch., Oxford; Queen's College, Cambridge (BA 1st cl. Hons Maths 1965; PhD 1969; ScD 1984). University of Newcastle upon Tyne: Lectr, 1971, Reader, 1981–86, Dept of Maths and Stats; Head, Div. of Applied Maths, 1985–95; Prof. of Fluid Dynamics, 1986–95. Visiting appointments: Courant Inst. of Mathematical Scis, NY, 1969–70; CIRES, Boulder, Colorado, 1970–71; IGPP, UCLA, 1977–78. Editor, Jl of Geophysical and Astrophysical Fluid Dynamics, 1991–. *Publications:* contribs to learned jls. *Recreations:* rock-climbing, running. *Address:* University of Exeter, The Queen's Drive, Exeter, Devon EX4 4QJ.

SOWDEN, John Percival; Chairman, Costain Group Ltd (formerly Richard Costain Ltd), 1972–80 (Director, 1967–82); Regional Director, Central London and City of London Regional Boards, Lloyds Bank, 1980–87; *b* 6 Jan. 1917; *s* of Percy Sowden and Gertrude Sowden (*née* Moss); *m* 1st, 1940, Ruth Dorothy Keane (marr. diss. 1969); one *s*; 2nd, 1969, Joyce Diana Timson. *Educ:* Silcoates Sch., Wakefield, Yorks; The Grammar Sch., Hebden Bridge, Yorks; City and Guilds Coll., Imperial Coll. of Science (BScEng, ACGI; FCGI 1973). FIStructE. Served War: commnd RE, with service in UK, ME and Italy, 1939–46 (despatches, 1943). Joined Richard Costain Ltd, 1948; Site Project Manager on various construction projects, incl. Festival of Britain, Apapa Wharf, Nigeria, and Bridgetown Harbour, Barbados, 1948–60; Joint Managing Director: Richard Costain (Associates) Ltd, 1961–62; Costain-Blankevoort Internat. Dredging Co. Ltd, 1963–65; Richard Costain Ltd: Manager, Civil Engrg Div., 1965–69; Board Member, 1967; Chief Executive, Internat. Area, 1969–70; Group Chief Executive, 1970–75. Member, Governing Body, Imperial Coll. of Science and Technology, 1971–, Fellow, 1980. FRSA 1983. *Recreations:* reading, joinery. *Address:* Below Star Cottage, East Tytherley Road, Lockerley, Romsey, Hants SO5 0LW. *T:* Romsey (01794) 41172. *Club:* Royal Automobile.

SOWDEN, Terence Cubitt; QC 1989; Juge d'Instruction, since 1994; HM's Solicitor General for Jersey, 1986–93; *b* 30 July 1929; *s* of George Henry Sowden, RNR, Master Mariner and Margaret Duncan Cubitt; *m* 1955, Doreen Mary Lucas (*d* 1983); one *s* two *d*. *Educ:* Victoria Coll. Prep. Sch.; Victoria Coll.; Hendon Tech. Coll., London. Called to the Bar, Middle Temple, 1951; Advocate, Royal Court of Jersey, 1951; in private practice in Jersey, 1951–85; Deputy for St Helier, States of Jersey, 1960–63; Sen. Partner, Crill Cubitt Sowden & Tomes, Advocates and Solicitors, 1962–83. *Publication:* (with Paul Matthews) The Jersey Law of Trusts, 1988, 3rd edn 1994. *Recreations:* writing, walking the low tide. *Address:* La Côte, Les Petits Sablons, Fauvic, Grouville, Jersey, CI JE3 9HG. *T:* Jersey (01534) 855395.

SOWREY, Air Marshal Sir Frederick (Beresford), KCB 1978 (CB 1968); CBE 1965; AFC 1954; *b* 14 Sept. 1922; *s* of late Group Captain Frederick Sowrey, DSO, MC, AFC; *m* 1946, Anne Margaret, *d* of late Captain C. T. A. Bunbury, OBE, RN; one *s* one *d*. *Educ:* Charterhouse. Joined RAF 1940; flying training in Canada, 1941; Fighter-reconnaissance Squadron, European theatre, 1942–44; Flying Instructors Sch., 1944; Airborne Forces, 1945; No 615 (Co. of Surrey) Squadron, RAuxAF ('Winston Churchill's Own'), 1946–48; Fighter Gunnery Sch., 1949–50, comdg 615 Sqdn, 1951–54; RAF Staff Coll., Bracknell, 1954; Chiefs of Staff Secretariat, 1955–58; comdg No 46 Sqdn, 1958–60; Personal Staff Officer to CAS, 1960–62; comdg RAF Abingdon, 1962–64; IDC 1965; SASO, Middle East Comd (Aden), 1966–67; Dir Defence Policy, MoD, 1968–70; SASO, RAF Trng Comd, 1970–72; Comdt, Nat. Defence Coll., 1972–75; Dir-Gen. RAF Training, 1975–77; UK Representative, Permanent Military Deputies Group CENTO, 1977–79. Research Fellow, IISS, 1980–81. Pres., Sussex Indust. Archaeology Soc., 1993– (Chm., 1981–93); Mem., Bd of Conservators, Ashdown Forest, 1984– (Vice Chm., 1991–93); Pres., Victory Services Assoc., 1989–93 (Chm., 1985–89); Chm., RAF Historical Soc., 1986–; Trustee: Guild of Aviation Artists, 1990–; Amberley Chalk Pits Museum, 1990–. *Publications:* (contrib.) D-Day Encyclopaedia, 1994; contribs, articles and book reviews for defence jls. *Recreations:* motoring sport (world class records 1956), veteran cars, mechanical devices of any kind and age. *Club:* Royal Air Force.

SOWRY, Dr (George Stephen) Clive, FRCP, FRCPEd; FFOM; Physician, Edgware General Hospital, 1953–82; *b* 26 Dec. 1917; *s* of Dr George H. Sowry and Mrs Stella Sowry; *m* 1943, Jeanne (*née* Adams); one *s* one *d*. *Educ:* Bilton Grange, near Rugby; Epsom Coll., Surrey; St Mary's Hosp. Med. Sch., London (MB, BS 1940; MD 1947). FRCP 1963 (MRCP 1946); FRCPEd 1986; FFOM 1987. Served War, RNVR, 1941–45 (Surg. Lieut). Med. appts, St Mary's Hosp., Brompton Hosp. and Hammersmith Hosp., until 1953; med. admin, Edgware Gen. Hosp., 1957–73. Royal College of Physicians: Pro Censor, 1975; Censor, 1976; Sen. Censor and Vice-Pres., 1978–79. Mem. Qualification Cttee, 1981–86, Examnr, 1981–86, Board Mem., 1987–92, Faculty of Occupational Medicine. Med. Sec., MRCP (UK) Pt 2 Exam. Bd., 1983–87; Member: Jt Academic Cttee, Conjoint Bd, 1983–89 (Chm., 1985–87); Med. Adv. Cttee, HSE, 1983–87. Silver Jubilee Medal, 1977. *Publication:* (jtly) article on aetiology of essential hypertension in Clin. Science. *Recreations:* sailing, singing. *Address:* 53 Aldenham Avenue, Radlett, Herts WD7 8JA. *T:* Radlett (01923) 856046.

SOYINKA, Wole; Nigerian writer; *b* 13 July 1934; *s* of Ayo and Eniola Soyinka; *m*; *c*. *Educ:* Univ. of Ibadan, Nigeria; Univ. of Leeds. Res. Fellow in Drama, Univ. of Ibadan,

1960–61; Lectr in English, Univ. of Ife, 1962–63; Sen. Lectr in English, Univ. of Lagos, 1965–67; political prisoner, 1967–69; Artistic Dir and Head of Dept of Theatre Arts, Univ. of Ibadan, 1969–72; Res. Prof. in Dramatic Literature, 1972, Prof. of Comparative Literature, 1976–85, Univ. of Ife; Goldwin Smith Prof. of Africana Studies and Theatre, Cornell Univ., 1988–92. Fellow, Churchill Coll., Cambridge, 1973–74. Hon. DLitt: Leeds, 1973; Yale, 1981; Paul Valéry, 1984; Morehouse Coll., 1988. Nobel Prize for Literature, 1986; AGIP/Enrico Mattei Award for the Humanities, 1986. *Publications: plays:* The Lion and the Jewel, 1959; The Swamp Dwellers, 1959; A Dance of the Forests, 1960; The Trials of Brother Jero, 1961; The Strong Breed, 1962; The Road, 1964; Kongi's Harvest, 1965; Madmen and Specialists, 1971; Before the Blackout, 1971; Jero's Metamorphosis, 1973; Camwood on the Leaves, 1973; The Bacchae of Euripides, 1974; Death and the King's Horsemen, 1975; Opera Wonyosi, 1978; A Play of Giants, 1984; From Zia with Love, 1992; A Scourge of Hyacinths, 1992; *novels:* The Interpreters, 1964; The Forest of a Thousand Daemons (trans.), Season of Anomy, 1973; *poetry:* Idanre and other poems, 1967; A Shuttle in the Crypt, 1972; (ed) Poems of Black Africa, 1975; Ogun Abibman, 1977; Mandela's Earth and other Poems, 1989; *non-fiction:* The Man Died (prison memoirs), 1972; Myth, Literature and the African World (lectures), 1972; Ake, the Years of Childhood (autobiog.), 1982; Art, Dialogue and Outrage (essays), 1988; Isara: a voyage around "Essay" (biog.), 1989.

SPACIE, Maj.-Gen. Keith, CB 1987; OBE 1974; Chairman: Sudbury Consultants Ltd, since 1989; LEaD Ltd, since 1989; *b* 21 June 1935; *s* of Frederick and Kathleen Spacie; *m* 1961, Valerie Rich; one *s*. Commnd Royal Lincolns, 1955; transf. Parachute Regt, 1959; Staff Coll., Camberley, 1966; DAA&QMG 16 Parachute Bde, 1968–70; Staff, RMA, Sandhurst, 1970–72; Comd, 3rd Bn Parachute Regt, 1973–75; SHAPE, 1976–78; Comdr 7 Field Force, 1979–81; RCDS, 1982; Mil. Comr and Comdr, British Forces Falkland Is, 1983–84; Dir of Army Training, 1984–87. *Recreations:* cross-country running, athletics, walking, battlefield touring, Victorian paintings. *Clubs:* Army and Navy; Thames Hare and Hounds.

SPACKMAN, Christopher John, FCIOB; Managing Director, Bovis Europe, since 1994; Chairman, Bovis Construction Ltd, since 1989 (Managing Director, 1985–93); *b* 21 May 1934; *s* of Eric Dickens Spackman, MB and Kathleen (*née* Crisp); *m* 1967, Marilyn Ann Rowland; one *s* two *d*. *Educ:* Sherborne Sch., Dorset; Brixton Sch. of Building (HND Building 1959); London Business Sch. FCIOB 1980. Commnd RA, 1952–54. Joined Bovis as trainee, 1955; Asst Contract Manager, then Contract Manager, 1959–64; Regl Dir, 1964; i/c Bovis Bristol Office, 1964–69; Harrow Office, 1969–73; Dir, Bovis Construction Ltd, 1973–; Asst Man. Dir, 1983–85. Chm., Deregulation Task Force for Construction, 1993. *Recreations:* squash, tennis. *Address:* Amberley, Bottom Lane, Seer Green, Beaconsfield, Bucks HP9 2UH. *T:* Beaconsfield (01494) 676855. *Clubs:* Beaconsfield Squash; Knotty Green Cricket.

SPACKMAN, Brig. John William Charles, PhD; Director: Management Information Systems, Government of Malta, since 1993; KFKI (CSC), Hungary, since 1993; *b* 12 May 1932; *s* of Lt-Col Robert Thomas Spackman, MBE and Ann (*née* Rees); *m* 1955, Jeanette Vera; two *s* one *d*. *Educ:* Cyfarthfa Castle Grammar School, Merthyr Tydfil; Wellington Grammar School; RMCS. BSc 1st cl. Hons London (external) 1960, PhD 1964; MSc (Management Sci.) UMIST, 1968. Nat. Service, 1950–52; Regular Commission, RAOC, 1952; Regtl appts, 1952–72; Project Wavell, 1969–72; RARDE, 1972–75; Senior Mil. Officer, Chem. Defence and Microbiological Defence Estab., Porton Down, 1975–78; Branch Chief, Inf. Systems Div., SHAPE, 1978–80; Dir, Supply Computer Services, 1980–83; retired from Army, 1983 (Brig.); Under Sec., and Dir, Social Security Operational Strategy, DHSS, 1983–87; Director: Computing and Information Services, BT, 1987–90; Europ. Telecommunications Informatics Services, 1991–93. FBCS 1987 (MBCS 1970); CEng 1990; MIMgt (MBIM 1970); MInstD 1983. Liveryman, Information Technologists' Co., 1989 (Mem., 1987). Freeman, City of London, 1987. *Recreations:* gardening, tennis, hill walking, opera. *Address:* 4 The Green, Evenley, Brackley, Northants NN13 5SQ. *T:* Brackley (01280) 703317. *Club:* Naval and Military.

SPACKMAN, Michael John; Gwilym Gibbon Research Fellow, Nuffield College, Oxford, 1995–Sept. 1996; *b* 8 Oct. 1936; *s* of late Geoffrey Spackman and Audrey (*née* Morecombe); *m* 1965, Judith Ann Leathem; two *s* two *d*. *Educ:* Malvern Coll.; Clare Coll., Cambridge (MA); Queen Mary Coll., London (MScEcon). Served RA (2nd Lieut), 1955–57; Physicist, UKAEA, Capenhurst, 1960–69; Sen. Physicist/Engr, Nuclear Power Gp Ltd, 1969–71; PSO, then Economic Advr, Dept of Energy, 1971–77; Economic Advr, HM Treasury, 1977–79; Dir of Econs and Accountancy, CS Coll., 1979–80; Hd of Public Services Econs Div., HM Treasury, 1980–85; Under Sec., 1985; Hd of Public Expenditure Econs Gp, HM Treasury, 1985–91 and 1993–95; Chief Economic Advr, Dept of Transport, 1991–93. *Recreations:* walking, climbing, children. *Address:* 44 Gibson Square, Islington, N1 0RA. *T:* 0171–359 1053.

SPAFFORD, Rev. Christopher Garnett Howsin; Provost and Vicar of Newcastle, 1976–89, retired; *b* 10 Sept. 1924; *s* of late Rev. Canon Douglas Norman Spafford and Frances Alison Spafford; *m* 1953, Stephanie Peel; three *s*. *Educ:* Marlborough Coll.; St John's Coll., Oxford (MA 2nd Cl. Hons Modern History); Wells Theological Coll. Curate of Brighouse, 1950–53; Curate of Huddersfield Parish Church, 1953–55; Vicar of Hebden Bridge, 1955–61; Rector of Thornhill, Dewsbury, 1961–69; Vicar of St Chad's, Shrewsbury, 1969–76. *Recreations:* reading, gardening, walking. *Address:* Low Moor, Elm Close, Leominster, Herefordshire HR6 8JX. *T:* Leominster (01568) 614395.

SPAFFORD, George Christopher Howsin; Chancellor, Manchester Diocese, since 1976; a Recorder of the Crown Court, 1975–88; *b* 1 Sept. 1921; *s* of Christopher Howsin Spafford and Clara Margaret Spafford; *m* 1959, Iola Margaret, 3rd *d* of Bertrand Leslie Hallward, *qv*; one *s* one *d*. *Educ:* Rugby; Brasenose Coll., Oxford (MA, BCL Hons); Univ of Wales Coll. of Cardiff (LLM 1994). Served RA, 1939–46 (Captain). Called to Bar, Middle Temple, 1948. Mem., Legal Adv. Commn of Gen. Synod, 1981–. Treasurer, Friends of the Manchester City Art Gall., 1986–92; Hon. Treasurer, RCA, 1995–; former Treasurer: Parish and People; Red Rose Guild of Designer Craftsmen. RCA 1989 (ARCamA 1986). Hon. LLM Manchester, 1992. *Recreation:* painting pictures. *Address:* 57 Hawthorn Lane, Wilmslow, Cheshire SK9 5DQ.

SPALDING, Prof. (Dudley) Brian, MA, ScD; FRS 1983; FEng 1989; FIMechE, FInstF; Professor of Heat Transfer, London University, 1958–88, now Emeritus, and Head, Computational Fluid Dynamics Unit, Imperial College of Science, Technology and Medicine, 1981–88; Managing Director, Concentration, Heat & Momentum Ltd, since 1975; *b* New Malden, Surrey, 9 Jan. 1923; *s* of H. A. Spalding; *m* 1st, Eda Ilse-Lotte (*née* Goericke); two *s* two *d*; 2nd, Colleen (*née* King); two *s*. *Educ:* King's College Sch., Wimbledon; The Queen's Coll., Oxford; Pembroke Coll., Cambridge. BA (Oxon) 1944; MA (Cantab) 1948, PhD (Cantab) 1951. Bataafsche Petroleum Matschapij, 1944–45; Ministry of Supply, 1945–47; National Physical Laboratory, 1947–48; ICI Research Fellow at Cambridge Univ., 1948–50; Cambridge University Demonstrator in Engineering, 1950–54; Reader in Applied Heat, Imperial College of Science and Technology, 1954–58. Man. Dir, Combustion, Heat and Mass Transfer Ltd, 1970–75; Chm., CHAM of N America Inc., 1977–91. *Publications:* Some Fundamentals of Combustion, 1955; (with E. H. Cole) Engineering Thermodynamics, 1958; Convective Mass Transfer, 1963; (with S. V. Patankar) Heat and Mass Transfer in Boundary Layers, 1967, rev. edn 1970; (co-author) Heat and Mass Transfer in Recirculating Flows, 1969; (with B. E. Launder) Mathematical Models of Turbulence, 1972; GENMIX: a general computer program for two-dimensional parabolic phenomena, 1978; Combustion and Mass Transfer, 1979; (jtly) Heat Exchanger Design Handbook, 1982; Numerical Prediction of Flow, Heat Transfer, Turbulence and Combustion (selected works), 1983; numerous scientific papers. *Recreations:* music, poetry. *Address:* Concentration, Heat & Momentum Ltd, Bakery House, 40 High Street, Wimbledon, SW19 5AU.

SPALDING, Frances, PhD; free-lance writer, since 1989; *b* 16 July 1950; *d* of Hedley Stinston Crabtree and Margaret (*née* Holiday); *m* 1974, Julian Spalding, *qv* (marr. diss. 1991); one *s*. *Educ:* Farringtons Sch.; Univ. of Nottingham (BA Hons 1972); PhD CNAA 1988. Lectr in Art Hist., Sheffield City Poly., 1978–88. Res. co-ordinator, Writers-in-Prison Cttee, English Centre of Internat. PEN, 1991–93. Mem. Council, Charleston Trust, 1990–; Editor, Charleston Mag., 1992–. Hon. Sec., Royal Orchestral Soc. for Amateur Musicians, 1992–94. FRSL 1984. *Publications:* Magnificent Dreams: Burne-Jones and the late Victorians, 1978; Whistler, 1979, rev. edn 1994; Roger Fry: art and life, 1980; Vanessa Bell, 1983; British Art since 1900, 1986; Stevie Smith: a critical biography, 1988; A Dictionary of 20th Century British Painters and Sculptors, 1990; Paper Darts: selected letters of Virginia Woolf, 1991; Dance Till the Stars Come Down: a biography of John Minton, 1991; contrib. TLS, Sunday Times, Burlington Mag., etc. *Recreation:* music. *Address:* c/o Coleridge & Rogers, 20 Powis Mews, W11 1JN. *T:* 0171–221 3717; The Flat, 70 Gloucester Crescent, NW1 7EG. *Club:* PEN.

SPALDING, Rear-Adm. Ian Jaffery L.; *see* Lees-Spalding.

SPALDING, John Oliver, CBE 1988; Vice President, National House-Building Council, since 1992 (Member, 1985–92; Chairman, 1988–92); *b* 4 Aug. 1924; *m* 1952, Mary Whitworth Hull; one *d* one *s*. *Educ:* William Hulme's Grammar School, Manchester; Jesus College, Cambridge (MA). Served War: Capt. RA, attached IA; served India, Burma, Singapore, Java. Admitted a Solicitor, 1952; service with Manchester Corporation and Hampshire CC, 1952–62; Halifax Building Society: Assistant Solicitor, 1962–64; Head Office Solicitor, 1964–74; General Manager, 1970; Director, 1975–88; Deputy Chief General Manager, 1981; Chief Exec., 1982–88. Member: BSA Legal Adv. Panel, 1965–80; Council of BSA, 1981–88; Chairman: Future Constitution and Powers of Bldg Socs Working Party (Spalding Cttee), 1981–83; Calderdale Small Business Advice Centre, 1983–88; Mem., Farrand Cttee investigating Conveyancing, 1984. Dir, NMW Computers Plc, 1989–92. *Recreations:* boats and bird-watching. *Address:* Water's Edge, Springe Lane, Swanley, Nantwich, Cheshire CW5 8NR.

SPALDING, Julian, FMA; Director, Glasgow Museums and Art Galleries, since 1989; *b* 15 June 1947; *s* of Eric Peter Spalding and Margaret Grace Savager; *m* 1st, 1974, Frances (*née* Crabtree) (*see* F. Spalding) (marr. diss. 1991); one *s*; 2nd, 1991, Gillian (*née* Tait), conservation advisor. *Educ:* Chislehurst and Sidcup Grammar Sch. for Boys; Univ. of Nottingham (BA Hons Fine Art). Dip. Museums Assoc., 1973; FMA 1983. Art Assistant: Leicester Museum and Art Gall., 1970; Durham Light Infantry Mus. and Arts Centre, 1971; Sheffield City Art Galleries: Keeper, Mappin Art Gall., 1972–76; Dep. Dir, 1976–82; Dir of Arts, Sheffield City Council, 1982–85; Dir, Manchester City Art Galls, 1985–89; Acting Dir, Nat. Mus. of Labour History, 1987–88. Art Panel Mem., Arts Council of GB, 1978–82 (Chm., Exhibns Sub-Cttee, 1981–82 and 1986–); Founder, Art Galleries Assoc., 1976, Mem. Cttee, 1976–, Chm., 1987–; Dir, Guild of St George (John Ruskin's Guild), 1983– (Companion, 1978); Member: Crafts Council, 1986– (Member: Projects and Orgn Cttee, 1985–87; Purchasing Cttee, 1986–; Exhibns Cttee, 1986–90), British Council, 1987– (Mem., Fine Arts Adv. Cttee, 1987–). Dir, Niki de Saint Phalle Foundn, 1994. BBC broadcaster (talks and reviews); Third Ear, BBC Radio Three, 1988. *Publications:* L. S. Lowry, 1979; Three Little Books on Painting, 1984; Is There Life in Museums?, 1990; pamphlets and exhibition catalogues, including: Modern British Painting 1900–1960, 1975; Fragments against Ruin, 1981; Francis Davison, 1983; George Fullard Drawings, 1984; The Forgotten Fifties, 1984; Modern Art in Manchester, 1986; The Art of Watercolour, 1987; L. S. Lowry, 1987; Ken Currie, 1988; Funfair or Church?, RSA, 1989; Glasgow's Great British Art Exhibition, 1990; contrib. Burlington Magazine. *Recreations:* cycling, gardening. *Address:* Art Gallery and Museum, Kelvingrove, Glasgow G3 8AG.

SPALVINS, Janis Gunars, (John); Chairman: Galufo Pty Ltd, since 1991; Westall Pty Ltd, since 1981; *b* 26 May 1936; *s* of Peter Spalvins and Hilda Blumentals; *m* 1961, Cecily Westall Rymill (*d* 1991); two *s*. *Educ:* Concordia College, Adelaide; Univ. of Adelaide (BEc). FCIS 1961; FASA 1967. Camelec Group of Cos, 1955–73 (Group Sec./Dir, subsidiary cos); Adelaide Steamship Co.: Asst Gen. Manager, 1973; Gen. Manager, 1977; Chief Gen. Manager and Dir, 1979; Man. Dir, 1981–91. Dir and Chief Exec., David Jones Ltd, 1980–91. Mem., Business Council of Australia, 1986–91. FAIM; MInstD Australia, 1981. *Recreations:* snow ski-ing, water ski-ing, tennis, sailing. *Address:* Galufo Pty, 2 Brookside Road, Springfield, SA 5062, Australia. *T:* (8) 3792965. *Clubs:* Cruising Yacht Club of SA, Royal SA Yacht Squadron (Adelaide); Ski Club of Victoria (Mount Buller).

SPANIER, Suzy Peta, (Mrs D. G. Spanier); *see* Menkes, S. P.

SPANKIE, Hugh Oliver; HM Diplomatic Service, retired 1986; *b* 11 Dec. 1936; *s* of late Col Hugh Vernon Spankie and Elizabeth Ursula (*née* Hills); *m* 1st, 1963, Anne Bridget Colville (marr. diss. 1981); one *s* one *d*; 2nd, 1988, Leena Marjatta Paloheimo. *Educ:* Tonbridge Sch. RM Officer, 1955–66; HM Diplomatic Service, 1967–: Helsinki, 1968–71; FCO, 1971–74; Helsinki, 1974–77; FCO and CSD, 1977–81; Counsellor, Copenhagen, 1981–85. *Address:* c/o Barclays Bank plc, 29 Stone Street, Cranbrook, Kent TN17 3HH.

SPANTON, (Harry) Merrik, OBE 1975; CEng; Chairman, British Coal Enterprise Ltd (formerly NCB (Enterprise) Ltd), 1984–91; *b* 27 Nov. 1924; *s* of late Henry Broadley Spanton and Edith Jane Spanton; *m* 1945, Mary Margaret Hawkins; one *s*. *Educ:* Eastbourne Coll.; Royal Sch. of Mines (BSc (Min) (Eng) 1945; ARSM). CEng, FIMinE 1957 (Hon. FIMinE 1986); CIMgt (CBIM 1979). Colliery Manager, 1950; Agent, 1954; Gp Man., 1956; Dep. Prodn Man., 1958; Dep. Prodn Dir, 1960; Asst Gen. Man., 1962; Gen. Man., 1964; Area Dir, 1967–80; Mem., NCB, 1980–85. Chairman: J. H. Sankey & Son, 1982–83; Coal Industry (Patents) Ltd, 1982–85; Director: British Mining Consultants Ltd, 1980–87 (Chm., 1981–83); Overseas Coal Develts Ltd, 1980–83; Compower, 1981–85 (Chm., 1984–85); NCB (Coal Products) Ltd, 1981–83; Coal Processing Consultants, 1981–83; Staveley Chemicals Ltd, 1981–83; NCB (Ancillaries) Ltd, 1982–85; British Fuel Co., 1983–87; Berry Hill Investments Ltd, 1984–85; CIBT Insurance Services Ltd, 1984–85; CIBT Developments Ltd, 1984–85; Coal Industry Social Welfare Orgn, 1983–85. Member: W European Coal Producers Assoc., 1980–85; CBI Overseas Cttee, 1981–85. Vice-Pres., Coal Trade Benevolent Assoc., 1979– (Chm., 1978). *Publications:*

articles in prof. jls. *Recreations:* travel, shooting, genealogy. *Address:* 4 Roselands Gardens, Canterbury, Kent CT2 7LP. *T:* Canterbury (01227) 769356.

SPÄRCK JONES, Karen Ida Boalth, FBA 1995; Reader in Computers and Information, Computer Laboratory, University of Cambridge, since 1994; *b* 26 Aug. 1935; *d* of A. Owen Jones and Ida Spärck; *m* 1958, Prof. Roger Michael Needham, *qv. Educ:* Girton Coll., Cambridge (BA, PhD). Cambridge University: Research Fellow, Newnham Coll., 1965–68; Royal Society Res. Fellow, 1968–73; Sen. Res. Associate, 1974–88; GEC Fellow, 1983–88; Asst Dir of Res., 1988–94. Fellow, Amer. Assoc. for Artificial Intelligence, 1993. *Publications:* Automatic Keyword Classification for Information Retrieval, 1971; (jtly) Linguistics and Information Science, 1973; (ed) Information Retrieval Experiment, 1981; (ed jtly) Automatic Natural Language Parsing, 1983; Synonymy and Semantic Classification, 1986; (ed jtly) Readings in Natural Language Processing, 1986; numerous papers. *Recreation:* art. *Address:* Computer Laboratory, University of Cambridge, New Museums Site, Pembroke Street, Cambridge CB2 3QG. *T:* Cambridge (01223) 334600.

SPAREY, John Raymond, MA; Director (Association of Municipal Engineers), Institution of Civil Engineers, 1984–85; Secretary-General, International Federation of Municipal Engineers, 1979–85; *b* 28 July 1924; *s* of late Henry Sparey and Lilian May (*née* Coles); *m* 1950, Audrie Kathleen (marr. diss. 1991), *d* of late Col E. J. W. Porter, OBE, TD, Portsmouth; two *s* one *d. Educ:* City of Bath Sch.; King's Coll., London; Trinity Coll., Cambridge (BA 1950, MA 1954). Royal Naval Scientific Service, 1944–47; Asst Secretary, Assoc. of Certified Accountants, 1952–69; Royal Institution of Chartered Surveyors: Dep. Sec., 1969–70; Sec. for Educn and Membership, 1970–74; Sec., Planning and Development Div., 1976; Sec., Instn of Municipal Engrs, 1977–84. *Recreations:* gardening, sailing. *Address:* 10 Elms Avenue, Great Shelford, Cambridge CB2 5LN. *T:* Cambridge (01223) 844572. *Club:* Seaview Yacht (Seaview, IoW).

SPARK, Dame Muriel (Sarah), DBE 1993 (OBE 1967); CLit 1991; writer; *b* Edinburgh; *d* of Bernard Camberg and Sarah Elizabeth Maud (*née* Uezzell); *m* 1937 (marr. diss.); one *s. Educ:* James Gillespie's School for Girls, Edinburgh; Heriot Watt Coll., Edinburgh. FO, 1944; General Secretary, The Poetry Society, Editor, The Poetry Review, 1947–49. FRSL 1963; FRSE 1995. Hon. Mem., Amer. Acad. of Arts and Letters, 1978. Hon. DLitt: Strathclyde, 1971; Edinburgh, 1989; Aberdeen, 1995; Heriot-Watt, 1995. Officier de l'Ordre des Arts et des Lettres, France, 1988. *Publications: critical and biographical:* (ed jtly) Tribute to Wordsworth, 1950; (ed) Selected Poems of Emily Brontë, 1952; Child of Light: a Reassessment of Mary Shelley, 1951, rev. edn, Mary Shelley, 1988; (ed jtly) My Best Mary: the letters of Mary Shelley, 1953; John Masefield, 1953, repr. 1992; (joint) Emily Brontë: her Life and Work, 1953; (ed) The Brontë Letters, 1954; (ed jointly) Letters of John Henry Newman, 1957; The Essence of the Brontës, 1993; *poems:* The Fanfarlo and Other Verse, 1952; Collected Poems I, 1967; Going Up to Sotheby's and other poems, 1982; *fiction:* The Comforters, 1957; Robinson, 1958; The Go-Away Bird, 1958; Memento Mori, 1959 (adapted for stage, 1964; televised, BBC, 1992); The Ballad of Peckham Rye, 1960 (Italia prize, for dramatic radio, 1962); The Bachelors, 1960; Voices at Play, 1961; The Prime of Miss Jean Brodie, 1961 (adapted for stage, 1966, filmed 1969, and BBC TV, 1978); Doctors of Philosophy (play), 1963; The Girls of Slender Means, 1963 (adapted for radio, 1964, and BBC TV, 1975); The Mandelbaum Gate, 1965 (James Tait Black Memorial Prize); Collected Stories I, 1967; The Public Image, 1968; The Very Fine Clock (for children), 1969; The Driver's Seat, 1970 (filmed 1974); Not to Disturb, 1971; The Hothouse by the East River, 1973; The Abbess of Crewe, 1974 (filmed 1977); The Takeover, 1976; Territorial Rights, 1979; Loitering with Intent, 1981; Bang-Bang You're Dead and other stories, 1982; The Only Problem, 1984; The Stories of Muriel Spark, 1987 (Scottish Book of Year Award); A Far Cry from Kensington, 1988; Symposium, 1990; Curriculum Vitae (autobiog.), 1992; The French Window and The Small Telephone (for children), 1993; Omnibus I, 1993; Omnibus II, 1994. *Recreations:* reading, travel. *Address:* c/o David Higham Associates Ltd, 5–8 Lower John Street, Golden Square, W1R 4HA.

SPARKES, Sir Robert Lyndley, Kt 1979; State President, National Party of Australia (formerly Country Party), Queensland, 1970–90; Managing Partner, Lyndley Pastoral Co., since 1974; *b* 30 May 1929; *s* of late Sir James Sparkes, Jandowae, Queensland; *m* 1953, June, *d* of M. Morgan; two *s. Educ:* Southport Sch., Queensland. Chairman: National Party (formerly Country Party) Lands Cttee, Queensland, 1966–; NPA Nominees Pty Ltd; Wambo Shire Council, 1967– (Mem., 1952–55 and 1964–). *Recreation:* reading. *Address:* Dundonald, PO Box 117, Jandowae, Queensland 4410, Australia. *T:* (76) 685196.

SPARKS, Arthur Charles, BSc (Econ); Under-Secretary, Ministry of Agriculture, Fisheries and Food, 1959–74; *b* 1914; *s* of late Charles Herbert and Kate Dorothy Sparks; *m* 1939, Betty Joan (*d* 1978), *d* of late Harry Oswald and Lilian Mary Simmons; three *d. Educ:* Selhurst Grammar Sch.; London School of Economics. Clerk, Ministry of Agriculture and Fisheries, 1931; Administrative Grade, 1936; National Fire Service, 1942–44; Principal Private Secretary to Minister of Agriculture and Fisheries, 1946–47; Asst Secretary, Ministry of Agriculture and Fisheries, 1947–49 and 1951–59; Asst Secretary, Treasury, 1949–51. Chm., Internat. Wheat Council, 1968–69. *Recreations:* reading, walking. *Address:* 2 Stratton Close, Merton Park, SW19 3JF. *T:* 0181–542 4827.

SPARKS, Rev. Hedley Frederick Davis, DD Oxon, 1949; FBA 1959; ATCL 1927; Oriel Professor of the Interpretation of Holy Scripture, University of Oxford, 1952–76; *b* 14 Nov. 1908; *s* of late Rev. Frederick Sparks and late Blanche Barnes Sparks (formerly Jackson); *m* 1953, Margaret Joan, *d* of late C. H. Davy; two *s* one *d. Educ:* St Edmund's Sch., Canterbury; BNC, Oxford (Colquitt Exhibnr, 1927; BA 1st Cl. Theol., 1930; Sen. Hulme Schol., 1930; Hon. Fellow, 1987); Ripon Hall, Oxford. Ordained deacon, 1933, priest, 1934; Curate of St Martin and All Saints, Oxford, and Chaplain of Ripon Hall, 1933–36; Lectr in Theol., 1936–46, and Censor of Hatfield Coll., 1940–46, Univ. of Durham; Prof. of Theol., 1946–52, and Dean, Faculty of Arts, 1949–52, Univ. of Birmingham; Rector of Wytham, 1961–68. Hon. DD: St Andrews, 1963; Birmingham, 1983. Hon. Fellow, Oriel Coll., Oxford, 1980. Jt Editor, Jl of Theol Studies, 1954–77. *Publications:* The Old Testament in the Christian Church, 1944; The Formation of the New Testament, 1952; A Synopsis of the Gospels, part I: The Synoptic Gospels with the Johannine Parallels, 1964, 2nd edn 1970; part II: The Gospel according to St John with the Synoptic Parallels, 1974, combined volume edn, 1977; *Editor:* The Apocryphal Old Testament, 1984; *Joint Editor:* Novum Testamentum Domini Nostri Iesu Christi Latine secundum editionem Sancti Hieronymi, Part ii, fasc. 5, 1937, fasc. 6, 1939, fasc. 7, 1941, Part iii, fasc. 2, 1949, fasc. 3, 1953; Biblia Sacra iuxta Vulgatam versionem, 1969, 4th edn 1994; *Contributor:* The Bible in its Ancient and English Versions, 1940, 2nd edn 1954; Studies in the Gospels, 1955; The Cambridge History of the Bible, vol. 1, 1970, 2nd edn, 1975. *Recreations:* music and railways. *Address:* 14 Longport, Canterbury, Kent CT1 1PE. *T:* Canterbury (01227) 766265.

SPARKS, Ian Leslie; Chief Executive, The Children's Society, since 1986; *b* 26 May 1943; *s* of Ronald Leslie and Hilda Sparks; *m* 1967, Eunice Jean; one *d. Educ:* Whitefield Road Primary School, Liverpool; Holt High School, Liverpool; Brunel Univ. (MA); AIB. Bank clerk, 1959–68; social worker, Liverpool, 1971–75; Asst Divl Dir, Barnardo's, 1975–80; Social Work Dir, The Children's Soc., 1981–86. Trustee: NCVCCO, 1995–; Nat. Children's Bureau; Chm., Christian Child Care Network, 1991–; Vice-Chm., Internat. Anglican Family Network, 1994–. *Recreations:* piano playing, gardening in miniature. *Address:* Edward Rudolf House, Margery Street, WC1X 0JL. *T:* 0171–837 4299.

SPARKS, Prof. (Robert) Stephen (John), FRS 1988; Chaning Wills Professor of Geology, Bristol University, since 1990 (Professor of Geology, since 1989); *b* 15 May 1949; *s* of Kenneth Grenfell Sparks and Ruth Joan Rugman; *m* 1971, Ann Elizabeth Talbot; two *s. Educ:* Imperial College London (BSc Hons 1971, PhD 1974). Postdoctoral fellowships, Lancaster Univ., 1974–76, Univ. of Rhode Island, 1976–78, studying physics of volcanic eruptions; Cambridge University: Demonstrator, 1978–82; Lectr in Geology, 1982–89; Fellow, Trinity Hall, 1981–89. Sherman Fairchild Dist. Scholar, Calif. Inst. of Technology, 1987; studies of volcanic eruptions: Heimaey, Iceland, 1973; Etna, 1975; Soufriere, WI, 1979; Mount St Helens, 1980. Pres., Geol Soc. of London, 1984–86. Wager Prize for Volcanology, Internat. Assoc. of Volcanology and Chemistry of Earth's Interior, 1983; Bigsby Medal, Geol Soc., 1985. *Publications:* numerous papers on physics of volcanic eruptions, geology of young volcanoes and origins of volcanism. *Recreations:* music, soccer, squash, travel, cooking. *Address:* Walnut Cottage, Brinsea Road, Congresbury, Bristol BS19 5JF.

SPARROW, (Albert) Charles; QC 1966; DL; barrister; *b* Kasauli, India, 16 Sept. 1925; *e s* of Captain Charles Thomas Sparrow, sometime Essex Regt, and Antonia Sparrow; *m* 1949, Edith Rosalie Taylor (*d* 1985); two *s* one *d. Educ:* Royal Grammar Sch., Colchester. Served Civil Defence, 1939–43; joined Army, 1943; posted as cadet to India, commnd into Royal Signals and served in Far East, 1944–47; OC, GHQ Signals, Simla, 1947. Admitted to Gray's Inn, 1947 (Holker Senior Scholar, Atkin Scholar, Lee Prizeman and Richards Prizeman); called to Bar, 1950, Master of the Bench, 1976; Master of Pictures and Silver, 1985, Treas., 1994, Gray's Inn (Vice-Treas., 1993); LLB London Univ., 1951; admitted to Lincoln's Inn, 1967; in practice in Chancery and before Parliament, 1950–. Member: General Council of the Bar, 1969–73; Senate of the Four Inns of Court, 1970–73; Incorp. Council of Law Reporting, 1977–83. Hon. Legal Adviser to Council for British Archæology (concerned notably with legal protection of antiquities and reform of treasure trove; produced two draft Antiquities Bills), 1966–. Chairman: independent Panel of Inquiry for affairs of RSPCA, 1973–74; independent Cttee of Inquiry for Girl Guides Rally at Crystal Palace, 1985. FSA 1972; Pres., Essex Archaeological Soc., 1975–78. Chm., Stock Branch, British Legion, 1970–75. Mem., Court, Univ. of Essex, 1985–. Advr to assocs of customary freemen, 1972–; Hon. Counsellor to Freemen of England, 1978–; Freeman, City of London; Hon. Life Mem., Gild of Freemen of City of York. KStJ 1993 (OStJ 1982; CStJ 1987); Mem. St John Council for Essex, 1977–; Comr for Essex, St John Ambulance Bde, 1983–90; Comdr, St John Ambulance for Essex, 1989–93. DL Essex, 1985. *Recreation:* Romano-British archæology. *Address:* 13 Old Square, Lincoln's Inn, WC2A 3UA. *T:* 0171–242 6105; Croyde Lodge, Stock, Essex CM4 9QB.

SPARROW, Bryan, CMG 1992; HM Diplomatic Service, retired; Ambassador to Croatia, 1992–94; *b* 8 June 1933; *m* 1958, Fiona Mary Mylechreest; one *s* one *d. Educ:* Hemel Hempstead Grammar Sch.; Pembroke Coll., Oxford (BA Hons). Served Army, 1951–53. Belgrade, 1958–61; FO, 1961–64; Moscow, 1964–66; Tunis, 1967–68; Casablanca, 1968–70; FO, 1970–72; Kinshasa, 1972–76; Prague, 1976–78; Counsellor (Commercial), Belgrade, 1978–81; Ambassador, United Republic of Cameroon, 1981–84, and concurrently to Republic of Equatorial Guinea and Central African Republic, 1982–84; Canadian Nat. Defence Coll., 1984–85; Consul-General: Toronto, 1985–89; Lyon, 1989–92. *Recreations:* gardening, travel. *Address:* c/o Midland Bank, 15 Crescent Road, Windermere, Cumbria LA23 1EF.

SPARROW, Charles; *see* Sparrow, A. C.

SPARROW, Sir John, Kt 1984; FCA; Chairman: Universities Superannuation Scheme Ltd, since 1988; Horserace Betting Levy Board, since 1991; Deputy Chairman, National & Provincial Building Society, since 1994 (Member, London Advisory Board, 1986–89; Director, since 1989); *b* 4 June 1933; *s* of Richard A. and Winifred R. Sparrow; *m* 1967, Cynthia Whitehouse. *Educ:* Stationers' Company's School; London School of Economics (BSc Econ; Hon. Fellow, 1994). FCA 1957. With Rawlinson & Hunter, Chartered Accountants, 1954–59; Ford Motor Co. Ltd, 1960; AEI-Hotpoint Ltd, 1960–63; United Leasing Corporation, 1963–64; Morgan Grenfell Group (formerly Morgan Grenfell & Co.), 1964–88; Dir, Morgan Grenfell Gp (formerly Morgan Grenfell Hldgs), 1971–88; Chm., Morgan Grenfell Asset Management, 1985–88; Morgan Grenfell Laurie Hldgs, 1985–88. Director: Federated Chemicals, 1969–78 (Chm., 1974–78); Harris Lebus, 1973–79; United Gas Industries, 1974–82 (Dep. Chm., 1981–82); Coalite Group plc, 1974–82, 1984–89; Gas and Oil Acreage, 1975–78; Tioxide Gp, 1977–78; Mather & Platt, 1979–81; Peterborough Develt Corp., 1981–88; Short Brothers plc, 1984–89 (Dep. Chm., 1985–89); ASW Holdings Plc, 1987–93; Regalian Properties PLC, 1990–93. Seconded as Head of Central Policy Review Staff, Cabinet Office, 1982–83. Chm., EDC for Process Plant Industry, 1984–85; Chm., National Stud, 1988–91. Vice-Chm., Governors, LSE, 1984–93 (Actg Chm., 1987–88); Pres., Old Stationers' Assoc., 1995–96. Hon. Fellow, Wolfson Coll., Cambridge, 1987. *Recreations:* cricket, crosswords, horse-racing. *Address:* 52 Grosvenor Gardens, SW1W 0AU. *T:* 0171–333 0043. *Club:* MCC.

SPAWFORTH, David Meredith, MA; Headmaster, Merchiston Castle School, Edinburgh, since April 1981; *b* 2 Jan. 1938; *s* of Lawrence and Gwen Spawforth, Wakefield, Yorks; *m* 1963, Yvonne Mary Gude; one *s* one *d. Educ:* Silcoates School; Hertford Coll., Oxford (Heath Harrison Travelling Schol.; MA ModLang). Assistant Master: Winchester Coll., 1961–64; Wellington Coll., 1964–80; Housemaster, Wellington Coll., 1968–80. British Petroleum Education Fellow, Keble Coll., Oxford, 1977. FRSA 1994. *Recreations:* gardening, France, history, theatre, walking. *Address:* Castle Gates, Merchiston Castle School, Colinton, Edinburgh EH13 0PU. *T:* 0131–441 3468.

SPEAIGHT, Anthony Hugh; QC 1995; *b* 31 July 1948; *s* of George Victor Speaight and Mary Olive Speaight (*née* Mudd); *m* 1991, Gabrielle Anne Kooy-Lister; one *s* one *d. Educ:* St Benedict's Sch., Ealing; Lincoln Coll., Oxford (MA; Sec., Oxford Union Soc., 1970). Called to the Bar, Middle Temple, 1973. Member: Bar Council, 1986–92; Bar Working Party on Televising Courts, 1990. Chm., Editl Bd, Counsel, jl of Bar of England and Wales, 1990–94. Schuman Silver Medal, FVS Foundn, Germany, 1976. *Publications:* (with G. Stone) The Law of Defective Premises, 1982; (ed jtly) Architects Legal Handbook, 3rd edn 1982 to 6th edn 1995. *Recreations:* theatre, cricket, foxhunting. *Address:* 12 King's Bench Walk, Temple, EC4Y 7EL. *T:* 0171–583 0811. *Clubs:* Carlton, Hurlingham.

SPEAKMAN-PITT, William, VC 1951; *b* 21 Sept. 1927; *m* 1st, 1956, Rachel Snitch; one *s*; 2nd, Jill; one *d. Educ:* Wellington Road Senior Boys' Sch., Altrincham. Entered Army as Private. Served Korean War, 1950–53 (VC), King's Own Scottish Borderers. *Recreations:* swimming, and ski-ing.

SPEAR, Harold Cumming, CBE 1976; Member, Electricity Council, 1972–76; *b* 26 Oct. 1909; *yr s* of late Rev. Edwin A. and Elizabeth Spear; *m* 1935, Gwendolen (*née*

Richards); one *s* one *d*. *Educ:* Kingswood Sch., Bath. Asst to Employment Manager, Gramophone Co. Ltd, 1928–33; Labour and Welfare Supervisor, Mitcham Works Ltd, 1933–35; Employment Supervisor, Hoover Ltd, 1935–38; Personnel Manager, Sperry Gyroscope Co. Ltd, 1938–40; appts with British Overseas Airways Corp., finally as Chief Personnel Officer, 1941–59; Dir of Personnel Management, Central Electricity Generating Bd, 1959–72; Mem., Central Arbitration Cttee, 1976–85. Pres., Inst. of Personnel Management, 1969–71; CIPM. *Recreation:* golf. *Address:* The Almonry, Newlands, Pershore, Worcs WR10 1BW. *Club:* Roehampton.

SPEAR, Prof. Walter Eric, PhD, DSc; FRS 1980, FRSE; Harris Professor of Physics, University of Dundee, 1968–90, now Emeritus Professor; *b* 20 Jan. 1921; *s* of David and Eva Spear; *m* 1952, Hilda Doris King; two *d*. *Educ:* Musterschule, Frankfurt/Main; Univ. of London (BSc 1947, PhD 1950, DSc 1967). Lecturer, 1953, Reader, 1967, in Physics, Univ. of Leicester; Vis. Professor, Purdue Univ., 1957–58. FRSE 1972; FInstP 1962. Max Born Prize and Medal, 1977; Europhysics Prize, 1977; Makdougal-Brisbane Medal, RSE, 1981; Rank Prize, 1988; Mott Award, Jl of Non-crystalline Solids, 1989; Rumford Medal, Royal Soc., 1990. *Publications:* numerous research papers on electronic and transport properties in crystalline solids, liquids and amorphous semiconductors. *Recreations:* literature, music (particularly chamber music), languages. *Address:* 20 Kelso Place, Dundee DD2 1SL. *T:* Dundee (01382) 667649.

SPEARING, Prof. Anthony Colin; William R. Kenan Professor of English, University of Virginia, since 1989 (Professor of English, since 1987); *b* 31 Jan. 1936; *s* of Frederick Spearing and Gertrude Spearing (*née* Calnin); *m* 1961, Elizabeth; one *s* one *d*. *Educ:* Alleyn's Sch., Dulwich; Jesus Coll., Cambridge (BA 1957; MA 1960). University of Cambridge: W. M. Tapp Res. Fellow, Gonville and Caius Coll., 1959–60; Univ. Asst Lectr in English, 1960–64; Supernumerary Fellow, Gonville and Caius Coll., 1960; Official Fellow, Queens' Coll., 1960–87; Univ. Lectr in English, 1964–85; Dir of Studies in English, Queens' Coll., 1967–85; Reader in Medieval English Literature, 1985–87; Life Fellow, Queens' Coll., 1987. Vis. Prof. of English, Univ. of Virginia, 1979–80, 1984. *Publications:* Criticism and Medieval Poetry, 1964, 2nd edn 1972; The Gawain-Poet: a critical study, 1970; Chaucer: Troilus and Criseyde, 1976; Medieval Dream-Poetry, 1976; Medieval to Renaissance in English Poetry, 1985; Readings in Medieval Poetry, 1987; The Medieval Poet as Voyeur, 1993; texts, articles in learned jls. *Address:* Department of English, Bryan Hall, University of Virginia, Charlottesville, VA 22903, USA.

SPEARING, George David; Technical Adviser, Institution of Highways and Transportation, 1984–86, retired; *b* 16 Dec. 1927; *s* of late George Thomas and Edith Lydia Anna Spearing; *m* 1951, Josephine Mary Newbould; two *s* one *d*. *Educ:* Rotherham Grammar Sch.; Sheffield Univ. BEng; MICE, FIHE. RAF, Airfield Construction Br., 1948. Asst Divl Surveyor, Somerset CC, 1951; Asst Civil Engr, W Riding of Yorks CC, 1953; Asst Engr, MoT, 1957; Supt. Engr, Midland Road Construction Unit, 1967; Asst Chief Engr, MoT, 1969; Regional Controller (Roads and Transportation), West Midlands, 1972; Dep. Chief Engr, DoE, 1973; Under Sec., DoE, 1974; Under Sec., Dept of Transport, and Dir Highways Planning and Management, 1974–78; Regional Dir, Eastern Reg., Depts of the Environment and Transport, and Chm., E Anglia Regional Bd, 1978–83. *Publications:* papers in Proc. Instn CE and Jl Instn HE. *Address:* 23 Colburn Avenue, Caterham, Surrey CR3 6HW. *T:* Caterham (01883) 347472.

SPEARING, Nigel John; MP (Lab) Newham South, since May 1974; *b* 8 Oct. 1930; *s* of late Austen and of May Spearing; *m* 1956, Wendy, *d* of Percy and Molly Newman, Newport, Mon; one *s* two *d*. *Educ:* Latymer Upper School, Hammersmith. Ranks and commission, Royal Signals, 1950–52; St Catharine's Coll., Cambridge, 1953–56. Tutor, Wandsworth School, 1956–68 (Sen. Geography Master, 1967–68); Director, Thameside Research and Development Group, Inst. of Community Studies, 1968–69; Housemaster, Elliott School, Putney, 1969–70. Chairman: Barons Court Labour Party, 1961–63; Hammersmith Local Govt Cttee of the Labour Party, 1966–68. Contested (Lab) Warwick and Leamington, 1964. MP (Lab) Acton, 1970–74; Secretary: Parly Lab. Party Educn Gp, 1971–74; Parly Inland Waterways Gp, 1970–74; Member Select Cttee: Overseas Develt, 1973–74, 1977–79; Members' Interests, 1974–75; Procedure, 1975–79; EEC Legislation, 1979– (Chm., 1983–92); Foreign and Commonwealth Affairs, 1980–87; Chair, Parly Affairs Cttee, PLP, 1989–. Vice-Pres., River Thames Soc.; Pres., Socialist Envt and Resources Assoc., 1977–86; Chm., British Anti-Common Market Campaign, 1977–83. Co-opted Mem. GLC Cttees, 1966–73. Mem. Bd, Christian Aid, 1987–91. *Publication:* The Thames Barrier-Barrage Controversy (Inst. of Community Studies), 1969. *Recreations:* rowing, reading. *Address:* House of Commons, SW1A 0AA. *T:* 0171–219 3000.

SPEARMAN, Sir Alexander Young Richard Mainwaring, 5th Bt *cr* 1840; *b* 3 Feb. 1969; *s* of Sir Alexander Bowyer Spearman, 4th Bt, and Martha, *d* of John Green, Naauwpoort, S Africa; *S* father, 1977; *m* 1994, Anne Stine, *d* of K. Munch. *Heir: uncle* Dr Richard Ian Campbell Spearman, FLS, FZS, *b* 14 Aug. 1926. *Address:* Zorguliet, 3 Sir George Grey Street, Oranjezicht 8001, Cape, S Africa.

SPEARMAN, Clement, CBE 1979; HM Diplomatic Service, retired; Ambassador and Consul-General to the Dominican Republic, 1975–79; *b* 10 Sept. 1919; *y s* of late Edward and Clara Spearman; *m* 1950, Olwen Regina Morgan; one *s* two *d*. *Educ:* Cardiff High School. RN (Air Arm), 1942–46. Entered Foreign (subseq. Diplomatic) Service, 1947; 3rd Sec., Brussels, 1948–49; 2nd Sec., FO, 1949–51; HM Consul, Skoplje, 1951–53; FO, 1953–56; 1st Sec., Buenos Aires, 1956–60; FO, 1960–62; Counsellor, CENTO, Ankara, 1962–65; Reykjavik, 1965–69; FCO, 1969–71; Manila, 1971–74; Toronto, 1974–75. *Recreations:* tennis, swimming. *Address:* 56 Riverview Gardens, SW13 9QZ. *T:* 0181–748 9339. *Clubs:* Naval, Roehampton.

SPEARMAN, John L.; Chief Executive, Classic FM, since 1992; *b* 25 Nov. 1941; *s* of Thomas and Elizabeth Alexandra Spearman; *m* 1st, 1966, Susan Elizabeth Henderson Elms (marr. diss. 1986); one *s* one *d*; 2nd, 1988, Angela Josephine van Praag. *Educ:* Trinity Coll., Dublin (MA). Unilever Grad. Trng Scheme; Lintas Ltd; London Press Exchange; Collett Dickenson Pearce, 1972–89: Man. Dir, 1982–83; Chm. and Chief Exec., 1983–89; Chairman: Playback Ltd, 1987–; Laser Sales (LWT), 1990–93. Member: Government Lead Body for Design, 1991–; Bd, RPO, 1994–. *Recreations:* music, sailing, ski-ing, walking, gardening. *Clubs:* Hurlingham; Royal Irish Yacht (Dublin).

SPECTOR, Prof. Roy Geoffrey, MD, PhD; FRCP, FRCPath; Professor of Applied Pharmacology, Guy's Hospital Medical School, 1972–89, now Emeritus; Hon. Physician, Guy's Hospital, since 1967; *b* 27 Aug. 1931; *s* of Paul Spector and Esther Cohen; *m* 1st, 1960, Evie Joan Freeman (marr. diss. 1979); two *s* one *d*; 2nd, 1986, Annette Skinner. *Educ:* Roundhay Sch., Leeds; Sch. of Medicine, Leeds Univ. (MB, ChB, MD); PhD Lond 1964, Dip. in Biochem. 1966. FRCP 1971; FRCPath 1976; FRSM. Lectr in Paediatric Res. Unit, Guy's Hosp., 1961–67; Guy's Hosp. Medical School, subseq. United Medical and Dental Schools of Guy's and St Thomas's Hosps: Reader in Pharmacology, 1968–71; Sub Dean for Admissions, 1975–89; Chm., Div. of Pharmacology, 1985–88. Vis. Prof. in Clin. Pharmacology, West China Med. Univ., Chengdu, 1986–87. External Examiner, Hong Kong Univ., 1994–95. Vice Chm., British Univs' Film Council, 1976–87. *Publications:* (jtly) The Nerve Cell, 1964, 2nd edn 1986; (jtly) Clinical Pharmacology in Dentistry, 1975, 6th edn 1995; (jtly) Mechanisms in Pharmacology and Therapeutics, 1976; (jtly) Aids to Pharmacology, 1980, 3rd edn 1993; (jtly) Textbook of Clinical Pharmacology, 1981, 2nd edn 1986; (jtly) Aids to Clinical Pharmacology and Therapeutics, 1984, 3rd edn 1993; (jtly) Common Drug Treatments in Psychiatry, 1984; Catechism in Clinical Pharmacology Therapeutics, 1986; (jtly) Drugs and Medicines, 1989; contributor: Textbook of Clinical Pharmacology, 1994; Handbook of Clinical Research, 1994; contribs to jls on pathology, medicine, gen. science, and applied pharmacology. *Recreation:* cookery. *Address:* 60 Crescent Drive, Petts Wood, Orpington, Kent BR5 1BD. *T:* Orpington (01689) 810069.

SPEDDING, Sir Colin (Raymond William), Kt 1994; CBE 1988; Professor of Agricultural Systems, 1975–90, and Pro-Vice-Chancellor, 1986–90, University of Reading, now Professor Emeritus; *b* 22 March 1925; *s* of Robert Kewley Spedding and Ilynn Spedding; *m* 1952, Betty Noreen George (*d* 1988); one *s* one *d* (and one *s* decd). *Educ:* London Univ. (External) (BSc 1951; MSc 1953; PhD 1955; DSc 1967). FIBiol 1967, CBiol 1984; FRASE 1984; FIHort 1986; FRAgS 1986; FLS 1995. Ilford Ltd, 1940–43; RNVR, 1943–46; Allen & Hanbury, 1948–49; Grassland Research Institute: joined 1949; Head of Ecology Div., 1967–75; Asst Dir, 1969–72; Dep. Dir, 1972–75; University of Reading: Visiting, then part-time Prof. of Agric. Systems, 1970–75; Head of Dept of Agric. and Horticl., 1975–83; Dean, Faculty of Agriculture and Food, 1983–86; Dir, Centre for Agricl Strategy, 1981–90, Consultant Dir, 1990–. Commonwealth Prestige Fellow, NZ, 1977; Vis. Prof., Univ. of Guelph, Canada, 1978. Mem., Programme Cttee, Internat. Livestock Centre for Africa, Addis Ababa, 1976–80, Vice Chm., 1980–83; Special Advr, H of C Select Cttee on Agric., 1980–83; Chairman: UK Register of Organic Food Standards Bd, 1987–; Farm Animal Welfare Council, 1988–; Apple and Pear Res. Council, 1989–; CSTI, 1994–. Dir, Lands Improvement Gp Ltd., 1986– (Dep. Chm., 1990–). President: European Assoc. of Animal Production Study Commn for Sheep and Goat Production, 1970–76; British Soc. for Animal Production, 1979–80; Inst. of Biology, 1992–94. Canadian Inst. of Agric. Recognition Award, 1971; Wooldridge Meml Medal, BVA, 1982. Governor: Royal Agricl Coll., 1982–88; Inst. of Grassland and Envmtl Res. (formerly Inst. for Grassland and Animal Production), 1987–91; Chm., Sci. Adv. Panel, WSPA, 1989–; Mem., Council of Management, PDSA, 1988–. Mem., Inst. of Dirs, 1992–. Hon. Life Mem., BSAS, 1990; Hon. FIBiol 1994; Hon. Associate, RCVS, 1994. George Hedley Award, 1971; Hawkesbury Centenary Medal of Honour, Univ. of Western Sydney, 1991; Massey Ferguson Nat. Agricl Award, 1991. Editor, Agricultural Systems, 1976–88. *Publications:* Sheep Production and Grazing Management, 1965, 2nd edn 1970; Grassland Ecology, 1971; (ed with E. C. Diekmahns) Grasses and Legumes in British Agriculture, 1972; The Biology of Agricultural Systems, 1975; An Introduction to Agricultural Systems, 1979, 2nd edn 1988; (ed) Vegetable Productivity, 1981; (with J. M. Walsingham and A. M. Hoxey) Biological Efficiency in Agriculture, 1981; (ed) Fream's Agriculture, 1983; (ed) Fream's Principles of Food and Agriculture, 1992; over 250 sci papers in learned jls. *Address:* Vine Cottage, Orchard Road, Hurst, Berks RG10 0SD. *Clubs:* Athenæum, Farmers'.

SPEDDING, David Rolland, CVO 1984; OBE 1980; HM Diplomatic Service; Counsellor, Foreign and Commonwealth Office, since 1987; *b* 7 March 1943; *s* of Lt Col Carlisle Montagu Rodney Spedding and Gwynfydd Joan Llewellyn; *m* 1970, Gillian Leslie Kinnear; two *s*. *Educ:* Sherborne School; Hertford College, Oxford (MA). Third Sec., FO, 1967; Middle East Centre for Arabic Studies, 1968; Second Sec., Beirut, 1970; Santiago, 1972; First Sec., FCO, 1974; Abu Dhabi, 1978; FCO, 1981–83; Counsellor, Amman, 1983–86. *Recreations:* golf, tennis, medieval history. *Address:* c/o Foreign and Commonwealth Office, King Charles Street, SW1A 2AH.

SPEED, Anthony James, QPM 1991; Assistant Commissioner, Central Area, Metrop[illegible] Police, since 1994; *b* 23 Feb. 1941; *m* 1961, Patricia Elizabeth Boyle; one *s* three [illegible] Thomas Calton Technical Sch., Dulwich. Metropolitan Police, 1957–: Personal P[illegible] Officer to the Prince of Wales, 1969; Scarman Inquiries into Red Lion Square D[illegible] 1974, Brixton Disorders, 1981; Divl Comdr, Brixton, 1981–83; posts in Wes[illegible] 1983–. *Recreation:* horse riding. *Address:* Metropolitan Police Central Area HQ[illegible] Embankment, SW1A 2JL. *T:* 0171–321 9008.

SPEED, Sir (Herbert) Keith, Kt 1992; RD 1967; MP (C) Ashford, since Oct. [illegible] March 1934; *s* of late Herbert Victor Speed and of Dorothy Barbara (*née* Mum[illegible] 1961, Peggy Voss Clarke; two *s* one *d* (and one *s* decd). *Educ:* Greenhill Sch., Eve[illegible] Bedford Modern Sch.; RNC, Dartmouth and Greenwich. Officer, RN, 1947–56; Lt-Comdr RNR, 1964–79. Sales Man., Amos (Electronics) Ltd, 1957–60; Marketing Man., Plysu Products Ltd, 1960–65; Officer, Conservative Res. Dept, 1965–68. MP (C) Meriden, March 1968–Feb. 1974; An Asst Govt Whip, 1970–71; a Lord Comr of HM Treasury, 1971–72; Parly Under-Sec. of State, DoE, 1972–74; Opposition spokesman on local govt, 1976–77, on home affairs, 1977–79; Parly Under Sec. of State for Defence for RN, 1979–81; Mem., Parly Select Cttee on Defence, 1983–87; UK Rep. to Parly Assembly of Council of Europe and WEU, 1987–. Parly Consultant, Professional Assoc. of Teachers, 1982–. Dir, Folkestone and District Water Co., 1986–. *Publications:* Blue Print for Britain, 1965; Sea Change, 1982; contribs to various political and defence jls. *Recreations:* classical music, reading. *Address:* House of Commons, SW1A 0AA. *Club:* Garrick.

See also J. J. M. Speed.

SPEED, Jeffery John Mumford, CBE 1991; Director of Fundraising and Treasurer's Department, Conservative Central Office, since 1995; *b* 3 Oct. 1936; *s* of late Herbert Victor Speed and of Dorothy Barbara Speed (*née* Mumford); *m* 1985, Hilary Anne Busfield, *d* of Haley Busfield, Mayfield, Sussex. *Educ:* Bedford Modern Sch. General Motors (Vauxhall), 1955–58; Sales Manager, later Sales Dir, Tompkins Moss Gp, 1959–65; Conservative Party Agent, 1965–78; Dep. Central Office Agent, S Eastern Area, 1978–82; Central Office Agent: E Midlands Area, 1982–88; Greater London Area, 1988–93; Dir, Constituency Services, Cons. Central Office, 1993–95. Mem., Inst. of Supervisory Mgt, 1993. FRSA 1993. *Recreations:* antique maps (especially those by John Speed, 1552–1629), oenology, travel, musical theatre and film. *Address:* Ashcombe Priory, Fordcombe, Kent TN3 9UR. *Clubs:* Carlton, St Stephen's Constitutional.

See also Sir H. K. Speed.

SPEED, Sir Robert (William Arney), Kt 1954; CB 1946; QC 1963; Counsel to the Speaker, 1960–80; *b* 18 July 1905; *s* of late Sir Edwin Arney Speed; *m* 1929, Phyllis (*d* 1991), *d* of Rev. P. Armitage; (one *s* one *d* decd). *Educ:* Rugby; Trinity College, Cambridge. Called to Bar, Inner Temple, 1928; Bencher, 1961; Principal Assistant Solicitor, Office of HM Procurator-General and Treasury Solicitor, 1945–48; Solicitor to the Board of Trade, 1948–60. *Address:* Upper Culham, Wargrave, Berks RG10 8NR. *T:* Henley-on-Thames (01491) 574271. *Club:* United Oxford & Cambridge University.

SPEELMAN, Sir Cornelis Jacob, 8th Bt *cr* 1686; BA; *b* 17 March 1917; *s* of Sir Cornelis Jacob Speelman, 7th Bt and Maria Catharina Helena, Castendijk; *S* father, 1949; *m* 1972, Julia Mona Le Besque (*d* 1978); *m* 1986, Irene Agnes van Leeuwen; two step *c*. Education Dept, Royal Dutch Army, 1947–49; with The Shell Company (Marketing Service Dept),

1950. Student, Univ. of Western Australia, 1952; formerly Master of Modern Languages at Clifton Coll., Geelong Grammar Sch.; Exeter Tutorial Coll.

SPEIGHT, Hon. Sir Graham (Davies), Kt 1983; Judge of the High Court of New Zealand, since 1966; *b* 21 July 1921; *s* of Henry Baxter and Anna May Speight; *m* 1947, Elisabeth Muriel Booth; one *s* one *d*. *Educ:* Auckland Grammar Sch.; Univ. of Auckland (LLB). Qualified barrister and solicitor, 1942; served 2nd NZ Expeditionary Force, Middle East and Italy, 1943–46: Lieut Royal NZ Artillery, 1943–46; Aide-de-Camp, General B. C. Freyberg, VC (later 1st Baron Freyberg), 1944–45; practising barrister, 1946–66. Justice of Appeal, Fiji, 1980–87; Chief Justice, Cook Is, 1982–87. Chairman: Eden Park Bd; Rothman Foundn. Chancellor, Univ. of Auckland, 1973–79; Hon. LLD Auckland, 1983. *Recreations:* golf, yachting. *Address:* 5/163 Victoria Avenue, Remvera, Auckland 5, New Zealand. *T:* (9) 5244464. *Clubs:* Auckland Golf, Royal New Zealand Yacht Squadron (Auckland) (Cdre 1961–63).

SPEIGHT, Johnny; writer; *b* 2 June 1920; *s* of John and Johanna Speight; *m* 1956, Constance Beatrice Barrett; two *s* one *d*. *Educ:* St Helen's RC School. Has written for: Arthur Haynes Show; Morecambe and Wise Show; Peter Sellers; Till Death Us Do Part (Screenwriters Guild Award, 1966, 1967, 1968); The Lady is a Tramp (Pye TV Award, 1982); In Sickness and in Health; with Ray Galton: Tea Ladies, 1979; Spooner's Patch, 1979. *Plays:* Compartment (Screenwriters Guild Award, 1962); Playmates; Salesman; Knackers Yard; If There Weren't any Blacks You Would Have to Invent Them (Prague Festival Award, 1969). Evening Standard Drama Award for Best Comedy. *Publications:* It Stands to Reason, 1974; The Thoughts of Chairman Alf, 1974; various scripts. *Recreation:* golf. *Address:* Fouracres, Heronsgate, Chorleywood, Herts. *T:* Chorleywood (019278) 2463. *Clubs:* 21; White Elephant; Stage Golf, Variety Golf, Pinner Hill Golf.

SPEIR, Sir Rupert (Malise), Kt 1964; *b* 10 Sept. 1910; *y s* of late Guy Thomas Speir and late Mary Lucy Fletcher, of Saltoun. *Educ:* Eton Coll.; Pembroke Coll., Cambridge (BA). Admitted Solicitor, 1936. Special Mem., Hops Marketing Board, 1958. Served in Army throughout War of 1939–45; commissioned in Intelligence Corps, Sept. 1939; retired with rank of Lt-Col, 1945. Contested (C) Linlithgow, 1945, Leek, 1950; MP (C) Hexham Div. of Northumberland, 1951–66, retired. Sponsor of: Litter Act, 1958; Noise Abatement Act, 1960; Local Government (Financial Provisions) Act, 1963; Parliamentary Private Secretary: to Minister of State for Foreign Affairs and to Parly Sec., CRO, 1956–59; to Parly and Fin. Sec., Admty and to Civil Lord of Admty, 1952–56. Hon. Fellow, Inst. of Public Cleansing; Vice-Pres., Keep Britain Tidy Group. *Recreations:* golf, shooting. *Address:* Birtley Hall, Hexham, Northumberland NE48 3HL. *T:* Bellingham (01434) 230275.

SPEIRS, Graham Hamilton; *b* 9 Jan. 1927; *s* of Graham Mushet Speirs and Jane (*née* McChesney); *m* 1954, Myra Reid (*née* Mills); one *s* one *d*. *Educ:* High Sch. of Glasgow Glasgow Univ. (MA 1950, LLB 1952). Anderson, Young and Dickson, Writers, Glasgow, 1950–52; Legal Asst, Dunbarton CC, 1952–54; Sen. Legal Asst, Stirling CC, 1954–59; Depute Sec., then Sec., Assoc. of County Councils in Scotland, 1959–75; Sec., Convention of Scottish Local Authorities, 1975–86, retd. Sec. Gen., Council of European Municipalities (British Section), 1980–84. Member: Scottish Legal Aid Bd, 1986; Bd, Bield Housing Assoc., 1986. *Recreation:* golf. *Address:* 3 Dirleton Avenue, North Berwick EH39 4AX. *T:* North Berwick (01620) 2801. *Club:* North Berwick Golf (North Berwick).

SPEIRS, William James McLaren; HM Diplomatic Service, retired; *b* 22 Nov. 1924; *s* of Alec McLaren Speirs and Olivia (*née* Petersen) *m* 1952, Jane Downing; two *s* one *d* (and one *d* decd). *Educ:* Clifton Coll.; Jesus Coll., Cambridge. Served Royal Signals, 1943–47; ADC to Governor of Singapore, 1946–47. HM Diplomatic Service, 1948–79: Rangoon, 1950; Jakarta, 1953; Berlin, 1957; Munich, 1963; Tel Aviv, 1970; Counsellor, FCO, [illegible]79. Gp Security Adviser, Gallaher Ltd, 1979–85; Sen. Advr, Sultanate of Oman, [illegible]94. *Recreations:* walking, collecting topographical books. *Address:* 24 Kingswood [illegible]rayshott, Hindhead, Surrey GU26 6ET. *Clubs:* Army and Navy, Special Forces.

[illegible]AR, John Francis; MP (Lab) Warley West, since 1992; *b* 5 Aug. 1947; *s* of William [illegible] and Phyllis Kathleen Spellar; *m* Anne Rosalind Wilmot; one *d*. *Educ:* Bromley [illegible]Primary Sch.; Dulwich Coll.; St Edmund's Hall, Oxford (BA PPE). Electrical, [illegible]nic, Telecommunication and Plumbing Union: Res. Officer, 1969–76; Nat. [illegible], 1976–92. Contested (Lab) Bromley, 1970; MP (Lab) Birmingham Northfield, [illegible]–83; contested (Lab) Birmingham Northfield, 1983, 1987. *Recreation:* gardening. [illegible]*dress:* House of Commons, SW1A 0AA. *T:* 0171–219 3000. *Clubs:* Bromley Labour; Rowley Regis and Blackheath Labour.

SPELLER, Antony; Senior Associate (Europe), Resource Planning and Management Systems Ltd, since 1992; Director, The Farm Villages Ltd, since 1992; *b* 12 June 1929; *s* of late John and Ethel Speller; *m* 1st, Margaret Lloyd-Jones (marr. diss.); two *s* one *d*; 2nd, 1960, Maureen R. McLellan; one *s* one *d*. *Educ:* Univ. of London (BScEcon); Univ. of Exeter (BA Social Studies); FHCIMA. Nat. Service, Subaltern, Devonshire Regt, 1951; Major, Devonshire Regt TA, 1965. Nigerian Produce Marketing Boards, 1952–54; Dir, Atlas Ltd, Nigeria, 1955–61. Chairman: Exeter Photo-Copying, 1963–93; EuroSpeedy Printing Centres UK, 1988–93; Copyshops of SW England, 1989–93. Vice Chairman: E Devon Water Bd, 1965–73; Devon River Authority, 1970–73. Councillor, Exeter CC, 1963–74 (Chairman: Public Works Cttee, 1965–69; Education Cttee, 1971–72). MP (C) N Devon, 1979–92; contested (C) N Devon, 1992. Mem., Select Cttee on Energy, 1982–88; Chairman: All-Party Alternative Energy Gp, 1984–92; W Africa Cttee, 1987–92; Treasurer: Anglo Nepal Gp, 1988–90; Anglo Korea Gp, 1989–90. Chm., W Country Cons. MPs, 1983–87. *Address:* 11 Newton House, Newton St Cyres, Exeter, Devon EX5 5BL. *Clubs:* Carlton, Royal Over-Seas League; Lagos Motor Boat (Nigeria).

SPELLER, Maj.-Gen. Norman Henry, CB 1976; Government Relations Adviser, ICL, 1976–86, retired; *b* 5 March 1921; *s* of late Col Norman Speller and Emily Florence Speller (*née* Lambert); *m* 1950, Barbara Eleanor (*née* Earle); two *s*. *Educ:* Wallingford Grammar School. Commnd RA, 1940; War Service N Africa; transf. to RAOC, 1945; psc 1952; DAA&QMG 39 Inf. Bde, 1953–55; Dirg Staff, Staff Coll., 1955–58; OC 20 Ordnance Field Park, 1958–60; Admin. Staff Coll., 1961; AA&QMG N Ireland, 1961–63; D/SPO COD Donnington, 1964–65; Col AQ 54 (EA) Div./District, 1965–66; AAG AG9, MoD, 1967; DDOS 1 British Corps, 1968–69; idc 1970; Dir of Systems Coordination, MoD, 1971–73; Dir of Ordnance Services, MoD, 1973–76, retired. Col Comdt, RAOC, 1978–83. Chm. Management Cttee, The Royal Homes for Officers' Widows and Daughters (SSAFA), 1987–94. *Recreations:* sailing, golf. *Address:* 1 Steeple Close, SW6 3LE. *Club:* Roehampton.

SPENCE, Prof. Alastair Andrew, CBE 1993; MD; FRCA, FRCSE, FRCPG, FRCPE, FRCS; Professor of Anaesthetics, University of Edinburgh, since 1984; *b* 18 Sept. 1936; *s* of James Glendinning Spence and Margaret Macdonald; *m* 1963, Maureen Isobel Aitchison; two *s*. *Educ:* Ayr Acad.; Glasgow Univ. FRCA (FFARCS 1964); FRCPG 1980; FRCSE 1991; FRCPE 1994; FRCS 1994. Western Infirmary, Glasgow, 1961–65; MRC Res. Fellow, Univ. of Glasgow Dept of Surgery, 1965–66; Steinberg Res. Fellow and Clinical Asst to Prof. of Anaesthesia, Univ. of Leeds, 1966–69; Sen. Lectr and Head of Dept of Anaesthesia, later Reader and Prof., Western Infirmary, Glasgow, 1969–84. Hon. Consultant Anaesthetist, Royal Infirmary of Edinburgh Trust, 1984–. Mem., Clinical Standards Adv. Gp, 1994–. Pres., Royal Coll. of Anaesthetists, 1991–94 (Vice-Pres., 1988–91). Hon. FDS 1994. Editor, British Jl of Anaesthesia, 1973–83 (Chm. Bd, 1983–91). *Publications:* books, chapters and papers on anaesthesia and respiratory care. *Recreations:* golf, gardening. *Address:* Harewood, Kilmacolm, Renfrewshire PA13 4HX. *T:* Kilmacolm (0150587) 2962; 3/9 Dun-Ard Garden, Oswald Road, Edinburgh EH9 2HZ. *T:* 0131–667 0231. *Club:* Caledonian.

SPENCE, Most Rev. Francis John; *see* Kingston (Ontario), Archbishop of.

SPENCE, Captain (Frederick) Michael (Alexander) T.; *see* Torrens-Spence.

SPENCE, Gabriel John; Under Secretary, Department of Education and Science, retired; *b* 5 April 1924; *s* of G. S. and D. A. Spence, Hope, Flints; *m* 1950, Averil Kingston (*née* Beresford); one *s* decd. *Educ:* Arnold House; King's Sch., Chester (King's Schol., Head of School); Wadham Coll., Oxon (Schol.). MA 1949; Stanhope Prize and Proxime, Gibbs Schol., Oxon, 1947; Haldane Essay Prize, Inst. Public Admin, 1959. Civil Service from 1949 (Min. of Works, Science Office, Min. of Housing and Local Govt, DES); Jt Sec., Adv. Council on Scientific Policy, 1959–62; Asst Sec., DES, 1964–73; Sec., Council for Scientific Policy, 1964–67; Under Sec., DES, 1973–81; Dep. Sec., UGC, 1978–81. Admin. Staff Coll., Henley, 1957. Trustee, The Oates Meml and Gilbert White Library and Museum, 1982–. *Recreations:* natural history, photography, golf. *Address:* Old Heath, Hillbrow Road, Liss, Hants GU33 7QD. *T:* Liss (01730) 893235.

SPENCE, Ian Richard; Under Secretary, and Director, International Division, Board of Inland Revenue, since 1991; *b* 15 Oct. 1938; *s* of John Jack Spence and Floretta Spence (*née* Bate); *m* 1971, Anne Kiggell; two *d*. *Educ:* Dulwich Coll.; Jesus Coll., Cambridge (BA Hist.). Joined Inland Revenue, 1962; seconded to DEA, 1966; Principal, 1967; seconded to CSSB, 1972; Asst Sec., 1975. Mem., Permanent Scientific Cttee, Internat. Fiscal Assoc., 1993–. *Recreations:* theatre, opera, tennis, golf. *Address:* Inland Revenue, Strand Bridge House, Strand, WC2R 1HH. *T:* 0171–438 6762. *Clubs:* Athenæum; Dulwich Sports.

SPENCE, Malcolm Hugh; QC 1979; a Recorder, since 1985; barrister-at-law, since 1958; *b* 23 March 1934; *s* of late Dr Allan William and Martha Lena Spence; *m* 1967, Jennifer Jane, *d* of Lt-Gen. Sir George Cole, KCB, CBE; one *s* one *d*. *Educ:* Summer Fields, Oxford; Stowe Sch.; Gonville and Caius Coll., Cambridge (MA, LLM). Gray's Inn: James Mould Schol., Holker Sen. Exhibnr, Lee Prizeman; called to the Bar, 1958; Bencher, 1988. Worcester Regt, First Lieut, 1954. Marshal to Mr Justice McNair, 1957; Pupil to Mr Nigel Bridge (now Lord Bridge of Harwich), 1958; entered chambers of Mr John Widgery, QC, 1958; practises mainly in Town and Country Planning and Compensation for Compulsory Purchase. Assistant Recorder, 1982–85. Chairman of Panel, Examination-in-Public of Hartlepool and Cleveland Structure Plans, 1979–. Chm., Local Govt Planning and Envmtl Bar Assoc., 1994–. *Publication:* (jtly) Rating Law and Valuation, 1961. *Recreations:* trout fishing, forestry and golf (Captain: Cambridge University Stymies, 1957; Old Stoic Golfing Soc., 1972; Semi-finalist, Scandinavian Amateur Championship, 1964). *Address:* (chambers) 2 Gray's Inn Square, WC1R 5JH. *T:* 0171–242 4986; 1 Gray's Inn Square, WC1R 5AA. *T:* 0171–405 4379; Scamadale, Arisaig, Inverness-shire PH39 4NS. *T:* Arisaig (01687) 450698. *Club:* Hawks (Cambridge).

SPENCE, Prof. Robert, FEng 1990; Professor of Information Engineering, Imperial College of Science, Technology and Medicine, since 1984; *b* 11 July 1933; *s* of Robert Whitehair Spence and Minnie Grace Spence (*née* Wood); *m* 1960, Kathleen Potts; one *s* one *d*. *Educ:* Hymers Coll., Hull; Hull Coll. of Technology (BScEng Hons London External 1954); Imperial College, London (DIC 1955; PhDEng 1959; DScEng 1983). FIEE, FIEEE, FCGI. Hull Corp. Telephones, 1950–51; General Dynamics/Electronics, Rochester, NY, 1959–62; Department of Electrical Engineering, Imperial College: Lectr, 1962–68; Reader, 1968–84; Prof., 1984–. Chm. and Founding Dir, Interactive Solutions Ltd, 1985–90. FRSA. Chevalier de l'Ordre des Palmes Académiques (France), 1985. *Publications:* Linear Active Networks, 1970; Tellegen's Theorem and Electrical Networks, 1970 (trans. Russian and Chinese); Resistive Circuit Theory, 1974; Modern Network Theory, 1978; Sensitivity and Optimization, 1980; Circuit Analysis by Computer, 1986; Tolerance Design of Electronic Circuits, 1988 (trans. Japanese); numerous papers in learned jls. *Recreations:* steel band (bass player), concrete aspects of gardening. *Address:* 1 Regent's Close, Whyteleafe, Surrey CR3 0AH. *T:* 0181–668 3649.

SPENCE, Stanley Brian; His Honour Judge Spence; a Circuit Judge, since 1991; *b* 3 May 1937; *s* of George Henry Spence and Sarah Spence (*née* Hoad); *m* 1961, Victoria Rosaleen Tapper; one *s* one *d*. *Educ:* Portsmouth Grammar Sch.; Britannia Royal Naval College, Dartmouth. Commissioned Supply and Secretariat Specialisation, RN, 1958; served: HMS Eagle; Staff of FO2 FEF; Portsmouth; 3rd Frigate Sqdn; HMS St Vincent; legal training, 1966–68; called to the Bar, Middle Temple, 1968; served: HMS Terror, Singapore; Staff of Commander FEF; 8th Frigate Sqdn; Legal Advr to C-in-C Naval Home Command and Flag Officer Spithead, 1974–75; retired from RN, 1975; DJA and AJAG, Office of Judge Advocate General of the Forces (Army and RAF), 1975–90; Recorder of the Crown Court, 1987–91. *Recreations:* maintaining a cottage in France, drinking wine, general DIY, enforced gardening, English history to 1485. *Address:* The Crown Court, Reading RG3 2JF.

SPENCER, family name of **Viscount Churchill** and of **Earl Spencer.**

SPENCER, 9th Earl *cr* 1765; **Charles Edward Maurice Spencer;** Baron and Viscount Spencer 1761; Viscount Althorp 1765; Viscount Althorp (UK) 1905; broadcaster; Reporter, NBC Super Channel, since 1995; *b* 20 May 1964; *s* of 8th Earl Spencer, LVO and of Hon. Frances Ruth Burke Roche, *yr d* of 4th Baron Fermoy; *S* father, 1992; *m* 1989, Victoria, *d* of John Lockwood; one *s* three *d* (incl. twin *d*). *Educ:* Maidwell Hall; Eton College; Magdalen Coll., Oxford. Page of Honour to HM the Queen, 1977–79; Contributing Correspondent, NBC News, 1987–91 and 1993–95; Reporter, Granada Television, 1991–93. *Heir:* *s* Viscount Althorp, *qv*. *Address:* Althorp, Northampton NN7 4HG. *Club:* Brooks's.

SPENCER, Alan Douglas, CIMgt; Director: Owen Owen plc, 1980–86; Johnson Wax (UK) Ltd, 1981–90; Member, East Midlands Electricity Board, 1976–86; *b* 22 Aug. 1920; *s* of Thomas Spencer and late Laura Spencer; *m* 1944, Dorothy Joan Harper; two *d*. *Educ:* Prince Henry's Grammar Sch., Evesham. FBIM 1975. Commnd Gloucester Regt, 1940; served War with Green Howards, 1940–45; Instr, Sch. of Infantry, 1945–47. Joined Boots Co., 1938; rejoined 1947; Dir, 1963–81, Man. Dir, 1975, Vice-Chm., 1978–80, Boots Co. Ltd; Man. Dir, 1977–79, Chm., 1977–80, Boots The Chemist Ltd. Pres., British Retailers' Assoc., 1983–84 (British Multiple Retailers Assoc., 1981–83). Governor, Trent Coll., 1979–90. *Recreation:* shooting. *Address:* Oakwood, Grange Road, Edwalton, Nottingham NG12 4BT. *T:* Nottingham (0115) 923 1722.

See also Sir G. M. Brown, P. J. Noest.

SPENCER, Comdt Anne Christine, CBE 1994; Director, Women's Royal Naval Service, 1991–93; *b* 15 Dec. 1938; *d* of late Ernest Spencer and Dora Harrie (*née*

Hauxwell). *Educ:* Newlands High Sch.; Yorks Coll. of Housecraft (HCIMA 1959). Direct Entry Officer, WRNS, 1962; commnd 1963; HMS Victory, 1963–64; HMS Dauntless, 1964–66; HMS Terror, Singapore, 1966–68; HMS St Vincent, 1968–69; HMS Nelson, 1969–70; Officer i/c WRNS, HMS Excellent, 1970–73; HMS Pembroke, 1973–74; Mess Manager, RNC, Greenwich, 1974–76; Defence Intelligence Staff, MoD, 1976–78; RNSC, 1978; Directorate of Naval Service Conditions, MoD, 1978–79; Terminology Co-ordinator, NATO HQ Brussels, 1979–81; WRNS Officers Appointer, MoD, 1981–83; Dep. Dir, WRNS, MoD, 1984–86; Naval Dir, NAAFI Bd of Management, 1986–88; Chief Staff Officer (Admin) to Flag Officer, Plymouth, 1988–91. ADC to HM Queen, 1991–93. *Recreations:* theatre, art, food, friends, Yorkshire. *Address:* c/o Drummonds, Royal Bank of Scotland, 49 Charing Cross, SW1A 2DX.

SPENCER, Prof. Anthony James Merrill, FRS 1987; Professor of Theoretical Mechanics, University of Nottingham, 1965–94, now Emeritus; *b* 23 Aug. 1929; *s* of James Lawrence Spencer and Gladys Spencer; *m* 1955, Margaret Bosker; three *s*. *Educ:* Queen Mary's Grammar Sch., Walsall; Queens' Coll., Cambridge (MA, PhD, ScD). Research Associate, Brown Univ., USA, 1955–57; Senior Scientific Officer, UKAEA, 1957–60; Lectr, Reader, Prof., Univ. of Nottingham, 1960–94. Visiting Professor: Brown Univ., 1966 and 1971; Lehigh Univ., 1978; Univ. of Queensland, 1982. *Publications:* Deformations of Fibre-reinforced Materials, 1972; (jtly) Engineering Mathematics, Vols I and II, 1977; Continuum Mechanics, 1980; Continuum Theory of the Mechanics of Fibre-reinforced composites, 1984; numerous articles in math. and eng. jls. *Address:* 43 Stanton Lane, Stanton-on-the-Wolds, Keyworth, Nottingham NG12 5BE. *T:* Nottingham (0115) 937 3134; Department of Theoretical Mechanics, The University, Nottingham NG7 2RD. *T:* Nottingham (0115) 951 3836.

SPENCER, Cyril; *b* 31 Aug. 1924; *s* of Isaac and Lily Spencer; *m* 1971, Wendy Lois Sutton; two *s* one *d* and two step *s* one step *d*. *Educ:* Christ Coll., Finchley; London Univ. (BSc). Joined Evans (Outsizes) Ltd, 1946: Managing Director, 1956; Chairman, 1969; Take Over of Evans by Burton Group Ltd, 1971; Head of Womenswear, 1972; Group Man. Dir and Chief Exec., 1976; Chairman, Burton Menswear, 1977; Exec. Chm., Burton Group Ltd, 1979–81; Chm., Waring and Gillow, 1985–88. *Recreations:* tennis, swimming, golf. *Address:* Eliot House, The Bishops Avenue, N2 0BA.

SPENCER, Cyril Charles, CMG 1951; First Deputy Executive Director, International Coffee Organisation, London, 1964–68; *b* 1 Feb. 1912; *s* of late Albert Edward Spencer, CBE, and Elsie Maud Spencer; *m* 1st, 1938; one *d*; 2nd, 1949, Catherine Dewar Robertson (*d* 1995). *Educ:* Royal Grammar Sch., Worcester; St John's Coll., Cambridge (BA 1934). Uganda: Asst Treas., 1935; Asst District Officer, 1937; Asst Financial Sec., 1946; Economic Sec., E Africa High Commission, 1948; Financial Sec., 1948; Acting Chief Sec. at various dates; Acting Governor, July 1951; Chairman: Uganda Lint Marketing Bd; Uganda Coffee Marketing Board; Member: Uganda Electricity Board; Uganda Development Corp.; Comr on Special Duty, Uganda, 1953–61; Sec.-Gen., Inter-African Coffee Organisation, Paris, 1961–64. *Recreations:* golf, fishing. *Address:* Flat No 2, Norton Garth, Station Road, Sidmouth, Devon EX10 8NY. *Club:* MCC.

SPENCER, Sir Derek (Harold), Kt 1992; QC 1980; MP (C) Brighton Pavilion, since 1992; Solicitor-General, since 1992; *b* 31 March 1936; *s* of Thomas Harold Spencer and Gladys Spencer (*née* Heslop); *m* 1st, 1960, Joan (*née* Nutter) (marr. diss.); two *s* one *d*; 2nd, 1988, Caroline Alexandra, *yr d* of Dr Franziskus Pärn, Hamburg; one *s*. *Educ:* Clitheroe Royal Grammar Sch.; Keble Coll., Oxford (MA, BCL). 2nd/Lieut King's Own Royal Regt, 1954–56; served in Nigeria. Part-time Law Tutor, Keble Coll., Oxford, 1960–64; called to the Bar, Gray's Inn, 1961 (Holt Scholar; Arden Scholar; Bencher, 1991); in practice SE Circuit; a Recorder, 1979–92. Councillor, London Borough of Camden, 1978–83; Dep. Leader, Conservative Party, London Borough of Camden, 1979–81. Contested (C) Leicester South, 1987. MP (C) Leicester South, 1983–87. PPS to: Home Office Ministers, 1986; the Attorney General, 1986–87. Joint Sec. Cons. Parly Legal Affairs Cttee, 1985–87. Vice-Chm., St Pancras North Cons. Assoc., 1977–78; Treas., City of London and Westminster Cons. Assoc., 1990–91. *Recreations:* reading, swimming, walking. *Address:* House of Commons, SW1A 0AA. *T:* 0171–219 3000.

SPENCER, Herbert, RDI 1965; DrRCA; Professor of Graphic Arts, Royal College of Art, 1978–85; *b* 22 June 1924; *m* 1954, Marianne Möls, Dordrecht; one *d*. DrRCA 1970; FSIA 1947. Sen. Res. Fellow, RCA, 1966–78, Hon. Fellow, 1985. Internat. Pres., Alliance Graphique Internat., 1971–74; Mem., PO Stamp Adv. Cttee, 1968–93; External advr to Design Cttee, British Telecom, 1981–83. Dir, Lund Humphries Publishers Ltd, 1970–88. Consultant: W. H. Smith Ltd (formerly W. H. Smith & Son Ltd), 1973–; Tate Gall., 1981–89; British Rail, 1984–86. Master, Faculty of Royal Designers for Industry, 1979–81; Vice-Pres., RSA, 1979–81. Governor, Bath Acad. of Art, Corsham, 1982–83. One-man exhibitions of paintings: Bleddfa Trust, 1986; Gallery 202, London, 1988–89 and 1990; Eva Jekel Gall., London, 1992; exhibition of photographs: Zelda Cheatle Gall., London, 1991; photographs in perm. collection of V & A Museum. Editor: Typographica, 1949–67; Penrose Annual, 1964–73. *Publications:* Design in Business Printing, 1952; London's Canal, 1961, 2nd edn 1976; Traces of Man, 1967; The Visible Word, 1968, 2nd edn 1969; Pioneers of Modern Typography, 1969, 2nd edn 1982, German edn 1970, Dutch edn 1983; (with Colin Forbes) New Alphabets A-Z, 1973, French edn 1974; (with Mafalda Spencer) The Book of Numbers, 1975; The Liberated Page, 1987, 2nd edn 1990. *Address:* 75 Deodar Road, Putney, SW15 2NU. *T:* and *Fax:* 0181–874 6352. *Club:* Chelsea Arts.

SPENCER, Isobel; *see* Johnstone, I. T.

SPENCER, James; QC 1991; a Recorder, since 1990; *b* 27 May 1947; *s* of James Henry Spencer and Irene Dulcie (*née* Wilson); *m* 1968, Patricia Johnson; two *s* one *d*. *Educ:* The King's Sch., Pontefract; Univ. of Newcastle upon Tyne (LLB). Admitted solicitor, 1971; called to the Bar, Gray's Inn, 1975. *Recreations:* watching Rugby League, playing golf. *Address:* 11 King's Bench Walk, Temple, EC4Y 7EQ. *T:* 0171–353 3337.

SPENCER, Mrs Joanna Miriam, CB 1971; CBE 1961; CompIGasE; *b* 26 July 1910; *d* of late Rev. R. S. Franks; *m* 1954, Frank Woolley Sim Spencer (*d* 1975). *Educ:* Redland High School for Girls, Bristol; Girton College, Cambridge (MA). Asst, Lancs County Library, 1934–35; Asst Librarian: Hull Univ. Coll., 1936–37; Regent Street Polytechnic, 1938; Librarian, Selly Oak Colls, 1938–42. Temp. Civil Servant, Min. of Aircraft Production, 1942–45. Principal, Min. of Supply, 1946; Assistant Secretary, Min. of Supply, 1949–55, Board of Trade, 1955–56, Min. of Power, 1957–64; Under-Secretary: Min. of Power, 1964–69; Min. of Technology, 1969–70; DTI, 1970–72. *Address:* 4 Rostrevor Road, SW19 7AP. *T:* 0181–946 4969.

SPENCER, John Loraine, TD; Headmaster, Berkhamsted School, 1972–83; Assistant Director, GAP Activity Projects Ltd, 1985–94; *b* 19 Jan. 1923; *s* of late Arthur Loraine Spencer, OBE, and Emily Maude Spencer, OBE, Woodford Green; *m* 1954, Brenda Elizabeth (*née* Loft); two *s* one *d*. *Educ:* Bancroft's Sch.; Gonville and Caius Coll., Cambridge (MA). 1st cl. hons Class. Tripos Pts I and II. War Service in Essex Regt, 1942–45 (Captain, despatches). Asst Master, Housemaster and Sixth Form Classics Master, Haileybury Coll., 1947–61; Headmaster, Lancaster Royal Grammar Sch., 1961–72. Mem. Chairman's Panel, Civil Service Selection Bds, 1985–90. Pres., Soc. of Schoolmasters, 1985–. Mem. Council, Lancaster Univ., 1968–72. *Address:* Crofts Close, 7 Aston Road, Haddenham, Bucks HP17 8AF. *T:* Haddenham (01844) 291235. *Club:* Royal Over-Seas League.

SPENCER, Dr Jonathan Page; Head, Insurance Division, Department of Trade and Industry, since 1991; *b* 24 April 1949; *s* of John Spencer and Doreen (*née* Page); *m* 1976, Caroline Sarah Armitage; one *s* two *d*. *Educ:* Bournemouth Sch.; Downing Coll., Cambridge (BA); Oxford Univ. (DPhil). ICI Res. Fellow, Oxford, 1973–74; joined Department of Trade and Industry, 1974: Principal, 1977; Principal Private Sec. to successive Secs of State, 1982–83; Asst Sec., 1983; Cabinet Office, 1987–89; DTI, 1989–91; Under Sec., 1991. *Recreations:* music, keeping the house up and the garden down. *Address:* Department of Trade and Industry, 1 Victoria Street, SW1H 0ET. *T:* 0171–215 0120.

SPENCER, Michael Gerald; QC 1989; a Recorder, since 1987; *b* 1 Dec. 1947; *s* of Dr Seymour J. G. Spencer and Margaret (*née* Behn); *m* 1969, Catherine Helen (*née* Dickinson); three *s*. *Educ:* Ampleforth Coll.; Hertford Coll., Oxford (MA Hons). Called to the Bar, Inner Temple, 1970. Mem., Oxford Circuit, 1971, Midland and Oxford Circuit, 1972–. Dir, Yattendon Investment Trust, 1992–. Member: Hertford Coll. Boat Club Soc.; Ampleforth Soc. *Publications:* (contrib.) Medical Negligence, 1990; (contrib.) Doctors, Patients and the Law, 1992. *Recreations:* Rugby football (coaching and referee), sailing, reading, classical music (16th century polyphony). *Address:* 1 Paper Buildings, Temple, EC4Y 7EP. *T:* 0171–583 7355. *Clubs:* Pegasus, Bar Yacht, Royal Thames Yacht; Chiltern Rugby Football.

SPENCER, Rosemary Jane, CMG 1991; HM Diplomatic Service; Minister and Head of British Embassy Berlin Office, since 1993; *b* 1 April 1941; *d* of Air Vice-Marshal Geoffrey Roger Cole Spencer, CB, CBE, and Juliet Mary Spencer (*née* Warwick). *Educ:* Upper Chine Sch., Shanklin, IoW; St Hilda's Coll., Oxford (BA Hons Modern Langs). Joined Foreign Office, 1962; FO, 1962–65; Third Secretary, Nairobi, 1965–67; Second Sec., FCO, 1967–70; Second Sec., UK Delegn to EEC, and Private Sec. to Hon. Sir Con O'Neill, Official Leader of UK negotiating team, 1970–71; First Sec., Office of UK Permanent Representative to EEC, Brussels, 1972–73; First Sec. (Economic), Lagos, 1974–77; First Sec., Asst Head of Rhodesia Dept, FCO, 1977–80; RCDS 1980; Counsellor (Agric. and Economic Affairs), Paris, 1980–84; Counsellor (External Relations), Office of UK Perm. Rep. to EEC, 1984–87; Hd of European Community Dept (External), FCO, 1987–89; Asst Under-Sec. of State, FCO, 1989–92. *Recreations:* country walking, travel, domestic arts. *Address:* c/o Foreign and Commonwealth Office, SW1A 2AH. *Clubs:* United Oxford & Cambridge University, Commonwealth Trust; International (Berlin).

SPENCER, Sarah Ann; Director, Human Rights Programme, Institute of Public Policy Research, since 1990; *b* 11 Dec. 1952; *d* of late Dr I. O. B. Spencer and of Dr Elspeth Wilkinson; *m* 1978, Brian Hackland; two *s*. *Educ:* Nottingham Univ. (BA Hons); University Coll. London (MPhil). Researcher, Law Faculty, UCL, 1977–79; Res. Officer, Cobden Trust (Civil Liberties Charity), 1979–84, Dir 1984–85; Gen. Sec., NCCL, 1985–89. Trustee, Cobden Trust, 1985–89. Editor, Rights Jl, 1979–84. *Publications:* Called to Account: police accountability in England and Wales, 1985; (jtly) The New Prevention of Terrorism Act, 1985; The Role of Police Authorities during the Miners' Strike, 1985; (jtly) A British Bill of Rights, 1990; (jtly) Accountable Policing: effectiveness, empowerment and equity, 1993; (ed) Strangers and Citizens: a positive approach to migrants and refugees, 1994; (ed) Immigration as an Economic Asset: the German experience, 1994. *Address:* 30–32 Southampton Street, WC2E 7HE.

SPENCER, Shaun Michael; QC 1988; a Recorder, since 1985; *b* 4 Feb. 1944; *s* of Edward Michael Spencer, Leeds and Barbara Spencer (*née* Williams); *m* 1971, Nicola, *e d* of F. G. Greenwood, Tockwith, York; three *s* two *d*. *Educ:* Middleton Boys' Sch., Leeds; Cockburn High Sch., Leeds; King's Coll., Newcastle (Univ. of Durham) LLB 1st cl. Hons 1965. Asst Lectr and Lectr in Law, Univ. of Sheffield, 1965–68; called to the Bar, Lincoln's Inn, 1968. *Recreations:* singing, cookery, books. *Address:* 34A Rutland Drive, Harrogate, N Yorks HG1 2NX.

SPENCER, Thomas Newnham Bayley, (Tom Spencer); Member (C) European Parliament, Surrey, since 1994 (Surrey West, 1989–94); *b* 10 April 1948; *s* of Thomas Henry Newnham Spencer and Anne Hester (*née* Readett-Bayley); *m* 1979, Elizabeth Nan Maltby, *er d* of late Captain Ronald Edgar Bath and of Doreen Lester (*née* Bush); two *d* and one step *d*. *Educ:* Nautical Coll., Pangbourne; Southampton Univ. (BSc Social Sciences). Peat, Marwick, Mitchell & Co., 1972–75; Asst to Dir, Britain-in-Europe Campaign, 1975; J. Walter Thompson & Co., 1975–79. Associate Dean, Templeton Coll., Oxford, 1984–89; Exec. Dir, Eur. Centre for Public Affairs, Oxford, 1987–89. Mem. (C) Derbyshire, European Parlt, 1979–84, contested same seat, 1984; European Democratic Group: Dep. Chief Whip, 1989–91; spokesman on: Social Affairs and Employment, 1979–81; External Econ. Relations, 1982–84; Social Affairs, 1993–; Member: Envmt, Public Health and Consumer Affairs Cttee, 1991–; Institutional Affairs Cttee, 1991–; Foreign Affairs Cttee, 1993–. Chm., British Section, EPP Gp, EP, 1993. Chm. EP delegn to Czech, Slovene and Slovak Republics, 1993–. Chm., European Union Cons. and Christian-Democratic Students, 1971–73. Mem., Global Legislators for a Balanced Environment, 1989–. Vice Pres., Globe Internat., 1993–. Robert Schuman Silver Medal, 1974. *Recreations:* gardening, swimming, opera. *Address:* Barford Court, Lampard Lane, Churt, Surrey GU10 2HJ. *Clubs:* Carlton, Brass Monkey.

SPENCER-CHURCHILL, family name of **Duke of Marlborough.**

SPENCER-NAIRN, Sir Robert (Arnold), 3rd Bt *cr* 1933; DL; *b* 11 Oct. 1933; *s* of Sir Douglas Spencer-Nairn, 2nd Bt, TD, and Elizabeth Livingston (*d* 1985), *d* of late Arnold J. Henderson; *S* father, 1970; *m* 1963, Joanna Elizabeth, *d* of late Lt-Comdr G. S. Salt, RN; two *s* one *d*. *Educ:* Eton College; Trinity Hall, Cambridge (MA). DL Fife, 1995. *Heir:* *s* James Robert Spencer-Nairn, *b* 7 Dec. 1966. *Address:* Barham, Cupar, Fife KY15 5RG. *Club:* Royal and Ancient Golf (St Andrews).

SPENCER PATERSON, Arthur; *see* Paterson, A. S.

SPENCER-SILVER, Prof. Peter Hele; S. A. Courtauld Professor of Anatomy in the University of London, at the Middlesex Hospital Medical School, 1974–82, now Emeritus; *b* 29 Oct. 1922; 2nd *s* of late Lt-Col J. H. Spencer Silver; *m* 1948, Patricia Anne, *e d* of late Col J. A. F. Cuffe, CMG, DSO, Wyke Mark, Winchester; two *s* one *d*. *Educ:* Harrow School; Middlesex Hosp. Med. School, Univ. of London. MRCS, LRCP; MB, BS London 1945; PhD London 1952. Res., Middlesex Hosp., 1945–46. RAF, 1946–48. Demonstrator in Anatomy, Middlesex Hosp. Med. Sch., 1948–57; Mem. 2nd Internat. Team in Embryology, Hübrecht Laboratory, Utrecht, Netherlands Govt Fellowship, 1956; Reader in Anatomy, Univ. of London, 1957; US Nat. Inst. of Health Post-doctoral Travelling Fellowship, 1961; Carnegie Inst. of Washington, Dept of Embryology, Baltimore, 1961–62; Prof. of Embryology, Mddx Hosp. Medical Sch., 1964–74, Sub-Dean, 1976–81. WHO Vis. Prof., 1976, 1979, 1981; Chm., Dept of Anatomy, King Saud

Univ. (Abha Br.), Saudi Arabia, 1984–86. FRSM. *Publications:* An Introduction to Human Anatomy, 1981; contribs to Jl Embryology and Experimental Morphology, Jl Physiol., Jl Anat., Lancet, etc. *Recreations:* music, George Myers. *Address:* c/o Barclays Bank, Jewry Street, Winchester, Hants SO23 8RG.

SPENCER SMITH, Prof. David, PhD; Hope Professor of Zoology/Entomology, University of Oxford, and Fellow of Jesus College, Oxford, since 1980; *b* 10 April 1934; *s* of Rev. Harry Chadwick Smith and Mary Edith (*née* Lupton); *m* 1st, 1964, Una Scully; one *d*; 2nd, 1974, Sylvia Hyder. *Educ:* Kingswood Sch.; Cambridge Univ. (BA, MA, PhD). Research Fellow: Rockefeller Univ., NY, 1958–61; St Catharine's Coll., Cambridge, 1961–63 (Res. Fellow); Asst Prof., Univ. of Virginia, 1963–66; Associate Prof. of Medicine and Biology, Univ. of Miami, Fla, 1966–70; Prof. of Medicine, Pharmacology and Biology, Univ. of Miami, 1970–80. Trustee, BM (Natural Hist.), 1984–88. Editor, Tissue & Cell, 1969–. *Publications:* Insect Cells: their structure and function, 1968; Muscle: a monograph, 1972; contrib. Standard Catalog of World Coins, annually, 1983–; papers and chapters in books and jls. *Recreations:* the ceramics and coinage of China; the coinage of the Indian subcontinent; cricket. *Address:* Jesus College, Oxford OX1 3DW.

SPENCER-SMITH, Sir John Hamilton, 7th Bt, *cr* 1804; quarantine kennel owner; *b* 18 March 1947; *s* of Sir Thomas Cospatric Hamilton-Spencer-Smith, 6th Bt, and Lucy Ashton, *o d* of late Thomas Ashton Ingram, Hopes, Norton-sub-Hamdon, Somerset; *S* father, 1959; *m* 1980, Christine (marr. diss. 1990), *d* of late John Theodore Charles Osborne, Durrington, Worthing, Sussex; one *d*. *Educ:* Milton Abbey; Lackham College of Agriculture, Wilts. *Recreations:* watching polo, ski-ing. *Heir: cousin* Michael Philip Spencer-Smith, *b* 2 April 1952. *Address:* Hazel House Quarantine Kennels, Elsted Marsh, Midhurst, West Sussex GU29 0JT. *T:* Midhurst (01730) 813616.

SPENCER WILLS; *see* Wills.

SPENDLOVE, Peter Roy, CVO 1981; HM Diplomatic Service, retired; consultant in development and public administration; Chairman, East Anglia Regional Ambulance Service NHS Trust, since 1993; *b* 11 Nov. 1925; *s* of H. A. Spendlove and Florence (*née* Jackson) *m* 1952, Wendy Margaret Valentine; two *s* three *d*. *Educ:* Chichester High Sch.; London Sch. of Economics; Edinburgh and Cambridge Univs. BScEcon Hons 1951. Called to Bar, Middle Temple, 1964. Served HM Forces, 1943–47: commnd, Indian Army/Royal Indian Artillery. LSE, 1948–51; Internat. Law Scholar at The Hague, 1951; Univ. of Cambridge, 1951–52. Apptd District Officer, Kenya, 1952; retired after serving in Provincial Admin and Central Govt, 1964. First Secretary, FCO, 1964; served in E Malaysia, Washington, Manila, FO, Jamaica; Counsellor, Economic, Commercial and Aid, Jakarta, 1977–80; Deputy High Comr, Sri Lanka, 1981–82; Dep. Chief Administrator, Broads Authority (E Anglia), 1983–86. Chm., Norfolk Ambulance Service NHS Trust, 1990–93. *Recreation:* riding. *Address:* 120 Newmarket Road, Norwich NR4 6SA.

SPENS, family name of **Baron Spens.**

SPENS, 3rd Baron *cr* 1959, of Blairsanquhar, Co. Fife; **Patrick Michael Rex Spens,** FCA; *b* 22 July 1942; *s* of 2nd Baron Spens and Joan Elizabeth (*d* 1994), *d* of late Reginald Goodall; *S* father, 1984; *m* 1966, Barbara Janet Lindsay, *d* of Rear-Adm. Ralph Lindsay Fisher, CB, DSO, OBE, DSC; one *s* one *d*. *Educ:* Rugby; Corpus Christi Coll., Cambridge (MA). FCA 1967. Director of Morgan Grenfell & Co. Ltd, 1972–82; Man. Dir, Henry Ansbacher & Co. Ltd, 1983–87. Proprietor, Patrick Spens & Co., Chartered Accountants. *Heir: s* Hon. Patrick Nathaniel George Spens, *b* 14 Oct 1968. *Address:* Gould, Frittenden, Kent TN17 2DT.

SPENS, Colin Hope, CB 1962; FICE, FIWEM; *b* 22 May 1906; *er s* of late Archibald Hope Spens, Lathallan, Fife and Hilda Constance Hooper; *m* 1941, Josephine, *d* of late Septimus Simond; two *s* one *d*. *Educ:* Lancing Coll.; Imperial College of Science and Technology. Consulting engineering experience, 1928–39. Served War of 1939–45 with Royal Signals, 1939–41; PA to Director of Works in Ministry of Works, 1941–44; Engineering Inspectorate of Min. of Health, 1944–51, Min. of Housing and Local Govt, 1951–60; Chief Engineer, Min. of Housing and Local Govt, 1960–67. Senior Consultant, Rofe, Kennard and Lapworth, 1967–76; Dep. Chm., Sutton District Water Co., 1971–83. Pres., IWES, 1974–75. Hon. FInstPHE. *Address:* 10 Ashbourne Court, Burlington Place, Eastbourne BN21 4AX. *T:* Eastbourne (01323) 638742.

SPENS, David Patrick; QC 1995; a Recorder of the Crown Court, since 1994; *b* 2 May 1950; *s* of Hugh Stuart Spens and Mary Jean Drake (*née* Reinhold); *m* 1979, Danièle Irving; two *d*. *Educ:* Rugby Sch.; Univ. of Kent at Canterbury (BA). Called to the Bar, Inner Temple, 1993; Junior Treasury Counsel, CCC, 1988–95. *Recreations:* opera, tennis, catamaran sailing, throwing parties. *Address:* 6 King's Bench Walk, Temple, EC4Y 7DR. *T:* 0171–583 0410.

SPENS, John Alexander, RD 1970; WS; Consultant, Maclay, Murray & Spens, Solicitors, Glasgow and Edinburgh (Partner, 1960–91); *b* 7 June 1933; *s* of Thomas Patrick Spens and Nancy F. Spens (*née* Anderson); *m* 1961, Finella Jane, *d* of Donald Duff Gilroy; two *s* one *d* (and one *s* decd). *Educ:* Cargilfield; Rugby School; Corpus Christi College, Cambridge (BA); Glasgow Univ. (LLB). WS 1977. Director: Scottish Amicable Life Assurance Soc., 1963– (Chairman, 1978–81); Standard Property Investment PLC, 1977–87. Carrick Pursuivant, 1974–85; Albany Herald, 1985–. *Recreations:* sailing, countryside and opera. *Address:* The Old Manse, Gartocharn, Dunbartonshire G83 8RX. *T:* Gartocharn (01389) 830329. *Clubs:* Naval; Western (Glasgow).

SPERRY, Rt. Rev. John Reginald, CD 1987; Bishop of The Arctic, 1974–90; National President, Canadian Bible Society, since 1990; *b* 2 May 1924; *s* of William Reginald Sperry and Elsie Agnes (*née* Priest); *m* 1952, Elizabeth Maclaren; one *s* one *d* (and one *d* decd). *Educ:* St Augustine's Coll., Canterbury; King's Coll., Halifax (STh). Deacon, 1950; priest, 1951; St Andrew's Mission, Coppermine, NWT, 1950–69; Canon of All Saints' Cathedral, Aklavik, 1957–59; Archdeacon of Coppermine, 1959–69; Rector of St John's, Fort Smith, NWT, 1969–73; Rector of Holy Trinity, Yellowknife, NWT, 1974. Hon. DD: Coll. of Emmanuel, St Chad, 1974; Wycliffe Coll., Toronto, 1979. *Publications:* translations into Copper Eskimo: Canadian Book of Common Prayer (1962), 1969; Four Gospels and Acts of the Apostles, 1972. *Address:* 1 Dakota Court, Yellowknife, Northwest Territories, X1A 2A4, Canada. *T:* (403) 8736163.

SPERRYN, Simon George; Chief Executive, London Chamber of Commerce and Industry, since 1992; *b* 7 April 1946; *s* of George Roland Neville Sperryn and Wendy Sperryn (*née* King). *Educ:* Rydal School; Pembroke College, Cambridge (MA); Cranfield School of Management (MBA). Birmingham Chamber of Commerce and Industry, 1967–77; Chief Executive: Northants Chamber of Commerce and Industry, 1979–85; Manchester Chamber of Commerce and Industry, 1986–92. Dir, BusinessLink London, 1995–. Pres., British Chambers of Commerce Executives, 1993– (Vice Pres., 1991–93); Mem., Nat. Council, ABCC, 1986–. FIMgt; FRSA; MIEx. *Recreations:* singing, reading, walking. *Address:* London Chamber of Commerce and Industry, 33 Queen Street, EC4R 1AP. *T:* 0171–248 4444; Deynes House, Deynes Lane, Debden, Saffron Walden, Essex CB1 3LG.

SPICER, Clive Colquhoun; retired; Honorary Research Fellow, Exeter University, 1979–91; Director, Medical Research Council Computer Unit, 1967–79; *b* 5 Nov. 1917; *s* of John Bishop Spicer and Marion Isobel Spicer; *m* 1st, 1941, Faith Haughton James, MB (marr. diss. 1979); one *s* two *d*; 2nd, 1979, Anne Nolan. *Educ:* Charterhouse Sch.; Guy's Hospital. Operational research on war casualties, 1941–46; Hon. Sqdn Leader, RAF; Staff, Imperial Cancer Research Fund, 1946–49; Dept of Biometry, University Coll., London, 1946–47; Public Health Laboratory Service, 1949–59; WHO Fellow, Univ. of Wisconsin, 1952–53; Vis. Scientist, US Nat. Insts of Health, 1959–60; Statistician, Imperial Cancer Research Fund, 1960–62; Chief Medical Statistician, General Register Office, 1962–66. Main interest has been in application of mathematical methods to medical problems. *Publications:* papers in scientific journals on epidemiology and medical statistics. *Recreations:* sailing, reading. *Address:* Churchtown, Michaelstow, St Tudy, Bodmin PL30 3PD.

SPICER, Sir James (Wilton), Kt 1988; MP (C) Dorset West since Feb. 1974; company director; *b* 4 Oct. 1925; *s* of James and Florence Clara Spicer; *m* 1954, Winifred Douglas Shanks; two *d*. *Educ:* Latymer. Regular army, 1943–57, retd (Major); commnd Royal Fusiliers, 1944; Para. Regt, 1951–57. Nat. Chm., CPC, 1968–71. Mem., Select Cttee on Agriculture, 1984–85. A Vice Chm., Cons. Party Orgn, and Chm., Internat. Office, 1985–92. Mem. (C) European Parlt, 1975–84 (elected Mem. for Wessex, 1979–84); Chief Whip, European Democratic Gp, 1975–79; Chairman: Cons. Group for Europe, 1975–78 (Dir, 1972–74); Conservatives Abroad, 1986–93; Westminster Foundn for Democracy, 1992–. *Recreations:* swimming, tennis. *Address:* Whatley, Beaminster, Dorset DT8 3SB. *T:* Beaminster (01308) 862337.

SPICER, Michael; *see* Spicer, W. M. H.

SPICER, Sir Nicholas (Adrian Albert), 5th Bt *cr* 1906, of Lancaster Gate, Paddington; general medical practitioner, since 1982; *b* 28 Oct. 1953; *o s* of (Sir) Peter James Spicer (4th Bt, but did not use the title) and of Margaret (*née* Wilson); *S* father, 1993; *m* 1992, Patricia Carol Dye; two *s*. *Educ:* Eton; Birmingham Univ. (MB ChB 1977). *Recreation:* amateur singing. *Heir: s* James Peter Warwick Spicer, *b* 12 June 1993. *Address:* 6 Linton Lane, Bromyard, Herefordshire HR7 4DQ; Lagafater, New Luce, Newton Stewart, Wigtownshire DG8 0BA.

SPICER, (William) Michael (Hardy); MP (C) South Worcestershire since Feb. 1974; *b* 22 Jan. 1943; *s* of late Brig. L. H. Spicer; *m* 1967, Patricia Ann Hunter; one *s* two *d*. *Educ:* Wellington Coll.; Emmanuel Coll., Cambridge (MA Econs). Asst to Editor, The Statist, 1964–66; Conservative Research Dept, 1966–68; Dir, Conservative Systems Research Centre, 1968–70; Man. Dir, Economic Models Ltd, 1970–80. PPS, Dept of Trade, 1979–81; Parly Under Sec. of State, 1984–87, and Minister for Aviation, 1985–87, Dept of Transport; Parly Under Sec. of State (Minister for Coal and Power), Dept of Energy, 1987–90; Minister of State (Minister for Housing and Planning), DoE, 1990. A Vice-Chm., 1981–83, Dep. Chm., 1983–84, Conservative Party. Chm., Parly OST, 1990; Dep. Chm., Parly and Scientific Cttee, 1994–; Chm., European Res. Gp, 1994–. Chm., Assoc. of Indep. Power Producers, 1991–. Gov., Wellington Coll., 1992–. *Publications:* A Treaty Too Far, 1992; *novels:* Final Act, 1981; Prime Minister Spy, 1986; Cotswold Manners, 1989; Cotswold Murders, 1990; Cotswold Mistress, 1992; Cotswold Moles, 1993; contrib. Jl Royal Inst. Public Admin. *Recreations:* painting, tennis, writing, travelling. *Address:* House of Commons, SW1A 0AA. *T:* 0171–219 3000. *Clubs:* Garrick, Pratt's.

SPICKERNELL, Rear-Adm. Derek Garland, CB 1974; CEng, FIMechE, FIEE, CIMgt, FIMarE; Chairman, Ritec Ltd, since 1987; Director General, British Standards Institution, 1981–86 (Technical Director, 1976–81); *b* 1 June 1921; *s* of late Comdr Sidney Garland Spickernell, RN, and Florence Elizabeth (*née* March); *m* 1946, Ursula Rosemary Sheila Money; one *s* one *d* (and one *s* decd). *Educ:* RNEC, Keyham. Served War, HM Ships Abdiel, Wayland, and Engr Officer HM Submarine Statesman, 1943–45. Engr Officer HM Submarines Telemachus, Tudor and Alcide, 1945–50; Submarine Trials Officer, 1950–51; Engrg Dept, HM Dockyard, Portsmouth, 1951–53; SEO: Portsmouth Frigate Sqdn, 1954–55; 2nd Submarine Sqdn, 1956–57; Supt, ULE, Bournemouth, 1958–59; Dep. Captain Supt, AUWE, Portland, 1959–62; Dep. Manager, Engrg Dept, HM Dockyard, Portsmouth, 1962–64; in command, HMS Fisgard, 1965–66; Dep. Dir, Naval Ship Production, 1967–70; Dep. Chief Exec., Defence Quality Assurance Bd, 1970–71; Dir-Gen., Quality Assurance, MoD (PE), 1972–75. Dir, James Martin Associates PLC, 1986–90; Bd Mem., Southern Water, 1987–89; Chm., Jeniva Landfill, 1987–92. Chm., Nat. Council for Quality and Reliability, 1973–75; A Vice-President: Inst. of Quality Assurance, 1974– (Hon. FIQA); Inst. of Trading Standards Admin, 1986–; Vice-Pres., Internat. Orgn for Standardisation, 1985–87; Bd Mem. for Internat. Affairs, BSI, 1986–87; Dir, Turkish Standards Inst., 1987–90; Member: Internat. Acad. of Quality Assurance, 1977–; Design Council, 1984–87; Council, Cranfield Inst. of Technol. FRSA. *Publications:* papers on Quality Assurance. *Recreation:* golf. *Clubs:* Hockley Golf; Chelworth Golf; Royal Fowey Yacht.

SPIEGL, Fritz; musician, writer, broadcaster; *b* 27 Jan. 1926; *s* of Rudolf Spiegl and Josefine Geiringer; *m* 1st, 1952, Bridget Fry; three *d*; 2nd, 1976, Ingrid Frances Romnes. *Educ:* Magdalen College Sch.; Royal Academy of Music (ARAM, FRAM 1986). Designer/typographer, Colman Prentis & Varley, 1941–46; Principal Flautist, Royal Liverpool Philharmonic, 1948–63 (Hon. Life Mem., 1988); sometime flautist: RPO; CBSO; Hallé; BBC NSO; Founder/Conductor, Liverpool Music Group, Liverpool Wind Ensemble, 1949–; Director, The Spieglers, 1975–. Founder, Scouse Press, 1965. Columnist: Liverpool Daily Post, 1970–; Classical Music, 1979–81; Classic CD, 1990–; Wordplay/Usage and Abusage columns, Daily Telegraph, 1989–; contributor to: Guardian; Independent; BBC Music Magazine, 1994–. Broadcaster in various capacities for BBC: Start the Week, 1972–80; Up to the Hour, 1977–78; Words, 1978; A–Z of Musical Curios, 1978–79; Fritz on Friday, 1978–80; Mainly for Pleasure, 1982–92; Wives of the Great Composers, 1985–86; Loves of the Great Composers, 1986–87; inflight music programmes, Swissair, Cathay Pacific, 1988–. *Quondam* question-setter, University Challenge. Pres., Merseyside Music Teachers' Assoc., 1991–. *Publications:* various edns of music; What the Papers Didn't Mean to Say, 1964; Lern Yerself Scouse, 1965; ABZ of Scouse, 1967; The Growth of a City, 1967; Liverpool Ballads, 1967; The Liverpool Manchester Railway, 1970; Slavers and Privateers, 1970; A Small Book of Grave Humour, 1971; Dead Funny, 1982; Keep Taking the Tabloids, 1983; Music Through the Looking-Glass, 1984; The Joy of Words, 1986; Fritz Spiegl's In-words & Out-words, 1987; Mediaspeak/Mediawrite, 1989; Scally Scouse, 1989; Sing the Titanic, 1993; Sick Notes: a hypochondriacs' dictionary, 1995; Wives, Lives and Loves of the Composers, 1995; Guinness Book of Musical Blunders, 1996; contrib. Grove's Dictionary of Music, New Grove Dictionary of Opera. *Recreations:* printing, cooking, inventing and several deadly sins. *Address:* 4 Windermere Terrace, Liverpool L8 3SB. *T:* 0151–727 2727, *Fax:* 0151–727 7272.

SPIELBERG, Steven; American film director and producer; *b* 18 Dec. 1947; *s* of Arnold Spielberg and Leah (*née* Posner); *m* 1985, Amy Irving (marr. diss.); one *s*; *m* Kate Capshaw; one *s* one *d*, and one adopted *s*. *Educ:* Calif State Coll. TV Director, Universal Pictures, 1968. Founder, Amblin Entertainment. Fellow, BAFTA, 1986. *Films include: directed:* Sugarland Express, 1974; Jaws, 1975; Close Encounters of the Third Kind, 1977; 1941, 1979; Raiders of the Lost Ark, 1981; (also produced) E.T., 1982; (also produced) Twilight Zone—the movie, 1983; Indiana Jones and the Temple of Doom, 1984; The Color Purple, 1985; Empire of the Sun, 1988; Indiana Jones and the Last Crusade, 1989; Hook, 1991; Jurassic Park, 1992; Schindler's List, 1994; *produced:* I Wanna Hold Your Hand, 1978; (also co-wrote) Poltergeist, 1982; Gremlins, 1984; Goonies, 1985; Young Sherlock Holmes, 1985; Back to the Future, 1986; Who Framed Roger Rabbit, 1988; Always, 1990; The Flintstones, 1994; Casper, 1995. *Publication:* (jtly) Close Encounters of the Third Kind. *Address:* Amblin Entertainment, 100 Universal City Plaza, Universal City, CA 91608, USA.

SPIERS, Sir Donald (Maurice), Kt 1993; CB 1987; TD 1966; aerospace consultant, since 1994; Director: Computing Devices Co. Ltd, since 1994; Meggitt plc, since 1995; *b* 27 Jan. 1934; *s* of Harold Herbert Spiers and Emma (*née* Foster); *m* 1958, Sylvia Mary Lowman; two *s*. *Educ:* Raynes Park County Grammar Sch.; Trinity Coll., Cambridge (MA). CEng, FRAeS. Commnd RE, 1952–54. de Havilland Engine Co., Hatfield, 1957–60; joined Air Min. as SSO, 1960; operational res. on deterrence, 1960–63; trials and analysis, Aden and Radfan, 1964; Kestrel evaluation trial, 1965; Scientific Adviser to FEAF, Singapore, 1967–70; Asst Chief Scientist (RAF), MoD, 1972–77; Asst Dir, Mil. Aircraft Projs, MoD (PE), 1978; Dir of Aircraft Post Design Services, MoD (PE), 1979–81; Dir Gen. Aircraft 1, MoD (PE), 1981–84; Dep. Controller Aircraft, MoD (PE), 1984–86; Controller of R&D Estabts, later of Estabts, Res. and Nuclear Programmes, and Hd of Profession Defence Engrg Service, MoD, 1986–89; Controller Aircraft, and Head of Profession Defence Sci. and Engrg, MoD, 1989–94. Vice Pres., 1993–95, Pres., 1995–, RAeS. Gold Medal, RAeS, 1989. *Recreations:* flying aeroplanes, mending cars. *Address:* 20 Paddock Close, Camberley, Surrey GU15 2BN. *Club:* Royal Air Force.

SPIERS, Ven. Graeme Hendry Gordon; Archdeacon of Liverpool, 1979–91, Archdeacon Emeritus, since 1991; *b* 15 Jan. 1925; *s* of Gordon and Mary Spiers; *m* 1958, Ann Chadwick; two *s*. *Educ:* Mercers Sch.; London College of Divinity. Westminster Bank, 1941–49; served RNVR, 1943–47. Deacon 1952, Priest 1953; Curate of Addiscombe, 1952–56; Succentor of Bradford Cathedral, 1956–58; Vicar of Speke, 1958–66; Vicar of Aigburth, 1966–80 and Rural Dean of Childwall, 1975–79. Hon. Canon, Liverpool Cathedral, 1977. *Recreation:* gardening. *Address:* 19 Barkfield Lane, Formby, Merseyside L37 1LY. *T:* Formby (017048) 72902.

SPIERS, John Raymond; Chairman: Trident Trust, since 1995; John Spiers Publishing Ltd, since 1988; Health Policy Adviser, The Social Market Foundation, since 1995; *b* 30 Sept. 1941; *s* of Horace Henry Spiers and Kate Dawson (*née* Root); *m* 1967, Prof. Margaret Ann Boden, *qv* (marr. diss. 1981); one *s* one *d*. *Educ:* Redhill Sch., E Sutton, Kent; Catford Coll. of Commerce; Univ. of Sussex (BA 1st Cl. Hons Hist. 1968). Writer and publisher, 1960–; Founder: Harvester Press Ltd (Chm., 1970–88); Harvester Press Microform Pubns Ltd (Chm., 1973–87) (Queen's Award for Export Achievement, 1986); Wheatsheaf Books Ltd (Chm., 1980–88). Special Advr to Dep. Chm., Cons. Party, 1989–90; Consultant Dir, Special Services Dept, Cons. Central Office, 1990–94; Mem., Citizens' Charter Adv. Panel to PM, 1995; Dep. Treas., Cons. Party SE England Area, 1990–92 (Mem., SE Area Council, 1990–92); Pres., Brighton Kemp Town Cons. Assoc., 1991–95. Founder and Chm., Brighton Business Gp, 1989–. Chairman: Brighton HA, 1991–92; Brighton Health Care NHS Trust, 1992–94; National Association of Health Authorities and Trusts: Mem., Nat. Council and Exec. Cttee, 1993–94; Chm., Nat. Conf. Cttee, 1993–94; Co-Chm., S Thames Network, 1994; Vice-Chm., Provider Cttee, 1993–94; Mem., NHS Mgt Exec. Adv. Gps, 1991–. Mem. Exec. Bd, Internat. Health Policy and Management Inst., 1994–. Co-Chm., The Radical Soc., 1991–. Vice-Chm., Grant Maintained Schools Foundn, 1992– (Trustee, 1992–). Trustee, Choice in Educn, 1990–92. Chm., Univ. of Sussex Alumni Soc., 1983–. FRSA 1994. DUniv Sussex, 1994. *Publications:* (with P. Coustillas) The Re-discovery of George Gissing, Novelist, 1971; The Invisible Hospital and the Secret Garden: an insider's commentary on the NHS reforms, 1995; (jtly) How to Be a Street-Wise Patient, 1995; contrib. Health Service Jl, British Jl of Health Management, Health Summary, Healthcare Today, Health Director. *Recreations:* collecting 19th century novels (and reading them), writing, walking, swimming (dutifully). *Address:* c/o John Spiers Publishing Ltd, 30 New Road, Brighton, Sussex BN1 1BN. *T:* Brighton (01273) 324163. *Club:* Carlton.

SPIERS, Air Cdre Reginald James, OBE 1972; FRAeS; *b* 8 Nov. 1928; *s* of Alfred James Oscar and Rose Emma Alice Spiers; *m* 1956, Cynthia Jeanette Williams; two *d*. *Educ:* Haberdashers' Aske's Sch.; RAF Coll., Cranwell. FRAeS 1975. Commissioned 1949; 247 and 64 Fighter Sqdns, 1950–54; Graduate, Empire Test Pilots' Sch., 1955; Fighter Test Sqdn, A&AEE, 1955–58; CO 4 Fighter Sqdn, 1958–61; PSO to C-in-C RAF Germany, 1961–63; RAF Staff Coll., 1964; FCO, 1965–67; CO RAF Masirah, 1967–68; Chief Test Flying Instructor, ETPS, 1968–71; Air Warfare Course, 1972; Air Secretary's Dept, MoD, 1972–73; MA to Governor of Gibraltar, 1973–75; CO Experimental Flying Dept, RAE Farnborough, 1975–78; Director, Defence Operational Requirements Staff, MoD, 1978–79; Comdt, A&AEE, Boscombe Down, 1979–83, retd. Marketing Exec., Marconi, later GEC, Avionics, 1984–91. *Recreations:* shooting, aviation. *Address:* Barnside, Penton Mewsey, near Andover, Hants SP11 0RQ. *T:* Weyhill (01264) 772376. *Club:* Royal Air Force.

SPIERS, Ronald Ian; consultant on international affairs, since 1992; Under-Secretary-General, Department of Political and General Assembly Affairs and Secretariat Services, United Nations, 1989–92; *b* 9 July 1925; *s* of Tomas H. and Blanca De P. Spiers; *m* 1949, Patience Baker; one *s* three *d*. *Educ:* Dartmouth Coll., New Hampshire (BA); Princeton Univ. (Master in Public Affairs, PhD). Mem., US Delegn to UN, 1956–60; US Department of State: Dir, Office of Disarmament and Arms Control, 1960–62; Dir, Office of NATO Affairs, 1962–66; Political Counsellor, London, 1966–69; Asst Sec. of State, Politico-Military Affairs, 1969–73; Ambassador to the Bahamas, 1973–74; Minister, London, 1974–77; Ambassador to Turkey, 1977–80; Asst Sec. of State, Bureau of Intelligence and Research, Dept of State, 1980–81; Ambassador to Pakistan, 1981–83; Under Sec. of State for Management, 1983–89. *Recreations:* swimming, music, theatre-going, gardening. *Address:* Middletown Road, South Londonderry, VT 05155, USA.

SPIERS, Shaun Mark; Member (Lab Co-op) for London South East, European Parliament, since 1994; *b* 23 April 1962; *s* of Charles Gordon Spiers and Ann Kathleen Spiers (*née* Hutton). *Educ:* St John's Coll., Oxford (BA Hons PPE); King's Coll. London (MA War Studies). Political Officer, SE Co-op, 1987–94. *Recreations:* music, sport. *Address:* Sunways House, 298 Broadway, Bexleyheath, Kent DA6 8AH. *Clubs:* Bromley Labour, Lewisham Labour.

SPIKINGS, Barry Peter; Partner, Pleskow/Spikings Partnership, international production and distribution of feature films, since 1992; *b* Boston, Lincs, 23 Nov. 1939; *m* 1st, 1962, Judith Anne Spikings; one *s* one *d*; 2nd, 1978, Dorothy Spikings; two step *d*. *Educ:* Boston Grammar School. Joint Managing Director: British Lion Films Ltd, 1973–75; EMI Films Ltd, 1975–78; Director, EMI Films Inc., 1975–78; Chm. and Chief Exec. Officer, EMI Film and Theatre Corp., 1978–80; Chm., Elstree Studios, 1978–82; Chm. and Chief Exec., Thorn EMI Films Worldwide, 1980–82; Pres. and Chief Operating Officer, Nelson Entertainment Inc., 1986–91. Oscar award as Producer of Best Picture of the Year, for The Deer Hunter, Acad. of Motion Picture Arts and Sciences, 1979. *Recreation:* making films. *Address:* 335 North Maple Drive, Suite 352, Beverly Hills, CA 90210, USA. *Club:* Mark's.

SPILLER, John Anthony Walsh, MBE 1979; Senior Consultant, Western Approaches PR Ltd, since 1993; *b* 29 Dec. 1942; *s* of C. H. Spiller and Sarah (*née* Walsh), Moycullen, Co. Galway, Eire; *m* 1972, Angela, *d* of Surtees Gleghorn; one *s* one *d*. *Educ:* County Secondary Sch., Bideford; North Devon College. Member Executive, Nat. League of Young Liberals, 1960–61; Organiser, Torrington Constituency Liberal Assoc., 1962–64; Divl Liberal Agent, Cornwall (Northern) Parly Constituency, 1965–71; Northern Regional Organiser (Election Agent, Rochdale By-Elec. 1972 and Berwick-upon-Tweed By-Elec. 1973), 1972–74; Nat. Agent, Liberal Central Assoc., 1974–76; Mem., Liberal Party Gen. Elec. Campaign Cttee, and Press Officer, Gen. Elections Feb. and Oct. 1974; Western Area Agent, 1977–80; Advisor, African Peoples Union, Independence Elections, Zimbabwe, 1980; By-Elec. and Marginal Seats Agent, Liberal Party Org. Headquarters, 1981–82; Sec. Gen., Liberal Party, 1983–85; Co. Liaison Officer, Devonshire PHAB Organisation UK, 1990–92; Chm., Lib Dem Campaign, Cornwall (Northern), Gen. Election 1992; Advr, Electoral Reform Soc., Democracy Conf., Lithuania, 1992, Estonia, 1995. Mem. Bd of Management, Gladstone Benevolent Fund, 1980– (Sec. 1980, Hon. Sec., 1993). *Recreations:* golf, walking in Connemara. *Address:* 5 Royston Road, Bideford, Devonshire EX39 3AN.

SPINK, Prof. Ian Walter Alfred; Professor of Music, London University at Royal Holloway; *b* 29 March 1932; *s* of William James Spink and Margaret Hamilton (*née* Anderson); *m* 1960, Margaret Storry Walton; three *s* four *d*. *Educ:* Mercers' Sch.; Trinity Coll. of Music (BMus 1953); Barber Inst. of Fine Arts, Univ. of Birmingham (MA 1957). Nat. Service, 1953–55, 2nd Lieut, RA. Overseas Examiner for Trinity Coll. of Music in Canada, NZ and Australia, 1958–59; Dir of Music, Westlain GS, Brighton, Sussex, 1960–62; Lectr, then Sen. Lectr, Univ. of Sydney, NSW, 1962–69; RHC, later RHBNC, now Royal Holloway, University of London: Head of Music Dept., 1969–92; Sen. Lectr, 1969–72; Reader, 1972–74; Prof., 1974–; Dean, Fac. of Arts, 1973–75 and 1983–85; Dean, Fac. of Music, and Mem. Senate, Univ. of London, 1974–78. *Publications:* English Song: Dowland to Purcell, 1974, 2nd edn 1986; The Seventeenth Century, Blackwell History of Music in Britain, vol. 3, 1992; Restoration Cathedral Music 1660–1714, 1995; editions of music in: The English Lute-songs, 2nd series, vol. 17, 1961, 2nd edn 1974, vol. 18, 1962, vol. 19, 1966; Musica Britannica, vol. 33, 1971, 2nd edn 1977, vol. 42, 1978; The Works of Henry Purcell, vol. 2, 1990, vol. 4, 1994; (contrib.) The New Grove, 1980; (contrib.) The New Oxford History of Music, vol. 6, 1986; (contrib.) Purcell Studies, 1995; articles in Acta Musicologica, Music and Letters, Proc. Royal Musical Assoc., etc. *Address:* Bridge House, Trumps Green Road, Virginia Water, Surrey GU25 4JA. *T:* Wentworth (01344) 843039.

SPINK, Dr Robert Michael; MP (C) Castle Point, since 1992; industrial engineer and management consultant, since 1984; *b* 1 Aug. 1948; *s* of George and Brenda Spink; *m* 1968, Janet Mary Barham; three *s* one *d*. *Educ:* Manchester Univ. (research and academic prizes; BSc 1st Cl. Hons Eng 1971); Cranfield Inst. of Technology (MSc Indust Eng 1974; PhD, Sch. of Management, 1989). CEng, MIProdE, MIIM, MIMgt, MIMC, CDipAF. Mill Boy (labourer), 1962–64; RAF, 1964–66; EMI Electronics, 1966–77 (Engrg Apprentice; EMI Graduate Apprentice of the Year, 1971); Management Consultant, 1977–; Dir and Co-Owner, Seafarer Navigation International, 1980–84; Dir, Bournemouth Internat. Airport, 1989–93. Dorset County Councillor, 1985–93 (Chm., Educn Policy Cttee, 1989–91); Mem., Dorset Police Authy, 1985–93. PPS to Min. of State, Dept of Employment, 1994–. Mem., Educn Select Cttee, 1992–; Vice Chm., Backbench Employment Cttee, 1993–94; Chm., All Party Parly Gp for Prisoners Abroad, 1995–. Dep. Chm., Poole Cons. Assoc., 1984–92; Mem. Nat. Exec., Baby Life Support Systems Charity, 1985–92. *Recreations:* golf (learning), squash, Bearded Collies. *Address:* House of Commons, SW1A 0AA. *T:* 0171–219 3000.

SPINKS, Mary Cecilia, RGN; health services consultant, specialising in risk management, audit and expert opinion on malpractice, since 1993; *b* 20 Sept. 1940; *d* of Francis and Mary Clark; *m* 1st, 1961, Robert Donn (marr. diss. 1975); 2nd, 1992, Leslie Oswald Spinks. *Educ:* St Vincent's Convent, Cork; Student Nurse, Whipps Cross Hosp. (RGN 1962); DipN London; William Rathbone Coll.; Thames Polytechnic (DMS). Post-graduate Staff Nurse, Charing Cross Hosp., 1962; Theatre Sister, St Mary's Hosp., Paddington, 1963–64; Theatre Sister, Nursing Officer, Sen. Nursing Officer, Bromley AHA, 1964–83; Dir, Nursing Services, Lewisham and N Southwark HA, 1983–84; Chief Nursing Officer and Dir, Consumer Affairs, Brighton HA, 1984–90; Regl Nursing Officer, NE Thames RHA, 1990–93. Former chm. and mem., nursing, health, editorial and advisory cttees; Chm., Nat. Assoc. of Theatre Nurses, 1975–78; Member: Maidstone HA, 1985–90; NHS Training Authy, 1988–91. MRSM 1992. *Publications:* numerous contribs to professional jls. *Recreations:* horse-racing, cricket, gardening. *Address:* 2 Somerford Close, Maidenhead, Berks SL6 8EJ. *T:* Maidenhead (01628) 75526.

SPITZ, Kathleen Emily, (Mrs Heinz Spitz); *see* Gales, Kathleen Emily.

SPITZ, Prof. Lewis, PhD; FRCS, FRCSE; Nuffield Professor of Paediatric Surgery, since 1979, and Head of Division of Surgery, since 1992, Institute of Child Health, London; Consultant Surgeon, Great Ormond Street Hospital for Children Trust (formerly Hospital for Sick Children, Great Ormond Street), since 1979; *b* 25 Aug. 1939; *s* of Woolf and Selma Spitz; *m* 1972, Louise Ruth Dyzenhaus; one *s* one *d*. *Educ:* Univ. of Pretoria (MB, ChB); Univ. of the Witwatersrand (PhD). FRCS (*ad eundem*) 1980; FRCSE 1969; Hon. FAAP 1987. Smith and Nephew Fellow, Liverpool and London, 1971; Paediatric Surgeon, Johannesburg, 1971–74; Consultant Paediatric Surgeon, Sheffield Children's Hosp., 1974–79. Hon. Consultant in Paediatric Surgery to the Army, 1983–. Windermere Vis. Prof., Univ. of Melbourne, 1988; Chafin-Snyder Vis. Prof., Children's Hosp., UCLA, 1992; Visiting Professor: Univ. of Hong Kong; Royal Coll. of Surgeons, Thailand, 1995. Lectures: Santuli, Babies Hosp., Columbia Univ., NY, 1992; Sulamaa, Children's Hosp., Univ. of Helsinki, 1993; Amer. Pediatric Surgical Assoc., 1995. Member: British Assoc. of Paediatric Surgeons; Assoc. of Surgeons of GB and Ireland; British Paediatric Assoc. (Mem. Acad. Bd, 1991–93); British Soc. of Gastroenterology; Chm., Specialist Adv. Cttee in Paediatric Surgery, 1994– (RCS Rep., 1991–); RCS Rep on Intercollegiate Bd of Paediatric Surgery, 1994–; MRSocMed. Hon. Mem., Paediatric Surgical Assocs of Switzerland, Austria, Greece, Asia and S Africa. Bronze Medal, Nordik Soc. of Paediatric Surgeons, 1990. Exec. Editor, Progress in Paediatric Surgery, 1982; Member, Editorial Board: Jl of Paediatric Surgery, 1980–; Archives of Diseases in Childhood, 1984–89; Turkish Jl of Paediatric Surgery, 1987–; Jl of RCSE, 1992–; Associate Editor, Pediatric Surgery International, 1986–. *Publications:* A Colour Atlas of Paediatric Surgical Diagnosis,

1981; A Colour Atlas of Surgery for Undescended Testes, 1984; (ed jtly and contrib.) Paediatric Surgery, 4th edn 1988 (Rob and Smith Operative Surgery series), 5th edn 1995; chapters in books on paediatrics and surgery; articles on oesophageal atresia, oesophageal replacement, gastro-oesophageal reflux, neonatal surgical conditions, and paediatric oncology. *Recreation:* tennis. *Address:* Institute of Child Health, 30 Guilford Street, WC1N 1EH. *T:* 0171–242 9789, 0171–829 8691; 0171–405 9200.

SPITZER, Prof. Lyman, (Jr), BA; PhD; Professor of Astronomy, 1947–82 (Charles A. Young Professor, 1952–82), Princeton University; Chairman of Astrophysical Sciences Department, and Director of Observatory, Princeton University, 1947–79; Chairman, Research Board, 1967–72; *b* 26 June 1914; *s* of Lyman Spitzer and Blanche B. (*née* Brumback); *m* 1940, Doreen D. Canaday; one *s* three *d*. *Educ:* Phillips Academy, Andover; Yale Univ. (BA); Cambridge Univ., England; Princeton Univ. (PhD). Instructor in Physics and Astronomy, Yale Univ., 1939–42; Scientist, Special Studies Group, Columbia Univ. Div. of War Research, 1942–44; Dir, Sonar Analysis Group, Columbia Univ. Div. of War Research, 1944–46; Assoc. Prof. of Astrophysics, Yale Univ., 1946–47. Dir Project Matterhorn, Princeton Univ., 1953–61; Chm. Exec. Cttee, Plasma Physics Lab., Princeton Univ., 1961–66; Principal Investigator, Princeton telescope on Copernicus satellite; Chm., Space Telescope Inst. Council, 1981–90. Member: Nat. Acad. of Sciences; American Academy of Arts and Sciences; American Philosophical Society; Internat. Acad. of Astronautics; Corr. Member, Société Royale des Sciences, Liège; Foreign Mem., Royal Soc., 1990; Foreign Associate, Royal Astronomical Soc.; Pres., American Astronomical Soc., 1959–61. Hon. Dr of Science: Yale Univ., 1958; Case Inst. of Technology, 1961; Harvard, 1975; Princeton, 1984; Hon. Dr of Laws, Toledo Univ., 1963. Rittenhouse Medal, Franklin Inst., 1957; NASA Medal, 1972; Bruce Medal, Astron. Soc. of the Pacific, 1973; Draper Medal, Nat. Acad. of Scis, 1974; Maxwell Prize, Amer. Physical Soc., 1975; Schwarzschild Medal, Deutsche Astron. Ges., 1975; Dist. Public Service Medal, NASA, 1976; Gold Medal, RAS, 1978; Nat. Medal of Science, 1980; Janssen Medal, Soc. Astron. de France, 1980; Franklin Medal, Franklin Inst., 1980; Crafoord Prize, Royal Swedish Acad. Sci., 1985; Madison Medal, Princeton Univ., 1989; Franklin Medal, Amer. Philosophical Soc., 1991. *Publications:* (ed) Physics of Sound in the Sea, 1946; Physics of Fully Ionized Gases, 1956 (2nd edn 1962); Diffuse Matter in Space, 1968; Physical Processes in the Interstellar Medium, 1978; Searching between the Stars, 1982; Dynamical Evolution of Globular Clusters, 1987; papers in Astrophysical Jl, Monthly Notices of Royal Astronomical Soc., Physical Review, Physics of Fluids, on interstellar matter, stellar dynamics, plasma physics, space astronomy, etc. *Recreations:* ski-ing, mountain climbing. *Address:* 659 Lake Drive, Princeton, NJ 08540, USA. *T:* (609) 9243007. *Clubs:* Alpine; American Alpine.

SPOCK, Dr Benjamin McLane; Professor of Child Development, Western Reserve University, USA, 1955–67, now lecturing, writing and working for peace; *b* New Haven, Connecticut, 2 May 1903; *s* of Benjamin Ives Spock and Mildred Louise (*née* Stoughton); *m* 1st, 1927, Jane Davenport Cheney (marr. diss. 1975); two *s*; 2nd, 1976, Mary Morgan; one step *d*. *Educ:* Yale Univ. (BA); Yale Medical Sch.; Coll. Physicians and Surgeons, Columbia Univ. (MD). In practice (Pediatrics) from 1933; Cornell Med. Coll.; NY Hospital; NYC Health Dept. Served, 1944–46 in US Navy. Subseq. on Staff of: Rochester (Minn) Child Health Inst., Mayo Clinic, University of Minnesota; Prof. of Child Development, University of Pittsburgh, 1951–55. *Publications:* The Pocket Book of Baby and Child Care (also published as The Common Sense Book of Baby and Child Care), 1946, 6th edn as Dr Spock's Baby and Child Care, 1992; (with John Reinhart and Wayne Miller) A Baby's First Year, 1955; (with Miriam E. Lowenberg) Feeding Your Baby and Child, 1955; Dr Spock Talks with Mothers, 1961; Problems of Parents, 1962; (with Marion Lerrigo) Caring for Your Disabled Child, 1964; (with Mitchell Zimmerman) Dr Spock on Vietnam, 1968; Decent and Indecent: our personal and political behaviour, 1970; A Young Person's Guide to Life and Love, 1971; Raising Children in a Difficult Time, 1974 (UK as Bringing Up Children in a Difficult Time, 1974); Dr Spock on Parenting, 1987; (with Mary Morgan) Spock on Spock, 1989; A Better World for Our Children, 1994. *Relevant publications:* The Trial of Doctor Spock, by Jessica Mitford, 1969; Dr Spock: biography of a conservative radical, by Lynn Z. Bloom, 1972. *Address:* PO Box 1268, Camden, ME 04843–1268, USA.

SPOKES, Ann; *see* Spokes Symonds, A. H.

SPOKES, John Arthur Clayton, QC 1973; *b* 6 Feb. 1931; 2nd *s* of late Peter Spencer Spokes and Lilla Jane Spokes (*née* Clayton), Oxford; *m* 1961, Jean, *yr d* of late Dr Robert McLean and Jean Symington McLean (*née* Barr), Carluke; one *s* one *d*. *Educ:* Westminster Sch.; Brasenose Coll., Oxford. BA 1954; MA 1959. Nat. Service, Royal Artillery, 1949–51 (commnd 1950). Called to Bar, Gray's Inn, 1955, Bencher, 1985; a Recorder, 1972–93. Chm., Data Protection Tribunal, 1985–. Chancellor, Dio. of Winchester, 1985–93. *Recreations:* gardening, walking. *Address:* 3 Pump Court, Temple, EC4Y 7AJ. *T:* 0171–353 0711. *Club:* Leander (Henley-on-Thames).

See also A. H. Spokes Symonds.

SPOKES SYMONDS, Ann (Hazel); Patron, Age Concern England, since 1994 (Chairman, 1983–86; Vice-President, 1987–94); *b* 10 Nov. 1925; *d* of Peter Spencer Spokes and Lilla Jane Spokes (*née* Clayton); *m* 1980, (John) Richard (Charters) Symonds, *qv*. *Educ:* Wychwood Sch., Oxford; Masters Sch., Dobbs Ferry, NY, USA; St Anne's Coll., Oxford (BA 1947; MA). Organising Secretary: Oxford Council of Social Service, 1959–74; Age Concern Oxford, 1958–80. Dir, ATV, 1978–81; Mem. W Midlands Bd, Central Indep. Television plc, 1981–92. Mem., Thames Valley Police Authy, 1973–85; Chm., No 5 Police Dist. Authy Cttee, 1982–85; Vice-Chm., Personal Social Services Council, 1978–80; Chm., Social Services Cttee, ACC, 1978–82; Mem. Bd, Anchor Housing Assoc., 1976–83, 1985–94; Member: Prince of Wales' Adv. Gp on Disability, 1983–90; Oftel Adv. Cttee for Disabled and Elderly People, 1985–91; Hearing Aid Council, 1986–89; Trustee, CERT, 1986–89. Member: Oxford City Council, 1957–95 (Lord Mayor, 1976–77); Oxfordshire CC, 1974–85 (Chm., 1981–83). Contested (C) NE Leicester, 1959, Brigg, 1966 and 1970. Mem., Soc. of Authors, 1992–. FRSA 1991. *Publications:* Celebrating Age: an anthology, 1987; Havens Across the Sea, 1990; The Great Grosvenor Hotel Scandal, 1993; Storks, Black Bags and Gooseberry Bushes, 1993. *Recreations:* lawn tennis, golf, photography, enjoying cats. *Address:* 43 Davenant Road, Oxford OX2 8BU. *T:* Oxford (01865) 515661.

See also J. A. C. Spokes.

SPOONER, Prof. Frank Clyffurde, MA, PhD, LittD; Professor of Economic History, University of Durham, 1966–85, now Emeritus; *b* 5 March 1924; *s* of Harry Gordon Morrison Spooner. *Educ:* Bromley Grammar Sch.; Christ's Coll., Cambridge. Hist. Tripos, 1st cl., Pt I 1947 and Pt II 1948; MA 1949; PhD 1953; LittD 1985. War Service, Sub-Lt (S) RNVR, 1943–46; Bachelor Research Scholar, 1948; Chargé de Recherches, CNRS, Paris, 1949–50; Allen Scholar, 1951; Fellow, Christ's Coll., Cambridge, 1951–57; Commonwealth Fund Fellow, 1955–57 at Chicago, Columbia, New York, and Harvard Univs; Ecole Pratique des Hautes Etudes, VI Section, Sorbonne, 1957–61; Lectr, Univ. of Oxford, 1958–59; Vis. Lectr in Econs, Harvard Univ., 1961–62; Irving Fisher Research Prof. of Econs, Yale Univ., 1962–63; Univ. of Durham: Lectr, 1963; Reader, 1964; Resident Tutor-in-charge, Lumley Castle, 1965–70; Dir, Inst. of European Studies, 1969–76; Leverhulme Fellow, 1976–78; Leverhulme Emeritus Fellow, 1985–86. FRHistS 1970; FSA 1983. Prix Limantour de l'Académie des Sciences Morales et Politiques, 1957; West European Award, British Academy, 1979; Ernst Meyer Award, 1983. *Publications:* L'économie mondiale et les frappes monétaires en France, 1493–1680, 1956, revised edn The International Economy and Monetary Movements in France, 1493–1725, 1972; Risks at Sea: Amsterdam insurance and maritime Europe 1766–1780, 1983; contribs to joint works and to jls. *Recreations:* music, photography, walking. *Club:* United Oxford & Cambridge University.

SPOONER, Sir James (Douglas), Kt 1981; Chairman, Morgan Crucible, since 1983 (Director, since 1978); Director, John Swire & Sons, since 1970; *b* 11 July 1932; *s* of late Vice-Adm. E. J. Spooner, DSO, and Megan Spooner (*née* Megan Foster, the singer); *m* 1958, Jane Alyson, *d* of late Sir Gerald Glover; two *s* one *d*. *Educ:* Eton Coll. (Fellow, 1990); Christ Church, Oxford. Chartered Accountant 1962; Partner, Dixon Wilson & Co., Chartered Accountants, 1963–72; Chm., Vantona Viyella, subseq. Coats Viyella, 1969–89. Chm., NAAFI, 1973–86 (Dir, 1968–86); Director: Abingworth, 1973–91; J. Sainsbury, 1981–94; Barclays Bank, 1983–94; Hogg Robinson Gp, 1971–85 (Dep. Chm., 1971–85); Dep. Chm., Royal Opera House, Covent Garden, 1992– (Dir, 1987–); Chm. of Trustees, British Telecom Pension Scheme, 1992–. Chm. Council, King's College London, 1986–. *Recreations:* music, history, shooting. *Address:* Swire House, 59 Buckingham Gate, SW1E 6AJ. *Clubs:* White's, Beefsteak.

SPORBORG, Christopher Henry; Deputy Chairman, Hambros PLC, since 1990 (Vice-Chairman, 1986–90); *b* 17 April 1939; *s* of late H. N. Sporborg and of Mary (*née* Rowlands); *m* 1961, Lucinda Jane (*née* Hanbury); two *s* two *d*. *Educ:* Rugby School; Emmanuel College, Cambridge (BA Hons). Nat. Service, Coldstream Guards, 1957–59 (Lieut). Hambros Bank, 1962–: Dir, 1970; Dep. Chm., 1983; Chm., Hambro Countrywide, 1986–, Hambro Insce Services Gp, 1993–, and Hambro overseas cos. Chm., United Racecourses (Hldgs), 1994–; Director: BMSS; Racecourse Hldgs Trusts; Mem., Jockey Club and Dir, Jockey Club Estates; Mem., Horserace Totalisator Bd, 1993–.Trustee: Develt Trust (for the Mentally Handicapped); Sir Jules Thorn Charitable Trust; Fitzwilliam Family Trusts. *Recreations:* hunting (Joint Master, Puckeridge Foxhounds), racing (owner and permit holder), bridge. *Address:* Brooms Farm, Upwick Green, Albury, Ware, Herts SG11 2JX. *T:* Albury (01279) 771444. *Club:* Boodle's.

SPOTSWOOD, Marshal of the Royal Air Force Sir Denis (Frank), GCB 1971 (KCB 1966; CB 1961); CBE 1946; DSO 1943; DFC 1942; *b* 26 Sept. 1916; *s* of late F. H. Spotswood and M. C. Spotswood; *m* 1942, Ann (*née* Child); one *s*. Commissioned in RAF, 1936; UK Service in Squadrons, 1937–41; No 209 Squadron, 1939–41. Served War of 1939–45 (despatches twice, DSO). Chief Instructor, Operation Training Unit, 1941–42; Officer Commanding No 500 (County of Kent) Squadron, RAuxAF, 1942–43; Director of Plans, HQ Supreme Allied Commander, South-East Asia, 1944–46; Directing Staff, RAF Staff Coll., 1946–48; Officer Commanding RAF (Fighter) Stations, Horsham St Faith and Coltishall, 1948–50; Directing Staff, Imperial Defence Coll., 1950–52; Exchange Duties, HQUSAF in USA, 1952–54; Officer Commanding RAF (Fighter) Station, Linton-on-Ouse, 1954–56; Deputy Director of Plans, Air Ministry, 1956–58; AOC and Commandant, RAF Coll., Cranwell, 1958–61; Assistant Chief of Staff (Air Defence), SHAPE, 1961–63; AOC No 3 Group, RAF Bomber Command, 1964–65; C-in-C RAF Germany, 1965–68; Commander, 2nd Allied Tactical Air Force, 1966–68; AOC-in-C, RAF Strike Command, 1968–71; Comdr, UK Air Defence Region, 1968–71; Chief of the Air Staff, 1971–74. Group Captain, 1954; Air Commodore, 1958; Air Vice-Marshal, 1961; Air Marshal, 1965; Air Chief Marshal, 1968; Marshal of the RAF, 1974. ADC to the Queen, 1957–61, Air ADC to the Queen, 1970–74. Vice-Chm. and Dir, Rolls Royce Ltd, 1974–80; Chm., Turbo Union Ltd, 1975–80; Director: RR/Turbomeca Ltd; Dowty Gp, 1980–87; Smiths Industries ADS, 1980–91 (Chm., 1980–82). Pres., SBAC, 1978–79. Chm. of Governors, Royal Star and Garter Home, 1981–85 (Gov., 1974–80); Vice-Patron, RAF Museum (Chm. of Trustees, 1974–80). FRAeS 1975. Officer of the Legion of Merit (USA). *Recreations:* golf, sailing, shooting, bridge. *Address:* Coombe Cottage, Hambleden, Henley-on-Thames, Oxon RG9 6SD. *Clubs:* Royal Air Force; Phyllis Court (Henley); Huntercombe Golf.

SPOTTISWOOD, Air Vice-Marshal James Donald, CB 1988; CVO 1977; AFC 1971; Vice President, Short's Support Services Division, since 1994; Managing Director, Airwork Ltd, Bournemouth International Airport, since 1989; *b* 27 May 1934; *s* of James Thomas Spottiswood and Caroline Margaret Spottiswood; *m* 1957, Margaret Maxwell (*née* Harrison); two *s* one *d*. *Educ:* West Hartlepool Grammar School; Boston Univ., USA (MA). Enlisted RAF, 1951, commissioned, 1952; 617 Sqn, 1962–64; Royal Naval Staff Coll., 1965; PSO to C-in-C Middle East, 1966–67; Commanded 53 Sqn, 1968–70; JSSC, 1970; Commanded: RAF Thorney Island, 1972–75; RAF Benson, 1975–76; Dep. Captain, the Queen's Flight, 1975–76; RCDS, 1978; Secretary to IMS, HQ NATO, 1980–83; DG of Trng, RAF, 1983–85; Air Officer Trng, RAF Support Comd, 1985–89, retired. Chm., British Gliding Assoc., 1989–. FIMgt (FBIM 1983). *Recreations:* gliding, sailing, golf. *Address:* Royal Bank of Scotland, 49–51 Old Christchurch Road, Bournemouth BH1 1EG. *Club:* Royal Air Force.

SPOTTISWOODE, Clare Mary Joan; Director General of Gas Supply, since 1993; *b* 20 March 1953; *d* of Charlotte and Tony Spottiswoode; *m* 1977, Oliver Richards; one *s* three *d*. *Educ:* Cheltenham Ladies' Coll.; Clare Coll., Cambridge (MA Maths Pt 1, Economics Pt 2); Yale Univ. (MPhil). HM Treasury, 1977–80; Spottiswoode Trading, 1980–84 (wholesale importing business); Chm. and Chief Exec., Spottiswoode and Spottiswoode (micro computer software), 1984–90. *Publications:* Quill, 1984; Abacus, 1984. *Recreations:* children, gardening, theatre. *Address:* Office of Gas Supply, Stockley House, 130 Wilton Road, SW1V 1LQ. *T:* 0171–932 1661.

SPRACKLING, Maj.-Gen. Ian Oliver John, OBE 1977; Associate Partner, Andersen Consulting, since 1992; Head of Andersen Consulting Russian practice, since 1993; *b* 3 Oct. 1936; *m* 1959, Ann Vonda (*née* Coote); two *s*. *Educ:* Bristol Grammar School; RMCS (BSc Eng); psc, RCDS. RMA Sandhurst, 1955; 2nd Lieut, Royal Corps of Signals, 1957; RMCS, 1958–61; served Far East, UK, BAOR, 1961–75; Staff Officer, Sultan of Oman's Armed Forces, 1975–77; CO, Electronic Warfare Regt, BAOR, 1977–79; Col, Cabinet Office, 1979–81; Comdr, Catterick Garrison, 1982–84; RCDS 1984; Dir, Mil. Assistance Overseas, 1985–86; Dir Gen., Management and Support of Intelligence, MoD, 1986–89, retired. *Recreations:* bridge, socialising, keep fit, watching Rugby. *Address:* 2 Arundel Street, WC2R 3LT. *Clubs:* Army and Navy; Clifton (Bristol); Fadeaways.

SPRAGGS, Rear-Adm. Trevor Owen Keith, CB 1983; CEng, FIEE; Chief of Staff to Commander-in-Chief, Naval Home Command, 1981–83; *b* 17 June 1926; *s* of Cecil James Spraggs and Gladys Maude (*née* Morey); *m* 1st, 1955, Mary Patricia Light (*d* 1983); two *s*; 2nd, 1986, Gwynedd Kate (*née* Adams) *widow* of Reginald A. W. Green, CEng, MIMechE. *Educ:* Portsmouth Grammar Sch.; St John's Coll., Southsea; Imperial College of Science and Technology, London (BScEng, ACGI). Joined Royal Navy, 1945; courses: HM Ships: King Alfred, Leander, Harrier, 1945–47; Admiralty Compass Obs., Slough,

1948; BRNC, Dartmouth, 1948–50; HM Ships: Dryad, Vanguard, Vernon, Collingwood, Ariel, Falcon, 1950–61; AEI, Manchester, 1962; RNEC, 1962–66; HMS Collingwood, 1966–69 and 1972–75; RNEC, 1969–72, and, as Dean, 1979–80; Dean, RNC, Greenwich, 1975–77; Dir of Naval Trng Support, Dir of Naval Educn and Trng Support, 1977–79; Chief Naval Instr Officer, 1981–83. ADC to the Queen, 1979. Member: Nautical Studies Bd of CNAA, 1975–80; Maritime Studies Adv. Cttee of Plymouth Polytech., 1979–80; Cttee of Management, Royal Hosp. Sch., Holbrook, 1981–83; Governor: Fareham Technical Coll., 1972–75; RN Sch. for Officers' Daughters, Haslemere, 1975–77. Pres., Combined Services and RN Amateur Athletic Assocs, 1981–83. *Recreations:* golf, sailing, gardening. *Address:* 46 Sinah Lane, Hayling Island, Hants PO11 0HH. *Clubs:* Royal Naval Sailing Association; Hayling Golf.

SPRAGUE, David Keith, MVO 1972; HM Diplomatic Service, retired; High Commissioner, Sierra Leone, 1991–93; *b* 20 Feb. 1935; *m* 1958, Audrey Mellon; two *s* one *d*. *Educ:* King Edward VI Grammar Sch., Camp Hill, Birmingham. Foreign Office, 1953; Nat. Service, 1953–55; FO, 1955, served Addis Ababa, Paris, Belgrade, Budapest, Kuala Lumpur, Abidjan, Sofia, and FCO; Dep. High Comr, Madras, 1986–89; Ambassador to Mongolia, 1989–91. *Recreation:* golf. *Address:* 5 Deepdene Drive, Dorking, Surrey RH5 4AD.

SPRATT, Prof. Brian Geoffrey, PhD; FRS 1993; Professor of Molecular Genetics and Wellcome Trust Principal Research Fellow, Sussex University, since 1989; *b* 21 March 1947; *s* of Clarence Albert Spratt and Marjory Alice (*née* Jeffreys); *m* 1986, Jennifer Broome-Smith (marr. diss. 1993); one *s*. *Educ:* Tonbridge Sch.; University Coll. London (BSc, PhD). Research Fellow: Princeton Univ., 1973–75; Leicester Univ., 1975–80; Sussex University: Lectr in Biochem., 1980–87; Reader in Molecular Genetics, 1987–89. *Publications:* numerous pubns on microbiol. and genetics in learned jls. *Address:* School of Biological Sciences, Sussex University, Brighton, Sussex BN1 9QG. *T:* Brighton (01273) 678309, *Fax:* (01273) 678433; Flat 4, 10 Fourth Avenue, Hove, Sussex BN3 2PH. *T:* Brighton (01273) 728984.

SPRATT, Sir Greville (Douglas), GBE 1987; TD 1962, Bar 1968; DL; JP; Underwriting Member of Lloyd's, since 1950; Lord Mayor of London, 1987–88; *b* 1 May 1927; *e s* of Hugh Douglas Spratt and Sheelah Ivy (*née* Stace); *m* 1954, Sheila Farrow Wade; three *d*. *Educ:* Leighton Park; Charterhouse. Served Coldstream Guards, 1945–46; commnd Oxfordshire and Bucks LI, 1946; seconded to Arab Legion; served Palestine, Trans Jordan and Egypt, 1946–48; GSO III (Ops and Intell.), 1948. Lloyd's, 1948–61; joined J. & N. Wade Gp of Electrical Distributors, 1961; Dir, 1969–76 and Man. Dir, 1972–76. Dir, 1989–92, Chm., 1991–92, City and West End Regl Adv. Bd, National Westminster Bank; Chairman: Forest Mere Ltd, 1993– (Dir, 1991–); Claremount Underwriting Agency, 1994–; Aimmedia Internat., 1994–; Director: Williams Lea Gp, 1989–; Charterhouse Enterprises Ltd, 1991–. Lieut of the City of London, 1972; Life Mem., Guild of Freemen, 1977 (Mem. Court, 1982–90); Liveryman, Ironmongers' Co., 1977– (Mem. Ct, 1982–; Master, 1995–96); Alderman, Castle Baynard Ward, 1978–; JP 1978; Sheriff of the City of London, 1984–85; DL Greater London, 1986; Mem., Police Cttee, 1989–91, Planning and Communications Cttee, 1990–91, Corp. of City of London. Joined HAC Infantry Bn as private, 1950; re-commnd 1950; CO, 1962–65; Regtl Col, 1966–70; Mem., Ct of Assts, HAC, 1960–70 and 1978–; ADC to the Queen, 1973–78; Mem., City TA&VRA, 1960– (Vice Chm., 1973–77, Chm., 1977–82); Chm., TA&VRA for Greater London, 1991– (Mem., Exec. and Finance Cttee, 1977–); Hon. Colonel: City and NE sector, London ACF, 1983–; 8th Bn, The Queen's Fusiliers (City of London), 1988–92; The London Regt, 1992–95. Church Comr, 1993–. Chm., Action Res. for the Crippled Child, 1989– (Mem. Council, 1982–; Mem. Haslemere Cttee, 1971–82); President: Royal British Legion, Haslemere (St James Vice Pres., 1991–); London Fedn of Old Comrades Assocs, 1983–; Vice President: Not Forgotten Assoc., 1990–; British Red Cross, 1993– (Dep. Pres., London, 1983–91); Mem. Council, Reserve Forces Assoc., 1981–84. Chm., Anglo Jordanian Soc., 1990–; Member: Cttee, Guildhall Sch. of Music and Drama, 1978–80 and 1989– (Hon. Mem., GSMD 1988); Court, City Univ., 1981– (Chancellor, 1987–88); Governing Bodies of Girls' Schs Assoc., 1982–90; Governor: St Ives Sch., 1976– (Vice Chm., 1977–86; Chm., 1986–90); King Edward's Sch., Witley, 1978– (Vice-Pres., 1989–); Christ's Hosp., 1978–; Bridewell Royal Hosp., 1978–; City of London Sch. for Girls, 1981–82; Malvern Girls' Coll., 1982–90; St Paul's Cathedral Choir Sch., 1985–; Charterhouse, 1985– (Chm. Governing Body, 1989–95); City of London Freemen's Sch., 1992–; Life Governor, Corp. of the Sons of the Clergy, 1985–; Patron: Internat. Centre for Child Studies, 1985–; Surrey Charity Gp, 1989–; Emily Appeal, 1992–. Mem., Surrey Scout Council, 1990–. Blackdown Cttee, Nat. Trust, 1977–87. Trustee: Chichester Theatre; Endowment of St Paul's Cathedral; Childrens' Research Internat. Carthusian Trust; Castle Baynard Educnl Trust; Ulysses Trust; Special Trustee, St Bartholomew's Hosp. FRSA. Hon. DLitt City Univ., 1988. KStJ 1987 (OStJ 1985). Chevalier de la Légion d'Honneur, 1961; Commandeur de l'Ordre National du Mérite, 1984; Commander, Order of the Lion, Malaŵi, 1985; Mem., Nat. Order of Aztec Eagle, Mexico, 1985; Order of St Olav, Norway, 1988; Order of Merit, Senegal, 1988. *Recreations:* tennis, music, military history, forestry. *Address:* Grayswood Place, Haslemere, Surrey GU27 2ET. *T:* Haslemere (01428) 644367. *Clubs:* City Livery, Guildhall, United Wards; Cowdray Park Golf and Polo.

SPRENT, Prof. Janet Irene, DSc; FRSE; Professor of Plant Biology, since 1989, and Head of Department of Biological Sciences, since 1992, University of Dundee; *b* 10 Jan. 1934; *d* of James William and Dorothy May Findlater; *m* 1955, Peter Sprent. *Educ:* Slough High Sch. for Girls; Imperial Coll. of Science and Technol., London (BSc; ARCS 1954); Univ. of Tasmania (PhD 1958); Univ. of London (DSc 1988). FRSE 1990. Scientific Officer, Rothamsted Expmtl Stn, 1954–55; ICIANZ Res. Fellow, Univ. of Tasmania, 1955–58; Botany Mistress, Rochester Girls' Grammar Sch., 1959–61; Lectr, subseq. Sen. Lectr, Goldsmiths' Coll., London, 1960–67; University of Dundee: successively Res. Fellow, Lectr, Sen. Lectr and Reader, 1967–89; Dean, Faculty of Science and Engrg, 1987–89. Hon. Res. Prof., Scottish Crop Res. Inst., 1991–. Extensive overseas collaboration, eg Australia, Brazil, Kenya, in nitrogen fixing crop and tree research. Member: Council, NERC, 1991–95; SHEFC, 1992–96; (indep.) JNCC, 1994–; Governing Body and Trustee, MacAuley Land Use Res. Inst., 1990– (Chm., 1995–). *Publications:* The Biology of Nitrogen Fixing Organisms, 1979; The Ecology of the Nitrogen Cycle, 1987; (with P. Sprent) Nitrogen Fixing Organisms: pure and applied aspects, 1990; (with P. Sprent) Suilven's World, 1995; papers in scientific jls and chapters in books and symposium vols. *Recreations:* flying (St John's Air Wing), hill-walking, gardening, music. *Address:* 32 Birkhill Avenue, Wormit, Newport on Tay, Fife DD6 8PW. *T:* Newport on Tay (01382) 541706.

SPREULL, Professor James (Spreull Andrew); William Dick Professor of Veterinary Surgery, at the University of Edinburgh, 1959–78, now Emeritus; *b* 2 May 1908; *s* of late Lt-Col Andrew Spreull, DSO, TD, MRCVS, and Effie Andrew Spreull; *m* 1951, Kirsten Brummerstedt-Hansen; three *s*. *Educ:* Dundee High Sch.; Edinburgh Univ. (PhD); Royal Dick Veterinary Coll. (MRCVS). Royal Dick Veterinary College: Demonstrator of Anatomy, 1930–34, Lecturer in Applied Anatomy, 1931–34. Engaged in general practice in Dundee, 1934–59. FRSE 1965. *Publications:* various contributions to Veterinary Journals. *Recreations:* agriculture, fishing, badminton, antiques. *Address:* 2 Marlee Road, Broughty Ferry, Dundee DD5 3HA. *T:* Dundee (01382) 75916.

SPRIDDELL, Peter Henry; Director: Capital & Counties Plc, since 1988; Royal Artillery Museums Ltd, 1990–94; *b* 18 Aug. 1928; *s* of Thomas Henry Spriddell and Eva Florence Spriddell; *m* 1952, Joyce Patricia (*née* Haycock); two *s* one *d*. *Educ:* Plymouth Coll.; Exeter Coll., Oxford (MA); Harvard Business Sch. Marks & Spencer: store management, 1951–68; Sen. Exec. Store Operations, 1968–70; Dir, 1970–88; Alternate Exec. Dir, 1970–72; Exec. Dir Personnel, 1972–75; Exec. Dir Store Operations, Transport, Building and Store Develt, Real Estate, 1975–88; Dir, NFC, 1978–82; non-exec. Mem., British Rail Property Bd, 1986–. Mem. Bd, British Council of Shopping Centres, 1983–95 (Pres., 1988–89). Mem. Council, Templeton Coll., Oxford (formerly Oxford Centre for Management Studies), 1978–; Vice-Pres., Devon Historic Bldgs Trust, 1978–. FRSA. Freeman, City of London; Liveryman, Worshipful Co. of Paviors, 1984. *Recreations:* music, golf. *Address:* 37 Main Avenue, Moor Park Estate, Northwood, Mddx HA6 2LH. *T:* Northwood (019238) 29654. *Club:* Moor Park Golf.

SPRIGGE, Prof. Timothy Lauro Squire, PhD; FRSE; Professor Emeritus and Endowment Fellow, University of Edinburgh, since 1989; *b* 14 Jan. 1932; *s* of Cecil and Katriona Sprigge; *m* 1959, Giglia Gordon; one *s* twin *d*. *Educ:* Gonville and Caius Coll., Cambridge (MA, PhD). FRSE 1993. Lecturer in Philosophy, University Coll. London, 1961–63; Lectr in Philosophy, 1963–70, Reader in Philosophy, 1970–79, Univ. of Sussex; Prof. of Logic and Metaphysics, Univ. of Edinburgh, 1979–89. Visiting Associate Professor, Univ. of Cincinnati, 1968–69. Member: Aristotelian Soc., 1960– (Pres., 1991–92); Mind Assoc., 1955–; Assoc. for the Advancement of Amer. Philosophy, 1978–; Scots Philosophical Club, 1979–. Chm., St Andrew Animal Fund, 1991–. *Publications:* ed, Correspondence of Jeremy Bentham, vols 1 and 2, 1968; Facts, Words and Beliefs, 1970; Santayana: an examination of his philosophy, 1974; The Vindication of Absolute Idealism, 1983; Theories of Existence, 1985; The Rational Foundations of Ethics, 1988; James and Bradley: American truth and British reality, 1993; contribs to various vols of philosophical essays and to periodicals, incl. Mind, Philosophy, Inquiry, Nous. *Recreation:* backgammon. *Address:* David Hume Tower, University of Edinburgh, George Square, Edinburgh EH8 9JX. *T:* 0131–667 1011.

SPRING, Sir Dryden (Thomas), Kt 1994; dairy farmer and company director; Director, since 1983, Chairman, since 1989, New Zealand Dairy Board; *b* 6 Oct. 1939; *s* of Maurice Spring and Violet Grace Spring; *m* 1960, Christine Margaret McCarthy; three *s* three *d*. *Educ:* Walton Primary Sch.; Matamata Coll. NZ Co-operative Dairy Co. Ltd: Dir, 1973–; Dep. Chm., 1979–82; Chm., 1982–89; Director: Rural Banking and Finance Corp., 1974–88; Maramarua Coalfields Ltd, 1978–84; Fernz Corp. Ltd, 1982–; Goodman Fielder Ltd, 1989–; Nat. Bank of NZ, and other cos; Dep. Chm., Ports of Auckland Ltd, 1988–94. Member: Prime Minister's Enterprise Council, 1991–; Adv. Bd, Japanese/NZ Business Council, 1994; Asian Pacific Econ. Co-operation Eminent Persons Gp, 1994–. Hon. Chm., NZ/Philippines Business Council. Patron, NZ/Thailand Business Council. Fellow, Inst. of Dirs in NZ, 1993. Life Mem., Federated Farmers of NZ (Waikato), 1987. NZ Commemoration Medal, 1990. *Recreations:* sport, reading, farming. *Address:* Eastport Road, RD 3, Te Aroha, New Zealand. *T:* (7) 8845817. *Clubs:* Wellington; Te Aroha; College Old Boys Rugby.

SPRING, Frank Stuart, FRS 1952; DSc (Manchester), PhD (Liverpool), FRSC; Director, Laporte Industries Ltd, London, W1, 1959–71; *b* 5 Sept. 1907; 3rd *s* of John Spring and Isabella Spring, Crosby, Liverpool; *m* 1932, Mary, 2nd *d* of Rev. John Mackintosh, MA and Mabelle Mackintosh, Heswall; one *s* one *d*. *Educ:* Waterloo Grammar Sch.; University of Liverpool. United Alkali Research Scholar, University of Liverpool, 1928–29; University Fellow, Liverpool, 1929–30. Assistant Lecturer, Lecturer and Senior Lecturer in Chemistry, University of Manchester, 1930–46; Freeland Professor of Chemistry, The Royal College of Science and Technology, Glasgow, 1946–59. Chemical Society, Tilden Lecturer, 1950. Hon. DSc: Salford, 1967; Strathclyde, 1981. *Publications:* papers (mostly jtly) in chemical journals. *Address:* Flat 26, 1 Hyde Park Square, W2 2JZ. *T:* 0171–262 8174.

SPRING, Richard, (Dick Spring); Member of the Dáil (TD) (Lab), North Kerry, since 1981; Deputy Prime Minister, 1982–87 and since 1993; Minister for Foreign Affairs, since 1993; *b* 29 Aug. 1950; *s* of Daniel and Anne Spring; *m* 1977, Kristi Lee Hutcheson; two *s* one *d*. *Educ:* Mt St Joseph Coll., Roscrea; Trinity Coll., Dublin (BA 1972). Called to the Bar, King's Inns, Dublin, 1975; in practice on Munster Circuit, 1977–81. Leader of Irish Labour Party, 1982–; Minister of State, Dept of Justice, 1981–82; Minister for the Environment, 1982–83; Minister for Energy, 1983–87. *Recreations:* swimming, reading, golf. *Address:* Dunroamin, Cloonanorig, Tralee, Co. Kerry, Ireland. *T:* Tralee (66) 25337, Dublin (1) 4784438.

SPRING, Richard John Grenville; MP (C) Bury St Edmunds, since 1992; *b* 24 Sept. 1946; *s* of late H. J. A. Spring and of Marjorie (*née* Watson-Morris); *m* 1979, Hon. Jane (marr. diss. 1993), *o d* of Baron Henniker, *qv*; one *s* one *d*. *Educ:* Rondebosch, Cape; Univ. of Cape Town; Magdalene Coll., Cambridge (MA Econs). Vice-Pres., Merrill Lynch Ltd, 1976–86; Dep. Man. Dir, E. F. Hutton Internat. Associates, 1986–88; Exec. Dir, Shearson Lehman Hutton, 1988–89; Man. Director, Xerox Furman Selz, 1989–92. Contested (C) Ashton-under-Lyne, 1983. Member: Employment Select Cttee, 1992–94; NI Select Cttee, 1994–; Health Select Cttee, 1995–; Vice Chairman: Cons. Backbench Arts and Heritage Gp, 1992–; NI Cons. Backbench Cttee, 1994–. Pres., Arts and Heritage Cttee, Bow Gp, 1992–. European Elections Campaign Co-ordinator, 1989; Chm., Westminster CPC, 1990; Vice-Chairman: Small Business Bureau (Chm., Parly Adv. Gp), 1992–; Cons. Industrial Fund, 1993–. *Recreations:* country pursuits, English watercolours. *Address:* c/o House of Commons, SW1A 0AA. *Clubs:* Boodle's; Bury St Edmunds Farmers'.

SPRING RICE, family name of **Baron Monteagle of Brandon.**

SPRINGER, Tobias; a Metropolitan Stipendiary Magistrate, 1963–82; Barrister-at-law; *b* 3 April 1907; *o c* of late Samuel Springer, MBE; *m* 1937, Stella Rauchwerger. *Educ:* Mill Hill Sch.; Caius Coll., Cambridge. Law Tripos 1928; called to Bar, Gray's Inn, 1929. Practised London and SE Circuit. Served War of 1939–45: 60th Rifles, 1940–45; Lt-Col GSO1, GHQ, H Forces, 1944. Returned to practise at Bar, 1945. Actg Dep. Chm., Co. London Sessions, periods 1962, 1963; sometime Dep. Circuit Judge. Life Governor: Mill Hill School; Metropolitan Hosp. Freedom, City of London, 1982. *Recreations:* travel, reading. *Address:* 82 Cholmley Gardens, Fortune Green Road, NW6 1UN. *T:* 0171–435 0817. *Clubs:* Old Mill Hillians; Porters Park Golf.

SPRINGETT, Jack Allan, CBE 1978; MA (Cantab); Education Officer, Association of Metropolitan Authorities, 1980–82; *b* 1 Feb. 1916; *s* of Arthur John and Agnes Springett; *m* 1950, Patricia Winifred Singleton; three *s* one *d*. *Educ:* Windsor Grammar Sch.; Fitzwilliam House, Cambridge. Asst Master, Christ's Hospital, Horsham, 1938–47. Served War, Royal Signals and Gen. Staff, 1940–46. Administrative Asst, North Riding, 1947–52;

Asst Educn Officer, Birmingham, 1952–62; Dep. Educn Officer, Essex, 1962–73; County Educn Officer, Essex, 1973–80. *Address:* 3 Roxwell Road, Chelmsford, Essex CM1 2LY. *T:* Chelmsford (01245) 258669.

SPRINGFORD, John Frederick Charles, CBE 1980 (OBE 1970); retired British Council Officer; *b* 6 June 1919; *s* of Frederick Charles Springford and Bertha Agnes Springford (*née* Trenery); *m* 1945, Phyllis Wharton; one *s* two *d. Educ:* Latymer Upper Sch.; Christ's College, Cambridge (MA). Served War 1940–46, RAC; seconded Indian Armoured Corps, 1942; Asst Political Agent II in Mekran, 1945. British Council Service, Baghdad and Mosul, Iraq, 1947–51, Isfahan, Iran, 1951–52; British Council Representative: Tanzania, 1952–57; Sudan, 1957–62; Dir, Overseas Students Dept, 1962–66; Representative: Jordan, 1966–69; Iraq, 1969–74; Canada, 1974–79, and Counsellor, Cultural Affairs, British High Commission, Ottawa. Mem. Council, British Sch. of Archaeology in Iraq, 1980–86. Hon. Sec., Sussex Heritage Trust, 1980–83; Chm., Sussex Eastern Sub-Area, 1981–85, Sussex Area, 1985–92, RSCM. Organist, St Mary's Church, Battle, 1986–. *Recreations:* archaeology, music. *Address:* Precinct, Crowhurst, Battle, East Sussex TN33 9AA. *T:* Crowhurst (01424) 830200.

SPRINGFORD, Prof. Michael, PhD; FInstP; Professor of Experimental Physics, since 1989, and Head of Department of Physics, since 1994, University of Bristol; *b* 10 Jan. 1936; *s* of Stanley Walter Springford and Lillian Springford (*née* Tyler); *m* 1st, 1958, Kathleen Elizabeth Wyatt (marr. diss. 1983); two *s* one *d*; 2nd, 1991, Maria Sergeevna Chakovskaya. *Educ:* Durham Univ. (BSc); Hull Univ. (PhD). Nat. Res. Council of Canada, 1962–64; Univ. of Sussex, 1964–89. *Publications:* (ed) Electrons at the Fermi Surface, 1980; The Quantum Properties of Condensed Matter; papers in learned jls. *Recreations:* music, sailing, walking. *Address:* H. H. Wills Physics Laboratory, University of Bristol, Tyndall Avenue, Bristol BS8 1TL. *T:* Bristol (0117) 928 8731.

SPROAT, Iain Mac Donald; MP (C) Harwich, since 1992; Minister of State, Department of National Heritage, since 1995 (Parliamentary Under-Secretary of State, 1993–95; Minister for Sport, since 1994); *b* Dollar, Clackmannanshire, 8 Nov. 1938; *s* of late William Bigham Sproat and Lydia Bain Sproat (*née* MacDonald); *m* 1979, Judith Mary Kernot (*née* King); one step *s. Educ:* St Mary's Sch., Melrose; Winchester Coll.; Univ. of Aix-en-Provence; Magdalen Coll., Oxford. Served RGJ (4th Bn), 1972–76. Chairman: Milner and Co., 1981 and 1983–93; Cricketers' Who's Who Ltd, 1980–81 and 1983–93. Contested (C) Roxburgh and Berwickshire, 1983. MP (C) Aberdeen South, 1970–83. PPS to Sec. of State for Scotland, 1973–74; Parly Under-Sec. of State, Dept of Trade (Minister: of Aviation and Shipping; of Tourism; responsible for Govt Statistics; Retail Trade; Distributive Trades; Video, Cinema and Film Industry), 1981–83; Special Advr to Prime Minister, Gen. Election, 1987. Leader, Cons. Gp, Scottish Select Cttee, 1979–81; Chm., Scottish Cons. Cttee, 1979–81; Chm., Soviet and E European Gp, Cons. Foreign Affairs Cttee, 1975–81. Member: British Parly Delegn to oversee S Vietnamese Elections, 1973; British Parly Delegn to Soviet Union, 1974; Leader, British Parly Delegn to Austria, 1980. Dist. Vis. Prof., Texas Univ., 1992. Lecturer: on guerilla warfare, RCDS, 1973; on Kurdish guerilla warfare in Iran/Iraq, RUSI, 1975. Trustee: African Med. and Res. Foundn (Flying Doctors), 1986–91; Scottish Self-Governing Schools Trust, 1989–. Chairman, Editorial Board: Oxford Univ. Press Hist. of the British Empire, 1987–92; Complete Works of Pushkin, 1987–93. Cricket Writer of the Year, Wombwell Cricket Lovers' Soc., 1983. *Publications:* (ed) Cricketers' Who's Who, annually 1980–93; Wodehouse at War, 1981; (contrib.) The British Prime Ministers. *Recreations:* collecting books, Rugby football, cricket. *Address:* c/o House of Commons, SW1A 0AA. *Clubs:* Cavalry and Guards, United Oxford & Cambridge University.

SPROT, Lt-Col Aidan Mark, MC 1944; JP; landed proprietor and farmer (Haystoun Estate); Lord-Lieutenant of Tweeddale, 1980–94; *b* 17 June 1919; *s* of Major Mark Sprot of Riddell. *Educ:* Stowe. Commissioned Royal Scots Greys, 1940; served: Middle East, 1941–43; Italy, 1943–44; NW Europe, 1944–45, and after the war in Germany, Libya, Egypt, Jordan and UK; Adjt 1945–46; CO, 1959–62, retired. Councillor, Peeblesshire CC, 1963–75; JP 1966, DL 1966–80, Peeblesshire. Member, Royal Company of Archers (Queen's Body Guard for Scotland), 1950–; Pres., Lowlands of Scotland, TAVRA, 1986–89. County Dir, 1966–74, Patron, 1983–, Tweeddale Br., British Red Cross Soc.; County Comr, 1968–73, Chm., 1975–80, Pres., 1980–94, Tweeddale Scout Assoc.; President: Borders Area Scout Assoc., 1994–; Lothian Fedn of Boys' Clubs, 1988–. Hon. Sec., Royal Caledonian Hunt, 1964–74. Freeman, Tweeddale Dist, 1994. Scout Medal of Merit, 1994. *Recreations:* country pursuits, motor cycle touring. *Address:* Crookston, Peebles EH45 9JQ. *T:* Kirkton Manor (01721) 740209. *Club:* New (Edinburgh).

SPRY, Christopher John; Regional Director, NHS Executive, South Thames, since 1994; *b* 29 Aug. 1946; *s* of late Reginald Charles Spry and Kathleen Edith Spry (*née* Hobart); *m* 1st, Jean Banks (marr. diss. 1989); two *s*; 2nd, 1989, Judith Christina (*née* Ryder). *Educ:* Sir Roger Manwood's Sch., Sandwich; Exeter Univ. (BA 1967). AHSM. Dep. Hosp. Sec., Lewisham Hosp., 1970; Hosp. Sec., Nottingham Gen. Hosp., 1973; Asst. Dist Administrator, S Nottingham, 1975, Dist Administrator, 1978; Dist Administrator, 1981, Dist Gen. Manager, 1984, Newcastle HA.; Regl Gen. Manager, SW Thames RHA, 1989–94. Member: ACARD Working Gp on UK Med. Equipment Industry, 1986; Working Party on Alternative Delivery and Funding of Health Services, 1988. *Publications:* (contrib.) The Future of Acute Services: doctors as managers, 1990; articles in health care management jls. *Recreations:* swimming, books, enjoying townscapes. *Address:* 36 King's Road, Wimbledon, SW19 8QW.

SPRY, Sir John (Farley), Kt 1975; President, British Antarctic Territory Court of Appeal, and Justice of Court of Appeal, Falkland Islands, since 1991; *b* 11 March 1910; *s* of Joseph Farley Spry and Fanny Seagrave Treloar Spry; *m* 1st (marr. diss. 1940); one *s* one *d*; 2nd, Stella Marie (*née* Fichat) (*d* 1995). *Educ:* Perse School and Peterhouse, Cambridge (MA). Solicitor, 1935; Asst Registrar of Titles and Conveyancer, Uganda, 1936–44; Chief Inspector of Land Registration, Palestine, 1944; Asst Director of Land Registration, Palestine, 1944–48; Registrar-General, Tanganyika 1948–50, Kenya 1950–52; Tanganyika: Registrar-Gen., 1952–56; Legal Draftsman, 1956–60; Principal Sec., Public Service Commn, 1960–61; Puisne Judge, 1961–64; Justice of Appeal, Court of Appeal for Eastern Africa, 1964–70; Vice-President, 1970–75; Chm., Pensions Appeal Tribunals, 1975–76; Chief Justice of Gibraltar, 1976–80, Justice of Appeal, 1980–83, Pres., Court of Appeal, 1983–91; Comr for Revision of Laws of Gibraltar, 1981–85; Chief Justice: British Indian Ocean Territory, 1981–87; St Helena and its Dependencies, 1983–92. *Publications:* Sea Shells of Dar es Salaam, Part I, 1961 (3rd edn 1968), Part II, 1964; Civil Procedure in East Africa, 1969; Civil Law of Defamation in East Africa, 1976. *Address:* 15 De Vere Gardens, W8 5AN.

SPUFFORD, Prof. (Honor) Margaret, PhD, DLittD; FRHistS; FBA 1995; Research Professor in Social and Local History, Roehampton Institute, London, since 1994; *b* 10 Dec. 1935; *d* of Leslie Marshall Clark and Mary (*née* Johnson); *m* 1962, Peter Spufford, *qv*; one *s* (one *d* decd). *Educ:* Univ. of Leicester (MA with Dist. 1963; PhD 1970); LittD Cantab 1986. FRHistS 1974. Calouste Gulbenkian Res. Fellow, Lucy Cavendish Coll., Cambridge, 1968–72; University of Keele: Hon. Lectr, 1974–79; Sen. Res. Fellow, 1978–79; Sen. Res. Associate, Faculty of Hist., Univ. of Cambridge, 1979–81; Fellow, Newnham Coll., Cambridge, 1980–92. Vis. Res. Fellow, Netherlands Inst. for Advanced Study, 1992–93; Vis. Prof., Rikkyo Univ., Tokyo, 1994. Earl Lectr, Univ. of Keele, 1993; James Ford Special Lectr, Univ. of Oxford, 1994. Founder, Bridget's Hostel for Disabled and Chronically Sick Students, Cambridge, 1987 (Chm., House Cttee, 1991–). *Publications:* (with P. Spufford) Eccleshall: the story of a Staffordshire market town, 1964; A Cambridgeshire Community: Chippenham from settlement to enclosure, 1966; Contrasting Communities: the English villager in the sixteenth and seventeenth centuries, 1974; Small Books and Pleasant Histories: popular fiction and its readership in seventeenth century England, 1981; The Great Reclothing of Rural England: petty chapmen and their wares in the seventeenth century, 1984; Celebration, 1989 (trans. Dutch, 1994, French, 1995); (ed) The World of Rural Dissenters, 1995; Poverty Portrayed: Gregory King and Eccleshall, Staffordshire, 1995; contrib. chapters in edited books, including: Literacy and Social Development in the West, 1981; Order and Disorder in Early Modern England, 1985; English Rural Society 1500–1800, 1990; A Miracle Mirror'd: the Dutch Republic in European Perspective, 1995; Spiritual Classics of the late Twentieth Century, 1995; contrib. articles in learned jls incl. Proc. Cambridge Antiquarian Soc., Agricl Hist. Rev., Studies in Church Hist., Theology. *Recreations:* Benedictine Anglican oblate, exploring countryside, vernacular architecture, listening to people. *Address:* Department of History, Digby Stuart College, Roehampton Institute, London, Roehampton Lane, SW15 5PH.

SPUFFORD, Dr Peter, FSA; FRHistS; FBA 1994; Reader in Economic History, University of Cambridge, since 1990; Fellow, Queens' College, Cambridge, since 1979; *b* 18 Aug. 1934; *s* of late Douglas Henry Spufford and Nancy Gwendoline Spufford (*née* Battagel); *m* 1962, Honor Margaret Clark (*see* H. M. Spufford); one *s* (one *d* decd). *Educ:* Kingswood Sch.; Jesus Coll., Cambridge (BA 1956; MA 1960; PhD 1963; LittD 1990). FRNS 1955; FRHistS 1968; FSG 1969; FSA 1990. Res. Fellow, Jesus Coll., Cambridge, 1958–60; Asst Lectr, Lectr, Sen. Lectr and Reader, Univ. of Keele, 1960–79; Lectr, Univ. of Cambridge, 1979–90. Visiting Fellow: Clare Hall, Cambridge, 1969–70; Netherlands Inst. for Advanced Study, 1992–93; Vis. Prof. of Burgundian Studies, 1972–73, Vis. Prof., Econ. Studies, 1993, Leuven. Chm., British Records Soc., 1985–; Hon. Mem., Koninklijk Genootschap voor Munt-en Penningkunde, 1992–. *Publications:* Origins of the English Parliament, 1967; Monetary Problems and Policies in the Burgundian Netherlands 1433–1496, 1970; Handbook of Medieval Exchange, 1986; (ed with N. J. Mayhew) Later Medieval Mints, 1988; Money and Its Use in Medieval Europe, 1988; (ed with G. H. Martin) Records of the Nation, 1990; chapters in: Cambridge Economic History of Europe, vol. 3, 1965, vol. 2, 2nd edn, 1987. *Address:* Queens' College, Cambridge CB3 9ET. *T:* Cambridge (01223) 332211.

SPURGEON, Maj.-Gen. Peter Lester, CB 1980; Chief Executive, Royal Agricultural Benevolent Institution, 1982–91; *b* 27 Aug. 1927; *s* of Harold Sidney Spurgeon and Emily Anne (*née* Bolton); *m* 1959, Susan Ann (*née* Aylward); one *s* one *d. Educ:* Merchant Taylors' Sch., Northwood. Commnd, 1946; 1949–66: HMS Glory; Depot, RM Deal; 40 Commando RM; ADC to Maj.-Gen. Plymouth Gp RM; DS Officers' Sch., RM; RAF Staff Coll., Bracknell; Staff of Comdt Gen. RM; 40 Commando RM; Jt Warfare Estab.; GS02 HQ: ME Comd, Aden, 1967; Army Strategic Comd, 1968–69; Second-in-Comd, 41 Commando RM, 1969–71; DS National Defence Coll., Latimer, 1971–73; CO RM Poole, 1973–75; Dir of Drafting and Records, RM, 1975–76; Comdr, Training Gp, RM, 1977–79 and Training and Reserve Forces, RM, 1979–80; retd 1980. Col Comdt, RM, 1987–90. Pres., RM Assoc., 1986–90. *Recreations:* golf, gardening. *Address:* c/o Lloyds Bank, 1 High Street, Oxford OX1 4AA. *Club:* Army and Navy.

SPURLING, (Susan) Hilary; writer and critic; *b* 25 Dec. 1940; *d* of Gilbert Alexander Forrest and Emily Maureen Forrest; *m* 1961, John Spurling; two *s* one *d. Educ:* Somerville Coll., Oxford (BA). Theatre Critic of the Spectator, 1964–70, Literary Editor, 1966–70. *Publications:* Ivy When Young: the early life of I. Compton-Burnett 1884–1919, 1974; Handbook to Anthony Powell's Music of Time, 1977; Secrets of a Woman's Heart: the later life of I. Compton-Burnett 1920–1969, 1984 (Duff Cooper Meml Prize, 1984; Heinemann Literary Award (jtly), 1985); Elinor Fettiplace's Receipt Book, 1986; Paul Scott, A Life, 1990; Paper Spirits, 1992. *Recreations:* reading, ratting, country walks. *Address:* c/o David Higham Associates, 5–8 Lower John Street, Golden Square, W1R 4HA.

SPURR, Margaret Anne, OBE 1994; Headmistress, Bolton School, Girls' Division, 1979–94; Governor, BBC, since 1993; *b* 7 Oct. 1933; *m* 1953, John Spurr; one *s* one *d. Educ:* Abbeydale Girls' Grammar Sch., Sheffield; Univ. of Keele. BA (Hons); PGCE. Tutor: Eng. Lit., Univ. of Glasgow, 1971; Eng. Lit. Dept, Adult Educn, Univ. of Keele, 1972–73. Chm., Scholaservices, 1990–. Sen. Examiner, Univ. of London, 1971–80. Pres., GSA, 1985–86. Chairman: Nat. ISIS Cttee, 1987–90; BBC English Nat. Forum, 1994–; Member: Adv. Cttee, American Studies Resources Centre, Polytechnic of Central London, 1977–90; Scholarship Selection Cttee, ESU, 1983–; CBI Schools Panel, 1985–89; Exec. Cttee, British-American-Canadian Associates, 1994–; Exec. Cttee, GBGSA, 1994–. Vice-Provost, Woodard Corp., 1994–; Fellow, Woodard Schs. Governor: Denstone Coll., 1989–; St Dominic's Sch., Stone, 1989–94; Kent Coll., Tunbridge Wells, 1993–; John Moores Univ., Liverpool, 1994–. Trustee, School Fees Trust Fund, 1994. Hon. DLitt Keele, 1995. FRSA 1991. *Publications:* (ed) A Curriculum for Capability, 1986; (ed) Girls First, 1987. *Recreations:* gardening, theatre, poetry, work, music. *Address:* The Old Vicarage, Croxden, Uttoxeter, Staffs ST14 5JQ. *T:* Hollington (01889) 507214, *Fax:* (01889) 507424. *Club:* Reform.

SPURRIER, Peter Brotherton; design consultant; Design Director, Maritime Insignia Ltd, since 1995; *b* 9 Aug. 1942; *s* of Eric Jack Spurrier, MBE and Frances Mary (*née* Brotherton); *m* 1973, Hon. Elizabeth Jane Maude, *d* of Baron Maude of Stratford-upon-Avon, TD, PC; two *s* one *d. Educ:* Chetham's Hosp. Sch., Manchester; Manchester Coll. of Art and Design (NDD 1965). MSIAD 1980. Designer for Wade Heath Pottery, Burslem, 1965–66; Asst Design Officer, DoE, 1966–71 (on design team for Investiture of HRH Prince of Wales, 1969); Dir, Dromas Design Ltd, 1971–79; Principal Designer, Idiom Design Ltd, 1979–81; Portcullis Pursuivant of Arms, 1981–93; York Herald of Arms, 1993. Hon. Asst Curator, Heralds' Mus. at Tower of London, 1981–83. Mem. Council, Heraldry Soc., 1981–90; Chm., Soc. of Heraldic Arts, 1991–. FRSA. Freeman, City of London, 1980; Freeman and Liveryman, Painter Stainers' Co., 1985. OStJ 1990. *Recreations:* painting, music, fishing. *Address:* 15 Morella Road, Wandsworth Common, SW12 8UQ.

SPY, James; Sheriff of North Strathclyde at Paisley, since 1988; *b* 1 Dec. 1952; *s* of James Spy and Jean Learmond; *m* 1980, Jennifer Margaret Malcolm; three *d. Educ:* Hermitage Acad., Helensburgh; Glasgow Univ. (LLB Hons). Admitted Solicitor, 1976; passed Advocate, 1979. *Recreations:* music, clocks, model ships, model trains. *Address:* St Ann's, 171 Nithsdale Road, Glasgow G41 5QS. *T:* 0141–423 5317.

SQUAIR, George Alexander; Non-executive Chairman, British Approvals Service For Cables, since 1993; *b* 26 July 1929; *s* of Alexander Squair and Elizabeth (*née* Macdonald); *m* 1953, Joy Honeybone; two *s* one *d. Educ:* Woolwich Polytechnic; Oxford Technical Coll.; Southampton Univ. CEng, FIEE 1986; CIMgt (CBIM 1984). Gen. distribution engrg posts, 1950–68; Southern, later South Eastern, Electricity Board, subseq. SEEBOARD: 1st Asst Dist Engr, 1968–69; Dist Engr, Swindon, 1969–70; Area Engr, Newbury, 1970–73; Dist Manager, Oxford, 1973–74; Area Manager, Newbury, 1974–78; Mem., Exec. Bd, 1976–78; Dep. Chm., 1978–83; Chm. and Chief Exec., 1983–92. *Recreations:* reading, golf. *Address:* Littlebury House, Storrington Road, Thakeham, Pulborough, West Sussex RH20 3ED.

SQUIRE, (Clifford) William, CMG 1978; LVO 1972; HM Diplomatic Service, retired; Development Director, University of Cambridge, since 1988; *b* 7 Oct. 1928; *s* of Clifford John Squire and Eleanor Eliza Harpley; *m* 1st, 1959, Marie José Carlier (*d* 1973); one *s* two *d* (and one *s* decd); 2nd, 1976, Sara Laetitia Hutchison; one *s* one *d*. *Educ:* Royal Masonic Sch., Bushey; St John's Coll., Oxford; Coll. of Europe, Bruges. PhD London 1979. British Army, 1947–49. Nigerian Admin. Service, 1953–59; FO, 1959–60; British Legation, Bucharest, 1961–63; FO, 1963–65; UK Mission to UN, New York, 1965–69; Head of Chancery, Bangkok, 1969–72; Head of SE Asian Dept, FCO, 1972–75; Extramural Fellow, Sch. of Oriental and African Studies, London Univ., 1975–76; Counsellor, later Head of Chancery, Washington, 1976–79; Ambassador to Senegal, 1979–82, concurrently to Cape Verde Is, Guinea (Bissau), Guinea (Conakry), Mali and Mauritania; Asst Under-Sec. of State, FCO, 1982–84; Ambassador to Israel, 1984–88. *Address:* Wolfson College, Cambridge CB3 9BB. *Clubs:* Travellers'; Cosmos (Washington, DC).

SQUIRE, Peter John; Headmaster, Bedford Modern School, since 1977; *b* 15 Feb. 1937; *s* of Leslie Ernest Squire and Doris Eileen Squire; *m* 1965, Susan Elizabeth (*née* Edwards); one *s* one *d*. *Educ:* King Edward's Sch., Birmingham; Jesus Coll., Oxford (BA 1960, MA 1964); Pembroke Coll. and Dept of Educn, Cambridge (Cert. in Educn 1961). Asst Master, Monkton Combe Sch., Bath, 1961–65; Haberdashers' Aske's Sch., Elstree, 1965–77: Sen. Boarding Housemaster, 1968–77; Sen. History Master, 1970–77. *Recreations:* foreign travel, gardening, antique collecting. *Address:* Bedford Modern School, Manton Lane, Bedford MK41 7NT. *T:* Bedford (01234) 364331.

SQUIRE, Air Vice-Marshal Peter Ted, DFC 1982; AFC 1979; Assistant Chief of the Air Staff, since 1994; *b* 7 Oct. 1945; *s* of late Wing Comdr Frank Squire and Margaret Pascoe Squire (*née* Trump); *m* 1970, Carolyn Joynson; three *s*. *Educ:* King's Sch., Bruton. psc(n). Flying and Staff appts include: commnd 1966; 20 Sqn, Singapore, 1968–70; 4 FTS, Anglesey, 1970–73; 3 (F) Sqn, Germany, 1975–78; OC1 (F) Sqn, 1981–83; Personal Staff Officer to AOC-in-C Strike Comd, 1984–86; Station Comdr, RAF Cottesmore, 1986–88; Dir Air Offensive, 1989–91; SASO, RAF Strike Comd, 1991–93. AOC No 1 Gp, 1993–94. Mem., GAPAN. Gov., King's Sch., Bruton, 1990–. *Recreations:* cricket, golf. *Address:* c/o National Westminster Bank, 5 South Street, Wincanton BA9 9DJ. *Club:* Royal Air Force.

SQUIRE, Rachel Anne; MP (Lab) Dunfermline, since 1992; *b* 13 July 1954; *d* of Louise Anne Squire (*née* Binder) and step *d* of Percy Garfield Squire; *m* 1984, Allan Lee Mason. *Educ:* Godolphin and Latymer Girls' Sch.; Durham Univ. (BA Hons); Birmingham Univ. (CQSW). Social worker, Birmingham, 1975–81; trade union officer, 1981–92. *Recreations:* reading, cooking, archaeology. *Address:* (office) 10–14 Douglas Street, Dunfermline, Fife KY12 7EB. *T:* Dunfermline (01383) 622889, *Fax:* (01383) 623500.

SQUIRE, Raglan, FRIBA, MSIA; Consultant, Raglan Squire & Partners, Architects, Engineers and Town Planners, since 1981 (Senior Partner, 1948–81); *b* 30 Jan. 1912; *e s* of late Sir John Squire, Kt; *m* 1st, 1938, Rachel, (*d* 1968), *d* of James Atkey, Oxshott, Surrey; two *s*; 2nd, 1968, Bridget Lawless. *Educ:* Blundell's; St John's Coll., Cambridge. Private practice in London, 1935–. War service with Royal Engineers, 1942–45. Founded firm of Raglan Squire & Partners, 1948. Principal projects: housing, educational and industrial work, 1935–41; pre-fabricated bldgs and industrial design, 1945–48; Eaton Sq. Conversion Scheme, 1945–56; Rangoon Univ. Engineering Coll., 1953–56; Associated Architect, Transport Pavilion, Festival of Britain Exhib., 1951; Town Planning Scheme for Mosul, Iraq, 1955; Bagdad airport report, 1955; factories at Weybridge, Huddersfield etc; office buildings London, Eastbourne, Bournemouth, etc; gen. practice at home and over-seas incl. major hotels at Teheran, Tunis, Nicosia, Malta and Singapore, Gibraltar, Caribbean and Middle East, 1955–81, retired from active practice. Sec. RIBA Reconstruction Cttee, 1941–42; Council of Architectural Assoc., 1951–52; Guest Editor Architects' Journal, 1947. *Publications:* Portrait of an Architect (autobiog.), 1985; articles in technical press on organisation of Building Industry, Architectural Education, etc. *Recreations:* gardening, chess, ocean racing and designing small yachts. *Address:* 1 Chester Row, SW1W 9JF. *T:* 0171–730 7275. *Clubs:* Royal Thames Yacht, Royal Ocean Racing; Royal Southern Yacht.

SQUIRE, Robin Clifford; MP (C) Hornchurch, since 1979; Parliamentary Under-Secretary of State, Department for Education and Employment (formerly Department for Education), since 1993; *b* 12 July 1944; *s* of late Sidney John Squire and Mabel Alice Squire (*née* Gilmore); *m* 1981, Susan Margaret Fey, *d* of late Arthur Frederick Branch and of Mahala Branch (*née* Parker); one step *s* one step *d*. *Educ:* Tiffin School, Kingston-upon-Thames. FCA. Qualified as Chartered Accountant, 1966; joined Lombard Banking Ltd (subsequently Lombard North Central Ltd) as Accountant, 1968, becoming Dep. Chief Accountant, 1972–79. Councillor, London Borough of Sutton, 1968–82; Chm., Finance Cttee, 1972–76; Leader of Council, 1976–79. Chm., Greater London Young Conservatives, 1973; Vice-Chm., Nat. Young Conservatives, 1974–75. Personal Asst to Rt Hon. Robert Carr, Gen. Election, Feb. 1974; contested (C) Havering, Hornchurch, Oct. 1974. PPS to Minister of State for Transport, 1983–85, to Rt Hon. Chris Patten, Chm. of Cons. Party, 1991–92; Parly Under-Sec. of State, DoE, 1992–93. Mem., Commons Select Cttee on Environment, 1979–83 and 1987–91, on European Legislation, 1985–88; Sec., Cons. Parly European Affairs Cttee, 1979–80; Vice-Chm., Cons. Parly Trade Cttee, 1980–83; Chm., Cons. Parly Environment Cttee, 1990–91 (Jt Vice-Chm., 1985–89); Originator of Local Govt (Access to Information) Act, 1985. Chm., Cons. Action for Electoral Reform, 1983–86 (Vice-Chm., 1982–83); Dep. Chm., Anglo-Asian Cons. Soc., 1982–83. Mem. Bd, Shelter, 1982–91; Dir, Link Assured Homes series of cos, 1988–92. *Publication:* (jtly) Set the Party Free, 1969. *Recreations:* films, bridge, modern music. *Address:* House of Commons, SW1A 0AA. *T:* 0171–219 4526.

SQUIRE, William; *see* Squire, C. W.

SRINIVASAN, Krishnan; Deputy Secretary-General, Commonwealth Secretariat, since 1995; *b* 15 Feb. 1937; *s* of late Captain C. Srinivasan, Indian Navy, and of Mrs Rukmani Chari; *m* 1975, Brinda Srinivasan; one *s*. *Educ:* Bedford Sch.; Christ Church, Oxford (MA). Joined Indian Foreign Service, 1959; Chargé d'Affaires, Tripoli, 1968–71; High Comr to Zambia and Botswana, 1974–77; Consul-Gen., NY, 1977–80; High Comr to Nigeria, and Ambassador to Benin and Cameroon, 1980–83; Ambassador, Netherlands, 1986–89; High Comr, Bangladesh, 1989–92; Perm. Sec., Min. of External Affairs, 1992–94; Foreign Secretary, 1994–95. *Publications:* Selections in Two Keys, 1974; The Water's Edge, 1975; The Eccentricity Factor, 1980; The Fourth Profile, 1991; A Fizzle Yield, 1992. *Recreations:* reading, writing, squash, jazz, watching sports. *Address:* Commonwealth Secretariat, Marlborough House, Pall Mall, SW1Y 5HX; Allegro, 194 2nd C Cross, Domlur II, Bangalore 560071, India. *T:* (080) 5261144. *Clubs:* Royal Over-Seas League; Vincent's (Oxford); Bengal (Calcutta); Delhi Gymkhana, Habitat Centre (New Delhi).

SRISKANDAN, Kanagaretnam, CEng, FICE, FIStructE, FIHT; consultant in highway and bridge engineering, since 1993; *b* 12 Aug. 1930; *s* of Kanagaretnam Kathiravelu and Kanmanyammal Kumaraswamy; *m* 1956, Dorothy (*née* Harley); two *s* one *d*. *Educ:* Royal College, Colombo; Univ. of Ceylon. BSc Hons London 1952. Junior Asst Engineer, PWD, Ceylon, 1953; Asst Engr, Sir William Halcrow and Partners, Cons. Engrs, London, 1956; Section Engr, Tarmac Civil Engineering Ltd, 1958; Asst Engr, West Riding of Yorkshire CC, 1959, left as Principal Engr; Department of Transport: Superintending Engr, Midland Road Construction Unit, 1968; Asst Chief Engr, 1971; Deputy Chief Highway Engr, 1976; Chief Highway Engr, 1980–87; Divl Dir, Mott, Hay and Anderson, subseq. Mott, MacDonald Gp, Consulting Engrs, 1988–93. *Publications:* papers on various engrg topics. *Recreation:* golf. *Address:* 21 Bonar Place, Chislehurst, Kent BR7 5RJ.

SRIVASTAVA, Chandrika Prasad, Padma Bhushan 1972; Hon. KCMG 1990; Secretary-General, International Maritime Organization (formerly IMCO), 1974–89; Chancellor, World Maritime University, 1983–90; *b* 8 July 1920; *s* of B. B. Srivastava; *m* 1947, Nirmala Salve; two *d*. *Educ:* Lucknow, India. 1st cl. BA 1940, 1st cl. BA Hons 1941, 1st cl. MA 1942, 1st cl. LLB 1944; gold medals for proficiency in Eng. Lit. and Polit. Science. Under-Sec., Min. of Commerce, India, 1948–49; City Magistrate, Lucknow, 1950; Addtl Dist. Magistrate, Meerut, 1951–52; Directorate-Gen. of Shipping, 1953; Dep. Dir-Gen. of Shipping, 1954–57; Dep. Sec., Min. of Transport, and Pvte Sec. to Minister of Transport and Communications, 1958; Sen. Dep. Dir-Gen. of Shipping, 1959–60; Man. Dir, Shipping Corp. of India, 1961–64; Jt Sec. to Prime Minister, 1964–66; Chm. and Man. Dir, Shipping Corp. of India, 1966–73; Director: Central Inland Water Transport Corp., 1967; Central Bd, Reserve Bank of India, 1972–73; Chm., Mogul Line Ltd, 1967–73. Vice-Pres., Sea Cadet Council, 1970–73. President: Indian Nat. Shipowners' Assoc., 1971–73; Inst. Mar. Technologists, India, 1972 (Hon. Mem., 1981); UN Conf. on Code of Conduct for Liner Confs, 1973–74; Internat. Maritime Lectrs' Assoc., 1980–; Chm., Cttee of Invisibles, 3rd UN Conf. on Trade and Develt, 1972; Member: Nat. Shipping Bd, 1959–73; Merchant Navy Trng Bd, 1959–73; Nat. Welfare Bd for Seafarers, 1966–73; Amer. Bureau of Shipping, 1969; Governing Body, Indian Inst. of Foreign Trade, 1970; State Bd of Tourism, 1970; Nat. Harbour Bd, 1970–73; Gen. Cttee, Bombay Chamber of Commerce and Ind., 1971; Governing Body Indian Inst. of Management, 1972–73; Adv. Bd, Seatrade Acad., 1978– (Chm. Awarding Body, Seatrade Annual Awards for Achievement, 1988); Europort Internat. Cttee of Honour, 1980–; Internat. Chamber of Commerce Internat. Maritime Bureau, 1981–; Bd of Dirs, ICC Centre for Maritime Co-operation, 1985–; Hon. Adv. Cttee, Internat. Congress on The Port—an Ecological Challenge, Hamburg, 1989–; Marine Soc., 1984. Vice Pres., Welsh Centre for Internat. Affairs, 1989–. FRSA 1981. Hon. Member: Master Mariners' Co., 1978; Royal Inst. of Navigation, 1984; Internat. Fedn of Shipmasters' Assocs, 1985; The Warsash Assoc., 1988; Internat. Maritime Pilots' Assoc., 1988; Hon. Fellow: Plymouth Polytech., 1979; Nautical Inst., 1985. Hon. LLD: Bhopal, 1984; Wales, 1987; Malta, 1988. Admiral Padilla Award, Colombia, 1978; Gran Amigo del Mar Award, Colombia, 1978; Gold Mercury Internat. Award Ad Personam, 1984; Award, Seatrade Acad., 1988. Commandeur du Mérite Maritime, France, 1982; Comdr, Order of St Olav, Norway, 1982; Grande Ufficiale dell'Ordine al Merito, Italy, 1983; Comdr, Order of Prince Henry the Navigator, Portugal, 1983; Gold Order of Distinguished Seafarers, Poland, 1983; Nautical Medal, 1st cl., Greece, 1983; Gran Cruz Distintivo Blanco, Orden Cruz Peruana al Mérito Naval, Peru, 1984; Gran Cruz, Orden de Manuel Amador Guerrero, Panama, 1985; Grande-Oficial, Ordem do Mérito Naval, Brazil, 1986; Commander's Cross, Order of Merit, Poland, 1986; Silver Medal of Honour, Malmö, Sweden, 1988; Kt Great Band, Order of Humane African Redemption, Liberia, 1989; Comdr's Cross of Order of Merit, FRG, 1989; Comdr Grand Cross, Royal Order of the Star of the North, Sweden, 1989. *Publications:* articles on shipping in newspapers and jls. *Recreation:* music. *Address:* c/o International Maritime Organization, 4 Albert Embankment, SE1 7SR. *Clubs:* Royal Anglo-Belgian; Willingdon (Bombay).

STABB, His Honour Sir William (Walter), Kt 1981; QC 1968; FCIArb; retired; a Circuit Judge (formerly Official Referee, Supreme Court of Judicature), 1969–78; Senior Official Referee, 1978–85; *b* 6 Oct. 1913; 2nd *s* of late Sir Newton Stabb, OBE and late Lady E. M. Stabb; *m* 1940, Dorothy Margaret Leckie; four *d*. *Educ:* Rugby; University Coll., Oxford. Called to the Bar, 1936; Master of the Bench, Inner Temple, 1964, Treasurer, 1985. Served with RAF, 1940–46, attaining rank of Sqdn Ldr. Junior Counsel to Ministry of Labour, 1960; Prosecuting Counsel to BoT, 1962–68. Chm. 1961–69, Dep. Chm. 1969–71, Bedfordshire QS. *Recreations:* fishing, golf. *Address:* Old Barn Cottage, Chipperfield, Kings Langley, Herts WD4 9BH. *T:* Kings Langley (01923) 263124; 1 King's Bench Walk, Temple, EC4Y 7DB. *T:* 0171–353 8436.

STABLE, His Honour (Rondle) Owen (Charles), QC 1963; a Circuit Judge, 1979–95; Senior Circuit Judge, Snaresbrook Crown Court, 1982–95; *b* 28 Jan. 1923; *yr s* of late Rt Hon. Sir Wintringham Norton Stable, MC, and Lucie Haden (*née* Freeman); *m* 1949, Yvonne Brook, *y d* of late Maj. L. B. Holliday, OBE; two *d*. *Educ:* Winchester. Served with Rifle Bde, 1940–46 (Captain). Barrister, Middle Temple, 1948; Bencher, 1969. Dep. Chm., QS, Herts, 1963–71; a Recorder of the Crown Court, 1972–79. Board of Trade Inspector: Cadco Group of Cos, 1963–64; H. S. Whiteside & Co Ltd, 1965–67; International Learning Systems Corp. Ltd, 1969–71; Pergamon Press, 1969–73. Sec. National Reference Tribunal for the Coal Mining Industry, 1953–64; Chancellor of Diocese of Bangor, 1959–88; Member, Governing Body of the Church in Wales, 1960–88; Licensed Parochial Lay Reader, Diocese of St Albans, 1961–; Member: General Council of the Bar, 1962–66; Senate of 4 Inns of Court, 1971–74; Senate of the Inns of Court and the Bar, 1974–75. Chm., Horserace Betting Levy Appeal Tribunal, 1969–74. JP Hertfordshire, 1963–71. *Publication:* (with R. M. Stuttard) A Review of Coursing, 1971. *Recreations:* listening to music, playing the flute. *Address:* Buckler's Hall, Much Hadham, Herts SG10 6EB. *T:* Much Hadham (01279) 842604. *Club:* Boodle's.

See also P. L. W. Owen.

STABLER, Arthur Fletcher; Board Member, Theatre Royal Trust Ltd, since 1987; *b* 7 Nov. 1919; *s* of Edward and Maggie Stabler; *m* 1948, Margaret Stabler; two *s*. *Educ:* Cruddas Park Sch. Engineer apprenticeship, Vickers Armstrong, 1935–39. Served War, Royal Northumberland Fusiliers, 1939–46. With Vickers Armstrong, 1946–78. Mem., Supplementary Benefits Commn, 1976–79. Newcastle upon Tyne: City Councillor, 1963–74; District Councillor, 1973–94; Dep. Lord Mayor, 1982–83; Lord Mayor, 1983–84; Chairman: Housing Renewals, 1975–76; Arts and Recreation, 1976–77; Case Work Sub-Cttee, 1974–77; Tenancy Relations Sub-Cttee, 1975–77; Community Develt Sub-Cttee, 1975–76; Town Moor Sub-Cttee, 1976–77; Personnel Sub-Cttee, 1982–; Area Housing Cttee, 1984–85; Priority Area Sub-Cttee, 1984–85; Health Adv. Cttee, 1986–87; District HA Jt Consultative Cttee; Festival Cttee, 1987–88; Public Works Cttee, 1987–88; Vice-Chairman: Social Services Cttee, 1974–76; Housing Management Cttee, 1975–76; Tyneside Summer Exhibn Cttee, 1982–; Tyne and Wear Jt Fire and Civil

Defence Cttee, 1986–89; Cityworks Cttee, 1989. Chm., Axwell Park Community Homes, 1978–79; Mem., numerous Tenants' Assocs. Chm., Newcastle upon Tyne Central Labour Party, 1965–78. Pres., No 6 Br., AUEW. Chm., Westerhope Golf Club Jt Sub-Cttee, 1976–77. President: Newcastle upon Tyne and District Allotments and Garden Council, 1980–; Elswick Park Bowling Club, 1980–; Cttee, Tyne Wear Polish Solidarity Club, 1981–. Life Mem., High Pitt Social Club; Hon. Member: Casino Royal Club, 1980; St Joseph's Club, 1983; Royal British Legion Club, 1983. *Publication:* Gannin Along the Scotswood Road, 1976. *Recreations:* social work, local history. *Address:* 10 Whitebeam Place, Elswick, Newcastle upon Tyne NE4 7EJ. *T:* 0191–273 2362. *Clubs:* Pineapple CIU, Polish White Eagle, Ryton Social, Tyneside Irish (Hon.), Maddison's (Hon.) (Newcastle upon Tyne).

STACEY, Air Vice-Marshal John Nichol, CBE 1971; DSO 1945; DFC 1942; *b* 14 Sept. 1920; *s* of Captain Herbert Chambers Stacey and Mrs May Stacey; *m* 1950, Veronica Satterly; two *d. Educ:* Whitgift Middle Sch., Croydon. Merchant Marine Apprentice, 1937–38; joined RAF, 1938; flying throughout War of 1939–45 (despatches thrice); comd No 160 Sqdn, 1944–45; Asst Air Attaché, Washington, 1947–48; psc 1949; on staff at Staff Coll., 1958–60; Chief of Air Staff, Royal Malayan Air Force, 1960–63 (JMN); comd RAF Laarbruch, Germany, 1963–66; AOC, Air Cadets, 1968–71; Dir, Orgn and Admin. Planning (RAF), MoD, 1971–74; AOA, Support Comd, 1974–75, retired. Dir, Stonham Housing Assoc., 1976–81; Member: Tunbridge Wells HA, 1981–86; RAFA Housing Assoc., 1982–86; Chm., High Weald Housing Assoc., 1992–. President: Royal British Legion Gondhurst Br., 1991–; Headcorn Br., RAFA; Trustee: Housing Assoc. Charitable Trust, 1978–86; Tunbridge Wells Cancer Help Centre; Bedgebury Sch., 1983–. *Recreations:* sailing, golf. *Address:* Riseden Cottage, Riseden, Goudhurst, Cranbrook, Kent TN17 1HJ. *T:* Goudhurst (01580) 211239. *Clubs:* Royal Air Force; Dale Hill Golf.

STACEY, Prof. Margaret; Professor of Sociology, University of Warwick, 1974–89, Emeritus Professor, 1989; *b* 27 March 1922; *d* of Conrad Eugene Petrie and Grace Priscilla Boyce; *m* 1945, Frank Arthur Stacey (*d* 1977); three *s* two *d. Educ:* City of London Sch. for Girls; London Sch. of Econs (BScEcon, 1st Cl. Hons Sociology). Labour Officer, Royal Ordnance Factory, 1943–44; Tutor, Oxford Univ., 1944–51; University Coll. of Swansea: Res. Officer and Fellow, 1961–63; Lectr in Sociol., 1963–70; Sen. Lectr in Sociol., 1970–74; Dir, Medical Sociol. Res. Centre, 1972–74. Lucille Petry Loene Vis. Prof. Univ. of Calif., San Francisco, 1988. British Sociological Association: Mem. Exec. Cttee, 1965–70, 1975–79; Hon. Gen. Sec., 1968–70; Chairperson, 1977–79; Pres., 1981–83; Mem. Women's Caucus, 1974–. Pres., Section N, BAAS, 1990. Scientific Advr to DHSS; Temp. Advr to Reg. Dir, WHO EURO. Pres., Assoc. for Welfare of Children in Hosp. (Wales), 1974–; Member: Assoc. for Welfare of Children in Hosp., 1960–; Welsh Hosp. Bd, 1970–74; Davies Cttee on Hosp. Complaints Procedure, 1971–73; GMC, 1976–84; Sociol. Cttee, SSRC, 1969–71; Health and Health Policy Cttee, SSRC, 1976–77. FRSM. Hon. Fellow, UC of Swansea, 1987. *Publications:* Tradition and Change: a study of Banbury, 1960, paperback 1970; (ed) Comparability in Social Research, 1969; (ed and jt author) Hospitals, Children and their Families: a study of the welfare of children in hospital, 1970; Methods of Social Research, 1970; (jtly) Power, Persistence and Change: a second study of Banbury, 1975; (ed) The Sociology of the NHS, 1976; (ed jtly and contrib.) Beyond Separation: further studies of children in hospital, 1979; (jtly) Women, Power and Politics, 1981 (Fawcett Book Prize, 1982); (ed jtly) Concepts of Health, Illness and Disease: a comparative perspective, 1986; Sociology of Health and Healing: a textbook, 1988; Regulating British Medicine: the General Medical Council, 1992; (ed) Changing Human Reproduction: social science perspectives, 1992; contrib. to Feminist Rev., Sociol Rev., Sociol., Brit. Jl of Sociol., Social Science and Med., Jl of Med. Ethics, and Sociol. of Health and Illness. *Recreations:* walking, gardening. *Address:* 8 Lansdowne Circus, Leamington Spa, Warwicks CV32 4SW. *T:* Leamington Spa (01926) 312094.

STACEY, Rear-Adm. Michael Lawrence, CB 1979; private consultant in marine pollution; Member: Advisory Committee on Protection of the Sea, since 1988; Committee of Management, Royal National Lifeboat Institution, since 1989; *b* 6 July 1924; *s* of Maurice Stacey and Dorice Evelyn (*née* Bulling); *m* 1955, Penelope Leana (*née* Riddoch); two *s. Educ:* Epsom Coll. Entered RN as Cadet, 1942; Normandy landings, HMS Hawkins, 1944; served on HM Ships Rotherham, Cambrian, Shoreham, Hornet, Vernon, Euryalus, Bermuda, Vigilant; Comdr 1958; staff of RN Staff Coll.; in comd HMS Blackpool, 1960–62; JSSC; Captain 1966; Chief Staff Officer to Admiral Commanding Reserves, 1966–68; in comd HMS Andromeda and Captain (F) Sixth Frigate Sqdn, 1968–70; Dep. Dir of Naval Warfare, 1970–73; in comd HMS Tiger, 1973–75; Asst Chief of Naval Staff (Policy), 1975–76; Flag Officer, Gibraltar, 1976–78. ADC to the Queen, 1975. Dir, Marine Emergency Ops, Marine Div., Dept of Trade, later Dept of Transport, 1979–87. FNI; FIMgt. Younger Brother, Trinity House, 1979. Liveryman, Shipwrights' Co., 1991. *Recreations:* fishing, yachting. *Address:* Little Hintock, 40 Lynch Road, Farnham, Surrey GU9 8BY. *T:* Farnham (01252) 713032. *Clubs:* Army and Navy, Royal Navy of 1765 and 1785, Royal Naval Sailing Association.

STACEY, Morna Dorothy, (Mrs W. D. Stacey); *see* Hooker, Prof. M. D.

STACEY, Rev. Nicolas David; Chairman, East Thames Housing Group (formerly East London Housing Association), since 1993; *b* 27 Nov. 1927; *s* of late David and of Gwen Stacey; *m* 1955, Hon. Anne Bridgeman, *er d* of 2nd Viscount Bridgeman, KBE, CB, DSO, MC; one *s* two *d. Educ:* RNC, Dartmouth; St Edmund Hall, Oxford (hons degree Mod. Hist.); Cuddesdon Theol Coll., Oxford. Midshipman, HMS Anson, 1945–46; Sub-Lt, 1946–48. Asst Curate, St Mark's, Portsea, 1953–58; Domestic Chap. to Bp of Birmingham, 1958–60; Rector of Woolwich, 1960–68; Dean of London Borough of Greenwich, 1965–68; Dep. Dir of Oxfam, 1968–70; Director of Social Services: London Borough of Ealing, 1971–74; Kent County Council, 1974–85; Dir, AIDS Policy Unit, sponsored by Citizen Action, 1988–89. Vice-Chm., TV South Charitable Trust, 1988–92. Six Preacher, Canterbury Cathedral, 1984–89. Sporting career: internat. sprinter, 1948–52, incl. British Empire Games, 1949, and Olympic Games, 1952 (semi-finalist 200 metres and finalist 4×400 metres relay); Pres., OUAC, 1951; winner, Oxf. v Cambridge 220 yds, 1948–51; Captain, Combined Oxf. and Camb. Athletic Team, 1951. *Publication:* Who Cares (autobiog.), 1971. *Address:* The Old Vicarage, Selling, Faversham, Kent ME13 9RD. *T:* Canterbury (01227) 752833, *Fax:* (01227) 752889. *Clubs:* Beefsteak; Royal St George's Golf (Sandwich, Kent).

STACK, (Ann) Prunella, (Mrs Brian St Quentin Power), OBE 1980; President, The Women's League of Health and Beauty, since 1982 (Member of Council, since 1950); *b* 28 July 1914; *d* of Capt. Hugh Bagot Stack, 8th Ghurka Rifles, and Mary Meta Bagot Stack, Founder of The Women's League of Health and Beauty; *m* 1st, 1938, Lord David Douglas-Hamilton (*d* 1944); two *s*; 2nd, 1950, Alfred G. Albers, FRCS (*d* 1951), Cape Town, S Africa; 3rd, 1964, Brian St Quentin Power. *Educ:* The Abbey, Malvern Wells. Mem. of the National Fitness Council, 1937–39. Vice-Pres., Outward Bound Trust, 1980–. *Publications:* The Way to Health and Beauty, 1938; Movement is Life, 1973; Island Quest, 1979; Zest for Life, 1988; Style for Life, 1990. *Recreations:* poetry, music, travel. *Address:* 14 Gertrude Street, SW10 0JN.

STACK, Rt. Rev. Mgr George; Administrator of Westminster Cathedral, since 1993; *b* 9 May 1946; *s* of Gerald Stack and Elizabeth (*née* McKenzie). *Educ:* St Aloysius Coll., Highgate; St Edmund's Coll., Ware; St Mary's Coll., Strawberry Hill. BEd (Hons). Ordained priest, 1972; Curate, St Joseph's, Hanwell 1972–75; Diocesan Catechetical Office, 1975–77; Curate, St Paul's, Wood Green, 1977–83; Parish Priest, Our Lady Help of Christians, Kentish Town, 1983–90; VG, Archdiocese of Westminster, 1990–93. Prelate of Honour to HH The Pope, 1993. *Address:* Cathedral Clergy House, 42 Francis Street, SW1P 1QW. *T:* 0171–834 7452.

STACK, Neville; international editorial consultant and syndicated political columnist, in South and South East Asia, Africa and the Caribbean, since 1989; *b* 2 Sept. 1928; *m* 1953, Molly Rowe; one *s* one *d. Educ:* Arnold School. Reporter: Ashton-under-Lyne Reporter, 1948; Express & Star, 1950; Sheffield Telegraph, and Kemsley National Papers, 1955; Northern News Editor, IPC national papers, 1971; Sub-editor, Daily Express, 1973; Editor, Stockport Advertiser, 1974; Editor, Leicester Mercury, 1974–87; Dir, F. Hewitt and Co. (1927) Ltd (Mercury Publishers), 1982–88; Editorial Consultant, Straits Times, Singapore, 1988–89. Columnist, The Hindu, Madras, 1990–; political commentator: Singapore Business Times, 1990–; NZ Herald, 1990–. Press Fellow, Wolfson Coll., Cambridge, 1987–88. Evaluator, RSA journalism qualification, 1992–; Co-organiser and Mem., Wolfson Coll. Regl Seminar for Editors, 1992–. Hon. MA Leicester, 1988. *Publications:* The Empty Palace, 1976; Editing for the Nineties, 1988. *Recreations:* writing, sailing, travel, flying. *Address:* 34 Main Street, Belton-in-Rutland, Leicestershire LE15 9LB. *T:* Belton (01572) 718718.

STACK, Prunella; *see* Stack, A. P.

STACPOOLE, John Wentworth; Deputy Secretary, Department of Health and Social Security, 1979–82; *b* 16 June 1926; *s* of late G. W. Stacpoole and of Mrs M. G. Butt; *m* 1954, Charmian, *d* of late J. P. Bishop and Mrs E. M. Bishop; one *s* one *d. Educ:* Sedbergh; Magdalen Coll., Oxford (Demy; MA). Army, 1944–47 (Lieut, Assam Regt). Colonial Office, 1951–68, Private Sec. to Sec. of State, 1964–65; transf. to Min. of Social Security, 1968; Under-Sec., DHSS, 1973. Mem., Maidstone HA, 1982–91. Chm., Maidstone Hospice Appeal, 1987–92. *Recreations:* reading, walking, sketching. *Address:* Fairseat Lodge, Fairseat, near Sevenoaks, Kent TN15 7LU. *T:* Fairseat (01732) 822201.

STADLEN, Nicholas Felix; QC 1991; *b* 3 May 1950; *s* of Peter Stadlen and Hedi (*née* Simon); *m* 1972, Frances Edith Howarth, *d* of T. E. B. and Margaret Howarth; three *s. Educ:* St Paul's School (Scholar); Trinity Coll., Cambridge (Open Scholarship and McGill Exhibition; BA Hons Classics Part 1, History Part 2). Pres., Cambridge Union Soc., 1970. First in order of merit, Part 1 Bar Exams, 1975; called to the Bar, Inner Temple, 1976. Mem., Bar Council Public Affairs Cttee, 1987. First Sec., British-Irish Assoc., 1972–74. *Publications:* (with Michael Barnes) Gulbenkian Foundation Reports on National Music and Drama Education, 1974–75; (contrib.) Convention: an account of the 1976 US Democratic Party Presidential Nominating Convention, 1976. *Recreation:* listening to classical music. *Address:* Fountain Court, Temple, EC4Y 9DH. *T:* 0171–583 3335.

STAFFORD, 15th Baron *cr* 1640; **Francis Melfort William Fitzherbert;** DL; *b* 13 March 1954; *s* of 14th Baron Stafford and of Morag Nada, *yr d* of late Lt-Col Alastair Campbell; *S* father, 1986; *m* 1980, Katharine Mary Codrington; two *s* two *d. Educ:* Ampleforth College; Reading Univ.; RAC, Cirencester. Director (non-executive): Tarmac Industrial Products Div., 1987–93; Mid Staffs Mental Health Foundn, 1990–; Hanley Economic BS, 1992–. Pro-Chancellor, Keele Univ., 1993–. Pres. and Patron various orgns in North Staffs. Governor, Harper Adams Agricl Coll., 1990–. DL Stafford, 1994. *Recreations:* shooting, cricket, golf. *Heir: s* Hon. Benjamin John Basil Fitzherbert, *b* 8 Nov. 1983. *Address:* Swynnerton Park, Stone, Staffordshire ST15 0QE. *T:* Swynnerton (01782) 796228. *Clubs:* Farmers'; Lord's Taverners.

STAFFORD, Bishop Suffragan of; *no new appointment at time of going to press.*

STAFFORD, Archdeaconry of; *see* Lichfield.

STAFFORD, David Valentine; Secretary, Economic and Social Research Council, 1988–90; *b* 14 Feb. 1930; *s* of Augustus Everard and Emily Blanche Stafford; *m* 1953, Aileen Patricia Wood; one *s* one *d. Educ:* Rutlish School, Merton. Dept of Educn and Science, 1951–88; Sec., Open Univ. Planning Cttee, 1967–69. Acting Chm., ESRC, Feb.–Sept. 1988. *Recreations:* reading, gardening, theatre, music. *Address:* Vallis, Lyncombe Vale Road, Bath, Avon BA2 4LS. *T:* Bath (01225) 312563.

STAFFORD, Godfrey Harry, CBE 1976; PhD; FRS 1979; FInstP; Master of St Cross College, Oxford, 1979–87; *b* 15 April 1920; *s* of Henry and Sarah Stafford; *m* 1950, Helen Goldthorp (*née* Clark); one *s* twin *d. Educ:* Rondebosch Boys High Sch., S Africa; Univ. of Cape Town; Gonville and Caius Coll., Cambridge. MSc Cape Town, 1941; Ebden Scholar, PhD Cantab 1950; MA Oxon 1971. South African Naval Forces, 1941–46. Harwell, 1949–51; Head of Biophysics Subdiv., CSIR, Pretoria, 1951–54; Cyclotron Gp, AERE, 1954–57; Rutherford Laboratory: Head of Proton Linear Accelerator Gp, 1957; Head of High Energy Physics Div., 1963; Dep. Dir, 1966; Dir, Rutherford Lab., Chilton, 1969–79; Dir Gen., 1979–81, Hon. Scientist, 1987–, Rutherford Appleton Laboratory; Fellow, St Cross Coll., Oxford, 1971–79 (Hon. Fellow, 1987). CERN appointments: UK deleg. to Council, 1973; Vice-Pres., Council, 1973; Scientific Policy Cttee, 1973, Vice-Chm., 1976, Chm., 1978. Vice-Pres. for meetings, Inst. of Physics, 1976; President: European Physical Soc., 1984–86 (Vice-Pres., 1982–84); Inst. of Physics, 1986–88. Governor: Oxford Centre for Post-Graduate Hebrew Studies, 1983–93; Westminster Coll., 1987–93. Glazebrook Prize and Medal, Inst. of Physics, 1981. Hon. DSc Birmingham, 1980. *Publications:* papers and articles in learned jls on: biophysics, nuclear physics, high energy physics. *Recreations:* walking, foreign travel, music. *Address:* Ferry Cottage, North Hinksey Village, Oxford OX2 0NA. *T:* Oxford (01865) 247621.

STAFFORD, John, OBE 1977; HM Diplomatic Service, retired; *b* 15 June 1920; *s* of late Frank and Gertrude Stafford, Sheffield; *m* 1949, Mary Jocelyn Goodwin, *d* of late Capt. J. G. Budge, RN. *Educ:* High Storrs Grammar Sch. Exchequer and Audit Dept, 1939. RAF, W/O Pilot, 1940. Board of Trade, 1946; Assistant Trade Commissioner, Delhi, Karachi, Bulawayo, 1946–56; Trade Commissioner, Karachi, Lahore, Bombay, Madras, Lahore, 1956–65; Dep. High Comr, Lahore, 1965–69; Consul, Houston, Texas, 1969–71; First Sec. (Commercial), New Delhi, 1974–77; Consul Gen., Brisbane, 1978–80. *Recreations:* cricket, tennis, theatre, music. *Address:* Leacroft, 268 Brooklands Road, Weybridge, Surrey KT13 0QX. *Clubs:* East India, Devonshire, Sports and Public Schools; Royal Bombay Yacht; Punjab (Lahore).

STAFFORD, Peter Moore, FCA; Member, Board of Partners, Touche Ross & Co., since 1990 (Chairman, 1992–95); *b* 24 April 1942; *s* of late Harry Shaw Stafford and May Alexandra (*née* Moore); *m* 1973, Elspeth Ann, *d* of James Steel Harvey; one *s* one *d. Educ:* Charterhouse. FCA 1976 (ACA 1965). Articled Clerk, Garnett Crewdson & Co., Manchester, 1960–64; Arthur Andersen, 1966–68; Partner, 1968–71, Garnett Crewdson & Co., merged with Spicer & Oppenheim: Partner, 1971–90; Managing Partner, 1990; merged with Touche Ross & Co. Mem., Council for Industry and Higher Educn, 1993–.

Governor, Terra Nova Sch., 1976–. *Recreations:* travel, gardening, restoring antique launches. *Address:* Holmes Chapel, Cheshire. *T:* Holmes Chapel (01477) 533339. *Clubs:* Royal Over-Seas League; St James's (Manchester).

STAFFORD-CLARK, Dr David, MD; FRCP; FRCPsych; DPM; Consultant Emeritus, Guy's Hospital and Joint Hospitals, Institute of Psychiatry, University of London; formerly Physician in Charge, Department of Psychological Medicine, and Director of The York Clinic, Guy's Hospital, 1954–73; Chairman, Psychiatric Division, Guy's Group, 1973–74; Consultant Physician, Bethlem Royal and Maudsley Hospitals and the Institute of Psychiatry, 1954–73; retired; *b* 17 March 1916; *s* of Francis and Cordelia Susan Stafford Clark; *m* 1941, Dorothy Stewart (*née* Oldfield); three *s* one *d. Educ:* Felsted; University of London. Guy's Hospital. MRCS, LRCP, 1939; MB, BS, 1939. Served War of 1939–45, RAFVR; trained as Medical Parachutist (despatches twice); demobilised 1945. Guy's Hosp., MRCP, Nuffield Med. Fellow, 1946; 3 years postgrad. trg appts, Inst. of Psychiatry, Maudsley Hosp.; MD London, 1947, DPM London, 1948; Registrar, Nat. Hosp., Queen Sq., 1948. Resident Massachusetts Gen. Hosp., Dept of Psychiatry, and Teaching Clinical Fellow, Harvard Med. School, 1949; First Asst, Professorial Unit, Maudsley Hosp., 1950; Mem. Assoc. for Research in Mental and Nervous Disorders, NY, 1950–53; Consultant Staff, Guy's Hosp., 1950; Lectureship, Psychology (Faculty of Letters), Reading Univ., 1950–54. Consultant, British Near East Forces, BMH Dhekelia and Princess Mary's Hosp., Akrotiri, Cyprus, 1975–80. Hon. Vis. Prof., Johns Hopkins Univ., USA, 1964; Gifford Lectr and Vis. Prof., St Andrews Univ., 1978. Member: Archbishop of Canterbury's Commn on Divine Healing; Council, Royal Medico-Psychological Assoc.; Council, Medico-Legal Soc.; Examr, RCP London and Cambridge MD; Editorial Bds, Guy's Hosp. Reports, and Mod. Med. of Gt Britain. Acted as adviser to various motion picture companies (Universal International etc) on medical aspects of their productions; has also acted as adviser and director on a large number of medical programmes on sound radio, and both BBC and Independent Television, including the "Lifeline" series of programmes for the BBC, and documentary programmes for ITV on the emotional and intellectual growth of normal children, and the life and work of Freud; Author of Brain and Behaviour Series in Adult Education Television Programmes on BBC Channel 2; Mind and Motive Series, 1966. FRCP, 1958; Mem., NY Acad. of Sciences; FRSA (Silver Medal), 1959; Hon. RCM, 1966; Foundn Fellow, RCPsych, 1972, Hon. Fellow, 1976; FRSM. Hon. Pres., Guy's Hosp. RUFC, 1972; Hon. Mem., Cambridge RUFC, 1972. Gate Prize for Poetry, 1933. *Publications: poetry:* Autumn Shadow, 1941; Sound in the Sky, 1944; *novel:* Soldier Without a Rifle, 1979; *medical:* Psychiatry Today (Pelican), 1951; Psychiatry for Students, 1964, 7th (rev.) edn, 1989; What Freud Really Said, 1965; Five Questions in Search of an Answer, 1970; chapters in: Emergencies in Medical Practice, 1st, 2nd and 3rd edns, 1948, 1950, 1952; Compendium of Emergencies, 1st and 2nd edns; Case Histories in Psychosomatic Medicine, 1952; Taylor's Medical Jurisprudence, 12th edn, 1965; Schizophrenia: Somatic Aspects, 1st edn, 1957; Frontiers in General Hospital Psychiatry, 1961; A Short Textbook of Medicine, 1963; The Pathology and Treatment of Sexual Deviation, 1964; Modern Trends in Psychological Medicine, 1970; Psychiatric Treatment, Concepts of, in Encyclopædia Britannica, 200th anniv. edn, 1973; contributions to various medical textbooks and to medical and scientific jls. *Recreations:* travel, reading, writing, making and watching films, theatre. *Club:* Royal Air Force.
See also M. Stafford-Clark.

STAFFORD-CLARK, Max; artistic director, Out of Joint Theatre Company, since 1993; *b* 17 March 1941; *s* of David Stafford-Clark, *qv*; *m* 1st, 1971, Carole Hayman; 2nd, 1981, Ann Pennington; one *d. Educ:* Felstead School; Riverdale Country Day School, NY; Trinity College, Dublin. Associate dir, Traverse, 1966, artistic dir, 1968–70; dir, Traverse Workshop Co., 1970–74; founder, Joint Stock Theatre Group, 1974; Artistic Dir, English Stage Company at Royal Court Theatre, 1979–93. *Publication:* Letters to George, 1989. *Address:* 7 Gloucester Crescent, NW1 7DS. *Club:* Groucho.

STAGG, Prof. Geoffrey Leonard, MBE 1945; Professor Emeritus, Department of Spanish and Portuguese, University of Toronto; *b* 10 May 1913; *s* of Henry Percy Stagg and Maude Emily Bradbury; *m* 1948, Amy Southwell, Wellesley Hills, Mass, USA; two *s* one *d. Educ:* King Edward's School, Birmingham (Scholar); Trinity Hall, Cambridge (Scholar). BA 1st cl. Hons Modern and Medieval Languages Tripos, 1934; MA 1946; Joseph Hodges Choate Mem. Fellow, Harvard Univ., 1934–36; AM (Harvard), 1935; Modern Languages Master, King Edward's School, Birmingham, 1938–40, 1946–47; served in Intelligence Corps, 1940–46; Lecturer in Spanish and Italian, Nottingham Univ., 1947–53, and Head of Dept of Spanish, 1954–56; Dept of Italian and Hispanic Studies, Toronto Univ.: Prof., 1956–78; Chm., 1956–66, 1969–78. Vice-Pres., Assoc. of Teachers of Spanish and Portuguese of GB and Ireland, 1948–; Pres., Canadian Assoc. of Hispanists, 1964–66, 1972–74; Vice-Pres., Internat. Assoc. of Hispanists, 1977–83; Chm., Local Organising Cttee, Sixth Congress of Internat. Assoc. of Hispanists, Toronto, 1977. Fellow, New Coll., Univ. of Toronto, 1962–; Senior Fellow, Massey Coll., Univ. of Toronto, 1965–70; Canada Council Senior Fellowship, 1967–68. *Publications:* articles on Spanish literature in learned jls. *Address:* 30 Old Bridle Path, Toronto, Ont M4T 1A7, Canada.

STAINFORTH, Maj.-Gen. Charles Herbert, CB 1969; OBE 1955; *b* 12 Dec. 1914; *s* of Lt-Col Stainforth, CMG, 4th Cavalry, IA, and Georgina Helen, *d* of Maj.-Gen. H. Pipon, CB; *m* Elizabeth, *d* of late John Tait Easdale; one *s* one *d. Educ:* Wellington Coll.; RMC, Sandhurst. Commnd into 2nd Royal Lancers, IA; transferred British Army, 1947; Chief of Staff, Southern Comd, 1965–66; GOC Aldershot District and SE Dist, 1966–69; Head of UK Future Command Structure, MoD, 1969–72. Col Comdt, RCT, 1970–72. Chm. Combined Cadet Forces, 1970–72. Consultant to Nat. Tourist Bds, 1973–75. Editor, Army Quarterly and Defence Journal, 1974–84. *Address:* Powderham House, Dippenhall, near Farnham, Surrey GU10 5EB. *Clubs:* Army and Navy, MCC.

STAINTON, Sir (John) Ross, Kt 1981; CBE 1971; retired; *b* 27 May 1914; *s* of late George Stainton and Helen Ross; *m* 1939, Doreen Werner; three *d. Educ:* Glengorse, Eastbourne; Malvern Coll., Worcestershire. Joined Imperial Airways as Trainee, 1933; served in Italy, Egypt, Sudan. Served with RAF in England, West Indies and USA, 1940–46. Man. N America, BOAC, 1949–53; General Sales Man. BOAC, and other Head Office posts, 1954–68; Dep. Man. Dir, 1968–71; Man. Dir, 1971–72; Mem., BOAC Bd, 1968, Chm. and Chief Exec., 1972, until merged into British Airways, 1974; Mem., 1971–, Dep. Chm. and Chief Exec., 1977–79, Chairman, 1979–80, British Airways Bd. Vice Pres., Private Patients Plan, 1986– (Dir, 1979–86). Hon. Treasurer, Air League Council, 1986–91. FCIT (Pres., 1970–71); CRAeS 1978. *Clubs:* Royal Air Force; Royal and Ancient Golf (St Andrews); Sunningdale Golf.

STAINTON, Keith; *b* 8 Nov. 1921; *m* 1946, Vanessa Ann Heald (marr. diss.); three *s* three *d*; *m* 1980, Frances Easton. *Educ:* Kendal Sch.; Manchester Univ. (BA (Com.) Dist. in Economics). Insurance clerk, 1936–39. Served War of 1939–45: Lieut, RNVR, Submarines and with French Resistance, 1940–46. Manchester Univ., 1946–49; Leader Writer, Financial Times, 1949–52; Industrial Consultant, 1952–57; joined Burton, Son & Sanders, Ltd, 1957, Man. Dir 1961–69, Chm. 1962–69; Chm. Scotia Investments Ltd, 1969–72. MP (C) Sudbury and Woodbridge, Dec. 1963–1983; Mem., House of Commons Select Cttees on Expenditure and Science and Technology. Mem. Council of Europe and WEU, 1979–83. Légion d'Honneur, Croix de Guerre avec Palmes, Ordre de l'Armée, 1943. *Address:* Little Bealings House, near Woodbridge, Suffolk IP13 6LX. *T:* Ipswich (01473) 624205.

STAINTON, Sir Ross; *see* Stainton, Sir J. R.

STAIR, 13th Earl of, *cr* 1703; **John Aymer Dalrymple,** KCVO 1978 (CVO 1964); MBE 1941; Bt 1664 and (Scot.) 1698; Viscount Stair, Lord Glenluce and Stranraer, 1690; Viscount Dalrymple, Lord Newliston, 1703; Baron Oxenfoord (UK) 1841; Colonel (retired) Scots Guards; Lord-Lieutenant of Wigtown, 1961–81; Captain General of the Queen's Body Guard for Scotland, Royal Company of Archers, 1973–88; *b* 9 Oct. 1906; *e s* of 12th Earl of Stair, KT, DSO, and Violet Evelyn (*née* Harford) (*d* 1968); *S* father, 1961; *m* 1960, Davina, DL, *d* of late Hon. Sir David Bowes-Lyon, KCVO; three *s. Educ:* Eton; Sandhurst. Bde Major, 3rd (London) Infantry Bde and Regimental Adjt Scots Guards, 1935–38; served Middle East, 1941; Bde Major, 16th Inf. Bde (despatches, MBE); Lieut-Colonel 1942; commanded 1st Scots Guards, 1942–43; AMS Headquarters AAI, 1944; Comd Trg Bn Scots Guards, 1945; Comd 2nd Scots Guards, 1946–49; Comd Scots Guards, Temp. Colonel, 1949–52; retired, 1953; retired as Hon. Colonel Scots Guards, 1953. *Heir: s* Viscount Dalrymple, *qv. Address:* Lochinch Castle, Stranraer, Wigtownshire DG9 8RT. *Club:* Cavalry and Guards.
See also Lady Jean Rankin.

STAKIS, Sir Reo (Argyros), Kt 1988; Founder, and Chairman, 1947–91, President, since 1986, Stakis plc; *b* 13 March 1913; *s* of Anastasis and Katerina Stakis; *m* 1946, Annitsa Petropoulos; two *s* four *d. Educ:* American Acad., Larnaca. Stakis plc includes hotels, restaurants, casinos, public houses and nursing homes. Hon. Comr for Cyprus at Glasgow, 1968–. Hon. LLD Strathclyde, 1986. *Recreations:* shooting, fishing. *Address:* (office) 58 West Regent Street, Glasgow G2 2QZ. *T:* 0141–332 7773; 54 Aytoun Road, Glasgow G41 5HE; Grant House, Dunblane, Perthshire.

STALLARD, family name of **Baron Stallard.**

STALLARD, Baron *cr* 1983 (Life Peer), of St Pancras in the London Borough of Camden; **Albert William Stallard;** *b* 5 Nov. 1921; *m* 1944, Sheila, *d* of W. C. Murphy; one *s* one *d. Educ:* Low Waters Public School; Hamilton Academy, Scotland. Engineer, 1937–65; Technical Training Officer, 1965–70. Councillor, St Pancras, 1953–59, Alderman, 1962–65; Councillor, Camden, 1965–70, Alderman, 1971–78. MP (Lab) St Pancras N, 1970–83; PPS to: Minister of State, Agriculture, Fisheries and Food, 1974; Minister of State for Housing and Construction, 1974–76; an Asst Govt Whip, 1976–78; a Lord Comr, HM Treasury, 1978–79. Chairman: Camden Town Disablement Cttee (Mem., 1951); Camden Assoc. for Mental Health. Mem., Inst. of Training Officers, 1971. AEU Order of Merit, 1968. *Address:* Flat 2, 2 Belmont Street, NW1 8HH.

STALLARD, Sir Peter (Hyla Gawne), KCMG 1961 (CMG 1960); CVO 1956; MBE 1945; Secretary to the Prime Minister of the Federation of Nigeria, 1958–61; *b* 6 March 1915; *y c* of Rev. L. B. Stallard and Eleanor, *e d* of Colonel J. M. Gawne; *m* 1941, Mary Elizabeth Kirke, CStJ; one *s* one *d. Educ:* Bromsgrove Sch.; Corpus Christi Coll., Oxford (MA). Cadet, Colonial Administrative Service, Northern Nigeria, 1937. Military Service, Nigeria, Gold Coast, Burma, 1939–45. Governor and Commander-in-Chief of British Honduras, 1961–66; Lt Governor of the Isle of Man, 1966–74. Pres., Devon and Cornwall Rent Assessment Panel, 1976–85. Pres., Somerset Assoc. of Boys Clubs, 1977–91; Chm., Dartmoor Steering Gp, 1978–89. KStJ 1961; Chapter-Gen., Order of St John, 1976–93. *Recreation:* golf. *Address:* 18 Henley Road, Taunton, Somerset TA1 5BJ. *T:* Taunton (01823) 331505. *Club:* Athenæum.
See also R. D. Wilson.

STALLWORTHY, Prof. Jon Howie, FBA 1990; Professor of English Literature, since 1992, and Fellow of Wolfson College, since 1986, Oxford University; *b* 18 Jan. 1935; *s* of Sir John (Arthur) Stallworthy; *m* 1960, Gillian Meredith (*née* Waldock); two *s* one *d. Educ:* The Dragon Sch., Oxford, Rugby Sch., Magdalen Coll., Oxford (MA, BLitt). Served RWAFF (pre-Oxford). At Oxford won Newdigate Prize, 1958 (runner-up, 1957). Joined Oxford Univ. Press, 1959, Dep. Head, Academic Div., 1975–77; John Wendell Anderson Prof. of English Lit., Cornell Univ., 1977–86; Reader in English Lit., Oxford Univ., 1986–92. Chatterton Lectr on an English Poet, British Academy, 1970; during a sabbatical year, 1971–72, was a Visiting Fellow at All Souls Coll., Oxford. FRSL, 1971. *Publications: poems:* (8 collections) The Astronomy of Love, 1961; Out of Bounds, 1963; Root and Branch, 1969; Positives, 1969; The Apple Barrel: selected poems, 1955–63, 1974; Hand in Hand, 1974; A Familiar Tree, 1978; The Anzac Sonata: new and selected poems, 1986; *criticism:* Between the Lines, W. B. Yeats's Poetry in the Making, 1963; Vision and Revision in Yeats's Last Poems, 1969; *biography:* Wilfred Owen, 1974 (winner of Duff Cooper Meml Prize, W. H. Smith Literary Award and E. M. Forster Award); Louis MacNeice, 1995; *translations:* (with Peter France) Alexander Blok: The Twelve and other poems, 1970; (with Jerzy Peterkiewicz) poems for 2nd edn of Five Centuries of Polish Poetry, 1970; (with Peter France) Boris Pasternak: Selected Poems, 1983; *edited:* The Penguin Book of Love Poetry, 1973; Wilfred Owen: Complete Poems and Fragments, 1983; The Oxford Book of War Poetry, 1984; The Poems of Wilfred Owen, 1985; First Lines: poems written in youth, from Herbert to Heaney, 1987; Henry Reed: Collected Poems, 1991; The War Poems of Wilfred Owen, 1994. *Address:* Wolfson College, Oxford OX2 6UD; Long Farm, Elsfield Road, Old Marston, Oxford OX3 0PR. *Club:* Vincent's (Oxford).

STAMENKOVIĆ, Dragi; Order of National Hero, Yugoslavia, 1952; Yugoslav Star with ribbon, 1981; Yugoslav Ambassador to the Court of St James's, 1981–85, retired; *b* 29 Feb. 1920; *s* of Todor Stamenković and Darinka Malešević; *m* 1945, Jelica Purić; two *s* one *d. Educ:* Belgrade Univ. Mem., Supreme HQ, Nat. Liberation Army for Serbia, 1941–45. Mem., Liberation Cttee for Belgrade Dist, 1945–48; Minister in Govt of Serbia, 1949–51; Pres., Fedn of Trade Unions of Serbia 1951–62; President: Exec. Council of Serbia, 1964–67; Working People of Serbia, 1967–71; Mem., Presidency of Yugoslavia, 1971–74; Ambassador to Brazil, 1974–78; Ambassador in Federal Secretariat for Foreign Affairs, 1978–81. Mem. Council, Fedn of Yugoslavia, 1985. Deputy of Fed. Assembly in three convocations, and of Republican Assembly in four; Mem., Presidency of Fed. Conf., Socialist Alliance of Working People of Yugoslavia; sometime head or mem., Yugoslav delegns abroad. Holder of many Yugoslav and foreign decorations. *Publications:* From Travels through China, 1955; contribs to jls and newspapers on economic and political affairs of Yugoslavia, 1945–75. *Recreations:* tennis, football. *Address:* Užička 10, 11040 Beograd, former Yugoslavia. *Club:* Hurlingham.

STAMER, Sir (Lovelace) Anthony, 5th Bt, *cr* 1809; MA; AMIMI; *b* 28 Feb. 1917; *s* of Sir Lovelace Stamer, 4th Bt, and Eva Mary (*d* 1974), *e d* of R. C. Otter; *S* father, 1941; *m* 1st, 1948, Stella Huguette (marr. diss., 1953), *d* of late Paul Burnell Binnie, Brussels; one *s* one *d*; 2nd, 1955, Margaret Lucy (marr. diss., 1959), *d* of late Major Belben and Mrs Stewart, Marandellas, Zimbabwe; 3rd, 1960, Marjorie June (marr. diss. 1968), *d* of late T. C. Noakes, St James, Cape; 4th, 1983, Elizabeth Graham Smith (*d* 1992), *widow* of G. P. H. Smith, Colyton, Devon. *Educ:* Harrow; Trinity Coll., Cambridge; Royal Agricultural

Coll., Cirencester. BA 1947; MA 1963; AMIMI 1963. Served RAF 1939–41; Officer in ATA 1941–45. Executive Director: Bentley Drivers Club Ltd, 1969–73; Bugatti & Ferrari Owners Club, 1973–75; Hon. Treasurer, Ferrari Owners' Club, 1975–81. *Heir: s* Peter Tomlinson Stamer, Sqn Leader, RAF, retd [*b* 19 Nov. 1951; *m* 1979, Dinah Louise Berry (marr. diss. 1989); one *s* one *d*]. *Address:* 5 Windrush Court, 175 The Hill, Burford, Oxon OX18 4RE.

STAMERS-SMITH, Eileen, MA; Headmistress, Malvern Girls' College, 1984–85; *b* 17 April 1929; *d* of Charles and May Fairey; *m* 1970, Henry Arthur Stamers-Smith, CBE, MA (*d* 1982). *Educ:* Castleford Grammar Sch., Yorks; Lady Margaret Hall, Oxford (BA Hons English Lang. and Lit., Cl. II, 1951; MA; DipEd). Asst English Teacher: Abbeydale Girls' Grammar Sch., Sheffield, 1952–57; Cheltenham Ladies' Coll., 1957–67; Headmistress, Bermuda Girls' High Sch., 1967–71. Tutor/lecturer in garden history, art history and English literature for Dept for Continuing Educn, Univ. of Oxford, Denman Coll., WI, WEA, English Sch. of Gardening, Inchbald Sch. of Design, V & A, etc., 1985–; Guest Lecturer: Swan's Hellenic Art Treasures Tours, 1990, 1992; Page & Moy, 1993. Mem. Council and Newsletter Editor, Garden Hist. Soc., 1986–; Editor, Garden Hist. Soc. Jl, 1989. *Publications:* monograph on R. Blomfield's designs for the garden at Lady Margaret Hall, Oxford, 1879–1929, 1991; The Gardens of Lady Margaret Hall 1929–1949, 1993; articles in Garden Hist. Soc. Jl and Newsletter, The Northern Gardener, HORTUS and Kipling Soc. Jl. *Recreations:* music, garden history, Venice, photography, calligraphy, writing poetry, collecting books. *Address:* 8 Mavor Close, Old Woodstock, Oxon OX20 1YL. *T:* Woodstock (01993) 811383.

STAMM, Temple Theodore, FRCS; Orthopædic Surgeon Emeritus, Guy's Hospital; *b* 22 Dec. 1905; *s* of Dr Louis Edward Stamm, Streatham, and Louisa Ethel (*née* Perry), Caterham, Surrey; *m* 1945, Pamela, *d* of Charles Russell, Chislehurst, Kent. *Educ:* Rose Hill Sch., Surrey; Haileybury Coll.; Guy's Hospital Medical School. MB, BS (London), 1930, MRCS, LRCP 1928, FRCS 1934. Fellow Royal Society of Medicine; Fellow British Orthopædic Assoc.; Member British Med. Assoc. Formerly: Orthopædic Surgeon, Bromley Hospital, 1941–66; Asst Orthopædic Surgeon and Orthopædic Registrar, Royal Nat. Orthopædic Hospital; Asst Orthopædic Surgeon, Orthopædic Registrar, Asst Anæsthetist and Demonstrator of Anatomy, Guy's Hospital. Major RAMC. *Publications:* Foot Troubles, 1957; Guide to Orthopædics, 1958; Surgery of the Foot, British Surgical Practice, Vol. 4; contributions to Blackburn and Lawrie's Textbook of Surgery, 1958; articles in: Lancet, Guy's Hospital Reports, Journal of Bone and Joint Surgery, Medical Press, etc. *Recreations:* farming, sailing, music. *Address:* Hambrook Lodge, West Ashling, Chichester, West Sussex PO18 8DQ.

STAMP, family name of **Baron Stamp.**

STAMP, 4th Baron *cr* 1938, of Shortlands; **Trevor Charles Bosworth Stamp**, MD; FRCP; Consultant Physician and Director, Department of Bone and Mineral Metabolism, Institute of Orthopaedics, Royal National Orthopaedic Hospital, since 1974; *b* 18 Sept. 1935; *s* of 3rd Baron Stamp, MD, FRCPath and of Frances Hammond, *d* of late Charles Henry Bosworth, Evanston, Illinois, USA; *S* father, 1987; *m* 1st, 1963, Anne Carolynn Churchill (marr. diss. 1971); two *d*; 2nd, 1975, Carol Anne, *d* of Robert Keith Russell; one *s* one *d*. *Educ:* The Leys School; Gonville and Caius Coll., Cambridge; Yale Univ.; St Mary's Hosp. Medical School. MSc (Yale) 1957; MD (Cantab) 1972; FRCP 1978. Qualified in medicine, 1960; Med. Registrar, Professorial Medical Unit, St Mary's Hosp., 1964–66; Hon. Senior Registrar 1968–73, and Hon. Sen. Lecturer 1972–73, Dept of Human Metabolism, University College Hosp. and Medical School; Hon. Consultant Physician and Sen. Lectr, Middlesex Hosp. and UCL School of Medicine, 1974–. Prix André Lichtwitz, France, 1973. *Publications:* numerous papers on disorders of mineral metabolism. *Recreations:* music, tennis, contract bridge. *Heir: s* Hon. Nicholas Charles Trevor Stamp, *b* 27 Feb. 1978. *Address:* Pennyroyal, Village Lane, Hedgerley, Bucks SL2 3UY. *T:* Farnham Common (01753) 642737.

STAMP, Gavin Mark, MA, PhD; architectural historian and writer; Lecturer, Mackintosh School of Architecture, Glasgow, since 1990; *b* 15 March 1948; *s* of Barry Hartnell Stamp and Norah Clare (*née* Rich); *m* 1982, Alexandra Frances Artley; two *d*. *Educ:* Dulwich Coll.; Gonville & Caius Coll., Cambridge (MA, PhD). Contributor to The Spectator, The Independent, Daily Telegraph, Private Eye, Architects' Jl, etc. Chm., Twentieth Century (formerly Thirties) Soc., 1983–; Founder and Chm., Alexander Thomson Soc., 1991–. Hon. FRIAS 1994. *Publications:* The Architect's Calendar, 1973; Silent Cities, 1977; (text only) Temples of Power, 1979; (jtly) The Victorian Buildings of London 1837–1887, 1980; Robert Weir Schultz and his work for the Marquesses of Bute, 1981; The Great Perspectivists, 1982; The Changing Metropolis, 1984; The English House 1860–1914, 1986; (jtly) The Church in Crisis, 1986; The Telephone Boxes, 1989; (ed jtly) Greek Thomson, 1994; articles in Arch. History, Arch. Design, Jl of RSA, etc. *Address:* 1 Moray Place, Strathbungo, Glasgow G41 2AQ. *T:* 0141–423 3747.

STAMP, Terence Henry; actor and director; *b* 22 July 1938; *s* of Thomas Stamp and Ethel Esther Perrott. *Educ:* Plaistow County Grammar School; Webber-Douglas Dramatic Acad. (Amehurst Webber Meml Schol., 1958). *Films include:* Billy Budd, 1962; The Collector, 1964; Far from the Madding Crowd, 1966; Blue, 1967; Spirits of the Dead, 1967; Theorem, 1968; Superman, 1977; Meetings with Remarkable Men, 1977; Superman 2, 1978; The Hit, 1984; Legal Eagles, 1985; Wall Street, 1987; Young Guns, 1988; The Sicilian, 1988; Alien Nation, 1989; Prince of Shadows, or Beltenebros, 1993; The Real McCoy, 1994; The Adventures of Priscilla the Queen of the Desert, 1994; *stage:* Alfie, Morosco, NY, 1965; Dracula, Shaftesbury, 1978; Lady from the Sea, Roundhouse, 1979. Hon. DArts East London, 1993. *Publications:* autobiography: Stamp Album, 1987; Coming Attractions, 1988; Double Feature, 1989; The Night (novel), 1992. *Address:* c/o Markham & Froggatt, 4 Windmill Street, W1P 1HF. *Club:* New York Athletic (New York).

STAMPER, John Trevor, MA; FEng, Hon. FRAeS, CIMgt; Corporate Technical Director, British Aerospace, 1977–85, retired; *b* 12 Oct. 1926; *s* of late Col Horace John Stamper and Clara Jane (*née* Collin); *m* 1950, Cynthia Joan Parsons; two *s* one *d*. *Educ:* Loughborough Grammar Sch.; Jesus Coll., Cambridge (MA 1951). FRAeS 1965 (Hon. FRAeS 1984); CEng 1966; FEng 1977; CIMgt (CBIM 1983). Blackburn Aircraft Ltd: Post-grad. apprenticeship, 1947; Dep. Head of Aerodynamics, 1955; Head of Structures, 1956; Flight Test Manager, 1960; Chief Designer (Buccaneer), 1961; Dir and Chief Designer, 1963; Hawker Siddeley Aviation Ltd (following merger): Exec. Dir Design (Military), 1966; Exec. Dir and Dep. Chief Engr (Civil), 1968; Tech. Dir, 1968–77. Member: Council, RAeS, 1971–77, 1978–88 (Pres., 1981–82); Tech. Bd, SBAC, 1966–85 (Chm., 1972–74); Council, SBAC, 1981–84; Council, Aircraft Res. Assoc., 1966–85 (Chm., 1976–78); Aeronautical Res. Council, 1971–74; Air Warfare Adv. Bd, Defence Scientific Adv. Council, 1973–84; Noise Adv. Council, 1975–78; Comité Technique et Industriel, Assoc. Européenne des Constructeurs de Matériel Aerospatial, 1971–81 (Chm., 1974–81); Airworthiness Requirements Bd, CAA, 1976–78, 1987–88. Hon. DSc Loughborough, 1986. Hodgeson Prize, RAeS, 1975 and 1986; British Gold Medal for Aeronautics, RAeS, 1976. *Publications:* (contrib.) The Future of Aeronautics, 1970; Air Power in the Next Generation, 1979; papers in Jl RAeS. *Recreations:* sailing, photography. *Address:* 7 Sycamore Close, The Mount, Fetcham, Surrey KT22 9EX. *T:* Fetcham (01372) 370336.

STANAGE, Rt. Rev. Thomas Shaun; *see* Bloemfontein, Bishop of.

STANBRIDGE, Air Vice-Marshal Sir Brian (Gerald Tivy), KCVO 1979 (MVO 1958); CBE 1974; AFC 1952; Director-General, Air Transport Users' Committee, 1979–85; *b* 6 July 1924; *s* of late Gerald Edward and Violet Georgina Stanbridge; *m* 1st, 1949, Kathleen Diana Hayes (marr. diss. 1983); two *d*; 2nd, 1984, Jennifer Anne Jenkins. *Educ:* Thurlestone Coll., Dartmouth. Served War: RAFVR, 1942; commnd, 1944; No 31 Sqdn (SE Asia), 1944–46; No 47 Sqdn, 1947–49; 2FTS/CFS, 1950–52; British Services Mission to Burma, 1952–54; The Queen's Flight (personal pilot and flying instructor to Duke of Edinburgh), 1954–58; Naval Staff Coll., 1958; PSO to AOC-in-C Coastal Comd, 1958–59; W/Cdr, Flying, RAF St Mawgan, 1960–62; jssc, 1962; RAFDS, Army Staff Coll., Camberley, 1962–63; Gp Captain on staff of NATO Standing Gp, Washington, DC, 1963–66; RAF Dir, Jt Anti-Submarine Sch., Londonderry, and Sen. RAF Officer, NI, 1966–68; Gp Captain Ops, HQ Coastal Comd, 1968–70; IDC, 1970; Air Cdre, 1970; Sec., Chiefs of Staff Cttee, MoD, 1971–73; Dep. Comdt, RAF Staff Coll., Bracknell, 1973–75; ADC to the Queen, 1973–75; Air Vice-Marshal, 1975; Defence Services Sec. to the Queen, 1975–79; retired 1979. Pres., No 31 Sqdn Assoc., 1992–. *Address:* 20 Durrant Way, Sway, Lymington, Hants SO41 6DQ. *Club:* Royal Air Force.

STANBRIDGE, Ven. Leslie Cyril; Archdeacon of York, 1972–88, Archdeacon Emeritus since 1988; *b* 19 May 1920. *Educ:* Bromley County Grammar Sch., Kent; St John's Coll., Durham Univ. (MA, DipTheol). Asst Curate of Erith Parish Church, Kent, 1949–51; Tutor and Chaplain, St John's Coll., Durham, 1951–55; Vicar of St Martin's, Hull, 1955–64; Examining Chaplain to the Archbishop of York, 1962–74; Rector of Cottingham, Yorks, 1964–72; Canon of York, 1968–; Succentor Canonicorum, 1988–; Rural Dean of Kingston-upon-Hull, 1970–72; Warden, York Diocesan Readers' Assoc., 1988–95. *Recreations:* fell walking, cycling. *Address:* 1 Deangate, York YO1 2JB. *T:* York (01904) 621174.

STANBROOK, Clive St George Clement, OBE 1987; QC 1989; Partner, Stanbrook & Hooper, since 1980; *b* 10 April 1948; *s* of Ivor Robert Stanbrook, *qv*; *m* 1971, Julia Suzanne Stanbrook; one *s* three *d*. *Educ:* Dragon Sch.; Westminster; University Coll. London. Called to the Bar, Inner Temple, 1972; called to Turks and Caicos Bar, 1986, New York Bar, 1988. Founded Stanbrook & Hooper, 1980. Pres., British Chamber of Commerce for Belgium and Luxembourg, 1985–87. *Publications:* Extradition: the law and practice, 1979; Dumping: manual of EEC rules, 1980; Dumping and Subsidies, 1985. *Recreations:* tennis, travel. *Address:* 42 Rue du Taciturne, Brussels 1040, Belgium.

STANBROOK, Ivor Robert; writer; *b* 13 Jan. 1924; *y s* of Arthur William and Lilian Stanbrook; *m* 1946, Joan (*née* Clement); two *s*. *Educ:* state schools; Univs of London (BSc (Econ) 1948), Oxford and East Anglia (PhD 1995). Served RAF, 1942–46. Colonial Administrative Service, Nigeria, 1950–60: Asst Sec., Council of Ministers, Lagos, 1956; Dist Officer, N Region, 1957–60. Called to the Bar, Inner Temple, 1960; practising barrister, 1960–90. Contested (C) East Ham, South, 1966. MP (C) Orpington, 1970–92. Chairman: All Party gps on Nigeria, 1979–92, Zambia, 1985–92, Southern Africa, 1987–92; Cons. parly cttees on constitutional affairs, 1985–92, on Northern Ireland, 1989–92; Member: Court of Referees, 1979–92; Select Cttee on Home Affairs, 1983–91; Exec., UK Br., CPA, 1988–89; UK Parly Observer, Zimbabwe independence elections, 1980. Founded Britain-Nigeria Assoc., 1961. Vice-Pres., Kent Opera, 1987–92. *Publications:* Extradition—the Law and Practice, 1979; British Nationality—the New Law, 1981; A Year in Politics, 1988; How to be an MP, 1993. *Recreations:* music, books. *Clubs:* Commonwealth Trust, Royal Over-Seas League.

See also C. St G. C. Stanbrook.

STANBURY, Richard Vivian Macaulay; HM Diplomatic Service, retired; *b* 5 Feb. 1916; *s* of late Gilbert Vivian Stanbury and Doris Marguerite (*née* Smythe); *m* 1953, Geraldine Anne, *d* of late R. F. W. Grant and of Winifred Helen Grant; one *s* one *d*. *Educ:* Shrewsbury Sch. (exhibnr); Magdalene Coll., Cambridge (exhibnr, 1st cl. Hons in Classical Tripos). Sudan Political Service, 1937–50 (District Comr in 12 districts, and Magistrate); HM Foreign (subseq. Diplomatic) Service, 1951–71: 2nd Sec., Cairo, 1951; FO 1954; Bahrain, Persian Gulf, 1956; FO 1959; Counsellor, Buenos Aires, 1968. *Recreations:* tennis, golf, and watching cricket (played for Somerset). *Address:* Shepherds House, Peasmarsh, near Rye, East Sussex TN31 6TF. *Clubs:* Naval & Military; Hawks (Cambridge); Rye Golf; Hurlingham (Buenos Aires).

STANBURY, Prof. Sydney William, MD, FRCP; Professor of Medicine, University of Manchester, 1965–84, now Emeritus; *b* 21 April 1919; *s* of F. A. W. Stanbury and A. B. Stanbury (*née* Rowe); *m* 1943, Helen, *d* of Harry and Patty Jackson; one *s* four *d*. *Educ:* Hulme Grammar Sch., Oldham; Manchester Univ. MB, ChB (1st Cl. Hons) 1942; MD (Gold Medal) 1948; MRCP 1947, FRCP 1958. Served RAMC, Burma and India, 1944–47. Beit Meml Res. Fellow, 1948–51; Rockefeller Travelling Fellow, 1951–52; Registrar, Lectr and Reader, Dept of Medicine, Manchester Royal Infirmary, 1947–65; Consultant Phys., United Manchester Hosps, 1959–. Member: Assoc. of Physicians; Bone and Tooth Soc. Visiting Professor: John Howard Means, Massachusetts Gen. Hosp., Boston, 1958; Henry M. Winans, Univ. of Texas, Dallas, 1958; W. T. Connoll, Queen's Univ., Kingston, Ont, 1978; Weild Lectr, RCP and S, Glasgow, 1958; Lumleian Lectr, RCP, 1981; Vis. Lectr: Univ. of Washington, Mayo Clinic, etc. *Publications:* contrib. European and American med. books and jls on: renal function, electrolyte metabolism, metabolic bone disease and vitamin D metabolism. *Recreation:* gardening. *Address:* Halamana, Gillan, Manaccan, Helston, Cornwall TR12 6HL. *T:* Manaccan (01326) 231586.

STANCIOFF, Ivan; Ambassador-at-Large for Bulgaria, since 1994; *b* 1 April 1929; *s* of late Ivan Robert Stancioff and Marion (*née* Mitchell); *m* 1st, 1957, Deirdre O'Donnell (marr. diss.); two *s* two *d*; 2nd, Alexandra Lawrence. *Educ:* Georgetown Univ., Washington (BA); New York Univ. Sch. of Business. Economist, Amer. and Foreign Power Corp., 1957–60; Dir Marketing, IBM World Trade Corp., São Paulo, 1961–63; Rio, 1963–65; Paris, 1965–70; Manager, ITT, Athens, 1970; Vice-Pres., ITEL Corp., London, 1971–74; Dir, Safestore Ltd, London, 1975–77; Vice-Pres., Storage Technol. Corp., London, 1977–81; Dir, Cresta Marketing SA, Geneva, 1981–90; Advr to UDF, Sofia, 1990–91; Ambassador to UK, 1991–94; Minister of Foreign Affairs, Bulgaria, 1994–95. Dir, Inst. for Intercultural Relations, Sofia, 1992. Mem. Bd, Friends of Bulgaria, 1990–. Mem., Sustrans, Bristol, 1989–. FLS; FRGS. Good Conduct Medal, US Army, 1956; Commander, Legion of Honour (France), 1994. *Recreations:* history, gardening, travel, painting. *Address:* 28 Cresswell Place, SW10 9RB. *Clubs:* Athenæum, Annabel's.

STANCLIFFE, Rt. Rev. David Staffurth; *see* Salisbury, Bishop of.

STANCLIFFE, Martin John, RIBA; Surveyor to the Fabric, St Paul's Cathedral, since 1990; *b* 28 Dec. 1944; *s* of Very Rev. Michael Staffurth Stancliffe and Barbara Elizabeth Tatlow; *m* 1979, Sara Judith Sanders; two *d*. *Educ:* Westminster Sch.; Magdalene Coll., Cambridge (MA, DipArch). Private architectural practice, 1975–; Architect to: Lichfield

Cath., 1983–; Southwell Minster, 1989–; Christ Church Cath., Oxford, 1990–. Member: Exec. Cttee, Council for the Care of Churches, 1980–91; Cathedrals' Fabric Commn for England, 1991–; Archbishops' Commn on Cathedrals, 1992–94; Historic Bldgs and Areas Adv. Cttee, English Heritage, 1995–. *Recreations:* the baroque oboe, old buildings, travel. *Address:* 29 Marygate, York YO3 7BH. *T:* York (01904) 644001.

See also Bishop of Salisbury.

STANDARD, Prof. Sir Kenneth (Livingstone), Kt 1982; CD 1976; MD, MPH; FFPHM; Professor, 1968, and Head of Department of Social and Preventive Medicine, 1966–89, University of the West Indies at Mona; Emeritus Professor, University of the West Indies, 1990; *b* 8 Dec. 1920; *m* 1955, Evelyn Francis; one *d*. *Educ:* UC of West Indies (MB BS); Univ. of Pittsburgh (MPH); Univ. of London (MD). FFPHM (FFCM 1972). Schoolmaster, Lynch's Secondary Sch., Barbados, 1940–48 (Headmaster, 1948); Med. House Officer, UCH of WI, 1956; MO, Nutrition Res., Jamaica, 1957–58; MOH, Barbados, 1958–61; MO, MRC Epidemiol. Res. Unit, Jamaica, 1961–66; Lectr, 1961–65, Sen. Lectr, 1965–68, Dept of Social and Preventive Medicine, Univ. of WI, Jamaica. Adjunct Prof. of Public Health, Grad. Sch. Public Health, Univ. of Pittsburgh, 1972–75; Stubenbord Vis. Prof., Cornell Univ. Med. Coll., USA, 1975–. Thomas Parran Lecture, Grad. Sch. of Public Health, Univ. of Pittsburgh, 1984. Member: WHO Adv. Cttee on Med. Res., 1969–72; WHO Expert Adv. Panel on Public Health Admin, 1969–. Foundn Pres., Caribbean Public Health Assoc., 1988–92. Fellow, Caribbean Coll. of Family Physicians, 1988. Fellowship, 1980, Medal, 1981, Jacques Parisot Foundn, WHO; Abraham Horwitz Award, Pan American Health and Educn Foundn, 1988; Health for All Medal, WHO, 1988; Medical Alumni Pioneer Award, Univ. of WI, 1988. *Publications:* (ed jtly) Manual for Community Health Workers, 1974, rev. edn 1983; Epidemiology and Community Health in Warm Climate Countries, 1976; Alternatives in the Delivery of Health Services, 1976; Four Decades of Advances in Health in the Commonwealth Caribbean, 1979. *Recreations:* reading, poetry, gardening. *Address:* Department of Social and Preventive Medicine, University of the West Indies, Mona, Kingston 7, Jamaica. *T:* 9272476. *Club:* Commonwealth Trust.

STANDING, John; *see* Leon, Sir J. R.

STANES, Ven. Ian Thomas; Archdeacon of Loughborough, since 1992; *b* 29 Jan. 1939; *s* of Sydney Stanes and Iris Stanes (*née* Hulme); *m* 1962, Sylvia Alice (*née* Drew); one *d* (one *s* decd). *Educ:* Sheffield Univ. (BSc 1962); Linacre Coll., Oxford (BA 1965; MA 1969); Wycliffe Hall, Oxford. Ordained: deacon, 1965; priest, 1966; Curate, Holy Apostles, Leicester, 1965–69; Vicar, Broom Leys, Coalville, Leicester, 1969–76; Priest Warden, Marrick Priory, Ripon, 1976–82; Willesden Area Officer for Mission, Ministry and Evangelism, London, 1982–92. Prebendary, St Paul's Cathedral, 1989–92. *Recreations:* hockey, rock climbing, walking, photography, music, drama, art appreciation. *Address:* The Archdeaconry, 21 Church Road, Glenfield, Leicester LE3 8DP. *T:* Leicester (0116) 231 1632.

STANESBY, Rev. Canon Derek Malcolm, PhD; SOSc; Canon of St George's Chapel, Windsor, since 1985; *b* 28 March 1931; *s* of Laurence J. C. Stanesby and late Elsie L. Stanesby (*née* Stean); *m* 1958, Christine A. Payne; three *s* one *d*. *Educ:* Orange Hill Central School, London; Northampton Polytechnic, London; Leeds Univ. (BA Hons); Manchester Univ. (MEd, PhD); College of the Resurrection, Mirfield. GPO Radio Research Station, Dollis Hill, 1947–51; RAF (Navigator), 1951–53. Ordained, 1958; Curate: Old Lakenham, Norwich, 1958–61; St Mary, Welling, Dio. Southwark, 1961–63; Vicar, St Mark, Bury, Dio. Manchester, 1963–67; Rector, St Chad, Ladybarn, Manchester, 1967–85. Mem., Archbishop's Commn on Christian Doctrine, 1986–91. FRSA 1993. *Publications:* Science, Reason and Religion, 1985; various articles. *Recreations:* hill walking, sailing, woodwork, idling. *Address:* 4 The Cloisters, Windsor Castle, Berks SL4 1NJ. *T:* Windsor (01753) 864142.

STANFIELD, Hon. Robert Lorne, PC (Canada) 1967; QC; Chairman, Institute for Research on Public Policy, 1981–86; *b* Truro, NS, 11 April 1914; *s* of late Frank Stanfield, sometime MLA and Lieutenant-Governor of NS, and Sarah (*née* Thomas); *m* 1st, 1940, N. Joyce (*d* 1954), *d* of C. W. Frazee, Vancouver; one *s* three *d*; 2nd, 1957, Mary Margaret (*d* 1977), *d* of late Hon. W. L. Hall, Judge of Supreme Court and formerly Attorney-Gen. of NS; 3rd, 1978, Anne Margaret Austin, *d* of Dr D. Nelson, Henderson, Toronto. *Educ:* Colchester County Academy, Truro; Ashbury Coll., Ottawa; Dalhousie Univ.; Harvard Law Sch. Southam Cup, Ashbury Coll.; BA Political Science and Economics 1936, Governor-General's Gold Medal, Dalhousie Univ.; LLB Harvard, 1939. War of 1939–45: attached Halifax Office of Wartime Prices and Trade Bd as Regional Rentals Officer, later as Enforcement Counsel. Admitted Bar of NS, 1940. Practised law, McInnes and Stanfield, Halifax, 1945–56; KC 1950. President, Nova Scotia Progressive Cons. Assoc., 1947–48; Leader, Nova Scotia Progressive Cons. Party, 1948–67; elected to Legislature of NS, 1949, Mem. for Colchester Co.; re-elected Mem., 1953, 1960, 1963, 1967; Premier and Minister of Education, NS, 1956; resigned as Premier of NS, 1967; MP (Progressive C): Colchester-Hants, NS, 1967–68; Halifax, NS, 1968–79; Leader, Progressive Cons. Party of Canada, and of Opposition in House of Commons, 1967–74. Ambassador at Large and special representative of Govt of Canada in Middle East, 1979–80. Dir, Canada Life. Chm., Commonwealth Foundn. Hon. LLD: University of New Brunswick, 1958; St Dunstan's Univ., PEI, 1964; McGill Univ., PQ, 1967; St Mary's Univ., NS, 1969; Dalhousie, 1982; Université Sainte-Anne, NS, Acadia Univ., NS, and Univ. of Toronto, 1987; Mount Allison Univ., 1990. Anglican. *Address:* 136 Acacia Avenue, Rockcliffe Park, Ottawa, Ontario K1M 0R1, Canada.

STANFORD, James Keith Edward; Director General, Leonard Cheshire Foundation, since 1991; *b* 12 April 1937; *s* of late Lt-Col J. K. Stanford, OBE, MC, author and naturalist, and Eleanor Stanford; *m* 1964, Carol Susan Harbord; one *s* one *d*. *Educ:* Rugby Sch.; RMA Sandhurst. 17th/21st Lancers, 1955–64; IBM Corp., 1965–72; industry and City, 1973–90; Chm., David Brown Corp., 1987–90. Dir, Aerospace Engrg, 1990–94. Gov., Holiday Care Service, 1991–. *Recreations:* country activities. *Address:* Grange Farm, Spratton, Northants NN6 8LA. *T:* Northampton (01604) 846500. *Club:* Cavalry and Guards.

STANFORD, Peter James; writer and broadcaster; *b* 23 Nov. 1961; *s* of Reginald James Hughes Stanford and Mary Catherine (*née* Fleming); *m* 1995, Siobhan, *d* of James and Celine Cross. *Educ:* St Anselm's Coll., Birkenhead; Merton Coll., Oxford (BA Hons 1983). Reporter, The Tablet, 1983–84; News Editor, 1984–88, Editor, 1988–92, The Catholic Herald. Chm., ASPIRE (Assoc. for Spinal Res., Reintegration and Rehabilitation), 1992–. Dir, CandCo Dance Co., 1994–. *Publications:* (ed) Hidden Hands: child workers around the world, 1988; (with Simon Lee) Believing Bishops, 1990; (ed) The Seven Deadly Sins, 1990; (with Kate Saunders) Catholics and Sex, 1992 (televised, 1992; Bronze Medal, NY TV Fest., 1993); Cardinal Hume and the changing face of English Catholicism, 1993; Lord Longford: an authorised life, 1994; (jtly) The Anatomy of the Catholic Church, 1994; (with Leanda de Liste) The Catholics and their Houses, 1995. *Recreations:* soap operas, vases, photography, credit cards. *Address:* 8 Healey Street, NW1 8SR. *T:* 0171–482 0364.

STANGER, David Harry, OBE 1987; IEng; FIQA; Secretary General, European Organisation for Testing and Certification, since 1993; *b* 14 Feb. 1939; *s* of Charles Harry Stanger, CBE and Florence Bessie Hepworth Stanger; *m* 1963, Jill Patricia (*née* Barnes); one *s* two *d*. *Educ:* Oundle Sch.; Millfield Sch. IEng (TEng 1971); FFB 1977; FIQA 1982; MSocIS 1982. Served Corps of RE, 1960–66; joined R. H. Harry Stanger, 1966; Partner, Al Hoty-Stanger Ltd, 1975; Chm. and Man. Dir, Harry Stanger Ltd, 1975–90 (Sen. Partner, 1972–85); non-exec. Chm., Stanger Consultants Ltd, 1990–93. Chm., Adv. Cttee, NAMAS, 1985–87. Sec. Gen., Union Internationale des Laboratoires Indépendants, 1983–93. Member: Steering Cttee, NATLAS, 1981–87; Adv. Council for Calibration and Measurement, 1982–87; Council, EUROLAB, 1990–93; Chairman: Standards, Quality and Measurement Adv. Cttee, 1988–92; British Measurement and Testing Assoc., 1990–93; Inst. of Quality Assurance, 1990–93 (a Vice-Pres., 1986–); Adv. Bd, Brunel Centre for Manufacturing Metrology, 1991–93. Pingat Peringatan, Malaysia, 1966. *Recreation:* collecting vintage wines. *Address:* EOTC, Egmont House, rue d'Egmonstraat 15, 1050 Brussels, Belgium. *T:* (2) 5024141; ave Louis Lepourte 116, 1060 Brussels, Belgium. *T:* (2) 3464371. *Club:* Carlton.

STANHOPE, family name of **Earl of Harrington.**

STANIER, Sir Beville (Douglas), 3rd Bt *cr* 1917, of Peplow Hall, Hodnet, Salop; farmer, since 1976; *b* 20 April 1934; *o s* of Brig. Sir Alexander Stanier, 2nd Bt, DSO, MC and Dorothy Gladys Miller (*d* 1973); *S* father, 1995; *m* 1963, Shelagh Sinnott; one *s* two *d*. *Educ:* Eton Coll. Joined Welsh Guards, 1952; commnd 2nd Lieut, 1953; Lieut, 1955; Captain, 1958; ADC to Governor-General of Australia, 1959–60. Stockbroker with Kitcat & Aitken, 1960–76 (Partner, 1968–76). *Recreations:* shooting, cricket. *Heir:* *s* Alexander James Sinnott Stanier, *b* 10 April 1970. *Address:* Kings Close House, Whaddon, Buckinghamshire MK17 0NG. *T:* Milton Keynes (01908) 501738. *Club:* MCC.

STANIER, Field Marshal Sir John (Wilfred), GCB 1982 (KCB 1978); MBE 1961; DL; Constable, HM Tower of London, since 1990; *b* 6 Oct. 1925; *s* of late Harold Allan Stanier and Penelope Rose Stanier (*née* Price); *m* 1955, Cicely Constance Lambert; four *d*. *Educ:* Marlborough Coll.; Merton Coll., Oxford. FRGS. Commd in 7th Queen's Own Hussars, 1946; served in N Italy, Germany and Hong Kong; comd Royal Scots Greys, 1966–68; comd 20th Armd Bde, 1969–70; GOC 1st Div., 1973–75; Comdt, Staff Coll., Camberley, 1975–78; Vice Chief of the General Staff, 1978–80; C-in-C, UKLF, 1981–82; CGS, 1982–85. ADC General to the Queen, 1981–85. Col, The Royal Scots Dragoon Guards, 1979–84; Col Comdt, RAC, 1982–85. Chm., RUSI, 1986–89. Pres., Hampshire Br., British Red Cross Soc., 1986–94. Mem. Council, Marlborough Coll., 1984–. DL Hampshire, 1987. *Recreations:* fishing, sailing, talking. *Address:* c/o Coutts & Co., Adelaide Branch, 440 Strand, WC2R 0QS. *Club:* Cavalry and Guards.

STANIFORTH, John Arthur Reginald, CBE 1969; Director: Constructors John Brown, 1947–84 (Chief Executive and Deputy Chairman, 1958–84); John Brown & Co., Ltd, 1965–84; John Brown Engineering (Clydebank) Ltd, 1968–84 (Chm., 1970–77); *b* 19 Sept. 1912; *o s* of Captain Staniforth, MC, Anston House, Anston, Yorks; *m* 1936, Penelope Cecile, *y d* of Maj.-Gen. Sir Henry Freeland; one *d* (one *s* decd). *Educ:* Marlborough Coll. With John Brown Group, 1929–84. Mem., Export Guarantees Adv. Council, 1971–76, Dep. Chm., 1975–76. Founder Chm., British Chemical Engrg Contractors Assoc., 1965–68; former Chm., Oil and Chemical Plant Assoc. Dir, St Wilfrid's Hospice (South Coast), 1981–92. Governor, Bryanston Sch., 1962–92. *Recreations:* golf, fishing. *Address:* 11 The Holdens, Old Bosham, West Sussex PO18 8LN. *T:* Bosham (01243) 572401. *Clubs:* MCC (Hon. Mem., 1991); Goodwood Golf and Country (Hon. Mem., 1994).

STANISZEWSKI, Stefan; Commander's Cross, Order of Polonia Restituta, and other orders; Ambassador of Poland to Libya, since 1990; *b* 11 Feb. 1931; *s* of Andrzej and Katarzyna Staniszewski; *m* 1953, Wanda Szuszkiewicz; one *d*. *Educ:* Warsaw Univ. (BA Philosophy); Jagiellonian Univ. (BA Pol. Sciences). Active in students' and social organizations, 1951–58; Head of Editorial Dept, ISKRY state publishing firm, 1958–60; entered foreign service, 1960; Minister's Cabinet, Min. of Foreign Affairs, 1960–63; successively 2nd Sec., 1st Sec. and Counsellor, Polish Embassy, Paris, 1963–69; Head of West European Dept and Mem. of Minister's Council, Min. of Foreign Affairs, 1969–72; Ambassador to Sweden, 1972–77; Head of Press, Cultural and Scientific Co-operation Dept, Min. of Foreign Affairs, 1977–81; Ambassador to UK, 1981–86, and to Ireland, 1984–86; Head of Press and Information Dept, 1986–90, and spokesman, 1988–90, Polish Min. of Foreign Affairs. Commander, Légion d'Honneur, 1972; Order of the Star of the North, Sweden, 1977; Commander, Order of the Aztec Eagle, Mexico, 1979. *Recreation:* swimming. *Address:* Embassy of the Republic of Poland, PO Box 519, 61 Shia Ben Ashour, Tripoli, Libya. *T:* (21) 607619.

STANLEY, family name of **Earl of Derby** and **Baron Stanley of Alderley.**

STANLEY OF ALDERLEY, 8th Baron (UK) *cr* 1839; **Thomas Henry Oliver Stanley;** Bt 1660; Baron Sheffield (Ire), 1783; Baron Eddisbury, 1848; DL; Captain (retired), Coldstream Guards; Tenant Farmer of New College, Oxford, since 1954; *b* 28 Sept. 1927; *s* of Lt-Col The Hon. Oliver Hugh Stanley, DSO, JP (3rd *s* of 4th Baron) (*d* 1952), and Lady Kathleen Stanley (*d* 1977), *e d* of 5th Marquess of Bath; *S* cousin (known as Baron Sheffield), 1971; *m* 1955, Jane Barrett, *d* of Ernest George Hartley; three *s* one *d*. *Educ:* Wellington College, Berks. Coldstream Guards, 1945–52; Guards Parachute Battalion and Independent Company, 1947–50; Northamptonshire Institute of Agriculture, 1952–53. Mem., Cttee of Management, RNLI, 1981–; Chm., Fund Raising Cttee, RNLI, 1985–94. Governor, St Edward's Sch., Oxford, 1979–. DL Gwynedd, 1985. *Recreations:* sailing, skiing, fishing. *Heir:* *e s* Hon. Richard Oliver Stanley, BSc [*b* 24 April 1956; *m* 1983, Carla, *er d* of Dr K. T. C. McKenzie, Solihull; three *d* (one *s* decd)]. *Address:* Trysglwyn Fawr, Amlwch, Anglesey LL68 9RF. *T:* Amlwch (01407) 830364; Rectory Farm, Stanton St John, Oxford OX9 1HF. *T:* Stanton St John (01865) 351214. *Club:* Farmers'.

STANLEY, Colin; *see* Stanley, G. C.

STANLEY, Derek Peter; His Honour Judge Stanley; a Circuit Judge, since 1994; *b* 7 Aug. 1947; *s* of Peter Stanley and Vera Stanley (*née* Sterry-Cooper); *m* 1971, Gabrielle Mary Tully; one *s* two *d*. *Educ:* Solihull Sch.; Inns of Court Sch. of Law. Called to the Bar, Gray's Inn, 1968; practised on Midland and Oxford Circuit, 1969–94; a Recorder, 1988–94. Mem., Bar Council, 1989–91. *Recreations:* squash, tennis, sailing, church music. *Address:* Birmingham Crown Court, Newton Street, Birmingham B4 7NA. *T:* 021–236 9751. *Club:* Edgbaston Priory (Birmingham).

STANLEY, Prof. Eric Gerald, MA (Oxford and Yale); PhD (Birmingham); FBA 1985; Rawlinson and Bosworth Professor of Anglo-Saxon in the University of Oxford, and Fellow of Pembroke College, Oxford, 1977–91; Emeritus Professor and Fellow, since 1991; *b* 19 Oct. 1923; *m* 1959, Mary Bateman, MD, FRCP; one *d*. *Educ:* Queen Elizabeth's Grammar Sch., Blackburn; University Coll., Oxford. Lectr in Eng. Lang. and Lit., Birmingham Univ., 1951–62; Reader in Eng. Lang. and Lit., 1962–64, Prof. of English, 1964–75, Univ. of London at QMC; Prof. of English, Yale Univ., 1975–76. Mem., Mediaeval Acad. of America, 1975–; Corresponding Member: Fryske Akad.,

Netherlands, 1991–; Bavarian Acad. of Scis, 1994–. Sir Israel Gollancz Meml Lectr, British Acad., 1984. Co-Editor, Notes and Queries, 1963–. *Publications:* (ed) The Owl and the Nightingale, 1960, 2nd edn 1972; The Search for Anglo-Saxon Paganism, 1975; A Collection of Papers with Emphasis on Old English Literature, 1987; In the Foreground: Beowulf, 1994; academic articles. *Recreations:* photography, travel. *Address:* Pembroke College, Oxford OX1 1DW. *Club:* Athenæum.

STANLEY, (Geoffrey) Colin; Director General, British Printing Industries Federation, 1988–95; Director, John Howitt Group Ltd; *b* 3 May 1937; *s* of Harold Bertram Smerdon Stanley and Ruth Mary (*née* Dunn); *m* 1962, Lesley Shadrach McWilliam; one *s* one *d*. *Educ:* Wallasey Grammar Sch. Joined Wiggins Teape, 1957: Director and General Manager: Wiggins Teape Toys & Crafts, 1976–78; Wiggins Teape Stationery Ltd, 1979–82; Dir and Manager, Wiggins Teape Paper Ltd, 1982–87; Dir, Wiggins Teape (UK) plc, 1983–85. Pres., Nat. Assoc. of Paper Merchants, 1986–88. Mem., Council, CBI, 1988–95 (Chm., Industrial Relns, Wages and Conditions Cttee, 1992–95; Mem., Employment Affairs Cttee, 1992–95). FRSA 1991. Freeman, City of London, 1985; Liveryman, Co. of Stationers & Newspaper Makers, 1987–. *Recreations:* squash, weekend gardening, music, reading. *Address:* 2 Abbey Hill Close, Winchester, Hants SO23 7AZ. *Club:* National Liberal.

STANLEY, Henry Sydney Herbert Cloete, CMG 1968; HM Diplomatic Service, retired; British High Commissioner to Trinidad and Tobago and (non-resident) to Grenada, 1977–80; *b* 5 March 1920; *er s* of late Sir Herbert Stanley, GCMG and Reniera (*née* Cloete), DBE; *m* 1941, Margaret (*d* 1994), *d* of late Professor H. B. Dixon, CBE, FRS; three *s*. *Educ:* Eton; Balliol College, Oxford. Served with King's Royal Rifle Corps, 1940–46 (Capt.); N-W Europe, 1944–46, also HQ, CCG. Appointed to Commonwealth Relations Office, 1947. Served in Pakistan, 1950–52; Swaziland and South Africa, 1954–57; USA, 1959–61; Tanganyika, 1961–63; Kenya, 1963–65; Inspector, HM Diplomatic Service, 1966–68, Chief Inspector, 1968–70; High Comr, Ghana, 1970–75; Asst Under Sec. of State, FCO, 1975–77; High Comr for the New Hebrides (non-resident), 1976–77. *Address:* 8 Birch Grove, W3 9SN.

STANLEY, Rev. Canon John Alexander; Vicar of Huyton, since 1974; Chaplain to the Queen, since 1993; *b* 20 May 1931; *s* of Edward Alexander Stanley and Lucy Vida Stanley; *m* 1956, (Flora) Elaine Wilkes; three *s* two *d*. *Educ:* Birkenhead Sch.; Tyndale Hall Theol Coll., Bristol. Assistant Curate: All Saints', Preston, 1956; St Mark's, St Helens, 1960; Vicar, St Cuthbert's, Everton, Liverpool, 1963; Priest in Charge, St Saviour, Everton, 1969; Vicar, St Saviour with St Cuthbert, Everton, 1970; Area Dean of Huyton, 1989–; Hon. Canon of Liverpool Cathedral, 1987–. Mem., Gen. Synod, and Proctor in Convocation, 1973–; Chm., Diocesan House of Clergy, 1979–85; Prolocutor, York Convocation, 1990–. A Church Comr, 1983– (Mem., Bd of Govs, 1989–); Mem., BCC, 1984–87; Trustee, Church Urban Fund, 1987–. *Recreations:* golf, bees, photography. *Address:* The Vicarage, Huyton, Merseyside L36 7SA. *T:* 0151–449 3900, *Fax:* 0151–480 6002.

STANLEY, John Mallalieu; Under Secretary (Legal), Department of Trade and Industry, since 1989; *b* 30 Sept. 1941; *s* of William and Rose Margaret Stanley; *m* 1968, Christine Mary Cunningham; two *s* one *d*. *Educ:* Welwyn Garden City Grammar Sch.; Clare College, Cambridge (MA). Solicitor. Church, Adams, Tatham & Co., 1965–68; Jaques & Co., 1968–75; Dept of Industry, later of Trade and Industry, 1975–. *Address:* Department of Trade and Industry, 10–18 Victoria Street, SW1H 0NN. *T:* 0171–215 3470.

STANLEY, Rt. Hon. Sir John (Paul), Kt 1988; PC 1984; MP (C) Tonbridge and Malling since Feb. 1974; *b* 19 Jan. 1942; *s* of Mr and Mrs H. Stanley; *m* 1968, Susan Elizabeth Giles; two *s* one *d*. *Educ:* Repton Sch.; Lincoln Coll., Oxford (MA). Conservative Research Dept with responsibility for Housing, 1967–68; Research Associate, Internat. Inst. for Strategic Studies, 1968–69; Rio Tinto-Zinc Corp. Ltd, 1969–79. PPS to Rt Hon. Margaret Thatcher, 1976–79; Minister of State (Minister for Housing and Construction), DoE, 1979–83; Minister of State: for the Armed Forces, MoD, 1983–87; Northern Ireland Office, 1987–88. Mem., Parly Select Cttee on Nationalised Industries, 1974, on Foreign Affairs, 1992–. Director: Conder Group plc, 1989–92; Henderson Highland Trust plc, 1990–. Trustee, ActionAid, 1989–. *Publication:* (jtly) The International Trade in Arms, 1972. *Recreations:* music, photography, sailing. *Address:* House of Commons, SW1A 0AA.

STANLEY, Martin Edward; Head of Vehicles, Metals and Minerals Division, Department of Trade and Industry, since 1992; *b* 1 Nov. 1948; *s* of Edward Alan and Dorothy Stanley; *m* 1971, Marilyn Joan Lewis (marr. diss. 1992); one *s*; lives with Janice Munday; one *s*. *Educ:* Royal GS, Newcastle upon Tyne; Magdalen Coll., Oxford (BA Hons). Inland Revenue, 1971–80; Department of Trade and Industry, 1980–: various posts, 1980–87; Head, Industry/Educn Unit, 1987–90; Principal Private Sec., 1990–92. *Recreations:* travelling slowly, including walking and sailing. *Address:* Department of Trade and Industry, 151 Buckingham Palace Road, SW1W 9SS. *T:* 0171–215 4193. *Club:* Hurlingham.

STANLEY, Oliver Duncan; Chairman, Rathbone Brothers (formerly Comprehensive Financial Services) PLC, since 1972; *b* 5 June 1925; *s* of Bernard Stanley and Mabel Best; *m* 1954, Ruth Brenner, JP, BA; one *s* three *d*. *Educ:* Christ Church, Oxford (MA); Harvard Univ., USA. Called to the Bar, Middle Temple, 1963. Served War, 8 Hussars, 1943–47. HM Inspector of Taxes, 1952–65; Dir, Gray Dawes Bank, 1966–72; founded Comprehensive Financial Services Gp of Cos, 1971. Chief Taxation Adviser, CLA, 1975–83 (Mem., Tax Cttee, 1983–). Dir, Axa Equity and Law, 1992–. Member: Soc. of Authors, 1967–; Council of Legal Educn, 1992–; Nat. Museums and Galls Develt Trust, 1994–. *Publications:* A Guide to Taxation, 1967; Taxology, 1971; Creation and Protection of Capital, 1974; Taxation of Farmers and Landowners, 1981, 6th edn 1995; Offshore Tax Planning, 1986; contrib. The Times and The Sunday Times, 1966–83; numerous articles in legal and agricultural periodicals. *Recreations:* music, tennis, French civilisation. *Address:* 5 The Park, NW11 7SR. *Club:* Travellers'.

STANLEY, Peter Ian; Chief Executive, Central Science Laboratory Agency, since 1992; *b* 25 June 1946. *Educ:* University College London. MAF, subseq. MAFF, 1970–. *Address:* Central Science Laboratory Agency, London Road, Slough SL3 7JH.

STANLEY PRICE, His Honour Peter, QC 1956; a Circuit Judge (formerly a Judge of the Central Criminal Court), 1969–83; President, National Reference Tribunal for the Coal Mining Industry, 1979–83; Judge of the Chancery Court of York, 1967–83; *b* 27 Nov. 1911; *s* of late Herbert Stanley Price and late Gertrude Rangeley S. P. (*née* Wightman); *m* 1st, 1946, Harriett Ella Theresa (*d* 1948), *o d* of late Rev. R. E. Pownall; two *s*; 2nd, 1950, Margaret Jane, *o d* of late Samuel Milkins (she *m* 1937, William Hebditch, RAF; he *d* 1941); one *d* one step *s*. *Educ:* Cheltenham; Exeter College, Oxford (1st cl. Final Hons Sch. of Jurisprudence, 1933). Barrister, Inner Temple, 1936, Master of the Bench, 1963. Served War of 1939–45, Lieut (S) RNVR. Recorder of Pontefract, 1954, of York, 1955, of Kingston-upon-Hull, 1958, of Sheffield, 1965–69. Dep. Chm., N Riding QS, 1955–58, 1970–71, Chm., 1958–70; Judge of Appeal, Jersey and Guernsey, 1964–69; Solicitor-General, County Palatine of Durham, 1965–69. Pres., Nat. Reference Tribunal, Officials Conciliation Scheme, 1967–79. *Recreations:* birds and trees; gardening, shooting. *Address:* Church Hill, Great Ouseburn, York YO5 9RH. *T:* Boroughbridge (01423) 330252. *Club:* Brooks's.

STANNARD, Ven. Colin Percy, TD 1966; Archdeacon of Carlisle and Residentiary Canon of Carlisle Cathedral, 1984–93, now Archdeacon and Canon Emeritus; *b* 8 Feb. 1924; *s* of Percy and Grace Adelaide Stannard; *m* 1950, Joan Callow; one *s* two *d*. *Educ:* Woodbridge School; Selwyn Coll., Cambridge (BA 1947, MA 1949); Lincoln Theological Coll. Deacon 1949, priest 1950; Curate, St James Cathedral, Bury St Edmunds, 1949–52; Priest-in-charge, St Martin's, Grimsby, 1952–55; CF (TA), 1953–67; Vicar: St James's, Barrow-in-Furness, 1955–64; St John the Baptist's, Upperby, 1964–70; Rector of Gosforth, 1970–75; RD of Calder, 1970–75; Hon. Canon of Carlisle, 1975–84; Priest-in-charge of Natland, 1975–76, Vicar, 1976–84; RD of Kendal, 1975–84. *Recreations:* walking, bringing order out of chaos—especially in gardens. *Address:* 51 Longlands Road, Carlisle, Cumbria CA3 9AE. *T:* Carlisle (01228) 38584.

STANSBY, John; Chairman: UIE (UK) Ltd, since 1974 (UK parent company of UIE Scotland Ltd and part of Bouygues Group); London Minsk Development Co. plc, since 1993; *b* 2 July 1930; *s* of late Dumon Stansby and Vera Margaret Main; *m* 1966, Anna Maria Kruschewsky; one *d* and one step *s* one step *d*. *Educ:* Oundle; Jesus Coll., Cambridge (Schol., MA). FInstPet, FCIT, FRSA. Commissioned, Queen's Royal Regt, 1949; Service, 1949–50, Somaliland Scouts. Shell Mex & BP Ltd, 1955–62; AIC Ltd, 1962–66; Dir, Rank Leisure Services, Rank Organisation, 1966–70; Dir, P&O Energy, P&OSN Co., 1970–74; Chm., Dumon Stansby & Co. Ltd, 1974–; Dep. Chm., London Transport Exec., 1978–80; Chairman: SAUR (UK) Ltd, 1986–89; Cementation–SAUR Water Services Ltd, 1986–88; Bouygues (UK) Ltd, 1987–89; SAUR UK Development PLC, 1989–91; Dep. Chm., Energy Resources Ltd, 1990–92; Director: Cambrian Environmental Services PLC, 1990–91; Stalwart Environmental Services PLC, 1989–91. European Bobsleigh Champion, 1952. *Address:* 19 Brook Green, W6 7BL. *T:* 0171–603 0886. *Club:* Travellers'.

STANSFIELD, George Norman, CBE 1985 (OBE 1980); HM Diplomatic Service, retired; *b* 28 Feb. 1926; *s* of George Stansfield and Martha Alice (*née* Leadbetter); *m* 1947, Elizabeth Margaret Williams. *Educ:* Liscard High Sch. Served War, RAF, 1944–47. Ministries of Food and Supply, 1948–58; Private Sec. to Dir-Gen. of Armament Prodn, 1958–61; CRO, 1961; Second Secretary: Calcutta, 1962–66; Port of Spain, 1966–68; First Secretary: FCO, 1968–71; Singapore, 1971–74; Consul, Durban, 1974–78; FCO, 1978; Counsellor, and Head of Overseas Estate Dept, 1980–82; High Comr, Solomon Islands, 1982–86. Training consultant, FCO, 1986–. *Recreations:* sailing, cine-photography, wildlife. *Address:* Deryn's Wood, 80 Westfield Road, Woking, Surrey GU22 9QA. *Club:* Royal Southampton Yacht.

STANSFIELD SMITH, Sir Colin, Kt 1993; CBE 1988; County Architect, Hampshire County Council, since 1973; Professor of Architectural Design, Portsmouth Polytechnic, since 1990; *b* 1 Oct. 1932; *s* of Stansfield Smith and Mary (*née* Simpson); *m* 1961, Angela Jean Earnshaw; one *s* one *d*. *Educ:* William Hulme's Grammar Sch., Manchester; Cambridge Univ. Sch. of Architecture (MA, DipArch). ARIBA. Schools Div., LCC, 1958–60; Sen. Asst then Associate Partner, Emberton Frank & Tardrew, Architects, 1960–65; Partner, Emberton Tardrew & Partners, 1965–71; Dep. County Architect, Cheshire CC, 1971–73. RIBA Royal Gold Medal, 1991. *Publications:* Hampshire Architecture (1974–1984), 1985; Schools of Thought, Hampshire Architecture (1974–1991), 1991; articles in Architects' Jl and Architectural Review. *Recreations:* golf, painting. *Address:* 8 Christchurch Road, Winchester, Hants SO23 9SR. *T:* Winchester (01962) 851970. *Club:* Hockley Golf (Twyford, Hants).

STANSGATE, Viscountcy of (*cr* 1942, of Stansgate); title disclaimed by 2nd Viscount (*see* Benn, Rt Hon. Tony).

STANTON, David; Director (Grade 3), Analytical Services Division, Department of Social Security, since 1992; *b* 5 Nov. 1942; *s* of Frederick Charles Patrick Stanton and Ethel (*née* Cout); *m* 1967, Isobel Joan Blair; one *s* one *d*. *Educ:* Bishops Stortford Coll.; Worcester Coll., Oxford (BA PPE 1965); LSE (MSc(Econ) 1971). ODI/Nuffield Fellow, Govt of Uganda, 1965–67; Lectr, Brunel Univ., 1967–70; Economic Adviser: Min. of Transport, 1970; Min. of Housing, then DoE, 1971–74; HM Treasury, 1974–75; Senior Economic Adviser: seconded to Hong Kong Govt, 1975–77; also Head of Unit for Manpower Studies, Dept of Employment, 1977–81; Econs Br., Dept of Employment, 1981–83; also Dir, Employment Market Res. Unit, 1983–87; Chief Economist (Grade 3), Dept of Employment, 1988–92. *Recreations:* people, dogs and other animals, singing. *Address:* Department of Social Security, Adelphi, 1–11 John Adam Street, WC2N 6HT; 5 Darell Road, Richmond, Surrey TW9 4LF. *T:* 0181–392 2107.

STANTON, Rev. John Maurice, MA; Rector of Chesham Bois, 1973–83; *b* 29 Aug. 1918; *s* of Frederick William Stanton, MInstCE and Maude Lozel (*née* Cole); *m* 1947, Helen Winifred (*née* Bowden); one *s* two *d*. *Educ:* King's School, Rochester; University College, Oxford (Gunsley Exhibnr; 2nd Class Hons, Final Hon. Sch. of Nat. Science, 1947; MA 1947). Commissioned Royal Artillery, 1940, 92nd Field Regt, RA, 1940–43. ISLD, CMF, 1943–46. Assistant Master, Tonbridge School, 1947–59; Headmaster, Blundell's School, 1959–71; Curate, St Matthew's, Exeter, 1972. Ordained Deacon, 1952; Priest, 1953. Sec., Oxford Diocesan Bd of Patronage, 1984–90. *Recreations:* water colour painting, gardening. *Address:* 37A St Andrew's Road, Old Headington, Oxford OX3 9DL. *T:* Oxford (01865) 65206.

STANYER, Maj.-Gen. John Turner, CBE 1971 (OBE 1967); *b* 28 July 1920; *s* of late Charles T. Stanyer and late Mrs R. H. Stanyer; *m* 1942, Mary Patricia Pattie; three *s* four *d*. *Educ:* Latymer Upper Sch., Hammersmith. Served War, 2/Lieut The Middlesex Regt, 1941; Lieut to Captain, The Middlesex Regt, 1941–47: Iceland, France, Germany, Palestine. Captain, Royal Army Ordnance Corps, 1947; Student, Staff Coll., Camberley, 1951; AA&QMG, UN Force in Cyprus, 1966; Dir of Ordnance Services, BAOR, 1968–71; Commandant, Central Ordnance Depot, Bicester, 1971–73; Comdr, Base Orgn, RAOC, 1973–75, retired. Col Comdt, RAOC, 1977–82. Dir Gen., Supply Co-ordination, MoD, 1975–80. Mem., Oxford City Council, 1983–87. *Recreation:* sailing. *Address:* Sandy House, Manor Close, Walberswick, Southwold, Suffolk IP18 6UQ. *T:* Southwold (01502) 724533.

STAPLE, Rev. David, OBE 1995; General Secretary, Free Church Federal Council, 1986–March 1996, subsequently General Secretary Emeritus; *b* 30 March 1930; *s* of William Hill Staple and Elsie Staple; *m* 1955, Margaret Lilian Berrington; one *s* three *d*. *Educ:* Watford Boys' Grammar Sch.; Christ's Coll., Cambridge (MA); Regent's Park Coll., Oxford; Wadham Coll., Oxford (MA); BD London (external). Baptist Minister: West Ham Central Mission, 1955–58; Llanishen, Cardiff, 1958–74; College Road, Harrow, 1974–86. Chm., Baptist Missionary Soc., 1981–82. Governor: Regent's Park Coll., Oxford, 1965–; Westhill Coll., Birmingham, 1986–. *Recreations:* fell walking, music. *Address:* 1 Althorp Road, St Albans, Herts AL1 3PH. *T:* St Albans (01727) 810009, *Fax:* (01727) 867888. *Club:* Penn.

STAPLE, George Warren; Director, Serious Fraud Office, since 1992; *b* 13 Sept. 1940; *s* of Kenneth Harry Staple and Betty Mary Staple; *m* 1968, Olivia Deirdre Lowry; two *s* two *d*. *Educ:* Haileybury. Solicitor, admitted 1964; articles, Walker Charlesworth and Jefferson, 1958–62; Associate with Condon and Forsyth, NY, 1963; Asst Solicitor, Clifford-Turner & Co., 1964–67; Partner, Clifford-Turner, later Clifford Chance, 1967–92. Legal Assessor, Disciplinary Cttee, Stock Exchange, 1978–92; DTI Inspector, Consolidated Gold Fields, 1986, Aldermanbury Trust, 1988; a Chairman, Authorisation and Disciplinary Tribunals: of The Securities Assoc., 1987–91; of Securities and Futures Authy, 1991–92; Mem., Commercial Court Cttee, 1977–92. Mem. Council, Law Soc., 1986– (Treas., 1989–92). Gov., London Guildhall Univ. (formerly City of London Polytechnic), 1982–94. *Recreations:* cricket, walking, gardening. *Address:* Serious Fraud Office, Elm House, 10–16 Elm Street, WC1X 0BJ. *Clubs:* Brooks's, City of London, MCC.

See also W. P. Staple.

STAPLE, William Philip; Director General, Takeover Panel, since 1994; *b* 28 Sept. 1947; *s* of Kenneth Harry Staple and Betty Mary Staple (*née* Lemon); *m* 1977, Jennifer Frances Walker (marr. diss. 1986); one *s* one *d*. *Educ:* Haileybury; Law Soc. Coll. of Law. Called to the Bar, Inner Temple, 1971; Executive at Cazenove, 1972–81; Asst Dir, 1981–86, Dir, 1986–, N. M. Rothschild. *Recreations:* various sports, theatre, reading. *Address:* c/o N. M. Rothschild & Sons, New Court, St Swithin's Lane, EC4P 4DU. *T:* 0171–280 5000. *Club:* White's.

See also G. W. Staple.

STAPLES, Brian Lynn; Chief Executive, North West Water Group, since 1994; *b* 6 April 1945; *s* of Stanley Holt Staples and Catherine Emma Annie Staples (*née* Walding); *m* 1st, Rosalind Louise McKay; one *d*; 2nd, Audrey Foster; one *s* two *d*; 3rd, Sonia Pearl Elizabeth Tuft. *Educ:* Sweyne Grammar Sch., Rayleigh. FIHT; Fellow, Instn of Civil Engineering Surveyors. Joined Tarmac Group, 1964, Chief Exec., 1991–94. Special Prof., Dept of Civil Engrg, Nottingham Univ., 1989. *Recreations:* music, theatre, hill walking. *Address:* North West Water, Dawson House, Warrington WA5 3LW; Warren Garth, 78 Orton Lane, Lower Penn, Wolverhampton WV4 4XB. *T:* Wolverhampton (01902) 895061.

STAPLES, Rev. Canon Edward Eric, CBE 1977 (OBE 1973); Chaplain to The Queen, 1973–80; Chaplain to the Anglican congregations in Helsinki and throughout Finland, in Moscow, Leningrad and elsewhere in the Soviet Union, and in Outer Mongolia, 1964–80; Hon. Chaplain, British Embassy: Helsinki, 1967–80, Moscow, 1968–80, Ulan Bator, 1970–81; Hon. Lecturer, English History, University of Helsinki, 1972–80; Hon. Canon of Gibraltar Cathedral, since 1974; *b* 15 Nov. 1910; *yr s* of Christopher Walter Staples and Esther Jane Staples; *m* 1962, Kate Ethel Thusberg (*née* Rönngren); two step *d*. *Educ:* Chichester Theol Coll. (earlier opportunities so misused that it is unwise to name the establishments concerned!). MA, PhD. Niger Company, 1932. Served with RNVR, 1939–46. Ordained 1948. Assistant of Court of Russia Company, 1977–89, Consul, 1978–88. Life Mem., Finnish-British Soc.; Mem., Anglo-Mongolian Soc. Medal of Univ. of Helsinki, 1980. Kt, Order of the Lion (Finland), 1976; Order of St Vladimir (Russian Orthodox Church), 1977. *Recreations:* climbing, cricket, fishing, gardening (no longer actively), historical research. *Address:* The Old Farmhouse, 13 Oxford Street, Ramsbury, Marlborough, Wilts SN8 2PG. *T:* Marlborough (01672) 521118. *Clubs:* MCC; Helsinki Cricket (Founder Mem.); Moscow Cricket (Founder Mem.); Ulan Bator Golf (Hon. Life Mem.).

STAPLES, (Hubert Anthony) Justin, CMG 1981; HM Diplomatic Service, retired; Ambassador to Finland, 1986–89; *b* 14 Nov. 1929; *s* of late Francis Hammond Staples, formerly ICS, and Catherine Margaret Mary Pownall; *m* 1962, Susan Angela Collingwood Carter; one *s* one *d*. *Educ:* Downside; Oriel Coll., Oxford. Served in RAF 1952–54 (Pilot Officer). Entered Foreign (later Diplomatic) Service, 1954; 3rd Sec., Bangkok, 1955; Foreign Office, 1959; 1st Sec., Berlin (Dep. Political Adviser), 1962; Vientiane, 1965 (acted as Chargé d'Affaires in 1966 and 1967); transf. to FO and seconded to Cabinet Office, 1968; Counsellor, UK Delegn to NATO, Brussels, 1971; Counsellor and Consul General, Bangkok, 1974 (acted as Chargé d'affaires, 1975 and 1977); Counsellor, Dublin, 1978–81; Ambassador to Thailand, 1981–86 and concurrently to Laos, 1985–86. Pres., Anglo-Finnish Soc., 1993–. *Recreations:* ski-ing, golf. *Address:* 48 Crescent Road, Kingston, Surrey KT2 7RF. *Clubs:* Travellers'; Roehampton; Royal Bangkok Sports (Bangkok).

STAPLES, Justin; *see* Staples, H. A. J.

STAPLES, Sir Thomas, 15th Bt *cr* 1628 (Ire.), of Lissan, Co. Tyrone; *b* 9 Feb. 1905; *s* of Thomas Staples (*d* 1963) (nephew of 10th Bt) and Mary Ussher (*d* 1966), *d* of Frederick Greer; *S* cousin, 1989; *m* 1952, Frances Ann Irvine (*d* 1981). *Heir: b* Gerald James Arland Staples [*b* 2 Dec. 1909; *m* 1951, Henrietta Owen, *d* of Arland Ussher; two *d*]. *Address:* 219, 3051 Shelbourne Street, Victoria, BC V8R 6T2, Canada.

STAPLETON, Air Vice-Marshal Deryck Cameron, CB 1960; CBE 1948; DFC; AFC; psa; *b* 1918; *s* of John Rouse Stapleton, OBE, Sarnia, Natal; *m* 1942, Ethleen Joan Clifford, *d* of late Sir Cuthbert William Whiteside. *Educ:* King Edward VI Sch., Totnes. Joined RAF, 1936; served Transjordan and Palestine (AFC), 1937–39; War of 1939–45 (DFC). Middle East, N Africa, Italy. Asst Sec. (Air), War Cabinet Offices, 1945–46; Secretary, Chiefs of Staff Cttee, Ministry of Defence, 1947–49; OC RAF, Odiham, 1949–51; subsequently, Plans, Fighter Comd HQ and Ops at AFCENT Fontainebleu; then OC, RAF, Oldenburg (Germany); Plans, Bomber Comd HQ, 1957–60; Air Ministry, 1960–62; Dir, Defence Plans, Min. of Defence, 1963–64; AOC No 1 Group, RAF Bomber Command, 1964–66; Comdt, RAF Staff Coll., Bracknell, 1966–68. BAC Area Manager, Libya, 1969–70; BAC Rep. CENTO Area, Tehran, later BAe Chief Exec. Iran, and Man. Dir, Irano-British Dynamics Co. Iran, 1970–79; Rep. BAe, Peking, China, and Chm., British Cos Assoc., Peking, 1979–83. Associate Fellow, British Interplanetary Soc., 1960. *Recreations:* most sports. *Address:* c/o National Westminster Bank, Leicester Square, WC2H 7LW.

STAPLETON, Guy, CB 1995; Chief Executive, Intervention Board Executive Agency (formerly Intervention Board for Agricultural Produce), since 1986; *b* 10 Nov. 1935; *s* of William Algernon Swann Stapleton and Joan Denise Stapleton (*née* Wilson). *Educ:* Malvern Coll. Clerical Officer, Min. of Transport and Civil Aviation, 1954–58; Exec. Officer, 1958; transf. to Min. of Aviation, 1959; Civil Aviation Asst, British Embassy, Rome, 1960–63; Private Sec. to Controller of National Air Traffic Control Services, 1963–65; Asst Principal, MAFF, 1965; Private Sec. to Jt Parly Sec., 1967–68; Principal, 1968; Asst Sec., 1973; Dept of Prices and Consumer Protection, 1974–76; Under Sec., 1981; European Secretariat, Cabinet Office, 1982–85; Dir of Establishments, MAFF, 1985–86. *Publications:* A Walk of Verse, 1961; (compiled) Poet's England: 2, Gloucestershire, 1977, 2nd edn 1982; 4, Avon and Somerset, 1981; 7, Devon, 1986; 9, Hertfordshire, 1988; 12, Leicestershire and Rutland, 1992; 13, Nottinghamshire, 1993; Vale of Moreton Churches, 1989; (ed) Memories of Moreton, 1989; Four Shire Memories, 1992. *Recreations:* local and family history, topographical verse. *Address:* c/o Fountain House, 2 Queen's Walk, Reading RG1 7QW. *T:* Reading (01734) 583626. *Clubs:* Civil Service, Royal Over-Seas League.

STAPLETON, Very Rev. Henry Edward Champneys; Dean of Carlisle, since 1988; *b* 17 June 1932; *s* of Edward Parker Stapleton and Frances Mary Champneys; *m* 1964, Mary Deborah Sapwell; two *d*. *Educ:* Lancing College; Pembroke Coll., Cambridge (BA 1954, MA 1958); Ely Theological Coll. Deacon 1956, priest 1957, York; Assistant Curate: St Olave with St Giles, 1956–59; Pocklington, 1959–61; Vicar of Seaton Ross with Everingham, Harswell and Bielby, 1961–67; RD of Weighton, 1966–67; Rector of Skelton, 1967–75; Vicar of Wroxham with Hoveton, 1975–81; Priest in Charge of Belaugh, 1976–81, with Hoveton St Peter, 1979–81; Canon Residentiary and Precentor of Rochester Cathedral, 1981–88; Warden of Readers, 1981–88. Church Comr, 1993–; Member: Council for the Care of Churches, 1965–91; Churches Conservation Trust (formerly Redundant Churches Fund), 1976–; Royal Commn on Historical Manuscripts, 1992–. FSA 1974. Editor, Cathedral, 1976–82. *Publications:* Skelton Village, 1971; Heirs without Title, 1974; The Skilful Master Builder, 1975; The Model Working Parson, 1976; (ed and contrib.) Churchyards Handbook, 2nd edn 1976, 3rd edn 1988; articles in Churchscape and other ecclesiastical jls. *Recreations:* visiting churches, second-hand bookshops. *Address:* The Deanery, Carlisle, Cumbria CA3 8TZ. *T:* Carlisle (01228) 23335.

STAPLETON, Prof. Richard Christopher, PhD; Wolfson Professor of Finance, Lancaster University, since 1989; *b* 11 Oct. 1942; *s* of Leonard Stapleton and Rosamund Kathleen May Stapleton; *m* 1968, Linda Cairns; one *s* one *d*. *Educ:* Univ. of Sheffield (BAEcon, PhD Business Studies); Open Univ. (BA Maths). Lectr in Business Finance, Sheffield Univ., 1965–73; Asst Prof. of Finance, New York Univ., 1973–76; Sen. Res. Fellow, 1976–77, Nat. West. Bank Prof. of Business Finance, 1977–86, Manchester Business Sch., Univ. of Manchester; Fellow, Churchill Coll., Cambridge, 1986–89. Hon. MBA Manchester, 1980. *Publications:* The Theory of Corporate Finance, 1970; International Tax Systems and Financing Policy, 1978; Capital Markets and Corporate Financial Decisions, 1980; contrib. Econ. Jl, Jl of Finance, Jl of Financial Econs, Qly Jl of Econs. *Recreations:* running, golf, reading, travel. *Address:* Lancaster University, University House, Lancaster LA1 4YW.

STAPLETON-COTTON, family name of **Viscount Combermere.**

STARK, Sir Andrew (Alexander Steel), KCMG 1975 (CMG 1964); CVO 1965; DL; HM Diplomatic Service, retired; Director, The Maersk Co., 1978–90 (Chairman, 1978–87); Adviser on European Affairs, Society of Motor Manufacturers and Traders, 1977–89; *b* 30 Dec. 1916; *yr s* of late Thomas Bow Stark and of late Barbara Black Stark (*née* Steel), Fauldhouse, West Lothian; *m* 1944, Helen Rosemary, *er d* of late Lt-Col J. Oxley Parker, TD, and Mary Monica (*née* Hills); two *s* (and one *s* decd). *Educ:* Bathgate Acad.; Edinburgh Univ. MA (Hons), Eng. Lit, Edinburgh, 1938. Served War of 1939–45, Green Howards and Staff appts. Major 1945. Entered Foreign Service, 1948, and served in Foreign Office until 1950; 1st Secretary, Vienna, 1951–53; Asst Private Sec. to Foreign Secretary, 1953–55; Head of Chancery: Belgrade, 1956–58; Rome, 1958–60; Counsellor: FO, 1960–64; Bonn, 1964–68; attached to Mission to UN with rank of Ambassador, Jan. 1968; British Mem., Seven Nation Cttee on Reorganisation of UN Secretariat; seconded to UN, NY, as Under-Secretary-General, Oct. 1968–1971; HM Ambassador to Denmark, 1971–76; Dep. Under-Sec. of State, FCO, 1976–78. Director: Scandinavian Bank Ltd, 1978–88; Carlsberg Brewery Ltd, 1980–87. Mem., CBI Europe Cttee, 1980–85. Chairman: Anglo-Danish Soc., 1983–; Anglo-Danish Trade Adv. Bd, 1983–93. President: British Assoc. of Former UN Civil Servants, 1989–94; Essex Physically Handicapped Assoc., 1979–; Chm., Rural Community Council of Essex, 1990–93. University of Essex: Mem. Council, 1978– (Chm. Council, 1983–89); Pro-Chancellor, 1983–95; DU 1990. DL Essex, 1981. Grosses Verdienstkreuz, German Federal Republic, 1965; Grand Cross, Order of the Dannebrog, Denmark, 1974. *Recreations:* tennis, shooting. *Address:* Fambridge Hall, White Notley, Witham, Essex CM8 1RN. *T:* Silver End (01376) 583117. *Clubs:* Travellers' (Chairman 1978–81), MCC.

STARK, George Robert, PhD; FRS 1990; Chairman, Research Institute, Cleveland Clinic Foundation, since 1992; *b* 4 July 1933; *s* of Jack and Florence Stark; *m* 1956, Mary Beck; one *s* one *d*. *Educ:* Columbia College, NY (BA 1955); Columbia Univ., NY (Chemistry; PhD 1959). Asst Prof., Rockefeller Univ., 1961; Stanford University: Asst Prof., 1963; Associate Prof., 1966; Prof. of Biochemistry, 1971; ICRF, 1983–92 (Associate Dir of Res., 1989–92). Member: Nat. Acad. of Scis, USA, 1987; European Molecular Biol. Orgn, 1985. *Publications:* contribs to scientific jls. *Recreations:* sports, stamps, books, records. *Address:* Cleveland Clinic Foundation, 9500 Euclid Avenue, Cleveland, OH 44195, USA. *T:* (216) 4443900, *Fax:* (216) 4443279.

STARKE, Hon. Sir John Erskine, Kt 1976; Judge of Supreme Court of Victoria, Australia, 1964–85; Trustee, Australian War Memorial, Canberra; *b* 1 Dec. 1913; *s* of Hon. Sir Hayden Starke, KCMG; *m* Elizabeth, *d* of late Colin Campbell. Admitted to Victorian Bar, 1939; QC 1955; Judge, 1946. *Address:* 16 Jacksons Road, Mount Eliza, Vic 3930, Australia.

STARKER, Janos; concert cellist, recording artist; Distinguished Professor of Music, Indiana University, since 1958; *b* 5 July 1924; *s* of F. Sandor and M. Margit; *m* 1944, Eva Uranyi; one *d*; *m* 1960, Rae D. Busch; one *d*. *Educ:* Franz Liszt Academy of Music, Budapest; Zrinyi Gymnasium, Budapest. Solo cellist: Budapest Opera and Philh., 1945–46; Dallas Symphony, 1948–49; Metropolitan Opera, 1949–53; Chicago Symphony, 1953–58; concert tours on all continents in recitals and as soloist with orchestras; numerous recordings. Grand Prix du Disque, 1948; George Washington Award, 1972; Sanford Fellowship Award, Yale, 1974; Herzl Award, 1978; Ed Press Award, 1983; Kodály Commemorative Medallion, NY, 1983; Arturo Toscanini Award, Toscanini Foundn, 1986; Tracy Sonneborn Award, Indiana Univ., 1986. Mem., Amer. Fedn Musicians; Hon. RAM, 1981. Hon. DMus: Chicago Conservatory Coll., 1961; Cornell, 1978; East-West Univ., 1982; Williams Coll., 1983; Lawrence Univ., 1990. Invented the Starker Bridge. *Publications:* Cello Method: an organised method of string playing, 1963; Bach Suites, 1971; Concerto Cadenzas, 1976; Beethoven Sonatas, 1978; Beethoven Variations, 1979; Bach Sonatas, 1979; Schubert-Starker Sonatina, 1980; Dvorak Concerto, 1981; Bottermund-Starker Variations, 1982; Encores, 1985; many articles and essays. *Recreations:* writing, swimming, staying alive. *Address:* Indiana University Music Department, Bloomington, IN 47405, USA.

STARKEY, Sir John (Philip), 3rd Bt *cr* 1935; DL; *b* 8 May 1938; *s* of Sir William Randle Starkey, 2nd Bt, and Irene Myrtle Starkey (*née* Francklin) (*d* 1965); *S* father, 1977; *m* 1966, Victoria Henrietta Fleetwood, *y d* of Lt-Col Christopher Fuller, TD; one *s* three *d*. *Educ:* Eton College; Christ Church, Oxford. Sloan Fellow, London Business School. A Church Commissioner and Mem. Commissioners' Assets Cttee, 1985–91; Mem., Archbishop's Commn on Rural Areas, 1988–90. Chairman: Notts Br., CLA, 1977–80; E Midlands Regional Cttee, Nat. Trust, 1986–. UK Vice Pres., Confedn of European Agriculture, 1989–; Pres., Newark Chamber of Commerce, 1980–82. Notts: DL, 1981; High Sheriff, 1987–88; JP Newark, 1981–88. FRSA 1990. *Recreations:* cricket, painting. *Heir: s* Henry John Starkey, *b* 13 Oct. 1973. *Address:* Norwood Park, Southwell, Notts NG25 0PF. *T:* Southwell (01636) 812762. *Club:* MCC.

STARLING, Keith Andrew; Headmaster, The Judd School, since 1986; *b* 12 June 1944; *s* of Stanley Ernest Starling and Gladys Joyce Starling; *m* 1968, Jacqueline Eagers; two *s*. *Educ:* The Perse Sch; Fitzwilliam Coll., Cambridge (MA, CertEd). Asst Master, Lancaster Royal Grammar Sch., 1968–71; Head of Geography, Sedbergh Sch., 1971–80; Dep. Headmaster, Portsmouth Grammar Sch., 1980–86. *Recreations:* music, walking, *Address:* The Judd School, Tonbridge, Kent. *T:* Tonbridge (01732) 770880.

STARMER-SMITH, Nigel Christopher; BBC TV Sports Commentator, since 1973; *b* 25 Dec. 1944; *s* of Harry Starmer-Smith and Joan Mary Starmer-Smith (*née* Keep); *m* 1973, Rosamund Mary Bartlett; two *s* (one *d* decd). *Educ:* Magdalen Coll. Sch., Oxford; University Coll., Oxford (MA). Schoolmaster, Epsom Coll., 1967; Producer and Reporter, BBC Radio Outside Broadcasts, 1971; BBC TV, 1973–; Presenter and Commentator, Rugby Special; commentator, hockey and other sports. Publisher and Editor, Rugby World and Post magazine, 1984–93. Former Rugby Union international: Harlequins, Oxford Univ., Barbarians, England. *Publications* include: The Barbarians, 1977; Rugby: a way of life, 1986. *Recreations:* family, tennis, piano playing, horse racing, gardening. *Address:* Berins Hill Wood, Ipsden, Wallingford, Oxon OX10 6QX. *T:* Wallingford (01491) 681822. *Clubs:* Vincent's (Oxford); Leander (Henley); Harlequins FC.

STASSEN, Harold Edward; lawyer, executive; politician, educator, United States; Chairman, International Law Committee of Philadelphia Bar Association, 1973; *b* W St Paul, Minn, 13 April 1907; *s* of William Andrew Stassen and Elsie Emma Mueller; *m* 1929, Esther G. Glewwe, artist; one *s* one *d*. *Educ:* Univ. of Minnesota Coll. (BA 1927; LLB 1929); Law School. Has several hon. degrees. Admitted to Minnesota Bar, 1929; practised South St Paul; County Attorney, Dakota County, 1930–38; thrice elected Governor of Minnesota, 1939–43; resigned for service with Navy; Lt Comdr, USN; Comdr on staff of Admiral Halsey in Pacific, 1943–45; Asst Chief of Staff, 1944; Capt., USNR; released to inactive duty, 1945. One of US delegates to San Francisco Conference, drafting and signing UN Charter, 1945. Pres., Minnesota Young Republicans; Delegate to Republican Convention, 1936; Temporary Chairman and Keynoter of Republican National Convention and floor manager for Wendell Wilkie, 1940; twice elected National Chairman National Governors' Conference, and of Council of State Governments, 1940–41. President, University of Pennsylvania, 1948–53; Director Foreign Operations Admin., 1953–55; Special Assistant to the President for Disarmament, 1955–58; Dep. US Rep. on Disarmament Commn, UN, 1955–58; Chief Consultant to ME Tech. Univ., Ankara, 1958; Mem., Nat. Security Council, 1953–58; Partner in law firm Stassen, Kephart, Sarkis and Scullin, later Stassen, Kostos and Mason, 1958–91. Chm., Constitutional Law Cttee, Amer. Bar. Assoc., 1950–51. President International Council of Religious Education, 1942, 1950; Vice-Pres. and a Founder, Nat. Council of Churches, 1951–52; President, Div. of Christian Educ. of Nat. Council of Churches, 1953. Mem., Horatio Alger Assoc., 1981. Delivered Godkind Lectures on Human Rights, Harvard Univ., 1946; candidate for Republican nomination for President of US, 1948. Chm., World Law Day, Geneva, 1968. Stassen Center for World Peace, Univ. of Minnesota, 1993. Adlai Stevenson World Peace Award, 1989. Bronze Star, 1944; Legion of Merit, Six Battle Stars (Western Pacific campaign), 1945. Baptist. Mason. *Publications:* Where I Stand, 1947; Man was meant to be Free, 1951; (jtly) Eisenhower: turning the world toward peace, 1991; United Nations: a working paper for restructuring in its 50th year 1995, 1993. *Address:* 310 Salem Church Road, Sunfish Lake, MN 55118, USA.

STATHAM, Sir Norman, KCMG 1977 (CMG 1967); CVO 1968; HM Diplomatic Service, retired; *b* Stretford, Lancs, 15 Aug. 1922; *s* of Frederick William and Maud Statham; *m* 1948, Hedwig Gerlich; one *s* one *d* (and one *s* decd). *Educ:* Seymour Park Council School, Stretford; Manchester Grammar School; Gonville and Caius College, Cambridge (MA). Intelligence Corps, 1943–47; Manchester Oil Refinery Ltd and Petrochemicals Ltd, 1948–50; Foreign Service, 1951: Foreign Office, 1951; Consul (Commercial), New York, 1954; First Secretary (Commercial), Bonn, 1958; Administrative Staff College, Henley, 1963; Foreign Office, 1964; Counsellor, Head of European Economic Integration Dept, 1965–68, 1970–71; Consul-General, São Paulo, 1968–70; Minister (Economic), Bonn, 1971; Asst Under Sec. of State, FCO, 1975; Dep. Under Sec. of State, FCO, 1975; Ambassador to Brazil, 1977–79. FCO Special Rep. for British-German Co-operation, 1984–86. Vice-Pres., British Chamber of Commerce in Germany, 1981–85; Pres., Council of British Chambers of Commerce in Continental Europe, 1982–84. *Recreations:* reading, birdwatching, calligraphy. *Address:* 11 Underhill Park Road, Reigate, Surrey RH2 9LU.

STATHATOS, Stephanos; Commander, Order of Phoenix; Officer, Order of George I; *b* 1922; *s* of Gerassimo and Eugenia Stathatos; *m* 1947, Thalia Mouzina. *Educ:* Law School, Athens Univ.; post graduate studies: Ecole des Sciences Politiques, Paris; LSE. Entered Greek Diplomatic Service, 1953; served Cairo, NATO, Paris, Athens, Washington; Dep. Perm. Rep. to UN, NY, 1968–72; Dir, Middle East Political Affairs, Min. of Foreign Affairs, 1972–74; Ambassador, Perm. Rep. to EEC, 1974–79; Ambassador, Paris, 1979–82; non-resident Ambassador to Holy See, 1981–82; Dep. Political Dir, 1982–84, Political Dir, 1984–85, Min. of Foreign Affairs; Ambassador to UK, 1986–89, and non-resident Ambassador to Iceland; Head of Prime Minister's Diplomatic Office, 1989–90. Pres., EU *ad hoc* Gp on Stability Pact, 1994. Vice-Pres., Hellenic Foundn for Defence and Foreign Policy, 1994– (Mem. Bd, 1992–); Mem., Adv. Cttee, Inst. of Internat. Affairs, 1992–. Holds numerous foreign orders and decorations. *Address:* 24 Ravinė Street, Athens 11521, Greece. *T:* (1) 7222004. *Club:* Athenæum.

STAUGHTON, Rt. Hon. Sir Christopher (Stephen Thomas Jonathan Thayer), Kt 1981; PC 1988; **Rt. Hon. Lord Justice Staughton;** a Lord Justice of Appeal, since 1987; *b* 24 May 1933; *yr s* of late Simon Thomas Samuel Staughton of Melbourne, Australia and Edith Madeline Jones of Halifax, Canada; *m* 1960, Joanna Susan Elizabeth, *er d* of late George Frederick Arthur Burgess; two *d*. *Educ:* Eton Coll. (Scholar); Magdalene Coll., Cambridge (Scholar; Hon. Fellow 1988). 2nd Lieut, 11th Hussars PAO, 1952–53; Lieut, Derbyshire Yeomanry TA, 1954–56. George Long Prize for Roman Law, Cambridge, 1955; BA 1956; MA 1961. Called to Bar, Inner Temple, 1957, Bencher, 1978; QC 1970; a Recorder of the Crown Court, 1972–81; a Judge of the High Court of Justice, QBD, 1981–87. Mem., Senate of the Inns of Court and the Bar, 1974–81; Chm., Code of Conduct sub-cttee, 1979–80. Chm., St Peter's Eaton Square Church of England Sch., 1974–83. *Publications:* (Jt Editor) The Law of General Average (British Shipping Laws vol. 7), 1964, new edn, 1975; (jtly) Profits of Crime and their Recovery, 1984; articles on plain English in the law. *Recreations:* bridge, growing dahlias. *Address:* Royal Courts of Justice, Strand, WC2A 2LL. *T:* 0171–936 6000.

STAUNTON, Marie; Publishing Director, Financial Times Law & Tax (formerly Longman Law Tax & Finance), since 1991; Editor, Solicitors' Journal, since 1990; *b* 28 May 1952; *d* of Ann and Austin Staunton; *m* 1986, James Albert Provan; two *d*. *Educ:* Lancaster Univ.; College of Law (BA). Solicitor. Head of casework for Simon Community Hostels for Addicts, Alcoholics and Homeless Families (England, NI and Eire), 1970–72; Articled Clerk and Solicitor in private practice and Law Centres, 1976–83; Legal Officer, NCCL, 1983–87; Dir, British Section, Amnesty Internat., 1987–90 (Vice-Chm., Internat. Exec. Cttee, 1993–95). *Publications:* Data Protection: putting the record straight, 1987; contribs to NCCL works; chapters in books on allied subjects. *Address:* (office) 21–27 Lambs Conduit Street, WC1N 3NJ. *T:* 0171–242 2548.

STAVELEY, Sir John (Malfroy), KBE 1980 (OBE 1972); MC 1941; FRCP; FRACPath; Haematologist, Auckland Hospital Board, 1950–64; Director, Auckland Blood Transfusion Service, 1965–76; *b* 30 Aug. 1914; *s* of William Staveley and Annie May Staveley (*née* Malfroy); *m* 1940, Elvira Cliafe Wycherley; one *s* one *d*. *Educ:* Univ. of Dunedin (MB ChB); Univ. of Edinburgh. FRCP 1958; FRACPath 1965. House Surgeon, Auckland Hosp., 1939; war service with 2NZEF, Middle East, 1940–45; post graduate educn, UK, 1946–47; Pathologist, Auckland Hosp., 1948–50. Landsteiner Award, USA, for medical research, 1980. *Publications:* papers in medical and scientific jls (British, American and NZ). *Recreations:* mountaineering, fishing, music. *Address:* 11 Matanui Street, Northcote, Auckland 9, New Zealand.

STAVELEY, Martin Samuel, CMG 1966; CVO 1966; CBE 1962 (MBE 1955); *b* 3 Oct. 1921; fourth *s* of late Herbert Samuel Staveley and Edith Ellen Staveley (*née* Shepherd); *m* 1942, Edith Eileen Baker; one *s* two *d*. *Educ:* Stamford School; Trinity College, Oxford. Appointed Cadet, Colonial Administrative Service, Nigeria, 1942; Secretary, Development and Welfare Organisation in the West Indies, 1946–57; Secretary to Governor-General, Federation of the West Indies, 1958–62; Administrator, British Virgin Islands, 1962–67; HM Diplomatic Service, 1967–74; Home Civil Service, 1974–84. *Address:* Church Barn Cottage, Sharrington, Norfolk NR24 2PF.

STAVELEY, Maj.-Gen. Robert; *b* 3 June 1928; *s* of Brig. Robin Staveley, DSO, and Ilys (*née* Sutherland); *m* 1958, Airlie, *d* of Maj.-Gen. W. H. Lambert, CB, CBE; one *s* one *d*. *Educ:* Wellington. RMA, Sandhurst, 1947; commissioned RA, 1948; served BAOR, 1949–51; ADC to GOC Malta, 1951–53; Air OP pilot, Malaya, 1954–57 (despatches); ADC to GOC-in-C Northern Command, 1957–58; Indian Staff Coll., 1959; Staff Officer and Missile Battery Comdr, BAOR, 1960–65; Instructor, Staff Coll., 1966–68; commanded 47 Lt Regt RA, UK and Hong Kong, 1969–71; CRA 2nd Div., BAOR, 1973–74; RCDS 1975; Director of Operational Requirements, MoD, 1976–79; C of S, Logistic Exec. (Army), 1979–82. Admin. Controller, Norton Rose, solicitors, 1983–91. Col Comdt, RA, 1982–87. Chm., Bd of Govs, Royal Sch., Hampstead, 1993–. FIMgt (FBIM 1983). *Recreations:* good food, sailing, skiing, music. *Address:* c/o Lloyds Bank (Cox's & King's Branch), 7 Pall Mall, SW1Y 5NA. *Clubs:* Army and Navy, Royal Ocean Racing; Royal Artillery Yacht (Commodore, 1980–83; Admiral, 1991–).

STAVELEY, Admiral of the Fleet Sir William (Doveton Minet), GCB 1984 (KCB 1981); DL; Chairman, North Thames Regional Health Authority, and Member, NHS Policy Board, since 1994; *b* 10 Nov. 1928; *s* of late Adm. Cecil Minet Staveley, CB, CMG, and Margaret Adela (*née* Sturdee); *m* 1954, Bettina Kirstine Shuter; one *s* one *d*. *Educ:* West Downs, Winchester; RN Colls, Dartmouth and Greenwich. Entered Royal Navy as Cadet, 1942; Midshipman, HMS Ajax, Mediterranean, 1946–47; Sub-Lieut/Lieut, HM Ships Nigeria and Bermuda, S Atlantic, 1949–51; Flag Lieut to Adm. Sir George Creasy, C-in-C Home Fleet, HM Ships Indomitable and Vanguard, 1952–54; Staff, Britannia, RNC, Dartmouth, 1954–56; HM Yacht Britannia, 1957; First Lieut, HMS Cavalier, Far East, 1958–59; Lt-Comdr, 1958; RN Staff Coll., 1959; Staff, C-in-C Nore and Flag Officer Medway, 1959–61; Comdr 1961; Sen. Officer, 104th and 6th Minesweeping Sqdn, HMS Houghton, Far East, 1962–63; Comdr, Sea Trng, Staff of Flag Officer, Sea Trng, Portland, 1964–66; comd HMS Zulu, ME and Home Station, 1967; Captain 1967; Asst Dir, Naval Plans, Naval Staff, 1967–70; Command: HM Ships Intrepid, Far and ME, 1970–72; Albion, Home Station, 1972; RCDS, 1973; Dir of Naval Plans, Naval Staff, 1974–76; Flag Officer, Second Flotilla, 1976–77; Flag Officer, Carriers and Amphibious Ships, and NATO Commander, Carrier Striking Group Two, 1977–78; Chief of Staff to C-in-C Fleet, 1978–80; Vice-Chief of Naval Staff, 1980–82; C-in-C, Fleet, and Allied C-in-C, Channel and E Atlantic, 1982–85; First Sea Lord and Chief of Naval Staff, 1985–89; First and Principal Naval ADC to the Queen, 1985–89. Chairman: Royal London Hosp. and Associated Community Services NHS Trust, 1991–92; NE Thames RHA, 1993–94. Chairman: Combined Services Equitation Assoc., 1980–82; Council, British Horse Soc., 1982; Member: London Adv. Cttee, English Heritage, 1990–; RHS; Royal Nat. Rose Soc; Gen. Council, King Edward VII Hosp. Fund for London, 1993–. Trustee: Florence Nightingale Mus. Trust, 1988–93; Chatham Historic Dockyard Trust, 1988–94 (Chm., 1991–); Special Trustee, Royal London Hosp., 1992. Pres., Kent Br., Royal British Legion, 1991–; a Vice Pres., Falkland Is Assoc., 1991. Dir, British Sch. of Osteopathy, 1990– (Chm., 1992–). Mem. Court, 1988–, Council, 1992–, Univ. of Kent; Governor, Sutton Valence Sch., 1990–92. A Younger Brother of Trinity House, 1973. CIMgt (CBIM 1983). Freeman, City of London, 1987; Liveryman and Hon. Freeman, Shipwrights' Co., 1987. DL Kent, 1992. *Recreations:* country sports, gardening. *Address:* North Thames Regional Health Authority, 40 Eastbourne Terrace, W2 3QR. *T:* 0171–725 3434, *Fax:* 0171–723 5739. *Clubs:* Boodle's; Royal Naval Sailing Association.

STAVERT, Rt. Rev. Alexander Bruce; *see* Quebec, Bishop of.

STEAD, Rev. Canon (George) Christopher, LittD; FBA 1980; Fellow, King's College, Cambridge, 1938–49 and 1971–85 (Professorial Fellow, 1971–80); Emeritus Fellow, Keble College, Oxford, since 1981; *b* 9 April 1913; *s* of Francis Bernard Stead, CBE, and Rachel Elizabeth, *d* of Rev. Canon G. C. Bell; *m* 1958, Doris Elizabeth Odom; two *s* one *d*. *Educ:* Marlborough Coll.; King's Coll., Cambridge (scholar). 1st cl. Classical Tripos Pt I, 1933; Pitt Scholar, 1934; 1st cl. Moral Science Tripos Pt II, 1935; BA 1935, MA 1938, LittD Cantab 1978; New Coll., Oxford (BA 1935); Cuddesdon Coll., Oxford, 1938. Ordained, 1938; Curate, St John's, Newcastle upon Tyne, 1939; Lectr in Divinity, King's Coll., Cambridge, 1938–49; Asst Master, Eton Coll., 1940–44; Fellow and Chaplain, Keble Coll., Oxford, 1949–71 (MA Oxon 1949); Ely Professor of Divinity, Cambridge, and Canon Residentiary of Ely Cathedral, 1971–80, Canon Emeritus, 1981. *Publications:* Divine Substance, 1977; Substance and Illusion in the Christian Fathers, 1985; Philosophie und Theologie I, 1990; Philosophy in Christian Antiquity, 1994; contributor to: Faith and Logic, 1957; New Testament Apocrypha, 1965; A New Dictionary of Christian Theology, 1983; Dizionario di Patristica, 1983; Theologische Realenzyklopädie, 1985, 1991; Augustinus-Lexikon, 1986–93; Reallexikon für Antike und Christentum, 1992; about 30 major articles in Jl of Theol Studies, Vigiliae Christianae, and various Festschriften. *Recreations:* walking, sailing, music. *Address:* 13 Station Road, Haddenham, Ely, Cambs CB6 3XD.

STEAD, Ian Mathieson, PhD; FSA; FBA 1991; Deputy Keeper, Department of Prehistoric and Romano-British Antiquities, British Museum, 1977–96 (Assistant Keeper, 1974–77); *b* 9 Jan. 1936; *er s* of Sidney William Stead and Edith Johann (*née* Mathieson); *m* 1962, Sheelagh Mary Johnson; one *s* one *d*. *Educ:* Nunthorpe Grammar Sch., York; Fitzwilliam House, Cambridge Univ. (MA; PhD 1965). FSA 1966. Asst Inspector of Ancient Monuments, 1962, Inspector, 1964–74, Min. of Works. Chairman: Herts Archaeol Council, 1970–75; Humberside Jt Archaeol Cttee, 1974–81; Sec., Prehistoric Soc., 1974–76. Hon. Life Mem., Yorks Philosophical Soc., 1982; Corresp. Mem., Deutsches Archäologisches Institut, 1976. *Publications:* La Tène Cultures of Eastern Yorkshire, 1965;

Winterton Roman Villa, 1976; Arras Culture, 1979; (with J.-L. Flouest) Iron Age Cemeteries in Champagne, 1979; Rudston Roman Villa, 1980; The Gauls, 1981; Celtic Art in Britain, 1985; Battersea Shield, 1985; (with J. B. Bourke and D. Brothwell) Lindow Man, the Body in the Bog, 1986; (with V. Rigby) Baldock, 1986; (with V. Rigby) Verulamium, the King Harry Lane Site, 1989; Iron Age Cemeteries in East Yorkshire, 1991; papers in learned jls. *Address:* Ratcliffe House, Ashwell, Herts SG7 5NP. *T:* Ashwell (01462) 742396.

STEAD, Ralph Edmund, FCA, FCMA; retired; Chairman, Eastern Region, British Gas Corporation, 1977–81; *b* 7 Jan. 1917; *s* of Albert Stead and Mabel Stead; *m* 1946, Evelyn Annie Ness; two *s* two *d*. *Educ:* Manchester Grammar Sch.; Ilford County High Sch. FCA 1949; FCMA 1952. Served War, RASC, 1940–46. Asst Divl Accountant, Cambridge Div., Eastern Gas Bd, 1949–50; N Eastern Gas Board: Asst Chief Accountant, 1950–53; Group Accountant, Bradford Gp, 1953–57; N Western Gas Board: Gp Accountant, Manchester Gp, 1957–61; Gen. Man., West Lancs Gp, 1961–65; Head of Management Services, 1966–71; Dir of Finance, 1971–73; Dep. Chm., Eastern Reg., British Gas Corp., 1973–77. Member: Financial Instns Gp, DoE, 1981–82; Management Cttee, Lazards Property Unit Trust, 1979–92; Rent Assessment Panel for Scotland, 1983–87. *Recreations:* golf, gardening, reading. *Address:* 12 Abbotsford Court, Colinton Road, Edinburgh EH10 5EH.

STEAD, Robert, CBE 1965; retired as Controller, BBC North Region, 1958–69; *b* 10 Aug. 1909; *s* of Charles Fearnley Stead and Mary Ellen Taylor; *m* 1932, Constance Ann Sharpley (*d* 1989); two *s*. *Educ:* Morley Grammar Sch. In journalism, 1926–40; served in RN, 1940–45. Talks Producer, BBC North Region, 1946–48; Head of North Regional Programmes, 1948–53; BBC Australian Representative, 1953–57. *Recreations:* golf, gardening, theatre. *Address:* 20 Fulshaw Court, Wilmslow, Cheshire SK9 5JB. *T:* Wilmslow (01625) 525536.

STEADMAN, Dr John Hubert; Head of Safety and Environmental Assurance, Unilever Plc, since 1993; *b* 10 Aug. 1938; *s* of late Dr Harry Hubert Steadman and Janet Gilchrist Steadman (*née* MacDonald); *m* 1972, Dr Anthea Howell; one *s* one *d*. *Educ:* Wimbledon Coll.; Guy's Hosp. (MB, BS); University Coll. London (MSc). University College Hospital, London: Beit Meml Fellowship, 1968–72; Sen. Registrar, Dept of Haematology, 1972–78, with secondments to Ahmadu Bello Univ. Hosp., Nigeria, 1973, and Royal Perth Hosp., WA, 1974; Cons. Haematologist, King George Hosp., Ilford, 1978–81; MO 1981, SMO 1982, PMO 1984, DHSS; SPMO, Head of Div. of Toxicology and Envmtl Health, subseq. Health Aspects of Envmt and Food, DoH, 1988–93. Expert Advr on food safety, WHO, 1988–93. *Publications:* articles in learned jls on regulatory toxicology, haematology and biochemistry. *Recreations:* cooking, political philosophy. *Address:* Research and Engineering Division, Unilever House, Blackfriars, EC4P 4BQ.

See also J. M. M. Curtis-Raleigh.

STEADMAN, Ralph Idris; freelance cartoonist, illustrator and writer; *b* 15 May 1936; *s* of Lionel Raphael Steadman (English), and Gwendoline (Welsh); *m* 1st, 1959, Sheila Thwaite (marr. diss. 1971); two *s* two *d*; 2nd, 1972, Anna Deverson; one *d*. *Educ:* Abergele Grammar Sch.; London Coll. of Printing and Graphic Arts. Apprentice, de Havilland Aircraft Co., 1952; Cartoonist, Kemsley (Thomson) Newspapers, 1956–59; freelance for Punch, Private Eye, Telegraph, during 1960s; Political Cartoonist, New Statesman, 1978–80; retired to work on book about Leonardo da Vinci; as a positive political statement, refuses to draw another politician; 15 Save the Children originals auctioned in aid of Ethiopia Fund, 1990. Retrospective exhibitions: Nat. Theatre, 1977; Royal Festival Hall, 1984; Wilhelm Busch Mus., Hannover, 1988; October Gall. (sculptures and silk screen prints), 1990, Gulf war collages, 1991; Peacock Gall., Aberdeen, 1993; Aberdeen City Art Gall., 1994. Designed set of stamps of Halley's Comet, 1986; opera libretto and concept, The Plague and the Moonflower, Exeter Cathedral and Festival, 1989 (artist-in-residence), St Paul's Cathedral, 1989, Canterbury Cathedral and Festival, 1990, performed as Hearts Betrayed, St Martin-in-the-Fields, 1993, televised 1995; artist-in-residence, Cheltenham Fest., 1994. Writer, dir and performer, TV film, Hanging Garden Centres of Kent, 1992. Hon. Fellow, Kent Inst. of Art and Design, 1993. Hon. DLitt Kent, 1995. D & AD Gold Award (for outstanding contribution to illustration), 1977, and Silver Award (for outstanding editorial illustration), 1977; Black Humour Award, France, 1986; W. H. Smith Illustration Award for best illustrated book for last five years, 1987; BBC Design Award for postage stamps, 1987. *Publications:* Jelly Book, 1968; Still Life with Raspberry: collected drawings, 1969; The Little Red Computer, 1970; Dogs Bodies, 1971; Bumper to Bumper Book, 1973; Two Donkeys and the Bridge, 1974; Flowers for the Moon, 1974; The Watchdog and the Lazy Dog, 1974; America: drawings, 1975; America: collected drawings, 1977 (rev. edn, Scar Strangled Banger, 1987); Between the Eyes, 1984; Paranoids, 1986; The Grapes of Ralph, 1992; Teddy! Where are you?, 1994; *written and illustrated:* Sigmund Freud, 1979 (as The Penguin Sigmund Freud, 1982); A Leg in the Wind and other Canine Curses, 1982; I, Leonardo, 1983; That's My Dad, 1986 (Critici in Erba Prize, 1987); The Big I Am, 1988; No Room to Swing a Cat, 1989; Near the Bone, 1990; Tales of the Weirrd, 1990; Still Life with Bottle, Whisky According to Ralph Steadman, 1994; Jones of Colorado, 1995; designed and printed, Steam Press Broadsheets; *illustrated:* Frank Dickens, Fly Away Peter, 1961; Mischa Damjan: The Big Squirrel and the Little Rhinoceros, 1962; The False Flamingoes, 1963; The Little Prince and the Tiger Cat, 1964; Richard Ingrams, The Tale of Driver Grope, 1964; Love and Marriage, 1964; Daisy Ashford, Where Love Lies Deepest, 1964; Fiona Saint, The Yellow Flowers, 1965; Alice in Wonderland, 1967; Midnight, 1967; Mischa Damjan, Two Cats in America, 1968; Tariq Ali, The Thoughts of Chairman Harold, 1968; Dr Hunter S. Thompson: Fear and Loathing in Las Vegas, 1972; The Curse of Lono, 1984; Contemporary Poets set to Music series, 1972; Through the Looking Glass, 1972; Night Edge: poems, 1973; The Poor Mouth, 1973; John Letts Limericks, 1974; The Hunting of the Snark, 1975; Dmitri Sidjanski, Cherrywood Cannon, 1978; Bernard Stone: Emergency Mouse, 1978; Inspector Mouse, 1980; Quasimodo Mouse, 1984; Ted Hughes, The Threshold (limited edn), 1979; Adrian Mitchell, For Beauty Douglas, 1982; Flann O'Brien, More of Myles, 1982; Wolf Mankowitz, The Devil in Texas, 1984; Treasure Island, 1985; The Complete Alice and The Hunting of the Snark, 1986; Friendship (short stories), 1990 (in aid of John McCarthy); Animal Farm, 50th anniv. edn, 1995. *Recreations:* gardening (planted vineyard), collecting, writing, sheep husbandry, fishing, guitar, trumpet. *Club:* Chelsea Arts.

STEAR, Air Chief Marshal Sir Michael (James Douglas), KCB 1990; CBE 1982; QCVSA 1969; Deputy Commander-in-Chief, Allied Forces Central Europe, since 1992; *b* 11 Oct. 1938; *s* of late Melbourne Douglas Stear and Barbara Jane Stear (*née* Fletcher); *m* 1966, Elizabeth Jane, *d* of late Donald Edward Macrae, FRCS and of Janet Wallace Macpherson Simpson; two *s* one *d*. *Educ:* Monkton Combe Sch.; Emmanuel Coll., Cambridge (MA; CU Air Sqn (RAFVR), 1959–62). Nat. Service, 1957–59. Joined RAF, 1962; served on 1 Sqn, 1964–67, on 208 Sqn, Persian Gulf, 1967–69; exchange tour with USAF, 1969–71; Air Sec.'s Br., MoD, 1972–74; OC 17 Sqn, Germany, 1974–76; OC 56 Sqn, RAF Wattisham, 1976; PSO to CAS, MoD, 1976–79; OC RAF Gutersloh, 1980–82; Asst C of S (Ops), HQ 2 ATAF, 1982; Air Cdre Plans, HQ Strike Command, 1982–85; AOC No 11 Gp, 1985–87; ACDS (Nato/UK), 1987–89; AOC No 18 Gp, and Comdr Maritime Air Eastern Atlantic and Channel, 1989–92. Mem., RUSI, 1989–. Member: Council, Malcolm Clubs, 1988–; RFU Cttee, 1987–; Pres., RAF RU, 1992– (Chm., 1983–86). Mem. Council, Epsom Coll., 1990–. *Recreations:* Rugby football, keeping sheep, gardening, fishing, shooting. *Address:* HQ AFCENT, BFPO 28. *Club:* Royal Air Force (Vice-Pres., 1990–).

STEARN, Dr William Thomas; botanical consultant; retired as Senior Principal Scientific Officer, Department of Botany, British Museum (Natural History), 1976; Editor, Annales Musei Goulandris, since 1976; *b* 16 April 1911; *e s* of late Thomas Stearn, Cambridge; *m* 1940, Eldwyth Ruth Alford, *d* of late Roger R. Alford, Tavistock; one *s* two *d*. *Educ:* Cambridge High Sch. for Boys; part-time research at Botany Sch., Cambridge; apprentice antiquarian bookseller, Bowes & Bowes, Cambridge, 1929–32. Librarian, Royal Horticultural Soc., 1933–41, 1946–52. Served RAF, in Britain, India and Burma, 1941–46. Botanist, British Museum (Natural History), 1952–76. Hon. Sec., Internat. Cttee for Nomenclature of Cultivated Plants, 1950–53; former Council Member: Botanical Soc. of British Isles (Vice-Pres., 1973–77); British Soc. for History of Science (Vice-Pres., 1969–72); British Soc. for History of Medicine; Field Studies Council; Garden History Soc. (Founder Mem., 1965; Pres., 1977–82); Linnean Soc. (Vice-Pres., 1961–62; Pres., 1979–82; Hon. Botanical Curator, 1959–85); Ray Soc. (Vice-Pres., 1964–67, 1970–73, Pres., 1974–77); Richmond Scientific Soc. (Pres., 1969–71); Soc. for Bibliography of Natural History (Founder Mem., 1936, Hon. Mem., 1976); Systematics Assoc.; Mem., Old Cantabrigian Soc. (Pres., 1984–85). Masters Meml Lectr, 1964; Sandars Reader in Bibliography, Cambridge, 1965; Vis. Prof., Dept of Botany and Agricl Botany, 1977–83, Hon. Res. Fellow, 1983, Univ. of Reading; Wilkins Lectr, Royal Soc., 1985. Botanical collections made in Europe, Jamaica, USA, Australia. Royal Horticultural Society: Hon. Fellow, 1946; Vice-Pres., 1986–; Veitch Meml Medal, 1964; Victoria Medal of Honour, 1965. FLS 1934; CBiol 1992, FIBiol 1967 (MIBiol 1965); Hon. Member: Kungl. Vetenskaps-Societeten i Uppsala, 1967; Svenska Linnésällskapet, 1971; Botanical Soc. of Amer., 1982; For. Mem., Royal Swedish Acad. of Sci., 1983; Corr. Mem., Amer. Soc. of Plant Taxonomists, 1980. Freeman, Gardeners' Co., 1982. Hon. Fellow, Sidney Sussex Coll., Cambridge, 1968. DSc *hc* Leiden, 1960; Hon. ScD Cantab, 1967; FilDr *hc* Uppsala, 1972. Boerhaave Commem. Medal, Leiden, 1969; Linnaeus Medal, Royal Swedish Acad. of Sciences, 1972; Linnean Gold Medal, Linnean Soc., 1976; Hutchinson Medal, Chicago Horticultural Soc., 1985; Founders Medal, Soc. for the Hist. of Natural Hist., 1986; Engler Medal in Gold, Internat. Assoc. Plant Taxonomy, 1993. Comdr, Order of the Star of the North (Sweden), 1980. *Publications:* (with W. Blunt) The Art of Botanical Illustration, 1950, new edn as sole author, 1994; (with H. B. D. Woodcock) Lilies of the World, 1950; (with E. Blatter and W. S. Millard) Some Beautiful Indian Trees, 1955; Introduction to the *Species Plantarum* of Carl Linnaeus, 1957; Early Leyden Botany, 1961; Botanical Latin, 1966, 4th edn 1992 (trans. Chinese, 1981); Three Prefaces on Linnaeus and Robert Brown, 1967; Humboldt, Bonpland, Kunth and Tropical American Botany, 1968; (with C. N. Goulimis and N. Goulandris) Wild Flowers of Greece, 1968; (with A. W. Smith) Gardener's Dictionary of Plant Names, 1972; (with W. Blunt) Captain Cook's Florilegium, 1973; (with M. Page) Culinary Herbs, 1974, 3rd edn 1992; (with W. Blunt) Australian Flower Paintings of Ferdinand Bauer, 1976; The Wondrous Transformation of Caterpillars: M. S. Merian (Biog.), 1978; (with H. Hara and L. H. J. Williams) Enumeration of Flowering Plants of Nepal, vol. 1, 1978; The Natural History Museum at South Kensington, 1981; (with E. Rücker) Merian in Surinam, 1982; Plant Portraits from the *Flora Danica*, 1983; (with E. Roberts and C. Opsomer) Livre des Simples Médicines, English trans. and commentaries, 1984; (with P. H. Davis) Peonies of Greece, 1984; (with M. Rix) Redouté's Fairest Flowers, 1987; (with C. Brickell and M. Grierson) An English Florilegium, 1987; (with A. T. Gage) A Bicentenary History of the Linnean Society of London, 1988; (with A. W. Roach) Hooker's Fairest Fruits, 1989; Flower Artists of Kew, 1990; Stearn's Dictionary of Plant Names for Gardeners, 1992; (with J. Stewart) The Orchid Paintings of Franz Bauer, 1993; (with J. Riddell) By Underground to Kew, 1994; (ed English text and contrib.): Siebold's Florilegium of Japanese Plants, 1995; C. P. Thunberg's Drawings of Japanese Plants, 1995; numerous bibliographical, biographical, botanical and horticultural contribs to learned jls (listed in Biological Jl of Linnean Soc. vol. 8, 1976, Botanical Jl of Linnean Soc., vol. 109, 1992), RHS Dictionary of Gardening, Chambers's Encyclopaedia, Dictionary of Scientific Biography, Flora Europaea, European Garden Flora, Flora of Australia, Mountain Flora of Greece, etc. *Recreations:* gardening, talking. *Address:* 17 High Park Road, Kew Gardens, Richmond, Surrey TW9 4BL.

STEDMAN, family name of **Baroness Stedman.**

STEDMAN, Baroness *cr* 1974 (Life Peer), of Longthorpe, Peterborough; **Phyllis Stedman,** OBE 1965; *b* 14 July 1916; *o d* of Percy and Emmie Adams; *m* 1941, Henry William Stedman (*d* 1989), OBE 1981. *Educ:* County Grammar Sch., Peterborough. Branch Librarian, Peterborough City Council, 1934–41; Group Officer, National Fire Service, 1942–45. Baroness-in-Waiting (a Govt Whip), 1975–79; Parly Under-Sec. of State, DoE, 1979; Govt spokesman for Transport, the Environment, Educn and Trade, 1975–79; Opposition spokesman on the environment, local govt, new towns and transport, 1979–81; Leader of SDP in House of Lords, 1988–91 (Mem., 1981–91, SDP Whip, 1982–86, SDP Chief Whip, 1986–88); cross-bencher, 1992–. County Councillor: Soke of Peterborough, 1946–65; Huntingdon and Peterborough, 1965–74; Cambridgeshire, 1974–76; Vice-Chm., Cambridgeshire County Council, 1974–76. Member: Board, Peterborough Development Corp., 1972–76; IBA, 1974–75; Board, Hereward Radio, 1979–85; Exec. Mem., Tripscope, 1994–; Vice-Chm., Nat. PHAB, 1978–; Vice-Pres., ACC, 1986–. Mem. Exec. Council, Fire Services Nat. Benevolent Fund, 1976–. *Address:* 1 Grovelands, Thorpe Road, Peterborough PE3 6AQ. *T:* Peterborough (01733) 61109.

STEEDMAN, Martha, (Mrs R. R. Steedman); *see* Hamilton, M.

STEEDMAN, Robert Russell, RSA 1979 (ARSA 1973); RIBA; FRIAS; ALI; Partner, Morris and Steedman, Architects and Landscape Architects, Edinburgh, since 1959; *b* 3 Jan. 1929; *s* of late Robert Smith Steedman and Helen Hope Brazier; *m* 1st, 1956, Susan Elizabeth (marr. diss. 1974), *d* of Sir Robert Scott, GCMG, CBE; one *s* two *d*; 2nd, 1977, Martha Hamilton, *qv*. *Educ:* Loretto Sch.; School of Architecture, Edinburgh College of Art (DA); Univ. of Pennsylvania (MLA). RIBA 1955; ALI 1979. Lieut, RWAFF, 1947–48. Worked in office, Alfred Roth, Zürich, 1953. Architectural works include: Principal's House, Univ. of Stirling; Head Offices for Christian Salvesen, Edinburgh; Administration Building for Shell UK Exploration and Production; Moss Morran Fife; Restoration of Old Waterworks, Perth, to form Tourist Information Centre and Offices; Nat. Lighthouse Mus., Fraserburgh. Ten Civic Trust Awards, 1963–88; British Steel Award, 1971; Saltire Award, 1971; RIBA Award for Scotland, 1974 and 1989; European Architectural Heritage Medal, 1975; Assoc. for Preservation of Rural Scotland Award, 1977 and 1989. Chm., Central Scotland Woodlands Project, 1984–87; Member: Countryside Commn for Scotland, 1980–88; Adv. Panel on Management of Popular Mountain Areas in Scotland, 1989; Royal Fine Art Commn for Scotland, 1984–; Sec., Royal Scottish Acad., 1983–90 (Mem. Council 1981–, Dep. Pres. 1982–83); Mem. Bd, Friends of Royal Scottish Acad., 1984–92; Governor, Edinburgh College of Art, 1974–88; Mem., Edinburgh Festival Soc., 1978–; past Mem. Council, RIAS and Soc. of Scottish

Artists. Hon. Senior, St Leonards Sch., 1987–. FRSA 1995. *Recreations:* skiing, sketching. *Address:* 11B Belford Mews, Edinburgh EH4 3BT; (office) 38 Young Street North Lane, Edinburgh EH2 4JD. *T:* 0131–226 6563. *Clubs:* New (Edinburgh); Royal & Ancient Golf (St Andrews).

STEEDS, Prof. John Wickham, FRS 1988; FInstP; Research Professor in Physics and Head of Microstructural Group, since 1985 and Director, Interface Analysis Centre, since 1990, Bristol University; *b* 9 Feb. 1940; *s* of John Henry William Steeds and Ethel Amelia Tyler; *m* 1969, Diana Mary Kettlewell; two *d. Educ:* University College London (BSc 1961); PhD Cantab 1965. FInstP 1991. Research Fellow, Selwyn Coll., Cambridge, 1964–67; IBM Res. Fellow, 1966–67; Fellow, Selwyn Coll., Cambridge, 1967; Lectr in Physics, 1967–77, Reader, 1977–85, Bristol Univ. Visiting Professor: Univ. of Santiago, Chile, 1971; Univ. of California, Berkeley, 1981. Chairman: Science Res. Foundn, Emersons Green, 1989–; Commn on Electron Diffraction, Internat. Union of Crystallography; Mem., Council, European Pole Univ., Lille. *Publications:* Introduction to Anistropic Elasticity Theory of Dislocations, 1973; (with J. F. Mansfield) Electron Diffraction of Phases in Alloys, 1984; (ed jtly) Thin Film Diamond, 1994; papers on electron diffraction, materials science and solid state physics. *Recreations:* tennis, cycling, overseas travel. *Address:* 21 Canynge Square, Clifton, Bristol BS8 3LA. *T:* Bristol (0117) 973 2183.

STEEL, Hon. Dame (Anne) Heather, (Dame Heather Beattie), DBE 1993; **Hon. Mrs Justice Steel;** a Judge of the High Court of Justice, Queen's Bench Division, since 1993; *b* 3 July 1940; *d* of late His Honour Edward Steel and Mary Evelyn Griffith Steel; *m* 1967, David Kerr-Muir Beattie; one *s* one *d. Educ:* Howell's School, Denbigh; Liverpool University (LLB). Called to the Bar, Gray's Inn, 1963, Bencher, 1993; practice on N Circuit; Prosecuting Counsel to DHSS on N Circuit, 1984–86; a Recorder, 1984–86; a Circuit Judge, 1986–93. Mem., Criminal Cttee, Judicial Studies Bd, 1992–95. President: Merseyside Medico Legal Soc., 1992–94; Law Faculty Assoc., Liverpool Univ. Mem. Council, Rossall Sch., 1990–. Freeman, City of London, 1993; Liveryman, Pattenmakers' Co. *Recreations:* theatre, gardening, art, antiques. *Address:* Royal Courts of Justice, Strand, WC2A 2LL.

STEEL, Very Rev. David; Minister of St Michael's, Linlithgow, 1959–76, now Minister Emeritus; Moderator of the General Assembly of the Church of Scotland, 1974–75; *b* 5 Oct. 1910; *s* of John S. G. Steel and Jane Scott, Hamilton; *m* 1937, Sheila Martin, Aberdeen; three *s* two *d. Educ:* Peterhead Academy; Robert Gordon's Coll., Aberdeen; Aberdeen Univ. MA 1932, BD 1935. Minister of Church of Scotland: Denbeath, Fife, 1936–41; Bridgend, Dumbarton, 1941–46; Home Organisation Foreign Mission Secretary, 1946–49; Minister of Parish of East Africa and of St Andrew's, Nairobi, 1949–57; Associate Minister, St Cuthbert's, Edinburgh, 1957–59. Vis. Prof., Columbia Theol Seminary, Atlanta, 1979–85. Chm. of Governors, Callendar Park Coll. of Educn, 1974–79; Vice-Pres., Boys' Brigade, 1974–79. Hon. Vice-President: Nat. Bible Soc. of Scotland; W Lothian History and Amenity Soc.; Boys' Brigade. Hon. DD Aberdeen 1964; Hon. LLD Dundee, 1977. *Publications:* History of St Michael's, Linlithgow, 1961; Preaching Through the Year, 1980; contrib. theological and church jls. *Recreation:* trout fishing. *Address:* 39 Newbattle Terrace, Edinburgh EH10 4SF. *T:* 0131–447 2180. *Club:* Aberdeen University Senior Common Room.

See also Rt Hon. Sir D. M. S. Steel.

STEEL, Sir David (Edward Charles), Kt 1977; DSO 1940; MC 1945; TD; Chairman, The Wellcome Trust, 1982–89; *b* 29 Nov. 1916; *s* of late Gerald Arthur Steel, CB; *m* 1956, Ann Wynne, *d* of Maj.-Gen. C. B. Price, CB, DSO, DCM, VD, CD; one *s* two *d. Educ:* Rugby School; University Coll., Oxford (BA; Hon. Fellow, 1981). Inns of Court Regt, 1938; Commissioned 9 QR Lancers, 1940; served 1940–45 France, Middle East, North Africa, Italy (DSO, MC, despatches thrice). Admitted a Solicitor, June 1948; Linklaters and Paines, 1948–50; Legal Dept of The British Petroleum Co. Ltd, 1950–56; Pres. BP (N Amer.) Ltd, 1959–61; Man. Dir, Kuwait Oil Co. Ltd, 1962–65; Man. Dir, 1965–75, a Dep. Chm., 1972–75 and Chm., 1975–81, BP. A Dir, Bank of England, 1978–85; Dir, Kleinwort Benson Gp (formerly Kleinwort, Benson, Lonsdale), 1985–92. Pres., London Chamber of Commerce and Industry, 1982–85. Trustee, The Economist, 1979–; Chairman: Lenta Educn Trust, 1986–90; London Educn Business Partnership, 1986–89; Governors, Rugby Sch., 1984–88. Hon. Freeman, Tallow Chandlers' Co., 1980. Hon. DCL City Univ., 1983. Order of Taj III, Iran, 1974; Comdr, Order of Leopold, Belgium, 1980. *Recreations:* gardening, golf. *Clubs:* Cavalry and Guards, MCC, Hurlingham; Royal and Ancient (St Andrews).

STEEL, Rt. Hon. Sir David (Martin Scott), KBE 1990; PC 1977; DL; MP Tweeddale, Ettrick and Lauderdale, since 1983 (Roxburgh, Selkirk and Peebles, 1965–83) (L 1965–88, Lib Dem, since 1988); Co-Founder, Social and Liberal Democrats, 1988; journalist and broadcaster; *b* Scotland, 31 March 1938; *s* of Very Rev. Dr David Steel, *qv*; *m* 1962, Judith Mary, *d* of W. D. MacGregor, CBE, Dunblane; two *s* one *d* and one adopted *s. Educ:* Prince of Wales School, Nairobi, Kenya; George Watson's College and Edinburgh University. MA 1960; LLB 1962. Rector, Edinburgh Univ., 1982–85. President: Edinburgh University Liberals, 1959; Students' Representative Council, 1960. Asst Secretary, Scottish Liberal Party, 1962–64; Youngest Member of 1964–66 Parliament, of Privy Council, 1977; Liberal Chief Whip, 1970–75; Mem. Parly Delegn to UN Gen. Assembly, 1967; Sponsor, Private Member's Bill to reform law on abortion, 1966–67. Leader of Liberal Party, 1976–88. Pres., Liberal International, 1994–. Pres., Anti-Apartheid Movement of GB, 1966–69; Chm., Shelter, Scotland, 1969–73. Member: British Council of Churches, 1971–75; Council of Management, Centre for Studies in Social Policy, 1971–76; Adv. Council, European Discussion Centre, 1971–76; Chubb Fellow, Yale Univ., 1987. BBC television interviewer in Scotland, 1964–65; Presenter of STV weekly religious programme, 1966–67, and for Granada, 1969, and BBC, 1971–76. FRSA 1990. DL Roxburgh, Ettrick and Lauderdale, 1990. Awarded Freedom of Tweeddale, 1988, of Ettrick and Lauderdale, 1990. DUniv Stirling, 1991; Hon. DLitt Buckingham. Commander's Cross, Order of Merit (Germany), 1992. *Publications:* Boost for the Borders, 1964; Out of Control, 1968; No Entry, 1969; The Liberal Way Forward, 1975; A New Political Agenda, 1976; Militant for the Reasonable Man, 1977; New Majority for a New Parliament, 1978; High Ground of Politics, 1979; A House Divided, 1980; (with Judy Steel) Border Country, 1985; (presenter) Partners in One Nation: a new vision of Britain 2000, 1985; (with Judy Steel) Mary Stuart's Scotland, 1987; Against Goliath: David Steel's story, 1989; contrib. to The Times, The Guardian, The Scotsman, other newspapers and political weeklies. *Recreations:* angling, vintage motoring. *Address:* House of Commons, SW1A 0AA; Aikwood Tower, Ettrick Bridge, Selkirkshire.

STEEL, David William, QC 1981; a Recorder, since 1991; a Deputy High Court Judge, since 1993; *b* 7 May 1943; *s* of Sir Lincoln Steel and late Barbara (*née* Goldschmidt); *m* 1970, Charlotte Elizabeth Ramsay; two *s. Educ:* Eton Coll.; Keble Coll., Oxford (MA Hons Jurisprudence). Called to the Bar, Inner Temple, 1966, Bencher, 1991. With Coudert Bros (Attorneys), New York, 1967–68; commenced practice in England, 1969; Junior Counsel to the Treasury (Common Law) 1978–81; Junior Counsel to the Treasury (Admiralty), 1978–81. Wreck Commissioner for England and Wales, 1982–; Mem., panel of Lloyd's Salvage Arbitrators, 1982–. Chm., Commercial Bar Assoc., 1990–91; Mem., Lord Chancellor's Adv. Cttee on Legal Educn and Conduct, 1994–. Chm., OUBC Trust Fund Cttee, 1990–93. *Publications:* Editor: Temperley: Merchant Shipping Acts, 1976–; Forms and Precedents: British Shipping Laws, 1977–; Kennedy: Salvage, 1981–. *Recreations:* shooting, fishing. *Address:* Chinnor Hill Manor, Chinnor, Oxford OX9 4BG. *T:* Kingston Blount (01844) 351469. *Club:* Turf.

STEEL, Donald MacLennan Arklay; golf correspondent and golf course architect; *b* 23 Aug. 1937; *s* of William Arklay Steel and Catherine Fanny (*née* Jacobs), internat. golfer; *m* 1988, Rachel Ellen. *Educ:* Fettes Coll; Christ's Coll., Cambridge (MA). Golf correspondent: Sunday Telegraph, 1961–90; Country Life, 1983–; golf course architect, 1965–: with C. K. Cotton, Pennink, Lawrie and Partners; with C. K. Cotton, Pennink, Steel & Co.; with Donald Steel & Co. President: British Inst. of Golf Course Architects, 1989–91 (Hon. Sec., 1971–83; Chm., 1983–86); Assoc. of Golf Writers, 1993–. *Publications:* (ed jtly) Shell World Encyclopaedia of Golf, 1975; (ed) Guinness Book of Golf Facts and Feats, 1980; Bedside Books of Golf, 1965, 1971; The Classic Links, 1992; (ed) 11 edns, The Golf Course Guide of the British Isles (Daily Telegraph). *Recreations:* cricket, wine. *Address:* 1 March Square, Chichester, West Sussex PO19 4AN. *T:* Chichester (01243) 528506. *Clubs:* MCC; Hawks (Cambridge); Royal and Ancient Golf.

STEEL, Elizabeth Mary, (Mrs Stuart Christie); Her Honour Judge Steel; DL; a Circuit Judge, since 1991; *b* 28 Nov. 1936; *d* of His Honour Edward Steel and Mary Evelyn Griffith Steel (*née* Roberts); *m* 1972, Stuart Christie; one *s* one *d. Educ:* Howells Sch., Denbigh; Liverpool Univ. (LLB). Admitted solicitor, 1960; Partner, John A. Behn Twyford & Co., 1968–80; Partner, Cuff Roberts, 1980–91; a Recorder, 1989. Member: Cripps Cttee, 1967–69; Race Relations Bd, 1970–78; Council, Radio Merseyside, 1974–78; Gen. Adv. Council, BBC, 1979–82 (Chm., NW Adv. Council). Member: Law Soc., 1960; Liverpool Law Soc., 1960 (Pres., 1989–90); Chm., Steering Cttee, Hillsborough Solicitors' Gp, 1989–91. Member: Royal Liverpool Univ. Hosp. NHS Trust, 1991; Liverpool Playhouse Bd, 1968–95 (Vice-Pres., 1995–). Nat. Vice-Chm., YCs, 1965–67. DL Merseyside, 1991. *Recreations:* theatre (amateur and professional), music, needlework, cooking. *Address:* Manchester Crown Court, Courts of Justice, Crown Square, Manchester M3 3FL. *T:* 0161–832 8393. *Clubs:* University Women's; Athenæum (Liverpool) (Associate Member).

STEEL, Henry, CMG 1976; OBE 1965; Principal Legal Adviser: Government of British Antarctic Territory, since 1989; Government of British Indian Ocean Territory, since 1991; Leader, UK Delegation to UN Human Rights Commission, 1987–92 and since 1994; consultant on international and commonwealth law; *b* 13 Jan. 1926; *yr s* of late Raphael Steel; *m* 1960, Jennifer Isobel Margaret, *d* of late Brig. M. M. Simpson, MBE; two *s* two *d. Educ:* Christ's Coll., Finchley; New Coll., Oxford. BA Oxon 1950. Military Service, RASC and Intell. Corps, 1944–47. Called to Bar, Lincoln's Inn, 1951; Legal Asst, Colonial Office, 1955; Senior Legal Asst, CO, 1960; Asst Legal Adviser, CRO, 1965; Legal Counsellor, FCO, 1967–73; Legal Adviser, UK Mission to UN, NY, 1973–76; Legal Counsellor, FCO, 1976–79; Asst Under-Sec. of State (on loan to Law Officers' Dept), 1979; Legal Adviser to Governor of Southern Rhodesia, 1979–80; Asst Legal Secretary (Under-Secretary), Law Officers' Dept, 1980–83, Legal Sec. (Dep. Sec.), 1983–86; Dir, Commonwealth Legal Adv. Service, British Inst. of Internat. and Comparative Law, 1986–87. *Address:* College Place, Chapel Lane, Bledington, Oxon OX7 6UZ.

STEEL, John Brychan; QC 1993; *b* 4 June 1954; *s* of John Exton Steel and Valentine Brychan-Rees; *m* 1981, Susan Rebecca Fraser; two *s* one *d. Educ:* Harrow Sch.; Durham Univ. (BSc Hons Chem.). Lieut, Inns of Court and City Yeomanry, 1977–81; called to the Bar, Gray's Inn, 1978; Attorney-General's Suppl. Panel (Common Law), 1989–93. Dir, Busoga Trust, 1983. *Recreations:* ski-ing, flying, walking. *Address:* 4–5 Gray's Inn Square, WC1R 5AY. *T:* 0171–404 5252; Great Rollright Manor, Chipping Norton, Oxon OX7 5RH. *T:* Chipping Norton (01608) 730131. *Clubs:* Royal Automobile; Kandahar (Chm., 1992), Ski of GB (Dep. Chm., 1989–91).

STEEL, Patricia Ann, OBE 1990; Public Affairs Adviser, Babtie Group, since 1992; *b* 30 Oct. 1941; *d* of Thomas Norman Steel and Winifred Steel. *Educ:* Hunmanby Hall, near Filey, Yorks; Exeter Univ. (BA). Parly Liaison, Chamber of Shipping of UK and British Shipping Fedn, 1968–71; Sec., Highway and Traffic Technicians Assoc., 1972–73; Sec., Instn of Highways and Transportation, 1973–90. Director: LRT, 1984–91; Docklands Light Railway, 1984–91 (Chm., 1988–89); Victoria Coach Station Ltd, 1988–91. Member: Occupational Pensions Bd, 1979–84; Transport Res. Lab. Management Bd, 1992–. Dir (non-exec.), Richmond, Twickenham and Roehampton Healthcare NHS Trust, 1992–. *Recreations:* music, travel, politics. *Address:* 7 The Strathmore, 27 Petersham Road, Richmond, Surrey TW9 3DQ.

STEEL, Robert, CBE 1979; Secretary-General, Royal Institution of Chartered Surveyors, 1968–85 (Fellow, 1961; Hon. Mem., 1985); *b* 7 April 1920; *e s* of late John Thomas Steel and Jane (*née* Gordon), Wooler, Northumberland; *m* 1943, Averal Frances, *d* of Arthur Pettitt; one *s* one *d. Educ:* Duke's Sch., Alnwick, Northumb.; Univ. of London (BSc 1945); Gray's Inn (Barrister, 1956). Surveyor, 1937–46; Asst Sec., Under Sec., Royal Instn of Surveyors, 1946–61; Dir of Town Development, Basingstoke, 1962–67. Sec.-Gen., Internat. Fedn of Surveyors, 1967–69, Vice-Pres., 1970–72, Hon. Mem., 1983; Sec., Commonwealth Assoc. of Surveying and Land Economy, 1969–90; Sec., Aubrey Barker Trust, 1970–94; Member: South East Economic Planning Council, 1974–76; Council, British Consultants Bureau, 1977–85. Chm., Geometers Liaison Cttee, EEC, 1972–86. Hon. Editor, Commonwealth Surveying and Land Economy, 1975–90. Founder Mem., 1977, Mem. Ct of Assts, 1977–, Master, 1988–89, Worshipful Co. of Chartered Surveyors. Organised national networks of beacons for Queen's Silver Jubilee celebrations, 1977, and for the Wedding of Prince Charles and Lady Diana Spencer, 1981. Raised: £71,210 for RICS Benev. Fund by sponsored walk of 1000 miles, John O'Groats to Land's End, 1979 (world record for largest sum raised by a single walker); £66,333 for RICS Benev. Fund and The Prince's Trust by walk of 1100 miles, Cape Wrath to Dover and London, 1985; £111,039 for Lord Mayor of London's Charity Appeal for Children, 1988, by walk of 1,200 miles from Strathy Point, Sutherland, to Portland Bill, Dorset, and London; £130,500 for National Trust Enterprise Neptune, 1990, by walk of 2,000 miles around the perimeter of England. Hon. Member: Bulgarian Mountain Rescue Service, 1964; Union Belge des Geomètres Experts, 1976; Hon. Fellow, Inst. of Surveyors, Malaysia, 1983. Hon. LLD Aberdeen, 1985. Distinguished Service Award, Surveyors Inst. of Sri Lanka, 1986. Silver Jubilee Medal, 1977. *Publications:* on Property Law; contrib. professional jls and internat. conferences. *Recreations:* mountain walking, travel, music. *Address:* 701 Hood House, Dolphin Square, SW1V 3NJ.

STEEL, Prof. Robert Walter, CBE 1983; BSc, MA Oxon; Principal, University College of Swansea, 1974–82; Vice-Chancellor, 1979–81, Emeritus Professor 1982, University of Wales; *b* 31 July 1915; *er s* of late Frederick Grabham and Winifred Barry Steel; *m* 1940, Eileen Margaret, *er d* of late Arthur Ernest and Evelyn Beatrice Page, Bournemouth; one *s* two *d. Educ:* Great Yarmouth Grammar Sch.; Cambridge and County High School for

Boys; Jesus College, Oxford (Open Exhibitioner in Geography; Hon. Fellow 1982). RGS Essay Prize, 1936. Drapers' Co. Research Scholarship for Geography, 1937–39, for work in Sierra Leone; Departmental Lectr in Geography, Univ. of Oxford, 1939–47; Naval Intelligence Div., Admiralty, 1940–45; attached to Sociological Dept of W African Inst. of Arts, Industry and Social Science as geographer to Ashanti Social Survey, Gold Coast, 1945–46; University of Oxford: Univ. Lectr in Commonwealth Geography, 1947–56; Lectr in Geography, St Peter's Hall, 1951–56; Official Fellow and Tutor in Geography, Jesus Coll., 1954–56 (Supernumary Welsh Fellow, 1974–75 and 1979–80; Hon. Fellow 1982); Univ. of Liverpool: John Rankin Prof. of Geography, 1957–74; Dean, Faculty of Arts, 1965–68, Pro-Vice-Chancellor, 1971–73. Murchison Grant (RGS), 1948; Council RGS, 1949–53, 1968–71; Inst. of Brit. Geographers: Council, 1947–60; Actg Sec., 1948, Asst Sec., 1949–50; Hon. Editor of Publications, 1950–60; Vice-Pres., 1966–67, Pres. 1968, Hon. Mem. 1974; President: Section E (Geography), BAAS, 1966; African Studies Assoc. of the UK, 1970–71 (Vice-Pres., 1969–70); Geographical Assoc., 1973 (Hon. Mem. 1982); Glamorgan Trust for Nature Conservation, 1982–86. Dir, Commonwealth Geographical Bureau, 1972–81; Member: Inter-Univ. Council for Higher Educn Overseas, 1974–81; Welsh Adv. Cttee, British Council, 1978–90; Cttee for Internat. Co-operation in Higher Educn, British Council (Higher Educn Div.), 1981–85; Chairman: Universities Council for Adult Educn, 1976–80; Governors, Westhill Coll., Birmingham, 1981–95; Bd, Wales Adv. Body for Local Authority Higher Educn, 1982–86; Swansea Festival of Music and the Arts, 1982–95; Lower Swansea Valley Develt Gp, 1979–88; Swansea Civic Soc., 1988–; Commonwealth Human Ecology Council, 1988–90; Pres., Council for Church and Associated Colls, 1990–94 (Vice-Chm., 1988–90); Mem., ESRC, 1983–86 (Chm., Internat. Activities Cttee, 1985–86). Member Council: National Univ. of Lesotho, 1981–85; Univ. of Swaziland, 1987–91. Vice-Pres., Royal African Soc., 1977–; Council, Nat. Inst. of Adult Educn, 1977–80. Vis. Prof., Univ. of Ghana, 1964; Canadian Commonwealth Vis. Fellow, Carleton Univ., 1970. Fellow, Selly Oak Coll., Birmingham, 1995. Hon. Fellow: UC Swansea, 1991; Trinity Coll., Carmarthen, 1995. Hon. DSc Salford, 1977; Hon. LLD: Wales, 1983; Liverpool, 1985; Birmingham, 1995; DUniv Open, 1987. *Publications:* ed (with A. F. Martin), and contrib. to The Oxford Region: a Scientific and Historical Survey, 1954; ed (with C. A. Fisher), and contrib. to Geographical Essays on British Tropical Lands, 1956; ed (with R. M. Prothero), and contrib. to Geographers and the Tropics: Liverpool Essays, 1964; ed (with R. Lawton), and contrib. to Liverpool Essays on Geography: a Jubilee Collection, 1967; (with Eileen M. Steel) Africa, 1974, 3rd edn 1982; ed, Human Ecology and Hong Kong: report for the Commonwealth Human Ecology Council, 1975; The Institute of British Geographers, the First Fifty Years, 1984; (contrib. and ed) British Geography 1918–1945, 1987; articles, mainly on tropical Africa, in Geographical Jl and other geog. jls. *Recreations:* walking, gardening, music. *Address:* 12 Cambridge Road, Langland, Swansea SA3 4PE. *T:* Swansea (01792) 369087. *Club:* Commonwealth Trust.

STEEL, Rupert Oliver; *b* 30 April 1922; *s* of Joseph Steel and Beatrice Elizabeth Courage; *m* 1st, Marigold Katharine, *d* of Percy Lowe; two *s*; 2nd, Lucinda Evelyn Tennant, *d* of Arthur James; one *s* one *d*. *Educ:* Eton. Served War of 1939–45 (despatches), Pilot, RNVR, Fleet Air Arm, 1941–46. Courage & Co. Ltd, 1946–78; Imperial Group Ltd, 1975–78; Chm., Everards Brewery Ltd, 1978–84; Director: Lloyds Bank Ltd, 1977–79; Lloyds Bank UK Management, 1979–85; Umeco plc, 1979–95; South Uist Estates Ltd, 1980–94. High Sheriff, Berks, 1985–86. *Recreation:* country. *Address:* Winterbourne Holt, Newbury, Berks RG20 8AP. *T:* Chieveley (01635) 248220. *Club:* Brooks's.

STEELE, Prof. Alan John; Professor of French, University of Edinburgh, 1972–80, retired; *b* Bellshill, Lanark, 11 April 1916; *s* of John Steele, MA, BD, and Anne (*née* Lawson); *m* 1947, Claire Alice Louise Belet; one *d* (one *s* decd). *Educ:* Royal Grammar School, Newcastle upon Tyne; Blyth Secondary School, Northumberland; Universities of Edinburgh, Grenoble and Paris. MA 1st Cl. Hons in French Language and Literature, Vans Dunlop Schol., Univ. of Edinburgh, 1938. Served War of 1939–45, at sea with 4th Maritime AA Regt, RA, 1941–42; commissioned, 1942, with 64th LAA Regt RA in Algeria, Italy and Greece. Lecturer in French, University of Edinburgh, 1946, Prof. of French Literature, 1961–72. Chairman: Scottish Central Cttee for Modern Languages, 1972–81; Assoc. of Univ. Profs of French, 1974–75; Consultative Cttee, Institut Français d'Ecosse, 1981–88; Vice-Pres., Franco-Scottish Soc., 1961–92. Mem., Church of Scotland Panel on Doctrine, 1978–86. Editor, Modern Language Review (French Section), 1971–79. Chevalier, Légion d'Honneur, 1973; Commandeur, Palmes Académiques, 1988. *Publications:* (with R. A. Leigh) Contemporary French Translation Passages, 1956; Three Centuries of French Verse, 1956, new edn, 1961; contrib. to collective volumes, Cahiers de l'Assoc. Internat. des Etudes françaises, Modern Language Review. *Recreation:* music. *Address:* 17 Polwarth Grove, Edinburgh EH11 1LY. *T:* 0131–337 5092.

STEELE, Dr Bernard Robert; Development and Property Director (formerly Property Secretary), Methodist Homes for the Aged, 1987–91; *b* 21 July 1929; *s* of Robert Walter and late Phyllis Mabel Steele; *m* 1953, Dorothy Anne Newman; one *s* two *d*. *Educ:* Oakham Sch.; Selwyn Coll., Cambridge (MA, PhD). Scientific Officer, Min. of Supply, 1953–55; Section Leader, UKAEA, Springfields, 1955–66; Building Research Station: Head, Materials Div., 1966–69; Asst Dir, 1969–72; Dep. Dir, Building Res. Estabt, 1972–75; Borough Housing Officer, Haringey, 1975–78; Dir, Science and Research Policy, DoE, 1978–82; Head, Housing Services, GLC, 1982–86. Vis. Prof., Bartlett Sch. of Architecture and Planning, UCL, 1987–89. Chm., Environment Cttee, SRC, later SERC, 1978–81. Pres., RILEM (Internat. Union of Testing and Res. Labs for Materials and Structures), 1974–75. Chm., Watford Churches Housing Assoc., 1975–78. *Publications:* contrib. numerous scientific publications on chemistry, materials science and building. *Recreations:* travelling, photography. *Address:* 1 Broom Grove, Watford WD1 3RY. *T:* Watford (01923) 241271.

STEELE, Frank Fenwick, OBE 1969; consultant; *b* 11 Feb. 1923; *s* of Frank Robert and Mary Fenwick Steele; *m*; one *s* one *d*. *Educ:* St Peter's Sch., York; Emmanuel Coll., Cambridge (MA). Army, 1943–47. HM Colonial Service, Uganda, 1948–50; joined HM Diplomatic Service, 1951; FO, 1951; Vice-Consul, Basra, 1951; Third, later Second Sec., Tripoli, 1953; Foreign Office, 1956; Second Sec., Beirut, 1958; FO, 1961; First Sec.: Amman, 1965; Nairobi, 1968; Counsellor and Dep. UK Rep., Belfast, 1971; FCO, 1973; resigned 1975. Joined Kleinwort, Benson as Adviser, 1975; Dir, and Hd of Export Finance Dept, Kleinwort Benson, 1985–87; Dir, cos in Cluff group, 1979–87; Chm., Network Television Ltd, 1981–87. Mem., Export Promotion Cttee, CBI, 1983–87. Dir, Arab British Chamber of Commerce, 1978–87; Member Council: Anglo-Jordanian Soc., 1980–88; Royal Soc. for Asian Affairs, 1981–88 (Vice-Pres., 1985–88); Royal Asiatic Soc., 1986–90 (Pres., 1988–90); Royal Geographical Soc., 1990–95 (Mem., F and GP Cttee, 1986–95; Vice-Pres., 1993–95); Mem. Cttee, Mount Everest Foundn, 1990–95. *Publications:* articles on Tibet. *Recreation:* travel. *Address:* 9 Ashley Gardens, SW1P 1QD. *T:* 0171–834 7596. *Clubs:* Beefsteak, Shikar, Travellers'.

STEELE, John Ernest, FInstPS; consultant to shipbuilding and allied industries, since 1989; Director, Morganite Special Carbons Ltd, since 1990; *b* 4 June 1935; *s* of William Steele and Amelia Steele (*née* Graham); *m* 1958, Lucy Wilkinson; one *s* three *d*. *Educ:* Rutherford College of Technology, Newcastle upon Tyne. MNECInst. Swan Hunter and Wigham Richardson Ltd: apprentice shipbuilder, 1951–56; Management Progression, 1956–68; Swan Hunter Shipbuilders Ltd: Local Dir, 1968–71; Purchasing Dir, 1971–74; Dep. Chm. and Dep. Chief Exec., 1974–78; Chief Exec., 1977–83; Chm. and Chief Exec., 1978–83; British Shipbuilders: Div. Man. Dir, Composite Yards, 1981–83; part time Bd Mem., 1979–82; Exec. Bd Mem., Offshore, 1982–84; a Corp. Man. Dir, Offshore, 1982–84; Exec. Bd Mem., Procurement, 1984–85; Corporate Man. Dir, Procurement and Special Projects, 1985–89; Commercial Dir, 1986–88, Man. Dir, 1988–89, North East Shipbuilders Ltd. Chairman: Cammell Laird Shipbuilders Ltd, 1981–84; V. O. Offshore Ltd, 1982–84; Scott Lithgow Ltd, 1983–84; Lyon Street Railway Ltd, 1977–84; Vosper Thorneycroft (UK) Ltd, 1984–86; Sunderland Forge Services, 1987–89; Exec. Cttee, Rigby Metal Components Ltd, 1990–91. British Cttee Mem., Det Norske Veritas, 1981–91. Director: Euroroute Construction Ltd, 1985–89; Sunderland Shipbuilders Ltd, 1988–89; Non-Exec. Dir, Gibraltar Shiprepair Ltd, 1987–90. Liveryman, Shipwrights' Co. *Recreations:* Rugby football, golf, reading.

STEELE, John Hamilton; Managing Director, Esso Exploration and Production UK, since 1995; *b* 13 March 1941. *Educ:* North Carolina State Univ. (BS Civil Engr, MS Engr). MInstPet. Exxon Corp., USA: joined 1965; Oil & Gas Production; Calif. Dist Manager, 1976–78; Production Manager, EPMI, Malaysia, 1978–82; Dir, Esso Exploration, Stavanger, 1982–85; EUSA: Div. Manager, New Orleans, 1985–92; Production Ops Manager, Houston, 1992–93; Vice-Pres., Production, Houston, 1993–94. Mem., Soc. of Petroleum Engineers. *Recreations:* golf, ballet, opera. *Address:* Esso House, 96 Victoria Street, SW1E 5JW. *T:* 0171–245 3280.

STEELE, Dr John Hyslop, FRS 1978; FRSE; President, Woods Hole Oceanographic Institution, Mass, 1986–92, now President Emeritus (Director, 1977–89); *b* 15 Nov. 1926; *s* of Adam Steele and Annie Hyslop Steele; *m* 1956, Margaret Evelyn Travis; one *s*. *Educ:* George Watson's Boys' Coll., Edinburgh (Higher Cert. of Educn); University Coll., London Univ. (BSc, DSc). FRSE 1968. Marine Lab., Aberdeen, Scotland: Marine Scientist, 1951–66; Sen. Principal Scientific Officer, 1966–73; Dep. Dir, 1973–77. Dir, Exxon Corp., 1989–. Mem., Cttee for Res. and Exploration, Nat. Geographic Soc., 1987–. Trustee, Robert Wood Johnson Foundn. Fellow, Amer. Acad. of Arts and Sciences, 1980; FAAAS 1985. Hon. Prof., Aberdeen Univ., 1993–. Agassiz Medal, Nat. Acad. of Sciences, USA, 1973. *Publications:* Structure of Marine Ecosystems, 1974; over 100 pubns in oceanographic and ecological jls. *Recreation:* sailing. *Address:* Woods Hole Oceanographic Institution, Woods Hole, MA 02543, USA. *T:* (508) 5481400.

STEELE, John Martin, CB 1995; OBE 1986 (MBE 1979); TD 1970; DL; Under Secretary, Northern Ireland Office, since 1987; *b* 20 May 1938; *s* of John and Margaret Steele; *m* 1st, 1961, Molly Fulton (*d* 1988); one *s* two *d*; 2nd, 1992, Margaret Norma Armstrong, ISO. *Educ:* Belfast High Sch.; Queen's Univ., Belfast. Various posts, NI Civil Service, 1962–66; staff of NI Parlt, 1966–72; Dept of Community Relations, 1972–73; Second Clerk Asst, NI Assembly, 1973–74; Co-Sec., Gardiner Cttee on measures to deal with terrorism in NI, 1974; Second Clerk Asst, NI Constitutional Convention, 1975–76; DoE, NI, 1976–78; DHSS, NI, 1978–82; Dir, NI Court Service, 1982–87. Mem., TA, 1958–85; formerly Dep. Comd 23 Artillery Bde and CO 102 Air Defence Regt, RA(V); Hon. Col, 102 AD Regt, 1987–93; Chm., RA Council of NI; Pres., Belfast Br., RAA. DL Belfast, 1992. *Recreations:* gardening, walking, reading, cooking. *T:* (office) Belfast (01232) 527012. *Clubs:* Army and Navy; Royal Ulster Yacht.

STEELE, John Roderic, CB 1979; transport consultant; Chairman, P & O European Transport Service, since 1989; Director: P & O Containers Ltd, since 1987; P & O Steam Navigation Co., since 1992; *b* 22 Feb. 1929; *s* of late Harold Graham Steele and Doris Steele (*née* Hall); *m* 1956, Margaret Marie, *d* of late Joseph and Alice Stevens; two *s* two *d*. *Educ:* Queen Elizabeth Grammar Sch., Wakefield; Queen's Coll., Oxford (MA). Asst Principal, Min. Civil Aviation, 1951; Private Sec. to Parly Sec., MTCA, 1954; Principal, Road Trans. Div., 1957; Sea Transport, 1960; Shipping Policy, 1962; Asst Sec., Shipping Policy, BoT, 1964, Counsellor (Shipping), British Embassy, Washington, 1967; Asst Sec., Civil Aviation Div., DTI, 1971, Under-Sec., Space Div., 1973, Shipping Policy Div., 1974, Gen. Div., 1975, Dept of Trade; Dep. Sec., Dept of Trade, 1976–80, Dept of Industry, 1980–81; Dir-Gen. for Transport, EEC, 1981–86. Mem., Dover Harbour Bd, 1990–92. *Recreations:* normal. *Address:* Brocas Oast, Hever, Edenbridge, Kent TN8 7LE; Square Ambiorix 30, Bte 30, 1040 Bruxelles, Belgium. *Clubs:* United Oxford & Cambridge University; Philippics.

STEELE, Kenneth Walter Lawrence, CBE 1980 (OBE 1967); KPM 1936; Chief Constable, Avon and Somerset Constabulary, 1974–79; *b* 28 July 1914; *s* of Walter and Susan Steele, Godalming, Surrey; *m* 1987, Irene Koh, Malaysia. *Educ:* Wellington Sch., Wellington, Somerset. Served War: with Somerset LI and Royal Northumberland Fusiliers, 1942–45. Asst Chief Constable, Buckinghamshire, 1953–55; Chief Constable: Somerset, 1955–66; Somerset and Bath, 1966–74. *Address:* Lloyds Bank Ltd, 31 Fore Street, Taunton, Somerset TA1 1HN.

STEELE, Maj.-Gen. Michael Chandos Merrett, MBE 1972; Chief of Joint Services Liaison Organization, Bonn, 1983–86; Regimental Comptroller, Royal Artillery, since 1989; *b* 1 Dec. 1931; *s* of late William Chandos Steele and Daisy Rhoda Steele (*née* Merrett); *m* 1961, Judith Ann Huxford; two *s* one *d*. *Educ:* Westminster School; RMA Sandhurst. Commissioned RA, 1952; Staff Coll., Camberley, 1962; BM RA, 53rd Welsh Div., 1965–67; BM, 8th Inf. Brigade, 1970–72; CO 22nd Light Air Defence Regt, RA, 1972–74; GSO1, HQ DRA, 1974–76; Comdr, 7th Artillery Brigade, 1976–78; Nat. Defence Coll., Canada, 1978–79; BGS, Defence Sales Organization, 1979–82. Col Comdt, RA, 1988–94. Hon. Col 104 Air Defence Regt, RA(V)TA, 1987–. Chm., Tree Council, 1994–. *Recreations:* lawn tennis, gardening. *Address:* Elders, Masons Bridge Road, Redhill, Surrey RH1 5LE. *T:* Redhill (01737) 763982.

STEELE, Sir (Philip John) Rupert, Kt 1980; Director, Trust Company of Australia Ltd (formerly Union Fidelity Trustee Co. of Australia), 1984–91; *b* 3 Nov. 1920; *s* of late C. Steele; *m* 1946, Judith, *d* of Dr Clifford Sharp; one *s* two *d*. *Educ:* Melbourne C of E Grammar School. Served RAAF and 115 Sqdn (Lancaster), RAF; POW 1944. Director: Steele & Co. Ltd, 1949–59; Carlton Brewery Ltd, 1964–73; Carlton and United Breweries, 1973–84. Mem. Council, Royal Agr. Soc. of Victoria, 1961–74. Pres., Prahan Football Club, 1980–85; Mem. Cttee, Victoria Racing Club, 1958–85, Hon. Treasurer, 1971–73, Vice-Chm., 1973–77, Chm., 1977–82; Mem., Racecourses Licensing Board, 1975–81. *Recreation:* racing thoroughbred horses. *Address:* 2/64 Irving Road, Toorak, Victoria 3142, Australia.

STEELE, Richard Charles, FIBiol, FICFor; Director General, Nature Conservancy Council, 1980–88; *b* 26 May 1928; *s* of Richard Orson Steele and Helen Curtis Steele (*née* Robertson); *m* 1966, Anne Freda Nelson; two *s* one *d*. *Educ:* Univ. of Wales (BSc Forestry and Botany); Univ. of Oxford. National Service, 1946–48. Assistant Conservator of Forests, Colonial Forest Service (later HMOCS), Tanganyika (later Tanzania), 1951–63; Head: Woodland Management Section, Nature Conservancy, Monks Wood, 1963–73; Terrestrial Life Sciences Section, Natural Environment Research Council, London,

1973–78; Division of Scientific Services, NERC Inst. of Terrestrial Ecology, Cambridge, 1978–80. Past Pres., Inst. of Foresters of Gt Britain; Mem., Southern Regl Cttee, NT. *Publications:* Wildlife Conservation in Woodlands, 1972; ed, Monks Wood: a nature reserve record, 1974; numerous papers on nature conservation, ecology and forestry in professional and scientific jls. *Recreations:* hill-walking, gardening, collecting books on natural history and E African travel. *Address:* Treetops, 20 Deepdene Wood, Dorking, Surrey, RH5 4BQ. *T:* Dorking (01306) 883106.

STEELE, Sir Rupert; *see* Steele, Sir P. J. R.

STEELE, Tommy, (Thomas Hicks), OBE 1979; actor; *b* Bermondsey, London, 17 Dec. 1936; *s* of late Thomas Walter Hicks and Elizabeth Ellen (*née* Bennett); *m* 1960, Ann Donoghue; one *d. Educ:* Bacon's Sch. for Boys, Bermondsey. First appearance on stage in variety, Empire Theatre, Sunderland, Nov. 1956; first London appearance, variety, Dominion Theatre, 1957; Buttons in Rodgers and Hammerstein's Cinderella, Coliseum, 1958; Tony Lumpkin in She Stoops to Conquer, Old Vic, 1960; Arthur Kipps in Half a Sixpence, Cambridge Theatre, London, 1963–64 and Broadhurst Theatre (first NY appearance), 1965; Truffaldino in The Servant of Two Masters, Queen's, 1969; Dick Whittington, London Palladium, 1969; Meet Me In London, Adelphi, 1971; Jack Point, in The Yeomen of the Guard, City of London Fest., 1978; London Palladium: The Tommy Steele Show, 1973; Hans Andersen, 1974 and 1977; one-man show, Prince of Wales, 1979; Singin' in the Rain (also dir.), 1983; Some Like It Hot, Prince Edward, (also dir.), 1992; *films:* Kill Me Tomorrow, 1956; The Tommy Steele Story; The Duke Wore Jeans; Tommy the Toreador; Touch It Light; It's All Happening; The Happiest Millionaire; Half a Sixpence; Finian's Rainbow; Where's Jack?; *television:* wrote and acted in Quincy's Quest, 1979. Composed and recorded, My Life, My Song, 1974; composed: A Portrait of Pablo, 1985; Rock Suite—an Elderly Person's Guide to Rock, 1987. *Publications:* Quincy, 1981; The Final Run, 1983. *Recreations:* squash, sculpture. *Address:* c/o Mark Furness Ltd, 10/12 Garrick Street, WC2E 9BH. *T:* 0171–836 7373.

STEELE-BODGER, Prof. Alasdair, CBE 1980; FRCVS; freelance consultant in forensic veterinary medicine; Professor of Veterinary Clinical Studies, University of Cambridge, 1979–90; *b* 1 Jan. 1924; *s* of late Harry Steele-Bodger, MRCVS, and Mrs K. Steele-Bodger (*née* MacDonald); *m* 1948, Anne, 2nd *d* of late Captain A. W. J. Finlayson, RN, and Mrs Nancy Finlayson; three *d. Educ:* Shrewsbury Sch.; Caius Coll., Cambridge (BA 1945, MA); Royal 'Dick' Veterinary Coll., Edinburgh Univ. (BSc, MRCVS 1948). Hon. FRCVS 1975; Scientific FZS 1989. Gen. vet. practice, Lichfield, Staffs, 1948–77; consultant practice, Fordingbridge, Hants, 1977–79. Hon. Vet. Consultant to British Agricl Export Council, 1967–. Vis. Prof., Univ. of Toronto, 1973. Pres., British Small Animal Vet. Assoc., 1962; Member: Horserace Scientific Adv. Cttee (formerly Jockey Club's Horserace Anti-Doping Cttee), 1973–92; UGC's Agricl and Vet. Sub-Cttee, 1973–81; Council: BVA, 1957–85 (Pres., 1966; Hon. Mem., 1985); RCVS, 1960–90 (Pres., 1972); Jt RCVS/BVA Cttee on Eur. Vet. Affairs, 1967–90; Eur. Liaison Gp for Agriculture, 1972–90; Cttee of Inquiry on Experiments on Animals, 1963–65; Council, Royal Agricl Soc. of England, 1967– (Hon. Fellow, 1993); Animal Feedingstuffs Industry/BVA/ADAS HQ Liaison Cttee, 1967–85. UK Deleg. to Fedn of Veterinarians of EEC, 1967–90; EEC Official Vet. Expert, 1974–; Member: EEC Adv. Cttee on Vet. Trng, 1981–90; Home Office Panel of Assessors under Animals (Scientific Procedures) Act, 1986–. Vice-Pres., Inst. of Animal Technology, 1988–. Dir, Bantin & Kingman Ltd, 1980–. Hon. Vet. Consultant, Nat. Cattle Breeders' Assoc., 1979–. Mem. Bd of Advisers, Univ. of London, 1984–. Gov., Cambs Coll. of Agric. and Hortic., 1989–90. Gen. Comr to Bd of Inland Revenue, 1969–81. Chairman: Editorial Bd, Veterinary Times (formerly Veterinary Drug), 1978–88; Adv. Bd, British Veterinary Formulary, 1987–. Ehrenbürger, Tierärztlich Hochschule, Hannover, 1992. Crookes' Prize, 1970; Dalrymple-Champneys Cup and Medal, 1972. Cambridge Triple Blue. *Publications:* Society of Practising Veterinary Surgeons Economics Report, 1961, and papers in vet. jls on clinical subjects and vet. econs. *Recreations:* swimming, fishing, travel. *Address:* The Old House, Walton-on-Trent, Derbyshire DE12 8LL. *T:* Barton-under-Needwood (01283) 716961. *Clubs:* Farmers'; Hawks (Cambridge).
See also M. R. Steele-Bodger.

STEELE-BODGER, Michael Roland, CBE 1990; veterinary surgeon in private practice, retired; *b* 4 Sept. 1925; *s* of late Henry William Steele-Bodger and Kathrine Macdonald; *m* 1955, Violet Mary St Clair Murray; two *s* one *d. Educ:* Rugby Sch.; Gonville and Caius Coll., Cambridge. MRCVS. Mem., Sports Council, 1976–82. England Rugby Selector, 1954–70; Pres., RFU, 1973–74; Mem., Internat. Rugby Football Bd, 1974–84; Chm., Four Home Rugby Unions' Tours Cttee, 1976–88; Pres., Barbarians FC, 1987–. Cambridge Univ. Rugby Blue, Captain 1946; England Rugby Internat., 1947–48. *Recreation:* interest in all sport. *Address:* Laxford Lodge, Bonehill, Tamworth, Staffs B78 3HY. *T:* Tamworth (01827) 251001. *Clubs:* East India, Devonshire, Sports and Public Schools; Hawks (Cambridge).
See also A. Steele-Bodger.

STEEN, Anthony David; MP (C) South Hams, since 1983 (Liverpool Wavertree, Feb. 1974–1983); barrister; youth leader; social worker; underwriter; *b* 22 July 1939; *s* of late Stephen Nicholas Steen; *m* 1965, Carolyn Padfield, educational psychologist; one *s* one *d. Educ:* Westminster Sch.; occasional student University Coll., London. Called to Bar, Gray's Inn, 1962; practising Barrister, 1962–74; Defence Counsel, MoD (Court Martials), 1964–68. Lectr in Law, Council of Legal Educn, 1964–67; Adv. Tutor, Sch. of Environment, Central London Poly, 1982–83. Youth Club Leader, E London Settlement, 1959–64; Founder, 1964, and First Director, 1964–68, Task Force to help London's old and lonely, with Govt support; Govt Foundn YVFF, tackling urban deprivation, 1968–74; Consultant to Canadian Govt on student and employment matters, 1970–71. PPS to Sec. of State for Nat. Heritage, 1992–. Member: Select Cttee on Race Relations, 1975–79; Select Cttee on the Envmt, 1991–. Chairman: Cons. Mems Parly Gp, 1974; Backbench gps on Youth and Young Children, 1976–79; Cons. Cttee on Cities, Urban and New Town Affairs, 1979–83; Parly Urban and Inner City Cttee, 1987–; All Party Friends of Cycling, 1979–88; Vice-Chm., Health and Social Services, 1979–80; Sec., Parly Caribbean Gp, 1979–; Chm., Chm's Unit Marginal Seats, Cons. Central Office, 1982–84; Vice-Chairman: Envmt Cttee, 1983–85; Deregulation Cttee, 1993–; Chairman: Parly PNG Gp, 1991–; Sane Planning Gp, 1989–; West Country Mems, 1992–94; Member: Parly Population and Develt Gp; Commons and Lord's Cycle Gp; Services Cttee; Jt Nat. Chm., Impact 80's Campaign. Member: Exec. Council, NPFA; Board, Community Transport; Council of Reference, Internat. Christian Relief; Council Mem., Anglo-Jewish Assoc.; Chm., Outlandos Charitable Trust; Vice-Chm., Task Force Trust; Vice-President: Ecology Bldg Soc.; Internat. Centre for Child Studies; Bentley Operatic Soc.; S Hams Young Farmers; Assoc. of District Councils; Marlborough with S Huish Horticultural Soc.; Devon CPRE; Trustee: Educn Extra; Dartington Summer Arts Foundn; Patron: Liverpool's Open Circle for Detached Youth Work; St Luke's Hospice, Plymouth; Pres., Devon Youth Assoc. *Publications:* New Life for Old Cities, 1981; Tested Ideas for Political Success, 1983, 2nd edn 1991; Plums, 1988. *Recreations:* piano, fell-walking, mountain climbing, cycling, wine-tasting. *Address:* House of Commons, SW1A 0AA; 1A Fore Street, Totnes, South Devon TQ9 5DA. *T:* Totnes (01803) 866069. *Clubs:* Royal Automobile; Churchill (Liverpool); Brixham; Totnes Conservative (South Hams).

STEER, David; QC 1993; a Recorder, since 1991; *b* 15 June 1951; *s* of Alcombe Steer and Nancy Steer; *m* 1974, Elizabeth May Hide; one *s. Educ:* Rainford High Sch.; Manchester Poly. (BA Hons Law). Called to the Bar, Middle Temple, 1974. Mem., Bar Council, 1995–. *Recreations:* carriage driving, Rugby League, horticulture. *Address:* 5th Floor, Corn Exchange Building, Fenwick Street, Liverpool L2 7QS. *T:* 0151–227 1081.

STEER, Prof. John Richardson, FSA 1981; Emeritus Professor of the History of Art, University of London; art-historian and director; *b* 14 Oct. 1928; *s* of Walter Wallis Steer and Elsie Gertrude (*née* Colman). *Educ:* Clayesmore Sch., Dorset; Keble Coll., Oxford (MA); Courtauld Inst. of Art, Univ. of London (BA). Gen. Asst, City Art Gall., Birmingham, 1953–56; Asst Lectr, Dept of Fine Art, Univ. of Glasgow, 1956–59; Lectr in Hist. of European Art, Univ. of Bristol, 1959–67; Prof. of Fine Arts, Univ. of St Andrews, 1967–80; Prof. of Hist. of Art, Birkbeck Coll., Univ. of London, 1980–84. Chm., Adv. Cttee on Validation, Heriot-Watt Univ./Edinburgh Coll. of Art, 1978–91; Chm., Art Historians Assoc. of GB, 1980–83; Vice-Chm., Scottish Theatre Ballet, 1969–71; Mem., Cttee for Art and Design, CNAA, 1977–82 (Chm., Hist. of Art/Design and Complementary Studies Bd, 1977–79); Member: Theatre Museum Adv. Council, 1981–83; Theatre Museum Cttee, V&A Mus., 1984–; Exec., Genius of Venice Exhibn, RA, 1983–84; Royal Fine Art Commn, 1992–. Chm., Theatre Manoeuvres Ltd, 1991–. Trustee, V&A Mus., 1991–. Adjudicator, National Student Drama Festival, 1977. Theatrical prodns include: The Seagull, St Andrews, 1971; And When Love Speaks, Edinburgh, 1975; The Privacy of the Patients, Edinburgh Fringe, 1977, ICA, 1978; Waiting for Godot, St Andrews, 1978; Minna von Barnhelm, plc, Theatre Co., Young Vic Studio, 1987. Hon. DLitt: St Andrews, 1990; Heriot-Watt, 1991. *Publications:* A Concise History of Venetian Painting, 1967; Mr Bacon's Titian (Selwyn Brinton Lecture, RSA), 1977; Alvise Vivarini, 1982; (with A. White) Atlas of Western Art History, 1994; contribs to Burlington Magazine, Art History. *Recreation:* travel. *Address:* 1 Cheriton Square, SW17 8AE.

STEER, Kenneth Arthur, CBE 1978; MA, PhD, FSA, FSAScot; Secretary, Royal Commission on the Ancient and Historical Monuments of Scotland, 1957–78; *b* 12 Nov. 1913; *o s* of Harold Steer and Emily Florence Thompson; *m* 1st, 1941, Rona Mary Mitchell (*d* 1983); one *d*; 2nd, 1985, Eileen Alice Nelson. *Educ:* Wath Grammar School; Durham University. Research Fellowship, 1936–38. Joined staff of Royal Commission on Ancient and Historical Monuments of Scotland, 1938. Intelligence Officer in Army, 1941–45 (despatches twice). Monuments, Fine Arts and Archives Officer, North Rhine Region, 1945–46. Corresponding Member, German Archæological Inst.; Horsley Memorial Lectr, Durham University, 1963; Rhind Lectr, Edinburgh, 1968. Pres., Soc. of Antiquaries of Scotland, 1972–75. Arts Council Literary Award, 1978. *Publications:* Late Medieval Monumental Sculpture in the West Highlands (with J. W. M. Bannerman), 1976; numerous articles in archæological journals. *Address:* 2 Morningside Courtyard, Idsall Drive, Prestbury, Cheltenham, Glos GL52 3BU.

STEER, Rt. Rev. Stanley Charles; Bishop of Saskatoon, 1950–70; *s* of S. E. and E. G. Steer; *m* 1936, Marjorie Slater. *Educ:* Guildford Gram. Sch.; Univ. of Saskatchewan (BA); Oxford Univ. (MA). Hon. DD: Wycliffe Coll., Toronto, 1947, Emmanuel Coll., Saskatoon, 1952; St Chad's Coll., Regina, 1964. Missionary at Vanderhoof, BC, 1929; Chaplain, St Mark's Church, Alexandria, 1931; Chaplain, University Coll., Oxford, 1932–33; St John's Hall, Univ. of London: Tutor, 1933; Vice-Principal, 1936. Chaplain, The Mercers' Company, City of London, 1937; Principal, Emmanuel Coll., Saskatoon, 1941; Hon. Canon of St John's Cathedral, Saskatoon, and CF (R of O), 1943. *Recreation:* tennis. *Address:* 2383 Lincoln Road, Victoria, BC V8R 6A3, Canada. *T:* (604) 5929888.

STEER, Wilfred Reed; QC 1972; *b* 23 Aug. 1926; *s* of George William and Dorothy Steer; *m* 1953, Jill Park; one *s* one *d*, and two step *s. Educ:* Bede Collegiate Sch., Sunderland, Co. Durham; London Sch. of Economics. LLB (Lond.) 1949. Called to the Bar, Gray's Inn, 1950. *Address:* Park Court Chambers, 40 Park Cross Street, Leeds LS1 2QH. *T:* Leeds (0113) 243 3277.

STEERE, Sir Ernest H. L.; *see* Lee-Steere, Sir E. H.

STEFF-LANGSTON, Group Captain John Antony, MBE 1959; Executive Secretary, Royal Astronomical Society, 1980–91; *b* 5 Nov. 1926; *s* of William Austen Paul Steff-Langston, organist and composer, and Ethel Maude (*née* Fletcher); *m* 1959, Joyce Marian Brown. *Educ:* Cathedral Choir Sch., Canterbury; King's Sch., Canterbury; Pembroke Coll., Cambridge. RAF Coll., 1945–46; 45 Sqn, Ceylon, 1948; 61 Gp, Kenley, 1949; 34 Sqn, 1950–51; 80 Sqn, Hong Kong, 1951–54; 540, 58 and 82 Sqns, Wyton and Singapore, 1955–57; HQ 3 Gp, 1957–59; 80 Sqn, Germany, 1959–62; Staff Coll., Andover, 1962–63; Air Sec.'s Dept, 1963–65; OC 114 Sqn, Benson, 1966–68; aws 1968; CO Northolt, 1969–71; Defence Advr to High Comrs to NZ and Fiji, 1971–74; sowc Greenwich, 1974–75; AMPs Dept, 1975–78; retd 1978. FIMgt (FBIM 1978); ARAeS 1987; FRAS 1992. Freeman, City of London, 1994; Liveryman, Fletchers' Co., 1994–. *Recreations:* ornithology, photography, travel, music, cricket. *Address:* 6 Beech Wood, Church Hill, Caterham, Surrey CR3 6SB. *T:* Caterham (01883) 344348. *Club:* Royal Air Force.

STEGGLE, Terence Harry, CMG 1990; HM Diplomatic Service, retired; Ambassador to Paraguay, 1989–91; *b* 4 March 1932; *s* of Henry Richard Steggle and Jane Steggle; *m* 1st, 1954, Odette Marie (*née* Audisio) (*d* 1988); two *d*; 2nd, 1989, Annemarie Klara Johanne (*née* Wohle). *Educ:* Chislehurst and Sidcup County Grammar School. Crown Agents, 1950–57; Lieut RA (TA), 1951–53; seconded to Govt of E Nigeria, 1957–58, 1960–62; FO 1963; served Laos, 1963, France, 1964, Zaire, 1970, Bolivia, 1978–82; Ambassador to Panama, 1983–86; Consul-Gen., São Paulo, 1986–87; Counsellor, FCO, 1987–89. *Recreations:* swimming, philately, bridge. *Address:* c/o Foreign and Commonwealth Office, SW1A 2AH. *Club:* Westminster East Rotary.

STEICHEN, René; Member, Commission of the European Communities, 1993–95; *b* Luxembourg, 27 Nov. 1942; *s* of Félix Steichen and Hélène Rausch; *m* 1975, Marianne Belche; two *s* one *d. Educ:* Lycée Classique, Diekirch; Cours Supérieurs, Luxembourg; Univ. of Aix-en-Provence; Univ. of Paris (LLD); Institut d'Etudes Politiques, Paris (Dip. Econs and Finance 1966). Qualified as notary, then solicitor, 1969; practised in Diekirch, 1969–84. Mem., Diekirch DC, 1969–84, Mayor, 1974–84. MP (Social Christian) North constituency, Luxembourg, 1979–93; Sec. of State for Agric. and Viticulture, 1984–89; Minister for Agric., Viticulture and Rural Develt and Minister for Cultural Affairs and Scientific Res., 1989–93. *Address:* 67 avenue Milcamps, 1040 Brussels, Belgium.

STEIN, Sheriff Colin Norman Ralph; Floating Sheriff of Tayside Central and Fife at Arbroath, since 1991; *b* 14 June 1948; *s* of late Colin Hunter Stein and of Margaret Lindsay Stein; *m* 1979, Dr Linda McNaught; one *s. Educ:* Glenalmond Coll.; Durham Univ. (BA Hons Modern History); Edinburgh Univ. (LLB). Admitted Member of Faculty of Advocates, 1975. Standing Jun. Counsel to MoD (RAF), Scotland, 1983–91; Temp. Sheriff, 1987–91. *Recreations:* angling, gardening. *Address:* c/o Sheriff Court, High Street, Arbroath DD11 1HC. *Club:* New (Edinburgh).

STEIN, Cyril; Chairman, St James's Club Ltd, since 1995; Ladbroke Group PLC, 1966–93; *b* 20 Feb. 1928; *s* of late Jack Stein and Rebecca Stein (*née* Selner); *m* 1949, Betty Young; two *s* one *d*.

STEIN, Prof. Peter Gonville, FBA 1974; JP; Regius Professor of Civil Law in the University of Cambridge, 1968–93, now Emeritus; Fellow of Queens' College, Cambridge, since 1968; *b* 29 May 1926; *o s* of late Walter Stein, MA, Solicitor, and Effie Drummond Stein (*née* Walker); *m* 1st, 1953, Janet Chamberlain; three *d*; 2nd, 1978, Anne M. Howard; one step *s*. *Educ:* Liverpool Coll. (Life Gov., 1976); Gonville and Caius Coll., Camb. (Classical Exhibitioner); University of Pavia. Served in RN, Sub-lieut (Sp) RNVR, 1944–47. Admitted a Solicitor, 1951; Italian Govt Scholar, 1951–52; Asst Lecturer in Law, Nottingham Univ., 1952–53; Lecturer in Jurisprudence, 1953–56, Prof. of Jurisprudence, 1956–68, Dean of Faculty of Law, 1961–64, Aberdeen Univ.; Chm., Faculty Bd of Law, Cambridge, 1973–76; Vice Pres., Queens' Coll., 1974–81 (Acting Pres., 1976 and 1980–81). Visiting Prof. of Law: Univ. of Virginia, 1965–66, 1978–79; Colorado, 1966; Witwatersrand, 1970; Louisiana State, 1974, 1977, 1983, 1985; Chicago, 1985, 1988, 1990, 1992, 1995; Padua and Palermo, 1991; Tulane, New Orleans, 1992; Salerno, 1994; Lectures: R. M. Jones, QUB, 1978; Irvine, Cornell, 1979; Sherman, Boston, 1979; Tucker, Louisiana State, 1985; David Murray, Glasgow, 1987. Fellow, Winchester Coll., 1976–91. Member: Council, Max Planck Inst. for European Legal History, Frankfurt, 1966–88; Council, Internat. Assoc. of Legal History, 1970– (Vice-Pres, 1985–); Internat. Acad. of Comparative Law, 1987–; Sec. of State for Scotland's Working Party on Hospital Endowments, 1966–69; Bd of Management, Royal Cornhill and Assoc. (Mental) Hospitals, Aberdeen, 1963–68 (Chm. 1967–68); UGC, 1971–75; US–UK Educnl Commn, 1985–91; Council, British Acad., 1988–90. Chm., Ely Diocesan Trust Cttee, 1987–94. Pres., Soc. of Public Teachers of Law, 1980–81; Vice-Pres., Selden Soc., 1984–87. Foreign Fellow: Accad. di Scienze morali e politiche, Naples, 1982; Accademia Nazionale dei Lincei, Rome, 1987; Corres. Fellow, Accademia degli Intronati, Siena, 1988; Fellow, Academia Europaea, 1989; Foreign Fellow, Koninklijke Academie voor Wetenschappen, Belgium, 1991. JP Cambridge, 1970 (Supplementary List, 1988). Hon. QC 1993. Hon. Dr jur Göttingen, 1980; Hon. Dott. Giur. Ferrara, 1991. *Publications:* Fault in the formation of Contract in Roman Law and Scots Law, 1958; editor, Buckland's Textbook of Roman Law, 3rd edn, 1963; Regulae Iuris: from juristic rules to legal maxims, 1966; Roman Law in Scotland in Ius Romanum Medii Aevi, 1968; Roman Law and English Jurisprudence (inaugural lect.), 1969; (with J. Shand) Legal Values in Western Society, 1974, Italian edn 1981; (ed jtly) Adam Smith's Lectures on Jurisprudence, 1978; Legal Evolution, 1980, Japanese edn 1987; (ed jtly) Studies in Justinian's Institutes, 1983; Legal Institutions: the development of dispute settlement, 1984, Italian edn 1987; The Character and Influence of the Roman Civil Law: historical essays, 1988; (with F. de Zulueta) The Teaching of Roman Law in England around 1200, 1990; (ed and contrib.) Notaries Public in England since the Reformation (English and Italian edns), 1991; articles in legal periodicals mainly on Roman Law and legal history. *Recreations:* hill walking, gardening. *Address:* Wimpole Cottage, 36 Wimpole Road, Great Eversden, Cambridge CB3 7HR. *T:* Cambridge (01223) 262349.

STEINBERG, Gerald Neil, (Gerry); MP (Lab) City of Durham, since 1987; *b* 20 April 1945; *s* of Harry and Esther Steinberg; *m* 1969, Margaret Cruddace Thornton; one *s* one *d*. *Educ:* St Margaret's Primary Sch.; Whinney Hill Secondary Sch.; Durham Johnston Sch.; Sheffield Coll. of Education; Newcastle Polytechnic. Cert. of Educn for Backward Children. Teacher, Dukeshouse Wood Camp Sch., Hexham, 1966–69; Teacher, Elemore Hall, 1969–75, Dep. Head, 1975–79; Head Teacher, Whitworth House Special Sch., 1979–87. Mem., Durham City Council, 1975–87 (Sec., Labour Gp, 1981–87). Mem., Parly Select Cttee on Education, 1987–; Chm., Labour Educn Cttee, 1990–. *Recreations:* Sunderland AFC supporter; cricket, squash, loves all sport (Pres., Bearpark Cricket Club; Vice Pres., Brandon AFC). *Address:* 20 Briardene, Durham DH1 4QU. *T:* Durham (0191) 3861082. *Clubs:* Sherburn Workman's, Sherburn Hill Workman's, Brandon Workman's, Crossgate Workman's, Nevilles Cross Workman's.

STEINBERG, Professor Hannah; Hon. Research Professor, Faculty of Social Science, Middlesex University, since 1992; *d* of late Michael Steinberg, doctor of law, and Marie (*née* Wein). *Educ:* Schwarzwaldschule, Vienna; Putney High School; Queen Anne's School, Caversham; Univ. of Reading (Cert. Comm.); Denton Secretarial Coll., London; University College London (BA 1st cl. Hons Psychology, PhD; Troughton Schol., 1948–50). FBPsS, CPsychol 1990. Pres., Univ. of London Union, 1947–48; Univ. of London Postgrad. Studentship, 1948–50. Sec. to Man. Dir, Omes Ltd, 1943–44. University College London: Asst Lectr in Pharmacology, 1954–55; Lectr, 1955–62; Reader in Psychopharmacology, 1962–70; Prof. of Psychopharmacology (first in W Europe), 1970–92; Head of Psychopharmacology Gp, Dept of Psychology, 1979–92; Hon. Res. Fellow, Dept of Psychology, 1992–; Prof. Emeritus, Univ. of London, 1989. Hon. consulting Clinical Psychologist, Dept of Psychological Medicine, Royal Free Hosp., 1970. Member MRC working parties on: Biochemistry and Pharmacology of Drug Dependence, 1968–73; Biological Aspects of Drug Dependence, 1971–75. Vice-President: Collegium Internationale Neuro-Psychopharmacologicum (CINP), 1968–74; Brit. Assoc. of Psychopharmacology, 1973–77 (Hon. Mem., 1989); Mem., Biological Council, 1977–80. Distinguished Affiliate of Amer. Psychol Assoc., Psychopharmacology Div., 1978; Member: British Pharmacol Soc.; Experimental Psychol. Soc.; Soc. for Study of Addiction; European Coll. of Neuropsychopharmacology; European Behavioural Pharmacol Soc.; European Health Psychol Soc., etc. Convener, Academic Women's Achievement Gp, 1979–92. Accredited Sports Psychologist, British Assoc. of Sports Scis, 1992. Special Trustee, Middx Hosp., 1989–92. Dir, Art, Research, Creativity and Health, 1992–. Past ed. of scientific jls. *Publications:* (trans. and ed jtly) Animals and Men, 1951; organiser of symposia and editor: Animal Behaviour and Drug Action (jt), 1963; Scientific Basis of Drug Dependence, 1968; Psychopharmacology, Sexual Disorders and Drug Abuse (jt), 1972; articles and reviews on psychopharmacology and physical exercise and mental health. *Address:* School of Psychology, Middlesex University, Queensway, Enfield, Mddx EN3 4SF. *T:* 0181–362 5000.

STEINBERG, Saul Phillip; Founder, 1961, and Chairman and Chief Executive Officer, since 1961, Reliance Group Holdings Inc.; *b* 13 Aug. 1939; *m* 3rd, 1984, Gayfryd McNabb; one *d* and one step *s*; and three *s* one *d* by previous marriages. *Educ:* Wharton School of Univ. of Pennsylvania (BScEcon). Director: Zenith National Insurance Corp.; Symbol Technologies Inc.; Chm. Bd, Telemundo Gp Inc. Dir, Long Island Jewish Medical Center. Mem., Bd of Overseers, Cornell Univ. Medical Coll.; Chm., Wharton Bd of Overseers; Trustee: Univ. of Pennsylvania; NY Public Library. *Address:* Park Avenue Plaza, 55 E 52 Street, New York, NY 10055, USA. *T:* (212) 9091110. *Club:* Glen Oaks (NY).

STEINBERGER, Prof. Jack; Professor of Physics, Scuola Normale Superiore, Pisa, since 1986; *b* 25 May 1921; *s* of Ludwig and Bertha Steinberger; *m* 1st, 1943, Joan Beauregard; two *s*; 2nd, 1962, Cynthia Eve Alff; one *s* one *d*. *Educ:* New Trier Township High Sch.; Armour Inst. of Technology; Univ. of Chicago (BS Chem 1942; PhD Phys 1948). Mem., Inst. of Advanced Study, Princeton, 1948–49; Asst, Univ. of California, Berkeley, 1949–50; Prof., Columbia Univ., 1950–68 (Higgins Prof., 1965–68); Physicist, CERN, Geneva, 1968–86. Member: Nat. Acad. of Sciences; Amer. Acad. of Arts and Sciences; Heidelberg Acad. of Science. (Jtly) President's Science Award, USA, 1988; (jtly) Nobel Prize for Physics, 1988; Matenzzi Medal, Soc. Italiana della Scienze, 1991. *Publications:* papers in learned jls on discoveries leading to better understanding of elementary particles. *Recreations:* flute; formerly mountaineering, tennis, yachting. *Address:* CERN, 1211 Geneva 23, Switzerland; 25 Ch. des Merles, 1213 Onex, Switzerland.

STEINBY, Prof. Eva Margareta; Professor of Archaeology of the Roman Empire, and Fellow of All Souls College, University of Oxford, since 1994; *b* 21 Nov. 1938; *d* of Kaarlo Erkki Wilén and Doris Margareta Steinby. *Educ:* Univ. of Helsinki (Hum. Kand. 1963; Fil. Kand. 1964; Fil. Lic. 1970; Fil. Dr 1976); MA Oxon 1995. Institutum Romanum Finlandiae, Rome: Asst, 1973–77; Dir, 1979–82 and 1992–94; Sen. Res. Fellow, Finnish Acad., Helsinki, 1985–92. Docent in History, Univ. of Helsinki, 1977–; Vis. Fellow, All Souls Coll., Oxford, 1990–91. Fellow, Suomen Historiallinen Seura, 1978; Corresp. Fellow, Pontificia Accademia Romana di Archeologia, 1982, Fellow, 1993; Fellow, Societas Scientiarum Fennica, 1983; Corresp. Fellow, Deutsches Archaologisches Institut, 1984. Medaglia d'Oro per Benemeriti Culturali (Italy) 1983. Officer, 1st Cl., Order of White Rose (Finland) 1991. *Publications:* La cronologia delle figlinae doliari urbane, 1976; Lateres signati Ostienses, Vol. I 1977, Vol. II 1978; Indici complementari ai bolli doliari urbani (CIL, XV, 1), 1987; (ed) Lacus Iuturnae I, 1989; (ed) Lexicon Topographicum Urbis Romae, 5 vols, 1993–; articles in Italian, German and Finnish learned jls. *Address:* University of Oxford Institute of Archaeology, 36 Beaumont Street, Oxford OX1 2PG. *T:* Oxford (01865) 278240; All Souls College, Oxford OX1 4AL. *T:* Oxford (01865) 279379.

STEINER, Prof. George, MA, DPhil; Extraordinary Fellow, Churchill College, Cambridge, since 1969; Weidenfeld Professor of Comparative Literature, and Fellow of St Anne's College, Oxford, 1994–95; *b* 23 April 1929; *s* of Dr F. G. and Mrs E. Steiner; *m* 1955, Zara Steiner (*née* Shakow); one *s* one *d*. *Educ:* Paris (BèsL); Univ. of Chicago (BA); Harvard (MA); Oxford (DPhil). Member, staff of the Economist, in London, 1952–56; Inst. for Advanced Study, Princeton, 1956–58; Gauss Lectr, Princeton Univ., 1959–60; Fellow of Churchill Coll., Cambridge, 1961–; Prof. of English and Comparative Literature, Univ. of Geneva, 1974–94, Prof. Emeritus, 1994–. Lectures: Massey, 1974; Leslie Stephen, Cambridge, 1986; W. P. Ker, 1986, Gifford, 1990, Univ. of Glasgow; Page-Barbour, Univ. of Virginia, 1987. Fulbright Professorship, 1958–69; Vis. Prof., Collège de France, 1992. Pres., English Assoc., 1975; Corresp. Mem., (Federal) German Acad. of Literature, 1981; Hon. Mem., Amer. Acad. of Arts and Scis, 1989. FRSL 1964. Hon. Fellow, Balliol Coll., Oxford, 1995. Hon. DLitt: East Anglia, 1976; Louvain, 1980; Mount Holyoke Coll., USA, 1983; Bristol, 1989; Glasgow, 1990; Liège, 1990; Ulster, 1993; Durham, 1995. O. Henry Short Story Award, 1958; Guggenheim Fellowship, 1971–72; Zabel Award of Nat. Inst. of Arts and Letters of the Us, 1970; Faulkner Stipend for Fiction, PEN, 1983; PEN Macmillan Fiction Prize, 1993. Chevalier de la Légion d'Honneur, 1984. *Publications:* Tolstoy or Dostoevsky, 1958; The Death of Tragedy, 1960; Anno Domini, 1964; Language and Silence, 1967; Extraterritorial, 1971; In Bluebeard's Castle, 1971; The Sporting Scene: White Knights in Reykjavik, 1973; After Babel, 1975 (adapted for TV as The Tongues of Men, 1977); Heidegger, 1978; On Difficulty and Other Essays, 1978; The Portage to San Cristobal of A. H., 1981; Antigones, 1984; George Steiner: a reader, 1984; Real Presences: is there anything in what we say?, 1989; Proofs and Three Parables, 1992. *Recreations:* music, chess, mountain walking. *Address:* 32 Barrow Road, Cambridge CB2 2AS. *T:* Cambridge (01223) 61200. *Clubs:* Athenæum, Savile; Harvard (New York).

STEINER, Rear-Adm. Ottokar Harold Mojmir St John, CB 1967; Assistant Chief of Defence Staff, 1966–68, retired; *b* 8 July 1916; *e s* of late O. F. Steiner; *m* 1st, 1940, Evelyn Mary Young (marr. diss. 1975); one *s* one *d*; 2nd, 1975, Eleanor, *widow* of Sqdn Leader W. J. H. Powell, RAF. *Educ:* St Paul's School. Special entry cadet, RN, 1935. Served War of 1939–45 (despatches twice), HMS Ilex, Havelock, Frobisher, Superb. Naval Staff Course, 1947; Staff of C-in-C, Far East Fleet, 1948–50; Comdr 1950; jssc 1953; HMS Ceylon, 1953–54; NATO Defence Coll., 1955; HMS Daedalus, 1955–56; Capt. 1956; Admiralty, 1956–58; in comd HMS Saintes and Capt. (D) 3rd Destroyer Squdn, 1958–60; Naval Adviser to UK High Commission, Canada, 1960–62; Senior Offrs War Course, 1962; in comd HMS Centaur, 1963–65; ADC to HM the Queen, 1965; Rear-Adm., 1966. Chm., Whitbread Round the World Race, 1972–82; Transglobe Expedition (Capt. of ship to Antarctica), 1979–80. Vice-Pres., Shipwrecked Fishermen and Mariners Royal Benevolent Soc. Freeman, City of London; Liveryman, Coachmakers and Coach Harness Makers. *Recreations:* sailing, golf. *Clubs:* Royal Cruising, Isle of Wight Motor Yacht (Adm.); Royal Naval Sailing Association; Union (Malta).

STEINER, Prof. Robert Emil, CBE 1979; Professor of Diagnostic Radiology, University of London, Royal Postgraduate Medical School, 1961–83, now Emeritus; *b* 1 Feb. 1918; *s* of Rudolf Steiner and Clary (*née* Nordlinger); *m* 1945, Gertrude Margaret Konirsch; two *d*. *Educ:* University of Vienna; University College, Dublin. Dep. Director, Dept of Radiology, Hammersmith Hosp.; Lecturer Diagnostic Radiology, Postgraduate Med. School of London, 1950, Sen. Lecturer, 1955, Director, 1955–. Vice-Chm., Nat. Radiological Protection Bd, 1972–83. Past Consultant Adviser in Radiology to DHSS; Past Civil Consultant in Radiology to Med. Dir-Gen., Navy. Warden of Fellowship, Faculty of Radiologists. Former Mem. Council, RCS; Past Pres., British Inst. Radiology; Pres., RCR, 1977–80. Hon. Fellow: Amer. Coll. of Radiology; Australian Coll. of Radiology; Faculty of Radiologists, RCSI. Hon. Member: Radiological Soc. of Finland; Radiological Soc. of N America; Amer. Roentgen Ray Soc.; Germany Roentgen Soc. Barclay Medal British Inst. of Radiology; Gold Medal, RCR, 1986. Former Editor, British Jl of Radiology. *Publications:* Clinical Disorders of the Pulmonary Circulation, 1960; Recent Advances of Radiology, vols 4–8, 1979–85; contrib. to British Journal of Radiology, Clinical Radiology, British Heart Jl, Lancet, BMJ, etc. *Address:* 12 Stonehill Road, East Sheen, SW14 8RW. *T:* 0181–876 4038. *Club:* Hurlingham.

STEINFELD, Alan Geoffrey; QC 1987; *b* 13 July 1946; *s* of Henry Chaim Steinfeld and Deborah Steinfeld; *m* 1976, Josephine Nicole (*née* Gros); two *s*. *Educ:* City of London Sch.; Downing Coll., Cambridge (BA Hons, LLB). Arnold McNair Schol. in Internat. Law, 1967; Whewell Schol. in Internat. Law, 1968. Called to the Bar, Lincoln's Inn, 1968; commenced pupillage at the Bar, 1968, practice at the Bar, 1969. *Recreations:* tennis, ski-ing, sailing, opera. *Address:* (chambers) 24 Old Buildings, Lincoln's Inn, WC2A 3UJ. *T:* 0171–404 0946. *Clubs:* Royal Automobile; Cumberland Lawn Tennis.

STELL, Prof. Philip Michael, FRCS, FRCSE; Professor of Oto-rhino-laryngology, University of Liverpool, 1979–92, now Emeritus; *b* 14 Aug. 1934; *s* of Frank Law Stell and Ada Stell; *m* 1959, Shirley Kathleen Mills; four *s* one *d*. *Educ:* Archbishop Holgate's Grammar Sch., York; Edinburgh Univ. (MB, ChB 1958). ChM Liverpool, 1976. FRCS 1966; FRCSE 1962. Jun. hosp. appts, Edinburgh and Liverpool, 1958–63; Fellow, Washington Univ., St Louis, USA, 1964–65; Sen. Lectr, Univ. of Liverpool, 1965–78. Hunterian Prof., RCS, 1976. President: Otorhinolaryngological Res. Soc., 1983–86; Assoc. of Head and Neck Oncologists of GB, 1986–89; Liverpool Med. Inst., 1986–87 and 1987–88; Sect. of Laryngology, RSM, 1990–91. Mem., Deutsche Akademie der Naturforscher Leopoldina, 1990. Hon. Life Member: Netherlands ENT Soc., 1992; N of England ENT Soc., 1993. Yearsley Gold Medal, 1980; Harrison Prize, RSM, 1982; Semon Medal, Univ. of London, 1986; George Davey Meml Prize, Univ. of London, 1987; Centenary Medal, Dudley Road Hosp., Birmingham, Gold Medal, Irish ENT Soc., 1988; Leegaard Medal, Norwegian ENT Soc., Gold Medal, Marie Curie Inst., Warsaw, Swedish Med. Assoc. Medal, Jobson Horne Prize, BMA, 1989; Gold Medal, German ENT Soc., 1991. *Publications:* approx. 20 books and over 300 articles in learned jls on surgery for cancer of head and neck. *Recreations:* history, gardening. *Address:* 69 The Village, Haxby, York YO3 3JE. *T:* York (01904) 761469.

STELLINI, Salv. John; High Commissioner for Malta in London, since 1991; *b* 19 July 1939; *s* of Joseph and Victoria Stellini; *m* 1969, Lucinda Flannery; one *s* one *d*. *Educ:* Royal Univ. of Malta (BA Hons); Univ. of Alberta (MA); LSE (Dip. Int. Rel.). Teacher, 1959–65; Maltese Diplomatic Service, 1966–80: 2nd Sec., New York, 1968–71; 1st Sec., London, 1974–79; Dir for Internat. Marketing, 1981–87; Ambassador to Washington DC, 1988–91. *Recreations:* reading, visiting historical sites, museums, films. *Address:* Malta High Commission, Malta House, 36–38 Piccadilly, W1V 0PQ. *T:* 0171–292 4800, *Fax:* 0171–734 1831.

STEMBRIDGE, David Harry, QC 1990; a Recorder of the Crown Court, since 1977; *b* 23 Dec. 1932; *s* of Percy G. Stembridge and Emily W. Stembridge; *m* 1956, Therese C. Furer; three *s* one *d*. *Educ:* St Chad's Cathedral Choir Sch., Lichfield; Bromsgrove Sch.; Birmingham Univ. (LLB Hons). Called to the Bar, Gray's Inn, 1955; practising barrister, 1956–. *Recreations:* organ playing, sailing. *Address:* 5 Fountain Court, Steelhouse Lane, Birmingham B4 6DR; 199 Strand, WC2R 1DR. *Club:* Bar Yacht.

STEMPLOWSKI, Ryszard, PhD; Polish Ambassador to the Court of St James's, since 1994; *b* 25 March 1939; *s* of Kazimierz Stemplowski and Eugenia Białecka; *m* 1st, 1964, Anita Zajaczkowska; 2nd, 1975, Irena Zasłona; two *d*. *Educ:* Tech. Lycée (Civil Build.), Bydgoszcz; Tech. Univ., Wrocław; Univ. of Wrocław (LLM 1968); Inst. of History, Polish Acad. of Scis (PhD 1973). Res. Fellow, Inst. of History, 1973–90; Chief of Chancellery of Sejm (Chamber of Deputies), Poland, 1990–93. Vis. Fellow, St Antony's Coll., Oxford, 1974; Vis. Prof., Oakland Univ., USA, 1976; Vis. Scholar and Alexander von Humboldt Fellow, Univ. of Cologne, 1981–82. *Publications:* Dependence and Defiance: Argentina and rivalries among USA, UK and Germany 1930–46, 1975; (jtly) History of Latin America 1850–1980, 3 vols, 1978–80; (jtly) The Slavic Settlers in Misiones 1897–1947, 1992; (jtly) Economic Nationalism in East Central Europe and South America 1918–39, 1990; numerous other works and translations in Polish, German, Spanish, English, French. *Recreations:* music, astrophysics. *Address:* Polish Embassy, 47 Portland Place, W1N 3AG. *T:* 0171–580 4327; 4 Templewood Avenue, NW3. *Clubs:* Athenæum, Army and Navy.

STENHAM, Anthony William Paul, (Cob), FCA; Chairman, Arjo Wiggins Appleton plc (formerly Wiggins Teape Appleton), since 1990; *b* 28 Jan. 1932; *s* of Bernard Basil Stenham and Annie Josephine (*née* Naylor); *m* 1st, 1966, Hon. Sheila Marion Poole (marr. diss.); 2nd, 1983, Anne Martha Mary O'Rawe; two *d*. *Educ:* Eton Coll.; Trinity Coll., Cambridge. MA. Qualified Accountant FCA 1958. Mem., Inner Temple, 1955. Price Waterhouse, 1955–61; Philip Hill Higginson Erlanger, 1962–64; William Baird & Co., 1964–69: Finance Dir and Jt Man. Dir; Unilever, 1969–86: Financial Dir, 1970–86, Corporate Develt Dir, 1984–86, Unilever PLC and Unilever NV; Chm., Unilever United States Inc., 1978–79; a Man. Dir, Bankers Trust Co. of NY, 1986–90 (Non-Exec. Chm., Bankers Trust UK and Europe). Director: Equity Capital for Industry, 1976–81; Capital Radio, 1982–94; Virgin Gp, 1986–89; Rank Organisation, 1987–; VSEL plc, 1987– (Dep. Chm., 1989–); Rothmans Internat., 1988–; Unigate, 1989–; STC, 1990–91; Arjomari Prioux, 1990–93; Colonial Mutual Gp (UK Hldgs), 1987–92; Standard Chartered, 1991–; Worms et Cie, 1991–; Trafalgar House, 1993–; Dep. Chm., Telewest Communications plc, 1994–. Institute of Contemporary Arts: Chm. Council, 1977–87; Chm., Adv. Bd, 1987–89; Mem. Council, Architectural Assoc., 1982–84; Royal Coll. of Art: Mem. Court, 1978–; Mem. Council, 1978–81; Chm. Council and Pro-Provost, 1979–81; Hon. Fellow, 1980. Governor: Museum of London, 1986–92; Theatres Trust, 1989–. Trustee, Design Mus., 1992–. FRSA. *Recreations:* cinema, opera, painting. *Address:* 4 The Grove, Highgate, N6 6JU. *T:* 0181–340 2266; 0171–839 7771. *Clubs:* White's, Beefsteak.

STENHOUSE, John Godwyn, TD with bar; FCIB; Chairman, Stenhouse Holdings plc, 1978–80 (Director, 1947–84); retired; *b* 16 Nov. 1908; *s* of Alexander Rennie Stenhouse and Hughina Cowan Stenhouse; *m* 1st, 1936, Margaret Constance Thornton (*d* 1965); two *d*; 2nd, 1967, Jean Ann Bennie (*née* Finlayson); one step *s*. *Educ:* Warristo Sch., Moffat; Kelvinside Acad., Glasgow. With an insurance co., 1927; joined A. R. Stenhouse & Partners, Ltd, Insurance Brokers (later Stenhouse Holdings Ltd), 1931. *Recreations:* sailing, mechanical engineering. *Address:* 2 St Germains, Bearsden, Glasgow G61 2RS. *T:* 0141–942 0151. *Club:* Royal Scottish Automobile (Glasgow).

STENHOUSE, Sir Nicol, Kt 1962; *b* 14 Feb. 1911; 2nd *s* of late John Stenhouse, Shanghai, China, and Tring, Hertfordshire; *m* 1951, Barbara Heath Wilson (*d* 1991); two *s* one *d*. *Educ:* Repton. Joined Andrew Yule & Co. Ltd, Calcutta, India, 1937; Managing Director, 1953–59; Chairman and Senior Managing Director, 1959–62; President: Bengal Chamber of Commerce and Industry, Calcutta, 1961–62; Associated Chambers of Commerce of India, Calcutta, 1961–62. *Recreation:* gardening. *Address:* 3 St Mary's Court, Sixpenny Handley, near Salisbury, Wilts SP5 5PH.

STENING, Sir George (Grafton Lees), Kt 1968; ED; Hon. Consultant Gynæcological Surgeon, Royal Prince Alfred Hosp., Sydney; Emeritus Consultant, St Luke's Hospital, Sydney; *b* 16 Feb. 1904; *s* of George Smith Stening and Muriel Grafton Lees; *m* 1935, Kathleen Mary Packer, DStJ; one *s* one *d*. *Educ:* Sydney High Sch.; Univ. of Sydney. MB, BS (Syd.) 1927 (Hons Cl. II); FRCS (Ed.) 1931; FRACS 1935; FRCOG 1947; FRACOG, 1980. Carnegie Trav. Fellow, 1948. Served War of 1939–45: Middle East, New Guinea, Australia; OC, 3rd Aust. Surgical Team, Libyan Desert, 1941; CO, 2/11 Aust. Gen. Hosp., 1941–44; CO, 113 Aust. Gen. Hosp., 1945. Hon. Col, RAAMC. GCStJ 1971; Chancellor, Order of St John, in Australia, 1961–82. Past Pres., Sen. Golfers' Soc. of Aust. *Publication:* A Text Book of Gynæcology (co-author), 1948. *Recreations:* golf, yachting. *Address:* 2/22 Wolseley Road, Point Piper, NSW 2027, Australia. *Clubs:* Royal Sydney Golf (Sydney); Australian Jockey.

STEPHEN, Barrie Michael Lace; *see* Stephen, M.

STEPHEN, David; *see* Stephen, J. D.

STEPHEN, Derek Ronald James, CB 1975; Deputy Under-Secretary of State, Ministry of Defence, 1973–82; *b* 22 June 1922; *s* of late Ronald James Stephen; *m* 1948, Gwendolen Margaret, *d* of late William James Heasman, CBE; two *s* one *d* (and one *s* decd). *Educ:* Bec Sch.; Christ's Coll., Cambridge (1st cl. Hons Classics). Served War, 1941–45; 11th Hussars and HQ 7th Armoured Div., N Africa, Italy, NW Europe; Captain. Asst Principal, War Office, 1946; Asst Private Sec. to Sec. of State for War, 1949–50; Principal, 1951; Private Sec. to Sec. of Cabinet, 1958–60; Asst Sec., WO (later MoD), 1960; IDC 1966; HM Treasury, 1968; Civil Service Dept (on its formation), 1968; Under-Sec., 1969–71; Asst Under-Sec. of State, MoD, 1972–73; Dep. Under-Sec. of State (Navy), MoD, and Mem. Admiralty Bd, 1973–78; Dep. Under-Sec. of State (Army), MoD, and Mem., Army Bd, 1978–82; Asst Sec., Royal Hosp., Chelsea, 1982–88. Army Benevolent Fund: Member: Grants Cttee, 1984–; Finance Cttee, 1988–; Mem. Council, Royal Cambridge Home for Soldiers' Widows, 1987–. Trustee, Tank Museum, 1982–. Gov., Royal Sch., Hampstead, 1984–. *Recreations:* music, opera, golf. *Club:* Naval and Military.

STEPHEN, Dr (George) Martin; High Master, Manchester Grammar School, since 1994; *b* 18 July 1949; *s* of Sir Andrew Stephen, MB, ChB and Lady Stephen (*née* Frances Barker); *m* 1971, Jennifer Elaine Fisher, JP; three *s*. *Educ:* Uppingham Sch.; Univ. of Leeds (BA); Univ. of Sheffield (Dip Ed, Dist., PhD; Hallam Prize for Educn, 1971). Child supervisor, Leeds and Oxford Remand Homes, 1966–67; Teacher of English, Uppingham, 1971–72, Haileybury, 1972–83 (and Housemaster); Second Master, Sedbergh, 1983–87; Headmaster, Perse Sch. for Boys, Cambridge, 1987–94. Member: ESRC, 1990–; Naval Review, 1992–; Community Service Volunteers' Educnl Adv. Council, 1994–; HMC/GSA Univ. Admissions Working Gp, 1994–; British Assoc. for Sport and Law, 1995–; Chm., HMC Community Service Cttee, 1992–95. Associate Mem., Combination Room, GCCC, 1988–94. Trustee, Project Trust, 1994–. Governor: Withington Sch., Manchester, 1994–; Pownall Hall Sch., Wilmslow, 1994–. *Publications:* An Introductory Guide to English Literature, 1984; Studying Shakespeare, 1984; British Warship Designs since 1906, 1985; English Literature, 1986, 3rd edn 1992; (ed) Never Such Innocence, 1988, 3rd edn 1993; Sea Battles in Close Up, 1988; The Fighting Admirals, 1991; (ed) The Best of Saki, 1993; Speaking for Themselves, 1995; contrib. York Notes series; articles and reviews for various jls. *Recreations:* writing, directing plays, pen and ink drawing, field and water sports, music. *Address:* Manchester Grammar School, Manchester M13 0XT. *Club:* East India (Hon. Mem.).

STEPHEN, Harbourne Mackay, CBE 1985; DSO 1941; DFC and bar 1940; AE 1943; Director, Telegraph plc (formerly Daily Telegraph), since 1963 (non-executive, since 1986); *b* 18 April 1916; *s* of Thomas Milne Stephen, JP, and Kathleen Vincent Park; *m* 1947, Sybil Erica Palmer; two *d*. *Educ:* Shrewsbury. Staff of Allied Newspapers, London, 1931; Evening Standard, 1936–39. RAFVR, 1937; served RAF, 1939–45 (destroyed numerous enemy aircraft): 605 and 74 Sqdns, 1939–40; at MAP, 1941, then joined 130 Sqdn and comd 234 Sqdn; served Far East, 1942–45; Wing Comdr (Flying) Dum Dum; RAF Jessore, Bengal; comd 166 Fighter Wing; then to Fighter Ops, 224 Gp Arakan; Ops "A" Air Comd SEA, 1945. Was OC 602 City of Glasgow (F) Sqdn RAuxAF, 1950–52. Returned to Beaverbrook Newspapers, Oct. 1945; worked on Scottish Daily Express, Scottish Sunday Express, and Evening Citizen in Glasgow, 1945–55; General Manager, Sunday Express, 1958; General Manager, Sunday Graphic, 1960, and thereafter General Manager, Thomson Papers, London; Man. Dir, Daily Telegraph and Sunday Telegraph, 1963–86; retired, 1986. Dir, Internat. Newspaper Colour Assoc., Darmstadt, 1964–69. Council Member: RSPB, 1972–73; Scientific Exploration Soc., 1992–; Operation Raleigh, 1992–; Trustee, Raleigh International, 1990–. *Recreations:* normal, occasionally. *Address:* Donnington Fields, Newbury, Berks RG16 9BA. *T:* Newbury (01635) 40105. *Clubs:* Naval and Military, Royal Air Force.

STEPHEN, Henrietta Hamilton, (Rita Stephen), MBE 1973; National Officer, GMB, 1989–91; *b* 9 Dec. 1925; *d* of late James Pithie Stephen, engine driver, Montrose and late Mary Hamilton Morton, South Queensferry. *Educ:* Wolseley Street and King's Park Elem. Schs, Glasgow; Queen's Park Sen. Secondary, Glasgow; Glasgow Univ. (extra-mural); LSE (TUC Schol.). McGill Univ. and Canada/US Travel, 1958–59. Law office junior, 1941; Clerk, Labour Exchange (Mem. MLSA), 1941–42; Post Office Telephonist, 1942–60; Officer and delegate, Union of Post Office Workers, Glasgow Br., 1942–60; Member: UPW Parly Panel, 1957; London and Home Counties Area Organiser, CAWU, 1960–65; Nat. Sec., CAWU, subseq. APEX, 1965–89. Negotiator in public and private sectors of industry, 1960–91; Editor, The Clerk, 1965–71; Union Educn Officer, 1965–72; Delegate: TUC; Labour Party Annual Confs; Member: EDC for Food and Drink Manufacturing, 1976–90; Food Standards Cttee, 1968–80; Mary Macarthur Educnl Trust, 1965–; Mary Macarthur Holiday Trust (Hon. Treas., 1991–); Distributive Industry Trng Bd, 1968–73; Monopolies and Mergers Commn, 1973–83; British Wool Marketing Bd, 1973–88; LSE Court, 1976–. Mem., TUC Women's Adv. Cttee, 1983; Chair, Nat. Jt Cttee of Working Women's Organisations, 1983–84; Jt Sec., British Coal Nat. Jt Council (Clerical), 1988–90. Life Mem., Industrial Soc., 1992 (former Mem. Council and Exec.). *Publications:* (jtly) Training Shop Stewards, 1968; (with Roy Moore) Statistics for Negotiators, 1973; contrib. Clerk, Industrial Soc. Jl, Target, etc. *Recreations:* food, walking, conversation, travel, theatre, reading. *Address:* 3 Pond Road, SE3 9JL. *T:* 0181–852 7797, 0181–947 3131.

STEPHEN, (John) David; Principal Officer, Executive Office of Secretary-General, United Nations, since 1992; *b* 3 April 1942; *s* of late John Stephen and Anne Eileen Stephen; *m* 1968, Susan Dorothy (*née* Harris); three *s* one *d*. *Educ:* Denbigh Road Primary Sch., Luton; Luton Grammar Sch.; King's Coll., Cambridge (BA Mod. Langs, 1964); Univ. of San Marcos, Lima, Peru; Univ. of Essex (MA Govt, 1968). Educn Officer, CRC, 1969–70; with Runnymede Trust, 1970–75 (Dir, 1973–75); Latin American Regional Rep., Internat. Univ. Exchange Fund, 1975–77; Special Adviser to Sec. of State for Foreign and Commonwealth Affairs, 1977–79; Editor, International Affairs, 1979–83; Dir, UK Immigrants Advisory Service, 1983–84; Commonwealth Development Corporation: Mem., Management Bd, 1985–92; Head of External Relations, 1985–89; Dir of Corporate Relns, 1989–92. Trustee, Action Aid, 1981–92. Contested (SDP-Liberal Alliance), N Luton, 1983, 1987. *Recreations:* the family, music, the countryside. *Address:* PO Box 20 (3850), United Nations, New York, NY 10163–0020, USA.

STEPHEN, John Low, ChM (Aberdeen), FRCSE, FRCS; Surgeon, St Mary's Hospital, W2, since 1958; Senior Surgeon, St Mary's Hospital, W9, 1948–77, retired; *b* 13 May 1912; 2nd *s* of late Dr J. H. Stephen, Aberdeen; *m* 1938, Mary Milne, MA, BSc; one *s* one *d*. *Educ:* Aberdeen Grammar School; Aberdeen and Edinburgh Universities. MA 1931, MB 1935, Aberd.; FRCSEd, 1937; ChM Aberd., 1945; FRCS (ad eundem), 1968. Various university and hospital appointments in Scotland and England. Associate Teacher in Surgery, St Mary's Hosp. Med. School, 1950–. FRSocMed. *Publications:* chapters in Operative Surgery (Smith and Rob); various articles on abdominal surgery in Brit. Jl of Surgery. *Recreations:* golf, motoring. *Address:* Luibeg, Groombridge, Tunbridge Wells TN3 9PR.

STEPHEN, His Honour Lessel Bruce; a Circuit Judge, 1972–89; *b* 15 Feb. 1920; *s* of L. P. Stephen, FRCS(E); *m* 1949, Brenda (*née* Tinkler). *Educ:* Marlborough; Sydney Sussex Coll., Cambridge (BA). Called to the Bar, Inner Temple, 1948; subsequently practised NE Circuit; Recorder, 1972. *Recreations:* golf, wine. *Address:* 2 Harcourt Buildings, Temple, EC4Y 9DB. *T:* 0171–353 2548.

STEPHEN, Martin; *see* Stephen, G. M.

STEPHEN, Michael; MP (C) Shoreham, since 1992; *b* 25 Sept. 1942; *s* of late Harry Lace Stephen and of Edna Florence Stephen; *m* 1989, Virginia Mary (*née* de Trensé). *Educ:*

King Henry VIII Sch., Coventry; Stanford Univ. (LLM 1971); Harvard Univ. Admitted Solicitor, 1964 (Dist. Company Law); called to the Bar, Inner Temple, 1966 (Hons); commissioned, The Life Guards, 1966–70; Harkness Fellowship in Internat. Law, 1970–72; Asst Legal Adviser, UK Delegn to UN, 1971; London Bar practice, 1973–87; Internat. Trade and Public Affairs Consultant, 1988–91. Mem., RIIA, 1984–. County Councillor, Dunmow, Essex, 1985–91; Mem., Nat. Exec., ACC, 1989–91; contested (C) Doncaster North, 1983. Mem., Select Cttee on the Environment, 1994–. Vice Chm., Cons. Parly Home Affairs and Legal Cttees. Author, Bail (Amendment) Act, 1993. *Publications:* numerous political pamphlets. *Recreations:* tennis, sailing, history, theatre. *Address:* House of Commons, SW1A 0AA. *T:* 0171–219 3000.

STEPHEN, Rt. Hon. Sir Ninian (Martin), KG 1994; AK 1982; GCMG 1982; GCVO 1982; KBE 1972; PC 1979; Judge, International War Crimes Tribunal for Yugoslavia, since 1993; *b* 15 June 1923; *o s* of late Frederick Stephen and Barbara Stephen (*née* Cruickshank); *m* 1949, Valery Mary, *d* of late A. Q. Sinclair and of Mrs G. M. Sinclair; five *d*. *Educ:* George Watson's Sch., Edinburgh; Edinburgh Acad.; St Paul's Sch., London; Chillon Coll., Switzerland; Scotch Coll., Melbourne; Melbourne Univ. (LLB). Served War, HM Forces (Australian Army), 1941–46. Admitted as Barrister and Solicitor, in State of Victoria, 1949; signed Roll of Victorian Bar, 1951; QC 1966. Appointed Judge of Supreme Court of Victoria, 1970; Justice of High Court of Australia, 1972–82; Gov.-Gen. of Australia, 1982–89; Australian Ambassador for the Envmt, 1989–92; Chm., Anglo-Irish Talks (2nd strand), 1992. Hon. Bencher Gray's Inn, 1981. Chm. , Nat. Liby of Aust., 1989–94. Hon. Liveryman, Clothworkers' Co., 1991. Hon. LLD: Sydney, 1984; Melbourne, 1985; Griffith, 1988; Hon. DLitt WA, 1993. KStJ 1982. Comdr, Legion of Honour (France), 1993. *Address:* Flat 12/1, 193 Domain Road, South Yarra, Vic 3141, Australia.

STEPHEN, Rita; *see* Stephen, H. H.

STEPHENS, Air Commandant Dame Anne, DBE 1961 (MBE 1946); Hon. ADC to the Queen, 1960–63; Director, Women's Royal Air Force, 1960–63; *b* 4 Nov. 1912; *d* of late General Sir Reginald Byng Stephens, KCB, CMG and late Lady Stephens. *Educ:* privately. Joined WAAF, 1939; served in UK, Belgium and Germany, 1939–45. Command WRAF Depot, Hawkinge, 1950–52; promoted Group Officer, 1951; Inspector WRAF, 1952–54; Deputy Director, 1954–57; Staff Officer, HQ 2nd TAF, 1957–59; promoted Air Commandant, 1960. *Address:* The Forge, Sibford Ferris, Banbury, Oxfordshire OX15 5RG. *T:* Swalcliffe (01295) 780452.

STEPHENS, Anthony William, CB 1989; CMG 1976; Deputy Under Secretary of State, Northern Ireland Office, 1985–90; *b* 9 Jan. 1930; *s* of late Donald Martyn Stephens and Norah Stephens (*née* Smith-Cleburne); *m* 1954, Mytyl Joy, *d* of late William Gay Burdett; four *d*. *Educ:* Bradfield Coll.; Bristol Univ. (LLB); Corpus Christi Coll., Cambridge. RM (commnd), 1948–50. Colonial Administrative Service, 1953; District Officer, Kenya, 1954–63; Home Civil Service, 1964; Principal, MoD, 1964–70; Asst Private Sec. to successive Secretaries of State for Defence, 1970–71; Asst Sec., 1971; Chief Officer, Sovereign Base Areas, Cyprus, 1974–76; Under Sec., NI Office, 1976–79; Asst Under Sec. of State, General Staff, 1979–83, Ordnance, 1983–84, MoD. *Recreations:* travel and the outdoor life, music, theatre. *Club:* Royal Over-Seas League.

STEPHENS, Barbara Marion, (Mrs T. J. Stephens); Director of Operations, West Cumbria Development Agency, since 1993; *b* 25 Aug. 1951; *d* of late Sydney and of Edna Webb; *m* 1970, Trevor James Stephens. *Educ:* Mid-Essex Technical Coll. (HNC Engrg); NE London Poly. (DMS); City Univ. (MBA Engrg Mgt). IEng; MIEIE 1976; MIET 1992. Mechanical technician apprentice, Marconi Co., 1969–73; various technical and managerial posts, Marconi Communication Systems Ltd, 1973–88; Industrial Advr, Electronic Applications, NEDO, 1988–92. Member: Engineering Council, 1990–; HEFCE, 1995–; Adv. Council for Devel of RN Personnel, 1995–. FIMgt 1994 (MBIM 1978); FRSA 1992. *Recreations:* embroidery, reading, letter-writing, encouraging women to pursue engineering careers. *Address:* Thirlmere Building, Lakes Road, Derwent Howe, Workington, Cumbria CA14 3YP. *T:* Workington (01900) 65656.

STEPHENS, Christopher Wilson T.; *see* Stephens, Wilson T.

STEPHENS, Prof. Kenneth Gilbert, CEng, FIEE; CPhys, FInstP; Professor of Electronic and Electrical Engineering, since 1978, and Dean of the Faculty of Engineering, since 1992, University of Surrey; *b* 3 May 1931; *s* of George Harry Stephens and Christiana Stephens; *m* 1980, Elizabeth Carolynn (*née* Jones); one *s* one *d*, and two step *s*. *Educ:* Bablake Sch., Coventry; Birmingham Univ. (BSc, PhD). Nuclear Reactor Res. Physicist, AEI Ltd, Aldermaston, 1955–62; Sen. Res. Engr, Pye Ltd, Cambridge, 1963–66; University of Surrey: Lectr 1966; Reader 1967; Head, Dept of Electronic and Electrical Engrg, 1983–91. *Publications:* (ed jtly) Low Energy Ion Beams (conf. procs), 1978, 1980; (ed jtly) Ion Implantation Technology (conf. procs), 1991; articles on ion beam effects on semiconductors in learned jls. *Recreations:* reading, music, gardening, watching sport, especially cricket. *Address:* 10 Brockway Close, Merrow, Guildford, Surrey GU1 2LW. *T:* Guildford (01483) 575087. *Clubs:* MCC; Blackheath Cricket.

STEPHENS, Malcolm George, CB 1991; Secretary-General, International Union of Credit and Investment Insurers (Berne Union), since 1992 (President, 1989–91); *b* 14 July 1937; *s* of Frank Ernest Stephens and Janet (*née* McQueen); *m* 1975, Lynette Marie Caffery, Brisbane, Australia. *Educ:* St Michael's and All Angels; Shooter's Hill Grammar Sch.; St John's Coll., Oxford (Casberd Scholar; BA 1st Cl. Hons PPE). National Service, RAOC, 1956–58. CRO, 1953; British High Commission: Ghana, 1959–62; Kenya, 1963–65; Export Credits Guarantee Dept, 1965–82: Principal, 1970; seconded to Civil Service Coll., 1971–72; Asst Sec., 1973; Estab. Officer, 1977; Under Sec., 1978; Head of Proj. Gp B, 1978–79; Principal Finance Officer, 1979–82; Internat. Finance Dir, Barclays Bank Internat. Ltd, 1982; Dir, Barclays Export Services, 1983–87; Export Finance Dir, Barclays Bank PLC, 1985–87; Chief Executive: ECGD, 1987–92; London Chamber of Commerce and Industry, 1991–92. Director: European Capital, 1992; Arab-British Chamber of Commerce, 1992. Member: Overseas Projects Bd, 1985; BOTB, 1987. FCIB (FIB 1984); FIEx 1987; MICM 1990. *Recreations:* gardening, reading, fitness centre, swimming. *Address:* 111 Woolwich Road, Bexleyheath, Kent DA7 4LP. *T:* 0181–303 6782. *Club:* Travellers'.

STEPHENS, Martin; *see* Stephens, S. M.

STEPHENS, Peter Norman Stuart; Director, News Group Newspapers, 1978–87, Editorial Director, 1981–87; *b* 19 Dec. 1927; *s* of J. G. Stephens; *m* 1950, Constance Mary Ratheram; two *s* one *d*. *Educ:* Mundella Grammar Sch., Nottingham. Newark Advertiser, 1945–48; Northern Echo, 1948–50; Daily Dispatch, 1950–55; Daily Mirror, Manchester, 1955–57; Asst Editor, Newcastle Journal, 1957–60; Asst Editor, Evening Chronicle, Newcastle, 1960–62, Editor 1962–66; Editor, Newcastle Journal, 1966–70; Asst Editor, The Sun, 1970–72, Dep. Editor 1972; Associate Editor, News of the World, 1973, Editor, 1974–75; Associate Editor, The Sun, 1975–81. *Publication:* Newark: the magic of malt, 1993. *Recreations:* the printed word, supporting Derby County Football Club. *Address:* The Friary, Newark on Trent, Notts NG24 1JY.

STEPHENS, Sir Robert (Graham), Kt 1995; actor; *b* 14 July 1931; *s* of Rueben Stephens and Gladys (*née* Deverell); *m* Tarn Bassett; one *d*; *m* 1967, Maggie Smith, (*see* Dame Maggie Smith) (marr. diss. 1975); two *s*; *m* 1995, Patricia Quinn. *Educ:* Bradford Civic Theatre School. Started with Caryl Jenner Mobile Theatre Co.; Mem. English Stage Co., Royal Court, 1956. *Stage:* The Crucible, Don Juan, The Death of Satan, Cards of Identity, The Good Woman of Setzuan and The Country Wife (also at Adelphi, 1957); The Apollo de Bellac, Yes-and After, The Making of Moo, How Can We Save Father?, The Waters of Babylon, Royal Court, 1957; The Entertainer, Palace, 1957; Epitaph for George Dillon, Royal Court, Comedy, Golden (NY), 1958 and Henry Miller, 1959; Look After Lulu (also at New) and The Kitchen (also 1961), Royal Court, 1959; The Wrong Side of the Park, Cambridge, 1960; The Sponge Room, Squat Betty, Royal Court, 1962; Chichester and Edinburgh Festival, 1963; Design for Living (Los Angeles), 1971; Private Lives, Queen's, 1972; The Seagull, Chichester, 1973; Apropos The Falling Sleet (dir.), Open Space, 1973; Ghosts, The Seagull, Hamlet, Greenwich, 1974; Sherlock Holmes, NY and Canada, 1975; Murderer, Garrick, 1975; Zoo Story, 1975, Othello, 1976, Open Air, Regent's Park; Pygmalion, Los Angeles, 1979; Othello, Cape Town, SA, 1982; WCPC, Half Moon, 1982; Light Up the Sky, Old Vic, 1985; Falstaff in Henry IV, parts I and II (Olivier Best Actor Award), Julius Caesar, 1991, King Lear, 1993, RSC (Shakespeare Globe Classic Best Actor Award; Variety Club Stage Actor Award); *National Theatre Company:* Hamlet, St Joan, The Recruiting Officer, 1963; Andorra, Play, The Royal Hunt of the Sun (also Chichester Fest.), Hay Fever, 1964; Much Ado About Nothing, Armstrong's Last Goodnight, Trelawny of the Wells (also Chichester Fest.), 1965; A Bond Honoured, Black Comedy, 1966; The Dance of Death, The Three Sisters (at Los Angeles, 1968), As You Like It, Tartuffe, 1967; Most Unwarrantable Intrusion (also dir.), Home and Beauty, 1968; Macrune's Guevara (also co-dir), 1969; The Beaux' Stratagem (also Los Angeles), Hedda Gabler, 1970; The Cherry Orchard, Brand, The Double Dealer, Has "Washington" Legs?, 1978; A Midsummer Night's Dream, Inner Voices, Cinderella, 1983; Passion Plays. *Films:* A Taste of Honey, 1961; The Small World of Sammy Lee, 1962; Cleopatra, 1963; The Prime of Miss Jean Brodie, 1967; The Private Life of Sherlock Holmes, 1969; Travels with my Aunt, 1972; The Asphyx, 1972; Luther, 1972; QBVII, 1973; Alexander the Great, 1980; Ill Fares The Land, 1982; High Season, 1986; Comrades, 1987; Empire of the Sun, 1987; The Fruit Machine, 1988; Henry V, 1989; Chaplin, 1992; The Dualists; The Shout; Ada in the Jungle; Children; Wings of Fame; Bonfire of the Vanities; Ferdy Duke; The Pope Must Die; Searching For Bobby Fischer, 1992; Century, 1993; Secret Rapture, 1993. *Television* includes: Vienna 1900 (6 part series), 1973; Tribute to J. B. Priestley, 1974; Kean, 1978; Voyage of Charles Darwin, 1978; Office Story, 1978; Friends in Space, 1979; Suez, 1979; The Executioner, 1980; Adelaide Bartlett (series), 1980; Winter's Tale, 1980; The Double Dealer, 1980; The Trial of Madame Farnay, 1980; Holocaust (USA), 1980; Eden End, 1981; The Year of the French (RTE), 1981; Anyone for Denis?, 1982; Tales Out of School, 1982; Box of Delights, 1984; Puccini, 1984; By the Sword Divided (series), 1984; Hells Bells (series), 1985; War and Remembrance (film series), 1986; Fortunes of War (series), 1986; Lizzie's Pictures (series), 1986; Shostokovich, 1987; Adam Bede; L. P. Hartley Trilogy; An Actor's Life For Me; Down Where the Buffalo Go; American Roulette; Fine Romance; Stolen; Greek Myths; In my own Defence; Roger Casement. *Radio* plays include: The Light Shines in the Darkness (BBC), 1985; Timon of Athens (BBC), 1989. Variety Club Award for stage actor, 1965. *Publication:* A Knight on the Tiles (autobiog.), 1995. *Recreations:* cooking, gymnastics, swimming. *Address:* c/o Michael Foster, ICM, Oxford House, 76 Oxford Street, W1N 0AX.

STEPHENS, (Stephen) Martin; QC 1982; **His Honour Judge Stephens;** a Circuit Judge, since 1986; *b* 26 June 1939; *s* of late Abraham Stephens and of Freda Stephens, Swansea; *m* 1965, Patricia Alison, *d* of late Joseph and of Anne Morris, Mapperley, Nottingham; one *s* one *d* (and one *s* decd). *Educ:* Swansea Grammar Sch.; Wadham Coll., Oxford (MA). Called to the Bar, Middle Temple, 1963; Wales and Chester Circuit; a Recorder, 1979–86. Mem., Parole Bd, 1995–. Mem., Criminal Cttee, Judicial Studies Bd, 1995–. *Recreations:* cricket, theatre. *Address:* c/o The Law Courts, St Helen's Road, Swansea SA1 4PF.

STEPHENS, William Henry, CB 1961; DSc, MSc, CEng, FRAeS; FBIS; retired; Non-Executive Director, General Technology Systems Ltd, 1987–89 (Senior Executive Director, 1973–87); *b* Kilkenny, Ireland, 18 March 1913; *s* of William Henry Stephens, MBE, and Helena Read Stephens (*née* Cantley); *m* 1938, Elizabeth Margaret Brown, BSc; one *s* one *d*. *Educ:* Methodist College and Queen's University, Belfast. Air Ministry, Royal Aircraft Establishment (Aerodynamic Research), 1935–38; War Office, Woolwich (Rocket Research), 1938–39; Ministry of Aircraft Prod., London (Air Defence Research), 1939–44; Asst Scientific Attaché and Asst Director, UK Scientific Mission, British Commonwealth Scientific Office, Washington, USA, 1944–47; Min. of Supply, RAE, Head of Guided Weapons Dept and later Dep. Director, 1947–58; Dir-Gen. Ballistic Missiles, Ministry of Aviation, 1959–62; Technical Dir, European Space Launcher Develt Organisation, Paris, 1962–69; Minister, Defence R&D, British Embassy, Washington, 1969–72; Special Advr (Internat. Affairs), Controllerate of Res., MoD, 1972–73. Mem., Internat. Acad. of Astronautics; Fellow, British Interplanetary Soc. *Publications:* contrib. to Jl Royal Aeronautical Soc.; Proc. Brit. Assoc.; Proc. Internat. Congress of Aeronautical Sciences. *Recreations:* travel, music, art, theatre. *Address:* Rosebrook House, Oriel Hill, Camberley, Surrey GU15 2JW. *Club:* Athenæum.

STEPHENS, Wilson (Treeve); Editor of The Field, 1950–77, Consultant 1987–90; Consultant, Countryweek, since 1991; *b* 2 June 1912; *s* of Rev. Arthur Treeve Stephens, Shepton Beauchamp, Somerset, and Margaret Wilson; *m* 1st, 1934, Nina, *d* of Arthur Frederick Curzon, Derby; two *d*; 2nd, 1960, Marygold Anne, *o d* of Major-General G. O. Crawford, CB, CBE; two *d*. *Educ:* Christ's Hosp. Formerly on editorial staffs of several provincial newspapers, and of The Daily Express. Served War of 1939–45, Royal Artillery. *Publications:* The Guinness Guide to Field Sports, 1979; Gundog Sense and Sensibility, 1982; Pigeon Racing, 1983; A Year Observed, 1984; Rivers of Britain (series) 1985–; contribs to numerous publications. *Recreations:* fly-fishing, shooting. *Address:* c/o Blake, Friedmann, 37–41 Gower Street, WC1E 6HH.

STEPHENSON, Ashley; *see* Stephenson, R. A. S.

STEPHENSON, Prof. Gordon, CBE 1967; FRIBA, FRTPI, LFRAIA, LFRAPI, FLI, DistTP; Professor Emeritus of Architecture, University of Western Australia; *b* 6 June 1908; *s* of Francis E. and Eva E. Stephenson, Liverpool; *m* 1938, Flora Bartlett Crockett (decd), Boston, USA; three *d*. *Educ:* Liverpool Institute; University of Liverpool; University of Paris; Massachusetts Institute of Technology. Elmes Scholar, Univ. of Liverpool, 1925–30; Holt Scholar, 1928; First Cl. Hons in Architecture, 1930; Chadwick Scholar at Brit. Inst. in Paris and Univ. of Paris, 1930–32; BArch; MCP(MIT). Lecturer and Studio Instructor in Architecture, University of Liverpool, 1932–36; Commonwealth Fellow and Medallist, Massachusetts Inst. of Technology, 1936–38; Studio Master, Architectural Assoc., School of Architecture, 1939–40; Lever Professor of Civic Design, School of Architecture, University of Liverpool, 1948–53; Professor of Town and Regional Planning in the University of Toronto, Canada, 1955–60; Prof. of Architecture, Univ. of WA, 1960–72. Architectural and Planning practice: asst to Corbett, Harrison and McMurray,

NY City, 1929; asst to Le Corbusier and Pierre Jeanneret, Paris, 1930–32; Div. Architect, with W. G. Holford, on Royal Ordnance Factory work, 1940–42; Research Officer, Sen. Research Officer, and Chief Planning Officer, Min. of Works and Planning, and Min. of Town and Country Planning, 1942–47; seconded to assist Sir Patrick Abercrombie on Greater London Plan, 1943–44; partner, Stephenson, Young and Partners, 1949–53; Cnslt Architect, Univ. of WA, 1960–69; in partnership with R. J. Ferguson, as architects and planners for Murdoch Univ., WA, 1972–76; in private practice, houses, militia camp, university bldgs, community centre, housing schemes, town and regional planning studies. Mem., Nat. Capital Planning Cttee, Canberra, 1967–73; Consultant, Perth Northwestern Suburbs Railway Project, 1989–90. Editor, Town Planning Review, 1949–54. Hon. MCIP 1960. Hon. LLD Univ. of WA, 1976; Hon. DArch Univ. of Melbourne, 1984; Hon. DSc Flinders Univ., 1987; DUniv Murdoch Univ., 1988. *Publications:* (with Flora Stephenson) Community Centres, 1941; (with F. R. S. Yorke) Planning for Reconstruction, 1944; (with J. A. Hepburn) Plan for the Metropolitan Region of Perth and Fremantle, 1955; a Redevelopment Study of Halifax, Nova Scotia, 1957; (with G. G. Muirhead) A Planning Study of Kingston, Ontario, 1959; The Design of Central Perth, 1975; Joondalup Regional Centre, 1977; Planning for the University of Western Australia: 1914–70, 1986; On a Human Scale, 1992; Compassionate Town Planning; articles and papers in British, Australian, Canadian Technical Professional Jls. *Recreations:* architectural practice, drawing and travel. *Address:* Unit 55, 14 Albert Street, St Louis Estate, Claremont, WA 6010, Australia. *T:* (9) 3852309.

STEPHENSON, Sir Henry Upton, 3rd Bt *cr* 1936; TD; Director: Stephenson, Blake (Holdings) Ltd; Thos Turton and Sons Ltd; *b* 26 Nov. 1926; *s* of Lt-Col Sir Henry Francis Blake Stephenson, 2nd Bt, OBE, TD, and of Joan, *d* of Major John Herbert Upton (formerly Upton Cottrell-Dormer); *S* father, 1982; *m* 1962, Susan, *o d* of Major J. E. Clowes, Ashbourne, Derbyshire; four *d*. *Educ:* Eton. Formerly Major, QO Yorkshire Dragoons. High Sheriff of Derbyshire, 1975. *Heir: cousin* Timothy Hugh Stephenson [*b* 5 Jan. 1930; *m* 1959, Susan Lesley, *yr d* of late George Arthur Harris; two *s*]. *Address:* Tissington Cottage, Rowland, Bakewell, Derbyshire DE4 1NR.

STEPHENSON, Prof. Hugh; writer and journalist; Professor of Journalism, City University, since 1986; *b* 18 July 1938; *s* of late Sir Hugh Stephenson; *m* 1st, 1962, Auriol Stevens (marr. diss. 1987); two *s* one *d*; 2nd, 1990, Diana Eden. *Educ:* Winchester Coll.; New Coll., Oxford (BA); Univ. of Calif, Berkeley. Pres., Oxford Union, 1962. HM Diplomatic Service, 1964–68; joined The Times, 1968; Editor, The Times Business News, 1972–81; Editor, The New Statesman, 1982–86. Mem., Cttee to Review Functioning of Financial Instns, 1977–80. Councillor, London Bor. of Wandsworth, 1971–78. Dir, History Today Ltd, 1981–. FRSA 1987. *Publications:* The Coming Clash, 1972; Mrs Thatcher's First Year, 1980; Claret and Chips, 1982. *Address:* Department of Journalism, City University, Northampton Square, EC1V 0HB.

STEPHENSON, (James) Ian (Love), RA 1986 (ARA 1975); painter; *b* 11 Jan. 1934; *o s* of James Stephenson and May (*née* Emery); *m* 1959, Kate, *o d* of James Brown; one *s* one *d*. *Educ:* King Edward VII School of Art, King's Coll., Univ. of Durham, Newcastle upon Tyne (3 prizes; Hatton Schol.; BA Dunelm 1956, 1st Class Hons in Fine Art). Tutorial Student, 1956–57, Studio Demonstrator, 1957–58, King's Coll., Newcastle upon Tyne (pioneered 1st foundn course in UK dedicated to new creativity in art); Boise Schol. (Italy), Univ. of London, 1958–59; Vis. Lectr, Polytechnic Sch. of Art, London, 1959–62; Vis. Painter, Chelsea Sch. of Art, 1959–66; Dir, Foundn Studies, Dept of Fine Art, Univ. of Newcastle, 1966–70 (introd alternating approach between perceptual and conceptual studies to academic syllabus for first time); Dir, Postgrad. Painting, Chelsea Sch. of Art, 1970–89 (attained Master's Degree status, 1974, the only CNAA Fine Art MA course in UK approved in nationwide survey, 1977–78); Internat. Course Leader, Voss Summer Sch., 1979. Member: Visual Arts Panel, Northern Arts Assoc., Newcastle, 1967–70; Fine Art Panel, NCDAD, 1972–74; Perm. Cttee, New Contemp. Assoc., 1973–75 (revived annual nat. student exhibns); Fine Art Board, CNAA, 1974–75; Adv. Cttee, Nat. Exhibn of Children's Art, Manchester, 1975–92; Working Party, RA Jubilee Exhbn, 1976–77; Selection Cttee, Arts Council Awards, 1977–78; Painting Faculty, Rome and Abbey Major Scholarships, 1978–82; Recommending Cttee, Chantrey Bequest, 1979–80; RA Steward, Artists' Gen. Benevolent Instn, 1979–80; Fine Art Advr, Canterbury Art Coll., 1974–79; 1st Specialist Advr, CNAA, 1980–83; Vice-Pres., Sunderland Arts Centre, 1982–86; Boise Scholarship Cttee, UCL, 1983; Cttee Chm., David Murray Studentship Fund, 1990. Examiner: Birmingham Poly., 1972–73; Portsmouth Poly., 1973–76; London Univ., 1975–83 (Sen. Postgrad. Examiner); Leicester Poly., 1976–78; Ulster Poly., 1979–82; Canterbury Art Coll., 1981–83; Newcastle Poly., 1982–85; Kingston Poly., 1985–88; Edinburgh Art Coll., 1989–. Juror: Contemporary Art, Portsmouth, 1966; Fedn N Art Socs, Newcastle, 1966; Pernod Competition NAA, Newcastle, 1970; Yorkshire Artists' Exhibn, Leeds, 1971; Open Field SAA, Reading, 1972; N Young Contemps, Manchester, 1973; British Painting, London, 1974; Winsor & Newton Award, Birmingham, 1975; Second Chance Charity Exhibn, London, 1977; RA Summer Exhibn, London, 1980; JM 12 Exhibn, Liverpool, 1980. Hon. Member: CAS, 1980–81; Accademia Italia, 1980–; Mark Twain Soc., 1978–. *Exhibitions include:* British Painting in the Sixties, London, 1963; Mostra di Pittura Contemporanea, Amsterdam and Europe, 1964–65; 9o Biennio, Lugano, 1966; 5e Biennale and 18e Salon, Paris, 1967; Recent British Painting, London and world tour, 1967–75; Junge Generation Grossbritannien, Berlin, 1968; Retrospective, Newcastle, 1970; La Peinture Anglaise Aujourd'hui, Paris, 1973; Elf Englische Zeichner, Baden Baden and Bremen, 1973; Recente Britse Tekenkunst, Antwerp, 1973; 13a Bienal, São Paulo and Latin America, 1975; Arte Inglese Oggi, Milan, 1976; Retrospective, London and Bristol, 1977; Englische Kunst der Gegenwart, Bregenz, 1977; British Painting 1952–77, London, 1977; Color en la Pintura Britanica, Rio de Janeiro and Latin America, 1977–79; Abstract Paintings from UK, Washington, 1978; Retrospective, Birmingham and Cardiff, 1978; Royal Acad. of Arts, Edinburgh, 1979–80; Art Anglais d'Aujourd'hui, Geneva, 1980; British Art 1940–80, London, 1980; Colour in British Painting, Hong Kong and Far East, 1980–81; Contemporary British Drawings, Tel-Aviv and Near East, 1980–82; The Deck of Cards, Athens and Arabia, 1980–82; A Taste of British Art Today, Brussels, 1982; Arteder Muestra Internacional, Bilbao, 1982; La Couleur en la Peinture Britannique, Luxembourg and Bucharest, 1982–83; 7th, 8th and 9th Internat. Print Biennales, Bradford, 1982, 1984 and 1986; 15a Bienale, Ljubljana, 1983; Peintiadau Prydeinig 1946–72, Penarth, 1985; Ready Steady Go, London and UK, 1992–93; *illustrations include:* Cubism and After (BBC film), 1962; Contemporary British Art, 1965; Private View, 1965; Blow Up (film), 1966; Art of Our Time, 1967; Recent British Painting, 1968; Adventure in Art, 1969; In Vogue, 1975; Painting in Britain 1525–1975, 1976; British Painting, 1976; Contemporary Artists, 1977, 1983 and 1989; Contemporary British Artists, 1979; Tendenze e Testimonianze, 1983; Dictionary of 20th Century British Artists, 1991; *work in collections:* Arnolfini Trust, Arts Council, Birmingham and Bristol City Art Galls, British Council, BP Chemicals and Co., Bury Art Gall., Contemp. Art Soc., Creasey Lit. Museum, DoE, Economist Newspaper, Granada TV, Gulbenkian Foundn, Hatton Gall., Hunterian Museum, Kettle's Yard, Leeds City Art Gall., Leicestershire Educn Authority, Madison Art Center, Marzotto Roma, Nat. West. Bank, Northern Arts Assoc., Nuffield Foundn, Queen Elizabeth II Conf. Centre, Stuyvesant Foundn, Sunderland Art Gall., Tate Gall., Unilever Ltd, Union Bank of Switzerland, V&A Museum, Victoria Nat. Gall., Welsh Nat. Museum, Whitworth Art Gall. *Prizes include:* Junior Section, Moores Exhibn, Liverpool, 1957; European Selection, Premio Marzotto, Valdagno, 1964; First, Northern Painters' Exhibn, 1966. *Address:* c/o Royal Academy of Arts, Piccadilly, W1V 0DS.

STEPHENSON, Jim; His Honour Judge Stephenson; a Circuit Judge, since 1983; *b* 17 July 1932; *s* of late Alex and Norah Stephenson, Heworth, Co. Durham; *m* 1964, Jill Christine, *d* of Dr Lindeck, Fairwarp, Sussex; three *s*. *Educ:* Royal Grammar Sch. and Dame Allan's Sch., Newcastle; Exeter Coll., Oxford (Exhibnr, BA). Pres., Oxford Univ. Law Society, Michaelmas, 1955. Called to Bar, Gray's Inn, 1957. Mem., General Council of the Bar, 1961–64; Junior, NE Circuit, 1961; a Recorder of the Crown Court, 1974–83. Pres., NE Br., Magistrates' Assoc., 1988–92. Additional Mem. of Bd, Faculty of Law, Newcastle Univ., 1984–90. Gov., Newcastle Prep. Sch., 1985–92. *Recreations:* reading, walking, history. *Address:* Crown Court, Quayside, Newcastle upon Tyne NE1 2LA.

STEPHENSON, Maj.-Gen. John Aubrey, CB 1982; OBE 1971; defence consultant, 1991–93; Managing Director, Weapon Systems Ltd, 1982–91; Deputy Master General of the Ordnance, 1980–81; *b* 15 May 1929; *s* of Reginald Jack Stephenson and Florence Stephenson; *m* 1953, Sheila Colbeck; two *s* one *d*. *Educ:* Dorchester Grammar School. Commnd RA, 1948; served Malaya (despatches, 1951), Libya, Canal Zone and Germany, 1949–58 (student pilot, 1953–54); student, RMCS, 1958–60; 39 Missile Regt, 1960–61; student, RMCS and Staff Coll., 1961–62; served UK and Germany, 1962–67; Staff, RMCS, 1967–69; CO 16 Light Air Defence Regt RA, 1969–71; Project Manager, 155mm Systems, Woolwich, 1971–73; student, RCDS, 1974; Comdr, 1st Artillery Bde, Germany, 1975–77; Sen. Mil. Officer, RARDE, 1977–78; Dir Gen. Weapons (Army), 1978–80. Dir, ATX Ltd, 1984–91. Col Comdt, RA, 1984–89; Hon. Regtl Col, 16 Regt, RA, 1989–. Governor, The Dorchester Thomas Hardye Sch. (formerly Hardye's Sch.), 1984–. FIMgt. *Recreations:* fishing, sailing, gardening, bridge, golf, military history. *Address:* Collingwood, 27 Trafalgar Way, Stockbridge, Hants SO20 6ET. *T:* Andover (01264) 810458. *Club:* Royal Over-Seas League.

STEPHENSON, Rt. Hon. Sir John (Frederick Eustace), PC 1971; Kt 1962; a Lord Justice of Appeal, 1971–85; *b* 28 March 1910; 2nd *s* of late Sir Guy Stephenson, CB, and of late Gwendolen, *d* of Rt Hon. J. G. Talbot; *m* 1951, Frances Rose, *yr d* of late Lord Asquith of Bishopstone, PC; two *s* two *d*. *Educ:* Winchester College (Schol.); New Coll., Oxford (Schol.); Hon. Fellow, 1979. 1st Cl. Hon. Mods. 1930, 1st Cl. Litt Hum. 1932, BA 1932, MA 1956. Called to Bar, Inner Temple (Entrance Scholarship), 1934; Bencher, 1962. Sapper RE (TA), 1938; War Office, 1940; Intelligence Corps, Captain 1943, Major 1944 and Lieut-Col 1946; Middle East and NW Europe; Regional Intelligence Officer, Hamburg, 1946; Recorder of Bridgwater, 1954–59; Recorder of Winchester, 1959–62; Chancellor of the Diocese: of Peterborough, 1956–62; of Winchester, 1958–62; QC 1960; Dep. Chm., Dorset QS, 1962–71; Judge of Queen's Bench Div., High Court of Justice, 1962–71. *Publication:* A Royal Correspondence, 1938. *Address:* 26 Doneraile Street, SW6 6EN. *T:* 0171–736 6782. *Clubs:* Hurlingham, MCC; Royal Wimbledon Golf.

STEPHENSON, Lt-Col John Robin, CBE 1994 (OBE (mil.) 1976); Secretary: Marylebone Cricket Club, 1987–93; International Cricket Council (formerly International Cricket Conference), 1987–93; *b* 25 Feb. 1931; *s* of John Stewart Stephenson and Edith Gerda Greenwell Stephenson; *m* 1962, Karen Margrethe Koppang; one *s* two *d*. *Educ:* Christ's Hospital; RMA Sandhurst. Commissioned Royal Sussex Regt, 1951; served Egypt, Korea, Gibraltar, Libya, Germany, N Ireland; Instructor, Mons Officer Cadet Sch., 1958–60; Infantry Rep., Sch. of Signals, 1968–70; SOWC, 1972–73; Comdg Officer, 5 (V) Queen's Regt, 1973–75; Dep. Pres., Regular Commissions Bd, 1976; Staff Officer, Cs-in-C Cttee, 1977–79. Asst Sec. (Cricket), MCC, 1979–86; managed MCC tours, Bangladesh, 1979–80, E Africa, 1980–81, Canada, 1985, Kenya, 1993. President: Forty Club, 1994–; Stragglers of Asia CC, 1994–. Governor: St Bede's Sch., Eastbourne, 1989–94; Clayesmore Sch., Dorset, 1989–. Order of Orange-Nassau, 1972. *Recreations:* Rugby football (RMA Sandhurst (Capt.), Richmond, Army, Sussex), cricket (RMA Sandhurst, MCC, IZ, FF, Army), golf, boating, gardening. *Address:* Plum Tree Cottage, Barford St Martin, Salisbury, Wilts SP3 4BL. *T:* Salisbury (01722) 743443. *Clubs:* East India, Farmers', MCC; IZ, Free Foresters, Stragglers of Asia.

STEPHENSON, Lynne, (Mrs Chaim Stephenson); *see* Banks, L. R.

STEPHENSON, Margaret Maud; *see* Tyzack, M. M.

STEPHENSON, Prof. Patrick Hay, MA, CEng, FIMechE; retired consultant Mechanical Engineer; *b* 31 March 1916; *e s* of late Stanley George Stephenson; *m* 1947, Pauline Coupland; two *s* one *d*. *Educ:* Wyggeston Sch., Leicester; Cambridge Univ. (MA). Apprenticeship and Research Engr, Brit. United Shoe Machinery Co., 1932–39. War Service as Ordnance Mechanical Engr and REME, India and Far East, 1939–45; held as POW by Japanese, 1942–45. Chief Mechanical Engr, Pye Ltd, 1949–67; Prof. of Mech. Engrg, Univ. of Strathclyde, 1967–79; Dir, Inst. of Advanced Machine Tool and Control Technology, Min. of Technology, 1967–70; Dir, Birniehill Inst. and Manufacturing Systems Group, DTI, 1970–72; Head of Research Requirements Branch 2, DoI, 1972–77. Research advisor to Institution of Mechanical Engineers; senior industrial advisor to the Design Council. Mem. Council, IMechE, 1960–68; Member: Bd, UKAC, 1964–73; Engrg Bd, SRC, 1973–. *Publications:* papers and articles in technical press. *Recreations:* music, vintage motoring. *Address:* Toft Lane, Great Wilbraham, Cambridge CB1 5JH. *T:* Cambridge (01223) 880405.

STEPHENSON, Paul; Regional Director, Wales and the West, Focus Consultancy Ltd; *b* 6 May 1937; *s* of Olive Stephenson; *m* 1965, Joyce Annikie; one *s* one *d*. *Educ:* Westhill Coll. of Educn, Selly Oak, Birmingham. MIPR 1978. Youth Tutor, St Paul's, Bristol, 1962–68; Sen. Community Relations Officer, Coventry, 1968–72; National Youth Trng Officer, Community Relations Commn, 1972–77; Sen. Liaison Officer, CRE, 1980–92. Chm., Muhammad Ali Sports Develt Assoc., Brixton and Lambeth, 1974–; Member: British Sports Council, 1976–82; Press Council, 1984–90. *Recreations:* travel, cinema, reading, international politics. *Address:* 12 Downs Park East, Westbury Park, Bristol BS6 7QD. *T:* Bristol (0117) 962 3638; Focus Consultancy Ltd, 444 Brixton Road, SW9 8EG.

STEPHENSON, (Robert) Ashley (Shute), LVO 1990 (MVO 1979); Bailiff of the Royal Parks, 1980–90; *b* 1 Sept. 1927; *s* of late James Stephenson and Agnes Maud Stephenson; *m* 1955, Isabel Dunn; one *s* one *d*. *Educ:* Walbottle Secondary Sch. Diploma in Horticulture, RHS, Wisley, 1954; MIHort 1987. Apprenticeship, Newcastle upon Tyne Parks Dept, 1942; served RASC, Palestine and Cyprus, 1946; Landscape Gardener, Donald Ireland Ltd, 1949; Student, RHS's gardens, Wisley, 1952; Royal Parks, 1954–: Supt, Regent's Park, 1969; Supt, Central Royal Parks, 1972. Gardening Correspondent, The Times, 1982–87. Pres., British Pelargonium and Geranium Soc., 1983–95; Member: Cttee, RHS, 1981–; London in Bloom Cttee, English Tourist Bd, 1980– (Vice-Chm., 1983); Chm., South East in Bloom, 1990–; Nat. Chm., Britain in Bloom, 1991–; Mem., The Queen's Anniversary Cttee 1952–92, 1992– (Chm., Horticl Cttee, 1992–). Contributor to television and radio programmes; regularly on BBC Radio Sussex gardening programmes; gardening correspondent to professional and amateur papers. *Publications:* The Garden Planner, 1981; contribs to nat. press. *Recreations:* sport, judging horticultural shows, natural history, walking, golf. *Address:* 17 Sandore Road, Seaford, E Sussex BN25 3PR. *Club:* Arts.

STEPHENSON, Stanley, CMG 1987; HM Diplomatic Service, retired; *b* 30 Sept. 1926; *s* of George Stephenson and Margaret Jane (*née* Nicholson); *m* 1957, Grace Claire Lyons (*d* 1987); one *s* one *d*. *Educ:* Bede Sch., Sunderland. Inland Revenue, 1942; Royal Navy, 1944–48; Foreign (later Diplomatic) Service, 1948–: Cairo, Jedda, Damascus, Curaçao, Ciudad Trujillo (now Santo Domingo), San José, Seoul, Santiago de Cuba, Bogotá (twice), Asunción, San Francisco, FCO; Diplomatic Service Inspector, 1978–80; Ambassador to Panama, 1981–83; Consul-Gen., Vancouver, 1983–86. *Recreations:* tennis, cricket, Rugby, theatre, gardening. *Address:* Marymount, Raggleswood, Chislehurst, Kent BR7 5NH. *T:* 0181–467 6066. *Clubs:* Civil Service; Crescent Lawn Tennis (Sidcup).

STEPHENSON, Air Vice-Marshal Tom Birkett, CB 1982; Assistant Chief of Defence Staff (Signals), 1980–82, retired; *b* 18 Aug. 1926; *s* of Richard and Isabel Stephenson; *m* 1951, Rosemary Patricia (*née* Kaye) (*d* 1984); one *s* three *d*. *Educ:* Workington Secondary Sch.; Manchester Univ.; Southampton Univ. (DipEl). Commissioned in RAF Engrg Branch, 1945; Staff Coll., 1962; Wing Comdr, Station and Staff appointments, until 1967; Command Electrical Engr, HQASC, 1967–69; Dep. Director Op. Requirements, 1969–72; AOEng, HQ NEAF, 1972–74; RCDS 1975; Director of Signals (Air), 1976–79. *Recreations:* sport, walking, reading. *Address:* c/o National Westminster Bank, High Street, Maidenhead SL6 1PY. *Club:* Royal Air Force.

STEPNEY, Area Bishop of; *no new appointment at time of going to press.*

STERLING, family name of **Baron Sterling of Plaistow.**

STERLING OF PLAISTOW, Baron *cr* 1991 (Life Peer), of Pall Mall in the City of Westminster; **Jeffrey Maurice Sterling,** Kt 1985; CBE 1977; Chairman, The Peninsular and Oriental Steam Navigation Company, since 1983; *b* 27 Dec. 1934; *s* of late Harry and of Alice Sterling; *m* 1985, Dorothy Ann Smith; one *d*. *Educ:* Reigate Grammar Sch.; Preston Manor County Sch.; Guildhall School of Music. Paul Schweder & Co. (Stock Exchange), 1955–57; G. Eberstadt & Co., 1957–62; Fin. Dir, General Guarantee Corp., 1962–64; Man. Dir, Gula Investments Ltd, 1964–69; Chm., Sterling Guarantee Trust plc, 1969–85, when it merged with P&O Steam Navigation Co. Mem., British Airways Bd, 1979–82. Special Advr to Sec. of State for Industry, later for Trade and Industry, 1982–90. Mem. Exec., 1966–, Chm. Organisation Cttee, 1969–73, World ORT Union; Chm., ORT Technical Services, 1974–; Vice-Pres., British ORT, 1978–; President: Gen. Council of British Shipping, 1990–91; EC Shipowners' Assocs, 1992–94. Dep. Chm. and Hon. Treasurer, London Celebrations Cttee, Queen's Silver Jubilee, 1975–83. Chm., Young Vic Co., 1975–83; Chm., of the Governors, Royal Ballet Sch., 1983–; Gov., Royal Ballet, 1986–; Chm., Motability (Chm. Exec., 1977–). Freeman, City of London. Hon. Captain, RNR, 1991. Elder Brother, Trinity House, 1991. Hon. FIMarE 1991; Hon. FICS 1992; Hon. MRICS 1993. *Recreations:* music, swimming, tennis. *Address:* The Peninsular and Oriental Steam Navigation Company, 79 Pall Mall, SW1Y 5EJ. *Clubs:* Garrick, Carlton, Hurlingham.

STERLING, Dr (Isobel Jane) Nuala, CBE 1993; FRCP; Consultant Physician in Geriatric Medicine, Royal South Hants Hospital, since 1979; *b* 12 Feb. 1937; *d* of Prof. F. Bradbury and Mrs J. Bradbury; *m* 1961, Dr G. M. Sterling; five *s* (one *d* decd). *Educ:* Friends' Sch., Saffron Walden; King's Coll. and St George's Hosp., London (MB BS 1960). MRCS LRCP 1960; MRCP 1971, FRCP 1981. House Officer and Registrar posts, St George's Hosp., 1960–67; in general practice: London, 1963–64; Oxford, 1968; Lectr in Medicine, Univ. of Calif., San Francisco, 1969–70; Sen. House Officer then Registrar, Oxford, 1970–71; Sen. Registrar and Lectr in Geriatric Medicine, Southampton Univ. Hosps, 1972–79. Member: Standing Med. Adv. Cttee to Sec. of State for Health, 1986–96 (Chm., 1990–94); Clinical Standards Adv. Gp, 1990–94. Royal College of Physicians: Chm., Standing Cttee of Mems, 1978–79; Mem., Jt Consultants Cttee, 1986–92; Pres., Medical Women's Fedn, 1989–90. *Publications:* research publications on immunology and cancer, endocrine and respiratory disorders in the elderly, provision of medical services and training. *Recreations:* music, modern art, growing orchids, watching cricket. *Address:* Royal South Hants Hospital, Southampton SO9 4PE.

STERLING, Michael John Howard, FEng 1991; FIEE; FInstMC; Vice-Chancellor and Principal, Brunel University, since 1990; *b* 9 Feb. 1946; *s* of Richard Howard Sterling and Joan Valeria Sterling (*née* Skinner); *m* 1969, Wendy Karla Anstead; two *s*. *Educ:* Hampton Grammar Sch., Middx; Univ. of Sheffield (BEng 1968; PhD 1971; DEng 1988). Student apprentice, AEI, 1964–68; research engineer, GEC-Eliott Process Automation, 1968–71; Sheffield University: Lectr in Control Engineering, 1971–78; Industrial Liaison Officer, 1976–80; Sen. Lectr in Control Engineering, 1978–80; Prof. of Engineering, Univ. of Durham, 1980–90 (Dir, Microprocessor Centre, 1980–85). Member: ESRC, 1987–89; SERC Engrg Bd, 1989–92; Cttee 2 for Internat. Co-op. in Higher Educn, British Council, 1991–; Quality Assessment Cttee, HEFCE, 1992–95; Royal Acad. Engrg Standing Cttee for Educn, Trng and Competence to Practise, 1993–; Engrg Council, 1994–; CVCP Council, 1994–; Chairman: OCEPS Ltd, 1990–; Higher Educn Statistics Agency, 1992–; Jt Performance Indicators Working Gp, Higher Educn Councils for England, Scotland and Wales, 1992–95. Nat. Pres., InstMC, 1988; Mem. Council, IEE, 1991–93. FRSA. Hon. DEng Sheffield, 1995. *Publications:* Power Systems Control, 1978; contribs to: Large Scale Systems Engineering Applications, 1980; Computer Control of Industrial Processes, 1982; Real Time Computer Control, 1984; Comparative Models for Electrical Load Forecasting, 1985; over 120 papers in learned jls. *Recreations:* gardening, DIY, computers, model engineering. *Address:* Brunel University, Uxbridge, Middx UB8 3PH. *T:* Uxbridge (01895) 274000.

STERLING, Nuala; *see* Sterling, I. J. N.

STERN, Isaac; violinist; *b* Kreminiecz, Russia, 21 July 1920; *s* of Solomon and Clara Stern; *m* 1948, Nora Kaye (*d* 1987); *m* 1951, Vera Lindenblit; three *c*. Studied San Francisco Conservatory, 1930–37. First public concert as guest artist San Francisco Symphony Orchestra, 1934; played with Los Angeles Philharmonic Orchestra and in concerts in Pacific Coast cities; New York début, 1937. Has since played in concerts throughout USA, in Europe, Israel, Australia, South America, Japan, China, India, The Philippines, Soviet Union and Iceland; has played with major American and European orchestras. Took part in Prades Festivals, 1950–52; Edinburgh and other major festivals in Europe and US. Film, Mao to Mozart: Isaac Stern in China (Best Full-length Documentary Acad. Award, 1981); (TV prodn) Carnegie Hall—The Grand Reopening, 1987 (Emmy Award). Chm., America-Israel Cultural Foundn, NY, 1964–; President, Carnegie Hall, NY, 1960–; Artistic Dir, Jerusalem Music Center. Hon. degrees from Univs of Columbia, Johns Hopkins, Dalhousie, Brown, Oxford, and San Francisco Conservatory of Music. Over 100 recordings for which many Grammy Awards received. Albert Schweitzer Music Award, 1975; Kennedy Center Honors, 1984. Commandeur, Légion d'Honneur (France), 1989. *Address:* c/o ICM Artists Ltd, 40 West 57th Street, New York, NY 10019, USA.

STERN, Linda Joy; QC 1991; a Recorder of the Crown Court, since 1990; *b* 21 Dec. 1941; *d* of Mrs L. R. Saville; *m* 1st, 1961, Michael Brian Rose (decd); two *s*; 2nd, 1978, Nigel Maurice Stern. *Educ:* St Paul's Girls' Sch. Called to the Bar, Gray's Inn, 1971; Mem., S Eastern Circuit. *Recreations:* music, theatre, reading, travel. *Address:* 5 King's Bench Walk, Temple, EC4Y 7DN. *T:* 0171–353 4713.

STERN, Michael Charles, FCA; MP (C) Bristol North West, since 1983; *b* 3 Aug. 1942; *s* of late Maurice Leonard Stern and of Rose Stern; *m* 1976, Jillian Denise Aldridge; one *d*. *Educ:* Christ's College Grammar School, Finchley. Mem. ICA 1964; FCA 1969. Partner, Percy Phillips & Co., Accountants, 1964–80; Partner, Halpern & Woolf, Chartered Accountants, 1980–92; Consultant, Cohen Arnold & Co., 1992–. Chm., The Bow Group, 1977–78; coopted Mem., Educn Cttee, Borough of Ealing, 1980–83. Contested (C) Derby S, 1979. PPS to Minister of State, HM Treasury, 1986–87, to Paymaster General, 1987–89, to Minister for Corporate Affairs, DTI, 1991. Chief Finance Officer, 1990–91, Vice-Chm., 1991–92, Cons. party. *Publications:* papers for The Bow Group. *Recreations:* fell walking, bridge, chess. *Address:* House of Commons, SW1A 0AA. *Clubs:* United and Cecil, Millbank, London Mountaineering.

STERN, Prof. Nicholas Herbert, FBA 1993; Sir John Hicks Professor of Economics, London School of Economics and Political Science, since 1986; Chief Economist, European Bank for Reconstruction and Development, since 1994; *b* 22 April 1946; *s* of Adalbert Stern and Marion Fatima Stern; *m* 1968, Susan Ruth (*née* Chesterton); two *s* one *d*. *Educ:* Peterhouse, Cambridge (BA Mathematics); Nuffield Coll., Oxford (DPhilEcon). Jun. Res. Fellow, The Queen's Coll., Oxford, 1969–70; Fellow/Tutor in Econs, St Catherine's Coll., and Univ. Lectr, Oxford, 1970–77; Prof. of Econs, Univ. of Warwick, 1978–85. Research Associate/Vis. Professor: MIT, 1972; Ecole Polytech., 1977; Indian Statistical Inst. (Overseas Vis. Fellow of British Acad., 1974–75, and Ford Foundn Vis. Prof., 1981–82); People's Univ. of China, Beijing, 1988. Fellow, Econometric Soc., 1978. Editor, Journal of Public Economics, 1980–. *Publications:* An Appraisal of Tea Production on Smallholdings in Kenya, 1972; (ed jtly) Theories of Economic Growth, 1973; (jtly) Crime, the Police and Criminal Statistics, 1979; (jtly) Palanpur: the economy of an Indian village, 1982; (jtly) The Theory of Taxation for Developing Countries, 1987; articles in Econ. Jl, Rev. of Econ. Studies, Jl of Public Econs, Jl of Develt Econs, and others. *Recreations:* reading novels, walking, watching sport, food. *Address:* EBRD, 1 Exchange Square, EC2A 3EH.

STERN, Vivien Helen, CBE 1992; Director, National Association for the Care and Resettlement of Offenders (NACRO), since 1977; *b* 25 Sept. 1941; *d* of Frederick Stern and Renate Mills. *Educ:* Kent Coll., Pembury, Kent; Bristol Univ. (BA, MLitt, CertEd). Lectr in Further Educn until 1970; Community Relations Commn, 1970–77. Member: Special Programmes Bd, Manpower Services Commn, 1980–82; Youth Training Bd, 1982–88; Gen. Adv. Council, IBA, 1982–87; Cttee on the Prison Disciplinary System, 1984–85; Adv. Council, PSI, 1993–. Vis. Fellow, Nuffield Coll., Oxford, 1984–91. Dir, S Thames TEC, 1992–. Hon. LLD Bristol, 1990. *Publications:* Bricks of Shame, 1987; Imprisoned by Our Prisons, 1989; Deprived of their Liberty, a report for Caribbean Rights, 1990. *Address:* National Association for the Care and Resettlement of Offenders, 169 Clapham Road, SW9 0PU.

STERNBERG, Sir Sigmund, Kt 1976; JP; Chairman: Martin Slowe Estates Ltd, since 1971; ISYS Ltd, since 1986; Lloyd's Underwriter, since 1969; *b* Budapest, 2 June 1921; *s* of late Abraham and Elizabeth Sternberg; *m* 1970, Hazel (*née* Everett Jones); one *s* one *d*, and one *s* one *d* from a previous marriage. Served War of 1939–45, Civil Defence Corps. Former Ring-Dealing Mem., London Metal Exchange. Instituted Res. Gp for Labour Shadow Cabinet, 1973–74; Econ. and Industry Cttee, Fabian Soc., 1976 (Chm., 1975–77, Treas., 1995–, Appeals Cttee); Dep. Chm., Labour Finance and Industry Gp, 1972–93. Chm., St Charles Gp, HMC, 1974; NW Metrop. RHB, 1974; Member: Camden and Islington AHA, 1974–77; Gen. Purposes Cttee, NAMH, 1972; Vice-Pres., Royal Coll. of Speech and Language Therapists; Chm., Inst. for Archaeo-Metallurgical Studies. Hon. Treas., Cruse Bereavement Care, 1981–92 (Pres., Friends of Cruse, 1993–). Chm., Exec. Cttee, Internat. Council of Christians and Jews; Mem., Board of Deputies of British Jews; Governor, Hebrew Univ. of Jerusalem; Trustee, Manor House Trust (Sternberg Centre for Judaism), 1984– (Chm., 1993–); Convenor, Religious Press Gp; Vice President: Reform Synagogues of GB, 1991; CCJ, 1992– (Hon. Treas., 1977–92); Life Mem., Magistrates' Assoc., 1965; Mem., Commonwealth Magistrates' and Judges' Assoc., 1985. Rotary Club: Speaker Chm., London, 1980–83, 1993–; Hon. Member: Highgate, 1990; Budapest, 1989; Paul Harris Fellow, Rotary Foundn of Rotary Internat., 1989. Mem., Court, Essex Univ. Liveryman, Co. of Horners; Freeman, City of London. JP Middlesex, 1965 (Middlesex Probation (Case) Cttee, 1973). FRSA 1979. Hon. FRSM 1981; Hon. FCST 1989. Judge, Templeton Foundn, 1988–92. Order of the Orthodox Hospitallers, First Class with Star and Badge of Religion, 1986; OStJ 1988. Brotherhood Award, Nat. Conf. of Christians and Jews Inc., 1980; KCSG 1985; Silver Pontifical Medal, 1986; Benemerenti Medal (Vatican), 1988, in Silver, 1990; Good Servant Medal, Canadian CCJ, 1991; Silver Jerusalem Mayoral Award, 1991; Man of Reconciliation Award, Polish CCJ, 1993; Medal of Merit, Warsaw Univ., 1995; Award, Hungarian CCJ, 1995. Order of Merit (Poland), 1989; Order of the Gold Star (Hungary), 1990; Medaglia d'Argento di Benemerenza, Sacred Mil. Constantinian Order of St George, 1991; Commander's Cross, 1st cl. (Austria), 1992; Commander's Cross, Order of Merit (Poland), 1992; Comdr of the Order of Civil Merit (Spain), 1993; Commander's Cross, Order of Merit (Germany), 1993. *Recreations:* golf, swimming. *Address:* 80 East End Road, N3 2SY. *Fax:* 0171–485 4512. *Clubs:* Reform, City Livery.

STERNE, Laurence Henry Gordon; *b* 2 July 1916; *o s* of late Henry Herbert Sterne and late Hilda Davey Stern; *m* 1944, Katharine Clover; two *d*. *Educ:* Culford Sch.; Jesus Coll. (Hon. Schol.), Oxford (MA). Royal Aircraft Establishment, 1940; Chief Supt at Bedford, 1955. Dir, von Karman Inst., Rhode Saint Genèse, Belgium, 1958; Research Policy Staff, MoD, 1962; Dir, Royal Naval Aircraft and Helicopters, 1964; Dep. Dir, Nat. Engineering Lab., E Kilbride, 1968–77. Vis. Prof., Strathclyde Univ., 1971–76. *Publications:* reports and memoranda of Aeronautical Research Council; ed jtly, early vols of Progress in Aeronautical Sciences. *Address:* 10 Trinity Street, Bungay, Suffolk NR35 1EH.

STEVAS; *see* St John-Stevas, family name of Baron St John of Fawsley.

STEVEN, Stewart; Editor, Evening Standard, since 1992; *b* 30 Sept. 1935; *s* of Rudolph and Trude Steven; *m* 1965, Inka Sobieniewska; one *s*. *Educ:* Mayfield Coll., Sussex. Political Reporter, Central Press Features, 1961–63; Political Correspondent, Western Daily Press, 1963–64; Daily Express: Political Reporter, 1964–65; Diplomatic Correspondent, 1965–67; Foreign Editor, 1967–72; Daily Mail: Asst Editor, 1972–74; Associate Editor, 1974–82; Ed., The Mail on Sunday, 1982–92. Director: The Mail on Sunday; Mail Newspapers plc; Associated Newspapers Holdings Ltd, 1989–. *Publications:* Operation Splinter-Factor, 1974; The Spymasters of Israel, 1976; The Poles, 1982. *Recreations:* classical guitar, writing, ski-ing. *Address:* Northcliffe House, 2 Derry Street, Kensington, W8 5EE. *Clubs:* Groucho; Surrey County Cricket.

STEVENS, family name of **Baron Stevens of Ludgate.**

STEVENS OF LUDGATE, Baron *cr* 1987 (Life Peer), of Ludgate in the City of London; **David Robert Stevens;** Chairman: United Newspapers plc, since 1981 (Director, since 1974); Express Newspapers, since 1985; *b* 26 May 1936; *s* of late (Arthur) Edwin Stevens, CBE; *m* 1st Patricia Rose (marr. diss. 1971); one *s* one *d*; 2nd, 1977, Melissa Milicevich (*d* 1989); 3rd, 1990, Meriza Giori. *Educ:* Stowe Sch.; Sidney Sussex Coll., Cambridge (MA Hons Econ). Management Trainee, Elliott Automation, 1959; Director: Hill Samuel Securities, 1959–68; Drayton Group, 1968–74. Chairman: Alexander Proudfoot Hldgs (formerly City & Foreign), 1976–95; Drayton Far East, 1976–93; English & International, 1976–79; Consolidated Venture (formerly Montagu Boston), 1979–93; Drayton Consolidated, 1980–92; Drayton Japan, 1980–88; Oak Industries, 1989–; Mid States, 1989–95; Chief Exec., 1980–87, Chm., 1980–93, Montagu Investment Management, subseq. INVESCO MIM Management; Dep. Chm., 1987–89, Chm., 1989–93, Britannia Arrow Hldgs, subseq. INVESCO MIM. Chm., EDC for Civil Engrg, 1984–86. *Recreations:* golf, gardening. *Address:* Ludgate House, 245 Blackfriars Road, SE1 9UY. *Clubs:* White's; Sunningdale Golf.

STEVENS, Prof. Anne Frances, PhD; Professor of European Studies and Chairman, School of European and Modern Language Studies, University of Kent at Canterbury, since 1991; *b* 28 Dec. 1942; *d* of Robert Ross, *qv* and Margaret Helen Ross (*née* Steadman); *m* 1966, Handley Michael Gambrell Stevens, *qv*; three *d*. *Educ:* Newnham Coll., Cambridge (BA 1964; MA 1975); LSE, Univ. of London (MSc Econ (with distinction) 1975; PhD 1980). Asst Principal, Dept of Technical Co-operation, ODM, 1964–66; part-time Lectr, Univ. of Malaya, 1966–68; HEO, British High Commn, Kuala Lumpur, 1968–69; School of European Studies, University of Sussex: Lectr in Politics, 1978–90; Dean, 1988–90. *Publications:* (jtly) Hostile Brothers: competition and closure in the European electronics industry, 1990; The Government and Politics of France, 1992; articles on comparative admin. *Recreations:* walking, English dancing, needlework. *Address:* School of European and Modern Language Studies, Cornwallis Building, University of Kent, Canterbury, Kent CT2 7NF. *T:* Canterbury (01227) 764000.

STEVENS, Anthony John; Post Graduate Veterinary Dean for London and South East England, Royal College of Veterinary Surgeons/British Veterinary Association, since 1986; engaged in consultancy and literary work; *b* 29 July 1926; *s* of John Walker Stevens and Hilda Stevens; *m* 1954, Patricia Frances, *d* of Robert Gill, Ponteland; one *s* two *d*. *Educ:* Liverpool and Manchester Univs; Magdalene Coll., Cambridge. MA, BVSc, MRCVS, DipBact. Veterinary Investigation Officer, Cambridge, 1956–65; Animal Health Expert for UNO, 1959–63; Suptg Veterinary Investigation Officer, Leeds, 1965–68; Ministry of Agriculture, Fisheries and Food: Dep. Dir, Central Vet. Lab., 1968–71; Asst Chief Vet. Officer, 1971–73; Dep. Chief Vet. Officer, 1973–78; Dir, Vet. Labs, MAFF, 1979–86. External Examr, Dublin, Liverpool and Edinburgh Univs., 1964–70. Past Pres., Veterinary Research Club. Vice Pres., Zoological Soc., 1989–90 (Mem. Council, 1987–91, 1994–). FRSA. *Publications:* UN/FAO Manual of Diagnostic Techniques; regular contributor to Veterinary Record, etc. *Recreations:* industrial archaeology particularly canals, riding, and all forms of livestock. *Address:* Marigold Cottage, Great Halfpenny Farm, Guildford, Surrey GU4 8PY. *T:* Guildford (01483) 65375.

STEVENS, Clifford David; Principal Establishment Officer, Welsh Office, since 1994; *b* 11 June 1941; *s* of late Robert Stevens and of Ivy (*née* White); *m* 1964, Mary Olive (*née* Bradford); one *s* two *d*. *Educ:* Stationers' Company's Sch., London. FO, 1959–63; BoT, 1963–64; DEA, 1964–70 (Private Sec. to successive Ministers, 1967–70); CSD, 1970–76; Cabinet Office, 1976–78; CSD, 1978–81; Management and Personnel Office, 1981–86; Welsh Office, 1986–; Dir, Industry Dept, 1987–94. *Recreations:* gardening, bowls. *Address:* c/o Welsh Office, Cathays Park, Cardiff CF1 3NQ. *T:* Cardiff (01222) 823307.

STEVENS, Prof. Denis William, CBE 1984; President and Artistic Director, Accademia Monteverdiana, since 1961; *b* 2 March 1922; *s* of William J. Stevens and Edith Driver; *m* 1st, 1949, Sheila Elizabeth Holloway; two *s* one *d*; 2nd, 1975, Leocadia Elzbieta Kwasny. *Educ:* Royal Grammar Sch., High Wycombe; Jesus College, Oxford. Served War of 1939–45, RAF Intelligence, India and Burma, 1942–46. Producer, BBC Music Div., 1949–54; Assoc. Founder and Conductor, Ambrosian Singers, 1952; Vis. Professor of Musicology, Cornell Univ., 1955, Columbia Univ., 1956; Secretary, Plainsong and Mediaeval Music Soc., 1958–63; Editor, Grove's Dictionary of Music and Musicians, 1959–63. Professor, Royal Acad. of Music, 1960. Vis. Prof. Univ. of California (Berkeley), 1962; Dist. Vis. Prof., Pennsylvania State Univ., 1962–63; Prof. of Musicology, Columbia Univ., 1964–76; Vis. Prof. Univ. of California (Santa Barbara), 1974–75; Brechemin Dist. Vis. Prof., Univ. of Washington, Seattle, 1976; Vis. Prof., Univ. of Michigan, Ann Arbor, 1977, San Diego State Univ., 1978. Lectures on music, especially British, and contrib. musicolog. confs, in England, France, Germany, Italy, USA and Russia; Organizer and Leader, Rockefeller Congress on Music, Bellagio, 1974; concerts, conducting own and ancillary ensembles at internat. festivals in GB (incl. 5 proms, the first introducing Monteverdi 1967), Europe and USA; TV and radio programmes in Europe and N America; first broadcast perfs of unknown works by Dufay, Dunstable and Telemann, of Charpentier's Medée and Monteverdi's Orfeo; cons. for films. FSA; Mem., Co. of Musicians. Hon. RAM, 1960. Hon.D, Humane Letters, Fairfield Univ., Connecticut, 1967. *Publications:* The Mulliner Book, 1952; Thomas Tomkins, 1957, rev. edn 1966; A History of Song, 1960, rev. edn, 1971; Tudor Church Music, 1966; A Treasury of English Church Music (I), 1965; (ed) First and Second Penguin Book of English Madrigals, 1967, 1971; Early Tudor Organ Music (II), 1969; Music in Honour of St Thomas of Canterbury, 1970; Monteverdi: sacred, secular and occasional music, 1978; Musicology: a practical guide, 1980; The Letters of Monteverdi, 1980, 2nd edn 1995; Renaissance Dialogues, 1981; The Worcester Fragments, 1981; Musicology in Practice, Pt I 1987, Pt II 1993; many edns of early music, including Monteverdi Vespers, 1961, 2nd edn 1994, and Orfeo; choral works by Gabrieli, Gesualdo, Lassus, Machaut, Tallis, Tomkins; contrib. Encyclopaedia Britannica, Amer. Acad. Encyclopedia, Grove's Dictionary, Die Musik in Geschichte und Gegenwart, Enciclopedia della Musica; reviews and articles in English and foreign journals; also many stereo recordings with Ambrosian Singers and Accademia Monteverdiana, ranging from plainsong to Beethoven. *Recreations:* travel, photography. *Address:* The Quadrangle, Morden College, SE3 0PW. *Club:* Garrick.

STEVENS, Handley Michael Gambrell; Under Secretary, Public Transport in London, Department of Transport, since 1991; *b* 29 June 1941; *s* of Ernest Norman Stevens and Kathleen Emily Gambrell; *m* 1966, Anne Frances Ross (*see* A. F. Stevens); three *d*. *Educ:* The Leys Sch., Cambridge; Phillips Acad., Andover, Mass (E-SU schol.); King's Coll., Cambridge (BA). Translator, Chrysler Internat., 1963; joined Foreign Office, 1964; Third, later Second, Sec., Kuala Lumpur, 1966; Asst Private Sec. to the Lord Privy Seal, 1970; Principal: CSD, 1971; DTI, 1973; Asst Sec., Dept of Trade, 1976; Under Sec., Internat. Aviation, 1983, Finance, 1988–91, Dept of Transport. *Recreations:* music, hill walking, travel. *Address:* Department of Transport, 2 Marsham Street, SW1P 3EB.

STEVENS, Jocelyn Edward Greville, CVO 1993; Chairman, English Heritage, since 1992; Deputy Chairman, Independent Television Commission, since 1991; *b* 14 Feb. 1932; *s* of late Major C. G. B. Stewart-Stevens and Mrs Greville Stevens; *m* 1956, Jane Armyne Sheffield (marr. diss. 1979); one *s* two *d* (and one *s* decd). *Educ:* Eton; Cambridge. Military service in Rifle Bde, 1950–52; Journalist, Hulton Press Ltd, 1955–56; Chairman and Managing Dir, Stevens Press Ltd, and Editor of Queen Magazine, 1957–68; Personal Asst to Chairman of Beaverbrook Newspapers, May–Dec. 1968; Director, 1971–81; Managing Director: Evening Standard Co. Ltd, 1969–72; Daily Express, 1972–74; Beaverbrook Newspapers, 1974–77; Express Newspapers, 1977–81 (Dep. Chm. and Man. Dir); Editor and Publisher, The Magazine, 1982–84; Dir, Centaur Communications, 1982–84; Rector and Vice Provost, RCA, 1984–92. Chm., Silver Trust, 1990–93; Trustee: Mental Health Foundn, 1972–94; Eureka! The Museum for Children, 1986–; Pres., Cheyne Walk Trust, 1989–93. Governor: Imperial Coll. of Science, Technology and Medicine, 1985–92; Winchester Sch. of Art, 1986–89. FRSA 1984; Senior Fellow RCA, 1990. Hon. FCSD 1990. Hon. DLitt Loughborough, 1989. *Address:* Testbourne, Longparish, near Andover, Hants SP11 6QT. *T:* Longparish (01264) 720232. *Clubs:* Buck's, Beefsteak, White's.

STEVENS, John Arthur, QPM 1992; Chief Constable of Northumbria, since 1991; *b* 21 Oct. 1942; *s* of C. J. and S. Stevens; *m*; two *s* one *d*. *Educ:* St Lawrence Coll., Ramsgate; Leicester Univ. (LLB Hons); Southampton Univ. (MPhil). Joined Metropolitan Police, 1963; DS, Police Staff Coll., 1983–84; Asst Chief Constable, Hampshire Constabulary, 1986–89; Dep. Chief Constable, Cambridgeshire Constab., 1989–91. Chairman: Jt Cttee on Offender Profiling, 1991; ACPO Crime Prevention Sub-Cttee, 1994. Chm., NI Enquiry into alleged collusion between paramil. and security forces (Stevens Enquiry), 1989–92. Advr, Forensic Sci. Service. Vis. Prof., CUNY, 1984–85. *Recreations:* walking, cricket, squash, Rugby. *Address:* Northumbria Police Headquarters, Ponteland, Newcastle upon Tyne NE20 0BL. *T:* Ponteland (01661) 72555.

STEVENS, John Christopher Courtenay; Member (C) Thames Valley, European Parliament, since 1989; *b* 23 May 1955; *s* of Sir John Melior Stevens, KCMG, DSO, OBE and of Anne Hely-Hutchinson. *Educ:* Winchester Coll.; Magdalen Coll., Oxford (BA Jurisprudence). Foreign exchange and Bond trader, Banque Indosuez, Paris, 1976–77; Bayerische Hypotheken und Wechselbank, Munich, 1977–78; Morgan Grenfell, London, 1979–89, Internat. Dir, 1986–89; Advr, St James's Place Capital plc, 1989–. *Recreations:* riding, ski-ing. *Address:* 27 St James's Place, SW1A 1NR. *T:* 0171–493 8111. *Club:* Carlton.

STEVENS, Prof. John Edgar, CBE 1980; PhD; FBA 1975; President of Magdalene College, Cambridge, 1983–88, Fellow, 1950–88, now Emeritus; Professor of Medieval and Renaissance English, University of Cambridge, 1978–88, now Emeritus; *b* 8 Oct. 1921; *s* of William Charles James and Fanny Stevens; *m* 1946, Charlotte Ethel Mary (*née* Somner); two *s* two *d*. *Educ:* Christ's Hospital, Horsham; Magdalene College, Cambridge (Schol.; MA, PhD). Served Royal Navy; Temp. Lieut RNVR. Cambridge University: Bye-Fellow 1948, Research Fellow 1950, Fellow 1953 and Tutor 1958–74, Magdalene Coll.; Univ. Lectr in English, 1954–74; Reader in English and Musical History, 1974–78. Vis. Dist. Prof. of Medieval Studies, Univ. of California, Berkeley, 1989. Chm., Plainsong and Medieval Music Soc., 1988–95. Hon. MusD Exeter, 1989. *Publications:* Medieval Carols (Musica Britannica vol. 4), 1952, 2nd edn 1958; Music and Poetry in the Early Tudor Court, 1961; Music at the Court of Henry VIII (Musica Britannica vol. 18), 1962, 2nd edn 1969; (with Richard Axton) Medieval French Plays, 1971; Medieval Romance, 1973; Early Tudor Songs & Carols (Musica Britannica vol. 36), 1975; Words and Music in the Middle Ages, 1986. *Recreations:* viol-playing, bricklaying. *Address:* 4 & 5 Bell's Court, Castle Street, Cambridge CB3 0AH.

STEVENS, Hon. John Paul; Associate Justice, Supreme Court of the United States, since 1975; *b* 20 April 1920; *s* of Ernest James Stevens and Elizabeth Stevens (*née* Street); *m* 1st, 1942, Elizabeth Jane Sheeren; one *s* three *d*; 2nd, 1979, Maryan Mulholland Simon. *Educ:* Univ. of Chicago (AB 1941); Northwestern Univ. (JD 1947). Served War, USNR, 1942–45 (Bronze Star). Law Clerk to US Supreme Ct Justice Wiley Rutledge, 1947–48; Associate, Poppenhusen, Johnston, Thompson & Raymond, 1948–50; Associate Counsel, sub-cttee on Study Monopoly Power, Cttee on Judiciary, US House of Reps, 1951; Partner, Rothschild, Hart, Stevens & Barry, 1952–70; US Circuit Judge, 1970–75. Lectr, anti-trust law, Northwestern Univ. Sch. of Law, 1953; Univ. of Chicago Law Sch., 1954–55; Mem., Attorney-Gen.'s Nat. Cttee to study Anti-Trust Laws, 1953–55. Mem., Chicago Bar Assoc. (2nd Vice-Pres. 1970). Order of Coif, Phi Beta Kappa, Psi Upsilon, Phi Delta Phi. *Publications:* chap. in book, Mr Justice (ed Dunham and Kurland); contrib. to Antitrust Developments: a supp. to Report of Attorney-Gen.'s Nat. Cttee to Study the Anti-trust Laws, 1955–68; various articles etc, in Ill. Law Rev., Proc. confs, and reports. *Recreations:* flying, tennis, bridge, reading, travel. *Address:* Supreme Court of the United States, Washington, DC 20543, USA.

STEVENS, John Williams, CB 1988; Member, 1989–90, Deputy Chairman, 1991–94, Civil Service Appeal Board; *b* 27 Feb. 1929; *s* of John Williams and Kathleen Stevens; *m* 1949, Grace Stevens; one *s* one *d*. *Educ:* St Ives School. Min. of Supply, 1952; UK Defence Res. and Supply Staff, Australia, 1958–61; HM Treasury, 1966; Civil Service Dept, 1969–73; Price Commn, 1973–74; Head of Personnel, Stock Exchange, 1975–76; Principal Private Sec. to Lord Pres. of the Council and Leader of the House of Commons, 1977–79, to Chancellor of Duchy of Lancaster and Leader of the House, 1979–80; Principal Estabts and Finance Officer, Cabinet Office, 1980–89; Under Sec. 1984. *Recreations:* Cornwall, reading, theatre. *Address:* 14 Highbury Crescent, Portsmouth Road, Camberley, Surrey GU15 1JZ. *Club:* Athenæum.

STEVENS, Kenneth Henry, CBE 1983; DL; Chief Executive Commissioner, The Scout Association, 1970–87; *b* 8 Oct. 1922; *s* of late Horace J. Stevens, CBE, sometime Senior Principal Inspector of Taxes, and late Nora Stevens (*née* Kauntze); *m* 1947, Yvonne Grace Ruth (*née* Mitchell); one *s* one *d*. *Educ:* Brighton Coll.; Brighton Technical Coll. South Coast Civil Defence, 1941–44. Alliance Assurance Co., 1944–47; Asst Dir of Adult Leader Training, Internat. Scout Training Centre, Gilwell Park, Chingford, 1947–56; Organising Comr, World Scout Jamboree, Indaba and Rover Moot, Sutton Coldfield, 1956–58; Dep. Dir of Adult Leader Training, Internat. Scout Training Centre, 1958–61; Asst Chief Exec. Comr, The Scout Assoc., 1961–63; Dep. Chief Exec. Comr, 1963–70. DL Surrey, 1989. *Publication:* Ceremonies of The Scout Movement, 1958. *Recreations:* motoring, gardening. *Address:* Drovers, Crampshaw Lane, Ashtead, Surrey KT21 2UF. *T:* Ashtead (01372) 277841. *Club:* MCC.

STEVENS, Prof. Kenneth William Harry; Professor of Theoretical Physics, 1958–87, now Emeritus, and Senior Research Fellow, 1987–88, University of Nottingham; *b* 17 Sept. 1922; *s* of Harry and Rose Stevens; *m* 1949, Audrey A. Gawthrop; one *s* one *d*. *Educ:* Magdalen College School, Oxford; Jesus and Merton Colleges, Oxford. MA 1947, DPhil 1949. Pressed Steel Company Ltd Research Fellow, Oxford University, 1949–53; Research Fellow, Harvard University, 1953–54; Reader in Theoretical Physics, University of Nottingham, 1953–58. Leverhulme Emeritus Fellow, 1990. Mem., IUPAP Commn on Magnetism, 1984–87. (Jointly) Maxwell Medal and Prize, 1968. *Publications:* contrib. to learned journals. *Recreations:* music, tennis, walking. *Address:* The University, Nottingham NG7 2RD.

STEVENS, Sir Laurence (Houghton), Kt 1983; CBE 1979; company director and business consultant; *b* 9 Jan. 1920; *s* of Laurence Stevens and Annie (*née* Houghton); *m* 1943, Beryl J. Dickson; one *s* two *d*. *Educ:* Auckland Boys' Grammar Sch.; Auckland Univ. (BCom). FCA NZ 1969; CMA 1966. Served War, Pacific (Tonga Defence Force) and ME (2NZEF). Joined Auckland Knitting Mills Ltd, 1946; Man. Dir, 1952; retd 1980. Chairman: Thorn EMI Gp of Cos, NZ, 1980–93; Chambard Property Develt (formerly Les Mills Corporation) Ltd, 1985–91; Fay Richwhite & Co. (formerly Capital Markets Ltd), 1986–96; Ascent Corp. Ltd, 1986–88; Auckland Internat. Airport Ltd, 1988–; Director: Guardian Royal Exchange, 1983–90; Wormald International NZ Ltd, 1983–90; Reserve Bank of New Zealand, 1978–86; Petroleum Corp. of New Zealand Ltd, 1984–88; R. W. Saunders Ltd, 1984–87; Petralgas Chemicals NZ Ltd, 1986–87; Wormald Pacific Ltd, 1987–90. Past President and Life Member: NZ Knitting Industries Fedn; Textile and Garment Fedn of NZ; Auckland Manufrs' Assoc.; Pres., NZ Manufrs' Fedn, 1970–71 and 1980–81; Chm., Auckland Agricl, Pastoral and Indust. Shows Bd, 1976–86; Mem., Melanesian Trust Bd, 1977–93. *Recreation:* tennis (Pres., Auckland Lawn Tennis Assoc., 1983–84). *Address:* 1/1 Watene Crescent, Orakei, Auckland 5, New Zealand. *T:* Auckland (9) 5210476. *Club:* Northern (Auckland).

STEVENS, Lewis David, MBE 1982; management and industrial engineering consultant (self-employed), since 1979; *b* 13 April 1936; *s* of Richard and Winnifred Stevens; *m* 1959, Margaret Eileen Gibson; two *s* one *d*. *Educ:* Oldbury Grammar Sch.; Liverpool Univ.; Lanchester Coll. RAF 1956–58. Various engrg cos, mainly in industrial engrg and production management positions, 1958–79. Mem., Nuneaton Borough Council, 1966–72. MP (C) Nuneaton, 1983–92; contested (C) Nuneaton, 1992. *Address:* 151 Sherbourne Avenue, Nuneaton, Warwicks CV10 9JN. *T:* Chapel End (01203) 396105.

STEVENS, Richard William, RDI 1973; BSc; FCSD; FCIBS; Partner, Richard Stevens Design Associates, 1987–94; *b* 1 Oct. 1924; *s* of William Edward Stevens and Caroline Alice (*née* Mills); *m* 1947, Anne Clara Hammond (*d* 1994); one *s* one *d*. *Educ:* Dorking County Grammar Sch.; Regent St Polytechnic (BSc). FCSD (FSIAD 1960); FCIBS 1977. Designer, then Chief Designer, Atlas Lighting Ltd, 1954–63; Industrial Design Manager, Standard Telephones and Cables Ltd, 1963–69; Design Manager, Post Office Telecommunications (later British Telecom), 1969–83. Pres., SIAD, 1972–73; Treasurer, ICSID, 1975–77. Gold Medal, Milan Triennale, 1957; three Design Centre Awards, London. *Recreations:* gardening, music, photography, walking. *Address:* Hazel Cottage, Ewood Lane, Newdigate, Dorking, Surrey RH5 5AR.

STEVENS, Dr Robert Bocking; Master, Pembroke College, Oxford, since 1993; *b* 8 June 1933; *s* of John Skevington Stevens and Enid Dorothy Stevens; *m* 1st, 1961, Rosemary Anne Wallace (marr. diss., 1982); one *s* one *d*; 2nd, 1985, Katherine Booth; one *d*. *Educ:* Oakham Sch.; Keble Coll., Oxford (BA 1956; BCL 1956; MA 1959; DCL 1984); Yale Univ. (LLM 1958). Called to the Bar, Gray's Inn, 1956. Yale University: Asst Prof. of Law, 1959–61; Associate Prof., 1961–65; Prof., 1965–76; Provost, Tulane Univ., 1976–78; Pres., Haverford Coll., 1978–87; Chancellor, Univ. of Calif., Santa Cruz, 1987–91; of Counsel, Covington and Burling, Washington and London, 1992–. Chm., Marshall Aid Commemoration Commn, 1995–. Gov., Abingdon Sch. Hon. LLD: NY Law Sch., 1984; Villanova, 1985; Pennsylvania, 1987; Hon. DLitt Haverford Coll., 1991. *Publications:* (with B. S. Yamey) The Restrictive Practices Court, 1965; (with B. Abel-Smith) Lawyers and the Courts, 1967; (with B. Abel-Smith) In Search of Justice, 1968; Income Security, 1970; (with R. A. Stevens) Welfare Medicine in America, 1974; Law and Politics, 1978; The American Law School, 1983; The Independence of the Judiciary, 1993. *Recreations:* walking, tennis, nineteenth century, politics. *Address:* The Master's Lodging, Pembroke College, Oxford OX1 1DW. *T:* Oxford (01865) 243482. *Club:* Reform.

STEVENS, Prof. Thomas Stevens, FRS 1963; FRSE 1964; Emeritus Professor of Chemistry, University of Sheffield; *b* 8 Oct. 1900; *o c* of John Stevens and Jane E. Stevens (*née* Irving); *m* 1949, Janet Wilson Forsyth (*d* 1994); no *c*. *Educ:* Paisley Grammar School; Glasgow Academy; Universities of Glasgow and Oxford. DPhil 1925. Assistant in Chemistry, Univ. of Glasgow, 1921–23, Lecturer, 1925–47; Ramsay Memorial Fellow, Oxford, 1923–25; Sen. Lectr in Organic Chemistry, Univ. of Sheffield, 1947–49, Reader, 1949–63, Prof., 1963–66; Visiting Prof. of Chemistry, Univ. of Strathclyde, Oct. 1966–Sept. 1967. Hon. DSc Glasgow, 1985. *Publications:* (with W. E. Watts) Selected Molecular Rearrangements, 1973; contrib. to Elsevier-Rodd, Chemistry of Carbon Compounds, 1957–60. Papers in scientific jls. *Recreation:* unsophisticated bridge. *Address:* 313 Albert Drive, Glasgow G41 5RP. *T:* 0141–423 6928

STEVENS, Timothy John; Assistant Director (Collections), Victoria & Albert Museum, since 1994; *b* 17 Jan. 1940; *s* of Seymour Stevens; *m* 1969, Caroline Sankey; twin *s*. *Educ:* King's Sch., Canterbury; Hertford Coll., Oxford (MA); Courtauld Inst., Univ. of London (Academic Diploma, History of Art). Walker Art Gallery: Asst Keeper of British Art, 1964–65; Keeper of Foreign Art, 1965–67; Dep. Dir, 1967–70; Dir, 1971–74; Dir, Merseyside CC Art Galls, 1974–86; Dep. Dir, Nat. Museums and Galleries on Merseyside, 1986–87; Keeper of Art, Nat. Mus. of Wales, 1987–94. Hon. LittD Liverpool, 1985. Chevalier de l'Ordre des Arts et des Lettres (France), 1988. *Recreation:* gardening. *Address:* c/o Victoria & Albert Museum, South Kensington, SW7 2RL.

STEVENS, Rt Rev. Timothy John; *see* Dunwich, Bishop Suffragan of.

STEVENS, William David; President and Chief Operating Officer, Mitchell Energy, Houston, since 1994; *b* USA, 18 Sept. 1934; *s* of Walter Gerald and Amy Grace Stevens; *m* 1st, 1954, Barbara Ann Duncan (marr. diss. 1994); one *s* three *d*; 2nd, 1994, Virginia L. Wilkinson. *Educ:* Texas A&I Univ. (BScEng). Joined Humble Oil, 1958: various assignments, US Gulf Coast, 1958–73; Exxon Corporation: Executive Asst to President, 1974; various assignments, New York, 1974–77; Vice Pres., Gas, 1977–78; Man. Dir, Esso UK Ltd, London, and Vice Pres. Upstream, Esso Europe, Inc., 1978–85; Executive Vice President: Esso Europe, 1985–86; Exxon Co., USA, Houston, 1986–87; Pres., Exxon Co., 1988–92, retired. *Recreations:* golf, shooting, hiking. *Address:* Mitchell Energy, PO Box 4000, The Woodlands, Houston, TX 77387–4000, USA. *T:* (713) 377 5500.

STEVENSON, Christopher Terence S.; *see* Sinclair Stevenson.

STEVENSON, Sir David; *see* Stevenson, Sir H. D.

STEVENSON, Prof. David John, PhD; FRS 1993; Professor of Planetary Science, California Institute of Technology, since 1984 (Chairman, Division of Geological and Planetary Sciences, 1989–94); *b* 2 Sept. 1948; *s* of Ian McIvor Stevenson and Gwenyth (*née* Carroll). *Educ:* Rongotai Coll.; Victoria Univ., Wellington, NZ (BSc, BSc Hons, MSc); Cornell Univ., NY (PhD). Res. Fellow, ANU, 1976–78; Asst Prof., UCLA, 1978–80; Associate Prof., CIT, 1980–84. Fellow, Amer. Geophysical Union, 1986 (Whipple Award, 1994). Urey Prize, Amer. Astronomical Soc., 1984. *Publications:* numerous papers in learned jls, principally in earth and planetary scis. *Recreations:* hiking, biking. *Address:* Division of Geological and Planetary Sciences, California Institute of Technology, Pasadena, CA 91125, USA. *T:* (818) 3956534.

STEVENSON, Dennis; *see* Stevenson, H. D.

STEVENSON, Dr Derek Paul, CBE 1972; MRCS, LRCP; *b* 11 July 1911; *s* of late Frederick Stevenson and Maud Coucher; *m* 1941, Pamela Mary, *d* of late Col C. N. Jervelund, OBE; two *s* one *d*. *Educ:* Epsom College; Guy's Hospital. MRCS, LRCP 1935; Lieut RAMC, 1935 (Montefiore Prize, Royal Army Med. Coll., 1935); Capt. RAMC 1936; Maj. 1942; Lt-Col 1943; service in China and Malaya. Asst Director-General Army Medical Service, War Office, 1942–46; Sec. Army Medical Advisory Bd 1943–46. War Office rep. on Central Med., War Cttee, 1943–46. British Medical Association: Asst Sec., 1946–48; Dep. Sec., 1948–58; Sec., 1958–76. Sec. Jt Consultants Cttee, 1958–76; Mem., Health Services Bd, and Scottish Cttee, 1977–80. Vice-Pres. British Medical Students Assoc.; Hon. Sec./Treas., British Commonwealth Med. Conf.; Delegate, Gen. Assembly World Medical Association: Sydney, 1968, Paris, 1969, Oslo, 1970, Ottawa, 1971, Amsterdam, 1972, Munich, 1973, Stockholm, 1974, Chm. Council, 1969, 1970–71 (Mem. Council, 1967–). Medical Sec. to Nat. Ophthalmic Treatment Board Assoc.; Mem. Council of London Hospital Service Plan; Mem. Cttee of Management: Medical Insurance Agency; Medical and Dental Retirement Adv. Service; Vice Pres., Private Patients Plan, 1984–. Adviser: Sterling Winthrop, Mediscope Jl; Mem. Adv. Bd, Allied Investments; Dir, Tavistock Computer Services; Gen. Comr, Inland Revenue. Hon. Sec. and Treas., British Commonwealth Medical Assoc., 1964; Sec. Gen., Permanent Cttee of Doctors, EEC, 1973–76; Member: Chichester HA; West Sussex Gen. Practitioners' Cttee; Hon. Sec., British Life Assurance Trust. Liaison Officer, MoD, 1964. Mem. Bd of Governors, Epsom College; Governor, Midhurst Grammar Sch.; Pres., Old Epsomian Club, 1974–75. Mem., Chichester Dio. Bd; Lay Chm., Rural Deanery. Mem., West Sussex CC, 1980–85. Fellow, Royal Commonwealth Soc., 1968; Fellow, BMA, 1976 (Gold Medal, 1976). Hon. FRCGP 1992. Hon. LLD Manchester, 1964. *Publications:* contrib. Irish Medical Jl; BMA Lecture delivered to Irish Medical Assoc.; contrib. Canadian Med. Assoc. Jl, and address at Centennial meeting, Montreal; NHS Reorganisation (in RSH Jl), address to RSH Congress 1973; regular contribs to Medical Interface. *Recreations:* golf, sailing, gardening. *Address:* 19 Marchwood Gate, Chichester, West Sussex PO19 4HA. *T:* Chichester (01243) 774237. *Clubs:* Athenæum, Commonwealth Trust.

STEVENSON, Prof. George Telford; Professor of Immunochemistry, Faculty of Medicine, University of Southampton, since 1974; *b* 18 April 1932; *s* of Ernest George Stevenson and Mary Josephine Madden; *m* 1963, Freda Kathryn Hartley; three *s*. *Educ:* North Sydney High Sch.; Univ. of Sydney (MB, BS; MD); Univ. of Oxford (DPhil). Resident MO, 1955–56, Resident Pathologist, 1957, Sydney Hosp.; Research Fellow, Dept of Medicine, Univ. of Sydney, 1958–61; Nuffield Dominions Demonstrator, Dept of Biochemistry, Univ. of Oxford, 1962–64; Sen. Research Fellow, Dept of Biochemistry, Univ. of Sydney, 1965–66; Scientific Staff, MRC Immunochemistry Unit, Univ. of Oxford, 1967–70; Dir, Tenovus Research Lab., Southampton Gen. Hosp., 1970–; Consultant Immunologist, Southampton Univ. Hosps, 1976–. Hammer Prize for Cancer Research (jtly) (Armand Hammer Foundn, LA), 1982. *Publications:* Immunological Investigation of Lymphoid Neoplasms (with J. L. Smith and T. J. Hamblin), 1983; research papers on immunology and cancer, considered mainly at molecular level. *Address:* 9 Meadowhead Road, Bassett, Southampton SO16 7AD. *T:* Southampton (01703) 769092.

STEVENSON, George William; MP (Lab) Stoke-on-Trent South, since 1992; *b* 30 Aug. 1938; *s* of Harold and Elsie May Stevenson; *m* 1958, Doreen June (decd); two *s* one *d*; *m* 1991, Pauline Brookes. *Educ:* Uttoxeter Road Primary School; Queensberry Road Secondary School, Stoke-on-Trent. Pottery caster, 1953–57; coal miner, 1957–66; transport driver, 1966–84; shop steward, TGWU 5/24 Branch, 1968–84 (Mem., 1964–; Chm., 1975–81). Member: Stoke-on-Trent City Council, 1972–86; Staffs County Council, 1981–85. MEP (Lab) Staffs East, 1984–94; Pres., Eur. Parlt Delegn for Relations with S Asia, 1989–92 (Vice-Pres., 1984–89). Mem., Select Cttee on Agric.; Chairman: All-Party Tibet Gp; PLP Agric. Cttee. *Recreations:* reading, crown green bowling. *Address:* (home) 823 Lightwood Road, Lightwood, Stoke-on-Trent ST3 6DD; (office) Stoke South Constituency Office, 2A Stanton Road, Meir, Stoke-on-Trent, Staffs ST3 6DD. *T:* Stoke-on-Trent (01782) 593393. *Club:* Meir Sports and Social.

STEVENSON, Henry Dennistoun, (Dennis Stevenson), CBE 1981; Chairman: SRU Group of companies, since 1972; Trustees of the Tate Gallery, since 1988; *b* 19 July 1945; *s* of Alexander James Stevenson and Sylvia Florence Stevenson (*née* Ingleby); *m* 1972, Charlotte Susan, *d* of Hon. Sir Peter Vanneck, *qv*; four *s*. *Educ:* Glenalmond; King's Coll., Cambridge (MA). Chm., Newton Aycliffe and Peterlee New Town Develt Corp., 1971–80; Dir, LDDC, 1981–88. Chairman: govt working party on role of voluntary movements and youth in the environment, 1971, '50 Million Volunteers' (HMSO); Indep. Advisory Cttee on Pop Festivals, 1972–76, 'Pop Festivals, Report and Code of Practice' (HMSO); Adviser on Agricultural Marketing to Minister of Agriculture, 1979–83. Mem., Panel on Takeovers and Mergers, 1992–. Mem. Admin. Council, Royal Jubilee Trusts, 1978–80. Chairman: Intermediate Technology Develt Gp, 1983–90; GPA Group, 1993–; Director: Nat. Building Agency, 1977–81; British Technology Gp, 1979–89; Tyne Tees Television, 1982–87; Pearson plc, 1986–; Manpower plc (formerly Blue Arrow), 1988–; Thames Television plc, 1991–93; J. Rothschild Assurance plc, 1991–. Chairman: NAYC, 1973–81; Sinfonia 21 (formerly Docklands Sinfonietta), 1990–. *Recreation:* home. *Clubs:* Brooks's, MCC.

STEVENSON, Hugh Alexander; Chairman, Mercury Asset Management Group plc, since 1992; *b* 7 Sept. 1942; *s* of William Hugh Stevenson and Elizabeth Margaret (*née* Wallace); *m* 1965, Catherine May Peacock; two *s* two *d*. *Educ:* Harrow Sch.; University Coll., Oxford (BA 1964); Harvard Business School (AMP 103). Admitted as Solicitor, 1967; with Linklaters & Paines, 1964–70; with S. G. Warburg & Co., 1970–92; Dir, S. G. Warburg Gp plc, 1986–. Dir, IMRO, 1995–. Hon. Treas., Inst. of Child Health, 1988–; Chm., The Sick Children's Trust, 1982–. *Address:* 33 King William Street, EC4R 9AS. *T:* 0171–280 2800.

STEVENSON, Vice-Adm. Sir (Hugh) David, AC 1976; KBE 1977 (CBE 1970); Royal Australian Navy, retired; *b* 24 Aug. 1918; *s* of late Rt Rev. William Henry Webster Stevenson, Bishop of Grafton, NSW, and Mrs Katherine Saumarez Stevenson; *m* 1st, 1944, Myra Joyce Clarke (*d* 1978); one *s* one *d*; 2nd, 1979, Margaret Wheeler Wright. *Educ:* Southport Sch., Qld; RAN Coll. psc RN 1956; idc 1966. Commnd, 1938; served War: Mediterranean, East Indies, Pacific; minesweeping post, SW Pacific; specialised in navigation, 1944 (HM Navigation Sch.); Commands: HMAS Tobruk and 10th Destroyer Sqdn, 1959–60; HMNZS Royalist, 1960–61; HMAS Sydney, 1964; HMAS Melbourne, 1965–66; Dir of Plans, 1962–63; Naval Officer i/c W Australian area, 1967; Dep. Chief of Naval Staff, 1968–69; Comdr Aust. Fleet, 1970–71; Chief of Naval Personnel, 1972–73; Naval Staff, 1973–76; retd 1976. Comdr 1952; Captain 1958; Cdre 1967; Rear-Adm. 1968; Vice-Adm. 1973–. Chm. for Territories, Queen Elizabeth Jubilee Fund for Young Australians, 1977; Patron, N Class Destroyers Assoc. (Qld), 1992–. *Publication:* (contrib.) The Use of Radar at Sea, 1952. *Recreations:* reading, opera, bridge. *Address:* PO Box 348, Palm Beach, Qld 4221, Australia. *T* and *Fax:* (75) 344103. *Clubs:* United Service (Brisbane), Twin Towns RSL (Tweed Heads).

STEVENSON, Dr Jim; Chief Executive, Educational Broadcasting Services Trust, since 1988; *b* 9 May 1937; *s* of George Stevenson and Frances Mildred Groat; *m* 1963, Brenda Cooley; one *s* one *d*. *Educ:* Kirkham Grammar Sch.; Univ. of Liverpool (BSc, PhD). NATO Res. Fellow, Univ. of Trondheim, 1963–65; Lectr in Biochemistry, Univ. of Warwick, 1965–69; BBC Open Univ. Production Centre: Producer, 1969–75; Exec. Producer, 1975–76; Editor (Science), 1976–79; Head of Programmes, 1979–82; Dep. Sec., BBC, 1982–83; Head of Educnl Broadcasting Services and Educn Sec., BBC, 1983–89. *Publications:* contribs to sci. jls and communications jls. *Recreations:* television, reading, drawing. *Address:* 34 Vallance Road, N22 4UB. *T:* 0181–889 6261.

STEVENSON, John, CBE 1987; Deputy Licensing Authority: South East Traffic Area, since 1987; Metropolitan Traffic Area, since 1989; Eastern Traffic Area, since 1990; Western Traffic Area, since 1991; *b* 15 June 1927; *s* of John and Harriet Esther Stevenson; *m* 1956, Kathleen Petch; one *s* one *d*. *Educ:* Durham Univ. (LLB); MA Oxon 1982. Solicitor. Legal Asst, Borough of Hartlepool, 1951; Junior Solicitor, County Borough of Sunderland, 1952; Solicitor, Hertfordshire CC, 1953, Asst Clerk, 1964; Clerk of the Peace and County Solicitor, Gloucestershire CC, 1969; Chief Executive, Buckinghamshire CC, 1974; Sec., ACC, 1980–87. Hon. Fellow, Inst. Local Govt Studies, Birmingham Univ., 1981–; Vis. Fellow, Nuffield Coll., Oxford, 1982–90. Vice President, Inst. of Trading Standards Administration, 1988. *Address:* 1 Hales Meadow, Lydekker Park, Harpenden, Herts AL5 4JB. *T:* Harpenden (01582) 761393.

STEVENSON, Joseph Aidan; Non-executive Director, Johnson Matthey plc, since 1991; Chairman, Young Group plc, since 1992; *b* 19 April 1931; *s* of Robert and Bridget Stevenson; *m* 1956, Marjorie Skinner; one *s* two *d*. *Educ:* Birmingham Univ. (BSc Hons Metallurgy). Instr Lieut, RN, 1955–58. Joined Johnson Matthey, 1958, as development metallurgist; held a number of sen. management, operating and div. dirships within the Johnson Matthey Gp; Gp Exec. Dir, 1982–91; Chief Exec. Officer, 1989–91. Chm. of Govs, Combe Bank Indep. Girls' Sch., Kent, 1985–91. Mem. Council, Royal London Soc. for the Blind, 1990–. FIM 1990 (Mem. Council, 1991–). Liveryman: Goldsmiths' Co.; Clockmakers' Co. Distinguished Achievement Award, Inst. of Precious Metals, 1989. *Recreations:* golf, sailing. *Address:* Johnson Matthey, 2–4 Cockspur Street, Trafalgar Square, SW1Y 5BQ. *Club:* Knole Park Golf (Sevenoaks).

STEVENSON, Juliet Anne Virginia; actress; Associate Artist, Royal Shakespeare Company; *b* 30 Oct. 1956; one *d*. *Educ:* RADA (Bancroft Gold Medal). With Royal Shakespeare Company, 1978–86: Les Liaisons Dangereuses; As You Like It; Troilus and Cressida; Measure for Measure; A Midsummer Night's Dream; The Witch of Edmonton; Money; Henry IV parts I and II; Once in a Lifetime; The White Guard; Hippolytus; Antony and Cleopatra; The Churchill Play; *other plays* include: Yerma, NT, 1987; Hedda Gabler, NT, 1989; Burn This, Hampstead, 1990; Death and the Maiden, Royal Court, transf. Albery, 1991; The Duchess of Malfi, Greenwich, transf. Wyndhams, 1995; *films* include: Drowning by Numbers, 1988; Ladder of Swords, 1990; Truly, Madly, Deeply, 1991; The Trial, 1993; The Secret Rapture, 1994; several television rôles. *Publication:* (jtly) Clamorous Voices, 1988. *Address:* c/o Markham and Froggatt Ltd, Julian House, 4 Windmill Street, W1P 1HF.

STEVENSON, Rt Rev. Kenneth William; *see* Portsmouth, Bishop of.

STEVENSON, Michael Charles; Secretary, British Broadcasting Corporation, since 1992; *b* 14 Aug. 1960; *s* of Michael Anthony and Ena Elizabeth Stevenson; *m* 1987, Deborah Frances Taylor; one *s* one *d*. *Educ:* Doncaster Grammar Sch.; Christ Church, Oxford (LitHum). British Broadcasting Corporation: trainee, 1983; Producer, Talks and Documentaries, Radio, 1984; Producer, News and Current Affairs, TV, 1988; Chief Assistant, Policy and Planning Unit, 1990; Dep. Editor, On The Record, 1991. Sir Huw Wheldon Fellow, Univ. of Wales, 1989. *Recreations:* music, tennis. *Address:* BBC Broadcasting House, W1A 1AA. *T:* 0171–580 4468. *Club:* Vanderbilt Racquet.

STEVENSON, Prof. Olive, CBE 1994; DLitt; Professor of Social Work Studies, University of Nottingham, 1984–94 (Head, School of Social Studies, 1987–91), now Professor Emeritus; Fellow, St Anne's College, University of Oxford, since 1970; *b* 13 Dec. 1930; *d* of John and Evelyn Stevenson. *Educ:* Purley County Grammar Sch. for Girls; Lady Margaret Hall, Oxford (BA EngLitt, MA 1955); London Sch. of Economics (Dip. in Social Studies, Dip. in Child Care); DLitt Nottingham, 1992. Tavistock Clinic; Child Care Officer, Devon CC, 1954–58; Lecturer in Applied Social Studies: Univ. of Bristol, 1959–61; Univ. of Oxford, 1961–68; Social Work Adviser, Supplementary Benefits Commn, 1968–70; Reader in Applied Social Studies, Univ. of Oxford, 1970–76; Prof. of Social Policy and Social Work: Univ. of Keele, 1976–82; Univ. of Liverpool, 1983–84. Member: Royal Commn on Civil Liability, 1973–78; Social Security Adv. Cttee, 1982–; Registered Homes Tribunal, 1985–90; Chairman: Adv. Cttee, Rent Rebates and Rent Allowances, 1977–83; Age Concern England, 1980–83; Councils of Voluntary Service Nat. Assoc., 1985–88; Care and Repair, 1993–. *Publications:* Someone Else's Child, 1965, rev. edn 1977; Claimant or Client?, 1970; Social Service Teams: the practitioner's view, 1978; Child Abuse: interprofessional communication, 1979; Specialisation in Social Service Teams, 1981; (with Fuller) Policies, Programmes and Disadvantage, 1983; Age and Vulnerability, a guide to better care, 1988; (ed) Child Abuse: public policy and professional practice, 1989; (jtly) Community Care and Empowerment, 1993. *Recreations:* music, cookery, conversation. *Address:* c/o School of Social Studies, University of Nottingham, Nottingham NG7 2RD.

STEVENSON, Maj.-Gen. Paul Timothy, OBE 1985 (MBE 1975); Clerk to Carpenters' Co., since 1992; *b* 9 March 1940; *s* of Ernest Stevenson and Dorothy Stevenson (*née* Trehearn); *m* 1965, Ann Douglas Drysdale; one *s* one *d*. *Educ:* Bloxham Sch. Commissioned Royal Marines 1958; 41 Commando, 1960; 45 Commando, Aden, 1962; HMS Mohawk, Gulf and W Indies, 1965–68; Army Staff Coll., 1972; 45 Commando, 1973–75; HMS Bulwark, 1975; Instructor, RN Staff Coll., 1978; SO Plans, HQ Land Forces, Falklands Campaign, 1982; CO 42 Commando, 1983; NATO Defence Coll., 1986; Dir, RM Personnel, 1987–88; RCDS 1989; Comdr, British Forces, Falkland Is, 1989–90. Modern Pentathlon British Team, 1962–69 (Olympic Team Manager, 1964); Biathlon British Team, 1965. *Recreations:* field sports, golf, gardening, ski-ing. *Address:* c/o Lloyds Bank, 23 Long Street, Wotton-under-Edge, Glos GL12 7DA. *Club:* Army and Navy.

STEVENSON, Robert Bryce; General President, National Union of Footwear Leather and Allied Trades, 1980–90, retired; *b* 26 June 1926; *s* of Daniel Liddle Stevenson and Christina Stevenson; *m* 1947, Margaret Eugenia; two *d*. *Educ:* Caldercruix Advanced Sch., Airdrie, Lanarks. Full-time Officer NUFLAT, Street, Som. Branch, 1961–80. Member, 1980–: Internat. Textile, Garment and Leather Workers Fedn Exec. Council and Cttee (Brussels); Jt Cttee, Footwear Industry in Europe (Brussels); Footwear Econ. Devélt Cttee, 1980–88; TUC Textile, Clothing and Footwear Industries Cttee; Council, Shoe and Allied Trades Res. Assoc.; Boot and Shoe Repairing Wages Council for GB; Bd of Management, Boot Trade Benevolent Soc.; Mem., Footwear Leather and Fur Skin Industry Trng Bd, 1980–82; Mem., TUC Gen. Council, 1984–. JP Wells and Glastonbury 1970 (on Supplementary List, Northants, 1981). *Recreations:* listening to and playing music, all sports.

STEVENSON, Robert Wilfrid, (Wilf); Director, British Film Institute, since 1988; *b* 19 April 1947; *s* of James Alexander Stevenson and Elizabeth Anne Stevenson (*née* Macrae); *m* 1st, 1972, Jennifer Grace Antonio (marr. diss. 1979); 2nd, 1991, Elizabeth Ann Minogue; one *s* two *d*. *Educ:* Edinburgh Academy; University College, Oxford (MA Natural Sciences, Chemistry); Napier Polytechnic. FCCA. Research Officer, Edinburgh Univ. Students' Assoc., 1970–74; Sec., Napier Coll., Edinburgh, 1974–87; Dep. Dir, BFI, 1987–88. *Recreations:* cinema, hill walking, bridge. *Address:* (office) 21 Stephen Street, W1P 1PL. *T:* 0171–255 1444.

STEVENSON, Sir Simpson, Kt 1976; DL; *b* 18 Aug. 1921; *s* of T. H. Stevenson, Greenock; *m* 1945, Jean Holmes Henry, JP, Port Glasgow. *Educ:* Greenock High Sch. Member: Greenock Town Council, 1949–67 and 1971– (Provost of Greenock, 1962–65); Inverclyde DC, 1974– (Provost, 1984–88); Vice-Chm., Clyde Port Authority, 1966–69; Chm., Greater Glasgow Health Bd, 1973–83; Chm., Scottish Health Services Common Service Agency, 1973–77, 1983–87. Member: Western Regional Hosp. Bd (Scotland), 1959–; Scottish Hosp. Administrative Staffs Cttee, 1965–74 (Chm., 1972–74); Chm., W Regional Hosp. Bd (Scotland), Glasgow, 1967–74; Member: Scottish Hosp. Endowments Commn, 1969–70; Scottish Health Services Planning Council; Royal Commn on the NHS, 1976–79. Chm., Consortium of Local Authorities Special Programme (CLASP), 1974. DL Renfrewshire, 1990. Hon. LLD Glasgow, 1982. *Recreations:* football, reading, choral singing. *Address:* 64A Reservoir Road, Gourock, Renfrewshire PA19 1YQ.

STEVENSON, Wilf; *see* Stevenson, R. W.

STEVENSON, William Trevor, CBE 1985; DL; *b* 21 March 1921; *o s* of late William Houston Stevenson and Mabel Rose Stevenson (*née* Hunt); *m* Alison Wilson (*née* Roy). *Educ:* Edinburgh Acad. Apprentice mechanical engineer, 1937–41; engineer, 1941–45; entered family food manufacturing business, Cottage Rusks, 1945; Man. Dir, 1948–54; Chm., 1954–59; Chief Executive, Cottage Rusks Associates, (following merger with Joseph Rank Ltd), 1959–69; Reg. Dir, Ranks Hovis McDougall, 1969–74; Dir, various cos in food, engrg, medical, hotel and aviation industries, 1974–; Chairman: Gleneagles Hotels, 1981–83; Scottish Transport Gp, 1981–86; Hodgson Martin Ventures, 1982–88; Alexander Wilkie, 1977–90. Master, Co. of Merchants of City of Edinburgh, 1978–80. DL City of Edinburgh, 1984. *Recreations:* flying, sailing, curling. *Club:* Caledonian.

STEWARD, Rear Adm. Cedric John, CB 1984; Director, Antric Park, since 1986; Horse Stud Owner, Antric Park, Auckland; Chief of Naval Staff, New Zealand, 1983–86, retired; *b* 31 Jan. 1931; *s* of Ethelbert Harold Steward and Anne Isabelle Steward; *m* 1952, Marie Antoinette Gurr; three *s*. *Educ:* Northcote College, Auckland, NZ; RNC Dartmouth; RNC Greenwich. Served: HMS Devonshire, 1950; HMS Illustrious, 1950; HMS Glory, 1951 (Korean Campaign and UN Medals, 1951); HMAS Australia, HMAS Barcoo, 1952; HM NZ Ships Hawea, 1953, Kaniere, 1954 (Korea), Tamaki, 1955–58, Stawell, 1958–59; HMAS Creswell (RAN College), 1959–62; HM NZ Ships Rotoiti, 1962–63 (Antarctic support), Tamaki, 1963–64, Royalist, 1965–66 (Confrontation), Philomel, 1966, Inverell (in Command), 1966–67; JSSC Latimer, 1968; Dep. Head, NZ Defence Liaison Staff, Canberra, 1969–73; in Command, HMNZS Otago, 1973–74; in Command and Captain F11, HMNZS Canterbury, 1974–75; Defence HQ, 1976–77; RCDS, 1978; Dep. Chief of Naval Staff, NZ, 1979–81; Commodore, Auckland, 1981–83. *Recreations:* rugby, golf, tennis, equestrian events, fishing, boating, philately, farming. *Clubs:* Helensville Golf (Kaukapakapa), Auckland Racing (Ellerslie).

STEWARD, Stanley Feargus, CBE 1947; CEng; FIEE; Director, George Thurlow and Sons (Holdings) Ltd; Chairman, ERA Technology Ltd, 1983–84; *b* 9 July 1904; *s* of late Arthur Robert and late Minnie Elizabeth Steward, Mundesley, Norfolk; *m* 1929, Phyllis Winifred, *d* of late J. Thurlow, Stowmarket, Suffolk; one *s* one *d*. *Educ:* The Paston Sch., North Walsham, Norfolk. Was apprenticed to East Anglian Engineering Co. (subseq. Bull Motors Ltd) and subseq. held positions of Chief Designer, Sales Manager and Managing Dir; Min. of Supply Electrical Adviser to Machine Tool Control, 1940; Director of Industrial Electrical Equipment, 1941–44; Dir Gen. of Machine Tools, 1944–45; Chm. Machine Tool Advisory Council, 1946–47; Chm. Gauge & Tool Advisory Council, 1946–47. Director: E. R. & F. Turner, Ltd, Ipswich, 1944–48. Chm., South Western Electricity Board, 1948–55; Man. Dir, Lancashire Dynamo Holdings Ltd, 1956–59 (Chm., 1957–58); Former Chm., Lancashire Dynamo and Crypto Ltd, Lancashire Dynamo Electronic Products Ltd and Lancashire Dynamo Group Sales; Chairman: William Steward (Holdings) Ltd and William Steward & Co. Ltd, 1970–80; Thurlow, Nunn & Sons Ltd, 1970–84; Dir, Bull Motors Ltd, 1981–85. Member: British Electricity Authority, 1952–53; Elect. Engineering EDC, 1962–71; Machine Tool EDC, 1971–80; Chm., British Electrical Development Assoc., 1954; President: Ipswich and District Electrical Assoc., 1964–67, 1972–78; Electrical Industries Club, 1966–67; Assoc. of Supervisory and Exec. Engineers, 1970–74; Electrical and Electronic Industries Benevolent Assoc., 1971–72; Instn of Engineers-in-Charge, 1982–84; Man. Dir, BEAMA, 1959–71; Pres., Exec. Cttee, Organisme de Liaison des Industries Metalliques Europeénes, 1963–67. Freeman of City of London; Master, Worshipful Company of Glaziers and Painters of Glass, 1964. *Publications:* Electricity and Food Production, 1953; British Electrical Manufacture in the National Economy, 1961; Twenty Five Years of South Western Electricity, 1973; The Story of the Dynamicables, 1983; The Story of Electrex, 1984; regular 'Personal View' contribs to Electrical Review and other jls. *Recreations:* books, music, watching cricket. *Address:* 41 Fairacres, Roehampton Lane, SW15 5LX. *T:* 0181–876 2457. *Clubs:* Athenæum, MCC.

STEWART, family name of **Earl of Galloway** and **Baron Stewartby**.

STEWART; *see* Vane-Tempest-Stewart, family name of Marquess of Londonderry.

STEWART, Sir Alan, KBE 1981 (CBE 1972); Vice-Chancellor of Massey University, 1964–83; *b* 8 Dec. 1917; *s* of Kenneth and Vera Mary Stewart; *m* 1950, Joan Cecily Sisam; one *s* three *d*. *Educ:* Massey Agricultural College; University College, Oxford. Sen. Lectr, Massey Agric. Coll., 1950–54; Chief Consulting Officer, Milk Marketing Board, England and Wales, 1954–58; Principal, Massey Agric. Coll., 1959–63. Hon. DSc Massey, 1984. *Address:* PO Box 3, Whakatane, New Zealand. *T:* (7) 3086619.

STEWART, Sir Alan (d'Arcy), 13th Bt *cr* 1623; yachtbuilder; *b* 29 Nov. 1932; *s* of Sir Jocelyn Harry Stewart, 12th Bt, and Constance Mary (*d* 1940), *d* of D'Arcy Shillaber; *S* father, 1982; *m* 1952, Patricia, *d* of Lawrence Turner; two *s* two *d*. *Educ:* All Saints College, Bathurst, NSW. *Heir:* *s* Nicholas Courtney d'Arcy Stewart, BSc, HDipEd, *b* 4 Aug. 1953. *Address:* One Acre House, Ramelton, Co. Donegal. *T:* Ramelton 82.

STEWART, Alastair James; presenter, London Tonight, since 1993, and GMTV, since 1994; *b* 22 June 1952; *s* of Group Captain James F. Stewart and Joan Mary Stewart (*née* Lord); *m* 1978, Sally Ann Jung; two *s* one *d*. *Educ:* St Augustine's Abbey Sch., Ramsgate; Univ. of Bristol. Dep. Pres., Nat. Union of Students, 1974–76. Reporter and presenter, Southern ITV, 1976–80; industrial corresp., ITN, 1980; presenter, ITN: News at Ten, 1981; Channel 4 News, 1983; News at One, 1985; News at 5.45, 1986; Parliament Programme, 1988; News at Ten, 1989, 1991–92; Washington corresp., 1990–91; presenter: BBC Radio, 1994; Missing, LWT, 1992–; Police, Camera, Action, Carlton

TV, 1994–. Commentator and presenter, numerous parly programmes and State occasions, UK and overseas, incl. first live transmission from House of Lords, 1985, House of Commons, 1989, Gulf War and liberation of Kuwait, 1991. *Recreations:* travel, cartography, a catholic taste in music. *Address:* London News Network, London Television Centre, Upper Ground, SE1 9LT. *T:* 0171–827 7700.

STEWART, Alastair Lindsay; Sheriff of Tayside, Central and Fife at Dundee, since 1990; *b* 28 Nov. 1938; *s* of Alexander Lindsay Stewart and Anna Stewart; *m* 1st, 1968, Annabel Claire Stewart (marr. diss. 1991), *yr d* of late Prof. W. McC. Stewart; two *s*; 2nd, 1991, Sheila Ann Mackinnon (*née* Flockhart), *o d* of David H. Flockhart. *Educ:* Edinburgh Academy; St Edmund Hall, Oxford (BA); Univ. of Edinburgh (LLB). Admitted to Faculty of Advocates, 1963; Tutor, Faculty of Law, Univ. of Edinburgh, 1963–73; Standing Junior Counsel to Registrar of Restrictive Trading Agreements, 1968–70; Advocate Depute, 1970–73; Sheriff of South Strathclyde, Dumfries and Galloway, at Airdrie, 1973–79, of Grampian, Highland and Islands, at Aberdeen and Stonehaven, 1979–90. Chairman: Grampian Family Conciliation Service, 1984–87 (Hon. Pres., 1987–90); Scottish Assoc. of Family Conciliation Services, 1986–89. Governor, Robert Gordon's Inst. of Technology, 1982–90 (Vice-Chm. of Governors, 1985–90). Editor, Scottish Civil Law Reports, 1992–. *Publications:* contrib. chapter in Sheriff Court Practice, by I. D. Macphail, 1988; The Scottish Criminal Courts in Action, 1990; various articles in legal jls. *Recreations:* reading, music, walking. *Address:* Sheriffs' Chambers, Sheriff Court House, PO Box 2, Dundee DD1 9AD. *T:* Dundee (01382) 26513.

STEWART, Sir Alastair (Robin), 3rd Bt *cr* 1960, of Strathgarry, Perth; *b* 26 Sept. 1925; 2nd *s* of Sir Kenneth Dugald Stewart, 1st Bt, GBE and Noel (*d* 1946), *yr d* of Kenric Brodribb, Melbourne; *S* brother, 1992; *m* 1953, Patricia Helen, *d* of late J. A. Merrett; one *s* three *d*. *Educ:* Marlborough Coll. Lieut, 1st Royal Gloucestershire Hussars, 1945–47. Dir, Neale & Wilkinson Ltd, 1947–71; Man. Dir, Stewart & Harvey Ltd, 1971–90. *Recreation:* gardening. *Heir: s* John Kenneth Alexander Stewart, *b* 15 Dec. 1961. *Address:* Walters Cottage, North Hill, Little Baddow, Chelmsford, Essex CM3 4TQ. *T:* Chelmsford (01245) 222445.

STEWART, Allan; *see* Stewart, J. A.

STEWART, Andrew Struthers, (Andy); farmer; Chairman, Agricultural Training Board, since 1992; *b* 27 May 1937; *s* of late James Stewart and of Elizabeth Stewart; *m* 1961, Louise Melvin (*née* Skimming); one *s* one *d*. *Educ:* Strathaven Acad., Scotland; West of Scotland Agricl Coll. Farming Beesthorpe Manor Farm, 1961–. Mem., Caunton Parish Council, 1973–83; Conservative Mem., Notts CC, 1975–83; Cons. spokesman on leisure services, 1981–83. MP (C) Sherwood, 1983–92; contested (C) Sherwood, 1992. PPS to Minister of Agriculture, Fisheries and Food, 1987–89, to Sec. of State for Educn and Science, 1989–90, to Lord Pres. of Council and Leader of H of C, 1990–92. Comr, Rural Develt Commn, 1993–. Chairman: Strathaven Br., Young Conservatives, 1957 and 1958; Caunton, Maplebeck and Kersall Cons. Br., 1970–73 (Founder Mem.). Member: Newark Br., NFU, 1961– (Mem., County Exec. Cttee, 1966–); Newark and Notts Agricl Soc.; Adv. Mem., Nottingham University Coll. of Agriculture, 1977–82 (formerly Chm., Notts Coll. of Agriculture Brackenhurst); formerly Chm., Governing Bd, Rufford Comprehensive Sch. Youth Club Leader, 1965–76; Life Vice President: Southwell Rugby Club; Caunton Cricket Club; Trustee, Southwell Recreation Centre, 1979–83. *Address:* Beesthorpe Manor Farm, Caunton, Newark, Notts NG23 6AT. *T:* Caunton (01636) 636270. *Clubs:* Farmers'; Bentinck Conservative (Hucknall, Notts).

STEWART, Angus; QC (Scot.); *b* 14 Dec. 1946; *s* of Archibald Ian Balfour Stewart, CBE, BL, FSAScot and Ailsa Rosamund Mary Massey; *m* 1975, Jennifer Margaret Stewart; one *d*. *Educ:* Edinburgh Acad.; Balliol Coll., Oxford (BA); Edinburgh Univ. (LLB). Called to the Scottish Bar, 1975. Keeper, Advocates' Liby, 1994–. Trustee: Nat. Liby of Scotland, 1994–; Stewart Heritage Trust, 1994–. *Address:* 8 Ann Street, Edinburgh EH4 1PJ. *T:* 0131–332 4083.

STEWART, Brian John, Group Chief Executive, Scottish and Newcastle plc (formerly Scottish & Newcastle Breweries), since 1991; *b* 9 April 1945; *m* 1971, Seonaid Duncan; two *s* one *d*. *Educ:* Edinburgh Univ. (MSc). Mem., Scottish Inst. of Chartered Accountants. Scottish and Newcastle Breweries: joined 1976; Finance Dir, 1988–91. Director: Booker, 1993–; Standard Life Assurance Co., 1993–. *Recreations:* golf, ski-ing. *Address:* Abbey Brewery, Holyrood Road, Edinburgh EH8 8YS. *T:* 0131–556 2591.

STEWART, Brian Thomas Webster, CMG 1969; Director of Operations (China), Racal Electronics, since 1982; *b* 27 April 1922; *s* of late Redvers Buller Stewart and Mabel Banks Sparks, Broich, Crieff; *m* 1946, Millicent Peggy Pollock (marr. diss. 1970); two *d*; *m* 1972, Sally Nugent; one *s* one *d*. *Educ:* Trinity Coll., Glenalmond; Worcester Coll., Oxford (MA). Commnd The Black Watch (RHR), 1942; served Europe and Far East (Capt.). Joined Malayan Civil Service, 1946; studying Chinese Macau, 1947; Asst Sec., Chinese Affairs, Singapore, 1949; Devonshire Course, Oxford, 1950; Asst Comr for Labour, Kuala Lumpur, 1951; Sec. for Chinese Affairs, Supt of Chinese Schs, Malacca and Penang, 1952–57; joined HM Diplomatic Service, 1957; served Rangoon, Peking, Shanghai, Manila, Kuala Lumpur, Hanoi; Asst Sec., Cabinet Office, 1968–72; Counsellor, Hong Kong, 1972–74; FCO, 1974–78. Special Rep., Rubber Growers Assoc., Malaysia, 1979–82. Hon. Lectr, Hong Kong Univ., 1986–. *Publication:* All Men's Wisdom (anthology of Chinese Proverbs), 1957. *Recreations:* climbing, sailing, ski-ing, chamber music, orientalia particularly chinoiserie. *Address:* c/o Royal Bank of Scotland, Crieff, Perthshire PH7 3RX. *Clubs:* Athenæum, Special Forces; Hong Kong.

STEWART, Campbell; *see* Stewart, W. A. C.

STEWART, Colin MacDonald, CB 1983; FIA, FSS; Directing Actuary, Government Actuary's Department, 1974–84; *b* 26 Dec. 1922; *s* of John Stewart and Lillias Cecilia MacDonald Fraser; *m* 1948, Gladys Edith Thwaites; three *d*. *Educ:* Queen's Park Secondary Sch., Glasgow. Clerical Officer, Rosyth Dockyard, 1939–42. Served War: Fleet Air Arm (Lieut (A) RNVR), 1942–46. Govt Actuary's Dept, London, 1946–84. Head of Actuarial Res., Godwins Ltd, 1985–88. FIA 1953. *Publications:* The Students' Society Log 1960–85, 1985; numerous articles on actuarial and demographic subjects in British and internat. jls. *Recreations:* genealogical research, foreign travel, grandchilding. *Address:* 8 The Chase, Coulsdon, Surrey CR5 2EG. *T:* 0181–660 3966.

STEWART, Sir David James H.; *see* Henderson-Stewart.

STEWART, Captain Sir David (John Christopher), 7th Bt *cr* 1803, of Athenree, Tyrone; *b* 19 June 1935; *s* of Sir Hugh Charlie Godfray Stewart, 6th Bt and his 1st wife, Rosemary Elinor Dorothy, *d* of Maj. George Peacocke; *S* father, 1994; *m* 1959, Bridget Anne, *er d* of late Patrick W. Sim; three *d*. *Educ:* Bradfield Coll.; RMA Sandhurst. Commnd Royal Inniskilling Fusiliers, 1956; seconded to Trucial Oman Scouts, 1957–58 (Jebel Akhdar Campaign, 1957); Adjt 1958; served in Trucial States, Oman and Muscat, 1957–58, Germany, 1958–59, Kenya, 1960–62 (Kuwait Operation, 1961), UN Peacekeeping Force, Cyprus, 1964; retd as Captain, 1965. Representative for E. S. & A. Robinson, Bristol, 1965–69; Director: Maurice James Holdings, Coventry, 1969–77; Papropak UK, 1977–79; self-employed, 1979–; owner, George Inn, Middlezoy, Somerset, 1982–85. *Recreations:* golf, cricket, crossword puzzles, picture restoration and framing, my grandchildren. *Heir:* half *b* Hugh Nicholas Stewart [*b* 20 April 1955; *m* 1976, Anna Leeke; one *s* three *d*]. *Address:* Tower View, 8 Silver Street, Wiveliscombe, Taunton, Somerset TA4 2PA. *Club:* MCC.

STEWART, Duncan Montgomery; Principal of Lady Margaret Hall, Oxford, 1979–95; *b* 14 Feb. 1930; *s* of William Montgomery Stewart and Mary Pauline (*née* Checkley); *m* 1961, Valerie Mary Grace, *er d* of Major E. H. T. Boileau, Rampisham, Dorset; one *s* one *d*. *Educ:* Greymouth Technical High Sch.; Christ's Coll., NZ; Canterbury University Coll., NZ (MA 1st Cl. French 1951, 1st Cl. Latin 1952; Pres., Students' Assoc., 1952); Rhodes Scholar, 1953; Queen's Coll., Oxford (1st Cl. Hons Mod. Langs 1955). Oxford University: Lectr, 1955, Fellow, 1956–79, Wadham Coll.; Mem., Gen. Bd of Faculties, 1972–79, 1985–88 (Vice-Chm., 1976–78); Mem., Hebdomadal Council, 1976–91; Vice-Chm., Libraries Bd, 1979–85; Curator, Bodleian Liby, 1979–83; Rhodes Trustee, 1986–; Sen. Mem., Univ. Wine Tasting Soc., 1974–85. Oxford Chm., Oxford and Cambridge Schs Exam. Bd, 1986–91. *Publications:* articles and revs on French Literature, esp. later medieval. *Recreations:* opera, wine. *Address:* 12 Dunstan Road, Oxford OX3 9BY; Place de la Résistance, 82270 Montpezat de Quercy, Tarn et Garonne, France.

STEWART, Sir Edward (Jackson), Kt 1980; Chairman, Stewarts Hotels Pty Ltd, since 1956; *b* 10 Dec. 1923; *s* of Charles Jackson Stewart and Jessie Stewart (*née* Dobbie); *m* 1956, Shirley Patricia Holmes; four *s*. *Educ:* St Joseph's College, Brisbane. Fellow Catering Inst. of Australia (FCIA); FAIM. Served with Australian Army, RAA, 1942–44. Chairman: Castlemaine Perkins Ltd, 1977–80 (Dir, 1970); Castlemaine Tooheys Ltd, 1980–85; Director: Birch Carroll & Coyle Ltd, 1967–92; Roadshow (Qld) Pty Ltd, 1970–92; Darwin Cinemas Pty Ltd, 1972–92; G. R. E. (Australia) Ltd, 1980–92; Besser (Qld) Ltd, 1981–87; Bank of Queensland Ltd, 1986–; QUF Industries Ltd, 1986–. President: Queensland Hotels Assoc., 1963–69; Aust. Hotels Assoc., 1966–69. Mem. Totalisator Administration Bd of Queensland, 1977–81. Chm., Queensland Inst. of Medical Research Trust, 1980–88. *Recreations:* reading, fishing and thoroughbred breeding. *Address:* 33 Eckersley Avenue, Buderim, Qld 4556, Australia. *Clubs:* Australian (Sydney); Brisbane, Tattersall's (Past Pres.) (Brisbane); Queensland Turf.

STEWART, Ewen; Sheriff at Wick, Caithness, 1962–92, at Dornoch, Sutherland and Tain, Ross and Cromarty, 1977–92, and at Stornoway, Western Isles, 1990–92; *b* 22 April 1926; *o s* of late Duncan Stewart and Kate Blunt, and *gs* of late Ewen Stewart, Kinlocheil; *m* 1959, Norma Porteous Hollands (*d* 1992), *d* of late William Charteris Hollands, Earlston; one *d*. *Educ:* Edinburgh University. BSc (Agric.) 1945; MA (Econ.) 1950; LLB 1952. Asst Agricultural Economist, East of Scotland Coll. of Agriculture, 1946–49; practised at Scottish Bar, 1952–62; lectr on Agricultural Law, Univ. of Edinburgh, 1957–62; former standing junior counsel, Min. of Fuel and Power. Parly Cand. (Lab.) Banffshire, 1962. *Address:* 16 Bignold Court, George Street, Wick, Caithness KW1 4DL.

STEWART, Prof. Sir Frederick (Henry), Kt 1974; FRS 1964; PhD Cantab; FRSE; FGS; Regius Professor of Geology, 1956–82, now Emeritus, Dean of Science Faculty, 1966–68, and Member, University Court, 1969–70, Edinburgh University; *b* 16 Jan. 1916; *o s* of Frederick Robert Stewart and Hester Alexander, Aberdeen; *m* 1945, Mary Florence Elinor Rainbow (*see* Mary Stewart); no *c*. *Educ:* Fettes Coll.; Univ. of Aberdeen (BSc); Emmanuel Coll., Cambridge. Mineralogist in Research Dept of ICI Ltd (Billingham Div.), 1941–43; Lectr in Geology, Durham Colls in the Univ. of Durham, 1943–56. Vice-Pres., Geological Soc. of London, 1965–66; Member: Council for Scientific Policy, 1967–71; Adv. Council for Applied R&D, 1976–79; Chairman: NERC, 1971–73 (Mem., Geol. Geophysics Cttee, 1967–70); Adv. Bd for Res. Councils, 1973–79 (Mem., 1972–73); Mem. Council, Royal Soc., 1969–70; Trustee, BM (Nat. Hist.), 1983–87; Mem. Council, Scottish Marine Biol Assoc., 1983–89. Lyell Fund Award, 1951, J. B. Tyrrell Fund, 1952, Geological Soc. of London; Mineralogical Soc. of America Award, 1952; Lyell Medal, Geological Soc. of London, 1970; Clough Medal, Edinburgh Geol. Soc., 1971; Sorby Medal, Yorks Geol. Soc., 1975. Hon. DSc: Aberdeen, 1975; Leicester, 1977; Heriot-Watt, 1978; Durham, 1983; Glasgow, 1988. *Publications:* The British Caledonides (ed with M. R. W. Johnson), 1963; Marine Evaporites, 1963; papers in Mineralogical Magazine, Jl of Geol. Soc. of London, etc., dealing with igneous and metamorphic petrology and salt deposits. *Recreation:* fishing. *Address:* 79 Morningside Park, Edinburgh EH10 5EZ. *T:* 0131–447 2620; House of Letterawe, Lochawe, Argyll PA33 1AH. *T:* Dalmally (01838) 200329. *Club:* New (Edinburgh).

STEWART, George Girdwood, CB 1979; MC 1945; TD 1954; Cairngorm Estate Adviser, Highlands and Islands Enterprise, since 1988; Associate Director, Oakwood Environmental, since 1990; *b* 12 Dec. 1919; *o s* of late Herbert A. Stewart, BSc, and of Janetta Dunlop Girdwood; *m* 1950, Shelagh Jean Morven Murray; one *s* one *d*. *Educ:* Kelvinside Academy, Glasgow; Glasgow Univ.; Edinburgh Univ. (BSc). Served RA, 1940–46 (MC, despatches); CO 278 (Lowland) Field Regt RA (TA), 1957–60. Dist Officer, Forestry Commn, 1949–61; Asst Conservator, 1961–67; Conservator, West Scotland, 1967–69; Comr for Forest and Estate Management, 1969–79; National Trust for Scotland: Mem., Council, 1975–79; Rep., Branklyn Garden, Perth, 1980–84; Regional Rep., Central and Tayside, 1984–88; Forestry Consultant, 1989–93. Specialist advr, Select Cttee on EEC Forestry Policy, 1986. Member: BR Bd Envt Panel, 1980–90; Countryside Commn for Scotland, 1981–88; Chm., Scottish Wildlife Trust, 1981–87; Cairngorm Recreation Trust, 1986–. Pres., Scottish Nat. Ski Council, 1988–94. Pres., Scottish Ski Club, 1971–75; Vice-Pres., Nat. Ski Fedn of GB; Chm., Alpine Racing Cttee, 1975–78. FRSA; FICFor; Hon. FLI. *Recreations:* ski-ing, tennis, studying Scottish painting. *Address:* Stormont House, 11 Mansfield Road, Scone, Perth PH2 6SA. *T:* Scone (01738) 551815. *Club:* Ski Club of Great Britain.

STEWART, (George Robert) Gordon, OBE 1984; Secretary, 1976–83, Legal Adviser 1983–89, Institute of Chartered Accountants of Scotland; *b* 13 Oct. 1924; *s* of David Gordon Stewart and Mary Grant Thompson or Stewart; *m* 1952, Rachel Jean Morrison; two *s* one *d*. *Educ:* George Watson's Coll., Edinburgh; Edinburgh Univ. (MA 1947, LLB 1949). WS. Mem., Law Soc. of Scotland, 1949–92. Served War, 1943–46: Captain, Royal Signals; Burma and SEAC. In practice as WS, Melville & Lindesay, WS, Edinburgh, 1950–59; Asst Sec., subseq. Sec., and Dir, Ideal-Standard Ltd, Hull, 1959–75. *Recreations:* aerobics, gardening. *Address:* 15 Hillpark Loan, Edinburgh EH4 7BH. *T:* 0131–312 7079. *Club:* University Staff (Edinburgh).

STEWART, Prof. George Russell, PhD; Professor of Botany, University of Queensland, Brisbane, since 1992; *b* 25 Feb. 1944; *s* of George and Isobella Stewart; *m* 1978, Janice Anne Grimes; three *d*. *Educ:* Pinner County Grammar Sch.; Univ. of Bristol (BSc 1965; PhD 1968). Lectr in Botany, Univ. of Manchester, 1968–81; London University: Prof. of Botany and Head of Dept, Birkbeck Coll., 1981–85; Quain Prof. of Botany, 1985–91 and Head of Dept of Biology, 1987–91, UCL; Dean of Faculty of Sci., 1990–91. Vis. Lectr, Dept of Biology, Univ. of Lagos, Nigeria; Visiting Professor: Dept of Botany, Univ. of Queensland, Aust.; Dept of Biology, Univ. of Campinas, Brazil; Dept of Biology, Univ. of WA. Member: Plants and Envmt Cttee, AFRC, 1989–91; Plants and Envmt Res. Bd,

AFRC (Chm., 1989–91); Agriculture Cttee, Long Ashton Res. Station, 1990–91; Inter-Agency Cttee on Res. into Global Envmtl Change (Working Gp 2), 1990–91; Inst. of Zoology Cttee, 1989–91. *Publications:* (ed jtly) The Genetic Manipulation of Plants and its Application to Agriculture, 1984; numerous scientific papers on plant physiology and metabolism and chapters in books and conf. proc. *Recreations:* cycling, cooking. *Address:* Department of Botany, University of Queensland, Brisbane, Qld 4072, Australia. *T:* (7) 33652728.

STEWART, Gillian Mary; Under-Secretary (part-time), Scottish Office Home and Health Department, responsible for criminal justice policy, parole, and life imprisonment, since 1992; *b* 2 June 1945; *d* of John Knott and Nora Elizabeth Knott; marr. diss.; two *s*. *Educ:* Blyth Grammar Sch.; Univ. of Durham (BA Hons Class 1 German). Scottish Office, 1970; posts in educn and social work; Asst Sec., 1984; posts in historic buildings and local govt. *Recreations:* swimming, walking, music, theatre. *Address:* St Andrews House, Edinburgh EH1 3DG. *T:* 0131–244 2131.

STEWART, Prof. Gordon Thallon, MD; Mechan Professor of Public Health, University of Glasgow, 1972–84, now Emeritus Professor; Hon. Consultant in Epidemiology and Preventive Medicine, Glasgow Area Health Board; *b* 5 Feb. 1919; *s* of John Stewart and Mary L. Thallon; *m* 1946, Joan Kego; two *s* two *d*; *m* 1975, Neena Walker. *Educ:* Paisley Grammar Sch.; Univs of Glasgow and Liverpool. BSc 1939; MB, ChB 1942; DTM&H 1947; MD (High Commendation) 1949; FRCPath 1964; FFCM 1972; MRCPGlas 1972; FRCPGlas 1975. House Phys. and House Surg., 1942–43; Surg. Lieut RNVR, 1943–46; Res. Fellow (MRC), Univ. of Liverpool, 1946–48; Sen. Registrar and Tutor, Wright-Fleming Inst., St Mary's Hosp., London, 1948–52; Cons. Pathologist, SW Metrop. Regional Hosp. Bd, 1954–63; Res. Worker at MRC Labs Carshalton, 1955–63; Prof. of Epidem. and Path., Univ. of N Carolina, 1964–68; Watkins Prof. of Epidem., Tulane Univ. Med. Center, New Orleans, 1968–72. Vis. Prof., Dow Med. Coll., Karachi, 1952–53 and Cornell Univ. Med. Coll., 1970–71; Cons. to WHO, and to NYC Dept of Health; Vis. Lectr and Examr, various univs in UK and overseas. Sen. Fellow, Nat. Science Foundn, Washington, 1964; Delta omega, 1969. *Publications:* (ed) Trends in Epidemiology, 1972; (ed jtly) Penicillin Allergy, 1970; Penicillin Group of Drugs, 1965; papers on chemotherapy of infectious diseases, drug allergy and epidemiology in various med. and sci. jls. *Recreations:* gardening, drawing, music. *Address:* Glenavon, The Promenade, Clifton, Bristol BS8 3HT. *T:* Bristol (0117) 973 6532.

STEWART, Prof. Harold Charles, CBE 1975; FRCP; FRSE; DL; Head of Pharmacology Department, St Mary's Hospital Medical School, 1950–74; Professor of Pharmacology in the University of London 1965–74, now Emeritus Professor (Reader, 1949–64); Consultant in Pharmacology to: St Mary's Hospital, 1946; Ministry of Defence (Army), since 1961; *b* 23 Nov. 1906; *s* of Bernard Halley Stewart, MA, MD, FRSE, FKC, Pres. of Sir Halley Stewart Trust, and Mabel Florence Wyatt; *m* 1st, 1929, Dorothy Irene Lowen (*d* 1969); one *s* one *d*; 2nd, 1970, Audrey Patricia Nicolle. *Educ:* Mill Hill Sch.; University Coll. London; Jesus Coll., Cambridge (BA 1928, MA 1934; MB, BCh 1931, MD 1935); University Coll. Hosp.; PhD London 1941; MRCP 1949. Gen. practice, Barnet, Herts, 1932–36. Sub-Dean, St Mary's Hospital Med. Sch., 1950–52; Gresham Prof. in Physic, City Univ., 1968–70. Examr now or formerly, Univs of London, Cambridge, Birmingham, Bristol and Wales, RCS, Soc. of Apothecaries. Research work, mainly on fat absorption and transport in the human subject, and on problems of pain and analgesia. Cons. in Pharmacology to Army; Med. Adviser and Mem. Commonwealth Council, Brit. Commonwealth Ex-Services League; Pres., Sir Halley Stewart Trust for Research, 1986– (Chm., 1979–86); Mem. Asthma Research Council; Dir-Gen., St John Ambulance Assoc., 1976–78 (Dep Dir-Gen., 1973–76; Dist Surg. for London, SJAB, 1950–64); Mem. Chapter-Gen., Order of St John (KStJ); Mem. Council, Stewart Soc.; Chm., Buttle Trust for Children, 1979–; Vice-Chairman: Med. Council of Alcoholism, 1986–87 (now Patron); St Christopher's Hospice for terminal cases, 1963–87 (Vice Pres., 1987); Sen. Vice-Pres. and British Rep., Assoc. Internat. de Sauvetage et de Premiers Secours en Cas d'Accidents, 1974–. Hon. Vice Pres., Stewart Soc., 1988. Liveryman, Soc. of Apothecaries of London; Freeman, City of London. Mem. Physiolog., Brit. Pharmacolog., Socs. FRCA (FFARCS 1969). FRSE 1974. RAMC, T, 1935; Mem. LDV, later Major and Med. Adviser, HG; comd and reformed Med. Unit, Univ. of London STC as Major RAMC, 1942–46. Defence Medal; Gen. Serv. Medal, 1939–46; Coronation Medal, 1953; Guthrie Meml Medal, 1974. DL Greater London, 1967–82. *Publications:* Drugs in Anæsthetic Practice (with F. G. Wood-Smith), 1962; (with W. H. Hughes) Concise Antibiotic Treatment, 2nd edn 1973; contribs to jls. *Recreations:* voluntary service; sport (lacrosse: Cambridge Half-Blue 1928; lawn tennis); genealogy and heraldry. *Address:* 41 The Glen, Green Lane, Northwood, Mddx HA6 2UR. *T:* Northwood (01923) 824893. *Club:* Athenæum.

See also Baron Stewartby.

STEWART, Sir Houston Mark S.; *see* Shaw-Stewart.

STEWART, Hugh Parker, FCA; Chairman: GB Glass Ltd, since 1994; Wellman plc, since 1995 (Director, since 1992); *b* 23 May 1934; *s* of George and Barbara Stewart; *m* 1960, Marion Gordon Cairns; one *s* one *d*. *Educ:* Sullivan Upper Sch., Holywood, Co. Down; Queen's Univ., Belfast (LLB Hons). Audit Manager, Hill Vellacott & Bailey, Belfast, 1959–62; Financial Comptroller, STC (NI) Ltd, Monkstown, 1962–67; Admin Manager, AMF Beaird, Belfast, 1967–70; Gp Financial Controller, Brightside Engrg Hldgs, Sheffield, 1970–71; SMM Ltd, Greenwich: Financial Dir., 1971–74; Overseas Dir, 1974–78; Man. Dir, SMM Foundries Ltd, Greenwich, 1978–79; Finance Dir, Westland plc, 1979–81; Finance Dir, Westland plc, and Exec. Dir, Westland Technologies Ltd, 1981–84; Man. Dir, Westland Technologies Ltd, 1984–85; Chief Exec., Westland Gp plc, 1985–88. Chm., Scheduling Technology Gp Ltd, 1989–90; Practice Chm., Aaron & Partners, Solicitors, 1989–91; Chairman: Programming Research Ltd, 1990–91; Wootton Jeffreys Consultants Ltd, 1991–94; Aerospace Systems & Technologies, 1993–95; Western Computer Gp, 1993–95; Director: DSK Systems Ltd, 1989–91; Cityflyer Express Ltd, 1991–; Chessington Computer Centre, 1995– (Mem., Ministerial Adv. Bd, 1995–). Governor, Sherborne Sch., 1982–. *Recreations:* classic cars, golf, gardening. *Address:* Ferncroft House, Walton Elm, Marnhull, Dorset DT10 1QG. *T:* Marnhull (01258) 820406; Flat 3, 80 Cambridge Street, SW1V 4QQ. *T:* 0171–931 0531. *Club:* Royal Automobile.

STEWART, Prof. Ian George; Professor of Economics, University of Edinburgh, 1967–84; *b* 24 June 1923; *s* of David Tweedie Stewart, MA and Ada Doris Montgomery Haldane; *m* 1949, Mary Katharine Oddie; one *s* two *d*. *Educ:* Fettes Coll.; Univ. of St Andrews (MA 1st Class Hons); MA Cantab 1954. Pilot, RAF, 1942–46. Commonwealth Fund Fellow, 1948–50. Research Officer, Dept of Applied Economics, Univ. of Cambridge, 1950–57; University of Edinburgh: Lectr in Economics, 1957–58; Sen. Lectr, 1958–61; Reader, 1961–67; Curator of Patronage, 1979–84. Vis. Associate Prof., Univ. of Michigan, 1962; Vis. Prof., Univ. of S Carolina, 1975. Dir, Scottish Provident Instn, 1980–90, Dep. Chm., 1983–85. Mem., British Library Bd, 1980–87. Governor, Fettes Coll., 1976–89. *Publications:* National Income of Nigeria (with A. R. Prest), 1953; (ed) Economic Development and Structural Change, 1969; articles in jls and bank reviews. *Recreations:* golf, fishing, gardening. *Address:* 571 Lanark Road West, Edinburgh EH14 7BL. *Club:* New (Edinburgh).

STEWART, Prof. Ian Nicholas, PhD; CMath; FIMA; Professor of Mathematics, University of Warwick, since 1990; *b* 24 Sept. 1945; *s* of Arthur Reginald Stewart and Marjorie Kathleen Stewart (*née* Diwell); *m* 1970, Avril Bernice Montgomery; two *s*. *Educ:* Cambridge Univ. (MA, PhD). FIMA 1993; CMath 1993. University of Warwick: Lectr, 1969–84; Reader, 1984–90. Humboldt Fellow, Tübingen, 1974; Vis. Fellow, Auckland, 1976; Associate Prof., Storrs, Conn, 1977–78; Professor: Carbondale, Ill, 1978; Houston, Texas, 1983–84; Gresham Prof. of Geometry, 1994. *Publications:* Galois Theory, 1973; Concepts of Modern Mathematics, 1975; Catastrophe Theory and its Applications, 1978; The Problems of Mathematics, 1987; Does God Play Dice?, 1989; Game Set & Math, 1991; Another Fine Math You've Got Me Into, 1992; Fearful Symmetry, 1992; The Collapse of Chaos, 1994; Nature's Numbers, 1995; From Here to Infinity, 1996. *Recreations:* science fiction, painting, guitar, keeping fish. *Address:* Mathematics Institute, University of Warwick, Coventry CV4 7AL. *T:* Coventry (01203) 523740.

STEWART, Jackie; *see* Stewart, John Young.

STEWART, James Cecil Campbell, CBE 1960; consultant; *b* 1916; *s* of late James Stewart and Mary Campbell Stewart; *m* 1946, Pamela Rouselle, *d* of William King-Smith; one *d*. *Educ:* Armstrong College and King's College, Durham University (BSc Physics). Telecommunications Research Establishment, 1939–46; Atomic Energy Research Establishment, Harwell, 1946–49; Industrial Group, UKAEA, 1949–63; Dep. Chm., British Nuclear Design and Construction, 1969–75; Member: UKAEA, 1963–69; Central Electricity Generating Bd, 1965–69; Dep. Chm., Nuclear Power Co. Ltd, 1975–80; Dir, National Nuclear Corp. Ltd, 1980–82. Chairman: British Nuclear Forum, 1974–92; Nuclear Power Co. Pension Trustee Ltd, 1979–92. Consultant, Internat. Adv. Cttee Concord, Denver, 1986–94. *Recreation:* tending a garden. *Address:* White Thorns, Higher Whitley, Cheshire WA4 4QJ. *T:* Norcott Brook (01925) 730377. *Clubs:* East India, Devonshire, Sports and Public Schools; Les Ambassadeurs.

STEWART, Sir James (Douglas), Kt 1983; agricultural consultant; Principal, Lincoln University College of Agriculture, 1974–84, retired; *b* 11 Aug. 1925; *s* of Charles Edward Stewart and Edith May Stewart (*née* Caldwell); *m* 1953, Nancy Elizabeth Dunbar; one *s* three *d*. *Educ:* Lincoln UC (Dip. Valuation and Farm Management); Canterbury Univ. (MA); Reading Univ. (DPhil). Lectr in Farm Management, Lincoln Coll., NZ, 1951–59; Research Fellow, Reading Univ., 1959–61; Sen. Lectr, Lincoln Coll., 1962–64; Prof. of Farm Management, Lincoln Coll., 1964–74. Chairman: NZ Vice-Chancellors Cttee, 1981–82; NZ Wheat Bd, 1986–87 (Dep. Chm., 1984–86); NZ Nat. Educn Qualifications Authority, 1989–95. Chm., Pyne Gould Guinness Internat. Ltd, 1987–95; Director: Pyne Gould Corp., 1982–95; Alpine Dairy Products Ltd, 1985–91. Chairman: Canterbury Develt Corp., 1983–89 (Dir, 1983–); Christchurch Sch. of Medicine, 1987–88; NZ Crown Res. Insts Implementation Cttee, 1991–. Silver Jubilee Medal, 1977. *Publications:* contrib. Jl Agricl Econs, Jl Farm Econs, Econ. Record, etc. *Recreations:* swimming, part-time farming. *Address:* Beach Road, RD 1, Amberley, New Zealand.

STEWART, James Harvey; management consultant; Chief Executive (formerly District General Manager), Barking and Havering (formerly Barking, Havering and Brentwood) Health Authority, 1985–95; *b* 15 Aug. 1939; *s* of Harvey Stewart and Annie (*née* Gray); *m* 1965, Fiona Maria Maclay Reid; three *s* one *d*. *Educ:* Peterhead Acad.; Aberdeen Univ. (MA 1962); Manchester Univ. (DSA 1964). Pres., Jun. Common Room, Crombie Hall, Aberdeen Univ., 1961–62. Hosp. Sec., Princess Margaret Rose Orthopaedic Hosp., Edinburgh, 1965–67; Principal Admin. Asst, 1967–68, and Dep. Gp Sec. and sometime Acting Gp Sec., 1968–73, York A HMC; Area Administrator, 1973–82, and Dist Administrator, 1982–83, Northumberland AHA; Regional Administrator, East Anglian RHA, 1983–85. Hon. Treasurer, Assoc. of Chief Administrators of Health Authorities in England and Wales, 1982–85 (Mem. Council, 1975–82). Mem., London Hosp. Officers Club, 1985–. *Recreations:* music, reading, walking, playing squash, watching Rugby. *Address:* White Cottage, Hardwick, Cambridge CB3 7QU. *T:* Madingley (01954) 210961. *Club:* Cambridge Univ. Rugby Union Football.

STEWART, James (Maitland), DFC with 2 oak leaf clusters (US); Air Medal with 3 oak leaf clusters; DSM (US); actor, stage and film; *b* Indiana, Pa, 20 May 1908; *s* of Alexander Maitland Stewart and Elizabeth Ruth (*née* Jackson); *m* 1949, Gloria McLean; two *s* twin *d*. *Educ:* Mercersburg Academy, Pa; Princeton University (BS Arch.). War Service, 1942–45: Lt-Col Air Corps; Europe, 1943–45 (Air Medal, DFC); Colonel, 1945. USAF Reserve; Brig.-Gen. 1959. Dir, Air Force Assoc. First New York appearance, Carry Nation, 1932; subseq. played in Goodbye Again, Spring in Autumn, All Good Americans, Yellow Jack, Divided by Three, Page Miss Glory, A Journey by Night. Entered films, 1935; *films include:* Murder Man, Next Time We Love, Seventh Heaven, You Can't Take It With You, Made for Each Other, Vivacious Lady, The Shopworn Angel, Mr Smith Goes to Washington, Destry Rides Again, No Time for Comedy, Philadelphia Story, The Shop around the Corner, Pot o' Gold, Ziegfeld Girl, Come Live with Me, It's a Wonderful Life, Magic Town, On Our Merry Way, You Gotta Stay Happy, Call Northside 777, Rope, The Stratton Story, Malaya, The Jackpot, Harvey, Winchester '73, Broken Arrow, No Highway in the Sky, Bend of the River, Carbine Williams, The Greatest Show on Earth, Thunder Bay, Naked Spur, The Glenn Miller Story, Rear Window, The Man from Laramie, The Far Country, Strategic Air Command, The Man Who Knew Too Much, Night Passage, Spirit of St Louis, Midnight Story, Vertigo, Bell, Book and Candle, Anatomy of a Murder, The FBI Story, The Mountain Road, The Man Who Shot Liberty Valance, Mr Hobbs Takes a Vacation, Take her, She's Mine, Cheyenne Autumn, Shenandoah, The Rare Breed, Firecreek, Bandalero, The Cheyenne Social Club, Fool's Parade, Dynamite Man from Glory Jail, The Shootist, Airport 77, The Big Sleep, Magic of Lassie. *Play:* Harvey (Broadway), 1970, (Prince of Wales), 1975. Holds many awards including: five Academy Award nominations; Oscar award as best actor of the year; Hon. Oscar Award; two NY Film Critics best actor awards; Venice Film Festival best actor award; France's Victoire Trophy for best actor; Screen Actors Guild award. Hon. degrees include: DLitt, Pennsylvania; MA, Princeton. *Address:* 9201 Wilshire Boulevard, Suite 204, Beverly Hills, CA 90210, USA.

STEWART, Sir (James) Moray, KCB 1995 (CB 1990); Second Permanent Under Secretary of State, Ministry of Defence, since 1990; *b* 21 June 1938; third *s* of James and Evelyn Stewart; *m* 1963, Dorothy May Batey, *o d* of Alan and Maud Batey; three *s*. *Educ:* Marlborough Coll.; Univ. of Keele (BA First Cl. Hons History and Econs). Sec., Univ. of Keele Union, 1960–61. Breakdown and Information Service Operator, AA, 1956–57; Asst Master, Northcliffe Sch., Bognor Regis, 1957–58; Asst Principal, Air Min., 1962–65; Private Sec. to 2nd Permanent Under Sec. of State (RAF), MoD, 1965–66; Principal, MoD, 1966–70; First Sec. (Defence), UK Delegn to NATO, 1970–73; Asst Sec., MoD, 1974–75; Private Sec. to successive Secs of State for NI, 1975–77; Dir, Naval Manpower Requirements, MoD, 1977; Dir, Defence Policy Staff, MoD, 1978–80; Asst Under Sec. of State, MoD, 1980–84; Asst Sec. Gen. for Defence Planning and Policy, NATO, 1984–86; Dep. Under Sec. of State, Personnel and Logistics, 1986–88, Defence

Procurement, 1988–90, MoD. Comr, Royal Hosp. Chelsea, 1986–88; Trustee, Imperial War Museum, 1986–88; Mem. Council, RUSI, 1988–92. Chm., Civil Service Medical Aid Assoc., 1993–. Vice Pres., Civil Service RFU, 1993–. Trustee, Pegasus Trust, 1993–. *Recreations:* reading, listening to music, walking. *Address:* Ministry of Defence, Whitehall, SW1A 2HB. *Club:* Royal Over-Seas League.

STEWART, James Robertson, CBE 1971 (OBE 1964); Principal, University of London, 1978–83; *b* 1917; *s* of James and Isabella Stewart; *m* 1941, Grace Margaret Kirsop (*d* 1992); two *s* one *d*. *Educ:* Perth Acad.; Whitley and Monkseaton High Sch.; Armstrong Coll. (later King's Coll.), Newcastle, Univ. of Durham. BA Dunelm (1st cl. hons Mod. History) 1937; DThPT (1st cl.) 1938; research in Canada (Canada Co.), 1938–39; awarded Holland Rose Studentship, Cambridge, and William Black Noble Fellowship, Durham, 1939; admitted to Christ's Coll., Cambridge, 1939; MA Dunelm 1941. Served Army, 1939–46: Royal Artillery (BEF); Combined Ops HQ; Directorate of Combined Ops, India and SE Asia; Major (Actg Lt-Col); Certif. of Good Service. Dep. Clerk of Court, Univ. of London, 1946–49, Clerk of Court, 1950–82. Dir, Charterhouse Venture Fund Management, 1984–94. Member, governing bodies: RPMS, 1983–89; Sch. of Pharmacy, London Univ., 1983– (Hon. Treas.); Wye Coll., 1983–91; Inst. of Educn, 1983–93; RVC, 1983– (Hon. Treas.); LSE, 1984–89; Brunel Univ., 1984–89; Inst. of Germanic Studies, 1984–92 (Chm.); Roedean Sch., 1984–; Sussex Univ., 1985–; Westfield Coll., London, 1985–89. Hon. Fellow: KCL, 1982; Sch. of Pharmacy, London Univ., 1982; Birkbeck Coll., London, 1982; LSE, 1982; UCL, 1982; Wye Coll., 1987; Queen Mary and Westfield Coll., London, 1989 (Westfield Coll., 1981); Inst. of Germanic Studies, 1993. Hon. LLD: London, 1983; Western Ontario, 1984. Symons Medal, ACU, 1983; Betts Prize, RVC, 1994. *Recreations:* military history, gardening, watching soccer and cricket. *Address:* 2 Hilltop, Dyke Road Avenue, Brighton, Sussex BN1 5LY. *T:* Brighton (01273) 551039. *Club:* Athenæum.

STEWART, James Simeon Hamilton, QC 1982; barrister; a Recorder of the Crown Court, since 1982; *b* 2 May 1943; *s* of late Henry Hamilton Stewart, MD, FRCS and of Edna Mary Hamilton Stewart; *m* 1972, Helen Margaret Whiteley; two *d*. *Educ:* Cheltenham Coll.; Univ. of Leeds (LLB Hons). Called to the Bar, Inner Temple, 1966, Bencher, 1992; a Dep. High Court Judge, 1993–. *Recreations:* cricket, golf, gardening. *Address:* 40 Park Cross Street, Leeds LS1 2QH. *Clubs:* Bradford (Bradford); Leeds Taverners (Leeds).

STEWART, (John) Allan; MP (C) Eastwood, since 1983 (East Renfrewshire, 1979–83); *b* 1 June 1942; *s* of Edward MacPherson Stewart and Eadie Barrie Stewart; *m* 1973, Marjorie Sally (Susie); one *s* one *d*. *Educ:* Bell Baxter High Sch., Cupar; St Andrews Univ. (1st Cl. Hons MA 1964); Harvard Univ. (Rotary Internat. Foundn Fellow, 1964–65). Lectr in Polit. Economy, St Andrews Univ., 1965–70 (Warden, John Burnet Hall, 1968–70); Confederation of British Industry: Head of Regional Develt Dept, 1971–73; Dep. Dir (Econs), 1973–76; Scottish Sec., 1976–78; Scottish Dir, 1978–79. Conservative Parly Candidate, Dundee E, 1970; Councillor, London Bor. of Bromley, 1975–76. PPS to Minister of State for Energy, 1981; Parly Under-Sec. of State, Scottish Office, 1981–86 and 1990–95. Mem., Select Cttee on Scottish Affairs, 1979–81 (Mem., Deregulation Cttee, 1995–). *Publications:* articles in academic and gen. pubns on econ. and polit. affairs. *Recreations:* bridge, hedgehogs. *Address:* House of Commons, SW1A 1AA. *T:* 0171–219 5110.

STEWART, Rt. Rev. John Craig; Assistant Bishop, diocese of Melbourne, since 1984; *b* 10 Aug. 1940; *s* of J. J. Stewart; *m* 1967, Janine (*née* Schahinger); two *s*. *Educ:* Newington Coll., Sydney; Wesley Coll., Melbourne; Ridley Theol Coll., Melbourne. Ordained: deacon, 1965; priest, 1966; Curate, S Australia, 1965–68; Asst Priest, St John's, Crawley, 1968–70; Vicar: St Aidan's, Parkdale, 1970–74; St Luke's, Frankston, 1974–79; Gen. Sec., Church Missionary Soc., Victoria, 1979–84. *Recreations:* music, genealogy, reading. *Address:* St Paul's Cathedral Building, Flinders Lane, Melbourne, Vic 3000, Australia.

STEWART, John Hall; Sheriff of South Strathclyde Dumfries and Galloway at Airdrie, since 1985; *b* 15 March 1944; *s* of Cecil Francis Wilson Stewart and Mary Fyfe Hall or Stewart; *m* 1968, Marion MacCalman; one *s* two *d*. *Educ:* Airdrie Acad.; St Andrews Univ. (LLB). Advocate. Enrolled solicitor, 1970–77; Mem. Faculty of Advocates, 1978–. *Recreations:* golf, spectator sports, his children. *Address:* 3 Fife Crescent, Bothwell, Glasgow G71 8DG. *T:* Bothwell (01698) 853854. *Club:* Uddingston Rugby (Past Pres.), Uddingston Cricket and Sports (Pres.).

STEWART, Sir (John) Simon (Watson), 6th Bt *cr* 1920, of Balgownie; MD, FRCP, FRCR; Consultant in Clinical Oncology at St Mary's Hospital and The Royal Postgraduate Medical School, since 1989; *b* 5 July 1955; *s* of Sir John Keith Watson Stewart, 5th Bt and of Mary Elizabeth, *d* of John Francis Moxon; *S* father, 1990; *m* 1978, Dr Catherine Stewart, *d* of H. Gordon Bond; one *s* one *d*. *Educ:* Uppingham Sch.; Charing Cross Hosp. Med. Sch. BSc (1st cl. Hons) 1977; MB BS Lond. 1980; MRCP 1983, FRCP 1994; FRCR 1986; MD 1989. Mem., Cavalhead Soc., 1978–. *Heir: s* John Hamish Watson Stewart, *b* 12 Dec. 1983. *Address:* 38 Dukes Avenue, Chiswick, W4 2AE. *T:* 0181–995 2213. *Club:* Oriental.

STEWART, John Young, (Jackie Stewart), OBE 1972; racing driver, retired 1973; developed Gleneagles Jackie Stewart Shooting School; Chairman, Paul Stewart Racing Team, since 1989; *b* 11 June 1939; *s* of late Robert Paul Stewart and of Jean Clark Young; *m* 1962, Helen McGregor; two *s*. *Educ:* Dumbarton Academy. First raced, 1961; competed in 4 meetings, 1961–62, driving for Barry Filer, Glasgow; drove for Ecurie Ecosse and Barry Filer, winning 14 out of 23 starts, 1963; 28 wins out of 53 starts, 1964; drove Formula 1 for BRM, 1965–67 and for Ken Tyrrell, 1968–73; has won Australian, New Zealand, Swedish, Mediterranean, Japanese and many other non-championship, major internat. Motor Races; set up new world record by winning his 26th World Championship Grand Prix (Zandvoort), July 1973, and 27th (Nurburgring), Aug. 1973; 3rd in World Championship, 1965; 2nd in 1968 and 1972; World Champion, 1969, 1971, 1973. BARC Gold Medal, 1971, 1973. Daily Express Sportsman of the Year, 1971, 1973; BBC Sports Personality of the Year, 1973; Scottish Sportsman of the Year, 1973; US Sportsman of the Year, 1973; Segrave Trophy, 1973. Hon. Dr Automotive Engrg, Lawrence Inst. of Technology, Mich, USA, 1986; DUniv Glasgow Caledonian, 1993. *Film:* Weekend of a Champion, 1972. *Publications:* World Champion, 1970 (with Eric Dymock); Faster!, 1972 (with Peter Manso); On the Road, 1983; Jackie Stewart's Principles of Performance Driving, 1986; The Jackie Stewart Book of Shooting, 1991. *Recreations:* golf, fishing, tennis, shooting (Mem. British Team for Clay Pigeon shooting; former Scottish, English, Irish, Welsh and British Champion; won Coupe des Nations, 1959 and 1960; reserve for two-man team, 1960 Olympics). *Address:* 24 route de Divonne, 1260 Nyon, Switzerland. *T:* Geneva (22) 3610152, *Fax:* (22) 3621096. *Clubs:* (Hon.) Royal Automobile, British Racing Drivers' (Vice-Pres.); (Hon.) Royal Scottish Automobile; (Pres.) Scottish Motor Racing (Duns); Royal and Ancient (St Andrews); Prestwick Golf; Geneva Golf.

STEWART, Kenneth Albert; Member (Lab) Merseyside West, European Parliament, since 1984; *b* Liverpool, 28 July 1925; *m* 1946, Margaret Robertson Vass; one *s* two *d*. *Educ:* local schs. Parachute Regt (Sgt). Former joiner. Former Member: Merseyside CC; Liverpool CC (Chm., Housing Cttee); former Chm. and Sec., Liverpool West Derby Labour Party. *Address:* 62 Ballantyne Road, Liverpool L13 9AL.

STEWART, Kenneth Hope, PhD; Director of Research, Meteorological Office, 1976–82; *b* 29 March 1922; *s* of Harry Sinclair Stewart and Nora Hassan Parry; *m* 1950, Hilary Guest (*d* 1993); four *s* four *d*. *Educ:* Trinity Coll., Cambridge (MA, PhD). Entered Meteorol Office, 1949; Dep. Dir, Physical Res., 1974. *Publications:* Ferromagnetic Domains, 1951; contrib. physical and meteorol jls. *Address:* 19 Harston Road, Newton, Cambridge CB2 5PA.

STEWART, Hon. Kevin James, AO 1989; Director, KJ Consulting Services, since 1989; Consultant, United Health Serv Pty Ltd, Sydney, since 1989; *b* 20 Sept. 1928; *m* 1952, Jean, *d* of late F. I. Keating; two *s* five *d*. *Educ:* Christian Brothers School, Lewisham, NSW; De La Salle College, NSW. Officer, NSW Govt Rlys, 1944–62 (Regional Pres., Aust. Transport Officers' Assoc. and Fedn, 1959–62). MLA for Canterbury, NSW, 1962–85; Exec., NSW Parly Labor Party and Spokesman on Health Matters, 1967; NSW State Exec., Aust. Labor Party, 1968; Minister, NSW: for Health, 1976–81; for Youth and Community Services, 1981–83; for Mineral Resources, 1983–84; for Local Govt, 1984–85. Mem., Labor Transport Cttee, 1965–76; Chm., Labor Health Cttee, 1968–76; Mem., Jt Cttee, Legislative Council upon Drugs. Agent General for NSW in UK, 1986–88. Life Mem., British-Australia Soc., 1988. Chm., Bd of Canterbury Hosp., 1955–76 (Dir, 1954). FRSA 1988. Freeman, City of London, 1987. Hon. Citizen of Tokyo, Japan, 1985. *Recreations:* supporter of community services, Rugby Football League, swimming, bowls. *Address:* 44 Chalmers Street, Belmore, NSW 2192, Australia. *T:* (2) 7597777. *Clubs:* International Nippon-Australia, Canterbury Bankstown League (Patron) (Sydney).

STEWART, Mary (Florence Elinor), (Lady Stewart); *b* 17 Sept. 1916; *d* of Rev. Frederick A. Rainbow, Durham Diocese, and Mary Edith (*née* Matthews), NZ; *m* 1945, Sir Frederick Henry Stewart, *qv*; no *c*. *Educ:* Eden Hall, Penrith, Cumberland; Skellfield School, Ripon, Yorks; St Hild's Coll., Durham Univ. BA 1938; MA 1941. Asst Lectr in English, Durham Univ., 1941–45; Part-time Lectr in English, St Hild's Training Coll., Durham, and Durham Univ., 1948–56. Hon. Fellow, Newnham Coll., Cambridge, 1986. *Publications: novels:* Madam, Will You Talk?, 1954; Wildfire at Midnight, 1956; Thunder on the Right, 1957; Nine Coaches Waiting, 1958; My Brother Michael, 1959; The Ivy Tree, 1961; The Moonspinners, 1962; This Rough Magic, 1964; Airs Above the Ground, 1965; The Gabriel Hounds, 1967; The Wind Off The Small Isles, 1968; The Crystal Cave, 1970 (Frederick Niven Award); The Little Broomstick, 1971; The Hollow Hills, 1973; Ludo and the Star Horse, 1974 (Scottish Arts Council Award); Touch Not the Cat, 1976; The Last Enchantment, 1979; A Walk in Wolf Wood, 1980; The Wicked Day, 1983; Thornyhold, 1988; Frost on the Window and Other Poems, 1990; Stormy Petrel, 1991; The Prince and the Pilgrim, 1995; also articles, radio plays. *Recreations:* gardening, music, painting. *Address:* 79 Morningside Park, Edinburgh EH10 5EZ. *T:* 0131–447 2620.

STEWART, Very Rev. Maurice Evan; Dean of St Patrick's Cathedral, Dublin, since 1991; *b* 8 Jan. 1929; *s* of Robert Carlisle and Annie Stewart; *m* 1965, Wendy Margaret McConnell; two *d*. *Educ:* Royal Belfast Academical Instn; Trinity Coll., Dublin (MA 1953; BD 1967); Queen's Univ., Belfast (PhD 1975). Ordained: deacon, 1952; priest, 1953; Curate, St James, Belfast, 1952–55; Chaplain, Bishop's Coll., Cheshunt, 1955–58; Head of TCD Mission in Belfast, 1958–61; Rector of Newcastle, Co. Down, 1961–69; Lectr, C of I Theol Coll., 1969–91; Lectr in Divinity, TCD, 1973–91; St Patrick's Cathedral, Dublin: Chancellor, 1980–89; Precentor, 1989–91. *Recreations:* Anglican theology, Swiftiana. *Address:* The Deanery, St Patrick's Close, Dublin 8. *T:* Dublin (1) 4543428. *Clubs:* Kildare Street and University, Friendly Brothers of St Patrick (Dublin).

STEWART, Michael James; Reader in Political Economy, University College, London University, 1969–94; *b* 6 Feb. 1933; *s* of late John Innes Mackintosh Stewart; *m* 1962, Frances Kaldor, *d* of Baron Kaldor, FBA; one *s* two *d* (and one *d* decd). *Educ:* Campbell Coll., Belfast; St Edward's Sch., Oxford; Magdalen Coll., Oxford. 1st cl. PPE (Oxon), 1955. Asst Res. Officer, Oxford Univ. Inst. of Statistics, 1955–56; Barnett Fellow, Cornell Univ., 1956–57; Econ. Asst, HM Treasury, 1957–60; Sec. to Council on Prices, Productivity and Incomes, 1960–61; Econ. Adviser, HM Treasury, 1961–62, Cabinet Office, 1964–67 (Senior Econ. Advr, 1967), Kenya Treasury, 1967–69; Special Adviser to Sec. of State for Trade, Apr.–Oct. 1974; Economic Adviser to Malta Labour Party, 1970–73; Special Econ. Advr to Foreign Sec., 1977–78. Guest Scholar, Brookings Instn, Washington, DC, 1978–79. Mem., Acad. Adv. Panel, Bank of England, 1977–83. Contested (Lab): Folkestone and Hythe, 1964; Croydon North-West, 1966. Asst Editor, Nat. Inst. Econ. Review, 1962–64. Consultant to various UN agencies, 1971–. *Publications:* Keynes and After, 1967; The Jekyll and Hyde Years: politics and economic policy since 1964, 1977; Controlling the Economic Future: policy dilemmas in a shrinking world, 1983; (with Peter Jay) Apocalypse 2000: economic breakdown and the suicide of democracy 1989–2000, 1987; Keynes in the 1990s: a return to economic sanity, 1993. *Recreations:* looking at paintings, eating in restaurants. *Address:* 79 South Hill Park, NW3 2SS. *T:* 0171–435 3686. *Club:* United Oxford & Cambridge University.

STEWART, Sir Moray; *see* Stewart, Sir J. M.

STEWART, Dame Muriel (Acadia), DBE 1968; Headmistress, Northumberland LEA, 1940–70; *b* 22 Oct. 1905; *d* of late James Edmund Stewart. *Educ:* Gateshead Grammar Sch.; Durham Univ. BA Hons 1926; MA 1929. Teacher: Newcastle upon Tyne, 1927–29; Northumberland, 1929–70 (a headteacher of Secondary Schools, 1940–69); Headmistress, Shiremoor Middle School, 1969–70. Nat. Pres., Nat. Union of Teachers, 1964–65; Chm., Schools Council, 1969–72. Vice-Chm., Bullock Cttee, 1972–74. Pres., Lib Dem Nat. Educn Assoc., 1991–. Hon. MEd Newcastle Univ., 1965. *Recreation:* music. *Address:* 102 Great North Road, Gosforth, Newcastle upon Tyne NE3 5JP. *T:* 0191–285 9902.

STEWART, Nicholas John Cameron; QC 1987; *b* 16 April 1947; *s* of John Cameron Stewart and Margaret Mary (*née* Botsford); *m* 1974, Pamela Jean Windham; one *s* two *d*. *Educ:* Bedford Modern Sch.; Worcester Coll., Oxford (BA). CDipAF. Called to the Bar, Inner Temple, 1971; a Dep. High Ct Judge, Chancery Div., 1991–. Chm., Bar Human Rights Cttee, 1994–. Narrator, No Further Questions?, BBC Radio series, 1993. 1995. *Recreations:* walking, Spain. *Address:* 4 New Square, Lincoln's Inn, WC2A 3RJ. *T:* 0171–404 3800, *Fax:* 0171–404 3900.

STEWART, Norman MacLeod; Senior Partner, Allan, Black & McCaskie; President, The Law Society of Scotland, May 1985–86; *b* 2 Dec. 1934; *s* of George and Elspeth Stewart; *m* 1959, Mary Slater Campbell; four *d*. *Educ:* Elgin Acad.; Univ. of Edinburgh (BL); SSC. Alex. Morison & Co., WS, Edinburgh, 1954–58; Allan, Black & McCaskie, Solicitors, Elgin, 1959–; Partner, 1961–. Law Society of Scotland: Mem. Council, 1976–87; Convener: Public Relations Cttee, 1979–81; Professional Practice Cttee, 1981–84; Vice-Pres., 1984–85. Chm., Elgin and Lossiemouth Harbour Bd, 1993–. Hon. Mem., American Bar Assoc., 1985–. *Recreations:* walking, golf, music, Spanish culture. *Address:* Argyll Lodge, Lossiemouth, Moray IV31 6QT. *T:* Lossiemouth (0134381) 3150. *Club:* New (Edinburgh).

STEWART, Lt-Col Robert Alexander, DSO 1993; Commanding Officer, 1st Battalion The Cheshire Regiment, since 1991; *b* 7 July 1949; *s* of late Sqdn Leader A. A. Stewart, MC and Marguerita Joan Stewart; *m* 1st (marr. diss. 1993); one *s* one *d*; 2nd, 1994, Claire Podbielski. *Educ:* Chigwell Sch.; RMA Sandhurst; Univ. of Wales, Aberystwyth (BSc 1st Cl. Hons Internat. Politics). Commnd, Cheshire Regt, 1969; Instructor, RMA, 1979–80; Army Staff Coll., 1981; Company Comdr, N Ireland, 1982–83; Staff Officer, MoD, 1984–85; 2 i/c 1st Bn Cheshire Regt, 1986–87; JSSC 1988; MA to Chm., NATO Mil. Cttee, HQ NATO, Brussels, 1989–91; UK, Germany, 1991–; Bosnia, 1991–92. *Publication:* Broken Lives, 1993. *Recreations:* painting, sub aqua, swimming. *Address:* c/o Royal Bank of Scotland, 51 Park Green, Macclesfield, Cheshire SK11 7NH. *Club:* Army and Navy.

STEWART, Lt-Col Robert Christie, CBE 1983; TD 1962; Lord Lieutenant of Clackmannan, since 1994; *b* 3 Aug. 1926; *m* 1953, Ann Grizel Cochrane; three *s* two *d*. *Educ:* Eton; University College, Oxford. Lt Scots Guards, 1945–49. Oxford Univ., 1949–51 (BA Agric.). TA, 7 Argyll and Sutherland Highlanders, 1948–66; Lt-Col Comdg 7 A & SH, 1963–66. Hon. Col, 1/51 Highland Volunteers, 1972–75. Chm. and Pres., Bd of Governors, E of Scotland Coll. of Agric., 1970–83. Lord-Lieutenant, Kinross-shire, 1966–74. DL Kinross 1956, VL 1958; Chairman Kinross County Council, 1963–73. *Address:* Arndean, by Dollar, Clackmannanshire FK14 7NH. *T:* Dollar (01259) 742527. *Club:* Royal Perth Golfing Society.

STEWART, Dr Robert William, OC 1979; FRS 1970; FRSC 1967; Adjunct Professor, School of Earth and Ocean Sciences, University of Victoria, since 1989; Hon. Professor of Physics and Oceanography, University of British Columbia, since 1971; Hon. Professor of Science, University of Alberta, since 1985; *b* 21 Aug. 1923; *m* 1st, 1948, V. Brande (marr. diss. 1972); two *s* one *d*; 2nd, 1973, Anne-Marie Robert; one *s*. *Educ:* Queen's Univ., Ontario. BSc 1945, MSc 1947, Queen's; PhD Cantab 1952. Canadian Defence Research Bd, 1950–61; Prof. of Physics and Oceanography, Univ. of British Columbia, 1961–70; Dir, Marine Scis Br., Pacific Reg., Environment Canada, 1970–74; Dir-Gen., Ocean and Aquatic Scis, Pacific Reg., Fisheries and Marine Service, Dept of Fisheries and Oceans, Canada, 1974–79; Dep. Minister, Ministry of Univs, Science and Communications, BC, Canada, 1979–84; Pres., Alberta Res. Council, 1984–87; Dir, Centre for Earth and Ocean Res., Univ. of Victoria, 1987–89. Vis. Professor: Dalhousie Univ., 1960–61; Harvard Univ., 1964; Pennsylvania State Univ., 1964; Commonwealth Vis. Prof., Cambridge Univ., 1967–68. Vice-Chm., 1968–72, Chm., 1972–76, Jt Organizing Cttee, Global Atmospheric Res. Program; Pres., Internat. Assoc. of Physical Scis of Ocean, 1975–79; Mem., Cttee on Climatic Changes and the Ocean, 1980–92 (Chm., 1983–87); Vice Chm., Sci. Cttee for Internat. Geosphere-Biosphere Prog., 1991–94. *Publications:* numerous, on turbulence, oceanography and meteorology. *Address:* School of Earth and Ocean Studies, University of Victoria, PO Box 1700, Victoria, British Columbia V8W 2Y2, Canada.

STEWART, Sir Robertson (Huntly), Kt 1979; CBE 1970; CEng, FIProdE, FPRI, FNZIM, FInstD; Executive Chairman: PDL Holdings Ltd (manufacturers of electrical and plastic products), since 1982 (Chairman and Managing Director, 1957–82); PDL (Asia), since 1975; *b* 21 Sept. 1913; *s* of Robert McGregor Stewart and Ivy Emily (*née* Grigg); *m* 1st, 1937, Ada Gladys Gunter; two *s* one *d*; 2nd, 1970, Ellen Adrienne Cansdale; two *s*. *Educ:* Christchurch Boys' High Sch.; Christchurch Technical Inst. CEng, FIEE (FIProdE 1967); FPRI 1960; FNZIM 1962; FInstD 1970. Introd plastics industry to NZ, 1936; commenced manuf. of electrical products in NZ, 1937; estabd PDL Gp of Cos, 1947. Led NZ Trade Missions, 1962, 1964, 1966, 1967, 1970 and 1972. Pres., NZ Manufrs Fedn, 1963–64. Hon. Malaysian Consul. *Recreations:* motor racing, tennis, fishing. *Address:* 127 Scarborough Road, Sumner, Christchurch, New Zealand. *T:* Christchurch (3) 3265213. *Club:* Canterbury (Christchurch).

STEWART, Robin Milton, QC 1978; a Recorder of the Crown Court, since 1978; *b* 5 Aug. 1938; *s* of late Brig. Guy Milton Stewart and of Dr Elaine Oenone Stewart, MD, BS; *m* 1962, Lynda Grace Medhurst; three *s*. *Educ:* Winchester; New Coll., Oxford (MA). Called to the Bar, Middle Temple, 1963, Bencher, 1988; called to the Irish Bar, King's Inns, Dublin, 1975. Prosecuting Counsel to Inland Revenue, NE Circuit, 1976–78. Freeman, City of London, 1966; Liveryman, Co. of Glaziers, 1966. *Recreations:* pictures, gardening, Scottish family history. *Address:* 199 Strand, WC2R 1DR. *T:* 0171–379 9779; Little Chart, 46 Oak Hill Road, Sevenoaks, Kent TN13 1NS. *T:* Sevenoaks (01732) 453475. *Club:* Oriental.

STEWART, Sir Ronald (Compton), 2nd Bt, *cr* 1937; DL; Chairman, London Brick Co. Ltd, 1966–79; *b* 14 Aug. 1903; *s* of Sir (Percy) Malcolm Stewart, 1st Bt, OBE, and Cordelia (*d* 1906,) *d* of late Rt Hon. Sir Joseph Compton Rickett, DL, MP; *S* father, 1951; *m* 1936, Cynthia, OBE, JP (*d* 1987), *d* of Harold Farmiloe. *Educ:* Rugby; Jesus College, Cambridge. High Sheriff of Bedfordshire, 1954, DL 1974. *Heir:* none. *Address:* Maulden Grange, Maulden, Bedfordshire MK45 2AU.

STEWART, Sir Simon; *see* Stewart, Sir J. S. W.

STEWART, Suzanne Freda; *see* Norwood, S. F.

STEWART, Theresa; Member (Lab), since 1970, and Leader, since 1993, Birmingham City Council; *b* 24 Aug. 1930; *d* of John Raisman and Ray Raisman (*née* Baker); *m* 1953, John Stewart; two *s* two *d*. *Educ:* Cowper Street Sch., Leeds; Allerton High Sch., Leeds; Somerville Coll., Oxford (MA). Member: Birmingham Regl Hosp. Bd, 1968–71; W Midland CC, 1974–77; Birmingham City Council: Chair: Birmingham Community Develt Project, 1973–76; Social Services Cttee, 1981–82 and 1984–87; Direct Labour Contract Services Cttee, 1989–93; Finance and Management Cttee. Vice-Chm., AMA Social Services Cttee, 1985–87. Chm., Assoc. of Direct Labour Orgns, 1994–95. *Recreations:* relaxing in a hot bath with a good book, walking, cooking. *Address:* 15 Selly Wick Road, Birmingham B29 7JJ. *T:* 0121–472 1512.

STEWART, Victor Colvin, FCA; Registrar General for Scotland, 1978–82; *b* 12 April 1921; *s* of Victor Stewart and Jean Cameron; *m* 1949, Aileen Laurie; one *s*. *Educ:* Selkirk High Sch.; Edinburgh Univ. (BCom). FCA 1954. Served War in RAF, Africa and ME, 1942–46. Joined Dept of Health for Scotland, 1938; Chief Exec. Officer, 1959; Principal, SHHD, 1963, Asst Sec. 1971; Dep. Registrar Gen. for Scotland, 1976. *Recreations:* golf, walking, bridge. *Address:* Tynet, Lodgehill Road, Nairn IV12 4QL. *T:* Nairn (01667) 452050. *Club:* Commonwealth Trust.

STEWART, Dr William, CB 1977; DSc; aerospace consultant, 1983–94; *b* Hamilton, 29 Aug. 1921; *m* 1955, Helen Cairney; two *d*. *Educ:* St John's Grammar Sch.; Hamilton Acad.; Glasgow Univ. BSc Hons (engin.); DSc 1958. RAE, Farnborough, 1942–53; British Jt Services Mission, Washington, 1953–56; Dep. Head of Naval Air Dept, RAE, Bedford, 1956–63; Imperial Defence College, 1964; Asst Dir, Project Time and Cost Analysis, 1965–66; Dir, Anglo-French Combat Trainer Aircraft Projects, 1966–70; Dir-Gen., Multi-Role Combat Aircraft, 1970–73; Dep. Controller, Aircraft A, 1973–78, Aircraft, 1978–81, MoD (PE). Silver Medal, RAeS, 1981. *Address:* 25 Brickhill Drive, Bedford MK41 7QA.

STEWART, Prof. (William Alexander) Campbell, MA, PhD; DL; Vice-Chancellor, University of Keele, 1967–79; *b* Glasgow, 17 Dec. 1915; *s* of late Thomas Stewart, Glasgow, and Helen Fraser, Elgin, Morayshire; *m* 1947, Ella Elizabeth Burnett, of Edinburgh; one *s* one *d*. *Educ:* Colfe's Grammar Sch., London; University Coll., and Inst. of Education, Univ. of London. Exhibitioner, University Coll., London., 1934–37; BA 1937; MA 1941; PhD 1947; Diploma in Education, 1938; Fellow, UCL, 1975. Sen. English Master: and Housemaster, Friends' School, Saffron Walden, Essex, 1938–43; Abbotsholme School, Derbyshire, 1943–44 (Member of Governing Body, 1960–80; Chm., Council, 1974–80); Asst Lectr and Lectr in Education, University Coll., Nottingham, 1944–47; Lectr in Education, Univ. of Wales (Cardiff), 1947–50; Prof. of Education, Univ. of Keele (formerly UC of N Staffs), 1950–67, Prof. Emeritus, 1979. Vis. Prof., McGill Univ., 1957, Univ. of Calif., Los Angeles 1959; Simon Vis. Prof., Univ. of Manchester, 1962–63; Prestige Fellow, NZ Univs, 1969; Hon. Vis. Professorial Fellow, 1979–84, Privy Council Mem. of Univ. Court, 1980–, Univ. of Sussex. Chairman: YMCA Educn Cttee, 1962–67; Nat. Adv. Council for Child Care, 1968–71; Univs Council for Adult Educn, 1969–73; Council, Roehampton Inst. of Higher Educn, 1979–88 (Fellow, 1988); Member: Inter-Univ. and Polytech. Council for Higher Education Overseas; Commonwealth Univ. Interchange Council, 1968–80; Adv. Council, Supply and Training of Teachers, 1974–78; US-UK Educnl Commn, 1977–81; Council: Univ. of Sierra Leone, 1968–83; Open Univ., 1973–80. Fellow, Internat. Inst. of Art and Letters. DL Stafford, 1973. Hon. DLitt: Ulster, 1973; Keele, 1981. *Publications:* Quakers and Education, 1953; (ed with J. Eros) Systematic Sociology of Karl Mannheim, 1957; (with K. Mannheim) An Introduction to the Sociology of Education, 1962; contrib. to The American College (ed Sanford), 1962; The Educational Innovators, Vol. 1, with W. P. McCann, 1967, Vol. 2, 1968; Progressives and Radicals in English Education 1750–1970, 1972; Higher Education in Postwar Britain, 1989. *Recreations:* talking and listening, theatre, music. *Address:* Flat 4, 74 Westgate, Chichester, West Sussex PO19 3HH. *T:* Chichester (01243) 785528. *Clubs:* Oriental; Federation House (Stoke on Trent).

STEWART, Sir William (Duncan Paterson), Kt 1994; PhD, DSc; FRS 1977; FRSE; Chief Scientific Adviser, Cabinet Office, 1990–95, and Head of Office of Science and Technology, 1992–95; Deputy Chairman, Council for Science and Technology, 1993–95; *b* 7 June 1935; *s* of John Stewart and Margaret (*née* Paterson); *m* 1958, Catherine MacLeod; one *s*. *Educ:* Bowmore Junior Secondary Sch., Isle-of-Islay; Dunoon Grammar Sch.; Glasgow Univ. (BSc, PhD, DSc). FRSE 1973. Asst Lectr, Univ. of Nottingham, 1961–63; Lectr, Westfield Coll., Univ. of London, 1963–68; University of Dundee: Hd of Dept of Biol Scis, 1968–83; Boyd Baxter Prof. of Biology, 1968–; Vice-Principal, 1985–87; Sec. and Chief Exec., AFRC, 1988–90. Vis. Res. Worker, Univ. of Wisconsin, 1966 and 1968; Vis. Professor: Univ. of Kuwait, 1980; Univ. of Otago, 1984. Chairman: Royal Soc. Biological Educn Cttee, 1977–80; Sci. Adv. Cttee, Freshwater Biol. Assoc., 1974–85; Royal Soc. Study Group on Nitrogen Cycle, 1979–84; Internat. Cttee on Microbial Ecology, 1983–86 (Sec., 1980–83); Royal Soc. Biotechnology and Educn Wkg Gp, 1980–81; Independent Adv. Gp on Gruinard Is., 1985–87; Vice-Pres., 1973–75, Pres., 1975–77, British Phycological Soc.; President: Section K, BAAS, 1984; Council, Scottish Marine Biol. Assoc., 1985–87 (Mem., 1969–74, 1982–); Vice-Pres., Freshwater Biol. Assoc., 1984–. Trustee, Estuarine and Brackish-Water Sciences Assoc., 1978–88. Member: Council, RSE, 1976–79; Council, Marine Biol. Assoc., 1973–76, 1977–80, 1981–84; Plants and Soils Res. Grants Bd, ARC, 1978–84; British Nat. Cttee for problems of environment, Royal Soc., 1979–85; UNESCO Panel on Microbiology, 1975–81; Council, NERC, 1979–85 (Chm., Aquatic Life Scis Grants Cttee, 1973–78, Marine Life Scis Preparatory Gp, 1982–85); Internat. Cell Res. Org., 1979–84; Royal Soc. Study Gp on Science Educn, 1981–82; Royal Soc. Study Gp on Pollution Control Priorities, 1987–88; Council, Royal Soc., 1984–86; Royal Commn on Environmental Pollution, 1986–88; Biol Sciences Sub-Cttee, UGC, 1988; DSAC, 1990–95. Chairman: Govt Technol. Foresight Steering Gp, 1993–; Govt Sci. and Engrg Base Co-ordinating Cttee, 1993–; Mem., DTI Link Steering Gp, 1990–94. Royal Soc. Assessor, AFRC, 1985–87; Assessor: ABRC, 1990–93 (Mem., 1988–90); ACOST, 1990–93. Member, Governing Body: Scottish Hort. Res. Inst., 1971–80; Scottish Crop Res. Inst., 1980–88; Macaulay Land Use Res. Inst., 1987–88. Lectures: Phycological Soc. of America Dist., 1977; Barton-Wright, Inst. Biol., 1977; Sir David Martin Royal Soc.-BAYS, 1979; Plenary, 2nd Internat. Symp. on Microbial Ecology, 1980; Holden, Nottingham Univ., 1983; Leeuwenhoek, Royal Soc., 1984; Plenary, 2nd Internat. Phycological Congress, Copenhagen, 1985; Diamond Jubilee, Hannah Res. Inst., 1989; Napier, 1992; Macaulay, 1992; British Geol Survey, 1993; Dainton, 1995; Bernal, Royal Soc., 1995. Fellow, QMW, 1993. Hon. DSc: Edinburgh, 1990; UEA, Glasgow, Nottingham, and Sheffield, 1991; Loughborough, Surrey and Westminster, 1992; Cranfield, Keele, 1993; Aberdeen, Buckingham, Birmingham, Sunderland, West of England, Glamorgan, 1994; Napier, Dundee, 1995; DUniv Stirling, 1991. *Publications:* Nitrogen Fixation in Plants, 1966; (jtly) The Blue-Green Algae, 1973; Algal Physiology and Biochemistry, 1974; (ed) Nitrogen Fixation by Free-living Organisms, 1975; (ed jtly) Nitrogen Fixation, 1980; (ed jtly) The Nitrogen Cycle of the United Kingdom, 1984; papers in learned jls of repute. *Recreations:* watching soccer, playing the bagpipes (occasionally). *Address:* 45 Fairfield Road, Broughty Ferry, Dundee DD5 1PL. *Clubs:* Athenæum, Farmers; Dundee United.

STEWART, William Ian; *see* Allanbridge, Hon. Lord.

STEWART-CLARK, Sir John, (Sir Jack), 3rd Bt *cr* 1918; Member (C) European Parliament, East Sussex and Kent South, since 1994 (Sussex East, 1979–94); a Vice-President, since 1992; *b* 17 Sept. 1929; *e s* of Sir Stewart Stewart-Clark, 2nd Bt, and Jane Pamela (*d* 1993), *d* of late Major Arundell Clarke; *S* father, 1971; *m* 1958, Lydia Frederike, *d* of J. W. Loudon, Holland; one *s* four *d*. *Educ:* Eton; Balliol College, Oxford; Harvard Business School. Commissioned with HM Coldstream Guards, 1948–49. Oxford, 1949–52. With J. & P. Coats Ltd, 1952–69; Managing Director: J. & P. Coats, Pakistan, Ltd, 1961–67; J. A. Carp's Garenfabrieken, Holland, 1967–69; Philips Electrical Ltd, London, 1971–75; Pye of Cambridge Ltd, 1975–79. Director: Low and Bonar plc; A. T. Kearney Ltd, 1979–92; Pioneer Concrete plc; TSB Scotland, 1986–89. Pres. Supervisory Bd, Eur. Inst. for Security, 1984–86; Mem. Council, RUSI, 1979–83. Dir and Trustee, Eur. Centre for Work and Society, 1982–; Chairman: Conf. of Regions of North Western Europe, 1986–92; Eur. Parliamentarians and Industrialists Council, 1990–. Treas., Eur. Democratic Group, 1979–92. Member Royal Company of Archers, Queen's Body Guard for Scotland. Contested (U) North Aberdeen, Gen. Election, 1959. *Publications:* Competition Law in the European Community, 1990; It's My Problem As Well: drugs prevention and education, 1993. *Recreations:* golf, tennis, photography, vintage cars. *Heir:* *s* Alexander Dudley Stewart-Clark, *b* 21 Nov. 1960. *Address:* Puckstye House, Holtye Common, Cowden, Kent TN8 7EL. *T:* Cowden (01342) 850541. *Clubs:* White's; Royal Ashdown Golf.

STEWART COX, Maj.-Gen. Arthur George Ernest, DFC 1952; General Officer Commanding Wales, 1978–80; *b* 11 April 1925; *s* of Lt-Col Arthur Stewart Cox and Mrs Dorothea Stewart Cox, *d* of Maj.-Gen. Sir Edward May; *m* 1953, Mary Pamela, *d* of Hon. George Lyttelton; three *s* one *d*. *Educ:* Marlborough Coll.; Aberdeen Univ. Commissioned RA, 1944; parachutist, RA regts, 1945–50; army pilot, Far East and Korea, 1950–52;

ADC to Comdt, RMA Sandhurst, 1954–56; Staff Coll., 1956; SO 99 Gurkha Inf. Bde, 1957–58; SO MoD, Malaya, 1963–65; CO 29 Commando Light Regt, RA, 1965–68; SO Sch. of Artillery, 1968–69; Comdr RA 4th Div., 1969–72; RCDS, 1973; Dep. Dir of Manning (Army), MoD, 1974–76. Col Comdt, RA, 1980–90; Hon. Colonel: 3rd Bn RWF, TAVR, 1980–85; 289 Commando Battery, RA, TAVR, 1983–91. *Recreations:* shooting, fishing, lepidoptery, gardening. *Address:* Long Mead, Brixton Deverill, Warminster, Wilts BA12 7EJ. *T:* Warminster (01985) 840872.

STEWART-JONES, Mrs Richard; *see* Smith, Emma.

STEWART-MOORE, Alexander Wyndham Hume; DL; Chairman, Gallaher Ltd, 1975–79 (Managing Director, 1966–75); Director, American Brands Inc., 1975–79; *b* 14 Feb. 1915; 2nd *s* of late James Stewart-Moore, DL, Ballydivity, Dervock, Co. Antrim, and of Katherine Marion (*née* Jackson); *m* 1948, Magdalene Clare, *y d* of Sir David Richard Llewellyn, 1st Bt, LLD, JP; three *s* one *d*. *Educ:* Shrewsbury. Joined Gallaher Ltd, Nov. 1934. Served War, Royal Artillery (Middle East and Italy), 1939–46. DL Co. Antrim, 1982. *Recreations:* farming, fishing, gardening. *Address:* Moyarget Farm, 98 Moyarget Road, Ballycastle, Co. Antrim, NI BT54 6HL. *T:* Ballycastle (012657) 62287.

STEWART-RICHARDSON, Sir Simon (Alaisdair), 17th Bt *cr* 1630; *b* 9 June 1947; *er s* of Sir Ian Rorie Hay Stewart-Richardson, 16th Bt, and of Audrey Meryl (who *m* 1975, P. A. P. Robertson, *qv*), *e d* of late Claude Odlum; *S* father, 1969; *m* 1990, Marilene Cabal do Nascimento; one *s* one *d*. *Educ:* Trinity College, Glenalmond. *Heir: b* Ninian Rorie Stewart-Richardson [*b* 20 Jan. 1949; *m* 1983, Joan Kristina, *d* of Howard Smee; two *s* one *d*]. *Address:* Lynedale, Longcross, near Chertsey, Surrey KT16 0DP. *T:* Ottershaw (01932) 872329.

STEWART-ROBERTS, Phyllida Katharine, OBE 1995; JP; DL; Superintendent-in-Chief, St John Ambulance Brigade, 1990–93; *b* 19 Aug. 1933; *d* of Lt-Col Walter Harold Bamfield, Royal Welch Fusiliers and Veronica Grissell; *m* 1955, Andrew Kerr Stewart-Roberts; one *s* one *d*. *Educ:* Tormead Sch.; RAM (Diploma). Primary sch. teacher, LCC, 1954–57; Love Walk Hostel for Disabled Workers: Mem., Management Cttee, 1972–; Vice Chm., 1980–83; Chm., 1983–89. Trustee: Community Service Volunteers, 1984–; Orders of St John Trust, 1994–; Member: Management Cttee, Habinteg Housing Assoc., 1988– (Chm., Southern Cttee, 1994–); St John Ambulance Brigade, Sussex, 1962–89 (County Pres., 1984–89); Chairman: Jt Cttee, Order of St John of Jerusalem and BRCS, 1991–; St John Council, Sussex, 1995–; Mem., Florence Nightingale Foundn (formerly Meml Cttee), 1990–; Pres., Love Walk, 1994–; Vice-Pres., VAD Assoc., 1991–. Mem. Council, Sussex Univ., 1995–. JP Inner London, 1980; Inner London Juvenile Panel, 1981–. DL E Sussex, 1991. DStJ 1993. *Recreations:* needlework, the gentler country pursuits. *Address:* Mount Harry Lodge, Offham, Lewes, E Sussex BN7 3QW.

STEWART-SMITH, Christopher Dudley, CBE 1995; Chairman: Healthcall Group plc, since 1991; Producer Responsibility Group, since 1994; Vice-President, Eurochambres, since 1994; *b* 21 Jan. 1941; *s* of late Ean Stewart-Smith and Edmee von Wallerstain und Marnegg; *m* 1964, Olivia Barstow (marr. diss. 1989); one *s* two *d*. *Educ:* Winchester; King's Coll., Cambridge (MA Mod Langs); MIT (SM Management). Courtaulds, 1962–65; McKinsey & Co. Management Consultants, 1966–71; joined Sterling Guarantee Trust, 1971, Dir, 1973; served on main bd after merger with Town & City Properties and later with P&OSNCo., until 1986; Chairman: Earls Court and Olympia Exhibns Gp, 1974–85; Sutcliffe Catering Gp, 1975–85; Butlers Warehousing & Distribution, 1971–85; Sterling Guards, 1974–85; P & O Cruises, Swan Hellenic, and Princess Cruises, 1985–86; Conder Group plc, 1987–92; Collett Dickenson Pearce Internat., 1990–91. Director: Outer London Reg. Bd, 1984–88, Southern Adv. Bd, 1988–92, Nat. Westminster Bank; Williamson Tea Holdings, 1986–94; Life Sciences Internat., 1987–; Erith plc, 1992–; Mem. Adv. Bd, Strategic Partnership, 1994–. Chm., London Chamber of Commerce and Industry, 1988–90 (Dep. Chm., 1986–88); Dep. Pres., 1990–92, Pres., 1992–94, ABCC. Member: Council, Worldaware (formerly Centre for World Develt Educn), 1988–; Council of Management, Acad. of St Martin in the Fields, 1990–93; Cttee, Royal Tournament, 1976–85; Vice-Pres., Olympia Internat. Showjumping, 1977–85; Hon. Mem., Royal Smithfield Club, 1985–. Mem. Ct of Assts, Grocers' Co., 1990. FRSA. *Recreations:* design of gardens and buildings, tennis, shooting, ski-ing. *Address:* 52 Westbourne Terrace, W2 3UJ. *T:* 0171–262 0514. *Club:* Travellers'.

STEWART-SMITH, Rev. Canon David Cree, MA; *b* 22 May 1913; 3rd *s* of late Thomas Stewart Stewart-Smith, JP, Heathlands, Kinver, Staffs, and Mabel (*née* McDougall); *m* 1943, Kathleen Georgiana Maule Ffinch, *d* of Rev. K. M. Ffinch, Ifield, Kent. *Educ:* Marlborough; King's Coll., Cambridge; Cuddesdon Theol. College. BA 1939, MA 1943. Vicar-Choral and Sacrist, York Minster, 1944–49; Vicar of Shadwell, Leeds, 1949–52; Warden, Brasted Place Coll., 1952–63; Dean of St George's Cath., Jerusalem, and Administrator of St George's Coll., 1964–67; Commissary for Archbishop in Jerusalem, 1968–76; Archdeacon of Bromley and Hon. Canon of Rochester, 1968–69; Archdeacon of Rochester and Canon Residentiary of Rochester Cathedral, 1969–76; Hon. Canon of Rochester, 1976–78, Canon Emeritus, 1978–; Director of Ordinands, dio. Rochester, 1968–74; Mem., C of E Pensions Bd, 1970–84; a Church Commissioner, 1973–78; Home Sec., Jerusalem and Middle East Church Assoc., 1976–78; Fellow of Woodard Corp.: Northern Div., 1949–52; Southern Div., 1959–64. *Recreations:* architecture, music, travel. *Address:* 16 Capel Court, Prestbury, near Cheltenham GL52 3EL. *T:* Cheltenham (01242) 510972.

STEWART-SMITH, (Dudley) Geoffrey; *b* 28 Dec. 1933; *s* of Dudley Cautley Stewart-Smith; *m* 1956, Kay Mary (marr. diss. 1990); three *s*. *Educ:* Winchester; RMA Sandhurst. Regular Officer, The Black Watch, 1952–60. Dir, Foreign Affairs Res. Inst., 1976–86. Director: Foreign Affairs Circle; Freedom Communications Internat. News Agency; Editor, East-West Digest; Dir, Foreign Affairs Publishing Co.; Financial Times, 1968. MP (C) Derbyshire, Belper, 1970–Feb 1974. Liveryman, Grocers' Co., 1962. *Publications:* The Defeat of Communism, 1964; No Vision Here: Non-Military Warfare in Britain, 1966; (ed) Brandt and the Destruction of NATO, 1973; The Struggle for Freedom, 1980; contribs to various foreign, defence and communist affairs jls at home and overseas. *Recreations:* walking, swimming, shooting and stalking.

STEWART-WILSON, Lt-Col Sir Blair (Aubyn), KCVO 1994 (CVO 1989; LVO 1983); Deputy Master of the Household and Equerry to Her Majesty, 1976–94, an Extra Equerry, since 1994; *b* 17 July 1929; *s* of late Aubyn Wilson and late Muriel Stewart Stevens; *m* 1962, Helen Mary Fox; three *d*. *Educ:* Eton; Sandhurst. Commnd Scots Guards, 1949, Atholl Highlanders, 1952; served with Regt in UK, Germany and Far East; Adjutant 2nd Bn, 1955–57; ADC to Viscount Cobham, Governor General and C-in-C, New Zealand, 1957–59; Equerry to late Duke of Gloucester, 1960–62; Regtl Adjutant, 1966–68; GSO1, Foreign Liaison Sect. (Army), MoD, 1970–73; Defence, Military and Air Attaché, British Embassy, Vienna, 1975–76. Captain, Atholl Highlanders, 1966. HM's Rep. Trustee, Bd of Royal Armouries, 1995–. *Address:* c/o Royal Bank of Scotland, 84 Atholl Road, Pitlochry PH16 5BJ. *Clubs:* Pratt's, White's.

STEWARTBY, Baron *cr* 1992 (Life Peer), of Portmoak in the District of Perth and Kinross; **Bernard Harold Ian Halley Stewart,** Kt 1991; PC 1989; RD 1972; FBA 1981; FRSE 1986; *b* 10 Aug. 1935; *s* of Prof. H. C. Stewart, *qv*; *m* 1966, Deborah Charlotte, JP, *d* of Hon. William Buchan and late Barbara Howard Ensor, JP; one *s* two *d*. *Educ:* Haileybury; Jesus Coll., Cambridge (MA; LittD 1978; Hon. Fellow, 1994). 1st cl. hons Class. Tripos Cantab. Nat. Service, RNVR, 1954–56; subseq. Lt-Cmdr RNR. Seccombe, Marshall & Campion Ltd, bill brokers, 1959–60; joined Brown, Shipley & Co. Ltd, 1960, Asst Man. 1963, Man. 1966, Dir 1971–83; Director: Brown Shipley Holdings Ltd, 1980–83; Victory Insurance Co. Ltd, 1976–83; Seccombe Marshall & Campion Hldgs Ltd, 1989–; Diploma plc, 1990–; Standard Chartered plc, 1990– (Dep. Chm., 1993–); Chairman: Throgmorton Trust, 1990–; Delian Lloyd's Investment Trust, 1993–95; Dep. Chm., Angerstein Underwriting Trust, 1995–. Mem., SIB, 1993–. MP (C) Hitchin, Feb. 1974–1983, N Herts, 1983–92. Opposition spokesman on Banking Bill, 1978–79; PPS to Chancellor of the Exchequer, 1979–83; Parly Under-Sec. of State for Defence Procurement, MoD, Jan.–Oct. 1983; Economic Sec. to HM Treasury, 1983–87; Minister of State: for the Armed Forces, MoD, 1987–88; NI Office, 1988–89. Jt Sec., Cons. Parly Finance Cttee, 1975–76, 1977–79; Member: Public Expenditure Cttee, 1977–79; Public Accounts Cttee, 1991–92. UK rep., Europ. Budget Council, 1983–85; responsible for: Trustee Savings Banks Act, 1985; Building Socs Act, 1986; Banking Act, 1987. Mem. British Academy Cttee for Sylloge of Coins of British Isles, 1967– (Chm., 1993–); Hon. Treas., Westminster Cttee for Protection of Children, 1960–70, Vice-Chm., 1975–92. FSA (Mem. Council 1974–76); FSAScot; Dir, British Numismatic Soc., 1965–75 (Sanford Saltus Gold Medal 1971); FRNS (Parkes Weber Prize); Numismatic advr, NACF, 1988–. Vice-Pres., Hertfordshire Soc., 1974–; Mem. Council, British Museum Soc., 1975–76. Life Governor, 1977, Mem. Council, 1980–, Haileybury; Trustee, Sir Halley Stewart Trust, 1978–. Hon. Vice-Pres., Stewart Soc. 1989–. County Vice-Pres., St John Ambulance for Herts, 1978–; KStJ 1992. *Publications:* The Scottish Coinage, 1955 (2nd edn 1967); Scottish Mints, 1971; (ed with C. N. L. Brooke and others) Studies in Numismatic Method, 1983; (with C. E. Blunt and C. S. S. Lyon) Coinage in Tenth-Century England, 1989; (with C. E. Challis and others) New History of the Royal Mint, 1992; many papers in Proc. Soc. Antiquaries of Scotland, Numismatic Chronicle, British Numismatic Jl, etc. *Recreations:* history; tennis (Captain CU Tennis Club, 1958–59; 1st string v Oxford, 1958 and 1959; winner Coupe de Bordeaux 1959; led 1st Oxford and Cambridge Tennis and Rackets team to USA, 1958; played squash for Herts); Homer. *Address:* House of Lords, SW1A 0PW. *Clubs:* Royal Automobile, MCC; Hawks, Pitt (Cambridge).

STEYN, family name of **Baron Steyn.**

STEYN, Baron *cr* 1995 (Life Peer), of Swafield in the county of Norfolk; **Johan Steyn;** Kt 1985; PC 1992; a Lord of Appeal in Ordinary, since 1995; *b* 15 Aug. 1932; *m* Susan Leonore (*née* Lewis); two *s* two *d* by previous *m*, and one step *s* one step *d*. *Educ:* Jan van Riebeeck Sch., Cape Town, S Africa; Univ. of Stellenbosch, S Africa (BA, LLB); University Coll., Oxford (MA; Hon. Fellow, 1995). Cape Province Rhodes Scholar, 1955; commenced practice at S African Bar, 1958; Sen. Counsel of Supreme Court of SA, 1970; settled in UK; commenced practice at English Bar, 1973 (Bencher, Lincoln's Inn, 1985); QC 1979; a Presiding Judge, Northern Circuit, 1989–91; Judge of the High Court, QBD, 1985–91; a Lord Justice of Appeal, 1992–95. Member: Supreme Court Rule Cttee, 1985–89; Deptl Adv. Cttee on Arbitration Law, 1986–89 (Chm., 1990–94); Chairman: Race Relations Cttee of the Bar, 1987–88; Lord Chancellor's Adv. Cttee on Legal Educn and Conduct, 1993–. Chm., Adv. Council, Centre for Commercial Law Studies, QMW, 1993–94. Pres., British Insce Law Assoc., 1992–94. *Address:* House of Lords, SW1A 0PW. *Club:* Garrick.

STIBBARD, Peter Jack; Director of Statistics, Department for Education and Employment (formerly Department of Employment), since 1989; *b* 15 May 1936; *s* of late Frederick Stibbard and Gladys Stibbard (*née* Daines); *m* 1964, Christine Fuller; two *d*. *Educ:* City of Norwich Grammar School; Hull Univ. (BSc Econ; MIS). Served RAF, 1954–56. Kodak Ltd, 1959–64; Thos Potterton Ltd, 1964–66; Greater London Council, 1966–68; Central Statistical Office, 1968–82; HM Treasury, 1982–85; Under Sec., Statistics Div. 2, DTI, 1985–89. *Publications:* articles in official and trade jls. *Address:* Department for Education and Employment, Caxton House, Tothill Street, SW1H 9NF.

STIBBE, Philip Godfrey, MA; Head Master of Norwich School, 1975–84; *b* 20 July 1921; *m* 1956, Mary Joy, *d* of late Canon C. G. Thornton; two *s* one *d*. *Educ:* Mill Hill Sch.; Merton Coll., Oxford (MA). Served War of 1939–45; joined Royal Sussex Regt, 1941; seconded King's (Liverpool) Regt, 1942; 1st Wingate Expedn into Burma (wounded, despatches), 1943; POW, 1943–45. Asst Master, 1948–75, Housemaster, 1953–74, Bradfield Coll. JP Norwich, 1979–84. *Publication:* Return via Rangoon, 1947, repr. 1994. *Recreations:* people, places, books. *Address:* 29A Bracondale, Norwich NR1 2AT. *T:* Norwich (01603) 630704.

STIBBON, Gen. Sir John (James), KCB 1988; OBE 1979; CEng, FICE; Chief Royal Engineer, since 1993; *b* 5 Jan. 1935; *s* of Jack Stibbon and Elizabeth Matilda Stibbon (*née* Dixon); *m* 1957, Jean Fergusson Skeggs, *d* of John Robert Skeggs and Florence Skeggs (*née* Hayes); two *d*. *Educ:* Portsmouth Southern Grammar School; Royal Military Academy; Royal Military College of Science. BSc (Eng). CEng 1989; FICE 1989. Commissioned RE, 1954; CO 28 Amphibious Engineer Regt, 1975–77; Asst Military Secretary, 1977–79; Comd 20 Armoured Brigade, 1979–81; Comdt, RMCS, 1983–85; ACDS Operational Requirements (Land Systems), 1985–87; Master Gen. of the Ordnance, 1987–91. Colonel Commandant: RAPC, 1985–92; RPC, 1986–91; RE, 1987–. Chairman: Bd of Govs, Royal Star & Garter Home, 1991–; Gordon Foundn, 1992–; Comr, Duke of York's Royal Mil. Sch., 1993–. Hon DSc Cranfield Inst. of Technology, 1989. *Recreations:* Association football, athletics, painting, palaeontology. *Club:* Lansdowne.

STIBBS, Prof. Douglas Walter Noble, MSc Sydney, DPhil Oxon; FRAS; FRSE; Napier Professor of Astronomy and Director of the University Observatory, 1959–89, Senior Professor Senatus Academicus, 1987–89, and Professor Emeritus, since 1990, University of St Andrews; Visiting Fellow, Mount Stromlo and Siding Spring Observatories, Australian National University, since 1990; *b* 17 Feb. 1919; 2nd *s* of Edward John Stibbs, Sydney, NSW; *m* 1949, Margaret Lilian Calvert, BSc, DipEd (Sydney), *er d* of Rev. John Calvert, Sydney, NSW; two *d*. *Educ:* Sydney High Sch.; Univ. of Sydney; New College, Oxford. Deas Thomson Scholar, Sch. of Physics, Univ. of Sydney, 1940; BSc (Sydney), 1st Class Hons, Univ. Medal in Physics, 1942; MSc (Sydney), 1943; DPhil (Oxon), 1954. Johnson Memorial Prize and Gold Medal for Advancement of Astronomy and Meteorology, Oxford Univ., 1956. Res. Asst, Commonwealth Solar Observatory, Canberra, ACT, 1940–42; Asst Lectr, Dept of Mathematics and Physics, New England University Coll., Armidale, NSW (now the Univ. of New England), 1942–45; Scientific Officer and Sen. Scientific Officer, Commonwealth Observatory, Canberra, ACT, 1945–51; Radcliffe Travelling Fellow in Astronomy, Radcliffe Observatory, Pretoria, S Africa, and Univ. Observatory, Oxford, 1951–54; PSO, UKAEA, 1955–59. Vis. Prof. of Astrophysics, Yale Univ. Observatory, 1966–67; British Council Vis. Prof., Univ. of Utrecht, 1968; Prof., Collège de France, 1975–76 (Médaille du Collège, 1976). Member: Internat. Astronomical Union, 1951– (Chm. Finance Cttee, 1964–67, 1973–76, 1976–79);

Amer. Astronomical Soc., 1956–73; Adv. Cttee on Meteorology for Scotland, 1960–69, 1972–75, 1978–80; Board of Visitors, Royal Greenwich Observatory, 1963–65; Council RAS, 1964–67, 1970–73 (Vice-Pres., 1972–73), Editorial Board, 1970–73; Council, RSE, 1970–72; National Cttee for Astronomy, 1964–76; SRC Cttees for Royal Greenwich Observatory, 1966–70, and Royal Observatory, Edinburgh, 1966–76, Chm., 1970–76; SRC Astronomy, Space and Radio Bd, 1970–76; SRC, 1972–76; S African Astron. Obs. Adv. Cttee, 1972–76; Chairman: Astronomy Policy and Grants Cttee, 1972–74; Northern Hemisphere Observatory Planning Cttee, 1972–75; Astronomy II Cttee, 1974–75; Mem., Centre National de la Recherche Scientifique Cttee, Obs. de Haute Provence, 1973–82. Life Member: Sydney Univ. Union, 1942; New Coll. Soc., 1953; New England Univ. Union, NSW, 1957. Mem., Western Province Masters Athletics Assoc., Cape Town, 1983–. Marathon Medals: Paris, Caithness, Edinburgh (3hrs 59mins), Flying Fox (British Veterans Championships), Honolulu, 1983; London, Loch Rannoch, and Aberdeen (Veterans Trophy Winner), 1984; Stoke-on-Trent (Potteries), Athens, Honolulu, 1985; London, Edinburgh (Commonwealth Games Peoples Marathon), Stoke-on-Trent (Potteries), Berlin, Honolulu, 1986; Boston, 1987; Half-marathons: 11 events incl. Windsor Great Park, Dundee, Dunfermline, Wagga (Australian Veterans Games, 1991, Gold Medallist), Canberra. *Publications:* The Outer Layers of a Star (with Sir Richard Woolley), 1953; contrib. Theoretical Astrophysics and Astronomy in Monthly Notices of RAS and other jls. *Recreations:* music, ornithology, photography, golf, long-distance running. *Address:* Mount Stromlo Observatory, Australian National University, Canberra, ACT 0200, Australia. *T:* Canberra (6) 2901773. *Club:* Royal and Ancient (St Andrews).

STIFF, Rt. Rev. Hugh Vernon; retired; *b* 15 Sept. 1916; unmarried. *Educ:* Univ. of Toronto (BA); Trinity Coll., Toronto (LTh). BD General Synod; Hon. DD, Trinity Coll., Toronto. Bishop of Keewatin, 1969–74; Rector of St James Cathedral and Dean of Toronto, 1974–86; Asst Bishop, Diocese of Toronto, 1977–86. *Address:* Apt #207, 83 Elm Avenue, Toronto, Ontario M4W 1P1, Canada.

STIGLITZ, Prof. Joseph Eugene, PhD; Member, Council of Economic Advisers to the President of the USA, since 1993; Professor of Economics, since 1988, Joan Kenney Professor of Economics, since 1992, Stanford University; *b* 9 Feb. 1943; *m* M. J. Hannaway; two *s* two *d*. *Educ:* Amherst Coll. (BA 1964); MIT (PhD 1966); Cambridge Univ. (MA 1970). Professor of Economics: Yale Univ. 1970–74; Stanford Univ., 1974–76; Drummond Prof. of Political Economy, Oxford Univ. and All Souls Coll., 1976–79; Prof. of Economics, Princeton Univ., 1979–88. Fellowships: Nat. Sci. Foundn, 1964–65; Fulbright, 1965–66; SSRC Faculty, 1969–70; Guggenheim, 1969–70; Oskar Morgenstern Distinguished Fellowship, Mathematica and Inst. for Advanced Study, Princeton, 1978–79. Consultant: Nat. Sci. Foundn, 1972–75; Ford Foundn Energy Policy Study, 1973; Dept of Labor (Pensions and Labor Turnover), 1974; Dept of Interior (Offshore Oil Leasing Programs), 1975; Federal Energy Admin (Intertemporal Biases in Market Allocation of Natural Resources), 1975–79; World Bank (Cost Benefit Analysis; Urban Rural Migration; Natural Resources), 1975–; Electric Power Res. Inst., 1976–; OECD; Office of Fair Trading; Treasury (Office of Tax Analysis), 1980; US AID (commodity price stabilization), 1977; Inter-American Development Bank; Bell Laboratories; Bell Communications Research; State of Alaska; Seneca Indian Nation. Internat. Prize, Academia Lincei, 1988; Union des Assurances de Paris Scientific Prize, 1989. Gen. Editor, Econometric Soc. Reprint Series; Associate Editor: Jl of Economic Theory, 1968–73; American Economic Rev., 1972–75; Jl of Economic Perspectives, 1988–; Co-editor, Jl of Public Economics, 1968–83; American Editor, Rev. of Economic Studies, 1968–76; Editorial Bd, World Bank Economic Review, The Geneva Papers, Revista de Econometrica, Assicurazioni. Vice-Pres., American Econ. Assoc., 1985. Fellow: Econometric Soc., 1972 (Sec./Treasurer, 1972–75); Amer. Acad. of Arts and Scis; Inst. for Policy Reform, 1990–; Sen. Fellow, Hoover Instn, 1988–. Corresp. FBA 1993. Hon. MA Yale, 1970; Hon. DHL Amherst, 1974. John Bates Clark Medal, Amer. Econ. Assoc. *Publications:* (ed) Collected Scientific Papers of P. A. Samuelson, 1965; (ed with H. Uzawa) Readings in Modern Theory of Economic Growth, 1969; (with A. B. Atkinson) Lectures in Public Finance, 1980; (with D. Newbery) The Economic Impact of Price Stabilization, 1980; Economics of the Public Sector, 1986; contribs on economics of growth, development, natural resources, information, uncertainty, imperfect competition, corporate finance and public finance in Amer. Econ. Rev., Qly Jl of Econs, Jl of Pol. Econ., Econometrica, Internat. Econ. Rev., Econ. Jl, Rev. of Econ. Studies, Jl of Public Econs, Jl of Econ. Theory, Oxford Econ. Papers. *Address:* Department of Economics, Stanford University, Stanford, CA 94305–6072, USA.

STILGOE, Richard Henry Simpson; songwriter, lyricist, entertainer and broadcaster, since 1962; *b* 28 March 1943; *s* of John Henry Tweedie Stilgoe and Joan Lucy Strutt Stilgoe; *m* 1st, 1964, Elizabeth Caroline Gross; one *s* one *d*; 2nd, 1975, Annabel Margaret Hunt; two *s* one *d*. *Educ:* Liverpool Coll.; Monkton Combe Sch.; Clare Coll., Cambridge (choral exhibnr). One-man show worldwide, incl. Windsor Castle, 1982 and British Embassy, Washington, 1986; Two-man show with Peter Skellern, London, 1985–86. Author and composer: Bodywork (children's musical), 1987; Brilliant the Dinosaur, 1991. Word-processor for Andrew Lloyd Webber on Cats, Starlight Express and Phantom of the Opera. Founder and Dir, Orpheus Trust (music and the disabled), 1985–; Pres., Surrey Care Trust, 1986–. Monaco Radio Prize, 1984, 1991; NY Radio Fest. Gold Award, 1989; Prix Italia, 1991. *Publications:* The Richard Stilgoe Letters, 1981; Brilliant The Dinosaur, 1994. *Recreations:* sailing, cricket, architecture, building, demolition, children. *Address:* c/o The Orpheus Trust, Trevereux Manor, Limpsfield Chart, Oxted, Surrey RH8 0TL. *Club:* Lord's Taverners.

STILLMAN, Dr Bruce William, FRS 1993; Director, Cold Spring Harbor Laboratory, New York, since 1994; *b* Melbourne, Australia, 16 Oct. 1953; *s* of Graham Leslie Stillman and Jessie May (*née* England); *m* 1981, Grace Angela Begley; one *s* one *d*. *Educ:* Glen Waverley High Sch.; Sydney Boys' High Sch.; Univ. of Sydney (BSc Hons); ANU (PhD). Cold Spring Harbor Laboratory, New York: Damon Runyon-Walter Winchell Postdoctoral Res. Fellow, 1979–80; Staff Investigator, 1981–82; Sen. Staff Investigator, 1983–85; Sen. Scientist, 1985–90; Asst Dir, 1990–93; Adjunct Prof. of Biochemistry and Adjunct Prof. of Microbiology, SUNY, 1982–. Damon Runyon-Walter Winchell Cancer Fund Fellow, 1979–80; Rita Allen Foundn Scholar, 1982–87. Harvey Soc. Lecture, 1993; Nieuwland Lectr, Univ. of Notre Dame, 1993. Commonwealth Postgrad. Award, 1976–80; Merit Award, NIH, 1986. *Publications:* numerous scientific pubns. *Address:* Cold Spring Harbor Laboratory, One Bungtown Road, Cold Spring Harbor, NY 11724, USA. *T:* (516) 3678383.

STIMSON, Robert Frederick, CBE 1992; Governor and Commander-in-Chief of St Helena and its Dependencies, 1987–91; *b* 16 May 1939; *s* of Frederick Henry and Gladys Alma Stimson (*née* Joel); *m* 1961, Margaret Faith Kerry; two *s* one *d*. *Educ:* Rendcomb Coll.; Queen Mary Coll., London (BSc First Cl. Hons; MSc (by thesis) mathematical physics). HM Diplomatic Service: FO, 1966–67; Saigon, 1967–68; Singapore, 1968–70; Cabinet Office, 1970–73; Mexico City, 1973–75; FCO, 1975–80; Counsellor, East Berlin, 1980–81; Head of Home Inspectorate, 1982–83; Counsellor and Hd of Chancery, Dublin, 1984–87. Order of Aztec Eagle, Mexico, 1975. *Publications:* contrib. Jl Physics and Chemistry of Solids. *Address:* c/o Foreign and Commonwealth Office, SW1A 2AH.

STINSON, His Honour David John; a Circuit Judge (formerly County Court Judge), 1969–86; President, Parents' Conciliation Trust, Suffolk, since 1988; *b* 22 Feb. 1921; *s* of late Henry John Edwin Stinson, MC, MA, LLB, Beckenham, Kent (sometime Chief Commoner of City of London, solicitor), and late Margaret Stinson (*née* Little); *m* 1950, Eleanor Judith (*née* Chance); two *s* two *d* (and one *s* decd). *Educ:* Eastbourne Coll.; Emmanuel Coll., Cambridge. MA 1946; Jesters Club, 1949 (Rugby Fives). Served War of 1939–45: Essex Yeomanry, Captain, RA, and Air OP, 1941–46 (despatches). Called to Bar, Middle Temple, 1947; Dep. Chm., Herts QS, 1965–71; Suffolk and Essex County Court Circuit, 1973–86. Chancellor, dio. of Carlisle, 1971–90. Chm., Ipswich Family Conciliation Service, 1982–88. *Recreations:* bird-watching, sailing. *Address:* Barrack Row, Waldringfield, Woodbridge, Suffolk IP12 4QX. *T:* Waldringfield (01473) 736280. *Club:* Waldringfield Sailing.

STIRLING, Sir Alexander (John Dickson), KBE 1981; CMG 1976; HM Diplomatic Service, retired; Chairman, SOS Sahel International—UK, since 1993; *b* 20 Oct. 1926; *e s* of late Brig. A. Dickson Stirling, DSO, MB, ChB, DPH, and Isobel Stirling, MA, DipEd, DipPsych, *d* of late Rev. J. C. Matthew (former senior Presidency Chaplain, Bombay); *m* 1955, Alison Mary, *y d* of Gp Capt. A. P. Campbell, CBE; two *s* two *d*. *Educ:* Edinburgh Academy; Lincoln Coll., Oxford (MA). RAFVR, 1945–48 (Egypt, 1945–47). Entered Foreign Office, 1951; Lebanon, 1952; British Embassy, Cairo, 1952–56 (Oriental Sec., 1955–56); FO, 1956–59; First Sec., British Embassy, Baghdad, 1959–62; First Sec. and Consul, Amman, 1962–64; First Sec., British Embassy, Santiago, 1965–67 (led UK Delegn to Fourth Antarctic Treaty Consultative Meeting, 1966); FO, 1967–69; British Political Agent, Bahrain, 1969–71, Ambassador, 1971–72; Counsellor, Beirut, 1972–75; RCDS 1976; Ambassador to Iraq, 1977–80, to the Tunisian Republic, 1981–84, to the Sudan, 1984–86. Chm., Soc. for Protection of Animals in N Africa, subseq. of Animals Abroad, 1989–92.

See also C. J. M. Stirling.

STIRLING, Sir Angus (Duncan Æneas), Kt 1994; Director-General, The National Trust, 1983–95 (Deputy Director-General, 1979–83); Chairman, Royal Opera House, Covent Garden, since 1991 (Member of the Board, since 1979); *b* 10 Dec. 1933; *s* of late Duncan Alexander Stirling and of Lady Marjorie Murray, *e d* of 8th Earl of Dunmore, VC, DSO, MVO; *m* 1959, Armyne Morar Helen Schofield, *e d* of late W. G. B. Schofield and Hon. Armyne Astley; one *s* two *d*. *Educ:* Eton Coll.; Trinity Coll., Cambridge; London Univ. (Extra Mural) (Dip. History of Art). Christie, Manson and Woods Ltd, 1954–57; Lazard Bros and Co. Ltd, 1957–66; Asst Dir, Paul Mellon Foundn for British Art, 1966–69 (Jt Dir, 1969–70); Dep. Sec.-General, Arts Council of GB, 1971–79. Mem., Govt Task Force on Tourism and the Envmt, 1991. Chm., Friends of Covent Garden, 1981–91; Dep. Chm., Royal Ballet Bd, 1988–91; a Gov., Royal Ballet, 1988–; Chm., RSCM, 1996–; Member: Crafts Council, 1980–85; Council of Management, Byam Shaw Sch. of Art, 1965–89; Management Cttee, Courtauld Inst. of Art, 1981–83 (Trustee, Home House (Courtauld Collection), 1983–); Adv. Council, London Symphony Orchestra, 1979–; Bd of Governors, Live Music Now, 1982–89; Bd of Trustees, The Theatres Trust, 1983–91; Bd of Trustees, Heritage of London Trust, 1983–. CIMgt; FRSA. *Recreations:* music, travel, walking, landscape photography. *Address:* 25 Ladbroke Grove, W11 3AY. *Clubs:* Garrick, Brooks's.

STIRLING, Prof. Charles James Matthew, FRS 1986; CChem, FRSC; Professor of Organic Chemistry, University of Sheffield, since 1990; *b* 8 Dec. 1930; *s* of Brig. Alexander Dickson Stirling, DSO, MB, ChB, DPH, RAMC, and Isobel Millicent Stirling, MA, DipPsych; *m* 1956, Eileen Gibson Powell, BA, MEd, *yr d* of William Leslie and Elsie May Powell; two *d* (and one *d* decd). *Educ:* Edinburgh Acad.; Univ. of St Andrews (Harkness Exhibn; BSc; Biochem. Medal 1951); Univ. of London (PhD, DSc). FRSC, CChem 1967. Civil Service Jun. Res. Fellowship, Porton, 1955, Sen. Fellowship, 1956; ICI Fellowship, Univ. of Edinburgh, 1957; Lectr, QUB, 1959; Reader in Org. Chem., KCL, 1965; University of Wales, Bangor: Prof. of Organic Chemistry, 1969–81; Dean of Faculty of Science, 1977–79; Hd of Dept of Chemistry, 1981–90; Sheffield University: Hd, Dept of Chemistry, 1991–94; Dir, Engrg and Physical Scis Div., Grad. Sch., 1994–; Public Orator, 1995–. Vis. Prof., Hebrew Univ. of Jerusalem, 1981. Royal Instn Christmas Lects, BBC TV, 1992. Mem., IUPAC Commn on Physical Organic Chemistry, 1992–95. Mem., Perkin Council, RSC, 1971–93 (Vice-Pres., 1985–88 and 1991–93, Pres., 1989–91); Pres., Section B (Chemistry), BAAS, 1990; Pres., Yorks and Humberside Sect., ASE, 1993–95. Hon. DSc St Andrews, 1994. Award for Organic Reaction Mechanisms, RSC, 1988. *Publications:* Radicals in Organic Chemistry, 1965; (ed) Organic Sulphur Chemistry, 1975; (ed) The Chemistry of the Sulphonium Group, 1981; (ed) The Chemistry of Sulphones and Sulphoxides, 1988; numerous res. papers mainly in Jls of RSC. *Recreations:* choral music, the collection of chiral objects, furniture restoration. *Address:* Department of Chemistry, University of Sheffield, Sheffield S3 7HF. *T:* Sheffield (0114) 276 8555; 114 Westbourne Road, Sheffield S10 2QT.

See also Sir A. J. D. Stirling.

STIRLING, Hamish; Sheriff of South Strathclyde, Dumfries and Galloway, since 1992; *b* 9 July 1938; *s* of late James Stirling, DSc, FRSE and Anne Wood Stirling; *m* 1963, Margaret Davidson Bottomley, RGN; two *s* one *d*. *Educ:* Liverpool Coll.; Robert Gordon's Coll., Aberdeen; Aberdeen Univ. (MA 1959; LLB 1961). Solicitor Assistant, Elgin, 1961–62; Procurator Fiscal Depute: Dundee, 1963–70; Borders, 1970–74; Glasgow, 1974–75; Scottish Bar, 1976. *Recreations:* golf, foreign travel, gardening, bridge, classic sports cars. *Address:* Sheriff's Chambers, Hamilton Sheriff Court, 4 Beckford Street, Hamilton ML3 6AA. *T:* Hamilton (01698) 282957.

STIRLING of Garden, Col James, CBE 1987; TD; FRICS; Lord-Lieutenant of Stirling and Falkirk (Central Region), since 1983; *b* 8 Sept. 1930; *s* of Col Archibald Stirling of Garden, OBE; *m* 1958, Fiona Janetta Sophia Wood Parker; two *s* two *d*. *Educ:* Rugby; Trinity Coll., Cambridge. BA; Dip. Estate Management. Chartered Surveyor in private practice. Partner, K. Ryden and Partners, Chartered Surveyors, 1962–89, Consultant, 1989–; Director: Local Bd, Scotland and N Ireland, Woolwich Building Soc., 1973–; Scottish Widows and Life Insurance Fund, 1975–. Chm., Highland TAVR Assoc., 1982–87 (Pres., 1992). DL 1970, Vice-Lieutenant 1979–83, Stirling. Hon. Col, 3/51st Highland Volunteers, TA, 1979–86. KStJ 1987. *Address:* Garden, Buchlyvie, Stirlingshire FK8 3NR. *T:* Buchlyvie (01360) 850212. *Club:* New (Edinburgh).

STIRLING, John Fullarton, JP; Librarian, University of Exeter, 1972–94; *b* 12 April 1931; *s* of Reginald Stirling and Jeanette Sybil (*née* Fullarton); *m* 1960, Sheila Mary Fane; two *d*. *Educ:* Waterloo Grammar sch.; Univ. of Liverpool (BA 1st Cl. Hons 1953; MA 1962). Asst, Liverpool Public Libraries, 1953–56; Asst Librarian, UCL, 1956–62; Sub-librarian, 1962–64, Dep. Librarian, 1964–66, Univ. of York; Librarian, Univ. of Stirling, 1966–71; Librarian designate, Univ. of Exeter, 1971–72. Member: various cttees, SCONUL, 1977–; UGC Working Gp on Liby Automation, 1986; British Liby Cttee for Bibliographic Services, 1987. JP Exeter, 1976. *Publications:* (ed) University Librarianship, 1981; contrib. various professional jls. *Address:* c/o Devon and Exeter Institution, 7 Cathedral Close, EX1 1EZ. *T:* Exeter (01392) 57413. *Club:* Devon and Exeter Institution (Exeter).

STIRLING, Rear-Adm. Michael Grote; Agent-General for British Columbia in the United Kingdom and Europe, 1968–75; *b* 29 June 1915; *s* of late Hon. Grote Stirling and late Mabel Katherine (*née* Brigstocke), Kelowna, British Columbia; *m* 1942, Sheelagh Kathleen Russell; two *s* one *d*. *Educ:* Shawnigan Lake School, BC; RNC Greenwich. Cadet, RCN, 1933; HMS Frobisher for training till 1934, then as Midshipman and Sub-Lt in RN, returning Canada Jan. 1938; Ships of RCN until 1941; specialized in Signals at HM Signal School, Portsmouth, then Home Fleet; Deputy Director, Signal Div., Naval Service HQ, Ottawa, 1942–43; SSO to C-in-C, Canadian North-West Atlantic, 1943–44; Commanded destroyers, 1944–46; Director Naval Communications, rank of Commander, 1949–51; promoted Captain and staff of Supreme Allied Commander Atlantic, Norfolk, Va, 1953–55; Commanded HMCS Cornwallis, 1955–57; 2nd Cdn Escort Sqdn, 1957–58; Naval Member of Directing Staff, Nat. Defence College as Commodore, 1958–61; Senior Canadian Officer Afloat, 1961–62; Chief of Naval Personnel, 1962–64; Maritime Comdr, Pacific, 1964–66. Rear-Adm. 1962. Dir, Univ. of Victoria Foundation, 1967–68. *Recreations:* golf, ski-ing. *Address:* 302–1280 Newport Avenue, Victoria, BC V8S 5E7, Canada. *Club:* Victoria Golf (Victoria, BC).

STIRLING of Fairburn, Captain Roderick William Kenneth, TD 1965; JP; Lord Lieutenant of Ross and Cromarty and Skye and Lochalsh, since 1988; *b* 17 June 1932; *s* of late Major Sir John Stirling, KT, MBE and Lady Marjory Kythé, *d* of Sir Kenneth Mackenzie, 7th Bt of Gairloch; *m* 1963, Penelope Jane Wright; four *d*. *Educ:* Wellesley House; Harrow. National Service, Scots Guards, 1950–52; commissioned 1951; TA Seaforth Highlanders and Queen's Own Highlanders (Seaforth and Cameron), 1953–69. Member: Ross and Cromarty County Council, 1970–74 (Chm. of Highways, 1973–74); Ross and Cromarty District Council, 1984–. Mem., Red Deer Commn, 1964–89 (Vice-Chm., 1975–89); Director: Moray Firth Salmon Fishing Co., 1973–91; Scottish Salmon and Whitefish Co., 1972–91 (Chm., 1980–). Mem., Scottish Council, NPFA, 1971–91 (Chm., Highland Cttee); President: Ross and Cromarty CVS, 1990–; Ross and Sutherland Scout Council, 1990–; Jun. Vice-Pres., Scottish Accident Prevention Council, 1991–92. JP Ross and Cromarty, 1975. *Recreations:* stalking, shooting, fishing, gardening, curling. *Address:* Arcan, Muir of Ord, Ross and Cromarty IV6 7UL. *T:* Urray (01997) 433207. *Club:* New (Edinburgh).

STIRLING-HAMILTON, Sir Malcolm William Bruce, 14th Bt *cr* 1673 (NS), of Preston, Haddingtonshire; *b* 6 Aug. 1979; *s* of Sir Bruce Stirling-Hamilton, 13th Bt and of Stephanie (who *m* 1990, Anthony Tinsley), *d* of Dr William Campbell, LRCP, LRCS; *S* father, 1989. *Educ:* Stowe. *Heir: cousin* Robert William Hamilton, *qv*. *Address:* Narborough Hall, King's Lynn, Norfolk PE32 1TE.

STIRRAT, Prof. Gordon Macmillan, MA, MD; FRCOG; Professor of Obstetrics and Gynaecology, since 1982, Pro-Vice-Chancellor, since 1993, University of Bristol (Dean of Faculty of Medicine, 1990–93); *b* 12 March 1940; *s* of Alexander and Caroline Mary Stirrat; *m* 1965, Janeen Mary (*née* Brown); three *d*. *Educ:* Hutcheson's Boys' Grammar Sch., Glasgow; Glasgow Univ. (MB, ChB). MA Oxon, MD London. FRCOG 1981. Jun. hosp. doctor appts, Glasgow and environs, and London, 1964–71; Lectr, St Mary's Hosp. Med. Sch., London, 1971–75; Clinical Reader, Univ. of Oxford, 1975–81. Dep. Chm., Bristol and Dist HA, 1991–. *Publications:* Legalised Abortion: the continuing dilemma, 1979; Obstetrics Pocket Consultant, 1981, 2nd edn 1986; (jtly) You and Your Baby—a Mother's Guide to Health, 1982; Aids to Reproductive Biology, 1982; Aids to Obstetrics and Gynaecology, 1983, 3rd edn 1991; (jtly) The Immune System in Disease, 1992. *Recreations:* fly-fishing, walking, writing. *Address:* Malpas Lodge, 24 Henbury Road, Westbury-on-Trym, Bristol BS9 3HJ. *T:* Bristol (0117) 950 5310.

STITT, (Thomas) Clive Somerville; HM Diplomatic Service; *b* 1 Jan. 1948; *m* 1977, Margaret Ann Milward; two *d*. FCO, 1970; Kabul, 1972; Third, then Second, Sec., New Delhi, 1974; First Sec., FCO, 1977; UK Mission to UN, Geneva, 1982; First Sec., then Counsellor, FCO, 1986; Counsellor, UK Mission to UN, NY, 1992–95. *Address:* c/o Foreign and Commonwealth Office, SW1A 2AH.

STOATE, Isabel Dorothy; HM Diplomatic Service, retired; Counsellor, Foreign and Commonwealth Office, 1980–82; *b* 31 May 1927; *d* of late William Maurice Stoate and Dorothy Evelyn Stoate (*née* French). *Educ:* Talbot Heath Sch., Bournemouth; St Andrews Univ. Athlone Press, London Univ., 1950–52; joined HM Diplomatic Service, 1952; served Cyprus, Vienna, Buenos Aires, Tokyo, Athens, Rio de Janeiro and FCO, 1952–80. *Recreations:* travel, tapestry. *Address:* 177 Gloucester Street, Cirencester, Glos GL7 2DP.

STOCK, Prof. Francis Edgar, CBE 1977 (OBE 1961); FRCS, FACS; Principal and Vice-Chancellor of the University of Natal, South Africa, 1970–77; now Emeritus Professor; *b* 5 July 1914; *o s* of late Edgar Stephen and Olive Blanche Stock; *m* 1939, Gwendoline Mary Thomas; two *s* one *d*. *Educ:* Colfe's Grammar Sch., Lewisham; King's Coll., London (Sambrooke schol.); King's Coll. Hosp., London (Jelf medal, Todd medal and prize in clin. med.; Hygiene and Psychological med. prizes); Univ. of Edinburgh. AKC, MB, BS (Lond.), FRCS, FACS, DTMH (Edin.). Ho. Surg., Cancer Research Registrar, Radium Registrar, King's Coll. Hosp., 1938–39; MO, Colonial Med. Service, Nigeria, 1940–45; Lectr and Asst to Prof. of Surg., Univ. of Liverpool, 1946–48; Prof. of Surgery, Univ. of Hong Kong, 1948–63; Cons. in Surg. to Hong Kong Govt, Brit. Mil. Hosps in Hong Kong, and Ruttonjee Sanatorium, 1948–63; Cons. Surg., RN, 1949–70; Dean, Fac. of Med., Univ. of Hong Kong, 1957–62; Med. Coun., Hong Kong, 1957–60; Pro-Vice-Chancellor, Univ. of Hong Kong, 1959–63; McIlrath Guest Prof., Royal Prince Alfred Hosp., Sydney, NSW, 1960 (Hon. Cons. Surg., 1960–); Prof. of Surg., Univ. of Liverpool, 1964–70; Cons. Surg., Liverpool Royal Infirmary and Liverpool Regional Hosp. Bd, 1964–70; Dean, Fac. of Med., Univ. of Liverpool, 1969–70. Visiting Prof. or Lectr: Univs of Alberta, Edinburgh, Qld, Singapore, W Australia, QUB, State Univ. of NY. Brit. Council Lectr: in Thailand, Burma, Fiji, Mauritius; Hunterian Prof., RCS London, 1948 and 1951. Member: BMA (Council 1964–69; Bd of Science and Educn, 1978–80); Bd of Governors, United Liverpool Hosps, 1967–70; Med. Adv. Council and Chm. Techn. Adv. Cttee on Surg., Liverpool Reg. Hosp. Bd, 1964–70; Gen. Med. Council, 1969–70; Med. Appeals Tribunals, Liverpool and N Wales, 1966–70; Council, Edgewood Coll. of Education, 1976–77; Univs Adv. Council, 1976–; Cttee of Univ. Principals, 1970–77 (Chm., 1976–77). Examr in Surgery: to Univs of Edinburgh, Glasgow, Liverpool, Hong Kong, Malaya, Singapore and NUI, at various times, 1949–70; to Soc. of Apothecaries, 1958–60; Mem. Ct of Examrs, RCS, 1965–69. Sen. Fellow, Assoc. of Surgeons of GB and Ire.; Sen. Mem. Pan Pacific Surg. Assoc. (past Mem. Coun. and Bd of Trustees). Mem., Board of Control, Nat. Inst. of Metallurgy, 1975–77. Liveryman, Soc. of Apothecaries. Hon. FACCP. *Publications:* Surgical Principles (with J. Moroney), 1968; chapters in: Surgery of Liver and Bile Ducts (ed Smith and Sherlock); Clinical Surgery (ed Rob and Smith); Scientific Foundations of Surgery (ed Wells and Kyle); Abdominal Operations (ed Maingot), and others; numerous articles in scientific jls. *Recreations:* swimming (Univ. of London colours, 1934, Kent Co. colours, 1935), sailing (Pres., Hong Kong Yacht Racing Assoc., 1961–63, Vice-Pres., Far East Yacht Racing Fedn, 1961–62), gardening, photography, music. *Address:* Pinewood Residential Home, Mont Millais, St Helier, Jersey, CI JE2 4RA. *T:* Jersey (01534) 888097. *Clubs:* Royal Over-Seas League; Royal Hong Kong Yacht (Cdre, 1957–63).

STOCK, His Honour Raymond, QC 1964; DL; a Circuit Judge (formerly Judge of County Courts), 1971–88; *b* 1913; *s* of late A. E. and M. E. Stock; *m* 1969, E. Dorothy Thorpe, JP. *Educ:* West Monmouth School; Balliol College, Oxford. Barrister-at-law, Gray's Inn, 1936, Bencher, 1969. Royal Artillery, 1939–45. Recorder: Penzance, 1962–64; Exeter, 1964–66; Southampton, 1966–71; Dep. Chm., Dorset QS, 1964–71. DL Hants, 1991. *Address:* Brambridge House, Bishopstoke, Hants SO50 6HL. *Clubs:* Athenæum; Hampshire (Winchester).

STOCKDALE, Sir (Arthur) Noel, Kt 1986; DFM 1942; Life President, ASDA (formerly ASDA–MFI), 1986 (Chairman, 1969–86); *b* 25 Dec. 1920; *s* of Arthur and Florence Stockdale; *m* 1944, Betty Monica Shaw; two *s*. *Educ:* Woodhouse Grove School; Reading University. Joined Hindells Dairy Farmers, 1939; RAF, 1940–46; rejoined Hindells Dairy Farmers, 1946, subseq. Associated Dairies & Farm Stores (Leeds) Ltd, 1949, Associated Dairies Group PLC, 1977 and ASDA–MFI Group PLC, 1985. Hon. LLD Leeds, 1986. *Recreations:* fishing, garden. *Address:* Granary Gap, Main Street, Linton, Wetherby, Yorks LS22 4HT. *T:* Wetherby (01937) 582970.

STOCKDALE, His Honour Eric; a Circuit Judge, 1972–94; *b* 8 Feb. 1929; *m* 1952, Joan (*née* Berry); two *s*. *Educ:* Collyers Sch., Horsham; London Sch. of Economics. LLB, BSc(Econ.), LLM, PhD (Lond.); MSc (Cranfield). 2nd Lieut, RA, 1947–49. Called to the Bar, Middle Temple, 1950; practised in London and on Midland Circuit until 1972; admitted to State Bar, Calif, 1983. Mem., Supreme Court Procedure Cttee, 1982–94. Tech. Advr, Central Council of Probation Cttees, 1979–84; Vice-Pres., NACRO, 1980–94 (Mem. Council, 1970–80); President: British Soc. of Criminology, 1978–81; Soc. of English and Amer. Lawyers, 1986–89 (Chm., 1984–86). Member: Central Council for Educn and Trng in Social Work, 1984–89; Parole Board, 1985–89; Criminal Injuries Compensation Bd, 1995–. Vis. Prof., Queen Mary and Westfield Coll., London Univ., 1989–93. Governor, 1977–89, Vis. Fellow, 1986–94, Vis. Prof., 1994–, Univ. of Hertfordshire (formerly Hatfield Poly.). Consultant Ed., Blackstone's Criminal Practice, 1991–. Hon. LLD Hertfordshire. *Publications:* The Court and the Offender, 1967; A Study of Bedford Prison 1660–1877, 1977; Law and Order in Georgian Bedfordshire, 1982; The Probation Volunteer, 1985; (with Keith Devlin) Sentencing, 1987; (with Silvia Casale) Criminal Justice Under Stress, 1992. *Address:* 20 Lyonsdown Road, Barnet, Herts EN5 1JE. *T:* 0181–449 7181. *Club:* Athenæum.

STOCKDALE, Sir Noel; *see* Stockdale, Sir A. N.

STOCKDALE, Sir Thomas (Minshull), 2nd Bt *cr* 1960, of Hoddington, Co. Southampton; barrister; *b* 7 Jan. 1940; *s* of Sir Edmund Villiers Minshull Stockdale, 1st Bt and Hon. Louise Fermor-Hesketh (*d* 1994), *er d* of 1st Lord Hesketh; *S* father, 1989; *m* 1965, Jacqueline Ha-Van-Vuong; one *s* one *d*. *Educ:* Eton; Worcester Coll., Oxford (MA). Called to Bar, Inner Temple, 1966. *Recreations:* shooting, travel. *Heir: s* John Minshull Stockdale, *b* 13 Dec. 1967. *Address:* Manor Farm, Weston Patrick, Basingstoke, Hants RG25 2NT; 73 Alderney Street, SW1V 4HH. *Clubs:* Turf, MCC.

STOCKER, Prof. Bruce Arnold Dunbar, FRS 1966; MD; Professor of Medical Microbiology in Stanford University, 1966–87, now Emeritus Active; *b* 26 May 1917. *Educ:* King's College, London; Westminster Hosp. Med. Sch. MB, BS, 1940; MRCS, LRCP, 1940; MD 1947. Guinness Prof. of Microbiology, Univ. of London, and Dir of Guinness-Lister Microbiological Research Unit, Lister Inst. of Preventive Med., until Dec. 1965. *Publications:* articles in scientific jls. *Address:* Department of Microbiology and Immunology, Stanford University School of Medicine, Stanford, CA 94305–5402, USA. *T:* (415) 7232006, *Fax:* (415) 7256757.

STOCKER, Rt. Hon. Sir John (Dexter), Kt 1973; MC; TD; PC 1986; a Lord Justice of Appeal, 1986–92; *b* 7 Oct. 1918; *s* of late John Augustus Stocker and Emma Eyre Stocker (*née* Kettle), Hampstead; *m* 1956, Margaret Mary Hegarty (*d* 1987); no *c*. *Educ:* Westminster Sch.; London University. 2nd Lt, QO Royal West Kent Regt, 1939; France, 1940; Middle East, 1942–43; Italy, 1943–46; Maj. 1943; Lt-Col 1945. LLB London 1947. Called to Bar, Middle Temple, 1948, Master of the Bench, 1971. QC 1965; a Recorder, 1972–73; Judge of the High Court, Queen's Bench Div., 1973–86; Presiding Judge, SE Circuit, 1976–79. *Recreations:* golf, cricket. *Address:* 20 Parkside Gardens, Wimbledon, SW19 5EU. *Clubs:* Naval and Military, Army and Navy, MCC; Royal Wimbledon Golf.

STOCKER, John Wilcox, PhD; FRACP; Director, Research and Innovation, Pratt Industries, Melbourne, since 1995; *b* 23 April 1945; *s* of W. R. Stocker and Gladys Noelle Davies; *m* 1973, Joanne Elizabeth Gross; two *d*. *Educ:* Wesley Coll., Univ. of Melbourne (MB BS BMedSc). FTS. RMO, Royal Melbourne Hosp., 1970–72; Res. Scientist, Walter & Eliza Hall Inst. of Med. Res., 1974–76; Mem., Basel Inst. of Immunology, 1976–78; Central Res. Unit, 1979–84; Dir, Pharm. Res., Hoffman-La Roche & Co., Basel, 1986–87; Dir, Vic. Govt Strategic Res. Foundn, 1988–; Chief Exec., CSIRO, 1990–95. Founding Man. Dir, AMRAD; Dir, Gene Shears Pty, 1992–. Mem., numerous Industry and Govt sci. orgns. *Publications:* scientific papers, contribs to learned jls. *Recreations:* tennis, tiling, gardening, reading. *Address:* Pratt Industries, 533 Little Lonsdale Street, Melbourne, Vic 3000, Australia. *T:* (3) 2474777. *Club:* Winzergenossenschaft zur Landskron (Switzerland).

STOCKHAUSEN, Karlheinz; composer and conductor; *b* 22 Aug. 1928; *s* of late Simon and Gertrud Stockhausen; *m* 1st, 1951, Doris Andreae; one *s* three *d*; 2nd, 1967, Mary Bauermeister; one *s* one *d*. *Educ:* Hochschule für Musik, and Univ., Cologne, 1947–51; studied with: Messiaen, 1952–53; Prof. Werner Meyer-Eppler, Bonn Univ., 1954–56. With Westdeutscher Rundfunk Electronic Music Studio, 1953–, Artistic Dir, 1963–77. Lectr, Internat. Summer Sch. for New Music, Darmstadt, 1953–74; Dir, Interpretation Group for live electronic music, 1964–; Founder, and Artistic Dir, Kölner Kurse für Neue Musik, 1963–68; Visiting Professor: Univ. of Pa, 1965; Univ. of Calif, 1966–67; Prof. of Composition, Cologne State Conservatory, 1971–77. Co-Editor, Die Reihe, 1954–59. First annual tour of 30 concerts and lectures, 1958, USA and Canada, since then throughout world. Has composed 250 individually performable works and made more than 100 records of his own works; since 1991 has been involved with production of complete issue of his works on CD. Member or Foreign Member: Akad. der Künste, Hamburg, 1968; Kungl. Musikaliska Akad., Sweden, 1970; Akad. der Künste, Berlin, 1973; Amer. Acad. and Inst. of Arts and Letters, 1977; Acad. Filarmonica Romana, 1979; Acad. Européenne des Sciences, des Arts et des Lettres, 1980; Hon. RAM 1987. Awards and Prizes from France, Germany, Italy and USA; Prix Ars Electronica, Cluiz, Austria, 1990; Picasso Medal, UNESCO, 1992. Bundesverdienstkreuz 1st class, 1974; Verdienstorden des Landes Nordrhein-Westfalen, 1992. *Publications:* Texte, 6 vols, 1963–89; Stockhausen on Music, 1989; *compositions:* Chöre für Doris, Drei Lieder, Choral, 1950–51; Sonatine, Kreuzspiel, Formel, 1951; Schlagtrio, Spiel für Orchester, Etude, 1952; Punkte, 1952, rev. 1962, Klavierstücke I-XI, 1952–56; Kontra-Punkte, 1953; Elektronische Studien I and II, 1953–54; Zeitmasze, Gesang der Jünglinge, 1956; Gruppen, 1957; Zyklus, Refrain, 1959; Carré, Kontakte für elektronische Klänge, Kontakte für elektronische Klänge, Klavier und Schlagzeug, 1960; Originale (musical play with Kontakte), 1961; Plus Minus, 1963; Momente, 1962–64, completed, 1969; Mixtur (new arr. 1967), Mikrophonie I, 1964; Mikrophonie II, Stop (new arr. 1969), 1965; Telemusik, Solo, Adieu, 1966; Hymnen,

Prozession, Ensemble, 1967; Kurzwellen, Stimmung, Aus den sieben Tagen, Spiral, Musik für ein Haus, 1968; Für Kommende Zeiten, 1968–70; Hymnen mit Orchester, Fresco, Dr K-Sextett, 1969; Pole, Expo, Mantra, 1970; Sternklang, Trans, 1971; Alphabet für Liège, Am Himmel wandre ich, (Indianerlieder), Ylem, 1972; Inori, 1973–74; Vortrag über Hu, Herbstmusik, Atmen gibt das Leben..., 1974; Musik im Bauch, Harlekin, Der Kleine Harlekin, 1975; Tierkreis, 1975–76; Sirius, 1975–77; Amour, 1976; Jubiläum, In Freundschaft, 1977; Licht, die sieben Tage der Woche (an operatic cycle for solo voices, solo instruments, solo dancers/choirs, orchestras, ballet and mimes/electronic and concrete music), 1977–: Donnerstag 1978–80 (Donnerstags-Gruss, or Michaels-Gruss, 1978; Unsichtbare Chöre, 1978–79; Michaels Jugend, 1979; Michaels Reise um die Erde, 1978; Michaels Heimkehr, 1980; Donnerstags-Abschied, 1980); Samstag, 1981–84 (Samstags-Gruss or Luzifers-Gruss, 1983; Luzifers Traum or Klavierstück XIII, 1981; Traum-Formel, 1981; Kathinkas Gesang als Luzifers Requiem, 1982–83; Luzifers Tanz, 1983; Luzifers Abschied, 1982); Montag, 1984–88 (Montags-Gruss, or Eva-Gruss, 1984/88; Evas Erstgeburt, 1987; Evas Zweitgeburt, 1984/87; Klavierstück XIV, 1984; Evas Zauber, 1986; Montags-Abschied, or Eva-Abschied, 1988); Dienstag, 1977/1990–91 (Jahreslauf, 1977–91; Invasion-Explosion mit Abschied, 1990–91); Freitag, 1992–94. *Address:* Stockhausen-Verlag, Kettenberg 15, 51515 Kürten, Germany.

STOCKING, Barbara Mary, (Mrs R. J. MacInnes); Chief Executive, Anglia and Oxford Regional Health Authority and Regional Director, NHS Executive, since 1994;' *b* 28 July 1951; *d* of Percy Frederick Stocking and Mary Stocking; *m* 1981, Dr R. John MacInnes; two *s*. *Educ:* New Hall, Cambridge (BA); Univ. of Wisconsin (MS). Teaching Asst, Dept of Physiology and Biophysics, Univ. of Illinois, 1972–73; Staff Associate, Nat. Acad. of Scis, Washington, 1974–76; Jt Research Fellow, Nuffield Provincial Hosps Trust and Centre for Med. Res., Univ. of Sussex, 1977–79; Sec., WHO Independent Commn on Long Term Prospects of Onchocerciasis Control Programme, LSHTM, 1979–91; Sen. Nuffield Res. Fellow, Centre for Med. Res., Univ. of Sussex, attached to Dept of Community Health, LSHTM, 1981–83; Fellow in Health Policy, Innovation and Evaluation, King's Fund Coll., 1983–86; Dir, King's Fund Centre for Health Services Develt, 1987–93; Chief Exec., Oxford RHA, 1993–94. Member: UK Harkness Fellowships Adv. and Selection Cttee, 1989–95; NHS Central R&D Cttee, 1992–. Mem., UK Forum, 1991–. *Publications:* (jtly) The Image and the Reality: a case study of the impacts of medical technology, 1978; (ed jtly and contrib.) Patterns for Uncertainty, 1979; Initiative and Inertia: case studies in the health services, 1985; (ed) In Dreams Begins Responsibility: a tribute to Tom Evans, 1987; (ed) Expensive Medical Technologies, 1988; (Series Editor) A Study of the Diffusion of Medical Technology in Europe, 3 vols, 1991; (jtly) Criteria for Change, 1991; Medical Advances: the future shape of acute services, 1991. *Recreation:* anything foreign. *Address:* 7 Dunstan Road, Oxford OX3 9BY. *T:* (work) Milton Keynes (01908) 844400.

STOCKPORT, Bishop Suffragan of, since 1994; **Rt. Rev. Geoffrey Martin Turner;** *b* 16 March 1934; *s* of Ernest Hugh Turner and Winifred Rose Turner (*née* Martin); *m* 1959, Gillian Chope; two *s* one *d*. *Educ:* Bideford Grammar Sch.; Sandhurst; Oak Hill Theol Coll. Ordained deacon, 1963, priest, 1964; Assistant Curate: St Stephen, Tonbridge, 1963–66; St John, Heatherlands, dio. of Salisbury, 1966–69; Vicar: St Peter, Derby, 1969–73; Christ Church, Chadderton, dio. of Manchester, 1973–79; Rector of Bebington, 1979–93; Rural Dean, Wirral North, 1989–93; Hon. Canon, Chester Cathedral, 1989–93; Archdeacon of Chester, 1993–94. *Recreations:* sport, spy fiction, fishing. *Address:* Bishop's Lodge, Dunham Town, Altrincham WA14 4SG. *T:* 0161–928 5611. *Club:* National Liberal.

STOCKTON, 2nd Earl of, *cr* 1984; **Alexander Daniel Alan Macmillan;** Viscount Macmillan of Ovenden, 1984; President, Macmillan Ltd, since 1990; *b* Oswestry, Shropshire, 10 Oct. 1943; *s* of Viscount Macmillan of Ovenden, PC, MP (*d* 1984) and of Katharine Viscountess Macmillan of Ovenden, DBE; *S* grandfather, 1986; *m* 1970, Hélène Birgitte (marr. diss. 1991), *o d* of late Alan D. C. Hamilton, Mitford, Northumberland; one *s* two *d*. *Educ:* Eton; Université de Paris, Strathclyde Univ. Contested (C) Bristol, Eur. Parly elecns, 1994. MIMgt (MBIM 1981); FRSA 1987. Liveryman: Worshipful Co. of Merchant Taylors, 1972 (Mem., Ct of Assts, 1987–; Master, 1992–93); Worshipful Co. of Stationers and Newspaper Makers, 1973. DUniv Strathclyde, Hon. DLitt De Montfort, 1993. *Heir: s* Viscount Macmillan of Ovenden, *qv*. *Address:* 25 Eccleston Place, SW1W 9NF. *Clubs:* Beefsteak, Buck's, Garrick, Pratt's, White's.

STOCKWELL, Air Cdre Edmund Arthur, CB 1967; MA; Command Education Officer, Training Command, 1968–72 (Flying Training Command, 1964–68); retired 1972; *b* 15 Dec. 1911; *e s* of Arthur Davenport Stockwell, Dewsbury; *m* 1937, Pearl Arber; two *d* (one *s* decd); *m* 1955, Lillian Gertrude Moore (*d* 1965), OBE, MRCP; two *s*; *m* 1970, Mrs Kathleen (Betty) Clarke, Chesham. *Educ:* Wheelwright Grammar School; Balliol Coll., Oxford (Williams Exhibnr; BA 1933; MA 1939). Entered RAF Educational Service, Cranwell, 1935; RAF Educn in India, 1936; Punjab and NW Frontier, 1936–38; RAFVR (Admin and Special Duties), 1939; Lahore, Simla, Delhi, 1939–44; Group Educn Officer, No 6 (RCAF) Group, 1944; Air Min., 1944–48; OC, RAF Sch. of Educn, 1948–51; Comd Educn Officer, Coastal Comd, 1951–53; Comd Educn Officer, Far East Air Force, 1953–55; Principal Educn Officer, Halton, 1956–59; Comd Educn Officer, Maintenance Comd, 1959–62; Dep. Dir of Educational Services, Air Min., 1962–64. Group Captain, 1954; Air Commodore, 1964. FRAeS 1963. *Recreations:* golf, gardening. *Address:* 95 Newland, Sherborne, Dorset DT9 3AS. *T:* Sherborne (01935) 815689.

STOCKWIN, Prof. James Arthur Ainscow; Nissan Professor of Modern Japanese Studies, Director of Nissan Institute of Japanese Studies, University of Oxford and Fellow, St Antony's College, Oxford, since 1982; *b* 28 Nov. 1935; *s* of Wilfred Arthur Stockwin and Edith Mary Stockwin; *m* 1960, Audrey Lucretia Hobson Stockwin (*née* Wood); one *s* two *d* (and one *s* decd). *Educ:* Exeter Coll., Oxford Univ. (MA); Australian Nat. Univ. (PhD). Australian National University: Lectr, Dept of Political Science, 1964–66; Sen. Lectr, 1966–72; Reader, 1972–81. Pres., British Assoc. of Japanese Studies, 1994–95. Gen. Ed., Nissan Inst.—Routledge Japanese Studies Series, 1984–. *Publications:* The Japanese Socialist Party and Neutralism, 1968; (ed) Japan and Australia in the Seventies, 1972; Japan, Divided Politics in a Growth Economy, 1975, 2nd edn 1982; Why Japan Matters, 1983; (jtly, also ed) Dynamic and Immobilist Politics in Japan, 1988; (trans.) Junji Banno, The Establishment of the Japanese Constitutional System, 1992; The Story of Tim, 1993; articles, largely on Japanese politics and foreign policy, in Pacific Affairs, Aust. Outlook, Aust. Jl Politics and History, Asian Survey, Japan Forum, etc. *Recreations:* languages, exercise. *Address:* Nissan Institute of Japanese Studies, 27 Winchester Road, Oxford OX2 6NA. *T:* Oxford (01865) 274570, *Fax:* (01865) 274574.

STODART, family name of **Baron Stodart of Leaston.**

STODART OF LEASTON, Baron *cr* 1981 (Life Peer), of Humbie in the District of East Lothian; **James Anthony Stodart;** PC 1974; *b* 6 June 1916; *yr s* of late Col Thomas Stodart, CIE, IMS, and of Mary Alice Coullie; *m* 1940, Hazel Jean Usher (*d* 1995). *Educ:* Wellington. Farming at Kingston, North Berwick, 1934–58, and now at Leaston, Humbie, East Lothian. Hon. Pres., Edinburgh Univ. Agricultural Soc., 1952; Pres. East Lothian Boy Scouts' Assoc., 1960–63. Contested: (L) Berwick and East Lothian, 1950; (C) Midlothian and Peebles, 1951; Midlothian, 1955; MP (C) Edinburgh West, 1959–Oct. 1974; Jt Under-Sec. of State, Scottish Office, Sept. 1963–Oct. 1964; An Opposition spokesman on Agriculture and on Scottish Affairs, 1966–69; Parly Sec., MAFF, 1970–72; Minister of State, MAFF, 1972–74; Vice-Chm., Conservative Agric. Cttee, House of Commons, 1962–63, 1964–65, 1966–70. Led Parly Delegns to Canada, 1974, 1983. Dir, FMC, 1980–82; Chm., Agricultural Credit Corp. Ltd, 1975–87. Chairman: Cttee of Inquiry into Local Govt in Scotland, 1980; Manpower Review of Vet. Profession in UK, 1984–85. *Publications:* (jt author) Land of Abundance, a study of Scottish Agriculture in the 20th Century, 1962; contrib. on farming topics to agricultural journals and newspapers. *Recreations:* music, playing golf and preserving a sense of humour. *Address:* Lorimers, North Berwick, East Lothian EH39 4NG. *T:* North Berwick (01620) 892457; Leaston, Humbie, E Lothian EH36 5DP. *T:* Humbie (01875) 833213. *Clubs:* Caledonian; New (Edinburgh); Hon. Company of Edinburgh Golfers.

STODDART, family name of **Baron Stoddart of Swindon.**

STODDART OF SWINDON, Baron *cr* 1983 (Life Peer), of Reading in the Royal County of Berkshire; **David Leonard Stoddart;** *b* 4 May 1926; *s* of Arthur Leonard Stoddart, coal miner, and Queenie Victoria Stoddart (*née* Price); *m* 1961, Jennifer Percival-Alwyn; two *s* (one *d* by previous marr.). *Educ:* elementary; St Clement Danes and Henley Grammar Schools. Youth in training, PO Telephones, 1942–44; business on own account, 1944–46; Railway Clerk, 1947–49; Hospital Clerk, 1949–51; Power Station Clerical Worker, 1951–70. Joined Labour Party, 1947; Member Reading County Borough Council, 1954–72; served at various times as Chairman of Housing, Transport and Finance Cttees; Leader of the Reading Labour Group of Councillors, 1962–70. Contested (Lab) Newbury, 1959 and 1964, Swindon, 1969, 1983. MP (Lab) Swindon, 1970–83; PPS to Minister for Housing and Construction, 1974–75; an Asst Govt Whip, 1975; a Lord Comr, HM Treasury, 1976–77; an opposition whip, and opposition spokesman on energy, House of Lords, 1983–88. Chm., Campaign for an Indep. Britain, 1985–. *Recreations:* gardening, music. *Address:* Sintra, 37A Bath Road, Reading, Berks RG1 6HL. *T:* Reading (01734) 576726.

STODDART, Anne Elizabeth; HM Diplomatic Service; Deputy Permanent Representative (Economic Affairs), UK Mission to the United Nations, Geneva, since 1991; *b* 29 March 1937; *d* of late James Stoddart and Ann Jack Stoddart (*née* Inglis). *Educ:* Kirby Grammar School, Middlesbrough; Somerville College, Oxford. MA. Entered Foreign Office, 1960; British Military Govt, Berlin, 1963–67; FCO, 1967–70; First Secretary (Economic), Ankara, 1970–73; Head of Chancery, Colombo, 1974–76; FCO, 1977–81; Dep. Permanent UK Rep. to Council of Europe, Strasbourg, 1981–87; seconded to External Eur. Policy Div., DTI, 1987–91. *Address:* c/o Foreign and Commonwealth Office, SW1A 2AH.

STODDART, Charles Norman, PhD; Sheriff of North Strathclyde at Paisley, since 1988; *b* 4 April 1948; *s* of Robert Stoddart and Margaret (*née* Allenby); *m* 1981, Anne Lees; one *d*. *Educ:* Edinburgh Univ. (LLB, PhD); McGill Univ. (LLM). Admitted Solicitor, 1972, practised, 1972–73, 1980–88; Lectr in Scots Law, Edinburgh Univ., 1973–80. Editor, Green's Criminal Law Bulletin, 1992–. *Publications:* (with H. Neilson) The Law and Practice of Legal Aid in Scotland, 1979, 4th edn 1994; (with C. H. W. Gane) A Casebook on Scottish Criminal Law, 1980, 2nd edn 1988; Bible John (crime documentary), 1980; (with C. H. W. Gane) Cases and Materials on Scottish Criminal Procedure, 1983, 2nd edn 1994; Criminal Warrants, 1991; contribs to professional jls. *Recreations:* music, foreign travel, ski-ing and other sport. *Address:* Sheriff's Chambers, Sheriff Court House, 106 Renfrew Road, Paisley PA3 4DD. *T:* 0141–887 5291.

STODDART, Christopher West; Managing Director, GMTV Ltd, since 1992; *b* 10 April 1950; *s* of Dr Ian West Stoddart and Bridget Stoddart (*née* Pilditch); *m* 1st, 1972, Deborah Ounsted (marr. diss. 1984); 2nd, 1985, Dr Hazel Grasmere, *d* of Hon. Robert and Evelyn Grasmere, USA. *Educ:* Winchester Coll.; Churchill Coll., Cambridge (BA Hons 1971). Joined CS, 1971; DoE, 1971–75; Research Sec., Centre for Envmtl Studies, 1976–80; Regl Companies Sec., 1980–81, Sec. 1981–82, ITCA; Tyne Tees Television: Gen. Manager, 1982–83; Dir of Resources, 1983–88; Man. Dir and Chief Exec., Satellite Information Services Ltd, 1988–92. *Publication:* The Inner City as Testing Ground for Government-funded Research, 1980. *Recreations:* mountaineering, wind-surfing, bad weather. *Address:* 7 Lyndhurst Terrace, NW3 5QA.

STODDART, Prof. John Little, CBE 1994; PhD, DSc; FIBiol; FRAgS; Director of Research, Institute of Grassland and Environmental Research, Agricultural and Food Research Council, 1988–93; *b* 1 Oct. 1933; *s* of John Little Stoddart and Margaret Pickering Dye; *m* 1957, Wendy Dalton Leardie; one *d* (one *s* decd). *Educ:* South Shields High Sch. for Boys; University Coll., Durham (BSc Botany 1954); University of Wales, Aberystwyth (PhD 1961); Durham Univ. (DSc 1973). FIBiol 1984; ARPS 1985; FRAgS 1993. Nat. Service, RA, UK, Hong Kong and Malaya, 1954–56. Fulbright-Hays Sen. Fellow, 1966–67; Res. Associate, Mich. State Univ./Atomic Energy Commn Plant Res. Lab., 1966–67; Welsh Plant Breeding Station: Dep. Dir, 1985–87; Dir, 1987–88; Head of Plants and Soils Div., 1985–88. Hon. Prof., Sch. of Agric. and Biol Scis, Univ. of Wales, 1988–. Chm., Plant Sci. Res. Adv. Cttee, ODA, 1995–. Mem. Council, NIAB, 1988–93. Non-exec. Dir, Derwen NHS Trust (W Wales), 1994–. Mem., Stapledon Meml Trust, 1988–. *Publications:* scientific articles, reviews and contribs to scientific books. *Recreations:* photography (pictorial), golf. *Address:* Institute of Biological Sciences, University of Wales, Aberystwyth, Dyfed SY23 3DA.

STODDART, John Maurice, CBE 1995; Principal, Sheffield Hallam University, since 1992 (Principal, Sheffield City Polytechnic, 1983–92); *b* 18 Sept. 1938; *s* of Gordon Stoddart and May (*née* Ledder). *Educ:* Wallasey Grammar Sch.; Univ. of Reading (BA Pol Econ.). FBIM 1977. Teacher, Wallasey GS, 1960–62; Lectr, Mid Cheshire Coll. of Further Educn, 1962–64; Lectr, Enfield Coll., 1964–70; Head, Dept of Econs and Business Studies, Sheffield Polytechnic, 1970–72; Asst Dir, NE London Polytechnic, 1972–76; Dir, Hull Coll. of Higher Educn (now Humberside Poly.), 1976–83. Dir, Sheffield Science Park Co. Ltd, 1988–. Chm., CNAA Cttee for Business and Management, 1985–88 (Chm., Undergrad. Courses Bd, 1976–83); Mem., CNAA, 1982–88, 1991–93; Chm., Cttee of Dirs of Polys, 1990–93 (Vice-Chm., 1988–90). Member: Sea Fisheries Trng Council, 1976–80; Architects Registration Council, UK, 1979–85; Council for Management Educn and Develt, 1988–; Council for Industry and Educn, 1989–; Council for Educn and Trng in Social Work, 1989–; BTEC, 1991–; Chm., Higher Educn Quality Council, 1992–. Member: Court, Univ. of Hull, 1976–83; Council, Univ. of Sheffield, 1983–92. Companion, British Business Graduates Soc., 1983; Hon. Fellow, Humberside Coll., 1983; FRSA 1977. CIMgt (CBIM 1990). Hon. DEd CNAA, 1992; Hon. DLitt Coventry, 1993; DUniv Middlesex, 1993. *Publications:* articles on business and management educn. *Address:* 58 Riverdale Road, Sheffield S10 3FB. *T:* Sheffield (0114) 268 3636. *Clubs:* Reform; Leander (Henley-on-Thames).

STODDART, Sir Kenneth (Maxwell), KCVO 1989; AE 1942; JP; DL; Lord-Lieutenant, Metropolitan County of Merseyside, 1979–89; *b* 26 May 1914; *s* of late Wilfrid Bowring

Stoddart and Mary Hyslop Stoddart (*née* Maxwell); *m* 1940, Jean Roberta Benson Young, DL; two *d*. *Educ:* Sedbergh; Clare Coll., Cambridge. Chairman: Cearns and Brown Ltd, 1973–84; United Mersey Supply Co. Ltd, 1978–81. Commissioned No 611 (West Lancashire) Sqdn, Auxiliary Air Force, 1936; served War, UK and Europe; comd W Lancashire Wing, Air Trng Corps, 1946–54; Vice-Chm. (Air) W Lancashire T&AFA, 1954–64. Pres., Merseyside Wing, ATC, 1991–. Chairman, Liverpool Child Welfare Assoc., 1965–81. DL Lancashire 1958 (transf. to Metropolitan County of Merseyside, 1974); JP Liverpool 1952; High Sheriff of Merseyside, 1974. Hon. Fellow, Liverpool Poly., 1989. Hon. LLD Liverpool, 1986. KStJ 1979. *Recreations:* gardening, walking. *Address:* The Spinney, Overdale Road, Willaston, South Wirral L64 1SY. *T:* 0151–327 5183. *Club:* Liverpool Racquet.

STODDART, Michael Craig, FCA; Chairman: Electra Investment Trust, since 1986; Electra Fleming Holdings (formerly Electra Kingsway), since 1988; *b* 27 March 1932; *s* of Frank Ogle Boyd Stoddart and Barbara Craig; *m* 1961, Susan Brigid (*née* O'Halloran); two *s* two *d*. *Educ:* Abberley Hall, Worcs; Marlborough Coll. Chartered Accountant 1955; joined Singer & Friedlander, 1955: resp. for opening provincial network; retired as Jt Chief Exec., 1973; Dep. Chm. and Chief Exec., Electra Investment Trust, 1974; pioneered into substantial unlisted investments, incl. developing venture capital arm. Non-executive Chairman: Sphere Drake, 1993– (Dir, 1987–); BSG plc, 1994–; non-executive Director: Bullough, 1968–; Next plc, 1974–; Summit Gp plc, 1990–, and other cos in UK and USA. *Recreations:* country pursuits, shooting, tennis, golf, theatre. *Address:* Compton House, Kinver, Worcs DY7 5LY. *Club:* Boodle's.

STOGDON, Norman Francis; a Recorder of the Crown Court, 1972–83; *b* 14 June 1909; *s* of late F. R. Stogdon and late L. Stogdon (*née* Reynolds); *m* 1959, Yvonne (*née* Jaques). *Educ:* Harrow; Brasenose Coll., Oxford (BA, BCL). Called to Bar, Middle Temple, 1932. War Service, Army, 1939–45: served with Royal Fusiliers, King's African Rifles, 1941–45; Staff Officer; sc Middle East 1944. Part-time Chairman: Mental Health Tribunal, 1960–81; Industrial Tribunal, 1975–83. Contested (Lab): Gosport, 1951; Banbury and N Oxford, 1955. ACIArb 1984. *Publications:* contrib. 2nd, 3rd and 4th edns Halsbury's Laws of England. *Recreations:* golf, ski-ing. *Address:* The Cloisters, Temple, EC4Y 7AA. *T:* 0171–353 2548. *Club:* Moor Park Golf.

STOICHEFF, Prof. Boris Peter, OC 1982; FRS 1975; FRSC 1965; Professor of Physics, 1964–89, now Emeritus, and University Professor, 1977–89, now Emeritus, University of Toronto; *b* 1 June 1924; *s* of Peter and Vasilka Stoicheff; *m* 1954, Lillian Joan Ambridge; one *s*. *Educ:* Univ. of Toronto, Faculty of Applied Science and Engineering (BASc), Dept of Physics (MA, PhD). McKee-Gilchrist Fellowship, Univ. of Toronto, 1950–51; National Research Council of Canada: Fellowship, Ottawa, 1952–53; Res. Officer in Div. of Pure Physics, 1953–64; Mem. Council, 1978–83. Exec. Dir, Ontario Laser and Lightware Res. Centre, 1988–91. Visiting Scientist, Mass Inst. of Technology, 1963–64. Chm., Engrg Science, Univ. of Toronto, 1972–77. Izaak Walton Killam Meml Scholarship, 1977–79; Senior Fellow, Massey Coll., Univ. of Toronto, 1979. H. L. Welsh Lecture, Univ. of Toronto, 1984; Elizabeth Laird Meml Lecture, Univ. Western Ontario, 1985; UK/Canada Rutherford Lectr, 1989. Pres., Canadian Assoc. of Physicists, 1983–84; Council Mem., Assoc. of Professional Engrs of Ontario, 1985–. Fellow, Optical Soc. of America, 1965 (Pres. 1976); Fellow, Amer. Phys. Soc., 1969; Geoffrey Frew Fellow, Australian Acad. of Science, 1980. Hon. Fellow: Indian Acad. of Scis, 1971; Macedonian Acad. of Sci. and Arts, 1981; Foreign Hon. Fellow, Amer. Acad. of Arts and Scis, 1989. Hon. DSc: York, Canada, 1982; Skopje, Yugoslavia, 1982; Windsor, Canada, 1989; Toronto, 1994. Gold Medal for Achievement in Physics of Canadian Assoc. of Physicists, 1974; William F. Meggers Award, Optical Soc. of America, 1981; Frederic Ives Medal, Optical Soc. of America, 1983; Henry Marshall Tory Medal, RSC, 1989. Centennial Medal of Canada, 1967. *Publications:* numerous scientific contribs to phys. and chem. jls. *Address:* Department of Physics, University of Toronto, Toronto, Ontario M5S 1A7, Canada. *T:* (416) 9782948.

STOKE-UPON-TRENT, Archdeacon of: *see* Ede, Ven. D.

STOKER, Dr Dennis James, FRCP, FRCS, FRCR; Consultant Radiologist, King Edward VII Hospital for Officers, London Clinic, and Royal National Orthopaedic Hospital, 1972–93; Senior Lecturer and Director of Radiological Studies, Institute of Orthopaedics, 1977–93; *b* 22 March 1928; *yr s* of Dr George Morris Stoker and Elsie Margaret Stoker (*née* Macqueen); *m* 1951, Anne Sylvia Nelson Forster; two *s* two *d*. *Educ:* Oundle Sch.; Guy's Hosp. Med. Sch. MB BS; DMRD; FRCP 1976; FRCS 1992. Guy's Hosp. appts, 1951–52; RAF Med. Branch, 1951–68; served Cyprus and Aden; Wing Cdr (retd). Consultant Physician, RAF, 1964–68; Registrar and Sen. Registrar, Diagnostic Radiology, St George's Hosp., London, 1968–72; Dean, Inst. of Orthopaedics, 1987–91. Royal Society of Medicine: Fellow, 1958; Mem. Council, Section of Radiol., 1975–77; Vice-Pres., 1978–80; Royal College of Radiologists: Fellow, 1976; Examr, 1981–84 and 1985–88; George Simon Lectr, 1988; Dean and Vice-Pres., 1989–91; Robert Knox Lectr, 1992. Fellow, British Orth. Assoc.; Mem., Internat. Skeletal Soc., 1974– (Medal, 1993). Editor, Skeletal Radiology, 1984–; Mem., Editl Bd, Clinical Radiology, 1974–84. *Publications:* Knee Arthrography, 1980; (jtly) Self Assessment in Orthopaedic Radiology, 1988; The Radiology of Skeletal Disorders, 1990; chapters in textbooks; papers on metabolic medicine, tropical disease and skeletal radiology. *Recreations:* philology, medical history. *Address:* 18 Llangar Grove, Crowthorne, Berks RG11 6EA. *T:* Crowthorne (01344) 777948. *Club:* Royal Air Force.

STOKER, John Francis; Regional Director, Government Office for Merseyside, since 1994; *b* 11 Sept. 1950; *s* of Francis Charles Stoker and Joyce Stoker (*née* Barnwell); *m* 1982, Julie Puddicombe. *Educ:* King Edward's Sch., Birmingham; Brasenose Coll., Oxford (BA Lit.Hum.). Department of the Environment: Admin Trainee, 1973–78; Principal, 1978; Tenant's Right to Buy, 1979–81; Alternatives to Rates, 1981–83; Cabinet Office, 1983–85; Grade 5, 1985; Envmt White Paper Div., 1990–92; Dir, Merseyside Task Force, Grade 3, 1992–94. *Recreations:* books, music, gardening. *Address:* Graeme House, Derby Square, Liverpool L2 7SU. *T:* 0151–224 6459. *Clubs:* Athenæum (Liverpool); Middlesex CC.

STOKER, Sir Michael (George Parke), Kt 1980; CBE 1974; FRCP 1979; FRS 1968; FRSE 1960; President of Clare Hall, Cambridge, 1980–87 (Fellow, 1978); *b* 4 July 1918; *e s* of Dr S. P. Stoker, Maypole, Monmouth; *m* 1942, Veronica Mary English; three *s* two *d*. *Educ:* Oakham Sch.; Sidney Sussex Coll., Cambridge (Hon. Fellow 1981); St Thomas' Hosp., London. MRCS, LRCP 1942; MB, BChir 1943; MD 1947. RAMC, 1942–47; Demonstrator in Pathology, Cambridge Univ., 1947–48; Univ. Lecturer in Pathology, 1948–50; Huddersfield Lecturer in Special Pathology, 1950–58; Asst Tutor and Dir of Medical Studies, Clare Coll., 1949–58; Fellow of Clare College, 1948–58, Hon. Fellow, 1976; Prof. of Virology, Glasgow Univ., and Hon. Dir, MRC Experimental Virus Research Unit, 1959–68; Dir, Imperial Cancer Res. Fund Laboratories, 1968–79. Hon. Consultant, ICRF Cell Interactions Lab., Cambridge Univ. Med. Sch., 1980–. WHO Travel Fellow, 1951; Rockefeller Foundn Travel Fellow, 1958; Vis. Prof., UCL, 1968–79. Royal Society: For. Sec., 1977–81; a Vice-Pres., 1977–81; Leeuwenhoek Lecture, 1971, Blackett Meml Lecture, 1980; Mendel Gold Medal, 1978. Dir, Celltech Ltd, 1980–86. Member: European Molecular Biology Organisation; Council for Scientific Policy, DES, 1970–73; Gen. Cttee, Internat. Council of Scientific Unions, 1977–81; Eur. Acad. of Arts, Scis and Humanities, 1980; Med. Res. Council, 1982–86; Chairman: UK Co-ordinating Cttee, Cancer Res., 1983–86; Scientific Cttee, Ludwig Inst. Cancer Res., 1985–. Foreign Hon. Member: Amer. Acad. of Arts and Scis, 1973; Czech Acad. of Scis, 1980. Chm. of Trustees, Strangeways Res. Lab., Cambridge, 1981–93. Hon. DSc Glasgow, 1982. *Publications:* various articles on cell biology and virology. *Recreation:* painting. *Address:* 3 Barrington House, South Acre Drive, Cambridge CB2 2TY. *Club:* United Oxford & Cambridge University.

STOKES, family name of **Baron Stokes.**

STOKES, Baron *cr* 1969 (Life Peer), of Leyland; **Donald Gresham Stokes,** Kt 1965; TD; DL; FEng, FIMechE; MSAE; FIMI; FCIT; FICE; Chairman, KBH Communications, since 1987; Chairman and Managing Director, 1968–75, Chief Executive, 1973–75, British Leyland Motor Corporation Ltd; President, BL Ltd, 1975–79; Consultant to Leyland Vehicles, 1979–81; *b* 22 March 1914; *o s* of Harry Potts Stokes; *m* 1939, Laura Elizabeth Courteney Lamb (*d* 1995); one *s*. *Educ:* Blundell's School; Harris Institute of Technology, Preston. Started Student Apprenticeship, Leyland Motors Ltd, 1930. Served War of 1939–45: REME (Lt-Col). Re-joined Leyland as Exports Manager, 1946; General Sales and Service Manager, 1950; Director, 1954; Managing Director, and Deputy Chairman, Leyland Motor Corp., 1963, Chm. 1967; Chm. and Man. Dir, British Leyland Ltd, 1973. Director: National Westminster Bank, 1969–81; London Weekend Television Ltd, 1967–71; Opus Public Relations Ltd, 1979–84; Scottish & Universal Investments Ltd, 1980–92; Dovercourt Motor Co. Ltd, 1982–90; Beherman Auto-Transport SA, 1983–89; GWR Gp, 1990–94. Vice-President, Empresa Nacional de Autocamiones SA, Spain, 1959–73. Chairman: British Arabian Adv. Co. Ltd, 1977–85; Two Counties Radio Ltd, 1978–84, 1990–94 (Pres., 1984–90); Jack Barclay Ltd, 1980–90; British Arabian Technical Co-operation Ltd, 1981–85; Reliant Group, 1990; Dutton Forshaw Motor Gp, 1980–90. Vice-Pres., Engineering Employers Fedn, 1967–75; President: SMMT, 1961–62; Motor Industry Res. Assoc., 1965–66; Manchester Univ. Inst. of Science and Technology, 1972–76 (Vice-Pres., 1967–71); IMechE, 1972 (Vice-Pres., 1971); Chm., EDC for Electronics Industry, 1966–67; Member: NW Economic Planning Council, 1965–70; IRC, 1966–71 (Dep. Chm. 1969); EDC for the Motor Manufacturing Industry, 1967–; Council, Public Transport Assoc.; Worshipful Co. of Carmen. Fellow, IRTE (Pres., 1983–84), Hon. FIRTE. DL Lancs 1968. Hon. Fellow, Keble Coll., Oxford, 1968. Hon. LLD Lancaster, 1967; Hon. DTech Loughborough, 1968; Hon. DSc: Southampton, 1969; Salford, 1971. Officier de l'Ordre de la Couronne (Belgium), 1964; Commandeur de l'ordre de Leopold II (Belgium), 1972. *Recreation:* sailing. *Address:* 2 Branksome Cliff, Westminster Road, Poole, Dorset BH13 6JW. *Clubs:* Army and Navy; Royal Motor Yacht (Commodore, 1979–81).

STOKES, Dr Adrian Victor, OBE 1983; CChem; CEng; FBCS; FInstD; MRSC; MIMgt; Principal Consultant, NHS Information Management Centre (formerly Centre for Information Technology), since 1989 (Consultant, on secondment, 1986–88); *b* 25 June 1945; *s* of Alfred Samuel and Edna Stokes; *m* (marr. diss.). *Educ:* Orange Hill Grammar School, Edgware; University College London. BSc 1966 (1st cl. Hons), PhD 1970; FBCS 1978; MIMgt (MBIM 1986); CEng 1990. Research Programmer, GEC-Computers Ltd, 1969–71; Research Asst, Inst. of Computer Science, 1971–73; Research Fellow, UCL, 1973–77; Sen. Research Fellow and Sen. Lectr, Hatfield Polytechnic, 1977–81; Dir of Computing, St Thomas' Hosp., 1981–88 (King's Fund Fellow, 1981–84); Chm., European Workshop for Open Systems Expert Gp on Healthcare, 1991–. Vis. Prof., Nene Coll., 1994–. Member: Silver Jubilee Cttee on Improving Access for Disabled People, 1977–78; Cttee on Restrictions Against Disabled People, 1979–81; Social Security Adv. Cttee, 1980–; Dept of Transport Panel of Advisers on Disability, 1983–85; Disabled Persons' Transport Adv. Cttee, 1986–89. Chm., Disabled Drivers' Motor Club, 1972–82, 1991–94, Vice-Pres., 1982–; Chm., Exec. Cttee, RADAR, 1985–92. Governor, Motability, 1978–; Trustee: PHAB, 1982–90; Indep. Living (1993) Fund, 1993–; Independent Living (Extension) Fund, 1993–. Freeman, City of London, 1988; Freeman, Co. of Information Technologists, 1988. Hon. DSc Hertfordshire, 1994. *Publications:* An Introduction to Data Processing Networks, 1978; Viewdata: a public information utility, 1979, 2nd edn 1980; The Concise Encyclopaedia of Computer Terminology, 1981; Networks, 1981; (with C. Saiady) What to Read in Microcomputing, 1982; Concise Encyclopaedia of Information Technology, 1982, 3rd edn 1986, USA edn 1983; Integrated Office Systems, 1982; (with M. D. Bacon and J. M. Bacon) Computer Networks: fundamentals and practice, 1984; Overview of Data Communications, 1985; The A to Z of Business Computing, 1986; Communications Standards, 1986; OSI Standards and Acronyms, 1987, 3rd edn 1991; (with H. de Glanville) The BJHc Abbreviary, 1995; numerous papers and articles, mainly concerned with computer technology. *Recreations:* philately, science fiction, collecting Elvis Presley records, computer programming. *Address:* 97 Millway, Mill Hill, NW7 3JL. *T:* 0181–959 6665; (mobile) 0385 502766, *Fax:* 0181–906 4137.

STOKES, Dr Alistair Michael; Director, Speywood Holdings, since 1995; Chief Executive Officer, Speywood Pharmaceuticals, since 1995; *b* 22 July 1948; *s* of Alan Philip and Janet Ross Stokes; *m* 1970, Stephanie Mary Garland; two *d*. *Educ:* University College, Cardiff (BSc, PhD). With Pharmacia AB (Sweden), 1974–76; Monsanto Co., St Louis, USA, 1976–82; Glaxo Pharmaceuticals, 1982–85; Regional Gen. Manager, Yorkshire RHA, 1985–87; Dir, Glaxo Pharmaceuticals, 1987–90; Dir and Chief Operating Officer, Porton Internat., 1990–95. Chm., E Berks Community Health NHS Trust, 1993–. *Publications:* Plasma Proteins, 1977; biochemical and scientific papers. *Recreations:* music, cricket, travel. *Address:* Speywood Pharmaceuticals, Sun Court, Moorbridge Road, Maidenhead SL6 8LT. *Club:* Naval and Military.

STOKES, David Mayhew Allen; QC 1989; a Recorder of the Crown Court, since 1985; *b* 12 Feb. 1944; *s* of Henry Pauntley Allen Stokes and Marjorie Joan Stokes; *m* 1970, Ruth Elizabeth, *d* of late Charles Tunstall Evans, CMG, Haywards Heath; one *s* one *d*. *Educ:* Radley College; Inst. de Touraine (Tours); Churchill College, Cambridge (MA History/Law). Admitted Student, Gray's Inn, 1964; Holt Scholar, 1966; called to the Bar, 1968. Mem., Gen. Council of the Bar, 1989–91; Chm., SE Circuit Liaison Cttee, 1991–. Vis. Instructor/Team Leader, Nat. Inst. Trial Advocacy Workshop, Osgoode Hall Law Sch., York Univ., Toronto, 1986–. Trustee/Dir, London Suzuki Gp, 1988–94. Chm., Cambridge Bar Mess, 1991–. *Recreations:* amateur dramatics, madrigals. *Address:* 5 Paper Buildings, Temple, EC4Y 7HB. *T:* 0171–583 6117. *Club:* Norfolk (Norwich).

See also M. A. Evans.

STOKES, Harry Michael; HM Diplomatic Service, retired; Counsellor, Foreign and Commonwealth Office, 1979–81; *b* 22 July 1926; *s* of late Wing Comdr Henry Alban Stokes, RAF, and Lilian Frances (*née* Ede); *m* 1951, Prudence Mary Watling; two *s* one *d*. *Educ:* Rossall Sch.; Worcester Coll., Oxford (BA, Dip. Slavonic Studies). Served RAF, 1944–47. Joined Foreign Service, 1951; attached Control Commission, Germany, 1952–55; Foreign Office, 1955; Singapore, 1958; FO, 1959; Washington, 1961; Copenhagen, 1963; FO 1965; New Delhi, 1976; FO, 1977. Chm., British Assoc. for

Cemeteries in S Asia, 1985–92. Dir, Indo-British Review, 1988–92. *Recreations:* walking, racquet games, photography, music. *Club:* Commonwealth Trust.

STOKES, John Fisher, MA, MD, FRCP; Physician, University College Hospital, since 1947; *b* 19 Sept. 1912; *e s* of late Dr Kenneth Stokes and Mary (*née* Fisher); *m* 1940, Elizabeth Joan, *d* of Thomas Rooke and Elizabeth Frances (*née* Pearce); one *s* one *d*. *Educ:* Haileybury (exhibitioner); Gonville and Caius Coll., Cambridge (exhibitioner); University Coll. Hosp. (Fellowes Silver Medal for clinical medicine). MB BChir (Cambridge) 1937; MRCP 1939; MD (Cambridge) 1947 (proxime accessit, Horton Smith prize); FRCP 1947; FRCPE 1975; Thruston Medal, Gonville and Caius Coll., 1948. Appointments on junior staff University Coll. Hosp. and Victoria Hosp. for Children, Tite St, 1937–42; RAMC 1942–46; served in Far East, 1943–46, Lt-Col (despatches). Examiner in Medicine, various Univs, 1949–70. Member of Council, Royal Soc. of Med., 1951–54, 1967–69. Vice-Pres., RCP, 1968–69; Harveian Orator, RCP, 1981. Trustee, Leeds Castle Foundn, 1984–. Amateur Squash Rackets Champion of Surrey, 1935, of East of England, 1936, Runner-up of British Isles, 1937; English International, 1938; Technical Adviser to Squash Rackets Assoc., 1948–52; Chm. Jesters Club, 1953–59. *Publications:* Examinations in Medicine (jtly), 1976; contrib. on liver disease and general medicine in medical journals. *Recreations:* music, tennis, painting. *Address:* Ossicles, Newnham Hill, near Henley-on-Thames, Oxon RG9 5TL. *Clubs:* Athenæum, Savile.

STOKES, Sir John (Heydon Romaine), Kt 1988; *b* 23 July 1917; *o* surv. *s* of late Victor Romaine Stokes, Hitchin; *m* 1st, 1939, Barbara Esmée (*d* 1988), *y d* of late R. E. Yorke, Wellingborough; one *s* two *d*; 2nd, 1989, Elsie Frances (*d* 1990), *widow* of John Plowman; 3rd, 1991, Ruth, *widow* of Sir Timothy Bligh, KBE, DSO, DSC. *Educ:* Temple Grove; Haileybury Coll.; Queen's Coll., Oxford. BA 1938; MA 1946. Hon. Agent and Treas., Oxford Univ. Conservative Assoc., 1937; Pres., Monarchist Soc., 1937; Pres., Mermaid Club, 1937. Asst Master, Prep. Sch., 1938–39. Served War, 1939–46: Dakar Expedn, 1940; wounded in N Africa, 1943; Mil. Asst to HM Minister Beirut and Damascus, 1944–46; Major, Royal Fusiliers. Personnel Officer, Imperial Chemical Industries, 1946–51; Personnel Manager, British Celanese, 1951–59; Dep. Personnel Manager, Courtaulds, 1957–59; Dir, Clive & Stokes, Personnel Consultants, 1959–80. Mem., Gen. Synod of C of E, 1985–90. Contested (C): Gloucester, 1964; Hitchin, 1966; MP (C) Oldbury and Halesowen, 1970–74, Halesowen and Stourbridge, 1974–92. Mem., Select Cttee on Parly Commn for Admin (Ombudsman), 1979–83. Leader, Parly delegations: to Portugal, 1980; to Falkland Islands, 1985; to Malta, 1988; to Trinidad and Tobago, 1991. Mem., Delegn to Council of Europe and WEU, 1983–92; Leader, Delegn from Council of Europe to observe elections in Albania, March 1992. Pres., W Midlands Cons. Clubs, 1971–84. Mem. Exec. Cttee, Oxford Soc.; Chm., Gen. Purposes Cttee, Primrose League, 1971–85; Vice-President: SSAFA, Bucks; Royal Stuart Soc.; Chairman: Trustee, Battlefields Trust; Acland Hosp. Support Gp, Oxford. Evelyn Wrench Speaker, ESU (USA), 1992. *Publications:* articles on political and historical subjects. *Recreations:* gardening, travel, English history, church affairs, writing to The Times. *Address:* 4 The Bradburys, Stratton Audley, near Bicester, Oxon OX6 9BW. *Clubs:* Buck's, Coningsby.

STOKES, Michael George Thomas; QC 1994; a Recorder, since 1990; *b* 30 May 1948; *e s* of late M. P. Stokes, Leyland, Lancs; *m* 1994, Alison Hamilton Pollock. *Educ:* Preston Catholic Coll.; Univ. of Leeds (LLB Hons 1970). Asst Lectr, Univ. of Nottingham, 1970–72; called to the Bar, Gray's Inn, 1971; in practice on Midland and Oxford Circuit, 1973–; Asst Recorder, 1986–90. *Recreations:* racing, ski-ing, trying to breed a Group 1 winner! *Address:* 1 King's Bench Walk, Temple, EC4Y 7DB. *T:* 0171–353 8436; Thornby Stud, Cold Ashby Road, Thornby, Northants NN6 8SH. *T:* Northants (01604) 740881. *Club:* Northampton and County (Northampton).

STOLLER, Anthony David; Chief Executive, Radio Authority, since 1995; *b* 14 May 1947; *s* of Louis and Pearl Stoller; *m* 1969, Andrea Lewisohn; one *s* one *d*. *Educ:* Hendon County Grammar Sch.; Gonville and Caius Coll., Cambridge (MA, LLB). Head of Radio Programming, IBA, 1974–79; Dir, Assoc. of Indep. Radio Contractors, 1979–81; Man. Dir, Thames Valley Broadcasting, 1981–85; John Lewis Partnership, 1985–95; Man. Dir, Tyrrell and Green, 1987–95. *Recreations:* cricket, sailing, music. *Address:* Radio Authority, Holbrook House, 14 Great Queen Street, WC2B 5DG. *T:* 0171–430 2724. *Clubs:* Penn, MCC; Island Sailing.

STOLLERY, Prof. John Leslie, CBE 1994; DScEng; FEng 1992; FRAeS; FCGI; FAIAA; Professor of Aerodynamics, 1973–95, and Head, College of Aeronautics, 1976–86, and 1992–95, Cranfield University (formerly Cranfield Institute of Technology); *b* 21 April 1930; *s* of George and Emma Stollery; *m* 1956, Jane Elizabeth, *d* of Walter and Mildred Reynolds; four *s*. *Educ:* East Barnet Grammar Sch.; Imperial Coll. of Science and Technol., London Univ. (BScEng 1951, MScEng 1953, DScEng 1973). DIC; CEng; FRAeS 1975; FCGI 1984; FAIAA 1988. Aerodynamics Dept, De Havilland Aircraft Co., 1952–56; Lectr, 1956, Reader, 1962, Aeronautics Dept, Imperial Coll., London; Dean, Faculty of Engrg, 1976–79, Pro Vice-Chancellor, 1982–85, Cranfield Inst. of Technol. Chairman: Aerospace Technology Bd, MoD, 1986–89; Aviation Cttee, DTI, 1986–94; Mem., Airworthiness Requirements Bd, 1990–. Pres., RAeS, 1987–88. Visiting Professor: Cornell Aeronautical Labs, Buffalo, USA, 1964; Aeronaut. Res. Lab., Wright Patterson Air Force Base, 1971; Nat. Aeronaut. Lab., Bangalore, India, 1977; Peking Inst. of Aeronautics and Astronautics, 1979; Univ. of Queensland, 1983. *Publications:* (Chief Editor) Shock Tube Research, 1971; papers in Jl of Fluid Mechanics, and various other aeronautical jls. *Recreations:* playing tennis, watching football, travelling. *Address:* 28 The Embankment, Bedford MK40 3PE. *T:* Bedford (01234) 355087.

STOLTENBERG, Gerhard, DrPhil; Member of the Bundestag, 1957–71 and since 1982; Minister of Defence, Federal Republic of Germany, 1989–92; *b* 29 Sept. 1928; *m* 1958, Margot Rann; one *s* one *d*. *Educ:* Bad Oldesloe; Kiel Univ. (DrPhil 1954). Military service, 1944–45; local govt, 1945–46; Asst Lectr, 1954–60, Lectr, 1960–65, Kiel Univ. Mem., CDU, 1947–: Dep. Chm., 1955–71, Chm., 1971–82, Schleswig-Holstein CDU; Nat. Dep. Chm., 1969–. Nat. Chm., Young Union, 1955–61. Schleswig-Holstein Parliament: Mem., 1954–57, 1971–82; Prime Minister, 1971–82. Bundestag: Minister of Scientific Research, 1965–69; Dep. Chm., CDU/CSU, 1969–71; Minister of Finance, 1982–89. *Publications:* The German Reichstag 1871–1873, 1954; Political Currents in Rural Schleswig-Holstein 1919–1933, 1960; State and Science, 1969; Schleswig-Holstein: present and future, 1978. *Address:* Bundeshaus, 53113 Bonn, Germany.

STOLTENBERG, Thorvald; *b* 8 July 1931; *s* of Emil and Ingeborg Stoltenberg; *m* 1957, Karin Heiberg; one *s* two *d*. *Educ:* Oslo Univ. (law degree). Joined Foreign Service, Norway, 1958; served: San Francisco, 1959–61; Belgrade, 1961–64; Press Secretary, Foreign Min., 1964–65; Executive Officer: Foreign Minister's Secretariat, 1965–70; Lagos, 1970; State Secretary: Foreign Min., 1971–72; MoD, 1973–74; Min. of Commerce and Shipping, 1974–76; Min. of Foreign Affairs, 1976–79; Defence Minister, 1979–81; Minister for Foreign Affairs, 1987–89; Ambassador to UN, NY, 1989–90; UN High Comr for Refugees, Jan.–Nov. 1990; Minister for Foreign Affairs, 1990–93; Special Rep. of UN Sec.-Gen. for Former Yugoslavia, 1993–94; UN Co-Chm., Steering Cttee of Internat. Conf. on Former Yugoslavia, 1994. Internat. Sec., Norwegian Fedn of Trade Unions, 1970–71, 1972–73 and 1981–83; active in local politics in Oslo, 1983–85; Dep. Mayor of Oslo, 1985–87. *Address:* c/o International Conference on the Former Yugoslavia, Palais des Nations, 1211 Geneva 10, Switzerland. *Fax:* (22) 9170079.

STONE, Sir Alexander, Kt 1994; OBE 1988; Chairman, Combined Capital Ltd, since 1978; Founder, and Chairman, since 1967, Alexander Stone Foundation; *b* 21 April 1907; *s* of Morris Stone and Rebecca (*née* Silverstone); *m* 1988, Phyllis Bette Fenton. *Educ:* Hutcheson's Grammar Sch., Glasgow; Univ. of Glasgow (BL). Estd Alexander Stone & Co., Lawyers, Glasgow, 1934; Chm., British Bank of Commerce Ltd, 1956–74; Director: Samuel Montague Ltd, 1961–65; James Finlay Corp. Ltd, 1975–79. Mem., CIB Scotland, 1991. Chm., Adv. Bd for Scotland and N of Eng., Bank Leumi, 1994–. Mem., Glasgow Univ. Investment Adv. Cttee, 1989–. Chm., Friends of Scottish Cons. Party, 1989–. Vice-Pres., Scottish Council for Spastics, 1984–. Hon. Life Mem., Law Soc. of Scotland, 1989. Hon. LLD Glasgow, 1986; Hon. DLitt Strathclyde, 1989. *Recreations:* reading, collecting antiquarian books, charitable activities. *Address:* The Lodge, 62 Sherbrooke Avenue, Glasgow G41 4RY. *T:* 0141–427 1567. *Club:* Western (Glasgow).

STONE, Andrew Zelig; Joint Managing Director, Marks and Spencer, since 1994; *b* 7 Sept. 1942; *s* of Sydney Stone and Louise Sophia Stone (*née* Gould); *m* 1973, Vivienne Wendy Lee; one *s* two *d*. *Educ:* Cardiff High School. Management Trainee, Marks and Spencer, 1966; Israel 1967; Merchandise Manager, 1973; PA to Chm., 1978–80; Divl Dir, 1986; Meanswear, Children's Wear, Ladies' Wear; Dir, 1990. Dir, Weizmann Inst. Foundn. FRSA. *Recreations:* reading, walking, thinking. *Address:* Marks & Spencer, Michael House, Baker Street, W1A 1DN. *T:* 0171–935 4422.

STONE, Maj.-Gen. Anthony Charles Peter, CB 1994; Director General Land Fighting Systems, Ministry of Defence (Procurement Executive), 1992–95; *b* 25 March 1939; *s* of Major (retd) Charles C. Stone and Kathleen M. Stone (*née* Grogan); *m* 1967, (Elizabeth) Mary, *d* of Rev. Canon Gideon Davies; two *s*. *Educ:* St Joseph's Coll.; RMA, Sandhurst; Staff Coll., Camberley. Commnd RA, 1960; served in light, field, medium, heavy, locating and air defence artillery in BAOR, FE and ME and in various general and weapons staff appts in MoD; commanded 5th Regt, RA, 1980–83; founded Special OP Troop, 1982; Col, Defence Progs Staff, MoD, 1983–84; Mil. Dir of Studies, RMCS, 1985–86; Ministry of Defence: Dir of Operational Requirements (Land), 1986–89; Dir of Light Weapons Projects, 1989–90; Dir Gen. Policy and Special Projects, 1990–92. Hon. Col, 5th Regt, RA, 1990–; Col Comdt, Royal Regt of Artillery, 1993–. *Recreations:* shooting (game), family, country pursuits, ski-ing. *Club:* Army and Navy.

STONE, Evan David Robert, QC 1979; a Recorder of the Crown Court, since 1979; *b* 26 Aug. 1928; *s* of Laurence George and Lillian Stone; *m* 1959, Gisela Bridget Mann; one *s*. *Educ:* Berkhamsted; Worcester Coll., Oxford (MA). National Service (commnd, Army), 1947–49; served Middle East and UK. Called to Bar, Inner Temple, 1954, Bencher, 1985; sometime HM Deputy Coroner: Inner West London; West Middlesex; City of London. Mem. Senate of Inns of Court and the Bar, 1985–86. Formerly Associate Editor, Medico-Legal Journal. Councillor, later Alderman, London Borough of Islington, 1969–74 (Dep. Leader, later Leader of Opposition). Chm., City and Hackney HA, 1984–92. Mem., Criminal Injuries Compensation Bd, 1989–. Governor: Moorfields Eye Hosp., 1970–79; Highbury Grove Sch., 1971–86 (Chm. of Governors, 1978–83). *Publications:* Forensic Medicine, 1987 (with Prof. H. Johnson); contrib. Social Welfare and the Citizen (paperback), 1957; contribs to Medico-Legal Jl and other professional jls. *Recreations:* reading, writing, sport, listening to music. *Address:* 60 Canonbury Park South, N1 2JG. *T:* 0171–226 6820; The Mill House, Ridgewell, Halstead, Essex CO9 4SR. *T:* Ridgewell (01440) 785338; (chambers) 29 Bedford Row, WC1R 4HE. *T:* 0171–831 2626. *Clubs:* Garrick, MCC; Norfolk (Norwich), Western (Glasgow).

STONE, Prof. (Francis) Gordon (Albert), CBE 1990; FRS 1976; Head of Department of Inorganic Chemistry, and Professor, Bristol University, 1963–90, now Professor Emeritus; Robert A. Welch Distinguished Professor of Chemistry, Baylor University, Texas, since 1990; *b* 19 May 1925; *s* of Sidney Charles and Florence Stone; *m* 1956, Judith M. Hislop, Sydney, Australia; three *s*. *Educ:* Exeter Sch.; Christ's Coll., Cambridge. BA 1948, MA and PhD 1952, ScD 1963, Cambridge. Fulbright Schol., Univ. of Southern Calif., 1952–54; Instructor and Asst Prof., Harvard Univ., 1954–62; Reader, Queen Mary Coll., London, 1962–63. Vis. Professor: Monash Univ., 1966; Princeton Univ., 1967; Univ. of Arizona, 1970; Carnegie-Mellon Univ., 1972; Texas A&M Univ., 1980; ANU, 1982; Guggenheim Fellow, 1961; Sen. Vis. Fellow, Australian Acad. of Sciences, 1966; A. R. Gordon Distinguished Lectr, Univ. of Toronto, 1977; Misha Strassberg Vis. Lectr, Univ. of WA, 1982. Lectures: Boomer, Univ. of Alberta, 1965; Firestone, Univ. of Wisconsin, 1970; Tilden, Chem. Soc., 1971; Ludwig Mond, RSC, 1982; Reilly, Univ. of Notre Dame, 1983; Waddington, Univ. of Durham, 1984; Sir Edward Frankland Prize, RSC, 1987; G. W. Watt, Univ. of Texas (Austin), 1988. Member: Council, Royal Soc. of Chemistry (formerly Chemical Soc.), 1968–70, 1981–83; Dalton Div. Council, 1971–74, 1981–85 (Vice-Pres. 1973 and 1984–85; Pres., 1981–83); Chemistry Cttee, SERC, 1982–85 (Mem., Chem. Cttee, SRC, 1971–74); Council, Royal Soc., 1986–88 (Vice-Pres., 1987–88). Hon. DSc: Exeter, and Waterloo, Canada, 1992; Durham, Salford, 1993; Zaragoza, 1994. Organometallic Chemistry Medal, 1972, Transition Metal Chemistry Medal, 1979, RSC; Chugaev Medal, Inst. of Inorganic Chem., USSR Acad. of Sciences, 1978; Amer. Chem. Soc. Award in Inorg. Chem., 1985; Davy Medal, Royal Soc., 1989; Longstaff Medal, RSC, 1990. *Publications:* Leaving no Stone Unturned (biog.); (Editor) Advances in Organometallic Chemistry, vols 1–37, 1964–92; (ed) Comprehensive Organometallic Chemistry, 1984, 1995; numerous papers in Jl Chem. Soc., Jl Amer. Chem. Soc., etc. *Recreation:* world travel. *Address:* 60 Coombe Lane, Bristol BS9 2AY. *T:* Bristol (0117) 968 6107; 1605 South 4th Street, Apt 106, Waco, TX 76706, USA. *T:* (817) 7527208.

STONE, Frederick Alistair, CBE 1988; DL; solicitor, now retired; Clerk and Chief Executive, Surrey County Council, 1973–88; *b* 13 Sept. 1927; *s* of Cyril Jackson and Elsie May Stone; *m* 1963, Anne Teresa Connor; one *s* one *d*. *Educ:* William Hulme's Grammar Sch.; Dulwich Coll.; Brasenose Coll., Oxford (BCL, MA). Asst Solicitor: Norwich City Council, 1954–58; Hampshire CC, 1958–60; Sen. Solicitor, CC of Lincoln (Parts of Lindsey), 1960–63; Asst Clerk, Hampshire CC, 1963–65; Dep. Clerk, Cheshire CC, 1965–73. Chairman: RIPA, 1979–81; Assoc. of County Chief Executives, 1986–87. Chm., Surrey Bd, Prince's Youth Business Trust, 1989–; Dep. Chm., Anchor Housing Assoc. and Trust, 1990–. DL Surrey, 1988. *Recreations:* music, walking, gardening. *Address:* North Lodge, Brockham Green, Betchworth RH3 7JS. *T:* Betchworth (01737) 842178.

STONE, Gerald Charles, PhD; FBA 1992; University Lecturer in non-Russian Slavonic Languages, Oxford University, and Fellow of Hertford College, Oxford, since 1972; *b* 22 Aug. 1932; *s* of Albert Leslie Stone and Grace Madeline Stone (*née* Varndell); *m* 1st, 1953, Charlotte Johanna Steinbach (marr. diss. 1973); two *s* one *d*; 2nd, 1974, Vera Fedorovna Konnova; one *d*. *Educ:* Windsor Grammar Sch.; School of Slavonic Studies, London Univ. (BA 1964; PhD 1969). Nat. service, Army, Trieste, 1951–53. Metropolitan Police, 1953–64; Asst Master, Bexhill Grammar Sch., 1964–65; Asst Lectr, 1966–67, Lectr, 1967–71, Nottingham Univ.; Asst Dir of Res., Cambridge Univ., 1971–72. General

Scientist and Gp Leader, Tube Investments Research Labs, 1960–78; Research Manager, Materials Dept, TI Research, 1978–88. Post-doctoral Res. Fellow, Ohio State Univ., 1962–63; Res. Fellow, Univ. of Minnesota, 1970. L. B. Pfeil Medal, Metals Soc., 1976; Sir Robert Hadfield Medal, Metals Soc., 1981. *Publications:* papers on electron microscopy, epitaxy, nucleation theory, superplasticity and physical metallurgy, in various jls. *Recreation:* music. *Address:* 1 Chalklands, Saffron Walden, Essex CB10 2ER. *T:* Saffron Walden (01799) 526486.

STOY, Prof. Philip Joseph; Professor of Dentistry, Queen's University of Belfast, 1948–73, now Professor Emeritus; *b* 19 Jan. 1906; *m* 1945, Isabella Mary Beatrice Crispin; two *s*. *Educ:* Wolverhampton School. Queen's Scholar, Birmingham Univ., 1929; LDS, RCS, 1931; BDS (Hons), Birmingham 1932; FDS, RCS, 1947; Fellow of the Faculty of Dentistry, RCSI, 1963 (FFDRCSI). Lectr in Dental Mechanics, Univ. of Bristol, 1934; Lectr in Dental Surgery, Univ. of Bristol, 1940. Hon. MD QUB, 1987. *Publications:* articles in British Dental Journal, Dental Record. *Recreations:* reading, painting, dental history, chess. *Address:* Westward Ho!, 57 Imperial Road, Exmouth, Devon EX8 1DQ. *T:* Exmouth (01395) 265113.

STOYLE, Roger John B.; *see* Blin-Stoyle.

STRABOLGI, 11th Baron of England, *cr* 1318; **David Montague de Burgh Kenworthy;** a Deputy Speaker and Deputy Chairman of Committees, House of Lords, since 1986; *b* 1 Nov. 1914; *e s* of 10th Baron Strabolgi and Doris Whitley (*d* 1988), *o c* of late Sir Frederick Whitley-Thomson, MP; *S* father, 1953; *m* 1961, Doreen Margaret, *e d* of late Alexander Morgan, Ashton-under-Lyne, and Emma Morgan (*née* Mellor). *Educ:* Gresham's School; Chelsea Sch. of Art; Académie Scandinave, Paris. Served with HM Forces, BEF, 1939–40; MEF, 1940–45, as Lt-Col RAOC. Mem. Parly Delegations to USSR, 1954, SHAPE, 1955, and France, 1981, 1983 and 1985; PPS to Minister of State, Home Office, 1968–69; PPS to Leader of the House of Lords and Lord Privy Seal, 1969–70; Asst Opposition Whip, and spokesman on the Arts, House of Lords, 1970–74; Captain of the Yeomen of the Guard (Dep. Govt Chief Whip), and Govt spokesman on Energy and Agriculture, 1974–79; Opposition spokesman on arts and libraries, 1979–85. Member: Jt Cttee on Consolidation Bills, 1986–; Select Cttee for Privileges, 1987–; Private Bills Cttee, 1987; Ecclesiastical Jt Cttee, 1991–; Select Cttee on Procedure, 1993–. A Vice-Pres., Franco-British Soc.; Member: British Sect., Franco-British Council, 1981; Council, Alliance Française in GB; Hon. Treas., Franco-British Parly Relations Cttee. Dir, Bolton Building Soc., 1958–74, 1979–87 (Dep. Chm., 1983, Chm., 1986–87). Hon. Life Mem., RPO, 1977. FIPR 1990. Freeman, City of London, 1960. Officier de la Légion d'Honneur, 1981. *Recreations:* books, music, travel. *Heir-pres: nephew* Andrew David Whitley Kenworthy, *b* 11 Feb. 1967. *Address:* House of Lords, SW1A 0PW. *Club:* Reform.

See also Sir Harold Hood, Bt.

STRACEY, Sir John (Simon), 9th Bt *cr* 1818; *b* 30 Nov. 1938; *s* of Captain Algernon Augustus Henry Stracey (2nd *s* of 6th Bt) (*d* 1940) and Olive Beryl (*d* 1972), *d* of late Major Charles Robert Eustace Radclyffe; *S* cousin, 1971; *m* 1968, Martha Maria, *d* of late Johann Egger; two *d*. *Heir: cousin* Henry Mounteney Stracey [*b* 24 April 1920; *m* 1st, 1943, Susanna, *d* of Adair Tracey; one *d*; 2nd, 1950, Lysbeth, *o d* of Charles Ashford, NZ; one *s* one *d*; 3rd, 1961, Jeltje, *y d* of Scholte de Boer]. *Address:* 14 Britts Farm Road, Buxted, East Sussex TN22 4LZ. *T:* and *Fax:* Buxted (01825) 732631.

STRACHAN, Alan Lockhart Thomson; theatre director; *b* 3 Sept. 1946; *s* of Roualeyn Robert Scott Strachan and Ellen Strachan (*née* Graham); *m* 1977, Jennifer Piercey-Thompson. *Educ:* Morgan Acad., Dundee; St Andrews Univ. (MA); Merton Coll., Oxford (B.Litt). Associate Dir, Mermaid Theatre, 1970–75; Artistic Director: Greenwich Th., 1978–88; Theatre of Comedy Co., 1991–; Churchill Theatre, Bromley, 1995–. *Productions directed include: Mermaid:* The Watched Pot, 1970; John Bull's Other Island, The Old Boys, 1971; (co-deviser) Cowardy Custard, 1972; Misalliance, 1973; Children, (co-deviser and dir) Cole, 1974; *Greenwich:* An Audience Called Edouard, 1978; The Play's the Thing, I Sent a Letter to my Love, 1979; Private Lives (transf. Duchess), Time and the Conways, 1980; Present Laughter (transf. Vaudeville), The Golden Age, The Doctor's Dilemma, 1981; Design for Living (transf. Globe), The Paranormalist, French Without Tears, 1982; The Dining Room, An Inspector Calls, A Streetcar Named Desire, 1983 (transf. Mermaid, 1984); The Glass Menagerie, Biography, 1985; One of Us, Relatively Speaking, For King and Country, 1986; The Viewing, The Perfect Party, 1987; How the Other Half Loves (transf. Duke of York's), 1988; *freelance:* Family and a Fortune, Apollo, 1975; (deviser and dir) Shakespeare's People, world tours, 1975–78; Confusions, Apollo, 1976; (also jt author) Yahoo, Queen's, 1976; Just Between Ourselves, Queen's, 1977; The Immortal Haydon, Mermaid, 1977 (transf. Greenwich, 1978); Bedroom Farce, Amsterdam, 1978; Noël and Gertie, King's Head, 1983, Comedy, 1989; (replacement cast) Woman in Mind, Vaudeville, 1987; The Deep Blue Sea, Haymarket, 1988; Re: Joyce!, Fortune, 1988 (transf. Vaudeville, 1989; USA, 1990), Vaudeville, 1991; (replacement cast) Henceforward . . ., Vaudeville, 1989; June Moon, Scarborough, 1989, Hampstead, transf. Vaudeville, 1992; Toekomstmuziek, Amsterdam, 1989; Alphabetical Order, Scarborough, 1990; (replacement cast) Man of the Moment, Globe, 1990; Other People's Money, Lyric, 1990; Taking Steps, NY, 1991; London Assurance, Dublin, 1993. *Producer/co-Producer:* Out of Order, tour, 1991; The Pocket Dream, Albery, 1992; Six Degrees of Separation, Royal Court, transf. Comedy, 1992; Hay Fever (also dir), Albery, 1992; Happy Families, tour, 1993; Hysteria, Royal Court, 1993; Under Their Hats (also devised), King's Head, 1994; The Prime of Miss Jean Brodie (also dir.), Strand, 1994; (exec. prod.) Love on a Branch Line, BBC1, 1994. *Publications:* contribs to periodicals. *Recreations:* music, tennis, travelling. *Address:* 11 Garlies Road, SE23 2RU. *T:* 0181–699 3360.

STRACHAN, Alexander William Bruce, OBE 1971; HM Diplomatic Service, retired; *b* 2 July 1917; *s* of William Fyfe and Winifred Orchar Strachan; *m* 1940, Rebecca Prince MacFarlane; one *s* one *d*. *Educ:* Daniel Stewart's Coll., Edinburgh; Allen Glen's High Sch., Glasgow. Served Army, 1939–46 (dispatches). GPO, 1935; Asst Postal Controller, 1949–64; Postal Adviser to Iraq Govt, 1964–66; First Sec., FCO, 1967–68; Jordan, 1968–72; Addis Ababa, 1972–73; Consul General, Lahore, 1973–74; Counsellor (Economic and Commercial) and Consul General, Islamabad, 1975–77. Order of Istiqlal, Hashemite Kingdom of Jordan, 1971.

STRACHAN, Major Benjamin Leckie, CMG 1978; HM Diplomatic Service, retired; Special Adviser (Middle East), Foreign and Commonwealth Office, 1990–91; *b* 4 Jan. 1924; *e s* of late Dr C. G. Strachan, MC FRCPE and Annie Primrose (*née* Leckie); *m* 1958, Lize Lund; three *s* and one step *s* one step *d*. *Educ:* Rossall Sch. (Scholar); RMCS. Royal Dragoons, 1944; France and Germany Campaign, 1944–45 (despatches); 4th QO Hussars, Malayan Campaign, 1948–51; Middle East Centre for Arab Studies, 1952–53; GSO2, HQ British Troops Egypt, 1954–55; Technical Staff Course, RMCS, 1956–58; 10th Royal Hussars, 1959–61; GSO2, WO, 1961; retd from Army and joined Foreign (subseq. Diplomatic) Service, 1961; 1st Sec., FO, 1961–62; Information Adviser to Governor of Aden, 1962–63; FO, 1964–66; Commercial Sec., Kuwait, 1966–69; Counsellor, Amman, 1969–71; Trade Comr, Toronto, 1971–74; Consul General, Vancouver, 1974–76; Ambassador to Yemen Arab Republic, 1977–78, and to Republic of Jibuti (non-resident), 1978, to the Lebanon, 1978–81, to Algeria, 1981–84. Principal, Mill of Strachan Language Inst., 1984–89. Vice Chm., Kincardine and Deeside Lib Dems, 1993–95; Chm., Kincardine and W Aberdeenshire Lib Dems, 1995. *Recreations:* golf, tennis, writing, fishing. *Address:* Mill of Strachan, Strachan, Kincardineshire AB31 3NS. *T:* Feughside (01330) 850663. *Club:* Lansdowne.

STRACHAN, Douglas Frederick; Chairman, Dartington Foods (UK) Ltd, since 1990; *b* 26 July 1933; *s* of Hon. Lord Strachan and Lady (Irene Louise) Strachan (*née* Warren); *m* 1st, 1956, Mary Scott Hardie (*d* 1976); four *s* one *d*; 2nd, 1980, Jane, *widow* of Lt-Col I. D. Corden-Lloyd, OBE, MC; three step *s*. *Educ:* Rugby Sch.; Corpus Christi Coll., Oxford (MA). Brewer, Arthur Guinness Son & Co. (Dublin) Ltd, 1956–67; Man. Dir, Cantrell & Cochrane Gp Ltd, Dublin, 1967–72; Dir, Showerings, Vine Products & Whiteways Ltd, 1972–77; Man. Dir, Allied Breweries Ltd, 1977–85; Dir, Allied-Lyons Plc, 1976–85; Dir (Chief Executive) PRO NED, 1985–89. Director: Cheltenham & Gloucester BS, 1991– (Vice-Chm., 1994–); Pascoe's Group (formerly Sheldon Jones), 1992– (Chm., 1992–95). Minsterstone (Wharf Lane) Ltd, 1993–. Chm., Somerset FHSA, 1989–93; Mem., South Western RHA, 1990–93. *Recreations:* gardening, music, shooting. *Address:* Hewletts Mill, Galhampton, Yeovil, Somerset BA22 7BG. *T:* North Cadbury (01963) 440308.

STRACHAN, Douglas Mark Arthur; QC 1987; a Recorder, since 1990; a Deputy High Court Judge, Queen's Bench Division, since 1993; *b* 25 Sept. 1946; *s* of William Arthur Watkin Strachan and Joyce Olive Strachan. *Educ:* Orange Hill Grammar Sch., Edgware, Middx; St Catherine's Coll., Oxford (Open Exhibnr in Eng. Lit.; BCL, MA); Nancy Univ. (French Govt Schol.). Called to the Bar, Inner Temple, 1969 (Major Schol. 1969–71); Asst Recorder, 1987–90. *Publications:* contributor to Modern Law Rev. *Recreations:* France, antiques, food.

STRACHAN, Michael Francis, CBE 1980 (MBE 1945); FRSE 1979; Chairman, Ben Line Steamers Ltd and Ben Line Containers Ltd, 1970–82; Director, Bank of Scotland, 1972–90; *b* 23 Oct. 1919; *s* of Francis William Strachan and Violet Blackwell (*née* Palmer); *m* 1948, Iris Hemingway; two *s* two *d*. *Educ:* Rugby Sch. (Scholar); Corpus Christi Coll., Cambridge (Exhibnr, MA). Served in Army, 1939–46; demobilised 1946 (Lt-Col). Joined Wm Thomson & Co., Edinburgh, Managers of Ben Line, 1946; Partner, 1950–64; Jt Man. Dir, Ben Line Steamers Ltd, 1964. Chm., Associated Container Transportation Ltd, 1971–75. Trustee: Nat. Galleries of Scotland, 1972–74; Nat. Library of Scotland, 1974– (Chm., 1974–90); Carnegie Trust for Univs of Scotland, 1976–; Hakluyt Soc., 1984–. Member of Queen's Body Guard for Scotland. *Publications:* The Life and Adventures of Thomas Coryate, 1962; (ed jtly) The East India Company Journals of Captain William Keeling and Master Thomas Bonner, 1615–1617, 1971; Sir Thomas Roe (1581–1644) A Life, 1989; (contrib.) Oxford Book of Military Anecdotes, 1987; The Ben Line 1825–1982, 1992; Esmond S. de Beer (1895–1990), Scholar and Benefactor, 1995; articles in Blackwood's, Hakluyt Society's Hakluyt Handbook, History Today, Jl Soc. for Nautical Research. *Recreations:* country pursuits, silviculture. *Address:* Glenhighton, Broughton, by Biggar ML12 6JF. *Club:* New (Edinburgh).

STRACHAN, Mrs Valerie Patricia Marie, CB 1991; Chairman, Board of Customs and Excise, since 1993 (a Deputy Chairman, 1987–93); *b* 10 Jan. 1940; *d* of John Jonas Nicholls and Louise Nicholls; *m* 1965, John Strachan; one *s* one *d*. *Educ:* Newland High Sch., Hull; Manchester Univ. (BA). Joined Customs and Excise, 1961; Dept of Economic Affairs, 1964; Home Office, 1966; Principal, Customs and Excise, 1966; Treasury, 1972; Asst Secretary, Customs and Excise, 1974, Comr, 1980; Head, Joint Management Unit, HM Treasury/Cabinet Office, 1985–87. CIMgt. Hon. LLD Manchester, 1995. *Address:* c/o Customs and Excise, New King's Beam House, 22 Upper Ground, SE1 9PJ.

STRACHAN, Walter, CBE 1967; CEng, FRAeS; Consulting Engineer since 1971; *b* 14 Oct. 1910; *s* of William John Strachan, Rothes, Morayshire, and Eva Hitchins, Bristol; *m* 1937, Elizabeth Dora Bradshaw, Aldershot; two *s*. *Educ:* Newfoundland Road Sch., Bristol; Merchant Venturers Technical Coll., Bristol. Bristol Aeroplane Co.: Apprentice, 1925; Aircraft Ground Engr, 1932; RAE, Farnborough, 1934; Inspector: Bristol Aeroplane Co., 1937. BAC Service Engr, RAF Martlesham Heath, 1938; BAC: Asst Service Manager, 1940; Asst Works Manager, 1942; Manager, Banwell, building Beaufort and Tempest aircraft, 1943; Gen.-Manager, Banwell and Weston Factories, manufrg Aluminium Houses, 1945; Gen. Manager, Banwell and Weston Factories, building helicopters and aircraft components, 1951; Managing Dir, Bristol Aerojet, Banwell, Rocket Motor Develt and Prod., 1958. Liveryman, Coachmakers' & Coach Harness Makers' Co., 1961. *Recreations:* golf, music, ornithology. *Address:* 18 Clarence Road East, Weston-super-Mare, Somerset BS23 4BW. *T:* Weston-super-Mare (01934) 623878. *Clubs:* Naval and Military; Royal Automobile.

STRACHEY, family name of **Baron O'Hagan.**

STRACHEY, Charles, (6th Bt *cr* 1801, but does not use the title); local government officer, retired; *b* 20 June 1934; *s* of Rt Hon. Evelyn John St Loe Strachey (*d* 1963) and Celia (*d* 1980), 3rd *d* of late Rev. Arthur Hume Simpson; *S* to baronetcy of cousin, 2nd Baron Strachie, 1973; *m* 1973, Janet Megan, *d* of Alexander Miller; one *d*. *Heir: kinsman* Henry Leofric Benvenuto Strachey, *b* 17 April 1947. *Address:* 31 Northchurch Terrace, N1 4EB. *T:* 0171–249 1055.

STRADBROKE, 6th Earl of, *cr* 1821; **Robert Keith Rous;** Bt 1660; Baron Rous 1796; Viscount Dunwich 1821; *b* 25 March 1937; *s* of 5th Earl of Stradbroke and Pamela Catherine Mabell (*d* 1972), *d* of Captain Hon. Edward James Kay-Shuttleworth; *S* father, 1983; *m* 1960, Dawn Antoinette (marr. diss. 1977), *d* of Thomas Edward Beverley, Brisbane; two *s* five *d*; 2nd, 1977, Roseanna Mary Blanche, *d* of late Francis Reitman, MD; six *s* two *d*. *Educ:* Harrow. *Recreation:* making babies. *Heir: s* Viscount Dunwich, *qv*. *Address:* Mount Fyans, RSD Darlington, Vic 3271, Australia. *T:* (55) 901294, *Fax:* (55) 901298.

See also Hon. Sir W. E. Rous.

STRADLING, Donald George; Group Personnel Director, John Laing & Son Ltd, then John Laing plc, 1969–89; *b* 7 Sept. 1929; *s* of George Frederic and Olive Emily Stradling; *m* 1955, Mary Anne Hartridge; two *d*. *Educ:* Clifton Coll.; Magdalen Coll., Oxford (Open Exhibnr; MA). CIPM. School Master, St Albans Sch., 1954–55; Group Trng and Educn Officer, John Laing & Son Ltd, Building and Civil Engrg Contractors, 1955. Vis. Prof., Univ. of Salford, 1989–94. Comr, Manpower Services Commn, 1980–82; Mem. Council, Inst. of Manpower Studies, 1975–81; Member: Employment Policy Cttee, CBI, 1978–84, 1986–91; Council, CBI, 1982–86; FCEC Wages and Industrial Cttee, 1978–; Council, FCEC, 1985–; National Steering Gp, New Technical and Vocational Educn Initiative, 1983–88; NHS Trng Authy, 1985–89. Director: Building and Civil Engrg Benefits Scheme (Trustee, 1984–); Building and Civil Engrg Holidays Scheme Management, 1984–; Construction ITB, 1985–90. Vice-Pres., Inst. of Personnel Management, 1974–76. Vice-Chm. of Governors, St Albans High Sch., 1977–95; Mem. Council, Tyndale House, 1977–. Liveryman, Glaziers' and Painters of Glass Co., 1983. Hon. PhD Internat. Management Centre, Buckingham, 1987; Hon. DSc Salford, 1995. *Publications:* contribs on music and musical instruments, et al. to New Bible Dictionary, 1962. *Recreations:* singing (St Albans Bach Choir), oboe (Abbey Gateway Orchestra), listening to music (espec. opera), walking. *Address:* Courts Edge, 12 The Warren, Harpenden, Herts AL5 2NH. *T:* Harpenden (01582) 712744. *Club:* Institute of Directors.

STRADLING, Rt. Rev. Leslie Edward, MA; *b* 11 Feb. 1908; *er s* of late Rev. W. H. Stradling; unmarried. *Educ:* King Edward VII Sch., Sheffield; The Queen's Coll., Oxford; Westcott House, Cambridge. Curate of St Paul's, Lorrimore Square, 1933–38; Vicar of St Luke's Camberwell, 1938–43; of St Anne's, Wandsworth, 1943–45; Bishop of Masasi, 1945–52; Bishop of South West Tanganyika, 1952–61; Bishop of Johannesburg, 1961–74. Hon. DCL Bishops' Univ., Lennoxville, Canada, 1968. *Publications:* A Bishop on Safari, 1960; The Acts through Modern Eyes, 1963; An Open Door, 1966; A Bishop at Prayer, 1971; Praying Now, 1976; Praying the Psalms, 1977. *Address:* Braehead House, Auburn Road, Kenilworth 7700, Republic of South Africa. *Club:* City and Civil Service (Cape Town).

STRAFFORD, 8th Earl of, *cr* 1847; **Thomas Edmund Byng;** Baron Strafford, 1835; Viscount Enfield, 1847; nurseryman, riverkeeper and artist's companion; *b* 26 Sept. 1936; *s* of 7th Earl of Strafford, and Maria Magdalena Elizabeth, *d* of late Henry Cloete, CMG, Alphen, S Africa; *S* father, 1984; *m* 1963, Jennifer Mary (marr. diss. 1981), *er d* of late Rt Hon. W. M. May, FCA, PC, MP, and of Mrs May, Mertoun Hall, Holywood, Co. Down; two *s* two *d*; 2nd, 1981, Mrs Julia Mary Howard, (Judy), *d* of Sir Dennis Pilcher, CBE. *Educ:* Eton; Clare Coll., Cambridge. Lieut, Royal Sussex Regt (National Service). Councillor, Winchester and District, 1983–87. *Recreations:* gardening, travelling. *Heir: s* Viscount Enfield, *qv*. *Address:* Apple Tree Cottage, Easton, Winchester, Hants SO21 1EF. *T:* Winchester (01962) 779467.

STRAKER, Rear-Adm. Bryan John, CB 1980; OBE 1966; Area Appeal Manager, Cancer Relief Macmillan Fund, 1993–94; *b* 26 May 1929; *s* of late George and Marjorie Straker; *m* 1954, Elizabeth Rosemary, *d* of Maj.-Gen. C. W. Greenway, CB, CBE, and Mrs C. W. Greenway; two *d*. *Educ:* St Albans Sch. FIMgt (FBIM 1978). Cadet, RNC Dartmouth, 1946; Flag Lieut to Flag Officer, Malayan Area, 1952–53; qual. in communications, 1955; CO: HMS Malcolm, 1962–63; HMS Defender, 1966–67; Asst Dir, Naval Operational Requirements, MoD, 1968–70; CO HMS Fearless, 1970–72; Dir of Naval Plans, MoD, 1972–74; Comdr British Forces Caribbean Area and Island Comdr, Bermuda, 1974–76; Asst Chief of Naval Staff (Policy), 1976–78; Sen. Naval Mem., DS, RCDS, 1978–80; RN retd, 1981. Hd of Personnel Services, ICRF, 1981–89; Appeal Dir, Macmillan (Cancer Relief) Service, Midhurst, 1990–93. Freeman, City of London. *Recreations:* tennis, gardening. *Address:* c/o National Westminster Bank, Petersfield, Hants. *Club:* Steep Lawn Tennis.

STRAKER, Major Ivan Charles; Chairman, Seagram Distillers plc, 1984–93 (Chief Executive, 1983–90); *b* 17 June 1928; *s* of Arthur Coppin Straker and Cicely Longueville Straker; *m* 1st, 1954, Gillian Elizabeth Grant (marr. diss. 1971); one *s* one *d* (and one *s* decd); 2nd, 1976, Sally Jane Hastings (marr. diss. 1986); one *s*. *Educ:* Harrow; RMA, Sandhurst. Commissioned 11th Hussars (PAO), 1948; served Germany, N Ireland, Middle East and Mil. Intell. Staff, War Office; left HM Armed Forces, 1962. Man. Dir, D. Rintoul & Co., 1964; Man. Dir, The Glenlivet and Glen Grant Agencies, 1964–71; apptd Main Board, The Glenlivet and Glen Grant Distillers, 1967; Chief Exec., The Glenlivet Distillers Ltd, 1971. Dir, Lothians Racing Syndicate Ltd, 1986–. Council Mem., Scotch Whisky Assoc., 1978–90 (Chm., Public Affairs Cttee, 1986–90). *Recreations:* fishing, shooting, golf, racing. *Address:* 33 Cluny Drive, Edinburgh EH10 6DT. *T:* 0131–447 6621. *Clubs:* Jockey, Cavalry and Guards, Boodle's, White's.

STRAKER, Sir Michael (Ian Bowstead), Kt 1984; CBE 1973; JP; DL; farmer, since 1951; Chairman, Go-Ahead Group plc, since 1987; *b* 10 March 1928; *s* of late Edward Charles Straker and Margaret Alice Bridget Straker. *Educ:* Eton. Served in Coldstream Guards, 1946–50. Dir, Newcastle and Gateshead Water Co., 1975–82 (Chm., 1979–82); Chairman: Northumbrian Water Authy, later Northumbrian Water Group plc, 1982–93; Aycliffe and Peterlee Develt Corps, 1980–88; Member, Board: Port of Tyne Authority, 1986–; British Shipbuilders, 1990–. Chairman: Newcastle upon Tyne AHA(T), 1973–81; Newcastle Univ. HMC, 1971; Mem. Newcastle Univ. Court and Council, 1972– (Chm. Council, 1983–93). Mem. Council, RASE, 1970–86. Chm., Northern Area Conservative Assoc., 1969–72. High Sheriff of Northumberland, 1977; JP, 1962, DL 1988, Northumberland. Hon. DCL Newcastle, 1987. *Address:* High Warden, Hexham, Northumberland NE46 4SR. *T:* Hexham (01434) 602083. *Club:* Northern Counties (Newcastle upon Tyne).

STRAND, Prof. Kenneth T.; Professor, Department of Economics, Simon Fraser University, 1968–86, now Emeritus; *b* Yakima, Wash, 30 June 1931; Canadian citizen since 1974; *m* 1960, Elna K. Tomaske; no *c*. *Educ:* Washington State Coll. (BA); Univ. of Wisconsin (PhD, MS). Woodrow Wilson Fellow, 1955–56; Ford Foundn Fellow, 1957–58; Herfurth Award, Univ. of Wisconsin, 1961 (for PhD thesis). Asst Exec. Sec., Hanford Contractors Negotiation Cttee, Richland, Wash, 1953–55; Asst Prof., Washington State Univ., 1959–60; Asst Prof., Oberlin Coll., 1960–65 (on leave, 1963–65); Economist, Manpower and Social Affairs Div., OECD, Paris, 1964–66; Assoc. Prof., Dept of Econs, Simon Fraser Univ., 1966–68; Pres., Simon Fraser Univ., 1969–74 (Acting Pres., 1968–69). Member: Industrial Relations Research Assoc.; Internat. Industrial Relations Assoc.; Canadian Industrial Relations Assoc. (Pres., 1983). Hon. LLD Simon Fraser Univ., 1983. FRSA 1972. *Publications:* Jurisdictional Disputes in Construction: The Causes, The Joint Board and the NLRB, 1961; contribs to Review of Econs and Statistics, Amer. Econ. Review, Industrial Relations, Sociaal Mannblad Arbeid. *Recreations:* fishing, ski-ing. *Address:* 3475 Main Avenue, Belcarra, BC V3H 4R2, Canada.

STRANG, family name of **Baron Strang.**

STRANG, 2nd Baron *cr* 1954, of Stonesfield; **Colin Strang;** Professor of Philosophy, University of Newcastle upon Tyne, 1975–82; Dean of the Faculty of Arts, 1976–79; retired 1982; *b* 12 June 1922; *s* of 1st Baron Strang, GCB, GCMG, MBE, and Elsie Wynne (*d* 1974), *d* of late J. E. Jones; *S* father, 1978; *m* 1st, 1948, Patricia Marie, *d* of Meiert C. Avis, Johannesburg; 2nd, 1955, Barbara Mary Hope Carr (*d* 1982); one *d*; 3rd, 1984, Mary Shewell. *Educ:* Merchant Taylors' School; St John's Coll., Oxford (MA, BPhil). *Heir:* none. *Address:* Stansfield Cottage West, Hole Bottom, Todmorton, W Yorks OL14 8DD.

STRANG, Gavin Steel; MP (Lab) Edinburgh East since 1970; *b* 10 July 1943; *s* of James Steel Strang and Marie Strang (*née* Finkle); *m*. *Educ:* Univs of Edinburgh and Cambridge. BSc Hons Edinburgh, 1964; DipAgricSci Cambridge, 1965; PhD Edinburgh, 1968. Mem., Tayside Econ. Planning Consultative Group, 1966–68; Scientist with ARC, 1968–70. Opposition front bench spokesman on Scottish affairs, 1972–73, on energy, 1973–74; Parly Under-Sec. of State, Dept of Energy, March-Oct. 1974; Parly Sec., MAFF, 1974–79; Opposition front bench spokesman on agriculture, 1979–82, on employment, 1987–89, on agriculture and rural affairs, 1992–. Chm., PLP Defence Group, 1984–87. *Publications:* articles in Animal Production. *Recreations:* golf, swimming, watching football. *Address:* House of Commons, SW1A 0AA. *T:* 0171–219 5155. *Clubs:* Jewel Miners' Welfare, Newcraighall Miners' Welfare (Edinburgh).

STRANG, William John, CBE 1973; PhD; FRS 1977; FEng 1977; FRAeS; Deputy Technical Director, British Aerospace, Aircraft Group, 1978–83, retired; *b* 29 June 1921; *s* of late John F. Strang and Violet Strang (*née* Terrell); *m* 1946, Margaret Nicholas Howells; three *s* one *d*. *Educ:* Torquay Grammar Sch.; King's Coll., London Univ. (BSc). Bristol Aeroplane Co., Ltd, Stress Office, 1939–46; King's Coll., London Univ., 1946–48; Aeronautical Research Lab., Melbourne, Aust., 1948–51; Bristol Aeroplane Co. Ltd: Dep. Head, Guided Weapons Dept, 1951–52; Head of Aerodynamics and Flight Research, 1952–55; Chief Designer, 1955–60; British Aircraft Corporation: Dir and Chief Engr, 1960–67, Technical Dir, 1967–71, Filton Div.; Technical Dir, Concorde, 1966–77; Technical Dir, 1971–77, Commercial Aircraft Div. Chm., Airworthiness Requirements Bd, 1983–90 (Mem., 1979–90). *Address:* April Cottage, Castle Combe, Wilts SN14 7HH. *T:* Castle Combe (01249) 782220.

STRANG STEEL, Major Sir (Fiennes) Michael, 3rd Bt *cr* 1938, of Philiphaugh, Selkirk; DL; *b* 22 Feb. 1943; *s* of Sir (Fiennes) William Strang Steel, 2nd Bt and Joan Strang Steel (*d* 1982), *d* of Brig-Gen. Sir Brodie Haldane Henderson, KCMG, CB; *S* father, 1992; *m* 1977, Sarah Jane Russell; two *s* one *d*. *Educ:* Eton. Major, 17/21 Lancers, 1962–80, retd. Forestry Comr, 1988–. DL Borders Region (Districts of Roxburgh, Ettrick & Lauderdale), 1990. *Heir: s* (Fiennes) Edward Strang Steel, *b* 8 Nov. 1978. *Address:* Philiphaugh, Selkirk TD7 5LX. *Club:* Cavalry and Guards.

STRANGE, Baroness (16th in line), *cr* 1628; **Jean Cherry Drummond;** *b* 17 Dec. 1928; *e c* of 15th Baron Strange (*d* 1982) and Violet Margaret Florence (*d* 1975), *d* of Sir Robert William Buchanan-Jardine, 2nd Bt; *S* (after termination of abeyance) 1986; *m* 1952, Captain Humphrey ap Evans, MC, who assumed name of Drummond of Megginch by decree of Lord Lyon, 1965; three *s* three *d*. *Educ:* St Andrews Univ. (MA 1951); Cambridge Univ. Pres., War Widows' Assoc. of GB, 1990–. *Publications:* Love from Belinda, 1960; Lalage in Love, 1962; Creatures Great and Small, 1968; Love is For Ever, 1988; The Remarkable Life of Victoria Drummond, Marine Engineer, 1994. *Heir: s* Hon. Adam Humphrey Drummond, Major Grenadier Guards [*b* 20 April 1953; *m* 1988, Mary Emma Dewar; one *s* one *d*]. *Address:* Megginch Castle, Errol, Perthshire PH2 7SW. *T:* Errol (01821) 642222; Tresco, 160 Kennington Road, SE11 6QR. *T:* 0171–735 3681.

STRANGE, Prof. Susan, (Mrs Clifford Selly); Professor of International Relations, Warwick University, since 1993; *b* 9 June 1923; *d* of Col Louis Strange and Marjorie Beath; *m* 1st, 1942, Dr Denis Merritt (marr. diss. 1955); one *s* one *d*; 2nd, 1955, Clifford Selly; two *s* one *d* (and one *s* decd). *Educ:* Royal Sch., Bath; Université de Caen; London Sch. of Econs (BScEcon). The Economist, 1944–46; The Observer, 1946–57 (Washington, UN, and Econ. Corresp.); Lectr in Internat. Relations, University Coll., London, 1949–64; Res. Fellow, RIIA, 1965–76; German Marshall Fund Fellow, 1976–78; Montague Burton Prof. of Internat. Relns, LSE, 1978–88; Prof. of Internat. Relns, European Univ. Inst., Florence, 1989–93. *Publications:* Sterling and British Policy, 1971; International Monetary Relations, 1976; (ed with R. Tooze) The International Politics of Surplus Capacity, 1981; (ed) Paths to International Political Economy, 1984; Casino Capitalism, 1986; States and Markets, 1988; (with J. Stopford) Rival States, Rival Firms, 1991. *Recreations:* cooking, gardening, tennis. *Address:* Weedon Hill House, Aylesbury, Bucks HP22 4DP. *T:* Aylesbury (01296) 22236.

STRANGWAYS; *see* Fox-Strangways, family name of Earl of Ilchester.

STRANRAER-MULL, Very Rev. Gerald; Dean of Aberdeen and Orkney, since 1988; Rector of Ellon and Cruden Bay, since 1972; *b* 24 Nov. 1942; *s* of Gerald and Lena Stranraer-Mull; *m* 1967, Glynis Mary Kempe; one *s* one *d* (and one *s* decd). *Educ:* Woodhouse Grove School, Apperley Bridge; King's College, London (AKC 1969); Saint Augustine's College, Canterbury. Journalist, 1960–66. Curate: Hexham Abbey, 1970–72; Corbridge, 1972; Editor of Aberdeen and Buchan Churchman, 1976–84, 1991–94; Director of Training for Ministry, Diocese of Aberdeen and Orkney, 1982–90; Canon of Saint Andrew's Cathedral, Aberdeen, 1981–. *Address:* The Rectory, Ellon, Aberdeenshire AB41 9NP. *T:* Ellon (01358) 720366.

STRATFORD, Neil Martin; Keeper of Medieval and Later Antiquities, British Museum, since 1975; *b* 26 April 1938; *s* of late Dr Martin Gould Stratford and Dr Mavis Stratford (*née* Beddall); *m* 1966, Anita Jennifer Lewis; two *d*. *Educ:* Marlborough Coll.; Magdalene Coll., Cambridge (BA Hons English 1961, MA); Courtauld Inst., London Univ. (BA Hons History of Art 1966). 2nd Lieut Coldstream Guards, 1956–58; Trainee Kleinwort, Benson, Lonsdale Ltd, 1961–63; Lecturer, Westfield Coll., London Univ., 1969–75. British Academy/Leverhulme Sen. Res. Fellow, 1991. Chm., St Albans Cathedral Fabric Cttee, 1995–; Conseil Scientifique, Société Française d'Archéologie, 1994–. Liveryman, Haberdashers' Company 1959–. Hon. Mem., Académie de Dijon, 1975; For. Mem., Société Nationale des Antiquaires de France, 1985. FSA 1976. *Publications:* La Sculpture Oubliée de Vézelay, 1984; Catalogue of Medieval Enamels in the British Museum, vol. II, Northern Romanesque Enamel, 1993; articles in French and English periodicals. *Recreations:* opera, food and wine, cricket and football. *Address:* 17 Church Row, NW3 6UP. *T:* 0171–794 5688. *Clubs:* Beefsteak, Garrick, MCC, I Zingari; University Pitt, Hawks (Cambridge).

STRATHALLAN, Viscount; John Eric Drummond; *b* 7 July 1935; *e s* of 17th Earl of Perth, *qv*; *m* 1963, Margaret Ann (marr. diss.), *o d* of Robin Gordon; two *s*; *m* 1988, Mrs Marion Elliot. *Heir: s* Hon. James David Drummond, *b* 24 Oct. 1965. *Address:* Stobhall, by Perth.

STRATHALMOND, 3rd Baron *cr* 1955; **William Roberton Fraser,** CA; Chairman, R. W. Sturge Ltd, 1991–94; *b* 22 July 1947; *s* of 2nd Baron Strathalmond, CMG, OBE, TD, and of Letitia, *d* of late Walter Krementz, New Jersey, USA; *S* father, 1976; *m* 1973, Amanda Rose, *yr d* of Rev. Gordon Clifford Taylor; two *s* one *d*. *Educ:* Loretto. Man. Dir, London Wall Members Agency Ltd, 1986–91 (Dir, 1985–91); Dir, London Wall Hldgs plc, 1986–91. *Heir: s* Hon. William Gordon Fraser, *b* 24 Sept. 1976. *Address:* Holt House, Elstead, near Godalming, Surrey GU8 6LF.

STRATHCARRON, 2nd Baron, *cr* 1936, of Banchor; **David William Anthony Blyth Macpherson;** Bt, *cr* 1933; Partner, Strathcarron & Co.; Director: Kirchhoff (London) Ltd; Seabourne World Express Group plc; Kent International Airport PLC; *b* 23 Jan. 1924; *s* of 1st Baron and Jill (*d* 1956), *o d* of Sir George Rhodes, 1st Bt; *S* father, 1937; *m* 1st, 1947, Valerie Cole (marr. annulled on his petition, 1947); 2nd, 1948, Mrs Diana Hawtrey Curle (*d* 1973), *o d* of Comdr R. H. Deane; two *s*; 3rd 1974, Mrs Eve Samuel, *o d* of late J. C. Higgins, CIE. *Educ:* Eton; Jesus College, Cambridge. Served War of 1939–45, RAFVR, 1942–47. Motoring Correspondent of The Field, 1954–. Member, British Parly Delegn to Austria, 1964. Pres., Inst. of Freight Forwarders, 1974–75. Mem. Council, Order of the Road, 1974–. President: Guild of Motoring Writers, 1971–; Guild of Experienced Motorists, 1980–86; National Breakdown Recovery Club, 1982–; Driving Instructors' Assoc., 1982–; Vehicle Builders' and Repairers' Assoc., 1983–; IRTE, 1990–. Fellow, Inst. of Advanced Motorists, 1993; FIMI 1989; FCIT 1991. *Publication:* Motoring overseas. Syndic, CUP, 1983. Vice-Pres., G. M. Hopkins Soc., 1971; Pres., Dickens Soc. of America, 1983–84. Governor: St Edward's, Oxford, 1959–69; Eastbourne Coll., 1965–69. Jt Gen. Editor, Letters of Dickens, Pilgrim edn, 1965–; General Editor: Cambridge Renaissance and Restoration Dramatists, 1975–89; Cambridge English Prose Texts, 1980–. *Publications:* Reuters' Century, 1951; Journals and Papers of G. M. Hopkins, 1959 (completed edn on death of Humphry House); (ed) A. P. Rossiter, Angel with Horns, 1961; (ed) Selected Verse and Prose of G. M. Hopkins, 1966; Letters of Charles Dickens, vol. I, 1965, vol. II, 1969, vol. III, 1974, vol. V, 1981, vol. VI, 1988 (ed jtly), vol. VII, 1993, (ed jtly); A Preface to Hopkins, 1981; (ed with Howard Erskine-Hill) Revolutionary Prose of the English Civil War, 1983; Bleak House (critical study), 1987; David Copperfield (critical study), 1991; contributions to: New Cambridge Bibliography, 1967; Writers and their Work, 1982; Dickens and Other Victorians, 1988; periodicals. *Recreations:* theatre, gardening, travel. *Address:* Trinity Hall, Cambridge CB2 1TJ. *T:* Cambridge (01223) 332500; Crown House, Caxton, Cambs CB3 8PQ. *T:* Caxton (01954) 719316.

STOREY, Jeremy Brian; QC 1994; a Recorder, since 1995; *b* 21 Oct. 1952; *s* of late Captain James Mackie Storey and Veronica Walmsley; *m* 1981, Carolyn Margaret Ansell; two *d*. *Educ:* Uppingham Sch.; Downing Coll., Cambridge (Scholar; BA Law 1st Class, MA). Called to the Bar, Inner Temple, 1974; Asst Recorder, 1991. Member: Western Circuit; Official Referees' Bar Assoc.; Cttee, London Common Law and Commercial Bar Assoc.; Commercial Bar Assoc.; Chm., Barristers' Overseas Advocacy Cttee. *Recreations:* travel, cricket, theatre. *Address:* 4 Pump Court, Temple, EC4Y 7AN. *T:* 0171–353 2656. *Clubs:* MCC; Glamorgan CC.

STOREY, Maude, CBE 1987; President, Royal College of Nursing, 1986–90; *b* 24 March 1930; *d* of late Henry Storey and of Sarah Farrimond Storey. *Educ:* Wigan and District Mining and Techn. Coll.; St Mary's Hosp., Manchester; Lancaster Royal Infirmary; Paddington Gen. Hosp.; Royal Coll. of Nursing, Edinburgh; Queen Elizabeth Coll., London. SRN 1952; SCM 1953; RCI (Edin.) 1962; RNT 1965. Domiciliary Midwife, Wigan County Borough, 1953–56; Midwifery Sister, St Mary's Hosp., Manchester, 1956–57; Charge Nurse, Intensive Therapy, Mayo Clinic, USA, 1957–59; Theatre Sister, Clinical Instructor, 1959–63, subseq. Nurse Tutor, 1965–68, Royal Albert Edward Infirmary, Wigan; Lectr in Community Nursing, Manchester Univ., 1968–71; Asst, subseq. Principal Regional Nursing Officer, Liverpool Regional Hosp. Bd, 1971–73; Regional Nursing Officer, Mersey RHA, 1973–77; Registrar, GNC for England and Wales, 1977–81; Registrar and Chief Exec., UKCC, 1981–87. Member: Standing Nursing and Midwifery Adv. Cttee, 1977–90; Wigan and Leigh HA, 1974–77; West Berks HA, 1982–93; Non-exec. Dir, Berks HA, 1993–; Chm., W Berks Ethics Res. Cttee, 1992–. Mem. Council, Reading Univ., 1988–. CStJ 1987. *Recreations:* travel, theatre. *Address:* 14 Conifer Drive, Long Lane, Tilehurst, Berks RG31 6YU. *T:* Reading (01734) 412082.

STOREY, Hon. Sir Richard, 2nd Bt *cr* 1960; Chairman of Portsmouth and Sunderland Newspapers plc, since 1973 (Director, since 1962); *b* 23 Jan. 1937; *s* of Baron Buckton (Life Peer) and Elisabeth (*d* 1951), *d* of late Brig.-Gen. W. J. Woodcock, DSO; *S* to baronetcy of father, 1978; *m* 1961, Virginia Anne, 3rd *d* of Sir Kenelm Cayley, 10th Bt; one *s* two *d*. *Educ:* Winchester; Trinity Coll., Cambridge (BA, LLB). National service commission, RNVR, 1956. Called to the Bar, Inner Temple, 1962. Director: One Stop Community Stores Ltd, 1971–; Reuters Hldgs PLC, 1986–92; Press Association Ltd, 1986– (Chm., 1991–95); Fleming Enterprise Investment Trust PLC, 1989–; Foreign & Colonial Smaller Cos PLC, 1993–. Chm., York Health Services Trust, 1991–. Member: Nat. Council and Exec., CLA, 1980–84, Yorks Exec., CLA (Chm., 1974–76); Employment Policy Cttee, CBI, 1984–88, CBI Regl Council, Yorks and Humberside, 1974–76; Press Council, 1980–86; Pres., Newspaper Soc., 1990–91 (Mem. Council, 1980–). Chm., Sir Harold Hillier Arboretum Management Cttee, 1989–. Trustee, Royal Botanic Gardens Kew Foundn, 1990–. Mem. Council: INCA-FIEJ Res. Assoc., 1983–88; European Newspaper Publishers' Assoc., 1991–. Contested (C): Don Valley, 1966; Huddersfield W, 1970. High Sheriff, N Yorks, 1992–93. Hon. Fellow, Univ. of Portsmouth, 1992. Hon. DLitt Sunderland Poly., 1989. *Recreations:* sport and silviculture, farms and administers land in Yorkshire. *Heir:* *s* Kenelm Storey, *b* 4 Jan. 1963. *Address:* Settrington House, Malton, Yorks YO17 8NP. *T:* North Grimston (01944) 768200, 7 Douro Place, W8 5PH. *T:* 0171–937 8823.

STORIE-PUGH, Col Peter David, CBE 1981 (MBE 1945); MC 1940; TD 1945 and 3 clasps; DL; Lecturer, University of Cambridge, 1953–82; Fellow of Wolfson College, Cambridge, since 1967; *b* 1 Nov. 1919; *s* of late Prof. Leslie Pugh, CBE, BSc, MA, FRCVS and Paula Storie; *m* 1st, 1946, Alison (marr. diss. 1971), *d* of late Sir Oliver Lyle, OBE; one *s* two *d*; 2nd, 1971, Leslie Helen, *d* of Earl Striegel; three *s* one *d*. *Educ:* Malvern; Queens' Coll., Cambridge (Hon. Foundn Scholar; MA, PhD); Royal Veterinary Coll., Univ. of London(FRCVS). CChem, FRSC. Served War of 1939–45, Queen's Own Royal W Kent Regt (escaped from Spangenberg and Colditz); comd 1st Bn, Cambs Regt, comd 1st Bn Suffolk and Cambs Regt; Col, Dep. Comdr, 161 Inf. Bde, ACF County Comdt. Wellcome Res. Fellow, Cambridge, 1950–52. Mem. Council, RCVS, 1956–84 (Chm. Parly Cttee, 1962–67, Pres., 1977–78); President: Cambridge Soc. for Study of Comparative Medicine, 1966–67; Internat. Pig Vet. Soc., 1967–69 (Life Pres., 1969); British Veterinary Assoc., 1968–69 and 1970–71 (Hon. Life Mem., 1984; Dalrymple-Champneys Cup and Medal, 1986); Mem. Exec. Cttee, Cambridgeshire Farmers Union, 1960–65; UK delegate, EEC Vet. Liaison Cttee, 1962–75 (Pres., 1973–75); UK Rep., Fedn of Veterinarians of EEC, 1975–83 (Pres. of Fedn, 1975–79); Chm., Eurovet, 1971–73; Mem. Jt RCVS/BVA Cttee on European Vet. Affairs, 1971–92; Observer, European Liaison Gp for Agric., 1972–80; Jt Pres., 1st European Vet. Congress, Wiesbaden, 1972; Permanent Mem. EEC Adv. Vet. Cttee, 1976–82; Mem. Council, Secrétariat Européen des Professions Libérales, 1976–80; Mem. Permanent Cttee, World Vet. Assoc., 1964–75. Member: Parly and Sci. Cttee, 1962–67; Home Sec.'s Adv. Cttee (Cruelty to Animals Act, 1876), 1963–80; Nat. Agric. Centre Adv. Bd, 1966–69; Production Cttee, Meat and Livestock Commn, 1967–70; Min. of Agriculture's Farm Animal Adv. Cttee, 1970–73; Econ. and Social Cttee, EEC, 1982–90. Chm., Nat. Sheep Breeders' Assoc., 1964–68; Vice-Pres., Agric. Section, British Assoc., 1970–71. Corresp. Mem., Bund Deutscher Veterinäroffiziere, 1979–. Robert von Ostertag Medal, German Vet. Assoc., 1972. DL Cambs, 1963. *Publications:* (and ed jtly) Eurovet: an Anatomy of Veterinary Europe, 1972; Eurovet-2, 1975. *Address:* Duxford Grange, Duxford, Cambridge CB2 4QF. *T:* Royston (01763) 208403.

STORMONT, Viscount; Alexander David Mungo Murray; junior representative, Grampian, Lothian and Tayside Regions, Christie's Scotland Ltd; *b* 17 Oct. 1956; *s* and *heir* of 8th Earl of Mansfield and Mansfield, *qv*; *m* 1985, Sophia Mary Veronica, *o d* of Biden Ashbrooke, St John, Jersey; one *s* two *d*. *Educ:* Eton. *Heir:* *s* Master of Stormont, *qv*. *Address:* Scone Palace, Perthshire PH2 6BE.

STORMONT, Master of; Hon. William Philip David Mungo Murray; *b* 1 Nov. 1988; *s* and *heir* of Viscount Stormont, *qv*.

STORMONTH DARLING, Sir James Carlisle, (Sir Jamie Stormonth Darling), Kt 1983; CBE 1972; MC 1945; TD; WS; Director, 1971–83, Vice-President Emeritus, since 1986, The National Trust for Scotland (Secretary, as Chief Executive, 1949–71); *b* 18 July 1918; *s* of late Robert Stormonth Darling, Writer to the Signet, Rosebank, Kelso, Roxburghshire, and late Beryl Madeleine Sayer, Battle, Sussex; *m* 1948, Mary Finella, BEM 1945, DL, *d* of late Lt.-Gen. Sir James Gammell, KCB, DSO, MC; one *s* two *d*. *Educ:* Winchester Coll.; Christ Church, Oxford; BA 1939, MA 1972; Edinburgh Univ.; LLB 1949. 2nd Lt KOSB (TA), 1938; War Service, 1939–46, in KOSB and 52nd (L) Reconnaissance Regt, RAC, of which Lt-Col comdg in 1945 (TD). Admitted Writer to the Signet, 1949. Member, Queen's Body Guard for Scotland (Royal Company of Archers), 1958–. Mem., Ancient Monuments Bd for Scotland, 1983–93. Dir, Scottish Widows Fund and Life Assce Soc., 1981–89. Vice-President: Scotland's Gardens Scheme, 1983–; Scottish Conservation Projects Trust, 1989– (Pres., 1984–89); Trustee: Scottish Churches Architectural Heritage Trust, 1983–; Edinburgh Old Town Charitable Trust, 1990– (Chm., 1985–91); Vice-Chm., Scotland's Churches Scheme, 1994–; Chm., Edinburgh Old Town Trust, 1985–91. Patron: Edinburgh Green Belt Trust, 1993–; Woodland Trust, 1993–. Hon. FRIAS 1982. DUniv Stirling, 1983; Hon. LLD Aberdeen, 1984. *Address:* Chapelhill House, Dirleton, East Lothian EH39 5HG. *T:* Dirleton (01620) 850296. *Clubs:* New, Hon. Co. of Edinburgh Golfers (Edinburgh).

STORMONTH DARLING, Peter; Director, Mercury Asset Management Group plc (formerly Warburg Investment Management Ltd) (Chairman, 1979–92); *b* 29 Sept. 1932; *s* of Patrick Stormonth Darling and Edith Mary Ormston Lamb; *m* 1st, 1958, Candis Hitzig; three *d*; 2nd, 1970, Maureen O'Leary. *Educ:* Winchester; New Coll., Oxford (MA). 2nd Lieut, Black Watch, 1950–53, served Korean War; RAFVR, 1953–56. Director: Deltec Panamerica, 1965–; S. G. Warburg & Co. Ltd, 1967–85 (Vice-Chm., 1977–85); S. G. Warburg Group plc, 1974–; First Hungary Fund, 1989–; Mercury Internat. Investment Trust, 1990–; Europe Fund, 1990–; Scottish Equitable Life Assurance Soc., 1992–; Keystone Investment Co., 1992–. Mem., UN Pension Fund Investments Cttee, 1990–. *Address:* 33 King William Street, EC4R 9AS.

See also R. A. Stormonth-Darling.

STORMONTH-DARLING, Robin Andrew; Chairman: Piper European Smaller Companies Trust, since 1994; Dumyat Investment Trust, since 1995; *b* 1 Oct. 1926; *s* of Patrick Stormonth-Darling and Edith Mary Ormston Lamb; *m* 1st, 1956, Susan Marion Clifford-Turner (marr. diss. 1970); three *s* one *d*; 2nd, 1974, Harriet Heathcoat-Amory (*née* Nye) (marr. diss. 1978); 3rd, 1981, Carola Marion Brooke, *er d* of Sir Robert Erskine-Hill, 2nd Bt. *Educ:* Abberley Hall; Winchester Coll. Served Fleet Air Arm (Pilot), 1945; 9th Queen's Royal Lancers, 1946–54: ADC to GOC-in-C Scotland, 1950–52; Officer Cadet Instr, 1952–54. Alexanders Laing & Cruickshank (formerly Laing & Cruickshank), 1954–87, Chm., 1980–87; Director: Austin Motor Co., 1959; British Motor Corp., 1960–68; British Leyland, 1968–75. Chm., Tranwood Gp, subseq. Tranwood, 1987–91. Director: London Scottish Bank (formerly London Scottish Finance Corp.), 1984–92; Mercantile House Holdings, 1984–87 (non-exec. Dep. Chm., 1987); GPI Leisure Corp. (Australia), 1986–90; Ptarmigan Internat. Capital Trust, 1993–. Stock Exchange: Mem., 1956–87; Mem. Council, 1978–86; Chairman: Quotations Cttee, 1981–85; Disciplinary Appeals Cttee, 1985–90. Dep. Chm., Panel on Take-Overs and Mergers, 1985–87; Mem., Securities and Investments Bd, 1985–87. Hon. Consul of Mexico at Edinburgh, 1993–. *Recreations:* shooting, ski-ing, flying, swimming. *Address:* Balvarran, Enochdhu, Blairgowrie, Perthshire PH10 7PA. *T:* Strathardle (01250) 881248. *Clubs:* White's, MCC, Hurlingham; Perth Hunt.

See also P. Stormonth Darling.

STORR, (Charles) Anthony, FRCP, FRCPsych; FRSL; writer and psychiatrist; Clinical Lecturer in Psychiatry, Faculty of Medicine, University of Oxford, 1974–84; Fellow, Green College, Oxford, 1979–84, now Emeritus; Hon. Consulting Psychiatrist, Oxford Health Authority, since 1986; *b* 18 May 1920; *y s* of Vernon Faithfull Storr, Subdean of Westminster and Katherine Cecilia Storr; *m* 1st, 1942, Catherine Cole; three *d*; 2nd, 1970, Catherine Barton (*née* Peters). *Educ:* Winchester Coll.; Christ's Coll., Cambridge; Westminster Hosp. Medical School. MB, BChir Cantab. FRSL 1990. Qual. in medicine, 1944; postgrad. trng in psychiatry, Maudsley Hosp., 1947–50; held various positions as psychiatrist in different hospitals; Consltnt Psychotherapist, Oxford AHA, 1974–84. Member: Parole Bd, 1976–77; Cttee on Obscenity and Film Censorship, 1977–79. Mem., NY Acad. of Scis, 1992. Hon. FRCPsych, 1993. *Publications:* The Integrity of the Personality, 1960; Sexual Deviation, 1964; Human Aggression, 1968; Human Destructiveness, 1972; The Dynamics of Creation, 1972; Jung, 1973; The Art of Psychotherapy, 1979; (ed) Jung: selected writings, 1983; Solitude, 1988; Freud, 1989; Churchill's Black Dog and Other Phenomena of the Human Mind, 1989; Music and the Mind, 1992; contrib. several books and jls. *Recreations:* music, broadcasting, journalism. *Address:* 45 Chalfont Road, Oxford OX2 6TJ. *T:* Oxford (01865) 53348. *Club:* Savile.

STOTHARD, Peter Michael; Editor of The Times, since 1992; *b* 28 Feb. 1951; *s* of Wilfred Max Stothard and Patricia J. Stothard (*née* Savage); *m* 1980, Sally Ceris Emerson; one *s* one *d*. *Educ:* Brentwood Sch., Essex; Trinity Coll., Oxford (BA Lit. Hum.; MA). BBC journalist, 1974–77; with Shell Internat. Petroleum, 1977–79; business and political writer, Sunday Times, 1979–80; The Times: Features Ed. and Leader writer, 1980–86; Dep. Ed., 1986–92; US Ed., 1989–92. *Recreation:* ancient and modern literature. *Address:* c/o The Times, 1 Pennington Street, E1 9XN. *T:* 0171–782 5000. *Club:* Reform.

STOTT, Rt. Hon. Lord; George Gordon Stott, PC 1964; Senator of College of Justice in Scotland, 1967–84; *b* 22 Dec. 1909; *s* of Rev. Dr G. Gordon Stott; *m* 1947, Nancy, *d* of A. D. Braggins; one *s* one *d*. *Educ:* Cramond Sch.; Edinburgh Acad.; Edinburgh Univ. Advocate 1936; QC (Scotland) 1950; Advocate-Depute, 1947–51; Editor, Edinburgh Clarion, 1939–44; Member, Monopolies Commission, 1949–56; Sheriff of Roxburgh, Berwick and Selkirk, 1961–64; Lord Advocate, 1964–67. *Publication:* Lord Advocate's Diary, 1991. *Address:* 12 Midmar Gardens, Edinburgh. *T:* 0131–447 4251.

STOTT, Sir Adrian, 4th Bt *cr* 1920; management consultant, since 1989; *b* 7 Oct. 1948; *s* of Sir Philip Sidney Stott, 3rd Bt, and of Cicely Florence, *o d* of Bertram Ellingham; *S* father, 1979. *Educ:* Univ. of British Columbia (BSc (Maths) 1968, MSc (Town Planning) 1974); Univ. of Waterloo, Ont (MMaths (Computer Science) 1971). Dir of Planning for a rural region of BC, 1974; formed own consulting practice, 1977; property develt, gen. management and town planning consultant, 1977–85; Manager: BC Govt Real Estate Portfolio, 1980; Islands Trust (coastal conservation and property develt control agency), 1985; Man. Dir, direct sales marketing company, 1986–88. Member: Cdn Inst. of Planners (MCIP); Assoc. for Computing Machinery. *Recreations:* music, inland waterways, computers, politics. *Heir:* *b* Vyvyan Philip Stott, *b* 5 Aug. 1952. *Address:* The Downs, Little Amwell, Herts.

STOTT, (Charlotte) Mary, OBE 1975; journalist, retired; *b* 1907; *d* of Robert Guy Waddington and Amalie Waddington (*née* Bates); *m* 1937, Kenneth Stott (*d* 1967); one *d*. *Educ:* Wyggeston Grammar Sch., Leicester. Leicester Mail, 1925–31; Bolton Evening News, 1931–33; Co-operative Press, Manchester, editing women's and children's publications, 1933–45; News sub-editor, Manchester Evening News, 1945–50; Women's Editor, The Guardian, 1957–72. Last Pres., Women's Press Club, 1970; Chm., Fawcett

Soc., 1980–82; Pres., Nat. Assoc. of Widows, 1993–. Hon. Fellow, Manchester Polytechnic, 1972. Hon. MA: Open, 1991; Leicester, 1995. *Publications:* Forgetting's No Excuse, 1973, rev. edn 1989; Organization Woman, 1978; Ageing for Beginners, 1981; Before I Go . . ., 1985; Women Talking, 1987. *Recreations:* committees, music (especially choir singing), painting (water colours), gardening. *Address:* 4/11 Morden Road, Blackheath, SE3 0AA. *T:* 0181–852 2901. *Club:* University Women's.

STOTT, Rt. Hon. George Gordon; *see* Stott, Rt Hon. Lord.

STOTT, Rev. John Robert Walmsley, MA Cantab; DD Lambeth; Director, London Institute for Contemporary Christianity, 1982–86, now President; Chaplain to the Queen, 1959–91, Extra Chaplain, since 1991; *b* 27 April 1921; *s* of late Sir Arnold W. Stott, KBE, physician, and late Emily Caroline Holland. *Educ:* Rugby Sch.; Trinity Coll., Cambridge; Ridley Hall, Cambridge. Curate of All Souls, Langham Place, 1945; Rector of All Souls, 1950–75 (with St Peter's, Vere Street, 1952), now Rector Emeritus. Hon. DD: Trinity Evangelical Divinity Sch., Deerfield, USA, 1971; Wycliffe Coll., Toronto, 1993. *Publications:* Men with a Message, 1954, revd edn with Stephen Motyer, 1994; What Christ Thinks of the Church, 1958; Basic Christianity, 1958; Your Confirmation, 1958, 2nd edn 1991; Fundamentalism and Evangelism, 1959; The Preacher's Portrait, 1961; Confess Your Sins, 1964; The Epistles of John, 1964; Canticles and Selected Psalms, 1966; Men Made New, 1966; Our Guilty Silence, 1967; The Message of Galatians, 1968; One People, 1969; Christ the Controversialist, 1970; Understanding the Bible, 1972; Guard the Gospel, 1973; Balanced Christianity, 1975; Christian Mission in the Modern World, 1975; Baptism and Fullness, 1975; The Lausanne Covenant, 1975; Christian Counter-Culture, 1978; Focus on Christ, 1979, 2nd edn as Life in Christ, 1991; God's New Society, 1979; I Believe in Preaching, 1982; The Bible Book for Today, 1982; Issues Facing Christians Today, 1984, 2nd edn 1991; The Authentic Jesus, 1985; The Cross of Christ, 1986; (with David Edwards) Essentials, 1988; The Message of Acts, 1990; The Message of I and II Thessalonians, 1991; The Contemporary Christian, 1992; The Message of Romans, 1994. *Recreations:* bird watching, photography. *Address:* 13 Bridford Mews, Devonshire Street, W1N 1LQ.

STOTT, Mary; *see* Stott, C. M.

STOTT, Richard Keith; Editor, Today, since 1993; *b* 17 Aug. 1943; *s* of late Fred B. Stott and Bertha Stott; *m* 1970, Penny, *yr d* of Air Vice-Marshal Sir Colin Scragg, KBE, CB, AFC; one *s* two *d*. *Educ:* Clifton College, Bristol. Bucks Herald, 1963–65; Ferrari Press Agency, 1965–68; Daily Mirror: Reporter, 1968–79; Features Editor, 1979–81; Asst Editor, 1981; Editor: Sunday People, 1984; Daily Mirror, 1985–89; The People, 1990–91; Daily Mirror, 1991–92. Dir, People Publishing Co., 1990–91. Reporter of the Year, British Press Awards, 1977; Editor of the Year, What the Papers Say Awards, 1993. *Recreations:* theatre, reading. *Address:* Today, 1 Virginia Street, E1 9BS.

STOTT, Roger, CBE 1979; MP (Lab) Wigan, since 1983 (Westhoughton, May 1973–1983); *b* 7 Aug. 1943; *s* of Richard and Edith Stott; *m* 1st, 1969, Irene Mills (marr. diss. 1982); two *s*; 2nd, 1985, Gillian Pye, Wigan; one *s* one *d*. *Educ:* Rochdale Tech. Coll. Served in Merchant Navy, 1959–64. Post Office Telephone Engineer, 1964–73. PPS to Sec. of State for Industry, 1975–76; PPS to the Prime Minister, 1976–79, to Leader of the Opposition, 1979; opposition spokesman on transport, 1980–83, 1984–86, on trade and industry, with special responsibility for IT, 1983–89, on NI, 1990–. Mem., Select Cttee on Agriculture, 1980–81. Pres., Bass Wingates Band, 1980–. *Recreations:* cricket, gardening, Rugby League. *Address:* House of Commons, SW1A 0AA; 26 Spelding Drive, Standish Lower Ground, Wigan WN6 8LW.

STOUGHTON-HARRIS, Anthony Geoffrey, CBE 1989; DL; FCA; Deputy Chairman, Nationwide Building Society, since 1990; *b* 5 June 1932; *s* of Geoffrey Stoughton-Harris and Kathleen Mary (*née* Baker Brown); *m* 1959, Elizabeth Thackery (*née* White); one *s* two *d*. *Educ:* Sherborne Sch., Dorset. FCA 1956. Partner, Norton Keen & Co., chartered accountants, 1958–74; Dir, Maidenhead & Berkshire Building Soc., subseq. re-named South of England, London & South of England, Anglia, Nationwide Anglia, then Nationwide Building Soc., 1967–; Man. Dir, London & South of England Building Soc., 1975; Chief Gen. Manager, Anglia Building Soc., 1983–87; Vice-Chm., Nationwide Anglia Building Soc., 1987–90. Chm., Electronic Funds Transfer Ltd, 1984–89; Director: Southern Electric, 1981– (Dep. Chm., 1993–); EftPos UK Ltd, 1988–89; Guardian Royal Exchange, 1990–. Gen. Comr, Inland Revenue, 1982–. Part-time Treasurer, W Herts Main Drainage Authority, 1964–70. Chairman: Metropolitan Assoc. of Building Socs, 1979–80; BSA, 1987–89; Northants TEC, 1990–. FRSA; FCBSI. DL Northants, 1994. *Recreations:* sport, gardening, DIY. *Address:* Old Farm House, Blackmile Lane, Grendon, Northants NN7 1JR. *T:* Wellingborough (01933) 664235.

STOURTON, family name of **Baron Mowbray, Segrave and Stourton.**

STOUT, Prof. David Ker; Director, Centre for Business Strategy, London Business School, since 1992; *b* Bangor, N Wales, 27 Jan. 1932; *s* of late Prof. Alan Ker Stout, FAHA, FASSA and of Evelyn Roberts; *m* 1956, Margaret Sugden; two *s* two *d*. *Educ:* Sydney High Sch.; Sydney Univ., NSW (BA 1st Cl. English Lit, Econs, and University Medal in Econs, 1953); NSW Rhodes Scholar 1954; Magdalen Coll., Oxford; George Webb Medley Jun. Scholar 1955, Sen. Scholar 1956; PPE 1st Cl. 1956; Nuffield Coll., Oxford (Studentship 1956); Magdalen Prize Fellow by Examination, 1958–59. Fellow and Lectr in Econs, University Coll., Oxford, 1959–76; Economic Dir, NEDO, 1971–72 and 1976–80; Tyler Prof. of Econs, Leicester Univ., 1980–82; Head of Econs, Unilever, 1982–92. Adviser on tax structure to Syrian Govt, 1965, and New Hebrides Condominium, 1966; Sen. Econ. Adviser to Monopolies Commn, 1969; Consultant on VAT, Nat. Bureau of Econ. Res., NY, 1970; Adviser to Australian Govt on Prices Justification, 1973, and on Wage Indexation, 1975–76. Member: Exec. Cttee, NIESR, 1974–82, 1992–; EEC Expert Gp on Community Planning, 1976–78, and on Adjustment Policy, 1979–80; ESRC, 1989–92 (Mem., Econ. Affairs Cttee, 1980–86; Chm., Industry, Economics and Envmt Cttee, 1989–92); Manufacturing Foresight Panel, OST, 1994–; Bd of Trustees, Strategic Planning Inst., Cambridge, Mass, 1983–87. Editor, Business Strategy Review, 1994–. *Publications:* papers on taxation policy, VAT, investment, incomes policy, trade performance, indust. policy, de-industrialisation, and European planning. *Recreations:* music, chess, bivalves. *Address:* London Business School, Regent's Park, NW1 4SA. *T:* and *Fax:* (home) Borough Green (01732) 780908.

STOUT, Prof. Robert William, MD, DSc; FRCP, FRCPE; Professor of Geriatric Medicine, since 1976, Dean, Faculty of Medicine, since 1991 and Provost for Health Sciences, since 1993, Queen's University, Belfast; *b* 6 March 1942; *s* of William Ferguson Stout, *qv* and Muriel Stout (*née* Kilner); *m* 1969, Helena Patricia Willis; two *s* one *d*. *Educ:* Campbell Coll., Belfast; Queen's Univ., Belfast (MD, DSc). FRCP 1979; FRCPE 1988; FRCPI 1989; FRCPSGlas 1994. MRC Eli Lilly Foreign Educnl Fellow, Univ. of Washington Sch. of Medicine, Seattle, 1971–73; Queen's University, Belfast: BHF Sen. Res. Fellow, 1974; Sen. Lectr in Medicine, 1975. Member, Health & Social Services Boards: Southern, 1982–91; Eastern, 1993–. Mem., GMC, 1991–. Mem., Bd of Govs, Methodist Coll., Belfast, 1983– (Chm., 1994–). *Publications:* Hormones and Atherosclerosis, 1982; Arterial Disease in the Elderly, 1984; Diabetes and Atherosclerosis, 1992; articles in scientific jls on geriatric medicine and related topics. *Recreations:* golf, gardening, reading. *Address:* 3 Larch Hill Drive, Craigavad, Co. Down BT18 0JS. *T:* Belfast (01232) 422253. *Club:* Royal Belfast Golf.

STOUT, Samuel Coredon; HM Diplomatic Service, retired; *b* 17 Feb. 1913; *m* 1st, Mary Finn (*d* 1965); two *s* one *d*; 2nd, 1966, Jill Emery. Ministry of National Insurance, 1937–40; Admiralty, 1940–46; Board of Trade, 1946–65 (Trade Commissioner, Singapore, Bombay and Melbourne); Counsellor (Commercial), Canberra, 1966–68; Dep. High Comr and Minister (Commercial), Karachi, 1968–70; Consul-Gen., St Louis, USA, 1970–72. *Address:* Clifton, Main Street, West Ashby, Lincs LN9 5PT.

STOUT, William Ferguson, CB 1964; Security Adviser to Government of Northern Ireland, 1971–72, retired; *b* Holywood, Co. Down, 22 Feb. 1907; *s* of late Robert and Amelia Stout; *m* 1938, Muriel Kilner; one *s* one *d*. *Educ:* Sullivan Upper Sch., Holywood; Queen's Univ., Belfast. Ministry of Home Affairs: Principal, 1943; Asst Sec., 1954; Senior Asst Sec., 1959; Permanent Sec., 1961–64; Permanent Secretary: Min. of Health and Local Govt, 1964; Min. of Development, 1965–71. *Recreation:* golf.
See also R. W. Stout.

STOUTE, Michael Ronald; race horse trainer, since 1972; *b* 22 Oct. 1945; *m*; one *s* one *d*. *Educ:* Harrison College, Barbados. Leading flat racing trainer, 1981, 1986, 1989 and 1994; trained: Derby winners, Shergar, 1981, Shahrastani, 1986; Irish Derby winners, Shergar, 1981, Shareef Dancer, 1983, Shahrastani, 1986; 1000 Guineas winner, Musical Bliss, 1989; Irish 1000 Guineas winner, Sonic Lady, 1986; 2000 Guineas Winners, Shadeed, 1985, Doyoun, 1988; Irish 2000 Guineas winner, Shaadi, 1989; Oaks winners, Fair Salinia, 1978, Unite, 1987; Irish Oaks winners, Fair Salinia, 1978, Colorspin, 1986, Unite, 1987, Melodist, 1988. *Recreations:* cricket, ski-ing. *Address:* Freemason Lodge, Bury Road, Newmarket, Suffolk CB8 7BT. *T:* Newmarket (01638) 663801.

STOW, Archdeacon of; *see* Wells, Ven. R. J.

STOW, Sir Christopher P.; *see* Philipson-Stow.

STOW, Sir John Montague, GCMG 1966 (KCMG 1959; CMG 1950); KCVO 1966; Governor-General of Barbados, 1966–67; retired, 1967; *b* 3 Oct. 1911; *s* of late Sir Alexander Stow, KCIE; *m* 1939, Beatrice Tryhorne; two *s*. *Educ:* Harrow School; Pembroke College, Cambridge. Administrative Officer, Nigeria, 1934; Secretariat, Gambia, 1938; Chief Sec., Windward Islands, 1944; Administrator, St Lucia, BWI, 1947; Dir of Establishments, Kenya, 1952–55; Chief Sec., Jamaica, 1955–59; Governor and C-in-C Barbados, 1959–66. With Stewart, Wrightson Ltd, 1967–77; Dir, Buckmaster Management Co. Ltd, 1981–83. Chm., Commonwealth Soc. for Deaf, 1983–85. KStJ 1959. *Recreations:* cricket, tennis. *Address:* 26a Tregunter Road, SW10 9LH. *T:* 0171–370 1921. *Clubs:* Caledonian, MCC.

STOW, (Julian) Randolph; writer; *b* Geraldton, W Australia, 28 Nov. 1935; *s* of Cedric Ernest Stow, barrister and Mary Stow (*née* Sewell). *Educ:* Guildford Grammar Sch., W Australia; Univ. of Western Australia. Lecturer in English Literature: Univ. of Leeds, 1962; Univ. of Western Australia, 1963–64; Harkness Fellow, United States, 1964–66; Lectr in English and Commonwealth Lit., Univ. of Leeds, 1968–69. Miles Franklin Award, 1958; Britannica Australia Award, 1966; Patrick White Award, 1979. *Publications: poems:* Outrider, 1962; A Counterfeit Silence, 1969; *novels:* To The Islands, 1958, rev. edn 1981; Tourmaline, 1963; The Merry-go-round in the Sea, 1965; Visitants, 1979; The Girl Green as Elderflower, 1980; The Suburbs of Hell, 1984; *music theatre* (with Peter Maxwell Davies): Eight Songs for a Mad King, 1969; Miss Donnithorne's Maggot, 1974; *for children:* Midnite, 1967. *Address:* c/o Richard Scott Simon Ltd, 43 Doughty Street, WC1N 2LF.

STOW, Ralph Conyers, CBE 1981; FCIS, FCIB; President and Chairman, Cheltenham & Gloucester Building Society, 1982–87 (Managing Director, 1973–82); *b* 19 Dec. 1916; *s* of Albert Conyers Stow and Mabel Louise Bourlet; *m* 1943, Eleanor Joyce Appleby; one *s* one *d*. *Educ:* Woodhouse Sch., Finchley. FCIS 1959; FBS 1952. Supt of Branches, Temperance Permanent Bldg Soc., 1950, Asst Manager 1958; Gen. Man. and Sec., Cheltenham & Gloucester Bldg Soc., 1962, Dir 1967. Pres., Bldg Socs Inst., 1971–72; Chm., Midland Assoc. of Bldg Socs, 1973–74; Chm., Bldg Socs Assoc., 1977–79. Mem., Glos AHA, 1973–81; Chm., Cheltenham DHA, 1981–88. *Recreations:* photography, oil painting. *Club:* Rotary (Cheltenham).

STOW, Randolph; *see* Stow, J. R.

STOW, Timothy Montague Fenwick; QC 1989; a Recorder, since 1989; *b* 31 Jan. 1943; *s* of Geoffrey Montague Fenwick Stow and Joan Fortescue Stow (*née* Flannery); *m* 1965, Alisoun Mary Francis Homberger; one *s* one *d*. *Educ:* Eton Coll. Called to the Bar, Gray's Inn, 1965; became a tenant in common law chambers of David Croom-Johnson, QC (later Lord Justice Croom-Johnson), 1966. *Recreations:* swimming, squash, tennis, foreign travel, music, looking after their country property. *Address:* 12 King's Bench Walk, Temple, EC4Y 7EL. *T:* 0171–583 0811.

STOW, William Llewelyn; Head of European Community and Trade Relations Division, Department of Trade and Industry, since 1994; *b* 11 Jan. 1948; *s* of Alfred Frank and Elizabeth Mary Stow; *m* 1976, Rosemary Ellen Burrows; two *s*. *Educ:* Eastbourne Grammar Sch.; Churchill Coll., Cambridge (MA). Joined DTI, 1971; seconded to FCO, 1980–83 (UK Delegn to OECD) and 1985–88 (UK Perm. Repn to EC, Brussels); Internal European Policy, DTI, 1988; Financial and Resource Management, DTI, 1991–94. *Recreations:* hill and coastal walking, bird-watching, cricket, reading. *Address:* Department of Trade and Industry, Kingsgate House, 66–74 Victoria Street, SW1E 6SW. *Club:* Mandarins Cricket.

STOWE, Sir Kenneth (Ronald), GCB 1986 (KCB 1980; CB 1977); CVO 1979; Chairman, Institute of Cancer Research, since 1987; *b* 17 July 1927; *er s* of Arthur and Emily Stowe; *m* 1949, Joan Frances Cullen (*d* 1995); two *s* one *d*. *Educ:* County High Sch., Dagenham; Exeter Coll., Oxford (MA; Hon. Fellow, 1989). Asst Principal, Nat. Assistance Board, 1951; Principal, 1956; seconded UN Secretariat, New York, 1958; Asst Sec., 1964; Asst Under-Sec. of State, DHSS, 1970–73; Under Sec., Cabinet Office, 1973–75, Dep. Sec., 1976; Principal Private Sec. to the Prime Minister, 1975–79; Permanent Under Sec. of State, NI Office, 1979–81; Perm. Sec., DHSS, 1981–87. Mem., President's Commn to review Public Service of Zimbabwe, 1987–89; Mem. Bd of Dirs, Commonwealth Assoc. for Public Admin and Management, 1994– (Chm., Founding Conf., PEI, 1994); Advr on admin. reform to HM Govt, UN Develt Prog., and Commonwealth Secretariat. Dir, Royal Marsden Hosp. NHS Trust, 1994–; Mem. Council, CRC, 1987–. Life Trustee, Carnegie UK Trust, 1988–; Chm., Carnegie Inquiry into The Third Age, 1989–93. *Recreations:* listening and thinking. *Club:* Athenæum.

STOWELL, Dr Michael James, FRS 1984; Research Director, Alcan International Ltd, 1990–94 (Principal Consulting Scientist, 1989–90); *b* 10 July 1935; *s* of Albert James Stowell and Kathleen Maud (*née* Poole); *m* 1962, Rosemary Allen (marr. diss. 1990); one *s* one *d*. *Educ:* St Julian's High Sch., Newport; Bristol Univ. (BSc 1957, PhD 1961). Res.

Editor, Oxford Slavonic Papers, 1983–94. *Publications:* The Smallest Slavonic Nation: the Sorbs of Lusatia, 1972; (with B. Comrie) The Russian Language since the Revolution, 1978; An Introduction to Polish, 1980, 2nd edn 1992; (ed with D. Worth) The Formation of the Slavonic Literary Languages, 1985. *Recreations:* gardening, walking, visiting pubs. *Address:* 6 Lathbury Road, Oxford OX2 7AU. *T:* Oxford (01865) 58227.

STONE, Gordon; *see* Stone, F. G. A.

STONE, Gregory; QC 1994; *b* 12 Dec. 1946; *s* of Frederick Albert Leslie Stone and Marion Gerda Stone (*née* Heller); *m* (separated); three *d. Educ:* Chislehurst and Sidcup Grammar Sch.; St Joseph's Coll., London; Université de Rennes; Queen's Coll., Oxford (MA); Univ. of Manchester (Dip. Econ. Develt (distinction) 1971; MA (Econ.) 1972). Sen. Economist, Morgan Grenfell, 1974–76; called to the Bar, Inner Temple, 1976; Standing Counsel to DTI for Criminal Matters on South Eastern Circuit, 1989–90. *Publications:* The Law of Defective Premises, 1982; The Architect's Legal Handbook, 2nd edn, to 5th edn 1990. *Recreations:* travel, music, walking. *Address:* 4–5 Gray's Inn Square, Gray's Inn, WC1R 5AY. *T:* 0171–404 5252.

STONE, Prof. Lawrence, MA Oxon; Dodge Professor of History, 1963–90, and Director, Shelby Cullom Davis Center for Historical Studies, 1968–90, Princeton University; *b* 4 Dec. 1919; *s* of Lawrence Frederick Stone and Mabel Julia Annie Stone; *m* 1943, Jeanne Caecilia, *d* of Prof. Robert Fawtier, Membre de l'Institut, Paris; one *s* one *d. Educ:* Charterhouse School, 1933–38; Sorbonne, Paris, 1938; Christ Church, Oxford, 1938–40, 1945–46. Lieut RNVR 1940–45. Bryce Research Student, Oxford Univ., 1946–47; Lectr, University Coll. Oxford, 1947–50; Fellow, Wadham Coll., Oxford, 1950–63 (Hon. Fellow, 1983); Mem. Inst. for Advanced Study, Princeton, 1960–61; Chm., Dept of History, 1967–70. Mem., Amer. Philosophical Soc., 1970. Fellow, Amer. Acad. of Arts and Sciences, 1968; Corresp. FBA 1983. Hon. DHL: Chicago, 1979; Pennsylvania, 1986; Hon. DLitt: Edinburgh, 1983; Glasgow, 1993; Oxford, 1994. *Publications:* Sculpture in Britain: The Middle Ages, 1955; An Elizabethan: Sir Horatio Palavicino, 1956; The Crisis of the Aristocracy, 1558–1641, 1965; The Causes of the English Revolution, 1529–1642, 1972; Family and Fortune: Studies in Aristocratic Finance in the 16th and 17th Centuries, 1973; (ed) The University in Society, 1975; (ed) Schooling and Society, 1977; Family, Sex and Marriage in England 1500–1800, 1977; The Past and the Present, 1981; An Open Elite? England 1540–1880, 1984; The Past and the Present Revisited, 1987; Road to Divorce: England 1530–1987, 1990; Uncertain Unions: marriage in England 1660–1753, 1992; Broken Lives: separation and divorce in England 1660–1857, 1993; (ed) An Imperial State at War: Britain from 1689 to 1815, 1994; numerous articles in History, Economic History Review, Past and Present, Archæological Jl, English Historical Review, Bulletin of the Inst. for Historical Research, Malone Soc., Comparative Studies in Society and History, History Today, etc. *Address:* 266 Moore Street, Princeton, NJ 08540, USA. *T:* (609) 9212717; 231A Woodstock Road, Oxford OX2 7AD. *T:* Oxford (01865) 59174.

STONE, Marcus; Sheriff of Lothian and Borders, 1984–93; Advocate; *b* 22 March 1921; *s* of Morris and Reva Stone; *m* 1956, Jacqueline Barnoin; three *s* two *d. Educ:* High Sch. of Glasgow; Univ. of Glasgow (MA 1940, LLB 1948). Served War of 1939–45, RASC: overseas service, West Africa, att. RWAFF. Admitted Solicitor, 1949; Post Grad. Dip., Psychology, Univ. of Glasgow, 1953; admitted Faculty of Advocates, 1965; apptd Hon. Sheriff Substitute, 1967, Sheriff, 1971–76, of Stirling, Dunbarton and Clackmannan, later N Strathclyde at Dumbarton; Sheriff of Glasgow and Strathkelvin, 1976–84. Accredited Mediator, Centre for Dispute Resolution, London, 1993 (Mem., Judicial Appraisal Panel for Scotland, 1993–); Man. Dir, Mediation Trng Seminars (Scotland) Ltd, and practising mediator, 1994–. MIMgt, 1993. *Publications:* Proof of Fact in Criminal Trials, 1984; Cross-examination in Criminal Trials, 1988, 2nd edn 1995; Fact-finding for Magistrates, 1990. *Recreations:* swimming, music. *Address:* 11 Grosvenor Crescent, Edinburgh EH12 5EL.

STONE, Prof. Norman; Professor of Modern History, and Fellow of Worcester College, University of Oxford, since 1984; *b* 8 March 1941; *s* of late Norman Stone and Mary Stone (*née* Pettigrew); *m* 1st, 1966, Nicole Aubry (marr. diss. 1977); two *s*; 2nd, 1982, Christine Margaret Booker (*née* Verity); one *s. Educ:* Glasgow Acad.; Gonville and Caius Coll., Cambridge (MA). Research student in Austria and Hungary, 1962–65; University of Cambridge: Research Fellow, Gonville and Caius Coll., 1965–67; Univ. Lectr in Russian History, 1967–84; Fellow and Dir of Studies in History, Jesus Coll., 1971–79; Fellow of Trinity Coll., 1979–84. Vis. Lectr, Sydney Univ., 1978. Trustee, Margaret Thatcher Foundn, 1991–. Order of Merit (Polish Republic), 1993. *Publications:* The Eastern Front 1914–1917, 1975, 3rd edn 1978 (Wolfson Prize for History, 1976); Hitler, 1980; Europe Transformed 1878–1919 (Fontana History of Europe), 1983; (ed jtly) Czechoslovakia, 1989; (jtly) The Other Russia, 1990; The Russian Chronicles, 1990. *Recreations:* Eastern Europe, music, languages, journalism. *Address:* 22 St Margaret's Road, Oxford OX2 6RX. *T:* Oxford (01865) 510457. *Clubs:* Beefsteak, Garrick, Polish.

STONE, Maj.-Gen. Patrick Philip Dennant, CB 1992; CBE 1984 (OBE 1981; MBE 1975); Director General, Personal Services (Army), 1988–91; *b* 7 Feb. 1939; *s* of Philip Hartley Stone and Elsie Maude Stone (*née* Dennant); *m* 1967, Christine Iredale Trent; two *s* one *d. Educ:* Christ's Hospital; psc 1972. Nat. Service, 1959; commissioned East Anglian Regt, 1959; seconded 6 KAR, 1960–62 (Tanganyika); served British Guyana and Aden, 1962–65; ADC to Governor of W Australia, 1965–67; RAF Staff Coll., 1972; Comd 2nd Bn, Royal Anglian Regt, 1977–80 (UK and Berlin); Chief of Staff, 1st Armoured Div., 1981–84; Comdr, Berlin Inf. Bde, 1985–86; Dep. Mil. Sec. (B), 1987. Dep. Col, Royal Anglian Regt, 1986–91, Col, 1991–; Col Comdt, Mil. Provost Staff Corps, 1988–92; Dep. Col Comdt, AGC, 1992–93. *Recreations:* country interests, travel, conservation. *Address:* c/o Lloyds Bank, 90A Mill Road, Cambridge. *Club:* Army and Navy.

STONE, Richard Frederick, QC 1968; *b* 11 March 1928; *s* of Sir Leonard Stone, OBE, QC, and Madeleine Marie (*née* Scheffler); *m* 1st, 1957, Georgina Maxwell Morris (decd); two *d*; 2nd, 1964, Susan van Heel; two *d. Educ:* Lakefield College Sch., Canada; Rugby; Trinity Hall, Cambridge (MA). Lt, Worcs Regt, 1946–48. Called to Bar, Gray's Inn, 1952, Bencher, 1974, Treasurer, 1992. Member: Panel of Lloyd's Arbitrators in Salvage Cases; Panel of Wreck Comrs. *Recreation:* sailing. *Address:* 5 Raymond Buildings, Gray's Inn, WC1R 5BP. *T:* 0171–242 2697; Orchard Gap, Wittering Road, Hayling Island, Hants PO11 9SP. *T:* Hayling Island (01705) 463645.

STONEFROST, Maurice Frank, CBE 1983; DL; Deputy Pro Chancellor and Vice-Chairman of the Council, City University, since 1992; *b* 1 Sept. 1927; *s* of Arthur and Anne Stonefrost, Bristol; *m* 1953, Audrey Jean Fishlock; one *s* one *d. Educ:* Merrywood Grammar Sch., Bristol (DPA). IPFA. Nat. Service, RAF, 1948–51; local govt finance: Bristol County Borough, 1951–54; Slough Borough, 1954–56; Coventry County Borough, 1956–61; W Sussex CC, 1961–64; Sec., Inst. of Municipal Treasurers and Accountants, 1964–73; Comptroller of Financial Services, GLC, 1973–84; Dir Gen. and Clerk, GLC, 1984–85; Chief Exec., BR Pension Fund, 1986–90; Chairman: Municipal Mutual Insce, 1990–93; CLF Municipal Bank, 1993–. President: Soc. of County Treasurers, 1982–83; CIPFA, 1984–85. Chm., Commn on Citizenship, 1989–90; Member: Marre Cttee on Future of Legal Profession, 1989–; Review Cttee of Finances of C of E, 1993. Member: Architectural Heritage Fund, 1990–; Foundn for Accountancy and Financial Management, Eastern Europe, 1993–. Chm., Dolphin Sq. Trust, 1993–. DL Greater London, 1986. Hon. DSc City Univ., 1987. *Recreation:* gardening. *Address:* 611 Hood House, Dolphin Square, SW1V 3LX. *T:* 0171–798 3247.

See also W. J. G. Keegan.

STONEHAM, Prof. Arthur Marshall, PhD; FRS 1989; Chief Scientist, UKAEA, since 1993; Massey Professor of Physics, and Director, Centre for Materials Research, University College London, since 1995; *b* 18 May 1940; *s* of Garth Rivers Stoneham and Nancy Wooler Stoneham (*née* Leslie); *m* 1962, Doreen Montgomery; two *d. Educ:* Univ. of Bristol (BSc 1961; PhD 1964). CPhys, FInstP 1981. Harwell Laboratory, UKAEA, 1964–: Group Leader, 1974; Individual Merit promotions to Band level, 1974, and Sen. level, 1979; Hd of Materials Physics and Metallurgy Div., 1989–90; Hd of Technical Area, Core and Fuel Studies, UKAEA, 1988–90; Dir of Res., AEA Industrial Technology, 1990–93. Wolfson Industrial Fellow, Oxford Univ., 1985–89; Fellow, Wolfson Coll., Oxford, 1989–95. Visiting Professor: Univ. of Illinois, 1969; Univ. of Connecticut, 1973; Univ. of Keele, 1988–; Univ. of Salford, 1992–; visiting scientist: Gen. Electric, Schenectady, 1969; Centre d'Etudes Nucléaires Grenoble, 1970; KFA Julich, 1973; IBM Yorktown Heights, 1982; PTB Braunschweig, 1985, etc. Member, Council: Royal Soc., 1994–; Inst. of Physics, 1994–. Dir, Inst. of Physics Publications; Editor, Jl of Physics C: Solid State Physics, 1983–88; Divl Associate Ed., Physical Review Letters, 1992–; mem. editl bds of other learned jls. *Publications:* Theory of Defects in Solids, 1975, new edn 1985 (Russian edn 1978); (with W. Hayes) Defects and Defect Processes in Non-Metallic Solids, 1985; (with M. G. Silk and J. A. G. Temple) Current Issues in Semiconductor Science, 1986; Current Issues in Condensed Matter Structure, 1987; Reliability of Non-Destructive Inspection, 1987; Ionic Solids at High Temperatures, 1989; Current Issues in Condensed Matter Spectroscopy, 1990; Materials Modelling: from theory to technology, 1992; (with S. C. Jain) GeSi Strained Layers and their Applications, 1995; research papers on defect properties of the solid state, quantum diffusion, and ordered structures in Jl Phys C: Solid State Phys, Phys Rev., Phys Rev. Lett., Procs of Royal Soc., etc. *Recreations:* music, esp. horn playing in orchestral and chamber music, musical scholarship, reading. *Address:* Riding Mill, Bridge End, Dorchester-on-Thames, Wallingford, Oxon OX10 7JP. *T:* Oxford (01865) 340066.

STONES, (Elsie) Margaret, AM 1988; MBE 1977; botanical artist; *b* 28 Aug. 1920; *d* of Frederick Stones and Agnes Kirkwood (*née* Fleming). *Educ:* Swinburne Technical Coll., Melbourne; Melbourne National Gall. Art Sch. Came to England, 1951; working independently as botanical artist, 1951–: at Royal Botanic Gardens, Kew; Nat. Hist. Museum; Royal Horticultural Soc., and at other botanical instns; Contrib. Artist to Curtis's Botanical Magazine, 1957–82. Drawings (water-colour): 20, Aust. plants, National Library, Canberra, 1962–63; 250, Tasmanian endemic plants, 1962–77; Basalt Plains flora, Melbourne Univ., 1975–76; Vis. Botanical Artist, Louisiana State Univ., 1977–86 (200 drawings of Louisiana flora, exhibited: Fitzwilliam, Cambridge, Royal Botanic Garden, Edinburgh, Ashmolean Mus., Oxford, 1991). Exhibitions: Colnaghi's, London, 1967–; retrospective, Melbourne Univ., 1976; Louisiana Drawings, Smithsonian, USA, 1980, Louisiana State Mus., 1985, Univ. of Virginia, 1993; Baskett & Day, 1984, 1989; Boston Athenæum, 1993; retrospective, Nat. Gall. of Victoria, Melbourne, 1996. Workshop, Cornell Univ., USA, 1990. Hon. DSc: Louisiana State Univ. Bâton Rouge, 1986; Melbourne Univ., 1989. Eloise Payne Luquer Medal, Garden Club of Amer., 1987; Gold Veitch Meml Medal, RHS, 1989. *Publications:* The Endemic Flora of Tasmania (text by W. M. Curtis), 6 Parts, 1967–78; Flora of Louisiana: water-colour drawings, 1991; illus. various books. *Recreations:* gardening, reading. *Address:* 1 Bushwood Road, Kew, Richmond, Surrey TW9 3BG. *T:* 0181–940 6183.

STONES, Sir William (Frederick), Kt 1990; OBE 1980; Senior Adviser, West Merchant Bank Ltd, Hong Kong, since 1993; Managing Director, China Light & Power Co., 1984–92 (Director, 1975–93); Chairman, Hong Kong Nuclear Investment Co., 1985–93; *b* 3 March 1923; *s* of Ralph William Stones and Ada Stones (*née* Armstrong); *m* 1st, 1946, Irene Mary Punter (marr. diss.); one *s* one *d*; 2nd, 1968, Margaret Joy Catton. *Educ:* Rutherford Coll., Newcastle upon Tyne. Chief Chemist, Michie & Davidson, 1948–51; Regional Res. Dir, CEGB NE Region, 1951–63; Supt, Ferrybridge Power Station, 1963–66; CEGB NE Region: Group Manager, 1966–68; Dir, Operational Planning, 1968–71; Dir, Generation, and Dep. Dir-Gen., 1971–75; Gen. Manager, China Light & Power Co., 1975–83. Dep. Chm., Guandong Nuclear Power Joint Venture Co., 1985–93. Commander, Order of Leopold II (Belgium), 1986. *Recreations:* fishing, country life. *Address:* Pirnie House, Kelso, Roxburghshire TD5 8NS. T: St Boswells (01835) 823854. *Clubs:* New (Edinburgh); Hong Kong.

STONEY, Brigadier Ralph Francis Ewart, CBE 1952 (OBE, 1943); Director-General, The Royal Society for the Prevention of Accidents, 1959–68; *b* 28 June 1903; *o s* of late Col R. D. S. Stoney, The Downs, Delgany, Co. Wicklow and Mrs E. M. M. Stoney; *m* 1st, 1939, Kathleen Nina (*née* Kirkland) (*d* 1973); one *d*; 2nd, 1979, Bridget Mary St John Browne. *Educ:* Royal Naval Colleges, Osborne and Dartmouth; Royal Military Academy, Woolwich. Commissioned Royal Engineers, 1923; Staff College, Camberley, 1937–38. Served War of 1939–45 as GSO, 1939–43 (OBE) and as CRE, 82 Div., 1943–46, in Burma (despatches twice). CRE 5th Div. and 2nd Div., 1947–48; Col GS (Intelligence), War Office, 1949–51; Brig. GS (Intelligence), Middle East, 1952–54. Retired, 1954. *Address:* Kinsale, Hook Heath Avenue, Woking, Surrey GU22 0HN.

STONHOUSE, Sir Philip (Allan), 18th Bt, *cr* 1628, and 14th Bt *cr* 1670; Assessor and Land Appraiser, Government of Alberta; *b* 24 Oct. 1916; *s* of Sir Arthur Allan Stonhouse, 17th Bt, and Beatrice C. Féron; *S* father, 1967; *m* 1946, Winnifred Emily Shield; two *s. Educ:* Western Canada Coll.; Queen's Univ., Kingston, Ontario. Gold Mining, 1936–40; General Construction, 1940–42; Ranching, 1942–54; Assessing, 1954–68. Is a Freemason. *Recreations:* water-fowl and upland game hunting, tennis, ski-ing. *Heir: s* Rev. Michael Philip Stonhouse, BA, LTh [*b* 4 Sept. 1948; *m* 1977, Colleen Coucill, Toronto; three *s. Educ:* Wycliffe Coll., Toronto]. *Address:* 521–12 Street SW, Medicine Hat, Alberta, Canada. *T:* (403) 5265832. *Club:* Medicine Hat Ski.

STONOR, family name of **Baron Camoys.**

STONOR, Air Marshal Sir Thomas (Henry), KCB 1989; Group Director and Controller, National Air Traffic Services, 1988–91; *b* 5 March 1936; *s* of Alphonsus and Ann Stonor; *m* 1964, Robin Antoinette, *er d* of late Wilfrid and Rita Budd; two *s* one *d. Educ:* St Cuthbert's High Sch., Newcastle upon Tyne; King's Coll., Univ. of Durham (BSc (Mech Eng) 1957). Commissioned, RAF, 1959; served No 3 Sqn, 2ATAF, 1961–64; CFS, 6 FTS and RAF Coll., Cranwell, 1964–67; No 231 Operational Conversion Unit, 1967–69; RAF Staff Coll., Bracknell, 1970; HQ, RAF Germany, 1971–73; OC 31 Sqn, 1974–76; Mil. Asst to VCDS, MoD, 1976–78; OC RAF Coltishall, 1978–80; RCDS, 1981; Inspector of Flight Safety, RAF, 1982–84; Dir of Control (Airspace Policy), NATS, 1985–86; Dep. Controller, NATS, 1986–88. Sen. Consultant, Siemens Plessey Systems, 1991–; Defence Advr, BT Defence Sales Sector, 1991–; Non-exec. Dir, COMAC Gp, 1994–. *Recreations:* gardening, music. *Address:* c/o Barclays Bank, Haymarket Branch, Newcastle upon Tyne NE1 7BH. *Club:* Royal Air Force.

STOPFORD, family name of **Earl of Courtown.**

STOPFORD, Viscount; James Richard Ian Montagu Stopford; *b* 30 March 1988; *s* and *heir* of Earl of Courtown, *qv.*

STOPFORD, Prof. John Morton, DBA; Professor of International Business, London Business School, since 1974; *b* 16 Sept. 1939; *s* of Rt Rev. and Rt Hon. Robert Wright Stopford, KCVO, CBE, DD and Winifred Sophia Stopford (*née* Morton); *m* 1966, Sarah Woodman; two *s. Educ:* Sherborne Sch.; Hertford Coll., Oxford (BA); MIT (SM); Harvard Univ. (DBA). Apprentice fitter, Baker Perkins, 1958; Engineer, Shell Chemicals, 1962–64; Acting Man. Dir, Guyana Stockfeeds, 1965; Sen. Lectr, Manchester Business Sch., 1968–70; Vis. Prof., Harvard Business Sch., 1970–71; Reader, London Business Sch., 1971–74. Non-Exec. Dir, Shell UK, 1973–77; Dir, InterMatrix, 1977–; Dep. Chm., Strategic Partnership, 1994–. Pres., Eur. Internat. Business Assoc., 1978–79; Vice-Pres., Acad. of Internat. Business, 1994–; UN Centre on Transitional Corps, NY, 1977–78. Visiting Professor: MIT, 1993; Stockholm Sch. of Econs, 1994–95; Aoyama Gakuin Univ., Tokyo, 1994–95. US Acad. of Management Book Prize, 1992. *Publications:* (with L. T. Wells) Managing the Multinational Enterprise, 1972; (with B. Garratt) Breaking down Barriers, 1980; Growth and Organisational Change, 1980; The Directory of Multinationals, 1980, 1992; (with J. H. Dunning) Multinationals, 1983; (with L. Turner) Britain and the Multinationals, 1985; (with S. Strange) Rival States, Rival Firms, 1991; (with C. Baden-Fuller) Rejuvenating the Mature Business, 1992, rev. edn 1994; contribs to learned jls. *Recreations:* hill-walking, tennis, reading. *Address:* London Business School, Sussex Place, Regent's Park, NW1 4SA; 6 Chalcot Square, NW1 8YB.

STOPFORD, Maj.-Gen. Stephen Robert Anthony, CB 1988; MBE 1971; Director, David Brown Vehicle Transmissions Ltd, since 1990; Director General Fighting Vehicles and Engineer Equipment, Ministry of Defence (Procurement Executive), 1985–89; *b* 1 April 1934; *s* of Comdr Robert Stopford, RN, and Elsie Stopford; *m* 1963, Vanessa (*née* Baron). *Educ:* Downside; Millfield. Graduate MIERE. Commissioned Royal Scots Greys, 1954; regimental service and various staff appts until 1977; Project Manager, MBT80, 1977–80; Military Attaché, Washington, 1983–85. *Recreations:* sailing, scuba diving, shooting. *Address:* 18 Thornton Avenue, SW2 4HG. *T:* 0181–674 1416.

STOPPARD, Miriam, MD, MRCP; writer and broadcaster; *b* 12 May 1937; *d* of Sydney and Jenny Stern; *m* 1972, Tom Stoppard, *qv* (marr. diss. 1992); two *s* and two step *s. Educ:* Newcastle upon Tyne Central High Sch. (State Scholar, 1955); Royal Free Hosp. Sch. of Medicine, Univ. of London (Prize for Experimental Physiol., 1958); King's Coll. Med. Sch. (Univ. of Durham), Newcastle upon Tyne (MB, BS Durham, 1961; MD Newcastle, 1966). MRCP 1964. Royal Victoria Infirmary, King's Coll. Hosp., Newcastle upon Tyne: House Surg., 1961; House Phys., 1962; Sen. House Officer in Medicine, 1962–63; Univ. of Bristol: Res. Fellow, Dept of Chem. Pathol., 1963–65 (MRC Scholar in Chem. Pathol.); Registrar in Dermatol., 1965–66 (MRC Scholar in Dermatol.); Sen. Registrar in Dermatol., 1966–68; Syntex Pharmaceuticals Ltd: Associate Med. Dir, 1968; Dep. Med. Dir, 1971; Med. Dir, 1974; Dep. Man. Dir, 1976; Man. Dir, 1977–81. TV series: Where There's Life (5 series), 1981–; Baby & Co. (2 series), 1984–; Woman to Woman, 1985–; Miriam Stoppard's Health and Beauty Show, 1988–; Dear Miriam, 1989. MRSocMed (Mem. Dermatol. Sect., Endocrinol. Sect.); Member: Heberden Soc.; Brit. Assoc. of Rheumatology and Rehabilitation. *Publications:* Miriam Stoppard's Book of Baby Care, 1977; (contrib.) My Medical School, 1978; Miriam Stoppard's Book of Health Care, 1979; The Face and Body Book, 1980; Everywoman's Lifeguide, 1982; Your Baby, 1982; Fifty Plus Lifeguide, 1982; Your Growing Child, 1983; Baby Care Book, 1983; Pregnancy and Birth Book, 1984; Baby and Child Medical Handbook, 1986; Everygirl's Lifeguide, 1987; Feeding Your Family, 1987; Miriam Stoppard's Health and Beauty Book, 1988; Every Woman's Medical Handbook, 1988; Lose 7 lb in 7 Days, 1990; Test Your Child, 1991; The Magic of Sex, 1991; Conception, Pregnancy and Birth, 1993; The Menopause, 1994; over 40 pubns in med. jls. *Recreations:* my family, gardening. *Address:* Iver Grove, Iver, Bucks SL0 0LB.

STOPPARD, Tom, CBE 1978; FRSL; playwright and novelist; *b* 3 July 1937; *yr s* of late Eugene Straussler and of Mrs Martha Stoppard; *m* 1st, 1965, Jose (marr. diss. 1972), *yr d* of John and Alice Ingle; two *s*; 2nd, 1972, Dr Miriam Moore-Robinson (*see* Miriam Stoppard) (marr. diss. 1992); two *s. Educ:* abroad; Dolphin Sch., Notts; Pocklington, Yorks. Journalist: Western Daily Press, Bristol, 1954–58; Bristol Evening World, 1958–60; freelance, 1960–63. Mem., Royal Nat. Theatre Bd, 1989–. Hon. degrees: Bristol, 1976; Brunel, 1979; Leeds, 1980; Sussex, 1980; London, 1982; Kenyon Coll., 1984; York, 1984. Shakespeare Prize, 1979. *Plays:* Enter a Free Man, London, 1968 (TV play, A Walk on the Water, 1963); Rosencrantz and Guildenstern are Dead, Nat. Theatre, 1967, subseq. NY, etc (Tony Award, NY, 1968; NY Drama Critics Circle Award, 1968); The Real Inspector Hound, London, 1968; After Magritte, Ambiance Theatre, 1970; Dogg's Our Pet, Ambiance Theatre, 1972; Jumpers, National Theatre, 1972 (Evening Standard Award); Travesties, Aldwych, 1974 (Evening Standard Award; Tony Award, NY, 1976); Dirty Linen, Newfoundland, Ambiance Theatre, 1976; Every Good Boy Deserves Favour (music-theatre), 1977; Night and Day, Phoenix, 1978 (Evening Standard Award); Dogg's Hamlet and Cahoot's Macbeth, Collegiate, 1979; Undiscovered Country (adaptation), NT, 1979; On the Razzle, NT, 1981; The Real Thing, Strand, 1982 (Standard Award), subseq. NY (Tony Award, 1984); Rough Crossing (adaptation), NT, 1984; Dalliance (adaptation), NT, 1986; Hapgood, Aldwych, 1988; Arcadia, NT, 1993 (Evening Standard Award; Olivier Award); Indian Ink, Aldwych, 1995; *radio:* The Dissolution of Dominic Boot, 1964; M is for Moon Among Other Things, 1964; If You're Glad I'll Be Frank, 1965; Albert's Bridge, 1967 (Prix Italia); Where Are They Now?, 1970; Artist Descending a Staircase, 1972; The Dog it was That Died, 1982 (Giles Cooper Award; televised 1988); In the Native State, 1991; *television:* A Separate Peace, 1966; Teeth, 1967; Another Moon Called Earth, 1967; Neutral Ground, 1968; (with Clive Exton) Boundaries, 1975; (adapted) Three Men in a Boat, 1976; Professional Foul, 1977; Squaring the Circle, 1984; *screenplays:* (with T. Wiseman) The Romantic Englishwoman, 1975; Despair, 1978; The Human Factor, 1979; (with Terry Gilliam and Charles McKeown) Brazil, 1985; Empire of the Sun, 1987; Rosencrantz and Guildenstern are Dead, 1990 (also dir); The Russian House, 1991; Billy Bathgate, 1991. John Whiting Award, Arts Council, 1967; Evening Standard Award for Most Promising Playwright, 1968. *Publications:* (short stories) Introduction 2, 1964; (novel) Lord Malquist and Mr Moon, 1965; *plays:* Rosencrantz and Guildenstern are Dead, 1967; The Real Inspector Hound, 1968; Albert's Bridge, 1968; Enter a Free Man, 1968; After Magritte, 1971; Jumpers, 1972; Artists Descending a Staircase, and, Where Are They Now?, 1973; Travesties, 1975; Dirty Linen, and New-Found-Land, 1976; Every Good Boy Deserves Favour, 1978; Professional Foul, 1978; Night and Day, 1978; Undiscovered Country, 1980; Dogg's Hamlet, Cahoot's Macbeth, 1980; On the Razzle, 1981; The Real Thing, 1983; The Dog it was that Died, 1983; Squaring the Circle, 1984; Four plays for radio, 1984; Rough Crossing, 1985; Dalliance and Undiscovered Country, 1986; (trans.) Largo Desolato, by Vaclav Havel, 1987; Hapgood, 1988; In the Native State, 1991; Arcadia, 1993; The Television Plays 1965–1984, 1993. *Address:* c/o Peters, Fraser & Dunlop, The Chambers, Chelsea Harbour, Lots Road, SW10 0XF.

STOPS, Timothy William Ashcroft J.; *see* Jackson-Stops.

STORAR, John Robert Allan Montague, CA; Chairman, Mitchell Cotts PLC, 1985–87 (Director, 1973–87; Deputy Chairman, 1978); *b* 6 Nov. 1925; *s* of James and Leonore Storar; *m* 1952, Catherine Swanson Henderson; two *s* one *d. Educ:* Dollar Academy. Dir 1960–74, Dep. Chief Exec. 1972–74, Drayton Corporation Ltd; Dir 1974–85, Dep. Chm. 1974–81, Man. Dir 1981–82, Samuel Montagu & Co. Ltd; Dir, Consolidated Gold Fields PLC, 1969–89. Chm., Assoc. of Investment Trust Cos, 1979–81. *Recreation:* fly fishing. *Address:* 3 Parkside Avenue, Wimbledon, SW19 5ES. *Club:* Caledonian.
See also L. E. T. Storar.

STORAR, Leonore Elizabeth Therese; retired; *b* 3 May 1920. Served HM Forces, 1942–46. Min. of Works, 1947; joined CRO, 1948; First Sec., Delhi and Calcutta, 1951–53; Salisbury, 1956–58; Colombo, 1960–62; Counsellor, 1963; Head of General and Migration Dept, CRO, 1962; Dep. Consul-Gen., NY, 1967; Consul-Gen., Boston, 1969; Head of Commonwealth Co-ordination Dept, FCO, 1971–75; Dir, Colombo Plan Bureau, Colombo, Sri Lanka, 1976–78. *Address:* Lavender Cottage, Dippenhall Street, Crondall, Farnham, Surrey GU10 5PF.
See also J. R. A. M. Storar.

STORER, David George; Under Secretary, Department of Social Security (formerly of Health and Social Security), 1984–89; *b* 27 June 1929; *s* of Herbert Edwards Storer; *m* 1960, Jean Mary Isobel Jenkin; one *s* two *d. Educ:* Monmouth School; St John's Coll., Cambridge (MA). Assistant Principal, Min. of Labour, 1952; Principal, 1957; Cabinet Office, 1963–66; Asst Secretary, Dept of Employment, 1966–73; Director, Training Opportunities Scheme, 1973–77; Dir of Corporate Services, MSC, 1977–84. *Recreations:* reading, walking. *Address:* Barclays Bank, 27 Regent Street, SW1.

STORER, James Donald, CEng, MRAeS; author and museum consultant; Keeper, Department of Science, Technology and Working Life, Royal Museum of Scotland, Edinburgh, 1985–88; *b* 11 Jan. 1928; *s* of James Arthur Storer and Elizabeth May Gartshore (*née* Pirie); *m* 1955, Shirley Anne (*née* Kent); one *s* one *d. Educ:* Hemsworth Grammar Sch., Yorks; Imperial Coll., London (BSc Hons, ACGI). Design Office, Vickers Armstrongs (Aircraft) Ltd, and British Aircraft Corporation, Weybridge, 1948–66; Dept of Technology, Royal Scottish Museum, 1966–85. Sec., British Aviation Preservation Council, 1990–; Chm., Friends of Ironbridge Gorge Museum, 1994–. MRAeS (AFRAeS 1958). *Publications:* Steel and Engineering, 1959; Behind the Scenes in an Aircraft Factory, 1965; It's Made Like This: Cars, 1967; The World We Are Making: Aviation, 1968; A Simple History of the Steam Engine, 1969; How to Run An Airport, 1971; How We Find Out About Flight, 1973; Flying Feats, 1977; Book of the Air, 1979; Great Inventions, 1980; (jtly) Encyclopedia of Transport, 1983; (jtly) East Fortune: Museum of Flight and history of the airfield, 1983; The Silver Burdett Encyclopedia of Transport: Air, 1984; Ship Models in the Royal Scottish Museum, 1986; The Conservation of Industrial Collections, 1989; (jtly) Fly Past, Fly Present, 1995. *Recreations:* aircraft preservation, industrial archaeology, gardening. *Address:* Stonewharf, 2 Dale Road, Coalbrookdale, Telford, Shropshire TF8 7DT. *T:* Ironbridge (01952) 433534.

STORER, Prof. Roy; Professor of Prosthodontics, 1968–92 and Dean of Dentistry, 1977–92 (Clinical Sub-Dean, 1970–77), The Dental School, University of Newcastle upon Tyne, Professor Emeritus, since 1992; *b* 21 Feb. 1928; *s* of late Harry and Jessie Storer; *m* 1953, Kathleen Mary Frances Pitman; one *s* two *d. Educ:* Wallasey Grammar Sch.; Univ. of Liverpool. LDS (Liverpool) 1950; FDSRCS 1954; MSc (Liverpool) 1960; DRD RCS Ed, 1978. House Surg., 1950, and Registrar, 1952–54, United Liverpool Hosps; Lieut (later Captain) Royal Army Dental Corps, 1950–52; Lectr in Dental Prosthetics, Univ. of Liverpool, 1954–61; Visiting Associate Prof., Northwestern Univ., Chicago, 1961–62; Sen. Lectr in Dental Prosthetics, Univ. of Liverpool, 1962–67; Hon. Cons. Dental Surgeon: United Liverpool Hosps, 1962–67; United Newcastle Hosps (later Newcastle Health Authority), 1968–92. Chm., Div. of Dentistry, Newcastle Univ. Hosps, 1972–75. Mem. Council and Sec., British Soc. for the Study of Prosthetic Dentistry, 1960–69 (Pres., 1968–69); Member: GDC, 1977–92 (Chm. Educn Cttee, 1986–91); Bd of Faculty, RCS, 1982–90; Dental Sub-Cttee, UGC, 1982–89; EC Dental Cttee for trng of dental practitioners, 1986–93; Med. Cttee, UFC, 1989–92. Pres., Med. Rugby Football Club (Newcastle), 1968–82; Mem. Bd of Dirs, Durham CCC, 1994–. Mem., Northern Sports Council, 1973–88; External Examiner in Dental Subjects: Univs of Belfast, Birmingham, Bristol, Dublin, Dundee, Leeds, London, Newcastle upon Tyne, RCS, and RCPSGlas. *Publications:* A Laboratory Course in Dental Materials for Dental Hygienists (with D. C. Smith), 1963; Immediate and Replacement Dentures (with J. N. Anderson), 3rd edn, 1981; papers on sci. and clin. subjects in dental and med. jls. *Recreations:* cricket, Rugby football, gardening. *Address:* 164 Eastern Way, Darras Hall, Ponteland, Newcastle upon Tyne NE20 9RH. *T:* Ponteland 823286. *Clubs:* Athenæum, MCC, East India.

STOREY, Christopher Thomas; QC 1995; *b* 13 Feb. 1945; *s* of Leslie Hall Storey and Joan Storey; *m* 1968, Hilary Johnston; two *s. Educ:* Rugby Sch. Chartered Accountant, 1967; Glass & Edwards, Liverpool, 1964–68; Price Waterhouse & Co., 1968–70; A. E. Smith Coggins Group, 1970–72; Stacey's, 1972–74; private practice as Chartered Accountant, 1974–82; called to the Bar, Lincoln's Inn, 1979; practising Barrister, NE Circuit, 1982–. *Recreations:* music, cricket, classic cars, flying light aircraft (instructor). *Address:* Pearl Chambers, 22 East Parade, Leeds LS1 5BU. *T:* Leeds (0113) 245 2702.

STOREY, David Malcolm; writer and dramatist; *b* 13 July 1933; *s* of Frank Richmond Storey and Lily (*née* Cartwright); *m* 1956, Barbara Rudd Hamilton; two *s* two *d. Educ:* Queen Elizabeth Grammar Sch., Wakefield, Yorks; Slade School of Fine Art, London; Fellow, UCL, 1974. *Plays:* The Restoration of Arnold Middleton, 1967 (Evening Standard Award); In Celebration, 1969 (Los Angeles Critics' Award); The Contractor, 1969 (Writer of the Year Award, Variety Club of GB, NY Critics' Award) (televised, 1989); Home, 1970 (Evening Standard Award, Critics' Award, NY); The Changing Room, 1971 (Critics' Award, NY); Cromwell, 1973; The Farm, 1973; Life Class, 1974; Mother's Day, 1976; Sisters, 1978; Early Days, 1980; The March on Russia, 1989; Stages, 1992. *Publications:* This Sporting Life, 1960 (Macmillan Fiction Award, US); Flight into Camden, 1960 (John Llewellyn Meml Prize, Somerset Maugham award); Radcliffe, 1963; Pasmore, 1972 (Geoffrey Faber Meml Prize, 1973); A Temporary Life, 1973; Edward, 1973; Saville, 1976 (Booker Prize, 1976); A Prodigal Child, 1982; Present Times, 1984; Storey's Lives: poems 1951–1991, 1992. *Address:* c/o Jonathan Cape Ltd, Random Century House, 20 Vauxhall Bridge Road, SW1V 2SA.

STOREY, Graham; Emeritus Reader in English, and Emeritus Fellow of Trinity Hall, Cambridge University, since 1988; *b* 8 Nov. 1920; *o surv. s* of late Stanley Runton Storey, LDS RCS and Winifred Storey (*née* Graham). *Educ:* St Edward's Sch., Oxford; Trinity Hall, Cambridge (MA 1944). Served War, RA, 1941–45; Lieut 1942; mentioned in despatches. Called to the Bar, Middle Temple, 1950, but did not practise. Cambridge University: Fellow, 1949–88, Sen. Tutor, 1958–68, Vice-Master, 1970–74, Trinity Hall; Univ. Lectr in English, 1965–81; Reader, 1981–88; Chm., Faculty Bd of English, 1972–74. Vis. Fellow, All Souls Coll., Oxford, 1968. Leverhulme Emeritus Res. Fellowship, 1988. Warton Lectr, British Acad., 1984; Lecture tours for British Council

for Pleasure, 1963. *Recreations:* motor-racing, sailing, motorcycling. *Heir:* *s* Hon. Ian David Patrick Macpherson, *b* 31 March 1949. *Address:* 22 Rutland Gate, SW7 1BB. *T:* 0171–584 1240; Otterwood, Beaulieu, Hants SO42 7YS. *T:* Beaulieu (01590) 612334. *Clubs:* Boodle's, Royal Air Force.

STRATHCLYDE, 2nd Baron *cr* 1955, of Barskimming; **Thomas Galloway Dunlop du Roy de Blicquy Galbraith;** PC 1995; Captain of the Hon. Corps of Gentlemen at Arms (Government Chief Whip in the House of Lords), since 1994; *b* 22 Feb. 1960; *s* of Hon. Sir Thomas Galloway Dunlop Galbraith, KBE, MP (*d* 1982) (*e s* of 1st Baron) and Simone Clothilde Fernande Marie Ghislaine (*d* 1991), *e d* of late Jean du Roy de Blicquy; *S* grandfather, 1985; *m* 1992, Jane, *er d* of John Skinner; one *d*. *Educ:* Wellington College; Univ. of East Anglia (BA 1982); Université d'Aix-en-Provence. Insurance Broker, Bain Dawes, subseq. Bain Clarkson Ltd, 1982–88. Contested (C) Merseyside East, European Parly Election, 1984. Spokesman for DTI, Treasury and Scotland; Govt Whip, 1988–89; Parly Under-Sec. of State, Dept of Employment, 1989–90, DoE, 1990, 1992–93, Scottish Office (Minister for Agric. and Fisheries), 1990–92, DTI, 1993–94; Minister of State, DTI, 1994. *Heir:* *b* Hon. Charles William du Roy de Blicquy Galbraith [*b* 20 May 1962; *m* 1992, Bridget, *d* of Brian Reeve, one *s*]. *Address:* House of Lords, SW1A 0AA. *T:* 0171–219 5353.

STRATHCONA AND MOUNT ROYAL, 4th Baron, *cr* 1900; **Donald Euan Palmer Howard;** *b* 26 Nov. 1923; *s* of 3rd Baron Strathcona and Mount Royal and Diana Evelyn (*d* 1985), twin *d* of 1st Baron Wakehurst; *S* father 1959; *m* 1st, 1954, Lady Jane Mary Waldegrave (marr. diss. 1977), 2nd *d* of 12th Earl Waldegrave, KG, GCVO; two *s* four *d*; 2nd, 1978, Patricia (*née* Thomas), *widow* of John Middleton. *Educ:* King's Mead, Seaford; Eton; Trinity Coll., Cambridge; McGill University, Montreal (1947–50). Served War of 1939–45: RN, 1942–47: Midshipman, RNVR, 1943; Lieutenant, 1945. With Urwick, Orr and Partners (Industrial Consultants), 1950–56. Lord in Waiting (Govt Whip), 1973–74; Parly Under-Sec. of State for Defence (RAF), MoD, 1974; Jt Dep. Leader of the Opposition, House of Lords, 1976–79; Minister of State, MoD, 1979–81. Dir, Computing Devices, Hastings, 1981–92. Chairman, Bath Festival Society, 1966–70. Dep. Chm., SS Great Britain Project, 1970–73; Founder Chm., Coastal Forces Heritage Trust, 1995–; President: Falkland Is Trust, 1982–; Steamboat Assoc. of GB, 1972–; Mem. Council, RN Mus., 1982–. *Recreations:* gardening, sailing. *Heir:* *s* Hon. Donald Alexander Smith Howard [*b* 24 June 1961; *m* 1992, Jane Maree, *d* of Shaun Gibb; one *s*]. *Address:* 16 Henning Street, SW11 3DR. *T:* 0171–223 2885; Kiloran, Isle of Colonsay, Argyll PA61 7YU. *T:* Colonsay (01951) 200301. *Clubs:* Brooks's, Pratt's; Royal Yacht Squadron.

STRATHEDEN, 6th Baron *cr* 1836, **AND CAMPBELL,** 6th Baron *cr* 1841; **Donald Campbell;** *b* 4 April 1934; *s* of 5th Baron Stratheden and Campbell and of Evelyn Mary Austen, *d* of late Col Herbert Austen Smith, CIE; *S* father, 1987; *m* 1957, Hilary Ann Holland (*d* 1991), *d* of Lt-Col William D. Turner; one *s* three *d*. *Educ:* Eton. *Heir:* *s* Hon. David Anthony Campbell, *b* 13 Feb. 1963. *Address:* Yalara, M5 401, Cooroy, Queensland 4563, Australia.

STRATHERN, Prof. Andrew Jamieson, PhD; Andrew Mellon Professor of Anthropology, University of Pittsburgh, since 1987; Emeritus Professor of Anthropology, University of London; Hon. Research Fellow, Institute of Papua New Guinea Studies, Port Moresby, since 1977 (Director, 1981–86); *b* 19 Jan. 1939; *s* of Robert Strathern and Mary Strathern (*née* Sharp); *m* 1963, Ann Marilyn Evans (marr. diss. 1986); two *s* one *d*; *m* 1990, Gabriele Stürzenhofecker. *Educ:* Colchester Royal Grammar Sch.; Trinity Coll., Cambridge (BA, PhD). Research Fellow, Trinity Coll., Cambridge, 1965–68; Research Fellow, then Fellow, Australian National Univ., 1969–72; Professor, later Vis. Professor, Dept of Anthropology and Sociology, Univ. of Papua New Guinea, 1973–77; Prof. of Anthropology and Hd of Dept of Anthropology, UCL, 1976–83. Hon. Mem., Phi Beta Kappa, 1993. Rivers Memorial Medal, RAI, 1976. 10th Independence Anniv. Medal (PNG), 1987. *Publications:* The Rope of Moka, 1971; One Father, One Blood, 1972; (with M. Strathern) Self-decoration in Mount Hagen, 1972; Melpa Amb Kenan, 1974; Myths and Legends from Mt Hagen, 1977; Beneath the Andaiya Tree, 1977; Ongka, 1979; (with Malcolm Kirk) Man as Art, 1981; Inequality in New Guinea Highlands Societies, 1982; Wiru Laa, 1983; A line of power, 1984; (ed jtly) Strauss, The Mi Culture of the Mount Hagen People, 1990; (with P. Birnbaum) Faces of Papua New Guinea, 1991; Landmarks: reflections on anthropology, 1993; Voices of Conflict, 1993; Ru, 1993; articles in Man, Oceania, Ethnology, Jl Polyn Soc., Amer. Anthropology, Amer. Ethnology, Mankind, Bijdragen, Jl de la Soc. des Océanistes, Oral History, Bikmaus, Pacific Studies, Ethos, Jl of Ethnomusicology. *Address:* Department of Anthropology, University of Pittsburgh, Pittsburgh, PA 15260, USA. *T:* (office) (412) 6487519.

STRATHERN, Prof. (Ann) Marilyn, FBA 1987; William Wyse Professor of Social Anthropology, University of Cambridge, since 1993; Fellow, Girton College, Cambridge, since 1993; *b* 6 March 1941; *d* of Eric Charles Evans and Joyce Florence Evans; *m* 1963, Andrew Jamieson Strathern, *qv* (marr. diss. 1986); twin *s* one *d*. *Educ:* Bromley High Sch (GPDST); Girton Coll., Cambridge (MA, PhD). Asst Curator, Mus. of Ethnology, Cambridge, 1966–68; Res. Fellow, ANU, 1970–72 and 1974–75; Bye-Fellow, Sen. Res. Fellow, then Official Fellow, Girton Coll., 1976–83; Fellow and Lectr, Trinity Coll., Cambridge, 1984–85; Prof. and Hd of Dept of Social Anthropology, Manchester Univ., 1985–93. Sen. Res. Fellow, ANU, 1983–84; Vis. Prof., Univ. of California, Berkeley, 1984. Hon. DSc (Soc Sci): Edinburgh, 1993; Copenhagen, 1994. Rivers Meml Medal, RAI, 1976. *Publications:* Self-Decoration in Mt Hagen (jtly), 1971; Women In Between, 1972; (co-ed) Nature, Culture and Gender, 1980; Kinship at the Core: an anthropology of Elmdon, Essex, 1981; (ed) Dealing With Inequality, 1987; The Gender of the Gift, 1988; Partial Connections, 1991; (ed) Big Men and Great Men in Melanesia, 1991; After Nature, 1992; Reproducing the Future, 1992; (jtly) Technologies of Procreation, 1993; (ed) Shifting Contexts, 1995. *Address:* Girton College, Cambridge CB3 0JG.

STRATHMORE AND KINGHORNE, 18th Earl of, *cr* 1677 (Scot.); Earl (UK) *cr* 1937; **Michael Fergus Bowes Lyon;** Lord Glamis, 1445; Earl of Kinghorne, Lord Lyon and Glamis, 1606; Viscount Lyon, Lord Glamis, Tannadyce, Sidlaw and Strathdichtie, 1677; Baron Bowes (UK), 1887; DL; Captain, Scots Guards; *b* 7 June 1957; *s* of 17th Earl of Strathmore and Kinghorne and of Mary Pamela, DL, *d* of Brig. Norman Duncan McCorquodale, MC; *S* father, 1987; *m* 1984, Isobel, *yr d* of Capt. A. E. Weatherall, Cowhill, Dumfries; three *s*. *Educ:* Univ. of Aberdeen (BLE 1979). Page of Honour to HM Queen Elizabeth The Queen Mother, 1971–73; commissioned, Scots Guards, 1980. A Lord in Waiting (Govt Whip), 1989–91; Captain of the Yeomen of the Guard (Dep. Govt Chief Whip), 1991–94. Director: Polypipe PLC, 1994–; Lancaster PLC, 1994–. Pres., Boys' Brigade, 1994–. DL Angus, 1993. *Heir:* *s* Lord Glamis, *qv*. *Address:* Glamis Castle, Forfar, Angus DD8 1QJ. *Clubs:* Turf, White's, Pratt's; Third Guards'; Perth (Perth).

STRATHNAVER, Lord; Alistair Charles St Clair Sutherland, DL; Master of Sutherland; with Sutherland Estates, since 1978; Vice Lord-Lieutenant of Sutherland, since 1993; *b* 7 Jan. 1947; *e s* of Charles Noel Janson, DL, and the Countess of Sutherland, *qv*; *heir* to mother's titles; *m* 1st, 1968, Eileen Elizabeth, *o d* of Richard Wheeler Baker, Jr, Princeton, NJ; two *d*; 2nd, 1980, Gillian, *er d* of Robert Murray, Gourock, Renfrewshire; one *s* one *d*. *Educ:* Eton; Christ Church, Oxford. BA. Metropolitan Police, 1969–74; with IBM UK Ltd, 1975–78. DL Sutherland, 1991. *Heir:* *s* Hon. Alexander Charles Robert Sutherland, *b* 1 Oct. 1981. *Address:* Sutherland Estates Office, Golspie, Sutherland KW10 6RR. *T:* Golspie (01408) 633268.

STRATHSPEY, 6th Baron *cr* 1884; **James Patrick Trevor Grant of Grant;** Bt (NS) 1625; *b* 9 Sept. 1943; *s* of 5th Baron and of his 1st wife, Alice, *o c* of late Francis Bowe; *S* father, 1992; *m* 1966, Linda (marr. diss. 1984), *d* of David Piggott; three *d*. *Heir:* half *b* Hon. Michael Patrick Francis Grant of Grant, *b* 22 April 1953.

STRATTON, Ven. Basil; Archdeacon of Stafford and Canon Residentiary of Lichfield Cathedral, 1959–74, Archdeacon Emeritus, since 1974; Chaplain to the Queen, 1965–76; *b* 27 April 1906; *s* of Reverend Samuel Henry Stratton and Kate Mabel Stratton; *m* 1934, Euphemia Frances Stuart; one *s* three *d*. *Educ:* Lincoln School; Hatfield College, Durham University. BA 1929, MA 1932. Deacon 1930; Priest 1931; Curate, St Stephen's, Grimsby, 1930–32; SPG Missionary, India, 1932–34; Indian Ecclesiastical Establishment, 1935–47. Chaplain to the Forces on service in Iraq, India, Burma and Malaya, 1941–46 (despatches); officiated as Chaplain-General in India, 1946. Vicar of Figheldean with Milston, Wilts, 1948–53; Vicar of Market Drayton, Shropshire, 1953–59. *Address:* The Ridge, Pettridge Lane, Mere, Wilts BA12 6DG. *T:* Mere (01747) 860235.

STRATTON, Air Vice-Marshal William Hector, CB 1970; CBE 1963; DFC 1939 and Bar 1944; company director; Chief of the Air Staff, RNZAF, 1969–71, retired 1971; *b* 22 July 1916; *s* of V. J. Stratton; *m* 1954, Dorothy M., *d* of J. D. Whyte; one *s* two *d*. *Educ:* Hawera Tech. High School, and privately. RAF, 1937–44. Appointments include: in comd RNZAF, Ohakea; Air Member for Personnel; assistant chief of Air Staff; Head NZ Defence Staff, Canberra; Head NZ Defence Staff, London. *Address:* 41 Goldsworthy Road, Claremont, Perth, WA 6010, Australia.

STRAUSS, Claude L.; *see* Levi-Strauss.

STRAUSS, Nicholas Albert; QC 1984; *b* 29 July 1942; *s* of late Walter Strauss and Ilse Strauss (*née* Leon); *m* 1972, Christine M. MacColl; two *d*. *Educ:* Highgate School; Jesus College, Cambridge. BA 1964; LLB 1965. Called to the Bar, Middle Temple, 1965; Harmsworth Scholar, 1965. *Address:* 1 Essex Court, Temple, EC4Y 9AR. *T:* 0171–583 2000.

STRAW, Alice Elizabeth, (Mrs J. W. Straw); *see* Perkins, A. E.

STRAW, Jack, (John Whitaker Straw); MP (Lab) Blackburn, since 1979; barrister; *b* 3 Aug. 1946; *s* of Walter Arthur Whitaker Straw and of Joan Sylvia Straw; *m* 1st, 1968, Anthea Lilian Weston (marr. diss. 1978); one *d* (decd); 2nd, 1978, Alice Elizabeth Perkins, *qv*; one *s* one *d*. *Educ:* Brentwood Sch., Essex; Univ. of Leeds. LLB 1967. Called to Bar, Inner Temple, 1972. Political Advr to Sec. of State for Social Services, 1974–76; Special Advr to Sec. of State for Environment, 1976–77; on staff of Granada TV (World in Action), 1977–79. Pres., Leeds Univ. Union, 1967–68; Pres., Nat. Union of Students, 1969–71; Mem., Islington Borough Council, 1971–78; Dep. Leader, Inner London Educn Authority, 1973–74; Mem., Labour Party's Nat. Exec. Sub-Cttee on Educn and Science, 1970–82; Chm., Jt Adv. Cttee on Polytechnic of N London, 1973–75. Vice-Pres., Assoc. of District Councils, 1984–. Contested (Lab) Tonbridge and Malling, Feb. 1974. Opposition spokesman on the Treasury, 1980–83, on the environment, 1983–87; Principal Opposition Spokesman on educn, 1987–92, on the envmt (local govt), 1992–94, on home affairs, 1994–. Mem., Shadow Cabinet, 1987–; Mem., NEC, Labour Pty, 1994–. Vis. Fellow, Nuffield Coll., Oxford, 1990–. Member, Council: Inst. for Fiscal Studies, 1983–; Lancaster Univ., 1988–91; Governor: Blackburn Coll., 1990–; Pimlico Sch., 1994–. *Publications:* Granada Guildhall Lecture, 1969; University of Leeds Convocation Lecture, 1978; Policy and Ideology, 1993; contrib. pamphlets, articles. *Recreations:* walking, cycling, cooking puddings, music. *Address:* House of Commons, SW1A 0AA.

STRAWSON, Maj.-Gen. John Michael, CB 1975; OBE 1964; idc, jssc, psc; Senior Military Adviser, Westland Aircraft Ltd, 1978–85 (Head of Cairo Office, 1976–78); *b* 1 Jan. 1921; *s* of late Cyril Walter and Nellie Dora Strawson; *m* 1960, Baroness Wilfried von Schellersheim; two *d*. *Educ:* Christ's Coll., Finchley. Joined Army, 1940; commnd, 1942; served with 4th QO Hussars in Middle East, Italy, Germany, Malaya, 1942–50, 1953–54, 1956–58; Staff Coll., Camberley, 1950; Bde Major, 1951–53; Instructor, Staff Coll. and Master of Drag Hounds, 1958–60; GSO1 and Col GS in WO and MoD, 1961–62 and 1965–66; comd QR Irish Hussars, Malaysia and BAOR, 1963–65; comd Inf. Bde, 1967–68; idc 1969; COS, Live Oak, SHAPE, 1970–72; COS, HQ UKLF, 1972–76. Col, Queen's Royal Irish Hussars, 1975–85. US Bronze Star, 1945. *Publications:* The Battle for North Africa, 1969; Hitler as Military Commander, 1971; The Battle for the Ardennes, 1972; The Battle for Berlin, 1974; (jtly) The Third World War, 1978; El Alamein, 1981; (jtly) The Third World War: the untold story, 1982; A History of the SAS Regiment, 1984; The Italian Campaign, 1987; Gentlemen in Khaki: the British Army 1890–1990, 1989; Beggars in Red: the British Army 1789–1889, 1991; The Duke and the Emperor, 1994. *Recreations:* equitation, shooting, reading. *Club:* Cavalry and Guards.

See also Sir P. F. Strawson.

STRAWSON, Sir Peter (Frederick), Kt 1977; FBA 1960; Fellow of Magdalen College, Oxford, 1968–87, Hon. Fellow, 1989; Waynflete Professor of Metaphysical Philosophy in the University of Oxford, 1968–87 (Reader, 1966–68); Fellow of University College, Oxford, 1948–68, Honorary Fellow since 1979; *b* 23 November 1919; *s* of late Cyril Walter and Nellie Dora Strawson; *m* 1945, Grace Hall Martin; two *s* two *d*. *Educ:* Christ's College, Finchley; St John's College, Oxford (scholar; Hon. Fellow, 1973). Served War of 1939–45, RA, REME, Capt. Asst Lecturer in Philosophy, University Coll. of N. Wales, 1946; John Locke Schol., Univ. of Oxford, 1946; Lecturer in Philosophy, 1947, Fellow and Praelector, 1948, University Coll., Oxford. Vis. Prof., Duke Univ., N Carolina, 1955–56; Fellow of Humanities Council and Vis. Associate Prof., Princeton Univ., 1960–61, Vis. Prof., 1972; Woodbridge Lectr, Columbia Univ., NY, 1983; Immanuel Kant Lectr, Munich, 1985; Vis. Prof., Collège de France, 1985. Mem., Academia Europaea, 1990; For. Hon. Mem., Amer. Acad. Arts and Scis, 1971. *Publications:* Introduction to Logical Theory, 1952; Individuals, 1959; The Bounds of Sense, 1966; (ed) Philosophical Logic, 1967; (ed) Studies in the Philosophy of Thought and Action, 1968; Logico-Linguistic Papers, 1971; Freedom and Resentment, 1974; Subject and Predicate in Logic and Grammar, 1974; Scepticism and Naturalism: some varieties, 1985; Analyse et Métaphysique, 1985; Analysis and Metaphysics, 1992; contrib. to Mind, Philosophy, Proc. Aristotelian Soc., Philosophical Review, etc. *Address:* 25 Farndon Road, Oxford OX2 6RT. *T:* Oxford (01865) 515026. *Club:* Athenæum.

See also J. M. Strawson.

STREAMS, Peter John, CMG 1986; HM Diplomatic Service, retired; Ambassador to Sudan, 1991–94; *b* 8 March 1935; *s* of Horace Stanley Streams and Isabel Esther (*née* Ellaway); *m* 1956, Margareta Decker; two *s* one *d*. *Educ:* Wallington County Grammar Sch. BoT, 1953; Bombay, 1960, Calcutta, 1962, Oslo, 1966; FCO, 1970; Mexico, 1973; FCO, 1977, Counsellor, 1979; Consul-Gen., Karachi, 1982; Counsellor, Stockholm,

1985; Ambassador to Honduras and concurrently to El Salvador, 1989. *Recreations:* walking, golf. *Address:* c/o Foreign and Commonwealth Office, SW1A 2AH.

STREATFEILD, Maj.-Gen. Timothy Stuart Champion, CB 1980; MBE 1960; Director, Royal Artillery, 1978–81; *b* 9 Sept. 1926; *s* of Henry Grey Champion and Edythe Streatfeild; *m* 1951, Annette Catherine, *d* of Sir John Clague, CMG, CIE, and Lady Clague; two *s* one *d*. *Educ:* Eton; Christ Church, Oxford. FIMgt. Commnd into RA, 1946; Instructor, Staff Coll., Camberley, 1963–65; Chief Instructor, Sudan Armed Forces Staff Coll., 1965–67; Commander, 7th Parachute Regt, RHA, 1967–69; Col Adjt and QMG, 4 Div., 1969–70; Commander, RA 2 Div., 1971–72; RCDS, 1973; Brigadier Adjt and QMG, 1st Corps, 1974–75; COS, Logistic Exec., MoD, 1976–78. Col. Commandant: RA, 1980–91; RHA, 1981–91. *Recreations:* fishing, sporting, the countryside, music. *Address:* Toatley Farm, Chawleigh, Chulmleigh, N Devon EX18 7HW. *T:* Lapford (01363) 83363. *Club:* Army and Navy.

STREATFEILD-JAMES, Captain John Jocelyn, RN retired; *b* 14 April 1929; *s* of late Comdr Rev. Eric Cardew Streatfeild-James, OBE, and Elizabeth Ann (*née* Kirby); *m* 1962, Sally Madeline (*née* Stewart); three *s* (one *d* decd). *Educ:* RNC, Dartmouth. Specialist in Undersea Warfare. FBIM; MNI 1982. Naval Cadet, 1943–47; Midshipman, 1947–49; Sub-Lt, 1949–51; Lieutenant: Minesweeping, Diving and Anti-Bandit Ops, Far East Stn, 1951; Officer and Rating Trng, Home Stn, 1952–53; specialised in Undersea Warfare, 1954–55; Ship and Staff Duties, Far East Stn, 1955–57; Exchange Service, RAN, 1957–59; Lieutenant-Commander: instructed Officers specialising in Undersea Warfare, 1960–61; Sea Duty, Staff Home Stn, 1962–63; Sen. Instr, Jt Anti-Submarine Sch., HMS Sea Eagle, 1964–65; Commander: Staff of C-in-C Western Fleet and C-in-C Eastern Atlantic Area, 1965–67; Jt Services Staff Coll., 1968; Staff of Comdr Allied Naval Forces, Southern Europe, Malta, 1968–71; HMS Dryad, 1971–73; Captain: Sen. Officers' War Course, RNC, Greenwich, 1974; Dir, OPCON Proj., 1974–77; HMS Howard (i/c), Head of British Defence Liaison Staff, Ottawa, and Defence Advr to British High Comr in Canada, 1978–80 (as Cdre); HMS Excellent (i/c), 1981–82; ADC to the Queen, 1982–83. *Recreations:* sailing, carpentry, painting. *Address:* South Lodge, Tower Road, Hindhead, Surrey GU26 6SP. *T:* Hindhead (01428) 606064. *Club:* Naval.

STREATOR, Edward James; consultant; *b* 12 Dec. 1930; *s* of Edward J. and Ella S. Streator; *m* 1957, Priscilla Craig Kenney; one *s* two *d*. *Educ:* Princeton Univ. (AB). US Naval Reserve, served to Lieut (jg), 1952–56; entered Foreign Service, 1956; Third Sec., US Embassy, Addis Ababa, 1958–60; Second Sec., Lome, 1960–62; Office of Intelligence and Research, Dept of State, 1962–64; Staff Asst to Sec. of State, 1964–66; First Sec., US Mission to NATO, 1966–69; Dep. Director, then Director, Office of NATO Affairs, Dept of State, 1969–75; Dep. US Permanent Representative to NATO, Brussels, 1975–77; Minister, US Embassy, London, 1977–84; US Ambassador to OECD, 1984–87. Mem., South Bank Bd, 1990–. Member: Council, RUSI, 1988–92; Exec. Cttee, IISS, 1988–; Bd, British Amer. Arts Assoc., 1989–; Develt Cttee, Nat. Gallery, 1991–; Fulbright Commn, 1995–. President: American Chamber of Commerce (UK), 1989–94; European Council, American Chambers of Commerce, 1992–. Mem. Exec. Cttee, The Pilgrims, 1984–; Governor: Ditchley Foundn, 1984–; ESU, 1989–95. Hon. FRSA. Benjamin Franklin Medal, RSA, 1992. *Recreation:* swimming. *Address:* 9 St Albans Mansion, Kensington Court Place, W8 5QH. *T:* 0171–937 4772. *Clubs:* White's, Beefsteak, Buck's, Garrick; Metropolitan (Washington); Mill Reef (Antigua).

STREEP, Meryl (Mary Louise); American actress; *b* 22 June 1949; *d* of Harry and Mary Streep; *m* 1978, Donald Gummer; one *s* two *d*. *Educ:* Vassar Coll. (BA 1971); Yale (MA 1975). *Stage appearances include:* New York Shakespeare Fest., 1976; Alice in Concert, NY Public Theater, 1981; *television appearances include:* The Deadliest Season (film), 1977; Holocaust, 1978; *films include:* The Deer Hunter, 1978; Manhattan, 1979; The Seduction of Joe Tynan, 1979; Kramer versus Kramer, 1979 (Academy Award, 1980); The French Lieutenant's Woman (BAFTA Award), 1981; Sophie's Choice (Academy Award), 1982; Still of the Night, 1982; Silkwood, 1983; Falling in Love, 1984; Plenty, 1985; Out of Africa, 1985; Heartburn, 1986; Ironweed, 1987; A Cry in the Dark, 1989; She-Devil, 1990; Postcards from the Edge, 1991; Defending your Life, 1991; Death Becomes Her, 1992; Before and After, 1993; The House of the Spirits, 1994; The River Wild, 1995; The Bridges of Madison County, 1995. Hon. DFA: Dartmouth Coll., 1981; Yale, 1983. *Address:* c/o International Creative Management, 40 West 57th Street, New York, NY 10019, USA.

STREET, Hon. Anthony Austin; manager and company director; *b* 8 Feb. 1926; *s* of late Brig. the Hon. G. A. Street, MC, MHR; *m* 1951, Valerie Erica, *d* of J. A. Rickard; three *s*. *Educ:* Melbourne C of E Grammar Sch. RAN, 1945–46. MP (L) Corangamite, Vic, 1966–84 (resigned); Mem., various Govt Mems Cttees, 1967–71; Mem., Fed. Exec. Council, 1971–; Asst Minister for Labour and Nat. Service, 1971–72; Mem., Opposition Exec., 1973–75 (Special Asst to Leader of Opposition and Shadow Minister for Labour and Immigration, March-Nov. 1975); Minister for Labour and Immigration, Caretaker Ministry after dissolution of Parliament, Nov. 1975; Minister for Employment and Industrial Relations and Minister Assisting Prime Minister in Public Service Matters, 1975–78; Minister for: Industrial Relations, 1978–80; Foreign Affairs, 1980–83. Chm., Fed. Rural Cttee, Liberal Party, 1970–74. *Recreations:* cricket, golf, tennis, flying. *Address:* 153 The Terrace, Ocean Grove, Vic 3226, Australia. *Clubs:* MCC; Melbourne; Royal Melbourne Golf, Barwon Heads Golf.

STREET, John Edmund Dudley, CMG 1966; retired; *b* 21 April 1918; *er s* of late Philip Edmund Wells Street and of Elinor Gladys Whittington-Ince; *m* 1st, 1940, Noreen Mary (*d* 1981), *o d* of Edward John Griffin Comerford and Mary Elizabeth Winstone; three *s* one *d*; 2nd, 1983, Mrs Patricia Curzon. *Educ:* Tonbridge School; Exeter College, Oxford. Served War of 1939–45, HM Forces, 1940–46. Entered Foreign Service, 1947; First Secretary: British Embassy, Oslo, 1950; British Embassy, Lisbon, 1952; Foreign Office, 1954; First Secretary and Head of Chancery, British Legation, Budapest, 1957–60; HM Ambassador to Malagasy Republic, 1961–62, also Consul-General for the Island of Réunion and the Comoro Islands, 1961–62; Asst Sec., MoD, 1967–76; Asst Under-Sec. of State, MoD, 1976–78. *Recreations:* reading, golf, bridge. *Address:* Cornerways, High Street, Old Woking, Surrey GU22 9JH. *T:* Guildford (01483) 764371.

STREET, Hon. Sir Laurence (Whistler), AC 1989; KCMG 1976; Lieutenant-Governor of New South Wales, 1974–89; Chief Justice of New South Wales, 1974–88; *b* Sydney, 3 July 1926; *s* of Hon. Sir Kenneth Street, KCMG; *m* 1st, 1952, Susan Gai, AM, *d* of E. A. S. Watt; two *s* two *d*; 2nd, Penelope Patricia, *d* of G. Ferguson; one *d*. *Educ:* Cranbrook Sch.; Univ. of Sydney (LLB Hons). FCIArb 1992. RANVR, incl. war service in Pacific, 1943–47. Comdr, Sen. Officer RANR Legal Br., 1964–65. Admitted to NSW Bar, 1951; QC 1963; Judge, Supreme Court of NSW, 1965; Judge of Appeal, 1972–74; Chief Judge in Equity, 1972–74. Dir, John Fairfax Holdings Ltd, 1991– (Chm., 1994–). Lectr in Procedure, Univ. of Sydney, 1962–63, Lectr in Bankruptcy, 1964–65; Member: Public Accountants Regn Bd, 1962–65; Companies Auditors Bd, 1962–65; Pres., Courts-Martial Appeal Tribunal, 1971–74; Chairman: Aust. Commercial Disputes Centre Planning Cttee, 1985–86; Aust. Govt Internat. Legal Services Adv. Council, 1990–. Mem. Court, London Court of Internat. Arbitration, 1988– (Pres., Asia-Pacific Council, 1989–). Pres., Aust. Br., 1990–, World Pres., 1990–92, Life Vice-Pres., 1992, Internat. Law Assoc.; Chm., Judiciary Appeals Bd, NSW Rugby League, 1989–. President: Sydney Univ. Law Grads Assoc., 1963–65; Cranbrook Sch. Council, 1966–74; Sydney Univ. Law Sch. Foundn, 1990–; St John Amb. Aust. (NSW), 1974–. Hon. Col, 1st/15th Royal NSW Lancers, 1986–. Fellow, Univ. of Technol., Sydney, 1990; Hon. FIArbA 1989. Hon. LLD: Sydney, 1984; Macquarie Univ., 1989. KStJ 1976. Grand Officer of Merit, SMO Malta, 1977. *Address:* 121 Macquarie Street, Sydney, NSW 2000, Australia. *Clubs:* Union (Sydney); Royal Sydney Golf.

STREET, Dr Peter Ronald; Director, Produce Studies Ltd, since 1992; *b* 4 May 1944; *s* of Leslie Arthur John and Winifred Marjorie Street; *m* 1969, Christine Hill; two *d*. *Educ:* Univ. of Reading (BScAgr, PhD Management and Econs). Lectr in Management and Econs, Faculty of Agricl Sci., Univ. of Nottingham, 1971–74; Tropical Products Institute: Principal Res. Officer, 1974–82; Sen. Principal Res. Officer and Head, Mkting and Industrial Econs Dept, 1982–85; Mem., Directorate Bd, 1982–85; Dir and Chief Economist, Produce Studies Ltd, 1985–89; Prof. of Agricl Systems and Head, Dept of Agriculture, Univ. of Reading, 1989–92. Numerous internat. consultancy assignments. MIMgt (MBIM 1972). *Publication:* (ed with J. G. W. Jones) Systems Theory Applied to Agriculture and the Food Chain, 1990. *Recreations:* gardening, fly fishing. *Address:* Merrowdown, Woodend Road, Crowe, Ringwood, Hants BH24 3DG. *T:* Ringwood (01425) 475222.

STREET, Prof. Robert, AO 1985; DSc; Vice-Chancellor, University of Western Australia, 1978–86, Hon. Research Fellow, since 1986; *b* 16 Dec. 1920; *s* of late J. Street, Allerton Bywater, Yorkshire, UK; *m* 1943, Joan Marjorie Bere; one *s* one *d*. *Educ:* Hanley High Sch.; King's Coll., London. BSc, MSc, PhD, DSc (London). MIEE, FInstP, FAIP, FAA. Scientific Officer, Dept of Supply, UK, 1942–45; Lectr, Dept of Physics, Univ. of Nottingham, 1945–54; Sen. Lectr, Dept of Physics, Univ. of Sheffield, 1954–60; Foundn Prof. of Physics, Monash Univ., Melbourne, Vic., 1960–74; Dir, Research Sch. of Physical Sciences, Aust. Nat. Univ., 1974–78. Former President: Aust. Inst. of Nuclear Science and Engrg; Aust. Inst. of Physics; Mem. and Chm., Aust. Research Grants Cttee, 1970–76; Chm., Nat. Standards Commn, 1967–78; Member: State Energy Adv. Council, WA, 1981–86; Australian Science and Technology Council, 1977–80; Council, Univ. of Technology, Lae, Papua New Guinea, 1982–84; Bd of Management, Royal Perth Hosp., 1978–85. Fellow, Aust. Acad. of Science, 1973 (Treas., 1976–77). Hon. DSc: Sheffield, 1986; Western Australia, 1988. *Publications:* research papers in scientific jls. *Recreation:* swimming. *Address:* Department of Physics, University of Western Australia, Nedlands, WA 6009, Australia. *Club:* Weld (Perth).

STREET-PORTER, Janet; journalist and broadcaster, since 1967; *b* 27 Dec. 1946; *m* 1st, 1967, Tim Street-Porter (marr. diss. 1975); 2nd, 1976, A. M. M. Elliott, *qv* (marr. diss. 1978); 3rd, 1978, Frank Cvitanovich (marr. diss. 1988; he *d* 1995). *Educ:* Lady Margaret Grammar Sch., Fulham; Architectural Assoc. TV presenter, 1975–; TV producer, 1981–; BBC TV, 1988–94; Man. Dir, Live TV, 1994–95; Dir, Mirror TV, 1994–95. Pres., Ramblers Assoc., 1994–. FRTS 1994. Award for originality, BAFTA, 1988; Prix Italia, 1993. *Publications:* The British Teapot, 1977; Scandal, 1981. *Recreations:* walking, talking, seeing friends; built my own house. *Address:* c/o Bob Storer, Harbottle & Lewis, 14 Hanover Square, W1R 0BE. *T:* 0171–629 7633.

STREETEN, Frank; *see* Streeten, R. H.

STREETEN, Paul Patrick, DLitt; Professor, Boston University, 1980–93, now Emeritus (Director: Center for Asian Development Studies, 1980–84; World Development Institute, 1984–90); *b* 18 July 1917; *e s* of Wilhelm Hornig, Vienna; changed name to Streeten under Army Council Instruction, 1943; *m* 1951, Ann Hilary Palmer, *d* of Edgar Higgins, Woodstock, Vermont; two *d* (and one step *s*). *Educ:* Vienna; Aberdeen Univ.; Balliol Coll., Oxford (Hon. Schol.); 1st cl. PPE, 1947; Student, Nuffield Coll., Oxford, 1947–48. DLitt Oxon, 1976. Mil. service in Commandos, 1941–43; wounded in Sicily, 1943. Fellow, Balliol Coll., Oxford, 1948–66 (Hon. Fellow, 1986); Associate, Oxford Univ. Inst. of Econs and Statistics, 1960–64; Dep. Dir-Gen., Econ. Planning Staff, Min. of Overseas Develt, 1964–66; Prof. of Econs, Fellow, Acting and Dep. Dir of Inst. of Develt Studies, Sussex Univ., 1966–68; Warden of Queen Elizabeth House, Dir, Inst. of Commonwealth Studies, Univ. of Oxford, and Fellow of Balliol Coll., 1968–78; Special Adviser, World Bank, 1976–79; Dir of Studies, Overseas Develt Council, 1979–80. Rockefeller Fellow, USA, 1950–51; Fellow, Johns Hopkins Univ., Baltimore, 1955–56; Fellow, Center for Advanced Studies, Wesleyan Univ., Conn.; Vis. Prof., Econ. Develt Inst. of World Bank, 1984–86; Jean Monnet Prof., European Univ. Inst., Florence, 1991. Sec., Oxford Econ. Papers, until 1961, Mem. Edit. Bd, 1971–78; Editor, Bulletin of Oxford Univ. Inst. of Econs and Statistics, 1961–64; Member: UK Nat. Commn of Unesco, 1966; Provisional Council of Univ. of Mauritius, 1966–72; Commonwealth Develt Corp., 1967–72; Statutory Commn, Royal Univ. of Malta, 1972–; Royal Commn on Environmental Pollution, 1974–76. Mem., Internat. Adv. Panel, Canadian Univ. Service Overseas. Vice-Chm., Social Sciences Adv. Cttee, 1971; Member, Governing Body: Queen Elizabeth House, Oxford, 1966–68; Inst. of Develt Studies, Univ. of Sussex, 1968–80 (Vice-Chm.); Dominion Students' Hall Trust, London House; Mem. Council, Overseas Develt Institute, until 1979. Pres., UK Chapter, Soc. for Internat. Develt until 1976. Mem., Phi Beta Delta. Hon. Fellow, Inst. of Develt Studies, Sussex, 1980. Raffaele Mattioli Lectr, Milan, 1991. Hon. LLD Aberdeen, 1980. Development Prize, Justus Liebig Univ., Giessen. Chm. Editorial Bd, World Develt, 1972–. *Publications:* (ed) Value in Social Theory, 1958; Economic Integration, 1961, 2nd edn 1964; (contrib.) Economic Growth in Britain, 1966; The Teaching of Development Economics, 1967; (ed with M. Lipton) Crisis in Indian Planning, 1968; (contrib. to) Gunnar Myrdal, Asian Drama, 1968; (ed) Unfashionable Economics, 1970; (ed, with Hugh Corbet) Commonwealth Policy in a Global Context, 1971; Frontiers of Development Studies, 1972; (ed) Trade Strategies for Development, 1973; The Limits of Development Research, 1975; (with S. Lall) Foreign Investment, Transnationals and Developing Countries, 1977; Development Perspectives, 1981; First Things First, 1981; (ed with Richard Jolly) Recent Issues in World Development, 1981; (ed with H. Maier) Human Resources, Employment and Development, 1983; What Price Food?, 1987; (ed) Beyond Adjustment, 1988; Mobilizing Human Potential, 1989; Paul Streeten in South Africa, 1992; Strategies for Human Development, 1994; (co-ed) The UN and the Bretton Woods Institutions, 1995; Thinking About Development, 1995; contribs to learned journals. *Address:* PO Box 92, Spencertown, NY 12165, USA. *Club:* United Oxford & Cambridge University.

STREETEN, Reginald Hawkins, (Frank), CBE 1991; Head of Statute Law Revision, Law Commission, 1978–93; *b* 19 March 1928; *s* of late Reginald Craufurd Streeten, BA, LLB and Olive Gladys Streeten (*née* Palmer); *m* 1962, Bodile Westergren, Lappland, Sweden; two *s*. *Educ:* Grey Coll., S Africa; Rhodes University Coll. (BA, LLB). Called to the Bar, S Rhodesia, 1959. Crown Counsel and Legal Draftsman, S Rhodesia and Fedn of Rhodesia and Nyasaland, 1952–63; Jun. Counsel for Fed. Govt at inquiry into aircraft accident involving late Dag Hammarskjöld, 1961; Parly Draftsman, Zambia, 1964–66; Mem. Legal Staff, 1967–93, Sec., 1981–82, Law Commn. Legal Mem., Med. Council of

S Rhodesia, 1959–63. Lawyer Mem., Dept of Transport Deregulation Rev. Gp, 1993–94. *Address:* 32 Holme Chase, St George's Avenue, Weybridge, Surrey KT13 0BZ. *T:* Weybridge (01932) 849937.

STREETER, Gary Nicholas; MP (C) Plymouth Sutton, since 1992; an Assistant Government Whip, since 1995; *b* 2 Oct. 1955; *s* of Kenneth Victor Streeter and Shirley Nellie (*née* Keable); *m* 1978, Janet Stevens; one *s* one *d*. *Educ:* Tiverton Grammar Sch.; King's Coll., London (LLB 1st cl. Hons). Articled at Coward Chance, London, 1978–80; admitted solicitor, 1980; joined Foot & Bowden, solicitors, Plymouth, 1980, Partner, 1984–. Plymouth City Council: Mem., 1986–92; Chm., Housing Cttee, 1989–91. PPS to Solicitor-General, 1993–95, and to Attorney-General, 1994–95. Mem., Select Cttee on Environment, 1992–93. *Recreations:* lover of cricket and Rugby. *Address:* House of Commons, SW1A 0AA. *T:* 0171–219 4070.

STREETER, His Honour John Stuart; DL; a Circuit Judge, 1972–86 (Deputy Chairman 1967–71, Chairman 1971, Kent Quarter Sessions); *b* 20 May 1920; *yr s* of late Wilfrid A. Streeter, osteopath, and late Mrs R. L. Streeter; *m* 1956, (Margaret) Nancy Richardson; one *s* two *d*. *Educ:* Sherborne. Served War of 1939–45 (despatches): Captain, Royal Scots Fusiliers, 1940–46. Called to Bar, Gray's Inn, Nov. 1947. Post Office Counsel SE Circuit, 1957; Treasury Counsel, London Sessions, 1959; Part-time Dep. Chm., Kent Quarter Sessions, 1963. Pres., Sherborne House Probation Centre, Bermondsey, 1993. Pres., Old Shirburnian Soc., 1990. DL Kent, 1986. *Recreation:* gardening. *Address:* Playstole, Sissinghurst, Cranbrook, Kent TN17 2JN. *T:* Cranbrook (01580) 712847.

STREETON, Sir Terence (George), KBE 1989 (MBE 1969); CMG 1981; HM Diplomatic Service, retired; Chairman: Healthco Pvt Ltd, Harare, since 1994; Director, Contact International Ltd, Harare, since 1992; *b* 12 Jan. 1930; *er s* of late Alfred Victor Streeton and Edith Streeton (*née* Deiton); *m* 1962, Molly Horsburgh; two *s* two *d*. *Educ:* Wellingborough Grammar School. Inland Revenue, 1946; Prison Commission, 1947; Government Communications Headquarters, 1952; Foreign Office (Diplomatic Wireless Service), 1953; Diplomatic Service, 1965–89: First Secretary, Bonn, 1966; FCO, 1970; First Secretary and Head of Chancery, Bombay, 1972; Counsellor and Head of Joint Admin Office, Brussels, 1975; Head of Finance Dept, FCO, 1979; Asst Under-Sec. of State and Prin. Finance Officer, FCO, 1982–83; High Comr to Bangladesh, 1983–89. Pres., Bangladesh-British Chamber of Commerce, 1993–. *Recreations:* walking, golf. *Address:* The Langtons, Beech Avenue, Olney, Bucks MK46 5AE. *T:* Bedford (01234) 711761. *Club:* Oriental.

STREISAND, Barbra Joan; singer, actress, director, producer, writer, composer, philanthropist; *b* Brooklyn, NY, 24 April 1942; *d* of Emanuel and Diana Streisand; *m* 1963, Elliott Gould (marr. diss. 1971); one *s*. *Educ:* Erasmus Hall High Sch. Nightclub début, Bon Soir, Greenwich Village, 1961; NY theatre début, Another Evening with Harry Stoones, 1961; musical comedy, I Can Get It For You Wholesale, 1962 (NY Critics' Best Supporting Actress Award, 1962); musical, Funny Girl, NY, 1964, London, 1966 (Best Foreign Actress, Variety Poll Award, 1966). Special Tony Award, 1970. *Films:* Funny Girl, 1968 (Golden Globe Award, Acad. Award, 1968); Hello Dolly, 1969; On a Clear Day You Can See Forever, 1970; The Owl and the Pussycat, 1971; What's Up Doc?, 1972; Up the Sandbox, 1972; The Way We Were, 1973; For Pete's Sake, 1974; Funny Lady, 1975; A Star is Born (also prod), 1976; The Main Event (also prod), 1979; All Night Long, 1981; Yentl (also co-wrote, dir. and prod), 1984 (Golden Globe Award for Best Picture and Best Dir); Nuts (also prod), 1987; The Prince of Tides (also dir. and prod), 1990. *Television specials:* My Name is Barbra, 1965 (5 Emmy Awards, Peabody Award); Color Me Barbra, 1966; Belle of 14th Street, 1967; A Happening in Central Park, 1968; Musical Instrument, 1973; One Voice, 1986; Barbra Streisand, the Concert (also prod and co-dir.), 1994 (Peabody Award, 3 Cable Ace Awards, 5 Emmy Awards); Serving in Silence: the Margarethe Cammermeyer story (exec. prod.), 1995. Began recording career, 1962; Grammy Awards for best female pop vocalist, 1963, 1964, 1965, 1977, 1986, for best songwriter (with Paul Williams), 1977; (jtly) Acad. Award for composing best song (Evergreen), 1976, awarded 37 gold and 21 platinum albums. *Albums include:* People, 1965, My Name is Barbra, 1965; The Way We Were, 1974; Guilty, 1980; The Broadway Album, 1986; Just for the Record (retrospective album), 1991; Back to Broadway, 1993; Barbra Streisand, the Concert (double album and video), 1994. *Address:* Barwood Productions, 433 N Camden Drive, Suite 500, Beverley Hills, CA 90210, USA.

STRETTON, Eric Hugh Alexander, CB 1972; Deputy Chief Executive in Property Services Agency, Department of the Environment, 1972–76, Deputy Chairman, 1973–76; *b* 22 June 1916; *y s* of Major S. G. Stretton, Wigston, Leicester; *m* 1946, Sheila Woodroffe Anderson, MB, BS, *d* of Dr A. W. Anderson, Cardiff (formerly of Ogmore Vale); one *s* one *d*. *Educ:* Wyggeston Sch; Pembroke Coll., Oxford. BA 1939, MA 1942. Leics Regt and 2/4 PWO Gurkha Rifles (Major), 1939–46. Asst Sec., Birmingham Univ. Appointments Board, 1946. Entered Ministry of Works, 1947; Prin. Private Sec. to Minister of Works, 1952–54; Asst Sec., 1954; Under-Secretary: MPBW, 1962–70; DoE, 1970–72; Dep. Sec., 1972. Chm., Structure Plan Examns in Public, Salop, 1979, Lincs, 1980, Central and N Lancs, 1981. *Publication:* Dacre Castle, 1994. *Address:* Dacre Castle, Penrith, Cumbria CA11 0HL. *T:* Pooley Bridge (017684) 86375.

STRETTON, Peter John; His Honour Judge Stretton; a Circuit Judge, since 1986; *b* 14 June 1938; *s* of Frank and Ella Stretton; *m* 1973, Eleanor Anne Wait; three *s* one *d*. *Educ:* Bedford Modern Sch. Called to the Bar, Middle Temple, 1962; Head of Chambers, 1985. A Recorder, 1982–86. *Recreations:* squash, gardening. *Address:* Derby Crown Court, Morledge, Derby DE1 2XE.

STRICK, Robert Charles Gordon; Clerk to the Drapers' Company, 1980–93 (Liveryman, Court of Assistants, 1994); *b* 23 March 1931; *m* 1960, Jennifer Mary Hathway; one *s* one *d*. *Educ:* Royal Grammar Sch., Guildford; Sidney Sussex Coll., Cambridge. MA. Served RA, 1949–51; TA, 1951–55. Spicers Ltd, 1954–55; joined HMOCS, 1955; Dist Officer, Fiji, 1955 59; Sec., Burns Commn into Natural Resources and Population Trends, 1959–60; Asst Sec., Suva, 1961–61; Sec. to Govt, Tonga, 1961–63; Develt Officer and Divl Comr, 1963–67, Sec. for Natural Resources, 1967–71, Fiji; retired 1971; Under Sec., ICA, 1971–72; Asst Sec.-Gen., RICS, 1972–80; Clerk, Chartered Surveyors' Co., 1977–80. Hon. Member: CGLI, 1991; Shrewsbury Co. of Drapers, 1992 (Court of Assts, 1993). Mem. Finance Cttee and Develt Trust, UCNW (Bangor), 1992–; Gov., QMC, 1980–89, Mem. Council, QMW, 1989–, Fellow, 1993; Chm., Foundn of Govs, Adam's Sch., Wem, 1994–; Governor: New England Coll., Arundel, 1991–; Royal GS, Guildford, 1994–. Hon. DLitt Coll. of William and Mary, Virginia, USA, 1993. *Recreations:* the countryside, walking, golf, gardening. *Address:* Highstead Corner, Lickfold, West Sussex GU28 9DX. *T:* Lodsworth (01798) 861367.

STRICKLAND, Benjamin Vincent Michael, FCA; Group Managing Director, Operations (including Group Strategy and Finances), and Director, Schroders PLC, 1983–91; *b* 20 Sept. 1939; *s* of Maj.-Gen. Eugene Vincent Michael Strickland, CMG, DSO, OBE, MM, and of Barbara Mary Farquharson Meares Lamb, *d* of Major Benjamin Lamb, RFA; *m* 1965, Tessa Mary Edwina, *d* of Rear-Adm. John Grant, *qv*; one *s* one *d*. *Educ:* Mayfield Coll.; University Coll., Oxford, 1960–63 (MA PPE; Pres., JCR); Harvard Business Sch. (AMPDip 1978). FCA 1967. Lieutenant: 17/21 Lancers, BAOR, 1959–60; Inns of Court and City Yeomanry, 1963–67. Jun. Man., Price Waterhouse & Co., 1963–68; joined J. Henry Schroder Wagg & Co. in Corp. Finance, 1968: Dir, Schroder Wagg, 1974; Chm., G. D. Peters Engineering, 1972–74; Dir, Property Hldgs Internat. (USA), 1974–75; Chm. and Chief Exec., Schroders Australia, 1978–82. Advr on strategy to leading City law firm, 1992–93, 1994–95, to leading media gp, 1993; Advr on mission and finances, Westminster Cathedral, 1991 (Chm., Planning and Finance Cttee, 1991–); Advr on private banking, 1994; Mem. steering gp, Vision for London, 1991–. Mem. Council, St George's Med. Sch., 1984–87. FRSA. *Publications:* Bow Group pamphlet on Resources of the Sea (with Laurance Reed), 1965; (contrib.) Financial Services Handbook, 1986. *Recreations:* travel, military and general history, shooting, theatre. *Address:* 6 Queen's Elm Square, Chelsea, SW3 6ED. *T:* 0171–351 0372. *Clubs:* Boodle's, Hurlingham.

STRICKLAND, Frank, OBE 1986; Vice-President, The Building Societies Association, since 1992 (Deputy Chairman, 1987–89; Chairman, 1989–91); *b* 4 Feb. 1928; *s* of Robert and Esther Strickland; *m* 1953, Marian Holt; one *d*. *Educ:* Harris Inst., Preston, Lancs. Asst Sec., Chorley and District Building Soc., 1952; Branch Manager, Hastings and Thanet Building Soc., 1955; Asst Sec., later Jt Sec., Corporation and Eligible Building Soc., 1965; Gen. Manager, Sunderland and Shields Building Soc., later North of England Building Soc., 1969; Chief Exec., 1975–89, Dir, 1982–92, Gen. Manager, 1986–89, Exec. Dep. Chm., 1989–91. Pres., European Fedn of Bldg Socs, 1989–91. *Recreations:* golf, cricket. *Address:* 43 Kewhurst Avenue, Cooden, Bexhill-on-Sea, East Sussex TN39 3BH. *T:* Bexhill (01424) 846795. *Club:* MCC.

STRICKLAND-CONSTABLE, Sir Frederic, 12th Bt *cr* 1641, of Boynton, Yorkshire; *b* 21 Oct. 1944; *er s* of Sir Robert Frederick Strickland-Constable, 11th Bt and of Lettice, *yr d* of Major Frederick Strickland; *S* father, 1994; *m* 1981, Pauline Margaret Harding, one *s* one *d*. *Educ:* Westminster; Corpus Christi Coll., Cambridge (BA); London Business Sch. (MSc). *Heir:* *s* Charles Strickland-Constable, *b* 10 Oct. 1985. *Address:* Beech House, Haxby, York YO3 3LH.

STRINGER, Donald Arthur, OBE 1975; Deputy Chairman, Associated British Ports (formerly British Transport Docks Board), 1982–85 (Member, 1969–85; Deputy Managing Director, 1967–71 and 1978–82; Joint Managing Director, 1982–85); *b* 15 June 1922; *s* of late Harry William Stringer and Helen Stringer; *m* 1945, Hazel Handley; one *s* one *d*. *Educ:* Dorking High Sch.; Borden Grammar Sch. FCIT; CIMgt. Joined Southern Railway Co., 1938; service with RAF, 1941–46; Docks Manager: Fleetwood, 1957–58; East Coast Scottish Ports, 1958–62; Chief Docks Man., Southampton, 1963–67, Port Director, 1970–77. Chairman: ABP (formerly BTDB) Bds: Southampton, 1972–85; Humber, 1978–85; Southampton Cargo Handling Co. Ltd, 1968–85; Nat. Assoc. of Port Employers, 1982–85 (Mem. Exec. Cttee, 1964–85); Mem., National Dock Labour Bd, 1976–85; Past Pres., Southampton Chamber of Commerce. Col, Engr and Transport Staff Corps, RE(TA). *Recreation:* gardening. *Address:* Hillcrest, Pinehurst Road, Bassett, Southampton SO16 7FZ. *T:* Southampton (01703) 768887. *Clubs:* Army and Navy; Royal Southampton Yacht.

STRINGER, Sir Donald (Edgar), Kt 1993; CBE 1987; *b* 21 Aug. 1930; *o s* of late Donald Bertram Frederick and Marjorie Stringer, Croydon; *m* 1957, Pamela Irene Totty; three *s*. *Educ:* Whitgift Sch., Croydon. Served Army, RMP, 1951–53. Conservative Party Agent, Fulham, Harrow and Hornsey, 1954–65; Conservative Central Office: Dep. Area Agent, W Midlands, 1965–71; Agent: Northern Area, 1971–73; Greater London Area, 1973–88; Wessex Area, 1988–93. Member: Cons. Agents Exam. Bd, 1987–93; Agents Employment Adv. Cttee, 1988–93. Vice-Chm., Salisbury Abbeyfield Soc. Mem., Guild of Freemen, City of London, 1988. *Recreations:* golf, walking, military history, philately. *Address:* Beech Cottage, Barford St Martin, Salisbury, Wilts SP3 4AS.

STRINGER, Pamela Mary; Headmistress, Clifton High School for Girls, 1965–85; *b* 30 Aug. 1928; *e d* of late E. Allen Stringer. *Educ:* Worcester Grammar Sch. for Girls; St Hugh's Coll., Oxford. MA (Hons Lit Hum). Asst Classics Mistress, Sherborne Sch. for Girls, 1950–59; Head of Classics Dept, Pate's Grammar Sch. for Girls, Cheltenham, 1959–64 (Dep. Head, 1963–64). Member: Exec. Cttee, Assoc. of Headmistresses, 1975–; Exec. Cttee, Girls Schools Assoc., 1975– (Pres., 1978–79; Chm., Educn Cttee, 1981–84); Council, Secondary Heads Assoc., 1978–79 (Pres. Area 7, 1978–79). *Recreations:* travel in Tuscany and Umbria, reading, arctophily, cooking. *Address:* 36 Henleaze Gardens, Bristol BS9 4HJ.

STROHM, Prof. Reinhard, PhD; FBA 1993; Professor of Historical Musicology, King's College London, 1991–Sept. 1996; Heather Professor of Music, and Fellow of Wadham College, Oxford University, from Oct. 1996; *b* 4 Aug. 1942. *Educ:* Tech. Univ., Berlin (PhD 1971). Lectr, then Reader, in Music, KCL, 1975–83; Prof. of Music Hist., Yale Univ., 1983–89; Reader in Histl Musicol., KCL, 1990–91. Edward J. Dent Medal, Royal Musical Assoc., 1977. *Publications:* Italienische Opernarien des frühen Settecento, 1976; Die italienische Oper im 18 Jahrhundert, 1979, 2nd edn 1991; Music in Late Medieval Bruges, 1985, 2nd edn 1990; Essays on Handel and Italian Opera, 1985; The Rise of European Music 1380–1500, 1993; many contribs to books and learned jls. *Recreations:* travel, mountaineering. *Address:* (until Sept. 1996) Institute of Advanced Musical Studies, King's College, WC2R 2LS. *T:* 0171–873 2576; (from Oct. 1996) Wadham College, Oxford OX1 3PN; 19 Hunt Close, Bicester, Oxon OX6 7HX.

STRONACH, David Brian, OBE 1975; FSA; Professor of Near Eastern Studies, since 1981, and Chair of Department, since 1994, University of California, Berkeley; Curator of Near Eastern Archaeology, Lowie Museum of Anthropology, Berkeley, since 1982; *b* 10 June 1931; *s* of Ian David Stronach, MB, FRCSE, and Marjorie Jessie Duncan (*née* Minto); *m* 1966, Ruth Vaadia; two *d*. *Educ:* Gordonstoun; St John's Coll., Cambridge (MA). Pres., Cambridge Univ. Archaeological Field Club, 1954. British Inst. of Archaeology at Ankara: Scholar, 1955–56; Fellow, 1957–58; Fellow, British Sch. of Archaeology in Iraq, 1957–60, Brit. Acad. Archaeological Attaché in Iran, 1960–61; Dir, British Inst. of Persian Studies, 1961–80, Hon. Vice Pres., 1981–. Asst on excavations at: Istanbul, 1954; Tell Rifa'at, 1956; Beycesultan, 1956–57; Hacilar, 1957–59; Nimrud, 1957–60; Charsada, 1958. Director, excavations at: Ras al'Amiya, 1960; Yarim Tepe, 1960–62; Pasargadae, 1961–63; Tepe Nush-i Jan, 1967–77; Nineveh, 1987–90; Co-director, excavations at: Shahr-i Qumis, 1967–78; Horom, 1992–. Mem., Internat. Cttee of Internat. Congresses of Iranian Art and Archaeology, 1968–80. Hagop Kevorkian Visiting Lectr in Iranian Art and Archaeology, Univ. of Pennsylvania, 1967; Lectures: Rhind, Edin., 1973; Norton, Amer. Inst. of Archaeology, 1980; Columbia in Iranian Studies, Columbia Univ., 1986; Leventritt, Harvard Univ., 1991; Cohodas, Hebrew Union Coll., Jerusalem, 1992; McNicoll, Univ. of Sydney, 1994. Vis. Prof. of Archaeology, Hebrew Univ., Jerusalem, 1977; Vis. Prof. of Archaeology and Iranian Studies, Univ. of Arizona, Tucson, 1980–81. Mem., German Archaeological Inst., 1973 (Corr. Mem., 1966); Associate Mem., Royal Belgian Acad., 1988–. Ghirshman Prize, Académie des Inscriptions et Belles-Lettres, Paris, 1979; Sir Percy Sykes Meml Medal, Royal Soc. for Asian Affairs, 1980. Adv. Editor: Jl of Mithraic Studies, 1976–79; Iran, 1980–; Iranica Antiqua, 1984–; Bulletin of Asia Inst., 1986–; Amer. Jl of Archaeol., 1989–. *Publications:*

Pasargadae, a Report on the Excavations conducted by the British Institute of Persian Studies, 1978; archaeological articles in: Jl of Near Eastern Studies; Iran; Iraq; Anatolian Studies, etc. *Recreations:* fly fishing, mediaeval architecture, tribal carpets; repr. Cambridge in athletics, 1953. *Address:* Department of Near Eastern Studies, University of California, Berkeley, CA 94720, USA. *Clubs:* Achilles; Hawks (Cambridge); Explorers' (New York).

STRONG, Air Cdre David Malcolm, CB 1964; AFC 1941; *b* 30 Sept. 1913; *s* of Theo Strong; *m* 1941, Daphne Irene Warren-Brown; two *s* one *d.* *Educ:* Cardiff High School. Pilot, under trng, 1936; Bomber Sqdn, 1937–41; POW, 1941–45. Station Commander, RAF Jurby, RAF Driffield, 1946–48; Staff Coll. (psa), 1949; Staff Officer, Rhodesian Air Trng Grp, 1949–51; Directing Staff, Staff Coll., 1952–55; Air Warfare Coll. (pfc), 1956; Station Comdr, RAF Coningsby, 1957–59; Dir of Personnel, Air Min., 1959–61; Senior Air Staff Officer, RAF Germany, 1962–63; Officer Commanding, RAF Halton, 1964–66. Retired, 1966. Chairman: RAF Rugby Union, 1954–56; RAF Golf Soc., 1964–66. *Recreation:* golf. *Address:* Old Coach House, Wendover, Bucks HP22 6EB. *T:* Wendover (01296) 624724. *Clubs:* Royal Air Force; Ashridge Golf.

STRONG, Jaqueline Ann Mary; Director of Education, Leicestershire County Council, since 1995; *b* 2 Oct. 1944; *d* of Donald Cameron McKeand and Gwendoline Mary Ann McKeand (*née* Graham); *m* 1966, Roger Francis Strong. *Educ:* Sexey's Grammar Sch.; Chipping Sodbury Grammar Sch.; Univ. of Wales (BSc, DipEd 1st cl.); Univ. of Bristol (MEd). Teacher, St Julian's Jun. High Sch., Newport, 1966–69; Lectr, Rhydyfelin Coll. of FE, 1967–70; teacher: Belfast, 1970–73; St Peter's Comp. Sch., Huntingdon, 1974, Dep. Head Teacher, 1974–81; Warden, The Village Coll., Bassingbourn, 1981–88; Asst Dir of Educn, Cambs CC, 1988–93; Dir of Educn, Leeds MDC, 1993–95. Mem., Exec. Bd, Encounter, 1984–. *Publications:* articles in educational magazines. *Recreations:* singing, exotic foreign travel, photography, walking, reading, concert and theatre going, taking in unwanted Great Danes. *Address:* County Hall, Glenfield, Leicester LE3 8RF.

STRONG, Dr John Anderson, CBE 1978 (MBE (mil.) 1942); MD; FRCP; FRCPE; FRSE; President, Royal College of Physicians of Edinburgh, 1979–82; *b* 18 Feb. 1915; *s* of Charles James Strong and Mabel Emma Strong (*née* Anderson); *m* 1939, Anne Frances Moira Heaney; one *s* two *d.* *Educ:* Monkton Combe Sch., Bath; Trinity Coll., Dublin (MB 1937, MA, MD). Served RAMC, UK, India and Burma, 1939–46 (despatches, Burma, 1945); Hon. Lt-Col RAMC, 1946. Senior Lecturer, Dept of Medicine, Univ. of Edinburgh, 1949; Hon. Cons. Phys., Western General Hosp., Edinburgh, 1949; Hon. Physician, MRC Clinical and Population Cytogenetics Unit, 1959–80; Professor of Medicine, Univ. of Edinburgh, 1966–80, Professor Emeritus, 1981. Mem., Medicines Commn, 1976–83; Chm., Scottish Health Educn Co-ordinating Cttee, 1986–88. Hon. FACP 1980; Hon. FRCPI 1980; Hon. Fellow: Coll. of Physicians of Philadelphia, 1981; TCD, 1982; Coll. of Physicians of S Africa, 1982; Fellow *ad eundem*, RCGP, 1982; Mem., Acad. of Medicine, Singapore, 1982. *Publications:* chapter on Endocrinology in Principles and Practice of Medicine, ed L. S. P. Davidson, 1952, 12th edn 1977; articles in general medical and endocrinological jls. *Recreations:* fishing, golf, stalking, natural history. *Address:* 12 Lomond Road, Edinburgh EH5 3JR. *T:* 0131–552 2865. *Clubs:* New (Edinburgh); Hon. Company of Edinburgh Golfers (Muirfield).

STRONG, John Clifford, CBE 1980; HM Diplomatic Service, retired; Governor, Turks and Caicos Islands, 1978–82; *b* 14 Jan. 1922; *m* 1942, Janet Browning (*d* 1992); three *d.* *Educ:* Beckenham Grammar Sch.; London Sch. of Economics and Political Science. LLB 1953. Served RN, 1942–46; HMOCS Tanzania, 1946–63; CRO, 1963; First Sec., Nairobi, 1964–68; FCO, 1968–73; Counsellor and Head of Chancery, Dar es Salaam, 1973–78. *Address:* Oakover, 24 Crescent Road, Beckenham BR3 2NE. *Club:* Royal Over-Seas League.

STRONG, Julia Trevelyan; *see* Oman, J. T.

STRONG, Liam; Chief Executive, Sears plc, since 1991; *b* 6 Jan. 1945; *s* of Gerald Strong and Geraldine Strong (*née* Crozier); *m* 1970, Jacqueline Gray; one *s* one *d.* *Educ:* Trinity Coll., Dublin. Procter & Gamble, 1967–71; Reckitt & Colman, 1971–86: Sunset Designs, USA, 1980–82; R & C Pharmaceuticals, 1982–86; Pres., Durkee French Foods, USA, 1986–88; Dir of Mktg and Ops, British Airways, 1988–91. Chm., London Health Partnership. Mem. Council, RCA. *Recreations:* film, shooting, walking, sailing.

STRONG, Maurice F., OC 1976; FRSC 1987; Chairman, Ontario Hydro, since 1993; *b* 29 April 1929; *s* of Frederick Milton Strong and late Mary Fyfe Strong; *m* 1st, 1950 (marr. diss. 1980); two *s* two *d*; 2nd, 1981, Hanne Marstrand; one foster *d.* *Educ:* Public and High Sch., Oak Lake, Manitoba, Canada. Served in UN Secretariat, 1947; worked in industry and Pres. or Dir, various Canadian and internat. corporations, 1948–66; Dir-Gen., External Aid Office (later Canadian Internat. Develt Agency), Canadian Govt, 1966–71; Under-Sec.-Gen. with responsibility for envmtl affairs, and Sec.-Gen. of 1972 Conf. on the Human Environment, Stockholm, 1971–72; Exec. Dir, UN Envmtl Programme, 1972–75; Pres., Chm. of Bd and Chm. of Exec. Cttee, Petro-Canada, 1976–78; Chm. of Bd, AZL Resources Inc., USA, 1978–83; Under-Sec.-Gen., UN, 1985–87 and 1989–92; Exec. Co-ordinator, UN Office for Emergency Ops in Africa, NY, 1985–87; Sec.-Gen., UN 1992 Conf. on Envmt and Develt, 1990–92. Dir, Massey Ferguson, Canada; Dir, Mem. Exec. Cttee and Vice Chm., Canada Develt Corp., Toronto. Chairman: Centre for Internat. Management Studies, Geneva, 1971–78; Strovest Hldgs, 1984; American Water Development, Denver, 1986; Internat. Energy Develt Corp., Geneva (also Special Advr); Canada Develt Investment Corp., Vancouver; World Economic Forum Council, 1988; Bd of Govs, Internat. Develt Res. Centre, 1977–78; Co-Chm., Interaction Policy Bd, Vienna; Vice-Chm. and Dir, Soc. Gén. pour l'Energie et les Ressources, Geneva, 1980–86; Member: Internat. Adv. Bd, Unisys Corp., USA; Bd, Bretton Woods Cttee, Washington; World Commn on Envmt and Develt; Alt. Gov., IBRD, ADB, Caribbean Develt Bank. President: World Fedn of UN Assocs, 1987; Better World Soc., 1988; Chairman: North South Energy Roundtable, Washington, DC; North South Energy Roundtable, Rome; Adv. Cttee, UN Univ., Tokyo, Japan. Dir, Lindisfarne Assoc.; Mem., Internat. Asia Soc., NY. Trustee: Rockefeller Foundn, 1971–78; Aspen Inst., 1971–; Internat. Foundn for Develt Alternatives. FRSA. Holds numerous hon. degrees from univs and colls in Canada, USA and UK. *Publications:* articles in various jls, including Foreign Affairs Magazine, Natural History Magazine. *Recreations:* swimming, skin-diving, farming, reading. *Address:* Ontario Hydro, 700 University Avenue, Toronto, Ont M5G 1X6, Canada. *Clubs:* Yale (New York); University (Vancouver).

STRONG, Sir Roy (Colin), Kt 1982; PhD, FSA; writer and historian, lecturer, critic, columnist, contributor to radio and television and organiser of exhibitions; Director, Oman Productions Ltd; *b* 23 Aug. 1935; *s* of G. E. C. Strong; *m* 1971, Julia Trevelyan Oman, *qv.* *Educ:* Edmonton Co. Grammar Sch.; Queen Mary Coll., London (Fellow, 1976); Warburg Inst., London. Asst Keeper, 1959, Director, Keeper and Secretary 1967–73, Nat. Portrait Gallery; Dir, Victoria and Albert Museum, 1974–87. Ferens Prof. of Fine Art, Univ. of Hull, 1972. Walls Lectures, Pierpont Morgan Library, 1974. Member: Fine Arts Adv. Cttee, British Council, 1974–87; Westminster Abbey Architectl Panel, 1975–89; Council, RCA, 1979–87; Arts Council of GB, 1983–87 (Chm., Arts Panel, 1983–87); Vice-Chm., South Bank Centre (formerly South Bank Bd), 1985–90. Trustee: Arundel Castle, 1974–86; Chevening, 1974–87; Sutton Place, 1982–84; Patron, Pallant House, Chichester, 1986– (Trustee, 1980–86). Writer and presenter, TV series incl. Royal Gardens 1992. Hon. DLitt: Leeds, 1983; Keele, 1984. Sen. Fellow, RCA, 1983. Shakespeare Prize, FVS Foundn, Hamburg, 1980. *Publications:* Portraits of Queen Elizabeth I, 1963; (with J. A. van Dorsten) Leicester's Triumph, 1964; Holbein and Henry VIII, 1967; Tudor and Jacobean Portraits, 1969; The English Icon: Elizabethan and Jacobean Portraiture, 1969; (with Julia Trevelyan Oman) Elizabeth R, 1971; Van Dyck: Charles I on Horseback, 1972; (with Julia Trevelyan Oman) Mary Queen of Scots, 1972; (with Stephen Orgel) Inigo Jones: the theatre of the Stuart court, 1973; contrib. Burke's Guide to the Royal Family, 1973; Splendour at Court: Renaissance Spectacle and the Theatre of Power, 1973; (with Colin Ford) An Early Victorian Album: the Hill-Adamson collection, 1974; Nicholas Hilliard, 1975; (contrib.) Spirit of the Age, 1975; The Cult of Elizabeth: Elizabethan Portraiture and Pageantry, 1977; And When Did You Last See Your Father?, 1978; The Renaissance Garden in England, 1979; (contrib.) The Garden, 1979; Britannia Triumphans: Inigo Jones, Rubens and Whitehall Palace, 1980; (introd.) Holbein, 1980; (contrib.) Designing for the Dancer, 1981; (jtly) The English Miniature, 1981; (with Julia Trevelyan Oman) The English Year, 1982; (contrib.) Pelican Guide to English Literature vol. 3, 1982; (with J. Murrell) Artists of the Tudor Court, 1983; The English Renaissance Miniature, 1983; (contrib.) Glyndebourne: a celebration, 1984; Art & Power, 1984; Strong Points, 1985; Henry, Prince of Wales and England's Lost Renaissance, 1986; (contrib.) For Veronica Wedgwood These, 1986; Creating Small Gardens, 1986; Gloriana, Portraits of Queen Elizabeth I, 1987; A Small Garden Designer's Handbook, 1987; Cecil Beaton: the Royal portraits, 1988; Creating Small Formal Gardens, 1989; (contrib.) British Theatre Design, 1989; Lost Treasures of Britain, 1990; (contrib.) Sir Philip Sidney's Achievements, 1990; (contrib.) England and the Continental Renaissance, 1990; (ed) A Celebration of Gardens, 1991; The Garden Trellis, 1991; Small Period Gardens, 1992; Royal Gardens, 1992; A Country Life, 1994; Successful Small Gardens, 1994; William Larkin: vanitù giacobite, Italy, 1994; The Tudor and Stuart Monarchy, vol. I, Tudor, 1995, vol. II, Elizabethan, 1995. *Recreations:* gardening, cooking, keeping fit. *Address:* The Laskett, Much Birch, Herefords HR2 8HZ. *Clubs:* Garrick, Grillions.

STRONGE, Christopher James; Partner, Coopers & Lybrand Deloitte, 1967–92; *b* 16 Aug. 1933; *s* of Reginald Herbert James Stronge and Doreen Marjorie Stronge; *m* 1964, Gabrielle; one *s* one *d.* *Educ:* Chigwell Sch.; Magdalene Coll., Cambridge (MA Math.). FCA. Deloitte Haskins & Sells: joined 1957; Partner 1967; Dep. Sen. Partner, 1985. Member: Accounting Standards Cttee, 1980–83; Internat. Accounting Standards Cttee, 1985–90; Treasurer, RIIA, 1981–91. *Recreations:* opera, golf, sailing. *Address:* 7 Woodhall Drive, SE21 7HJ. *T:* 0181–693 6778. *Club:* Little Ship.

STRONGE, Sir James Anselan Maxwell, 10th Bt *cr* 1803; *b* 17 July 1946; *s* of Maxwell Du Pré James Stronge (*d* 1973) (*g g s* of 2nd Bt) and Eileen Mary (*d* 1976), *d* of Rt Hon. Maurice Marcus McCausland, PC, Drenagh, Limavady, Co. Londonderry; *S* cousin, 1981. *Heir:* none. *Address:* Camphill Community Clanabogan, 15 Drudgeon Road, Clanabogan, Omagh, Co. Tyrone BT78 1TJ.

STROUD, Sir (Charles) Eric, Kt 1989; FRCP; Professor of Child Health, King's College School of Medicine and Dentistry (formerly King's College Hospital Medical School), and Director, Department of Child Health, 1968–88; Paediatric Consultant to RAF, since 1976; *b* 15 May 1924; *s* of Frank Edmund and Lavinia May Stroud; *m* 1950, June, *d* of Harold Neep; one *s* two *d.* *Educ:* Cardiff High Sch. for Boys; Welsh National Sch. of Medicine. BSc 1945, MB, BCh 1948 (Wales); MRCP 1955, DCH 1955, FRCP 1968 (London). Sqdn Ldr, RAF, 1950–52. Med. Qual., 1948; Paediatric Registrar, Welsh Nat. Sch. of Med.; Sen. Registrar, Great Ormond Street Children's Hosp., 1957–61; Paediatrician, Uganda Govt, 1958–60; Asst to Dir, Dept of Child Health, Guy's Hosp., 1961–62; Cons. Paediatrician, King's Coll. Hosp., 1962–68. Med. Advr, Eastern Hemisphere, Variety Clubs Internat., 1985–; Hon. Med. Dir, Children Nationwide Med. Res. Fund. FKC 1989. *Publications:* chapters in Textbook of Obstetrics, 1958; Childhealth in the Tropics, 1961; various articles in med. jls, mainly on sickle cell anaemia, nutrition and health of ethnic minorities. *Recreations:* bad golf, good fishing, cheap antiques, planning for retirement. *Address:* 84 Copse Hill, Wimbledon, SW20 0EF. *T:* 0181–947 1336.

STROUD, Derek H.; *see* Hammond-Stroud.

STROUD, Dorothy Nancy, MBE 1968; Assistant Curator, Sir John Soane's Museum, 1945–84; *b* London, 11 Jan. 1910; *o c* of late Nancy and Alfred Stroud, London. *Educ:* Claremont, Eastbourne; Edgbaston High Sch. On staff of: Country Life, 1930–41; National Monuments Record, 1941–45. Vice-Pres., Garden History Soc., 1982–; Mem., Historic Buildings Council, 1974–82. FSA 1951; Hon. RIBA, 1975. *Publications:* Capability Brown, 1950, new edn 1975; The Thurloe Estate, 1959; The Architecture of Sir John Soane, 1961; Humphry Repton, 1962; Henry Holland, 1966; George Dance, 1971; The South Kensington Estate of Henry Smith's Charity, 1975; Sir John Soane, Architect, 1984. *Address:* 24 Onslow Square, SW7 3NS.

STROUD, Sir Eric; *see* Stroud, Sir C. E.

STROUD, Ven. Ernest Charles Frederick; Archdeacon of Colchester, since 1983; *b* 20 May 1931; *s* of Charles Henry and Irene Doris Stroud; *m* 1959, Jeanne Marguerite Evans; two *d.* *Educ:* Merrywood Grammar School; Merchant Venturers' Technical College; St Chad's Coll., Univ. of Durham. BA (Hons Theology), Diploma in Theology, Diploma in Rural Ministry and Mission. Esso Petroleum Co. Ltd, 1947–55. Deacon 1960, priest 1961, dio. Wakefield; Asst Curate, All Saints, S Kirkby, Yorks, 1960–63; Priest-in-Charge, St Ninian, Whitby, 1963–66; Minister of Conventional District, and first Vicar, All Saints, Chelmsford, 1966–75; Vicar of St Margaret of Antioch, Leigh on Sea, 1975–83; Asst RD of Southend, 1976–79; RD of Hadleigh, 1979–83; Hon. Canon of Chelmsford, 1982–. Member: General Synod, 1981–; C of E Pensions Bd, 1984– (Vice-Chm., Finance and Investment Cttee, 1990–). Chairman: Additional Curates Soc., 1988–; Church Union, 1989–; Dr George Richard's Charity, 1990–. *Publication:* contrib. on ministry of healing to Christian. *Recreations:* travel, music, theatre. *Address:* 63 Powers Hall End, Witham, Essex CM8 1NH. *T:* Witham (01376) 513130, *Fax:* Witham (01376) 500789.

STROWGER, (Gaston) Jack, CBE 1976; Managing Director, Thorn Electrical Industries, 1970–79; *b* 8 Feb. 1916; *s* of Alfred Henry Strowger, Lowestoft boat-owner, and Lily Ellen Tripp; *m* 1939, Katherine Ellen Gilbert; two *s* one *d.* *Educ:* Lowestoft Grammar School. Joined London Electrical Supply Co., 1934; HM Forces, 1939–43. Joined TEI, as an Accountant, 1943; Group Chief Accountant, 1952; joined Tricity Finance Corp. as Dir, 1959; Exec. Dir, TEI, 1961; full Dir 1966; Financial Dir 1967; Dep. Chm., Tricity Finance Corp., 1968; Chm., Thorn-Ericsson, 1974–81. Dir (non-exec.), Hornby Hobbies (Chm., 1981–93). FIMgt. *Recreations:* gardening, bowling. *Address:* The Penthouse, 46 Maplin Close, Eversley Park Road, Winchmore Hill, N21 1NB.

STROYAN, Ronald Angus Ropner, QC 1972; **His Honour Judge Stroyan;** a Circuit Judge, since 1975; a Senior Circuit Judge and Hon. Recorder of Newcastle upon Tyne, since 1993; *b* 27 Nov. 1924; *e s* of Ronald S. Stroyan of Boreland, Killin; *m* 1st, 1952,

Elisabeth Anna Grant (marr. diss. 1965), *y d* of Col J. P. Grant of Rothiemurchus; one *s* two *d*; 2nd, 1967, Jill Annette Johnston, *d* of late Sir Douglas Marshall; one *s* (and two step *s* two step *d*). *Educ:* Harrow School; Trinity College, Cambridge; BA(Hons). Served 1943–45 with The Black Watch (NW Europe); attd Argyll and Sutherland Highlanders, Palestine, 1945–47 (despatches); Captain; later with Black Watch TA. Barrister-at-Law, 1950, Inner Temple. Dep. Chm., North Riding QS, 1962–70, Chm., 1970–71; a Recorder of the Crown Court, 1972–75. Mem. Gen. Council of the Bar, 1963–67, 1969–73 and 1975. Chm., West Rannoch Deer Management Gp, 1989–. *Recreations:* shooting, stalking, fishing. *Address:* Chapel Cottage, Whashton, near Richmond, Yorks DL11 7JW; Boreland, Killin, Perthshire FK21 8TT. *T:* Killin (0156) 820252. *Clubs:* Caledonian; Yorkshire (York).

STRUDWICK, Air Cdre Arthur Sidney Ronald, CB 1976; DFC 1945; *b* 16 April 1921; *s* of Percival and Mary Strudwick; *m* 1941, Cissily (*d* 1983); two *s* one *d*. *Educ:* Guildford Tech. Coll.; RAF Colls. Joined RAF 1940; War Service as Fighter Pilot, 1941–43; POW Germany, 1944; Test Flying, Canada, 1948–50; CO No 98 Sqdn, 1951–53; Staff Coll., Camberley, 1954; Commanded Jt Services Trials Unit, Woomera, 1956–59; JSSC, 1959–60; MoD Planning Staff, 1960–62; Dir of Plans, Far East, 1962–64; Commanded RAF Leuchars, 1965–67; Air Cdre Plans, Strategic Comd, 1967–69; IDC 1969; Dir of Flying (R&D), MoD PE, 1970–73; AOC Central Tactics and Trials Orgn, 1973–76, retired 1976. Defence Liaison Officer, Singer Co., Link-Miles Div., 1976–86. *Recreations:* golf, gardening. *Club:* Royal Air Force.

STRUTHERS, Alastair James, OBE 1995; *b* 25 July 1929; *s* of Alexander Struthers and Elizabeth Struthers (*née* Hutchison); *m* 1967, Elizabeth Henderson; three *d*. *Educ:* Stowe; Trinity Coll., Cambridge (MA). Chairman: J. & A. Gardner & Co. Ltd, 1962–; Scottish National Trust plc, 1983–; Caledonian MacBrayne Ltd, 1990–94. Chm., Steamship Mutual Underwriting Assoc., 1988–. Comr, Northern Lighthouse Bd, 1980–. Dep. Sen. Steward, Jockey Club, 1990–94. *Recreations:* racing, shooting, golf. *Address:* Craigmaddie, Milngavie, by Glasgow G62 8LB. *T:* 0141–956 1262. *Club:* Western (Glasgow).

STRUTT, family name of **Barons Belper** and **Rayleigh.**

STRUTT, Sir Nigel (Edward), Kt 1972; TD; DL; *b* 18 Jan. 1916; *yr s* of late Edward Jolliffe Strutt and Amélie, *d* of Frederic Devas. *Educ:* Winchester; Wye Agricultural College (Fellow, 1970). Essex Yeomanry (Major), 1937–56. Member: Eastern Electricity Bd, 1964–76; Agricultural Advisory Council, 1963– (Chm. 1969–73; Chm., Adv. Council for Agriculture and Horticulture, 1973–80); NEDC for Agriculture, 1967–82. President: Country Landowners' Association, 1967–69; British Friesian Cattle Soc., 1974–75; Royal Agricultural Soc. of England, 1982–83. Master, Farmers' Co., 1976–77. DL Essex 1954; High Sheriff of Essex, 1966. Hon. FRASE, 1971. Hon. DSc Cranfield, 1979; DU Essex, 1981; Hon. DPhil Anglia Polytech. Univ., 1993. Massey Ferguson Award, 1976. Von Thünen Gold Medal, Kiel Univ., 1974. *Recreations:* shooting, travelling. *Address:* Sparrows, Terling, Essex CM3 2QY. *T:* Terling (01245) 233213. *Clubs:* Brooks's, Farmers'.

STUART, family name of **Earl Castle Stewart, Earl of Moray** and **Viscount Stuart of Findhorn.**

STUART; *see* Crichton-Stuart, family name of Marquess of Bute.

STUART; *see* Mackenzie Stuart, family name of Baron Mackenzie-Stuart.

STUART, Viscount; Andrew Richard Charles Stuart; *b* 7 Oct. 1953; *s* and *heir* of 8th Earl Castle Stewart, *qv*; *m* 1973, Annie Le Poulain, St Malo, France; one *d*. *Educ:* Wynstones, Glos; Millfield, Som. *Recreations:* flying, sailing. *Address:* Combe Hayes Farm, Buckerell, near Honiton, Devon EX14 0ET.

STUART OF FINDHORN, 2nd Viscount *cr* 1959; **David Randolph Moray Stuart;** *b* 20 June 1924; *s* of 1st Viscount Stuart of Findhorn, PC, CH, MVO, MC, and Lady Rachel Cavendish, OBE (*d* 1977), 4th *d* of 9th Duke of Devonshire; *S* father, 1971; *m* 1st, 1945, Grizel Mary Wilfreda (*d* 1948), *d* of D. T. Fyfe and *widow* of Michael Gillilan; one *s*; 2nd, 1951, Marian Emelia (marr. diss. 1979), *d* of Gerald H. Wilson; one *s* three *d*; 3rd, 1979, Margaret Anne, *yr d* of Comdr Peter Du Cane, CBE, RN. *Educ:* Eton; Cirencester Agricultural College. FRICS. Page of Honour to HM George VI, 1937–39. Served KRRC LI, 1942–47. Later RWF Major, TA. DL Caernarvonshire (retired). *Heir: s* Hon. James Dominic Stuart [*b* 25 March 1948; *m* 1979, Yvonne Lucienne, *d* of Edgar Després, Ottawa]. *Address:* Findhorn, Forres, Moray IV36 0YE.

STUART, Andrew Christopher, CMG 1979; CPM 1961; HM Diplomatic Service, retired; Chairman, Centre for British Teachers, since 1991; Consultant to Voluntary Service Overseas, since 1990; *b* 30 Nov. 1928; *s* of late Rt Rev. Cyril Edgar Stuart and Mary Summerhayes; *m* 1959, Patricia Kelly; two *s* one *d*. *Educ:* Bryanston; Clare Coll., Cambridge (MA). Royal Navy, 1947–49. Colonial Admin. Service, Uganda, 1953; retd from HMOCS as Judicial Adviser, 1965. Called to Bar, Middle Temple, 1965. Entered HM Diplomatic Service, 1965; 1st Sec. and Head of Chancery, Helsinki, 1968; Asst, S Asian Dept, FCO, 1971; Head of Hong Kong and Indian Ocean Dept, FCO, 1972–75; Counsellor, Jakarta, 1975–78; British Resident Comr, New Hebrides, 1978–80; Ambassador to Finland, 1980–83. Principal, United World Coll. of the Atlantic, 1983–90. Governor: ESU, 1991–; Lancing Coll., 1991–. Order of the Lion (Finland), 1990. *Recreations:* sailing, gliding. *Address:* Long Hall, North Street, Wareham, Dorset BH20 4AG. *T:* Wareham (01929) 551658, *Fax:* (01929) 551712. *Clubs:* United Oxford & Cambridge University, Alpine; Jesters; Royal Naval Sailing Association.

STUART, Antony James Cobham E.; *see* Edwards-Stuart.

STUART, (Charles) Murray, CBE 1995; Chairman, Scottish Power, since 1992 (Director, since 1990); *b* 28 July 1933; *s* of Charles Maitland Stuart and Grace Forrester Stuart (*née* Kerr); *m* 1963, Netta Caroline; one *s* one *d*. *Educ:* Glasgow Acad.; Glasgow Univ. (MA, LLB). Scottish Chartered Accountant; CA. With P. & W. McLellan, Ford Motor Co., Sheffield Twist Drill & Steel Co., and Unicorn Industries, 1961–73; Finance Dir, Hepworths, 1973–74; Finance Dir and Dep. Man. Dir, ICL, 1974–81; Metal Box, subseq. MB Group: Finance Dir, Dir—Finance, Planning and Admin, 1981–86; Man. Dir, Dec. 1986–Dec. 1987; Gp Chief Exec., 1988–89; Chm., 1989–90; Finance Dir, 1990–91, Chief Exec., 1991, Berisford International. Vice Chm., CMB Packaging SA, 1989–90; Vice-Chm. and Dir, Hill Samuel, 1992–93; Chairman: Hill Samuel Scotland, 1993–94; Intermediate Capital Group PLC, 1993–; Non-exec. Director: Save & Prosper Insurance, 1987–91; Save & Prosper Securities, 1988–91; Hunter Saphir, 1991–92; Clerical Medical & General Life Assurance Soc., 1993–. Dep. Chm., Audit Commn, 1991–95 (Mem., 1986–95). Mem., W Surrey and NE Hants HA, 1990–93. *Recreations:* sailing, tennis. *Address:* Scottish Power plc, 1 Atlantic Quay, Glasgow G2 8SP. *T:* 0141–248 8200. *Club:* Western (Glasgow).

STUART, Duncan, CMG 1989; HM Diplomatic Service, retired; Chairman and Chief Executive, Cyrus International Ltd, since 1994; *b* 1 July 1934; *s* of late Ian Cameron Stuart and Patricia Forbes; *m* 1961, Leonore Luise Liederwald; one *s* one *d*. *Educ:* Rugby Sch.; Brasenose Coll., Oxford (MA). Served 1st Bn Oxfordshire and Bucks LI, 1955–57 (2nd Lieut). Joined Foreign, later Diplomatic, Service, 1959; Office of Political Advr, Berlin, 1960–61; FO, 1961–64; Helsinki, 1964–66; Head of Chancery, Dar-es-Salaam, 1966–69; FCO, 1969–70; Helsinki, 1970–74; FCO, 1974–80; Bonn, 1980–83; FCO, 1983–86; Counsellor, Washington, 1986–88; FCO, 1988–92. Gov., St Clare's, Oxford, 1991–. *Address:* c/o C. Hoare & Co., 37 Fleet Street, EC4P 4DQ. *Clubs:* Boodle's, United Oxford & Cambridge University, MCC.

STUART, Francis; *b* Queensland, Australia, 1902; *s* of Henry and Elizabeth Stuart, Co. Antrim, Ireland; *m* 1st, 1920, Iseult Gonne; one *s* one *d*; 2nd, 1954, Gertrude Meiszner; 3rd, 1987, Finola Graham. *Educ:* Rugby. First book, poems, which received an American prize and also award of the Royal Irish Academy, published at age of 21; first novel published in 1931 at age of 29; contributor to various newspapers and periodicals. *Publications: novels:* Women and God, 1931; Pigeon Irish, 1932; The Coloured Dome, 1933; Try the Sky, 1933; Glory, 1934; The Pillar of Cloud, 1948; Redemption, 1949; The Flowering Cross, 1950; Good Friday's Daughter, 1951; The Chariot, 1953; The Pilgrimage, 1955; Victors and Vanquished, 1958; Angels of Providence, 1959; Black List, Section H, 1971; Memorial, 1973; A Hole in the Head, 1977; The High Consistory, 1980; Faillandia, 1985; The Abandoned Snail Shell, 1987; A Compendium of Lovers, 1990; *short stories:* Selected Stories, 1983; *poetry:* We Have Kept the Faith, 1923; Night Pilot, 1988; Collected Poems, 1992; *autobiography:* Things to Live For, 1936. *Recreations:* horse-racing, golf. *Address:* 2 Highfield Park, Dublin 14, Ireland.

STUART, Rev. Canon Herbert James, CB 1983; Canon Emeritus of Lincoln Cathedral, since 1983 (Canon, 1980–83); *b* 16 Nov. 1926; *s* of Joseph and Jane Stuart; *m* 1955, Adrienne Le Fanu; two *s* one *d*. *Educ:* Mountjoy School, Dublin; Trinity Coll., Dublin (BA Hons, MA). Priest, 1950; served in Church of Ireland, 1950–55; Chaplain, RAF, 1955; Asst Chaplain-in-Chief, RAF, 1973; Chaplain-in-Chief and Archdeacon, RAF, 1980–83; QHC, 1978–83; Rector of Cherbury, 1983–87. *Recreations:* gardening, travel, books. *Address:* Abbots Walk, Lechlade Park, Lechlade, Glos GL7 3DB. *Club:* Royal Air Force.

STUART, Sir (James) Keith, Kt 1986; Chairman: Associated British Ports Holdings PLC, since 1983; SEEBOARD plc, since 1992 (Director, since 1990); *b* 4 March 1940; *s* of James and Marjorie Stuart; *m* 1966, Kathleen Anne Pinder (*née* Woodman); three *s* one *d*. *Educ:* King George V School, Southport; Gonville and Caius College, Cambridge (MA). FCIT, CIMgt, FRSA. District Manager, South Western Electricity Bd, 1970–72; British Transport Docks Board: Sec., 1972–75; Gen. Manager, 1976–77; Man. Dir, 1977–82; Dep. Chm., 1980–82; Chm., 1982–83. Dir, Internat. Assoc. of Ports and Harbors, 1983–, Vice-Pres., 1985–87; Pres., Inst. of Freight Forwarders, 1983–84. Director: Royal Ordnance Factories, 1983–85; BAA Plc, 1986–92. Chm., UK-S Africa Trade Assoc., 1988–93; Vice-Chm., UK-Southern Africa Business Assoc., 1994–95. Chartered Inst. of Transport: Mem. Council, 1979–88; Vice-Pres., 1982–83; Pres., 1985–86. Liveryman, Clockmakers' Co., 1987. Governor, Trinity Coll. of Music, 1991– (Dir, 1992). *Recreation:* music. *Address:* Associated British Ports Holdings PLC, 150 Holborn, EC1N 2LR. *T:* 0171–430 1177. *Clubs:* Brooks's, United Oxford & Cambridge University (Trustee, 1989–94).

STUART, Prof. John Trevor, FRS 1974; Professor of Theoretical Fluid Mechanics, Imperial College of Science, Technology and Medicine, University of London, 1966–94, now Emeritus; Dean, Royal College of Science, 1990–93; *b* 28 Jan. 1929; *s* of Horace Stuart and Phyllis Emily Stuart (*née* Potter); *m* 1957, Christine Mary (*née* Tracy); two *s* one *d*. *Educ:* Gateway Sch., Leicester; Imperial Coll., London. BSc 1949, PhD 1951. Aerodynamics Div., Nat. Physical Lab., Teddington, 1951–66; Sen. Principal Scientific Officer (Special Merit), 1961; Hd, Maths Dept, Imperial Coll., London, 1974–79, 1983–86. Vis. Lectr, Dept of Maths, MIT, 1956–57; Vis. Prof. of Maths, MIT, 1965–66; Vis. Prof. of Theoretical Fluid Mechanics, Brown Univ., 1978–; Hon. Prof., Tianjin Univ., China, 1983–. Member: Council, Royal Soc., 1982–84; SERC, 1989–93 (Chm., Mathematics Cttee, 1985–88). 1st Stewartson Meml Lectr, Long Beach, Calif., 1985; 1st DiPrima Meml Lectr, Troy, NY, 1985; Ludwig Prandtl Meml Lectr, Dortmund, 1986. Hon. ScD; Brown Univ., 1986; East Anglia, 1987. Senior Whitehead Prize, London Mathematical Soc., 1984; Otto Laporte Award, Amer. Physical Soc., 1987. *Publications:* (contrib.) Laminar Boundary Layers, ed L. Rosenhead, 1963; articles in Proc. Royal Soc., Phil. Trans Royal Soc., Jl Fluid Mech., Proc. 10th Int. Cong. Appl. Mech., Jl Lub. Tech. (ASME). *Recreations:* theatre, music, gardening, reading, do-it-yourself, ornithology. *Address:* Mathematics Department, Imperial College, SW7 2AZ. *T:* 0171–594 8535; 3 Steeple Close, Wimbledon, SW19 5AD. *T:* 0181–946 7019.

STUART, Joseph B.; *see* Burnett-Stuart.

STUART, Sir Keith; *see* Stuart, Sir J. K.

STUART, Prof. Sir Kenneth (Lamonte), Kt 1977; MD, FRCP, FRCPE, FACP, FFPM, FFPHM, DTM&H; Hon. Medical and Scientific Adviser, Barbados High Commission, since 1991; *b* 16 June 1920; *s* of Egbert and Louise Stuart; *m* 1958, Barbara Cecille Ashby; one *s* two *d*. *Educ:* Harrison Coll., Barbados; Queen's Univ., Belfast (MB, BCh, BAO 1948). Consultant Physician, University Coll. Hospital of the West Indies, 1954–76; University of the West Indies: Prof. of Medicine, 1966–76; Dean, Medical Faculty, 1969–71; Head, Dept of Medicine, 1972–76; Mem. Council, 1971–76; Medical Adviser, Commonwealth Secretariat, 1976–84. Rockefeller Foundation Fellow in Cardiology, Massachusetts Gen. Hosp., Boston, 1956–57; Wellcome Foundation Research Fellow, Harvard Univ., Boston, 1960–61; Gresham Prof. of Physic, 1988–92. Consultant to WHO on Cardiovascular Disorders, 1969–. Chm., Commonwealth Caribbean MRC, 1989–. Chm., Court of Governors, LSHTM, 1982–86; Member: Council, Liverpool Sch. of Tropical Medicine, 1980–; Council, UMDS Guy's and St Thomas's Hosps, 1994–; Court of Governors, Internat. Develt Res. Centre of Canada, 1985–90; Council, London Lighthouse, 1994–. Trustee, Schools Partnership Worldwide, 1986–; Chm., Errol Barrow Meml Trust, 1989–. Hon. DSc QUB, 1986. *Publications:* articles on hepatic and cardiovascular disorders in medical journals. *Recreations:* tennis, music. *Address:* Barbados High Commission, 1 Great Russell Street, WC1B 3JY.

STUART, Marian Elizabeth; Under Secretary, Cabinet Office; on secondment as Resident Chairman, Civil Service Selection Board, since 1993; *b* 17 July 1944; *d* of William and Greta Stuart; one *s* one *d*. *Educ:* Eye Grammar School, Suffolk; Mount Grace Comprehensive School, Potters Bar; Leicester Univ. (MA). Joined Min. of Health as Asst Principal, 1967; Principal, DHSS, 1971; Asst Sec., 1979; Dep. Chief Inspector of Social Services, 1988; Under Sec., Finance Div., DoH, 1989–93. *Recreations:* reading, bridge, ski-ing. *Address:* Cabinet Office, 24 Whitehall, SW1A 2ED.

STUART, Mark M.; *see* Moody-Stuart.

STUART, Michael Francis Harvey; Treasury Adviser, UK Mission to the United Nations, 1974–82, retired; *b* 3 Oct. 1926; *s* of late Willoughby Stuart and Ethel Candy; *m* 1961, Ruth Tennyson-d'Eyncourt; one *s* one *d*. *Educ:* Harrow; Magdalen Coll., Oxford. Air Min., 1950–65; DEA, 1965–69; HM Treasury, 1969–74. Mem., UN Adv. Cttee on Administrative and Budgetary Questions, 1975–80. *Recreations:* music, golf. *Address:*

Bourne House, Chertsey Road, Chobham, Woking, Surrey GU24 8NB. *T:* Chobham (01276) 857954.

STUART, Murray; *see* Stuart, C. M.

STUART, Nicholas Willoughby, CB 1990; Director General for Employment and Lifetime Learning, Department for Education and Employment, since 1995; *b* 2 Oct. 1942; *s* of Douglas Willoughby Stuart and Margaret Eileen Stuart; *m* 1st, 1963, Sarah Mustard (marr. diss. 1974); one *d* (one *s* decd); 2nd, 1975, Susan Jane Fletcher; one *s* one *d*. *Educ:* Harrow Sch.; Christ Church Coll., Oxford (MA). Asst Principal, DES, 1964–68; Private Sec. to Minister for the Arts, 1968–69; Principal, DES, 1969–73; Private Secretary to: Head of the Civil Service, 1973; Prime Minister, 1973–76; Asst Sec., DES, 1976–78; Advr, Cabinet of Pres. of EEC, 1978–80; Under Sec., 1981–87, Dep. Sec., 1987–92, DES; Dir of Resources and Strategy, Dept of Employment, 1992–95. *Recreation:* collecting Tunbridgeware.

STUART, Sir Phillip (Luttrell), 9th Bt *cr* 1660; late F/O RCAF; President, Agassiz Industries Ltd; *b* 7 September 1937; *s* of late Luttrell Hamilton Stuart and late Irene Ethel Jackman; *S* uncle, Sir Houlton John Stuart, 8th Bt, 1959; *m* 1st, 1962, Marlene Rose Muth (marr. diss. 1968); two *d*; 2nd, 1969, Beverley Clare Pieri; one *s* one *d*. *Educ:* Vancouver. Enlisted RCAF, Nov. 1955; commnd FO (1957–62). *Heir: s* Geoffrey Phillip Stuart, *b* 5 July 1973.

[*But his name does not, at the time of going to press, appear on the official Roll of Baronets.*

STUART-FORBES, Sir Charles Edward; *see* Forbes.

STUART-HARRIS, Sir Charles (Herbert), Kt 1970; CBE 1961; MD; FRCP; Fogarty Scholar-in-Residence, National Institutes of Health, Bethesda, Maryland, USA, 1979–80; Postgraduate Dean of Medicine, University of Sheffield, 1972–77, Professor of Medicine, 1946–72, now Emeritus Professor; Physician, United Sheffield Hospitals, 1946–74; *b* 12 July 1909; *s* of late Dr and Mrs Herbert Harris, Birmingham; *m* 1937, Marjorie, *y d* of late Mr and Mrs F. Robinson, Dulwich; two *s* one *d*. *Educ:* King Edward's School, Birmingham; St Bartholomew's Hospital Medical School. MB, BS London 1931 (Gold Medal); MD 1933 (Gold Medal); FRCP 1944. House-Physician and Demonstrator in Pathology, St Bartholomew's Hosp.; First Asst, Dept of Medicine, Brit. Postgrad. Medical Sch., 1935; Sir Henry Royce Research Fellow. Univ. of London, 1935; Foulerton Research Fellow, Royal Society, 1938. War Service, 1939–46; Specialist Pathologist Comdg Mobile Bacteriological, Command and Field Laboratories; Colonel RAMC, 1945. Goulstonian Lectr, Royal College of Physicians, 1944; Visiting Prof. of Medicine, Albany Medical Coll., New York, 1953; Sir Arthur Sims Commonwealth Travelling Prof., 1962. Vis. Professor of Medicine: Vanderbilt Univ., Tennessee, 1961; Univ. of Southern California, Los Angeles, 1962; Croonian Lectr, Royal Coll. of Physicians, 1962; Henry Cohen Lectr, Hebrew Univ. of Jerusalem, 1966; Waring Prof., Univ. of Colorado and Stanford Univ., Calif., 1967; Harveian Orator, RCP, 1974. Member: MRC, 1957–61; Public Health Lab. Service Bd, 1954–66; UGC 1968–77 (Chm., Med. Sub-Cttee, 1973–77); UPGC, Hong Kong, 1978–84. Pres., Assoc. of Physicians of GB and Ireland, 1971. Hon. Member: Assoc. of Amer. Physicians; Infectious Diseases Soc. of Amer. Hon. DSc: Hull, 1973; Sheffield, 1978. *Publications:* (co-author) Chronic bronchitis emphysema and cor pulmonale, 1957; Influenza and other virus infections of the respiratory tract, 1965; (co-author) Virus and Rickettsial Diseases, 1967; (co-author) Influenza—the Viruses and the Disease, 1976, 2nd edn 1985; (contrib.) Topley and Wilson, Principles of Bacteriology, Virology and Immunity, vol. 4, Virology, 8th edn 1990; papers in med. and scientific jls on influenza, typhus and bronchitis. *Recreation:* music. *Address:* 28 Whitworth Road, Sheffield S10 3HD. *T:* Sheffield (0114) 230 1200.

STUART-MENTETH, Sir James; *see* Menteth.

STUART-MOORE, Michael, QC 1990; **Hon. Mr Justice Stuart-Moore;** a Judge of the High Court of Hong Kong, since 1993; a Recorder of the Crown Court, since 1985; *b* 7 July 1944; *s* of (Kenneth) Basil Moore and Marjorie (Elizabeth) Moore; *m* 1973, Katherine Ann, *d* of William and Ruth Scott; one *s* one *d*. *Educ:* Cranleigh School. Called to the Bar, Middle Temple, 1966. *Recreations:* photography, travel, music, tennis. *Address:* 1 Hare Court, Temple, EC4Y 7BE. *T:* 0171–353 5324.

STUART-PAUL, Air Marshal Sir Ronald (Ian), KBE 1990 (MBE 1967); RAF, retired; Director General, Saudi Air Force Project, 1985–92; *b* 7 Nov. 1934; *s* of Dr J. G. Stuart-Paul and Mary (*née* McDonald); *m* 1963, Priscilla Frances (*née* Kay); one *s* one *d*. *Educ:* Dollar Acad.; RAF Coll., Cranwell. Served 14, 19, 56 and 92 Sqns and 11 and 12 Groups, 1957–73; Defence Attaché, Saudi Arabia, 1974–75; Stn Comdr, RAF Lossiemouth, 1976–78; RCDS, 1979; Dep. Comdr, NAEW Force, SHAPE, 1980–82; Dir of Ops Air Defence, RAF, 1982–83; AO Training, RAF Support Command, 1984–85. *Recreations:* golf, campanology, sailing, rug-making. *Address:* Sycamore House, Gaunts Common, Wimborne, Dorset BH21 4JP. *T:* Witchampton (01258) 840430. *Club:* Royal Air Force.

STUART-SHAW, Max, CBE 1963; Executive Director, Olympic Airways, 1969–71; *b* 20 Dec. 1912; *e s* of Herman and Anne Louise Stuart-Shaw; *m* 1967, Janna Job, *d* of C. W. Howard. *Educ:* Belmont School, Sussex; St Paul's, London. Imperial Airways/BOAC, 1931–46; Aer Lingus Irish Airlines; Traffic Manager, Commercial Manager, Asst Gen. Manager, 1947–57; Chief Exec. and Gen. Manager Central African Airways, Salisbury, Rhodesia, 1958–65; Man. Dir, BUA, 1966–67; Vice-Chairman, British United Airways, 1967–68. FCIT. *Recreation:* air transport.

STUART-SMITH, James, CB 1986; QC 1988; Judge Advocate General, 1984–91 (Vice Judge Advocate General, 1979–84); a Recorder, 1985–91; *b* 13 Sept. 1919; *s* of James Stuart-Smith and Florence Emma (*née* Armfield); *m* 1957, Jean Marie Therese Young Groundsell, *d* of Hubert Young Groundsell, Newport, IoW; one *s* one *d*. *Educ:* Brighton Coll.; London Hospital. Medical student, 1938. Served War of 1939–45: commnd KRRC, 1940; served ME and Italy, and staff appointments in UK; demobilised 1947. Called to Bar, Middle Temple, 1948; practised in London, 1948–55; Legal Asst, JAG's Office, 1955; Dep. Judge Advocate, 1957; Asst Judge Advocate General, 1968; Dep. Judge Advocate, Middle East Comd (Aden), 1964–65; Dep. Judge Advocate General, British Forces Germany, 1976–79. Hon. Pres., Internat. Soc. for Military Law and the Law of War, 1991– (Vice-Pres., 1979–85; Pres., 1985–91). *Publications:* contribs to Internat. Soc. for Military Law and Law of War Rev. and Law Qly Rev., on history and practice of British military law. *Recreations:* composing letters, mowing lawns. *Address:* The Firs, Copthorne, Sussex RH10 4HH. *T:* Copthorne (01342) 712395. *Club:* Royal Air Force.

STUART-SMITH, Rt. Hon. Sir Murray, Kt 1981; PC 1988; **Rt. Hon. Lord Justice Stuart-Smith;** a Lord Justice of Appeal, since 1988; *b* 18 Nov. 1927; *s* of Edward Stuart-Smith and Doris Mary Laughland; *m* 1953, Joan Elizabeth Mary Motion, BA, JP, DL (High Sheriff of Herts, 1983); three *s* three *d*. *Educ:* Radley; Corpus Christi Coll., Cambridge (Foundn Scholar; 1st Cl. Hons Law Tripos, Pts I and II; 1st Cl. Hons LLM; MA; Hon. Fellow 1994). 2nd Lieut, 5th Royal Inniskilling Dragoon Guards, 1947. Called to the Bar, Gray's Inn, 1952 (Atkin Scholar), Bencher 1977; QC 1970; a Recorder of the Crown Court, 1972–81; a Judge of the High Court of Justice, QBD, 1981–88; Presiding Judge, Western Circuit, 1983–87. Jt Inspector into Grays Bldg Soc., 1979. Mem., Criminal Injuries Compensation Bd, 1980–81. *Recreations:* playing 'cello, shooting, building, playing bridge. *Address:* Royal Courts of Justice, Strand, WC2A 2LL. *Club:* Beefsteak.

STUART TAYLOR, Sir Nicholas (Richard), 4th Bt *cr* 1917; solicitor; *b* 14 Jan. 1952; *s* of Sir Richard Laurence Stuart Taylor, 3rd Bt, and of Iris Mary, *d* of Rev. Edwin John Gargery; *S* father, 1978; *m* 1984, Malvena Elizabeth Sullivan, BSc, MB, BS, FRCA, *d* of late Daniel David Charles Sullivan and Kathleen Sullivan; two *d*. *Educ:* Bradfield. Admitted Solicitor, 1977. *Recreations:* ski-ing and other sports. *Heir:* none. *Address:* 3 Horseshoe Drive, Romsey, Hampshire SO51 7TP. *Club:* Ski Club of Great Britain.

STUART-WHITE, Hon. Sir Christopher (Stuart), Kt 1993; **Hon. Mr Justice Stuart-White;** a Judge of the High Court of Justice, Family Division, since 1993; *b* 18 Dec. 1933; *s* of Reginald Stuart-White and Catherine Mary Wigmore Stuart-White (*née* Higginson); *m* 1957, Pamela (*née* Grant); one *s* two *d*. *Educ:* Winchester; Trinity Coll., Oxford (BA). Called to Bar, Inner Temple, 1957, Bencher 1993. Barrister on the Midland and Oxford Circuit, 1958–78; a Recorder of the Crown Court, 1974–78; a Circuit Judge, 1978–93. Chairman: Magisterial Cttee, Judicial Studies Bd, 1985–90; County Court Rule Cttee, 1988–92. *Recreation:* gardening. *Address:* Royal Courts of Justice, Strand, WC2A 2LL.

STUBBLEFIELD, Sir (Cyril) James, Kt 1965; FRS 1944; FGS; FZS; DSc (London); ARCS; formerly Director, Geological Survey of Great Britain and Museum of Practical Geology, 1960–66; Director, Geological Survey in Northern Ireland, 1960–66; *b* Cambridge, 6 Sept. 1901; *s* of James and Jane Stubblefield; *m* 1932, Muriel Elizabeth, *d* of L. R. Yakchee; two *s*. *Educ:* The Perse Sch.; Chelsea Polytechnic; Royal College of Science, London (Royal Scholar); London Univ. Geology Scholar, 1921. Demonstrator in Geology, Imperial College of Science and Technology, 1923–28; Warden of pioneer Imperial Coll. Hostel, 1926–28. Apptd Geological Survey as Geologist, 1928; Chief Palæontologist, 1947–53; Asst Director, 1953–60. Mem., Anglo-French Commn of Surveillance, Channel Tunnel, 1964–67. Pres. Geological Soc. of London, 1958–60; Bigsby Medallist, 1941; Murchison Medallist, 1955. Sec. of Palæontographical Soc., 1934–48; Pres., 1966–71, Hon. Mem., 1974. Member Council Brit. Assoc. for Advancement of Science, 1946–52, 1958–63; Pres. Section C (Geology), Oxford, 1954. Pres. Cambrian Subcommn, Internat. Geol. Union's Commn on Stratigraphy, 1964–72. Pres. Internat. Congress Carboniferous Stratigraphy and Geology, 6th Session, Sheffield, 1967, and Editor, 4 vol. Compte rendu, 1968–72. Vice-Pres. International Paleontological Union, 1948–56. Corresp. Paleont. Soc. (USA), 1950–; Corresp. Mem. Geol. Soc. Stockholm, 1952–; Senckenbergische Naturforschende Gesellschaft, 1957–. Member: Gov. Body (later Council), Chelsea Coll. of Science and Technology, 1958–82; Council, Royal Soc., 1960–62. Hon. Fellow: Pal. Soc. India, 1961–; Chelsea Coll., 1985; KCL, 1985–. Fellow Imperial Coll., 1962–; Hon. Member: Geologists' Assoc., 1973–; Liverpool Geol. Soc., 1960–; Petroleum Exploration Soc. GB, 1966–; For. Corr., Geol. Soc., France, 1963–, For. Vice-Pres., 1966. Hon. DSc Southampton, 1965. *Publications:* papers in journals, on Palæozoic fossils and rocks; also contributions to: Geological Survey Memoirs; Trilobita, Zoological Record, 1938–51, 1965–77. Joint Editor of the Handbook of the Geology of Great Britain, 1929; Reviser, Introduction to Palæontology (A. Morley Davies), 3rd edn, 1961. *Address:* 35 Kent Avenue, Ealing, W13 8BE. *T:* 0181–997 5051.

STUBBS, Sir James (Wilfrid), KCVO 1979; TD 1946; Grand Secretary, United Grand Lodge of England, 1958–80; *b* 13 Aug. 1910; *s* of Rev. Wilfrid Thomas Stubbs and Muriel Elizabeth (*née* Pope); *m* Richenda Katherine Theodora Streatfeild (*d* 1995); one *s* (and one *d* decd). *Educ:* Charterhouse (Junior and Senior Scholar); Brasenose Coll., Oxford (Scholar; MA). Assistant Master, St Paul's Sch., London, 1934–46. Served War, Royal Signals, 1941–46: Captain 1941, Major 1945, Lt-Col 1946 (2nd Lieut, SR, 1932, Lieut 1935). Asst Grand Sec., United Grand Lodge of England, 1948–54; Dep. Grand Sec., 1954–58. *Publications:* Grand Lodge 1717–1967, 1967; The Four Corners, 1983; Freemasonry in My Life, 1985. *Recreations:* family history, travel. *Address:* 5 Pensioners Court, The Charterhouse, EC1M 6AU. *T:* 0171–253 1982. *Club:* Athenæum.

STUBBS, John F. A. H.; *see* Heath-Stubbs.

STUBBS, Prof. Michael Wesley, PhD; Professor of English Linguistics, University of Trier, Germany, since 1990; *b* 23 Dec. 1947; *s* of late Leonard Garforth Stubbs and Isabella Wardrop (*née* McGavin). *Educ:* Glasgow High Sch. for Boys; King's Coll., Cambridge (MA); Univ. of Edinburgh (PhD 1975). Res. Associate, Univ. of Birmingham, 1973–74; Lectr in Linguistics, Univ. of Nottingham, 1974–85; Prof. of English in Educn, Inst. of Educn, Univ. of London, 1985–90. Vis. Prof. of Linguistics, Univ. of Tübingen, Germany, 1985; Hon. Sen. Res. Fellow, Univ. of Birmingham, 1994–. *Publications:* Language, Schools and Classrooms, 1976, 2nd edn 1983; Language and Literacy, 1980; Discourse Analysis, 1983; Educational Linguistics, 1986; articles in Lang. and Educn, Applied Linguistics, Jl of Pragmatics. *Recreation:* walking. *Address:* FB2 Anglistik, University of Trier, 54286 Trier, Germany. *T:* (651) 2012278.

STUBBS, Thomas, OBE 1980; HM Diplomatic Service, retired; *b* 12 July 1926; *s* of Thomas Stubbs and Lillian Marguerite (*née* Rumball, formerly Bell); *m* 1951, Dorothy Miller; one *s* one *d*. *Educ:* Heaton Tech. Sch., Newcastle upon Tyne. Served in Army, 1944–48. Joined Min. of Nat. Insce, later Min. of Pensions and Nat. Insce, 1948; transf. to CRO, 1960; New Delhi, 1962; CRO, 1964; Wellington, NZ, 1965; Vice-Consul, Düsseldorf, 1970; seconded to BOTB, 1974; First Sec. (Commercial) and Consul, Addis Ababa, 1977; Consul, Hannover, 1980; Dep. High Comr, Madras, 1983–86. Mayor, Borough of Spelthorne, 1992–93 (Mem. Council, 1987–; Vice-Chm., Leisure and Amenities Cttee, 1987–89; Chairman: Personnel Cttee, 1989–91; Resources Cttee, 1995–; Dep. Mayor, 1991–92). Hon. Pres., County of Middlesex Trust, 1992–. *Recreations:* reading, golf. *Address:* 17 Chester Close, Ashford Common, Middlesex TW15 1PH.

STUBBS, William Frederick, QC 1978; *b* 27 Nov. 1934; *s* of William John Stubbs and Winifred Hilda (*née* Johnson); *m* 1961, Anne Katharine (*d* 1966), *d* of late Prof. W. K. C. Guthrie, FBA; one *s* one *d*. *Educ:* The High Sch., Newcastle-under-Lyme, Staffs; Gonville and Caius Coll., Cambridge; Harvard Law Sch. Open Minor Scholar in Nat. Sci., Gonville and Caius Coll., 1951; Student, Gray's Inn, 1953; 1st Cl. Hons Law Tripos Pt I, and George Long Prize for Roman Law, Cambridge, 1954; Major Scholar, Gonville and Caius Coll., 1954; 1st Cl. Hons with Distinction Law Tripos Pt II, Cambridge, 1955; LLB 1st Cl. Hons with Dist., and Chancellor's Medal for English Law, Cambridge, 1956; Tapp Post-Grad. Law Scholar, Gonville and Caius Coll., 1956 (also awarded Schuldham Plate); Joseph Hodges Choate Meml Fellow, Harvard Coll., 1957; Bar Final Exam., 2nd Cl. Hons Div. 1, 1957; Holker Sen. Scholar and Macaskie Scholar, Gray's Inn, 1957; called to the Bar, Gray's Inn, 1957, Bencher, 1987. Has practised in Courts of Malaysia, Singapore, Hong Kong and Cayman Is. *Recreations:* reading, walking, natural history. *Address:* Erskine Chambers, 30 Lincoln's Inn Fields, WC2A 3PF. *T:* 0171–242 5532; 3 Atherton Drive, SW19 5LB. *T:* 0181–947 3986. *Club:* MCC.

STUBBS, Sir William (Hamilton), Kt 1994; Chief Executive, Further Education Funding Council, since 1992; *b* 5 Nov. 1937; *s* of Joseph Stubbs and Mary Stubbs (*née* McNicol); *m* 1963, Marie Margaret Pierce; three *d*. *Educ:* Workington Grammar Sch.; St Aloysius

Coll., Glasgow; Glasgow Univ. (BSc, PhD). Res. Associate, Univ. of Arizona, 1963–64; with Shell Oil Co., San Francisco, 1964–67; teaching, 1967–72; Asst Dir of Educn, Carlisle, 1972–74; Asst Dir of Educn, 1974–76, Second Dep. Dir of Educn, 1976–77, Cumbria; Second Dep. Educn Officer, 1977–79, Dir of Educn (Schools), 1979–82, Educn Officer and Chief Exec., 1982–88, ILEA; Chief Exec., PCFC, 1988–93. Mem. Council, CRAC, 1993–. Hon. Prof., Dept of Continuing Educn, Univ. of Warwick, 1993. DUniv Open, 1995. CIMgt; FRSA. *Address:* Lockes Cottage, Manor Road, West Adderbury, near Banbury, Oxon OX17 3EL.

STÜCKLEN, Richard; Grosskreuz des Verdienstordens der Bundesrepublik Deutschland; Bayerischer Verdienstorden; Vice-President of the Bundestag, Federal Republic of Germany, 1976–79 and 1983–90 (President, 1979–83); *b* 20 Aug. 1916; *s* of Georg Stücklen and Mathilde (*née* Bach); *m* 1943, Ruth Stücklen (*née* Geissler); one *s* one *d*. *Educ:* primary sch.; technical sch.; engineering sch. Industrial Dept Manager and Manager in family business, 1945–49. Mem. of Bundestag, 1949–; Dep. Chm., CDU/Christian Social Union and Party Leader, Christian Social Union, 1953–57 and 1967–76; Federal Minister of Posts and Telegraphs, 1957–66. *Publications:* Bundestagsreden und Zeitdokumente, 1979; and others. *Recreations:* skating, chess, soccer. *Address:* Bundeshaus, 53113 Bonn, Germany. *T:* (228) 162912. *Club:* Lions.

STUCLEY, Sir Hugh (George Coplestone Bampfylde), 6th Bt *cr* 1859; Lieut Royal Horse Guards, retired; *b* 8 Jan. 1945; *s* of Major Sir Dennis Frederic Bankes Stucley, 5th Bt, and of Hon. Sheila Bampfylde, *o d* of 4th Baron Poltimore; *S* father, 1983; *m* 1969, Angela Caroline, *e d* of Richard Charles Robertson Toller, MC, Theale, Berks; two *s* two *d*. *Educ:* Milton Abbey School; Royal Agricultural College, Cirencester. *Heir:* *s* George Dennis Bampfylde Stucley, *b* 26 Dec. 1970. *Address:* Affeton Castle, Worlington, Crediton, Devon EX17 4TU. *Club:* Sloane.

STUDD, Sir Edward (Fairfax), 4th Bt *cr* 1929; Chairman, Gray Dawes Travel, and director of other companies; *b* 3 May 1929; *s* of Sir Eric Studd, 2nd Bt, OBE, and Stephana (*d* 1976), *o d* of L. J. Langmead; *S* brother, 1977; *m* 1960, Prudence Janet, *o d* of Alastair Douglas Fyfe, OBE, Riding Mill, Northumberland; two *s* one *d*. *Educ:* Winchester College. Lieutenant Coldstream Guards, London and Malaya, 1947–49; Macneill & Barry Ltd, Calcutta, 1951–62; Inchcape & Co. Ltd, London, 1962–86 (Dir, 1974–86). Master, Merchant Taylor's Co., 1987–88 and 1993–94. *Recreations:* walking, shooting, fishing. *Heir:* *s* Philip Alastair Fairfax Studd [*b* 27 Oct. 1961; *m* 1987, Georgina, *d* of Roger Neville; one *s* one *d*].

STUDD, Sir Peter Malden, GBE 1971; KCVO 1979; Kt 1969; DL; MA, DSc; *b* 15 Sept. 1916; *s* of late Brig. Malden Augustus Studd, DSO, MC and Netta Cramsie; *m* 1943, Angela Mary Hamilton (*née* Garnier) (*d* 1995); two *s*. *Educ:* Harrow; Clare Coll., Cambridge (MA). Captain of cricket, Harrow and Cambridge Univ. Served War of 1939–45, Royal Artillery, ME and European campaigns. De La Rue Co., 1939–81. Alderman, Cripplegate Ward, City of London, 1959–76; Sheriff, 1967–68; Lord Mayor of London, 1970–71; Hon. DSc City Univ., 1971. Chm., King George's Jubilee Trust, 1972; Dep. Chm., Queen's Silver Jubilee Trust, 1976–80; Vice-Pres., Britain-Australia Bicentennial Cttee '88, 1985–; Pres., British Chiropractic Advancement Assoc., 1987–90; Vice-Pres., The Arts Educational Schools, 1984–; Trustee, Royal Jubilee Trusts, 1980–95. Liveryman, Merchant Taylors' Co., 1959 (Asst, 1959–, Master, 1973–74); Hon. Liveryman, Worshipful Cos of Fruiterers and Plaisterers. DL Wilts, 1983. KStJ 1968. *Recreations:* gardening, fishing, shooting, 'lighting up the Thames'. *Address:* c/o Messrs C. Hoare & Co., 37 Fleet Street, EC4P 4DQ. *Clubs:* MCC, I Zingari; Hawks (Cambridge); Houghton (Stockbridge).

STUDHOLME, Sir Henry (William), 3rd Bt *cr* 1956, of Perridge, Co. Devon; *b* 31 Jan. 1958; *s* of Sir Paul Henry William Studholme, 2nd Bt and Virginia (*d* 1990), *yr d* of Sir (Herbert) Richmond Palmer, KCMG, CBE; *S* father, 1990; *m* 1988, Sarah Lucy Rosita (*née* Deans-Chrystall); two *s* one *d*. *Educ:* Eton; Trinity Hall, Cambridge (MA). ACA, ATII. *Heir:* *s* Joshua Henry Paul Studholme, *b* 2 Feb. 1992. *Address:* Halscombe Farm, Ide, near Exeter EX2 9TQ. *Club:* Brooks's.

STURDEE, Rear-Adm. Arthur Rodney Barry, CB 1971; DSC 1945; *b* 6 Dec. 1919; *s* of Comdr Barry V. Sturdee, RN, and Barbara (*née* Sturdee); *m* 1953, Marie-Claire Amstoutz (*d* 1995), Mulhouse, France; one *s* one *d*. *Educ:* Canford Sch. Entered Royal Navy as Special Entry Cadet, 1937. Served War of 1939–45: Midshipman in HMS Exeter at Battle of the River Plate, 1939; Lieut, 1941; specialised in Navigation, 1944; minesweeping in Mediterranean, 1944–45 (DSC). Lt-Comdr, 1949; RN Staff Coll., 1950–51; Staff of Navigation Sch., 1951–52; Comdr, 1952; JSSC, 1953; BJSM, Washington, 1953–55; Fleet Navigating Officer, Medit., 1955–57; Exec. Officer, RNAS, Culdrose, 1958–59; Captain 1960; NATO Defence Coll., 1960–63; Queen's Harbour-Master, Singapore, 1963–65; Staff of Chief of Defence Staff, 1965–67; Chief of Staff to C-in-C, Portsmouth (as Cdre), 1967–69; Rear-Adm. 1969; Flag Officer, Gibraltar, 1969–72; retired 1972. ADC to the Queen, 1969. *Address:* 3 Tibberton Mews, Tibberton Road, Malvern, Worcestershire WR14 3AS. *T:* Malvern (01684) 575402.

STURDY, Henry William, OBE 1975 (MBE 1968); HM Diplomatic Service, retired; Deputy Consul General and Counsellor Commercial, Chicago, 1976–78; *b* 17 Feb. 1919; *s* of late Henry William Dawson Sturdy and Jemima Aixill; *m* 1945, Anne Jamieson Marr; one *s* one *d*. *Educ:* Woolwich Polytechnic (Mechanical Engineering). Served War in Middle East, 1939–45; Allied Control Commission, Germany, 1946. Executive Branch of Civil Service and Board of Trade, 1951; tour in Trade Commission Service, 1953; appointments: Pakistan, Bangladesh, Sri Lanka, Canada. First Secretary, Diplomatic Service, 1965; Counsellor, Korea, 1976. Defence Medal; 1939–45 Medal; General Service Medal, 1939, with Palestine Clasp, 1945. *Recreations:* squash, bridge, reading, argument, international cuisine. *Address:* 17 Clock Tower Court, Park Avenue, Bexhill-on-Sea, E Sussex TN39 3HP.

STURDY, Robert William; Member (C) Cambridgeshire, European Parliament, since 1994; *b* 22 June 1944; *s* of late Gordon Sturdy and of Kathleen Sturdy (*née* Wells); *m* 1969, Elizabeth Hommes; one *s* one *d*. *Educ:* Ashville Coll., Harrogate. Accountant; Partner, G. E. Sturdy & Son, North Deighton Farms, 1965–. European Parliament: Cons. Agric. spokesman; Vice-Pres., Delegn to SE Europe. *Recreations:* fishing, tennis, ski-ing, cricket. *Address:* 153 St Neots Road, Hardwick, Cambridge CB3 7QJ.

STURGE, Maj.-Gen. (Henry Arthur) John, CB 1978; *b* 27 April 1925; *s* of Henry George Arthur Sturge and Lilian Beatrice Sturge; *m* 1953, Jean Ailsa Mountain; two *s* one *d*. *Educ:* Wilson's Sch., (formerly) Camberwell, London; Queen Mary Coll., London. Commissioned, Royal Signals, 1946; UK, 1946–50; Egypt, 1950–53; UK, incl. psc, 1953–59; Far East, 1959–62; jssc, 1962; BAOR, 1963–64; RMA, Sandhurst, 1965–66; BAOR, incl. Command, 1966–69; Min. of Defence, 1970–75; Chief Signal Officer, BAOR, 1975–77; ACDS (Signals), 1977–80. Col Comdt, Royal Corps of Signals, 1977–85. Colonel, Queen's Gurkha Signals, 1980–86. Gen. Manager, 1981–84, Dir, 1983–84, Marconi Space and Defence Systems; Man. Dir, 1984–85, Chm., 1985–86, Marconi Secure Radio Systems; Prin. Consultant, Logica Space and Defence Systems, 1986–90; Chm., Logica Defence and Civil Government Ltd, 1991–94. Vice Chm., Governors, Wilson's Sch., 1979–. *Recreations:* sailing, (formerly) Rugby. *Address:* 18 High Street, Odiham, Hampshire RG25 1LG. *Club:* Army and Navy.

STURKEY, (Robert) Douglas, CVO 1995; Official Secretary to the Governor-General of Australia, since 1990; Secretary of the Order of Australia, since 1990; *b* 7 Sept. 1935; *s* of late James Robert Sturkey and Jessie Grace (*née* Meares). *Educ:* Wesley Coll., S Perth; Univ. of WA (BA Hons). Mem., Australian Diplomatic Service, 1957–90: service abroad at Wellington, Lagos, Suva, Malta, Calcutta; Counsellor, later Dep. Perm. Rep., UN, New York, 1974–77; Ambassador to Saudi Arabia (also concurrently to countries of Arabian peninsula), 1979–84; Head, S Asia, Africa and ME Br., Dept of Foreign Affairs, Canberra, 1984–87; Principal Advr, Asia Div., Dept of Foreign Affairs and Trade, Canberra, 1987–90. CStJ 1992. *Recreations:* opera, music, theatre. *Address:* Government House Cottage, Canberra, ACT 2600, Australia. *T:* (62) 833533.

STURROCK, Philip James; Chairman and Managing Director, Cassell, since 1986; *b* 5 Oct. 1947; *s* of James Cars Sturrock and Joyce Sturrock (*née* Knowles); *m* 1972, Susan Haycock; one *s* two *d*. *Educ:* Queen Mary's School, Walsall; Trinity College, Oxford (MA); Manchester Business School (MBA). Managing Director: IBIS Informatin Services, 1972–80; Pitman Books, 1980–83; Group Man. Dir, Routledge & Kegan Paul, 1983–85. Governor, Pusey House, Oxford, 1975–. FRSA 1992. Liveryman, Glaziers' Co., 1983–. *Recreations:* reading, walking, music. *Address:* 14, 11 Avenue Road, St Albans, Herts AL1 3QG. *T:* St Albans (01727) 832469. *Club:* Athenæum.

STUTTAFORD, Dr (Irving) Thomas; medical practitioner; *b* 4 May 1931; 2nd *s* of late Dr W. J. E. Stuttaford, MC, Horning, Norfolk and Mrs Marjorie Stuttaford (*née* Royden); *m* 1957, Pamela, *d* of late Col Richard Ropner, TD, DL, Tain; three *s*. *Educ:* Gresham's Sch.; Brasenose Coll., Oxford; West London Hosp. 2nd Lieut, 10th Royal Hussars (PWO), 1953–55; Lieut, Scottish Horse (TA), 1955–59. Qualif. MRCS, LRCP, 1959; junior hosp. appts, 1959 and 1960. Gen. Med. practice, 1960–70. Mem. Blofield and Flegg RDC, 1964–66; Mem., Norwich City Council, 1969–71. MP (C) Norwich S, 1970–Feb. 1974; Mem. Select Cttee Science and Technology, 1970–74. Contested (C) Isle of Ely, Oct. 1974, 1979. Physician, BUPA Medical Centre; Clinical Assistant to: The London Hosp., 1975–93; Queen Mary's Hosp. for East End, 1974–79; Moorfields Eye Hosp., 1975–79. Member: Council, Research Defence Soc., 1970–79; Birth Control Campaign Cttee, 1970–79; British Cancer Council, 1970–79. Medical Adviser: Rank Organisation, 1980–85; Barclays Bank, Standard Chartered Bank, Hogg Robinson, Rank Hotels and other cos; Medical Corresp. to The Times, 1982–91; medical columnist The Times; Contributor to: Elle, For Him, Oldie, Options, etc. *Recreation:* country life. *Address:* 123/4 Houghton St Giles, Walsingham, Norfolk NR22 6AQ. *T:* Walsingham (01328) 820947; 8 Devonshire Place, W1N 1PB. *T:* 0171–935 5011. *Clubs:* Athenæum, Reform, Cavalry and Guards, Beefsteak; Norfolk (Norwich).

See also Sir W. R. Stuttaford.

STUTTAFORD, Sir William Royden, Kt 1995; CBE 1989 (OBE 1983); Director, Invesco plc, since 1993; *b* 21 Nov. 1928; *s* of Dr William Joseph Edward Stuttaford and Mary Marjorie Dean Stuttaford; *m* 1st, 1958, Sarah Jane Legge; two *s* two *d*; 2nd, 1974, Susan d'Esterre Grahame (*née* Curteis). *Educ:* Gresham's Sch., Holt; Trinity Coll., Oxford (MA Nat. Scis). 2nd Lieut, 10th Royal Hussars (PWO), 1952–53. Mem. Stock Exchange, 1959–92; Chairman: Framlington Unit Management, 1974–87; Framlington Gp, 1983–89; Senior Partner, Laurence, Prust & Co., 1983–86. Director: Gen. Portfolio Gp, 1988–; Brown Shipley Hldgs, 1990–93; Towry Law, 1993–. Chm., Unit Trust Assoc., 1987–89. Chairman: Conservative Political Centre, 1978–81; Eastern Area Cons. Council, 1986–89; Pres., Nat. Union of Cons. and Unionist Assocs, 1994–95 (Jt Vice-Chm., 1991–94). *Address:* Moulshams Manor, Great Wigborough, Colchester, Essex CO5 7RL. *T:* Colchester (01206) 735330. *Club:* Cavalry and Guards.

See also I. T. Stuttaford.

STYLE, Lt-Comdr Sir Godfrey (William), Kt 1973; CBE 1961; DSC 1941; RN; Governor, Queen Elizabeth's Foundation, since 1975; Director, Star Centre for Youth, Cheltenham, since 1967; also Member of a number of allied advisory bodies and panels; an External Member of Lloyd's, since 1943; *b* 3 April 1915; *er s* of Brig.-Gen. R. C. Style (*y s* of Sir William Henry Marsham Style, 9th Bt), and Hélène Pauline, *d* of Herman Greverus Kleinwort; *m* 1st, 1942, Jill Elizabeth Caruth (marr. diss. 1951); one *s* two *d*; 2nd, 1951, Sigrid Elisabeth Julin (*née* Carlberg) (*d* 1985); one *s*; 3rd, 1986, Valerie Beauclerk (*née* Hulton-Sams), *widow* of W. D. McClure. *Educ:* Eton. Joined Royal Navy as a Regular Officer, 1933; served in Royal Yacht Victoria and Albert, 1938. Served War, Flag-Lieut to C-in-C, Home Fleet, 1939–41 (despatches, DSC, 1941); wounded, 1942, in Mediterranean); despatches, 1943; invalided from Royal Navy, due to war wounds and injuries, 1945. Dep. Underwriter at Lloyd's, 1945–55; Mem., National Advisory Council on Employment of Disabled People, 1944–74 (Chm., 1963–74). Mem. Council, Sir Oswald Stoll Foundn, 1975–84. *Recreations:* the field sports, horticulture, lapidary work. *Address:* 30 Carlyle Court, Chelsea Harbour, SW10 0UQ. T: 0171–352 6512. *Club:* Naval and Military.

STYLE, Sir William Frederick, 13th Bt *cr* 1627, of Wateringbury, Kent; *b* 13 May 1945; *s* of Sir William Montague Style, 12th Bt, and of La Verne, *d* of late T. M. Comstock; *S* father, 1981; *m* 1st, 1968, Wendy Gay (marr. diss. 1971), *d* of Gene Wittenberger, Hartford, Wisconsin, USA; two *d*; 2nd, 1986, Linnea Lorna, *d* of Donn Erickson, Sussex, Wisconsin, USA; two *d*. *Heir:* *b* Frederick Montague Style [*b* 5 Nov. 1947; *m* 1971, Sharon (marr. diss. 1988), *d* of William H. Kurz; two *d*].

STYLER, Granville Charles; His Honour Judge Styler; a Circuit Judge, since 1992; *b* 9 Jan. 1947; *s* of Samuel Charles Styler and Frances Joan Styler (*née* Clifford); *m* 1971, Penelope Darbyshire; three *d*. *Educ:* King Edward VI Sch., Stratford-on-Avon. Called to the Bar, Gray's Inn, 1970; a Recorder, 1988–92. *Recreations:* carriage driving, tennis, gardening, point to point racing. *Address:* c/o Courts Administrator's Office, Kemley House, 2 Victoria Road, Stafford ST16 2AE.

STYLES, (Frank) Showell, FRGS; author; *b* 14 March 1908; *s* of Frank Styles and Edith (*née* Showell); *m* 1954, Kathleen Jane Humphreys; one *s* two *d*. *Educ:* Bishop Vesey's Grammar Sch., Sutton Coldfield. Served Royal Navy, 1939; retd (Comdr), 1946. Professional author, 1946–76, retd. Led two private Arctic expedns, 1952–53; led private Himalayan expedn, 1954. FRGS 1954. *Publications:* 123 books: *travel*, incl. Mountains of the Midnight Sun, 1954; Blue Remembered Hills, 1965; *biography*, incl. Mr Nelson's Ladies, 1954; Mallory of Everest, 1967; *mountain guidebooks*, incl. The Mountains of North Wales, 1973; The Glyder Range, 1973; *instructional books*, incl. Modern Mountaineering, 1964; Introduction to Mountaineering, 1955; *naval historical fiction*, incl. Stella and the Fireships, 1985; The Lee Shore, 1986; Gun-brig Captain, 1987; HMS Cracker, 1988; Nelson's Midshipman, 1990; *children's fiction*, incl. Kami the Sherpa, 1957; The Shop in the Mountain, 1961; *detective fiction* (under *pen-name*, Glyn Carr), incl. Death under Snowdon, 1954; The Corpse in the Crevasse, 1957. *Recreations:* mountaineering, gardening, music. *Address:* Trwyn Cae Iago, Borth-y-Gest, Porthmadog, Gwynedd LL49

9TW. *T:* Porthmadog (01766) 2849. *Club:* Midland Association of Mountaineers (Birmingham).

STYLES, Fredrick William, BEM 1943; Director, Royal Arsenal Co-operative Society, 1968–84 (Chairman, 1975–79); *b* 18 Dec. 1914; *s* of Henry Albert Styles and Mabel Louise (*née* Sherwood); *m* 1942, Mary Gwendoline Harrison; one *s* three *d.* *Educ:* LCC elementary sch.; London Univ. (Dipl. economics); NCLC (Dipls Local and Central Govt). Salesman, Co-op, 1929–39. RAFVR Air Sea Rescue Service, 1939–46. Royal Humane Soc. Silver Medal, 1939; BEM for gallantry, 1943. Trade union official, NUPE (London divisional officer), 1946–52; social worker, hospital, 1952–58; social worker, LCC and GLC, 1958–68. Mem. Exec., 1973, Vice-Chm., 1974–79, Chm., 1979–80, Bexley and Greenwich AHA. Mem. for Greenwich, GLC, 1974–81; Mem., Greenwich Borough Council, 1971–78; Mem., 1971–81, Vice-Chm., 1974–75, Chm., 1975–76, ILEA; Chm. Staff and General Cttee, ILEA, 1977–81; Chm., ILEA schools, 1983–92 (Vice Chm., 1976–83): Nansen (partially sighted), now incorporated into Hawthorn Cottage (physically handicapped), and Rose Cottage (educationally sub-normal). Chm., Co-operative Metropolitan Industrial Relations Cttee, 1979–85 (Exec. Mem., 1970; Vice-Chm., 1973); first Chm., Heronsgate Community Centre, Thamesmead, 1982–92; Sen. Vice-Chm. 1986–, Chm., 1988–, Governors, Greenwich Univ. (formerly Thames Polytechnic); Chm. Governors, Avery Hill Teachers Trng Coll. (incorporated in Thames Polytechnic, 1986), 1971–86; Governor: Woolwich Coll., 1971–92 (Vice-Chm., 1983–92); Thameside Inst., 1971–92 (Vice Chm., 1983–87, Chm., 1987). DUniv Greenwich, 1994. *Recreations:* problems, people, pensioners, politics. *Address:* 49 Court Farm Road, Mottingham, SE9 4JN. *T:* 0181–857 1508.

STYLES, Lt-Col George; *see* Styles, Lt-Col S. G.

STYLES, Showell; *see* Styles, F. S.

STYLES, Lt-Col (Stephen) George, GC 1972; retired; company director, since 1974; *b* 16 March 1928; *s* of Stephen Styles and Grace Lily Styles (*née* Preston) *m* 1952, Mary Rose Styles (*née* Woolgar); one *s* two *d.* *Educ:* Collyers Sch., Horsham; Royal Military Coll. of Science. Ammunition Technical Officer, commissioned RAOC, Nov. 1947; seconded to 1 Bn KOYLI, 1949–51 (despatches, 1952); RMCS, 1952–56; HQ Ammunition Organisation, 1956–58; OC 28 Commonwealth Bde, Ordnance Field Park, Malaya, 1958–61; 2i/c 16 Bn RAOC, Bicester, 1961–64; OC Eastern Command Ammunition Inspectorate, 1964–67; Sen. Ammo Tech. Officer, 3 BAPD, BAOR, 1967–68; OC 1(BR) Corps Vehicle Company, 1968–69; Sen. Ammo Tech. Officer, Northern Ireland, 1969–72; Chief Ammo Tech. Officer (EOD), HQ DOS (CILSA), 1972–74. Member: Royal Soc. of St George, NRA, NSRA. *Publications:* Bombs Have No Pity, 1975; contrib. Proc. ICE, Jl of Forensic Science Soc. *Recreation:* rifle and game shooting, cartridge collector. *Address:* c/o Barclays Bank, Abingdon.

STYLES, Dr William McNeil, OBE 1995; FRCGP; Chairman, Royal College of General Practitioners, 1993–Nov. 1996; Principal in General Practice, since 1969; *b* 22 March 1941; *s* of Sydney James Styles and Mary McCallum Styles; *m* 1967, Jill Manderson; one *s* three *d.* *Educ:* City of Bath Boys' Sch.; St Catharine's Coll., Cambridge (MA); St Mary's Hosp. Med. Sch., London. MB, BChir. FRCGP 1980. Regl Advr in General Practice, NW Thames RHA, 1983–. Royal College of General Practitioners: Hon. Sec., 1983–89; Chm., Commn on Primary Care, 1992–. Hon. Sec., Jt Cttee on Postgrad. Trng for General Practice, 1984–93. Mem. Council, and Chm., GP Adv. Bd, Med. Protection Soc., 1990–. *Publications:* papers on medical educn for general practice. *Recreations:* reading, horse-riding, family. *Address:* The Grove Health Centre, 95 Goldhawk Road, W12 8EJ; 86 Park Road, Chiswick, W4 3HL. *T:* 0181–995 2952.

SUAREZ, Juan L.; *see* Lechin-Suarez.

SUBAK-SHARPE, Prof. John Herbert, CBE 1991; FRSE 1970; Professor Emeritus and Hon. Senior Research Fellow, University of Glasgow, since 1994 (Professor of Virology, 1968–94); Hon. Director, Medical Research Council Virology Unit, 1968–94; *b* 14 Feb. 1924; *s* of late Robert Subak and late Nelly (*née* Bruell), Vienna, Austria; *m* 1953, Barbara Naomi Morris; two *s* one *d.* *Educ:* Humanistic Gymnasium, Vienna; Univ. of Birmingham. BSc (Genetics) (1st Cl. Hons) 1952; PhD 1956. Refugee from Nazi oppression, 1939; farm pupil, 1939–44; HM Forces (Parachute Regt), 1944–47. Asst Lectr in Genetics, Glasgow Univ., 1954–56; Mem. scientific staff, ARC Animal Virus Research Inst., Pirbright, 1956–60; Nat. Foundn Fellow, California Inst. of Technology, 1961; Mem. Scientific staff of MRC, in Experimental Virus Research Unit, Glasgow, 1961–68. Visiting Professor: US Nat. Insts of Health, Bethesda, Md, 1967; US Univ. of Health Services, Bethesda, Md, 1985; Vis. Fellow, Clare Hall, Cambridge, 1986–87. Sec., Genetical Soc., 1966–72, Vice-Pres. 1972–75, Trustee 1971–. Member: European Molecular Biology Orgn, 1969– (Chm., Course and Workshops Cttee, 1976–78); Genetic Manipulation Adv. Gp, 1976–80; Biomed. Res. Cttee, SHHD Chief Scientist Orgn, 1979–84; British Nat. Cttee of Biophysics, 1970–76; Governing Body, W of Scotland Oncological Orgn, 1974–; Scientific Adv. Body, W German Cancer Res. Centre, 1977–82; Governing Body, Animal Virus Res. Inst., Pirbright, 1986–87; MRC Training Awards Panel, 1985–89 (Chm., 1986–89); Scientific Adv. Gp of Equine Virology Res. Foundn, 1987–; MRC Cell and Disorders Bd, 1988–92. CIBA Medal, Biochem. Soc., 1993. *Publications:* articles in scientific jls on genetic studies with viruses and cells. *Recreations:* travel, hill walking, bridge. *Address:* 63 Kelvin Court, Glasgow G12 0AG. *T:* 0141–334 1863. *Club:* Athenæum.

SUBBA ROW, Raman, CBE 1991; Chairman, Test and County Cricket Board, 1985–90; *b* 29 Jan. 1932; *s* of Panguluri Venkata Subba Row and Doris Mildred Subba Row; *m* 1960, Anne Dorothy (*née* Harrison); two *s* one *d.* *Educ:* Whitgift Sch., Croydon; Trinity Hall, Cambridge (MA Hons). Associate Dir, W. S. Crawford Ltd, 1963–69; Man. Dir, Management Public Relations Ltd, 1969–92. *Recreation:* golf. *Address:* Leeward, Manor Way, South Croydon, Surrey CR2 7BT. *T:* 0181–688 2991. *Clubs:* Royal Air Force, Institute of Directors, MCC, Surrey County Cricket; Addington Golf; Cricket of India (Bombay); Kingston Cricket (Jamaica).

SUBRAMANIAM, Chidambaram; Chairman, Rajaji International Institute of Public Affairs and Administration, since 1980; President, Madras Voluntary Health Services, since 1987; Governor of Maharashtra, Bombay, 1990–93; *b* 30 Jan. 1910; *s* of Chidambara Gounder and Valliammal; *m* 1945, Sakuntala; one *s* two *d.* *Educ:* Madras (BA, LLB). Set up legal practice, Coimbatore, 1936; took active part in freedom movt, imprisoned 1932, 1941 and again 1942; Pres., District Congress Committee, Coimbatore; Mem. Working Cttee of State Congress Cttee; Mem. Constituent Assembly; Minister of Finance, Educn and Law, Govt of Madras, 1952; MP 1962; Minister of Steel, 1962–63; Minister of Steel, Mines and Heavy Engrg, 1963–64; Minister of Food and Agric., 1964–66; Minister of Food and Agriculture, CD and Coopn, 1966–67; Chm. Cttee on Aeronautics Industry, 1967–69; Interim Pres., Indian Nat. Congress, July-Dec. 1969; Chm. Nat. Commn on Agric., 1970; Minister of Planning and Dep. Chm., Planning Commn, 1971; also i/c Dept of Science and Technology; Minister of Industrial Develt and Science and Technology, 1972 (also Agric., temp., 1974); Minister of Finance, 1974–77; Minister of Defence, 1979. Hon. Pres., Internat. Inst. of Public Enterprises, Ljubljana, 1985–87; Pres., Bharatiya Vidya Bhavan, Bombay, 1985–. Hon. DLitt: Wattair; Sri Venkateswara; Madurai; Madras; Annamalai; Hon. LLD Andhra. Jawaharlal Nehru Award, 1991. *Publications:* Nan Sendra Sila Nadugal (travelogues), 1961; War on Poverty, 1963; Ulagam Sutrinen (in Tamil); India of My Dreams (in English), 1972; Strategy Statement for Fighting Protein Hunger in Developing Countries; The New Strategy in Indian Agriculture, 1979; Hand of Destiny (memoirs): vol. 1, The Turning Point, 1993, vol. 2, The Green Revolution, 1995. *Recreation:* yoga. *Address:* River View, Kotturpuram, Madras 600085, India. *T:* (44) 414208. *Clubs:* Cosmopolitan, Gymkhana (Madras); Cosmopolitan (Coimbatore).

SUCH, Frederick Rudolph Charles; a Recorder of the Crown Court, since 1979; *b* 19 June 1936; *s* of Frederick Sidney Such and Anne Marie Louise (*née* Martin); *m* 1961, Elizabeth, *d* of late Judge Norman and Mrs Harper, Cloughton, Yorkshire; one *s* one *d.* *Educ:* Mbeya Sch., Tanganyika Territory, E Africa (Tanzania); Taunton Sch.; Keble Coll., Oxford (MA). Called to the Bar, Gray's Inn, 1960; practised: London, 1960–69, then North Eastern Circuit, 1969–. *Recreations:* theatre, opera, hockey, squash, tennis. *Address:* The Rift Barns, Wylam, Northumberland NE41 8BL. *T:* Wylam (01661) 852763. *Club:* Northern Counties (Newcastle upon Tyne).

SUCHET, David; actor; associate artiste, Royal Shakespeare Co.; *b* 2 May 1946; *s* of Jack and late Joan Suchet; *m* 1976, Sheila Ferris, actress; one *s* one *d.* *Educ:* Wellington Sch.; LAMDA (Best Drama Student, 1968). *Stage:* repertory theatres, incl. Chester, Birmingham, Exeter, Worthing, Coventry, 1969–73; for Royal Shakespeare Co.: Romeo and Juliet (Mercutio and Tybalt), As You Like It (Orlando), Once in a Lifetime (Glogauer), Measure for Measure (Angelo), The Tempest (Caliban), King Lear, King John, Merchant of Venice (Shylock), Troilus and Cressida (Achilles), Richard II (Bolingbroke), Every Good Boy Deserves Favour, 1983, Othello (Iago), 1986, Timon of Athens (title rôle), 1991; Separation, Comedy, 1988; Oleanna, Royal Court, 1993 (Variety Club Award for Best Actor, 1994); *films include:* Falcon and the Snowman, 1983; Thirteen at Dinner, 1985; Song for Europe, 1985; Harry and the Hendersons, 1986; When the Whales came, 1990; serials and series for *television:* Oppenheimer, 1978; Reilly, 1981; Saigon, 1982; Freud, 1983; Blott on the Landscape, 1984; Oxbridge Blues, 1984; Playing Shakespeare, 1985; Great Writers, 1988; Agatha Christie's Hercule Poirot, 1989, 1991, 1992, 1993; The Secret Agent, 1992; numerous radio parts. Mem. Council, LAMDA, 1985–. Lectr, US Univs; Vis. Prof., Univ. of Nebraska, 1975. Numerous awards, incl. Best Actor, RTS, 1986. *Publications:* (contrib.) Players of Shakespeare, 2 vols, 1985 and 1988; essays on interpretation of roles. *Recreations:* clarinet, photography, reading, ornithology, theology. *Address:* c/o ICM Ltd, Oxford House, 76 Oxford Street, W1N 0AX.

See also J. A. Suchet.

SUCHET, John Aleck; television journalist, Independent Television News, since 1972; *b* 29 March 1944; *s* of Jack and late Joan Suchet; *m* 1st, 1968, Moya Hankinson (marr. diss. 1985); three *s*; 2nd, 1985, Bonnie Simonson. *Educ:* Uppingham; Univ. of St Andrews (MA Hons). Reuters News Agency, 1967–71; BBC TV News, 1971–72; Independent Television News, 1972–: reporter, 1976–86; Washington corresp., 1981–83; newscaster, 1986–. TV Journalist of the Year, RTS, 1986. *Publication:* TV News: the inside story, 1989. *Recreations:* classical music, photography. *Address:* ITN, 200 Gray's Inn Road, WC1X 8XZ. *T:* 0171–833 3000.

See also D. Suchet.

SUCKLING, Dr Charles Walter, CBE 1989; FRS 1978; FRSC; *b* 24 July 1920; *s* of Edward Ernest and Barbara Suckling (*née* Thomson); *m* 1946, (Eleanor) Margaret Watterson; two *s* one *d.* *Educ:* Oldershaw Grammar Sch., Wallasey; Liverpool Univ. (BSc, PhD). ICI: joined Gen. Chemicals Div., 1942; R&D Director, Mond Div., 1967; Dep. Chairman, Mond Div., 1969; Chairman, Paints Div., 1972; Gen. Man., Res. and Technol., 1977–82; Chm., Bradbury, Suckling and Partners, 1982–93; Dir, Albright and Wilson, 1982–89. Hon. Vis. Prof., Univ. of Stirling, 1968–93. Member: BBC Science Consultative Gp, 1980–85; Royal Commn on Environmental Pollution, 1982–92; Electricity Supply Res. Council, 1983–90; ABRC/NERC Gp into Geol Surveying, 1985–87; Cttee of Inquiry into Teaching of English Language, 1987–88; Nat. Curriculum English Working Gp, 1988–89; Nat. Curriculum Mod. For. Langs Wkg Gp, 1989–90; Council, RCA, 1981–90 (Treasurer, 1984–90); Chm., Roy. Soc. Study Gp on Pollution Control Priorities, 1988–92; Mem., Nat. Adv. Gp on Eco-labelling, 1990–92. Bicentennial Lecture, Washington Coll., Maryland, 1981; Robbins Lecture, Stirling Univ., 1990; Joseph Clover Lecture, Royal Coll. of Anaesthetists, 1994. Senior Fellow, RCA, 1986. Hon. DSc Liverpool, 1980; DUniv Stirling, 1985. Liverpool Univ. Chem. Soc. Medal, 1964; John Scott Medal, City of Philadelphia, 1973; Medal, Royal Coll. of Anaesthetists, 1992. *Publications:* (with A. Baines and F. R. Bradbury) Research in the Chemical Industry, 1969; (with C. J. Suckling and K. E. Suckling) Chemistry through Models, 1978; papers on anaesthetics, industrial research and strategy in journals. *Recreations:* music, gardening, languages, writing. *Address:* 1 Desborough Drive, Tewin, Welwyn, Herts AL6 0HQ. *T:* Bulls Green (01438) 798250.

SUCKSDORFF, Mrs Åke; *see* Jonzen, Mrs Karin.

SUDBURY, Archdeacon of; *see* Cox, Ven. J. S.

SUDDABY, Arthur, CBE 1980; PhD, MSc; CChem, FRSC; CEng, MIChemE; scientific consultant on the carriage of goods by sea, until 1990; Provost, City of London Polytechnic, 1970–81; *b* 26 Feb. 1919; *e s* of George Suddaby, Kingston-upon-Hull, Yorks; *m* 1944, Elizabeth Bullin Vyse (decd), *d* of Charles Vyse; two *s.* *Educ:* Riley High Sch., Kingston-upon-Hull; Hull Technical Coll.; Chelsea Polytechnic; Queen Mary Coll. London. Chemist and Chemical Engr, in industry, 1937–47; Lectr in Physical Chemistry, and later Sen. Lectr in Chem. Engrg, West Ham Coll. of Technology, 1947–50; Sir John Cass Coll.: Sen. Lectr in Physics, 1950–61; Head of Dept of Physics, 1961–66; Principal, 1966–70. Chm., Cttee of Directors of Polytechnics, 1976–78; Member: Chem. Engrg Cttee, 1948–51; London and Home Counties Regional Adv. Council, 1971–; Bd of Examrs and Educn Cttee, Inst. of Chem. Engrs, 1948–51; CNAA: Chem. Engrg Bd, 1969–75; Nautical Studies Bd, 1972–75; Chm., Standing Conf. of Approved Coll. Res. Deg. Cttees, 1979–81; Court of the City University, 1967–81; Vis. Cttee, Cranfield Inst. of Technology, 1979–85; Chm., Assoc. of Navigation Schs, 1972. *Publications:* various original research papers in theoretical physics, in scientific jls; review articles. *Recreations:* country sports, music. *Address:* Flat 3, 16 Elm Park Gardens, Chelsea, SW10 9NY. *T:* 0171–352 9164; Castle Hill House, Godshill Wood, near Fordingbridge, Hants SP6 2LU. *T:* Fordingbridge (01425) 652234. *Club:* Athenæum.

SUDDARDS, Roger Whitley, CBE 1987; DL; Consultant, Hammond Suddards, solicitors, 1988–95; Chairman, Hammond Suddards Research Ltd, 1989–94; *b* 5 June 1930; *s* of John Whitley Suddards, OBE and Jean Suddards (*née* Rollitt); *m* 1963, Elizabeth Anne Rayner; two *d.* *Educ:* Bradford Grammar Sch. Admitted solicitor, 1952; Sen. Partner, Last Suddards, 1952–88; Dir, Yorkshire BS, 1985–95 (Chm., 1988–91). Vis. Lectr, Leeds Sch. of Town Planning, 1964–74; Planning Law Consultant: to UN, 1974–77; to Govt of Mauritius, 1981–82 and 1989–94. Former Chairman: Examinations Bd, ISVA; Adv. Cttee for Land Commn for Yorks and Humberside; Chm., Working Party on Future of Bradford

Churches, 1978–79. Member: Law Society Bye-Laws Revision Cttee, 1984–87; Law Society Planning Law Cttee, 1964–81; Pres., Bradford Law Soc., 1969; Legal Mem., RTPI (Hon. Solr and Hon. Sec., 1991–95). Sec., Hand Knitting Assoc., 1958–75. Chm., Bradford Disaster Appeal Trust, 1985–89. Mem. Cttee, Nat. Mus. Photography, Film and TV, 1984–; Comr, English Heritage, 1992–95; Dir, Mus. Trng Inst. (Dep. Chm., 1987–93); Member: W Yorks Residuary Body, 1986–89; Civic Trust, 1988–. Chm., Educn Assets Bd, 1994–. Pro-Chancellor, 1987–93, and Chm. of Council, 1987–93, Bradford Univ. Mem. of Bd, 1979–86, Vice Chm. and Chm, 1985–88, Bradford Grammar Sch. Hon. FSVA. DL W Yorks, 1990. Hon. LLD Bradford, 1993. *Publications:* Town Planning Law of West Indies, 1974; History of Bradford Law Society, 1975; Listed Buildings, 1982, 3rd edn 1995; A Lawyer's Peregrination, 1984, 2nd edn 1987; Bradford Disaster Appeal, 1986; articles in Jl of Planning and Environmental Law, and Law Society Gazette. *Recreations:* theatre, music, reading, travel. *Address:* Low House, High Eldwick, Bingley, West Yorks BD16 3AZ. *T:* Bradford (01274) 564832, 532233. *Clubs:* Arts; Bradford (Bradford).

SUDELEY, 7th Baron *cr* 1838; **Merlin Charles Sainthill Hanbury-Tracy,** FSA; *b* 17 June 1939; *o c* of late Captain Michael David Charles Hanbury-Tracy, Scots Guards, and Colline Ammabel (*d* 1985), *d* of late Lt-Col C. G. H. St Hill and *widow* of Lt-Col Frank King, DSO, OBE; *S* cousin, 1941; *m* 1980, Hon. Mrs Elizabeth Villiers (marr. diss. 1988), *d* of late Viscount Bury (*s* of 9th Earl of Albemarle). *Educ:* at Eton and in the ranks of the Scots Guards. Chm., Monday Club; Vice-Chancellor, Monarchist League. Patron: Assoc. of Bankrupts; Anglican Assoc.; Lay Patron, Prayer Book Soc. *Publications:* (jtly) The Sudeleys—Lords of Toddington, 1987; (contrib.) The House of Lords: a thousand years of British tradition, 1994; contribs to Quarterly Review, Contemporary Review, Family History, Trans of Bristol and Gloucestershire Archaeol. Soc., Montgomeryshire Collections, Bull. of Manorial Soc., Die Waage (Zeitschrift der Chemie Grünenthal), Monday Club Jl. *Recreations:* ancestor worship; cultivating his sensibility. *Heir: kinsman* Desmond Andrew John Hanbury-Tracy [*b* 30 Nov. 1928; *m* 1st, 1957, Jennifer Lynn (marr. diss. 1966), *d* of Dr R. C. Hodges; one *s*; 2nd, 1967, Lillian, *d* of Nathaniel Laurie; one *s*; 3rd, 1988, Mrs Margaret Cecilia White, *d* of late Alfred Henry Marmaduke Purse]. *Address:* 25 Melcombe Court, Dorset Square, NW1 6EP. *Club:* Brooks's.

SUENENS, His Eminence Cardinal Leo Joseph, DTheol, DPhil; Cardinal since 1962; Archbishop of Malines-Brussels and Primate of Belgium, 1961–79; *b* Ixelles (Brussels), 16 July 1904. *Educ:* primary sch., Inst. of Marist Brothers, Brussels; secondary sch., St Mary's High Sch., Brussels; Gregorian Univ., Rome (BCL, DPhil, DrTheol). Priest, 1927; Teacher, St Mary's High Sch., Brussels, 1929; Prof. of Philosophy, Diocesan Seminary, Malines, 1930; Vice-Rector, Cath. Univ. of Louvain, 1940; Vicar-Gen., Archdio. of Malines, 1945; Auxiliary Bp to Archbp of Malines, 1945. Moderator of Second Vatican Council, 1962–65; Pres., Belgian Bishops' Conf.; Internat. Pastoral Delegate for Catholic Charismatic Renewal. Templeton Prize for Religion, 1976. *Publications:* L'Eglise en état de mission, 1955, 4th edn 1957; Théologie de l'apostolat de la Légion de Marie, 1954, 7th edn 1957 (Theology of the Apostolate of the Legion of Mary, 1951); Une héroïne de l'apostolat: Edel Quinn, 1952, 4th edn 1954 (English trans. 1952); Que faut-il penser du Réarmement moral?, 1953 (The Right View on Moral Rearmament, 1953); (ed) The Gospel to Every Creature, 1955; La Question scolaire, 1956; Quelle est Celle-ci?, 1957; (ed) Mary the Mother of God, 1957; Un problème crucial: amour et maîtrise de soi, 5th edn 1959 (Love and Control, 1961); Vie quotidienne, vie chrétienne, 2nd edn 1962 (Christian Life Day by Day, 1961); La Promotion apostolique de la religieuse, 1962 (The Nun in the World, 1962); The Church in Dialogue, 1965; La Coresponsabilité dans l'Eglise d'aujourd'hui, 1968 (Co-responsibility in the Church, 1968); (ed with Archbishop Ramsey) L'Avenir de l'Eglise, 1971 (The Future of the Christian Church, 1971); Une nouvelle Pentecôte, 1974 (A New Pentecost?, 1975); Ways of the Spirit, 1976; (with Archbishop Ramsey) Come Holy Spirit, 1976; Essays on Renewal, 1976; Your God?, 1978; Pour l'Eglise de demain, 1979; Open the Frontiers, 1980; La Promesse légionnaire, 1982; Renewal and the Powers of Darkness, 1982; Nature and Grace, 1986; Itinéraire spirituel, 1990 (Spiritual Journey, 1990); Souvenirs et Espérances, 1991 (Memories and Hopes, 1992); Les Imprévus du Dieu, 1993. *Address:* Boulevard de Smet de Mayer 570, 1020 Bruxelles, Belgium. *T:* (2) 4791950.

SUENSON-TAYLOR, family name of **Baron Grantchester.**

SUFFIAN, Tun Mohamed, SSM 1975 (PSM 1967); SPCM 1978; SPMK 1989; DIMP 1969; JMN 1961; SMB 1959; PJK 1963; Judge, Administrative Tribunal, World Bank, Washington DC, 1985–94; Vice President, International Labour Organisation Administrative Tribunal, Geneva, 1987–92 (Judge, 1986–87); *b* 12 Nov. 1917; *s* of late Haji Mohamed Hashim and Zaharah binti Ibrahim; *m* 1946, Dora Evelina Grange. *Educ:* Gonville and Caius Coll., Cambridge (MA Hons, LLM); SOAS; LSE. Called to the Bar, Middle Temple, 1941 (Hon. Bencher, 1984). All India Radio, New Delhi, 1942–45; BBC, London, 1945–46; Malayan Civil Service, 1948; Malayan Judicial and Legal Service, 1949–61; Solicitor General, 1959; High Court Judge, 1961; Federal Judge, 1968; Chief Justice of Malaya, 1973; Lord Pres., Federal Court, 1974–82. Advr, Standard Chartered Bank in Malaysia, 1982–90. Pro-Chancellor, Univ. of Malaya, 1963–86. President: Commonwealth Magistrates Assoc., 1979–85; Asean Law Assoc., 1982–84. Pres., Malaysian Br., Royal Asiatic Soc., 1978–92. Fellow, Univ. Coll. at Buckingham, 1979. Hon. LLD: Singapore, 1975; Buckingham, 1983; Hon. DLitt Malaya, 1975; DUniv Murdoch, WA, 1988. Ramon Magsaysay Foundn Award for Government Service, 1975. *Publications:* Malayan Constitution (official trans.), 1963; An Introduction to the Constitution of Malaysia, 1972, 2nd edn 1976; (ed jtly) The Constitution of Malaysia: its development 1957–1977, 1978; Introduction to the Legal System of Malaysia, 1987, 2nd edn 1989. *Recreations:* gardening, swimming, reading. *Address:* Suite 1B, Bangunan Dato Zainal, 23 Jalan Melaka, 50100 Kuala Lumpur, Malaysia. *T:* (3) 2920527, *Fax:* (3) 2987237. *Clubs:* Lake, Bankers' (Kuala Lumpur).

SUFFIELD, 11th Baron *cr* 1786; **Anthony Philip Harbord-Hamond,** Bt, *cr* 1745; MC 1950; Major, retired, 1961; *b* 19 June 1922; *o s* of 10th Baron and Nina Annette Mary Crawfuird (*d* 1955), *e d* of John Hutchison of Laurieston and Edingham, Stewartry of Kirkcudbright; *S* father 1951; *m* 1952, Elizabeth Eve (*d* 1995), *er d* of late Judge Edgedale; three *s* one *d*. *Educ:* Eton. Commission, Coldstream Guards, 1942; served War of 1939–45, in North African and Italian campaigns, 1942–45; Malaya, 1948–50. One of HM Hon. Corps of Gentlemen-at-Arms, 1973–92 (Harbinger, 1990–92). *Recreations:* normal. *Heir: s* Hon. Charles Anthony Assheton Harbord-Hamond [*b* 3 Dec. 1953; *m* 1983, Lucy (marr. diss. 1990), *yr d* of Comdr A. S. Hutchinson. Commissioned Coldstream Guards, 1972, RARO 1979]. *Address:* Gardeners Cottage, Gunton Park, Hanworth, Norfolk NR11 7HL. *T:* Cromer (01263) 768423. *Clubs:* Army and Navy, Pratt's.

SUFFIELD, Sir (Henry John) Lester, Kt 1973; Head of Defence Sales, Ministry of Defence, 1969–76; *b* 28 April 1911; *m* 1940, Elizabeth Mary White (*d* 1985); one *s* one *d*. *Educ:* Camberwell Central, LCC. Served with RASC, 1939–45 (Major). LNER, 1926–35; Morris Motors, 1935–38 and 1945–52; Pres., British Motor Corp., Canada and USA, 1952–64; Dep. Man. Dir, British Motor Corp., Birmingham, 1964–68; Sales Dir, British Leyland Motor Corp., 1968–69. Freeman of City of London, 1978; Liveryman, Coachmakers and Coach Harness Makers Co. *Recreation:* golf. *Address:* 16 Glebe Court, Fleet, Hants GU13 8NJ. *T:* Fleet (01252) 616861. *Clubs:* Royal Automobile; Royal Wimbledon Golf.

SUFFOLK AND BERKSHIRE, 21st Earl of, *cr* 1603; **Michael John James George Robert Howard;** Viscount Andover and Baron Howard, 1622; Earl of Berkshire, 1626; *b* 27 March 1935; *s* of 20th Earl (killed by enemy action, 1941) and Mimi (*d* 1966), *yr d* of late A. G. Forde Pigott; *S* father 1941; *m* 1st, 1960, Mme Simone Paulmier (marr. diss. 1967), *d* of late Georges Litman, Paris; (one *d* decd); 2nd, 1973, Anita (marr. diss. 1980), *d* of R. R. Fuglesang, Haywards Heath, Sussex; one *s* one *d*; 3rd, 1983, Linda Viscountess Bridport; two *d*. Owns 5,000 acres. *Heir: s* Viscount Andover, *qv*. *Address:* Charlton Park, Malmesbury, Wilts SN16 9DG.

SUFFOLK, Archdeacon of; *see* Arrand, Ven. G. W.

SUGAR, Alan Michael; Chairman, Amstrad plc, since 1968; *b* 24 March 1947; *s* of Nathan and Fay Sugar; *m* 1968, Ann Simons; two *s* one *d*. *Educ:* Brooke House School, London. Chm. of Amstrad since formation in 1968. Chm., Tottenham Hotspur plc, 1991–. Hon. DSc City, 1988. *Recreation:* tennis. *Address:* 169 King's Road, Brentwood, Essex CM14 4EF. *T:* Brentwood (01277) 228888.

SUGDEN, Sir Arthur, Kt 1978; Chief Executive Officer, Co-operative Wholesale Society Ltd, 1974–80; Chairman: Co-operative Bank Ltd, 1974–80; Co-operative Commercial Bank Ltd, 1974–80; *b* 12 Sept. 1918; *s* of late Arthur and Elizabeth Ann Sugden; *m* 1946, Agnes Grayston; two *s*. *Educ:* Thomas Street, Manchester. Certified Accountant, Chartered Secretary. FIB 1975. Served War of 1939–45, Royal Artillery; CPO 6th Super Heavy Battery; Adjt 12th Medium Regt; Staff Captain 16th Army Group. CWS Ltd: Accountancy Asst, 1946; Office Man., 1950; Factory Man., 1954; Group Man., Edible Oils and Fats Factories, 1964; Controller, Food Div., 1967; Dep. Chief Exec. Officer, 1971. Chairman, 1974–80: FC Finance Ltd; CWS (Longburn) Ltd; CWS (New Zealand) Holdings Ltd; CWS Marketing Ltd; CWS (India) Ltd; Ocean Beach Freezing Co. Ltd; Shaw's Smokers' Products Ltd; Former Director: Co-operative City Investments Ltd; Co-operative Pension Funds Unit Trust Managers' Ltd; Associated Co-operative Creameries Ltd; CWS Svineslagterier A/S Denmark; CWS (Overseas) Ltd; Tukuyu Tea Estates Ltd; Spillers French Holdings Ltd; J. W. French (Milling & Baking Holdings) Ltd; North Eastern Co-operative Soc. Ltd; Manchester Ship Canal Ltd, 1978–87; Manchester Chamber of Commerce. Former Vice-President: Inst. of Bankers; Inst. of Grocery Distribution Ltd. Member: Central Cttee, Internat. Co-operative Alliance; Management Bds, Euro-Coop and Inter-Coop (Pres., 1979–80). Pres., Co-operative Congress, 1978. CIMgt; FIGD. *Recreations:* music, reading, walking. *Address:* 56 Old Wool Lane, Cheadle Hulme, Cheadle, Cheshire SK8 5JA.

SUGDEN, Maj.-Gen. Francis George, CB 1991; CBE 1989 (OBE 1980); Lieutenant Governor and Secretary, Royal Hospital, Chelsea, since 1992; *b* IOM, 27 July 1938; *s* of Maj.-Gen. Sir Henry H. C. Sugden, KBE, CB, DSO and Joan Morgan Sugden (*née* Francis); *m* 1964, Elizabeth Blackburn Bradbury; two *s* one *d*. *Educ:* Wellington Coll. Commnd RE, 1958; service on Christmas Is, in England and Germany; sc 1970; GSO2 Defence Secretariat 6, MoD, 1971–72; OC 4 Field Sqn RE, BAOR, 1973–74; GSO2 RE HQ 1 (BR) Corps, 1974–77; GSO1 Staff of CDS, MoD, 1977–78; CO 22 Engr Regt, UK and Rhodesia, 1978–80; Col GS HQ 1 (BR) Corps, 1980–83; RCDS, 1984; Comdr Engr HQ 1 (BR) Corps and Comdr Hameln Garrison, 1985–86; GS Dir, MoD, 1986–89; COS, HQ BAOR, 1989–91. Chm., Management Cttee, Royal Homes for Officers' Widows and Daughters, 1994–. Zimbabwe Independence Medal, 1980. *Recreations:* golf, gardening, ski-ing.

SUGDEN, John Goldthorp, MA; ARCM; Headmaster, Wellingborough School, 1965–73; *b* 22 July 1921; *s* of A. G. Sugden, Brighouse, Yorkshire; *m* 1954, Jane Machin; two *s*. *Educ:* Radley; Magdalene College, Cambridge. War Service, Royal Signals, 1941–46. Asst Master, Bilton Grange Prep. School, 1948–52; Asst Master, The King's School, Canterbury, 1952–59; Headmaster, Foster's School, Sherborne, 1959–64. *Publication:* Niccolo Paganini, 1980. *Recreations:* music, golf. *Address:* Woodlands, 2 Linksview Avenue, Parkstone, Poole, Dorset BH14 9QT. *T:* Parkstone (01202) 707497.

SUGG, Aldhelm St John, CMG 1963; retired as Provincial Commissioner, Southern Province of Northern Rhodesia, August 1963; *b* 21 Oct. 1909; *s* of H. G. St J. Sugg; *m* 1935, Jessie May Parker (*d* 1994); one *s* one *d*. *Educ:* Colchester Royal Grammar School. Palestine Police, 1930–31; Northern Rhodesia Police, 1932–43; Colonial Administrative Service, in N Rhodesia, 1943–63. Retired to England, 1963. *Recreations:* sailing, field sports. *Address:* Bushbury, Blackboys, Uckfield, East Sussex TN22 5JE. *T:* Framfield (01825) 890282. *Club:* Commonwealth Trust.

SUHARTO, Gen.; *see* Soeharto.

SUIRDALE, Viscount; John Michael James Hely Hutchinson; company director since 1981; *b* 7 Aug. 1952; *s* and *heir* of 8th Earl of Donoughmore, *qv*; *m* 1976, Marie-Claire Carola Etienne van den Driessche; one *s* two *d*. *Educ:* Harrow. *Recreations:* golf, fishing, etc. *Heir: s* Hon. Richard Gregory Hely-Hutchinson, *b* 3 July 1980. *Address:* 38 Thornton Avenue, Chiswick W4 1QG.

See also Hon. T. M. Hely Hutchinson.

SULLIVAN, David Douglas Hooper, QC 1975; author and historian; *b* 10 April 1926; *s* of Michael and Maude Sullivan; *m* 1st, 1951, Sheila, *d* of Henry and Georgina Bathurst; three *d*; 2nd, 1981, Ann Munro, *d* of Malcolm and Eva Betten. *Educ:* Haileybury (schol.); Christ Church, Oxford (schol.). MA 1949, BCL 1951. Served War, with RNVR (Sub-Lieut), 1944–46. Called to Bar, Inner Temple, 1951, Bencher, 1984, retired 1988. Mem., Central Policy Cttee, Mental Health Act Commn, 1983–86. Author of various plays and media programmes, including: radio: Shadows are Realities to me; A right-royal Burglary; Straw and Steel; stage: John Constable and Maria. *Publication:* The Westminster Corridor, 1994. *Recreations:* painting, medieval history. *Address:* Well Mount Cottage, Well Road, NW3 1LJ. *T:* 0171–431 3433.

SULLIVAN, Sir Desmond (John), Kt 1985; Chief District Court Judge, New Zealand, 1979–85, retired; Member, Treaty of Waitangi Tribunal, since 1986; *b* 3 March 1920; *s* of Patrick James Sullivan and Annie Sullivan; *m* 1947, Phyllis Maude Mahon; two *s* four *d* (and one *s* decd). *Educ:* Timaru Marist; Timaru Boys' High Sch.; Canterbury Univ. (LLB). Served NZ Army and Navy, 1940–45. Barrister and solicitor: Westport, 1949–59; Palmerston North, 1960–66; Stipendiary Magistrate, Wellington, 1966–79. Member, Westport Bor. Council, 1955–59; Chairman: NZ Council for Recreation and Sport, 1973–76; Film Industry Board, 1962–85. *Publication:* (jtly) Violence in the Community, 1975. *Recreations:* golf, swimming, reading. *Address:* 208 Whites Line East, Lower Hutt, New Zealand. *T:* (4) 5695440.

SULLIVAN, Prof. (Donovan) Michael; Professor of Oriental Art, 1966–85, Christensen Professor, 1975–85, Stanford University, California; Fellow, St Catherine's College, Oxford, 1979–90, now Emeritus Fellow; *b* 29 Oct. 1916; *s* of Alan Sullivan and Elisabeth

Hees; *m* 1943, Khoan, *d* of Ngo Eng-lim, Kulangsu, Amoy, China; no *c*. *Educ:* Rugby School; Corpus Christi College, Cambridge (MA); Univ. of London (BA Hons); Harvard Univ. (PhD); LittD Cambridge, 1966; MA, DLitt Oxon, 1973. Chinese Govt Scholarship, Univ. of London, 1947–50; Rockefeller Foundn Travelling Fellowship in USA, 1950–51; Bollingen Foundn Research Fellowship, 1952–54; Curator of Art Museum and Lectr in the History of Art, Univ. of Malaya (now Univ. of Singapore), Singapore, 1954–60; Lectr in Asian Art, Sch. of Oriental and African Studies, Univ. of London, 1960–66. Vis. Prof. of Far Eastern Art, Univ. of Michigan (Spring Semester), 1964; Slade Prof. of Fine Art, Oxford Univ., 1973–74, Cambridge Univ., 1983–84; Guggenheim Foundn Fellowship, 1974; Vis. Fellow, St Antony's Coll., Oxford, 1976–77; Nat. Endowment for the Humanities Fellowship, 1976–77; Professorial Fellow, Corpus Christi Coll., Cambridge, 1983–84; Vis. Fellow, Humanities Centre, ANU, 1987. Fellow, Amer. Acad. of Arts and Sciences, 1977. *Publications:* Chinese Art in the Twentieth Century, 1959; An Introduction to Chinese Art, 1961; The Birth of Landscape Painting in China, 1962; Chinese Ceramics, Bronzes and Jades in the Collection of Sir Alan and Lady Barlow, 1963; Chinese and Japanese Art, 1965; A Short History of Chinese Art, 1967, 3rd edn as The Arts of China, 1973, rev. edns 1977, 1984, 1986; The Cave Temples of Maichishan, 1969; The Meeting of Eastern and Western Art, 1973, rev. and expanded edn 1989; Chinese Art: recent discoveries, 1973; The Three Perfections, 1975; Chinese Landscape Painting, vol. II, The Sui and T'ang Dynasties, 1979; Symbols of Eternity: the art of landscape painting in China, 1979; Studies in the Art of China and South-East Asia, vol. 1, 1991, vol. 2, 1992; contrib. to learned journals, Encyclopedia Britannica, Chambers's Encyclopædia, etc. *Address:* St Catherine's College, Oxford OX1 3UJ.

SULLIVAN, Edmund Wendell, FRCVS; Chief Veterinary Officer, Department of Agriculture for Northern Ireland, 1983–90; *b* 21 March 1925; *s* of Thomas Llewellyn Sullivan and Letitia Sullivan; *m* 1957, Elinor Wilson Melville; two *s* one *d*. *Educ:* Portadown College; Queen's University, Belfast; Royal (Dick) Veterinary College. MRCVS 1947, FRCVS 1991. General Veterinary Practice, Appleby, Westmoreland, 1947; joined staff of State Veterinary Service, Dept. of Agriculture for N Ireland, 1948; Headquarters staff, 1966–90. *Recreations:* hill walking, wood craft, following rugby and cricket. *Address:* Kinfauns, 26 Dillon's Avenue, Newtownabbey, Co. Antrim BT37 0SX. *T:* Belfast (01232) 862323.

SULLIVAN, Jeremy Mirth; QC 1982; a Recorder, since 1989; a Deputy High Court Judge, since 1993; Attorney General to the Prince of Wales, since 1994; *b* 17 Sept. 1945; *s* of late Arthur Brian and of Pamela Jean Sullivan; *m* 1st, 1970, Ursula Klara Marie Hildenbrock (marr. diss. 1993); two *s*; 2nd, 1993, Dr Sandra Jean Farmer. *Educ:* Framlingham Coll.; King's Coll., London. LLB 1967, LLM 1968; LAMTPI 1970, LMRTPI 1976. 2nd Lieut, Suffolk & Cambs Regt (TA), 1963–65. Called to the Bar, Inner Temple, 1968, Bencher, 1993; Lectr in Law, City of London Polytechnic, 1968–71; in practice, Planning and Local Govt Bar, Parly Bar, 1971–. Mem. Council, RTPI, 1984–87. Gov., Highgate Sch., 1991–. *Publications:* contribs to Jl of Planning Law. *Recreations:* creating wildflower meadows, walking, railways, canals, reading history. *Address:* 4–5 Gray's Inn Square, WC1R 5JA. *T:* 0171–404 5252.

SULLIVAN, Linda Elizabeth, (Mrs J. W. Blake-James); QC 1994; a Recorder, since 1990; *b* 1 Jan. 1948; *d* of Donal Sullivan and Esmé Beryl Sullivan (*née* McKenzie); *m* 1972, Dr Justin Wynne Blake-James (marr. diss. 1994); one *s* twin *d*. *Educ:* St Leonard's-Mayfield Sch.; Univ. of Kent (BA Hons Phil. and English 1969); St Hilda's Coll., Oxford (Cert Ed 1970). Called to the Bar, Middle Temple, 1973, Bencher, 1993; Mem., Western Circuit. *Address:* 35 Essex Street, Temple, WC2R 3AR.

SULLIVAN, Prof. Michael; *see* Sullivan, D. M.

SULLIVAN, Michael Frederick, MBE 1981; HM Diplomatic Service; Consul-General, Hamburg, since 1994; *b* 22 June 1940; *s* of late Frederick Franklin Sullivan and of Leonora Mary Sullivan; *m* 1967, Jennifer Enid Saunders. *Educ:* King's Sch., Canterbury; Jesus Coll., Oxford (BA). CRO 1962–66; Moscow, 1967; Ulan Bator, Mongolia, 1967–69; Sydney, 1970–74; FCO, 1975–77; First Sec., W Indian and Atlantic Dept, FCO, 1977–79; Consul (Industrial Develt), British Trade Develt Office, NY, 1979–81; Cultural Attaché, Moscow, 1981–85; Assistant Head: Personnel Services Dept, FCO, 1985–86; Energy, Sci. and Space Dept, FCO, 1986–88; Counsellor (Cultural Affairs), Moscow, 1988–89; Counsellor, Export Promotion Policy Unit, DTI, 1989–90; Hd of Nationality, Treaty and Claims Dept, FCO, 1990–93. *Recreations:* piano playing, music and the arts, tennis, jogging, swimming. *Address:* c/o Foreign and Commonwealth Office, SW1A 2AH.

SULLIVAN, Richard Arthur, (9th Bt *cr* 1804, but does not use the title); Project Manager, Dow Environmental; *b* 9 Aug. 1931; *s* of Sir Richard Benjamin Magniac Sullivan, 8th Bt, and Muriel Mary Paget (*d* 1988), *d* of late Francis Charles Trayler Pineo; *S* father, 1977; *m* 1962, Elenor Mary, *e d* of late K. M. Thorpe; one *s* three *d*. *Educ:* Univ. of Cape Town (BSc); Massachusetts Inst. of Technology (SM). Chartered Engineer, UK; Professional Engineer, Ontario, Texas and Louisiana. *Publications:* technical papers to international conferences and geotechnical journals. *Recreation:* tennis. *Heir: s* Charles Merson Sullivan, MA Cantab, MRCVS, *b* 15 Dec. 1962. *Address:* PO Box 1954, Tustin, CA 92681, USA.

SULLIVAN, Tod; Executive Secretary, Immigration Appeals Advisory Service, 1993; *b* 3 Jan. 1934; *s* of Timothy William and Elizabeth Sullivan; *m* 1963, Patricia Norma Roughsedge; one *s* three *d*. *Educ:* Fanshawe Crescent Sch., Dagenham. Merchant Navy, 1950–52; RAF, 1952–55; Electrician, 1955–60; Children's Journalist, 1960–68; Industrial Relations Officer: ATV, 1968–71; CIR, 1971–72; Gen. Sec., Union of Kodak Workers, 1973–74 (until transfer of engagements to TGWU); Nat. Sec., Admin., Clerical, Tech. and Supervisory Staffs, TGWU, 1974–92. *Recreations:* reading, music, golf. *Address:* Windchimes, 48 Westlands, Pickering, N Yorks YO18 7HJ.

SULSTON, John Edward, PhD; FRS 1986; Staff Scientist, MRC Laboratory of Molecular Biology, Cambridge, since 1969; Director, The Sanger Centre (for genome research), Hinxton, Cambridge, since 1992; *b* 27 March 1942; *s* of late Rev. Canon Arthur Edward Aubrey Sulston and of Josephine Muriel Frearson (*née* Blocksidge); *m* 1966, Daphne Edith Bate; one *s* one *d*. *Educ:* Merchant Taylors' School; Pembroke College, Cambridge (BA, PhD). Postdoctoral Fellow, Salk Inst., San Diego, 1966–69. *Publications:* articles on organic chemistry, molecular and developmental biology in sci. jls. *Recreations:* gardening, walking, avoiding people. *Address:* 39 Mingle Lane, Stapleford, Cambridge CB2 5BG. *T:* Cambridge (01223) 842248.

SULZBERGER, Arthur Ochs; Chairman, New York Times Co., 1973–92; Publisher of The New York Times, 1963–92; *b* 5 Feb. 1926; *s* of late Arthur Hays Sulzberger; *m* 1st, 1948, Barbara Grant (marr. diss. 1956); one *s* one *d*; 2nd, 1956, Carol Fox Fuhrman; one *d* (and one adopted *d*). *Educ:* Browning School, New York City; Loomis School, Windsor, Conn; Columbia University, NYC. Reporter, Milwaukee Journal, 1953–54; Foreign Correspondent, New York Times, 1954–55; Asst to the Publisher, New York Times, 1956–57; Asst Treasurer, New York Times, 1957–63. Chm., Bd of Trustees, Metropolitan Mus. of Art; Trustee Emeritus, Columbia Univ. Hon. LLD: Dartmouth, 1964; Bard, 1967; Hon LHD: Montclair State Coll.; Tufts Univ., 1984. *Recreation:* fishing. *Address:* 229 West 43rd Street, New York, NY 10036, USA. *T:* (212) 5561771. *Clubs:* Overseas Press, Explorers (New York); Metropolitan (Washington, DC).

SUMBERG, David Anthony Gerald; MP (C) Bury South, since 1983; *b* 2 June 1941; *s* of Joshua and Lorna Sumberg; *m* 1972, Carolyn Ann Rae Franks; one *s* one *d*. *Educ:* Tettenhall Coll., Staffs; Coll. of Law, London. Qualified as a Solicitor, 1964. Mem. (C) Manchester City Council, 1982–84. Contested (C) Manchester, Wythenshawe, 1979. PPS to: Solicitor-General, 1986–87; Attorney-General, 1987–90. Member: Home Affairs Select Cttee, 1991–92; Foreign Affairs Select Cttee, 1992–. Mem., Adv. Council on Public Records, 1993–. *Recreation:* family. *Address:* 19 New Road, Radcliffe, Manchester M26 9LS. *T:* 0161–723 3457.

SUMMERFIELD, Prof. Arthur, BSc Tech; BSc; CPsychol, FBPsS, FInstD; Chairman, LearnIT Ltd, since 1991; Professor of Psychology, University of London, 1961–88, now Emeritus, and Head of the Department of Psychology at Birkbeck College, 1961–88; *b* 31 March 1923; *s* of late Arthur and Dora Gertrude Summerfield; *m* 1st, 1946, Aline Whalley; one *s* one *d*; 2nd, 1974, Angela Barbara, MA Cantab, PhD London, CPsychol, FBPsS, *d* of late George Frederick and Estelle Steer. *Educ:* Manchester Grammar Sch.; Manchester Univ.; University Coll. London (1st cl. hons Psychology). Served War of 1939–45, Electrical Officer, RNVR, 1943–46: Naval Air Stations, 1943–46; Dept of Sen. Psychologist to the Admiralty, 1946. Asst Lectr in Psychology, University Coll. London, 1949–51, Lectr, 1951–61, Hon. Research Associate, 1961–70, Hon. Research Fellow, 1970–; first Dean, Fac. of Econs, Birkbeck Coll., 1971–72, Governor, 1982–86; Hon. Lectr in Psychology, Westminster Med. Sch., 1974–76. Member: Univ. of London Bd of Studies in Psychology, 1956–88 (Chm., 1967–70); Special Adv. Cttee on Ergonomics, 1968–88 (Chm., 1983–88); Acad. Adv. Bd in Medicine, 1974–88; Acad. Council Standing Sub-Cttee on Science and Engrg, 1974–77. Hon. Life Mem., British Psychological Soc., 1993 (Mem. Council, 1953–65, 1967–75, 1977–84; Hon. Gen. Sec., 1954–59; Pres., 1963–64; Vice-Pres., 1964–65; first Chm., Scientific Affairs Bd, 1974–75); Member: Cttee on Internat. Relations in Psychology, Amer. Psychological Assoc., 1977–79; Bd of Dirs, European Coordination Centre for Res. and Documentation in Social Scis (Vienna Centre), 1977–81; ICSU Study Gp on biol, med. and physical effects of large scale use of nuclear weapons, 1983–87; Pres., International Union of Psychological Science, 1976–80 (Mem., Exec. Cttee, 1963–84, Assembly, 1957–84; Vice-Pres., 1972–76); Pres., Section J (Psychology) BAAS, 1976–77; Pres., Internat. Soc. Sci. Council, 1977–81 (Mem. Prog. Cttee, 1973–83; Mem. Exec. Cttee, 1977–83); Chm., DES Working Party on Psychologists in Educn Services, 1965–68 (Summerfield report). Member: DSIR Human Sciences Res. Grants Cttee, 1962–65; SSRC, 1979–81; Psychology Cttee, SSRC, 1979–81. Vis. Prof., Univ. of California (at Dept of Psychobiology, Irvine Campus), 1968. Governor, Enfield Coll. of Technology, 1968–72. Dir, British Jl of Educnl Psychology Ltd, 1976–93; Asst Editor, Brit. Jl Psychology (Statistical Section), 1950–54; Editor, British Journal of Psychology, 1964–67; Scientific Editor, British Med. Bulletin issues on Experimental Psychology, 1964, Cognitive Psychology, 1971, (with D. M. Warburton) Psychobiology, 1981. *Publications:* (trans. and ed jtly) Animals and Men, 1951; articles on perception, memory, statistical methods and psycho-pharmacology in scientific periodicals. *Address:* Rose Bank, Sutton-under-Whitestonecliffe, Thirsk, N Yorks YO7 2PR. *T:* Thirsk (01845) 597395; (office) (01845) 597097, *Fax:* 597005. *Club:* Athenæum.

SUMMERFIELD, Sir John (Crampton), Kt 1973; CBE 1966 (OBE 1961); Judge of the Grand Court and Chief Justice of the Cayman Islands, 1977–87, retired; *b* 20 Sept. 1920; *s* of late Arthur Fred Summerfield and late Lilian Winifred Summerfield (*née* Staas); *m* 1945, Patricia Sandra Musgrave; two *s* two *d*. *Educ:* Lucton Sch., Herefordshire. Called to Bar, Gray's Inn, 1949. Served War, 1939–46: East Africa, Abyssinia, Somaliland, Madagascar; Captain, Royal Signals. Crown Counsel, Tanganyika (now Tanzania), 1949; Legal Draftsman, 1953; Dep. Legal Sec., EA High Commission, 1958. Attorney-Gen., Bermuda, 1962; QC (Bermuda) 1963; MEC, 1962–68, and MLC, 1962–68 (Bermuda); Chief Justice of Bermuda, 1972–77; Judge of Supreme Court, Turks and Caicos Islands, 1977–82; Justice of Appeal for Bermuda, 1979–87; Pres., Ct of Appeal for Belize, 1982–84. *Publications:* Preparation of Revised Laws of Bermuda, 1963 and 1971 edns. *Recreations:* photography, chess, sailing. *Address:* 3 The Corniche, Sandgate, Folkestone, Kent CT20 3TA. *Club:* Commonwealth Trust.

SUMMERHAYES, Dr Colin Peter; Director, Institute of Oceanographic Sciences Deacon Laboratory, since 1988; *b* 7 March 1942; *s* of late Leonard Percy Summerhayes and of Jessica Adelaide (*née* Crump); *m* 1st, 1966 (marr. diss. 1977); one *s* one *d*; 2nd, 1981, Diana Ridley (*née* Perry); one step *s* one step *d*. *Educ:* Slough Grammar Sch.; UCL (BSc 1963); Keble Coll., Oxford; Victoria Univ., Wellington, NZ (MSc 1967; DSc 1986); Imperial Coll., London (DIC; PhD 1970). Scientific Officer, DSIR, NZ Oceanographic Inst., 1964–67; Res. Asst, Geol. Dept, Imperial Coll., London, 1967–70; Sen. Scientific Officer, CSIR, Marine Geosci. Unit, Univ. of Cape Town, 1970–72; Asst Scientist, Geol. and Geophys Dept, Woods Hole Oceanographic Instn, 1972–76; Research Associate/Project Leader: Geochem. Br., Exxon Prodn Res. Centre, Houston, 1976–82; Global Paleoreconstruction Sect., Stratigraphy Br., BP Res. Centre, 1982–85; Manager and Sen. Res. Associate, Stratigraphy Br., BP Res. Centre, 1985–88. Vis. Prof., UCL, 1987–95. Member: Geol Soc.; Challenger Soc. for Marine Sci.; Soc. for Underwater Technology; RSPB. MIMgt. *Publications:* 100 papers in various geol, geochem., oceanographic jls, 3 on seabirds. *Recreations:* ornithology, jogging, reading, films and theatre. *Address:* Institute of Oceanographic Sciences Deacon Laboratory, Brook Road, Wormley, Godalming, Surrey GU8 5UB. *T:* Wormley (01428) 684141.

SUMMERHAYES, David Michael, CMG 1975; HM Diplomatic Service, retired; Disarmament Adviser, Foreign and Commonwealth Office, 1983–92; *b* 29 Sept. 1922; *s* of Sir Christopher Summerhayes, KBE, CMG and late Anna (*née* Johnson); *m* 1959, June van der Hardt Aberson; two *s* one *d*. *Educ:* Marlborough; Emmanuel Coll., Cambridge. Served War of 1939–45 in Royal Artillery (Capt.) N Africa and Italy. 3rd Sec., FO, 1948; Baghdad, 1949; Brussels, 1950–53; 2nd Sec., FO, 1953–56; 1st Sec. (Commercial), The Hague, 1956–59; 1st Sec. and Consul, Reykjavik, 1959–61; FO, 1961–65; Consul-General and Counsellor, Buenos Aires, 1965–70; Head of Arms Control and Disarmament Dept, FCO, 1970–74; Minister, Pretoria/Cape Town, 1974–78; Ambassador and Leader, UK Delegn to Cttee on Disarmament, Geneva, 1979–82. Hon. Officer, Order of Orange Nassau. *Recreations:* golf, walking. *Address:* Ivy House, South Harting, Petersfield, Hants GU31 5QQ. *Club:* United Oxford & Cambridge University.

SUMMERHAYES, Gerald Victor, CMG 1979; OBE 1969; *b* 28 Jan. 1928; *s* of Victor Samuel and Florence A. V. Summerhayes. Administrative Service, Nigeria, 1952–81; Permanent Secretary: Local Govt, North Western State, 1975–76, Sokoto State, 1976–77; Cabinet Office (Political and Trng), 1977–79; Dir of Trng, Cabinet Office, Sokoto, 1979–81. *Address:* Bridge Cottage, Bridge Street, Sidbury, Devon EX10 0RU. *T:* Sidbury (01395) 597311; PO Box 172, Sokoto, Nigeria.

SUMMERS, (Sir) Felix Roland Brattan, 2nd Bt *cr* 1952; does not use the title and his name is not on the Official Roll of Baronets.

SUMMERS, Henry Forbes, CB 1961; Under-Secretary, Department of the Environment (formerly Ministry of Housing and Local Government), 1955–71; *b* 18 August 1911; *s* of late Rev. H. H. Summers, Harrogate, Yorks; *m* 1937, Rosemary, *d* of late Robert L. Roberts, CBE; two *s* one *d*. *Educ:* Fettes Coll., Edinburgh; Trinity College, Oxford. *Publications:* Smoke After Flame, 1944; Hinterland, 1947; Tomorrow is my Love, 1978; The Burning Book, 1982. *Address:* Folly Fields, Tunbridge Wells, Kent TN2 5QU. *T:* Tunbridge Wells (01892) 527671.
See also N. Summers.

SUMMERS, Janet Margaret, (Mrs L. J. Summers); *see* Bately, J. M.

SUMMERS, Nicholas; Under Secretary, Department for Education and Employment (formerly of Education and Science, then for Education), since 1981; *b* 11 July 1939; *s* of Henry Forbes Summers, *qv*; *m* 1965, Marian Elizabeth Ottley; four *s*. *Educ:* Tonbridge Sch.; Corpus Christi Coll., Oxford. Min. of Educn, 1961–64; DES, 1964–74; Private Sec. to Minister for the Arts, 1965–66; Cabinet Office, 1974–76; DES, subseq. Dept for Educn, 1976–. FRSA 1993. *Recreations:* family, music. *Address:* c/o Department for Education and Employment, Sanctuary Buildings, Great Smith Street, SW1P 3BT.

SUMMERSCALE, David Michael, MA; Head Master of Westminster School, since 1986; *b* 22 April 1937; *s* of late Noel Tynwald Summerscale and Beatrice (*née* Wilson); *m* 1975, Pauline, *d* of Prof. Michel Fleury, Président de l'Ecole des Hautes Etudes, Paris, Directeur des Antiquités Historiques de l'Ile-de-France; one *s* one *d*. *Educ:* Northaw; Sherborne Sch.; Trinity Hall, Cambridge. Lectr in English Literature and Tutor, St Stephen's Coll., Univ. of Delhi, 1959–63; Charterhouse, 1963–75 (Head of English, Housemaster); Master of Haileybury, 1976–86. Dir, Namdang Tea Co. (India) Ltd, 1991–. Oxford and Cambridge Schs Examination Bd Awarder and Reviser in English. Vice-Chm., E-SU Scholarship Cttee, 1982–; Member: Managing Cttee of Cambridge Mission to Delhi, 1965; C. F. Andrews Centenary Appeal Cttee, 1970; HMC Academic Policy Sub-Cttee, 1982–86; Council, Charing Cross and Westminster Med. Sch., 1986–. Governor: The Hall Sch., Hampstead, 1986–; Arnold House Sch., St John's Wood, 1988–; King's House Sch., Richmond, 1991–; Staff Advr, Governing Body, Westminster Abbey Choir Sch., 1989–; Nominated Mem., Sch. Cttee, Merchant Taylors' Co., 1988–; Consultant and Gov., Assam Valley Sch., India, 1989–; Member Council: Queen's Coll., London, 1991–; Book Aid Internat. (formerly Ranfurly Library Service), 1992–. Trustee, Criterion Theatre Trust, 1992–. FRSA 1984. *Publications:* articles on English and Indian literature; dramatisations of novels and verse. *Recreations:* music, reading, mountaineering, games (squash (Mem. SRA), cricket, tennis, rackets (Mem. Tennis and Rackets Assoc.), golf. *Address:* 17 Dean's Yard, SW1P 3PB. *Clubs:* Athenæum, I Zingari, Free Foresters, Jesters; Club Alpin Suisse.

SUMMERSCALE, Peter Wayne; HM Diplomatic Service, retired; *b* 22 April 1935; *s* of Sir John Summerscale, KBE; *m* 1st, 1964, Valerie Turner (marr. diss. 1983); one *s* two *d*; 2nd, 1985, Cristina Fournier (marr. diss. 1986); 3rd, 1989, Elizabeth Carro. *Educ:* Rugby Sch.; New Coll., Oxford Univ. (Exhibnr; 1st Cl. Hons Modern History); Russian Res. Centre, Harvard Univ. FO, 1960–62; Polit. Residency, Bahrain, 1962–65; 1st Sec., Tokyo, 1965–68; FCO, 1968–69; Cabinet Office, 1969–71; 1st Sec. and Head of Chancery, Santiago, Chile, 1971–75; Head of CSCE Unit, FCO, 1976–77; Dep. Leader, UK Delegn, Belgrade Rev. Conf., 1977–78; Counsellor and Head of Chancery, Brussels, 1978–79; Vis. FCO Res. Fellow, RIIA, Chatham House, 1979–81; Head of Civilian Faculty, Nat. Defence Coll., 1981–82; Ambassador to Costa Rica, 1982–86, and concurrently (non-resident) to Nicaragua; Dep. Leader, UK Delegn to CSCE, 1986–88; Hd, CSCE Unit, FCO, 1989–90. Hd UK Delegn, 1992, Belgrade Regl Centre, 1995–, EC Monitoring Mission, Yugoslavia; UK expert, EC Programme for Human Rights in Central America, 1992–. *Publications:* (jtly) Soviet—East European Dilemmas, 1981; The East European Predicament, 1982; articles on E Europe and communism. *Recreations:* sailing, skiing, walking. *Address:* 17 Chester Road, N19 5DE.

SUMMERSKILL, Dr the Hon. Shirley Catherine Wynne; Medical Practitioner; Medical Officer in Blood Transfusion Service, 1983–91; *b* London, 9 Sept. 1931; *d* of late Dr E. J. Samuel and Baroness Summerskill, CH, PC. *Educ:* St Paul's Girls' Sch.; Somerville Coll., Oxford; St Thomas' Hospital. MA, BM, BCh., 1958. Treas., Oxford Univ. Labour Club, 1952. Resident House Surgeon, later House Physician, St Helier Hosp., Carshalton, 1959; Partner in Gen. Practice, 1960–68. Contested (Lab): Blackpool North by-election, 1962; Halifax, 1983. MP (Lab) Halifax, 1964–83; opposition spokesman on health, 1970–74; Parly Under-Sec. of State, Home Office, 1974–79; opposition spokesman on home affairs, 1979–83. Vice-Chm., PLP Health Gp, 1964–69, Chm., 1969–70; Mem., Labour Party NEC, 1981–83. UK delegate, UN Status of Women Commn, 1968 and 1969; Mem. British delegn, Council of Europe and WEU, 1968, 1969. *Publications:* A Surgical Affair (novel), 1963; Destined to Love (novel), 1986. *Recreations:* music, fiction.

SUMMERSON, Hugo Hawksley Fitzthomas; Director, Palatine Properties, since 1983; Consultant, Amhurst Properties Ltd, since 1992; Principal, Speaker Skills Training, since 1994; *b* 21 July 1950; *s* of late Thomas Hawksley Summerson, OBE and of Joan Florence Summerson; *m* 1989, Rosemary (marr. diss. 1992), *d* of late John Pitts, Exeter. *Educ:* Harrow School; Royal Agricultural College. FRICS; MRAC. Land Agent with Knight, Frank and Rutley, 1973–76; travel in S America, 1977; self-employment, 1978–83. Contested (C): Barking, 1983; Walthamstow, 1992. MP (C) Walthamstow, 1987–92. Mem., Select Cttee on Envmt, 1991–92; Treas., British Latin-American Parly Gp, 1990; Vice-Chm., All-Party Parly Gp on Child Abduction, 1991–92; Sec., Cons. Back Bench Agriculture Cttee, 1991–92. Chm., Greater London Area Adopted Parly Candidates Assoc., 1986; Vice-Pres., Greater London Area, Nat. Soc. of Cons. and Unionist Agents, 1989; Mem. Council, British Atlantic Gp of Young Politicians, 1989; Parly Advr to Drinking Fountain Assoc., 1989. Fellow, Industry and Parlt Trust, 1991. Sir Anthony Berry Meml Scholar, 1985. *Recreations:* fishing, music, cricket. *Address:* 14c York House, Highbury Crescent, N5 1RP. *T:* 0171–607 8269. *Club:* Royal Over-Seas League.

SUMMERTON, Dr Neil William; Under Secretary, Water, Department of the Environment, since 1991; *b* 5 April 1942; *s* of H. E. W. Summerton and Nancy Summerton; *m* 1965, Pauline Webb; two *s*. *Educ:* Wellington Grammar Sch., Shropshire; King's Coll., London (BA History 1963; PhD War Studies 1970). Min. of Transport, 1966–69; PA to Principal, 1969–71, Asst Sec. (Co-ordination), 1971–74, KCL; DoE, 1974–; Asst Sec., heading various housing Divs, 1978–85; Under Sec., Planning Land-Use Policy Directorate, 1985–87; Under Sec., Planning and Develt Control Directorate, 1987–88; Under Sec., Local Govt Finance Policy Directorate, 1988–91. Attended HM Treasury Centre for Admin. Studies, 1968–69; Civil Service Top Management Programme, 1985. Non-exec. Dir, Redland Bricks Ltd, 1988–91; Director: Partnership (UK) Ltd, 1994–; Christian Impact Ltd, 1989–; London Christian Housing plc, 1990–; Christian Research Assoc., 1992–. Member: Cttee of Management, Council on Christian Approaches to Defence and Disarmament, 1983– (Hon. Sec., 1984–91); Council, Evangelical Alliance, 1990–. Elder of a Christian congregation; other Christian activities. *Publications:* A Noble Task: eldership and ministry in the local church, 1987, 2nd edn 1994; articles and essays on historical, theological and ethical matters.

SUMNER, Christopher John; His Honour Judge Sumner; a Circuit Judge, since 1987; *b* 28 Aug. 1939; *s* of His Honour W. D. M. Sumner, OBE, QC; *m* 1970, Carole Ashley Mann; one *s* two *d*. *Educ:* Charterhouse; Sidney Sussex Coll., Cambridge (MA). Called to the Bar, Inner Temple, 1961, Bencher, 1994; Asst Recorder, 1983; Recorder, 1986. Mem., Judicial Studies Bd, 1991–. *Recreations:* reading, sport, theatre, listening to music. *Club:* Hurlingham.

SUMPTION, Anthony James Chadwick, DSC 1944; *b* 15 May 1919; *s* of late John Chadwick Sumption and late Winifred Fanny Sumption; *m* 1946, Hedy Hedigan (marr. diss. 1979); two *s* two *d*. *Educ:* Cheltenham Coll.; London Sch. of Economics. Served RNVR, 1939–46; HM Submarines, 1941–45: comd Varangian, 1944; Upright, 1945. Solicitor, 1946; called to the Bar, Lincoln's Inn, 1971; a Recorder of the Crown Court, 1980–84. Member (C): LCC, 1949–52; Westminster City Council, 1953–56. Contested (C): Hayes and Harlington, March 1953; Middlesbrough W, 1964. *Publications:* Taxation of Overseas Income and Gains, 1973, 4th edn 1982; Tax Planning, (with Philip Lawton) 6th edn 1973–8th edn 1979, (with Giles Clarke) 9th edn 1981–10th edn 1982; Capital Gains Tax, 1981. *Recreations:* painting, angling. *Address:* c/o Coutts & Co., 188 Fleet Street, EC4A 2AH. *Club:* Garrick.
See also J. P. C. Sumption.

SUMPTION, Jonathan Philip Chadwick; QC 1986; a Recorder, since 1993; *b* 9 Dec. 1948; *s* of Anthony James Chadwick Sumption, *qv*; *m* 1971, Teresa Mary (*née* Whelan); one *s* two *d*. *Educ:* Eton; Magdalen College, Oxford (MA). Fellow (in History) of Magdalen College, Oxford, 1971–75; called to the Bar, Inner Temple, 1975, Bencher, 1990. *Publications:* Pilgrimage: an image of medieval religion, 1975; The Albigensian Crusade, 1978; The Hundred Years' War, 1990. *Recreations:* music, history. *Address:* 34 Crooms Hill, Greenwich, SE10 8ER. *T:* 0181–858 4444.

SUMRAY, Monty; CBE 1989; Chairman, FII Group, since 1965 (Managing Director, 1965–95); *b* 12 Oct. 1918; *m* 1939, Catherine Beber; one *s* one *d*. *Educ:* Upton House, London. Royal Berkshire Regt, 1939–46; served in Burma (Captain). UK footwear manufacturing, 1934–; Dir, FII Group. Pres., British Footwear Manufacturers' Fedn, 1976–77, formerly: Member: Footwear Industry Study Steering Gp (Chm., Home Working Cttee); Footwear Economic Develt Cttee (4 years); Pres., London Footwear Manufacturers' Assoc.; Chm., London Branch, British Boot & Shoe Instn. FCFI 1974; FInstD 1981; FRSA 1993. *Recreations:* tennis, reading, social and charitable work. *Address:* 11 Neville Drive, N2 0QS. *T:* 0181–458 2788.

SUMSION, John Walbridge, OBE 1991; Director, Library and Information Statistics Unit, Loughborough University, since 1991; *b* 16 Aug. 1928; *s* of late Dr Herbert Sumsion, CBE; *m* 1st, 1961, Annette Dorothea Wilson (marr. diss. 1979); two *s* two *d*; 2nd, 1979, Hazel Mary Jones (*née* English). *Educ:* St George's Choir Sch., Windsor Castle; St Thomas' Choir Sch., New York City; Rendcomb Coll., Cirencester; Clare Coll., Cambridge (BA (Hons) History); Yale Univ., USA (MA Economics); Cornell Univ., USA (Teaching Fellow). FIMgt. Somervell Brothers (K Shoemakers) Ltd: Graduate trainee, 1954; Production Manager (Women's Shoes), 1959; Director, 1962–81; Registrar, Public Lending Right, 1981–91. Dir, TeleOrdering Ltd, 1992–94. Mem., Library and Information Services Council (England), 1992–95. Hon. FLA 1990. *Publications:* Setting Up Public Lending Right, 1984; PLR in Practice, 1988, 2nd edn 1991; Practical Performance Indicators, 1992; various statistical reports. *Recreations:* music (flute, singing), tennis. *Address:* Library and Information Statistics Unit, Loughborough University, Leics LE11 3TU. *T:* Loughborough (01509) 223071. *Club:* United Oxford & Cambridge University.

SUNDERLAND, Earl of; George Spencer-Churchill; *b* 28 July 1992; *s* and *heir* of Marquess of Blandford, *qv*.

SUNDERLAND, (Arthur) John; Commissioner-in-Chief, St John Ambulance Brigade, 1986–90; *b* 24 Feb. 1932; *s* of George Frederick Irvon Sunderland and Mary Katharine Sunderland; *m* 1958, Audrey Ann Thompson (*d* 1992); three *s*. *Educ:* Marlborough Coll. Served Army, RE, 1953–55 (2nd Lieut). Director: James Upton Ltd, 1963–69; Surrey Fine Art Press Ltd, 1963–69; Sunderland Print Ltd, 1969–84; Randall Bros Ltd, 1970–84; Alday Green & Welburn, 1978–84; Foxplan Ltd, 1984–; Rapidflow Ltd, 1985–91; SADC Ltd, 1986–. Dep. County Comr, 1976–78, County Comr, 1978–86, St John Ambulance Bde, W Midlands; KStJ 1986 (CStJ 1982; OStJ 1978). Chm., Ladypool Road Neighbourhood Centre, Balsall Heath, 1970–76. Governor, West House Sch., Birmingham, 1973–91. *Recreations:* walking, sport generally. *Address:* Rowans, Grafton Flyford, Worcs WR7 4PJ. *T:* Himbleton (01905) 391281.

SUNDERLAND, Prof. Eric, PhD; FIBiol; Principal, later Vice-Chancellor, University College of North Wales, Bangor, 1984–95; *b* 18 March 1930; *s* of Leonard Sunderland and Mary Agnes (*née* Davies); *m* 1957, Jean Patricia (*née* Watson); two *d*. *Educ:* Amman Valley Grammar Sch.; Univ. of Wales (BA, MA); Univ. of London (PhD). FIBiol 1975. Commnd Officer, RA, 1955–56. Res. Asst, UCL, 1953–54; Res. Scientist, NCB, 1957–58; Univ. of Durham: Lectr, 1958–66; Sen. Lectr, 1966–71; Prof. of Anthropology, 1971–84; Pro Vice-Chancellor, 1979–84; Vice-Chancellor, Univ. of Wales, 1989–91. Welsh Supernumerary Fellow, Jesus Coll., Oxford, 1987–88. Sec.-Gen., Internat. Union of Anthropol and Ethnol Sciences, 1978–; President, Royal Anthropol Inst., 1989–91 (Hon. Sec., 1978–85; Hon. Treasurer, 1985–89); Chm., Biosocial Soc., 1981–85. Member: Welsh Language Bd, 1988–; Ct of Govs, Nat. Mus. of Wales, 1991–94; Gen. Cttee, ICSU, 1993–; Vice Pres., Internat. Social Sci. Council, 1994–; Chairman: Welsh Language Educn Develt Cttee, 1987–94; Local Govt Boundary Commn for Wales, 1994–. Hon. Mem., The Gorsedd, 1985. *Publications:* Elements of Human and Social Geography: some anthropological perspectives, 1973; (ed jtly) Genetic Variation in Britain, 1973; (ed jtly) The Operation of Intelligence: biological preconditions for the operation of intelligence, 1980; (ed jtly) Genetic and Population Studies in Wales, 1986; contrib. Annals of Human Biol., Human Heredity, Man, Human Biol., Nature, Amer. Jl of Phys. Anthropol., and Trans Royal Soc. *Recreations:* travel, gardening, book collecting, reading. *Address:* University of Wales, Bangor, Gwynedd LL57 2DG. *T:* Bangor (01248) 382000; Bryn, Ffriddredd Road, Bangor, Gwynedd LL57 2EM. *T:* Bangor (01248) 353265. *Club:* Athenæum.

SUNDERLAND, (Godfrey) Russell, CB 1991; FRAeS; Director, Air Miles Travel Promotions Ltd; *b* 28 July 1936; *s* of Allan and Laura Sunderland; *m* 1965, Greta Jones; one *s* one *d*. *Educ:* Heath Grammar Sch., Halifax; The Queen's College, Oxford (MA). FRAeS 1993. Ministry of Aviation: Asst Principal, 1962; Asst Private Sec. to Minister, 1964; Principal, 1965; HM Diplomatic Service: First Sec. (Civil Air), Beirut, and other Middle East posts, 1969; Principal, Board of Trade, 1971; Asst Sec., DTI, 1973; Under Sec., DTI, 1979; Dir of Shipping Policy and Emergency Planning, Dept of Transport, 1984; Dep. Sec., Aviation, Shipping and Internat., Dept of Transport, 1988–94. Chairman: Consultative Shipping Group, 1984–88; Maritime Transport Cttee, OECD, 1992–94. Mem., Policy Cttee, CIT, 1995–. FRSA 1991. *Recreations:* garden, piano, amateur theatre. *Address:* Windrush, Silkmore Lane, West Horsley, Leatherhead, Surrey KT24 6JQ. *T:* Guildford (01483) 282660.

SUNDERLAND, John; *see* Sunderland, A. J.

SUNDERLAND, Russell; *see* Sunderland, G. R.

SUPHAMONGKHON, Dr Konthi, Kt Grand Cordon of the White Elephant, Kt Grand Cordon, Order of the Crown of Thailand; Kt Grand Commander, Order of Chula Chom Klao; Hon. GCVO 1972; *b* 3 Aug. 1916; *m* 1951, Dootsdi Atthakravi; two *s* one *d*. *Educ:* Univ. of Moral and Political Sciences, Bangkok (LLB); Univ. of Paris (Dr-en-Droit). Joined Min. of Foreign Affairs, 1941; Second Sec., Tokyo, 1942–44; Chief of Polit. Div., 1944–48; Dir-Gen., Western Affairs Dept, 1948–50; UN Affairs Dept, 1950–52; Minister to Australia, 1952–56, Ambassador, June 1956–59, and to New Zealand, Oct. 1956–59; Dir-Gen. of Internat. Organizations, 1959–63; Adviser on Foreign Affairs to the Prime Minister, 1962–64; Sec.-Gen., SEATO, 1964–65; Ambassador to Federal Republic of Germany, 1965–70, and to Finland, 1967–70; Ambassador to Court of St James's, 1970–76. Frequent Lecturer, 1944–; notably at Thammasat Univ., 1944–52, at National Defence Coll., 1960–62, and at Army War Coll., Bangkok, 1960–63. Member: Internat. Law Assoc.; IISS; RIIA. Holds foreign decorations, incl. Grosskreuz des Verdienstordens (Germany), 1970. *Publications:* Thailand and her relations with France, 1940 (in French); Account of a return journey from Marseilles to Singapore, 1965 (in French); Thai Foreign Policy, 1984 (in Thai). *Recreations:* tennis, golf, swimming. *Address:* Kanta Mansion, 73 Soi 26, Sukhumvit Road, Bangkok, Thailand; 60 Kensington Court, Kensington, W8 5DG. *Clubs:* Siam Society, Royal Sport of Bangkok, Royal Turf (Bangkok).

SUPPERSTONE, Michael Alan; QC 1991; an Assistant Recorder, since 1992; *b* 30 March 1950; *s* of late Harold Bernard Supperstone and Muriel Supperstone; *m* 1985, Dianne Jaffe; one *s* one *d*. *Educ:* St Paul's School; Lincoln College, Oxford (MA, BCL). Called to the Bar, Middle Temple, 1973; in practice, 1974. Vis. Scholar, Harvard Law Sch., 1979–80; Vis. Lectr, Nat. Univ. of Singapore, 1981, 1982. Vice-Chm., Administrative Law Bar Assoc., 1995– (Sec., 1986–91; Treas., 1991–94). Trustee, Internat. Centre for Public Law, 1993–. *Publications:* Brownlie's Law of Public Order and National Security, 2nd edn, 1981; Immigration: the law and practice, 1983, 3rd edn 1994; (principal contributor) Administrative Law Title in Halsbury's Laws of England, 4th edn reissue, 1989; (ed jtly and contrib.) Judicial Review, 1992; articles on public law. *Recreations:* playing tennis, watching Association Football. *Address:* 11 King's Bench Walk, Temple, EC4Y 7EQ. *T:* 0171–583 0610. *Clubs:* Garrick, Royal Automobile, Roehampton.

SUPPLE, Prof. Barry Emanuel, FRHistS; FBA 1987; Director, Leverhulme Trust, since 1993; Professor of Economic History, University of Cambridge, 1981–93, now Professor Emeritus; *b* 27 Oct. 1930; *s* of Solomon and Rose Supple; *m* 1958, Sonia (*née* Caller); two *s* one *d*. *Educ:* Hackney Downs Grammar Sch.; London Sch. of Econs and Polit. Science (BScEcon 1952); Christ's Coll., Cambridge (PhD 1955). LittD Cambridge, 1993. FRHistS 1972. Asst Prof. of Business History, Grad. Sch. of Business Admin, Harvard Univ., 1955–60; Associate Prof. of Econ. Hist., McGill Univ., 1960–62; University of Sussex: Lectr, Reader, then Prof. of Econ. and Social Hist., 1962–78; Dean, Sch. of Social Sciences, 1965–68; Pro-Vice-Chancellor (Arts and Social Studies), 1968–72; Pro-Vice-Chancellor, 1978; University of Oxford: Reader in Recent Social and Econ. Hist., 1978–81; Professorial Fellow, Nuffield Coll., 1978–81; Professorial Fellow, 1981–83, Hon. Fellow, 1984, Christ's Coll., Cambridge; Master of St Catharine's Coll., Cambridge, 1984–93 (Hon. Fellow, 1993). Hon. Fellow, Worcester Coll., 1986; Associate Fellow, Trumbull Coll., Yale, 1986. Chm., Consultative Cttee of Assessment of Performance Unit, DES, 1975–80; Member: Council, SSRC, 1972–77; Social Science Fellowship Cttee, Nuffield Foundn, 1974–95. Pres., Econ. Hist. Soc., 1992–95. Foreign Sec., British Acad., 1995–July 1996. Co-editor, Econ. Hist. Rev., 1973–82. *Publications:* Commercial Crisis and Change in England, 1600–42, 1959; (ed) The Experience of Economic Growth, 1963; Boston Capitalists and Western Railroads, 1967; The Royal Exchange Assurance: a history of British insurance, 1720–1970, 1970; (ed) Essays in Business History, 1977; History of the British Coal Industry: vol. 4, 1914–46, The Political Economy of Decline, 1987; (ed) The State and Economic Knowledge: the American and British experience, 1990; (ed) The Rise of Big Business, 1992; articles and revs in learned jls. *Recreations:* tennis, photography. *Address:* Leverhulme Trust, 15–19 New Fetter Lane, EC4A 1NR. *T:* 0171–822 6938.

SURR, Jeremy Bernard, CB 1993; consultant; Director Operations (South and East), Training Enterprise and Education Directorate, Department of Employment, 1990–92; *b* 23 Jan. 1938; *s* of Thomas Bernard Surr, ISO, and Mabel Edith Moore; *m* 1965, Gillian Mary Lapage. *Educ:* Rutlish Sch., Wimbledon; Bury Grammar Sch., Lancs. National Service, RCS, 1956–58. Min. of Labour, 1959–65; computer systems analyst, 1965–70; Asst Private Sec. to Sec. of State for Employment, 1971–74; Principal, Employment Protection, Incomes Policy and Res. and Planning, 1974–78; on secondment to Australian Dept of Employment and Industrial Relations, 1978–80; joined MSC as Head of Sheltered Employment and Employment Rehabilitation Br., 1980; Head of Special Measures Br., 1982–85; Dir of Special Measures, 1985–86; Chief Exec., Employment and Enterprise Gp, 1986–87; Dir of Adult Programmes, 1987–89, Dir, Operations and Trng and Enterprise Councils Devlt, 1989–90, Training Agency (formerly MSC, later Training Commn). Dir, Energy Action Grants Agency, 1993–. Trustee, Drive for Youth, 1993–. FRSA 1993. *Recreations:* golf, walking, gardening, DIY. *Address:* 48 Oak Hill Road, Nether Edge, Sheffield S7 1SH. *T:* Sheffield (0114) 255 7554. *Clubs:* East India, Devonshire, Sports and Public Schools; Royal Cinque Ports Golf; Abbeydale Golf (Sheffield).

SURREY, Archdeacon of; *no new appointment at time of going to press.*

SURTEES, John, MBE 1961; controls companies in automotive research and development and property development; *b* 11 Feb. 1934; *s* of late John Norman and Dorothy Surtees; *m* 1st, 1962, Patricia Phyllis Burke (marr. diss. 1979); 2nd, 1987, Jane A. Sparrow; one *s* two *d*. *Educ:* Ashburton School, Croydon. 5 year engineering apprenticeship, Vincent Engrs, Stevenage, Herts. Motorcycle racing, 1952–60; British Champion, 1954, 1955; World 500 cc Motorcycle Champion, 1956; World 350 and 500 cc Motorcycle Champion, 1958, 1959, 1960. At end of 1960 he retd from motorcycling; motor racing, 1961–72; with Ferrari Co., won World Motor Racing title, 1964; 5th in World Championship, 1965 (following accident in Canada due to suspension failure); in 1966 left Ferrari in mid-season and joined Cooper, finishing 2nd in World Championship; in 1967 with Honda Motor Co. as first driver and develt engr (1967–68); 3rd in World Championship; with BRM as No 1 driver, 1969; designed and built own Formula 1 car, 1970. *Publications:* Motorcycle Racing and Preparation, 1958; John Surtees Book of Motorcycling, 1960; Speed, 1963; Six Days in August, 1968; John Surtees—World Champion, 1991; (jtly) The Pirelli Album of Motor Racing Heroes, 1992. *Recreations:* music, architecture; interested in most sports. *Address:* c/o John Surtees Ltd, Enterprise Way, Edenbridge, Kent TN8 6EW. *T:* Edenbridge (01732) 863773.

SUTCH, Peter Dennis Antony, CBE 1995; FRAeS; Chairman: John Swire & Sons (HK) Ltd, since 1992; Cathay Pacific Airways Ltd; *b* 8 April 1945; *s* of Ronald Antony Sutch and Kathleen (*née* Roden); *m* 1968, Rosemary Aisling Langan (separated); three *s* one *d*. *Educ:* Downside Sch., Stratton-on-Fosse; Exeter Coll., Oxford Univ. (MA Hist.). Joined John Swire & Sons Ltd, Hong Kong, 1966: Shipping Division: Hong Kong, 1966–67; Japan, 1967–69; Cathay Pacific Airways: Manager, W Japan, 1970–72; Passenger Sales Manager, Hong Kong, 1972–76; Gen. Manager, Japan, 1976–81; Dep. Dir and Gen. Manager, Hong Kong, 1981–83; Dep. Man. Dir, 1983–84; Man. Dir, 1984–88; Dep. Chm. and Man. Dir, 1988; Dep. Chm., John Swire & Sons (HK) Ltd and Swire Pacific Ltd, 1988–92; Chairman: Hong Kong Aircraft Engrg Co. Ltd, 1987–95; Swire Gp, Hong Kong, 1992–; Swire Pacific Ltd. Board Member: Hongkong & Shanghai Banking Corp.; Lee Gardens Internat. Hldgs; Community Chest of Hong Kong. Council Mem., Univ. of Hong Kong. Member: Governor's Business Council; Aviation Adv. Bd; Gen. Cttee, Hong Kong Gen. Chamber of Commerce; Hong Kong Trade Develt Council; CIT in Hong Kong. Mem., Barristers Disciplinary Tribunal Panel, Hong Kong. *Recreations:* golf, travel, boating, fishing. *Address:* John Swire & Sons (HK) Ltd, GPO Box 1, Hong Kong; 25 Peak Road, Hong Kong. *T:* 28494433. *Clubs:* Royal Automobile; Hong Kong, Royal Hong Kong Jockey, Royal Hong Kong Golf, China, Shek O Country (Hong Kong).

SUTCLIFFE, Allan; a Director, British Gas plc, 1986–91; *b* 30 Jan. 1936; *s* of Bertie and May Sutcliffe; *m* 1983, Pauline, *d* of Mark and Lilian Abrahams; one *s* one *d* by a previous marr. *Educ:* Neath Grammar Sch.; University Coll. London (LLB); FCMA, CIGasE. Graduate trainee, BR, 1957–60; various positions in Finance in Western, Eastern and Southern Regions and at HQ, BR, 1960–70; Wales Gas Board: Chief Accountant, 1970; Dir of Finance, 1972; Deputy Chairman: British Gas W Midlands, 1980; British Gas N Thames, 1983; British Gas plc: Man. Dir, Finance, 1987; Gp Man. Dir, Finance, 1991, retd. *Recreations:* music, reading, old buildings. *Address:* Manor Cottage, 106 Kenilworth Road, Knowle, Solihull, W Midlands B93 0JD. *T:* Knowle (01564) 771538. *Club:* Royal Automobile.

SUTCLIFFE, Geoffrey Scott, OBE 1944; TD 1952; *b* 12 June 1912; *o s* of late John Walton Sutcliffe and late Alice Mary Sutcliffe (*née* Scott); *m* 1946, Mary Sylvia, *d* of late George Herbert Kay; two *s* one *d*. *Educ:* Repton. TA 2nd Lieut, 1939; Lt-Col, 1943; GSO1, AFHQ, N Africa and Italy; served France and Belgium, 1940; N Africa and Italy, 1943–45 (despatches, OBE). Ferodo Ltd, 1932: Works Dir, 1947; Home Sales Dir, 1952; Man. Dir, 1955; Chm., 1956–67; Turner & Newall Ltd: Dir, 1957–75; Jt Man. Dir, 1963–74; Dep. Chm., 1967–74. *Recreations:* gardening, reading. *Address:* Crosswinds, 25b Coopers Drive, Bridport, Dorset DT6 4JU. *Club:* Army and Navy.

SUTCLIFFE, Gerard; MP (Lab) Bradford South, since June 1994; *b* 13 May 1953; *s* of Henry and Margaret Sutcliffe; *m* 1972, Maria Holgate; three *s*. *Educ:* Cardinal Hinsley Grammar Sch.; Bradford Coll. Salesperson, Brown Muff dept store, 1969–71; display advertising clerk, Bradford Telegraph and Argus, 1971–75; Field Printers, 1975–80; Dep. Sec., SOGAT, subseq. GPMU, 1980–94. Bradford Metropolitan District Council: Councillor, 1982–88 and 1990–94; Leader, 1992–94. *Recreations:* sport, music, politics. *Address:* House of Commons, SW1A 0AA. *T:* 0171–219 3247; (office) Bradford (01274) 7549721.

SUTCLIFFE, John Harold Vick, CBE 1994; DL; company director; Chairman, Great Fosters (1931) Ltd, since 1958; Member Board, Teesside Development Corporation, since 1987; *b* 30 April 1931; *o s* of late Sir Harold Sutcliffe and Emily Theodora Cochrane; *m* 1959, Cecilia Mary, *e d* of Ralph Meredyth Turton; three *s* one *d*. *Educ:* Winchester Coll.; New Coll., Oxford (MA). 2nd Lieut RA, 1950–51. Called to Bar, Inner Temple, 1956; practised until 1960, Midland Circuit. Chairman: North Housing Ltd, 1985–93; North Housing Association Ltd, 1985–94; Director: Allied Investors Trusts Ltd, 1958–69; Norton Junction Sand & Gravel Ltd, 1958–64; Tyne Tees Waste Disposal Ltd, 1964–71. Manager, Kildale Estate, 1965–. Mem., Housing Corp., 1982–88. Mem. Bd, Civic Trust, 1989–93; Chm., North East Civic Trust (Northern Heritage), 1989–93 (Chm., Northern Heritage Trust, 1981–89; Vice-Chm., Civic Trust NE, 1977–89). Contested (C): Oldham West, 1959; Chorley, Lancs, 1964; Middlesbrough West, 1966. MP (C) Middlesbrough W, 1970–Feb. 1974. Contested (C) Teesside Thornaby, Oct. 1974. Chairman: Country Endeavour, 1983–88; Bow Street Project, Guisborough, 1988–; Pres., N Yorks Youth Clubs, 1984–93 (Chm., 1966–70); Mem., N Yorks Moors Nat. Park Cttee, 1982–88. DL Cleveland, 1983; High Sheriff, N Yorks, 1987–88. *Recreations:* woodlands, gardening, travel, shooting. *Address:* Chapelgarth, Great Broughton, Middlesbrough, N Yorks TS9 7ET. *T:* Stokesley (01642) 712228.

SUTCLIFFE, Linda, (Mrs P. B. Walker); Her Honour Judge Sutcliffe; a Circuit Judge, since 1993; *b* 2 Dec. 1946; *d* of James Loftus Woodward and Florence Woodward; *m* 1st, 1968, David Iain Sutcliffe (marr. diss. 1979); 2nd, 1987, Peter Brian Walker. *Educ:* Eccles Grammar Sch.; LSE (LLB Hons 1968). Called to the Bar, Gray's Inn, 1975; Lectr in Law, Univ. of Sheffield, 1968–76, part-time 1976–81; in practice at the Bar, 1976–93; a Recorder, 1991–93. Part-time Chm., Industrial Tribunals, 1983–92. FRSA. *Recreations:* music, gardening. *Address:* c/o The Courts Administrator, Lord Chancellor's Department, 10th Floor, Pennine Centre, 20/22 Hawley Centre, Sheffield S1 2EA.

SUTER, Michael; Chief Executive, Shropshire County Council, 1987–92; *b* 21 Jan. 1944; *s* of Robert and Rose Suter; *m* 1963, Sandra Harrison; two *s*. *Educ:* Liverpool Collegiate Sch.; Liverpool Univ. (LLB). Solicitor. Dep. Chief Exec., Notts CC, 1980–87. *Recreations:* music, gardening, watching old Hollywood films, visiting Spain. *Address:* Redcliffe House, Weston-under-Redcastle, Shrewsbury, Shropshire SY4 5UX.

SUTHERLAND, family name of **Countess of Sutherland.**

SUTHERLAND, 6th Duke of, *cr* 1833; **John Sutherland Egerton,** TD; DL; Bt 1620; Baron Gower, 1703; Earl Gower, Viscount Trentham, 1746; Marquis of Stafford (county), 1786; Viscount Brackley and Earl of Ellesmere, 1846; *b* 10 May 1915; *o s* of 4th Earl of Ellesmere and Violet (*d* 1976), *e d* of 4th Earl of Durham; *S* father, 1944; *S* kinsman as Duke of Sutherland, 1963; *m* 1st, 1939, Lady Diana Percy (*d* 1978), *yr d* of 8th Duke of Northumberland; 2nd, 1979, Evelyn, *e d* of late Maj. Robert Moubray. Served War of 1939–45 (prisoner). DL Berwickshire, 1955. *Heir: c* Francis Ronald Egerton [*b* 18 Feb. 1940; *m* 1974, Victoria Mary, *d* of Maj.-Gen. Edward Alexander Wilmot Williams, CB, CBE, MC; two *s*]. *Address:* Mertoun, St Boswell's, Melrose, Roxburghshire TD6 0EA; Lingay Cottage, Hall Farm, Newmarket CB8 0TX. *Clubs:* White's, Turf; Jockey (Newmarket).

See also J. M. E. Askew, Lady M. Colville, Baron Home of the Hirsel.

SUTHERLAND, Countess of (24th in line) *cr* (*c*) 1235; **Elizabeth Millicent Sutherland;** Lady Strathnaver (*c*) 1235; Chief of Clan Sutherland; *b* 30 March 1921; *o c* of Lord Alistair St Clair Sutherland-Leveson-Gower, MC (*d* 1921; 2nd *s* of 4th Duke), and Baroness Osten Driesen (*d* 1931); *niece* of 5th Duke of Sutherland, KT, PC; *S* (to uncle's Earldom of Sutherland and Lordship of Strathnaver), 1963; *m* 1946, Charles Noel Janson (DL, 1959–93), late Welsh Guards; two *s* one *d* (and one *s* decd). *Educ:* Queen's College, Harley Street, W1, and abroad. Land Army, 1939–41; Laboratory Technician: Raigmore Hospital, Inverness, 1941–43; St Thomas' Hospital, SE1, 1943–45. Chm., Dunrobin Castle Ltd. *Recreations:* reading, swimming. *Heir: e s* Lord Strathnaver, *qv*. *Address:* Dunrobin Castle, Sutherland; House of Tongue, by Lairg, Sutherland; 39 Edwardes Square, W8 6HJ. *T:* 0171–603 0659.

SUTHERLAND, Hon. Lord; Ronald Iain Sutherland; a Senator of the College of Justice in Scotland, since 1985; *b* 23 Jan. 1932; *s* of J. W. and A. K. Sutherland, Edinburgh; *m* 1964, Janice Mary, *d* of W. S. Miller, Edinburgh; two *s*. *Educ:* Edinburgh Academy; Edinburgh University. MA 1951, LLB 1953. Admitted to Faculty of Advocates, 1956; QC (Scot.) 1969. Advocate Depute, 1962–64, 1971–77; Standing Junior Counsel to Min. of Defence (Army Dept), 1964–69. Mem., Criminal Injuries Compensation Bd, 1977–85. *Recreations:* sailing, shooting. *Address:* 38 Lauder Road, Edinburgh EH9 1UE. *T:* 0131–667 5280. *Clubs:* New (Edinburgh); Hon. Company of Edinburgh Golfers.

SUTHERLAND, Anthony (Frederic Arthur); Under-Secretary, Department of Employment, retired; *b* 19 Oct. 1916; *e s* of Bertram and Grace Sutherland; *m* 1940, Betty Josephine Glass; one *s* two *d*. *Educ:* Christ's Hosp.; Gonville and Caius Coll., Cambridge (Classical Schol.). 1st cl. hons Classics, 1938; MA 1944. HM Forces, 1940–45 (Major, Mddx Regt). Asst Prin., Min. of Labour, 1938; Prin., 1943; Prin. Private Sec. to Ministers of Labour, 1948–53; Counsellor (Labour), British Embassy, Rome, 1953–55; Asst Sec., 1955; Imp. Def. Coll., 1960; Under-Sec., 1967. Coronation Medal, 1953; Silver Jubilee Medal, 1977. *Recreations:* philately, bird watching. *Address:* 53 Wieland Road, Northwood, Mddx HA6 3QX. *T:* Northwood (01923) 822078. *Club:* Civil Service.

SUTHERLAND, Colin John MacLean; QC (Scot.) 1990; *b* 20 May 1954; *s* of Eric Alexander Cruickshank Sutherland and Mary Macaulay or Sutherland; *m* 1988, Jane Alexander Turnbull or Sutherland; two *s*. *Educ:* Hurst Grange Prep. Sch., Stirling; Edinburgh Acad.; Edinburgh Univ. (LLB Hons). Advocate, 1977; Advocate Depute, 1986–89. Treas., Faculty of Advocates, 1994–. *Address:* 10 Eton Terrace, Edinburgh EH4 1QD. *T:* 0131–332 6725. *Club:* Scottish Arts (Edinburgh).

SUTHERLAND, Euan Ross, CB 1993; Parliamentary Counsel, since 1989; *b* 24 Nov. 1943; *s* of Dr Alister Sutherland and Margaret Sutherland; *m* 1967, Katharine Mary Jenkins, *qv*; one *s* one *d*. *Educ:* Kingswood Sch., Bath; Balliol Coll., Oxford (BA Hist.). Called to the Bar, Inner Temple, 1969; Office of the Parliamentary Counsel, 1974–; seconded to: Govt of Solomon Is, 1979–81; Law Commn, 1986–88. *Recreations:* music, gardening, hill-walking. *Address:* Office of the Parliamentary Counsel, 36 Whitehall, SW1A 2AY.

SUTHERLAND, Ian, MA; Director of Education and Training to Health Education Council, 1971–86; *b* 7 July 1926; *m* 1951, Virginia Scovil Bliss (marr. diss. 1978); one *s* one *d*. *Educ:* Wyggeston Grammar School, Leicester; Sidney Sussex College, Cambridge. Assistant Professor of Classics, Univ. of New Brunswick, NB, Canada, 1949–50; Asst Master: Christ's Hospital, 1951–52; Harrow School, 1952–60; Head Master, St John's School, Leatherhead, 1960–70; Dir of Educn, Health Educn Council, 1970–71. Mem., Wandsworth HA, 1986–89. Governor, Reeds Sch., 1980–93. *Publications:* From Pericles to Cleophon, 1954; (ed) Health Education: perspectives and choices, 1979; Health Education, Half a Policy: the rise and fall of the Health Education Council, 1987; Around the World by Train, 1991. *Recreations:* painting, cricket. *Address:* 14 The Green, Great Bowden, Market Harborough, Leics LE16 7EU. *Clubs:* United Oxford & Cambridge University, MCC, Free Foresters'.

SUTHERLAND, Dr Ian Boyd; Senior Administrative Medical Officer, South Western Regional Hospital Board, 1970–73; Regional Medical Officer, South Western Regional Health Authority, 1973–80; *b* 19 Oct. 1926; *s* of William Sutherland and Grace Alexandra Campbell; *m* 1950, Charlotte Winifred Cordin; two *d*. *Educ:* Bradford Grammar Sch.; Edinburgh Univ. MB, ChB; FRCPE, FFCM, DPH. Medical Officer, RAF, 1950–52; Asst MOH, Counties of Roxburgh and Selkirk, 1953–55; Dep. MOH, County and Borough of Inverness, 1955–59; Dep. County MOH, Oxfordshire CC, 1959–60; Asst SMO, Leeds Regional Hosp. Bd, 1960–63; Dep. Sen. Admin. MO, SW Regl Hosp Bd, 1963–70; Community Medicine Specialist, Lothian Health Bd, 1980–86. Research Fellow, Dept of Clin. Surgery, Univ. of Edinburgh, 1986–88. *Recreations:* reading, art. *Address:* 8 Chesterfield Road, Eastbourne, E Sussex BN20 7NU.

SUTHERLAND, James, CBE 1974; Partner, McClure Naismith, Anderson & Gardiner (formerly McClure Naismith), Solicitors, Glasgow and Edinburgh, 1951–87; *b* 15 Feb. 1920; *s* of James Sutherland, JP and Agnes Walker; *m* 1st, 1948, Elizabeth Kelly Barr; two *s*; 2nd, 1984, Grace Williamson Dawson. *Educ:* Queens Park Secondary Sch., Glasgow; Glasgow Univ. MA 1940, LLB 1948; Hon. LLD 1985. Served Royal Signals, 1940–46. Examr in Scots Law, 1951–55 and Mercantile Law and Industrial Law, 1968–69, Glasgow Univ.; Chm., Glasgow South Nat. Insce Tribunal, 1964–66; Member: Bd of Management, Glasgow Maternity and Women's Hosps, 1964–74 (Chm. 1966–74); Council, Law Soc. of Scotland, 1959–77 (Vice-Pres. 1969–70; Pres. 1972–74); Council, Internat. Bar Assoc., 1972– (Chm., Gen. Practice Section, 1978–80; Sec.-Gen., 1980–84; Pres., 1984–86); GDC, 1975–89; Scottish Dental Estimates Bd, 1982–87; Vice-Chm., Glasgow Eastern Health Council, 1975–77; Deacon, Incorporation of Barbers, Glasgow, 1962–63; Sec., Local Dental Cttee, City of Glasgow, 1955–65; Dean, Royal Faculty of Procurators in Glasgow, 1977–80. Mem. Court, Univ. of Strathclyde, 1977–92. *Recreation:* golf. *Address:* Greenacres, 20/1 Easter Belmont Road, Edinburgh EH12 6EX. *T:* 0131–337 1888. *Clubs:* Western (Glasgow); Royal and Ancient.

SUTHERLAND, Sir James (Runcieman), Kt 1992; FBA 1953; MA, BLitt; Emeritus Professor of Modern English Literature, University College, London (Lord Northcliffe Professor, 1951–67); *b* Aberdeen, 26 April 1900; *s* of Henry Edward Sutherland, Stockbroker; *m* 1st, 1931, Helen (*d* 1975) *d* of Will H. Dircks; 2nd, 1977, Eve Betts, *widow* of Ernest Betts. *Educ:* Aberdeen Grammar Sch.; Univ. of Aberdeen; Oxford Univ. BLitt Oxford, 1927. Lecturer in English, Univ. of Saskatchewan, 1921–23; Merton Coll., Oxford, 1923–25; Chancellor's English Essay Prize, Oxford, 1925; Lecturer in English, University College, Southampton, 1925; Lecturer in English, University of Glasgow, 1925–30; Senior Lecturer in English, University College, London, 1930–36; Professor of English Literature, Birkbeck College, London, 1936–44; Prof. of English Language and Literature, Queen Mary College, London, 1944–51. Warton lecturer on English Poetry to the British Academy, 1944; editor of The Review of English Studies, 1940–47. Visiting Professor: Harvard Univ., 1947; Indiana Univ., 1950–51, UCLA, 1967–68; Mellon Prof., Univ. of Pittsburgh, 1965; Berg Prof., NY Univ., 1969–70. Sir Walter Scott Lectures, Edinburgh University, 1952; Clark Lectures, Cambridge University, 1956; Alexander Lectures, Toronto University, 1956; Public Orator, University of London, 1957–62; W. P. Ker Memorial Lecture, Glasgow Univ., 1962; Clark Library Fellow, Univ. of California, Los Angeles, 1962–63. Hon. Mem. Modern Language Assoc. of America, 1960. Hon. LLD Aberdeen, 1955; Hon. DLitt Edinburgh, 1968; Hon. Doctor, Liège, 1974. *Publications:* Leucocholy (Poems), 1926; Jasper Weeple, 1930; The Medium of Poetry, 1934; Defoe, 1937; Background for Queen Anne, 1939; (ed) The Dunciad, 1943; English in the Universities, 1945; A Preface to Eighteenth Century Poetry, 1948; The English Critic, 1952; The Oxford Book of English Talk, 1953; On English Prose, 1957; English Satire, 1958; English Literature of the late Seventeenth Century, 1969; Daniel Defoe: a critical study, 1971; editions of plays by Nicholas Rowe, Thomas Dekker, John Dryden, William Shakespeare, and of Lucy Hutchinson's Memoirs of the Life of Colonel Hutchinson, 1973; (ed) The Oxford Book of Literary Anecdotes, 1975; The Restoration Newspaper and its Development, 1986; contributions to various literary journals. *Recreations:* fishing, second-hand book catalogues. *Address:* Oaken Holt Residential Home, Farmoor, Eynsham, Oxford OX2 9NL.

SUTHERLAND, Dame Joan, OM 1991; AC 1975; DBE 1979 (CBE 1961); soprano; *b* 7 Nov. 1926; *d* of McDonald Sutherland, Sydney, NSW, and Muriel Alston Sutherland; *m* 1954, Richard Bonynge, *qv*; one *s*. *Educ:* St Catherine's, Waverley, Sydney. Début as Dido in Purcell's Dido and Aeneas, Sydney, 1947; subsequently concerts, oratorios and broadcasts throughout Australia. Came to London, 1951; joined Covent Garden, 1952, where she remained resident soprano for 7 years; won international fame with début as Lucia di Lammermoor, Covent Garden, 1959, and by early 1960s had sung throughout the Americas and Europe. Has specialised throughout her career in the popular and lesser-known bel canto operatic repertoire of 18th and 19th centuries, and has made many recordings. Hon. DMus: Sydney, 1984; Oxon, 1992. *Publication:* The Joan Sutherland Album (autobiog., with Richard Bonynge), 1986; *Relevant publications:* Joan Sutherland, by R. Braddon, 1962; Joan Sutherland, by E. Greenfield, 1972; La Stupenda, by B. Adams, 1980; Joan Sutherland, by Norma Major, 1987. *Recreations:* reading, gardening, needlepoint. *Address:* c/o Ingpen & Williams, 14 Kensington Court, W8 5DN.

SUTHERLAND, John Alexander Muir; Chief Executive, Celtic Films Ltd, since 1986; *b* 5 April 1933; *m* 1970, Mercedes Gonzalez; two *s*. *Educ:* India; Trinity Coll., Glenalmond; Hertford Coll., Oxford (MA). 2nd Lieut, HLI, 1952–53. Economist, Fed. Govt of Nigeria, 1957–58; film production, Spain and Portugal, 1958–62; Head of Presentation and Programme Planning, Border TV, 1963–66; Programme Co-Ordinator: ABC TV, 1966–68; Thames TV, 1968–72; Controller of Programme Sales, Thames TV, 1973–74; Man. Dir, 1975–82, Dep Chm., 1982–86, Thames TV Internat.; Dir of Programmes, Thames TV, 1982–86. Dir, Border TV, 1986–. Executive Producer: Red Fox, 1991; Sharpe series, 1992–95. *Address:* Celtic Films Ltd, 1–2 Bromley Place, W1P 5HB. *T:* 0171–637 7651.

SUTHERLAND, Prof. John Andrew, PhD; FRSL; Lord Northcliffe Professor of Modern English Literature, University College London, since 1992; *b* 9 Oct. 1938; *s* of Jack Sutherland and Elizabeth (*née* Salter); *m* 1967, Guilland Watt; one *s*. *Educ:* Colchester Royal Grammar Sch.; Leicester Univ. (BA 1964; MA 1966); Edinburgh Univ. (PhD 1973). FRSL 1991. Nat. Service, 2nd Lieut, Suffolk Regt, 1958–60. Lectr in English, Univ. of Edinburgh, 1965–72; Lectr, then Reader in English, UCL, 1972–84; Prof. of English, CIT, 1984–92. *Publications:* Thackeray at Work, 1974; Victorian Novelists and Publishers, 1976; Fiction and the Fiction Industry, 1978; Bestsellers, 1980; Offensive Literature, 1982; The Longman Companion to Victorian Fiction, 1989; Mrs Humphry Ward, 1992; The Life of Walter Scott: a critical biography, 1995; Victorian Fiction: writers, publishers, readers, 1995. *Recreation:* walking. *Address:* Department of English, University College London, Gower Street, WC1E 6BT. *T:* 0171–387 7050. *Club:* Athenæum.

SUTHERLAND, John Brewer; (3rd Bt *cr* 1921, but does not use the title); *b* 19 Oct. 1931; *s* of Sir (Benjamin) Ivan Sutherland, 2nd Bt, and Marjorie Constance Daniel (*d* 1980), *yr d* of Frederic William Brewer, OBE; *S* father, 1980; *m* 1st, 1958, Alice Muireall (*d* 1984), *d* of late W. Stamford Henderson, Kelso; three *s* one *d*; 2nd, 1988, Heather, *d* of late David A. Gray, Chester-le-Street. *Educ:* Sedbergh; St Catharine's Coll., Cambridge. *Heir:* *s* Peter William Sutherland, *b* 18 May 1963.

SUTHERLAND, John Menzies, CEng, FICE, FIStructE, FASCE; Secretary, Joint Board of Moderators, Institution of Civil Engineers, 1985–93; *b* 19 June 1928; *s* of John Menzies and Margaret Rae Sutherland; *m* 1962, Margaret Mary (*née* Collins); one *s* one *d*. *Educ:* Royal Technical Coll., Glasgow. Eur. Ing. 1988. Indentured Civil Engineer, City Engineer, Glasgow, 1945–51; Engineer, Costains Group, 1952–56; Site Agent, Pakistan and Chief Engineer, Middle East, Gammon Group, 1956–61; Engineer Adviser (Colombo Plan), new capital city, Islamabad, Pakistan, 1962–66; Associate Partner, Bullen & Partners, 1966–69; Chief Civil Engineer, overseas plant construction, Union International Co. (Vestey Gp Holding Co.), 1970–74; Board Dir and Dir Engineering Projects, Internat Military Services Ltd, 1974–83 (2 years Malaysia); Gen. Manager, BTR-Swire Projects, Singapore, 1983–85. *Publication:* Naval Bases and Infrastructure, 1979. *Recreations:* music, collecting Victorian ceramics. *Address:* 13 Ravenshill, Chislehurst, Kent BR7 5PD. *T:* 0181–467 0037. *Clubs;* Royal Over-Seas League; Chislehurst Golf.

SUTHERLAND, Sir Maurice, Kt 1976; Member, Cleveland County Council, 1973–93 (Leader, 1973–77 and 1981–85; Leader of Opposition, 1977–81); *b* 12 July 1915; *s* of Thomas Daniel and Ada Sutherland; *m* 1st, 1941, Beatrice (*née* Skinner); one *s*; 2nd, 1960, Jane Ellen (*née* Bell); one step-*d*; 3rd, Ellen Margaret (*née* Guy). *Educ:* Stockton Secondary Sch. War service with Green Howards and RCS, N Africa and NW Europe. Solicitor, 1937–. Mem. Stockton Borough Council, 1957–67; Chm., Teesside Steering Cttee, 1966–67; Leader of Labour Party, Teesside County Borough Council, 1967–74; Mayor of Teesside, 1972–73. Chm., Northern Econ. Planning Council, 1977–79. Hon. LLM Teesside, 1994. *Recreations:* cricket, walking, chess, politics. *Address:* 8 Manor Close, Low Worsall, Yarm, Cleveland TS15 9QE. *T:* Eaglescliffe (01642) 782799.

SUTHERLAND, Muir; *see* Sutherland, J. A. M.

SUTHERLAND, Prof. (Norman) Stuart, MA, DPhil; Professor of Experimental Psychology, University of Sussex, 1965–92, now Professor Emeritus; *b* 26 March 1927; *s* of Norman McLeod Sutherland; *m* 1966, Jose Louise Fogden; two *d*. *Educ:* Magdalen Coll., Oxford. BA Hons Lit. Hum. 1949 and PPP 1953; John Locke Scholar 1953. Fellow; Magdalen Coll., 1954–58; Merton Coll., 1962–64; Oxford Univ. Lectr in Exper. Psychol., 1960–64. Vis. Prof., MIT, 1961–62, 1964–65. Director: William Schlackman Ltd, 1968–81; Deedland Ltd, 1987–. *Publications:* Shape Discrimination by Animals, 1959; (ed jtly) Animal Discrimination Learning, 1969; (with N. J. Mackintosh) Mechanisms of Animal Discrimination Learning, 1971; Breakdown: a personal crisis and a medical dilemma, 1976, 2nd edn 1987; (ed) Tutorial Essays in Psychology, vol. 1, 1977, vol. 2, 1979; Discovering the Human Mind, 1982; Men Change Too, 1987; Macmillan Dictionary of Psychology, 1989; Irrationality: the enemy within, 1992; scientific papers mainly on perception and learning. *Address:* Centre for Research on Perception and Cognition, Sussex University, Brighton BN1 9QG. *T:* Brighton (01273) 678304.

SUTHERLAND, Peter Denis, SC; Partner and Chairman, Goldman Sachs International, since 1995; Deputy Chairman, The British Petroleum Co. plc, since 1995; *b* 25 April 1946; *s* of W. G. Sutherland and Barbara Sutherland (*née* Nealon); *m* 1971, Maria Del Pilar Cabria Valcarcel; two *s* one *d*. *Educ:* Gonzaga Coll.; University Coll. Dublin (BCL). Called to Bar: King's Inns, 1968; Middle Temple, 1976; Attorney of New York Bar, 1981; Attorney and Counsellor of Supreme Court of USA, 1986. Tutor in Law, University Coll., Dublin, 1968–71; practising member of Irish Bar, 1968–81, and 1981–82; Senior Counsel 1980; Attorney General of Ireland, June 1981–Feb. 1982 and Dec. 1982–Dec. 1984; Mem. Council of State, 1981–82 and 1982–84; Comr for Competition and Comr for Social Affairs and Educn, EEC, 1985–86, for Competition and Relns with European Parliament, 1986–88; Chm., Allied Irish Banks, 1989–93; Dir Gen., GATT, 1993–94. Director: GPA, 1989–93; CRH plc, 1989–93; James Crean plc, 1989–93; Delta Air Lines

Inc., 1990–93; Investor, 1995–. Chm., Bd of Govs, Eur. Inst. of Public Admin, 1991–. Hon. LLD: St Louis, 1985; NUI, 1990; Dublin City, 1992; Holy Cross, Mass, 1994. Gold Medal, Eur. Parlt, 1988. Grand Cross, King Leopold II (Belgium), 1989; Grand Cross of Civil Merit (Spain), 1989; Chevalier, Légion d'Honneur (France), 1993. *Publications:* Premier Janvier 1993 ce qui va changer en Europe, 1988; contribs to law jls. *Recreations:* sports generally, reading. *Address:* Goldman Sachs International, Peterborough Court, 133 Fleet Street, EC4A 2BB. *Clubs:* Hibernian United Service, Fitzwilliam Lawn Tennis (Dublin); Lansdowne FC.

SUTHERLAND, Ranald Iain; *see* Sutherland, Hon. Lord.

SUTHERLAND, Prof. Sir Stewart (Ross), Kt 1995; FBA 1992; FRSE; Principal and Vice-Chancellor, University of Edinburgh, since 1994; *b* 25 Feb. 1941; *s* of late George A. C. Sutherland and of Ethel (*née* Masson); *m* 1964, Sheena Robertson; one *s* two *d*. *Educ:* Woodside Sch.; Robert Gordon's Coll.; Univ. of Aberdeen (MA); Corpus Christi Coll., Cambridge (Hon. Schol.; MA; Hon. Fellow, 1989). FRSE 1995. Asst Lectr in Philosophy, UCNW, 1965; Lectr in Philosophy, 1968, Sen. Lectr, 1972, Reader, 1976, Univ. of Stirling; King's College London: Prof. of Hist. and Philos. of Religion, 1977–85, Titular Prof., 1985–94; Vice-Principal, 1981–85; Principal, 1985–90; FKC 1983.; Vice-Chancellor, London Univ., 1990–94; Chief Inspector of Schools, 1992–94. Vis. Fellow, ANU, 1974; Gillespie Vis. Prof., Wooster Ohio, 1975. Lectures: Hope, Stirling, 1979; Ferguson, Manchester, 1982; Wilde, Oxford, 1981–84; Boutwood, Cambridge, 1990; F. D. Maurice, KCL, 1993; Drummond, Stirling, 1993; St George's, Windsor, 1993; Debrabant, Southampton, 1994; Ballard Matthews, Bangor, 1994. Chairman: British Acad. Postgrad. Studentships Cttee, 1987–95; Royal Inst. of Philosophy, 1988–; London Conf. on Overseas Students, 1989–94; Vice-Chm., CVCP, 1989–92. Member: C of E Bd of Educn, 1980–84; Arts Sub-Cttee, UGC, 1983–85; City Parochial Foundn, 1988–90; Council for Sci. and Technology, 1993–; Humanities Res. Bd, Brit. Acad., 1994–95. Member: NW Thames RHA, 1992–94; N Thames RHA, 1994. Pres., Soc. for the Study of Theology, 1985, 1986. Chm., Ethiopian Gemini Trust, 1987–92. Editor, Religious Studies, 1984–90; Member, Editorial Board: Scottish Jl of Religious Studies, 1980–; Modern Theology, 1984–91. Associate Fellow, Warwick Univ., 1986–94; Hon. Fellow, UCNW, 1990. FCP 1994. Hon. LHD: Wooster, Ohio, 1986; Commonwealth Univ. of Virginia, 1992; Hon. LLD: Aberdeen, 1990; NUI, 1992; Hon. DLitt Richmond, 1995; DUniv Stirling, 1993; Dr *hc* Uppsala, 1995. *Publications:* Atheism and the Rejection of God, 1977, 2nd edn 1980; (ed with B. L. Hebblethwaite) The Philosophical Frontiers of Christian Theology, 1983; God, Jesus and Belief, 1984; Faith and Ambiguity, 1984; (ed) The World's Religions, 1988; (ed with T. A. Roberts) Religion, Reason and the Self, 1989; articles in books and learned jls. *Recreations:* Tassie medallions, theatre, jazz. *Address:* University of Edinburgh, Old College, South Bridge, Edinburgh EH8 9YL. *T:* 0131–650 1000. *Club:* Athenæum.

SUTHERLAND, Prof. Stuart; *see* Sutherland, Prof. N. S.

SUTHERLAND, Veronica Evelyn, (Mrs A. J. Sutherland), CMG 1988; HM Diplomatic Service; Ambassador to the Republic of Ireland, since 1995; *b* 25 April 1939; *d* of late Lt-Col Maurice George Beckett, KOYLI, and of Constance Mary Cavenagh-Mainwaring; *m* 1981, Alex James Sutherland. *Educ:* Royal Sch., Bath; London Univ. (BA); Southampton Univ. (MA). Joined HM Diplomatic Service, 1965; Second, later First Sec., Copenhagen, 1967–70; FCO, 1970–75; First Sec., New Delhi, 1975–78; FCO, 1978–80; Counsellor, 1981; Perm. UK Deleg. to UNESCO, 1981–84; Counsellor, FCO, 1984–87; Ambassador to Côte d'Ivoire, 1987–90; Asst Under-Sec. of State (Personnel), FCO, 1990–95. *Recreations:* theatre, painting. *Address:* c/o Foreign and Commonwealth Office, SW1A 2AH.

SUTHERLAND, Sir William (George MacKenzie), Kt 1988; QPM 1981; Chief Constable, Lothian and Borders Police, since 1983; *b* 12 Nov. 1933; *m* 1957, Jennie Abbott; two *d*. *Educ:* Inverness Technical High Sch. Cheshire Police, 1954–73; Surrey Police, 1973–75; Hertfordshire Police, 1975–79; Chief Constable of Bedfordshire, 1979–83. Hon. Sec., ACPO in Scotland, 1985–; Chm., British Police Athletic Assoc., 1991– (Chm., Squash Section, 1984–; Chm., Ski Section, 1992–). FRSA 1992. *Recreations:* squash, hill walking. *Address:* Police Headquarters, Fettes Avenue, Edinburgh EH4 1RB. *T:* 0131–311 3131.

SUTHIWART-NARUEPUT, Dr Owart; Kt Grand Cordon: Order of Crown of Thailand, 1981; Order of White Elephant, 1985; Hon. CMG 1972; Lecturer, since 1987, Director, Language Institute, since 1990, Thammasat University; Member, Constitutional Tribunal, since 1992; *b* 19 Sept. 1926; *s* of Luang Suthiwart-Narueput and Mrs Khae; *m* 1959, Angkana (*née* Sthapitanond); one *s* one *d*. *Educ:* Thammasat Univ., Thailand (BA Law); Fletcher Sch. of Law and Diplomacy, Tufts Univ., USA (MA, PhD); Nat. Defence Coll. Joined Min. of For. Affairs, 1945; Asst Sec. to Minister, 1958; SEATO Res. Officer, 1959; Protocol Dept, 1963; Econ. Dept, 1964; Counsellor, Thai Embassy, Canberra, 1965; Dir-Gen. of Inf. Dept, 1969; Ambassador to India, Nepal, Sri Lanka, and Minister to Afghanistan, 1972; Ambassador to Poland, E Germany and Bulgaria, 1976; Dir-Gen. of Political Dept, 1977; Under-Sec. of State (Permanent Sec.) for For. Affairs, 1979; Ambassador to France and Perm. Representative to UNESCO, 1980; Ambassador: to Switzerland and to Holy See, 1983; to UK, 1984–86, concurrently to Ireland, 1985–86. Chm. Adv. Gp, Thai Investors Assoc., 1990–. Mem. Exec. Cttee, Internat. Understanding Program, Inst. Asian Studies, Chulalongkorn Univ., 1988–. Commander: Order of Phoenix, Greece, 1963; Order of Orange-Nassau, Netherlands, 1963; Bintang Djasa (1st Cl.), Indonesia, 1970; Order of Merit, Poland, 1979; Grand Officier, L'Ordre Nat. du Mérite, France, 1983. *Publication:* The Evolution of Thailand's Foreign Relations since 1855: from extraterritoriality to equality, 1955. *Recreations:* reading, music. *Address:* 193 Lane 4 Navathanee, Sukha-Pibarn 2 Road, Kannayao, Bunggum, Bangkok 10230, Thailand. *Clubs:* Old England Students' Assoc., Amer. Univs Alumni Assoc. (Bangkok).

SUTTIE, Sir (George) Philip Grant-, 8th Bt, *cr* 1702; *b* 20 Dec. 1938; *o s* of late Maj. George Donald Grant-Suttie and Marjorie Neville, *d* of Capt. C. E. Carter, RN, of Newfoundland; *S* cousin, 1947; *m* 1962, Elspeth Mary (marr. diss. 1969), *e d* of Maj.-Gen. R. E. Urquhart, CB, DSO; one *s*. *Educ:* Sussex Composite High School, NB, Canada; Macdonald College, McGill University, Montreal. *Recreations:* flying, fishing, farming, forestry. *Heir: s* James Edward Grant-Suttie [*b* 29 May 1965; *m* 1989, Emma Jane, *yr d* of Peter Craig]. *Address:* (seat) Balgone, North Berwick EH39 5PB; The Granary, Sheriff Hall, North Berwick, East Lothian EH39 5PB. *T:* North Berwick (01620) 2569, (office) 3750.

SUTTILL, Dr Margaret Joan, (Mrs G. A. Rink); *d* of Ernest Montrose and Caroline Hyde; *m* 1st, 1935, F. A. Suttill, DSO, LLB (*d* 1945); two *s*; 2nd, 1949, G. A. Rink, QC (*d* 1983). *Educ:* Royal Free Hospital Medical School. MB, BS; MRCP 1972. Director, Medical Dept, and Chief Medical Advr, British Council, retired. Vice Pres. and Mem. Court, DGAA, 1995– (Mem. Council, 1984–95). *Recreations:* music, reading, walking, consumer problems. *Address:* 173 Oakwood Court, W14 8JE. *T:* 0171–602 2143.

SUTTON, Alan John; Founder Chairman and Chief Executive, Anglolink Ltd, since 1985; *b* 16 March 1936; *s* of William Clifford Sutton and Emily Sutton (*née* Batten); *m* 1957, Glenis (*née* Henry); one *s* one *d*. *Educ:* Bristol Univ. BSc (Hons) Elec. Engrg; MIEE. Design, Production and Trials Evaluation of Guided Missiles, English Electric Aviation Ltd, 1957–63; Design, Production, Sales and General Management of Scientific Digital, Analogue and Hybrid Computers, Solartron Electronic Group Ltd, 1963–69; International Sales Manager, Sales Director, of A. B. Electronic Components Ltd, 1969–73; Managing Director, A. B. Connectors, 1973–76; Industrial Dir, Welsh Office, 1976–79; Welsh Development Agency: Exec. Dir (Industry and Investment), 1979–83; Exec. Dir (Marketing), 1983–85; Sen. Vice-Pres., USA W Coast Div., WINvest, 1985–88. *Recreation:* golf. *Address:* 56 Heol-y-Delyn, Lisvane, Cardiff CF4 5SR. *T:* Cardiff (01222) 753194.

SUTTON, Barry Bridge, JP; Headmaster, Taunton School, since 1987; *b* 21 Jan. 1937; *s* of Albert and Ethel Sutton; *m* 1961, Margaret Helen (*née* Palmer); one *s* two *d*. *Educ:* Eltham Coll.; Peterhouse, Cambridge (MA Hist. Tripos); Bristol Univ. (PGCE). Asst Master and Housemaster, Wycliffe College, 1961–75; Headmaster, Hereford Cathedral School, 1975–87. Chm. Cttee, Scout Assoc. Council, 1994–. JP Hereford, 1982, Taunton, 1987. *Recreations:* hill-walking, scouting. *Address:* Taunton School, Taunton, Somerset TA2 6AD. *T:* Taunton (01823) 284596. *Club:* East India and Public Schools.

SUTTON, Colin Bertie John, QPM 1985; Director, Police Scientific Development Branch, Home Office, since 1992; *b* 6 Dec. 1938; *s* of Bertie Sidney Russell Sutton and Phyllis May; *m* 1960, Anne Margaret Davis. *Educ:* King Edward VI Grammar School, Stratford-upon-Avon; University College London (LLB 1970). Police Constable, 1957, Sergeant, 1964, Inspector, 1966, Warwicks County Police; Chief Inspector, 1970, Supt, 1972, Chief Supt, 1974, Warwicks and Coventry Constabulary; Chief Supt, W Midlands Police, 1974–77; Asst Chief Constable, Leics Constabulary, 1977; Metropolitan Police: Dep. Asst Comr, 1983–84; Asst Comr, 1984–88; Dir, Police Requirements Support Unit, Home Office, 1988–91. Freeman, City of London, 1988; Liveryman, Fletchers' Co., 1989. SBStJ 1990. *Recreations:* golf, angling, squash, music, art, literature. *Address:* Woodcock Hill, Sandridge, St Albans AL4 9HQ. *T:* St Albans (01727) 865051.

SUTTON, Sir Frederick (Walter), Kt 1974; OBE 1971; Founder and Chairman of Directors of the Sutton Group of Companies; *b* 1 Feb. 1915; *s* of late William W. Sutton and Daisy Sutton; *m* 1934; three *s*; *m* 1977, Morna Patricia Smyth. *Educ:* Sydney Technical College. Motor Engineer, founder and Chief Executive of the Sutton group of Companies; Mem. Bd of Directors, and life Governor, Royal New South Wales Inst. for Deaf and Blind Children. *Recreations:* flying, going fishing, boating. *Address:* (office) 114 Bourke Street, Potts Point, Sydney, NSW 2011, Australia. *T:* (2) 3571777. *Clubs:* Royal Aero of NSW (Life Member); Royal Automobile of Australia; Royal Automobile of Victoria; American (Sydney).

SUTTON, Dr Howard Michael, CChem, FRSC; Director, Trade and Industry, West Midlands, since 1994; *b* 12 Nov. 1942; *s* of Albert Sutton and Constance Olive Sutton (*née* Topham); *m* 1967, Diane Cash; one *s* one *d*. *Educ:* Univ. of Edinburgh (BSc 1965; PhD 1968). Res. Fellow, Univ. of Kent at Canterbury, 1968–70; Warren Spring Laboratory: Materials Handling Div., 1970–78; Head, Planning and Marketing, 1978–85; Dep. Dir, 1985–88; Department of Trade and Industry: Head, Shipbuilding and Marine Engineering, 1988–91; Head, Single Market Unit, 1991–93; Head, Mech. Engrg Sponsorship, 1993–94. *Publications:* contribs to learned jls. *Recreations:* writing, drama, music. *Address:* Government Office for West Midlands, 77 Paradise Circus, Queensway, Birmingham B1 2DT. *T:* 0121–212 5206; 161 Moor Green Lane, Birmingham B13 8NT.

SUTTON, Air Marshal Sir John (Matthias Dobson), KCB 1986 (CB 1981); Chairman, Arrow and Inter Management Groups of Companies, since 1995; Chairman, Armed Forces Resettlement Initiative, since 1995; *b* 9 July 1932; *s* of late Harry Rowston Sutton and Gertrude Sutton; *m* 1954 (marr. diss. 1968); one *s* one *d*; *m* 1969, Angela Faith Gray; two *s*. *Educ:* Queen Elizabeth's Grammar Sch., Alford, Lincs. Joined RAF, 1950; pilot trng, commnd, 1951; served on Fighter Sqdns, UK and Germany; Staff Coll., 1963; OC 249 Sqdn, 1964–66; Asst Sec., Chiefs of Staff Cttee, 1966–69; OC 14 Sqdn, 1970–71; Asst Chief of Staff (Policy and Plans), HQ 2 ATAF, 1971–73; Staff, Chief of Def. Staff, 1973–74; RCDS, 1975; Comdt Central Flying Sch., 1976–77; Asst Chief of Air Staff (Policy), 1977–79; Dep. Comdr, RAF Germany, 1980–82; ACDS (Commitments), 1982–84; ACDS (Overseas), 1985; C-in-C, RAF Support Comd, 1986–89; Lt-Gov. and C-in-C, Jersey, 1990–95. KStJ 1990. *Recreations:* golf, ski-ing. *Address:* Pantiles, Stretton, Rutland LE15 7QZ. *Clubs:* Royal Air Force; Colonels (founder Mem.); Luffenham Heath Golf.

SUTTON, John Sydney; General Secretary, Secondary Heads Association, since 1988; *b* 9 June 1936; *s* of Sydney and Mabel Sutton; *m* 1961, Carmen Grandoso Martinez; three *s*. *Educ:* King Edward VI Sch., Southampton; Univ. of Keele (BA Hons, MA). Asst Teacher, Christopher Wren Sch., London, 1958–60; Asst Master, later Head of History, Bemrose Sch., Derby, 1960–68; Head, Social Studies Dept, Sir Wilfrid Martineau Sch., Birmingham, 1968–73; Headmaster: Corby Grammar Sch., 1973; Southwood Sch., Corby, 1973–82; Queen Elizabeth Sch., Corby, 1982–88. Mem. Council, Hansard Soc. for Parly Govt, 1973–. *Publications:* American Government, 1974; Understanding Politics in Modern Britain, 1977; (with L. Robbins and T. Brennan) People and Politics in Britain, 1985; (jtly) School Management in Practice, 1985. *Recreations:* wine appreciation, Geddington Volunteer Fire Brigade. *Address:* 24 Bright Trees Road, Geddington, Kettering, Northants NN14 1BS. *T:* Kettering (01536) 742559. *Clubs:* Royal Over-Seas League; Rotary (Kettering Huxloe).

SUTTON, Rt. Rev. Keith Norman; *see* Lichfield, Bishop of.

SUTTON, Rt. Rev. Peter (Eves), CBE 1990; Bishop of Nelson, New Zealand, 1965–90; Senior Anglican Bishop, 1979–90; Acting Primate, New Zealand, 1985–86; *b* Wellington, NZ, 7 June 1923; *m* 1956, Pamela Cherrington, *e d* of R. A. Dalley, Patin House, Kidderminster; one *s* one *d*. *Educ:* Wellesley Coll.; Nelson Coll.; University of New Zealand. BA 1945; MA 1947; LTh 1948. Deacon, 1947; Priest, 1948 (Wellington); Curate of Wanganui, New Zealand, 1947–50; St John the Evangelist, Bethnal Green, 1950–51; Bishops Hatfield, Diocese of St Albans (England), 1951–52; Vicar of St Cuthberts, Berhampore (NZ), 1952–58; Whangarei, Diocese of Auckland, New Zealand, 1958–64; Archdeacon of Waimate, 1962–64; Dean of Dunedin and Vicar of St Paul's Cathedral, Dunedin, 1964–65. Chm., Cawthron Inst., 1977–90, 1991–93. Founding Mem., Nelson Civic Trust; Founder: Protect our Heritage, Nelson; Friends of Nelson City; Life Mem., Founder's Mus., Nelson; Rep., Provincial Mus. Cttee, 1989–; Patrons' Rep., Suter Art Gall. Bd, 1990–93; NZ Co-ordinator, All Religions, Amnesty Internat.; NZ Rep., St Deiniol's Library, Hawarden, 1988–. Governor, St John's Coll., Auckland, 1965–90. ChStJ 1986; Sub-Prelate, Order of St John, NZ, 1987–. Silver Jubilee Medal, 1977; NZ Commemoration Medal, 1990. *Publication:* Freedom for Convictions, 1971. *Recreation:* golf (Canterbury Univ. Blue). *Address:* 3 Ngatiawa Street, Nelson, New Zealand. *Club:* Nelson (New Zealand).

SUTTON, Dr Peter Morgan; Director, Public Health Laboratory Service Centre for Applied Microbiology and Research, Porton Down, 1979–92; *b* 21 June 1932; *s* of Sir Graham Sutton, CBE, FRS and late Lady Sutton (*née* Doris Morgan); *m* 1959, Helen Ersy Economides; two *s* two *d*. *Educ:* Bishop Wordsworth Sch., Salisbury; Wrekin Coll., Wellington; University Coll. (Fellow, 1985) and University Coll. Hosp. Med. Sch., London. House Surgeon and House Physician, UCH, 1956–57; Graham Scholar in Pathology, Univ. of London, 1958–59; on academic staff of UCH Med. Sch., 1960–65; Vis. Asst Prof. of Pathology, Univ. of Pittsburg, USA, 1966–67; Hon. Consultant Pathologist, UCH, 1967–79; Reader in Pathology, Univ. of London, 1971–79; Vice-Dean, UCH Med. Sch., 1973–78. Vis. Prof., Dept of Biochemical Pathology, UCL, 1983–. Sometime Examr in Pathology, Univ. of London and RCS. *Publications:* The Nature of Cancer, 1962; various papers on fibrinolytic enzymes and novel antiviral compounds. *Recreations:* English literature, history of science. *Address:* Manderley, 34 Bower Gardens, Salisbury, Wilts SP1 2RL. *T:* Salisbury (01722) 323902.

SUTTON, Philip John, RA 1989 (ARA 1977); *b* 20 Oct. 1928; *m* 1954; one *s* three *d*. *Educ:* Slade Sch. of Fine Art, UCL. One-man exhibitions: Roland Browse and Delbanco (now Browse and Darby) Gallery, London, 1958–81; Leeds City Art Gallery, 1960; Newcastle-on-Tyne, 1962; Bradford, 1962; Edinburgh, 1962; Sydney, 1963, 1966, 1970, 1973; Perth, 1963, 1972; Royal Acad. (Diploma Gall.), London, 1977; David Jones Gall., Sydney, 1980; Bonython Art Gall., Adelaide, 1981; Norwich, Bath and New York, 1983; Lichfield Fest., 1985; Beaux Arts Gall., Bath, 1985; Galerie Joël Salaün, Paris, 1988; exhibn of ceramics, Oditte Gilbert Gall., London, 1987; Agnews, London, 1992; touring exhibn, Wales, 1993–94. Designed Post Office 'Greetings' stamps, 1989. *Recreations:* swimming, running. *Address:* 3 Morfa Terrace, Manorbier, Tenby, Dyfed SA70 7TH.

SUTTON, Dr Richard, DSc (Med); FRCP, FACC, FESC; Consultant Cardiologist: Royal Brompton National Heart and Lung Hospital, since 1993; Chelsea and Westminster Hospital (formerly Westminster Hospital), since 1976; British Airways, since 1976; *b* 1 Sept. 1940; *s* of late Dick Brasnett Sutton and of Greta Mary (*née* Leadbeter); *m* 1964, Anna Gunilla (*née* Cassö); one *s*. *Educ:* Gresham's Sch.; King's Coll., London; King's Coll. Hosp. (MB, BS 1964); DSc (Med) London 1988. FRCP 1983 (MRCP 1967); FACC 1975; FESC 1990. Gen. medical trng followed graduation; career in cardiology began at St George's Hosp., London, 1967; Fellow in Cardiol., Univ. of NC, 1968–69; Registrar, Sen. Registrar, then Temp. Consultant, National Heart Hosp., London, 1970–76. Consultant Cardiologist, St Stephen's Hosp., 1976–89; Hon. Consultant Cardiologist: Italian Hosp., London, 1977–89; St Luke's Hosp., London, 1980–. Member: British Medical Assoc.; British Cardiac Soc.; British Pacing and Electrophysiology Group (Co-Founder, Mem. Council, Past Pres. and Hon. Sec.). Governors' Award, Amer. Coll. of Cardiol., 1979 (Scientific Exhibit, Physiol Cardiac Pacing), and 1982 (1st Prize; Scientific Exhibit, 5 yrs of Physiol Cardiac Pacing). Editor in Chief, European Jl of Cardiac Pacing and Electrophysiology, 1991–. *Publications:* Foundations of Cardiac Pacing, pt 1, 1991, pt 2, 1995; articles on many aspects of cardiology incl. cardiac pacing, coronary artery disease, left ventricular function, and assessment of pharm. agents, in Circulation, Amer. Jl of Cardiol., Amer. Heart Jl, Brit. Heart Jl, Pace, Lancet, BMJ, and Oxford Textbook of Medicine, 1967–. *Recreations:* opera, foreign travel, tennis. *Address:* 149 Harley Street, W1N 1HG. *T:* 0171–935 4444.

SUTTON, Richard Lewis; Regional Director, Northern Region, Department of Industry, 1974–81; *b* 3 Feb. 1923; *s* of William Richard Sutton and Marina Susan Sutton (*née* Chudleigh); *m* 1944, Jean Muriel (*née* Turner). *Educ:* Ealing County Grammar Sch. Board of Trade, 1939. Served War: HM Forces (Lieut RA), 1942–47. Asst Trade Comr, Port of Spain, 1950–52; BoT, 1953–62; Trade Comr, Kuala Lumpur, 1962–66; Monopolies Commn, 1966; BoT, 1967–68; Dir, British Industrial Develt Office, New York, 1968–71; Regional Dir, West Midland Region, Dept of Trade and Industry, 1971–74. *Recreations:* music, walking, bridge. *Address:* Barton Toft, Dowlish Wake, Ilminster, Somerset TA19 0QG. *T:* Ilminster (01460) 57127.

SUTTON, Sir Richard (Lexington), 9th Bt *cr* 1772; farmer; *b* 27 April 1937; *s* of Sir Robert Lexington Sutton, 8th Bt, and of Gwynneth Gwladys, *o d* of Major Arnold Charles Gover, MC; *S* father, 1981; *m* 1959, Fiamma, *o d* of G. M. Ferrari, Rome; one *s* one *d*. *Educ:* Stowe. *Recreations:* ski-ing, sailing, swimming, tennis. *Heir:* *s* David Robert Sutton [*b* 26 Feb. 1960; *m* 1992, Annette, *o d* of B. David]. *Address:* Moorhill, Langham, Gillingham, Dorset SP8 5NY. *T:* Gillingham (01747) 862665.

SUTTON, Richard Patrick; QC 1993; a Recorder, since 1994 (Assistant Recorder, 1991–94); *b* 13 Nov. 1944; *s* of Jack Doherty Sutton and Beryl Clarisse Scholes Sutton (*née* Folkard); *m* 1978, Jean Folley; one *s* one *d*. *Educ:* Culford Sch.; Wadham Coll., Oxford (BA Hons Jurisprudence). Called to the Bar, Middle Temple, 1969. *Recreations:* playing guitar, meeting people.

SUTTON, Robert William, CB 1962; OBE 1946; retired as Superintendent and Chief Scientific Officer, Services Electronics Research Laboratories, Baldock, Herts, 1946–70; *b* 13 Nov. 1905; *s* of late William Sutton; *m* 1951, Elizabeth Mary, *d* of George Maurice Wright, CBE, Chelmsford; one *s* two *d*. *Educ:* Brighton College; Royal College of Science, London University. Formerly with Ferranti Ltd, and then with E. K. Cole Ltd until 1938. Admiralty, 1939–68. *Address:* 32 High Street, Cottenham, Cambridge CB4 4SA.

SUTTON, Shaun Alfred Graham, OBE 1979; television producer and writer; Head of Drama Group, BBC Television, 1969–81; Consultant Director and Associate, Prime Time Television, since 1987; *b* 14 Oct. 1919; *s* of Eric Graham Sutton and Beryl Astley-Marsden; *m* 1948, Barbara Leslie; one *s* three *d*. *Educ:* Latymer Upper Sch.; Embassy Sch. of Acting, London. Actor and Stage Manager, Q, Embassy, Aldwych, Adelphi, Arts, Criterion Theatres, 1938–40. Royal Navy, 1940–46, Lieut RNVR. Stage Dir, Embassy and provincial theatres, 1946–48; Producer, Embassy, Buxton, Croydon Theatres, 1948–50; toured S Africa as Producer, 1950; Producer, Embassy, Ipswich, Buxton, 1951–52; entered BBC TV Service, 1952; produced and wrote many children's TV plays and serials; directed many series incl. Z Cars, Softly Softly, Sherlock Holmes, Kipling, etc.; Head of BBC Drama Serials Dept, 1966–69; dramatised Rogue Herries and Judith Paris for BBC Radio, 1971; Producer: BBC TV Shakespeare series, 1982–84; Theatre Night series, BBC 2, including Season's Greetings, Make and Break, The Devil's Disciple, What the Butler Saw, Absent Friends, The Master Builder, Strife, The Miser, The Rivals, Journey's End, When We are Married, Once in a Lifetime, Benefactors, The Contractor, The Winslow Boy, Relatively Speaking, Merlin, Re-Joyce. Fellow, Royal TV Soc.; Mem., BAFTA. *Publications:* A Christmas Carol (stage adaptation), 1949; Queen's Champion (children's novel), 1961; The Largest Theatre in the World, 1982. *Recreations:* gardening, walking. *Address:* 15 Corringham Court, Corringham Road, NW11 7BY. *T:* 0181–455 5417; The Cottage, Brewery Road, Trunch, Norfolk NR28 0PU.

SUVA, Archbishop of, (RC), since 1976; **Most Rev. Petero Mataca;** *b* 28 April 1933; *s* of Gaberiele Daunivucu and Akeneta Taina. *Educ:* Holy Name Seminary, Dunedin, NZ; Propaganda Fidei, Rome. Priest, Rome, 1959; Vicar-Gen. of Archdiocese of Suva, 1966; Rector of Pacific Regional Seminary, 1973; Auxiliary Bishop of Suva, 1974. Pres., Episcopal Conf. of South Pacific, 1981. *Address:* Archbishop's House, Box 393, Suva, Fiji. *T:* 301955.

SUYIN; *see* Han Suyin.

SUZMAN, Mrs Helen, Hon. DBE 1989; *b* 7 Nov. 1917; *d* of late Samuel Gavronsky; *m* Dr M. M. Suzman, FRCP (*d* 1994); two *d*. *Educ:* Parktown Convent, Johannesburg; Univ. of Witwatersrand (BCom). Lectr in Economic History, Univ. of Witwatersrand, 1944–52. Elected MP for Houghton, RSA, 1953; United Party 1953–61; Progressive Party (later Progressive Reform Party and Progressive Federal Party), 1961–89. Pres., SA Inst. of Race Relns, 1991–93. Hon. Fellow: St Hugh's Coll., Oxford, 1973; London Sch. of Economics, 1975; New Hall, Cambridge, 1990. Hon. DCL Oxford, 1973; Hon. LLD: Harvard, Witwatersrand, 1976; Columbia, Smith Coll., 1977; Brandeis, 1981; Jewish Theological Seminary, NY, Cape Town, 1986; Ohio, Western Ontario, 1989; Rhodes, S Africa, Cambridge, Glasgow, Nottingham, Warwick, Ulster, 1990; Indiana, Rutgers, 1992; Hon. DHL: Denison, 1982; New Sch. for Social Res., NY, Sacred Heart Univ., USA, 1984; DUniv Brunel, 1991. UN Human Rights Award, 1978; Roger E. Joseph Award, Hebrew Union Coll., NY, 1986; Moses Mendelssohn Prize, Berlin Senate, 1988; B'Nai B'Rith Dor L'Dor Award, 1992; Notre Dame Univ. Award, 1995. *Publication:* In No Uncertain Terms (autobiog.), 1993. *Recreations:* swimming, fishing, bridge. *Address:* 52 2nd Avenue, Illovo, Sandton, Transvaal 2196, South Africa. *T* and *Fax:* (11) 7882833. *Clubs:* Lansdowne; Inanda, Wanderers (Johannesburg).

See also Prof. J. L. Jowell.

SUZMAN, Janet; actress; *b* 9 Feb. 1939; *d* of Saul Suzman; *m* 1969, Trevor Nunn, *qv* (marr. diss. 1986); one *s*. *Educ:* Kingsmead Coll., Johannesburg; Univ. of the Witwatersrand (BA); London Acad. of Music and Dramatic Art. Hon. Associate Artist, RSC. Vis. Prof of Drama Studies, Westfield Coll., London, 1983–84. Lectures: Spencer, Harvard Univ., 1988; Tanner, Brasenose Coll., Oxford, 1995. Vice-Chm., LAMDA Council, 1992– (Mem., 1978–). Rôles played for *Royal Shakespeare Co.* incl.: Joan La Pucelle in The Wars of the Roses, 1963–64; Lulu in The Birthday Party, Rosaline, Portia, 1965; Ophelia, 1965–66; Katharina, Celia, and Berinthia in The Relapse, 1967; Beatrice, Rosalind, 1968–69; Cleopatra and Lavinia, 1972–73; Clytemnestra and Helen of Troy in The Greeks, 1980; *other rôles* incl.: Kate Hardcastle, and Carmen in The Balcony, Oxford Playhouse, 1966; Hester in Hello and Goodbye, King's Head Theatre, 1973; Masha in Three Sisters, Cambridge, 1976; Good Woman of Setzuan, Newcastle, 1976, Royal Court, 1977; Hedda Gabler, Duke of York's, 1977; Boo-hoo, Open Space, 1978; The Duchess of Malfi, Birmingham, 1979; Cowardice, Ambassadors, 1983; Boesman and Lena, Hampstead, 1984; Vassa, Greenwich, 1985; Andromache, Old Vic, 1988; Another Time, Wyndham's, 1989; Hippolytus, Almeida, 1991; The Sisters Rosenweig, Greenwich, 1994, Old Vic, 1994–95; *director:* Othello, Market Theatre, Johannesburg, 1987 (Best Prodn, Vita Awards, 1988); A Dream of People, The Pit, 1990; The Cruel Grasp, Edinburgh Fest., 1991; No Flies on Mr Hunter, Chelsea Centre, 1992; Death of a Salesman, Theatr Clywd, 1993 (Liverpool Echo and Daily Post Arts Awards, Best Production, 1994). *Films:* A Day in the Death of Joe Egg, 1970; Nicholas and Alexandra, 1971; The Priest of Love, 1980; The Draughtsman's Contract, 1981; E la Nave Va, 1983; A Dry White Season, 1990; Nuns on the Run, 1990; Leon the Pig Farmer, 1993; *television:* plays for BBC and ITV incl.: St Joan, 1968; Three Sisters, 1969; Macbeth, 1970; Hedda Gabler, 1972; Twelfth Night, 1973; Antony and Cleopatra, 1974; Miss Nightingale, 1974; Clayhanger, serial, 1975–76; Mountbatten—The Last Viceroy, 1986; The Singing Detective, 1986, The Miser, 1987; dir., Othello, 1988; Cripples, 1989; The Amazon, 1989; master class on Shakespearean comedy, BBC, 1990. Acad. Award Nomination, Best Actress, 1971; Evening Standard Drama Awards, Best Actress, 1973, 1976; Plays and Players Award, Best Actress, 1976. Hon. MA Open, 1984; Hon. DLitt: Warwick, 1990; Leicester, 1992. *Address:* William Morris (UK) Ltd, 31/32 Soho Square, W1V 5DG. *T:* 0171–434 2191.

SVENSON, Dame Beryl; *see* Grey, Dame Beryl.

SVETLANOV, Yevgeny Fyodorovich; Principal Conductor, Russia (formerly USSR) State Symphony Orchestra, since 1965; composer; *b* 6 Sept. 1928. *Educ:* Moscow Conservatoire. Conductor, 1955–63, Chief Conductor, 1963–65, Bolshoi Theatre. Prin. Guest Conductor, LSO, 1979–. *Compositions* include: Concerto, 1951; Siberian Fantasy, 1953; Rhapsody, 1954; Symphony, 1957; sonatas, sonatinas. *Address:* Apt 41, Stanislavsky Str. 14, 103009 Moscow, Russia.

SVOBODA, Prof. Josef, RDI 1989; Chief Scenographer, National Theatre, Prague, since 1948; Professor at Academy of Applied Arts, since 1968; *b* Čáslav, 10 May 1920; *m* 1948, Libuše Svobodová; one *d*. *Educ:* Gymnasium; special sch. for interior architecture; Academy of Applied Arts (architecture). EXPO 58, Brussels: success with Laterna Magica; EXPO 67, Montreal: polyvision, polydiaekran. He co-operates with many theatres all over the world (Metropolitan Opera, New York; Covent Garden; Geneva; Bayreuth; Frankfurt, etc); Chief of Laterna Magica, experimental scene of National Theatre, Prague, 1973–. Hon. RA 1969. Hon. DFA: Denison, Ohio, 1978; Western Michigan, 1984. Internat. Theatre Award, ATA, 1976; Internat. Prize for scenery and costumes, Teatro de l'Europa, 1984. Laureate of State Prize, 1954; Merited Artist of CSSR, 1966; National Artist of CSSR, 1968; Chevalier, Ordre des Arts et des Lettres (France), 1976. *Publications:* relevant monographs: Josef Svoboda (by Theatre Inst.) 1967 (Prague); Josef Svoboda (by Denis Bablet) 1970 (France); The Scenography of J. Svoboda (by Jarka Burian) 1971, 1974 (USA); Teatr Josefa Svobody (by V. Berjozkin) 1973 (USSR). *Recreations:* theatre, photography, creative arts, music, literature. *Address:* Filmařská 535/17, 15200 Prague 5, Czech Republic.

SWABY, Peter; County Treasurer, Derbyshire County Council, since 1991; *b* 8 Oct. 1947; *s* of late Arthur Swaby and of Mona Swaby; *m* 1974, Yvette Shann; one *s* one *d*. *Educ:* Longcroft Sch., Beverley. CIPFA 1973. E Riding CC, 1967; Humberside CC, 1974, Chief Internal Auditor, 1983; Asst County Treasurer, S Glam CC, 1985. *Recreation:* classical guitarist (ALCM). *Address:* Yellow Grove House, Moor Lane, Youlgrave, Bakewell, Derbys DE45 1US. *T:* Bakewell (01629) 636165.

SWAFFIELD, Sir James (Chesebrough), Kt 1976; CBE 1971; RD 1967; DL; Chairman, British Rail Property Board, 1984–91; solicitor, retired; *b* 16 Feb. 1924; *s* of Frederick and Kate Elizabeth Swaffield, Cheltenham; *m* 1950, Elizabeth Margaret Ellen, 2nd *d* of A. V. and K. E. Maunder, Belfast; two *s* two *d*. *Educ:* Cheltenham Grammar Sch.; Haberdashers' Aske's Hampstead Sch.; London Univ. (LLB); MA Oxon 1974. RNVR, 1942–46. Articled Town Clerk, Lincoln, 1946–49; Asst Solicitor: Norwich Corp., 1949–52; Cheltenham Corp., 1952–53; Southend-on-Sea Corp., 1953–56; Dep. Town Clerk, subseq. Town Clerk and Clerk of Peace, Blackpool, 1956–62; Sec., Assoc. of Municipal Corps, 1962–72; Dir-Gen. and Clerk to GLC, Clerk to ILEA and Clerk of Lieutenancy for Greater London, 1973–84. Chairman: St Paul's Cathedral Ct of Advrs; London Marathon Charitable Trust; Vice-President: Age Concern, London; RSNC; Trustee: Outward Bound Trust; Civic Trust; Patron, Age Resource. Gov., Dulwich Coll. FRSA. Hon. Fellow, Inst. Local Govt Studies, Birmingham Univ. DL Greater London, 1978. OStJ. Dist. Service Award (Internat. City Management Assoc.), 1984. *Address:* 10 Kelsey Way, Beckenham, Kent BR3 3LL. *Clubs:* Reform, Naval.

SWAIN, Henry Thornhill, CBE 1971; RIBA; County Architect, Nottinghamshire County Council, 1964–88, retired; *b* 14 Feb. 1924; *s* of Thornhill Madge Swain and Bessie Marion Swain; *m*; three *d. Educ:* Bryanston Sch.; Architectural Assoc. (Hons Dipl.). Served with RN, 1943–46. Herts County Architect's Dept, 1949; worked in primary school group; Notts CC, 1955; Group Leader i/c initial develt of CLASP construction; Dep. County Architect, 1958. *Publications:* many articles in architectural jls. *Recreation:* sailing. *Address:* 50 Loughborough Road, West Bridgford, Nottingham NG2 7JJ. *T:* Nottingham (0115) 981 8059.

SWAINE, Edward Thomas William, CMG 1968; MBE 1952; Director, Exhibitions Division, Central Office of Information, 1961–71, retired; *b* 17 July 1907; *s* of Edward James Swaine; *m* 1942, Ruby Louise (*née* Ticehurst) (*d* 1974). Entered Govt Service, Min. of Information, 1940; Festival of Britain, 1948–52; Dir of Exhibns, British Pavilion, Montreal World Exhibn, 1967; UK Dep. Comr-Gen. and Dir of Exhbns, Japan World Exhibn, 1970. *Recreation:* photography. *Address:* 6/12 Northwood Hall, Highgate, N6 5PN. *T:* 0181–340 4392.

SWAINE, Sir John (Joseph), Kt 1995; CBE 1987 (OBE 1980); QC (Hong Kong) 1975; JP; President, Legislative Council, Hong Kong, since 1993; *b* 22 April 1932; *s* of Henry Edward Swaine, MBE and Gladys Elizabeth Luke Swaine; *m* 1959, Fatima Gwendoline Jorge Cotton; four *s* one *d. Educ:* Univ. of Hong Kong (BA). Admin. Officer, Hong Kong Govt, 1952–57; called to the Bar, Lincoln's Inn, 1960, Hong Kong, 1960; in practice, 1960–. Non-exec. Dir, Hong Kong & Shanghai Banking Corp. Ltd, 1986–. JP Hong Kong, 1975. Hon. LLD: Baptist, HK, 1992; City, HK, 1993; Hon. PhD (Hum) Lingnan Coll., HK, 1994. *Recreation:* breeding and racing thoroughbred horses. *Address:* Office of the President, Legislative Council, Legislative Council Building, 8 Jackson Road, Hong Kong. *T:* 28699461; 704D Admiralty Centre, Tower 1, 18 Harcourt Road, Hong Kong. *Clubs:* Royal Hong Kong Jockey (Chm., 1993–), Country (Hong Kong).

SWAINSON, Eric, CBE 1981; Vice-Chairman: Fairey Group, since 1987; Lloyds Bank plc, since 1992 (Director, since 1986); Director, AMEC, since 1987; *b* 5 Dec. 1926; *m* 1953, Betty Heywood; two *d. Educ:* Sheffield Univ. (BMet 1st cl. Hons; W. H. A. Robertson medal, 1959). Joined Imperial Chemical Industries Metals Div. (now IMI), 1946; Technical Officer, Res. Dept, 1946–53; Manager, Titanium Melting Plant, 1953–56; Asst Manager, Technical Dept, 1956–59; Gen. Manager and Man. Dir, Lightning Fasteners, 1961–69; Dir, IMI, 1969–86; Asst Man. Dir, 1972–74; Man. Dir, 1974–86; Dep. Chm., Pegler-Hattersley plc, 1986. Director: Birmingham Broadcasting, 1973–92; Midlands Radio Hldgs, 1988–92; Lloyds Merchant Bank Hldgs, 1989–93; Cheltenham & Gloucester Bldg Soc., 1995–; Chm., Birmingham and West Midlands Reg. Bd, Lloyds Bank, 1985–91 (Reg. Dir, 1979–91). Chm., W Midlands Industrial Develt Bd, 1985–90; Member: Review Bd for Govt Contracts, 1978–93; NEDC Cttee on Finance for Industry, 1978–86; Council, CBI, 1975–86; W Midlands Reg. Council, CBI, 1973–83 (Chm. 1976–78); Industrial Develt Adv. Bd, 1982–88. Pro-Chancellor, Aston Univ., 1981–86. FRSA 1985. Hon. DSc Aston, 1986. *Address:* Paddox Hollow, Norton Lindsey, Warwick CV35 8JA.

SWAINSON, Roy; Chief Executive and Director General, Merseytravel, since 1990; *b* 15 April 1947; *s* of William Swainson and Florence Swainson (*née* Moss); *m* 1973, Irene Ann Shearson; one *s* one *d. Educ:* Merchant Taylors' Sch., Crosby; Univ. of Manchester (LLB). Southport County Borough Council: Asst Solicitor, 1969–71; Sen. Asst Solicitor, 1971–74; Asst Borough Solicitor and Sec., Sefton MBC, 1974–82; Dep. City Solicitor and Sec., Liverpool CC, 1982–90. Chm., Mersey Ferries Ltd, 1990–; Co. Sec., Liverpool Airport PLC, 1990–. *Recreations:* reading, theatre, travel. *Address:* 24 Hatton Garden, Liverpool L3 2AN. *T:* 0151–227 5181.

SWALLOW, Comdt Patricia; *see* Nichol, Comdt D. P.

SWALLOW, Sydney; Senior Director, Procurement, Post Office, 1977–81; Chief Procurement Officer, British Telecommunications, 1981–83; *b* 29 June 1919; *s* of William and Charlotte Lucy Swallow; *m* 1950, Monica Williams; one *s. Educ:* Woking County Sch.; St Catharine's Coll., Cambridge (Scholar; BA 1st cl. Hons 1940, MA). Mines Dept, Board of Trade, 1940–42. Served War: Royal Engineers (Survey), 1942–46. Nat. Coal Bd, 1946–59; Central Electricity Generating Bd, 1959–65; Associated Electrical Industries Ltd, 1965–68; General Electric Co. Ltd, 1968; Dir of Supplies, GLC, 1968–77. Chm., Educn Cttee, Inst. of Purchasing and Supply, 1967–77; Visiting Prof., Univ. of Bradford Management Centre, 1972–75; Vis. Fellow, ASC, 1976–80. FCIPS. *Publications:* various articles on purchasing and supply in professional jls. *Recreations:* gardening, cricket. *Address:* 101 Muswell Hill Road, N10 3HT. *T:* 0181–444 8775.

SWALLOW, Sir William, Kt 1967; FIMechE; *b* 2 Jan. 1905; *s* of William Turner Swallow, Gomersal, Yorks; *m* 1929, Kathleen Lucy Smith; no *c. Educ:* Batley and Huddersfield Technical Colleges. Draughtsman, Karrier Motors Ltd, 1923; senior draughtsman, chief body designer, Short Bros, 1926; Gilford Motors Ltd, 1930; development engineer, Pressed Steel Co., 1932; chief production engineer, Short Bros, 1943; development engineer, General Motors Overseas Operations, New York, 1947; i/c manufacturing staff, General Motors Ltd, 1948; gen. man., A. C. Sphinx Spark Plug Div. of Gen. Motors Ltd, 1950; Managing Director, General Motors Ltd, 1953, Chairman, 1958; Chm., Vauxhall Motors Ltd, Luton, Beds, 1961–66 (Man. Dir, 1961–65). Mem., Advisory Council on Technology, 1968–70; Chairman: NPL Adv. Bd, 1969–; Shipbuilding and Shiprepairing Council, 1967–71; EDC for Hotel and Catering Industry, 1966–72; Shipbuilding Industry Bd, 1966–71. Governor, Ashridge Coll., 1965–72. ARAeS; MSAE. President: SMMT, 1964–65 (Dep. Pres. 1966–67); Inst. Road Tspt Engrs, 1966–68. *Address:* Alderton Lodge, Ashridge Park, Berkhamsted, Herts HP4 1NA. *T:* Little Gaddesden (01442) 842284.

SWAMINATHAN, Dr Monkombu Sambasivan, FRS 1973; Chairman, M. S. Swaminathan Research Foundation, since 1990; *b* 7 Aug. 1925; *m* Mina Swaminathan; three *d. Educ:* Univs of Kerala, Madras and Cambridge. BSc Kerala, 1944; BSc (Agric.) Madras, 1947; Assoc. IARI 1949; PhD Cantab, 1952. Responsible for developing Nat. Demonstration Project, 1964, and for evolving Seed Village concept; actively involved in develt of High Yielding Varieties, Dryland Farming and Multiple Cropping Programmes. Vice-Pres., Internat. Congress of Genetics, The Hague, 1963; Gen. Pres., Indian Science Congress, 1976; Mem. (Agriculture), Planning Commn, 1980–82 (formerly Dir-Gen., Indian Council of Agricultural Research); Dir-Gen., Internat. Rice Res. Inst., Manila, 1982–88; Pres., IUCN, 1984–90. First Zakir Hussain Meml Lectr, 1970; UGC Nat. Lectr, 1971; lectures at many internat. scientific symposia. Foreign Associate, US Nat. Acad. of Scis; For. Mem., All Union Acad. of Agricl Scis, USSR; Hon. Mem., Swedish Seed Assoc.; Hon. Fellow, Indian Nat. Acad. of Sciences. FNA; Fellow, Italian Nat. Sci. Acad. Hon. DSc from thirty-three universities. Shanti Swarup Bhatnagar Award for contribs in Biological Scis, 1961; Mendel Centenary Award, Czechoslovak Acad. of Scis, 1965; Birbal Sahni Award, Indian Bot. Soc., 1965; Ramon Magsaysay Award for Community Leadership, 1971; Silver Jubilee Award, 1973, Meghnath Saha Medal, 1981, Indian Nat. Science Acad.; R. B. Bennett Commonwealth Prize, RSA, 1984; Albert Einstein World Science Award, 1986; World Food Prize, 1987; Tyler Prize for Envmtl Achievement, 1991; Honda Prize for Eco-technology, 1991; Jawaharlal Nehru Centenary Award, 1993; Sasakawa Envmt Prize, UN, 1994. Padma Shri, 1967; Padma Bhushan, 1972; Padma Vibhushan, 1989. *Publications:* numerous scientific papers. *Address:* 11 Rathna Nagar, Teynampet, Madras 600018, India.

SWAN, Sir Conrad (Marshall John Fisher), KCVO 1994 (CVO 1986; LVO 1978); PhD; Garter Principal King of Arms, 1992–95; Genealogist: of Order of the Bath, since 1972; of Grand Priory, OStJ, since 1976; First Hon. Genealogist, Order of St Michael and St George, since 1989; *b* 13 May 1924; *yr s* of late Dr Henry Peter Swan, Major RAMC and RCAMC, of BC, Canada and Colchester, Essex, and of Edna Hanson Magdalen (*née* Green), Cross of Honour Pro Ecclesia et Pontifice *m* 1957, Lady Hilda Susan Mary Northcote, Dame of Honour and Devotion, SMO Malta, 1979, and of Justice of SMO of Constantine St George, 1975, *yr d* of 3rd Earl of Iddesleigh; one *s* four *d. Educ:* St George's Coll., Weybridge; Sch. of Oriental and African Studies, Univ. of London; Univ. of Western Ontario (BA 1949; MA 1951); Peterhouse, Cambridge (PhD 1955). Served Europe and India (Capt. Madras Regt, IA), 1942–47. Assumption Univ. of Windsor, Ont.: Lectr in History, 1955–57; Asst Prof. of Hist., 1957–60; Univ. Beadle, 1957–60. Rouge Dragon Pursuivant of Arms, 1962–68; York Herald of Arms, 1968–92; Registrar and Sen. Herald-in-Waiting, College of Arms, 1982–92. Inspector of Regimental Colours, 1993–. On Earl Marshal's staff for State Funeral of Sir Winston Churchill, 1965 and Investiture of HRH Prince of Wales, 1969. In attendance: upon HM The Queen at Installation of HRH Prince of Wales as Great Master of Order of the Bath, 1975; during Silver Jubilee Thanksgiving Service, 1977; on Australasian Tour, 1977; at Commonwealth Heads of Govt Conf., 1987; Gentleman Usher-in-Waiting to HH the Pope, GB visit, 1982. Woodward Lectr, Yale, 1964; Centennial Lectr, St Thomas More Coll., Univ. of Saskatchewan, 1967; Inaugural Sir William Scott Meml Lectr, Ulster-Scot Hist. Foundn, 1968; 60th Anniv. Lectr, St Joseph's Coll., Univ. of Alberta, 1987; first Herald to execute duties across Atlantic (Bermuda, 1969) and in S Hemisphere (Brisbane, Qld, 1977) (both in tabard) and in Canada in attendance upon the Sovereign (Vancouver, 1987), to visit Australia, 1970, S America, 1972, Thailand, Japan, 1973, NZ, 1976, Poland, 1991, Lithuania, 1994. World lecture tours, 1970, 1973, 1976. Adviser to PM of Canada on establishment of Nat. Flag of Canada and Order of Canada, 1964–67; at invitation of Sec. of State of Canada participated in nat. forum on heraldry in Canada, 1987. Co-founder (with Lady Hilda Swan), Heraldic Garden, Boxford, Suffolk, 1983. Hon. Citizen, State of Texas; Freemanships in USA; Freeman: St George's, Bermuda, 1969; City of London, 1974. Fellow, 1976, Hon. Vice-Pres. and a Founder, Heraldry Soc. of Canada; Fellow, Geneal. Soc. of Victoria (Australia), 1970; FSA 1971; FZS 1986. Master, Gunmakers' Co., 1993 (Liveryman and Freeman, 1974; Mem., Ct of Assts, 1983). KStJ 1976. Kt of Honour and Devotion, SMO of Malta, 1979 (Kt of Grace and Devotion, 1964) (Genealogist Br. Assoc., 1974–); Cross of Comdr of Order of Merit, SMO of Malta, 1983. *Publications:* Heraldry: Ulster and North American Connections, 1972; Canada: Symbols of Sovereignty, 1977; (jtly) Blood of the Martyrs, 1993; many articles in learned jls on heraldic, sigillographic and related subjects. *Recreations:* hunting, driving (horse drawn vehicles), rearing ornamental pheasants and waterfowl, marine biology. *Address:* Boxford House, Suffolk CO10 5JT. *T:* Boxford (01787) 210208.

SWAN, Dermot Joseph, MVO 1972; HM Diplomatic Service, retired; HM Consul-General, Marseilles, 1971–77; *b* 24 Oct. 1917; *s* of Dr William Swan and Anne Cosgrave; *m* 1947, Jeanne Labat; one *d. Educ:* St George's, Weybridge; University Coll., London Univ. BA (Hons) French and German. Served War, HM Forces, 1939–46. HM Foreign (later Diplomatic) Service: Vice-Consul, Marseilles, 1947; Saigon, 1949; Foreign Office, 1951; Brazzaville, 1951; Budapest, 1953; FO 1955; First Sec., 1958; Head of Chancery, Phnom Penh, 1959, and Budapest, 1961; UK Mission, New York, 1963; FO (later FCO), 1967; Counsellor, Special Asst to Sec.-Gen. of CENTO, Ankara, 1969. *Recreations:* ice-skating, skiing, swimming. *Address:* Résidence du Golf, 66120 Font Romeu, France. *Club:* Roehampton.

SWAN, Hon. Sir John (William David), KBE 1990; JP; MP (United Bermuda Party) Paget East, since 1972; Premier of Bermuda, 1982–95; *b* 3 July 1935; *s* of late John N. Swan and of Margaret E. Swan; *m* 1965, Jacqueline A. D. Roberts; one *s* two *d. Educ:* West Virginia Wesleyan Coll. (BA). Salesman, Real Estate, Rego Ltd, 1960–62; Founder, Chairman and Chief Exec., John W. Swan Ltd, 1962–. Minister for: Marine and Air Services; Labour and Immigration, 1977–78; Home Affairs, 1978–82; formerly: Parly Sec. for Finance; Chairman: Bermuda Hosps Bd; Dept of Civil Aviation; Young Presidents' Organization, 1974–86. Member: Chief Execs Orgn; World Business Council, 1986. Mem. and Fellow, Senate, Jun. Chamber Internat., 1992. Hon. Freeman of London, 1985. Hon. LLD: Univ. of Tampa, Fla, 1985; W Virginia Wesleyan Coll., 1987; Atlantic Union Coll., Mass, 1991. Internat. Medal of Excellence (1st recipient), Poor Richard Club of Philadelphia, 1987; Outstanding Learning Disabled Achiever Award, Lab Sch. of Washington, 1992. *Recreations:* sailing, tennis. *Address:* 11 Grape Bay Drive, Paget PG 06, Bermuda. *T:* 361303. *Clubs:* Hamilton Rotary, Royal Bermuda Yacht (Bermuda); Bohemian (San Francisco); Chevy Chase (Maryland).

SWANN, Benjamin Colin Lewis; Controller, Finance, British Council, 1975–79, retired; *b* 9 May 1922; *s* of Henry Basil Swann and Olivia Ophelia Lewis; *m* 1946, Phyllis Julia Sybil Lewis; three *s* one *d. Educ:* Bridgend County School. CA. RAFVR, 1941; Transatlantic Ferry, 1942; Flt Lieut, Transport Command, 1944; Flt Supervisor, BOAC, 1946. Apprentice Chartered Accountant, 1950; Audit Asst, George A. Touche & Co., 1953; Treasury Acct, Malaya, 1954; Financial Adviser, Petaling Jaya, 1956; Partner, Milligan Swann & Co., Chartered Accountants, Exeter, 1957; British Council, 1960; Regional Acct, SE Asia, 1961; Dep. Dir Audit, 1965; Asst Representative, Delhi, 1970; Director, Budget, 1972; Dep. Controller, Finance, 1972. *Recreations:* cuisine, lepidoptery. *Address:* Les Malardeaux, St Sernin de Duras 47120, France.

SWANN, Julian Dana Nimmo H.; *see* Hartland-Swann.

SWANN, Sir Michael (Christopher), 4th Bt *cr* 1906, of Prince's Gardens, Royal Borough of Kensington; TD 1979; Director: GVG Financial Services Ltd, since 1988; Partner, Smith Swann & Co., since 1992; *b* 23 Sept. 1941; *s* of Sir Anthony Swann, 3rd Bt, CMG, OBE and of Jean Margaret, *d* of late John Herbert Niblock-Stuart; *S* father, 1991; *m* 1st, 1965, Hon. Lydia Hewitt (marr. diss. 1985), *e d* of 8th Viscount Lifford; two *s* one *d*; 2nd, 1988, Marilyn Ann Morse (*née* Tobitt). *Educ:* Eton Coll. APMI 1978. Lt KRRC (The Royal Green Jackets), 1960–63; T&AVR 4th Bn The Royal Green Jackets, 1964–79 (Brevet Lt-Col 1979). Director: Wright Deen (Life and Estate Duty), 1964–74; Richards Longstaff (Holdings) Ltd, 1974–86; Richards Longstaff Ltd, 1974–88. Vice-Chm., Gabbitas Truman and Thring, 1987–. General Comr of Income Tax, 1988–. *Recreations:* cricket, golf, ski-ing, gardening, growing orchids, racing. *Heir: s* Jonathan Christopher Swann [*b* 17 Nov. 1966; *m* 1994, Polly, *d* of Comdr David Baston]. *Address:* 100 Hurlingham Road, SW6 3NR. *T:* 0171–731 5601. *Clubs:* Hurlingham, IZ, MCC; Rye Golf.

SWANNELL, Nicola Mary, (Mrs Graham Swannell); *see* Pagett, N. M.

SWANSEA, 4th Baron *cr* 1893; **John Hussey Hamilton Vivian,** Bt 1882; DL; *b* 1 Jan. 1925; *s* of 3rd Baron and Hon. Winifred Hamilton (*d* 1944), 4th *d* of 1st Baron Holm Patrick; *S* father, 1934; *m* 1st, 1956, Miriam Antoinette (marr. diss. 1973; she *d* 1975), 2nd *d* of A. W. F. Caccia-Birch, MC, of Guernsey Lodge, Marton, NZ; one *s* two *d*; 2nd, 1982, Mrs Lucy Temple-Richards (*née* Gough). *Educ:* Eton; Trinity Coll., Cambridge. DL Powys (formerly Brecknock), 1962. CStJ 1994. *Recreations:* shooting, fishing, rifle shooting. *Heir: s* Hon. Richard Anthony Hussey Vivian, *b* 24 Jan. 1957. *Address:* Chapel House Cottage, Alltmawr, Builth Wells, Powys LD2 3LX. *Club:* Carlton.

SWANSEA and BRECON, Bishop of; since 1988; **Rt. Rev. Dewi Morris Bridges;** *b* 18 Nov. 1933; *s* of Harold Davies Bridges and Elsie Margaret Bridges; *m* 1959, Rhiannon Williams; one *s* one *d*. *Educ:* St David's University College, Lampeter (BA 1954, 1st cl. Hons History); Corpus Christi Coll., Cambridge (BA 1956 II 1, Pt 2 Theol. Tripos, MA 1960); Westcott House, Cambridge. Assistant Curate: Rhymney, Gwent, 1957–60; Chepstow, 1960–63; Vicar of St James', Tredegar, 1963–65; Lecturer and Senior Lectr, Summerfield Coll. of Education, Kidderminster, 1965–69; Vicar of Kempsey, Worcester, 1969–79; RD of Upton-upon-Severn, 1974–79; Rector of Tenby, Pembs, 1979–88; RD of Narberth, 1980–82; Archdeacon of St Davids, 1982–88. Member: Court and Council, UCW, Swansea, 1989–; Council, St David's UC, Lampeter, 1992–. *Recreations:* walking, gardening, photography. *Address:* Ely Tower, Brecon, Powys, LD3 9DE. *T:* Brecon (01874) 622008.

SWANSON, Prof. Sydney Alan Vasey, FEng 1987; Professor of Biomechanics, since 1974, and Pro Rector (Educational Quality), since 1994, Imperial College, University of London; *b* 31 Oct. 1931; *s* of Charles Henry William Swanson and Hannah Elizabeth Swanson (*née* Vasey); *m* 1956, Mary Howarth; one *s* one *d*. *Educ:* Scarborough Boys' High Sch.; Imperial Coll., London. DSc (Eng), PhD, DIC, FCGI, FIMechE. Engineering Laboratories, Bristol Aircraft Ltd, 1955–58; Imperial College, London: Lectr, Mechanical Engineering, 1958–69; Reader in Biomechanics, 1969–74; Dean, City and Guilds Coll., 1976–79; Head of Mechanical Engineering Dept, 1978–83; Pro Rector, 1983–86. FRSA. *Publications:* Engineering Dynamics, 1963; Engineering in Medicine (with B. M. Sayers and B. Watson), 1975; (with M. A. R. Freeman) The Scientific Basis of Joint Replacement, 1977; papers on bone, cartilage and joints in learned jls. *Recreations:* photography, cycling, fell-walking. *Address:* Mechanical Engineering Department, Imperial College, SW7 2BX. *T:* 0171–594 5008. *Club:* Lyke Wake (Northallerton).

SWANSTON, Roy; Chairman, Local Government Residuary Board (England), since 1995. President, Royal Institution of Chartered Surveyors, 1994–95; *b* 31 Oct. 1940; *s* of Robert Trotter Swanston and Margaret Ann Swanston (*née* Paxton); *m* 1963, Doreen Edmundson; one *s* one *d*. *Educ:* Berwick-upon-Tweed Grammar Sch.; FRICS, FIMgt. County Borough of Sunderland, 1958–67; Clasp Develt Gp, Nottingham, 1967–71; Notts CC, 1971–74; Durham CC, 1974–75; Dir of Building Economics, 1975–82, of Dept of Architecture, 1982–87, Cheshire CC; Sen. Management Consultant, Peat Marwick McLintock, 1987–88; Dir of Develt, Bucknall Austin, 1988–90; Dir, Properties in Care, 1990–93, Res. and Professional Services, 1993–95, English Heritage. Vis. Fellow, Salford Univ., 1986–. Hon. Treasurer, RICS, 1987–90 (Pres., QS Div., 1982–83). Mem., Barnardo's Council. Methodist Local Preacher. FRSA. Hon. DSc Salford, 1994. *Recreations:* supporter of Sunderland AFC, fell walking.

SWANTON, Ernest William, CBE, 1994 (OBE 1965); author; Cricket and Rugby football Correspondent to the Daily Telegraph, retired 1975; BBC Commentator, 1934–75; *b* 11 Feb. 1907; *s* of late William Swanton; *m* 1958, Ann, *d* of late R. H. de Montmorency and *widow* of G. H. Carbutt. *Educ:* Cranleigh. Evening Standard, 1927–39. Played Cricket for Middlesex, 1937–38. Served 1939–46; captured at Singapore, 1942; POW Siam, 1942–45; Actg Maj. Bedfordshire Yeomanry (RA). Joined Daily Telegraph staff, 1946. Covered 20 Test tours to Australia, W Indies, S Africa, New Zealand and India; managed own XI to West Indies, 1956 and 1961 and to Malaya and Far East, 1964. Pres., The Cricketer, 1988– (Editorial Director, 1967–88). Hon. Life Vice-Pres., MCC, 1989 (Mem. Cttee, 1975–84). Mem. Cttee, Kent CCC, 1971–91 (Pres., 1981); President: Sandwich Town CC, 1976–; Cricket Soc., 1976–83; Forty Club, 1983–86. *Publications:* (with H. S. Altham) A History of Cricket, 1938, 4th edn 1962; Denis Compton, A Cricket Sketch, 1948; Elusive Victory, 1951; Cricket and The Clock, 1952; Best Cricket Stories, 1953; West Indian Adventure, 1954, Victory in Australia, 1954/5, 1955; Report from South Africa, 1957; West Indies Revisited, 1960; The Ashes in Suspense, 1963; Cricket from all Angles, 1968; Sort of a Cricket Person (memoirs), 1972; Swanton in Australia, 1975; Follow On (memoirs), 1977; As I Said at the Time: a lifetime of cricket, 1983; Gubby Allen: Man of Cricket, 1985; (with C. H. Taylor) Kent Cricket: a photographic history 1744–1984, 1985; Back Page Cricket, 1987; The Essential E. W. Swanton (anthol.), 1990; General Editor, The World of Cricket, 1966, revised as Barclays World of Cricket, 1980, 3rd edn 1986; Arabs in Aspic, 1993. *Recreations:* cricket, golf. *Address:* Delf House, Sandwich, Kent CT13 9HB. *Clubs:* Army and Navy, MCC; Vincent's (Oxford); Royal St George's Golf.

SWANWICK, Sir Graham Russell, Kt 1966; MBE 1944; Judge of the High Court of Justice (Queen's Bench Division), 1966–80; Presiding Judge, Midland and Oxford Circuit, 1975–78; *b* 24 August 1906; *s* of Eric Drayton Swanwick and Margery Eleanor (*née* Norton), Whittington House, Chesterfield; *m* 1st, 1933, Helen Barbara Reid (marr. diss., 1945; she *d* 1970); two *s*; 2nd, 1952, Audrey Celia Parkinson (*d* 1987). *Educ:* Winchester Coll.; University Coll., Oxford (BA). Called to Bar, Inner Temple, 1930, Master of the Bench, 1962; QC 1956; Leader Midland Circuit, 1961–65. Wing Comdr RAFVR, 1940–45 (MBE, despatches). Recorder: City of Lincoln, 1957–59; City of Leicester, 1959–66; Judge of Appeal, Channel Islands, 1964–66; Derbyshire QS: Chm., 1963–66; Dep. Chm., 1966–71. *Recreation:* country pursuits. *Address:* Burnett's Ashurst, Steyning, West Sussex BN44 3AY. *T:* Partridge Green (01403) 710241. *Club:* Royal Air Force.

SWARBRICK, Prof. James, PhD, DSc; FRSC, CChem; FRPharmS; Vice President, Research and Development, Applied Analytical Industries Inc., since 1993; *b* 8 May 1934; *s* of George Winston Swarbrick and Edith M. C. Cooper; *m* 1960, Pamela Margaret Oliver. *Educ:* Sloane Grammar Sch.; Chelsea Coll., Univ. of London (BPharm Hons 1960; PhD 1964; DSc 1972). FRSC (FRIC 1970); FRPharmS (FPS 1978; MPS 1961). Asst Lectr, 1962, Lectr, 1964, Chelsea Coll.; Vis. Asst Prof., Purdue Univ., 1964; Associate Prof., 1966, Prof. and Chm. of Dept of Pharmaceutics, 1969, Asst Dean, 1970, Univ. of Conn; Dir of Product Develt, Sterling-Winthrop Res. Inst., NY, 1972; first Prof. of Pharmaceutics, Univ. of Sydney, 1975–76; Dean, Sch. of Pharmacy, Univ. of London, 1976–78; Prof. of Pharmacy and Chm., Res. Council, Univ. of S California, Los Angeles, 1978–81; Prof. of Pharmaceutics and Chm., Div. of Pharmaceutics, Univ. of N Carolina, 1981–93. Vis. Scientist, Astra Labs, Sweden, 1971; Vis. Prof., Shanghai Med. Univ., 1991–92. Indust. Cons., 1965–72, 1975–; Cons., Aust. Dept. of Health, 1975–76; Mem., Cttee on Specifications, National Formulary, 1970–75; Chm., Jt US Pharmacopoeia-Nat. Formulary Panel on Disintegration and Dissolution Testing, 1971–75. Member: Cttee on Grad. Programs, Amer. Assoc. of Colls of Pharmacy, 1969–71; Practice Trng Cttee, Pharm. Soc. of NSW, 1975–76; Academic Bd, Univ. of Sydney, 1975–76; Collegiate Council, 1976–78; Educn Cttee, Pharmaceutical Soc. of GB, 1976–78; Working Party on Pre-Registration Training, 1977–78. Pharmaceutical Manufacturers Assoc. Foundation: Mem., Basic Pharmacology Adv. Cttee, 1982–91; Chm., Pharmaceutics Adv. Cttee, 1986–; Mem., Scientific Adv. Cttee, 1986–; Mem., Generic Drugs Adv. Cttee, Food and Drug Admin, 1993– (Chm., 1995–). FAAAS 1966; Fellow: Acad. of Pharm. Sciences, 1973; Amer. Assoc. of Pharmaceutical Scientists, 1987. Kenan Res. Study Award, 1988. Mem. Editorial Board: Jl of Biopharmaceutics and Pharmacokinetics, 1973–79; Drug Development Communications, 1974–82; Pharmaceutical Technology, 1978–; Biopharmaceutics and Drug Disposition, 1979–; series Editor, Current Concepts in the Pharmaceutical Sciences, Drugs and the Pharmaceutical Sciences. *Publications:* (with A. N. Martin and A. Cammarata) Physical Pharmacy, 2nd edn 1969, 3rd edn 1983; (ed jtly) Encyclopedia of Pharmaceutical Technology; contributed: American Pharmacy, 6th edn 1966 and 7th edn 1974; Remington's Pharmaceutical Sciences, 14th edn 1970 to 19th edn 1993; contrib. Current Concepts in the Pharmaceutical Sciences: Biopharmaceutics, 1970; res. contribs to internat. sci. jls. *Recreation:* woodworking, listening to music, golf. *Address:* AAI Inc., 1206 North 23rd Street, Wilmington, NC 28405, USA. *T:* (910) 2516433, *Fax:* (910) 7639633.

SWARTZ, Rt. Rev. George Alfred; Bishop of Kimberley and Kuruman, 1983–91; *b* 8 Sept. 1928; *s* of Philip and Julia Swartz; *m* 1957, Sylvia Agatha (*née* George); one *s* one *d*. *Educ:* Umbilo Road High Sch., Durban; Univ. of the Witwatersrand, Johannesburg; Coll. of the Resurrection, Mirfield, Yorks; St Augustine's Coll., Canterbury. BA, Primary Lower Teacher's Cert., Central Coll. Dip. (Canterbury). Asst Teacher, Sydenham Primary Sch., 1951–52; Deacon, 1954; Priest, 1955; Asst Curate, St Paul's Church, Cape Town, 1955–56; Priest in Charge, Parochial Dist of St Helena Bay, Cape, 1957–60; St Augustine's Coll., Canterbury, 1960–61; Dir, Cape Town Dio. Mission to Muslims, 1962–63; Dir, Mission to Muslims and Rector St Philip's Church, Cape Town, 1963–70; Regional Dean of Woodstock Deanery, 1966–70; Priest in Charge, Church of the Resurrection, Bonteheuwel, Cape, 1971–72; a Bishop Suffragan of Cape Town, 1972–83; Canon of St George's Cathedral, Cape Town, 1969–72. Dean of the Province, Church of the Province of Southern Africa, 1986–89. *Recreations:* cinema, music (traditional jazz; instruments played are guitar and saxophone). *Address:* 11 Tanglin, Thomas Road, Kenilworth, Cape Town, 7700, Republic of South Africa. *T:* (21) 7979079.

SWARTZ, Col Hon. Sir Reginald (William Colin), KBE 1972 (MBE (mil.) 1948); ED; FAIM, FIMgt, FAICD; retired parliamentarian and company director (director of nine companies, 1973–83); *b* 14 April 1911; *s* of late J. Swartz, Toowoomba, Qld; *m* 1936, Hilda, *d* of late G. C. Robinson; two *s* one *d*. *Educ:* Toowoomba and Brisbane Grammar Schs. Commonwealth Military Forces, 1928–40, Lieut, 1934. Served War of 1939–45: Captain 2–26 Bn, 8 Div., AIF, 1940; Malaya (PoW): Singapore, Malaya, Thailand (Burma-Thailand Rly); CMF, in Darling Downs Regt, Lt-Col, AQMG, CMF, N Comd, Col (RL), 1961. Hon. Col Australian Army Aviation Corps, 1969–75. MHR (L) Darling Downs, Qld, 1949–72; Parly Under-Sec. for Commerce and Agric., 1952–56; Parly Sec. for Trade, 1956–61; Minister: (of State) for Repatriation, Dec. 1961–Dec. 1964; for Health, 1964–66; for Social Services, 1965; for Civil Aviation, 1966–69; for Nat. Develt, 1969–72; Leader, House of Representatives, Canberra, 1971–72. Leader of many delegns overseas incl. Aust. Delegn to India, 1967, and Trade Mission to SE Asia, 1958; Parly Delegn to S and SE Asia, 1966. Patron and/or Vice-Pres. or Mem. of numerous public organizations. Life Chm. of Trustees, Australian Army Aviation Corps. Past Chm., Inst. of Dirs (Queensland). Member, RSL. *Recreation:* bowls. *Address:* 39/110 King Street, Doncaster East, Victoria 3109, Australia. *Clubs:* United Service (Brisbane); Royal Automobile Club of Victoria; Twin Towns Services (Tweed Head); Darling Downs Aero; Probus (Doncaster) (Foundation Pres.); Templestowe Bowling (Melbourne).

SWARUP, Prof. Govind, PhD; FRS 1991; Director, Giant Metrewave Radio Telescope Project, Tata Institute of Fundamental Research, Bombay since 1986; *b* 29 March 1929; *m* Bina Jain; one *s* one *d*. *Educ:* Allahabad Univ. (BSc 1948; MSc 1950); Stanford Univ., USA (PhD 1961). Sec., Radio Res. Cttee, CSIR, Nat. Physical Lab., New Delhi, 1950–53; Colombo-Plan Fellowship, CSIRO, Sydney, 1953–55; Res. Associate, Harvard Univ., 1956–57; Grad. Student, Stanford Univ., USA, 1957–60, Asst Prof. 1961–63; Tata Institute of Fundamental Research, Bombay: Reader, 1963–65; Associate Prof., 1965–70; Prof., 1970–79; Sen. Prof., 1979–90; Prof. of Eminence, 1990–94; Prof. Emer., 1994–. Visiting Professor: Univ. of Md, USA, 1980; Univ. of Groningen, Netherlands, 1980–81; Univ. of Leiden, Netherlands, 1981. Chm., Indian Nat. Cttee, URSI, 1986–88, 1994–. Fellow: Indian Nat. Sci. Acad.; Indian Acad. Scis; Nat. Acad. Scis, India; Indian Geophysical Union. Associate, RAS; Member: Astronomical Soc. India (Pres., 1975–77); IAU (Pres., Radio Astronomical Cttee, 1979–82); Indian Physics Assoc.; Indian Physical Soc. Member Editorial Board: Indian Jl Radio and Space Physics; Nat. Acad. of Science, India. Numerous awards, incl. Tskolovosky medal, Fedn of Cosmonautics, USSR. *Publications:* (ed jtly) Quasars, 1986; (ed jtly) History of Oriental Astronomy, 1987. *Address:* National Centre for Radio Astrophysics, Tata Institute of Fundamental Research, Poona University Campus, Post Bag 3, Ganeshkhind, Pune 411007, India. *T:* (office) (212) 356111; (home) (212) 351632.

SWASH, Stanley Victor, MC 1917 and Bar 1918; *b* 29 February 1896; British; *s* of A. W. Swash, JP and Sylvia Swash; *m* 1924; *m* 1955, Jane Henderson. *Educ:* Llandovery College; St John's College, Oxford; Lincoln's Inn. Served European War, 1915–19, RFA. MA (Mathematics); short period in Ministry of Pensions; served Royal Navy as Lieut Inst., 1921–24; worked in Woolworth Company, 1924–55; Director, 1939, Chairman, 1951–55; retired 1955. Called to Bar, Lincoln's Inn, 1938. OC 57 County of London Home Guard Battalion, Lieut-Colonel, 1940–45. Chairman, Horticultural Marketing Advisory Council, 1958; Member Milk Marketing Board, 1957–63; Chm. BOAC/MEA Cttee of Enquiry, 1963–64. *Recreations:* swimming, bridge. *Address:* Park Avenue, St Andrews, Malta. *Club:* United Oxford & Cambridge University.

SWAYTHLING, 4th Baron, *cr* 1907; **David Charles Samuel Montagu;** Bt 1894; Chairman, Rothmans International plc, since 1988; *b* 6 Aug. 1928; *e s* of 3rd Baron Swaythling, OBE, and Mary Violet, *e d* of Major Levy, DSO; *S* father, 1990; *m* 1951, Christiane Françoise (Ninette), *d* of Edgar Dreyfus, Paris; one *s* one *d* (and one *d* decd). *Educ:* Eton; Trinity Coll., Cambridge. Exec. Dir, 1954, Chm., 1970–73, Samuel Montagu & Co. Ltd; Chm. and Chief Exec., Orion Bank, 1974–79; Chm., Ailsa Investment Trust plc, 1981–88; Director: J. Rothschild Holdings PLC, 1983–89; The Telegraph plc, 1985–; Chelsfield plc, 1993–. Mem., Bd of Banking Supervision, Bank of England, 1990–. Dir, British Horseracing Bd, 1993–. *Recreations:* shooting, racing, theatre. *Heir: s* Hon. Charles Edgar Samuel Montagu, *b* 20 Feb. 1954. *Address:* 14 Craven Hill Mews, Devonshire Terrace, W2 3DY. *T:* 0171–724 7860; (office) 15 Hill Street, W1X 7FB. *T:* 0171–491 4366. *Clubs:* White's, Portland, Pratt's.

SWEANEY, William Douglas, CMG 1965; retired 1972, as Establishment Officer, Overseas Development Administration, Foreign and Commonwealth Office; *b* 12 Nov. 1912; *s* of late Lt-Comdr William Sweaney, MBE, RN, and late Elizabeth Bridson; *m* 1939, Dorothy Beatrice Parsons; one *s*. *Educ:* Gillingham County Sch.; London Sch. of Economics. BSc(Econ). Clerical Officer, Inland Revenue (Special Comrs of Income Tax), 1929; Officer of Customs and Excise, 1932; seconded to Colonial Office, 1943 (promoted Surveyor of Customs and Excise *in absentia*); transferred to Colonial Office, 1948; Principal, 1948; Private Sec. to Minister of State for Colonial Affairs, 1953; Asst Sec., 1955; Dept of Technical Co-operation, 1961; ODM, later ODA, FCO, 1964–72; Establishment Officer,

1965. Panel of Chairmen, Agricl Dwelling House Adv. Cttees, 1977–86. *Recreations:* travel, ornithology. *Address:* 1 Beech Hurst Close, Haywards Heath, West Sussex RH16 4AE. *T:* Haywards Heath (01444) 450341.

SWEENEY, Nigel Hamilton; Senior Prosecuting Counsel to the Crown at the Central Criminal Court, since 1992; *b* 18 March 1954; *s* of Alan Vincent Sweeney and Dorothy Sweeney; *m* 1985, Joanna Clair Slater; one *s* one *d. Educ:* Wellington Sch., Som; Nottingham Univ. (LLB 1975). Called to the Bar, Middle Temple, 1976 (Harmsworth Schol. 1976); Jun. Prosecuting Counsel to the Crown, CCC, 1987–91, First Jun. Prosecuting Counsel, 1991–92. *Recreations:* golf, tennis, the arts. *Address:* 6 King's Bench Walk, Temple, EC4Y 7DR. *T:* 0171–583 0410. *Club:* Woking Golf.

SWEENEY, Thomas Kevin; Senior Medical Officer, Department of Health and Social Security, 1983–88, retired; *b* 10 Aug. 1923; *s* of John Francis and Mildred Sweeney; *m* 1950, Eveleen Moira Ryan; two *s* two *d. Educ:* O'Connell Sch., Dublin; University Coll., Dublin (MB, BCh, BAO NUI; DTM&H London; TDD Wales). FFPHM (FFCM 1983). Principal Med. Officer, Colonial Medical Service, 1950–65, retd; Asst Sen. Med. Officer, Welsh Hosp. Bd, 1965–68; Department of Health and Social Security: Med. Officer, 1968–72; Sen. Med. Officer, 1972–79; SPMO, 1979–83. QHP 1984–87. *Publication:* contrib. BMJ. *Recreations:* gardening, golf, cathedrals. *Address:* Tresanton, Wych Hill Way, Woking, Surrey GU22 0AE. *T:* Woking (01483) 760414.

SWEENEY, Timothy Patrick; Director General, British Bankers Association, since 1994; *b* 2 June 1944; *s* of John Edward Sweeney and Olive Bridget (*née* Montgomery-Cunningham); *m* 1965, Carol Ann Wardle; one *s* one *d. Educ:* Pierrepont School; Sussex Univ. (MA Philosophy); Surrey Univ. (MSc Econs). With Bank of England, 1967–94. *Recreations:* music, archery, walking. *Address:* 10 Lombard Street, EC3V 9EL. *T:* 0171–623 4001.

SWEENEY, Walter Edward; MP (C) Vale of Glamorgan, since 1992; *b* Dublin, 23 April 1949; *s* of Patrick Anthony Sweeney, veterinary surgeon and Jane Yerbury Sweeney, retired head teacher; *m* 1992, Dr Nuala Maire Kennan. *Educ:* Church Lawford Primary Sch.; Lawrence Sheriff Sch., Rugby; Univ. of Aix-Marseille; Univ. of Hull (BA Hons); Darwin Coll., Cambridge (MPhil); Cert. Ed. TEFL. Admitted Solicitor, 1976. Mem., Vale of Glam CHC, 1991–92. Joined Cons. Party, 1964; Chairman: Rugby Div. YCs, 1965; Church Lawford Cons. Br., 1969; Rugby Cons. Political Centre, 1970. Member: Church Lawford Parish Council, 1971–74; Rugby BC, 1974–77; Beds CC, 1981–89 (Vice-Chm. and Gp spokesman on Police Cttee). Contested (C) Stretford, 1983. Member, Select Committee: on Welsh Affairs, 1992–; on Home Affairs, 1995–; on Channel Tunnel Rail Link, 1995–; Vice Chm., All-Party Penal Affairs Cttee, 1993– (Sec., 1992–93); Secretary: Cons. back bench Legal Affairs Cttee, 1994–; Cons. back bench Home Affairs Cttee, 1994–. *Recreations:* walking, swimming, flying, theatre, reading. *Address:* House of Commons, SW1A 0AA. *Club:* Bedford (Bedford).

SWEET, Prof. Peter Alan, MA, PhD; FRAS; Regius Professor of Astronomy in the University of Glasgow, 1959–82; retired; *b* 15 May 1921; *s* of David Frank Sweet; *m* 1947, Myrtle Vera Parnell; two *s. Educ:* Kingsbury County Grammar School, London; Sidney Sussex College, Cambridge. Open Maj. Schol. in Maths, Sidney Sussex Coll., 1940–42, Wrangler, 1942, BA Cantab 1943. Junior Scientific Officer, Min. of Aircraft Prod., 1942–45; BA Scholar, at Sidney Sussex Coll., 1945–47; MA Cantab 1946; Mayhew Prizeman, 1946, PhD Cantab 1950. FRAS 1949. Lectr in Astronomy, Univ. of Glasgow, 1947–52; Lectr in Astronomy and Asst Director of the Observatory, Univ. of London, 1952–59; Dean, Faculty of Science, Univ. of Glasgow, 1973–75. Visiting Asst Professor of Astronomy, Univ. of California, Berkeley, 1957–58; Vis. Sen. Res. Fellow, NASA Inst. for Space Studies, NY, 1965–66. *Publications:* papers on Stellar Evolution, Cosmic Magnetism, and Solar Flares in Monthly Notices of Royal Astronomical Soc., etc. *Recreations:* music, gardening. *Address:* 17 Westbourne Crescent, Glasgow G61 4HB. *T:* 0141–942 4425.

SWEETBAUM, Henry Alan; Chairman and Chief Executive, Wickes plc, since 1982; *b* 22 Nov. 1937; *s* of late Irving and Bertha Sweetbaum; *m* 1st, 1960, Suzanne Milberg (decd); three *s*; 2nd, 1971, Anne Betty Leonie de Vigier; one *s. Educ:* Wharton School, Univ. of Pennsylvania (BS Econ 1959). Underwood Corp., 1960; Exec. Vice-Pres. and Dir, Reliance Corp., 1962–70; Exec. Dir, Plessey Corp., 1970; Non-Exec. Dir, Huntingdon Securities, 1971–; Data Recording Instrument Co.: Non-Exec. Dir, 1973–76; Chm., 1976–82. University of Pennsylvania Wharton School Board Member: Graduate Bd; European Adv. Bd; SEI Center for Advanced Management Studies; Management Educn Council. *Publication:* Restructuring the Management Challenge, 1990. *Recreations:* swimming, shooting, Keep Fit. *Address:* Wickes plc, 19/21 Mortimer Street, W1N 7RJ. *T:* 071–631 1018. *Club:* Reform.

SWEETMAN, Jennifer Joan, (Mrs Ronald Andrew); *see* Dickson, J. J.

SWEETMAN, John Francis, CB 1991; TD 1964; Clerk of Committees of the House of Commons, 1990–95; *b* 31 Oct. 1930; *s* of late Thomas Nelson Sweetman and Mary Monica (*née* D'Arcy-Reddy); *m* 1st, 1959, Susan Margaret Manley; one *s* one *d*; 2nd, 1983, Celia Elizabeth, *yr d* of Sir William Nield, GCMG, KCB; two *s. Educ:* Cardinal Vaughan Sch.; St Catharine's Coll., Cambridge (MA Law). 2nd Lieut, RA, Gibraltar, 1949–51; TA (City of London RA) and AER, 1951–65. A Clerk, House of Commons, 1954–95: Clerk of Select Cttees on Nationalised Industries and on Sci. and Technol., 1962–65, 1970–73; Second Clerk of Select Cttees, 1979–83; Clerk of the Overseas Office, 1983–87; Clerk Asst of H of C, 1987–90; Clerk of Select Cttees on Sittings of the House, 1991–92. Mem., Assoc. of Secs-Gen. of Parliaments, IPU, 1987–95. Mem., Oxford and Cambridge Catholic Educn Bd, 1964–84. *Publications:* contrib. to: Erskine May's Parliamentary Practice; Halsbury's Laws of England, 4th edn; Council of Europe, Procedure and Practice of the Parliamentary Assembly, 9th edn 1990. *Address:* 41 Creffield Road, W5 3RR. *T:* 0181–992 2456. *Clubs:* Garrick, MCC.

SWEETNAM, Sir (David) Rodney, KCVO 1992; CBE 1990; MA; FRCS; Orthopaedic Surgeon to the Queen, 1982–92; President, Royal College of Surgeons of England, since 1995; Consultant Surgeon to: The Middlesex Hospital, 1960–92; King Edward VII Hospital for Officers, London, since 1964; *b* 5 Feb. 1927; second *s* of late Dr William Sweetnam and Irene (*née* Black); *m* 1959, Patricia Ann, *er d* of late A. Staveley Gough, OBE, FRCS; one *s* one *d. Educ:* Clayesmore; Peterhouse, Cambridge (Titular Scholar; BA 1947, MA 1951); Middlesex Hosp. Med. Sch. (MB, BChir 1950). FRCS 1955. Surg. Lieut RNVR, 1950–52. Jun. appts, Mddx Hosp., London Hosp. and Royal National Orthopaedic Hosp. Hon. Civil Consultant in Orth. Surgery to the Army, 1974–92; Hon. Consultant Orthopaedic Surgeon, Royal Hosp., Chelsea, 1974–92. Consultant Advisor in Orth. Surgery to DHSS, 1981–90; Hon. Consultant Surgeon, Royal Nat. Orthopaedic Hosp., 1983–92. Dir, Medical Sickness Annuity and Life Assce Soc. Ltd, 1982–; Dir and Vice-Chm., Permanent Insurance Co., 1989–95. Chairman: DHSS Adv. Gp on Orthopaedic Implants, 1973–81; MRC's Working Party on Bone Sarcoma, 1980–85. Royal College of Surgeons: Mem. Council, 1985– (Vice-Pres., 1992–94); Jacksonian Prize, 1966; Hunterian Prof., 1967; Gordon Taylor Meml Lectr, 1982; Stanford Cade Meml Lectr, 1986; Bradshaw Lectr, 1992; Robert Jones Lectr, 1993. President: Combined Services Orthopaedic Soc., 1983–86; British Orthopaedic Assoc., 1984–85. Mem. Exec. Cttee, Arthritis and Rheumatism Council, 1985–93; Mem. Res. Adv. Cttee, Royal Hosp. and Home, Putney (formerly Royal Hosp. for Incurables), 1985–. Trustee: Develt Trust, Queen Elizabeth Foundn for the Disabled, 1984–; Smith & Nephew Charitable Trust 1988–. Fellow, UCL, 1993. Chm., British Editorial Soc. of Bone and Joint Surgery, 1992– (Sec. and Treas., 1975–92). *Publications:* (ed jtly) The Basis and Practice of Orthopaedics, 1980; contrib. med. books and jls in field of gen. orth. surgery, trauma and bone tumours. *Recreation:* gardening. *Address:* 23 Wimpole Street, W1M 7AD. *T:* 0171–580 5409.

SWIFT, Caroline Jane, (Mrs C. P. L. Openshaw); QC 1993; a Recorder, since 1995; *b* 30 May 1955; *d* of late Vincent Seymour Swift and of Amy Ruth Swift; *m* 1979, Charles Peter Lawford Openshaw, *qv*; one *s* one *d. Educ:* Lancaster Girls' Grammar Sch.; Univ. of Durham (BA Hons Law). Pres., Durham Union Soc., 1975. Called to the Bar, Inner Temple, 1977; practised on Northern Circuit, 1978–; Asst Recorder, 1992–95. *Publication:* (jtly) Ribchester: 100 years in photographs, 1994. *Recreations:* home and family, participating in parish affairs, cooking, ski-ing. *Address:* 25 Byrom Street, Manchester M3 4PF. *T:* 0161–834 5238; 61 Fleet Street, EC4Y 1JU.

SWIFT, Clive Walter; actor, author, teacher; initiator, 1980, and co-Chair, Actor's Centre; *b* 9 Feb. 1936; *s* of Abram Swift and Lillie (*née* Greenman); *m* 1960, Margaret Drabble, *qv* (marr. diss. 1975); two *s* one *d. Educ:* Clifton Coll., Bristol; Caius Coll., Cambridge (MA Hons Eng. Lit.). Teaching at LAMDA and RADA, 1967–79; teaching verse-speaking at Actor's Centre, 1980–. *Theatre:* début, Nottingham Playhouse, 1959; RSC, 1960–68; Man and Superman, Arts, Vaudeville, and Garrick, 1965; The Young Churchill, Duchess, 1969; Dirty Linen, Arts, 1976; Inadmissible Evidence, Royal Court, 1978; The Potsdam Quartet, Lyric, Hammersmith, 1980; Messiah, Hampstead, Aldwych, 1982; The Genius, Royal Court, 1983; The Sisterhood, New End, 1987; An Enemy of the People, Young Vic, Playhouse, 1988; Othello, Other Place, Young Vic, 1990; Pooter, in Mr and Mrs Nobody, nat. tour, 1993–94; Chichester Festival theatre seasons, 1965 and 1971; *director:* at LAMDA: The Wild Goose Chase, 1969; The Cherry Orchard, 1973; The Lower Depths, 1969; *television:* Love Story, 1961; Dombey & Son, 1968; Waugh on Crime, 1970; The Exorcism, 1972; South Riding, 1974; Gibbon, 1975; Barchester Chronicles, 1982; Pickwick Papers, 1984; First Among Equals, 1985; Keeping up Appearances, 5 series, 1990–; *radio:* reader, Fielding's Tom Jones, 1963; Young Churchill, 1969; Radio Rep, 1973; Sword of Honour, 1974; narrator, Babar, 1986; Getting Stratford (monologue), 1987; Heavy Roller, 1988; From the depths of Waters, 1990 (Sony Award Winner); Madame Bovary, 1992; Black Box, 1993; The Double Dealer, 1995; *films:* Catch us if You Can, 1963; Frenzy, 1971; The National Health, 1972; Excalibur, 1980; A Passage to India, 1984; Sir Horace Jones, in Tower Bridge Permanent Exhibn film, 1994. Cyprus Medal, 1956. *Publications:* The Job of Acting, 1976, 2nd edn 1985; The Performing World of the Actor, 1981. *Recreations:* playing and listening to music, watching Lancashire CCC and Arsenal. *Address:* c/o Roxane Vacca, Vacca Management, 8 Silver Place, W1R 3LJ. *T:* 0171–734 8085. *Club:* Groucho.

SWIFT, Graham Colin, FRSL; author; *b* 4 May 1949; *s* of Sheila Irene Swift and Lionel Allan Stanley Swift. *Educ:* Dulwich Coll.; Queens' Coll., Cambridge (MA); Univ. of York. *Publications: novels:* The Sweet Shop Owner, 1980; Shuttlecock, 1981 (Geoffrey Faber Meml Prize, 1983); Waterland, 1983 (Winifred Holtby Award, RSL, 1983; Guardian Fiction Prize, 1983; Premio Grinzane Cavour, 1987); Out of This World, 1988; Ever After, 1992 (Prix du Meilleur Livre Etranger, 1994); Last Orders, 1996; *short stories:* Learning to swim and other stories, 1982; (ed with David Profumo) The Magic Wheel (anthology), 1985. *Recreation:* fishing. *Address:* c/o A. P. Watt, 20 John Street, WC1N 2DR.

SWIFT, John Anthony; QC 1981; Rail Regulator, Office of the Rail Regulator, since 1993; *b* 11 July 1940; *s* of late Jack Swift and Clare Medcalf; *m* 1972, Jane Carol Sharples; one *s* one *d. Educ:* Birkenhead Sch.; University Coll., Oxford (MA); Johns Hopkins Univ.; Bologna. Called to the Bar, Inner Temple, 1965, Bencher, 1992. FCIT 1994. *Recreations:* theatre, walking, gardening, golf. *Address:* Wittenham House, Little Wittenham, Abingdon, Oxon OX14 4RA; Office of the Rail Regulator, 1 Waterhouse Square, 138–142 Holborn, EC1N 2SU. *Clubs:* Reform; Huntercombe Golf.

SWIFT, Lionel, QC 1975; JD; Barrister, since 1961; a Recorder of the Crown Court, since 1979; *b* Bristol, 3 Oct. 1931; *s* of late Harris and Bessie Swift, Hampstead; *m* 1966, Elizabeth (*née* Herzig) (Liz E, London fashion writer); one *d. Educ:* Whittinghame Coll., Brighton; University Coll., London (LLB 1951); Brasenose Coll., Oxford (BCL 1959); Univ. of Chicago (Juris Doc, 1960). Solicitor, Natal, S Africa, 1954; called to the Bar, Inner Temple, 1959, Bencher, 1984. British Commonwealth Fellow, Univ. of Chicago Law Sch., 1960; Amer. Social Science Res. Council Grant for work on admin of criminal justice, 1960. Jun. Counsel to Treasury in Probate Matters, 1974. Chm., Inst. of Laryngology and Otology, 1985–86. *Publication:* The South African Law of Criminal Procedure (Gen. Editor, A. B. Harcourt, QC), 1957. *Address:* (chambers) 4 Paper Buildings, Temple, EC4Y 7EX.

SWIFT, Malcolm Robin Farquhar; QC 1988; a Recorder, since 1987; *b* 19 Jan. 1948; *s* of Willie Swift and Heather May Farquhar Swift, OBE (*née* Nield); *m*; one *s* two *d. Educ:* Colne Valley High Sch., Yorks; King's Coll. London (LLB, AKC). Called to the Bar, Gray's Inn, 1970. Co-opted Mem., Remuneration Cttee of Bar Council, 1978–89 (rep. NE Circuit); Mem., Public Affairs Cttee, Bar Council, 1995–. *Recreations:* music ("Count One and the t.i.cs"), theatre, cycling, re-cycling. *Address:* Park Court Chambers, Park Cross Street, Leeds LS1 2QH. *T:* Leeds (0113) 243 3277; 6 Gray's Inn Square, Gray's Inn, WC1R 5EZ. *T:* 0171–242 1052.

SWIFT, Michael Charles, MC 1943; Member, Economic and Social Committee of the European Communities, 1983–86; Secretary-General, British Bankers' Association, 1978–82; *b* 29 Aug. 1921; *s* of late Comdr C. C. Swift, OBE, RN; *m* 1957, (Dorothy) Jill, *d* of late R. G. Bundey; one *s* one *d. Educ:* Radley College. Served War, Royal Artillery (Captain), 1940–45. Bank of England, 1946–58; Committee of London Clearing Bankers, 1958–75; Dep. Sec., British Bankers' Assoc., 1975–78. UK Rep., European Communities Banking Fedn Central Cttee, 1978–82, Chm. 1980–82. Gen. Comr for City of London, 1982–87. *Recreations:* golf, birdwatching. *Club:* Royal West Norfolk Golf.

SWINBURN, Lt-Gen. Sir Richard (Hull), KCB 1991; farmer; Director: Friarsgrove Management Services, since 1995; Glancal Property Co., since 1990; *b* 30 Oct. 1937; *s* of late Maj.-Gen. H. R. Swinburn, CB, OBE, MC and Naomi Barbara Swinburn, *d* of late Maj.-Gen. Sir Amyatt Hull, KCB, and *sister* of late Field Marshal Sir Richard Hull, KG, GCB, DSO; *m* 1964, Jane Elise Brodie, *d* of late Antony Douglas Brodie and of Juliane (*née* Falk). *Educ:* Wellington Coll.; RMA Sandhurst. Commnd 17th/21st Lancers, 1957; Adjt, Sherwood Rangers Yeomanry and 17th/21st Lancers, 1963–65; sc 1968–69; MA to VCGS, 1971–72; Instructor, Staff Coll., 1975–76; MA to COS AFCENT, 1976–78; Comdr 17th/21st Lancers, UK and BAOR, 1979–81; Col ASD 2, MoD, Falklands Campaign, 1982; Comdr, 7th Armoured Bde, BAOR, 1983–84; rcds 1985; Dir Army Plans, 1986–87; GOC 1st Armoured Div., BAOR, 1987–89; ACGS, MoD, 1989–90; Lt-

Gen., 1990; GOC SE Dist, 1990–92; GOC Southern Dist, 1992–94; Dep. C-in-C, UKLF, Comdr, UK Field Army, and Inspector Gen., TA, 1994–95, retd. Col, Queen's Royal Lancers, 1995–; Hon. Col, Exeter Univ. OTC, 1994–. Mem. Council, RUSI, 1991–95. Comr, Duke of York's Royal Mil. Sch., 1990–94. Huntsman: RMA Sandhurst Beagles, 1956–57; Dhekelia Draghounds, Cyprus, 1971; (and Master) Staff Coll. Draghounds, 1975–76; Chm., Army Beagling Assoc., 1988–94. *Recreations:* hunting, country pursuits. *Address:* Stone, Exford, Somerset TA24 7NX. *Club:* Cavalry and Guards.

SWINBURN, Walter Robert John; *b* 7 Aug. 1961; *s* of Walter Swinburn. Joined Frenchie Nicholson, 1977; rode 1st winner, Kempton, 1978; first jockey for Michael Stoute, 1981, for Sheikh Maktoum Al Maktoum, 1993. Won on Shergar, 1981, Chester Vase, Derby and King George VI and Queen Elizabeth Diamond Stakes; Irish Derby, 1983, on Shareef Dancer; Derby and Irish Derby, 1986, on Sharastani; Derby, 1995, on Lammtarra; Irish 1,000 Guineas, 1986, on Sonic Lady, 1992, on Marling; Oaks, 1987, on Unite; 2,000 Guineas, 1988, on Doyoun; 1,000 Guineas, 1989, on Musical Bliss, 1992, on Hatoof, 1993, on Sayyedati; Irish 2,000 Guineas, 1989, on Shaadi; Prix de l'Arc de Triomphe, 1983, on All Along.

SWINBURNE, Nora; actress; retired from stage and films, 1975; *b* Bath, 24 July 1902; *d* of H. Swinburne Johnson; *m* 1st, Francis Lister (marr. diss.); one *s*; 2nd, Edward Ashley-Cooper (marr. diss.); 3rd, 1946, Esmond Knight (*d* 1987). *Educ:* Rossholme College, Weston-super-Mare; Royal Academy of Dramatic Art. First West End appearance, 1916; went to America, 1923; returned to London stage, 1924; New York, again, 1930; continuous successes in London, from 1931; went into management, 1938, in addition to acting. Played as Diana Wentworth in The Years Between (which ran for more than a year), Wyndhams, 1945; Red Letter Day, Garrick; A Woman of No Importance, Savoy, 1953; The Lost Generation, Garrick, 1955; Fool's Paradise, Apollo, 1959; Music at Midnight, Westminster, 1962; All Good Children, Hampstead, 1964; Family Reunion, 1973, The Cocktail Party, 1975, Royal Exchange, Manchester. *Films include:* Jassy, Good Time Girl, The Blind Goddess, Fanny by Gaslight, They Knew Mr Knight, Quartet, Christopher Columbus, My Daughter Joy, The River (made in India), Quo Vadis, also Helen of Troy (made in Italy), Third Man on the Mountain, Conspiracy of Hearts, Music at Midnight, Interlude, Anne of the Thousand Days. Has appeared on television (incl. Forsyte Saga, Post Mortem, Kate serial, Fall of Eagles). *Address:* 52 Cranmer Court, SW3 3HW.

SWINBURNE, Prof. Richard Granville, FBA 1992; Nolloth Professor of Philosophy of Christian Religion, University of Oxford, since 1985; *b* 26 Dec. 1934; *s* of William Henry Swinburne and Gladys Edith Swinburne (*née* Parker); *m* 1960, Monica Holmstrom (separated 1985); two *d*. *Educ:* Exeter College, Oxford (Scholar). BPhil 1959, MA 1961, DipTheol 1960. Fereday Fellow, St John's Coll., Oxford, 1958–61; Leverhulme Res. Fellow in Hist. and Phil. of Science, Univ. of Leeds, 1961–63; Lectr in Philosophy, then Sen. Lectr, Univ. of Hull, 1963–72; Prof. of Philosophy, Univ. of Keele, 1972–84. Vis. Associate Prof. of Philosophy, Univ. of Maryland, 1969–70; Dist. Vis. Schol., Univ. of Adelaide, 1982; Vis. Prof. of Philosophy, Syracuse Univ., 1987; Vis. Lectr, Indian Council for Philosophical Res., 1992; Lectures: Wilde, Oxford Univ., 1975–78; Forwood, Liverpool Univ., 1977; Marrett Meml, Exeter Coll., Oxford, 1980; Gifford, Univ. of Aberdeen, 1982–84; Edward Cadbury, Univ. of Birmingham, 1987; Wade, St Louis Univ., 1990; Dotterer, Pennsylvania State Univ., 1992. *Publications:* Space and Time, 1968, 2nd edn 1981; The Concept of Miracle, 1971; An Introduction to Confirmation Theory, 1973; The Coherence of Theism, 1977, rev. edn 1993; The Existence of God, 1979, rev. edn 1991; Faith and Reason, 1981; (with S. Shoemaker) Personal Identity, 1984; The Evolution of the Soul, 1986; Responsibility and Atonement, 1989; Revelation, 1992; The Christian God, 1994; articles and reviews in learned jls. *Address:* Oriel College, Oxford OX1 4EW. *T:* Oxford (01865) 276589.

SWINBURNE, Prof. Terence Reginald; Professor of Horticultural Development, Wye College, London University, since 1994; *b* 17 July 1936; *s* of Reginald and Gladys Swinburne; *m* 1958, Valerie Parkes; two *s*. *Educ:* Imperial Coll., Univ. of London (DSc, ARCS, DIC, PhD); FIHort. Plant Pathology Res. Div., Min., later Dept, of Agriculture for NI, 1960–80; Scientific Officer, 1960–62; Sen. Scientific Officer, 1962–71; PSO, 1971–79; SPSO, 1979–80; Queen's University, Belfast: Asst Lectr, Faculty of Agriculture, 1961–64; Lectr, 1965–77; Reader, 1977–80; Head of Crop Protection Div., E Malling Res. Stn, 1980–85; Dir, Inst. of Hortl Res., AFRC, 1985–90; Sen. Res. Fellow, Wye Coll., London Univ., 1990–94. Kellogg Fellow, Oregon State Univ., 1964–65; Vis. Prof., Dept of Pure and Applied Biology, Imperial Coll., London, 1986–. *Publication:* Iron Siderophores and Plant Diseases, 1986. *Recreation:* sailing. *Address:* Tan House, 15 Frog Lane, West Malling, Kent ME19 6LN. *T:* West Malling (01732) 846090. *Club:* Farmers'.

SWINDELLS, Maj.-Gen. (George) Michael (Geoffrey), CB 1985; Controller, Army Benevolent Fund, since 1987; *b* 15 Jan. 1930; *s* of late George Martyn Swindells and Marjorie Swindells; *m* 1955, Prudence Bridget Barbara Tully; one *s* two *d*. *Educ:* Rugby School. Nat. Service Commission, 5th Royal Inniskilling Dragoon Guards, 1949; served in Germany, Korea and Canal Zone; Adjutant, Cheshire Yeomanry, 1955–56; Staff Coll., 1960; transfer to 9th/12th Royal Lancers, to command, 1969–71; Comdr 11th Armd Brigade, 1975–76; RCDS course, 1977; Dir of Op. Requirements (3), MoD, 1978–79; Chief of Jt Services Liaison Organisation, Bonn, 1980–83; Dir of Management and Support of Intelligence, 1983–85. Col, 9th/12th Royal Lancers, 1990–95. Chairman: Royal Soldiers' Daughters Sch., 1985–89; BLESMA, 1991–. *Recreations:* country life, gardening. *Club:* Cavalry and Guards.

SWINDELLS, Heather Hughson, (Mrs R. Inglis); QC 1995; a Recorder, since 1994; *b* 26 March 1950; *d* of Mrs Debra Hughson Swindells; *m* 1976, Richard Inglis; one *s*. *Educ:* Nottingham High Sch. for Girls; St Anne's Coll., Oxford (MA Lit.Hum. 1972). Called to the Bar, Middle Temple, 1974. *Recreations:* books, music, art, archaeology. *Address:* The Ropewalk Chambers, 24 The Ropewalk, Nottingham NG1 5EF. *T:* Nottingham (0115) 947 2581.

SWINDEN, (Thomas) Alan, CBE 1971; Executive Chairman, Institute of Manpower Studies, 1978–86; *b* 27 Aug. 1915; *s* of Thomas and Ethel Swinden; *m* 1941, Brenda Elise Roe; one *d*. *Educ:* Rydal Sch.; Sheffield Univ. (BEng). With Rolls-Royce, 1937–55; seconded to AFV Div., Min. of Supply, 1941–45; with Engrg Employers Fedn, 1955–65, Dir, 1964–65; Dir, Engrg Industry Trng Bd, 1965–70; Confederation of British Industry: Dep. Dir Gen. (Industrial Relations), 1970–74; Chief Advr, Social Affairs, 1974–78; Consultant, 1978–81; Chm., 1974–85, Dir, 1980–84, Kingston Regional Management Centre. Chm., Derby No 1 HMC, 1953–55. Council Member: British Employers Confedn, 1955–65; ACAS, 1974–84; British Assoc. for Commercial and Industrial Educn, 1982–94; Inst. for Employment Studies (formerly of Manpower Studies), 1986–; Mem., BBC Consultative Gp on Industrial and Business Affairs, 1977–83. *Address:* 85 College Road, Epsom, Surrey KT17 4HH. *T:* Epsom (01372) 720848. *Club:* Royal Automobile.

SWINDON, Bishop Suffragan of, since 1994; **Rt. Rev. Michael David Doe;** *b* Lymington, Hants, 24 Dec. 1947; *s* of late Albert Henry Doe and of Violet Nellie Doe (*née* Curtis). *Educ:* Brockenhurst Grammar Sch.; Durham Univ. (BA 1969); Ripon Hall Theol Coll., Oxford. Ordained deacon, 1972, priest, 1973; Asst Curate, 1972–76, Hon. Curate, 1976–81, St Peter, St Helier, Morden; Youth Sec., BCC, 1976–81; Priest-Missioner, 1981–88, Vicar, 1988–89, Blackbird Leys LEP, Oxford; RD, Cowley, 1986–89; Social Responsibility Advr, dio. of Portsmouth, and Canon Residentiary, Portsmouth Cathedral, 1989–94. Mem., Gen. Synod of C of E, 1990–94. *Recreations:* travel, radio, television. *Address:* Mark House, Field Rise, Swindon, Wilts SN1 4HP. *T:* Swindon (01793) 538654.

SWINDON, Archdeacon of; *see* Middleton, Ven. M. J.

SWINFEN, 3rd Baron *cr* 1919; **Roger Mynors Swinfen Eady;** *b* 14 Dec. 1938; *s* of 2nd Baron Swinfen and of Mary Aline (*see* M. A. Siepmann); *S* father, 1977; *m* 1962, Patricia Anne, *o d* of late F. D. Blackmore, Dundrum, Dublin; one *s* three *d*. *Educ:* Westminster; RMA, Sandhurst. ARICS 1970. Mem., Direct Mail Services Standards Bd, 1983–. Mem., Select Cttee on EC Sub-Cttee C (Envmtl and Social Affairs), 1991–94. Chm., Parly Gp, Video Enquiry Working Party, 1983–85. Pres. SE Reg., British Sports Assoc. for the Disabled, 1986–. Fellow, Industry and Parlt Trust. *Heir:* *s* Hon. Charles Roger Peregrine Swinfen Eady, *b* 8 March 1971. *Address:* House of Lords, SW1A 0PW.

SWINGLAND, Owen Merlin Webb, QC 1974; Barrister-at-Law; *b* 26 Sept. 1919; *er s* of Charles and Maggie Eveline Swingland; *m* 1941, Kathleen Joan Eason (*née* Parry), Newport, Mon; one *s* two *d*. *Educ:* Haberdashers' Aske's Hatcham Sch.; King's Coll., London. LLB 1941, AKC. Called to Bar, Gray's Inn, 1946, Bencher, 1985; practice at Chancery Bar, 1948–88; Barrister of Lincoln's Inn, 1977. A Church Comr, 1982–90. Past Pres., British Insurance Law Assoc. Mem., Court of Assts, Haberdashers' Co. (Master, 1987–88); Freeman of the City of London. *Recreations:* music, theatre, fishing, reading; interested in competitive sports. *Address:* Redwings House, Bayleys Hill, Weald, Sevenoaks, Kent TN14 6HS. *T:* Sevenoaks (01732) 451667.

SWINGLER, Bryan Edwin, CBE 1979; British Council Representative in France, 1980–84, retired; *b* 20 Sept. 1924; *s* of late George Edwin Swingler, Birmingham, and Mary Eliza Frayne; *m* 1954, Herta (*d* 1993), *er d* of late Edwin Jaeger, Schoenlinde; one *d*. *Educ:* King Edward's Sch., Birmingham; Peterhouse, Cambridge (Sen. Schol.); Charles Univ., Prague. BA 1948, MA 1953. Served War, Royal Navy (Leading Signalman), 1943–46. Apptd to British Council, 1949; Vienna, 1949–52; Lahore, 1952–55; Karachi, 1955–56; Oslo, 1956–59; Berlin, 1959–61; Cologne, 1961–63; Dir, Scholarships, 1963–67; Dep. Controller, Commonwealth Div., 1967–68; Rep. Indonesia, Djakarta, 1968–71; Controller Finance, 1972–73; Controller, Home, 1973–75; Asst Dir-Gen., 1975–77; Head of British Council Div., India, and Minister (Educn), British High Commn, New Delhi, 1977–80. Vice-Chm., British Council Staff Assoc., 1965–67; Member: British-Austrian Mixed Commn, 1973–77; British-French Mixed Commn, 1976–77, 1980–84. *Recreations:* tending Rebel a border terrier, reading, writing, arithmetic, music, painting, oriental ceramics. *Address:* Brackenside Granary, Bowsden, Berwick-upon-Tweed TD15 2TQ. *T:* Lowick (01289) 388302; 5 quai Commandant Mages, 34300 Agde, France. *T:* 67944621. *Club:* Travellers'.

SWINGLER, Raymond John Peter; editorial consultant, since 1992; *b* 8 Oct. 1933; *s* of Raymond Joseph and Mary Swingler; *m* 1960, Shirley (*d* 1980), *e d* of Frederick and Dorothy Wilkinson, Plymouth; two *d*. *Educ:* St Bede's Coll., Christchurch, NZ; Canterbury Univ. Journalist, The Press, Christchurch, NZ, 1956–57; Marlborough Express, 1957–59; Nelson Mail, 1959–61; freelance Middle East, 1961–62; Cambridge Evening News, 1962–79. Press Council: Mem., 1975–78; Mem., Complaints Cttee, 1976–78; Sec. and conciliator, 1980–91; Asst Dir, 1989–91; Asst Dir, Press Complaints Commn, 1991. Member: Nat. Exec. Council, Nat. Union of Journalists, 1973–75, 1978–79; Provincial Newspapers Industrial Council, 1976–79; Chm., General Purposes Cttee (when journalists' Code of Professional Conduct (revised) introduced), 1974–75. *Recreations:* horses, and horsewomen. *Address:* 11A Church Path, E17 9QR.

SWINLEY, Margaret Albinia Joanna, OBE 1980; British Council Service, retired; *b* 30 Sept. 1935; *er* twin *d* of late Captain Casper Silas Balfour Swinley, DSO, DSC, RN and of Sylvia Jocosa Swinley, 4th *d* of late Canon W. H. Carnegie. *Educ:* Southover Manor Sch., Lewes; Edinburgh Univ. (MA Hons Hist.). English Teacher/Sec., United Paper Mills, Jämsänkoski, Finland, 1958–60; joined British Council, 1960; Birmingham Area Office, 1960–63; Tel Aviv, 1963; Lagos, 1963–66; seconded to London HQ of VSO, 1966–67; New Delhi, 1967–70; Dep. Rep., Lagos, 1970–73; Dir, Tech. Assistance Trng Dept, 1973–76; Rep., Israel, 1976–80; Asst, then Dep., Controller, Educn, Medicine and Science Div., 1980–82; Controller, Africa and Middle East Div., 1982–86; Controller, Home Div., 1986–89. Trustee, Lloyd Foundn; Adviser on Overseas Projects, HelpAge Internat.; Mem., Council of Govs, Internat. Students' House, London; Governor: Westbury-on-Severn C of E Primary Sch. (Chm., 1990–); Hosting for Overseas Students. *Recreations:* theatre-going, country life, keeping dogs and Shire horses. *Clubs:* Commonwealth Trust, Soroptimist International of Greater London (Pres., 1988–89).

SWINNERTON-DYER, Prof. Sir (Henry) Peter (Francis), 16th Bt *cr* 1678; KBE 1987; FRS 1967; Chief Executive, Universities Funding Council, 1989–91; *b* 2 Aug. 1927; *s* of Sir Leonard Schroeder Swinnerton Dyer, 15th Bt, and Barbara (*d* 1990), *d* of Hereward Brackenbury, CBE; *S* father, 1975; *m* 1983, Dr Harriet Crawford, *er d* of Rt Hon. Sir Patrick Browne, *qv*. *Educ:* Eton; Trinity College, Cambridge (Hon. Fellow 1981). University of Cambridge: Research Fellow, 1950–54, Fellow, 1955–73, Dean, 1963–73, Trinity Coll.; Master, St Catharine's Coll., 1973–83 (Hon. Fellow, 1983); Univ. Lectr, 1960–71 (at Mathematical Lab., 1960–67); Prof. of Maths, 1971–88; Vice-Chancellor, 1979–81. Commonwealth Fund Fellow, Univ. of Chicago, 1954–55. Vis. Prof., Harvard Univ., 1971. Hon. Fellow, Worcester Coll., Oxford, 1980. Chairman: Cttee on Academic Organisation, Univ. of London, 1980–82; Meteorological Cttee, 1983–; UGC, 1983–89; CODEST, 1986–91. Chm., Sec. of State for Nat. Heritage's Adv. Cttee, Liby and Inf. Services Council, 1992–. Hon. DSc: Bath, 1981; Ulster, Wales, 1991; Birmingham, Nottingham, 1992; Warwick, 1993; Hon. LLD Aberdeen, 1991. *Publications:* numerous papers in mathematical journals. *Recreation:* gardening. *Heir:* *kinsman* John Swinnerton Dyer-Bennet [*b* 17 April 1915; *m* 1951, Mary Abby Randall; one *s* one *d*]. *Address:* The Dower House, Thriplow, Royston, Herts SG8 7RJ. *T:* Fowlmere (01763) 208220.

SWINSON, Christopher, FCA; Partner, BDO Stoy Hayward, since 1993; *b* 27 Jan. 1948; *s* of Arthur Montagu Swinson and Jean Swinson; *m* 1972, Christine Margaret Hallam; one *s*. *Educ:* Wadham Coll., Oxford (MA). FCA 1979 (ACA 1974). Price Waterhouse, 1970–77; Hacker Young, 1977–79; with Binder Hamlyn, 1979–92 (Nat. Man. Partner, 1989–92). Treasurer: Navy Records Soc., 1987–94; Soc. for Nautical Res., 1991–95; NCVO, 1993–. FRSA 1992. *Publications:* Companies Act 1989, 1990; Regulation of Auditors, 1990; Delivering a Quality Service, 1992; Group Accounts, 1993. *Recreation:* model railway construction. *Address:* 2 Seymour Close, Hatch End, Pinner, Mddx HA5 4SB. *T:* 0181–421 0951, *Fax:* 0181–421 3344. *Club:* Athenæum.

SWINSON, Sir John (Henry Alan), Kt 1984; OBE 1974; Commercial Director (Ireland), Forte (formerly Trusthouse Forte) plc, since 1965; *b* 12 July 1922; *s* of Edward Alexander

Stanley Swinson and Mary Margaret McLeod; *m* 1944, Margaret Sturgeon Gallagher; two *s*. *Educ:* Royal Belfast Academical Institution. Founded J. H. A. Swinson and Co. Ltd, 1946; Man. Dir (also of associated cos), until 1959; merged with Lockhart Gp, 1959, which merged with Trust Houses (later Trusthouse Forte plc), 1965. Chairman: Catering Industry Training Board, 1966–75; NI Training Executive, 1975–83; Livestock Marketing Commn (NI), 1970–85; NI Tourist Bd, 1979–88 (Mem., 1970–88); Member: Council, NIHCA, 1961– (Past Pres.); Catering Wages Council, 1965–82; NI Economic Council, 1977–81; Industrial Forum for NI, 1980–83. *Recreation:* sailing. *Address:* 10 Circular Road East, Cultra, Co. Down BT18 0HA. *T:* (office) Belfast (01232) 612101; (home) Holywood (01232) 422494.

SWINTON, 2nd Earl of, *cr* 1955; **David Yarburgh Cunliffe-Lister,** JP; DL; Viscount Swinton, 1935; Baron Masham, 1955; Director, Leeds Permanent Building Society, since 1987; *b* 21 March 1937; *s* of Major Hon. John Yarburgh Cunliffe-Lister (*d* of wounds received in action, 1943) and Anne Irvine (*d* 1961), *yr d* of late Rev. Canon R. S. Medlicott (she *m* 2nd, 1944, Donald Chapple-Gill); *S* grandfather, 1972; *m* 1959, Susan Lilian Primrose Sinclair (*see* Baroness Masham of Ilton); one *s* one *d* (both adopted). *Educ:* Winchester; Royal Agricultural College. Member: N Riding Yorks CC, 1961–74; N Yorks CC, 1973–77. Captain of the Yeoman of the Guard (Dep. Govt Chief Whip), 1982–86. Mem., Countryside Commn, 1987–93. JP North (formerly NR) Yorks, 1971; DL North Yorks, 1978. *Heir: b* Hon. Nicholas John Cunliffe-Lister [*b* 4 Sept. 1939; *m* 1966, Hon. Elizabeth Susan, *e d* of Viscount Whitelaw, *qv*; two *s* one *d*]. *Address:* Dykes Hill House, Masham, N Yorks HG4 4NS. *T:* Ripon (01765) 689241; 46 Westminster Gardens, SW1P 4JG. *T:* 0171–834 0700. *Clubs:* White's, Pratt's; Leyburn Market (N Yorks).

SWINTON, Countess of; *see* Masham of Ilton, Baroness.

SWINTON, Maj.-Gen. Sir John, KCVO 1979; OBE 1969; JP; Lord-Lieutenant of Berwickshire, since 1989; *b* 21 April 1925; *s* of late Brig. A. H. C. Swinton, MC, Scots Guards; *m* 1954, Judith, *d* of late Harold Killen, Merribee, NSW; three *s* one *d*. *Educ:* Harrow. Enlisted, Scots Guards, 1943, commissioned, 1944; served NW Europe, 1945 (twice wounded); Malaya, 1948–51 (despatches); ADC to Field Marshal Sir William Slim, Governor-General of Australia, 1953–54; Staff College, 1957; DAA&QMG 1st Guards Brigade, 1958–59; Regimental Adjutant Scots Guards, 1960–62; Adjutant, RMA Sandhurst, 1962–64; comd 2nd Bn Scots Guards, 1966–68; AAG PS12 MoD, 1968–70; Lt Col Comdg Scots Guards, 1970–71; Comdr, 4th Guards Armoured Brigade, BAOR, 1972–73; RCDS 1974; Brigadier Lowlands and Comdr Edinburgh and Glasgow Garrisons, 1975–76; GOC London Dist and Maj.-Gen. Comdg Household Divn, 1976–79; retired 1979. Mem., Queen's Body Guard for Scotland (Royal Co. of Archers), 1954– (Brig., 1977–); Hon. Col 2nd Bn 52nd Lowland Volunteers, 1983–90. Pres., Lowland TA & VRA, 1992–; Nat. Chm., Royal British Legion Scotland, 1986–89 (Nat. Vice-Chm., 1984–86); Trustee, Cairn Housing Assoc., 1989–; Mem. Council, British Commonwealth Ex-Services League, 1984–. Mem., Central Adv. Cttee on War Pensions, 1986–89. Pres., Borders Area SSAFA, 1993–. Trustee: Army Museums Ogilby Trust, 1978–90; Scottish Nat. War Meml, 1984– (Vice-Chm., 1987–); Chm., Thirlestane Castle Trust, 1984–90. Borders Liaison Officer, Duke of Edinburgh's Award Scheme, 1982–84. Chairman: Berwicks Civic Soc., 1982–; Roxburgh and Berwickshire Cons. Assoc., 1983–85; Jt Management Cttee, St Abb's Head Nat. Nature Reserve, 1991–. Pres., RHAS, 1993–94. DL, 1980–89, JP, 1989–, Berwickshire. *Address:* Kimmerghame, Duns, Berwickshire TD11 3LU. *T:* Duns (01361) 883277.

SWIRE, Sir Adrian (Christopher), Kt 1982; DL; Chairman, John Swire and Sons Ltd, since 1987 (Director, 1961; Deputy Chairman, 1966–87); Director: Swire Pacific Ltd; Cathay Pacific Airways; HSBC Holdings plc, since 1995; *b* 15 Feb. 1932; *yr s* of late John Kidston Swire and Juliet Richenda, *d* of Theodore Barclay; *m* 1970, Lady Judith Compton, *e d* of 6th Marquess of Northampton, DSO; two *s* one *d*. *Educ:* Eton; University Coll., Oxford (MA). Served Coldstream Guards, 1950–52; RAFVR and Royal Hong Kong AAF (AE 1961). Joined Butterfield & Swire in Far East, 1956. Director: Brooke Bond Gp, 1972–82; NAAFI, 1972–87 (Dep. Chm., 1982–85); Chm., China Navigation Co. Ltd, 1968–88; Mem., Internat. Adv. Council, China Internat. Trust and Investment Corp., 1995–. Mem., Gen. Cttee, Lloyd's Register, 1967–. Pres., General Council of British Shipping, 1980–81; Chm., Internat. Chamber of Shipping, 1982–87. Elder Brother, Trinity House, 1990. Vis. Fellow, Nuffield Coll., Oxford, 1981–89. Trustee, RAF Museum, 1983–91. Hon. Air Cdre, No 1 (Co. Hertford) Maritime HQ Unit, RAuxAF, 1987–. Pro-Chancellor, Southampton Univ., 1995–. Mem. Council, Wycombe Abbey Sch., 1988–95. Hon. CRAeS 1991. Liveryman: Fishmongers' Co., 1962; GAPAN, 1986. DL Oxon, 1989. Hon. DSc Cranfield, 1995. *Address:* Swire House, 59 Buckingham Gate, SW1E 6AJ. *Clubs:* White's, Brooks's, Pratt's; Hong Kong (Hong Kong).
See also Sir J. A. Swire.

SWIRE, Sir John (Anthony), Kt 1990; CBE 1977; Hon. President, and Director, John Swire & Sons Ltd, since 1987 (Chairman, 1966–87, Executive Director, 1955–92); *b* 28 Feb. 1927; *er s* of late John Kidston Swire and Juliet Richenda, *d* of Theodore Barclay; *m* 1961, Moira Cecilia Ducharne; two *s* one *d*. *Educ:* Eton; University Coll., Oxford (MA). Served Irish Guards, UK and Palestine, 1945–48. Joined Butterfield & Swire, Hong Kong, 1950; Director: Swire Pacific Ltd, 1965–92; Royal Insurance plc, 1975–80; British Bank of the Middle East, 1975–79; James Finlay plc, 1976–92; Ocean Transport & Trading plc, 1977–83; Shell Transport and Trading Co., 1990–95. Chairman: Hong Kong Assoc., 1975–87; Cook Soc., 1984. Member: London Adv. Cttee, Hongkong and Shanghai Banking Corp., 1969–89; Euro-Asia Centre Adv. Bd, 1980–91; Adv. Council, Sch. of Business, Stanford Univ., 1981–90; Council, Univ. of Kent at Canterbury, 1989– (Dep. Pro-Chancellor, 1993–). Hon. Fellow: St Antony's Coll., Oxford, 1987; University Coll., Oxford, 1989. Hon. LLD Hong Kong Univ., 1989. *Address:* Swire House, 59 Buckingham Gate, SW1E 6AJ. *T:* 0171–834 7717. *Clubs:* Brooks's, Pratt's, Cavalry and Guards, Flyfishers' (Pres., 1988–89); Union (Sydney); Hong Kong (Hong Kong).
See also Sir A. C. Swire.

SWISS, Sir Rodney (Geoffrey), Kt 1975; OBE 1964; JP; FDSRCS; President, General Dental Council, 1974–79 (Member, 1957–79); *b* 4 Aug. 1904; *e s* of Henry H. Swiss, Devonport, Devon, and Emma Jane Swiss (*née* Williams); *m* 1928, Muriel Alberta Gledhill (*d* 1985). *Educ:* Plymouth Coll.; Dean Close Sch., Cheltenham; Guy's Hosp. LDSRCS 1926, FDSRCS 1978. General dental practice, Harrow, Mddx, 1930–69 (Hon. dental surgeon, Harrow Hosp., 1935–67). NHS Mddx Exec. Council, 1947–74 (Chm., 1970–71); Chm., Visiting Cttee and Bd of Visitors, Wormwood Scrubs Prison, 1958–63; Mem., Central Health Services Council, 1964–74; Chairman: Standing Dental Advisory Cttee, 1964–74; Hendon Juvenile Court, 1959–64; Gore Petty Sessional Div., 1965–67 and 1970–74; Management Cttee, Sch. for Dental Auxiliaries, 1972–74. JP Mddx area, 1949. *Publications:* contribs to dental press. *Recreation:* philately. *Address:* Shrublands, 23 West Way, Pinner, Mddx HA5 3NX.

SWITZER, Barbara; Assistant General Secretary, Manufacturing Science Finance, since 1988; *b* 26 Nov. 1940; *d* of Albert and Edith McMinn; *m* 1973, John Michael Switzer. *Educ:* Chorlton Central Sch., Manchester; Stretford Technical Coll. City & Guilds Final Cert. for Electrical Technician. Engrg apprentice, Metropolitan Vickers, 1957–62; Draughtswoman: GEC, Trafford Park, 1962–70; Cableform, Romiley, 1970–71; Mather & Platt, 1972–76; Divisional Organiser 1976–79, National Organiser 1979–83, AUEW (TASS); Dep. Gen. Sec., TASS—The Manufacturing Union, 1983–87. Pres., CSEU, 1995–; Mem., TUC Gen. Council, 1993–. Associate Mem., Women's Engineering Soc. TUC Women's Gold Badge for services to Trade Unionism, 1976. *Address:* 16 Follett Drive, Abbots Langley, Herts WD5 0LP. *T:* Garston (01923) 674662.

SWORD, John Howe; Director, Oral History Project, University of Toronto, 1981–90; a Vice-President, Associated Medical Services Inc., 1984–92; *b* Saskatoon, Saskatchewan, 22 Jan. 1915; *m* 1947, Constance A. Offen; one *s* one *d*. *Educ:* public and high schs, Winnipeg; Univ. of Manitoba (BA); Univ. of Toronto (MA). Served War, RCAF, Aircrew navigation trg and instr in Western Canada. Taught for six years, before War, in Roland, Teulon and Winnipeg, Manitoba. Secretary, Manitoba Royal Commn on Adult Educn, 1945–46. Univ. of Toronto: Asst Sec. and Sec., Sch. of Grad. Studies, 1947–60; Exec. Asst to the President, 1960–65; Vice-Provost, 1965–67; Actg Pres., 1967–68; Exec. Vice-Pres. (Academic), and Provost, 1968–71; Actg Pres., 1971–72; Vice-Pres., Institutional Relations and Planning, 1972–74; Special Asst to the President, Institutional Relations, 1974–80, retired; Acting Dir, Sch. of Continuing Studies, 1980–81 and 1983–84. Chm., Art Cttee, 1980–83, Finance Cttee, 1983–88, Mem. Bd of Stewards, 1988–94, Hart House, Univ. of Toronto. Chm., Certificate Review Adv. Cttee, Ministry of Educn, 1984–94. Member: Bd, Addiction Res. Foundn of Ont, 1981–88; Council, Royal Canadian Inst., Toronto, 1981–93. Dir, Toronto Dist Heating Corp., 1983–87. Chm., Toronto Round Table, 1991–93; Mem. Management Bd, Geneva Park YMCA, 1972–85; Trustee: Toronto Sch. of Theology, 1978–83; Wychwood Pk Heritage Conservation Dist, 1986–90. Mem., United Church. Hon. LLD: Univ. of Manitoba, 1970; Univ. of Toronto, 1988. Silver Jubilee Medal, 1977. *Recreations:* tennis, swimming. *Address:* 8 Wychwood Park, Toronto, Ontario M6G 2V5, Canada. *T:* (416) 6565876. *Clubs:* Faculty (Univ. of Toronto); Arts and Letters, Queen's.

SWYNNERTON, Sir Roger (John Massy), Kt 1976; CMG 1959; OBE 1951; MC 1941; former consultant in tropical agriculture and development; Director, Booker Agriculture International Ltd, 1976–88; *b* S Rhodesia, 16 Jan. 1911; *s* of late C. F. M. Swynnerton, CMG, formerly Dir, Tsetse Research, Tanganyika, and Mrs N. A. G. Swynnerton (*née* Watt Smyth); *m* Grizel Beryl Miller, *d* of late R. W. R. Miller, CMG, formerly Member for Agriculture and Natural Resources, Tanganyika; two *s*. *Educ:* Lancing Coll.; Gonville and Caius Coll., Cambridge (BA Hons 1932; DipAgric 1933); Imperial Coll. of Tropical Agriculture, Trinidad. AICTA 1934. O/c CUOTC Artillery Bty, 1932–33; TARO, 1933–60. Entered Colonial Agricultural Service as Agric. Officer and Sen. Agric. Officer, 1934–50, in Tanganyika Territory. Served War, 1939–42, with 1/6 Bn KAR (Temp. Capt. and Adjt, 1941–42); Abyssinian Campaign. Seconded to Malta on Agric. duty, 1942–43. Transferred to Kenya on promotion, Asst Director of Agric., 1951, Dep. Dir, 1954, Director, 1956. Nominated Member of Kenya Legislative Council, 1956–61; Permanent Sec., Min. of Agriculture, 1960–62; Temp. Minister for Agriculture, Animal Husbandry and Water Resources, 1961, retd 1963. Mem. Advisory Cttee on Development of Economic Resources of S Rhodesia, 1961–62; Agric. Adviser and Mem. Exec. Management Bd, Commonwealth Develt Corp., 1962–76. Vis. Lectr, 1977–88, and Mem. Adv. Bd, Inst. of Irrigation Studies, 1980–88, Southampton Univ. President: Swinnerton Family Soc., 1982–93; Tropical Agriculture Assoc., 1983–89. *Publications:* All About KNCU Coffee, 1948; A Plan to Intensify the Development of African Agriculture in Kenya, 1954; various agricultural and scientific papers. *Address:* Cherry House, 2 Vincent Road, Stoke D'Abernon, Cobham, Surrey KT11 3JB. *Clubs:* Commonwealth Trust, Royal Over-Seas League.

SYDNEY, Archbishop of, and Metropolitan of New South Wales, since 1993; **Most Rev. Richard Henry Goodhew, (Harry);** *b* 19 March 1931; *s* of Baden Powell Richard Goodhew and Christina Delgarno Goodhew (*née* Fraser); *m* 1958, Pamela (*née* Coughlan); two *s* two *d*. *Educ:* Univ. of Wollongong (MA Hons; DLitt *hc*, 1993); Moore Theol Coll. (ThL 2nd cl. Hons, Diploma 2nd cl. Hons). Ordained 1958; Curate, St Matthew's, Bondi, NSW, 1958; Curate-in-charge, St Bede's, Beverly Hills, NSW, 1959–63; with Bush Church Aid, Ceduna, SA, 1963–66; Rector: St Paul's, Carlingford, NSW, 1966–71; St Stephen's, Coorparoo, Qld, 1971–76; Rector and Senior Canon, St Michael's Cathedral, Wollongong, 1976–79; Archdeacon of Wollongong and Camden, 1979–82; Bishop of Wollongong, Asst Bishop in dio. of Sydney, 1982–93. *Recreations:* jogging, reading, tennis, swimming. *Address:* St Andrew's House, Sydney Square, NSW 2000, Australia. *T:* (2) 2651555.

SYDNEY, Archbishop of, (RC), since 1983; **His Eminence Cardinal Edward Bede Clancy,** AC 1992 (AO 1984); *b* 13 Dec. 1923; *s* of John Bede Clancy and Ellen Lucy Clancy (*née* Edwards). *Educ:* Marist Brothers Coll., Parramatta, NSW; St Patrick's Coll., Manly, NSW; Biblical Inst., Rome (LSS); Propaganda Fide Univ., Rome (DD). Ordained to priesthood, 1949; parish ministry, 1950–51; studies in Rome, 1952–54; parish ministry, 1955–57; seminary staff, 1958–61; studies in Rome, 1962–64; seminary staff, Manly, 1966–73; Auxiliary Bishop, Sydney, 1974–78; Archbishop of Canberra and Goulburn, 1979–82. Cardinal, 1988. Chancellor, Aust. Catholic Univ., 1990–. *Publications:* The Bible—The Church's Book, 1974; contribs to Australian Catholic Record. *Recreation:* golf. *Address:* St Mary's Cathedral, Sydney, NSW 2000, Australia. *T:* (2) 2200400.

SYDNEY, NORTH, Bishop of; *see* Barnett, Rt Rev. P. W.

SYDNEY, SOUTH, Bishop of; *see* Watson, Rt Rev. P. R.

SYDNEY, Assistant Bishops of; *see* Barnett, Rt Rev. P. W.; King, Rt Rev. B. F. V.; Piper, Rt Rev. R. J.; Smith, Rt Rev R. G.; Watson, Rt Rev. P. R.

SYKES, Bonar Hugh Charles; farmer; formerly Counsellor in HM Diplomatic Service; *b* 20 Dec. 1922; *s* of late Sir Frederick Sykes, GCSI, GCIE, GBE, KCB, CMG, and of Isabel, *d* of Andrew Bonar Law; *m* 1949, Mary, *d* of late Sir Eric Phipps, GCB, GCMG, GCVO, and of Frances Phipps; four *s*. *Educ:* Eton; The Queen's Coll., Oxford. War service in Navy (Lieut RNVR), 1942–46. Trainee with Ford Motor Co. (Tractor Div.), 1948–49. Joined Foreign Service, 1949: served in Prague, Bonn, Tehran, Ottawa, FCO; retired 1970. Pres., Wiltshire Archaeological and Natural History Soc., 1975–85 (Trustee, 1947–). Chm., Bd of Visitors of Erlestoke Prison, 1983–85 (Mem., 1977–87); Member: Area Museums Council (SW), 1976–86; Council, Museums Assoc., 1981–84. FSA 1986. High Sheriff, Wilts, 1988. *Address:* Conock Manor, Devizes, Wiltshire SN10 3QQ. *T:* Devizes (01380) 840227.

SYKES, Dr Donald Armstrong; Principal of Mansfield College, Oxford, 1977–86; *b* 13 Feb. 1930; *s* of late Rev. Leonard Sykes and Edith Mary Sykes (*née* Armstrong); *m* 1962, Marta Sproul Whitehouse; two *s*. *Educ:* The High Sch. of Dundee; Univ. of St Andrews (MA 2nd cl. Classics 1952; Guthrie Scholar); Mansfield Coll., Oxford (BA 1st cl. Theol. 1958; MA 1961; DPhil 1967); Univ. of Glasgow (DipEd). Fellow in Theology, 1959–77, Senior Tutor, 1970–77, and Sen. Res. Fellow, 1986–89, Mansfield Coll., Oxford. Vis.

Professor in Classics and Religion, St Olaf Coll., Northfield, Minn, 1969–70, 1987. Hon. DD St Olaf, 1979. *Publications:* (contrib.) Studies of the Church in History: essays honoring Robert S. Paul, ed Horton Davies, 1983; articles and reviews in Jl Theological Studies, Studia Patristica, Byzantinische Zeitschrift. *Recreations:* gramophone records, walking. *Address:* 23 Weyland Road, Headington, Oxford OX3 8PE. *T:* Oxford (01865) 61576.

SYKES, Edwin Leonard, CMG 1966; *b* 1 May 1914; *m* 1st, 1946, Margaret Elizabeth McCulloch (*d* 1973); 2nd, 1976, Dorothy Soderberg. *Educ:* Leys School, Cambridge (Schol.); Trinity Coll., Cambridge (Senior Schol.). Entered Dominions Office, 1937; Asst Priv. Sec. to Secretary of State, 1939. Served War, 1939–45 (despatches). Served in British High Commissions, Canada, 1945–47, India, 1952–54; idc 1955; Dep. UK High Commissioner in Federation of Rhodesia and Nyasaland, 1956–59; Asst Under-Sec. of State, CRO, 1964–65; Dep. UK High Commissioner in Pakistan, 1965–66; Sec., Office of the Parly Comr for Administration, 1967–74. *Address:* 7 Upper Rose Hill, Dorking, Surrey RH4 2EB.

SYKES, Sir (Francis) John (Badcock), 10th Bt *cr* 1781, of Basildon, Berkshire; Partner, Townsends, solicitors, Swindon and Newbury, since 1972; *b* 7 June 1942; *s* of Sir Francis Godfrey Sykes, 9th Bt and Lady Eira Betty Sykes (*née* Badcock) (*d* 1970); *S* father, 1990; *m* 1966, Susan Alexandra, *er d* of Adm. of the Fleet Sir E. B. Ashmore, *qv*; three *s*. *Educ:* Shrewsbury; Worcester Coll., Oxford (MA). Admitted solicitor, 1968; Assistant Solicitor: Gamlens, Lincoln's Inn, 1968–69; Townsends, 1969–71. Pres., Swindon Chamber of Commerce, 1981. Governor: Swindon Coll., 1982–90; Swindon Enterprise Trust, 1982–89. Trustee: Roman Research Trust, 1990–; Merchant's House (Marlborough) Trust, 1991–; Wilts Community Foundn, 1993–. Mem., HAC. *Recreations:* local and Anglo-Indian history. *Heir: s* Francis Charles Sykes, *b* 18 June 1968. *Address:* Kingsbury Croft, Kingsbury Street, Marlborough, Wilts SN8 1HU.

SYKES, (James) Richard, QC 1981; *b* 28 May 1934; *s* of late Philip James and Lucy Barbara Sykes; *m* 1959, Susan Ethne Patricia Allen, *d* of late Lt-Col J. M. and Mrs E. M. B. Allen, Morrinsville, NZ; one *s* three *d*. *Educ:* Charterhouse; Pembroke Coll., Cambridge. BA 1957, MA 1971. Nat. Service, 2nd Lieut RASC, 1952–54. Called to the Bar, Lincoln's Inn, 1958, Bencher, 1989. Member: City Company Law Cttee, 1974–79; City Capital Markets Cttee, 1980–94; Chairman: Judging Panel, Accountant and Stock Exchange Annual Awards, 1982–90; Judging Panel, Stock Exchange and Inst. of Chartered Accountants Awards, 1990–. Mem. Management Cttee, Internat. Exhibn Co-operative Wine Soc. Ltd, 1986–. Mem. Council, VSO, 1987– (Mem. Exec., 1987–93). *Publications:* (Consultant Editor) Gore-Browne on Companies, 42nd edn 1972, 43rd edn 1977, 44th edn 1986; (ed jtly) The Conduct of Meetings, 20th edn 1966, 21st edn 1975. *Address:* Erskine Chambers, 30 Lincoln's Inn Fields, WC2A 3PF. *T:* 0171–242 5532.

SYKES, Sir John; *see* Sykes, Sir F. J. B.

SYKES, Rev. Canon John; Vicar, St Mary with St Peter, Oldham and Team Rector, Parish of Oldham, since 1987; Chaplain to the Queen, since 1995; *b* 20 March 1939; *s* of George Reginald Sykes and Doris Sykes (*née* Briggs); *m* 1967, Anne Shufflebotham; one *s* one *d*. *Educ:* St James C of E Sch., Slaithwaite; Royds Hall Grammar Sch., Huddersfield; W Bridgford Grammar Sch., Nottingham; Manchester Univ. (BA); Ripon Hall, Oxford. Ordained deacon, 1963, priest, 1964; Curate: St Luke's, Heywood, 1963–67; i/c Holy Trinity, Bolton, 1967–71; Lectr, Bolton Inst. of Technol., 1967–71; Chaplain to Bolton Colls of Further Educn, 1967–71; Rector, St Elisabeth, Reddish, 1971–78; Vicar, Saddleworth, 1978–87. Proctor in Convocation and Mem., Gen. Synod of C of E, 1980–90. Council for the Care of Churches: Mem., 1986–90; Vice-Chm., Art and Design Sub-cttee, 1988–90. Mem., various Manchester Diocesan Cttees and Councils, 1968–93. Chaplain to: Coliseum Theatre, Oldham, 1987–; three Mayors of Oldham, 1989–92; High Sheriff of Gtr Manchester, 1993–94; Gtr Manchester Police, Q Div., 1995–. Hon. Canon, Manchester Cathedral, 1991–. *Recreations:* architecture, fine arts, music, walking. *Address:* Oldham Vicarage, 15 Grotton Hollow, Grotton, Oldham OL4 4LN. *T:* and *Fax:* 0161–678 6767. *Club:* Manchester Pedestrians.

SYKES, Sir John (Charles Anthony le Gallais), 3rd Bt *cr* 1921; *b* 19 April 1928; *er s* of Stanley Edgar Sykes (*d* 1963) (2nd *s* of 1st Bt) and Florence Anaise le Gallais (*d* 1955); *S* uncle, 1974; *m* (marr. diss.). *Educ:* Churchers College. Export merchant, retired. Mem., British Epicure Soc. *Recreations:* wine, food, travel. *Heir: nephew* David Michael Sykes [*b* 10 June 1954; *m* 1st 1974, Susan Elizabeth (marr. diss. 1987), 3rd *d* of G. W. Hall; one *s*; 2nd, 1987, Margaret Lynne, *o d* of J. McGreavy; one *d*].

SYKES, John David; MP (C) Scarborough, since 1992; *b* 24 Aug. 1956; *m* 1981, Jane Aspinall; one *s* two *d*. *Educ:* St David's Prep. Sch., Huddersfield; Giggleswick Sch., N Riding. Joined Shaw Fuels Ltd (family company), 1974: graduated through every company dept, specialising in sales and transport; Dir, 1978–79; Man. Dir, Gp Petroleum Retail Div., 1981–; also Dir, subsid. cos. Mem., Select Cttee on Deregulation, 1995–; Vice Chm., Backbench Deregulation Cttee, 1995– (Sec., 1993–95). *Recreations:* walking, reading, Rugby Union, playing piano. *Address:* The Old Vicarage, North Street, Scalby, Scarborough, N Yorks YO13 0RP.

SYKES, Joseph Walter, CMG 1962; CVO 1953; Chairman, Fiji Public Service Commission, 1971–80, retired 1981; *b* 10 July 1915; *s* of Samuel Sykes and Lucy M. Womack; *m* 1940, Elima Petrie, *d* of late Sir Hugh Hall Ragg; three *s* two *d*. *Educ:* De La Salle Coll., Sheffield; Rotherham Gram. Sch.; Jesus Coll., Oxford. Colonial Administrative Service, Fiji; Cadet, 1938; Dist Officer, 1940; District Commissioner, 1950; Deputy Secretary for Fijian Affairs, 1952; Assistant Colonial Secretary, 1953; transferred to Cyprus as Dep. Colonial Sec., Nov. 1954; Admin. Sec., Cyprus. 1955–56; Colonial Sec., Bermuda, 1956–68; Chief Sec., Bermuda, 1968–71; retired. *Publication:* The Royal Visit to Fiji 1953, 1954. *Recreations:* gardening, carpentry. *Address:* 8 Dorking Road, City Beach, Perth, WA 6015, Australia.

SYKES, Prof. Keble Watson; Vice-Principal, 1978–86, Professor of Physical Chemistry, 1956–86, Queen Mary College, University of London; now Emeritus Professor; *b* 7 Jan. 1921; *s* of Watson and Victoria May Sykes; *m* 1950, Elizabeth Margaret Ewing Forsyth; three *d* (and one *s* decd). *Educ:* Seascale Preparatory Sch.; St Bees Sch.; The Queen's Coll., Oxford, MA, BSc, DPhil (Oxon.). ICI Research Fellow, Physical Chemistry Lab., Oxford, 1945–48; Lecturer, 1948–51, and Senior Lecturer in Chemistry, 1951–56, University Coll. of Swansea, Univ. of Wales; Head of Chemistry Dept, 1959–78, and Dean, Fac. of Science, 1970–73, QMC, subseq. QMW London (Fellow, 1987). Mem., Physical Scis Subcttee, UGC, 1980–85. Hon. Sec. Chemical Soc. of London, 1960–66, Vice-Pres., 1966–69, Mem. Council, 1977–80. Member Council, Westfield College, University of London, 1962–77; Governor, Highgate Sch., 1986–91. *Publications:* scientific papers in journals of Royal Society, Faraday Soc. and Chem. Soc. *Address:* 58 Wood Vale, Muswell Hill, N10 3DN. *T:* 0181–883 1502.

SYKES, Sir Keith; *see* Sykes, Sir M. K.

SYKES, Sir (Malcolm) Keith, Kt 1991; Nuffield Professor of Anaesthetics, University of Oxford, 1980–91, Emeritus Professor since 1991; Supernumary Fellow of Pembroke College, Oxford, since 1991 (Fellow, 1980–91); *b* 13 Sept. 1925; *s* of Joseph and Phyllis Mary Sykes; *m* 1956, Michelle June (*née* Ratcliffe); one *s* three *d*. *Educ:* Magdalene Coll., Cambridge (MA, MB, BChir); University Coll. Hosp., London (DA; FFARCS). RAMC, 1950–52. House appointments, University Coll. and Norfolk and Norwich Hosps, 1949–50; Sen. House Officer, Registrar and Sen. Registrar in anaesthetics, UCH, 1952–54 and 1955–58; Rickman Godlee Travelling Scholar and Fellow in Anesthesia, Mass. General Hosp., Boston, USA, 1954–55; RPMS and Hammersmith Hosp., 1958–80: Lectr and Sen. Lectr, 1958–67; Reader, 1967–70; Prof. of Clinical Anaesthesia, 1970–80. Vis. Prof., univs in Canada, USA, Australia, NZ, Malaysia, Europe. Eponymous lectures: Holme, 1970; Clover, 1976; Weinbren, 1976; Rowbottom, 1978; Gillespie, 1979; Gillies, 1985; Wesley Bourne, 1986; Husfeldt, 1986; Della Briggs, 1988; E. M. Papper, 1991; BOC Healthcare, 1992; Harold Griffith, 1992; Sir Robert Macintosh, 1992. Mem. Bd, Fac. of Anaesthetists, 1969–85; Pres., Section of Anaesthetics, RSM, 1989–90; Vice Pres., Assoc. of Anaesthetists, 1990–92 (Mem. Council, 1967–70); Senator and Vice Pres., European Acad. of Anaesthesiology, 1978–85. Hon. FANZCA (Hon. FFARACS 1979); Hon. FFA (SA) 1989. Dudley Buxton Prize, Fac. of Anaesthetists, 1980; Fac. of Anaesthetists Medal, 1987; John Snow Medal, Assoc. of Anaesthetists, 1992. *Publications:* Respiratory Failure, 1969, 2nd edn 1976; Principles of Measurement for Anaesthetists, 1970; Principles of Clinical Measurement, 1980; Principles of Measurement and Monitoring in Anaesthesia and Intensive Care, 1991; Respiratory Support, 1995; chapters and papers on respiratory failure, intensive care, respiratory and cardiovascular physiology applied to anaesthesia, etc. *Recreations:* sailing, walking, birdwatching, gardening, music. *Address:* 10 Fitzherbert Close, Iffley, Oxford OX4 4EN. *T:* Oxford (01865) 771152.

SYKES, Richard; *see* Sykes, J. R.

SYKES, Sir Richard (Brook), Kt 1994; Deputy Chairman and Chief Executive, Glaxo Wellcome plc, since 1995; *b* 7 Aug. 1942; *s* of late Eric Sykes and of Muriel Mary Sykes; *m* 1969, Janet Mary Norman; one *s* one *d*. *Educ:* Queen Elizabeth Coll., London (1st Cl. Hons Microbiol.); Bristol Univ. (PhD Microbial Biochem.); DSc London, 1993. Glaxo Res. UK (Head of Antibiotic Res. Unit), 1972–77; Squibb Inst. for Med. Res., USA, 1977–86 (Vice-Pres., Infectious and Metabolic Diseases, 1983–86); Glaxo Group Research: Dep. Chief Exec., 1986; Chm. and Chief Exec., 1987–93; Glaxo Holdings: Group R&D Dir, 1987–93; Dep. Chm., 1993–94; Chief Exec., 1993–95; Chm., 1994–95. Member: CEST, 1990–; Internat. Adv. Panel, Nat. Sci. and Technol. Bd, 1991–; Central R & D Cttee for NHS, 1991–93; Council for Sci. and Technol., 1993–; Adv. Cttee on Human Genome Res., 1993–; Adv. Council, Save British Science, 1993–. Mem., President's Cttee, CBI, 1995–. Chairman: Business Leader Gp, British Lung Foundn, 1993–; British Red Cross Corporate Club, 1994–. Mem. Bd of Govs, Univ. of Herts (formerly Hatfield Poly.), 1988–. Fleming Fellow, Lincoln Coll., Oxford, 1992. MInstD 1995. HonFRCP. Hon. DPharm Madrid, 1993; Hon. DSc: Brunel; Hull; Hertfordshire; Bristol; Newcastle; Hon. MD Birmingham. *Recreations:* opera, tennis, swimming. *Address:* Glaxo Wellcome plc, Lansdowne House, Berkeley Square, W1X 6BP. *T:* 0171–493 4060.

SYKES, Rt. Rev. Stephen Whitefield; *see* Ely, Bishop of.

SYKES, Sir Tatton (Christopher Mark), 8th Bt *cr* 1783; landowner; *b* 24 Dec. 1943; *s* of Sir (Mark Tatton) Richard Tatton-Sykes, 7th Bt and Virginia (*d* 1970), *d* of late John Francis Grey Gilliat; *S* father, 1978; granted use of additional arms of Tatton, 1980. *Educ:* Eton; Univ. d'Aix-Marseille; Royal Agric. Coll., Cirencester. *Heir: b* Jeremy John Sykes [*b* 8 March 1946; *m* 1982, Pamela June, *o d* of Thomas Wood]. *Address:* Sledmere, Driffield, East Yorkshire YO25 0XG.

SYLVESTER, (Anthony) David (Bernard), CBE 1983; writer on art, etc; editing catalogue raisonné of René Magritte; *b* 21 Sept. 1924; *s* of Philip Silvester and Sybil Rosen; *m* Pamela Briddon; three *d*. *Educ:* University Coll. Sch. Arts Council of Great Britain: Mem., 1980–82; Mem., Art Panel, 1962–70, 1972–77, Chm., 1980–82. Mem., BFI Prodn Bd, 1966–69; Mem., Commn d'Acquisitions, Musée Nat. d'Art Moderne, Paris, 1984–; Trustee, Tate Gall., 1967–69. Vis. Lecturer: Slade Sch. of Fine Art, 1953–57, RCA, 1960–70; Swarthmore Coll., Pa, 1967–68. Hon. FRA 1986. Golden Lion of Venice, for film criticism, 1993. *Exhibitions:* Henry Moore, Tate, 1951; Alberto Giacometti, Arts Council, 1955; Chaim Soutine, Tate, 1963; Giacometti, Tate, 1965; Moore, Tate, 1968; René Magritte, Tate, 1969; (with M. Compton) Robert Morris, Tate, 1971; (with J. Drew) Henri Laurens, Hayward, 1971; Joan Miró bronzes, Hayward, 1972; Islamic carpets, Hayward, 1972; Willem de Kooning, Serpentine, 1977; Dada and Surrealism Reviewed (Chm. of Cttee), Hayward, 1978; Moore, Serpentine, 1978; Magritte, Palais des Beaux-Arts, Brussels, and Musée National d'Art Moderne, Paris, 1978–79; Giacometti, Serpentine, 1981; (with D. King) The Eastern Carpet in the Western World, Hayward, 1983, etc; *films and TV:* Ten Modern Artists (writer/presenter of series), 1964; Giacometti (writer/producer), 1967; Matisse and His Model (writer), 1968; Magritte: The False Mirror (dir), 1970, etc; *radio:* many interviews, talks and discussions for BBC. *Publications:* Henry Moore, 1968; Magritte, 1969; Interviews with Francis Bacon, 1975, enlarged edn 1980; Looking at Giacometti, 1994; exhibn catalogues; articles, incl. some on films or sport, 1942–, in Tribune, New Statesman, Burlington Mag., Listener, Encounter, The Times, Observer, Sunday Times Mag., etc. *Fax:* 071–229 4078.

SYLVESTER-EVANS, Alun, CB 1975; Deputy Chief Executive, Property Services Agency, Department of the Environment, 1973–78, retired; Member, Chairman's Panel of Assessors, Civil Service Selection Boards, 1980–88; *b* 21 April 1918; *o c* of Daniel Elias Evans and Esther Evans, Rhymney, Mon.; *m* 1945, Joan Maureen, *o c* of A. J. Sylvester, CBE; two *s*. *Educ:* Lewis' School, Pengam; University of Wales, Aberystwyth. Armed services, 1940–46. Asst Research Officer, Min. of Town and Country Planning, 1946–47; Asst Principal, 1947–48; Principal Private Sec. to Minister of Housing and Local Govt, 1954–57; Asst Secretary, 1957–66, Under-Sec., 1966–73, Min. of Housing and Local Govt, later DoE. *Recreation:* golf. *Address:* Rudloe Cottage, Rudloe, Corsham, Wilts SN13 0PG. *T:* Hawthorn (01225) 810375. *Club:* Commonwealth Trust.

SYME, Dr James, FRCP, FRCPE, FRCPGlas; Consultant Paediatrician, Edinburgh, 1965–94, retired; *b* 25 Aug. 1930; *s* of James Wilson Syme and Christina Kay Syme (*née* Marshall); *m* 1956, Pamela McCormick; one *s* one *d*. *Educ:* University of Edinburgh (MB ChB). FRCPE 1967; FRCPGlas 1978; FRCP 1991. House Officer posts, 1954–55; Captain, RAMC, 1955–57; Royal Infirmary, Edinburgh, 1957–62; Senior Registrar in Paediatrics, Glasgow, 1962–65. Royal College of Physicians of Edinburgh: Secretary, 1971–75; Mem. Council, 1976–85; Vice-Pres., 1985–89. Chm., Part II MRCP Bd of three Royal Colls of Physicians of UK, 1989–95. External examnr, London, Glasgow, Dundee, Nigeria, Hong Kong, Dublin, Singapore. *Publications:* contribs to Textbook of Paediatrics (Forfar & Arneil), 1st edn, 1973 to 4th edn, 1992; papers in med. jls on paediatric topics. *Recreations:* travel, visiting churches, gardening. *Address:* Holme Barn, Airton, by Skipton, North Yorks BD23 4AL. *T:* Airton (01729) 830579. *Clubs:* New, Aesculapian, Harveian Society (Edinburgh).

SYMES, (Lilian) Mary; Clerk to Justices, 6 Divisions in Suffolk, 1943–74; Chairman, Norfolk and Suffolk Rent Tribunal, 1974–83; *b* 18 Oct. 1912; *d* of Walter Ernest and Lilian May Hollowell; *m* 1953, Thomas Alban Symes (*d* 1984); one *s*. *Educ:* St Mary's

Convent, Lowestoft; Great Yarmouth High School. Articled in Solicitor's Office; qualified as Solicitor, 1936. Became first woman Clerk to Justices (Stowmarket), 1942; first woman Deputy Coroner, 1945; Clerk to the Justices, Woodbridge, 1946, Bosmere and Claydon, 1951; first woman Coroner, 1951; Deputy Coroner, Northern District, Suffolk, 1956–82. *Recreations:* Worcester porcelain, gardening. *Address:* Leiston Old Abbey, Leiston, Suffolk IP16 4RF.

SYMINGTON, Prof. Sir Thomas, Kt 1978; MD; FRSE; Director, 1970–77, and Professor of Pathology, 1970–77, Institute of Cancer Research, Royal Cancer Hospital; *b* 1 April 1915; *m* 1943, Esther Margaret Forsyth, MB, ChB; two *s* one *d. Educ:* Cumnock Academy; Glasgow Univ. BSc 1936; MB ChB, 1941; MD 1950. Maj., RAMC (Dep. Asst Dir Pathology, Malaya, 1947–49). St Mungo (Notman) Prof. of Pathology, Univ. of Glasgow, 1954–70. Visiting Prof. of Pathology, Stanford Univ., Calif., 1965–66. Member, Medical Research Council, 1968–72. FRSE, 1956; FRIC, 1958 (ARIC, 1951); FRCP(G), 1963; FRFPS (G), 1958; FRCPath, 1964. Hon. MD Szeged Univ., Hungary, 1971; Hon. DSc McGill Univ., Canada, 1983. *Publications:* Functional Pathology of the Human Adrenal Gland, 1969; Scientific Foundations of Oncology, 1976; numerous papers on problems of adrenal glands in Journals of Endocrinology and Pathology. *Recreation:* golf. *Address:* Greenbriar, 2 Lady Margaret Drive, Troon KA10 7AL. *T:* Troon (01292) 315707.

SYMMERS, Prof. William St Clair, senior; MD; retired; Emeritus Professor of Histopathology, University of London, since 1986; *b* 16 Aug. 1917; *s* of William St Clair Symmers, Columbia, S Carolina (Musgrave Professor of Pathology and Bacteriology, QUB) and Marion Latimer (*née* Macredie), Sydney, NSW; *m* 1941, Jean Noble (*d* 1990), *d* of Kenyon and Elizabeth Wright, Paisley, Renfrewshire; one *s. Educ:* Royal Belfast Academical Instn; Queen's Univ. of Belfast (MB, BCh, BAO 1939; Johnson Symington Medal in Anatomy, 1936; Sinclair Medal in Surgery, 1939; MD 1946); Univ. of Freiburg, Breisgau, Germany. PhD Birmingham, 1953; DSc London, 1979; FRCP, FRCPI, FRCPE; FRCS; FRCPA; FRCPath; FFPath, RCPI. Surg.-Lieut, RNVR, 1940–46. Demonstrator in Pathology and pupil of Prof. G. Payling Wright, Guy's Hosp. Med. Sch., 1946–47; Registrar in Clinical Pathology, Guy's Hosp., 1946–47; Deptl Demonstrator of Pathology, Univ. of Oxford, 1947; Sen. Asst Pathologist, 1947–48, Consultant, 1948, Radcliffe Infirmary, Oxford; Sen. Lectr in Pathology, Univ. of Birmingham, England, 1948–53; Hon. Consultant Pathologist: United Birmingham Hosps, 1948–53; Birmingham Regional Hosp. Bd, 1949–53; Prof. of Morbid Anatomy, later of Histopathology, Univ. of London at Charing Cross Hosp. Med. Sch., 1953–82; Hon. Consultant Pathologist, Charing Cross Hosp., 1953–82, Hon. Consulting Pathologist, 1983–. Pres., Section of Pathology, RSM, 1969–70. Hon. FRCPA 1980; Hon. FACP 1982. Hon. DSc QUB, 1990. Dr Dhayagude Meml Prize, Seth GS Med. Sch., Univ. of Bombay, 1967; Yamagiwa Medal, Univ. of Tokyo, 1969; Scott-Heron Medal, Royal Victoria Hosp., Belfast, 1975; Morgagni Medal, Univ. of Padua, 1979. *Publications:* Systemic Pathology, 1966 (ed with late Prof. G. Payling Wright), (ed) 2nd edn, 6 vols, 1976–80, (gen. editor) 3rd edn, 15 vols, 1986–; Curiosa, 1974; Exotica, 1984. *Address:* Woodbine Cottage, 10 Kingsmeadows Road, Peebles, Scotland EH45 9EN. *T:* Peebles (01721) 723100.

SYMMONDS, Algernon Washington, GCM 1980; QC (Barbados) 1995; solicitor and attorney-at-law; *b* 19 Nov. 1926; *s* of late Algernon F. Symmonds and Olga Ianthe (*née* Harper); *m* 1954, Gladwyn Ward; one *s* one *d. Educ:* Combermere Sch.; Harrison Coll.; Codrington Coll., Barbados. Solicitor, Barbados, 1953, enrolled in UK, 1958; in practice as Solicitor, Barbados, 1953–55; Dep. Registrar, Barbados, 1955–59; Crown Solicitor, Barbados, 1959–66; Permanent Secretary: Min. of Home Affairs, 1966–72; Min. of Educn, 1972–76; Min. of External Affairs and Head of Foreign Service, 1976–79; appointed to rank of Ambassador, 1977; High Comr in UK, 1979–83 and non-resident Ambassador to Denmark, Finland, Iceland, Norway and Sweden, 1981–83, and to the Holy See, 1982–83; Perm. Sec., Prime Minister's Office, Barbados, 1983–86; Head of CS, 1986. President: Barbados CS Assoc., 1958–65; Fedn of British CS Assocs in Caribbean, 1960–64; Dep. Mem. Exec., Public Services Internat., 1964–66. Chairman: Disciplinary Cttee, Barbados Bar Assoc., 1991–; Barbados Br., WI Cttee, 1992–; Dep. Chm., Caribbean Examinations Council, 1973–76. Past Pres., Barbados Lawn Tennis Assoc. *Recreations:* tennis, cricket broadcasting (represented Barbados in football, lawn tennis, basketball). *Address:* Melksham, Margaret Terrace, Pine, St Michael, Barbados, WI; Equitas Chambers, Pinfold Street, Bridgetown, Barbados, WI. *Clubs:* Bridgetown, Empire (Cricket and Football) (Life Mem. and Past Vice-Pres.), Summerhayes Tennis (Past Pres.) (Barbados).

SYMON, Prof. Lindsay, CBE 1994; TD 1967; FRCS, FRCSE; Professor of Neurological Surgery, Institute of Neurology, London University and the National Hospital, Queen Square, since 1978; *b* 4 Nov. 1929; *s* of William Lindsay Symon and Isabel Symon; *m* 1954, Pauline Barbara Rowland; one *s* two *d. Educ:* Aberdeen Grammar Sch.; Aberdeen Univ. (MB, ChB Hons). FRCSE 1957; FRCS 1959. House Physician and Surgeon, Aberdeen Royal Infirmary, 1952–53; Jun. Specialist in Surgery, RAMC, 1953–55; Surgical Registrar, Aberdeen Royal Infirmary, 1956–58; Neurosurgical Registrar, Middlesex and Maida Vale Hosps, 1958–61, Sen. Neurosurgical Registrar, 1962–65; Mem., External Scientific Staff, MRC, 1965–78; Consultant Neurosurgeon: Nat. Hosp. for Nervous Diseases, Queen Square and Maida Vale, 1965–78; St Thomas' Hosp., 1970–78. Hon. Consultant Neurological Surgeon, St Thomas' Hosp., Hammersmith Hosp., Royal Nose, Throat and Ear Hosp., 1978–; Hon. Consultant Neurosurgeon, Nat. Hosp. for Neurology and Neurosurgery, 1978–; Civilian Advr in Neurological Surgery to RN, 1979–. Adjunct Prof., Dept of Surgery, Southwestern Med. Sch., Dallas, 1982–. Rockefeller Travelling Fellow in Medicine, Wayne State Univ., Detroit, 1961–62. Hon. Pres., World Fedn Neurosurgical Socs, 1993– (Pres., 1989–93). *Publications:* Operative Surgery/Neurosurgery, 1976, 2nd edn 1986; Advances and Technical Standards in Neurosurgery, 1972, 18th edn 1991; numerous papers on cerebral circulation and metabolism, brain tumours, general neurosurgical topics, etc. *Recreation:* golf. *Address:* Department of Neurological Surgery, Institute of Neurology, Queen Square, WC1N 3BG. *T:* 0171–278 1091; Cairngorm, 42 Granville Road, Barnet, Herts EN5 4DS. *T:* 0181–449 5842. *Clubs:* Caledonian; Royal & Ancient (St Andrews).

SYMON, Rev. Canon Roger Hugh Crispin; Canon Residentiary, Canterbury Cathedral, since 1994; *b* 25 Oct. 1934; *s* of Rev. Alan Symon and Margaret Sarah Symon (*née* Sharp); *m* 1963, Daphne Mary Roberts; two *d. Educ:* King's Sch., Canterbury; St John's Coll., Cambridge (MA); Coll. of the Resurrection, Mirfield. Curate, St Stephen's, Westminster, 1961–66; Priest-in-Charge, St Peter's, Hascombe, 1966–68; Chaplain, Univ. of Surrey, Guildford, 1966–74; Vicar, Christ Church, Lancaster Gate, 1974–79, with St James, Sussex Gardens, 1977–79; Home Staff, USPG, 1980–86; Actg Sec. for Anglican Communion Affairs to Archbp of Canterbury, 1987–91, Sec., 1991–94. *Address:* 19 The Precincts, Canterbury, Kent CT1 2EP.

SYMONDS, Ann Hazel S.; *see* Spokes Symonds.

SYMONDS, Jane Ursula; *see* Kellock, J. U.

SYMONDS, (John) Richard (Charters); Senior Research Associate, Queen Elizabeth House, Oxford, since 1979; *b* 2 Oct. 1918; *s* of Sir Charles Putnam Symonds, KBE, CB, DM, FRCP, and Janet (*née* Poulton); *m* 1980, Ann Hazel Spokes (*see* A. H. Spokes Symonds); two *s* by a previous marriage. *Educ:* Rugby Sch.; Corpus Christi Coll., Oxford (Scholar in Mod. History, MA); Secretary Elect, Oxford Union, 1939. Friends Amb. Unit, 1939–44; Dep. Dir Relief and Rehab., Govt of Bengal, 1944–45; UNRRA, Austria, 1946–47; Friends Service Unit, Punjab and Kashmir, 1947–48; UN Commn for India and Pakistan (Kashmir), 1948–49; UN Technical Assistance Board: New York, 1950–51; Liaison Officer in Europe, 1952–53; Resident Rep., Ceylon, 1953–55, Yugoslavia, 1955–58; Rep. in Europe, 1959–62; Reg. Rep., E Africa, 1961. Sen. Res. Officer, Oxford Univ. Inst. of Commonwealth Studies, 1962–65; Reg. Rep. in Southern Africa, UNTAB, 1964–65; Professorial Fellow, IDS, Univ. of Sussex, 1966–69, later Vis. Prof.; Consultant, UN Population Div., 1968–69; Rep. in Europe, UNITAR, 1969–71; UNDP Resident Rep. in Greece, 1972–75, and in Tunisia, 1975–78; Sen. Adviser, UNDP and UN Fund for Population Activities, NY, 1978–79; Sen. Associate Mem., St Antony's Coll., Oxford, 1979–92; Hon. Dir, UN Career Records Project, 1989–92; Consultant: Commonwealth Foundn, 1980; WHO, 1981. Mem. Council, Royal Commonwealth Soc., 1983–86. *Publications:* The Making of Pakistan, 1950; The British and their Successors, 1966; (ed) International Targets for Development, 1970; (with M. Carder) The United Nations and the Population Question, 1973; Oxford and Empire—the last lost cause?, 1986; Alternative Saints: the post Reformation British people commemorated by the Church of England, 1988; Far Above Rubies: the women uncommemorated by the Church of England, 1993. *Recreations:* walking, travel. *Address:* 43 Davenant Road, Oxford OX2 8BU. *T:* Oxford (01865) 515661. *Club:* Royal Over-Seas League.

See also R. C. Symonds.

SYMONDS, Matthew John; columnist, Sunday Express, since 1995; *b* 20 Dec. 1953; *s* of Lord Ardwick and Anne Symonds; *m* 1981, Alison Mary Brown; one *s* two *d. Educ:* Holland Park, London; Balliol College, Oxford (MA). Graduate trainee, Daily Mirror, 1976–78; Financial Times, 1978–81; economics and defence leader writer, economics columnist, Daily Telegraph, 1981–86; Director, Newspaper Publishing plc, 1986–94; The Independent: Dep. Editor, 1986–94; Exec. Editor, 1989–94. Res. Fellow, Social Market Foundn, 1995–. *Recreations:* history, looking at churches and pictures, novels, theatre, boating, tennis, family. *Address:* 16 St Peter's Road, St Margarets, Twickenham, Middx TW1 1QX.

SYMONDS, Richard; *see* Symonds, J. R. C.

SYMONDS, Ronald Charters, CB 1975; *b* 25 June 1916; *e s* of Sir Charles Symonds, KBE, CB, and late Janet (*née* Poulton); *m* 1939, Pamela Painton; two *s* one *d. Educ:* Rugby Sch.; New Coll., Oxford. British Council, 1938–39 and 1946–51. Military Service, 1939–45. War Office, later MoD, 1951–76, retired. Advr, Royal Commn on Gambling, 1976–78. Consultant, ICI Ltd, 1978–81. United States Bronze Star, 1948. *Recreations:* walking, ornithology. *Address:* 10 Bisham Gardens, N6 6DD.

See also J. R. C. Symonds.

SYMONS, Christopher John Maurice; QC 1989; a Recorder, since 1993 (an Assistant Recorder, 1990–93); *b* 5 Feb. 1949; *s* of Clifford Louis Symons and Pamela Constance Symons; *m* 1974, Susan Mary Teichmann; one *s* one *d. Educ:* Sherborne Prep. Sch.; Clifton Coll.; Kent Univ. (BA Hons (Law)). Called to the Bar, Middle Temple, 1972; called to the Bar of Gibraltar, 1985, to the Irish Bar, 1988, to the NI Bar, 1990. Jun. Crown Counsel (Common Law), 1985–89. *Recreation:* hitting balls. *Address:* 3 Gray's Inn Place, Gray's Inn, WC1R 5EA. *T:* 071–831 8441. *Clubs:* Hurlingham, Roehampton; Woking; Sotogrande (Spain).

SYMONS, Elizabeth Conway; General Secretary, Association of First Division Civil Servants, since 1989; *b* 14 April 1951; *d* of Ernest Vize Symons, CB and Elizabeth Megan Symons (*née* Jenkins); partner, Philip Alan Bassett; one *s. Educ:* Putney High Sch. for Girls; Girton Coll., Cambridge (MA). Research, Girton Coll., Cambridge, 1972–74; Administration Trainee, DoE, 1974–77; Asst Sec. 1977–78, Dep. Gen. Sec., 1988–89, Inland Revenue Staff Fedn. Mem., Employment Appeal Tribunal, 1995–. Member: Gen. Council, TUC; Council, RIPA; Exec. Council, Campaign for Freedom of Information, 1989–; Hansard Soc. Council, 1992–; Council, Industrial Soc., 1994–; Trustee, IPPR, 1993–; Exec. Mem., Involvement and Participation Assoc., 1992–. Member: Council, Open Univ., 1994–; Adv. Council, Civil Service Coll., 1992–; Governor: Polytechnic of North London, 1989–94; London Business Sch., 1993–. FRSA. Hon. Associate, Nat. Council of Women, 1989. *Recreations:* reading, gardening, friends. *Address:* Association of First Division Civil Servants, 2 Caxton Street, SW1H 0QH. *T:* 0171–222 6242.

SYMONS, Prof. Martyn Christian Raymond, FRS 1985; Visiting Research Professor, De Montfort University, since 1993; *b* 12 Nov. 1925; *s* of Marjorie LeBrasseur and Stephen White Symons; *m* 1950, Joy Lendon (decd); one *s* one *d. Educ:* Battersea Polytechnic (BSc, PhD, DSc London); CChem, FRSC. Army, 1945–48. Lecturer: Battersea Polytechnic, 1948–53; Southampton Univ., 1953–60; Leicester University: Prof. of Physical Chem., 1960–88; Res. Prof. of Chem., CRC Sen. Fellow, and Dir, CRC Electron Spin Resonance Res. Gp, 1988–93. Royal Soc. of Chemistry: Vice Pres., Faraday Div., 1985–87; Bruker Lectr (first), 1986; R. A. Robinson Lectr, 1987. FRSA. *Publications:* The Structure of Inorganic Radicals (with P. W. Atkins), 1967; Chemical and Biochemical Aspects of Electron Spin Resonance Spectroscopy, 1978; (jtly) Techniques in Free Radical Research, 1992; over 1000 scientific articles mainly in chem. jls. *Recreations:* watercolour landscape painting, piano playing. *Address:* 324 Old Heath Road, Colchester, Essex CO2 8BW.

SYMONS, Sir Patrick (Jeremy), KBE 1986; Chairman, Chichester Priority Care Services NHS Trust, since 1994; *b* 9 June 1933; *s* of Ronald and Joanne Symons; *m* 1961, Elizabeth Lawrence; one *s* one *d. Educ:* Dartmouth Royal Naval College. Commissioned 1951; in command, HMS Torquay, 1968–70, HMS Birmingham, 1976–77, HMS Bulwark, 1980–81; Naval Attaché, Washington, 1982–84; C of S to Comdr, Allied Naval Forces Southern Europe, 1985–88; SACLANT's Rep. in Europe, 1988–92; retired in rank of Vice-Adm. *Recreations:* sailing, skiing, swimming. *Address:* c/o Lloyds Bank, Cox's and King's Branch, 7 Pall Mall, SW1Y 5NA. *Club:* Royal Naval Sailing Association (Portsmouth).

SYMONS, Prof. Robert Henry, FRS 1988; FAA 1983; Professor, Department of Plant Science, University of Adelaide, since 1991 (Professor of Biochemistry, 1987–90); *b* 20 March 1934; *s* of Irene Olivette Symons (*née* Wellington) and Henry Officer Symons; *m* 1958, Verna Helen Lloyd; two *s* two *d. Educ:* Univ. of Melbourne (BAgSc 1956; PhD 1963). Senior Demonstrator, Univ. of Melbourne, 1958–60 ; Post-Doctoral Fellow, UK, 1961–62; Lectr, Sen. Lectr, Reader, Dept of Biochemistry, Univ. of Adelaide, 1962–87. Hon. DSc Macquarie, 1992. Lemberg Medal, Aust. Biochem. Soc., 1985. *Publications:* papers to learned jls on nucleic acid biochemistry and allied subjects. *Recreations:* gardening, wine, establishing wine vineyard. *Address:* Department of Plant Science, Waite Agricultural Research Institute, University of Adelaide, Glen Osmond, SA 5064, Australia. *T:* (8) 3037423, *Fax:* (8) 3037102.

SYMS, John Grenville St George, OBE 1981; QC 1962; Barrister-at-Law; a Recorder of the Crown Court, 1972–80; *b* 6 Jan. 1913; *s* of late Harold St George Syms and

Margaret (*née* Wordley); *m* 1st, 1951, Yvonne Yolande Rigby (marr. diss. 1971); one *s*; 2nd, 1971, Anne Jacqueline, *d* of Brig. J. B. P. Willis-Fleming, CBE, TD. Educ: Harrow; Magdalen College, Oxford (BA). Called to the Bar, 1936. Dep. Chm., Huntingdon and Peterborough QS, 1965–71. Chm., SE Agricultural Land Tribunal, 1972–83. Served in RAFVR, 1940–45 (despatches); Wing Commander, 1944. *Recreations:* fishing, shooting. *Address:* Brook Lodge, Brook, Albury, near Guildford, Surrey GU5 9DJ. *T:* Shere (01483) 202393.

SYNGE, Henry Millington; Chairman, Union International Co. Ltd, 1969–88 (Director 1955–88); Consultant, Tilney (Stockbrokers); *b* 3 April 1921; *s* of Richard Millington Synge, MC, Liverpool and Eileen Hall; *m* 1947, Joyce Helen, *d* of Alexander Ross Topping and Mrs Topping (*née* Stileman); two *s* one *d*. *Educ:* Shrewsbury School. Mercantile Marine: Radio Officer, 1941; Purser, Bibby Line, 1943; demobilised, 1946. Partner, Sing White & Co. (Stockbrokers), 1947. Manager, Liverpool Trustee Savings Bank, 1957, Chm. 1968–69; Regional Bd Mem., Trustee Savings Bank, England and Wales, 1970–85. *Recreations:* private flying, fishing, amateur radio. *Address:* Lake Cottage, Llynclys Hill, Oswestry, Shropshire SY10 8LL. *T:* Oswestry (01691) 830845.

SYNGE, Sir Robert Carson, 8th Bt, *cr* 1801; Manager and Owner, Rob's Furniture; *b* 4 May 1922; *s* of late Neale Hutchinson Synge (2nd *s* of 6th Bt) and Edith Elizabeth Thurlow (*d* 1933), Great Parndon, Essex; *S* uncle, 1942; *m* 1944, Dorothy Jean Johnson, *d* of T. Johnson, Cloverdale; two *d*. *Heir: cousin* Neale Francis Synge [*b* 28 Feb. 1917; *m* 1939, Kathleen Caroline Bowes; one *s* one *d*].

SYNNOT, Adm. Sir Anthony (Monckton), KBE 1979 (CBE 1972); AO 1976; Hon. JMN 1965; Hon. PSM 1982; *b* 5 Jan. 1922; *m* 1st, 1959, M. Virginia (*d* 1965), *d* of late Dr W. K. Davenport; two *d*; 2nd, 1968, E. Anne, *d* of late E. W. Manifold, MC. *Educ:* Geelong Grammar School. Joined RAN, 1939; served War of 1939–45 in HMA Ships Canberra, Stuart, Quiberon; HM Ships Barham, Punjabi; CO HMAS Warramunga, 1956–57; HMAS Vampire, 1961–62; OC Royal Malaysian Navy, 1962–65; CO HMAS Sydney, 1966, HMAS Melbourne, 1967; IDC 1968; Chief of Naval Personnel, 1970; Dep. Chief of Naval Staff, 1971–72; Commanding HM Australian Fleet, 1973; Director Joint Staff, 1974–76; Chief of Naval Staff, 1976–79; Chief of Defence Force Staff, 1979–82, retired. Chm., Australian War Meml Council, 1982–85. *Address:* Ballymoyer, Barton Highway, Yass, NSW 2582, Australia. *Clubs:* Commonwealth (Canberra); Melbourne (Melbourne).

SYNNOTT, Hilary Nicholas Hugh; HM Diplomatic Service; Minister and Deputy High Commissioner, New Delhi, since 1993; *b* 20 March 1945; *s* of late Commander Jasper Nicholas Netterville Synnott, DSC, RN and Florence England Synnott (*née* Hillary); *m* 1973, Anne Penelope Clarke; one *s* decd. *Educ:* Beaumont College; Dartmouth Naval College (scholar); Peterhouse, Cambridge (MA); RN Engineering College. CEng; MIEE 1971–76. RN 1962–73 (HM Submarines, 1968–73). Joined HM Diplomatic Service, FCO, 1973; UK Delegn to OECD, Paris, 1975; Bonn, 1978; FCO, 1981; Head of Chancery, Amman, 1985; Head of Western European Dept, FCO, 1989; Head of Security Co-ordination Dept, FCO, 1991. *Address:* c/o Foreign and Commonwealth Office, King Charles Street, SW1A 2AH. *Club:* United Oxford & Cambridge University.

SYSONBY, 3rd Baron, *cr* 1935, of Wonersh; **John Frederick Ponsonby;** *b* 5 Aug. 1945; *s* of 2nd Baron Sysonby, DSO and Sallie Monkland, *d* of Dr Leonard Sanford, New York; *S* father 1956. *Address:* c/o Friars, White Friars, Chester CH1 1XS.

SYTHES, Percy Arthur, CB 1980; retired 1980; Comptroller and Auditor General for Northern Ireland, 1974–80; *b* 21 Dec. 1915; *s* of William Sythes and Alice Maud Grice; *m* 1941, Doreen Smyth Fitzsimmons; three *d*. *Educ:* Campbell Coll., Belfast; Trinity Coll., Dublin. Exhibr, Scholar; BA (Mod. Lit.), 1st cl. hons Gold Medal 1938; Vice-Chancellor's Prizeman 1939. Asst Master: Royal Sch., Dungannon, 1939; Portadown Coll., 1940. Royal Artillery, 1940–46 (Major); GSO2, 1946. Asst Principal, NI Civil Service, 1946; Asst Sec. 1963; Dep. Sec. 1971. Chm., Bd of Governors, Strathearn Sch., 1982–91 (Mem., 1966–91). *Recreations:* gardens, family. *Address:* Malory, 37 Tweskard Park, Belfast BT4 2JZ. *T:* Belfast (01232) 63310.

SZASZY, Dame Miraka Petricevich, (Dame Mira), DBE 1990 (CBE 1976); QSM 1975; JP; *b* 7 Aug. 1921; *d* of Lovré (Lawrence) Cvitanov Petricevich and Mákeretá Raharuhi; *m* 1956, Albert Szaszy (decd); two *s*. *Educ;* Te Hapua Primary Sch.; Queen Victoria Maori Girls' Sch., Auckland; Auckland Girls' Grammar Sch.; Auckland Teachers' Training Coll. (BCert 1942); Auckland Univ. (BA 1945); Univ. of Hawaii (Dip. Soc. Sci. 1949). Teacher, 1946, 1968–70; social welfare work, 1946–48, Employment Officer, 1951–52, Maori Affairs Dept; Exec. Sec., Maori Women's Welfare League, 1952–57; Lecturer: Teachers' Training Coll., 1972 and 1974–79; Ardmore Trng Coll., 1973; Dir, Community Dept, Ngatapuwae Sec. Sch., 1980–84; returned to tribal home in north of NZ, 1984; helped re-establish Iwi tribal roots of Ngati Kuri through Waananga (study of history, genealogy and lore), 1989. Member: Wellington UN Club; SE Asian and Pacific Women's Assoc.; Board of Trustees, Queen Victoria and St Stephen's Schs; Anglican Church and Soc. Commn, 1970; Bishopric of Aotearoa, 1988–; NZ Anglican Synod, 1989–; NZ Race Relations Council, 1969–70; Bd, NZ Broadcasting Council (Mem., Northern NZ Broadcasting Council, 1969–70; Dep. Chm., Radio NZ); NZ Council, Protection Citizens Rights (Vice-Pres.); Social Welfare Commn, 1988–90; Maori Educn Foundn Trust Board; Maori Fisheries Commn, 1990–; Shellfish Recovery Trust, 1993–; Women's Adv. Cttee on estabt of Ministry of Women's Affairs; Maori Women's Gp which estabd Te Ohu Whakatupu (Maori Women's Secretariat) within Women's Ministry; Maori Women's Develt Trust Fund, 1988–; Muriwhenua Runanga, 1986; Muriwhenua Incorporation, 1991–; Te Orangikaupapa Trust, 1987–; Ngati Kuri Trust Bd, 1993–; Telethon Family Trust Cttee, 1982–85; Managing Trustee, Waiora Papakainga Trust, 1989–; Chm., Waiora Marae Trustees, 1988–; Maori Women's Welfare League: Rep., 1962–70; 1st Vice-Pres., 1971; Pres., 1974–77; Mem., 1st Delegn to Govt on Equal Pay for Women; Delegate: Maori Congress, 1990; Taitokerau Forum, 1990. Pres., Three Combined Tribes, 1988. LLD *hc* Victoria Univ. of Wellington, 1993. Silver Jubilee Medal, 1977. *Recreations:* tennis, basketball (rep. Auckland Univ., rep. North Island), reading, gardening. *Address:* Ngataki, RD4, Kaitaia, New Zealand. *T:* (9) 4098558.

SZÉLL, Patrick John; Head, International and EC Environmental Law Division, since 1985, and Under Secretary (Legal) since 1992, Department of the Environment; *b* Budapest, Hungary, 10 Feb. 1942; *s* of Dr János Széll and late Vera Széll (*née* Beckett); *m* 1967, Olivia (*née* Brain), JP; two *s* one *d*. *Educ:* Reading Sch.; Trinity Coll., Dublin (MA, LLB; Julian Prize 1964). Called to the Bar, Inner Temple, 1966. Joined Min. of Housing and Local Govt as Legal Asst, 1969; Department of the Environment: Sen. Legal Asst, 1973–85; Asst Solicitor, 1985–92. Legal Advr to UK Delegns at internat. envmtl negotiations, 1974–, including: Vienna Convention for Protection of Ozone Layer and Montreal Protocol, 1982–; Basle Convention on Transboundary Movements of Hazardous Wastes, 1988–; Climate Change Convention, 1990–; Biodiversity Convention, 1990–. Member: Internat. Council of Envmtl Law, Bonn, 1982–; IUCN Commn on Envmtl Law, 1994–. *Recreations:* travel, hockey, butterflies. *Address:* Department of the Environment, 2 Marsham Street, SW1P 3EB.

SZEMERÉNYI, Prof. Oswald John Louis, DrPhil (Budapest); FBA 1982; Professor of Indo-European and General Linguistics, University of Freiburg-im-Breisgau, 1965–81, now Emeritus Professor; *b* London, 7 Sept. 1913; *m* 1940, Elizabeth Kövér; one *s*. *Educ:* Madách Imre Gimnázium; University of Budapest. Classics Master in Beregszász and Mátyásföld, 1939–41; Lecturer in Greek, 1942–45, Reader, 1946, Professor of Comparative Indo-European Philology in University of Budapest, 1947–48. Came to England, Oct. 1948; employed in industry, 1949–52; Research Fellow, Bedford Coll., London, 1952–53; Asst Lecturer, 1953–54, Lecturer, 1954–58, Reader, 1958–60, in Greek at Bedford College; Professor of Comparative Philology, University College, London, 1960–65. Collitz Prof., Linguistic Inst., USA, 1963; Vis. Prof., Seattle, 1964. Corresp. Mem., Hungarian Acad. of Scis, 1948 (restitution, 1989), Ordinary Mem., 1991; Hon. Mem., Linguistic Soc. of Amer., 1989. *Publications:* The Indo-European liquid sonants in Latin, 1941; Studies in the Indo-European System of Numerals, 1960; Trends and Tasks in Comparative Philology, 1962; Syncope in Greek and Indo-European, 1964; Einführung in die vergleichende Sprachwissenschaft, 1970 (trans. Spanish, 1978, Russian, 1980, Italian, 1985), 4th edn 1991; Richtungen der modernen Sprachwissenschaft, part I, 1971 (trans. Spanish, 1979), part II, 1982 (trans. Spanish, 1986); (contrib.) Comparative Linguistics in: Current Trends in Linguistics 9, 1972; The Kinship Terminology of the Indo-European Languages, 1978; Four Old Iranian Ethnic Names, 1980; An den Quellen des Lateinischen Wortschatzes, 1989; Scripta Minora: selected essays in Indo-European, Greek and Latin, I–III, 1987, IV, 1991, V, 1992; Summing up a Life, 1992; contribs to British and foreign learned jls; *festschriften:* Studies in Diachronic, Synchronic and Typological Linguistics, ed Bela Brogyanyi, 1979; General Linguistics, Historical Philology I–III, ed B. Brogyanyi and R. Lipp, 1992–93. *Recreation:* motoring. *Address:* Caspar Schrenk Weg 14, 79117 Freiburg-im-Breisgau, Germany. *T:* (761) 66117.

SZWARC, Michael M., FRS 1966; Distinguished Professor of Chemistry of the State University of New York, 1966–79, now Professor Emeritus; *b* 9 June 1909; Polish; *m* 1933, Marja Frenkel; one *s* two *d*. *Educ:* Warsaw Inst. of Technology (Chem. Eng. 1933); Hebrew Univ., Jerusalem (PhD 1942). University of Manchester (Lecturer), 1945–52; PhD (Phys. Chem.) 1947; DSc 1949; State University Coll. of Environmental Scis at Syracuse, NY, 1952–82: Prof. of Physical and Polymer Chemistry; Research Prof.; Distinguished Prof. of Chemistry; Dir, Polymer Research Inst. Baker Lectr, Cornell Univ., 1972. Nobel Guest Prof., Univ. of Uppsala, 1969–72; Visiting Professor: Univ. of Leuven, 1974; Univ. of Calif, San Diego, 1979–80. Foreign Mem., Polish Acad. of Scis, 1988. Hon. Dr: Leuven, Belgium, 1974; Uppsala, Sweden, 1975; Louis Pasteur Univ., France, 1978. Amer. Chem. Soc. Award for Outstanding Achievements in Polymer Chemistry, 1969; Gold Medal, Soc. of Plastic Engrs, 1972; Gold Medal, Benjamin Franklin Inst., 1978; Herman Mark Award, Amer. Chem. Soc., 1990; Kyoto Award, 1991. *Publications:* Carbanions, Living Polymers and Electron Transfer Processes, 1968; Ions and Ion-pairs in Organic Chemistry, Vol. I, 1972, Vol. II, 1974; Ionic Polymerization and Living Polymers, 1993; numerous contribs to Jl Chem. Soc., Trans Faraday Soc., Proc. Royal Soc., Jl Am. Chem. Soc., Jl Chem. Phys., Jl Phys. Chem., Jl Polymer Sci., Nature, Chem. Rev., Quarterly Reviews, etc. *Address:* 1176 Santa Luisa Drive, Solana Beach, CA 92075, USA. *T:* (619) 4811863.

T

TABACHNIK, Eldred, QC 1982; *b* 5 Nov. 1943; *s* of Solomon Joseph Tabachnik and Esther Tabachnik; *m* 1966, Jennifer Kay Lawson; two *s* one *d*. *Educ:* Univ. of Cape Town (BA, LLB); Univ. of London (LLM). Called to the Bar, Inner Temple, 1970, Bencher, 1988. Lectr, UCL, 1969–72. Pres., Bd of Deputies of British Jews, 1994–. *Recreation:* reading. *Address:* 11 King's Bench Walk, Temple, EC4Y 7EQ. *T:* 0171–583 0610. *Club:* Reform.

TABBARA, Hani Bahjat; Hon. GCVO 1984; Ambassador of the Hashemite Kingdom of Jordan to Australia, since 1993; *b* 10 Feb. 1939; *s* of Bahjat and Nimat Tabbara; *m* 1980, Wafa; three *s*. *Educ:* University of Alexandria. Entered Govt service, 1963; Jordan Embassy, London, 1971–73; Counsellor, Foreign Ministry, Amman, 1973; Minister Plenipotentiary, Jordan Embassy, London, 1973–76; Private Sec. to Prime Minister, Amman, 1976–77; Ambassador: Morocco, 1977–80; Romania, 1980–82; Saudi Arabia, 1982–84; UK, 1984–85; Turkey, 1985–87; Yugoslavia, 1987–92. Order of El Istiqlal (Jordan), 1988. *Address:* c/o Ministry of Foreign Affairs, Amman, Jordan.

TABONE, Dr Vincent, (Censu), FRCSE; President of Malta, 1989–94; *b* 30 March 1913; *s* of Elisa Calleja and Nicolo Tabone; *m* 1948, Maria Wirth; four *s* five *d* (and one *c* decd). *Educ:* St Aloysius Coll.; Univ. of Malta. Dip. Opth. Oxford 1946; FRCSE 1948; Dip. RCP; Dip. RCS; Dip. in Med. Jurisp., Soc. of Apothecaries of London 1963. Surgeon Captain, Royal Malta Artillery (campaign medals), 1939–45 War. WHO Consultant on Trachoma in Taiwan, Indonesia, Iraq; Dep., Internat. Panel of Trachoma Experts, WHO, 1956; Lectr in Clinical Ophthalmology, Dept of Surgery, Univ. of Malta, 1960. MP, 1966–89; Minister of Labour, Employment and Welfare, 1966–71; Minister of Foreign Affairs, 1987–89. Mem., Council of Europe Cttees; Chm., Council of Ministers, 1988. Founded Medical Officers Union of Malta, 1954. Hon. LLD Univ. of Malta, 1989. Awarded UN Testimonial for service to UN Programme on Aging, 1989. *Recreations:* reading, watch repairing, travel. *Address:* 33 Carmel Street, St Julian's, Malta. *Clubs:* Casino Maltese (1852), Sliema Band.

TABOR, Prof. David, PhD, ScD; FRS 1963; Professor of Physics in the University of Cambridge, 1973–81, now Emeritus; Head of Physics and Chemistry of Solids, Cavendish Laboratory, 1969–81; Fellow of Gonville and Caius College, Cambridge, since 1957; *b* 23 Oct. 1913; *s* of Charles Tabor and Rebecca Weinstein; *m* 1943, Hannalene Stillschweig; two *s*. *Educ:* Regent St Polytechnic; Universities of London and Cambridge. BSc London 1934; PhD Cambridge 1939; ScD Cambridge 1956. Reader in Physics, Cambridge Univ., 1964–73. Vis. Prof., Imperial Coll., London, 1981–. For. Associate, US NAE, 1995. Hon. DSc Bath, 1985. Inaugural Gold Medal of Tribology, Instn of Engrs, 1972; Guthrie Medal, Inst. Physics, 1975. *Publications:* The Hardness of Metals, 1951; Gases, Liquids and Solids, 1969, 3rd edn 1991; (with F. P. Bowden) Friction and Lubrication of Solids, Part I, 1950, rev. edn 1954, repr. 1986; Part II, 1964; contributions to learned jls on friction, adhesion, lubrication and hardness. *Recreation:* Judaica. *Address:* Cavendish Laboratory, Madingley Road, Cambridge CB3 0HE; Gonville and Caius College, Cambridge CB2 1TA; 8 Rutherford Road, Cambridge CB2 2HH. *T:* Cambridge (01223) 841336.

TABOR, Maj.-Gen. David John St Maur, CB 1977; MC 1944; late Royal Horse Guards; GOC Eastern District, 1974–77, retired; *b* 5 Oct. 1922; *y s* of late Harry Tabor, Hitchin, Herts; *m* 1st 1955, Hon. Pamela Roxane (*d* 1987), 2nd *d* of 2nd Baron Glendyne; two *s*; 2nd, 1989, Marguerite, *widow* of Col Peter Arkwright. *Educ:* Eton; RMA, Sandhurst. Served War: 2nd Lieut, RHG, 1942; NW Europe, 1944–45 (wounded, 1944); Major, 1946. Lt-Col Comdg RHG, 1960; Lt-Col Comdg Household Cavalry, and Silver Stick in Waiting, 1964; Col, 1964; Brig., 1966; Comdr Berlin Infty Bde, 1966; Comdr, British Army Staff and Mil. Attaché, Washington, 1968; RCDS, 1971; Maj.-Gen., 1972; Defence Attaché, Paris, 1972–74. *Recreations:* shooting, fishing, sailing, golf, gardening. *Address:* Lower Farm, Compton Abdale, Cheltenham, Glos GL54 4DS. *T:* Cheltenham (01242) 890234. *Clubs:* Turf, Royal Automobile, MCC.

See also Baron Glendyne.

TACKABERRY, John Antony, QC 1982; FCIArb, FFB; a Recorder, since 1988; *b* 13 Nov. 1939; *s* of late Thomas Raphael Tackaberry and Mary Catherine (*née* Geoghegan); *m* 1966, Penelope Holt (*d* 1994); two *s*. *Educ:* Downside; Trinity Coll., Dublin; Downing Coll., Cambridge (MA, LLB). Called to the Bar, Gray's Inn, 1967. FCIArb 1973; FFB 1979. Teacher in China, 1964–65 and in London, 1965–67. Adjunct Prof. of Law, Qld Univ. of Technology, 1989. Chm., CIArb, 1990–91 (Mem. Council, 1985–94); President: Soc. of Construction Law, 1983–85; Eur. Soc. of Construction Law, 1985–87. Registered Arbitrator, 1993; Mem., many panels of internat. arbitrators. *Recreations:* good food, good wine, good company. *Address:* Arbitration Chambers, 22 Willes Road, NW5 3DS. *T:* 0171–267 2137.

TACON, Air Cdre Ernest William, CBE 1958; DSO 1944; LVO 1950; DFC 1940 (Bar 1944); AFC 1942 (Bar 1953); *b* 6 Dec. 1917; *s* of Ernest Richard Tacon, Hastings, New Zealand; *m* 1st, 1949, Clare Keating (*d* 1956), *d* of late Michael Keating, Greymouth, NZ; one *s* two *d*; 2nd, 1960, Bernardine, *d* of Cecil Leamy, Wellington, NZ; three *s*. *Educ:* St Patrick's College, Silverstream, New Zealand. Joined RNZAF, 1938. Served with RAF, 1939–46. Transferred to RAF, 1946. CO, King's Flight, Benson, 1946–49. Overseas Services since War: Canal Zone, 1951–53; Cyprus, 1956–58; Persian Gulf, 1961–63; Commandant, Central Fighter Establishment, 1963–65; Air Cdre, Tactics, HQ Fighter Comd, 1966–67; AOC Military Air Traffic Ops, 1968–71, retired. MBIM. *Address:* 69 McLeans Road, Bucklands Beach, Auckland, NZ.

TADIÉ, Prof. Jean-Yves, Chevalier de l'Ordre National du Mérite, 1974; Officier des Palmes académiques, 1988; Professor of French Literature, Université de Paris-Sorbonne, since 1991; *b* 7 Sept. 1936; *s* of Henri Tadié and Marie (*née* Férester); *m* 1962, Arlette Khoury; three *s*. *Educ:* St Louis de Gonzague, Paris; Lycée Louis-le-Grand; Ecole Normale Supérieure (Agrégé de lettres); DèsL Sorbonne 1970; MA Oxford 1988. Lectr, Univ. of Alexandria, 1960–62; Asst Prof., Faculté des Lettres de Paris, 1964; Professor: Univ. de Caen, 1968–69; Univ. de Tours, 1969–70; Univ. de la Sorbonne nouvelle, Paris III, 1970; Hd of French Dept, Cairo Univ., 1972–76; Dir, French Inst., London, 1976–81; Marshal Foch Prof. of French Literature, and Fellow, All Souls Coll., Oxford Univ., 1988–91. Corresp. FBA, 1991. Grand Prix de l'Acad. française, 1988. Officier de l'Ordre de la Couronne de Belgique, 1979. *Publications:* Introduction à la vie littéraire du XIXe Siècle, 1970; Lectures de Proust, 1971; Proust et le Roman, 1971; Le Récit poétique, 1978; Le Roman d'aventures, 1982; Proust, 1983; La Critique littéraire au XXe Siècle, 1987; (ed) M. Proust, A la Recherche du Temps perdu (Bibl. de la Pléiade), 1987–89; Portrait de l'Artiste, 1990; Le Roman du XXe Siècle, 1990; Marcel Proust: a biography, 1996. *Recreations:* tennis, opera, cinema. *Address:* Université de Paris-Sorbonne, 1 rue Victor Cousin, 75005 Paris, France.

TAFROV, Stefan Lubomirov; Ambassador of Bulgaria to the Court of St James's, since 1995; *b* Sofia, 11 Feb. 1958; *s* of Lubomir Tafrov and Nadezhda Tafrova. *Educ:* Sofia Univ. (MA in Journalism). Foreign News Editor, Democratzia, newspaper, Jan. 1990; Chief, Foreign Affairs Dept, Union of Democratic Forces, Feb.–Aug. 1990; Foreign Affairs Advr to Pres. of Bulgaria, 1990–92; First Dep. Minister of Foreign Affairs, 1992–93; Ambassador to Italy, 1993–95. *Recreation:* music. *Address:* 29 Hyde Park Gate, SW7 5HL. *T:* 0171–584 9400.

TAFT, William Howard, IV; Partner, Fried, Frank, Harris, Shriver & Jacobson, since 1992; *b* 13 Sept. 1945; *s* of William Howard Taft, III and Barbara Bradfield Taft; *m* 1974, Julia Ann Vadala; one *s* two *d*. *Educ:* St Paul's Sch., Concord, NH; Yale Coll. (BA 1966); Harvard Univ. (JD 1969). Attorney, Winthrop, Stimson, Putnam & Roberts, NY, 1969–70; Attorney Advr to Chm., Federal Trade Commn, 1970; Principal Asst to Dep. Dir, Office of Management and Budget, 1970–72, Exec. Asst to Dir, 1972–73; Exec. Asst to Sec., Health, Educn and Welfare, 1973–76; Gen. Counsel, Dept of Health, Educn and Welfare, 1976–77; Partner, Leva, Hawes, Symington, Martin & Oppenheimer, 1977–81; General Counsel 1981–84, Dep. Sec. of Defense 1984–89, US Dept of Defense; US Perm. Rep. on N Atlantic Council, 1989–92. Mem., DC Bar Assoc., Washington. Bd Mem., Washington Opera, 1977–81, 1992–. Woodrow Wilson Vis. Teaching Fellow, Woodrow Wilson Foundn, 1977–81. Dir, Atlantic Council, 1993–. *Publication:* contrib. Indiana Law Jl. *Recreation:* tennis. *Address:* 1001 Pennsylvania Avenue NW, Washington, DC 20004–2505, USA. *T:* (202) 6397000. *Clubs:* Cosmos, Leo, Literary Society (Washington, DC).

TAFTI, Rt. Rev. Hassan Barnaba D.; *see* Dehqani-Tafti.

TAGER, Romie; QC 1995; *b* 19 July 1947; *s* of Osias Tager and Minnie Tager (*née* Mett); *m* 1971, Esther Marianne Sichel; twin *s*. *Educ:* Hasmonean Grammar Sch., Hendon; University Coll. London (Hurst prize; LLB 1st Cl. Hons 1969). Called to the Bar, Middle Temple, 1970. Hon. Sec., Jewish Book Council, 1990–. *Recreations:* opera, theatre, travel. *Address:* Hardwicke Building, New Square, Lincoln's Inn, WC2A 3SB. *T:* 0171–242 2523.

TAGG, Alan; freelance designer/theatre designer; *b* 13 April 1928; *s* of Thomas Bertram Tagg and Edith Annie Hufton. *Educ:* Mansfield Coll. of Art; Old Vic Theatre Sch. Worked as asst to Cecil Beaton, Oliver Messel, etc; first play, Charles Morgan's The River Line, 1952; worked for H. M. Tennent Ltd; Founder Mem., English Stage Co., 1956: designed first prodn of Look Back in Anger, 1956; designed The Entertainer (with Laurence Olivier), 1957; also 15 other prodns at Royal Court Theatre; designed 4 prodns for RSC, including Graham Greene's The Return of A. J. Raffles, 1975; designed 12 prodns at Chichester Festival Theatre, including: Dear Antoine (with Edith Evans), 1971; Waters of the Moon (with Ingrid Bergman), 1977; 9 plays by Alan Ayckbourn; designed: 10 prodns for NT; 93 West End prodns, including: Billy Liar, 1959; How the Other Half Loves, 1970; The Constant Wife, 1973; Alphabetical Order, 1975; Donkeys Years, 1976; The Kingfisher, 1977; Candida, 1977; The Millionairess, 1978; Peter Shaffer's Lettice and Lovage (with Maggie Smith), 1987; 11 prodns on Broadway, including Peter Shaffer's Black Comedy, 1967, Lettice and Lovage, 1990 (US tour 1992); Look Back in Anger, Moscow Arts Theatre, 1957; Sleuth, Berlin, 1991; directors worked with include Lindsay Anderson, Michael Blakemore, John Dexter, John Gielgud, Tony Richardson and Michael Rudman; exhibitions designed include: Shakespeare, Stratford-upon-Avon, 1964; Hector Berlioz, 1969; 25 Years of Covent Garden, V&A Museum, 1971; Byron, 1974. *Recreation:* living in France. *Address:* 19 Parsons Green, SW6 4UL. *T:* 071–731 2787; Chemin de Masmolène, Vallabrix, 30700 Uzès, France. *T:* 66226393. *Club:* Groucho.

TAHOURDIN, John Gabriel, CMG 1961; HM Diplomatic Service, retired; *b* 15 Nov. 1913; *s* of late John St Clair Tahourdin; *m* 1957, Margaret Michie; one *s* one *d*. *Educ:* Merchant Taylors' School; St John's College, Oxford. Served HM Embassy, Peking, 1936–37; Private Secretary to HM Ambassador at Shanghai, 1937–40; BoT, 1940–41; Vice-Consul, Baltimore, 1941; Foreign Office, 1942; Private Secretary to Parliamentary Under-Secretary of State, 1943, and to Minister of State, 1945; Athens, 1946; returned to Foreign Office, 1949; Counsellor, British Embassy, The Hague, 1955; Foreign Office, 1957; Minister, UK Delegn to 18 Nation Disarmament Conf., Geneva, 1963–66; HM Ambassador to: Senegal, 1966–71, and concurrently to Mauritania, 1968–71, to Mali, 1969–71, and to Guinea, 1970–71; Bolivia, 1971–73. Mem., Internat. Inst. for Strategic Studies. Price Commission, 1975–77; Kleinwort Benson, 1977–79. *Recreations:* music cinematography, foreign languages, travel. *Address:* Diana Lodge, Little Kineton, Warwick CV35 0DL. *T:* Kineton (01926) 640276; Le Clos des Oliviers, 1007 Bar-sur-Loup, 06620 France. *Clubs:* Athenæum, Travellers', Beefsteak; Norfolk.

TAIN, Paul Christopher; Stipendiary Magistrate for East and West Sussex, since 1992; *b* 18 Feb. 1950; *s* of Reginald Tain and Kathleen (*née* Hoffland); *m* 1971, Angela Margaret Kirkup; four *s*. *Educ:* London Univ. (BA Hist.); Inst. of Judicial Admin, Birmingham Univ. (MJur). Admitted solicitor, 1975; solicitor, Wolverhampton MBC and N Yorks County Council, 1976–80; private practitioner, 1980–92; Dep. Stipendiary Magistrate, 1989–92. *Publications:* Childcare Law, 1993; Criminal Justice Act, 1994. *Recreations:* sailing, sailing and sailing. *Address:* The Law Courts, Edward Street, Brighton, Sussex BN2 2LG.

TAIT, Dr Alan Anderson; Director, International Monetary Fund in Geneva, since 1995; *b* 1 July 1934; *s* of Stanley Tait and Margaret Ruth (*née* Anderson); *m* 1963, Susan Valerie Somers; one *s*. *Educ:* Heriot's Sch., Edinburgh; Univ. of Edinburgh (MA); Trinity Coll., Dublin (PhD). Lectr, Trinity Coll., Dublin, 1959–71 (Fellow, 1968, Sen. Tutor, 1970); Visiting Prof., Univ. of Illinois, 1965–66. Economic adviser to Irish Govt on industrial develt and taxation and chief economic adviser to Confedn of Irish Industry, 1967–71; economic consultant to Sec. of State for Scotland, 1972–77; International Monetary Fund: Visiting Scholar, 1972; Consultant, 1973 and 1974; Chief, Fiscal Analysis Div., 1976–79; Asst Dir, 1979–82; Dep. Dir, Fiscal Affairs Dept, 1982–94. Prof. of Money and Finance, Univ. of Strathclyde, 1971–77. *Publications:* The Taxation of Personal Wealth, 1967; (with J. Bristow) Economic Policy in Ireland, 1968; (with J. Bristow) Ireland: some problems of a developing economy, 1971; The Value Added Tax, 1972; The Value Added Tax: international practice and problems, 1988; (ed) Value Added Tax: administrative and policy issues, 1991; articles on public finance in Rev. of Economic Studies, Finanzarchiv, Public Finance, Staff Papers, etc. *Recreations:* sailing, painting. *Address:* 58 Rue de Moillebeau, 1209 Geneva, Switzerland. *T:* (22) 7343000, *Fax:* (22) 7343388. *Club:* Cosmos (Washington DC).

TAIT, Adm. Sir (Allan) Gordon, KCB 1977; DSC 1943; Chief of Naval Personnel and Second Sea Lord, 1977–79; Chairman, Lion Nathan Ltd (incorporating NZ Breweries Ltd, Lion Breweries Ltd and Lion Corporation), since 1984; *b* 30 Oct. 1921; *s* of Allan G. Tait and Ann Gordon, Timaru, NZ; *m* 1952, Philippa, *d* of Sir Bryan Todd; two *s* two *d*. *Educ:* Timaru Boys' High Sch.; RNC Dartmouth; War Service, Atlantic and N Russia Convoys, 1939–42; Submarines, Mediterranean and Far East, 1942–45 (despatches); Commanded HM Submarines: Teredo, 1947; Solent, 1948; ADC to Governor-General of New Zealand (Lt-Gen. Lord Freyberg, VC), 1949–51; commanded HM Submarines: Ambush, 1951; Aurochs, 1951–53; Tally Ho, 1955; Sanguine, 1955–56; Asst Naval Adviser, UK High Commn, Canada, 1957–59; commanded HM Ships: Caprice, 1960–62; Ajax, 1965–66; Maidstone, 1967; commanded: 2nd Destroyer Squadron (Far East), 1965–66; 3rd Submarine Sqdn, 1967–69; Chief of Staff, Submarine Comd, 1969–70; commanded, Britannia RNC, 1970–72; Rear-Adm., 1972; Naval Secretary, MoD, 1972–74; Vice-Adm., 1974; Flag Officer, Plymouth, Port Admiral, Devonport, NATO Comdr, Central Sub Area, Eastern Atlantic, 1975–77; Adm., 1978. Naval ADC to the Queen, 1972. Director: NZ Bd, Westpac Banking Corp., 1981–93; Todd Bros Ltd, 1981–87; Todd Corp., 1987– (Dep. Chm.); Owens Gp Ltd, 1984–93; AGC (NZ) Ltd, 1987–93. Pres., and Chm. of Trustees, NZ Sports Foundn, 1981–86; Chairman: NZ Family Trust, 1983–; NZ Internat. Yachting Trust, 1989–94; Business Council, Auckland Maritime Mus., 1990–; Trustee, NZ Nat. Maritime Mus., 1990–; Mem., Spirit of Adventure Trust Board, 1982–91. *Address:* 22 Orakei Road, Auckland 5, New Zealand; Waikopou Bay, Waiheke Island, New Zealand. *Clubs:* White's; Royal Yacht Squadron; Northern (Auckland).

TAIT, Andrew Wilson, OBE 1967; Deputy Chairman, Barratt plc, since 1991 (Director, since 1988); Chairman, National House-Building Council, 1984–87 (Director-General, 1967–84); *b* 25 Sept. 1922; *s* of late Dr Adam and Jenny Tait; *m* 1954, Elizabeth Isobel Maclennan; three *d*. *Educ:* George Watson's Coll., Edinburgh; Edinburgh Univ. (MA 1st Class Hons History). Served Army, 1942–45. Leader writer, The Scotsman, 1947–48; Scottish Office, 1948–64; Chm., Housing Res. Foundn, 1969–85. Chairman: Internat. Housing and Home Warranty Assoc., 1984–87; Jt Land Requirements Cttee, 1981–87; Home Buyers Adv. Service, 1985–; Bridging the Gap, 1986–; New Homes Mktg Bd, 1988–89; Johnson Fry Property, 1988–; New Homes Envmtl Gp, 1988–91. Mem., Lloyd's, 1985– . *Recreations:* golf, tennis, chess. *Address:* Orchard Croft, Grimmshill, Great Missenden, Bucks HP16 9BA. *T:* Great Missenden (01494) 862061. *Club:* Caledonian.

TAIT, Arthur Gordon; Secretary-General, Institute of Actuaries, since 1991; *b* 28 July 1934; *s* of George Aidan Drury Tait and Margaret Evelyn Tait (*née* Gray); *m* 1958, Ann Sutcliffe Gilbert; two *s* two *d* (and one *s* decd). *Educ:* Eton Coll.; St John's Coll., Cambridge (BA Hist., MA). FIPD. Commnd KRRC, 1953–54. Imperial Chemical Industries, 1957–91: Personnel Dir, Mond Div., 1976–82; Internat. Personnel Manager, 1983–91. FRSA. *Recreations:* family, swimming, travel, friends who visit, following most sports. *Address:* 39 Hollywood Road, SW10 9HT. *T:* 0171–352 5127.

TAIT, Eric, MBE 1980; Director of European Operations, since 1989 and International Executive Director, since 1992, Pannell Kerr Forster, Chartered Accountants; *b* 10 Jan. 1945; *s* of William Johnston Tait and Sarah Tait (*née* Jones); *m* 1967, Agnes Jean Boag (*née* Anderson); one *s* one *d*. *Educ:* George Heriot's Sch., Edinburgh; RMA Sandhurst; RMCS Shrivenham (BSc Eng); Churchill Coll., Cambridge (MPhil); 2nd Lieut, Royal Engineers, 1965; despatches 1976; student, RAF Staff Coll., Bracknell, 1977; OC 7 Field Sqn, RE, 1979–81; Lt-Col 1982; Directing Staff, Staff Coll., Camberley, 1982–83, retired, at own request, 1983; Sec., Inst. of Chartered Accountants of Scotland, 1984–89. Mem. of Exec., Scottish Council (Develt and Industry), 1984–89. Editor in Chief, The Accountant's Magazine, 1984–89. Chm., European Forum, Nottingham Trent Univ., 1993–. *Recreations:* swimming, hill walking, reading. *Address:* Pannell Kerr Forster, New Garden House, 78 Hatton Garden, EC1N 8JA. *T:* 0171–831 7393.

TAIT, Prof. James Francis, PhD; FRS 1959; engaged in writing review of emdocrine subject; Emeritus Professor, University of London, since 1982; *b* 1 December 1925; *s* of Herbert Tait and Constance Levinia Brotherton; *m* 1956, Sylvia Agnes Simpson (*née* Wardropper) (*see* S. A. S. Tait). *Educ:* Darlington Grammar Sch.; Leeds Univ. Lectr in Medical Physics, Middlesex Hospital Medical School, 1948–55; External Scientific Staff, Medical Research Council, Middlesex Hospital Medical School, 1955–58; Senior Scientist, Worcester Foundation for Experimental Biology, USA, 1958–70; Joel Prof. of Physics as Applied to Medicine, Univ. of London, 1970–82; Co-Dir, Biophysical Endocrinology Unit, Physics Dept, Middlesex Hosp. Med. Sch., 1970–85. (With S. A. S. Tait) R. Douglas Wright Lectr and Medallion, Univ. of Melbourne, 1989. Hon. DSc Hull, 1979. Society for Endocrinology: Medal, 1969 and Sir Henry Dale Medal, 1979; Tadeus Reichstein Award, Internat. Soc. of Endocrinology, 1976; CIBA Award, Amer. Heart Assoc. for Hypertension Research, 1977. *Publications:* papers on medical physics, biophysics and endocrinology. *Recreations:* gardening, photography, chess. *Address:* Moorlands, Main Road, East Boldre, near Brockenhurst, Hants SO42 7WT. *T:* East End (01590) 626312.

TAIT, Sir James (Sharp), Kt 1969; DSc, LLD, PhD, BSc(Eng), CEng, FIEE; Vice-Chancellor and Principal, The City University, 1966–74, retired (formerly Northampton College of Advanced Technology, London, of which he was Principal, 1957–66); *b* 13 June 1912; *s* of William Blyth Tait and Helen Sharp; *m* 1939, Mary C. Linton; two *s* one *d*. *Educ:* Royal Technical College, Glasgow; Glasgow Univ. (BSc (Eng.), PhD). Lecturer, Royal Technical Coll., Glasgow, 1935–46; Head of Electrical Engineering Department: Portsmouth Municipal Coll., 1946–47; Northampton Polytechnic, EC1, 1947–51; Principal, Woolwich Polytechnic, SE18, 1951–56. Member: Adv. Council on Scientific Policy, 1959–62; National Electronics Council, 1964–76, Hon. Mem., 1976. Pres., Inst. of Information Scientists, 1970–72. Hon. Fellow: Inst. of Measurement and Control, 1970; Inst. of Inf. Scientists, 1973. Hon. LLD Strathclyde, 1967; Hon. DSc City, 1974. *Recreation:* open-air pursuits. *Address:* 23 Trowlock Avenue, Teddington, Mddx TW11 9QT. *T:* 0181–977 6541.

TAIT, Michael Logan, CMG 1987; LVO 1972; HM Diplomatic Service; Ambassador to Tunisia, since 1992; *b* 27 Sept. 1936; *s* of William and Dorothea Tait; *m* 1968, Margaret Kirsteen Stewart (marr. diss. 1990); two *s* one *d*. *Educ:* Calday Grange Grammar Sch.; New College, Oxford. Nat. service, 2nd Lieut Royal Signals, 1955–57. Foreign Office, 1961; served MECAS, 1961; Bahrain, 1963; Asst Political Agent, Dubai, Trucial States, 1963; FO, 1966; Private Sec. to Minister of State, FO, later FCO, 1968; First Sec. and Hd of Chancery, Belgrade, 1970; First Sec. (Political), Hd of Chancery and Consul, Amman, 1972; FCO, 1975; Counsellor and Hd of Chancery, Baghdad, 1977; Counsellor, FCO, 1978; Dep. Hd of Delegn, CSCE, Madrid, 1980; Dep. Hd of Delegn and Counsellor (Econ. and Finance), OECD, Paris, 1982; Hd of Economic Relns Dept, FCO, 1984; Ambassador to UAE, 1986–89; Asst Under-Sec. of State with responsibility for Soviet Union and Eastern Europe, 1990–92. *Recreations:* languages, mountains, sailing. *Address:* c/o Foreign and Commonwealth Office, SW1A 2AH. *Clubs:* Garrick; Vanderbilt.

TAIT, Sir Peter, KBE 1975 (OBE 1967); JP; *b* Wellington, NZ, 5 Sept. 1915; *s* of John Oliver Tait and Barbara Ann Isbister; *m* 1946, Lilian Jean Dunn; one *s* one *d*. *Educ:* Wellington Coll., NZ. MP, New Zealand National Party, 1951–54; Mayor, City of Napier, 1956–74; Pres., NZ Municipal Assoc., 1968–69. Chairman: Napier Fire Bd, 1956–75; Hawke's Bay Airport Authority, 1962–74. Freeman, City of Napier. JP 1956–. *Recreations:* bowls, gardening. *Address:* 1 Avon Terrace, Taradale, Napier, New Zealand. *T:* (70) 8445266. *Clubs:* Lions, (Hon.) Cosmopolitan (Napier).

TAIT, Richard Graham, DPhil; Editor-in-Chief, Independent Television News, since 1995; *b* 22 May 1947; *s* of Dr William Graham Tait and Isabella Dempster Tait (*née* Cumiskey); *m* 1st, 1980, Sandra Janine McKenzie McIntosh (marr. diss. 1984); 2nd, 1995, Kathryn Jane Ellison. *Educ:* Bradfield Coll.; New Coll,, Oxford (BA Mod. Hist.; MA; DPhil 1978). St Edmund Jun. Res. Fellow, St Edmund Hall, Oxford, 1972–74; BBC Television: Researcher, Money Prog., 1974–75; Producer, Nationwide, 1976–82; Editor: People and Power, 1982; Money Prog., 1983–85; Newsnight, 1985–87; General Election Results Prog., 1987; Independent Television News: Editor: Channel Four News, 1987–90; Channel Four progs, 1990–95. *Recreations:* history, ballet, opera, tennis, ski-ing. *Address:* Independent Television News, 200 Gray's Inn Road, WC1X 8XZ. *T:* 0171–833 3000.

TAIT, Mrs Sylvia Agnes Sophia, (Mrs James F. Tait), FRS 1959; Honorary Research Associate and Co-Director, Biophysical Endocrinology Unit, Physics Department, Middlesex Hospital Medical School, 1982; biochemist; distinguished for her work on the hormones controlling the distribution of salts in the body; *m* 1956, James Francis Tait, *qv*. Research Asst, Courtauld Inst. of Biochemistry, Middlesex Hosp. Med. Sch., 1944–45; External Scientific Staff, MRC, Middlesex Hosp. Med. Sch., 1955–58; Senior Scientist, Worcester Foundn for Experimental Biology, USA, 1958–70; Research Associate and Co-Director, Biophysical Endocrinology Unit, Dept of Physics as Applied to Medicine, Middlesex Hosp. Med. School, 1970–82. (With Prof. J. F. Tait) R. Douglas Wright Lecture and Medallion, Univ. of Melbourne, 1989. Hon. DSc Hull, 1979. Tadeus Reichstein Award, Internat. Endocrine Society, 1976; Gregory Pincus Meml Medal, 1977; CIBA Award, American Heart Assoc. for Hypertension Research, 1977; Sir Henry Dale Medal of Soc. for Endocrinology, 1979. *Address:* Moorlands, Main Road, East Boldre, Brockenhurst, Hants SO42 7WT. *T:* East End (01590) 626312.

TAK; *see* Drummond, T. A. K.

TALBOT OF MALAHIDE, 10th Baron *cr* 1831 (Ire.); **Reginald John Richard Arundell;** DL; Hereditary Lord Admiral Malahide and Adjacent Seas; *b* 9 Jan. 1931; *s* of Reginald John Arthur Arundell (*g g g s* of 1st Baroness) (who assumed by Royal Licence, 1945, names and arms of Arundell in lieu of Talbot, and *d* 1953), and Winifred (*d* 1954), *d* of R. B. S. Castle; *S* cousin, 1987; *m* 1st, 1955, Laura Duff (*d* 1989), *d* of late Group Captain Edward John Tennant, DSO, MC; one *s* four *d*; 2nd, 1992, Patricia Mary Blundell-Brown, *d* of late J. Riddell, OBE. *Educ:* Stonyhurst. DL Wilts. KStJ 1988 (CStJ 1983; OStJ 1978); Chm., St John Council for Wilts, 1976–. Knight of Malta, 1977. Hon. Citizen, State of Maryland, USA, 1984. *Heir: s* Hon. Richard John Tennant Arundell [*b* 28 March 1957; *m* 1984, Jane Catherine, *d* of Timothy Heathcote Unwin; four *d*]. *Address:* Park Gate, Donhead, Shaftesbury, Dorset SP7 9EU. *Clubs:* Pratt's, Farmers'.

TALBOT, Vice-Adm. Sir (Arthur Allison) FitzRoy, KBE 1964; CB 1961; DSO 1940 and Bar 1942; DL; Commander-in-Chief, Plymouth, 1965–67; retired; *b* 22 October 1909; *s* of late Henry FitzRoy George Talbot, Captain Royal Navy, and of Susan Blair Athol Allison; *m* 1st, 1940, Joyce Gertrude Linley (*d* 1981); two *d*; 2nd, 1983, Lady (Elizabeth) Durlacher. *Educ:* RN College, Dartmouth. Served War of 1939–45: Comd 10th A/S Striking Force, North Sea, 1939, and 3rd MGB Flotilla, Channel, 1940–41 (DSO); Comd HMS Whitshed, East Coast, 1942 (Bar to DSO); Comd HMS Teazer, Mediterranean, 1943–44. Comdr 1945; Chief Staff Officer, Commodore Western Isles, 1945; Staff Officer Ops to C-in-C Brit. Pacific Fleet and Far East Station, 1947–48; Comd HMS Alert, 1949. Capt. 1950; Naval Attaché, Moscow and Helsinki, 1951–53. Imperial Defence College, 1954. Capt. (D) 3rd Destroyer Squadron, 1955–57; Commodore RN Barracks Portsmouth, 1957–59; Rear-Adm. 1960; Flag Officer: Arabian Seas and Persian Gulf, 1960–61; Middle East, 1961–62; Vice-Adm. 1962; Commander-in-Chief, S Atlantic and S America, 1963–65. DL Somerset, 1973. *Recreations:* riding, shooting. *Address:* Wootton Fitzpaine Manor, Bridport, Dorset, DT6 6NE. *T:* Charmouth (01297) 560455. *Club:* Army and Navy.

TALBOT, Vice-Adm. Sir FitzRoy, *see* Talbot, Vice-Adm. Sir A. A. F.

TALBOT, Godfrey Walker, LVO 1960; OBE 1946; author, broadcaster, lecturer, journalist; Senior News Reporter and Commentator on staff of British Broadcasting Corporation, 1946–69; official BBC observer accredited to Buckingham Palace, 1948–69; *b* 8 Oct. 1908; *s* of Frank Talbot and Kate Bertha Talbot (*née* Walker); *m* 1933, Bess, *d* of Robert and Clara Owen, Bradford House, Wigan; one *s* (and one *s* decd). *Educ:* Leeds Grammar School. Joined editorial staff on The Yorkshire Post, 1928; Editor of The Manchester City News, 1932–34; Editorial Staff, Daily Dispatch, 1934–37. Joined BBC, 1937; War of 1939–45: BBC war correspondent overseas, 1941–45 (despatches, OBE); organised BBC Home Reporting Unit, as Chief Reporter, after the war. BBC Commentator, Royal Commonwealth Tour, 1953–54, and other overseas visits by HM the Queen. Pres., Queen's English Soc., 1982–. *Publications:* Speaking from the Desert, 1944; Ten Seconds from Now, 1973; Queen Elizabeth the Queen Mother, 1973; Permission to Speak, 1976; Royal Heritage, 1977; Royalty Annual, 1952, 1953, 1954,

1955, 1956; The Country Life Book of Queen Elizabeth The Queen Mother, 1978, 3rd edn 1989; The Country Life Book of the Royal Family, 1980, new edn 1983; Forty Years The Queen, 1992. *Recreation:* keeping quiet. *Address:* Holmwell, Hook Hill, Sanderstead, Surrey CR2 0LA. *T:* 0181–657 3476. *Club:* Royal Over-Seas League (Vice-Chm., 1985–).

TALBOT, Sir Hilary Gwynne, Kt 1968; a Judge of the High Court of Justice, Queen's Bench Division, 1968–83; Judge of the Employment Appeals Tribunal, 1978–81; *b* 22 Jan. 1912; *s* of late Rev. Prebendary A. T. S. Talbot, RD, and Mrs Talbot; *m* 1963, Jean Whitworth (JP Wilts), *o d* of late Mr and Mrs Kenneth Fisher. *Educ:* Haileybury Coll.; Worcester Coll., Oxford. MA Oxon. Served War of 1939–45; Captain, RA. Called to Bar by Middle Temple Jan. 1935, Bencher, 1968. Dep. Chm., Northants QS, 1948–62; Chm., Derbyshire QS, 1958–63; Dep. Chm. Hants QS, 1964–71; Judge of County Courts, 1962–68; a Presiding Judge, Wales and Chester Circuit, 1970–74. Mem., Parole Bd, 1980–82. Dep. Chm., Boundary Commn for Wales, 1980–83. Formerly Dep. Chm., Agricultural Land Tribunals. *Recreations:* fishing, walking, bird-watching. *Address:* Old Chapel House, Little Ashley, Bradford-on-Avon, Wilts BA15 2PN.

TALBOT, John Andrew, FCA; Partner, Arthur Andersen, since 1983 (Director, Worldwide Corporate Recovery Practice, since 1993); *b* 2 Aug. 1949; *s* of Robert Talbot and Lucy E. Talbot (*née* Jarvis); *m* 1st, 1969, Susan Hollingbery (marr. diss.); one *s* one *d*; 2nd, 1983, Jennifer Anne Houghton; one *s* two *d*. CA 1971; accountant in manufacturing, 1972–73; Bernard Phillips & Co., Accountants, 1973–75; Spicer & Pegler, 1975–83, Partner, 1979; joined Arthur Andersen, 1983: Hd, UK Insolvency Practice, 1988; Administrator, Maxwell Private Cos, 1991–; Receiver: Leyland DAF, 1993; Ferranti, 1994. Chm., Insolvency Licensing Cttee, ICAEW, 1992–94. Hon. Treas., English Nat. Ballet, 1990–. *Recreations:* contemporary art, antiquarian books, snooker, modern history, modern and classical dance. *Address:* c/o Arthur Andersen, 1 Surrey Street, WC2R 2NT. *T:* 0171–438 3739. *Club:* Royal Automobile.

TALBOT, Commandant Mary (Irene), CB; Director, Women's Royal Naval Service, 1973–76; *b* 17 Feb. 1922. *Educ:* Bristol Univ. BA Hons, Philosophy and Economics. Joined WRNS as a Naval recruiting asst, Nov. 1943; Officer training course, 1944, and apptd to HMS Eaglet, in Liverpool, as an Educn and Resettlement Officer; served on staffs of C-in-Cs: Mediterranean; the Nore; Portsmouth, 1945–61; First Officer, and apptd to staff of Dir Naval Educn Service, 1952; subseq. served HMS Condor, Dauntless and Raleigh; Chief Officer, and apptd Sen. WRNS Officer, the Nore, 1960; on staff of Dir Naval Manning, 1963–66, and then became Asst Dir, WRNS; Superintendent, and served on staff of C-in-C Naval Home Command, 1969; Supt in charge, WRNS training estabt, HMS Dauntless, near Reading, 1972–73. Hon. ADC, 1973–76. Hon. LLD Bristol, 1993. *Recreations:* bridge, gardening, racing. *Address:* Sonning Cottage, Pound Lane, Sonning-on-Thames RG4 0XE. *T:* Reading (01734) 693323; Flat 2, 35 Buckingham Gate, SW1 6PA. *T:* 0171–834 2579.

TALBOT, Very Rev. Maurice John; Dean Emeritus of Limerick; *b* 29 March 1912; 2nd *s* of late Very Rev. Joseph Talbot, sometime Dean of Cashel; *m* 1942, Elisabeth Enid Westropp (*d* 1975); four *s*; 2nd, 1980, Reta Soames. *Educ:* St Columba's College; Trinity College, Dublin (MA). Curate of Nantenan, 1935; Rector of Rathkeale, 1942; Rector of Killarney, 1952; Dean of Limerick, 1954–71; Prebendary of Taney, St Patrick's Nat. Cathedral, Dublin; Bishop's Curate, Kilmallock Union of Parishes, 1971–73; Rector of Drumcliffe, 1980–84. *Publications:* Pictorial Guide to St Mary's Cathedral, Limerick, 1969; contrib. to North Munster Studies, 1967; The Monuments of St Mary's Cathedral, 1976. *Recreations:* tennis, shooting, fishing. *Address:* 4 Meadow Close, Caherdavin, Limerick, Ireland.

TALBOT, Prof Michael Owen, FBA 1990; James and Constance Alsop Professor of Music, University of Liverpool, since 1986; *b* 4 Jan. 1943; *s* of Alan and Annelise Talbot; *m* 1970, Shirley Ellen Mashiane; one *s* one *d*. *Educ:* Welwyn Garden City Grammar Sch.; Royal Coll. of Music (ARCM); Clare Coll., Cambridge (Open, later Meml Scholar; MusB Hons 1963; MA; PhD 1968). Lectr in Music, 1968, Sen. Lectr, 1979, Reader, 1983–86, Univ. of Liverpool. Corresp. Mem., Ateneo Veneto, Venice, 1986. Order of Merit (Italy), 1980. *Publications:* Vivaldi, 1978 (Italian, German and Polish edns); Vivaldi, 1979 (Japanese, Brazilian and Spanish edns); Albinoni: Leben und Werk, 1980; Antonio Vivaldi: a guide to research, 1988 (Italian edn); Tomaso Albinoni: the Venetian composer and his world, 1990; Benedetto Vinaccesi: a musician in Brescia and Venice in the age of Corelli, 1994. *Recreations:* chess, reading novels, travel. *Address:* 36 Montclair Drive, Liverpool L18 0HA. *T:* 0151–722 3328.

TALBOT, Patrick John; QC 1990; *b* 28 July 1946; *s* of John Bentley Talbot, MC, and late Marguerite Maxwell Talbot (*née* Townley); *m* 1976, Judith Anne Urwin; one *s* two *d*. *Educ:* Charterhouse (Foundn Schol.); University Coll., Oxford (MA). Called to Bar, Lincoln's Inn, 1969; in practice at Chancery Bar, 1970–. Member: Senate of Inns of Court and the Bar, 1976–78; Council of Legal Educn, 1977– (Vice-Chm., 1992–). Affiliate British Trustee, British Amer. Educnl Foundn, 1984–. Hon. Life Mem., Nat. Union of Students, 1982. *Recreations:* cricket, ski-ing, collecting toys, bridge. *Address:* 22 West Park Road, Kew, Richmond, Surrey TW9 4DA. *T:* 0181–878 3516. *Clubs:* MCC, Wimbledon Wanderers CC.

TALBOYS, Rt. Hon. Sir Brian (Edward), Hon. AC 1982; CH 1981; KCB 1991; PC 1977; *b* Wanganui, 1921; *m*; two *s*. *Educ:* Wanganui Collegiate Sch.; Univ. of Manitoba; Victoria Univ., Wellington (BA). Served war of 1939–45, RNZAF. MP for Wallace, NZ, 1957–81; Dep. Leader, National Party, 1974–81; Parly Under-Sec. to Minister of Trade and Industry, 1960; Minister of Agriculture, 1962–69; Minister of Science, 1964–72; Minister of Education, 1969–72; Minister of Overseas Trade and Trade and Industry, 1972; Minister of Nat. Develt, 1975–77; Dep. Prime Minister and Minister of For. Affairs and Overseas Trade, 1975–81. Leader of a number of NZ delegns to overseas confs; NZ Rep., Standing Cttee of Pacific Economic Co-operation Conf., 1983–90. Grand Cross 1st Class, Order of Merit, Fed. Republic of Germany, 1978. Hon. DSc Massey Univ., 1981; Hon. DLitt Chung-Ang Univ., Seoul, 1981. *Address:* 1 Hamilton Avenue, Winton, New Zealand.

TALINTYRE, Douglas George; Director, Office of Manpower Economics, 1989–92; *b* 26 July 1932; *o s* of late Henry Matthew Talintyre and Gladys Talintyre; *m* 1956, Maureen Diana Lyons; one *s* one *d*. *Educ:* Harrow County Grammar School; London School of Economics. BSc (Econ.) 1956; MSc (Industrial Relns and Personnel Management) 1983. Joined National Coal Board, 1956: Administrative Assistant, 1956–59; Marketing Officer, Durham Div., 1959–61; Head of Manpower Planning and Intelligence, HQ, 1961–62; Dep. Head of Manpower, HQ, 1962–64; Head of Wages and Control, NW Div., 1964–66. Entered Civil Service, 1966: Principal, Naval Personnel (Pay) Div., MoD, 1966–69; Senior Industrial Relations Officer, CIR, 1969–71; Director of Industrial Relations, CIR, 1971–74; Asst Secretary, Training Services Agency, 1974–75; Counsellor (Labour), HM Embassy, Washington DC, 1975–77; Head of Policy and Planning, Manpower Services Commn, 1977–80; Department of Employment: Hd of Health and Safety Liaison, 1980–83; Asst Sec., Industrial Relations Div., 1983–86; Under Sec., 1986; Dir of Finance and Resource Management, and Principal Finance Officer, 1986–89. Freeman, Co. of Cordwainers, Newcastle upon Tyne, 1952. *Address:* Woodwards, School Lane, Cookham Dean, Berks SL6 9PQ. *Club:* Reform.
See also P. A. Rowan.

TALLBOYS, Richard Gilbert, CMG 1981; OBE 1974; FCA; FCIS; FCPA; international trade consultant; Chief Executive, World Coal Institute, London, 1988–93; *b* 25 April 1931; *s* of late Harry Tallboys; *m* 1954, Margaret Evelyn, *d* of late Brig. H. W. Strutt, DSO, ED, Hobart; two *s* two *d*. *Educ:* Palmer's School. LLB (London), BCom (Tasmania). Merchant Navy apprentice, 1947–51; Third/Second Mate, Australian coast, 1952–55; Lt-Comdr, RANR, retd 1991. Accounting profession in Australia, 1955–62; Alderman, Hobart City Council, 1958–62; Australian Govt Trade Commissioner, Johannesburg, Singapore, Jakarta, 1962–68. HM Diplomatic Service, 1968–88: First Secretary i/c Brasilia, 1969; Head of Chancery, Phnom Penh, 1972 (Chargé d'Affaires *ai* 1972, 1973); FO, 1973; Counsellor Commercial, Seoul, 1976–80 (Chargé d'Affaires *ai* 1977, 1978, 1979); Consul-General, Houston, 1980–85; Ambassador to Vietnam, 1985–87. Mem., Internat. Trade Cttee, and Mem. Council, London Chamber of Commerce and Industry, 1990–93, 1995–. Mem. Council, RIIA, 1995–. Freeman, City of London, 1985. *Recreations:* squash, ski-ing, cautious adventuring. *Address:* 7 Chapel Side, W2 4LG; 5/362 Sandy Bay Road, Hobart, Tas 7005, Australia. *Clubs:* Travellers'; Tasmanian (Hobart); Royal Australian Naval Sailing Assoc.

TALLING, John Francis, DSc; FRS 1978; Research Fellow, Freshwater Biological Association, since 1991; *b* 23 March 1929; *s* of Frank and Miriam Talling; *m* 1959, Ida Björnsson; one *s* one *d*. *Educ:* Sir William Turner's Sch., Coatham; Univ. of Leeds. BSc, PhD, DSc. Lecturer in Botany, Univ. of Khartoum, 1953–56; Visiting Research Fellow, Univ. of California, 1957; Plant Physiologist (SPSO), Freshwater Biological Assoc., 1958–89; Hon. Reader, 1979–84, Vis. Prof., 1992–, Univ. of Lancaster. *Publications:* co-author, Water Analysis: some revised methods for limnologists, 1978; papers in various learned jls. *Recreation:* country walking. *Address:* 18 Brow Crescent, Windermere, Cumbria LA23 2EZ. *T:* Windermere (015394) 42836.

TAMBLIN, Air Cdre Pamela Joy, CB 1980; retired; Director, Women's Royal Air Force, 1976–80; *b* 11 Jan. 1926; *d* of late Albert Laing and Olga Victoria Laing; *m* 1970, Douglas Victor Tamblin; one step *s* one step *d*. *Educ:* James Gillespie's High Sch., Edinburgh; Heaton High Sch., Newcastle upon Tyne; Durham Univ. (BA Hons). ATS, 1943–45. Essex County Council Planning Officer, 1949–51. Joined Royal Air Force, 1951; served Education Branch, 1951–55: RAF Locking; RAF Stanmore Park; RAF Wahn, Germany; Secretarial (now Administrative) Branch, 1955–76; Schools Liaison Recruiting, 1955–59; Accountant Officer, RAF St Mawgan and RAF Steamer Point, Aden, 1959–61; Staff College, 1962–63; MoD, Air Secretary's Dept, 1963–66; Sen. Trng Officer, RAF Spitalgate, 1966–68; Admin. Plans Officer, HQ Maintenance Comd, 1968–69; Command WRAF Admin. Officer, HQ Strike Comd, 1969–71; Station Comdr, RAF Spitalgate, 1971–74; Command Accountant, HQ Strike Comd, 1974–76. Chm., Cttee on Women in Nato Forces, 1977–79. Pres., E Cornwall Branch, RAFA, 1984–; Chm., S Western Area Council, RAFA, 1991–93 (Mem., 1986–; Vice-Chm., 1988–91). FBIM 1977, CBIM 1979; FRSA 1979. *Recreations:* various charitable works, tapestry work, handbell ringing. *Address:* Trecairne, 3 Plaidy Park Road, Looe, Cornwall PL13 1LG. *Club:* Royal Air Force.

TAMBUNTING, Jesus Paraiso; Ambassador of the Philippines to the Court of St James's, and concurrently to Ireland, since 1993; *b* 21 Dec. 1937; *s* of Antonio Tambunting and Aurora Paraiso Tambunting; *m* 1967, Margarita Ansaldo; two *s* two *d*. *Educ:* Univ. of Maryland (BS, BA Econs). Chairman: Planters Development Bank, 1975–; Planters DB Leasing Corp., 1992–. Perm. Rep. of Philippines to IMO, 1993–. Hon. Pres., British–Philippine Soc., 1993–. *Recreations:* tennis, golf. *Address:* Philippine Embassy, 9A Palace Green, W8 4QE. *T:* 0171–937 1600. *Clubs:* Army and Navy; Roehampton Golf.

TAME, William Charles, CB 1963; Deputy Secretary, Ministry of Agriculture, Fisheries and Food, 1967–71; *b* 25 June 1909; *s* of late Charles Henry Tame, Wimbledon, Surrey; *m* 1935, Alice Margaret, *o d* of late G. B. Forrest, Witherslack, Cumbria; one *s* one *d*. *Educ:* King's College School, Wimbledon; Hertford College, Oxford. Entered Ministry of Agriculture as Assistant Principal, 1933. Chairman: International Whaling Commission, 1966–68; Fisheries R&D Bd, 1972–78. Member: Council, Royal Veterinary Coll., Univ. of London, 1972–80 (Vice-Chm., 1973–80); Governing Body, Animal Virus Res. Inst., 1972–76. *Recreation:* music.

TAMMADGE, Alan Richard; Headmaster, Sevenoaks School, 1971–81; *b* 9 July 1921; *m* 1950, Rosemary Anne Broadribb; two *s* one *d*. *Educ:* Bromley County Sch.; Dulwich Coll.; Emmanuel Coll., Cambridge. BA (Maths) 1950; MA 1957. Royal Navy Special Entry, 1940; resigned, 1947 (Lt); Cambridge, 1947–50; Lectr, RMA Sandhurst, 1950–55; Asst Master, Dulwich College, 1956–58; Head of Mathematics Dept, Abingdon School, 1958–67; Master, Magdalen College School, Oxford, 1967–71. Royal Instn Mathematics Master Classes, 1982–94. Pres., Mathematical Assoc., 1978–79. FIMA 1965. *Publications:* Complex Numbers, 1965; (jtly) School Mathematics Project Books 1–5, 1965–69; (jtly) General Education, 1969; Parents' Guide to School Mathematics, 1976; articles in Mathemat. Gazette, Mathematics Teacher (USA), Aspects of Education (Hull Univ.). *Recreations:* music, gardens. *Address:* 20 Claverham Way, Battle, East Sussex TN33 0JE.

TAMUNO, Prof. Tekena Nitonye, DLit; Emeritus Professor, University of Ibadan, since 1994; Distinguished Fellow, National Institute for Policy and Strategic Studies, Kuru, Nigeria, 1992–94 (Research Professor in History, 1990–92); *b* 28 Jan. 1932; *s* of late Chief Mark Tamuno Igbiri and Mrs Ransoline I. Tamuno; *m* 1963, Olu Grace Tamuno (*née* Esho); two *s* two *d*. *Educ:* University Col Ibadan; Birkbeck Coll., Univ. of London; Columbia Univ., New York City. BA (Hons) History, PhD History, DLit (London). University of Ibadan: Professor of History, 1971; Head, Dept of History, 1972–75; Dean of Arts, 1973–75; Chairman, Cttee of Deans, 1974–75; Vice-Chancellor, 1975–79; Res. Prof. in History, Inst. of African Studies, 1979–90. Principal, University Coll., Ilorin, Oct.-Nov. 1975; Pro-Chancellor and Chm. Council, Rivers State Univ. of Sci. and Technol., Port-Harcourt, 1981–88; Vis. Prof. in History, Nigerian Defence Acad., Kaduna, 1989–90. Chairman: Presidential Panel on Nigeria Since Independence History Project, 1980–; Bd of Dirs, New Nigerian Newspapers Ltd, 1984–89. Nat. Vice-Pres., Historical Soc. of Nigeria, 1974–78 (Fellow, 1992). Gen. Ed., African Leadership Forum Biographical Series, 1991. JP Ibadan, 1976. *Publications:* Nigeria and Elective Representation, 1923–1947, 1966; The Police in Modern Nigeria, 1961–1965, 1970; The Evolution of the Nigerian State: The Southern Phase, 1898–1914, 1972; (ed, with Prof. J. F. A. Ajayi) The University of Ibadan, 1948–1973: A History of the First Twenty-Five Years, 1973; History and History-makers in Modern Nigeria, 1973; Herbert Macaulay, Nigerian Patriot, 1975; (ed with E. J. Alagoa) Eminent Nigerians of the Rivers State, 1980; (ed) Ibadan Voices: Ibadan University in Transition, 1981; Songs of an Egg-Head (poems), 1982; (ed) National Conference on Nigeria since Independence: addresses at the formal opening, 1983; (ed) Proceedings of the National Conference on Nigeria since Independence, Zaria, March 1983, Vol. III: The Civil War Years, 1984; Nigeria Since

Independence: The First Twenty-Five Years: (ed with J. A. Atanda) Vol. III, Education, 1989; (ed with J. A. Atanda) Vol. IV, Government and Public Policy, 1989; (ed with S. C. Ukpabi) Vol. VI, The Civil War Years, 1989; (ed with E. J. Alagoa) Land and People of Nigeria: Rivers State, 1989; Peace and Violence in Nigeria, 1991. *Recreations:* music, photography, swimming, horse-riding, gardening, domestic pets. *Address:* Institute of African Studies, University of Ibadan, Ibadan, Nigeria. *T:* (22) 410352. *Club:* University Senior Staff (Ibadan).

TAMWORTH, Viscount; Robert William Saswalo Shirley, FCA; Director, Ruffer Investment Management Ltd, since 1994; *b* 29 Dec. 1952; *s* and *heir* of 13th Earl Ferrers, *qv*; *m* 1980, Susannah, *y d* of late C. E. W. Sheepshanks, Arthington Hall, Yorks; two *s* one *d*. *Educ:* Ampleforth. Teaching in Kenya, under CMS's Youth Service Abroad Scheme, 1971–72. Articled to Whinney Murray & Co, CA, 1972–76; employed at Ernst & Whinney, 1976–82, Asst Manager, 1981–82; Gp Auditor, 1982–85, Sen. Treasury Analyst, 1986, BICC plc; Director: Viking Property Gp Ltd, 1987–88 (Financial Controller and Company Sec., 1986–87); Ashby Securities, subseq. Norseman Hldgs, 1987–92. Admitted to Inst. of Chartered Accountants of England and Wales, 1976. *Recreations:* the British countryside and related activities, gardening. *Heir: s* Hon. William Robert Charles Shirley, *b* 10 Dec. 1984. *Address:* The Old Vicarage, Shirley, Ashbourne, Derbyshire DE6 3AZ. *T:* Ashbourne (01335) 360815. *Club:* Boodle's.

TAN, Melvyn; pianist; *b* 13 Oct. 1956; *s* of Keng Hian Tan and Sov Yuen Wong. *Educ:* Anglo-Chinese Sch.; Yehudi Menuhin Sch.; Royal Coll. of Music. Performer of classical piano repertoire on period instruments, 1983–; solo career, 1985–; performs in internat. music festivals, incl. Austria, Germany, Holland, France, Scandinavia, UK, USA, Japan; pioneered interest in keyboard music of 18/19th centuries, incl. tour with Beethoven's own Broadwood piano, 1992; cycle of complete Beethoven sonatas, Japan, 1994; numerous recordings. *Recreations:* swimming, wine, travelling to places where free of performing. *Address:* Valerie Barber Management, 5th Floor, 24 Chancery Lane, WC2A 1LS.

TANBURN, Jennifer Jephcott; research consultant, 1984–94, retired; *b* 6 Oct. 1929; *d* of late Harold Jephcott Tanburn and Elise Noel Tanburn (*née* Armour). *Educ:* St Joseph's Priory, Dorking; Settrington Sch., Hampstead; University Coll. of the South West, Exeter (BSc (Econ)). Market Research Dept, Unilever Ltd, 1951–52; Research and Information, Lintas Ltd, 1952–66, Head of Div., 1962–66, Head of Special Projects, 1966–74; British Airways Board, 1974–76; Head of Res. and Consumer Affairs, Booker McConnell Food Distbn Div., 1975–76 (a Dir, 1976–83). Member: Marketing Policy Cttee, 1977–80, and Potato Product Gp, 1980–82, Central Council for Agricl and Hortl Co-operation; Market Research Soc.; Marketing Gp of GB; Packaging Council, 1978–82; Chm., Consumers' Cttees for GB and England and Wales under Agricl Marketing Act of 1958, 1982–91. Hon. Fellow, Durham Univ. (Business Sch.), 1991–94. FRSA 1991. *Publications:* Food, Women and Shops, 1968; People, Shops and the '70s, 1970; Superstores in the '70s, 1972; Retailing and the Competitive Challenge: a study of retail trends in the Common Market, Sweden and the USA, 1974; Food Distribution: its impact on marketing in the '80s, 1981; articles on retailing and marketing subjects. *Recreations:* travel, golf, gardening, dressmaking, television viewing, reading. *Address:* 8 Ellwood Rise, Vache Lane, Chalfont St Giles, Bucks HP8 4SU. *T:* Chalfont St Giles (01494) 875205. *Club:* Beaconsfield Golf.

TANCRED, Sir H. L.; *see* Lawson-Tancred.

TANFIELD, Jennifer Bridget; Librarian, House of Commons, since 1993; *b* 19 July 1941; *d* of Doylah and Phyllis Tanfield. *Educ:* Abbots Bromley; LSE (BSc Econ 1962). House of Commons: Library Clerk, 1963–72; Head, Econ. Affairs Section, later Statistical Section, 1972–87; Head, Parly Div., 1987–91; Dep. Librarian, 1991–93. *Publication:* In Parliament 1939–1951, 1991. *Recreations:* opera, theatre, travel, squash. *Address:* The Library, House of Commons, SW1A 0AA. *T:* 0171–219 3635.

TANGAROA, Hon. Sir Tangaroa, Kt 1987; MBE 1984; Queen's Representative, Cook Islands, 1984–90; *b* 6 May 1921; *s* of Tangaroa and Mihiau; *m* 1941; two *s* seven *d*. *Educ:* Avarua Primary School, Rarotonga. Radio operator, 1939–54; Shipping Clerk, A. B. Donald Ltd and J. & P. Ingram Ltd, 1955–65; MP for Penrhyn, 1958–84; Minister of Educn, Works, Survey, Printing and Electric Power Supply; Minister of Internal Affairs, 1978–80; retired from politics, 1984. Pres., Cook Is Crippled Children's Soc., 1966–; Deacon, Cook Is Christian Church (served 15 years in Penrhyn, 28 years in Avarua); former community positions: Mem., Tereora Coll. Sch. Cttee for 20 years and 10 as Sec./Treasurer; Pres., Cook Is Boys Brigade for 15 years; delegate to Cook Is Sports Assoc. *Address:* Tukao, Manihiki, Cook Islands. *Clubs:* Rarotonga Rotary; Avatiu (formerly Treasurer).

TANGE, Sir Arthur (Harold), AC 1977; Kt 1959; CBE 1955 (OBE 1953); retired civil servant; *b* 18 August 1914; 2nd *s* of late Charles L. Tange, Solicitor, Gosford, New South Wales; *m* 1940, Marjorie Florence, 2nd *d* of late Professor Edward O. G. Shann; one *s* one *d*. *Educ:* Gosford High School; Western Australia University (BA; 1st Cl. Hons Economics). Joined Bank of NSW, 1931; Economist, Bank of NSW, 1938; Economic Research in Commonwealth Depts, Canberra, 1942–46. Entered Australian Diplomatic Service, 1946; First Secretary, Australian Mission to United Nations, 1946–48; Counsellor, United Nations Division, Canberra, 1948–50; Assistant Secretary, Department of External Affairs, Canberra, 1950–53; Minister at Australian Embassy, Washington, 1953–54; Secretary of Dept of External Affairs, Canberra, 1954–65; High Comr in India and Ambassador to Nepal, 1965–70; Sec., Dept of Defence, 1970–79. Represented Australia at many international diplomatic, economic, trade and defence conferences, 1944–79. *Publications:* (jointly) Australia Foots the Bill, 1942; various articles and collected lectures on defence and public administration. *Recreation:* stream fishing. *Address:* 32 La Perouse Street, Griffith, ACT 2603, Australia. *T:* (6) 2958879. *Club:* Commonwealth (Canberra).

TANKERVILLE, 10th Earl of, *cr* 1714; **Peter Grey Bennet;** Baron Ossulston, 1682; *b* 18 Oct. 1956; *s* of 9th Earl of Tankerville, and of Georgiana Lilian Maude, *d* of late Gilbert Wilson, MA, DD, PhD; *S* father, 1980. *Educ:* Oberlin Conservatory, Ohio (Bachelor of Music); San Francisco State Univ. (Master of Music). Working as musician, San Francisco. *Heir: uncle* Rev. the Hon. George Arthur Grey Bennet [*b* 12 March 1925; *m* 1957, Hazel Glyddon, *d* of late E. W. G. Judson; two *s* one *d*]. *Address:* 139 Olympia Way, San Francisco, CA 94131, USA. *T:* (415) 8266639.

TANLAW, Baron *cr* 1971 (Life Peer), of Tanlawhill, Dumfries; **Simon Brooke Mackay;** Chairman and Managing Director, Fandstan Ltd, since 1973; *b* 30 March 1934; *s* of 2nd Earl of Inchcape; *m* 1st, 1959, Joanna Susan, *d* of Major J. S. Hirsch; one *s* two *d* (and one *s* decd); 2nd, 1976, Rina Siew Yong Tan, *d* of late Tiong Cha Tan and Mrs Tan; one *s* one *d*. *Educ:* Eton College; Trinity College, Cambridge (MA 1966). Served as 2nd Lt XII Royal Lancers, Malaya. Inchcape Group of Companies, India and Far East, 1960–66; Managing Director, Inchcape & Co., 1967–71, Dir 1971–92; Chm., Thwaites & Reed Ltd, 1971–74; Chm. and Man. Dir, Fandstan Group of private cos, 1973–. Chm., Building Cttee, Univ. of Buckingham (formerly UC at Buckingham), 1973–78, Mem. Council of Management 1973–, Hon. Fellow, 1981, DUniv 1983; Mem. Ct of Governors, LSE, 1980–. Mem., Lord Chancellor's Inner London Adv. Cttee on Justices of the Peace, 1972–83. Contested (L) Galloway, by-election and gen. election, 1959, and gen. election, 1964. Mem., EC Cttee Sub-Cttee F (Energy, Transport Technology and Research), 1980–83; Chm., Parly Liaison Gp for Alternative Energy Strategies, 1981–83. Joint Treasurer, 1971–72, Dep. Chm., 1972, Scottish Liberal Party. Pres., Sarawak Assoc., 1973–75. Chm., Nat. Appeal, Elizabeth FitzRoy Homes for the mentally handicapped, 1985–. Mem. Consultative Panel, British Horological Inst. *Publications:* article, The Case for a British Astro-physical Master Clock; paper, Horology and Space-Time. *Recreations:* normal. *Address:* Tanlawhill, Eskdalemuir, By Langholm, Dumfriesshire DG13 0PQ. *T:* Eskdalemuir (013873) 73273; 31 Brompton Square, SW3 2AE. *Clubs:* White's, Oriental, Buck's; Puffin's (Edinburgh).

TANNER, Brian Michael; Chief Executive, Somerset County Council, since 1990; *b* 15 Feb. 1941; *s* of Gerald Evelyn Tanner and Mary Tanner; *m* 1963, June Ann Walker; one *s* one *d*. *Educ:* Acklam Hall Grammar Sch., Middlesbrough; Bishop Vesey Grammar Sch., Sutton Coldfield; Bristol Univ. (BA 1st class Hons). CIPFA. Trainee Accountant, Birmingham CBC, 1962–66; Economist, Coventry CBC, 1966–69; Chief Accountant, Teesside CBC, 1969–71; Warwickshire County Council: Asst County Treasurer, 1971–73; Asst Chief Exec., 1973–75; County Treasurer, Somerset CC, 1975–90; Treasurer, Avon and Somerset Police Authy, 1975–91. Advr, ACC Cttees on agric, educn, nat. parks, finance, policy, police, 1976–92; Mem., Accounting Standards Cttee, 1982–85; Chief Negotiator with Central Govt on Rate Support Grant, 1985–88; Mem., Investment Cttee, Nat. Assoc. of Pension Funds, 1988–91. Director: Avon Enterprise Fund, 1988–; Somerset TEC, 1990–. Trustee, Central Bureau for Educnl Visits and Exchanges, 1981–92. Governor: Millfield Sch., 1989–; Bridgwater Coll., 1994–. Freeman, City of London, 1990. *Publication:* Financial Management in the 1990's, 1989. *Recreations:* squash, gardening, golf, philately, antiques. *Address:* County Hall, Taunton, Somerset TA1 4DY. *T:* Taunton (01823) 255000; 8 Broadlands Road, Taunton, Somerset TA1 4HQ. *T:* Taunton (01823) 337826. *Club:* Sloane.

TANNER, David Williamson, DPhil; Under Secretary, Head of Science Branch, Department of Education and Science, 1981–89; *b* 28 Dec. 1930; *s* of late Arthur Bertram Tanner, MBE and of Susan (*née* Williamson); *m* 1960, Glenis Mary (*née* Stringer); one *s* two *d*. *Educ:* Raynes Park County Grammar Sch.; University Coll., Oxford. MA, DPhil (Oxon). Univ. of Minnesota (post-doctoral research), USA, 1954–56; Dept of Scientific and Industrial Research (Fuel Research Station and Warren Spring Lab.), 1957–64; Dept of Educn and Science, 1964–89. *Publications:* papers on physical chem. in Trans. Faraday Soc., Jl Applied Chem., Jl Heat and Mass Transfer, etc. *Recreations:* family, philosophy, sociology. *Address:* The Limes, Market Place, Kenninghall, Norwich, Norfolk NR16 2AH. *T:* Quidenham (01953) 887666.

See also P. A. Tanner.

TANNER, Dr John Benedict Ian, CBE 1979; Founding Director: Royal Air Force Museum, 1963–88; Battle of Britain Museum, 1978–88; Cosford Aero-Space Museum, 1978–88; Bomber Command Museum, 1982–88; Hon. Archivist, since 1980, Senior Research Fellow, since 1982, Pembroke College, Oxford; *b* London, 2 Jan. 1927; *o s* of R. A. and I. D. M. Tanner; *m* 1st, 1953, April Rothery (marr. diss. 1972, and subseq. by RC Tribunal); one *d*; 2nd, 1991, Andrea Isobel Duncan. *Educ:* City of London Library Sch.; Universities of London, Nottingham (MA, PhD) and Oxford (MA). Reading Public Library, 1950; Archivist-Librarian, Kensington Library, 1950–51; Leighton House Art Gall. and Museum, 1951–53; Curator, Librarian and Tutor, RAF Coll., 1953–63; Hon. Sec., Old Cranwellian Assoc., 1956–64; Extra-mural Lectr in History of Art, Univ. of Nottingham, 1959–63. Walmsley Lectr, City Univ., 1980. Vis. Fellow, Wolfson Coll., Cambridge, 1983–; Prof., The Polish Univ., 1987–94, now Emeritus. Mem., Adv. Council, Inst. of Heraldic and Genealogical Studies. Chm., Internat. Air Museum Cttee; Vice-President: Guild of Aviation Artists; Croydon Airport Museum Soc.; Trustee, Manchester Air and Space Museum; Mem. Founding Cttee, All England Lawn Tennis Museum; Mem. Br. Cttee, Caen Musée pour la Paix; President: Anglo-American Ecumenical Assoc; USAF European Meml Foundn; Mem. Bd of Advrs, Battle Harbour Foundn's Anglican Service, Training and Religious Orgn. Life Vice-Pres., Friends of RAF Mus. FLA, FMA, FRHistS, FRAeS, FSA. Freeman, City of London, 1966; Liveryman: Worshipful Co. of Gold and Silver Wyre Drawers, 1966; Scriveners' Co., 1978. Freeman, Guild of Air Pilots and Air Navigators, 1979. Hon. Mem. Collegio Araldico of Rome, 1963. Hon. DLitt City, 1982; Hon. LLD The Polish Univ., 1989; Hon. DCL Assumption Coll., Worcester, Mass, 1993. Tissandier Award, Fedn Aeronautique Internat., 1977. KStJ 1978 (OStJ 1964; St John Service Medal, 1985); KCSG 1977; KCSG, with Star, 1985; Cross of Merit, Order of Malta, 1978. Grand Comdr, OM Holy Sepulchre (Vatican); Order of Polonia Restituta (Poland), 1985; Nile Gold Medal (Egypt), 1987. *Publications:* (ed) List of Cranwell Graduates, 2nd edn, 1963; (jtly) Encyclopedic Dictionary of Heraldry, 1968; How to trace your Ancestors, 1971; Man in Flight (limited edn), 1973; The Royal Air Force Museum: one hundred years of aviation history, 1973; (with W. E. May and W. Y. Carman) Badges and Insignia of the British Armed Services, 1974; Charles I, 1974; Who's Famous in Your Family: a Reader's Digest guide to genealogy, 1975, 2nd edn 1979; Wings of the Eagle (exhibition catalogue), 1976; (ed) They Fell in the Battle, 1980 (limited edn, to commemorate 40th anniv. of Battle of Britain); Sir William Rothenstein: an RAF Museum exhibition catalogue, 1985; RAF Museum — a combined guide, 1987; Editor, RAF Museum Air Publication series, 10 vols; General Editor: Museums and Libraries (Internat. Series); Studies in Air History; reviews and articles in professional and other jls. *Recreations:* cricket, opera, reading. *Address:* Flat One, 57 Drayton Gardens, SW10 9RU. *Clubs:* Athenæum, Reform, MCC.

TANNER, John W., CBE 1983; FRIBA, FRTPI; Director, United Nations Relief and Works Agency for Palestine Refugees, Jordan, 1971–83 (accorded rank of Ambassador to Hashemite Kingdom of Jordan, 1973); *b* 15 Nov. 1923; *s* of Walter George Tanner and Elizabeth Wilkes Tanner (*née* Humphreys); *m* 1948, Hazel Harford Harford-Jones; one *s* two *d*. *Educ:* Clifton Coll.; Liverpool Univ. Sch. of Architecture and Dept of Civic Design. MCD, BArch (Hons). Sen. Planning Officer, Nairobi, 1951; Architect, Nairobi, 1953; Hon. Sec., Kenya Chapter of Architects, 1954; UN Relief and Works Agency: Architect and Planning Officer, Beirut, 1955; Chief Techn. Div., 1957. Past Mem. Cttee, Fedn of Internat. Civil Servants Assoc., 1968–70. *Buildings:* vocational and teacher training centres (Damascus, Syria; Siblin, Lebanon; Ramallah; Wadi Seer; Amman, Jordan); schools; low cost housing and health centres; E African Rugby Union HQ, Nairobi. *Publications:* The Colour Problem in Liverpool: accommodation or assimilation, 1951; Building for the UNRWA/UNESCO Education and Training Programme, 1968. *Recreations:* formerly: Rugby football (Waterloo, Lancs, 1950; Kenya Harlequins, Kenya and E Africa); skiing, board sailing. *Address:* 69B La Pleta, Ordino, Andorra. *Club:* Royal Automobile.

TANNER, Mary Elizabeth, (Mrs J. B. Tanner); Secretary, Council for Christian Unity, General Synod of the Church of England, since 1991; *b* 23 July 1938; *d* of Harold Fussell and Marjorie (*née* Teucher); *m* 1961, John Bryan Tanner; one *s* one *d*. *Educ:* Colston's Girls' Sch., Bristol; Birmingham Univ. (BA Hons). Lecturer in: OT and Hebrew, Hull Univ., 1960–67; OT and Hebrew, Bristol Univ., 1972–75; OT, Westcott House, Cambridge, 1978–82; Theol Sec., Bd for Mission and Unity, C of E, 1982–91. DD

Lambeth, 1988; Hon. DD, General Seminary, NY, 1991. Officer's Cross, Order of Merit (Germany), 1991. *Publications:* essays in: Feminine in the Church, 1984; The Study of Anglicanism, 1988; Runcie by His Friends, 1989; Women and Church, 1991; articles in Theology, Ecumenical Rev., One in Christ, etc. *Recreations:* music, gardening. *Address:* Highclere, Camp End Road, Weybridge, Surrey KT13 0NW. *T:* Weybridge (01932) 842786. *Club:* Commonwealth Trust.

TANNER, Meg; *see* Beresford, M.

TANNER, Prof. Paul Antony, (Tony); Professor of English and American Literature, since 1989, and Fellow of King's College, since 1960, University of Cambridge; *b* 18 March 1935; *s* of late Arthur Bertram Tanner, MBE and of Susan Williamson; *m* 1979, Nadia Fusini. *Educ:* Raynes Park County Grammar Sch.; Jesus Coll., Cambridge (MA, PhD). ACLS Fellow, Univ. of California, Berkeley, 1962–63; Univ. Lectr, Cambridge, 1966–80; Fellow, Center for Advanced Studies in Behavioral Sciences, Stanford, 1974–75; Reader in Amer. Lit., Cambridge Univ., 1980–89. *Publications:* The Reign of Wonder, 1965; City of Words, 1970; Adultery in the Novel, 1979; Thomas Pynchon, 1982; Henry James, 1985; Jane Austen, 1986; Scenes of Nature, Signs of Men, 1987; Venice Desired, 1992. *Recreations:* travelling, talking. *Address:* King's College, Cambridge CB2 1ST. *T:* Cambridge (01223) 350411.
See also D. W. Tanner.

TANSEY, Rock Benedict; QC 1990; a Recorder, since 1995; *b* 22 July 1939; *m* 1964, Wendy Carver; one *s* two *d*. *Educ:* Bristol Univ. (LLB Hons; Dip. Social Studies). Called to the Bar, Lincoln's Inn, 1966. *Recreations:* politics, theatre, opera, football, tennis, golf. *Address:* 3 Gray's Inn Square, Gray's Inn, WC1R 5AH.

TANTUM, Geoffrey Alan, CMG 1995; OBE 1981; HM Diplomatic Service, retired; Middle East Consultant; *b* 12 Nov. 1940; *s* of George Frederick Tantum and Margaret Amelia Tantum (*née* Goozée); *m* 1977, Caroline Kent; three *d*. *Educ:* Hampton Grammar Sch.; RMA Sandhurst; St John's Coll., Oxford (MA 1st Class Hons Oriental Studies (Arabic)). MIL. HM Forces, 1959–66; joined Diplomatic Service, 1969; Kuwait, 1970–72; Aden, 1972–73; FCO, 1973–76; Amman, 1977–80; FCO, 1980–85; Counsellor, Rome, 1985–88; FCO, 1988–95. Chm., Bd of Dirs, Internat. Community Sch. (Jordan) Ltd, 1978–80. *Publication:* Muslim Warfare: Islamic arms and armour, 1979. *Recreations:* sailing, oriental studies. *Club:* Travellers'.

TANZANIA, Archbishop of, since 1984; **Most Rev. John Acland Ramadhani;** Bishop of Zanzibar and Tanga, since 1980; *b* 1932. *Educ:* Univ. of Birmingham (DipTh 1975); Univ. of Dar-es-Salaam (BA 1967); Queen's Coll., Birmingham. Deacon 1975, Birmingham; priest 1976, Dar-es-Salaam; Asst Chaplain, Queen's Coll., Birmingham, 1975–76; Warden, St Mark's Theol Coll., Dar-es-Salaam, 1976–80. *Address:* PO Box 35, Korogwe, Tanzania.

TAPLIN, Dr Oliver Paul, FBA 1995; Tutorial Fellow in Classics, Magdalen College, Oxford, since 1973; Reader in Greek Literature, Oxford University, since 1994; *b* 2 Aug. 1943; *s* of Walter Taplin and Susan (*née* Rosenberg); *m* 1964, Kim Stampfer (separated 1989); one *s* one *d*. *Educ:* Sevenoaks Sch.; Corpus Christi Coll., Oxford (MA; DPhil 1974). Fellow by Examination, Madgalen Coll., Oxford, 1968–72; Fellow, Center for Hellenic Studies, Washington, 1970–71; Lectr, Bristol Univ., 1972–73. Visiting Professor: Dartmouth Coll., 1981; UCLA, 1987, 1990. *Publications:* The Stagecraft of Aeschylus, 1977; Greek Tragedy in Action, 1978; Greek Fire, 1989; (with Beaty Rubens) An Odyssey Round Odysseus, 1990; Homeric Soundings, 1992; Comic Angels, 1993. *Recreations:* theatre, surf-boarding, Greece. *Address:* Madgalen College, Oxford OX1 4AU. *T:* Oxford (01865) 276069.

TAPP, David Robert George; Provincial Stipendiary Magistrate, County of Merseyside, since 1992; *b* 13 Oct. 1948; *s* of Victor George Tapp and May Allen Tapp. *Educ:* Stockport Sch.; Manchester Univ. (LLB Hons). Solicitor. Articled Clerk, Wigan Magistrates' Court, 1971–73; Principal Asst, Eccles Magistrates' Court, 1973–80; Dep. Justices' Clerk, 1980–83, Justices' Clerk, 1983–92, Stoke-on-Trent Magistrates' Court. Mem., British Pottery Manufrs' Fedn Club. *Recreations:* watching sport, waterfowl, music, Manchester City FC, Lancashire CCC. *Address:* 45 East Quay, Wapping Dock, Liverpool L3 4BU. *T:* 0151–707 1608; Magistrates' Court, 107/111 Dale Street, Liverpool L2 2JQ. *T:* 0151–236 5871. *Club:* Athenæum (Liverpool).

TAPPER, Prof. Colin Frederick Herbert; Professor of Law, since 1992, and Fellow of Magdalen College, since 1965, Oxford University; Special Consultant on Computer Law to Messrs Masons (Solicitors), since 1990; *b* 13 Oct. 1934; *s* of Herbert Frederick Tapper and Florence Gertrude Tapper; *m* 1961, Margaret White; one *d*. *Educ:* Bishopshalt Grammar Sch.; Magdalen Coll., Oxford. Lectr, LSE, 1959–65; All Souls Reader in Law, Oxford Univ., 1979–92. Visiting Professor, Universities of: Alabama, 1970; NY, 1970; Stanford, 1975; Monash, 1984; Northern Kentucky, 1986; Sydney, 1989; Western Australia, 1991. *Publications:* Computers and the Law, 1973; Computer Law, 1978, 4th edn 1990; (ed) Crime Proof and Punishment, 1981; (ed) Cross on Evidence, 6th edn 1985, to 8th edn 1995; (ed) Cross and Wilkins Introduction to Evidence, 6th edn 1986; (ed) Handbook of European Software Law, 1993. *Recreations:* reading, computing, writing. *Address:* Corner Cottage, Stonesfield, Oxford OX8 8QA. *T:* Stonesfield (01993) 891284.

TAPPIN, Michael; Member (Lab) Staffordshire West and Congleton, European Parliament, since 1994; *b* 22 Dec. 1946; *s* of Thomas and Eileen Tappin; *m* 1971, Angela Florence (*née* Reed); one *s* one *d*. *Educ:* Univ. of Essex; LSE; Strathclyde Univ. Lectr in Politics, Dept of American Studies, Univ. of Keele, 1974–. Dist Cllr, Newcastle-under-Lyme BC, 1980–84; Staffordshire County Council: Councillor (Lab), 1981–; Chairman: Planning Cttee, 1985–89; Enterprise and Econ. Develt Cttee, 1989–94; European Cttee, 1990–94. Dep. Chm., Staffs Develt Assoc., 1985–94. Chm., W Midlands Regl Forum of Local Authorities, 1993–94. *Publication:* (jtly) American Politics Today, 1980, 3rd edn 1993. *Recreations:* squash, reading, cinema, theatre. *Address:* Europa House, 28–30 Hartshill Road, Stoke-on-Trent, Staffs ST4 7QU. *T:* Stoke-on-Trent (01782) 414771, *Fax:* (01782) 414805.

TAPPS GERVIS MEYRICK; *see* Meyrick.

TAPSELL, Sir Peter (Hannay Bailey), Kt 1985; MP (C) East Lindsey (Lincs), since 1983 (Nottingham West, 1959–64; Horncastle, Lincs, 1966–83); *b* Hove, Sussex, 1 Feb. 1930; *s* of late Eustace Bailey Tapsell (39th Central India Horse) and Jessie Maxwell (*née* Hannay); *m* 1st, 1963, Hon. Cecilia Hawke (marr. diss. 1971), 3rd *d* of 9th Baron Hawke; one *s* decd; 2nd, 1974, Mlle Gabrielle Mahieu, *e d* of late Jean and Bathelde Mahieu, Normandy, France. *Educ:* Tonbridge Sch.; Merton Coll., Oxford (1st Cl. Hons Mod. Hist., 1953; Hon. Postmaster, 1953; MA 1957; Hon. Fellow, 1989). Nat. Service, Subaltern, Royal Sussex Regt, 1948–50 (Middle East). Librarian of Oxford Union, 1953; Rep. Oxford Union on debating tour of United States, 1954 (Trustee, Oxford Union, 1985–93). Conservative Research Department, 1954–57 (Social Services and Agriculture). Personal Asst to Prime Minister (Anthony Eden) during 1955 General Election Campaign. Contested (C) Wednesbury, bye-election, Feb. 1957. Opposition front bench spokesman on Foreign and Commonwealth affairs, 1976–77, on Treasury and economic affairs, 1977–78. Mem., Trilateral Commn, 1979–. London Stock Exchange, 1957–90. Internat. investment advr to several central banks, foreign banks and trading cos; Hon. Mem., Brunei Govt Investment Adv. Bd, 1976–83; Hon. Dep. Chm., Mitsubishi Trust Oxford Foundn, 1988–; Member: Council, Inst. for Fiscal Studies; Court, Univ. of Nottingham, 1959–64; Univ. of Hull, 1966–. Chm., Coningsby Club, 1957–58. Jt Chm., British-Caribbean Assoc., 1963–64. Mem. Organising Cttee, Zaire River Expedn, 1974–75. Vice Pres., Tennyson Soc., 1966–. Hon. Life Mem., 6th Sqdn RAF, 1971. Brunei Dato, 1971. *Recreations:* travel in Third World, walking in mountains, reading history. *Address:* c/o House of Commons, SW1A 0AA. *T:* 0171–219 3000. *Clubs:* Athenæum, Carlton, Hurlingham.

TARBAT, Viscount; Colin Ruaridh Mackenzie; *b* 7 Sept. 1987; *s* and *heir* of Earl of Cromartie, *qv*.

TARGETT, Prof. Geoffrey Arthur Trevor, PhD, DSc; Professor of Immunology of Protozoal Diseases, since 1983 and Head of Department of Medical Parasitology, since 1988, London School of Hygiene and Tropical Medicine; *b* 10 Dec. 1935; *s* of Trevor and Phyllis Targett; *m* 1958, Sheila Margaret Gibson (*d* 1988); two *s* three *d*. *Educ:* Nottingham Univ. (BSc Hons Zool. 1957); London Univ. (PhD 1961; DSc 1982). Research Scientist: MRC Bilharzia Res. Gp, 1957–62; Nat. Inst. for Med. Res., 1962–64; Lectr, Dept of Natural History, St Andrews Univ., 1964–70; London School of Hygiene and Tropical Medicine: Sen. Lectr, 1970–76; Reader, 1976–83. *Publications:* Malaria: waiting for the vaccine, 1991; numerous papers in internat. med. and scientific jls. *Recreations:* golf, music, travel. *Address:* London School of Hygiene and Tropical Medicine, Keppel Street, WC1E 7HT. *T:* 0171–636 8636.

TARJANNE, Pekka; Secretary General, International Telecommunication Union, since 1989; *b* 19 Sept. 1937; *s* of P. K. Tarjanne and Annu Tarjanne; *m* 1962, Aino Kairamo; two *s* one *d* (and one *d* decd). *Educ:* Helsinki Univ. of Technology (Dr Tech. 1962). Prof. of Theoretical Physics, Univ. of Oulu, 1965–66, Univ. of Helsinki, 1967–77. MP, Finland, 1970–77; Minister of Communications, 1972–75; Dir. Gen., Posts and Telecommunications, 1977–89. Commander, Order of White Rose of Finland. *Address:* International Telecommunication Union, Place des Nations, 1211 Geneva 20, Switzerland. *T:* (22) 7305115.

TARN, Prof. John Nelson, OBE 1992; Roscoe Professor of Architecture, since 1974, Pro-Vice-Chancellor, 1988–91 and since 1994, University of Liverpool; *b* 23 Nov. 1934; *s* of Percival Nelson Tarn and Mary I. Tarn (*née* Purvis); unmarried. *Educ:* Royal Grammar Sch., Newcastle upon Tyne; Univ. of Durham (BArch); Univ. of Cambridge (PhD). 1st cl. hons Dunelm; FRIBA, FRSA, FRHistS, FSA. Lectr in Architecture, Univ. of Sheffield, 1963–70; Prof. of Architecture, Univ. of Nottingham, 1970–73; Actg Vice-Chancellor, 1991–92, Public Orator, 1994–, Liverpool Univ. Member: Professional Literature Cttee, RIBA, 1968–77; RIBA Educn Cttee, 1978– (Vice-Chm., 1983–; Chm., Moderators and Examiners Cttee, 1975–); Council, RIBA, 1987–93; Council, ARCUK, 1980–90 (Vice-Chm., 1986–87; Chm., 1987–90; Vice-Chm., Bd of Educn, 1981–83, Chm., 1983–86); Technology Sub-Cttee, UGC, 1974–84; Adv. Cttee on Architectural Educn to EEC, Brussels, 1987–; CNAA Built Environment Bd, 1987–90; Ministerial nominee, Peak Park Jt Planning Bd, 1973–82, a rep. of Greater Manchester Council, PPJPB, 1982–86 (Vice-Chm. of Bd, 1981–86; co-opted Mem., Planning Control Cttee and Park Management Cttee, 1986–; Chm., Planning Control Cttee, 1979–); Mem., National Parks Review Cttee, 1990. Chm., Art and Architecture Dept, Liturgy Commn, Archdio. of Liverpool, 1978–; Member: Design and Planning Cttee, Central Council for Care of Churches, 1981–86; Diocesan Adv. Cttee for Derby, 1979–93; Liverpool Cathedral Adv. Cttee, 1992–. *Publications:* Working Class Housing in Nineteenth Century Britain, 1971; The Peak District National Park: its architecture, 1971; Five Per Cent Philanthropy, 1974; (adv. ed.) Sir Banister Fletcher's History of Architecture, 19th edn, 1987. *Recreations:* music, cooking. *Address:* University of Liverpool, PO Box 147, Liverpool L69 3BX. *Club:* Athenæum.

TARR, Robert James; Director General, Centro (The West Midlands Passenger Transport Executive), 1987–95; *b* 8 June 1944; *s* of Jack William Tarr; *m* 1966, Linda Andrews. *Educ:* Whytemead and Downsbrook Schools, Worthing; Worthing High Sch. for Boys. IPFA 1967; BSc(Econ) Hons London, 1977; BA Open Univ.,1979. FCIT 1989. W Sussex CC, Worthing BC, Denbighshire CC, Sunderland Met. BC to 1975; Corporate Planning Co-ordinator and Head of Policy Unit, Bradford Met. Council, 1975–81; Chief Exec., Royal Borough of Kingston upon Thames, 1981–83; Chief Exec. and Town Clerk, Coventry City Council, 1983–87. *Publications:* contribs to jls and conf. papers. *Recreations:* viticulture and wine-making, soaking up sun and scenery, the Pre-Raphaelites and Victorian architecture, mountains and alpine flowers, canal-boating, photography, computing, amateur radio (call sign G3PUR), keeping fit. *Address:* Oakfield, Warwick Avenue, Coventry CV5 6DJ.

TARUA, Ilinome Frank, CBE 1988 (OBE 1980); Consultant specialising on Papua New Guinea and South Pacific, since 1993; *b* 23 Sept. 1941; *s* of Peni Frank Tarua and Anaiele Tarua; *m* 1970, Susan Christine (*née* Reeves); two *d*. *Educ:* Sydney University; University of Papua New Guinea (BL 1971). Legal Officer, Dept of Law, 1971–72; Legal Constitutional Advisor to Prime Minister, 1972–76; Dep. Perm. Head, Prime Minister's Dept, 1977–78; Secretary to Cabinet, 1978–79; High Commissioner to NZ, 1980; Ambassador to UN, 1980–81; Perm. Head, Dept of Public Service, 1982; Perm. Head, Prime Minister's Dept, 1982–83; High Comr in London, 1983–89, concurrently Ambassador to Greece, Israel and Italy; Consul Gen., Sydney, 1989–91; Consultant Lawyer with Gadens Ridgeway Lawyers, Australia and PNG, 1991–93. *Recreations:* cricket, squash, golf. *Address:* c/o Gadens Ridgeway Lawyers, Skygarden Building, 77 Castlereagh Street, Sydney, NSW 2000, Australia.

TASMANIA, Bishop of, since 1982; **Rt. Rev. Phillip Keith Newell,** AO 1993; *b* 30 Jan. 1930; *s* of Frank James and Ada Miriam Newell; *m* 1959, Merle Edith Callaghan; three *s*. *Educ:* Univ. of Melbourne; Trinity Coll., Melbourne. BSc 1953; DiplEd(Hons) 1954; ThL(Hons) 1959; BEd 1960; MEd 1969; FACE 1990. Mathematics Master: Melbourne High School, 1954–56; University High School, 1957–58; Tutor in Physics, Secondary Teachers' Coll., 1957; Assistant Curate: All Saints, East St Kilda, Melbourne, 1960–61; S Andrew's, Brighton, Melbourne, 1962–63; Asst Priest, S James, King Street, Sydney, 1963–67; Chaplain, Sydney Hosp., 1963–67; Rector, Christ Church, St Lucia, Brisbane, 1967–82; Residentiary Canon, S John's Cathedral, Brisbane, 1973–82; Archdeacon of Lilley, Brisbane, 1976–82. KStJ 1981. *Publication:* Body Search, 1993. *Recreations:* education; music (classical and light opera); singing; choral conducting; wine making; travel; cricket (spectator); tennis (occasional game). *Address:* GPO Box 748H, Hobart, Tas 7001, Australia. *T:* (02) 238811. *Club:* Tasmanian (Hobart).

TATA, Dr Jamshed Rustom, FRS 1973; Head, Division of Developmental Biochemistry, National Institute for Medical Research, since 1973; *b* 13 April 1930; *s* of Rustom and Gool Tata; *m* 1954, Renée Suzanne Zanetto; two *s* one *d*. *Educ:* Univ. of Bombay (BSc); Univ. of Paris, Sorbonne (D-ès-Sc). Post-doctoral Fellow, Sloan-Kettering Inst., New

York, 1954–56; Beit Memorial Fellow, Nat. Inst. for Med. Research, 1956–60; Vis. Scientist, Wenner-Gren Inst., Stockholm, 1960–62; Mem., Scientific Staff, MRC, Nat. Inst. for Med. Research, 1962–. Visiting Professor: King's Coll., London, 1968–69, and 1970–77; Univ. of California, Berkeley, 1969–70; Vis. Senior Scientist, Nat. Institutes of Health, USA, 1977; Fogarty Scholar, NIH, USA, 1983, 1986, 1989. Chm., Cell and Molecular Panel, 1990–92, Mem., Basic Sci. Gp, 1992–93, The Wellcome Trust. Fellow: Indian Nat. Science Acad., 1978; Third World Acad. of Sci., 1986. Van Meter Award, 1954; Colworth Medal, 1966; Medal of Soc. for Endocrinology, 1973; Jubilee Medal, Indian Inst. of Sci., 1985. *Publications:* (jtly): The Thyroid Hormones, 1959; The Chemistry of Thyroid Diseases, 1960; Metamorphosis, 1996; papers in jls of: Biochemistry; Developmental Biology. *Address:* 15 Bittacy Park Avenue, Mill Hill, NW7 2HA. *T:* 0181–346 6291.

TATE, Francis Herbert; Vice-Chairman, Tate & Lyle Ltd, 1962–78; *b* 3 April 1913; 2nd *s* of late Alfred Herbert Tate and late Elsie Tate (*née* Jelf Petit); *g g s* of Sir Henry Tate, Bt, founder of Henry Tate & Sons (now Tate & Lyle, Ltd) and donor of the Tate Gallery; *m* 1937, Esther, *d* of late Sir John Bromhead-Matthews, KC, JP, and late Lady Matthews, JP; one *s* two *d*. *Educ:* Private Tutor; Christ Church Oxford (BA 1934, MA 1963). Called to the Bar, Inner Temple, 1937. War Service, 1940–46, Royal Corps of Military Police (Lt-Col). Joined Tate & Lyle Ltd, 1946; Man. Dir, 1949. Chairman: British Sugar Bureau, 1966–78; Council, London Chamber of Commerce, 1962–64 (Vice-Pres., 1964–); Federation of Commonwealth Chambers of Commerce, 1964–69. Dir, Lloyds Bank, Southern Region, 1977–83; a Managing Trustee, Bustamente Foundn, 1979–. General Comr for Income Tax, Woking Div., 1980–88. Dep. Chm., Royal Commonwealth Soc. for the Blind, 1984–89; Chm. Central Council, Royal Commonwealth Soc., 1969–72; Mem. Council, Australia Soc., 1974–78. Governor, Commonwealth Inst., 1975–88. Master of Mercers' Company, 1967–68. *Recreations:* golf (played for Oxford, 1934–35); motoring. *Address:* Little Wissett, Hook Heath, Woking, Surrey GU22 0QG. *T:* Woking (01483) 760532. *Club:* Woking Golf (Pres., 1986–).

TATE, Sir (Henry) Saxon, 5th Bt *cr* 1898, of Park Hill, Streatham; CBE 1991; Chairman, London Futures and Options Exchange (formerly London Commodity Exchange Co. Ltd), 1985–91; Director, Tate & Lyle Ltd, since 1956; *b* 28 Nov. 1931; *er s* of Lt-Col Sir Henry Tate, 4th Bt, TD and his 1st wife, Nairne (*d* 1984), *d* of Saxon Gregson-Ellis, JP; *S* father, 1994; *m* 1st, 1953, Sheila Ann (marr. diss. 1975; she *d* 1987), *e d* of Duncan Robertson; four *s* (incl. twin *s*); 2nd, 1975, Virginia Sturm. *Educ:* Eton; Christ Church, Oxford. FIMgt (FBIM 1975). National Service, Life Guards (Lieut), 1949–50. Joined Tate & Lyle Ltd, 1952, Director, 1956; Pres. and Chief Executive Officer, Redpath Industries Ltd, Canada, 1965–72; Tate & Lyle Ltd: Chm., Executive Cttee, 1973–78; Man. Dir, 1978–80; Vice Chm., 1980–82. Chief Executive, Industrial Development Bd of NI, 1982–85. Fellow, Amer. Management Assoc., 1972. *Recreations:* various. *Heir:* *s* Edward Nicholas Tate, *b* 2 July 1966. *Address:* 26 Cleaver Square, SE11 4EA.

TATE, Dr Jeffrey Philip, CBE 1990; Principal Conductor, English Chamber Orchestra, since 1985; *b* 28 April 1943; *s* of Cyril Henry Tate and Ivy Ellen Naylor (*née* Evans). *Educ:* Farnham Grammar Sch.; Christ's Coll., Cambridge (MA; MB, BChir; Hon. Fellow, 1989); St Thomas' Hosp., London. Trained as doctor of medicine, 1961–67; left medicine for London Opera Centre, 1969; joined Covent Garden Staff, 1970; assisted conductors who included Kempe, Krips, Solti, Davies, Kleiber, for performances and recordings; records made as harpsichordist, 1973–77; Assistant to Boulez for Bayreuth Ring, 1976–81; joined Cologne Opera as assistant to Sir John Pritchard, 1977; conducted Gothenberg Opera, Sweden, 1978–80; NY Metropolitan Opera début, USA, 1979; Covent Garden début, 1982; Salzburg Fest. début (world première Henze/Monteverdi), 1985; Principal Conductor, Royal Opera House, Covent Garden, 1986–91, Principal Guest Conductor, 1991–94; Chief Conductor and Artistic Dir, Rotterdam Phil. Orch., 1991–94; Chief Guest Conductor, Geneva Opera, 1983–95; Principal Guest Conductor, Orchestre National de France, 1989–. Appearances with major symph. orchs in Europe and Amer.; numerous recordings with English Chamber Orch. President: ASBAH, 1989–; Music Space, 1991–. Hon. DMus Leicester, 1993. Chevalier de l'Ordre des Arts et des Lettres, France, 1990. *Recreation:* church-crawling, with gastronomic interludes.

TATE, Prof. Robert Brian, FBA 1980; FRHistS; Professor and Head of Department of Hispanic Studies, Nottingham University, 1958–83, retired; *b* 27 Dec. 1921; *s* of Robert and Jane Grantie Tate; *m* 1951, Beth Ida Lewis; one *s* one *d*. *Educ:* Royal Belfast Academical Instn; Queen's Univ. Belfast (MA, PhD). FRHistS 1990. Asst Lectr, Manchester Univ., 1949–52; Lectr, QUB, 1952–56; Reader in Hispanic Studies, Nottingham Univ., 1956–58. Vis. Prof., Univs of Harvard, Cornell, SUNY at Buffalo, Texas and Virginia. Corresponding Fellow: Institut d'Estudis Catalans, Barcelona, 1964; Real Academia de Historia, Madrid, 1974; Real Academia de Buenas Letras de Barcelona, 1980. *Publications:* Joan Margarit i Pau, Cardinal Bishop of Gerona: a biographical study, 1954; Ensayos sobre la historiografia peninsular del siglo XV, 1970; The Medieval Kingdoms of the Iberian Peninsula, in P. E. Russell, Spain: a companion to Spanish studies, 1973; El Cardenal Joan Margarit, vida i obra, 1976; (with Marcus Tate) The Pilgrim Route to Santiago, 1987; Pilgrimages to St James of Compostella from the British Isles during the Middle Ages, 1990; *edited:* (with A. Yates) Actes del Colloqui internacional de llengua i literatura catalanes, 1976; Essays on Narrative Fiction in the Iberian Peninsula, 1982; (with T. Turville Petre) Two Pilgrim Itineraries of the Later Middle Ages, 1995; *edited with introduction and notes:* Fernán Pérez de Guzmán, Generaciones y Semblanzas, 1965; Fernando del Pulgar, Claros varones de Castilla, 1971, rev. edn 1985; (with I. R. Macpherson) Don Juan Manuel, Libro de los estados, 1974, rev. edn 1991; Anon, Directorio de príncipes, 1977; Alfonso de Palencia, Epistolario, 1983; contrib. articles in numerous learned jls. *Recreations:* architecture and the history of art, jazz. *Address:* 11 Hope Street, Beeston, Nottingham NG9 1DJ. *T:* Nottingham (0115) 925 1243.

TATE, Sir Saxon; *see* Tate, Sir H. S.

TATHAM, David Everard, CMG 1991; HM Diplomatic Service; Governor, Falkland Islands, and Commissioner for South Georgia and South Sandwich Islands, since 1992; *b* 28 June 1939; *s* of Lt-Col Francis Everard Tatham and Eileen Mary Wilson; *m* 1963, Valerie Ann Mylechreest; three *s*. *Educ:* St Lawrence Coll., Ramsgate; Wadham Coll., Oxford (BA History). Entered HM Diplomatic Service, 1960; 3rd Sec., UK Mission to the UN, New York, 1962–63; Vice-Consul (Commercial), Milan, 1963–67; ME Centre for Arabic Studies, 1967–69; Jeddah, 1969–70; FCO, 1971–74; Muscat, 1974–77; Asst Head of ME Dept, FCO, 1977–80; Counsellor, Dublin, 1981–84; Ambassador to Yemen Arab Republic, also accredited to Republic of Djibouti, 1984–87; Hd of Falkland Is Dept, FCO, 1987–90; Ambassador to Lebanese Republic, 1990–92. *Recreation:* walking uphill. *Address:* c/o Foreign and Commonwealth Office, SW1A 2AH. *Club:* Athenæum.

TATHAM, Francis Hugh Currer; Editor of Whitaker's Almanack, 1950–81; *b* 29 May 1916; *s* of late Harold Lewis Tatham, Gravesend, Kent, and late Frances Eva (*née* Crook); *m* 1945, Nancy Margaret, *d* of John Robins, Newton Abbot; two *s*. *Educ:* Charterhouse; Christ Church, Oxford. Missioner, Shrewsbury School Mission, Liverpool, 1939–42; Sub-Warden, Mary Ward Settlement, 1942–45; Army Cadet Force, 1943–45; Editor, Church of England Newspaper, 1945–47. Vice-Pres., Harrow RFC. *Recreations:* watching cricket, travel. *Address:* 27 Montacute Road, Lewes, East Sussex BN7 1EN. *T:* Lewes (01273) 473585. *Club:* MCC.

TATLOW, John Colin, PhD, DSc (Birmingham); CChem; FRSC; consultant; Professor of Organic Chemistry, University of Birmingham, 1959–82, now Emeritus; *b* 19 Jan. 1923; *s* of Thomas George and Florence Annie Tatlow, Cannock, Staffs; *m* 1946, Clarice Evelyn Mabel, *d* of Eric Millward and Mabel Evelyn Joiner, Sutton Coldfield; two *d*. *Educ:* Rugeley Grammar School, Staffs; University of Birmingham. Scientific Officer, Min. of Supply, 1946–48; University of Birmingham: Lectr in Chemistry, 1948–56; Sen. Lectr, 1956–57; Reader in Organic Chemistry, 1957–59; Head of Dept of Chemistry, 1974–81. Council of Chemical Society, 1957–60. Examiner, Royal Inst. of Chemistry, 1963–67. ACS Award for creative work in fluorine chemistry, 1990. *Publications:* over 300 scientific papers on fluorine chemistry, mainly in Jl of Chem. Soc., Tetrahedron, Nature, and Jl of Fluorine Chem.; Editor, Jl of Fluorine Chemistry. *Address:* 30 Grassmoor Road, King's Norton, Birmingham B38 8BP. *T:* 0121–458 1260.

TATTERSALL, Geoffrey Frank; QC 1992; a Recorder, since 1989; *b* 22 Sept. 1947; *s* of Frank Tattersall and Margaret (*née* Hassall); *m* 1971, Hazel Shaw; one *s* two *d*. *Educ:* Manchester Grammar Sch.; Christ Church, Oxford (MA Jurisprudence). Called to the Bar, Lincoln's Inn, 1970 (Tancred Studentship in Common Law); in practice, Northern Circuit, 1970–; called to the Bar, NSW, 1992. Lay Chm., Bolton Deanery Synod, 1993–; Chm., House of Laity and Vice Pres., Manchester Diocesan Synod, 1994–. *Recreations:* family, music, travel. *Address:* 25 Byrom Street, Manchester M3 4PF. *T:* 0161–834 5238.

TATTON BROWN, William Eden, CB 1965; ARIBA; retired architect; *b* 13 Oct. 1910; *m* 1936, Aileen Hope Johnston Sparrow; two *s* one *d* (and one *d* decd). *Educ:* Wellington Coll.; King's Coll., Cambridge (MA); Architectural Association School, London; School of Planning, London. Special Final Examination of Town Planning Institute. Chief Design Asst, Messrs Tecton, Architects, 1934–38; private practice, 1938–40; Finsbury Borough Council, 1940–41. Served in HM Forces, Major, Royal Engineers, 1941–46. Asst Regional Planning Officer, Min. of Town and Country Planning, 1946–48; Dep. County Architect, Herts CC, 1948–59; Chief Architect, Min. of Health, later Dept of Health and Social Security, 1959–71. Steuben-Corning Research Fellowship, Travelling Scholarship to USA, 1957. Guest Lectr, Internat. Hosp. Confs: Finland, 1966; Holland, 1967; Australia, 1967; Düsseldorf, 1969; Tunisia, 1969; Sweden, 1970; Canada, 1970; S Africa, 1971; WHO Commn to Madrid, 1968. Lecturer and broadcaster. *Publications:* (with Paul James) Hospitals: design and development, 1986; contributor to technical and national press. *Recreation:* painting. *Address:* 47 Lansdowne Road, W11 2LG. *T:* 0171–727 4529.

TAUBE, Prof. Henry, PhD; Professor, Department of Chemistry, Stanford Univeristy, since 1962; *b* 30 Nov. 1915; *s* of Samuel and Albertina (Tiledetski) Taube; *m* 1952, Mary Alice Wesche; two *s* two *d*. *Educ:* Univ. of Saskatchewan (BS 1935, MS 1937); Univ. of California, Berkeley (PhD 1940). Instructor, Univ. of California, Berkeley, 1940–41; Instructor and Asst Prof., Cornell Univ., 1941–46; Asst Prof., Associate Prof., Prof., Univ. of Chicago, 1946–61; Chm., Dept. of Chemistry, Univ. of Chicago, 1956–59; Chm., Stanford Univ., 1972–74 and 1978–79. Foreign Mem., Royal Soc., 1988; Hon. Member: Canadian Soc. for Chemistry, 1986; Hungarian Acad. of Scis, 1988; Corresponding Member: Brazilian Acad. of Scis, 1991; Australian Acad. of Sci., 1991; Foreign Associate, Engrg Acad. of Japan, 1991. Hon. FRSC 1989; Hon. Fellow, Indian Chem. Soc., 1989. Hon. LLD Saskatchewan, 1973; Hon. PhD Hebrew Univ. of Jerusalem, 1979; Hon. DSc: Chicago, 1983; Polytechnic Inst., NY, 1984; State Univ. of NY, 1985; Guelph Univ., 1987; Seton Hall Univ., 1988; Lajos Kossuth Univ., Debrecen, Hungary, 1988. Guggenheim Fellow, 1949, 1955. ACS Award for Nuclear Applications in Chemistry, 1955; ACS Award for Distinguished Service in the Advancement of Inorganic Chemistry, 1967; Willard Gibbs Medal, Chicago Section, ACS, 1971; Nat. Medal of Science, Washington DC, 1977; T. W. Richards Medal of the Northwestern Section, ACS, 1980; ACS Award in Inorganic Chemistry of the Monsanto Co., 1981; Nat. Acad. of Sciences Award in Chemical Sciences, 1983; Robert A. Welch Foundn Award in Chemistry, 1983; Nobel Prize for Chemistry, 1983; Priestly Medal, ACS, 1985; Dist. Achievement Award, Internat. Precious Metals Inst., 1986. *Publications:* numerous papers in scientific jls on the reactivity of coordination compounds. *Recreations:* gardening, collecting classical vocal records. *Address:* 441 Gerona Road, Stanford, CA 94305, USA. *T:* (415) 3282759.

TAUNTON, Bishop Suffragan of, since 1992; **Rt. Rev. (John Hubert) Richard Lewis;** *b* 10 Dec. 1943; *s* of John Wilfred and Winifred Mary Lewis; *m* 1968, Sara Patricia Hamilton; three *s*. *Educ:* Radley; King's Coll., London (AKC). Curate of Hexham, 1967–70; Industrial Chaplain, Diocese of Newcastle, 1970–77; Communications Officer, Diocese of Durham, 1977–82; Agricultural Chaplain, Diocese of Hereford, 1982–87; Archdeacon of Ludlow, 1987–92; Prebendary, Wells Cathedral, 1992–. Nat. Chm., Small Farmers' Assoc., 1984–88. Mem., Gen. Synod of C of E, 1987–92. *Publication:* (ed jtly) The People, the Land and the Church, 1987. *Recreations:* bricklaying, bumble bees, kit car building. *Address:* Sherford Farm House, Sherford, Taunton TA1 3RF. *T:* Taunton (01823) 288759, *Fax:* (01823) 257085.

TAUNTON, Archdeacon of; *see* Frith, Ven. R. M. C.

TAUSKY, Vilem, CBE 1981; FGSM 1968; conductor; Director of Opera, Guildhall School of Music, 1966–87; *b* 20 July 1910; *s* of Emil Tausky, MD, Prerov, Czechoslovakia, and Josefine Ascher, opera singer; *m* 1948, Margaret Helen Powell (*d* 1982). *Educ:* Univ. of Brno; Janáček Conservatoire, Brno; Meisterschule, Prague. Military Service in France and England, 1939–45. National Opera House, Brno, Czechoslovakia, 1929–39; Musical Director, Carl Rosa Opera, 1945–49; Artistic Dir, Phoenix Opera Co., 1967. BBC Conductor, 1950. Guest Conductor: Royal Opera House, Covent Garden, 1951–; Sadler's Wells Opera, 1953–. Freeman, City of London, 1979. Czechoslovak Military Cross, 1944; Czechoslovak Order of Merit, 1945. *Publications:* Czechoslovak Christmas Carols, 1942; Oboe Concerto, 1957; Concertino for harmonica and orchestra, 1963; Divertimento for strings, 1966; Soho: Scherzo for orchestra, 1966; Concert Overture for Brass Band, 1969; Cakes and Ale: Overture for Brass Band, 1971; Ballad for Cello and Piano; From Our Village: orchestral suite, 1972; Sonata for Cello and Piano, 1976; Suite for Violin and Piano, 1979; String Quartet, 1981; (book) Vilem Tausky Tells his Story, 1979; Leoš Janáček, Leaves from his Life, 1982; contribs to: Tension in the Performance of Music, 1979; The Spectator, 1979. *Recreation:* country life. *Address:* 44 Haven Green Court, W5 2UY. *T:* 0181–997 6512.

TAVAIQIA, Ratu Sir Josaia (Nasorowale), KBE 1986; JP; First Vice President, Republic of Fiji, since 1993 (Second Vice President, 1992–93); *b* 25 Dec. 1930; *s* of Ratu Josaia Tavaiqia and Adi Lusiana Ratu; *m* 1955, Adi Lady Merewalesi Naqei; three *d*. *Educ:* Queen Victoria Sch.; Natabua Indian Secondary Sch., Fiji (Sen. Cambridge Examination). Custom Officer, Custom Dept, Fiji, 1949–59; Hotel Manager, 1961–75; Minister of State for Forests, 1977–89. Pres., Rural Youth Council of Fiji, 1979–92. Traditional role as Tui (Chief) of Vuda, with tradit. title of Tui Vuda (Chief of Vuda). *Recreation:* Rugby

management. *Address:* Viseisei, Vuda, Fiji. *T:* 661273. *Clubs:* Commonwealth Trust, Union.

TAVARÉ, Andrew Kenneth; Special Commissioner of Income Tax, 1976–88 (Deputy Special Commissioner, April–Oct. 1988); *b* 10 Jan. 1918; *s* of late L. A. Tavaré, Bromley, Kent; *m* 1950, June Elinor Attwood, Beckenham, Kent; three *s*. *Educ:* Chatham House School, Ramsgate; King's College, London University. LLB (London). Solicitor of the Supreme Court. Served War with 79th HAA Regt (Hertfordshire Yeomanry), RA, 1940–45; N Africa and Italy, rank of Captain. Admitted Solicitor, 1948; Solicitor's Office, Inland Revenue, 1953–; Assistant Solicitor, 1965–75. Consultant Editor of Sergeant on Stamp Duties, 4th edition 1963, to 8th edition 1982. *Publications:* (contrib.) Simon's Taxes, 2nd edn, 1965, and 3rd edn, 1970.
See also Sir J. Tavaré.

TAVARÉ, Sir John, Kt 1989; CBE 1983; CEng; Chairman, Luxonic Lighting plc, since 1986; *b* 12 July 1920; *s* of Leon Alfred Tavaré and Grace Tavaré; *m* 1949, Margaret Daphne Wray; three *s* (and one *s* decd). *Educ:* Chatham House, Ramsgate; Bromley Grammar Sch.; King's Coll., London (BScEng 1946). MIMechE 1954; FInstD 1983; FIWEM 1991. Trainee, Thames Board Mills Ltd, 1938–43; Works Manager, Wm C. Jones. Ltd, 1946–48; Personnel Administration Ltd, UK, Australia and NZ, 1949–58; Thames Board Mills Ltd (Unilever), 1958–68: Sales and Marketing Dir, 1960–65; Vice-Chm., 1966–68; Paper, Plastics and Packaging Bd, Unilever, 1968–70; Whitecroft plc, 1970–85: Gp Man. Dir, 1973–76; Chm. and Gp Man. Dir, 1976–85. Chm., Mersey Basin Campaign, DoE, 1985–92. Member: Nat. Council, CBI, 1978–85 (Chm., NW Reg., 1980–82); Nat. Rivers Authy Adv. Bd, NW Region, 1989–92. *Recreations:* golf, garden, environment, business. *Address:* The Gables, 4 Macclesfield Road, Prestbury, Macclesfield, Cheshire SK10 4BN. *T:* Macclesfield (01625) 829778.
See also A. K. Tavaré.

TAVENER, John; composer; *b* 28 Jan. 1944; *m* 1991, Maryanna (*née* Schaefer); one *d*. *Educ:* Highgate Sch.; Royal Academy of Music (LRAM). Hon. FRAM, Hon. FTCL, Hon. FRSCM. Russian Orthodox religion. Dr *hc* New Delhi, 1990. Apollo Award, Friends of Greek Nat. Opera, 1993. *Compositions:* Piano Concerto; Three Holy Sonnets (Donne); Cain and Abel (1st Prize, Monaco); Chamber Concerto; The Cappe-makers; Three Songs of T. S. Eliot; Grandma's Footsteps; In Memoriam Igor Stravinsky; Responsorium in memory of Annon Lee; The Whale; Introit for March 27th; Three Surrealist Songs; In Alium; Celtic Requiem; Ultimos Ritos; Thérèse (opera); A Gentle Spirit (opera); Kyklike Kinesis; Palin; Palintropos: Canticle of the Mother of God; Divine Liturgy of St John Chrysostom; The Immurement of Antigone; Lamentation, Last Prayer and Exaltation; Six Abbasid Songs; Greek Interlude; Akhmatova: Rékviem; Sappho: Lyrical Fragments; Prayer for the World; The Great Canon of St Andrew of Crete; Trisāgion; Risen!; Mandelion; The Lamb (a Christmas carol); Mandoodles; Towards the Son; 16 Haiku of Seferis; Ikon of Light; All-Night Vigil Service of the Orthodox Church; Eis Thanaton (a ritual); Two Hymns to the Mother of God; Ikon of St Cuthbert; Akathist (Glory to God for everything); Meditation on the Light; Panikhida (Orthodox Burial Service); The Protecting Veil; Ikon of St Seraphim; Let not the Prince be silent; The Tyger; Resurrection; The Uncreated Eros; Lament of the Mother of God; The Hidden Treasure (string quartet); Today the Virgin; Eonia; Psalm 121, I Will Lift Up Mine Eyes unto the Hills; Thunder Entered Her (a divine allegory); Ikon of the Trinity; Do Not Move; A Christmas Round; The Repentant Thief (dance-lament); Thrinos (for solo 'cello); Mary of Egypt (chamber opera); A Village Wedding; Theophany; Eternal Memory; The Apocalypse; We Shall See Him As He Is; Annunciation; Song for Athene; The World is Burning; The Myrrh-Bearer; Hymns of Paradise; Akhmatova Songs; The Child Lived; The Last Sleep of the Virgin. *Publication:* (jtly) Ikons: meditations in words and music, 1994. *Address:* c/o Chester Music, 8–9 Frith Street, W1V 5TZ.

TAVERNE, Dick, QC 1965; President, PRIMA Europe Ltd, since 1993 (Director, since 1987; Chairman, 1991–93); *b* 18 Oct. 1928; *s* of Dr N. J. M. and Mrs L. V. Taverne, *m* 1955, Janice Hennessey; two *d*. *Educ:* Charterhouse School; Balliol College, Oxford (First in Greats). Oxford Union Debating tour of USA, 1951. Called to Bar, 1954. MP (Lab) Lincoln, March 1962–Oct. 1972, resigned; MP (Democratic Lab) Lincoln, March 1973–Sept. 1974; Parliamentary Under-Secretary of State, Home Office, 1966–68; Minister of State, Treasury, 1968–69; Financial Secretary to the Treasury, 1969–70. Chm., Public Expenditure (General) Sub-Cttee, 1971–72. Institute for Fiscal Studies: First Dir, 1970; Dir-Gen., 1979–81; Chm., 1981–82; Chm., Public Policy Centre, 1984–87. Chm., OLIM Investment Trust, 1989–; Dir, Axa Equity and Law; Dep. Chm., Central European Growth Fund. Mem., Internat. Ind. Review Body to review workings of European Commn, 1979. Member: Nat. Cttee, SDP, 1981–87; Federal Policy Cttee, Liberal Democrats, 1989–90. Contested (SDP): Southwark, Peckham, Oct. 1982; Dulwich, 1983. *Publication:* The Future of the Left: Lincoln and after, 1973. *Recreations:* marathon running, sailing. *Address:* 60 Cambridge Street, SW1V 4QQ.

TAVISTOCK, Marquess of; Henry Robin Ian Russell, DL; a Director, Berkeley Govett & Co. Ltd, since 1985; *b* 21 Jan. 1940; *s* and *heir* of 13th Duke of Bedford, *qv*; *m* 1961, Henrietta Joan, *d* of late Henry F. Tiarks; three *s*. *Educ:* Le Rosey, Switzerland; Harvard University. Partner, De Zoete and Bevan, 1970–82; Chairman: Cedar Investment Trust, 1977–82; Berkeley Develt Capital Ltd, 1984–92; TR Property Investment Trust, 1982–89 (Dir, 1982–91); Director: Touche, Remnant Holdings, 1977–88; Trafalgar House Ltd, 1977–91; United Racecourses, 1977–94. Hon. Trustee, Kennedy Memorial Trust (Chm., 1985–90). Pres., Woburn Golf and Country Club. DL Beds, 1985. *Heir: s* Lord Howland, *qv*. *Address:* Woburn Abbey, Woburn, Bedfordshire MK43 0TP. *T:* Woburn (01525) 290666. *Clubs:* White's; Jockey Club Rooms; The Brook (New York).

TAYLER, (Harold) Clive, QC 1979; **His Honour Judge Tayler;** a Circuit Judge, since 1984; *b* 4 Nov. 1932; *m* 1959, Catherine Jane (*née* Thomas); two *s* one *d*. *Educ:* Solihull Sch.; Balliol Coll., Oxford. BCL and BA (Jurisprudence). Called to the Bar, Inner Temple, 1956; in practice, Birmingham, 1958–84, and London, 1979–84; a Recorder of the Crown Court, 1974–84; Midland and Oxford Circuit. *Address:* c/o Midland and Oxford Circuit Administrators' Office, 2 Newton Street, Birmingham B4 7LU.

TAYLER, Prof. Roger John, OBE 1990; PhD; FRS 1995; Professor of Astronomy, University of Sussex, 1967–95; *b* 25 Oct. 1929; *s* of Richard Henry Tayler and Frances Florence Bessie Tayler (*née* Redrup); *m* 1955, Moya Elizabeth Fry. *Educ:* Solihull Sch.; Clare Coll., Cambridge (MA, PhD). Commonwealth Fund Fellow, CIT and Princeton, 1953–54; AEA Harwell and Culham, 1955–61; Dept of Applied Maths and Theoretical Physics, Cambridge Univ., and Fellow, Corpus Christi Coll., Cambridge, 1961–67. Royal Astronomical Society: Sec., 1971–79; Treas., 1979–87; Pres., 1989–90. *Publications:* The Stars: their structure and evolution, 1970, 2nd edn 1994; The Origin of the Chemical Elements, 1972; Galaxies: structure and evolution, 1978, 2nd edn 1993; (ed) History of the Astronomical Society, vol. 2, 1987; The Hidden Universe, 1991; (ed) Stellar Astrophysics, 1992. *Recreations:* walking, gardening. *Address:* 17 Prince Edward's Road, Lewes, East Sussex BN7 1BJ. *T:* Lewes (01273) 472181.

TAYLOR; *see* Suenson-Taylor, family name of Baron Grantchester.

TAYLOR, family name of **Barons Ingrow, Taylor of Blackburn, Taylor of Gosforth** and **Taylor of Gryfe.**

TAYLOR, Lady, (Charity), MB, BS, MRCS, LRCP; retired as Assistant Director and Inspector of Prisons (Women), (1959–66); Member, BBC General Advisory Council, 1964–67; President, Newfoundland and Labrador Social Welfare Council, 1968–71; *b* Sept. 1914; *d* of W. George and Emma Clifford; *m* 1939, Stephen J. L. Taylor (later Lord Taylor) (*d* 1988); two *s* one *d*. *Educ:* The Grammar School, Huntingdon; London (Royal Free Hospital) School of Medicine for Women. HS Royal Free Hospital; HS Elizabeth Garrett Anderson Hospital; Assistant Medical Officer HM Prison, Holloway; Medical Officer, HM Prison Holloway; Governor, HM Prison, Holloway, 1945–59. *Recreation:* conversation. *Address:* Flat 10, Clover Court, Church Road, Haywards Heath, West Sussex RH16 3UF.

TAYLOR OF BLACKBURN, Baron *cr* 1978 (Life Peer), of Blackburn in the County of Lancashire; **Thomas Taylor,** CBE 1974 (OBE 1969); JP; DL; Consultant, Shorrock Security Systems Ltd, and other companies; *b* 10 June 1929; *s* of James and Edith Gladys Taylor; *m* 1950, Kathleen Nurton; one *s*. *Educ:* Mill Hill Primary Sch.; Blakey Moor Elementary Sch. Mem., Blackburn Town Council, 1954–76 (Leader, chm. of cttees and rep. on various bodies). Chm., Electricity Cons. Council for NW and Mem. Norweb Bd, 1977–80; Member: NW Econ. Planning Council; NW AHA (Chm. Brockhall HMC, 1972–74, Vice-Chm. Blackburn HMC, 1964–74); Council for Educational Technology in UK; Nat. Foundn for Educn Research in Eng. and Wales; Schools Council; Regional Rent Tribunal. Chairman: Govt Cttee of Enquiry into Management and Govt of Schools; Nat. Foundn for Visual Aids. Former Mem., Public Schools Commn; past Pres., Assoc. of Educn Cttees. Dir, Councils and Education Press. University of Lancaster: Founder Mem. and Mem. Council; author of Taylor Report on problems; Dep. Pro-Chancellor. Former Dep. Dir, Central Lancs Family and Community Project. Director: EDS (Consultant, 1994–); Tricapital. Elder, URC; Pres., Free Church Council, 1962–63. JP Blackburn, 1960, DL Lancs, 1994; former Chm., Juvenile Bench. Freeman, Blackburn, 1992. *Address:* 34 Tower Road, Feniscliffe, Blackburn BB2 5LE. *T:* Blackburn (01254) 202808.

TAYLOR OF GOSFORTH, Baron *cr* 1992 (Life Peer), of Embleton in the County of Northumberland; **Peter Murray Taylor,** Kt 1980; PC 1988; Lord Chief Justice of England, since 1992; *b* 1 May 1930; *s* of Herman Louis Taylor, medical practitioner and Raie Helena Taylor (*née* Shockett); *m* 1956, Irene Shirley (*d* 1995), *d* of Lionel and Mary Harris; one *s* three *d*. *Educ:* Newcastle upon Tyne Royal Gram. Sch.; Pembroke Coll., Cambridge (Exhibr; Hon. Fellow, 1992). Called to Bar, Inner Temple, 1954, Bencher, 1975; QC 1967; Vice-Chm. of the Bar, 1978–79, Chm., 1979–80. Recorder of: Huddersfield, 1969–70; Teesside, 1970–71; Dep. Chm., Northumberland QS, 1970–71; a Recorder of the Crown Court, 1972–80; a Judge of the High Court of Justice, QBD, 1980–88. North Eastern Circuit: Leader, 1975–80; Presiding Judge, 1984–88; a Lord Justice of Appeal, 1988–92. Pres., Inns of Court Council, 1990–92. Chm., Inquiry into Hillsborough Football Club Disaster, 1989. Controller, Royal Opera House Develt Land Trust, 1990–. Chm., Trinity Coll. of Music, 1991–92. Hon. Member: Amer. Bar Assoc., 1980–; Canadian Bar Assoc., 1980–. Hon. LLD: Newcastle upon Tyne, 1990; Liverpool, 1993; Northumbria, 1993; Nottingham, 1994; Leeds, 1995. *Recreation:* music. *Address:* Royal Courts of Justice, Strand, WC2A 2LL. *Club:* Garrick.

TAYLOR OF GRYFE, Baron *cr* 1968 (Life Peer), of Bridge of Weir; **Thomas Johnston Taylor;** DL; FRSE 1977; Chairman, Morgan Grenfell (Scotland) Ltd, 1973–85; *b* 27 April 1912; *m* 1943, Isobel Wands; two *d*. *Educ:* Bellahouston Acad., Glasgow. Member: British Railways Bd, 1968–80 (Chm., Scottish Railways Board, 1971–80); Board of Scottish Television Ltd, 1968–82; Forestry Commn, 1963–76 (Chm., 1970–76). President, Scottish CWS, 1965–70; Mem., Scottish Economic Council, 1971–74. Director: Whiteaway Laidlaw & Co. Ltd, 1971–89; Friends' Provident Life Office, 1972–82; Scottish Metropolitan Property Co. Ltd, 1972–88; BR Property Bd, 1972–82; Mem., Internat. Adv. Council, Morgan Grenfell. Chm., Economic Forestry Group, 1976–81. Trustee, Dulverton Trust, 1980–; Chm., Scottish Action on Dementia, 1989–. DL Renfrewshire, 1970. Hon. LLD Strathclyde, 1974. Comdr's Cross, OM (FRG), 1992. *Recreations:* theatre, golf, walking. *Address:* 33 Seagale, Kingsbarns, Fife KY16 8SR. *T:* Boarhills (01334) 880430. *Clubs:* Caledonian; Royal and Ancient (St Andrews).

TAYLOR, Alan; *see* Taylor, Robert A.

TAYLOR, Alan Broughton; His Honour Judge Alan Taylor; a Circuit Judge, since 1991; *b* 23 Jan. 1939; *yr s* of Valentine James Broughton Taylor and Gladys Maud Taylor; *m* 1964, Diana Hindmarsh; two *s*. *Educ:* Malvern Coll.; Geneva Univ.; Birmingham Univ. (LLB); Brasenose Coll., Oxford (BLitt, re-designated MLitt 1979). Called to the Bar, Gray's Inn, 1961; barrister on Oxford Circuit, subseq. Midland and Oxford Circuit, 1963–91; a Recorder, 1979–91. Gov., St Matthew's Sch., Sandwell, 1988–92. FCIArb 1994. *Publication:* (contrib.) A Practical Guide to the Care of the Injured, ed P. S. London, 1967. *Recreations:* philately, fell walking. *Address:* c/o Circuit Administrator's Office, 2 Newton Street, Birmingham B4 7LU.

TAYLOR, Lt-Gen. Sir Allan (Macnab), KBE 1972; MC 1944; Deputy Commander-in-Chief, United Kingdom Land Forces, 1973–76, retired; *b* 26 March 1919; *s* of Alexander Lawrence Taylor and Winifred Ethel (*née* Nisbet); *m* 1945, Madeleine Turpin (marr. diss. 1963); two *d*. *Educ:* Fyling Hall School, Robin Hood's Bay. Joined TA, 1938; Troop Leader, 10th R Tank Regt, 1940; Squadron Leader, 7th R Tank Regt, 1942; 6th R Tank Regt, 1946; Staff College, 1948; GSO, 2, 56 London Armoured Div., 1949; Bde Major 20 Armoured Bde, 1952; Instructor, Staff College, 1954; Squadron Leader, 1st R Tank Regt, 1957; Second in Comd 5th RTR, 1959; Comdg Officer: 5th RTR, 1960 and 3rd, 1961; AA & QMG, 1st Div., 1962; Commandant, RAC Gunnery School, 1963; Comd Berlin Brigade, 1964; Imperial Defence College, 1967; Comdr, 1st Div., 1968; Commandant, Staff College, Camberley, 1969–72; GOC South East District, April–Dec. 1972. Chm., Cttee on Regular Officer Training, 1972–. Col Comdt, RTR, 1973–77. *Recreation:* golf. *Address:* 4 Mill Close, Middle Assendon, Henley-on-Thames, Oxon RG9 6BA. *T:* Henley (01491) 575167.

TAYLOR, Andrew James, CBE 1965; Chairman, British Manufacturing and Research Co., Grantham, Lincs, 1968–73; *b* 1902; *s* of late Alfred George Ralph Meston Taylor, Broughty Ferry, Dundee; *m* 1925, Mary Ann Symmers, *d* of George Cowie, Aberdeen; one *s* one *d* (and two *s* decd). *Educ:* Robert Gordon's Coll., Aberdeen. Dir of Manufacture and Exec. Dir, Ford Motor Co. Ltd, 1962–65; Deputy Managing Director, 1965–67. *Recreations:* photography, fishing. *Address:* 2 Drummond Road, Blairgowrie, Perthshire PH10 6PD. *T:* Blairgowrie (01250) 873358. *Club:* Royal Automobile.
See also R. O. Taylor.

TAYLOR, Ann; *see* Taylor, (Winifred) Ann.

TAYLOR, Arnold Joseph, CBE 1971; DLitt, MA; Docteur *hc* Caen; FBA 1972; FSA; Hon. Vice-President, Society of Antiquaries, since 1978 (Vice-President, 1963–64; Secretary, 1964–70; Director, 1970–75; President, 1975–78); *b* 24 July 1911; *y s* of late John George Taylor, Headmaster of Sir Walter St John's School, Battersea; *m* 1940,

Patricia Katharine, *d* of late S. A. Guilbride, Victoria, BC; one *s* one *d*. *Educ:* Merchant Taylors' School; St John's College, Oxford (MA). Assistant master, Chard School, Somerset, 1934; Assistant Inspector of Ancient Monuments, HM Office of Works, 1935. Served War of 1939–45, Intelligence Officer, RAF, 1942–46. Inspector of Ancient Monuments for Wales, Min. of Works, 1946–54, Asst Chief Inspector, 1954–61; Chief Inspector of Ancient Monuments and Historic Buildings, MPBW, later DoE, 1961–72. Commissioner: Royal Commissions on Ancient and Historical Monuments (Wales and Monmouthshire), 1956–83; Historical Monuments (England), 1963–78; Mem., Ancient Monuments Board: for England, 1973–82; for Scotland, 1974–79; for Wales, 1974–82. Member: Cathedrals Advisory Cttee, 1964–80; Adv. Bd for Redundant Churches, 1973–82 (Chm., 1975–77); Westminster Abbey Architectural Adv. Panel, 1979–92; Vice-President: English Place-Name Soc., 1986–; British Archaeol Assoc., 1993; Hon. Vice-President: Flintshire Hist. Soc., 1953; Royal Archaeol Inst., 1979– (Vice-Pres., 1968–72); Surrey Archaeol Soc., 1979; President: Oxford Univ. Archaeol Soc., 1932; Cambrian Archaeol Assoc., 1969; London and Mddx Archaeol Soc., 1971–74; Soc. for Medieval Archaeology, 1972–75; Friends of Lydiard Tregoze, 1983–86; Sir Walter St John's Old Boys' Assoc., 1969–70 (Hon. Life Patron, 1992); Old Merchant Taylors' Soc., 1985–86. Mem., Sir Walter St John's Schools Trust, 1970. Reckitt Lectr, British Acad., 1977. Hon. Corres. Mem., Société Jersiaise, 1983. Hon. Pres., Colloque Internat. du Château Gaillard, 1992. Hon. DLitt Wales, 1970; Docteur *hc* Caen, 1980. Reginald Taylor Prize, British Archaeol Assoc., 1949; G. T. Clark Prize, Cambrian Archaeol Assoc., 1956; Gold Medal, Soc. of Antiquaries, 1988. Médaille d'Honneur de la Ville de Saint-Georges d'Espéranche, 1988. Silver Jubilee Medal, 1977. *Publications:* Records of the Barony and Honour of the Rape of Lewes, 1940; official guides to various historical monuments in care Ministry of Works (now DoE), 1939–80; chapter on Military Architecture, in vol. Medieval England, 1958; (part author) History of the King's Works, 1963; Four Great Castles, 1983; Studies in Castles and Castle-Building, 1986; contribs on medieval architectural history in Eng. Hist. Rev., Antiquaries Jl, Archaeologia Cambrensis, etc. *Recreations:* reading and using records, resisting iconoclasts. *Address:* Rose Cottage, Lincoln's Hill, Chiddingfold, Surrey GU8 4UN. *T:* Wormley (01428) 682069.

TAYLOR, Sir (Arthur) Godfrey, Kt 1980; DL; Chairman, London Residuary Body, since 1985; *b* 3 Aug. 1925; *s* of Fred and Lucy Taylor; *m* 1945, Eileen Dorothy Daniel; one *s* three *d*. *Educ:* Stockport Secondary School. Sutton and Cheam Borough Council: Councillor, 1951–62; Alderman, 1962–65; London Bor. of Sutton: Alderman, 1964–78; Councillor, 1978–82; Hon. Freeman, 1978. Managing Trustee, Municipal Mutual Insurance Ltd, 1979–86; Chm., Southern Water Authority, 1981–85. Chm., Assoc. of Metropolitan Authorities, 1978–80. Chm., London Bor. Assoc., 1968–71. High Sheriff, 1984, DL, 1988, Greater London. *Recreation:* golf. *Address:* 23 Somerhill Lodge, Somerhill Road, Hove, E Sussex BN3 1RU. *T:* Brighton (01273) 776161.

TAYLOR, Arthur Robert; President, Muhlenberg College, Pennsylvania, since 1992; *b* 6 July 1935; *s* of Arthur Earl Taylor and Marian Hilda Scott; *m* Kathryn Pelgrift; three *d* by previous marriage. *Educ:* Brown Univ., USA (AB, MA). Asst Dir, Admissions, Brown Univ., June 1957–Dec. 1960; Vice-Pres./Dir, The First Boston Co., Jan. 1961–May 1970; Exec. Vice-Pres./Director, Internat. Paper Co., 1970–72; Pres., CBS Inc., 1972–76; Chm., Arthur Taylor & Co. Inc., 1977–92. Dean, Grad. Sch. of Business, Fordham Univ., 1985–89. Director: Louisiana Land & Exploration Co.; Pitney Bowes; Nomura Pacific Basin Fund, Inc.; Trustee, Drucker Foundn; Trustee Emeritus, Brown Univ. Hon. degrees: Dr Humane Letters: Simmons Coll., 1975; Rensselaer Polytechnic Inst., 1975; Dr of Humanities, Bucknell Univ., 1975. *Publications:* contrib. chapter to The Other Side of Profit, 1975; articles on US competitiveness and corporate responsibility in jls. *Recreations:* sailing, tennis, riding. *Address:* (office) Muhlenberg College, 2400 Chew Street, Allentown, PA 18104–5586, USA. *Clubs:* Century (New York); Metropolitan (Washington); California (Los Angeles).

TAYLOR, Arthur Ronald, MBE (mil.) 1945; DL; Chairman, Willis Faber plc, 1978–81; Vice-Chairman, Legal and General Group plc, 1984–86 (Director, 1982–86); *b* 13 June 1921; *yr s* of late Arthur Taylor and Kathleen Frances (*née* Constable Curtis); *m* 1949, Elizabeth Josephine Kiek; three *s*. *Educ:* Winchester Coll.; Trinity Coll., Oxford. Served Grenadier Guards, 1940–53 (despatches); sc; Bde Major 32nd Guards Bde. Laurence Philipps & Co. (Insurance) Ltd, 1953–58; Member of Lloyd's, 1955; Director, Willis, Faber and Dumas Ltd, 1959; Dep. Chm., Willis Faber Ltd, 1974. Vice-President: Corporation of Insurance Brokers, 1967–78; British Insurance Brokers Assoc., 1978–81. DL Hants, 1994. *Recreations:* golf, shooting. *Address:* Coutts & Co., 15 Lombard Street, EC3V 9AU.

TAYLOR, Bernard David, CBE 1993; Chairman, Medeva plc, since 1990; *b* 17 Oct. 1935; *s* of Thomas Taylor and Winifred (*née* Smith); *m* 1959, Nadine Barbara; two *s* two *d*. *Educ:* Univ. of Wales, Bangor (BSc Zoology). Science Teacher, Coventry Educn Authority, 1958; Sales and Marketing, SK&F, 1960; Sales and Marketing Manager, Glaxo NZ, 1964; New Products Manager, Glaxo UK, 1967; Man. Dir, Glaxo Australia, 1972; Dir, Glaxo Holdings plc, and Man. Dir, Glaxo Pharmaceuticals UK, 1984; Chief Exec., Glaxo Holdings, 1986–89. Councillor and Vice-Pres., Aust. Pharm. Manufrs' Assoc., 1974–79; Councillor, Victorian Coll. of Pharmacy, 1976–82. Member: CBI Europe Cttee, 1987–89; BOTB, 1987–. Trustee, WWF (UK), 1990–. CIMgt (CBIM 1986). Fellow, London Business Sch., 1988. *Address:* Medeva plc, 10 St James's Street, SW1A 1EF.

TAYLOR, Brian Arthur Edward; Assistant Under-Secretary of State, Civilian Management (Policy), since 1994; *b* 10 Jan. 1942; *s* of Arthur Frederick Taylor and Gertrude Maclean Taylor (*née* Campbell); *m* 1967, Carole Ann Smith; three *s* one *d*. *Educ:* St Benedict's Sch., Ealing; Corpus Christi Coll., Oxford (MA LitHum). Ministry of Defence, 1965–: Asst Private Sec. to Sec. of State, 1969–70; Private Sec. to Chief of Air Staff, 1973–75; Head, Management Services Div., 1977–79; Head, Naval Personnel Div., 1979–81; RCDS 1982; Central Policy Review Staff, Cabinet Office, 1983; Head, Civilian Management Div., MoD, 1984–86; Asst Under-Sec. of State (Quartermaster), 1986–88, Air (PE) 1988–91; Head of Personnel Policy Gp (Under Sec.), HM Treasury, 1992–94. *Recreations:* sport, music, reading, family. *Address:* Ministry of Defence, Northumberland House, Northumberland Avenue, WC2N 5BP. *Club:* Richmond Football.

TAYLOR, Brian Hyde; Secretary General, Committee of Vice-Chancellors and Principals, 1983–88; *b* 18 Aug. 1931; *s* of late Robert E. Taylor and late Ivy Taylor (*née* Wash), Woodford, Essex; *m* 1960, Audrey Anne Barnes; two *s*. *Educ:* Buckhurst Hill County High Sch.; SW Essex Technical Coll.; LSE (BSc (Econ)). Nat. Service, commnd RASC, 1954–56. Clerk, Corp. of Lloyd's, 1947–48; Personal Asst to Principal, Univ. of London, 1956–59; administrative posts, Univ. of London, 1959–66; Asst Sec., ACU (and Vice-Chancellors Cttee), 1966; Exec. Sec., Cttee of Vice-Chancellors and Principals, 1973; Sec., Univ. Authorities Panel, 1980. Mem., Bd of Dirs, Busoga Trust, 1990–; Treasurer, Council for Educn in Commonwealth, 1991–. *Recreations:* travel, browsing in bookshops. *Address:* Sylverstone, Ashley Park Road, Walton-on-Thames, Surrey KT12 1JN. *T:* Walton-on-Thames (01932) 225397. *Club:* Athenæum.

TAYLOR, Brian William; Under Secretary, Civil Service Commission, retired; Resident Chairman, Recruitment and Assessment Services, Office of Minister for Civil Service, 1990–93; *b* 29 April 1933; *s* of late Alan Taylor and Betty Taylor; *m* 1959, Mary Evelyn Buckley; two *s* two *d*. *Educ:* Emanuel School. Entered Ministry of Nat. Insurance (subseq. DHSS, then DSS) as Exec. Officer, 1952; Higher Exec. Officer, 1963; Principal, 1968; Asst Sec., 1976; Under Sec., 1982; on loan from DSS, 1990–93. *Recreations:* music, theatre, literature, tennis.

TAYLOR, Cavan; Senior Partner, Lovell White Durrant, since 1991; *b* 23 Feb. 1935; *s* of late Albert William Taylor and Constance Muriel (*née* Horncastle); *m* 1962, Helen Tinling; one *s* two *d*. *Educ:* King's Coll. Sch., Wimbledon; Emmanuel Coll., Cambridge (BA 1958; LLM 1959). 2nd Lieut, RASC, 1953–55. Articled with Herbert Smith & Co., 1958–61; qualified as solicitor, 1961; Legal Dept, Distillers' Co. Ltd, 1962–65; Asst Solicitor, Piesse & Sons, 1965–66, Partner, 1966; by amalgamation, Partner, Durrant Piesse and Lovell White Durrant; Dep. Sen. Partner, Lovell White Durrant, 1990–91. Gov., King's Coll. Sch., Wimbledon, 1970– (Chm., 1973–90). *Publications:* articles in legal jls. *Recreations:* reading, gardening, conversation with my children. *Address:* (office) 65 Holborn Viaduct, EC1A 2DY. *T:* 0171–236 0066, *Fax:* 0171–248 4212. *Club:* Travellers'.

TAYLOR, Dr Charity; *see* Taylor, Lady.

TAYLOR, Prof. Charles Margrave, DPhil; FBA 1979; Professor of Political Science, McGill University, since 1982; *b* 5 Nov. 1931; *s* of Walter Margrave Taylor and Simone Beaubien; *m* 1956, Alba Romer; five *d*. *Educ:* McGill Univ. (BA History); Oxford Univ. (BA PPE, MA, DPhil). Fellow, All Souls Coll., Oxford, 1956–61; McGill University: Asst Prof., later Associate Prof., later Prof. of Polit. Science, Dept of Polit. Science, 1961–76; Prof. of Philosophy, Dept. of Philos., 1973–76; Chichele Prof. of Social and Political Theory, and Fellow of All Souls Coll., Oxford Univ., 1976–81; Mem., Sch. of Social Science, Inst. for Advanced Study, Princeton, 1981–82. Prof. asst, later Prof. agrégé, later Prof. titulaire, Ecole Normale Supérieure, 1962–64, Dept de Philos., 1963–71, Univ. de Montréal. Vis. Prof. in Philos., Princeton Univ., 1965; Mills Vis. Prof. in Philos., Univ. of Calif, Berkeley, 1974. For. Hon. Mem., Amer. Acad. of Arts and Scis, 1986. *Publications:* The Explanation of Behavior, 1964; Pattern of Politics, 1970; Hegel, 1975; Erklarung und Interpretation in den Wissenschaften vom Menschen, 1975; Social Theory as Practice, 1983; Philosophical Papers, 1985; Negative Freiheit, 1988; Sources of the Self, 1989; The Ethics of Authenticity, 1992. *Recreations:* skiing, swimming. *Address:* 344 Metcalfe Avenue, Montréal, PQ H3Z 2J3 Canada.

TAYLOR, Christopher Charles, FSA; FBA 1995; Head, Archaeological Survey, Royal Commission on Historical Monuments, 1985–93, retired; *b* 7 Nov. 1935; *s* of R. H. Taylor and A. M. Taylor; *m* 1st, 1961, Angela Ballard (*d* 1983); one *s* one *d*; 2nd, 1985, Stephanie, *d* of Wing Comdr R. J. S. Spooner; one step *d*. *Educ:* King Edward VI Sch., Lichfield; Univ. of Keele (BA 1958); Inst. of Archaeol., Univ. of London (Dip. Archaeol. 1960). FSA 1966; MIFA 1987. Investigator, Sen. Investigator and Principal Investigator, RCHM, 1960–93. Mem., English Heritage Historic Parks and Gardens Adv. Cttee, 1987–. Pres., Cambridge Antiquarian Soc., 1994–. *Publications:* Dorset, 1970; The Making of the Cambridgeshire Landscape, 1973; Fieldwork in Medieval Archaeology, 1974; Fields in the English Landscape, 1975, 3rd edn 1987; Roads and Tracks in Britain, 1979, 2nd edn 1982; The Archaeology of Gardens, 1983; Village and Farmstead, 1983; (ed) W. G. Hoskins, The Making of the English Landscape, rev. edn 1988; contrib. to various pubns of RCHM; papers in learned jls on archaeol. and landscape hist. *Recreations:* gardening, garden history. *Address:* 13 West End, Whittlesford, Cambridge CB2 4LX.

See also D. H. C. Taylor.

TAYLOR, Prof. Christopher Malcolm, FIMechE; Professor of Tribology, since 1990, and Head of Department of Mechanical Engineering, since 1992, University of Leeds; *b* 15 Jan. 1943; *s* of William Taylor and Esther Hopkinson; *m* 1st, 1968, Gillian Walton (marr. diss. 1986); one *d*; 2nd, 1994, Diane Shorrocks. *Educ:* King's College London (BScEng), Univ. of Leeds (MSc, PhD, DEng). Research Engineer, English Electric Co.; Sen. Engr, Industrial Unit of Tribology, Leeds, 1968–71; Academic Staff, Univ. of Leeds, 1971–. Tribology Trust Silver Medal, 1992; Donald Julius Groen Prize, IMechE, 1993. Editor, Part J, Procs IMechE; Co-Editor, Procs annual Leeds–Lyon Symposium on Tribology. *Publications:* numerous contribs to learned jls. *Recreations:* walking, cycling. *Address:* Department of Mechanical Engineering, The University, Leeds LS2 9JT. *T:* Leeds (0113) 233 2156.

TAYLOR, Claire Mavis, RRC 1994 (ARRC 1977); QHNS 1994; Principal Nursing Officer and Matron-in-Chief, Queen Alexandra's Royal Naval Nursing Service, since 1994; *b* 26 May 1943; *d* of late William Taylor and Sybil (*née* Matthews). *Educ:* George Dixon Grammar Sch., Edgbaston. SRN 1964; SCM 1967; RNT 1977. Served QARNNS, 1967–73; Nursing Sister, Papua New Guinea, 1973–74; rejoined QARNNS 1975. OStJ. *Recreations:* travel, reading. *Address:* c/o Barclays Bank, 69 West Street, Fareham, Hants PO16 0AW.

TAYLOR, Clifford; management consultant; Director, Resources Television, BBC, 1988–93 (Deputy Director, 1987–88); *b* 6 March 1941; *s* of Fred Taylor and Annie Elisabeth (*née* Hudson); *m* 1962, Catherine Helen (*née* Green); two *d*. *Educ:* Barnsley and District Holgate Grammar Sch.; Barnsley College of Mining and Technology. ACMA. NCB, 1957–65; Midlands Counties Dairies, 1965–68; BBC: Radio Cost Accountant, 1968–71; Television Hd of Costing, 1971–76; Chief Accountant, Corporate Finance, 1976–77 and 1982–84; Chief Acct, Engineering, 1977–82; Dep. Dir, Finance, 1984–86. *Recreations:* sport — plays squash, golf, enjoys horse racing. *Address:* 35 Hare Hill Close, Pyrford, near Woking, Surrey GU22 8UH. *T:* Byfleet (01932) 348301. *Clubs:* MCC (Associate Mem.), BBC.

TAYLOR, Sir Cyril (Julian Hebden), Kt 1989; Chairman: City Technology Colleges Trust, since 1987; American Institute for Foreign Study, since 1964; *b* 14 May 1935; *s* of Cyril Eustace Taylor and Margaret Victoria (*née* Hebden); *m* 1965, June Judith Denman; one *d*. *Educ:* St Marylebone Grammar Sch.; Trinity Hall, Cambridge (MA); Harvard Business Sch. (MBA). National Service, Officer with KAR in Kenya during Mau Mau Emergency, 1954–56 (seconded from E Surrey Regt). Brand Manager in Advertising Dept, Proctor & Gamble, Cincinnati, Ohio, 1961–64; Founder Chm., American Institute for Foreign Study, 1964–: group cos include: Amer. Inst. for Foreign Study; Richmond Coll.; Amer. Council for Internat. Studies; Camp America; Au Pair in America. Advr to Sec. of State for Educn and Science, 1987–. Mem. for Ruislip Northwood, GLC, 1977–86: Chm., Professional and Gen. Services Cttee, 1979–81; Opposition spokesperson for employment, 1981–82, transport, 1982–85, policy and resources, 1985–86; Dep. Leader of the Opposition, 1983–86; Mem., Wkg Party reviewing legislation to abolish GLC and MCCs, 1983–86. Pres., Ruislip Northwood Cons. Assoc., 1986–; contested (C): Huddersfield E, Feb. 1974; Keighley, Oct. 1974. Member: Bd of Dirs, Centre for Policy Studies, 1984–; Council, Westfield Coll., Univ. of London, 1983–89; Council, RCM, 1988–95; Bd of Governors, Holland Park Comprehensive Sch., 1971–74. Chm., Lexham Gdns Residents' Assoc., 1986–. Pres., Harvard Business Sch. Club, London, 1990–93; Vice Pres., Alumni Council, Harvard Business Sch., 1994– (Mem., 1993–).

FRSA 1990. Hon. LLD New England, 1991. *Publications:* (jtly) The New Guide to Study Abroad, USA 1969, 4th edn 1976; Peace has its Price, 1972; No More Tick, 1974; The Elected Member's Guide to Reducing Public Expenditure, 1980; A Realistic Plan for London Transport, 1982; Reforming London's Government, 1984; Quangoes Just Grow, 1985; London Preserv'd, 1985; Bringing Accountability Back to Local Government, 1985; Employment Examined: the right approach to more jobs, 1986; Raising Educational Standards, 1990. . *Recreations:* keen tennis player, swimmer, gardener, theatre-goer. *Address:* 1 Lexham Walk, W8 5JD. *T:* 0171–370 2081; American Institute for Foreign Study, 37 Queen's Gate, SW7 5HR. *T:* 0171–581 7391, *Fax:* 0171–581 7388. *Clubs:* Carlton, Hurlingham, Chelsea Arts; Harvard, Racquet (New York).

TAYLOR, Dr Daniel Brumhall Cochrane; JP; Vice-Chancellor, Victoria University of Wellington, New Zealand, 1968–82; Referee of the Small Claims Tribunal, Wellington, 1985–88; *b* 13 May 1921; *s* of Daniel Brumhall Taylor, Coleraine, NI and Anna Martha Taylor (*née* Rice); *m* 1955, Elizabeth Page, Christchurch, NZ; one *s* one *d*. *Educ:* Coleraine Academical Instn, NI; Queen's Univ., Belfast. BSc (Mech. Engrg) 1942, BSc (Elec. Engrg) 1943, MSc 1946, PhD 1948, QUB; MA Cantab 1956; FIMechE 1968. Lecturer in Engineering: Liverpool Univ., 1948–50; Nottingham Univ., 1950–53; ICI Fellow, Cambridge Univ., 1953–56; Lectr in Mechanical Sciences, Cambridge Univ., 1956–68; Fellow of Peterhouse, 1958–68, Fellow Emeritus, 1968; Tutor of Peterhouse, 1958–65, Senior Tutor, 1965–68. Member: NZ/USA Educnl Foundn, 1970–82; Council, Assoc. of Commonwealth Univs, 1974–77 (Chm., 1975–76); Chm., NZ Vice-Chancellors' Cttee, 1975–77. JP New Zealand, 1985. Hon. LLD Victoria Univ. of Wellington, 1983. *Publications:* numerous engrg and metallurgical papers. *Recreation:* golf. *Address:* PO Box 5280720, Trentham, New Zealand. *T:* (4) 5267904. *Club:* Leander (Henley-on-Thames).
See also M. J. Kelly.

TAYLOR, David George Pendleton, CBE 1993; Governor of Montserrat, West Indies, 1990–93; *b* 5 July 1933; *s* of George James Pendleton Taylor and Dorothy May Taylor (*née* Williams). *Educ:* Clifton College; Clare College, Cambridge (MA). Nat. Service as Sub-Lieut (Special) RNVR, 1952–54; Admin. Officer, HMOCS Tanganyika, 1958–63; joined Booker McConnell, 1964; Chm. and Chief Exec., Bookers (Malaŵi) Ltd, 1976–77; Director: Consumer Buying Corp. of Zambia, 1978; National Drug Co., Zambia, 1978; Bookers (Zambia), 1978; Minvielle & Chastanet Ltd, St Lucia, 1979; United Rum Merchants Ltd, 1981; Estate Industries Ltd, Jamaica, 1981; seconded full time to Falkland Is Govt, Dec. 1983; Chief Exec., Falkland Islands Govt and Exec. Vice Chm., FI Develt Corp., 1983–87 and 1988–89 (sometime acting Governor). Dir, Booker Agric. Internat., 1987–88. Member: Royal African Soc., 1986–; RIIA, 1988–. Governor, Clifton Coll., 1987–; Pres., Old Cliftonian Soc., 1993–95. FRGS 1990. *Recreations:* water colour painting, travel, rural France. *Address:* 53 Lillian Road, Barnes, SW13 9JF. *Clubs:* United Oxford & Cambridge University, Commonwealth Trust, MCC, British Sportsman's.

TAYLOR, David John; writer and editor; *b* 17 March 1947: *s* of John Whitfield Taylor and Alice Elaine Oldacre; *m* 1972, Ann Robinson; two *d*. *Educ:* High Sch., Newcastle-under-Lyme; Magdalene Coll., Cambridge (MA (English)). Reporter, Staffordshire Evening Sentinel, 1966; Editor, Varsity, 1969; BBC TV, Late Night Line-Up, 1969; Asst Editor, 1970–78, Dep. Editor, 1978–87, Editor, 1988, Punch; Editor, Business Life, 1988–93. Radio and TV broadcaster; columnist, Daily Telegraph. *Recreations:* bell-ringing, golf, personal computers. *Address:* Premier Magazines, Haymarket House, 1 Oxendon Street, SW1Y 4EE.

TAYLOR, David Wilson; Chief Executive, English Partnerships, since 1993; *b* 9 May 1950; *s* of Eric and Sybil Taylor; *m* 1980, Brenda Elizabeth Birchall; two *s*. *Educ:* Galashiels Acad.; Dundee Univ. Sch. of Architecture; Architectural Assoc. (DipArch, Dip. Urban and Regl Planning). Research and journalism, 1979–81; Advisor on regl policy to John Prescott, MP, 1981–83; Lancashire Enterprises Ltd: Dep. Man. Dir, 1983–85; Man. Dir, 1985–89; AMEC plc: Man. Dir, AMEC Regeneration, 1989–92; Man. Dir, AMEC Develts, 1992–93. *Recreations:* football (British and American), Rugby (Union and League). *Address:* 16/18 Old Queen Street, SW1H 9HP. *T:* 0171–976 7070. *Club:* Manchester United Football.

TAYLOR, Derek, CBE 1992; FEng 1988; Managing Director, NNC Ltd (formerly National Nuclear Corporation), 1987–94; Chairman, European Nuclear Assistance Consortium, since 1992; *b* 25 April 1930; *s* of Ambrose and Joyce Taylor; *m* 1955, Lorna Margaret Ross; two *s* one *d*. *Educ:* Egerton Boys' School, Knutsford; Salford Royal Tech. Coll. FIMechE; FINucE 1988. Engineer, Ministry of Supply, 1951; UKAEA, 1955; Asst Chief Engineer, UKAEA, 1968; Eng. Manager, Nuclear Power Gp, 1969; Project Gen. Manager, Nuclear Power Co., 1980; Project Dir, Nat. Nuclear Corp., 1984–87. Non-exec. Dir, PWR Power Projects Ltd, 1988–. *Publications:* papers on nuclear engineering. *Recreations:* golf, gardening. *Address:* 68 Glebelands Road, Knutsford, Cheshire WA16 9DZ. *T:* Knutsford (01565) 633907.

TAYLOR, Desmond S.; *see* Shawe-Taylor.

TAYLOR, Douglas Hugh Charles, PhD; FEng; independent consultant on internal combustion engines, since 1992; *b* 4 April 1938; *s* of Richard Hugh Taylor and Alice Mary Davies; *m* 1970, Janet Elizabeth Scott; two *d*. *Educ:* King Edward VI Grammar Sch., Lichfield; Loughborough University of Technology. PhD, BTech; FEng, 1987; FIMechE. Ruston & Hornsby/GEC Ruston Diesels, 1962–72, Chief Research Engineer, 1968; Ricardo Consulting Engineers, 1972–90: Head of Large Engines, 1973; Dir, 1977; Man. Dir, 1984–90; Chm., 1987–90; Gp Man. Dir, Ricardo Internat., 1990–91. Vis. Prof., Loughborough Univ., 1994–. *Recreations:* campanology, flying. *Address:* Ellington House, 20 Coombe Drove, Bramber, Steyning, Sussex BN44 3PW. *T:* Steyning (01903) 813566.

TAYLOR, Sir Edward Macmillan, (Sir Teddy), Kt 1991; MP (C) Southend East, since March 1980; journalist, consultant and company director; *b* 18 April 1937; *s* of late Edward Taylor and of Minnie Hamilton Taylor; *m* 1970, Sheila Duncan; two *s* one *d*. *Educ:* Glasgow High School and University (MA (Hons) Econ. and Politics). Commercial Editorial Staff of Glasgow Herald, 1958–59; Industrial Relations Officer on Staff of Clyde Shipbuilders' Assoc., 1959–64. Director: Shepherds Foods, 1968–; Ansvar (Temperance) Insurance, 1970–; Adviser: John Lawrence (Glasgow) Ltd, 1970–; Port of London Police Fedn, 1972–. MP (C) Glasgow, Cathcart, 1964–79; Parly Under-Sec. of State, Scottish Office, 1970–71, resigned; Parly Under-Sec. of State, Scottish Office, 1974; Opposition spokesman on Trade, 1977, on Scotland affairs, 1977–79. Vice-Chm., Cons. Parly Party Home Affairs Cttee, 1992–94 (Sec., 1983–92). *Publications:* (novel) Hearts of Stone, 1968; contributions to the press. *Address:* 12 Lynton Road, Thorpe Bay, Southend-on-Sea, Essex SS1 3BE. *T:* Southend (01702) 586282.

TAYLOR, Prof. Edwin William, FRS 1978; Louis Block Professor of Molecular Genetics and Cell Biology, University of Chicago, since 1984 (Professor, Department of Biophysics, since 1975); *b* Toronto, 8 June 1929; *s* of William Taylor and Jean Taylor (*née* Christie); *m* 1956, Jean Heather Logan; two *s* one *d*. *Educ:* Univ. of Toronto (BA 1952); McMaster Univ. (MSc 1955); Univ. of Chicago (PhD 1957). Asst Prof., 1959–63, Associate Prof., 1963–67, Prof., 1967–72, Univ. of Chicago; Prof. of Biology, King's College and MRC Unit, London, 1972–74; Associate Dean, Div. of Biol Sci and Medicine, 1977–79, Prof. and Chm., Dept of Biology, 1979–84, Chicago Univ. Rockefeller Foundn Fellow, 1957–58; Nat. Insts of Health Fellow, 1958–59, cons. to NIH, 1970–72, 1976–80. Member: Amer. Biochem. Soc.; Biophysical Soc. *Address:* Cummings Life Sciences Center, University of Chicago, 920 East 58th Street, Chicago, IL 60637, USA. *T:* (312) 7021660; 5634 South Harper Avenue, Chicago, IL 60637, USA. *T:* (312) 9552441.

TAYLOR, Elizabeth (Rosemond); film actress; *b* London, 27 Feb. 1932; *d* of late Francis Taylor and Sara (*née* Sothern); *m* 1st, 1950, Conrad Nicholas Hilton, Jr (marr. diss.; he *d* 1969); 2nd, 1952, Michael Wilding (marr. diss.; he *d* 1979); two *s*; 3rd, 1957, Mike Todd (*d* 1958); one *d*; 4th, 1959, Eddie Fisher (marr. diss. 1964); 5th, 1964, Richard Burton, CBE (*d* 1984) (marr. diss.; remarried 1975; marr. diss. 1976); 7th, 1976, Senator John Warner (marr. diss. 1982); 8th, 1991, Larry Fortensky. *Educ:* Byron House, Hampstead; Hawthorne School, Beverly Hills; Metro-Goldwyn-Mayer School; University High School, Hollywood. First film, There's One Born Every Minute, 1942. *Films include:* Lassie Come Home, The White Cliffs of Dover, 1943; Jane Eyre, National Velvet, 1944; Courage of Lassie, Life with Father, 1946; Cynthia, 1947; A Date With Judy, 1948; Julia Misbehaves, 1948; The Big Hangover, 1949; Father's Little Dividend, Little Women, The Conspirator, Father of the Bride, 1950; A Place in the Sun, Love is Better than Ever, 1951; Ivanhoe, 1952; Beau Brummel, Elephant Walk, Rhapsody, 1954; Last Time I Saw Paris, 1955; Giant, 1956; Raintree County, 1957; Cat on a Hot Tin Roof, 1958; Suddenly Last Summer, 1959; Holiday in Spain, Butterfield 8 (Academy Award for Best Actress), 1960; Cleopatra, The VIPs, 1963; The Sandpiper, 1965; Who's Afraid of Virginia Woolf? (Academy Award for Best Actress), 1966; The Taming of the Shrew, Doctor Faustus, 1967; Boom!, The Comedians, Reflections in a Golden Eye, Secret Ceremony, 1968; The Only Game in Town, 1970; Under Milk Wood, Zee and Co., Hammersmith is Out, 1972; Night Watch, 1973; Ash Wednesday, 1974; The Driver's Seat, Blue Bird, 1975; A Little Night Music, 1977; Winter Kills, 1979; The Mirror Crack'd, 1980; Between Friends, 1983; Young Toscanini, 1988; The Flintstones, 1994. Stage debut as Regina in The Little Foxes, NY, 1981, London stage debut, Victoria Palace, 1982; Private Lives, NY, 1983. Initiated Elizabeth Taylor-Ben Gurion Univ. Fund for Children of the Negev, 1982; founded American Foundn for AIDS Res., 1985, Internat. Fund, 1985. Aristotle S. Onassis Foundn Award, 1988; Humanitarian Award, American Academy, 1993. Comdr of Arts and Letters (France), 1985; Legion of Honour (France), 1987. *Publications:* (with Richard Burton) World Enough and Time, 1964; Elizabeth Taylor, 1966; Elizabeth Takes Off, 1988. *Address:* Chen Sam & Associates Inc., 506 East 74th Street, Suite 3E, New York, NY 10021–3486, USA. *Fax:* (212) 4399438.

TAYLOR, Eric; a Recorder of the Crown Court, since 1978; *b* 22 Jan. 1931; *s* of Sydney Taylor and Sarah Helen (*née* Lea); *m* 1958, Margaret Jessie Taylor, *qv*. *Educ:* Wigan Grammar Sch.; Manchester Univ. (LLB 1952; Dauntesey Sen. Legal Scholar; LLM 1954). Admitted solicitor, 1955. Partner, Temperley Taylor Chadwick, Middleton, Manchester, 1957–. Part-time Lectr in Law, Manchester Univ., 1958–80, Hon. Special Lectr in Law, 1980–. Examr, (Old) Law Soc. Final Exams, 1968–81, Chief Examr, (New) Law Soc. Final Exams, 1978–83; Moderator, Qualified Lawyers' Transfer Test, 1990–; Chief Examr for solicitors qualifying to appear as advocates, 1993–. Pres., Oldham Law Assoc., 1970–72. Chairman: Manchester Young Solicitors' Gp, 1963; Manchester Nat. Insurance Appeal Tribunal, 1967–73; Disciplinary Cttee, Architects Registration Council, 1989–95. Member: Council, Law Soc., 1972–91 (Chm., Educn and Trng Cttee, 1980–83; Chm., Criminal Law Cttee, 1984–87); CNAA Legal Studies Bd, 1975–84; Lord Chancellor's Adv. Cttee on Trng of Magistrates, 1974–79. Governor: Coll. of Law, 1984–; Bd, Common Professional Examn, 1990–. *Publications:* Modern Conveyancing Precedents, 1964, 2nd edn 1989; Modern Wills Precedents, 1969, 2nd edn 1987; contrib. legal jls. *Recreations:* equestrian sports. *Address:* 10 Mercers Road, Heywood, Lancs OL10 2NP. *T:* Heywood (01706) 366630. *Club:* Farmers'.

TAYLOR, Eric W., RE 1948 (ARE 1935); ARCA 1934; ASIA (Ed) 1965; printmaker, painter and sculptor; *b* 6 Aug. 1909; *s* of Thomas John and Ethel Annie Taylor; *m* 1939, Alfreda Marjorie Hurren; one *s* one *d*. *Educ:* William Ellis School, Hampstead; Royal College of Art, South Kensington. Worked for 3 years in London Studio; then as a free-lance illustrator; won British Inst. Scholarship, 1932; runner-up in Prix de Rome, 1934, while at Royal College of Art. Exhibited: Royal Academy; Royal Scottish Academy; Doncaster Art Gallery; New York; Brooklyn; Chicago; London Group; New English Art Club. Pictures in permanent Collections of Stockholm Art Gallery, Art Inst. of Chicago, Washington Art Gallery, War Museum, London, V&A and British Museum Print Rooms, Ashmolean Mus., Leeds Art Gall., Bradford Art Gall., Inst. of Contemp. History, Wiener Liby, Kirkleatham Old Hall Mus., Redcar, Leeds Univ. Art Gall. Logan Prize for best Etching in International Exhibition of Etching and Engraving at Art Institute of Chicago, 1937. Selected by British Council to exhibit in Scandinavian Exhibition, 1940, S America, 1942–44, Spain and Portugal, 1942–44, Turkey, 1943–45, Iceland, 1943, Mexico, 1943–45, China, 1945, Czechoslovakia, 1948, and Rotterdam, 1948. Associate Chicago Society of Etchers, 1937. War pictures bought by National Gallery Advisory Committee for Imperial War Museum, 1945. Volunteered for RA, Nov. 1939. Instructor at Northern Command Camouflage School, 1941–43; Royal Engineers, France and Germany, 1943–45; Normandy Landing, Falaise Gap, Battle of Caen, crossings of Rhine and Maas. Instructing for Educational Corps Germany, 1946; Art Instructor Camberwell School of Art, 1936–39; Willesden School of Art, 1936–49; Central School of Art, 1948–49; Examiner: Bristol Univ., 1948–51; Durham Univ., 1971–74; Min. of Education NDD Pictorial Subjects, 1957–59. Designer and Supervisor of Lubeck School of Art for the Services, 1946. Head of the Design School, Leeds Coll. of Art, 1949–56, Principal, 1956–69, Organiser and Administrator of revolutionary Leeds Basic Course which played considerable part in changing whole direction of British art education; Asst Dir, Leeds Polytechnic, 1969–71; disagreed with organization of Art Faculties in Polytechnics and returned to work as full-time artist, 1971. Leverhulme Research Awards, 1958–59, visiting Colleges of Art in Austria, Germany, Holland, Denmark and Italy. Study of Mosaics, Italy, 1965, prior to execution of large mural on Leeds Meirion Centre. Representative Exhibitions: Wakefield Art Gall., 1960; Goosewell Gall., Menston, 1972, 1973, 1976; Middlesbrough Art Gall., 1972; Northern Artists Gall., Harrogate, 1977; Linton Ct Gall., Settle, 1983; Design Innovation Centre, Leeds, 1992; retrospective, Leeds Univ. Art Gall., 1994; group exhibn, Staithes Gall., Nottingham, and Scarborough Art Gall., 1994. Extensive experimental ceramic work, 1980–. British Representative Speaker, International Design Conference, Karachi, 1962. Print selected by Royal Soc. of Painter Etchers for Presentation to Print Collections Club, 1947. Mem. of Senefelder Club, 1947. Picture purchased by British Council, 1948. *Publications:* etchings published in Fine Prints of the Year, 1935, 1936, 1937, and in 1939 and 1940 issues of Print Collectors Quarterly. *Address:* Linton Springs Farm, Sicklinghall Road, near Wetherby, W Yorks LS22 4AQ. *T:* Wetherby (01937) 588143.

TAYLOR, Frank, CBE 1969; QFSM 1965; fire consultant; Chief Fire Officer, Merseyside County Fire Brigade, 1974–76, retired (Liverpool Fire Brigade, 1962–74); *b* 6 April 1915; *s* of Percy and Beatrice Taylor; *m* 1940, Nancy (*née* Hefford); two *s* two *d*; *m* 1976, Florence Mary Latham. *Educ:* Council Sch., Sheffield. Fireman, Sheffield Fire Bde,

1935–41; Instr, NFS West Riding, 1941–42; Company Officer up to Station Officer (ops), NFS in Yorkshire, 1942–49; Chief Officer, Western Fire Authority, NI, 1949–51; Divl Officer NI Fire Authority, 1951–57; Belfast: Dep. Chief Officer, 1958–60; Chief Officer, 1960–62. *Recreations:* football, gardening. *Address:* Onchan, Hall Lane, Wrightington, near Wigan, Lancs WN6 9EQ.

TAYLOR, Dr Frank; Deputy Director and Principal Keeper, The John Rylands University Library of Manchester, 1972–77; Hon. Lecturer in Manuscript Studies, University of Manchester, 1967–77. *Educ:* Univ. of Manchester (MA, PhD). FSA. Served with RN, 1942–46: Lieut, RNVR, 1943–46. Research for Cttee on History of Parlt, 1934–35; Keeper of Western Manuscripts, 1935–49, Keeper of Manuscripts, 1949–72, Librarian, 1970–72, John Rylands Library. Jt. Hon. Sec., Lancs Parish Record Soc., 1937–56, Hon. Sec., 1956–82; Registrar of Research, Soc. of Architectural Historians, 1978–82. Member: British Acad. Oriental Documents Cttee, 1974–80; British Acad. Medieval Latin Dictionary Cttee, 1973–83. Editor, Bulletin of the John Rylands Univ. Lib. of Manchester, 1948–87. *Publications:* various Calendars of Western Manuscripts and Charter Room collections in the Rylands Library, 1937–77; The Chronicle of John Strecche for the Reign of Henry 5, 1932; An Early Seventeenth Century Calendar of Records Preserved in Westminster Palace Treasury, 1939; The Parish Registers of Aughton, 1541–1764, 1942; contrib. to Some Twentieth Century Interpretations of Boswell's Life of Johnson (ed J. L. Clifford), 1970; The Oriental Manuscript Collections in the John Rylands Library, 1972; (ed with J. S. Roskell) Gesta Henrici Quinti, 1975; (with G. A. Matheson) Hand-List of Personal Papers from the Muniments of the Earl of Crawford and Balcarres, 1976; revised edn of M. R. James's Descriptive Catalogue of Latin Manuscripts in the John Rylands Library (1921), 1980; (ed) Society of Architectural Historians, Research Register No 5, 1981; The John Rylands University Library of Manchester, 1982; articles in Bulletin of John Rylands Library, Indian Archives.

TAYLOR, Frank Henry; Principal, Frank H. Taylor & Co., City of London, Chartered Accountants; *b* 10 Oct. 1907; 2nd *s* of George Henry Taylor, Cambridgeshire; *m* 1936, Margaret Dora Mackay (*d* 1944), Invernesshire; one *d*; *m* 1948, Mabel Hills (*d* 1974), Hertfordshire; two *s*; *m* 1978, Glenys Mary Edwards, MBE, Bethesda, N Wales. *Educ:* Rutlish School, Merton, Surrey, FCIS 1929; FCA 1930. Commenced in practice as Chartered Accountant, 1930; Ministry of Food Finance Director of Tea, Coffee, Cocoa and Yeast, 1942; Min. of War Transport Finance Rep. overseas, 1944; visited over 40 countries on financial and political missions. Lt-Colonel comdg 1st Caernarvonshire Bn Home Guard, 1943. Contested (C) Newcastle under Lyme, 1955, Chorley, 1959; MP (C) Manchester, Moss Side, Nov. 1961–Feb. 1974. Mem. Council, London World Trade Centre, 1982–. Governor of Rutlish School, 1951–89. Liveryman, City of London. Master, Bakers' Co., 1981–82; Mem., GAPAN. *Publication:* Called to Account (autobiog.), 1993. *Recreations:* numerous including Rugby (for Surrey County), sculling (Thames Championship), punting (several Thames championships), golf (Captain RAC 1962). *Address:* 4 Barrie House, Lancaster Gate, W2 3QJ. *T:* 0171–262 5684. *Clubs:* City Livery, Royal Automobile, British Sportsman's, Dinosaurs.

TAYLOR, Dr Frank Henry; Director, Libraries, Books and Information Division, British Council, 1990–92; *b* 20 Jan. 1932; *s* of Frank Taylor and Norah (*née* Dunn). *Educ:* Frimley and Camberley Co. Grammar Sch.; King's Coll., London (BSc 1953; PhD 1957). Beit Meml Fellow for Med. Res., Imperial Coll., London and Pasteur Inst., Paris, 1957–60; British Council, 1960–92: Science Officer, 1960–61; Asst Cultural Attaché, Cairo, 1961–64; Asst Regl Rep., Calcutta, 1965–69; Science Officer, Rio de Janeiro, 1970–74; Dir, Science and Technology Dept, 1974–78; Rep., Saudi Arabia, 1978–81; Head Operations, Technical Educn and Trng in Overseas Countries, and Dep. Controller, Science, Technology and Education Div., 1981–84; Counsellor, British Council and Cultural Affairs, Ankara, 1984–87; Dep. Controller, Asia and Pacific Div., then S and W Asia Div., 1987–88; Controller, Africa and ME Div., 1989–90. *Publications:* articles on surface chemistry and reviews in Proc. Royal Soc., etc. *Recreations:* music, bridge, travel, Middle East. *Address:* c/o British Council, 10 Spring Gardens, SW1A 2BN. *T:* 071–930 8466.

TAYLOR, Prof. Fredric William, DPhil; Professor of Atmospheric Physics, since 1990, Head of Department, since 1979, Oxford University; Fellow, Jesus College, Oxford, since 1979; *b* 24 Sept. 1944; *s* of William Taylor and Ena Lloyd (*née* Burns); *m* 1969, Doris Jean Buer. *Educ:* Duke of Northumberland's Sch.; Univ. of Liverpool (BSc 1966): Univ. of Oxford (DPhil 1970; MA 1983). Resident Res. Associate, US Nat. Res. Council, 1970–72; Sen. Scientist, Jet Propulsion Lab., CIT, 1972–79; Reader in Atmospheric Physics, Oxford Univ., 1983–89. *Publications:* Cambridge Atlas of the Planets, 1982, 2nd edn 1986 (trans. German 1984, Italian 1988); Remote Sounding of Atmospheres, 1984, 2nd edn 1987; contrib. to learned jls. *Recreations:* walking, theatre, poker, literature, history, railways. *Address:* Clarendon Laboratory, Oxford OX1 3PU; Jesus College, Oxford OX1 3DW. *T:* Oxford (01865) 272903.

TAYLOR, Geoffrey H.; *see* Handley-Taylor.

TAYLOR, Geoffrey William, FCIB; Director, Daiwa Europe Bank PLC, since 1987 (Chairman, 1987–93); *b* 4 Feb. 1927; *s* of late Joseph William and Doris Taylor; *m* 1951, Joyce (*née* Walker); three *s* one *d*. *Educ:* Heckmondwike Grammar School; Univ. of London. BComm. Joined Midland Bank Ltd, 1943; Gen. Man. and Man. Dir, Midland Bank Finance Corp. Ltd, 1967–76; Asst Chief General Manager, 1974–80, Dep. Group Chief Exec., 1980–82, Group Chief Exec., 1982–86, Dir, 1982–87, Vice-Chm., 1986–87, Midland Bank Plc. Dir, Y. J. Lovell (Hldgs) PLC, 1987–; Chm., Foster Brother Meanswear Ltd, 1992–. Member: Internat. Adv. Council, Wells Fargo & Co., 1987–; Internat. Adv. Bd, Govt of Malta, 1989–. Mem., Banking Law Review, (Jack), Cttee, 1987–90. *Recreations:* golf, reading, music. *Address:* c/o Liberty Capital Ltd, 46 New Broad Street, EC2M 1JD. *Clubs:* City of London; Burhill Golf.

TAYLOR, Sir Godfrey; *see* Taylor, Sir A. G.

TAYLOR, Gordon; Chief Executive, Professional Footballers' Association, since 1981; *b* 28 Dec. 1944; *s* of Alec and Mary Taylor; *m* 1968, Catharine Margaret Johnston; two *s*. *Educ:* Ashton-under-Lyne Grammar Sch.; Bolton Technical Coll.; Univ. of London (BScEcon Hons (ext.)). Professional footballer with: Bolton Wanderers, 1960–70; Birmingham City, 1970–76; Blackburn Rovers, 1976–78; Vancouver Whitecaps (N American Soccer League), 1977; Bury, 1978–80, retd. Professional Footballers Association: Mem., Management Cttee, 1971; Chm., 1978–80; (full-time) Asst Sec., 1980; Sec./Treasurer, 1981. Hon. MA Loughborough Univ. of Technol., 1986 (for services to football). *Recreations:* theatre, dining-out, squash, watching football, reading. *Address:* (office) 2 Oxford Court, Bishopsgate, Manchester M2 3WQ. *T:* 0161–236 0575.

TAYLOR, Dr Gordon William; Managing Director, Firemarket Ltd, since 1988; *b* 26 June 1928; *s* of William and Elizabeth Taylor; *m* 1954, Audrey Catherine Bull; three *s* two *d*. *Educ:* J. H. Burrows Sch., Grays, Essex; Army Apprentice Sch.; London Univ. (BScEng Hons, PhDEng). MICE, MIMechE, AMIEE, MIBC. Kellogg Internat. Corp., 1954–59; W. R. Grace, 1960–62; Gen. Man., Nalco Ltd, 1962–66; BTR Industries, 1966–68; Managing Director: Kestrel Chemicals, 1968–69; Astral Marketing, 1969–70; Robson Refractories, 1970–87. Greater London Council: Alderman, 1972–77; Mem. for Croydon Central, 1977–80; Chairman: Public Services Cttee, 1977–78; London Transp. Cttee, 1978–79. *Recreations:* theatre, reading, tennis. *Address:* 33 Royal Avenue, Chelsea, SW3 4QE. *Club:* Holland Park Lawn Tennis.

TAYLOR, Graham; Manager, Wolverhampton Wanderers Football Club, since 1994; *b* Worksop, Notts, 15 Sept. 1944; *s* of Tommy Taylor; *m* 1965, Rita Cowling; two *d*. *Educ:* Scunthorpe Grammar Sch. Professional football player: Grimsby Town, 1963–68; Lincoln City, 1968–72; Manager: Lincoln City, 1972–77; Watford, 1977–87; Aston Villa, 1987–90; England Football Team, 1990–93. *Address:* c/o Wolverhampton Wanderers Football Club, Molineux Stadium, Waterloo Road, Wolverhampton WV1 4QR.

TAYLOR, Harold McCarter, CBE 1955; TD 1945; retired, 1967; *b* Dunedin, New Zealand, 13 May 1907; *s* of late James Taylor, and late Louisa Urquhart Taylor; *m* 1st, 1933, Joan (*d* 1965), *d* of late George Reginald Sills, Lincoln; two *s* two *d*; 2nd, 1966, Dorothy Judith, *d* of late Charles Samuel, Liverpool. *Educ:* Otago Boys' High School and Univ. of Otago, NZ; Clare Coll., Cambridge. MSc New Zealand, 1928; MA, PhD Cambridge, 1933. Allen Scholar and Smith's Prizeman, 1932. Fellow of Clare College, Cambridge, 1933–61; Hon. Fellow, 1961–; Lecturer in Mathematics, University of Cambridge, 1934–45; Treasurer of the University, 1945–53; Secretary General of the Faculties, 1953–61; Vice-Chancellor, University of Keele, 1962–67 (Principal, University College of North Staffordshire, 1961–62); Rede Lecturer, Cambridge University, 1966. Mem., Royal Commn on Historical Monuments (England), 1972–78. Pres., Royal Archaeol Inst., 1972–75; Vice-Pres., Soc. of Antiquaries of London, 1974–77 (Frend Medal, 1981). Hon. LLD Cambridge, 1967; Hon. DLitt: Keele, 1968; Birmingham, 1983. Commissioned in TA, NZ, 1925; served War of 1939–45 as Major and Lieut-Col RA; Instructor and Senior Instructor in Gunnery at School of Artillery, Larkhill; J. H. Lefroy Medal, RA, 1946. *Publications:* Anglo-Saxon Architecture, vols I and II (with Joan Taylor), 1965, vol. III, 1978; many articles in nat. and county archaeological jls. *Recreations:* mountaineering and ski-ing; Anglo-Saxon art and architecture; photography. *Address:* 192 Huntingdon Road, Cambridge CB3 0LB. *T:* Cambridge (01223) 276324.

TAYLOR, Henry George, DSc(Eng); Director of Electrical Research Association, 1957–69, retired; *b* 4 Nov. 1904; *m* 1931, Gwendolyn Hilda Adams; one *s* two *d*. *Educ:* Taunton School; Battersea Polytechnic Inst., City and Guilds Engineering College. Metropolitan Vickers, 1929–30; Electrical Research Assoc., 1930–38; Copper Development Assoc., 1938–42; Philips Lamps Ltd, 1942–47; British Welding Research Assoc., 1947–57. *Publications:* contribs to: Instn of Electrical Engineers Jl, Jl of Inst. of Physics, etc. *Recreation:* walking.

TAYLOR, Hermon, MA, MD, MChir, FRCS; retired; formerly Consulting Surgeon: London Hospital, E1; King George Hospital, Ilford; *b* 11 May 1905; *s* of Enoch Oliver Taylor and L. M. Taylor (*née* Harrison); *m* 1st, 1932, Méarie Amélie Pearson (*d* 1981); three *s* two *d*; 2nd, 1983, Mrs Noreen Cooke. *Educ:* Latymer School, Edmonton; St John's Coll., Cambridge (scholar); St Bartholomew's Hospital (Entrance Scholar). BA 1926; MRCS, LRCP 1929; MB, ChB Cantab. 1930; FRCS Eng. 1930. House Surgeon, Demonstr of Pathology, St Bart's Hosp.; Res. Surgical Officer: Hertford Co. Hosp., Lincoln Co. Hosp.; Surgical Registrar, Prince of Wales' Hosp., Tottenham. MChir Cantab 1932; MD Cantab 1934; Horton Smith Prize, Univ. Cantab; Luther Holden Research Scholar, St Bartholomew's Hospital; BMA Research Scholar, Surgical First Assistant London Hospital. Moynihan Fellow, Assoc. of Surgeons of GB and Ireland; Hunterian Professor, RCS. Past President, British Society of Gastro-enterology; Hon. Member Amer. Gastro-enterological Assoc. Hon. Fellow, London Hosp. Med. Coll., 1988. *Publications:* Carcinoma of the Stomach, in Modern Trends in Gastro-Enterology, 1952; contrib. to BMJ, Lancet, etc, 1942–. *Address:* Coppice Field, Bosham Hoe, Chichester, West Sussex PO18 8ET. *T:* Chichester (01243) 573385. *Club:* Athenæum.

See also J. Hermon-Taylor.

TAYLOR, Hugh Henderson; Under Secretary and Head of Management Development Group, Cabinet Office, since 1993; *b* 22 March 1950; *s* of Leslie Henderson Taylor and Alison Taylor; *m* 1989, Diane Bacon; two *d*. *Educ:* Brentwood Sch.; Emmanuel Coll., Cambridge (BA). Joined Home Office, 1972; Private Sec. to Minister of State, 1976–77; Principal Private Sec. to Home Sec., 1983–85; Asst Sec., 1984; Prison Service, 1985–88 and 1992–93; seconded to Cabinet Office, 1988–91. *Recreations:* arts, sport. *Address:* c/o Office of Public Service and Science, Cabinet Office, Horse Guards Road, SW1P 3AL.

TAYLOR, Rt. Rev. Humphrey Vincent; *see* Selby, Bishop Suffragan of.

TAYLOR, Ian Colin, MBE 1974; MP (C) Esher, since 1987; Parliamentary Under-Secretary of State for Trade and Technology, Department of Trade and Industry, since 1994; *b* 18 April 1945; *s* of late Horace Stanley Taylor and Beryl Taylor (*née* Harper); *m* 1974, Hon. Carole Alport, *d* of Baron Alport, *qv*; two *s*. *Educ:* Whitley Abbey Sch., Coventry; Keele Univ. (BA); London School of Economics (Res. Schol.). Corporate financial adviser; Dir, Mathercourt Securities Ltd, 1980–90. Nat. Chm., Fedn of Cons. Students, 1968–69; Chm., Europ. Union of Christian Democratic and Cons. Students, 1969–70; Hon. Sec., Brit. Cons. Assoc. in France, 1976–78; Chairman: Commonwealth Youth Exchange Council, 1980–84; Cons. Foreign and Commonwealth Council, 1990–; Nat. Chm., Cons. Gp for Europe, 1985–88. Contested (C) Coventry SE, Feb. 1974. Parliamentary Private Secretary: FCO, 1990; to Sec. of State for Health, 1990–92; to Chancellor of Duchy of Lancaster, 1992–94. Mem., Select Cttee on Foreign Affairs, 1987–90; Chm., Cons. Parly European Affairs Cttee, 1988–89. Vice-Chm., Assoc. of Cons. Clubs, 1988–92. AIIMR, 1972; FInstD 1983; FRSA 1991. *Publications:* various pamphlets; contrib. to various jls, etc, on politics and business. *Recreations:* cricket, opera, lawnmowing, shooting. *Address:* House of Commons, SW1A 0AA. *T:* 0171–219 5221. *Clubs:* Carlton; Molesey Working Men's.

TAYLOR, Prof. Ian Galbraith, CBE 1987; Ellis Llwyd Jones Professor of Audiology and Education of the Deaf, University of Manchester, 1964–88, now Emeritus; *b* 24 April 1924; *s* of David Oswald Taylor, MD, and Margaret Ballantine Taylor; *m* 1954, Audrey Wolstenholme; two *d*. *Educ:* Manchester Grammar Sch.; Univ. of Manchester. MB, ChB, DPH Manchester; MD (Gold Medal) Manchester 1963; MRCP 1973; FRCP 1977. Ho. Surg., Manchester Royal Infirm., 1948; DAD, Army Health of N Regional Canal Zone, and OC Army Sch. of Hygiene, ME, 1949–51; Asst MO, City of Manchester, 1951–54. Univ. of Manchester: Hon. Special Lectr and Ewing Foundn Fellow, Dept of Education of the Deaf, 1956–60; Lectr in Clinical Audiology, 1963–64. Consultant in Audiological Medicine, United Manchester Hosps, 1968. Pres., Hearing Concern (formerly British Assoc. of the Hard of Hearing), 1981–. *Publication:* Neurological Mechanisms of Hearing and Speech in Children, 1964. *Recreations:* gardening, fishing. *Address:* Croft Cottage, The Beeches, Whitegate, near Northwich, Cheshire CW8 2BL.

TAYLOR, His Honour Ivor Ralph, QC 1973; a Circuit Judge, 1976–94; *b* 26 Oct. 1927; *s* of late Abraham and Ruth Taylor; *m* 1st, 1954, Ruth Cassel (marr. diss. 1974); one *s* one *d* (and one *d* decd); 3rd, 1984, (Audrey) Joyce Goldman (*née* Wayne). *Educ:* Stand

Grammar Sch., Whitefield; Manchester Univ. Served War of 1939–45, AC2 in RAF, 1945. Called to Bar, Gray's Inn, 1951. Standing Counsel to Inland Revenue, N Circuit, 1969–73; a Recorder of the Crown Court, 1972–76. Chm., Inquiry into Death of Baby Brown at Rochdale Infirmary, 1974. Chm., PTA, Dept of Audiology, Manchester Univ., 1966–67. Pres., Manchester and District Medico Legal Soc., 1974, 1975. Gov., Royal Manchester Children's Hosp., 1967–70; Mem. Management Cttee, Salford Hosp., 1967–70. *Recreations:* walking, indifferent golfing. *Address:* 5 Eagle Lodge, 19 Harrop Road, Hale, Altrincham, Cheshire WA15 9DA.

TAYLOR, Dame Jean (Elizabeth); *see* Dowling, Dame J. E.

TAYLOR, Jessie; *see* Taylor, M. J.

TAYLOR, Rt Rev. John Bernard; Bishop of St Albans, 1980–95; Lord High Almoner to HM the Queen, since 1988; *b* 6 May 1929; *s* of George Ernest and Gwendoline Irene Taylor; *m* 1956, Linda Courtenay Barnes; one *s* two *d. Educ:* Watford Grammar Sch.; Christ's Coll., Cambridge; Jesus Coll., Cambridge. MA Cantab. Vicar of Henham and Elsenham, Essex, 1959–64; Vice-Principal, Oak Hill Theological Coll., 1964–72; Vicar of All Saints', Woodford Wells, 1972–75; Archdeacon of West Ham, 1975–80. Examining Chaplain to Bishop of Chelmsford, 1962–80. Chm., Gen. Synod's Cttee for Communications, 1986–93. Member: Churches' Council for Covenanting, 1978–82; Liturgical Commn, 1981–86; Doctrine Commn, 1989–95. Chairman Council: Haileybury Coll., 1980–95; Wycliffe Hall, Oxford, 1985–. President: Hildenborough Evangelistic Trust, 1985–; Garden Tomb Assoc., Jerusalem, 1986–. Took his seat in House of Lords, 1985. *Publications:* A Christian's Guide to the Old Testament, 1966; Evangelism among Children and Young People, 1967; Tyndale Commentary on Ezekiel, 1969; Preaching through the Prophets, 1983; Preaching on God's Justice, 1994. *Address:* 22 Conduit Head Road, Cambridge CB3 0EY.

TAYLOR, Prof. John Bryan, FRS 1970; Fondren Professor of Plasma Theory, University of Texas at Austin, 1989–94; *b* 26 Dec. 1928; *s* of Frank and Ada Taylor, Birmingham; *m* 1951, Joan M. Hargest; one *s* one *d. Educ:* Oldbury Grammar Sch.; Birmingham Univ., 1947–50 and 1952–55. RAF, 1950–52. Atomic Weapons Research Establishment, Aldermaston, 1955–59 and 1960–62; Harkness Fellow, Commonwealth Fund, Univ. of California (Berkeley), 1959–60; Culham Laboratory (UKAEA), 1962–69 and 1970–89 (Head of Theoretical Physics Div., 1963–81; Chief Physicist, 1981–89); Inst. for Advanced Study, Princeton, 1969. FInstP 1969. Fellow, Amer. Phys. Soc., 1984. Maxwell Medal, IPPS, 1971; Max Born Medal, German Phys. Soc., 1979; Award for Excellence in Plasma Physics Res., Amer. Phys. Soc., 1986. *Publications:* contribs to scientific learned jls. *Recreations:* gliding, model engineering. *Address:* Radwinter, Winterbrook Lane, Wallingford OX10 9EJ. *T:* Wallingford (01491) 837269.

TAYLOR, John Charles; QC 1983; *b* 22 April 1931; *s* of late Sidney Herbert and Gertrude Florence Taylor, St Ives, Cambs; *m* 1964, Jean Aimée Monteith; one *d. Educ:* Palmers Sch., Grays, Essex; Queens' Coll., Cambridge (MA, LLB); Harvard Law School (LLM). Called to the Bar, Middle Temple, 1958. Mem., Stephens Cttee on Minerals Planning Control, 1972–74. Contested (C) Kettering, 1970. *Recreations:* country pursuits, art, boardsailing, motorcycling. *Address:* Clifton Grange, Clifton, Shefford, Beds SG17 5EW. *Clubs:* Athenæum, Travellers'.

TAYLOR, John Clayton, PhD; FRS 1981; Professor of Mathematical Physics, Cambridge University, and Fellow of Robinson College, Cambridge, 1980–95, now Fellow Emeritus; *b* 4 Aug. 1930; *s* of Leonard Taylor and Edith (*née* Tytherleigh); *m* 1959, Gillian Mary (*née* Schofield); two *s. Educ:* Selhurst Grammar Sch., Croydon; Cambridge Univ. (MA). Lectr, Imperial Coll., London, 1956–60; Lectr, Cambridge Univ., and Fellow of Peterhouse, 1960–64; Reader in Theoretical Physics, Oxford Univ., and Fellow of University Coll., Oxford, 1964–80 (Hon. Fellow, 1989). *Publication:* Gauge Theories of Weak Interactions, 1976. *Recreation:* pottering about. *Address:* 9 Bowers Croft, Cambridge CB1 4RP.

TAYLOR, John D.; *see* Debenham Taylor.

TAYLOR, Rt. Hon. John David, PC (N Ire.) 1970; MP (UU) Strangford, since 1983 (resigned seat Dec. 1985 in protest against Anglo-Irish Agreement; re-elected Jan. 1986); *b* 24 Dec. 1937; *er s* of George D. Taylor and Georgina Baird; *m* 1970, Mary Frances Todd; one *s* five *d. Educ:* Royal Sch., Armagh; Queen's Univ. of Belfast (BSc). CEng; AMInstHE, AMICEI. MP (UU) S Tyrone, NI Parlt, 1965–73; Mem. (UU), Fermanagh and S Tyrone, NI Assembly, 1973–75; Mem. (UU), North Down, NI Constitutional Convention, 1975–76; Parly Sec. to Min. of Home Affairs, 1969–70; Minister of State, Min. of Home Affairs, 1970–72; Mem. (UU), North Down, NI Assembly, 1982–86. Mem. (UU) NI, Europ. Parlt, 1979–89. Partner, G. D. Taylor and Associates, Architects and Civil Engineers, 1966–74; Director: West Ulster Estates Ltd, 1968–; Bramley Apple Restaurant Ltd, 1974–; West Ulster Hotels Co. Ltd, 1976–86; Gosford Housing Assoc. Ltd, 1977–; Tontine Rooms Ltd, 1978–; Ulster Gazette (Armagh) Ltd, 1983–; Cerdac (Belfast) Ltd, 1986–; Tyrone Printing Co. Ltd, 1986–; Tyrone Courier Ltd, 1986–; Sovereign Properties (NI) Ltd, 1989–; Carrickfergus Advertiser Ltd, 1992–. *Publication:* (jtly) Ulster—the facts, 1982. *Recreation:* foreign travel. *Address:* Mullinure, Portadown Road, Armagh, Northern Ireland BT61 9EL. *T:* Armagh (01861) 522409, 0171–931 7211. *Clubs:* Farmers'; Armagh County (Armagh).

TAYLOR, John Derek, CBE 1992; Vice President, National Union of Conservative Associations, since 1994; *b* 12 Nov. 1943; *s* of Percy Otto Taylor and Ethel Taylor (*née* Brocklehurst); *m* 1968, Julia Aileen Cunnington, *d* of late Leslie and Evelyn Cunnington, Bedford; two *s. Educ:* Holbeach Primary Sch.; St Felix Sch., Felixstowe; Bedford Sch. Dir, family horticultural and farming businesses, 1968–. Director: Springfields Horticl Soc. Ltd, 1990–; Publicity for British Bulbs Ltd, 1990–. Chairman: EC Working Party on European Bulb Industry, 1982; NFU Bulb Sub-cttee, 1982–87. Governor: Glasshouse Crops Res. Inst., 1984–88; Inst. of Horticl Res., 1987–90; Mem., Horticl Develt Council, 1986–91. Member, Minister of Agriculture's Regional Panel: Eastern Reg., 1990–92; E Midlands Reg., 1992–. Chm., Holbeach and E Elloe Hosp. Charitable Trust, 1989–. Mem., Lincoln Diocesan Bd of Finance, 1995–. East Midlands Conservative Council: Mem., Exec. Cttee, 1966–; Hon. Treas., 1984–89; Chm., 1989–94; Mem., Cons. Bd of Finance, 1985–89; National Union of Conservative Associations: Member: Exec. Cttee, 1966–68 and 1984–; Gen. Purposes Cttee, 1988–; Standing Rev. Cttee, 1988–; Agents Employment Adv. Cttee, 1988–94; Agents Exam Bd, 1994–. Founder Chm., local Young Cons. Br., 1964; Mem., Holland with Boston Cons. Assoc., 1964–95 (formerly Treas., Vice Chm., Chm. and Pres.); Pres., S Holland and The Deepings Cons. Assoc., 1995–. Contested (C): Chesterfield, Feb. and Oct. 1974; Nottingham, EP elections, 1979. Editor, In Touch with the National Union, 1993–. FRSA 1994. *Publication:* (ed) Taylor's Bulb Book, 1994. *Recreations:* English landscape and vernacular buildings, travel, particularly in France, literature, arts, music. *Address:* The Manor, Washway Road, Holbeach, Lincs PE12 7PP. *Club:* Farmers'.

TAYLOR, Prof. John Gerald; Professor of Mathematics, King's College, University of London, since 1971; *b* 18 Aug. 1931; *s* of William and Elsie Taylor; *m* Pamela Nancy (*née* Cutmore); two *s* three *d. Educ:* King Edward VI Grammar Sch., Chelmsford; Mid-Essex Polytechnic, Chelmsford; Christ's Coll., Cambridge. Fellow, Inst. for Advanced Study, Princeton, NJ, USA, 1956–58 (Mem., 1961–63); Fellow, Christ's Coll., Cambridge, 1958–60; Asst Lectr, Faculty of Mathematics, Univ. of Cambridge, 1959–60. Dir, Centre for Neural Networks, KCL, 1990–. Member: Inst. des Hautes Etudes Scient., Paris, 1960; Res. Inst. Advanced Study, Baltimore, Md, USA, 1960. Sen. Res. Fellow, Churchill Coll., Cambridge, 1963–64; Prof. of Physics, Rutgers Univ., New Brunswick, NJ, 1964–66; Fellow, Hertford Coll., Oxford, and Lectr, Math. Inst., Oxford, 1966–67; Reader in Particles and Fields, Queen Mary Coll., London, 1967–69; Prof. of Physics, Univ. of Southampton, 1969–71. Chm., 1982–87, Vice-Chm., 1988–, Mathematical Physics Gp, Inst. of Physics. Chm., Jt European Neural Net Initiative, 1990–91; Convener, British Neural Networks Soc., 1989–; President: European Neural Network Soc., 1993– (Vice-Pres., 1991–93); Internat. Neural Network Soc., 1995–; Dir, NEURONET EC Networks of Excellence in Neural Networks, 1994–. European Editor-in-Chief, Neural Networks, 1991–. *Publications:* Quantum Mechanics, an Introduction, 1969; The Shape of Minds to Come, 1970; The New Physics, 1972; Black Holes: the end of the Universe?, 1973; Superminds, 1975; Special Relativity, 1975; Science and the Supernatural, 1980; The Horizons of Knowledge, 1982; Finite Superstrings, 1992; The Promise of Neural Networks, 1993; When the Clock Struck Zero, 1994; *edited:* Supergravity, 1981; Supersymmetry and Supergravity, 1982; Tributes to Paul Dirac, 1987; Recent Developments in Neural Computation, 1990; Coupled Oscillating Neurons, 1992; Theory and Applications of Neural Networks, 1992; also scientific papers in Proc. Royal Soc., Phys. Rev., Proc. Camb. Phil. Soc., Jl Math. Phys. etc. *Recreations:* listening to music, walking. *Address:* 33 Meredyth Road, Barnes, SW13 0DS. *T:* 0181–876 3391.

TAYLOR, John H.; *see* Hermon-Taylor.

TAYLOR, Sir John Lang, (Sir Jock Taylor), KCMG 1979 (CMG 1974); HM Diplomatic Service, retired; Chairman: Klöckner INA Industrial Plants Ltd, since 1985; Siemens Ltd, since 1986; Director, Schering Holdings Ltd, since 1986; *b* 3 Aug. 1924; *y s* of Sir John William Taylor, KBE, CMG; *m* 1952, Molly, *o d* of James Rushworth; five *s* three *d. Educ:* Prague; Vienna; Imperial Services Coll., Windsor; Baltimore Polytechnic Inst., Md; Cornell Univ.; Trinity Coll., Cambridge. RAFVR, 1944–47 (Flt-Lt 1946). Joined HM Foreign (now Diplomatic) Service, 1949; served in: FO, 1949–50 and 1957–60; Saigon, 1950–52; Hanoi, 1951; Beirut, 1952–55; Prague, 1955–57; Montevideo, 1960–64; Bonn, 1964–69; Minister (Commercial), Buenos Aires, 1969–71; RCDS, 1972; Head of Industry, Science and Energy Dept, FCO, 1972–73; Asst Under-Sec. of State, FCO, 1973–74; Under-Sec., Dept of Energy, 1974–75; Ambassador to: Venezuela, 1975–79; the Netherlands, 1979–81; FRG, 1981–84. Chm., Latin Amer. Trade Adv. Gp, BOTB, 1986–89. Vice-Chm., Hispanic and Luso-Brazilian Councils (Canning House), 1987; Trustee, Anglo-German Foundn for the Study of Industrial Soc., 1988. *Address:* The Old Flint, Boxgrove, near Chichester, W Sussex. *Club:* Travellers'.

TAYLOR, John Mark; MP (C) Solihull, since 1983; Parliamentary Secretary, Lord Chancellor's Department, since 1992; *b* 19 Aug. 1941; *s* of Wilfred and Eileen Martha Taylor. *Educ:* Eversfield Prep. School; Bromsgrove School and College of Law. Admitted Solicitor, 1966; Senior Partner, John Taylor & Co., 1983–88. Member: Solihull County Borough Council, 1971–74; W Midlands Metropolitan County Council, 1973–86 (Opposition (Conservative) Leader, 1975–77; Leader, 1977–79). PPS to Chancellor of Duchy of Lancaster and Minister for Trade and Industry, 1987–88; an Asst Govt Whip, 1988–89; a Lord Comr of HM Treasury (Govt Whip), 1989–90; Vice Chamberlain of HM Household, 1990–92. Mem., Select Cttee on the Environment, 1983–87; Sec., Cons. Back-bench Cttee on Eur. Affairs, 1983–86 (Vice-Chm., 1986–87); Vice-Chm., Cons. Back-bench Cttee on Sport, 1986–87. Vice-Pres., AMA, 1979– (Dep. Chm., 1978–79). Mem., W Midlands Economic Planning Council, 1978–79; Governor, Univ. of Birmingham, 1977–81. Contested (C) Dudley East, Feb. and Oct. 1974. Mem. (C) Midlands E, European Parlt, 1979–84; European Democratic Group spokesman on Community Budget, 1979–81, Group Dep. Chm., 1981–82. *Recreations:* fellowship, cricket, golf, reading. *Address:* Northampton House, Poplar Road, Solihull, West Midlands B91 3AW. *T:* (office) 0121–704 3071. *Clubs:* Carlton, MCC.

TAYLOR, (John) Martin; Chief Executive, Barclays Bank, since 1994; *b* 8 June 1952; *m* 1976, Janet Davey; two *d. Educ:* Eton; Balliol Coll., Oxford. Reuters, 1974–78; Financial Times, 1978–82; Courtaulds plc, 1982–90 (Dir, 1987–90); Courtaulds Textiles plc, 1990–93 (Chief Exec., 1990–93; Chm., 1993). *Address:* Barclays Bank, 54 Lombard Street, EC3P 3AH.

TAYLOR, Rt. Rev. John Mitchell; *see* Glasgow and Galloway, Bishop of.

TAYLOR, John Russell; Art Critic, The Times, since 1978; *b* 19 June 1935; *s* of Arthur Russell and Kathleen Mary Taylor (*née* Picker). *Educ:* Dover Grammar Sch.; Jesus Coll., Cambridge (MA); Courtauld Inst. of Art, London. Sub-Editor, Times Educational Supplement, 1959; Editorial Asst, Times Literary Supplement, 1960; Film Critic, The Times, 1962–73. Lectr on Film, Tufts Univ. in London, 1970–71; Prof., Div. of Cinema, Univ. of Southern California, 1972–78. Editor, Films and Filming, 1983–90. *Publications:* Anger and After, 1962; Anatomy of a Television Play, 1962; Cinema Eye, Cinema Ear, 1964; Penguin Dictionary of the Theatre, 1966; The Art Nouveau Book in Britain, 1966; The Rise and Fall of the Well-Made Play, 1967; The Art Dealers, 1969; Harold Pinter, 1969; The Hollywood Musical, 1971; The Second Wave, 1971; David Storey, 1974; Directors and Directions, 1975; Peter Shaffer, 1975; Hitch, 1978; The Revels History of Drama in English, vol. VII, 1978; Impressionism, 1981; Strangers in Paradise, 1983; Ingrid Bergman, 1983; Alec Guinness, 1984; Vivien Leigh, 1984; Portraits of the British Cinema, 1985; Hollywood 1940s, 1985; Orson Welles, 1986; Edward Wolfe, 1986; Great Movie Moments, 1987; Post-war Friends, 1987; Robin Tanner, 1989; Bernard Meninsky, 1990; Impressionist Dreams, 1990; Liz Taylor, 1991; Ricardo Cinalli, 1993; Igor Mitoraj, 1993; Muriel Pemberton, 1993; Claude Monet, 1995. *Address:* c/o The Times, 1 Pennington Street, E1 9XN.

TAYLOR, Rt. Rev. John Vernon; *b* 11 Sept. 1914; *s* of late Bishop J. R. S. Taylor and Margaret Irene Taylor (*née* Garrett); *m* 1940, Margaret Wright; one *s* two *d. Educ:* St Lawrence Coll., Ramsgate; Trinity Coll., Cambridge (Hon. Fellow, 1987); St Catherine's Soc., Oxford; Wycliffe Hall, Oxford; Institute of Education, London. Curate, All Souls, Langham Place, W1, 1938–40; Curate in Charge, St Andrew's Church, St Helens, Lancs, 1940–43; Warden, Bishop Tucker College, Mukono, Uganda, 1945–54; Research Worker, Internat. Missionary Council, 1955–59; Africa Sec., CMS, 1959–63; Gen. Sec., CMS, 1963–74; Bishop of Winchester, 1975–85. Chm., Doctrine Commn of C of E, 1978–85. Examng Chap. to Bishop of Truro, 1974–75. Hon. Canon of Namirembe Cathedral, 1963–74. Hon. Fellow: New Coll., Oxford, 1985; Magdalen Coll., Oxford, 1986; Selly Oak Colls, Birmingham, 1987; Trinity Coll., Cambridge, 1988. Hon. DD Wycliffe Coll., Toronto, 1964; Hon. DLitt CNAA, 1991. *Publications:* Man in the Midst, 1955; Christianity and Politics in Africa, 1957; The Growth of the Church in Buganda, 1958; African Passion, 1958; Christians of the Copperbelt, 1961; The Primal Vision, 1963; For All the World, 1966; Change of Address, 1968; The Go-Between God, 1972; Enough is Enough, 1975; Weep not for Me, 1986; A Matter of Life and Death, 1986; Kingdom

Come, 1989; A Christmas Sequence and Other Poems, 1989; The Christlike God, 1992. *Recreations:* theatre, music. *Address:* 65 Aston Street, Oxford OX4 1EW. *T:* Oxford (01865) 248502.

TAYLOR, John William Ransom, OBE 1991; author; Editor Emeritus, Jane's All the World's Aircraft, since 1990; *b* 8 June 1922; *s* of late Victor Charles Taylor and late Florence Hilda Taylor (*née* Ransom); *m* 1946, Doris Alice Haddrick; one *s* one *d*. *Educ:* Ely Cathedral Choir Sch.; Soham Grammar Sch., Cambs. FRAeS, FRHistS, AFAIAA. Design Dept, Hawker Aircraft Ltd, 1941–47; Editorial Publicity Officer, Fairey Aviation Gp, 1947–55; Jane's All the World's Aircraft: Editl Asst, 1955; Asst Compiler, 1956–59; Editor, 1959–84; Editor-in-Chief, 1985–89. Air Corresp., Meccano Magazine, 1943–72; Editor, Air BP Magazine, British Petroleum, 1956–72; Jt Editor, Guinness Book of Air Facts and Feats, 1974–83; Contributing Editor: Air Force Magazine (USA), 1971–; Jane's Defence Weekly (formerly Jane's Defence Review), 1980–87; Specialist Correspondent, Jane's Intelligence Review (formerly Soviet Intelligence Review), 1989–. Member: Académie Nat. de l'Air et de l'Espace, France, 1985–; CFS Assoc. (Hon. Mem., 1987–). Pres., Chiltern Aviation Soc.; Gov., Horse Rangers Assoc.; Vice-President: Guild of Aviation Artists; Croydon Airport Soc.; Surbiton Scout Assoc. Warden, Christ Church, Surbiton Hill, 1976–80. Freeman, 1983, Liveryman, 1987, GAPAN; Freeman, City of London, 1987. Hon. DEng Kingston, 1993. C. P. Robertson Memorial Trophy, 1959; Cert. of Honour, Commn of Bibliography, History and Arts, Aero Club de France, 1971; Order of Merit, World Aerospace Educn Organization, 1981; Tissandier Diploma, FAI, 1990; Lauren D. Lyman Award, Aviation Space Writers Assoc., USA, 1990. *Publications:* Spitfire, 1946; Aircraft Annual, 1949–75; Civil Aircraft Markings, 1950–78; Wings for Tomorrow, 1951; Military Aircraft Recognition, 1952–79; Civil Airliner Recognition, 1953–79; Picture History of Flight, 1955; Science in the Atomic Age, 1956; Rockets and Space Travel, 1956; Best Flying Stories, 1956; Jane's All the World's Aircraft, 1956–89; Helicopters Work Like This, 1957; Royal Air Force, 1957; Fleet Air Arm, 1957; Jet Planes Work Like This, 1957; Russian Aircraft, 1957; Rockets and Missiles, 1958; CFS, Birthplace of Air Power, 1958, rev. edn 1987; Rockets and Spacecraft Work Like This; British Airports, 1959; US Military Aircraft, 1959; Warplanes of the World, 1959, rev. as Military Aircraft of the World; BP Book of Flight Today, 1960; Combat Aircraft of the World, 1969; Westland 50, 1965; Pictorial History of the Royal Air Force, 3 vols 1968–71, rev. 1980; Aircraft Aircraft, 1967, 4th edn 1974; Encyclopaedia of World Aircraft, 1966; The Lore of Flight, 1971; Rockets and Missiles, 1971; Light Plane Recognition, 1970; Civil Aircraft of the World, 1970–79; British Civil Aircraft Register, 1971; (with M. J. H. Taylor) Missiles of the World, 1972–79; (with D. Mondey) Spies in the Sky, 1972; (with K. Munson) History of Aviation, 1973, 2nd edn, 1978; Jane's Aircraft Pocket Books, 1973–87; History of Aerial Warfare, 1974; (with S. H. H. Young) Passenger Aircraft and Airlines, 1975; Jets, 1976; (with M. J. H. Taylor) Helicopters of the World, 1976–79; (with Air Vice-Marshal R. A. Mason) Aircraft, Strategy and Operations of the Soviet Air Force, 1986; Soviet Wings, 1991. *Recreations:* historical studies, travel. *Address:* 36 Alexandra Drive, Surbiton, Surrey KT5 9AF. *T:* 0181–399 5435. *Clubs:* City Livery, Royal Aero, Royal Air Force (Hon.); Avro 504 (Manchester).

TAYLOR, Jonathan Francis; Chairman, Booker plc, since 1993 (Chief Executive, 1984–93); *b* 12 Aug. 1935; *s* of Sir Reginald Taylor, CMG and Lady Taylor; *m* 1965, Anthea Gail Proctor; three *s*. *Educ:* Winchester College; Corpus Christi College, Oxford (Schol.; BA Mod. Hist.; MA). Joined Booker, 1959; Chm., Agricultural Div., 1976–80; Dir, Booker plc, 1980; Pres., Ibec Inc. (USA), 1980–84; Dir, Arbor Acres Farm Inc., 1980– (Dep. Chm., 1985–90; Chm., 1990–). Director: Sifida Investment Bank, Geneva, 1978–90; Tate & Lyle, 1988–; MEPC, 1992–; Equitable Life Assurance Soc., 1995–; Chm., Ellis & Everard, 1993–. Mem., Adv. Council, UNIDO, 1986–93; Director: Foundn for Develt of Polish Agric., 1991–; Internat. Agribusiness Management Assoc., 1991– (Pres., 1993–94); Winrock Internat. Inst. for Agricl Develt (US), 1991–. Governor, SOAS, London Univ., 1988–90. Co-opted Curator, Bodleian Library, 1989–. *Recreations:* collecting water colours, ski-ing, travel. *Address:* Booker plc, Portland House, Stag Place, SW1E 5AY. *Clubs:* Travellers'; Knickerbocker (NY).

TAYLOR, Judy, (Julia Marie), (Judy Hough), MBE 1971; writer and publisher; *b* 12 Aug. 1932; adopted *d* of Gladys Spicer Taylor; *m* 1980, Richard Hough, *qv*. *Educ:* St Paul's Girls' Sch. Joined The Bodley Head, 1951, specialising in children's books; Director: The Bodley Head Ltd, 1967–84 (Dep. Man. Dir, 1971–80); Chatto, Bodley Head & Jonathan Cape Ltd, 1973–80; Chatto, Bodley Head & Jonathan Cape Australia Pty Ltd, 1977–80. Publishers Association: Chm., Children's Book Gp, 1969–72; Mem. Council, 1972–78; Member: Book Develt Council, 1973–76; Unicef Internat. Art Cttee, 1968–70, 1976, 1982–83; UK Unicef Greeting Card Cttee, 1982–85. Consultant to Penguin (formerly to Frederick Warne) on Beatrix Potter, 1981–87, 1989–92; Associate Dir, Weston Woods Inst., USA, 1984–; Consulting Ed., Reinhardt Books, 1988–93. Chm., Beatrix Potter Soc., 1990–; Mem., London Cttee, Volunteer Reading Help, 1993–. FRSA 1991. *Publications:* Sophie and Jack, 1982; Sophie and Jack Help Out, 1983; My First Year: a Beatrix Potter baby book, 1983; Sophie and Jack in the Snow, 1984; Beatrix Potter: artist, storyteller and countrywoman, 1986; Dudley and the Monster, 1986; Dudley Goes Flying, 1986; Dudley in a Jam, 1986; Dudley and the Strawberry Shake, 1986; That Naughty Rabbit: Beatrix Potter and Peter Rabbit, 1987; My Dog, 1987; My Cat, 1987; Dudley Bakes a Cake, 1988; Beatrix Potter and Hawkshead, 1988; Sophie and Jack in the Rain, 1989; Beatrix Potter and Hill Top, 1989; Beatrix Potter's Letters: a selection, 1989; (ed) Letters to Children from Beatrix Potter, 1992; (ed) So I Shall Tell You a Story: encounters with Beatrix Potter, 1993; The Choyce Letters: Beatrix Potter to Louie Choyce 1916–1943, 1994; numerous professional articles. *Recreations:* collecting early children's books, growing things. *Address:* 31 Meadowbank, Primrose Hill Road, NW3 3AY. *T:* 0171–722 5663, *Fax:* 0171–722 7750.

TAYLOR, Keith Breden, MA, DM; FRCP; Vice-Chancellor, St George's University School of Medicine, 1989–90, and since 1992; George de Forest Barnett Professor of Medicine, Stanford University, 1966–81 and 1982–89, now Emeritus; *b* 16 April 1924; *yr s* of Francis Henry Taylor and Florence (*née* Latham); *m* 1st, 1949, Ann Gaynor Hughes Jones (*d* 1971); three *s* one *d* (and one *s* decd); 2nd, 1972, Kym Williams (*d* 1992), Adelaide, Aust. *Educ:* King's College Sch., Wimbledon; Magdalen Coll., Oxford (Exhibnr; BA Hons Physiology 1946, BM BCh 1949). Member, SHAEF Nutrition Survey Team, 1945; RAMC (Major), 1951–53; Dir Gen., Health Educn Council, 1981–82. Late Hon. Consultant, Central Middlesex Hosp.; Mem., MRC Gastroenterology Research Unit; Asst in Nuffield Dept Clin. Med., Oxford. Radcliffe Travelling Fellow, 1953; Rockefeller Foundn Fellow, 1959; Guggenheim Fellow, 1971; Fogarty Sen. Fellow, USPHS, 1978–79. Cons., US National Insts of Health; Mem., USPHS Trng Grants Cttee in Gastroenterology and Nutrition, 1965–70; Chm., Stanford Univ. Cttee on Human Nutrition, 1974–81; Vis. Professorships include: Rochester, NY, 1966; Columbia-Presbyterian, NY, 1969; Univ. of Adelaide, 1971; Academic Medical Unit, Royal Free Hosp., 1978–79. *Publications:* contribs to scientific jls, also texts, espec. in biochemistry and physiology of vitamin B12, immunological and other aspects of gastrointestinal disease and nutrition. *Recreations:* theatre, tennis, walking, gardening. *Address:* The Chancellory, St George's University School of Medicine, PO Box 7, St George's, Grenada, West Indies. *Club:* Athenæum.

TAYLOR, Keith Henry, PhD; FEng; Chairman and Chief Executive, Esso UK plc, since 1993 (Managing Director, 1985–93); *b* 25 Oct. 1938; *s* of George Henry Philip Taylor and Vera May (*née* Jones); *m* 1964, Adelaide Lines; one *s* one *d*. *Educ:* King Edward VI Sch., Stratford upon Avon; Birmingham Univ. (BSc, PhD Chem. Engrg). FEng 1994. Joined Esso, 1964, holding variety of positions in Refining, Research, Marine and Planning Functions of Co., 1964–80; Division Operations Man., Exxon Co. USA, New Orleans, 1980; Production Man., Esso Exploration and Production UK Ltd, London, 1982; Exec. Asst to Chm., Exxon Corp., New York, 1984. Pres., UKOOA, 1988–89; Vice Pres., Inst. of Petroleum, 1991–; Mem., Offshore Industry Adv. Bd, 1989–. Mem. Bd, Lloyd's Register of Shipping, 1994–. Member: Adv. Council, Prince's Youth Business Trust, 1993–; Council, Inst. of Business Ethics, 1993–. Gov., NIESR, 1993–. FIChemE 1991 (Vice Pres., 1995–). *Address:* Esso House, Victoria Street, SW1E 5JW *T:* 0171–245 3294.

TAYLOR, Kenneth, OBE 1981; FEng, FIMechE, FIEE; FCIT; consultant on railway mechanical and electrical engineering; Director of Mechanical and Electrical Engineering, British Railways Board, 1977–82; *b* 29 Sept. 1921; *s* of Charles Taylor and Amy (*née* Booth); *m* 1945, Elsie Armitt; one *d*. *Educ:* Manchester Coll. of Technol. FIMechE, FIEE 1971; FCIT 1977; FEng 1981. Principal appts with British Railways: Electric Traction Engr, Manchester, 1956; Electrical Engr, LMR, 1963; Chief Mech. and Elec. Engr, LMR, 1970; Traction Engr, BR Bd HQ, 1971. *Recreations:* golf, gardening. *Address:* 137 Burley Lane, Quarndon, Derby DE22 5JS. *T:* Derby (01332) 550123.

TAYLOR, Prof. Kenneth MacDonald, MD; FRCSE, FRCSGlas; FSAScot; British Heart Foundation Professor of Cardiac Surgery, University of London, since 1983, and Professor and Chief of Cardiac Surgery, Royal Postgraduate Medical School, Hammersmith Hospital, since 1983; *b* 20 Oct. 1947; *s* of Hugh Baird Taylor and late Mary Taylor; *m* 1971, Christine Elizabeth (*née* Buchanan); one *s* one *d*. *Educ:* Jordanhill College School; Univ. of Glasgow (MB ChB, MD; Cullen Medal, 1968; Gairdner Medal, 1969; Allan Hird Prize, 1969). Univ. of Glasgow: Hall Fellow in Surgery, 1971–72, Lectr and Sen. Lectr in Cardiac Surgery, 1975–83; Consultant Cardiac Surgeon, Royal Infirmary and Western Infirmaries, Glasgow, 1979–83. Chm., Specialist Adv. Cttee in Cardiothoracic Surgery, 1992–95 (Mem., 1986–92); Dir, UK Heart Valve Registry, 1986–; Clin. Dir, UK Sch. of Perfusion Science, 1987–. Member: Exec. Cttee, Soc. of Cardiothoracic Surgeons of GB and Ire., 1992–95; Wkg Gp on Cardiac Waiting Times, DoH, 1994–95; Chairman: Database Cttee, European Assoc. for Cardiothoracic Surgery, 1994–; UK Cardiac Audit Steering Gp, 1994–. Member: British Cardiac Soc., 1983–; Amer. Soc. of Thoracic Surgeons, 1984–; Amer. Assoc. for Thoracic Surgery, 1988–; European Assoc. for Cardiothoracic Surgery, 1988–; Pres., Soc. of Perfusionists of GB and Ire., 1989–; Hon. Mem., Amer. Acad. of Cardiovascular Perfusion, 1993. Governor, Drayton Manor High Sch., London, 1989–. Editor, Perfusion, 1986–; Member, Advisory Editorial Board: Annals of Thoracic Surgery, 1990–; Jl of Cardiovascular Anaesthesia, 1993–; Jl of Heart Valve Disease, 1993–. Peter Allen Prize, Soc. of Thoracic and Cardiovascular Surgeons, 1975; Patey Prize, Surgical Res. Soc., 1977; Fletcher Prize, RCSG, 1977; Watson Prize, RCSG, 1982. *Publications:* Pulsatile Perfusion, 1979, 2nd edn 1982; Handbook of Intensive Care, 1984; Cardiopulmonary Bypass, 1986; Cardiac Surgery, 1987; Principles of Surgical Research, 1989, 2nd edn 1995; The Brain and Cardiac Surgery, 1992; numerous articles on cardiac surgery. *Recreations:* family, church, music. *Address:* 129 Argyle Road, Ealing, W13 0DB.

TAYLOR, Kim; *see* Taylor, L. C.

TAYLOR, Prof. Laurie, (Laurence John); Visiting Professor, Birkbeck College, University of London, since 1994; Professor of Sociology, University of York, 1974–93; *s* of Stanley Douglas Taylor and Winifred Agnes (*née* Cooper); marr. diss.; one *s*. *Educ:* St Mary's Coll., Liverpool; Rose Bruford College of Drama, Kent; Birkbeck Coll., Univ. of London (BA); Univ. of Leicester (MA). Librarian, 1952–54; Sales Asst, 1954–56; Professional Actor, 1960–61; English Teacher, 1961–64; Lectr in Sociology, 1965–73, Reader in Sociology, 1973–74, Univ. of York. *Publications:* Deviance and Society, 1971; (jtly) Psychological Survival, 1972; (jtly) Crime, Deviance and Socio-Legal Control, 1972; (ed jtly) Politics and Deviance, 1973; Man's Experience of the World, 1976; (jtly) Escape Attempts, 1976, 2nd edn 1992; (jtly) Prison Secrets, 1978; (jtly) In Whose Best Interests?, 1980; In the Underworld, 1984; (jtly) Uninvited Guests, 1986; Professor Lapping Sends His Apologies, 1987; The Tuesday Afternoon Time Immemorial Committee, 1989; Laurie Taylor's Guide to Higher Education, 1994; articles, reviews, broadcasts, TV series. *Address:* 42 Witley Court, Coram Street, WC1N 1HD. *T:* 0171–837 5996.

TAYLOR, Len Clive, (Kim); Director, Calouste Gulbenkian Foundation (UK Branch), 1982–88, retired; *b* 4 Aug. 1922; *s* of late S. R. Taylor, Calcutta, India; *m* 1951, Suzanne Dufault, Spencer, Massachusetts, USA; one *s* two *d*. *Educ:* Sevenoaks School; New College, Oxford; Chicago University. New College, Oxford; 1st Cl. Hons Mod. Hist.; Commonwealth Fund Fellowship. Assistant Master, St Paul's School, Darjeeling, India, 1940–42 and 1945–46; Indian Army Intelligence Corps, 1942–45; New College, Oxford, 1946–49; Chicago University, 1949–50; Senior History Master, Repton School, 1950–54; Headmaster, Sevenoaks School, 1954–68; Dir, Nuffield Foundn 'Resources for Learning' Project, 1966–72; Principal Administrator, Centre for Educnl Res. and Innovation, OECD, Paris, 1972–77; Head of Educnl Prog. Services, IBA, 1977–82. Comdr, Order of Henry the Navigator (Portugal), 1989. *Publications:* Experiments in Education at Sevenoaks, 1965; Resources for Learning, 1971. *Address:* 43 The Drive, Sevenoaks, Kent TN13 3AD. *T:* Sevenoaks (01732) 451448.

TAYLOR, Leon Eric Manners; Research Analyst; *b* 28 Oct. 1917; *s* of late Leon Eric Taylor and Veronica Dalmahoy (*née* Rogers); *m* 1963, Margaret Betty Thompson; no *c*. *Educ:* Fettes Coll., Edinburgh; Oriel Coll., Oxford. Captain RA (Service, 1939–46). Asst Principal, 1945, Principal, 1948, in Bd of Trade until 1963. First Sec., UK Delegn to the European Communities, 1963–66; Econ. Counsellor, British High Commn, Kuala Lumpur, 1966–70. Called to Bar, Inner Temple, 1951. Attended Joint Services Staff College, 1952. Hon. Visiting Fellow, Centre for Contemporary European Studies, University of Sussex, 1970–71; Counsellor (Commercial), The Hague, 1971–72; Research Fellow, Univ. of Sussex, 1973–75. *Recreations:* walking, amateur theatre, golf. *Address:* Sam's Hill Cottage, 47 North Street, Middle Barton, Chipping Norton, Oxon OX7 7BH. *T:* Steeple Aston (01869) 47256.

TAYLOR, Malcolm; *see* McDowell, M.

TAYLOR, (Margaret) Jessie, OBE 1989; Headmistress, Whalley Range High School for Girls, 1976–88; *b* 30 Nov. 1924; *d* of Thomas Brown Gowland and Ann Goldie Gowland; *m* 1958, Eric Taylor, *qv*. *Educ:* Queen Elizabeth's Grammar Sch., Middleton; Manchester Univ. (BA Hons, DipEd). Jun. Classics Teacher, Cheadle Hulme Sch., 1946–49; North Manchester Grammar School for Girls: Sen. Classics Teacher, 1950; Sen. Mistress, 1963; Actg Headmistress, Jan.–July 1967; Dep. Head Teacher, Wright Robinson Comprehensive High Sch., 1967–75. Voluntary worker, UNICEF, 1988–. Dir, Piccadilly Radio, 1979–. Chm., Manchester High Sch. Heads Gp, 1984–88; Member: Council and Exams Cttee, Associated Lancs Schs Examining Bd, 1976–91 (Mem. Classics Panel, 1968–72); Exams

Cttee, Northern Exams Assoc., 1988–92; Nursing Educn Cttee, S Manchester Area, 1976–84; Home Office Cttee on Obscenity and Film Censorship, 1977–79; Consultant Course Tutor, NW Educnl Management Centre, Padgate, 1980–82. Mem. Court, Salford Univ., 1982–88; Gov., William Hulme's Grammar Sch., 1989–. FRSA 1980. *Recreations:* music, riding. *Address:* 10 Mercers Road, Hopwood, Heywood, Lancs OL10 2NP. *T:* Heywood (01706) 366630.

TAYLOR, Mark Christopher; Director, Museums Association, since 1989; *b* 24 Nov. 1958; *s* of Norman and June Taylor; *m* 1989, Debra Howes; two *s* one *d*. *Educ:* Loughborough Grammar Sch.; Birmingham Univ. (BA Medieval and Modern Hist.); Leeds Poly. (postgrad. Hotel Management qualification). Hotel Management, Norfolk Capital Hotels, 1981–84; Conf. Manager, Museums Assoc., 1984–89. Mem. Council, Nat. Campaign for the Arts, 1990–. *Recreations:* sport, films, food. *Address:* Museums Association, 42 Clerkenwell Close, EC1R 0PA. *T:* 0171–250 1789.

TAYLOR, Martin; *see* Taylor, J. M.

TAYLOR, Martin Gibbeson, CBE 1993; FCA; Vice Chairman, Hanson plc, 1988–95; *b* 30 Jan. 1935; *s* of late Roy G. Taylor and Vera Constance (*née* Farmer); *m* 1960, Gunilla Chaterina Bryner; two *s*. *Educ:* Haileybury; St Catharine's Coll., Cambridge (MA 1962). Company Sec. and Asst, Dow Chemical, 1963–69; joined Hanson plc, 1969, Dir 1976–95. Chm., National Westminster Life Assce, 1992–; Non-executive Director: Vickers plc, 1986–; National Westminster Bank plc, 1990–; Securities Assoc., 1987–90; UGI plc, 1979–82. Confederation of British Industry: Mem. Council, 1981–; Mem., Companies Cttee, 1981–94 (Chm., 1990–94); City/Industry Task Force, 1987; Mem., President's Cttee, 1990–94; Mem., Steering Gp on Long Termism & Corporate Governance, 1990–92; Rep. on Takeover Panel. Industrial Develt Adv. Bd. Hon. Treas., Snapshot Appeal, Nat. Assoc. for Epilepsy. Governor, Mall Sch. Trust. *Recreations:* art, books, sport, theatre. *Address:* c/o 1 Grosvenor Place, SW1X 7JH. *T:* 0171–245 1245. *Club:* MCC.

TAYLOR, Matthew Owen John; MP Truro, since March 1987 (L 1987–88, Lib Dem since 1988); *b* 3 Jan. 1963; *s* of Ken Taylor and Jill Taylor (*née* Black). *Educ:* Treliske School, Truro; University College School; Lady Margaret Hall, Oxford (Scholar; BA Hons). Pres., Oxford Univ. Student Union, 1985–86. Economic policy researcher to Parly Liberal Party (attached to David Penhaligon, MP), 1986–87. Parly spokesman on energy, 1987–88, on local govt, 1988–89, on trade and industry, 1989–90, on educn, 1990–92, on citizen's charter, 1992–94, on environment, 1994–. Communications Chm. for Lib Dems, 1989–92; Lib Dem Chm. of Campaigns and Communications, 1992–94. *Address:* House of Commons, SW1A 0AA. *T:* 0171–219 6686.

TAYLOR, Rt. Rev. Maurice; *see* Galloway, Bishop of, (RC).

TAYLOR, Rev. Michael Hugh; JP; Director, Christian Aid, since 1985; *b* 8 Sept. 1936; *s* of Albert Ernest and Gwendoline Louisa Taylor; *m* 1960, Adèle May Dixon; two *s* one *d*. *Educ:* Northampton Grammar School; Univ. of Manchester (BA, BD, MA); Union Theological Seminary, NY (STM). Baptist Minister, N Shields, 1961–66, Birmingham Hall Green, 1966–69; Principal, Northern Baptist Coll., Manchester, 1970–85; Lectr, Univ. of Manchester, 1970–85. Chm., Assoc. of Protestant Devlt Agencies in Europe, 1991–94; Mem., WCC Commn on Sharing and Service, 1991–. JP Manchester, 1980. *Publications:* Variations on a Theme, 1973; Sermon on the Mount, 1982; (ed) Christians and the Future of Social Democracy, 1982; Learning to Care, 1983; Good for the Poor, 1990; Christianity and the Persistence of Poverty, 1991; contribs to books and jls. *Recreations:* walking, cooking, theatre. *Address:* c/o Christian Aid, PO Box 100, SE1 7RT.

TAYLOR, Neville, CB 1989; Principal Associate, Defence Public Affairs Consultants Ltd, since 1989; *b* 17 Nov. 1930; *y s* of late Frederick Taylor and of Lottie Taylor; *m* 1954, Margaret Ann, *y d* of late Thomas Bainbridge Vickers and Gladys Vickers; two *s*. *Educ:* Sir Joseph Williamson's Mathematical Sch., Rochester; Coll. of Commerce, Gillingham, Kent. Junior Reporter, Chatham News Group, 1947; Royal Signals, 1948–50; Journalism, 1950–58; Asst Information Officer, Admiralty, 1958; Information Officer (Press), Admiralty, 1960; Fleet Information Officer, Singapore, 1963; Chief Press Officer, MoD, 1966; Information Adviser to Nat. Economic Develt Office, 1968; Dep. Dir, Public Relns (Royal Navy), 1970; Head of Information, Min. of Agriculture, Fisheries and Food, 1971; Dep. Dir of Information, DoE, 1973–74, Dir of Information, 1974–79; Dir of Information, DHSS, 1979–82; Chief of Public Relations, MOD, 1982–85; Dir-Gen., COI and Hd of Govt Inf. Service, 1985–88. *Recreation:* fishing. *Address:* Crow Lane House, Crow Lane, Rochester, Kent ME1 1RF. *T:* Medway (01634) 842990.

TAYLOR, Nicholas George Frederick, CMG 1970; FIPR; Development Director, East Caribbean, Higgs & Hill (UK) Ltd, 1973–80; Chairman: Higgs & Hill (St Kitts) Ltd, 1973–80; West Indies General Insurance Co., since 1979; Caribbean (East) Currency Authority, 1983 (Director, since 1981); Director, Cariblue Hotels Ltd, St Lucia, since 1968; Local Adviser, Barclays Bank International, St Lucia, since 1974; *b* 14 Feb. 1917; 3rd *s* of Louis Joseph Taylor and Philipsie (*née* Phillip); *m* 1952, Morella Agnes, *e d* of George Duncan Pitcairn and Florence (*née* La Guerre); two *s* two *d*. *Educ:* St Mary's Coll., St Lucia; LSE, London; Gonville and Caius Coll., Cambridge. Clerk, various Depts, St Lucia, 1937–46; Asst Social Welfare Officer, 1948–49; Public Relations and Social Welfare Officer, 1949–54; District Officer, and Authorised Officer, Ordnance Area, St Lucia, 1954–57; Dep. Dir St Lucia Br., Red Cross Soc., 1956–57; Perm. Sec., Min. of Trade and Production, 1957–58 (acted Harbour Master in conjunction with substantive duties); Commn for W Indies in UK: Administrative Asst, 1959; Asst Sec.-Chief Community Development Officer, Migrants Services Div., 1961; Commn in UK for Eastern Caribbean Govts: Officer-in-Charge, 1962–63; Actg Comr, 1964–66; Comr for E Caribbean Govts in UK, 1967–73. Dir, St Lucia (Co-operative) Bank Ltd, 1973–74. Mem., Civil Service Appeals Bd, 1973–77. Vice-Chm. Commonwealth Assoc., Bexley, Crayford and Erith, 1965–67; a Patron, British-Caribbean Assoc., 1962–73. Member: West India Committee Executive, 1968–; Bd of Governors, Commonwealth Inst., 1968–73. Assoc. Mem. 1951, Mem. 1962, Fellow, 1973, (British) Inst. of Public Relations. Chairman: Central Library Bd, 1973–81, Nat. Insurance Scheme, 1979–81, St Lucia; Central Housing Authority, St Lucia, 1975–77; Income Tax Comrs Appeals Bd, 1980–; St Lucia Boy Scouts Assoc., 1977–79. Vice-Chm., Nat. Develt Corp., 1979–. Founder Life Mem., Cambridge Soc., 1976. JP 1948. Coronation Medal, 1953; British Red Cross Medal, 1949–59. *Recreations:* cricket, lawn tennis, reading. *Clubs:* Commonwealth Trust, Travellers'.

TAYLOR, Sir Nicholas Richard S.; *see* Stuart Taylor.

TAYLOR, Peter, BScEcon, FCIS; Clerk of Convocation, since 1991, Esquire Bedell, since 1994, University of London; *b* 5 Jan. 1924; *s* of late Frederick and Doris Taylor; *m* 1948, Jeannette (*née* Evans); two *d*. *Educ:* Salt Boys' High Sch., Saltaire, Yorks; Bradford Technical Coll. BSc(Econ) London, 1949. FCIS 1959. Served War, FAA, 1942–46. WR Treasurer's Dept, 1940–50; Registrar, Lincoln Technical Coll., 1950–58; Secretary: Wolverhampton and Staffs Coll. of Technol., 1959–60; Chelsea Coll., Univ. of London, 1961–77; Clerk of Senate, Univ. of London, 1977–89. Pres., Assoc. of Coll. Registrars, 1970–72. Treas., Soc. for Promotion of Hellenic Studies, 1989–93. Hon. FKC, 1985. *Address:* April Cottage, 52 Wattleton Road, Beaconsfield, Bucks HP9 1SD.

TAYLOR, Peter John Whittaker, OBE 1990; Director, Spain, British Council, since 1995; *b* 22 April 1939; *s* of late Claud Whittaker Taylor and of Mary Elizabeth Taylor (*née* Garlick); *m* 1987, Carolina Haro; one *d* by previous marriage. *Educ:* Solihull Sch.; St Catharine's Coll., Cambridge (MA Hons English); Reading Univ. (MA Applied Linguistics). Dir, Internat Lang. Centre, Paris, 1970–78; British Council, 1978–: Eng. Lang. Officer, Mexico, 1979–81; Regl Dir, Valencia, Spain, 1981–85; Dep. Dir, Saudi Arabia, 1985–87; Dir, Morocco, 1987–90; Dep. Dir, Africa and ME Div., 1990–93; Regl Dir, ME and N Africa, 1993–94. *Recreations:* books, classical music. *Address:* British Council, Paseo del General Martinez Campos 31, 28010 Madrid, Spain.

TAYLOR, Peter William Edward, QC 1981; *b* 27 July 1917; *s* of late Peter and Julia A. Taylor; *m* 1948, Julia Mary Brown, *d* of Air Cdre Sir Vernon Brown, CB, OBE; two *s*. *Educ:* Peter Symonds' Sch., Winchester; Christ's Coll., Cambridge (MA; Wrangler, Math. Tripos, Part II; 1st Class, Law Tripos, Part II). Served RA, 1939–46: France and Belgium, 1939–40; N Africa, 1942–43; NW Europe, 1944–45 (mentioned in dispatches); Actg Lt-Col 1945; transferred to TARO as Hon. Major, 1946. Called to the Bar, Inner Temple, 1946; Lincoln's Inn, *ad eundem*, 1953 (Bencher, 1976); practice at the Bar, 1947–94; Occasional Lectr, LSE, 1946–56; Lectr in Construction of Documents, Council of Legal Educn, 1952–70; Conveyancing Counsel of the Court, 1974–81. Member: General Council of the Bar, 1971–74; Senate of Inns of Court and the Bar, 1974–75; Inter-Professional Cttee on Retirement Provision, 1974–92; Land Registration Rule Cttee, 1976–81; Standing Cttee on Conveyancing, 1985–87; Incorporated Council of Law Reporting, 1977–91 (Vice-Chm., 1987–91); Council, Selden Soc., 1977–. *Recreations:* sailing, shooting, music. *Address:* 46 Onslow Square, SW7 3NX. *T:* 0171–589 1301; Carey Sconce, Yarmouth, Isle of Wight PO41 0SB.

TAYLOR, Philippe Arthur; Managing Director, Seatrain Sailing; *b* 9 Feb. 1937; *s* of Arthur Peach Taylor and Simone Vacquin; *m* 1973, Margaret Nancy Wilkins; two *s*. *Educ:* Trinity College, Glenalmond; St Andrews University. Procter & Gamble, 1963; Masius International, 1967; British Tourist Authority, 1970; Chief Executive, Scottish Tourist Board, 1975–80; Man. Dir, Taylor and Partners, 1980–82; Chief Exec., Birmingham Convention and Visitor Bureau Ltd, 1982–94. Vice-Chm., Ikon Gall., 1982–92; Chm., British Assoc. of Conf. Towns, 1987–90. *Publications:* childrens' books; various papers and articles on tourism. *Recreations:* sailing, making things, tourism, reading. *Address:* Bridge House, Mill Road, Friston, Saxmundham, Suffolk IP17 1NW. *Clubs:* Royal Yachting Association; Royal Northumberland Yacht (Blyth); Orford Sailing.

TAYLOR, Phyllis Mary Constance, MA; Honorary Associate, Institute of Education, London, 1983–85; *b* 29 Sept. 1926; *d* of Cecil and Constance Tedder; *m* 1949, Peter Royston Taylor; one *s*. *Educ:* Woodford High Sch.; Sudbury High Sch., Suffolk; Girton Coll., Cambridge (State Scholar; BA Hons History, 1948; MA 1951). Asst Hist. Mistress, Loughton High Sch., 1948–51, Head of Hist., 1951–58; Teacher of Hist. and Religious Educn, Lancaster Royal Grammar Sch. for Boys, 1959; Head of Hist., Casterton Sch. (private boarding), Kirby Lonsdale, 1960; Teacher of Gen. Subjects, Lancaster Girls' Grammar Sch., 1960–61, Head of Hist., 1961–62; Dep. Headmistress, Carlisle Sch., Chelsea, 1962–64; Headmistress: Walthamstow High Sch. for Girls, 1964–68; Walthamstow Sen. High Sch., 1968–75; Wanstead High Sch., London Borough of Redbridge, 1976–82. Consultant Head to NE London Polytechnic (Counselling/Careers sect.), 1974–78; Moderator, Part-time Diploma, Pastoral Care and Counselling, 1979–85. Pres., Essex Sector, Secondary Heads' Assoc., 1978–79. Member: UGC, 1978–83 (Mem., Educn Sub-Cttee, 1978–85, and Wkg Party on Continuing Educn, 1983); Teacher Trng Sub-Cttee, Adv. Cttee on Supply and Educn of Teachers, 1980–85; former Mem., Nat. Exec., Assoc. of Head Mistresses. Mem., RAM Foundn Appeals Cttee, 1985–86. Parish Councillor, High Roding, 1995–. Chm., Dunmow Liberals, 1986–88. Governor, Rodings Primary Sch., 1988–90. *Publications:* (as Julianne Royston) The Penhale Saga: The Penhale Heiress, 1988; The Penhale Fortune, 1989. *Recreations:* music, theatre, bridge, horses, country life, ecology. *Address:* White Horses, High Roding, Great Dunmow, Essex CM6 1NS. *T:* Great Dunmow (01371) 873161.

TAYLOR, Prof. Richard Edward; Professor, Stanford Linear Accelerator Center, Stanford University, since 1968; *b* 2 Nov. 1929; *s* of Clarence Richard Taylor and Delia Alena Taylor (*née* Brunsdale); *m* 1951, Rita Jean Bonneau; one *s*. *Educ:* Univ. of Alberta (BS 1950; MS 1952); Stanford Univ. (PhD 1962). Boursier Lab. de l'Accelerateur Linéaire, France, 1958–61; physicist, Lawrence Berkeley Lab., Berkeley, Calif., 1961–62; staff mem., 1962–68, Associate Dir, 1982–86, Stanford Linear Accelerator Center. Distinguished Prof., Univ. of Alberta, 1992–. Fellow: Guggenheim Foundn, 1971–72; Amer. Phys. Soc (W. K. H. Panofsky Prize, Div. of Particles and Fields, 1989); FRSC; FAAAS 1992; Fellow, Amer. Acad. of Arts and Scis, 1992. Hon DSc: Paris-Sud, 1980; Alberta, 1991; Lethbridge, 1993; Victoria, 1994; Hon. LLD Calgary, 1993. Von Humboldt Award, 1982; Nobel Prize in Physics, 1990. *Address:* Stanford Linear Accelerator Center, PO Box 4349–MS 96, Stanford, CA 94309, USA. *T:* (415) 9262417.

TAYLOR, Prof. Richard Lawrence, PhD; FRS 1995; Savilian Professor of Geometry, and Fellow of New College, Oxford University, since 1995; *b* 19 May 1962; *s* of John Clayton Taylor and Gillian Mary Taylor (*née* Schofield); *m* 1995, Christine Jiayou Chang. *Educ:* Magdalen Coll. Sch., Oxford; Clare Coll., Cambridge (BA); Princeton Univ. (PhD). Fellow, Clare Coll., Cambridge, 1988–95; Asst Lectr, 1989–92, Lectr, 1992–94, Reader, 1994–95, Cambridge Univ. *Recreation:* hill walking. *Address:* Mathematics Institute, Oxford University, 24–29 St Giles, Oxford OX1 3LB. *T:* Oxford (01865) 273525.

TAYLOR, (Robert) Alan; Chief Executive and Town Clerk, Royal Borough of Kensington and Chelsea, since 1990; *b* 13 Sept. 1944; *s* of Alfred Taylor and Hilda Mary (*née* Weekley); *m* 1st, 1965, Dorothy Joan Walker (*d* 1986); two *s*; 2nd, 1987, Margaret Susanne Barnes. *Educ:* Thornbury Grammar Sch., Thornbury, Glos.; King's Coll., Univ. of London (LLB). Solicitor. Asst Solicitor, Plymouth CBC, 1970–74; Plymouth City Council: Dep. City Solicitor and Sec., 1974–76; Asst Town Clerk, 1976–81; Chief Exec., London Borough of Sutton, 1981–90. Clerk, NE Surrey Crematorium Bd, 1983–90; Director: Sutton Enterprise Agency Ltd, 1987–90; S London TEC, 1989–90. Hon. Sec., SOLACE, 1992–95. *Recreations:* theatre, books, walking. *Address:* 2 Morden Grange Cottages, The Street, Betchworth, Surrey RH3 7DJ. *T:* Betchworth (01737) 843237.

TAYLOR, Robert Carruthers; His Honour Judge Robert Taylor; a Circuit Judge, since 1984; *b* 6 Jan. 1939; *o s* of late John Taylor, CBE and Barbara Mary Taylor; *m* 1968, Jacqueline Marjorie, *er d* of Nigel and Marjorie Chambers; one *s* one *d*. *Educ:* Wycliffe Coll.; St John's Coll., Oxford. MA 1967. Called to Bar, Middle Temple, 1961; Member, NE Circuit, 1962–84; a Recorder, 1976–84. Chm., Agricl Land Tribunal, Yorks and Lancs, Yorks and Humberside Areas, 1979–. Mem., W Yorks Probation Cttee, 1991–. *Recreations:* reading, music, spectating, gardening, domestic life. *Address:* The Courthouse, 1 Oxford Row, Leeds LS1 3BE. *T:* Leeds (0532) 830040. *Clubs:* Commonwealth Trust; Ilkley Book (Ilkley).

TAYLOR, Robert Richard, OBE 1989 (MBE (mil.) 1972); JP; Lord Lieutenant, County of West Midlands, since 1993; *b* 14 June 1932; *s* of Sydney Arthur Taylor and Edith Alice Taylor; *m* 1957, Sheila Welch. *Educ:* Yardley Grammar Sch., Birmingham. Pilot then

Sqdn Leader, RAF, 1950–73. Progressive Properties, Birmingham, 1973–74; Asst Dir, 1974–76, Airport Dir, 1976–86, Man. Dir, 1986–94, Birmingham Airport plc. JP W Midlands, 1994. DUniv Central England, 1993. KStJ 1994. QCVSA 1966. *Recreations:* garden, literature, people. *Address:* Lieutenancy Office, The Coach House, Barston, Solihull B92 0JL. *Club:* Royal Air Force.

TAYLOR, (Robert) Ronald, CBE 1971; FIM; Former Chairman: Robert Taylor (Holdings) Ltd (formerly Robert Taylor Ironfounders (Holdings) Ltd); Forth Alloys Ltd; *b* 25 Aug. 1916; *e s* of late Robert Taylor, ironfounder, Larbert; *m* 1941, Margaret, *d* of late William Purdie, Coatbridge; two *s* two *d*. *Educ:* High Sch., Stirling. FIM 1970. Chm., Glenrothes Develt Corp., 1964–78 (Dep. Chm., 1960–64). Rep. of Sec. of State for Scotland to Scottish Council Develt and Industry, 1966–82 (Fellow of Council, 1986). Chm. Council, British Cast Iron Res. Assoc., 1970–71; Member: Extra Parly Panel, 1967–87; Scottish Industrial Adv. Bd, 1978–83. Mem. Court, St Andrews Univ., 1968–71; Trustee and Mem., Exec. Cttee, Carnegie Trust for Scottish Univs, 1976–85. E. J. Fox Gold Medal, Inst. of British Foundrymen, 1967. *Recreations:* fishing, stalking, golf. *Address:* Beoraid, Caledonian Crescent, Auchterarder, Perthshire PH3 1NG. *Club:* Army and Navy.

TAYLOR, Dr Robert Thomas, CBE 1990; Chairman, Management Interviewing and Research Institute, since 1993; Visiting Senior Fellow, Manchester Business School, since 1993; *b* 21 March 1933; *s* of George Taylor and Marie Louise Fidler; *m* 1965, Rosemary Janet Boileau; three *s* one *d*. *Educ:* Boteler Grammar Sch., Warrington; University Coll., Oxford (Open Exhbnr; BA 1954, MA 1957; DPhil 1957). Fulbright Scholar. Research Associate, Randall Lab. of Physics, Univ. of Michigan, USA, 1957–58; ICI Research Fellow, 1958–59, Lectr, Physics Dept, 1959–61, Univ. of Liverpool; Chief Examr for NUJMB, GCE Physics (Scholarship Level), 1961; British Council: Asst Regional Rep., Madras, 1961–64; Science Officer, Madrid, 1964–69; Dir, Staff Recruitment Dept, 1969–73; Regional Educn Advr, Bombay, 1973–77; Rep., Mexico, 1977–81; Controller, Personnel, 1981–86; Rep., Greece, 1986–90; Asst Dir-Gen., British Council, 1990–93. *Publications:* contrib. to Chambers Encyclopaedia, 1967 edn; papers in scientific jls. *Recreations:* computers, war and war gaming. *Address:* Mark Haven, High Street, Cranbrook, Kent TN17 3EW. *T:* Cranbrook (01580) 714212.

TAYLOR, Roger Miles Whitworth; Director, Newchurch and Company, since 1994; *b* 18 May 1944; *s* of Richard and Joan Taylor; *m* 1969, Georgina Lucy Tonks; two *s* two *d*. *Educ:* Repton School; Birmingham University (LLB). Solicitor, admitted 1968; Asst Sol., Cheshire CC, 1969–71; Asst County Clerk, Lincs parts of Lindsey, 1971–73; Dep. County Secretary, Northants CC, 1973–79; Dep. Town Clerk, 1979–85, Town Clerk and Chief Exec., 1985–88, City of Manchester; Chief Exec., Birmingham CC, 1988–94. Mem., Farrand Cttee on Conveyancing, 1983–84; Clerk, Greater Manchester Passenger Transport Authy, 1986–88. Sec., W Midlands Jt Cttee, 1988–94. Chairman: Birmingham Marketing Partnership, 1993–94; Birmingham Common Purpose, 1994; Local Govt Television Adv. Bd, 1994–; Dir, Birmingham TEC, 1990–93. Mancunian of the Year, Manchester Jun. Chamber of Commerce, 1988. *Publications:* contribs to Local Govt Chronicle, Municipal Review, Municipal Jl. *Recreations:* sailing, walking. *Address:* Newchurch and Company, 12 Charterhouse Square, EC1M 6AX.

TAYLOR, Ronald; *see* Taylor, R. R.

TAYLOR, Ronald George, CBE 1988; Director-General, Association of British Chambers of Commerce, since 1984; *b* 12 Dec. 1935; *s* of Ernest and May Taylor; *m* 1960, Patricia Stoker; one *s* two *d*. *Educ:* Jesus College, Oxford (BA Modern Langs). Commnd Royal Signals, 1957–59. Leeds Chamber of Commerce and Industry: joined, 1959; Asst Sec., 1964–74; Director, 1974–84. Reg. Sec., Assoc. of Yorks and Humberside Chambers of Commerce, 1974–84. *Recreations:* Rugby Union, bridge. *Address:* 2 Holly Bush Lane, Harpenden, Herts AL5 4AP. *T:* Harpenden (01582) 712139.

TAYLOR, Ronald Oliver; Managing Director, Vickers, 1988–90; *b* 12 Aug. 1931; *s* of Andrew James Taylor, *qv*; *m* 1961, Frances Sylvia Howcroft; three *s* one *d*. *Educ:* Grove Academy, Dundee. Mem., Inst. of Chartered Accountants of Scotland. Joined Vickers as Accountant, 1958: Managing Dir, Printing Machinery Group, 1969–72; Chief Exec., Howson-Algraphy Group, 1972–85; Director, 1977; Jt Dep. Managing Dir, 1984; Jt Managing Dir, 1987. Mem., CBI Europe Cttee, 1987–89. *Recreations:* golf, walking. *Address:* Ryburn, Crabtree Green, Collingham, near Wetherby, West Yorks LS22 5AB. *T:* Wetherby (01937) 572135.

TAYLOR, Prof. Ronald Wentworth, MD; FRCOG; Professor Emeritus of Obstetrics and Gynaecology, United Medical and Dental Schools of Guy's and St Thomas' Hospitals, since 1989; *b* 28 Oct. 1932; *s* of George Richard and Winifred Taylor; *m* 1962, Mary Patricia O'Neill; three *s* one *d*. *Educ:* St Mary's Coll., Crosby; Liverpool Univ. (MB ChB 1958; MD 1972). MRCOG 1965, FRCOG 1975. Jun. House Officer posts, Liverpool, 1958–59; Sen. House Officer posts, Preston, 1960, Manchester, 1962; GP, Ormskirk, Lancs, 1962–63; Registrar, Whittington Hosp., London, 1963–64; St Thomas' Hospital: Lectr, 1965–67; Sen. Lectr, 1968–76; Prof., 1977–89, subseq. at UMDS of Guy's and St Thomas' Hosps. *Publications:* Gynaecological Cancer, 1975; "Ten Teachers" Obstetrics and Gynaecology, 14th edn 1985; (ed) Confidential Enquiry into Perinatal Deaths, 1988; Endometrial Cancer, 1988. *Recreations:* fell walking, sailing, silversmithing, restoration of furniture, photography. *Address:* Keld Head, Keld Shap, Penrith, Cumbria CA10 3QF. *T:* Penrith (01931) 716553. *Club:* Royal Society of Medicine.

TAYLOR, Selwyn Francis, DM, MCh, FRCS; Dean Emeritus and Fellow, Royal Postgraduate Medical School, London; Senior Lecturer in Surgery, and Surgeon, Hammersmith Hospital; Emeritus Consultant to Royal Navy; Member, Armed Forces Medical Advisory Board; Examiner in Surgery, Universities of Oxford, London, Manchester, Leeds, National University of Ireland, West Indies, Makerere and Society of Apothecaries; *b* Sale, Cheshire, 16 Sept. 1913; *s* of late Alfred Petre Taylor and Emily Taylor, Salcombe, Devon; *m* 1939, Ruth Margaret, 2nd *d* of late Sir Alfred Howitt, CVO; one *s* one *d*. *Educ:* Peter Symonds, Winchester; Keble College, Oxford; King's College Hospital. BA (Hons) Oxford, 1936; Burney Yeo Schol., King's Coll. Hosp., 1936; MA Oxon; MRCS, LRCP, 1939; FRCS 1940; MCh, 1946; DM 1959. Surgical Registrar, King's Coll. Hosp., 1946–47; Oxford Univ. George Herbert Hunt Travelling Schol., Stockholm, 1947; Rockefeller Travelling Fellow in Surgery, 1948–49; Research Fellow, Harvard Univ., and Fellow in Clin. Surgery, Massachusetts Gen. Hosp., Boston, Mass, USA, 1948–49. RNVR, 1940–46; Surgeon Lt-Comdr; Surgeon Specialist, Kintyre, East Indies, Australia; Surgeon: Belgrave Hosp. for Children, 1946–65; Hammersmith Hosp., 1947–78; King's Coll. Hospital, 1951–65. Bradshaw Lectr, RCS, 1977; Legg Meml Lectr, KCH, 1979; Keats Lectr, Soc. of Apothecaries, 1987. President: Harveian Soc., 1969; Internat. Assoc. Endocrine Surgeons, 1979–81; Member: Council, RCS, 1966– (Senior Vice-Pres., 1976–77 and 1977–78; Joll Prize, 1976); GMC, 1974–83; Surgical Research Soc.; Internat. Soc. for Surgery; Fellow Assoc. Surgeons of GB; FRSM; Hon. FRCSE 1976; Hon. FCS (S Africa) 1978; Corresp. Fellow Amer. Thyroid Assoc.; Pres., London Thyroid Club and Sec., Fourth Internat. Goitre Conference. Mem., Senate of London Univ., 1970–75. Chm., Heinemann Medical Books, 1972–83. *Publications:* books and papers on surgical subjects and thyroid physiology. *Recreations:* sailing, tennis, wine. *Address:* Trippets, Bosham, West Sussex PO18 8JE. *T:* Bosham (01243) 573387. *Clubs:* Garrick, Hurlingham; Bosham Sailing.

TAYLOR, Sir Teddy; *see* Taylor, Sir E. M.

TAYLOR, Maj.-Gen. Walter Reynell, CB 1981; Director, EST Ltd; *b* 5 April 1928; *s* of Col Richard Reynell Taylor and Margaret Catherine Taylor (*née* Holme); *m* 1st, 1954, Doreen Myrtle Dodge; one *s* one *d*; 2nd, 1982, Mrs Rosemary Gardner (*née* Breed); one *s*. *Educ:* Wellington; RMC, Sandhurst. Commanded: 4th/7th Royal Dragoon Guards, 1969–71; 12 Mechanised Bde, 1972–74; rcds 1975; Brig., Mil. Operations, MoD, 1976–78; Administrator, Sovereign Base Areas of Cyprus, 1978–80; COS, HQ BAOR, 1980–84. Dir, ME Centre for Management Studies, Nicosia, Cyprus, 1984–86. *Recreation:* sailing. *Address:* Blake's Farm, Halse, Taunton TA4 3AG. *Clubs:* Special Forces; Royal Armoured Corps Yacht.

TAYLOR, Wendy Ann, CBE 1988; sculptor; Member, Royal Fine Art Commission, since 1981; *b* 29 July 1945; *d* of Edward Philip Taylor and Lilian Maude Wright; *m* 1982, Bruce Robertson; one *s*. *Educ:* St Martin's School of Art. LDAD (Hons). One-man exhibitions: Axiom Gall., London, 1970; Angela Flowers Gall., London, 1972; 24th King's Lynn Fest., Norfolk, and World Trade Centre, London, 1974; Annely Juda Fine Art, London, 1975; Oxford Gall., Oxford, 1976; Oliver Dowling Gall., Dublin, 1976 and 1979; Building Art—the process, Building Centre Gall., 1986; Austin, Desmond and Phipps, 1992. Shown in over 100 group exhibitions, 1964–82. Represented in collections in GB, USA, NI, Eire, NZ, Germany, Sweden, Qatar, Switzerland, Seychelles. Major commissions: The Travellers 1970, London; Gazebo (edn of 4) 1970–71, London, New York, Suffolk, Oxford; Triad 1971, Oxford; Timepiece 1973, London; Calthae 1978, Leicestershire; Octo 1980, Milton Keynes; Counterpoise 1980, Birmingham; Compass Bowl 1980, Basildon; Sentinel 1981, Reigate; Bronze Relief 1981, Canterbury; Equatorial Sundial 1982, Bletchley; Essence 1982, Milton Keynes; Opus 1983, Morley Coll., London; Gazebo 1983, Golder's Hill Park, London; Network, 1985, London; Roundacre Improvement Scheme Phase I, 1985–88, Phase II, 1989–90, Basildon; Geo I & Geo II 1986, Stratford-Upon-Avon; Landscape, and Tree of the Wood 1986, Fernhurst, Surrey; Pharos 1986, Peel Park, E Kilbride; Ceres 1986, Fernhurst, Surrey; Nexus 1986, Corby, Northants; Globe Sundial 1987, Swansea Maritime Quarter; Spirit of Enterprise 1987, Isle of Dogs, London; Silver Fountain 1988, Continuum 1990, Guildford, Surrey; The Whirlies 1988, Pharos II 1989, Phoenix 1989–90, E Kilbride; Pilot Kites 1988, Norwich Airport; Fireflow 1988, Strathclyde Fire Brigade HQ, Hamilton; Armillary Sundial 1989, The New Towns, Essex; Globe Sundial II 1990, London Zool Gdns; Butterfly Mosaic 1990, Barking and Dagenham Council; Square Piece 1991, Plano, Ill; Sundial Meml 1991, Sheffield; Anchorage 1991, Salford Quays, Manchester; Wyvern 1992, Leics; stained glass window, St George's Church, Sheffield Univ., 1994; The Jester, Emmanuel Coll., Cambridge, 1994; Challenge, Stockley Park, 1995. Mem., CNAA, 1980–85 (Specialist Advr, 1985–93; Mem., Cttee for Art and Design, 1987–91); Consultant, New Town Commn (Basildon) (formerly Basildon Develt Corp.), 1985–; Mem., Design Adv. Gp, LDDC, 1989–; Design Consultant, London Borough of Barking and Dagenham, 1989–93. Mem., Adv. Gp, PCFC, 1989–90. Examiner, Univ. of London, 1982–83; Mem. Court, RCA, 1982–; Mem. Council, Morley Coll., 1984–88. FZS 1989; FRBS 1995; Fellow, QMW, 1993. Awards: Walter Neurath, 1964; Pratt, 1965; Sainsbury, 1966; Arts Council, 1977; Duais na Riochta (Kingdom Prize), 1977; Gold Medal, Eire, 1977; 1st Prize Silk Screen, Barcham Green Print Comp., 1978. *Recreation:* gardening. *Address:* 73 Bow Road, Bow E3 2AN. *T:* 0181–981 2037.

TAYLOR, Sir William, Kt 1990; CBE 1982; Chairman of Convocation, University of London, since 1994; Visiting Professor of Education, Oxford University, since 1991; *b* 31 May 1930; *s* of Herbert and Maud E. Taylor, Crayford, Kent; *m* 1954, Rita, *d* of Ronald and Marjorie Hague, Sheffield; one *s* two *d*. *Educ:* Erith Grammar Sch., London Sch. of Economics; Westminster Coll., Oxford (Hon. Fellow, 1990); Univ. of London Inst. of Educn. BSc Econ 1952, PhD 1960. Teaching in Kent, 1953–56; Deputy Head, Slade Green Secondary Sch., 1956–59; Sen. Lectr, St Luke's Coll., Exeter, 1959–61; Head of Educn Dept, Bede Coll., Durham, 1961–64; Tutor and Lectr in Educn, Univ. of Oxford, 1964–66; Prof. of Educn and Dir of Sch. of Educn, Univ. of Bristol, 1966–73; Dir, Univ. of London Inst. of Educn, 1973–83; Principal, Univ. of London, 1983–85; Vice-Chancellor: Univ. of Hull, 1985–91; Univ. of Huddersfield, 1994–95. Research Consultant, Dept of Educn and Science (part-time), 1968–73; Chairman: European Cttee for Educnl Research, 1969–71; UK Nat. Commn for UNESCO, 1975–83 (Mem., 1973–83); Educnl Adv. Council, IBA, 1974–82; UCET, 1976–79; Cttee on Training of Univ. Teachers, 1981–88; NFER, 1983–88; CATE, 1984–93; Univs Council for Adult and Continuing Educn, 1986–90; N of England Univs Management and Leadership Prog., 1987–91; Studies in Education, 1991–. Member: UGC Educn Cttee, 1971–80; British Library Res. and Develt Cttee, 1975–79; Open Univ. Academic Adv. Cttee, 1975–82; SSRC Educnl Research Board, 1976–80 (Vice-Chm., 1978–80); Adv. Cttee on Supply and Training of Teachers, 1976–79; Working Gp on Management of Higher Educn, 1977–78; Steering Cttee on Future of Examinations at 16+, 1977–78; Cttee of Vice-Chancellors and Principals, 1980–91; Adv. Cttee on Supply and Educn of Teachers (Sec. of State's nominee), 1980–83. UK Rep., Permanent Educn Steering Cttee, Council of Europe, 1971–73; Rapporteur, OECD Review of Educn in NZ, 1982–83. Member: Senate, Univ. of London, 1977–85; Cttee of Management, Inst. of Advanced Legal Studies, 1980–83; Council, Open Univ., 1984–88; Council, Coll of Preceptors, 1987–89; Editl Adv. Bd, World Book Internat., 1989–; CBI Educn Foundn, 1993–. Commonwealth Vis. Fellow, Australian States, 1975; NZ UGC Prestige Fellowship, 1977; Hon. Vis. Fellow, Green Coll., Oxford, 1991–. President: Council for Educn in World Citizenship, 1979–90; English New Educn Fellowship, 1979–86; Comparative Educn Soc. of GB, 1981–84; Assoc. of Colls of Further and Higher Educn, 1984–88; European Assoc. for Institnl Res., 1990–92; Univs of N of England Consortium for Internat. Develt, 1991–94; N of England Educn Conference, 1992; Inst. of Educn Soc., 1990–93; Vice President: Soc. for Research in Higher Educn, 1983–; British Educnl Admin, and Management Soc., 1985–; Council for Internat. Educn, 1992–. Chm., NFER/Nelson Publishing Co., 1985–86, 1987–; Dir, Fenner plc, 1988–93. Trustee, Forbes Trust, 1987–88. Governor: Wye Coll., 1981–83; Hymers Coll., Hull, 1985–91; Westminster Coll., Oxford, 1991–; Univ. of Glamorgan (formerly Poly. of Wales), 1991–; Sevenoaks Sch., 1994–. Freeman, City of London, 1985. Yeoman, 1982–87, Liveryman, 1988–, Worshipful Soc. of Apothecaries of London. Hon. FCP 1977; Hon. FCCEA 1980. Hon. Fellow: Thames Polytechnic, 1991; Inst. of Educn, Univ. of London, 1995. Hon. DSc Aston (Birmingham), 1977; Hon. LittD Leeds, 1979; Hon. DCL Kent, 1981; DUniv Open, 1983; Hon. DLitt Loughborough, 1984; Hon. LLD Hull, 1992; Hon. DEd: Kingston, 1993; Oxford Brookes, 1993; Plymouth, 1993; UWE, 1994. *Publications:* The Secondary Modern School, 1963; Society and the Education of Teachers, 1969; (ed with G. Baron) Educational Administration and the Social Sciences, 1969; Heading for Change, 1969; Planning and Policy in Post Secondary Education, 1972; Theory into Practice, 1972; Research Perspectives in Education, 1973; (ed with R. Farquhar and R. Thomas) Educational Administration in Australia and Abroad, 1975; Research and Reform in

Teacher Education, 1978; (ed with B. Simon) Education in the Eighties: the central issues, 1981; (ed) Metaphors of Education, 1984; Universities Under Scrutiny, 1987; Policy and Strategy for Higher Education: collaboration between business and higher eduction, 1989; articles and papers in professional jls. *Recreations:* writing, walking. *Address:* Office of Chairman of Convocation, University of London, Senate House, Malet Street, WC1E 7HU. *T:* 0171–636 8000, *Fax:* 0171–631 3047.

TAYLOR, William, QPM 1991; Commissioner, City of London Police, since 1994; *b* 25 March 1947; *s* of late William Taylor and Margaret Taylor; *m* 1978, Denise Lloyd; two step *s*. *Educ:* Blairgowrie High Sch.; Nat. Police Coll. (8th Special Course and 16th Sen. Command Course). Joined Metropolitan Police Service, 1966; served Central London locations as Det. Constable, Sergeant and Inspector, and Chief Inspector, 1966–76; New Scotland Yard: Community Relations Branch, 1976–78; Det. Supt, Central Drugs Squad, 1978–79; Staff Officer to Comr of Police, 1980–82 (Det. Chief Supt); Comdr CID NE London, then Uniform Comdr, Hackney; Comdr Robbery Squad (Flying Squad) and Regional Crime Squad, 1982–85; Asst Comr, City of London Police, 1985–89; Dep. Chief Constable, Thames Valley Police, 1989–90; Asst Comr, Specialist Ops, Metropolitan Police, 1990–94. Police Long Service and Good Conduct Medal, 1988. *Recreations:* reading (travel, management and historical), hill walking, horse riding, collecting some Dalton ware. *Address:* 26 Old Jewry, EC2R 8DJ. *T:* 0171–601 2004.

TAYLOR, William Bernard; Public Sector Specialist Adviser: Invesco Asset Management Ltd (formerly MIM, subseq. Invesco MIM Ltd), since 1986; Sedgwick UK Ltd, since 1986; Baronsmead PLC, since 1993; Underwriting Member, Lloyd's, since 1988; *b* 13 Dec. 1930; *s* of Frank and Elizabeth Taylor; *m* 1956, Rachel May Davies; one *s* two *d*. *Educ:* Dynevor Sch., Swansea; Univ. of Kent. MA; IPFA, FRSA. Nat. Service, RN, 1949–51; commnd RNVR; served in coastal forces. District Audit Service, 1951–61; Llwchwr UDC, 1961–70; Asst Educn Officer, Manchester Corp., 1970–72; Asst County Treasurer, 1972–73, Dep. County Treasurer, 1973–80, County Treasurer, 1980–86, Kent. Financial Adviser: Social Servs Cttee, ACC, 1983–86; Standing Conf. of Planning Auths in SE England, 1983–86; Hon. Treas., SE England Tourist Bd, 1980–86; Chm., wkg party of Council of Europe on borrowing by municipalities of member states, 1982–84. Dir, Interlake DRC Ltd., 1989–94. Public Sector Specialist Advisor: to Ernst & Young, 1986–91; to Lombard North Central, 1986–92. Gov., and Chm. F and GP (formerly Finance Cttee), Kent Inst. of Art and Design, 1989–95; Non-exec. Mem., and Chm. Finance and Rev. Cttee, Medway HA, 1990–93; Vice-Chm., Medway NHS Health Trust, 1994–. Pres., Maidstone Rotary Club, 1995–June 1996. *Publications:* The Management of Assets: terotechnology in the pursuit of economic life cycle costs, 1980; The Financial Management of Local Authorities, 1993; contribs to local govt and other learned journals. *Recreations:* cricket, rugby, public speaking. *Address:* Selby Shaw, Heath Road, Boughton Monchelsea, near Maidstone, Kent ME17 4JE. *T:* Maidstone (01622) 745022. *Club:* Maidstone (Maidstone).

TAYLOR, William Edward Michael; His Honour Judge William Taylor; a Circuit Judge, Western Circuit, since 1989; Resident Judge for Plymouth and Cornwall, since 1990; *b* 27 July 1944; *s* of William Henry Taylor and Winifred Mary (*née* Day); *m* 1969, Caroline Joyce Gillies; two *d*. *Educ:* Denstone Coll., Uttoxeter, Staffs; Council of Legal Educn. Called to the Bar, Inner Temple, 1968. Practised from 2 Harcourt Bldgs, Temple; a Recorder, 1987–89; Liaison Judge for Devon and Plymouth. Lectr, Council of Legal Educn, 1976–89. Mem., Shadow Probation Bd, Devon. Hon. Pres., Univ. of Plymouth Law Soc. *Recreations:* music, opera, fishing, vintage cars, wine. *Address:* c/o Court Administrator, The Castle, Exeter, Devon EX4 3TH. *T:* Exeter (01392) 74876. *Club:* Royal Western Yacht (Plymouth).

TAYLOR, Lt-Comdr William Horace, GC 1941; MBE 1973; Commissioner of the Scout Association, 1946–74; *b* 23 Oct. 1908; *s* of William Arthur Taylor; *m* 1946, Joan Isabel Skaife d'Ingerthorpe; one *s* three *d*. *Educ:* Manchester Grammar Sch. Junior Partner, 1929; Managing Dir, 1937. Served War: Dept of Torpedoes and Mines, Admiralty, 1940 (despatches, 1941); Founder Mem., Naval Clearance Divers, HMS Vernon (D), 1944. Travelling Commissioner for Sea Scouts of UK, 1946; Field Commissioner for SW England, Scout Association, 1952–74, Estate Manager, 1975–84. *Recreations:* scouting, boating, music. *Address:* 3 Hanover Court, Station Road, Banchory, Kincardineshire AB31 3ZA. *T:* Banchory (01330) 824038. *Clubs:* Naval; Manchester Cruising Association.

TAYLOR, William James; QC (Scot) 1986; *b* 13 Sept. 1944; *s* of Cecil Taylor and Ellen Taylor (*née* Daubney). *Educ:* Robert Gordon's College, Aberdeen; Aberdeen Univ. (MA Hons 1966; LLB 1969); Glasgow Univ. (Cert. in European Law (French) 1990). Admitted Faculty of Advocates, 1971; called to the Bar, Inner Temple, 1990. Standing Junior Counsel to DHSS, 1978–79, to FCO, 1979–86. Contested (Lab) Edinburgh W, Feb. and Oct. 1974; Regional Councillor (Lab), 1973–82. *Recreations:* the arts, ski-ing, sailing, Scottish mountains, swimming, travel. *Address:* Hill House, 69 Dirleton Avenue, North Berwick, E Lothian EH39 4QL. *T:* North Berwick (01620) 895111. *Clubs:* Scottish Arts, Traverse Theatre (Edinburgh).

TAYLOR, William McCaughey; Chairman, Northern Ireland Coal Importers Association, 1986–91, retired; *b* 10 May 1926; *s* of William and Georgina Lindsay Taylor; *m* 1955, June Louise Macartney; two *s* two *d*. *Educ:* Campbell College, Belfast; Trinity College, Oxford (MA 1950). Lieut, Royal Inniskilling Fusiliers, 1944–47. International Computers Ltd, 1950–58; Lobitos Oilfields Ltd, 1958–60; HM Vice Consul, New York, 1960–63, HM Consul, 1963–65; NI Dept of Commerce, 1965–79; Sec. and Chief Exec., NI Police Authy, 1979–86. *Recreations:* golf, bridge, gardening, piano. *Club:* Royal Belfast Golf.

TAYLOR, William Rodney E.; *see* Eatock Taylor.

TAYLOR, Mrs (Winifred) Ann; MP (Lab) Dewsbury, since 1987; *b* Motherwell, 2 July 1947; *m* 1966, David Taylor; one *s* one *d*. *Educ:* Bolton Sch.; Bradford Univ.; Sheffield Univ. Formerly teaching. Past part-time Tutor, Open Univ.; interested in housing, regional policy, and education. Monitoring Officer, Housing Corp., 1985–87. Member: Association of Univ. Teachers; APEX; Holmfirth Urban District Council, 1972–74. MP (Lab) Bolton W, Oct. 1974–1983; PPS to Sec. of State for Educn and Science, 1975–76; PPS to Sec. of State for Defence, 1976–77; an Asst Govt Whip, 1977–79; Opposition frontbench spokesman on education, 1979–81, on housing, 1981–83, on home affairs, 1987–90 (Shadow Water Minister, 1988), on environment, 1990–92, on education, 1992–. Contested (Lab): Bolton W, Feb. 1974; Bolton NE, 1983. Hon. Fellow, Birkbeck Coll. *Address:* Glyn Garth, Stoney Bank Road, Thongsbridge, Huddersfield, Yorks HD7 2SL.

TAYLOR THOMPSON, (John) Derek, CB 1985; Commissioner of Inland Revenue, 1973–87; Secretary, Churches' Main Committee, since 1990; *b* 6 Aug. 1927; *o s* of late John Taylor Thompson and Marjorie (*née* Westcott); *m* 1954, Helen Laurie Walker; two *d*. *Educ:* St Peter's Sch., York; Balliol Coll., Oxford. MA. Asst Principal, Inland Revenue, 1951; Private Sec. to Chm., 1954; Private Sec. to Minister without Portfolio, 1962; Asst Sec., Inland Revenue, 1965. Chm., Fiscal Affairs Cttee, OECD, 1984–89. Chm., Legislation—Monitoring Service for Charities, 1991–. *Recreations:* rural pursuits, reading, historical writing. *Address:* Jessops, Nutley, Sussex TN22 3PD. *Club:* United Oxford & Cambridge University.

TAYLORSON, John Brown; Chairman, International Service Industry Search, since 1990; Managing Director: John Taylorson Associates, since 1990; Inflight Marketing Services, since 1990; *b* 5 March 1931; *s* of John Brown Taylorson and Edith Maria Taylorson; *m* 1st, 1960, Barbara June (*née* Hagg) (marr. diss.); one *s* one *d*; 2nd, 1985, Helen Anne (*née* Parkinson); one *s*. *Educ:* Forest School, Snaresbrook; Hotel School, Westminster. Sales Director, Gardner Merchant Food Services Ltd, 1970–73; Managing Director: International Division, Gardner Merchant Food Services, 1973–77; Fedics Food Services, 1977–80; Chief Executive, Civil Service Catering Organisation, 1980–81; Hd of Catering Servs, British Airways, 1981–89. Pres., Internat. Flight Catering Assoc., 1983–85; Chm., Inflight Services Gp, Assoc. of European Airlines, 1983–85. *Recreations:* golf, theatre, crossword puzzles. *Address:* Deer Pond Cottage, Highfields, East Horsley, Surrey KT24 5AA. *Clubs:* Old Foresters; Burhill Golf.

TAYLOUR, family name of **Marquess of Headfort.**

TEAGLE, Vice-Adm. Sir Somerford (Francis), KBE 1994; Chief of Defence Force, New Zealand, 1991–95; *b* 9 June 1938; *s* of Leonard Herbert Teagle and Muriel Frances Teagle; *m* 1961, Leonie Marie Maire; one *s* one *d*. *Educ:* Christ's Coll., Christchurch, NZ; Royal Naval Coll., Dartmouth. Royal New Zealand Navy: Sea and Staff appts, 1958–85: Commanding Officer HMNZS: Manga, 1962–64; Taranaki, 1977; jssc, Canberra, 1977; HMNZS Canterbury, 1978–79; Captain, Naval Trng, 1981–84; ndc, Canada, 1983; Cdre, Auckland, 1986–87; Dep. Chief of Naval Staff, 1988–89; Chief of Naval Staff, 1989–91. *Recreations:* gardening, farming. *Address:* 67 Pretoria Street, Lower Hutt, New Zealand. *Clubs:* Wellington, Wellesley (Wellington).

TEAR, Robert, CBE 1984; concert and operatic tenor; first Professor of International Singing, Royal Academy of Music, since 1985; *b* 8 March 1939; *s* of Thomas Arthur and Edith Tear; *m* 1961, Hilary Thomas; two *d*. *Educ:* Barry Grammar Sch.; King's Coll., Cambridge (MA; Hon. Fellow 1989). Hon. RCM, RAM. Mem., King's Coll. Choir, 1957–60; subseq. St Paul's Cathedral and solo career; joined English Opera Group, 1964. By 1968 worked with world's leading conductors, notably Karajan, Giulini, Bernstein and Solti; during this period created many rôles in operas by Benjamin Britten. Has appeared in all major festivals; close association with Sir Michael Tippett, 1970–; Covent Garden: début, The Knot Garden, 1970, closely followed by Lensky in Eugène Onégin; Fledermaus, 1977; Peter Grimes, 1978; Rake's Progress, 1979; Thérèse, 1979; Loge in Rheingold, 1980; Admetus in Alceste, 1981; David in Die Meistersinger, 1982; Captain Vere in Billy Budd, 1982; appears regularly with Royal Opera. Glyndebourne: Marriage of Figaro, and Rake's Progress, 1994. Started relationship with Scottish Opera (singing in La Traviata, Alceste, Don Giovanni), 1974. Paris Opera: début, 1976; Lulu 1979. Début as conductor with Thames Chamber Orchestra, QEH, 1980. Has conducted Minneapolis Orch., ECO, LSO, Philharmonia, London Mozart Players. Has worked with every major recording co. and made numerous recordings (incl. solo recital discs). Sermon, King's Coll. Chapel, Cambridge Univ., 1990. *Publications:* Victorian Songs and Duets, 1980; Tear Here (autobiog.), 1990; Singer Beware, 1995. *Recreations:* any sport; interested in 18th and 19th century English water colours. *Club:* Arts.

TEARE, Andrew Hubert; Group Chief Executive, English China Clays plc, since 1990; *b* 8 Sept. 1942; *s* of Arthur Hubert Teare and Rosalind Margaret Baker; *m* 1964, Janet Nina Skidmore; three *s*. *Educ:* Kingswood School, Bath; University College London (BA Hons Classics 1964). Turner & Newall, 1964–72; CRH, 1972–83 (Gen. Manager Europe, 1978–83); Rugby Group, 1983–90 (Asst Man. Dir, 1983–84; Man. Dir, 1984–90). Non-Executive Director: Heiton Holdings, 1984–90; NFC, 1989–; Prudential Corp., 1992–. Pres., Nat. Council of Building Material Producers, 1990–92. CBIM. *Recreations:* ski-ing, mountain walking, reading. *Address:* English China Clays plc, 125 Wood Street, EC2V 7AQ. *T:* 0171–696 9229. *Club:* Hibernian United Service (Dublin).

TEARE, Nigel John Martin; QC 1991; *b* 8 Jan. 1952; *s* of Eric John Teare and Mary Rackham Teare; *m* 1975, Elizabeth Jane Pentecost; two *s* one *d*. *Educ:* King William's Coll., Isle of Man; St Peter's Coll., Oxford (BA 1973; MA 1975). Called to the Bar, Lincoln's Inn, 1974; practising barrister, 1975–; Jun. Counsel to Treasury in Admiralty matters, 1989–91. *Recreations:* collecting Manx paintings, squash, tennis. *Address:* 2 Essex Court, Temple, EC4Y 9AP. *T:* 0171–583 8381. *Club:* Royal Automobile.

TE ATAIRANGIKAAHU, Arikinui, ONZ 1987; DBE 1970; Arikinui and Head of Maori Kingship, since 1966; *b* 23 July 1931; *o d* of King Koroki V; *m* 1952, Whatumoana; two *s* five *d*. *Educ:* Waikato Diocesan School, Hamilton, NZ. Elected by the Maori people as Head of the Maori Kingship on the death of King Koroki, the fifth Maori King, with title of Arikinui (Queen), in 1966. Hon. Dr Waikato, 1979. OStJ 1986. *Recreation:* the fostering of all aspects of Maori culture and traditions. *Address:* Turongo House, Turangawaewae Marae, Ngaruawahia, New Zealand.

TEBALDI, Renata; Italian Soprano; *b* Pesaro, Italy, 1 Feb. 1922; *o c* of Teobaldo and Giuseppina (Barbieri) Tebaldi. Studied at Arrigo Boito Conservatory, Parma; Gioacchino Rossini Conservatory, Pesaro; subsequently a pupil of Carmen Melis and later of Giuseppe Pais. Made professional début as Elena in Mefistofele, Rovigo, 1944. First sang at La Scala, Milan, at post-war reopening concert (conductor Toscanini), 1946. Has sung at Covent Garden and in opera houses of Naples, Rome, Venice, Pompeii, Turin, Cesana, Modena, Bologna and Florence; toured England, France, Spain and South America. American début in title rôle Aïda, San Francisco, 1950; Metropolitan Opera House Season, New York, 1955. Recordings of complete operas include: Otello; Adriana Lecouvreur; Il Trittico; Don Carlo; La Gioconda; Un Ballo in Maschera; Madame Butterfly; Mefistofele; La Fanciulla Del West; La Forza Del Destino; Andrea Chenier; Manon Lescaut; La Tosca; Il Trovatore; Aida, La Bohème. *Address:* c/o Marks Management Ltd, 14 New Burlington Street, W1X 1FF.

TEBBIT, family name of **Baron Tebbit**.

TEBBIT, Baron *cr* 1992 (Life Peer), of Chingford, in the London Borough of Waltham Forest; **Norman Beresford Tebbit,** CH 1987; PC 1981; Director: Sears (Holdings) PLC, since 1987; British Telecommunications plc, since 1987; BET, since 1987; Spectator (1828) Ltd, since 1989; journalist; *b* 29 March 1931; 2nd *s* of Leonard and Edith Tebbit, Enfield; *m* 1956, Margaret Elizabeth Daines; two *s* one *d*. *Educ:* Edmonton County Grammar Sch. Embarked on career in journalism, 1947. Served RAF: commissioned GD Branch; qualif. Pilot, 1949–51; Reserve service RAuxAF, No 604 City of Mddx Sqdn, 1952–55. Entered and left publishing and advertising, 1951–53. Civil Airline Pilot, 1953–70 (Mem. BALPA; former holder various offices in that Assoc.). Active mem. and holder various offices, Conservative Party, 1946–. MP (C) Epping, 1970–74, Chingford, 1974–92; PPS to Minister of State, Dept of Employment, 1972–73; Parly Under Sec. of State, Dept of Trade, 1979–81; Minister of State, Dept of Industry, 1981; Secretary of State for: Employment, 1981–83; Trade and Industry, 1983–85; Chancellor of the Duchy of Lancaster, 1985–87; Chm., Conservative Party, 1985–87. Former Chm., Cons.

Members Aviation Cttee; former Vice-Chm. and Sec., Cons. Members Housing and Construction Cttee; Sec. House of Commons New Town Members Cttee. Dir, J. C. Bamford Excavators, 1987–91. Co-presenter, Target, Sky TV, 1989–; columnist, The Sun, 1995–. *Publications:* Upwardly Mobile (autobiog.), 1988; Unfinished Business, 1991. *Address:* c/o House of Lords, SW1A 0PW.

TEBBIT, Sir Donald (Claude), GCMG 1980 (KCMG 1975; CMG 1965); HM Diplomatic Service, retired; *b* 4 May 1920; *m* 1947, Barbara Margaret Olson Matheson; one *s* three *d*. *Educ:* Perse School; Trinity Hall, Cambridge (MA). Served War of 1939–45, RNVR. Joined Foreign (now Diplomatic) Service, 1946; Second Secretary, Washington, 1948; transferred to Foreign Office, 1951; First Secretary, 1952; transferred to Bonn, 1954; Private Secretary to Minister of State, Foreign Office, 1958; Counsellor, 1962; transferred to Copenhagen, 1964; Commonwealth Office, 1967; Asst Under-Sec. of State, FCO, 1968–70; Minister, British Embassy, Washington, 1970–72; Chief Clerk, FCO, 1972–76; High Comr in Australia, 1976–80. Chairman: Diplomatic Service Appeals Bd, 1980–87; E-SU, 1983–87; Mem., Appeals Bd, Council of Europe, 1981–90. Dir, RTZ Corp., 1980–90. Dir Gen., British Property Fedn, 1980–85. Pres. (UK), Australian-British Chamber of Commerce, 1980–90; Chairman: Zimbabwe Tech. Management Training Trust, 1983–91; Marshall Aid Commemoration Commn, 1985–95; Jt Commonwealth Socs Council, 1987–93. Governor, Nuffield Hospitals, 1980–90, Dep. Chm., 1985–90. President: Old Persean Soc., 1981–82; Trinity Hall Assoc., 1984–85. *Address:* Priory Cottage, Toft, Cambridge CB3 7RH.

TEBBIT, Kevin Reginald; HM Diplomatic Service; Assistant Under-Secretary of State (Resources) and Chief Inspector, Foreign and Commonwealth Office, since 1994; *b* 18 Oct. 1946; *s* of R. F. J. Tebbit and N. M. Tebbit (*née* Nichols); *m* 1969, Elizabeth Alison, *d* of John and Elizabeth Tinley; one *s* one *d*. *Educ:* Cambridgeshire High Sch.; St John's Coll., Cambridge (Schol.; BA Hons 1969). Asst Principal, MoD, 1969–72; Asst Private Sec. to Sec. of State for Defence, 1973–74; Principal, MoD, 1974–79; First Sec., UK Delegn to NATO, 1979–82; transferred to FCO, 1982; E European and Soviet Dept, 1982–84; Hd of Chancery, Ankara, 1984–87; Dir, Cabinet of Sec. Gen. of NATO, 1987–88; Counsellor (Politico-Mil.), Washington, 1988–91; Hd, Econ. Relns Dept, FCO, 1992–94. *Address:* c/o Foreign and Commonwealth Office, King Charles Street, SW1A 2AH.

TEBBLE, Norman, DSc; FRSE; CBiol, FIBiol; Director, Royal Scottish Museum, 1971–84; *b* 17 Aug. 1924; 3rd *s* of late Robert Soulsby Tebble and Jane Ann (*née* Graham); *m* 1954, Mary Olivia Archer, *o d* of H. B. and J. I. Archer, Kenilworth; two *s* one *d*. *Educ:* Bedlington Grammar School; St Andrews Univ.; BSc (1st cl. Hons Zool.) 1950, DSc 1968; MA, Merton Coll., Oxford, 1971. FIBiol 1971, CBiol 1986; FRSE 1976. St Andrews Univ. Air Squadron, 1942–43; Pilot, RAFVR, Canada, India and Burma, 1943–46. Scientific Officer, British Museum (Natural History), 1950, Curator of Annelida; John Murray Travelling Student in Oceanography, Royal Soc., 1958; Vis. Curator, Univ. of California, Scripps Inst. of Oceanography, 1959; Curator of Molluscs, British Museum, 1961; Univ. Lecturer in Zoology and Curator, zoological collection, Univ. of Oxford, 1968; Curator, Oxford Univ. Museum, 1969. Member Council: Marine Biological Assoc., UK, 1963–66; Scottish Marine Biological Assoc., 1973–78; Museums Assoc., 1972–75 (Vice-Pres., 1976–77; Pres., 1977–78); Mem., Tyne and Wear Museums Cttee, 1986–92. *Publications:* (ed jtly) Speciation in the Sea, 1963; British Bivalve Seashells, 1966, 2nd edn 1976; (ed jtly) Bibliography British Fauna and Flora, 1967; scientific papers on Systematics of Annelida and Distribution in the World Oceans. *Recreations:* Tebbel-Tebble genealogy, ornithology, walking grandsons on Camelback, Arizona and Arthur's Seat. *Address:* Vale Bank, 48 Forth Street, North Berwick, E Lothian EH39 4JQ. *T:* North Berwick (01620) 892595.

TEDDER, family name of **Baron Tedder.**

TEDDER, 3rd Baron *cr* 1946, of Glenguin, Co. Stirling; **Robin John Tedder;** *b* 6 April 1955; *er s* of 2nd Baron Tedder and of Peggy Eileen Growcott; *S* father, 1994; *m* 1st, 1977, Jennifer Peggy (*d* 1978), *d* of John Mangan, NZ; 2nd, 1980, Rita Aristeia, *yr d* of John Frangidis, Sydney, NSW; two *s* one *d*. *Heir:* *s* Hon. Benjamin John Tedder, *b* 23 April 1985. *Address:* 11 Kardinia Road, Clifton Gardens, Sydney, NSW 2088, Australia.

TEDFORD, Prof. David John, ScD; CEng, FIEE; CPhys, FInstP; Professor of Electrical Engineering, University of Strathclyde, since 1972; *b* 12 July 1931; *s* of Thomas Tedford and Eliza Jane (*née* Yates); *m* 1956, Mary White Gardner; three *s* one *d*. *Educ:* Coatbridge High Sch.; Royal Tech. Coll. (ARCST 1952); Glasgow Univ. (BSc 1952; PhD 1955). CEng, FIEE 1970; CPhys, FInstP 1970. Res. Engr, Ferranti Ltd, Edinburgh, 1955–57; Strathclyde University: Lectr, 1957–64; Sen. Lectr, 1964–69; Reader, 1969–72; Dep. Principal, 1982–84; Vice-Principal, 1984–88; Dep. Principal (Internat. Affairs), 1988–91; Special Advr to Principal, 1991–92. Sec. of State Scientific Advr to Scottish Office Industry Dept, 1992–; Chief Scientific Advr to Sec. of State for Scotland, 1994–. Member: Brit. Nat. Cttee and Exec. Cttee, CIGRE 1985–; Standing Conf. on Univ. Entrance, 1989–93; Scottish Exam. Bd, 1986–; Mgt Bd, SCOTVEC, 1993–; Mgt Bd, Bell Coll. of Technol., Hamilton, 1990–. Member: Educn Cttee and Internat. Relns Cttee, Royal Soc., 1991–; Council, IEE, 1992–; Vice-Pres., RSE, 1992–; SMIEE, 1982. FRSE 1978; FRSA 1983. Hon. ScD Lodz, 1988. Order of Merit (Poland), 1985. *Publications:* numerous in scientific and engrg jls. *Recreations:* hill-walking, tennis, music, amateur astronomy. *Address:* Department of Electronic and Electrical Engineering, Strathclyde University, Royal College, 204 George Street, Glasgow G1 1XW. *T:* 0141–552 4400.

TEELOCK, Dr Boodhun; High Commissioner for Mauritius in London, 1989–91; *b* 20 July 1922; *s* of Ramessur Teelock and Sadny Teelock; *m* 1956, Riziya; three *d*. *Educ:* Edinburgh Univ. (MB ChB 1950); Liverpool Univ. (DTM&H 1951). DPH. Ministry of Health, Mauritius: School MO, 1952–58; Senior School MO, 1958–59; Principal MO, 1960–68; World Health Organisation: Regional Adviser, Public Health Administration, Brazzaville, 1968–71; Chief of Mission, Tanzania, 1971–74, Kenya and Seychelles, 1974–79; Immunisation MO, Air Mauritius, 1980–88. *Recreation:* reading. *Address:* 12 Labourdonnais Avenue, Quatre Bornes, Mauritius.

TEESDALE, Edmund Brinsley, CMG 1964; MC 1945; DPhil; *b* 30 Sept. 1915; *s* of late John Herman Teesdale and late Winifred Mary (*née* Gull); *m* 1947, Joyce, *d* of late Walter Mills and of Mrs J. T. Murray; three *d*. *Educ:* Lancing; Trinity College, Oxford. DPhil CNAA, 1987. Entered Colonial Administrative Service, Hong Kong, 1938. Active Service in Hong Kong, China, India, 1941–45. Subsequently various administrative posts in Hong Kong; Colonial Secretary, Hong Kong, 1963–65. Dir, Assoc. of British Pharmaceutical Industry, 1965–76. *Publications:* The Queen's Gunstonemaker, 1984; Gunfounding in the Weald in the Sixteenth Century, 1991. *Recreations:* gardening, swimming, reading. *Address:* The Hogge House, Buxted, East Sussex TN22 4AY.

TEGNER, Ian Nicol, CA; Chairman: Control Risks Group, since 1992; Crest Packaging, since 1993; Director: Arjo Wiggins Appleton (formerly Wiggins Teape Appleton) since 1990; Teesside Power Ltd, since 1993; English Touring Opera (formerly Opera 80), since 1991; *b* 11 July 1933; *s* of Sven Stuart Tegner, OBE, and Edith Margaret Tegner (*née* Nicol): *m* 1961, Meriel Helen, *d* of Brig. M. S. Lush, CB, CBE, MC; one *s* one *d*. *Educ:* Rugby School. CA. Clarkson Gordon & Co., Toronto, 1958–59; Manager 1959–65, Partner 1965–71, Barton Mayhew & Co., Chartered Accts; Finance Dir, Bowater Industries, 1971–86; Chm., Cayzer Steel Bowater, 1981–86; Dir, Gp Finance, Midland Bank, 1987–89. Institute of Chartered Accountants of Scotland: Mem. Council 1981–86; Pres., 1991–92; Mem., Accounting Standards Cttee of CCAB, 1984–86; Chm., Hundred Gp of Finance Dirs, 1988–90. *Publications:* articles on accountancy in various jls and pubns. *Recreations:* book collecting, travel, hill-walking, choral singing, family life. *Address:* 44 Norland Square, W11 4PZ.

TE HEUHEU, Sir Hepi (Hoani), KBE 1979; New Zealand sheep and cattle farmer; Paramount Chief of Ngati-Tuwharetoa tribe of Maoris; *b* 1919; *m*; six *c*. Chairman: Tuwharetoa Maori Trust Board; Puketapu 3A Block (near Taupo); Rotoaira Lake Trust; Rotoaira Forest Trust; Tauranga-Taupo Trust; Motutere Point Trust; Turamakina Tribal Cttee; Lake Taupo Forest Trust; Oraukura 3 Block; Hauhungaroa 1C Block; Waihi Pukawa Block; Mem., Tongariro National Park Board (great grandson of original donor). OStJ. *Address:* Pungapunga Road, Ngapuke, Taumarunui, New Zealand.

TEI ABAL, Sir, Kt 1976; CBE 1974; MHA, PNG; *b* 1932; *m*; six *c*. Became a tea-planter and trader in Papua New Guinea; a Leader of the Engi Clan in Western Highlands. Member for Wabag, open electorate, PNG; Former Member (Ministerial) in 1st, 2nd and 3rd Houses of Assembly; Leader of the Opposition, UP, and later Minister of Public Utilities, 1979–80, in Somare Govt. *Address:* c/o PO Box 3534, Port Moresby, Papua New Guinea; Wabag, Papua New Guinea.

TEJAN-SIE, Sir Banja, GCMG 1970 (CMG 1967); Governor-General of Sierra Leone, 1970–71 (Acting Governor-General, 1968–70); international business and legal consultant; *b* 7 Aug. 1917; *s* of late Alpha Ahmed Tejan-Sie; *m* 1946, Admira Stapleton; three *s* one *d*. *Educ:* Bo Sch., Freetown; Prince of Wales Sch., Freetown; LSE, London University. Called to Bar, Lincoln's Inn, 1951. Station Clerk, Sierra Leone Railway,1938–39; Nurse, Medical Dept, 1940–46; Ed., West African Students' Union, 1948–51; Nat. Vice-Pres., Sierra Leone People's Party, 1953–56; Police Magistrate: Eastern Province, 1955; Northern Province, 1958; Sen. Police Magistrate Provinces, 1961; Speaker, Sierra Leone House of Representatives, 1962–67; Chief Justice of Sierra Leone, 1967–70. Mem. Keith Lucas Commn on Electoral Reform, 1954. Hon. Sec. Sierra Leone Bar Assoc., 1957–58. Chm. Bd of Management, Cheshire Foundn, Sierra Leone, 1966. Has led delegations and paid official visits to many countries throughout the world. Hon. Treasurer, Internat. African Inst., London, 1978–. Pres., Freetown Golf Club, 1970–. GCON (Nigeria), 1970; Grand Band, Order of Star of Africa (Liberia), 1969; Special Grand Cordon, Order of propitious clouds (Taiwan), 1970; Grand Cordon, Order of Knighthood of Pioneers (Liberia), 1970; Order of Cedar (Lebanon), 1970. *Recreations:* music, reading. *Address:* 3 Tracy Avenue, NW2 4AT. *T:* 0181–452 2324. *Club:* Commonwealth Trust.

TE KANAWA, Dame Kiri (Jeanette), ONZ 1995; DBE 1982 (OBE 1973); opera singer; *b* Gisborne, New Zealand, 6 March 1944; *m* 1967, Desmond Stephen Park; one *s* one *d*. *Educ:* St Mary's Coll., Auckland, NZ; London Opera Centre. Major rôles at Royal Opera House, Covent Garden, include: the Countess, in Marriage of Figaro; Elvira, in Don Giovanni; Mimi, in La Bohème; Desdemona, in Otello; Marguerite, in Faust; Amelia, in Simon Boccanegra; Fiordiligi, in Così Fan Tutte; Tatiana, in Eugene Onegin; title rôle in Arabella; Rosalinde, in Die Fledermaus; Violetta, in La Traviata; Manon, in Manon Lescaut. Has sung leading rôles at Metropolitan Opera, New York, notably, Desdemona, Elvira, and Countess; also at the Paris Opera, Elvira, Fiordiligi, and Pamina in Magic Flute, title rôle in Tosca; at San Francisco Opera, Amelia and Pamina; at Sydney Opera House, Mimi, Amelia, and Violetta in La Traviata; Elvira, with Cologne Opera; Amelia at la Scala, Milan; Countess in Le Nozze di Figaro at Salzburg fest. Hon. Fellow, Somerville Coll., Oxford, 1983; Hon. DMus Oxford, 1983. *Publication:* Land of the Long White Cloud: Maori myths and legends, 1989. *Recreations:* golf, swimming, tennis. *Address:* c/o Jules Haefliger, Impresario AG, Postfach 4113, 6002 Lucerne, Switzerland.

TELFER, Robert Gilmour Jamieson, (Rab), CBE 1985; PhD; Executive Chairman, BSI Standards, 1989–92; Director, Manchester Business School, 1984–88; *b* 22 April 1928; *s* of late James Telfer and Helen Lambie Jamieson; *m* 1953, Joan Audrey Gunning; three *s*. *Educ:* Bathgate Academy (Dawson Trust Bursary); Univ. of Edinburgh (Mackay-Smith Prize; Blandfield Prize; BSc (Hons 1st cl.) 1950, PhD 1953). Shift Chemist, AEA, 1953–54; Imperial Chemical Industries Ltd: Res. Chemist, Billingham Div., 1954–58; Heavy Organic Chemicals Div., 1958–71; Fibre Intermediates Dir and R & D Dir, 1971–75; Div. Dep. Chm., 1975–76, Div. Chm., 1976–81, Petrochemicals Div.; Chm. and Man. Dir, 1981–84, Dir, 1984, Mather & Platt Ltd; Chm., European Industrial Services Ltd, 1988–89. Mem. Bd, Philips-Imperial Petroleum Ltd, 1975–81; Director: Renold PLC, 1984– (Chm., Audit Cttee, 1993–); Volex PLC, 1986– (Chm., Audit Cttee, 1993–); Teesside Hldgs Ltd, 1993–. Sen. Vis. Fellow, Manchester Business Sch., 1988–. Group Chm., Duke of Edinburgh's Study Conf., 1974; Mem., ACORD for Fuel and Power, 1981–87; Chm., Adv. Council on Energy Conservation, 1982–84. Personal Adviser to Sec. of State for Energy, 1984–87. British Standards Institution: Mem. Main Bd, and Mem. Finance Cttee, 1988–92; non-exec. Chm., Standards Bd and Testing Bd, 1988–89. Member: Civil Service Coll. Adv. Council, 1986–89; HEFCE, 1992– (Chm., Audit Cttee, 1993–). Governor, Univ. of Teesside (formerly Teesside Polytechnic), 1989– (Chm., Govs, 1992–; Chm., Resources Cttee, 1989–92). CIMgt. Hon. MBA Manchester, 1989. *Publications:* papers in Jl Chem. Soc. and Chemistry and Industry. *Recreations:* walking, swimming, poetry, decorative egg collecting, supporting Middlesbrough FC. *Address:* Downings, Upleatham Village, Redcar, Cleveland TS11 8AG. *Club:* Caledonian.

TELFORD, Sir Robert, Kt 1978; CBE 1967; DL; FEng, FIEE; CIMgt; FRSA; Life President, The Marconi Company Ltd, 1984 (Managing Director, 1965–81; Chairman, 1981–84, retired); *b* 1 Oct. 1915; *s* of Robert and Sarah Annie Telford; *m* 1st, 1941 (marr. diss. 1950); one *s*; 2nd, 1958, Elizabeth Mary (*née* Shelley); three *d*. *Educ:* Quarry Bank Sch., Liverpool; Queen Elizabeth's Grammar Sch., Tamworth; Christ's Coll., Cambridge (MA). Manager, Hackbridge Works, The Marconi Co. Ltd, 1940–46; Man. Dir, Companhia Marconi Brasileira, 1946–50; The Marconi Company Ltd: Asst to Gen. Manager, 1950–53; Gen. Works Manager, 1953–61; Gen. Manager, 1961–65; Man. Dir, GEC-Marconi Electronics Ltd, 1968–84; Chm., GEC Avionics Ltd, 1982–86; Director: The General Electric Co., 1973–84; Canadian Marconi Co., Montreal, 1968–84; Ericsson Radio Systems AB (formerly SRA Communications, AB), Stockholm, 1969–85. Chairman: DRI Hldgs Ltd, 1984–88; Prelude Technology Investments, 1985–91; CTP Investments, 1987–90; Diametric, 1988–89; Dir, BAJ Hldgs, 1985–87. Visitor, Hatfield Polytech., 1986–91. President: Electronic Engrg Assoc., 1963–64; IProdE, 1982–83; Chairman: Electronics and Avionics Requirement Bd, DTI, 1980–85; Alvey Steering Cttee, 1983–88; SERC Teaching Company Management Cttee, 1984–87; Commonwealth Engineers' Council, 1989–93; Member: Electronics EDC, 1964–67, 1981–85; Engrg Industry Trng Bd, 1968–82; Council, Industrial Soc., 1982–86; Council, Fellowship of Engrg, 1983–86; BTEC, 1984–86; SERC Engrg Bd, 1985–88; Engrg Council, 1985–89; IT Adv. Gp, DTI, 1985–88. Advr to Comett Programme of European Community, 1987–; Mem., Industrial R & D Adv. Cttee to European Community,

1988–92. Mem., Council of Sen. Advrs to Internat. Assoc. of Univ. Presidents, 1992. Mem., Council, 1981–88, and Court, 1981–, Univ. of Essex. DL Essex, 1981. Freeman, City of London, 1984. Hon. FIMechE, 1983; Hon. FIEE, 1987; Hon. FICE 1992. Hon. Fellow, Hatfield Poly., 1991. Hon. DSc: Salford, 1981; Cranfield, 1983; Bath, 1984; Aston, 1985; Hon. DEng: Bradford, 1986; Birmingham, 1986; Hon. DTech Anglia Inst., 1989. Leonardo da Vinci Medal, SEFI, 1992. *Address:* Rettendon House, Rettendon, Chelmsford, Essex CM3 8DW. *T:* Wickford (01268) 733131. *Club:* Royal Air Force.

TELFORD BEASLEY, John, CBE 1988; Chairman, PS Ltd, since 1991; Director, MGM Assurance, since 1987; *b* 26 March 1929; *s* of James George and Florence Telford Beasley; *m* (marr. diss.); one *s* two *d*. *Educ:* Watford Grammar School; Open Univ. (BA). Dep. Chm., Cadbury Ltd, 1970–73; Chm., Cadbury Schweppes Food Ltd, 1973–75; Dir, Cadbury Schweppes, 1973–77; Chm., Schweppes Ltd, 1975–77; Regional Pres., Warner Lamber Co., 1977–84; Dir, LRT, 1984–92; Chm., London Buses Ltd, 1985–92. *Recreations:* golf, cricket. *Address:* 3 Monmouth Square, Winchester, Hants SO22 4HY.

TELLER, Prof. Edward; Senior Research Fellow, Hoover Institution, since 1975; University Professor, University of California, Berkeley, 1971–75, now Emeritus (Professor of Physics, 1960–71); Chairman, Department of Applied Science, University of California, 1963–66; Associate Director, Lawrence Radiation Laboratory, University of California, 1954–75, now Emeritus; *b* Budapest, Hungary, 15 January 1908; *s* of a lawyer; became US citizen, 1941; *m* 1934, Augusta Harkanyi; one *s* one *d*. *Educ:* Karlsruhe Technical Inst., Germany; Univ. of Munich; Leipzig (PhD). Research Associate, Leipzig, 1929–31; Research Associate, Göttingen, 1931–33; Rockefeller Fellow, Copenhagen, 1934; Lectr, Univ. of London, 1934–35; Prof. of Physics, George Washington Univ., Washington, DC, 1935–41; Prof. of Physics, Columbia Univ., 1941–42; Physicist, Manhattan, Engineer District, 1942–46, Univ. of Chicago, 1942–43; Los Alamos Scientific Laboratory, 1943–46; Prof. of Physics, Univ. of Chicago, 1946–52; Asst Dir, Los Alamos (on leave, Chicago), 1949–52; Consultant, Livermore Br., Univ. of Calif, Radiation Laboratory, 1952–53; Prof. of Physics, Univ. of Calif, 1953–60; Dir, Livermore Br., Lawrence Livermore Lab., Univ. of Calif, 1958–60, now Dir Emeritus. Mem. Nat. Acad. of Sciences, etc. Holds several hon. degrees, 1954–. Has gained awards, 1957–, incl. Enrico Fermi Award, 1962; Harvey Prize, Israel, 1975; Gold Medal, Amer. Coll. of Nuclear Med., 1980; Man of the Year, Achievement Rewards for College Scientists, 1980; Nat. Medal of Science, 1983. *Publications:* The Structure of Matter, 1949; Our Nuclear Future, 1958; The Legacy of Hiroshima, 1962; The Reluctant Revolutionary, 1964; The Constructive Uses of Nuclear Explosives, 1968; Great Men of Physics, 1969; Nuclear Energy in a Developing World, 1977; Energy from Heaven and Earth, 1979; Pursuit of Simplicity, 1980; Better a Shield than a Sword, 1987; Conversations on the Dark Secrets of Physics, 1991. *Address:* Stanford, CA 94305, USA.

TELLO, Manuel, CMG (Hon.) 1975; Permanent Representative of Mexico to the United Nations, 1993–94 and since 1995; *b* 15 March 1935; *s* of late Manuel Tello and Guadalupe M. de Tello; *m* 1983, Rhonda M. de Tello. *Educ:* schools in Mexico City; Georgetown Univ.; Sch. for Foreign Service, Washington, DC; Escuela Libre de Derecho; Institut de Hautes Etudes Internationales, Geneva. Equivalent of BA in Foreign Service Studies; post-grad. studies in Internat. Law. Joined Mexican Foreign Service, 1957; Asst Dir Gen. for Internat. Organizations, 1967–70, Dir Gen., 1970–72; Dir for Multilateral Affairs, 1972–74; Dir for Political Affairs, 1975–76; Ambassador to UK, 1977–79; Under Sec., Dept of Foreign Affairs, Mexico, 1979–82; Perm. Rep. of Mexico to Internat. Orgns, Geneva, 1983–89; Ambassador to France, 1989–92; Minister of Foreign Affairs, 1994–95. Alternate Rep. of Mexico to: OAS, 1959–63; Internat. Orgs, Geneva, 1963–65; Conf. of Cttee on Disarmament, Geneva, 1963–66; Rep. of Mexico to: Org. for Proscription of Nuclear Weapons in Latin America, 1970–73; 3rd UN Conf. on Law of the Sea, 1971–76 and 1982. Has attended several Sessions of UN Gen. Assembly. Holds decorations from Chile, Ecuador, Egypt, France, Italy, Jordan, Panama, Senegal, Sweden, Venezuela, Yugoslavia. *Publications:* contribs to learned jls in the field of international relations. *Recreations:* tennis, theatre, music. *Address:* 2 UN Plaza, 28th Floor, New York, NY 10017, USA.

TEMIRKANOV, Yuri; Principal Conductor, Royal Philharmonic Orchestra, since 1992 (Principal Guest Conductor, 1981–92); Music Director and Principal Conductor, St Petersburg (formerly Leningrad) Philharmonic Orchestra, since 1988; *b* 10 Dec. 1938. *Educ:* Leningrad Conservatory (graduated violinist, 1962, conductor, 1965). Musical Dir, Leningrad Symphony Orch., 1969–77; Artistic Dir and Chief Conductor, Kirov Opera, Leningrad, 1977–88. Principal Guest Conductor, Dresden Philharmonic Orch., 1994–. Has conducted: Berlin Philharmonic; Boston Symphony; Dresden State; Los Angeles Philharmonic; New York Philharmonic; Orchestre de Paris; Philadelphia; Pittsburgh Symphony; Royal Concertgebouw; Vienna Philharmonic, etc. Recordings of major orchestral works of Tchaikovsky, Stravinsky, Prokofiev and Mussorgsky. *Address:* c/o IMG Artists Europe, 3 Burlington Lane, W4 2TH. *T:* 0181–233 5800.

TEMKIN, Prof. Jennifer, (Mrs G. J. Zellick); Professor of Law, University of Sussex, since 1992; Director, Centre for Legal Studies, since 1994; *b* 6 June 1948; *d* of late Michael Temkin and Minnie Temkin (*née* Levy); *m* 1975, Prof. Graham Zellick, *qv*; one *s* one *d*. *Educ:* S Hampstead High Sch. for Girls; LSE (LLB, LLM (Dist.)); Inns of Court Sch. of Law. Called to the Bar, Middle Temple, 1971; Lectr in Law, LSE, 1971–89; Prof. of Law and Dean, Sch. of Law, Univ. of Buckingham, 1989–92. Vis. Prof., Univ. of Toronto, 1978–79. Mem., Cttee of Heads of Univ. Law Schs, 1989–92, 1994–. Member: Scrutiny Cttee on Draft Criminal Code, CCC, 1985–86; Home Sec's Adv. Gp on Use of Video Recordings in Criminal Proceedings, 1988–89; NCH Cttee on Children Who Abuse Other Children, 1990–92. Patron, Standing Cttee on Sexually Abused Children, 1993–. Gov., S Hampstead High Sch. for Girls, 1991–. FRSA 1989. Member: Editl Adv. Gp, Howard Jl of Criminal Justice, 1984–; Editl Bd, Jl of Criminal Law, 1986–. *Publications:* Rape and the Legal Process, 1987; articles in Mod. Law Rev., Criminal Law Rev., Cambridge Law Jl, Law Qly Rev., Internat. and Comparative Law Qly and other learned and professional jls. *Address:* Centre for Legal Studies, University of Sussex, Falmer, Brighton, Sussex BN1 9QN. *T:* Brighton (01273) 606755.

TEMKO, Edward James, (Ned); Editor, Jewish Chronicle, since 1990; *b* 5 Nov. 1952; *s* of Stanley L. Temko and Francine (*née* Salzman); *m* 1st, 1980, Noa Weiss (marr. diss. 1984); 2nd, 1986, Astra Bergson Kook; one *s*. *Educ:* Williams Coll., USA (BA Hons Pol Sci. and Econs). Reporter, Associated Press, Lisbon, 1976; United Press International: Europe, ME and Africa Editl Desk, Brussels, 1977; Correspondent, ME Office, Beirut, 1977–78; Christian Science Monitor: Chief ME Correspondent, Beirut, 1978–80; Moscow Correspondent, 1981–83; ME Correspondent, Jerusalem, 1984–85; SA Correspondent, Johannesburg, 1986–87; Sen. TV Correspondent for Europe, ME and Africa in London, World Monitor TV, 1989–90. *Publications:* To Win or To Die: a biography of Menachem Begin, 1987. *Recreations:* tennis, reading, computers, travel. *Address:* 25 Furnival Street, EC4A 1JT. *T:* 071–405 9252.

TEMPANY, Myles McDermott, OBE 1984; Vice-Principal (External Affairs), King's College London, 1986–88; *b* 31 March 1924; *y s* of late Martin Tempany and Margaret (*née* McDermott); *m* 1951, Pamela Allan; one *s* one *d*. *Educ:* St Muredach's College, Ballina, Co. Mayo; Intermediate and University College, Dublin. Military service, 1944–47. King's College London: Asst Acct, 1948–70; Acct, 1970–73; Finance Officer and Acct, 1973–77; FKC 1975; Bursar, 1977–81; Head of Admin and Bursar, 1981–83; Secretary, 1983–85; Mem. Council, 1986–89. Mem. Delegacy, King's Coll. Sch. of Medicine and Dentistry, 1986–88; Founder Chm., St Raphael's Training Centre Develt Trust, 1978–83; Mem., Governing Body, Univ. of Hertfordshire (formerly Hatfield Polytechnic), 1985–; Chm., Bd of Governors, Pope Paul Sch., Potters Bar, 1986–. KHS 1972, KCHS 1978; KSG 1983. President's Award, Develt Bd, Univ. of Texas Health Science Center, Houston, 1986. *Recreations:* golf, watching Association Football. *Address:* 18 Tiverton Road, Potters Bar, Herts EN6 5HY. *T:* Potters Bar (01707) 656860. *Clubs:* Institute of Directors; Brookman's Park Golf.

TEMPLE OF STOWE, 8th Earl *cr* 1822; **Walter Grenville Algernon Temple-Gore-Langton;** *b* 2 Oct. 1924; *s* of Comdr Hon. Evelyn Arthur Temple-Gore-Langton, DSO, RN (*d* 1972) (*y s* of 4th Earl) and Irene (*d* 1967), *d* of Brig.-Gen. Cavendish Walter Gartside-Spaight; *S* cousin, 1988; *m* 1st, 1954, Zillah Ray (*d* 1966), *d* of James Boxall; two *s* one *d*; 2nd, 1968, Margaret Elizabeth Graham, *o d* of late Col H. W. Scarth of Breckness. *Heir: s* Lord Langton, *qv*.

TEMPLE, Anthony Dominic Afamado; QC 1986; a Recorder, since 1989; *b* 21 Sept. 1945; *s* of Sir Rawden Temple, *qv*; *m* 1st, 1975 (marr. diss.); 2nd, 1983, Suzie Bodansky; two *d*. *Educ:* Haileybury and ISC; Worcester College, Oxford (Hon. Sec., OU Modern Pentathlon Assoc.). Called to the Bar, Inner Temple, 1968, Bencher, 1995; Crown Law Office, Western Australia, 1969; Assistant Recorder, 1982; a Dep. High Ct Judge, 1994–. *Recreations:* modern pentathlon, travel, history. *Address:* 4 Pump Court, EC4Y 7AN.
See also V. B. A. Temple.

TEMPLE, His Honour Sir (Ernest) Sanderson, Kt 1988; MBE; MA; QC 1969; a Circuit Judge, 1977–91; Honorary Recorder of Kendal, since 1972, of Liverpool, 1978–91, and of Lancaster, since 1987; *b* 23 May 1921; *o s* of Ernest Temple, Oxenholme House, Kendal; *m* 1946, June Debonnaire (*d* 1995), *o d* of W. M. Saunders, JP, Wennington Hall, Lancaster; one *s* two *d*. *Educ:* Kendal School; Queen's Coll., Oxford. Served in Border Regt in India and Burma, attaining temp. rank of Lt-Col (despatches, 1945). Barrister-at-Law, 1943. Joined Northern Circuit, 1946; Dep. Recorder of Salford, 1962–65; Dep. Chm., Agricultural Land Tribunal (Northern), 1966–69; Chm., Westmorland QS, 1969–71 (Dep. Chm., 1967); a Recorder of the Crown Court, 1972–77; Mem., Bar Council, 1965. Chairman: Arnside/Silverdale Landscape Trust, 1987–; NW Area Point-to-Point Assoc., 1987–; Pres., British Harness Racing Club, 1991–. Jt Master, Vale of Lune Hunt, 1963–85. Hon. FICW. Hon. Citizen of Kendal, 1992. *Recreations:* farming and horses. *Address:* Yealand Hall, Yealand Redmayne, near Carnforth, Lancs LA5 9TD. *T:* Burton (Cumbria) (01524) 781200.

TEMPLE, Rt. Rev. Frederick Stephen; Honorary Assistant Bishop, Diocese of Bristol, since 1983; *b* 24 Nov. 1916; *s* of Frederick Charles and Frances Temple; *m* 1947, Joan Catharine Webb; one *s* one *d* (and one *s* decd). *Educ:* Rugby; Balliol Coll., Oxford; Trinity Hall, Cambridge; Westcott House, Cambridge. Deacon, 1947, Priest, 1948; Curate, St Mary's, Arnold, Notts, 1947–49; Curate, Newark Parish Church, 1949–51; Rector, St Agnes, Birch, Manchester, 1951–53; Dean of Hong Kong, 1953–59; Senior Chaplain to the Archbishop of Canterbury, 1959–61; Vicar of St Mary's, Portsea, 1961–70; Archdeacon of Swindon, 1970–73; Bishop Suffragan of Malmesbury, 1973–83. Proctor, Canterbury Convocation, 1964; Hon. Canon, Portsmouth Cathedral, 1965. *Publication:* (ed) William Temple, Some Lambeth Letters, 1942–44, 1963. *Recreations:* gardening, theatre, television. *Address:* 7 The Barton, Wood Street, Wootton Bassett, Wilts SN4 7BG. *T:* Swindon (01793) 851227.

TEMPLE, Ven. George Frederick; Archdeacon of Bodmin, 1981–89, Archdeacon Emeritus since 1989; *b* 16 March 1933; *s* of George Frederick and Lilian Rose Temple; *m* 1961, Jacqueline Rose Urwin; one *s* one *d*. *Educ:* St Paul's, Jersey; Wells Theological College. Deacon 1968, priest 1969, Guildford; Curate: St Nicholas, Great Bookham, 1968–70; St Mary the Virgin, Penzance, 1970–72; Vicar of St Just in Penwith with Sancreed, 1972–74; Vicar of St Gluvias, Penryn, 1974–81; Vicar of Saltash, 1982–85. Mem., General Synod of C of E, 1981–85; Chm., House of Clergy, Truro Diocesan Synod, 1982–85; Diocesan Dir of Ordinands, 1985–87. Hon. Canon of Truro, 1981–89. *Recreations:* poetry, history, walking. *Address:* 50 Athelstan Park, Bodmin, Cornwall PL31 1DT.

TEMPLE, Nicholas John; Chairman, IBM United Kingdom Ltd, since 1994 (Chief Executive, 1992–94); Vice President, Industries, IBM Europe, since 1995; *b* 2 Oct. 1947; *s* of late Leonard Temple and of Lilly Irene Temple (*née* Thornton); *m* 1975, Janet Perry; one *s* two *d*. *Educ:* King's Sch., Glos. Joined IBM, 1965. Council Mem., Foundn for Mfg and Ind., 1993–. Chm., Action: Employees in the Community, 1993–. Mem., President's Adv. Gp, Spastics' Soc., 1993–. *Recreations:* rowing, ski-ing, opera. *Address:* (office) South Bank, 76/78 Upper Ground, SE1 9PZ. *T:* 0171–202 3000.

TEMPLE, Sir Rawden (John Afamado), Kt 1980; CBE 1964; QC 1951; Chief Social Security (formerly National Insurance) Commissioner, 1975–81 (a National Insurance Commissioner, 1969); a Referee under Child Benefit Act, 1975, since 1976; *b* 1908; *m* 1936, Margaret Jessie Wiseman (*d* 1980), *d* of late Sir James Gunson, CMG, CBE; two *s*. *Educ:* King Edward's School, Birmingham; The Queen's College, Oxford. BA 1930; BCL, 1931; called to Bar, 1931; Master of the Bench, Inner Temple, 1960 (Reader, 1982; Treasurer, 1983); Vice-Chairman, General Council of the Bar, 1960–64. Mem., Industrial Injuries Adv. Council, 1981–84. War Service, 1941–45. Liveryman Worshipful Company of Pattenmakers, 1948. *Recreations:* fishing; collecting portraits and oriental rugs. *Address:* 3 North King's Bench Walk, Temple, EC4Y 7DQ.
See also A. D. A. Temple, V. B. A. Temple.

TEMPLE, Reginald Robert, CMG 1979; HM Diplomatic Service, retired; Oman Government Service, 1979–85; *b* 12 Feb. 1922; *s* of Lt-Gen. R. C. Temple, CB, OBE, RM, and Z. E. Temple (*née* Hunt); *m* 1st, 1952, Julia Jasmine Anthony (marr. diss. 1979); one *s* one *d*; 2nd, 1979, Susan McCorquodale (*née* Pick); one *d* (one step *s* one step *d*). *Educ:* Wellington College; Peterhouse, Cambridge. HM Forces, 1940–46, RE and Para Regt; Stockbroking, 1947–51; entered HM Foreign Service, 1951; Office of HM Comr Gen. for SE Asia, 1952–56; 2nd Sec., Beirut, 1958–62; 1st Sec., Algiers, 1964–66, Paris, 1967–69; FCO, 1969–79; Counsellor 1975. Director: Shearwater Securities Ltd, I of M, 1989–92; City and International Securities Ltd, I of M, 1993–. American Silver Star, 1944; Order of Oman, 3rd Class, 1985. *Recreations:* sailing, fishing. *Address:* Scarlett House, near Castletown, Isle of Man IM9 1TB. *Clubs:* Army and Navy, Royal Cruising, Royal Ocean Racing.

TEMPLE, Sir Richard Anthony Purbeck, 4th Bt, *cr* 1876; MC 1941; *b* 19 Jan. 1913; *s* of Sir Richard Durand Temple, 3rd Bt, DSO; *S* father, 1962; *m* 1st, 1936, Lucy Geils (marr. diss., 1946), 2nd *d* of late Alain Joly de Lotbinière, Montreal; two *s*; 2nd, 1950, Jean, *d* of late James T. Finnie, and *widow* of Oliver P. Croom-Johnson; one *d*. *Educ:* Stowe; Trinity Hall, Cambridge; Lausanne University. Served War of 1939–45 (wounded,

MC). Sometime Major, KRRC. *Recreation:* sailing. *Heir:* *s* Richard Temple [*b* 17 Aug. 1937; *m* 1964, Emma Rose, 2nd *d* of late Maj.-Gen. Sir Robert Laycock, KCMG, CB, DSO; three *d*]. *Address:* c/o National Westminster Bank, 55 Kensington High Street, W8 5ED.

TEMPLE, Sir Sanderson; *see* Temple, Sir E. S.

TEMPLE, Victor Bevis Afoumado; QC 1993; a Recorder of the Crown Court, since 1989; *b* 23 Feb. 1941; *s* of Sir Rawden Temple, CBE, QC and of late Lady Temple; *m* 1974, Richenda Penn-Bull; two *s*. *Educ:* Shrewsbury Sch.; Inns of Court Sch. of Law. TA, Westminster Dragoons, 1960–61. Marketing Exec., 1960–68. Called to the Bar, Inner Temple, 1971; Jun. Prosecuting Counsel to the Crown, 1985–91, Sen. Treasury Counsel, 1991–93, CCC. DTI Inspector into Nat. Westminster Bank Ltd, 1992. Mem. Panel of Chairmen, Police Discipline Tribunals, 1993–. *Recreations:* rowing, carpentry. *Address:* 6 King's Bench Walk, Temple, EC4Y 7DR. *T:* 0171–583 0410. *Club:* Thames Rowing.

See also A. D. A. Temple.

TEMPLE-GORE-LANGTON, family name of **Earl Temple of Stowe.**

TEMPLE-MORRIS, Peter; MP (C) Leominster since Feb. 1974; Solicitor, Payne Hicks Beach, since 1989; *b* 12 Feb. 1938; *o s* of His Honour Sir Owen Temple-Morris, QC and Lady (Vera) Temple-Morris (*née* Thompson); *m* 1964, Taheré, *e d* of HE Senator Khozeimé Alam, Teheran; two *s* two *d*. *Educ:* Hillstone Sch., Malvern; Malvern Coll.; St Catharine's Coll., Cambridge (MA). Chm., Cambridge Univ. Conservative Assoc., 1961; Mem. Cambridge Afro-Asian Expedn, 1961. Called to Bar, Inner Temple, 1962. Judge's Marshal, Midland Circuit, 1958; Mem., Young Barristers' Cttee, Bar Council, 1962–63; in practice on Wales and Chester Circuit, 1963–66; London and SE Circuit, 1966–76; 2nd Prosecuting Counsel to Inland Revenue, SE Circuit, 1971–74; admitted a solicitor, 1989. Contested (C): Newport (Mon), 1964 and 1966; Norwood (Lambeth), 1970. PPS to Minister of Transport, 1979. Member: Select Cttee on Agriculture, 1982–83; Select Cttee on Foreign Affairs, 1987–90. Chairman: British-Lebanese Parly Gp, 1983–94 (Vice-Chm., 1994–); British-Netherlands Parly Gp, 1988–; British-Iranian Parly Gp, 1989– (Sec., 1974–89); British-South Africa (formerly British-Southern Africa) All-Party Gp, 1992–; British-Russian All-Party Gp, 1992–94; British-Spanish All-Party Gp, 1994–; House of Lords and Commons Solicitors Gp, 1992–; Co-Chm., Working Party to establish British-Irish Inter-Parly Body, 1988–90, first British Co-Chm., 1990–; Secretary: Conservative Parly Transport Cttee, 1976–79; Cons. Parly Legal Cttee, 1977–78; Vice-Chairman: Cons. Parly Foreign and Commonwealth Affairs Cttee, 1982–90 (Sec., 1979–82); Cons. Parly NI Cttee, 1989–92; British-Argentina Parly Gp, 1990–94; European-Atlantic Gp, 1991–. Mem. Exec. British Branch, IPU, 1977– (Chm., 1982–85); British delegate, IPU fact-finding mission on Namibia, 1977; Mem., 1980, Leader, 1984, Parly Delegation to UN Gen. Assembly; Mem., Argentine-British Conf., 1991. Chm., Hampstead Conservative Political Centre, 1971–73; Society of Conservative Lawyers: Chm., 1995–; Mem., 1968–71, 1990–, and Chm., 1995–, Exec. Cttee; Vice-Chm., Standing Cttee on Criminal Law, 1976–79; Chm., F&GP Cttee, 1992–95. Chm., Bow Gp Standing Cttee on Home Affairs, 1975–79. Chm., Afghanistan Support Cttee, 1981–82; Vice-Chm., GB-Russian Centre (formerly GB-USSR Assoc.), 1993– (Mem. Council, 1982–92); Member: Council, Iran Soc., 1968–80; RIIA. Nat. Treas., UNA, 1987–. Freeman, City of London; Liveryman: Basketmakers' Co.; Barbers' Co., 1993. Governor: Malvern Coll., 1975– (Council Mem., 1978–); Wilton Park Conf. Centre (FCO), 1990–. Fellow, Industry and Parlt Trust, Barclays Bank, 1988. Hon. Associate, BVA, 1976. Chevalier du Tastevin, 1991. *Recreations:* shooting; wine and food; family relaxation. *Address:* House of Commons, SW1A 0AA. *T:* 0171–219 4181. *Clubs:* Carlton; Cardiff and County.

TEMPLEMAN, family name of **Baron Templeman.**

TEMPLEMAN, Baron *cr* 1982 (Life Peer), of White Lackington in the County of Somerset; **Sydney William Templeman;** Kt 1972; MBE 1946; PC 1978; a Lord of Appeal in Ordinary, 1982–94; *b* 3 March 1920; *s* of late Herbert William and Lilian Templeman; *m* 1946, Margaret Joan (*née* Rowles) (*d* 1988); two *s*. *Educ:* Southall Grammar School; St John's College, Cambridge (Schol.; MA 1944; Hon. Fellow 1982). Served War of 1939–45: commnd 4/1st Gurkha Rifles, 1941; NW Frontier, 1942; Arakan, 1943; Imphal, 1944; Burma with 7 Ind. and 17 Ind. Divisions, 1945 (despatches; Hon. Major). Called to the Bar, 1947; Harmsworth and MacMahon schols; Mem., Middle Temple and Lincoln's Inn; Mem., Bar Council, 1961–65, 1970–72; QC 1964; Bencher, Middle Temple, 1969 (Treasurer, 1987). Attorney Gen. of the Duchy of Lancaster, 1970–72; a Judge of the High Court of Justice, Chancery Div., 1972–78; a Lord Justice of Appeal, 1978–82. Member: Tribunal to inquire into matters relating to the Vehicle and General Insurance Co., 1971; Adv. Cttee on Legal Education, 1972–74; Royal Commn on Legal Services, 1976–79; Chm., Bishop of London's Commn on City Churches, 1992–94. Treasurer, Senate of the Four Inns, 1972–74; Pres., Senate of the Inns of Court and the Bar, 1974–76. President: Bar Assoc. for Commerce, Finance and Industry, 1982–85; Bar European Gp, 1987–. Pres., Holdsworth Club, 1983–84. Hon. Member: Canadian Bar Assoc., 1976; Amer. Bar Assoc., 1976; Newfoundland Law Soc., 1984. Hon. DLitt Reading, 1980; Hon. LLD: Birmingham, 1986; CNAA, 1990; Exeter, 1991; W of England, 1993; Nat. Law Sch. of India, 1994. *Address:* Manor Heath, Knowl Hill, Woking, Surrey GU22 7HL. *T:* Woking (01483) 761930.

TEMPLEMAN, Michael; Group Tax Director, J Henry Schroder (formerly J Henry Schroder Wagg) & Co. Ltd, since 1994; *b* 6 May 1943; *s* of Geoffrey Templeman and Dorothy May Templeman (*née* Heathcote); *m* 1970, Jane Margaret Willmer Lee; four *d*. *Educ:* King Edward's Sch., Birmingham; Selwyn Coll., Cambridge (MA). Inland Revenue, 1965–93: Inspector of Taxes, 1965; Dist Inspector, Cannock, 1971–72; Head Office Specialist, Oil Taxation, 1972–78; Dist. Inspector, Luton, 1978–81; Head Office Specialist, Financial Concerns, 1981–89; Controller, Oil Taxation Office, 1989–92; Dir, Financial Institutions Div., 1992–93. *Recreations:* distance running, cricket, classical music, cooking. *Address:* (office) 120 Cheapside, EC2V 6DS. *T:* 0171–382 6450.

TEMPLER, Maj.-Gen. James Robert, CB 1989; OBE 1978 (MBE 1973); retired; *b* 8 Jan. 1936; *s* of Brig. Cecil Robert Templer, DSO and Angela Mary Templer (*née* Henderson); *m* 1963 (marr. diss. 1979); two *s* one *d*; 2nd, 1981, Sarah Ann Evans (*née* Rogers). *Educ:* Charterhouse; RMA Sandhurst. RCDS, psc. Commissioned Royal Artillery, 1955; Instructor, Staff Coll., 1974–75; Comd 42nd Regt, 1975–77; Comd 5th Regt, 1977–78; CRA 2nd Armd Div., 1978–82; RCDS 1983; ACOS Training, HQ UKLF, 1983–86; ACDS (Concepts), MoD, 1986–89. Mem., British Cross Country Ski Team, 1958; European 3 Day Event Champion, 1962; Mem., British Olympic 3 Day Event Team, 1964. FBIM 1988. *Recreations:* sailing, ski-ing, riding, gardening, fishing, beekeeping, DIY. *Address:* c/o Lloyds Bank, Crediton, Devon EX17 3AH.

TEMPLETON, Prof. (Alexander) Allan, FRCOG; Professor of Obstetrics and Gynaecology, University of Aberdeen, since 1985; *b* 28 June 1946; *s* of Richard and Minnie Templeton; *m* 1980, Gillian Constance Penney; three *s* one *d*. *Educ:* Aberdeen Grammar School; Univ. of Aberdeen (MB ChB 1969; MD Hons 1982); MRCOG 1974, FRCOG 1987. Resident and Registrar, Aberdeen Hosps, 1969–75; Lectr and Sen. Lectr, Dept of Obst. and Gyn., Univ. of Edinburgh, 1976–85. *Publications:* clinical and sci. articles on human infertility and *in vitro* fertilisation. *Recreation:* mountaineering. *Address:* Knapperna House, Udny, Aberdeenshire AB4 0SA. *T:* Udny (01651) 842481.

TEMPLETON, Darwin Herbert, CBE 1975; *b* 14 July 1922; *s* of Malcolm and Mary Templeton; *m* 1950; two *s* one *d*. *Educ:* Rocavan Sch.; Ballymena Academy. FICAI. Qualified as Chartered Accountant, 1945. Partner, Ashworth Rowan, 1947; Senior Partner, Price Waterhouse Northern Ireland (formerly Ashworth Rowan Craig Gardner), 1967–82. Chm., Ulster Soc. of Chartered Accountants, 1961–62; Pres., ICAI, 1970–71. Mem., Royal Commn on Legal Services, 1976–79. Chairman: Northern Publishing Office (UK) Ltd; Ballycassidy Sawmills Ltd; Director: Larne Harbour Ltd; Boxmore International plc. *Recreations:* music, golf, motor racing. *Address:* 4 Cashel Road, Broughshane, Ballymena, Co. Antrim, Northern Ireland BT42 4PL. *T:* Broughshane (01266) 861017. *Club:* Royal Scottish Automobile.

TEMPLETON, Mrs Edith; author, since 1950; *b* 7 April 1916; *m* Edmund Ronald, MD (*d* 1984); one *s*. *Educ:* Prague and Paris; Prague Medical University. During War of 1939–45 worked in American War Office, in office of Surgeon General. Conference (1945–46) and Conference Interpreter for British Forces in Germany, rank of Capt. *Publications:* Summer in the Country, 1950 (USA 1951), repr. 1985; Living on Yesterday, 1951, repr. 1986; The Island of Desire, 1952, repr. 1985; The Surprise of Cremona, 1954 (USA 1957), repr. 1985; This Charming Pastime, 1955; (as Louise Walbrook) Gordon, 1966 (US edn as The Demon's Feast, 1968); Three (USA 1971); Murder in Estoril, 1992; contributor to The New Yorker, Holiday, Atlantic Monthly, Vogue, Harper's Magazine. *Recreation:* travel, with the greatest comfort possible. *Address:* 76 Corso Europa, 18012 Bordighera, Italy.

TEMPLETON, Sir John (Marks), Kt 1987; Secretary, John Templeton Foundation, since 1985; Chairman, Templeton, Galbraith and Hansberger Ltd, 1986–92; Chairman Emeritus, Templeton International, Inc.; chartered financial analyst, 1965–92; *b* 29 Nov. 1912; *s* of Harvey Maxwell Templeton and Vella Templeton (*née* Handly); *m* 1st, 1937, Judith Dudley Folk (*d* 1950); two *s* one *d*; 2nd, 1958, Irene Reynolds Butler; one step *s* one step *d*. *Educ:* Yale Univ. (BA *summa cum laude*); Balliol Coll., Oxford (MA; Rhodes Scholar). Vice Pres., Nat. Geophysical Co., 1937–40; President: Templeton Dobbrow and Vance Inc., 1940–60; Templeton Growth Fund Ltd, 1954–85; Templeton Investment Counsel Ltd of Edinburgh, 1976–92; Templeton World Fund Inc., 1978–87; Founder: Templeton Prizes for Progress in Religion, 1972; Templeton UK Project Trust, 1984; Trustee, Templeton Educn and Charity Trust, 1991–; Pres., Bd of Trustees, Princeton Theol Seminary, 1967–73 and 1979–85; Mem., Bd of Trustees, Westminster Abbey Trust, 1991–. Mem. Council, Templeton College (formerly Oxford Centre for Management Studies), 1983– (Hon. Fellow, 1991). Hon. LLD: Beaver Coll., 1968; Marquette Univ., 1980; Jamestown Coll., 1983; Maryville Coll., 1984; Stone Hill Coll., 1995; Hon. LHD Wilson Coll., 1974; Hon. DD Buena Vista Coll., 1979; Hon. DCL Univ. of the South, 1984; Hon. DLitt Manhattan Coll., 1990; Hon. Dr Rhodes Coll., Babson Coll., Florida Southern Coll., Univ. of Dubuque, and Univ. of Rochester, 1992. *Publications:* The Humble Approach, 1982; Riches for the Mind and Spirit, 1990; (jtly) The God Who Would Be Known, 1990; Is God the Only Reality, 1993; (ed) Evidence of Purpose, 1994; Discovering the Laws of Life, 1994; articles in professional jls. *Recreations:* swimming, gardening. *Address:* Lyford Cay, Nassau, Bahamas. *T:* 3624295. *Clubs:* Athenæum, White's, United Oxford & Cambridge University; University (NY); Lyford Cay (Bahamas).

TEMPLETON-COTILL, Rear-Adm. John Atrill, CB 1972; retired; *b* 4 June 1920; *s* of late Captain Jack Lionel Cottle, Tank Corps. *Educ:* Canford Sch.; New Coll., Oxford. Joined RNVR, 1939; served war 1939–45; HMS Crocus, 1940–41; British Naval Liaison Officer, French warship Chevreuil, 1941–42; staff, GOC New Caledonia (US), 1942; US Embassy, London, 1943; Flag Lieutenant to Vice-Adm., Malta, 1943–44; 1st Lieut, MTB 421, 1944–45; ADC to Governor of Victoria, 1945–46; served in HMS London, Loch Quoich, Whirlwind, Jutland, Barrosa and Sparrow, 1946–55; Comdr 1955; comd HMS Sefton and 108th Minesweeping Sqdn, 1955–56; jssc 1956; Comdr-in-Charge, RN School of Work Study, 1957–59; HMS Tiger, 1959–61; Captain 1961; British Naval Attaché, Moscow, 1962–64; comd HMS Rhyl and Captain (D), 23rd Escort Sqdn, 1964–66; Senior Naval Mem., Defence Operational Analysis Estabt, 1966–68; comd HMS Bulwark, 1968–69; Rear-Adm. Jan. 1970; Chief of Staff to Comdr Far East Fleet, 1970–71; Flag Officer, Malta, and NATO Comdr, SE Area Mediterranean, 1971–73; Comdr, British Forces Malta, 1972–73. Director: Sotheby Parke Bernet (France), 1974–81; Sotheby Parke Bernet (Monaco), 1975–81. *Recreations:* gardening, riding, shooting, travel, skiing. *Address:* Moulin de Fontvive, Ribas, par 30290 Laudun, France. *T:* 66794737.

TENBY, 3rd Viscount *cr* 1957, of Bulford; **William Lloyd-George;** Chairman, St James Public Relations, since 1990; *b* 7 Nov. 1927; 2nd *s* of 1st Viscount Tenby, TD, PC, and Edna Gwenfron (*d* 1971), *d* of David Jones, Gwynfa, Denbigh; *S* brother, 1983; *m* 1955, Ursula Diana Ethel, *y d* of late Lt-Col Henry Edward Medlicott, DSO; one *s* two *d*. *Educ:* Eastbourne College; St Catharine's Coll., Cambridge (Exhibnr; BA 1949). Captain, Royal Welch Fusiliers, TA. Dir, Williams Lea & Co., 1988–. JP Hants (Chm., Odiham Bench, 1990–). *Heir:* *s* Hon. Timothy Henry Gwilym Lloyd-George, *b* 19 Oct. 1962. *Address:* Triggs, Crondall, near Farnham, Surrey.

TENCH, David Edward, OBE 1987; Head of Legal Department, 1988–94, Director of Legal Affairs, 1991–94, Consumers' Association (publishers of Which?); consultant on business lobbying and consumer law, since 1994; *b* 14 June 1929; *s* of late Henry George Tench and Emma Rose (*née* Orsborn); *m* 1st, 1957, Judith April Seaton Gurney (*d* 1986); two *s* one *d*; 2nd, 1988, Elizabeth Ann Irvine Macdonald. *Educ:* Merchant Taylors' Sch., Northwood, Mddx. Solicitor, 1952. Private practice, 1954–58; Office of Solicitor of Inland Revenue, 1958–69. Chm., Domestic Coal Consumers' Council, 1976–87; Energy Comr, 1977–79. Broadcaster on consumer affairs, 1964–. *Publications:* The Law for Consumers, 1962; The Legal Side of Buying a House, 1965 (2nd edn 1974); Wills and Probate, 1967 (6th edn 1977); How to Sue in the County Court, 1973; Towards a Middle System of Law, 1981. *Recreations:* music, bland gardening. *Address:* Pleasant View, The Platt, Amersham, Bucks HP7 0HX. *T:* Amersham (01494) 724974.

See also W. H. Tench.

TENCH, William Henry, CBE 1980; retired; Chief Inspector of Accidents, Department of Trade, 1974–81; *b* 2 Aug. 1921; *s* of Henry George Tench and Emma Rose Tench (*née* Orsborn); *m* 1944, Margaret Ireland; one *d*. *Educ:* Portsmouth Grammar School. CEng, FRAeS. Learned to fly in Fleet Air Arm, 1940; pilot with oil co. in S America, 1947 and 1948; joined KLM Royal Dutch Airlines, W Indies Div., 1948; transf. to Holland, 1951, flying N and S Atlantic, S African, ME and European routes; joined Min. of Transport and Civil Aviation as Inspector of Accidents, 1955. Consultant on aircraft accident investigation, MoD, 1986–87; Special Advr on air safety to EEC Comr for Transport,

1986–88. *Publication:* Safety is no Accident, 1985. *Recreations:* music, sailing. *Address:* Seaways, Restronguet Point, Feock, Cornwall TR3 6RB.
See also D. E. Tench.

TENISON; *see* Hanbury-Tenison.

TENISON; *see* King-Tenison.

TENNANT, family name of **Baron Glenconner.**

TENNANT, Sir Anthony (John), Kt 1992; Chairman, Christie's International plc, since 1993; *b* 5 Nov. 1930; *s* of late Major John Tennant, TD and Hon. Antonia, *d* of 1st Baron Charnwood and later Viscountess Radcliffe; *m* 1954, Rosemary Violet Stockdale; two *s. Educ:* Eton; Trinity College, Cambridge (BA). National Service, Scots Guards (Malaya). Mather & Crowther, 1953–66 (Dir, 1959); Marketing Consultancy, 1966–70; Dir, 1970, then Dep. Man. Dir, Truman Ltd; Dir, Watney Mann & Truman Brewers, 1972–76; Man. Dir, 1976–82, Chm., 1983–87, International Distillers & Vintners Ltd; Gp Chief Exec., 1987–89, Chm., 1989–92, Guinness plc; Deputy Chairman: Forte plc, 1992–; Wellcome plc, 1994–95; Sen. Advr and Dir, Morgan Stanley UK Gp, 1993–. Director: Exploration Co. plc, 1967–89; El Oro Mining and Exploration Co. plc, 1967–89; Grand Metropolitan PLC, 1977–87; Close Brothers Group plc, 1980–90; Guardian Royal Exchange, 1989–; Guardian Assurance, 1989–; BNP UK Hldgs Ltd, 1990–; Mem., Supervisory Bd, LVMH Moet Hennessy Louis Vuitton, Paris, 1988–92. Dir (non-exec.), Internat. Stock Exchange of UK and Republic of Ireland Ltd, 1991–94. Chm., Priorities Bd for R & D in Agric. and Food, 1992–93; Mem. Council, Food From Britain, 1983–86. Trustee, RA Trust, 1994–. Medal, City of Paris, 1989. Chevalier, Légion d'Honneur (France), 1991. *Address:* 18 Hamilton House, Vicarage Gate, W8 4HL. *T:* 0171–937 6203. *Club:* Boodle's.
See also M. I. Tennant of Balfluig.

TENNANT, Bernard; Director of Retail, British Chambers of Commerce, 1993–95; *b* 14 Oct. 1930; *s* of Richard and Phyllis Tennant; *m* 1956, Marie (*née* Tonge); two *s* one *d. Educ:* Farnworth Grammar Sch.; Open Univ. (BA Govt and Modern European Hist.). Nat. Service, RAF, 1949. Local authority admin, Worsley and Bolton, 1950; Secretary: Bolton Chamber of Trade, 1960–74; Bolton Chamber of Commerce and Industry, and numerous trade associations, 1968–74; National Chamber of Trade, 1975–92, Dir Gen., 1987–92. Member: British Retail Consortium Council, 1986–95; Home Office Standing Cttee on Crime Prevention, 1986–92; Dept of Employment Retail Price Index Adv. Cttee, 1988–92. Magistrate, Bolton, 1968–75; Reading, 1975–78. Founder Sec., Moorside Housing Gp of charitable housing assocs, 1964–75. Editor, NCT News, 1986–92. *Publications:* articles in professional and trade jls. *Recreations:* music, photography, collating historical chronology.

TENNANT, Lady Emma; Chairman, National Trust Gardens Advisory Panel, since 1984; Member, Council, National Trust, since 1990; *b* 26 March 1943; *d* of Duke of Devonshire, *qv*; *m* 1963, Hon. Tobias William Tennant, *y s* of 2nd Baron Glenconner; one *s* two *d. Educ:* St Elphins' Sch., Darley Dale; St Anne's Coll., Oxford (BA History 1963). *Publication:* Rag Rugs, 1992. *Recreations:* gardening, painting. *Address:* Shaws, Newcastleton, Roxburghshire TD9 0SH. *T:* Steele Road (013873) 76241.

TENNANT, Emma Christina, FRSL 1982; writer; *b* 20 Oct. 1937; *d* of 2nd Baron Glenconner and Elizabeth Lady Glenconner; one *s* two *d. Educ:* St Paul's Girls' School. Freelance journalist to 1973; became full time novelist, 1973; founder Editor, Bananas, 1975–78; general editor: In Verse, 1982–; Lives of Modern Women, 1985–. TV film script, Frankenstein's Baby, 1990. *Publications:* The Colour of Rain (pseud. Catherine Aydy), 1963; The Time of the Crack, 1973; The Last of the Country House Murders, 1975; Hotel de Dream, 1976; (ed) Bananas Anthology, 1977; (ed) Saturday Night Reader, 1978; The Bad Sister, 1978; Wild Nights, 1979; Alice Fell, 1980; Queen of Stones, 1982; Woman Beware Woman, 1983; Black Marina, 1985; Adventures of Robina by Herself, ed Emma Tennant, 1986; Cycle of the Sun: The House of Hospitalities, 1987, A Wedding of Cousins, 1988; The Magic Drum, 1989; Two Women of London, 1989; Sisters and Strangers, 1990; Faustine, 1991; Tess, 1993; Pemberley, 1993; An Unequal Marriage, 1994; (contrib.) Novelists in Interview (ed John Haffenden), 1985; (contrib.) Women's Writing: a challenge to theory (ed Maria Monteith), 1986; *for children:* The Boggart (with Mary Rayner), 1979; The Search for Treasure Island, 1981; The Ghost Child, 1984. *Recreation:* walking about. *Address:* c/o Faber & Faber, 3 Queen Square, WC1N 3AU. *T:* 071–465 0045.

TENNANT, Harry; Commissioner of Customs and Excise, 1975–78; *b* 10 Dec. 1917; *s* of late Robert and Mary Tennant; *m* 1944, Bernice Baker; one *s. Educ:* Oldham High School. Appointed Officer of Customs and Excise, 1938; Inspector, 1960; Principal Inspector, 1970; Asst Sec., 1971; Dep. Chief Inspector, 1973; Mem., CS Appeal Bd, 1980–87. *Publications:* Back to the Bible, 1962, repr. 1984; Moses My Servant, 1966, repr. 1990; The Man David, 1968, repr. 1983; The Christadelphians: what they believe and preach, 1986. *Recreations:* walking, travel. *Address:* Strathtay, Alexandra Road, Watford, Herts WD1 3QY. *T:* Watford (01923) 222079.

TENNANT, Sir Iain (Mark), KT 1986; JP; Lord-Lieutenant of Morayshire, 1963–94; Crown Estate Commissioner, 1970–90; Lord High Commissioner to General Assembly, Church of Scotland, 1988–89; *b* 11 March 1919; *e s* of late Col Edward Tennant, Innes, Elgin and Mrs Georgina Tennant; *m* 1946, Lady Margaret Helen Isla Marion Ogilvy, 2nd *d* of 12th Earl of Airlie, Kt, GCVO, MC; two *s* one *d. Educ:* Eton College; Magdalene College, Cambridge. Scots Guards, 1939–46. Caledonian Cinemas, 1947; Chm., Grampian Television Ltd, 1968–89; Director: Times Publishing Co. Ltd, 1962–66; Clydesdale Bank Ltd, 1968–89; The Seagram Co. Ltd, Montreal, 1978–81; Moray Enterprise Trust Ltd, 1986–94; Chairman: The Glenlivet Distillers Ltd, 1964–84; Seagram Distillers, 1979–84. Mem. Newspaper Panel, Monopolies and Mergers Commn, 1981–86. Chm. Bd of Governors, Gordonstoun School, 1954–71. Lieut, Queen's Body Guard for Scotland (Royal Company of Archers), 1981–. FRSA 1971; CIMgt (CBIM 1983). DL Moray, 1954; JP Moray, 1961. Freeman, Dist of Moray, 1994. Hon. LLD Aberdeen, 1990. *Recreations:* shooting, fishing; formerly rowing (rowed for Eton, 1937). *Address:* Lochnabo, Lhanbryde, Moray IV30 3QY. *T:* Lhanbryde (01343) 842228, *Fax:* (01343) 842696.

TENNANT of Balfluig, Mark Iain; Master of the Supreme Court, Queen's Bench Division, since 1988; Baron of Balfluig; *b* 4 Dec. 1932; *s* of late Major John Tennant, TD, KStJ and Hon. Antonia Mary Roby Benson, *d* of 1st Baron Charnwood and later Viscountess Radcliffe; *m* 1965, Lady Harriot Pleydell-Bouverie, *y d* of 7th Earl of Radnor; one *s* one *d. Educ:* Eton College; New College, Oxford (MA 1959). Lieut, The Rifle Brigade (SRO). Called to the Bar, Inner Temple, 1958, Bencher, 1984; Recorder, 1987. Restored Balfluig Castle, 1967 (barony of Balfluig *cr* of Charles II, 1650). Chm., Royal Orchestral Soc. for Amateur Musicians, 1989–. *Recreations:* music, architecture, books, shooting. *Address:* Royal Courts of Justice, Strand, WC2A 2LL; Balfluig Castle, Aberdeenshire AB33 8EJ. *Club:* Brooks's.
See also Sir A. J. Tennant.

TENNANT, Maj.-Gen. Michael Trenchard, CB 1994; Head of External Communications, Royal Ordnance Division, British Aerospace, since 1994; *b* 3 Sept. 1941; *s* of Lt-Col Hugh Trenchard Tennant, MC and Mary Isobel Tennant (*née* Wilkie); *m* 1964, Susan Daphne (*d* 1993), *d* of Lt-Col Frank Beale, LVO; three *s. Educ:* Wellington College. psc†. Commissioned RA 1961; served Bahrain, Aden, BAOR, Hong Kong, UK, 1962–71; Staff College, 1972–73; MoD, 1974–75; Bty Comdr, 127 (Dragon) Bty, BAOR, 1976–78; Directing Staff, Staff Coll., 1978–80; CO, 1 RHA, UK and BAOR, 1980–83; Comdr British Training Team, Nigeria, 1983–85; CRA 3 Armd Div., BAOR, 1985–87; CRA UKLF, 1988–91; Dir, RA, 1991–94. Col Comdt, RA, 1994–; Hon. Col, 1 RHA, 1994–. Pres., Army Cricket, 1992–93. *Recreations:* bridge, golf, tennis, cricket. *Address:* British Aerospace Defence, Lancaster House, PO Box 87, Farnborough Aerospace Centre, Hants GU14 6YU. *Clubs:* Army and Navy; Fadeaways.

TENNANT, Sir Peter (Frank Dalrymple), Kt 1972; CMG 1958; OBE 1945; Director-General, British National Export Council, 1965–71; Industrial Adviser, Barclays Bank International Ltd, 1972–81; Director: Prudential Assurance Company Ltd, 1973–81; Prudential Corporation plc, 1979–86; C. Tennant Sons & Company Ltd, 1972–80; Anglo-Romanian Bank, 1973–81; Northern Engineering Industries (International) Ltd, 1979–82; International Energy Bank, 1981–84; *b* 29 Nov. 1910; *s* of G. F. D. Tennant and Barbara Tennant (*née* Beck); *m* 1st, 1934 (marr. diss. 1952), Hellis, *d* of Professor Fellenius, Stockholm; one *s* two *d*; 2nd, 1953, Galina Bosley (*d* 1995), *d* of K. Grunberg, Helsinki; one step *s. Educ:* Marlborough; Trinity College, Cambridge. Sen. Mod. Languages Scholar, Trinity College, Cambridge, 1929; Cholmondely Studentship, Lincoln's Inn; 1st Cl. Hons Mod. Langs Tripos, 1931; BA 1931, MA 1936, Cambridge. Cambridge Scandinavian Studentship, Oslo, Copenhagen, Stockholm, 1932–33; Fellow Queens' College, Cambridge, and University Lecturer, Scandinavian Languages, 1933; Press Attaché, British Legation, Stockholm, 1939–45; Information Counsellor, British Embassy, Paris, 1945–50; Deputy Commandant, British Sector, Berlin, 1950–52; resigned Foreign Service to become Overseas Director, FBI, 1952–63. Deputy Director-General, FBI, 1963–65. Special Advr, CBI, 1964–65. Mem., Council of Industrial Design, 1954–71; Acting Chm., Wilton Park Academic Council, 1969–71; Mem. Bd, Centre for Internat. Briefing, Farnham Castle, 1954–72; Chm., Gabbitas Thring Educational Trust, 1971–91; Pres., London Chamber of Commerce and Industry, 1978–79 (Chm., 1976–78); Chm., British Cttee, European Cultural Foundn, 1975–90; Mem., Impact Foundn Council, 1974–91; Trustee, Heinz Koeppler Trust, 1985–. Vis. Fellow, St Cross Coll., Oxford, 1982. MA Oxford, 1982. *Publications:* Ibsen's Dramatic Technique, 1947; The Scandinavian Book, 1952; (in Swedish) Touchlines of War, 1989, English edn 1992. *Recreations:* writing, talking, painting, travel, languages, sailing, country life. *Address:* Blue Anchor House, Linchmere Road, Haslemere, Surrey GU27 3QF. *T:* Haslemere (01428) 643124. *Club:* Travellers'.

TENNSTEDT, Klaus; Principal Conductor and Music Director, The London Philharmonic, 1983–87, now Conductor Laureate; *b* 6 June 1926; *s* of Hermann and Agnes Tennstedt; *m* 1960, Ingeborg Fischer. *Educ:* Leipzig Conservatory (violin, piano). Conductor at: Landersoper, Dresden, 1958–62; Staatstheater, Schwerin, 1962–70; Operhaus, Kiel, 1972–76; guest conductor with Boston, Chicago, New York Philharmonic, Cleveland, Philadelphia, Berlin and Israel Philharmonic Orchestras. Hon. RAM, 1990. Hon. DMus: Colgate Hamilton, NY State, 1984; Oxford, 1994. Officer's Cross, Order of Merit (FRG), 1986. *Recreations:* astronomy, hot air ballooning. *Address:* c/o The London Philharmonic, 35 Doughty Street, WC1N 2AA. *T:* 0171–833 2744.

TENNYSON, family name of **Baron Tennyson.**

TENNYSON, 5th Baron *cr* 1884; **Comdr Mark Aubrey Tennyson,** DSC 1943; RN retd; *b* 28 March 1920; *s* of 3rd Baron and Hon. Clarissa Tennant (*d* 1960), *o d* of 1st Baron Glenconner; *S* brother, 1991; *m* 1964, Deline Celeste Budler (*d* 1995). *Educ:* RNC Dartmouth. RN, 1937–60; served war 1939–45 on destroyers in action in Atlantic and Mediterranean (despatches 1945). Production Manager, Rowntree-Mackintosh (S Africa), 1960–67; Export Sales Dir, Joseph Terry & Sons (UK), 1968–82. Skied for RN, 1947–51; Captain, RN Cresta Run team, 1951–54. *Heir: cousin* Lt-Comdr James Alfred Tennyson, DSC, RN retd [*b* 26 Nov. 1913; *m* 1954, Beatrice Aventon, *e d* of Alexander Tolhurst Young; two *s*]. *Address:* 304 Grosvenor Square, Duke Road, Rondebosch, Cape Town 7700, South Africa. *Clubs:* White's, Royal Automobile; Royal Yacht Squadron (Cowes).

TENNYSON-d'EYNCOURT, Sir Mark (Gervais), 5th Bt *cr* 1930, of Carter's Corner Farm, Herstmonceux; *b* 12 March 1967; *o s* of Sir Giles Gervais Tennyson-d'Eyncourt, 4th Bt and of Juanita, *d* of late Fortunato Borromeo; *S* father, 1989. *Heir:* none. *Educ:* Charterhouse; Kingston Polytechnic (BA Hons Fashion). Freeman, City of London, 1989.

TENZIN GYATSO; The Dalai Lama XIV; spiritual and temporal leader of Tibet, since 1940; *b* 6 July 1935; named Lhamo Thondup; *s* of Chokyong Tsering and Diki Tsering. *Educ:* Monasteries of Sera, Drepung and Gaden, Lhasa; traditional Tibetan degree equivalent to Dr in Buddhist philosophy, 1959. Enthroned Dalai Lama, Lhasa, 1940; given name Jetsun Jampel Ngawang Losang Yeshi Tenzin Gyatso Sisum Wang-gyur Tsungpa Mepai De Pel Sangpo. Fled to Chumbi, South Tibet, on Chinese invasion, 1950; negotiated with China, 1951; fled to India after abortive revolt of Tibetan people against Communist Chinese, 1959, and established govt-in-exile in Dharamsala. Awards include: Magsaysay, Philippines, 1959; Lincoln, USA, 1960; Albert Schweitzer Humanitarian, USA, 1987; numerous other awards, hon. doctorates, hon. citizenships from France, Germany, India, Mongolia, Norway, USA; Nobel Peace Prize, 1989. *Publications:* My Land and My People, 1962; The Opening of the Wisdom Eye, 1963; An Introduction to Buddhism, 1965; Key to the Middle Way, 1971; Universal Responsibility and Good Heart, 1977; Four Essential Buddhist Commentaries, 1982; A Human Approach to World Peace, 1984; Kindness, Clarity and Insight, 1987; Freedom in Exile, 1990. *Address:* Thekchen Choeling, Mcleod Ganj 176219, Dharamsala, HP, India.

TEŌ, Sir (Fiatau) Penitala, GCMG 1979; GCVO 1982; ISO 1970; MBE 1956; Governor-General of Tuvalu, 1978–86; *b* 23 July 1911; *s* of Teō Veli, Niutao, and Tilesa Samuelu, Funafuti; *m* 1st, 1931, Muniara Apelu, Vaitupu; one *d* (one *s* decd); 2nd, 1949, Uimai Tofiga, Nanumaga; eight *s* three *d* (and one *d* decd). *Educ:* Elisefou, Vaitupu, Tuvalu. Asst Sch. Master, Elisefou, 1930–32; Clerk and Ellice Interpreter: Dist Admin, Funafuti, 1932–37; Resident Comr's Office, Ocean Is., 1937–42; under Japanese Occupation (Ocean Is. and Tarawa), 1942–43 (1939–45 Star, Pacific Star and War Medal); re-joined Res. Comr's Office, 1943 (i/c Labour Force), Special Clerk 1944; Asst Admin. Officer and Mem., Gilbert and Ellice Is Defence Force (2nd Lieut), 1944; Asst and Actg Dist Officer for Ellice Is, 1944–50; transf. to Tarawa to re-organise Information Office, 1953; Acting Colony Marine Supt., 1953; Dep. Comr for Western Pacific, 1960; Officer i/c, Betio, 1960; Lands Officer for Gilbert and Ellice Is, 1960–62; District Commissioner: Ocean Is., 1963; (acting) Gilbert and Ellice Is, 1965; Ellice Is, 1967–69; Asst and Actg Supt of Labour, British Phosphate Comrs, Ocean Is., 1971–78. ADC to High Comr of Western Pacific during tours, 1954 and 1957; Dist Officer for visit of Prince Philip to Vaitupu Is., Ellice Is, 1959; ADC to Res. Comr, 1963. Represented Gilbert and Ellice Is at confs, and Festival of Britain, 1951. Scout Medal of Merit, 1971. Coronation Medal,

1953. *Recreations:* formerly fishing, cricket, football, Rugby, local games. *Address:* Alapi, Funafuti, Tuvalu, S Pacific.

TERESA, Mother, (Agnes Gonxha Bojaxhiu), MC; Hon. OM 1983; Hon. OBE 1978; Padma Shri, 1962; Bharat Ratna (Jewel of India), 1980; Roman Catholic nun; *b* Skopje, Yugoslavia, 27 Aug. 1910; *d* of Albanian parents. *Educ:* government school in Yugoslavia. Joined Sisters of Loretto, Rathfarnam, Ireland, 1929; trained at Loretto insts in Ireland and India; came to Calcutta, 1929; Principal, St Mary's High School, Calcutta. Founded the Missionaries of Charity (Sisters), 1950, Missionary Brothers of Charity, 1963, the Internat. Co-Workers of Mother Teresa, 1969, Missionaries of Charity, Sisters Contemplatives, 1976, Brothers of the Word Contemplatives, 1979, and Missionaries of Charity Fathers, 1983, to give free service to the poor and the unwanted, irrespective of caste, creed, nationality, race or place; she has set up: slum schools; orphanages; Nirmol Hridoy (Pure Heart) Homes for sick and dying street cases; Shishu Bhavan Homes for unwanted, crippled and mentally-retarded children; mobile gen. clinics and centres for malnourished; mobile clinics and rehabilitation centres for leprosy patients; homes for drug addicts and alcoholics; night shelters for the homeless. Hon. DD Cambridge, 1977; Hon. DrMed: Catholic Univ. of Sacred Heart, Rome, 1981; Catholic Univ. of Louvain, 1982. Ramón Magsaysay Internat. Award, 1962; Pope John XXIII Peace Prize, 1971; Kennedy Internat. Award, 1971; Jawaharlal Nehru Internat. Award, 1972; Templeton Foundation Prize, 1973; first Albert Schweitzer Internat. Prize, 1975; Nobel Peace Prize, 1979, and many other awards too numerous to mention. Hon. Citizen, Assisi, 1982. *Publications:* Gift for God, 1975; Heart of Joy, 1988; Living the Word, 1990; Loving Jesus, 1991; *relevant publications* include: Something Beautiful for God, by Malcolm Muggeridge; Mother Teresa, her people and her works, by Desmond Doig; Such a Vision of the Street, by Eileen Egan. *Address:* 54A Acharya Jagadish Chandra Bose Road, Calcutta 700016, India. *T:* (33) 297115.

TERESHKOVA, Valentina N.; *see* Nikolayeva-Tereshkova.

ter HAAR, Roger Eduard Lound; QC 1992; *b* 14 June 1952; *s* of Dirk ter Haar and Christine Janet ter Haar; *m* 1977, Sarah Anne Martyn; two *s* one *d*. *Educ:* Felsted Sch.; Magdalen Coll., Oxford (BA 1973). Called to the Bar, Inner Temple, 1974, Bencher, 1993. *Recreations:* gardening, reading. *Address:* 2 Crown Office Row, Temple, EC4Y 7HB. *T:* 0171–797 8100. *Club:* Brooks's.

TERLEZKI, Stefan, CBE 1992; *b* Ukraine, 29 Oct. 1927; *s* of late Oleksa Terlezki and Olena Terlezki; *m* 1955, Mary; two *d*. *Educ:* Cardiff Coll. of Food Technol. and Commerce. Member: Hotel and Catering Inst., 1965–80; Chamber of Trade, 1975–80. Member: Cardiff CC, 1968–83 (Press Officer, 1970–83; Chairman: Licensing Cttee, 1975–78; Environment Services Cttee, 1978–80; Housing Liaison Cttee, 1978–80); S Glam CC, 1973–85; S Wales Police Auth., 1975–80; Welsh Jt Educn Cttee, 1975–85; Chm., Jt Consultative Cttee, S Glam Health Auth., 1978–79; Member: Educn Authority for Cardiff CC and S Glam CC, 1969–85; Planning, Finance and Policy Cttee, 1965–83. Member: Welsh Tourist Council, 1965–80; Welsh Games Council, 1974–80; Cardiff Wales Airport Authy, 1979–83; Adv. Bd of Internat. Politics, Univ. of Wales, Aberystwyth, 1993–. Contested (C): Cardiff South East, Feb. and Oct. 1974; Cardiff West, 1987; South Wales, European Parly elecn, 1979. MP (C) Cardiff West, 1983–87. Mem., Parly Select Cttee on Welsh Affairs, 1983–87. Chairman: Keep Britain in Europe Campaign, 1973–75; Cons. Gp for European Movement, 1973–75; Foreign Affairs Forum, 1974–. Vice-Pres., Wales Area Young Conservatives, 1975–80; Member: Central Council, CPC, 1979–83; Official Nat. Speaking Panels of Cons. Party, European Movement, and Eur. Parlt; British delegn, Council of Europe, 1985–87 (UK Rep. Mem., Convention Cttee for the Prevention of Torture and In-Human or Degradation Treatment and Punishment, 1989–); WEU, 1985–87; Industry and Parlt Trust; IPU, 1987–; UN Temple of Peace, Cardiff, 1979–87; Rapporteur, Assembly of Western European Community for Parly and Public Relns, 1986–87. Life Mem., CPA. Chairman: Cardiff City Football Club, 1975–77; Cardiff High Sch. Bd of Governors, 1975–83. Languages: Ukrainian, Polish, Russian, German (basic). Radio and television broadcasts; occasional journalism. Silver Jubilee Medal, 1977. *Recreations:* human rights, foreign affairs, defence, European Community, East-West Relations, glasnost and perestroika, law and order, senior citizens, debates, sport, travel. *Address:* 16 Bryngwyn Road, Cyncoed, Cardiff CF2 6PQ. *T:* Cardiff (01222) 759524.

TERRAINE, John Alfred, FRHistS; author; *b* 15 Jan. 1921; *s* of Charles William Terraine and Eveline Holmes; *m* 1945, Joyce Eileen Waite; one *d*. *Educ:* Stamford Sch.; Keble Coll., Oxford (Hon. Fellow, 1986). Joined BBC, 1944; Pacific and S African Programme Organiser, 1953–63; resigned from BBC, 1964. Associate producer and chief scriptwriter of The Great War, BBC TV, 1963–64; part-scriptwriter The Lost Peace, BBC TV, 1965; scriptwriter, The Life and Times of Lord Mountbatten, Rediffusion/Thames TV, 1966–68; scriptwriter, The Mighty Continent, BBC TV, 1974–75. Founder Pres., Western Front Assoc., 1980–; Mem. Council, RUSI, 1976–84. FRHistS 1987. Chesney Gold Medal, RUSI, 1982. C. P. Robertson Meml Trophy, Air Public Relations Assoc., 1985. *Publications:* Mons: The Retreat to Victory, 1960; Douglas Haig: The Educated Soldier, 1963; The Western Front, 1964; General Jack's Diary, 1964; The Great War: An Illustrated History, 1965 (NY), unillustrated reprint, The First World War, 1983; The Life and Times of Lord Mountbatten, 1968; Impacts of War 1914 and 1918, 1970; The Mighty Continent, 1974; Trafalgar, 1976; The Road to Passchendaele, 1977; To Win a War: 1918 The Year of Victory, 1978; The Smoke and the Fire, 1980; White Heat: The New Warfare 1914–1918, 1982; The Right of the Line: the Royal Air Force in the European War 1939–45, 1985 (Yorkshire Post Book of the Year Award, 1985); Business in Great Waters: the U-Boat Wars 1916–1945, 1989. *Recreation:* convivial and congenial conversation. *Address:* 74 Kensington Park Road, W11 2PL. *T:* 0171–229 8152.

TERRELL, Richard Deane; Vice Chancellor, Australian National University, since 1994; *b* 22 April 1936; *s* of Norman Walter Terrell and Dorothy Ismay Terrell; *m* 1961, Jennifer Anne Kathleen, *d* of Lenard Spencer and Margaret Rose Doman; two *s* one *d*. *Educ:* St Peter's Coll., Adelaide; Adelaide Univ. (Rhodes Scholar; BEc, MEc Hons); Oxford Univ.; ANU (PhD). Teaching appts, Univ. of Adelaide and MIT, 1959–64; Australian National University: Lectr, 1964–70; Sen. Lectr, Stats, 1970; Prof. of Econometrics, 1971–89; Head, Dept of Stats, 1979–82, 1989–91; Acting Dep. Vice-Chancellor, and Dep. Vice-Chancellor, 1991–93. Vis. Prof., Princeton and LSE, 1972–73. *Publications:* numerous articles in professional jls. *Recreations:* farming, football, cricket. *Address:* Australian National University, Canberra, ACT 0200, Australia. *Club:* Commonwealth (Canberra).

TERRELL, Colonel Stephen, OBE 1952; TD; QC 1965; DL. Called to the Bar, Gray's Inn, 1946; Bencher, Gray's Inn, 1970. South Eastern Circuit. Pres., Liberal Party, 1972. Contested (L) Eastbourne, Feb. 1974. DL Middlesex, 1961.

TERRINGTON, 4th Baron, *cr* 1918, of Huddersfield; **James Allen David Woodhouse;** former Member, Stock Exchange; Partner in Sheppards and Chase, 1952–80; *b* 30 December 1915; *er s* of 3rd Baron Terrington, KBE, and Valerie (*née* Phillips) (*d* 1958), Leyden's House, Edenbridge, Kent; *S* father, 1961; *m* 1942, Suzanne, *y d* of Colonel T. S. Irwin, DL, JP, late Royal Dragoons, Justicetown, Carlisle, and Mill House, Holton, Suffolk; three *d*. *Educ:* Winchester; Royal Military College, Sandhurst. Commnd Royal Norfolk Regiment, TA, 1936. Farming in Norfolk, 1936–39. Served War of 1939–45 in India, North Africa (1st Army, Tunisia) and Middle East (wounded); ADC to GOC Madras, 1940; Staff Coll., Haifa, 1944; psc 1944; GSOII, Allied Force HQ Algiers, Ninth Army, Lebanon, Middle East, and War Office, Military Operations; GSO, India (during Partition), 1947; retired as Major, 1948; joined Queen's Westminster Rifles (KRRC), TA. Joined Messrs Chase Henderson and Tennant, 1949 (now Sheppards). Deputy Chairman of Cttees, House of Lords, 1961–63; Mem., Select Cttee on Commodity Prices, 1976. Member: Ecclesiastical Cttee, 1979–; Exec. Cttee, Wider Shareownership Council, 1981– (former Dep. Chm. of Council); Dep. Chm., Nat. Listening Library (Talking Books for the Disabled), 1977–. Vice-Pres., Small Farmers' Assoc., 1986–. Mem. Internat. Adv. Bd, American Univ., Washington DC, 1985–. *Heir: b* Hon. Christopher Montague Woodhouse, *qv*. *Address:* c/o House of Lords, SW1A 0PW. *Club:* Boodle's.

See also Earl Alexander of Tunis.

TERRY, Air Vice-Marshal Colin George, CB 1995; OBE 1983; Chief of Staff, Royal Air Force Logistics Command, since 1995; *b* 8 Aug. 1943; *e s* of George Albert Terry and Edna Joan Terry (*née* Purslow); *m* 1966, Gillian, *d* of late Conrad Glendor Grindley and Muriel Grace Grindley (*née* Duffield); two *s* one *d*. *Educ:* Bridgnorth Grammar Sch.; RAF Coll.; Imperial Coll., London. CEng, BScEng, ACGI, FRAeS. Commnd, Engr Br., RAF, 1962; served Abingdon, RAF Coll., Church Fenton, Leeming, Oakington, Finningley, RNAY Belfast, Laarbruch, Wildenrath, HQ Strike Comd; Student, RAF Coll., 1978; OC Eng Wing, RAF Coltishall, 1979–82; Eng Authy Staff, HQ Strike Comd, 1982–84; OC Eng Wing, RAF Stanley, 1982–83; Dep. Comd Engr, HQ Strike Comd, 1985–86; Station Comdr, RAF Abingdon, 1986–88; RCDS 1989; Dir, Support Management and Sen. Dir, MoD Harrogate, 1990–92; Dir Gen., Support Management, RAF, 1993–95. *Recreations:* sailing (Commodore, RAF Sailing Assoc.), flying, ski-ing, modern languages, music. *Address:* Headquarters Logistics Command, RAF Brampton, Huntingdon PE18 8QL. *T:* Huntingdon (01480) 52151. *Club:* Royal Air Force.

TERRY, (John) Quinlan, FRIBA 1962; architect in private practice, since 1967; *b* 24 July 1937; *s* of late Philip and of Phyllis Terry; *m* 1961, Christine de Ruttié; one *s* four *d*. *Educ:* Bryanston School; Architectural Association; Rome Scholar. Assistant to Raymond Erith, RA, FRIBA, 1962, Partner 1967–, Erith & Terry; work includes: new country houses in classical style; Ionic, Veneto and Gothick Villas, Regent's Park for Crown Estate Comrs; Common Room Building, Gray's Inn; offices, shops, flats and public gardens at Richmond Riverside; new Lecture Theatre and new Library, Downing Coll., Cambridge; new Brentwood Cathedral; restoration of the three State Drawing Rooms, 10 Downing Street; restoration of St Helen's, Bishopsgate. Mem., Royal Fine Art Commn, 1994–. *Recreation:* the Pauline epistles. *Address:* Old Exchange, High Street, Dedham, Colchester, Essex CO7 6HA. *T:* Colchester (01206) 323186.

TERRY, Sir Michael Edward Stanley I.; *see* Imbert-Terry.

TERRY, Air Chief Marshal Sir Peter (David George), GCB 1983 (KCB 1978; CB 1975); AFC 1968; QCVSA 1959 and 1962; *b* 18 Oct. 1926; *s* of James George Terry and Laura Chilton Terry (*née* Powell); *m* 1946, Betty Martha Louisa Thompson; one *s* one *d* (and one *s* decd). *Educ:* Chatham House Sch., Ramsgate. Joined RAF, 1945; commnd in RAF Regt, 1946; Pilot, 1953. Staff Coll., 1962; OC, No 51 Sqdn, 1966–68; OC, RAF El Adem, 1968–70; Dir, Air Staff Briefing, MoD, 1970–71; Dir of Forward Policy for RAF, 1971–74; ACOS (Policy and Plans), SHAPE, 1975–77; VCAS, 1977–79; C-in-C RAF Germany and Comdr Second Allied Tactical Air Force, 1979–81; Dep. C-in-C, Allied Forces Central Europe, Feb.–April 1981; Dep. Supreme Allied Commander, Europe, 1981–84; Governor and C-in-C, Gibraltar, 1985–89. Vice-Pres., Re-Solv, 1985–. KStJ 1986. *Recreation:* golf. *Club:* Royal Air Force.

TERRY, Quinlan; *see* Terry, J. Q.

TESH, Robert Mathieson, CMG 1968; HM Diplomatic Service, retired; Ambassador to Ethiopia, 1979–82; *b* 15 Sept. 1922; *s* of late E. Tesh, Hurst Green, Surrey; *m* 1950, Jean Bowker; two *s* one *d*. *Educ:* Queen Elizabeth's, Wakefield; Queen's College, Oxford (MA). Oxford, 1940–42 and 1945–47; Rifle Brigade, 1942–45; HM Foreign Service, 1947: New Delhi, 1948–50; FO, 1950–53 and 1957–60; Delegation to NATO, Paris, 1953–55; Beirut, 1955–57; Bangkok, 1960–64; Dep. High Comr, Ghana, 1965–66; Lusaka, 1966; Consul-General British Interests Section, Canadian Embassy, Cairo, 1966–67; Counsellor, British Embassy, Cairo, 1968; IDC, 1969; Head of Defence Dept, FCO, 1970–72; Ambassador to Bahrain, 1972–75; Ambassador to: the Democratic Republic of Vietnam, 1976; the Socialist Republic of Vietnam, 1976–78; FCO, 1978–79. *Recreations:* music, theatre, golf. *Address:* Ashenden, 10 Albany Close, Esher, Surrey KT10 9JR. *T:* Esher (01372) 464192. *Club:* Travellers'.

TESLER, Brian, CBE 1986; Deputy Chairman, LWT (Holdings) plc, 1990–94; Chairman: London Weekend Television Ltd, 1984–92 (Managing Director, 1976–90; Deputy Chairman, 1982–84; Deputy Chief Executive, 1974–76); The London Studios Ltd (formerly LWT Production Facilities Ltd), 1989–92; LWT International Ltd, 1990–92; LWT Programmes Ltd, 1990–92; *b* 19 Feb. 1929; *s* of late David Tesler and of Stella Tesler; *m* 1959, Audrey Mary Maclean; one *s*. *Educ:* Chiswick County School for Boys; Exeter Coll., Oxford (State Schol.; MA). Theatre Editor, The Isis, 1950–51; Pres., Oxford Univ. Experimental Theatre Club, 1951–52. British Forces Broadcasting Service, 1947–49; Producer/Director: BBC Television, 1952; ATV, 1957; ABC Television: Head of Features and Light Entertainment, 1960; Programme Controller, 1961; Dir of Programmes, 1962; Dir of Programmes, Thames Television, 1968. Chairman: ITV Superchannel Ltd, 1986–88; ITCA, 1980–82; Indep. TV Network Prog. Cttee, 1976–78, 1986–88; LWT Programme Adv. Bd, 1990–92; ITCA Cable and Satellite Television Wkg Party, 1981–88; ITV Film Purchase Cttee, 1989–90; The Magazine Business Ltd, 1992–. Director: ITN Ltd, 1979–90; Channel Four Television Ltd, 1980–85; Oracle Teletext Ltd, 1980–; Services Sound and Vision Corp. (formerly Services Kinema Corp.), 1981–. Chm., Lord Chancellor's Adv. Cttee on JPs, 1993– (Mem., 1991–); Member: British Screen Adv. Council, 1985–94 (Wkg Party on Future of British Film Industry, 1975–77; Interim Action Cttee on Film Industry, 1977–85); TRIC, 1979– (Pres., 1979–80); Vice-Pres., RTS, 1984–94 (FRTS 1992). Governor: Nat. Film and TV Sch. (formerly Nat. Film Sch.), 1977–; BFI, 1986– (Dep. Chm., 1993–). Daily Mail Nat. TV Award, 1954; Guild of Television Producers and Directors Award, 1957; Lord Willis Trophy for Outstanding Services to Television, Pye Television Award, 1986; Presidential Award, TRIC, 1991. *Recreations:* books, theatre, cinema, music.

TESTAFERRATA, Marquis; *see* San Vincenzo Ferreri, Marquis of.

TETLEY, Glen; choreographer, since 1948; *b* 3 Feb. 1926; *s* of Glenford Andrew Tetley and Mary Eleanor (*née* Byrne). *Educ:* Franklyn and Marshal Coll., Lancaster, USA (pre-med); New York Univ. (BSc). Studied medicine, then dance with Hanya Holm, Antony Tudor, Martha Graham. Danced with Holm's Co., 1946–51; New York City Opera, 1952–54; John Butler Dance Theatre, 1955; Joffrey Ballet, 1956–57; Martha Graham Co., 1958; American Ballet Theatre, 1960; Robbins Ballets USA, 1961. Joined Netherlands

Dance Theatre as dancer and choreographer, 1962, eventually becoming artistic co-director; directed own company, 1969; Dir, Stuttgart Ballet, 1974–76. *Choreography:* Pierrot Lunaire, own company, 1962, Ballet Rambert, 1985; Netherlands Dance Theatre: The Anatomy Lesson, 1964; Circles, 1968; Imaginary Film, 1970; Mutations, 1970; Summer's End, 1980; American Ballet Theatre (formerly Company): Ricercare, 1966; Nocturne, 1977; Sphinx, 1977; Contredances, 1979; Ballet Rambert: Freefall, 1967; Ziggurat, 1967; Embrace Tiger and Return to Mountain, 1968; Rag Dances, 1971; Praeludium, 1978; The Tempest, first full-length work, 1979; Murderer, Hope of Women, 1983; Royal Ballet: Field Figures, 1970; Laborintus, 1972; Dances of Albion, 1980; Stuttgart Ballet: Voluntaries, 1973; Daphnis and Chloe, 1975; Greening, 1975; National Ballet of Canada: Alice, 1986; La Ronde, 1987; Tagore, 1989; Oracle, 1994; also: Le Sacre du Printemps, Munich State Opera Ballet, 1974; Tristan, Paris Opera, 1974; Firebird, Royal Danish Ballet, 1981; Revelation and Fall, Australian Dance Theatre, 1984; Pulcinella, Festival Ballet, 1984; Dream Walk of the Shaman, Aterballetto, 1985; Orpheus, Australian Ballet, 1987; Dialogues, Dance Theatre of Harlem, 1991. Queen Elizabeth Coronation Award, Royal Acad. of Dancing, 1980; Prix Italia, 1982; Ohioana Career Medal, 1986; NY Univ. Achievement Award, 1988. *Address:* 15 West Ninth Street, New York, NY 10011, USA. *T:* (212) 4754604.

TETLEY, Sir Herbert, KBE 1965; CB 1958; Government Actuary, 1958–73; *b* 23 April 1908; *s* of Albert Tetley, Leeds; *m* 1941, Agnes Maclean Macfarlane Macphee; one *s*. *Educ:* Leeds Grammar School; The Queen's College, Oxford. Hastings Scholar, Queen's College, 1927–30; 1st Cl. Hons Mods (Mathematics), 1928; 1st Cl. Final Hons School of Mathematics, 1930. Fellow of Institute of Actuaries, 1934; Fellow of Royal Statistical Society; served with London Life Assoc., 1930–36; Scottish Provident Instn, 1936–38; National Provident Instn, 1938–51 (Joint Actuary). Joined Government Actuary's Dept as Principal Actuary, 1951; Deputy Government Actuary, 1953; Chairman: Civil Service Insurance Soc., 1961–73; Cttee on Economics Road Research Board, 1962–65; Cttee on Road Traffic Research, 1966–73. Pres., Inst. of Actuaries, 1964–66. *Publications:* Actuarial Statistics, Vol. I, 1946; (jtly) Statistics, An Intermediate Text Book, Vol. I, 1949, Vol. II, 1950. *Recreations:* gardening, music, fell-walking. *Address:* 37 Upper Brighton Road, Surbiton, Surrey KT6 6QX. *T:* 0181–399 3001.

TETLEY, Air Vice-Marshal John Francis Humphrey, CB 1987; CVO 1978; *b* 5 Feb. 1932; *s* of Humphrey and Evelyn Tetley; *m* 1960, Elizabeth, *d* of Wing Comdr Arthur Stevens; two *s*. *Educ:* Malvern College. RAF Coll., Cranwell, 1950–53; served No 249 Sqn, No 204 Sqn and HQ Coastal Command, 1955–64; RAF Staff Coll., 1964; HQ Middle East Command, 1965–67; OC No 24 Sqn, 1968–70; JSSC 1970; MoD (Air), 1971–72; RAF Germany, 1973–75; Dir Air Staff Briefing, MoD (Air), 1975–76; Silver Jubilee Project Officer, 1977; RCDS, 1978; SASO HQ 38 Group, 1979–82; Dir of Ops (Air Support), RAF, 1982–83; AO Scotland and NI, 1983–86; Sen. Directing Staff (Air), RCDS, 1986–87; retired 1987. Mem. Exec. Cttee, RNLI, 1993–. *Recreations:* gardening, photography, boating. *Club:* Royal Air Force.

TETLOW, Christopher Bruce; His Honour Judge Tetlow; a Circuit Judge, since 1992; *b* 27 Feb. 1943; *s* of George Wilfred Tetlow and Betty Tetlow; *m* 1981, Rosalind Jane Cope; two *s* one *d*. *Educ:* Stowe Sch.; Magdalene Coll., Cambridge (MA). Called to the Bar, Middle Temple, 1969. *Club:* St James's (Manchester).

TETT, Sir Hugh (Charles), Kt 1966; ARCS, BSc, DIC; *b* Exeter, Devon, 28 Oct. 1906; *e s* of late James Charles Tett and late Florence Tett (*née* Lihou); *m* 1st, 1931, Katie Sargent (*d* 1948); one *d*; 2nd, 1949, Joyce Lilian (*née* Mansell) (*d* 1979); one *d*; 3rd, 1980, Barbara Mary (*née* Mackenzie). *Educ:* Hele's School, Exeter; University College, Exeter; Royal College of Science (Kitchener's Scholar). Joined Esso Petroleum Co. Ltd, 1928; Technical Advisory Committee, Petroleum Board, 1940–45; Lieut-Colonel, Combined Intelligence Objectives Sub-Cttee, 1944–45; Chairman of Council, Institute of Petroleum, 1947–48; Managing Director, Esso Research Ltd, 1947–49; Director, Esso Petroleum Co. Ltd, 1951, Chairman, 1959–67. Member: Council for Scientific and Industrial Research, 1961–64; Advisory Council, Ministry of Technology, 1964–67. Chairman, Economic Development Cttee for Motor Manufacturing Industry, 1967–69. Pro-Chancellor, Univ. of Southampton, 1967–79. Fellow, Imperial Coll. of Science and Technology, 1964. Hon. DSc: Southampton, 1965; Exeter, 1970. *Address:* Primrose Cottage, Bosham, Chichester, West Sussex PO18 8HZ. *T:* Bosham (01243) 572705. *Club:* Athenæum.

TETTENBORN, Richard Garstin, OBE 1993; Treasurer, Staffordshire County Council, since 1992; *b* 23 Sept. 1940; *s* of Philip Arthur de Gleichen Tettenborn and Helena Louise Tettenborn (*née* Sharpe); *m* 1983, Susan Margaret Wrigley (*née* Crew); one *s*. *Educ:* Herbert Strutt Sch., Belper; Brasenose Coll., Oxford (MA). IPFA 1967. Trainee accountant, Derbyshire CC, 1963–67; Sen. Accountant, London Borough of Sutton, 1967–70; Asst Treas., W Sussex CC, 1970–76; Dep. Treas., Mid Glamorgan CC, 1976–79; Treas., S Glamorgan CC, 1980–92. Financial Advr, Welsh Counties Cttee, 1984–91; Comr, Public Works Loan Bd, 1991–95. President: Soc. of Co. Treasurers, 1992–93; CIPFA, 1994–95. *Recreations:* family, golf, watching sport, theatre. *Address:* County Buildings, Eastgate Street, Stafford ST16 2NF. *T:* Stafford (01785) 276300; Sweetbriar, 68 Weeping Cross, Stafford ST17 0DL. *T:* Stafford (01785) 661072. *Club:* United Oxford & Cambridge University.

TEUSNER, Hon. Berthold Herbert, CMG 1972; JP; Solicitor, 1931–71; Speaker, South Australian Parliament, 1956–62; *b* 16 May 1907; *s* of Carl Theodor Teusner and Agnes Sophie Elisabeth Teusner (*née* Christian); *m* 1934, Viola Hilda Kleeman; two *s*. *Educ:* Immanuel Coll., Adelaide; Univ. of Adelaide (LLB). Legal Practice at Tanunda, SA, 1932–71. MP for Angas, S Australian Parlt, 1944–70; Govt Whip, 1954–55; Dep. Speaker and Chm. of Cttees: 1955–56, 1962–65 and 1968–70. Councillor, Dist. Council of Tanunda, 1936–56 (Chm. for 17 years); JP, 1939–. Member: Bd of Governors, Adelaide Botanical Gdns, 1956–70; SA Nat. Fitness Council, 1953–70; Royal Adelaide Hosp. and Queen Elizabeth Hosp. Advisory Cttees (Chm., 1962–65); Immanuel Coll. Council, 1933–71; Hon. Assoc. Life Mem., SA Br. of Commonwealth Parly Assoc.; Mem., Transport Control Bd of SA, 1971–74. *Recreations:* bowls, gardening. *Address:* 18 Elizabeth Street, Tanunda, SA 5352, Australia. *T:* 632422.

TEVERSON, Robin; Member (Lib Dem) Cornwall and West Plymouth, European Parliament, since 1994; *b* 31 March 1952; *s* of Dr Crofton Teverson and Joan Teverson; *m* 1975, Rosemary Anne Young; two *d*. *Educ:* Exeter Univ. (BA Hons Econs). Managing Director: SPD Ltd and Dir, Exel Logistics, 1987–89; Supply Chain Consultancy (Rationale Ltd), 1989–94. *Recreations:* history, riding, astronomy, travel, music. *Address:* Newton Farm, Metherell, Callington, Cornwall PL17 8DQ. *T:* Liskeard (01579) 51234.

TEVIOT, 2nd Baron, *cr* 1940, of Burghclere; **Charles John Kerr;** genealogist; *b* 16 Dec. 1934; *s* of 1st Baron Teviot, DSO, MC, and Florence Angela (*d* 1979), *d* of late Lt-Col Charles Walter Villiers, CBE, DSO; *S* father, 1968; *m* 1965, Patricia Mary Harris; one *s* one *d*. *Educ:* Eton. Bus Conductor and Driver; genealogical and historical record agent. Director: Debrett's Peerage Ltd, 1977–83; Burke's Peerage Research, 1983–85; Burke's Peerage Ltd, 1984–85. Mem., Adv. Council on Public Records, 1974–83. Fellow, Soc. of Genealogists, 1975. *Recreations:* reading, walking. *Heir:* *s* Hon. Charles Robert Kerr, *b* 19 Sept. 1971. *Address:* The Knoll, Stockcroft Road, Balcombe, West Sussex RH17 6LG. *T:* Haywards Heath (01444) 811654.

TEW, Prof. John Hedley Brian, OBE 1988; PhD; External Professor, Economics Department, University of Loughborough, since 1982; Midland Bank Professor of Money and Banking, University of Nottingham, 1967–82; *b* 1 Feb. 1917; *s* of Herbert and Catherine Mary Tew; *m* 1944, Marjorie Hoey Craigie; one *s* one *d*. *Educ:* Mill Hill School, Leicester; University College, Leicester; Peterhouse, Cambridge. BSc (Econ.) London; PhD Cantab. Iron and Steel Control, 1940–42; Ministry of Aircraft Production, 1942–45; Industrial and Commercial Finance Corp., 1946; Professor of Economics, Univ. of Adelaide (Australia), 1947–49; Professor of Economics, University of Nottingham, 1950–67. Part-time Member: Iron and Steel Board, 1964–67; East Midlands Electricity Board, 1965–76; Tubes Div., BSC, 1969–73; Mem., Cttee of Enquiry on Small Firms, Dept of Trade and Industry, 1969–71. *Publications:* Wealth and Income, 1950; International Monetary Co-operation 1952; (jt editor) Studies in Company Finance, 1959; Monetary Theory, 1969; The Evolution of the International Monetary System, 1977. *Address:* 121 Bramcote Lane, Wollaton, Notts NG8 2NJ.

TEWKESBURY, Bishop Suffragan of, since 1996; **Rt Rev. John Stewart Went;** *b* 11 March 1944; *s* of Douglas and Barbara Went; *m* 1968, Rosemary Evelyn Amy (*née* Dunn); three *s*. *Educ:* Corpus Christi Coll., Cambridge (1st Cl Classics Pt I, starred 1st Theology Pt II; MA). Curate, Emmanuel, Northwood, Mddx, 1969–75; Vicar, Holy Trinity, Margate, 1975–83; Vice-Principal, Wycliffe Hall, Oxford, 1983–89; Archdeacon of Surrey, 1989–95. Chm., Diocesan Council for Unity and Mission, Guildford, 1990–95. *Recreations:* music, photography, crosswords. *Address:* Green Acre, 166 Hempsted Lane, Gloucester GL2 6LG. *T:* Gloucester (01452) 521824, *Fax:* (01452) 505554.

TEYNHAM, 20th Baron *cr* 1616; **John Christopher Ingham Roper-Curzon;** *b* 25 Dec. 1928; *s* of 19th Baron Teynham, DSO, DSC, and Elspeth Grace (who *m* 2nd, 1958, 6th Marquess of Northampton, DSO, and *d* 1976), *e d* of late William Ingham Whitaker; *S* father, 1972; *m* 1964, Elizabeth, *yr d* of Lt-Col the Hon. David Scrymgeour-Wedderburn, DSO, Scots Guards (killed on active service 1944), and of Patricia, Countess of Dundee; five *s* five *d* (of whom one *s* one *d* are twins). *Educ:* Eton. A Land Agent. Late Captain, The Buffs (TA), formerly Coldstream Guards; active service in Palestine, 1948. ADC to Governor of Bermuda, 1953 and 1955; ADC to Governor of Leeward Islands, 1955; Private Secretary and ADC, 1956; ADC to Governor of Jamaica, 1962. Pres., Inst. of Commerce, 1972–; Vice Pres., Inst. of Export. Member of Council, Sail Training Association, 1964–. OStJ. Lord of the Manors of South Baddesley and Sharpricks. *Recreations:* shooting and fishing. *Heir:* *s* Hon. David John Henry Ingham Roper-Curzon [*b* 5 Oct. 1965; *m* 1985, Lydia Lucinda, *d* of Maj.-Gen. Sir Christopher Airy, *qv*; one *s* one *d*]. *Address:* Pylewell Park, Lymington, Hants SO41 5SJ. *Clubs:* Turf; House of Lords Yacht; Ocean Cruising; Puffin's (Edinburgh).

THACKER, David Thomas; Director-in-Residence, Royal Shakespeare Company, since 1993; *b* 21 Dec. 1950; *s* of Thomas Richard Thacker and Alice May (*née* Beaumont); *m* 1983, Margot Elizabeth Leicester; three *s* one *d*. *Educ:* Wellingborough Grammar Sch.; Univ. of York (BA English and Related Lit.; MA Shakespeare). Theatre Royal, York: Asst Stage Manager, Dep. Stage Manager and Stage Manager, 1974–75; Asst Dir, 1975–76; Gateway Theatre, Chester: Arts Council Asst Dir, 1975–76; Associate Dir, 1977–78; Arts Council Associate Dir, Duke's Playhouse, 1978–79; Director: Lancaster Theatre, 1980–84; Young Vic Theatre, 1984–93. Dir of the Year, Laurence Olivier Awards, 1991. *Recreations:* sport, family, film and television, reading. *Address:* 55 Onslow Gardens, Muswell Hill, N10 3JY. *T* and *Fax:* 0181–444 8436.

THAIN, Eric Malcolm, PhD; FRSC; Director, Tropical Development and Research Institute, Overseas Development Administration, 1983–86; Hon. Research Fellow, Chemistry Department, University College London, since 1986; *b* 29 Nov. 1925; *s* of late Arthur Robert Thain and Olive Grace (*née* Parsons); *m* 1954, Nancy Garbutt Key *d* of late Mr and Mrs T. G. Key; one *s* one *d*. *Educ:* St Dunstan's Coll., Catford; Univ. of London (BSc, PhD). Lister Institute of Preventive Medicine, 1949: ICI Research Fellow, 1953–54; Royal Society/National Academy of Science Research Fellow, Univ. of California, Berkeley, 1954–55; ICI Research Fellow, University Coll. London, 1955–57; Tropical Products Institute: Member, Scientific Staff, 1957; Asst Director, 1963; Dep. Director, 1969; Director, 1981–86. Member: WHO and FAO Expert Committees on Pesticides, 1961–; Executive Cttee, Essex Bird Watching and Preservation Soc., 1950– (Chm. 1970–73); Quekett Microscopical Club (Pres., 1980–81). Mem. Council, Norfolk and Norwich Naturalists' Soc., 1994–. *Publications:* research papers on organic chemistry and pesticides in jls of various learned societies. *Recreations:* natural history, visiting museums. *Address:* 36 Friars Quay, Norwich, Norfolk NR3 1ES. *T:* Norwich (01603) 625017.

THATCHER, family name of **Baroness Thatcher**.

THATCHER, Baroness *cr* 1992 (Life Peer), of Kesteven in the County of Lincolnshire; **Margaret Hilda Thatcher,** LG 1995; OM 1990; PC 1970; FRS 1983; Chancellor: University of Buckingham, since 1992; William and Mary College Virginia, since 1993; *b* 13 Oct. 1925; *d* of late Alfred Roberts, Grantham, Lincs; *m* 1951, Denis Thatcher (*see* Sir Denis Thatcher, Bt); one *s* one *d* (twins). *Educ:* Kesteven and Grantham Girls' School; Somerville College, Oxford (MA, BSc). Research Chemist, 1947–51; called to the Bar, Lincoln's Inn, 1954, Hon. Bencher, 1975. MP (C) Finchley, 1959–92; Joint Parly Sec., Min. of Pensions and National Insurance, Oct. 1961–64; Sec. of State for Educn and Sci., 1970–74; Leader of the Opposition, 1975–79; Prime Minister and First Lord of the Treasury, 1979–90. Co-Chm., Women's Nat. Commn, 1970–74. Hon. Fellow, Somerville Coll., Oxford, 1970. Freedom of Borough of Barnet, 1980, of City of London, 1989. Donovan Award, USA, 1981. *Publications:* In Defence of Freedom, 1986; *memoirs:* The Downing Street Years 1979–90, 1993; The Path to Power, 1995. *Recreations:* music, reading. *Address:* PO Box 1466, SW1X 9HY. *Club:* Carlton.

THATCHER, Anthony Neville, CEng, FIMechE; Vice Chairman, Thyssen-Bornemisza Group SAM, since 1993 (President and Chief Executive Officer, Thyssen-Bornemisza Group, 1991–92); *b* 10 Sept. 1939; *s* of Edwin Neville Thatcher and Elsie May Webster; *m* 1968, Sally Margaret Clark. *Educ:* Sir John Lawes Sch., Harpenden; Luton Tech. Coll.; Manchester Univ. (MSc). Student apprentice, Haywards Tyler & Co., Luton, 1956–64; Project Engineer, Smiths Industries, 1964–67; Ultra Electronics: Operations Res. Asst, Acton, 1967–69; Vice-Pres., Sales, USA, 1970–73; Marketing Dir, Acton, 1973–77; Managing Dir, Ultra Electronic Controls, 1977; Managing Director: Dowty Electronic Controls, 1978–82; Electronics Div., Dowty Gp, 1982; Dir, 1983–91, Chief Exec., 1986–91, Dowty Gp. Member: Avionics Cttee, Electronics and Avionics Requirements Bd, DTI, 1981–85; Council, Electronics Engineering Assoc., 1983–91 (Pres., 1986–87); RARDE Management Bd (Indust.), 1986–91; Innovation Adv. Bd, DTI, 1988–91; Engrg Markets Adv. Bd, DTI, 1988–90; Engrg Council, 1989–91. Council Mem., Cheltenham Ladies' Coll., 1988–91. Freeman, City of London; Liveryman, Glass Sellers' Co. *Recreations:* art, jazz piano, opera, fishing, gardening, bird watching. *Address:* 12 Gayfere Street, SW1P 3HP.

THATCHER, Arthur Roger, CB 1974; Director, Office of Population Censuses and Surveys, and Registrar General for England and Wales, 1978–86; *b* 22 Oct. 1926; *s* of Arthur Thatcher and Edith Mary Ruth (*née* Dobson); *m* 1950, Mary Audrey Betty (*née* Street); two *d. Educ:* The Leys Sch.; St John's Coll., Cambridge (MA). Instr Lieut, Royal Navy, 1947–49. North Western Gas Board, 1949–52; Admiralty, 1952–61; Cabinet Office, 1961–63; Ministry of Labour, 1963–68; Director of Statistics, Dept of Employment, 1968–78, Dep. Sec., 1972–78. *Publications:* official publications; articles in jls. *Address:* 129 Thetford Road, New Malden, Surrey KT3 5DS. *Club:* Army and Navy.

THATCHER, Sir Denis, 1st Bt *cr* 1991, of Scotney in the County of Kent; MBE (mil.) 1944; TD 1946; company director; *b* 10 May 1915; *m* 1951, Margaret Hilda Roberts (*see* Baroness Thatcher); one *s* one *d* (twins). *Educ:* Mill Hill Sch. Major, RA, 1938–46. Man. Dir, Atlas Preservative Co., 1949; Director: Castrol, 1963; Burmah Oil Trading Ltd, 1969–; non-exec. Dir, various cos, 1975–. *Recreation:* golf. *Heir: s* Hon. Mark Thatcher [*b* 15 Aug. 1953; *m* 1987, Diane Bergdorf, Dallas, Texas; one *s* one *d*]. *Clubs:* Carlton, Buck's, Pratt's.

THAW, John Edward, CBE 1993; actor; *b* 3 Jan. 1942; *s* of John Edward Thaw and Dorothy (*née* Abblott); *m* 1st (marr. diss.); one *d*; 2nd, 1973, Sheila Hancock, *qv*; one *d* one step *d. Educ:* Ducie Technical High Sch., Manchester; RADA (Vanbrugh Award; Liverpool Playhouse Award). *Theatre* appearances include: A Shred of Evidence, Liverpool Playhouse, 1960; The Fire Raisers, Royal Court, 1961; Women Beware Women, Arts, 1962; Semi-Detached, Saville, 1962; So What About Love?, Criterion, 1969; Random Happenings in the Hebrides, Edinburgh Fest., 1970; The Lady from the Sea, Greenwich, 1971; Collaborators, Duchess, 1973; Absurd Person Singular (tour), 1976; Night and Day, Phoenix, 1978; Sergeant Musgrave's Dance, NT, 1982; Twelfth Night, The Time of Your Life, Henry VIII, RSC, 1983; Pygmalion, Shaftesbury, 1984; All My Sons, Royal Exchange, Manchester, 1988; The Absence of War, Royal NT, 1993; *television* appearances include: Redcap, 1965–66; Thick As Thieves, 1973; The Sweeney, 1974–78; Sir Francis Drake, 1981; Mitch, 1983; The Life and Death of King John, 1984; Home to Roost, 1985–89; Inspector Morse, 1986–93; Stanley and the Women, 1991; A Year in Provence, 1993; Kavanagh QC, 1994; The Absence of War, 1995; *films* include: The Bofors Gun, 1968; The Sweeney, 1976; The Sweeney II, 1977; The Grass is Singing, 1982; Cry Freedom, 1987; Charlie, 1992. *Address:* c/o John Redway Associates, 5 Denmark Street, WC2H 8LP.

THAW, Sheila, (Mrs John Thaw); *see* Hancock, S.

THEAKSTON, John Andrew; Chief Executive, Higgs & Hill plc, since 1991; *b* 23 May 1952; *s* of Robert Francis Theakston and Jane Hawley (*née* Boyle); *m* 1977, Elizabeth Jane Morgan; one *s* one *d. Educ:* Sedbergh Sch., Yorks; Worcester Coll., Oxford (MA Mod. History); Durham Univ. (MSc). Trainee, T. & R. Theakston, Brewers, 1975–77; Donald Macpherson Group: Corporate Planning Manager, 1977–81; Overseas Div. Manager, 1981–84; Higgs & Hill plc: Business Develt Manager, 1985–87; Gp Finance Dir, 1987–89; Jt Gp Man. Dir. 1989–90. Dir, Black Sheep Brewery. *Recreations:* sailing, walking, trout fishing. *Address:* Higgs & Hill, Crown House, Kingston Road, New Malden, Surrey KT3 3ST. *T:* 0181–942 8921.

THELLUSSON, family name of **Baron Rendlesham.**

THELWELL, Norman; freelance artist-cartoonist since 1957; *b* Birkenhead, 3 May 1923; *s* of Christopher Thelwell and Emily (*née* Vick); *m* 1949, Rhona Evelyn Ladbury; one *s* one *d. Educ:* Rock Ferry High Sch., Birkenhead; Liverpool Coll. of Art. Nat. Diploma of Art; ATD. Teacher of Art, Wolverhampton Coll. of Art, 1950–57. Regular contributor to Punch, 1952–; cartoonist for: News Chronicle, 1956–60; Sunday Dispatch, 1960–61; Sunday Express, 1962–. Drawings for general publications, advertising, book jackets, illustrations, etc. *Publications:* Angels on Horseback, 1957; Thelwell Country, 1959; A Place of Your Own, 1960; Thelwell in Orbit, 1961; A Leg at Each Corner, 1962; The Penguin Thelwell, 1963; Top Dog, 1964; Thelwell's Riding Academy, 1965; Drawing Ponies, 1966; Up the Garden Path, 1967; Thelwell's Compleat Tangler, 1967; Thelwell's Book of Leisure, 1968; This Desirable Plot, 1970; The Effluent Society, 1971; Penelope, 1972; Three Sheets in the Wind, 1973; Belt Up, 1974; Thelwell Goes West, 1975; Thelwell's Brat Race, 1977; A Plank Bridge by a Pool, 1978; Thelwell's Gymkhana, 1979; Thelwell Annual, 1980; A Millstone Round My Neck, 1981; Thelwell Annual, 1981; Pony Cavalcade, 1981; How to Draw Ponies, 1982; Some Damn Fool's Signed the Rubens Again, 1982; Thelwell's Magnificat, 1983; Thelwell's Sporting Prints, 1984; Wrestling with a Pencil: the life of a freelance artist, 1986; Play It As It Lies: Thelwell's golfing manual, 1987; Penelope Rides Again, 1988; The Cat's Pyjamas, 1992. *Recreations:* trout and salmon angling, painting. *Address:* Herons Mead, Timsbury, Romsey, Hants SO51 0NE. *T:* Braishfield (01794) 68238.

THEOBALD, George Peter, JP; company director, since 1958; *b* 5 Aug. 1931; *s* of late George Oswald Theobald and Helen (*née* Moore); *m* 1955, Josephine Mary (*née* Boodle); two *s* three *d. Educ:* Betteshanger Sch.; Harrow. National Service commission, 5 Regt RHA, 1950–52; 290 (City of London) RA (TA), 1953–59. Robert Warner Ltd, 1953–74: Director, 1958; Man. Dir, Chm. Gp subsidiaries, 1965; private company director, 1974–; Tea Clearing House, 1959–72 (Chm., 1970–72); Moran Holdings (formerly Moran Tea Holdings) plc, 1980– (Chm., 1992–); Moran Tea Co. (India) plc, 1981– (Chm., 1992–). City of London (Queenhithe Ward): Chm., Ward Club, 1966–68; Common Councilman, 1968–74; Alderman, 1974–79. Member: Transport Users' Consultative Cttee for London, 1969–84 (Dep. Chm. 1978); London Regional Passengers Cttee, 1984–90. Governor: Bridewell Royal Hosp., 1974–93; King Edward's Sch., Witley, 1974–93 (Trustee, Educational Trust, 1977–); Donation Governor, Christ's Hosp., 1976–91; Governor, St Leonards-Mayfield Sch., 1982–88; Chm., St John's Sch., Northwood, 1990–; Mem. Cttee, Langford Cross Children's Home, 1976–90; Trustee: National Flood and Tempest Distress Fund, 1977–; Harrow Club W10, 1978–. Church Commissioner for England, 1978–79. Master, Merchant Taylors' Co., 1989–90, 1991–92. JP City of London, 1974. *Recreations:* gardening, transport, walking. *Address:* Towerhill Manor, Gomshall, Guildford, Surrey GU5 9LP. *T:* Guildford (01483) 202381. *Clubs:* Oriental, City Livery, Guildhall, MCC.

THEOCHAROUS, Archbishop Gregorios; His Eminence The Most Rev. Gregorios; Greek Orthodox Archbishop of Thyateira and Great Britain, since 1988; *b* 1929. *Educ:* High Sch., Lefkoniko, Famagusta; Pan Cyprian Gymnasium, Nicosia; Theol Faculty, Univ. of Athens. Monk in the Sacred Monastery, Stavrovouni, Cyprus; ordained: deacon, 1953; presbyter, 1959; asst parish priest and later parish priest, All Saints, London, 1959–69; Archdiocese of Thyateira: Chancellor, 1965–79; Asst Bishop to Archbishop Athenagoras, 1970–79; locum tenens on death of Archbishop Athenagoras, 1979; Bishop of Tropaeou, 1970–88; spiritual oversight of Community of St Barnabas, Wood Green, 1970–88. Dr *hc* North London, 1993. *Address:* Thyateira House, 5 Craven Hill, W2 3EN. *T:* 0171–723 4787, *Fax:* 0171–224 9301.

THÉODORE, Jean-François; Chief Executive Officer, since 1990 and Chairman, since 1991, SBF-Paris Bourse; Chairman, SICOVAM, since 1993; *b* 5 Dec. 1946; *m* 1976, Claudine Lefebvre; one *s* two *d. Educ:* Univ. of Paris (Licencé); Institut d'Etudes Politiques; Ecole Nationale d'Administration. Asst Hd, State Holdings Bureau, French Treasury, 1974–78; seconded to Credit National, as Mem., Exec. Bd, 1978–80; Treasury: Hd, African States-Franc Zone Bureau, 1980–82; Hd, Foreign Investment Bureau, 1982–84; Dep. Dir i/c, Banking Dept, 1984–86; Dep. Dir, Investments, State Participations and Public Corps Dept, 1986–93. Pres., Internat. Fedn of Stock Exchanges, 1993–94. Chevalier, Légion d'Honneur, 1994. *Address:* 39 rue Cambon, 75001 Paris, France. *T:* 49271102. *Clubs:* Paris-Europlace, Bourse (Paris).

THEROUX, Paul Edward, FRSL; FRGS; writer; *b* 10 April 1941; *s* of Albert Eugene Theroux and Anne Dittami Theroux; *m* 1967, Anne Castle (marr. diss. 1993); two *s. Educ:* Univ. of Massachusetts (BA). Lecturer: Univ. of Urbino, 1963; Soche Hill Coll., Malawi, 1963–65; Makerere Univ., Kampala, Uganda, 1965–68; Univ. of Singapore, 1968–71; Writer-in-Residence, Univ. of Virginia, 1972. Mem., AAIL, 1984. Hon. DLitt: Trinity Coll., Washington DC, 1980; Tufts Univ., Mass, 1980; Univ. of Mass, 1988. *Publications: novels:* Waldo, 1967; Fong and the Indians, 1968; Girls at Play, 1969; Murder in Mount Holly, 1969; Jungle Lovers, 1971; Sinning with Annie, 1972; Saint Jack, 1973 (filmed, 1979); The Black House, 1974; The Family Arsenal, 1976; Picture Palace, 1978 (Whitbread Award, 1978); A Christmas Card, 1978; London Snow, 1980; The Mosquito Coast, 1981 (James Tait Black Prize, 1982; filmed, 1987); Doctor Slaughter, 1984 (filmed as Half Moon Street, 1987); O-Zone, 1986; My Secret History, 1989; Chicago Loop, 1990; Doctor de Marr, 1990; Millroy the Magician, 1993; *short stories:* The Consul's File, 1977; World's End, 1980; The London Embassy, 1982 (televised, 1987); *play:* The White Man's Burden, 1987; *criticism:* V. S. Naipaul, 1972; *travel:* The Great Railway Bazaar, 1975; The Old Patagonian Express, 1979; The Kingdom by the Sea, 1983; Sailing through China, illus. Patrick Procktor, 1983; Sunrise with Seamonsters: travels and discoveries 1964–84, 1985; The Imperial Way, 1985; Riding the Iron Rooster, 1988; Travelling The World, 1990; The Happy Isles of Oceania, 1992; The Pillars of Hercules, 1995; *screenplay:* Saint Jack, 1979; reviews in The Sunday Times, New York Times, etc. *Recreation:* rowing. *Address:* c/o Hamish Hamilton Ltd, 27 Wrights Lane, W8 5TZ.

THESIGER, family name of **Viscount Chelmsford.**

THESIGER, Roderic Miles Doughty; Director, P. & D. Colnaghi and Co. Ltd, 1955–71; *b* 8 Nov. 1915; *y s* of late Hon. Wilfred Thesiger, DSO, and Mrs Reginald Astley, CBE; *m* 1st, 1940, Mary Rose (marr. diss. 1946; she *d* 1962), *d* of Hon. Guy Charteris; 2nd, 1946, Ursula, *d* of A. W. Whitworth, Woollas Hall, Pershore; one *s* one *d. Educ:* Eton; Christ Church, Oxford; Courtauld Institute. Served War of 1939–45, Welsh Guards, 1939–41; 1st Parachute Bde, 1941–44 (twice wounded, POW). Assistant, Tate Gallery, 1945–46; afterwards worked with Messrs Sotheby and privately until 1954. *Recreations:* visiting Italy and France. *Address:* The Paddocks, Lucton, Leominster, Herefordshire HR6 9PG. *T:* Yarpole (01568) 780327.

See also Sir W. P. Thesiger.

THESIGER, Sir Wilfred (Patrick), KBE 1995 (CBE 1968); DSO 1941; MA Oxon; *b* 3 June 1910; *e s* of late Hon. Wilfred Thesiger, DSO, and Mrs Reginald Astley, CBE. *Educ:* Eton; Magdalen College, Oxford (MA; Hon. Fellow, 1982). Repres. Oxford at boxing, 1930–33; Captain Oxford Boxing Team, 1933; Hon. Attaché Duke of Gloucester's Mission to Abyssinia, for Haile Selassi's coronation, 1930; served Middle East, 1941 (DSO); explored Danakil country of Abyssinia and the Aussa Sultanate, 1933–34 (awarded Back Grant by RGS, 1935); Sudan Political Service, Darfur-Upper Nile, 1935–40; served in Ethiopian, Syrian and Western Desert campaigns with SDF and SAS regiment with rank of Major; explored in Southern Arabia, 1945–49; twice crossed the Empty Quarter. Hon. Vice-Pres., RSAA. FRSL; Hon. FBA 1982; Hon. DLitt: Leicester, 1967; Bath, 1992. Founder's Medal, RGS, 1948; Lawrence of Arabia Medal, RCAS, 1955; Livingstone Medal, RSGS, 1962; W. H. Heinemann Award (for 1964), RSL, 1965; Burton Memorial Medal, Roy. Asiatic Soc., 1966. 3rd Class Star of Ethiopia, 1930. *Publications:* Arabian Sands, 1959; The Marsh Arabs, 1964; Desert, Marsh and Mountain: the world of a nomad, 1979; The Life of my Choice (autobiog.), 1987; Visions of a Nomad, 1987; My Kenya Days, 1994. *Recreations:* travelling, photography. *Address:* 15 Shelley Court, Tite Street, SW3 4JB. *T:* 0171–352 7213. *Clubs:* Travellers' (Special Mem.), Beefsteak (Hon. Life Mem.).

See also R. M. D. Thesiger.

THETFORD, Bishop Suffragan of, since 1992; **Rt. Rev. Hugo Ferdinand de Waal;** *b* 16 March 1935; *s* of Bernard Hendrik and Albertine Felice de Waal; *m* 1960, Brigit Elizabeth Townsend Massingberd-Mundy; one *s* three *d. Educ:* Tonbridge School; Pembroke Coll., Cambridge (MA), Münster Univ., Germany, Ridley Hall, Cambridge. Curate, St Martin's-in-the Bull Ring, Birmingham, 1960; Chaplain, Pembroke Coll., Cambridge, 1964–68; Rector of Dry Drayton, Cambs, 1964–73; with Bar Hill Ecumenical Area, 1967–73; Vicar of St John's, Blackpool Parish Church, 1974–78; Principal, Ridley Hall Theol Coll., Cambridge, 1978–91. Hon. Canon, Ely Cathedral, 1986–91. *Recreations:* music, tennis and squash, fly-fishing. *Address:* Rectory Meadow, Bramerton, Norwich NR14 7DW. *T:* Surlingham (01508) 538251.

THIAN, Robert Peter; Director, Celltech Group plc, since 1991; *b* 1 Aug. 1943; *s* of Clifford Peter Thian and Frances Elizabeth (*née* Stafford-Bird); *m* 1964, Liselotte Borges; two *d. Educ:* Geneva Univ. (Lic. en Droit 1967). Called to the Bar, Gray's Inn, 1971. Glaxo Group plc: Legal Advr, 1967–71; Man. Dir, Portugal, 1972–80; Abbott Laboratories (USA): European Business Develt Dir, 1981–84; Regional Dir, Europe, 1985–87; Vice Pres., Internat. Operations, Novo Industri A/S (Denmark), 1987–89; Gp Chief Exec., North West Water Group, 1990–93. *Recreations:* horses, golf, reading. *Clubs:* East India and Sports, Lansdowne.

THIMANN, Prof. Kenneth Vivian; Professor of Biology, 1965–72, and Provost of Crown College, 1966–72, Emeritus Professor, recalled to duty 1972–87, University of California, Santa Cruz, Calif, USA; *b* 5 Aug. 1904; *s* of Phoebus Thimann and Muriel Kate Thimann (*née* Harding); *m* 1929, Ann Mary Bateman, Sutton Bridge, Lincs; three *d. Educ:* Caterham Sch., Surrey; Imperial Coll., London. BSc, ARCS 1924; DIC 1925; PhD 1928. Beit Memorial Res. Fellow, 1927–29; Demonstr in Bacteriology, King's Coll. for Women, 1926–28; Instr in Biochem., Calif Inst. of Techn., 1930–35; Harvard University: Lectr on Botany, 1935; (Biology): Asst Prof., 1936, Associate Prof., 1939, Prof., 1946, and Higgins Prof., 1962–65, now Prof. Emeritus. Vis. Professor: Sorbonne, 1954; Univ. of Massachusetts, 1974; Univ. of Texas, 1976. Scientific Consultant, US Navy, 1942–45. Dir, Amer. Assoc. for Adv. of Science, 1968–71. Pres., XIth Internat. Botanical Congress, Seattle, USA, 1969; 2nd Nat. Biol Congress, Miami, 1971. Hon. AM Harvard, 1940; PhD (Hon.) Univ. of Basle, 1959; Doctor (Hon.) Univ. of Clermont-Ferrand, 1961; DSc (Hon.) Brown Univ., 1989. Fellow: Nat. Acad. of Scis (Councillor, 1967–71); Amer. Acad. of Arts and Scis; Amer. Philosophical Soc. (Councillor, 1973–76); and professional biological socs in USA and England; Foreign Member: Royal Society (London); Institut de France (Acad. des Sciences, Paris); Académie d'Agriculture; Accademia Nazionale dei Lincei (Rome); Leopoldina Akademie (Halle); Roumanian Academy (Bucharest); Botanical Societies of Japan and Netherlands. Silver Medal, Internat. Plant Growth

Substance Assoc.; Balzan Prize, 1983. *Publications:* (in USA) Phytohormones (with F. W. Went), 1937; The Action of Hormones in Plants and Invertebrates, 1948; The Life of Bacteria, 1955, 2nd edn 1963 (German edn 1964); L'Origine et les Fonctions des Auxines, 1956; The Natural Plant Hormones, 1972; Hormones in the Whole Life of Plants, 1977; (ed) Senescence in Plants, 1980; (with J. Langenheim) Botany: Plant Biology in relation to Human Affairs, 1981; over 300 papers in biological and biochemical jls. *Recreations:* music (piano), gardening. *Address:* The Quadrangle, 3300 Darby Road, Apt 3314, Haverford, PA 19041, USA. *Club:* Harvard Faculty (Cambridge, Mass).

THIMONT, Bernard Maurice, CB 1979; Secretary, Churches' Main Committee, 1981–90; *b* 1 July 1920; *s* of Georges André Thimont; *m* 1949, Joy Rowe; one *s* one *d*. *Educ:* St Ignatius Coll., London. Served War of 1939–45, in Army (Major), 1939–48. Foreign Office, 1948–50; HM Treasury, 1950–65; IDC, 1966; Cabinet Office, 1967; HM Treasury, 1967–68; Civil Service Dept, 1968–77; Controller, HM Stationery Office and Queen's Printer of Acts of Parlt, 1977–80. MA Lambeth, 1990. *Recreations:* music, building. *Address:* Trusham, Kingsnorth Close, Bridport, Dorset DT6 4BZ. *T:* Bridport (01308) 425426.

THIRD, Rt. Rev. Richard Henry McPhail; Assistant Bishop, Diocese of Bath and Wells, since 1992; *b* 29 Sept. 1927; *s* of Henry McPhail and Marjorie Caroline Third; *m* 1966, Helen Illingworth; two *d*. *Educ:* Alleyn's Sch.; Reigate Grammar Sch.; Emmanuel Coll., Cambridge (BA 1950, MA 1955); Lincoln Theological Coll. Deacon 1952, priest 1953; Southwark; Curate: S Andrew, Mottingham, 1952–55; Sanderstead (in charge of St Edmund, Riddlesdown), 1955–59; Vicar of Sheerness, 1959–67; Vicar of Orpington, 1967–76; RD of Orpington, 1973–76; Hon. Canon of Rochester, 1974–76; Proctor in Convocation, 1975–76 and 1980–85; Bishop Suffragan: of Maidstone, 1976–80; of Dover, 1980–92. Chm. of Govs, Christ Church Coll., Canterbury, 1986–92. Hon. DCL Kent, 1990. *Recreations:* music, walking, reading, gardening. *Address:* 25 Church Close, Martock, Somerset TA12 6DS. *T:* Martock (01935) 825519.

THIRKETTLE, (William) Ellis, CBE 1959; Principal, London College of Printing, 1939–67; *b* 26 July 1904; *s* of William Edward Thirkettle; *m* 1930, Alva (*d* 1987), *d* of Thomas Tough Watson; two *s*. *Educ:* Tiffin School. Principal, Stow College of Printing, Glasgow, 1936–39. *Address:* 21 Astley Close, Hollybush Lane, Pewsey, Wilts SN9 5BD.

THIRLWALL, Air Vice-Marshal George Edwin, CB 1976; retired; *b* 24 Dec. 1924; *s* of Albert and Clarice Editha Thirlwall; *m* 1st, 1949, Daphne Patricia Wynn Giles (*d* 1975); 2nd, 1977, Louisa Buck Russell (*née* Cranston). *Educ:* Sheffield Univ.; Cranfield Inst. of Technology. BEng, MSc. Joined RAF, 1950; OC RAF Sealand, 1969; Dir Air Guided Weapons, MoD, 1972; AO Ground Trng, RAF Trng Comd, 1974–76; AO Engineering, Strike Command, 1976–79. Director: Ceramics, Glass and Mineral ITB, 1979–82; Sand and Gravel Assoc., 1983–89. *Recreations:* gardening, golf. *Address:* Che Sara Sara, Gosmore Road, Hitchin, Herts SG4 9AR. *T:* Hitchin (01462) 434182. *Club:* Royal Air Force.

THIRSK, Dr (Irene) Joan, CBE 1994; FBA 1974; Reader in Economic History in the University of Oxford, and Fellow of St Hilda's College, Oxford, 1965–83 (Hon. Fellow, 1983); *b* 19 June 1922; *d* of William Henry Watkins and Daisy (*née* Frayer); *m* 1945, James Wood Thirsk; one *s* one *d*. *Educ:* Camden School for Girls, NW5; Westfield Coll., Univ. of London. BA, PhD London; MA Oxford. Subaltern, ATS, Intelligence Corps, 1942–45. Asst Lectr in Sociology, LSE, 1950–51; Sen. Res. Fellow in Agrarian History, Dept of English Local History, Leicester Univ., 1951–65. Ford Lectr in English History, Oxford, 1975. Sen. Mellon Fellow, Nat. Humanities Centre, 1986–87. Member: Royal Commn on Historical Monuments (England), 1977–86; Econ. and Social Hist. Cttee, SSRC, 1978–82; Royal Commn on Historical Manuscripts, 1989–. Mem. Council, Economic Hist. Soc., 1955–83; Vice-Chm., Standing Conf. for Local Hist., 1965–82; President: British Agricl Hist. Soc., 1983–86 (Mem. Exec. Cttee, 1953–83, Chm. Exec. Cttee, 1974–77); Edmonton Hundred Historical Soc., 1978–; Oxfordshire Local Hist. Assoc., 1981–86 (Vice-Pres., 1980–81); Conf. of Teachers of Regional and Local Hist. in Tertiary Educn, 1981–82; British Assoc. for Local Hist., 1986–92; Kent Hist. Fedn, 1990–; Vice-Pres., Soc. for Lincs Hist. and Archaeol., 1979–; Foreign Mem., Amer. Philos. Soc., 1982–; Corresp. Mem., Colonial Soc. of Massachusetts, 1983–. Editor, Agricultural History Review, 1964–72; Gen. Editor, The Agrarian History of England and Wales, 1974– (Dep. Gen. Ed., 1966–74); Mem. Editorial Bd, Past and Present, 1956–92. Hon. DLitt: Leicester, 1985; East Anglia, 1990; Kent, 1993; Sussex, 1994; DUniv Open, 1991; Hon. DAgric. Wageningen Agricl Univ., Netherlands, 1993. *Publications:* English Peasant Farming, 1957; Suffolk Farming in the Nineteenth Century, 1958; Tudor Enclosures, 1959; The Agrarian History of England and Wales: vol. IV, 1500–1640, 1967; vol. V, 1640–1750, 1984; (with J. P. Cooper) Seventeenth-Century Economic Documents, 1972; The Restoration, 1976; Economic Policy and Projects, 1978; The Rural Economy of England (collected essays), 1985; England's Agricultural Regions and Agrarian History 1500–1750, 1987; articles in Economic History Rev., Agric. History Rev., Past and Present, History, Jl Modern History, etc. *Recreations:* gardening, sewing, machine-knitting. *Address:* 1 Hadlow Castle, Hadlow, Tonbridge, Kent TN11 0EG.

THISELTON, Prof. Rev. Canon Anthony Charles, PhD, DD; Professor of Christian Theology and Head of Department of Theology, University of Nottingham, since 1992; Canon Theologian, Leicester Cathedral, since 1994; *b* 13 July 1937; *s* of Eric Charles Thiselton and Hilda Winifred (*née* Kevan); *m* 1963, Rosemary Stella Harman; two *s* one *d*. *Educ:* City of London School; King's Coll., London. BD 1959; MTh 1964 (London); PhD (Sheffield) 1977; DD (Durham) 1993. Curate, Holy Trinity, Sydenham, 1960–63; Lectr and Chaplain, Tyndale Hall, Bristol, 1963–67, Sen. Tutor, 1967–70; Recognised Teacher in Theology, Univ. of Bristol, 1965–71; University of Sheffield: Sir Henry Stephenson Fellow, 1970–71; Lectr in Biblical Studies, 1971–79; Sen. Lectr, 1979–86; Principal, St John's Coll., Nottingham and Special Lectr in Theology, Univ. of Nottingham, 1986–88; Principal, St John's Coll. with Cranmer Hall, Univ. of Durham, 1988–92. Visiting Professor: Calvin Coll., Grand Rapids, USA, 1982–83; Regent Coll., Vancouver, 1983; Fuller Theolog. Seminary, Pasadena, Calif, 1984; North Park Coll. and Seminary, Chicago, 1984. Exam. Chaplain to Bishop of Sheffield, 1977–80, to Bishop of Leicester, 1979–89 and 1993–. Member: C of E Faith and Order Adv. Group, 1971–81, 1987–90; Doctrine Commn, 1977–90 (Vice-Chm., 1987–90). Council for National Academic Awards: Vice-Chm., Bd of Theol and Religious Studies, 1984–87; Mem., Cttee for Humanities, 1987–89. Mem., Working party on Revised Catechism, 1988–89. Adv. Editor, Jl for Study of NT, 1981–91; Mem. Editl Bd, Biblical Interpretation (Brill, Leiden), 1992–. *Publications:* The Two Horizons: New Testament Hermeneutics and Philosophical Description, 1980; (with C. Walhout and R. Lundin) The Responsibility of Hermeneutics, 1985; New Horizons in Hermeneutics: theory and practice of transforming biblical reading, 1992; Interpreting God and the Postmodern Self, 1995; contribs to learned jls and other books on New Testament, doctrine, and philosophical hermeneutics. *Recreation:* choral and organ music. *Address:* Department of Theology, University of Nottingham, University Park, Nottingham NG7 2RD. *T:* Nottingham (0115) 951 5852, *Fax:* (0115) 951 5887.

THISTLETHWAITE, Prof. Frank, CBE 1979; Emeritus Professor, University of East Anglia; founding Vice-Chancellor, 1961–80; *b* 24 July 1915; *s* of late Lee and Florence Nightingale Thistlethwaite; *m* 1940, Jane (*d* 1992), *d* of H. Lindley Hosford, Lyme, Connecticut, USA; one *s* three *d* (and one *s* decd). *Educ:* Bootham School; St John's College, Cambridge (Exhibitioner and Scholar). BA 1938, MA 1941. FRHistS. Editor, The Cambridge Review, 1937. Commonwealth Fund Fellow, University of Minnesota, 1938–40; British Press Service, New York, 1940–41. RAF, 1941–45; seconded to Office of War Cabinet (Joint-Amer. Secretariat), 1942–45. Fellow, St John's College, Cambridge, 1945–61; at various times, Tutor, Praelector, Steward; University Lecturer in Faculty of Economics and Politics, 1949–61. Visiting Prof. of American Civilization, Univ. of Pennsylvania, 1956; Vis. Fellow, Henry E. Huntington Library, Calif, 1973; Leverhulme Emeritus Fellow, 1981; Hill Vis. Prof., Univ. of Minnesota, 1986; British Acad. Research Leave Award, 1995–96. Chairman: British Assoc. for Amer. Studies, 1955–59; Cttee of Management, Inst. of US Studies, Univ. of London, 1966–80; IUPC (formerly IUC), 1977–81 (Mem., 1962–81); Member: Inst. for Advanced Study, Princeton, 1954; Academic Adv. Cttee, Open Univ., 1969–74; Provisional Council, Univ. of Zambia, 1965–69; Univ. of Malaŵi, 1971–75; Univ. of Mauritius, 1974–84; Marshall Aid Commemoration Commn, 1964–80; US-UK Educnl (Fulbright) Commn, 1964–79; European Adv. Council, Salzburg Seminar in Amer. Studies, 1969–74; Bd, British Council, 1971–82; British Cttee of Award, Harkness Fellowships, 1974–80; Adviser to Nat. Council of Higher Educn, Ceylon, 1967. Governor, Sedbergh Sch., 1958–73. Pres., Friends of Cambridge Univ. Library, 1983–. Hon. Fellow, St John's Coll., Cambridge, 1974. Hon. Prof. of History, Univ. of Mauritius, 1981. Hon. FRIBA 1985. Hon. LHD Colorado, 1972; Hon. DCL East Anglia, 1980; Hon. DSc Minnesota, 1994. *Publications:* The Great Experiment: An Introduction to the History of the American People, 1955 (trans. 14 languages); The Anglo-American Connection in the Early Nineteenth Century, 1958; Dorset Pilgrims: the story of West Country pilgrims who went to New England in the 17th century, 1989; Migration from Europe Overseas in the Nineteenth and Twentieth Centuries, in, A Century of European Migrations 1830–1930, 1991; contrib. New Cambridge Modern History and other historical works and journals; New Universities in the Modern World (ed M. G. Ross). *Recreation:* music. *Address:* 15 Park Parade, Cambridge CB5 8AL; Island Cottage, Winson, Glos GL7 5ER. *Club:* Athenæum.

See also J. H. Pellew.

THODAY, Prof. John Marion, BSc Wales, PhD, ScD Cantab; FRS 1965; Arthur Balfour Professor of Genetics, Cambridge University, 1959–83, now Emeritus; Life Fellow of Emmanuel College, 1983 (Fellow, 1959); *b* 30 Aug. 1916; *s* of Professor D. Thoday, FRS; *m* 1950, Doris Joan Rich, PhD (Fellow, Lucy Cavendish College); one *s* one *d*. *Educ:* Bootham School, York; University Coll. of N Wales, Bangor; Trinity College, Cambridge. Photographic Intelligence, Royal Air Force, 1941–46; Cytologist, Mount Vernon Hospital, 1946–47; Asst Lectr, then Lectr for Cytogenetics, Departments of Botany and Zoology, University of Sheffield, 1947–54; Head of Department of Genetics: Sheffield, 1954–59; Cambridge, 1959–82. Leverhulme Emeritus Res. Fellow, 1984–86. Director, OECD Project for reform of secondary school Biology teaching 1962, 1963. Chm., UK Nat. Cttee for Biology, 1982–88. Pres., Genetical Soc., 1975–78. *Publications:* (with J. N. Thompson) Quantitive Genetics, 1979; articles on radiation cytology, experimental evolution, the genetics of continuous variables, biological progress and on genetics and society. *Address:* 7 Clarkson Road, Cambridge CB3 0EH.

THODE, Dr Henry George, CC (Canada) 1967; MBE 1946; FRS 1954; FRSC 1943; FCIC 1948; Professor Emeritus, McMaster University, Canada, since 1979; *b* 10 September 1910; Canadian; *m* 1935, Sadie Alicia Patrick; three *s*. *Educ:* University of Saskatchewan (BSc 1930, MSc 1932); University of Chicago (PhD 1934). Research Asst, Columbia Univ., 1936–38; Research Chemist, US Rubber Co., 1938; McMaster University: Asst Prof. of Chem., 1939–42; Assoc. Prof. of Chem., 1942–44; Prof. of Chem., 1944–79; Head, Department of Chemistry, 1948–52; Dir of Res., 1947–61; Principal of Hamilton Coll., 1949–63; Vice-Pres., 1957–61; Pres. and Vice-Chancellor, 1961–72. California Inst. of Technology, Pasadena, Calif: Nat. Science Foundn Sen. Foreign Res. Fellow, 1970; Sherman Fairchild Distinguished Scholar, 1977. National Research Council, War Research-Atomic Energy, 1943–45. Member: Nat. Research Council, 1943–45; Defence Research Bd, 1955–61; Commn on Atomic Weights (SAIC), IUPAC, 1965–73; Board of Governors, Ontario Research Foundn, 1955–82; Director: Atomic Energy of Canada Ltd, 1966–81; Stelco Inc., 1969–85. Hon. Fellow, Chemical Inst. of Canada, 1972; Shell Canada Merit Fellowship, 1974. Hon. DSc: Universities: Toronto, 1955; BC, Acadia, 1960; Laval, 1963; RMC, 1964; McGill, 1966; Queen's, 1967; York, 1972; McMaster, 1973. Hon. LLD: Sask., 1958; Regina, 1983. Medal of Chemical Inst. of Canada, 1957; Tory Medal, 1959, Centenary Medal, 1982, Sir William Dawson Medal, 1989, Royal Soc. of Canada; Arthur L. Day Medal, Geological Soc. of America, 1980; Montreal Medal, Chem. Inst. of Canada, 1993. Order of Ontario, 1989. *Publications:* numerous publications on nuclear chemistry, isotope chemistry, isotope abundances in terrestrial and extraterrestrial material, separation of isotopes, magnetic susceptibilities, electrical discharges in gases, sulphur concentrations and isotope ratios in lunar materials. *Recreations:* swimming, farming. *Address:* Department of Chemistry, Nuclear Research Building, McMaster University, 1280 Main Street West, Hamilton, Ontario L8S 4K1, Canada. *T:* (905) 5259140. *Club:* Rotary (Hamilton, Ont.).

THODY, Prof. Philip Malcolm Waller; Professor of French Literature, University of Leeds, 1965–93, now Professor Emeritus; *b* Lincoln, 21 March 1928; *s* of Thomas Edwin Thody and Florence Ethel (*née* Hart); *m* 1954, Joyce Elizabeth Woodin; two *s* two *d*. *Educ:* Lincoln Sch.; King's Coll., Univ. of London. FIL 1982. Temp. Asst Lectr, Univ. of Birmingham, 1954–55; Asst Lectr, subseq. Lectr, QUB, 1956–65; Chairman: Dept of French, Univ. of Leeds, 1968–72, 1975–79, 1982–85, 1987–93; Bd of Faculties of Arts, Social Studies and Law, Univ. of Leeds, 1972–74. Visiting Professor: Univ. of Western Ontario, Canada, 1963–64; Berkeley Summer Sch., 1964; Harvard Summer Sch., 1968; Virginia Summer Sch., 1990; Stamford Univ., 1993–94; Centenary Vis. Prof., Adelaide Univ., 1974; Canterbury Vis. Fellow, Univ. of Canterbury, NZ, 1977, 1982; Vis. Fellow, Univ. of WA, 1988. Pres., Modern Languages Assoc., 1980, 1981. Officier dans l'Ordre des Palmes Académiques, 1981. *Publications:* Albert Camus, a study of his work, 1957; Jean-Paul Sartre, a literary and political study, 1960; Albert Camus, 1913–1960, 1961; Jean Genet, a study of his novels and plays, 1968; Jean Anouilh, 1968; Choderlos de Laclos, 1970; Jean-Paul Sartre, a biographical introduction, 1971; Aldous Huxley, a biographical introduction, 1973; Roland Barthes: a conservative estimate, 1977; A True Life Reader for Children and Parents, 1977; Dog Days in Babel (novel), 1979; (jtly) Faux Amis and Key Words, 1985; Marcel Proust, novelist, 1987; Albert Camus, novelist, 1989; French Caesarism from Napoleon 1er to Charles de Gaulle, 1989; Jean-Paul Sartre, novelist, 1992; The Conservative Imagination, 1993; Le Franglais, 1995; Twentieth-Century Literature: critical issues and themes, 1996; contribs to French Studies, Times Literary Supplement, Times Higher Educational Supplement, Modern Languages Review, London Magazine, Twentieth Century, Encounter, Yorkshire Post. *Recreations:* talking, golf, Wodehouse inter-war first editions. *Address:* 6 The Nook, Primley Park, Alwoodley, Leeds LS17 7JU. *T:* Leeds (0113) 2687350.

THOM, Kenneth Cadwallader; HM Diplomatic Service, retired; *b* 4 Dec. 1922; *m* 1948, Patience Myra (*née* Collingridge); three *s* one *d*. *Educ:* University College School, London;

St Andrews Univ.; MA(Hons). Army Service, 1942–47; Assistant District Officer, then District Officer, Northern Nigerian Administration, 1950–59; 1st Secretary: FO, 1959; UK Mission to UN, NY, 1960–63; FO, 1963–66; Budapest, 1966–68; FCO, 1968–72; Counsellor, Dublin, 1972–74; Counsellor, FCO, 1974–78; Consul-General: Hanover, 1978–79; Hamburg, 1979–81; retired, and re-employed, FCO, 1981–85. FIL 1981. *Address:* Heybrook, Lower Backway, Bruton, Somerset BA10 0EA.

THOMAS; *see* Elis-Thomas.

THOMAS, family name of **Viscount Tonypandy** and **Barons Thomas of Gwydir, Thomas of Swynnerton** and **Baroness Thomas of Walliswood**.

THOMAS OF GWYDIR, Baron *cr* 1987 (Life Peer), of Llanrwst in the county of Gwynedd; **Peter John Mitchell Thomas;** PC 1964; QC 1965; a Recorder of the Crown Court, 1974–88; *b* 31 July 1920; *o s* of late David Thomas, Solicitor, Llanrwst, Denbighshire, and Anne Gwendoline Mitchell; *m* 1947, Frances Elizabeth Tessa (*d* 1985), *o d* of late Basil Dean, CBE and Lady Mercy Greville; two *s* two *d. Educ:* Epworth College, Rhyl; Jesus College, Oxford (MA). Served War of 1939–45, in RAF (Bomber Comd); Prisoner of War (Germany), 1941–45. Called to Bar, Middle Temple, 1947 (Master of the Bench 1971, Emeritus 1991); Member of Wales and Chester Circuit; Deputy Chairman: Cheshire QS, 1966–70; Denbighshire QS, 1968–70. Arbitrator, Court of Arbitration, Internat. Chamber of Commerce, Paris, 1974–88. MP (C): Conway Div. of Caernarvonshire, 1951–66; Hendon South, 1970–87; PPS to the Solicitor-General, 1954–59; Parly Secretary, Min. of Labour, 1959–61; Parly Under-Sec. of State, Foreign Office, 1961–63; Minister of State for Foreign Affairs, 1963–64; Opp. Front Bench Spokesman on Foreign Affairs and Law, 1964–66; Sec. of State for Wales, 1970–74. Member: Select Cttee on Conduct of Members, 1976–77; Select Cttee on Procedure (Supply), 1981–83 (Chm.); Select Cttee on Foreign Affairs, 1983–87 (Dep. Chm.); Select Cttee on Privileges, 1984–87; Chairman: Select Cttee on Members' Salaries, 1981–82; Select Cttee on Revision of Standing Orders, 1982–83. Chm., Cons. Party Organisation, 1970–72. Pres., Nat. Union of Conservative and Unionist Assocs, 1974 and 1975. Mem., Council of Europe and WEU, 1957–59. Member, Historic Buildings Council for Wales, 1965–67. *Address:* 37 Chester Way, SE11 4UR. *T:* 0171–735 6047; Millicent Cottage, Elstead, Surrey GU8 6HD. *T:* Elstead (01252) 702052. *Club:* Carlton.

THOMAS OF SWYNNERTON, Baron *cr* 1981 (Life Peer), of Notting Hill in Greater London; **Hugh Swynnerton Thomas;** historian; King Juan Carlos I Professor, New York University, 1995; *b* 21 Oct. 1931; *s* of Hugh Whitelegge Thomas, CMG, Colonial Service, Gold Coast (Ghana) and Margery Swynnerton; *m* 1962, Vanessa Jebb, *d* of 1st Baron Gladwyn, *qv*; two *s* one *d. Educ:* Sherborne; Queens' Coll., Cambridge (Scholar); Sorbonne, Paris. Pres. Cambridge Union, 1953. Foreign Office, 1954–57; Sec. to UK delegn to UN Disarmament Sub-Cttee, 1955–56; Lectr at RMA Sandhurst, 1957; Prof. of History, 1966–76, and Chm., Grad. Sch. of Contemp. European Studies, 1973–76, Univ. of Reading. Ansken Lectr, Frick Mus., NY, 1991; Yaseen Lectr, Met. Mus. of Art, NY, 1995. Chm., Centre for Policy Studies, 1979–90. Corresp. Mem., Real Acad. de la Historia, Madrid, 1994. Somerset Maugham Prize, 1962; Arts Council prize for History (1st Nat. Book Awards), 1980. Commander, Order of Isabel la Católica, Spain, 1986; Order of Aztec Eagle, Mexico, 1994. *Publications:* (as Hugh Thomas) The World's Game, 1957; The Spanish Civil War, 1961, rev. edn 1977, rev. illustrated edn, Spain, 1979; The Suez Affair, 1967; Cuba, or the Pursuit of Freedom, 1971; (ed) The selected writings of José Antonio Primo de Rivera, 1972; Goya and The Third of May 1808, 1972; Europe, the Radical Challenge, 1973; John Strachey, 1973; The Cuban Revolution, 1977; An Unfinished History of the World, 1979, rev. edn 1982 (US 1979, A History of the World); The Case for the Round Reading Room, 1983; Havannah (novel), 1984; Armed Truce, 1986; A Traveller's Companion to Madrid, 1988; Klara (novel), 1988; Ever Closer Union: Britain's destiny in Europe, 1991; The Conquest of Mexico, 1993. *Address:* c/o House of Lords, SW1A 0PW.

THOMAS OF WALLISWOOD, Baroness *cr* 1994 (Life Peer), of Dorking in the County of Surrey; **Susan Petronella Thomas,** OBE 1989; Vice Chairman, Surrey County Council, since 1993 (Member (Lib Dem), since 1985); *b* 20 Dec. 1935; *m* 1958, David Churchill Thomas, *qv* (separated); one *s* two *d. Educ:* Cranborne Chase Sch.; Lady Margaret Hall, Oxford. Chief Exec., British Clothing Industries Council for Europe, 1974–78. Chm. and Treas., Richmond Liberal Assoc., 1974; former Pres., Women Lib Dems. Chm., Highways and Transport Cttee, Surrey CC, 1993–. Contested: (Lib Alliance) Mole Valley, 1983 and 1987; (Lib Dem) Surrey, Eur. Parly elecns, 1994. *Address:* Weathertop, Tower Hill, Dorking, Surrey RH4 2AP. *T:* Dorking (01306) 885590, *Fax:* (01306) 883874.

See also Hon. D. W. P. Thomas.

THOMAS, Prof. Adrian Tregerthen; Hamilton Harty Professor of Music, Queen's University of Belfast, since 1985; *b* 11 June 1947; *s* of Owen George Thomas and Jean Tregerthen. *Educ:* Univ. of Nottingham (BMus 1969); University Coll., Cardiff (MA 1971). Lectr in Music, 1973–82, Sen. Lectr, 1982–85, QUB. Hd of Music, BBC Radio 3, 1990–93. Medal of Polish Composers' Union, for Distinguished Service to Contemporary Polish Music, 1989. *Publications:* Grazyna Bacewicz: chamber and orchestral music, USA 1985; (contrib.) Cambridge Companion to Chopin, 1992; (contrib.) New Grove Dictionary of Opera, 1993; (contrib.) New Grove Dictionary of Women Composers, 1994; Górecki, 1995; contrib. Music Rev., THES, Contemp. Music Rev., Music and Letters. *Recreations:* poetry, oriental arts, hill-walking. *Address:* School of Music, Queen's University of Belfast, Belfast BT7 1NN. *T:* Belfast (01232) 335105.

THOMAS, Sir Alan; *see* Thomas Sir J. A.

THOMAS, Alston Havard Rees; Finance and Property Writer, Bristol Evening Post, 1985 (Diary Editor, 1970–85); *b* Dinas, Pembrokeshire, 8 July 1925. Trainee and reporter, West Wales Guardian, 1939–44; Dist Reporter, Wilts Times, 1944–46; joined Bristol Evening Post, 1946, successively Industrial, Speedway, Municipal, Ecclesiastical, Crime and Med. correspondent. Institute of Journalists: Mem., 1974–; Chm. Nat. Exec., 1981–84; Pres., 1985–86; Chm. SW Region, 1975–; Mem., Press Council, 1979–90. Mem., St John Council (Avon Co., 1974–). *Recreations:* rugby union, music, travel, gardening. *Address:* Havene, Maysmead Lane, Langford, Avon BS18 7HX. *T:* Weston-super-Mare (01934) 862515. *Club:* Savages (Bristol).

THOMAS, Ambler Reginald, CMG 1951; Under-Secretary, Ministry of Overseas Development, retired 1975; *b* 12 Feb. 1913; *s* of late John Frederick Ivor Thomas, OBE, MICE, MIME and Elizabeth Thomas; *m* 1943, Diana Beresford Gresham; two *s* three *d. Educ:* Gresham's School, Holt; Corpus Christi College, Cambridge. Entered Home Civil Service as Asst Principal and apptd to Ministry of Agriculture and Fisheries, 1935; transferred to Colonial Office, 1936. Asst Private Sec. to Sec. of State for Colonies, 1938–39; Principal, Colonial Office, 1939; Asst Sec., 1946; Chief Sec. to Govt of Aden, 1947–49; Establishment and Organization Officer, Colonial Office, 1950–52; Assistant Under-Sec. of State, Colonial Office, 1952–64; Under-Sec., Min. of Overseas Develt, and Overseas Develt Administration, 1964–73. Member, Exec. Cttee, British Council, 1965–68. Chairman: Commn of Inquiry into Gilbert Is Develt Authority, 1976; Corona Club. *Address:* Champsland, North Chideock, Bridport, Dorset DT6 6JZ. *Club:* United Oxford & Cambridge University.

THOMAS, Aneurin Morgan; Director, Welsh Arts Council, 1967–84; *b* 3 April 1921; *s* of Philip Thomas and Olwen Amy Thomas (*née* Davies); *m* 1947, Mary Dineen; one *s* one *d. Educ:* Ystalyfera Intermediate Sch., Glamorgan; Swansea School of Art and Crafts. British and Indian Armies, 1941–46 (Major). Lecturer, later Vice-Principal, Somerset College of Art, 1947–60; Vice-Principal, Hornsey College of Art, 1960–67. Member, Board of Governors: Loughborough Coll. of Art and Design, 1980–89; S Glamorgan Inst. of Higher Educn, 1985–89 (Chm., Faculty of Art and Design Adv. Cttee, 1985–90); Carmarthenshire Coll. of Tech. and Art, 1985– (Chm., Faculty of Art and Design Adv. Cttee, 1985–); Vice-President: Nat. Soc. for Art Educn, 1967–68; Llangollen Internat. Music Eisteddfod, 1970–. Chm., Assoc. of Art Instns, 1977–78. *Publications:* periodic contribs to books and professional jls. *Recreation:* observing with interest and humour but with increasing bewilderment. *Address:* Netherwood, 8 Lower Cwrt-y-vil Road, Penarth, South Glamorgan CF64 3HQ. *T:* Penarth (01222) 702239.

THOMAS, (Anthony) Richard, CMG 1995; HM Diplomatic Service; High Commissioner, Jamaica, since 1995; *b* 11 July 1939; *s* of Frederick James Thomas and Winifred Kate Apthorpe Webb; *m* 1976, Ricky Parks Prado, London and Lima; one *s* one *d. Educ:* Ampleforth; Peterhouse, Cambridge (MA). FO 1962; served Caracas, Budapest, Washington, Madrid and FCO; Counsellor, Dep. Consul-Gen., Johannesburg, 1981; Minister Counsellor and Consul-Gen., Brasilia, 1985; FCO 1989; Ambassador to Angola, São Tomé and Principe, 1993. *Recreations:* listening to music, reading, theatre, visual arts, cooking. *Address:* c/o Foreign and Commonwealth Office, SW1A 2AH.

THOMAS, Prof. (Antony) Charles, CBE 1991; DL; DLitt; FSA; FRHistS; FBA 1989; Professor of Cornish Studies, University of Exeter, 1971–91, Professor Emeritus, 1993; Director, Institute of Cornish Studies, 1971–91; *b* 24 April 1928; *s* of late Donald Woodroffe Thomas and Viva Warrington Thomas; *m* 1959, Jessica Dorothea Esther, *d* of late F. A. Mann, CBE, FBA, Hon. QC; two *s* two *d. Educ:* Winchester; Corpus Christi Coll., Oxon (BA Hons Jurisp.); Univ. of London (Dipl. Prehist. Archaeol.; Fellow, UCL, 1993); DLitt Oxon, 1983. Lectr in Archaeology, Univ. of Edinburgh, 1957–67; Prof. of Archaeology, Univ. of Leicester, 1967–71. Leverhulme Fellowship, 1965–67; Sir John Rhys Fellow, Univ. of Oxford, and Vis. Sen. Res. Fellow, Jesus Coll., 1985–86; Emeritus Leverhulme Fellowship, 1993–95. Lectures: Dalrymple, Univ. of Glasgow, 1991; (first) Whithorn Trust, 1992. President: Council for British Archaeology, 1970–73; Royal Instn of Cornwall, 1970–72; Cornwall Archaeol. Soc., 1984–88; Soc. for Medieval Archaeology, 1986–89; Soc. for Landscape Studies, 1993–. Chairman: BBC SW Reg. Adv. Council, 1975–80; DoE Area Archaeol Cttee, Cornwall and Devon, 1975–79; Cornwall Cttee Rescue Archaeol., 1976–88; Mem., Royal Commn on Historical Monuments (England), 1983– (Acting Chm., Feb. 1988–Oct. 1989; Vice Chm., 1991–). Hon. Mem., Royal Irish Acad., 1973; Hon. Fellow: RSAI, 1975, St David's Univ. Coll. Lampeter, 1992. DL Cornwall, 1988. William Frend Medal, Soc. of Antiquaries, 1982. *Publications:* Christian Antiquities of Camborne, 1967; The Early Christian Archaeology of North Britain, 1971; Britain and Ireland in Early Christian Times, 1971; (with A. Small and D. Wilson) St Ninian's Isle and its Treasure, 1973; (with D. Ivall) Military Insignia of Cornwall, 1974; Christianity in Roman Britain to AD 500, 1981; Exploration of a Drowned Landscape, 1985; Celtic Britain, 1986; Views and Likenesses: photographers in Cornwall and Scilly 1839–70, 1988; Tintagel, Arthur and Archaeology, 1993; And Shall These Mute Stones Speak?: post-Roman inscriptions in Western Britain, 1994. *Recreations:* military history, archaeological fieldwork. *Address:* Lambessow, St Clement, Truro, Cornwall TR1 1TB.

THOMAS, Cedric Marshall, CBE 1991 (OBE 1983); consultant on business, health and safety; Chairman, Jesse Shirley & Son Ltd, since 1991; Deputy Chairman, Thomas William Lench Ltd, since 1993 (Director, since 1991); Director, Poplars Resource Management Co. Ltd, since 1992; *b* 26 May 1930; *s* of David J. Thomas and Evis (*née* Field); *m* 1st, 1954, Dora Ann Pritchard (*d* 1975); one *s* one *d*; 2nd, 1976, Margaret Elizabeth (*née* Crawley); one step *s* three step *d. Educ:* King Edward's Sch., Birmingham; Univ. of Birmingham (BSc Hons, PhD). CEng; FIMinE; FMES (Pres., 1969–71); CIMgt. NCB, 1954–60; Johnson Progress Group, 1961–77 (Chief Exec., 1970–77); Business Consultant, 1977–80; Benjamin Priest Group, 1980–84 (Chief Exec., 1983); Dir and Chief Exec., Engrg Employers' W Midlands Assoc., 1984–91. Member: Management Bd, Engrg Employers' Fedn, 1974–80, 1983–84; HSC, 1980–90; Engrg Employers' Fedn Council, 1992–95; Chairman: Special Programmes Area Bd, 1978–83; Area Manpower Bd, 1986–88. Pres., Engineering Employers' W Midlands Assoc., 1976–78. Governor, N Staffs Polytechnic, 1973–80. Hon. FFOM 1992. *Recreations:* Rugby football, tennis, theatre, walking. *Address:* Parkfields House, Tittensor, Staffs ST12 9HQ. *T:* Barlaston (01782) 373677.

THOMAS, Charles; *see* Thomas, A. C.

THOMAS, Ven. Charles Edward; Archdeacon of Wells, 1983–93; *b* 1927. *Educ:* St David's College, Lampeter (BA 1951); College of the Resurrection, Mirfield. Deacon 1953, priest 1954; Curate of Ilminster, 1953–56; Chaplain and Asst Master, St Michael's Coll., Tenbury, 1956–57; Curate of St Stephen's, St Albans, 1957–58; Vicar, St Michael and All Angels, Boreham Wood, 1958–66; Rector, Monksilver with Elworthy, 1966–74, with Brompton Ralph and Nettlecombe, 1969–74 (Curate-in-charge of Nettlecombe, 1968–69); Vicar of South Petherton with the Seavingtons, 1974–83. RD of Crewkerne, 1977–82. *Address:* Geryfelin, Pentre, Tregaron, Dyfed SY25 6NF. *T:* Tregaron (01974) 298102.

THOMAS, (Christopher) Paul; Director, Quality Assurance Division, Department for Education and Employment, since 1994; *b* 9 Feb. 1951; *s* of Donald Thomas and Rita Thomas (*née* Kershaw); *m* 1981, Colleen Doey. *Educ:* Hutton Grammar Sch.; Bridlington Sch.; Keble Coll., Oxford (MA PPE). Joined Civil Service, 1973; has served in Customs & Excise, HM Treasury, Cabinet Office and Dept of Employment. *Recreations:* squash, cricket, walking, sailing, jazz. *Address:* Croft Head, Aston Lane, Hope, Derbys S30 2RA. *T:* Hope Valley (01433) 621764.

THOMAS, Christopher Sydney; QC 1989; PhD; FCIArb; *b* 17 March 1950; *s* of late John Raymond Thomas and of Daphne May Thomas; *m* 1979, Patricia Jane Heath; one *s* one *d. Educ:* King's Sch., Worcester; Univ. of Kent at Canterbury (BA Hons, 1st Cl.); Faculté International de Droit Comparé, Paris (Diplôme de Droit Comparé (avec mérite), 1972); King's Coll., London (PhD 1994). FCIArb 1994. Hardwick Scholar and Jenkins Scholar, Lincoln's Inn; called to the Bar, Lincoln's Inn, 1973; Asst Recorder, 1993–. Called to Gibraltar Bar, 1989. *Recreation:* farming. *Address:* 10 Essex Street, Outer Temple, WC2R 3AA. *T:* 0171–240 6981.

THOMAS, Clarence; Associate Justice of the Supreme Court of the United States, since 1991; *b* 23 June 1948. *Educ:* Yale Univ. (JD). Asst to Attorney Gen., State of Missouri, 1974–77; attorney in private practice, 1977–79; Legislative Asst, US Senate, 1979–81; Asst Sec. for Civil Rights, Dept of Educn, Washington, 1981–82; Chm., Equal Employment

Opportunity Commn, Washington, 1982–90; Judge, US Court of Appeals, 1990–91. *Address:* United States Supreme Court, 1 First Street NE, Washington, DC 20543, USA.

THOMAS, Colin Agnew; chartered accountant; *b* 14 Feb. 1921; *s* of Harold Alfred Thomas and Nora (*née* Williams); *m* 1947, Jane Jardine Barnish, *d* of Leonard Barnish, FRIBA; one *s* one *d*. *Educ:* Oundle School. Lieut, RNVR, 1941–46. Finance Comptroller, Lloyd's, 1964–75, Sec.-Gen., 1976–79. Member: Dorking Art Club; Leatherhead Art Club. *Recreations:* golf, gardening, sketching. *Address:* 33 Cobham Road, Leatherhead, Surrey KT22 9AY. *T:* Leatherhead (01372) 374335; 15 Ravenspoint, Trearddur Bay, Anglesey LL65 2AJ. *T:* Trearddur Bay (01407) 860091. *Clubs:* Effingham Golf; Trearddur Bay Sailing.

THOMAS, Rev. Canon David; Vicar of St Peter's, Newton, Swansea, since 1987; Residentiary Canon, Brecon Cathedral, since 1994; *b* 22 July 1942; *s* of late Rt Rev. John James Absalom Thomas; *m* 1967, Rosemary Christine Calton; one *s* one *d*. *Educ:* Christ College, Brecon; Keble College, Oxford; St Stephen's House, Oxford. MA Oxon. Curate of Hawarden, 1967–69; Tutor, St Michael's College, Llandaff, Cardiff, 1969–70, Chaplain 1970–75; Secretary, Church in Wales Liturgical Commn, 1970–75; Vice-Principal, St Stephen's House, Oxford, 1975–79; Vicar of Chepstow, 1979–82; Principal, St Stephen's House, Oxford, 1982–87. Mem., Standing Doctrinal Commn, 1975–93, Standing Liturgical Adv. Commn, 1987–, Church in Wales. *Publication:* (contrib.) The Ministry of the Word (ed G. J. Cuming), 1979. *Recreations:* music, walking. *Address:* St Peter's Vicarage, Mary Twill Lane, Newton, Swansea SA3 4RB. *T:* Swansea (01792) 368348.

THOMAS, Prof. David; Professor of Geography, University of Birmingham, 1978–95, now Professor Emeritus; *b* 16 Feb. 1931; *s* of William and Florence Grace Thomas; *m* 1955, Daphne Elizabeth Berry; one *s* one *d*. *Educ:* Bridgend Grammar School; University College of Wales, Aberystwyth (BA, MA); PhD London. Asst Lectr, Lectr, Reader, University College London, 1957–70; Prof. and Head of Dept, St David's University College, Lampeter, 1970–78; Birmingham University: Head of Dept of Geography, 1978–86; Head of Sch. of Geog., 1991–93; Pro Vice-Chancellor, 1984–89. Pres., IBG, 1988 (Hon. Sec., 1976–78); Mem., Council, RGS, 1988–91. *Publications:* Agriculture in Wales during the Napoleonic Wars, 1963; London's Green Belt, 1970; (ed) An Advanced Geography of the British Isles, 1974; (with J. A. Dawson) Man and his world, 1975; (ed) Wales: a new study, 1977; (with P. T. J. Morgan) Wales: the shaping of a nation, 1984; articles in learned jls. *Recreations:* music, wine, spectating. *Address:* 6 Plymouth Drive, Barnt Green, Birmingham B45 8JB. *T:* 0121–445 3295.

THOMAS, David Bowen, PhD; Keeper, Department of Physical Sciences, Science Museum, 1984–87 (Keeper, Department of Physics, 1978–84); *b* 28 Dec. 1931; *s* of Evan Thomas and Florence Annie Bowen. *Educ:* Tredegar Grammar Sch.; Manchester Univ. (BSc). Research Fellow, Wayne Univ., Detroit, USA, 1955–57; Research Scientist, Min. of Agriculture, Fisheries and Food, Aberdeen, 1957–61; Asst Keeper, Science Museum, Dept of Chemistry, 1961–73; Keeper, Dept of Museum Services, 1973–78. *Publications:* The First Negatives, 1964; The Science Museum Photography Collection, 1969; The First Colour Motion Pictures, 1969. Hon. FRPS 1985. *Recreation:* country walking. *Address:* Tanglewood, Moushill Lane, Milford, Godalming, Surrey GU8 5BQ.

THOMAS, David Churchill, CMG 1982; HM Diplomatic Service, retired; Assistant Under Secretary of State, Foreign and Commonwealth Office, 1984–86; *b* 21 Oct. 1933; *o s* of late David Bernard Thomas and Violet Churchill Thomas (*née* Quicke); *m* 1958, Susan Petronella Arrow (*see* Baroness Thomas of Walliswood) (separated); one *s* two *d*. *Educ:* Eton Coll.; New Coll., Oxford (Exhibnr). Mod. Hist. 1st Cl., 1957. Army, 2nd Lieut, Rifle Brigade, 1952–54. Foreign Office, 1958; 3rd Sec., Moscow, 1959–61; 2nd Sec., Lisbon, 1961–64; FCO, 1964–68; 1st Sec. (Commercial), Lima, 1968–70; FCO, 1970–73; Head of South West European Dept, 1974; Asst Sec., Cabinet Office, 1973–78; Counsellor (Internal Affairs), Washington, 1978–81; Ambassador to Cuba, 1981–84. Advr on Overseas Scholarships Funding, FCO, 1989–. Mem. Council, RIIA, 1988–94. Mem. Bd, Inst. of Latin American Studies, Univ. of London, 1988–93. Associate Fellow, Centre for Caribbean Studies, Warwick Univ., 1990–. *Publications:* essays and review articles on Latin American affairs. *Recreations:* photography, listening to music. *Address:* 11 Crookham Road, SW6 4EG. *T:* 0171–736 9096.

See also Hon. D. W. P. Thomas.

THOMAS, David (Edward); Member (Lab) Suffolk and South West Norfolk, European Parliament, since 1994; *b* 12 Jan. 1955; *m* 1975, Janet Elizabeth Whatrup; one *s* one *d*. *Educ:* Univ. of East Anglia (BA). Served RN, 1972–80; Suffolk Constabulary, 1980–88. Mem. (Lab) Suffolk CC, 1993. Mem., Police Authy. *Address:* European Parliament, 97 Rue Belliard, 1040 Brussels, Belgium.

THOMAS, David Emrys; management and personnel consultant, since 1991; Member, Local Government Commission for England, since 1992; *b* Ewell, 9 July 1935; *s* of Emrys and Elsie Florence Thomas; *m* 1957, Rosemary, *d* of Alexander and Kathleen De'Ath of Hampton, Middx; two *s* one *d*. *Educ:* Tiffin Grammar Sch., Kingston upon Thames. Dip. Mun. Admin; FIPM. Local Govt Administrator, 1951–63; Indust. Relations Officer, LACSAB, 1963–68; Chief Admin. Officer, LGTB, 1968–69; Dep. Estab. Officer, Surrey CC, 1969–70; County Personnel Officer, Surrey, 1970–77; Under-Sec. (Manpower), AMA, 1977–81; Dep. Sec., 1981–87, Sec., 1987–91, LACSAB; Employers' Sec. to nat. jt negotiating councils in local govt, 1987–91; Official Side Sec., Police Negotiating Bd, 1987–91; Sec., UK Steering Cttee on Local Govt Superannuation, 1987–91. Founder Pres., Soc. of Chief Personnel Officers in Local Govt, 1975. *Recreations:* unskilled gardening, the musical theatre. *Address:* The White House, Three Pears Road, Merrow, Guildford, Surrey GU1 2XU. *T:* Guildford (01483) 69588.

THOMAS, Prof. David Glyndor Treharne, FRCSE, FRCP, FRCPG; Professor of Neurological Surgery and Head of Gough Cooper Department of Neurological Surgery, Institute of Neurology, National Hospital, Queen Square, since 1995; *b* 14 May 1941; *s* of Dr John Glyndor Treharne Thomas, MC and Ellen Thomas (*née* Geldart); *m* 1970, Dr Hazel Agnes Christina Cockburn, FFARCS; one *s*. *Educ:* Perse Sch., Cambridge; Gonville and Caius Coll., Cambridge (BA, MA); St Mary's Hosp. Med. Sch. (MB BChir). Hosp. appts at St Mary's to 1969 and Asst Lectr in Anatomy, 1967–68; Sen. House Officer in Surgery, 1970, Registrar in Cardio-Thoracic Surgery, 1970–71, RPMS; Registrar, Sen. Registrar and Lectr in Neurosurgery, Inst. of Neur. Scis, Glasgow, 1972–76; Sen. Lectr, 1976–92, Prof. of Neurosurgery, 1992–95, Inst. of Neurology; Consultant Neurosurgeon: Nat. Hosp. for Neurology and Neurosurgery and Northwick Park Hosp., Harrow, 1976–; St Mary's Hosp., 1994–. Vice-President: Eur. Assoc. of Neurosurgical Socs, 1991–95; Eur. Soc. for Stereotactic and Functional Neurosurgery, 1994–. *Publications:* (ed with D. I. Graham) Brain Tumours, 1980; (ed with M. D. Walker) Biology of Brain Tumour, 1986; (ed) Neuro-oncology: primary brain tumours, 1989; (ed) Stereotactic and Image Directed Surgery of Brain Tumours, 1993; (ed with D. I. Graham) Malignant Brain Tumours, 1995. *Recreation:* military and naval history. *Address:* The National Hospital, Queen Square, WC1N 3BG. *T:* 0171–829 8755; 34 Oppidans Road, Primrose Hill, NW3 3AG. *T:* 0171–586 2262. *Clubs:* Athenæum, Royal Society of Medicine.

THOMAS, David Hamilton Pryce, CBE 1977; solicitor, retired; Chairman, Land Authority for Wales, 1980–86 (Deputy Chairman, 1975–80); President, Rent Assessment Panel for Wales, 1971–89 (Member, 1966); *b* 3 July 1922; *s* of Trevor John Thomas and Eleanor Maud Thomas; *m* 1948, Eluned Mair Morgan; two *s* one *d*. *Educ:* Barry County Sch.; University College, Cardiff. Served War of 1939–45; British and Indian Armies, terminal rank T/Captain (GSO III), 1941–46. Qualified as Solicitor, 1948, with hons; Partner in J. A. Hughes & Co., Solicitors, Barry, 1950–75; Notary Public, 1953. Director 1962–67, Vice-Chm. 1967–71, Chm. 1971–78, Barry Mutual Building Society; Vice Chm., 1978, Chm., 1982–84, Glam. Building Soc.; Chm., Wales Area Bd, Bradford and Bingley Bldg Soc., 1984–87; Vice-Chm., Building Socs Assoc. for Wales, 1983; Mem., Adv. Cttee on Fair Rents, 1973; Chm., E Glam. Rent Tribunal, 1967–71; District Comr of Scouts, Barry and District, 1963–70; Chm., Barry District Scout Assoc. 1971–81; Vice-Chm., S Glam. Scout Council, 1975–81. *Recreations:* books, music. *Address:* 34 Camden Road, Brecon, Powys LD3 7RT.

See also M. C. P. Thomas, R. L. Thomas.

THOMAS, David (John), MD; FRCP; Senior Consultant Neurologist, St Mary's Hospital, London, since 1978; *b* 7 Dec. 1943; *s* of Jack and Rachel Lloyd Thomas, Cwmgorse; *m* 1966, Celia Margaret Barratt, *d* of Sir Charles and Lady Barratt; two *s* three *d*. *Educ:* Alleyn's Sch.; Clare Coll., Cambridge (BA Nat. Sci. 1966; BChir 1969; MA, MB 1970); Univ. of Birmingham Med. Sch. (MD 1977). MRCP 1972, FRCP 1985. Consultant Neurologist: King Edward VII Hosp., Windsor, Heatherwood Hosp., Ascot, Wexham Park Hosp., Slough and St Mark's Hosp., Maidenhead, 1978–; Sen. Lectr in Neurology, Inst. of Neurology and Hon. Consultant Neurologist, Nat. Hosp. for Neurology and Neurosurgery, 1979–, and Chalfont Centre for Epilepsy, 1995–. Sec. and Chm., Special Adv. Cttee on Neurology to RCP, 1985–91. Member: Council, Stroke Assoc., 1992–; Stroke Council, Amer. Heart Assoc., 1992–; European Stroke Council, 1993–. Chm., Charitable Assoc. Supplying Hosps, 1984–. *Publications:* Strokes and their Prevention, 1988; The Eye and Systemic Disease, 1989; Neurology: what shall I do?, 1990; papers on cerebrovascular disease, arachnoiditis and other neurological subjects. *Recreations:* photography, lecturing. *Address:* Woolletts, Fulmer, Bucks SL3 6JE. *T:* Fulmer (01753) 662147. *Club:* Royal Society of Medicine.

THOMAS, David Monro; retired; *b* 31 July 1915; *s* of late Henry Monro and Winifred Thomas, East Hagbourne, Berks; *m* 1948, Ursula Mary, *d* of late H. W. Liversidge; two *s* one *d*. *Educ:* St Edward's School, Oxford; St Edmund Hall, Oxford. Oxford House, 1937; Army, 1939, Major, Royal Welch Fusiliers; Head of Oxford House, 1946–48; Secretary of Greek House, 1948–51; Legal & General Assurance Soc. Ltd, 1951–75; YWCA, 1975–80; Co. Sec., YWCA, 1977–80. *Address:* Watcombe Corner, Watlington, Oxford OX9 5QJ. *T:* Watlington (01491) 612403.

THOMAS, David Owen, QC 1972; a Recorder of the Crown Court, since 1972; *b* 22 Aug. 1926; *s* of late Emrys Aeron Thomas and Dorothy May Thomas; *m* 1967, Mary Susan Atkinson; three *d* (and one *d* decd). *Educ:* Queen Elizabeth's, Barnet; John Bright Sch., Llandudno; Queen's Univ., Belfast. Served War, HM Forces, 1943–45 and to 1948. Called to the Bar, Middle Temple, 1952, Bencher, 1980; Dep. Chairman, Devon QS, 1971. Mem., Criminal Injuries Compensation Bd, 1987. Freeman, City of London; Liveryman, Needlemakers' Co. *Recreations:* acting, cricket, Rugby football. *Address:* 2 King's Bench Walk, Temple, EC4Y 7DE. *T:* 0171–353 1746; 9 Devereux Court, WC2R 3JJ. *T:* 0171–583 4245. *Clubs:* Garrick, MCC; Hampshire (Winchester); Western (Glasgow).

THOMAS, Hon. David (William Penrose); author, journalist; Television Critic, Sunday Express, since 1991; *b* 17 Jan. 1959; *s* of David Churchill Thomas, *qv* and Baroness Thomas of Walliswood, *qv*; *m* 1986, Clare Jeremy; two *d*. *Educ:* Eton; King's College, Cambridge (BA History of Art). Freelance journalist, 1980–84; Editor, The Magazine, 1984–85; Editor, Extra Magazine, Sunday Today, 1986; Asst Editor and Chief Feature Writer, You Magazine, Mail on Sunday, 1986–89; Ed., Punch, 1989–92. Young Journalist of the Year (British Press Awards), 1983; Columnist of the Year (Magazine Publishing Awards), 1989. *Publications:* Not Guilty: in defence of the modern man, 1993; Great Sporting Moments, 1990; Girl (novel), 1995; with Ian Irvine: Bilko: the Fort Baxter Story, 1985; Fame and Fortune, 1988; Sex and Shopping, 1988. *Recreations:* if only . . . . *Address:* c/o Christopher Little Literary Agency, 48 Walham Grove, SW6 1QR. *T:* 0171–386 1800. *Club:* Groucho.

THOMAS, Derek John, IPFA; Chief Executive, Surrey County Council, 1988–95; *b* 3 Dec. 1934; *s* of late James Llewellyn Thomas and Winifred Mary Thomas; *m* 1st (marr. diss.); three *d*; 2nd, 1978, Christine (*née* Brewer); one *s*. *Educ:* Hele's Sch., Exeter. Formerly: Treasurer's Depts: Devon CC; Corby Development Corporation; Bath CC; Taunton Bor. Council; Sen. Asst Bor. Treasurer, Poole Bor. Council; Asst County Treasurer, Gloucestershire CC; Principal Asst County Treasurer, Avon CC; County Treasurer, Surrey CC. CIPFA: Mem. Council, 1977–78, 1985–87; Chm., Local Management in Schools Initiative, 1988–93. Member: Bd, Surrey TEC, 1990–; Council, Surrey Univ., 1994– (Chm., F and GP Cttee, 1995–). CIMgt. *Address:* Squirrels Leap, 14 Lime Avenue, Camberley, Surrey GU15 2BS. *T:* Camberley (01276) 684433.

THOMAS, Sir Derek (Morison David), KCMG 1987 (CMG 1977); Director, N. M. Rothschild & Sons, since 1991; *b* 31 Oct. 1929; *s* of K. P. D. Thomas and Mali McL. Thomas; *m* 1956, Lineke van der Mast; two *c*. *Educ:* Radley Coll., Abingdon; Trinity Hall, Cambridge (MA). Mod. Langs Tripos. Articled apprentice, Dolphin Industrial Developments Ltd, 1947. Entered HM Foreign Service, 1953; Midshipman 1953, Sub-Lt 1955, RNVR; FO, 1955; 3rd, later 2nd, Sec., Moscow, 1956–59; 2nd Sec., Manila, 1959–61; UK Delegn to Brussels Conf., 1961–62; 1st Sec., FO, 1962; Sofia, 1964–67; Ottawa, 1967–69; seconded to Treasury, 1969–70; Financial Counsellor, Paris, 1971–75; Head of N American Dept, FCO, 1975–76; Asst Under Sec. of State, FCO, 1976–79; Minister Commercial and later Minister, Washington, 1979–84; Dep. Under Sec. of State for Europe and Political Dir, FCO, 1984–87; Amb. to Italy, 1987–89. European Advr to N M Rothschild & Sons, 1990–; Director: Rothschild Italia, 1990–; Christow Consultants, 1990–; Nexus Marketing Consultancy, 1991–92; Associate, CDP Nexus, 1990–92. Chm., Liberalisation of Trade in Services Cttee, BI, 1992–; Mem., Export Guarantees Adv. Cttee, 1992–. Member, Council: RIIA, 1994–; Reading Univ., 1991–. *Recreations:* listening to people and music; being by, in or on water. *Address:* Flat 1, 12 Lower Sloane Street, SW1W 8BJ. *Clubs:* United Oxford & Cambridge University; Leander.

See also Sir E. W. Gladstone, Bt.

THOMAS, His Honour Dewi Alun, MBE; a Circuit Judge, 1972–90; *b* 3 Dec. 1917; *e s* of late Joshua and Martha Ann Thomas; *m* 1952, Doris Maureen Smith, Barrister; one *s* one *d*. *Educ:* Christ Coll., Brecon; Jesus Coll., Oxford (MA). Served War of 1939–45 (MBE, despatches): mobilised with TA (RA), 1939; served Sicily, Italy, the Balkans; Major, No 2 Commando. Called to Bar, Inner Temple, 1951, Bencher 1969. *Recreations:* golf, watching Rugby football. *Address:* c/o Law Courts, Barker Road, Maidstone, Kent ME16 8EW.

THOMAS, Donald Martin; *see* Thomas, Martin.

THOMAS, Donald Michael; poet and novelist; *b* Redruth, Cornwall, 27 Jan. 1935; *s* of Harold Redvers Thomas and Amy (*née* Moyle); two *s* one *d*. *Educ:* Redruth Grammar Sch.; Univ. High Sch., Melbourne; New Coll., Oxford (BA 1st cl. Hons in English; MA). School teacher, Teignmouth Grammar Sch., 1959–63; Lectr, Hereford Coll. of Educn, 1964–78; full-time author, 1978–. *Publications: poetry:* Penguin Modern Poets 11, 1968; Two Voices, 1968; Logan Stone, 1971; Love and Other Deaths, 1975; The Honeymoon Voyage, 1978; Dreaming in Bronze, 1981; Selected Poems, 1983; *novels:* The Flute-Player, 1979; Birthstone, 1980; The White Hotel, 1981; Russian Nights, a quintet (Ararat, 1983; Swallow, 1984; Sphinx, 1986; Summit, 1987; Lying Together, 1990); Flying in to Love, 1992; Pictures at an Exhibition, 1993; Eating Pavlova, 1994; *translations:* Requiem and Poem without a Hero, Akhmatova, 1976; Way of All the Earth, Akhmatova, 1979; Bronze Horseman, Pushkin, 1982; *memoirs:* Memories and Hallucinations, 1988. *Recreations:* travel, Russia and other myths, the culture and history of Cornwall, the life of the imagination. *Address:* The Coach House, Rashleigh Vale, Truro, Cornwall TR1 1TJ.

THOMAS, Donnall; *see* Thomas, Edward D.

THOMAS, Dudley Lloyd; Metropolitan Stipendiary Magistrate, since 1990; Member: Family Proceedings Court Panel, since 1991; Youth Court Panel, since 1994; *b* 11 Jan. 1946; *s* of late Myrddin Lloyd Thomas and Marjorie Emily (*née* Morgan); *m* 1970, Dr Margaret Susan Early; three *s*. *Educ:* King Edward's Sch., Bath; Coll. of Law, London. Justices Clerk's Asst, 1966–71; admitted as solicitor, 1971; Partner, Trump & Partners, Bristol, 1973–88; called to the Bar, Gray's Inn, 1988; Mem., Western Circuit. Member: Bristol Medico-Legal Soc.; Cadw. Friend, Royal Acad. of Arts. *Recreations:* Rugby football, cricket, music, theatre, travel, classic motor cars, dogs and walking. *Address:* c/o West London Magistrates' Court, Southcombe Street, Kensington, W14 0RD. *T:* 0171–371 1222. *Club:* Royal Over-Seas League.

THOMAS, Prof. (Edward) Donnall, MD; Member, Fred Hutchinson Cancer Research Center, Seattle, since 1974 (Director, Medical Oncology, 1974–89; Associate Director, Clinical Research Programs, 1982–89); Professor Emeritus of Medicine, University of Washington School of Medicine, Seattle, since 1990; *b* Mart, Texas, 15 March 1920; *m* 1942, Dorothy Martin; two *s* one *d*. *Educ:* Univ. of Texas, Austin (BA 1941; MA 1943); Harvard Medical Sch. (MD 1946). Assignments in internal medicine, US Army, 1948–50; Nat. Res. Council Postdoctoral Fellow in Medicine, Dept of Biol., MIT, 1950–51; Chief Med. Resident and Sen. Asst Resident, Peter Bent Brigham Hosp., Seattle, 1951–53, Hematologist, 1953–55; Instructor in Medicine, Harvard Med. Sch. and Res. Associate, Cancer Res. Foundn, Children's Med. Center, Boston, 1953–55; Physician-in-Chief, Mary Imogene Bassett Hosp., Cooperstown, NY and Associate Clinical Prof. of Medicine, Coll. of Physicians and Surgeons, Columbia Univ., NY, 1955–63; Prof. of Medicine, Univ. of Washington Sch. of Medicine, Seattle, 1963–90, Hd, Div. of Oncology, 1963–85. Consulting Physician, Children's Orthopedic Hosp. and Med. Center, Seattle, 1963–90; Attending Physician, Seattle: Univ. of Washington Hosp., 1963–90; Harborview Med. Center, 1963–90; Veterans Admin Hosp., 1963–90; Providence Med. Center, 1973–90; Swedish Hosp., 1975–90. Member Editorial Board: Blood, 1962–75, 1977–82; Transplantation, 1970–76; Procs Soc. Exptl Biol. and Medicine, 1974–81; Leukemia Res., 1977–87; Hematological Oncology, 1982–87; Jl Clinical Immunology, 1982–87; Amer. Jl Hematology, 1985–; Bone Marrow Transplantation, 1986–. Member: Amer. Assoc. Cancer Res.; Amer. Assoc. Physicians; Amer. Fedn Clinical Res.; Amer. Soc. Clinical Oncology; Amer. Soc. Clinical Investigation; Amer. Soc. Hematology (Pres., 1987–88); Nat. Acad. Scis and other foreign socs on related subjects. Lectures in US and UK on hematology and cancer res. Numerous awards from instns in N America and abroad incl. Nobel Prize for Physiology or Medicine, 1990; Presidential Medal of Science, 1990. *Recreations:* hunting, fishing, hiking. *Address:* c/o Fred Hutchinson Cancer Research Center, Room 172, 1124 Columbia Street, Seattle, WA 98104, USA.

THOMAS, Elizabeth; *see* Thomas, M.E.

THOMAS, Elizabeth Marjorie; Secretary General, 1979–83, Literary Consultant, 1984–85, The Authors' Lending and Copyright Society; *b* 10 Aug. 1919; *d* of Frank Porter and Marjorie Porter (*née* Pascall); *m* 1941, George Thomas; one *s* one *d*. *Educ:* St George's Sch., Harpenden; Girton Coll., Cambridge (BA 1st Cl.). Journalist, 1951–59 and Literary Editor, 1959–71, Tribune; Asst Literary Editor, New Statesman, 1971–76; Political Adviser to Rt Hon. Michael Foot, MP, Lord Pres. of the Council and Leader of the House of Commons, 1976–79. Mem., Arts Council, 1974–77 (Mem., Literature Panel, 1971–77); Chm., Literature Panel, Eastern Arts Assoc., 1978–84; Member: Ethnic Minority Arts Cttee, Commission for Racial Equality, 1979–82; British Council Bd, 1982–88. *Publication:* (ed) Tribune 21, 1959. *Address:* 27 Delavale Road, Winchcombe, Glos GL54 5YL. *T:* Cheltenham (01242) 602788.

THOMAS, Emyr, CBE 1980; LLB, LMTPI; DL; General Manager, Telford New Town Development Corporation, 1969–80; Chairman, Telford Community Council, 1980–84; *b* 25 April 1920; *s* of late Brinley Thomas, MA, Aldershot; *m* 1947, Barbara J. May; one *d*. *Educ:* Aldershot County High School. Served War of 1939–45, RASC. Admitted Solicitor, 1947. Asst Solicitor, Exeter City Council, 1947–50; Sen. Asst Solicitor, Reading County Borough Council, 1950–53; Dep. Town Clerk, West Bromwich County Borough Council, 1953–64; Sec. and Solicitor, Dawley (later Telford) Development Corp., 1964–69. First Hon. Sec., 1968–89, Hon. Curator and Vice-Pres., 1989–, Ironbridge Gorge Museum Trust. DL Salop, 1979. *Recreation:* industrial archaeology. *Address:* 8 Vixen Walk, New Milton, Hampshire BH25 5RU. *T:* New Milton (01425) 628826.

THOMAS, Rt. Rev. Eryl Stephen; Hon. Assistant Bishop of Swansea and Brecon, since 1988; *b* 20 Oct. 1910; *s* of Edward Stephen and Margaret Susannah Thomas; *m* 1939, Jean Mary Alice Wilson; three *s* one *d*. *Educ:* Rossall Sch.; St John's Coll., Oxford; Wells Theological Coll. BA 2nd Class Hon. Theology, Oxford, 1932; MA 1935. Curate of Colwyn Bay, 1933–38, of Hawarden, 1938–43; Vicar of Risca, Mon, 1943–48; Warden of St Michael's Theological Coll., Llandaff, 1948–54; Dean of Llandaff, 1954–68; Bishop of Monmouth, 1968–71, of Llandaff, 1971–75. Chaplain and Sub-Prelate, Order of St John of Jerusalem, 1969. *Address:* 17 Orchard Close, Gilwern, Abergavenny, Gwent NP7 0EN. *T:* Gilwern (01873) 831050.

THOMAS, Frank; *see* Thomas, J. F. P.

THOMAS, Franklin Augustine; President, Ford Foundation, since 1979; *b* 27 May 1934; *s* of James Thomas and Viola Thomas (*née* Atherley); *m* (mar diss.); two *s* two *d*. *Educ:* Columbia College, New York (BA 1956); Columbia Univ. (LLB 1963). Admitted to NY State Bar, 1964; Attorney, Fed. Housing and Home Finance Agency, NYC, 1963–64; Asst US Attorney for Southern District, NY, 1964–65; Dep. Police Comr, charge legal matters, NYC, 1965–67; Pres., Chief Exec. Officer, Bedford Stuyvesant Restoration Corp., Brooklyn, 1967–77. Hon. LLD: Yale, 1970; Fordham, 1972; Pratt Institute, 1974; Pace, 1977; Columbia, 1979. *Address:* The Ford Foundation, 320 East 43rd Street, New York, NY 10017, USA. *T:* (212) 5735383.

THOMAS, Sir Frederick William, Kt 1959; Councillor, City of Melbourne, 1953–65 (Lord Mayor, 1957–59); *b* 27 June 1906; *s* of F. J. Thomas; *m* 1968, Dorothy Alexa Gordon; three *s* by former marr. *Educ:* Melbourne Grammar School. Served War of 1939–45, RAAF (Air Efficiency Award, two bars); Group Captain. Comdr Order of Orange Nassau with swords (Holland), 1943. *Recreation:* golf. *Address:* 35 Hitchcock Avenue, Barwon Heads, Victoria 3227, Australia. *Clubs:* Naval and Military, Royal Automobile of Victoria (Melbourne); Barwon Heads Golf, Melbourne Cricket.

THOMAS, Dr Geoffrey Price; Director, University of Oxford Department for Continuing Education, since 1986; President, Kellogg College (formerly Rewley House), since 1990; *b* 3 July 1941; *s* of Richard Lewis Thomas and Aerona (*née* Price); *m* 1965, Judith Vaughan, *d* of Arsul John Williams; two *d*. *Educ:* Maesteg Grammar Sch.; UC of Swansea (BSc 1st Cl. Hons Physics); Churchill Coll., Cambridge (PhD 1966); Univ. of Oxford (MA). Post-doctoral res., Cavendish Lab., Univ. of Cambridge, 1966–67; Staff Tutor, UC of Swansea, 1967–78; Dep. Dir, Dept of Ext. Studies, Univ. of Oxford, 1978–86; Fellow, Linacre Coll., Oxford, 1978–90. Hon. Fellow, 1990. Co-Chm., Council on Scientific Literacy, Chicago Acad. of Sci., 1993–. Visiting Scholar: Smithsonian Instn, 1986; Northern Illinois Univ., 1986; Univ. of Calif, Berkeley, 1993; Univ. of Washington, 1993; Harvard Univ., 1993. *Publications:* (ed jtly) The Nuclear Arms Race, 1982; (ed jtly) Science and Sporting Performance, 1982; numerous articles on public understanding of science, and on continuing educn policy. *Address:* University of Oxford Department for Continuing Education, 1 Wellington Square, Oxford OX1 2JA. *T:* Oxford (01865) 270376, *Fax:* (01865) 270309.

THOMAS, Sir (Godfrey) Michael (David), 11th Bt, *cr* 1694; Member of Stock Exchange, London, 1959–88; *b* 10 Oct. 1925; *o s* of Rt Hon. Sir Godfrey Thomas, PC, GCVO, KCB, CSI, 10th Bt, and Diana, *d* of late Ven. B. G. Hoskyns (*d* 1985); *S* father 1968; *m* 1956, Margaret Greta Cleland, *yr d* of John Cleland, Stormont Court, Godden Green, Kent; one *s* two *d*, of whom one *s* one *d* are twins. *Educ:* Harrow. The Rifle Brigade, 1944–56. *Heir: s* David John Godfrey Thomas, *b* 11 June 1961. *Address:* 2 Napier Avenue, SW6 3PT. *T:* 0171–736 6896. *Clubs:* MCC, Hurlingham.

See also Sir Peter Hutchison, Bt.

THOMAS, Graham Stuart, OBE 1975; VMH 1968; Gardens Consultant to National Trust, since 1974; *b* 3 April 1909; *s* of W. R. Thomas and L. Thomas. *Educ:* horticultural and botanical training, Cambridge Univ. Botanic Garden, 1926–29. Six Hills Nursery, Stevenage, 1930; Foreman, later Manager, T. Hilling & Co., Chobham, 1931–55; Manager, Sunningdale Nurseries, Windlesham, 1956, Associate Dir, 1968–71; Gardens Adviser, National Trust, 1955–74. Vice-President: RHS; Garden History Soc.; British Hosta and Hemerocallis Soc.; Vice-Patron, Royal Nat. Rose Soc. (Dean Hole Medal, 1976); Hon. Mem., Irish Garden Plant Soc. Veitch Meml Medal, RHS, 1966. *Publications:* The Old Shrub Roses, 1955, 5th edn 1978; Colour in the Winter Garden, 1957, 3rd edn 1984; Shrub Roses of Today, 1962, rev. edn 1980; Climbing Roses Old and New, 1965, new edn 1983; Plants for Ground Cover, 1970, rev. edn 1989; Perennial Garden Plants, 1976, rev. and enlarged edn 1990; Gardens of the National Trust, 1979; Three Gardens, 1983; Trees in the Landscape, 1983; The Art of Planting, 1984; A Garden of Roses, 1987; The Complete Flower Paintings and Drawings of Graham Stuart Thomas, 1987; The Rock Garden and its Plants, 1989; An English Rose Garden, 1991; Ornamental Shrubs, Climbers and Bamboos, 1992; The Graham Stuart Thomas Rose Book, 1994. *Recreations:* horticulture, music, painting and drawing plants. *Address:* 21 Kettlewell Close, Horsell, Woking, Surrey GU21 4HY.

THOMAS, Gwyn Edward Ward; *see* Ward Thomas.

THOMAS, Harvey; *see* Thomas, J. H. N.

THOMAS, Prof. Howard Christopher, FRCP; FRCPGlas; FRCPath; Professor of Medicine, St Mary's Hospital Medical School and Imperial College of Science, Technology and Medicine, London University, since 1987; *b* 31 July 1945; *s* of Harold Thomas and Hilda Thomas; *m* 1975, Dilys Ferguson; two *s* one *d*. *Educ:* Univ. of Newcastle (BSc Physiol; MB, BS); PhD Glasgow. MRCPath 1983, FRCPath 1992; MRCP 1969, FRCP 1983; FRCPGlas 1984. Lectr in Immunology, Glasgow Univ., 1971–74; Royal Free Hospital Medical School, London: Lectr in Medicine, 1974–78; Sen. Wellcome Fellow in Clin. Sci., 1978–83; Reader in Medicine, 1983–84; Titular Prof. of Medicine, 1984–87. Sec., Scientific Adv. Cttee, British Liver Trust. Member: Educn Cttee, European Assoc. for the Study of the Liver; MRC Adv. Gp on Hepatitis; DHSS Adv. Gp on Hepatitis. Editor, Jl of Viral Hepatitis. Humphry Davy Rolleston Lectr, RCP, 1986. British Soc. of Gastroenterology Res. Medal, 1984; Hans Popper Internat. Prize for Distinction in Hepatology, 1989. *Publications:* Clinical Gastrointestinal Immunology, 1979; (ed jtly) Recent Advances in Hepatology, Vol. 1, 1983, vol. 2, 1986; Viral Hepatitis, 1994; pubns in Hepatology. *Recreations:* fishing, golf. *Address:* Department of Medicine, St Mary's Hospital Medical School, Praed Street, W2 1PG. *T:* 0171–725 1606.

THOMAS, Hugh; *see* Thomas of Swynnerton, Baron.

THOMAS, Prof. Hywel Rhys, PhD; Professor and Head of School of Education, University of Birmingham, since 1993; *b* 11 Jan. 1947; *s* of John Howard Thomas and Eva Beryl Thomas (*née* James); *m* 1st, 1968, Patricia Anne Beard (marr. diss.); 2nd, 1980, Christine MacArthur; one *s* two *d*. *Educ:* Llanelli Boys' Grammar Sch.; Univ. of Manchester (BA, MEd, PGCE); Univ. of Birmingham (PhD 1988). Parkinson Cowan Ltd, 1968–69; teacher: New Mills Sch., Derbys, 1970–73; Kersal High Sch., Salford, 1974–79; University of Birmingham: Lectr, 1979–89; Sen. Lectr, 1989–91; Reader, 1991–93. *Publications:* Managing Education: the system and the institution, 1985; Economics and Education Management, 1986; Education Costs and Performance, 1990; Financial Delegation and Local Management of Schools, 1990. *Recreations:* running, sailing. *Address:* School of Education, University of Birmingham, Edgbaston, Birmingham B15 2TT; 30 Linden Road, Bournville, Birmingham B30 1JU.

THOMAS, Prof. Jean Olwen, CBE 1993; ScD; FRS 1986; Professor of Macromolecular Biochemistry, University of Cambridge, since 1991; Fellow, New Hall, Cambridge, since 1969; *b* 1 Oct. 1942; *o c* of John Robert Thomas and Lorna Prunella Thomas (*née* Harris). *Educ:* Llwyn-y-Bryn High School for Girls, Swansea; University Coll., Swansea, Univ. of Wales (BSc and Ayling Prize, 1964; PhD and Hinkel Research Prize, 1967 (Chem.)); MA Cantab 1969; ScD Cantab 1985. CChem, MRSC. Beit Meml Fellow, MRC Lab. of Molecular Biology, Cambridge, 1967–69; Demonstrator in Biochemistry, 1969–73, Lectr, 1973–87, Reader in the Biochemistry of Macromolecules, 1987–91, Univ. of Cambridge; Tutor, 1970–76, Vice-Pres., 1983–87, Coll. Lectr, 1969–91, New Hall, Cambridge. Chm., Cambridge Centre for Molecular Recognition, 1993–. Member: SERC, 1990–94; Council, Royal Soc., 1990–92; EPSRC, 1994–; Council and Scientific Adv. Cttee, ICRF, 1994–; Scientific Adv. Cttee, Lister Inst., 1994–. Trustee, BM, 1994–. Member: EMBO, 1982; Academia Europaea, 1991. Hon. Fellow, UCW, Swansea, 1987. Hon. DSc Wales, 1992. K. M. Stott Research Prize, Newnham Coll., Cambridge, 1976. *Publications:* Companion to Biochemistry: selected topics for further study, vol. 1, 1974, vol. 2, 1979 (ed jtly and contrib.); papers in sci. jls, esp. on histones and chromatin structure. *Recreations:* reading, music, walking. *Address:* Department of Biochemistry, Tennis Court Road,

Cambridge CB2 1QW. *T:* Cambridge (01223) 333670; 26 Eachard Road, Cambridge CB3 0HY. *T:* Cambridge (01223) 62620.

THOMAS, Jenkin; HM Diplomatic Service, retired; Deputy UK Permanent Representative and Counsellor (Economic and Financial), OECD, Paris, 1990–94; *b* 2 Jan. 1938; *s* of late William John Thomas and of Annie Muriel (*née* Thomas). *Educ:* Maesydderwen Sch.; University Coll. London (BA Hons); Univ. of Michigan, Ann Arbor (MA). Joined HM Foreign (subseq. Diplomatic) Service, 1960; Foreign Office, 1960–63; Pretoria/Cape Town, 1963–66; Saigon, 1966–68; FCO, 1968–73; Washington, 1973–77; FCO, 1977–79; Cabinet Office, 1979–80; Tokyo, 1980–82; Athens, 1982–87; Head of Claims Dept, FCO, 1987–90. *Recreations:* reading, music. *Address:* c/o Foreign and Commonwealth Office, SW1A 2AH.

THOMAS, Sir Jeremy (Cashel), KCMG 1987 (CMG 1980); HM Diplomatic Service, retired; Chairman, Chichester Harbour Conservancy Advisory Committee, since 1992; *b* 1 June 1931; *s* of Rev. H. C. Thomas and Margaret Betty (*née* Humby); *m* 1957, Diana Mary Summerhayes; three *s*. *Educ:* Eton; Merton Coll., Oxford. 16th/5th Lancers, 1949–51. Entered FO, 1954; served Singapore, Rome and Belgrade; Dep. Head, Personnel Ops Dept, FCO, 1970–74; Counsellor and Head of Chancery, UK Mission to UN, NY, 1974–76; Head of Perm. Under-Sec.'s Dept, FCO, 1977–79; Ambassador to Luxembourg, 1979–82; Asst Under-Sec. of State, FCO, 1982–85; Ambassador to Greece, 1985–89. *Recreations:* sailing, fishing. *Address:* East Manor Farm, Pook Lane, East Lavant, near Chichester, West Sussex PO18 0AH. *T:* Chichester (01243) 531661. *Clubs:* United Oxford & Cambridge University, Flyfishers'; Itchenor Sailing, Bosham Sailing.

THOMAS, Jeremy Jack; film producer; Chairman, British Film Institute, since 1993; *b* 26 July 1949; *s* of Ralph Philip Thomas, *qv*; *m* 1st, 1977, Claudia Frolich (marr. diss. 1981); one *d*; 2nd, 1982, Vivien Coughman; two *s*. *Educ:* Millfield. Has worked in most aspects of film prodn, esp. in editing dept before becoming a producer. Producer: Mad Dog Morgan, 1974; The Shout, 1977; The Great Rock 'n Roll Swindle, 1979; Bad Timing, 1980; Merry Christmas, Mr Lawrence, 1982; Eureka, 1982; The Hit, 1984; Insignificance, 1985; The Last Emperor, 1987 (Acad. Award for Best Film); Everybody Wins, 1990; The Sheltering Sky, 1990; The Naked Lunch, 1991; Let Him Have It, 1991; Little Buddha, 1992. Special Award for Outstanding Contribn to Cinema, Evening Standard, 1990; Michael Balcon Award for Outstanding Contribn to Cinema, BAFTA, 1991. *Address:* Recorded Picture Co. Ltd, 24 Hanway Street, W1P 9DD. *T:* 0171–439 0607. *Club:* Royal Automobile.

THOMAS, Sir (John) Alan, Kt 1993; Chairman: Firth Holdings (formerly G. M. Firth (Holdings)) plc, since 1994; Raytheon Europe, since 1995; *b* 4 Jan. 1943; *s* of Idris Thomas and Ellen Constance Thomas (*née* Noakes); *m* 1966, Angela Taylor; two *s*. *Educ:* Dynevor Sch.; Nottingham Univ. (Richard Thomas & Baldwins Industrial Schol.; BSc Mech. Engrg). FCMA (First Prizewinner); CEng; FIEE. Chief Exec., Data Logic, 1973–85; Vice Pres., Raytheon Co. (US), 1985–89; Pres. and Chief Exec. Officer, Raytheon Europe, 1985–89; Chm., Tag Semi-Conductors (US), 1985–89; Dir, Eur. subsids, 1978–89; seconded to MoD as Head of Defence Export Services Orgn, 1989–94. Mem., Engrg Council, 1994–. Polytechnic of Central London, now University of Westminster: Vis. Prof., 1981–; Gov., 1989–, Dep. Chm., Ct of Govs, 1995–. Pres., Computing Services Assoc., 1980–81. Freeman, City of London, 1988. *Recreations:* music, sport. *Address:* (office) 40 Catherine Place, SW1E 6HL. *T:* 0171–828 9989. *Club:* Athenæum.

THOMAS, Dr John Anthony Griffiths; Managing Director, BBC International Television Ltd, since 1993; Deputy Chairman, BBC Publishing Ltd, since 1994; *b* 28 Aug. 1943; *s* of late William and Bernice Thomas; *m* 1965, Sylvia Jean Norman; two *d*. *Educ:* Leeds Univ. (BSc Chem. 1965); Univ. of Keele (PhD 1968). Teacher of Chemistry, Leeds Grammar Sch., 1968–69; Reed Business Publishing Ltd: Editor, 1969–75; Editorial Dir, 1975–77; Publishing Dir, 1977–84; Divisional Man. Dir, Med. Div., 1984–86; BBC Enterprises Ltd: Dir, BBC Magazines and Electronic Publishing Gp, 1986–93; Man. Dir, 1993–94; Chairman: Redwood Publishing Ltd, 1988–93; Frontline Ltd, 1990–94; BBC Haymarket Exhibns Ltd, 1992–94; Galleon Ltd, 1993–94; Dir, Periodicals Publishing Assoc., 1989–94. Stanford Univ. Alumni, 1991. *Publications:* (ed) Energy Modelling, 1974; Energy Today, 1977; (ed) Energy Analysis, 1977; The Quest for Fuel, 1978. *Recreations:* reading, music, walking. *Address:* BBC International Television Ltd, 80 Wood Lane, W12 0TT.

THOMAS, Prof. John David, PhD; FBA 1989; Professorial Fellow in Papyrology, University of Durham, 1990–92, now Emeritus Professor; *b* 23 June 1931; *s* of Henry Thomas and Elsie Thomas (*née* Bruin); *m* 1956, Marion Amy Peach; two *s*. *Educ:* Wyggeston Grammar Sch., Leicester; Worcester Coll., Oxford (MA); PhD Wales. Lectr in Classics, UCW, Aberystwyth, 1955–66; University of Durham: Lectr, then Sen. Lectr in Palaeography, 1966–77; Reader in Papyrology, 1977–90. Vis. Fellow, Wolfson Coll., Oxford, 1981. Member: Inst. for Advanced Study, Princeton, 1972; Comité Internat. de Papyrologie, 1983–. *Publications:* Greek Papyri in the Collection of W. Merton III, 1967; The Epistrategos in Ptolemaic and Roman Egypt, Pt I 1975, Pt II 1982; (with A. K. Bowman) Vindolanda: the Latin writing tablets, 1983; (with A. K. Bowman) The Vindolanda writing-tablets: Tabulae Vindolandenses II, 1994; contribs to the Oxyrhynchus Papyri XXXVIII, XLIV, XLVII, L, LVII; articles and reviews in learned jls. *Recreations:* music, bird watching, fell walking. *Address:* 39 Wearside Drive, Durham DH1 1LE. *T:* Durham (0191) 3861723.

THOMAS, (John) Frank (Phillips); Telecommunications Consultant to British Telecom, international industry and commerce; *b* 11 April 1920; *s* of late John and Catherine Myfanwy Phillips Thomas; *m* 1942, Edith V. Milne; one *s* one *d*. *Educ:* Christ's Coll., Finchley; Univ. of London (BSc). CEng, MIEE. Joined Post Office Research Dept, 1937; trans-oceanic telephone cable system develt, 1947–63; planning UK inland telephone network, 1963–69; Dep. Dir London Telephone Region, 1969–71; Dep. Dir Engrg, Network Planning Dept, 1971; Dir, Network Planning Dept, 1972–79; Dir, Overseas Liaison and Consultancy Dept, Post Office, 1979–81. *Publications:* contrib. scientific and technical jls on telecommunications subjects. *Recreations:* fly fishing, automated horticulture. *Address:* 24 Moneyhill Road, Rickmansworth, Herts WD3 2EQ. *T:* Rickmansworth (01923) 772992. *Club:* Rickmansworth Lawn Tennis (Vice-Pres.).

THOMAS, (John) Harvey (Noake), CBE 1990; international public relations consultant, since 1976; Consultant Director of Presentation, Conservative Party, 1986–91; *b* 10 April 1939; *s* of John Humphrey Kenneth Thomas and Olga Rosina Thomas (*née* Noake); *m* 1978, Marlies (*née* Kram); two *d*. *Educ:* Westminster School; Northwestern Bible College, Minneapolis; Univs of Minnesota and Hawaii. Billy Graham Evangelistic Assoc., 1960–75; Dir of Press and Communications, Conservative Party, 1985–86. Mem., Bd of Dirs, London Cremation Co., 1984–. FIPR, FCIJ, MACE. *Publications:* In the Face of Fear, 1985; Making an Impact, 1989; If they haven't heard it—you haven't said it, 1995. *Recreations:* travel, family. *Address:* 23 The Service Road, Potters Bar, Herts EN6 1QA. *T:* Potters Bar (01707) 649910, *Fax:* (01707) 662653. *Club:* Institute of Directors.

THOMAS, Sir (John) Maldwyn, Kt 1984; President, Welsh Liberal Party, 1985–86; *b* 17 June 1918; *s* of Daniel and Gwladys Thomas; *m* 1975, Maureen Elizabeth. *Educ:* Porth Rhondda Grammar Sch. FCIS. Called to Bar, Gray's Inn, 1953; Solicitor, 1965; readmitted to Gray's Inn, 1987. Lewis & Tylor Ltd, Cardiff, 1940–56; Signode Ltd, Swansea, 1956–59; Commercial Agreements Manager, UKAEA, 1959–63; Rank Xerox Ltd: Sec., 1964–70; Man. Dir, 1970–72; Chm., 1972–79; Dir, Xerox Corp., USA, 1974–79. Chm., European Govt Business Relations Council, 1978–79; Dir, Westland PLC, 1985–94. Contested (L) Aberavon, 1950. Pres., London Welsh Assoc. and Trust; Vice-Pres., London Welsh Rugby Club. Trustee, London Welsh Sch. *Address:* 9 Chester Terrace, Regent's Park, NW1 4ND. *Clubs:* Reform, National Liberal.

THOMAS, Sir John Meurig, Kt 1991; MA, PhD, DSc; FRS 1977; Master of Peterhouse, Cambridge, since 1993; *b* Llanelli, Wales, 15 Dec. 1932; *s* of David John and Edyth Thomas; *m* 1959, Margaret (*née* Edwards); two *d*. *Educ:* Gwendraeth Grammar Sch. (State Scholar); University College of Swansea (Hon. Fellow, 1985); Queen Mary Coll., London. Scientific Officer, UKAEA, 1957–58; Asst Lectr 1958–59, Lectr 1959–65, Reader 1965–69, in Chemistry, UCNW, Bangor; Prof. and Head of Dept of Chemistry, UCW, Aberystwyth, 1969–78; Prof. and Head of Dept of Physical Chemistry, and Fellow of King's Coll., Univ. of Cambridge, 1978–86; Dir, Royal Instn of GB, and Davy Faraday Res. Lab., 1986–91; Resident Prof. of Chemistry, 1986–88, Fullerian Prof. of Chemistry, 1988–94, Royal Instn of GB; Dep. Pro-Chancellor, Univ. of Wales, 1991–94. Visiting appointments: Tech. Univ. Eindhoven, Holland, 1962; Penna State Univ., USA, 1963, 1967; Tech. Univ. Karlsruhe, Germany, 1966; Weizmann Inst., Israel, 1969; Univ. of Florence, Italy, 1972; Amer. Univ. in Cairo, Egypt, 1973; IBM Res. Center, San José, 1977; Harvard, 1983; Ecole Nat. Sup. de Chimie de Paris, 1991. Ind. Mem., Radioactive Waste Management Cttee, 1978–80; Member: Chem. SRC, 1976–78; SERC, 1986–90; Adv. Cttee, Davy-Faraday Labs, Royal Instn, 1978–80; Scientific Adv. Cttee, Sci. Center, Alexandria, 1979–; ACARD (Cabinet Office), 1982–85; COPUS, 1986–92; Bd of Governors, Weizmann Inst., 1982–; Academia Europaea, 1989. Comr, Royal Commn for Exhibn of 1851, 1995–. Chm., Chemrawn (Chem. Res. Applied to World Needs), IUPAC, 1987–; President: Chem. Section, BAAS, 1988–89; London Internat. Youth Sci. Fortnight, 1989–93. Trustee: BM (Natural Hist.), 1987–92; Science Mus., 1990–. Vice-President: Cambridge Univ. Musical Soc., 1994–; Cambridge Philosophical Soc., 1994–. Hon. Visiting Professor: in Physical Chem., QMC, 1986–; of Chem., Imperial Coll., London, 1986–91; Academia Sinica, Beijing; Inst. of Ceramic Sci., Shanghai, 1986–. Lectures: BBC Welsh Radio Annual, 1978; Gerhardt Schmidt Meml, Weizmann Inst., 1979; Baker, Cornell Univ., 1982–83; Hund-Klemm, Max Planck Ges., Stuttgart, 1987; Christmas Lectures, Royal Instn, 1987 (televised, 1988); First Kenneth Pitzer, Coll. of Chem., Univ. of Calif, Berkeley, 1988; Van't Hoff, Royal Dutch Acad. of Arts and Scis, 1988; Bakerian, Royal Soc., 1990; Bruce Preller Prize, RSE, 1990; Sir Krishnan Meml, Delhi, 1991; Watson Centennial, CIT, 1991; Birch, ANU Canberra, 1992; Liversidge, Univ. of Sydney, 1992; Sir Joseph Larmor, Cambridge Philos. Soc., 1992; Patten, Indiana Univ., 1993; Rutherford Meml, Royal Soc., 1995; Hon. FRSE 1993; Hon. Fellow: Indian Acad. of Science, 1980; UMIST, 1984; UCNW, Bangor, 1988; RMS, 1989; Queen Mary and Westfield Coll., London, 1990; Foreign Fellow, INA, 1985; Hon. Foreign Member: Amer. Acad. of Arts and Scis, 1990; Venezuelan Acad. of Scis, 1994; Hon. For. Assoc., Engrg Acad. of Japan, 1991; For. Mem., Amer. Philosophical Soc., 1993; Hon. For. Fellow, Russian Acad. of Scis, 1994. Hon. Bencher, Gray's Inn, 1987. Hon. LLD Wales, 1984; Hon. DLitt CNAA, 1987; Hon. DSc: Heriot-Watt, 1989; Birmingham, 1991; Complutense, Madrid, 1994; Western Ontario, Glamorgan, 1995; DUniv Open, 1991; Dr *hc* Lyon, 1994. Corday Morgan Silver Medal, Chem. Soc., 1967; first Pettinos Prize, American Carbon Soc., 1969; Tilden Medal and Lectr, Chem. Soc., 1973; Chem. Soc. Prizewinner in Solid State Chem., 1978; Hugo Müller Medal, RSC, 1983; Faraday Medal and Lectr, RSC, 1989; Messel Medal, SCI, 1992; Davy Medal, Royal Soc., 1994; Gibbs Gold Medal, ACS, 1995. Crystals and Lasers, TV series, 1987; Dylanwadau, radio series, 1990. *Publications:* (with W. J. Thomas) Introduction to the Principles of Heterogeneous Catalysis, 1967 (trans. Russian, 1970); Pan edrychwyf ar y nefoedd, 1978; Heterogeneous Catalysis: theory and practice, 1991; Michael Faraday and the Royal Institution: the genius of man and place, 1991 (trans. Japanese, 1994); (with K. I. Zamaraev) Perspectives in Catalysis, 1992; numerous articles on solid state and surface chemistry, catalysis and influence of crystalline imperfections, in Proc. Royal Soc., Jl Chem. Soc., etc. *Recreations:* ancient civilizations, bird watching, hill walking, Welsh literature. *Address:* Master's Lodge, Peterhouse, Cambridge CB2 1QY.

THOMAS, Kathrin Elizabeth, (Mrs E. V. Thomas); JP; Vice Lord-Lieutenant, Mid Glamorgan, since 1994; *b* 20 May 1944; *d* of Dillwyn Evans and Dorothy Nelle (*née* Bullock); *m* 1967, Edward Vaughan Thomas; two *s*. *Educ:* Cheltenham Ladies' Coll. Chairman: Mid Glamorgan FHSA, 1990–94; Mid Glamorgan HA, 1994–. Mid Glamorgan: JP 1983; High Sheriff 1986–87; DL 1989. *Recreations:* farming, talking, reading. *Address:* Gelli Hir, Nelson, Treharris, Mid Glamorgan CF46 6PL.

THOMAS, Keith Henry Westcott, CB 1982; OBE 1962; FEng, FRINA, FIMgt; RCNC; Chief Executive, Royal Dockyards, and Head of Royal Corps of Naval Constructors, 1979–83; *b* 20 May 1923; *s* of Henry and Norah Thomas; *m* 1946, Brenda Jeanette Crofton; two *s*. *Educ:* Portsmouth Southern Secondary Sch.; HM Dockyard Sch., Portsmouth; RNC, Greenwich. Asst Constructor, Admiralty Experiment Works, Haslar, 1947–49; Constructor: Admty, London, 1949–56; Large Carrier Design Section, Admty, Bath, 1956–60; Submarines and New Construction, HM Dockyard, Portsmouth, 1960–63; Project Leader, Special Refit HMS Hermes, Devonport, 1963–66; Dep. Planning Manager, HM Dockyard, Devonport, 1966–68; Project Man., Ikara Leanders, MoD(N), 1968–70; Dir-Gen. of Naval Design, Dept of Navy, Canberra, Aust. (on secondment), 1970–73; Planning Man., 1973–75, Gen. Man., 1975–77, HM Dockyard, Rosyth; Gen. Manager, HM Dockyard, Devonport, 1977–79. Pres., Portsmouth Royal Dockyard Historical Soc., 1988–. *Recreations:* music, lapidary, painting. *Address:* 6 Wyborn Close, Hayling Island, Hants PO11 9HY. *T:* Hayling Island (01705) 463435.

THOMAS, Sir Keith (Vivian), Kt 1988; FBA 1979; President of Corpus Christi College, Oxford, since 1986; President, British Academy, since 1993; *b* 2 Jan. 1933; *s* of late Vivian Jones Thomas and Hilda Janet Eirene Thomas (*née* Davies); *m* 1961, Valerie Little; one *s* one *d*. *Educ:* Barry County Grammar Sch.; Balliol Coll., Oxford (Brackenbury Schol.; 1st Cl. Hons Mod. History, 1955; Hon. Fellow 1984). Oxford University: Senior Scholar, St Antony's Coll., 1955; Fellow of All Souls Coll., 1955–57; Fellow of St John's Coll., 1957–86 (Tutor, 1957–85; Hon. Fellow, 1986); Reader in Modern Hist., 1978–85; Prof. of Modern Hist., Jan.–Sept. 1986; Pro-Vice-Chancellor, 1988–; Mem., Hebdomadal Council, 1988–. Vis. Professor, Louisiana State Univ., 1970; Vis. Fellow, Princeton Univ., 1978. Joint Literary Director, Royal Historical Soc., 1970–74, Mem. Council, 1975–78, Vice-Pres., 1980–84. Member: ESRC, 1985–90; Reviewing Cttee on Export of Works of Art, 1989–92; Royal Commn on Historical Manuscripts, 1992–; Trustee, Nat. Gall., 1991–. Delegate, OUP, 1980– (Chm., Finance Cttee, 1988–). Lectures: Stenton, Univ. of Reading, 1975; Raleigh, British Acad., 1976; Neale, University Coll. London, 1976; G. M. Trevelyan, Univ. of Cambridge, 1978–79; Sir D. Owen Evans, University Coll. of Wales, Aberystwyth, 1980; Kaplan, Univ. of Pennsylvania, 1983; Creighton, Univ. of London, 1983; Ena H. Thompson, Pomona Coll., 1986; Prothero, RHistS, 1986; Merle Curti, Univ. of Wisconsin-Madison, 1989; Spinoza, Univ. of Amsterdam, 1992. For.

Hon. Mem., Amer. Acad. of Arts and Scis, 1983. Hon. Fellow, Univ. of Wales Coll. of Cardiff, 1995. Hon. DLitt: Kent, 1983; Wales, 1987; Hull, 1995; Hon. LLD Williams Coll., Mass, 1988; Hon. LittD: Sheffield, 1992; Cantab, 1995. Cavaliere Ufficiale, Ordine al Merito della Repubblica Italiana, 1991. Gen. Editor, Past Masters Series, OUP, 1979–. *Publications:* Religion and the Decline of Magic, 1971 (Wolfson Lit. Award for History, 1972); Rule and Misrule in the Schools of Early Modern England, 1976; Age and Authority in Early Modern England, 1977; ed (with Donald Pennington), Puritans and Revolutionaries, 1978; Man and the Natural World, 1983; contribs to historical books and jls. *Recreation:* visiting secondhand bookshops. *Address:* Corpus Christi College, Oxford OX1 4JF. *T:* Oxford (01865) 276739.

THOMAS, Kenneth Rowland, OBE 1995; General Secretary, Civil and Public Services Association, 1976–82; *b* 7 Feb. 1927; *s* of William Rowland Thomas and Anne Thomas; *m* 1955, Nora (*née* Hughes); four *s*. *Educ:* St Joseph's Elementary Sch., Penarth; Penarth Grammar Sch. Trainee Reporter, South Wales Echo and Western Mail, 1943–44; Civil Servant, 1944–54; Asst Sec., Civil and Public Services Assoc., 1955, Dep. Gen. Sec., 1967. Mem., TUC Gen. Council, 1977–82. Member: Occupational Pensions Bd, 1981–; CSAB, 1984–91; Law Soc. Professional Purposes Cttee, 1984–86; Solicitors Complaints Bureau, 1986–92; Trustee: Post Office Pension Fund, 1969–84; London Develt Capital Fund, 1984–; British Telecommunications Fund, 1983–; Charity Aid Foundn, 1982–92; Director: Postel, 1982–95; West Midlands Enterprise Bd, 1982–; Univ. of Warwick Sci. Park, 1986–; Warwickshire Venture Capital Fund, 1988–91; Coventry Venture Capital Fund, 1988–91. *Recreations:* music, anything Welsh. *Address:* Penycoed Hall, Dolgellau, Gwynedd LL40 2YP. *T:* Dolgellau (01341) 423403.

THOMAS, Prof. Lancelot, FInstP; Professor of Physics, University of Wales, Aberystwyth, since 1981 (Head of Department, 1981–94); *b* 4 Aug. 1930; *s* of Evan Lancelot Redvers Thomas and Olive Margaretta Thomas; *m* 1955, Helen McGraith Reilly; two *s* one *d*. *Educ:* Port Talbot Secondary Grammar Sch.; University College of Swansea (BSc, PhD, DSc). FRMetS. Flying Officer, RAF, 1954–56; Royal Soc. post-doctoral appt, UC of Swansea, 1956–58; SERC Appleton Lab., 1959–65, 1966–81; Guest Worker, Envmtl Res. Labs, Nat. Oceanic and Atmospheric Admin, Boulder, Colorado, 1965–66. Chm., British Nat. Cttee for Solar Terrestrial Physics, Royal Soc., 1982–87; Member: Astronomy and Planetary Sci. Bd, SERC, 1989–93; Astronomy Cttee, PPARC, 1994–; Council, Inst. of Physics, 1994–. Charles Chree Medal and Prize, Inst. of Physics, 1991. *Publications:* (ed jtly) Space Research X, 1970; numerous papers in learned jls on atmospheric and ionospheric physics. *Recreations:* music, modern history, golf. *Address:* Branas, Lôn Tyllwyd, Llanfarian, Aberystwyth, Dyfed SY23 4UH. *T:* Aberystwyth (01970) 617223.

THOMAS, Leslie John, FRSL; author; *b* 22 March 1931; *s* of late David James Thomas and late Dorothy Hilda Court Thomas, Newport (Mon); *m* 1st, 1956, Maureen Crane (marr. diss.); two *s* one *d*; 2nd, 1970, Diana Miles; one *s*. *Educ:* Dr Barnardo's, Kingston-upon-Thames; Kingston Technical Sch.; SW Essex Technical Coll., Walthamstow. Local Newspapers, London area, 1948–49 and 1951–53; Army, 1949–51 (rose to Lance-Corporal); Exchange Telegraph News Agency, 1953–55; Special Writer, London Evening News, 1955–66; subseq. author. FRSL 1994. Hon. MA Wales, 1995. *Publications: autobiography:* This Time Next Week, 1964; In My Wildest Dreams, 1984; *novels:* The Virgin Soldiers, 1966; Orange Wednesday, 1967; The Love Beach, 1968; Come to the War, 1969; His Lordship, 1970; Onward Virgin Soldiers, 1971; Arthur McCann and All His Women, 1972; The Man with Power, 1973; Tropic of Ruislip, 1974; Stand up Virgin Soldiers, 1975; Dangerous Davies, 1976; Bare Nell, 1977; Ormerod's Landing, 1978; That Old Gang of Mine, 1979; The Magic Army, 1981; The Dearest and the Best, 1984; The Adventures of Goodnight and Loving, 1986; Dangerous in Love, 1987; Orders For New York, 1989; The Loves and Journeys of Revolving Jones, 1991; Arrivals and Departures, 1992; Dangerous by Moonlight, 1993; Running Away, 1994; *non-fiction:* Some Lovely Islands, 1968; The Hidden Places of Britain, 1981; A World of Islands, 1983; Short Singles, 1986; TV Plays and Documentaries, etc, incl. Channel Four series, Great British Isles (also presented), 1989, also short stories. *Recreations:* islands, antiques, cricket. *Address:* The Walton Canonry, The Close, Salisbury, Wilts SP1 2EN. *Clubs:* MCC, Wig and Pen, Lord's Taverners.

THOMAS, Sir Maldwyn; *see* Thomas, Sir J. M.

THOMAS, Margaret, Women's International Art Club, 1940; RBA 1947; NEAC 1950; Contemporary Portrait Society, 1970; RWA 1971; Practising Artist (Painter); *b* 26 Sept. 1916; *d* of late Francis Stewart Thomas and of Grace Whetherly. *Educ:* privately; Slade Sch.; RA Schools. Slade Scholar, 1936. Hon. Sec. Artists International Assoc., 1944–45; FRSA 1971. Group exhibitions, Wildensteins, 1946, 1949 and 1962; First one-man show at Leicester Galls, 1949, and subsequently at same gallery, 1950; one-man shows in Edinburgh (Aitken Dotts), 1952, 1955, 1966, and at Outlook Tower, Edinburgh, during Internat. Fest., 1961; RBA Galleries, London, 1953; at Canaletto Gall. (a barge, at Little Venice), 1961; Exhibition of Women Artists, Wakefield Art Gall., 1961; Howard Roberts Gallery Cardiff, 1963, The Minories, Colchester, 1964, QUB, 1967, Mall Galls, London, 1972; Octagon Gall., Belfast, 1973; Court Lodge Gallery, Kent, 1974; Gallery Paton, Edinburgh, 1977; Scottish Gall., Edinburgh (major retrospective), 1982; Sally Hunter, London, 1988, 1991 and 1995; RWA, 1992; regular exhibitor Royal Academy and Royal Scottish Academy. Official purchases: Prince Philip, Duke of Edinburgh; Chantrey Bequest; Arts Council; Exeter College, Oxford; Min. of Education; Min. of Works; Wakefield, Hull, Paisley and Carlisle Art Galleries; Edinburgh City Corporation; Nuffield Foundation Trust; Steel Co. of Wales; Financial Times; Mitsukoshi Ltd, Tokyo; Scottish Nat. Orchestra; Robert Flemming collection; Lloyd's of London; Sock Shop Internat.; GLC and county education authorities in Yorks, Bucks, Monmouth, Derbyshire, Hampshire and Wales. Coronation painting purchased by Min. of Works for British Embassy in Santiago. Winner, Hunting Gp Award for best oil painting of the year, 1981. *Publications:* work reproduced in: Daily Telegraph, News Chronicle, Listener, Studio, Scottish Field, Music and Musicians, The Lady, Arts Review, Western Mail; Illustrated London News, The Artist, The Spectator, Eastern Daily Press. *Recreations:* antique collecting, gardening, vintage cars. *Address:* Ellingham Mill, near Bungay, Suffolk NR35 2EP. *T:* Kirby Cane (01508) 518656; 8 North Bank Street, Edinburgh EH1 2LP. *T:* 0131–225 3343; 13A North Road, Highgate Village, N6 4BD. *T:* 0181–340 2527.

THOMAS, Martin, OBE 1982; QC 1979; a Recorder of the Crown Court, since 1976; *b* 13 March 1937; *s* of Hywel and Olwen Thomas; *m* 1961, Nan Thomas (*née* Kerr); three *s* one *d*. *Educ:* Grove Park Grammar Sch., Wrexham; Peterhouse, Cambridge. MA, LLB (Cantab). Solicitor at Wrexham, 1961–66; Lectr in Law, 1966–68; called to the Bar, Gray's Inn, 1967, Bencher, 1989; Barrister, Wales and Chester Circuit, 1968–; Dep. Circuit Judge, 1974–76; Dep. High Court Judge, 1985–. Mem., Criminal Injury Compensation Bd, 1985–93. Contested (L): W Flints, 1964, 1966, 1970; Wrexham, Feb. and Oct. 1974, 1979, 1983, 1987; Vice Chm., Welsh Liberal Party, 1967–69, Chm. 1969–74; President: Wrexham Liberal Assoc., 1975–; Welsh Liberal Party, 1977, 1978, 1979; Welsh Liberal Democrats, 1993– (Vice-Pres., 1991–93). Chm., Marcher Sound, 1991– (ind. local radio for NE Wales and Cheshire) (Vice Chm., 1983–91). *Recreations:* Rugby football, rowing, golf, music-making, fishing. *Address:* Glasfryn, Gresford, Wrexham, Clwyd LL12 8RG. *T:* Gresford (01978) 832205. *Clubs:* Reform; Western (Glasgow); Wrexham Rugby Football.

THOMAS, (Mary) Elizabeth; with Shropshire Music Service (part-time), since 1993; Director, West Midlands Board, Central Television plc, 1982–92 (Member, Regional Advisory Council, 1993); *b* 22 March 1935; *d* of Kathleen Mary Thomas (*née* Dodd) and David John Thomas; *m* 1962, Brian Haydn Thomas; two *d*. *Educ:* Dr Williams' School, Dolgellau; Talbot Heath School, Bournemouth; Royal Acad. of Music. ARCM, GRSM. Head of Music, High Sch., Totnes, 1958–61; Music Lectr, Ingestre Hall, Stafford, 1962; Berkshire Music Schs, 1964–66; Adult Educn Lectr, Bridgnorth Coll. of Further Educn, 1966–69. Chm., Pentabus Arts Ltd, 1983–87. Arts Council of Great Britain: Member, 1984–88; Chm., Regl Adv. Cttee, 1984–86; Chm., Planning and Develt Bd, 1986–88. Chairman: W Midlands Arts, 1980–84; Council, Regional Arts Assocs, 1982–85; Nat. Assoc. of Local Arts Councils, 1980–82 (Vice-Pres., 1982); City of Birmingham Touring Opera, 1987–92. *Recreations:* collecting antique glass, gardening, string quartet playing. *Address:* Cutters House, 48 Sheinton Street, Much Wenlock, Shropshire TF13 6HU.

THOMAS, Rt. Rev. Maxwell McNee, ThD; Warden of St Paul's College, Sydney, since 1985; Lecturer in History and Thought of Christianity, University of Sydney, since 1986; *b* 23 Aug. 1926; *s* of Rev. Charles Elliot Thomas, ThL, and Elsie Frances Thomas (*née* McNee); *m* 1952, Elaine Joy Walker; two *s* one *d*. *Educ:* St Paul's Coll., Univ. of Sydney (MA, BD); General Theological Seminary, New York (ThD). Lectr in Theology and Greek, St John's Coll, Morpeth, NSW, 1950; deacon, 1950; priest, 1952; Curate: St Peter's, E. Maitland, 1951–52; St Mary Magdalene, Richmond, Surrey, 1952–54; All Saints', Singleton, NSW, 1955. Priest-in-Charge and Rector, The Entrance, NSW, 1955–59; Fellow and Tutor, General Theol. Seminary, NY, 1959–63; Hon. Chaplain to Bishop of New York, 1959–63, Chaplain, 1963–64; Chaplain, Univ. of Melbourne and of Canterbury Fellowship, 1964–68; Consultant Theologian to Archbishop of Melbourne, Stewart Lectr in Divinity, Trinity Coll. and Chaplain of Canterbury Fellowship, 1968–75; Bishop of Wangaratta, 1975–85. Member: Gen. Synod's Commn on Doctrine, 1970– (Chm., 1976–); Faith and Order Commn, WCC, 1977–79; Anglican-Orthodox Jt Doctrinal Discussion Gp, 1978. *Address:* St Paul's College, Sydney, NSW 2006, Australia. *Clubs:* Melbourne, Royal Automobile of Victoria; Australian (Sydney).

THOMAS, Sir Michael, 3rd Bt; *see* Thomas, Sir W. M. M.

THOMAS, Sir Michael, 11th Bt; *see* Thomas, Sir G. M. D.

THOMAS, Michael Christopher Pryce; Legal Adviser, Department of Transport, since 1993; *b* 31 Oct. 1949; *s* of David Hamilton Pryce Thomas, *qv* and Eluned Mair Thomas (*née* Morgan); *m* 1978, Pauline Marie Buckman. *Educ:* St John's Coll., Oxford (BA); Univ. of Sussex (MA). Admitted solicitor, 1976; in private practice as asst solicitor, 1976–79; Legal Dept, MAFF, 1980–86; Law Officers' Dept, 1986–88; Grade 5, Legal Dept, MAFF, 1988–92. Mem., ICA. *Recreations:* music, theatre, ski-ing. *Address:* Department of Transport, Great Minster House, 76 Marsham Street, SW1P 4DR. *T:* 0171–276 5700.

THOMAS, Michael David, CMG 1985; QC 1973; barrister in private practice; Attorney-General of Hong Kong, 1983–88; Member, Executive and Legislative Councils, Hong Kong, 1983–88; Chairman, Law Reform Commission, Hong Kong, 1983–88; *b* 8 Sept. 1933; *s* of late D. Cardigan Thomas and Kathleen Thomas; *m* 1st, 1958, Jane Lena Mary (marr. diss. 1978), *e d* of late Francis Neate; two *s* two *d*; 2nd, 1981, Mrs Gabrielle Blakemore (marr. diss. 1986); 3rd, 1988, Hon. Lydia Dunn (*see* Baroness Dunn). *Educ:* Chigwell Sch., Essex; London Sch. of Economics. LLB (Hons) 1954. Called to Bar, Middle Temple, 1955 (Blackstone Entrance Schol., 1952; Harmsworth Schol., 1957); Bencher, 1981. Nat. Service with RN, Sub-Lt RNVR, 1955–57. In practice at Bar from 1958. Junior Counsel to Minister of Defence (RN) and to Treasury in Admty matters, 1966–73. Wreck Commissioner under Merchant Shipping Act 1970; one of Lloyd's salvage arbitrators, 1974. Governor, Chigwell Sch., 1971–83. *Publications:* (ed jtly) Temperley: Merchant Shipping Acts, 6th edn 1963 and 7th edn 1974. *Recreations:* music, travel. *Address:* 4 Essex Court, Temple, EC4Y 9AJ; Temple Chambers, 16F One Pacific Place, 88 Queensway, Hong Kong. *Clubs:* Garrick; Hong Kong (Hong Kong).

THOMAS, Col Michael John Glyn; private consultant in transfusion medicine, since 1995; Clinical Director, Blood Care Foundation, since 1995; Director, MG & SJ Enterprises, since 1995; *b* 14 Feb. 1938; *s* of Glyn Pritchard Thomas and Mary Thomas (*née* Moseley); *m* 1969, Sheelagh Thorpe; one *d*. *Educ:* Haileybury and ISC; Trinity College, Cambridge; St Bartholomew's Hosp. MA, MB, BChir, LMSSA, DTM&H. Qualified 1962; House Surgeon, Essex County Hosp. and House Physician, St James, Balham, 1963; Regtl MO, 2nd Bn The Parachute Regt, 1965; Trainee Pathologist, BMH Singapore, 1968; Specialist in Pathology, Colchester Mil. Hosp., 1971; Senior Specialist in Pathology, Army Blood Supply Depot, 1977; Exchange Pathologist, Walter Reed Army Inst. of Research, 1982–84; Officer in Charge of Leishman Lab., Cambridge Mil. Hosp., 1985–87; CO, Army Blood Supply Depot, 1987–95. Hon. Consultant Haemotologist, UCH/Middlesex Hosp., 1987. Member: Council, BMA, 1974–82 (Chm., Junior Mems Forum, 1974–75; Chm., Central Ethical Cttee, 1978–82; Mem., expert panel on AIDS, 1986–; Mem., Bd of Sci. and Educn, 1987–93; Fellow, 1995); Cttee on Transfusion Equipment, BSI; Economic and Social Cttee, EEC, 1989–; Founder Chm., Autologous Transfusion Special Interest Gp, British Blood Transfusion Soc., 1992–. *Publications:* contribs to ref. books, reports and jls on Medical Ethics, Haematology and Blood Banking, Malariology and subjects of general medical interest. *Recreations:* sailing, travel, photography, philately. *Address:* The White Cottage, Warren Corner, Ewshot, Farnham, Surrey GU10 5AT. *Club:* Tanglin (Singapore).

THOMAS, Rear-Adm. Michael Richard, BSc (Eng); CEng, FIEE; President of the Ordnance Board, and Director General Technical Services, since 1994. Joined RN 1960; served HMS Lincoln, Dido, and Andromeda; subseq. HM Dockyards Devonport and Portsmouth; Naval Sec's Dept, MoD; Naval Asst to Chief of Fleet Support; Supt Ships, Devonport; comd HMS Drake, 1992. Comdr 1977; Capt. 1985; Cdre 1993. Mem., Devon Scout Council; Life Vice-President: Plymouth Scouts; Sea Cadet Corps. FIMgt; MInstD. *Recreation:* Rugby administration. *Address:* Ordnance Board, Empress State Building, Lillie Road, SW6 1TR.

THOMAS, Michael Stuart, (Mike Thomas); Chairman and Managing Director, Corporate Communications Strategy, since 1988; Chairman, Media Audits Ltd, since 1990; *b* 24 May 1944; *s* of Arthur Edward Thomas. *Educ:* Latymer Upper Sch.; King's Sch., Macclesfield; Liverpool Univ. (BA). Pres., Liverpool Univ. Guild of Undergraduates, 1965–66; Past Mem. Nat. Exec., NUS. Head of Research Dept, Co-operative Party, 1966–68; Sen. Res. Officer, Political and Economic Planning (now PSI), 1968–73; Dir, Volunteer Centre, 1973–74; Dir of Public Relations and Public Affairs, Dewe Rogerson, 1984–88; Mem., BR Western Reg. Bd, 1985–92. MP (Lab and Co-op 1974–81, SDP 1981–83) Newcastle upon Tyne E, Oct. 1974–1983. Mem., Select Cttee on Nationalised Industries, 1975–79; Chm., PLP Trade Gp, 1979–81; SDP spokesman on health and social services, 1981–83; Member: SDP Nat. Cttee, 1981–90; SDP Policy Cttee, 1981–90; Chairman: Organisation Cttee of SDP, 1981–88; By-election Cttee, SDP, 1984–88; SDP

Finance Working Gp, 1988–90; a Vice-Pres., SDP, 1988–90; Mem., Alliance Strategy Cttee, 1983–87. Contested: (SDP) Newcastle upon Tyne East, 1983; (SDP/Alliance) Exeter, 1987. Mem., USDAW; founder of parly jl The House Magazine. *Publications:* Participation and the Redcliffe Maud Report, 1970; (ed) The BBC Guide to Parliament, 1979, 1983; various PEP pamphlets, contribs, etc, 1971–; various articles, reviews, etc. *Recreations:* collecting historical pottery and medals relating to elections, theatre, music, cooking. *Address:* 16 Dufours Place, W1V 1FE. *T:* 0171–836 1111.

THOMAS, Michael T.; *see* Tilson Thomas.

THOMAS, Neville; *see* Thomas, R. N.

THOMAS, Norman, CBE 1980; HM Chief Inspector of Schools, 1973–81; Specialist Professor in Primary Education, University of Nottingham, 1987–88; *b* 1 June 1921; *s* of Bowen Thomas and Ada Thomas (*née* Redding); *m* 1942, Rose Henshaw; one *s* one *d*. *Educ:* Latymer's Sch., Edmonton; Camden Coll. Qual. Teacher. Commerce and Industry, then primary schs in London and Herts, 1948–56; Head, Longmeadow Sch., Stevenage, 1956–61; HM Inspector of Schools, Lincs and SE England, 1962–68; HMI, Staff Inspector for Primary (Junior and Middle) Schs, 1969–73. Chm., Cttee of Enquiry on Primary Educn in ILEA, 1983–84. Adviser to Parly Cttee on Educn, Science and Art, 1984–86, on Educn, 1994–. Visiting Professor: NE London Polytechnic, 1984–86; Univ. of Herts (formerly Hatfield Poly.), 1991–; Hon. Prof., Univ. of Warwick, 1986–94. Hon. FCP, 1988. *Publications:* Primary Education from Plowden to the 1990s, 1990; chapters in books and articles in professional jls. *Recreations:* photography, reading. *Address:* 19 Langley Way, Watford, Herts WD1 3EJ. *T:* Watford (01923) 223766.

THOMAS, Patricia Anne; Commissioner for Local Administration in England, since 1985; Vice-Chairman, Commission for Local Administration in England, since 1994; *b* 3 April 1940; *d* of Frederick S. Lofts and Ann Elizabeth Lofts; *m* 1968, Joseph Glyn Thomas; one *s* two *d*. *Educ:* King's College London. LLB, LLM. Lectr in Law, Univ. of Leeds, 1962–63, 1964–68; Teaching Fellow, Univ. of Illinois, 1963–64; Sen. Lectr, then Principal Lectr, Head of Sch. of Law and Prof., Lancashire Polytechnic, 1973–85. Mem., 1976–84, Vice-Pres., 1984, Pres., 1985, Greater Manchester and Lancashire Rent Assessment Panel; Chm., Blackpool Supplementary Benefit Appeal Tribunal, 1980–85. Hon. Fellow, Lancashire Polytech., 1991. *Publication:* Law of Evidence, 1972. *Recreations:* farming, family. *Address:* Commission for Local Administration in England, Beverley House, Shipton Road, York YO3 6FZ. *T:* York (01904) 663200.

THOMAS, Paul; *see* Thomas, C. P.

THOMAS, Prof. Phillip Charles, FRSE; FIBiol; Principal, Scottish Agricultural College, since 1990, and Professor of Agriculture, University of Glasgow, since 1987; *b* 17 June 1942; *s* of William Charles Thomas and Gwendolen (*née* Emery); *m* 1967, Pamela Mary Hirst; one *s* one *d*. *Educ:* University College of North Wales, Bangor (BSc, PhD). FIBiol 1983; FRSE 1993. Lectr in animal nutrition and physiology, Univ. of Leeds, 1966–71; progressively, SSO to SPSO, Hannah Research Inst., 1971–87; Principal, West of Scotland Coll., 1987–90. Hon. Prof., Edinburgh Univ., 1990–. *Publications:* (with J. A. F. Rook) Silage for Milk Production, 1982; (with J. A. F. Rook) Nutritional Physiology of Farm Animals, 1983. *Address:* Scottish Agricultural College, Central Office, West Mains Road, Edinburgh EH9 3JG. *T:* 0131–662 1303. *Club:* Farmers'.

THOMAS, Quentin Jeremy, CB 1994; Deputy Secretary, Northern Ireland Office, since 1991; *b* 1 Aug. 1944; *s* of late Arthur Albert Thomas and Edith Kathleen Thomas (*née* Bigg); *m* 1969, Anabel Jane, *d* of late J. H. Humphreys; one *s* two *d*. *Educ:* Perse School, Cambridge; Gonville and Caius College, Cambridge. Home Office, 1966; Private Sec. to Perm. Under-Sec. of State, 1970; Crime Policy Planning Unit, 1974–76; Sec. to Royal Commn on Gambling, 1976–78; Civil Service (Nuffield and Leverhulme) Travelling Fellowship, 1980–81; Head, Broadcasting Dept, Home Office, 1984–88; Under Sec., NI Office, 1988–91. *Address:* Northern Ireland Office, Whitehall, SW1A 2AZ.
See also R. C. Thomas.

THOMAS, Ralph Philip, MC 1942; Film Director; *b* Hull, Yorks, 10 Aug.; *m* 1944, Joy Spanjer; one *s* one *d*. *Educ:* Tellisford School, Clifton. Entered film industry, 1932, and worked in all production depts, particularly editing, until 1939. Served War of 1939–45, as Regimental Officer 9th Lancers until 1944; thereafter Instructor Royal Military College. Returned to Film Industry, in Rank Organisation Trailer Dept, 1946; Joined Gainsborough Pictures, 1948, and directed Once Upon a Dream, Traveller's Joy. Films directed at Pinewood Studios: The Clouded Yellow, Appointment with Venus, The Venetian Bird, A Day to Remember, Doctor in the House, Mad About Men, Above Us The Waves, Doctor at Sea, The Iron Petticoat, Checkpoint, Doctor at Large, Campbell's Kingdom, A Tale of Two Cities, The Wind Cannot Read, The 39 Steps, Upstairs and Downstairs, Conspiracy of Hearts, Doctor in Love, No My Darling Daughter, No Love for Johnnie, The Wild and the Willing, Doctor in Distress, Hot enough for June, The High Bright Sun, Doctor in Clover, Deadlier than the Male, Nobody Runs Forever, Some Girls Do, Doctor in Trouble, Quest, Percy, It's a 2 foot 6 inch Above the Ground World, Percy's Progress, A Nightingale Sang in Berkeley Square, Doctors' Daughters, Pop Pirates. *Address:* Kirtin House, Blyton Close, Beaconsfield, Bucks HP9 2LX. *T:* Beaconsfield (01494) 671856. *Club:* Garrick.
See also J. J. Thomas.

THOMAS, Dr Reginald; Ambassador; Inspector General in the Ministry of Foreign Affairs, Vienna, 1988–93; *b* 28 Feb. 1928; *s* of Dr Leopold Thomas and Irma Thomas (*née* von Smekal); *m* 1960, Ingrid Renate Leitner; three *s* one *d*. *Educ:* Univ. of Vienna (Dr jur 1950). Entered Austrian Foreign Service, 1951; Austrian Legation, Bern, 1952–56; Dep. Legal Adviser on Internat. Law, Min. of Foreign Affairs, Vienna, 1956–59; Austrian Embassy, Tokyo, 1959–62; Head of Office of Sec. Gen. for Foreign Affairs, Vienna, 1962–68; Ambassador to Pakistan and concurrently accredited to Union of Burma, 1968–71; Ambassador to Japan and concurrently accredited to Republic of Korea, 1971–75; Head of Dept of Administration, Min. of Foreign Affairs, Vienna, 1975–82; concurrently Dep. Sec. Gen. for Foreign Affairs, Vienna, 1978–82; Austrian Ambassador to UK, 1982–87. Mem., Austrian Assoc. for Foreign Policy and Internat. Relations, Vienna, 1978–82. Knight Comdr's Cross (Austria), 1993; Foreign orders include: Grand Cross: Order of the Rising Sun (Japan); Order of Diplomatic Service (Korea); Independence Order (Jordan); Order of F. de Miranda (Venezuela); Hilal-i-Qaid-i-Azam (Pakistan). *Recreation:* sports. *Address:* Schwarzenbergstrasse 8, 1010 Wien, Austria. *Club:* Queen's (Life Mem.).

THOMAS, Richard; *see* Thomas, A. R.

THOMAS, Adm. Sir Richard; *see* Thomas, Adm. Sir W. R. S.

THOMAS, Richard, CMG 1990; HM Diplomatic Service; High Commissioner to Barbados, Grenada, St Vincent and the Grenadines, St Lucia, Dominica, Antigua and Barbuda, and St Kitts and Nevis, since 1994; *b* 18 Feb. 1938; *s* of Anthony Hugh Thomas, JP and Molly Thomas, MBE; *m* 1966, Catherine Jane Hayes, Sydney, NSW; one *s* two *d*. *Educ:* Leighton Park; Merton Coll., Oxford (MA). Nat. Service, 2nd Lt, RASC, 1959–61. Asst Principal, CRO, 1961; Private Sec. to Parly Under Sec., 1962–63; Second Secretary: Accra, 1963–65; Lomé, 1965–66; (later First Sec.) UK Delegn NATO, Paris and Brussels, 1966–69; First Secretary: FCO, 1969–72; (Economic), New Delhi, 1972–75; and Asst Head of Dept, FCO, 1976–78; FCO Visiting Res. Fellow, RIIA, 1978–79; Counsellor, Prague, 1979–83; Ambassador, Iceland, 1983–86; Overseas Inspector, 1986–89; Ambassador to Bulgaria, 1989–94. *Publication:* India's Emergence as an Industrial Power: Middle Eastern Contracts, 1982. *Recreations:* foreign parts, gossip, gardening, skiing. *Address:* c/o Foreign and Commonwealth Office, SW1A 2AH. *Clubs:* United Oxford & Cambridge University, Royal Over-Seas League.

THOMAS, Richard James, LLB; Director, Public Policy Group, Clifford Chance, since 1992; *b* 18 June 1949; *s* of Daniel Lewis Thomas, JP, and Norah Mary Thomas; *m* 1974, Julia Delicia, *d* of Dr E. G. W. Clarke; two *s* one *d*. *Educ:* Bishop's Stortford Coll.; Univ. of Southampton (LLB Hons); College of Law. Admitted Solicitor, 1973. Articled clerk and Asst Solicitor, Freshfields, 1971–74; Solicitor, CAB Legal Service, 1974–79; Legal Officer and Hd of Resources Gp, Nat. Consumer Council, 1979–86; Under Sec. and Dir of Consumer Affairs, OFT, 1986–92. Chm., British Univs N America Club, 1970–71; Trustee, W London Fair Housing Gp, 1976–79; Member: Management Cttee, Gtr London CAB Service, 1977–79; Legal Services Gp, Nat. Assoc. of CABx, 1978–86; Management Cttee, Royal Courts of Justice CAB, 1992–; London Electricity Cons. Council, 1979–84; European Consumer Law Gp, 1981–86; European Commn Working Party on Access to Justice, 1981–82; Cttee of City of Westminster Law Soc., 1984–86; Lord Chancellor's Adv. Cttee on Civil Justice Rev., 1985–88; Council, Office of Banking Ombudsman, 1992–. FRSA 1992. *Publications:* reports, articles and broadcasts on range of legal and consumer issues. *Recreations:* family, maintenance of home and garden, travel. *Address:* Clifford Chance, 200 Aldersgate Street, EC1A 4JJ.

THOMAS, Sir Robert (Evan), Kt 1967; DL, JP; Leader, Greater Manchester Metropolitan County Council, 1973–77; Deputy Chairman, Manchester Ship Canal, 1971–74; *b* 8 Oct. 1901; *s* of Jesse and Anne Thomas; *m* 1924, Edna Isherwood; one *s* one *d*. *Educ:* St Peter's, Leigh, Lancs. Miner, 1914; served Army, 1919–21; Bus Driver, 1924–37; Trade Union Official, 1937–66; Member, Manchester City Council, 1944–74; Lord Mayor of Manchester, 1962–63. Chairman: Assoc. of Municipal Corps, 1973–74; Assoc. of Metropolitan Authorities, 1974–77; British Sector, Internat. Union of Local Authorities, 1974–77. JP Manchester, 1948; DL: County Palatine of Lancaster, 1967–73, County Palatine of Greater Manchester, 1974. Hon. MA Manchester, 1974. *Recreations:* dancing, gardening, golf. *Address:* 29 Milwain Road, Manchester M19 2PX. *T:* 0161–224 5778.

THOMAS, (Robert) Neville, QC 1975; barrister-at-law; a Recorder of the Crown Court, 1975–82; *b* 31 March 1936; *s* of Robert Derfel Thomas and Enid Anne Thomas; *m* 1970, Jennifer Anne Brownrigg; one *s* one *d*. *Educ:* Ruthin Sch.; University Coll., Oxford (MA, BCL). Called to Bar, Inner Temple, 1962, Bencher, 1985. *Recreations:* fishing, walking, reading. *Address:* Glansevern, Berriew, Welshpool, Powys SY21 8AH. *Club:* Garrick.

THOMAS, Prof. Roger Christopher, FRS 1989; Professor of Physiology, University of Bristol, since 1986; *b* 2 June 1939; *e s* of late Arthur Albert Thomas and Edith Kathleen (*née* Bigg); *m* 1964, Monica Mary, *d* of late Lt-Comdr William Peter Querstret, RN; two *s*. *Educ:* Perse Sch., Cambridge; Univ. of Southampton (BSc, PhD). Res. Associate, Rockefeller Univ., NY, 1964–66; Hon. Res. Asst, Biophysics, UCL, 1966–69; Bristol University: Lectr, 1969–77; Reader in Physiology, 1977–86; Hd of Dept of Physiology, 1985–90; Dean, Faculty of Science, 1990–93. Vis. Prof., Yale Univ., 1979–80. *Publications:* Ion-Sensitive Intracellular Microelectrodes, 1978; many papers on ion transport in learned jls. *Recreations:* cooking, ski-ing. *Address:* Department of Physiology, School of Medical Sciences, The University, Bristol BS8 1TD. *T:* Bristol (0117) 928 7821, *Fax:* (0117) 928 7628.
See also Q. J. Thomas.

THOMAS, Roger Humphrey; Chairman and Managing Director, Black & Decker, since 1983; *b* 12 April 1942; *s* of Cyril Lewis Thomas and Phyllis Amy Thomas; *m* 1962, Myfanwy Ruth, (Nikki), Nicholas; three *s*. *Educ:* Slough Grammar School. FCCA. Black & Decker, 1970–. *Recreations:* theatre, DIY, golf. *Address:* Black & Decker, Westpoint, The Grove, Slough, Berks SL1 1QQ. *T:* Slough (01753) 824744.

THOMAS, Roger John Laugharne; QC 1984; a Recorder, since 1987; *b* 22 Oct. 1947; *s* of Roger Edward Laugharne Thomas and Dinah Agnes Thomas; *m* 1973, Elizabeth Ann Buchanan; one *s* one *d*. *Educ:* Rugby School; Trinity Hall, Cambridge (BA); Univ. of Chicago (Commonwealth Fellow; JD). Called to Bar, Gray's Inn, 1969, Bencher, 1992. Asst Teacher, Mayo College, Ajmer, India, 1965–66. Faculty Fellow, Law Sch., Univ. of Southampton, 1990–. DTI Inspector, Mirror Gp Newspapers plc, 1992–. *Publications:* papers and articles on maritime law and insurance and reinsurance law. *Recreations:* gardens, walking, travel. *Address:* Essex Court Chambers, 24 Lincoln's Inn Fields, WC2A 3ED. *T:* 0171–813 8000, *Fax:* 0171–813 8080.

THOMAS, Roger Lloyd; Senior Clerk (Acting), Committee Office, House of Commons, 1979–84 and Clerk, Select Committee on Welsh Affairs, 1982–84, retired; *b* 7 Feb. 1919; *er s* of Trevor John Thomas and Eleanor Maud (*née* Jones), Abercarn, Mon; *m* 1945, Stella Mary, *d* of Reginald Ernest Willmett, Newport, Mon; three *s* one *d*. *Educ:* Barry County Sch.; Magdalen Coll., Oxford (Doncaster Schol.; Heath Harrison Trav. Schol.). BA 2nd Mod. Langs, 1939; MA 1946. Pres., OU Italian Soc., 1938–39. Served 1939–46, RA and Gen. Staff (Major GSO2) in India, Middle East, N Africa, Italy and Germany. Civil Servant, 1948–70: Min. of Fuel and Power, Home Office, Treasury, Welsh Office and Min. of Housing and Local Govt; Private Sec. to Perm. Under-Sec. of State, Home Office, 1950 and to successive Parly Under-Secs of State, 1951–53; Sec., Interdeptl Cttee on powers of Subpoena, 1960; Asst Sec., 1963; Sec., Aberfan Inquiry Tribunal, 1966–67; Chm., Working Party on Building by Direct Labour Organisations, 1968–69; Gen. Manager, The Housing Corporation, 1970–73; Asst Sec., DoE, 1974–79. *Publications:* sundry reports. *Recreation:* growing flowers. *Address:* 5 Park Avenue, Caterham, Surrey CR3 6AH. *T:* Caterham (01883) 342080. *Club:* Union (Oxford).
See also D. H. P. Thomas.

THOMAS, Roger Lloyd; QC 1994; *b* 7 Feb. 1947; *s* of David Eyron Thomas, CBE and Marie Lloyd Thomas; *m* 1974, Susan Nicola Orchard; one *s* one *d*. *Educ:* Cathays High Sch., Cardiff; University Coll. of Wales Aberystwyth (LLB). Called to the Bar, Gray's Inn, 1969; Recorder, 1987. *Recreations:* tennis, music, reading. *Address:* 9 Park Place, Cardiff CF1 3DP. *T:* Cardiff (01222) 382731. *Club:* Cardiff Lawn Tennis.

THOMAS, Roger R.; *see* Ridley-Thomas, R.

THOMAS, Ronald Richard; *b* March 1929. *Educ:* Ruskin Coll. and Balliol Coll., Oxford (MA). Sen. Lectr, Econ. and Indust. Studies, Univ. of Bristol. Contested (Lab): Bristol North-West, Feb. 1974; Bristol East, 1987; MP (Lab) Bristol NW, Oct. 1974–1979. Former Mem., Bristol DC. Mem. ASTMS. *Address:* 64 Morris Road, Lockleaze, Bristol BS7 9TA.

THOMAS, Rev. Ronald Stuart; poet; *b* 29 March 1913; *m* Mildred E. Eldridge; one *s*. *Educ:* University of Wales (BA); St Michael's College, Llandaff. Ordained deacon, 1936; priest, 1937. Curate of Chirk, 1936–40; Curate of Hanmer, in charge of Talarn Green, 1940–42; Rector of Manafon, 1942–54; Vicar of Eglwysfach, 1954–67; Vicar of St Hywyn, Aberdaron, with St Mary, Bodferin, 1967–78, and Rector of Rhiw with Llanfaelrhys, 1972–78. First record, reading his own poems, 1977. Queen's Gold Medal for Poetry, 1964; Cholmondeley Award, 1978. *Publications: poems:* Stones of the Field (privately printed), 1947; Song at the Year's Turning, 1955 (Heinemann Award of the Royal Society of Literature, 1956); Poetry for Supper, 1958; Tares, 1961; Bread of Truth, 1963; Pietà, 1966; Not That He Brought Flowers, 1968; H'm, 1972; Selected Poems 1946–1968, 1974; Laboratories of the Spirit, 1976; Frequencies, 1978; Between Here and Now, 1981; Later Poems 1972–1982, 1983; Experimenting with an Amen, 1986; Welsh Airs, 1987; The Echoes Return Slow, 1988; Counterpoint, 1990; Mass for Hard Times, 1992; Collected Poems 1945–1990, 1993; No Truth with the Furies, 1995; *autobiography:* Neb, 1985; *edited:* A Book of Country Verse, 1961; Penguin Book of Religious Verse, 1963; Edward Thomas: Selected Poems, 1964; George Herbert, A Choice of Verse, 1967; A Choice of Wordsworth's Verse, 1971. *Address:* Cefn Du Ganol, Llanfairynghornwy, Holyhead LL65 4LG. *T:* Llanfaethlu (01407) 730943.

THOMAS, Roydon Urquhart; QC 1985; a Recorder, since 1986; *b* 17 May 1936; *s* of Rowland Daniel Thomas and Jean Milne Thomas; *m* (marr. diss.); one *s* one *d* (and one *s* decd). *Educ:* Fettes College; Sidney Sussex College, Cambridge (BA). Called to the Bar, Middle Temple, 1960, Bencher, 1993; South Eastern Circuit. *Publication:* (Asst Editor) Tolstoy on Divorce, 1964. *Recreations:* golf, fishing. *Address:* 1 Essex Court, Temple, EC4Y 9AR. *T:* 0171–583 2000. *Clubs:* Hurlingham; High Post Golf.

THOMAS, Rt. Hon. Sir Swinton (Barclay), Kt 1985; PC 1994; **Rt. Hon. Lord Justice Swinton Thomas;** a Lord Justice of Appeal, since 1994; *b* 12 Jan. 1931; *s* of late Brig. William Bain Thomas, CBE, DSO, and Mary Georgina Thomas; *m* 1967, Angela, Lady Cope; one *s* one *d*. *Educ:* Ampleforth Coll.; Lincoln Coll., Oxford (Scholar) (MA). Served with Cameronians (Scottish Rifles), 1950–51, Lieut. Called to Bar, Inner Temple, 1955 (Bencher, 1983); QC 1975; a Recorder of the Crown Court, 1975–85; a Judge of the High Court of Justice, Family Div., 1985–90, QBD, 1990–94. A Presiding Judge, Western Circuit, 1987–90. Member: General Council of the Bar, 1970–74; Criminal Injuries Compensation Bd, 1984–85; Vice-Chm., Parole Bd, 1994 (Mem., 1992–95). *Recreations:* reading, travel. *Address:* Royal Courts of Justice, Strand, WC2A 2LL. *T:* 0171–936 6884. *Club:* Garrick.

THOMAS, Victor Gerald B.; *see* Bulmer-Thomas.

THOMAS, Vivian Elliott Sgrifan, OBE 1992; Chairman, British Standards Institution, since 1992; *b* 13 March 1932; *s* of William Edward Thomas and Cicely (*née* Elliott); *m* 1962, Valerie Slade Thomas; one *s* one *d*. *Educ:* Swindon High Sch.; Southampton Univ. (1st Class Marine Engrg). Engr Officer, Union Castle Line, 1953–58; with British Petroleum plc, 1959–92; Chief Exec. Officer, BP Oil UK Ltd, 1989–92. Director: Southern Water plc, 1992–; Jaguar Ltd, 1992–; Gowrings Plc, 1992–. *Recreations:* golf, music, theatre. *Address:* Camelot, Bennett Way, West Clandon, Surrey GU4 7NN. *T:* Woking (01483) 222665. *Club:* Royal Automobile.

THOMAS, Maj.-Gen. Walter Babington, CB 1971; DSO 1943; MC and Bar, 1942; Commander, HQ Far East Land Forces, Nov. 1970–Nov. 1971 (Chief of Staff, April–Oct. 1970); retired Jan. 1972; *b* Nelson, NZ, 29 June 1919; *s* of Walter Harington Thomas, Farmer; *m* 1947, Iredale Edith Lauchlan (*née* Trent); three *d*. *Educ:* Motueka Dist High Sch., Nelson, NZ. Clerk, Bank of New Zealand, 1936–39. Served War of 1939–45 (despatches, MC and Bar, DSO): 2nd NZEF, 1940–46, in Greece, Crete, Western Desert, Tunis and Italy; Comd 23 (NZ) Bn, 1944–45; Comd 22 (NZ) Bn, in Japan, 1946; transf. to Brit. Army, Royal Hampshire Regt, 1947; Bde Major, 39 Inf. Bde Gp, 1953 55 (despatches); GSO2, UK JSLS, Aust., 1958–60; AA&QMG, HQ 1 Div. BAOR, 1962–64; Comd 12 Inf. Bde Gp, 1964–66; IDC, 1967; GOC 5th Div., 1968–70. Silver Star, Medal, 1945 (USA). *Publications:* Dare to be Free, 1951; Touch of Pitch, 1956. *Recreation:* riding. *Address:* Kerry Road, M/S 413, Beaudesert, Qld 4285, Australia.

THOMAS, William David; Stipendiary Magistrate for South Yorkshire, since 1989; *b* 10 Oct. 1941; *s* of Arnold and Ada Thomas; *m* 1966, Cynthia Janice Jackson; one *s* two *d*. *Educ:* Whitcliffe Mount Grammar Sch., Cleckheaton; LSE (LLB Hons 1963); Part II, Law Society Finals, 1964. Admitted Solicitor, 1966. Asst Solicitor 1966, Partner, 1967–89, Finn Gledhill & Co., Halifax. *Publications:* contribs to Yorkshire Ridings Magazine and Pennine Radio, Bradford. *Recreations:* Rugby, theatre, ballet, gardening. *Address:* Rotherham Magistrate's Court, PO Box 15, The Statutes, Rotherham S60 1YW. *T:* Rotherham (01709) 839339. *Club:* Halifax Rugby Union Football.

THOMAS, William Fremlyn Cotter; His Honour Judge Thomas; a Circuit Judge, since 1990; *b* 18 March 1935; *s* of Stephen Kerr Thomas and Nâdine Dieudonnée Thomas (*née* March); *m* 1st, 1960, Mary Alanna Mudie; one *d*; 2nd, 1968, Thalia Mary Edith Myers; 3rd, 1978, Ursula Nancy Eden; one *s* one *d*. *Educ:* Bryanston Sch., Dorset; University Coll., Oxford. National Service in 1st NRR, Malaya, 2nd Lieut, 1954–56. Called to the Bar, Inner Temple, 1961; SE Circuit; a Recorder, 1986. *Recreations:* music, carpentry, architecture. *Address:* The Crown Court, Canbury Park Road, Kingston upon Thames, Surrey KT2 6JU.

THOMAS, Sir William James Cooper, 2nd Bt, *cr* 1919; TD; JP; DL; Captain RA; *b* 7 May 1919; *er s* of Sir William James Thomas, 1st Bt, and Maud Mary Cooper, Bexhill-on-Sea; *S* father 1945; *m* 1947, Freida Dunbar (*d* 1990), *yr d* of late F. A. Whyte; two *s* one *d*. *Educ:* Harrow; Downing Coll., Cambridge. Barrister, Inner Temple, 1948. Member TA, 1938. Served War of 1939–45. Monmouthshire: JP 1958; DL 1973; High Sheriff, 1973. *Heir: s* William Michael Thomas, *b* 5 Dec. 1948. *Address:* Tump House, Llanrothal, Monmouth, Gwent NP5 3QL. *T:* Monmouth (01600) 712757.

THOMAS, Ven. William Jordison; Archdeacon of Northumberland, 1983–92, Archdeacon Emeritus 1993; *b* 16 Dec. 1927; *s* of Henry William and Dorothy Newton Thomas; *m* 1954, Kathleen Jeffrey Robson, *d* of William Robson, Reaveley, Powburn, Alnwick. *Educ:* Holmwood Prep. School, Middlesbrough; Acklam Hall Grammar School, Middlesbrough; Giggleswick School; King's Coll., Cambridge (BA 1951, MA 1955); Cuddesdon College. National Service, RN, 1946–48. Assistant Curate: St Anthony of Egypt, Newcastle upon Tyne, 1953–56; Berwick Parish Church, 1956–59; Vicar: Alwinton with Holystone and Alnham and the Lordship of Kidland, 1959–70; Alston with Garrigill, Nenthead and Kirkhaugh, 1970–80, i/c Knaresdale, 1973–80; Industrial Chaplain, 1972–80; Team Rector of Glendale, 1980–82; RD of Bamburgh and Glendale, 1980–82. Hon. Chaplain, Actors' Church Union, 1953–56. Harbour Comr, N Sunderland, 1990–92. *Recreations:* sailing own dinghy and other people's yachts, making pictures, travelling and making magic. *Address:* Wark Cottage, Whittingham, Alnwick, Northumberland NE66 4RB. *T:* Whittingham (01665) 574300. *Clubs:* Victory Services; Northern Constitutional (Newcastle upon Tyne).

THOMAS, Sir (William) Michael (Marsh), 3rd Bt *cr* 1918; *b* 4 Dec. 1930; *s* of Sir William Eustace Rhyddlad Thomas, 2nd Bt, and Enid Helena Marsh; *S* father 1957; *m* 1957, Geraldine Mary, *d* of Robert Drysdale, Anglesey; three *d*. *Educ:* Oundle School, Northants. Formerly Man. Dir, Gors Nurseries Ltd. *Address:* Belan, Rhosneigr, Gwynedd LL64 5JE.

THOMAS, Adm. Sir (William) Richard (Scott), KCB 1987; KCVO 1995; OBE 1974; Gentleman Usher of the Black Rod, and Serjeant-at-Arms, House of Lords, and Secretary to the Lord Great Chamberlain, 1992–95; *b* 22 March 1932; *s* of late Comdr William Scott Thomas, DSC, RN and Mary Hilda Bertha Hemelryk, Findon, Sussex; *m* 1959, Patricia (Paddy) Margaret, *d* of late Dr and Mrs J. H. Cullinan, Fressingfield, Suffolk; three *s* four *d* (and one *s* decd). *Educ:* Penryn Sch., Ross-on-Wye; Downside Sch., Bath. psc 1963, jssc 1966, rcds 1979. Midshipman, 1951–52; Sub-Lt and Lieut, 1953–62 (CO HM Ships Buttress, Wolverton and Greetham); CO HMS Troubridge, 1966–68; Staff Officer Ops to Flag Officer First Flotilla and Flag Officer Scotland and NI, 1970–74; Directorate of Naval Plans, MoD, 1974–77; CO HMS Fearless, 1977–78; Dir of Office Appts (Seamen), 1980–83; Naval Sec., 1983–85; Flag Officer Second Flotilla, 1985–87; Dep. SACLANT, 1987–89; UK Mil. Rep. to NATO, 1989–92. Mem. Cttee, Royal Humane Soc., 1992–. Pres., Havant Dist Scouts, 1992–. *Recreations:* family, gardening, golf. *Address:* Holmwood House, King Street, Emsworth, Hants PO10 7AZ.

THOMAS, Wyndham, CBE 1982; Chairman, Inner City Enterprises, 1983–92; Board Member, Muxton Grange Leisure Ltd, since 1992; *b* 1 Feb. 1924; *s* of Robert John Thomas and Hannah Mary; *m* 1947, Elizabeth Terry Hopkin; one *s* three *d*. *Educ:* Maesteg Grammar School. Served Army (Lieut, Royal Welch Fusiliers), 1943–47. Schoolmaster, 1950–53; Director, Town and Country Planning Association, 1955–67; Gen. Manager, Peterborough New Town Develt Corp., 1968–83. Member: Land Commission, 1967–68; Commission for the New Towns, 1964–68; Property Adv. Gp, DoE, 1978–90; London Docklands Develt Corp., 1981–88. Chm., House Builders' Fedn Commn of Inquiry into Housebuilding and the Inner Cities, 1986–87 (report published 1987). Mayor of Hemel Hempstead, 1958–59. Hon. MRTPI 1979 (Mem. Council, 1989–). Officer of the Order of Orange-Nassau (Netherlands), 1982. *Publications:* many articles on town planning, housing, etc, in learned jls. *Recreations:* collecting old furniture, work, golf. *Address:* 8 Westwood Park Road, Peterborough PE3 6JL. *T:* Peterborough (01733) 64399.

THOMASON, Prof. George Frederick, CBE 1983; Montague Burton Professor of Industrial Relations, University College, Cardiff, 1969–85, now Emeritus; *b* 27 Nov. 1927; *s* of George Frederick Thomason and Eva Elizabeth (*née* Walker); *m* 1953, Jean Elizabeth Horsley; one *s* one *d*. *Educ:* Kelsick Grammar Sch.; Univ. of Sheffield (BA); Univ. of Toronto (MA); PhD (Wales). CIPM, FBIM; FCIT. University College, Cardiff: Research Asst, 1953; Asst Lectr, 1954; Research Associate, 1956; Lectr, 1959; Asst Man. Dir, Flex Fasteners Ltd, Rhondda, 1960; University College, Cardiff: Lectr, 1962; Sen. Lectr, 1963; Reader, 1969; Dean, Faculty of Economics, 1971–73; Dep. Principal (Humanities), 1974–77. Member: Doctors' and Dentists' Pay Review Body, 1979–; Pay Rev. Body for Nurses, Midwives, Health Service Visitors and Professions allied to Medicine, 1983–. Dir, Enterprise Develt and Trng Ltd. *Publications:* Welsh Society in Transition, 1963; Personnel Manager's Guide to Job Evaluation, 1968; Professional Approach to Community Work, 1969; The Management of Research and Development, 1970; Improving the Quality of Organization, 1973; Textbook of Personnel Management, 1975, 5th edn as Textbook of Human Resource Management, 1988; Job Evaluation: Objectives and Methods, 1980; Textbook of Industrial Relations Management, 1984. *Recreation:* gardening. *Address:* Ty Gwyn, 149 Lake Road West, Cardiff CF2 5PJ. *T:* Cardiff (01222) 754236.

THOMASON, (Kenneth) Roy, OBE 1986; MP (C) Bromsgrove, since 1992; solicitor; *b* 14 Dec. 1944; *s* of Thomas Roger and Constance Dora Thomason; *m* 1969, Christine Ann (*née* Parsons); two *s* two *d*. *Educ:* Cheney Sch., Oxford; London Univ. (LLB). Admitted Solicitor, 1969; Partner, 1970–91, Sen. Partner, 1979–91, Horden & George, Bournemouth. Mem., Bournemouth Council, 1970–92 (Leader, 1974–82; past Chm. Policy, Ways and Means, and Finance Cttees). Association of District Councils: Mem. Council, 1979–91; Leader, 1981–87; Chm., 1987–91; Chm., Housing and Environmental Health Cttee, 1983–87. Mem., Cons. Nat. Local Govt Adv. Cttee, 1981–; various Cons. Party positions at constituency and area level, 1966– (Constituency Chm., 1981–82); contested (C) Newport E, 1983. Member: Envmt Select Cttee, 1992–; Jt Statutory Instrument Cttee, 1992–; Sec., All-Party Export Gp, 1993–; Vice Chm., Cons. Parly Envmt Cttee, 1993–. FRSA. *Recreations:* walking, reading, architectural history. *Address:* c/o House of Commons, SW1A 0AA. *Club:* Carlton.

THOMPSON; *see* Pullein-Thompson.

THOMPSON, Alan, CB 1978; Chairman, Review Group on the Youth Service, 1981–82; *b* 16 July 1920; *s* of Herbert and Esther Thompson; *m* 1944, Joyce Nora Banks; two *s* one *d*. *Educ:* Carlisle Grammar Sch.; Queen's Coll., Oxford. Joined Min. of Education, 1946; Private Sec. to Minister of Education, 1954–56; Asst Sec., Further Education Br., 1956–64; Under Sec., UGC, 1964–71; Under Sec., Science Br., DES, 1971–75; Dep. Sec., DES, 1975–80. *Address:* 1 Haven Close, Wimbledon, SW19 5JW.

THOMPSON, Prof. Alan Eric; Professor of the Economics of Government, 1972–87, Professor Emeritus, since 1987, Heriot-Watt University; *b* 16 Sept. 1924; *o c* of late Eric Joseph Thompson and of Florence Thompson; *m* 1960, Mary Heather Long; three *s* one *d*. *Educ:* University of Edinburgh (MA 1949, MA (Hons Class I, Economic Science), 1951, PhD 1953, Carnegie Research Scholar, 1951–52). FSAScot 1995. Served army (including service with Central Mediterranean Forces), World War II. Asst in Political Economy, 1952–53, Lectr in Economics (formerly Political Economy), 1953–59, and 1964–71, Univ. of Edinburgh. Parly Adviser to Scottish Television, 1966–76; Scottish Governor, BBC, 1976–79. Visiting Professor, Graduate School of Business, Stanford Univ., USA, 1966, 1968. Contested (Lab) Galloway, 1950 and 1951; MP (Lab) Dunfermline, 1959–64. Mem., Speaker's Parly Delegn to USA, 1962. Chm., Adv. Bd on Economics Educn (Esmée Fairbairn Research Project), 1970–76; Jt Chm., Scottish-Soviet Co-ordinating Cttee for Trade and Industry, 1985–; Member: Scottish Cttee, Public Schools Commn, 1969–70; Cttee enquiring into conditions of service life for young servicemen, 1969; Scottish Council for Adult Educn in HM Forces, 1973–; Jt Mil. Educn Cttee, Edinburgh and Heriot-Watt Univs, 1975–; Local Govt Boundary Commn for Scotland, 1975–82; Royal Fine Art Commn for Scotland, 1975–80; Adv. Bd, Defence Finance Unit, Heriot-Watt Univ., 1987–90; Chm., Northern Offshore (Maritime) Resources Study, 1974–77; Chm., Edinburgh Cttee, Peace Through NATO, 1984–. Parly Adviser, Pharmaceutical Gen. Council (Scotland), 1984–. Hon. Vice-Pres., Assoc. of Nazi War Camp Survivors, 1960–; Pres., Edinburgh Amenity and Transport Assoc., 1970–75; Dir, Scottish AIDS Res. Foundn, 1988–. Chm. of Governors, Newbattle Abbey Coll., 1980–82 (Governor, 1975–82); Governor, Leith Nautical Coll., 1981–;85 Trustee, Bell's Nautical Trust, 1981–85. Has broadcast and appeared on TV (economic and political talks and discussions) in Britain and USA. FRSA 1972. *Publications:* Development of Economic Doctrine (jtly), 1980; contribs to learned journals. *Recreations:* writing children's stories and plays, bridge, croquet. *Address:* 11 Upper Gray Street, Edinburgh EH9 1SN. *T:* 0131–667 2140; Ardtrostan Cottage, St Fillans, Perthshire PH6 2NL. *T:* St Fillans (01764) 685275. *Clubs:* New, Edinburgh University Staff (Edinburgh); Loch Earn Sailing.

THOMPSON, Anthony Arthur Richard; QC 1980; **His Honour Judge Anthony Thompson;** a Circuit Judge, since 1992; Liaison Judge for Cornwall, since 1993; *b* 4 July 1932; *s* of late William Frank McGregor Thompson and Doris Louise Thompson (*née* Hill); *m* 1958, Françoise Alix Marie Reynier; two *s* one *d* (and one *s* decd). *Educ:* Latymer Upper Sch.; University Coll., Oxford; La Sorbonne. FCIArb 1991. Called to the Bar, Inner Temple, 1957, Bencher, 1986; admitted to Paris Bar, 1988; a Recorder, 1985–92. Chm., Bar European Gp, 1984–86 (Vice-Chm., 1982–84); Mem., Internat. Relations Cttee, Bar Council, 1984–86. QC, St Vincent and the Grenadines, 1986. Contested (Lab) Arundel and Shoreham, Oct. 1964. *Recreations:* food and wine, lawn tennis, theatre, cinema, 19th century music, 20th century painting. *Address:* Truro Combined Court Centre, Courts of Justice, Edward Street, Truro, Cornwall TR1 2PB. *Club:* Roehampton.

THOMPSON, Aubrey Gordon D.; *see* Denton-Thompson.

THOMPSON, Charles Allister; HM Diplomatic Service, retired; *b* 21 July 1922; *yr s* of late Herbert Ivie and Margaret (*née* Browne-Webber) Thompson, Managua, Nicaragua; *m* 1950, Jean Margaret, *er d* of late Alexander Bruce Dickson; one *s* two *d* (and one *s* decd). *Educ:* Haileybury; Hertford Coll., Oxford (MA, BLitt). War Service, 1942–46, 1st King's Dragoon Guards. Joined Foreign Service (now Diplomatic Service), 1947, and served in FO until 1949; 3rd Sec., Prague, 1949–50; 2nd Sec. (Commercial), Mexico City, 1950–53; FO 1953–56; 1st Sec., Karachi, 1956–59; Head of Chancery, Luxembourg, 1959–62; FO, 1962–65; Counsellor, 1965; Dep. Consul-Gen., New York, 1965–67; Dep. High Comr, Port of Spain, 1967–70; HM Consul-Gen., Philadelphia, 1970–74; Vis. Fellow, Centre for Internat. Studies, LSE, 1974–75; Head of Training Dept, FCO, and Dir, Diplomatic Service Language Centre, 1975–76. Founding Chm., HELP Jávea, 1978. *Recreations:* gardening, golf, gerontology. *Address:* Calle Carrasquetes 17, MGCA 212, Jávea, 03737 Alicante, Spain. *T:* (6) 5792283.

THOMPSON, Charles Norman, CBE 1978; CChem; FRSC; Head of Research and Development Liaison, and Health, Safety and Environment Administration, Shell UK Ltd, 1978–82, retired; Consultant to Shell UK Ltd, since 1982; *b* 23 Oct. 1922; *s* of Robert Norman Thompson and Evelyn Tivendale Thompson (*née* Wood); *m* 1946, Pamela Margaret Wicks; one *d*. *Educ:* Birkenhead Institute; Liverpool Univ. (BSc). Research Chemist, Thornton Research Centre (Shell Refining & Marketing Co. Ltd), 1943; Lectr, Petroleum Chemistry and Technology, Liverpool Coll. of Technology, 1947–51; Personnel Supt and Dep. Associate Manager, Thornton Research Centre, Shell Research Ltd, 1959–61; Dir (Res. Admin), Shell Research Ltd, 1961–78. Mem. Council, 1976–82, Vice Pres., 1977–80, 1981–82, Inst. of Petroleum (Chm., Res. Adv. Cttee, 1973–82). Pres., RIC, 1976–78. Chairman: Professional Affairs Bd, 1980–84, Water Chemistry Forum, 1987–90, RSC; Council of Science and Technology Insts, 1981–83 (Chm., Health Care Scientific Adv. Cttee, 1986–94); Bd Mem., Thames Water Authority, 1980–87; Member: Technician Educn Council, 1980–83; Ct, Univ. of Surrey, 1980–; Parly and Scientific Cttee, 1976–. *Publications:* Reviews of Petroleum Technology, vol. 13: insulating and hydraulic oils, 1953; numerous papers in Jl Inst. Petroleum, Chem. and Ind., Chem. in Brit., on hydrocarbon dielectrics, insulating oils, diffusion as rate-limiting factor in oxidation, antioxidants in the oil industry, mechanism of copper catalysis in insulating oil oxidation, scientific manpower, etc. *Recreations:* golf, bowls. *Address:* Delamere, Horsell Park, Woking, Surrey GU21 4LW. *T:* Woking (01483) 714939.

THOMPSON, Maj.-Gen. Christopher Noel, CB 1988; *b* 25 Dec. 1932; *s* of late Brig. William Gordon Starkey Thompson and Kathleen Elizabeth (*née* Craven); *m* 1964, Margaret (*née* Longsworth); one *s* twin *d*. *Educ:* Wellington College; RMA Sandhurst; Sidney Sussex College, Cambridge (BA); University College London. Commissioned RE, 1953; served BAOR, 1957–59; Bomb Disposal, UK, 1959–62; Aden, 1963–66; Canada, 1966–68; OC 13 Field Survey Sqn, 1969–70; USA, 1971–75; CO 42 Survey Engr Regt, 1975–77; Dep. Dir, Planning and Develt, Ordnance Survey, 1978–79; Dir, Surveys and Production, Ordnance Survey, 1980–83; Dir of Mil. Survey, MoD, 1984–87. Col Comdt, RE, 1987–92. Pres., Commission D, European Organisation for Experimental Photogrammetric Research, 1980–87. *Publications:* articles on surveying and mapping in Chartered Surveyor, Photogrammetric Record. *Recreations:* sailing, tennis, gardening, house restoration. *Address:* Burgh House, Burgh-by-Sands, Carlisle CA5 6AN.

THOMPSON, Lt-Col Sir Christopher (Peile), 6th Bt *cr* 1890; charity consultant, since 1993; non-executive Chairman, Nuclear Decommissioning Ltd, since 1995 (Director, 1994–95); *b* 21 Dec. 1944; *s* of Sir Peile Thompson, 5th Bt, OBE, and Barbara Johnson (*d* 1993), *d* of late H. J. Rampling; *S* father, 1985; *m* 1969, Anna Elizabeth, *d* of Major Arthur Callander; one *s* one *d*. *Educ:* Marlborough; RMA Sandhurst. Commnd 11th Hussars (PAO), 1965; Tank Troop Leader and Reconnaissance Troop Leader, 11th Hussars, 1965–69; Gunnery Instructor, RAC Gunnery Sch., 1970–72; Sqdn Second i/c, A Sqdn, Royal Hussars, 1972–75; GSO 3 Intelligence, Allied Staff, Berlin, 1975–76; RMCS Shrivenham, 1977; Staff Coll., Camberley, 1978; DAAG (a) M2 (A) (Officer Manning), MoD, 1978–81; C Sqdn Ldr, Royal Hussars, 1981–83; GSO 2 (Operational Requirements), HQ DRAC, 1983–85; CO, Royal Hussars (PWO), 1985–87; SO1, Sen. Officers Tactics Div., 1987–90, retd. Equerry to HRH Prince Michael of Kent, 1989– (Private Sec., 1990–92). Dir, Hyde Park Appeal, 1990–; Trustee: Bike Aid, 1990–; Queen Elizabeth Gate Appeal, 1990–; Tusk, 1994–; Antigua Trust, 1995–. *Recreations:* fishing, shooting, ski-ing, reading, gardening, sailing, Cresta Run, golf. *Heir: s* Peile Richard Thompson, *b* 3 March 1975. *Address:* c/o Barclays Bank, PO Box 8, 13 Library Place, St Helier, Jersey. *Clubs:* Cavalry and Guards, Woodroffe's; St Moritz Tobogganing.

THOMPSON, Christopher Ronald; Senior Partner, Aldenham Business Services Ltd, since 1984; *b* 14 Dec. 1927; *s* of late Col S. J. Thompson, DSO, DL and Margaret Thompson (née Green); *m* 1949, Rachael Meynell; one *s* one *d* (and one *s* decd). *Educ:* Shrewsbury School; Trinity College, Cambridge. 1st Bn KSLI (Lieut), 1946–48. Dir, John Thompson Ltd, 1954–68, Chm., 1969; Dir, Rockwell-Thompson Ltd, 1973–74; Vice-Pres., Rockwell Europe, 1974–78. Chairman: NEI Internat., 1979–84; Wynn Electronics, 1983–87; Hoccum Developments Ltd, 1985–; John Sutcliffe Shipping Ltd, 1986–89; Director: Saraswati Syndicate pte India, 1954–; Barclays Bank Birmingham Bd, 1974–87; G. T. Japan Investment Trust, 1983–; Isotron plc, 1984–; Craven Grain Storage Ltd, 1984–; Plessey Co. plc, 1988–89. Member: Overseas Projects Bd, BOTB, 1981–84; Sino-British Trade Council, 1983–85.; Indo-British Industrial Forum, 1987–. Pres., BEAMA, 1984–85. Vice-Chm., CLA Cttee for Shropshire, 1993–. Chm., Anglo-Venezuelan Soc., 1981–85. Trustee: Hereford Cathedral Trust, 1984–; Mappa Mundi Trust, 1990–. High Sheriff, Shropshire, 1984–85. *Recreations:* flyfishing, shooting, forestry. *Address:* Aldenham Park, near Bridgnorth, Shropshire WV16 4RN. *T:* Morville (01746) 714218. *Club:* Boodle's.

THOMPSON, Clive Hepworth; Director, John Russell Associates, since 1995; Deputy Chairman, Audit Commission, since 1995 (Member, since 1990); *b* 7 July 1937; *s* of late Sidney Hepworth Thompson and Vera Wynne; *m* 1962, Joan Mary Kershaw; two *s*. *Educ:* Holywell Grammar Sch.; Manchester Univ. (BTech, MSc); Harvard Business Sch. BP Chemicals: Technical and Management appts; Works Gen. Manager, Barry Plant, 1975–78, Baglan Bay Plant, 1978–82; Gen. Manager, later Dir, Worldwide Petrochemicals, Production and Human Resources, 1982–90; Vice-Pres., Ops and Supply, Arco Chemical Europe, 1990–95. Member: Welsh Water Authy, 1980–82; Chem. Industries Assoc. Cttees, 1985–; Chm., Inter-Company Productivity Group, 1987–90 (Mem., 1983–90). Liveryman, Horners' Co. (Mem., Ct of Assts, 1995–). *Publications:* contribs to newspapers and learned jls on petrochemicals, environment policy and costs, quality management. *Recreations:* hill walking, opera, music, golf, reading history. *Address:* Dwr Golau, 13 Heronscourt, Lightwater, Surrey GU18 5SW. *T:* Bagshot (01276) 476410. *Club:* Harvard Business School.

THOMPSON, Colin Edward, CBE 1983; FRSE 1978; Director, National Galleries of Scotland, 1977–84; *b* 2 Nov. 1919; *s* of late Edward Vincent Thompson, CB, and Jessie Forbes Cameron; *m* 1950, Jean Agnes Jardine O'Connell; one *s* one *d*. *Educ:* Sedbergh Sch.; King's College, Cambridge; Chelsea Polytechnic Sch. of Art. MA (Cantab). FMA. FS Wing CMP, 1940–41; Foreign Office, 1941–45. Lectr, Bath Acad. of Art, Corsham, 1948–54; Asst Keeper, 1954, Keeper, 1967, National Gall. of Scotland. Sen. Adviser, Res. Centre in Art Educn, Bath Acad. of Art, 1962–65; Chm., Scottish Museums Council, 1984–87; Member: Scottish Arts Council, 1976–83; Edinburgh Fest. Council, 1979–82; Bd of Governors, Edinburgh Coll. of Art, 1985–91 (Chm., 1989–91); Scottish Mining Museum Trust, 1987– (Chm., 1992–). DUniv Edinburgh, 1985. *Publications:* (with Lorne Campbell) Hugo van der Goes and the Trinity Panels in Edinburgh, 1974; Exploring Museums: Scotland, 1990; guide books, catalogues and a history of the National Gallery of Scotland; articles in Burlington Magazine, Museums Jl, etc. *Address:* Edenkerry, Lasswade, Midlothian EH18 1LW. *T:* 0131–663 7927.

See also D. C. Thompson.

THOMPSON, David Brian; Chairman, Union Square plc, 1987–91; *b* 4 April 1936; *s* of Bernard Thompson and Rosamund Dee; *m* 1962, Patricia Henchley; one *s* two *d*. *Educ:* Haileybury and ISC. Jt Man. Dir, B. Thompson Ltd, 1960–70; Chm. and co-founder, 1974–84, Jt Chm., 1984–87, Dir, 1987–89, Hillsdown Holdings plc. *Recreations:* family, business, breeding and racing of bloodstock, swimming. *Address:* 1 Dover Street, W1X 3PJ. *T:* 0171–491 8839.

THOMPSON, David Richard, CB 1974; QC 1980; Master of the Crown Office and Queen's Coroner and Attorney, Registrar of Criminal Appeals and of the Courts Martial Appeal Court, 1965–88; *b* 11 Feb. 1916; *s* of William George Thompson; *m* 1952, Sally Jennifer Rowntree Thompson (*née* Stockton); two *s* four *d*. *Educ:* Alleyn's Sch., Dulwich; Jesus Coll., Oxford. BA Physics 1938. Royal Corps of Signals, 1939–46 (despatches). Called to Bar, Lincoln's Inn, 1946, Bencher, 1982. Office of DPP, 1948–54; Dep. Asst Registrar, then Asst Registrar, Court of Criminal Appeal, 1954–65. *Publications:* (with H. W. Wollaston) Court of Appeal Criminal Division, 1969; (with Morrish and McLean) Proceedings in the Criminal Division of the Court of Appeal, 1979. *Recreation:* personal computer word processor. *Address:* 54 Highbury Grove, N5 2AG. *T:* 0171–226 6514.

THOMPSON, David Robin Bibby, TD 1987; Director, Bibby Line Ltd, 1974–87; Deputy Chairman, Rural Development Commission, since 1992 (Member, since 1986); *b* 23 July 1946; *s* of Noel Denis Thompson and Cynthia Joan (*née* Bibby); *m* 1971, Caroline Ann Foster; one *s* one *d*. *Educ:* Uppingham Sch.; Mons Officer Cadet Sch. Short service commn, QRIH, 1965; comd Queen's Own Yeomanry (TA), 1984–87; Hon. ADC to the Queen, 1987–90. Member: Council, Royal Agricl Soc. of England, 1985–91; Bd, Housing Corp., 1989–; Chm., S Shropshire Housing Assoc., 1991–. High Sheriff, Shropshire, 1989. *Recreations:* ski-ing, horses, conservation. *Address:* Sansaw Hall, Clive, Shrewsbury, Shropshire SY4 3JR. *Club:* Cavalry and Guards.

THOMPSON, Dennis Cameron; Founder, Journal of World Trade (formerly Journal of World Trade Law), 1967 (Editor, 1977–86); *b* 25 Oct. 1914; *s* of late Edward Vincent Thompson, CB, and late Jessie Forbes; *m* 1959, Maria von Skramlik; one *d*. *Educ:* Oundle; King's Coll., Cambridge. Nat. Sci. Tripos Pt I, Law Pt II; MA 1949. RAF, 1940–45: Sqdn-Ldr, personnel staff, Desert Air Force, and Germany. Called to Bar, Inner Temple, 1939; practised London and Midland Circuit, 1946–63; Asst Dir (European Law), British Inst. of Internat. and Comparative Law, 1963–66; Legal Adviser, Secretariat of EFTA, Geneva, 1967–73; participated in negotiations for European Patent Convention, 1969–73; Dir, Restrictive Practices and Dominant Positions, EEC, 1973–76; Consultant to UNCTAD on Restrictive Business Practices and Transfer of Technol., 1977–82. Convenor, Geneva Conf., Antarctica, the Environment and the Future, 1992; Pres., Internat. Cttee for Cryosphere Ecosystems, Geneva, 1993–; Mem. Council, Geneva Internat. Peace Res. Inst., 1991–. Vis. Prof., Georgia Univ. Sch. of Law, Athens, GA, 1978. Trustee, Federal Trust, 1962–71. *Publications:* (ed) Kennedy, CIF Contracts, 3rd edn 1959; (with Alan Campbell) Common Market Law, 1962; The Proposal for a European Company, 1969; articles in Internat. and Compar. Law Quarterly; (ed jtly) Common Market Law Review, 1963–67. *Recreations:* walking, Antarctic studies. *Address:* 8 rue des Belles Filles, 1299 Crans, Switzerland. *T:* (22) 7761687, *Fax:* (22) 7767303. *Club:* United Oxford & Cambridge University.

See also C. E. Thompson.

THOMPSON, Sir Donald, Kt 1992; MP (C) Calder Valley, since 1983 (Sowerby, 1979–83); *b* 13 Nov. 1931; *s* of Geoffrey and Rachel Thompson; *m* 1957, Patricia Ann Hopkins; two *s*. Formerly Dir, Halifax Farmers' Trading Assoc.; Man. Dir, Armadillo Plastics (Glass Fibre Manufacturers), 1974–79, Dir, 1979–. Member: WR CC, 1967–74; W Yorks CC, 1974–75; Calderdale Dist Council, 1975–79. Contested (C): Batley and Morley, 1970; Sowerby, Feb. and Oct. 1974. An Asst Govt Whip, then a Lord Comr of HM Treasury, 1981–86; Parly Sec., MAFF, 1986–89. A Govt Whip, Council of Europe and WEU, 1990–. Chm., Cons. Candidates' Assoc., 1972–74. *Recreations:* Rugby football, poor golf, conversation. *Address:* House of Commons, SW1A 0AA. *T:* 0171–219 6215. *Clubs:* Beefsteak, St Stephen's Constitutional; Brodleians (Hipperholme); Octave (Elland).

THOMPSON, Donald Henry, MA Oxon; Headmaster, Chigwell School, Essex, 1947–71; *b* 29 Aug. 1911; *s* of H. R. Thompson, solicitor, Swansea; *m* 1942, Helen Mary Wray; four *s*. *Educ:* Shrewsbury School; Merton College, Oxford. Postmaster in Classics, Merton Coll., Oxford, 1930; 1st Class Hon. Mod., 1932; 1st Class Literae Humaniores, 1934; Asst Master Haileybury Coll., Hertford, 1934–46. Served War of 1939–45, RA, 1940–45. JP Essex, 1955–81. *Recreations:* cricket, bird-watching, conservation. *Address:* Glasses Farm, Holcombe Bath, Somerset BA3 5EQ. *T:* Stratton-on-Fosse (01761) 232322.

THOMPSON, Emma; actor; *b* 15 April 1959; *d* of Eric Norman Thompson and Phyllida Ann Law; *m* 1989, Kenneth Charles Branagh, *qv*. *Educ:* Newnham College, Cambridge (MA). *Stage:* Footlights, Australia, 1982; Me and My Girl, 1984; Look Back in Anger, 1989; King Lear, 1989; A Midsummer Night's Dream, 1989; *films:* Henry V, 1988; The Tall Guy, 1988; Impromptu, 1989; Dead Again, 1990; Howards End, 1992 (BAFTA Best Actress, 1993; Academy Award, 1993); Peter's Friends, 1992; Much Ado About Nothing, 1993; The Remains of the Day, 1993; In the Name of the Father, 1993; Junior, 1994; Carrington, 1995; *television series and serials:* Alfresco, 1983; Tutti Frutti, 1986 (BAFTA

Best Actress); Fortunes of War, 1986 (BAFTA Best Actress); Thompson, 1987. *Recreations:* reading, walking, cooking, acting. *Address:* Lorraine Hamilton Management, 19 Denmark Street, Soho, WC2H 8NA.

THOMPSON, Eric John, CB 1995; Deputy Director, Office of Population Censuses and Surveys, 1989–94; *b* Beverley, E Yorks, 26 Sept. 1934; *o s* of late Herbert William Thompson and Florence Thompson (*née* Brewer). *Educ:* Beverley Grammar Sch.; London School of Economics (BScEcon). National Service: Pilot Officer in Dept of Scientific Adviser to Air Ministry, 1956–58. Operations Planning Dept, International Computers and Tabulators Ltd, 1958–60; Supply and Planning Dept, Shell International Petroleum Co. Ltd, 1960–65; Head of Regional Demography Unit, General Register Office, 1965–67; Head of Population Studies Section, 1967–72, Asst Dir of Intelligence, 1972–74, GLC Research and Intelligence Unit; Head of Social Monitoring Branch, Central Statistical Office, 1975–80; Dir of Statistics, Dept of Transport, 1980–89. Royal Statistical Society: Fellow, 1956; Mem. Council 1981–85; Vice-Pres., 1982–83; Chm., Official Stats Section, 1992–94. Member: Data Archive Adv. Cttee, ESRC, 1993–; British Computer Soc., 1959–76 (MBCS 1968). Member: East Yorkshire Local History Soc., 1974–; Housman Soc., 1976–; Richard III Soc., 1979– (Mem. Cttee, 1984–); Selden Soc., 1987–; Friends of British Library, 1989–; Tolkien Soc., 1989–; London Topographical Soc., 1991–; Trustee, Richard III and Yorkist Hist. Trust, 1985–. *Publications:* ed, Social Trends, Nos 6–10, 1975–80; contrib. chapters in books on regional and urban planning and on statistical computing; articles and reviews in GLC Intelligence Unit's quarterly bulletin and various statistical jls; article on historical bibliography in The Ricardian. *Recreations:* reading and collecting books, British mediæval history, English literature. *Address:* 120 Melrose Avenue, NW2 4JX.

THOMPSON, Ernest; *see* Thompson, R. E.

THOMPSON, Prof. Francis Michael Longstreth, CBE 1992; FBA 1979; Director, Institute of Historical Research, and Professor of History in the University of London, 1977–90, now Emeritus Professor; *b* 13 Aug. 1925; *s* of late Francis Longstreth-Thompson, OBE; *m* 1951, Anne Challoner; two *s* one *d*. *Educ:* Bootham Sch., York; Queen's Coll., Oxford (Hastings Schol.; MA, DPhil). ARICS 1968. War service, with Indian Artillery, 1943–47; James Bryce Sen. Schol., Oxford, 1949–50; Harmsworth Sen. Schol., Merton Coll., Oxford, 1949–51; Lectr in History, UCL, 1951–63; Reader in Economic History, UCL, 1963–68; Prof. of Modern Hist., Univ. of London, and Head of Dept of Hist., Bedford Coll., London, 1968–77. Joint Editor, Economic History Review, 1968–80. Sec., British Nat. Cttee of Historical Scis, 1978–94; British Mem., Standing Cttee for Humanities, European Sci. Foundn, 1983–93; President: Economic Hist. Soc., 1983–86; RHistS, 1988–92 (Fellow, 1964); British Agricl Hist. Soc., 1989–92; Hon. Treas., Internat. Econ. History Assoc., 1986–94. Member: Senate and Academic Council, Univ. of London, 1970–78; Senate and Collegiate Council, 1981–89. Ford's Lectr, Oxford Univ., 1994. Fellow, RHBNC, 1992–94. DUniv. *Publications:* English Landed Society in the Nineteenth Century, 1963; Chartered Surveyors: the growth of a profession, 1968; Victorian England: the horse-drawn society, 1970; Countrysides, in The Nineteenth Century, ed Asa Briggs, 1970; Hampstead: building a borough, 1650–1964, 1974; introd. to General Report on Gosford Estates in County Armagh 1821, by William Greig, 1976; Britain, in European Landed Elites in the Nineteenth Century, ed David Spring, 1977; Landowners and Farmers, in The Faces of Europe, ed Alan Bullock, 1980; 2 chapters in The Victorian Countryside, ed G. E. Mingay, 1981; (ed) The Rise of Suburbia, 1982; (ed) Horses in European Economic History, 1983; Towns, Industry and the Victorian Landscape, in The English Landscape, ed S. R. J. Woodell, 1985; Private Property and Public Policy, in Salisbury: The Man and his Policies, ed Lord Blake and Hugh Cecil, 1987; Rise of Respectable Society: a social history of Victorian Britain, 1988; (ed) The Cambridge Social History of Britain 1750–1950, vol. 1 Regions and Communities, vol. 2 People and their Environment, vol. 3 Social Agencies and Social Institutions, 1990; (ed) The University of London and the World of Learning 1836–1986, 1990; (ed) Landowners, Capitalists, and Entrepreneurs: essays for Sir John Habakkuk, 1994; numerous articles in Economic History Review, History, English Historical Review, etc. *Recreations:* gardening, walking, carpentry, tennis. *Address:* Holly Cottage, Sheepcote Lane, Wheathampstead, Herts AL4 8NJ. *T:* Wheathampstead (01582) 833129.

THOMPSON, Dr Frank Derek, FRCP; Senior Consultant Nephrologist, St Peter's Group of Hospitals, since 1981; Dean, Institute of Urology, London University, since 1985; *b* 18 May 1939; *s* of Frank and Irene Thompson; *m* 1964, Elizabeth Ann Sherwood; two *s* one *d*. *Educ:* St Catharine's College, Cambridge (MA, MB BChir); St Mary's Hosp., London. FRCP 1983. Sen. Lectr, Inst. of Urology, 1974; Consultant Nephrologist to Harefield and Mount Vernon Hosps, 1979–; Hon. Consultant Nephrologist to Nat. Heart Hosp., 1980–; Vice-Dean, Faculty of Clinical Science, University College and Middx Sch. of Medicine, 1990–. *Publications:* Disorders of the Kidney and Urinary Tract, 1987; contribs to BMJ, Clinical Nephrology. *Recreations:* golf, gardening, ornithology. *Address:* 27 Moor Park Road, Northwood, Middx HA6 2DL. *T:* Northwood (019274) 27361. *Club:* Moor Park Golf.

THOMPSON, Rt. Rev. Geoffrey Hewlett; *see* Exeter, Bishop of.

THOMPSON, Rev. George H.; Administrator, St Margaret of Scotland, Irvine, since 1993; *b* Sept. 1928. *Educ:* Dalry Sch.; Kirkcudbright Acad.; Edinburgh Univ. Teacher, modern languages, Kirkcudbright Academy; Principal Teacher of French, 1979–85, Principal Teacher of Modern Languages, 1985–86, Annan Acad., Dumfriesshire. Contested (SNP): Galloway, Feb. 1974, 1979; Galloway and Upper Nithsdale, 1983. Former SNP Asst Nat. Sec.; MP (SNP) Galloway, Oct. 1974–1979; SNP Spokesman: on health, Oct. 1974–79; on forestry, 1975. Deacon, RC dio. of Galloway, 1989, priest 1989; Asst Priest, St Teresa's, Dumfries, 1989–93. *Address:* St Margaret of Scotland, Castlepark, Irvine KA12 9PR. *T:* Irvine (01294) 272852.

THOMPSON, Sir Gilbert (Williamson), Kt 1993; OBE 1985; Chief Executive, 1981–93, and Board Member, 1986–93, Manchester Airport plc; *b* 1 March 1930; *s* of Henry Gordon Thompson and Isabella Thompson; *m* 1954, Dorothy Millar; two *d*. *Educ:* London Business Sch.; Manchester Business Sch. British European Airways, later British Airways: mgt trainee, Belfast, 1950; Regl Manager, Los Angeles, 1965–67; Manager, Irish Republic, 1967–69; General Manager: USA, 1969–72; Scotland, 1972–74; N of England, 1974–81. Non-executive Chairman: Sunset Holidays, 1994–; Global Forum; Credit & Investment Reconstruction Ltd; non-executive Director: Eurocamp; Fortune Radio 1458. Pres., British Amer. Business Gp; Member: British Amer. Business Council; Commonwealth Bid Cttee; Olympic Bid Cttee. Vice Pres., Sports Aid Soc. Hon. DLitt Salford, 1993. *Recreations:* golf, bridge, soccer, jogging, keep fit. *Address:* Longridge, 29 Hilltop Hale, Cheshire WA15 0NN. *T:* 0161–980 1429.

THOMPSON, Godfrey; *see* Thompson, W. G.

THOMPSON, Sir Godfrey James M.; see Milton-Thompson.

THOMPSON, Rt. Rev. Hewlett; *see* Thompson, Rt Rev. G. H.

THOMPSON, Howard; *see* Thompson, James H.

THOMPSON, Vice-Adm. Sir Hugh (Leslie Owen), KBE 1987; FEng 1989; FIMechE; Deputy Controller of the Navy and Chief Above-Water Systems Executive (formerly Deputy Controller Warships), Ministry of Defence, 1986–89; Chief Naval Engineer Officer, 1987–89; retired; *b* 2 April 1931; *s* of Hugh Thompson and Elsie Standish (*née* Owen); *m* 1st, 1957, Sheila Jean Finch (*d* 1974); one *s* two *d*; 2nd, 1977, Rosemary Ann (*née* Oliver). *Educ:* Royal Belfast Academical Institution; RNC Dartmouth; RNEC Manadon. Asst Dir, Submarines Mechanical, 1976–79; RCDS, 1980; Dep. Dir, Systems 1, 1981–83; Dir Gen., Marine Engineering, 1983–84; Dir Gen. Surface Ships, MoD, 1984–86. *Recreations:* railways, woodwork. *Clubs:* Army and Navy; Bath and County (Bath).

THOMPSON, (Hugh) Patrick; MP (C) Norwich North, since 1983; *b* 21 Oct. 1935; *s* of late Gerald Leopold Thompson and of Kathleen Mary Landsdown Thompson; *m* 1962, Kathleen Howson. *Educ:* Felsted Sch., Essex; Emmanuel Coll., Cambridge (MA). MInstP 1964. Nat. Service, 2nd Lieut, KOYLI, 1957–59; TA, Manchester, 1960–65; Gresham's Sch., CCF, 1965–82 (CFM 1980); Major, retd. Engr, English Electric Valve Co., Chelmsford, 1959–60; Sixth Form Physics Master: Manchester Grammar Sch., 1960–65; Gresham's Sch., Holt, 1965–83. Parliamentary Private Secretary: to Minister of State for Transport, 1987–88; to Minister of State, Dept of Social Security, 1988–89; to Minister for Health, 1992–94. Member: Parly and Scientific Cttee, 1983–; Select Cttee, Educn, Science and the Arts, 1991–92; Speaker's Panel of Chairmen, 1994–; Founder Mem., All Party Gp for Engrg Develt, 1985–; Secretary: Cons. Back Bench Energy Cttee, 1986–87; Cons. Back Bench European Cttee, 1991–92. *Publication:* Elementary Calculations in Physics, 1963. *Recreations:* travel, music, gardening. *Address:* c/o House of Commons, SW1A 0AA. *Club:* Norfolk (Norwich).

THOMPSON, Sir (Humphrey) Simon M.; *see* Meysey-Thompson.

THOMPSON, Ian; County Treasurer, Berkshire County Council, since 1993; *b* 20 May 1951; *s* of Eber Edward Thompson and Edith (*née* Gilchrist); *m* 1972, Anne Rosalind Clouston (marr. diss. 1995); one *d*. *Educ:* Workington Grammar Sch.; Univ. of Hull (BSc). IPFA. With Humberside CC, 1974–80; Northamptonshire County Council, 1980–89; Chief Acctnt, 1986–88; Sen. Asst Educn Officer, 1988–89; Sen. Asst Co. Treas., Berks CC, 1989–93. *Recreations:* fell-walking, playing squash, playing trains. *Address:* PO Box 900, Shire Hall, Reading, Berks RG2 9XA. *T:* Reading (01734) 234100.

THOMPSON, Dr (Ian) McKim; Deputy Secretary, British Medical Association, since 1985 (Senior Under Secretary, 1969–85); *b* 19 Aug. 1938; *s* of late J. W. Thompson and of Dr E. M. Thompson; *m* 1962, Dr Veronica Jane Richards; two *s* one *d*. *Educ:* Epsom Coll.; Birmingham Univ. (MB, ChB 1961). FRSM 1987. Lectr in Pathology, Univ. of Birmingham, 1964–67; Sen. Registrar, Birmingham RHB, 1967–69. Consulting Forensic Pathologist to HM Coroner, City of Birmingham, 1966–. Part time Tutor, Dept of Adult and Continuing Educn, Keele Univ., 1985–. Member: GMC, 1979–94; Birmingham Med. Inst. Hon. Collegian, Med. Colls of Spain, 1975. *Publications:* (ed) The Hospital Gazeteer, 1972; (ed) BMA Handbook for Hospital Junior Doctors, 1977, 5th edn 1990; (ed) BMA Handbook for Trainee Doctors in General Practice, 1982, 3rd edn 1985; various medical scientific papers. *Recreations:* inland waterways, rambling. *Address:* Weir Cottage, Millbank, Fladbury, Pershore, Worcs WR10 2QA. *T:* Evesham (01386) 860668.

THOMPSON, James, FLA; University Librarian, University of Birmingham, 1987–95; *b* 11 Jan. 1932; *s* of James Thompson and Mary Margaret Thompson (*née* Harland); *m* 1st, 1958, Mary Josephine McAndrew (marr. diss. 1987); one *s* one *d*; 2nd, 1988, Susan Lesley Challans. *Educ:* St Cuthbert's Grammar Sch.; Univ. of Durham (BA 1st Cl. Hons English). FLA 1963. Newcastle City Libraries, 1948–59; Nottingham Univ. Liby, 1959–63; Sen. Asst Librarian, UEA, 1963–65; Dep. Librarian, Univ. of Glasgow, 1965–67; Univ. Librarian, Univ. of Reading, 1967–87. Member: Council, LA, 1972–74; Berks Co. Liby Sub-cttee, 1973–87; SCONUL Council, 1983–86. Pres., Reading AUT, 1981–83. Project Hd, Location Register of Twentieth Century English Literary MSS and Letters, 1982–87. *Publications:* The Librarian and English Literature, 1968, 2nd edn as English Studies, 1971; Books: an anthology, 1968; An Introduction to University Library Administration, 1970, 4th edn 1987 (Spanish edn 1989); Library Power, 1974; A History of the Principles of Librarianship, 1977; (ed) University Library History, 1980; The End of Libraries, 1982; Redirection of Academic Library Management, 1991; contribs to books, conf. proceedings and jls. *Recreation:* gardening. *Address:* 189 Redditch Road, Kings Norton, Birmingham B38 8RH. *T:* 0121–459 2897.

THOMPSON, James Craig; Chairman and Managing Director, Harvest Publications Ltd, since 1983; *b* 27 Oct. 1933; *s* of Alfred Thompson and Eleanor (*née* Craig); *m* 1957, Catherine (*née* Warburton); one *s* one *d*. *Educ:* Heaton Grammar Sch., Newcastle upon Tyne; Rutherford Coll., Newcastle upon Tyne. Commercial Exec., Belfast Telegraph, Newcastle Chronicle and Journal, Scotsman Publications, Liverpool Post and Echo, 1960–76; Advertising and Marketing Manager, Kent Messenger Gp, 1976–79, Dir, 1972–79; Man. Dir, South Eastern Newspapers, 1975–79; Chm. and Man. Dir, 1973–89, Consultant Dir, 1989–92, Adverkit Internat. Ltd. Dir, Weekly Newspaper Advtg Bureau, 1977. Dir, Ad Builder Ltd, 1971–89. Dir and Chief Exec., Maidstone and Mid Kent Chamber of Commerce and Industry, 1994–. Life Governor, Kent County Agricl Soc., 1976. Hon. Life Mem., Kent CCC, 1978; Mem., Catenian Assoc. (Pres., Maidstone Circle, 1974–75). Chm., Maidstone United Football Club, 1970–92; Pres., Maidstone Invicta Football Club, 1992–. Chm., Southern Football League, 1977–79 (Life Mem., 1985); Pres., The Football Conf., 1989–; Mem. Council, Football Assoc., 1982–92. FInstD; MInstM; MIMgt. Liveryman, Worshipful Co. of Stationers and Newspaper Makers; Freeman, City of London. Distinguished Service Award, Internat. Classified Advertising Assoc., Baltimore, 1968. *Publications:* numerous articles on commercial aspects of newspaper publishing and Association football. *Recreations:* walking, Northumbrian history. *Address:* Prescott House, Otham, Kent ME15 8RL. *T:* Maidstone (01622) 861606. *Clubs:* MCC; Maidstone (Maidstone).

THOMPSON, (James) Howard, OBE 1984; British Council Director in Egypt, since 1993; *b* 26 March 1942; *s* of James Alan Thompson and Edna (*née* Perkins); *m* 1965, Claire Marguerite Dockrell; one *s* one *d*. *Educ:* Northampton Grammar Sch.; Magdalene Coll., Cambridge (BA); Stanford Univ. (MA). English Language Officer, British Council, Yugoslavia, 1966–69; Associate Prof., Punjab Univ., 1970–73; Dep. Representative, British Council, Kenya, 1974–78; Advr, Schs and Further Educn Dept, 1978–80; Educn Attaché, British Embassy, Washington, 1980–84; Dep. Controller, 1984–87, Controller, 1987–89, Science, Technology and Educn Div., British Council; Chm., Educn and Trng Export Cttee, 1988–89; British Council Dir, Indonesia, 1989–92. *Publication:* Teaching English, 1972. *Recreations:* photography, travel. *Address:* 1 Homefield Road, W4 2LN; c/o British Council, 10 Spring Gardens, SW1A 2BN.

THOMPSON, Rt. Rev. James Lawton; *see* Bath and Wells, Bishop of.

THOMPSON, Janet, DPhil; Director General, Forensic Science Service, since 1988; *b* 23 Oct. 1941. *Educ:* Brighton Coll. of Technol. (BSc 1963); Univ. of Oxford (DPhil 1968).

Address: Home Office, 50 Queen Anne's Gate, SW1H 9AT; Priory House, Gooch Street North, Birmingham B5 6QQ.

THOMPSON, Jeff; *see* Thompson, John J.

THOMPSON, John; MP (Lab) Wansbeck, since 1983; *b* 27 Aug. 1928; *s* of Nicholas and Lilian Thompson; *m* 1952, Margaret Clarke; one *s* one *d*. *Educ:* Bothal Sch.; Ashington Mining Coll. Electrical Engr, 1966–83. Councillor: Wansbeck DC, 1974–79; Northumberland CC, 1974–85 (Leader, and Chm., Policy and Resources, and Employment Cttees, 1981–83). An Opposition Whip, 1990–. Mem., Select Cttee on Educn, Science and Arts, 1985–87; Chm., Northern Labour MPs, 1991–92 (Sec., 1985–90). Member: Council of Europe (Chm., Fisheries Sub Cttee, 1995–); WEU (Chm., Rules and Privileges Cttee, 1992–). *Address:* 20 Falstone Crescent, Ashington, Northumberland NE63 0TY. *T:* Ashington (01670) 817830.

THOMPSON, John, MBE 1975; HM Diplomatic Service; Deputy Consul-General and Director of Trade, New York, since 1992; *b* 28 May 1945; *s* of Arthur Thompson and Josephine (*née* Brooke); *m* 1966, Barbara Hopper; one *d*. *Educ:* Whiteheath County Primary Sch., Ruislip, Mddx; St Nicholas Grammar Sch., Northwood, Mddx; Polytechnic of Central London (DMS). Joined FO, 1964; Vice-Consul, Düsseldorf, 1966–69; Consular Officer, later Vice-Consul, Abu Dhabi, 1969–72; Vice-Consul, Phnom Penh, 1972–74; seconded to DTI, 1975–77; First Sec., FCO, 1977–79; First Sec., Hd of Chancery and Consul, Luanda, 1979–81; Consul (Commercial), São Paulo, 1981–85; Assistant Head: S Pacific Dept, FCO, 1985–87; Aid Policy Dept, FCO, 1987–88; High Comr to Vanuatu, 1988–92. *Recreations:* philately, walking, reading, bridge. *Address:* c/o Foreign and Commonwealth Office, King Charles Street, SW1A 2AH. *Club:* Commonwealth Trust.

THOMPSON, John Alan, CMG 1974; HM Diplomatic Service, retired; *b* 21 June 1926; *m* 1956, Maureen Sayers. *Educ:* Bromsgrove Sch.; Brasenose Coll., Oxford. Control Commission for Germany, 1952; Vice-Consul, Hanoi, 1954; Second Sec., Saigon, 1956; Warsaw, 1959; Foreign Office, 1961; First Sec. (Commercial), Havana, 1964; First Sec., FO (later FCO), 1966–75; Counsellor, 1973. *Recreations:* music, mountains. *Address:* Sun House, Hall Street, Long Melford, Suffolk CO10 9HZ. *T:* Sudbury (01787) 378252.

THOMPSON, John Brian, CBE 1980; Director of Radio, Independent Broadcasting Authority, 1973–87; *b* 8 June 1928; *y s* of late John and Lilian Thompson; *m* 1957, Sylvia, *d* of late Thomas Waterhouse, CBE, and of Doris Waterhouse (*née* Gough); two *s* one *d*. *Educ:* St Paul's; Pembroke College, Oxford (BA; MA). Eileen Power Studentship, LSE, 1950; Glaxo Laboratories Ltd, 1950–54; Masius & Fergusson Ltd, 1955; Asst Editor, Truth, 1956–57; Daily Express, 1957–59 (New York Correspondent; Drama Critic); ITN, 1959–60 (Newscaster/Reporter); Editor, Time and Tide, 1960–62; News Editor, The Observer, 1962–66; Editor, Observer Colour Magazine, 1966–70; Publisher and Editorial Dir, BPC Publishing Ltd, 1971; Editor, The Viewer, 1988–90. Vis. Prof., Sch. of Media, Lancashire Poly., 1987–90. Sen. Advr on Radio to Minister of Posts and Telecommunications, 1972; Mem., MoD Study Group on Censorship, 1983. Director: Worlds End Productions Ltd, 1987–; The Observer, 1989–93; Dep. Chm., Zabaxe Gp, 1988–90. Vice-Chm. (radio), EBU, 1986–88. Mem. Delegacy, Goldsmiths' Coll., London, 1986–. Associate Mem., Nuffield Coll., Oxford, 1988–90. Judge, Booker Fiction Prize, 1987; Panel of Selection Bd Chairmen, CS Commn/RAS, 1988–93. Sony Radio special award, 1983. *Address:* 1 Bedwyn Common, Great Bedwyn, Marlborough, Wilts SN8 3HZ. *T:* Marlborough (01672) 870641; 46 Holland Road, W14 8BB. *T:* 0171–602 5276. *Clubs:* Garrick, Groucho.

See also Hon. Sir R. G. Waterhouse.

THOMPSON, (John) Derek T.; *see* Taylor Thompson.

THOMPSON, Prof. John Griggs, PhD; FRS 1979; Rouse Ball Professor of Mathematics, University of Cambridge, 1971–93; Fellow of Churchill College, Cambridge, since 1968; *b* Kansas, 13 Oct. 1932; *s* of John and Eleanor Thompson; *m* 1960, Diane Oenning; one *s* one *d*. *Educ:* Yale (BA 1955); Chicago (PhD 1959); MA Cantab 1972. Prof. of Mathematics, Chicago Univ., 1962–68; Vis. Prof. of Mathematics, Cambridge Univ., 1968–70. Hon. DSc Oxon, 1987. Cole Prize, 1966; Field Medal, 1970; Berwick Prize, London Math. Soc., 1982; Sylvester Medal, Royal Soc., 1985; Wolf Prize, 1992; Poincaré Medal, 1992. *Address:* 16 Millington Road, Cambridge CB3 9HP.

THOMPSON, John Handby, CB 1988; CVO 1994; Ceremonial Officer, Cabinet Office, and Secretary, Political Honours Scrutiny Committee, 1988–94; *b* 21 Feb. 1929; *s* of late Rev. John Thomas Thompson and Clara Handby. *Educ:* Silcoates Sch., Wakefield; St John's Coll., Oxford (MA); Sheffield Univ. (PhD 1991). Served Intell. Corps, 1947–49. HM Inspector of Taxes, 1953–63; Dept of Educn and Science, 1964–88: Schs Council, 1971–73; Asst Sec., 1973; Mem., Prep. Cttee of European Univ. Inst., 1973–75; Dep. Accountant-Gen., 1976–78; Under Sec., 1978; Head of Schs Br. 1, 1978–80; Head of Further and Higher Educn Br. 1, 1980–84; Dir of Estabts and Orgn, 1985–88. Gov., Univ. (formerly Poly.) of N London, 1989–. *Recreations:* reading about Albania, Nonconformist history. *Club:* Reform.

THOMPSON, Prof. John Jeffrey, (Jeff), CBE 1989; PhD; CChem, FRSC; Professor of Education, since 1979, and Director, Centre for the Study of Education in an International Context, since 1992, University of Bath; *b* 13 July 1938; *s* of John Thompson and Elsie May Thompson (*née* Wright); *m* 1963, Kathleen Audrey Gough; three *d*. *Educ:* King George V Sch., Southport; St John's Coll., Cambridge (MA); Balliol Coll., Oxford (MA); PhD (CNAA); DipEd (Oxon). Asst Master, Blundell's Sch., 1961–65; Head of Chemistry, Watford Grammar Sch., 1965–69; Lectr in Educn, KCL, 1968–69; Shell Fellow, UCL, 1969–70; Lectr and Tutor, Dept of Educnl Studies, Oxford Univ., 1970–79; Lectr in Chemistry, Keble Coll., Oxford, 1970–76; Pro-Vice-Chancellor, Univ. of Bath, 1986–89. Chief Examnr, Internat. Baccalaureate, 1970– (Chm., Bd of Chief Examnrs, 1985–89). Chairman: Assoc. for Science Educn, 1981; Nat. Curriculum Science Working Gp, 1987–88. Mem., Council, 1988–92, Dep. Chm., 1989–92, School Exams and Assessment Council; Member: Nat. Commn on Educn, 1991–93; English Nat. Bd for Nursing, Midwifery and Health Visiting, 1993–. Pres., Educn Div., Royal Soc. of Chemistry, 1983–85; Vice-Pres. and Gen. Sec., BAAS, 1985–91 (Chm., Council 1991–). Mem., Educn Cttee, Royal Soc., 1989–. Mem. Council, Wildfowl Trust, 1981–91. FRSA 1983. Freeman: Goldsmiths' Co., 1992; City of London, 1992. Gen. Editor, Bath Science series, age gps 16–19 (10 titles), and 5–16 (78 titles). *Publications:* Introduction to Chemical Energetics, 1967; European Curriculum Studies; Chemistry, 1972; (ed) Practical Work in Sixthform Science, 1976; Foundation Course in Chemistry, 1982; Modern Physical Chemistry, 1982; (ed) Dimensions of Science (9 titles), 1986; The Chemistry Dimension, 1987. *Recreations:* music (brass bands and blue grass), North Country art, collecting sugar wrappers. *Address:* University of Bath, Claverton Down, Bath BA2 7AY.

THOMPSON, John Keith Lumley, CMG 1982; MBE (mil.) 1965; TD 1961; President, Lumley Associates, since 1983; *b* 31 March 1923; *s* of late John V. V. and Gertrude Thompson; *m* 1950, Audrey Olley; one *s*. *Educ:* Wallsend Grammar Sch.; King's Coll., Durham Univ. (BSc). FIMgt (FBIM; MBIM 1975); MSAE 1983. Served War of 1939–45: Officer in REME, 1942–47, NW Europe; BEME 44 Para Bde (V), 1948–70. Dep. Inspector, REME (V) Southern Comd, 1970–72 (Lt-Col); Dep. Comdr, 44 Para Bde (V), 1972–75 (Col). Road Research Lab., DSIR, 1948–55; AWRE, Aldermaston, 1955–64; Staff of Chief Scientific Adviser, MoD, 1964–65; Head of E Midlands Regional Office, Min. Tech., 1965–70; Head, Internat. Affairs, Atomic Energy Div., Dept of Energy, 1972–74; Regional Dir, W Midlands and Northern Regional Offices, DoI, 1970–72 and 1974–78; Counseller (Sci. and Tech.), Washington, 1978–83. ADC to the Queen (TAVR), 1974–78. *Publications:* papers on vehicle behaviour, crash helmets and implosion systems; numerous articles on American science and technology. *Recreations:* outdoor activities, reading. *Address:* c/o Lumley Associates, 7 School Lane, Baston, Peterborough PE6 9PD. *T:* Greatford (01778) 560374.

THOMPSON, John Leonard C.; *see* Cloudsley-Thompson.

THOMPSON, John Michael Anthony, FMA; museums and heritage consultant, since 1991; Director, Art Galleries and Museums, Tyne and Wear County Museums, 1975–91; *b* 3 Feb. 1941; *s* of George Thompson and Joan Smith; *m* 1965, Alison Sara Bowers; two *d*. *Educ:* William Hulme's Grammar Sch., Manchester; Univ. of Manchester. BA, MA; FMA 1980. Research Asst, Whitworth Art Gall., 1964–66; Keeper, Rutherston Collection, City Art Gall., Manchester, 1966–68; Director: North Western Museum and Art Gall. Service, 1968–70; Arts and Museums, Bradford City Council, 1970–74; Chief Arts and Museums Officer, Bradford Metropolitan Council, 1974–75. Councillor, Museums Assoc., 1977–80, 1984–87 (Chm., Accreditation Cttee, 1978–80); Advisor to Arts and Recreation Cttee, AMA, 1981–91; Pres., Museums North, 1977, and 1991–92; Chm., Soc. of County Museum Dirs, 1982–86; Founder Mem. and Hon. Sec., Gp of Dirs of Museums in the British Isles, 1985–91. Dir, Museums and Galleries Consultancy Ltd, 1992–; Mem. Bd, Jarrow 700 AD Ltd, 1992–. Chm., Gosforth Adult Educn Assoc., 1994–. *Publications:* (ed) The Manual of Curatorship: a guide to museum practice, 1984, 2nd edn 1993; Contracting Culture: museums and local government, 1994; articles in Museums Jl, Penrose Annual, Connoisseur. *Recreations:* classical guitar, long distance running, walking. *Address:* 21 Linden Road, Gosforth, Newcastle upon Tyne NE3 4EY. *T:* 0191–284 2797.

THOMPSON, Prof. John Michael Tutill, FRS 1985; Professor of Nonlinear Dynamics, Department of Civil Engineering, and Director, Centre for Nonlinear Dynamics and Its Applications, University College London, since 1991; Chairman, ES-Consult (Consulting Engineers), Copenhagen, since 1995; *b* 7 June 1937; *s* of John Hornsey Thompson and Kathleen Rita Thompson (*née* Tutill); *m* 1959, Margaret Cecilia Chapman; one *s* one *d*. *Educ:* Hull Grammar Sch.; Clare Coll., Cambridge (MA, PhD, ScD). FIMA. Research Fellow, Peterhouse, 1961–64; Vis. Res. Associate, Stanford (Fulbright grant), 1962–63; Lectr, 1964–68, Reader, 1968–77, Prof. of Structural Mechanics, 1977–91, UCL; Chm., Bd of Studies in Civil and Mech. Eng., Univ. of London, 1984–86. Vis. Prof., Faculté des Sciences, Univ. Libre de Bruxelles, 1976–78; Vis. Mathematician, Brookhaven Nat. Lab., 1984; Vis. Res. Fellow, Centre for Nonlinear Studies, Univ. of Leeds, 1987–; Sen. Fellow, SERC, 1988–93. Mem. Council, IMA, 1989–92 (Organizer, Conf. on Chaos, UCL, 1990). Cambridge University Prizes: Rex Moir, 1957; Archibald Denny, 1958; John Winbolt, 1960; OMAE Award, ASME, 1985; James Alfred Ewing Medal, ICE, 1992. Organizer and Editor, IUTAM Symposium: on Collapse: the buckling of structures in theory and practice, 1982; on non-linearity and chaos in engrg dynamics, 1993; Actg Ed., Phil. Trans Roy. Soc., Series A, 1990 (Ed. and Organizer, first Theme Issue, 1990); sci. contribs to radio and TV, 1975–. *Publications:* (with G. W. Hunt) A general theory of elastic stability, 1973; Instabilities and catastrophes in science and engineering, 1982; (with G. W. Hunt) Elastic instability phenomena, 1984; (with H. B. Stewart) Nonlinear dynamics and chaos, 1986; articles in learned jls (and mem., editl bds). *Recreations:* walking, music, tennis, table tennis. *Address:* 31 Hillside Road, Bushey, Herts WD2 2HB. *T:* Watford (01923) 229803.

THOMPSON, (John) Peter (Stuart); Director, Solicitors' Complaints Bureau, 1986–90; *b* 6 July 1925; *s* of Frederick Charles Victor Thompson and Hilda Mary (*née* Hampton); *m* 1956, Valerie Merriel (*née* Harman). *Educ:* Burton Grammar Sch.; Royal Naval Coll., Dartmouth; Royal Naval Engineering Coll., Devonport; Univ. of Birmingham, 1952–55 (LLB). Admitted Solicitor, 1966. Served Royal Navy, 1943–47. Arts Council Drama Dept and associated theatres: Actor/Stage Dir, 1947–52. Asst Company Sec., Saunders-Roe Ltd, Aircraft Manufrs, 1955–61; articled clerk, Helder Roberts & Co., Solicitors, London, 1961–66, Partner 1966–70; Law Soc. Professional Purposes Dept, 1971–86. *Recreations:* gardening, marine technology, 18th Century music, flora and fauna of tropical islands. *Address:* Parkhurst Lodge, Abinger Common, Dorking, Surrey RH5 6LL. *T:* Dorking (01306) 730522.

THOMPSON, John William McWean, CBE 1986; Editor, Sunday Telegraph, 1976–86; *b* 12 June 1920; *s* of Charles and Charlotte Thompson; *m* 1947, Cynthia Ledsham; one *s* one *d*. *Educ:* Roundhay Sch., Leeds. Previously on staffs of Yorkshire Evening News, Evening Standard, London, and The Spectator (Dep. Editor); joined Sunday Telegraph, 1970; Asst Editor, 1975. *Publication:* (as Peter Quince) Country Life, 1975. *Address:* Corner Cottage, Burnham Norton, Norfolk PE31 8DS. *T:* Fakenham (01328) 738396. *Club:* Travellers'.

See also D. B. Johnson.

THOMPSON, Rear-Adm. John Yelverton, CB 1960; retired 1961; *b* 25 May 1909; *s* of late Sir John Perronet Thompson, KCSI, KCIE, and Ada Lucia, Lady Thompson (*née* Tyrrell); *m* 1934, Barbara Helen Mary Aston Key; two *s*. *Educ:* Mourne Grange, Kilkeel, Co. Down; RN College, Dartmouth. Midshipman: HMS Repulse and Berwick, 1926–29; Sub-Lieutenant: HMS Warspite, 1931; Lieutenant: HMS Queen Elizabeth, 1931–32, Restless 1933, Excellent 1933–34, Queen Elizabeth 1935, Glasgow 1936–39; Lieut-Commander: HMS Excellent 1939–41, Anson 1941–43; Commander: Admiralty, Naval Ordnance Dept, 1943–45; US Fifth Fleet, 1946; HMS Liverpool, 1947; HMS Newcastle, 1948; Captain: Ordnance Board, 1948–50; HMS Unicorn, 1951–52; Director, Gunnery Division, Naval Staff, 1952–54; Imperial Defence College, 1955; Commodore: Royal Naval Barracks, Portsmouth, 1956–57; Rear-Admiral: Admiralty Interview Boards, 1958; Adm. Superintendent, HM Dockyard, Chatham, 1958–61. ADC to the Queen, 1957. Governor, Aldenham Sch., 1967–73. DL: Hertfordshire, 1966–73; Cornwall, 1973–88. American Legion of Merit, 1953. *Address:* The Old Vicarage, Moulsford, Wallingford OX10 9JB.

THOMPSON, Julian; *see* Thompson, R. J. de la M.

THOMPSON, Maj.-Gen. Julian Howard Atherden, CB 1982; OBE 1978; Senior Research Fellow in Logistics and Armed Conflict in the Modern Age, King's College London, since 1987; *b* 7 Oct. 1934; *s* of late Major A. J. Thompson, DSO, MC and Mary Stearns Thompson (*née* Krause); *m* 1960, Janet Avery, *d* of late Richard Robinson Rodd; one *s* one *d*. *Educ:* Sherborne School. 2nd Lieut RM, 1952; served 40, 42, 43, 45 Commandos RM, 1954–69; Asst Sec., Chiefs of Staff Cttee, 1970–71; BM, 3 Cdo Brigade, 1972–73; Directing Staff, Staff Coll., Camberley, 1974–75; CO 40 Cdo RM, 1975–78; Comdr 3 Cdo Brigade, 1981–83, incl. Falklands campaign (CB); Maj.-Gen. Comdg Trng Reserve Forces and Special Forces RM, 1983–86, retired. Pres., British Assoc. for Physical Training, 1988–. *Publications:* No Picnic: 3 Commando Brigade in the

South Atlantic 1982, 1985; Ready for Anything: The Parachute Regiment at War 1940–1982, 1989; (contrib.) Military Strategy in a Changing Europe, 1991; (contrib.) Fallen Stars, 1991; The Lifeblood of War, 1991; The Imperial War Museum Book of Victory in Europe: North West Europe 1944–45, 1994. *Recreations:* sailing, shooting, history, cross-country ski-ing, ballet, opera, jazz. *Address:* c/o Lloyds Bank, Royal Parade, Plymouth, Devon PL1 1HB. *Clubs:* Army and Navy; Royal Marines Sailing.

THOMPSON, Julian O.; *see* Ogilvie Thompson.

THOMPSON, Keith Bruce; Vice-Chancellor, Staffordshire University, 1992–95; *b* 13 Sept. 1932; *m* 1956, Kathleen Reeves; one *s* one *d*. *Educ:* Bishopshalt School, Hillingdon; New College, Oxford (Sec./Librarian, Oxford Union). PPE 1955, Dip Educn (distn), 1956, MA 1959; MEd Bristol, 1968. Schoolmaster, City of Bath Boys' School, 1956–62; Lectr, Newton Park Coll., Bath, 1962–67; Head of Dept, Philippa Fawcett Coll., Streatham, 1967–72; Principal, Madeley Coll. of Educn, 1972–78; Dep. Dir, 1978–86, Dir, 1987–92, N Staffs, later Staffs Poly. Chairman: Standing Conf. on Studies in Educn, 1980–82; Undergraduate Initial Training Bd (Educn), CNAA, 1981–85; Chm., Polytechnics Central Admissions System, 1989–93; Dep. Chm., UCAS, 1993–95; Member: Bd, Nat. Adv. Body for Public Sector Higher Educn, 1983–88 (Chm., Teacher Educn Gp, 1983–85). Editor, Educn for Teaching, 1968–74. *Publications:* Education and Philosophy, 1972; (jtly) Curriculum Development, 1974; articles on educn, philosophy, physical educn. *Recreations:* sport, music. *Address:* Hawthorn House, Little Tixall Lane, Great Haywood, Staffs ST18 0SE. *T:* Little Haywood (01889) 881874.

THOMPSON, Hon. Lindsay Hamilton Simpson, AO 1990; CMG 1975; Premier of Victoria, 1981–82; Leader of the Opposition, Victoria, 1982; *b* 15 Oct. 1923; *s* of Arthur K. Thompson and Ethel M. Thompson; *m* 1950, Joan Margaret Poynder; two *s* one *d*. *Educ:* Caulfield Grammar Sch., Victoria (Captain and Dux 1941); Melbourne Univ. (BA Hons, BEd). MACE. AIF, New Guinea, 1942–45. MP (Lib.) in Victorian Legislative Council: Higinbotham Prov., 1955–67; Monash Prov., 1967–70; MLA Malvern, 1970–82; Member of Cabinet, 1956–82; Parly Sec. of Cabinet, 1956–58; Asst Chief Sec. and Asst Attorney-Gen., 1958–61; Asst Minister of Transport, 1960–61; Minister of Housing and Forests, 1961–67; Dep. Leader of Govt in Legislative Council, 1962–70; Minister in charge of Aboriginal Welfare, 1965–67; Minister of Educn, 1967–79 (longest term ever in this portfolio); Leader of Legislative Assembly, 1972–79; Dep. Premier of Victoria, 1972–81; Minister for Police and Emergency Services, 1979–81; Treasurer, 1979–82; served longest period as Cabinet Minister in history of Victoria. Director: Mutual Friendly Soc., 1986–; Composite Benefits Soc., 1986–92. State Govt Rep., Melbourne Univ. Council, 1955–59. Dep. Chm., Aust. Advertising Standards Council, 1990– (Mem., 1988–90). Pres., Royal Life Saving Soc., 1970–. Trustee: Melb. Cricket Ground, 1967– (Chm., 1987–); Nat. Tennis Centre Trust, 1986– (Chm., 1994–); Patron: Victorian Cricket Assoc.; Prahran CC; Aust. Quadriplegic Assoc.; Richmond FC. Bronze Medal, Royal Humane Soc., 1974. *Publications:* Australian Housing Today and Tomorrow, 1965; Looking Ahead in Education, 1969; A Fair Deal for Victoria, 1981; I Remember, 1989. *Recreations:* cricket, golf, tennis. *Address:* 19 Allenby Avenue, Glen Iris, Victoria 3146, Australia. *T:* (3) 8856191. *Clubs:* Melbourne (Melbourne), Kingston Heath Golf, Sorrento Golf.

THOMPSON, Sir Lionel; *see* Thompson, Sir T. L. T., Bt.

THOMPSON, McKim; *see* Thompson, I. McK.

THOMPSON, Marjorie Ellis; Head of Communications, Commission for Racial Equality, since 1993; *b* St Louis, Mo, 8 June 1957; *d* of John William Thompson, III and Janet Ann (*née* Neubeiser); *m* 1982, Kevin Mark Williams (marr. diss. 1992); partner 1984–92, Dafydd Elis Thomas (now Baron Elis-Thomas). *Educ:* Woodrow Wilson High Sch., Long Beach, California; Colorado Coll., Colorado Springs (BSc Hons 1978); LSE (MSc Econ 1979). Volunteer, Georgetown Centre for Strategic and Internat. Studies, Washington, 1980–81; PA, Energy and Lang. Services Depts, World Bank, 1980–81; Legislative Corresp., office of Congressman Gerald B. Solomon, 1981–82; Lobbyist, Nat. Energy Educn Day Project, Washington, 1982; Administrator, Boston Univ. US Naval Support Facility, Holy Loch, Scotland, 1982–83; Asst to political reporters, HTV, General Election, 1983; Volunteer, Medical Campaign Against Nuclear Weapons, CBC Radio Action Line, Cardiff, 1983; Campaign for Nuclear Disarmament: Parly Officer, 1983–86; Hd of Press and Public Relns, 1986–87; Vice-Chair, 1987–90; Chair, 1990–93; Researcher for Ann Clwyd, MP, 1987; Royal College of Nursing: Parly Officer, 1988–91; Advr, Dept of Nursing Policy and Practice, 1991–93. Co-Chair, Cttee to Stop War in the Gulf, 1990–91; Hon. Pres., Cttee for Just Peace in ME, 1991; Hon. Vice-Pres., Scottish CND, 1994–. Executive Management Board: New Directions Camden (mental health); Totem Theatre Co. Mem., IISS, 1992–94. Fellow, British–American Project. *Publications:* (contrib.) Nursing: the hidden agenda, 1993; contrib. New Statesman & Society, Tribune. *Recreations:* travel, biography and contemporary fiction, theatre, cinema. *Address:* c/o Commission for Racial Equality, Elliot House, 10/12 Allington Street, SW1E 5EH. *T:* 0171–932 5280, *Fax:* 0171–828 5680.

THOMPSON, Mark; *see* Thompson, O. M.

THOMPSON, Mark John Thompson; Head of Factual Programmes, BBC Television, since 1994; *b* 31 July 1957; *s* of Duncan John Thompson and Sydney Columba Corduff Thompson; *m* 1987, Jane Emilie Blumberg; one *s* one *d*. *Educ:* Stonyhurst Coll.; Merton Coll., Oxford (BA). BBC Television: Research Asst Trainee, 1979–80; Asst Producer, Nationwide, 1980–82; Producer, Breakfast Time, 1982–84; Output Editor: London Plus, 1984–85; Newsnight, 1985–87; Editor: Nine O'Clock News, 1988–90, Panorama, 1990–92; Head of Features, 1992–94. *Recreations:* walking, cooking. *Address:* c/o BBC Television, Wood Lane, W12 8QT. *T:* 0181–743 8000.

THOMPSON, Michael Harry Rex, OBE 1992; FCIB; Deputy Chairman, Lloyds Bank Plc, 1991–95 (Director, 1986–95); *b* 14 Jan. 1931; *s* of William Henry Thompson and late Beatrice Hilda Thompson (*née* Heard); *m* 1958, Joyce (*née* Redpath); one *s* one *d*. *Educ:* St John's Sch., Leatherhead, Surrey. Joined Lloyds Bank, 1948; Dep. Chief Exec., 1987–91; Director: National Bank of New Zealand, 1978–82, 1991–95; Lloyds Abbey Life 1991–95; Chm., German Investment Trust, 1990–95. *Recreation:* Rugby football.

THOMPSON, Michael Jacques, CMG 1989; OBE 1977; HM Diplomatic Service; Counsellor, Foreign and Commonwealth Office, since 1985; *b* 31 Jan. 1936; *s* of late Christopher Thompson and of Colette Jeanne-Marie Thompson; *m* 1967, Mary Susan (*née* Everard); one *s* one *d*. *Educ:* Uppingham; Christ's Coll., Cambridge (Law Tripos, 1956–60; MA). National Service, Kenya, Aden and Cyprus, 1954–56. HMOCS, Kenya, 1960–63; FCO, 1964; served Kuala Lumpur, Saigon, Lusaka and FCO, 1965–79; Counsellor, Kuala Lumpur, 1979–82; seconded to Comdr, British Land Forces, Hong Kong, 1982–85. Mem., Royal Asia Soc. Mem., Co. of Barbers. *Recreations:* squash, tennis, golf, gardening. *Address:* c/o Foreign and Commonwealth Office, SW1A 2AH. *Clubs:* United Oxford & Cambridge University; Hong Kong; Huntercombe Golf.

THOMPSON, Prof. Sir Michael (Warwick), Kt 1991; DSc; FInstP; Vice-Chancellor and Principal, University of Birmingham, since 1987; *b* 1 June 1931; *s* of Kelvin Warwick Thompson and Madeleine Thompson; *m* Sybil (*née* Spooner); two *s*. *Educ:* Rydal Sch.; Univ. of Liverpool (BSc, DSc). Research scientist, AERE, Harwell, 1953–65; Sussex University: Prof. of Experimental Physics, 1965–80; Pro-Vice-Chancellor, 1973–77, actg Vice-Chancellor, 1976; Vis. Prof., 1980–86; Vice-Chancellor, UEA, 1980–86. Chm., Physics Cttee, SRC, 1975–79; Member: E Sussex AHA, 1974–79; E Sussex Educn Cttee, 1973–78; non-exec. Dir, W Midlands RHA, 1987–. Member: Council, Birmingham Chamber of Industry and Commerce, 1987–; Council, CNAA, 1989–91; Council for Internat. Co-operation in Higher Educn, 1989–91; Council, CVCP, 1990–93, 1994–; Council for Industry and Higher Educn, 1991–; Council, ACU, 1991–. Dep. Chm., Alliance & Leicester Building Soc., 1995– (Dir, 1985–; Dir, Alliance Building Soc., 1979–85); Dir, Cobuild Ltd, 1987–. Mem. Council, Eastbourne Coll., 1977–. Trustee, Barber Inst. of Fine Arts, 1987–. Mem., Lunar Soc., 1991–. Oliver Lodge Prizewinner, Univ. of Liverpool, 1953; Prizewinner, Materials Science Club, 1970; C. V. Boys Prizewinner, Inst. of Physics, 1972. *Publications:* Defects and Radiation Damage in Metals, 1969; (jtly) Channelling, 1973; over 90 papers in sci. jls. *Recreations:* the arts, navigation in small ships. *Address:* University of Birmingham, Edgbaston, Birmingham B15 2TT. *Clubs:* Athenæum; Royal Fowey Yacht.

THOMPSON, Nicolas de la Mare; Chairman: Copyright Licensing Agency Ltd, since 1994; Publishers Licensing Society, since 1992; Director, International Book Development Ltd, since 1991; *b* 4 June 1928; *s* of Rupert Spens Thompson and Florence Elizabeth Thompson (*née* de la Mare); *m* 1956, Erica Pennell (*d* 1993); two *s* one *d*. *Educ:* Eton; Christ Church, Oxford (MA). Managing Director, George Weidenfeld and Nicolson, 1956–70; Publishing Dir, Pitman, 1970–85; Managing Dir, Heinemann Gp of Publishers, 1985–87; Director: Octopus Publishing Gp, 1985–92; Reed Internat. Books, 1990–93; Chairman: Heinemann Educational Books, 1985–91; Ginn & Co., 1985–91; Heinemann Professional Publishing, 1986–90; George Philip & Son, 1988–90; Mitchell Beazley, 1988–90. Chm., Book Development Council, 1984–86; Treas., Publishers Assoc., 1986–88. Dir, Almeida Theatre Co. Ltd, 1993–. *Address:* 8 Ennismore Gardens, SW7 1NL. *Club:* Garrick.

THOMPSON, Dr Noel Brentnall Watson, CEng; Consultant and Visiting Professor of Educational Development, Luton University, since 1993; Chief Executive, National Council for Educational Technology, 1988–92; *b* 11 Dec. 1932; *s* of George Watson Thompson and Mary Henrietta Gibson; *m* 1957, Margaret Angela Elizabeth Baston; one *s*. *Educ:* Manchester Grammar School; Cambridge Univ. (MA); Imperial College, London (MSc Eng, PhD). National Service, RN (Sub-Lieut), 1951–53. Research, Imperial Coll., 1958–61; Lectr in Physical Metallurgy, Univ. of Birmingham, 1961–65; Dept of Education and Science, 1966–67, 1969–77 and 1979–88 (Under Sec., 1980–88; Head of Higher and Further Educn II Br., 1980–86; Head of Schools 2 Br. and Internat. Relations, 1986–88); Secretary, National Libraries Cttee, 1967–69; Cabinet Office, 1977–79. *Publications:* papers in professional journals. *Recreations:* railways of all sizes, mechanics, music, modern history, photography, walking. *Address:* 101 Woodcock Hill, Kenton, Harrow HA3 0JJ. *T:* 0181–907 1716. *Clubs:* other people's.

THOMPSON, Norman Sinclair, CBE 1980; Chairman: Vaile Sinclair & Co. Ltd (formerly Vaile & Co. (Dorset)), since 1991; Horsemaster Ltd, since 1991; Portland Port Ltd, since 1995; *b* 7 July 1920; *s* of Norman Whitfield Thompson and Jane Thompson (*née* Robinson); *m* 1945, Peggy Sivil; two *s* (one *d* decd). *Educ:* Middlesbrough High Sch. Qual. Chartered Accountant, 1947 (FCA); Cost and Management Accountant (ACMA), 1949. Served War, Merchant Seaman, 1940–45. Asst Sec., Paton's and Baldwin's Ltd, 1947; Commercial Manager, Cowan's Sheldon & Co. Ltd, 1955; Group Secretary, Richardson's Westgarth & Co. Ltd, 1957; Financial Dir, David Brown & Sons (Huddersfield) Ltd, 1961; Gen. Manager, Malta Drydocks, Swan Hunter Group Ltd, 1963; apptd Swan Hunter Bd, 1964; Overseas Dir, 1967; Dep. Managing Dir, 1969; The Cunard Steam-Ship Co. Ltd: Man. Dir, Cargo Shipping, 1970; Man. Dir, 1971–74; Chairman: Mass Transit Railway Corp., Hong Kong, 1975–83; Poole Harbour Comrs, 1984–86; Dep. Chm., New Hong Kong Tunnel Co., 1986–92; Director: Hong Kong and Shanghai Banking Corp., 1978–86; British Shipbuilders, 1983–86. *Recreations:* dogs, music. *Address:* Shadrach House, Burton Bradstock, Bridport, Dorset DT6 4QG. *Clubs:* Oriental; Hong Kong, Royal Hong Kong Yacht, Royal Hong Kong Jockey.

THOMPSON, (Owen) Mark; theatre designer; *b* 12 April 1957; *s* of Owen Edgar Thompson and Barbara Adele (*née* Lister). *Educ:* Radley Coll.; Birmingham Univ. (BA Hons Drama and Theatre Arts). Worked in rep. at Worcester, Exeter, Sheffield and Leeds; designs for: The Scarlet Pimpernel, Chichester, 1985 (transf. Her Majesty's); Cabaret, Strand, 1986; The Sneeze, Aldwych, 1988; Ivanov, and Much Ado About Nothing, Strand, 1989; A Little Night Music, Piccadilly, 1989; Shadowlands, Queen's, 1989 (transf. NY); Joseph and the Amazing Technicolor Dreamcoat, Palladium and Canadian, Australian and American tours, 1991 (Set Design Olivier Award, 1992); Six Degrees of Separation, Royal Court, 1992 (transf. Comedy); *for Royal Exchange Manchester:* Jumpers, 1984; The Country Wife, Mumbo Jumbo, 1986; The School for Scandal, 1990; *for RSC:* Measure for Measure, 1987; The Wizard of Oz, Much Ado About Nothing, 1988; The Comedy of Errors, 1990 (Set Design and Costume Design Olivier Awards, 1992); *for Almeida:* Volpone, 1990; Betrayal, Party Time, 1991; *for Royal National Theatre:* The Wind in the Willows, 1990 (Olivier Award, Plays and Players Award, Critics Circle Award, 1991); The Madness of George III, 1991 (costume design for film, 1994); Arcadia, 1993; Hysteria, 1994 (Olivier Award for Set Design); Pericles, 1994; *opera:* Montag aus Licht, La Scala, 1989 (costume design only); Falstaff, Scottish Opera, 1991; Peter Grimes, Opera North, 1989; Ariadne auf Naxos, Saltzburg, 1991; Il Viaggio a Reims, Royal Opera, 1992; Hansel and Gretel, Sydney, 1992; The Two Widows, ENO, 1993; *ballet:* Don Quixote, Royal Ballet, 1993. *Recreations:* cooking, gardening. *Address:* c/o Simpson Fox Associates, 52 Shaftesbury Avenue, W1V 7DE. *T:* 0171–434 9167.

THOMPSON, Patrick; *see* Thompson, H. P.

THOMPSON, Sir Paul (Anthony), 2nd Bt *cr* 1963; company director; *b* 6 Oct. 1939; *s* of Sir Kenneth Pugh Thompson, 1st Bt, and Nanne (*d* 1994), *yr d* of Charles Broome, Walton, Liverpool; *S* father, 1984; *m* 1971, Pauline Dorothy, *d* of Robert O. Spencer, Bolton, Lancs; two *s* two *d*. *Educ:* Aldenham School, Herts. *Heir: s* Richard Kenneth Spencer Thompson, *b* 27 Jan. 1976. *Address:* The Old Vicarage, Church Road, Bickerstaffe, Ormskirk, Lancs L39 0EB.

THOMPSON, Prof. Paul Richard, DPhil; social historian; Research Professor in Social History, University of Essex, since 1988; Director, National Life Story Collection, since 1987; *b* 1935; *m* 1st, Thea Vigne; one *s* one *d*; 2nd, Natasha Burchardt; one *d*. *Educ:* Bishop's Stortford Coll., Corpus Christi Coll., Oxford; The Queen's Coll., Oxford (Junior Research Fellow, 1961–64). MA, DPhil 1964. University of Essex: Lectr in Sociology, 1964–69; Sen. Lectr, 1969–71; Reader, 1971–88; Sen. Res. Fellow, Nuffield Coll., Oxford, 1968–69; Vis. Prof. of Art History, Johns Hopkins Univ., 1972; Hoffman Wood Prof. of Architecture, Univ. of Leeds, 1977–78; Benjamin Meaker Prof., Univ. of Bristol,

1987. Editor: Victorian Soc. Conf. Reports, 1965–67; Oral History, 1970–; Life Stories, 1985–89; International Yearbook of Oral History and Life Stories, 1992–. *Publications:* History of English Architecture (with Peter Kidson and Peter Murray), 1965, 2nd edn 1979; The Work of William Morris, 1967, 3rd edn 1991; Socialists, Liberals and Labour: the struggle for London 1880–1914, 1967; The Edwardians: the remaking of British Society, 1975, 2nd edn 1992; The Voice of the Past: Oral History, 1978, 2nd edn 1988; Living the Fishing, 1983; I Don't Feel Old: the experience of later life, 1990; The Myths We Live By, 1990; The Nineties, 1993; Listening for a Change, 1993. *Recreations:* cycling, drawing, music, friendship, travel. *Address:* 18 Lonsdale Road, Oxford OX2 7EW. *T:* Oxford (01865) 510840.

THOMPSON, Peter; *see* Thompson, J. P. S.

THOMPSON, Sir Peter (Anthony), Kt 1984; FCIT; Chairman: Community Hospitals plc, since 1981; Child Base Ltd, since 1989; FI Group plc, since 1990; M–31, since 1991; M–33, since 1991; Douglas Stewart Ltd, since 1992; *b* 14 April 1928; *s* of late Herbert Thompson and Sarah Jane Thompson; *m* 1st, 1958, Patricia Anne Norcott (*d* 1983); one *s* two *d*; 2nd, 1986, Lydia Mary Kite (*née* Hodding); two *d*. *Educ:* Royal Drapers Sch.; Bradford Grammar Sch.; Leeds Univ. (BA Econ). Unilever, 1952–62; GKN, 1962–64; Transport Controller, Rank Organisation, 1964–67; Head of Transport, BSC, 1967–72; Group Co-ordinator, BRS Ltd, 1972–75; Exec. Vice-Chm. (Operations), Nat. Freight Corp., 1975–77; Chief Exec., Nat. Freight Corp., later Nat. Freight Co., 1977–80; Dep. Chm. and Chief Exec., 1980–82, Chm. and Chief Exec., 1982–84, Exec. Chm., 1984–90, Pres., 1991–93, NFC. Dir, 1989–90, Dep. Chm., 1989–90, Chm., March–July 1990, British & Commonwealth Hldgs; Dep. Chm., Wembley plc, 1991–95; Director: Granville & Co. Ltd, 1984–90; Pilkington plc, 1985–93; Kenning Motor Group, 1985–86; Smiths Industries PLC, 1986–; Meyer International, 1988–92; Aegis plc, 1993–; Brewin Dolphin Gp, 1994–; Pres., ProShare, 1994– (Chm., 1992–94). Mem., Nat. Trng Task Force, 1989–93. President: Inst. of Freight Forwarders, 1982–83; Inst. of Logistics and Distribn Management (formerly Inst. of Physical Distribn Management), 1988–93 (Chm., 1985–88); Vice-Pres., CIT, 1982–85; Chm., CBI Wider Share Ownership Task Force, 1990. CIMgt. Hon. LLD: Leeds, 1991; Nottingham, 1991; Hon. DTech Bradford, 1991; Hon. DSc Cranfield Inst. of Technol., 1992. Hambro Businessman of the Year, 1983; BIM Gold Medal, 1991. *Publication:* Sharing the Success: the story of the NFC, 1990. *Recreations:* golf, walking, music. *Address:* The Mill House, Mill Street, Newport Pagnell, Bucks MK16 8ER. *Club:* Royal Automobile.

THOMPSON, Prof. Peter John; Education and Training Consultant, and Visiting Professor, School of Management, Open University, since 1991; *b* 17 April 1937; *s* of late George Kenneth Thompson and Gladys Pamela (*née* Partington), W Midlands; *m* 1961, Dorothy Ann Smith; one *s* one *d*. *Educ:* Aston Univ. (BSc 1st Cl. Hons MechEngrg; MSc); CNAA (DTech). Whitworth Soc. Prize. CEng, FIMechE, FIEE, FIPlantE; FITD. With Tube Investments, 1952–61; Lectr 1961, Sen. Lectr 1968–70, Harris Coll., Preston; Sen. Sci. Officer, UKAEA, Preston, 1965–68; Prin. Lectr, Sheffield City Poly., 1970–77; Hd of Dept and Dean of Engrg, Trent Poly., Nottingham, 1977–83; Pro Rector, then Dep. Rector, Poly. of Central London, 1983–86; Professor: Trent Poly., 1980–83; Poly. of Central London, 1983–86; Chief Exec., NCVQ, 1986–91. Mem., then Chm., Manufacturing Bd, CNAA, 1978–86; Mem., Cttee for Sci. and Technology, CNAA, 1982–86; Mem. then Chm., Cttee for Engrg in Polytechnics, 1981–86; Member: Engrg Adv. Cttee, NAB, 1980–84; Engrg Scis Divl Bd of IMechE, 1984–86; Chm., Materials Tech. Activities Cttee, IMechE, 1984–86; Mem., Council, Open Coll., 1987–90. Sen. Awards Consultant, C&G, 1992–. Hon. Mem., C&G, 1991. FRSA. *Publications:* numerous papers on engrg manufacture and vocational educn and trng, 1968–, incl. papers on hydrostatic extension, lubrication, cutting tool wear and mechanics and metal forming; patents. *Recreations:* genealogy, numismatics, golf. *Address:* Open University, Milton Keynes, MK7 6AA. *T:* Milton Keynes (01908) 655888.

THOMPSON, Peter Kenneth James; Solicitor to Departments of Health and of Social Security, since 1989; *b* 30 July 1937; *s* of Kenneth George Thompson and Doreen May Thompson; *m* 1970, Sandy Lynne Harper; two *d*. *Educ:* Worksop Coll.; Christ's Coll., Cambridge (MA, LLB). Called to the Bar, Lincoln's Inn, 1961; practised at Common Law Bar, 1961–73; Lawyer in Govt Service: Law Commission, 1973–78; Lord Chancellor's Dept, 1978–83; Under Sec., DHSS, 1983. *Publications:* The Unfair Contract Terms Act 1977, 1978; The Recovery of Interest, 1985; *radio plays:* A Matter of Form, 1977; Dormer and Grand-Daughter, 1978. *Recreation:* writing. *Address:* Departments of Health and Social Security, Room 401, New Court, Carey Street, WC2A 2LS.

THOMPSON, Pratt; *see* Thompson, W. P.

THOMPSON, Prof. Raymond, CBE 1988; PhD; FRSC; FEng 1985, FIMM; Deputy Chairman, Borax Research Ltd, 1986–90 (Managing Director, 1980–86); Director: RTZ Chemicals (formerly Borax Consolidated) (Borides) Ltd, 1986–89; Boride Ceramics and Composites Ltd, 1990–92; Azmat Ltd, since 1993; *b* 4 April 1925; *s* of late William Edward Thompson and Hilda Thompson (*née* Rowley). *Educ:* Longton High Sch.; Univ. of Nottingham (MSc 1950, PhD 1952); Imperial Coll., Univ. of London (DIC 1953). Research Manager, Borax Consolidated, 1961; Res. Dir, 1969–86, Business Develt Dir, 1986–87, Scientific Advr, 1987–, RTZ Borax and Minerals Ltd (formerly Borax Hldgs Ltd). Consultant: RTZ Chemicals Ltd, 1988–89; CRA Ltd, 1988–91; Rhône-Poulenc, 1989–92. Special Professor of Inorganic Chemistry, Univ. of Nottingham, 1975–; Hon. Prof., Molecular Sciences, Univ. of Warwick, 1975–94. Member Council: Royal Inst. of Chemistry, 1969–72; Chemical Soc., 1977–80 (Chm., Inorganic Chemicals Gp, 1972–83); RSC, 1983–88 (Vice-Pres., Industrial Div., 1981–83, Pres., 1983–85 and 1988–89). Governor, Kingston-upon-Thames Polytechnic, 1978–88. Hon. Associate, RHC, London Univ., 1984. Liveryman: Glass Sellers' Co.; Engineers' Co. Freeman, City of London. Industrial Chemistry Award, Chem. Soc., 1976. *Publications:* (ed) The Modern Inorganic Chemicals Industry, 1977; (ed) Mellors Comprehensive Treatise, Boron Supplement, Part A, 1979, Part BI, 1981; (ed) Speciality Inorganic Chemicals, 1981; (ed) Energy and Chemistry, 1981; (ed) Trace Metal Removal From Aqueous Solution, 1986; (ed) The Chemistry of Wood Preservation, 1991; Industrial Inorganic Chemicals: production and uses, 1995; various papers on inorganic boron and nitrogen chemistry. *Recreation:* gardening. *Address:* The Garth, 7 Winchester Close, Esher, Surrey KT10 8QH. *T:* Esher (01372) 464428.

THOMPSON, Reginald Aubrey, CMG 1964; *b* 22 Nov. 1905; *s* of John and Alice Thompson, Mansfield; *m* 1932, Gwendoline Marian Jackson (*d* 1978); one *s*. *Educ:* Brunts Sch., Mansfield; University Coll., Nottingham. BSc London (1st Cl. Hons Chemistry), 1927. Research, Organic Chemistry, 1927–29; Science Master, various grammar schools, 1929–41; Scientific Civil Service, Min. of Supply, 1941–46; transf. to Admin. Class (Principal), 1946; Asst Sec., 1953; Assistant Secretary, Department of Education and Science (formerly Office of Minister of Science), 1956–64; Ministry of Technology, 1964; retd, 1966. Led UK Delegn at Confs on: liability of operators of nuclear ships, Brussels Convention, 1962; liability for nuclear damage, Vienna Convention, 1963. *Recreations:* reading, music, crosswords. *Address:* 81 Bentsbrook Park, North Holmwood, Dorking, Surrey RH5 4JL. *T:* Dorking (01306) 882289.

THOMPSON, Sir Richard (Hilton Marler), 1st Bt *cr* 1963; *b* Calcutta, India, 5 Oct. 1912; *s* of late Richard Smith Thompson and Kathleen Hilda (*née* Marler); *m* 1939, Anne Christabel de Vere, *d* of late Philip de Vere Annesley, MA, and Mrs Annesley, BEM; one *s*. *Educ:* Malvern College. In business in India, Burma and Ceylon, 1930–40; travelled in Tibet, Persia, Iraq, Turkey, etc. Served in RNVR, 1940–46, volunteering as ordinary seaman; commissioned, 1941 (despatches, 1942); Lieut-Comdr 1944. MP (C) Croydon West, 1950–55; Assistant-Government Whip, 1952; Lord Commissioner of the Treasury, 1954; MP (C) Croydon South, 1955–66 and 1970–Feb. 1974; Vice-Chamberlain of HM Household, 1956; Parly Sec., Ministry of Health, 1957–59; Under-Secretary of State, CRO, 1959–60; Parly Sec., Ministry of Works, Oct. 1960–July 1962. Mem., Public Accounts Cttee, 1973–74. A Cottonian family Trustee of the British Museum, 1951–63, a Prime Minister's Trustee, 1963–84; Trustees' representative on Council of Nat. Trust, 1978–84. Chm., Overseas Migration Bd, 1959; led UK delegation to ECAFE in Bangkok, 1960; signed Indus Waters Agreement with India, Pakistan and World Bank for UK, Sept. 1960; led UK Parly Delegn to Tanganyika, to present Speaker's chair, Jan. 1963. Chm., Capital and Counties Property Co., 1971–77, retired; Pres., British Property Fedn, 1976–77; Director, British Museum Publications Ltd. Chm., British Museum Society, 1970–74. *Recreations:* gardening, collecting, study of history. *Heir:* *s* Nicholas Annesley Marler Thompson [*b* 19 March 1947; *m* 1982, Venetia, *y d* of Mr and Mrs John Heathcote, Conington; three *s* one *d*]. *Address:* Rhodes House, Sellindge, Kent TN25 6JA. *Clubs:* Carlton, Army and Navy.

THOMPSON, Richard Paul Hepworth, DM; FRCP; Physician to the Queen and Head of HM Medical Household, since 1993 (Physician to the Royal Household, 1982–93); Consultant Physician, St Thomas' Hospital, since 1972; Physician, King Edward VII Hospital for Officers, since 1982; *b* 14 April 1940; *s* of Stanley Henry and Winifred Lilian Thompson; *m* 1974, Eleanor Mary Hughes. *Educ:* Epsom Coll.; Worcester Coll., Oxford (MA, DM); St Thomas's Hosp. Med. Sch. MRC Clinical Res. Fellow, Liver Unit, KCH, 1967–69; Fellow, Gastroenterology Unit, Mayo Clinic, USA, 1969–71; Lectr, Liver Unit, KCH, 1971–72. Mem., Lambeth, Southwark and Lewisham AHA, 1979–82. Examiner in Medicine: Soc. of Apothecaries, 1976–80; Faculty of Dental Surgery, RCS, 1980–86. Governor, Guy's Hosp. Med. Sch., 1980–82; Member Cttee of Management: Inst. of Psychiatry, 1981–; King Edward VII Hosp. Fund, 1985–89, 1992– (Mem., Gen. Council, 1985–). *Publications:* Physical Signs in Medicine, 1980; Lecture Notes on the Liver, 1986; papers and reviews in med. jls. *Address:* 36 Dealtry Road, SW15 6NL. *T:* 0181–789 3839.

THOMPSON, Robert Henry Stewart, CBE 1973; MA, DSc, DM, BCh; FRS 1974; FRCP; FRCPath; Courtauld Professor of Biochemistry, Middlesex Hospital Medical School, University of London, 1965–76; now Emeritus Professor; Trustee, Wellcome Trust, 1963–82; *b* 2 Feb. 1912; *s* of Dr Joseph Henry Thompson and Mary Eleanor Rutherford; *m* 1938, Inge Vilma Anita Gebert; one *s* two *d*. *Educ:* Epsom College; Trinity College, Oxford; Guy's Hospital Medical School. Millard Scholar, Trinity College, Oxford, 1930; Theodore Williams Scholar in Physiology, Oxford, 1932; 1st Class Animal Physiology, Oxford, 1933; Senior Demy, Magdalen College, Oxford, 1933; Univ. Scholar, Guy's Hosp. Med. School, 1933; Adrian Stokes Travelling Fellowship to Hosp. of Rockefeller Inst., New York, 1937–38; Gillson Research Scholar in Pathology, Soc. of Apothecaries of London, 1938; Fellow of University Coll., Oxford, 1938–47, Hon. Fellow, 1983; Demonstrator in Biochemistry, Oxford, 1938–47; Dean of Medical School, Oxford, 1946–47; Prof. of Chemical Pathology, Guy's Hosp. Medical School, Univ. of London, 1947–65; Secretary-General International Union of Biochemistry, 1955–64; Hon. Sec. Royal Society of Medicine, 1958–64; Mem. of Medical Research Council, 1958–62; Mem., Bd of Governors, Middlesex Hosp., 1972–74. Governor, Epsom Coll., 1982–. Hon. Mem., Biochemical Soc., 1986. Radcliffe Prize for Medical Research, Oxford, 1943. Served War of 1939–45, Major, RAMC, 1944–46. *Publications:* (with C. W. Carter) Biochemistry in relation to Medicine, 1949; Joint Editor (with E. J. King) Biochemical Disorders in Human Disease, 1957; numerous papers on biochemical and pathological subjects in various scientific journals. *Recreation:* gardening. *Address:* 7 The Cedars, Milford, Godalming, Surrey GU8 5DH. *T:* Godalming (01483) 427516. Orchard's Almshouses, Launcells, N Cornwall EX23 9NG. *T:* Bude (01288) 353817. *Club:* Athenæum.

THOMPSON, (Rupert) Julian (de la Mare); Chairman, Sotheby's Asia, since 1992; *b* 23 July 1941; *s* of Rupert Spens Thompson and Florence Elizabeth (*née* de la Mare); *m* 1965, Jacqueline Mary Ivimy; three *d*. *Educ:* Eton Coll.; King's Coll., Cambridge (MA). Joined Sotheby's, 1963: appointed a Director, 1969; Chm., 1982–86; Dep. Chm., 1987–92; Chm., Sotheby's International, 1982–85, 1987–88. *Address:* 43 Clarendon Road, W11 4JD. *T:* 0171–727 6039.

See also N. de la M. Thompson.

THOMPSON, (Russell) Ernest; Chief Executive, Society of Motor Manufacturers and Traders, since 1993; *b* 18 Feb. 1936; *s* of Russell Thompson and Madge Edith Mary Thompson; *m* 1958, Muriel June; one *s* one *d*. *Educ:* Brighton, Hove and Sussex Grammar Sch.; Corpus Christi Coll., Oxford (MA Mod. Hist.). Joined Ford Motor Co. Ltd, 1960: Director: Car Sales, 1973–82; Marketing, 1982–86; Sales, 1986–93. *Recreations:* golf, reading, walking. *Address:* Forbes House, Halkin Street, SW1X 7DS. *T:* 0171–235 7000.

THOMPSON, Sir (Thomas) Lionel (Tennyson), 5th Bt, *cr* 1806; Barrister-at-Law; *b* 19 June 1921; *s* of Lt-Col Sir Thomas Thompson, 4th Bt, MC, and of Milicent Ellen Jean, *d* of late Edmund Charles Tennyson-d'Eyncourt, Bayons Manor, Lincolnshire; *S* father, 1964; *m* 1955, Mrs Margaret van Beers (marr. diss. 1962), *d* of late Walter Herbert Browne; one *s* one *d*. *Educ:* Eton. Served War of 1939–45: Royal Air Force Volunteer Reserve, 1940; Flying Officer, 1942 (invalided, 1944); Able Seaman, Royal Fleet Auxiliary, 1944–46. Awarded 1939–45 Star, Aircrew (Europe) Star, Defence and Victory Medals. Called to the Bar, Lincoln's Inn, 1952. *Recreations:* shooting, sailing, photography. *Heir:* *s* Thomas d'Eyncourt John Thompson, *b* 22 Dec. 1956. *Address:* 16 Old Buildings, Lincoln's Inn, WC2A 3UP. *T:* 0171–405 7929.

THOMPSON, Vernon Cecil, MB, BS London; FRCS; retired 1970 as Surgeon to Department of Thoracic Surgery, The London Hospital; Surgeon, London Chest Hospital; Hon. Consulting Thoracic Surgeon to: West London Hospital, Hammersmith; King Edward VII Hospital, Windsor; Harefield Hospital, Middlesex; Broomfield and Black Notley Hospitals, Essex; *b* 17 Sept. 1905; 2nd *s* of Dr C. C. B. Thompson, Tidenham, Glos; *m* 1942, Jean, *d* of late H. J. Hilary; one *s* one *d*. *Educ:* Monmouth School; St Bartholomew's Hospital. Resident House appointments followed by First Assistant to a Surgical Unit, St Bartholomew's Hospital, 1929–37. Dorothy Temple Cross Travelling Fellowship, Vienna, and University Hosp., Ann Arbor, Michigan, USA, 1937. President, Soc. of Thoracic Surgeons of Great Britain and Ireland, 1966; Hon. Mem. Amer. Soc. for Thoracic Surgery, 1967. *Publications:* contrib. on surgical diseases of the chest to jls and text books. *Recreations:* fishing, shooting, gardening. *Address:* 2 Elms Road, SW4 9EU.

THOMPSON, William Bell, MA, PhD; Professor of Physics, University of California, 1965–90, now Emeritus; Chairman, Department of Physics, University of California at San Diego, 1969–72; *b* N Ireland, 27 Feb. 1922; *m* 1953, Gertrud Helene Goldschmidt, PhD (marr. diss. 1972); one *s* one *d*; *m* 1972, Johanna Elzelina Ladestein Korevaar. *Educ:* Universities of British Columbia and Toronto, Canada. BA 1945, MA 1947, Univ. of BC; PhD Toronto, 1950. AERE Harwell: Senior Research Fellow, 1950; Deputy Chief Scientist, 1959. Visiting Prof., Univ. of California, 1961; Head, Theoretical Physics Division, Culham Laboratory, UKAEA, 1961–63; Prof. of Theoretical Plasma Physics, Oxford Univ., 1963–65. *Publications:* Introduction to Plasma Physics, 1962; numerous papers in learned journals, on controlled thermonuclear research, plasma physics, kinetic theory, etc. *Recreations:* music, walking. *Address:* Physics Department, University of California at San Diego, La Jolla, CA 92093, USA.

THOMPSON, (William) Godfrey, MA; FSA, FLA, FRSA; library planning consultant, since 1983; *b* 28 June 1921; *s* of late A. and E. M. Thompson, Coventry; *m* 1946, Doreen Mary Cattell; one *s*. *Educ:* King Henry VIII Sch., Coventry. MA Loughborough, 1977. Served with Royal Signals and Indian Signal Corps, 1941–46. Entered Library Service, Coventry, 1937; Dep. Borough Librarian, Chatham, 1946; Dep. City Librarian: Kingston-upon-Hull, 1952; Manchester, 1958; City Librarian, Leeds, 1963; Guildhall Librarian, Director of Libraries and Art Galleries, City of London, 1966–83; Cultural Consultant, UAE, Abu Dhabi, 1983–86. Organiser, City Treasurer's exhibns in Brussels, Vienna, San Francisco etc. Hon. Librarian to Clockmakers' Co., Gardeners' Co., Charles Lamb Soc.; Pres., Assoc. of Assistant Librarians, 1962. Member: Council, Library Assoc., 1968–81 (Hon. Treasurer, 1974–77; Pres., 1978); Council, Aslib, 1968–71; Founding Hon. Sec. Internat. Assoc. Metropolitan Libraries, 1968–70; Adv. Bd, New Library World; Libraries Specialist, Architects' Jl, 1968–74. Member: Adv. Panel to Sec. of State on allocation of books received under Capital Transfer Tax; Adv. Panel to Sec. of State on Export of Works of Art. Mem. Exec. Cttee, Friends of the Nat. Libraries. Governor, St Bride Foundn. Consultant on libraries to more than 20 overseas governments, including the planning of eleven nat. libraries. *Recreation:* reading — at last. *Publications:* London's Statues, 1971; Planning and Design of Library Buildings, 1972, 3rd edn 1989; (ed) London for Everyman, 1969; (ed) Encyclopædia of London, 1969. *Address:* Southdown, Down Lane, Compton, Surrey GU3 1DN.

THOMPSON, (William) Pratt; consultant and director, various companies; *b* 9 Feb. 1933; *s* of Philip Amos Thompson and Regina Beatrice (*née* Kirby); *m* 1963, Jenny Frances Styles; two *d*. *Educ:* Princeton Univ.; Columbia Univ. (BA Econ *magna cum laude*, Phi Beta Kappa); University of Geneva (MBA). AMF Incorporated, 1959–73: executive assignments in NYC, Geneva, Tokyo, Hong Kong and London; Vice Pres., 1968; Dep. Managing Director, Bowthorpe Holdings Ltd, 1973–78; BL Limited, 1978–81: Man. Dir, Jaguar Rover Triumph Ltd, 1978–79; Chm., BL Internat. Ltd, 1979–81; Dir, Metalurgica de Santa Ana SA (Madrid), 1978–81; Vice-Chm., Colbert Gp (Geneva), 1981–84; Chairman: AIDCOM International plc, 1983–86 (Dir, 1982–); AIDCOM Technology Ltd, 1982–86; Husky Computers Ltd, 1982–86; Gallex Ltd, 1989–91; Dir, 1987–93, Man. Dir, 1989–93, Unitech plc. Member: Council, SMM&T, 1978–81; Council on Foreign Relations (USA), 1980–89. Advisor, Internat. Centre for Child Studies, Bristol Univ., 1982–84. *Recreations:* various. *Address:* Trinity Hall, Castle Hedingham, Essex CO9 3EY. *Clubs:* Brooks's; Hong Kong (Hong Kong).

THOMPSON, Willoughby Harry, CMG 1974; CBE 1968 (MBE 1954); *b* 3 Dec. 1919; *m* 1963, Sheelah O'Grady; no *c*. Served War: RA, and E African Artillery, 1939–47. Kenya Govt Service, 1947–48; Colonial Administrative Service, Kenya, 1948–63; Colonial Sec., Falkland Islands, 1963–69 (Actg Governor, 1964 and 1967); Actg Judge, Falkland Islands and Dependencies Supreme Court, 1965–69; Actg Administrator, British Virgin Islands, May-July 1969; HM Commissioner in Anguilla, July 1969–71; Governor of Montserrat, 1971–74.

THOMPSON HANCOCK, P(ercy) E(llis); *see* Hancock.

THOMPSON-McCAUSLAND, Benedict Maurice Perronet, FCA; Partner, Temax Associates, since 1991; Group Managing Director, National & Provincial Building Society, 1987–90; *b* 5 Feb. 1938; *s* of late Lucius P. Thompson-McCausland, CMG and of Helen Laura McCausland; *m* 1964, Frances Catherine Fothergill Smith; three *d*. *Educ:* Eton Coll.; Trinity Coll., Cambridge (MA; Rowing Blue). FCA 1974. Articled to Coopers & Lybrand, Chartered Accountants, 1961–64; Arbuthnot Latham & Co. Ltd, 1964–80: Asst to Dirs, 1964; Banking Manager, 1967; Dir, 1968; Dep. Chm., 1978; London Life Association Ltd: Dir, 1976–81; Vice-Pres., 1979–87; Chief Exec., 1981–87. Dir, Advanced Personnel Technology, 1993–; formerly Director: Western Trust & Savings Ltd; Concord Internat.; First National Finance Corp. plc. Chm., Lombard Assoc., 1979–81. Director: British Sch. of Osteopathy, 1991–; Harefield Hosp. NHS Trust, 1992–. Mem. Council, 1987–, and Mem. Exec. Cttee, 1988–91, Industrial Soc. Mem., Council of Management, Arnolfini Gall., 1983–86. *Publications:* (with Derek Biddle) Change, Business Performance and Values, 1985; (with J. Bergwerk) Leading to Success: how leaders unlock energy, 1994; articles in business jls. *Recreations:* windsurfing, ski-ing, walking. *Address:* 91 Blenheim Crescent, W11 2EQ. *T:* 0171–727 1266. *Clubs:* Leander (Henley-on-Thames); Hawks (Cambridge).

THOMSON, family name of **Barons Thomson of Fleet** and **Thomson of Monifieth.**

THOMSON OF FLEET, 2nd Baron *cr* 1964; **Kenneth Roy Thomson;** newspaper proprietor; Chairman of the Board, The Thomson Corporation; Chairman of the Board and Director: The Thomson Corporation; The Thomson Corporation Plc; The Woodbridge Co. Ltd; Thomson US Inc.; *b* Toronto, Ont., 1 Sept. 1923; *s* of 1st Baron Thomson of Fleet, GBE, founder of Thomson Newspapers, and Edna Alice (*d* 1951), *d* of John Irvine, Drayton, Ont.; *S* father, 1976; *m* 1956, Nora Marilyn, *d* of A. V. Lavis; two *s* one *d*. *Educ:* Upper Canada Coll.; Univ. of Cambridge, England (MA). Served War of 1942–45 with RCAF. Began in editorial dept of Timmins Daily Press, Timmins, Ont., 1947; Advertising Dept, Galt Reporter, Cambridge, Ont, 1948–50, General Manager, 1950–53; returned to Toronto Head Office of Thomson Newspapers to take over direction of Company's Canadian and American operations. Pres. and Dir: Thomson Works of Art Ltd; Director: Hudson's Bay Co.; IBM Canada; Markborough Properties Inc.; Toronto-Dominion Bank. Dep. Chm., 1966–67, Chm., 1968–70, Co-Pres., 1971–81, Times Newspapers Ltd. Member, Baptist Church. *Recreations:* collecting paintings and works of art, walking. *Heir:* *s* Hon. David Kenneth Roy Thomson, *b* 12 June 1957. *Address:* (home) 8 Castle Frank Road, Toronto, Ont M4W 2Z4, Canada; 8 Kensington Palace Gardens, W8; (office) The Thomson Corporation, 65 Queen Street West, Toronto, Ont. M5H 2M8, Canada; The Thomson Corporation Plc, The Quadrangle, PO Box 4YG, 180 Wardour Street, W1A 4YG. *Clubs:* York Downs, National, Toronto, Granite, York, Toronto Hunt (Toronto).

THOMSON OF MONIFIETH, Baron *cr* 1977 (Life Peer), of Monifieth, Dundee; **George Morgan Thomson,** KT 1981; PC 1966; DL; Chairman, Independent Broadcasting Authority, 1981–88 (Deputy Chairman, 1980); Chancellor, Heriot Watt University, 1977–91; *b* 16 Jan. 1921; *s* of late James Thomson, Monifieth; *m* 1948, Grace Jenkins; two *d*. *Educ:* Grove Academy, Dundee. Served War of 1939–45, in Royal Air Force, 1940–46. Assistant Editor, Forward, 1946, Editor, 1948–53. Contested (Lab) Glasgow, Hillhead, 1950; MP (Lab) Dundee East, July 1952–72. Joint Chm., Council for Education in the Commonwealth, 1959–64; Adviser to Educational Institute of Scotland, 1960–64. Minister of State, Foreign Office, 1964–66; Chancellor of the Duchy of Lancaster, 1966–67; Joint Minister of State, Foreign Office, 1967; Secretary of State for Commonwealth Affairs, Aug. 1967–Oct. 1968; Minister Without Portfolio, 1968–69; Chancellor of the Duchy of Lancaster, 1969–70; Shadow Defence Minister, 1970–72. Chm., Labour Cttee for Europe, 1972–73; Commissioner, EEC, 1973–Jan. 1977. Mem., Lib Dems, 1989– (spokesman on foreign affairs and broadcasting, H of L). Chairman: European Movement in Britain, 1977–80; Advertising Standards Authority, 1977–80; European TV and Film Forum, 1989–91. First Crown Estate Comr, 1978–80. Director: Royal Bank of Scotland Gp, 1977–90; ICI plc, 1977–89; Woolwich Equitable Building Soc., 1979–91 (Dep. Chm., 1988–91); Chairman: Value and Income Trust, 1988–; Grant Leisure, 1990–94; Woolwich Europe, 1990–92. President: Hist. of Advertising Trust, 1985–; Prix Italia, 1989–91; Dir, ENO, 1987–93. Chm., Suzy Lamplugh Trust, 1990–93; Dep. Chm., Ditchley Foundn, 1983–87; Pilgrims Trustee, 1977–; Trustee: Thomson Foundn, 1977–; Leeds Castle Foundn, 1978– (Chm., 1994–). FRSE 1985; FRTS 1990 (Vice-Pres., 1982–89). DL Kent, 1992. Hon. LLD Dundee, 1967; Hon. DLitt: Heriot-Watt, 1973; New Univ. of Ulster, 1984; Hon. DSc Aston, 1976. *Address:* House of Lords, SW1A 0PW. *Club:* Brooks's.

THOMSON, Sir Adam, Kt 1983; CBE 1976; Chairman and Chief Executive, British Caledonian Group (formerly The Caledonian Aviation Group plc), 1970–88 (formerly Airways Interests (Thomson) Ltd, Chairman and Managing Director, 1964–70); Chairman and Chief Executive, British Caledonian Airways Ltd, 1970–88; *b* 7 July 1926; *s* of Frank Thomson and Jemina Rodgers; *m* 1948, Dawn Elizabeth Burt; two *s*. *Educ:* Rutherglen Acad.; Coatbridge Coll.; Royal Technical Coll., Glasgow. Pilot; Fleet Air Arm, 1944–47; Flying Instructor/Commercial Pilot, 1947–50; BEA, West African Airways, Britavia, 1951–59. Caledonian Airways: Man. Dir, 1961–64; Chm. and Man. Dir, 1964–70; Chairman: Caledonian Airmotive Ltd, 1978–87; Caledonian Hotel Holdings, 1971–87. Dep. Chm., Martin Currie Pacific Trust PLC, 1985–92; Director: Williams & Glyn's Bank Ltd, 1978–82; Royal Bank of Scotland Gp, 1982–91; Otis Elevators Ltd, 1978–84; MEPC plc, 1982–89. Chairman: Assoc. of European Airlines, 1977–78; Inst. of Directors, 1988–91 (Mem., 1977–). FRAeS; FCIT; FIMgt. Hon. LLD: Glasgow, 1979; Sussex, 1984; Strathclyde, 1986. Businessman of the Year, Hambro Award, 1970; first Scottish Free Enterprise Award, Aims for Freedom and Enterprise, 1976. *Publication:* High Risk: the politics of the air, 1990. *Recreations:* golf, sailing. *Address:* 5 Green Ridge, Westdene, Brighton BN1 5LT.

THOMSON, Prof. Andrew James, DPhil; FRS 1993; CChem, FRSC; Professor of Chemistry, School of Chemical Sciences, University of East Anglia, since 1985; *b* 31 July 1940; *s* of Andrew Henderson Thomson and late Eva Frances Annie (*née* Moss); *m* 1966, Anne Marsden; two *s*. *Educ:* Steyning Grammar Sch.; Wadham Coll., Oxford (MA, DPhil). FRSC 1990. Res. Asst Prof., Dept of Biophysics, Michigan State Univ., 1967; School of Chemical Sciences, University of East Anglia: Demonstrator, 1967–68; Lectr, 1968–77; Sen. Lectr, 1977–83; Reader, 1983–85; Hd of Inorganic Chem. Sector, 1984. *Publications:* articles in Biochem. Jl, Jl Chem. Soc., Dalton Trans. *Recreations:* hill walking, singing. *Address:* 12 Armitage Close, Cringleford, Norwich NR4 6XZ. *T:* Norwich (01603) 504623.

THOMSON, Prof. Andrew William John, PhD; OBE 1993; Professor, School of Management, Open University, since 1988; *b* 26 Jan. 1936; *s* of Andrew Edward Thomson and Helen Thomson; *m* 1st, 1966, Joan Marjorie Hughes (marr. diss. 1980); two *s*; 2nd, 1992, Rosemary Joy Hetherington Smith, *d* of Captain A. H. Shakeshaft, OBE. *Educ:* St Bees Sch.; St Edmund Hall, Oxford (BA Hons PPE 1959); Cornell Univ. (MS 1961; PhD 1968). 2nd Lieut, RA, 1954–56; Lieut, Parachute Regt TA, 1958–63; Brand Manager, Lever Brothers, 1961–65; University of Glasgow: Lectr, Sen. Lectr and Reader, 1968–78; Prof. of Business Policy, 1978–87; Dean: Scottish Business Sch., 1983–87; Sch. of Management, Open Univ., 1988–93. Prof., Univ. of Chicago, 1973, 1977. Mem. and former Mem., numerous govt, industry and research councils, cttees and boards. *Publications:* (with L. C. Hunter) The Nationalised Transport Industries, 1973; (with S. R. Engleman) The Industrial Relations Act, 1975; (with V. V. Murray) Grievance Procedures, 1976; (with P. B. Beaumont) Collective Bargaining in the Public Sector, 1978; (ed with M. Warner) The Behavioural Sciences and Industrial Relations, 1981; (ed with M. B. Gregory) A Portrait of Pay, 1990. *Recreations:* golf, paddling the Net. *Address:* The Willow House, Daventry Road, Norton, Northants NN11 5ND. *T:* Daventry (01327) 79147. *Club:* West Park Golf.

THOMSON, Brian Harold, TD 1947; DL; Chairman, since 1974, Joint Managing Director, since 1948, D. C. Thomson & Co. Ltd; *b* 21 Nov. 1918; *e s* of late William Harold Thomson of Kemback and Helen Irene, *d* of Sir Charles Ballance; *m* 1947, Agnes Jane Patricia Cunninghame (*d* 1991); one *s* four *d*. *Educ:* Charterhouse. Served War of 1939–45: 1st Fife and Forfar Yeomanry, and on Staff, DAQMG 1st Armoured Div., N Africa and Italy, 1943–44. GSO2 Instructor, Staff Coll., Haifa, 1944–46; Lt-Col Comdg Fife and Forfar Yeomanry TA, 1953–56. Entered D. C. Thomson & Co. Ltd, 1937. Director: John Leng & Co. Ltd, 1948–; Southern Television, 1959–88; Alliance Trust and Second Alliance Trust, 1961–89. DL Fife, 1988. *Recreations:* golf, shooting. *Club:* Royal and Ancient Golf (St Andrews).

THOMSON, Sir David; *see* Thomson, Sir F. D. D.

THOMSON, David Paget, RD 1969; Member, Monopolies and Mergers Commission, since 1984; Chairman, F & C Germany Investment Trust, since 1990; Director General, British Invisible Exports Council, 1987–90; *b* 19 March 1931; *s* of Sir George Paget Thomson, FRS, Nobel Laureate, and Kathleen Buchanan Smith; *m* 1959, Patience Mary, *d* of Sir William Lawrence Bragg, CH, OBE, MC, FRS, Nobel Laureate; two *s* two *d*. *Educ:* Rugby Sch.; Grenoble Univ.; Trinity Coll., Cambridge (scholar; BA 1953, MA 1957). Nat. Service, RN (Sub-Lieut), 1953–55; subseq. Lieut-Comdr RNR. Senior Scholar, Trinity Coll., Cambridge, 1955; Lazard Bros & Co., 1956, Director, 1965–86; seconded to HM Diplomatic Service, 1971–73, as Counsellor (Economic), Bonn. Dep. Chm., City Communications Centre, 1987–89. Chm., Jufcrest, 1984–89; Director: Finance Co. Viking, Zurich, 1969–87; Richard Daus & Co., bankers, Frankfurt, 1974–81; Applied Photophysics, 1976–87; Medical Sickness Annuity and Life Assurance Soc. Ltd, 1990–. Member: Council, Brunel Univ., 1974–85; Court of Governors, Henley Management Coll. (formerly Admin. Staff Coll.), 1979–; Dir, Henley Distance Learning Ltd, 1985. Hon. Treasurer, British Dyslexia Assoc., 1984–86. Chairman: Fitzwilliam Mus. Trust, 1988–; Portsmouth Naval Base Property Trust, 1992; Royal Institution: Treasurer, 1976–81; Chm. Council, 1985. CC Oxon 1985–89. Master, Plumbers' Co., 1980–81. *Recreations:* hill-walking, gardening, historical biography. *Address:* Little Stoke House, Wallingford, Oxon OX10 6AX. *T:* Wallingford (01491) 37161. *Club:* Athenæum.

See also S. L. Bragg, Sir J. A. Thomson.

THOMSON, Maj.-Gen. David Phillips, CB 1993; CBE 1989; MC 1965; Senior Army Member, Royal College of Defence Studies, 1992–95; *b* 30 Jan. 1942; *s* of Cyril Robert William Thomson and Louise Mary Thomson (*née* Phillips). *Educ:* Eastbourne Coll.; RMA Sandhurst. Commnd, Argyll and Sutherland Highlanders, 1962; despatches, 1968; Bde Major, 6th Armd Bde, 1975; Instr, Staff Coll., 1980; CO, 1st Bn, A and SH, 1982; Chief of Staff: RMCS, 1985; 1st Armd Div., 1986; Comdr, 1st Inf. Bde/UK Mobile Force, 1987; despatches, 1992. Col, Argyll and Sutherland Highlanders, 1992–. Captain, Royal Castle of Tarbert, 1992–. FRGS 1993. *Recreations:* golf, historical research. *Address:* Regimental HQ, Argyll and Sutherland Highlanders, The Castle, Stirling FK8 1EH. *T:* Stirling (01786) 475165. *Club:* Caledonian.

THOMSON, Rt. Hon. David Spence, CMG 1993; MC 1942; ED; PC 1981; *b* Stratford, 14 Nov. 1915; *s* of Percy Thomson, MBE; *m* 1942, June Grace Adams; one *s* three *d*. *Educ:* Stratford Primary and High Sch. Territorial Army, 1931–; served Middle East, 19th Inf. Bat. 1st Echelon, 1939–42; 2nd NZED, 1939–45; POW 1942; Hon. Col, 5 RNZIR, 1955–81; Brigadier (Reserve of Officers), 2nd Inf. Brig., 1959–60. Dairy farmer; Pres., NZ Federated Farmers Central Taranaki Exec., 1959–63. MP (Nat.) Stratford/Taranaki, 1963–84; Minister of Defence, War Pensions and Rehabilitation, 1966–72, and 1980–84; Minister of Tourism, 1966–69; Minister of Police, 1969–72; Minister of Labour and Immigration, 1972; Minister of Justice, 1975–78; Minister of State Services and Leader, House of Reps, 1978–84. *Recreations:* golf, gardening, classical music. *Address:* 22 Bird Road, Stratford, New Zealand.

THOMSON, Prof. Derick Smith, FBA 1992; FRSE; Professor of Celtic, University of Glasgow, 1963–91, now Emeritus; *b* 5 Aug. 1921; *s* of James and Christina Thomson; *m* 1952, Carol Mac Michael Galbraith; five *s* one *d*. *Educ:* Nicolson Inst., Stornoway; Univ. of Aberdeen (MA); University College of North Wales, Bangor; Emmanuel Coll., Cambridge (BA 1948). Asst in Celtic, Univ. of Edinburgh, 1948–49; Lectr in Welsh, Univ. of Glasgow, 1949–56; Reader in Celtic, Univ. of Aberdeen, 1956–63. Chm., Gaelic Books Council, 1968–91; Pres., Scottish Gaelic Texts Soc. Editor: Scottish Gaelic Studies, 1962–76; Gairm, 1952–. Hon. DLitt: Wales, 1987; Aberdeen, 1994. First recipient, Ossian Prize, FVS Foundn, Hamburg, 1974. *Publications:* The Gaelic Sources of Macpherson's Ossian, 1952; Branwen Verch Lyr, 1961, 2nd edn 1968; An Introduction to Gaelic Poetry, 1974, 2nd edn 1990; The Companion to Gaelic Scotland, 1983, 3rd edn 1994; The MacDiarmid MS Anthology, 1992; Gaelic Poetry in the Eighteenth Century, 1993; *poetry:* (ed) Creachadh Na Clàrsaich (Plundering the Harp), 1982; Smeur an Dòchais (Bramble of Hope), 1992; Meall Garbh (The Rugged Mountain), 1995. *Recreations:* writing, travel, politics, gardening. *Address:* 263 Fenwick Road, Giffnock, Glasgow G46 6JX. *T:* 0141–638 0957. *Clubs:* Glasgow Art, Town and Gown (Glasgow).

THOMSON, Dick; HM Diplomatic Service; Ambassador to the Dominican Republic, since 1995; *b* 18 Dec. 1942; *s* of Adam and Janet Alexander Thomson; *m* 1972, Jacqueline Margaret Dunn; one *s* one *d*. *Educ:* Port Glasgow High Sch.; Greenock High Sch. With Ministry of Transport, 1961–66; entered FCO, 1966; served: Havana, 1969–70; Athens, 1970–71; Rome, 1971–72; Warsaw, 1972–73; Personnel Dept, FCO, 1973–76; San Francisco, 1976–80; Consul, Algiers, 1980–83; Near East and N Africa Dept, FCO, 1984–87; First Sec., Copenhagen, 1988–92; Head of Parly Relns Unit, FCO, 1992–95. *Recreations:* mainly sport—soccer, tennis, swimming. *Address:* c/o Foreign and Commonwealth Office, SW1A 2AH.

THOMSON, Duncan, PhD; Keeper, Scottish National Portrait Gallery, since 1982; *b* 2 Oct. 1934; *s* of Duncan Murdoch Thomson and Jane McFarlane Wilson; *m* 1964, Julia Jane Macphail; one *d*. *Educ:* Airdrie Acad.; Univ. of Edinburgh (MA 1956, PhD 1970); Edinburgh Coll. of Art (Cert. of Coll.; Post-Dip. Scholarship); Moray House Coll. of Educn. Teacher of Art, 1959–67; Asst Keeper, Scottish National Portrait Gall., 1967–82. Scottish Arts Council: Mem., Art Cttee, 1983–89; Chm., Exhibn Panel, 1985–89. *Publications:* The Life and Art of George Jamesone, 1974; Sir Henry Raeburn, 1994; Arikha, 1994; *exhibition catalogues:* A Virtuous and Noble Education, 1971; Painting in Scotland 1570–1650, 1975; Eye to Eye, 1980; (jtly) John Michael Wright, 1982; (jtly) The Queen's Image, 1987. *Recreation:* reading poetry (and thinking about writing it). *Address:* 3 Eglinton Crescent, Edinburgh EH12 5DH. *T:* 0131–225 6430.

THOMSON, Francis Paul, OBE 1975; CEng, MIEE; Consultant on Post Office and Bank Giro Systems, 1968–85; *b* Corstorphine, Edinburgh, 17 Dec. 1914; *y s* of late William George and Elizabeth Hannah Thomson, Goring-by-Sea; *m* 1954, E. Sylvia, *e d* of late Lokförare J. Erik Nilsson, Bollnäs, Sweden. *Educ:* Friends' Sch., Sibford Ferris; Sch. of Engrg, Polytechnic, London; in Denmark and Sweden. TV and radar research, 1935–42; Special Ops Exec., 1942–44; Sen. Planning Engr, Postwar research and reconstruction, communications industry; founded British Post Giro Campaign, 1946 and conducted Campaign to victory in Parlt, 1965; Lectr, Stockholm Univ. Extension, 1947–49; Founder, and Man. Editor, English Illustrated, 1950–61; techn. exports promotion with various firms, esp. electronic equipment, 1950–60; pioneered electronic language laboratory equipment and methods, 1930–; Bank Computerisation Consultant, 1967–80. Governor, Watford Coll. of Technology, 1965–70 (Engrg and Sci. Dept Adv. Cttee, 1972–91); Mem., Communication of Technical Information Adv. Cttee, CGLI; Advr to PO Users' Nat. Council's Giro Sub Cttee, 1975; Founder and first Hon. Sec., SW Herts Post Office Adv. Cttee, 1976–90; First British Cttee Mem., Internat. Centre for Ancient and Modern Tapestry (CITAM), Lausanne, 1974–80. Founder and Hon. Sec., St Andrews Residents' Assoc. (Watford). Mem., Soc. of Authors, 1990–; MIMgt; FIQA 1978. Hon. Fellow, Inst. of Scientific and Technical Communicators, 1975. Life Member: Corstorphine Trust; Anglo-Swedish Soc.; House of Gordon Assoc.; Friends of Chichester Cathedral; Voice of Listener & Viewer. Has donated research papers, book copyrights and mss to Scottish univ. libraries, IEE, Royal Coll. of Art, V&A etc. *Publications:* Giro Credit Transfer Systems, 1964; Money in the Computer Age, 1968; (ed jtly) Banking Automation, 1971; (ed with E. S. Thomson) rev. repr. of A History of Tapestry (2nd edn), by W. G. Thomson, 1973; Tapestry: mirror of history, 1979; numerous papers in European and other learned jls. *Recreations:* gardening, archaeology, walking, Swedish hospitals and healthcare.

THOMSON, Sir (Frederick Douglas) David, 3rd Bt *cr* 1929; Chairman: Jove Investment Trust, since 1983; Britannia Steam Ship Insurance Association Ltd, since 1986 (Director, since 1965); Through Transport Marine Mutual Assurance Association (Burmuda), since 1983 (Director, since 1973); Ptarmigan International Capital Trust (formerly The Castle Cairn Investment Trust Co.), since 1990; Abtrust European Index (formerly Abtrust New European) Investment Trust, since 1990; *b* 14 Feb. 1940; *s* of Sir James Douglas Wishart Thomson, 2nd Bt, and of Evelyn Margaret Isabel, (Bettina), *d* of Lt-Comdr D. W. S. Douglas, RN; *S* father, 1972; *m* 1967, Caroline Anne (marr. diss. 1994), *d* of Major Timothy Stuart Lewis; two *s* one *d*. *Educ:* Eton; University College, Oxford (BA Agric). Worked for Ben Line, 1961–89. Director: Cairn Energy, 1971–; Danae Investment Trust, 1979–; Martin Currie Pacific Trust, 1985–; Kynoch Gp (formerly G. & G. Kynoch), 1990–; James Fisher, 1993–; Laurence J. Smith, 1993–; Asset Management Investment Trust, 1994–. Member: Queen's Body Guard for Scotland, Royal Company of Archers. *Recreations:* shooting, ski-ing, music. *Heir:* *s* Simon Douglas Charles Thomson, *b* 16 June 1969. *Address:* Holylee, Walkerburn, Peeblesshire EH43 6BD. *T:* Walkerburn (01896) 870673.

THOMSON, Garry, CBE 1983; Scientific Adviser to the Trustees and Head of the Scientific Department, National Gallery, London, 1960–85; *b* 13 Sept. 1925; *s* of late Robert Thomson and Mona Spence; *m* 1954, M. R. Saisvasdi Svasti; four *s*. *Educ:* Charterhouse; Magdalene College, Cambridge (MA). Editorial Staff of A History of Technology, 1951; Research Chemist, National Gallery, 1955; Hon. Editor, Studies in Conservation, 1959–67; Pres., Internat. Inst. for Conservation of Historic and Artistic Works, 1983–86. Vice-Pres., Buddhist Soc., London, 1978–88. Trustee, Nat. Museums and Galls on Merseyside, 1986–91. *Publications:* Recent Advances in Conservation (ed), 1963; Museum Climatology (ed), 1967; The Museum Environment, 1978; Reflections on the Life of the Buddha, 1982; The Sceptical Buddhist, 1995. *Address:* Squire's Hill, Tilford, Surrey GU10 2AD. *T:* Runfold (01252) 782206.

THOMSON, George Malcolm, OBE 1990; author and journalist; *b* Leith, Scotland, 2 Aug. 1899; *e s* of Charles Thomson, journalist, and Mary Arthur, *d* of John Eason; *m* 1926, Else (*d* 1957), *d* of Harald Ellefsen, Tœnsberg, Norway; one *s* one *d*; *m* 1963, Diana Van Cortlandt Robertson. *Educ:* Daniel Stewart's College, Edinburgh; Edinburgh University. Journalist. *Publications:* Caledonia, or the Future of the Scots, 1927; A Short History of Scotland, 1930; Crisis in Zanat, 1942; The Twelve Days, 1964; The Robbers Passing By, 1966; The Crime of Mary Stuart, 1967; Vote of Censure, 1968; A Kind of Justice, 1970; Sir Francis Drake, 1972; Lord Castlerosse, 1973; The North-West Passage, 1975; Warrior Prince: Prince Rupert of the Rhine, 1976; The First Churchill: the life of John, 1st Duke of Marlborough, 1979; The Prime Ministers, 1980; The Ball at Glenkerran, 1982; Kronstadt '21, 1985. *Address:* 5 The Mount Square, NW3 6SY. *T:* 0171–435 8775. *Club:* Garrick.

THOMSON, Very Rev. Ian; *see* White-Thomson.

THOMSON, Ian Mackenzie, WS; President, Industrial Tribunals (Scotland), 1989–91; *b* 16 Feb. 1926; *s* of Donald Hugh Thomson and Doris Emma (*née* Moseley); *m* 1950, Elizabeth Marie Wallace; two *s* one *d*. *Educ:* George Watson's Coll.; Edinburgh Univ., 1947–50 (BL). Served Royal Navy, 1944–47. Admitted: Solicitor, 1951; Writer to the Signet, 1958; Partner, Davidson and Syme, WS, and after merger, Dundas and Wilson, CS, 1958–75; full-time Chm., Industrial Tribunals, 1975; Regl Chm., 1978; Temp. Sheriff, 1987. *Recreations:* swimming, walking, reading, occasional fishing. *Club:* Drumsheugh Baths (Edinburgh).

THOMSON, Prof. James Leonard, CBE 1955; Professor Emeritus in Civil Engineering, Royal Military College of Science, Shrivenham, since 1970; *b* 9 Aug. 1905; *s* of James Thomson, Liverpool. *Educ:* University of Manchester; St John's College, Cambridge. Mather & Platt, Ltd, Manchester, 1923–26; Univ. of Manchester, 1926–30 (BSc (Tech.) 1st Cl. Hons and Stoney Prizeman); Lecturer, Technical College, Horwich, 1930–32; Whitworth Senior Scholar, 1931; St John's Coll., Cambridge, 1932–34 (BA 1934, MA 1938); Research Engineer, ICI, Billingham-on-Tees, 1934–38; Lecturer, Dept of Civil and Mechanical Engineering, Univ. of London, King's College, 1938. Seconded for War-time Service: Managing Engineer, HM Royal Ordnance Factory, Pembrey, Carms, 1940–42; Principal Technical Officer, School of Tank Technology, 1942–46. Royal Military College of Science, Shrivenham: Prof. of Mechanical Engrg and Head of Dept of Civil and Mechanical Engrg, 1946–61; Prof. of Civil Engrg and Head of Dept of Civil Engrg, 1965–70; seconded to ME Technical Univ., Ankara, Turkey, 1961–65 : Consultant Dean and Mechanical Engrg Specialist; later Chief Technical Adviser for UNESCO project in Turkey. *Publications:* various scientific papers dealing with High Pressure Techniques. *Recreations:* mountaineering, sailing. *Address:* c/o 33 West Street, Bridport, Dorset DT6 3QW.

THOMSON, James Phillips Spalding, FRCS; Consultant Surgeon, since 1974 and Clinical Director, since 1990, St Mark's Hospital (Northwick Park and St Mark's NHS Trust); *b* 2 Oct. 1939; *s* of Peggy Marion Thomson (*née* Phillips) and James Laing Spalding Thomson, MB ChB; *m* 1968, Dr Anne Katharine (*née* Richards), MB BS, MRCP; one *s* three *d*. *Educ:* Haileybury and Imperial Service Coll.; Middlesex Hosp. Med. Sch., Univ. of London (MB BS 1962; MS 1974); LRCP, MRCS, 1962, FRCS 1969; DObst RCOG 1964. Jun. med. and surgical appts, 1962–71; Demonstrator, Dept of Anatomy, Middlesex Hosp. Med. Sch., 1964–66; Consultant Surgeon: Royal Northern Hosp., 1975–77; Hackney Hosp., 1977–86; Homerton Hosp., 1986–90. Hon. Consultant Surgeon: St John's Hosp. for Diseases of the Skin, 1973–75; St Mary's Hosp., 1982–; St Luke's Hosp. for the Clergy, 1976–; Civil Cons. in Surgery, RAF, 1984–; Civilian Cons. in Colorectal Surgery, RN, 1986–; Hon. Lectr in Surgery, Bart's Hosp. Med. Coll., 1977–94; Hon. Clin. Sen. Lectr in Surgery, St Mary's Hosp. Med. Sch., Imperial Coll., London, 1994–. Hon. Cons. Advr in Surgery, Ileostomy Assoc., 1986–. Examr in Surgery, Univs of Cambridge, Liverpool and London; Mem., Court of Examrs, RCS, 1986–92. Vice-Chm. of Council and Trustee, St Luke's Hosp. for the Clergy, 1992–; Governor, Corp. of Sons of the Clergy, 1988–. Liveryman: Apothecaries' Soc., 1980–; Barbers' Co., 1992–. DM Lambeth, 1987. *Publications:* (jtly) Colorectal Disease, 1981; (jtly) Frontiers in Colorectal Disease, 1986; (jtly) Updates in Coloproctology, 1992; contribs to books and learned jls. *Recreations:* church music, railways, canals. *Address:* The Rowans, 1 Seaforth Gardens, Winchmore Hill, N21 3BT. *T:* 0181–886 3960; Northwick Park and St Mark's NHS Trust, Watford Road, Harrow, Middx HA1 3UJ. *T:* 0181–235 4000; 149 Harley Street, W1N 1HQ. *T:* 0171–935 3137. *Club:* Royal Society of Medicine.

THOMSON, Sir John, KBE 1972; TD 1944; MA; Chairman, Morland and Co. Ltd, 1979–83; Director: Barclays Bank Ltd, 1947–78 (Chairman, 1962–73); Union Discount Company of London Ltd, 1960–74; *b* 1908; *s* of late Guy Thomson, JP, Woodperry, Oxford; *m* 1st, 1935, Elizabeth, JP (*d* 1977), *d* of late Stanley Brotherhood, JP, Thornhaugh Hall, Peterborough; no *c*; 2nd, 1979, Eva Elizabeth (*d* 1993), *d* of Marcus Ralph Russell, and *widow* of Tom Dreaper. *Educ:* Winchester; Magdalen College, Oxford. Commanded Oxfordshire Yeomanry Regt, RATA, 1942–44 and 1947–50. Deputy High Steward of Oxford University; a Curator of Oxford University Chest, 1949–74; Chairman: Nuffield Medical Benefaction, 1951–82 (Trustee, 1947–82); Nuffield Orthopædic Centre Trust, 1949–81. President, British Bankers' Association, 1964–66 (Vice-President, 1963–64); FIB. Mem. Royal Commn on Trade Unions and Employers' Assocs, 1965–68; Mem. BNEC, 1968–71. Hon. Fellow St Catherine's Coll., Oxford. Hon. Colonel: 299 Fd Regt RA (TA), 1964–67; Oxfordshire Territorials, 1967–75; Bt Col, 1950. DL Oxfordshire, 1947–57; High Sheriff of Oxfordshire, 1957; Vice-Lieut, 1957–63; Lord-Lieut, 1963–79. A Steward, Jockey Club, 1974–77. Hon. DCL Oxford, 1957. KStJ 1973. *Address:* Manor Farm House, Spelsbury, Oxford OX7 3LG. *T:* Charlbury (011608) 810266. *Clubs:* Cavalry and Guards, Overseas Bankers' (Vice-Pres., 1969–; Pres., 1968–69).

THOMSON, Sir John (Adam), GCMG 1985 (KCMG 1978; CMG 1972); MA; HM Diplomatic Service, retired; Director, ANZ Grindlays Bank, since 1987; Chairman: Minority Rights Group International, since 1991; Fleming Emerging Markets Investment Trust, since 1991; *b* 27 April 1927; *s* of late Sir George Thomson, FRS, Master of Corpus Christi Coll., Cambridge, 1952–62 (*s* of Sir J. J. Thomson, OM, FRS, Master of Trinity

Coll., Cambridge, 1919–40), and late Kathleen, *d* of Very Rev. Sir George Adam Smith, DD, LLD, Principal of Aberdeen Univ., 1909–35; *m* 1st, 1953, Elizabeth Anne McClure (*d* 1988), *d* of late Norman McClure, Pres. of Ursinus Coll., Penn, USA; three *s* one *d*; 2nd, 1992, Judith Ogden Bullitt, *d* of late John Stanley Ogden, NY, and Olga Geddes Bradshaw, Melbourne. *Educ:* Phillips Exeter Acad., USA; Univ. of Aberdeen; Trinity Coll., Cambridge. Foreign Office, 1950; Third Sec., Jedda, 1951; Damascus, 1954; FO, 1955; Private Sec. to Permanent Under-Secretary, 1958–60; First Sec., Washington, 1960–64; FO, 1964; Acting Head of Planning Staff, 1966; Counsellor, 1967; Head of Planning Staff, FO, 1967; seconded to Cabinet Office as Chief of Assessments Staff, 1968–71; Minister and Dep. Permanent Rep. to N Atlantic Council, 1972–73; Head of UK Delegn to MBFR Exploratory Talks, Vienna, 1973; Asst Under-Sec. of State, FCO, 1973–76; High Comr to India, 1977–82; UK Perm. Rep. to UN, 1982–87. Mem., Howie Cttee on Scottish Secondary Educn, 1990–93. Trustee, Nat. Museums of Scotland, 1991–. Principal Dir, 21st Century Trust, 1987–90; Dir, Minority Rights Gp, USA, 1993–. Member: Council, IISS, 1987–; Council, ODI, 1987–; Governing Body, IDS, 1987–. Dir and Visitor, IAS, Princeton, 1995–. Trustee, Indian Nat. Trust, 1989–. Associate Mem., Nuffield Coll., Oxford, 1987–91. Hon. LLD: Ursinus Coll., Penn, 1984; Aberdeen, 1986; Hon. DHL Allegheny Coll., Penn, 1985. *Publication:* Crusader Castles (with R. Fedden), 1956. *Recreations:* carpets, castles, walking. *Clubs:* Athenæum; Century (New York).

See also Janet Adam Smith (Mrs John Carleton), D. P. Thomson.

THOMSON, Sir John Sutherland, (Sir Ian), KBE 1985 (MBE (mil.) 1944); CMG 1968; retired, 1987; *b* 8 Jan. 1920; *s* of late William Sutherland Thomson and of Jessie McCaig Malloch; *m* 1st, 1945, Nancy Marguerite Kearsley (*d* 1988), Suva, Fiji; seven *s* one *d*; 2nd, 1989, Nancy Caldwell (*née* McColl). *Educ:* High Sch. of Glasgow; Univ. of Glasgow (MA Hons). Served War of 1939–45: Black Watch, 1940; Fiji Military Forces, 1941–45 (Captain). Appointed Cadet, Colonial Administrative Service, Fiji and Western Pacific, 1941; District Administration and Secretariat, Fiji, 1946–54; Seconded to Colonial Office, 1954–56; Dep. Comr, Native Lands and Fisheries, Fiji, 1957–58; Comr of Native Reserves and Chairman, Native Lands and Fisheries Commission, Fiji, 1958–62; Divisional Commissioner, Fiji, 1963–66; Administrator, British Virgin Islands, 1967–71; Acting Governor-Gen., Fiji, 1980–83 on occasions. Indep. Chm., Fiji Sugar Industry, 1971–84; Chairman: Fiji Coconut Bd, 1973–83; Economic Develt Bd, Fiji, 1980–86; Fiji Liquor Laws Review Cttee, 1985; Fiji Nat. Tourism Assoc., 1984–87; Chairman: Sedgwick (Fiji) Ltd, 1984–87; Air Pacific Ltd, 1984–87; Thomson Pacific Resources Ltd, 1988–92. *Publication:* Fiji in the Forties and Fifties, 1994. *Recreations:* golf, gardening. *Address:* 1/4 Fettes Rise, Edinburgh EH4 1QH. *T:* 0131–552 6421.

THOMSON, Prof. Joseph McGeachy; Regius Professor of Law, University of Glasgow, since 1991; *b* 6 May 1948; *s* of James Thomson and Catherine (*née* McGeachy). *Educ:* Keil Sch., Dumbarton; Univ. of Edinburgh (LLB 1970). Lectr in Law, Univ. of Birmingham, 1970–74; Lectr in Laws, King's Coll., London, 1974–84; Prof. of Law, Univ. of Strathclyde, 1984–90. Dep. General Editor, Stair Meml Encyclopaedia of Laws of Scotland, 1984–. *Publications:* Family Law in Scotland, 1987, 2nd edn 1991; Delictual Liability, 1994; contribs to Law Qly Review, Modern Law Review, Juridical Review, Scots Law Times, etc. *Recreations:* opera, ballet, wine and food. *Address:* Department of Law, Stair Building, The University, Glasgow G12 8QQ. *T:* 0141–339 8855; 140 Hyndland Road, Glasgow G12 9PN. *Club:* Glasgow Art.

THOMSON, Malcolm George; QC (Scot.) 1987; *b* 6 April 1950; *s* of late George Robert Thomson, OBE, and of Daphne Ethel Thomson; *m* 1978, Susan Gordon Aitken; two *d*. *Educ:* Edinburgh Acad.; Edinburgh Univ. (LLB). Advocate 1974; called to the Bar, Lincoln's Inn, 1991. Standing Junior Counsel to Dept of Agriculture and Fisheries for Scotland and Forestry Commn in Scotland, 1982–87. *Recreations:* sailing, ski-ing. *Address:* 2 Gamekeeper's Park, Edinburgh EH4 6PA. *T:* 0131–336 5261. *Club:* New (Edinburgh).

THOMSON, Sir Mark (Wilfrid Home), 3rd Bt *cr* 1925, of Old Nunthorpe, Co. York; Chairman, Moorgate Investment Management Ltd; *b* 29 Dec. 1939; *s* of Sir Ivo Wilfrid Home Thomson, 2nd Bt and Sybil Marguerite, *yr d* of C. W. Thompson; *S* father, 1991; *m* 1976, Lady Jacqueline Rufus Isaacs, *o d* of 3rd Marquess of Reading, MBE, MC; three *s* one *d* (incl. twin *s*). *Heir: s* Albert Mark Home Thomson, *b* 3 Aug. 1979. *Address:* 42 Glebe Place, SW3 5JE.

THOMSON, Nigel Ernest Drummond, CBE 1993; Sheriff of Lothian and Borders, at Edinburgh and Peebles, since 1976; *b* 19 June 1926; *y s* of late Rev. James Kyd Thomson, and late Joan Drummond; *m* 1964, Snjólaug Magnússon, *yr d* of late Consul-General Sigursteinn Magnússon; one *s* one *d*. *Educ:* George Watson's College, Edinburgh; Univs of St Andrews and Edinburgh. Served with Scots Guards and Indian Grenadiers, 1944–47. MA (St Andrews) 1950; LLB (Edin.) 1953. Called to Scottish Bar, 1953. Standing Counsel to Scottish Educn Dept, 1961–66; Sheriff of Lanarkshire, later S Strathclyde, Dumfries and Galloway, at Hamilton, 1966–76. Chm., Music Cttee, Scottish Arts Council, 1978–83; Chm., Edinburgh Youth Orchestra, 1986–92. Convenor, Council for Music in Hosps in Scotland. Pres., Speculative Soc., Edinburgh, 1960; Vice President: Tenovus-Scotland, 1985–; British Assoc. for Counselling, 1992–; Hon. Pres., Scottish Assoc. for Counselling, 1978–88. *Recreations:* music, woodwork, golf. *Address:* 50 Grange Road, Edinburgh. *T:* 0131–667 2166. *Clubs:* New (Edinburgh); Arts (Strathaven); Bruntsfield Golf (Edinburgh).

THOMSON, Peter Alexander Bremner, CVO 1986; HM Diplomatic Service; High Commissioner, the Seychelles, since 1995; *b* 16 Jan. 1938; *s* of Alexander Thomson, financial journalist, and Dorothy (*née* Scurr); *m* 1965, Lucinda Sellar; three *s*. *Educ:* Canford School; RN College, Dartmouth; Sch. of African and Oriental Studies, London (BA 1970; MPhil 1975; MA 1991). Sub Lieut and Lieut RN in HM Ships Albion, Plover, Tiger, Ark Royal, Eagle; Lt Comdr ashore in Taiwan and Hong Kong; joined Diplomatic Service, 1975; First Sec., FCO, Lagos, Hong Kong, 1975–84; Counsellor, Peking, 1984–87; High Comr, Belize, 1987–90; Counsellor, FCO, 1991–95. *Recreations:* sailing, walking, 19th century fiction. *Address:* c/o Foreign and Commonwealth Office, SW1A 2AH. *Clubs:* Travellers'; Thames Barge Sailing; Hong Kong.

THOMSON, Robert Howard Garry; *see* Thomson, Garry.

THOMSON, Robert John Stewart, CMG 1969; MBE 1955; Ministry of Defence, 1969–81; *b* 5 May 1922; *s* of late John Stewart Thomson, FRIBA, and late Nellie Thomson (*née* Morris). *Educ:* Bromsgrove Sch.; Worcester Coll., Oxford. Service with Sudan Defence Force, 1943–45. Sudan Political Service, 1943–54 (District Commissioner, 1950–54). Attached Ministry of Defence, 1955–56; First Sec., British High Commission, Accra, 1956–60, 1962–64, Counsellor, 1966–69. *Recreations:* gardening, singing. *Address:* Ardgowan, 119 Lenthay Road, Sherborne, Dorset DT9 6AQ.

THOMSON, Prof. Robert William, PhD; FBA 1995; Calouste Gulbenkian Professor of Armenian Studies and Fellow of Pembroke College, Oxford, since 1992; *b* 24 March 1934; *s* of late David William Thomson and Lilian (*née* Cramphorn); *m* 1963, Judith Ailsa Cawdry; two *s*. *Educ:* George Watson's Boys' Coll., Edinburgh; Sidney Sussex Coll., Cambridge (BA 1955); Trinity Coll., Cambridge (PhD 1962). Halki Theol Coll., Istanbul, 1955–56; Jun. Fellow, Dumbarton Oaks, Washington, 1960–61; Louvain Univ., 1961–62; Harvard University: Instructor, then Asst Prof. of Classical Armenian, Dept of Near Eastern Langs, 1963–69; Mashtots Prof. of Armenian Studies, 1969–92; Chm., Dept of Near Eastern Langs, 1973–78, 1980–81. Dir, Dumbarton Oaks, Washington DC, 1984–89. *Publications:* (ed with J. N. Birdsall) Biblical and Patristic Studies in Memory of Robert Pierce Casey, 1963; Athanasiana Syriaca, 4 parts, 1965–77; Athanasius: Contra Gentes and De Incarnatione, 1971; The Teaching of Saint Gregory, 1971; Introduction to Classical Armenian, 1975; Agathangelos: history of the Armenians, 1977; (with K. B. Bardakjian) Textbook of Modern Western Armenian, 1977; Moses Khorenatsi: history of the Armenians, 1978; Elishe: history of Vardan, 1982; (ed with N. G. Garsoian and T. J. Mathews) East of Byzantium, 1982; (with B. Kendall) David the Invincible Philosopher, 1983; Thomas Artsruni: history of the Artsruni House, 1985; The Armenian Version of Dionysius the Areopagite, 2 vols, 1987; Lazar Parpetsi: history of the Armenians, 1991; Studies in Armenian Literature and Christianity, 1994; The Syriac Version of the Hexaemeron by Basil of Caesarea, 1995; contribs to Jl Theol Studies, Le Muséon, Revue des études arméniennes, Dumbarton Oaks Papers, Oxford Dictionary of Byzantium, Encyclopedia Iranica. *Address:* Oriental Institute, Pusey Lane, Oxford OX1 2LE.

THOMSON, Rosemary Edith Robertson, OBE 1992; JP; Chairman of the Council, Magistrates' Association, since 1993; *b* 3 Oct. 1934; *d* of James Heggie and Cecilia (*née* Walker); *m* 1958, Peter Thomson; one *s* one *d*. *Educ:* Watford Grammar Sch. for Girls; Girton Coll., Cambridge (MA); McGill Univ., Montreal. Open University: Tutor-counsellor, 1974–; counsellor to students in Broadmoor Hosp., 1974–84. Feltham Young Offenders' Institution: Mem., 1980–86; Chm., Bd of Visitors, 1984–86. Mem., Berks Probation Cttee, 1987–. Magistrates' Association: Mem. Council, 1975–; Chm., Trng Cttee, 1981–87; Chm., Berks Br., 1987–92; Dep. Chm., Council, 1987–93. Member: Lord Chancellor's Adv. Cttee on Trng of Magistrates, 1981–84; Judicial Studies Bd, 1985–88; Criminal Justice Consultative Council, 1992–; Magistrates' Courts Consultative Council, 1992–; Council, Commonwealth Magistrates and Judges Assoc., 1991– (Mem., Trng Cttee, 1987–). JP Maidenhead, 1971. Hon. Dr Central England, 1995. *Publications:* numerous articles on magisterial matters mostly in The Magistrate. *Recreations:* sedentary and literary pursuits, looking at pictures, family life. *Address:* Little Lodge, Lower Cookham Road, Maidenhead, Berks SL6 8JT. *T:* Maidenhead (01628) 26816.

THOMSON, Sir Thomas (James), Kt 1991; CBE 1984 (OBE 1978); FRCPGlas, FRCP, FRCPEd, FRCPI; retired; Chairman, Greater Glasgow Health Board, 1987–93; Consultant Physician and Gastroenterologist, Stobhill General Hospital, Glasgow, 1961–87; Hon. Lecturer, Department of Materia Medica, University of Glasgow, 1961–87; *b* 8 April 1923; *s* of Thomas Thomson and Annie Jane Grant; *m* 1948, Jessie Smith Shotbolt; two *s* one *d*. *Educ:* Airdrie Acad.; Univ. of Glasgow (MB, ChB 1945). FRCPGlas 1964 (FRFPSG 1949); FRCP 1969 (MRCP 1950); FRCPEd 1982; FRCPI 1983. Lectr, Dept of Materia Medica, Univ. of Glasgow, 1953–61; Postgrad. Adviser to Glasgow Northern Hosps, 1961–80. Sec., Specialist Adv. Cttee for Gen. Internal Medicine for UK, 1970–74; Chairman: Medico-Pharmaceutical Forum, 1978–80 (Chm., Educn Adv. Bd, 1979–84); National Med. Consultative Cttee for Scotland, 1982–87; Conf. of Royal Colls and Faculties in Scotland, 1982–84; Hon. Sec., 1965–73, Pres., 1982–84, RCPSGlas. Active participation in postgrad. med. educnl cttees, locally, nationally and in EEC. Mem. Ct, Strathclyde Univ., 1993–. Hon. FACP 1983. Hon. LLD Glasgow, 1988. *Publications:* (ed jtly) Dilling's Pharmacology, 1969; Gastroenterology—an integrated course, 1972, 3rd edn 1983; pubns related to gen. medicine, gastroent. and therapeutics. *Recreations:* swimming, golfing. *Address:* 1 Varna Road, Glasgow G14 9NE. *T:* 0141–959 5930. *Club:* Royal Air Force.

THOMSON, William Oliver, MD, DPH, DIH; Chief Administrative Medical Officer, Lanarkshire Health Board, 1973–88; *b* 23 March 1925; *s* of William Crosbie Thomson and Mary Jolie Johnston; *m* 1956, Isobel Lauder Glendinning Brady; two *s*. *Educ:* Allan Glen's Sch., Glasgow; Univ. of Glasgow (MB ChB, MD). DPA; FFCM; FRCPGlas 1988 (MRCPGlas 1986). Chronic student of Gray's Inn, London. Captain, RAMC, 1948–50. Hospital appointments, 1951–53; appointments in Public Health, Glasgow, 1953–60; Admin. MO, Western Regional Hospital Bd, 1960–70; Group Medical Superintendent, Glasgow Maternity and Women's Hospitals, 1970–73; Mem., Health Services Ind. Adv. Cttee, 1980–86. Visiting Lecturer: Univ. of Michigan, Ann Arbor; Ministry of Health, Ontario; Hon. Lectr, Univ. of Glasgow. Med. Advr, Scottish TV, 1992–. Diploma of Scottish Council for Health Educn (for services to health educn), 1979. *Publications:* (jtly) In England Now, 1989; articles on clinical medicine, community medicine, general practice, occupational health and health education, in various medical jls; humorous pieces in The Lancet, BMJ, etc. *Recreations:* walking, talking, writing. *Address:* Flat 7, Silverwells Court, Silverwells Crescent, Bothwell, Glasgow G71 8LT. *T:* Bothwell (01698) 852586.

THONEMANN, Peter Clive, MSc, DPhil; Professor Emeritus, Department of Physics, University College, Swansea (Professor and Head of Department, 1968–84); *b* 3 June 1917. *Educ:* Melbourne Church of England Grammar Sch., Melbourne; Sydney and Oxford Univs. BSc Melbourne, 1940; MSc Sydney, 1945; DPhil Oxford, 1949. Munition Supply Laboratories, Victoria, Australia, 1940; Amalgamated Wireless, Australia, 1942; University of Sydney, Commonwealth Research Fellow, 1944; Trinity Coll. and Clarendon Laboratory, Oxford, ICI Research Fellow, 1946; initiated research for controlled fusion power, 1947–49; United Kingdom Atomic Energy Authority: Head of Controlled Fusion Res., 1949–60; with Res. Unit, 1960–64, Head of B Div., 1964–67, Dep. Dir, 1967–68, Culham Laboratory. *Publications:* many contributions to learned journals. *Address:* Department of Physics, University College of Swansea, Singleton Park, Swansea, Wales SA2 8PP; 130 Bishopston Road, Swansea SA3 3EU. *T:* Swansea (01792) 232669.

THORBURN, Andrew, BSc; FRTPI; FTS; Chairman, Thorburns, since 1990; Principal, Andrew Thorburn Associates, since 1985; *b* 20 March 1934; *s* of James Beresford Thorburn and Marjorie Clara Burford; *m* Margaret Anne Crack; one *s* two *d*. *Educ:* Bridport Grammar Sch.; Univ. of Southampton (BSc). MRTPI 1959, FRTPI 1969. National Service, RN, 1954–56. Planning Asst, Kent CC, 1957–59; Planning Officer, Devon CC, 1959–63; Asst County Planning Officer, Hampshire CC, 1963–68; Dir, Notts and Derbyshire Sub-Region Study, 1968–70; Dep. County Planning Dir, Cheshire CC, 1970–73; County Planning Officer, E Sussex CC, 1973–83; Chief Exec., English Tourist Bd, 1983–85; Head of Tourism and Leisure Div., Grant Thornton, 1986–90. Pres., RTPI, 1982; Mem. Exec., Town and Country Planning Assoc., 1969–81; Founder Trustee, Sussex Heritage Trust, 1978–; Fellow, Tourism Soc., 1983–. *Publication:* Planning Villages, 1971. *Recreations:* sailing, countryside appreciation. *Address:* Hyde Manor, Kingston, Lewes, East Sussex BN7 3PB.

THORLEY, Charles Graham; *b* 4 Jan. 1914; *s* of Charles Lord Thorley; *m* 1958, Peggy Percival Ellis (*née* Boor); one step *s* one step *d*. *Educ:* Manchester Grammar Sch.; King's Coll., Cambridge (Mod. Lang. Scholar). Served War of 1939–45, Eritrea and Cyrenaica (Lt-Col). Entered Civil Service as Economist, Bd of Trade, 1936; attached to British Embassy, China, 1936–38; Mem. British Economic Mission to Belgian Congo, 1940–41; HM Treasury, 1940–57; served on UK financial delegns and missions in Japan, US, Egypt, France, Switzerland, W Germany, etc; Min. of Power, 1957; Under-Secretary and Head of Coal Div., 1965–69; Acct-Gen. and Dir of Finance, 1969. Chm., NATO Petroleum Planning Cttee, 1962–65; Under-Sec., Min. of Technology and DTI, 1969–74. Specialist Advr, House of Lords, 1975–79. *Address:* Preston House, Corton Denham, Sherborne, Dorset DT9 4LS. *T:* Corton Denham (01963) 220269.

THORLEY, Simon Joe; QC 1989; *b* 22 May 1950; *s* of Sir Gerald Bowers Thorley, TD and of Beryl, *d* of G. Preston Rhodes; *m* 1983, Jane Elizabeth Cockcroft; two *s* one *d.* *Educ:* Rugby Sch.; Keble Coll., Oxford (MA Jurisprudence). Called to the Bar, Inner Temple, 1972. Pupilled to William Aldous; in practice at Patent Bar. Chm., Patent Bar Assoc., 1995–; Mem. Council, British Gp, Internat. Assoc. for Protection of Industrial Property, 1993–. *Publication:* (co-ed) Terrell on The Law of Patents, 13th edn 1982, 14th edn 1994. *Recreations:* family, tennis, shooting, opera. *Address:* 3 New Square, Lincoln's Inn, WC2A 3RS. *T:* 0171–405 1111.

THORN, E. Gaston; Politician, Luxembourg; President: Banque Internationale, Luxembourg, since 1985; Mouvement Européen International, since 1985; President—Director General, RTL Luxembourg, since 1987; Member, Public Review Board, Arthur Andersen & Co.; *b* 3 Sept. 1928; *s* of Edouard Thorn and Suzanne Weber; *m* 1957, Liliane Petit; one *s.* *Educ:* Univs of Montpellier, Lausanne, and Paris. DenD. Admitted to Luxembourg Bar; Pres., Nat. Union of Students, Luxembourg, 1959; Member, European Parlt, 1959–69, Vice-Pres., Liberal Group; Pres., Democratic Party, Luxembourg, 1969; Minister of Foreign Affairs and of Foreign Trade, also Minister of Physical Educn and Sport, 1974–77; Prime Minister and Minister of State, 1974–79; Minister of Nat. Econ. and Middle Classes, 1977; of Justice, 1979; Dep. Prime Minister, and Minister of Foreign Affairs, July 1979–1980; Pres., EEC, 1981–85. Pres., 30th Session of UN Gen. Assembly, 1975–76. President: Liberal International, 1970–82; Fedn of Liberal and Democratic Parties of European Community, 1976–80. Decorations include Grand Cross of Orders of Adolphe de Nassau, Couronne de Chêne, and Mérite (Luxembourg), Grand Cross of Légion d'Honneur (France), GCVO and GCMG (GB) and other Grand Crosses. *Recreations:* tennis, reading. *Address:* 1 rue de la Forge, Luxembourg.

THORN, John Leonard, MA; writer and educational consultant; Headmaster of Winchester College, 1968–85; *b* 28 April 1925; *s* of late Stanley and Winifred Thorn; *m* 1955, Veronica Laura, *d* of late Sir Robert Maconochie, OBE, QC; one *s* one *d.* *Educ:* St Paul's School; Corpus Christi College, Cambridge. Served War of 1939–45, Sub-Lieutenant, RNVR, 1943–46. 1st Class Historical Tripos, Parts I and II. Asst Master, Clifton Coll., 1949–61; Headmaster, Repton School, 1961–68. Dir, Winchester Cathedral Trust, 1986–89. Dir, Royal Opera House, Covent Garden, 1971–76. Chm., Headmasters' Conference, 1981. Member: Bd, Securities Assoc., 1987–91; Exec. Cttee, Cancer Res. Campaign, 1987–90; Chm., Hants Bldgs Preservation Trust, 1992– (Vice-Chm., 1989–92); Trustee: British Museum, 1980–85; Oakham Sch., 1985–89. Governor, Stowe Sch., 1985–90; Chm. of Governors, Abingdon Sch., 1991–94. *Publications:* (joint) A History of England, 1961; The Road to Winchester (autobiog.), 1989; various articles. *Address:* 6 Chilbolton Avenue, Winchester SO22 5HD. *T:* Winchester (01962) 855990. *Club:* Garrick.

THORN, Sir John (Samuel), Kt 1984; OBE 1977; Mayor, Port Chalmers Borough Council, 1956–89 (Member, 1938–41, 1947–50 and 1950–53); *b* 19 March 1911; *s* of J. S. Thorn; *m* 1936, Constance Maud, *d* of W. T. Haines; one *s.* *Educ:* Port Chalmers School; King Edward Technical College. Served 1939–45 war, 3rd Div. Apprentice plumber, later plumbing contractor and land agent; Manager, Thorn's Bookshop, 1950–80. Chairman: Municipal Insce Co.; Coastal N Otago United Council. Pres., Municipal Assoc., 1974–; Dep. Chm., Nat. Roads Board, 1974–83. *Address:* 94C Stevenson Avenue, Sawyers Bay, Dunedin, New Zealand.

THORN, Roger Eric; QC 1990; *b* 23 March 1948; twin *s* of James Douglas 'Pat' Thorn and Daphne Elizabeth (*née* Robinson). *Educ:* Mill Hill Sch.; Newcastle Univ. (LLB Hons). Called to the Bar, Middle Temple, 1970 (Harmsworth Schol. and Major Exhibn); NE Circuit, 1970–. Mem., Bd of Faculty of Law, Newcastle Univ., 1990–94. Life Gov., Mill Hill Sch., 1994. *Publications:* A Practical Guide to Road Traffic Accident Claims, 1987, 2nd edn 1991; legal contributor to Negotiating Better Deals, by J. G. Thorn (twin *b*), 1988. *Recreations:* theatre, music, walking, local Amenity Society (Chairman). *Address:* 199 Strand, WC2R 1DR. *T:* 0171–379 9779; New Court Chambers, 3 Broad Chare, Quayside, Newcastle upon Tyne NE1 3DQ. *T:* 0191–232 1980; Whitton Grange, Rothbury, via Morpeth, Northumberland NE65 7RL. *Clubs:* National Liberal; Durham County.

THORNBURGH, Richard Lewis; Partner, Kirkpatrick & Lockhart, 1987–88, 1991–92 and since 1994; *b* 16 July 1932; *s* of Charles G. and Alice S. Thornburgh; *m* 1955, Virginia Hooton (decd); *m* 1963, Virginia Judson; four *s.* *Educ:* Yale Univ. (BEng 1954); Univ. of Pittsburgh Sch. of Law (LLB 1957). Staff Counsel, Aluminum Co. of America, 1957–59; Associate, Kirkpatrick, Pomeroy, Lockhart & Johnson, 1959–69; US Attorney, Western District, Pennsylvania, 1969–75; Asst Attorney General, Criminal Div., US Dept of Justice, 1975–77; Partner, Kirkpatrick Lockhart, Johnson & Hutchison, 1977–79; Governor, Commonwealth of Pennsylvania, 1979–87; Attorney Gen. of the USA, 1988–91; Under-Sec.-Gen. for Admin and Management, UN, 1992–93. Dir, Inst. of Politics, John F. Kennedy Sch. of Govt, 1987–88. Numerous hon. degrees. *Publications:* articles in professional jls. *Address:* 2540 Massachusetts Avenue NW, Washington, DC 20008, USA; Kirkpatrick & Lockhart, 1800 M Street NW, Suite 900, South Lobby, Washington, DC 20036–5891, USA.

THORNE, Benjamin, CMG 1979; MBE 1966; consultant on Far East trade; *b* 19 June 1922; *m* 1949, Sylvia Una (*née* Graves); one *s* two *d.* *Educ:* St Marylebone Grammar Sch.; Regent Street Polytechnic. Served War, RAF, 1940–46. Joined Civil Service, 1946; British Trade Commission: India, 1950–54; Ghana, 1954–58; Nigeria, 1958–61; Hong Kong, 1964–68; Dir, British Week in Tokyo, 1968–69; Commercial Counsellor, Tokyo, 1973–79, retd. Japanese Order of the Sacred Treasure, 3rd cl., 1975. *Recreations:* cricket, travel, gardening, reading. *Address:* 34 Quarry Hill Road, Borough Green, Sevenoaks, Kent TN15 8RH. *T:* Borough Green (01732) 882547. *Clubs:* Civil Service; Hong Kong (Hong Kong); Foreign Correspondents' (Tokyo); Yokohama Country and Athletic.

THORNE, Maj.-Gen. Sir David (Calthrop), KBE 1983 (CBE 1979; OBE 1975); CVO 1995; Director General, Commonwealth Trust, since 1989; *b* 13 Dec. 1933; *s* of Richard Everard Thorne and Audrey Ursula (*née* Bone); *m* 1962, Susan Anne Goldsmith; one *s* two *d.* *Educ:* St Edward's Sch., Oxford; RMA, Sandhurst. Staff Coll., Camberley, 1963; jssc 1967; Defence Intelligence Staff, MoD, 1968–70; Instructor, RAF Staff Coll., 1970–72; CO 1 Royal Anglian, 1972–74; Col, General Staff, MoD, 1975–77; Comdr, 3rd Inf. Bde, NI, 1978–79; RCDS 1980; VQMG, 1981–82; Comdr, British Forces Falkland Islands, July 1982–April 1983; Comdr, 1st Armoured Div., 1983–85. Dep. Col, Royal Anglian Regt, 1981–86; Col Comdt, Queen's Div., 1986–88; Dir of Infantry, 1986–88. Dir, W Suffolk Hosps NHS Trust, 1993–. Pres., Norfolk CCC, 1993–. *Recreations:* cricket, squash, butterfly collecting. *Address:* c/o Barclays Bank, 52 Abbeygate Street, Bury St Edmunds, Suffolk IP33 1LL. *Clubs:* Army and Navy, MCC.

THORNE, Rear-Adm. (retd) Edward Courtney, CB 1975; CBE 1971; Chairman, Manuahi Enterprises; Chairman, New Zealand Fire Service Commission, 1976–86; Chief of Naval Staff, New Zealand, 1972–75; *b* 29 Oct. 1923; *s* of Ernest Alexander Thorne and Ethel Violet Thorne; *m* 1949, Fay Bradburn (*née* Kerr); three *s.* *Educ:* Rongotai Coll.; Nelson Coll., NZ. IDC 1966. Chm., Nat. Council, United World Colls, 1982–94; Mem., Nat. Council, Duke of Edinburgh Award Scheme, 1976–89; Pres., Sea Cadet Assoc. of NZ, 1990–. Hon. FIFireE 1983. *Recreations:* golf, gardening, walking. *Address:* 75 Hatton Street, Karori, Wellington 5, New Zealand.

THORNE, Sir Neil (Gordon), Kt 1992; OBE 1980; TD 1969; DL; *b* 8 Aug. 1932; *s* of late Henry Frederick Thorne and Ivy Gladys Thorne. *Educ:* City of London Sch.; London Univ. BSc. FRICS. Asst Adjt, 58 Med. Regt, RA, BAOR, 1957–59. Sen. Partner, Hull & Co., Chartered Surveyors, 1962–76. Councillor, London Borough of Redbridge, 1965–68, Alderman, 1975–78; Mem., GLC and Chm., Central Area Bd, 1967–73. MP (C) Ilford South, 1979–92; Founder and first Chm., Unpaired Members Gp, 1982–85; Chairman: British Nepalese Parly Gp, 1983–92; British Korean Parly Gp, 1988–92; Vice Chm., UK Br., IPU, 1987–90; Member: Defence Select Cttee, 1983–92; Court of Referees, 1987–92. Chm., H of C Motor Club, 1985–91; Founder and Chairman: Armed Forces Parly Scheme, 1988–; Police Service Parly Scheme, 1994–. Chm., Britain-Nepal Soc., 1992–. Mem., TA, 1952–82; CO, London Univ. OTC, 1976–80. Fellow, Industry and Parliament Trust, 1980 and 1990. Chairman: Nat. Council for Civil Defence, 1982–86; St Edward's Housing Assoc., 1986–93; Ilford Age Concern, 1984–87; President: Redbridge Parkinson's Disease Soc., 1982–; Ilford Arthritis Care, 1986–; Gtr London Dist, St John Ambulance, 1992–; Vice Pres., Ilford Tuberculosis and Chest Care Assoc., 1987–; Patron, Jubilee Club for Visually Handicapped, 1986–; Trustee, Children In Distress (Romanian Children's Hospices charity). Chm., Lord Mayor's Appeal for St Paul's Cathedral, 1993–94. Jun. Grand Warden, United Grand Lodge of England, 1994–95; Prov. Grand Master for Essex, 1995–. DL Greater London, 1991. CStJ 1992 (Mem., Chapter Gen., 1989–; Almoner, 1995–). Silver Jubilee Medal, 1977. HQA (Pakistan), 1991; GDB (Nepal), 1991. *Publications:* Pedestrianised Streets: a study of Europe and America, 1973; Highway Robbery in the Twentieth Century: policy reform for compulsory purchase, 1990. *Address:* 60 Gyllyngdune Gardens, Ilford IG3 9HY. *T:* 0181–590 3262. *Clubs:* St John House; Ilford Conservative.

THORNE, Sir Peter (Francis), KCVO 1981; CBE 1966; ERD; Serjeant at Arms, House of Commons, 1976–82; *b* 1914; *y s* of late Gen. Sir Andrew Thorne, KCB, CMG, DSO; *m* 1959, Lady Anne Pery, MA, DPhil, Senior Res. Fellow, Imperial College of Science and Technology, *d* of 5th Earl of Limerick, GBE, CH, KCB, DSO, TD; one *s* three *d.* *Educ:* Eton; Trinity Coll., Oxford. Served War of 1939–45: with 3rd Bn Grenadier Guards (wounded), 1939–41; HQ 2nd Div., 1941–42; Staff College, Quetta, 1942; on staff of India Command and HQ, SACSEA, 1943–45; demobilised with rank of Hon. Lieut-Col, 1946. With Imperial Chemical Industries Ltd, 1946–48. Assistant Serjeant at Arms, House of Commons, 1948–57, Dep. Serjeant at Arms, 1957–76. *Publications:* The Royal Mace in the House of Commons, 1990; various HMSO pamphlets and articles in parly and historical pubns. *Address:* Chiddinglye Farmhouse, West Hoathly, East Grinstead, West Sussex RH19 4QS. *T:* Sharpthorne (01342) 810338. *Clubs:* Cavalry and Guards; Royal Yacht Squadron.

THORNE, Robin Horton John, CMG 1966; OBE 1963; HM Overseas Service, retired; *b* 13 July 1917; *s* of late Sir John Anderson Thorne; *m* 1946, Joan Helen Wadman; one *s.* *Educ:* Dragon Sch., Oxford; Rugby (open scholar); Exeter College, Oxford (open scholar; MA). War Service, Devonshire Regiment and King's African Rifles, 1939–46. Colonial Administrative Service (now HM Overseas Civil Service), 1946–67; Tanganyika Administration, 1946–58; Aden, 1958–67; Asst Chief Sec. (Colony), MLC and Mem. of Governor's Exec. Coun., 1959–63; Ministerial Sec. to Chief Minister, 1963–65; Assistant High Commissioner, 1966–67. With Vice-Chancellors' Cttee, 1967–77; part-time admin. work, Univ. of Sussex, 1978–81. Trustee of Aden Port Trust, 1959–66; Chm., Staines Trust, 1979–85; Mem., Management Cttee, Sussex Housing Assoc. for the Aged, 1983–87. *Recreations:* various. *Address:* The Old Vicarage, Old Heathfield, East Sussex TN21 9AD. *T:* Heathfield (01435) 863160. *Club:* Commonwealth Trust.

THORNE, Stanley George; *b* 22 July 1918; *s* of postman and dressmaker; *m* Catherine Mary Rand; two *s* three *d.* *Educ:* Ruskin Coll., Oxford; Univ. of Liverpool. Dip. Social Studies Oxon 1968; BA Hons Liverpool 1970. 30 yrs in industry and commerce: coal-miner, semi-skilled fitter, chartered accountant's clerk, rly signalman, office manager, auditor, commercial manager, etc; lectr in govt and industrial sociology. MP (Lab): Preston South, Feb. 1974–1983; Preston 1983–87. *Recreations:* chess, bridge, golf. *Address:* 26 Station Road, Gateacre, Liverpool L25 3PZ.

THORNELY, Gervase Michael Cobham; Headmaster of Sedbergh School, 1954–75; *b* 21 Oct. 1918; *er s* of late Major J. E. B. Thornely, OBE, and late Hon. Mrs M. H. Thornely; *m* 1954, Jennifer Margery, *d* of late Sir Hilary Scott, Knowle House, Addington, Surrey; two *s* two *d.* *Educ:* Rugby Sch.; Trinity Hall, Cambridge. Organ Scholar; 2nd Cl. Hons, Modern and Mediæval Languages Tripos; BA, 1940; MA, 1944. FRSA 1968. Assistant Master, Sedbergh School, 1940. *Recreations:* music, fly-fishing. *Address:* High Stangerthwaite, Killington, Sedbergh, Cumbria LA10 5EP. *T:* Sedbergh (015396) 20444.

THORNHILL, Andrew Robert; QC 1985; *b* 4 Aug. 1943; *s* of Edward Percy Thornhill and Amelia Joy Thornhill; *m* 1971, Helen Mary Livingston; two *s* two *d.* *Educ:* Clifton Coll. Prep. Sch.; Clifton Coll.; Corpus Christi Coll., Oxford. Called to the Bar, Middle Temple, 1969; entered chambers of H. H. Monroe, QC, 1969. *Publications:* (ed) Potter & Monroe: Tax Planning with Precedents, 7th edn 1974, to 9th edn 1982; (jtly) Tax Planning Through Wills, 1981, 1984; (jtly) Passing Down the Family Farm, 1982; (jtly) Passing Down the Family Business, 1984. *Recreations:* dinghy sailing, squash, walking. *Address:* 37 Canynge Road, Clifton, Bristol BS8 3LD. *T:* Bristol (0117) 974 4015. *Clubs:* United Oxford & Cambridge University; Tamesis (Teddington); Bristol Avon Sailing.

THORNHILL, Lt-Col Edmund Basil, MC 1918; *b* 27 Feb. 1898; *e s* of late E. H. Thornhill, Manor House, Boxworth, Cambridge; *m* 1934, Diana Pearl Day Beales (*d* 1983), *d* of late Hubert G. D. Beales, Hambleden and Cambridge; two *s* one *d.* *Educ:* St Bees School; Royal Military Academy. 2nd Lieut Royal Artillery, 1916; served European War, 1914–18, France and Belgium (wounded, MC); served War of 1939–45, France, Western Desert (Eighth Army) and Italy (despatches); psc 1934; Lt-Col 1945; retd 1948. Chm., Cambs and I of Ely TA & AFA, 1957–62. DL Cambs and Isle of Ely, 1956, Vice-Lieut, 1965–75. *Address:* Manor House, Boxworth, Cambridge CB3 8NF. *T:* Elsworth (01954) 267209. *Club:* Army and Navy.

See also Lt-Col H. W. Davies.

THORNING-PETERSEN, Rudolph; Knight Commander, Order of the Dannebrog, 1994; Ambassador of Denmark to the Court of St James's, since 1989; *b* 17 July 1927; *s* of Erik Thorning-Petersen, FRDanAA, architect, and Helga (*née* Westergaard); *m* 1949, Britta Leyssac; one *s* one *d.* *Educ:* Copenhagen Univ. (LLM 1952). Entered Royal Danish Foreign Service, 1952; alternating service, Min. of Foreign Affairs and at Danish Embassies in Cairo, Moscow and Stockholm, 1952–75; Ambassador to Lebanon, Syria, Jordan, Iraq and Cyprus (resident Beirut), 1975; to People's Republic of China, 1980, to USSR, 1983–89 Knight Grand Cross, Order of Cedar (Lebanon); Order of Independence (Jordan); Comdr, Order of Polar Star (Sweden). *Recreations:* modern history, genealogy, history of art. *Address:* Royal Danish Embassy, 55 Sloane Street, SW1X 9SR. *T:* 0171–333 0200. *Clubs:* Travellers', Royal Automobile.

THORNTON, Allan Charles; Chairman, Environmental Investigation Agency, since 1988 (Co-Founder and Director, 1984–86); *b* 17 Nov. 1949; *s* of Robert Charles Thornton and Jessie (Waldram) Thornton. *Educ:* Banff Centre of Fine Art, Banff, Canada. Co-ordinator of Banff Centre Creative Writing Programme, 1976, 1977; established Greenpeace UK, 1977; Exec. Dir, 1977–81 and 1986–88; co-founder of Greenpeace vessel, Rainbow Warrior, 1978; Internat. Project Co-ordinator with Greenpeace International, 1981. *Recreation:* saving African elephants and viewing them in the wilds of Tanzania and other African countries. *Address:* c/o Environmental Investigation Agency, 2 Peartree Court, EC1R 0DS. *T:* 0171–490 7040.

THORNTON, Anthony Christopher Lawrence; QC 1988; **His Honour Judge Thornton;** a Circuit Judge, since 1994; *b* 18 Aug. 1947; *s* of Richard Thornton and Margery Alice (*née* Clerk); *m* 1983, Lyn Christine Thurlby; one *s*. *Educ:* Eton Coll.; Keble Coll., Oxford (BCL, MA). AIArb. Called to the Bar, Middle Temple, 1970, Bencher, 1992. A Recorder, 1992–94. Chairman: Fulham Legal Advice Centre, 1973–78; Hammersmith and Fulham Law Centre, 1975–78. External Moderator, Centre of Construction and Project Management, KCL, 1987–; Hon. Sen. Vis. Fellow, Centre for Commercial Law Studies, QMC, 1987–. Mem., Gen. Council of the Bar, 1988–94 (Treas., 1990–92; Chm., Professional Standards Cttee, 1992–93). Dir, Apex Trust, 1991–94. Liveryman, Leathersellers' Co., 1976–. Jt Editor, Construction Law Jl, 1984–. *Publications:* (ed jtly) Building Contracts, in Halsbury's Laws of England, vol. 4, 1973, repr. 1992; (contrib.) Construction Disputes: liability and the expert witness, 1989; (ed jtly) Fay's Official Referees' Business, 2nd edn 1995; contribs to Construction Law Jl. *Recreations:* cricket, opera. *Address:* Official Referees' Courts, St Dunstan's House, EC4A 1HD. *T:* 0171–404 0102. *Club:* Royal Automobile.

THORNTON, Clive Edward Ian, CBE 1983; LLB (Lond); FInstLEx, FCBSI; Chairman: Gabriel Communications (formerly Universe Publications) Ltd, since 1986; Melton Mowbray Building Society, since 1991 (Director, since 1988); Armstrong Capital Holdings Ltd, since 1988; *b* 12 Dec. 1929; *s* of Albert and Margaret Thornton; *m* 1956, Maureen Carmine (*née* Crane); one *s* one *d*. *Educ:* St Anthony's Sch., Newcastle upon Tyne; Coll. of Commerce, Newcastle upon Tyne; College of Law, London; LLB London. Solicitor. FInstLEx 1958; FCBSI 1970. Associate, Pensions Management Inst. Articled to Kenneth Hudson, solicitor, London, 1959; admitted solicitor of Supreme Court, 1963. Asst Solicitor, Nationwide Building Soc., 1963; Solicitor, Cassel Arenz Ltd, Merchant Bankers, 1964–67; Abbey National Building Society: Chief Solicitor, 1967; Dep. Chief Gen. Man., 1978; Chief Gen. Manager, 1979–83; Dir, 1980–83; Partner, Stoneham Langton and Passmore, Solicitors, 1985–88. Chm., Metropolitan Assoc. of Building Socs, 1981–82. Chairman: Mirror Group Newspapers, 1984; Financial Weekly, 1985–87; Thamesmead Town Ltd, 1986–90; Dir, Investment Data Services Ltd, 1986–90; Proprietor, Thorndale Devon Cattle, 1983–. Member: Law Soc. (Chm., Commerce and Industry Gp, 1974); Council, Chartered Bldg Socs Inst., 1973–81; Council, Building Socs Assoc., 1979–83; Bd, Housing Corp., 1980–86. Chairman: SHAC, 1983–86; Belford Hall Management Co. Ltd, 1990–93. Mem. Council, St Mary's Hosp. Med. Sch., 1984–. Freeman, City of London; Liveryman, Worshipful Co. of Bakers. *Publications:* Building Society Law, Cases and Materials, 1969 (3rd edn 1988); History of Devon Cattle, 1994. *Recreations:* antique collecting, music, reading, farming. *Address:* Keythorpe Grange, East Norton, Leics LE7 9XL.

THORNTON, Sir (George) Malcolm, Kt 1992; MP (C) Crosby, since 1983 (Liverpool, Garston, 1979–83); *b* 3 April 1939; *s* of George Edmund and Ethel Thornton; *m* 1st, 1962; one *s*; 2nd, 1972, Shirley Ann, (Sue) (*née* Banton) (*d* 1989); 3rd, 1990, Rosemary (*née* Hewitt). *Educ:* Wallasey Grammar Sch.; Liverpool Nautical Coll. Liverpool Pilot Service, 1955–79 (Sen. 1st cl. Licence holder). Member: Wallasey County Borough Council, 1965–74 (Chm., Transport Cttee, 1968–69); Wirral Metropolitan Council, 1973–79 (Council Leader, 1974–77); Chairman: Merseyside Metropolitan Districts Liaison Cttee, 1975–77; Educn Cttee, AMA, 1978–79 (Mem., 1974–79); Council of Local Educn Authorities, 1978. Mem., Burnham (Primary and Secondary) Cttee, 1975–79. PPS to Sec. of State for Industry, 1981–83, for the Environment, 1983–84. Chm., Select Cttee on Educn, Sci. and the Arts, 1989– (Mem., 1985–). FRSA. Hon. DEd De Montfort, 1994. *Recreations:* fishing, sailing, cooking. *Address:* House of Commons, SW1A 0AA. *T:* 0171–219 4489. *Club:* Wyresdale Anglers.

THORNTON, Helen Ann Elizabeth, (Mrs J. E. C. Thornton); *see* Meixner, H. A. E.

THORNTON, Jack Edward Clive, CB 1978; OBE 1964 (MBE 1945); *b* 22 Nov. 1915; *s* of late Stanley Henry Thornton and Elizabeth Daisy (*née* Baxter); *m* 1st, Margaret, JP, *d* of late John David and Emily Copeland, Crewe, Cheshire; 2nd, Helen Ann Elizabeth Meixner, *qv*. *Educ:* Solihull Sch.; Christ's Coll., Cambridge (Open Exhibnr 1936; BA 1938). Cert. Educn 1939; MA 1942. Served in RASC, 1939–46 (despatches, 1946); Lt-Col 1944. Teaching in UK, 1946–47; Asst, then Dep. Educn Officer, City of York, 1947–51; Asst Educn Officer, WR Yorks, 1951–54; Dep. Dir of Educn, Cumberland, 1954–62; Sec., Bureau for External Aid for Educn, Fed. Govt of Nigeria, 1962–64; Educn Consultant, IBRD, 1964–65; Adviser on Educn in W Africa and Controller Appts Div., British Council, 1965–68; Dep. Educn Adviser, 1968–70, Chief Educn Adviser and Under Sec., 1970–77, Ministry of Overseas Devlt (now Overseas Devlt Admin in FCO). Lectr, Dept of Educn in Developing Countries, Inst. of Educn, Univ. of London, 1978–79. Chm., PNEU World-wide Educn Service, 1979–90; Member: Exec. Cttee, Council for Educn in the Commonwealth, 1978– (Chm., 1979–85; Dep. Chm., 1985–90); Lloyd Foundn, 1981– (Vice-Chm., 1988–95); Educational Panel, Independent Schs Tribunal, 1978–; Charlotte Mason Coll. Higher Educn Corp., 1986–92; Trustee, Christopher Cox Meml Fund, 1983–. *Recreations:* books, conservation, gardens, mountains, music, railways, travel. *Address:* 131 Dalling Road, W6 0ET. *T:* 0181–748 7692; 15 Chepstow House, Chepstow Street, Manchester M1 5JF. *T:* 0161–237 1407.

THORNTON, John Henry, OBE 1987; QPM 1980; Deputy Assistant Commissioner, Metropolitan Police, 1981–86; *b* 24 Dec. 1930; *s* of late Sidney Thornton and Ethel Thornton (*née* Grinnell); *m* 1st, 1952, Norma Lucille, *d* of Alfred and Kate Scrivenor (marr. diss. 1972); two *s*; 2nd, 1972, Hazel Ann, *d* of William and Edna Butler; one *s* one *d* (and one *s* decd). *Educ:* Prince Henry's Grammar School. Evesham. RN 1949–50. Metropolitan Police, 1950; Head of Community Relations, 1977–80; RCDS, 1981; Dep. Asst Commissioner, 1981; Dir of Information, 1982–83; Hd of Training, 1983–85; NW Area, 1985–86. Vice-Pres., British Section, Internat. Police Assoc., 1969–79. Chm., Breakaway Theatre Co., St Albans, 1987–94; Chm., St Albans Internat. Organ Fest., 1988–91. Chm. of Govs, Townsend C of E Sch., St Albans, 1990–. Lay Canon and Cathedral Warden, St Albans, 1988–94. Liveryman, Glaziers' Co., 1983. CStJ 1984. *Recreations:* music, gardening, classics. *Address:* c/o Barclays Bank, 16 High Street, Harpenden, Herts AL5 2TD.

THORNTON, Lt-Gen. Sir Leonard (Whitmore), KCB 1967 (CB 1962); CBE 1957 (OBE 1944); *b* Christchurch, 15 Oct. 1916; *s* of late Cuthbert John Thornton and Frances Caverhill Thornton; *m* 1942, Gladys Janet Sloman, Wellington; three *s*; *m* 1971, Ruth Leicester, Wellington. *Educ:* Christchurch Boys' High Sch.; Royal Military Coll., Duntroon, Australia. Commissioned in New Zealand Army, 1937. Served War of 1939–45 (despatches twice, OBE), Middle East and Italy in 2nd New Zealand Expeditionary Force; Commander, Royal Artillery, 2 New Zealand Division. Commander, Tokyo Sub-area, 1946; Deputy Chief of General Staff, 1948; idc 1952; Head, New Zealand Joint Service Liaison Staff, 1953 and 1954; QMG, New Zealand, 1955; AG, 1956–58; Chief, SEATO Planning Office, Thailand, 1958–59; Chief of General Staff, NZ, 1960–65; Chief of Defence Staff, NZ, 1965–71; Ambassador for New Zealand in S Vietnam and Khmer Republic, 1972–74. Chm., Alcoholic Liquor Adv. Council, 1977–83. *Recreation:* fishing. *Address:* 20 Beauchamp Street, Wellington 5, New Zealand. *Club:* Wellington (Wellington).

THORNTON, Sir Malcolm; *see* Thornton, Sir G. M.

THORNTON, Neil Ross; Head, Exports to Europe and the Americas Division, Department of Trade and Industry, since 1993; *b* 11 Feb. 1950; *s* of George and Kay Thornton; *m* 1977, Christine Anne Boyes; two *d*. *Educ:* Sedbergh Sch.; Pembroke Coll., Cambridge (BA Eng. 1971). Private Sec. to Perm. Sec., DoI, 1975; HM Treasury, 1979; Asst Sec., DTI, 1984; Principal Private Sec. to Sec. of State for Trade and Industry, 1988–90; Under Sec., DTI, 1990. *Recreations:* literature, choral singing, golf. *Address:* Department of Trade and Industry, 66–74 Victoria Street, SW1E 6SW. *T:* 0171–215 5000.

THORNTON, Sir Peter (Eustace), KCB 1974 (CB 1971); Permanent Secretary, Department of Trade, 1974–77; *b* 28 Aug. 1917; *s* of Douglas Oscar Thornton and Dorothy (*née* Shepherd); *m* 1946, Rosamond Hobart Myers, US Medal of Freedom, Sewanee, Tennessee; two *s* one *d*. *Educ:* Charterhouse; Gonville and Caius Coll., Cambridge. Served with RA, mainly in Middle East and Italy, 1940–46. Joined Board of Trade, 1946. Secretary, Company Law Cttee (Jenkins Cttee), 1959–62; Assistant Under-Secretary of State, Department of Economic Affairs, 1964–67; Under-Sec., 1967–70, Dep. Sec., 1970–72, Cabinet Office, with central co-ordinating role during British negotiations for membership of EEC; Dep. Sec., DTI, March-July 1972; Sec. (Aerospace and Shipping), DTI, 1972–74; Second Permanent Sec., Dept of Trade, 1974. Director: Hill Samuel Gp, 1977–83; Rolls Royce, 1977–85; Courtaulds, 1977–87; Laird Gp, 1978–92; Superior Oil, 1980–84. Mem., Megaw Cttee of Inquiry into Civil Service Pay, 1981–82. Pro-Chancellor, Open Univ., 1979–83 (DUniv 1984). Governor, Sutton's Hosp., Charterhouse, 1980–89.

THORNTON, Peter Kai, FSA 1976; Curator of Sir John Soane's Museum, 1984–95; *b* 8 April 1925; *s* of Sir Gerard Thornton, FRS, and of Gerda, *d* of Kai Nørregaard, Copenhagen; *m* 1950, Mary Ann Rosamund, *d* of E. A. P. Helps, Cregane, Rosscarbery, Co. Cork; three *d*. *Educ:* Bryanston Sch.; De Havilland Aeronautical Technical Sch.; Trinity Hall, Cambridge. Served with Army, Intelligence Corps, Austria, 1945–48; Cambridge, 1948–50; Voluntary Asst Keeper, Fitzwilliam Museum, Cambridge, 1950–52; Joint Secretary, National Art-Collections Fund, London, 1952–54; entered Victoria and Albert Museum as Asst Keeper, Dept of Textiles, 1954; transf. to Dept of Woodwork, 1962; Keeper, Dept of Furniture and Woodwork, 1966–84. Sen. Vis. Res. Fellow, St John's Coll., Oxford, 1985–86; Leverhulme Emeritus Res. Fellow, 1988–89. Chm., Furniture History Soc., 1974–84; Member: Council, Nat. Trust, 1983–85; London Adv. Cttee, English Heritage, 1986–88. *Publications:* Baroque and Rococo Silks, 1965; Seventeenth Century Interior Decoration in England, France and Holland, 1978 (Alice Davis Hitchcock Medallion, Soc. of Architectural Historians of GB, 1982); (jtly) The Furnishing and Decoration of Ham House, 1981; Musical Instruments as Works of Art, 1982; Authentic Décor: the domestic interior 1620–1920, 1984 (Sir Bannister Fletcher Prize, RIBA, 1985); (jtly) The Italian Renaissance Interior 1400–1600, 1992 (Prix Vasari International du Livre d'Art for French edn, 1992); (jtly) A Miscellany of Objects from Sir John Soane's Museum, 1992. *Address:* 102 West Kensington Court, W14 9AB; Ballycahane, Castletownshend, Co. Cork, Eire.

See also Hon. P. Jay.

THORNTON, Peter Ribblesdale; QC 1992; an Assistant Recorder, since 1994; *b* 17 Oct. 1946; *s* of Robert Ribblesdale Thornton, *qv*; *m* 1981, Susan Margaret Dalal; one *s* one *d*. *Educ:* Clifton Coll.; St John's Coll., Cambridge (BA). Called to the Bar, Middle Temple, 1969. Chairman: NCCL, 1981–83; Civil Liberties Trust, 1991–. *Publications:* (contrib.) Civil Liberties 1984, 1984; We Protest: Public Order Debate, 1985; The Civil Liberties of the Zircon Affair, 1987; Public Order Law, 1987; (contrib.) The Polygraph Test, 1988; Decade of Decline: Civil Liberties in the Thatcher Years, 1989; (ed jtly) Penguin Civil Liberty Guide, 1989; (jtly) Justice on Trial, 1992; (ed jtly) Archbold's Criminal Pleadings, Evidence and Practice, 1994. *Address:* Doughty Street Chambers, 11 Doughty Street, WC1N 2PG. *T:* 0171–404 1313.

THORNTON, Richard Eustace, OBE 1980; JP; HM Lord Lieutenant of Surrey, since 1986; *b* 10 Oct. 1922; *m* 1954, Gabrielle Elizabeth Sharpe; four *d*. *Educ:* Eton Coll.; Trinity Coll., Cambridge (MA). Member: Thames Conservancy, 1968–74; TWA, 1974–80; Royal Commission on Environmental Pollution, 1977–84. Chm., Mount Alvernia Management Trust, 1992–. Chm. Govs, Bishop Reindorp Sch., 1985–; Mem. Governing Body, Charterhouse Sch. (Chm., 1981–89). Surrey: DL; High Sheriff 1978–79; JP. KStJ 1986. *Address:* Hampton, Seale, near Farnham, Surrey GU10 1JE. *T:* Guildford (01483) 810208.

THORNTON, Robert John, CB 1980; Assistant Under Secretary of State and Director General of Supplies and Transport (Naval), Ministry of Defence, 1977–81; *b* 23 Dec. 1919; *s* of Herbert John Thornton and Ethel Mary Thornton (*née* Dunning); *m* 1944, Joan Elizabeth Roberts; three *s*. *Educ:* Queen Elizabeth Grammar School, Atherstone. MBIM 1970. Joined Naval Store Dept, Admiralty, as Asst Naval Store Officer, 1938; Singapore, 1941; Dep. Naval Store Officer, Colombo, 1942; Support Ship Hong Siang, 1943; Naval Store Officer, Admiralty, 1945; Gibraltar, 1951; Asst Dir of Stores, 1955; Superintending Naval Store Officer, Portsmouth, 1960; Dep. Dir of Stores, 1964; Dir of Victualling, 1971; Dir of Supplies and Transport (General Stores and Victualling), 1971. *Recreations:* bowls, fly fishing, gardening.

THORNTON, Robert Ribblesdale, CBE 1973; DL; solicitor; Deputy Chairman, Local Government Boundary Commission for England, 1982 (Member, 1976–82); *b* 2 April 1913; *s* of Thomas Thornton and Florence Thornton (*née* Gatenby); *m* 1940, Ruth Eleonore Tuckson; one *s* one *d*. *Educ:* Leeds Grammar Sch.; St John's Coll., Cambridge (MA, LLM). Asst Solicitor, Leeds, 1938–40 and 1946–47. Served War, 1940–46. Asst Solicitor, Bristol, 1947–53; Dep. Town Clerk, Southampton, 1953–54; Town Clerk: Salford, 1954–66; Leicester, 1966–73; Chief Exec., Leicestershire CC, 1973–76. Pres.,

Soc. of Town Clerks, 1971. Treasurer, Leicester Univ., 1980–85. Hon. LLD Leicester, 1987. DL Leicestershire, 1974–85. French Croix de Guerre, 1946. *Recreations:* music, sport. *Address:* 16 St Mary's Close, Winterborne Whitechurch, Blandford Forum, Dorset DT11 0DJ. *T:* Milton Abbas (01258) 880980.

See also P. R. Thornton.

THORNTON, Sally; *see* Burgess, Sally.

THORNTON, Dr William Dickson, CB 1990; Deputy Chief Medical Officer, Department of Health and Social Services, Northern Ireland, 1978–90, retired; *b* 9 July 1930; *s* of late William J. Thornton and of Elfreda Thornton (*née* Dickson); *m* 1957, Dr Maureen Gilpin; one *s* three *d. Educ:* Portora Royal School; Trinity College Dublin (BA, MD). FFPHM. General medical practitioner, 1955–65; NI Hospitals Authy, 1966–72; Dept of Health and Social Services (NI), 1973–90. Civil QHP, 1990–92. *Recreations:* yachting, reading, gardening. *Address:* 54 Deramore Park South, Belfast BT9 5JY. *T:* Belfast (01232) 660186.

THOROGOOD, Alfreda, (Mrs D. R. Wall), ARAD (PDTC); Artistic Advisor, Royal Academy of Dancing, since 1989; *b* 17 Aug. 1942; *d* of Alfreda and Edward Thorogood; *m* 1967, David Wall, *qv*; one *s* one *d. Educ:* Lady Eden's Sch.; Royal Ballet Sch., Jun. and Sen. Royal Ballet Company, 1960–80: Soloist, Aug. 1965; Principal Dancer, 1968; Bush Davies School: Sen. Teacher, 1982–84; Dep. Ballet Principal, 1984–89; Dir, 1988–89; Sen. Teacher, Elmhurst Ballet Sch., 1992–. *Recreations:* listening to music, cooking, interior design, art, painting. *Address:* 34 Croham Manor Road, S Croydon CR2 7BE.

THOROGOOD, Rev. Bernard George, OBE 1992; General Secretary, United Reformed Church, 1980–92; *b* 21 July 1927; *s* of Frederick and Winifred Thorogood; *m* 1952, Jannett Lindsay Paton (*née* Cameron) (*d* 1988); two *s*; *m* 1991, Joan Tierney. *Educ:* Glasgow Univ. (MA); Scottish Congregational College. Ordained in Congregational Church, 1952; missionary appointment under London Missionary Society in South Pacific Islands, 1953–70; Gen. Sec., Council for World Mission, 1971–80. Moderator, Exec. Cttee, BCC, 1984–90; Mem., Central Cttee, WCC, 1984–91. DD Lambeth 1992. *Publications:* Not Quite Paradise, 1960; Guide to the Book of Amos, 1971; Our Father's House, 1983; Risen Today, 1987; The Flag and The Cross, 1988; No Abiding City, 1989; On Judging Caesar, 1990; One Wind Many Flames, 1991; Looking at Leisure: a European view, 1991; (ed) Glass of Change, 1994. *Recreation:* sketching. *Address:* 2 Ashmore Avenue, Pymble, NSW 2073, Australia. *T:* (2) 441822.

THOROGOOD, Kenneth Alfred Charles; *b* 1924; *s* of Albert Jesse and Alice Lucy Thorogood; *m* 1st, 1947, José Patricia Smith; two *d*; 2nd, 1979, Mrs Gaye Lambourne. *Educ:* Highbury County Grammar School. Pilot, RAF, 1941–46. Chm., Tozer Kemsley & Millbourn (Holdings) plc, 1972–82; Dep. Chm. and Dir, Felixstowe Dock and Railway Co., 1976–81; Director: Alexanders Discount Co. Ltd, to 1983; Royal Insurance Co. Ltd; Abelson Plant (Holdings) Ltd; Spicer-Firgos Ltd; Welbeck Finance plc, 1984–88. Chairman, Brit. Export Houses Assoc., 1968–70; Mem., Cttee of Invisibles, 1968–70. *Recreations:* aviation, music. *Address:* Flat 1, 18 Lowndes Square, SW1X 9HB. *Clubs:* Travellers', City of London, Royal Air Force, MCC; Wanderers (Johannesburg).

THOROLD, Captain Sir Anthony (Henry), 15th Bt, *cr* 1642; OBE 1942; DSC 1942, and Bar 1945; JP; RN Retired; *b* 7 Sept. 1903; *s* of Sir James (Ernest) Thorold, 14th Bt; *S* father, 1965; *m* 1939, Jocelyn Elaine Laura (*d* 1993), *er d* of late Sir Clifford Heathcote-Smith, KBE, CMG; one *s* two *d. Educ:* Royal Naval Colleges Osborne and Dartmouth. Entered RN 1917; qualified as Navigating Officer, 1928; psc 1935; Commander, 1940; served in Mediterranean and Home Fleets, 1939–40; Staff Officer Operations to Flag Officer Commanding Force 'H', 1941–43; in command of Escort Groups in Western Approaches Comd, 1944–45; Captain, 1946; Naval Assistant Secretary in Cabinet Office and Ministry of Defence, 1945–48; Sen. Officer, Fishery Protection Flotilla, 1949–50; Captain of HMS Dryad (Navigation and Direction Sch.), 1951–52; Commodore in Charge, Hong Kong, 1953–55; ADC to the Queen, 1955–56; retired, 1956. DL Lincs, 1959–95; JP Lincolnshire (Parts of Kesteven), 1961; High Sheriff of Lincolnshire, 1968. Chairman: Grantham Hospital Management Cttee, 1963–74; Lincoln Diocesan Trust and Board of Finance, 1966–71; Community Council of Lincs, 1974–81; CC Kesteven, 1958–74; Leader, Lincs County Council, 1973–81. *Recreation:* shooting. *Heir: s* (Anthony) Oliver Thorold [*b* 15 April 1945; *m* 1977, Genevra M., *y d* of John Richardson, Midlothian; one *s* one *d*]. *Address:* Syston Old Hall, Grantham, Lincs NG32 2BX. *T:* Loveden (01400) 250270. *Club:* Army and Navy.

THORP, David; Chairman: Unipalm Group plc, since 1994 (Chairman, Unipalm Ltd, 1992–94); Patientline plc, since 1994; Director, Baronsmead plc, since 1995; *b* 22 July 1945; *s* of John and Kathleen Mary Thorp; *m* 1969, Christine Janice Kenyon; three *s. Educ:* Portsmouth Grammar Sch.; Queens' College, Cambridge (MA Natural Scis); London Business School (MBA). Alcan (UK), 1967–69; Investors in Industry plc, 1971, Dir, 1985–91; Dir-Gen, ESU, 1991–94. Non-Exec. Dir, Royal Surrey County Hosp., 1990–. MInstD 1986 (Mem., Corporate Governance Cttee, 1986–). *Recreations:* cricket, tennis, singing. *Address:* Larks Hill, 16 Longdown, Guildford, Surrey GU4 8PP. *T:* Guildford (01483) 572851.

THORP, Jeremy Walter; HM Diplomatic Service; Head, Resource and Finance Department, Foreign and Commonwealth Office, since 1993; *b* 12 Dec. 1941; *s* of Walter and Dorothy Bliss Thorp; *m* 1973, Estela Lessa Guyer. *Educ:* Corpus Christi Coll., Oxford (MA). HM Treasury, 1963–67; DEA, 1967–69; HM Treasury, 1969–71; First Sec. (Financial), HM Embassy, Washington, 1971–73; HM Treasury, 1973–78; FCO, 1978–82; Head of Chancery, Lima, 1982–86; FCO, 1986–88; Dep. Hd of Mission, Dublin, 1988–92. *Recreations:* music, travel, 20th century history, walking. *Address:* c/o Foreign and Commonwealth Office, King Charles Street, SW1A 2AH. *Club:* Kildare Street and University (Dublin).

THORPE, Adrian Charles, CMG 1994; MA; HM Diplomatic Service; Ambassador to the Philippines, since 1995; *b* 29 July 1942; *o s* of late Prof. Lewis Thorpe and of Dr Barbara Reynolds, *qv*; *m* 1968, Miyoko Kosugi. *Educ:* The Leys Sch., Cambridge; Christ's Coll., Cambridge (MA). HM Diplomatic Service, 1965–: Tokyo, 1965–70; FCO, 1970–73; Beirut, 1973–76 (Head of Chancery, 1975–76); FCO, 1976; Tokyo, 1976–81; FCO, 1981–85, Hd of IT Dept, 1982–85; Counsellor (Econ.), Bonn, 1985–89; Dep. High Comr, Kuala Lumpur, 1989–91; Minister, Tokyo, 1991–95. FRSA. *Publications:* articles in journals. *Recreations:* opera, travel, bookshops, comfort. *Address:* c/o Foreign and Commonwealth Office, SW1A 2AH. *Clubs:* Tokyo, Foreign Correspondents' (Tokyo).

THORPE, Anthony Geoffrey Younghusband; His Honour Judge Thorpe; a Circuit Judge, since 1990; *b* 21 Aug. 1941; *s* of G. J. Y. Thorpe, MBE; *m* 1966, Janet Patricia; one *s* one *d. Educ:* Highgate School; Britannia Royal Naval College (scholarship); King's College London. Royal Navy: served HM Ships Hermes, Ark Royal, Vidal, Blake; Captain 1983; Chief Naval Judge Advocate, 1983–86; retired from RN 1990. Called to the Bar, Inner Temple, 1972 (Treasurer's Prize); Asst Recorder, 1984–89, Recorder, 1989–90. Pres., Indep. Tribunal Service, 1992–94 (Social Security, Medical, Disability, and Vaccine Damage Appeals, Child Support Appeals). *Publications:* articles in learned jls. *Recreations:* sailing. *Address:* c/o Lloyds Bank, 4 West Street, Havant PO9 1PE. *Club:* Naval.

THORPE, Brian Russell, CBE 1987; Deputy Chairman, Southern Water PLC (formerly Southern Water Authority), 1983–93 (Chief Executive, 1973–88); *b* 12 July 1929; *s* of late Robert and Florrie Thorpe; *m* 1955, Ann Sinclair Raby; three *d. Educ:* Rastrick Grammar Sch. LLB London, LLM Leeds. Solicitor, 1952. Asst Prosecuting Solicitor, Bradford CC, 1954–55; Asst Solicitor, later Asst Town Clerk, Southampton CC, 1955–61; Dep. Town Clerk, Blackpool, 1961–65; Gen. Man., Sussex River Authority, 1965–73. Churchill Fellow, 1972. *Recreations:* golf, gardening, foreign travel. *Address:* First Avenue, Worthing. *Club:* Worthing Golf.

THORPE, Rt. Hon. (John) Jeremy, PC 1967; Chairman, Jeremy Thorpe Associates (Development Consultants in the Third World), since 1984; *b* 29 April 1929; *s* of late J. H. Thorpe, OBE, KC, MP (C) Rusholme, and Ursula, *d* of Sir John Norton-Griffiths, 1st Bt, KCB, DSO, sometime MP (C); *m* 1st, 1968, Caroline (*d* 1970), *d* of Warwick Allpass, Kingswood, Surrey; one *s*; 2nd, 1973, Marion, *d* of late Erwin Stein. *Educ:* Rectory Sch., Connecticut, USA; Eton Coll.; Trinity Coll., Oxford, Hon. Fellow, 1972. President, Oxford Union Society, Hilary, 1951; Barrister, Inner Temple, 1954. Member Devon Sessions. Contested (L) N Devon, 1955; MP (L) Devon N, 1959–79. Hon. Treasurer, Liberal Party Organisation, 1965–67; Leader, Liberal Party, 1967–76; Pres., N Devon Liberal Democrats (formerly N Devon Liberal Assoc.), 1987–. United Nations Association: Chm., Exec., 1976–80; Chm., Political Cttee, 1977–85. FRSA. Hon. LLD Exeter, 1974. *Publications:* (jtly) To all who are interested in Democracy, 1951; Europe: the case for going in, 1971; contrib. to newspapers and periodicals. *Recreations:* music; collecting Chinese ceramics. *Address:* 2 Orme Square, W2 4RS. *Clubs:* National Liberal; N Devon Liberal.

THORPE, Hon. Sir Mathew Alexander, Kt 1988; **Hon. Mr Justice Thorpe;** a Judge of the High Court of Justice, Family Division, since 1988; *b* 1938; *s* of late Michael Alexander Thorpe and of Dorothea Margaret Lambert; *m* 1st, 1966, Lavinia Hermione Buxton (marr. diss. 1989); three *s*; 2nd, 1989, Mrs Carola Millar. *Educ:* Stowe; Balliol Coll., Oxford. Called to the Bar, Inner Temple, 1961, Bencher, 1985; QC 1980; a Recorder, 1982–88. *Address:* Royal Courts of Justice, Strand, WC2A 2LL.

THORPE, Nigel James, CVO 1991; HM Diplomatic Service; Head, Central European Department, Foreign and Commonwealth Office, since 1992; *b* 3 Oct. 1945; *s* of Ronald Thorpe and Glenys (*née* Robilliard); *m* 1969 (marr. diss. 1976); two *s*; *m* 1978, Susan Bamforth; two *d. Educ:* East Grinstead Grammar Sch.; University Coll. of S Wales and Monmouthshire (BA Hons). Joined HM Diplomatic Service, 1969; Warsaw, 1970–72; Dacca, 1973–74; FCO, 1975–79; Ottawa, 1979–81; seconded to Dept of Energy, 1981–82; Asst Hd of Southern Africa Dept, FCO, 1982–85; Counsellor, Warsaw, 1985–88; Dep. High Comr, Harare, 1989–92. *Recreations:* my family, keeping fit, carpentry. *Address:* c/o Foreign and Commonwealth Office, King Charles Street, SW1A 2AH.

THORPE, Phillip Andrew; Chief Executive, Investment Management Regulatory Organisation Ltd, since 1993; *b* 26 Aug. 1954; *s* of Reginald Thorpe, OBE and Fay Eglantine Thorpe; *m* 1st, 1976, Isabell Hanna Henkel (marr. diss. 1989); one *s* two *d*; 2nd, 1990, Melinda Kilgour Lowis; one *s* one *d. Educ:* Victoria Univ., Wellington, NZ (BA Pol Sci., LLB); Univ. of Hong Kong (MSocSc Dist.). Admitted Barrister and Solicitor of Supreme Court of NZ and as Solicitor and Notary Public, Republic of Nauru. Solicitor, Beyer Christie O'Regan & Partners, Wellington, NZ, 1976–79; Legal Officer and Public Prosecutor, Govt of Republic of Nauru, 1979–81; Solicitor, Registrar-General's Dept, Hong Kong Govt, 1981–83; Hong Kong Securities Commission: Sen. Legal Advr, 1983–86; Asst Comr, 1986–88; Dep. Comr, 1988–89; Exec. Vice-Chm. and Chief Exec., Hong Kong Futures Exchange, 1987–89; Chief Exec., Assoc. of Futures Brokers and Dealers Ltd, 1989–91; Exec. Dir and Dep. Chief Exec., SFA Ltd, 1991–93; Exec. Dir and Chief Exec., London Commodity Exchange (1986) Ltd, 1991–92. *Publication:* (Country Editor for Hong Kong) International Securities Regulation, 1986. *Recreations:* viticulture, bricolage, long distance driving. *Club:* Hong Kong Cricket.

THORPE, Prof. Stephen Austen, PhD; FRS 1991; Professor of Oceanography, University of Southampton, since 1986. *Educ:* Rutherford Coll., Newcastle (BSc); Trinity Coll., Cambridge (BA 1961; PhD 1966). SPSO, Inst. of Oceanographic Scis, NERC, until 1986. Mem., NERC, 1991–94 (Mem., Marine Scis Cttee). Pres., RMetS, 1990–92. *Publications:* contribs to learned jls. *Address:* Department of Oceanography, The University, Southampton SO9 5NH. *T:* Southampton (01703) 593755; Merrie Meade, Birch Road, Chilworth, Southampton SO1 7LN.

THORPE-TRACEY, Stephen Frederick; Controller, Newcastle Central Office, Department of Social Security (formerly of Health and Social Security), 1986–89, retired; *b* 27 Dec. 1929; *s* of Rev. and Mrs J. S. V. Thorpe-Tracey; *m* 1955, Shirley Byles; one *s* two *d. Educ:* Plymouth Coll. Emergency Commn, 1948; Short Service Commn, 1950; Regular Commn, DLI, 1952; Staff Coll., Camberley, 1960 (psc); GS02, Defence Operational Res. Estabt, 1961–64; Training Major, 8 DLI (TA), 1964–65; Major, 1 DLI, 1965–66; GSO2, MoD, 1966–70; direct entry, Home Civil Service, 1970; Principal, DHSS, 1970; Asst Sec., 1977; Under Sec., 1986. Chm., Northern Gp, RIPA, 1988–90. Mem., Prescription Pricing Authy, 1990–93. Chm., Grantlands Residents' Assoc., 1993–; Vice Chm., Carr-Gomm (Tyneside) Housing Assoc. Ltd, 1990–91. Hon. Sec., Mid Devon Div., SSAFA and FHS, 1992–. Mem., Uffculme Parish Council, 1995–. Chm., Uffculme Soc., 1994–. Sec. Trustees, Childharbour Mill, 1994–. Hon. Sec., Civil Service Chess Assoc., 1974–77; Chm., Tiverton Chess Club, 1994–; Cdre, Goring Thames Sailing Club, 1981–82. *Publications:* T^2 series of articles in military jls. *Recreations:* chess, golf, fell-walking. *Address:* 9 Grantlands, Uffculme, Cullompton, Devon EX15 3ED. *T:* Cullompton (01884) 841864.

THOULESS, Prof. David James, FRS 1979; Professor of Physics, University of Washington, since 1980; *b* 21 Sept. 1934; *s* of late Robert Henry Thouless; *m* 1958, Margaret Elizabeth Scrase; two *s* one *d. Educ:* Winchester Coll.; Trinity Hall, Cambridge (BA); Cornell Univ. (PhD). Physicist, Lawrence Radiation Laboratory, Berkeley, Calif, 1958–59; ICI Research Fellow, Birmingham Univ., 1959–61; Lecturer, Cambridge Univ., and Fellow of Churchill Coll., 1961–65; Prof. of Mathematical Physics, Birmingham Univ., 1965–78; Prof. of Applied Science, Yale Univ., 1979–80; Royal Soc. Res. Prof., and Fellow of Clare Hall, Cambridge Univ., 1983–86. Mem., US Nat. Acad. Scis, 1995. Wolf Prize for Physics, Wolf Foundn, Israel, 1990; Dirac Prize, Inst. of Physics, 1993. *Publication:* Quantum Mechanics of Many-Body Systems, 1961, 2nd edn 1972. *Address:* Department of Physics FM-15, University of Washington, Seattle, WA 98195, USA.

THOURON, Sir John (Rupert Hunt), KBE 1976 (CBE 1967); *b* 10 May 1908; *m* 1st, 1930, Lorna Ellett (marr. diss. 1939); one *s*; 2nd, 1953, Esther duPont (*d* 1984). *Educ:* Sherborne School, Dorset. Served War of 1939–45; Major, Black Watch. With Lady Thouron, Founder of the Thouron University of Pennsylvania Fund for British-American Student Exchange, 1960. *Recreations:* shooting, fishing, golf, gardening. *Address:* Unionville,

Chester County, PA 19375, USA. *T:* (215) 3845542; (winter) 416 South Beach Road, Hobe Sound, FL 33455, USA. *T:* (407) 5463577. *Clubs:* White's; Brook (NY); Sunningdale Golf; Royal St George Golf; Wilmington, Wilmington Country, Vicmead (all Delaware); Pine Valley, British Officers Club of Philadelphia (Pennsylvania); Seminole Golf, Island Club of Hobe Sound (Florida).

THRELFALL, David; actor; *b* 12 Oct. 1953. *Educ:* Wilbraham Comprehensive Sch.; Sheffield Art Coll.; Manchester Polytechnic Sch. of Theatre. *Stage:* Bed of Roses, Royal Court; 3 years with RSC, incl. Savage Amusement, Nicholas Nickleby, 1980 (Clarence Derwent Award, British Theatre Assoc., SWET Award); Not Quite Jerusalem, Royal Court, 1982; Hamlet, Edinburgh Fest., 1986; Bussy D'Ambois, Old Vic, 1988; Wild Duck, Phoenix, 1990; Count of Monte Cristo, Royal Exchange, 1994; Richard II, Cottesloe, RNT, 1995; *television:* The Kiss of Death, 1976; Nicholas Nickleby, 1984; Paradise Postponed, 1985; The Marksman, 1988; Jumping the Queue, 1989; Nightingales, 1990–; Titmuss Regained, 1991; Clothes in the Wardrobe, Statement of Affairs, 1993; Diana: Her True Story, 1993; Men of the World, 1994; *films:* When the Whales Came, 1989; The Russia House, 1990; Patriot Games, 1992. Plays and Players Promising Newcomer, 1978. *Recreations:* motor bike, squash, gym, friends. *Address:* c/o James Sharkey Associates, 21 Golden Square, W1R 8RU.

THRELFALL, Richard Ian, QC 1965; *b* 14 Jan. 1920; *s* of William Bernhard and Evelyn Alice Threlfall; *m* 1948, Annette, *d* of George C. H. Matthey; two *s* three *d* (and one *s* decd). *Educ:* Oundle; Gonville and Caius Coll., Cambridge. War service, 1940–45 (despatches twice); Indian Armoured Corps (Probyn's Horse) and Staff appointments. Barrister, Lincoln's Inn, 1947, Bencher 1973. FSA, 1949. Mem. Court of Assistants, Worshipful Co. of Goldsmiths (Prime Warden, 1978–79). *Address:* Pebble Hill House, Limpsfield, Surrey RH8 0EA. *T:* Oxted (01883) 712452.

THRING, Rear-Adm. George Arthur, CB 1958; DSO 1940 and Bar 1952; DL; *b* 13 Sept. 1903; *s* of late Sir Arthur Thring, KCB; *m* 1929, Betty Mary (*d* 1983), *er d* of Colonel Stewart William Ward Blacker, DSO; two *s* two *d*. *Educ:* Royal Naval Colleges, Osborne and Dartmouth. Commander, 1941; Captain, 1946; Rear-Admiral, 1956; retired, 1958. Commanded: HMS Deptford, 1940–41; 42nd and 20th Escort Groups, Atlantic, 1943–45; HMS Ceylon, 1951–52; Flag Officer, Malayan Area, 1956–58. Officer, Legion of Merit (USA), 1945. DL Somerset, 1968. *Recreations:* golf, shooting and fishing. *Address:* Alford House, Castle Cary, Somerset BA7 7PN. *T:* Wheathill (01963) 240329.

THRING, Prof. Meredith Wooldridge, ScD; FEng; Professor of Mechanical Engineering, Queen Mary College, London University, 1964–81; *b* 17 Dec. 1915; *s* of Captain W. H. C. S. Thring, CBE, RN, and Dorothy (*née* Wooldridge); *m* 1940, Alice Margaret Hooley (*d* 1986), two *s* one *d*. *Educ:* Malvern Coll., Worcs; Trinity Coll., Cambridge (Senior Scholar, 1937). Hons Degree Maths and Physics, 1937; ScD, 1964. Student's Medal, Inst. of Fuel, for work on producer gas mains, 1938; British Coal Utilisation Research Assoc.: Asst Scientific Officer, 1937; Senior Scientific Officer and Head of Combustion Research Laboratory, 1944; British Iron and Steel Research Assoc.: Head of Physics Dept, 1946; Superintendent, 1950; Assistant Director, 1953; Prof. of Fuel Technology and Chemical Engineering, Sheffield Univ., 1953–64. General Superintendent International Flame Radiation Research Foundn, 1951–76. Visitor: Production Engineering Research Assoc., 1967; Machine Tool Industry Research Assoc., 1967. Member Clean Air Council, 1957–62; Fuel Research Board, 1957–58; Fire Research Board, 1961–64; BISRA Council, 1958–60; President, Inst. of Fuel, 1962–63 (Vice-President, 1959–62); Member: Adv. Council on Research and Development, Ministry of Power, 1960–66; Acad. Adv. Council, University of Strathclyde, 1962–67; Education Cttee, RAF, 1968–76; Unesco Commn to Bangladesh, 1979. FInstP 1944; FInstF 1951; FIChemE 1972 (MIChemE 1956); FIMechE 1968 (MIMechE 1964), FIEE 1968 (MIEE 1964); FEng 1976 (a Founder Fellow); FRSA 1964; MRI 1965; FRAeS 1969. Elected Mem., Royal Norwegian Scientific Soc., 1974; Corresp. Mem., Nat. Acad. of Engineering of Mexico, 1977. Lectures: Parsons Meml on Magnetohydrodynamics, 1961; First Wenca, Lagos, 1989. DUniv Open, 1982. Sir Robert Hadfield medal of Iron and Steel Inst. for studies on open hearth furnaces, 1949. *Publications:* The Science of Flames and Furnaces, 1952, 2nd edn, 1960; (with J. H. Chesters) The Influence of Port Design on Open Hearth Furnace Flames (Iron and Steel Institute Special Report 37), 1946; (with R. Edgeworth Johnstone) Pilot Plants, Models and Scale-up Methods in Chemical Engineering, 1957; (ed.) Air Pollution, 1957; Nuclear Propulsion, 1961; Man, Machines and Tomorrow, 1973; Machines—Masters or Slaves of Man?, 1973; (ed with R. J. Crookes) Energy and Humanity, 1974; (with E. R. Laithwaite) How to Invent, 1977; The Engineer's Conscience, 1980; Robots and Telechirs, 1983. *Recreations:* arboriculture, wood-carving. *Address:* Bell Farm, Brundish, Suffolk IP13 8BL. *Club:* Athenæum.

THROCKMORTON, Clare McLaren, (Mrs Andrew McLaren); *see* Tritton, E. C.

THRUSH, Prof. Brian Arthur, FRS 1976; Professor of Physical Chemistry, University of Cambridge, 1978–Sept. 1995; Fellow, Emmanuel College, Cambridge, since 1960; *b* Hampstead Garden Suburb, 23 July 1928; *s* of late Arthur Albert Thrush and late Dorothy Charlotte Thrush (*née* Money); *m* 1958, Rosemary Catherine Terry, *d* of late George and Gertrude Terry, Ottawa; one *s* one *d*. *Educ:* Haberdashers' Aske's Sch.; Emmanuel Coll., Cambridge (Schol. 1946–50). BA 1949, MA, PhD 1953, ScD 1965. University of Cambridge: Demonstrator in Physical Chemistry, 1953; Asst Dir of Research, 1959; Lectr in Physical Chemistry, 1964, Reader, 1969; Hd of Dept of Physical Chemistry, 1986–88; Head of Dept of Chemistry, 1988–93; Tutor, 1963–67, Dir of Studies in Chemistry, 1963–78, Vice-Master, 1986–90 and Acting Master, 1986–87, Emmanuel Coll. Consultant Physicist, US Nat. Bureau of Standards, Washington, 1957–58; Sen. Vis. Scientist, Nat. Res. Council, Ottawa, 1961, 1971, 1980. Tilden Lectr, Chem. Soc., 1965; Vis. Prof., Chinese Acad. of Science, 1980–; Member: Faraday Council, Chem. Soc., 1976–79; US Nat. Acad. of Scis Panel on Atmospheric Chemistry, 1975–80; Lawes Agric. Trust Cttee, 1979–89; NERC, 1985–90; Council, Royal Soc., 1989–91; NATO Panel on Global Change, 1989–92. Pres., Chemistry Sect., BAAS, 1986. Mem., Academia Europaea, 1990 (Mem., Council, 1992–). M. Polanyi Medal, RSC, 1980; Rank Prize for Opto-Electronics, 1992. *Publications:* papers on gas kinetics and spectroscopy in Proc. Royal Soc., Trans Faraday Soc., etc. *Recreations:* wine, walking. *Address:* Brook Cottage, Pemberton Terrace, Cambridge CB2 1JA. *T:* Cambridge (01223) 357637. *Club:* Athenæum.

THUBRON, Colin Gerald Dryden; travel writer and novelist, since 1966; *b* 14 June 1939; *s* of late Brig. Gerald Ernest Thubron, DSO, OBE, and of Evelyn (*née* Dryden). *Educ:* Eton Coll. Editorial staff, Hutchinson & Co., 1959–62; freelance television film maker, Turkey, Japan, Morocco, 1962–64; Editorial staff, Macmillan Co., New York, 1964–65. FRSL 1969. *Publications:* non-fiction: Mirror to Damascus, 1967; The Hills of Adonis, 1968, 2nd edn 1987; Jerusalem, 1969, 2nd edn 1986; Journey into Cyprus, 1975; The Royal Opera House, 1982; Among the Russians, 1983; Behind the Wall, 1987 (Thomas Cook Award, Hawthorden Prize, 1988); The Lost Heart of Asia, 1994; novels: The God in the Mountain, 1977; Emperor, 1978; A Cruel Madness, 1984 (Silver Pen Award, 1985); Falling, 1989; Turning Back the Sun, 1991; contribs The Times, TLS, The Independent, The Spectator, Sunday Telegraph. *Address:* Garden Cottage, 27 St Ann's Villas, W11 4RT. *T:* 0171–602 2522.

THUILLIER, Maj.-Gen. Leslie de Malapert, (Pete), CB 1958; CVO 1966; OBE 1944; writer; freelance journalist; *b* 26 Sept. 1905; *s* of late Lt-Col L. C. Thuillier, Indian Army; *m* 1936, Barbara Leonard Rawlins; one *s* two *d*. *Educ:* Berkhamsted Sch.; Royal Military Academy, Woolwich. Commissioned as 2nd Lieut, Royal Corps of Signals, 1926; Lieut, 1929; Captain, 1937; Staff Coll., Camberley, 1939; Temp. Major, 1940; Temp. Lt-Col, 1941; Temp. Colonel, 1945; Colonel, 1949, Brigadier, 1951; Maj.-Gen., 1955. War Office, 1940–41; Middle East and Italy, 1941–45; Chief Signal Officer, Northern Ireland District, 1945–46; British Troops in Egypt, 1951–53; Northern Command, 1954–55; Director of Telecommunications, War Office, 1955–58; Asst Sec., Cabinet Office, 1958–67. Leader, UK Govtl Mission to USA to discuss experimental civil mil. satellite communications systems, 1960; Mem., UK Delegn to Internat. Conf. in Paris, Rome and London to discuss estabt of internat. communication satellite systems, 1963–65. Consultant, Airwork Services Ltd, 1969–84. *Recreation:* gardening. *Address:* The Red Barn, Patney, Devizes, Wilts SN10 3RA. *T:* Devizes (01380) 840669. *Club:* Naval and Military.

THURLOW, 8th Baron *cr* 1792; **Francis Edward Hovell-Thurlow-Cumming-Bruce,** KCMG 1961 (CMG 1957); Governor and C-in-C of the Bahamas, 1968–72; *b* 9 March 1912; *s* of 6th Baron Thurlow and Grace Catherine, *d* of Rev. Henry Trotter; *S* brother, 1971; *m* 1949, Yvonne Diana Aubyn Wilson, CStJ 1969 (*d* 1990); one *s* two *d* (and one *s* decd). *Educ:* Shrewsbury Sch.; Trinity Coll., Cambridge. Asst Principal, Dept of Agriculture for Scotland, 1935; transferred to Dominions Office, 1937; Asst Private Sec. to Sec. of State, 1939; Asst Sec., Office of UK High Comr in NZ, 1939; Asst Sec., Office of UK High Comr in Canada, 1944; Secretariat, Meeting of Commonwealth Prime Ministers in London, 1946; served with UK Delegn at Paris Peace Conf., 1946, and at UN Gen. Assemblies, 1946 and 1948; Principal Private Sec. to Sec. of State, 1946; Asst Sec., CRO, 1948; Head of Political Div., Office of UK High Comr in New Delhi, 1949; Establishment Officer, CRO, 1952; Head of Commodities Dept, CRO, 1954; Adviser on External Affairs to Governor of Gold Coast, 1955; Deputy High Comr for the UK in Ghana, 1957; Asst Under-Sec. of State, CRO, April 1958; Deputy High Comr for the UK in Canada, 1958; High Comr for UK: in New Zealand, 1959–63; in Nigeria, 1964–67; Dep. Under-Sec. of State, FCO, 1964. KStJ 1969. *Heir:* *s* Hon. Roualeyn Robert Hovell-Thurlow-Cumming-Bruce [*b* 13 April 1952; *m* 1980, Bridget Anne, *o d* of H. B. Ismay Cheape, Fossoway Lodge, Kinross; two *s* two *d*]. *Address:* 102 Leith Mansions, Grantully Road, W9 1LJ. *T:* 0171–289 9664; Philham Water, Hartland, Bideford EX69 6EZ. *T:* Bideford (01237) 441433. *Club:* Travellers'.

See also Rt Hon. Sir J. R. H.-T.-Cumming-Bruce.

THURNHAM, Peter Giles; MP (C) Bolton North-East, since 1983; Chairman, Wathes Group of Cos (formerly First and Third Securities Ltd), since 1972; *b* 21 Aug. 1938; *s* of late Giles Rymer Thurnham and Marjorie May (*née* Preston); *m* 1963, Sarah Janet Stroude; one *s* three *d* and one adopted *s*. *Educ:* Oundle Sch.; Peterhouse, Cambridge (MA 1967); Cranfield Inst. of Technol. (Dip. in Advanced Engrg, 1967); SRC/NATO Scholarship, Harvard Business Sch., Harvard Univ. (MBA 1969). CEng 1967; FIMechE 1985. Design Engr, NEI Parsons Ltd, 1957–66; Divl Dir, British Steam Specialties Ltd, 1967–72. Parliamentary Private Secretary: to Sec. of State for Employment, 1987–90; to Eric Forth, MP and Robert Jackson, MP, 1991–92; to Sec. of State for the Envmt, 1992–. Mem., Select Cttee on Employment, 1983–87. Treas., All-Party Parly Gp, Chemical Industry, 1985–87; Vice Chairman: All-Party Parly Gp for Children, 1986–; All Party Disability Gp, 1992–. Conservative Back Bench 1922 Committees: Vice-Chairman: Smaller Business Cttee, 1985–87; Home Improvement Sub-Cttee, 1986–87; Secretary: Employment Cttee, 1986–87; Social Security Cttee, 1990–91; Founder and Chm., Cons. Disability Gp, 1989–. Mem. Council, PSI, 1985–89. Founder Mem., 1985 and Mem. Cttee, 1985–, Progress, Campaign for Res. into Reproduction; Founder and Vice Pres., Campaign for Inter Country Adoption, 1991–. Patron, Stork, Assoc. of Families who have Adopted from Abroad. *Publications:* discussion papers; contrib. technical jls. *Recreation:* Lake District family life. *Address:* Hollin Hall, Crook, Kendal, Cumbria LA8 9HP. *T:* Staveley (01539) 821382; 4 North Court, Great Peter Street, SW1P 3LL. *T:* 0171–799 5859.

THURSO, 3rd Viscount *cr* 1952, of Ulbster; **John Archibald Sinclair;** Bt 1786; Managing Director, Fitness & Leisure Holdings, since 1995; *b* 10 Sept. 1953; *er s* of 2nd Viscount Thurso and of Margaret Beaumont Sinclair (*née* Robertson); *S* father, 1995; *m* 1976, Marion Ticknor (*née* Sage); two *s* one *d*. *Educ:* Summerfields; Eton Coll. FHCIMA 1991; Master Innholder 1991. Savoy Hotel plc: Trainee, 1972; Gen. Manager and Dir, Lancaster Hotel, Paris, 1981–85; Gen. Manager and Dir, Cliveden, 1985–92; Chief Exec. Officer, Granfel Hldgs, 1992–95; non-exec. Director: Savoy Hotel plc; Lochdhu Hotels Ltd; Thurso Fisheries Ltd. *Recreations:* shooting, fishing, food and wine. *Heir:* *s* Hon. James Alexander Robin Sinclair, *b* 14 Jan. 1984. *Address:* Home Farm, Little Horsted, East Sussex TN22 5TS. *T:* Isfield (01825) 750503. *Club:* New (Edinburgh).

THURSTON, Thea; *see* King, T.

THWAITE, Ann Barbara, FRSL 1987; writer; *b* London, 4 Oct. 1932; *d* of A. J. Harrop, LittD, PhD and H. M. Valentine of New Zealand; *m* 1955, Anthony Simon Thwaite, *qv*; four *d*. *Educ:* Marsden School, Wellington, NZ; Queen Elizabeth's Girls' Grammar Sch., Barnet; St Hilda's Coll., Oxford (MA 1959). Vis. Prof., Tokyo Women's Univ., 1985–86; Helen Stubbs Meml Lectr, Toronto Public Library, 1990; Ezra Jack Keats Meml Lectr, Univ. of Southern Mississippi, 1992. Churchill Travelling Fellowship, 1993. Regular reviewer of children's books; TLS, 1963–85; Guardian; TES. Governor: St Mary's Middle Sch., Long Stratton, Norfolk, 1990–; Hapton VC Primary Sch., Norfolk, 1995–. *Publications:* Waiting for the Party: the life of Frances Hodgson Burnett, 1974; (ed) My Oxford, 1977; Edmund Gosse: a literary landscape, 1984 (Duff Cooper Meml Prize, 1985); A. A. Milne: his life, 1990 (Whitbread Biography Award); (ed) Portraits from Life: essays by Edmund Gosse, 1991; The Brilliant Career of Winnie-the-Pooh, 1992; *children's books include:* The Camelthorn Papers, 1969; Tracks, 1978; (ed) Allsorts 1–7, 1968–75; Allsorts of Poems, 1978; The Ashton Affair, 1995. *Recreations:* other people's lives, messing about on the river. *Address:* The Mill House, Low Tharston, Norfolk NR15 2YN. *T:* Fundenhall (01508) 489569. *Club:* Society of Authors.

THWAITE, Anthony Simon, OBE 1990; FRSL 1978; poet; Editorial Consultant, André Deutsch Ltd, 1992–95 (Director, 1986–92); *b* 23 June 1930; *s* of late Hartley Thwaite, JP, FSA, and of Alice Evelyn Mallinson; *m* 1955, Ann Barbara Harrop (*see* A. B. Thwaite); four *d*. *Educ:* Kingswood Sch.; Christ Church, Oxford (MA). Vis. Lectr in English, Tokyo Univ., 1955–57; Producer, BBC, 1957–62; Literary Editor, The Listener, 1962–65; Asst Prof. of English, Univ. of Libya, 1965–67; Literary Editor, New Statesman, 1968–72; co-editor, Encounter, 1973–85. Henfield Writing Fellow, Univ. of East Anglia, 1972; Vis. Prof., Kuwait Univ., 1974; Japan Foundn Fellow, Tokyo Univ., 1985–86; Poet-in-Residence, Vanderbilt Univ., 1992. Chm. of Judges, Booker Prize, 1986. Hon. Fellow, Westminster Coll., Oxford, 1990. Hon. DLitt Hull, 1989. Cholmondeley Poetry Award, 1983. *Publications:* *poetry:* Home Truths, 1957; The Owl in the Tree, 1963; The Stones of Emptiness, 1967 (Richard Hillary Memorial Prize, 1968); Inscriptions, 1973; New

Confessions, 1974; A Portion for Foxes, 1977; Victorian Voices, 1980; Poems 1953–1983, 1984; Letter from Tokyo, 1987; Poems 1953–1988, 1989; The Dust of the World, 1994; *criticism:* Contemporary English Poetry, 1959; Poetry Today, 1973, rev. and expanded, 1985; Twentieth Century English Poetry, 1978; Six Centuries of Verse, 1984 (companion to Thames TV/Channel 4 series); *travel:* (with Roloff Beny) Japan, 1968; The Deserts of Hesperides, 1969; (with Roloff Beny and Peter Porter) In Italy, 1974; (with Roloff Beny) Odyssey: Mirror of the Mediterranean, 1981; *editor:* (with Geoffrey Bownas) Penguin Book of Japanese Verse, 1964; (with Peter Porter) The English Poets, 1974; (with Fleur Adcock) New Poetry 4, 1978; Larkin at Sixty, 1982; (with John Mole) Poetry 1945 to 1980, 1983; Collected Poems of Philip Larkin, 1988; Selected Letters of Philip Larkin, 1992; *for children:* Beyond the Inhabited World, 1976. *Recreations:* archaeology, travel. *Address:* The Mill House, Low Tharston, Norfolk NR15 2YN. *T:* Fundenhall (01508) 489569.

THWAITES, Prof. Sir Bryan, Kt 1986; MA, PhD; FIMA; Hon. Professor, Southampton University, since 1983; *b* London, 6 December 1923; *e s* of late Ernest James and Dorothy Marguerite Thwaites; *m* 1948, Katharine Mary (*d* 1991), 4th *c* of late H. R. Harries and late Mrs L. Harries, Longhope, Glos; four *s* two *d*. *Educ:* Dulwich College; Winchester College; Clare College, Cambridge (Wrangler, 1944). Scientific Officer, National Physical Laboratory, 1944–47; Lecturer, Imperial College, London, 1947–51; Assistant Master, Winchester College, 1951–59; Professor of Theoretical Mechanics, Southampton Univ., 1959–66; Principal, Westfield Coll., London, 1966–83 (Hon. Fellow, 1983; Hon. Fellow, QMW, 1990). Gresham Prof. in Geometry, City Univ., 1969–72. Co-founder and Co-Chm., Education 2000, 1982–86. Hon. Sec. and Treas., Dulwich College Mission, 1946–57; inventor of the Thwaites Flap, 1947. Chm. and Mem. ARC Cttees, 1948–69. Special Lecturer, Imperial College, 1951–58. Chm., Southampton Mathematical Conf., 1961. Founding Director of the School Mathematics Project, 1961–75, Chm. of Trustees, 1966–83, Life Pres., 1984; Chm. of Internat. Mathematical Olympiad, first in UK, 1979; Chm. Adv. Council, ICL/CES, 1968–84. Member: Approved Sch. Cttee, Hampshire CC, 1954–58, 1961–66; US/UK (Fulbright) Commn, 1966–76; Davies Cttee on CSSB, 1969–70; Council, Kennedy Inst. of Rheumatology, 1969–71; Ct of London Univ., 1975–81; Council, Middlesex Hosp. Med. Sch., 1975–83; Court, Southampton Univ., 1981–94. Chairman: Collegiate Council, London Univ., 1973–76; Delegacy, Goldsmiths' Coll., 1975–80. Mem. Acad. Advisory Committee: Univ. of Bath, 1964–71; Open Univ., 1969–75. Chairman of: Council of C of E Colleges of Education, 1969–71; Church of England Higher Educn Cttee, 1974–76; Northwick Park Hosp. Management Cttee, 1970–74; Brent and Harrow AHA, 1973–82; Wessex RHA, 1982–88; King's Fund Enquiry into Sen. Management Trng in NHS, 1975–76; Nat. Staff Cttee for Admin. and Clerical Staff, NHS, 1983–86; Enquiry into Radiotherapy Incident, Exeter Hosp., 1988. Founding Chm., British False Memory Soc., 1993. Chairman: Govs, Heythrop Coll., 1978–82; Friends of Winchester Coll., 1989–91; Govs, More House, 1993–; Trustee: Westfield Coll. Develt Trust, 1979–83; Southampton Med. Sch. Trust, 1982–88; Richmond Coll., 1987–93 (Academic Gov., 1992–); City Tech. Colls Trust, 1987–; Forbes Trust, 1987–; Patron, Winchester Detached Youth Project, 1990–. Mercier Lectr, Whitelands Coll., 1973; Foundn Lectr, Inst. of Health Policy Studies, Southampton Univ., 1987; 25th Anniv. Lectr, Nuffield Inst., Leeds Univ., 1988. Shadow Vice-Chancellor, Independent Univ., July-Nov. 1971. Hon. Life Mem., Math. Assoc., 1962. JP, Winchester City Bench, 1963–66. A Vice-Pres., Friends of GPDST, 1975–95. Mem. Council, 1964–94, Pres., 1966–67, Institute of Mathematics and its Applications. Sponsor, Family and Youth Concern (formerly The Responsible Society), 1979– (Trustee, 1992–). *Publications:* (ed) Incompressible Aerodynamics, 1960; (ed) On Teaching Mathematics, 1961; The SMP: the first ten years, 1973; (ed) Hypotheses for Education in AD 2000, 1983; numerous contributions to Proc. Royal Soc., Reports and Memoranda of Aeronautical Research Council, Quart. Jl of Applied Mech., Jl of Royal Aeronautical Soc., etc. *Recreations:* music, sailing. *Address:* Milnthorpe, Winchester, Hants SO22 4NF. *T:* Winchester (01962) 852394. *Club:* Royal Over-Seas League.

THWAITES, Jacqueline Ann; *see* Duncan, J. A.

THWAITES, Ronald; QC 1987; *b* 21 Jan. 1946; *e s* of Stanley Thwaites and Aviva Thwaites; *m* 1972, Judith Myers; three *s* one *d*. *Educ:* Richard Hind Secondary Tech. Sch.; Grangefield Grammar Sch., Stockton-on-Tees; Kingston Coll. of Technol. (subseq. Polytechnic, now Univ.); LLB London (external) 1968. Called to the Bar, Gray's Inn, 1970. *Recreations:* squash, swimming, lighting bonfires. *Address:* (chambers) 10 King's Bench Walk, Temple, EC4Y 7EB. *T:* 0171–353 2501.

THWAITES, Roy; Deputy Director, South Yorkshire Branch, British Red Cross Society, 1990; *b* 13 Aug. 1931; *s* of Walter and Emily Alice Thwaites; *m* 1st, 1954, Margaret Anne (*née* Noble) (marr. diss.); one *s*; 2nd, 1991, Mary (*née* Appleby). *Educ:* Southey Green Secondary Sch.; Sheffield Central Technical Sch. City Councillor, Sheffield, 1965–74, Chief Whip and Chm. of Transport Cttee, 1969–74; South Yorkshire County Council: Councillor, 1973–86; Chief Whip and Chm. Passenger Transport Authority, 1973–78; Dep. Leader, 1978–79; Leader, and Chm. of Policy Cttee, 1979–86. Dep. Chm. and Dir, SYT Ltd, 1986–93. Member: E Midlands Airport Consultative Gp, 1982–86; Industrial Tribunals, 1987–. Vice-Chm., 1979–84, Dep. Chm., 1984–86, AMA; Member: Local Authorities' Conditions of Service Adv. Bd, 1979–86; Yorks and Humberside County Councils Assoc., 1983–86; Vice-Chm., 1982–85, Chm., 1985–86, NJC Local Govt Manual Workers Employers. Mem., Special Employment Measures Adv. Gp, MSC, 1983–86. Director: Yorks Mining Museum Trust, 1986–92; Northern Racing Sch. Trust, 1986–. Hon. Fellow, Sheffield City Poly., 1982. *Recreations:* walking, reading, photography. *Address:* 2 Borough Road, Sheffield S6 2AY.

THYATEIRA AND GREAT BRITAIN, Archbishop of; *see* Theocharous, Archbishop Gregorios.

THYNE, Malcolm Tod, MA; FRSE; Headmaster, Fettes College, Edinburgh, since 1988; *b* 6 Nov. 1942; *s* of late Andrew Tod and Margaret Melrose Thyne; *m* 1969, Eleanor Christine Scott; two *s*. *Educ:* The Leys Sch., Cambridge; Clare Coll., Cambridge (MA Nat. Scis with Pt II in Chem.; Cert. of Educn). FRSE 1994. Asst Master, Edinburgh Acad., 1965–69; Asst Master, Oundle Sch., 1969–72, Housemaster, 1972–80; Headmaster, St Bees School, 1980–88. *Publications:* Periodicity, Atomic Structure and Bonding (Revised Nuffield Chemistry), 1976; contrib: Revised Nuffield Chemistry Handbook for Pupils, 1978; Revised Nuffield Chemistry Teachers' Guides, Vols II and III, 1978. *Recreation:* mountaineering. *Address:* The Lodge, Fettes College, Edinburgh EH4 1QX. *T:* 0131–332 2281. *Club:* New (Edinburgh).

THYNN, family name of **Marquess of Bath.**

THYNN, Alexander; *see* Bath, Marquess of.

THYNNE, John Corelli James, CB 1990; PhD, DSc; Director, Newbridge Networks Corporation, since 1992; *b* 27 Nov. 1931; *s* of Corelli James Thynne and Isabel Ann (*née* Griffiths). *Educ:* Milford Haven Grammar Sch.; Nottingham Univ. (BSc, PhD); Edinburgh Univ. (DSc). Res. Chemist, English Electric Co. (Guided Missile Div.), 1956–58; Fellow: Nat. Res. Council, Ottawa, 1958–59; UCLA, 1959–60; Univ. of Leeds, 1960–63; Lectr in Chemistry and Dir of Studies, Univ. of Edinburgh, 1963–70; Principal, DTI, 1970–73; Counsellor (Scientific), British Embassy, Moscow, 1974–78; Asst Sec., IT Div., DoI, 1978–83; Department of Trade and Industry: Regl Dir, NW Reg., 1983–86; Under Sec., 1986; Electronic Applications Div., 1986–87; IT Div., 1987–89; Dir, Information Engrg Directorate, 1989–90; Head, IT Div., 1990. Dir Gen., Electronic Components Industry Fedn, 1991–94. Chm., ComCare Systems Ltd, 1992–94; Dir, Camrose Consultancy Services, 1991–; Sen. Advr, InterMatrix Gp, 1991–; Director: LTW Ltd, 1993–; Celtic House Investment Partners Ltd, 1993–. Member: Exec. Cttee, Nat. Electronics Council, 1986–90; NEDO Electronics Industries Sector Gp, 1986–90; Council, Nat. Interactive Video Centre, 1987–89; Management Bd, Science and Engrg Policy Studies Unit, 1991–94; Welsh Funding Councils Res. Gp, 1992–94; Radiocommunications Agency Bd, 1994–. Mem. Council, Salford Univ., 1984–87; Gov., Univ. of Glamorgan (formerly Poly. of Wales), 1991–95. Vice Chm. Trustees, Mus. of Sci. and Industry, 1991–. *Publications:* contribs on physical chemistry to scientific journals. *Recreation:* cricket. *Address:* Newbridge Networks Corporation, 600 March Road, Kanata, Ont K2K 2E6, Canada. *T:* (613) 5913600; 5 Eldon Grove, NW3 5PS. *T:* 0171–794 1356, *Fax:* 0171–794 1821. *Clubs:* Athenæum, MCC.

THYSSEN BORNEMISZA de KASZON, Baron Hans Heinrich; Swiss industrialist and administrator; *b* The Hague, 13 April 1921; *s* of Dr Heinrich Thyssen-Bornemisza and Margit Bornemisza de Kaszon; *m* 1985, Carmen Cervera; one adopted *s*, and three *s* one *d* by former marrs. *Educ:* Realgymnasium, The Hague; Fribourg Univ. Chm. and Hon. Pres., Supervisory Bd, Thyssen-Bornemisza Gp; Hon. Chm., Bremer Vulkan, Bremer; Member: Trustee Council, Nat. Gallery of Art, Washington DC; Sotheby's Holdings Adv. Bd; Hon. President: Mauritshuis, The Hague; Fundación Thyssen-Bornemisza, Madrid. Corresp. Mem., Acad. of Fine Arts, San Fernando, Madrid; owner of collection of paintings and works of art housed in Museo Thyssen-Bornemisza, Madrid, Monasterio de Pedralbes, Barcelona and Villa Favorita, Lugano. Gran Cruz, Orden Carlo III (Spain), 1988. *Address:* Camino del Golf, 3 La Moraleja, 28109 Madrid, Spain; 56 Chester Square, SW1W 9EA; Villa Favorita, 6976, Castagnola, Switzerland. *Clubs:* Corviglia (St Moritz); Knickerbocker (NY).

TIBBER, Anthony Harris; His Honour Judge Tibber; a Circuit Judge, since 1977; *b* 23 June 1926; *s* of Maurice and Priscilla Tibber; *m* 1954, Rhona Ann Salter; three *s*. *Educ:* University College School, London; Magdelen College School, Brackley. Served in Royal Signals, 1945–48; called to the Bar, Gray's Inn, 1950; a Recorder of the Crown Court, 1976. Member: Matrimonial Causes Rule Cttee, 1980–84; Matrimonial Causes Procedure Cttee (Booth Cttee), 1983–85. *Recreations:* cultivating, idling, pottering. *Address:* c/o Edmonton County Court, 59 Fore Street, N18 2TM. *T:* (home) 0181–348 3605.

TIBBITS, Captain Sir David (Stanley), Kt 1976; DSC 1942; FNI; RN retired; Deputy Master and Chairman of Board, Trinity House, 1972–76; *b* 11 April 1911; *s* of late Hubert Tibbits, MB, BCh, Warwick, and Edith Lucy (*née* Harman) Tibbits; *m* 1938, Mary Florence Butterfield, Hamilton, Bermuda; two *d*. *Educ:* Wells House, Malvern Wells; RNC, Dartmouth. RN Cadet 1925; navigation specialist, 1934; served War, 1939–45, HMS York, Devonshire and Anson; Comdr 1946; Captain 1953; Dir, Radio Equipment Dept, Admty, 1953–56; in comd, HM Ships Manxman, Dryad and Hermes, 1956–61; retd. Trinity House: Elder Brother, 1961; Warden, 1969. Hon. Sec., King George's Fund for Sailors, 1974–80; Lay Vice-Pres., Missions to Seamen, 1972–. Engaged in various voluntary activities in Bermuda including: Mem., Marine Board and Port Authy, 1978–92; Chm., Pilotage Commn, 1978–92; Pres., Sea Cadet and Sail Trng Assoc., 1978–87; Chm. and Pres., Bermuda Soc. for Blind, 1982– (Mem. Cttee, 1977–). Mem. Court, Worshipful Co. of Shipwrights, 1976–. Trustee, National Maritime Museum, 1974–77. Governor, Pangbourne Coll., 1973–78. Founder Mem., 1972, Fellow 1979–, Nautical Inst. CStJ 1993 (Mem. Council for Bermuda, 1978–). *Recreations:* sailing, colour photography, classical music. *Address:* Harting Hill, PO Box HM 1419, Hamilton, Bermuda HM FX; c/o Trinity House, Tower Hill, EC3N 4DH. *Clubs:* Army and Navy, Hurlingham; Royal Yacht Squadron (Naval Mem.); Royal Bermuda Yacht (Bermuda).

TIBBS, Craigie John, FRICS; Head of Estates and Planning Department, BBC, 1980; *b* 17 Feb. 1935; *s* of Arthur and Gladys Tibbs; *m* 1959, Carol Ann (*née* Linsell); two *d* *Educ:* King George V School, Southport; Heaton Grammar School, Newcastle upon Tyne; RMA Sandhurst; London University. BSc; FRICS. Trainee Estates Officer, London Transport, 1959–62; Valuer and Senior Valuer, Luton Corp., 1962–67; Chief Valuer and Surveyor, London Borough of Newham, 1967–71; Development Officer, City of Birmingham, 1971–73; County Estates Officer, Hants County Council, 1973–76; Under Sec. (Dir of Land Economy), Depts of Environment and Transport, 1976–80. *Recreations:* music, reading, writing, walking, swimming, golf, the Well Game.

TIBBS, (Geoffrey) Michael (Graydon), OBE 1987; Secretary of the Royal College of Physicians, 1968–86 (Secretary of Joint Faculty of Community Medicine, 1971–72 and of Faculty of Occupational Medicine, 1978–86); *b* 21 Nov. 1921; *s* of Rev. Geoffrey Wilberforce Tibbs, sometime Chaplain RN and Vicar of Lynchmere, Sussex, and Margaret Florence Tibbs (*née* Skinner); *m* 1951, Anne Rosemary Wortley; two *s*. *Educ:* Berkhamsted Sch.; St Peter's Hall, Oxford. BA Hons Geography, 1948; MA 1952. FInstAM; MIPM; FRGS. Served RNVR, Ordinary Seaman/Lieut, 1940–46 (despatches), HMS Cottesmore, HMS Sheffield, HM S/M Tantalus, HM S/M Varne. Sudan Political Service, Kordofan Province, 1949–55: seconded to MECAS, 1950; Dist Comr, Dar Messeria District, 1953. Various appointments in personnel, organisation and overseas services depts, Automobile Assoc., 1955–68. Hon. Mem., Soc. of Occupational Medicine, 1983; Hon. FRCP 1986; Hon. FFOM 1986; Hon. FFCM 1987. Freeman, City of London, 1986. *Publication:* A Look at Lynchmere, 1990. *Recreations:* producing pantomimes, parish affairs, making bonfires. *Address:* Welkin, Lynchmere Ridge, Haslemere, Surrey GU27 3PP. *T:* Haslemere (01428) 643120, 642176. *Club:* Naval.

TICEHURST, Maj.-Gen. Arthur Christopher; Medical Officer, Army Medical Directorate (Medico-Legal), since 1994; *b* 22 April 1933; *s* of late Arthur William Ticehurst and of Edith Violet Ticehurst (*née* Adams); *m* 1959, Valerie Jean Hughes; four *s*. *Educ:* Chichester High Sch.; King's Coll. London; Westminster Hosp. (MB BS 1955). MFCM 1977; FFPHM 1990. House appointments, Westminster Hosp., 1955–56; National Service, RAMC, 1958–60; Regular Commn, 1961; Medical Officer: Kent, Cyprus, 1958–61; Singapore, Brunei, Thailand, 1962–65; CO, 11 Field Dressing Station, BAOR, 1965–67; Instructor, RAMC Trng Centre, 1967–68; Army Staff Coll., 1968–69; MoD, 1970–72; CO, 4 Armoured Field Ambulance, 1972–74; ndc, 1974–75; Army Med. Directorate, MoD, 1976–80; Chief Instructor, RAMC Trng Centre, 1980–83; Comdr, Med. HQ, NE Dist, 1983–84; Dep. Comdr, Med. HQ, BAOR, 1984–87; Asst Surgeon Gen., MoD, 1987–90; Dir, Med. Ops and Plans, MoD, 1990; Comdr Med., HQ UKLF, 1990–93. QHS 1991–93. FIMgt (FBIM 1992). OStJ 1972. *Publications:* articles on use of medical services in disaster relief to professional jls. *Recreations:* tennis, squash, board sailing, military history, maps, water colours. *Address:* c/o Lloyds Bank, 19 Obelisk Street, Camberley, Surrey.

TICKELL, Sir Crispin (Charles Cervantes), GCMG 1989; KCVO 1983 (MVO 1958); HM Diplomatic Service, retired; Warden, Green College, since 1990, and Director, Green College Centre for Environmental Policy and Understanding, since 1992, University of Oxford; *b* 25 Aug. 1930; *s* of late Jerrard Tickell and Renée (*née* Haynes); *m* 1st, 1954, Chloë (marr. diss. 1976), *d* of late Sir James Gunn, RA, PRP; two *s* one *d*; 2nd, 1977, Penelope, *d* of late Dr Vernon Thorne Thorne. *Educ:* Westminster (King's Schol.; Hon. Fellow, 1993); Christ Church, Oxford (Hinchliffe and Hon. Schol.). 1st Cl. Hons Mod. Hist. 1952. Served with Coldstream Guards, 1952–54; entered HM Diplomatic Service, 1954. Served at: Foreign Office, 1954–55; The Hague, 1955–58; Mexico, 1958–61; FO (Planning Staff), 1961–64; Paris, 1964–70; Private Sec. to successive Ministers responsible for British entry into the European Community, 1970–72; FCO, 1972–75; Fellow, Center for Internat. Affairs, Harvard Univ., 1975–76; Chef de Cabinet to Pres. of Commn of European Community, 1977–81; Vis. Fellow, All Souls Coll., Oxford, 1981; Ambassador to Mexico, 1981–83; Dep. Under-Sec. of State, FCO, 1983–84; Perm. Sec., ODA, 1984–87; British Perm. Rep. to UN, 1987–90. Director: IBM (UK), 1990–95 (Mem. IBM Adv. Bd, 1995–); BOC Envmtl Foundn, 1990–; Govett Mexican Horizons, 1991–. Chairman: Internat. Inst. for Envmt and Develt, 1990–94; Climate Inst. of Washington, 1990–; Earthwatch (Europe), 1990–; Adv. Cttee on the Darwin Initiative for the Survival of Species, 1992–. Trustee: Natural Hist. Mus., 1992–; WWF (UK), 1993. Pres., Marine Biol. Assoc., 1990–; Vice Pres., RGS, 1993– (Pres., 1990–93). Convenor, Govt Panel on Sustainable Develt, 1994–. Mem., Global 500 (UN Roll of Honour for Envmtl Achievement), 1991. Mem. (Dr *hc*), Mexican Acad. of Internat. Law, 1983 (Orden Academico del Derecho, de la Cultura y de la Paz, 1989). Hon. LLD: Massachusetts, 1990; Bristol, 1991; Birmingham, 1991; Hon. DSc: UEA, 1990; Sussex, 1991; Cranfield, 1992; Loughborough, 1995; Dr *hc*: Central London Poly., 1990; Stirling, 1990. Officer, Order of Orange Nassau (Netherlands), 1958; Order of Aztec Eagle with sash (Mexico), 1994. *Publications:* (contrib.) The Evacuees, 1968; (contrib.) Life After Death, 1976; Climatic Change and World Affairs, 1977, 1986 (contrib.) The United Kingdom/The United Nations, 1990; (contrib.) Sustaining Earth, 1990; (contrib.) Monitoring the Environment, 1992; (contrib.) Threats Without Enemies, 1993; (contrib.) Science for the Earth, 1995. *Recreations:* climatology; palæohistory; art, especially pre-Columbiana; mountains. *Address:* Warden's Lodgings, Green College, Oxford OX2 6HG. *Club:* Brooks's.

TICKELL, Maj.-Gen. Marston Eustace, CBE 1973 (MBE 1955); MC 1945; CEng, FICE; Commandant Royal Military College of Science, 1975–78, retired; *b* 18 Nov. 1923; *er s* of late Maj.-Gen. Sir Eustace Tickell, KBE, CB, MC; *m* 1961, Pamela Vere, *d* of Vice-Adm. A. D. Read, CB; no *c*. *Educ:* Wellington Coll.; Peterhouse, Cambridge (MA). Commnd in RE, 1944; NW Europe Campaign and Middle East, 1944–45; psc 1954; Mil. Ops, MoD, 1955–57; served in Libya, Cyprus and Jordan, 1958–59; US Armed Forces Staff Coll. and Instructor RMCS and Staff Coll., 1959–62; Defence Planning Staff, MoD, 1962–64; CRE 4th Div., 1964–66; comd 12 Engr Bde, 1967–69; Indian Nat. Defence Coll., 1970; COS Northern Ireland, 1971–72; E-in-C, MoD, 1972–75. Col Comdt, RE, 1978–83. Hon. Col, Engr and Transport Staff Corps, 1983–88. Lord Chancellor's Panel of Independent Inspectors, 1979–93. Pres., Instn of Royal Engrs, 1979–82. FICE 1974. *Recreation:* sailing. *Address:* The Old Vicarage, Branscombe, Seaton, Devon EX12 3DW. *Clubs:* Army and Navy; Royal Ocean Racing.

TICKLE, Brian Percival, CB 1985; Senior Registrar of the Family Division, High Court of Justice, 1982–88 (Registrar, 1970–88); *b* 31 Oct. 1921; *s* of late William Tickle and Lucy (*née* Percival); *m* 1945, Margaret Alice Pendrey (*d* 1994); one *s* one *d*. *Educ:* The Judd Sch., Tonbridge. Entered Civil Service, 1938. Served War, Royal Signals, 1941–46. Civil Service, 1946–70. Member: Matrimonial Causes Rules Cttee, 1982–88; Independent Schs Tribunal, 1988–93. *Publications:* Rees Divorce Handbook, 1963; Atkin's Court Forms and Precedents (Probate), 2nd edn 1974, rev. edn 1984. *Recreations:* golf, watching cricket and Rugby. *Address:* Hillbrow Court, 1A Royal Chase, Tunbridge Wells, Kent TN4 8AX.

TIDBURY, Sir Charles (Henderson), Kt 1989; DL; Chairman, Whitbread PLC, 1978–84; *b* 26 Jan. 1926; *s* of late Brig. O. H. Tidbury, MC, and Beryl (*née* Pearce); *m* Anne, *d* of late Brig. H. E. Russell, DSO, and of Lady O'Connor; two *s* three *d*. *Educ:* Eton Coll. Served KRRC, 1943–52: Palestine, 1946–48 (despatches); Queen's Westminsters TA, 1952–60. Joined Whitbread & Co. Ltd, 1952; a Man. Dir, 1959; Chief Exec., 1974; Dep. Chm., 1977; Dir, 1984–88. Chm., Brickwoods Brewery Ltd, 1966–71. Dep. Chm., INSPEC plc, 1994–; Director: Whitbread Investment Co. PLC, 1975–93; Barclays Bank PLC, 1978–91; Mercantile Gp plc, 1985–91; Nabisco Gp Ltd, 1985–88; Vaux Gp plc, 1985–91; ICL (Europe, formerly UK), 1985–; Pearl Assurance PLC, 1985–94; Gales Brewery, Horndean, 1990–. Dir, Centre for Policy Studies, 1988–93. Pres., Inst. of Brewing, 1976–78; Chm., 1982–84, Vice-Pres., 1985–, Brewers' Soc.; President: Shire Horse Soc., 1985–87; British Inst. of Innkeeping, 1985–92 (Vice-Pres., 1992–); Brewing Res. Foundn Internat. (formerly Brewing Res. Foundn), 1993– (Chm., 1985–93). Chairman: Mary Rose Development Trust, 1980–86; William and Mary Tercentenary Trust, 1986–93; Hampshire Business Liaison Exec. Bd, 1993–; Mem., Portsmouth and SE Hants Health Commn, 1992–; Trustee, Nat. Maritime Museum, 1984–. Governor: Nat. Heart and Chest Hosps, 1988–90; Portsmouth Univ. (formerly Polytechnic), 1988–; Portsmouth High Sch., 1992– (Chm., 1992–). Master, Brewers' Co., 1988–89. DL Hampshire, 1989. *Recreations:* my family, sailing, countryside. *Address:* Crocker Hill Farm, Forest Lane, Wickham, Hants PO17 5DW. *Clubs:* Brooks's; Royal Yacht Squadron, Bembridge Sailing.

TIDY, Morley David; Assistant Under-Secretary of State (Personnel) (Air), Ministry of Defence, 1990–92; *b* 23 April 1933; *s* of James Morley and Winnie Tidy; *m* 1957, Wendy Ann Bennett; one *s* two *d*. *Educ:* Hove County Grammar School; Magdalene College, Cambridge (MA). National Service, RAF, 1951–53. Dept of Employment, 1956–57; HM Inspector of Taxes, Inland Revenue, 1957–66; MoD, 1966; Manchester Business School, 1967; First Sec. (Defence), UK Delegn to NATO, 1969–72; MoD, 1973; RCDS, 1977; Chief Officer, SBAA, Cyprus, 1980–83; Asst Under-Sec., Air Staff, MoD, 1984; Asst Under Sec. (Ordnance), MoD, 1985; Asst Under Sec., Defence Export Services, Administration, MoD, 1988. *Recreations:* tennis, cricket, golf, jigsaws.

TIDY, William Edward, (Bill); freelance cartoonist, since 1958; writer, playwright, television and radio presenter; Managing Director, Bill Tidy, since 1989; *b* 9 Oct. 1933; *s* of William Edward Tidy and Catherine Price; *m* 1960, Rosa Colotti; two *s* one *d*. *Educ:* Anfield Road Jun. Sch., Liverpool; St Margaret's Sen. Sch., Anfield, Liverpool. Shipping office boy, R. P. Houston, Liverpool, 1950–51. Served RE, 1952–55. Layout artist, Pagan Smith Advertising Agency, 1956–58. Presented for BBC TV: Tidy Up Walsall; Tidy Up Naples; My City; Draw Me; radio broadcasting includes: The News Quiz (also Guest Presenter); Midweek (also Guest Presenter); I'm Sorry I Haven't a Clue; Back to Square One; The Law Game; Trivia Test Match; Down Your Way; radio adaptation, The Fosdyke Saga (with John Junkin). *Publications: (written and illustrated):* Sporting Chance, 1961; O Cleo, 1962; Laugh with Bill Tidy, 1966; Up the Reds, Up the Blues, 1968; Tidy's World, 1969; The Cloggies, 1969; Tidy Again, 1970; The Fosdyke Saga (14 vols), 1972–85; The Cloggies Dance Back, 1973; The Great Eric Ackroyd Disaster, 1976; The Cloggies Are Back, 1977; Mine's a Pint, What's Yours (The Kegbuster Story), 1981; Robbie and the Blobbies, 1982; Bill Tidy's Little Rude Book, 1984; A Day at Cringemound School, 1985; Bill Tidy's Book of Classic Cockups, 1985; The World's Worst Golf Club, 1987; The Incredible Bed, 1990; Draw me 387 Baked Beans in 10 seconds, 1991; Save Daring Waring with a pencil, 1993; Is there any news of the Iceberg? (autobiog.), 1995; has also illustrated over seventy other books; contrib. to Gen. Practioner. *Recreation:* cricket (Lord's Taverners). *Address:* The Yews, 59 High Street, Kegworth, Derby DE74 2DA. *T:* Kegworth (01509) 673939. *Clubs:* Cartoonist of Great Britain; Nottinghamshire County Cricket.

TIERNEY, Sydney; JP; President, 1977–81, and 1983–91, and National Officer, 1979–91, Union of Shop, Distributive and Allied Workers; Chairman, Labour Party, 1986–87 (Vice-Chairman, 1985–86); *b* 16 Sept. 1923; *m* 1985, Margaret Olive (*née* Hannah); two *d*. *Educ:* Secondary Modern Sch., Dearne; Plater Coll., Oxford. Mem., Co-operative Party; an Official and Member, USDAW. Vice-Chm., W Midlands Labour Gp of MPs, 1974–79; Mem., Labour Party NEC, to 1990. MP (Lab) Birmingham, Yardley, Feb. 1974–1979; PPS to Min. of State for Agriculture, 1976–79. JP Leicester, 1966. *Address:* Rocklands, 56 Priory Lane, Kents Bank, Grange Over Sands, Cumbria LA11 7BJ.

TIETMEYER, Dr Hans; President, Deutsche Bundesbank, since 1993 (Vice-Governor, 1991–93); *b* 18 Aug. 1931; *s* of Bernhard and Helene Tietmeyer; *m* 1st, Marie-Luise Floßdorf (*d* 1978); one *s* one *d*; 2nd, 1980, Maria-Therese Kalff. *Educ:* Univs of Münster, Bonn and Cologne (Dr Rer Pol). Sec., Bishöfliche Studienforderung Cusanuswerk, 1959–62; Fed. Min. of Economics, 1962–82, Head of Div. of Gen. Economic Policy, 1973–82; Mem., Econ. Policy Cttee of EC and OECD, 1972–82; Sec. of State, Min. of Finance, 1982–89; Mem., Bd of Dirs, Deutsche Bundesbank, 1990–. *Publications:* numerous articles on economics. *Recreation:* sport. *Address:* Deutsche Bundesbank, Wilhelm Epstein Strasse, 60431 Frankfurt, Germany.

TIKARAM, Sir Moti, KBE 1980; **Hon. Justice Sir Moti Tikaram;** Justice of the Court of Appeal, Fiji, since 1988; President, Fiji Court of Appeal, since 1994; *b* 18 March 1925; *s* of Tikaram and Singari; *m* 1944, Satyawati (*d* 1981); two *s* one *d*. *Educ:* Marist Brothers High Sch., Suva; Victoria Univ., Wellington, NZ (LLB 1954). Started law practice, 1954; Stipendiary Magistrate, 1960; Puisne Judge, 1968; acted as Chief Justice, 1971 and 1990. Ombudsman, Fiji, 1972–87. Patron, Fiji Lawn Tennis Assoc. Scouting Medal of Merit, 1986. *Publications:* articles in The Pacific Way and in Recent Law 131. *Recreation:* tennis. *Address:* (home) PO Box 514, 45 Domain Road, Suva, Fiji. *T:* 302005; (office) PO Box 2215, Government Buildings, Suva. *T:* 211489. *Clubs:* Fiji, Fiji Golf (Suva).

TILBERIS, Elizabeth Jane; Editor in Chief, Harper's Bazaar magazine, since 1992; *b* 7 Sept. 1947; *d* of Thomas Stuart-Black Kelly and Janet Storrie Kelly; *m* 1971, Andrew Tilberis; two *s*. *Educ:* Malvern Girl's Coll.; Jacob Kramer Coll., Leeds; Leicester College of Art (BA Art and Design). Vogue Magazine: Fashion Asst, 1970; Fashion Editor, 1973; Exec. Fashion Editor, 1985; Fashion Dir, 1986; Editor in Chief, 1987–92. Dir, Condé Nast Publications, 1991–. *Recreations:* gardening, music. *Address:* The Hearst Corp., 1700 Broadway, New York, NY 10019, USA.

TILEY, Prof. John; Professor of the Law of Taxation, University of Cambridge, since 1990; Fellow, since 1967, Vice-President, since 1988, Queens' College, Cambridge; a Recorder of the Crown Court, since 1989; *b* 25 Feb. 1941; *s* of William Arthur Tiley, OBE and Audrey Ellen (*née* Burton); *m* 1964, Jillinda Millicent Draper; two *s* one *d*. *Educ:* Winchester Coll.; Lincoln Coll., Oxford (BA 1962; BCL 1963; MA 1967). Called to the Bar, Inner Temple, 1964, Hon. Bencher, 1993. Lecturer: Lincoln Coll., Oxford, 1963–64; Univ. of Birmingham, 1964–67; University of Cambridge: Asst Lectr, 1967–72; Lectr, 1972–87; Reader in Law of Taxation, 1987–90. Visiting Professor: Dalhousie Univ., 1972–73, Univ. of W Ontario, 1978–79; Univ. of Melbourne, 1979; Case Western Reserve Univ., 1985–86. Gen. Editor, Butterworth's UK Tax Guide, 1982–. *Publications:* A Casebook on Equity and Succession, 1968; Revenue Law, 1976, 3rd edn 1981; contrib. to legal jls. *Recreations:* walking, cricket, music. *Address:* Queens' College, Cambridge CB3 9ET. *T:* Cambridge (01223) 335546.

TILL, Barry Dorn; Principal of Morley College, London, 1965–86; Adviser, 1973–86, Director, 1986–92, Baring Foundation; *b* 1 June 1923; *s* of John Johnson and Hilda Lucy Till; *m* 1st, 1954, Shirley Philipson (marr. diss. 1965); two *s*; 2nd, 1966, Antonia, *d* of Sir Michael Clapham, *qv*; two *d*. *Educ:* Harrow; Jesus College and Westcott House, Cambridge. 1st Class Theology Pt III, 1949; Lightfoot Scholar, 1949. Served War, Coldstream Guards, 1942–46; Italian campaign. Deacon, 1950; Priest, 1951; Asst Curate, Bury Parish Church, Lancs, 1950–53; Fellow of Jesus Coll., Cambridge, 1953–60, Chaplain, 1953–56, Dean, 1956–60, Tutor, 1957–60; Univ. Preacher, Cambridge, 1955; Examining Chaplain to Bishop of Lichfield, 1957–60; Dean of Hong Kong, 1960–64. Chm., Asia Christian Colleges Assoc., 1968–76, Vice-Pres., 1976–. Governor, British Inst. of Recorded Sound, 1967–72; Mem., Adv. Council, V&A Museum, 1977–83. Chairman: Greater London AACE, 1976–82; Work-Out, 1986–89; Mary Ward Settlement, 1987–. Founder Mem., Exec. Cttee, Assoc. of Charitable Foundns, 1989–91. Governor, St Olaf's Grammar Sch., 1973–82 (Chm., 1980–82); Member: Cultural Cttee, European Culture Foundn, 1976–78; Council, London Sinfonietta, 1992–. Trustee: Thomas Cubitt Trust, 1978–; LentA Educnl Trust, 1987–92 (Chm., 1990–92); Open Coll. of the Arts, 1992–; Charity House, 1992–; Transport 2000, 1992–; London Educn Business Partnership, 1992–; Fitzwilliam Mus. Trust, 1993–. *Publications:* contrib. to The Historic Episcopate, 1954; Change and Exchange, 1964; Changing Frontiers in the Mission of the Church, 1965; contrib. to A Holy Week Manual, 1967; The Churches Search for Unity, 1972. *Recreations:* travel, gardening, opera. *Address:* 44 Canonbury Square, N1 2AW. *T:* 0171–359 0708. *Club:* Brooks's.

TILL, Ven. Michael Stanley; Archdeacon of Canterbury, since 1986; *b* 19 Nov. 1935; *s* of Stanley Brierley Till and Mary Till; *m* 1965, Tessa, *d* of Capt. Stephen Roskill; one *s* one *d*. *Educ:* Brighton, Hove and Sussex Grammar School; Lincoln Coll., Oxford (BA, History 1960, Theology 1962; MA 1967); Westcott House, Cambridge. Curate, St John's, St John's Wood, NW8, 1964–67; Chaplain 1967–70, Dean and Fellow 1970–81, King's College, Cambridge; Vicar of All Saints', Fulham, 1981–86; Area Dean, Hammersmith and Fulham, 1984–86. *Address:* 29 The Precincts, Canterbury, Kent CT1 2EP. *T:* Canterbury (01227) 463036.

TILLER, Rev. Canon John; Chancellor and Canon Residentiary of Hereford Cathedral, since 1984; Diocesan Director of Training, Hereford, since 1991; *b* 22 June 1938; *s* of Harry Maurice Tiller and Lucille Maisie Tiller; *m* 1961, Ruth Alison (*née* Watson); two *s* one *d*. *Educ:* St Albans Sch.; Christ Church, Oxford (MA, 2nd Cl. Mod. Hist.); Bristol Univ. (MLitt). Ordained deacon 1962, priest 1963, St Albans. Asst Curate: St Cuthbert, Bedford, 1962–65; Widcombe, Bath, 1965–67; Chaplain and Tutor, Tyndale Hall, Bristol, 1967–71; Lectr in Church History and Worship, Trinity Coll., Bristol, 1971–73; Priest-in-Charge, Christ Church, Bedford, 1973–78; Chief Sec., ACCM, 1978–84. Hon. Canon of St Albans Cathedral, 1979–84. *Publications:* The Service of Holy Communion and its Revision (with R. T. Beckwith), 1972; A Modern Liturgical Bibliography, 1974; The

Great Acquittal, 1980; Puritan, Pietist, Pentecostalist, 1982; A Strategy for the Church's Ministry, 1983; The Gospel Community, 1987; contribs to: The New International Dictionary of the Christian Church, 1974; Anglican Worship Today, 1980; New Dictionary of Christian Theology, 1988; The Parish Church?, 1988. *Recreations:* walking, bird-watching, spuddling. *Address:* Canon's House, 3 St John Street, Hereford HR1 2NB. *T:* Hereford (01432) 265659.

TILLEY, John Vincent; Parliamentary Secretary of the Co-operative Union, since 1988; *b* June 1941; *m* Kathryn Riley; two *d.* Mem., Wandsworth Borough Council, 1971–78. Mem., Co-operative Party. MP (Lab) Lambeth Central, Apr. 1978–83. Contested (Lab): Kensington Div. of Kensington and Chelsea, Feb. and Oct. 1974; Southwark and Bermondsey, 1983. Chief Economic Advisor, London Borough of Hackney, 1983–88. *Address:* 35 Point Hill, SE10 8QW.

TILLEY, Olwen Mary, (Mrs A. Tilley); *see* Rice, O. M.

TILLING, George Henry Garfield; Chairman, Scottish Postal Board, 1977–84, retired; *b* 24 Jan. 1924; *s* of late Thomas and Anne Tilling; *m* 1956, Margaret Meriel, *d* of late Rear-Adm. Sir Alexander McGlashan, KBE, CB, DSO; two *s* two *d.* *Educ:* Hardye's Sch., Dorchester; University Coll., Oxford (Open Exhibnr, Kitchener Schol., Farquharson Prizeman, MA). Served War of 1939–45, NW Europe: Captain, Dorset Regt, 1943–46. Post Office: Asst Principal, 1948; Principal, 1953; Private Sec. to Postmaster General, 1964; Dep. Dir of Finance, 1965; Dir, Eastern Postal Region, 1967; Sec. of the Post Office, 1973–75; Dir of Postal Ops, 1975–77. Mem. Council, Lord Kitchener Nat. Meml Fund, 1979–90. Order of St John: Mem. Council, London, 1975–77; Mem. Cttee of the Order for Edinburgh, 1978–87; Mem., Scottish Priory Chapter, 1993–. Trustee, Bield Retirement Housing Trust, 1988–. Hon. Mem., St Andrew's Ambulance Assoc., 1980. KStJ. FSAScot; FCIT. *Recreations:* orders and medals, heraldry, uniforms. *Address:* Standpretty, Gorebridge, Midlothian EH23 4QG. *T:* Gorebridge (01875) 822409.

TILLINGHAST, Charles Carpenter, Jr; aviation and financial consultant; *b* 30 Jan. 1911; *s* of Charles Carpenter Tillinghast and Adelaide Barrows Shaw; *m* 1935, Elizabeth (Lisette) Judd Micoleau; one *s* three *d.* *Educ:* Horace Mann Sch.; Brown Univ. (PhB); Columbia Univ. (JD). Associate, Hughes, Schurman & Dwight, 1935–37; Dep. Asst Dist Attorney, NY County, 1938–40; Associate, Hughes, Richards, Hubbard & Ewing, 1940–42; Partner, Hughes, Hubbard and Ewing (and successor firm, Hughes, Hubbard, Blair & Reed), 1942–57; Vice-Pres. and Dir, The Bendix Corp., 1957–61; Pres. and Chief Exec. Officer, Trans World Airlines Inc., 1961–69 (Director, 1961–81; Chm. and Chief Exec. Officer, 1969–76); Vice-Chm., White, Weld & Co. Inc., 1977–78; Man. Dir, Merrill Lynch White Weld Capital Markets Gp, 1978–83; Vice-Pres., Merrill Lynch Pierce Fenner & Smith Inc., 1978–84; Director: Amstar Corp., 1964–83; Merck & Co., 1962–83; Trustee: Mutual Life Ins. Co. of NY, 1966–84; Brown Univ., 1954–61, 1965–79 (Chancellor, 1968–79; Fellow, 1979–); Mem. IATA Executive Cttee, 1969–76. Hon. Degrees: LHD, South Dakota Sch. of Mines and Tech., 1959; LLD: Franklin Coll., 1963; Univ. of Redlands, 1964; Brown Univ., 1967; Drury Coll., 1967; William Jewell Coll., 1973. *Recreations:* golf, shooting, gardening, woodworking, reading, Philharmonic and opera. *Address:* 355 Blackstone Boulevard, Apt 530, Providence, RI 02906, USA. *T:* (401) 8616676. *Clubs:* Brown Faculty, Wings (NY); Hope (RI); Sakonnet Golf (all in USA).

TILLOTSON, Maj.-Gen. Henry Michael, CB 1983; CBE 1976 (OBE 1970, MBE 1956); *b* 12 May 1928; *er s* of Henry Tillotson, Keighley, Yorks; *m* 1956, Angela, *d* of Bertram Wadsworth Shaw, E Yorks; two *s* one *d.* *Educ:* Chesterfield Sch.; RMA Sandhurst. Commnd E Yorks Regt, 1948; served: Austria, 1948–50; Germany, 1951–52; Indo-China (attached French Union Forces), 1953; Malaya, 1953–55; Staff Coll., Camberley, 1958; JSSC, Latimer, 1963–64; Malaysia, 1964–65; S Arabia, 1965–67 (Queen's Commendation); GSO 1 Defence Intelligence, MoD, 1967–69; CO 1st Bn Prince of Wales's Own Regt of Yorks, Cyprus, 1969–71; Col GS, Hong Kong, 1974–76; Chief of Staff UN Force, Cyprus, and Comdr British Contingent, 1976–78; Dep. Dir, Army Staff Duties, MoD, 1978–79; Chief of Staff to C-in-C UKLF, 1980–83. Col, Prince of Wales's Own Regt of Yorks, 1979–86. Regl Dir, SE Asia, Internat. Mil. Services Ltd, 1983–86. Associate Mem., Council for Arms Control, 1989–92. Fellow, RSPB, 1981. *Publications:* Finland at Peace and War 1918–1993, 1993; With the Prince of Wales's Own, 1995. *Recreations:* travel, birds, listening to music. *Address:* BP 08, 50520 Juvigny Le Tertre, France. *Clubs:* Army and Navy; Cercle National des Armées (Paris).

TILLOTSON, Prof. Kathleen Mary, CBE 1991 (OBE 1983); MA, BLitt; FRSL 1984; FBA 1965; Hildred Carlile Professor of English in the University of London, at Bedford College, 1958–71, now Emeritus; *b* 3 April 1906; *e d* of late Eric A. Constable, BLitt (Durham), journalist, and Catherine H. Constable, Berwick-on-Tweed and Birmingham; *m* 1933, Geoffrey Tillotson, FBA (*d* 1969); two adopted *s.* *Educ:* Ackworth School; Mount School, York; Somerville College, Oxford (Exhibitioner and Shaw Lefevre Scholar). Charles Oldham Shakespeare Scholarship, 1926; BA 1927; temporary tutor, Somerville College, 1928–29; BLitt 1929; teaching at Somerville and St Hilda's Colleges, 1929–39; part-time Assistant, later Junior Lecturer, 1929, Lecturer, 1939, Fellow, 1971, Bedford College; Reader in the University of London at Bedford College, 1947–58. General Editor, Clarendon Dickens, 1957–; nine novels published by 1994. Vice-President: Dickens Fellowship; Brontë Soc.; Trustee: Wordsworth Trust; Bosanquet Trust. Warton Lecture, British Academy, 1956; Annual Brontë Lecture, 1966, 1986; Dickens Meml Lecture, 1970; Annual Tennyson Lecture, 1974; Robert Spence Watson Lecture, 1978. James Bryce Memorial Lecturer, Somerville College, Oxford, 1963, Hon. Fellow, 1965. Hon. DLit Belfast, 1972; Hon. DLitt: Oxon, 1982; London, 1982. Rose Mary Crawshay prize, British Academy, 1943, 1988. *Publications:* (with J. W. Hebel and B. H. Newdigate) Works of Michael Drayton, vol. V, 1941; Novels of the Eighteen-Forties, 1954; Matthew Arnold and Carlyle (Warton Lecture), 1957; (with John Butt) Dickens at Work, 1957; Introductions to Trollope's Barsetshire novels, 1958–75; The Tale and the Teller (inaug. lect.), 1959; Vanity Fair (ed with G. Tillotson), 1963; Mid-Victorian Studies (with G. Tillotson), 1965; Letters of Charles Dickens (General Editor, 1978–), vol. 1, 1965 (Mem., Editl Cttee), vol. 2, 1969 (Associate Editor), vol. 3, 1974 (Associate Editor), vol. 4, 1977, vol. 5, 1981, vol. 6, 1988 (Joint Editor), vol. 7, 1993 (Joint Editor), vol. 8, 1995; (ed) Oliver Twist, 1966; (ed with A. Trodd) The Woman in White, 1969; (ed) Oliver Twist (World's Classics), 1982; James Kinsley (memoir, British Acad.), 1989; contributions to periodicals. *Address:* 23 Tanza Road, NW3 2UA. *T:* 0171–435 5639. *Club:* University Women's.

TILLSLEY, Gen. Bramwell Harold; General of the Salvation Army, 1993–94; *b* 18 Aug. 1931; *s* of Harold Tillsley and Doris Tillsley (*née* Lawrence); *m* 1953, Maude Pitcher; two *s* one *d.* *Educ:* Kitchener-Waterloo Collegiate; Univ. of Western Ontario (BA); Wycliffe Coll., Toronto; Salvation Army Trng Coll., Toronto. Social worker, Children's Aid Soc., Kitchener, Ont., 1952–55; Salvation Army: Windsor, Nova Scotia, 1956–58; Oakville, Ont., 1958–59; on staff, Salvation Army Coll., Toronto, 1959–65; Divl Youth Sec., Saskatchewan, 1965–66; N Toronto Congregation, 1966–71; Training Principal: Newfoundland, 1971–74; NY, 1974–77; Provincial Comdr, Newfoundland, 1977–79; Divl Comdr, Metro-Toronto, 1979–81; Trng Principal, London, 1981–85; Chief Sec., USA, South, 1985–89; Territorial Comdr, Australian Southern Territory, 1989–91; COS, Internat. HQ, London, 1991–93. Mem., Rotary Club, Toronto, Melbourne and London. Queen's Medal (Canada), 1978. *Publications:* Life in the Spirit, 1966; Life More Abundant, 1968; Manpower for the Master, 1970; This Mind in You, 1989. *Recreations:* music, golf, sports (ice hockey in youth). *Address:* 65 Spring Garden Avenue, Unit 604, North York, Ont M2N 6H9, Canada.

TILNEY, Charles Edward, CMG 1956; Minister for Finance and Economics, Tanganyika, 1957–60; *b* 13 April 1909; *yr s* of late Lt-Col N. E. Tilney, CBE, DSO, and Mrs Tilney; *m* 1952, Rosalind Hull (*d* 1993), *e d* of late Lt-Col E. C. de Renzy-Martin, CMG, DSO, MC, and Mrs de Renzy-Martin; two *s.* *Educ:* Rugby School; Oriel College, Oxford. Ceylon Civil Service, 1932; Tanganyika: Asst Chief Secretary (Finance), 1948; Dep. Financial Secretary, 1948; Secretary for Finance, 1950; Member for Finance and Economics, 1953. Retd from E Africa, 1960. *Address:* 8 Butts Close, Biddestone, Chippenham, Wilts SN14 7DZ. *T:* Corsham (01249) 714770.

TILNEY, Dame Guinevere, DBE 1984; Adviser to Rt Hon. Margaret Thatcher, MP, 1975–83; UK Representative on United Nations Commission on Status of Women, 1970–73; *b* 8 Sept. 1916; *y d* of late Sir Hamilton Grant, 12th Bt, KCSI, KCIE, and late Lady Grant; *m* 1st, 1944, Captain Lionel Hunter (*d* 1947), Princess Louise Dragoon Guards; one *s*; 2nd, 1954, Sir John Tilney, TD (*d* 1994). *Educ:* Westonbirt. WRNS, 1941–45; Private Sec. to Earl of Selborne, 1949–54; Vice-Chm., SE Lancs Br., British Empire Cancer Campaign, 1957–64; Founder Mem., 1st Chm., 1st Pres., Merseyside Conservative Ladies Luncheon Club, 1957–75, now 1st Hon. Life Mem.; Nat. Council of Women of Great Britain: Vice-Pres., 1958–61, Pres., 1961–68, Liverpool and Birkenhead Br.; Sen. Nat. Vice-Pres., 1966–68; Nat. Pres., 1968–70; Co-Chm., Women's Nat. Commn, 1969–71; Mem., North Thames Gas Consultative Council, 1967–69; Mem., BBC Gen. Adv. Council, 1967–76. Co-Chm., Women Caring Trust, 1972–75. DL: Co. Palatine of Lancaster, 1971–74; Co. Merseyside, 1974–76. *Recreations:* reading, making soup, writing. *Address:* 3 Victoria Square, SW1W 0QZ. *T:* 0171–828 8674.

TILSON, Joseph Charles, (Joe), RA 1991 (ARA 1985); painter, sculptor and printmaker; *b* 24 Aug. 1928; *s* of Frederick Albert Edward Tilson and Ethel Stapley Louise Saunders; *m* 1956, Joslyn Morton; one *s* two *d.* *Educ:* St Martin's School of Art; Royal Coll. of Art (ARCA); British School at Rome (Rome Scholar). RAF, 1946–49. Worked in Italy and Spain, 1955–59; Vis. Lectr, Slade Sch., Univ. of London and King's Coll., Univ. of Durham, 1962–63; taught at Sch. of Visual Arts, NY, 1966; Vis. Lectr, Staatliche Hochschule für Bildende Kunste, Hamburg, 1971–72. Mem., Arts Panel, Arts Council, 1966–71. Exhib. Venice Biennale, 1964; work at Marlborough Gall., 1961–77, later at Waddington Galls; retrospective exhibitions: Boymans Van Beuningen Mus., Rotterdam, 1973; Vancouver Art Gall., 1979; Volterra, 1983. Biennale Prizes: Krakow, 1974; Ljubljana, 1985. Subject of TV films, 1963, 1968, 1974. *Recreation:* planting trees. *Address:* The Old Rectory, Christian Malford, Wilts SN15 4BW. *T:* Seagry (01249) 720223.

TILSON THOMAS, Michael; Principal Guest Conductor, London Symphony Orchestra, since 1995 (Principal Conductor, 1988–95); Artistic Director (formerly Artistic Adviser), New World Symphony, since 1988; concert pianist; *b* 21 Dec. 1944; *s* of Theodor and Roberta Thomas; *g s* of Boris and Bessie Thomashefsky, founders of Yiddish Theater, United States. *Educ:* Univ. of Southern California (Master of Music). Conductor, Young Musicians' Foundn Orchestra, LA, and conductor and pianist, Monday Evening Concerts, 1963–68; musical asst, Bayreuth, 1966–67; Koussevitzky Prize, Tanglewood, 1968; Asst then Principal Guest Conductor, Boston Symphony, 1969–74; NY début, 1969; London début, with LSO, 1970; Music Director: Buffalo Philharmonic, 1971–79; televised NY Philharmonic Young Peoples' Concerts, 1971–77; Principal Guest Conductor, LA Philharmonic, 1981–85; Music Dir, Great Woods Festival, 1985; guest conductor with orchestras and opera houses in US and Europe; numerous recordings. *Address:* c/o Columbia Artists, 7A Fitzroy Park, N6 6HS. *Club:* St Botolph (Boston).

TILT, (Robin) Richard; Director of Security and Programmes, HM Prison Service, since 1995; *b* 11 March 1944; *s* of Francis Arthur Tilt and Mary Elizabeth (*née* Ashworth); *m* 1966, Kate Busby; two *s* one *d.* *Educ:* King's Sch., Worcester; Univ. of Nottingham (BA Hons); Open Univ. (Dip). HM Prison Service: Asst Governor, HM Borstal, Wellingborough, 1968–71; Tutor, Prison Service Staff Coll., 1971–74; Governor, HM Borstal, Pollington, 1974–75; Deputy Governor: Ranby, 1975–78; Gartree, 1978–80; Governor, Bedford, 1980–82; Hd, Manpower Section, HQ, 1982–84; Governor, Gartree, 1984–88; Dep. Regl Dir, Midlands, 1988–89; Hd, Industrial Relns, HQ, 1989–92; Hd of Finance, Police Dept, 1992–94; Dir of Services, 1994. Churchill Fellow, 1991. Friend of RA. *Recreations:* walking, reading, theatre, art. *Address:* HM Prison Service, Cleland House, Page Street, SW1P 4LN. *T:* 0171–217 6393.

TIMBERLAKE, Herman Leslie Patterson, (Tim); Director, Abbey National Building Society, 1972–84 (Chief General Manager, 1971–79; Deputy Chairman, 1976–79); *b* 3 Feb. 1914; *s* of William Walter and Mabel Timberlake; *m* 1940, Betty (*née* Curtis); two *s.* *Educ:* Watford Grammar Sch. FCIS; FCIB; CIMgt. Served War of 1939–45. Joined Abbey Road Building Soc., 1930; Asst Branch Manager, Watford, 1936; became Abbey National Building Soc., 1944; Branch Manager appts, 1946–59; Manager: Branches Admin. Dept, 1959; Investments Admin. Dept, 1964; Branches and Agencies, 1966; Jt General Manager, 1968. Mem. Council, Building Societies Assoc., 1975–79; Pres., Building Societies Institute, 1977–78. *Address:* 1 Rochester Drive, Pinner, Mddx HA5 1DA. *T:* 0181–866 1554.

TIMBURY, Morag Crichton, MD, PhD; FRSE; FRCP, FRCPGlas, FRCPath; Director, Central Public Health Laboratory, Public Health Laboratory Service, 1988–95; *b* 29 Sept. 1930; *d* of William McCulloch and Dr Esther Sinclair McCulloch (*née* Hood); *m* 1954, Dr Gerald Charles Timbury, FRCPE, FRCPGlas, FRCPsych (decd); one *d.* *Educ:* St Bride's Sch.; Univ. of Glasgow (MB ChB; MD; PhD). MRCPath 1964, FRCPath 1976; MRCPGlas 1972, FRCPGlas 1974; FRCP 1994; FRSE 1979.University of Glasgow: Maurice Bloch Res. Fellow in Virology, 1960–63; Lectr in Bacteriology, 1963–65; Sen. Lectr in Virology, 1966–76; Reader, 1976–78; Prof. of Bacteriology and William Teacher Lectr, 1978–88. Hon. Cons. in Bacteriology and Virology, 1966–88. Member Council: RCPSG, 1985–88; RCP, 1987–90. External examiner in med. microbiol., 1973–88, variously at QUB, Univs of Aberdeen, Cambridge, Dundee, Edinburgh, Newcastle. Vis. Associate Prof. in Virology, Baylor College of Medicine, Houston, Texas, 1975; Vis. Mayne Guest Prof., Univ. of Queensland, Brisbane, 1990; Hon. Vis. Prof. (Virology) RPMS, 1990–; Hon. Sen. Lectr, Royal Free Hosp. and Hon. Lectr in Virology, St Bartholomew's Hosp., 1990–. Mem., RSM, 1986–. *Publications:* Notes on Medical Virology, 1967, 10th edn 1994; (with J. D. Sleigh) Notes on Medical Bacteriology, 1981, 4th edn 1994; (co-ed) vol. 4, Virology, Topley and Wilson's Principles of Bacteriology, Virology and Immunity, 1929, 8th edn 1990; sci. papers on bacterial and viral infections, genetics of herpes simplex virus type 2. *Recreations:* military history, theatre. *Address:* Flat 9, 2 Antrim Grove, Belsize Park, NW3 4XR. *T:* 0171–722 5588.

TIMMER, Jan Dirk; President and Board Chairman, Philips, since 1990; *b* Lienden, 20 Feb. 1933. Joined Philips, 1952; Philips Ethiopia, 1963; Head, Regl Bureau, Tropical

Africa, 1968; Corporate Staff Bureau, 1970, Dir, 1973; Head, Philips South Africa, 1977; Mem., Gp Management Cttee and Chm., Consumer Electronics Div., 1987–90; Chief Exec., PolyGram, 1983. *Address:* Philips, 5600 AM Eindhoven, Netherlands.

TIMMINS, Col John Bradford, OBE (mil.) 1973; TD 1968 (1st Clasp 1974); JP; Lord Lieutenant of Greater Manchester, since 1987; Chairman, Warburton Properties Ltd, since 1973; *b* 23 June 1932; *s* of John James Timmins and Janet Gwendoline (*née* Legg); *m* 1956, Jean Edwards; five *s* one *d*. *Educ:* Dudley Grammar Sch.; Wolverhampton Technical Coll.; Univ. of Aston-in-Birmingham (MSc). Building and Civil Engrg Industry, 1949–80; NW Regional Pres., Nat. Fedn of Building Trade Employers, 1974–75. Commnd RE, 1954; National Service, 1954–56; TA, 1956–80; comd 75 Eng. Regt(V), 1971–73, Hon. Col of the Regt, 1980–90; Hon. Colonel: Manchester and Salford Univ. OTC, 1990–; Gtr Manchester ACF, 1991–. Pres., TA&VRA for NW England, 1994– (Vice-Chm., 1983–87; Vice-Pres., 1987–94). ADC to the Queen, 1975–80. High Sheriff of Gtr Manchester, 1986–87. JP Trafford, 1987. KStJ 1988. Hon. DSc Salford, 1990. *Recreations:* sailing, good food and good wine. *Address:* The Old Rectory, Warburton, Lymm WA13 9SS. *Clubs:* Army and Navy; St James's (Manchester).

TIMMS, Dr Cecil, DEng, CEng, FIMechE, FIProdE; former Engineering Consultant, Department of Trade and Industry, later Department of Industry, retired; *b* 13 Dec. 1911; *m*; no *c*. *Educ:* Liverpool Univ. Head of Metrology, Mechanisms and Noise Control Div., 1950–61, Supt of Machinery Group, 1961–65, National Engrg Laboratory; Head of Machine Tools Branch, Min. of Technology, later DTI, 1965–73. *Publications:* contribs to Proc. IMechE, Metalworking Prod. and Prod. Engr. *Address:* Broom House, Ballsdown, Chiddingfold, Surrey GU8 4XJ. *T:* Wormley (01428) 682014.

TIMMS, Ven. George Boorne; Archdeacon of Hackney, 1971–81, now Emeritus; Vicar of St Andrew, Holborn, 1965–81; *b* 4 Oct. 1910; *s* of late George Timms and Annie Elizabeth Timms (*née* Boorne); unmarried. *Educ:* Derby Sch.; St Edmund Hall, Oxford; Coll. of the Resurrection, Mirfield. MA Oxon. Deacon, 1935; Priest, 1936; Curate: St Mary Magdalen, Coventry, 1935–38; St Bartholomew, Reading, 1938–49; Oxford Diocesan Inspector of Schools, 1944–49; Sacrist of Southwark Cath., 1949–52; Vicar of St Mary, Primrose Hill, NW3, 1952–65; Rural Dean of Hampstead, 1959–65; Prebendary of St Paul's Cathedral, 1964–71. Proctor in Conv., 1955–59, 1965–70, 1974–80; Member: Standing Cttee Church Assembly, 1968–70; Anglican-Methodist Unity Commn, 1965–69. Dir of Ordination Trg, and Exam. Chap. to Bp of London, 1965–81; Chm., Alcuin Club, 1968–87. Pres., Sion Coll., 1980–81. Papal Medallion for services to Christian Unity, 1976. *Publications:* Dixit Cranmer, 1946; The Liturgical Seasons, 1965; (jtly) The Cloud of Witnesses, 1982; contributor to A Manual for Holy Week, 1967; (ed) English Praise, 1975; (ed) The New English Hymnal, 1985. *Address:* Cleve Lodge, Minster-in-Thanet, Ramsgate, Kent CT12 4BA. *T:* Thanet (01843) 821777.

TIMMS, Prof. Noel Walter; Professor of Social Work and Director, School of Social Work, University of Leicester, 1984–89, now Emeritus Professor; *b* 25 Dec. 1927; *s* of Harold John Timms and Josephine Mary Cecilia Timms; *m* 1956, Rita Caldwell; three *s* three *d*. *Educ:* Cardinal Vaughan School; Univ. of London (BA Hons History; MA Sociology); Univ. of Oxford. Social Worker, Family Service Units, 1952–54; Psychiatric social worker, 1955–57; Lectr, Dept of Social Science, Cardiff University Coll., 1957–61; Lectr, LSE, 1963–69; Prof. of Applied Social Studies, Bradford Univ., 1969–75; Prof. of Social Studies, Newcastle upon Tyne Univ., 1975–84. *Publications:* Social Casework, Principles and Practice, 1964; Language of Social Casework, 1968; (with John Mayer) The Client Speaks, 1970; (with Rita Timms) Dictionary of Social Welfare, 1982; Social Work Values: an enquiry, 1983; Family and Citizenship, 1992; (jtly) Secure Accommodation in Child Care, 1993; (jtly) Mediation: the making and remaking of co-operative relationships, 1994. *Recreations:* Evensong; looking at old furniture and at performances of Don Giovanni. *Address:* 706 Kenilworth Road, Balsall Common, near Coventry CV7 7HD. *T:* Berkswell (01676) 534593.

TIMMS, Stephen Creswell; MP (Lab) Newham North East, since June 1994; *b* 29 July 1955; *s* of late Ronald James Timms and of Margaret Joyce Timms (*née* Johnson); *m* 1986, Hui-Leng Lim. *Educ:* Farnborough Grammar Sch.; Emmanuel Coll., Cambridge (MA, MPhil). Consultant, Logica, 1978–86; Ovum: Principal Consultant, 1986–94; Manager, Telecommunications Reports, 1994. Sec., Newham NE Labour Party, 1981–84. Newham Borough Council: Councillor (Lab), 1984–; Chm., Planning Cttee, 1987–90; Leader, 1990–94. Member: Plaistow Christian Fellowship; Christian Socialist Movement. Mem., Ramblers' Assoc. Hon. Pres., Telecommunications Users' Assoc., 1995–. *Publications:* Broadband Communications: the commercial impact, 1986; ISDN: customer premises equipment, 1988; Broadband Communications: market strategies, 1992. *Address:* 94 Katherine Road, E6 1EN. *T:* 0181–471 7090.

TIMMS, Vera Kate, (Mrs E. W. Gordon); Principal Finance Officer, Ministry of Agriculture, Fisheries and Food, since 1995; *b* 8 Oct. 1944; *d* of late Kenneth Timms and of Elsie Timms (*née* Cussans); *m* 1977, Ernest William Gordon; one step *d*. *Educ:* Queen Anne Grammar School, York; St Hilda's College, Oxford (PPE hons). Economic Asst, NEDO, 1966–70; Ministry of Agriculture, Fisheries and Food, 1970; Asst Private Sec. to Minister of Agric., 1974–75; seconded to European Secretariat of Cabinet Office, 1976–79; Principal Private Sec. to Minister of Agric. 1980–82; Asst Sec. responsible for marketing policy, MAFF, 1982–84; Counsellor, Paris, seconded to HM Diplomatic Service, 1984–88; Asst Sec. and Head of Sugar and Oilseeds Div., MAFF, 1988–89; Under Sec., Arable Crops Gp, MAFF, 1989–90; Minister (Agriculture), Office of the UK Perm. Rep., Brussels, 1990–95. Ordre du Mérite Agricole (France), 1988. *Address:* Holly House, 62A London Street, Swaffham, Norfolk PE37 7DJ. *T:* Swaffham (01760) 723034; 42 The Foreshore, SE8 3AG. *T:* 0181–691 0823.

TIMPSON, John Harry Robert, OBE 1987; writer and broadcaster; *b* 2 July 1928; *s* of late John Hubert Victor Timpson and Caroline (*née* Willson); *m* 1951, (Muriel) Patricia Whale; two *s*. *Educ:* Merchant Taylors' Sch. National Service, RASC, 1946–49. Reporter: Wembley News, 1945–46 and 1949–51; Eastern Daily Press, 1951–59; BBC News Staff, 1959–87; BBC Dep. Court Correspondent, 1962–67 (reporting Australian, Ethiopian and other Royal tours); Presenter: Newsroom, BBC-2, 1968–70; Tonight, BBC-1, 1976–78; Today, BBC Radio 4, 1970–76, 1978–86; Chm., Any Questions, BBC Radio 4, 1984–87. Hon. MA UEA, 1991. Sony Gold Award for outstanding services to radio, 1986. *Publications:* Today and Yesterday (autobiog.), 1976; The Lighter Side of Today, 1983; The Early Morning Book, 1986; Timpson's England—A Look beyond the Obvious, 1987; Paper Trail (novel), 1989; Timpson's Towns, 1989; Timpson's Travels in East Anglia, 1990; Sound Track (novel), 1991; Timpson's English Eccentrics, 1991; Little Trains of Britain, 1992; Timpson's English Villages, 1992; Timpson's Other England, 1993; Timpson's Timepaths, 1994; Timpson's English Country Inns, 1995. *Recreation:* enjoying Norfolk. *Address:* Ark Cottage, Wellingham, Weasenham St Peter, King's Lynn, Norfolk PE32 2TH.

TIMS, Sir Michael (David), KCVO 1992 (CVO 1984; LVO 1973; MVO 1963); Serjeant-at-Arms to HM The Queen, 1987–92, retired; *b* 14 Sept. 1931; *s* of late William Edward Tims and Eva Ida Tims; *m* 1959, Jacqueline Lily Clark; one *s*. *Educ:* Christ's Hosp. The Queen's Household: Dep. Comptroller of Supply, 1953–68; Asst to the Master of the Household, 1968–92. Mem., Bd of Green Cloth, 1988–. FRSA 1992. JP Inner London, 1984–91. Freeman, City of London, 1986; Liveryman, Co. of Cooks, 1993–. Various hon. foreign awards. *Publications:* articles on fishing in national magazines. *Recreations:* battling with and painting big game fish. *Address:* Clock Tower House, The Royal Paddocks, Hampton Court Road, E Molesey, Surrey KT8 9DA.

TIMSON, Penelope Anne Constance; *see* Keith, P. A. C.

TINDAL-CARILL-WORSLEY, Air Commodore Geoffrey Nicolas Ernest, CB 1954; CBE 1943; Royal Air Force, retired; *b* 8 June 1908; *s* of late Philip Tindal-Carill-Worsley; *m* 1st, 1937, Berys Elizabeth Gilmour (marr. diss., 1951; she *d* 1962); one *s*; 2nd, 1951, Dorothy Mabel Murray Stanley-Turner (*d* 1995). *Educ:* Eton; RAF Coll., Cranwell. Commanding Officer, RAF Station, Halton, Bucks, 1954–56; Sen. Technical Staff Officer, Far East Air Force, 1956–59; Director of Technical Training, Air Ministry, 1959; retired 1960. *Recreation:* country life.

TINDALE, Gordon Anthony, OBE 1983; public relations consultant, Washington, since 1994; *b* 17 March 1938; *s* of George Augustus Tindale and Olive Sarah Collier; *m* 1960, Sonia Mary Soper; one *s* one *d*. *Educ:* Highgate Sch.; Trinity Coll., Oxford (BA (Mod. Hist)); Birkbeck Coll., London (MA (Int. Relations)). Nat. Service, 1956–58. Joined British Council, 1961; postings in Iraq, Jordan, London and Egypt; Representative: Lesotho, Botswana and Swaziland, 1975–78; Zambia, 1979–83; Controller, Management Div., 1984–87; Representative, Egypt, 1987–89; Cultural Counsellor (formerly Cultural Attaché), Washington, 1989–94. *Recreations:* music, golf. *Address:* 4450 South Park Avenue, Apt 1619, Chevy Chase, Maryland 20815, USA. *T:* (301) 2157132; 23 Heath Hurst Road, Hampstead, NW3 2RU. *Club:* Hendon Golf.

TINDALE, Lawrence Victor Dolman, CBE 1971; CA; Chairman, North British Canadian Investment Trust, 1979–94; *b* 24 April 1921; *s* of late John Stephen and Alice Lilian Tindale; *m* 1946, Beatrice Mabel (Betty) Barton; one *s* one *d*. *Educ:* Latymer Upper Sch., Hammersmith; Inst. of Chartered Accountants of Scotland. Apprenticed McClelland Ker, 1938. Served War, Army, in E Africa and Burma, 1941–45. Returned to McClelland Ker, and qualified, 1946; Partner, 1951. Invited to join ICFC Ltd as Asst Gen. Manager, 1959; Dir and Gen. Manager, 1966–72; on secondment, DTI, as Dir of Industrial Development, 1972–74; Dep. Chm., FFI, subseq. Investors in Industry Gp, then 3i Gp, 1974–91. Member: DTI Cttee of Inquiry on Small Firms, 1969–71; Adv. Council on Energy Conservation, 1977–80; British Technology Gp (NRDC, 1974–91; NEB, 1981–91); Chm., EDC for Mechanical Engrg Industry, 1968–72. Director: Commodore Shipping Co. Ltd, 1969–; Guernsey Gas Light Co. Ltd, 1970–91; Investment Trust of Guernsey Ltd, 1970–94; Edbro plc (Chm.), 1974–91; Northern Engineering Industries plc, 1974–89 (Dep. Chm., 1986–89); Flextech (Holdings) Ltd, 1975–93 (Chm., 1984–86); London Atlantic Investment Trust plc (Chm.), 1977–91; Transpec Holdings Ltd, 1980–87; Dewrance MacNeil Ltd, 1980–88; British Caledonian Gp (formerly Caledonian Airways) plc, 1980–88; BNOC, 1980–84; Britoil, 1984–88; Penspen Ltd, 1985–89; Polly Peck (International) plc, 1985–91; Shandwick plc, 1985–92; C. & J. Clark, 1986–91 (Chm., 1986–91); Barnsley Partnership Ltd, 1991–. Mem. Council: Consumers' Assoc., 1970–87 (Vice Chm., 1981–85); BIM, 1974–84 (Chm. 1982–84; Vice-Pres., 1984–); Soc. for Protection of Ancient Buildings (Hon. Treasurer), 1974–; Mem., Management Cttee, Ex-Services Mental Welfare Soc. CA; CIMgt; FRSA 1989. *Recreation:* opera. *Address:* 3 Amyand Park Gardens, Twickenham, TW1 3HS. *T:* 0181–892 9457. *Clubs:* Reform; St James's (Manchester).

TINDALE, Patricia Randall; architect; Chief Architect, Department of the Environment, 1982–86; *b* 11 March 1926; *d* of Thomas John Tindale and May Tindale (*née* Uttin). *Educ:* Blatchington Court, Seaford, Sussex; Architectural Assoc. Sch. of Architecture (AADip.). ARIBA. Architect, Welsh Dept, Min. of Educn, 1949–50; Min. of Educn Develt Gp, 1951–60; Min. of Housing and Local Govt R&D Gp, 1960–70; DoE Housing Develt Gp, 1970–72; Head, Building Regulations Professional Div., DoE, 1972–74; Dir, Housing Develt Directorate, DoE, 1974–81; Dir, Central Unit of Built Environment, DoE, 1981–82. Member: Building Regulations Adv. Cttee, 1993; British Bd of Agrément, 1993–; Anchor Housing Assoc., 1993–. Mem., AA Council, 1965–68. *Publication:* Housebuilding in the USA, 1966. *Recreations:* weaving, travelling. *Address:* 34 Crescent Grove, SW4 7AH. *T:* 0171–622 1926. *Club:* Reform.

TINDALL, Rev. Canon Frederick Cryer, BD 1923; FKC 1950 (AKC 1922); Principal Emeritus of Salisbury Theological College since 1965; Canon and Prebendary Emeritus of Salisbury Cathedral since 1981; *b* 2 July 1900; *s* of late Frederick and Frances Tindall, Hove, Sussex; *m* 1942, Rosemary Phyllis, *d* of late Frank and Katharine Alice Newman, Woking; one *s* (one *d* decd). *Educ:* Brighton Grammar Sch.; King's Coll., London; Ely Theological College. Curate of S Cyprian, S Marylebone, 1924–28; Lecturer and Bursar, Chichester Theological College, 1928–30, Vice-Principal, 1930–36; Warden of Connaught Hall and Lecturer in Theology, Southampton Univ., 1936–39; Vicar of St Augustine, Brighton, 1939–50; Principal, Salisbury Theological Coll., 1950–65 (Sabbatical Year 1965–66). Proctor in Convocation for Diocese of Chichester, 1936–45, 1949–50; Examining Chaplain to Bishop of Chichester, 1941–50, Canon and Prebendary of Chichester Cathedral, 1948–50; Canon and Prebendary of Salisbury Cathedral, 1950–81; Proctor in Convocation for Diocese of Salisbury, 1950–75; Vice-Pres. and Chm. House of Clergy, Salisbury Diocesan Synod, 1970–76; Chm., Salisbury Diocesan Liturgical Cttee, 1973–81; Member: Commn for Revision of the Catechism, 1958; Church Assembly Standing Orders Cttee, 1963; Archbishop's Commn on London and SE England, 1965; Greater London Area Liaison Cttee, 1968; Pastoral Measure Appeal Tribunal, 1969–75; General Synod Standing Orders Cttee, 1970–75. Clerical Judge, Court of Arches, Canterbury, 1969–80. Pro-Prolocutor, Lower House of Convocation of Canterbury, 1959–75. Trustee, St John's Hosp., Heytesbury, 1968–83. *Publications:* England Expects, 1946; a History of S Augustine's Brighton, 1946; Christian Initiation, Anglican Principles and Practice, 1951; contributor to: History of Christian Thought, 1937; Encyclopædia Britannica Year Book, 1939; Baptism To-Day, 1949; Theology, Church Quarterly Review, Guardian, etc. *Recreations:* music, travelling, golf, gardening. *Address:* 16 The Close, Salisbury, Wilts SP1 2EB. *T:* Salisbury (01722) 322373. *Clubs:* Athenæum, Commonwealth Trust, Ski Club of Great Britain.

TINDALL, Gillian Elizabeth; novelist, biographer, historian; *b* 4 May 1938; *d* of D. H. Tindall and U. M. D. Orange; *m* 1963, Richard G. Lansdown; one *s*. *Educ:* Univ. of Oxford (BA 1st cl., MA). Freelance journalism: occasional articles and reviews for Observer, Guardian, New Statesman, London Evening Standard, The Times, Encounter, New Society, and Independent. Occasional broadcasts, BBC. *Publications: novels:* No Name in the Street, 1959; The Water and the Sound, 1961; The Edge of the Paper, 1963; The Youngest, 1967; Someone Else, 1969, 2nd edn 1975; Fly Away Home, 1971 (Somerset Maugham Award, 1972); The Traveller and His Child, 1975; The Intruder, 1979; Looking Forward, 1983; To the City, 1987; Give Them All My Love, 1989; Spirit Weddings, 1992; *short stories:* Dances of Death, 1973; The China Egg and Other Stories, 1981; Journey of a Lifetime and Other Stories, 1990; *biography:* The Born Exile (George

Gissing), 1974; *other non-fiction:* A Handbook on Witchcraft, 1965; The Fields Beneath, 1977; City of Gold: the biography of Bombay, 1981, 2nd edn 1992; Rosamond Lehmann: an Appreciation, 1985; (contrib.) Architecture of the British Empire, 1986; Countries of the Mind: the meaning of place to writers, 1991; Célestine: voices from a French village, 1995. *Recreations:* keeping house, foreign travel. *Address:* c/o Curtis Brown Ltd, 28/29 Haymarket, SW1Y 4SP.

TINDALL, Prof. Victor Ronald, CBE 1992; FRCSE, FRCOG; Professor of Obstetrics and Gynaecology, University of Manchester at St Mary's Hospital, since 1972; *b* 1 Aug. 1928; *m* 1955, Brenda Fay; one *s* one *d*. *Educ:* Wallasey Grammar Sch.; Liverpool Univ. (MB ChB; MD); Manchester Univ. (MSc). Sen. Lectr and Consultant, Welsh Nat. Sch. of Medicine, Cardiff, 1965–70; Consultant Obstetrician and Gynaecologist, Univ. Hosp. of Wales, 1970–72. Sen. Vice-Pres., RCOG, 1990–93. FRCS by election, 1991. *Publications:* MCQ Tutor, MRCOG Part I, 1977, 2nd edn 1985, combined edn 1987; (jtly) Practical Student Obstetrics, 1980; Colour Atlas of Clinical Gynaecology, 1981; Essential Sciences for Clinicians, 1981; Clinical Gynaecology, 1986; (ed) Jeffcoates' Principles of Gynaecology, 5th edn 1987; Diagnostic Picture Tests in Obstetrics and Gynaecology, 1986; (ed jtly) Current Approaches to Endometrial Carcinoma, 1988; (jtly) Preparations and Advice for the Members of the Royal College of Obstetricians and Gynaecologists, 1989; Illustrated Textbook of Gynaecology, 1991; reports for DHSS on maternal deaths in the UK. *Recreations:* ex Rugby international, international sporting activities. *Address:* 4 Planetree Road, Hale, Altrincham, Cheshire WA15 9JL. *T:* 0161–980 2680; St Mary's Hospital, Whitworth Park, Manchester M13 0JH. *Clubs:* Royal Society of Medicine, Royal College of Obstetricians and Gynaecologists.

TINDEMANS, Leo; Member (EPP) European Parliament, 1979–81, and since 1989; President, Group of the European People's Party, since 1992; Member (Christian Democratic Party), House of Representatives, Belgium, 1961–89; *b* Zwijndrecht, 16 April 1922; *m* 1960, Rosa Naesens; two *s* two *d*. *Educ:* State Univ., Ghent; Catholic Univ., Louvain. Minister: for Community Relations, 1968–71; of Agriculture and Middle Class Affairs, 1972–73; Dep. Prime Minister and Minister for the Budget, 1973–74; Prime Minister of Belgium, 1974–78; Minister of Foreign Relations, 1981–89. Mayor of Edegem, 1965–76. President: Christian Democratic Party, 1979–81; European People's Party, 1976–85. Prof., Faculty of Social Scis, Catholic Univ., Louvain; first holder, Jacques Delors Chair, Maastricht. Hon. DLitt: City Univ., 1976; Heriot-Watt Univ., 1978; Georgetown Univ., Washington, 1984; Univ. de Deusto, Bilbao, 1991. Charlemagne Prize, 1976; St Liborius Medaille für Einheit und Frieden, 1977; Stresemann Medaille, 1979; Schuman Prize, 1980; Médaille d'Or du Cercle Chateaubriand, 1992; Heinrich Brauns Prize, 1994. *Publications:* L'autonomie culturelle, 1971; Een handvest voor woelig België, 1972; Dagboek van de werkgroep Eyskens, 1973; European Union, 1975; Europe, Ideal of our Generation, 1976; Atlantisch Europa, 1981; Europa zonder Kompas, 1987; L'Europe de l'Est vue de Bruxelles, 1989; Duel met de Minister, 1991; De toekomst van een idee, 1993. *Recreations:* reading, writing, walking. *Address:* Jan Verbertlei 24, B-2650 Edegem, Belgium.

TINDLE, David, RA 1979 (ARA 1973); painter; *b* 29 April 1932; *m* 1969, Janet Trollope (marr. diss. 1992); one *s* two *d*. *Educ:* Coventry Sch. of Art. MA Oxon 1985. Worked as scene painter and commercial artist, 1946–51; subseq. taught at Hornsey Coll. of Art; Vis. Tutor, Royal Coll. of Art, 1972–83, Fellow, 1981, Hon. FRCA, 1984; Ruskin Master of Drawing, Oxford Univ., and Professorial Fellow, St Edmund Hall, Oxford, 1985–87 (Hon. Fellow, 1988). RE, 1988–91. Hon. RBSA 1989. First showed work, Archer Gall., 1952 and 1953; regular one-man exhibns, Piccadilly Gall., from 1954; one-man exhibns at many public and private galleries in Gt Britain incl. Fischer Fine Art, 1985, 1989, 1992; Redfern Gall., London, 1994; Galerie du Tours, San Francisco and Los Angeles, 1964; Gallerie Vinciana, Milan, 1968; Galleria Carbonesi, Bologna, 1968; Gallery XX, Hamburg, 1974, 1977, 1980; rep. in exhibns at: Piccadilly Gall., 1954–; Royal Acad.; Internat. Biennale of Realist Art, Bruges, 1958 and Bologna, 1967; British Exhibn Art, Basel, 1958; John Moores, 1959 and 1961; Arts Council Shows: British Self-Portraits; Painters in East Anglia; Thames in Art; The British Art Show, 1979–80; Salon de la Jeune Peinture, Paris, 1967; Mostra Mercato d'Arte Contemporanea, Florence, 1967; British Painting 1974, Hayward Gall.; British Painting 1952–77, RA; Six English Painters—Eros in Albion, Arezzo, Italy, 1989; Portrait of the Artist, Tate Gall., 1989. Set of 3 Mural decorations for Open Univ., Milton Keynes, 1977–78. Designed sets for Iolanta, Aldeburgh Fest., 1988. Work rep. in numerous public and private collections, incl. Nat. Portrait Gall.; Chantrey Bequest purchases, 1974 and 1975, now in Tate Gall. Critic Prize, 1962; Europe Prize for Painting, 1969; Critics' Choice, Tooths, 1974; Waddington Prize, Chichester Nat. Art Exhibn, 1975; Johnson Wax Award, RA, 1983. *Address:* Redfern Gallery, 20 Cork Street, W1X 2HL.

TINDLE, Sir Ray (Stanley), Kt 1994; CBE 1987 (OBE 1973); DL; Chairman: Tindle Newspapers Ltd, since 1972; Surrey Advertiser Newspaper Holdings Ltd, since 1978; *b* 8 Oct. 1926; *s* of late John Robert Tindle and Maud Tindle; *m* 1949, Beryl Julia (*née* Ellis), MA, DipEd; one *s*. *Educ:* Torquay Grammar Sch.; Strand Sch. FCIS; FCIArb. War service, Devonshire Regt (Captain), 1944–47. Asst to Dir, Newspaper Soc., 1952–58; Managing Director: Surrey Mirror Newspapers, 1959–63; Surrey Advertiser Newspapers, 1963–78. Pres., Newspaper Soc., 1971–72; Vice Pres. and Chm. of Appeal, Newspaper Press Fund, 1990; Member: Newspaper Panel, Monopolies and Mergers Commn, 1987–93; Council, CPU, 1987–; Press Bd of Finance, 1990–. Founder, Tindle Enterprise Centres for the Unemployed, 1984–. Master, Stationers' and Newspaper Makers' Co., 1985–86. DL Surrey, 1989. *Publication:* The Press Today and Tomorrow, 1975. *Recreations:* veteran cars, newspapers, boating. *Address:* 114 West Street, Farnham, Surrey GU9 7HL. *Clubs:* Veteran Car, City Livery Yacht.

TING, Prof. Samuel Chao Chung; Thomas D. Cabot Institute Professor, Massachusetts Institute of Technology, since 1977; *b* 27 Jan. 1936; *s* of K. H. Ting and late T. S. Wang; *m*; two *d*; *m* 1985, Susan Carol Marks; one *s*. *Educ:* Univ. of Michigan (PhD). Ford Fellow, CERN, Geneva, 1963; Asst Prof. of Physics, Columbia Univ., 1965; Prof. of Physics, MIT, 1969. Assoc. Editor, Nuclear Physics B, 1970; Mem. Editorial Board: Nuclear Instruments and Methods, 1977; Mathematical Modeling, 1980. Hon. Professor: Beijing Normal Coll., 1984; Jiatong Univ., Shanghai, 1987. Member: US Nat. Acad. of Science, 1976; European Physical Soc.; Italian Physical Soc.; Foreign Member: Pakistan Acad. of Science, 1984; Academia Sinica (Republic of China), 1975; Soviet Acad. of Science, 1988; Fellow, Amer. Acad. of Arts and Science, 1975. Hon. ScD: Chinese Univ. of Hong Kong, 1987; Bologna, 1988; Columbia, 1990; Univ. of Sci. and Technol. of China, 1990; Moscow State Univ., 1991. Nobel Prize for Physics (jt), 1976; Ernest Orlando Lawrence Award, US Govt, 1976; A. E. Eringen Medal, Soc. of Engineering Science, USA, 1977; Gold Medal in Science, City of Brescia, Italy, 1988; De Gasperi Prize, Italian Republic, 1988. Hon. ScD Michigan, 1978. *Publications:* articles in Physical Review and Physical Review Letters. *Address:* 51 Vassar Street, Cambridge, MA 02139–4308, USA. *Club:* Explorers' (NY).

TINKER, Prof. Hugh Russell; Professor of Politics, University of Lancaster, 1977–82, now Emeritus; *b* 20 July 1921; *s* of late Clement Hugh Tinker and Gertrude Marian Tinker; *m* 1947, Elisabeth McKenzie (*née* Willis); two *s* (and one *s* killed in action). *Educ:* Taunton Sch.; Sidney Sussex Coll., Cambridge (BA Scholar). Indian Army, 1941–45; Indian civil admin, 1945–46. Lectr, Reader and Prof., SOAS, 1948–69; Dir, Inst. of Race Relations, 1970–72; Sen. Fellow, Inst. of Commonwealth Studies, Univ. of London, 1972–77. Prof., Univ. of Rangoon, 1954–55; Prof., Cornell Univ., USA, 1959. Vice-Pres., Ex-Services Campaign for Nuclear Disarmament. Contested (L): Barnet, gen. elecs 1964 and 1966; Morecambe and Lonsdale, 1979. *Publications:* The Foundations of Local Self-Government in India, Pakistan and Burma, 1954; The Union of Burma, a Study of the First Years of Independence, 1957 (4th edn 1967); India and Pakistan, a Political Analysis, 1962; Ballot Box and Bayonet, People and Government in Emergent Asian Countries, 1964; Reorientations, Studies on Asia in Transition, 1965; South Asia, a Short History, 1966; Experiment with Freedom, India and Pakistan 1947, 1967; (ed and wrote introduction) Henry Yule: Narrative of the Mission to the Court of Ava in 1855, 1969; A New System of Slavery: the export of Indian labour overseas 1830–1920, 1974; Separate and Unequal: India and the Indians in the British Commonwealth 1920–1950, 1976; The Banyan Tree: overseas emigrants from India, Pakistan and Bangladesh, 1977; Race, Conflict and the International Order: from Empire to United Nations, 1977; The Ordeal of Love: C. F. Andrews and India, 1979; A Message from the Falklands: the life and gallant death of David Tinker, 1982; (ed) Burma: the struggle for independence, vol. I 1944–1946, 1983, vol. II 1946–1948, 1984; Men Who Overturned Empires: fighters, dreamers, schemers, 1987. *Recreation:* pottering. *Address:* Montbegon, Hornby, near Lancaster LA2 8JZ.

TINKER, Dr Jack, FRCP, FRCSGlas; Dean of Postgraduate Medicine, University of London and North Thames Regional Health Authority, since 1988; *b* 20 Jan. 1936; *s* of Lawrence and Jessie Tinker; *m* 1961, Maureen Ann Crawford; two *s*. *Educ:* Manchester Univ. (BSc (Hons), MB ChB); DIC. Dir, Intensive Therapy Unit, Middlesex Hosp., 1974–88; Hon. Cons. Physician, Middlesex Hosp., 1988–; Hon. Sen. Clin. Lectr, UCL Med. Sch. (formerly UCMSM), 1988–; Hon. Sen. Lectr, St Bartholomew's Hosp. Med. Coll., 1991–. Sen. Med. Cons. Sun Life of Canada, 1983–; Med. Advr, RTZ Gp, 1986–. FRSM 1989. Editor in Chief, British Jl of Hospital Medicine, 1985– Man. Editor, Intensive Care Medicine, 1973–88. *Publications:* A Course in Intensive Therapy Nursing, 1980; Care of the Critically Ill Patient, 1982, 2nd edn 1991; A Pocket Book for Intensive Care, 1986, 2nd edn 1990; contribs to intensive care and cardiological jls. *Recreations:* road running, cricket. *Address:* 1 Rectory Road, Barnes, SW13 9HH. *T:* 0181–878 0159. *Clubs:* Royal Automobile, MCC; Scarborough.

TINKER, Dr Philip Bernard Hague, FIBiol, FRSC; Director of Terrestrial and Freshwater Science, Natural Environment Research Council, 1985–92; *b* 1 Feb. 1930; *s* of Philip and Gertrude Tinker; *m* 1955, Maureen Ellis; one *s* one *d*. *Educ:* Rochdale High Sch.; Sheffield Univ. (BSc); PhD 1955; MA, DSc 1984, Oxon. FIBiol 1974; FRSC 1985. Overseas Res. Service, 1955–62; Sen. Scientific Officer, Rothamsted Experimental Stn, 1962–65; Lectr, Oxford Univ., 1965–71; Prof. of Agricultural Botany, Leeds Univ., 1971–77; Head of Soils Div., 1977–85, and Dep. Dir, 1981–85, Rothamsted Experimental Stn. Fellow, 1969–72, Sen. Res. Fellow, 1988–, St Cross Coll., Oxford. Hon. Vis. Prof., Imperial Coll., 1992–95. Lectures: Regents, Univ. of California, 1979; Hannaford Meml, Adelaide, 1990; Francis New Meml and Medal, Fertilizer Soc., 1991. Chairman: UK Man and Biosphere Cttee, 1990–93; UK Cttee for Internat. Geosphere-Biosphere Prog., 1992–. Member: UNESCO Adv. Cttee for Biosphere Reserves, 1992–; IGPP Scientific Cttee, 1992–96. Pres., British Soil Sci. Soc., 1983–84; Gov., Macaulay Land Use Res. Inst., Aberdeen, 1990–. Fellow, Norwegian Acad. of Science and Letters, 1987; Hon. FRASE, 1990. Busk Medal, RGS, 1994. *Publications:* (with F. E. Sanders and B. Mosse) Endomycorrhisas, 1975; (with P. H. Nye) Solute Movement in the Soil-root System, 1977; Soil and Agriculture—Critical Reviews, 1980; (with A. Läuchli) Advances in Plant Nutrition, vol. I, 1984, vol. II, 1986, vol. III, 1988; *c* 140 papers. *Recreations:* reading, gardening, map collecting. *Address:* The Glebe House, Broadwell, Lechlade, Glos GL7 3QS. *T:* Faringdon (01367) 860436. *Club:* Farmers'.

TINN, James; *b* 23 Aug. 1922; *s* of James Tinn and Nora (*née* Davie). *Educ:* Consett Elementary School; Ruskin College; Jesus College, Oxford. Cokeworker until 1953; Branch official, Nat. Union of Blastfurnacemen. Full-time study for BA (PPE Oxon). Teacher, secondary modern school, 1958–64. MP (Lab): Cleveland, 1964–74; Redcar, 1974–87. PPS to Sec. of State for Commonwealth (formerly for Commonwealth Relations), 1965–66, to Minister for Overseas Development, 1966–67; an Asst Govt Whip, 1976–79; an Opposition Whip, 1979–82. Mem. Exec. Cttee, CPA. *Address:* 1 Norfolk Road, Moorside, Consett, Co. Durham DH8 8DD. *T:* Consett (01207) 509313. *Club:* United Oxford & Cambridge University.

TINNISWOOD, Maurice Owen; *b* 26 March 1919; *y s* of late Robert Tinniswood, OBE; *m* 1946, Anne Katharine, *yr d* of late Rev. J. Trevor Matchett; one *s* one *d*. *Educ:* Merchant Taylors' School. Served with Royal Hampshire Regt, 1939–46 (Major). Joined PO, 1938 as Executive Officer, Principal, 1949; Asst Secretary, 1958; Imperial Defence College, 1963; Director of Establishments and Organisation, 1965; Director of Reorganization, 1966; Secretary to the Post Office, 1969–70; Dir of Personnel, BBC, 1970–77. Chm., Kingston, Richmond and Esher Community Health Council, 1980–81; Mem., Kingston and Esher HA, 1982–85. CIMgt. *Address:* Little Croft, Weston Green Road, Thames Ditton, Surrey KT7 0HY. *T:* 0181–398 4561.

TINSON, Dame Susan (Myfanwy), DBE 1990; Associate Editor, Independent Television News, since 1989; *b* 15 Jan. 1943; *d* of John and Kathleen Thomas; *m* 1968, Trevor James Tinson (marr. diss. 1979). *Educ:* South Hampstead High Sch.; Hull Univ. (BA Hons Social Studies). Independent Television News: trainee, 1964; Sub-editor, field co-ordinator, 1967; Chief Sub Editor, News at Ten, 1975; Senior Editor, News at Ten and Asst Editor, ITN, 1982; Head of Special Events, 1989–, and of External Affairs, ITN; programmes include: elections, UK and abroad; Royal occasions; revolutions and wars. *Address:* c/o ITN, 200 Gray's Inn Road, WC1X 8XZ. *T:* 0171–430 4546.

TINSTON, Robert Sydney; Chief Executive, North West Regional Health Authority, since 1994; *b* 29 March 1951; *s* of Sydney Tinston and Rita (*née* Jardine); *m* 1975, Catherine Mary Somers; one *s* one *d*. *Educ:* Stockport Sch.; Edinburgh Univ. (BSc). DipHSM 1979; MHSM 1979. Assistant Sector Administrator: Withington Hosp., Manchester, 1976–78; King's Coll. Hosp., London, 1978–79; Hosp. Sec., Cookridge Hosp., Leeds, 1979–83; Commissioning Officer, Clarendon Wing, Leeds, 1983–86; Gen. Manager, Leeds General Infirmary, 1986–89; Chief Exec., Royal Liverpool Hosp., 1989–91; Dep. Chief Exec., then Chief Exec., Mersey RHA, 1991–94. FRSA 1994. *Recreations:* astronomy, genealogy, Stockport County Football Club. *Address:* The Thatched Cottage, Utkinton, Tarporley, Cheshire CW6 0LL.

TIPPET, Vice-Adm. Sir Anthony (Sanders), KCB 1984; Chief Executive, Great Ormond Street Hospital for Children NHS Trust, 1994–95; *b* 2 Oct. 1928; *s* of W. K. R. Tippet and H. W. P. Kitley (*née* Sanders); *m* 1950, Lola Bassett; two *s* one *d* (and one *s* decd). *Educ:* West Buckland Sch., Devon. Called to the Bar, Gray's Inn, 1959. Entered RN, 1946; Lieut 1950; HM Ships Ceres, Superb, Staff C-in-C Mediterranean; Lt Comdr

1958; HMS Trafalgar, Britannia RNC; Comdr 1963; Secretary: to Director of Naval Intelligence; to Flag Officer Middle East; CO HMS Jufair, Supply Officer, HMS Eagle; Captain 1970: Asst Director Naval Plans (Warfare), 1970–72; CSO (Administration) to Flag Officer Plymouth, 1972–74; Director of Naval Officers' Appointments (Supply and WRNS Officers), 1974–76; Captain HMS Pembroke and Flag Captain to Flag Officer Medway, 1976–79; Rear-Adm. 1979; Asst Chief of Fleet Support, MoD, 1979–81; Flag Officer and Port Admiral, Portsmouth, and Chief Naval Supply and Secretariat Officer, 1981–83; Chief of Fleet Support, 1983–86. Gen. Manager, Hospitals for Sick Children, London, 1987–94. Chm., RN Benevolent Soc., 1995–; Chairman: Children in Hospitals, 1990–; Write Away, 1990–. Chm. of Govs, West Buckland Sch., 1989–95. CIMgt. Hon. Fellow, Inst. of Child Health, 1995. *Recreations:* sailing, hill walking. *Clubs:* Anchorites; Royal Naval Sailing Association (Portsmouth).

TIPPETT, Sir Michael (Kemp), OM 1983; CH 1979; Kt 1966; CBE 1959; Composer; *b* 2 Jan. 1905; *s* of Henry William Tippett and Isabel Kemp. *Educ:* Stamford Grammar Sch.; Royal College of Music (Foley Scholar; FRCM 1961). Ran Choral and Dramatic Society, Oxted, Surrey, and taught French at Hazelwood School, till 1931. Entered Adult Education work in music (LCC and Royal Arsenal Co-operative Soc. Educn Depts), 1932. Director of Music at Morley College, London, 1940–51. Sent to prison for 3 months as a conscientious objector, June 1943. A Child of Our Time first performed March 1944, broadcast Jan. 1945. 1st Symphony performed Nov. 1945 by Liverpool Philharmonic Society. Artistic Dir, Bath Festival, 1969–74. President: Kent Opera Company, 1979–; London Coll. of Music, 1983–. Hon. Mem., Amer. Acad. of Arts and Letters, 1973; Extraordinary Mem., Akad. der Künste, Berlin, 1976. Honorary degrees include: MusD Cambridge, 1964; DMus: Trinity Coll., Dublin, 1964; Leeds, 1965; Oxford, 1967; London, 1975; Keele, 1986; DUniv York, 1966; DLitt Warwick, 1974. Cobbett Medal for Chamber Music, 1948; Gold Medal, Royal Philharmonic Society, 1976; Prix de Composition Musicale, Fondation Prince Pierre de Monaco, 1984. Commandeur de l'Ordre des Arts et des Lettres (France), 1988. *Works include:* String Quartet No 1, 1935; Piano Sonata, 1937; Concerto for Double String Orchestra, 1939; A Child of Our Time, Oratorio, 1941; Fantasia on a theme of Handel for Piano and Orchestra, 1942; String Quartet, No 2, 1943; Symphony No 1, 1945; String Quartet No 3, 1946; Little Music for Strings, 1946; Suite in D, 1948; Song Cycle, The Heart's Assurance, 1951; Opera, The Midsummer Marriage, 1952 (first performed 1955); Ritual Dances, excerpts from the Opera for Orchestra, 1953; Fantasia Concertante on a Theme of Corelli for String Orchestra, 1953 (commnd for Edinburgh Festival); Divertimento, 1955; Concerto for piano and orchestra, 1956 (commnd by City of Birmingham Symphony Orch.); Symphony No 2, 1957 (commnd by BBC); Crown of the Year (commnd by Badminton School), 1958; Opera, King Priam (commnd by Koussevitsky Foundation of America), 1961; Magnificat and Nunc Dimittis (commnd by St John's Coll., Cambridge), 1961; Piano Sonata No 2, 1962; Incidental music to The Tempest, 1962; Praeludium for Brass etc (commnd by BBC), 1962; Cantata, The Vision of St Augustine, 1966; The Shires Suite, 1970; Opera, The Knot Garden, 1970; Songs for Dov, 1970; Symphony No 3, 1972; Piano Sonata no 3, 1973; Opera, The Ice Break, 1977; Symphony No 4, 1977 (commnd by Chicago SO); String Quartet No 4, 1979; Triple Concerto, 1979 (commnd by LSO with Ralph Vaughan Williams Trust); The Mask of Time, 1983 (commnd by Boston SO); The Blue Guitar, 1983 (commnd by Ambassador Internat. Cultural Foundn); Festal Brass with Blues, 1983 (commnd by Hong Kong Fest.); Piano Sonata No 4, 1984 (commnd by LA Philharmonic Assoc.); Opera, New Year, 1989 (commnd by Houston Grand Opera, Glyndebourne Fest. Opera and BBC); Byzantium, for soprano solo and orchestra, 1989 (commnd by Chicago Symphony Orch. and Carnegie Hall for their centennials); String Quartet No 5, 1991 (commnd by Lindsay String Quartet), The Rose Lake, 1993 (commnd by LSO, Boston and Toronto SOs). *Publications:* Moving into Aquarius, 1959, rev. edn 1974; Music of the Angels, 1980; Those Twentieth Century Blues (autobiog.), 1991; Tippett on Music, 1995. *Recreation:* walking. *Address:* 5 Thirsk Road, SW11 5SU. *T:* 0171–228 0465, *Fax:* 0171–738 2790.

TIPPETTS, Rutherford Berriman; *b* 8 Feb. 1913; *s* of late Percy William Berriman Tippetts and Katherine Brown Rutherford; *m* 1948, Audrey Helen Wilson Cameron; one *s* one *d*. *Educ:* Rugby; Trinity Coll., Oxford (MA). Asst Principal, BoT, 1936; Principal Private Sec. to Ministers of Supply and Presidents of BoT, 1941–45; idc 1954; Chief Exec., Dollar Exports Council, 1959–61; served in Commercial Relations and Exports, Industry and Tourism Divs of BoT; Under-Sec., Export Services Div., DTI, 1970–73. Mem., Council, CGLI. Master, Worshipful Co. of Armourers and Brasiers, 1975–76. *Address:* 74 Ebury Mews East, SW1W 9QP. *T:* 0171–730 6464; Linden Lodge, Linden Hill Lane, Kiln Green, Berks RG10 9XS. *T:* Wargrave (01734) 401621. *Clubs:* Carlton, Royal Wimbledon.

TIPPING, Sir David Gwynne E.; *see* Evans-Tipping.

TIPPING, Simon Patrick, (Paddy); MP (Lab) Sherwood, since 1992; *b* 24 Oct. 1949; *m* 1970, Irene Margaret Quinn; two *d*. *Educ:* Hipperholme Grammar Sch.; Nottingham Univ. (BA 1972; MA 1978). Social Worker, Notts, 1972–79; Project Leader, C of E Children's Soc., Nottingham, 1979–83. Mem. (Lab) Notts CC, 1981–93 (Chm., Economic Develt and Finance Cttees); Director: Notts Co-op. Develt Agency, 1983–92; Nottingham Develt Enterprise, 1987–93. Contested (Lab) Rushcliffe, 1987. *Recreations:* running, walking, gardening. *Address:* House of Commons, SW1A 0AA.

TIPPLER, John; Director, Network, British Telecom, UK Communications Division, 1986–89, retired; *b* 9 Aug. 1929; *s* of George Herbert and Sarah Tippler, Spalding, Lincs; *m* 1st, 1952, Pauline Taylor (marr. diss. 1983); two *s*; 2nd, 1992, Martha Elisabet Berg, psychoanalyst, Stockholm. *Educ:* Spalding Grammar School. Architect's Dept, Spalding RDC, 1945; Post Office Telephone Service, 1947; Royal Signals, 1949–50; Staff Mem., PO Central Engineering Sch., 1954–59; PO Engineering Develt, 1960–80; Dir, Exchange and Data Systems Op. and Develt, 1980; Dir of Engrg, BT, 1982–86. Dir, IT Inst., 1982–86. *Recreations:* music, country walking, motor-cycling, cinema, theatre. *Address:* 227 Broadgate, Weston Hills, Spalding, Lincs PE12 6DQ.

TIRVENGADUM, Sir Harry (Krishnan), Kt 1987; Chevalier, Ordre National de la Légion d'Honneur 1986; Chairman and Managing Director, Air Mauritius, since 1981; *b* 2 Sept. 1933; *s* of late Govinden Tirvengadum and Meenatchee Sangeelee; *m* 1970, Elahe Amin Amin; three *d*. *Educ:* Royal College, Mauritius; Oxford Univ. Asst Sec., Min. of Works, 1952–67; Principal Assistant Secretary: Min. of Communications, in charge of Depts of Civil Aviation, Telecommunications, Marine Services, Posts & Telegraphs and Meteorological Services, 1968–72; Min. of Commerce and Industry, 1970; Air Mauritius: Gen. Manager, 1972–78; Dep. Chm. and Dep. Man. Dir, 1978–81. Chairman: Rodrigues Hotel, 1981–; New Airport Catering Services, 1988–; Mauritius Shopping Paradise Ltd, 1984–93; Director: Mauritius Hotels Gp, 1973–81; Plaisance Airlift Catering Unit, 1980–92; Mauritius Telecom, 1984–; Mauritius Estate Development & Co., 1986–; Mauritius Commercial Bank, 1989–; State Bank Internat., 1990–. Chm., Municipal Commn, Quatre-Bornes, 1974–77. Chief delegate of Mauritius, Triennial Assemblies, ICAO, 1971–; Rep. of Employers on Employment of Disabled Persons Bd, 1988–. Member: Exec. Cttee, IATA, 1988–91 (Chm., 1992–93); Nat. Educn Award Panel, 1988. Pres., African Airlines Assoc., 1995–96. FCIT; FInstD. Citoyen d'Honneur, Town of Beau Bassin/Rose Hill, Mauritius, 1986. Chevalier, Légion d'Honneur (France), 1986. *Recreations:* bridge, swimming, walking. *Address:* Dr Arthur De Chazal Lane, Floréal, Mauritius. *T:* 6966003. *Club:* Mauritius Gymkhana.

TISHLER, Gillian, (Mrs Richard Wood); Chief Executive, Young Women's Christian Association of Great Britain, since 1993; *b* 27 March 1958; *d* of Harry and Joyce Tishler; *m* 1991, Richard Wood. *Educ:* King Edward VI Sch., Morpeth; St Anne's Coll., Oxford (BA Hons Mod. Langs). Ministry of Agriculture, Fisheries and Food: fast stream trainee, 1979; Private Office (Private Sec. to Parly Sec.), 1986–87; Royal National Institute for the Blind: Parly Officer, 1987–89; Head of Public Affairs, 1989–93. *Recreations:* theatre, singing, walking. *Address:* Young Women's Christian Association of Great Britain, Clarendon House, 52 Cornmarket Street, Oxford OX1 3EJ. *T:* Oxford (01865) 726110.

TITCHELL, John, RA 1991 (ARA 1986); ARCA; professional painter, since 1951; *b* 1926; *s* of Arthur Titchell and Elsie Catt; *m* 1947, Audrey Ward; one *s* one *d*. *Educ:* Crayford Elem. Sch.; Sidcup Sch. of Art; Royal Coll. of Art (ARCA 1951). *Recreations:* reading, listening to music. *Address:* Frith Farm, Pluckley, Ashford, Kent TN27 0SY.

TITCHENER, Alan Ronald, CB 1993; Managing Director, Resource (Science and Technology Expertise) Ltd, since 1993; *b* 18 June 1934; *s* of Edmund Hickman Ronald Titchener and Minnie Ellen Titchener; *m* 1959, Joyce Blakesley; two *s*. *Educ:* Harrow County Grammar Sch.; London School of Economics. BSc(Econ) 1962. RAF, 1952. Colonial Office, 1954; Min. of Transport, 1962; Board of Trade, 1964; HM Consul New York, 1969; Dept of Trade, 1973; HM Consul-Gen., Johannesburg, 1978; Under Secretary, Department of Trade and Industry, 1982–93: Overseas Trade Div., 1982; Head of Enterprise Initiative Div., 1987; Head of Personnel, 1991. FRSA 1993. *Address:* Resource (Science and Technology Expertise) Ltd, 1–3 Birdcage Walk, SW1H 9JH. *Club:* Royal Air Force.

TITCHENER, (John) Lanham (Bradbury), CMG 1955; OBE 1947; *b* 28 Nov. 1912; *s* of late Alfred Titchener and late Alicia Marion Leonora Bradbury; *m* 1937, Catherine Law Clark (*decd*) (marr. diss. 1958); no *c*; *m* 1958, Rikke Marian Lehmann (*née* Bendixsen), *e d* of late Frederik Carl Bendixsen and Kammerherreinde Nina Grandjean of Vennerslund, Falster, Denmark; two step *s*. *Educ:* City of London Sch.; Royal College of Music. Nat. Council of Education of Canada, 1934; BBC 1938–43; War of 1939–45: served HM Forces, Jan.-Aug. 1943; Psychological Warfare Branch, Allied Force HQ, Algiers, 1943; 15th Army Group HQ, Italy, 1944–45; Asst Dep. Director, Political Warfare Div., SACSEA, 1945; Political Warfare Adviser to C-in-C, Netherlands East Indies, 1945–46; First Secretary, HM Foreign Service, 1947; served in FO until 1950, when transferred to HM Embassy, Moscow; then at HM Embassy, Ankara, 1953–54; Economic Counsellor, HM Embassy, Tehran, 1954–56, Chargé d'Affaires, 1955. Resigned HM Foreign Service, 1957. *Recreations:* music, gardening, fishing. *Address:* 3 Impasse du Château, 06190 Roquebrune Village, France. *T:* 93350785; Weysesgade 13, 2100 Copenhagen, Denmark. *T:* 31200871. *Club:* Travellers'.

TITCHENER-BARRETT, Sir Dennis (Charles), Kt 1981; TD 1953, 2 bars; Chairman, Woodstock (London) Ltd (industrial minerals), 1962–89; *m* 1940, Joan Wilson; one *s* three *d*. Served War, RA, 1939–46; commanded 415 Coast Regt RA (TA), 1950–56; Mem., Kent T&AFA, 1950–56. An Underwriting Member of Lloyd's, 1977–. ILEA School Governor, 1956–73; Member: Gtr London Central Valuation Panel, 1964–75; Cons. Bd of Finance, 1968–75; Cons. Policy Gp for Gtr London, 1975–78; National Union of Conservative Associations: Mem., Central Council and Exec. Cttee, 1968–81; Treasurer, 1968–75, Chm., 1975–78, Vice-Pres., 1978–, Gtr London Area; Vice-Pres., Nat. Soc. of Cons. Agents, Gtr London Area, 1975–; Chm., S Kensington Cons. Assoc., 1954–57; Trustee, Kensington Cons. Assoc., 1975–94 (Pres., 1975–89). Mem., RUSI, 1947–. Fellow, Inst. of Dirs, 1952. High Sheriff of Greater London, 1977–78. *Address:* 8 Launceston Place, W8 5RL. *T:* 0171–937 0613. *Club:* Carlton.

TITCHMARSH, Alan Fred; writer and broadcaster; *b* 2 May 1949; *s* of Alan Titchmarsh and Bessie Titchmarsh (*née* Hardisty); *m* 1975, Alison Margaret Needs; two *d*. *Educ:* Ilkley County Secondary Sch.; Shipley Art and Tech. Inst.; Herts Coll. of Agric. and Hortic. (Nat. Cert. Hort.); Royal Botanic Gardens, Kew (DipHort). Apprentice gardener, Parks Dept, Ilkley UDC, 1964–68; Supervisor, Staff Trng, Royal Botanic Gardens, 1972–74; Asst Editor, gardening books, Hamlyn Publishing, 1974–76; Asst Editor and Dep. Editor, Amateur Gardening, 1976–79; freelance writer and broadcaster, 1979–; gardening correspondent: Woman's Own, 1980–85; Daily Mail, 1985–; gardening editor, Homes & Gardens, 1985–89. *BBC radio series include:* You and Yours, Down to Earth, A House in a Garden, Alan Titchmarsh Show; numerous other progs; *BBC TV:* Nationwide, Breakfast Time, Open Air, Daytime Live; Chelsea Flower Show, 1983–; Songs of Praise, 1989–94; Pebble Mill, 1991–; Sweet Inspiration, 1993–94. Vice-Pres., Wessex Cancer Trust, 1988–; Patron: Rainbow Trust, 1993–; Kaleidoscope Theatre, 1995–; President: Gardening for Disabled Trust, 1989–; Telephones for the Blind, 1993–. Freeman, City of London; Liveryman, Gardeners' Co. Gardening Writer of the Year, 1980, 1983; RHS Gold Medal, Chelsea Flower Show, 1985. *Publications:* Starting With House Plants, 1976; Gardening Under Cover, 1979, 2nd edn 1985; Guide to Greenhouse Gardening, 1980; Climbers and Wall Plants, 1980; Everyone's Book of House Plants, 1981; (with R. C. M. Wright) Complete Book of Plant Propagation, 1981; Gardening Techniques, 1981; Pocket Indoor Gardener, 1982; Hamlyn Guide to House Plants, 1982; Pest-Free Plants, 1982; The Allotment Gardener's Handbook, 1982, 2nd edn 1993; The Rock Gardener's Handbook, 1983; How to be a Supergardener, 1983, 3rd edn 1993; (ed) 1,000 Handy Gardening Hints, 1983; Alan Titchmarsh's Avant Gardening, 1984, 2nd edn 1994; Alan Titchmarsh's Gardening Guides, 1984; The Gardener's Logbook, 1985; (ed) A–Z of Popular Garden Plants, 1985; Pocket Guide to Gardening, 1987, (cons. ed.) All Your Gardening Questions Answered, 1988; Daytime Live Gardening Book, 1990; The English River, 1993; My Favourite Gardens, 1995. *Recreations:* theatre, reading, gardening, riding, boating. *Address:* c/o Arlington Enterprises, 1–3 Charlotte Street, W1P 1HD. *Clubs:* Lord's Taverners; Birmingham Press.

TITE, Prof. Michael Stanley, DPhil; FSA; Edward Hall Professor of Archaeological Science, Director of Research Laboratory for Archaeology and History of Art, and Fellow of Linacre College, University of Oxford, since 1989; *b* 9 Nov. 1938; *s* of late Arthur Robert Tite and Evelyn Frances Violet Tite (*née* Endersby); *m* 1967, Virginia Byng Noel; two *d*. *Educ:* Trinity Sch. of John Whitgift, Croydon; Christ Church, Oxford (MA, DPhil). FSA 1977. Research Fellow in Ceramics, Univ. of Leeds, 1964–67; Lectr in Physics, Univ. of Essex, 1967–75; Keeper, Dept of Scientific Res. (formerly Res. Lab.), British Museum, 1975–89. *Publications:* Methods of Physical Examination in Archaeology, 1972; papers on scientific methods applied to archaeology in various jls. *Recreations:* travelling with "The Buildings of England", gardening. *Address:* 7 Kings Cross Road, Oxford OX2 7EU. *T:* Oxford (01865) 58422; Research Laboratory for Archaeology and History of Art, 6 Keble Road, Oxford OX1 3QJ.

TITFORD, Rear-Adm. Donald George, CEng, FRAeS; retired 1978; Deputy Controller of Aircraft, Ministry of Defence, 1976–78; *b* 15 June 1925; *s* of late Percy Maurice Titford and Emily Hannah Titford (*née* McLaren). *Educ:* Highgate Sch Royal Naval Engineering Coll.; Coll. of Aeronautics, Cranfield. MSc. Entered RN as Cadet, 1943; Comdr 1959; Air Engr Officer, HMS Victorious, 1965; Captain 1967; comd, RN Air Station, Lee-on-Solent, 1972–74; Comd Engr Officer, Naval Air Comd, 1974–76. *Recreations:* modern pentathlon, old English watercolours. *Address:* Merry Hill, North Road, Bath BA2 6HD. *T:* Bath (01225) 462132.

TITHERIDGE, Roger Noel, QC 1973; a Recorder of the Crown Court since 1972; Barrister-at-Law; *b* 21 Dec. 1928; *s* of Jack George Ralph Titheridge and Mabel Titheridge (*née* Steains); *m* 1963, Annabel Maureen (*née* Scott-Fisher); two *d. Educ:* Midhurst Grammar Sch.; Merton Coll., Oxford (Exhibnr). MA (History and Jurisprudence). Called to the Bar, Gray's Inn, 1954; Holker Sen. Scholar, Gray's Inn, 1954; Bencher, Gray's Inn, 1985; Leader, Western Circuit, 1989–92. *Recreations:* tennis, sailing. *Address:* 1 Paper Buildings, Temple, EC4Y 7EP. *T:* 0171–353 3728; 13 The Moat, Traps Lane, New Malden, Surrey KT3 4SB. *T:* 0181–942 2747.

TITLEY, Gary; Member (Lab) Greater Manchester West, European Parliament, since 1989; *b* 19 Jan. 1950; *s* of Wilfred James and Joyce Lillian Titley; *m* 1975, Maria, (Charo), Rosario; one *s* one *d. Educ:* York Univ. (BA Hons Hist./Educn, 1973; PGCE 1974). TEFL, Bilbao, 1973–75; taught History, Earls High Sch., Halesowen, 1976–84; Personal Assistant to MEP, 1984–89. Mem., W Midlands CC, 1981–86 (Vice-Chair: EDC, 1981–84; Consumer Services Cttee, 1984–86). Dir, W Midlands Enterprise Bd, 1982–89; Chairman: W Midlands Co-op Finance Co., 1982–89; Black Country Co-op Develt Agency, 1982–88. Contested (Lab): Bromsgrove, 1983; Dudley W, 1987. Pres., Eur. Parlt delegn for relations with Finland, 1992–94; rapporteur, accession of Finland to EU. Pres., EEA Jt Parly Assembly, 1994–95; Vice-Pres., delegn for relns with Czech, Slovak and Slovenia Repubs. Commander, White Rose (Finland), 1995. *Recreations:* family, reading, sport. *Address:* (office) 16 Spring Lane, Radcliffe, Manchester M26 2TQ. *T:* 0161–724 4008. *Club:* Little Lever (Bolton).

TITLEY, Commandant Nursing Officer Jane, CBE 1995; RRC 1990 (ARRC 1986); Director of Defence Nursing Services, 1992–95; *b* 22 April 1940; *d* of Louis and Phyllis Myra (Josephine) Titley. *Educ:* St Catherine's Convent, Nottingham; St Bartholomew's Hosp.; Sussex Maternity Hosp. SRN 1962; SCM 1963. Joined QARNNS, 1965; served in Naval hosps and estabts in UK, Malta, Singapore, Naples and Gibraltar; Matron, 1986; Dep. Matron-in-Chief, 1988; Matron-in-Chief, 1990–94; QHNS, 1990–94. OStJ 1990. *Recreations:* 'to stand and stare', personal correspondence, gardening, dress-making. *Address:* Sixpenny Cottage, 55 Gosport Road, Lee-on-the-Solent, Hants PO13 9EJ.

TITMAN, Sir John (Edward Powis), KCVO 1991 (CVO 1982; LVO 1966; MVO 1957); JP; DL; Secretary of the Lord Chamberlain's Office, 1978–91; Serjeant-at-Arms to the Queen, 1982–91; *b* 23 May 1926; *s* of late Sir George Titman, CBE, MVO, sometime Secretary, Lord Chamberlain's Office, and Lady Titman; *m* 1953, Annabel Clare (*née* Naylor); two *s. Educ:* City of London School. Entered Lord Chamberlain's Office, 1947; State Invitations Asst, 1956; Asst Sec., 1976; retired 1991. Master, Wax Chandlers' Co., 1984. JP Surrey, 1971, DL Surrey, 1991. *Address:* Friars Garth, The Parade, Epsom, Surrey KT18 5DH. *T:* Epsom (01372) 722302. *Clubs:* Royal Automobile, MCC.

TIVERTON, Viscount; *see* Giffard, A. E.

TIWARI, Narayan Datt; Chief Minister, Uttar Pradesh, 1976–77, 1984–85, March–Sept. 1985 and 1988–89; Member, National Working Committee, Indian National Congress; *b* Balyuti, UP, 18 Oct. 1925; *s* of Poorna Nand Tiwari and Chandrawati Devi Tiwari; *m* 1954, Dr Sushila Tiwari. *Educ:* Allahabad Univ., UP (Golden Jubilee Schol. 1948; MA Diplomacy and Internat. Affairs; LLB; Pres., Students' Union). Studied Scandinavian Econ. and Budgetary Systems in Sweden, 1959; Congressional Practices and Procedures in USA, 1964; Whitley Council System, UK, and Co-op. Banking System in Germany, Dairy Develt in Denmark. Joined Freedom Movement, 1938, and Quit India Movement, 1942, resulting in 15 months in jail, 1942. MLA (Socialist) UP, 1952, re-elected 1957, 1969, 1977, 1987. State Govt appts, 1969–77: Chm., Public Accts Cttee; Minister for Finance, Heavy Industry, Sugar Cane Develt; Dep. Chm., State Planning Commn, 1980. Leader of Opposition in UP, 1977; MP (Lower House), 1980–; Union Minister for Planning and Labour and Dep. Chm., Planning Commn, India, 1980; Union Minister: for Industry and Steel and Mines, 1981–84; of Industry, Petroleum and Natural Gas, Ext. Affairs, Finance and Commerce, 1985–87; of Finance and Commerce, India, 1987–88. Editor, Prabhat (a Hindi Monthly magazine). *Publications:* European Miscellany; hundreds of articles as a journalist. *Recreations:* playing cricket, hockey, chess; reading. *Address:* Village Padampuri, PO Padampuri, Dist Nainital, UP, India; B 315, Sector B, Mahanagar, Lucknow, UP. *T:* (522) 384859, (522) 385719.

TIZARD, Prof. Barbara, PhD, FBPsS; Professor of Education, Institute of Education, University of London, 1982–90, now Emeritus; Director, Thomas Coram Research Unit, Institute of Education, 1980–90; *b* 16 April 1926; *d* of late Herbert Parker and Elsie Parker (*née* Kirk); *m* 1947, Jack Tizard (*d* 1979); one *s* two *d* (and two *s* decd). *Educ:* St Paul's Girls' School; Somerville College, Oxford. BA Oxon, PhD London. Lectr, Dept of Experimental Neurology, Inst. of Psychiatry, 1963–67; Res. Officer then Senior Res. Fellow, Inst. of Education, 1967–77, Reader in Education, 1978–80. Chm., Assoc. of Child Psychology and Psychiatry, 1976–77. Co-editor, British Jl of Psychology, 1975–79; Mem., Editorial Bd, Jl of Child Psychology and Psychiatry, 1979–. *Publications:* Early Childhood Education, 1975; Adoption: a second chance, 1977; (with J. Mortimore and B. Burchell) Involving Parents in Nursery and Infant Schools, 1981; (with M. Hughes) Young Children Learning, 1984; (jtly) Young Children at School in the Inner City, 1988; (jtly) Black, White or Mixed Race? Race and racism in the lives of young people of mixed parentage, 1993; articles on transracial and intercountry adoption, children in care, child development and early education. *Address:* The Garden Flat, 6 Hampstead Hill Gardens, NW3 2PL.

See also M.C. Parker.

TIZARD, Dame Catherine (Anne), GCMG 1990; DBE 1985; Governor-General of New Zealand, 1990–March 1996; *b* 4 April 1931; *d* of Neil Maclean and Helen Montgomery Maclean; *m* 1951, Rt Hon. Robert James Tizard, *qv* (marr. diss. 1983); one *s* three *d. Educ:* Matamata College; Auckland University (BA). Tutor in Zoology, Univ. of Auckland, 1967–84. Member: Auckland City Council, 1971–83 (Mayor of Auckland, 1983–90); Auckland Regional Authy, 1980–83. *Recreations:* music, reading, drama, scuba diving, cryptic crosswords. *Address:* (until March 1996) Government House, Wellington, New Zealand. *T:* (4) 3898055; 8 Glendowie Road, Auckland 5, New Zealand.

TIZARD, Rt. Hon. Robert James, PC (NZ) 1985; MP for Tamaki, Otahuhu, Pakuranga, and Panmure, New Zealand, 1957–90; Minister of Defence, Science and Technology, 1987–90; retired; *b* 7 June 1924; *s* of Henry James and Jessie May Tizard; *m* 1951, Catherine Anne Maclean (*see* Dame Catherine Tizard) (marr. diss. 1983); one *s* three *d*; *m* 1983, Mary Christina Nacey; one *s. Educ:* Auckland Grammar Sch.; Auckland Univ. MA, Hons Hist., 1949. Served War: RNZAF, 1943–46, incl. service in Canada and Britain; (commnd as a Navigator, 1944). Pres., Students' Assoc., Auckland Univ., 1948; Lectr in History, Auckland Univ., 1949–53; teaching, 1954–57 and 1961–62. MP 1957–60 and 1963–90; Minister of Health and State Services, 1972–74; Dep. Prime Minister and Minister of Finance, 1974–75; Dep. Leader of the Opposition, 1975–79; Minister of Energy, Science and Technol., and Statistics, and Minister i/c Audit Dept, 1984–87. *Recreation:* golf. *Address:* 8 Glendowie Road, Auckland 5, New Zealand.

TOBIAS, Dr Jeffrey Stewart, FRCP, FRCR; Clinical Director, Meyerstein Institute of Oncology, Middlesex Hospital, since 1992 and Consultant in Radiotherapy and Oncology, University College and Middlesex Hospitals, since 1981; *b* 4 Dec. 1946; *s* of Gerald Joseph Tobias and Sylvia Tobias (*née* Pearlberg); *m* 1973, Dr Gabriela Jill Jaecker; two *s* one *d. Educ:* Hendon Grammar Sch.; Gonville and Caius Coll., Cambridge (MA, MD, BChir); St Bartholomew's Hosp. Med. Sch. Junior hosp. posts, St Bartholomew's, Whittington, UCH and Hammersmith Hosps, 1971–74; Research Fellow in Oncology, Harvard Med. Sch., 1975–76; Fellow in Oncology, St Bartholomew's and Royal Marsden Hosps, 1976–80. Chairman: CRC New Studies Breast Cancer Working Party; UK Co-ordinating Cttee for Cancer Research Head and Neck Working Party. Founder Sec., British Oncological Assoc., 1986; Mem. Council, RCR, 1992–94; Pres., Assoc. of Head and Neck Oncologists, 1996. *Publications:* (with M. J. Peckham) Primary Management of Breast Cancer, 1985; (with R. L. Souhami) Cancer and its Management, 1986, 2nd edn 1995; (with C. J. Williams) Cancer, a Colour Atlas, 1993; (with P. R. Thomas) Current Radiation Oncology, 2 vols, 1994, 1995; Cancer: what every patient needs to know, 1995; contribs to learned jls. *Recreations:* nothing too strenuous; music, cycling, ski-ing, reading, writing, theatre, food and drink. *Address:* Meyerstein Institute of Oncology, Middlesex Hospital, Mortimer Street, W1N 8AA. *T:* 0171–380 9214, 0171–637 1214, *Fax:* 0171–637 1201; 48 Northchurch Road, N1 4EJ. *Clubs:* Royal Society of Medicine, Les Six; Albatros Wind and Water.

TOBIN, Prof. James, PhD; Sterling Professor of Economics, Yale University, 1957–88, now Emeritus; *b* 5 March 1918; *s* of Louis Michael and Margaret Edgerton Tobin; *m* 1946, Elizabeth Fay Ringo; three *s* one *d. Educ:* Harvard Univ. AB 1939 (*summa cum laude*); MA 1940; PhD 1947. Economist, Office of Price Admin, and Civilian Supply and War Production Bd, Washington, 1941–42; line officer, destroyer, USN, 1942–46. Teaching Fellow in Econs, 1946–47, Jun. Fellow, Soc. of Fellows, 1947–50, Harvard Univ.; Yale University: Associate Prof. of Econs, 1950–55; Prof. of Econs, 1955–88; Dir, Cowles Foundn for Res. in Econs, 1955–61; Chm., Dept of Econs, 1968–69, 1974–78. Vis. Prof., Univ. of Nairobi, 1972–73; Ford Vis. Res. Prof. of Econs, Univ. of Calif, Berkeley, 1983; P. K. Seidman Vis. Dist. Prof. of Internat. Studies, Rhodes Coll., 1992. Mem., Pres.'s Council of Econ. Advrs, 1961–62. Corresp. FBA 1984. LLD *hc* Syracuse Univ., 1967; Univ. of Illinois, 1969; Dartmouth Coll., 1970; Swarthmore Coll., 1980; New Sch. for Social Res., and New York Univ., 1982; Univ. of Hartford, 1984; Colgate Univ., 1984; Western Maryland Coll., 1984; Univ. of New Haven, 1986; DEcon *hc* New Univ. of Lisbon, 1980; Hon. DHL: Bates Coll., 1982; Hofstra Univ., 1983; Gustavus Adolphus Coll., 1986; Sacred Heart Univ., 1990; DSocSc *hc* Helsinki, 1986. Foreign Associate, Acad. of Sciences, Portugal, 1980. Nobel Prize in Economics, 1981; Centennial Medal, Harvard Univ. Graduate Sch., 1989. Grand Cordon, Order of the Sacred Treasure (Japan), 1988. *Publications:* (jtly) The American Business Creed, 1956; National Economic Policy, 1966; Essays in Economics: vol. 1, Macroeconomics, 1971; vol. 2, Consumption and Econometrics, 1975; vol. 3, Theory and Policy, 1982; The New Economics One Decade Older, 1974; Asset Accumulation and Economic Activity, Reflections on Contemporary Macroeconomic Theory, 1980; Policies for Prosperity, 1987; contribs to professional jls. *Recreations:* tennis, ski-ing, sailing, canoeing, fishing, chess. *Address:* Cowles Foundation for Research in Economics, Yale University, Box 208281, New Haven, CT 06520–8281, USA. *T:* (203) 4323720. *Clubs:* Yale (New York); Mory's Association, The Club (New Haven).

TOD, Sir John Hunter H.; *see* Hunter-Tod.

TOD, John Mackenzie, OBE 1987; Director, Arts Division, British Council, since 1993; *b* 24 Oct. 1944; *s* of John Alexander Tod and Eleanor May Tod (*née* Darrah); *m* 1970, Christiane Teytaud; two *s* one *d. Educ:* Calday Grange GS; King's Coll., Cambridge (BA); Leeds Univ. (postgrad. Dip. TESL 1969); Inst. of Educn, London Univ. (MA Ed 1983). VSO, Malaita, Solomon Is, 1963–64; teacher, Ruffwood Comp. Sch., Kirby, 1965; joined British Council, 1968: Ghana, 1969–72; Brazil, 1972–74; Asst Dir (Educn), Kano, Nigeria, 1975–78; Asst Dir, Overseas Educnl Appts Dept, 1978–82; Rep., Senegal, 1983–88; Regl Dir and Supt Gen., Sociedade Brasileira de Cultura Inglesa, São Paulo, 1988–93. *Recreations:* choral music, literature, theatre, sailing. *Address:* British Council, 10 Spring Gardens, SW1A 2BN. *T:* 0171–930 8466.

TOD, Vice-Adm. Jonathan James Richard, CBE 1982; Deputy Commander Fleet, since 1994; *b* 26 March 1939; *e s* of late Col Richard Logan Tod and Elizabeth Allan Tod; *m* 1962, Claire Elizabeth Russell Dixon; two *s. Educ:* Gordonstoun Sch. BRNC, Dartmouth, 1957–59; Flying trng, 1961; Hal Far (Malta), 1963; HM Ships: Ark Royal, Hermes, Eagle, RNAS, Lossiemouth, 1962–70; BRNC, Dartmouth, 1970–72; Exec. Officer, HMS Devonshire, 1972–74; Naval Staff, 1975–77; Comd HMS Brighton, 1978–80; Cabinet Office, 1980–82; RCDS 1983; Comd HMS Fife, 1984–85; Dir, Defence Programme, 1986–88; Comd HMS Illustrious, 1988–89; Flag Officer Portsmouth and Naval Base Comdr Portsmouth, 1989–90; ACDS (Policy and Nuclear), MoD, 1990–94. *Recreations:* sailing, driving pony and trap. *Address:* Eastbury Park, Northwood, Middx HA6 3HP.

TODD, family name of **Baron Todd.**

TODD, Baron, *cr* 1962, of Trumpington (Life Peer); **Alexander Robertus Todd,** OM 1977; Kt 1954; FRS 1942; DSc Glasgow; Dr Phil nat Frankfurt; DPhil Oxon; MA Cantab; FRSC; Master of Christ's College, Cambridge, 1963–78 (Fellow, 1944); Professor of Organic Chemistry, University of Cambridge, 1944–71; (first) Chancellor, University of Strathclyde, Glasgow, 1965–91 (Fellow, 1990); *b* Glasgow, 2 Oct. 1907; *e s* of Alexander Todd, JP, Glasgow; *m* 1937, Alison Sarah (*d* 1987), *e d* of Sir H. H. Dale, OM, GBE, FRS; one *s* two *d. Educ:* Allan Glen's Sch.; University of Glasgow. Carnegie Research Scholar, University of Glasgow, 1928–29; Univ. of Frankfurt a M, 1929–31; 1851 Exhibition Senior Student, Univ. of Oxford, 1931–34; Assistant in Medical Chemistry, 1934–35, and Beit Memorial Research Fellow, 1935–36, University of Edinburgh; Member of Staff, Lister Institute of Preventive Medicine, London, 1936–38; Reader in Biochemistry, University of London, 1937–38; Visiting Lecturer, California Institute of Technology, USA, 1938; Sir Samuel Hall Professor of Chemistry and Director of Chemical Laboratories, University of Manchester, 1938–44. Visiting Professor: University of Chicago, 1948; University of Sydney, 1950; Mass. Inst. Tech., 1954. Chemical Society, Tilden Lecturer, 1941, Pedler Lecturer, 1946; Meldola Medal, 1936; Leverhulme Lecturer, Society of Chemical Industry, 1948; Visitor, Hatfield Polytechnic, 1978–86. Dir, Fisons Ltd, 1963–78. President: Chemical Soc., 1960–62; Internat. Union of Pure and Applied Chemistry, 1963–65; BAAS, 1969–70; Royal Soc., 1975–80; Soc. of Chem. Industry, 1981–82. Chairman: Adv. Council on Scientific Policy, 1952–64; Royal Commn on Medical Education, 1965–68; Board of Governors, United Cambridge Hospitals, 1969–74.

Member Council, Royal Society, 1967–70; Mem., NRDC, 1968–76. Hon. Member French, German, Spanish, Belgian, Swiss, Japanese Chemical Societies; Foreign Member: Nat. Acad. Sciences, USA; American Acad. of Arts and Sciences; Akad. Naturf. Halle; American Phil. Soc.; Australian, Austrian, Indian, Iranian, Japanese, New York, Russian and Polish Academies of Science. Hon. Fellow: Australian Chem. Institute; Manchester College Technology; Royal Society Edinburgh. Chairman, Managing Trustees, Nuffield Foundation, 1973–79 (Trustee, 1950–79); Pres., Croucher Foundn (Hong Kong), 1988– (Trustee, 1979–; Chm., Trustees, 1980–88); Pres., Parly and Scientific Cttee, 1983–86. Lavoisier Medallist, French Chemical Society, 1948; Davy Medal of Royal Society, 1949; Bakerian Lecturer, 1954; Royal Medal of Royal Society, 1955; Nobel Prize for Chemistry, 1957; Cannizzaro Medal, Italian Chemical Society, 1958; Paul Karrer Medal, Univ. Zürich, 1962; Stas Medal, Belgian Chemical Society, 1962; Longstaff Medal, Chemical Society, 1963; Copley Medal, Royal Society, 1970; Lomonosov Medal, USSR Acad. Sci., 1979; Copernicus Medal, Polish Acad. Sci., 1979; Hanbury Medal, Pharmaceutical Soc., 1986. Hon. FRCP 1975; Hon. FRCPS(Glas) 1980; Hon. FIMechE 1976. Hon. Fellow: Oriel Coll., Oxford, 1955; Churchill Coll., Cambridge, 1971; Darwin Coll., Cambridge, 1981. Hon. LLD: Glasgow, Melbourne, Edinburgh, Manchester, California, Hokkaido, Chinese Univ. of Hong Kong; Hon. Dr rer nat Kiel; Hon. DSc: London, Madrid, Exeter, Leicester, Aligarh, Sheffield, Wales, Yale, Strasbourg, Harvard, Liverpool, Adelaide, Strathclyde, Oxford, ANU, Paris, Warwick, Durham, Michigan, Cambridge, Widener, Philippines, Tufts, Hong Kong; Hon. DLitt Sydney. Pour le Mérite, German Federal Republic, 1966; Order of Rising Sun (Japan), 1978. Master, Salters' Company, 1961. *Publications:* A Time to Remember (autobiog.), 1983; numerous scientific papers in chemical and biochemical journals. *Recreations:* fishing, golf. *Address:* 9 Parker Street, Cambridge CB1 1JL. *T:* Cambridge (01223) 356688.

TODD, Rev. Alastair, CMG 1971; *b* 21 Dec. 1920; *s* of late Prof. James Eadie Todd, MA, FRHistS (formerly Prof. of History, Queen's University, Belfast) and Margaret Simpson Johnstone Maybin; *m* 1952, Nancy Hazel Buyers; two *s* two *d. Educ:* Royal Belfast Academical Institution; Fettes Coll., Edinburgh; Corpus Christi Coll., Oxford; London Univ. (External); Salisbury and Wells Theological Coll. BA (Oxon), DipTheol (London). Served War, Army, 1940–46, Capt. RHA. Apptd Colonial Administrative Service, Hong Kong, 1946; Joint Services Staff Coll., 1950; Defence Sec., Hong Kong, 1957–60; Dep. Colonial Sec., Hong Kong, 1963–64; Dir of Social Welfare, also MLC, 1966–68; and, again, Defence Sec., 1968–71, retd. Ordained Deacon by Bishop of Chichester, 1973 and Priest, 1974; Asst Curate, Willingdon, 1973–77; Vicar, St Augustine's, Brighton, 1978–86. *Recreations:* reading, walking, embroidery, gardening. *Address:* 59 Park Avenue, Eastbourne BN21 2XH. *T:* Eastbourne (01323) 505843.

TODD, Rev. Andrew Stewart; Minister of St Machar's Cathedral, Old Aberdeen, 1967–93; Chaplain to the Queen in Scotland, since 1991; *b* 26 May 1926; *s* of late William Stewart Todd and Robina Victoria Fraser; *m* 1953, Janet Agnes Brown Smith, *d* of late John Smith, JP, DL, Glasgow and Symington; two *s* two *d.* *Educ:* High Sch. of Stirling; Edinburgh Univ. (MA Hons, Classics 1947); New Coll., Edinburgh (BD 1950); Basel Univ. Asst Minister, St Cuthbert's, Edinburgh, 1951–52; ordained, 1952; Minister: Symington, Lanarkshire, 1952–60; North Leith, 1960–67. Convenor, Gen. Assembly's Cttee on Public Worship and Aids to Devotion, 1974–78; Moderator, Aberdeen Presbytery, 1980–81; Convenor, Panel on Doctrine, 1990–; Member: Church Hymnary Cttee, 1963–73; Church Hymnary Trust. Hon. President: Church Service Soc.; Scottish Church Soc. Hon. DD Aberdeen, 1982. *Publications:* jt translator, Oscar Cullmann, Early Christian Worship, 1953; translator: Ludwig Koehler, Old Testament Theology, 1957; Ernst Lohmeyer, Lord of the Temple, 1961; contributions to liturgical jls. *Recreations:* music, gardening. *Address:* Culearn, Balquhidder, Lochearnhead, Perthshire FK19 8PB. *Club:* Royal Over-Seas League.

TODD, Prof. Sir David, Kt 1995; CBE 1990 (OBE 1982); FRCP, FRCPE, FRCPGlas, FRACP, FRCPath; Professor of Medicine, University of Hong Kong, since 1972; *b* 17 Nov. 1928; *s* of Paul J. Todd and Margaret S. Todd. *Educ:* Univ. of Hong Kong (MB BS, MD). University of Hong Kong: Lectr, Sen. Lectr and Reader, 1958–72; Head of Dept, 1974–89; Sub-Dean of Medicine, 1976–78; Pro-Vice-Chancellor, 1978–80. Hong Kong Government: Consultant in Medicine, 1974–89; Chm., Research Grants Council, Hong Kong, 1991–93. President: Hong Kong Coll. of Physicians, 1986–92; Hong Kong Acad. of Medicine, 1992–; Chm., Council for Aids Trust Fund, Hong Kong, 1993–96. Hon. FAMS Singapore, 1986. Hon DSc Chinese Univ. of Hong Kong, 1990; Hon DSc Univ. of Hong Kong, 1992. *Publications:* articles on: haematological disorders in liver disease and splenomegaly; thalassaemia; G6PD deficiency; lymphoma; leukaemia; med. educn and physician training. *Recreations:* swimming, travelling, classical music. *Address:* University Department of Medicine, Queen Mary Hospital, Pokfulam Road, Hong Kong. *T:* 28554251, *Fax:* 28162863. *Clubs:* Royal Hong Kong Golf, Hong Kong Country.

TODD, Hon. Sir Garfield; *see* Todd, Hon. Sir R. S. G.

TODD, Sir Ian (Pelham), KBE 1989; FRCS; Consulting Surgeon: King Edward VII Hospital for Officers, since 1989 (Consultant Surgeon, 1972–89); St Bartholomew's Hospital, since 1981 (Consultant Surgeon, 1958–81); St Mark's Hospital, since 1986 (Consultant Surgeon, 1954–86); *b* 23 March 1921; *s* of Alan Herepath and Constance Todd; *m* 1946, Jean Audrey Ann Noble; two *s* three *d.* *Educ:* Sherborne Sch.; St Bartholomew's Hosp. Med. Coll.; Toronto Univ. (Rockefeller studentship, 1941–43; MD 1945; MS 1956). MRCS, LRCP 1944; DCH 1947; FRCS 1949. Served RAMC, Captain (AER Major). Wellcome Res. Fellow, 1955–56. Lectures: Wilson-Hay Meml, Perth, 1978; Howard H. Frykman Meml, Minneapolis, 1979; Patrick Hanley Meml, New Orleans, 1982; Gordon Watson, St Bart's Hosp., 1982; Purdue Frederick, New Orleans, 1984; Zachary Cope Meml, RCS, 1985; Henry Floyd Meml, Stoke Mandeville, 1986; John Clive Meml, Calif., 1986; Pybus Meml, Durham, 1988; Chesledon, St Thomas' Hosp., 1988; Cutait Oration, São Paulo, 1991. Visiting Professorships incl.: Montevideo; Ribeirao Preto; La Paz; Vellore; New Orleans; Minneapolis; Madras; Detroit. Examiner in Surgery: Univ. of London, 1958–64; Cambridge Univ., 1988; Dhaka, 1990; Ex-civilian Cons. (Proctology), RN, 1970–86. President: Sect. Colo-proctology, RSM, 1970–71; Med. Soc. of London, 1984–85; RCS, 1986–89 (Mem. Council, 1975–89; Hunterian Prof., 1953; Arris and Gale Lectr, 1957–58); British Colostomy Assoc., 1991–; Vice-President: Imperial Cancer Res. Fund, 1986–89; Internat. Fedn of Surgical Colls, 1990–93. Founder, Leeds Castle Polyposis Gp, 1983. Fellow, Assoc. of Surgeons of GB and Ire., 1960; Founder Mem., Surgical Sixty Club; Hon. Member: Amer. Soc. of Colon and Rectal Surgs, 1974; RACS, 1974; Soc. Gastroent. Belge, 1964; Ileostomy Soc. of GB and Ire.; Surgical Res. Soc. of SA; Hellenic Surgical Assoc.; Assoc. of Surgs of India; Acad. of Medicine of Malaysia; NY State Surgical Soc., and S Amer. socs. FRGS 1986; Hon. FCMSA 1987; Hon. FRACS 1988; Hon. FACS 1988; Hon. FRCSCan 1989; Hon. FRCPSGlas 1989; FCPS (Bangladesh) 1990; Hon. Fellow, Colo-rectal Soc. of Sydney. Lister Prize in Surgery, Toronto, 1956. Star of Jordan, 1973. *Publications:* Intestinal Stomas, 1978; (ed) Rob and Smith, Operative Surgery, vol. 3, 1982; many articles on surgery of colon and rectum in Brit. and Amer. jls. *Recreations:* ski-ing, travel, philately, music. *Address:* 4 Longmead Close, Farleigh Road, Norton St Philip, Bath BA3 6NS.

TODD, Prof. Janet Margaret, PhD; Professor of English Literature, University of East Anglia, since 1990; *b* 10 Sept. 1942; *d* of George and Elizabeth Dakin; *m* 1966 (marr. diss.); one *s* one *d.* *Educ:* Newnham Coll., Cambridge (BA 1964); Univ. of Leeds; Univ. of Florida (PhD). Lectr, Univ. of Cape Coast, Ghana, 1966–67; Asst Prof. of English, Univ. of Puerto Rico, 1972–74; Asst, Associate, Full Prof. of English, Rutgers Univ., NJ, 1974–83; Fellow in English, Sidney Sussex Coll., Cambridge, 1983–89. Vis. Prof. Univ. of Southampton, 1982–83. Numerous awards. *Publications:* In Adam's Garden: a study of John Clare, 1973; Mary Wollstonecraft: an annotated bibliography, 1976; Women's Friendship in Literature, 1980; (jtly) English Congregational Hymns in the 18th Century, 1983; Sensibility, 1986; Feminist Literary History, 1988; The Sign of Angellica: women writing and fiction 1660–1800, 1989; (ed jtly) The Complete Works of Mary Wollstonecraft, 1989; (ed) A Dictionary of British Women Writers, 1989; (ed) The Works of Aphra Behn, vol. I, 1992, vols II and III, 1993, vols IV–VII, 1994; (ed) Aphra Behn's Oroonoko, The Rover and Other Works, 1993; Gender, Art and Death, 1993. *Address:* 14 Friars Quay, Norwich NR3 1ES.

TODD, Prof. John Francis James, PhD; CEng; CChem, FRSC; Professor of Mass Spectroscopy, University of Kent at Canterbury, since 1991 (Director, University Chemical Laboratory, 1991–94); *b* 20 May 1937; *o s* of late Eric Todd and Annie Lewin Todd (*née* Tinkler); *m* 1963, Mavis Georgina Lee; three *s.* *Educ:* Leeds Grammar Sch.; Leeds Univ. (BSc, Cl. 1 Hons Chem.). FInstMC; MIEnvSci; CEng. Research Fellow: Leeds Univ., 1962–63; Yale Univ., USA, 1963–65; University of Kent at Canterbury: Asst Lectr in Chemistry, 1965–66; Lectr in Chemistry, 1966–73; Sen. Lectr, 1973–89; Reader in Physical Chemistry, Faculty of Natural Scis, 1990; Master of Rutherford Coll., 1975–85. CIL Distinguished Vis. Lectr, Trent Univ., Canada, 1988. J. B. Cohen Prizeman, Leeds Univ., 1963; Fulbright Research Scholar, 1963–65. Chm., Canterbury and Thanet HA, 1982–86. Chairman: Kent Section of Chem. Soc., 1975; British Mass Spectroscopy Soc., 1980–81 (Treas., 1990–93); Titular Mem., IUPAC Commn on Molecular Structures and Spectroscopy, 1979–91; Nat. Mem. Council, RSC, 1993–95. Mem., Kent Educn Cttee, 1983–88. Member: Clergy Orphan Corp., 1985–; Council, Strode Park Foundn for the Disabled, 1986–90. Governor: S Kent Coll. of Technology, 1977–89; Canterbury Christ Church Coll., 1994–. Mem., Amer. Soc. of Sigma Xi, Yale Chapter. Jt Editor, Internat. Jl of Mass Spectrometry and Ion Processes, 1985–. *Publications:* Dynamic Mass Spectrometry, vol. 4, 1975, vol. 5, 1978, vol. 6, 1981; Advances in Mass Spectrometry 1985, 1986; reviews and papers, mainly on mass spectrometry, in Jl of Chem. Soc. and Jl of Physics, etc. *Recreations:* music, travel. *Address:* University Chemical Laboratory, University of Kent at Canterbury, CT2 7NH. *T:* Canterbury (01227) 823518; West Bank, 122 Whitstable Road, Canterbury, Kent CT2 8EG. *T:* Canterbury (01227) 769552.

TODD, John Rawling, CVO 1972; OBE 1985; Secretary for Housing, Hong Kong Government, 1986–88; *b* 15 Feb. 1929; *s* of William Rawling Todd and Isabella May Todd; *m* 1960, Ingrid von Rothermann; one *s* one *d.* *Educ:* Durham Univ. (BSc). Nat. Service, RA, 1952. Joined HMOCS; Admin. Officer, Gambia, 1955; New Hebrides, 1962; Administrator, British Indian Ocean Territory, 1966; Dep. Governor, Seychelles, 1970; seconded to FCO, 1974; Hong Kong: Dep. Sec., 1976; Dir of Lands, 1982. Sen. British Rep., Sino-British Land Commn, 1984–88; Chm., Special Cttee on Compensation and Betterment, Hong Kong, 1991. *Recreations:* reading, gardening, walking, croquet. *Address:* A2822, Erlach, NO, Gut Harrathof, Austria. *Club:* Commonwealth Trust.

TODD, Prof. Malcolm, FSA 1970; Professor of Archaeology, University of Exeter, since 1979; *b* 27 Nov. 1939; *s* of Wilfrid and Rose Evelyn Todd; *m* 1964, Molly Tanner; one *s* one *d.* *Educ:* Univ. of Wales (BA, DLitt); Brasenose Coll., Oxford (Dip. Class. Archaeol (Dist.)). Res. Assistant, Rheinisches Landesmus., Bonn, 1963–65; Lectr 1965–74, Sen. Lectr 1974–77, Reader in Archaeology 1977–79, Univ. of Nottingham. Vis. Prof., New York Univ., 1979; Visiting Fellow: All Souls Coll., Oxford, 1984; Brasenose Coll., Oxford, 1990–91; Sen. Res. Fellow, British Acad./Leverhulme Trust, 1990–91. Vice-Pres., Roman Soc., 1985–; Member: RCHM, 1986–92; Council, National Trust, 1987–91. Trustee, Roman Res. Trust, 1994–. Corr. Mem., German Arch. Inst., 1977–. Editor, Britannia, 1984–89. *Publications:* The Northern Barbarians, 1975, 2nd edn 1987; The Walls of Rome, 1978; Roman Britain, 1981, 2nd edn 1985; The South-West to AD 1000, 1987; (ed) Research on Roman Britain, 1960–89, 1989; Les Germains: aux frontières romaines, 1990; The Early Germans, 1992; papers in Germania, Britannia, Antiquaries Jl, Antiquity, Amer. Jl of Arch. *Recreations:* reading, writing, travel on foot. *Address:* The University, Exeter, Devon EX4 4QH. *T:* Exeter (01392) 264351.

TODD, Mary Williamson Spottiswoode, MA; Headmistress of Harrogate College, 1952–73; *b* 11 June 1909; *d* of John and Mary Todd, Oxford. *Educ:* Oxford High School; Lady Margaret Hall, Oxford. MA Hons Oxon. Final Hon. Sch.: Mathematics, 1932, Nat. Science, 1933; London Diploma in Theology, 1941. Various teaching posts: St Felix School, Southwold, 1933–37; Clifton High School, Bristol, 1937–39; Westonbirt School, Glos, 1939–46; Headmistress of Durham, 1946–52. *Address:* 93 Oakdale, Harrogate, North Yorks HG1 2LT. *T:* Harrogate (01423) 566411.

TODD, Hon. Sir (Reginald Stephen) Garfield, Kt 1986; *b* 13 July 1908; *s* of late Thomas and Edith C. Todd; *m* 1932, Jean Grace Wilson; three *d.* *Educ:* Otago Univ.; Glen Leith Theol Coll., NZ; University of Witwatersrand. Superintendent Dadaya Mission, 1934–53, Chm. Governing Bd 1963–85. MP for Shabani, 1946–58; Prime Minister of S Rhodesia, 1953–58; Mem. Senate, Parlt of Zimbabwe, 1980–85. First Vice-President, World Convention of Churches of Christ, 1955–60; awarded Citation for Christian Leadership in Politics and Race Relations; former Member Executive: United Coll. of Educn, Bulawayo; Rhodesian Christian Council. Arrested by Smith regime in 1965 and confined to Hokonui Ranch for one year; arrested by Smith regime in 1972 and imprisoned, then detained, Jan 1972–June 1976. Received medal acknowledging efforts for peace and justice in Rhodesia, from Pope Paul, 1973. Holds hon. doctorates, NZ and USA. Knighted for services to NZ and Africa. *Address:* Box FM 693, Famona, Bulawayo, Zimbabwe. *Club:* Bulawayo.

See also Baron Acton.

TODD, Richard, (Richard Andrew Palethorpe-Todd), OBE 1993; actor; *b* 11 June 1919; *s* of Major A. W. Palethorpe-Todd, Castlederg, Co. Tyrone, and Marvil Agar-Daly, Ballymalis Castle, Kerry; *m* 1st, 1949, Catherine Stewart Crawford Grant-Bogle (marr. diss. 1970); one *s* one *d;* 2nd, 1970, Virginia Anne Rollo Mailer (marr. diss. 1992); two *s.* *Educ:* Shrewsbury; privately. Entered the theatre in 1937. Served in King's Own Yorkshire Light Infantry and The Parachute Regt, 1940–46; GSO iii (Ops), 6 Airborne Div., 1944–45. *Films* since War of 1939–45 include: The Hasty Heart, 1949; Stage Fright, 1950; Robin Hood, 1952; Rob Roy, 1953; A Man Called Peter, 1954; The Dambusters, 1954; The Virgin Queen, 1955; Yangtse Incident, 1957; Chase a Crooked Shadow, 1957; The Long and the Short and the Tall, 1960; The Hellions, 1961; The Longest Day, 1962; Operation Crossbow, 1964; Coast of Skeletons, 1964; The Love-Ins (USA), 1967; Subterfuge, 1968; Dorian Grey, 1969; Asylum, 1972; Secret Agent 008, 1976; The House of the Long Shadows, 1982; The Olympus Force, 1988. *Stage* appearances include: An Ideal Husband, Strand, 1965–66; Dear Octopus, Haymarket, 1967; USA tour, The Marquise, 1972; Australia tour, Sleuth, 1973; led RSC N American tour, 1974; Equus,

Australian Nat. Theatre Co., 1975; On Approval (S Africa), 1976; nat. tour of Quadrille, and The Heat of the Moment, 1977; Nightfall (S Africa), 1979; This Happy Breed (nat. tour), 1980; The Business of Murder, Duchess, 1981, Mayfair, 1982–88; The Woman in Black, Sydney Opera House, Liverpool Playhouse, 1991; nat. tour of Sweet Revenge, 1993; nat. tour of Brideshead Revisited, 1995. *Television:* H. G. Wells, in Beautiful Lies, 1991; series, Virtual Murder, 1992. Formed Triumph Theatre Productions, 1970. Past Grand Steward, Past Master, Lodge of Emulation No 21. *Publications:* Caught in the Act (autobiog.), 1986; In Camera (autobiog.), 1989. *Recreations:* shooting and farming. *Address:* Chinham Farm, Faringdon, Oxon SN7 8EZ; Little Ponton House, near Grantham, Lincs NG33 5BS. *Club:* Army and Navy.

TODD, Ronald; General Secretary, Transport and General Workers' Union, 1985–92; *b* 11 March 1927; *s* of late George Thomas Todd and of Emily Todd; *m* 1945, Josephine Tarrant; one *s* two *d*. *Educ:* St Patrick's Sch., Walthamstow, E17. Served with Royal Marine Commandos; spent considerable time in China. Joined TGWU: worked at Ford Motor Co., 1954–62, latterly Dep. Convener; full-time officer of TGWU, 1962; Regional Officer, 1969; Reg. Sec., 1976; Nat. Organiser, 1978. Mem., TUC Gen. Council, 1984–92; Chm., TUC Internat. Cttee, 1985–92. Chm. (TU side), Ford Nat. Jt Council, 1978–85; Jt Sec., Nat. Jt Council for Stable Staff (Workpeople's side), 1978–85. Member: NEDC, 1985–92; MSC, 1986–88. Member: Unity Trust, 1986– (Pres., 1986–89); Council for Charitable Support, 1988–. Hon. Vice-President: CND; BDA. Patron, Margaret Centre Macmillan Appeal. *Recreations:* collecting Victorian music covers, archaeology. *Address:* 65 Surrey Road, Dagenham, Essex RM10 8ET.

TOFFOLO, Rt. Rev. Mgr. Adrian Titian; Rector, Venerable English College, Rome, since 1991; *b* 22 Sept. 1944; *s* of Sante Battista Toffolo and Ethel Elizabeth (*née* Hanniford-Hill). *Educ:* St Boniface's Coll., Plymouth; Gregorian Univ., Rome (PhL, STL). Asst Priest, Penzance, 1969–72; Prof. of Theology, Oscott Coll., 1972–76; Assistant Priest: Torquay, 1976–80; Plymouth, 1980–84; Parish Priest: St Austell, 1984–85; Truro, 1985–91. Prelate of Honour, 1992. *Recreations:* mountain walking, music, D-I-Y. *Address:* Ven. Collegio Inglese, Via di Monserrato 45, 00186 Roma, Italy. *T:* (6) 6864185, (6) 6865808.

TOFT, Dr Anthony Douglas, CBE 1995; FRCPE; Consultant Physician, Royal Infirmary, Edinburgh, since 1978; *b* 29 Oct. 1944; *s* of William Vincent Toft and Anne Laing; *m* 1968, Maureen Margaret Darling; one *s* one *d*. *Educ:* Perth Academy; Univ. of Edinburgh (BSc Hons, MD). FRCPE 1980; FCPS(Pak) 1990; FRCP 1992; FRCPI 1993; FRCPGlas 1993; FRCSE (*ad hominem*), 1994. House Physician and House Surgeon, Royal Infirmary, Edinburgh, 1969–70. Chief Medical Adviser, Scottish Equitable Life Assurance Soc., 1989–. Royal Coll. of Physicians of Edinburgh: Chm., Collegiate Members' Cttee, 1977; Mem. Council, 1986–88; Vice-Pres., 1990–91; Pres., 1991–94. Chairman: Scottish Royal Colls, 1993–94; Jt Cttee on Higher Med. Trng; Vice-Chm., UK Conf. of Med. Royal Colls, 1993–94. Mem., Assoc. of Physicians of GB and Ireland, 1983–; Sec., Harveian Soc., 1980–94. Hon. Mem., Acad. of Medicine of Malaysia, 1993. Hon. FACP 1993; Hon. FRACP 1993; Hon. FRCSC 1994; Hon. FRCGP 1994; Hon. FFPM 1994; Hon. Fellow, Acad. of Medicine of Singapore, 1994. *Publications:* Diagnosis and Management of Endocrine Diseases, 1982; papers on thyroid disease. *Recreations:* golf, gardening, hill-walking. *Address:* 41 Hermitage Gardens, Edinburgh EH10 6AZ. *T:* 0131–447 2221. *Club:* New (Edinburgh).

TOGANIVALU, Ratu Josua Brown, CBE 1980; JP; Chairman, Fiji Broadcasting Commission, 1988–94; Chairman, Fiji Care Insurance Ltd, 1995; *b* Fiji, 2 May 1930; *m*; two *s* one *d*. *Educ:* Levuka Public Sch.; Marist Brothers Sch., Suva; Queensland Agricultural Coll.; Royal Agricultural Coll., Cirencester. With Native Lands Trust Board, 1953–71; MP Fiji, 1966–77: Minister for Lands, Mines and Mineral Resources, 1972–73; Minister for Agriculture, Fisheries and Forests, 1974–77; High Commissioner for Fiji: to New Zealand, 1978–81; in London, 1981–85. Chm., Fiji Public Service Commn, 1989–92. Represented Fiji at ACP Meeting, Guyana, 1975, ACP Meeting, Malawi, 1976, ACP/EEC Sugar Meetings, Brussels, 1976. JP (Fiji) 1968. *Recreations:* cricket, Rugby, boxing. *Address:* Box 13326, Suva, Fiji. *Clubs:* United, Defence (Fiji).

TOH CHIN CHYE, Nila Utama, 1st class, 1990; BSc, PhD, DipSc; *b* 10 Dec. 1921; *m*. *Educ:* Raffles Coll., Singapore; University College, London; Nat. Inst. for Medical Research, London. Reader in Physiology, 1958–64, Research Associate 1964, Vice-Chancellor, 1968–75, Univ. of Singapore. Chm., People's Action Party, 1954–81 (a Founder Mem.); MP, Singapore, 1959–88; Dep. Prime Minister of Singapore, 1959–68; Minister for Science and Technology, 1968–75; Minister for Health, 1975–81. Chm., Applied Res. Corp., 1973–75. Chairman, Board of Governors: Singapore Polytechnic, 1959–75; Regional Inst. of Higher Educn and Devélt, 1970–75; Mem. Admin. Bd, Assoc. of SE Asian Insts of Higher Learning, 1968–75. DLitt (*hc*) Singapore, 1976. *Publications:* papers in Jl of Physiology and other relevant jls. *Address:* 23 Greenview Crescent, Singapore 1128.

TOKATY, Prof. Grigori Alexandrovich; Professor Emeritus, City University; *b* North Caucasus, Russia; Ossetian by mother tongue. *Educ:* Leningrad Rabfak, 1929–30; Rykov Rabfak of Moscow Higher Technical Coll. MVTU, 1930–32; Zhukovsky Air Force Academy of Aeronautics, Moscow, 1932–37. DEng, PhD, DAeSc, CEng, CanTechSc. Lt Col, Air Force. Zhukovsky Academy: Aeronautical Research Engineer, 1937–38; Head of Aeronautics Laboratory, 1938–41; Dep. Head of Res. Dept, 1941; Lectr in Aerodynamics and Aircraft Design, 1941–45; Acting Prof. of Aviation, Moscow Engrg Inst, 1939–45; Rocket research and development, 1944–45; Rocket scientist, Berlin, 1945–47. Varied work for HM Govt, London, 1948–52; Imperial Coll., and Coll. of Aeronautics, Cranfield, 1953–56; work on theoretical rocket dynamics and orbital flight mechanics associated with Apollo programme, 1956–68; Reader in Aeronautics and Astronautics, Northampton Coll. of Advanced Technology, 1960–61; Head, 1961–75, and Prof., 1967–75, Dept of Aeronautics and Space Technology, Northampton Coll. of Advanced Technology and City Univ. Chief Scientific Adviser, WTI, 1976–78. Visiting Professor: Univs of the US, Jordan, Nigeria, Iran, Turkey, Holland. FRAeS, FAIAA, FIMA. *Publications:* numerous, including seven books: Rocketdynamics, 1961; The History of Rocket Technology (jt), 1964; A History and Philosophy of Fluid Mechanics, 1971; Cosmonautics-Astronautics, 1976; Higher Education, 1982; Scientific Technological Education for the shape of things to come, 1988; Theoretic Principles of Spaceship Design, 1989; articles and booklets (alone or jointly) in the fields of fluid mechanics, gasdynamics, rocketdynamics, theory and philosophy of educn, and non-scientific subjects. *Recreations:* writing, broadcasting, travelling. *Address:* Centre for Aeronautics, City University, Northampton Square, EC1V 0HB. *Club:* National Liberal.

TOLER; *see* Graham-Toler, family name of Earl of Norbury.

TOLER, Maj.-Gen. David Arthur Hodges, OBE 1963; MC 1945; DL; *b* 13 Sept. 1920; *s* of Major Thomas Clayton Toler, DL, JP, Swettenham Hall, Congleton; *m* 1951, Judith Mary, *d* of James William Garden, DSO, Aberdeen; one *s* one *d*. *Educ:* Stowe; Christ Church, Oxford (MA). 2nd Lieut Coldstream Guards, 1940; served War of 1939–45, N Africa and Italy; Regimental Adjt, Coldstream Guards, 1952–54; Bde Major, 4th Gds Bde, 1956–57; Adjt, RMA Sandhurst, 1958–60; Bt Lt-Col 1959; comd 2nd Bn Coldstream Guards, 1962–64; comd Coldstream Guards, 1964–65; comd 4th Guards Bde, 1965–68; Dep. Comdt, Staff Coll., Camberley, 1968–69; GOC E Midland Dist, 1970–73; retired 1973. Dep. Hon. Col, Royal Anglian Regt (Lincolnshire) TAVR, 1979–84. Emergency Planning Officer, Lincolnshire CC, 1974–77. Chm., Lincoln Dio. Adv. Cttee, 1981–86. Pres., SSAFA, Lincs, 1978–. DL Lincs, 1982. *Recreations:* shooting, fishing, gardening. *Address:* Rutland Farm, Fulbeck, Grantham, Lincs NG32 3LG. *Club:* Army and Navy.

TOLHURST, Rear-Adm. John Gordon, CB 1995; Flag Officer Sea Training, 1992–April 1996; *b* 22 April 1943; *s* of Virgil George Tolhurst and Elizabeth Mary Tolhurst; *m* 1975, Susan Jayne Spencer; one *s* one *d*. *Educ:* Sevenoaks Sch. Joined RN 1961; Commanding Officer: HMS Berwick, 1977; HMS Exeter, 1984; Asst Dir, Naval Warfare, 1986; Commodore, HMS Nelson, 1988; CO HMS Invincible, 1990; ADC to the Queen, 1990. *Recreations:* classic cars, shooting, gardening. *Address:* (until April 1996) Rodney House, Portland, Dorset. *T:* Portland (01305) 820311.

TOLLEMACHE, family name of **Baron Tollemache.**

TOLLEMACHE, 5th Baron *cr* 1876; **Timothy John Edward Tollemache;** Vice Lord-Lieutenant of Suffolk, since 1994; Director, Fortis (UK) (formerly AMEV (UK)) Ltd, since 1980, and other companies; farmer and landowner; *b* 13 Dec. 1939; *s* of 4th Baron Tollemache, MC, DL, and of Dinah Susan, *d* of late Sir Archibald Auldjo Jamieson, KBE, MC; *S* father, 1975; *m* 1970, Alexandra Dorothy Jean, *d* of late Col Hugo Meynell, MC; two *s* one *d*. *Educ:* Eton. Commissioned into Coldstream Guards, 1959; served Kenya, Persian Gulf and Zanzibar, 1960–62; Course of Estate Management at Sandringham, Norfolk, 1962–64. President: Suffolk Assoc. of Local Councils, 1978–; NW Agronomy, 1983–; E Anglian Productivity Assoc., 1984–88; Suffolk Agricl Assoc., 1988; The Milk Gp, 1994–; Chm., CLA, Suffolk, 1990–93. Vice Pres., Cheshire Red Cross, 1980–; Chm., St John's Council for Suffolk, 1982–89. President: Friends of Ipswich Museums, 1980–; Suffolk Family History Soc., 1988–; Chairman: HHA (E Anglia), 1979–83; Bury St Edmunds Cathedral Appeal, 1986–90; Vice Patron, Suffolk Preservation Soc., 1992–. Patron: Suffolk Accident Rescue Service, 1983–; E Suffolk Assoc. for the Blind, 1992–. DL Suffolk, 1984. CStJ 1988. *Recreations:* shooting, fishing, natural history. *Heir:* *s* Hon. Edward John Hugo Tollemache, *b* 12 May 1976. *Address:* Helmingham Hall, Stowmarket, Suffolk IP14 6EF. *Clubs:* White's, Pratt's, Special Forces.

TOLLEMACHE, Sir Lyonel (Humphry John), 7th Bt *cr* 1793, of Hanby Hall; JP; DL; *b* 10 July 1931; *s* of Maj.-Gen. Sir Humphry Tollemache, 6th Bt, CB, CBE, DL and Nora Priscilla (*d* 1990), *d* of John Taylor; *S* father, 1990; *m* 1960, Mary Joscelyne, *d* of late William Henry Whitbread, TD; two *s* two *d*. *Educ:* Uppingham Sch.; RMA Sandhurst; RAC Cirencester. FRICS. Major, Coldstream Guards, retd 1963. Mem., Leics CC, 1985–. Gov., Royal Star and Garter Home, Richmond, 1985–. High Sheriff 1978–79, JP 1978, DL 1980, Leics. *Heir:* *s* Lyonel Thomas Tollemache, *b* 23 Jan. 1963. *Address:* Buckminster Park, Grantham NG33 5RU.

TOLLEY, Rev. Canon George; Hon. Canon, since 1976, and Hon. Assistant, since 1990, Sheffield Cathedral; Chairman, Central Sheffield University Hospitals NHS Trust, since 1992; *b* 24 May 1925; *s* of George and Elsie Tolley, Old Hill, Staffordshire; *m* 1947, Joan Amelia Grosvenor; two *s* one *d*. *Educ:* Halesowen Grammar Sch.; Birmingham Central Tech. Coll. (part-time); Princeton Univ., USA; Lincoln Theol Coll., 1965–67; Sheffield Univ. (MA). BSc, MSc, PhD (London); FRSC; FIM; CIMgt. Rotary Foundation Fellow, Princeton Univ., 1949–50. Head, Department of Chemistry, College of Advanced Technology, Birmingham, 1954–58; Head of Research and Experimental Dept, Allied Ironfounders Ltd, 1958–61; Principal, Worcester Tech. College, 1961–65; Senior Director of Studies, Royal Air Force Coll., Cranwell, 1965–66; Principal, Sheffield Coll. of Technology, 1966–69, Sheffield City Polytechnic, 1969–82; Manpower Services Commission: Dir, Open Tech Unit, 1983–84; Head, Quality Branch, 1984–85; Chief Officer, Review of Vocational Qualifications, 1985–86; Advr, NCVQ, 1986–88; Advr, Trng Commn, then Trng Agency, 1988–90. Ordained deacon, 1967, priest, 1968; Curate, St Andrew's, Sharrow, 1967–90. Chairman: Council, Plastics Inst., 1959–61; Further Educn Adv. Cttee, Food, Drink and Tobacco Ind. Trng Bd, 1974–78; Bd, Further Educn Curriculum Unit, 1978–82; BTec Continuing Educn Cttee, 1983–85; Council of the Selly Oak Colls, Birmingham, 1984–92; Adv. Bd, Pitman Exams Inst., 1987–92; Pres., Inst. of Home Economics, 1987–90; Vice-Pres., Educn 2000, 1990–92; Hon. Sec., Assoc. of Colleges of Further and Higher Educn, 1975–82; Member: CNAA (Chm., Cttee for Business and Management Studies, 1972–83); Yorks and Humberside Economic Planning Council, 1976–79; RAF Trng and Educn Cttee, 1975–80; Governing Body, Derbyshire Coll. of Higher Educn, 1984–87. Member Council: PSI, 1981–89; RSA, 1983–92. Dep. Chm., S Yorks Foundn, 1986–90. Sheffield Church Burgess. Hon. FCP; Hon. Fellow: Sheffield City Polytechnic, 1982; Columbia—Pacific Univ., 1983; CGLI, 1984; Inst. of Trng and Devélt, 1989. Hon. DSc: Sheffield, 1984; CNAA, 1986; DUniv Open, 1984. *Publications:* Meaning and Purpose in Higher Education, 1976; many papers relating to plastics and education in British and foreign journals. *Recreations:* music, hill walking, bird watching. *Address:* 74 Furniss Avenue, Dore, Sheffield S17 3QP. *Club:* Athenæum.

TOLOLO, Sir Alkan, KBE 1985 (CBE); High Commissioner for Papua New Guinea in Malaysia, 1986; *m* Nerrie Tololo, MBE; two *s* two *d*. Teaching, 1957–61; supervisory teacher, 1963–65; Superintendent of Schools, 1967–69; Mem., Public Service Board, 1969–70; First Comr, PNG Teaching Service, 1971–73; Dir of Education, 1973–79; Chm., Public Services Commn, 1979–80; Consul-General Sydney, 1981; High Comr in Australia, 1983–86. Former Mem. or Chm. of numerous Boards and Cttees on education, culture and employment, PNG. Hon. LLD 1982, Hon. DTech 1982, Univ. of Papua New Guinea. *Address:* c/o Ministry for Foreign Affairs, Central Government Offices, Post Office, Wards Strip, Waigani, Papua New Guinea.

TOLSTOY, Dimitry, (Dimitry Tolstoy-Miloslavsky), QC 1959; Barrister-at-Law; *b* 8 Nov. 1912; *s* of late Michael Tolstoy-Miloslavsky and Eileen May Hamshaw; *m* 1st, 1934, Frieda Mary Wicksteed (marr. diss.); one *s* one *d*; 2nd, 1943, Natalie Deytrikh; one *s* one *d*. *Educ:* Wellington; Trinity Coll., Cambridge. President of Cambridge Union, 1935. Called to Bar, Gray's Inn, 1937. Lecturer in Divorce to Inns of Court, 1952–68. *Publications:* Tolstoy on Divorce, 1946–7th edn 1971; The Tolstoys: genealogy and origin, 1991; articles in legal periodicals.

TOMALIN, Claire; writer; *b* 20 June 1933; *d* of Emile Delavenay and Muriel Herbert; *m* 1st, 1955, Nicholas Osborne Tomalin (*d* 1973); one *s* two *d* (and one *s* one *d* decd); 2nd, 1993, Michael Frayn, *qv*. *Educ:* Hitchin Girls' Grammar Sch.; Dartington Hall Sch.; Newnham Coll., Cambridge (MA). Publishers' reader and editor, Messrs Heinemann, Hutchinson, Cape, 1955–67; Evening Standard, 1967–68; New Statesman: Asst Literary Editor, 1968–70; Literary Editor, 1974–77; Literary Editor, Sunday Times, 1979–86. Stage play, The Winter Wife, Nuffield, Southampton, 1991. Trustee, Nat. Portrait Gallery, 1992–. Registrar, Royal Literary Fund, 1984– (Mem. Cttee, 1974–). FRSL (Mem. Council, 1993–). *Publications:* The Life and Death of Mary Wollstonecraft, 1974; Shelley and his World, 1980; Parents and Children, 1981; Katherine Mansfield: a secret life, 1987; The Invisible Woman: the story of Nelly Ternan and Charles Dickens, 1990

(NCR, Hawthornden, and James Tait Black Prizes, 1991); Mrs Jordan's Profession, 1994; literary journalism. *Recreations:* travelling in Europe, walking in Regent's Park. *Address:* c/o Peters, Fraser & Dunlop, 503/4 The Chambers, Chelsea Harbour, SW10 0XF.

TOMBS, family name of **Baron Tombs.**

TOMBS, Baron *cr* 1990 (Life Peer), of Brailes in the county of Warwickshire; **Francis Leonard Tombs,** Kt 1978; FEng 1977; FRAeS; Chairman: Rolls-Royce, 1985–92 (Director, 1982–92); Old Mutual South Africa Trust, since 1994; *b* 17 May 1924; *s* of Joseph and Jane Tombs; *m* 1949, Marjorie Evans; three *d. Educ:* Elmore Green Sch., Walsall; Birmingham Coll. of Technology; BSc (Econ) Hons, London. FRAeS 1994. GEC, 1939–45; Birmingham Corp., 1946–47; British Electricity Authority, Midlands, then Central Electricity Authority, Merseyside and N Wales, 1948–57; Gen. Man., GEC, Erith, 1958–67; Dir and Gen. Man., James Howden & Co., Glasgow, 1967–68; successively Dir of Engrg, Dep. Chm., Chm., South of Scotland Electricity Bd, 1969–77; Chm., Electricity Council, 1977–80. Chairman: Weir Group, 1981–83; Turner & Newall, subseq. T & N, 1982–89; Director: N. M. Rothschild & Sons, 1981–94; Shell-UK, 1983–94. Pres., Molecule Theatre Ltd, 1993– (Chm., 1985–92). Member: Nature Conservancy Council, 1978–82; Standing Commn on Energy and the Environment, 1978–; SERC, 1982–85; Chairman: Engrg Council, 1985–88; ACARD, 1985–87 (Mem., 1984–87); ACOST, 1987–90. Chm., H of L Select Cttee on Sustainable Develt, 1994–. Pres., IEE, 1981–82; formerly Vice-Pres., Fellowship of Engrg; Vice-Pres., Engineers for Disaster Relief, 1985–94. Chm., Assoc. of British Orchestras, 1982–86. Hon. FIChemE 1985; Hon. FICE 1986; Hon. FIProdE 1986; Hon. FIMechE 1989; Hon. FIEE 1991; Hon. Mem., British Nuclear Energy Soc. Pro-Chancellor and Chm. Council, Cranfield Inst. of Technol., 1985–91; Chancellor, Strathclyde Univ., 1991– (Hon. LLD 1976; DUniv 1991). Freeman, City of London, 1980; Liveryman, 1981–, and Prime Warden, 1994–95, Goldsmiths' Co. Hon. DTech Loughborough, 1979; Hon. DSc: Aston, 1979; Lodz, Poland, 1980; Cranfield, 1985; Bradford, 1986; City, 1986; Surrey, 1988; Nottingham, 1989; Warwick, 1990; Cambridge, 1990; DSc(Eng) QUB, 1986; DEd CNAA, 1989. *Recreations:* music, golf, sailing. *Address:* Honington Lodge, Honington, Shipston-upon-Stour, Warwickshire CV36 5AA.

TOMKINS, Sir Edward Emile, GCMG 1975 (KCMG 1969; CMG 1960); CVO 1957; Grand Officiér, Légion d'Honneur, 1984; HM Diplomatic Service, retired; HM Ambassador to France, 1972–75; *b* 16 Nov. 1915; *s* of late Lt-Col E. L. Tomkins; *m* 1955, Gillian Benson; one *s* two *d. Educ:* Ampleforth Coll.; Trinity Coll., Cambridge. Foreign Office, 1939. Military service, 1940–43. HM Embassy, Moscow, 1944–46; Foreign Office, 1946–51; HM Embassy, Washington, 1951–54; HM Embassy, Paris, 1954–59; Foreign Office, 1959–63; HM Embassy, Bonn, 1963–67; HM Embassy, Washington, 1967–69; Ambassador to the Netherlands, 1970–72. Mem., Bucks CC, 1977–85. *Address:* Winslow Hall, Winslow, Bucks. *T:* Winslow (01296) 712323. *Club:* Garrick.

TOMKYS, Sir (William) Roger, KCMG 1991 (CMG 1984); HM Diplomatic Service, retired; Master of Pembroke College, Cambridge, since 1992; *b* 15 March 1937; *s* of late William Arthur and Edith Tomkys; *m* 1963, Margaret Jean Abbey; one *s* one *d. Educ:* Bradford Grammar Sch.; Balliol Coll., Oxford (Domus Scholar; 1st cl. Hons Lit. Hum.). Entered Foreign Service, 1960; MECAS, 1960; 3rd Sec., Amman, 1962; 2nd Sec., FCO, 1964; 1st Sec., Head of Chancery, Benghazi, 1967; Planning Staff, FCO, 1969; Head of Chancery, Athens, 1972; Counsellor, seconded to Cabinet Office, 1975; Head of Near East and North Africa Dept, FCO, 1977–80; Counsellor, Rome, 1980–81; Ambassador: to Bahrain, 1981–84; to Syria, 1984–86; Asst Under Sec. of State and Principal Finance Officer, FCO, 1987–89; Dep. Under Sec. of State, FCO, 1989–90; High Comr, Kenya, 1990–92. Commendatore dell'Ordine al Merito, 1980; Order of Bahrain, 1st cl., 1984. *Address:* The Master's Lodge, Pembroke College, Cambridge CB2 1RF. *Clubs:* Royal Blackheath Golf; Royal & Ancient Golf (St Andrews).

TOMLINSON, Prof. (Alfred) Charles; Professor of English, University of Bristol, 1982–92, now Emeritus; *b* 8 Jan. 1927; *s* of Alfred Tomlinson and May Lucas; *m* 1948, Brenda Raybould; two *d. Educ:* Longton High School; Queens' Coll., Cambridge (MA; Hon. Fellow, 1974); Royal Holloway and Bedford Colls, Univ. of London (MA; Hon. Fellow RHBNC, 1991). Lecturer, 1957–68, Reader in English poetry, 1968–82, Bristol Univ. Visiting Prof., Univ. of New Mexico, 1962–63; O'Connor Prof., Colgate Univ., NY, 1967–68 and 1989; Vis. Fellow, Princeton Univ., 1981; Lamont Prof., Union Coll., NY, 1987; Vis. Prof., McMaster Univ., Canada, 1987; Hon. Prof. of English, Keele Univ., 1989. Arts Council Poetry Panel, 1964–66. Lectures: Witter Bynner, Univ. of New Mexico, 1976; Clark, Cambridge, 1982; Edmund Blunden, Hong Kong, 1987; Stubbs, Tononto, 1992; St Jerome, London, 1995. Exhibition of Graphics: Ely House, OUP, London, 1972; Clare Coll., Cambridge, 1975; Arts Council touring exhibn, 1978–80; Poetry Soc., 1983; Regent's Coll. Gall., 1986; in Surrealism in English Art, touring exhibn, 1986–87; Colby Coll., Maine, USA, 1987; McMaster Univ. Gall., Canada, 1987. FRSL 1974. Hon. DLitt: Keele, 1981; Colgate, 1981; New Mexico, 1986. Cholmondeley Award, 1979; Wilbur Award, 1982; Citadella Premio Europeo, 1991; Bennett Award, NY, 1993. *Publications: poetry:* Relations and Contraries, 1951; The Necklace, 1955, repr. 1966; Seeing is Believing, 1960 (US 1958); A Peopled Landscape, 1963; Poems, 1964; American Scenes, 1966; The Poem as Initiation, (US) 1968; The Way of a World, 1969; Poems, in Penguin Modern Poets, 1969; Renga (France) 1970, (US) 1972, (England) 1979; Written on Water, 1972; The Way In, 1974; Selected Poems, 1978; The Shaft, 1978; (with Octavio Paz) Air Born, 1981 (Mexico 1979); The Flood, 1981; Notes from New York and other Poems, 1984; Collected Poems, 1985, expanded repr., 1987; The Return, 1987; Nella pienezza del tempo (Italy), 1987; Annunciations, 1989; Selected Poems, 1989; The Door in the Wall, 1992; Poemas (Portugal), 1992; Charles Tomlinson: sette poesie (Italy), 1993; Gedichte (Germany), 1994; (authology) La insistencia de las cosas (Spain), 1994; La huella del cievo (Spain), 1994; En la plenitud del tiempo (Spain), 1994; *prose:* Some Americans: a personal record, 1980 (US); Poetry and Metamorphosis, 1983; The Letters of William Carlos Williams and Charles Tomlinson (US), 1992; *graphics:* Words and Images, 1972; In Black and White, 1975; Eden, 1985; *translations:* (with Henry Gifford): Versions from Fyodor Tyutchev, 1960; Castilian Ilexes: Versions from Antonio Machado, 1963; Ten Versions from Trilce by César Vallejo, (US) 1970; Translations, 1983; Attilio Bertolucci: selected poems, 1993; *edited:* Marianne Moore: A Collection of Critical Essays, (US) 1969; William Carlos Williams: A Collection of Critical Essays, 1972; William Carlos Williams: Selected Poems, 1976, rev. edn (US) 1985; Octavio Paz: Selected Poems, 1979; The Oxford Book of Verse in English Translation, 1980; George Oppen: selected poems, 1990; Eros Englished: erotic poems from the Greek and Latin, 1992; contribs to: Essays in Criticism, Hudson Review, Modern Painters, Poetry (Chicago), Poetry Nation Review, Sewanee Review, Times Lit. Supp., Vuetta. *Recreations:* music, walking. *Address:* Ozleworth, Glos GL12 7QB.

TOMLINSON, Sir Bernard (Evans), Kt 1988; CBE 1981; DL; MD; FRCP, FRCPath; Chairman, Northern Regional Health Authority, 1982–90; Emeritus Professor of Pathology, University of Newcastle upon Tyne, since 1985; Consultant Neuropathologist, Newcastle Health Authority (formerly Area Health Authority), since 1976; *b* 13 July 1920; *s* of James Arthur Tomlinson and Doris Mary (*née* Evans); *m* 1944, Betty Oxley; one *s* one *d. Educ:* Brunts Sch., Mansfield; University Coll. and University Coll. Hosp., London (BS 1943, MD 1962). FRCP 1965; FRCPath 1964. Trainee Pathologist, EMS, 1943–47; served RAMC as Specialist Pathologist, 1947–49 (Major). Newcastle upon Tyne General Hospital: Sen. Registrar, Pathology, 1949–50; Consultant Pathologist, 1950–53; Sen. Consultant Pathologist, 1953–82; Hon. Lectr in Path., Univ. of Newcastle upon Tyne, 1960–71, Hon. Prof., 1973–85. Hon. Mem. Scientific Staff, MRC Neurochemical Pathology Unit, 1987–. Chm., Jt Planning Appts Cttee, DHSS, 1986–90; Mem., Disablement Services Authority, 1987–91. Leader of indep. enquiry into London's health services, 1991–92; Non-exec. Dir, Newcastle City Health Trust, 1994–95. Privy Council Mem., RPharmS, 1990–95. Pres., NE Alzheimer Disease Soc., 1985–. Chm., Friends of Durham Cathedral, 1991–94. DL Tyne and Wear 1988. Gold medal Sci. Award, 3rd Internat. Conf. on Alzheimer's Disease, Padua, 1992. *Publications:* articles and book chapters on neuropath., partic. on path. of brain injury, brain changes in old age and on dementia. *Recreations:* gardening, golf, music, walking. *Address:* Greyholme, Wynbury Road, Low Fell, Gateshead, Tyne and Wear NE9 6TS.

TOMLINSON, Charles; *see* Tomlinson, A. C.

TOMLINSON, David (Cecil MacAlister); actor; *b* 7 May 1917; *s* of C. S. Tomlinson, Solicitor, Folkestone, Kent, and F. E. Tomlinson (*née* Sinclair-Thomson); *m* Audrey Freeman, actress; four *s. Educ:* Tonbridge Sch. Guardsman, Grenadier Guards, 1935–36; served War of 1939–45, Flight Lieut, Pilot, RAF; demobilised, 1946. Chief roles include: Henry, in The Little Hut, Lyric, Aug. 1950–Sept. 1953; Clive, in All for Mary, Duke of York's, June 1954–May 1955; David, in Dear Delinquent, Westminster and Aldwych, June 1957–July 1958; Tom, in The Ring of Truth, Savoy, July 1959; Robert in Boeing Boeing, Apollo, 1962; acted and directed: Mother's Boy (Nero), Globe, 1964; A Friend Indeed, Cambridge, 1966; The Impossible Years, Cambridge, 1966; On the Rocks (Prime Minister), Dublin Festival, 1969; A Friend Indeed, and A Song at Twilight, South Africa, 1973–74; The Turning Point, Duke of York's, 1974. First appeared in films, 1939; since then has appeared, in leading roles, in over 50 films. *Publication:* Luckier than Most (autobiog.), 1990. *Recreation:* putting my feet up. *Address:* Brook Cottage, Mursley, Bucks MK17 0RS. *Club:* Boodle's.

TOMLINSON, John; operatic bass; *b* 22 Sept. 1946; *s* of Rowland and Ellen Tomlinson; *m* 1969, Moya (*née* Joel); one *s* two *d. Educ:* Manchester Univ. (BSc Civil Engrg); Royal Manchester Coll. of Music. Since beginning career with Glyndebourne in 1970, has sung over 100 operatic bass roles with ENO, Royal Opera, Covent Garden, Opera North, Scottish Opera, and in Geneva, Lisbon, Milan, Copenhagen, Amsterdam, Stuttgart, Bayreuth, Berlin, Tokyo, Vienna, Paris, Bordeaux, Avignon, Aix-en-Provence, Orange, San Diego, San Francisco, Pittsburgh, Vancouver, NY, Munich, Chicago and Salzburg; best known for interpretations of Wagner bass and bass-baritone rôles, incl. Hans Sachs, Wotan, Hagen, Gurnemanz in Berlin, Covent Garden and Bayreuth Fest., 1988–94. *Address:* c/o Music International, 13 Ardilaun Road, Highbury, N5 2QR. *T:* 0171–359 5183.

TOMLINSON, John Edward; Member (Lab) Birmingham West, European Parliament, since 1984; European Parliamentary Labour Party Spokesman on Budgetary Control, since 1989; *b* 1 Aug. 1939; *s* of Frederick Edwin Tomlinson, headmaster, and Doris Mary Tomlinson; *m* 1963, Marianne Solveig Sommar, Stockholm; three *s* one *d. Educ:* Westminster City Sch.; Co-operative Coll., Loughborough; Nottingham Univ. (Dip. Polit. Econ. Social Studies); MA (Industrial Relations) Warwick, 1982. Sec., Sheffield Co-operative Party, 1961–68; Head of Research Dept, AUEW, 1968–70; Lectr in Industrial Relations, 1970–74. MP (Lab) Meriden, Feb. 1974–1979; PPS to Prime Minister, 1975–76; Parly Under-Sec. of State, FCO, 1976–79, and ODM, 1977–79. Sen. Lectr in Industrial Relations and Management, later Hd of Social Studies, Solihull Coll. of Tech., 1979–84. Vice Chm., Hansard Soc. Trustee, Industry and Parlt Trust. Contested (Lab) Warwicks N, 1983. *Publication:* Left, Right: the march of political extremism in Britain, 1981. *Address:* 34 Bridge Street, Walsall, WS1 1JQ. *Club:* West Bromwich Labour.

TOMLINSON, Prof. John Race Godfrey, CBE 1983; MA; Professor of Education and Director, Institute of Education, University of Warwick, since 1985; *b* 24 April 1932; *s* of John Angell Tomlinson and Beatrice Elizabeth Race Godfrey; *m* 1954, Audrey Mavis Barrett; two *s* two *d. Educ:* Stretford Grammar Sch.; Manchester Univ. (MA); London Inst. of Historical Research. Flt Lt, RAF, 1955–58. Teaching, 1958–60; Admin. Asst, Salop LEA, 1960–63; Asst Educn Officer, Lancs LEA, 1963–67; Dep. Dir of Educn, Cheshire LEA, 1967–72; Dir of Educn, Cheshire CC, 1972–84. Chairman: Schools Council, 1978–81; NICEC, 1985–89; Arts in Education Project, SCDC, 1985–90. Member: Court Cttee on Child Health Services, 1973–76; Gulbenkian enquiries into Drama, Music and Dance, 1974–78; Founder Chm., Further Educn Curriculum Review and Develt Unit, 1976; Member: Special Programmes Bd, MSC, 1977–82; Delegacy for Continuing Educn, Open Univ., 1978–81; Study Commn on the Family, 1978–83; Adv. Cttee on Supply and Trng of Teachers, 1979–82; Council, Foundn for Educn Business Partnerships, 1990–91; Educn Advr, RNCM, 1972–85. Chairman: Exec. Cttee and Trustees, Nat. Schs Curriculum Award, 1982–; MSC TVEI Quality and Standards Gp, 1986–88; Enquiry into Freedom of Information, ILEA, 1986–87; Gen. Teaching Council initiative, 1991–; FEFC Enquiry, Disability and Learning Difficulties, 1993–96. Royal Society of Arts: Vice-Pres., 1986; Chm., Exams Bd, 1986–89; Chm. Council, 1989–91 (Mem. Council, 1982–); FRSA 1976. Pres., Soc. of Educn Officers, 1982; Trustee, Community Service Volunteers, 1981–89; Edward Boyle Trust, 1988–; Comino Foundn, 1989–; Governor: Chetham's Sch., Manchester, 1984–92; Menuhin Sch., 1987–89. Hon. Prof., Dept of Educn, Keele Univ., 1981–84. Lectures: Wilfred Fish Meml, GDC, 1978; Charles Gittens Meml, Univ. of Wales, 1980; Lockyer, RCP, 1980; Schools Council, BAAS, 1981; Standing Conf. on Schools' Science and Technology Annual, 1987; Barry and Tye Meml, 1987; Internat. Schs Distinguished, 1994. FIMgt (MBIM 1976); FCP 1980. Hon. RNCM 1980. Freeman, City of London, 1989; Liveryman, Goldsmiths' Co., 1991– (Mem., Educn Cttee, 1982–89, 1994–). *Publications:* Additional Grenville Papers 1763–65, 1962; (ed) The Changing Government of Education, 1986; Teacher Appraisal: a nationwide approach, 1989; The Control of Education, 1993; School Co-operation: new forms of governance, 1994; articles in various jls. *Recreations:* family and garden, music and walking, a relentless search for good bitter. *Address:* Institute of Education, University of Warwick, Coventry CV4 7AL; Barn House, 76 Birmingham Road, Allesley, Coventry CV5 9GX. *Clubs:* Athenæum, Army and Navy.

TOMLINSON, Maj.-Gen. Michael John, CB 1981; OBE 1973 (MBE 1964); Secretary, The Dulverton Trust, 1984–94; Director Royal Artillery, 1981–84, retired; *b* 20 May 1929; *s* of late Sidney Tomlinson and Rose Hodges; *m* 1955, Patricia, *d* of late Lt-Col A. Rowland; one *s* one *d. Educ:* Skinners' Sch.; Royal Military Academy. Commissioned, RA, 1949; served in Brunei (despatches, 1962); GSO2 to Dir of Ops Borneo, 1962–64; DAMS, MoD, 1966–68; GSO1, Staff Coll. Camberley, 1968–70; CO, 2 Field Regt RA, 1970–72; Col GS, Staff Coll. Camberley, 1972–73; CRA 3rd Div., 1973–75; Student, RCDS, 1976; Dep. Mil. Sec. (B), MoD, 1976–78; Dir of Manning, Army, 1978–79; Vice-Adjt Gen., 1979–81. Col Comdt, RA, 1982–91; Hon. Colonel: 2 Field Regt, RA, 1985–89; 104 Regt RA (Volunteers), 1985–87. FIMgt (FBIM 1984); FRSA 1985.

Recreations: music, gardening. *Address:* c/o Lloyds Bank, 82 Mount Pleasant Road, Tunbridge Wells, Kent TN1 1RP. *Club:* Army and Navy.

TOMLINSON, Michael John; Director of Inspection, Office for Standards in Education, since 1995 (Deputy Director, 1992–95); *b* 17 Oct. 1942; *s* of Edith Cresswell and Jack Tomlinson; *m* 1965, Maureen Janet; one *s* one *d*. *Educ:* Oakwood Technical High Sch., Rotherham; Bournemouth Boys' Sch.; Durham Univ. (BSc Hons Chem.); Nottingham Univ. (post-grad. Cert Ed (First Div.)). Chemistry teacher, Henry Mellish GS, Nottingham, 1965–69; Head of Chemistry, Ashby-de-la-Zouch GS, 1969–77; School/Industry Liaison Officer, ICI (secondment), 1977; Chief Inspector (Schools), HM Inspectorate of Schs, 1989–92. Chem. Soc. Award in Chem. Educn (Bronze Medal), 1975. Silver Jubilee Medal, 1977. *Publications:* New Movements in the Study and Teaching of Chemistry, 1975; Organic Chemistry: a problem-solving approach, 1977; Mechanisms in Organic Chemistry: case studies, 1978; BP educn service contribs, 1974–78; articles in professional jls. *Recreations:* gardening, food and wine, reading. *Address:* Brooksby, Mayhall Lane, Chesham Bois, Amersham, Bucks HP6 5NR. *T:* Amersham (01494) 726967.

TOMLINSON, Prof. Richard Allan, FSA; Director, British School at Athens, since 1995; *b* 25 April 1932; *s* of James Edward Tomlinson and Dorothea Mary (*née* Grellier); *m* 1957, Heather Margaret Murphy; three *s* one *d*. *Educ:* King Edward's Sch., Birmingham; St John's Coll., Cambridge (BA, MA). FSA 1970. Asst, Dept of Greek, Univ. of Edinburgh, 1957; University of Birmingham: Asst Lectr 1958, Lectr 1961, Sen. Lectr 1969, Prof., 1971–95, Dept of Ancient History and Archaeology; Head of Sch. of Antiquity, 1988–91. British School at Athens: Editor, Annual, 1978–91; Chm. Managing Cttee, 1991–95. *Publications:* Argos and the Argolid, 1972; Greek Sanctuaries, 1976; Epidaurus, 1983; (ed) Greek Architecture, by A. W. Lawrence, 4th edn 1983; (contrib.) Sir Banister Fletcher, A History of Architecture, 19th edn, 1987; Greek Architecture, 1989; The Athens of Alma-Tadema, 1991; From Mycenae to Constantinople, 1992; Greek and Roman Architecture, 1995; articles in Annual of British Sch. at Athens, Jl of Hellenic Studies, Amer. Jl of Archaeology, etc. *Recreations:* architecture, walking. *Address:* British School at Athens 52 Sonedias, Athens 10676, Greece.

TOMLINSON, Prof. Sally, PhD; Goldsmiths' Professor of Policy and Management in Education, since 1992, and Pro Warden, since 1994, Goldsmiths' College, London University; *b* 22 Aug. 1936; *d* of Clifford Gilmore Entwistle and Alice Nora Stubbs; *m* 1957, Brian Joseph Tomlinson, Sqdn Ldr, RAF (retd); one *s* two *d*. *Educ:* Macclesfield Grammar Sch.; Liverpool Univ. (BA Hons); Birmingham Univ. (MSocSci); Warwick Univ. (PhD); Manchester Univ. (PGCE). Lectr and Sen. Lectr, West Midlands Coll. of Educn, 1970–74; Sen. Res. Fellow, Warwick Univ., 1974–78; Lectr, then Sen. Lectr, later Prof. of Educn, Lancaster Univ., 1978–91; Prof. of Educn, UC Swansea, 1991–92; Dean, Faculty of Educn, Goldsmiths' Coll., London Univ., 1992–95. Sen. Associate Mem., St Antony's Coll., Oxford, 1984–85. Trustee: Africa Educational Trust; Learning from Experience Trust; Foundn for After School Activities. *Publications:* (with John Rex) Colonial Immigrants in a British City, 1979; Education Subnormality, 1981; A Sociology of Special Education, 1982; Ethnic Minorities in British Schools, 1983; Home and School in Multicultural Britain, 1984; (ed with Len Barton) Special Education and Social Interests, 1984; (with David Smith) The School Effect, 1989; Multicultural Education in White Schools, 1990; Educational Reform and its consequences, 1994; (jtly) The Assessment of Special Educational Needs: whose problem?, 1994; (ed with Maurice Craft) Ethnic Relations and Schooling, 1995; many contribs to books and learned jls. *Recreations:* riding, walking, politics. *Address:* Goldsmiths' College, University of London, New Cross, SE14 6NW. *T:* 0171–919 7301.

TOMLINSON, Stephen Miles; QC 1988; a Recorder, since 1995; *b* 29 March 1952; *s* of Enoch Tomlinson and Mary Marjorie Cecilia Tomlinson (*née* Miles); *m* 1980, Joanna Kathleen Greig; one *s* one *d*. *Educ:* King's Sch., Worcester (schol.); Worcester Coll., Oxford (schol.; Eldon Law Schol.; MA). Called to the Bar, Inner Temple, 1974, Bencher, 1990. Lectr in Law, Worcester Coll., Oxford, 1974–76. *Recreations:* gardening, family, cricket. *Address:* 7 King's Bench Walk, Temple, EC4Y 7DS. *T:* 0171–583 0404. *Club:* MCC.

TOMPKINS, Prof. Frederick Clifford, FRS 1955; Professor in Physical Chemistry, Imperial College of Science and Technology, SW7, 1959–77, now Emeritus; Editor and Secretary of Faraday Division of The Chemical Society (formerly The Faraday Society), 1950–77, President, 1978; *b* 29 Aug. 1910; *m* 1936, Catherine Livingstone Macdougal; one *d*. *Educ:* Yeovil Sch.; Bristol Univ. Asst Lectr, King's Coll., Strand, 1934–37; Lectr and Senior Lectr, Natal Univ., Natal, S Africa, 1937–46; ICI Fellow, King's College, Strand, 1946–47; Reader in Physical Chemistry, Imperial College of Science and Technology, 1947; Hon. ARCS 1964. Hon. DSc Bradford, 1975. *Publications:* Chemisorption of Gases on Metals, 1978; contributions to Proc. Royal Society, Journal Chem. Soc., Trans Faraday Soc., Jl Chem. Physics, Zeitung Elektrochem.

TOMS, Carl, OBE 1969; First Head of Design, and Associate Director, for the Young Vic at the National Theatre, since 1970; *b* 29 May 1927. *Educ:* High Oakham Sch., Mansfield, Nottingham; Mansfield College of Art; Royal Coll. of Art; Old Vic Sch. Designing for theatre, films, opera, ballet, etc, on the London stage, 1957–; also for productions at Glyndebourne, Edinburgh Festival, Chichester Festival, and Aldeburgh (world première of Midsummer Night's Dream, 1960). *Theatre designs include:* Vivat! Vivat Regina!, Chichester and London, 1970, NY 1972; Sherlock Holmes, London, 1974, NY 1974 (Tony Award and Drama Desk Award for Theatre Design); Travesties, London, 1974, NY 1975, Vienna Burgtheater, 1976; Long Day's Journey into Night, LA 1977; Man and Superman, Malvern Festival and London, 1977; The Devil's Disciple, LA 1977, NY 1978; Look After Lulu, Chichester, 1978, Haymarket, 1978; Night and Day, Phoenix, 1978, NY, 1979; Stage Struck, Vaudeville, 1979; Windy City, Victoria Palace, 1982; The Real Thing, Strand, 1982; The Winslow Boy, Lyric, 1983; A Patriot for Me, Chichester and Haymarket, 1983, LA, 1984 (Hollywood Dramalogue Critics Award); The Hothouse, Vienna Burgtheater, 1983; Jeeves Takes Charge, NY, 1983; Hay Fever, Queen's, 1983; The Aspern Papers, 1984; Jumpers, Aldwych, 1985; The Dragon's Tail, Apollo, 1985; Blithe Spirit, Vaudeville, 1986; Wildfire, Phoenix, 1986; The Importance of Being Earnest, Royalty, 1987; Hapgood, Aldwych, 1988; The Browning Version, Royalty, 1988; Artist Descending a Staircase, Duke of York's, 1988; Richard II, Phoenix, 1988; Richard III, Phoenix, 1989; Hapgood, LA, 1989; Noël and Gertie, Comedy, 1989; Thark, Lyric, Hammersmith, 1989; Look Look!, Aldwych, 1990; The Silver King, Chichester, 1990; Private Lives, Aldwych, 1990; Painting Churches, Playhouse, 1991; Preserving Mr Panure, Chichester, 1991; It's Ralph, Comedy, 1991; Straight and Narrow, Wyndhams, 1992; An Ideal Husband, Globe, 1992; Separate Tables, Albery, 1993; She Stoops to Conquer, Queen's, 1993; Three Tall Women, Wyndham's, 1994; Indian Ink, Aldwych, 1995; *for Royal Opera House, Covent Garden,* include: Gala perf. for State Visit of King and Queen of Nepal, 1960; Iphigénie en Tauride, 1961; Ballet Imperial, 1963; Swan Lake, 1963; Die Frau ohne Schatten (costumes), 1967; Fanfare for Europe, 1973; Queen's Silver Jubilee Gala, 1977; Fanfare for Elizabeth, 1986; *for London Festival Ballet:* Swan Lake, 1982; for Sadler's Wells: Cenerentola, 1959; The Barber of Seville, 1960; Our Man in Havana, 1963; *for English National Ballet:* Swan Lake 1995; *for National Theatre:* Edward II, Love's Labour's Lost, 1968; Cyrano de Bergerac, 1970; For Services Rendered, 1979; Playbill, The Provok'd Wife, 1980 (SWET Designer of the Year award); The Second Mrs Tanqueray, On the Razzle, 1981; Rough Crossing, 1984; Brighton Beach Memoirs, Dalliance, The Magistrate, 1986; Six Characters in Search of an Author, Fathers and Sons, The Ting Tang Mine, 1987; *for RSC:* The Happiest Days of Your Life, 1984; The Man Who Came to Dinner, 1989; The Strange Case of Dr Jekyll and Mr Hyde, 1991; *for Vienna Nat. Theatre:* Travesties, 1977; She Stoops to Conquer, 1978; Betrayal, 1978; The Guardsman, 1979; Night and Day, 1980; *for Vienna State Opera:* Macbeth, 1982; Faust, 1985; *for NY City Opera:* Die Meistersinger von Nürnberg, 1975; The Marriage of Figaro, 1977; The Voice of Ariadne, 1977; Der Freischutz, 1981; Rigoletto, 1988; *for NY Metropolitan Opera:* Thais, 1978; *for San Diego Opera Co.:* Norma, 1976; La Traviata, 1976; The Merry Widow, 1977; Hamlet, 1978; Romeo and Juliet, 1982; *for San Francisco Opera:* Peter Grimes, 1973; Thais, 1976; The Italian Girl in Algiers (costumes), Geneva, 1984; Lucia di Lammermoor (costumes), Cologne Opera, 1985; Oberon, Edinburgh Fest. and Frankfurt, 1986; The Importance of Being Earnest, Royal Th., Copenhagen, 1987; Making it Better, Josephstadt Th., Vienna, 1991; Arcadia, Zurich, 1993. Other companies and theatres designed for include Old Vic, Young Vic, Welsh Nat. Opera, NY State Opera. Completed re-designing of: Theatre Royal, Windsor, 1965; Theatre Royal, Bath, 1982; Richmond Theatre, 1991; design consultant for Investiture of Prince of Wales, Caernarvon Castle, 1969. Has designed sets and costumes for numerous films; work has incl. decoration of restaurants, hotels, houses, etc; has also designed exhibns, programmes, cards, etc. FRSA 1987. *Publications:* Winter's Tale (designs for stage prod.), 1975; Scapino (designs for stage prod.), 1975. *Recreations:* gardening, travel. *Address:* The White House, Beaumont, near Wormley, Broxbourne, Herts EN10 7QJ. *T:* Hoddesdon (01992) 63961.

TOMS, Edward Ernest; Director, Porcelain & Pictures Ltd, since 1983; *b* 10 Dec. 1920; *s* of Alfred William and Julia Harrington Toms; *m* 1946, Veronica Rose, Dovercourt, Essex; three *s* one *d*. *Educ:* St Boniface's Coll.; Staff Coll., Camberley (psc), Nat. Defence Coll. (jssc). War service 1939–45; Captain Seaforth Highlanders; Special Forces, W Desert, Italy, Balkans, NW Europe; Regular Army, 1946, Seaforth Highlanders and QO Highlanders; Brigade Major, Berlin, 1959–61; Col GS (UK Cs-in-C Cttee), 1967–69. Principal, Home Civil Service, 1969; Asst Sec., Dept of Employment, 1973; seconded to Diplomatic Service as Counsellor, Bonn and Vienna, 1977–81; Internat. Labour Advr, FCO, 1981–83. *Recreation:* hill-walking (founder Mem., Aberdeen Mountain Rescue Assoc., 1964). *Address:* c/o Clydesdale Bank, 5 Castle Street, Aberdeen AB9 8AX. *Club:* Special Forces.

TOMSETT, Alan Jeffrey, OBE 1974; Director, Associated British Ports Holdings PLC, 1983–92 (Finance Director, 1983–87); chartered accountant; *b* 3 May 1922; *s* of Maurice Jeffrey Tomsett and Edith Sarah (*née* Mackelworth); *m* 1948, Joyce May Hill; one *s* one *d*. *Educ:* Trinity School of John Whitgift, Croydon; Univ. of London (BCom). JDipMA. Hodgson Harris & Co., Chartered Accountants, London, 1938. Served War, with RAF, 1941–46 (Middle East, 1942–45). Smallfield Rawlins & Co., Chartered Accountants, London, 1951; Northern Mercantile & Investment Corp. Ltd, 1955; William Baird & Co. Ltd, 1962–63. British Transport Docks Board, later Associated British Ports: Dep. Chief Accountant, 1963; Chief Accountant, 1964; Financial Controller, 1970; Bd Mem., 1974–87 (Finance Dir, 1974–85). Churchwarden, St John's, Shirley, 1988–92. FCA, FCMA, IPFA, FCIS, FCIT (Hon. Treasurer, 1982–88); FRSA 1969. *Address:* 102 Ballards Way, Croydon, Surrey CR0 5RG. *T:* 0181–657 5069.

TONBRIDGE, Bishop Suffragan of, since 1993; **Rt. Rev. Brian Arthur Smith;** *b* 15 Aug. 1943; *s* of late Arthur and of Doris Marion Smith; *m* 1970, Elizabeth Berring (*née* Hutchinson); two *d*. *Educ:* George Heriot's School, Edinburgh; Edinburgh Univ. (MA Mental Philosophy 1966); Fitzwilliam Coll., Cambridge (BA Theology 1968, MA 1972); Westcott House, Cambridge; Jesus Coll., Cambridge (MLitt 1973). Curate of Cuddesdon, 1972–79; Tutor in Doctrine, Cuddesdon Coll., Oxford, 1972–75; Dir of Studies, Ripon Coll., Cuddesdon, 1975–78, Senior Tutor 1978–79. Diocese of Wakefield: Priest-in-charge of Cragg Vale, 1979–85; Dir of In-Service Training, 1979–81; Dir of Ministerial Trng, 1981–87; Warden of Readers, 1981–87; Sec. of Dio. Board of Ministry, 1979–87; Hon. Canon of Wakefield, 1981–87; Proctor in Convocation, 1985–87; Archdeacon of Craven, 1987–93. Vice-Chairman, Northern Ordination Course, 1985–93. A Director, Scottish Jl of Theology, 1977–81. *Recreations:* browsing in junk shops, walking, reading, music, short-wave radio listening. *Address:* Bishop's Lodge, 48 St Botolph's Road, Sevenoaks, Kent TN13 3AG. *T:* Sevenoaks (01732) 456070.

TONBRIDGE, Archdeacon of; *no new appointment at time of going to press.*

TONČIĆ-SORINJ, Dr Lujo; Secretary-General, Council of Europe, 1969–74; *b* Vienna, 12 April 1915; *s* of Dušan Tončić-Sorinj (formerly Consul-Gen. in service of Imperial Ministry for Foreign Affairs), and Mabel (*née* Plason de la Woesthyne); *m* 1956, Renate Trenker; one *s* four *d*. *Educ:* Secondary sch. (Gymnasium), Salzburg. Studied law and philosophy at Univs of Vienna and Agram (Zagreb), 1934–41, also medicine and psychology (LLD Vienna); political science, Institut d'Etudes Politiques, Paris. Head of Polit. Dept of Austrian Research Inst. for Economics and Politics in Salzburg and Editor of Berichte und Informationen (political periodical published by Austrian Research Inst. for Economics and Politics), 1946–49. MP for Land Salzburg, 1949–66; Chairman: Legal Cttee of Austrian Parl., 1953–56; For. Affairs Cttee, 1956–59; in charge of For. Affairs questions, Austrian People's Party, 1959–66. Austrian Parly Observer to Consultative Assembly of Council of Europe, 1953–56; Austrian Mem., Consultative Assembly, 1956–66; Vice-Pres., Council of Europe; Vice-Pres., Political Commn, 1961–62; Minister for Foreign Affairs, Austria, 1966–68. Permanent Rep. of Austrian People's Party to Christian-Democratic Gp, European Parlt, 1980–; Rep. of Republic of Croatia to European Parlt, 1991–. Chm., Austrian Assoc. of UN, 1978–92; Pres., Union Internationale de la Propriété Immobilière, 1987–. Grand Cross of several orders including Order of St Michael and St George, Great Britain (Hon. GCMG). *Publications:* Erfüllte Träume (autobiog.), 1982; Am Abgrund vorbei, 1992; over 350 articles and essays on politics, economics, internat. law and history. *Recreations:* swimming, diving, history, geography. *Address:* 5020 Salzburg, Schloss Fürberg, Pausingerstrasse 11, Austria. *T:* (662) 642886.

TONEGAWA, Prof. Susumu; Professor of Biology, Center for Cancer Research and Department of Biology, Massachusetts Institute of Technology, since 1981; *b* Nagoya, 5 Sept. 1939; *s* of Tsutomo and Miyoko Tonegawa; *m* 1985, Mayumi Yoshinari; three *s*. *Educ:* Kyoto Univ. (BS); Univ. of San Diego (PhD). Postgraduate work: Univ. of California, San Diego, 1968–69; Salk Inst., San Diego, 1969–70; Mem., Basel Inst. of Immunology, 1971–81. Avery Landsteiner Prize, Ges. für Immunologie, 1981; Gairdner Foundn Internat. Award, 1983; Nobel Prize for Physiology or Medicine, 1987. *Address:* Massachusetts Institute of Technology, 77 Massachusetts Avenue, Cambridge, MA 02139–4307, USA.

TONGA, HM the King of; **King Taufa'ahau Tupou IV,** Hon. GCMG 1977 (Hon. KCMG 1968); Hon. GCVO 1970; Hon. KBE 1958 (Hon. CBE 1951); *b* 4 July 1918; *s* of Prince Uiliami Tupoulahi Tungi and Queen Salote Tupou of Tonga; *S* mother, 1965; *m* 1947, Halaevalu Mata'aho 'Ahome'e; three *s* one *d*. *Educ:* Tupou College, Tonga;

Newington College, Sydney; Wesley College, Sydney University. Minister for Health and Education, Tonga, 1943–50; Prime Minister, 1950–65. *Heir:* *s* HRH Prince Tupouto'a, *b* 4 May 1948. *Address:* The Palace, Nukualofa, Tonga. *T:* 21000.
See also HRH Prince Fatafehi Tu'ipelehake.

TONGE, Brian Lawrence, PhD; Director, Oxford Polytechnic, 1981–85; *b* 19 April 1933; *s* of Lawrence and Louisa Tonge; *m* 1955, Anne Billcliff; one *d*. *Educ:* Bury High Sch.; London Univ. (BSc 1st Cl. Chemistry); Manchester Univ. (PhD). FRIC 1964. Scientific Officer, Hirst Research Centre, GEC Ltd, 1956–59; Chemist, Medical Research Council Carcinogenic Substances Research Unit, Exeter Univ., 1959; Lectr in Chemistry, Plymouth Coll. of Technology, 1960–63; Research Manager, Pure Chemicals Ltd, 1963–65; Principal Lectr in Chemistry, West Ham Coll. of Technology, 1965–67; Head of Dept of Applied Science and Dean of Faculty of Science, Wolverhampton Polytechnic, 1967–71; Dep. Director, Oxford Polytechnic, 1971–81. Member, Wolfson Coll., Oxford, 1975–85. *Publications:* numerous contribs to learned jls and articles in scientific and educnl press. *Recreations:* gardening, reading, music. *Address:* 9 Ashleigh Park, Bampton, Devon EX16 9LF. *T:* Bampton (01398) 331122.

TONGUE, Carole; Member (Lab) London East, European Parliament, since 1984; *b* 14 Oct. 1955; *d* of Muriel Esther Lambert and Walter Archer Tongue; *m* 1990, Chris Pond, *qv*. *Educ:* Brentwood County High School; Loughborough University of Technology (BA Govt (Hons) and French). Asst Editor, Laboratory Practice, 1977–78; courier/guide in France with Sunsites Ltd, 1978–79; Robert Schuman scholarship for research in social affairs with European Parlt, Dec. 1979–March 1980; sec./admin. asst., Socialist Group of European Parlt, 1980–84. Dep. Leader, Eur. PLP, 1989–91. Bd Mem., Westminster Foundn for Democracy, 1992–. Sen. Vis. Fellow, Dept European Studies, Loughborough Univ. Member: CND; Co-operative Party; Fabian Soc.; World Women Parliamentarians for Peace. Trustee, CSV. *Recreations:* piano, cello, tennis, squash, horse riding, cinema, theatre, opera. *Address:* London East European Constituency Office, 97A Ilford Lane, Ilford, Essex IG1 2RJ. *T:* 0181–514 0198.

TONKIN, Hon. David Oliver, AO 1993, FRACO; Secretary-General, Commonwealth Parliamentary Association, 1986–92; *b* 20 July 1929; *s* of Oliver Athelstone Prisk Tonkin and Bertha Ida Louise (*née* Kennett); *m* 1954, Prudence Anne Juttner; three *s* three *d*. *Educ:* St Peter's Coll., Adelaide; Univ. of Adelaide (MB, BS 1953); Inst. of Ophthalmology, London (DO 1958). FRACO 1974. In private ophthalmic practice, 1958–70. Vis. staff, Royal Adelaide Hosp., 1958–68. Mem., Social Adv. Council, SA Govt, 1968–70; MLA (L) for Bragg, SA, 1970–83; Leader, Liberal Party of SA, 1975–82; Leader of the Opposition, 1975–79; Premier, Treasurer, Minister of State Development and of Ethnic Affairs, SA, 1979–82. Chm., Patient Care Review Cttee, Adelaide Children's Hosp., 1984–86. Chairman: State Opera of SA, 1985; SA Film Corp., 1994–. Hon. Consul of Belgium for SA and NT, 1984–85. Governor: Commonwealth Trust, 1990–94; Royal Commonwealth Soc. for the Blind, 1990–94; Trustee, Vision Aid Overseas, 1990–93. Governor, Queen Elizabeth House, Oxford, 1986–94. Freeman, City of London, 1981; Liveryman, Spectacle Makers' Co., 1992–. *Publications:* Sex Discrimination Bill, 1973; Patient Care Review: quality assurance in health care, 1985. *Recreations:* the family, music, film and theatre. *Address:* 5A Glenferrie Avenue, Myrtle Bank, SA 5064, Australia. *T:* (8) 3790419, *Fax:* (8) 3795001. *Clubs:* East India; Adelaide.

TONKIN, Derek, CMG 1982; HM Diplomatic Service, retired; Chairman: Beta Viet Nam Fund Ltd, since 1993; Beta Mekong Fund Ltd, since 1994; *b* 30 Dec. 1929; *s* of Henry James Tonkin and Norah Wearing; *m* 1953, Doreen Rooke; one *s* two *d* (and one *s* decd). *Educ:* High Pavement Grammar Sch., Nottingham; St Catherine's Society, Oxford (MA). HM Forces, 1948–49; FO, 1952; Warsaw, 1955; Bangkok, 1957; Phnom Penh, 1961; FO, 1963; Warsaw, 1966; Wellington, 1968; FCO, 1972; East Berlin, 1976; Ambassador to Vietnam, 1980–82; Minister, Pretoria, 1983–86; Ambassador to Thailand, and concurrently to Laos, 1986–89. Chairman: Ockenden Venture Gen. Cttee, 1990–; Adv. Bd, Centre for SE Asia Studies, SOAS, 1990–93; Thai–British Business Assoc., 1991–93; Vietnam-Britain Business Assoc., 1993–94. *Recreations:* tennis, music. *Address:* Heathfields, Berry Lane, Worplesdon, Guildford, Surrey GU3 3PU. *Club:* Royal Over-Seas League.

TONYPANDY, 1st Viscount *cr* 1983, of Rhondda in the County of Mid Glamorgan; **Thomas George Thomas;** PC 1968; *b* 29 Jan. 1909; *s* of Zacharia and Emma Jane Thomas. *Educ:* University Coll., Southampton. Schoolmaster. MP (Lab): Cardiff Central, 1945–50; Cardiff West, 1950–83; Speaker of the House of Commons, 1976–83; PPS, Min. of Civil Aviation, 1951; Mem., Chairman's Panel, H of C, 1951–64; Jt Parly Under-Sec. of State, Home Office, 1964–66; Minister of State: Welsh Office, 1966–67; Commonwealth Office, 1967–68; Secretary of State for Wales, 1968–70; Dep. Speaker and Chm. of Ways and Means, House of Commons, 1974–76. First Chm., Welsh Parly Grand Cttee, 1951; Chairman: Welsh PLP, 1950–51; Jt Commonwealth Societies' Council, 1984–87. Chm., Bank of Wales, 1985–91. Vice-Pres., Methodist Conf., 1960–61; President: Nat. Brotherhood Movement, 1955; Luton Methodist Industrial Coll., 1982; College of Preceptors, 1984–87; National Children's Home, 1990–95 (Chm., 1983–89). A Vice Pres., Macmillan Fund for Cancer Relief, 1994–. Life Governor, ICRF, 1994. Hon. Mem., Ct of Assts, Blacksmiths' Co., 1980. Freeman: Borough of Rhondda, 1970; City of Cardiff, 1975; City of London, 1980; Hon. Freeman: Paphos, Cyprus, 1989; Port Talbot, 1990. Hon. Master Bencher, Gray's Inn, 1982; Hon. Fellow: UC Cardiff, 1972; College of Preceptors, 1977; Polytechnic of Wales, 1982; St Hugh's Coll., Oxford, 1983; Hertford Coll., Oxford, 1983; Faculty of Bldg, 1983; Westminster Coll., Oxford, 1990; Trinity Coll., Carmarthen, 1994; Hon. Companion, Leicester Polytechnic, 1989. Hon. DCL Oxford, 1983; Hon. LLD: Asbury Coll., Kentucky, 1976; Southampton, 1977; Wales, 1977; Birmingham, 1978; Oklahoma, 1981; Liverpool, 1982; Leeds, 1983; Keele, 1984; Warwick, 1984; DUniv Open, 1984; Hon. DD Centenary Univ., Louisiana, 1982. William Hopkins Bronze Medal, St David's Soc., New York, 1982; Rhondda Rotary Paul Harris Award, 1992. Dato Setia Negara, Brunei, 1971; Grand Cross of the Peruvian Congress, 1982; Gold Medal for Democratic Services, State of Carinthia, Austria, 1982; Silver Medal of St Paul and St Barnabas, Cyprus, 1989. *Publications:* The Christian Heritage in Politics, 1960; George Thomas, Mr Speaker, 1985; My Wales, 1986. *Heir:* none. *Address:* House of Lords, SW1A 0AA. *Clubs:* Travellers', Reform, English-Speaking Union, United Oxford & Cambridge University; County (Cardiff).

TOOHEY, Mrs Joyce, CB 1977; Under-Secretary, Department of the Environment, 1970–76; *b* 20 Sept. 1917; *o d* of Louis Zinkin and Lena Zinkin (*née* Daiches); *m* 1947, Monty I. Toohey, MD, MRCP, DCH (*d* 1960); two *d*. *Educ:* Brondesbury and Kilburn High Sch.; Girton Coll., Cambridge; London Sch. of Economics. BA 1938, MA 1945, Cambridge. Asst Principal, Min. of Supply, 1941; transferred to Min. of Works, 1946; Principal, 1948; Asst Secretary, MPBW, 1956; Under-Secretary, 1964. Harvard Business Sch., 1970. *Recreations:* reading, walking. *Address:* 11 Kensington Court Gardens, W8 5QE. *T:* 0171–937 1559.

TOOK, John Michael Exton, MBE 1964; Controller, Europe and North Asia Division, British Council, 1983–86, retired; Director, United Kingdom Committee of the European Cultural Foundation, since 1992; *b* 15 Sept. 1926; *s* of late George Took, Dover, and Ailsa Clowes (*née* Turner); *m* 1964, Judith Margaret, *d* of late Brig. and Mrs W. J. Birkle; two *d*. *Educ:* Dover Coll.; Jesus Coll., Cambridge (MA, Mod. and Med. Langs Tripos). Served Indian Army, 1944–47, Captain. HM Colonial Admin. Service (later HMOCS), N Rhodesia, 1950–57; Min. of External Affairs, Fedn of Rhodesia & Nyasaland, 1957–63; Min. of External Affairs, Republic of Zambia, 1964–65; joined British Council, 1965; Asst Reg. Dir, Frankfurt, 1965–67; Reg. Dir, Cape Coast, 1967–69; Rep., Cyprus, 1971–74; Cultural Attaché, British Embassy, Budapest, 1974–77; Dep. Controller, European Div., 1977–80; Rep., Greece, 1980–83. *Publications:* Common Birds of Cyprus, 1973, 4th edn 1986; Birds of Cyprus, 1992; contribs to ornithological jls. *Recreations:* ornithology, fishing, natural history. *Address:* Pilgrims, Appledore, near Ashford, Kent TN26 2AE. *T:* Appledore (01233) 758215. *Club:* United Oxford & Cambridge University.

TOOKEY, Richard William, CBE 1984; Director and Group Public Affairs Co-ordinator, Shell International Petroleum Co. Ltd, 1984–93; *b* 11 July 1934; *s* of Geoffrey William Tookey, QC and Rosemary Sherwell Tookey (*née* Clogg); *m* 1st, 1956, Jill (*née* Ransford) (marr. diss. 1994); one *s* one *d* (and one *s* decd); 2nd, 1994, Colleen (*née* Channon). *Educ:* Charterhouse. National Service, 2nd Lieut, 1st King's Dragoon Guards, 1952–54; Lanarkshire Yeomanry (TA), 1954–56; Inns of Court Regt/Inns of Court and City Yeomanry (TA), 1957–64. Joined Royal Dutch/Shell Group, 1954; posts in internat. oil supply and trading, 1954–73; Head of Supply Operations, 1973–75; Vice-Pres., Shell Internat. Trading Co., 1975–77; Man. Dir, Shell Tankers (UK) Ltd, 1978–79, Chm., 1980–84; Man. Dir, Shell Internat. Marine Ltd, 1980–84; Marine Co-ordinator, Shell Internat. Petroleum Co. Ltd, 1980–84. Part-time Mem., BRB, 1985–90; Mem., Gen. Cttee, Lloyd's Register of Shipping, 1978–85; Pres., Gen. Council of British Shipping, 1983–84. Liveryman, Shipwrights' Co., 1983–, Mem. Ct of Assts, 1987–. *Recreations:* home, garden. *Address:* Corner Cottage, Broad Oak, Heathfield, E Sussex TN21 8UE. *T:* Heathfield (01435) 862420.

TOOLEY, Sir John, Kt 1979; Arts consultant, since 1988; General Director, Royal Opera House, Covent Garden, 1980–88; *b* 1 June 1924; *yr s* of late H. R. Tooley; *m* 1st, 1951, Judith Craig Morris (marr. diss., 1965); three *d*; 2nd, 1968, Patricia Janet Norah Bagshawe (marr. diss. 1990), 2nd *d* of late G. W. S. Bagshawe; one *s*. *Educ:* Repton; Magdalene Coll., Cambridge. Served The Rifle Brigade, 1943–47. Sec., Guildhall School of Music and Drama, 1952–55; Royal Opera House, Covent Garden: Asst to Gen. Administrator, 1955–60; Asst Gen. Administrator, 1960–70; Gen. Administrator, 1970–80. Chairman: Nat. Music Council Executive, 1970–72; HEFCE Music Conservatories Adv. Gp, 1993–. Chm., Almeida Th., 1990–; Director: Britten Estate Ltd, 1989–; South Bank Bd, 1991–; Compton Verney Opera Project, 1991–; WNO, 1992–; Consultant: Internat. Management Gp, 1988–; Ballet Opera House, Toronto, 1989–90; Trustee: Wigmore Hall; SPNM; Britten Pears Foundn, 1989–; Dartington Summer Sch., 1989–; Purcell Tercentenary Trust, 1991–; Pres., Salisbury Festival, 1988–; Chm., Salisbury Cathedral Fabric Cttee, 1990–. Gen. Advr, Internat. Istanbul Fest, 1993–. Governor, Repton Sch., 1984–94. Hon. FRAM; Hon. GSM; Hon. RNCM. Commendatore, Italian Republic, 1976. *Recreations:* walking, theatre. *Address:* 23 Warwick Square, SW1V 2AB. *T:* 0171–630 9711, *Fax:* 0171–233 7045. *Clubs:* Garrick, Arts.

TOOMEY, Ralph; Under-Secretary, Department of Education and Science, 1969–78; *b* 26 Dec. 1918; *s* of late James and Theresa Toomey; *m* 1951, Patricia Tizard; two *d*. *Educ:* Cyfarthfa Grammar Sch., Merthyr Tydfil; University Coll., London; Univ. of Caen. Served British and Indian Army, 1940–46. Teacher, Enfield Grammar Sch., 1947; Lecturer, Univ. of London, at Sch. of Oriental and African Studies, 1948. Min. of Education, 1948–60 and 1963–78 (seconded to Govt of Mauritius, 1960–63, Principal Asst Sec. in Colonial Secretary's Office and Min. of Local Govt and Co-operative Develt). A UK Rep., High Council, European Univ. Inst., Florence, 1974–78. DUniv Open, 1979. *Address:* 8 The Close, Montreal Park, Sevenoaks, Kent TN13 2HE. *T:* Sevenoaks (01732) 452553. *Club:* Knole Park Golf (Sevenoaks).

TOOTH, Geoffrey Cuthbert, MD, MRCP, DPM; Visiting Scientist, National Institute of Mental Health, USA, 1968–71; *b* 1 Sept. 1908; *s* of late Howard Henry Tooth, CB, CMG, MD, FRCP, and late Helen Katherine Tooth, OBE (*née* Chilver); *m* 1st, 1934, Princess Olga Galitzine (*d* 1955), *d* of Prince Alexander Galitzine, MD; 2nd, 1958, HSH Princess Xenia of Russia, *d* of Prince Andrew of Russia. *Educ:* Rugby Sch.; St John's Coll., Cambridge; St Bartholomew's Hosp.; Johns Hopkins Hosp., Baltimore, Md, USA. MRCS, LRCP 1934, MA Cantab 1935, MD Cantab 1946, DPM 1944; MRCP 1965. Asst Psychiatrist, Maudsley Hosp., 1937–39. Surg. Lt-Comdr, RNVR, Neuropsychiatric Specialist, 1939–45. Colonial Social Science Research Fellow, 1946–53; Comr, Bd of Control, 1954–60; transf. to Min. of Health, and retd as Sen. PMO, Head of Mental Health Section, Med. Div., 1968. Mem. Expert Advisory Panel (Mental Health), WHO. *Publications:* Studies in Mental Illness in the Gold Coast, 1950; various reports to learned societies; articles and papers in med. jls. *Recreations:* sailing, gardening, metal work, photography. *Address:* Grand Prouillac, Plazac, 24580 Rouffignac, France.

TOOTH, Sir (Hugh) John L.; *see* Lucas-Tooth.

TOOZE, Dr John, FRS 1994; Director of Support Services, Imperial Cancer Research Fund, since 1994; *b* 16 May 1938; *s* of Reginald John Tooze and Doris Edith Tooze (*née* Bull); *m* 1st, 1962, Sarah Margaret Wynn (marr. diss.); two *s* one *d*; 2nd, 1983, Sharon Ann Queally; one *s* one *d*. *Educ:* Handsworth Grammar Sch., Birmingham; Jesus Coll., Cambridge (BA 1961); King's Coll. London (PhD 1965); Harvard Univ. Served Army, 1956–58. King's College London: Asst Lectr in Biophysics, 1961–65; Lectr, 1965–68; Wellcome Res. Fellow, Harvard Univ., 1965–67; Dep. Editor, Nature, 1968–70; Res. Administrator, ICRF, 1970–73; Exec. Sec., EMBO, Heidelberg, 1973–94; Associate Dir, EMBL, 1993–94. Editor: Trends in Biochemistry, 1979–85, EMBO Jl, 1982–. Trustee, Darwin Trust of Edinburgh, 1991–. EMBO Medal, 1986. *Publications:* Molecular Biology of Tumor Viruses, 1973; DNA Tumor Viruses, 1980; (with J. D. Watson) The DNA Story, 1982; (with C. I. Branden) Introduction to Protein Structure, 1991. *Recreations:* numismatics, English history, gardening. *Address:* Imperial Cancer Research Fund, PO Box No 123, Lincoln's Inn Fields, WC2A 3PX. *T:* 0171–242 0200. *Club:* Athenæum.

TOPE, family name of **Baron Tope.**

TOPE, Baron *cr* 1994 (Life Peer), of Sutton in the London Borough of Sutton; **Graham Norman Tope,** CBE 1991; Leader of Council, London Borough of Sutton, since 1986; President, London Liberal Democrats, since 1991; *b* 30 Nov. 1943; *s* of late Leslie Tope, Plymouth and Winifred Tope (*née* Merrick), Bermuda; *m* 1972, Margaret East; two *s*. *Educ:* Whitgift Sch., S Croydon. Company Sec., 1965–72; Insce Manager, 1970–72; Dep. Gen. Sec., Voluntary Action Camden, 1975–90. Pres., Nat. League of Young Liberals, 1973–75 (Vice-Chm., 1971–73); Mem., Liberal Party Nat. Council, 1970–76; Exec. Cttee, London Liberal Party, 1981–84. Sutton Council: Councillor 1974–; Leader, Lib Dem (formerly Soc & Lib Dem) Group, 1988– (Liberal Gp, 1974–83, Liberal/SDP Alliance Gp, 1983–88); Leader of Opposition, 1984–86. MP (L) Sutton and Cheam, 1972–Feb. 1974; Liberal Party spokesman on environment, Dec. 1972–1974; contested (L) Sutton and Cheam, Oct. 1974. Mem., Policy Cttee, AMA, 1989–; Chm., Policy and

Finance Cttee, London Boroughs Assoc., 1994–95; UK Rep., EU Cttee of the Regions, 1994–. Lib Dem spokesman on educn, H of L. Mem. Leaders' Cttee, Assoc. of London Govt, 1995–. *Publication:* (jtly) Liberals and the Community, 1974. *Address:* 88 The Gallop, Sutton, Surrey SM2 5SA. *T:* 0181–770 7269.

TOPHAM, Surgeon Captain Lawrence Garth, RN (Retd); Consultant Physician in Geriatric Medicine, Central Hampshire District Winchester and Andover Hospitals, 1974–83; *b* 14 Nov. 1914; *s* of late J. Topham and late Mrs Topham; *m* 1943, Olive Barbara Marshall (VAD), *yr d* of late J. Marshall and late Mrs Marshall; one *s* one *d*. *Educ:* Bradford Grammar Sch.; Univ. of Leeds. MB, ChB 1937; MD 1946; MRCPE 1957; FRCPE 1967; MRCP 1969. Joined RN 1938. Served War: HMS Newcastle and HMS Milford, 1939–41; USN Flight Surgeon's Wings, 1943; RN Fleet Air Arm Pilot's Wings, 1944. Pres., Central Air Med. Bd, 1949; HMS Sheffield, 1951; Med. Specialist and Consultant in Medicine, at RN Hosps, Trincomalee, Haslar and Plymouth, 1952–66; Prof. of Med., RN, and RCP, 1966–71; QHP 1970; retd at own request, from RN, 1971. House Governor and Medical Superintendent, King Edward VII Convalescent Home for Officers, Osborne, IoW, 1971–74. Member: British Nat. Cttee, Internat. Soc. of Internal Medicine; British Geriatric Soc.; Wessex Physicians Club. OStJ (Officer Brother) 1970. *Publications:* several articles in med. jls, especially on subject of diseases of the chest. *Recreations:* Rugby football refereeing, rowing, photography, Oriental cookery. *Address:* Tilings, 3 Holt Close, Wickham, Hants PO17 5EY. *T:* Wickham (01329) 832072.

TOPLEY, Keith; *see* Topley, W. K.

TOPLEY, Kenneth Wallis Joseph, CMG 1976; Secretary for Education and Manpower, Hong Kong, 1981–83, retired; *b* 22 Oct. 1922; *s* of William Frederick Topley, MC and Daisy Elizabeth (*née* Wellings); *m* 1st, 1949, Marjorie Doreen Wills (marr. diss.); two *s* two *d*; 2nd, 1989, Barbara Newman Hough. *Educ:* Dulwich Coll.; Aberdeen Univ.; London Sch. of Econs and Pol. Science (BScEcon 1949). Served War, RAFVR, 1941–46 (Flt Lieut). Westminster Bank, 1939–41; Mass-Observation, 1941; Malayan Civil Service, 1950–55: Econ. Affairs Secretariat, Comr Gen.'s Office, and Labour Dept; Hong Kong Civil Service, 1955–83: various appts, 1955–62; Comr for Co-operative Develt and Fisheries, 1962–64; Sec., UGC, 1965–67; Comr for Census and Statistics, 1970–73; Dir of Social Welfare, 1973–74; Dir of Educn, 1974–80; Chm., Cttee to Review Post-Secondary and Technical Educn, 1980–81. Secretary: Univ. of E Asia, Macau, 1984–88; E Asia Open Inst, 1988–90. Commandeur de l'Ordre des Arts et des Lettres (France), 1987. *Recreations:* walking, study of society. *Address:* Chantry Cottage, One the Square, Chilham, Kent CT4 8BY. *Club:* Royal Hong Kong Jockey (Hong Kong).

TOPLEY, (William) Keith, MA; Senior Master of the Supreme Court (Queen's Bench Division) and Queen's Remembrancer, since 1990; Admiralty Registrar of the Supreme Court, 1986–92; *b* 19 Jan. 1936; *s* of late Bryan Topley and Grizel Hester (*née* Stirling); *m* 1980, Clare Mary Pennington; one *s* by former marriage. *Educ:* Bryanston School; Trinity Coll., Oxford (MA). Called to Bar, Inner Temple, 1959, Bencher, 1990; Master of Supreme Court, QBD, 1980–90. Mem., Bar Council, 1967–68. Mem. Adv. Bd, Coll. of Law, 1992–. Freeman, City of London, 1993; Mem., Watermen and Lightermen's Co., 1993–. *Publication:* (ed jtly) Supreme Court Practice, 1988, 1991. *Recreations:* golf, sailing. *Address:* 22 Queens Road, Cowes, Isle of Wight PO31 8BJ. *T:* Cowes (01983) 299742. *Clubs:* Garrick; Royal Yacht Squadron, Royal London Yacht (Cowes); Bar Yacht (Cdre, 1992–95); New Zealand Golf.

TOPOLSKI, Daniel; freelance writer and broadcaster; photo-journalist; Oxford Boat-Race coach, 1973–87 and 1995; *b* 4 June 1945; *s* of late Feliks Topolski and Marion Everall; partner, Susan Gilmore; two *d*. *Educ:* Lycée Français, London; Westminster Sch.; New Coll., Oxford (BA, Geography 1967; DipSoc Anthropology 1968, MA 1970). Writer and TV broadcaster on travel and sport; BBC TV Researcher and Producer, 1969–73; TV and Radio presenter and commentator, 1982–; expedition leader: Brazil, 1963; Iran (Marco Polo), 1973–74; travel in Africa, North and South America, India, Himalayas, China, Middle East, SE Asia, Australia. Rowing Competitor: Boat Race, Oxford, 1967, 1968; World Championships, 1969–78 (Gold medal 1977); Henley Regatta (4 victories); Rowing Coach: Oxford Boat Race Crew, 1973–87 (12 victories, record 10 in a row); Nat. Women's Squad, 1979–80; Nat. Men's Pair and Women's Pair, 1982; Nat. Men's Pair, Olympics, 1984. Churchill Fellow, 1980. Radio Travel Prog. of the Year award for Topolski's Travels, 1993. *Publications:* Muzungu: one man's Africa, 1976; (with Feliks Topolski) Travels with my Father: journey through South America, 1983; Boat Race, 1985; (with Patrick Robinson) True Blue, 1989 (Sports Book of the Year, 1990); Henley: the Regatta, 1989. *Recreations:* theatre, cinema, rowing (Steward, Henley Regatta), ski-ing, travel, family. *Address;* 69 Randolph Avenue, W9 1DW. *T:* 0171–289 8939. *Clubs:* Morton's; London Rowing (Putney); Leander (Henley).

TOPP, Air Commodore Roger Leslie, AFC 1950 (Bar 1955, 2nd Bar 1957); independent consultant, aviation and defence; *b* 14 May 1923; *s* of William Horace Topp and Kathleen (*née* Peters); *m* 1945, Audrey Jane Jeffery; one *s* one *d*. *Educ:* North Mundham Sch.; RAF, Cranwell. Served War: Pilot trg, Canada, 1943–44, commissioned 1944; 'E' Sqdn Glider Pilot Regt, Rhine Crossing, 1945. Nos 107 and 98 Mosquito Sqdns, Germany, 1947–50; Empire Test Pilots' Sch. and RAE Farnborough, 1951–54; Commanded No 111 Fighter Sqdn (Black Arrows) Aerobatic Team, 1955–58; Allied Air Forces Central Europe, Fontainbleau, 1959; Sector Operational Centre, Brockzetel, Germany, 1959–61; jssc, Latimer, 1961–62; commanded Fighter Test Sqdn, Boscombe Down, 1962–64; Station Cmdr, RAF Coltishall, 1964–66; Nat. Def. Coll., Canada, 1966–67; Opl Requirements, MoD (Air), London, 1967–69; Multi-role Combat Aircraft Project, Munich, 1969–70; HQ No 38 Gp, Odiham, 1970; Commandant, Aeroplane and Armament Experimental Estabt, Boscombe Down, 1970–72; Dep. Gen. Man., Multi-role Combat Aircraft Develt and Production Agency, Munich, 1972–78; retd from RAF, 1978. Consultant to Ferranti Defence Systems Ltd, Scotland (Aviation and Defence, FRG), 1978–88. *Recreations:* golf, sailing. *Address:* Cedar Lodge, Meadow Drive, Hoveton St John, Norfolk NR12 8UN. *Clubs:* Royal Air Force; Royal Fowey Yacht.

TOPPING, Rev. Frank; actor, author and broadcaster; *b* 30 March 1937; *s* of late Frank and Dorothy Topping; *m* 1958, June Berry; two *s* one *d*. *Educ:* St Anne's Convent Sch., Birkenhead; St Anselm's Christian Brother Coll., Birkenhead; North West School of Speech and Drama; Didsbury Coll., Bristol. Served RAF, Cyprus, 1955–57. Leatherhead Rep. Th., 1957–59; Royal Court, Chelsea, 1959; Wolverhampton Rep. Th., 1959; Granada TV, 1960–64; read Theology at Didsbury Coll., Bristol, 1964–67; asst minister at Dome Methodist Mission, Brighton, and methodist univ. chaplain at Sussex, 1967–70; also freelance broadcaster, BBC Radio Brighton, 1967–70; ordained 1970; staff producer, BBC, 1970–80. Song-writing partnership with Donald Swann, 1973–81; two man show, Swann with Topping, played in Jersey, London fringe theatre, then at Ambassadors; presented three one-man plays, Edinburgh Fest. Fringe, 1986. TV appearances: own series, Sunday Best, 1981, and Topping on Sunday, 1982–84; The 5 Minute Show (weekday series), TVS, 1989–90. Author of radio plays: On the Hill, 1974 (Grace Wyndham Goldie UNDA Dove award, 1975); A Particular Star, 1977. Formed Emmaus Theatre Prodns with wife, 1993. *Publications:* Lord of the Morning, 1977; Lord of the Evening, 1979; Lord of my Days, 1980; Working at Prayer, 1981; Pause for Thought with Frank Topping, 1981; Lord of Life, 1982; The Words of Christ: forty meditations, 1983; God Bless You—Spoonbill, 1984; Lord of Time, 1985; An Impossible God, 1985; Wings of the Morning, 1986; Act Your Age, 1989; Laughing in my Sleep (autobiog.), 1993; All the Days of my Life, 1994. *Recreations:* sailing, travel, photography, late night conversation. *Address:* 34 Eastland Road, Thornbury, Bristol BS12 1DS. *T:* (0850) 261539. *Clubs:* Naval; Hurst Castle Sailing (Keyhaven, Hants).

TORDOFF, family name of **Baron Tordoff.**

TORDOFF, Baron *cr* 1981 (Life Peer), of Knutsford in the County of Cheshire; **Geoffrey Johnson Tordoff;** President of the Liberal Party, 1983–84; Lib Dem Chief Whip, House of Lords, 1988–94 (Liberal Chief Whip, 1984–88; Deputy Chief Whip, 1983–84); *b* 11 Oct. 1928; *s* of Stanley Acomb Tordoff and Annie Tordoff (*née* Johnson); *m* 1953, Mary Patricia (*née* Swarbrick); two *s* three *d*. *Educ:* North Manchester School; Manchester Grammar School; Univ. of Manchester. Contested (L), Northwich 1964, Knutsford 1966, 1970. Chairman: Liberal Party Assembly Cttee, 1974–76; Liberal Party, 1976–79 (and its Campaigns and Elections Cttee, 1980, 1981); Member, Liberal Party Nat. Executive, 1975–84. Principal Dep. Chm. of Cttees and Chm., H of L Select Cttee on the EC, 1994–. Chm., ME Cttee, Refugee Council, 1990–95. Mem., Press Complaints Commn, 1995–. *Address:* House of Lords, SW1A 0PW.

TORNARITIS, Criton George, QC (Cyprus); LLB (Hons, Athens); Attorney-General of the Republic of Cyprus, 1960–84 (Attorney-General, Cyprus, 1952); seconded as Commissioner for Consolidation of the Cyprus Legislation, 1956; Special Legal Adviser of the President of the Republic of Cyprus; *b* 27 May 1902; *m* 1934, Mary (*née* Pitta) (*d* 1973); one *s*. *Educ:* Gymnasium of Limassol; Athens University; Gray's Inn. Advocate of the Supreme Court of Cyprus, 1924; District Judge, Cyprus, 1940; President District Court, Cyprus, 1942; Solicitor-General, Cyprus, 1944; Attorney-General, Cyprus, 1952. Attached to Legal Div. of the Colonial Office, 1955. Legal Adviser to Greek-Cypriot Delegation on the Mixed Constitutional Commission, 1959; Greek-Cypriot delegate to Ankara for initialling of Constitution of Republic of Cyprus, 1960. Prize of Academy of Athens, 1984. *Publications:* The Laws of Cyprus, rev. edn, 1959; The individual as a subject of international law, 1972; The Turkish invasion of Cyprus and legal problems arising therefrom, 1975; The European Convention of Human Rights in the Legal Order of the Republic of Cyprus, 1975; The Ecclesiastical Courts especially in Cyprus, 1976; Cyprus and its Constitutional and other Legal Problems, 1977, 2nd edn 1980; Federalism and Regionalism in the Contemporary World, 1979; The State Law of the Republic of Cyprus, 1982; Constitutional Review of the Laws in the Republic of Cyprus, 1983; The Legal System in the Republic of Cyprus, 1984; The Legal Position of the Church in the Republic of Cyprus, 1989; contributions to legal journals and periodicals. *Recreations:* walking, reading. *Address:* 11 Penelope Delta Street, Nicosia, Cyprus. *T:* (2) 376252.

TORNEY, Thomas William; JP; *b* London, 2 July 1915; *m* (wife decd); one *d*; *m* 2nd, 1987. *Educ:* elementary school. Joined Labour Party, 1930; Election Agent: Wembley North, 1945; Derbyshire West, 1964. Derby and Dist Area Organizer, USDAW, 1946–70. Member: (Past Chm.) North Midland Regional Joint Apprenticeship Council for catering industry, 1946–68; Local Appeals Tribunal, Min. of Social Security, 1946–68. MP (Lab) Bradford South, 1970–87. Member: Parly Select Cttee on Race Relations and Immigration, 1970–79; Parly Select Cttee on Agriculture, 1979–87; Chm., PLP Gp on Agriculture, Fish and Food, 1981–87. Especially interested in education, social security, industrial relations, agriculture and food. JP Derby, 1969. Chevalier, Commanderie of GB, Confrérie des Chevaliers du Sacavan d'Anjou, 1976.

ToROBERT, Sir Henry Thomas, KBE 1981; Governor and Chairman of the Board of the Bank of Papua New Guinea since its formation, 1973–93; Partner, Deloitte Touche Tohmatsu, PNG, since 1993; Chairman, Credit Corporation (PNG) Ltd, since 1993; *b* Kokopo, 1942. *Educ:* primary educn in East New Britain; secondary educn in Qld, Australia; Univ. of Sydney, Aust. (BEcon. 1965). Asst Research Officer, Reserve Bank of Australia, Port Moresby, 1965 (one of first local officers to join the bank); Dep. Manager, Port Moresby Branch, 1971; Manager of the Reserve Bank, 1972 (the first Papua New Guinean to hold such a position at a time when all banks were branches of the Aust. commercial banks). Member of the cttee responsible for working out a PNG banking system which came into effect by an act of parliament in 1973; Chairman: Management Bd, PNG Bankers' Coll., 1973–; PNG Currency Working Group advising the Govt on arrangements leading to the introduction of PNG currency, the Kina; ToRobert Cttee to look into problems of administration in PNG Public Service, 1979 (ToRobert Report, 1979); Council, PNG Inst. of Applied Social and Econ. Res., 1975–82; Govt Super Task Force on project implementation, 1994–. Pres., PNG Amateur Sports Fedn and PNG Olympic and Commonwealth Games Cttee, 1980–. *Address:* PO Box 898, Port Moresby, Papua New Guinea.

TORONTO, Archbishop of, (RC), since 1990; **Most Rev. Aloysius Matthew Ambrozic;** *b* 27 Jan. 1930; *s* of Aloysius Ambrozic and Helena (*née* Pecar). *Educ:* St Augustine's Seminary, Scarborough, Ont; Angelicum Rome (STL); Biblicum, Rome, 1957–60 (SSL); Univ. of Würzburg, Germany (ThD). Ordained, 1955; Curate, St Teresa's, Port Colborne, Ont, 1955–57; Professor: St Augustine's Seminary, Scarborough, Ont, 1960–67; Toronto Sch. of Theol., 1970–76; Auxiliary Bishop of Toronto, 1976–86; Coadjutor Archbishop of Toronto, 1986–90. *Publications:* The Hidden Kingdom, 1972; Remarks on the Canadian Catechism, 1974; Oce, posvečeno bodi tvoje ime, 1980. *Recreations:* hiking, swimming. *Address:* 355 Church Street, Toronto, Ontario M5B 1Z8, Canada. *T:* (416) 9771500.

TORONTO, Bishop of, since 1989; **Rt. Rev. Terence Edward Finlay;** *b* 19 May 1937; *s* of Terence John Finlay and Sarah McBryan; *m* 1962, Alice-Jean Cracknell; two *d*. *Educ:* Univ. of Western Ontario (BA); Huron Coll., London, Ont (BTh); Cambridge Univ., Eng. (MA). Deacon1961, priest 1962; Dean of Residence, Renison Coll., Waterloo, Canada; Incumbent: All Saints, Waterloo, 1964–66; St Aidan's, London, Canada, 1966–68; Rector: St John the Evangelist, London, 1968–78; Grace Church, Brantford, 1978–82; Archdeacon of Brant, 1978–82; Incumbent, St Clement's, Eglinton, Toronto, 1982–86; a Suffragan Bishop, Diocese of Toronto, 1986; Coadjutor Bishop, 1987. DD: (*jure dignitatis*) Huron Coll., 1987; (*hc*) Wycliffe Coll., 1988; (*hc*) Trinity Coll., 1989. *Recreations:* music, ski-ing, travel. *Address:* Synod Office, 135 Adelaide Street E, Toronto, Ont M5C 1L8, Canada. *T:* (416) 3636021.

TORONTO, Bishops Suffragan of; *see* Bedford-Jones, Rt Rev. M.; Blackwell, Rt Rev. D. C.; Matthews, Rt Rev. V.; Pryce, Rt Rev. J. T.

TORPHICHEN, 15th Lord *cr* 1564; **James Andrew Douglas Sandilands;** *b* 27 Aug. 1946; *s* of 14th Lord Torphichen, and Mary Thurstan, *d* of late Randle Henry Neville Vaudrey; *S* father, 1975; *m* 1976, Margaret Elizabeth, *o d* of late William A. Beale and of Mrs Margaret Patten Beale, Peterborough, New Hampshire, USA; four *d*. *Heir: cousin* Douglas Robert Alexander Sandilands [*b* 31 Aug. 1926; *m* 1949, Ethel Louise Burkitt; one *s*; *m* Suzette Véva (*née* Pernet); two *s*]. *Address:* Calder House, Mid-Calder, West Lothian EH53 0HN.

TORRANCE, Rev. Professor James Bruce; Professor of Systematic Theology, King's College, University of Aberdeen, and Christ's College, Aberdeen, 1977–89 (Dean of the Faculty of Divinity, 1978–81), now Professor Emeritus; *b* 3 Feb. 1923; *s* of late Rev. Thomas Torrance and Annie Elizabeth Sharp; *m* 1955, Mary Heather Aitken, medical practitioner; one *s* two *d*. *Educ:* Royal High School, Edinburgh; Edinburgh Univ. (MA Hons Philosophy, 1st Cl.); New Coll., Edinburgh (BD Systematic Theol., Distinction); Univs of Marburg, Basle and Oxford. Licensed Minister of Church of Scotland, 1950; parish of Invergowrie, Dundee, 1954; Lectr in Divinity and Dogmatics in History of Christian Thought, New Coll., Univ. of Edinburgh, 1961; Sen. Lectr in Christian Dogmatics, New Coll., 1972. Visiting Professor: of New Testament, Union Theol. Seminary, Richmond, Va, 1960; of Theology, Columbia Theol. Seminary, Decatur, Ga., 1965, and Vancouver Sch. of Theology, BC, 1974–75; Fuller Theol Seminary, Pasadena, 1982, 1984, 1987, 1989, 1991; S Africa, 1980, 1984, 1986; univs and theol schs in Melbourne, Adelaide and Sydney, 1990. *Publications:* (trans. jtly) Oscar Cullmann's Early Christian Worship, 1953; contribs: Essays in Christology for Karl Barth (Karl Barth's Festschrift), 1956; Where Faith and Science Meet, 1954; Calvinus Ecclesiae Doctor, 1978; Incarnation (on Nicene-Constantinopolitan Creed, 381 AD), 1981; The Westminster Confession in the Church Today, 1982; Calvinus Reformator, 1982; articles to Biblical and Biographical Dictionaries, Scottish Jl of Theology, Interpretation, Church Service Society Annual, and other symposia; *festschrift:* Christ in Our Place (ed T. Hart and D. Timell), 1991. *Recreations:* beekeeping, fishing, gardening, swimming. *Address:* 3 Greenbank Crescent, Edinburgh EH10 5TE. *T:* 0131–447 3230.

See also Very Rev. Prof. T. F. Torrance.

TORRANCE, Very Rev. Prof. Thomas Forsyth, MBE 1945; DLitt, DTh, DThéol, Dr Teol, DD, DSc; FRSE 1979; FBA 1983; Professor of Christian Dogmatics, University of Edinburgh, and New College, Edinburgh, 1952–79; Moderator of General Assembly of Church of Scotland, May 1976–77; *b* 30 Aug. 1913; *e s* of late Rev. T. Torrance, then of Chengtu, Szechwan, China; *m* 1946, Margaret Edith, *y d* of late Mr and Mrs G. F. Spear, The Brow, Combe Down, Bath; two *s* one *d*. *Educ:* Chengtu Canadian School; Bellshill Academy; Univs of Edinburgh, Oxford, Basel. MA Edinburgh 1934; studies in Jerusalem and Athens, 1936; BD Edinburgh 1937; post-grad. studies, Basel, 1937–38; DLitt Edinburgh 1971. Prof. of Theology, Auburn, NY, USA, 1938–39; post-grad. studies, Oriel Coll., Oxford, 1939–40; ordained minister of Alyth Barony Parish, 1940; Church of Scotland chaplain (with Huts and Canteens) in MEF and CMF, 1943–45; returned to Alyth; DTh Univ. of Basel, 1946; minister of Beechgrove Church, Aberdeen, 1947; Professor of Church History, Univ. of Edinburgh, and New Coll., Edinburgh, 1950–52. Participant, World Conf. on Faith and Order, Lund, 1952; Evanston Assembly of WCC, 1954; Faith and Order Commn of WCC, 1952–62; Participant in Conversations between: Church of Scotland and Church of England, 1950–58; World Alliance of Reformed Churches and Greek Orthodox Church, 1979–. Lectures: Hewett, 1959 (NY, Newton Center and Cambridge, Mass); Harris, Dundee, 1970; Anderson, Presbyterian Coll., Montreal, 1971; Taylor, Yale, 1971; Keese, Univ. of Mississippi, Chattanooga, 1971; Cummings, McGill Univ., Montreal, 1978; Richards, Univ. of Virginia at Charlottesville, 1978; Staley, Davidson Coll., NC, 1978; Cosgrove, Glasgow, 1981; Warfield, Princeton, 1981; Payton, Pasadena, 1981; Didsbury, Manchester, 1982; Staley, Regent Coll., Vancouver, 1982; William Lyall Meml, Montreal, 1990; Warburton, Lincoln's Inn, 1995. Mem., Académie Internationale des Sciences Religieuses, 1965 (Pres., 1972–81); For. Mem., Société de l'Histoire du Protestantisme Français, 1968; Mem. Soc. Internat. pour l'Etude de la Philosophie Médiévale, 1969; Hon. President: Soc. for Study of Theology, 1966–68; Church Service Soc. of the Church of Scotland, 1970–71; New Coll. Union, 1972–73. Vice-Pres., Inst. of Religion and Theology of GB and Ireland, 1973–76 (Pres., 1976–78); Mem., Center of Theol Inquiry, Princeton, 1982–. Protopresbyter of Greek Orthodox Church (Patriarchate of Alexandria), 1973. Curator: Deutsches Institut für Bildung und Wissen, 1982–; Europäische Akademie für Umweltfragen, 1986–. Membre d'honneur, Acad. Internat. de Philosophie des Scis, 1976. DD (*hc*) Presbyterian Coll., Montreal, 1950; DThéol (*hc*) Geneva, 1959; DThéol (*hc*) Paris, 1959; DD (*hc*) St Andrews, 1960; Dr Teol (*hc*) Oslo, 1961; Hon. DSc Heriot-Watt, 1983. Templeton Foundn Prize, 1978. Cross of St Mark (first class), 1970. *Publications:* The Modern Theological Debate, 1942; The Doctrine of Grace in the Apostolic Fathers, 1949; Calvin's Doctrine of Man, 1949; Royal Priesthood, 1955, 2nd edn 1993; Kingdom and Church, 1956; When Christ Comes and Comes Again, 1957; The Mystery of the Lord's Supper (Sermons on the Sacrament by Robert Bruce), 1958; ed Calvin's Tracts and Treatises, Vols I–III, 1959; The School of Faith, 1959; Conflict and Agreement in the Church, Vol. I, Order and Disorder, 1959; The Apocalypse Today, 1959; Conflict and Agreement in the Church, Vol. II, The Ministry and the Sacraments of the Gospel, 1960; Karl Barth: an Introduction to his Early Theology, 1910–1930, 1962; ed (with D. W. Torrance) Calvin's NT Commentaries, 1959–73; Theology in Reconstruction, 1965; Theological Science, 1969 (Collins Religious Book Award; trans. French, 1990); Space, Time and Incarnation, 1969; God and Rationality, 1971; Theology in Reconciliation: Essays towards Evangelical and Catholic Unity in East and West, 1975; The Centrality of Christ, 1976; Space, Time and Resurrection, 1976; The Ground and Grammar of Theology, 1980; Christian Theology and Scientific Culture, 1980; (ed) Belief in Science and in Christian Life, 1980; (ed) The Incarnation: ecumenical studies in the Nicene Constantinopolitan Creed, 1981; Divine and Contingent Order, 1981; Reality and Evangelical Theology, 1982; Juridical Law and Physical Law, 1982; (ed) James Clerk Maxwell: A Dynamical Theory of the Electromagnetic Field, 1982; The Meditation of Christ, 1983, 2nd edn 1992; Transformation and Convergence in the Frame of Knowledge, 1984; The Christian Frame of Mind, 1985, 2nd enlarged edn (subtitled Reason, Order and Openness in Theology and Natural Science), 1989; Reality and Scientific Theology, 1985; (ed) Theological Dialogue between Orthodox and Reformed Churches, vol. 1, 1985, vol. 2, 1993; The Trinitarian Faith: the Evangelical Theology of the Ancient Catholic Church, 1988; The Hermeneutics of John Calvin, 1988; (ed) Thomas Torrance, China's First Missionaries, Ancient Israelites, 1988; Karl Barth, Biblical and Evangelical Theologian, 1990; Senso del divino e scienza moderna, 1992; Divine Meaning: studies in Patristic Hermaneutics, 1993; Trinitarian Perspectives: towards doctrinal agreement, 1993; Preaching Christ Today: the Gospel and scientific thinking, 1994; Divine Meaning: studies in patristic hermeneutics, 1995; The Christian Doctrine of God, One Being, Three Persons, 1995; Editor, Theology and Science at the Frontiers of Knowledge, series, 1985–91; Jt Editor, Church Dogmatics, Vols 1, 2, 3 and 4, by Karl Barth, 1956–69; Emeritus Editor: Scottish Jl Theology; SJT Monographs. *Recreations:* golf, fishing. *Address:* 37 Braid Farm Road, Edinburgh EH10 6LE. *Clubs:* New, University (Edinburgh).

See also Rev. Prof. J. B. Torrance.

TORRENS-SPENCE, Captain (Frederick) Michael (Alexander), DSO 1941; DSC 1941; AFC 1944; Royal Navy retired; Lord Lieutenant of County Armagh, 1981–89; *b* 10 March 1914; *s* of Lt-Col Herbert Frederick Torrens-Spence and Mrs Eileen Torrens-Spence; *m* 1944, Rachel Nora Clarke; three *s* one *d*. *Educ:* RNC, Dartmouth. Commnd Sub Lieut, 1934; specialised as pilot, 1936; Battle of Taranto, 1940; commanded 815 Naval Air Sqdn, 1941; Battle of Matapan, 1941; Chief Instructor, Empire Test Pilots Sch., 1947–48; Dep. Dir, Air Warfare Div., Naval Staff, 1952–54; commanded HMS Delight, 1955–56, HMS Albion, 1959–61; ADC to the Queen, 1961. Comdr 1946, Captain 1952. Co. Comdt, Ulster Special Constabulary, 1961–70; commanded 2nd (Co. Armagh) Bn, Ulster Defence Regt, 1970–71. High Sheriff, Co. Armagh, 1979. DFC, Greece, 1941. *Address:* Drumcullen House, Ballydugan, Downpatrick, Co. Down BT30 8HZ. *Club:* MCC.

TORRINGTON, 11th Viscount, *cr* 1721; **Timothy Howard St George Byng;** Bt 1715; Baron Byng of Southill, 1721; *b* 13 July 1943; *o s* of Hon. George Byng, RN (*d* on active service, 1944; *o s* of 10th Viscount) and Anne Yvonne Wood (she *m* 2nd, 1951, Howard Henry Masterton Carpenter; 3rd, 1990, Michael Ingram Bostock); *S* grandfather, 1961; *m* 1973, Susan, *d* of M. G. T. Webster, *qv*; three *d*. *Educ:* Harrow; St Edmund Hall, Oxford. Mem., Select Cttee on EEC, H of L, 1984–87 (Chm., Sub-Cttee B (Energy, Transport and Broadcasting), 1985–87). Director: Alliance Resources, 1993–; Conrad, 1993–. *Recreation:* travel. *Heir: kinsman,* John Launcelot Byng, MC [*b* 18 March 1919; *m* 1955, Margaret Ellen Hardy; one *s* two *d*]. *Address:* Great Hunts Place, Owslebury, Winchester, Hants SO21 1JL. *Clubs:* White's, Pratt's; Muthaiga (Nairobi).

TORTELIER, Yan Pascal; Principal Conductor, BBC Philharmonic, since 1992; *b* 19 April 1947; *s* of late Paul Tortelier and of Maud (*née* Martin); *m* 1970, Sylvie Brunet-Moret; two *s*. *Educ:* Paris Conservatoire; general musical studies with Nadia Boulanger; studied conducting with Franco Ferrara in Sienna. Leader and Associate Conductor, Orchestre du Capitole de Toulouse, 1974–82; Principal Conductor and Artistic Dir, Ulster Orchestra, 1989–92. Has conducted all major British orchestras and toured extensively in USA, Canada, Japan, Australia, Scandinavia, E and W Europe. Numerous recordings incl. complete symphonic works of Debussy and Ravel with Ulster Orch., and Hindemith and Dutilleux series with BBC Philharmonic. Hon. DLitt Ulster, 1992. *Publication:* Première orchestration of Ravel's Piano Trio, 1992. *Recreations:* ski-ing, windsurfing, scuba diving, nature. *Address:* c/o IMG Artists Europe, Media House, 3 Burlington Lane, Chiswick, W4 2TH.

TORVILL, Jayne, (Mrs P. L. Christensen), MBE 1981; professional ice skater; *b* 7 Oct. 1957; *d* of George Henry Torvill and Betty (*née* Smart); *m* 1990, Philip Lee Christensen. *Educ:* Clifton Hall Grammar Sch. for Girls, Nottingham. Ice dancer, with Christopher Dean, *qv*; British Champions, 1978, 1979, 1980, 1981, 1982, 1983 and 1994; European Champions, 1981, 1982, 1984 and 1994; World Champions, 1981, 1982, 1983 and 1984; Olympic Champions, 1984; Olympic Bronze Medallists, 1994. Hon. MA Nottingham Trent, 1993. *Recreations:* dance, theatre, caring for Freddy, my dog. *Address:* c/o 59 Goodwin Avenue, Swalecliffe, Kent CT5 2RA. *T:* Canterbury (01227) 793721.

TORY, Sir Geofroy (William), KCMG 1958 (CMG 1956); HM Diplomatic Service, retired; *b* 31 July 1912; *s* of William Frank Tory and Edith Wreghitt; *m* 1st, 1938, Emilia Strickland; two *s* one *d*; 2nd, 1950, Hazel Winfield (*d* 1985). *Educ:* King Edward VII Sch., Sheffield; Queens' Coll., Cambridge. Apptd Dominions Office, 1935; Private Sec. to Perm. Under-Sec. of State, 1938–39; served War, 1939–43, in Royal Artillery; Prin. Private Sec. to Sec. of State, 1945–46; Senior Sec., Office of UK High Comr, Ottawa, 1946–49; Prin. Sec., Office of UK Rep. to Republic of Ireland, 1949–50; Counsellor, UK Embassy, Dublin, 1950–51; idc 1952; Dep. High Comr for UK in Pakistan (Peshawar), 1953–54, in Australia, 1954–57; Asst Under-Sec. of State, CRO, 1957; High Comr for UK in Fedn of Malaya, 1957–63; Ambassador to Ireland, 1964–66; High Commissioner to Malta, 1967–70. PMN (Malaysia) 1963. *Recreations:* painting, music. *Address:* Cliff Top, Harbour View, Kilbrittain, Co. Cork, Ireland.

TOSELAND, Ronald James, OBE 1991; Deputy Controller, National Air Traffic Services, 1988–91, retired; *b* 7 March 1933; *s* of W. M. and E. M. Toseland; *m* 1954, Joan Mary, *d* of A. R. and D. M. Pickett; two *s*. *Educ:* Kettering Boys' School. RAF Navigator, 1951–61; Air Traffic Control Officer, 1961–91; i/c Heathrow ATC, 1981–83; Dir, Civil Air Traffic Ops, 1983–87; Joint Field Commander, NATS, 1987–88. *Recreations:* music, walking. *Address:* 1 Marshall Place, Oakley Green, Windsor SL4 4QD. *T:* Windsor (01753) 863313.

TOTNES, Archdeacon of; *no new appointment at time of going to press.*

TOTTENHAM, family name of **Marquess of Ely.**

TÖTTERMAN, Richard Evert Björnson, Kt Comdr, Order of the White Rose of Finland; Hon. GCVO 1976 (Hon. KCVO 1969); Hon. OBE 1961; DPhil; Finnish Ambassador, retired; *b* 10 Oct. 1926; *s* of Björn B. Tötterman and Katharine C. (*née* Wimpenny); *m* 1953, Camilla Susanna Veronica Huber; one *s* one *d*. *Educ:* Univ. of Helsinki (Jur. lic.); Brasenose Coll., Oxford (DPhil; Hon. Fellow, 1982). Entered Finnish Foreign Service, 1952: served Stockholm, 1954–56; Moscow, 1956–58; Ministry for Foreign Affairs, Finland, 1958–62; Berne, 1962–63; Paris, 1963–66; Dep. Dir, Min. for For. Affairs, Helsinki, 1966; Sec.-Gen., Office of the President of Finland, 1966–70; Sec. of State, Min. for For. Aff., 1970–75; Ambassador: UK, 1975–83; Switzerland, 1983–90, and (concurrently) to the Holy See, 1988–90. Chm. or Mem. of a number of Finnish Govt Cttees, 1959–75, and participated as Finnish rep. in various internat. negotiations; Chm., Multilateral Consultations preparing Conf. on Security and Co-operation in Europe, 1972–73. Holds numerous foreign orders (Grand Cross, Kt Comdr, etc). *Recreations:* music, outdoor life. *Address:* Parkgatan 9 A 11, 00140 Helsinki, Finland.

TOTTLE, Prof. Charles Ronald; Professor of Medical Engineering, University of Bath, 1975–78, now Emeritus, a Pro Vice-Chancellor, 1973–77; Director, Bath Institute of Medical Engineering, 1975–78; Editor, Materials Science, Research Studies Press, since 1977; *b* 2 Sept. 1920; *m* 1944, Eileen P. Geoghegan; one *s* one *d*. *Educ:* Nether Edge Grammar School; University of Sheffield (MMet). English Electric Co. Ltd, 1941–45; Lecturer in Metallurgy, University of Durham, King's College, 1945–50; Ministry of Supply, Atomic Energy Division, Springfields Works, 1950–51; Culcheth Laboratories, 1951–56 (UKAEA); Head of Laboratories, Dounreay, 1956–57; Deputy Director, Dounreay, 1958–59; Prof. of Metallurgy, 1959–67, Dean of Science, 1966, Univ. of Manchester; Prof. and Head of School of Materials Science, Univ. of Bath, 1967–75; Man. Dir, South Western Industrial Research Ltd, 1970–75. Resident Research Associate, Argonne Nat. Laboratory, Illinois, USA, 1964–65. Vice-Pres., Instn of Metallurgists, 1968–70; Jt Editor, Institution of Metallurgists Series of Textbooks, 1962–70. Governor, Dauntsey's Sch., 1979–88. CEng 1978; FIM; FInstP 1958, CPhys 1985. Hon. MSc Manchester. *Publications:* The Science of Engineering Materials, 1965; An Encyclopaedia of Metallurgy and Materials, 1984; various contribs to metallurgical and engineering jls. *Recreations:* music, model making, gardening. *Address:* Parkview, 47 Queens Road, Devizes, Wilts SN10 5HP.

TOUCHE, Sir Anthony (George), 3rd Bt *cr* 1920; Deputy Chairman, Friends' Provident Life Office, since 1983; *b* 31 Jan. 1927; *s* of Donovan Meredith Touche (*d* 1952) (2nd *s* of 1st Bt) and of Muriel Amy Frances (*d* 1983), *e d* of Rev. Charles R. Thorold Winckley; *S* uncle, 1977; *m* 1961, Hester Christina, *er d* of Dr Werner Pleuger; two *s* one *d* (and one *s* decd). *Educ:* Eton College. FCA. Partner in George A. Touche & Co. (later Touche Ross

& Co.), 1951; Director of investment trust companies, 1952–90; retired from Touche Ross & Co., 1968; Touche, Remnant Holdings Ltd, 1965–89. Dir, 1968–90, Dep. Chm., 1977–87, National Westminster Bank. Chairman, Assoc. of Investment Trust Companies, 1971–73. Prime Warden, Goldsmiths' Co., 1987. *Recreations:* music, reading, walking. *Heir: s* William George Touche [*b* 26 June 1962; *m* 1987, Elizabeth Louise, *y d* of Allen Bridges; two *s*]. *Address:* Stane House, Ockley, Dorking, Surrey RH5 5TQ. *T:* Oakwood Hill (01306) 627397.

TOUCHE, Sir Rodney (Gordon), 2nd Bt *cr* 1962; *b* 5 Dec. 1928; *s* of Rt Hon. Sir Gordon Touche, 1st Bt, and of Ruby, Lady Touche (formerly Ruby Ann Macpherson) (*d* 1989); *S* father 1972; *m* 1955, Ouida Ann, *d* of F. G. MacLellan, Moncton, NB, Canada; one *s* three *d*. *Educ:* Marlborough; University Coll., Oxford. *Heir: s* Eric MacLellan Touche [*b* 22 Feb. 1960; *m* 1990, Leeanne Marie Stringer; one *s* one *d*]. *Address:* 2403 Westmount Place, 1100 8th Avenue SW, Calgary, Alta T2P 3T9, Canada. *T:* (403) 2338800.

TOUHIG, James Donnelly, (Don); MP (Lab) Islwyn, since 1995; *b* 5 Dec. 1947; *s* of Michael Touhig and Catherine Touhig (*née* Corten); *m* 1968, Jennifer Hughes; two *s* two *d*. *Educ:* St Francis Sch., Aberyschan; E Monmouth Coll., Pontypool. Journalist, 1968–95; Editor, Free Press of Monmouthshire, 1976–88; General Manager: Free Press Gp, 1988–92; (Business Develt) Bailey Gp, 1992–93; Bailey Print, 1993–95. KSS 1991. *Recreations:* reading, cooking for family and friends, walking. *Address:* House of Commons, SW1A 0AA. *T:* 0171–219 6435.

TOULMIN, John Kelvin, CMG 1994; QC 1980; barrister-at-law; a Recorder, since 1984; *b* 14 Feb. 1941; *s* of late Arthur Heaton Toulmin and B. Toulmin (*née* Fraser); *m* 1967, Carolyn Merton (*née* Gullick), barrister-at-law; one *s* two *d*. *Educ:* Winchester Coll.; Trinity Hall, Cambridge (Patterson Law Scholar, 1959; BA 1963, MA 1966); Univ. of Michigan (Ford Foundn Fellow and Fulbright Scholar, 1964; LLM 1965). Middle Temple: Harmsworth Exhibnr, 1960; Astbury Scholar, 1965; called to the Bar, 1965; Bencher, 1986; Western Circuit; a Dep. High Court Judge, 1994–; called to Bar of NI, 1989, to Irish Bar, 1991. Cambridge Univ. Debating Tour, USA, 1963. Chm., Young Barristers, 1973–75; Member: Bar Council, 1971–77, 1978–81 and 1987–90 (Chm., Internat. Practice Cttee, 1987); Supreme Court Rules Cttee, 1976–80; Council of Legal Educn, 1981–83; DHSS Enquiry into Unnecessary Dental Treatment in NHS (Report, 1986). Mem., Internat. Panel of Dist. Mediators, CPR Inst. for Dispute Resolution, NY, 1993; William W. Bishop Jr Fellow, Univ. of Michigan Law Sch., 1993. Council of Bars and Law Societies of Europe: Mem. UK delegn, 1983–90, Leader, 1987–90; Chm. of the cttee at European Courts of Justice, 1990–93; Vice-Pres., 1991–92; Pres., 1993. Member: Bd of Governors, Maudsley and Bethlem Royal Hosps, 1979–82; SHA, 1982–87; Cttee of Management, Inst. of Psychiatry, 1982–. Trustee: Pro Corda, 1992–; Europäische Rechtsakademie, Trier, 1993– (Vice-Chm., 1994–). Hon. Mem., Law Soc., 1994. Grand Decoration for Merit (Austria), 1995. *Publications:* (contrib.) The Influence of Litigation in Medical Practice, 1977; European Ed., Encyclopaedia of Banking Law, 1990; Consulting Ed., European Legal Systems, 1992; EFTA Legal Systems, 1993. *Recreations:* cricket, music, theatre. *Address:* 3 Gray's Inn Place, Gray's Inn, WC1R 5EA. *T:* 0171–831 8441, *Fax:* 0171–831 8479. *Clubs:* Pilgrims, MCC; Surrey County Cricket.

TOULMIN, Stephen Edelston, MA, PhD; Henry R. Luce Foundation Professor, Center for Multiethnic and Transnational Studies, University of Southern California, since 1993; Avalon Foundation Professor in the Humanities, Northwestern University, 1986–92, now Emeritus; *b* 25 March 1922; *s* of late G. E. Toulmin and Mrs E. D. Toulmin; *m*; two *s* two *d*. *Educ:* Oundle School; King's College, Cambridge. BA 1943; MA 1946; PhD 1948; MA (Oxon) 1948. Junior Scientific Officer, Ministry of Aircraft Production, 1942–45; Fellow of King's College, Cambridge, 1947–51; University Lecturer in the Philosophy of Science, Oxford, 1949–55; Acting Head of Department of History and Methods of Science, University of Melbourne, Australia, 1954–55; Professor of Philosophy, University of Leeds, 1955–59; Visiting Prof. of Philosophy, NY Univ. and Stanford Univ. (California) and Columbia Univ. (NY), 1959–60; Director, Nuffield Foundation Unit for History of Ideas, 1960–64; Prof. of Philosophy, Brandeis Univ., 1965–69, Michigan State Univ., 1969–72; Provost, Crown College, Univ. of California, Santa Cruz, 1972–73; Prof. in Cttee on Social Thought, Chicago Univ., 1973–86. Counsellor, Smithsonian Institution, 1966–75; Mem., Consejo Cientifico, Instituto Internacional de Estudios Avanzados, Carácas, 1985–. Hon. DTech Royal Inst. of Technol., Stockholm, 1991. *Publications:* The Place of Reason in Ethics, 1950; The Philosophy of Science: an Introduction, 1953; Metaphysical Beliefs (3 essays: author of one of them), 1957; The Uses of Argument, 1958; Foresight and Understanding, 1961; The Ancestry of Science, Vol. I (The Fabric of the Heavens) 1961, Vol. II (The Architecture of Matter), 1962, Vol. III (The Discovery of Time), 1965; Night Sky at Rhodes, 1963; Human Understanding, vol. 1, 1972; Wittgenstein's Vienna, 1973; Knowing and Acting, 1976; An Introduction to Reasoning, 1979; The Return to Cosmology, 1982; The Abuse of Casuistry, 1987; Cosmopolis, 1989; also films, broadcast talks and contribs to learned jls and weeklies. *Address:* Center for Multiethnic and Transnational Studies, University of Southern California, Los Angeles, CA 90089-7724, USA.

See also M. E. P. Jones.

TOULSON, Elizabeth; National Chairman, Womens' Royal Voluntary Service, since 1993; *b* 10 Nov. 1948; *d* of Henry Bertram Chrimes, *qv* and Suzanne Isabel Chrimes (*née* Corbett-Lowe); *m* 1973, Roger Grenfell Toulson, *qv*; two *s* two *d*. *Educ:* Liverpool Univ.; Clare Hall, Cambridge (LLB). Called to the Bar, Inner Temple, 1974. Womens' Royal Voluntary Service: Trustee, 1981–; Vice-Chm., 1989–93. *Recreations:* reading, music, walking, tennis, swimming, ski-ing. *Address:* Billhurst Farm, White Hart Lane, Wood Street Village, Guildford, Surrey GU3 3DZ.

TOULSON, Roger Grenfell; QC 1986; a Recorder, since 1987; *b* 23 Sept. 1946; *s* of late Stanley Kilsha Toulson and Lilian Mary Toulson; *m* 1973, Elizabeth Chrimes (*see* E. Toulson); two *s* two *d*. *Educ:* Mill Hill School; Jesus College, Cambridge (MA, LLB). Called to the Bar, Inner Temple, 1969. *Recreations:* ski-ing, tennis, gardening. *Address:* Billhurst Farm, Wood Street Village, near Guildford, Surrey GU3 3DZ. *T:* Worplesdon (01483) 235246. *Club:* Old Millhillians.

TOUT, Herbert, CMG 1946; MA; Reader in Political Economy, University College, London, 1947–68, retired; *b* Manchester, 20 April 1904; *e s* of Professor T. F. Tout, Manchester University, and Mary Johnstone; unmarried. *Educ:* Sherborne School; Hertford College, Oxford. Instructor in Economics, University of Minnesota, USA, 1929–35; Assistant Lecturer, University College, London, 1936; Colston Research Fellow and Director of University of Bristol Social Survey, 1936–38; Lecturer, University of Bristol, 1938–47; Temp. Principal, Board of Trade, 1940–41; Assistant Secretary, 1941–45. *Recreation:* reading. *Address:* Brooklands Nursing Home, Wych Cross, East Sussex RH18 5JN. *T:* Nutley (01825) 712005.

TOVELL, Laurence, FCA; Chief Inspector of Audit, Department of the Environment, 1977–79; *b* 6 March 1919; *s* of William Henry Tovell and Margaret Tovell (*née* Mahoney); *m* 1945, Iris Joan (*née* Lee); two *s* one *d*. *Educ:* Devonport High School. Entered Civil Service as Audit Assistant, District Audit Service, 1938. Served War, 1940–46; Lieut RNVR, 1942–46. District Auditor, No 4 Audit District, Birmingham, 1962. *Recreation:* do-it-yourself. *Address:* White Lions, Links Road, Bramley, Guildford, Surrey GU5 0AL. *T:* Guildford (01483) 892702.

TOVEY, Sir Brian (John Maynard), KCMG 1980; Chairman: Cresswell Associates Ltd, since 1988; Fujitsu Europe Telecoms R & D Centre Ltd, since 1990; IES Group PLC, since 1993; Deputy Chairman, Advanced Media Group plc, since 1994; *b* 15 April 1926; *s* of Rev. Collett John Tovey (Canon, Bermuda Cathedral, 1935–38) and Kathleen Edith Maud Tovey (*née* Maynard); *m* 1989, Mary Helen (*née* Lane). *Educ:* St Edward's Sch., Oxford; St Edmund Hall, Oxford, 1944–45; School of Oriental and African Studies, London, 1948–50. BA Hons London. Service with Royal Navy and subseq. Army (Intelligence Corps and RAEC), 1945–48. Joined Government Communications Headquarters as Jun. Asst, 1950; Principal, 1957; Asst Sec., 1967; Under Sec., 1975; Dep. Sec., 1978; Dir, 1978–83, retired. Defence Systems Consultant, 1983–85, and Defence and Political Adviser, 1985–88, Plessey Electronic Systems Ltd; Dir, Plessey Defence Systems Ltd, 1983–85. Vice-Pres. (Information and Communications Technology), Fedn of Electronics Industry, 1995–. *Recreations:* music, walking, history of art (espec. 16th Century Italian). *Address:* 8 Cresswell Gardens, SW5 0BJ. *Club:* Naval and Military (Vice-Pres., 1995–).

TOVUE, Sir Ronald, Kt 1987; OBE 1981; Premier, Provincial Government of East New Britain Province, Papua New Guinea, 1981; Member of Provincial Assembly, since 1979; *b* 14 Feb. 1933; *s* of Apmeledi To Palanga and Rachael Warurui; *m* 1969, Suluet Tinvil; two *s* one *d*. *Educ:* Pilapila Community Sch.; Kerevat High Sch. Teacher, 1957–65; Magistrate, 1965–74; Commissioner, 1974–76. *Recreations:* golf, reading, gardening, church activities. *Address:* Ratavul, Rabaul, Papua New Guinea. *T:* 921301 B/H; PO Box 354, Rabaul, Papua New Guinea. *T:* 927216 A/H. *Club:* Rabaul Golf (Rabaul).

TOWER, Maj.-Gen. Philip Thomas, CB 1968; DSO 1944; MBE 1942; National Trust Administrator, Blickling Hall, 1973–82; *b* 1 March 1917; *s* of late Vice-Admiral Sir Thomas Tower, KBE, CB and late Mrs E. H. Tower; *m* 1943, Elizabeth, *y d* of late Thomas Ralph Sneyd-Kynnersley, OBE, MC and late Alice Sneyd-Kynnersley. *Educ:* Harrow; Royal Military Acad., Woolwich. 2nd Lt Royal Artillery, 1937; served in India, 1937–40; served War of 1939–45 (despatches); Middle East, 1940–42; POW Italy, 1942–43; escaped, 1943; Arnhem, 1944; Norway, 1945; Staff Coll., 1948; Instructor at RMA Sandhurst, 1951–53; comd J (Sidi Rezegh) Bty RHA in Middle East, 1954–55; Joint Services Staff Coll., 1955–56; GSO1 Plans, BJSM Washington, DC, 1956–57; comd 3rd Regt RHA, 1957–60; Imperial Defence Coll., 1961; Comd 51 Inf. Bde Gp, 1961–62; Comd 12 Inf. Bde Gp, BAOR, 1962–64; Director of Public Relations (Army), 1965–67; GOC Middle East Land Forces, 1967 (despatches); Comdt, RMA Sandhurst, 1968–72, retd 1972. Col Comdt, Royal Regt of Artillery, 1970–80. County Comr (Norfolk), SJAB, 1975–78. OStJ 1977. *Recreations:* shooting, gardening. *Address:* Hall Farm, East Raynham, Fakenham, Norfolk NR21 7EE. *T:* Fakenham (01328) 864904; Studio A, 414 Fulham Road, SW6 1EB. *T:* 0171–385 8538. *Club:* Army and Navy.

TOWERS, John, CBE 1995; FEng, FIMechE; Chief Executive, Rover Group Holdings PLC, since 1994; *b* 30 March 1948; *s* of Jack Towers and Florence Towers (*née* Abley); *m* 1990, Bethanie Williams; one *s* one *d*. *Educ:* Durham Johnston Sch.; Univ. of Bradford (BSc Hons Mech. Engrg). CEng 1974; FEng 1992; FIMechE 1992; FIIM 1989. Joined Perkins Engines as student apprentice, 1966: Quality Engr, later Mfg Dir and Gen. Manager, 1983–86; Vice-Pres., Internat. Services, Varity Corp. (Canada), 1986–87; Man. Dir, Massey Ferguson Tractors, 1987–88; Rover Group, 1988–: Mfg Dir, Land Rover, 1988–89; Product Develt Dir, 1989–90; Dir, 1990–91, Man. Dir, Jan.–Dec. 1991, Product Supply; Gp Man. Dir, 1991–94. Vis. Prof., Warwick Univ., 1993. Mem., Council for Sci. and Technol., 1993–. DUniv Central England in Birmingham, 1994. *Recreations:* golf, music. *Address:* Rover Group Holdings PLC, International House, Bickenhill, Birmingham B37 7HQ. *T:* 0121–781 7114.

TOWNDROW, Ven. Frank Noel; Archdeacon of Oakham, 1967–77, now Archdeacon Emeritus; Residentiary Canon of Peterborough, 1966–77, now Canon Emeritus; a Chaplain to the Queen, 1975–81; *b* 25 Dec. 1911; *e s* of F. R. and H. A. Towndrow, London; *m* 1947, Olive Helen Weinberger (*d* 1978); one *d* (one *s* decd). *Educ:* St Olave's Grammar Sch.; King's Coll., Cambridge; Coll. of Resurrection, Mirfield. Curate, Chingford, E4, 1937–40; Chaplain, RAFVR, 1940–47; Rector of Grangemouth, Stirlingshire, 1947–51; Vicar of Kirton Lindsey, Lincs, 1951–53; Rector of Greenford, Middx, 1953–62; Vicar of Ravensthorpe, E Haddon and Rector of Holdenby, 1962–66. *Recreation:* modern history. *Address:* 17 Croake Hill, Swinstead, Grantham, Lincs NG33 4PE. *T:* Corby Glen (01476) 550478.

TOWNELEY, Sir Simon (Peter Edmund Cosmo William), KCVO 1994; Lord-Lieutenant and Custos Rotulorum of Lancashire, since 1976; *b* 14 Dec. 1921; *e s* of late Col A. Koch de Gooreynd, OBE and Baroness Norman, CBE; assumed surname and arms of Towneley by royal licence, 1955, by reason of descent from *e d* and senior co-heiress of Col Charles Towneley of Towneley; *m* 1955, Mary, 2nd *d* of Cuthbert Fitzherbert; one *s* six *d*. *Educ:* Stowe; Worcester Coll., Oxford (MA, DPhil; Ruffini Scholar). Served War of 1939–45, KRRC. Lectr in History of Music, Worcester Coll., Oxford, 1949–55. Mem., Agricultural Lands Tribunal, 1960–92. Dir, Granada Television, 1981–92. CC Lancs, 1961–64; JP 1956; DL 1970; High Sheriff of Lancashire, 1971. Mem. Council, Duchy of Lancaster, 1986–. Patron, Nat. Assoc. for Mental Health (North-West). President: Community Council of Lancashire; Mid-Pennine Assoc. for the Arts; Lancashire Playing Field Assoc.; NW of England and IoM TA&VRA, 1987–92; Chm., Northern Ballet Theatre, 1969–86; Member: Bd of Governors, Royal Northern Coll. of Music; Court and Council, Univ. of Manchester; Trustee: Historic Churches Preservation Trust, 1984–93; British Museum, 1988–93. Hon. Col, Duke of Lancaster's Own Yeomanry, 1979–88. CRNCM 1990; Hon. Fellow, Lancashire Polytechnic, 1987. Hon. DMus Lancaster, 1994. KStJ; KCSG. *Publications:* Venetian Opera in the Seventeenth Century, 1954 (repr. 1968); contribs to New Oxford History of Music. *Address:* Dyneley, Burnley, Lancs BB11 3RE. *T:* Burnley (01282) 23322. *Clubs:* Boodle's, Pratt's, Beefsteak.

See also Sir P. G. Worsthorne.

TOWNEND, James Barrie Stanley; QC 1978; a Recorder of the Crown Court, since 1979; *b* 21 Feb. 1938; *s* of late Frederick Stanley Townend and Marjorie Elizabeth Townend (*née* Arnold); *m* 1970, Airelle Claire (*née* Nies); one step *d*. *Educ:* Tonbridge Sch.; Lincoln Coll., Oxford (MA). National Service in BAOR and UK, 1955–57: 2nd Lieut, 18th Medium Regt, RA. Called to Bar, Middle Temple, 1962, Bencher, 1987. Chairman: Sussex Crown Court Liaison Cttee, 1978–89; Family Law Bar Assoc., 1986–88; Member: Kingston and Esher DHA, 1983–86; Bar Council, 1984–88; Supreme Court Procedure Cttee, 1986–88. *Recreations:* sailing, fishing, writing verse. *Address:* 1 King's Bench Walk, Temple, EC4Y 7DB. *T:* 0171–583 6266. *Club:* Bar Yacht.

TOWNEND, John Coupe; Deputy Director, Bank of England, since 1994; *b* 24 Aug, 1947; *s* of Harry Norman Townend and Joyce Dentith (*née* Coupe); *m* 1969, Dorothy Allister; three *s*. *Educ:* Liverpool Inst. High Sch. for Boys; London Sch. of Economics (BSc

Econ; MSc). With Bank of England, 1968–: First Head, Wholesale Markets Supervision Div., 1986–90; Head, Gilt-Edged and Money Markets Div., 1990–94. *Publications:* articles in econ. jls. *Recreations:* running, trekking, opera, birds. *Address:* Bank of England, Threadneedle Street, EC2R 8AH. *T:* 0171–601 4541.

TOWNEND, John Ernest; MP (C) Bridlington, since 1979; *b* 12 June 1934; *s* of Charles Hope Townend and Dorothy Townend; *m* 1963, Jennifer Ann; two *s* two *d.* *Educ:* Hymers Coll., Hull. FCA (Plender Prize). Articled Clerk, Chartered Accountants, 1951–56; National Service: Pilot Officer, RAF, 1957–59; J. Townend & Sons Ltd (Hull) Ltd: Co. Sec./Dir, 1959–67; Man. Dir, 1967–77; Chm., 1977–; Vice-Chm., Surrey Building Soc., 1984–93; Dir, AAH Hldgs, 1989–. Mem., Hull City Council, 1966–74 (Chm., Finance Cttee, 1968–70); Chm., Humber Bridge Bd, 1969–71; Member, Humberside County Council, 1973–79: Cons. Leader of Opposition, 1973–77; Leader, 1977–79; Chm., Policy Cttee, 1977–79. Mem., Policy Cttee, Assoc. of County Councils, 1977–79. PPS to Minister of State for Social Security, 1981–83. Mem., Treasury and Civil Service Select Cttee, 1983–92; Chm., Cons. Small Business Cttee, 1988–; Chm., Cons. backbench Finance Cttee, 1993– (Vice-Chm., 1983–91). Chm., Merchant Vintners Co., 1964–. *Recreations:* swimming, tennis. *Address:* Sigglesthorne Hall, Sigglesthorne, Hull, North Humberside HU11 5QA. *Club:* Carlton.

TOWNEND, John Philip; His Honour Judge Townend; a Circuit Judge, since 1987; *b* 20 June 1935; *o s* of Luke and Ethel Townend; *m* 1st, 1959; two *s* one *d*; 2nd, 1981, Anne Glover; one step *s* one step *d.* *Educ:* St Joseph's Coll., Blackpool; Manchester Univ. (LLB). National Service, 1957–58. Called to the Bar, Gray's Inn, 1959; Lectr in Law, Gibson and Weldon College of Law, 1960–65; Asst Legal Advr, Pilkington Bros, 1966–68; Legal Advr, Honeywell Ltd and G. Dew Ltd, 1968–70; joined chambers of Mr Stewart Oakes, Manchester, 1970. *Publications:* articles in various jls on legal topics. *Recreations:* classical music, jazz, food and wine, a decreasing number of active games, mountain walking. *Address:* c/o The Crown Court, Crown Square, Manchester M60 9DJ. *Clubs:* Fairhaven Golf; Lytham Tennis and Hockey.

TOWNES, Charles Hard; University Professor of Physics, University of California, USA, 1967–86, now Emeritus; *b* Greenville, South Carolina, 28 July 1915; *s* of Henry Keith Townes and Ellen Sumter (*née* Hard); *m* 1941, Frances H. Brown; four *d.* *Educ:* Furman Univ. (BA, BS); Duke Univ. (MA); California Institute of Technology (PhD). Assistant in Physics, California Inst. of Technology, 1937–39; Member Techn Staff, Bell Telephone Labs, 1939–47; Associate Prof. of Physics, Columbia Univ., 1948–50; Prof. of Physics, Columbia Univ., 1950–61; Exec. Director, Columbia Radiation Lab., 1950–52; Chairman, Dept of Physics, Columbia Univ., 1952–55; Vice-President and Director of Research, Inst. for Defense Analyses, 1959–61; Provost and Professor of Physics, MIT, 1961–66; Institute Professor, MIT, 1966–67. Guggenheim Fellow, 1955–56; Fulbright Lecturer, University of Paris, 1955–56, University of Tokyo, 1956; Lecturer, 1955, 1960, Dir, 1963, Enrico Fermi Internat. Sch. of Physics; Scott Lecturer, University of Cambridge, 1963. Centennial Lecturer, University of Toronto, 1967. Dir, Bulletin of Atomic Scientists, 1964–69. Board of Editors: Review of Scientific Instruments, 1950–52; Physical Review, 1951–53; Journal of Molecular Spectroscopy, 1957–60; Columbia University Forum, 1957–59. Fellow: American Phys. Society (Richtmyer Lecturer, 1959; Member Council, 1959–62, 1965–71; President, 1967); Inst. of Electrical and Electronics Engrs; Chairman, Sci. and Technology Adv. Commn for Manned Space Flight, NASA, 1964–69; Member: President's Science Adv. Cttee, 1966–69 (Vice-Chm., 1967–69); Scientific Adv. Bd, US Air Force, 1958–61; Soc. Française de Physique (Member Council, 1956–58); Nat. Acad. Scis (Mem. Council, 1969–72); American Acad. Arts and Sciences; American Philos. Society; American Astron. Society; American Assoc. of Physics Teachers; Société Royale des Sciences de Liège; Pontifical Acad., 1983; Foreign Member: Royal Society, 1976; Russian Acad. of Scis, 1994; Hon. Mem., Optical Soc. of America. Trustee: Salk Inst. for Biological Studies, 1963–68; Rand Corp., 1965–70; Carnegie Instn of Washington, 1965–; Calif Inst. of Technol., 1979–. Chairman: Space Science Bd, Nat. Acad. of Sciences, 1970–73; Science Adv. Cttee, General Motors Corp., 1971–73; Bd of Dirs, General Motors, 1973–86; Perkin-Elmer Corp., 1966–85. Trustee: Pacific Sch. of Religion, 1983–93; California Acad. of Scis, 1987–; Grad. Theol Union, 1993–; Enshrinee, Engrg and Sci. Hall of Fame, Ohio, 1983. Holds numerous honorary degrees. Nobel Prize for Physics (jointly), 1964. Research Corp. Annual Award, 1958; Comstock Prize, Nat. Acad. of Sciences, 1959; Stuart Ballantine Medal, Franklin Inst., 1959, 1962; Rumford Premium, Amer. Acad. of Arts and Sciences, 1961; Thomas Young Medal and Prize, Inst. of Physics and Physical Soc., England, 1963; Medal of Honor, Inst. of Electrical and Electronics Engineers, 1967; C. E. K. Mees Medal, Optical Soc. of America, 1968; Churchman of the Year Award, Southern Baptist Theological Seminary, 1967; Distinguished Public Service Medal, NASA, 1969; Michelson-Morley Award, 1970; Wilhelm-Exner Award (Austria), 1970; Medal of Honor, Univ. of Liège, 1971; Earle K. Plyler Prize, 1977; Niels Bohr Internat. Gold Medal, 1979; Nat. Medal of Sci., 1983; Commonwealth Award, 1993. National Inventors Hall of Fame, 1976; S Carolina Hall of Fame, 1977. Officier, Légion d'Honneur (France), 1990. *Publications:* (with A. L. Schawlow) Microwave Spectroscopy, 1955; (ed) Quantum Electronics, 1960; (ed with P. A. Miles) Quantum Electronics and Coherent Light, 1964; many scientific articles on microwave spectroscopy, molecular and nuclear structure, quantum electronics, radio and infra-red astrophysics; fundamental patents on masers and (with A. L. Schawlow) lasers. *Address:* Department of Physics, University of California, Berkeley, CA 94720, USA. *T:* (510) 6421128. *Clubs:* Cosmos (Washington, DC); Bohemian (San Francisco).

TOWNSEND, Albert Alan, FRS 1960; PhD; Reader (Experimental Fluid Mechanics), Cavendish Laboratory, University of Cambridge, 1961–85 (Assistant Director of Research, 1950–61); Fellow of Emmanuel College, Cambridge, since 1947; *b* 22 Jan. 1917; *s* of A. R. Townsend and D. Gay; *m* 1950, V. Dees; one *s* two *d.* *Educ:* Telopea Park IHS; Melbourne and Cambridge Universities. PhD 1947. *Publications:* The Structure of Turbulent Shear Flow, 1956; papers in technical journals. *Address:* Emmanuel College, Cambridge CB2 3AP.

TOWNSEND, Bryan Sydney, CBE 1994; Chairman, Midlands Electricity plc (formerly Midlands Electricity Board), since 1986 (Chief Executive, 1990–92); *b* 2 April 1930; *s* of Sydney and Gladys Townsend; *m* 1951, Betty Eileen Underwood; one *s* two *d.* *Educ:* Wolverton Technical Coll. CEng, FIEE; FIMgt. Trainee, Northampton Electric Light & Power Co., 1946–50; successive appts, E Midlands, Eastern and Southern Electricity Bds, 1952–66; Southern Electricity Board: Swindon Dist Manager, 1966–68; Newbury Area Engr, 1968–70; Asst Chief Engr, 1970–73; Dep. Chief Engr, SE Electricity Bd, 1973–76; Chief Engr, S Wales Electricity Bd, 1976–78; Dep. Chm., SW Electricity Bd, 1978–86. *Recreation:* golf. *Address:* Midlands Electricity plc, Mucklow Hill, Halesowen, West Midlands B62 8BP. *T:* 0121–423 2345.

TOWNSEND, Dr Christina, CPsychol; FIPD; Chief Executive and Main Board Director, Business & Technology Education Council, since 1994; *b* 10 Jan. 1947; *d* of Sidney Townsend and Vera (*née* Wallis). *Educ:* Dursley Grammar Sch., Glos; Leeds Univ. (BSc Psychol.); Birmingham Univ. (MSc); UWIST (PhD). CPsychol 1969; FIPD (FIPM 1991). Lectr, UWIST, 1973–75; Sen. Res. Officer, MSC, 1976–78; Asst Dir, Ashridge Mgt Coll., 1978–80; Hd of Div., Inst. of Manpower Studies, 1981–84; NHS Training Authority, subseq. Directorate: Dir, Res. Educn and Trng, 1984–88; Chief Exec., 1988–91; Nat. Trng Dir and Chief Exec., 1991–93. Dep. Chm., Personnel Standards Lead Body, 1991–94; Director: City Technol. Colls Trust, 1994–; Mgt Charter Initiative, 1994–; Further Educn Develt Agency, 1994–. Trustee, Learning from Experience Trust, 1991–94. MInstD 1991 (Mem., Nat. Employment Cttee, 1991–); CIMgt 1994; FRSA 1992. *Recreations:* sailing, hill-walking, theatre, circuit training. *Address:* Business & Technology Education Council, Central House, Upper Woburn Place, WC1H 0HH. *T:* 0171–413 8400. *Club:* Royal Society of Medicine.

TOWNSEND, Cyril David; MP (C) Bexleyheath since Feb. 1974; *b* 21 Dec. 1937; *s* of Lt-Col Cyril M. Townsend and Lois (*née* Henderson); *m* 1976, Anita, MA, *d* of late Lt-Col F. G. W. Walshe and of Mrs Walshe; two *s.* *Educ:* Bradfield Coll.; RMA Sandhurst. Commnd into Durham LI; served in Berlin and Hong Kong; active service in Cyprus, 1958 and Borneo, 1966; ADC to Governor and C-in-C Hong Kong, 1964–66; Adjt 1DLI, 1966–68. A Personal Asst to Edward Heath, 1968–70; Mem. Conservative Research Dept, 1970–74. PPS to Minister of State, DHSS, 1979; Member: Select Cttee on Violence in the Family, 1975; Select Cttee on Foreign Affairs, 1982–83; Vice-Chairman: Cons. Parly Defence Cttee, 1985– (Jt Sec., 1982–85); Cons. Parly Foreign Affairs Cttee, 1991–; Chairman: Select Cttee on Armed Forces Bill, 1981; British-Cyprus Parly Gp, 1983–92; All-Party Freedom for Rudolf Hess Campaign, 1977–87; Bow Gp Standing Cttee on Foreign Affairs, 1977–84; (and Co-Founder) South Atlantic Council, 1983–; Organizing Cttee, Argentine-British Conference, 1988–90; UN Parly Gp, 1992–; Jt Chm., Council for Advancement of Arab-British Understanding, 1982–92; Chm., Cons. ME Council, 1992– (Jt Vice-Chm., 1988–92); Vice-Chairman: Friends of Cyprus, 1980–92 (Mem., Exec. Cttee); Hansard Soc., 1988–; Mem. Exec. Cttee, UK Branch, CPA, 1992–93; Mem., Nat. Cttee, British-Arab Univ. Assoc. Mem., SE London Industrial Consultative Gp, 1975–83. Pres., Bexley Arthritis Care. Trustee, Lord Caradon Lecture Trust. Fellow, Industry and Parliament Trust, 1982. Introduced Protection of Children Act, 1978. *Publications:* Helping Others to Help Themselves: voluntary action in the eighties, 1981; Cyprus and NATO's Southern Flank, 1986; contribs to Contemporary Review and political jls. *Recreations:* books, music, exercise, exploring Cornwall. *Address:* House of Commons, SW1A 0AA.

TOWNSEND, Jean Ann, (Mrs P. B. Townsend); *see* Corston, J. A.

TOWNSEND, Mrs Joan, MA, MSc; Headmistress, Oxford High School, GPDST, since 1981; *b* 7 Dec. 1936; *d* of Emlyn Davies and Amelia Mary Davies (*née* Tyrer); *m* 1960, Prof. William Godfrey Townsend, RMCS, Shrivenham; two *d.* *Educ:* Somerville Coll., Oxford (Beilby Schol.; BA (Cl.I), MA); University College of Swansea, Univ. of Wales (MSc). School teaching and lecturing of various kinds, including: Tutor, Open University, 1971–75; Lectr, Oxford Polytechnic, 1975–76; Head of Mathematics, School of S Helen and S Katharine, Abingdon, 1976–81. FRSA 1986. *Publication:* paper in Qly Jl Maths and Applied Mech., 1965. *Address:* Silver Howe, 62 Iffley Turn, Oxford OX4 4HN. *T:* Oxford (01865) 715807.

TOWNSEND, Mrs Lena Moncrieff, CBE 1974; Member, Race Relations Board, 1967–72; *b* 3 Nov. 1911; twin *d* of late Captain R. G. Westropp, Cairo, Egypt; *m* (twice); two *s* one *d.* *Educ:* Downe House, Newbury; Somerville Coll., Oxford; Heidelberg Univ., Germany. During War of 1939–45 was an Organiser in WVS and in Women's Land Army, and then taught at Downe House. Mem. for Hampstead, LCC, 1955–65; Alderman, London Borough of Camden, 1964–67; Mem. for Camden, GLC, 1967–70; Alderman, GLC, 1970–77, and Dep. Chm., 1976–77; Inner London Education Authority: Dep. Leader, later Leader, 1967–70; Leader of the Opposition, 1970–71; Chm., Management Panel, Burnham Cttee, 1967–70; Mem., Women's European Cttee, 1972–75. Pres., Anglo-Egyptian Assoc., 1961–87 (when wound-up); Executive Member: British Section, European Union of Women, 1970–81; National Council, European Movement (British Council), 1970–86 (Mem., Speaker's Panel); Cons. Gp for Europe, 1967–88 (Founder Mem.); British Section, Internat. Union of Local Authorities and Council of European Municipalities, 1975– (rep. on Jt Twinning Cttee, 1975–83); London Europe Soc., 1977– (Vice-Pres. 1981–); Arkwright Arts Trust, 1971–84 (Chm., 1971–73). Mem., House Cttee, New End Hosp., then Hampstead Cttee, Royal Free Hosp., 1953–65. Mem. Exec. Cttee, Contemporary Dance Trust, 1968–75. Chm., Students' Accommodation Cttee, Univ. of London, 1977–86 (and Mem., Intercollegiate Halls Management Cttee); Member: Council, Westfield Coll., London Univ., 1965–89; Cons Nat. Adv. Cttee on Education, 1976–82; Governor, Barrett Street Coll., later London Coll. of Fashion, 1958–86 (Chm., 1967–86); Old Vic Trust, 1976–88; Hampstead Parochial Primary Sch., 1979–93. Patron, Lewis Carroll Soc. Hon. Fellow, QMW (Hon. Fellow, Westfield Coll., 1983). *Recreations:* once foreign languages, travel, the arts, gardening; now knitting, sewing, entertaining grandchildren and watching television. *Address:* 16 Holly Mount, NW3 6SG. *T:* 0171–435 8555.

TOWNSEND, Rear-Adm. Sir Leslie (William), KCVO 1981; CBE 1973; Member: Lord Chancellor's Panel of Independent Inspectors, since 1982; Lord Chancellor's Services Pensions Appeals Tribunal, since 1985; *b* 22 Feb. 1924; *s* of Ellen (*née* Alford) and William Bligh Townsend; *m* 1947, Marjorie Bennett; one *s* three *d.* *Educ:* Regent's Park School, Southampton. Joined RN, 1942; served in HMS Durban, 1942–43; Commissioned, 1943; HM Ships Spurwing, Astraea, Liverpool, Duke of York, Ceres, 1944–53; HMS Ceylon, 1956–58; Secretary to ACNS, 1959, to VCNS, 1967, to First Sea Lord, 1970; MA to CDS, 1971–73, to Chm. NATO Mil. Cttee, 1974; Dir, Naval and WRNS Officers' Appointments, 1977; Rear-Adm. 1979; Defence Services Sec., 1979–82. *Recreations:* fishing, cooking. *Clubs:* Army and Navy; Royal Naval and Royal Albert Yacht.

TOWNSEND, Prof. Peter Brereton; Professor of Social Policy, University of Bristol, 1982–93, now Emeritus; *b* 6 April 1928; *s* of late Philip Brereton Townsend and Alice Mary Townsend (*née* Southcote); *m* 1st, 1949, Ruth (*née* Pearce); four *s*; 2nd, 1977, Joy (*née* Skegg); one *d*; 3rd, 1985, Jean Ann Corston, *qv*; one step *s* one step *d.* *Educ:* Fleet Road Elementary Sch., London; University Coll. Sch., London; St John's Coll., Cambridge Univ.; Free Univ., Berlin. Research Sec., Political and Economic Planning, 1952–54; Research Officer, Inst. of Community Studies, 1954–57; Research Fellow and then Lectr in Social Administration, London Sch. of Economics, 1957–63; Prof. of Sociology, 1963–81, Pro-Vice-Chancellor (Social Policy), 1975–78, Univ. of Essex; Dir, Sch. of Applied Social Studies, Bristol Univ., 1983–85 and 1988–93. Vis. Prof. of Sociology, Essex Univ., 1982–86; Michael Harrington Distinguished Vis. Prof. of Social Sci., CUNY, 1991–92. Chm., 1965–66, Vice Pres., 1989–, Fabian Society (Chairman: Social Policy Cttee, 1970–82; Res. and Pubns Cttee, 1983–86). President: Psychiatric Rehabilitation Assoc., 1968–83; Child Poverty Action Gp, 1989– (Chm., 1969–89); SW Region, MENCAP, 1989–93; Chm., Disability Alliance, 1974–. Member: Chief Scientist's Cttee, DHSS, 1976–78; Govt Working Gp on Inequalities and Health, 1977–80; MSC Working Gp on Quota Scheme for Disabled, 1983–85. UNESCO consultant on poverty and development, 1978–80; Consultant: to GLC on poverty and the labour market in London, 1985–86; to Northern RHA on Inequalities of Health, 1985–86; to a consortium of 7 metropolitan boroughs on deprivation and shopping centres in Greater Manchester,

1987–88; to Islington Borough Council on deprivation and living standards, 1987–88; to UN for world summit on social develt, 1994–95; to UNDP on social safety net in Georgia, 1994; to UNDP and IILS on patterns and causes of social exclusion, 1994. DU Essex, 1990; DLitt Teeside, 1994; DUniv Open, 1994. *Publications:* The Family Life of Old People, 1957; National Superannuation (co-author), 1957; Nursing Homes in England and Wales (co-author), 1961; The Last Refuge: a survey of residential institutions and homes for the aged in England and Wales, 1962; The Aged in the Welfare State (co-author), 1965; The Poor and the Poorest (co-author), 1965; Old People in Three Industrial Societies (co-author), 1968; (ed) The Concept of Poverty, 1970; (ed) Labour and Inequality, 1972; The Social Minority, 1973; Sociology and Social Policy, 1975; Poverty in the United Kingdom: a survey of household resources and standards of living, 1979; (ed) Labour and Equality, 1980; Inequalities in Health (co-author), 1980; Manifesto (co-author), 1981; (ed jtly) Disability in Britain, 1981; The Family and Later Life, 1981; (ed jtly) Responses to Poverty: lessons from Europe, 1984; (jtly) Inequalities of Health in the Northern Region, 1986; Poverty and Labour in London, 1987; (jtly) Health and Deprivation: inequalities and the North, 1987; (jtly) Service Provision and Living Standards in Islington, 1988; (jtly) Inequalities in Health: the Black report and the health divide, 1988, 3rd edn 1993; The International Analysis of Poverty, 1993. *Recreation:* athletics.

TOWNSEND, Susan, (Sue); writer; *b* 2 April 1946. *Educ:* South Wigston Girls' High Sch. Writer and Presenter, Think of England, BBC TV, 1991. *Publications:* The Secret Diary of Adrian Mole Aged 13¾, 1982; The Growing Pains of Adrian Mole, 1984; Bazaar and Rummage, Groping for Words, and Womberang (plays), 1984; The Great Celestial Cow (play), 1985; The Secret Diary of Adrian Mole (play), 1985; Rebuilding Coventry, 1988; Mr Bevans Dream, 1989; Ten Tiny Fingers, Nine Tiny Toes (play), 1989; Adrian Mole From Minor to Major, 1991; The Queen and I, 1992 (adapted for stage, 1994); Adrian Mole—the Wilderness Years, 1993. *Recreations:* mooching about, reading, looking at pictures, canoeing. *Address:* Bridge Works, Knighton Fields Road West, Leicester LE2 6LH. *T:* Leicester (0116) 283 1176. *Club:* Groucho.

TOWNSHEND, family name of **Marquess Townshend.**

TOWNSHEND, 7th Marquess *cr* 1787; **George John Patrick Dominic Townshend;** Bt 1617; Baron Townshend of Lynn Regis, 1661; Viscount Townshend of Raynham, 1682; *b* 13 May 1916; *s* of 6th Marquess and Gladys Ethel Gwendolen Eugenie (*d* 1959), *e d* of late Thomas Sutherst, barrister; *S* father, 1921; *m* 1st, 1939, Elizabeth (marr. diss. 1960; she *m* 1960, Brig. Sir James Gault, KCMG, MVO, OBE; she *d* 1989), *o d* of Thomas Luby, ICS; one *s* two *d*; 2nd, 1960, Ann Frances (*d* 1988), *d* of Arthur Pellew Darlow; one *s* one *d*. Norfolk Yeomanry TA, 1936–40; Scots Guards, 1940–45. Chairman: Anglia Television Gp plc, 1971–86; Anglia Television Ltd, 1958–86; Survival Anglia, 1971–86; Anchor Enterprises Ltd, 1967–88; AP Bank Ltd, 1975–87; East Coast Grain Ltd, 1982–90; D. E. Longe & Co. Ltd, 1982–90; Norfolk Agricultural Station, 1973–87; Raynham Farm Co. Ltd, 1957–; Vice-Chairman: Norwich Union Life Insurance Society Ltd, 1973–86; Norwich Union Fire Insurance Society Ltd, 1975–86; Director: Scottish Union & National Insurance Co., 1968–86; Maritime Insurance Co. Ltd, 1968–86; London Merchant Securities plc, 1964–; Norwich Union (Holdings) plc, 1981–86; Napak Ltd, 1982–90; Riggs Nat. Corp., Washington, 1987–89. Chairman, Royal Norfolk Agricultural Association, 1978–85. Hon. DCL East Anglia, 1989. DL Norfolk, 1951–61. *Heir: s* Viscount Raynham, *qv*. *Address:* Raynham Hall, Fakenham, Norfolk NR21 7EP. *T:* Fakenham (01328) 862133. *Clubs:* White's, MCC; Norfolk (Norwich).

TOWNSING, Sir Kenneth (Joseph), Kt 1982; CMG 1971; ISO 1966; Director: Western Mining Corporation Ltd, 1975–87; Central Norseman Gold Corporation, 1982–87; *b* 25 July 1914; *s* of J. W. and L. A. Townsing; *m* 1942, Frances Olive Daniel; two *s* one *d*. *Educ:* Perth Boys' Sch.; Univ. of Western Australia. Treasury Officer, 1933–39. Served War, AIF (Middle East), 1940–46, Major. Public Service Inspector, 1946–49; Sec., Public Service Commissioner's Office, 1949–52; Dep. Under Treasurer, 1952–57; Public Service Comr, 1958–59; Under Treasurer (Permanent Head), 1959–75. Chm., Salaries and Allowances Tribunal, 1975–84. Mem. Senate, Univ. of Western Australia, 1954–70 (Chm. Finance Cttee, 1956–70; Pro-Chancellor, 1968–70); Comr, Rural and Industries Bank, 1959–65; Member: Jackson Cttee on Tertiary Educn, 1967; Tertiary Educn Commn, 1971–74; Past Mem. numerous other Bds and Cttees. Fellow, W Australian Museum, 1975; Hon. Zoo Associate, 1979. FCPA. Hon. LLD Univ. of W Australia, 1971; DUniv Murdoch, 1982. *Recreation:* gardening. *Address:* 22 Robin Street, Mount Lawley, WA 6050, Australia. *T:* (9) 2721393. *Club:* University House (Perth).

TOWRY, Peter; *see* Piper, Sir D. T.

TOY, Rev. Canon John, PhD; Chancellor of York Minster, since 1983 (also Librarian and Guestmaster); Prebendary of Laughton-en-le-Morthen, since 1994; *b* 25 Nov. 1930; *e s* of late Sidney Toy, FSA and late Violet Mary (*née* Doudney); *m* 1963, Mollie *d* of Eric and Elsie Tilbury; one *s* one *d*. *Educ:* Epsom County Grammar Sch.; Hatfield Coll., Durham (BA 1st cl. Hons. Theol. 1953, MA 1962). PhD Leeds, 1982. Ordained deacon, 1955, priest, 1956; Curate, St Paul's, Lorrimore Sq., Southwark, 1955–58; Student Christian Movement Sec. for S of England, 1958–60; Chaplain: Ely Theol Coll., 1960–64; St Andrew's Church, Gothenburg, Sweden, 1965–69; St John's College, York: Lectr in Theology, 1969; Sen. Lectr, 1972; Principal Lectr, 1979–83; Prebendary of Tockerington, 1983–94. *Publications:* Jesus, Man for God, 1988; contrib. to learned jls and cathedral booklets. *Recreations:* music, history, architecture. *Address:* 4 Minster Yard, York YO1 2JF. *T:* York (01904) 620877.

TOY, Sam, OBE 1994; Chairman and Managing Director, Ford Motor Co. Ltd, 1980–86; Chairman, Norman Cordiner Ltd, Inverness, since 1991; *b* 21 Aug. 1923; *s* of Edward and Lillian Toy; *m* 1st, 1944, Jean Balls; one *s*; 2nd, 1950, Joan Franklin Rook; two *s* one *d*; 3rd, 1984, Janetta McMorrow. *Educ:* Falmouth Grammar Sch.; Fitzwilliam Coll., Cambridge (MA; Hon. Fellow, 1984). Pilot (Flt Lieut), RAF, 1942–48. Graduate trainee, Ford Motor Co. Ltd, 1948; thereafter, all business career with Ford Motor Co. Ltd. Mem. Council, SMMT, 1975– (Vice-Pres., 1982–86; Pres., 1986–87; Dep. Pres., 1987–88). Chm., UK 2000 Scotland, 1988–. *Recreations:* trout and salmon fishing, golf. *Address:* 1 Primrose Bay, Invermoriston, Inverness IV3 6YD; 35 Stanhope Terrace, Lancaster Gate, W2 2UA. *Clubs:* Lord's Taverners', Eccentric.

TOYE, Bryan Edward; JP; Chairman, Toye & Co. and associated companies, since 1969; *b* 17 March 1938; *s* of Herbert Graham Donovan Toye and Marion Alberta Toye (*née* Montignani); *m* 1982, Fiona Hogg; two *s* one *d*. *Educ:* St Andrew's Prep. Sch., Eastbourne; Stowe Sch. Joined Toye & Co., 1956; Dir, Toye Kenning & Spencer, 1962–; Dir, Toye & Co., 1966. Non-exec. Director: Futurama Signs Ltd; Trehaven Trust Ltd. Alderman, Ward of Lime Street, City of London, 1983– (Pres., Lime Street Ward Club); Pres., City Livery Club, 1988–89; Master, Gold and Silver Wyre Drawers' Co., 1984; Member, Court of Assistants: Broderers' Co.; Guild of Freemen of City of London; Mem., Court of Assistants, Goldsmiths' Co., 1992–; Hon. Mem., Court of Assistants, Hon. Artillery Co.; Pres., Royal Warrant Holders' Assoc., 1991–92 (Mem. Council, 1982–). Governor: Bridewell Royal Hosp., 1989–93; Christ's Hosp.; Estates and Sch. Governor, King Edward's Sch., Witley, 1988–93; Trustee: Queen Elizabeth Scholarship Trust; Britain–Australia Bicentennial Trust; Black Country Museum London Gp; Vice Pres., British Red Cross, 1993– (Dep. Pres. and Trustee, 1993). Steward, Henley Royal Regatta, 1980. Hon. Col, 124 Havering Petroleum Sqn (V), RLC. JP City of London, 1983. FInstD, FIMgt, MInstPS, FRSA. OStJ. *Recreations:* swimming, tennis, gardening, music, Rugby, entertaining. *Address:* Toye & Co., 19/21 Great Queen Street, WC2B 5BE. *T:* 0171–242 0471. *Clubs:* Wig and Pen, Royal Automobile, MCC; Middlesex Co. RFC; Wasps FC (Vice-Pres.); Leander (Henley).

TOYE, Prof. John Francis Joseph; Director, Institute of Development Studies, University of Sussex, since 1987; *b* 7 Oct. 1942; *s* of John Redmond Toye and Adele Toye (*née* Francis); *m* 1967, Janet Reason; one *s* one *d*. *Educ:* Christ's Coll., Finchley; Jesus Coll., Cambridge (schol.; MA); Harvard Univ. (Frank Knox Vis. Fellow); Sch. of Oriental and African Studies, Univ. of London (MScEcon; PhD). Asst Principal, HM Treasury, 1965–68; Res. Fellow, SOAS, Univ. of London, 1970–72; Fellow (later Tutor), Wolfson Coll., Cambridge, 1972–80, and Asst Dir of Develt Studies, Cambridge Univ., 1977–80; Dir, Commodities Res. Unit Ltd, 1980–85; Prof. of Develt Policy and Planning and Dir, Centre for Develt Studies, University Coll. of Swansea, 1982–87. Hon. Fellow, Univ. of Birmingham, Inst. of Local Govt Studies, 1986. Member: Council, ODI, 1988–; Adv. Cttee on Econ. and Social Res., ODA, 1989–. *Publications:* (ed) Taxation and Economic Development, 1978; (ed) Trade and Poor Economies, 1979; Public Expenditure and Indian Development Policy 1960–70, 1981; Dilemmas of Development, 1987; (jtly) Does Aid Work in India?, 1990; (jtly) Aid and Power, 1991; Structural Adjustment and Employment Policy, 1995; numerous articles in acad. jls. *Recreations:* walking, music. *Address:* c/o Institute of Development Studies, University of Sussex, Falmer, Brighton, Sussex BN1 9RE. *T:* Brighton (01273) 606261.

TOYE, Wendy, CBE 1992; theatrical and film director; choreographer, actress, dancer; *b* 1 May 1917. First professional appearance as Peasblossom in A Midsummer Night's Dream, Old Vic, 1929; principal dancer in Hiawatha, Royal Albert Hall, 1931; Marigold, Phœbe in Toad of Toad Hall and produced dances, Royalty, Christmas, 1931–32; in early 1930s performed and choreographed for the very distinguished Carmargo Society of Ballet; guest artist with Sadler's Wells Ballet and Mme Rambert's Ballet Club; went to Denmark as principal dancer with British Ballet, organized by Adeline Genée, 1932; danced in C. B. Cochran's The Miracle, Lyceum, 1932; masked dancer in Ballerina, Gaiety, 1933; member of Ninette de Valois' original Vic Wells Ballet, principal dancer for Ninette de Valois in The Golden Toy, Coliseum, 1934; toured with Anton Dolin's ballet (choreog. for divertissements and short ballets), 1934–35; in Tulip Time, Alhambra, then Markova-Dolin Ballet as principal dancer and choreog., 1935; in Love and How to Cure It, Globe, 1937. Arranged dances and ballets for many shows and films including most of George Black's productions for next 7 years, notably Black Velvet in which also principal dancer, 1939. Shakespearean season, Open Air Theatre, 1939. *Theatre productions:* Big Ben, Bless the Bride, Tough at the Top (for C. B. Cochran), Adelphi; The Shepherd Show, Prince's; Co-Director and Choreographer, Peter Pan, New York; And So To Bed, New Theatre; Co-Director and Choreographer, Feu d'Artifice, Paris; Night of Masquerade, Q; Second Threshold, Vaudeville; Choreography for Three's Company in Joyce Grenfell Requests the Pleasure, Fortune; Wild Thyme, Duke of York's; Lady at the Wheel, Lyric, Hammersmith; Majority of One, Phœnix; Magic Lantern, Saville; As You Like It, Old Vic; Virtue in Danger, Mermaid and Strand; Robert and Elizabeth, Lyric; On the Level, Saville; Midsummer Night's Dream, Shakespeare quatercentenary Latin American tour, 1964; Soldier's Tale, Edinburgh Festival, 1967; Boots with Strawberry Jam, Nottingham Playhouse, 1968; The Great Waltz, Drury Lane, 1970; Showboat, Adelphi, 1971; She Stoops to Conquer, Young Vic, 1972; Cowardy Custard, Mermaid, 1972; Stand and Deliver, Roundhouse, 1972; R loves J, Chichester, 1973; The Confederacy, Chichester, 1974; The Englishman Amused, Young Vic, 1974; Follow The Star, Chichester, 1974, Westminster Theatre, 1976; Made in Heaven, Chichester, 1975; Make Me a World, Chichester, 1976; Once More with Music (with Cicely Courtneidge and Jack Hulbert), 1976; Oh, Mr Porter, Mermaid, 1977; Dance for Gods, Conversations, 1979; Colette, Comedy, 1980; Gingerbread Man, Water Mill, 1981; This Thing Called Love, Ambassadors, 1983; (Associate Prod.) Singin' in the Rain, Palladium, 1983; (dir and narr.) Noel and Gertie, Monte Carlo and Canada; (Associate Prod.) Barnham, Manchester, 1984, Victoria Palace, 1985; Birds of a Feather, 1984, and Mad Woman of Chaillot, 1985, Niagara-on-the-Lake; Gala for Joyce Grenfell Tribute, 1985; (Associate Prod.) Torvill and Dean World Tour, 1985; Once Upon a Mattress, Watermill Theatre, 1985; Kiss Me Kate, Aarhus and Copenhagen, 1986; Unholy Trinity, Stephenville Fest., 1986; Laburnam Grove, Palace Th. Watford, 1987; Miranda, Chichester Fest., 1987; Get the Message, Molecule, 1987; Songbook, Watermill, 1988; Mrs Dot, Watford, 1988; When That I Was, Manitoba, 1988; Oh! Coward, Hong Kong, 1989; Cinderella, Palace Th., Watford, 1989; Penny Black, Wavendon, 1990; Moll Flanders, Watermill, 1990; Heaven's Up, Playhouse, 1990; Mrs Pat's Profession (workshop with Cleo Laine), Wavendon, 1991; The Drummer, Watermill, 1991; Sound of Music, Sadler's Wells, 1992; See How They Run, Watermill, 1992; Vienna, 1993; Under their Hats, King's Head, 1994, Vienna, 1995; The Anastasia File, Watermill, 1994; Lloyd George Knew My Father, Watermill, 1995; *Opera Productions:* Bluebeard's Castle (Bartok), Sadler's Wells and Brussels; The Telephone (Menotti), Sadler's Wells; Russalka (Dvořák), Sadler's Wells; Fledermaus, Coliseum and Sadler's Wells; Orpheus in the Underworld, Sadler's Wells and Australia; La Vie Parisienne, Sadler's Wells; Seraglio, Bath Festival, 1967; The Impresario, Don Pasquale (for Phoenix Opera Group), 1968; The Italian Girl in Algiers, Coliseum, 1968; La Cenerentola; Merry Widow, 1979, Orpheus in the Underworld, 1981, ENO North; The Mikado, Nat. Opera Co., Ankara, 1982; Italian Girl in Algiers, ENO, 1982; La Serva Padrona and Der Apotoker, Aix-en-Provence Fest., 1991. *Films directed:* The Stranger Left No Card; The Teckman Mystery; Raising a Riot; The Twelfth Day of Christmas; Three Cases of Murder; All for Mary; True as a Turtle; We Joined the Navy; The King's Breakfast; Cliff in Scotland; A Goodly Manor for a Song; Girls Wanted—Istanbul; Trial by Jury (TV). Retrospectives of films directed: Festival de Films des Femmes International, Créteil, Paris, 1990; Tokyo Film Fest., 1991. Productions for TV, etc, inc. Golden Gala, ATV, 1978; Follow the Star, BBC2, 1979; Stranger in Town, Anglia, 1981. Dir concert, Till We Meet Again, RFH, 1989. Advisor, Arts Council Trng Scheme, for many years; Member: Council, LAMDA; (original) Accreditation Bd instig. by Nat. Council of Drama Training for acting courses, 1981–84; Grand Council, Royal Acad. of Dancing; 1st directors' rep. on Equity Council, 1974– (Dir, Sub-Cttee, 1971–). Committee Member: Wavendon Allmusic Scheme; Vivian Ellis Award Scheme; Richard Stilgoe Award Scheme. Trained with Euphen MacLaren, Karsavina, Dolin, Morosoff, Legat, Rambert. Silver Jubilee Medal, 1977.

TOYN, His Honour Richard John; a Circuit Judge 1972–92; *b* 24 Jan. 1927; *s* of Richard Thomas Millington Toyn and Ethel Toyn; *m* 1955, Joyce Evelyn Goodwin; two *s* two *d*. *Educ:* Solihull Sch.; Bristol Grammar Sch.; Bristol Univ. (LLB). Royal Army Service Corps, 1948–50. Called to the Bar, Gray's Inn, 1950. Mem., Parole Bd, 1978–80. Contributing Ed., Butterworths County Court Precedents and Pleadings, 1985. *Recreations:* music, drama, photography.

TOYNBEE, Polly; Associate Editor and columnist, Independent, since 1995; writer; *b* 27 Dec. 1946; *d* of late Philip Toynbee, and of Anne Powell; *m* 1970, Peter Jenkins (*d* 1992);

one *s* two *d* and one step *d*. *Educ:* Badminton Sch.; Holland Park Comprehensive; St Anne's Coll., Oxford. Reporter, The Observer, 1968–71; Editor, The Washington Monthly, USA, 1972–73; Feature Writer, The Observer, 1974–76; Columnist, The Guardian, 1977–88; Social Affairs Editor, News and Current Affairs, BBC, 1988–95. Contested (SDP) Lewisham E, 1983. Gov., LSE, 1988–. Catherine Pakenham Award for Journalism, 1975; British Press Award, 1977, 1982, 1986 (Columnist of the Year). *Publications:* Leftovers, 1966; A Working Life, 1970 (paperback 1972); Hospital, 1977 (paperback 1979); The Way We Live Now, 1981; Lost Children, 1985. *Address:* Independent, 1 Canada Square, Canary Wharf, E14 5AP.

TOYNE, Prof. Peter, DL; Vice-Chancellor, Liverpool John Moores University, since 1992 (Rector, Liverpool Polytechnic, 1986–92); *b* 3 Dec. 1939; *s* of Harold and Doris Toyne; *m* 1969, Angela Wedderburn; one *s*. *Educ:* Ripon Grammar Sch.; Bristol Univ. (BA); The Sorbonne. FRSA; CBIM. Res. Asst, Univ. of Lille, 1964; Univ. of Exeter: Lectr in Geography, 1965–76; Sen. Lectr in Geography and Sub Dean of Social Studies, 1976–78; Dir, DES Credit Transfer Feasibility Study, 1978–80; Hd of Bishop Otter Coll., Chichester, and Dep. Dir (Academic), W Sussex Inst. of Higher Educn, 1980–83; Dep. Rector, NE London Polytechnic, 1983–86. Dir, Liverpool Playhouse, 1987–91. Chairman: Initial Training Panel, Council for Educn and Training in Youth and Community Work, 1984–87; Credit Accumulation and Transfer Scheme Cttee, CNAA, 1986–90; CNAA/DES Cttee on Recognition of Access Courses, 1988–92; ECCTIS 2000 Adv. Gp, 1990–; BBC Radio Merseyside Adv. Council, 1988–92; BBC North Adv. Council, 1992–; DES Expert Cttee on Envmtl Educn, 1992; Higher Educn Quality Council, Div. of Credits and Access, 1992–; Liverpool Compact, 1990–; Vice-Chairman: Cttee of Dirs of Polytechnics, 1990–92; Cttee on Internat. Co-operation in Higher Educn, British Council, 1991–; CVCP, 1992–; Member: BBC NW Regional Council, 1988–92; Merseyside Enterprise Forum, 1986–; Business Opportunities on Merseyside, 1986–93; Bd, Merseyside Innovation Centre, 1987–; Council, Merseyside Chamber of Commerce and Industry, 1990–; Rover Learning Business Bd, 1991–; Open Learning (formerly Poly.) Bd, 1991–93; PCEF Bd, 1991–; Bd, Liverpool Inst. for Performing Arts, 1991–; Higher Educn Quality Council Bd, 1992–; Further and Higher Educn Cttee, Gen. Synod Bd of Educn, 1985–92; Central Services Unit, Careers in Higher Educn, 1989–93; Theol Coll. Inspector, House of Bishops, 1980–; Trustee: Farringdon Trust, 1982–; St Luke's Trust, 1984–89; Higher Educn Foundn, 1988–91. Hon. DEd CNAA, 1992. DL Merseyside, 1990. *Publications:* World Problems, 1970; Techniques in Human Geography, 1971; Organisation, Location and Behaviour, 1974; Recreation and Environment, 1974; Toyne Report: Credit Transfer, 1979; Toyne Report: Environmental Education, 1993; numerous articles in geographical, educnl jls, festschriften and popular press. *Recreations:* railways (model and real), liturgy, music (especially sacred). *Address:* 2 Rodney Street, Liverpool L3 5UX. *T:* 0151–709 3676. *Club:* Athenæum (Liverpool).

TOYNE SEWELL, Maj.-Gen. Timothy Patrick; Director, The London Goodenough Trust for Overseas Graduates, since 1995; *b* 7 July 1941; *s* of late Brig. E. P. Sewell, CBE and of E. C. M. Sewell, MBE (*née* Toyne); *m* 1965, Jennifer Lesley Lunt; one *s* one *d*. *Educ:* Bedford Sch.; RMA, Sandhurst. psc 1973; jsdc 1985; rcds 1988. Commnd KOSB, 1961; ADC to Governor of Aden, 1962–63; helicopter pilot, 2 RGJ and 2 Para, 1966–69; Staff College, 1973; GSO 1, staff of CDS, 1979–81; CO, 1 KOSB, 1981–83; CoS, British Forces Falkland Is, 1983–84; Sen. Directing Staff (Army), JSDC, 1984–85; Comdr, 19 Infantry Bde, 1985–87; RCDS, 1988; Comdr, British Mil. and Adv. Team, Zimbabwe, 1989–91; Comdt, RMA, 1991–94; Team Leader, Tri-Service Study into Services Recruiting Orgns, 1994–95, retired. *Recreations:* racquet sports, golf, fishing, music. *Address:* c/o Lloyds Bank, Cox's & King's Branch, PO Box 1190, 7 Pall Mall, SW1Y 5NA. *Club:* Army and Navy.

TRACEY, Prof. Ian; Organist and Master of the Choristers, Liverpool Cathedral, since 1980; Professor, Fellow and Organist, Liverpool John Moores University (formerly Liverpool Polytechnic), since 1988; *b* 27 May 1955; *s* of William Tracey and Helene Mignon Tracey (*née* Harris). *Educ:* Trinity Coll. of Music, London (FTCL); St Katharine's Coll., Liverpool (PGCE). Chorus Master, Royal Liverpool Philharmonic Soc., 1985–; Liverpool City Organist (formerly Consultant Organist, City of Liverpool), 1986–. FRSA 1988. NW Arts Award for Classical Music, 1994. *Address:* 6 Cathedral Close, Liverpool Cathedral, Liverpool L1 7BR. *T:* 0151–708 8471. *Club:* Artists' (Liverpool).

TRACEY, Richard Patrick, JP; MP (C) Surbiton, since 1983; *b* 8 Feb. 1943; *o s* of late P. H. (Dick) Tracey and of Hilda Tracey; *m*, Katharine Gardner; one *s* three *d*. *Educ:* King Edward VI Sch., Stratford-upon-Avon; Birmingham Univ. (LLB Hons). Leader Writer, Daily Express, 1964–66; Presenter/Reporter, BBC Television and Radio, 1966–78: internat. news and current affairs (The World at One, PM, Today, Newsdesk, 24 Hours, The Money Prog.); feature programmes (Wheelbase, Waterline, Motoring and the Motorist, You and Yours, Checkpoint); also documentaries; Public Affairs Consultant/Advisor, 1978–83. Member: Econ. Res. Council, 1981–; ISIS Assoc., 1981–92. Various Conservative Party Offices, 1974–81; Dep. Chm., Greater London Cons. Party, 1981–83; Mem., Cons. National Union Exec. Cttee, 1981–83. PPS to Min. of State for Trade and Industry (IT), 1984–85; Parly Under Sec. of State, DoE (with special responsibility for sport), 1985–87. Member: Select Cttee on Televising H of C, 1988–92; Selection Cttee, 1992–94; Public Accounts Cttee, 1994–. Chm., Cons. Parly Greater London MP's Cttee, 1990– (Jt Sec., 1983–84); Sec., Cons. Parly Media Cttee, 1983–84. Contested (C) Northampton N, Oct. 1974. JP SW London (Wimbledon PSD), 1977. Freeman, City of London, 1984. *Publications:* (with Richard Hudson-Evans) The World of Motor Sport, 1971; (with Michael Clayton) Hickstead—the first twelve years, 1972; articles, pamphlets. *Recreations:* riding, boating, debating. *Address:* House of Commons, SW1A 0AA. *T:* 0171–219 5196. *Club:* Wig and Pen.

TRACEY, Stanley William, OBE 1986; professional pianist, composer and arranger, since 1943; *b* 30 Dec. 1926; *s* of Stanley Clark Tracey and Florence Louise Tracey; *m* 1st, 1946, Joan; 2nd, 1954, Jean; 3rd, 1960, Florence Mary, (Jackie); one *s* one *d*. *Educ:* Tooting, Graveney and Ensham Schools. Leading own small group, 1965–, orchestra, 1969–. Hon. RAM 1984. Fellow, City of Leeds Coll. of Music, 1993. Numerous records of own compositions and arrangements; compositions include: Under Milk Wood suite, 1965; Genesis, 1986; 500 other titles. Awards include: BASCA Award, 1984; voted best jazz composer, Wire/Guardian, 1989; voted best album of year, Big Band, 1989; pianist of the year, British Jazz Awards, 1992; Best arranger/composer, British Jazz Awards, 1995. *Address:* 12 Cotlandswick, London Colney, Herts AL2 1EE. *T:* Bowmansgreen (01727) 823286.

TRACEY, Stephen Frederick T.; *see* Thorpe-Tracey.

TRACY; *see* Hanbury-Tracy, family name of Baron Sudeley.

TRACY, Rear-Adm. Hugh Gordon Henry, CB 1965; DSC 1945; *b* 15 Nov. 1912; *e s* of Comdr A. F. G. Tracy, RN; *m* 1938, Muriel, *d* of Maj.-Gen. Sir R. B. Ainsworth, CB, DSO, OBE; two *s* one *d*. *Educ:* Nautical Coll., Pangbourne. Joined RN, 1929; Lieut, 1934; served in HMS Shropshire, Hawkins and Furious, in Admiralty and attended Advanced Engineering course before promotion to Lt-Comdr, 1942; Sen. Engineer, HMS Illustrious, 1942–44; Asst to Manager, Engineering Dept, HM Dockyard Chatham, 1944–46; Comdr 1946; served in HMS Manxman, Admiralty, RN Engineering Coll. and HM Dockyard Malta; Captain, 1955; Asst Director of Marine Engineering, Admiralty, 1956–58; CO HMS Sultan, 1959–60; Imperial Defence Coll., 1961; CSO (Tech.) to Flag Officer, Sea Training, 1962–63; Rear-Admiral, 1963; Director of Marine Engineering, Ministry of Defence (Navy), 1963–66; retired, 1966. Pres., Wilts Gardens Trust, 1992– (Chm., 1985–89). *Recreations:* gardening, plant ecology. *Address:* 21a Sion Hill, Bath BA1 2UL.

TRAFFORD; *see* de Trafford.

TRAFFORD, Ian Colton, OBE 1967; Publisher, The Times Supplements, 1981–88, retired; *b* 8 July 1928; *s* of late Dr Harold Trafford and Laura Dorothy Trafford; *m* 1st, 1949, Nella Georgara (marr. diss. 1964); one *d*; 2nd, 1972, Jacqueline Carole Trenque. *Educ:* Charterhouse; St John's Coll., Oxford. Feature writer and industrial correspondent, The Financial Times, 1951–58; UK Correspondent, Barrons Weekly, New York, 1954–60; Director, Industrial and Trade Fairs Holdings Ltd, 1958–71, Managing Director, 1966–71; Director-General British Trade Fairs in: Peking, 1964; Moscow, 1966; Bucharest, 1968; Sao Paulo, 1969; Buenos Aires, 1970; Man. Dir, Economist Newspaper, 1971–81; Chm., Economist Intelligence Unit, 1971–79; Dep. Chm., Times Books Ltd, 1981–86. Local Dir, W London Board, Commercial Union Assce, 1974–83. OBE awarded for services to exports. *Address:* Grafton House, 128 Westhall Road, Warlingham, Surrey CR6 9HF. *T:* Upper Warlingham (01883) 622048.

TRAHAIR, John Rosewarne, CBE 1990; DL; Chairman, Plymouth District Health Authority, 1981–90; *b* 29 March 1921; *s* of late Percy Edward Trahair and Edith Irene Trahair; *m* 1948, Patricia Elizabeth (*née* Godrich); one *s* one *d*. *Educ:* Leys Sch.; Christ's Coll., Cambridge (MA). FCIS. Served with Royal Artillery, 1941–46 (Captain). Finance Dir, Farleys Infant Food Ltd, 1948–73; Dir 1950–74, Dep. Chm. 1956–74, Western Credit Holdings Ltd. Chairman: Moorhaven HMC, 1959–66; Plymouth and District HMC, 1966–74; Member: SW Regional Hosp. Bd, 1965–74 (Vice-Chm. 1971–73, Chm. 1973–74); South Western RHA, 1974–81. Mem., Devon CC, 1977–81. Pres., Devon County Agricl Assoc., 1993–. High Sheriff, Devon, 1987–88; DL Devon, 1989. *Recreations:* sailing, walking. *Address:* West Park, Ivybridge, South Devon PL21 9JP. *T:* Plymouth (01752) 892466. *Club:* Royal Western Yacht.

TRAILL, Sir Alan Towers, GBE 1984; QSO 1990; Managing Director, Colburn Traill Ltd, since 1989; Underwriting Member of Lloyd's, 1963–89; *b* 7 May 1935; *s* of George Traill and Margaret Eleanor (*née* Matthews); *m* 1964, Sarah Jane (*née* Hutt); one *s*. *Educ:* St Andrew's Sch., Eastbourne; Charterhouse; Jesus Coll., Cambridge (MA). ACIArb 1991. British Insurance Brokers Association: Mem. Council, 1978–79; Chairman: Reinsurance Brokers Cttee, 1978–79; UK/NZ 1990 Cttee, 1989–90. Member, Court of Common Council, City of London, 1970; Alderman for Langbourn Ward, 1975–; Sheriff, 1982–83; Lord Mayor of London, 1984–85. Master, Worshipful Co. of Cutlers, 1979–80; Dir, City Arts Trust, 1980–; Chm. Trustees, Waitangi Foundn, 1991–. Trustee, Morden Coll., 1995–. Mem. Adv. Cttee, LSO. Governor: Royal Shakespeare Co., 1982–; Treloar Coll., 1986–; Almoner, Christ's Hosp. Foundn, 1980–. KStJ 1985. *Recreations:* shooting, skiing, DIY, travel, opera, assisting education. *Address:* 19/21 Great Tower Street, EC3R 5AQ. *T:* 0171–283 7442.

TRAIN, Christopher John, CB 1986; Deputy Under Secretary of State, Home Office, and Director-General, Prison Service, 1983–91; *b* 12 March 1932; *s* of late Keith Sydney Sayer Train and Edna Ashby Train; *m* 1957, Sheila Mary Watson; one *s* one *d*. *Educ:* Nottingham High Sch.; Christ Church Oxford (BA Lit. Hum., MA). Served Royal Navy, 1955–57; Assistant Master, St Paul's Sch., W Kensington, 1957–67; Principal, Home Office, 1968; Asst Sec., Home Office, 1972; Secretary, Royal Commn on Criminal Procedure, 1978–80; Asst Under Sec. of State, Home Office, 1980–83. Vis. Prof., Dept of Management Sci., Strathclyde Univ., 1992–. Pres., Suffolk Horse Soc., 1989–90. *Recreations:* collecting and writing cricket books, jogging, playing the piano. *Club:* Vincent's (Oxford).

TRAIN, David, MC 1945; PhD; FCGI, FRPharmS, FRSC; FEng, FIChemE; Partner, 1961–82, Senior Partner, 1980–82, Senior Consultant, 1982–88, Cremer and Warner, Consulting Engineers and Scientists; *b* 27 Feb. 1919; *s* of Charles and Elsie Louisa Train; *m* 1943, Jeanne Catherine, *d* of late William R. and M. M. Edmunds; two *s*. *Educ:* Lady Hawkins' Grammar Sch., Kington; School of Pharmacy, Univ. of London; Northampton Coll. of Advanced Technology; Imperial Coll., Univ. of London. Fairchild Schol. 1940, MPS 1941, Hewlett Exhibn 1941; BPharm 1942, PhC 1942; BScChemEng 1949, PhD 1956, DIC 1956. ARIC 1949; FRSH 1972; FCGI 1982 (ACGI 1949); FEng 1983. Apprenticed to F. T. Roper and Daughter, Kington, 1935–38. War service: St John's Hosp. Reserve, 1939; RAMC (non-med.), NW Europe, 1942–45; 212 Fd Amb. 53rd Welsh (Lieut). Lectr in Pharmaceutical Engrg Science, 1949–59, Reader, 1959–61, Fellow, 1991–, Sch. of Pharmacy, London; Vis. Prof., Univ. of Wisconsin, 1959. Examiner: for Pharm. Soc. of Gt Brit., 1949–56; IChemE, 1956–66; Mem. Bd of Studies in Chem. Engrg, Univ. of London, 1958–94. Jt Hon. Secretary: Brit. Pharm. Conf., 1958–64; IChemE, 1972–77; Member: Adv. Cttee on Oil Pollution of the Sea, 1973–84; Parly Gp for Engrg Devel, 1987–; Air Pollution Control Assoc., USA, 1971–84; Fédn Internat. Pharmaceutique, 1970–82. Gov., Bromley Coll. of Further Educn, 1987–95. Liveryman: Worshipful Soc. of Apothecaries, 1975–; Worshipful Co. of Engineers, 1983–. *Publications:* various, on compression of powders, protection of the environment, acidic emissions, hazards in medicaments, preventative toxicology. *Recreations:* gardening, travelling. *Address:* 3 Grayland Close, Bromley, Kent BR1 2PA. *T:* 0181–464 4701.

TRANT, Gen. Sir Richard (Brooking), KCB 1982 (CB 1979); Chairman: Hunting Engineering Ltd, 1988–93; Defence Division, Hunting Plc, since 1989; Irvin Aerospace Ltd, since 1993; Deputy Chairman, Wilson's Hogg Robinson Ltd, since 1988; *b* 30 March 1928; *s* of Richard Brooking Trant and Dora Rodney Trant (*née* Lancaster); *m* 1957, Diana Clare, 2nd *d* of Rev. Stephen Zachary and Ruth Beatrice Edwards; one *s* two *d*. Commissioned RA 1947; served Korean War, 1952–53; Defence Services Staff Coll., India, 1961–62; S Arabia, 1962–65; Jt Services Staff Coll., 1965; commanded 3rd Regt RHA, 1968–71, 5th Airportable Brigade, 1972–74; Dep. Mil. Sec., MoD (Army), 1975–76; Comdr Land Forces, NI, 1977–79; Dir, Army Staff Duties, 1979–82; GOC South East District, 1982–83, Land Dep. C-in-C Fleet during S Atlantic Campaign, 1982; QMG, 1983–86. Col Comdt: RAEC, 1979–86; RA, 1982–87; RAOC, 1984–88; HAC (TA), 1984–92. Special Comr, Duke of York's Royal Mil. Sch., Dover, 1987–93; Comr, Royal Hosp. Chelsea, 1988–. Defence Advisor, Short Bros, 1987–88; Dir, Eastern Region Technology Centre, 1989–93. Member: Armed Forces Pay Rev. Body, 1988–; Council, SBAC, 1988–; Vice Pres., Defence Manufacturers' Assoc., 1989–. Pres., Beds Chamber of Commerce and Industry, 1993–; Dir, S Beds Community Health Trust, 1991–. Pres., RA Hunt and RA Saddle Club, 1984–90; Admiral, Army Sailing Assoc., 1984–87. Trustee, Cornwall Heritage Trust, 1991–. CIMgt (CBIM 1985); MInstD 1987. Freeman, City of London, 1984. Order of South Arabia, 3rd Class, 1965. *Recreations:* golf, field sports, natural history, sailing. *Address:* c/o Lloyds Bank, Newquay, Cornwall TR7 1JB. *Clubs:* Army and Navy; Royal Fowey Yacht.

TRANTER, Nigel Godwin, OBE 1983; novelist and author since 1936; *b* Glasgow, 23 Nov. 1909; *yr s* of Gilbert T. Tranter and Eleanor A. Cass; *m* 1933, May Jean Campbell Grieve (*d* 1979); one *d* (one *s* decd). *Educ:* St James Episcopal Sch., Edinburgh; George Heriot's Sch., Edinburgh. Served War of 1939–45, RASC and RA. Accountancy trng, then in small family insce co., until could live on writing, after war service; much and actively interested in Scottish public affairs; Chm., Scottish Convention, Edinburgh Br., 1948–51; Vice-Convener, Scottish Covenant Assoc., 1951–55; Pres., E Lothian Liberal Assoc., 1960–76; Chm., Nat. Forth Road Bridge Cttee, 1953–57; Pres., Scottish PEN, 1962–66, Hon. Pres., 1973–; Chm., Soc. of Authors, Scotland, 1966–72; Pres., E Lothian Wildfowlers' Assoc., 1952–73; Chm., St Andrew Soc. of E Lothian, 1966–; Chm., Nat. Book League, Scotland, 1972–77; Hon. Vice-Pres., Scottish Assoc. of Teachers of History, 1989; Hon. Pres., Saltire Soc., 1991; Mem., Cttee of Aberlady Bay Nature Reserve, 1953–76, etc. Hon. Member: Mark Twain Soc. of Amer., 1976; Scottish Soc. of Memphis, Tennessee. Hon. Freeman, Blackstone, Va, 1980. Hon. MA Edinburgh, 1971; Hon. DLitt Strathclyde, 1990. Scot of the Year, BBC Radio Scotland, 1989. Chevalier, Order of St Lazarus of Jerusalem, 1961 (Vice-Chancellor of the Order, Scotland, 1980, Chancellor, 1986). *Publications: fiction:* 80 novels, from Trespass, 1937, including: Bridal Path, 1952; Macgregor's Gathering, 1957; the Master of Gray trilogy: The Master of Gray, 1961; The Courtesan, 1963; Past Master, 1965; Chain of Destiny, 1964; the Robert the Bruce trilogy: The Steps to the Empty Throne, 1969; The Path of the Hero King, 1970; The Price of the King's Peace, 1971; The Young Montrose, 1972; Montrose: the Captain General, 1973; The Wisest Fool, 1974; The Wallace, 1975; Lords of Misrule, 1976; A Folly of Princes, 1977; The Captive Crown, 1977; Macbeth the King, 1978; Margaret the Queen, 1979; David the Prince, 1980; True Thomas, 1981; The Patriot, 1982; Lord of the Isles, 1983; Unicorn Rampant, 1984; The Riven Realm, 1984; James, By the Grace of God, 1985; Rough Wooing, 1986; Columba, 1987; Cache Down, 1987; Flowers of Chivalry, 1988; Mail Royal, 1989; Warden of the Queen's March, 1989; Kenneth, 1990; Crusader, 1991; Children of the Mist, 1992; Druid Sacrifice, 1993; Tapestry of the Boar, 1993; Price of a Princess, 1994; Lord in Waiting, 1994; Highness in Hiding, 1995; Honours Even, 1995; 12 children's novels; *non-fiction:* The Fortalices and Early Mansions of Southern Scotland, 1935; The Fortified House in Scotland (5 vols), 1962–71; Pegasus Book of Scotland, 1964; Outlaw of the Highlands: Rob Roy, 1965; Land of the Scots, 1968; Portrait of the Border Country, 1972; Portrait of the Lothians, 1979; The Queen's Scotland Series: The Heartland: Clackmannan, Perth and Stirlingshire, 1971; The Eastern Counties: Aberdeen, Angus and Kincardineshire, 1972; The North East: Banff, Moray, Nairn, East Inverness and Easter Ross, 1974; Argyll and Bute, 1977; Nigel Tranter's Scotland, 1981; Scottish Castles: tales and traditions, 1982, revd edn 1993; Scotland of Robert the Bruce, 1986; The Story of Scotland, 1987; Footbridge to Enchantment, 1992; contribs to many jls, on Scots history, topography, castellated architecture, etc. *Recreations:* walking, historical research, helping to restore Scottish castles. *Address:* Quarry House, Aberlady, East Lothian EH32 0QB. *T:* Aberlady (01875) 870258. *Club:* PEN.

TRAPNELL, Barry Maurice Waller, CBE 1982; DL; MA, PhD Cantab; Headmaster of Oundle School, 1968–84; Chairman, Cambridge Occupational Analysts, since 1986; *b* 18 May 1924; *s* of Waller Bertram and late Rachel Trapnell; *m* 1951, Dorothy Joan, *d* of late P. J. Kerr, ICS; two *d. Educ:* University College Sch., Hampstead; St John's Coll., Cambridge (Scholar). Research in physical chemistry in Department of Colloid Science, Cambridge, 1945–46, and Royal Institution, London, 1946–50; Commonwealth Fund Fellow, Northwestern Univ., Ill., 1950–51; Lecturer in chemistry: Worcester Coll., Oxford, 1951–54; Liverpool Univ., 1954–57; Headmaster, Denstone Coll., 1957–68. Visiting Lecturer, American Association for Advancement of Science, 1961. Pres., Independent Schools Assoc. Inc., 1984–; Member: Adv. Cttee on Supply and Training of Teachers; C of E Commn on Religious Education. E Anglian Regl Dir, Index, 1985–92. Mem. Governing Body, Roedean Sch., 1987–92. Director: Southend Estates Gp plc, 1984–86; Thomas Wall Trust, 1984–92. Hon. FCP, 1995. DL: Staffs, 1967; Northants, 1974–84. Hon. Liveryman, Worshipful Co. of Grocers, 1984. *Publications:* Chemisorption, 1955 (Russian edition, 1958; 2nd English edition, 1964); Learning and Discerning, 1966; papers in British and American scientific journals. *Recreations:* several games (represented Cambridge *v* Oxford at cricket and squash rackets, and Gentlemen *v* Players at cricket; won Amateur Championships at Rugby Fives), English furniture and silver. *Address:* 6 Corfe Close, Cambridge CB2 2QA. *T:* Cambridge (01223) 249278. *Clubs:* The 100, United Oxford & Cambridge University; Hawks (Cambridge); Vincent's (Oxford).

TRAPNELL, John Arthur; Under-Secretary, Departments of Trade and Industry, 1973–77; *b* 7 Sept. 1913; *s* of Arthur Westicote Trapnell and Helen Trapnell (*née* Alles); *m* 1939, Winifred Chadwick Rushton; two *d. Educ:* privately; Law Soc.'s Sch. of Law. Admitted Solicitor 1938; private practice until 1940; served HM Army, 1940–46: commnd Som. LI, 1943; served with 82nd W African Div. (Major). Civil Service from 1946: Board of Trade, Solicitors Dept. Mem. Law Soc. *Recreations:* golf, bridge. *Address:* 29 Connaught Road, New Malden, Surrey KT3 3PZ. *T:* 0181–942 3183.

TRAPP, Prof. Joseph Burney, CBE 1990; FSA; FBA 1980; Director, Warburg Institute (University of London) and Professor of the History of the Classical Tradition, 1976–90; *b* 16 July 1925; *s* of H. M. B. and Frances M. Trapp; *m* 1953, Elayne M. Falla; two *s. Educ:* Dannevirke High Sch. and Victoria University Coll., Wellington, NZ (MA). FSA 1978. Alexander Turnbull Library, Wellington, 1946–50; Jun. Lectr, Victoria University Coll., 1950–51; Asst Lectr, Reading Univ., 1951–53; Warburg Institute: Asst Librarian, 1953–66; Librarian, 1966–76; Hon. Fellow, 1990. Visiting Professor: Univ. of Toronto, 1969; Univ. of Melbourne, 1980; Iowa State Univ., Princeton Univ., 1984; Univ. of Warwick, 1992–. J. H. Gray Lectr, Univ. of Cambridge, 1990; Panizzi Lectr, British Liby, 1990; J. P. R. Lyell Reader in Bibliography, Oxford Univ., 1994. Member: Advisory Council: V&A Museum, 1977–83; British Library, 1980–87; Exec. Cttee, British Sch. at Rome, 1983–87, Council, 1984–95; Foreign Sec., British Academy, 1988–95 (Vice-Pres., 1983–85). *Publications:* (ed) The Apology of Sir Thomas More, 1979; Essays in the Renaissance and the Classical Tradition, 1990; Erasmus, Colet and More . . . (Panizzi Lectures), 1991; articles in learned jls. *Address:* c/o Warburg Institute, Woburn Square, WC1H 0AB.

TRASENSTER, Michael Augustus Tulk, CVO 1954; Photographer, ARPS 1979; *b* 26 Jan. 1923; *er s* of late Major William Augustus Trasenster, MC, and late Brenda de Courcy Trasenster; *m* 1950, Fay Norrie Darley, *d* of late Thomas Bladworth Darley, Cantley Hall, Yorkshire; two *d. Educ:* Winchester. Served with 4th/7th Royal Dragoon Guards, 1942–; NW Europe (Tanks, D-Day to V-E Day), 1944; Middle East, 1946; ADC to Governor of South Australia, 1947–49; School of Tank Technology, 1951; Military Secretary and Comptroller to the Governor General of New Zealand, 1952–55. Chevalier of Order of Leopold II of Belgium, with palm, 1944; Belgian Croix de Guerre, with palm, 1944. *Recreations:* painting, reading. *Address:* c/o Royal Bank of Scotland, High Street, Winchester, Hants SO23 9DA.

TRASLER, Prof. Gordon Blair, PhD; FBPsS; JP; first Professor of Psychology, University of Southampton, 1964–94, now Emeritus; Leverhulme Emeritus Fellow, since 1995; *b* 7 March 1929; *s* of Frank Ferrier Trasler and Marian (*née* Blair); *m* 1953, Kathleen Patricia Fegan. *Educ:* Isleworth Grammar Sch.; Bryanston Sch.; University Coll., Exeter (MA); London Univ. (BSc, PhD). FBPsS 1963; CPsychol. Tutorial Asst, UC, Exeter, 1952–53; Psychologist, HM Prisons, Wandsworth and Winchester, 1955–57; Lectr, Southampton Univ., 1957–64. Visiting Lecturer: LSE, 1962–63; Inst. of Criminology, Cambridge Univ., 1968–; Vis. Prof., Univ. of Alberta at Edmonton, 1977. Mem., Winchester Health Authority, 1981–89. Vice-Pres., Inst. for Study and Treatment of Delinquency, 1987– (Chm., 1981–87); Chm., Div. of Criminolog. and Legal Psychol., BPsS, 1980–83. Chief Scientist's Advr, DHSS, 1977–80 and 1983–; Member: Adv. Council on Penal System, 1968–74; Wootton Cttee on Non-custodial penalties, 1968–70; Younger Cttee on Young Adult Offenders, 1970–74; Lord Chancellor's Adv. Cttee for Southampton, 1988–. Editor-in-chief, British Jl of Criminology, 1980–85. JP Hants, 1978. Sellin-Glueck Award (for outstanding scholarly contribs to criminology), Amer. Soc. of Criminology, 1990. *Publications:* In Place of Parents, 1960; The Explanation of Criminality, 1962; The Shaping of Social Behaviour, 1967; (jtly) The Formative Years, 1968; (with D. P. Farrington) Behaviour Modification with Offenders, 1980; many papers in jls and chapters on psychology and criminology. *Recreations:* reading, photography, writing. *Address:* Fox Croft, Old Kennels Lane, Oliver's Battery, Winchester SO22 4JT. *T:* Winchester (01962) 52345.

TRAVERS, Basil Holmes, AM 1983; OBE 1943; BA (Sydney); MA (Oxon); BLitt (Oxon); FACE; FRSA; FAIM; Headmaster of Sydney Church of England Grammar School, North Sydney, NSW, 1959–84; *b* 7 July 1919; *m* 1942, Margaret Emily Marr; three *d. Educ:* Sydney Church of England Grammar Sch.; Sydney Univ.; New Coll., Oxford Univ. Rhodes Scholar for NSW, 1940. Served War of 1939–45 (despatches, OBE); AIF, 2/2 Australian Infantry Battalion; ADC to Maj.-Gen. Sir I. G. Mackay, 1940; Brigade Major, 15 Aust. Inf. Bde, 1943–44; psc 1944; GSO 2, HQ, 2 Aust. Corps, 1944–45. Assistant Master, Wellington Coll., Berks, England, 1948–49; Assistant Master, Cranbrook Sch., Sydney, 1950–52; Headmaster, Launceston Church Grammar Sch., Launceston, Tasmania, 1953–58. Chm., Headmasters' Conf. of Australia, 1971–73. Lt-Col commanding 12 Inf. Bn (CMF), 1955–58. Member: Soldiers' Children Education Board, 1959–; NSW Cttee, Duke of Edinburgh's Award Scheme in Australia, 1959–88 (Chm., 1979–84). Col Comdt, Royal Australian Army Educn Corps, 1984–88. *Publications:* Let's Talk Rugger, 1949; The Captain General, 1952. *Recreations:* cricket (Oxford Blue, 1946, 1948), swimming, rugby (Oxford Blue, 1946, 1947), athletics (Half Blue, 1947); also Sydney Blue, football, cricket; Rugby Union International for England, 1947, 1948, 1949; represented NSW, 1950. *Address:* 19 Edward Street, Gordon, NSW 2072, Australia. *T:* (2) 4984661. *Club:* Rugby Union (Sydney).

TRAVERS, Sir Thomas (à Beckett), Kt 1972; Consulting Ophthalmologist, Royal Melbourne Hospital, 1962–63 (Hon. Ophthalmologist, 1946–62); *b* 16 Aug. 1902; *s* of late Walter Travers, Warragul, Vic and late Isabelle Travers; *m* Mercy, (Tone), *d* of H. Smith and *widow* of R. S. Burnard; no *c. Educ:* Melbourne Grammar School. MB, BS 1925, DSc 1941, Melbourne; MRCP 1928; DOMS London 1928; FRACS. Asst Ophthalmologist, Alfred Hosp., 1930–39; Consultant, RAAF, 1939–45. *Publications:* various on strabismus. *Recreation:* gardening. *Address:* 6 Barrup Street, Carlton, Vic 3053, Australia. *T:* 3476286. *Club:* Melbourne (Melbourne).

TRAVERSE-HEALY, Prof. Thomas Hector, (Tim), OBE 1989; FIPR, FPA; Professor of Public Relations, University of Stirling, since 1988; Senior Partner, Traverse-Healy Ltd, 1947–93; *b* 25 March 1923; *s* of John Healy, MBE, and Gladys Traverse; *m* 1946, Joan Thompson; two *s* three *d. Educ:* Stonyhurst Coll.; St Mary's Hosp., London Univ. DipCAM. Served War, Royal Marines Commandos and Special Forces, 1941–46. Chairman: Traverse-Healy & Regester Ltd, 1985–87; Charles Barker Traverse-Healy, 1987–89; Non-exec. Dir, Charles Barker Hldgs, 1990–92. Mem., Public and Social Policy Cttee, National Westminster Bank, 1974–92; Professional Advr, Corporate Communications, 1990–92; Specialist Advr, CNAA, 1990–92. Visiting Professor: Baylor Univ., Texas, 1988; Univ. of Wales, 1990–. President: Internat. PR Res. and Educn Foundn, 1983–86; Internat. Foundn for PR Studies, 1987–89; Chm., (UK) PR Educn Trust, 1990–92; Mem., Professional Practices Cttee, PR Consultants Assoc., 1987–91; Dir, Centre for PR Studies, 1994–; Sec., PR Res. Network, 1994–. Institute of Public Relations: Mem. 1948, Fellow 1956; Pres. 1967–68; Tallents Gold Medal, 1985; Hon. Fellow 1988; European PR Federation: Vice-Pres. 1965–69; Internat. PR Assoc.: Sec. 1950–61, Pres. 1968–73, Mem. Emeritus, 1982; Presidential Gold Medal, 1985. FRSA 1953; FIPA 1957. Member, US Public Affairs Council, 1975–; Board Mem., Centre for Public Affairs Studies, 1969–; Pres., World PR Congress: Tel Aviv, 1970; Geneva, 1973. Congress Foundn Lecture: Boston, 1976; Bombay, 1982; Melbourne, 1988. PR News Award, 1983; PR Week Award, 1987; Page Soc. Award, 1990. *Publications:* numerous published lectures and articles in professional jls. *Recreations:* French politics, Irish Society. *Address:* PO Box LDN 810, SE24 9NQ. *T:* 0171–738 3044. *Clubs:* Athenæum; Philippics.

TREACHER, Adm. Sir John (Devereux), KCB 1975; Director, Meggitt PLC, 1989–95; *b* Chile, 23 Sept. 1924; *s* of late Frank Charles Treacher, Bentley, Suffolk; *m* 1st, 1953, Patcie Jane (marr. diss. 1968), *d* of late Dr F. L. McGrath, Evanston, Ill; one *s* one *d*; 2nd, 1969, Kirsteen Forbes, *d* of late D. F. Landale; one *s* one *d. Educ:* St Paul's School. War service in HM Ships Nelson, Glasgow, Keppel and Mermaid in Mediterranean, Russian convoys; qual. Fleet Air Arm pilot, 1947; CO: 778 Sqdn 1951, 849 Sqdn 1952–53; CO, HMS Lowestoft, 1964–66; CO, HMS Eagle, 1968–70; Flag Officer Carriers and Amphibious Ships and Comdr Carrier Striking Gp 2, 1970–72; Flag Officer, Naval Air Comd, 1972–73; Vice-Chief of Naval Staff, 1973–75; C-in-C Fleet, and Allied C-in-C Channel and Eastern Atlantic, 1975–77. Chief Exec., 1977–81, and Dir, 1977–85, Nat. Car Parks; Chm., Westland Inc., 1983–89; Dep. Chm., Westland Gp, 1986–89 (Dir. 1978–89). Non-press Mem., Press Council, 1978–81; Dir, SBAC, 1983–89. FRAeS 1973. *Recreations:* shooting, photography. *Address:* 22 Newton Road, W2 5LT. *Clubs:* Boodle's, Institute of Directors.

TREACY, Colman Maurice; QC 1990; a Recorder, since 1991; *b* 28 July 1949; *s* of Dr Maurice Treacy and Mary Treacy; *m* (marr. diss.); one *s* one *d. Educ:* Stonyhurst Coll.; Jesus Coll., Cambridge (Open Scholar in Classics; MA). Called to the Bar, Middle Temple, 1971; an Asst Recorder, 1988–91. *Address:* 3 Fountain Court, Steelhouse Lane, Birmingham B4 6DR. *T:* 0121–236 5854.

TREADGOLD, Hazel Rhona; JP; Central President of the Mothers' Union, 1983–88; *b* 29 May 1936; *m* 1959, Very Rev. John David Treadgold, *qv*; two *s* one *d*. Mothers' Union: has held office, Dioceses of Southwell, Durham and Chichester, and at HQ; Chm., Central Young Families Cttee, 1971–76; a Central Vice-Pres., 1978–83; Vice-Pres., Chichester dio., 1992–. Archbishop of Canterbury's Co-ordinator, Bishops' Wives Conf., Lambeth, 1988; Member: Women's Nat. Commn, 1980–83; Exec., Women's Council, 1989–91. Vice-Pres., Chichester Relate. Gov., Bishop Luffa C of E Comprehensive Sch., 1990–. JP Chichester, 1991. *Recreations:* travel, reading, flower arranging, swimming, dog walking. *Address:* The Deanery, Chichester, West Sussex PO19 1PX. *T:* Chichester (01243) 783286, *Fax:* (01243) 536190. *Clubs:* Parrot; Chichester Festival.

TREADGOLD, Very Rev. John David, LVO 1990; Dean of Chichester, since 1989; Chaplain to the Queen, 1983–89; *b* 30 Dec. 1931; *s* of Oscar and Sybil Treadgold; *m* 1959, Hazel Rhona Bailey (*see* H. R. Treadgold); two *s* one *d*. *Educ:* Nottingham Univ. (BA); Wells Theological College. Deacon 1959, priest 1960; Vicar Choral, Southwell Minster, 1959–64; Rector of Wollaton, Nottingham, 1964–74; Vicar of Darlington, 1974–81; Canon of Windsor and Chaplain to Windsor Great Park, 1981–89. Chaplain, TA, 1962–67; TAVR, 1974–78; Chaplain to High Sheriff: of Nottinghamshire, 1963–64 and 1975–76; of Durham, 1978–79. Chm., Chichester DAC for the Care of Churches. Chm. of Govs, Prebendal Sch., Chichester, 1989–. Governor: Slindon Coll., 1995–; Wycombe Abbey Sch., 1995–. FRSA 1991. *Recreations:* musical appreciation; church architecture. *Address:* The Deanery, Chichester, West Sussex PO19 1PX. *T:* Chichester (01243) 783286.

TREADGOLD, Sydney William, FCA; Secretary: Financial Reporting Council, since 1990; Financial Reporting Review Panel, since 1991; *b* 10 May 1933; *s* of Harold Bryan Treadgold and Violet Gladys Watson; *m* 1961, Elizabeth Ann White; two *s*. *Educ:* Larkmead Sch., Abingdon. Chartered accountant (ACA 1960, FCA 1970). Served RAF, 1951–53 (Navigator). Wenn Townsend & Co., Chartered Accountants, 1954–62; Asst Finance Officer, Univ. of Liverpool, 1963–65; Principal: Min. of Aviation, 1965–67; Min. of Technol., 1967–71; Asst Sec., DTI, 1972–78; Under Secretary: Price Commn, 1978–79; Depts of Industry and Trade, 1979–83; DTI, 1983–89; Mem., Accounting Standards Task Gp, 1989–90; Sec., Accounting Standards Bd, 1990–93. FRSA 1988. *Recreations:* nothing serious. *Address:* Holborn Hall, 100 Gray's Inn Road, WC1X 8AL.

TREADWELL, Charles James, CMG 1972; CVO 1979; HM Diplomatic Service, retired; *b* 10 Feb. 1920; *s* of late C. A. L. Treadwell, OBE, Barrister and Solicitor, Wellington, NZ. *Educ:* Wellington Coll., NZ; University of New Zealand (LLB). Served with HM Forces, 1939–45. Sudan Political Service and Sudan Judiciary, 1945–55; FO, 1955–57; British High Commn, Lahore, 1957–60; HM Embassy, Ankara, 1960–62; HM Embassy, Jedda, 1963–64; British Dep. High Comr for Eastern Nigeria, 1965–66; Head of Joint Information Services Department, Foreign Office/Commonwealth Office, 1966–68; British Political Agent, Abu Dhabi, 1968–71; Ambassador, United Arab Emirates, 1971–73; High Comr to Bahamas, 1973–75; Ambassador to Oman, 1975–79. *Address:* Cherry Orchard Cottage, Buddington Lane, Midhurst, W Sussex GU29 0QP.

TREASE, Geoffrey; *see* Trease, R. G.

TREASE, (Robert) Geoffrey, FRSL 1979; *b* 11 Aug. 1909; *s* of George Albert Trease and Florence (*née* Dale); *m* 1933, Marian Haselden Granger Boyer (*d* 1989); one *d*. *Educ:* Nottingham High Sch.; Queen's Coll., Oxford (schol.). Chm., 1972–73, Mem. Council, 1974–, Society of Authors. *Publications:* Walking in England, 1935; Such Divinity, 1939; Only Natural, 1940; Tales Out of School, 1949; Snared Nightingale, 1957; So Wild the Heart, 1959; The Italian Story, 1963; The Grand Tour, 1967; (ed) Matthew Todd's Journal, 1968; Nottingham, a biography, 1970; The Condottieri, 1970; A Whiff of Burnt Boats, an early autobiography, 1971; Samuel Pepys and his World, 1972; Laughter at the Door, a continued autobiography, 1974; London, a concise history, 1975; Portrait of a Cavalier: William Cavendish, first Duke of Newcastle, 1979; *for young readers:* Bows Against the Barons, 1934; Cue for Treason, 1940; Trumpets in the West, 1947; The Hills of Varna, 1948; No Boats on Bannermere, 1949; The Seven Queens of England, 1953; This Is Your Century, 1965; The Red Towers of Granada, 1966; Byron, A Poet Dangerous to Know, 1969; A Masque for the Queen, 1970; Horsemen on the Hills, 1971; D. H. Lawrence: the Phoenix and the Flame, 1973; Popinjay Stairs, 1973; Days to Remember, 1973; The Iron Tsar, 1975; The Chocolate Boy, 1975; When the Drums Beat, 1976; Violet for Bonaparte, 1976; The Field of the Forty Footsteps, 1977; Mandeville, 1980; A Wood by Moonlight and Other Stories, 1981; Saraband for Shadows, 1982; The Cormorant Venture, 1984; The Edwardian Era, 1986; Tomorrow is a Stranger, 1987; The Arpino Assignment, 1988; A Flight of Angels, 1988; Shadow Under the Sea, 1990; Calabrian Quest, 1990; Aunt Augusta's Elephant, 1991; Song for a Tattered Flag, 1992; Fire on the Wind, 1993; Bring Out the Banners, 1994; No Horn at Midnight, 1994; Curse on the Sea, 1996, and many others; *plays:* After the Tempest, 1938 (Welwyn Fest. award); Colony, 1939. *Recreations:* walking, the theatre. *Address:* 1 Yomede Park, Newbridge Road, Bath BA1 3LS.

TREASURE, Prof. John Albert Penberthy, PhD; *b* 20 June 1924; *s* of Harold Paul Treasure and Constance Frances Treasure; *m* 1954, Valerie Ellen Bell; three *s*. *Educ:* Cardiff High Sch.; University Coll., Cardiff (BA 1946); Univ. of Cambridge (PhD 1956). Joined British Market Research Bureau Ltd, 1952, Man. Dir 1957; Marketing Dir, J. Walter Thompson Co. Ltd, 1960, Chm. 1967; Dir, J. Walter Thompson Co. USA, 1967, Vice Chm. 1974; Vice-Chm., Saatchi & Saatchi Advertising Ltd (formerly Saatchi & Saatchi Compton Ltd), 1983–89. Chm., Taylor Nelson AGB plc, 1992–; Director: Rowntree Mackintosh plc, 1976–88; Assi Packaging (UK) Ltd (formerly AFIH Ltd), 1984–94; Household Mortgage Corp. plc, 1986–94. Dean and Prof. of Marketing, City Univ. Business Sch., 1978–82. President: Inst. of Practitioners in Advertising, 1975–77; Market Res. Soc., 1975–78; Nat. Advertising Benevolent Soc., 1977–78; Chm., History of Advertising Trust, 1985–90. *Publications:* articles on marketing, market research and economics in Financial Times, Times, New Soc., Econ. Jl, Commentary, and Advertising Qly. *Recreations:* golf, tennis. *Address:* 20 Queensberry House, Friars Lane, Richmond, Surrey TW9 1NT. *T:* (office) 0181–967 4132. *Clubs:* Caledonian, Queen's, Hurlingham; Royal Mid-Surrey Golf (Richmond).

TREDINNICK, David Arthur Stephen; MP (C) Bosworth, since 1987; *b* 19 Jan. 1950; *m* 1983, Rebecca Jane Shott; one *s* one *d*. *Educ:* Ludgrove Sch., Wokingham; Eton; Mons Officer Cadet Sch.; Graduate Business Sch., Capetown Univ. (MBA); St John's Coll., Oxford (MLitt 1987). Trainee, E. B. Savoury Milln & Co, Stockbrokers, 1972; Account Exec., Quadrant International, 1974; Salesman, Kalle Infotec UK, 1976; Sales Manager, Word Processing, 1977–78; Consultant, Baird Communications, NY, 1978–79; Marketing Manager, Q1 Europe Ltd, 1979–81; Res. asst to Kenneth Warren, MP, and Angela Rumbold, CBE, MP, 1981–87; Manager, Malden Mitcham Properties (family business), 1985–. PPS to Minister of State, Welsh Office, 1991–94. Treasurer: All-Party Parly Gp for Alternative and Complementary Medicine, 1991–; Parly Gp for World Govt, 1991–; Secretary: Cons. backbench Defence Cttee, 1990–91; Cons. backbench Foreign Affairs Cttee, 1990–91. Chm., British Atlantic Gp of Young Politicians, 1989–91; Co-Chm., Future of Europe Trust, 1991–94; Chairman: Anglo East European Trade Co., 1990–; Ukraine Business Agency, 1992–. Contested (C) Cardiff S and Penarth, 1983. *Address:* House of Commons, SW1A 0AA. *T:* 0171–219 4514.

TREFGARNE, family name of **Baron Trefgarne.**

TREFGARNE, 2nd Baron, *cr* 1947, of Cleddau; **David Garro Trefgarne;** PC 1989; *b* 31 March 1941; *s* of 1st Baron Trefgarne and of Elizabeth (who *m* 1962, Comdr A. T. Courtney (from whom she obt. a divorce, 1966); *m* 1971, H. C. H. Ker (*d* 1987), Dundee), *d* of C. E. Churchill; *S* father, 1960; *m* 1968, Rosalie, *d* of Baron Lane of Horsell, *qv*; two *s* one *d*. *Educ:* Haileybury; Princeton University, USA. Opposition Whip, House of Lords, 1977–79; a Lord in Waiting (Govt Whip), 1979–81; Parly Under Sec. of State, DoT, 1981, FCO, 1981–82, DHSS, 1982–83, (Armed Forces) MoD, 1983–85; Minister of State: for Defence Support, 1985–86; for Defence Procurement, 1986–89; DTI, 1989–90. Dir of various companies. Chm., Engrg Trng Authority, 1994–. Pres., Popular Flying Assoc., 1992–; Hon. President: METCOM, 1990–; British Assoc. of Aviation Consultants, 1994–. Vice Chm., ACF Assoc., 1992–. Gov., Guildford Sch. of Acting, 1992–; Life Gov., Haileybury, 1992. Trustee, Mary Rose Trust, 1994–. Awarded Royal Aero Club Bronze Medal (jointly) for flight from England to Australia and back in light aircraft, 1963. *Recreation:* photography. *Heir:* *s* Hon. George Garro Trefgarne, *b* 4 Jan. 1970. *Address:* House of Lords, SW1A 0PW.

TREFUSIS; *see* Fane Trefusis, family name of Baron Clinton.

TREGARTHEN JENKIN, Ian Evers; *see* Jenkin.

TREGEAR, Mary, FBA 1985; Keeper of Eastern Art, Ashmolean Museum, Oxford, 1987–91; *b* 11 Feb. 1924; *d* of late Thomas R. and Norah Tregear. *Educ:* Sidcot Sch., Somerset; West of England Coll. of Art (ATD 1946); London Univ. (BA); MA Oxon. Taught Art, Wuhan, China, 1947–50; Curator/Lectr, Hong Kong Univ., 1956–61; Sen. Asst Keeper, Chinese, Ashmolean Museum, 1961–87. *Publications:* Arts of China, vol. 1 (co-ordinating ed.), 1968; Catalogue of Chinese Greenwares in the Ashmolean Museum, 1976; Chinese Art, 1980; Song Ceramics, 1982; Tesori d'Arte in Cina, 1994.

TREGLOWN, Prof. Jeremy Dickinson; Professor of English, University of Warwick, since 1993; *b* 24 May 1946; *s* of late Rev. Geoffrey and of Beryl Treglown; *m* 1st, 1970, Rona Bower (marr. diss. 1982); one *s* two *d*; 2nd, 1984, Holly Eley (*née* Urquhart). *Educ:* Bristol Grammar Sch.; St Peter's Coll., Oxford. MA, BLitt Oxon; PhD London. Lecturer: Lincoln Coll., Oxford, 1974–77; University College London, 1977–80; Times Literary Supplement: Asst Editor, 1980–82; Editor, 1982–90. Vis. Fellow: All Souls Coll., Oxford, 1986; Huntington Library, San Marino, Calif, 1988; Mellon Vis. Associate, Calif Inst. of Technol., 1988; Hon. Res. Fellow, UCL, 1991–; Ferris Vis. Prof., Princeton Univ., 1991–92. Mem. Council, RSL, 1989–96; FRSL 1991 (Hon. FRSL 1989). FRSA 1990. Chm. of Judges, Booker Prize, 1991. Contributing Editor, Grand Street, NY, 1991–. *Publications:* Roald Dahl, 1994; edited: The Letters of John Wilmot, Earl of Rochester, 1980; Spirit of Wit, 1982; The Lantern Bearers, Essays by Robert Louis Stevenson, 1988; various articles and book introductions. *Address:* 102 Savernake Road, NW3 2JR; Gardens Cottage, Ditchley Park, Enstone, near Chipping Norton, Oxon OX7 4EP.

TREHANE, Sir (Walter) Richard, Kt 1967; Chairman of the Milk Marketing Board, 1958–77; *b* 14 July 1913; *s* of James Trehane and Muriel Yeoman Cowl; *m* 1948, Elizabeth Mitchell; two *s*. *Educ:* Monkton Combe School, Somerset; University of Reading (BSc (Agric.)). On staff of School of Agriculture, Cambridge, 1933–36; Manager of Hampreston Manor Farm, Dorset, 1936–. Member: Dorset War Agric. Exec. Cttee, later Dorset Agricl Cttee, 1942–52 (Dep. Chm., 1947–52); MMB, 1947–77 (Vice-Chm., 1952–58; Chm., 1958–77); Mem. (later Vice-Chm.) Avon and Stour Catchment Bd, subseq. Avon & Dorset Rivers Bd, 1944–53; Mem. Dorset County Council and Chm. Secondary Education Cttee, 1946–49; Chm. Dorset National Farmers' Union, 1947–48; Member, Nat. Milk Publicity Council, 1954–77 (1st Pres. 1954–56); Chm. English Country Cheese Council, 1955–77; Pres. British Farm Produce Council, 1963–78 (Chm. 1960–63). Chm. Govg Body, Grassland Research Institute, Hurley, Berks, 1959–78 (Hon. Fellow, 1981); Chm. and Pres. European Cttee on Milk/Butterfat Recording, 1957–60; Director of British Semen Exports Ltd, 1960–77; Vice-President: World Assoc. Animal Production, 1965–68; President: European Assoc. Animal Prodn, 1961–67 (Hon. Pres., 1967–); British Soc. Animal Prodn, 1954, 1961; British Friesian Cattle Soc., 1969–70; Royal Assoc. British Dairy Farmers, 1968, 1977; Internat. Dairy Fedn, 1968–72, Hon. Pres., 1972–76. Chm., UK Dairy Assoc., 1963–69. Chm., Alfa-Laval Co. Ltd, 1982–84 (Dir, 1977–84); Director: Southern Television, 1969–81; The Rank Organisation Ltd, 1970–84; Beaumont UK, 1980–83. Trustee, UK Farming Scholarship Trust, 1970. Governor: Monkton Combe School, 1957–83; British Nutrition Foundn, 1975–77. FRAgSs 1970. Hon. DSc Reading, 1976. Justus-von-Liebig Prize, Kiel Univ., 1968; Gold Medal, Soc. of Dairy Technology, 1969; Massey-Fergusson Award, 1971. Comdr du Mérite Agricole, 1964. *Address:* Hampreston Manor Farm, Wimborne, Dorset BH21 7LX. *Clubs:* Farmers'; Royal Motor Yacht (Poole).

TREISMAN, Dr Richard Henry, FRS 1994; Principal Scientist and Head, Transcription Laboratory, Imperial Cancer Research Fund, since 1988; *b* 7 Oct. 1954; *s* of Walter Benjamin Treisman and Marjorie Elizabeth (*née* Grounsell); *m* 1993, Kathleen Mary Weston. *Educ:* Haberdashers' Aske's Sch.; Christ's Coll., Cambridge (BA 1977); ICRF/UCL (PhD 1981). Postdoctoral Fellow, Harvard Univ., 1981–84; Mem., Scientific Staff, Lab. of Molecular Biol., Cambridge, 1984–88. Mem., EMBO, 1987. Mem., Festiniog Railway Soc., Porthmadog, 1967–. *Publications:* papers in scientific jls. *Recreations:* piano playing, fell-walking. *Address:* Transcription Laboratory, Room 528, Imperial Cancer Research Fund, 44 Lincoln's Inn Fields, WC2A 3PX. *T:* 0171–269 3271.

TREITEL, Prof. Guenter Heinz, DCL; FBA 1977; QC 1983; Vinerian Professor of English Law, Oxford University, since 1979; Fellow of All Souls College, Oxford, since 1979; *b* 26 Oct. 1928; *s* of Theodor Treitel and Hanna Lilly Treitel (*née* Levy); *m* 1957, Phyllis Margaret Cook; two *s*. *Educ:* Kilburn Grammar School; Magdalen College, Oxford. BA 1949, BCL 1951, MA 1953, DCL 1976. Called to the Bar, Gray's Inn, 1952, Hon. Bencher, 1982. Asst Lectr, LSE, 1951–53; Lectr, University Coll., Oxford, 1953–54; Fellow, Magdalen Coll., Oxford, 1954–79, Fellow Emeritus, 1979; All Souls Reader in English Law, Univ. of Oxford, 1964–79. Vis. Lectr, Univ. of Chicago, 1963–64; Visiting Professor: Chicago, 1968–69 and 1971–72; W Australia, 1976; Houston, 1977; Southern Methodist, 1978, 1988–89 and 1994; Virginia, 1978–79 and 1983–84; Santa Clara, 1981; Vis. Scholar, Ernst von Caemmerer Gedächtnisstiftung, 1990. Trustee, British Museum, 1983–; Mem. Council, National Trust, 1984–93. *Publications:* The Law of Contract, 1962, 9th edn 1995; An Outline of the Law of Contract, 1975, 5th edn 1995; Remedies for Breach of Contract: a comparative account, 1988; edited jointly: Dicey's Conflict of Laws, 7th edn 1958; Dicey and Morris, Conflict of Laws, 8th edn 1967; Chitty on Contracts, 23rd edn 1968 to 27th edn 1994; Benjamin's Sale of Goods, 1974, 4th edn 1992; Unmöglichkeit, "Impracticability" und "Frustration" im anglo-amerikanischen Recht, 1991; Frustration and Force Majeure, 1994. *Recreations:* music, reading. *Address:* All Souls College, Oxford OX1 4AL. *T:* Oxford (01865) 279379.

TRELAWNY, Sir John Barry Salusbury-, 13th Bt *cr* 1628; Director, Goddard Kay Rogers and Associates Ltd, since 1984; Chairman, GKR Group Ltd, since 1993; *b* 4 Sept. 1934; *s* of Sir John William Robin Maurice Salusbury-Trelawny, 12th Bt and of his 1st wife, Glenys Mary (*d* 1985), *d* of John Cameron Kynoch; *S* father, 1956; *m* 1958, Carol Knox, *yr d* of late C. F. K. Watson, The Field, Saltwood, Kent; one *s* three *d*. *Educ:* HMS Worcester. Subseq. Sub-Lt RNVR (National Service). Dir, The Martin Walter Group Ltd, 1971–74; various directorships, 1974–; Dir, 1978–83, Jt Dep. Man. Dir 1981–83, Korn/Ferry Internat. Inc. FInstM 1974. JP 1973–78. *Heir:* *s* John William Richard Salusbury-Trelawny [*b* 30 March 1960; *m* 1st, 1980, Anita (marr. diss. 1986), *d* of Kenneth Snelgrove; one *s* one *d*; 2nd, 1987, Sandra (marr. diss. 1993), *d* of Joseph Thompson; one s]. *Address:* Beavers Hill, Rectory Lane, Saltwood, Kent CT21 4QA. *T:* Hythe (01303) 266476. *Clubs:* Army and Navy, Buck's.

TRELFORD, Donald Gilchrist; writer, broadcaster and media consultant; Professor of Journalism Studies, Sheffield University, since 1994; Editor, The Observer, 1975–93; *b* 9 Nov. 1937; *s* of Thomas and Doris Trelford (*née* Gilchrist); *m* 1st, 1963, Janice Ingram; two *s* one *d*; 2nd, 1978, Katherine Louise, *d* of Mr and Mrs John Mark, Guernsey, and *g d* of late John Mark and Louisa (*née* Hobson); one *d*. *Educ:* Bablake Sch., Coventry (School Captain, 1956); Open exhibnr in English, Selwyn Coll., Cambridge; MA; University rugby and cricket. Pilot Officer, RAF, 1956–58. Reporter and Sub-Editor, Coventry Standard and Sheffield Telegraph, 1960–63; Editor, Times of Malawi, 1963–66; Correspondent in Africa for The Observer, The Times, and BBC, 1963–66; The Observer: Dep. News Editor, 1966; Asst Man. Editor, 1968; Dep. Editor, 1969; Chief Exec., The Observer Ltd, 1992–93. Acting Editor, The Oldie, 1994; Sports columnist, Daily Telegraph, 1993–. Director: Optomen Television, 1988–; Observer Films, 1989–93; Central Observer TV, 1990–93; media consultant, Beacon Millenium, 1994–. Mem. Editorial Adv. Gp, Bloomsbury Publishing, 1987–. Chairman, Globenet Syndication Ltd, 1995–; Creative Management Partnership, 1994–95. Dir, St Cecilia Internat. Festival of Music, 1995–. Member: British Executive Cttee, IPI, 1976–; Council, Media Soc., 1981–; Assoc. of British Editors, 1984–; Guild of British Newspaper Editors, 1985– (Mem., Parly and Legal Cttee, 1987–91); Defence, Press and Broadcasting Cttee, 1986–93; Vice-Pres., Newspaper Press Fund, 1992– (Appeals Chm., 1991). Member: judging panel, British Press Awards, 1981–; judging panel, Scottish Press Awards, 1985; Olivier Awards Cttee, SWET, 1984–93; Sony Radio Awards, 1994; Adv. Bd, London Choral Soc., 1991–. Vice-Pres., British Sports Trust, 1988–. Liveryman, Worshipful Co. of Stationers and Newspaper Makers, 1986; Freeman, City of London, 1986. FRSA 1988. Hon. DLitt Sheffield, 1990. Granada Newspaper of the Year Award, 1983, 1993; commended, Internat. Editor of the Year, World Press Rev., NY, 1984. Frequent broadcasts (writer, interviewer and panellist) on TV and radio; presenter: Running Late (C4); LBC Morning Report, 1990–; TV interviews include: Rajiv Gandhi, Lord Goodman, Sir Leonard Hutton, Gromyko; speaker at internat. media confs in Spain, Egypt, W Germany, USA, India, Turkey, S Africa, Argentina, Kenya, Trinidad, Lebanon, Canada and Korea. *Publications:* Siege, 1980; (ed) Sunday Best, 1981, 1982, 1983; (contrib.) County Champions, 1982; Snookered, 1986; (contrib.) The Queen Observed, 1986; (with Garry Kasparov) Child of Change, 1987; (contrib.) Saturday's Boys, 1990; (contrib.) Fine Glances, 1991; Len Hutton Remembered, 1992; (contrib.) One Over Par, 1992; (with Daniel King) World Chess Championship, 1993; (contrib.) Animal Passions, 1994. *Recreations:* golf, snooker. *Address:* 20 Richmond Crescent, N1 0LZ. *T:* 0171–607 5346. *Clubs:* Garrick, Beefsteak, Groucho, Royal Air Force, MCC (Mem., Cttee, 1988–91).
See also J. Mark, Sir R. Mark.

TREMAIN, Rose, FRSL 1983; novelist and playright; *b* 2 Aug. 1943; *d* of Viola Mabel Thomson and Keith Nicholas Home Thomson; *m* 1st, 1971, Jon Tremain (marr. diss.); one *d*; 2nd, 1982, Jonathan Dudley (marr. diss.). *Educ:* Sorbonne, Paris; Univ. of East Anglia (BA Hons Eng. Lit.). Dylan Thomas Prize, 1984; Giles Cooper Award, Best Radio Play, 1984. *Publications: novels:* Sadler's Birthday, 1976; Letter to Sister Benedicta, 1978; The Cupboard, 1981; The Swimming Pool Season, 1984; Restoration, 1989 (Sunday Express Book of the Year Award); Sacred Country, 1992 (James Tait Black Meml Prize, 1993; Prix Femina Etranger (France), 1994); *short stories:* The Colonel's Daughter, 1982; The Garden of the Villa Mollini, 1986; Evangelista's Fan, 1994; *for children:* Journey to the Volcano, 1985. *Recreations:* gardening, swimming, yoga. *Address:* 2 High House, South Avenue, Thorpe St Andrew, Norwich NR7 0EZ. *T:* Norwich (01603) 39682.

TREMAINE, Prof. Scott Duncan, PhD; FRS 1994; FRSC 1994; Professor of Physics and Astronomy and Director, Canadian Institute for Theoretical Astrophysics, University of Toronto, since 1985; *b* 25 May 1950; *s* of Vincent Joseph Tremaine and Beatrice Delphine (*née* Sharp). *Educ:* McMaster Univ. (BSc); Princeton Univ. (MA, PhD). Postdoctoral Fellow, CIT, 1975–77; Res. Associate, Inst. of Astronomy, Cambridge, 1977–78; Long-term Mem., Inst. for Advanced Study, Princeton, 1978–81; Associate Prof., MIT, 1981–85. Foreign Hon. Mem., Amer. Acad. of Arts and Scis, 1992. *Publications:* (with J. J. Binney) Galactic Dynamics, 1987; papers in jls of physics and astronomy. *Address:* Canadian Institute for Theoretical Astrophysics, McLennan Laboratories, University of Toronto, 60 St George Street, Toronto, Ont M5S 1A7, Canada. *T:* (416) 9786477. *Club:* Alpine.

TREMBLAY, Dr Marc-Adélard, OC 1980; Professor of Anthropology, Université Laval, Québec, since 1956; *b* Les Eboulements, Qué., 24 April 1922; *s* of Willie Tremblay and Lauretta (*née* Tremblay); *m* 1949, Jacqueline Cyr; one *s* five *d*. *Educ:* Montréal Univ. (AB, LSA (Agricl Sci.)); Laval (MA Sociol.); Cornell Univ. (PhD Anthropol.). Research Associate, Cornell Univ., 1953–56; Université Laval: Vice-Dean, Faculty Social Scis, 1969–71; Head, Anthropology Dept, 1970; Dean, Graduate Sch., 1971–79. Pres., RSC, 1982–85. Hon. LLD: Ottawa, 1982; Guelph, 1984; Univ. of Northern BC, 1994; Carleton Univ., 1995. Innis-Gerin Medal, RSC, 1979; Centennial Medal, RSC, 1982; Molson Prize, Canada Council, 1987; Marcel Vincent Medal, French Canadian Assoc. for Advancement of Science, 1988; Internat. Order of Merit, Internat. Biog. Inst., 1990; Esdras Minville Prize in Soc. Scis, Soc. St Jean-Baptiste, 1991. Grand Officier, Order of Québec, 1995. *Publications:* The Acadians of Portsmouth, 1954; (jtly) People of Cove and Woodlot, 1960; (jtly) Les Comportements économiques de la famille salariée, 1964; Les Fondements Sociaux de la Maturation chez l'enfant, 1965; (jtly) Rural Canada in Transition, 1966; (jtly) A Survey of Contemporary Indians of Canada, 1967; Initiation à la recherche dans les sciences humaines, 1968; (jtly) Etude sur les Indiens contemporains du Canada, 1969; (jtly) Les Changements socio-culturels à Saint-Augustin, 1969; (jtly) Famille et parenté en Acadie, 1971; (jtly) Communautés et Culture, 1973 (Eng. trans. 1973); (jtly) Patterns of Amerindian Identity, 1976; (jtly) The Individual, Language and Society in Canada, 1977; L'Identité Québécoise en péril, 1983; (jtly) Conscience et Enquête, 1983; L'Anthropologie à l'Université Laval: fondements historiques, pratiques académiques, dynamismes d'évolution, 1989; Les fondements historiques et théoriques de la practique professionnelle en anthropologie, 1990; over one hundred and seventy-five scientific articles. *Recreations:* gardening, cross-country skiing. *Address:* 835 Nouvelle-Orléans, Sainte Foy, Québec G1X 3J4, Canada. *T:* (418) 6535411.

TREMLETT, Ven. Anthony Frank; Archdeacon of Exeter, since 1994; *b* 25 Aug. 1937; *s* of Frank and Sally Tremlett; *m* 1958, Patricia Lapthorn; two *s* one *d*. *Educ:* Plymouth College. Certificated Transport Manager; MIMgt. Clerk, Management Trainee (Traffic Apprentice), Area Manager, 1953–68, British Rail; Traffic Manager, District Manager, Operations Director, 1968–80, National Carriers (Nat. Freight Corporation). Asst Curate, Southway, Plymouth, 1981–82; Priest-in-Charge, 1982–84; Vicar, 1984–88; RD of Moorside, Plymouth, 1986–88; Archdeacon of Totnes, 1988–94. *Recreations:* music, home and family, housing policy. *Address:* St Matthew's House, 45 Spicer Road, Exeter EX1 1TA. *T:* Exeter (01392) 425432.

TREMLETT, George William, OBE 1981; author, journalist and bookseller; Director, Corran Books Ltd, since 1981; Founder Chairman, George Tremlett Ltd, since 1965; *b* 5 Sept. 1939; *s* of late Wilfred George and of Elizabeth Tremlett; *m* 1971, Jane, *o c* of late Benjamin James Mitchell and Mrs P. A. Mitchell; three *s*. *Educ:* Taunton School; King Edward VI School, Stratford upon Avon. Member of Richmond upon Thames Borough Council, 1963–74; Chairman: Further Education Cttee, 1966–68; Barnes School Governors, 1967–73; Schools Cttee, 1972–73; Shene VIth Form Coll. Governors, 1973–74; Housing Cttee, 1972–74; Thames Water Authority, 1973–74. Greater London Council: Mem. for Hillingdon, 1970–73, for Twickenham, 1973–86; Opposition Housing Spokesman, 1974–77; Leader of Housing Policy Cttee, 1977–81. Consultant: Nat. Assoc. of Voluntary Hostels, 1980–84; Local Govt Inf. Unit, 1985–86; Appeal Dir, SHAC and Help the Homeless National Appeal, 1985–. Member: Housing Minister's Adv. Cttee on Co-operatives, 1977–79; Housing Consultative Council for England, 1977–81; Northampton Develt Corp., 1979–83; Stonham Housing Assoc., 1978–92; Chiswick Family Rescue Appeal Fund, 1979–80; Bd, Empty Property Unit, 1985–86; Adv. Panel, BBC Community Prog. Unit, 1985–. Founder Chm., Dylan Thomas Meml Trust, 1985–90. Governor, Kingston Polytechnic and Twickenham Coll. of Technology, 1967–70; Court of City Univ., 1968–74. *Publications:* 17 biographies of rock musicians, 1974–77—on John Lennon, David Bowie, 10cc, Paul McCartney, The Osmonds, Alvin Stardust, Cat Stevens, Cliff Richard, Slade, The Who, David Essex, Slik, Gary Glitter, Marc Bolan, Rod Stewart, Queen and the Rolling Stones (published in many different countries); Living Cities, 1979; (with Caitlin Thomas) Life with Dylan Thomas, 1986; Clubmen, 1987; Homeless but for St Mungo's, 1989; Little Legs, 1989; Rock Gold, 1990; Dylan Thomas: in the mercy of his means, 1991; Gadaffi: the desert mystic, 1993; David Bowie, 1995. *Recreations:* ornithology, exploring old churches, local history, rock 'n' roll music. *Address:* Corran House, Laugharne, Carmarthen, Dyfed SA33 4SJ. *T:* Laugharne (01994) 427444. *Clubs:* Carlton, Wig and Pen, United and Cecil; Laugharne RFC.

TRENAMAN, Nancy Kathleen, (Mrs M. S. Trenaman); Principal of St Anne's College, Oxford, 1966–84 (Hon. Fellow, since 1984); *b* 1919; *d* of Frederick Broughton Fisher and Edith Fisher; *m* 1967, M. S. Trenaman. *Educ:* Bradford Girls' Grammar School; Somerville College, Oxford (Hon. Fellow, 1977). Board of Trade, 1941–51; Assistant Secretary, Ministry of Materials, 1951–54; Counsellor, British Embassy, Washington, 1951–53; Board of Trade, 1954–66, Under-Sec. 1962–66. Mem., Commn on the Constitution, 1969–73. Chm., Exec. Cttee, LEPRA, 1992–95. *Address:* 4 Fairlawn End, Oxford OX2 8AR. *T:* Oxford (01865) 57723. *Club:* United Oxford & Cambridge University.

TRENCH, family name of **Baron Ashtown.**

TRENCH, *see* Le Poer Trench, family name of Earl of Clancarty.

TRENCH, John; Master of the Supreme Court, Queen's Bench Division, since 1986; *b* 15 Sept. 1932; *s* of late Prince Constantine Lobanow-Rostovsky and Princess Violette Lobanow-Rostovsky (*née* Le Poer Trench); *m* 1st, 1955, Roxane Bibica-Rosetti (marr. diss.); two *s* one *d*; 2nd 1980, Patricia Margaret Skitmore. *Educ:* Oundle; Christ's College, Cambridge (MA). Nat. Service, 1950–52; commissioned The Duke of Wellington's Regt. Called to the Bar, Lincoln's Inn, 1956, practised at the Bar, in London and on the Oxford Circuit, 1956–86. *Recreations:* painting, collecting antique handwriting equipment. *Address:* Royal Courts of Justice, Strand WC2A 2LL.

TRENCH, Sir Peter (Edward), Kt 1979; CBE 1964 (OBE (mil.) 1945); TD 1949; *b* 16 June 1918; *s* of James Knights Trench and Grace Sim; *m* 1940, Mary St Clair Morford; one *s* one *d*. *Educ:* privately; London Sch. of Economics, London Univ.; St John's Coll., Cambridge Univ. BSc (Econ.) Hons. Served in The Queen's Royal Regt, 1939–46: Staff Coll., 1942; AAG, HQ 21 Army Gp, 1944–45 (OBE). Man. Dir, Bovis Ltd, 1954–59; Director: Nat. Fedn of Bldg Trades Employers, 1959–64; Nat. Bldg Agency, 1964–66; Part-time Mem., Nat. Bd for Prices and Incomes, 1965–68. Chm., Y. J. Lovell (Holdings) plc, 1972–83; Director, 1970–83: LEP plc; Haden plc; Capital & Counties plc; Builder Gp plc; Crendon Ltd; Nationwide Building Soc. Vis. Prof. in Construction Management, Reading Univ., 1981–88. Chm., Construction and Housing Res. Adv. Council, 1973–79; Pres., Construction Health Safety Gp, 1974–80; Vice-President: NHBC, 1984– (Chm., 1978–84); Building Centre, 1976–; Member: Review of Housing Finance Adv. Gp, 1975–76; Council, CBI, 1981–83; Council, RSA, 1981–83. Mem. Court of Governors, LSE; Hon. Mem., Architectural Assoc.; Hon. Treasurer, St Mary's Hosp. Med. Sch. JP Inner London, 1963–71. Hon. FCIOB; Hon. FFB; FCIArb; FRSA; CIMgt; Hon. FRIBA; Hon. Mem. CGLI. Hon. DSc Reading, 1986. *Recreations:* tennis, swimming, travelling. *Address:* 4 Napier Close, Napier Road, W14 8LG. *T:* 0171–602 3936. *Club:* MCC.

TRENCHARD, family name of **Viscount Trenchard.**

TRENCHARD, 3rd Viscount *cr* 1936, of Wolfeton; **Hugh Trenchard;** Bt 1919; Baron 1930; Director, Kleinwort Benson Ltd, since 1986; *b* 12 March 1951; *s* of 2nd Viscount Trenchard, MC and of Patricia, *d* of Admiral Sir Sidney Bailey, KBE, CB, DSO; *S* father, 1987; *m* 1975, Fiona Elizabeth, *d* of Hon. James Morrison, *qv*; two *s* two *d*. *Educ:* Eton; Trinity Coll., Cambridge. Captain, 4th Royal Green Jackets, TA, 1973–80. Entered Kleinwort Benson Ltd, 1973; Chief Rep. in Japan, 1980–85; Gen. Man., Kleinwort Benson Internat. Inc., Tokyo Br., 1985–88; Pres., 1988–95, Rep. in Japan, 1993–95, Dep. Chm., 1995–, Kleinwort Benson Internat. Incorporated; Director: KB Berkeley Japan Development Capital Ltd, 1987–; Dover Japan Inc., 1985–87. Chm., Securities Cttee, 1993–95, Vice Chm. Council, 1995,European Business Community (Japan); Director: Japan Securities Dealers' Assoc., 1994–95; Bond Underwriters' Assoc. of Japan, 1994–95; Member: Japan Assoc. of Corporate Executives, 1987–95; Council, Japan Soc., 1992–93. Hon. Treas., H of L All-Party Defence Study Gp, 1992–93. Mem. Council, RAF Benevolent Fund, 1991–. *Heir:* *s* Hon. Alexander Thomas Trenchard, *b* 26 July 1978. *Address:* Standon Lordship, Ware, Herts SG11 1PR.

TREND, Hon. Michael (St John); MP (C) Windsor and Maidenhead, since 1992; a Deputy Chairman, Conservative Party, since 1995; *b* 19 April 1952; *e s* of Baron Trend, PC, GCB, CVO and Patricia Charlotte, *o d* of Rev. Gilbert Shaw; *m* 1987, Jill Elizabeth Kershaw; one *s* two *d*. *Educ:* Tormore Sch., Upper Deal, Kent; Westminster; Oriel Coll., Oxford; Greek Govt Scholar. Toynbee Hall, 1975–76; Sub-Editor, then Managing Editor, TLS, 1976–81; Editor: History Today, 1981–82; Parliamentary House Magazine, 1984–87; Home Editor, Spectator, 1987–90; Chief Leader Writer, Daily Telegraph, 1990–92. PPS to Minister of State, DoH, 1993–94, to Sec. of State for Transport, 1994–95. Member: Select Cttee on Health, 1992–93; Speaker's Adv. Cttee on Works of Art, 1993–. Mem. Bd, Victoria County History, 1992–. *Publication:* The Music Makers, 1985. *Recreations:* music, hill walking. *Address:* House of Commons, SW1A 0AA. *T:* 0171–219 6929. *Club:* Athenæum.

TRENDALL, Prof. Arthur Dale, AC 1976; CMG 1961; MA, LittD; FSA; FBA; FAHA; Resident Fellow, Menzies College, La Trobe University; Emeritus Professor, University of Sydney, 1954; *b* Auckland, NZ, 28 March 1909; *s* of late Arthur D. Trendall and late Iza W. Uttley-Todd; unmarried. *Educ:* King's College, Auckland; Univs. of Otago (MA 1929; LittD 1936); Cambridge Univ. (MA 1937; LittD 1968); DLitt La Trobe, 1991. NZ Post-Graduate Scholar in Arts, 1931; Rome Scholar in Archæology, 1934–35; Fellow of

Trinity Coll., Cambridge, 1936–40; Librarian British School at Rome, 1936–38; FSA 1939; Professor of Greek, Univ. of Sydney, 1939–54; Dean, Faculty of Arts, 1947–50; Chairman Professorial Board, 1949–50, 1952; Acting Vice-Chancellor, 1953; Master of Univ. House, ANU, 1954–69, retd; Hon. Fellow, 1969. Hon. Curator, Greek and Roman Section, Nicholson Museum, 1954, and Hon. Consultant, National Gallery of Victoria, 1957; Deputy Vice-Chancellor, ANU, 1958–64; Mem. Royal Commn on Univ. of Tas., 1955. Geddes-Harrower Professor of Greek Art and Archæology, Aberdeen Univ., 1966–67; Guest Scholar, J. Paul Getty Mus., 1985. Chm. Aust. Humanities Research Council, 1957–59. Mem., Nat. Capital Planning Cttee, 1958–67; Mem. Australian Universities Commission, 1959–70. Member: Accademia dei Lincei, Rome, 1971; Athens Acad., 1973; Corresp. Mem., Pontifical Acad. of Archaeology, Rome, 1973; Life Mem., Nat. Gall. of Victoria, 1976; For. Mem., Royal Netherlands Acad., 1977; Hon. Member: Hellenic Soc., 1982; Archaeol Inst. of Amer., 1987. Hon. Fellow: Athens Archaeological Soc., 1975; British School at Rome, 1983. FBA 1968. Hon. LittD: Melbourne, 1956; ANU 1970; Hon. DLitt: Adelaide, 1960; Sydney, 1972; Tasmania, 1979; Hon. Dott. in Lettere, Lecce, 1981. For. Galileo Galilei Prize for Archaeology, 1971; Cassano Gold Medal for Magna Graecia Studies, 1971; Britannica Award (Australia), 1973; Kenyon Medal, British Acad., 1983. KCSG, 1956; Commendatore, Ordine al Merito, Republic of Italy, 1965 (Cav. Uff. 1961). *Publications:* Paestan Pottery, 1936; Frühitaliotische Vasen, 1938; Guide to the Cast Collection of the Nicholson Museum, Sydney, 1941; The Shellal Mosaic, 1942, 4th edn 1973; Handbook to the Nicholson Museum (editor), 2nd edn 1948; Paestan Pottery, Supplement, 1952; Vasi Italioti del Vaticano, vol. i, 1953; vol. ii, 1955; The Felton Greek Vases, 1958; Phlyax Vases, 1959, 2nd edn 1967; Paestan Addenda, 1960; Apulian Vase Painters of the Plain Style (with A. Cambitoglou), 1962; South Italian Vase Painting (British Museum Guide), 1966, 2nd edn 1976; The Red-figured Vases of Lucania, Campania and Sicily, 1967, Supplement I, 1970, Supplement II, 1973, Supplement III, 1983; Greek Vases in the Felton Collection, 1968, 2nd edn 1978; Greek Vases in the Logie Collection, Christchurch, NZ, 1971; Illustrations of Greek Drama (with T. B. L. Webster), 1971; Early South Italian Vase-painting, 1974; Eine Gruppe Apulischer Grabvasen in Basel (with M. Schmidt and A. Cambitoglou), 1976; Vasi antichi dipinti del Vaticano—Collezione Astarita: (iii) Vasi italiòti, 1976; (with A. Cambitoglou) The Red-figured Vases of Apulia, 2 vols, 1978, 1982, Supplement I, 1983, Supplement II, 1991; (with Ian McPhee) Greek Red-figured Fish-plates, 1987; The Red-figured Vases of Paestum, 1987; Red-figure Vases of South Italy and Sicily, 1989, German edn 1991; (with Marit Jentoft Nilsen) Corpus Vasorum Antiquorum, Malibu, J. Paul Getty Museum, vol. 3, 1990, vol. 4, 1991, vol. 5, 1994; several articles in learned periodicals. *Address:* Menzies College, La Trobe University, Bundoora, Vic 3083, Australia.

TRENTHAM, Dr David Rostron, FRS 1982; Head of Physical Biochemistry Division, National Institute for Medical Research, Mill Hill, since 1984; *b* 22 Sept. 1938; *s* of John Austin and Julia Agnes Mary Trentham; *m* 1966, Kamalini; two *s*. *Educ:* Univ. of Cambridge (BA Chemistry, PhD Organic Chemistry). Biochemistry Dept, University of Bristol: Jun. Research Fellow (Medical Research Council), 1966–69; Research Associate, 1969–72; Lectr in Biochemistry, 1972–75; Reader in Biochemistry, 1975–77; Edwin M. Chance Prof., Biochemistry and Biophysics Dept, Univ. of Pennsylvania, 1977–84. Colworth Medal (an annual award), Biochemical Soc., UK, 1974; Wilhelm Feldberg Prize, Feldberg Foundn Bd for Anglo-German Scientific Exchange, 1990. *Publications:* numerous research papers in scientific jls. *Address:* Physical Biochemistry Division, National Institute for Medical Research, The Ridgeway, Mill Hill, NW7 1AA. *T:* 0181–959 3666.

TREPTE, Paul, FRCO; Organist and Master of the Choristers, Ely Cathedral, since 1990; *b* 24 April 1954; *s* of Harry and Ruth Trepte; *m* 1981, Sally Lampard; one *d*. *Educ:* New College, Oxford (MA). Asst Organist, Worcester Cathedral, 1976; Dir of Music, St Mary's, Warwick, 1981; Organist and Master of the Choristers, St Edmundsbury Cathedral, 1985. *Publications:* choral works. *Address:* The Old Sacristy, The College, Ely CB7 4JU. *T:* Ely (01353) 665669.

TRESCOWTHICK, Sir Donald (Henry), AC 1991; KBE 1979; Chairman: Charles Davis Ltd, since 1972; Signet Group Holdings Pty Ltd, since 1978; *b* 4 Dec. 1930; *s* of Thomas Patrick and Elsie May Trescowthick; *m* 1952, Norma Margaret Callaghan; two *s* two *d*. FCPA. Chairman: Co-operative Motors, 1972–89; Harris Scarfe, 1976–93; G. P. FitzGerald & Co., 1981–92. Founder Chm., Victorian Div. and Exec. Dir, Aust. Olympic Team Fund; Chairman: Minus Children's Fund, 1975–; Sir Donald and Lady Trescowthick Foundn; Inaugural Chm. and Patron, Melbourne to Hobart Yacht Race Cttee, 1972–88; Dir, Aust. Ballet Develt, 1978–93. Pres., Peter MacCallum Cancer Inst. Appeal, 1991–94; Patron: DOXA Youth Welfare Foundn; Special Olympics Australia, 1992–; Team Equestrian Australia, 1993–. Olympic OM, 1981; CLJ 1982; Knight of Magistral Grace, SMO, Malta, 1984. *Recreations:* travel, reading. *Address:* PO Box 93, Toorak, Vic. 3142, Australia. *T:* (3) 98266933. *Clubs:* Les Ambassadeurs; Athenæum, Victoria Racing, Victorian Amateur Turf (Melbourne); Moonee Valley Racing, Tasmanian Turf, Tasmanian Racing (Hobart); Geelong Football.

TRESIDDER, Gerald Charles, FRCS; Lecturer, Department of Anatomy, University of Leicester, retired; *b* Rawalpindi, 5 Dec. 1912; *s* of late Lt-Col A. G. Tresidder, CIE, MD, MS, FRCS; *m* 1940, Marguerite Bell; one *s* two *d*. *Educ:* Haileybury; Queen Mary College and The London Hospital Medical College, Univ. of London. LRCP, MRCS 1937; MB, BS London 1938; FRCS 1946. Surgical Specialist, Major, Indian Medical Service, 1940–46. Surgeon, 1951–64, Urologist, 1964–76, at The London Hospital; Lectr in Surgery and part-time Sen. Lectr in Anatomy, The London Hosp. Med. Coll., 1951–76; Senior Lectr, Human Morphology, Univ. of Southampton, 1976–80. Past Pres., Section of Urology, RSocMed; Senior Mem., British Assoc. of Urological Surgeons; Sen. Fellow, British Assoc. of Clinical Anatomists; formerly Examr in Anatomy for Primary FRCSEng and Ed. *Publications:* contributions to: Rob and Smith's Operative Surgery; Smith and Aitkenhead's Textbook of Anaesthesia, 1985; British Jl of Surgery; British Jl of Urology; Lancet; BMJ. *Recreations:* walking and talking. *Address:* Woodspring, 4 Penny Long Lane, Derby DE22 1AW. *T:* Derby (01332) 558026.

TRESS, Ronald Charles, CBE 1968; BSc (Econ.) London, DSc Bristol; Director, The Leverhulme Trust, 1977–84; *b* Upchurch, Sittingbourne, Kent, 11 Jan. 1915; *er s* of S. C. Tress; *m* 1942, Josephine Kelly (*d* 1993), *d* of H. J. Medland; one *s* two *d*. *Educ:* Gillingham (Kent) County School; Univ. College, Southampton. Gladstone Student, St Deiniol's Library, Hawarden, 1936–37; Drummond Fraser Research Fellow, Univ. of Manchester, 1937–38; Asst Lecturer in Economics, Univ. Coll. of the S West, Exeter, 1938–41; Economic Asst, War Cabinet Offices, 1941–45; Economic Adviser, Cabinet Secretariat, 1945–47; Reader in Public Finance, Univ. of London, 1947–51; Prof. of Political Economy, Univ. of Bristol, 1951–68; Master of Birkbeck Coll., 1968–77, Fellow, 1977–; Mem., Univ. of London Senate, 1968–77, and Court, 1976–77. Managing Editor, London and Cambridge Economic Service, 1949–51; Member: Reorganisation Commn for Pigs and Bacon, 1955–56; Nigeria Fiscal Commn, 1957–58; Departmental Cttee on Rating of Charities, 1958; Develt Commn, 1959–81; Financial Enquiry, Aden Colony, 1959; East Africa Economic and Fiscal Commn, 1960, Uganda Fiscal Commn, 1962; Kenya Fiscal Commn (Chm.), 1962–63; National Incomes Commn, 1963–65; Chm., SW Economic Planning Council, 1965–68; Mem., Cttee of Inquiry into Teachers' Pay, 1974; Chm., Cttee for Univ. Assistance to Adult Educn in HM Forces, 1974–79; Lay Mem., Solicitors' Disciplinary Tribunal, 1975–79; Chm., Lord Chancellor's Adv. Cttee on Legal Aid, 1979–84. Trustee, City Parochial Foundn, 1974–77, 1979–89; Governor, Christ Church Coll., Canterbury, 1975–91; Mem. Council, Kent Univ., 1977–92. Royal Economic Society: Council, 1960–70, Sec.-Gen., 1975–79, Vice-Pres., 1979–. Hon. LLD: Furman Univ., S Carolina, 1973; Exeter, 1976; DUniv Open Univ., 1974; Hon. DSc (SocSc) Southampton, 1978; Hon. DCL Kent, 1984. *Publications:* articles and reviews in Economic Journal, Economica, LCES Bulletin, etc. *Address:* The Red House, 29 Palace Road, East Molesey, Surrey KT8 9DJ. *T:* 0181–979 0605. *Club:* Athenæum.

TRETHOWAN, Prof. Sir William (Henry), Kt 1980; CBE 1975; FRCP, FRACP; Professor of Psychiatry, University of Birmingham, 1962–82, Emeritus since 1983; Hon. Consultant Psychiatrist: Hollymoor Hospital, 1964–82; Midland Centre for Neurosurgery, 1975–82; Central Birmingham Health District, since 1983; *b* 3 June 1917; *s* of William Henry Trethowan and Joan Durham Trethowan (*née* Hickson); *m* 1st, 1941, Pamela Waters (*d* 1985); one *s* two *d*; 2nd, 1988, Heather Dalton (*née* Gardiner). *Educ:* Oundle Sch.; Clare Coll., Cambridge; Guy's Hosp. Med. Sch. MA, MB, BChir (Cantab) 1943; MRCP 1948; FRACP 1961; FRCP 1963; FRCPsych 1971 (Hon. Fellow 1983). Served War, RAMC: Major, Med. Specialist, 1944–47. Psychiatric Registrar, Maudsley Hosp., 1948–50; Psychiatric Resident, Mass Gen. Hosp., and Hon. Teaching Fellow, Harvard, 1951; Lectr and Sen. Lectr in Psychiatry, Univ. of Manchester, 1951–56; Prof. of Psychiatry, Univ. of Sydney, and Hon. Consultant Psychiatrist, Royal Prince Alfred and Royal North Shore Hosps, Sydney, 1956–62. Mem. GMC, 1969–81 (Treasurer, 1978–81); Cons. Adviser in Psychiatry, DHSS, 1964–78; Dean, Univ. of Birmingham Med. Sch., 1968–74; Chm., Standing Mental Health Adv. Cttee, 1968–74; Mem., UGC Med. Subcttee, 1974–81. Member: Birmingham Reg. Hosp. Bd, 1964–74; Standing Med. Adv. Cttee, 1966–82 (Chm., 1976); Central Health Services Council, 1966–80 (Vice-Chm., 1976–80); W Midlands Regional Health Authority, 1974–76. Chm., Med. Acad. Adv. Cttee, Chinese Univ. of Hong Kong, 1976–86. FRSocMed; Hon. Fellow, Royal Aust. and NZ Coll. of Psychiatry (FRANZCP 1962); Corresp. Fellow, Amer. Psychiatric Assoc. Hon. DSc Chinese Univ. of Hong Kong, 1979. Hon. FRCPsych. *Publications:* Psychiatry, 2nd edn (with Prof. E. W. Anderson), 1967, 5th edn (with Prof. A. C. P. Sims), 1983; Uncommon Psychiatric Syndromes, 1967, 3rd edn (with M. D. Enoch), 1991; numerous scientific and other articles in various jls; book reviews, etc. *Recreations:* music, cooking, natural history. *Address:* 31 High Point, Richmond Hill Road, Birmingham B15 3RU.

TREUHERZ, Julian Benjamin; Keeper of Art Galleries, National Museums and Galleries on Merseyside (Walker Art Gallery, Lady Lever Art Gallery and Sudley), since 1989; *b* 12 March 1947; *s* of Werner Treuherz and Irmgard (*née* Amberg). *Educ:* Manchester Grammar Sch.; Christ Church, Oxford (MA); Univ. of East Anglia (MA). Dip. Museums Assoc. 1974. Manchester City Art Gallery: Trainee, 1971; Asst Keeper, 1972–74, Keeper, 1974–89, of Fine Art. Member: Victorian Soc. (Hon. Sec., Manchester Gp, 1972–79, Chm., 1980–83); Cttee, Fine Arts Sub-Gp, Liverpool Univ., 1989–; Cttee, Whitworth Art Gall., 1993–. *Publications:* Pre-Raphaelite Paintings from the Manchester City Art Gallery, 1981; Hard Times: social realism in Victorian art, 1987; (with Peter de Figueiredo) Country Houses of Cheshire, 1988; Victorian Painting, 1993; articles in art-historical jls. *Recreations:* playing the piano, cooking, opera. *Address:* Walker Art Gallery, William Brown Street, Liverpool L3 8EL.

TREVELYAN, (Adye) Mary; *see* Fedden, A. M.

TREVELYAN, Dennis John, CB 1981; MA; FIPM; Principal, Mansfield College, Oxford, since 1989; *b* 21 July 1929; *s* of John Henry Trevelyan; *m* 1959, Carol Coombes; one *s* one *d*. *Educ:* Enfield Grammar Sch.; University Coll., Oxford (Scholar). Entered Home Office, 1950; Treasury, 1953–54; Sec. to Parly Under-Sec. of State, Home Office, 1954–55; Principal Private Sec. to Lord President of Council and Leader of House, 1964–67; Asst Sec., 1966; Asst Under-Sec. of State, NI Office, 1972–76; Home Office: Asst Under-Sec. of State, Broadcasting Dept, 1976–77; Dep. Under-Sec. of State and Dir-Gen., Prison Service, 1978–83; First CS Comr and Dep. Sec., Cabinet Office, 1983–89, retd. Secretary: Peppiatt Cttee on a Levy on Betting on Horse Races, 1960; Lord Radcliffe's Cttee of Privy Counsellors to inquire into D Notice Matters, 1967. Vice-Chm., CS Sports Council, 1981–; Vice-Pres., Industrial Participation Assoc., 1987–; Member: Bd of Management, Eur. Inst. of Public Admin, Maastricht, 1984–89; Council, City Univ. Business Sch., 1986–89; ECCTIS Adv. Group, 1990–; Governor: Ashridge Management Coll., 1985–89; Contemporary Dance Trust, 1986–89; Oxford Centre for Postgraduate Hebrew Studies, 1992–; Trustee, Dancers Resettlement Fund, 1987–91. FRSA 1986. *Recreation:* music. *Address:* Mansfield College, Mansfield Road, Oxford OX1 3TF. *Clubs:* Athenæum, MCC; Vincent's (Oxford).

TREVELYAN, Sir George (Lowthian), 4th Bt, *cr* 1874; Hon. President, Wrekin Trust (Founder, 1971; Director, 1971–86); *b* 5 Nov. 1906; *e s* of Rt Hon. Sir C. P. Trevelyan, 3rd Bt; *S* father 1958; *m* 1940, Editha Helen (*d* 1994), *d* of Col John Lindsay-Smith; one adopted *d*. *Educ:* Sidcot School; Trinity College, Cambridge (MA). Worked as artist-craftsman with Peter Waals workshops, fine furniture, 1929–31. Trained and worked in F. M. Alexander re-education method, 1932–36. Taught at Gordonstoun School and Abinger Hill School, 1936–41. Served War, 1941–45, Captain, Home Guard Training. Taught No 1 Army Coll., Newbattle Abbey, 1945–47. Principal, Shropshire Adult College, Attingham Park, Shrewsbury, 1947–71; mounted and ran Wrekin Trust courses, 1971–86; now lecture tours on holistic themes. *Publications:* A Vision of the Aquarian Age, 1977; The Active Eye in Architecture, 1977; Magic Casements, 1980; Operation Redemption, 1981; Summons to a High Crusade, 1986; Exploration into God, 1991. *Heir: b* Geoffrey Washington Trevelyan [*b* 4 July 1920; *m* 1947, Gillian Isabel, *d* of late Alexander Wood; one *s* one *d*]. *Address:* The Barn, Hawkesbury, near Badminton, Avon GL9 1BW. *T:* Chipping Sodbury (01454) 238359.

TREVELYAN, Sir Norman Irving, 10th Bt *cr* 1662; *b* 29 Jan. 1915; *s* of Edward Walter Trevelyan (*d* 1947), and of Kathleen E. H., *d* of William Irving; *S* kinsman, Sir Willoughby John Trevelyan, 9th Bt, 1976; *m* 1951, Jennifer Mary, *d* of Arthur E. Riddett, Burgh Heath, Surrey; two *s* one *d*. *Educ:* The Cate School, Carpinteria, California (grad. 1932); Harvard Univ., Cambridge, Mass (grad. 1936). *Heir: s* Edward Norman Trevelyan, *b* 14 Aug. 1955. *Address:* 1041 Adella Avenue, Coronado, California 92118, USA.

[*But his name does not, at the time of going to press, appear on the Roll of the Baronetage.*

TREVELYAN OMAN, Julia; *see* Oman.

TREVES, Vanni Emanuele; Senior Partner, Macfarlanes, Solicitors, since 1987; Chairman: BBA Group PLC, since 1989; McKechnie plc, since 1991; *b* 3 Nov. 1940; *s* of Giuliano Treves (killed in action, 1944), and of Marianna Treves (*née* Baer); *m* 1971, Angela Veronica Fyffe; two *s* one *d*. *Educ;* St Paul's Sch. (Foundn Scholar); University Coll. Oxford (MA); Univ. of Illinois (LLM; Fulbright Scholar). Articled clerk and Solicitor, Macfarlanes, 1963–68; Vis. Attorney, White & Case, New York, 1968–69; Partner, Macfarlanes, 1970–87. Director: Oceonics Group, 1984–, Saatchi & Saatchi, 1987–90. Chm., Fledgeling Equity and Bond Funds, 1992–. Solicitor to RA, 1992–. Chm., Develt

Cttee, Nat. Portrait Gall., 1991–; Mem., Develt Bd, London Business Sch., 1992–. Trustee: J. Paul Getty Jr Charitable Trust, 1985–; 29th May 1961 Charitable Trust, 1970–. Vice-Pres., London Fedn of Clubs for Young People (formerly of Boys' Clubs), 1991– (Hon. Treas., 1976–95). Gov., Hall Sch., Hampstead, 1983–94. *Recreations:* walking, eating, English watercolours. *Address:* 10 Norwich Street, EC4A 1BD. *T:* 0171–831 9222. *Clubs:* Boodle's, City of London.

TREVETHIN, 4th Baron **AND OAKSEY,** 2nd Baron; *see under* Oaksey, 2nd Baron.

TREVETT, Peter George; QC 1992; *b* 25 Nov. 1947; *s* of George Albert Trevett and of late Janet Trevett; *m* 1972, Vera Lucia dos Santos Ferreira; two *s* one *d*. *Educ:* Kingston Grammar Sch.; Queens' Coll., Cambridge (MA, LLM). Called to the Bar, Lincoln's Inn, 1971 (Mansfield Schol.); in practice at Revenue Bar, 1973–. *Publications:* contribs to legal pubns. *Recreations:* golf, reading, collecting cactaceae, gardening. *Address:* 11 New Square, Lincoln's Inn, WC2A 3QB. *T:* 0171–242 4017. *Club:* Woking Golf.

TREVIS, Diane Ellen; theatre director; *b* 8 Nov. 1947; *d* of late Joseph Trevis and of Marjorie Trevis; *m* 1986, Dominic John Muldowney, *qv*; one *d*. *Educ:* Waverley Grammar Sch., Birmingham; Sussex Univ. Actress and dir, Glasgow Citizens' Theatre, 1972–80; Arts Council Associate Dir, Palace Theatre, Westcliff, 1982; Director: Royal Shakespeare Company: Taming of the Shrew, Happy End, 1985–86; The Revenger's Tragedy, 1987; Much Ado About Nothing, 1988; Elgar's Rondo, 1993; Royal National Theatre: Irish-Hebrew Lesson, 1981; The Mother, Yerma, School for Wives, A Matter of Life and Death, 1985–86; The Resistible Rise of Arturo Ui, 1991; Inadmissible Evidence, 1993; Gawain, Royal Opera House, 1991; Voyage in the Dark, 1995. *Recreations:* meals, movies, long mountain walks. *Address:* c/o National Theatre, South Bank, SE1 9PX.

TREVOR, 4th Baron *cr* 1880; **Charles Edwin Hill-Trevor,** JP; *b* 13 Aug. 1928; *e s* of 3rd Baron and Phyllis May, 2nd *d* of J. A. Sims, Ings House, Kirton-in-Lindsey, Lincolnshire; *S* father, 1950; *m* 1967, Susan Janet Elizabeth, *o d* of Dr Ronald Bence; two *s*. *Educ:* Shrewsbury. Royal Forestry Society: Mem. Council and Trustee; Chm., N Wales Div. Trustee, Robert Jones and Agnes Hunt Orthopaedic Hosp. Inst. Cttee. JP Clwyd (formerly Denbighshire) 1959; Chm., Berwyn PSD. CStJ. *Recreations:* shooting, fishing. *Heir: s* Hon. Marke Charles Hill-Trevor, *b* 8 Jan. 1970. *Address:* Brynkinalt, Chirk, Wrexham, Clwyd LL14 5NS. *T:* Chirk (01691) 773425; Auch, Bridge of Orchy, Argyllshire. *T:* Tyndrum (01838) 400282. *Clubs:* East India, Flyfishers'.

TREVOR, Brig. Kenneth Rowland Swetenham, CBE 1964 (OBE 1952); DSO 1945; Brigadier (retired 1966); *b* 15 April 1914; 2nd *s* of late Mr and Mrs E. S. R. Trevor, formerly of The Acres, Upton Heath, Chester; *m* 1st, 1941, Margaret Baynham (*d* 1988), *er d* of late Reverend J. H. Baynham, ACG; two *s*; 2nd, 1989, Jeanne Alexander (*née* Holmes Henderson). *Educ:* Rossall; RMC, Camberley. Joined 22nd (Cheshire) Regt, 1934; served in India and with RWAFF in Nigeria. War of 1939–45 (despatches and DSO): No. 1 Commando, N Africa and Burma, 1941–45, as CO, 1943–45; Staff College, Camberley, 1945–46; Bde Major, 29 Infantry Brigade Group, 1949–51; served Korea, 1950–51 (despatches, OBE); GSO1 and Chief Instructor, RMA, Sandhurst, 1954–56; Commanded 1st Bn Cheshire Regt, 1956–58; Malaya, 1957–58 (despatches); Deputy Commander, 50 Infantry Brigade Group/Central Area, Cyprus, 1959; Brigade Col Mercian Brigade, 1960–61; Commander, 2 Infantry Brigade Group and Devon/Cornwall Sub District, 1961–64; Commander, British Guiana Garrison, 1963; Inspector of Boys' Training (Army), 1964–66. With Runcorn Develt Corp., 1966–78. Vice-Pres., The Commando Assoc. *Address:* Barrelwell Hill, Chester CH3 5BR. *Club:* Army and Navy.

TREVOR, Meriol; Author; *b* 15 April 1919; *d* of Lt-Col Arthur Prescott Trevor and Lucy M. E. Trevor (*née* Dimmock). *Educ:* Perse Girls' Sch., Cambridge; St Hugh's Coll., Oxford. FRSL. *Publications: novels:* The Last of Britain, 1956; The New People, 1957; A Narrow Place, 1958; Shadows and Images, 1960; The City and the World, 1970; The Holy Images, 1971; The Fugitives, 1973; The Two Kingdoms, 1973; The Marked Man, 1974; The Enemy at Home, 1974; The Forgotten Country, 1975; The Fortunate Marriage, 1976; The Treacherous Paths, 1976; The Civil Prisoners, 1977; The Fortunes of Peace, 1978; The Wanton Fires, 1979; The Sun with a Face, 1984; The Golden Palaces, 1986; *poems:* Midsummer, Midwinter, 1957; *biography:* Newman: The Pillar of the Cloud, 1962; Newman: Light in Winter, 1962 (James Tait Black Meml Prize); Apostle of Rome, 1966; Pope John, 1967; Prophets and Guardians, 1969; The Arnolds, 1973; The Shadow of a Crown: the life story of James II of England and VII of Scotland, 1988; also books for children. *Address:* 41 Fitzroy House, Pulteney Street, Bath, Avon BA2 4DW.

TREVOR, William, (William Trevor Cox), CBE (Hon.) 1977; CLit 1994; writer; *b* 24 May 1928; *er s* of J. W. Cox; *m* 1952, Jane, *yr d* of C. N. Ryan; two *s*. *Educ:* St Columba's College, Co. Dublin; Trinity College, Dublin. Mem., Irish Acad. Letters. Television plays include: The Mark-2 Wife; O Fat White Woman; The Grass Widows; The General's Day; Love Affair; Last Wishes; Matilda's England; Secret Orchards; Autumn Sunshine. Radio plays include: The Penthouse Apartment; Beyond the Pale (Giles Cooper award, 1980); Travellers; Autumn Sunshine (Giles Cooper award, 1982); Events at Drimaghleen. Allied Irish Banks Award for Literature, 1976. Hon. DLitt: Exeter, 1984; TCD, 1986; Cork, 1990; Hon. DLit Belfast, 1989. *Publications:* A Standard of Behaviour, 1956; The Old Boys, 1964 (Hawthornden Prize; as play, produced Mermaid, 1971); The Boarding-House, 1965; The Love Department, 1966; The Day We Got Drunk on Cake, 1967; Mrs Eckdorf in O'Neill's Hotel, 1969; Miss Gomez and the Brethren, 1971; The Ballroom of Romance, 1972 (adapted for BBC TV, 1982); Going Home (play), 1972; A Night with Mrs da Tanka (play), 1972; Marriages (play), 1973; Elizabeth Alone, 1973; Angels at the Ritz, 1975 (RSL award); The Children of Dynmouth, 1976 (Whitbread Novel Award; televised, 1987); Lovers of Their Time, 1978; Other People's Worlds, 1980; Beyond the Pale, 1981 (televised, 1989); Scenes from an Album (play), 1981; Fools of Fortune, 1983 (Whitbread Novel Award); A Writer's Ireland, 1984; The News from Ireland and other stories, 1986; Nights at the Alexandra, 1987; The Silence in the Garden, 1988; (ed) The Oxford Book of Irish Short Stories, 1989; Family Sins and other stories, 1989; Two Lives, 1991; Juliet's Story (for children), 1992; Excursions in the Real World, 1993; Felicia's Journey, 1994 (Whitbread Book of the Year Award; Sunday Express Book of the Year Award). *Address:* c/o A. D. Peters, 5th Floor, The Chambers, Chelsea Harbour, SW10 0XF.

TREVOR COX, Major Horace Brimson; *b* 14 June 1908; *o s* of late C. Horace Cox, Roche Old Court, Winterslow, Wilts and formerly of Whitby Hall, nr Chester; *m* 1957, Gwenda Mary, *d* of Alfred Ellis, Woodford, Essex; one *d*. *Educ:* Eton (played football for Eton Field and Wall game, 1926 and 1927, boxed for Eton, 1925, 1926, 1927); Germany and USA. Major late Welsh Guards (SR); served in France with BEF, 1939–40, and on General Staff, 1940–44; Major AA Comd. HQ, 1944–46, RARO, 1946–61. Studied commercial and political conditions in Germany, 1927–29, in America and Canada, 1929–30, and in Near East (Egypt and Palestine), 1934; contested (C) NE Derbyshire, 1935, Stalybridge and Hyde, 1937; MP (C) County of Chester, Stalybridge and Hyde, 1937–45; Parliamentary Private Secretary to: Rt Hon. Sir Ronald Cross when Under-Secretary Board of Trade, 1938–39, and when Minister of Economic Warfare, 1939–40; Minister of Health Rt Hon. H. U. Willink, 1945. Hon. Treasr, Russian Relief Assoc., 1945–47. Contested (C) Stalybridge and Hyde, 1945, Birkenhead, 1950; Parly Candidate (C) for Romford and Brentwood, Essex, 1953–55; contested (Ind) Salisbury by-election, 1965; later joined Labour Party; contested (Lab): RDC, Wilts, 1970; Wilts CC, 1973. Member of Exec. County Committee, British Legion, Wilts, 1946–62; Chairman: Salisbury and S Wilts Branch, English-Speaking Union, 1957–63; Salisbury Road Safety Cttee, 1985 (Mem., 1977–85); Mem. Exec. Cttee, CLA, for Wilts, Hants, IoW and Berks. Farmer and landowner. Lord of Manor of East Winterslow. *Address:* Roche Old Court, Winterslow, Wilts SP5 1BG. *Club:* Brooks's.

TREVOR-ROPER, family name of **Baron Dacre of Glanton.**

TREVOR-ROPER, Patrick Dacre, MA, MD, BChir Cantab; FRCS, DOMS England; Hon. FCOphth; FZS; FRGS; Consultant Ophthalmic Surgeon: Westminster Hospital, 1947–82; Moorfields Eye Hospital, 1961–81; King Edward VII Hospital for Officers, 1964–86; Teacher of Ophthalmology, University of London, 1953–82; *b* 1916; *yr s* of Dr B. W. E. Trevor-Roper, Alnwick, Northumberland; unmarried. *Educ:* Charterhouse (senior classical schol.); Clare Coll., Cambridge (exhibitioner); Westminster Hospital Medical Sch. (scholar). Served as Captain, NZ Medical Corps, 1943–46, in Central Mediterranean Forces. Held resident appointments, Westminster Hospital and Moorfields Eye Hospital. Vice-Pres., Ophthalmol Soc. of UK; Chm., Ophth. Qualifications Cttee, 1974–; Founder Mem., Internat. Acad. of Ophthalmology, 1976; FRSocMed (Pres., Ophthalmol Sect., June 1978–80). Formerly: Examnr for Diploma of Ophthalmology, RCS; Mem., Ophth. Group Cttee, BMA; Mem., London Med. Cttee. Hon. Member: Brazilian Society of Ophthalmology, 1958; Ophthalmological Soc. of NZ, 1975; Hon. dipl., Peruvian and Columbian Societies of Otolaryngology and Ophthalmology, 1958; President, etc., of various clubs in connection with sports, music and drama, both hospital and county. Freeman, City of London; Liveryman, Soc. of Spectaclemakers. Doyne medal, 1980; (first) de Lancey medal, RSocMed; Lettsomian Medal, Med. Soc. of London, 1994. Editor, Trans Ophthalmol Soc., UK, 1949–88; Member Editorial Board: Modern Medicine, 1975–; Annals of Ophth., 1972–86; The Broadway, 1946–83. *Publications:* (ed) Music at Court (Four 18th century studies by A. Yorke-Long), 1954; Ophthalmology, a Textbook for Diploma Students, 1955, new edn 1962; Lecture-notes in Ophthalmology, 1960, 7th edn 1986 (trans. French, Spanish, Portuguese, Malay); (ed) International Ophthalmology Clinics VIII, 1962; The World Through Blunted Sight: an inquiry into the effects of disordered vision on character and art, 1971, 3rd edn 1990; The Eye and Its Disorders, 1973, new edn 1984; (ed) Recent Advances in Ophthalmology, 1975; (ed) The Bowman Lectures, 1980; (ed) Procs 6th Congress of European Ophth. Soc., 1980; Ophthalmology (pocket consultant series), 1981, 2nd edn 1985; miscellaneous articles in medical and other journals. *Recreations:* music, travel. *Address:* 3 Park Square West, Regent's Park, NW1 4LJ. *T:* 0171–935 5052; Long Crichel House, near Wimborne, Dorset BH21 5JU. *Clubs:* Athenæum, Beefsteak.

See also Baron Dacre of Glanton.

TREW, Francis Sidney Edward, CMG 1984; HM Diplomatic Service, retired; Ambassador to Bahrain, 1984–88; *b* 22 Feb. 1931; *s* of Harry Francis and Alice Mary Trew; *m* 1958, Marlene Laurette Regnery; three *d*. *Educ:* Taunton's Sch., Southampton. Served Army, 1949–51; 2nd Lieut, Royal Hampshire Regt. FO, 1951; Lebanon, 1952; Amman, 1953; Bahrain, 1953–54; Jedda, 1954–56; Vice-Consul, Philadelphia, 1956–59; Second Sec., Kuwait, 1959–62; FO, 1962; seconded as Sec., European Conf. on Satellite Communications, 1963–65; Consul, Guatemala City, 1965–70; First Sec., Mexico City, 1971–74; FCO, 1974–77; Consul, Algeciras, 1977–79; FCO, 1980–81; High Comr at Belmopan, Belize, 1981–84. Mem. Management Cttee, Devon Community Housing Soc., 1994–. Order of Aztec Eagle (Mexico), 1975. *Recreations:* carpentry, fishing. *Address:* The Orchard, Higher Trickeys, Morebath, Devon EX16 9AL.

TREW, Peter John Edward, FCIS, FCT, FCIArb, MICE; Director, Rush & Tompkins Group plc, 1973–90 (Chairman of Executive Committee, 1986–87); *b* 30 April 1932; *s* of Antony Trew, DSC; *m* 1st, 1955, Angela (marr. diss. 1985; she *d* 1991), *d* of Kenneth Rush, CBE; two *s* one *d*; 2nd, 1985, Joan, *d* of Allan Haworth. *Educ:* Diocesan Coll., Rondebosch, Cape. Royal Navy, 1950–54; served HMS Devonshire, Unicorn and Charity. Chartered Inst. of Secretaries Sir Ernest Clarke Prize, 1955. Contested (C) Dartford, 1966; MP (C) Dartford, 1970–Feb. 1974; Jt Sec., Cons. Parly Finance Cttee, 1972–74; Mem., Select Cttee on Tax Credits, 1972–73. Chm., Kent West Cons. European Constituency Council, 1978–80. Mem. Council, CBI, 1975–83 (Mem., Econ. and Fin. Policy Cttee, 1980–86). Foundn FCT, 1979; FCIArb 1989. *Address:* 1 Painshill House, Cobham, Surrey KT11 1DL. *T:* Cobham (01932) 863315.

TREWBY, Vice-Adm. Sir (George Francis) Allan, KCB 1974; FEng 1978; retired; *b* Simonstown, S Africa, 8 July 1917; *s* of late Vice-Admiral G. Trewby, CMG, DSO, and Dorothea Trewby (*née* Allan); *m* 1942, Sandra Coleridge Stedham; two *s*. *Educ:* RNC, Dartmouth; RNEC, Keyham; RNC, Greenwich. Naval Cadet, Dartmouth, 1931 (King's Dirk, 1934). Served in HMS: Frobisher, Barham, Nelson, Duke of York, Dido, Cadiz, Albion. Comdg Officer, HMS Sultan, 1963–64; IDC, 1965; Captain of Naval Base, Portland, 1966–68; Asst Controller (Polaris), MoD, 1968–71; Chief of Fleet Support and Member of Board of Admiralty, 1971–74. Commander, 1950; Captain, 1959; Rear-Adm., 1968; Vice-Adm., 1971. Naval ADC to HM the Queen, 1968. FIMechE; FIMarE; CBIM. Akroyd Stuart Award of InstMarE for 1954–55. *Publications:* papers on naval marine engineering, in UK, USA, Sweden and Italy. *Address:* 2 Radnor Close, Henley-on-Thames RG9 2DA. *T:* Henley (01491) 577260. *Clubs:* Naval, MCC, Ebury Court; Phyllis Court (Henley).

TRIBE, Geoffrey Reuben, OBE 1968; Controller, Higher Education Division, British Council, 1981–83, retired; *b* 20 Feb. 1924; *s* of late Harry and Olive Tribe; *m* 1st, 1946, Sheila Mackenzie (marr. diss. 1977); 2nd, 1978, Malvina Anne Butt. *Educ:* Southern Grammar Sch., Portsmouth; University Coll. London (BA). Served War, Royal Hampshire Regt (Lieut), 1942–45. Teaching, 1948–58. Appointed to British Council, 1958; Asst Regional Rep., Madras, 1958–63; Regional Dir, Mwanza, 1963–65; Regional Rep., E Nigeria, 1965–67; Asst Controller, Personnel and Staff Recruitment, 1968–73; Controller, Arts Div., 1973–79; Representative, Nigeria, 1979–81. *Recreations:* sailing, walking. *Address:* Seacrest, 74 Trefusis Road, Flushing, Falmouth, Cornwall TR11 5TY. *T:* Falmouth (01326) 377613.

TRIBE, Rear-Admiral Raymond Haydn, CB 1964; MBE 1944; DL; *b* 9 April 1908; *s* of Thomas and Gillian Ada Tribe; *m* 1938, Alice Mary (*née* Golby); no *c*. Served War of 1939–45 (MBE, despatches twice). Commander, 1947; Captain, 1955; Rear-Admiral, 1962. Inspector-General, Fleet Maintenance, and Chief Staff Officer (Technical) to C-in-C Home Fleet, 1962–65; retired from Royal Navy, Sept. 1965. Distinguished Battle Service Medal of Soviet Union, 1943. CC Berks, 1970–77. DL Berks, 1975. *Recreations:* gardening, painting. *Address:* Oak Cottage, Compton, near Newbury, Berks. *T:* Compton (01635) 578253.

TRICKER, Prof. Robert Ian, DLitt; FCA; FCMA; Professor of Finance and Accounting, University of Hong Kong, since 1986; Director, International Corporate Policy Group (formerly Corporate Policy Group, Oxford), since 1979; *b* 14 Dec. 1933; *s* of Ralph

Edward Tricker, Coventry; *m* 1st, 1958, Doreen Murray (marr. diss. 1982); two *d*; 2nd, 1982, Gretchen Elizabeth Bigelow. *Educ:* King Henry VIII Sch., Coventry; Harvard Business Sch., USA. MA, JDipMA; DLitt CNAA, 1983. Articled Clerk, Daffern & Co., 1950–55; Sub-Lt, RNVR, 1956–58; Controller, Unbrako Ltd, 1959–64; Directing Staff, Iron & Steel Fedn Management Coll., 1965; Barclays Bank Prof. of Management Information Systems, Univ. of Warwick, 1968–70. Director, Oxford Centre for Management Studies, 1970–79, Professorial Fellow, 1979–84 (P. D. Leake Res. Fellow, 1966–67); Res. Fellow, Nuffield Coll., Oxford, 1979–84 (Vis. Fellow, 1971–79); Dir, Management Develt Centre of Hong Kong, 1984–86. Institute of Chartered Accountants in England and Wales: Mem. Council, 1979–84; Mem. Educn and Trng Directorate, 1979–82; Chairman: Examination Cttee, 1980–82; Tech. and Res. Cttee, 1982–84. Member: Council, ICMA, 1969–72; Management and Industrial Relations Cttee, SSRC, 1973–75; Chm., Independent Inquiry into Prescription Pricing Authority for Minister for Health, 1976. Member: Nuffield Hosp. Management Cttee, 1972–74; Adv. Panel on Company Law, Dept of Trade, 1980–83; Company Affairs Cttee, Inst. of Directors, 1980–84; Standing Commn on CS Salaries and Conditions of Service, Hong Kong, 1989–. Editor, Corporate Governance—an international review, 1992–. *Publications:* The Accountant in Management, 1967; Strategy for Accounting Research, 1975; Management Information and Control Systems, 1976, 2nd edn 1982; The Independent Director, 1978; Effective Information Management, 1982; Governing the Institute, 1983; Corporate Governance, 1984; The Effective Director, 1986; The Director's Manual, 1990; International Corporate Governance, 1993; Harnessing Information Power, 1994. *Address:* University of Hong Kong Business School, Hong Kong.

TRICKETT, Jon Hedley; Leader, Leeds City Council, since 1989; *b* 2 July 1950; *s* of Lawrence and Rose Trickett; *m* 1969 (marr. diss.); one *s* one *d*; *m* 1994, Sarah Balfour. *Educ:* Hull Univ. (BA Politics); Leeds Univ. (MA Pol Sociol). Builder/plumber, to 1985. Joined Labour Party, 1971; Leeds City Council: Councillor, Beeston Ward, 1985; Chair: Finance Cttee, 1986–89; Housing Cttee, 1988–89. Chm., Leeds City Development Co., 1989–; Member of Board: Leeds Development Corp., 1992–; Leeds Health Care,1992–; Director: Leeds/Bradford Airport, 1988–; Leeds Playhouse, 1988–; Leeds Theatre Co., 1988–. Mem., GMBATU. *Recreations:* cycling, Leeds United. *Address:* 268 Cross Flatts Grove, Leeds LS11 7BS. *T:* Leeds (0113) 277 3108. *Club:* Cyclists Touring.

TRICKETT, (Mabel) Rachel; Principal, St Hugh's College, Oxford, 1973–91; *b* 20 Dec. 1923. *Educ:* Lady Margaret Hall, Oxford, 1942–45 (BA Hons 1st Cl. in English; MA 1947; Hon. Fellow, 1978). Asst to Curator, Manchester City Art Galleries, 1945–46; Asst Lectr in English, Univ. of Hull, 1946–49; Commonwealth Fund Fellow, Yale Univ., 1949–50; Lectr in English, Hull Univ., 1950–54; Fellow and Tutor in English, St Hugh's Coll., Oxford, 1954–73, Hon. Fellow, 1991. *Publications:* The Honest Muse (a study in Augustan verse), 1967; *novels:* The Return Home, 1952; The Course of Love, 1954; Point of Honour, 1958; A Changing Place, 1962; The Elders, 1966; A Visit to Timon, 1970. *Address:* Flat 4, 18 Norham Gardens, Oxford OX2 6QB. *T:* Oxford (01865) 56121.

TRICKEY, Edward Lorden, FRCS; Dean, Institute of Orthopaedics, London University, 1981–87, retired; Consultant Orthopaedic Surgeon, Royal National Orthopaedic Hospital, London, and Edgware General Hospital, 1960–85, retired; *b* 22 July 1920; *s* of E. G. W. Trickey and M. C. Trickey; *m* 1944, Ivy Doreen Harold; two *s* one *d*. *Educ:* Dulwich College; King's College, London Univ. (MB BS). Consultant Orthopaedic Surgeon, Ashton under Lyne, 1957–60. *Publications:* various articles on orthopaedic trauma and knee joint surgery. *Recreations:* cricket, bridge. *Address:* 43 Beverley Gardens, Stanmore, Mddx HA7 2AP. *T:* 0181–863 6964. *Clubs:* MCC, Middlesex CC.

TRICKEY, Very Rev. (Frederick) Marc; Dean of Guernsey, since 1995; Rector of St Martin de la Bellouse, Guernsey, since 1977; *b* 16 Aug. 1935; *s* of Alan Paul Trickey and Isabella Livingston Gunn; *m* 1963, Elisabeth Marriette Plummer; one *s* one *d*. *Educ:* Bristol Grammar Sch.; St John's Coll., Univ. of Durham (BA (Hons) Psychol. 1962; DipTh 1964). Commercial trainee, Nat. Smelting Co. Ltd, Avonmouth, Bristol, 1954–59. Ordained deacon, 1964, priest, 1965; Asst Curate, St Lawrence, Alton, Hants, 1964–68; Rector of St John with Winnall, Winchester, 1968–77. Hon. Canon of Winchester Cathedral, 1996–. *Publication:* Your Marriage, 1987. *Recreations:* singing, embroidery, walking, photography. *Address:* St Martin's Rectory, Guernsey, Channel Islands GY4 6RR. *T:* Guernsey (01481) 38303.

TRIER, Peter Eugene, CBE 1980; MA; FEng, FIEE; FInstP, FIMA; Pro-Chancellor, Brunel University, since 1980; Director of Research and Development, Philips Electronics UK, 1969–81, retired; *b* Darmstadt, 12 Sept. 1919; *s* of Ernst and Nellie Trier; *m* 1946, Margaret Nora Holloway; three *s*. *Educ:* Mill Hill Sch.; Trinity Hall, Cambridge (Wrangler 1941). Royal Naval Scientific Service, 1941–50; Mullard Research Labs, 1950–69, Dir, 1953–69. Dir, Mullard Ltd and other Philips subsidiaries, 1957–85; Main Bd Dir, Philips Electronics, 1969–85. Specialist Advr, House of Lords Select Cttee on Sci and Technol., 1982–84; Member: Electronics Res. Council, MoD, 1963–80 (Chm., 1976–80); Defence Scientific Adv. Council, 1975–85 (Chm., 1981–85); ACARD sub-group on Annual Review of Govt-funded R&D, 1984–86. (Chm., 1985–86). IEE: Vice-Pres., 1974–77; Faraday Lectr, 1968–69; Chm., Electronics Div. Bd, 1971–72; Pres., IMA, 1982–83. FEng 1978 (Hon. Sec. for Electrical Engrg, 1985–87; Chm., Membership Cttee, 1987–90); Pres., Electronic Engrg Assoc., 1980–81; Member: Management Cttee, Royal Instn, 1978–81; Adv. Bd, RCDS, 1980–90. Brunel University: Mem. Council, 1969– (Chm., 1973–78); Chm., Supervisory Bd, Brunel Inst. of Bio-Engineering, 1983–; Chairman: Engrg Adv. Cttee, UWIST, 1983–86; Technol. Faculty Adv. Bd, Polytechnic South West, subseq. Plymouth Univ., 1989–93; External Examr in Maths: Polytechnic of Central London, 1983–86; Coventry Polytechnic, 1986–92. Mem. Editorial Bd, Interdisciplinary Science Reviews, 1975–. Mem., Management Cttee, The Wine Soc., 1977–92. Liveryman, Co. of Scientific Instrument Makers, 1968–. Hon. DTech Brunel, 1975. Glazebrook Medal and Prize, Inst. of Physics, 1984. *Publications:* Strategic Implications of Microelectronics, 1982; Mathematics and Information, 1983; papers in scientific and technical jls. *Recreations:* travel, mathematics, Trier family history, railway history. *Address:* Yew Tree House, Bredon, Tewkesbury, Glos GL20 7HF. *T:* Bredon (01684) 772200. *Club:* Old Millhillians.

TRIESMAN, David Maxim; General Secretary, Association of University Teachers, since 1993; *b* 30 Oct. 1943; *s* of Michael Triesman and Rita (*née* Lubran). *Educ:* Stationers' Co. Sch., London; Univ. of Essex (BA Hons, MA Philosophy); King's Coll., Cambridge. FSS 1984. Res. Officer in Addiction, Inst. of Psychiatry, 1970–74; ASTMS secondment, 1974–75; Sen. Lectr and co-ord. postgrad. res., Poly. of S Bank, 1975–84; Dep. Sec. Gen. (Nat. Negotiating Sec.), NATFHE, 1984–93. Vis. Prof. in Social Econ., S Lawrence Univ., 1977. Member: Greater London Manpower Bd, 1981–86; Home Office Consultative Cttee on Prison Educn, 1980–83; Burnham Further and Higher Educn Cttee, 1980–84; Univ. Entrance and Schs Exams Bd for Soc. Sci., 1980–84. Mem., Kensington, Chelsea and Westminster AHA, 1976–82. Member: Fabian Soc., 1974–; Charles Rennie Mackintosh Soc., Glasgow, 1986–; Highgate Literary and Scientific Inst., 1990–. FRSA 1990. *Publications:* The Medical and Non-Medical Use of Drugs, 1969; (with G. Viani) Football Mania, 1972; Football in London, 1985; (jtly) College Administration, 1988; Managing Change, 1991. *Recreations:* football, art, reading, walking. *Address:* Association of University Teachers, United House, 9 Pembridge Road, W11 3JY. *T:* 0171–221 4370. *Clubs:* Middlesex CC; Tottenham Hotspurs' Supporters.

TRIGGER, Ian James Campbell; His Honour Judge Trigger; a Circuit Judge, since 1993; *b* 16 Nov. 1943; *s* of late Walter James Trigger and Mary Elizabeth Trigger; *m* 1971, Jennifer Ann Downs; two *s*. *Educ:* Ruthin Sch.; UCW, Aberystwyth (LLB); Downing Coll., Cambridge (MA, LLM). Called to the Bar, Inner Temple, 1970 (major scholarship, 1967); Lectr in Law, UWIST, 1967–70; practice on Northern Circuit, 1970–93. Pt-time Pres., Mental Health Review Tribunal, 1995–. Hon. Chm., Vale of Clwyd Alliance. *Recreations:* gardening, walking, spending time with family. *Address:* Queen Elizabeth II Law Courts, Derby Square, Liverpool L2 1XA. *T:* 0151–473 7373.

TRIMBLE, David; *see* Trimble, W. D.

TRIMBLE, Jenifer, (Mrs M. R. Trimble); *see* Wilson-Barnett, J.

TRIMBLE, (William) David; MP (UU) Upper Bann, since May 1990; Leader, Ulster Unionist Party, since 1995; *b* 15 Oct. 1944; *s* of William and Ivy Trimble; *m* 1978, Daphne Orr; two *s* two *d*. *Educ:* Bangor Grammar Sch.; Queen's University Belfast (LLB). Called to the Bar of Northern Ireland, 1969; Lectr, 1968, Sen. Lectr, 1977, Faculty of Law, QUB. Mem., Constitutional Convention, 1975–76. *Publications:* Northern Ireland Housing Law, 1986; NI Law Reports, 1975–90. *Recreations:* music, reading. *Address:* House of Commons, SW1A 0AA.

TRIMLESTOWN, 20th Baron *cr* 1461 (Ire.); **Anthony Edward Barnewall;** *b* 2 Feb. 1928; *s* of 19th Baron and Muriel (*d* 1937), *d* of Edward Oskar Schneider; *S* father, 1990; *m* 1st, 1963, Lorna Margaret Marion (marr. diss. 1973; she *d* 1988), *d* of late Douglas Ramsay; 2nd, 1977, Mary Wonderly, *e d* of late Judge Thomas F. McAllister, Grand Rapids, Mich. *Educ:* Ampleforth. Irish Guards, 1946–48. Naval architect with Jack Jones, 1949–53; European Sales Exec., P&O Shipping Co., 1965–74. *Recreation:* travel. *Heir:* *b* Hon. Raymond Charles Barnewall, *b* 29 Dec. 1930. *Address:* PO Box 215, Ada, MI 49301, USA.

TRINDER, Frederick William; Charity Commissioner, 1984–85; *b* 18 Nov. 1930; *s* of Charles Elliott Trinder and Grace Johanna Trinder (*née* Hoadly); *m* 1964, Christiane Friederike Brigitte Dorothea (*née* Hase) (*d* 1994); one *s*. *Educ:* LSE, Univ. of London (BSc). Admitted Solicitor, 1966; Legal Asst/Sen. Legal Asst, Charity Commn, 1966–74; Dep. Charity Comr, 1974–84. Mem., BBC and IBA Central Appeals Adv. Cttees, 1986–92. Trustee, Charities Official Investment Fund, 1988–. *Recreations:* travel, gardening, music. *Address:* 37 The Common, West Wratting, Cambridge CB1 5LR. *T:* Cambridge (01223) 290469. *Club:* Royal Over-Seas League.

TRIPP, Rt. Rev. Howard George; an Auxiliary Bishop and Vicar General in Southwark, (RC), since 1980; Titular Bishop of Newport, since 1980; *b* 3 July 1927; *s* of late Basil Howard Tripp and Alice Emily Tripp (*née* Haslett). *Educ:* John Fisher School, Purley; St John's Seminary, Wonersh. Priest, 1953; Assistant Priest: Blackheath SE3, 1953–56; East Sheen, 1956–62; Asst Diocesan Financial Sec., 1962–68; Parish Priest, East Sheen, 1965–71; Director, Southwark Catholic Children's Soc., 1971–80. Chm., London Churches Gp, 1993–. *Recreation:* vegetable gardening. *Address:* 8 Arterberry Road, SW20 8AJ. *T:* 0181–946 4609.

TRIPP, (John) Peter, CMG 1971; Consultant, Al-Tajir Bank, since 1986; *b* 27 March 1921; *s* of Charles Howard and Constance Tripp; *m* 1948, Rosemary Rees Jones; one *s* one *d*. *Educ:* Bedford Sch.; Sutton Valence Sch.; L'Institut de Touraine. Served War of 1939–45: Royal Marines, 1941–46. Sudan Political Service, 1946–54. Foreign (subsequently Diplomatic) Service, 1954–81; Political Agent, Trucial States, 1955–58; Head of Chancery, Vienna, 1958–61; Economic Secretary, Residency Bahrain, 1961–63, Counsellor 1963; Political Agent, Bahrain, 1963–65; sabbatical year at Durham Univ., 1965; Amman, 1966–68; Head of Near Eastern Dept, FCO, 1969–70; Ambassador to Libya, 1970–74; High Comr in Singapore, 1974–78; Ambassador to Thailand, 1978–81. Political Adviser, Inchcape Gp, 1981–86; Chm., Private Investment Co. for Asia (UK), 1981–84. County Councillor (Ind.), Powys, 1985–87. Chairman: Anglo-Thai Soc., 1983–88; Montgomeryshire Br., CPRW, 1990–94. *Recreations:* theatre, gardening. *Address:* Tanyffridd, Llanfechain, Powys SY22 6UE.

TRIPPIER, Sir David (Austin), Kt 1992; RD 1983; JP; DL; Chairman: Envirosystems Ltd, since 1992; Davenham Group, since 1994; *b* 15 May 1946; *s* of late Austin Wilkinson Trippier, MC and Mary Trippier; *m* 1975, Ruth Worthington, Barrister; three *s*. *Educ:* Bury Grammar School. Commnd Officer, Royal Marines Reserve, 1968. Member of Stock Exchange, 1968–; Chm., W. H. Ireland, Stockbrokers. Mem., Rochdale Council, 1969–78, Leader Cons. Gp, 1974–76. MP (C) Rossendale, 1979–83, Rossendale and Darwen, 1983–92; contested (C) Rossendale and Darwen, 1992. Sec., Cons. Parly Defence Cttee, 1980–82; PPS to Minister for Health, 1982–83; Parliamentary Under-Secretary of State: (Minister for Small Firms and Enterprise) DTI, 1983–85; Dept of Employment, 1985–87; DoE, 1987–89; Minister of State (Minister for the Envmt and Countryside), DoE, 1989–92. Dep. Chm., Cons. Party, 1990. Nat. Vice Chm., Assoc. of Cons. Clubs, 1980–84. Chm., Tepnel Diagnostics PLC, 1992–94; Director, 1992–: Dunlop Heywood & Co.; St Modwen Properties; Sir David Trippier & Associates; P & P; Consultant, 1992–: Halliwell Landau; Waste Management; Halliday Meecham. Pres., Northern Reg., RM Assoc., 1988–93. JP Rochdale, 1975; DL Lancs, 1994. *Publications:* Defending the Peace, 1982; New Life for Inner Cities, 1989. *Recreations:* gardening, tennis. *Address:* Dowry Head, Helmshore, Rossendale, Lancs BB4 4AE. *Club:* St James's (Manchester).

TRITTON, Alan George; DL; Director, Barclays Bank Ltd, 1974–91; India Adviser, Barclays Bank, since 1992; Chairman: Plantation and General Investments, since 1994; University Life Assurance Society, since 1994; a Vice-President, Equitable Life Assurance Society, since 1983 (Director, since 1976); *b* 2 Oct. 1931; *s* of George Henton Tritton, Lyons Hall, Essex, and Iris Mary Baillie, Lochloy; *m* 1st, 1958, Elizabeth Clare d'Abreu (marr. diss.); two *s* one *d*; 2nd, 1972, Diana Marion Spencer. *Educ:* Eton. Member of British Schools Exploring Soc. Expedn, Arctic Norway, 1949. Lt, 1st Batt. Seaforth Highlanders, active service Pahang, Malaya, 1950–52. Leader, S Orkneys Base, Falkland Islands Dependencies Survey, 1952–54; entered Barclays Bank Ltd, 1954; local Dir, 54 Lombard Street, 1964; Dir, Barclays Bank UK Management Ltd, 1972. A Vice-Pres., Royal Geographical Soc., 1983– (Mem. Council, 1975–, Hon. Treas., 1984). Member: Cttee, British Trans-Arctic Expedn, 1966–69; Cttee, British Everest SW Face Expedn, 1974–75; Cttee of Management, Mount Everest Foundn, 1976–80; Friends' Cttee, Scott Polar Research Inst., 1976–80. Chairman: Westminster Abbey Investment Cttee, 1976–94; Calcutta Tercentenary Trust, 1989; Member: Council, Internat. Chamber of Commerce, 1975–90 (Hon. Treas. 1985); Council, Foundn for Aviation and Sustainable Tourism, New Delhi, 1994–. High Sheriff, 1992, DL 1993, Essex. *Recreations:* travelling, shooting. *Clubs:* Boodle's, Pratt's, Antarctic, Geographical, Essex; Tollygunge (Calcutta).

TRITTON, Major Sir Anthony (John Ernest), 4th Bt *cr* 1905; *b* 4 March 1927; *s* of Sir Geoffrey Ernest Tritton, 3rd Bt, CBE, and Mary Patience Winifred (*d* 1960), *d* of John Kenneth Foster; *S* father, 1976; *m* 1957, Diana, *d* of Rear-Adm. St J. A. Micklethwait, CB, DSO, and of Clemence Penelope Olga Welby-Everard; one *s* one *d*. *Educ:* Eton. Commissioned 3rd Hussars, Oct. 1945; retired as Major, 1962, The Queen's Own Hussars. *Recreations:* shooting, fishing. *Heir: s* Jeremy Ernest Tritton, *b* 6 Oct. 1961. *Address:* River House, Heytesbury, Wilts BA12 0EE. *Club:* Cavalry and Guards.

TRITTON, (Elizabeth) Clare, (Clare McLaren-Throckmorton; Mrs Andrew McLaren); QC 1988; Chief Executive, Throckmorton Estates; *b* 18 Aug. 1935; *d* of Prof. Alfonsus d'Abreu and Elizabeth d'Abreu (*née* Throckmorton); *m* 1st, 1958, Alan Tritton, *qv* (marr. diss. 1971); two *s* one *d*; 2nd, 1973, Andrew McLaren; name changed to McLaren-Throckmorton by deed poll, 1991, following death of uncle, Sir Robert Throckmorton, 11th Bt. *Educ:* Convent of the Holy Child Jesus, Mayfield, St Leonards; Univ. of Birmingham (BA Hons English). Called to the Bar, Inner Temple, 1968. Lived and worked in USA, France, Germany and Italy, intermittently, 1952–86; Centre Organiser, WVS, 1963–64; Charlemagne Chambers, Brussels, 1985–89; founded own Chambers, practising overseas as European Law Chambers, 1987. Chm., Bar European Group, 1982–84; Vice Chm., Internat. Practice Cttee, Gen. Council of the Bar, 1988–91; Chm., Sub Cttee on Eur. Legislation, Hansard Commn on Legislative Reform, 1991–93. Member: Council, Bow Gp, 1963–65; Eur. Cttee, British Invisible Exports Council, 1989–93; Monopolies and Mergers Commn, 1993–. Dir, Severn Trent plc, 1991–. Indep. Mem., Council, FIMBRA, 1991–. Founder, Bar European News, 1983. *Publications:* articles in law magazines on EEC and private internat. law. *Recreations:* reading, gardening, travel, cooking, children. *Address:* Coughton Court, Alcester, Warwicks B49 5JA. *T:* Alcester (01789) 400777; Manor House, Molland, South Molton, North Devon EX36 3ND. *T:* South Molton (01769) 550325.

TROLLOPE, Andrew David Hedderwick; QC 1991; a Recorder of the Crown Court, since 1989; *b* 6 Nov. 1948; *s* of Arthur George Cecil Trollope and Rosemary (*née* Hodson); *m* 1978, Anne Forbes; two *s*. *Educ:* Charterhouse; Univ. of Nancy. Called to the Bar, Inner Temple, 1971; Asst Recorder, 1985–89. Member: South Eastern Circuit Cttee, 1990–93, 1994–; Cttee, Criminal Bar Assoc., 1991–. *Recreations:* opera, jazz, swimming, tennis, sailing, travel. *Address:* 1 Middle Temple Lane, Temple, EC4Y 9AA. *T:* 0171–583 0659. *Club:* Hurlingham.

See also J. Trollope.

TROLLOPE, Sir Anthony (Simon), 17th Bt *cr* 1642, of Casewick, Lincolnshire; Marketing Executive with Ricegrowers Co-operative Ltd; *b* 31 Aug. 1945; *s* of Sir Anthony Owen Clavering Trollope, 16th Bt and of Joan Mary Alexis, *d* of Alexis Robert Gibbs; *S* father, 1987; *m* 1969, Denise, *d* of Trevern and Vida Thompson; two *d*. *Educ:* Univ. of Sydney (BA 1969). Breeder, in partnership with his wife, of Anglo-Arabian horses and Rhodesian Ridgeback dogs. Mem., Australian Marketing Inst., 1988–. *Heir: b* Hugh Irwin Trollope [*b* 31 March 1947; *m* 1971, Barbara Anne, *d* of William Ian Jamieson; one *s* two *d*]. *Address:* 28 Midson Road, Oakville, NSW 2765, Australia. *Clubs:* Gordon Rugby, Rhodesian Ridgeback, Arab Horse Society of Australia, Castle Hill RSL (Sydney).

TROLLOPE, Joanna, (Mrs Ian Curteis); writer; *b* 9 Dec. 1943; *er d* of Arthur George Cecil Trollope and Rosemary Trollope (*née* Hodson); *m* 1st, 1966, David Roger William Potter, *qv*; two *d*; 2nd, 1985, Ian Bayley Curteis, *qv*; two step *s*. *Educ:* Reigate County Sch. for Girls; St Hugh's Coll., Oxford (Gamble Scholar; MA 1972). Inf. and Research Dept, Foreign Office, 1965–67; teaching posts, 1967–79, incl. Farnham Girls' Grammar Sch., adult educn, English for foreigners and at Daneshill Sch. *Publications:* Eliza Stanhope, 1978; Parson Harding's Daughter, 1979; Leaves from the Valley, 1980; The City of Gems, 1981; The Steps of the Sun, 1983; Britannia's Daughters: a study of women in the British Empire, 1983; The Taverners' Place, 1986; The Choir, 1988 (televised, 1995); A Village Affair, 1989; A Passionate Man, 1990; The Rector's Wife, 1991 (televised, 1994); The Men and the Girls, 1992; A Spanish Lover, 1993; (ed) The Country Habit: an anthology, 1993; The Best of Friends, 1995; *as Caroline Harvey:* Legacy of Love, 1992; A Second Legacy, 1993; A Castle in Italy, 1993; contribs to newspapers and magazines. *Recreations:* reading, conversation, very long baths. *Address:* c/o Peters, Fraser & Dunlop, Fifth Floor, The Chambers, Chelsea Harbour, SW10 0XF.

See also A. D. H. Trollope.

TROSS, Jonathan Edward Simon; Grade 2, Director Resource Management and Planning Group, Department of Social Security, since 1994; *b* 21 Jan. 1949; *s* of late Francis Tross and Audrey (*née* Payne); *m* 1972, Ann Humphries; one *s* one *d*. *Educ:* Chislehurst and Sidcup Grammar Sch.; University Coll., Oxford (BA Hons Modern Hist., 1970). Teacher in Kenya, 1971; Department of Health and Social Security: grad. trainee, 1972; Principal, 1977–84; Asst Sec., Supplementary Benefits Review, 1984–87; Asst Dir, Corporate Div., Barclays Bank, on secondment, 1987–90; Head of Pharmaceutical Industry Br., DoH, 1990–91; G3, Head of Planning and Finance Div., DSS, 1991–94. *Recreations:* football, reading, theatre, photography, allotment. *Address:* Department of Social Security, Richmond House, 79 Whitehall, SW1A 2NS. *T:* 0171–210 5470. *Club:* Fulham Football.

TROTMAN-DICKENSON, Sir Aubrey (Fiennes), Kt 1989; PhD, DSc; Principal, University of Wales College of Cardiff, 1988–93; Vice-Chancellor, University of Wales, 1975–77, 1983–85 and 1991–93; *b* 12 Feb. 1926; *s* of late Edward Newton Trotman-Dickenson and Violet Murray Nicoll; *m* 1953, Danusia Irena Hewell; two *s* one *d*. *Educ:* Winchester Coll.; Balliol Coll., Oxford. MA Oxon, BSc Oxon; PhD Manchester; DSc Edinburgh. Fellow, National Research Council, Ottawa, 1948–50; Asst Lecturer, ICI Fellow, Manchester Univ., 1950–53; E. I. du Pont de Nemours, Wilmington, USA, 1953–54; Lecturer, Edinburgh Univ., 1954–60; Professor, University College of Wales, Aberystwyth, 1960–68; Principal; UWIST, Cardiff, 1968–88; UC Cardiff, 1987–88. Chm., Job Creation Programme, Wales, 1975–78. Member: Welsh Council, 1971–79; Planning and Transport Res. Adv. Council, DoE, 1975–79. Tilden Lectr, Chem. Soc., 1963. Hon. LLD Wales, 1995. *Publications:* Gas Kinetics, 1955; Free Radicals, 1959; Tables of Bimolecular Gas Reactions, 1967; (ed) Comprehensive Inorganic Chemistry, 1973; contrib. to learned journals. *Address:* Syston Court, Bristol BS17 3LU. *T:* Bristol (0117) 937 2109.

TROTTER, David; *see* Trotter, W. D.

TROTTER, Neville Guthrie, JP; FCA; MP (C) Tynemouth, since Feb. 1974; *b* 27 Jan. 1932; *s* of Captain Alexander Trotter and Elizabeth Winifred Trotter (*née* Guthrie); *m* 1983, Caroline, *d* of Captain John Farrow, RN retd and Oona Farrow (*née* Hall); one *d*. *Educ:* Shrewsbury; King's Coll., Durham (BCom). Short service commn in RAF, 1955–58. Partner, Thornton Baker & Co., Chartered Accountants, 1962–74, now Consultant with Grant Thornton; Dir, Romag Plc; Consultant: Bowring; Northern General Transport; British Marine Equipment Council; British Transport Police Fedn. Mem., Newcastle City Council, 1963–74 (Alderman, 1970–74; Chm., Finance Cttee, Traffic Highways and Transport Cttee, Theatre Cttee). Mem., CAA Airline Users Cttee, 1973–79. Mem., Tyne and Wear Metropolitan Council, 1973–74; Vice-Chm., Northumberland Police Authority, 1970–74. Chm., Cons. Party Shipping and Shipbuilding Cttee, 1979–85, 1994– (Vice-Chm., 1976–79); Secretary: Cons. Party Industry Cttee, 1981–83; Cons. Party Transport Cttee, 1983–84; Mil. Sec., Cons. Party Aviation Cttee, 1976–79; Member: Industry Sub-Cttee, Select Cttee on Expenditure, 1976–79; Select Cttee on Transport, 1983–92; Select Cttee on Defence, 1993–; Parly Defence Study Group, 1980–; Atlantic Council of UK; Chm., All-Party Gp for Prevention of Solvent Abuse. Private Member's Bills: Consumer Safety, 1978; Licensing Amendment, 1980; Intoxicating Substances Supply (Glue Sniffing), 1985. Former Member: Northern Economic Planning Council; Tyne Improvement Commn; Tyneside Passenger Transport Authority; Industrial Relations Tribunal; Council, RUSI. Mem., US Naval Inst. Freeman, City of London, 1978; Mem., Worshipful Co. of Chartered Accountants, 1978. JP Newcastle upon Tyne, 1973. *Recreations:* aviation, gardening, fell-walking, study of foreign affairs, defence and industry. *Address:* c/o House of Commons, SW1A 0AA. *Clubs:* Royal Air Force; Northern Counties (Newcastle upon Tyne); Tynemouth and Whitley Bay Conservative.

TROTTER, Sir Ronald (Ramsay), Kt 1985; FCA; New Zealand business executive; Chairman, Fletcher Challenge Ltd, 1981–95 (Chief Executive, 1981–87); *b* Hawera, 9 Oct. 1927; *s* of Clement George Trotter, CBE and Annie Euphemia Trotter (*née* Young); *m* 1955, Margaret Patricia, *d* of James Rainey; three *s* one *d*. *Educ:* Collegiate School, Wanganui; Victoria Univ. of Wellington; Lincoln Coll., Canterbury (BCom, Cert. in Agric.). FCA 1976. Wright Stephenson & Co., 1958–72: Dir, 1962–68; Man. Dir, 1968–70; Chm. and Man. Dir, 1970–72; Chm. and Man. Dir, Challenge Corp., 1972–81. Chairman: Telecom Corp. of New Zealand Ltd, 1987–90; Post Office Bank, 1989; Ciba-Geigy New Zealand Ltd, 1990–; Wrightson Ltd, 1993–; Toyota New Zealand Ltd, 1994– (Dir, 1990–94); Director: Reserve Bank of NZ, 1986–88; Australia and New Zealand Banking Gp, 1988– (Inaugural Mem., Internat. Bd of Advice, 1986–93); Air New Zealand Ltd, 1989–; Ciba-Geigy Australia Ltd, 1991–; Wrightson Farmers Finance Ltd, 1993–; Mem., Internat. Adv. Bd, Proudfoot plc, 1992–. Trustee and Chm., NZ Inst. of Economic Research, 1973–86; Chairman: Overseas Investment Commn, 1974–77; NZ Business Roundtable, 1985–90; Pacific Basin Econ. Council, 1985–90 (Internat. Pres., 1986–88). Mem., Project Develt Bd, Museum of NZ, 1988–92. Hon. LLD Victoria Univ. of Wellington, 1984. Bledisloe Medal, Lincoln Coll., 1988. Silver Jubilee Medal, 1977; NZ Commemoration Medal, 1990. *Address:* 16 Wesley Road, Wellington 1, New Zealand. *T:* (4) 4726628, *Fax:* (4) 4990051. *Club:* Wellington (Wellington, NZ).

TROTTER, Thomas Andrew, FRCO; Organist, St Margaret's Church, Westminster Abbey, since 1982; Organist to the City of Birmingham, since 1983; *b* 4 April 1957; *s* of late His Honour Richard Stanley Trotter and Ruth Elizabeth Trotter. *Educ:* Malvern Coll.; Royal Coll. of Music, 1974–76 (schol.; ARCM) (organ schol., St George's Chapel, Windsor, 1975–76); King's Coll., Cambridge (organ schol., 1976–79; MA). John Stewart of Rannock Schol. in Sacred Music, Cambridge Univ., 1979; Countess of Munster schol. for further organ studies with Marie-Claire Alain in Paris. Début at Royal Fest. Hall, 1980; Prom. début, 1986; regular broadcasts for Radio 2 and Radio 3; has performed at fests throughout UK and in Europe; concert tours to Australia, USA and Far East; organ recordings. Walford Davies Prize, RCM, 1976; First prize and Bach prize, St Albans Internat. Organ Competition, 1979; Prix de Virtuosité, Conservatoire Rueil-Malmaison, 1981. *Address:* c/o The Town Hall, Birmingham B3 3DQ. *T:* 0121–235 3942.

TROTTER, Prof. (Wilfred) David, PhD; Quain Professor of English Language and Literature, University College London, since 1991; *b* 25 July 1951; *s* of Wilfred Robert Trotter and Enid Beatrice Trotter (*née* Roulston). *Educ:* Gonville and Caius Coll., Cambridge (BA, PhD). Res. Fellow, Magdalene Coll., Cambridge, 1975–77; University College London: Lectr in English, 1977–87; Reader, 1987–90; Prof. of English, 1990–91. Vis. Prof., CIT, 1988–89. *Publications:* The Poetry of Abraham Cowley, 1979; The Making of the Reader, 1984; Circulation: Defoe, Dickens and the economies of the novel, 1988; The English Novel in History 1895–1920, 1993. *Address:* Department of English, University College London, Gower Street, WC1E 6BT. *T:* 0171–387 7050.

TROUBRIDGE, Sir Thomas (Richard), 7th Bt *cr* 1799, of Plymouth; FCA; Partner, Price Waterhouse, since 1989; *b* 23 Jan. 1955; *s* of Sir Peter Troubridge, 6th Bt and of Hon. Venetia Daphne, *d* of 1st Baron Weeks; *S* father, 1988; *m* 1984, Hon. Rosemary Douglas-Pennant, *yr d* of Baron Penrhyn, *qv*; two *s* one *d*. *Educ:* Eton College; Durham Univ. (BSc Eng). ACA 1980, FCA 1991. Joined Price Waterhouse, 1977. *Recreations:* sailing, ski-ing. *Heir: s* Edward Peter Troubridge, *b* 10 Aug. 1989. *Address:* 28 Lilyville Road, SW6 5DW. *T:* 0171–736 5739. *Clubs:* Royal Automobile; Itchenor Sailing.

TROUGHTON, Peter, PhD; Chairman, Marine-Air Systems, since 1993; Director, Electricity Supply Industry Reform Unit, Victoria, Australia, since 1993; *b* 26 Aug. 1943; *s* of late Frank Sydney Troughton and of Joan Vera Troughton (*née* Root); *m* 1967, Joyce Uncles; two *s*. *Educ:* City Univ. (BSc Eng); University College London (PhD). Technical apprentice, Plessey Co., then Post Office apprentice, 1959; PO scholarship, 1964; research for PhD, 1967; develt of microprocessor techniques for control of telephone switching systems, 1970; Dep. Gen. Manager, South Central Telephone Area, 1977; Head of Ops, Prestel, 1979; Gen. Manager, City Telephone Area, 1980; Regional Dir, British Telecom London, 1983; Man. Dir, British Telecom Enterprises, 1984–86; Dir and Partner, Alan Patricof Associates, 1986–88, non-exec. Dir, 1988–90; Man. Dir and Chief Exec. Officer, Telecom Corp. of NZ, 1988–92; Dir, Crown Health Enterprise Develt Unit, NZ, 1992–93; Chm., Trans Power (NZ National Power Grid) Estabt Bd, 1990–92. Advr to NZ govt, 1993–94. Mem., State Owned Enterprises Steering Cttee, 1992–93. Mem., NZ Business Round Table, 1988–92; Chm., Twyford and Dist Round Table, 1981–82. NZ Chief Exec. of the Year Award, 1991. NZ Commemoration Medal, 1990. *Publications:* articles and papers on microwave systems, computers and communications. *Recreations:* travel, archaeology, bridge. *Clubs:* Wellesley, Wellington (NZ).

TROUNSON, Rev. Ronald Charles, MA; Rector (non-stipendiary), Easton-on-the-Hill, since 1994 (Rector, Easton-on-the-Hill and Collyweston with Duddington and Tixover, 1989–94); Rural Dean of Barnack, 1991–94; *b* 7 Dec. 1926; *s* of Edwin Trounson and Elsie Mary Trounson (*née* Bolitho); *m* 1952, Leonora Anne Keate; two *s* three *d*. *Educ:* Plymouth Coll.; Emmanuel Coll., Cambridge (Schol.); Ripon Hall, Oxford (MA). Deacon, 1956; Priest, 1957. National Service, RAF, 1948–50. Asst Master, Scaitcliffe Sch., Englefield Green, Surrey, 1950–52; Sixth Form Classics Master, Plymouth Coll., 1953–58; Asst Curate, St Gabriel's, Plymouth, 1956–58; Chaplain, Denstone Coll., 1958–76; Second Master, 1968–76, Bursar, 1976–78; Principal of St Chad's College and Lectr in Classics, Univ. of Durham, 1978–88. Chm., of Governors, Durham High Sch., 1990–94. Fellow, Woodard Corporation, 1983. FRSA 1984. *Address:* The Rectory, Easton-on-the-Hill, Stamford PE9 3LS. *T:* Stamford (01780) 62616.

TROUP, Alistair Mewburn; His Honour Judge Troup; a Circuit Judge, since 1980; *b* 23 Nov. 1927; *y s* of late William Annandale Troup, MC, MD, and Margaret Loïs Troup (*née* Mewburn); *m* 1969, Marjorie Cynthia (*née* Hutchinson); one *s* three *d* by previous marriages. *Educ:* Merchant Taylor's School; New College, Oxford (BA). Served Army, 1946–48. Called to the Bar, Lincoln's Inn, 1952; Crown Counsel, Tanganyika, 1955–62, Sen. Crown Counsel, 1962–64; returned to practice at English bar, 1964; Dep. Circuit

Judge, 1975–77; a Recorder of the Crown Court, 1977–80. Member Panel of Counsel: for Courts Martial Appeals Court, 1970–80; for Comrs of Customs and Excise at VAT Tribunals, 1973–80; Inspector for Dept of Trade, Hartley-Baird Ltd Inquiry, 1974–76. *Recreations:* golf, gardening. *Address:* c/o Lewes Crown Court, The Law Courts, High Street, Lewes, East Sussex BN7 1YB. *Clubs:* Sloane; Seaford Golf.

TROUP, Sir Anthony; *see* Troup, Sir J. A. R.

TROUP, Vice-Adm. Sir (John) Anthony (Rose), KCB 1975; DSC and Bar; *b* 18 July 1921; *s* of late Captain H. R. Troup, RN and N. M. Troup (*née* Milne-Thompson); *m* 1st, 1943, B. M. J. Gordon-Smith (marr. diss. 1952); two *s* one *d*; 2nd, 1953, C. M. Hope; two *s* one *d*. *Educ:* Naut. Trng Coll., HMS Worcester, 1934; RNC Dartmouth, 1936; war service includes: Submarines Turbulent and Strongbow, 1941–45 (dispatches, 1942); HMS Victorious, 1956–59; Comd 3rd Submarine Sqdn, 1961–63; HMS Intrepid, 1966–68; Flag Officer Sea Training, 1969–71; Comdr Far East Fleet, 1971; Flag Officer Submarines and NATO Comdr Submarines, Eastern Atlantic, 1972–74; Flag Officer, Scotland and NI, and NATO Comdr Norlant, 1974–77. *Recreations:* sailing, shooting, gardening. *Address:* Bridge Gardens, Hungerford, Berks RG17 0DL. *Clubs:* Army and Navy; Royal Yacht Squadron.

TROWBRIDGE, George William Job, CBE 1969; CEng; Chairman, AMT (Birmingham) Ltd, since 1981; *b* 21 July 1911; *s* of George Clarke Trowbridge and Thirza Lampier Trowbridge (*née* Dingle); *m* 1938, Doris Isobel Morrison (decd); one *s*. *Educ:* Southall Technical Coll. Works Manager, Gays (Hampton) Ltd, 1938–45; Works Dir, Kingston Instrument Co. Ltd, 1945–52; Wickman Ltd, Coventry, 1952–79: London Area Manager, 1952–57; General Sales Manager, 1957–62; General Sales Dir, 1962–64; Dep. Man. Dir, 1966–79; Man. Dir, Machine Tool Sales Ltd, 1964–79; Director: John Brown & Co. Ltd, 1969–79; Machine Tools (India) Ltd, Calcutta, 1976–79; Drury Wickman Ltd, Johannesburg, 1976–79; Wickman (Australia) Ltd, Melbourne, 1976–79; Chairman: Wickman Machine Tools Inc., USA; Wickman Machine Tools SA, France. President: Machine Tool Trades Assoc., 1975–77; Comité Européen de Coopération des Industries de la Machine-Outil, 1975–77; Mem., Economic Develt Cttee for Machine Tools, 1968–79. MIProdE. *Publications:* A Handbook for Marketing Machinery, 1970; A Financial Study of British Machine Tool Companies, 1974. *Recreations:* walking, fishing. *Address:* 6 Moultrie Road, Rugby CV21 3BD. *T:* Rugby (01788) 560946. *Club:* Institute of Directors.

TROWBRIDGE, Martin Edward O'Keeffe, CBE 1987; FCGI; public affairs, environmental, regulatory and EC counsellor; Chairman, since 1973, and Chief Executive, since 1987, Martin Trowbridge Ltd; *b* 9 May 1925; *s* of late Edward Stanley Trowbridge and Ida Trowbridge (*née* O'Keeffe); *m* 1946, Valerie Ann Glazebrook; one *s*. *Educ:* Royal College of Science; Imperial Coll. of Science and Technology, London Univ. (BSc Eng (Chem. Eng); ACGI 1946); Amer. Management Assoc. Coll., NYC (Dip. Bus. Studies). Technical Officer, ICI (Billingham Div.) Ltd, 1946–48; Division Manager, HWP/Fluor, 1948–53; Technical Dir, Sharples Co., 1953–57; Man. Dir, Sharples Co., 1957–59; Internat. Man. Dir, Sharples Corp., 1959–63; Group Managing Director: Pennwalt International Corp., 1963–72; Pegler-Hattersley Ltd, 1972–73; Dir Gen., Chemical Industries Assoc., 1973–87. Member: Process Plant Working Party, NEDO, 1970–77; Chemicals EDC, NEDO, 1973–87; Process Plant EDC, NEDO, 1977–80; CBI Council; CBI Heads of Sector Group; CBI Europe Cttee; Eur. Chem. Ind. PR Cttee, Brussels; CEFIC R&D Cttee, Brussels; Anglo-German Gp for Chem. Ind.; Anglo-French Gp for Chem. Ind.; ESRC Govt Industry Relns Cttee, 1973–87; Adv. Cttee, Eur. Business Inst., 1984–90; Bd, NRPB, 1987–91; IMRO Ltd, 1988–95. Chm., NEDO Task-Group on Tech., Research and Develt; Pres., Conseil d'Administration/CEFIC, Brussels, 1984–87 (Mem., 1973–87). Chm., Professional Develt Cttee, IChemE; Mem. Council, IChemE, 1987–89. Trustee, Chemical Ind. Museum, 1985–89. Hinchley Medal, IChemE, 1946; Internat. Medal, SCI, 1987. *Publications:* Purification of Oils for Marine Service, 1960; Scaling Up Centrifugal Separation Equipment, 1962; Collected Poems, 1963; Centrifugation, 1966, Exhibiting for Profit, 1969; Market Research and Forecasting, 1969; The Financial Performance of Process and Plant Companies, 1970; Poems for the Second Half, 1975; The Particular World of Directors General, 1987. *Recreations:* having fun, painting, shooting, mineralogy, print making, kitsch, wooden containers. *Address:* 51A Moreton Terrace, SW1V 2NS. *Club:* Frensham Gun.

TROWBRIDGE, Rear-Adm. Sir Richard (John), KCVO 1975; Governor of Western Australia, 1980–83; *b* 21 Jan. 1920; *s* of A. G. Trowbridge, Andover, Hants; *m* 1955, Anne Mildred Perceval; two *s*. *Educ:* Andover Grammar Sch.; Royal Navy. Joined RN as Boy Seaman, 1935. War of 1939–45: commissioned as Sub Lieut, Dec. 1940 (despatches Aug. 1945). Comdr, 1953; commanded Destroyer Carysfort, 1956–58; Exec. Officer, HMS Bermuda, 1958–59, and HMS Excellent, 1959–60; Captain, 1960; commanded Fishery Protection Sqdn, 1962–64; completed course IDC, 1966; commanded HMS Hampshire, 1967–69; Rear-Adm., 1970; Flag Officer Royal Yachts, 1970–75. An Extra Equerry to the Queen, 1970–. Younger Brother of Trinity Hse, 1972. KStJ 1980. *Recreations:* fishing, sailing, golf; most outdoor pursuits. *Address:* Old Idsworth Garden, Finchdean, Portsmouth PO8 0BA. *T:* Rowlands Castle (01705) 412714. *Club:* Army and Navy.

TROWELL, Prof. Brian Lewis, PhD; Heather Professor of Music and Fellow of Wadham College, University of Oxford, 1988–Oct. 1996; *b* 21 Feb. 1931; *s* of Richard Lewis and Edith J. R. Trowell; *m* 1958, Rhianon James; two *d*. *Educ:* Christ's Hospital; Gonville and Caius Coll., Cambridge. MA 1959; PhD 1960. Asst Lectr, later Lectr, in Music, Birmingham Univ., 1957–62; freelance scholar, conductor, opera producer, lecturer and editor, 1962–67; Head of BBC Radio opera, 1967–70; Reader in Music, 1970, Professor of Music, 1973, King Edward Prof. of Music, 1974–88, KCL. Regents' Prof., Univ. of California at Berkeley, 1970; Vis. Gresham Prof. of Music, City Univ., 1971–74. Pres., Royal Musical Assoc., 1983–88. Hon. RAM, 1972; Hon. FGSM, 1972, FRCM 1977; FTCL 1978; Fellow, Curwen Inst., 1987. Chm., Editorial Cttee, Musica Britannica, 1983–93. *Publications:* The Early Renaissance, Pelican History of Music vol. ii, 1963; Four Motets by John Plummer, 1968; (ed jtly) John Dunstable: Complete Works, ed M. F. Bukofzer, 2nd edn, 1970; (ed) Invitation to Medieval Music, vol. 3 1976, vol. 4 1978; opera translations; contrib. dictionaries of music and articles in learned journals. *Recreations:* theatre, reading, gardening. *Address:* (until Oct. 1996) Faculty of Music, St Aldate's, Oxford OX1 1DB; 5 Tree Lane, Iffley Village, Oxford OX4 4EY.

TROYAT, Henri; Légion d'Honneur; writer; Member of the French Academy, 1959; *b* Moscow, 1 Nov. 1911; *m* 1948, Marguerite Saintagne; one *s* one *d*. *Educ:* Paris. *Publications: novels:* l'Araigne (Prix Goncourt, 1938) (The Web, 1984); Les Semailles et les Moissons (5 vols), 1957; Tant que la Terre durera (3 vols), 1960; La Lumière des Justes (5 vols), 1963; Viou, 1980; Le Pain de l'Etranger, 1982 (The Children, 1983); Le Bruit solitaire du Coeur, 1985; A demain, Sylvie, 1986; Le Troisième Bonheur, 1987; Treachery, 1990; Aliocha, 1991; Youri, 1992; Le Défi d'Olga, 1995; *biographies:* Pushkin, Dostoievsky, Tolstoi, Gogol, Catherine la Grande, Pierre le Grand, Alexandre 1er, Ivan le Terrible, Tchekhov, Gorki, Flaubert, Turgenev, Maupassant, Zola, Verlaine, Nicolas II, Baudelaire. *Address:* Académie Française, Quai de Conti, Paris.

TRUBSHAW, (Ernest) Brian, CBE 1970 (OBE 1964); MVO 1948; FRAeS; aviation consultant; *b* 29 Jan. 1924; *s* of late Major H. E. Trubshaw, DL, and Lumly Victoria (*née* Carter); *m* 1973, Mrs Yvonne Edmondson, *widow* of Richard Edmondson, and *d* of late J. A. Clapham, Harrogate, Yorks. *Educ:* Winchester College. Royal Air Force, 1942–50: Bomber Command, 1944; Transport Command, 1945–46; The King's Flight, 1946–48; Empire Flying School, 1949; RAF Flying Coll., 1949–50. Joined Vickers-Armstrongs (Aircraft) Ltd as Experimental Test Pilot, 1950; Dep. Chief Test Pilot, 1953; Chief Test Pilot, 1960; Dir of Flight Test, 1966–80; Divl Dir and Gen. Man. (Filton), Civil Aircraft Div., BAe plc, 1980–86. Mem. Bd (part-time), CAA, 1986–93. Warden, Guild of Air Pilots, 1958–61; Fellow, Society Experimental Test Pilots, USA. Hon. DTech Loughborough, 1986. Derry and Richards Memorial Medal, 1961 and 1964; Richard Hansford Burroughs Memorial Trophy (USA), 1964; R. P. Alston Memorial Medal, 1964; Segrave Trophy, 1970; Air League Founders' Medal, 1971; Iven C. Kinchloe Award, USA, 1971; Harmon Aviation Trophy, 1971; Bluebird Trophy, 1973; French Aeronautical Medal, 1976. *Recreation:* gardening. *Address:* The Garden House, Dodington, Chipping Sodbury, Avon BS17 6SG. *T:* Chipping Sodbury (01454) 323951. *Clubs:* Royal Air Force, MCC.

TRUDEAU, Rt. Hon. Pierre Elliott, CC 1985; CH 1984; PC (Can.); QC (Can.) 1969; FRSC; Prime Minister of Canada, 1968–79 and 1980–84; Leader of Liberal Party of Canada, 1968–84; Senior Consultant, Heenan Blaikie, since 1984; *b* Montreal, 18 Oct. 1919; *s* of Charles-Emile Trudeau and late Grace Elliott; *m* 1971, Margaret Joan (marr. diss. 1984), *d* of late James Sinclair and of Kathleen Bernard; three *s*. *Educ:* Jean-de-Brébeuf College, Montreal; University of Montreal; Harvard University; Ecole des Sciences Politiques, Paris; London School of Economics. Called to Bar: Quebec, 1944; Ontario 1967; practised law, Quebec; co-founder of review Cité Libre; Associate Professor of Law, University of Montreal, 1961–65. MP (L) Mount Royal, Montreal, 1965–84. Parliamentary Secretary to Prime Minister, Jan. 1966–April 1967; Minister of Justice and Attorney General, April 1967–July 1968; Leader of the Opposition, 1979. Mem., Bars of Provinces of Quebec and Ontario. Founding Member, Montreal Civil Liberties Union. Freeman of City of London, 1975. Hon. Dean, Faculty of Law, Univ. of Poitiers, 1975. Hon. Fellow, LSE, 1969. Hon. degrees and awards from many universities in Canada, US, Japan, Macau. *Publications:* La Grève de l'Amiante, 1956; (with Jacques Hébert) Deux Innocents en Chine Rouge, 1961 (Two Innocents in Red China, 1969); Le Fédéralisme et la Société canadienne-française, 1968 (Federalism and the French Canadians, 1968); Réponses, 1968; Memoirs, 1994. *Recreations:* swimming, ski-ing, flying, scuba diving, canoeing. *Address:* c/o Heenan Blaikie, 1250 boulevard René-Lévesque Ouest, Bureau 2500, Montreal, Que H3B 4Y1, Canada.

TRUDGILL, Prof. Peter John, FBA 1989; Professor of English Linguistics, University of Lausanne, since 1993; *b* 7 Nov. 1943; *s* of John Trudgill and Hettie Jean Trudgill (*née* Gooch), *m* 1980, Jean Marie Hannah. *Educ:* City of Norwich Sch.; King's Coll., Cambridge (BA; MA 1966); Edinburgh Univ. (Dip Gen Linguistics 1967; PhD 1971). Asst Lectr, Lectr, Reader, Prof., Dept of Linguistic Sci., Univ. of Reading, 1970–86; Reader, 1986–87, Prof. of Sociolinguistics, 1987–92, Essex Univ. Vis. Prof. at Univs of Hong Kong, Bergen, Aarhus, Illinois, Stanford, Osmania, Tokyo International Christian, ANU, Texas Austin, Toronto, Canterbury (NZ). Fellow, Norwegian Acad. of Sci and Letters, 1995. Hon PhD Uppsala, 1995. *Publications:* The Social Differentiation of English in Norwich, 1974; Sociolinguistics: an introduction, 1974, 2nd edn 1983; Accent, Dialect and the School, 1975; Sociolinguistic Patterns in British English, 1978; (with A. Hughes) English Accents and Dialects, 1979; (with J. K. Chambers) Dialectology, 1980; (with J. M. Hannah) International English, 1982, 3rd edn 1994; On Dialect, 1983; Coping with America, 1983, 2nd edn 1985; Language in the British Isles, 1984; Applied Sociolinguistics, 1984; Dialects in Contact, 1986; The Dialects of England, 1990; (with J. K. Chambers) English Dialects: studies in grammatical variation, 1991; (with L. Andersson) Bad Language, 1991; Introducing Language and Society, 1992, Dialects, 1994. *Recreations:* Norwich City FC, playing the 'cello. *Address:* Section d'anglais, Université de Lausanne, BFSH 2, 1015 Lausanne, Switzerland. *T:* (21) 6922994.

TRUEMAN, Prof. Edwin Royden; Beyer Professor of Zoology, University of Manchester, 1974–82, now Emeritus; *b* 7 Jan. 1922; *s* of late Sir Arthur Trueman, KBE, FRS, and late Lady (Florence Kate) Trueman (*née* Offler); *m* 1945, Doreen Burt; two *d*. *Educ:* Bristol Grammar Sch.; Univ. of Glasgow. DSc Glasgow, MSc Manchester. Technical Officer (Radar), RAF, 1942–46. Asst Lectr and Lectr, Univ. of Hull, 1946–58, Sen. Lectr and Reader, 1958–68; Dean, Faculty of Science, Univ. of Hull, 1954–57; Prof. of Zoology, Univ. of Manchester, 1969–74. R. T. French Vis. Prof., Univ. of Rochester, NY, 1960–61; Nuffield Travelling Fellowship in Tropical Marine Biology, Univ. of West Indies, Jamaica, 1968–69; Leverhulme Emeritus Fellowship, 1983–85. *Publications:* Locomotion of Soft-bodied Animals, 1975; (ed) Aspects of Animal Movement, 1980; (ed) vols 10–12 of series The Mollusca, 1985–88; articles on animal locomotion, littoral physiology and Mollusca. *Address:* Heron's Creek, Yealm View Road, Newton Ferrers, Plymouth, Devon PL8 1AN. *T:* Plymouth (01752) 872775.

TRUEMAN, Frederick Sewards, OBE 1989; writer and broadcaster; *b* Stainton, Yorks, 6 Feb. 1931; *s* of late Alan Thomas Trueman; *m* 1st, 1955, Enid (marr. diss.); one *s* two *d* (incl. twin *s* and *d*); 2nd, Veronica. *Educ:* Maltby Secondary Sch. Apprentice bricklayer, 1946; worked in tally office of Maltby Main pit, 1948–51; Nat. service, RAF, 1951–53. Played club cricket, 1945–48; Yorks Fedn cricket tour, 1948; played for Yorks CCC, 1949–68 (took 2304 wickets in first class games, incl. 100 wickets in a season twelve times; also made 3 centuries); county cap, 1951; captained Yorkshire 31 times, 1962–68; played 6 one day matches for Derby CCC, 1972; first Test series, against India, 1952; MCC tours to WI, 1953–54, 1959–60, and to Australia, 1958–59, 1962–63 (took a total of 307 Test wickets, 1952–65, incl. 10 in a match and 7 in an innings three times, and was first bowler to take 300 Test wickets, 1963). Journalist, Sunday People, 1957–; anchorman, Indoor League series, Yorks TV; cricket commentator for BBC. *Publications:* Fast Fury, 1961; Cricket, 1963; Book of Cricket, 1964; The Freddie Trueman Story, 1966; Ball of Fire (autobiog.), 1976; (with John Arlott) On Cricket, 1977; Thoughts of Trueman Now, 1978; (with Frank Hardy) You Nearly Had Him That Time, 1978; My Most Memorable Matches, 1982; (with Trevor Bailey) From Larwood to Lillee, 1983; (with Don Mosey) Fred Trueman's Yorkshire, 1984; (with Trevor Bailey) The Spinners' Web, 1988; (with Peter Grosvenor) Fred Trueman's Cricket Masterpieces: classic tales from the pavilion, 1990; (with Don Mosey) Champion Times, 1994. *Recreations:* ornithology, working for children's charities. *Address:* c/o BBC, Broadcasting House, W1A 1AA. *Clubs:* Yorkshire County Cricket (Hon. Life Mem.), MCC (Hon. Life Mem.), Lord's Taverners, Variety of GB, Forty, Saint Cricket; Ilkley Golf.

TRUMPINGTON, Baroness *cr* 1980 (Life Peer), of Sandwich in the County of Kent; **Jean Alys Barker;** PC 1992; a Baroness in Waiting (Government Whip), since 1992; *d* of late Arthur Edward Campbell-Harris, MC and late Doris Marie Robson; *m* 1954, William Alan Barker (*d* 1988); one *s*. *Educ:* privately in England and France. Land Girl to Rt Hon. David Lloyd George, MP, 1940–41; Foreign Office, Bletchley Park, 1941–45; European Central Inland Transport Orgn, 1945–49; Sec. to Viscount Hinchingbrooke, MP,

1950–52. Conservative Councillor, Cambridge City Council, Trumpington Ward, 1963–73; Mayor of Cambridge, 1971–72; Deputy Mayor, 1972–73; Conservative County Councillor, Cambridgeshire, Trumpington Ward, 1973–75; Hon. Councillor of the City of Cambridge, 1975–. Baroness in Waiting (Government Whip), 1983–85; Parly Under-Sec. of State, DHSS, 1985–87, MAFF, 1987–89; Minister of State, MAFF, 1989–92. UK Delegate to UN Status of Women Commn, 1979–82. Member: Air Transport Users' Cttee, 1972–80 (Dep. Chairman 1978–79, Chm. 1979–80); Bd of Visitors to HM Prison, Pentonville, 1975–81; Mental Health Review Tribunal, 1975–81. Gen. Commissioner of Taxes, 1976–83. Pres., Assoc. of Heads of Independent Schs, 1980–89. Steward, Folkestone Racecourse, 1980–92. Hon. Fellow, Lucy Cavendish Coll., Cambridge, 1980. Hon. FRCPath 1992; Hon. ARCVS 1994. JP Cambridge, 1972–75, South Westminster, 1976–82. *Recreations:* bridge, racing, collecting antiques, needlepoint. *Address:* House of Lords, SW1A 0PW. *Clubs:* Farmers', Grillions.

TRURO, Bishop of, since 1990; **Rt. Rev. Michael Thomas Ball,** CGA; *b* 14 Feb. 1932; *s* of Thomas James Ball and Kathleen Bradley Ball *Educ:* Lancing Coll., Sussex; Queens' Coll., Cambridge (BA 1955, MA 1959). Schoolmastering, 1955–76; Co-Founder, Community of the Glorious Ascension, 1960; Prior at Stroud Priory, 1963–76; Curate, Whitehall, Stroud, Glos, 1971–76; Priest-in-charge of Stanmer with Falmer, and Senior Anglican Chaplain to Higher Education in Brighton, including Sussex Univ., 1976–80; Bishop Suffragan of Jarrow, 1980–90. *Recreations:* music, sport, Boxers, housework. *Address:* Lis Escop, Truro, Cornwall TR3 6QQ. *T:* Truro (01872) 862657.
See also Rt Rev. P. J. Ball.

TRURO, Dean of; *see* Shearlock, Very Rev. D. J.

TRUSCOTT, Sir George (James Irving), 3rd Bt *cr* 1909; *b* 24 Oct. 1929; *s* of Sir Eric Homewood Stanham Truscott, 2nd Bt, and Lady (Mary Dorcas) Truscott (*née* Irving) (*d* 1948); *S* father, 1973; *m* 1962, Yvonne Dora (*née* Nicholson); one *s* one *d*. *Educ:* Sherborne School. *Heir: s* Ralph Eric Nicholson Truscott, *b* 21 Feb. 1966. *Address:* BM QUILL, London WC1N 3XX.

TRUSCOTT, Dr Peter; Member (Lab) Hertfordshire, European Parliament, since 1994; *b* 20 March 1959; *s* of late Derek Truscott and of Dorothy Truscott; *m* 1991, Svetlana, *d* of Col Prof. Nicolai Chernicov and Svetlana Chernicova. *Educ:* Newton Abbot Grammar Sch.; Exeter Coll., Oxford (History Prize; BA 1981, MA 1985, DPhil 1986, Modern History). Labour Party Organiser, 1986–89; NACRO, 1989–94. Mem. Cttee, Herts Assoc., NACRO, 1993–94. Councillor, Colchester Borough Council, 1988–92; contested (Lab) Torbay, 1992. Member: TGWU, 1986–; Co-op Party, 1987–; posts in Trade Union and Labour movements. European Parliament: Vice-Pres., Cttee on Security and Disarmament, 1994–; Mem., Foreign Affairs Cttee, 1994–; Substitute Mem., Regl Policy Cttee, 1994–. Sch. governor, 1988–92. *Publications:* newspaper articles. *Recreations:* walking, music, country dancing, swimming, leafletting. *Address:* Euro Office, Weltech Centre, Ridgeway, Welwyn Garden City, Herts AL7 2AA. *T:* Welwyn Garden City (01707) 336969. *Club:* William Morris Labour (South Oxhey).

TRUSTRAM EVE; *see* Eve, family name of Baron Silsoe.

TRUSWELL, Prof. (Arthur) Stewart, MD, FRCP, FFPHM, FRACP; Boden Professor of Human Nutrition, University of Sydney, since 1978; *b* 18 Aug. 1928; *s* of George Truswell and Molly Truswell (*née* Stewart-Hess); *m* 1st, 1956, Sheila McGregor (marr. diss. 1983); four *s*; 2nd, 1986, Catherine Hull; two *d*. *Educ:* Ruthin Sch., Clwyd; Liverpool and Cape Town Univs. MB, ChB 1952, MD 1959; FRCP 1975; FFCM 1979; FRACP 1980. Registrar in Pathology, Cape Town Univ., 1954; Registrar in Med., Groote Schuur Hosp., 1955–57; Research Bursar, Clin. Nutrition Unit, Dept. of Med., Cape Town Univ., 1958 and 1959; Adams Meml Trav. Fellowship to London, 1960; Sen. Fellow, Clin. Nutrition, Tulane Univ., USA, 1961; Res. Officer, Clin. Nutrition Unit, Cape Town Univ., 1962; Sen. Mem., Scientific Staff, MRC Atheroma Research Unit, Western Infirmary, Glasgow, 1963 and 1964; full-time Lectr, then Sen. Lectr in Med. and Consultant Gen. Physician, Cape Town Univ. and Groote Schuur Hosp., 1965–71; Warden of Med. Students' Residence, Cape Town Univ., 1967–69; Prof. of Nutrition and Dietetics, Queen Elizabeth Coll., London Univ., 1971–78. Vice-Pres., Internat. Union of Nutritional Sciences, 1985–93; Member, numerous cttees, working parties, editorial bds and socs related to nutrition. *Publications:* Human Nutrition and Dietetics, 7th edn (with S. Davidson, R. Passmore, J. F. Brock), 1979; ABC of Nutrition, 1986, 2nd edn 1992; numerous research papers in sci. jls on various topics in human nutrition and medicine. *Recreations:* gardening, walking (esp. on mountains). *Address:* 23 Woonona Road, Northbridge, NSW 2063, Australia; Human Nutrition Unit, Department of Biochemistry, Sydney University, Sydney, NSW 2006, Australia. *T:* (2) 3513726, *Fax:* (2) 3516022.

TRYON, family name of **Baron Tryon.**

TRYON, 3rd Baron *cr* 1940, of Durnford; **Anthony George Merrik Tryon;** DL; *b* 26 May 1940; *s* of 2nd Baron Tryon, PC, GCVO, KCB, DSO, and of Etheldreda Josephine, *d* of Sir Merrik Burrell, 7th Bt, CBE; *S* father, 1976; *m* 1973, Dale Elizabeth, *d* of Barry Harper; two *s* two *d* (of whom one *s* one *d* are twins). *Educ:* Eton. Page of Honour to the Queen, 1954–56. Captain Wessex Yeomanry, 1972. Dir, Lazard Bros & Co. Ltd, 1976–83; Chairman: English & Scottish Investors Ltd, 1977–88; Swaine Adeney Brigg, 1991–93. Chm., Salisbury Cathedral Spire Trust, 1985–. Pres., Anglers Conservation Assoc., 1985–. DL Wilts, 1992. *Recreations:* fishing and shooting. *Heir: s* Hon. Charles George Barrington Tryon, *b* 15 May 1976. *Address:* The Manor House, Great Durnford, near Salisbury, Wilts SP4 6BB. *T:* Middle Woodford (01722) 782225. *Clubs:* White's, Pratt's.

TRYON-WILSON, Brig. Charles Edward, CBE 1945 (MBE 1943); DSO 1944; Vice Lord-Lieutenant of Cumbria, 1980–83; *b* 20 Sept. 1909; 2nd *s* of late Charles Robert Tryon; *m* 1st, 1937, Cicely Joan (*d* 1969), *y d* of Captain Henry Whitworth; one *d* (and one *d* decd); 2nd, 1975, Rosemary Lucas. *Educ:* Shawnigan Lake School, BC; Trinity Coll., Glenalmond. Served 60th Rifles, 1927–30, Royal Fusiliers, 1930–36 and 1938–46 (N Africa, Italy, Austria; despatches twice). DL Westmorland (later Cumbria), 1971–85. *Recreations:* shooting, fishing. *Address:* Dallam Tower, Milnthorpe, Cumbria LA7 7AG. *T:* Milnthorpe (015395) 63368. *Clubs:* Army and Navy, Lansdowne; Flyfishers' (Buck's).

TRYTHALL, Maj.-Gen. Anthony John, CB 1983; Director of Army Education, 1980–84; Director: Brassey's (UK) Ltd (formerly Brassey's Defence Publishers Ltd), since 1984 (Managing Director, 1984–87; Executive Deputy Chairman, 1988–95); Brassey's (US) Inc., 1984–95; *b* 30 March 1927; *s* of Eric Stewart Trythall and Irene (*née* Hollingham); *m* 1952, Celia Haddon; two *s* one *d*. *Educ:* Lawrence Sheriff Sch., Rugby; St Edmund Hall, Oxford (BA Hons Mod. Hist., 1947, DipEd 1951); Institute of Education, London Univ. (Academic DipEd 1962); King's College, London (MA in War Studies, 1969). National Service as RAEC Officer, UK, Egypt and Akaba, 1947–49; teaching, 1951–53; Regular RAEC Officer, 1953; seconded to Malay Regt for service at Fedn Mil. Coll., Port Dickson, 1953–56; WO, 1957–62; BAOR, 1962–66; Inspector, 1967–68; Educn Adviser, Regular Commns Bd, 1969–71; Head of Officer Educn Br., 1971–73; Chief Inspector of Army Educn, and Col Res., 1973–74; MoD, 1974–76; Chief Educn Officer, UKLF, 1976–80. Col Comdt, RAEC, 1986–89. Member: Council, Royal United Services Instn for Def. Studies, 1978–84; London Univ. Bd of War Studies, 1983–; Chm., Gallipoli Meml Lecture Trust, 1986–89 (Trustee, 1984–). 1st Prize, Trench-Gascoigne Essay Competition, 1969. *Publications:* Boney Fuller: the intellectual general, 1977 (USA, as Boney Fuller: soldier, strategist and writer); (contrib.) The Downfall of Leslie Hore-Belisha in the Second World War, 1982; Fuller and the Tanks in Home Fires and Foreign Fields, 1985; articles in Army Qly, Jl of RUSI, British Army Rev., and Jl of Contemp. Hist. *Address:* c/o Royal Bank of Scotland, Holt's Branch, Lawrie House, Victoria Road, Farnborough, Hants GU14 7NR. *Club:* Naval and Military.

TS'ONG, Fou; *see* Fou Ts'ong.

TSUI, Prof. Lap-Chee, OC 1991; PhD; FRS 1991; FRSC 1989; Staff Geneticist and Senior Research Scientist, since 1983, Sellers Professor in Cystic Fibrosis Research, since 1989, Hospital for Sick Children, Toronto; Professor, Department of Molecular and Medical Genetics, since 1990, University Professor, since 1994, University of Toronto; *b* 21 Dec. 1950; *s* of Jing-Lue Hsue and Hui-Ching Wang; *m* 1977, Lan Fong (Ellen); two *s*. *Educ:* Chinese Univ. of Hong Kong (BSc Biol. 1972; MPhil 1974); Univ. of Pittsburgh (PhD Biol Scis 1979). Asst Prof. 1983–88, Associate Prof. 1988–90, Depts of Med. Genetics and Med. Biophysics, Univ. of Toronto. Trustee, Educn Foundn, Fedn of Chinese Canadian Professionals, Ontario. Hon. DCL: Univ. of King's Coll., Halifax, 1991; St Francis Xavier, Antigonish, NS, 1994; Hon. DSc: Univ. of New Brunswick, Fredericton, 1991; Chinese Univ. of Hong Kong, 1992. Paul di Sant'Agnese Distinguished Scientific Achievement Award, Cystic Fibrosis Foundn, USA, 1989; Gold Medal of Honor, Pharmaceutical Manufacturers' Assoc., Canada, 1989; Centennial Award, RSCan, 1989; Maclean's Honor Roll, 1989; Award of Excellence, Genetic Soc. Canada, 1990; Courvoisier Leadership Award, 1990; Gairdner Internat. Award, 1990; Cresson Medal, Franklin Inst., 1992; Mead Johnson Award, 1992; Sarsdedt Res. Prize, 1993; Sanremo Internat. Award, 1993; Lecocq Prize, Acad. des Scis, Inst de France, 1994; Henry Friesen Award, 1995. *Publications:* numerous papers in learned jls and invited papers and reviews. *Recreations:* cooking, travel, sightseeing. *Address:* Department of Genetics, Hospital for Sick Children, 555 University Avenue, Toronto, Ont M5G 1X8, Canada. *T:* (416) 8136015, *Fax:* (416) 8134931.

TUAM, Archbishop of, (RC), since 1987; **Most Rev. Joseph Cassidy;** *b* 29 Oct. 1933; *s* of John Cassidy and Mary Gallagher. *Educ:* St Nathy's College, Maynooth; University College, Galway. Professor, Garbally College, Ballinasloe, 1959–77, President 1977–79; Coadjutor Bishop of Clonfert, 1979–82; Bishop of Clonfert, 1982–87; Spokesman for Irish Bishops' Conference, 1980–88. *Publications:* plays, articles and homilies. *Address:* Archbishop's House, Tuam, Co. Galway, Ireland. *T:* Tuam (93) 24166.

TUAM, KILLALA AND ACHONRY, Bishop of, since 1986; **Rt. Rev. John Robert Winder Neill;** *b* 17 Dec. 1945; *s* of Eberto Mahon Neill and Rhoda Anne Georgina Neill; *m* 1968, Betty Anne (*née* Cox); three *s*. *Educ:* Sandford Park School, Dublin; Trinity Coll., Dublin (Foundation Schol., BA 1st Cl., MA); Jesus Coll., Cambridge (MA, Gardiner Memorial Schol., Univ. of Cambridge); Ridley Hall, Cambridge (GOE). Curate Asst, St Paul's, Glenageary, Dublin, 1969–71; Lectr (Old Testament) in Divinity Hostel, 1970–71; Bishop's Vicar and Dio. Registrar, Kilkenny, 1971–74; Rector of Abbeystrewry, Skibbereen, Co. Cork, 1974–78; Rector of St Bartholomew's, and Leeson Park, Dublin, 1978–84; Lectr (Liturgy) in Theological Coll., 1982–84; Exam. Chaplain to Archbishop of Dublin, 1982–84; Dean of Christ Church Cathedral, Waterford, 1984–86; Archdeacon of Waterford, 1984–86. Sec., Irish House of Bishops, 1988–95; Mem., Central Cttee, WCC, 1994–. *Publications:* contribs to Theology, New Divinity, Search, Doctrine and Life and Intercom. *Recreations:* photography, travel. *Address:* Bishop's House, Knockglass, Crossmolina, Co. Mayo, Ireland. *T:* Ballina (96) 31317, *Fax:* (96) 31775.

TUBBS, Ralph, OBE 1952; FRIBA; architect; *b* 9 Jan. 1912; *s* of late Sydney W. Tubbs and Mabel Frost; *m* 1946, Mary Taberner; two *s* one *d*. *Educ:* Mill Hill School; Architectural Assoc. School (Hons Dip.). Sec. MARS Group (Modern Architectural Research), 1939; Member: Council and Executive Committee of RIBA, 1944–50, re-elected Council, 1951; Vice-Pres. Architectural Assoc., 1945–47; Associate Institute of Landscape Architects, 1942–. Member Presentation Panel and Design Group for 1951 Festival of Britain, and architect of Dome of Discovery in London Exhibn (then the largest dome in world, 365 ft diam.). Other works include: Baden-Powell House for Boy Scouts' Assoc., London; Indian Students' Union building, Fitzroy Sq., London; Granada TV Centre and Studios, Manchester; Cambridge Inst. Educn; Halls of residence for University Coll., London, Residential Areas at Harlow and Basildon New Towns; Industrial Buildings. Architect for new Charing Cross Hospital and Med. Sch., London; Consultant for Hospital Develt, Jersey, CI. Pres., British Entomological and Natural Hist. Soc., 1977; Vice-Pres., Royal Entomol Soc. of London, 1982–84. *Publications:* Living in Cities, 1942; The Englishman Builds, 1945. *Recreation:* study of the natural world. *Address:* 9 Lingfield Road, Wimbledon, SW19 4QA. *T:* 0181–946 2010.

TUCK, Anthony; *see* Tuck, J. A.

TUCK, Sir Bruce (Adolph Reginald), 3rd Bt, *cr* 1910; *b* 29 June 1926; *o s* of Major Sir (William) Reginald Tuck, 2nd Bt, and Gladys Emily Kettle (*d* 1966), *d* of late N. Alfred Nathan, Wickford, Auckland, New Zealand, and *widow* of Desmond Fosberry Kettle, Auckland Mounted Rifles; *S* father 1954; *m* 1st, 1949, Luise (marr. diss., in Jamaica, 1964), *d* of John C. Renfro, San Angelo, Texas, USA; two *s*; 2nd, 1968, Pamela Dorothy Nicholson, *d* of Alfred Nicholson, London; one *d*. *Educ:* Canford School, Dorset. Lieutenant, Scots Guards, 1945–47. *Heir: s* Richard Bruce Tuck, *b* 7 Oct. 1952. *Address:* PO Box 274, Montego Bay, Jamaica.

TUCK, Clarence Edward Henry; Civil Service Commissioner, 1977–83; *b* 18 April 1925; *s* of Frederick and May Tuck; *m* 1950, Daphne Robinson; one *s* one *d*. *Educ:* Rendcomb Coll., Cirencester; Merton Coll., Oxford. BA 1949. Served in Royal Signals, 1943–47. Inland Revenue, 1950; Min. of Supply, 1950–55; seconded to Nigerian Federal Govt, Lagos, 1955–57; Ministry of: Supply, 1957–59; Aviation, 1959–60; Defence, 1960–62; Aviation, 1962–66; IDC, 1967; Min. of Technology, 1968–70; Trade and Industry, 1970; CSD, 1971; Trade and Industry, 1973; Dept of Energy, 1974; Civil Service Dept, 1976; Management and Personnel Office, 1981; Dir, Civil Service Selection Board, 1977–81. Asst Principal, 1950; Principal, 1953; Asst Sec., 1962; Under-Sec., 1970.

TUCK, Prof. (John) Anthony, MA, PhD; FRHistS; Professor of Medieval History, University of Bristol, 1990–93, now Emeritus; *b* 14 Nov. 1940; *s* of Prof. John Philip Tuck, *qv*; *m* 1976, Amanda, *d* of Dr L. J. Cawley, Carlton Husthwaite, near Thirsk, Yorks; two *s*. *Educ:* Newcastle upon Tyne Royal Grammar Sch.; Jesus Coll., Cambridge (BA, MA, PhD). FRHistS 1987. Lecturer in History, 1965–75, Sen. Lectr, 1975–78, Univ. of Lancaster; Master of Collingwood Coll., and Hon. Lectr in History, Univ. of Durham, 1978–87; Reader in Medieval History, Univ. of Bristol, 1987–90. *Publications:* Richard II and the English Nobility, 1973; Crown and Nobility 1272–1461, 1985; contribs to English

Historical Rev., Northern History, etc. *Recreations:* walking, gardening. *Address:* 7 High Street, Teversham, Cambridge CB1 5AF.
See also R. F. Tuck.

TUCK, Prof. John Philip; Professor of Education, University of Newcastle upon Tyne (formerly King's College, University of Durham) 1948–76, now Emeritus; *b* 16 April 1911; *s* of late William John and Annie Tuck, Uplyme, Lyme Regis; *m* 1936, Jane Adelaide, *d* of late George William Wall and Maria Ellen Wall, Ulceby, N Lincs; two *s*. *Educ:* Strand School; Jesus College, Cambridge. BA Hons English and History, Class I, 1933; Cambridge certificate in Education, 1934; Adelaide Stoll Bachelor Research Scholar, Christ's College, 1935; MA 1937. English Master: Gateshead Grammar School, 1936; Manchester Central High School, 1938; Wilson's Grammar School, 1939 and 1946. Served War of 1939–45, East Surrey Regt, and Army Education Corps, N Africa, Sicily, Italy, Austria. Lecturer in Education, King's College, Newcastle upon Tyne, 1946–48. Mem. Council, GPDST, 1976–84. FRSA 1970. Hon. Fellow, Coll. of Speech Therapists, 1966. *Address:* 7 Chesterford House, Southacre Drive, Chaucer Road, Cambridge CB2 2TZ. *T:* Cambridge (01223) 324655.
See also J. A. Tuck, R. F. Tuck.

TUCK, Dr Richard Francis, FBA 1994; Lecturer in History, Cambridge University, since 1977; Fellow of Jesus College, Cambridge, since 1971; *b* 9 Jan. 1949; *s* of Prof. John Philip Tuck, *qv*; *m* 1st, 1970, Mary Polwarth (marr. diss. 1993); two *s*; 2nd, 1993, Anne Malcolm; one *d*. *Educ:* Royal Grammar Sch., Newcastle upon Tyne; Jesus Coll., Cambridge (BA 1970; PhD 1976). Research Fellow, Jesus Coll., Cambridge, 1970; Univ. Asst Lectr in History, Cambridge, 1973–77. Vis. Fellow, Princeton Univ., 1989; Carlyle Lectr, Oxford, 1991. Foreign Hon. Mem., Amer. Acad. of Arts and Scis, 1992. *Publications:* Natural Rights Theories, 1979; Hobbes, 1989; Hobbes' Leviathan, 1991; Philosophy and Government 1572–1651, 1993. *Recreations:* repairing houses, looking after children. *Address:* Jesus College, Cambridge CB5 8BL; 9 Park Terrace, Cambridge CB1 1JH.

TUCK, Prof. Ronald Humphrey; Professor of Agricultural Economics, University of Reading, 1965–86 (part-time, 1982–86), now Emeritus; *b* 28 June 1921; *s* of Francis Tuck and Edith Ann Tuck (*née* Bridgewater); *m* Margaret Sylvia Everley (*d* 1990); one *s* two *d*. *Educ:* Harrow County Sch.; Corpus Christi Coll., Oxford. War Service, RAOC and REME, mainly N Africa and Italy, 1941–45 (despatches). Univ. of Reading, Dept of Agric. Economics: Research Economist, 1947–49; Lecturer, 1949–62; Reader, 1962–65; Head of Dept of Agricultural Economics and Management, Univ. of Reading, and Provincial Agricultural Economist (Reading Province), 1965–81; Dean, Faculty of Agriculture and Food, Univ. of Reading, 1971–74. *Publications:* An Essay on the Economic Theory of Rank, 1954; An Introduction to the Principles of Agricultural Economics, 1961 (Italian trans., 1970); reviews etc in Jl of Agric. Economics and Economic Jl. *Recreations:* reading, music, drawing, walking. *Address:* 211 Kidmore Road, Caversham, Reading RG4 7NW. *T:* Reading (01734) 473426.

TUCKER, Brian George, CB 1976; OBE 1963; Deputy Secretary, Department of Energy, 1974–81; Member, UKAEA, 1976–81; *b* 6 May 1922; *s* of late Frank Ernest Tucker and May Tucker; *m* 1948, Marion Pollitt; three *d*. *Educ:* Christ's Hospital. Entered Home Civil Service, 1939, as Clerical Officer, Admty; successive postings at home, in Africa, the Middle East, Ceylon and Hong Kong till 1953; promoted Executive Officer, 1945; Higher Executive Officer, 1949. Min. of Power, Asst Principal, 1954, Principal, 1957; seconded to HMOCS, 1957–62, Asst Sec., Govt of Northern Rhodesia; returned to MOP, 1962, Principal Private Sec. to Minister, 1965–66, Asst Sec., 1966, Under-Sec., Ministry of Technology, 1969–70, Cabinet Office, 1970–72, DTI, 1972–73; Dep. Sec., 1973. *Recreations:* gardening, music. *Address:* 1 Sondes Place Drive, Dorking, Surrey RH4 3ED. *T:* Dorking (01306) 884720.

TUCKER, Clive Fenemore; Under Secretary, Department for Education and Employment (formerly Department of Employment), since 1987; *b* 13 July 1944; *s* of William Frederick Tucker and Joan Tucker; *m* 1978, Caroline Elisabeth Macready; two *d*. *Educ:* Cheltenham Grammar Sch.; Balliol Coll., Oxford (BA). Entered Ministry of Labour, 1965; Private Sec. to Perm. Sec., 1968–70; Department of Employment: Principal, 1970; Asst Sec., 1978; Grade 4, 1986. Non-exec. Dir, RTZ Chemicals, 1987–90. *Recreations:* opera, looking at pictures, tennis. *Address:* c/o Department for Education and Employment, Caxton House, Tothill Street, SW1H 9NF.

TUCKER, Elizabeth Mary; Head Mistress, Headington School, Oxford, 1982–Aug. 1996; *b* 20 July 1936; *d* of Harold and Doris Tucker. *Educ:* Cheltenham Ladies' College; Newnham College, Cambridge (MA Classical Tripos; Associate, 1988); King's College London (PGCE). Assistant Mistress, Queen Anne's School, Caversham, 1959–64; Head of Classics, Notting Hill and Ealing High School, GPDST, 1964–72; Head Mistress, Christ's Hospital, Hertford, 1972–82. Member, Council: St Hugh's Sch., Faringdon, 1987–; Channing Sch., Highgate, 1995–. Corporate Mem., Cheltenham Ladies' Coll., 1994. Trustee, Bloxham Project, 1982–. *Recreations:* music (piano, spinet, singing), art and architecture (sketching), travel. *Address:* (until Aug. 1996) Headington School, Oxford OX3 7TD. *T:* Oxford (01865) 62711; (from Aug. 1996) 78 Manor Drive, N20 0DU. *Club:* University Women's.

TUCKER, (Henry John) Martin, QC 1975; **His Honour Judge Tucker;** a Circuit Judge, since 1981; Resident Judge, Winchester Combined Court Centre, since 1994; *b* 8 April 1930; *s* of late P. A. Tucker, LDS, RCS and Mrs Dorothy Tucker (*née* Hobbs); *m* 1957, Sheila Helen Wateridge, LRAM; one *s* four *d*. *Educ:* St Peter's Sch., Southbourne; Downside Sch.; Christ Church, Oxford (MA). Called to Bar, Inner Temple, 1954; Dep. Chm., Somerset QS, 1971; a Recorder of the Crown Court, 1972–81. Pres., Council of HM Circuit Judges, 1993. *Recreations:* walking occasionally; gardening gently; listening to music. *Address:* Chingri Khal, Sleepers Hill, Winchester, Hants SO22 4NB. *T:* Winchester (01962) 853927. *Club:* Hampshire (Winchester).

TUCKER, Herbert Harold, OBE 1965; HM Diplomatic Service, retired; Secretary, Roberts Centre; Consultant, Dulverton Trust, since 1989; *b* 4 Dec. 1925; *o s* of late Francis Tucker and late Mary Ann Tucker; *m* 1948, Mary Stewart Dunlop; three *s*. *Educ:* Queen Elizabeth's, Lincs; Rossington Main, Yorks. Western Morning News, Sheffield Telegraph, Nottingham Journal, Daily Telegraph, 1944–51; Economic Information Unit, Treasury, 1948–49; FO, later FCO, 1951; Counsellor (Information) and Dir, British Information Services, Canberra, 1974–78; Consul-General, Vancouver, 1979–83; Disarmament Information Coordinator, FCO, 1983–84. Consultant, Centre for Security and Conflict Studies, 1986–89. *Publication:* (ed) Combating the Terrorists, 1988. *Recreations:* gardening, reading, watercolouring. *Address:* Pullens Cottage, Leigh Hill Road, Cobham, Surrey KT11 2HX. *T:* Cobham (01932) 864461. *Clubs:* Travellers', Commonwealth Trust.

TUCKER, Martin; *see* Tucker, H. J. M.

TUCKER, Peter Louis; practising barrister, Sierra Leone; Commissioner/Chairman, Sierra Leone Population Census, since 1984; *b* 11 Dec. 1927; *s* of Peter Louis Tucker and Marion Tucker; *m* 1st, 1955, Clarissa Mary Harleston; three *s* one *d* (and one *d* decd); 2nd, 1972, Teresa Josephine Ganda; one *s*. *Educ:* Fourah Bay Coll., Sierra Leone (MA Latin, Dunelm); Jesus Coll., Oxford (MA Jurisp.); DipEd. Called to Bar, Gray's Inn, 1970. Teacher, 1952–57; Education Officer, 1957–61; Secretary, Training and Recruitment, Sierra Leone Civil Service, 1961–63; Establishment Sec., 1963–66; Sec. to the Prime Minister and Head of Sierra Leone Civil Service, 1966–67; Asst Director, UK Immigrants Advisory Service, 1970–72; Principal Admin. Officer, Community Relations Commn, 1972–74, Dir of Fieldwork and Admin., 1974–77; Dir of Legal and Gen. Services, and Sec., 1977, Chief Exec., 1977–82, CRE; Special Envoy on Foreign Aid to Sierra Leone and Chm., Nat. Aid Co-ordinating Cttee, 1986; Chm., National Constitutional Review Commn, 1990–91. DCL (*hc*) Sierra Leone. Papal Medal Pro Ecclesia et Pontifice, 1966. *Publications:* miscellaneous booklets, articles and reports for Community Relations Commission and Govt of Sierra Leone. *Recreations:* photography, listening to music. *Address:* 1 Forest Road Hill Station, Free Town, Sierra Leone. *T:* Sierra Leone (22) 24868; (home) (22) 236414.

TUCKER, Hon. Sir Richard (Howard), Kt 1985; **Hon. Mr Justice Tucker;** a Judge of the High Court of Justice, Queen's Bench Division, since 1985; *b* 9 July 1930; *s* of Howard Archibald Tucker, later His Honour Judge Tucker, and Margaret Minton Tucker; *m* 1st, 1958, Paula Mary Bennett Frost (marr. diss. 1974); one *s* two *d*; 2nd, 1975, Wendy Kate Standbrook (*d* 1988); 3rd, 1989, Jacqueline Suzanne Rossvell Thomson, *widow* of William Thomson, artist. *Educ:* Shrewsbury Sch.; The Queen's Coll., Oxford (MA; Hon. Fellow, 1992). Called to Bar, Lincoln's Inn, 1954; Bencher, 1979. QC 1972; a Recorder, 1972–85; Mem. Senate, Inns of Court and the Bar, 1984–86; Dep. Leader, 1984–85, and Presiding Judge, 1986–90, Midland and Oxford Circuit. Mem., Employment Appeal Tribunal, 1986–. *Recreations:* sailing, shooting, gardening. *Address:* Royal Courts of Justice, Strand, WC2A 2LL. *Clubs:* Garrick; Leander (Henley-on-Thames); Bar Yacht; Ariel Rowing (Bristol).

TUCKEY, Andrew Marmaduke Lane; Chairman, Baring Brothers & Co., Ltd, 1989–95; Deputy Chairman, Barings plc, 1989–95; Adviser, Baring Brothers Ltd, since 1995; *b* 28 Aug. 1943; *s* of late Henry Lane Tuckey and of Aileen Rosemary Newson Tuckey; *m* 1967, Margaret Louise (*née* Barnes); one *s* two *d*. *Educ:* Plumtree Sch., Zimbabwe. Chartered Accountant, 1966. Dixon Wilson, Chartered Accountants, 1962–66; British American Tobacco, 1966–68; Baring Brothers & Co., Ltd, 1968–95: Dir, 1973–81; Man. Dir, 1981–89. Dir, Dillon, Read Holding Inc., 1991–. Member: Federal Reserve Bank of New York Internat. Capital Markets Adv. Cttee, 1992–; Financial Law Panel, 1993–; Council, Baring Foundn, 1994–. Dir and Treasurer, Friends of Covent Garden, 1981–; Dir, Royal Opera House, 1992–; Trustee: Esmée Fairbairn Charitable Trust, 1986–; Classic FM Charitable Trust, 1992–. *Recreations:* music, tennis. *Address:* Baring Brothers Ltd, 8 Bishopsgate, EC2N 4AE. *Clubs:* White's, City of London, Roehampton.
See also Hon. Sir S. L. Tuckey.

TUCKEY, Hon. Sir Simon (Lane), Kt 1992; **Hon. Mr Justice Tuckey;** a Judge of the High Court of Justice, Queen's Bench Division, since 1992; a Judge, Employment Appeal Tribunal, since 1993; *b* 17 Oct. 1941; *s* of late Henry Lane Tuckey and of Aileen Rosemary Newsom Tuckey; *m* 1964, Jennifer Rosemary (*née* Hardie); one *s* two *d*. *Educ:* Plumtree School, Zimbabwe. Called to Bar, Lincoln's Inn, 1964, Bencher, 1989; QC 1981; a Recorder, 1984–92; Presiding Judge, Western Circuit, 1995–. Chm., Review Panel, Financial Reporting Council, 1990–92. Mem., Judicial Studies Bd, 1993–95 (Chm., Civil and Family Cttee, 1993–95). *Recreations:* sailing, tennis. *Address:* Royal Courts of Justice, Strand, WC2A 2LL.
See also A. M. L. Tuckey.

TUCKMAN, Frederick Augustus, (Fred), OBE 1990; FCIS, FIPM; *b* 9 June 1922; *s* of Otto and Amy Tina Tuchmann (*née* Adler); *m* 1966, Patricia Caroline Myers; two *s* one *d*. *Educ:* English and German schools; London School of Economics, 1946–49 (BScEcon). Served RAF, 1942–46. Commercial posts, 1950–65; Management Consultant and Partner, HAY Gp, 1965–85; Managing Director, HAY GmbH, Frankfurt, 1970–80; Partner, HAY Associates, 1975–85; Chm., Suomen HAY, OY, Helsinki, 1973–81; consultant assignments in Europe, Africa and N America. Hon. Sec., Bow Gp, 1958–59; Councillor, London Borough of Camden, 1965–71 (Chm., Library and Arts, 1968–71). Mem. (C) Leicester, European Parliament, 1979–89; contested (C) Leicester, Eur. Parly elecn, 1989. Mem. Council, Inst. of Personnel Management, 1963–70. Chm., Greater London Area, CPC, 1968–70. European Parliament: Budget Cttee, 1979–81; Social and Employment Cttee, 1981–89 (Cons. spokesman, 1984–89); substitute Mem., Economic and Monetary Cttee, 1979–87; substitute Mem., Budgetary Control Cttee, 1984–87; First Vice Pres., Latin American Delegn, 1982–85; Mem., Israel Delegn, 1987–89; Chm., Internat. Gp on Small Business, 1985–86. UK Chm., European Year of Small Business, 1983; Vice Chm., Small Business Bureau, London, 1985–89. Pres., Anglo-Jewish Assoc., 1989– (Vice-Pres., 1988–89); Vice Pres., Eur. Medium and Small Units, 1985–. Cross, Order of Merit (FRG), 1989. *Recreations:* reading, arguing, travel, swimming; priority—family. *Address:* 6 Cumberland Road, Barnes, SW13 9LY. *T:* 0181–748 2392. *Clubs:* Athenæum, Carlton.

TUCKWELL, Anthony David, MA; Headmaster, King Edward VI Grammar School, Chelmsford, since 1984; *b* 4 July 1943; *s* of Alec William Tuckwell and Muriel Florence Tuckwell (*née* Green); *m* 1967, Kathleen Olivia Hatton. *Educ:* St Peter's Coll., Oxford (MA); Oxford Univ. Dept of Educn (DipEd); MBA Leeds 1995. History Master, Southern Grammar Sch. for Boys, Portsmouth, 1966–69; St John's College, Southsea: Hd of Hist., 1970–73; Sen. Teacher (Curriculum Co-ordinator), 1973–78; Dep. Headmaster, Sale Co. Grammar Sch. for Boys, 1979–83. FRSA 1994. *Recreations:* music, literature, gardening, travel. *Address:* 28 Oaklands Crescent, Chelmsford, Essex CM2 9PP.

TUCKWELL, Barry Emmanuel, AC 1992; OBE 1965; horn soloist; conductor; Conductor and Music Director, Maryland Symphony Orchestra, since 1982; *b* 5 March 1931; *s* of late Charles and Elizabeth Tuckwell, Australia; *m* 1st, 1958, Sally Eelin Newton; one *s* one *d*; 2nd, 1971, Hilary Jane Warburton; one *s*; 3rd, 1992, Susan Terry Levitan. *Educ:* various schs, Australia; Sydney Conservatorium. FRCM 1993. Melbourne Symph. Orch., 1947; Sydney Symph. Orch., 1947–50; Hallé Orch., 1951–53; Scottish Nat. Orch., 1953–54; Bournemouth Symphony Orch., 1954–55; London Symph. Orch., 1955–68; founded Tuckwell Wind Quintet, 1968; Conductor, Tasmanian Symphony Orch., 1979–83; Guest Conductor, Northern Sinfonia, 1993–. Mem. Chamber Music Soc. of Lincoln Center, 1974–81; Horn Prof., Royal Academy of Music, 1963–74; Pres., Internat. Horn Soc., 1969–77, 1992–. Plays and conducts annually throughout Europe, Gt Britain, USA and Canada; has appeared at many internat. festivals, incl. Salzburg and Edinburgh; took part in 1st Anglo-Soviet Music Exchange, Leningrad and Moscow, 1963; toured: Far East, 1964 and 1975; Australia, 1970–; S America, 1976; USSR, 1977; People's Republic of China, 1984. Many works dedicated to him; has made numerous recordings. Editor, complete horn literature for G. Schirmer Inc. Hon. RAM, 1966; Hon. GSM, 1967. Harriet Cohen Internat. Award for Solo Instruments, 1968; Grammy Award Nominations. *Publications:* Playing the Horn, 1978; The Horn, 1981. *Club:* Athenæum.

TUDBALL, Peter Colum, CBE 1993; Chairman, Baltic Exchange, since 1991; Managing Director, Graig Shipping PLC, since 1979; *b* 5 July 1933; *s* of Colum Tudball and Annie (*née* Critchett); *m* 1960, Carole Maureen Thompson; one *s* two *d*. *Educ:* Cardiff High Sch. Joined Idwal Williams, Managers of Graig Shipping PLC, 1953. Mem., Baltic Exchange,

1954–. *Recreations:* sport, walking, acting. *Address:* Cleaver House, Headley, Surrey KT18 6NR. *T:* Leatherhead (01372) 377314. *Club:* Cardiff and County.

TUDHOPE, David Hamilton, CMG 1984; DFC 1944, and Bar 1944; Chairman, National Bank of New Zealand, 1983–92; *b* 9 Nov. 1921; *s* of William and Sybil Tudhope; *m* 1946, Georgina Charity Lee; two *s* two *d.* *Educ:* Wanganui Collegiate Sch., NZ; King's Coll., Cambridge (MA, LLB). Served War, 1941–45: Pilot RNZAF, UK (Flt Lieut) (DFC and Bar, Pathfinder Force, Bomber Comd). Barrister and Solicitor, NZ, 1947–49; Shell Oil, NZ, 1949–60; Gen. Manager, Shell Oil Rhodesia, N Rhodesia and Nyasaland, 1960–62; Area Co-ordinator, Shell London, 1962–67; Chm. and Chief Exec., Shell Interests in NZ, 1967–81; Chm., Shell BP & Todd Oil Services, 1967–81; Chm. (in rotation), NZ Oil Refinery, 1969, 1974, 1980, and Maui Development, 1975, 1980; Chm., National Mutual Life Assoc., 1983–88; Director: Shell Holdings Ltd, 1981–87; Commercial Union Insurance, 1982–88; Steel & Tube, 1986–93. Dep. Chm., Crown Corp., 1984–86. Chm., Pukeiti Rhododendron Trust, 1981–90. *Recreations:* gardening, golf. *Address:* 7 Cluny Avenue, Kelburn, Wellington, New Zealand. *T:* Wellington (4) 4759358. *Club:* Wellington (Pres., 1992–94).

TUDHOPE, James Mackenzie, CB 1987; Chairman of Social Security Appeal Tribunals, 1987–91; *b* 11 Feb. 1927; *m* Margaret Willock Kirkwood, MA Glasgow; two *s.* *Educ:* Dunoon Grammar School; Univ. of Glasgow (BL 1951). Admitted Solicitor, 1951. Private legal practice, 1951–55; Procurator Fiscal Depute, 1955, Senior PF Depute, 1962, Asst PF, 1968–70, Glasgow; PF, Kilmarnock, 1970–73, Dumbarton, 1973–76; Regional Procurator Fiscal: S Strathclyde, Dumfries and Galloway at Hamilton, 1976–80; for Glasgow and Strathkelvin, 1980–87. Hon. Sheriff, N Strathclyde, 1989–. Mem. Council, Law Soc. of Scotland, 1983–86. *Recreation:* serendipity. *Address:* Point House, Dundonald Road, Kilmarnock, Ayrshire KA1 1TY.

TUDOR, Rev. Dr (Richard) John, BA; Superintendent Minister, Westminster Central Hall, London, since 1981; *b* 8 Feb. 1930; *s* of Charles Leonard and Ellen Tudor; *m* 1956, Cynthia Campbell Anderson; one *s* one *d.* *Educ:* Clee Grammar Sch., Grimsby; Queen Elizabeth's, Barnet; Univ. of Manchester, 1951–54 (BA Theology). Served RAF, 1948–51. Junior Methodist Minister, East Ham, London, 1954–57; Ordained, Newark, 1957; Minister, Thornton Cleveleys, Blackpool, 1957–60; Superintendent Minister: Derby Methodist Mission, 1960–71: Chaplain to Mayor of Derby, Factories and Association with Derby Football Club; Coventry Methodist Mission, 1971–75; Chaplain to Lord Mayor; Brighton Dome Mission, 1975–81; Free Church Chaplain, Westminster Hosp., 1982–93; Chaplain to Ancient Order of Foresters Charity Stewards, 1989–, to Lord Mayor of Westminster, 1993–94. Hon. DD Texas Wesleyan Univ., Fort Worth, USA, 1981; Hon. Texan, 1965; Freeman of Fort Worth, 1970. *Publication:* Word for all Seasons, 1992. *Recreations:* motoring, cooking, photography, the delights of family life. *Address:* The Methodist Church, Central Hall, Westminster, SW1H 9NP. *T:* 0171–222 8010.

TUDOR EVANS, Sir Haydn, Kt 1974; a Judge of the High Court of Justice, Queen's Bench Division, 1978–94 (Family Division, 1974–78); *b* 20 June 1920; 4th *s* of John Edgar Evans and Ellen Stringer; *m* 1947, Sheilagh Isabella Pilkington; one *s.* *Educ:* Cardiff High Sch.; West Monmouth School; Lincoln College, Oxford. RNVR, 1940–41. Open Scholar, Lincoln Coll., Oxford (Mod. History), 1940; Stewart Exhibitioner, 1942; Final Hons Sch., Mod. History, 1944; Final Hons Sch., Jurisprudence, 1945. Cholmeley Scholar, Lincoln's Inn, 1946; called to the Bar, Lincoln's Inn, 1947, Bencher 1970. QC 1962; Dep. Chm., Kent QS, 1968–72; Recorder of Crown Court, 1972–74; a Judge, Employment Appeal Tribunal, 1982–88. *Recreation:* watching Rugby, racing and cricket. *Address:* 30 Stanford Road, Kensington, W8 5PZ. *Clubs:* Garrick, Royal Automobile, MCC.

TUDWAY QUILTER, David C.; *see* Quilter.

TUFFIN, Alan David, CBE 1993; General Secretary, Union of Communication Workers, 1982–93; *b* 2 Aug. 1933; *s* of Oliver Francis and Gertrude Elizabeth Tuffin; *m* 1957, Jean Elizabeth Tuffin; one *s* one *d.* *Educ:* Eltham Secondary Sch., SE9. Post Office employment, London, 1949–69; London Union Regional Official for UCW, 1957–69; National Official, 1969; Deputy General Secretary, 1979. Member: TUC Gen. Council, 1982–93 (Pres., 1992–93); HSC, 1986–; Employment Appeal Tribunal, 1995–. Dir, Trade Union Fund Managers Ltd (formerly Trade Union Unit Trust), 1985–. FRSA 1990. *Recreations:* reading, squash, West Ham United FC. *Address:* c/o UCW House, Crescent Lane, SW4 9RN.

TUFNELL, Col Greville Wyndham; DL; Development Officer, National Star Centre for Disabled Youth, since 1982; Lieutenant, Queen's Body Guard of the Yeomen of the Guard, since 1993; *b* 7 April 1932; *s* of K. E. M. Tufnell, MC and E. H. Tufnell (*née* Du Faur); *m* 1962, Hon. Anne Rosemary Trench (*d* 1992), *d* of 5th Baron Ashtown, OBE and *widow* of Capt. Timothy Patrick Arnold Gosselin; three *d*, and one step *d*; *m* 1994, Susan Arnot Burrows. *Educ:* Eton; RMA, Sandhurst. Commnd Grenadier Guards, 1952; Adjt, 2nd Bn, 1959–61; GSO 3, War Office, 1962–63; Staff Coll., 1964; Maj. 1965; DAQMG, London Dist, 1966–67; GSO 2, HQ 2 Div., 1969–71; Lt Col 1971; comdg 1st Bn, 1971–73 (despatches, 1972); Bde Maj., Household Div., 1974–76; Col 1976; Lt Col comdg Grenadier Guards, 1976–78; retd 1979. Queen's Body Guard of Yeomen of the Guard: Exon, 1979; Ensign, 1985; Clerk of the Cheque and Adjutant, 1987. Freeman, City of London, 1961; Liveryman, Grocers' Co., 1965–. DL Glos, 1994. *Recreations:* shooting, fishing, gardening. *Address:* The Manor House, Ampney St Peter, Cirencester, Glos GL7 5SH. *Clubs:* Cavalry and Guards; MCC.

TUFTON, family name of **Baron Hothfield.**

TUGENDHAT, family name of **Baron Tugendhat.**

TUGENDHAT, Baron *cr* 1993 (Life Peer), of Widdington in the County of Essex; **Christopher Samuel Tugendhat,** Kt 1990; Chairman, Abbey National plc, since 1991; Director: The BOC Group, since 1985; Eurotunnel plc, since 1991; *b* 23 Feb. 1937; *er s* of late Dr Georg Tugendhat; *m* 1967, Julia Lissant Dobson; two *s.* *Educ:* Ampleforth Coll.; Gonville and Caius Coll., Cambridge (Pres. of Union). Financial Times leader and feature writer, 1960–70. MP (C) City of London and Westminster South, 1974–76 (Cities of London and Westminster, 1970–74); Mem., 1977–85, a Vice-Pres., 1981–85, EEC Commn. Director: Sunningdale Oils, 1971–76; Phillips Petroleum International (UK) Ltd, 1972–76; National Westminster Bank, 1985–91 (Dep. Chm., 1990–91); Commercial Union Assce, 1988–91; LWT (Hldgs), 1991–94. Chm., CAA, 1986–91. Chm., RIIA (Chatham House), 1986–95; Governor, Council of Ditchley Foundn, 1986–; Vice-Pres., Council of British Lung Foundn, 1986–. *Publications:* Oil: the biggest business, 1968; The Multinationals, 1971 (McKinsey Foundn Book Award, 1971); Making Sense of Europe, 1986; (with William Wallace) Options for British Foreign Policy in the 1990s, 1988; various pamphlets and numerous articles. *Recreations:* being with his family, reading, conversation. *Address:* 35 Westbourne Park Road, W2 5QD. *Clubs:* Buck's, Royal Anglo-Belgian.

See also M. G. Tugendhat.

TUGENDHAT, Michael George; QC 1986; a Recorder, since 1994; *b* 21 Oct. 1944; *s* of late Georg Tugendhat and Maire Littledale; *m* 1970, Blandine de Loisne; four *s.* *Educ:* Ampleforth Coll.; Gonville and Caius Coll., Cambridge (Scholar; MA); Yale Univ. Henry Fellowship. Called to the Bar, Inner Temple, 1969, Bencher, 1988. Mem., Bar Council, 1992–94. *Address:* 5 Raymond Buildings, Gray's Inn, WC1R 5BP. *T:* 0171–242 2902. *Club:* Brooks's.

See also Baron Tugendhat.

TU'IPELEHAKE, HRH Prince Fatafehi, Hon. KBE 1977 (Hon. CBE); Prime Minister of Tonga, 1965–91, and Minister for Agriculture, Fisheries and Forests, and Marine Affairs; *b* 7 Jan 1922; *s* of HRH Prince Viliami Tupoulahi Tungi and HM Queen Salote of Tonga; *m* 1947, Princess Melenaite Topou Moheofo; two *s* four *d.* *Educ:* Newington College, Sydney; Gatton Agricultural College, Queensland. Governor of Vava'u, 1949–51. Chm., Commodities Board. 'Uluafi Medal, 1982. *Address:* c/o Office of the Prime Minister, Nuku'alofa, Tonga.

See also HM King of Tonga.

TUITA, Sir Mariano (Kelesimalefo), KBE 1992 (OBE 1975); Cross of Solomon Islands, 1985; Managing Director, L. K. P. Hardware Ltd, since 1985; *b* Solomon Is, 12 Nov. 1932; *s* of late Joachim Alick and Ann Maria Tangoia Hagota; *m* 1957, Luisa Mae; three *s* six *d.* *Educ:* St Joseph's Sch., Tenaru on Guadacanal. Mem. for Lau, Malaita Local Govt Council, 1958–60; Pres., Malaita Council, 1960–68; Member: first Solomon Is Legislative Council, 1960–65; for N Malaita Constituency, 1965–67; for NE Malaita Constituency, 1967–69; Governing Council for Lau and Baelelea, 1970–73; for Lau and Baelelea, Legislative Assembly, Solomon Is Nat. Parlt, 1976–80. *Address:* L. K. P. Hardware Ltd, PO Box 317, Honiara, Solomon Islands. *T:* 22594 and 23848.

TUITE, Sir Christopher (Hugh), 14th Bt *cr* 1622; Controller, The Nature Conservancy; *b* 3 Nov. 1949; *s* of Sir Dennis George Harmsworth Tuite, 13th Bt, MBE, and of Margaret Essie, *d* of late Col Walter Leslie Dundas, DSO; *S* father, 1981; *m* 1976, Deborah Ann, *d* of A. E. Martz, Punxsutawney, Pa; two *s.* *Educ:* Univ. of Liverpool (BSc Hons); Univ. of Bristol (PhD). Research Officer, The Wildfowl Trust, 1978–81. *Publications:* contribs to Jl of Animal Ecology, Jl of Applied Ecology, Freshwater Biology, Wildfowl. *Heir:* *s* Thomas Livingstone Tuite, *b* 24 July 1977. *Address:* c/o The Midland Bank, 33 The Borough, Farnham, Surrey GU9 7NJ.

TUIVAGA, Hon. Sir Timoci (Uluiburotu), Kt 1981; **Hon. Mr Justice Tuivaga;** Chief Justice of Fiji, 1980–87, and since 1988; *b* 21 Oct. 1931; *s* of Isimeli Siga Tuivaga and Jessie Hill; *m* 1958, Vilimaina Leba Parrott Tuivaga; three *s* one *d.* *Educ:* Univ. of Auckland (BA). Called to Bar, Gray's Inn, 1964, and NSW, 1968. Native Magistrate, 1958–61; Crown Counsel, 1965–68; Principal Legal Officer, 1968–70; Acting Director of Public Prosecutions, 1970; Crown Solicitor, 1971; Puisne Judge, 1972; Acting Chief Justice, 1974; sometime Acting Gov.-Gen., 1983–87. *Recreations:* golf, gardening. *Address:* 228 Ratu Sukuna Road, Suva, Fiji. *T:* 301782. *Club:* Fiji Golf (Suva).

TUKE, Sir Anthony (Favill), Kt 1979; Chairman, Savoy Hotel, 1984–94 (Director, 1982–94); Director, Barclays Bank International, since 1966 (Chairman, 1972–79; Vice-Chairman, 1968–72); *b* 22 Aug. 1920; *s* of late Anthony William Tuke; *m* 1946, Emilia Mila; one *s* one *d.* *Educ:* Winchester; Magdalene Coll., Cambridge. Scots Guards, 1940–46. Barclays Bank Ltd, 1946–90 (Dir, 1965–90; Vice-Chm, 1972–73; Chm., 1973–81); Dir, Barclays Bank UK, 1971–81. Dep. Chm., Royal Insurance, 1985–92 (Dir, 1978–92); Director: Merchants Trust, 1969–94; RTZ Corp., 1980–91 (Chm., 1981–85); Whitbread Investment Company PLC, 1984–93. Vice-President: Inst. of Bankers, 1973–81; British Bankers' Assoc., 1977–81; Chm., Cttee of London Clearing Bankers, 1976–78 (Dep. Chm., 1974–76); Pres., Internat. Monetary Conference, 1977–78. Mem., Trilateral Commn, 1973–91. Chm., 1980 British Olympic Appeal; Pres., MCC, 1982–83. Mem., Stevenage Develt Corp., 1959–64. Governor, Motability, 1978–85. Mem. Council, Warwick Univ., 1966–73; Treas., English-Speaking Union, 1969–73. *Recreation:* gardening. *Address:* Freelands, Wherwell, near Andover, Hants SP11 7JS. *Club:* MCC.

TULLY, (William) Mark, OBE 1985; freelance journalist and broadcaster, since 1994; *b* 24 Oct. 1935; *s* of late William Scarth Carlisle Tully, CBE and of Patience Treby Tully; *m* 1960, Frances Margaret (*née* Butler); two *s* two *d.* *Educ:* Twyford School, Winchester; Marlborough College; Trinity Hall, Cambridge (MA; Hon. Fellow, 1994). Regional Dir, Abbeyfield Soc., 1960–64; BBC, 1964–94: Asst, Appointments Dept, 1964–65; Asst, then Actg Rep., New Delhi, 1965–69; Prog. Organiser and Talks Writer, Eastern Service, 1969–71; Chief of Bureau, Delhi, 1972–93; South Asia Correspondent, 1993–94. Padma Shri (India), 1992. *Publications:* (with Satish Jacob) Amritsar: Mrs Gandhi's last battle, 1985; (with Z. Masani) From Raj to Rajiv, 1988; No Full Stops in India, 1991; The Heart of India (short stories), 1995. *Recreations:* fishing, bird watching, reading. *Address:* 1 Nizamuddin (East), New Delhi 110 013, India. *T:* Delhi (11) 616108/616102. *Clubs:* Oriental; Press, India International, Gymkhana (Delhi), Bengal (Calcutta).

TULVING, Prof. Endel, PhD; FRS 1992; FRSC; Tanenbaum Chair in Cognitive Neuroscience, Rotman Research Institute, Baycrest Centre, Toronto, since 1992; University Professor Emeritus in Psychology, University of Toronto, since 1992; *b* 26 May 1927; *s* of Juhan Tulving and Linda (*née* Soome); *m* 1950, Ruth Mikkelsaar; two *d.* *Educ:* Hugo Treffner Gymnasium; Univ. of Heidelberg; Univ. of Toronto (BA, MA); Harvard Univ. (Foundn Fellow, 1954–55; PhD). FRSC 1979. Teaching Fellow, Harvard Univ., 1955–56; University of Toronto: Lectr, 1956–59; Asst Prof. of Psychol., 1959–62; Associate Prof., 1962–65; Prof., 1965–70; Prof. of Psychol., Yale Univ., 1970–75; University of Toronto: Prof. of Psychol., 1972–92; Chm., Dept of Psychol., 1974–80; Univ. Prof., 1985–92. Vis. Scholar, Univ. of Calif., Berkeley, 1964–65; Fellow, Center for Advanced Study in Behavioural Scis, Stanford, Calif., 1972–73; Commonwealth Vis. Prof., Univ. of Oxford, 1977–78; Distinguished Res. Prof. of Neurosci., Univ. of Calif., Davis, 1993–. Izaak Walton Killam Meml Scholarship, 1976; Guggenheim Fellow, 1987–88; William James Fellow, Amer. Psychol Soc., 1990. For. Hon. Mem., Amer. Acad. Arts and Scis, 1986; For. Associate, Nat. Acad. Scis, USA, 1988; For. Mem., Royal Swedish Acad. Scis, 1991. Hon. MA Yale, 1969; Hon. PhD Umeå, Sweden, 1982; Hon. DLitt: Waterloo, Canada, 1987; Laurentian, Canada, 1988; Hon. DPsych Tartu, Estonia, 1989. Warren Medal, Soc. of Exptl Psychologists, 1982; Dist. Scientific Contrib. Award, Amer. Psychol Assoc., 1983; Award for Dist. Contribs to Psychol. as a Science, Canadian Psychol Assoc., 1983; Izaak Walton Killam Prize in Health Scis, Canada Council, 1994; Gold Medal Award, Amer. Psychol Foundn, 1994. *Publications:* Elements of Episodic Memory, 1983; (ed jtly) Organization of Memory, 1972; Memory Systems 1994, 1994; articles in scientific jls. *Recreations:* tennis, walking, chess, bridge. *Address:* 45 Bâby Point Crescent, Toronto, Ont M6S 2B7, Canada. *T:* (416) 7623736.

TUMIM, Stephen; His Honour Judge Tumim; a Circuit Judge, since 1978; HM's Chief Inspector of Prisons for England and Wales, 1987–95; *b* 15 Aug. 1930; *yr s* of late Joseph Tumim, CBE (late Clerk of Assize, Oxford Circuit) and late Renée Tumim; *m* 1962, Winifred, OBE 1992, *er d* of late Col A. M. Borthwick; three *d.* *Educ:* St Edward's Sch., Oxford; Worcester Coll., Oxford (Scholar; Hon. Fellow, 1994). Called to Bar, Middle Temple, 1955, Bencher, 1990. A Recorder of the Crown Court, 1977–78; a Judge of

Willesden County Court, 1980–87. Chm., Nat. Deaf Children's Soc., 1974–79. Chairman: Friends of Tate Gall., 1983–90; British Art Market Standing Cttee, 1990–; Koestler Award Trust, 1993–; Pres., Royal Lit. Fund, 1990–. Fellow, Royal Philanthropic Soc., 1994. Hon. FRCPsych 1993; Hon. Fellow: LSE, 1993; UEA, 1994; Hon. Sen. Fellow, Cayman Is Law Sch., 1994. DUniv Stirling, 1993; Hon. LLD: Leicester, UWE, 1994; Birmingham, Essex, Southampton, 1995. *Publications:* Great Legal Disasters, 1983; Great Legal Fiascos, 1985; occasional reviews. *Recreations:* books and pictures. *Address:* c/o Home Office, Queen Anne's Gate, SW1H 9AT. *Clubs:* Garrick, Beefsteak.

TUNBRIDGE, William Michael Gregg, MD; FRCP; Director of Postgraduate Medical Education and Training, Oxford University, since 1994; Professorial Fellow of Wadham College, Oxford, since 1994; *b* 13 June 1940; *s* of Sir Ronald Ernest Tunbridge, OBE and of Dorothy (*née* Gregg); *m* 1965, Felicity Katherine Edith Parrish; two *d. Educ:* Kingswood Sch., Bath; Queens' Coll., Cambridge (MA, MD); University Coll. Hosp. House appointments: UCH, 1964–65; Mpilo Hosp., Bulawayo, 1965–66; Manchester Royal Infirmary, 1967–68; Tutor in Medicine, Univ. of Manchester, 1969–70; Registrar, Hammersmith Hosp., 1970–72; Sen. Res. Associate, Univ. of Newcastle, 1972–75; Sen. Registrar in Medicine, Durham, 1975–76; MRC Travelling Fellow, Liège, 1976–77; Consultant Physician, Newcastle Gen. Hosp. and Sen. Lectr in Medicine, Univ. of Newcastle upon Tyne, 1977–94; Hon. Consultant Physician, Radcliffe Infirmary, Oxford, 1994–. *Publications:* (with P. D. Home) Diabetes and Endocrinology in Clinical Practice, 1991; (with R. I. S. Bayliss) Thyroid Disease: the facts, 2nd edn, 1991; (ed) Rationing of Health Care in Medicine, 1993. *Recreation:* walking. *Address:* Coppermill, Church Lane, Weston on the Green, Bicester, Oxon OX6 8QS. *T:* Bicester (01869) 350691. *Club:* Athenæum.

TUNC, Prof. André Robert; Croix de Guerre 1940; Officier de la Légion d'Honneur 1984; Professor, University of Paris, since 1958; *b* 3 May 1917; *s* of Gaston Tunc and Gervaise Letourneur; *m* 1941, Suzanne Fortin. *Educ:* Law Sch., Paris. LLB 1937, LLM 1941. Agrégé des Facultés de Droit, 1943. Prof., Univ. of Grenoble, 1943–47; Counsellor, Internat. Monetary Fund, 1947–50; Prof., Univ. of Grenoble, 1950–58; Legal Adviser, UN Economic Commn for Europe, 1957–58. Hon. Doctorates: Free Univ. of Brussels, 1958; Cath. Univ. of Louvain, 1968; LLD Cambridge, 1986; DCL: Oxford, 1970; Stockholm, 1978; Geneva, 1984; Gent, 1986; Saarbrück, 1988; MA Cantab, 1972; Corr. FBA (London), 1974; Corresp. Fellow, Royal Acad. of Belgium, 1978; Foreign Member: Royal Acad. of the Netherlands, 1980; Amer. Acad. of Arts and Scis; Istituto Lombardo, 1993. Officier de l'Ordre d'Orange-Nassau, 1965. *Publications:* Le contrat de garde, 1941; Le particulier au service de l'ordre public, 1942; (with Suzanne Tunc) Le Système constitutionnel des Etats-Unis d'Amérique, 2 vols, 1953, 1954; (with Suzanne Tunc) Le droit des Etats-Unis d'Amérique, 1955; (with François Givord) (tome 8) Le louage: Contrats civils, du Traité pratique de droit civil français de Planiol et Ripert, 2nd edn 1956; Traité théorique et pratique de la responsabilité civile de Henri et Léon Mazeaud, vols, 1957, 1958, 1960, 5th edn, and 6th edn (Vol. I) 1965; Les Etats-Unis—comment ils sont gouvernés, 1958, 3rd edn 1974; Dans un monde qui souffre, 1962, 4th edn 1968; Le droit des Etats-Unis (Que sais-je?), 1964, 5th edn 1989; La sécurité routière, 1965; Le droit anglais des sociétés anonymes, 1971, 3rd edn 1987; Traffic Accident Compensation: Law and Proposals (Internat. Encycl. of Comparative Law, Vol. XI: Torts, chap. 14), 1971; Introd. to Vol. XI: Torts (Internat. Encycl. of Comparative Law), 1974; La cour judiciaire suprême: une enquête comparative, 1978; La responsabilité civile, 1981, 2nd edn 1990; Pour une loi sur les accidents de la circulation, 1981; Le droit américain des sociétés anonymes, 1985; Jalons, dits et écrits d'André Tunc, 1991; articles in various legal periodicals. *Address:* 112 rue de Vaugirard, 75006 Paris, France.

TUNNELL, Hugh James Oliver Redvers; HM Diplomatic Service, retired; Ambassador to Bahrain, 1992–95; *b* 31 Dec. 1935; *s* of Heather and Oliver Tunnell; *m* 1st, 1958, Helen Miller (marr. diss.); three *d*; 2nd, 1979, Margaret, *d* of Sir Richard John Randall; two *d. Educ:* Chatham House Grammar School, Ramsgate. Royal Artillery, 1954–56. FO, 1956–59; Amman, 1959–62; Middle East Centre for Arab Studies, 1962–63; served FO, Aden, CRO, Damascus and FO, 1964–67; UK Delegn to European Communities, 1968–70; FCO, 1970–72; Kuwait, 1972–76; FCO, 1976–79; Head of Chancery, Muscat, 1979–83; Consul Gen., Brisbane, 1983–88; Comr-Gen., British Section, EXPO 88, 1987–88; Consul Gen., Jedda, 1989–92. *Recreations:* water sports, tennis. *Address:* c/o Foreign and Commonwealth Office, SW1A 2AH. *Clubs:* Royal Over-Seas League; Brisbane (Brisbane).

TUNNICLIFFE, Denis, CBE 1993; Managing Director, London Underground Ltd, since 1988; Member of Board, London Transport, since 1993; *b* 17 Jan. 1943; *s* of Arthur Harold and Ellen Tunnicliffe; *m* 1968, Susan Dale; two *s. Educ:* Henry Cavendish Sch., Derby; University Coll. London (State Schol.; BSc (Special)); College of Air Training, Hamble. Pilot, BOAC, 1966–72; British Airways, 1972–86; Chief Exec., International Leisure Group, Aviation Div., 1986–88. Councillor, Royal Bor. of New Windsor, 1971–75; Councillor, Royal County of Berkshire, 1974–77; Dist Councillor, Bracknell, 1979–83. FCIT 1990; CIMgt (CBIM 1991). *Recreations:* flying, boating, church, travelling. *Address:* London Underground Ltd, 55 Broadway, SW1H 0BD. *Clubs:* Royal Air Force, Royal Automobile.

TUOHY, John Francis, (Frank Tuohy); FRSL 1965; novelist; short story writer; *b* 2 May 1925; *s* of late Patrick Gerald Tuohy and Dorothy Marion (*née* Annandale). *Educ:* Stowe Sch.; King's College, Cambridge. Prof. of English Language and Literature, Univ. of São Paulo, 1950–56; Contract Prof., Jagiellonian Univ., Cracow, Poland, 1958–60; Visiting Professor: Waseda Univ., Tokyo, 1964–67; Rikkyo Univ., Tokyo, 1983–89; Writer-in-Residence, Purdue Univ., Indiana, 1970–71, 1976, 1980. Hon. DLitt Purdue, 1987. Bennett Award, Hudson Review, 1994. *Publications:* The Animal Game, 1957; The Warm Nights of January, 1960; The Admiral and the Nuns, short stories (Katherine Mansfield Memorial Prize), 1962; The Ice Saints (James Tait Black and Geoffrey Faber Memorial Prizes), 1964; Portugal, 1970; Fingers in the Door, short stories (E. M. Forster Meml Award, 1972), 1970; Yeats: a biographical study, 1976; Live Bait, short stories, 1978 (Heinemann Award, 1979); Collected Stories, 1984. *Recreation:* travel. *Address:* Shatwell Cottage, Yarlington, near Wincanton, Somerset BA9 8DL.

TUOHY, Thomas, CBE 1969; Managing Director, British Nuclear Fuels Ltd, 1971–73; *b* 7 Nov. 1917; *s* of late Michael Tuohy and Isabella Tuohy, Cobh, Eire; *m* 1949, Lilian May Barnes (*d* 1971); one *s* one *d. Educ:* St Cuthberts Grammar Sch., Newcastle; Reading Univ. (BSc). Chemist in various Royal Ordnance Factories, 1939–46. Manager: Health Physics, Springfields Nuclear Fuel Plant, Dept Atomic Energy, 1946; Health Physics, Windscale Plutonium Plant, 1949; Plutonium Piles and Metal Plant, Windscale, 1950; Works Manager: Springfields, 1952; Windscale, UKAEA, 1954; Windscale and Calder Hall: Dep. Gen. Manager, 1957; Gen. Manager, 1958; Man. Dir, Production Gp, UKAEA, 1964–71. Managing Director: Urenco, 1973–74; Vorsitzender der Geschäftsführung Centec GmbH, 1973–74; Dep. Chm., Centec, 1973–74; former Dir, Centec-Algermann Co. Mem. Council, Internat. Inst. for Management of Technology, 1971–73. *Publications:* various technical papers on reactor operation and plutonium manufacture. *Recreations:* gardening, travel. *Address:* Ingleberg, Beckermet, Cumbria CA21 2XX. *T:* Beckermet (01946) 841226.

TUPMAN, William Ivan, DPhil; Director General of Internal Audit, Ministry of Defence, 1974–81; *b* 22 July 1921; *s* of Leonard and Elsie Tupman; *m* 1945, Barbara (*née* Capel); two *s* one *d. Educ:* Queen Elizabeth's Hosp., Bristol; New Coll., Oxford (Exhibnr; MA, DPhil). Served War, 1942–45, RN (Lieut RNVR). Entered Admiralty as Asst Principal, 1948; Private Sec. to Parly Sec., 1950–52; Principal, 1952; Civil Affairs Adviser to C-in-C, Far East Station, 1958–61; Private Sec. to First Lord of the Admiralty, 1963; Asst Sec., 1964; IDC, 1967.

TUPPER, Sir Charles Hibbert, 5th Bt *cr* 1888, of Armdale, Halifax, Nova Scotia; retired; *b* 4 July 1930; *o s* of Sir James Macdonald Tupper, 4th Bt, formerly Assistant Commissioner, Royal Canadian Mounted Police, and of Mary Agnes Jean Collins; *S* father, 1967; *m* (marr. diss. 1976); one *s. Heir: s* Charles Hibbert Tupper [*b* 10 July 1964; *m* 1987, Elizabeth Ann Heaslip; one *d*]. *Address:* 955 Marine Drive, Apt 1101, West Vancouver, BC V7T 1A9, Canada.

TURBERVILLE, Geoffrey, MA; Principal, Leulumoega High School, Samoa, 1959–62, (retired); *b* 31 Mar. 1899; *o s* of A. E. Turberville, FCA, Stroud Green, London; *m* Jane Campbell Lawson. *Educ:* Westminster Sch. (King's Scholar); Trinity College, Cambridge (Exhibitioner). 2nd Lieut, Queen's Royal West Surrey Regt, 1917–19; Senior Classical Master, Liverpool Collegiate School, 1921–25; Senior Classical Master, Epsom College, 1925–30; Headmaster of Eltham College, 1930–59. Chm. Dorset Congregational Assoc., 1970–71. *Publications:* Cicero and Antony; Arva Latina II; Translation into Latin. *Address:* 4 Spiller's House, Shaftesbury, Dorset SP7 8EP.

TURBOTT, Sir Ian (Graham), Kt 1968; CMG 1962; CVO 1966; Foundation Chancellor, University of Western Sydney, since 1989; *b* Whangarei, New Zealand, 9 March 1922; *s* of late Thomas Turbott and late E. A. Turbott, both of New Zealand; *m* 1952, Nancy Hall Lantz, California, USA; three *d. Educ:* Takapuna Grammar School, Auckland, NZ; Auckland University; Jesus College, Cambridge; London University. NZ Forces (Army), 1940–46: Solomon Is area and 2 NZEF, Italy. Colonial Service (Overseas Civil Service): Western Pacific, Gilbert and Ellice Is, 1948–56; Colonial Office, 1956–58; Administrator of Antigua, The West Indies, 1958–64; also Queen's Representative under new constitution, 1960–64; Administrator of Grenada and Queen's Representative, 1964–67; Governor of Associated State of Grenada, 1966–68. Partner, Spencer Stuart and Associates Worldwide, 1973–84; Chairman: Spencer Stuart and Associates Pty Ltd, 1970–84; Chloride Batteries Australia Ltd, 1978–85; TNT Security Pty Ltd; Stuart Brooke Consultants Pty Ltd, Sydney, 1974–82; 2MMM Broadcasting Co. Pty Ltd; Melbourne F/M Radio Pty Ltd, 1986–93; Penrith Lakes Develt Corp., 1980–; Essington Ltd, 1984–89; New World Pictures (Aust.) Ltd, 1986–89; Triple M FM Radio Group, 1986–93; Cape York Space Agency Ltd, 1987–89; Chm., Hoyts Media Ltd, 1991–93; Dir, Hoyts Entertainment Ltd, 1990–93; Dep. Chm., Adv. Bd, Amer. Internat. Underwriting (Aust.) Ltd; Director: Standard Chartered Bank Australia Ltd, 1980–91; Capita Financial Gp, 1979–91; Newcastle F/M P/L, 1983–94. Chairman: Internat. Piano Competition Ltd, Sydney, 1977–84; Duke of Edinburgh's Award Scheme, NSW, 1984–. Governor, NSW Conservatorium of Music, 1974–89. FRSA. Hon Consul for Cook Is in Australia, 1995. JP. Hon. DLitt Western Sydney, 1993. Silver Jubilee Medal, 1977. Holds 1939–45 Star, Pacific Star, Italy Star, Defence Medal, War Medal, New Zealand Service Medal. CStJ 1964. *Publications:* various technical and scientific, 1948–51, in Jl of Polynesian Society (on Pacific area). *Recreations:* boating, farming, cricket, fishing. *Address:* 27 Amiens Road, Clontarf, NSW 2093, Australia; 38 MacMasters Parade, MacMasters Beach, NSW 2251, Australia. *Clubs:* Australian (Sydney); Royal Sydney Yacht.

TURCAN, Henry Watson; a Recorder of the Crown Court, since 1985; *b* 22 Aug. 1941; *s* of late Henry Hutchison Turcan and Lilias Cheyne; *m* 1969, Jane Fairrie Blair; one *s* one *d. Educ:* Rugby School, Trinity College, Oxford (BA, MA). Called to the Bar, Inner Temple, 1965; Bencher, 1992. Legal Assessor to General Optical Council, 1983. *Recreations:* hunting, shooting, fishing, golf. *Address:* 4 Paper Buildings, Temple, EC4Y 7EX. *T:* 0171–353 3420. *Clubs:* Royal and Ancient Golf (St Andrews); Hon. Company of Edinburgh Golfers (Muirfield).

TURCAN, William James; Chief Executive, Harrisons & Crosfield plc, since 1994; *b* 4 Jan. 1943; *m* 1967, Elisabeth Margaret Stewart; three *s* one *d. Educ:* Rugby Sch.; Trinity Coll., Oxford (MA). ACA. Binder Hamlyn, 1965–70; Pauls Malt, 1970–86; Finance Dir, Pauls plc, 1986–88; Finance Dir, Harrisons & Crosfield, 1988–94. Bd Mem., Glenrothes New Town Develt Corp., 1983–86. *Address:* (office) One Great Tower Street, EC3R 5AH. *T:* 0171–711 1400.

TURCOTTE, His Eminence Cardinal Jean-Claude; *see* Montreal, Archbishop of, (RC).

TURECK, Rosalyn; concert artist; conductor; writer; teacher; *b* Chicago, 14 Dec. 1914; *d* of Samuel Tureck and Monya (*née* Lipson); *m* 1964, George Wallingford Downs (*d* 1964). *Educ:* Juilliard Sch. of Music, NY. Member Faculty: Philadelphia Conservatory of Music, 1935–42; Mannes School, NYC, 1940–44; Juilliard School of Music, 1943–53; Columbia University, NY, 1953–55; Professor of Music: Univ. of California, San Diego, 1966–72; Univ. of Maryland, 1981–85; Yale Univ., 1991–93. Vis. Prof., Washington Univ., 1963–64; Visiting Fellow: St Hilda's Coll., Oxford, 1974 (Hon. Life Fellow, 1974); Wolfson Coll., Oxford, 1975; Lectures: educnl instns in USA, S America, Canada and Europe; Royal Instn, and Boston Univ., 1993; Smithsonian Instn, 1994; Regents' Lectr, Univ. of Calif, 1995. Has appeared as soloist and conductor of leading orchestras in US, Europe and Israel, and toured US, Canada, South Africa, South America; début solo recital, Chicago, 1924; European début, Copenhagen, 1947, since when has toured extensively in Europe, and played at festivals in Edinburgh, Venice, Holland, Wexford, Schaffhausen, Bath, Brussels World Fair, Glyndebourne, Barcelona, Puerto Rico, etc, and in major Amer. festivals including Mostly Mozart Festival, NY, Caramoor, Detroit, etc; extensive tours: India, Australia and Far East, 1971; S America, 1986–; Spain, 1986–. Founder: Composers of Today, 1949–53; also Director: Tureck Bach Players, London, 1957 (conductor, 1960–72), NY, 1981; Internat. Bach Soc., Inst. for Bach Studies, 1968; Tureck Bach Inst. Inc., 1981; Tureck Bach Res. Foundn, Oxford, 1994. Hon. Member, GSMD, London, 1961; Member: Royal Musical Assoc., London; Inc. Soc. of Musicians, London; Amer. Musicological Soc; Amer. Br., New Bach Soc. Editor, Tureck/Bach Urtext series, 1979–. Numerous recordings. Hon. Dr of Music, Colby Coll., USA, 1964; Hon. DMus: Roosevelt Univ., 1968; Wilson Coll., 1968; Oxon, 1977; Music and Arts Inst. of San Francisco, 1987. Has won several awards. Officer's Cross, Order of Merit, Fed. Republic of Germany, 1979. *Television films:* Fantasy and Fugue: Rosalyn Tureck plays Bach, 1972; Rosalyn Tureck plays on Harpsichord and Organ, 1977; Joy of Bach, 1978; Bach and Tureck at Ephesus, 1985; also many appearances, US. *Publications:* An Introduction to the Performance of Bach, 1960; Authenticity, 1994; (contrib.) Music and Mathematics, 1995; edited: Bach: Sarabande, C minor, 1950; (transcribed) Paganini: Moto Perpetuo, 1950; (Urtext and performance edns) Bach: Italian Concerto, 1983, 2nd edn 1991; J. S. Bach, Lute Suite in E minor, set for classical guitar, 1984, Lute Suite in C minor, 1985; Authenticity, 1994; many articles. *Address:* c/o Lies Askonas, 6 Henrietta Street, WC2E 8LA; Tureck Bach Research Foundation, Windrush House, Davenant Road, Oxford OX2 8BX; Tureck Bach Institute, 215 E 68th Street, New York, NY 10021, USA. *Club:* Century (NY).

TURING, Sir John Dermot, 12th Bt *cr* 1638 (NS), of Foveran, Aberdeenshire; solicitor; *b* 26 Feb. 1961; *s* of John Ferrier Turing (*d* 1983) and of Beryl Mary Ada, *d* of late Herbert Vaughan Hann; *S* kinsman, Sir John Leslie Turing, 11th Bt, 1987; *m* 1986, Nicola J., *er d* of M. D. Simmonds; two *s*. *Educ:* Sherborne School, Dorset; King's College, Cambridge; New College, Oxford. *Heir: s* John Malcolm Ferrier Turing, *b* 5 Sept. 1988. *Address:* 55 Shirley Avenue, Southampton SO15 5NH.

TURMEAU, Prof. William Arthur, CBE 1989; PhD; FRSE; CEng, FIMechE; Principal and Vice-Chancellor, Napier University, 1992–94 (Principal, Napier College, subseq. Napier Polytechnic of Edinburgh, 1982–92); *b* 19 Sept. 1929; *s* of Frank Richard Turmeau and Catherine Lyon Linklater; *m* 1957, Margaret Moar Burnett, MA, BCom; one *d*. *Educ:* Stromness Acad., Orkney; Univ. of Edinburgh (BSc); Moray House Coll. of Educn; Heriot-Watt Univ. (PhD). FIMechE, CEng, 1971; FRSE 1990. Royal Signals, 1947–49. Research Engr, Northern Electric Co. Ltd, Montreal, 1952–54; Mechanical Engr, USAF, Goose Bay, Labrador, 1954–56; Contracts Manager, Godfrey Engrg Co. Ltd, Montreal, 1956–61; Lectr, Bristo Technical Inst., 1962–64; Napier College: Lectr and Sen. Lectr, 1964–68; Head, Dept of Mechanical Engrg, 1968–75; Asst Principal and Dean, Faculty of Technology, 1975–82. Member: Scottish Econ. Council, 1987–; CICHE, British Council, 1982–92; CVCP, 1992–94 (Mem., Cttee of Dirs of Polytechnics, 1982–92); Standing Conf. of Rectors and Vice-Chancellors of European Univs, 1990–94; Cttee of Scottish Univ. Principals, 1992–94; Council for Industry and Higher Educn, 1992–; Scottish Div. Cttee, Inst. of Dirs, 1992–94. Mem. Court, Edinburgh Acad., 1993–. Dr *hc* Edinburgh, 1992. *Publications:* various papers relating to higher educn. *Recreations:* modern jazz, Leonardo da Vinci. *Address:* 71 Morningside Park, Edinburgh EH10 5EZ. *T:* 0131–447 4639. *Club:* Caledonian.

TURNAGE, Mark-Anthony; composer; *b* 1960. *Educ:* Royal College of Music. Mendelssohn Scholar, Tanglewood, USA, 1983. Composer in Residence, Nat. Centre for Orchestral Studies, 1985–86; Composer in Association with the City of Birmingham Symphony Orchestra, 1989–93. *Compositions include: stage:* Greek, 1988 (BMW prizes for best opera and best libretto, Munich Biennale, 1988); Killing Time, 1991; *choral:* One Hand in Brooklyn Heights, 1986; Leaving, 1990; *vocal:* Lament for a Hanging Man, 1983; Greek Suite, 1989; Some Days, 1989; Her Anxiety, 1991; *orchestral:* Night Dances, 1981; Gross Intrusion, 1987; Three Screaming Popes, 1989; Momentum, 1991; Drowned Out, 1993; Your Rockaby (saxophone concerto), 1994; *ensemble:* After Dark, 1983; On All Fours, 1985; Kai, 1990; Three Farewells, 1990; Are You Sure?, 1990; *instrumental:* Sleep on, 1992. *Address:* c/o Schott, 48 Great Marlborough Street, W1V 2BN. *T:* 0171–437 1246.

TURNBERG, Sir Leslie Arnold, Kt 1994; MD; FRCP; Professor of Medicine, University of Manchester, since 1973; Hon. Consultant Physician, Salford Health Authority, since 1973; President, Royal College of Physicians, since 1992; *b* 22 March 1934; *s* of Hyman and Dora Turnberg; *m* 1968, Edna Barme; one *s* one *d*. *Educ:* Stand Grammar Sch., Whitefield; Univ. of Manchester (MB, ChB 1957, MD 1966). MRCP 1961, FRCP 1973; FRCPE 1993; FRCP(I); FRCPSGlas; FCPS(Pak). Junior medical posts: Manchester Jewish Hosp.; Northern Hosp.; Ancoats Hosp.; Manchester Royal Infirmary, 1957–61 and 1964–66; Registrar, UCH, 1961–64; Lectr, Royal Free Hosp., 1967; Res. Fellow, Univ. of Texas South-Western Med. Sch., Dallas, Texas, 1968; University of Manchester: Lectr, then Sen. Lectr, 1968–73; Dean, Fac. of Medicine, 1986–89. Member: Salford HA, 1974–81 and 1990–92; NW RHA, 1986–89. Royal College of Physicians: Mem. Council, 1989–; Chairman: Educn Cttee, 1990–92; Wking Gp on Communication, 1991–92; British Society of Gastroenterology: Mem. Council, 1989–; Chm., Res. Cttee, 1991–92; Pres., Med. Section, Manchester Med. Soc., 1992–93. Hon. FRACP; Hon. FFOM; Hon. FFPM; Hon. Fellow: Acad. of Medicine, Singapore; Coll. of Medicine, S Africa. *Publications:* Electrolyte and Water Transport Across Gastro-intestinal Epithelia, 1982; Clinical Gastroenterology, 1989; pubns on mechanisms of intestinal absorption and secretion in health and disease and on clinical gastroenterology. *Recreations:* reading, antiquarian books, walking, talking. *Address:* Department of Medicine, Hope Hospital, Salford M6 8HD. *T:* 0161–787 4363.

TURNBULL, Andrew, CB 1990; CVO 1992; Permanent Secretary, Department of the Environment, since 1994; *b* 21 Jan. 1945; *s* of Anthony and Mary Turnbull; *m* 1967, Diane Clarke; two *s*. *Educ:* Enfield Grammar Sch.; Christ's Coll., Cambridge (BA). ODI Fellow working as economist, Govt of Republic of Zambia, Lusaka, 1968–70; Asst Principal, HM Treasury, 1970; Principal, 1972; on secondment to staff of IMF, 1976–78; Asst Sec., HM Treasury, 1978; Private Sec. to the Prime Minister, 1983–85; Under Sec., 1985; Hd of Gen. Expenditure Policy Gp, HM Treasury, 1985–88; Principal Private Sec. to Prime Minister, 1988–92; Dep. Sec. (Public Finance), HM Treasury, 1992; Second Permanent Sec. (Public Expenditure), HM Treasury, 1993–94. *Recreations:* walking, running, opera. *Address:* Department of the Environment, 2 Marsham Street, SW1P 3EB. *Club:* Tottenham Hotspur.

TURNBULL, Rt. Rev. (Anthony) Michael (Arnold); *see* Durham, Bishop of.

TURNBULL, Ven. David Charles; Archdeacon of Carlisle, and Canon Residentiary, Carlisle Cathedral, since 1993; *b* 16 March 1944. *Educ:* Leeds Univ. (BA 1965); Chichester Theol Coll.; Sheffield Univ. (MEd 1992). Ordained deacon, 1969, priest, 1970; Curate of Jarrow, 1969–74; Vicar, Carlinghow, 1974–83; Vicar of Penistone, 1983–86, and Priest in charge of Thurlstone, 1985–86, Team Rector of Penistone and Thurlstone, 1986–93; RD of Barnsley, 1988–93. Hon. Canon, Wakefield, 1993. *Address:* 2 The Abbey, Carlisle CA3 8TZ. *T:* Carlisle (01228) 23026.

TURNBULL, Jeffrey Alan, CBE 1991; FEng 1992; FICE, FIHT; Consultant, Mott MacDonald Group Ltd, since 1994 (Chairman and Director, 1989–94); *b* 14 Aug. 1934; *s* of Alan Edward Turnbull and Alice May (*née* Slee); *m* 1957, Beryl (*née* Griffith); two *s* one *d*. *Educ:* Newcastle upon Tyne Royal Grammar Sch.; Liverpool Coll. of Technology. DipTE 1964; CEng; FIHT 1966; FICE 1973. National Service, RE, 1956–58. Jun. Engr, Cheshire CC, 1951–55; Engr, Herefordshire CC, 1955–59; Resident Engr, Berks CC, 1959–66; Mott Hay & Anderson, 1966–: Chief Designer (Roads), 1968; Associate, 1973; Dir, Mott Hay & Anderson International Ltd, 1975–88; Dir, Mott Hay & Anderson, 1978–88; Dir, 1983–88, Chief Exec., 1987–88, Mott Hay & Anderson Holdings Ltd. *Publication:* (contrib.) Civil Engineer's Reference Book, 4th edn 1988. *Recreations:* walking, France. *Address:* c/o Mott MacDonald Group Ltd, 20/26 Wellesley Road, Croydon, Surrey CR9 2UL. *T:* 0181–686 5041; 63 Higher Drive, Banstead, Surrey SM1 1PW. *T:* 0181–393 1054. *Club:* Royal Automobile.

TURNBULL, John William; Chief Executive, Hereford and Worcester County Council, since 1993; *b* 12 May 1934; *s* of Henry W. Turnbull and Janet Turnbull; *m* 1956, Sheila Batey; two *d*. *Educ:* Westminster Coll.; LSE (BScEcon); London Inst. of Educn (MA, DipEd). Teacher, 1957–68; Lectr, 1968–70; Educn Officer, 1970–76; Dep. County Educn Officer, Leics, 1977–83; County Educn Officer, Hereford and Worcester, 1984–93. FRSA. *Publications:* articles on educn and administration. *Recreations:* reading, playing piano. *Address:* County Hall, Spetchley Road, Worcester WR5 2NP.

TURNBULL, Malcolm Bligh; Managing Director, Turnbull & Partners Ltd, Investment Bankers, Sydney, since 1987; Principal, Turnbull & Co., Solicitors, since 1987; *b* 24 Oct. 1954; *s* of late Bruce Bligh Turnbull and Coral (*née* Lansbury); *m* 1980, Lucinda Mary Forrest Hughes; one *s* one *d*. *Educ:* Sydney Grammar Sch.; Sydney Univ. (BA, LLB); Brasenose Coll., Oxford (Rhodes Schol. (NSW) 1978, BCL 1980). Journalist, Nation Review, 1975; Political Correspondent: TCN–9, Sydney, 1976; The Bulletin, 1977–78; Journalist, Sunday Times, London, 1979; admitted to NSW Bar, 1980; Barrister, Sydney, 1980–82; Gen. Counsel and Secretary, Consolidated Press Holdings Ltd, 1983–85; Partner, Turnbull McWilliam, Solicitors, Sydney, 1986–87; Jt Man. Dir, Whitlam Turnbull & Co. Ltd, Investment Bankers, Sydney, 1987–90. Chairman: Republic Adv. Cttee, 1993–; Australian Republican Movement, 1993– (Dir, 1991–). Chm., Axiom Forest Resources Ltd, 1991–92; Director: Muswellbrook Energy and Minerals Ltd, 1985–87; Communications and Entertainment Ltd, 1986–87; Nine Network Australia Ltd, 1990; Star Mining Corp. NL, 1993–; Sydney Grammar School Foundn Ltd, 1988–. Chm., Centre for Immunology, St Vincent's Hosp., Sydney, 1991–93. *Publications:* The Spycatcher Trial, 1988; The Reluctant Republic, 1993. *Recreations:* riding, swimming. *Address:* Turnbull & Partners Ltd, 8th Floor, 1 Chifley Square, Sydney, NSW 2000, Australia. *T:* (2) 2235899. *Clubs:* Australian, Tattersall's, University and Schools (Sydney); Athenæum (Philadelphia).

TURNBULL, Rt. Rev. Michael; *see* Durham, Bishop of.

TURNBULL, Sir Richard (Gordon), GCMG 1962 (KCMG 1958, CMG 1953); *b* 7 July 1909; *s* of Richard Francis Turnbull; *m* 1939, Beatrice (*d* 1986), *d* of John Wilson, Glasgow; two *s* one *d*. *Educ:* University College School, London; University College, London; Magdalene Coll., Cambridge. Colonial Administrative Service, Kenya: District Officer, 1931–48; Provincial Comr, 1948–53; Minister for Internal Security and Defence, 1954; Chief Secretary, Kenya, 1955–58; Governor and C-in-C, Tanganyika, 1958–61; Governor-General and Commander-in-Chief, 1961–62; Chairman, Central Land Board, Kenya, 1963–64; High Commissioner for Aden and the Protectorate of South Arabia, 1965–67. Fellow of University College, London; Hon. Fellow, Magdalene College, Cambridge, 1970–. KStJ 1958. *Address:* Friars Neuk, Jedburgh, Roxburghshire TD8 6BN. *T:* Jedburgh (01835) 62589.

TURNER, family name of **Baron Netherthorpe** and **Baroness Turner of Camden.**

TURNER OF CAMDEN, Baroness *cr* 1985 (Life Peer), of Camden in Greater London; **Muriel Winifred Turner;** *b* 18 Sept. 1927; *m* 1955, Reginald Thomas Frederick Turner, MC, DFC. Asst Gen. Sec., ASTMS, 1970–87. Member: Occupational Pensions Board, 1978–93; Central Arbitration Cttee, 1980–90; TUC General Council, 1981–87; Equal Opportunities Commission, 1982–88. Junior Spokesperson on Social Security, 1986–, Principal Opposition Spokesperson on Employment, 1988–, H of L. Chm., Ombudsman Council, PIA, 1994–. Hon. LLD Leicester, 1991. *Address:* House of Lords, SW1A 0PW.

TURNER, Adair; *see* Turner, J. A.

TURNER, Alan B.; *see* Brooke Turner.

TURNER, Amédée Edward, QC 1976; *b* 26 March 1929; *s* of Frederick William Turner and Ruth Hempson; *m* 1960, Deborah Dudley Owen; one *s* one *d*. *Educ:* Temple Grove, Heron's Ghyll, Sussex; Dauntsey Sch., Wilts; Christ Church, Oxford (MA). Called to Bar, Inner Temple, 1954; practised patent bar, 1954–57; Associate, Kenyon & Kenyon, patent attorneys, NY, 1957–60; London practice, 1960–; Sen. Counsel, APCO Europe, Brussels, 1995–; of Counsel, Oppenheimer Wolff and Donnelly, Brussels, 1994–. Contested (C) Norwich N, gen. elections, 1964, 1966, 1970. European Parliament: MEP (C) Suffolk, 1979–94; contested (C) Suffolk and SW Norfolk, 1994; Hon. MEP, 1994; EDG spokesman on energy res. and technol., 1984–89; Chief Whip, EDG, 1989–92; joined EPP Gp, 1992; Mem., EPP Gp Bureau, 1992–94; Chm., Civil Liberties and Internal Affairs Cttee, 1992–94; Vice Chm., Legal Cttee, 1979–84; Member: Economic and Monetary Cttee, 1979–84; ACP Jt Cttee, 1980–94; Transport Cttee, 1981–84; Energy Cttee, 1984–94; Legal Affairs Cttee, 1984–89. *Publications:* The Law of Trade Secrets, 1962, supplement, 1968; The Law of the New European Patent, 1979; many Conservative Party study papers on defence, oil and Middle East. *Recreations:* garden design, art deco collection, fish keeping, oil painting, Annexe 3A Royal Festival Hall. *Address:* 3 Montrose Place, SW1X 7DU. *T:* 0171–235 2894, 0171–235 3191, *Fax:* 0171–235 9237; 250 Avenue Louise, Brussels 1050, Belgium. *T:* (2) 6260072, *Fax:* (2) 6260075; 1 Essex Court, Temple, EC4Y 9AR. *T:* 0171–936 3030; The Barn, Westleton, Saxmundham, Suffolk IP17 3AN. *T:* Westleton (01728) 648235; La Combe de la Boissière, St Maximin, Uzès 30700, France. *Clubs:* Carlton, Coningsby, United & Cecil.

TURNER, Ven. Antony Hubert Michael; Archdeacon of the Isle of Wight, since 1986; *b* 17 June 1930; *s* of Frederick George and Winifred Frances Turner; *m* 1956, Margaret Kathleen (*née* Phillips); one *s* two *d*. *Educ:* Royal Liberty Grammar School, Romford, Essex; Tyndale Hall, Bristol. FCA 1963 (ACA 1952); DipTh (Univ. of London), 1956. Deacon, 1956; Priest, 1957; Curate, St Ann's, Nottingham, 1956–59; Curate in Charge, St Cuthbert's, Cheadle, Dio. Chester, 1959–62; Vicar, Christ Church, Macclesfield, 1962–68; Home Sec., Bible Churchmen's Missionary Soc., 1968–74; Vicar of St Jude's, Southsea, 1974–86; RD of Portsmouth, 1979–84. Church Commissioner, 1983–93. Vice Chm., C of E Pensions Bd, 1988–. *Recreations:* photography, caravanning. *Address:* 3 Beech Grove, Ryde, Isle of Wight PO33 3AN. *T:* Isle of Wight (01983) 565522.

TURNER, Air Vice-Marshal Cameron Archer, CB 1968; CBE 1960 (OBE 1947); Royal New Zealand Air Force, retired; *b* Wanganui, NZ, 29 Aug. 1915; *s* of James Oswald Turner and Vida Cathrine Turner; *m* 1941, Josephine Mary, *d* of George Richardson; two *s*. *Educ:* New Plymouth Boys' High Sch.; Victoria University of Wellington; Massey Univ., Palmerston North, NZ. CEng, FIEE, FRAeS. Commn RAF, 1936–39; commn RNZ Air Force, 1940; served War of 1939–45, UK, NZ, and Pacific; comd RNZAF Station Nausori, Fiji, 1944; comd RNZAF Station, Guadalcanal, Solomon Islands, 1944; Director of Signals, 1945–47; psa 1947; RNZAF Liaison Officer, Melbourne, Australia, 1948–50; comd RNZAF Station, Taieri, NZ, 1950–52; Director of Organization, HQ, RNZAF, 1953–56; comd RNZAF Station Ohakea, NZ, 1956–58; Asst Chief of Air Staff, HQ, RNZAF, 1958; Air Member for Personnel, HQ, RNZAF, 1959; idc 1960; AOC HQ, RNZAF, London, 1961–63; Air Member for Supply, HQ, RNZAF, 1964–65; Chief of Air Staff, HQ RNZAF, 1966–69. Dir, NZ Inventions Develt Authority, 1969–76. Pres., RNZAF Assoc., 1972–81. *Recreations:* fishing, Polynesian and religious studies. *Address:* 37a Parkvale Road, Wellington 5, New Zealand. *T:* (4) 4766063. *Clubs:* Wellington (Wellington); Taranaki (New Plymouth).

TURNER, Prof. Cedric Edward, CBE 1987; FEng 1989; Emeritus Professor and Senior Research Fellow, Imperial College, London, since 1991; *b* 5 Aug. 1926; *s* of Charles

Turner and Mabel Evelyn (*née* Berry); *m* 1953, Margaret Dorothy (*née* Davies); one *s* two *d*. *Educ:* Brockenhurst Grammar Sch.; University Coll., Southampton (now Univ. of Southampton) (BScEng); DScEng, PhD London. CEng, FIMechE. Res. Asst, Imperial Coll., 1948–52; Academic Staff, Imperial Coll., 1952–76 and 1979–: Prof. of Materials in Mech. Engrg, 1975–91; seconded NPL and Brit. Aerospace, 1976–78. Hon. Prof., Shenyang Inst. of Aeronautical Engrg, Shenyang, China, 1987; Leverhulme Emeritus Fellow, 1990–92. Silver Medal, Plastics Inst., 1963; James Clayton Prize, IMechE, 1981. *Publications:* Introduction to Plate and Shell Theory, 1965; (jtly) Post Yield Fracture Mechanics, 1979, 2nd edn 1984; contribs to Proc. Royal Soc., Proc. IMechE, Jl Strain Anal., Amer. Soc. Test & Mat., etc. *Recreations:* fracture mechanics, travel, reading. *Address:* The Corner House, 17 Meadway, Epsom, Surrey KT19 8JZ. *T:* Epsom (01372) 722989.

TURNER, Rev. Christopher Gilbert; Hon. Assistant Curate, Hook Norton with Great Rollright, Swerford and Wigginton, since 1992; Headmaster, Stowe School, 1979–89; *b* 23 Dec. 1929; *s* of late Theodore F. Turner, QC; *m* 1961, Lucia, *d* of late Prof. S. R. K. Glanville (Provost of King's Coll., Cambridge); one *s* one *d* (and one *d* decd). *Educ:* Winchester Coll. (Schol.); New Coll., Oxford (Exhibnr, MA); Oxford Ministry Course. Asst Master, Radley Coll., 1952–61; Senior Classics Master, Charterhouse, 1961–68; Headmaster, Dean Close Sch., 1968–79. Schoolmaster Student at Christ Church, Oxford, 1967. Foundation Member of Council, Cheltenham Colleges of Educn, 1968. Mem., HMC Cttee, 1974–75, 1987–88; Chm., Common Entrance Cttee, 1976–80; Chm. of Governors: Aldro Sch.; Elstree Sch.; Great Rollright Sch. Ordained deacon, 1992, priest, 1993. *Publications:* chapter on History, in Comparative Study of Greek and Latin Literature, 1969; chapter on Dean Close in the Seventies, in The First Hundred Years, 1986. *Recreations:* music (violin-playing), reading, walking, different forms of manual labour; OUBC 1951. *Address:* Rosemullion, High Street, Great Rollright, near Chipping Norton, Oxon OX7 5RQ. *T:* Chipping Norton (01608) 737359; 78 Vista Green, King's Norton, Birmingham B38 9PD. *T:* 0121–459 3863.

See also Hon. Sir M. J. Turner.

TURNER, Christopher John, CBE 1990 (OBE 1977); Managing Director, McLane (UK), since 1993; Vice President Development, McLane International, since 1994; *b* 17 Aug. 1933; *s* of Arthur Basil Turner and Joan Meddows (*née* Taylor); *m* 1961, Irene Philomena de Souza; two *d* (one *s* decd). *Educ:* Truro Cathedral Sch.; Jesus Coll., Cambridge (MA). Served RAF, Pilot Officer (Navigator), 1951–53. Tanganyika/Tanzania: Dist Officer, 1958–61; Dist Comr, 1961–62; Magistrate and Regional Local Courts Officer, 1962–64; Sec., Sch. Admin, 1964–69; Anglo-French Condominium of New Hebrides: Dist Agent, 1970–73; Develt Sec., 1973; Financial Sec., 1975; Chief Sec., 1977–80; Admin. Officer (Staff Planning), Hong Kong, 1980–82; Governor: Turks and Caicos Islands, 1982–87; Montserrat, WI, 1987–90. Manager, Internat. Business Develt, 1990–92, consultant on regl business develt, Santa Domingo, 1990–91, McLane (Wal Mart), Texas. Vanuatu Independence Medal, 1981. *Recreations:* ornithology, photography, diving, tropical gardening. *Address:* 98 Christchurch Road, Winchester SO23 9TE. *T:* Winchester (01962) 870775; (office) 22 Shirlock Road, NW3 2HS. *T:* 0171–284 4154.

TURNER, Colin Francis; Senior District Judge (formerly Senior Registrar), Family Division of High Court, 1988–91, retired (Registrar, 1971–88); *b* 11 April 1930; *s* of Sidney F. and Charlotte C. Turner; *m* 1951, Josephine Alma Jones; two *s* one *d*. *Educ:* Beckenham Grammar Sch.; King's Coll., London. LLB 1955. Entered Principal Probate Registry, 1949; District Probate Registrar, York, 1965–68. MBOU. *Publications:* (ed jtly) Rayden on Divorce, 9th, 11th, 12th and 13th edns, consulting editor to 14th edn; an editor of Supreme Court Practice, 1972–90; (jtly) Precedents in Matrimonial Causes and Ancillary Matters, 1985. *Recreations:* birding, fishing. *Address:* Lakers, Church Road, St Johns, Redhill, Surrey RH1 6QA. *T:* Redhill (01737) 761807.

TURNER, Colin William; Rector, Glasgow Academy, 1983–94; *b* 10 Dec. 1933; *s* of William and Joyce Turner; *m* 1958, Priscilla Mary Trickett; two *s* two *d*. *Educ:* Torquay Grammar Sch.; King's Coll., London (BSc; AKC). Edinburgh Academy: Asst Master, 1958–82; OC CCF, 1960–74; Head, Maths Dept, 1973–75; Housemaster, 1975–82. *Recreations:* mountaineering, gardening, local history. *Address:* Leat, Lower Down, Bovey Tracey, Devon TQ13 9LF. *T:* Bovey Tracey (01626) 832266.

TURNER, Sir Colin (William Carstairs), Kt 1993; CBE 1985; DFC 1944; President, The Colin Turner Group, International Media Representatives and Marketing Consultants, since 1988 (Chairman, 1985–88); *b* 4 Jan. 1922; *s* of late Colin C. W. Turner, Enfield; *m* 1949, Evelyn Mary, *d* of late Claude H. Buckard, Enfield; three *s* one *d*. *Educ:* Highgate Sch. Served War of 1939–45 with RAF, 1940–45, Air observer; S. Africa and E Africa, 223 Squadron; Desert Air Force, N. Africa, 1942–44; commissioned, 1943; invalided out as Flying Officer, 1945, after air crash; Chm., 223 Squadron Assoc., 1975–93; Pres., Enfield Br., 1979–93, Chm., Sheringham and Dist Br., 1994–, RAFA. Mem., Enfield Borough Council, 1956–58. Pres., Overseas Press and Media Association, 1965–67, Life Pres., 1982 (Hon. Secretary, 1967; Hon. Treasurer, 1974–82; Editor, Overseas Media Guide, 1968, 1969, 1970, 1971, 1972, 1973, 1974); Chm., PR Cttee, Commonwealth Press Union, 1970–87; Chm., Cons. Commonwealth and Overseas Council, 1976–82 (Dep. Chm. 1975); Vice-Pres., Cons. Foreign and Commonwealth Council, 1985–94; Mem., Nat. Exec., Cons. Party, 1946–53, 1968–73, 1976–82; Pres., Enfield North Cons. Assoc., 1984–93 (Chm., 1979–84); Chm., Cons. Europ. Constituency Council, London N, 1984–89. Contested (C) Enfield (East), 1950 and 1951; MP (C) Woolwich West, 1959–64. Editor, The Cholmeleian, 1982–95 (Pres., Old Cholmeleian Soc., 1985–86). *Recreations:* gardening, do-it-yourself, sailing, fishing. *Address:* The Thatched House, Balfour Road, West Runton, Norfolk NR27 9QJ. *T:* West Runton (01263) 837229.

TURNER, David Andrew; QC 1991; a Recorder of the Crown Court, since 1990; *b* 6 March 1947; *s* of James and Phyllis Turner; *m* 1978, Mary Christine Moffatt; two *s* one *d*. *Educ:* King George V Sch., Southport; Queens' Coll., Cambridge (MA, LLM). Called to the Bar, Gray's Inn, 1971, Asst Recorder, 1987–90. *Recreations:* squash, music. *Address:* Pearl Assurance House, Derby Square, Liverpool L2 9XX. *T:* 0151–236 7747. *Club:* Liverpool Racquet.

TURNER, Prof. David Warren, FRS 1973; Fellow of Balliol College, Oxford, 1967–94, now Emeritus Fellow; Professor of Electron Spectroscopy, Oxford, 1985–94, now Emeritus Professor; *b* 16 July 1927; *s* of Robert Cecil Turner and Constance Margaret (*née* Bonner); *m* 1954, Barbara Marion Fisher; one *s* one *d*. *Educ:* Westcliff High Sch.; Univ. of Exeter. MA, BSc, PhD, DIC. Lectr, Imperial Coll., 1958; Reader in Organic Chemistry, Imperial Coll., 1965; Oxford University: Lectr in Physical Chem., 1968; Reader in Physical Chemistry, 1978; Reader in Electron Spectroscopy, 1984. Lectures: Kahlbaum, Univ. of Basle, 1971; Van Geuns, Univ. of Amsterdam, 1974; Harkins, Chicago Univ., 1974; Kistiakowski, Harvard, 1979; Liversidge, RSC, 1981–82. Tilden Medal, Chemical Soc., 1967; Harrison Howe Award, Amer. Chem. Soc., 1973. Hon. DTech, Royal Inst., Stockholm, 1971; Hon. DPhil Basle, 1980. *Publications:* Molecular Photoelectron Spectroscopy, 1970; contrib. Phil. Trans Royal Soc., Proc. Royal Soc., Jl Chem. Soc., etc. *Recreations:* music, gardening, tinkering with gadgets. *Address:* Balliol College, Oxford OX1 3BJ.

TURNER, Dennis; MP (Lab) Wolverhampton South East, since 1987; *b* 26 Aug. 1942; *s* of Mary Elizabeth Peasley and Thomas Herbert Turner; *m* 1976, Patricia Mary Narroway; one *s* one *d*. *Educ:* Stonefield Secondary Modern School, Bilston; Bilston College of Further Education; Bilston Black Country. Office boy, salesman, market trader, steel worker, partner in worker co-operative. Mem. (Lab), Wolverhampton BC, 1966–86 (Chairman of Committees: Social Services, 1972–79; Educn, 1979–86; Econ. Develt, 1982–85; Housing, 1985–86). An Opposition Whip, 1993–. Mem., Educn Select Cttee, 1989–94; Chm., All-Party Gps on Further Educn and Housing Co-ops. *Address:* House of Commons, SW1A 0AA. *T:* 0171–219 4210; Ambleside, King Street, Bradley, Bilston, W Midlands WV14 8PQ. *Club:* Springvale Sports and Social (Bilston).

TURNER, Donald William, CEng, FICE; Director: Turner Associates, since 1986; Lydd Airport Group, since 1987; Atlantic Ltd, since 1994; *b* 17 Aug. 1925; *s* of William John Turner and Agnes Elizabeth Jane (*née* Bristow); *m* 1947, Patricia (*née* Stuteley); one *s* one *d*. *Educ:* Wanstead County High Sch.; Birmingham Univ. Served War, Army, 1943–45. Subseq. completed engrg trng in Britain; then took up post in Australia with Qld Railways, 1949. Left Qld, 1954; joined firm of UK consulting engrs and then worked in W Africa on rly and highway construction until 1960. Returned to UK, but remained with consultants until 1966, when joined BAA; Chief Engr, Heathrow Airport, 1970; Dir of Planning and Bd Mem., 1973; Dir of Privatisation, 1985–86; Chm., British Airports International, 1984–87. Dir, London Underground, 1985–93. *Address:* 18 Osborne Villas, Hove, Sussex BN3 2RE.

TURNER, Dudley Russell Flower, CB 1977; Secretary, Advisory, Conciliation and Arbitration Service, 1974–77; *b* 15 Nov. 1916; *s* of Gerald Flower Turner and Dorothy May Turner (*née* Gillard), Penang; *m* 1941, Sheila Isobel Stewart; one *s* one *d*. *Educ:* Whitgift Sch.; London Univ. (BA Hons). Served RA (Captain), 1940–46. Entered Ministry of Labour, 1935; HM Treasury, 1953–56; Principal Private Secretary to Minister of Labour, 1956–59; Assistant Secretary: Cabinet Office, 1959–62; Ministry of Labour, 1962–64, 1966; Under-Sec., Ministry of Labour, 1967; Asst Under-Sec. of State, Dept of Employment and Productivity, 1968–70; Under-Sec., Trng Div., 1970–72, Manpower Gen. Div., 1972–73, Dept of Employment; Sec., Commn on Industrial Relations, 1973–74. Imperial Defence Coll., 1965. Pres., East Surrey Decorative and Fine Arts Soc., 1986– (Chm., 1980–86). *Recreations:* music, gardening. *Address:* 9 Witherby Close, Croydon, Surrey CR0 5SU. *Club:* Civil Service.

TURNER, Captain Ernest John Donaldson, CBE 1968; DSO 1942; DSC 1941, RN retd; French Croix de Guerre 1941; Vice Lord-Lieutenant of Dunbartonshire, since 1986; *b* 21 March 1914; *s* of Ernest Turner (*d* 1916, HMS Hampshire) and Margaret Donaldson; *m* 1940, Catherine Chalmers; one *d*. *Educ:* Hermitage Academy; Glasgow Technical College; Royal Navy; sowc, IDC. Joined Merchant Navy as Cadet, 1930; RN from RNR, 1937; specialised in submarines, 1939; served in submarines, 1941–68; Commodore, Submarines, 1964; Captain i/c Clyde, 1965–68, during building of Faslane Polaris Base; officer recruitment (after retiring), 1968–80; PA to Chm., Whyte & Mackay Distillers Ltd, 1980–82. *Recreations:* hockey and golf, holidays abroad. *Address:* Langcroft, Buchanan Castle, Drymen, by Glasgow G63 0HX. *T:* Drymen (01360) 60274. *Clubs:* Victory; Buchanan Castle Golf.

TURNER, Rt. Rev. Geoffrey Martin; *see* Stockport, Bishop Suffragan of.

TURNER, Prof. Grenville, FRS 1980; Professor of Isotope Geochemistry, Manchester University, since 1988; *b* 1 Nov. 1936; *o s* of Arnold and Florence Turner, Todmorden, Yorks; *m* 1961, Kathleen, *d* of William and Joan Morris, Rochdale, Lancs; one *s* one *d*. *Educ:* Todmorden Grammar Sch.; St John's Coll., Cambridge (MA); Balliol Coll., Oxford (DPhil). Asst Prof., Univ. of Calif at Berkeley, 1962–64; Lectr, Sheffield Univ., 1964–74, Sen. Lectr, 1974–79, Reader, 1979–80, Prof. of Physics, 1980–88. Vis. Associate in Nuclear Geophysics, Calif Inst. of Technol., 1970–71. Mem. Council, Royal Soc., 1990–92. *Publications:* scientific papers. *Recreations:* photography, walking, theatre. *Address:* 42 Edgehill Road, Sheffield S7 1SP. *T:* (office) 0161–275 3800.

TURNER, Harry Edward; Managing Director, Television South West PLC, 1985–92; *b* 28 Feb. 1935; *s* of Harry Turner and Bessie Elizabeth Jay; *m* 1956, Carolyn Bird; one *s* one *d*. *Educ:* Sloane Grammar Sch., Chelsea. Served Middlesex Regt, Austria, 2nd Lieut, 1953–55. Sales Representative, Crosse & Blackwell Foods, 1955–56; Advertising Executive: Daily Herald, 1956–58; Kemsley Newspapers, 1958–60; Feature Writer and Advtsg Manager, TV International Magazine, 1960–62; Sales Dir, Westward Television, 1962–80; Dir of Marketing, Television South West, 1980–85; Dir, ITN, 1987–. Dir, Prince of Wales Trust, 1988–. FRSA 1986. *Publications:* The Man Who Could Hear Fishes Scream (short stories), 1978; The Gentle Art of Salesmanship, 1985; So You Want To Be a Sales Manager, 1987; Innocents in the Boardroom, 1991. *Recreations:* tennis, riding, skiing, literature, travel. *Address:* Four Acres, Lake Road, Deepcut, Surrey GU16 6RB. *T:* Deepcut (01252) 835527; Villa Providencia, 9 Flores de Calahonda, Marbella, Spain. *Clubs:* English-Speaking Union, White Elephant, Tramp.

TURNER, Rev. Professor Henry Ernest William, DD; Canon Residentiary, Durham Cathedral, 1950–73, now Canon Emeritus; Treasurer, 1956–73; Sub-Dean, 1959–73; Acting Dean, 1973; Van Mildert Professor of Divinity, Durham University, 1958–73, now Emeritus; *b* 14 Jan. 1907; *o s* of Henry Frederick Richard and Ethel Turner, Sheffield; *m* 1936, Constance Parker, *d* of Dr E. P. Haythornthwaite, Rowrah, Cumberland; two *s*. *Educ:* King Edward VII Sch., Sheffield; St John's Coll., Oxford; Wycliffe Hall, Oxford. MA 1933; BD 1940; DD 1955. Curate, Christ Church, Cockermouth, 1931–34; Curate, Holy Trinity, Wavertree, 1934–35; Fellow, Chaplain and Tutor, Lincoln Coll., Oxford, 1935–50; Chaplain, RAFVR, 1940–45; Librarian, Lincoln Coll., 1945–48; Senior Tutor, Lincoln Coll., 1948–50; Lightfoot Prof. of Divinity, Durham Univ., 1950–58. Select Preacher, Oxford Univ., 1950–51; Bampton Lectr, Oxford, 1954. Member: Anglican delegation to Third Conference of World Council of Churches, Lund, 1952; Doctrine Commn of the Church of England, 1967–76; formerly Mem., Anglican-Presbyterian Conversations; Theological Consultant to Anglican Roman Catholic Conversations, 1970. *Publications:* The Life and Person of Jesus Christ, 1951; The Patristic Doctrine of Redemption, 1952; Jesus Master and Lord, 1953; The Pattern of Christian Truth (Bampton Lectures), 1955; Why Bishops?, 1955; The Meaning of the Cross, 1959; (jt author with H. Montefiore) Thomas and the Evangelists, 1962; Historicity and the Gospels, 1963; Jesus the Christ, 1976; contributions to the Guardian, Theology and Church Quarterly Review. *Address:* Realands, Eskdale, near Holmrook, Cumbria CA19 1TW. *T:* Eskdale (019467) 23321.

TURNER, Prof. Herbert Arthur (Frederick), BSc Econ London, PhD Manchester, MA Cantab; Montague Burton Professor of Industrial Relations, University of Cambridge, 1963–83, now Professor Emeritus; Fellow of Churchill College, Cambridge, since 1963; *b* 11 Dec. 1919; *s* of Frederick and May Turner. *Educ:* Henry Thornton Sch., Clapham; LSE (Leverhulme Schol., then Leverhulme Res. Student, 1936–40; BSc (Econ) 1939); PhD Manchester, 1960. Army, then naval staff, 1940–44. Member, Trades Union Congress Research and Economic Department, 1944; Assistant Education Secretary, TUC, 1947; Lecturer, 1950, Senior Lecturer, 1959, University of Manchester; Council of

Europe Res. Fellow, 1957–58; Montague Burton Professor of Industrial Relations, University of Leeds, 1961–63. Mem., NBPI, 1967–71. Visiting Professor: Lusaka, 1969; Harvard and MIT, 1971–72; Sydney Univ., 1976–77; Hong Kong Univ., 1978–79 and 1985–87; Monash Univ., 1982; Bombay and Lucknow Univs, 1983; South China Univ. of Technology, 1986; Zhongshan Univ., 1987; Leverhulme Sen. Res. Fellow, 1985–88. Sometime Adviser to Govts of Congo, Zaïre, Egypt, Tanzania, Fiji, Papua New Guinea, Zambia and other developing countries; Chm., Incomes Policies Commn of E African Community, 1973; ILO Adviser: Malawi, 1967; Iran, 1975; Labour Adviser, UNECA, 1980; World Bank Consultant, China, 1988. *Publications:* Arbitration, 1951; Wage Policy Abroad, 1956; Trade Union Growth, Structure and Policy, 1962; Wages: the Problems for Underdeveloped Countries, 1965, 2nd edn 1968; Prices, Wages and Incomes Policies, 1966; Labour Relations in the Motor Industry, 1967; Is Britain Really Strike-Prone?, 1969; Do Trade Unions Cause Inflation?, 1972, 3rd edn 1978; Management Characteristics and Labour Conflict, 1978; The Last Colony: labour in Hong Kong, 1980; The ILO and Hong Kong, 1986; Between Two Societies: Hong Kong labour in transition, 1990; Studies of Labour in Hong Kong, 1991; various reports of ILO, monographs, papers and articles on labour economics and statistics, industrial relations, developing countries. *Recreations:* minimal but mostly excusable. *Address:* Churchill College, Cambridge CB3 0DS; 129 Route de Bourgogne, Veneux-les-Sablons 77250, France. *Club:* United Oxford & Cambridge University.

TURNER, Hugh Wason, CMG 1980; Director, National Gas Turbine Establishment, 1980–83, retired; *b* 2 April 1923; *s* of Thomas W. Turner and Elizabeth P. Turner (*née* Pooley); *m* 1950, Rosemary Borley; two *s* two *d*. *Educ:* Dollar Academy; Glasgow University. BSc Hons (Mech. Eng); CEng; FRAeS. Aeroplane and Armament Experimental Establishment, 1943–52; Chief Tech. Instructor, Empire Test Pilots School, 1953; A&AEE (Prin. Scientific Officer), 1954–64; Asst Director, RAF Aircraft, Min. of Technology, 1965–68; Superintendent, Trials Management, A&AEE, 1968–69; Division Leader, Systems Engineering, NATO MRCA Management Agency (NAMMA), Munich, 1969–74; Chief Superintendent, A&AEE, 1974–75; DGA1 (Dir Gen., Tornado), MoD (PE), 1976–80. *Recreations:* ski-ing, model building, photography, DIY. *Address:* Lavender Cottage, 1 Highcliff Road, Lyme Regis, Dorset DT7 3EW. *T:* Lyme Regis (01297) 442310.

TURNER, Prof. James Johnson, FRS 1992; Research Professor of Chemistry, University of Nottingham, since 1995 (Professor of Inorganic Chemistry, 1979–95); *b* 24 Dec. 1935; *s* of Harry Turner and Evelyn Turner (*née* Johnson); *m* 1961, Joanna Margaret Gargett; two *d*. *Educ:* Darwen Grammar Sch.; King's Coll., Cambridge (MA, PhD 1960; ScD 1985). CChem; FRSC. Research Fellow, King's Coll., Cambridge, 1960; Harkness Fellow, Univ. of Calif, Berkeley, 1961–63; University of Cambridge: Univ. Demonstrator, 1963–68; Univ. Lectr, 1968–71; College Lectr, 1963–71, Admissions Tutor, 1967–71, King's Coll.; Prof. and Head of Dept of Inorganic Chemistry, Univ. of Newcastle upon Tyne, 1972–78; Nottingham University: Hd of Chem. Dept, 1982–85, 1991–93; Pro-Vice-Chancellor, 1986–90. Visiting Professor: Univ. of Western Ontario, 1975; Texas, 1977; MIT, 1984; Chicago, 1986. Science and Engineering Research Council (formerly SRC): Mem., 1974–77, Chm., 1979–82, Chemistry Cttee; Mem., Science Bd, 1979–86; Mem. Council, 1982–86. Royal Society of Chemistry: Mem., 1974–77, Vice-Pres., 1982–84 and 1991–93, Pres., 1993–, Dalton Council; Tilden Lectr, 1978; Liversidge Lectr, 1991. *Publications:* papers mainly in jls of Chem. Soc. and Amer. Chem. Soc. *Recreation:* walking. *Address:* Department of Chemistry, University of Nottingham, University Park, Nottingham NG7 2RD. *T:* Nottingham (0115) 951 3490.

TURNER, Janet; *see* Kear, J.

TURNER, Hon. Joanna Elizabeth, (Hon. Mrs Turner), MA; Classics Teacher, Ellesmere College, Salop, 1975–80; *b* 10 Jan. 1923; 2nd *d* of 1st Baron Piercy, CBE, and Mary Louisa, *d* of Hon. Thomas Pelham; *m* 1968, James Francis Turner (*d* 1983), *er s* of late Rev. P. R. Turner. *Educ:* St Paul's Girls' Sch.; Somerville Coll., Oxford (Sen. Classics Schol.). Asst Classics Mistress: Downe House, Newbury, 1944–46; Gordonstoun Sch., 1947–48; Badminton Sch., Bristol, 1948–65, Headmistress, Badminton Sch., Bristol, 1966–69. JP Inner London (Juvenile Courts), 1970–75. *Publications:* B. M. Sanderson and Badminton School 1947–1966, 1988; Quarries and Craftsmen of the Windrush Valley, 1988. *Address:* Gable Cottage, 55 Witney Street, Burford, Oxon OX18 4RX. *T:* Burford (01993) 822368.

TURNER, John; Under Secretary, Employment Department Group (formerly Department of Employment), since 1988; Government Regional Director for Eastern Region, since 1994; *b* 22 April 1946; *s* of late William Cecil Turner and Hilda Margaret Turner; *m* 1971, Susan Georgina Kennedy; two *s* one *d*. *Educ:* Ramsey Abbey Grammar Sch.; Northwood Hills Grammar Sch. Entered Civil Service, 1967; Principal, DoI, 1979; MSC, 1981–84; Asst Sec., Dept of Employment, 1985; Prin. Pvte Sec. to Rt. Hon. Lord Young of Graffham and Rt. Hon. Norman Fowler, 1986–87; Small Firms and Tourism Div., Dept of Employment, 1989; Dep. Chief Exec., Employment Service, 1989–94. *Recreations:* music, motoring, the outdoors. *Address:* 24 Rutland Park, Sheffield S10 2PB. *T:* Sheffield (0114) 266 1067.

TURNER, Prof. John Derfel; Sarah Fielden Professor of Education, University of Manchester, 1985–94, now Professor Emeritus; *b* 27 Feb. 1928; *s* of Joseph Turner and Dorothy Winifred Turner; *m* 1951, Susan Broady Hovey; two *s*. *Educ:* Manchester Grammar Sch.; Univ. of Manchester. BA 1948, MA 1951, Teacher's Diploma 1951. Education Officer, RAF, 1948–50; teacher, Prince Henry's Grammar Sch., Evesham, 1951–53; Lectr in English, 1953–56, Sen. Lectr in Educn, 1956–61, Nigerian Coll. of Arts, Science and Technology; Lectr in Educn, Univ. of Exeter Inst. of Education, 1961–64; Prof. of Educn and Dir, Sch. of Educn, 1964–70, and Pro-Vice-Chancellor, 1966–70, Univ. of Botswana, Lesotho and Swaziland, Emeritus Prof., 1970; University of Manchester: Prof. of Educn and Dir of Sch. of Educn, 1970–76; Dean, Faculty of Educn, 1972–74 and 1986–91; Prof. of Adult and Higher Educn, 1976–85; Pro Vice-Chancellor, 1981–94. Rector, University Coll. of Botswana, Univ. of Botswana and Swaziland, 1981–82 and Vice-Chancellor, Univ. of Botswana, 1982–84. Chairman: Univs Council for Educn of Teachers, 1979–81 and 1988–91 (Vice-Chm., 1976–79); Council of Validating Univs, 1990–94; Presidential Commn on Higher Educn in Namibia, 1991–92; Member: UK Nat. Commn for UNESCO, 1975–81; IUC Working Parties on East and Central Africa and on Rural Development, 1975–81; Educn Sub-Cttee, UGC, 1980–81; Educn Cttee and Further Educn Bd, CNAA, 1979–81; Chm., European Develt Fund/IUC Working Party on Academic Develt of Univ. of Juba, 1977–78; Chm. and Mem. Council, Social Studies Adv. Cttee, Selly Oak Colleges, 1975–81. Chm., Bd of Governors, Abbotsholme Sch., 1980–. Chm., Editl Bd, Internat. Jl of Educn and Develt, 1978–81. Hon. FCP 1985 (Pres., 1994–); Hon. Fellow, Bolton Inst. of Higher Educn, 1988. Hon. LLD Ohio Univ., 1982. *Publications:* Introducing the Language Laboratory, 1963; (ed with A. P. Hunter) Educational Development in Predominantly Rural Countries, 1968; (ed with J. Rushton) The Teacher in a Changing Society, 1974; (ed with J. Rushton) Education and Deprivation, 1975; (ed with J. Rushton) Education and Professions, 1976; (ed) The Reform of Educational Systems to Meet Local and National Needs, 1994; school text books and contribs to edited works and to jls. *Recreations:* reading, music, theatre, walking; Methodist local preacher. *Address:* 13 Firswood Mount, Gatley, Cheadle, Cheshire SK8 4JY. *T:* 0161–428 2734. *Club:* Commonwealth Trust.

TURNER, Rt. Hon. John Napier, PC (Can.) 1965; CC (Can.) 1995; QC (Can.); Leader of the Liberal Party of Canada, and Leader of the Opposition, 1984–90; Partner, Miller Thomson, Toronto, since 1990; *b* 7 June 1929; *s* of Leonard Turner and Phyllis Turner (*née* Gregory); *m* 1963, Geills McCrae Kilgour; three *s* one *d*. *Educ:* Normal Model Public Sch., Ottawa, Ont.; Ashbury Coll., 1939–42; St Patrick's Coll., 1942–45; Univ. of BC; Oxford Univ. BA (PolSci, Hons) BC, 1949; Rhodes Scholar, Oxford Univ., BA (Juris.) 1951; BCL 1952; MA 1957. Joined Stikeman, Elliott, Tamaki, Mercier & Turner, Montreal, Quebec; practised with them after being called to English Bar, 1953, Bar of Quebec, 1954 and Bar of Ont., 1968; QC (Ont and Que) 1968; with McMillan Binch, Toronto, 1976–84. MP for Montreal-St Lawrence-St Georges, 1962–68, Ottawa-Carleton, 1968–76, Vancouver Quadra, 1984–93; Parly Sec. to Minister of Northern Affairs and Nat. Resources, 1963–65; Minister without Portfolio, Dec. 1965–April 1967; Registrar-Gen. of Canada, April 1967–Jan. 1968; Minister of Consumer and Corporate Affairs, Dec. 1967–July 1968; Solicitor-Gen., April–July 1968; Minister of Justice and Attorney-Gen. of Canada, July 1968–Jan. 1972; Minister of Finance, Jan. 1972–Sept. 1975; resigned as MP, Feb. 1976; Prime Minister of Canada, June–Sept. 1984. Barbados Bar, 1969; Yukon and Northwest Territories, 1969; Trinidad Bar, 1969; British Columbia, 1969. Hon. Dr of Laws: Univ. of New Brunswick, 1968; York Univ., Toronto, 1969; Hon. Dr of Civil Law, Mt Allison Univ., NB, 1980. *Publications:* Senate of Canada, 1961; Politics of Purpose, 1968. *Recreations:* tennis, canoeing, ski-ing; Canadian Track Field Champion 1948, Mem. English Track and Field Team. *Address:* (office) 20 Queen Street West, Suite 2700, Toronto, Ont M5H 3S1, Canada; (home) 27 Dunloe Road, Toronto, Ont M4W 2W4, Canada.

TURNER, Prof. John Stewart, FAA 1979; FRS 1982; Professor of Geophysical Fluid Dynamics, Australian National University, since 1975; *b* Sydney, Aust., 11 Jan. 1930; *s* of Ivan Stewart Turner and Enid Florence (*née* Payne); *m* 1959, Sheila Lloyd Jones; two *s* one *d*. *Educ:* North Sydney Boys' High Sch.; Wesley Coll., Univ. of Sydney (BSc, MSc); Trinity Coll., Univ. of Cambridge (PhD). FInstP 1969. Research Officer, CSIRO cloud physics group, 1953–54 and 1960–61; 1851 Exhibition Overseas Schol., 1954–57; postdoctoral research post, Univ. of Manchester, 1958–59; Rossby Fellow, then Associate Scientist, Woods Hole Oceanographic Instn, 1962–66; Asst Director of Research, then Reader, Dept of Applied Mathematics and Theoretical Physics, Univ. of Cambridge, 1966–75; Fellow of Darwin Coll., Cambridge, 1974; Foundation Prof. of Geophysical Fluid Dynamics in the Research Sch. of Earth Sciences, ANU, 1975–; Overseas Fellow, Churchill Coll., Cambridge, 1985; Fairchild Scholar, CIT, 1993. Matthew Flinders Lectr, Aust. Acad. of Science, 1990. Member, Australian Marine Sciences and Technologies Adv. Cttee (AMSTAC), 1979–84. Associate Editor, Journal of Fluid Mechanics, 1975–; Mem. Editorial Adv. Board, Deep-Sea Research, 1974–84. *Publications:* Buoyancy Effects in Fluids, 1973, paperback 1979; papers in various scientific jls. *Recreations:* bushwalking, photography, home handyman. *Address:* (office) Research School of Earth Sciences, Australian National University, Canberra, ACT 0200, Australia. *T:* (6) 2494530; (home) 2/28 Black Street, Yarralumla, ACT 2600, Australia.

TURNER, John Turnage; His Honour Judge Turner; a Circuit Judge, since 1976; Resident Judge at Ipswich, since 1984; *b* 12 Nov. 1929; *s* of Wilfrid Edward and May Martha Turner; *m* 1956, Gillian Mary Rayner; two *d*. *Educ:* Earls Colne Grammar School. Called to the Bar, Inner Temple, 1952. *Recreations:* music appreciation, travelling, watching cricket. *Address:* The Crown Court, Ipswich IP1 2DX. *Club:* MCC.

TURNER, (Jonathan) Adair; Director General, Confederation of British Industry, since 1995; *b* 5 Oct. 1955; *s* of Geoffrey Vincent Turner and Kathleen Margaret (*née* Broadhurst); *m* 1985, Orna Ni Chionna; two *d*. *Educ:* Gonville and Caius Coll., Cambridge (MA Hist. and Econs). BP, 1979; with Chase Manhattan Bank, 1979–82; McKinsey & Co., 1982–95: Principal, 1988; Dir, 1994–95. Mem., RIIA. *Recreations:* ski-ing, opera, gardening, children. *Address:* c/o Confederation of British Industry, Centre Point, 103 New Oxford Street, WC1A 1DU. *T:* 0171–379 7400.

TURNER, Lloyd Charles; livestock farmer, Kent, since 1986; Director, Messenger Nationwide, since 1988; Assistant Editor, Today, since 1990; *b* 2 Oct. 1938; *s* of Charles Thomas and Lily Turner; *m* 1st, 1961, Rosemary Munday (marr. diss. 1966); 2nd, 1967, Jennifer Anne Cox (marr. diss. 1972); 3rd, 1973, Jill Marguerite King. *Educ:* Giants Creek Primary Sch., Australia; The Armidale Sch., Armidale, Australia. Newcastle Morning Herald, Australia: Cadet journalist, 1956; Chief Crime Reporter, 1960; Features Editor, 1961; Picture Editor, 1962; Asst Editor, 1964; Industrial Correspondent, Manchester Evening News, 1968; Daily Express: Sub-Editor, 1968; Asst Chief Sub-Editor, 1974; Dep. Chief Sub-Editor, 1975; Asst Night Editor, 1976; Dep. Night Editor, 1977; Night Editor, 1979; Editor: The Daily Star, subseq. The Star, 1980–87; The Post, 1988; Editor-in-Chief, Messenger TV, 1988; Director: Express Newspapers plc, 1982–87; Daily Star plc, 1982–87. CPU Scholar, 1966. Pres., Australian Journalists Assoc. (Provincial), 1962–65; Chm., (Father), Daily Express/Sunday Express NUJ Chapel, 1969–74. Hon. Mem., NSPCC, 1989. *Recreations:* gardening, horse-racing. *Address:* 1 Virginia Street, E1 9BS. *Clubs:* St James's; Journalists' (Sydney).

TURNER, Hon. Sir Michael (John); Hon. Mr Justice Turner; Kt 1985; a Judge of the High Court of Justice, Queen's Bench Division, since 1985; *b* 31 May 1931; *s* of late Theodore F. Turner, QC; *m* 1st, 1956, Hon. Susan Money-Coutts (marr. diss. 1965); one *s* one *d*; 2nd, 1965, Frances Deborah (marr. diss.), *d* of Rt Hon. Sir David Croom-Johnson, *qv*; two *s*; 3rd, 1995, Ingrid Maria Fear (*née* Ortner). *Educ:* Winchester; Magdalene Coll., Cambridge (BA). Called to Bar, Inner Temple, 1954 (Bencher 1981); a Recorder, 1972–85; QC 1973–85. Chm., E Mids Agricultural Tribunal, 1979–82. Mem., Judicial Studies Bd, 1988–93 (Co-Chm., Civil and Family Cttee, 1988–93). *Recreations:* horses, listening to music. *Address:* Royal Courts of Justice, Strand, WC2A 2LL.
See also C. G. Turner.

TURNER, Michael Ralph, FRSA; Group Managing Director, 1976–88, Chief Executive, 1982–88, Associated Book Publishers PLC; Chairman, Associated Book Publishers (UK) Ltd, 1977–90; *b* 26 Jan. 1929; *s* of Ralph Victor Turner and May Turner; *m* 1955, Ruth Baylis; two *s* two *d*. *Educ:* Newport Sch., Essex; Trinity Coll., Cambridge (BA Hons). Served RAF, Transport Comd, 1947–49. Jun. Editor, J. M. Dent & Sons, 1949–50; Methuen & Co.: Jun. Editor, 1953; subseq. Publicity and Promotion Manager, and Dir; Associated Publishers Ltd: Marketing Dir, 1973; Asst Gp Man. Dir, 1975; Gp Man. Dir, 1976. Chm., Methuen Inc., New York, 1981–88; Pres., Carswell Co. Ltd, Toronto, 1982–84; Dir, ABP Investments (Aust.) Pty Ltd, 1976–88; Sen. Vice-Pres., Publishing Information Gp, Internat. Thomson Orgn Ltd, 1987–89. Chairman: Book Marketing Council, 1981–84; Book Trust, 1990–92; Member: Book Trade Working Party, 1973–74; Council, Publishers Assoc., 1981–90 (Vice-Pres., 1985–87 and 1989–90; Pres., 1987–89; Chm., Home Trade and Services Council, 1989–90); National Council and Exec., NBL, 1980–87; British Library Adv. Council, 1989–94; Centre for the Book Adv. Cttee, 1990–;

Publishing Bd, Design Council, 1991–94. Chm., Soc. of Bookmen, 1992–94. FRSA 1984. *Publications:* The Bluffer's Guide to the Theatre, 1967; Parlour Poetry, 1967; (with Antony Miall) The Parlour Song Book, 1972; (with Antony Miall) Just a Song at Twilight, 1975; (with Antony Miall) The Edwardian Song Book, 1982; (with Michael Geare) Gluttony, Pride and Lust and Other Sins from the World of Books, 1984; (with Leslie Lonsdale-Cooper) translations of Hergé's Tintin books, 1958–95. *Recreations:* reading, music, theatre, maritime painting and models. *Address:* Paradise House, Boscastle, Cornwall PL35 0BL. *T:* Boscastle (01840) 250250. *Club:* Garrick.

TURNER, Norman Henry, CBE 1977; Official Solicitor to the Supreme Court of Judicature, 1970–80; *b* 11 May 1916; *s* of late Henry James Turner, MA and Hilda Gertrude Turner; *m* 1st, 1939, Dora Ardella (*née* Cooper) (*d* 1990); three *s* two *d*; 2nd, 1991, Mona Florence Mackenzie. *Educ:* Nottingham High School. Articled, Nottingham, 1933; admitted Solicitor (Hons), 1938; joined Official Solicitor's Dept, 1948; Asst Official Solicitor, 1958. *Address:* 62 Walcote Drive, West Bridgford, Nottingham NG2 7GS. *T:* Nottingham (0115) 923 3565.

TURNER, Patricia, OBE 1981; Head of National Equal Rights Department, and National Industrial Officer, General, Municipal, Boilermakers and Allied Trades Union (formerly General and Municipal Workers' Union), 1971–89; Member, General Council, TUC, 1981–89; *b* 14 May 1927; *d* of John Richard and Maire Collins; *m* 1954, Donald Turner, BSc (Econ). *Educ:* London School of Economics (BSc (Econ), MSc (Econ)). Industrial Sociology Lectr, 1965–69; Consultant, Manpower and Productivity Service (Dept of Employment and Productivity), 1969–70; Sen. Industrial Relations Officer, Commn on Industrial Relations, 1970–71. Member: Confedn of Shipbuilding and Engineering Unions Exec. Council, 1971–89 (Pres., 1982–83); Engineering Industry Training Bd, 1971–89; Women's Nat. Commn, 1973–89; Central Arbitration Cttee, 1976–93; Dept of Employment Adv. Cttee on Women's Employment, 1980–89; Equal Opportunities Commn, 1985–91; Employment Appeal Tribunal, 1987–. *Recreations:* reading, theatre. *Address:* 22 Kenilworth Road, Edgware, Middlesex HA8 8YG.

TURNER, Peter; *see* Turner, T. P.

TURNER, Air Vice-Marshal Peter, CB 1979; MA; Bursar and Steward, Wolfson College, Cambridge, 1979–89; *b* 29 Dec. 1924; *s* of late George Allen and of Emma Turner; *m* 1949, Doreen Newbon; one *s*. *Educ:* Tapton House Sch., Chesterfield. Served War of 1939–45; 640 Sqdn, 1943–45; Nos 51, 242 and 246 Sqdns, 1945–48; psa 1961; NATO staff, 1963–67; jssc 1967; Chief Equipment and Secretarial Instructor, RAF Coll., Cranwell, 1967–68; Comd Accountant, HQ Air Support Comd, 1968–69; Station Comdr, RAF Uxbridge, 1969–71; RCDS, 1972; Dir of Personnel (Ground) (RAF), MoD, 1973–75; AOA, HQ RAF Support Command, 1975–79, and Head of RAF Admin. Branch, 1976–79. MA Cantab 1979. *Recreation:* retrospective contemplation. *Address:* Hedge End, Potton Road, Hilton, Cambs PE18 9NG. *Club:* Royal Air Force.

TURNER, Peter William; District Secretary, Hereford and Worcester, Transport and General Workers' Union, 1969–91, retired; *m* Maureen Ann Turner (*née* Hill), Councillor, JP. *Educ:* Bordesley Green Infant and Junior Sch.; Saltley Grammar Sch. (until 1940); various Trade Union weekend courses. Appointed District Officer, TGWU, 1969; District Sec., CSEU, 1974–76; seconded as Industrial Advr to DoI, 1976–78. Member of various cttees including: Chemical Industry Area Productivity Cttee, 1969–76 (Vice-Chm., 1970–72, Chm., 1972–74); TUC Regional Educn Adv. Cttee, 1970–76; Birmingham Crime Prevention Panel, 1973–76; W Midlands Consultative Cttee on Race Relations, 1974–76; DoE Working Party on Race Relations, 1974–76; Teaching Co. Management Cttee, 1977–82. Member: Birmingham Trades Council, 1956–76; Local Appeals Tribunal, 1969–74. *Recreations:* motoring, motor cycling, caravanning, do-it-yourself, reading, electronics. *Address:* 2 Oakleigh Road, Droitwich, Worcs WR9 0RP.

TURNER, Phil; Member, since 1971, and Chair of Leisure and Community Services, since 1995, Camden Borough Council; *b* 7 June 1939; *s* of William Morris Turner and Eileen Lascelles Turner; *m* 1963, Gillian Sharp (*d* 1988); one *s* two *d* (and one *s* decd). *Educ:* Beckenham and Penge Grammar School for Boys; University Coll. London (BScEcon). National Coal Board, later British Coal: Management Trainee, 1961–63; Hd of Information, Purchasing and Stores, 1963–65; O & M Officer, 1965–66; Hd of Admin, R & D Dept, 1966–68; Hd of Manpower Planning, 1968–73; Staff Manager, Opencast Exec., 1973–78; Hd of Conditions of Service, 1978–80; Dep. Dir of Staff Pay and Conditions, 1980–86; Head of Employment Policy, 1986–89. Joined Labour Party, 1963; Chairman, Hampstead Labour Party, 1968–70; Camden Borough Council, 1971–: Chm., Building Works and Services Cttee, 1978–80 and 1986–89; Chair: Staff and Management Services Cttee, 1990–93; Leisure Services Cttee, 1993–95; Leader of Council, 1982–86, Dep. Leader, 1992–93 and 1994–95. Member: Assoc. of London Authorities, 1983–86 and 1994–; Policy Cttee, AMA, 1984–86. Contested (Lab): Cities of London and Westminster South, Feb. and Oct. 1974; (Lab) Hampstead and Highgate, 1987. Mem., Hampstead Theatre Bd, 1994–. *Recreations:* family, travelling, book collecting, Woodcraft Folk camps. *Address:* 33 Minster Road, NW2 3SH. *T:* 0171–794 8805.

TURNER, Philip, CBE 1975; LLB (London); in private practice with Infields, Hampton Wick, Surrey, 1978–91; *b* 1 June 1913; *er s* of late George Francis and late Daisy Louise Turner (*née* Frayn), Alverstoke, Hants; *m* 1938, Hazel Edith, *d* of late Douglas Anton and late Edith Ada Benda; one *d* (one *d* decd). *Educ:* Peter Symonds, Winchester. Admitted Solicitor, 1935. Entered General Post Office Solicitor's Dept, 1935. Served in Royal Navy, 1940–46 (Lt-Comdr). Asst Solicitor to General Post Office, 1953; Principal Asst Solicitor, 1962–72, Solicitor to the Post Office, 1972–75; temp. mem. of legal staff, DoE, 1976–77. Chm., Civil Service Legal Soc., 1957–58; Chm., Internat. Bar Assoc.'s Cttee on Public Utility Law, 1972–77. FRSA 1955. *Recreations:* piano, golf. *Address:* 8 Walters Mead, Ashtead, Surrey KT21 2BP. *T:* Ashtead (01372) 273656. *Clubs:* Naval, Royal Automobile, Law Society; Hampshire County Cricket, Surrey County Cricket.

TURNER, Surgeon Rear-Admiral (D) Philip Stanley, CB 1963; QHDS 1960–64; Director of Dental Services, RN, Admiralty, Nov. 1961–64; *b* 31 Oct. 1905; *s* of Frank Overy Turner and Ellen Mary Turner, Langton Green, Tunbridge Wells; *m* 1934, Marguerite Donnelly (*d* 1990); one *d* (and one *s* decd). *Educ:* Cranbrook Coll.; Guy's Hospital. LDS, RCS 1927. Surgeon Lieut (D) Royal Navy, 1928; Surgeon Captain (D) 1955; Surgeon Rear-Admiral (D), 1961; Senior Specialist in Dental Surgery, 1946–61. Served in: HMS Ramillies, Vanguard, Implacable, Indomitable; HMHS Maine, Tjitjalengka; RN Hospitals Haslar, Plymouth; RN Barracks Portsmouth, etc; Naval HQ, Malta. Foundation Fellow, British Assoc. of Oral Surgeons, 1962.

TURNER, Robert Lockley; Master of the Supreme Court, Queen's Bench Division, since 1984; *b* 2 Sept. 1935; *s* of James Lockley Turner and Maud Beatrice Turner; *m* 1963, Jennifer Mary Leather; one *s* one *d*. *Educ:* Clifton Coll.; St Catharine's Coll., Cambridge (BA 1957, MA 1973). Called to the Bar, Gray's Inn, 1958. Commnd Gloucestershire Regt (28th/61st), 1959 (2nd Lieut); transf. to Army Legal Services, 1960 (Captain); Major 1962; retd from Army, 1966 (GSM with clasp South Arabia, 1966). Practised at Common Law Bar in London and on Midland and Oxford Circuit, 1967–84; a Recorder of the Crown Court, 1981–84. Hon. Steward, Westminster Abbey, 1985–; Churchwarden, St Matthew's, Midgham, 1990–92. *Recreations:* gardening, gothic churches. *Publications:* (ed jtly) Supreme Court Practice, 1988; The Office of the Queen's Bench Master, 1990; (ed jtly) Chitty and Jacob, Queen's Bench Forms, 1992; (ed jtly) High Court Litigation Manual, 1992; Annual Practice, 1995. *Address:* Royal Courts of Justice, WC2A 2LL; Midgham Green, Berks RG7 5TT. *Clubs:* Army and Navy; Royal Fowey Yacht (Fowey).

TURNER, Stephen Gordon; General Secretary, British Association of Journalists, since 1992; *b* 27 July 1935; *s* of John Turner and Lillian Turner (*née* Wiseman); *m* 1st, 1955, Jean Florence Watts (marr. diss. 1978); two *s* one *d*; 2nd, 1979, Deborah Diana Thomas; one *d*. *Educ:* Triptons Secondary Modern Sch., Dagenham; Royal Liberty Grammar Sch., Romford. Royal Signals radio mechanic, 1953–55. Reporter: Romford Times, 1955–56; Ilford Recorder, 1956; Bristol Evening World, 1957; freelance journalist, 1958–68; News sub-editor: Ipswich Evening Star, 1969; Daily Mail, 1969–71; Features sub-editor, 1971–73, Public Opinion Editor, 1973–90, Daily Mirror; Gen. Sec., NUJ, 1990–92. Independent Councillor, Colchester BC, 1967–68. Mem., NUJ, 1955–92; Father of the Chapel, Daily Mirror, 1976–78, 1986–90. *Address:* 1 Priory Grove, Dover, Kent CT17 0AB.

TURNER, Theodora, OBE 1961; ARRC 1944; retired as Matron of St Thomas' Hospital and Superintendent Nightingale Training School (1955–65); *b* 5 Aug. 1907; *er d* of H. E. M. Turner. *Educ:* Godolphin School, Salisbury; Edinburgh School of Domestic Economy. Ward Sister, St Thomas' Hosp., 1935–38; Administrative Course, Florence Nightingale Internat. Foundn, 1938–39. QAIMNS Reserve, 1939–45. Administrative Sister, St Thomas' Hosp., 1946–47; Matron Royal Infirmary, Liverpool, 1948–53; Education Officer, Educn Centre, Royal College of Nursing, Birmingham, 1953–55. President: Florence Nightingale Internat. Nurses Assoc., 1971–74; Royal Coll. of Nursing and Nat. Council of Nurses of UK, 1966–68. Mem., Argyll and Clyde Health Bd, 1974–75. *Recreations:* gardening and painting.

TURNER, (Thomas) Peter; Evaluation Consultant, since 1985; *b* 8 May 1928; *s* of Thomas Turner and Laura Crawley; *m* 1952, Jean Rosalie Weston; one *s* one *d*. *Educ:* Ilford County High Sch.; London University. BSc (1st Class Hons), Maths and Physics. GEC, North Wembley, 1947–50; Armament Design Establishment, 1950–54; Air Ministry (Science 3), 1954–58 and 1962–63; Chief Research Officer, RAF Maintenance Command, 1958–62; Police Research and Development Branch, Home Office, 1963–68; Civil Service Dept (OR), 1968–73; Head of Treasury/CSD Joint Operational Research Unit, 1973–76; Head of Operational Res., CSD, 1977–81, HM Treasury, 1981–84. *Address:* 8 Waring Drive, Green St Green, Orpington, Kent BR6 6DW. *T:* Farnborough (Kent) (01689) 851189.

TURNER, Wilfred, CMG 1977; CVO 1979; HM Diplomatic Service, retired; Director, Transportation Systems and Market Research Ltd (Transmark), 1987–90; *b* 10 Oct. 1921; *s* of late Allen Turner and Eliza (*née* Leach); *m* 1947, June Gladys Tite; two *s* one *d*. *Educ:* Heywood Grammar Sch., Lancs; London Univ. BSc 1942. Min. of Labour, 1938–42. Served War, REME, 1942–47. Min. of Labour, 1947–55; Brit. High Commn, New Delhi (Asst Lab. Adviser), 1955–59; Senior Wages Inspector, Min. of Labour, 1959–60; Min. of Health (Sec., Cttee on Safety of Drugs, 1963–66), 1960–66. Joined HM Diplomatic Service, 1966; Commonwealth Office, 1966; First Sec.: Kaduna, Nigeria, 1966–69; Kuala Lumpur, 1969–73; Dep. High Comr, and Commercial/Economic Counsellor, Accra, 1973–77; High Comr to Botswana, 1977–81. Dir, Southern Africa Assoc., 1983–88. Member: Cttee, Zambia Soc., 1983–91; Central Council, Royal Commonwealth Soc., 1987–94; RIIA, 1987–; Royal African Soc., 1987–. *Recreation:* hill walking. *Address:* 44 Tower Road, Twickenham TW1 4PE. *T:* 0181–892 1593. *Club:* Commonwealth Trust.

TURNER, Dr William; Regional Medical Officer, Yorkshire Regional Health Authority, 1976–86, retired; *b* 23 Feb. 1927; *s* of Clarence and Mabel Turner; *m* 1950, Patricia Bramham Wilkinson; one *s* two *d*. *Educ:* Prince Henry's Grammar Sch., Otley, Yorks; Leeds Univ. MB, ChB; DPH, FFCM; LLB. House Officer, Leeds Gen. Infirmary, 1950–51; RAMC, 1951–53; Gen. Practitioner, 1953–55; Public Health Trng, 1955–60; Medical Officer of Health: Hyde, 1960–63; Huddersfield, 1963–67; Bradford, 1967–74; Area MO, Bradford, 1974–76. Member: Standing Med. Adv. Cttee, 1978–82; NHS Steering Gp on Health Services Inf., 1979–84. *Publications:* contrib. BMJ, Medical Officer. *Address:* Bentcliffe, 1 Premiere Park, Ilkley, West Yorks LS29 9RQ. *T:* Ilkley (01943) 600114.

TURNER CAIN, Maj.-Gen. George Robert, CB 1967; CBE 1963; DSO 1945; President, Anglia Maltings (Holdings) Ltd, since 1982 (Chairman, 1976–82); Chairman: Anglia Maltings Ltd, 1976–82; F. & G. Smith Ltd, 1962–82; Walpole & Wright Ltd, 1968–82; Director: Crisp Maltings Ltd, 1967–82; Crisp Malt Products Ltd, 1968–82; Edme Ltd, 1972–82; *b* 16 Feb. 1912; *s* of late Wing Comdr G. Turner Cain; *m* 1938, Lamorna Maturin, *d* of late Col G. B. Hingston; one *s* one *d*. *Educ:* Norwich Sch.; RMC Sandhurst. 2nd Lt Norfolk Regt, 1932; 1st Bn Royal Norfolk Regt, India, 1933–38; Waziristan Campaign, 1937. Served War of 1939–45 with 1st Royal Norfolk and 1st Hereford Regt, BLA, 1944–45. Comd 1st Royal Norfolk Regt, Berlin, 1947–48; Hong Kong and UK, 1953–55; Comd Tactical Wing, School of Infantry, 1955–57; Comd 1st Fed. Inf. Bde, Malaya, in operations in Malaya, 1957–59; BGS, HQ, BAOR, 1961; Maj.-Gen. Administration, GHQ FARELF, 1964–67, retired; ADC, 1961–64. Dep. Col, Royal Anglian Regt, 1971–74. Croix de Guerre avec Palm, 1945; Star of Kedah (Malaya), 1959. *Recreation:* shooting. *Address:* Holbreck, Hollow Lane, Stiffkey, Wells-next-the-Sea, Norfolk NR23 1QG.

TURNER-SAMUELS, David Jessel, QC 1972; Barrister-at-Law; *b* 5 April 1918; *s* of late Moss Turner-Samuels, QC, MP, and Gladys Deborah Turner-Samuels (*née* Belcher); *m* 1939, Norma Turner-Samuels (*née* Verstone) (marr. diss. 1975); one *s* one *d*; *m* 1976, Norma Florence Negus, *qv*. *Educ:* Westminster Sch. Called to Bar, Middle Temple, 1939 (Bencher 1980); admitted to Trinidad bar, 1976. Served War of 1939–45, in Army, 1939–46. *Publication:* (jointly) Industrial Negotiation and Arbitration, 1951. *Recreation:* getting away from it all. *Address:* Cherry Tree Cottage, Petworth Road, Anstead Brook, Haslemere, Surrey GU27 3BG. *T:* Haslemere (01428) 651970; New Court, Temple, EC4Y 9BE. *T:* 0171–353 7613.

TURNER-SAMUELS, Norma Florence, (Mrs D. J. Turner-Samuels); *see* Negus, N. F.

TURNER-WARWICK, Prof. Dame Margaret (Elizabeth Harvey), DBE 1991; MA, DM, PhD; FRCP; Chairman, Royal Devon and Exeter Health Care NHS Trust, since 1992; President, Royal College of Physicians, 1989–92; Consultant Physician, Brompton Hospital, since 1965 (Professor of Medicine (Thoracic Medicine), 1972–87, Dean, 1984–87, Cardiothoracic Institute, now Emeritus Professor); *b* 19 Nov. 1924; *d* of William Harvey Moore, QC, and Maud Baden-Powell; *m* 1950, Richard Trevor Turner-Warwick, *qv*; two *d*. *Educ:* St Paul's Sch.; Lady Margaret Hall, Oxford (Open Schol. 1943; Hon. Fellow, 1990). DM Oxon, 1956; PhD London, 1961; FRCP 1969; FFOM 1983; FRACP

1983; FRCPE 1990; FFPHM 1990; FRCPGlas 1991; FRCGP 1991; FRCPI 1992. University Coll. Hosp., 1947–50: Tuke silver medal, Filliter exhibn in Pathology, Magrath Schol. in Medicine, Atchison Schol.; Postgrad. trng at UCH and Brompton Hosp., 1950–61; Cons. Physician: (Gen. Med.), Elizabeth Garrett Anderson Hosp., 1961–67; Brompton and London Chest Hosps, 1967–72. Sen. Lectr, Inst. of Diseases of the Chest, 1961–72. Lectures: Marc Daniels, 1974, Phillip Ellman, 1980, Tudor Edwards, 1985, RCP; Lettsomian, Med. Soc. of London, 1982. Pres., British Thoracic Soc., 1982–85; Chairman: Central Academic Council, BPMF, 1982–85; Asthma Res. Council (Chm., Med, Res. Cttee, 1982–); Conf. of Colleges and their Faculties in UK, 1990–; UKCCCR, 1991–; Member: MRC Systems Bd (DHSS nomination), 1982–85; Council, British Lung Foundn, 1984–; Gen. Council, King's Fund, 1991; Mem. Council and Vice-Pres., ASH, 1990–. University of London: Mem. Senate, 1983–87; Mem., Academic Council, 1983–87; Mem., Scholarships Cttee, 1984–87; Mem., Cttee of Extramural Studies, 1984–. Fellow, UCL, 1991. Hon. FACP 1988; Hon. FRCP&S (Canada) 1990; Hon. FRCAnaes 1991; Hon. FCMSA 1991; Hon FRCPath 1992; Hon. FRCS 1993; Hon. FRCR 1994. Hon. Bencher, Middle Temple, 1990. Hon. Member: Assoc. of Physicians of GB and Ireland, 1991; S German and Australasian Thoracic Socs; Member; Alpha Omega Alpha, USA, 1987; Acad. of Malaysia, 1991. Hon. DSc: New York, 1985; Exeter, 1990; London, 1990; Hull, 1991; Sussex, 1992; Oxford, 1992; Cambridge, 1993. *Publications:* Immunology of the Lung, 1978; (jtly) Occupational Lung Diseases: research approaches and methods, 1981; chapters in various textbooks on immunology and thoracic medicine, particularly fibrosing lung disorders and asthma; contrib. original articles: Lancet, BMJ, Quarterly Jl Med., Thorax, Tubercle, Jl Clin. Experimental Immunology, etc. *Recreations:* her family and their hobbies, gardening, country life, watercolour painting, music. *Address:* Pynes House, Thorverton, Exeter EX5 5LT.

TURNER-WARWICK, Richard Trevor, CBE 1991; MA, BSc, DM Oxon, MCh; Hon. DSc; FRCP, FRCS, FRCOG, FACS; Hon. FRACS; specialist in reconstruction and functional restoration of the urinary tract; Emeritus Surgeon and Urologist to the Middlesex Hospital (Senior Surgeon, 1969–90), St Peter's Hospital and Royal National Orthopædic Hospital; Senior Urological Surgeon to King Edward VII Hospital for Officers; Senior Lecturer, London University Institute of Urology, since 1962; Hon. Consultant Urologist, Royal Prince Alfred Hospital, Sydney, since 1980; Robert Luff Foundation Fellow in Reconstrucive Surgery, since 1990; *b* 21 Feb. 1925; *s* of W. Turner Warwick, FRCS; *m* 1950, Margaret Elizabeth Harvey Moore (*see* Dame Margaret Turner-Warwick); two *d. Educ:* Bedales School; Oriel Coll., Oxford; Middlesex Hosp. Medical School. Pres. OUBC, 1946; Mem. Univ. Boat Race Crew, Isis Head of River crew and Univ. Fours, 1946; Winner OU Silver Sculls, 1946; BSc thesis in neuroanatomy, 1946. Sen. Broderip Schol., Lyell Gold Medallist and Freeman Schol., Middx Hosp., 1949; surgical trng at Middx Hosp. and St Paul's Hosp., London, and Columbia Presbyterian Med. Centre, NY, 1959. Hunterian Prof. of RCS, 1957, 1976; Comyns Berkeley Travelling Fellowship to USA, 1959. British Assoc. of Urological Surgeons: Mem. Council, 1975–78 and 1982–92; Pres., 1988–90; Fellow, 1961; St Peter's Medal, 1978; Member: Council, Royal Coll. of Surgeons, 1980–92; RCOG, 1990–92; Internat. Soc. of Urology, 1966–; European Soc. of Urology; Soc. of Pelvic Surgeons, 1963; Founder Mem., 1969, Pres., 1985, Internat. Continence Soc.; Corresp. Member: Amer. Assoc. of Genito Urinary Surgeons, 1972; American and Australasian Urological Assocs. Fellow UCL, 1992. Fellow: Assoc. of Surgeons of GB and Ireland, 1960; Australasian Soc. Urology, 1989; Hon. FRACS, 1981. Hon. DSc New York, 1985. Moynihan Prize of Assoc. of Surgeons, 1957; Victor Bonney Prize, RCOG, 1987; Valentine Medal, NY Acad. of Medicine, 1992. *Publications:* various articles in scientific jls, contributing to surgery, to develt of operative procedures for the reconstruction and restoration of function of the urinary tract, and to design of surgical instruments. *Recreations:* water, family, fishing, gardening. *Address:* Pynes House, 9 Silver Street, Thorverton, Exeter EX5 5LT. *T:* Exeter (01392) 861173, *Fax:* (01392) 860940; 77 Harley House, NW1 5HL. *T:* 0171–935 2550. *Clubs:* Vincent's (Oxford); The Houghton (Stockbridge); Leander (Henley); Ottery St Mary Fly Fishers.

TURNEY, Alan Harry, CB 1991; Assistant Under Secretary of State, Fire and Emergency Planning Department, Home Office, 1986–92; *b* 20 Aug. 1932; *s* of late Harry Landry Turney and Alice Theresa Turney (*née* Bailey); *m* 1957, Ann Mary Dollimore. *Educ:* St Albans Grammar Sch.; London School of Economics (BScEcon). Asst Principal, Home Office, 1961; Asst Private Sec. to Home Sec., 1962–65; Principal, 1965; Asst Sec., Broadcasting Dept, 1976; Rayner Review of Forensic Science Service, 1981; Criminal Dept, 1981–82; Prison Dept, 1982–86. *Recreations:* Rugby Union football, touring provincial France, enjoying the garden. *Address:* 74 Kimpton Road, Blackmore End, Wheathampstead, Herts AL4 8LX. *T:* Kimpton (01438) 832636.

TURNOUR, family name of **Earl Winterton.**

TURNQUEST, Sir Orville (Alton), GCMG 1995; QC (Bahamas) 1992; Governor-General of the Bahamas, since 1995; *b* 19 July 1929; *y s* of late Robert Turnquest and Gwendolyn Turnquest; *m* 1955, Edith Louise Thompson; one *s* two *d. Educ:* Govt High Sch.; Univ. of London (LLB). Articled 1947–53; called to Bahamas Bar, 1953; called to the Bar, Lincoln's Inn, 1960; Counsel and Attorney of Supreme Ct; Notary Public; private practice, 1953–92; stipendiary and circuit magistrate and coroner, 1959; law tutor and Mem., Exam. Bd, Bahamas Bar, 1965–92. Chancellor, Dio. of Nassau and Bahamas. Sec.-Gen., Progressive Liberal Party, 1960–62; MP South Central, Nassau, 1962–67, Montagu, 1982–94; Opposition Leader in Senate, 1972–79; Dep. Leader, Free Nat. Movement, 1987–94; Attorney-Gen., 1992–94; Minister of Justice, 1992–93, of Foreign Affairs, 1992–94; Dep. Prime Minister, 1993–94. Pres., Bahamas Bar Assoc.; Chm., Bahamas Bar Council, 1970–72. Pres., CPA, 1992–93. Member: Anglican Central Educnl Authy; Nat. Cttee of United World Colls; Bd of Govs, St John's Coll. and St Anne's High Sch. Patron, Bahamas Games. *Recreations:* tennis, swimming, music, reading. *Address:* Government House, PO Box N-8301, Nassau, Bahamas.

TURPIN, James Alexander, CMG 1966; HM Diplomatic Service, retired; *b* 7 Jan. 1917; *s* of late Samuel Alexander Turpin; *m* 1942, Kathleen Iris Eadie; one *d. Educ:* King's Hosp., Dublin; Trinity Coll., Dublin (schol., 1st cl. Hons, Gold Medal, MA). Asst Lectr, Trinity College, Dublin, 1940. Served Army (Royal Irish Fusiliers), 1942–46. Joined Foreign Service, 1947; Mem., UK Delegn to OEEC, Paris, 1948; 1st Sec., 1949; FO, 1950; Warsaw, 1953; Tokyo, 1955; Counsellor, 1960; seconded to BoT, 1960–63; Counsellor (Commercial), The Hague, 1963–67; Minister (Economic and Commercial), New Delhi, 1967–70; Asst Under-Sec. of State, FCO, 1971–72; Ambassador to the Philippines, 1972–76; retired, 1977. Chm., British-Philippine Soc., 1986–88. *Publications:* New Society's Challenge in the Philippines, 1980; The Philippines: problems of the ageing New Society, 1984. *Recreations:* tennis, music, swimming, wine, cookery. *Address:* 12 Grimwood Road, Twickenham, Middlesex TW1 1BX.

TURPIN, Kenneth Charlton; Provost of Oriel College, Oxford, 1957–80, and Hon. Fellow since 1980; Vice-Chancellor, Oxford University, 1966–69 (Pro-Vice Chancellor, 1964–66, 1969–79); Member, Hebdomadal Council, 1959–77; *b* 13 Jan. 1915; *e s* of late Henry John Turpin, Ludlow. *Educ:* Manchester Grammar Sch.; Oriel College, Oxford. Treasury, 1940–43; Asst Private Sec. to C. R. Attlee, Lord President and Dep. Prime Minister, 1943–45; 2nd Asst Registrar, University Registry, Oxford, 1945–47; Sec. of Faculties, Univ. of Oxford, 1947–57; professorial fellow, Oriel Coll., 1948; Hon. Fellow Trinity Coll., Dublin, 1968. A Church Commissioner, 1984–89. *Recreations:* gardening, walking. *Address:* 13 Apsley Road, Oxford OX2 7QX. *Clubs:* Athenæum; Vincent's (Oxford).

TURPIN, Maj.-Gen. Patrick George, CB 1962; OBE 1943; FCIT; *b* 27 April 1911; 3rd *s* of late Rev. J. J. Turpin, MA, BD, late Vicar of Misterton, Somerset; *m* 1947, Cherry Leslie Joy, *d* of late Major K. S. Grove, York and Lancaster Regiment; one *s* one *d. Educ:* Haileybury Coll., Hertford; Exeter College, Oxford (Sen. Classical Schol.). BA (Hons) Oxford (Lit. Hum.), 1933; MA 1963. Commd RASC, 2nd Lt, 1933; Lt 1936; Capt. 1941; Major 1946; Lt-Col 1949; Col 1953; Brig. 1959; Maj.-Gen. 1960. Served War of 1939–45 (despatches twice, OBE): Adjt, 1939–40; AQMG, 30 Corps, W Desert, 1943; AA&QMG, 5th Div., Italy, 1943–44; DA&QMG (Brig.), 1 Corps, BLA, 1945; Brig. A, 21 Army Gp, 1945–46; Comd 6 Training Bn, RASC, 1947; ADS&T, WO, 1948; AA&QMG (Plans), HQ, BTE (Egypt), 1950; GSO1 (instructor), Jt Services Staff Coll., 1951–53; ADS&T (Col), WO, 1953–54; DAG, HQ, BAOR, 1956–59; Brig. i/c Adm., 17 Gurkha Div., Malaya, 1959–60; DST, 1960–63; Dir of Movements, MoD (Army), 1963–66; psc 1941; jssc 1949; idc 1955; Col Comdt, Royal Corps of Transport, 1965–71; Col Gurkha Army Service Corps, 1960–65; Col Gurkha Transport Regt, 1965–73. Sec.-Gen., Assoc. of British Travel Agents, 1966–69. Pres., Army Lawn Tennis Assoc., 1968–73. Governor, Royal Sch. for Daughters of Officers of the Army, Bath, 1963–83. FCIT (MInstT 1961). *Publication:* The Turn of the Wheel, 1988. *Recreations:* lawn tennis (Somerset County Champion, 1948, Army Colours, 1952); squash rackets (Bucks County Colours, 1952); golf. *Clubs:* Oxford Union Society; All England Lawn Tennis; International Lawn Tennis; Escorts Squash Rackets.

TURTON, Eugenie Christine, (Genie); Director, Citizen's Charter Unit, Cabinet Office, since 1994; *b* 19 Feb. 1946; *d* of Arthur Turton and Georgina (*née* Fairhurst); *m* 1st, 1968, Richard Gordon (marr. diss. 1972); 2nd, 1974, Gerry Flanagan (marr. diss. 1978). *Educ:* Nottingham Girls' High Sch. (GPDST); Girton Coll., Cambridge (schol.; MA). Research student (G. C. Winter Warr Studentship), Univ. of Cambridge, 1967–70; joined CS as Asst Principal, MoT (later DoE), 1970; Private Sec. to Parly Under Sec. of State, 1973–74; Principal, 1974–80; Prin. Private Sec. to successive Secretaries of State for Transport, 1978–80; Asst Sec., 1980–86; seconded to Midland Bank International, 1981–82, and to Cabinet Office/MPO (Machinery of Govt Div.), 1982–85; Under Sec., DoE, 1986–91; Director: Heritage and Royal Estate (formerly Ancient Monuments and Historic Bldgs), 1987–90; Inner Cities, 1990–91; Dep. Sec., DoE, 1991–94. Non-Exec. Dir, Woolwich Building Soc., 1987–91. Trustee, Pilgrim Trust, 1991–. *Recreations:* books, music, shopping, gardening. *Address:* c/o Citizen's Charter Unit, Government Offices, Horseguards Road, SW1P 3AL.

TURTON, Victor Ernest; Managing Director: V. E. Turton (Tools) Ltd; V. E. Turton (Wholesalers) Ltd; *b* 29 June 1924; *s* of H. E. Turton; *m* 1951, Jean Edith Murray; two *d. Educ:* Paget Secondary Modern Sch.; Aston Techn. Coll.; Birmingham Central Techn. Coll. Birmingham City Councillor (Lab) Duddeston Ward, 1945–63; Saltley Ward, 1970–71; Alderman, Birmingham, 1963–70 and 1971–74, Hon. Alderman, 1974–; Lord Mayor of Birmingham, 1971–72, Dep. Lord Mayor, 1972–73; West Midlands County Council: Mem., 1974–77, 1981–86; Vice-Chm., 1983–84, Chm., 1984–85; Chm., Airport Cttee, 1974–77; Member: Airport and Fire Bde Cttee; Transportation Cttee. Chm., Birmingham Airport, 1959–66; Dir, Birmingham Exec. Airways, 1983–89. Chairman: Smallholdings and Agric. Cttee, 1954–58; West Midlands Regional Adv. Cttee for Civil Aviation, 1966–72; Jt Airports Cttee of Local Authorities, 1975–77. Vice Pres., Heart of England Tourist Bd, 1977– (Chm., 1975–77). Chm., Hall Green Div. Labour Party, 1957–59. Former Governor, Coll. of Technology (now Univ. of Aston in Birmingham). *Recreations:* football, cricket, table tennis, philately. *Address:* 121 Maypole Lane, King's Heath, Birmingham B14 4PF. *Club:* Rotary (Birmingham).

TURVEY, Garry, CBE 1991; Director-General, Freight Transport Association, 1984–93; *b* 11 Oct. 1934; *s* of Henry Oxley Turvey and Annie Maud Braley; *m* 1960, Hilary Margaret Saines; three *s. Educ:* Morecambe Grammar School. FCIS; FCIT. Metropolitan Vickers Ltd, Manchester, 1956–58; AEI Manchester Ltd, 1958–60; Asst Sec., 1960–67, Sec., 1967–69, Traders' Road Transport Assoc.; Sec., 1969–84 and Dep. Dir-Gen., 1974–84, Freight Transport Assoc. Freeman, City of London, 1994; Liveryman, Carmen's Co., 1994. *Recreations:* cricket, gardening. *Address:* 139 Imberhorne Lane, East Grinstead, West Sussex RH19 1RP. *T:* East Grinstead (01342) 325829. *Clubs:* Royal Automobile, MCC.

TURVEY, Ralph, DSc (Econ); economist; Visiting Professor of Economics, London School of Economics, 1973–75 and since 1990; *b* 1 May 1927; *s* of John and Margaret Turvey; *m* 1957, Sheila Bucher (*d* 1987); one *s* one *d. Educ:* Sidcot School; London School of Economics; Uppsala University. Lectr, then Reader, in Economics, at London School of Economics, 1948–64, with interruptions. Vis. Lectr, Johns Hopkins Univ., 1953; Ford Foundation Vis. Res. Prof., Univ. of Chicago, 1958–59; Economic Section, HM Treasury, 1960–62; Center of Economic Research, Athens, 1963. Chief Economist, The Electricity Council, 1964–67. Member, NBPI, 1967–71, Jt Dep. Chm. 1968–71; Economic Advr, Scientific Control Systems Ltd, 1971–75; Economic Advr, then Chief Statistician, ILO, 1975–89; Dir, Dept of Labour Information and Statistics, ILO, until 1989; Res. Fellow, Statistics Canada, 1989–90. Mem., Nat. Water Council, 1974–75. Governor, Kingston Polytechnic, 1972–75. Member: Inflation Accounting Cttee, 1974–75; NZ Adv. Cttee on price indices, 1991; RPI Adv. Cttee, 1992–94; Canadian and Swedish adv. cttees on consumer price indices. *Publications:* The Economics of Real Property, 1957; Interest Rates and Asset Prices, 1960; (joint author) Studies in Greek Taxation, 1964; Optimal Pricing and Investment in Electricity Supply, 1968; Economic Analysis and Public Enterprises, 1971; Demand and Supply, 1971; (joint author) Electricity Economics, 1977; Consumer Price Indices, 1989; (ed and joint author) Developments in International Labour Statistics, 1989; papers on applied welfare economics in Economic Jl, Amer. Economic Review, etc. *Recreations:* economic history of Victorian London, walking. *Address:* 30 Sloane Gardens, SW1W 8DJ. *Club:* Reform.

TUSA, John; Managing Director, Barbican Centre, since 1995; *b* 2 March 1936; *s* of late John Tusa, OBE and of Lydia Sklenarova; *m* 1960, Ann Hilary Dowson; two *s. Educ:* Trinity Coll., Cambridge (BA 1st Cl. Hons History). BBC general trainee, 1960; Producer, BBC External Services, 1962; freelance radio journalist, 1965; Presenter: BBC Radio 4 The World Tonight, 1968; BBC2 Newsnight, 1979–86; Man. Dir, World Service, BBC, 1986–92; Presenter, One O'Clock News, BBC TV, 1993–95. Chm., London News Radio, 1993–94. Pres., Wolfson Coll., Cambridge, 1993. Chairman: Adv. Cttee, Govt Art Collection, 1993–; BBC Marshall Plan of the Mind Trust, 1992–; Member: Council, RIIA, 1984–90, 1991–; Board, Public Radio Internat. (formerly American Public Radio), 1990–; Adv. Cttee, London Internat. String Quartet Competition, 1991– (Vice-Chm. of Board, 1995–); Board, ENO, 1994–; Trustee: Nat. Portrait Gall., 1988–; Thomson Foundn, 1992–; Wigmore Hall Trust, 1993–. Hon. LLD London, 1993; DUniv Heriot-

Watt, 1993. TV Journalist of the Year, RTS 1983; Richard Dimbleby Award, BAFTA, 1984; BPG Award for outstanding contribn to radio, 1991. *Publications:* Conversations with the World, 1990; A World in Your Ear, 1992; (with Ann Tusa): The Nuremberg Trial, 1983; The Berlin Blockade, 1988. *Recreations:* tennis, chamber music, listening. *Address:* 21 Christchurch Hill, NW3 1JY. *T:* 0171–435 9495.

TUSHINGHAM, Rita; actress; *b* 14 March 1942; *d* of John Tushingham; *m* 1962, Terence William Bicknell (marr. diss. 1976); two *d*; *m* 1981, Ousama Rawi. *Educ:* La Sagesse Convent, Liverpool. Student, Liverpool Playhouse, 1958–60. BBC Personality of the Year, Variety Club of GB, 1988. *Stage appearances:* Royal Court Theatre: The Changeling, 1960; The Kitchen, 1961; A Midsummer Night's Dream, 1962; Twelfth Night, 1962; The Knack, 1962; other London theatres: The Giveaway, 1969; Lorna and Ted, 1970; Mistress of Novices, 1973; My Fat Friend, 1981; Children, Children, 1984. *Films:* A Taste of Honey, 1961 (Brit. Film Acad. and Variety Club awards for Most Promising Newcomer, 1961; NY Critics, Cannes Film Festival and Hollywood Foreign Press Assoc. awards); The Leather Boys, 1962; A Place to Go, 1963; Girl with Green Eyes, 1963 (Variety Club award); The Knack, 1964 (Silver Goddess award, Mexican Assoc. of Film Corresps); Dr Zhivago, 1965; The Trap, 1966; Smashing Time, 1967; Diamonds For Breakfast, 1967; The Guru, 1968; The Bed-Sitting Room, 1970; Straight on till Morning, 1972; Situation, 1972; Instant Coffee, 1973; Rachel's Man, 1974; The Human Factor, 1976; Pot Luck, 1977; State of Shock, 1977; Mysteries, 1978; Incredible Mrs Chadwick, 1979; The Spaghetti House Siege, 1982; Flying, 1984; A Judgement in Stone, 1986; Single Room, 1986; Resurrected, 1989; Dante and Beatrice in Liverpool, 1989; Hard Days' Hard Nights, 1990; Paper Marriage, 1991; Rapture of Deceit, 1991; Desert Lunch, 1992; An Awfully Big Adventure, 1994. *TV appearances include:* Red Riding Hood (play), 1973; No Strings (own series), 1974; Don't Let Them Kill Me on Wednesday, 1980; Confessions of Felix Krull, 1980; Seeing Red, 1983; Pippi Longstocking, 1984; The White Whale — The Life of Ernest Hemingway (film), 1987; cameo appearance in Bread, 1988; Sunday Pursuit; Gütt, Ein Journalist, 1991; Hamburg Poison, 1992; Family Secrets (film), 1995. *Recreations:* interior decorating, cooking, watercolour painting. *Address:* c/o Grizelda Burgess, London Management, 2–4 Noel Street, W1V 3RB.

TUSTIN, Rt. Rev. David; *see* Grimsby, Bishop Suffragan of.

TUTI, Rt Rev. Dudley, KBE 1988 (OBE 1974); Paramount Chief of Santa Ysabel, since 1975; Chairman, Solomon Islands Credit Union, since 1982; Member, Law Reform Commission, Solomon Islands, since 1995; *b* 1919; *s* of John Tariniu and Daisy Mele Pago; *m* 1957, Naomi Tate; one *s* seven *d* (and one *s* decd). *Educ:* St John's Coll., Auckland, NZ. Deacon, 1946; priest, 1954. Headmaster, Vureas Boys' Sch., 1954–56; District Priest and Rural Dean of Santa Ysabel, 1956–63; consecrated Bishop (by the Archbishop of NZ), 1963; Asst Bishop, dio. of Melanesia, 1963–75; Bishop and Archdeacon, Central Solomons, 1968–75; Vicar-General, dio. of Melanesia, 1971–75; Bishop of Santa Ysabel, 1975–82. *Address:* Jejevo, Santa Ysabel, Solomon Islands. *T:* 35135.

TUTIN, Dorothy, CBE 1967; actress (stage and films); *b* 8 April 1931; *d* of late John Tutin, DSc, and Adie Evelyn Tutin; *m* 1963, Derek Barton-Chapple (stage name Derek Waring); one *s* one *d*. *Educ:* St Catherine's, Bramley, Surrey; RADA. Began career, 1950; Stratford Festival, 1958, 1960. *Parts include:* Rose, in The Living Room; Katherine, in Henry V; Sally Bowles, in I am a Camera; St Joan, in The Lark; Catherine, in The Gates of Summer; Hedwig, in The Wild Duck; Viola, in Twelfth Night; Juliet, in Romeo and Juliet; Ophelia, in Hamlet; during Shakespeare Memorial Theatre tour of Russia, 1958, played parts of Ophelia, Viola and Juliet; Dolly, in Once More, With Feeling (New), 1959; Portia, Viola, Cressida (S-on-A), 1960; Sister Jeanne, in The Devils (Aldwych), 1961, 1962; Juliet, Desdemona (S-on-A), 1961; Varya, in The Cherry Orchard (S-on-A, and Aldwych), 1961; Cressida, Prioress, in The Devils (Edinburgh), 1962; Polly Peachum, in The Beggar's Opera (Aldwych), 1963; The Hollow Crown (New York), 1963; Queen Victoria, in Portrait of a Queen, Vaudeville, 1965; Rosalind, As You Like It, Stratford, 1967, Los Angeles, 1968; Portrait of a Queen, NY, 1968; Play on Love, St Martin's, 1970; Old Times, Aldwych, 1971; Peter Pan, Coliseum, 1971, 1972; What Every Woman Knows, 1973, Albery, 1974; Natalya Petrovna, in A Month in the Country, Chichester, 1974, Albery, 1975; Cleopatra, in Antony and Cleopatra, Edinburgh, 1977; Madame Ranevsky, The Cherry Orchard, Lady Macbeth, in Macbeth, Lady Plyant, in The Double Dealer (SWET Award, 1978), Nat. Theatre, 1978; Undiscovered Country, Nat. Theatre, 1979; Reflections, Theatre Royal, Haymarket, 1980; The Provok'd Wife, Nat. Theatre, 1980; Hester, in The Deep Blue Sea, Greenwich, 1981; After the Lions, Royal Exchange, Manchester, 1982; Ballerina, Churchill Theatre, Bromley, 1984; A Kind of Alaska, Duchess Theatre, 1985; The Chalk Garden, Chichester, 1986; Are you sitting comfortably, Watford, 1986; Brighton Beach Memoirs, Aldwych, 1987; Thursday's Ladies, Apollo, 1987, Harlequinade and The Browning Version (double-bill), Royalty, 1988; A Little Night Music, Chichester Fest., transf. Piccadilly, 1989; Henry VIII, Chichester, 1991; Getting Married, Chichester, 1993. *Films:* Cecily, in The Importance of Being Earnest, 1951; Polly Peachum, in The Beggar's Opera, 1954; Lucie Manette, in A Tale of Two Cities, 1956; Henrietta Maria in Cromwell; Sophie Breska in Savage Messiah (Variety Club of GB Film Actress Award, 1972); The Shooting Party; Great Moments in Aviation, 1992; The Great Kandinsky. Has appeared on television. *Recreations:* music; Isle of Arran. *Address:* c/o Michael Whitehall, 125 Gloucester Road, SW7 4TE.

TUTIN, Mrs Winifred Anne, (Winifred Pennington), PhD; FRS 1979; Principal Scientific Officer, Freshwater Biological Association, 1967–81, retired; *b* 8 Oct. 1915; *d* of Albert R. Pennington and Margaret S. Pennington; *m* 1942, Thomas Gaskell Tutin, FRS (*d* 1987); one *s* three *d*. *Educ:* Barrow-in-Furness Grammar Sch.; Reading Univ. (BSc, PhD). Research posts with Freshwater Biological Assoc., 1940–45; Demonstrator and Special Lectr, Univ. of Leicester, 1947–67; Hon. Reader in Botany, Univ. of Leicester, 1971–79, Hon. Professor, 1980–. Foreign Member, Royal Danish Academy, 1974. *Publications:* (as Winifred Pennington): The History of British Vegetation, 1969, 2nd edn 1974; (with W. H. Pearsall) The Lake District, 1973; papers in New Phytologist, Jl of Ecology, Phil. Trans of Royal Society, and others. *Recreations:* gardening, plain cooking. *Address:* Priory Cottage, North Street, Kingsclere, Newbury, Berks RG20 5QY.

TUTT, Prof. Norman Sydney; Executive Director, Social Information Systems, since 1993; *b* 8 June 1944; *s* of Sydney Robert Tutt and Stella May Tutt; *m* 1966, Diana Patricia Hewitt; two *s*. *Educ:* Chislehurst and Sidcup Grammar Sch.; Univ. of Keele (BA); Univ. of Leeds (MSc); Univ. of Nottingham (PhD). Clin. Psychologist, Nottingham, 1966–69; Resident Psychologist, St Gilbert's Approved Sch., 1969–73; Professional Advr, Northampton Social Services, 1973–74; Sen. Develt Officer, London Boroughs Children Reg. Planning Cttee, 1974–75; Principal Social Work Services Officer, DHSS, 1975–79; Prof. of Applied Social Studies, 1979–92 (on leave of absence, 1989–92), and Hon. Prof., 1992–95, Lancaster Univ.; Dir of Social Services, Leeds CC, 1989–93. Vis. Prof., Faculty of Community Health Scis, Cardiff Inst., 1994. *Publications:* Care or Custody, 1975; (ed) Violence, 1975; (ed) Alternative Strategies for Coping with Crime, 1978; (ed) A Way of Life for the Handicapped, 1983; Children in Custody, 1987; contributor to other pubns. *Recreations:* work, wine, walks, cracking jokes. *Address:* Styche Hall, Market Drayton, Salop TF9 3RB; Le Grand Margantinet, 61330 Torchamp, France. *Clubs:* as with Groucho Marx he would not join a club which would have him as a member.

TUTTE, Prof. William Thomas, FRS 1987; FRSC 1958; Professor of Mathematics, University of Waterloo, Ontario, 1962–85, Professor Emeritus since 1985; *b* 14 May 1917; *s* of William John Tutte and Annie Tutte (*née* Newell); *m* 1949, Dorothea Geraldine Mitchell. *Educ:* Cambridge and County High Sch.; Cambridge Univ. (BA, MA, PhD). Fellow of Trinity Coll., Cambridge, 1942–49; Lectr to Associate Prof., Univ. of Toronto, 1948–62. *Publications:* Connectivity in Graphs, 1966; Introduction to the Theory of Matroids, 1971; Graph Theory, 1984; papers in mathematical jls. *Address:* 16 Bridge Street, West Montrose, Ont N0B 2V0, Canada. *T:* (519) 6692475.

TUTU, Most Rev. Desmond Mpilo; *see* Cape Town, Archbishop of.

TUZO, Gen. Sir Harry (Craufurd), GCB 1973 (KCB 1971); OBE 1961; MC 1945; DL; *b* 26 Aug. 1917; *s* of John Atkinson Tuzo and Annie Katherine (*née* Craufurd); *m* 1943, Monica Patience Salter; one *d*. *Educ:* Wellington Coll.; Oriel Coll., Oxford (Hon. Fellow 1977). BA Oxon 1939, MA 1970. Regimental Service, Royal Artillery, 1939–45; Staff appts, Far East, 1946–49; Royal Horse Artillery, 1950–51 and 1954–58; Staff at Sch. of Infantry, 1951–53; GSO1, War Office, 1958–60; CO, 3rd Regt, RHA, 1960–62; Asst Comdt, Sandhurst, 1962–63; Comdr, 51 Gurkha Infantry Bde, 1963–65; Imp. Def. Coll., 1966; Maj.-Gen. 1966; Chief of Staff, BAOR, 1967–69; Director, RA, 1969–71; Lt-Gen. 1971; GOC and Dir of Operations, NI, 1971–73; Gen. 1973; Comdr Northern Army Gp and C-in-C BAOR, 1973–76; Dep. Supreme Allied Comdr, Europe, 1976–78. ADC (Gen.) to the Queen, 1974–77. Colonel Commandant: RA, 1971–83; RHA, 1976–83; Master Gunner, St James's Park, 1977–83. Chm., Marconi Space and Defence Systems, 1979–83; Dir, Oceonics, 1988–91. Chm., RUSI, 1980–83; Member: Council, IISS, 1978–87; Council, Inst. for Study of Conflict, later Res. Inst. for Study of Conflict and Terrorism, 1979–91. Chairman: Fermoy Centre Foundn, Kings Lynn, 1982–87; Imperial War Mus. Redevelt Appeal, 1984–88; Council, Pensthorpe Waterfowl Trust, 1988–; Pres., Norfolk Soc., CPRE, 1987–92. DL Norfolk, 1983. Dato Setia Negeri Brunei, 1965. *Recreations:* gardening, music, theatre. *Club:* Army and Navy.
See also Sir William Garthwaite, Bt.

TWEEDDALE, 13th Marquis of, *cr* 1694; **Edward Douglas John Hay;** Lord Hay of Yester, 1488; Earl of Tweeddale, 1646; Viscount Walden, Earl of Gifford, 1694; Baron Tweeddale (UK), 1881; Hereditary Chamberlain of Dunfermline; insurance broker; *b* 6 Aug. 1947; *s* of 12th Marquis of Tweeddale, GC, and of Sonia Mary, *d* of 1st Viscount Ingleby; *S* father, 1979. *Educ:* Milton Abbey, Blandford, Dorset; Trinity Coll., Oxford (BA Hons PPE). *Heir: yr* twin *b* Lord Charles David Montagu Hay, *b* 6 Aug. 1947. *Address:* House of Lords, SW1A 0PW.

TWEEDIE, Sir David (Philip), Kt 1994; Chairman, Accounting Standards Board, since 1990; *b* 7 July 1944; *s* of Aidrian Ian Tweedie and Marie Patricia Tweedie (*née* Phillips); *m* 1970, Janice Christine Brown; two *s*. *Educ:* Grangemouth High Sch.; Edinburgh Univ. (BCom, PhD). CA 1972. Accountancy trng, Mann, Judd, Gordon (Glasgow), 1969–72; Edinburgh University: Lectr in Accounting, 1973–78; Associate Dean, Fac. of Social Scis, 1975–78; Technical Dir, Inst. of Chartered Accountants, Scotland, 1978–81; Nat. Res. Partner, KMG Thomson McLintock, 1982–87; Nat. Tech. Partner, KPMG Peat Marwick McLintock, 1987–90. Visiting Professor of Accounting: Univ. of Lancaster, 1978–88; Univ. of Bristol, 1988–. UK and Irish Tech. Advr, Internat. Accounting Standards Cttee, 1979–81; UK and Irish Rep., Internat. Auditing Practices Cttee, 1983–88; Auditing Practices Committee, Consultative Committee of Accountancy Bodies: Mem., 1985–90; Vice-Chm., 1986–88; Chm., 1989–90. Institute of Chartered Accountants in England and Wales: Mem. Council, 1989–91; Mem., Financial Reporting Council, 1990–; Chm., Urgent Issues Task Force, 1990–. Hon. DSc (Econ) Hull, 1993; Hon. LLD Lancaster, 1993. *Publications:* (with T. A. Lee) The Private Shareholder and the Corporate Report, 1977; Financial Reporting, Inflation and the Capital Maintenance Concept, 1979; (with T. A. Lee) The Institutional Investor and Financial Information, 1981; (with G. Whittington) The Debate on Inflation Accounting, 1984; contribs to professional and acad. accounting jls and books. *Recreations:* athletics and Rugby (watching, not participating, sadly), walking, gardening. *Address:* c/o Accounting Standards Board, 100 Gray's Inn Road, WC1X 8AL. *T:* 0171–404 8818.

TWEEDSMUIR, 2nd Baron, *cr* 1935, of Elsfield; **John Norman Stuart Buchan,** CBE 1964 (OBE (mil.) 1945); CD 1964; FRSE; Lt-Col Canadian Infantry Corps, retired; *b* 25 November 1911; *e s* of 1st Baron and Susan Charlotte (*d* 1977), *d* of Hon. Norman Grosvenor; *S* father, 1940; *m* 1st, 1948, Priscilla Jean Fortescue, later Baroness Tweedsmuir of Belhelvie, PC (*d* 1978); one *d*; 2nd, 1980, Jean Margherita, *widow* of Sir Francis Grant, 12th Bt. *Educ:* Eton; Brasenose Coll., Oxford (BA 1933; MA 1987). Asst District Comr, Uganda Protectorate, 1934–36; joined Hudson's Bay Company, 1937; wintered in their service at Cape Dorset, Baffin Land, Canadian Arctic, 1938–39; served War of 1939–45 in Canadian Army (wounded, despatches twice, OBE (mil.) 1945, Order of Orange-Nassau, with swords); comd Hastings and Prince Edward Regt in Sicily and Italy, 1943; Hon. Col, 1955–60. Rector of Aberdeen Univ., 1948–51; Chm., Joint East and Central African Board, 1950–52; UK Delegate: UN Assembly, 1951–52; Council of Europe, 1952; Pres., Commonwealth and British Empire Chambers of Commerce, 1955–57; a Governor: Commonwealth Inst., 1958–77, Trustee, 1977–; Ditchley Foundn; Pres., Inst. of Export, 1964–67; Mem. Board, BOAC, 1955–64; Chairman: Advertising Standards Authority, 1971–74; Council on Tribunals, 1973–80. Mem., Scottish Cttee, Nature Conservancy, 1971–73. President: Institute of Rural Life at Home and Overseas, 1951–85; British Schools Exploring Society, 1964–85; Chm., British Rheumatism and Arthritis Assoc., 1971–78, Pres., 1978–86. Chancellor, Primrose League, 1969–75. FRSA. Hon. LLD: Aberdeen, 1949; Queen's (Canada) 1955. *Publications:* (part author) St Kilda papers, 1931; Hudson's Bay Trader, 1951; Always a Countryman, 1953; One Man's Happiness, 1968. *Recreations:* fishing, shooting, falconry. *Heir: b* Hon. William de l'Aigle Buchan, RAFVR [*b* 10 Jan. 1916; *m* 1st, Nesta (marr. diss. 1946), *o d* of Lt-Col C. D. Crozier; one *d*; 2nd, 1946, Barbara (marr. diss. 1960), 2nd *d* of E. N. Ensor, late of Hong Kong; three *s* three *d*; 3rd, 1960, Sauré Cynthia Mary, *y d* of late Major G. E. Tatchell, Royal Lincolnshire Regt; one *s*. *Educ:* Eton; New College, Oxford]. *Address:* Kingston House, Kingston Bagpuize, Oxon OX13 5AX. *T:* Longworth (01865) 820259. *Clubs:* Carlton, Travellers', Flyfishers'.
See also Lord James Douglas-Hamilton.

TWEEDY, Colin David; Director General, Association for Business Sponsorship of the Arts, since 1983; *b* 26 Oct. 1953; *s* of Clifford Harry Tweedy, of Abbotsbury, Dorset and Kitty Audrey (*née* Matthews). *Educ:* City of Bath Boys' Sch.; St Catherine's Coll., Oxford (MA). Manager, Thorndike Theatre, Leatherhead, 1976–78; Corporate Finance Officer, Guinness Mahon, 1978–80; Asst Dir, Streets Financial PR, 1980–83. Dir, ABSA Consulting. Vice Chm., Comité Européen pour le Rapprochement de l'Economie et de la Culture; Mem. Council, Japan Festival, 1991; Director: Covent Garden Festival; Oxford Stage Co.; Crusaid; Member: UK Nat. Cttee, European Cinema and TV Year, 1988–89; Council for Charitable Support; Nat. Cinema Centenary Cttee. Trustee, Serpentine Gall.

Freeman, City of London, 1978. FRSA. *Publication:* A Celebration of Ten Years' Business Sponsorship of the Arts, 1987. *Recreations:* the arts in general, opera, theatre and contemporary art in particular, food, travel. *Address:* Association for Business Sponsorship of the Arts, Nutmeg House, 60 Gainsford Street, SE1 2NY. *T:* 0171–378 8143. *Club:* United Oxford & Cambridge University.

TWELVETREE, Eric Alan; designer silversmith, since 1991; Director, Chelmsford Hospice, since 1991; Member, Executive Committee, Field Studies Council, since 1978; *b* 26 Dec. 1928; *m* 1953, Patricia Mary Starkings; two *d. Educ:* Stamford Sch., Lincs; qualif. IPFA and ACCA. Served with Borough Councils: Gt Yarmouth, Ipswich, Stockport, Southampton; County Councils: Gloucestershire, Kent; County Treasurer, Essex CC, 1974–87. Pres., Soc. of County Treasurers, 1986–87. *Address:* 17 Bishopscourt Gardens, Chelmsford, Essex CM2 6AZ.

TWIGG, Patrick Alan; QC 1986; a Recorder, since 1987; *b* 19 May 1943; *s* of late Alan Oswald Twigg and of Gwendoline Mary Twigg; *m* 1974, Gabrielle Madeline Bay Green; one *s* one *d. Educ:* Repton Sch., Derbyshire; Universities of: The Sorbonne, Paris; Perugia, Italy; Bristol (LLB); Virginia, USA (LLM). Called to the Bar, Inner Temple, 1967; Mem., Western Circuit. Dir, Canterbury Festival, 1991–. Pres., Bishopsbourne Cricket Club, 1989–. *Recreations:* family, landscape and other gardening, music (particularly piano and chamber music), musical composition, amateur dramatics (Mem. Old Stagers 1969–), travel, lawn tennis. *Address:* 2 Temple Gardens, Temple, EC4Y 9AY. *T:* 0171–583 6041, *Fax:* 0171–583 2094. *Club:* Delta Theta Phi Fraternity (Charlottesville, Virginia).

TWIGGY; *see* Lawson, Lesley.

TWIN, Prof. Peter John, OBE 1991; FRS 1993; Professor of Experimental Physics, University of Liverpool, since 1987; *b* 26 July 1939; *s* of Arthur James and Hilda Ethel Twin; *m* 1963, Jean Esther Leatherland; one *s* one *d. Educ:* Sir George Monoux Grammar Sch., Walthamstow; Univ. of Liverpool (BSc Hons, PhD). University of Liverpool: Lectr, 1964–73; Sen. Lectr, 1973–79; Reader, 1979–87; Head, Nuclear Structure Facility, Daresbury Lab., SERC, 1983–87. Vis. Prof., Univ. of Alberta, 1968–69. Reader, dio. of Chester, 1991–. Tom Bonner Prize, APS, 1991; John Price Wetherill Medal, Benjamin Franklin Inst., USA, 1991. *Publications:* numerous papers in learned jls. *Address:* Oliver Lodge Laboratory, University of Liverpool, Liverpool L69 3BX. *T:* 0151–794 3378.

TWINING, Prof. William Lawrence; Quain Professor of Jurisprudence, University College London, since 1983; *b* 22 Sept. 1934; *s* of Edward Francis Twining and Helen Mary Twining (*née* Dubuisson); *m* 1957, Penelope Elizabeth Wall Morris; one *s* one *d. Educ:* Charterhouse School; Brasenose College, Oxford (BA 1955; MA 1960; DCL 1990); Univ. of Chicago (JD 1958). Lectr in Private Law, Univ. of Khartoum, 1958–61; Sen. Lectr in Law, University Coll., Dar-es-Salaam, 1961–65; Prof. of Jurisprudence, The Queen's Univ., Belfast, 1965–72; Prof. of Law, Univ. of Warwick, 1972–82. Mem., Cttee on Legal Educn in N Ireland, 1972–74; President: Soc. of Public Law Teachers of Law, 1978–79; UK Assoc. for Legal and Social Philosophy, 1980–83; Chairman: Bentham Cttee, 1982–; Commonwealth Legal Educn Assoc., 1983–93; vis. appts in several Univs. Hon. LLD: Univ. of Victoria, BC, 1980; Edinburgh, 1994. General Editor: Law in Context series, 1966–; Jurists series, 1979–. *Publications:* The Karl Llewellyn Papers, 1968; Karl Llewellyn and the Realist Movement, 1973; (with David Miers) How to Do Things with Rules, 1976, 3rd edn 1991; (with J. Uglow) Law Publishing and Legal Information, 1981; (ed) Facts in Law, 1983; Theories of Evidence, 1985; (ed) Legal Theory and Common Law, 1986; (ed with R. Tur) Essays on Kelsen, 1986; (ed jtly) Learning Lawyers' Skills, 1989; (ed jtly) Access to Legal Education and the Legal Profession, 1989; Rethinking Evidence, 1990; (ed) Issues of Self-determination, 1991; (with T. Anderson) Analysis of Evidence, 1991; (with E. Quick) Legal Records in the Commonwealth, 1994; Blackstone's Tower: the English Law School, 1994. *Address:* 10 Mill Lane, Iffley, Oxford OX4 4EJ.

TWINN, Ian David, PhD; MP (C) Edmonton, since 1983; *b* 26 April 1950; *s* of David Twinn and Gwynneth Irene Twinn; *m* 1973, Frances Elizabeth Holtby; two *s. Educ:* Netherhall Secondary Modern School, Cambridge; Cambridge Grammar School; University College of Wales, Aberystwyth (BA hons); University of Reading (PhD). Senior Lecturer in Planning, Polytechnic of the South Bank, 1975–83. PPS to Minister of State for Industry, 1985–86, to Dep. Chm. of Cons. Party, 1986–88, to Minister of State for Energy, 1987–90, to Minister of State for the Environment, 1990–92, to Paymaster Gen., 1992–94. Vice Chm., British Caribbean Assoc., 1986–. FRSA 1989; FRGS. *Recreations:* collecting secondhand books, renovating antique furniture. *Address:* House of Commons, SW1A 0AA. *T:* 0171–219 3000.

TWINN, John Ernest; Director General Guided Weapons and Electronics, Ministry of Defence, 1978–81, retired; *b* 11 July 1921; *s* of late Col Frank Charles George Twinn, CMG and Lilian May Twinn (*née* Tomlinson); *m* 1950, Mary Constance Smallwood; three *d. Educ:* Manchester Grammar Sch.; Christ's Coll., Cambridge (MA). FIEE 1981. Air Min., 1941; Telecommunications Research Estabt (later Royal Radar Estabt), 1943; Head of Guided Weapons Gp, RRE, 1965; Head of Space Dept, RAE, 1968; Head of Weapons Dept, RAE, 1972; Asst Chief Scientific Advr (Projects), MoD, 1973; Dir Underwater Weapons Projects (Naval), 1976. *Recreations:* sailing, music, genealogy. *Address:* Timbers, 9 Woodway, Merrow, Guildford, Surrey GU1 2TF. *T:* Guildford (01483) 68993.

TWISK, Russell Godfrey; Editor-in-Chief, British Reader's Digest, since 1988; *b* 24 Aug. 1941; *s* of K. Y. Twisk and Joyce Brunning; *m* 1965, Ellen Elizabeth Banbury; two *d. Educ:* Salesian Coll., Farnborough. Harmsworth Press, Dep. Editor, Golf Illustrated, 1960; Sub Editor, Sphere; freelance journalist, 1962; joined BBC, editorial staff Radio Times, 1966; Deputy Editor, Radio Times, 1971; Development Manager, BBC, 1975; Editor, The Listener, 1981–87. Has edited numerous BBC publications; radio critic for The Observer, 1989–94; Publisher, BBC Adult Literacy Project; devised Radio Times Drama Awards. Director: Reader's Digest, 1988–; Berkeley Magazines Ltd, 1990–. Governor, London College of Printing, 1967–87 (Chm., 1974, 1978). Mem. Adv. Council, ASH. Chm., Reader's Digest Trust, 1988–. Chm., National Campaign Cttee, Charities Aid Foundn, 1991–94. Pres., Media Soc., 1993–95. *Recreations:* running, map reading, watching horses race. *Address:* The Old Barn, Harting, near Petersfield, Hants GU31 5LZ. *Clubs:* Reform, Groucho.

TWISLETON-WYKEHAM-FIENNES; *see* Fiennes.

TWISLETON-WYKEHAM-FIENNES, Sir John (Saye Wingfield), KCB 1970 (CB 1953); QC 1972; First Parliamentary Counsel, 1968–72, retired; *b* 14 April 1911; *s* of Gerard Yorke Twisleton-Wykeham-Fiennes and Gwendolen (*née* Gisborne); *m* 1937, Sylvia Beatrice, *d* of Rev. C. R. L. McDowall; two *s* one *d. Educ:* Winchester; Balliol College, Oxford. Called to Bar, Middle Temple, 1936; Bencher, 1969. Joined parliamentary counsel office, 1939; Second Parly Coun., Treasury, 1956–68. Parliamentary Counsel, Malaya, 1962–63 (Colombo Plan). With Law Commission, 1965–66. *Address:* Mill House, Preston, Sudbury, Suffolk CO10 9ND.

TWISS, (Lionel) Peter; OBE 1957; DSC 1942 and Bar 1943; marine consultant; Director and General Manager, Hamble Point Marina Ltd, 1978–88; formerly Chief Test Pilot of Fairey Aviation Ltd; *b* 23 July 1921; *m* 1950, Mrs Vera Maguire (marr. diss.); one *d* (and one *d* decd), one step *s* one step *d*; *m* 1960, Cherry (marr. diss.), *d* of late Sir John Huggins, GCMG, MC; one *d*; *m* 1964, Mrs Heather Danby (*d* 1988), Titchfield; one step *s* one step *d. Educ:* Sherborne Sch. Joined Fleet Air Arm, 1939; served on catapult ships, aircraft-carriers, 1941–43; night fighter development, 1943–44; served in British Air Commn, America, 1944. Empire Test Pilots School, Boscombe Down, 1945; Test Pilot, Fairey Aviation Co. Ltd, 1946, Chief Test Pilot, 1957–60. Dir, Fairey Marine Ltd, 1968–78. Mem., Lasham Gliding Soc. Holder of World's Absolute Speed Record, 10 March 1956. *Publication:* Faster than the Sun, 1963. *Address:* Nettleworth, 33 South Street, Titchfield, Hants PO14 4DL. *T:* Titchfield (01329) 843146. *Clubs:* Royal Southern Yacht; Surrey and Hants Gliding.

TWIST, Henry Aloysius, CMG 1966; OBE 1947; company director; *b* 18 June 1914; *s* of John Twist, Preston; *m* 1941, Mary Monica, *yr d* of Nicholas Mulhall, Manchester; one *s* one *d. Educ:* Liverpool Univ. (BA). Senior Classics Master, St Chad's Coll., Wolverhampton, 1936–40; Lecturer in English, South Staffordshire High School of Commerce, 1939–40. Served War of 1939–45 with RASC and RAEC, 1940–46; released with rank of Lt-Col, 1946. Principal, Dominions Office, 1946; Official Secretary, British High Commission in Ceylon, 1948–49; British High Commission in Australia, 1949–52; Commonwealth Relations Office, 1952–54; Secretariat, Commonwealth Economic Conference, London, 1952; Deputy High Commissioner for the United Kingdom in Bombay, 1954–57; Assistant Secretary, Commonwealth Relations Office, 1957–60; British Deputy High Commissioner, Kaduna, Northern Region, Federation of Nigeria, 1960–62; Commonwealth Service representative on the 1963 Course at Imperial Defence College; Commonwealth Office, 1964; Asst Under-Sec., 1966; Dep. High Comr, 1966–70, Minister (Commercial), 1968–70, Rawalpindi; retired 1970. Dir of Studies, RIPA, 1973–82. *Recreation:* gardening. *Address:* Pine Lodge, Woodham Lane, Woking, Surrey GU21 5SP. *Club:* Commonwealth Trust.

TWIST, Kenneth Lyndon, CEng, FIMinE; HM Chief Inspector of Mines, since 1992; *b* 13 Jan. 1938; *s* of Joseph and Sarah Ellen Twist; *m* 1959, Emily Owens; three *s. Educ:* Wigan and Dist Mining & Technical Coll. (Dip. Mining Engrg). Colliery Manager's Cert., 1963. FIMinE 1979. Dep. General Manager, Agecroft, 1969–76; Health and Safety Executive: Inspector of Mines, 1976–87; Principal Dist Inspector of Mines, 1987–91; Dep. Chief Inspector of Mines, 1991–92. Chm., Safety in Mines Res. Adv. Bd, HSC, 1992–. FRSA. *Publications:* papers in Mining Engineer, Jl of Instn of Mining Engrs. *Recreations:* gardening, reading, computing. *Address:* Ridgeway, Sunnyridge Avenue, Marford, Clwyd LL12 8TE. *T:* Gresford (01978) 855638.

TWITCHETT, Prof. Denis Crispin, FBA 1967; Gordon Wu Professor of Chinese Studies, Princeton University, 1980–94; *b* 23 Sept. 1925; *m* 1956, Umeko (*née* Ichikawa); two *s. Educ:* St Catharine's Coll., Cambridge. Lectr in Far-Eastern History, Univ. of London, 1954–56; Univ. Lectr in Classical Chinese, Univ. of Cambridge, 1956–60; Prof. of Chinese, SOAS, London Univ., 1960–68; Prof. of Chinese, Univ. of Cambridge, 1968–80. Vis. Prof., Princeton Univ., 1973–74, 1978–79. Principal Editor, Cambridge History of China, 1977–. *Publications:* (ed with A. F. Wright) Confucian Personalities, 1962; The Financial Administration under the T'ang dynasty, 1963, 2nd edn 1971; (ed with A. F. Wright) Perspectives on the T'ang, 1973; (ed with P. J. M. Geelan) The Times Atlas of China, 1975; (ed) Cambridge History of China, Vol. 10 1978, Vol. 3 1979, Vol. 11 1980, Vol. 12 1983, Vol. 1 1986, Vol. 13 1986, Vol. 7 1987, Vol. 14 1987, Vol. 15 1990, Vol. 6 1994; Printing and Publishing in Medieval China, 1983; Reader in T'ang History, 1986; The Writing of Official History in T'ang China, 1992. *Address:* 24 Arbury Road, Cambridge CB4 2JE; 211 Jones Hall, Princeton, NJ 08544, USA.

TWITE, Robin, OBE 1982; Projects Director, Israel-Palestine Center for Research and Information, Jerusalem, since 1993; Director, Conflict Resolution Project, Leonard Davis Institute for International Relations, Hebrew University, since 1994; *b* 2 May 1932; *s* of Reginald John Twite and May Elizabeth Walker; *m* 1st, 1958, Sally Randall (marr. diss.); 2nd, 1980, Sonia Yaari; one *s* three step *d. Educ:* Lawrence Sheriff School, Rugby; Balliol College, Oxford (BA History 1955). Asst Editor, Schoolmaster, weekly jl of NUT, 1956–58; British Council, 1958–73: served in Israel and London as Sec., Overseas Students Fees Awards Scheme; Sec., Open Univ. of Israel, 1973–76; British Council, 1976–88: adviser on adult and further educn, 1977–79; regional rep., Calcutta, 1980–84; Controller, Books, Libraries and Inf. Div., 1984–88. Advr to Chm., Res. Authy, Hebrew Univ., Jerusalem, 1988–91; Develt Advr, Truman Res. Inst. for Peace, Hebrew Univ., 1991–93. *Publications:* (ed) The Future of Jerusalem, 1993; (ed) Israeli-Arab Negotiations, 1993; (ed) Our Shared Environment: environmental problems of Israel, the West Bank and Gaza. *Recreations:* international relations, local history. *Address:* 36 Ezor Gimel, Ein Kerem, Jerusalem, Israel. *T:* Jerusalem (2) 410023.

TWYCROSS, Dr Robert Geoffrey, FRCP; Consultant Physician, Sir Michael Sobell House, Churchill Hospital, since 1976; Macmillan Clinical Reader in Palliative Medicine, Oxford University, since 1988, and Fellow of St Peter's College, Oxford, since 1987; Director, WHO Collaborating Centre for Palliative Cancer Care, since 1988; *b* 29 Jan. 1941; *s* of Jervis and Irene Twycross; *m* 1964, Deirdre Maeve, *d* of John Richard Campbell; two *s* three *d. Educ:* St John's Sch., Leatherhead; St Peter's Coll., Oxford (BA 1962; BM BCh 1965; MA 1965; DM 1977). MRCP 1969, FRCP 1980; FRSocMed 1989. Hosp. appts, Oxford, Lancaster, Epsom and Manchester, 1966–71; Res. Fellow, St Christopher's Hospice, London, 1971–76; Vis. MO, St Joseph's Hospice, London, 1971–76. Visiting Professor: RSocMed of USA Foundation, 1979; Sir Ernest Finch, Sheffield, 1994; Lectures: Abbott, Amer. Soc. of Regl Anaesthesia, 1980; Rendle Short, Christian Med. Fellowship, 1984; Archbishop Dwyer Meml, 1993. Chm., Internat. Sch. for Cancer Care, 1987; Member: WHO Expert Adv. Panel on Cancer, 1985; Acad. Scientiarum et Artium Europaea, 1992; Bd, Pallium Foundn, Netherlands, 1993; founder mem., numerous internat. care assocs. Aid and Co-operation Medal, Poland, 1993; Founder's Award, Nat. Hospice Orgn, USA, 1994; Serturner Prize, Serturner Soc., 1995. *Publications:* The Dying Patient, 1975; (ed) Pain Relief in Cancer, vol. 3 No 1, 1984; A Time to Die, 1984; (ed) Edinburgh Symposium on Pain Control and Medical Education, 1989; Pain Relief in Advanced Cancer, 1994; Introducing Palliative Care, 1995; Symptom Management in Advanced Cancer, 1995; with S. A. Lack: Symptom Control in Far-Advanced Cancer, 1983; Therapeutics in Terminal Cancer, 1984; Oral Morphine in Advanced Cancer, 1984; Control of Alimentary Symptoms in Far-Advanced Cancer, 1986; Oral Morphine: information for patients, families and friends, 1987, rev. edn 1993; contribs to learned jls. *Recreations:* gardening, walking, sailing, reading, theatre. *Address:* Tewsfield, Netherwoods Road, Risinghurst, Oxford OX3 8HF.

TWYFORD, Donald Henry, CB 1990; Under Secretary, Export Credits Guarantee Department, 1981–89, Director and Chairman of Project Group Board, 1986–89; *b* 4 Feb. 1931; *s* of Henry John Twyford and Lily Hilda (*née* Ridler). *Educ:* Wembley County School. Joined Export Credits Guarantee Dept, 1949; Principal, 1965; seconded to Dept of Trade: Principal (Commercial Relations with East Europe), 1972–75; Asst Secretary

(Country Policy), 1976; Establishment Officer, 1979–81; Under Secretary, Head of Services Group (internat. and country policy), ECGD, 1981–85; Hd of Project Underwriting Gp, 1985–89. Chairman, European Policy Coordination Group, 1981. *Recreations:* gardening (especially growing citrus fruit), music, travel. *Address:* Cansala Lluca 16, Javea 03739, Alicante, Spain.

TWYMAN, Paul Hadleigh; management consultant; Executive Chairman, Political Strategy Ltd, since 1988; Director: Nationwide (formerly Nationwide Anglia) Building Society, since 1987 (Anglia Building Society, 1983–87); D'Arcy Masius Benton & Bowles, since 1990; *s* of late Lawrence Alfred Twyman and of Gladys Mary (*née* Williams). *Educ:* Leyton County High Sch.; Chatham House Sch., Ramsgate; Univ. of Sheffield (BAEcon); London Sch. of Econs and Pol Science (MScEcon). Schoolteacher, 1964; Asst Principal, BoT, 1967; Secretariat, Commn on Third London Airport, 1969; Private Sec. to Sec. of State for Trade and Industry, 1971; Dept of Industry, 1975; Anti-Dumping Unit, Dept of Trade, 1976; Asst Sec., and Head of Overseas Projects Group, Dept of Trade, 1978; Dept of Transport, 1983; Cabinet Office, 1984; Under Sec., and Dir, Enterprise and Deregulation Unit, Dept of Employment, 1985. Contested (C) Greater Manchester W, European Parly elecn, 1989. Econ. Adviser to Chm. of Conservative Party, and Head of Econ. Section, Cons. Res. Dept, 1987. Chm., N Thanet Conservative Assoc., 1989–91; Mem., SE Area Council and Gen. Purposes Cttee, Cons. Nat. Union, 1990–. Councillor, Thanet DC, 1991–95. Mem., British Pteridological Soc. FIMgt; MCIT; FRSA. *Recreations:* family and friends, gardening, hill walking, observing gorillas. *Address:* 123 Buckingham Palace Road, SW1W 9SR.

TYACKE, Maj.-Gen. David Noel Hugh, CB 1970; OBE 1957; Controller, Army Benevolent Fund, 1971–80; *b* 18 Nov. 1915; *s* of Capt. Charles Noel Walker Tyacke (killed in action, March 1918) and late Phoebe Mary Cicely (*née* Coulthard), Cornwall; *m* 1940, Diana, *d* of Aubrey Hare Duke; one *s*. *Educ:* Malvern Coll.; RMC Sandhurst. Commissioned DCLI, 1935; India, 1936–39; France and Belgium, 1939–40; India and Burma, 1943–46; Instructor, Staff Coll., Camberley, 1950–52; CO 1st Bn DCLI, 1957–59; Comdr 130 Inf. Bde (TA), 1961–63; Dir of Administrative Planning (Army), 1963–64; Brig. Gen. Staff (Ops), Min. of Defence, 1965–66; GOC Singapore Dist., 1966–70, retired. Col, The Light Infantry, 1972–77. Mem., Malvern Coll. Council, 1978–88. *Recreations:* walking, motoring, bird-watching. *Address:* c/o Lloyds Bank, Cox's & King's Branch, 7 Pall Mall, SW1Y 5NA.

See also S. J. Tyacke.

TYACKE, Sarah Jacqueline, (Mrs Nicholas Tyacke), FSA; Chief Executive and Keeper of Public Records, Public Record Office, since 1992; *b* 29 Sept. 1945; *d* of late Colin Walton Jeacock and Elsie Marguerite Stanton; *m* 1971, Nicholas, *s* of Maj.-Gen. D. N. H. Tyacke, *qv*; one *d*. *Educ:* Chelmsford County High Sch.; Bedford Coll., London (BA Hons History). FSA 1985. Asst Keeper, Map Room, BM, 1968; Dep. Map Librarian, British Liby, 1973–85; undertook govt scrutiny of BL preservation (under Efficiency Unit, Cabinet Office), 1985–86; Director of Special Collections, British Library, 1986–91. Chm., European Co-ordinating Bd, Internat. Congress on Archives, 1992–; Jt Hon. Sec., Hakluyt Soc., 1984–; Vice-Chm., Professional Bd, IFLA, 1987–89. Dir, Imago Mundi 1987–; Trustee, Mappa Mundi, 1989–. *Publications:* Copernicus and the New Astronomy (with H. Swiderska), 1973; (ed jtly with H. M. Wallis) My Head is a Map: essay and memoirs in honour of R. V. Tooley, 1973; London Map-Sellers 1660–1720, 1978; (with John Huddy) Christopher Saxton and Tudor map-making, 1980; (ed) English map-making 1500–1650: historical essays, 1983; Catalogue of maps, charts and plans in the Pepys Library, Magdalene College, Cambridge, 1989; contribs to archival, library and cartographic jls, incl. The Library, Imago Mundi, Cartographic Jl. *Recreations:* the sea, travel, hill-walking, painting. *Address:* Public Record Office, Ruskin Avenue, Kew, Richmond, Surrey TW9 4DU.

TYBULEWICZ, Albin, CPhys, FInstP; Scientific Editor, Quantum Electronics, since 1994; *b* Poland, 1 March 1929; *s* of Julian and Elżbieta Tybulewicz (*née* Świgost); *m* 1959, Tuliola Sylwina Bryl; one *s* one *d*. *Educ:* schools in Poland, Russia, Iran, India; St Mary's High Sch., Bombay. BSc London 1952. Research Officer, BICC, 1953–56; Asst Editor, 1956–63, Editor, 1963–67, Physics Abstracts and Current Papers in Physics; Editor: Soviet Physics—Semiconductors, 1967–92; Soviet Jl of Quantum Electronics, 1970–92; Soviet Physics—Solid State (jtly with Prof. L. Azaroff), 1982–92. Founder and Chm., Food for Poland Fund, 1980–84. FIL; FIInfSc; Fellow: Amer. Phys. Soc.; Inst. of Translation and Interpreting (Mem. Council, 1986–94). Natthorst Non-Literary Prize, Fedn Internat. des Traducteurs, 1990. *Publications:* American Institute of Physics Translation Manual, 1983; trans of numerous Russian physics monographs; contribs to physics and professional jls on language and translation. *Recreations:* theatre, reading, Polish community affairs in England, politics in Poland. *Address:* 2 Oak Dene, West Ealing, W13 8AW. *T:* 0181–997 8822. *Club:* Wig and Pen.

TYDEMAN, Col Frank William Edward, CMG 1966; CIE 1945; Port Consultant; *b* 20 January 1901; *s* of Harvey James and Kate Mary Anne Tydeman; *m* 1924, Jessie Sarah Mann (*d* 1947); one *s* (and one *s* decd). *Educ:* London University. BSc (Eng) London 1920. Chartered Civil Engineer. FICE, FIMechE, FIStructE, FIEAust, FCIT. Served Palestine; Haifa Harbour, 1930; Jaffa Port, 1934; Singapore Harbour Board, 1937; Indian Army, 1942; Colonel, Deputy Director Transportation, India, Burma and Malaya, 1944; reconstructed Bombay Port and Town after disastrous explosion, 1945; Port Consultant, Australia, to Commonwealth and WA govts and port authorities, on develt of ports of Fremantle, Bunbury, Townsville, Davenport, Mackay, Lae, Tjilatjap, 1946; Fremantle Harbour Trust, 1950; retired 1965. *Recreation:* music. *Address:* c/o ANZ Banking Group Ltd, 77 St George's Terrace, Perth, WA 6000, Australia. *Club:* Naval and Military (Perth).

TYDEMAN, John Peter; Head of BBC Radio Drama, 1986–94; *b* 30 March 1936; *s* of George Alfred Tydeman and Gladys (*née* Johnson). *Educ:* Feltonfleet; Hertford GS; Trinity Coll., Cambridge (MA). Nat. Service, 2 Lieut RA, 1954–56. Joined BBC, 1959; producer, 1962–80; Asst Head, Radio Drama, 1980–86. Dir of stage, radio and television plays. Prix Italia, 1970; Prix Futura, 1979 and 1983; Broadcasting Press Guild Award, 1983; Sony Award, 1994. *Recreations:* theatre, travel, reading, the company of friends. *Address:* Flat 7, 88 Great Titchfield Street, W1P 7AG. *T:* 0171–636 3886. *Clubs:* Garrick, Rugby.

TYE, Alan Peter, RDI 1986; Partner, Alan Tye Design (Industrial & Product Designers), since 1962; *b* 18 Sept. 1933; *s* of Chang Qing Tai and Emily Tai (*née* Thompson); *m* 1966, Anita Birgitta Göethe Tye; three *s* two *d*. *Educ:* Regent Street Polytechnic Sch. of Architecture. RIBA 1959; FCSD (FSIAD 1979). Qualified as architect, 1958; with Prof. Arne Jacobsen, Copenhagen, 1960–62; formed Alan Tye Design, 1962; incorporated HID Ltd, 1977; launched Healthy Individual Design Practice Method (HID), 1992. Mem., Selection Cttee, Council of Industrial Design, 1967; Civic Trust Award Assessor, 1968, 1969; Vis. Tutor, RCA, 1978–83, External Examr, 1987–90; Specialist Adviser on Industrial Design, CNAA, 1980; London Region Assessor, RIBA, 1981 and 1988; RSA Bursary Judge, 1983–. Convenor, Faculty of RDI, RSA, 1991–. Internat. Design Prize, Rome, 1962; Council of Industrial Design Award, 1965, 1966, 1981; British Aluminium Design Award, 1966; 1st Prize, GAI Award, 1969; Observer (London) Design Award, 1969; Ringling Mus. of Art (Fla) Award, 1969; Gold Medal, Graphic Design, 1970; 1st Prize, GAI Award, Internat. Bldg Exhibn, 1971; British Aluminium Eros Trophy, 1973; 4 Awards for Design Excellence, Aust., 1973; Commendation for Arch., 1977; Internat. Award, Inst. of Business Designers (NY), 1982; Internat. Bldg Exhibits Top Design Award, 1983, 1985; Resources Council of America Design Award, 1987; other design awards. *Publication:* (with Dermot O'Flynn) Healthy Industrial Design, 1995. *Recreations:* tai chi, aikido, badminton, fly-fishing. *Address:* Great West Plantation, Tring, Herts HP23 6DA. *T:* Tring (01442) 825353.

TYE, James; Director-General, British Safety Council, since 1968; *b* 21 Dec. 1921; *s* of late Benjamin Tye and Rose Tye; *m* 1950, Mrs Rosalie Hooker; one *s* one *d*. *Educ:* Upper Hornsey LCC Sch. Served War of 1939–45; RAF, 1940–46. Advertising Agent and Contractor, 1946–50; Managing Dir, 1950–62: Sky Press Ltd; Safety Publications Ltd. Joined British Safety Council as Exec. Dir, 1962. Chairman: Bd of Governors, Internat. Inst. of Safety Management, 1975–; British Wellness Council, 1990–. FIMgt; Hon. Vice-Pres., Inst. of Occupational Safety and Health; Member: Amer. Soc. of Safety Engineers; Amer. Safety Management Soc.; Vice-Pres., Jamaica Safety Council; Fellow, Inst. of Accident Prevention, Zambia. FRSA. Freeman, City of London, 1976; Liveryman, Worshipful Co. of Basketmakers; Mem., Guild of Freemen of City of London. *Publications:* Communicating the Safety Message, 1968; Management Introduction to Total Loss Control, 1971; Safety-Uncensored (with K. Ullyett, JP), 1971; (with Bowes Egan) The Management Guide to Product Liability, 1979; *handbooks:* Industrial Safety Digest, 1953; Skilful Driving, 1952; Advanced Driving, 1954; International Nautical Safety Code (with Uffa Fox), 1961; Why Imprison Untrained Drivers?, 1980; Workplace Wellness; Papers and Reports to Parly Groups and British Safety Council Members on: product liability, training safety officers, vehicle seat belts, anti-jack knife devices for articulated vehicles, lifejackets and buoyancy aids, motorway safety barriers, Britain's filthy beaches, back pain, insurance costs, dangers of: mini fire extinguishers, safety in fairgrounds, drip feed oil heaters, children's flammable nightwear, vehicle recall procedures, need for a nat. vehicle defects hotline, brain injuries caused by boxing and recommendations to improve the rules, pollution caused by diesel engines, safe toys, introduction of defensive driving techniques, risk management — stress at work, incr. risk of accidents thereof, use of colour in envmt to promote safety and productivity, dangers of smoke masks, fire prevention — recommendations to industry. *Recreations:* squash, badminton, ski-ing, golf, sailing. *Address:* 55 Hartington Road, Chiswick, W4 3TS. *T:* 0181–995 3206. *Clubs:* City Livery, Royal Automobile.

TYE, Dr Walter, CBE 1966; CEng; *b* 12 Dec. 1912; *s* of Walter and Alice Tye; *m* 1939, Eileen Mary Whitmore; one *s* one *d*. *Educ:* Woodbridge Sch.; London Univ. (BScEng). Fairey Aviation Co., 1934; RAE, 1935–38; Air Registration Bd, 1938–39; RAE, 1939–44; Air Registration Bd, 1944–72 (Chief Techn. Officer, 1946, Chief Exec., 1969); Mem., CAA (Controller Safety), 1972–74. Hon. FRAeS; Hon. DSc Cranfield Inst. of Technology, 1972. *Publications:* articles, lectures and contrib. Jl RAeS. *Address:* 12 Bramble Rise, Cobham, Surrey KT11 2HP. *T:* Cobham (01932) 863692.

TYLER, Anne; writer; *b* 25 Oct. 1941; *d* of Lloyd Parry Tyler and Phyllis Mahon Tyler (*née* Mahon); *m* 1963, Taghi M. Modarressi, MD; two *d*. *Educ:* Duke Univ. (BA). Mem., AAIL. AAIL Award for Literature, 1977; Nat. Book Critics Circle Award for fiction, 1985; Pulitzer Prize for fiction, 1989. *Publications:* If Morning Ever Comes, 1964; The Tin Can Tree, 1965; A Slipping Down Life, 1970; The Clock Winder, 1972; Celestial Navigation, 1974; Searching for Caleb, 1976; Earthly Possessions, 1977; Morgan's Passing, 1980; Dinner at the Homesick Restaurant, 1982; The Accidental Tourist, 1985; Breathing Lessons, 1988; Saint Maybe, 1991; Ladder of Years, 1995. *Address:* 222 Tunbridge Road, Baltimore, MD 21212, USA.

TYLER, Brig. Arthur Catchmay, CBE 1960; MC 1945; DL; a Military Knight of Windsor, since 1978 (Supernumerary, 1991); *b* 20 Aug. 1913; 4th *s* of Hugh Griffin Tyler and Muriel Tyler (*née* Barnes); *m* 1938, Sheila, *d* of James Kinloch, Meigle, Perthshire; three *s* one *d*. *Educ:* Allhallows Sch.; RMC, Sandhurst. Commissioned, The Welch Regt, 1933. Served War of 1939–45: Africa, India and Burma (despatches). Staff Coll., 1946; JSSC, 1951; Sec., BJSM, Washington, 1952–54; Bt Lt-Col, 1953; Comd 4th (Carms) Bn The Welch Regt, 1954–57; Col, 1957; AAG, War Office, 1957–60; Brig. 1960; Senior UK Liaison Officer and Military Adviser to High Commissioner, Canada, 1960–63; Asst Chief of Staff (Ops and Plans), Allied Forces Central Europe, 1963–65. Sec., Council, TA&VR Assocs, 1967–72. Hon. Col., 7th(V) Bn, The Queen's Regt, T&AVR, 1971–75. Governor, Allhallows Sch., 1968, Chm., 1977–80. DL Surrey, 1968. *Address:* 17 Fosters Way, Bude, Cornwall EX23 8HF.

TYLER, Maj.-Gen. Christopher, CB 1989; CEng, FIMechE; Director of Fundraising, Airborne Forces Charities Development Trust, since 1995; *b* 9 July 1934; *s* of Maj.-Gen. Sir Leslie Tyler, KBE, CB, and late Louie Teresa Tyler (*née* Franklin); *m* 1958, Suzanne, *d* of Eileen Whitcomb and late Patrick Whitcomb; one *s* three *d*. *Educ:* Beaumont College; RMA Sandhurst; Trinity Coll., Cambridge (MA). Commissioned REME, 1954; served UK and BAOR, 1959–65; Army Staff Course, 1966–67; Weapons Staff, 1968–70 and 1972–74; CO 1st Parachute Logistic Regt, 1974–76; MoD, 1976–80; Chief Aircraft Engineer, Army Air Corps, 1980–82; DEME (Management Services), Logistic Exec., 1982–83; Comd Maint., HQ 1 (BR) Corps, 1983–85; Dep. Comdt, RMCS, 1985–87; DCS (Support), HQ Allied Forces N Europe, 1987–89. Resident Gov. and Keeper of the Jewel House, HM Tower of London, 1989–94. Col Comdt, REME, 1989–94; Hon. Col, REME (V), 1994–. External Mem. of Council, Parachute Regt, 1993–; Trustee: Tower Hill Imp Trust, 1990–; Ulysses Trust, 1992–94. Gov., St Mary's Sch., Ascot, 1995–. Liveryman, Turners' Co., 1979– (Mem., Ct of Assts, 1991–; Chm., Educn Cttee, 1994–). *Recreations:* Rugby football (RFU Panel Referee, 1957–59 and 1967–73 and Chm., Army and Combined Services, 1985–86), tennis, squash. *Address.* Oak Cottage, Stratfield Saye, Reading, Berks RG7 2EB.

TYLER, Cyril, DSc, PhD, FRSC; Professor of Physiology and Biochemistry, University of Reading, 1958–76, now Emeritus; Deputy Vice-Chancellor, 1968–76; *b* 26 Jan. 1911; *er s* of John and Annie Tyler; *m* 1st, 1939, Myra Eileen (*d* 1971), *d* of George and Rosa Batten; two *s* one *d*; 2nd, 1971, Rita Patricia, *d* of Sidney and Lilian Jones. *Educ:* Ossett Grammar Sch.; Univ. of Leeds. BSc 1st Class Hons 1933, PhD 1935, DSc 1959, Leeds. Lectr in Agricultural Chemistry. RAC, Cirencester, 1935–39; Univ. of Reading: Lecturer in Agricultural Chemistry, 1939–47; Professor, 1947–58; Dean of the Faculty of Agriculture, 1959–62. Playing Mem., Glos CCC, 1936–39. *Publications:* Organic Chemistry for Students of Agriculture, 1946; Animal Nutrition (2nd edn), 1964; Wilhelm von Nathusius 1821–1899 on Avian Eggshells, 1964; numerous papers on poultry metabolism and egg shells in scientific journals. *Recreations:* gardening, history of animal nutrition. *Address:* 22 Belle Avenue, Reading, Berks RG6 2BL.

TYLER, Ven. Leonard George; Rector of St Michael and St Mary Magdalene, Easthampstead, 1973–85, retired; *b* 15 April 1920; *s* of Hugh Horstead Tyler and Mabel Adam Stewart Tyler; *m* 1946, Sylvia May Wilson; one *s* two *d*. *Educ:* Darwen Grammar School; Liverpool University; Christ's College, Cambridge; Westcott House. Chaplain,

Trinity College, Kandy, Ceylon, 1946–48; Principal, Diocesan Divinity School, Colombo, Ceylon, 1948–50; Rector, Christ Church, Bradford, Manchester, 1950–55; Vicar of Leigh, Lancs, 1955–66 (Rural Dean, 1955–62); Chaplain, Leigh Infirmary, 1955–66; Archdeacon of Rochdale, 1962–66; Principal, William Temple College, Manchester, 1966–73. Anglican Adviser to ABC Television, 1958–68. *Publications:* contributor to Theology. *Address:* 11 Ashton Place, Kintbury, Hungerford, Berks RG17 9XS. *T:* Kintbury (01488) 658510.

TYLER, Prof. Lorraine Komisarjevsky, PhD; FBA 1995; Professor of Psychology, and Co-Director, Centre for Speech and Language, Birkbeck College, London University, since 1990; *b* 11 Jan. 1945; *d* of James and Anne Komisarjevsky; *m* 1982, William D. Marslen-Wilson; one *s* one *d*. *Educ:* Leicester Univ. (BA); Chicago Univ. (PhD 1977). Sen. Res. Fellow, Max Planck Inst. for Psycholinguistics, 1977–85; Lectr, Dept of Psychology, Cambridge Univ., 1985–90. *Publications:* Spoken Language Comprehension, 1992; contrib. Brain and Lang., Jl of Memory and Lang., Psychological Rev., Cognition, etc. *Address:* Department of Psychology, Birkbeck College, Malet Street, WC1E 7HX. *T:* 0171–631 6589.

TYLER, Paul Archer, CBE 1985; MP (Lib Dem) North Cornwall, since 1992; public affairs consultant; Director, Western Approaches Public Relations Ltd, Launceston, Cornwall, since 1987 (Managing Director, 1987–92); *b* 29 Oct. 1941; *s* of Oliver Walter Tyler and Ursula Grace Gibbons Tyler (*née* May); *m* 1970, Nicola Mary Ingram; one *s* one *d*. *Educ:* Mount House Sch., Tavistock; Sherborne Sch.; Exeter Coll., Oxford (MA). Pres., Oxford Univ. Liberal Club, 1962. Royal Inst. of British Architects: Admin. Asst, 1966; Asst Sec., 1967; Dep. Dir Public Affairs, 1971; Dir Public Affairs, 1972. Man. Dir, Cornwall Courier newspaper gp, 1976–81; Exec. Dir, Public Affairs Div., Good Relations plc, 1982–84; Chief Exec., 1984–86, Chm., 1986–87, Good Relations Public Affairs Ltd; Dir, Good Relations plc, 1985–88; Sen. Consultant, Good Relations Ltd, 1987–92. County Councillor, Devon, 1964–70; Mem., Devon and Cornwall Police Authority, 1965–70; Vice-Chm., Dartmoor Nat. Park Cttee, 1965–70; Chm., CPRE Working Party on the Future of the Village, 1974–81; Vice-President: ACRE; ACC; BTCV; Mem. Bd of Shelter (Nat. Campaign for the Homeless), and rep. in Devon and Cornwall, 1975–76. Sec., L/SDP Jt Commn on Employment and Industrial Recovery, 1981–82. Chm., Devon and Cornwall Region Liberal Party, 1981–82; Chm., Liberal Party NEC, 1983–86. Campaign Adviser to Rt Hon. David Steel, and Mem., Alliance Campaign Planning Gp, 1986–87. Contested (L): Totnes, 1966; Bodmin, 1970, 1979; Beaconsfield, 1982; contested (Soc & Lib Dem) Cornwall and Plymouth, European Parly Election, 1989; MP (L) Bodmin, Feb.–Sept. 1974; Parly Liberal spokesman on housing and transport, 1974; Parly adviser to RIBA, 1974; Lib Dem spokesman on agriculture and rural affairs, 1992–, on transport, 1994–. Chm., All Party Coastal Gp, 1993–; Hon. Officer: All Party Tourism Gp, 1993–; All Party Water Gp, 1993–. *Publication:* A New Deal for Rural Britain (jtly), 1978. *Recreations:* sailing, gardening, walking. *Address:* Church Stile, Launceston, Cornwall PL15 8AT. *Clubs:* National Liberal; Launceston Liberal Democrat (Cornwall).

TYNAN, Prof. Michael John, MD, FRCP; Professor of Paediatric Cardiology, Guy's Hospital, since 1982; *b* 18 April 1934; *s* of late Jerry Joseph Tynan and Florence Ann Tynan; *m* 1958, Eirlys Pugh Williams. *Educ:* Bedford Modern School; London Hospital. MD, BS. Senior Asst Resident, Children's Hosp., Boston, Mass, 1962; Registrar, Westminster Hosp., 1964; Registrar, later Lectr, Hosp. for Sick Children, Great Ormond St, 1966; consultant paediatric cardiologist, Newcastle Univ. Hospitals, 1971, Guy's Hosp., 1977. *Publications:* (jtly) Paediatric Cardiology, a textbook, vol. 5, 1983; articles on nomenclature and classification of congenital heart disease and on heart disease in children. *Recreations:* singing, watching cricket, playing snooker. *Address:* 5 Ravensdon Street, SE11 4AQ. *T:* 0171–735 7119. *Clubs:* Athenæum; Borth and Ynyslas Golf.

TYNDALE-BISCOE, Rear-Adm. Alec Julian, CB 1959; OBE 1946; lately Chairman of Blaw Knox Ltd; *b* 10 Aug. 1906; *s* of late Lt-Col A. A. T. Tyndale-Biscoe, Aubrey House, Keyhaven, Lymington, Hants; *m* 1st, 1939, Emma Winifred Haselden (*d* 1974); four *d*; 2nd, 1974, Hugolyne Cotton Cooke, *widow* of Captain Geoffrey Cotton Cooke. *Educ:* RN Colleges Osborne and Dartmouth. Entered RN, 1920. Served War, 1939–46; HMS Vanguard, 1947–49; Captain, 1949; Asst Engineer-in-Chief, Fleet, 1950–53; Comdg RN Air Station, Anthorn, 1953–55; Fleet Engr Officer, Mediterranean, 1955–57; Rear-Adm. 1957; Flag-Officer Reserve Aircraft, 1957–59, retired. *Address:* Bunces Farm Gardens, Birch Grove, Haywards Heath, West Sussex RH17 7BT.

TYNDALL, Nicholas John; Chief Officer, National Marriage Guidance Council, 1968–86; *b* 15 Aug. 1928; *s* of Rev. Edward Denis Tyndall and Nora Mildred Tyndall; *m* 1953, Elizabeth Mary (*née* Ballard); two *s* two *d*. *Educ:* Marlborough College; Jesus College, Cambridge. BA. HM Prison and Borstal Service, 1952–68; Training Officer, Cruse-Bereavement Care, 1987–91, retd. Dir, Council of Europe Co-ordinated Research Fellowship on Marriage Guidance and Family Counselling, 1973–75; Mem., Home Office/DHSS Working Party on Marriage Guidance, 1976–78; Chairman: British Assoc. for Counselling, 1976–78; Marriage and Marriage Guidance Commn of Internat. Union of Family Organisations, 1971–86. Mem., Gen. Synod of Church of England, 1981–88. *Publication:* Counselling in the Voluntary Sector, 1993. *Recreations:* Morris dancing, children. *Address:* 18 Stanford Road, Faringdon, Oxon SN7 7AQ.

See also Rev. T. Tyndall.

TYNDALL, Rev. Canon Timothy; Chief Secretary, Advisory Council for the Church's Ministry, 1985–90; *b* 24 April 1925; *s* of Rev. Denis Tyndall and Nora Tyndall; *m* 1953, Dr Ruth Mary Turner; two *s* twin *d*. *Educ:* Jesus Coll., Cambridge (BA). Parish Incumbent: Newark, 1955; Nottingham, 1960; Sunderland, 1975. *Address:* 29 Kingswood Road, Chiswick, W4 5EU. *T:* 0181–994 4516.

See also N. J. Tyndall.

TYREE, Sir (Alfred) William, Kt 1975; OBE 1971; electrical engineer, chief executive and chairman; *b* Auckland, NZ, 4 Nov. 1921; *s* of J. V. Tyree and A. Hezeltine (who migrated to Australia, 1938); *m* 1946, Joyce, *d* of F. Lyndon; two *s* one *d*. *Educ:* Auckland Grammar School; Sydney Technical Coll. (Dip. in Elec. Engrg). FIE (Aust) 1968 (Peter Nicol Russell Mem. Award 1985); FIProdE 1983 (James N. Kirby Medal 1980). Founded Tyree Industries Ltd and Westralian Transformers and subsids, 1956; Founder and Chairman: Alpha Air (Sydney) Pty Ltd; Technical Components Pty Ltd; Tycan Australia Pty Ltd; Tyree Holdings Pty Ltd; A. W. Tyree Transformers Pty Ltd; Wirex Pty Ltd; A. W. Tyree Foundation. Mem., Inst. of Dirs in Aust.; Councillor: Metal Trades Industries Assoc. (Mem., Nat. Exec.); Aust. Chamber of Manufrs. Hon. Fellow, Univ. of Sydney, 1985; Hon. Life Governor, Aust. Postgrad. Fedn in Medicine, 1985. Hon. DSc Univ. of NSW, 1986. IEEE Centennial Medal and Cert., 1984. *Recreations:* ski-ing, photography, water ski-ing, yachting, tennis, music, golf, sail board riding. *Address:* 60 Martin Place, Sydney, NSW 2000, Australia; (home) 3 Lindsay Avenue Darling Point, NSW. *Clubs:* Royal Aero, American National, Royal Automobile (NSW); Royal Prince Alfred Yacht, Royal Motor Yacht, Cruising Yacht, Kosciusko Alpine, Australian Alpine, RAC, Australian Golf.

TYRELL-KENYON; *see* Kenyon.

TYRER, Christopher John Meese; His Honour Judge Tyrer; a Circuit Judge, since 1989; *b* 22 May 1944; *s* of late Jack Meese Tyrer and of Margaret Joan Tyrer (*née* Wyatt); *m* 1974, Jane Beckett, JP, LLB, MA, barrister; one *s* one *d*. *Educ:* Wellington College; Bristol University. LLB hons. Called to the Bar, Inner Temple, 1968. Asst Recorder, 1979–83; a Recorder, 1983–89. Governor: St John's Sch., Lacey Green, 1984–92; Speen Sch., 1984– (Chm., 1989–91); Misbourne Sch., 1993–. Mem., Bucks Assoc. of Govs of Primary Schs, 1989–90. *Recreations:* music, growing fuchsias, photography. *Address:* Randalls Cottage, Loosley Row, Princes Risborough, Bucks HP27 0NU. *T:* Princes Risborough (01844) 344650; Milton Keynes County Court, 351 Silbury Boulevard, Witan Gate East, Central Milton Keynes MK9 2DT. *T:* Milton Keynes (01908) 668855.

TYRIE, Peter Robert; Managing Director, Balmoral International Hotels, since 1989; *b* 3 April 1946; *m* 1972, Christine Mary Tyrie; three *s* (and one *d* decd). *Educ:* Westminster College Hotel Sch. (BSc Hotel Admin). Manager, Inverurie Hotel, Bermuda, 1969–71; Resident Man., Portman Hotel, London, 1971–73; Project Dir, Pannell Kerr Forster, 1973–77; Operations Dir, Penta Hotels, 1977–80; Managing Director: Gleneagles Hotels plc, 1980–86; Mandarin Oriental Hotel Gp, 1986–89. Director: Bell's Whisky, 1983; Dragon Trust, 1989–, New Tiger Trust, 1994–, Edinburgh Fund Managers. FHCIMA 1977. *Recreations:* squash, shooting, fishing, Rugby, classic cars. *Address:* Ravelston Brae, 36 Ravelston Dykes Road, Edinburgh EH4 3NZ. *T:* 0131–346 7874.

TYRONE, Earl of; Henry Nicholas de la Poer Beresford; *b* 23 March 1958; *s* and *heir* of 8th Marquess of Waterford, *qv*; *m* 1986, Amanda, *d* of Norman Thompson; two *s*. *Educ:* Harrow School. *Heir:* *s* Baron Le Poer, *qv*.

TYROR, John George, JP; Director of Safety, United Kingdom Atomic Energy Authority, 1990–92, retired; *b* 5 Nov. 1930; *s* of John Thomas Tyror and Nora Tyror (*née* Tennant); *m* 1956, Sheila Wylie; one *s* one *d*. *Educ:* Manchester Univ. (BSc 1st cl. Hons Maths, MSc); Trinity Hall, Cambridge. FInstP. Asst Lectr, Univ. of Leeds, 1955–56; AEA Harwell, 1956–59; Atomic Energy Estabt, Winfrith, 1959–63; Reactor Develt Lab., Windscale, 1963–66; Winfrith, 1966–87 (Asst Dir, 1979–87); Dir, Safety and Reliability Directorate, Culcheth, 1987–90. JP Macclesfield, 1976. *Publication:* An Introduction to the Neutron Kinetics of Nuclear Power Reactors, 1970. *Recreations:* tennis, golf, food and wine, antique map collecting, grandfather. *Clubs:* Lancashire CC, Knutsford Golf, Broadstone Golf, East Dorset Lawn Tennis and Croquet.

TYRRELL, Alan Rupert, QC 1976; FCIArb; a Recorder of the Crown Court, since 1972; Barrister-at-Law; *b* 27 June 1933; *s* of Rev. T. G. R. Tyrrell, and Mrs W. A. Tyrrell, MSc; *m* 1960, Elaine Eleanor Ware, LLB; one *s* one *d*. *Educ:* Bridport Grammar Sch.; London Univ. (LLB). FCIArb 1993. Called to the Bar, Gray's Inn, 1956, Bencher, 1986; Chm. of the Bar Eur. Gp, 1986–88; Chm. of the Internat. Practice Cttee, Bar Council (co-opted to Bar Council), 1988. Lord Chancellor's Legal Visitor, 1990–. Dir, Papworth Hosp. NHS Trust, 1993–. Council Mem., Med. Protection Soc., 1990–. Chm. London Reg., and Mem. Nat. Exec., Nat. Fedn of Self-Employed, 1978–79. Mem. (C) London E, European Parlt, 1979–84; contested same seat, 1984, 1989. *Publications:* (ed) Moore's Practical Agreements, 10th edn 1965; Students' Guide to Europe, 1984; The Legal Professions in the New Europe, 1992. *Recreations:* bridge, budgerigars. *Address:* 15 Willifield Way, Hampstead Garden Suburb, NW11 7XU. *T:* 0181–455 5798; Francis Taylor Building, Temple, EC4Y 7BY. *T:* 0171–797 7250; 205 Boulevard St Germain, 75007 Paris, France. *T:* 44392919. *Clubs:* Athenæum; Hampshire (Winchester).

TYRRELL, Dr David Arthur John, CBE 1980; FRCP, FRCPath; FRS 1970; Director, MRC Common Cold Unit, 1982–90, retired; *b* 19 June 1925; *s* of Sidney Charles Tyrrell and Agnes Kate (*née* Blewett); *m* 1950, Betty Moyra Wylie; two *d* (one *s* decd). *Educ:* Sheffield University. FRCP 1965. Junior hosp. appts, Sheffield, 1948–51; Asst, Rockefeller Inst., New York, 1951–54; Virus Research Lab., Sheffield, 1954–57; MRC Common Cold Unit, Salisbury, 1957–90; Dep. Dir of Clin. Res. Centre, Northwick Park, Harrow, and Head of Div. of Communicable Diseases, 1970–84. Chairman: (first), Adv. Cttee on Dangerous Pathogens, 1981–91; Consultative Cttee on Res. into Spongiform Encephalopathies, 1989–90; Spongiform Encephalopathy Adv. Cttee, 1990–; Biol Sub-Cttee, Cttee on Safety of Medicines, 1989–92. Managing Trustee, Nuffield Foundn, 1977–92. Sir Arthur Sims Commonwealth Travelling Prof., 1985. Hon. DSc Sheffield, 1979; Hon. DM Southampton, 1990. Stewart Prize, BMA, 1977; Ambuj Nath Bose Prize, 1983, Conway Evans Prize, 1986, RCP. *Publications:* Common Colds and Related Diseases, 1965; Interferon and its Clinical Potential, 1976; (jtly) Microbial Diseases, 1979; The Abolition of Infection: hope or illusion?, 1982; numerous papers on infectious diseases and viruses. *Recreations:* music-making, gardening, walking; various Christian organizations. *Address:* (office) Centre for Applied Microbiology and Research, Porton Down, Salisbury SP4 0JG. *T:* Amesbury (01980) 612682, *Fax:* (01980) 611384; Ash Lodge, Dean Lane, Whiteparish, Salisbury, Wilts SP5 2RN. *T:* Whiteparish (01794) 884352.

TYRRELL, Prof. (Henry John) Valentine, FRSC; Vice-Principal, King's College London (KQC), 1985–87, retired; *b* 14 Feb. 1920; *s* of John Rice Tyrrell and Josephine (*née* McGuinness); *m* 1st, 1947, Sheila Mabel (*née* Straw) (*d* 1985); three *s* three *d*; 2nd, 1986, Dr Bethan Davies. *Educ:* state schools; Jesus Coll., Oxford. DSc. Chemical Industry, 1942–47; Sheffield Univ., 1947–65; Chelsea College: Professor of Physical and Inorganic Chemistry, 1965–84; Head of Dept, 1972–82; Vice-Principal, 1976–84; Principal, 1984–85. Royal Institution of Great Britain: Sec., 1978–84; Vice-Pres., 1978–84, 1987–89, 1991–94; Chm. Council, 1987–89. *Publications:* Diffusion and Heat Flow in Liquids, 1961; Thermometric Titrimetry, 1968; Diffusion in Liquids, 1984; papers in chemical and physical jls. *Recreations:* foreign travel, gardening. *Address:* Fair Oaks, Coombe Hill Road, Kingston-on-Thames KT2 7DU. *Clubs:* Athenæum, Royal Institution.

TYRRELL, Robert James; Executive Chairman, Henley Centre for Forecasting, since 1995 (Managing Director, 1986–92; Chief Executive, 1992–95); *b* 6 June 1951; *s* of Peter John Tyrrell and Mair (*née* Harries); *m* 1983, Jean Linda McKerrow; two *d*. *Educ:* St Peter's Coll., Oxford (MA, PPE), LSE (MSc Phil with dist.). Academic research, Sussex and Glasgow Univs, 1972–74; joined James Morrell & Associates, 1974; Perkins Engines, 1977; Futures Group, USA, 1980. Special Advisor, Open Univ., 1989; Vis. Prof., City Univ. Business Sch., 1994–. Member: NEDO Tourism and Leisure Competitiveness Working Party, 1991; Adv. Council of Demos, 1992–; Steering Cttee, Econ. Beliefs and Behaviour Prog., ESRC, 1994–. FRSA. *Publications:* (ed jtly) Britain in the 1980s, 1974; (ed jtly) Britain 2001, 1977; (ed jtly) Planning for Social Change, 1991. *Recreations:* cycling, ski-ing, theatre, reading, family, holistic thinking. *Address:* 27 Marchmont Road, Richmond, Surrey TW10 6HQ. *T:* 0181–948 8275.

TYRRELL, Valentine; *see* Tyrrell, H. J. V.

TYRWHITT, Brig. Dame Mary (Joan Caroline), DBE 1949 (OBE 1946); TD; *b* 27 Dec. 1903; *d* of Admiral of the Fleet Sir Reginald Tyrwhitt, 1st Bt, GCB, DSO; unmarried. Senior Controller, 1946 (rank altered to Brigadier, 1950); Director, ATS, 1946–49, Women's Royal Army Corps, 1949–50, retired Dec. 1950; Hon. ADC to the King, 1949–50. *Address:* 12A Tiddington Court, Tiddington, Stratford-on-Avon CV37 7AP.

TYRWHITT, Sir Reginald (Thomas Newman), 3rd Bt, *cr* 1919; *b* 21 Feb. 1947; *er s* of Admiral Sir St John Tyrwhitt, 2nd Bt, KCB, DSO, DSC and Bar (*d* 1961), and of Nancy (Veronica) Gilbey (who *m* 1965, Sir Godfrey Agnew, *qv*); *S* father, 1961; *m* 1972, Sheila Gail (marr. diss. 1980 and annulled 1984), *d* of William Alistair Crawford Nicoll, Liphook, Hants; *m* 1984, Charlotte, *o d* of late Captain Angus Hildyard and of Hon. Mrs Angus Hildyard, The White Hall, Winestead, Kingston-upon-Hull; one *s* one *d*. *Educ:* Downside. 2nd Lieut, RA, 1966, Lieut 1969; RARO 1969. *Recreations:* shooting, fishing, drawing. *Heir: s* Robert St John Hildyard Tyrwhitt, *b* 15 Feb. 1987.

See also Dame Mary Tyrwhitt.

TYSOE, John Sidney; Chairman, Yorkshire Electricity Group, 1992–94; *b* 14 March 1932; *s* of Florence Alice Tysoe (*née* Gypps) and late Sidney George Tysoe; *m* 1953, Ann Dunham; two *s* one *d*. *Educ:* Harrow Weald County Grammar Sch.; City of London Coll. FCCA, IPFA, CompIEE. Nat. Service Commn, RN, 1950–52. Exchequer and Audit Dept, 1953–65; Southern Electricity Bd, 1966–67; Head, Special Investigations and Asst Management Accountant, BR, 1967–68; Asst and Dep. Financial Advr, Electricity Council, 1969–77; Chief Accountant and Financial Dir, Southern Electricity Bd, 1978–85; Dep. Chm., Yorkshire Electricity Bd, 1985–89; Gp Man. Dir, Yorkshire Electricity Gp, 1989–92. Mem. Council, CBI, 1993–94. *Recreations:* walking, woodcarving, theatre.

TYSON, Dr Alan Walker, CBE 1989; FBA 1978; musicologist; Fellow of All Souls College, Oxford, 1952–94, Senior Research Fellow, 1971–94; *b* 27 Oct. 1926; *e s* of Henry Alan Maurice Tyson and Dorothy (*née* Walker). *Educ:* Rugby School; Magdalen College, Oxford; University College Hospital Medical School, London. BA 1951, MA 1952; MB, BS 1965; MRCPsych 1972. Vis. Lectr in Psychiatry, Montefiore Hosp., NY, 1967–68; Lectr in Psychopathology and Developmental Psychology, Oxford Univ., 1968–70. Vis. Prof. of Music, Columbia Univ., 1969; James P. R. Lyell Reader in Bibliography, Oxford Univ., 1973–74; Ernest Bloch Prof. of Music, Univ. of California at Berkeley, 1977–78; Mem., Inst. for Advanced Study, Princeton, 1983–84; Vis. Prof. of Music, Graduate Center, City Univ. of New York, 1985. Hon. Mem., British Psychoanalytical Soc., 1989–. Hon. DLitt St Andrews, 1989. On editorial staff, Standard Edition of Freud's Works, 1952–74. *Publications:* The Authentic English Editions of Beethoven, 1963; (with O. W. Neighbour) English Music Publishers' Plate Numbers, 1965; (ed) Selected letters of Beethoven, 1967; Thematic Catalogue of the Works of Muzio Clementi, 1967; (ed) Beethoven Studies, Vol. 1, 1973, Vol. 2, 1977, Vol. 3, 1982; (with D. Johnson and R. Winter) The Beethoven Sketchbooks, 1985; Mozart: studies of the autograph scores, 1987; (with A. Rosenthal) Mozart's Thematic Catalogue: a facsimile, 1990; Pictures of the Watermarks in Mozart's autographs, and their probable dates, 1992. *Address:* 7 Southcote Road, N19 5BJ. *T:* 0171–609 2981.

TYSON, Monica Elizabeth; Editor, A La Carte, 1986–87, retired; *b* 7 June 1927; *d* of F. S. Hill and E. Hill; *m* 1st, 1950, P. M. Lyon (marr. diss. 1958); one *d*; 2nd, 1960, R. E. D. Tyson. *Educ:* George Watson's Ladies Coll.; Edinburgh Coll. of Domestic Science (Dip. in Dom. Sci.). Asst Home Editor, Modern Woman, 1958–60; Ideal Home: Domestic Planning Editor, 1960–64; Asst Editor, 1964–68; Editor, 1968–77; Editor: Woman's Realm, 1977–82; Special Assignments, IPC Magazines, 1982–84; Mother, 1984–86. *Recreations:* travelling, reading. *Address:* 29 Fisher Street, Sandwich, Kent CT13 9EJ.

TYZACK, Margaret Maud, OBE 1970; *b* 9 Sept. 1931; *d* of Thomas Edward Tyzack and Doris Moseley; *m* 1958, Alan Stephenson; one *s*. *Educ:* St Angela's Ursuline Convent; Royal Academy of Dramatic Art. Trained at RADA (Gilbert Prize for Comedy). First engagement, Civic Theatre, Chesterfield. Vassilissa in The Lower Depths, Royal Shakespeare Co., Arts Theatre, 1962; Lady MacBeth, Nottingham, 1962; Miss Frost in The Ginger Man, Royal Court, London, 1964; Madame Ranevsky in The Cherry Orchard, Exeter and Tour, 1969; Jacqui in Find Your Way Home, Open Space Theatre, London, 1970; Queen Elizabeth in Vivat! Vivat Regina!, Piccadilly, 1971; Tamora in Titus Andronicus, Portia in Julius Caesar and Volumnia in Coriolanus, Royal Shakespeare Co., Stratford-on-Avon, 1972; Portia in Julius Caesar, and Volumnia in Coriolanus, RSC, Aldwych, 1973; Maria Lvovna in Summerfolk, RSC, Aldwych, and NY, 1974–75; Richard III, All's Well That Ends Well, Ghosts, Stratford, Ont., 1977; People Are Living There, Manchester Royal Exchange, 1979; Martha, in Who's Afraid of Virginia Woolf?, Nat. Theatre, 1981 (SWET Best Actress in a Revival Award); Countess of Rossilion, in All's Well That Ends Well, RSC Barbican and NY, 1983; An Inspector Calls, Greenwich, 1983; Tom and Viv, Royal Court, 1984, also New York, 1985; Mornings at Seven, Westminster, 1984; Night Must Fall, Greenwich, 1986; Lettice and Lovage, Globe, 1987 (Variety Club of GB Award for Best Stage Actress), and New York, 1990 (Tony award); The Importance of Being Earnest, Aldwych, 1993; An Inspector Calls, Aldwych, 1994; Indian Ink, Aldwych, 1995. *Films:* Ring of Spies, 2001: A Space Odyssey, The Whisperers, A Clockwork Orange, The Legacy, The King's Whore. *Television series include:* The Forsyte Saga; The First Churchills; Cousin Bette, 1970–71; I, Claudius, 1976; Quatermass, 1979; The Winter's Tale; Young Indiana Jones, 1992. Actress of the Year Award (BAFTA) for Queen Anne in The First Churchills, 1969. *Address:* c/o Representation Joyce Edwards, 275 Kennington Road, SE11 6BY. *T:* 0171–735 5736, *Fax:* 0171–820 1845.

U

U, Hla Maung; Ambassador of the Union of Myanmar to the Court of St James's, since 1992, concurrently accredited to Denmark, Norway and Sweden; *b* 8 Nov. 1932; *s* of U Pya and Daw Amar; *m* 1955, Daw Khin Myint; four *s* two *d*. *Educ:* Univ. of Yangon (BA Econs); Vanderbilt Univ., USA (MA Econs; Dip. in Econ. Develt). Ministry of Planning and Finance, Yangon: Asst Dir, 1966–72; Dir-Gen., 1972–78; Asian Development Bank, Manila: Alternate Exec. Dir, 1978–80; Exec. Dir, 1981–83; Dir-Gen., Min. of Planning and Finance, Yangon, 1983–84; Ambassador to: Philippines, 1984–87; Yugoslavia, 1987–92. Kyein Wut Pi Pya Ye/Taya U Pade So Mo Ye Tazeik, 1989; Pyi Thu Wun Htan Taziek, 1989; Naingngandaw Ayechan Thayarye Tazeik, 1989; Pyi Thu Wun Htan Kaung Taziek, 1992. *Publications:* articles on econs to Myanmar monthly jls. *Recreations:* reading, swimming. *Address:* Embassy of the Union of Myanmar, 19A Charles Street, W1X 8ER. *T:* 0171–629 9531.

UATIOA, Dame Mere, DBE 1978; *b* 19 Jan. 1924; *d* of Aberam Takenibeia and Bereti Bamatang; *m* 1950, Reuben K. Uatioa, MBE (*d* 1977); three *s* one *d*. *Educ:* Hiram Bingham High School, Beru Island. Widow of Reuben K. Uatioa, MBE, a leading Gilbertese nationalist and former Speaker, House of Assembly, Gilbert Islands; supported her husband throughout his long public service, demonstrating those qualities of wife and mother which are most admired in the Pacific. After his death, she devoted herself to her family. *Recreations:* social and voluntary work for Churches. *Address:* Erik House, Antebuka, Tarawa, Kiribati.

UBEE, Air Vice-Marshal Sydney Richard, CB 1952; AFC 1939; Royal Air Force; retired as Air Officer Commanding, No 2 Group, 2nd Tactical Air Force, Germany (1955–58); *b* 5 March 1903; *s* of late Edward Joseph Ubee, London; *m* 1942, Marjorie Doris (*d* 1954), *d* of George Clement-Parker, Newport, Mon; two step *s*. *Educ:* Beaufoy Technical Institute. Joined RAF, 1927, with short service commission; permanent commission, 1932; test pilot, Royal Aircraft Establishment, Farnborough, 1933–37; served in India, Iraq, Burma, and Ceylon, 1937–43; Airborne Forces Experimental Establishment, 1943–45; Comdg Officer, Experimental Flying, RAE Farnborough, 1946–47; Commandant Empire Test Pilots' Sch., Cranfield, Bucks, and Farnborough, 1947–48; Deputy Director Operational Requirements, Air Min., 1948–51; Commandant RAF Flying Coll., Manby, 1951–54; Director-General of Personnel (II), Air Ministry, 1954–55. *Address:* Harwood Lodge, 100 Lodge Hill Road, Lower Bourne, Farnham, Surrey GU10 3RD. *Club:* Royal Air Force.

UCHIDA, Mitsuko; pianist; *b* 20 Dec. 1948; *d* of Fujio and Yasuko Uchida. *Educ:* Hochschule für Musik, Vienna. First recital at age of 14 in Vienna; performs regularly with orchestras worldwide incl. Berlin Philharmonic, Vienna Philharmonic, Cleveland, etc.; performed complete Mozart piano sonatas in London, 1982, Tokyo, 1983, and NY, 1991; Schubert and Schönberg recitals in Salzberg, London, Vienna, NY, Tokyo, etc, 1994–96; repertoire ranges from J. S. Bach to Messiaen. Recordings include: complete piano sonatas and concertos of Mozart; Beethoven's piano concertos; Debussy's Etudes; Schumann's Carnaval. Has won many prizes for recordings. *Recreations:* sleeping, listening to music. *Address:* c/o Van Walsum Management, 26 Wadham Road, SW15 2LR. *T:* 0181–874 6344.

ud-DIN, Rt. Rev. Khair-; Church Missionary Society Mission Partner in Britain, since 1990; *b* 7 Feb. 1921; *s* of Sharam-ud-Din and Barkat Bibi; *m* 1963, Daphne Dionys. *Educ:* Punjab Univ., Lahore (BA Hons Oriental Langs); theol studies in India, Canada, UK. Ordained Deacon, 1948, priest, 1949. Mem., St John's Divinity Sch., 1952. Pattoki, Okara and Clarkabad mission dists, Punjab, 1948–64; Vicar: St John's, Peshawar, 1964–68; Cath. Church of the Resurrection, Lahore, 1968–77; Associate Priest, St Martin in the Bullring, Birmingham, 1973; Archdeacon of Lahore and Dean of Frontier Regions, Lahore Dio., 1977–82; Bishop of Peshawar, 1982–90. Official rep. of Danish Missionary Soc. in Pakistan, as Dean of Frontier Regions. Radio and TV broadcaster in Pakistan. Reviewer of books of poetry and prose in oriental lit., 1969–85. Hon. DD Theol Seminary, Gujranwala, Pakistan, 1987. Gold Medallist for outstanding servs in Dio. Lahore, 1979. *Publications:* Guidebook for Youth Workers, 1966; ed. Sunday Sch. courses, 1962–66. *Recreations:* gardening, antiques. *Address:* 60 St Leonards Road, Headington, Oxford OX3 8AB. *Club:* St Clement's Family Centre (Oxford).

UDEN, Martin David; HM Diplomatic Service; Political Counsellor and Consul-General, Seoul, since 1994; *b* 28 Feb. 1955; *s* of Rodney Frederick Uden and Margaret Irene Uden (*née* Brunt); *m* 1982, Fiona Jane Smith; two *s*. *Educ:* Ravensbourne Sch. for Boys; Queen Mary Coll., London Univ. (LLB). Called to the Bar, Inner Temple, 1977; joined FCO, 1977; Second Sec., Seoul, 1978–81; Second, later First Sec., FCO, 1981–86; First Sec., Bonn, 1986–90; FCO, 1990–93; Dep. Head, CSCE Unit, FCO, 1993–94. *Address:* c/o Foreign and Commonwealth Office, King Charles Street, SW1A 2AH.

UDOMA, Hon. Sir (Egbert) Udo, CFR 1978; Kt 1964; Justice, Supreme Court of Nigeria, Lagos, 1969–82, retired; Commissioner for Law Reform, Cross River State, Nigeria, 1985–88; *b* 21 June 1917; *s* of Chief Udoma Inam of Ibekwe Ntanaran Akama of Opobo (now Ikot Abasi, Akwa Ibom State), Nigeria; *m* 1950, Grace Bassey; six *s* one *d* (and one *s* decd). *Educ:* Methodist Coll., Uzuakoli, Nigeria; Trinity Coll., Dublin; St Catherine's Coll., Oxford. BA 1942; LLB 1942; PhD 1944; MA 1945. President, Dublin Univ. Philosophical Society, 1942–43. Called to Bar, Gray's Inn, 1945; practised as Barrister-at-Law in Nigeria, 1946–61; Member, House of Representatives, Nigeria, 1952–59; Judge of High Court of Federal Territory of Lagos, Nigeria, 1961–63. Member Nigeria Marketing Board and Director Nigeria Marketing Co. Board, 1952–54; Member Managing Cttee, West African Inst. for Oil Palm Research, 1953–63; Nat. President, Ibibio State Union, 1947–61; Vice-President, Nigeria Bar Assoc., 1957–61; Member: Internat. Commn of Jurists; World Assoc. of Judges; Chief Justice, High Court, Uganda, 1963–69; Acting Gov.-Gen., Uganda, 1963; Vice-President, Uganda Sports Union, 1964; Chairman, Board of Trustees, King George V Memorial Fund, 1964–69; Chancellor, Ahmadu Bello Univ., Zaria, 1972–75. Chm., Constituent Assembly for Nigerian Constitution, 1977–78; Dir, Seminar for Judges, 1980–82. Patron, Nigerian Soc. of Internat. Law, 1968–82; Mem., Nigerian Inst. of Internat. Affairs, 1979–. Grand Patron, Ikot Abasi dio. Methodist church, 1993. LLD (*hc*): Ibadan, 1967; Zaria, 1972; TCD, 1973. Awarded title of Obong Ikpa Isong Ibibio, 1961. Kt of John Wesley, Methodist Conf., Nigeria, 1994. *Publications:* The Lion and the Oil Palm and other essays, 1943; (jtly) The Human Right to Individual Freedom—a Symposium on World Habeas Corpus, ed by Luis Kutner, 1970; The Story of the Ibibio Union, 1987; History and the Law of the Constitution of Nigeria, 1994. *Recreations:* billiards, tennis, gardening. *Address:* Mfut Itiat Enin, 8 Dr Udoma Street, PO Box 47, Ikot Abasi, Akwa Ibom State, Nigeria, West Africa. *Clubs:* Island, Metropolitan (Lagos); Yoruba Tennis (Vice-Patron, 1982–) (Lagos).

UFF, Prof. John Francis, PhD, CEng, FICE, FCIArb; QC; international arbitrator, advocate and engineer; Nash Professor of Engineering Law, University of London, since 1991; Director, Centre of Construction Law and Management, King's College London, since 1987; *b* 30 Jan. 1942; *s* of Frederick and Eva Uff; *m* 1967, Diana Muriel Graveson; two *s* one *d*. *Educ:* Stratton Sch.; King's College London. BSc (Eng), PhD. Asst engineer, Rendel Palmer & Tritton, 1966–70; Vis. Lectr in civil engineering, 1963–68; called to the Bar, Gray's Inn, 1970, Bencher, 1993; practice at Bar, Keating Chambers, 1970–, Head of Chambers, 1992–; Asst Recorder, 1993; arbitrator in construction disputes; lectr to professional bodies in engineering law and arbitration. Bldg Users Insurance against Latent Defects Cttee, DoE, 1986–88; Adv. Cttee on arbitration law, DTI, 1993–95. Member, Council: ICE, 1982–85; Soc. Construction Law, 1990–. Vice-Pres., KCL Assoc., 1993–95. Prin. Ed., book series of Centre of Construction Law and Mgt, KCL, on construction law, management, environment law and dispute resolution, 1988–. *Publications:* Construction Law, 1974, 5th edn 1991; Commentary on ICE Conditions, 1978, 1991, 1995; (jtly) ICE Arbitration Practice, 1986; (jtly) Methods of Procurement in Ground Investigation, 1986; technical papers in civil engineering; papers and articles in engineering law and procedure. *Recreations:* playing and making violins, farming. *Address:* 10 Essex Street, Outer Temple, WC2R 3AA. *T:* 0171–240 6981; Ashtead Farm, Selside, Cumbria. *Club:* Ronnie Scott's.

UFFEN, Kenneth James, CMG 1977; HM Diplomatic Service, retired; Ambassador and UK Permanent Representative to OECD, Paris, 1982–85; *b* 29 Sept. 1925; *s* of late Percival James Uffen, MBE, former Civil Servant, and late Gladys Ethel James; *m* 1954, Nancy Elizabeth Winbolt; one *s* two *d*. *Educ:* Latymer Upper Sch.; St Catharine's Coll., Cambridge. HM Forces (Flt-Lt, RAFVR), 1943–48; St Catharine's Coll., 1948–50; 3rd Sec., FO, 1950–52; Paris, 1952–55; 2nd Sec., Buenos Aires, 1955–58; 1st Sec., FO, 1958–61; 1st Sec. (Commercial), Moscow, 1961–63; seconded to HM Treasury, 1963–65; FCO, 1965–68; Counsellor, Mexico City, 1968–70; Economic Counsellor, Washington, 1970–72; Commercial Counsellor, Moscow, 1972–76; Res. Associate, IISS, 1976–77; Ambassador to Colombia, 1977–82. *Recreations:* music, gardens. *Address:* 40 Winchester Road, Walton-on-Thames, Surrey KT12 2RH.

ULANOVA, Galina Sergeyevna; Order of Lenin, 1953, 1970; Hero of Socialist Labour, 1974, 1980; People's Artist of the USSR, 1951; Order of Red Banner of Labour, 1939, 1951, 1959, 1967; Order of People's Friendship, 1986; Badge of Honour, 1940; Prima Ballerina, Bolshoi Theatre, Moscow, 1944–60, retired; ballet-mistress at the Bolshoi Theatre since 1963; *b* 8 Jan. 1910; *d* of Sergei Nikolaevich Ulanov and Maria Feodorovna Romanova (dancers at Mariinsky Theatre, Petersburg). *Educ:* State School of Choreography, Leningrad. Kirov Theatre of Opera and Ballet, Leningrad, 1928–44 (début, 1928); danced Odette-Odile in Swan Lake, 1929; Raimonda, 1931; Solweig in The Ice Maiden, 1931; danced Diane Mirelle in first performance of Flames of Paris, 1932; Giselle, 1933; Masha in The Nutcracker Suite, 1933; The Fountain of Bakhchisarai, as Maria, 1934; Lost Illusions, as Coralie, 1936; Romeo and Juliet, as Juliet, 1940; with Bolshoi: Cinderella, as Cinderella, 1945; Parasha in The Bronze Horseman, 1949; Tao Hua in The Red Poppy, 1950; Katerina in The Stone Flower, 1954. Visited London with the Bolshoi Theatre Ballet, 1956. Member, Academies of Arts of USA, GB and France. Winner of first Anna Pavlova Prize; awarded State Prize, 1941; for Cinderella, 1946; for Romeo and Juliet, 1947; for Red Poppy, 1950. Awarded Lenin prize for outstanding achievement in ballet, 1957. FRAD 1963. *Address:* Bolshoi Theatre, Moscow. *Clubs:* Union of Theatrical Workers, Central House of Workers in the Arts.

ULLENDORFF, Prof. Edward, MA Jerusalem, DPhil Oxford; FBA 1965; Professor of Semitic Languages, School of Oriental and African Studies, University of London, 1979–82, now Professor Emeritus (Professor of Ethiopian Studies, 1964–79; Head of Africa Department, 1972–77); *b* 25 Jan. 1920; *s* of late Frederic and Cilli Ullendorff; *m* 1943, Dina Noack. *Educ:* Gymnasium Graues Kloster; Universities of Jerusalem and Oxford. Chief Examiner, British Censorship, Eritrea, 1942–43; Editor, African Publ., British Ministry of Information, Eritrea-Ethiopia, 1943–45; Assistant Political Secretary, British Military Admin, Eritrea, 1945–46; Asst Secretary, Palestine Government, 1947–48; Research Officer and Librarian, Oxford Univ. Inst. of Colonial Studies, 1948–49; Scarbrough Senior Research Studentship in Oriental Languages, 1949–50; Reader (Lectr, 1950–56) in Semitic Languages, St Andrews Univ., 1956–59; Professor of Semitic Languages and Literatures, University of Manchester, 1959–64. Carnegie Travelling Fellow to Ethiopia, 1958; Research Journeys to Ethiopia, 1964, 1966, 1969. Catalogued Ethiopian Manuscripts in Royal Library, Windsor Castle. Chairman: Assoc. of British Orientalists, 1963–64; Anglo-Ethiopian Soc., 1965–68 (Vice-Pres. 1969–77); Pres., Soc. for Old Testament Study, 1971; Vice-Pres., RAS, 1975–79, 1981–85. Joint Organizer, 2nd Internat. Congress of Ethiopian Studies, Manchester, 1963. Chm., Editorial Bd, Bulletin of SOAS, 1968–78; Mem., Adv. Bd, British Library, 1975–83. Vice-Pres., British

Acad., 1980–82; Schweich Lectr, British Acad., 1967. FRAS; Hon. Fellow, SOAS, 1985. Imperial Ethiopian Gold Medallion, 1960; Haile Sellassie Internat. Prize for Ethiopian studies, 1972. MA Manchester, 1962; Hon. DLitt St Andrews, 1972; Hon. Dr Phil Hamburg, 1990. *Publications:* The definite article in the Semitic languages, 1941; Exploration and Study of Abyssinia, 1945; Catalogue of Ethiopian Manuscripts in the Bodleian Library, Oxford, 1951; The Semitic Languages of Ethiopia, 1955; The Ethiopians, 1959, 3rd edn 1973; (with Stephen Wright) Catalogue of Ethiopian MSS in Cambridge University Library, 1961; Comparative Semitics in Linguistica Semitica, 1961; (with S. Moscati and others) Introduction to Comparative Grammar of Semitic Languages, 1964; An Amharic Chrestomathy, 1965, 2nd edn 1978; The Challenge of Amharic, 1965; Ethiopia and the Bible, 1968; (with J. B. Pritchard and others) Solomon and Sheba, 1974; annotated and trans., Emperor Haile Sellassie, My Life and Ethiopia's Progress (autobiog.), 1976; Studies in Semitic Languages and Civilizations, 1977; (with M. A. Knibb) Book of Enoch, 1978; The Bawdy Bible, 1979; (jtly) The Amharic Letters of Emperor Theodore of Ethiopia to Queen Victoria, 1979; (with C. F. Beckingham) The Hebrew Letters of Prester John, 1982; A Tigrinya Chrestomathy, 1985; Studia Aethiopica et Semitica, 1987; The Two Zions, 1988; From the Bible to Enrico Cerulli, 1990; H. J. Polotsky (1905–1991), 1992; From Emperor Haile Sellassie to H. J. Polotsky, 1995; Joint Editor of Studies in honour of G. R. Driver, 1962; Joint Editor of Ethiopian Studies, 1964; articles and reviews in journals of learned societies; contribs to Encyclopaedia Britannica, Encyclopaedia of Islam, etc; Joint Editor, Journal of Semitic Studies, 1961–64. *Recreations:* music, motoring in Scotland. *Address:* 4 Bladon Close, Oxford OX2 8AD.

ULLMANN, Liv (Johanne); actress; *b* Tokyo, 16 Dec. 1938; *d* of late Viggo Ullmann and of Janna (*née* Lund), Norway; *m* 1960, Dr Gappe Stang (marr. diss. 1965). *Educ:* Norway; London (dramatic trng). Stage début, The Diary of Anne Frank (title role), Stavanger, 1956; major roles, National Theatre and Norwegian State Theatre, Oslo; Amer. stage début, A Doll's House, New York Shakespeare Festival, 1974–75; Anna Christie, USA, 1977; The Bear, La Voix humaine, Australia, 1978; I Remember Mama, USA, and Ghosts (Ibsen), Broadway, 1979; British theatre début, Old Times, Guildford, 1985. Wrote and dir. short film, Parting, 1981. Eight Hon. doctorates, including Brown, Smith Coll., Tufts and Haifa. *Films:* Pan, 1965; The Night Visitor, 1971; Pope Joan, 1972; The Emigrants, 1972 (Golden Globe Award); The New Land, 1973 (Best Actress, Nat. Soc. of Film Critics, USA); Lost Horizon, 1973; 40 Carats, 1973; Zandy's Bride, 1973; The Abdication, 1974; The Wild Duck, 1983; The Bay Boy, 1985; Let's Hope it's a Girl, 1987; Mosca Addio, 1987; Time of Indifference, 1987; La Amiga, 1987; The Ox, 1993; *director:* Sophie, 1993; (*dir. by Ingmar Bergman*): Persona, 1966; The Hour of the Wolf, 1968 (Best Actress, Nat. Soc. of Film Critics, USA); Shame, 1968 (Best Actress, Nat. Soc. of Film Critics, USA); The Passion of Anna, 1969; Cries and Whispers, 1972; Scenes from a Marriage, 1974; Face to Face, 1976; The Serpent's Egg, 1977; The Autumn Sonata, 1978. Peer Gynt Award, Norway (1st female recipient). Commander, Order of St Olav (Norway), 1994. *Publications:* (autobiog.) Changing, 1977; Choices, 1984. *Address:* c/o Robert Lantz, 888 Seventh Avenue, New York, NY 10106, USA; c/o London Management, 235 Regent Street, W1.

ULLSTEIN, Augustus Rupert Patrick Anthony; QC 1992; *b* 21 March 1947; *s* of Frederick Charles Leopold Ullstein and Patricia (*née* Guinness); *m* 1970, Pamela Margaret Wells; two *s* two *d*. *Educ:* Bradfield Coll., Berks; LSE (LLB Hons). Called to the Bar, Inner Temple, 1970; in practice as barrister, 1970–. Dir, Saxon Radio, 1980–82. *Publications:* (Supervising Editor) Pelling and Purdie, Matrimonial Injunctions, 1982. *Recreations:* my children, after dinner speaking. *Address:* 29 Bedford Row, Holborn, WC1R 4HE. *T:* 0171–831 2626.

ULLSWATER, 2nd Viscount *cr* 1921, of Campsea Ashe, Suffolk; **Nicholas James Christopher Lowther;** PC 1994; Minister of State (Minister for Construction and Planning), Department of the Environment, 1994–95; *b* 9 Jan. 1942; *s* of Lieut John Arthur Lowther, MVO, RNVR (*d* 1942), and Priscilla Violet (*d* 1945), *yr d* of Reginald Everitt Lambert; *S* great-grandfather, 1949; *m* 1967, Susan, *d* of James Howard Weatherby; two *s* two *d*. *Educ:* Eton; Trinity Coll., Cambridge. Captain, Royal Wessex Yeomanry, T&AVR, 1973–78. A Lord in Waiting (Govt Whip), H of L, 1989–90; Parly Under-Sec. of State, Dept of Employment, 1990–93; Capt. of Corps of Gentlemen at Arms (Govt Chief Whip), H of L, 1993–94. *Heir: s* Hon. Benjamin James Lowther, *b* 26 Nov. 1975. *Address:* The Old Rectory, Docking, King's Lynn, Norfolk PE31 8LJ. *T:* Docking (01485) 518822.

ULRICH, Walter Otto; Deputy Secretary, Department of Education and Science, 1977–87; *b* 1 April 1927. Ministry of Works: Asst Principal, 1951; Principal, 1955; Treasury 1958–60; Principal Private Sec. to Minister of Public Building and Works, 1963–65; Asst Sec., 1965; Min. of Housing and Local Govt, 1966; DoE, 1970; Under-Sec., 1972; Cabinet Office, 1974–76. *Address:* 41 Beechwood Avenue, St Albans, Herts AL1 4XR. *T:* St Albans (01727) 834024.

ULSTER, Earl of; Alexander Patrick Gregers Richard Windsor; *b* 24 Oct. 1974; *s* of HRH the Duke of Gloucester and HRH the Duchess of Gloucester.

See under Royal Family.

UNDERHILL, Herbert Stuart; President, Victoria (BC) Press, 1978–79; Publisher, Victoria Times, 1971–78, retired; *b* 20 May 1914; *s* of Canon H. J. Underhill and Helena (*née* Ross); *m* 1937, Emma Gwendolyn MacGregor; one *s* one *d*. *Educ:* University Sch., Victoria, BC. Correspondent and Editor, The Canadian Press, Vancouver, BC, Toronto, New York and London, 1936–50; Reuters North American Editor, 1950; Asst General Manager, Reuters, 1958; Managing Editor, 1965–68; Dep. Gen. Manager, with special responsibility for North and South America and Caribbean, 1963–70. Director: Canadian Daily Newspaper Publishers' Assoc., 1972–76; The Canadian Press, 1972–78. *Publication:* The Iron Church, 1984. *Recreations:* travel, reading. *Address:* 308 Beach Drive, Victoria, BC, V8S 2M2, Canada.

UNDERHILL, Nicholas Edward; QC 1992; a Recorder, since 1994; *b* 12 May 1952; *s* of late Judge Underhill, QC and Rosalie Jean Underhill (who *m* 1989, William Anderson Beaumont, *qv*); *m* 1987, Nina Grunfeld; one *s* two *d*. *Educ:* Winchester Coll.; New Coll., Oxford (MA Hons). Called to the Bar, Gray's Inn, 1976. *Publication:* The Lord Chancellor, 1978. *Address:* Fountain Court, Temple, EC4Y 9DH. *T:* 0171–583 3335.

UNDERWOOD, John Morris; Partner, Clear Communication, since 1991; Editor, New Century, since 1993; *b* 8 Nov. 1953; *s* of John Edward Underwood and Ella Lillian Morris Underwood; *m* 1987, Susan Clare Inglish; two *s*. *Educ:* Univ. of Sheffield (BSc hons); University Coll., Cardiff (Graduate Dip. in Journalism). BBC trainee journalist, 1976–78; regional TV reporter, 1978–80; TV reporter, ITN, 1980–82; home affairs corresp., ITN, 1982–83; freelance TV producer and presenter, 1983–89; Exec. Producer, House of Commons Cttee TV, 1989–90; Dir of Campaigns and Communications, Labour Party, 1990–91. *Publication:* The Will to Win: John Egan and Jaguar, 1989. *Recreations:* theatre, walking. *Address:* 10 Percival Road, SW14 7QE. *T:* 0181–876 8884.

UNERMAN, Sandra Diane; Deputy Solicitor, Department of the Environment, since 1992; *b* 23 Aug. 1950; *d* of Cecil Unerman and Renee Unerman (*née* Goldberg). *Educ:* Gartlett Sch.; Orange Hill Grammar Sch.; Bristol Univ. (BA Hons History). Called to the Bar, Inner Temple, 1973; Legal Dept, DoE, 1974–. UK Civil Service Fellow, Humphrey Inst., Univ. of Minnesota, 1989–90. *Publication:* Trial of Three (novel), 1979. *Recreations:* writing, reading, listening to music, theatre going, folklore, needlework, conversation. *Address:* Department of the Environment, P3/132, 2 Marsham Street, SW1P 3EB.

UNGER, Michael Ronald; Editor, Manchester Evening News, since 1983; Director, The Guardian and Manchester Evening News plc, since 1983; Trustee, Scott Trust, since 1986; *b* 8 Dec. 1943; *s* of Ronald and Joan Maureen Unger; *m* 1st, 1966, Eunice Dickens (marr. diss. 1992); one *s* (one *d* decd); 2nd, 1993, Noorah Ahmed. *Educ:* Wirral Grammar School. Trainee journalist, Thomson Regional Newspapers, Stockport, 1963; Reading Evening Post, 1965–67; Perth Daily News, W Australia, 1967–71; Daily Post, Liverpool, 1971, Editor, 1979–82; Editor, Liverpool Echo, 1982–83. Chm., NW Arts Bd, 1991–93. *Publication:* (ed) The Memoirs of Bridget Hitler, 1979. *Recreation:* reading. *Address:* 164 Deansgate, Manchester M60 2RD. *T:* 0161–832 7200.

UNGERER, Tomi; writer and graphic artist; Chargé de Mission, Jack Lang, Ministre de la Culture, commission inter-ministérielle Franco-Allemande, since 1987; *b* Strasbourg, 28 Nov. 1931; *s* of Theo Ungerer and Alice (*née* Essler); *m* 1970, Yvonne Wright; two *s* one *d*. *Educ:* Colmar; Ecole Municipale des Arts Décoratifs, Strasbourg. Moved to USA, 1956; joined Harper's, 1957; worked for Amer. magazines and in advertising; moved to Nova Scotia, 1971, to Ireland, 1976; exhibitions: (first) Berlin, 1962; Strasbourg, 1975; Louvre, Paris, 1981; RFH, London, 1985. Pres. and Founder, Culture Bank, Strasbourg, 1990. Burckhardt Prize, Goethe Foundn, 1983. Commandeur des Arts et des Lettres (France), 1985; Chevalier, Légion d'Honneur (France), 1990; Cross of Merit (Germany), 1992; numerous other prizes and awards. *Films include:* The Three Robbers, 1972; Beast of Monsieur Racine, 1975. *Publications:* over 100 books in English, French and German, including: Horrible, 1958; Inside Marriage, 1960; The Underground Sketchbook, 1964; The Party, 1966; Fornicon, 1970; Compromises, 1970; The Poster Art of Tomi Ungerer, 1971; Testament, 1985; Once in a Lifetime, 1985; Far Out is not Far Enough, 1985; Joy of Frogs, 1985; *for children:* The Mellops series: The Mellops go Diving for Treasure; Crictor, 1958; Adelaide, 1959; Christmas Eve at the Mellops', 1960; Emile, 1960; Rufus, 1961; The Three Robbers, 1962; Snail, Where Are You?, 1962; One, Two, Where's My Shoe?, 1964; The Brave Vulture Orlando, 1966; Moon Man, 1967; Zeralda's Ogre, 1967; Ask Me a Question, 1968; The Hat, 1970; The Beast of Monsieur Racine, 1971; I am Papa Snap and These are My Favourite No Such Stories, 1971; No Kiss for Mother, 1973; Allumette, 1974. *Address:* Diogens Verlag AG, Sprecherstrasse 8, 8032 Zürich, Switzerland; Centre Tomi Ungerer, Musées de Strasbourg, 4 rue de la Haute Montée, Strasbourg 67000, France.

UNSWORTH, Barry Forster; author; *b* 10 Aug. 1930; *s* of Michael Unsworth and Elsie (*née* Forster); *m* 1st, 1959, Valerie Irene Moor (marr. diss. 1991); three *d*; 2nd, 1992, Aira Pohjanvaara-Buffa. *Educ:* Stockton Grammar Sch.; Manchester Univ. (BA Hons English). FRSL 1973. *Publications:* The Partnership, 1966; The Greeks Have a Word for It, 1967; The Hide, 1970; Mooncranker's Gift (Heinemann Award), 1973; The Big Day, 1976; Pascali's Island, 1980; The Rage of the Vulture, 1982; Stone Virgin, 1985; Sugar and Rum, 1990; Sacred Hunger (jtly, Booker Prize), 1992; Morality Play, 1995. *Recreations:* gardening, viticulture, bird-watching. *Address:* Casella Postale 24, Agello, Magiore, Perugia, Italy. *T:* (75) 5050084.

UNSWORTH, Sir Edgar (Ignatius Godfrey), Kt 1963; CMG 1954; QC (N Rhodesia) 1951; *b* 18 April 1906; *yr s* of John William and Minnie Unsworth; *m* 1964, Eileen, *widow* of Raymond Ritzema. *Educ:* Stonyhurst Coll.; Manchester Univ. (LLB Hons). Barrister-at-Law, Gray's Inn, 1930; private practice, 1930–37. Parly Cand. (C) for Farnworth, General Election, 1935. Crown Counsel: Nigeria, 1937; N Rhodesia, 1942; Solicitor-General: N Rhodesia, 1946; Fedn of Malaya, 1949; Chm. of Cttees, N Rhodesia, 1950; Attorney-General, N Rhodesia, 1951–56. Acting Chief Sec. and Dep. to Governor of N Rhodesia for periods during 1953, 1954 and 1955; Attorney-General, Fedn of Nigeria 1956–60; Federal Justice of Federal Supreme Court of Nigeria, 1960–62; Chief Justice, Nyasaland, 1962–64; Director of a Course for Government Officers from Overseas, 1964–65; Chief Justice of Gibraltar, 1965–76; Justice of Appeal, Gibraltar, 1976–81. Member Rhodesia Railways Arbitration Tribunal, 1946; Chm., Commn of Enquiry into Central African Airways Corp., 1947; Mem., British Observers' Group, Independence Elections, Rhodesia, 1980 (submitted independent report). *Publication:* Laws of Northern Rhodesia (rev. edn), 1949. *Recreations:* gardening, bridge. *Address:* 12 Brock Street, Bath BA1 2LW; Pedro El Grande 9, Sotogrande, Provincia de Cadiz, Spain. *Clubs:* Bath and County (Bath); Royal Gibraltar Yacht.

UNWIN, Sir Brian; *see* Unwin, Sir J. B.

UNWIN, Rev. Canon Christopher Philip, TD 1963; MA; Archdeacon of Northumberland, 1963–82; *b* 27 Sept. 1917; *e s* of Rev. Philip Henry and Decima Unwin. *Educ:* Repton Sch.; Magdalene Coll., Cambridge; Queen's Theological Coll., Birmingham. Deacon, 1940, Priest, 1941. Asst Curate of: Benwell, 1940–43; Sugley, 1944–47; Vicar of: Horton, Northumberland, 1947–55; Benwell, 1955–63. *Recreations:* reading, walking. *Address:* 60 Sandringham Avenue, Benton, Newcastle upon Tyne NE12 8JX. *T:* 0191–270 0418.

UNWIN, David Charles; QC 1995; *b* 12 May 1947; *s* of Peter Unwin and Rosemary (*née* Locket); *m* 1969, Lorna Bullivant; one *s* one *d*. *Educ:* Clifton Coll.; Trinity Coll., Oxford. Called to the Bar, Middle Temple, 1971; Jun. Counsel to Attorney Gen. in charity matters, 1987–95. *Recreations:* music, mountaineering, windsurfing. *Address:* 7 Stone Buildings, Lincoln's Inn, WC2A 3SZ. *Club:* Climbers'.

UNWIN, David Storr; author; *b* 3 Dec. 1918; *e s* of late Sir Stanley Unwin, KCMG; *m* 1945, Periwinkle, *yr d* of late Captain Sidney Herbert, RN; twin *s* and *d*. *Educ:* Abbotsholme. League of Nations Secretariat, Geneva, 1938–39; George Allen & Unwin Ltd, Publishers, 1940–44. *Publications:* The Governor's Wife, 1954 (Authors' Club First Novel Award, 1955); A View of the Heath, 1956; Fifty Years with Father: a Relationship (autobiog.), 1982; *for children:* (under pen name David Severn) Rick Afire!, 1942; A Cabin for Crusoe, 1943; Waggon for Five, 1944; Hermit in the Hills, 1945; Forest Holiday, 1946; Ponies and Poachers, 1947; Dream Gold, 1948; The Cruise of the Maiden Castle, 1948; Treasure for Three, 1949; My Foreign Correspondent through Africa, 1950; Crazy Castle, 1951; Burglars and Bandicoots, 1952; Drumbeats!, 1953; The Future Took Us, 1958; The Green-eyed Gryphon, 1958; Foxy-boy, 1959; Three at the Sea, 1959; Clouds over the Alberhorn, 1963; Jeff Dickson, Cowhand, 1963; The Girl in the Grove, 1974; The Wishing Bone, 1977. *Recreations:* travel, gardening. *Address:* Garden Flat, 31 Belsize Park, NW3 4DX. *Club:* PEN.

See also R. S. Unwin.

UNWIN, Eric Geoffrey; Chief Operating Officer, Cap Gemini Sogeti, since 1993; Executive Chairman, Hoskyns Group, since 1988; *b* 9 Aug. 1942; *s* of Maurice Doughty

Unwin and Olive Milburn (*née* Watson); *m* 1967, Margaret Bronia Element; one *s* one *d*. *Educ:* Heaton Grammar School, Newcastle upon Tyne; King's College, Durham Univ. (BSc Hons Chemistry). Cadbury Bros, 1963–68; joined John Hoskyns & Co., 1968; Managing Dir, Hoskyns Systems Development, 1978; Dir, 1982, Man. Dir, 1984, Hoskyns Group. Chm., Cap Programmator AB, 1993–; Non-Exec. Dir, Volmac Software Groep NV, 1992–. Pres., Computing Services Assoc., 1987–88. Mem., ITAB, 1988–91. CIMgt (CBIM 1984; Mem., Bd., 1990–94). Freeman, City of London, 1987; Founder Mem., and Liveryman, Co. of Information Technologists, 1987. *Recreations:* golf, riding, ski-ing, sailing. *Address:* 17 Park Village West, NW1 4AE. *Club:* Royal Automobile.

UNWIN, Sir (James) Brian, KCB 1990 (CB 1986); President, European Investment Bank, since 1993; Chairman, Supervisory Board, European Investment Fund, since 1994; *b* 21 Sept. 1935; *s* of Reginald Unwin and Winifred Annie Walthall; *m* 1964, Diana Susan, *d* of Sir D. A. Scott, *qv*; three *s*. *Educ:* Chesterfield School; New College, Oxford (MA); Yale University (MA). Asst Principal, CRO, 1960; Private Sec. to British High Commissioner, Salisbury, 1961–64; 1st Secretary, British High Commission, Accra, 1964–65; FCO, 1965–68; transferred to HM Treasury, 1968; Private Sec. to Chief Secretary to Treasury, 1970–72; Asst Secretary, 1972; Under Sec., 1976; seconded to Cabinet Office, 1981–83; Dep. Sec., HM Treasury, 1983–85; Dir, Eur. Investment Bank, 1983–85; Dep. Sec., Cabinet Office, 1985–87; Chm., Bd of HM Customs and Excise, 1987–93. Pres., Customs Co-operation Council, 1991–92. Chm., Civil Service Sports Council, 1989–93. Member: IMPACT Adv. Bd, 1990–93; Bd of Dirs, ENO, 1993–94 (Sec., 1987–93). *Recreations:* opera, bird watching, Wellingtoniana, cricket. *Address:* European Investment Bank, 100 boulevard Konrad Adenauer, 2950 Luxembourg. *Clubs:* Reform; Kingswood Village (Surrey).

UNWIN, Ven. Kenneth; Archdeacon of Pontefract, 1981–92, now Emeritus; *b* 16 Sept. 1926; *s* of Percy and Elsie Unwin; *m* 1958, Beryl Riley; one *s* four *d*. *Educ:* Chesterfield Grammar School; St Edmund Hall, Oxford (MA Hons); Ely Theological Coll. Assistant Curate: All Saints, Leeds, 1951–55; St Margaret, Durham City (in charge, St John's, Neville's Cross), 1955–59; Vicar: St John Baptist, Dodworth, Barnsley, 1959–69; St John Baptist, Royston, Barnsley, 1969–73; St John's, Wakefield, 1973–82. Hon. Canon, Wakefield Cathedral, 1980–92. RD of Wakefield, 1980–81. Proctor in Convocation, 1972–82. *Address:* 2 Rockwood Close, Skipton, Yorks BD23 1UG. *T:* Skipton (01756) 791323.

UNWIN, Dr (Peter) Nigel (Tripp), FRS 1983; Scientist, Medical Research Council Laboratory of Molecular Biology, Cambridge, 1968–80 and since 1987; Senior Research Fellow, Trinity College, Cambridge, since 1988; *b* 1 Nov. 1942; *s* of Peter Unwin and Cara Unwin (*née* Pinckney); *m* 1968, Janet Patricia Ladd; one *s* one *d*. *Educ:* Univ. of Otago, NZ (BE); Univ. of Cambridge (PhD 1968). Prof. of Structural Biol., then Cell Biol., Stanford Univ. Sch. of Medicine, Calif, 1980–87. Hon. FRMS 1989. Ernst Ruska Award, Ernst Ruska Foundn, 1980; Rosenstiel Award, Brandeis Univ., Mass, 1991. *Recreation:* mountaineering. *Address:* 19/20 Portugal Place, Cambridge CB5 8AF.

UNWIN, Peter William, CMG 1981; HM Diplomatic Service, retired; Director, David Davies Memorial Institute of International Studies, since 1995; *b* 20 May 1932; *s* of Arnold and Norah Unwin; *m* 1955, Monica Steven; two *s* two *d*. *Educ:* Ampleforth; Christ Church, Oxford. Army, 1954–56; FO, 1956–58; British Legation, Budapest, 1958–61; British Embassy, Tokyo, 1961–63; FCO, 1963–67; British Information Services, NY, 1967–70; FCO, 1970–72; Bank of England, 1973; British Embassy, Bonn, 1973–76; Head of Personnel Policy Dept, FCO, 1976–79; Fellow, Center for Internat. Affairs, Harvard, 1979–80; Minister (Economic), Bonn, 1980–83; Ambassador to: Hungary, 1983–86; Denmark, 1986–88; a Dep. Sec. Gen. of the Commonwealth, 1989–93. Chairman: British-Hungarian Soc., 1993–; Abbeyfield Internat., Apr. 1996– (Vice Chm., 1994–96). *Publications:* Voice in the Wilderness: Imre Nagy and the Hungarian Revolution, 1991; contrib. The European, Evening Standard, Independent, International Affairs, The [illegible]r, The Times and The Tablet. *Address:* 30 Kew Green, Richmond, Surrey TW9 [illegible]: 0181–940 8037. *Club:* United Oxford & Cambridge University.

[illegible]N, Rayner Stephens, CBE 1977; Chairman, Unwin Enterprises, since 1986; [illegible]tor, Allen and Unwin Australia, since 1990; *b* 23 Dec. 1925; *s* of late Sir Stanley [illegible]vin and Mary Storr; *m* 1952, Carol Margaret, *d* of Harold Curwen; one *s* three *d*. [illegible]c: Abbotsholme Sch.; Trinity Coll., Oxford (MA); Harvard, USA (MA). Sub-Lt, [illegible]NVR, 1944–47. Entered George Allen & Unwin Ltd, 1951; Chm., 1968–86; Chm., [illegible]986–88, Vice-Chm., 1988–90, Unwin Hyman. Mem. Council, Publishers' Assoc., [illegible]965–85 (Treasurer, 1969; Pres., 1971; Vice-Pres., 1973); Chm., British Council Publishers' Adv. Cttee, 1981–88; Dir, Book House Training Centre, 1976–. Pres., Book Trade Benevolent Soc., 1989–95; Vice-Pres., Book Trust, 1991–. Chm., Little Missenden Festival, 1981–88. *Publications:* The Rural Muse, 1954; The Defeat of John Hawkins, 1960; A Winter away from Home, 1995. *Recreations:* mountains, birds and gardens. *Address:* Limes Cottage, Little Missenden, near Amersham, Bucks HP7 0RG. *T:* Great Missenden (01494) 862900. *Club:* Garrick.

See also D. S. Unwin.

UPDIKE, John Hoyer; freelance writer; *b* 18 March 1932; *s* of late Wesley R. and Linda G. Updike; *m* 1st, 1953, Mary E. Pennington (marr. diss.); two *s* two *d*; 2nd, 1977, Martha Bernhard. *Educ:* Harvard Coll. Worked as journalist for The New Yorker magazine, 1955–57. *Publications: poems:* Hoping for a Hoopoe (in America, The Carpentered Hen), 1958; Telephone Poles, 1968; Midpoint and other poems, 1969; Tossing and Turning, 1977; Facing Nature, 1985; Collected Poems, 1993; *novels:* The Poorhouse Fair, 1959; Rabbit, Run, 1960; The Centaur, 1963; Of the Farm, 1966; Couples, 1968; Rabbit Redux, 1972; A Month of Sundays, 1975; Marry Me, 1976; The Coup, 1979; Rabbit is Rich (Pulitzer Prize), 1982; The Witches of Eastwick, 1984 (filmed 1987); Roger's Version, 1986; S., 1988; Rabbit at Rest, 1990 (Pulitzer Prize 1991); Memories of the Ford Administration, 1993; Brazil, 1994; *short stories:* The Same Door, 1959; Pigeon Feathers, 1962; The Music School, 1966; Bech: A Book, 1970; Museums and Women, 1973; Problems, 1980; Bech is Back, 1982; (ed) The Year's Best American Short Stories, 1985; Trust Me, 1987; The Afterlife and other stories, 1995; *miscellanies:* Assorted Prose, 1965; Picked-Up Pieces, 1976; Hugging the Shore, 1983; Just Looking: essays on art, 1989; Odd Jobs: essays and criticism, 1991; *autobiography:* Self-Consciousness: Memoirs, 1989; *play:* Buchanan Dying, 1974. *Address:* Beverly Farms, MA 01915, USA.

UPJOHN, Maj.-Gen. Gordon Farleigh, CB 1966; CBE 1959 (OBE 1955); *b* 9 May 1912; *e s* of late Dudley Francis Upjohn; *m* 1946, Rita Joan, *d* of late Major Clarence Walters; three *d*. *Educ:* Felsted School; RMC Sandhurst. 2nd Lieut, The Duke of Wellington's Regt; RWAFF, 1937; Adjt 3rd Bn The Nigeria Regt, 1940; Staff Coll., 1941; GSO2 Ops GHQ Middle East, 1941; Bde Maj. 3 WA Inf. Bde, 1942 (despatches); Lt-Col Comd 6 Bn The Nigeria Regt, 1944 (despatches); DAA&QMG Southern Comd India, 1946; GSO2 Mil. Ops Directorate WO, 1948; Lt-Col Chief Instructor RMA Sandhurst, 1951; Lt-Col Comd WA Inf. Bn, 1954; Bde Comdr 2 Inf. Bde Malaya, 1957 (despatches; Meritorious Medal (Perak Malaya)); Provost Marshal WO, 1960; GOC Yorkshire District, 1962–65. Automobile Assoc., 1965–76. *Recreations:* golf, cricket, field sports. *Address:* c/o Lloyds Bank, Grayshott, Hindhead, Surrey GU26 6LG.

UPWARD, Mrs Janet; Commissioning Project Manager, Primary Care Commissioning and Investment Group, Birmingham Family Health Services Authority, since 1993. *Educ:* Newnham College, Cambridge (BA (Geog. Hons) 1961; MA 1966); Univ. of Birmingham (MSocSci 1993). Sec., National Fedn of Consumer Gps, 1972–82; Mem., 1978–84, Dep. Chm., 1978–83, Domestic Coal Consumers' Council; Chm., National Consumer Congress, 1981–83; Chief Officer, S Birmingham CHC, 1983–90; Quality Assurance Review Officer, Birmingham FHSA, 1991–93. *Address:* 61 Valentine Road, Birmingham B14 7AJ. *T:* 0121–444 2837.

URE, James Mathie, OBE 1969; British Council Representative, India, and Minister (Education), British High Commission, New Delhi, 1980–84; *b* 5 May 1925; *s* of late William Alexander Ure, and of Helen Jones; *m* 1950, Martha Walker Paterson; one *s* one *d*. *Educ:* Shawlands Acad., Glasgow; Glasgow Univ. (MA); Trinity Coll., Oxford (BLitt). Army Service, 1944–47. Lectr, Edinburgh Univ., 1953–59; British Council: Istanbul, 1956–57; India, 1959–68; Dep. Controller, Arts Div., 1968–71; Rep., Indonesia, 1971–75; Controller, Home Div., 1975–80. *Publications:* Old English Benedictine Office, 1952; (with L. A. Hill) English Sounds and Spellings, 1962; (with L. A. Hill) English Sounds and Spellings—Tests, 1963; (with J. S. Bhandari and C. S. Bhandari) Read and Act, 1965; (with C. S. Bhandari) Short Stories, 1966.

URE, Sir John (Burns), KCMG 1987 (CMG 1980); LVO 1968; HM Diplomatic Service, retired; author; company director; *b* 5 July 1931; *s* of late Tam Ure; *m* 1972, Caroline, *d* of Charles Allan, Roxburghshire; one *s* one *d*. *Educ:* Uppingham Sch.; Magdalene Coll., Cambridge (MA); Harvard Business Sch. (AMP). Active Service as 2nd Lieut with Cameronians (Scottish Rifles), Malaya, 1950–51; Lieut, London Scottish (Gordon Highlanders) TA, 1952–55. Book publishing with Ernest Benn Ltd, 1951–53; joined Foreign (subseq. Diplomatic) Service, 1956; 3rd Sec. and Private Sec. to Ambassador, Moscow, 1957–59; Resident Clerk, FO, 1960–61; 2nd Sec., Leopoldville, 1962–63; FO, 1964–66; 1st Sec. (Commercial), Santiago, 1967–70; FCO, 1971–72; Counsellor, and intermittently Chargé d'Affaires, Lisbon, 1972–77; Head of South America Dept, FCO, 1977–79; Ambassador to Cuba, 1979–81; Asst Under-Sec. of State, FCO, 1981–84; Ambassador to Brazil, 1984–87, to Sweden, 1987–91. UK Comr Gen., Expo 92, 1990–92. Director: Thomas Cook Group, 1991–; Sotheby's Scandinavia AB, 1991–; CSE Aviation, 1992–94; Consultant, Robert Flemings (merchant bankers), 1995–. Chairman: Anglo-Swedish Soc., 1992–; Anglo-Brazilian Chamber of Commerce, 1994–. Trustee, Leeds Castle Foundn, 1995–. Life Fellow and Mem. Council, RGS, 1982–84. Thomas Cook lecture on Literary Travellers, RGS, 1988; regular guest lectr on foreign tours. Comdr, Mil. Order of Christ, Portugal, 1973. *Publications:* Cucumber Sandwiches in the Andes, 1973 (Travel Book Club Choice); Prince Henry the Navigator, 1977 (History Guild Choice); The Trail of Tamerlane, 1980 (Ancient History Club Choice); The Quest for Captain Morgan, 1983; Trespassers on the Amazon, 1986; Central and South America sections, in RGS History of World Exploration, 1990; A Bird on the Wing: Bonnie Prince Charlie's flight from Culloden retraced, 1992; Diplomatic Bag, 1994; book reviews in TLS. *Recreation:* travelling uncomfortably in remote places and writing about it comfortably afterwards. *Address:* Netters Hall, Hawkhurst, Kent TN18 5AT. *T:* Hawkhurst (01580) 752191. *Clubs:* White's, Beefsteak, Pilgrims.

URIE, Wing Comdr (John) Dunlop, AE 1942; bar 1945; *b* 12 Oct. 1915; *s* of late John Urie, OBE, Glasgow; *m* 1939, Mary Taylor, *d* of Peter Bonnar, Dunfermline; one *s* two *d*. *Educ:* Sedbergh; Glasgow Univ. Served War of 1939–45: with RAuxAF, in Fighter Command and Middle East Command; Wing Comdr, 1942. DL Co. of Glasgow, 1963. OStJ. *Address:* 80 Westbrook Avenue, Wahroonga, NSW 2076, Australia. *Club:* Royal Northern and Clyde Yacht.

URMSON, James Opie, MC 1943; Emeritus Professor of Philosophy, Stanford University; Emeritus Fellow of Corpus Christi College, Oxford; *b* 4 March 1915; *s* of Rev. J. O. Urmson; *m* 1940, Marion Joyce Drage; one *d*. *Educ:* Kingswood School, Bath; Corpus Christi College, Oxford. Senior Demy, Magdalen College, 1938; Fellow by examination, Magdalen College, 1939–45. Served Army (Duke of Wellington's Regt), 1939–45. Lecturer of Christ Church, 1945–46; Student of Christ Church, 1946–55; Professor of Philosophy, Queen's College, Dundee, University of St Andrews, 1955–59; Fellow and Tutor in Philosophy, CCC, Oxford, 1959–78. Visiting Associate Prof., Princeton Univ., 1950–51. Visiting Lectr, Univ. of Michigan, 1961–62, 1965–66, and 1969; Stuart Prof. of Philosophy, Stanford, 1975–80. *Publications:* Philosophical Analysis, 1956; The Emotive Theory of Ethics, 1968; Berkeley, 1982; Aristotle's Ethics, 1988; The Greek Philosophical Vocabulary, 1990; edited: Encyclopedia of Western Philosophy, 1960; J. L. Austin: How to Do Things with Words, 1962; (with G. J. Warnock) J. L. Austin: Philosophical Papers, 2nd edn, 1970; translations from ancient Greek; articles in philosophical jls. *Recreations:* gardening, music. *Address:* 5 Appleton Road, Cumnor, Oxford OX2 9QH. *T:* Oxford (01865) 862769.

URQUHART, Sir Brian (Edward), KCMG 1986; MBE 1945; Scholar-in-Residence, Ford Foundation, since 1986; an Under-Secretary-General, United Nations, 1974–86; *b* 28 Feb. 1919; *s* of Murray and Bertha Urquhart; *m* 1st, 1944, Alfreda Huntington (marr. diss. 1963); two *s* one *d*; 2nd, 1963, Sidney Damrosch Howard; one *s* one *d*. *Educ:* Westminster; Christ Church, Oxford (Hon. Student, 1985). British Army: Dorset Regt and Airborne Forces, N Africa, Sicily and Europe, 1939–45; Personal Asst to Gladwyn Jebb, Exec. Sec. of Preparatory Commn of UN, London, 1945–46; Personal Asst to Trygve Lie, 1st Sec.-Gen. of UN, 1946–49; Sec., Collective Measures Cttee, 1951–53; Mem., Office of Under-Sec.-Gen. for Special Political Affairs, 1954–71; Asst Sec.-Gen., UN, 1972–74; Exec. Sec., 1st and 2nd UN Conf. on Peaceful Uses of Atomic Energy, 1955 and 1958; active in organization and direction of UN Emergency Force in Middle East, 1956; Dep. Exec. Sec., Preparatory Commn of Internat. Atomic Energy Agency, 1957; Asst to Sec.-Gen.'s Special Rep. in Congo, July–Oct. 1960; UN Rep. in Katanga, Congo, 1961–62; responsible for organization and direction of UN peace-keeping ops and special political assignments. Hon. LLD: Yale, 1981; Tufts, 1985; Grinnell, 1986; State Univ. NY, 1986; Warwick, 1989; DUniv: Essex, 1981; City Univ. NY, 1986; Hon. DCL Oxford, 1986; Hon. DHL Colorado, 1987; Hon. DLitt Keele, 1987. *Publications:* Hammarskjold, 1972; A Life in Peace and War (autobiog.), 1987; Decolonization and World Peace, 1989; (with Erskine Childers) A World in Need of Leadership: tomorrow's United Nations, 1990; Ralph Bunche: an American life, 1993; (with Erskine Childers) Renewing the United Nations System, 1994; various articles and reviews on internat. affairs. *Address:* 50 West 29th Street, New York, NY 10001, USA; Howard Farm, Tyringham, MA 01264, USA. *T:* (212) 6796358. *Club:* Century (New York).

URQUHART, James Graham, CVO 1983; FCIT, FIMH; Chairman, Fiox Ltd, 1990–92 (Director, 1988–90); *b* 23 April 1925; *s* of James Graham Urquhart and Mary Clark; *m* 1949, Margaret Hutchinson; two *d*. *Educ:* Berwickshire High Sch. Served War, RAF, 1941–44. Management Trainee, Eastern Region, BR, 1949–52; Chief Controller, Fenchurch Street, 1956–59; Dist Traffic Supt, Perth, 1960–62; Divl Operating Supt,

Glasgow, 1962–64; Divl Manager, Glasgow and SW Scotland, 1964–67; Asst Gen. Man., Eastern Reg., 1967–69; BR Bd HQ: Chief Ops Man., 1969–72; Exec. Dir, Personnel, 1972–75; Gen. Manager, London Midland Reg., BR, 1975–76; BR Bd: Exec. Mem., Operations and Productivity, 1977–83; Mem., Exports, 1983–85; Chairman: British Transport Police, 1977–86; BRE-Metro, 1978–86; BR Engrg Ltd, 1979–85; Freightliners, 1983–85; Transmark, 1983–86. Director: Waterslides PLC, 1987–89; Park Air Electronics Ltd, 1987–91; Systems Connection Group PLC, 1988–92; CVC Ltd, 1988–91; Sonic Tape PLC, 1988–90. Mem., Industrial Tribunal, 1987–90. MIPM, MInstM, CIMgt. *Recreations:* golf, travel, gardening. *Address:* 10 Wychcotes, Caversham, Reading RG4 7DA. *T:* Reading (01734) 479071.

URQUHART, Lawrence McAllister, CA; Chairman, Burmah Castrol (formerly Burmah Oil) plc, since 1990; *b* 24 Sept. 1935; *s* of Robert and Josephine Urquhart; *m* 1961, Elizabeth Catherine Burns; three *s* one *d. Educ:* Strathallan; King's Coll., London (LLB). Price Waterhouse & Co., 1957–62; Shell International Petroleum, 1962–64; P. A. Management Consultants, 1964–68; Charterhouse Gp, 1968–74; TKM Gp, 1974–77; Burmah Oil, subseq. Burmah Castrol, 1977–: Gp Man. Dir, 1985–88; Chief Exec., 1988–93. Chairman: English China Clays, 1995– (Dir, 1991–); Scottish Widows' Fund and Life Assurance Soc., 1995– (non-exec. Dir, 1992–); Non-executive Director: BAA, 1993–; Kleinwort Benson plc, 1994–. *Recreations:* golf, music. *Address:* Burmah Castrol plc, Burmah Castrol House, Pipers Way, Swindon, Wilts SN3 1RE. *T:* Swindon (01793) 511521. *Clubs:* Frilford Heath Golf; La Cala (Andalucia).

URQUHART, Peter William Gordon; His Honour Judge Urquhart; a Circuit Judge, since 1992; *b* 18 March 1934; *s* of Gordon Eldridge Urquhart and Constance Margaret (*née* Taylor); *m* 1965, Carolyn Hemingway Hines; one *s* one *d. Educ:* Liverpool Coll.; Peterhouse, Cambridge (MA, LLB). Admitted solicitor, 1960. Member: Lord Chancellor's Legal Aid Adv. Cttee, 1974–80; Equal Opportunities Commn, 1977–82. *Recreations:* book collecting, reading, gardening, early music, jazz. *Address:* Braehead, 19 Poplar Road, Birkenhead, Merseyside L43 5TB. *T:* 0151–652 4043. *Club:* Athenæum (Liverpool).

URSELL, Prof. Fritz Joseph, FRS 1972; Emeritus Professor of Applied Mathematics, Manchester University, since 1990 (Beyer Professor of Applied Mathematics, 1961–90); *b* 28 April 1923; *m* 1959, Katharina Renate (*née* Zander); two *d. Educ:* Clifton; Marlborough; Trinity College, Cambridge (BA 1943; MA 1947; ScD 1957). Admiralty Service, 1943–47; ICI Fellow in Applied Mathematics, Manchester Univ., 1947–50. Fellow (Title A), Trinity Coll., Cambridge, 1947–51; Univ. Lecturer in Mathematics, Cambridge, 1950–61; Stringer Fellow in Natural Sciences, King's Coll., Cambridge, 1954–60. Georg Weinblum Lectr in Ship Hydrodynamics, Hamburg and Washington, 1986; Stewartson Lectr in Fluid Mechanics, 1991. FIMA 1964 (Gold Medal, 1994). MSc Manchester, 1965. *Publication:* Collected Papers 1946–1992, 1994. *Address:* 28 Old Broadway, Manchester M20 3DF. *T:* 0161–445 5791.

URSELL, Rev. Philip Elliott; Principal of Pusey House, Oxford, since 1982; *b* 3 Dec. 1942; *o s* of late Clifford Edwin Ursell and Hilda Jane Ursell (*née* Tucker). *Educ:* Cathays High Sch.; University Coll. Cardiff (Craddock Wells Exhibnr; BA); St Stephen's House, Oxford. MA Oxon. Curate of Newton Nottage, Porthcawl, 1968–71; Asst Chaplain of University Coll. Cardiff, 1971–77; Chaplain of Polytechnic of Wales, 1974–77; Chaplain, Fellow and Dir of Studies in Music, Emmanuel Coll., Cambridge, 1977–82. Select Preacher, Harvard Univ., 1982, 1983; Univ. Preacher, Harvard Summer Sch., 1985. Warden, Soc. of Most Holy Trinity, Ascot Priory, 1985–. Examining Chaplain to the Bishop of London, 1987–. Mem. Governing Body, Church in Wales, 1971–77. *Recreations:* fly-fishing, Jane Austen. *Address:* Pusey House, Oxford OX1 3LZ. *T:* Oxford (01865) 278415; Ascot Priory, Berks SL5 8RT. *T:* Ascot (01344) 885157; 8 Raglan House, Castle Court, Westgate Street, Cardiff CF1 1DN. *T:* Cardiff (01222) 665775.

URUGUAY, Bishop of, since 1988; **Rt. Rev. (Harold) William Godfrey;** Assistant Presiding Bishop, Province of the Southern Cone of America, 1989–95; *b* 21 April 1948; *s* of Charles Robert Godfrey and Irene Eva Godfrey (*née* Kirk); *m* 1968, Judith Moya (*née* Fenton); one *s* two *d. Educ:* Chesterfield School; King's Coll., Univ. of London (AKC); St Augustine's Coll., Canterbury. VSO, Isfahan, Iran, 1966–67; Asst Curate, Warsop with Sookholme, Diocese of Southwell, 1972–75; Team Vicar of St Peter and St Paul, Hucknall Torkard, 1975–86; Bishop of Southwell's Ecumenical Officer, 1981–82; Rector of Montevideo, 1986–88, Archdeacon of Montevideo, 1986–87; Asst Bishop of Argentina and Uruguay, 1987–88. Founder Mem., Jesus Caritas Fraternity (Anglican Communion), 1974. *Recreations:* walking, guitar, bird watching, hockey (University, Derbyshire and Midland colours). *Address:* CC 6108, 11000 Montevideo, Uruguay. *T:* (2) 959627, 954037, *Fax:* (2) 962519.

URWICK, Sir Alan (Bedford), KCVO 1984; CMG 1978; Serjeant at Arms, House of Commons, 1989–95; *b* 2 May 1930; *s* of late Col Lyndall Fownes Urwick, OBE, MC and Joan Wilhelmina Saunders (*née* Bedford); *m* 1960, Marta, *o d* of Adhemar Montagne; three *s. Educ:* Dragon Sch.; Rugby (Schol.); New Coll., Oxford (Exhibr). 1st cl. hons Mod. History 1952. Joined HM Foreign (subseq. Diplomatic) Service, 1952; served in: Brussels, 1954–56; Moscow, 1958–59; Baghdad, 1960–61; Amman, 1965–67; Washington, 1967–70; Cairo, 1971–73; seconded to Cabinet Office as Asst Sec., Central Policy Review Staff, 1973–75; Head of Near East and N Africa Dept, FCO, 1975–76; Minister, Madrid, 1977–79; Ambassador to Jordan, 1979–84; Ambassador to Egypt, 1985–87; High Comr to Canada, 1987–89. KStJ 1982. Grand Cordon, first class, Order of Independence (Jordan), 1984.

URWIN, Harry, (Charles Henry); Associate Fellow, Industrial Relations Research Unit, Warwick University, since 1981; Member, TUC General Council, 1969–80; Deputy General-Secretary, Transport and General Workers Union, 1969–80; Chairman, TUC Employment Policy and Organisation Committee, 1973–80; *b* 24 Feb. 1915; *s* of Thomas and Lydia Urwin; *m* 1941, Hilda Pinfold; one *d. Educ:* Durham County Council Sch. Convenor, Machine Tool Industry, until 1947; Coventry Dist Officer, TGWU, 1947–59; Coventry Dist Sec., Confedn of Shipbuilding and Engineering Unions, 1954–59; Regional Officer, TGWU, 1959–69; Member: Industrial Develt Adv. Bd, Industry Act, 1972–79; Sir Don Ryder Inquiry, British Leyland Motor Corp., 1974–75; Manpower Services Commn, 1974–79; Nat. Enterprise Bd, 1975–79; Energy Commn, 1977–79; Council, ACAS, 1978–80; Standing Cttee on Pay Comparability, 1979–80. *Recreation:* swimming. *Address:* 4 Leacliffe Way, Aldridge, Walsall WS9 0PW.

URWIN, Rt. Rev. Lindsay Goodall; *see* Horsham, Bishop Suffragan of.

URWIN, (Terence) Peter; Director of Administration and County Solicitor, Northumberland County Council, since 1990; *b* 28 Oct. 1948; *s* of John Robson Urwin; *m* 1971, Mary Theresa Smith; one *d. Educ:* Durham Johnston Sch.; Liverpool Univ. (LLB Hons). Solicitor. Durham County Council: Asst Solicitor, 1973–74; Asst Clerk of the Council, 1974–86; Dep. County Solicitor, 1986–90. Clerk to the Lieutenancy, Northumberland, 1990–. Secretary, Northumberland Advisory Committee: Justices of the Peace, 1990–; Gen. Comrs of Income Tax, 1990–. *Recreations:* Rugby, walking, crosswords. *Address:* Buckburns, Brancepeth Village, Durham City DH7 8DT. *T:* Durham (0191) 3783086.

USBORNE, Henry Charles, MA; Founder, Parliamentary Group for World Government, 1946; *b* 16 Jan. 1909; *s* of Charles Frederick Usborne and Janet Lefroy; *m* 1936; two *s* two *d. Educ:* Bradfield; Corpus Christi, Cambridge. MP (Lab) Yardley Div. of Birmingham, 1950–59 (Acock's Green Div. of Birmingham, 1945–50). JP Worcs, 1964–79. *Address:* Totterdown, Evesham, Worcs WR11 5JP.

See also R. A. Usborne.

USBORNE, Richard Alexander; writer; *b* 16 May 1910; *s* of Charles Frederick Usborne, ICS, and Janet Muriel (*née* Lefroy); *m* 1938, Monica (*d* 1986), *d* of Archibald Stuart MacArthur, Wagon Mound, New Mexico, USA; one *s* one *d. Educ:* Summer Fields Preparatory Sch.; Charterhouse; Balliol Coll., Oxford. BA Mods and Greats; MA 1981. Served War, 1941–45: Army, SOE and PWE, Middle East, Major, Gen. List. Advertising agencies, 1933–36; part-owner and Editor of What's On, 1936–37; London Press Exchange, 1937–39; BBC Monitoring Service, 1939–41; Asst Editor, Strand Magazine, 1946–50; Dir, Graham & Gillies Ltd, Advertising, retd, 1970; Custodian, National Trust, 1974–81. *Publications:* Clubland Heroes, 1953 (rev. 1975, 1983); (ed) A Century of Summer Fields, 1964; Wodehouse at Work, 1961, rev. edn, as Wodehouse at Work to the End, 1977; (ed) Sunset at Blandings, 1977; (ed) Vintage Wodehouse, 1977; A Wodehouse Companion, 1981; (ed) Wodehouse 'Nuggets', 1983; (ed) The Penguin Wodehouse Companion, 1988; After Hours with P. G. Wodehouse, 1991; adaptations of Wodehouse novels and stories for BBC radio serials. *Recreations:* reading, writing light verse. *Address:* The Charterhouse, Charterhouse Square, EC1M 6AN. *T:* 0171–608 0140.

See also H. C. Usborne.

USHER, Sir Leonard (Gray), KBE 1986 (CBE 1971); JP; Secretary, Fiji Press Council, 1985–94; Chairman, Suva Stock Exchange, 1978–92; *b* 29 May 1907; *s* of Robert Usher and Mary Elizabeth (*née* Johnston); *m* 1st, 1940, Mary Gertrude Lockie; one *s* one *d*; 2nd, 1962, Jane Hammond Derné (*d* 1984). *Educ:* Auckland Grammar Sch., NZ; Auckland Training Coll. (Trained Teachers Cert. B); Auckland Univ. (BA). Headmaster, Levuka Public Sch., Provincial Schs, Queen Victoria Sch., 1930–43; Fiji Govt PRO, 1943–56; Exec. Dir, Fiji Times and Herald Ltd, 1957–73; Editor, Fiji Times, 1958–73; Org. Dir, Pacific Is News Assoc., 1974–85 (Councillor and Life Mem., 1985–). Chm., Fiji Develt Bank, 1978–82; Dep. Chm., Nat. Bank of Fiji, 1974–83. Mem., Suva CC, 1962–71, 1975–77; Mayor of Suva, 1966–70, 1975–76. *Publications:* Satellite Over The Pacific, 1975; 50 Years in Fiji, 1978; (jtly) Suva—a history and guide, 1978; Levuka School Century, 1979; (jtly) This is Radio Fiji, 1979; The Lodge of Fiji 1882–1982, 1982; (ed) Pacific News Media, 1986; Mainly About Fiji, 1987; 60 Years in Fiji, 1988; Letters From Fiji 1987–1990, 1992; More Letters from Fiji 1990–1994, 1994. *Recreations:* reading, computer programmes, conversation. *Address:* 24 Des Voeux Road, Suva, Fiji. *T:* 302025, *Fax:* 303025; PO Box 13250, Suva, Fiji. *Clubs:* Defence, Fiji, United, Ex-Servicemen's (Fiji); Royal Automobile (Sydney).

USHER, Sir William John Tevenar, 7th Bt *cr* 1899, of Norton, Ratho, Midlothian, and of Wells, Hobkirk, Roxburghshire; *b* 18 April 1940; *er s* of William Dove Usher (*d* 1969), 5th *s* of Sir Robert Usher, 2nd Bt, and of Christa Elizabeth, *d* of Bruno von Tevenar; *S* kinsman, 1994; *m* 1962, Rosemary Margaret (marr. diss. 1990), *d* of Col Sir Reginald Douglas Henry Houldsworth, 4th Bt, OBE, TD; two *s* one *d. Educ:* Uppingham. *Heir: s* Andrew John Usher [*b* 8 Feb. 1963; *m* 1987, Charlotte Louise Alexandra, *o d* of R. B. Eldridge; two *s*].

USTINOV, Sir Peter (Alexander), Kt 1990; CBE 1975; FRSA, FRSL; actor, dramatist, film director; Chancellor, Durham University, since 1992; Rector of the University of Dundee, 1968–74; Goodwill Ambassador for UNICEF, 1969; *b* London, 16 April 1921; *s* of late Iona Ustinov and Nadia Benois, painter; *m* 1st, 1940, Isolde Denham (marr. diss. 1950); one *d*; 2nd, 1954, Suzanne Cloutier (marr. diss. 1971); one *s* two *d*; 3rd, 1972, Hélène du Lau d'Allemans. *Educ:* Westminster School. Served in Army, Royal Sussex Regt and RAOC, 1942–46. Author of plays: House of Regrets, 1940 (prod Arts Theatre 1942); Blow Your Own Trumpet, 1941 (prod Playhouse [Old Vic] 1943); Beyond, 1942 (prod Arts Theatre, 1943); The Banbury Nose, 1943 (prod Wyndham's 1944); The Tragedy of Good Intentions, 1944 (prod Old Vic, Liverpool, 1945); The Indifferent Shepherd (prod Criterion, 1948); Frenzy (adapted from Swedish of Ingmar Bergman, prod and acted in St Martin's, 1948); The Man in the Raincoat (Edinburgh Festival, 1949); The Love of Four Colonels (and acted in, Wyndham's, 1951); The Moment of Truth (Adelphi, 1951); High Balcony, 1952 (written 1946); No Sign of the Dove (Savoy, 1953); The Empty Chair (Bristol Old Vic, 1956); Romanoff and Juliet (Piccadilly, 1956, film, 1961; musical, R loves J, Chichester, 1973); Photo Finish (prod and acted in it, Saville, 1962); The Life in My Hands, 1963; The Unknown Soldier and his Wife, 1967 (prod and acted in it, Chichester, 1968, New London, 1973); Halfway up the Tree (Queen's), 1967; compiled, prod and acted in The Marriage, Edinburgh, 1982; wrote and acted in Beethoven's Tenth (Vaudeville, 1983, 1987–88); An Evening with Peter Ustinov, (Haymarket), 1990, 1991, 1994. Co-Author of film: The Way Ahead, 1943–44. Author and Director of films: School for Secrets, 1946; Vice-Versa, 1947. Author, director, producer and main actor in film Private Angelo, 1946; acted in films: One Of Our Aircraft is Missing, 1941; The Way Ahead, 1944; Odette, Quo Vadis, Hotel Sahara, 1950; Beau Brummell, The Egyptian, We're No Angels, 1954; Lola Montez, 1955; The Spies, 1955; I Girovaghi, 1956; An Angel Flew Over Brooklyn, 1957; Spartacus, 1960 (Academy Award, Best Supporting Actor, 1961); The Sundowners, 1961; Romanoff and Juliet, 1961; Topkapi (Academy Award, Best Supporting Actor), 1964; John Goldfarb, Please Come Home, 1964; Blackbeard's Ghost, 1967; The Comedians, 1968; Hot Millions, 1968; Viva Max, 1969; Big Truck and Poor Clare, 1971; One of our Dinosaurs is Missing, 1974; Logan's Run, 1975; Treasure of Matecumbe, 1977, Un Taxi Mauve, 1977; The Last Remake of Beau Geste, 1977, Death on the Nile, 1978 (Best Film Actor, Variety Club of GB); Ashanti, The Thief of Baghdad, 1979; Charlie Chan and the Curse of the Dragon Queen, 1981; Evil under the Sun, 1981; Appointment with Death, 1988; The French Revolution, 1989; Lorenzo's Oil, 1992; The Phoenix and the Magic Carpet, 1994; director, producer and actor in film Billy Budd, 1961; director and actor in films: Hammersmith is Out, 1971; Memed My Hawk, 1984. Directed operas at: Covent Garden, 1962; Hamburg Opera, 1968; Paris Opera, 1973; Edinburgh Fest., 1973, 1981; Berlin Opera, 1978; Piccola Scala, Milan, 1981, 1982; Hamburg Opera, 1985, 1987; Dresden Opera, 1993. Master's Course (opera direction), Salzburg, 1986. Acted in: revues: Swinging the Gate, 1940, Diversion, 1941; plays: Crime and Punishment, New Theatre, 1946; Love in Albania, St James's, 1949; King Lear, Stratford, Ont, 1979; Beethoven's Tenth, Berlin, 1987; directed Lady L, 1965; *television:* Omnibus: the life of Samuel Johnson (Emmy Award), 1957–58; Barefoot in Athens (Emmy Award), 1966; Storm in Summer (Emmy Award), 1970; The Mighty Continent (series), 1974; Einstein's Universe (series), 1979; 13 at Dinner, 1985; Dead Man's Folly, 1985; World Challenge (series), 1985; Peter Ustinov's Russia (series), 1987; Peter Ustinov in China, 1987 (ACE Award, 1988); Around the World in 80 Days, 1988–89; Secret Identity of Jack the Ripper, 1989; Ustinov aboard the Orient Express, 1992; Ustinov Meets Pavarotti, 1993; Inside the Vatican, 1994;

The Old Curiosity Shop, 1995; Haydn Gala, 1995; Sir Peter Ustinov in Thailand, Sir Peter Ustinov in Hong Kong, 1995; Paths of Gods, 1995. Member: British Film Academy; Acad. of Fine Arts, Paris, 1988. Pres., World Federalist Movt, 1992–96; Mem., British USA Bicentennial Liaison Cttee, 1973–. Hon. doctorates include: Hon. DMus Cleveland Inst. of Music, 1967; Hon. DHL Georgetown Univ., 1988; Hon. LLD Ottawa, 1991; Hon. DLitt Durham, 1992. Benjamin Franklin Medal, Royal Society of Arts, 1957; UNICEF award, 1978, 1995; Gold Medal, City of Athens, 1990; Medal of the Greek Red Cross, 1990; Medal of Honour, Charles Univ., Prague, 1991; Grammy Award; Britannia Award, LA Br., BAFTA, 1992; Critics' Circle Award, 1993. Order of the Smile (for dedication to idea of internat. assistance to children), Warsaw, 1974; Commandeur des Arts et des Lettres (France), 1985; Order of El Istiglal (Jordan); Order of Yugoslav Flag (Yugoslavia); Ordem Nacional do Cruzerio do Sul (Brazil), 1994. *Publications:* House of Regrets, 1943; Beyond, 1944; The Banbury Nose, 1945; Plays About People, 1950; The Love of Four Colonels, 1951; The Moment of Truth, 1953; Romanoff and Juliet (Stage and Film); Add a Dash of Pity (short stories), 1959; Ustinov's Diplomats (a book of photographs), 1960; The Loser (novel), 1961; The Frontiers of the Sea, 1966; Krumnagel, 1971; Dear Me (autobiog.), 1977; Overheard (play), 1981; My Russia, 1983; Ustinov in Russia, 1987; The Disinformer, 1989; The Old Man and Mr Smith, 1990; Ustinov at Large (compilation of articles in The European), 1991; Still at Large (compilation of articles in The European), 1993, 1995; contributor short stories to Atlantic Monthly. *Recreations:* lawn tennis, squash, collecting old masters' drawings, music. *Address:* 11 rue de Silly, 92100 Boulogne, France. *Clubs:* Garrick, Savage, Royal Automobile, Arts Theatre, Queen's.

UTEEM, Cassam; President, Republic of Mauritius, since 1992; *b* 22 March 1941; *s* of Aisha Uteem and Omar Farook; *m* 1967, Zohra Uteem; two *s* one *d*. *Educ:* Univ. of Mauritius (Dip. Soc. Work); Univ. of Paris VII (LèsL, MPsychol). Mem., Municipal Council, Port Louis, 1969, 1977–79, 1986–88 (Lord Mayor, 1986); MLA Port Louis East/Maritime, 1982–92; Minister of Employment, Social Security and National Solidarity, 1982–83; Opposition Whip, 1983–87; Chm., Public Accounts Cttee, 1988–90; Dep. Prime Minister and Minister of Industry and Industrial Technol., 1990–92. Hon. DCL Mauritius, 1994; Dr *hc* Aix Marseilles III, 1994. Grand Commander, Order of Star and Key of the Indian Ocean, 1993. *Recreations:* reading, walking. *Address:* State House, Le Reduit, Mauritius. *T:* 4543021.

UTLEY, (Clifton) Garrick; journalist and broadcaster, since 1964; Chief Foreign Correspondent, ABC News, since 1993; *b* 19 Nov. 1939; *s* of late Clifton Maxwell Utley and of Frayn Garrick Utley; *m* 1973, Gertje Rommeswinkel. *Educ:* Carleton Coll., Northfield, Minn, USA (BA 1961); Free Univ., Berlin. Correspondent, NBC News: Saigon, Vietnam, 1964–65; Berlin, Germany, 1966–68; Paris, France, 1969–71; NY, 1971–72; London (Senior European Correspondent), 1973–79; New York (Chief Foreign Correspondent), 1980–93. Numerous documentary films on foreign affairs. Hon. LLD Carleton Coll., 1979. *Recreations:* music, conversation, languages. *Address:* ABC News, 8 Carburton Street, W1P 7DT. *T:* 0171–637 9222.

UTLEY, Prof. James Henry Paul; Professor of Organic Chemistry, since 1983, and Head of Organic Section, since 1994, Queen Mary and Westfield College (formerly at Queen Mary College), University of London; *b* 11 Sept. 1936; *s* of Victor Eric Utley and Lena Beatrice Utley; *m* 1959, Hazel Wendler (*née* Brown); two *s* two *d*. *Educ:* E. P. Collier Sch., Reading; Univ. of Hull (BSc, PhD); Technische Hogeschool, Delft; University College London; DSc London. CChem, FRSC. NATO Research Fellowships, 1961–62; Queen Mary, later Queen Mary and Westfield College, London: Lectr, 1963–76; Reader in Organic Chemistry, 1976–83; Head of Chemistry, 1987–91; Dean, Faculty of Natural Scis, 1991–94; Mem. Council, 1991–94. Guest Professor: Univ. of Aarhus, 1973; Univ. of Münster, 1985; Ecole Normale Supérieure, Paris, 1994; Univ. of Texas at Austin, 1995. *Publications:* research and review articles in internat. learned jls. *Recreations:* walking, bowls, jazz. *Address:* 23 Frewin Road, Wandsworth Common, SW18 3LR. *T:* 0181–874 2939. *Club:* Heathfield (Wandsworth Common).

UTTING, Sir William (Benjamin), Kt 1991; CB 1985; Chairman, National Institute for Social Work, since 1991; *b* 13 May 1931; *s* of John William Utting and Florence Ada Utting; *m* 1954, Mildred Jackson; two *s* one *d*. *Educ:* Great Yarmouth Grammar Sch.; New Coll., Oxford; Barnett House, Oxford. MA Oxon. Probation Officer: Co. Durham, 1956–58; Norfolk, 1958–61; Sen. Probation Officer, Co. Durham, 1961–64; Principal Probation Officer, Newcastle upon Tyne, 1964–68; Lectr in Social Studies, Univ. of Newcastle upon Tyne, 1968–70; Dir of Social Services, Kensington and Chelsea, 1970–76; Chief Social Work Officer, DHSS, 1976–85; Chief Inspector, Social Services Inspectorate, DHSS, subseq. DoH, 1985–91. Member: Chief Scientist's Res. Cttee, DHSS, 1973–76; SSRC, 1979–83; ESRC, 1984; Cttee on Standards in Public Life, 1994–. Mem. Council, Goldsmiths' Coll., 1993–. Trustee: Mental Health Foundn, 1988–; Joseph Rowntree Foundn, 1991–; CSV, 1991–. Hon. DLitt UEA, 1992. *Publications:* contribs to professional jls. *Recreations:* literature, music, art. *Address:* 76 Great Brownings, College Road, SE21 7HR. *T:* 0181–670 1201.

UVAROV, Dame Olga (Nikolaevna), DBE 1983 (CBE 1978); DSc, FRCVS; Vice-President, Universities Federation for Animal Welfare, 1986–92; *d* of Nikolas and Elena Uvarov. *Educ:* Royal Vet. Coll. (Bronze Medals for Physiol. and Histol.). MRCVS 1934; FRCVS 1973. Asst in gen. mixed practice, 1934–43; own small animal practice, 1944–53; licence to practice and work at greyhound stadium, 1945–68; clinical res., Pharmaceutical industry, 1953–70; Head of Vet. Adv. Dept, Glaxo Laboratories, 1967–70; BVA Technical Inf. Service, 1970–76; Advr on Tech. Inf., BVA, 1976–78; Mem. MAFF Cttees under Medicines Act (1968), 1971–78. RCVS: Mem. Council, 1968–88; Chm. Parly Cttee, 1971–74; Jun. Vice-Pres., 1975; Pres., 1976–77; Sen. Vice-Pres., 1977–78; President: Soc. Women Vet. Surgeons, 1947–49 (Sec., 1946); Central Vet. Soc., 1951–52; Assoc. Vet. Teachers and Res. Workers, 1967–68 (Pres. S Reg., 1967–68); Section of Comparative Medicine, RSocMed, 1967–68 (Sec., 1965–67; Sec. for Internat. Affairs, 1971–78, 1983–92); Lab. Animal Science Assoc., 1984–86 (Vice-Pres., 1983–84); Vice-Pres., Inst. of Animal Technicians, 1983–; Member Council: BVA, 1944–67; RSocMed, 1968–70 (Hon. Fellow, 1982); Res. Defence Soc., 1968–82 (Hon. Sec., 1978–82; Vice-Pres., 1982–); Member: Medicines Commn, 1978–82; Vet. Res. Club, 1967–; British Small Animal Vet. Assoc.; British Codex Sub-Cttee, Pharmaceutical Soc., 1970–71. FRVC 1979; Hon. FIBiol, 1983; Hon. DSc Guelph, 1976. Victory Gold Medal, Central Vet. Soc., 1965. *Publications:* contribs to: The Veterinary Annual; International Encyclopaedia of Veterinary Medicine, 1966; also papers in many learned jls. *Recreations:* work, travel, literature, flowers. *Address:* 30 Elm Park Court, Elm Park Road, Pinner, Middx HA5 3LJ. *Club:* Royal Society of Medicine.

UXBRIDGE, Earl of; Charles Alexander Vaughan Paget; *b* 13 Nov 1950; *s* and *heir* of 7th Marquess of Anglesey, *qv*; *m* 1986, Georganne Elizabeth Elliott, *d* of Col John Alfred Downes, MBE, MC; one *s* one *d*. *Educ:* Dragon School, Oxford; Eton; Exeter Coll., Oxford. *Heir:* *s* Lord Paget de Beaudesert, *qv*. *Address:* Plâs-Newydd, Llanfairpwll, Gwynedd LL61 6DZ.

UZIELL-HAMILTON, Adrianne Pauline; Her Honour Judge Uziell-Hamilton; a Circuit Judge, since 1990; *b* 14 May 1932; *e d* of late Dr Marcus and Ella Grantham; *m* 1952, Mario Reginald Uziell-Hamilton (*d* 1988); one *s* one *d*. *Educ:* Maria Gray's Academy for Girls and privately. Called to the Bar, Middle Temple, 1965; *ad eundem* Mem., Inner Temple, 1976–; Head of Chambers, 1976–90; a Recorder, 1985–90. Vice-Chm., Ethics Cttee, Nat. Hosp., 1993– (Mem., 1991–); Member: Legal Aid Panel, 1969–; Parole Bd, 1994–; General Council of the Bar, 1970–74 (Exec. Cttee, 1973–74). Pres., Mental Health Review Tribunals, 1988. Gov., North London Univ. (formerly Polytechnic of N London), 1986–. FRSA. *Publications:* articles on marriage contracts. *Recreations:* collecting ballet and theatre costume design, cooking for friends, conversation.

V

VACHON, His Eminence Cardinal Louis-Albert, CC (Canada) 1969; OQ 1985; FRSC 1974; Officier de l'Ordre de la fidélité française, 1963; Archbishop (RC) of Quebec and Primate of Canada, 1981–90; *b* 4 Feb. 1912; *s* of Napoléon Vachon and Alexandrine Gilbert. *Educ:* Laval Univ. (PhD Philosophy, 1947); PhD Theology, Angelicum, Rome, 1949. Ordained priest, 1938; Prof. of Philosophy, 1941–47, Prof. of Theology, 1949–55, Laval Univ. Superior, Grand Séminaire de Québec, 1955–59; Superior General, 1960–77; Auxiliary Bishop of Quebec, 1977–81; Cardinal, 1985. Vice-Rector of Laval Univ., 1959–60, Rector, 1960–72. Mem., Royal Canadian Soc. of Arts. Hon. FRCP&S (Canada), 1972. Hon. doctorates: Montreal, McGill and Victoria, 1964; Guelph, 1966; Moncton, 1967; Queen's, Bishop's and Strasbourg, 1968; Notre-Dame (Indiana), 1971; Carleton, 1972; Laval, 1982. Centennial Medal, 1967. KHS 1985; KM 1987. *Publications:* Espérance et Présomption, 1958; Vérité et Liberté, 1962; Unité de l'Université, 1962; Apostolat de l'universitaire catholique, 1963; Mémorial, 1963; Communauté universitaire, 1963; Progrès de l'université et consentement populaire, 1964; Responsabilité collective des universitaires, 1964; Les humanités aujourd'hui, 1966; Excellence et loyauté des universitaires, 1969; Pastoral Letters, 1981. *Recreations:* reading, beaux arts. *Address:* 1 rue des Remparts, Quebec G1R 5L7, Canada.

VAEA, Baron of Houma; Prime Minister of Tonga, since 1991; Minister: of Agriculture and Forestry, of Fisheries, for Marine and Ports, responsible for Telecommunications, since 1991; Chairman, National Reserve Bank Board, since 1989; *b* 15 May 1921; *s* of Viliami Vilai Tupou and Tupou Seini Vaea; *m* 1952, Tuputupu Ma'afu; three *s* three *d*. *Educ:* Wesley College, Auckland, NZ. RNZAF, 1942–45; Tonga Civil Service, 1945–53; ADC to HM Queen Salote, 1954–59; Governor of Ha'apai, 1959–68; Commissioner and Consul in UK, 1969; High Comr in UK, 1970–72; Minister for Labour, Commerce and Industries, 1973–91; Actg Dep. Prime Minister, 1986. Chairman: Tonga Telecommunications Commn, 1991–; Tonga Broadcasting Commn, 1991–; Port Admin Cttee, 1991–; Shipping Corp. of Polynesia. Chm., Tonga Investment Ltd, 1991–. Given the title Baron Vaea of Houma by HM The King of Tonga, 1970. *Recreations:* fishing, tennis. *Heir: e s* Albert Tu'ivanuavou Vaea, *b* 19 Sept. 1957. *Address:* PO Box 262, Nuku'alofa, Tonga. *T:* (office) 24644, *Fax:* 23888, *Telex:* 676 66269.

VAES, Baron Robert, Hon. KCMG 1966; LLD; Grand Officer, Order of Leopold, Belgium; Director of Sotheby's, since 1984; *b* Antwerp, 9 Jan. 1919; created Baron, 1985; *m* 1947, Anne Albers; one *d*. *Educ:* Brussels Univ. (LLD; special degree in Commercial and Maritime Law). Joined Diplomatic Service, 1946: postings to Washington, Paris, Hong Kong, London, Rome and Madrid; Personal Private Sec. to Minister of Foreign Trade, 1958–60; Dir-Gen. of Polit. Affairs, 1964–66; Permanent Under-Sec., Min. of For. Affairs, For. Trade and Develt Cooperation, 1966–72; Ambassador: to Spain, 1972–76; to UK, 1976–84. Numerous foreign decorations including: Grand Officer, Legion of Honour (France); Grand Cross, Order of Isabela la Católica (Spain). *Recreation:* bridge. *Address:* 45 Gloucester Square, W2 2TQ. *Clubs:* White's, Pratt's, Royal Anglo-Belgian; Royal Yacht of Belgium.

VAISEY, David George, FSA; FRHistS; Bodley's Librarian, Oxford, since 1986; Professorial Fellow, Exeter College, Oxford, since 1975; *b* 15 March 1935; *s* of William Thomas Vaisey and Minnie Vaisey (*née* Payne); *m* 1965, Maureen Anne (*née* Mansell); two *d*. *Educ:* Rendcomb Coll., Glos (schol.); Exeter Coll., Oxford (Exhibnr; BA Mod. Hist., MA). 2nd Lieut, Glos Regt and KAR, 1955–56. Archivist, Staffordshire CC, 1960–63; Asst then Sen. Asst Librarian, Bodleian Liby, 1963–75; Dep. Keeper, Oxford Univ. Archives, 1966–75; Keeper of Western Manuscripts, Bodleian Liby, 1975–86. Vis. Prof., Liby Studies, UCLA, 1985. Hon. Res. Fellow, Dept of Library, Archive and Information Studies, UCL, 1987–. Member: Royal Commn on Historical Manuscripts, 1986–; Adv. Council on Public Records, 1989–94; Chm., Nat. Council on Archives, 1988–91. FRHistS 1973; FSA 1974. Encomienda, Order of Isabel the Catholic (Spain), 1989. *Publications:* Staffordshire and The Great Rebellion (jtly), 1964; Probate Inventories of Lichfield and District 1568–1680, 1969; (jtly) Victorian and Edwardian Oxford from old photographs, 1971; (jtly) Oxford Shops and Shopping, 1972; (jtly) Art for Commerce, 1973; Oxfordshire: a handbook for students of local history, 1973, 2nd edn 1974; The Diary of Thomas Turner 1754–65, 1984; articles in learned jls and collections. *Address:* Bodleian Library, Oxford OX1 3BG. *T:* Oxford (01865) 277000.

VAIZEY, Lady; Marina Vaizey; writer and art critic; Editor, National Art Collections Fund Publications, 1991–94 (Editorial Consultant, 1994–95); *b* 16 Jan. 1938; *o d* of late Lyman Stansky and Ruth Stansky; *m* 1961, Lord Vaizey (*d* 1984); two *s* one *d*. *Educ:* Brearley Sch., New York; Putney Sch., Putney, Vermont; Radcliffe Coll., Harvard Univ. (BA Medieval History and Lit.); Girton Coll., Cambridge (BA, MA). Art Critic: Financial Times, 1970–74; Sunday Times, 1974–91; Dance Critic, Now!, 1979–81. Member: Arts Council, 1976–78 (Mem. Art Panel, 1973–78, Dep. Chm., 1976–78); Advisory Cttee, DoE, 1975–81; Paintings for Hospitals, 1974–; Cttee, Contemporary Art Soc., 1975–79, 1980–94 (Hon. Sec., 1988–94); Hist. of Art and Complementary Studies Bd, CNAA, 1978–82; Photography Bd, CNAA, 1979–81; Fine Art Bd, CNAA, 1980–83; Passenger Services Sub-Cttee, Heathrow Airport, 1979–83; Visual Arts Adv. Cttee, British Council, 1987–; Crafts Council, 1988–94; Art Wkg Gp, National Curriculum, DES, 1990–91; Gov., South Bank Bd, 1993–; Trustee: Nat. Museums and Galleries on Merseyside, 1986– (Pres., Friends of NMGM, 1994–); Geffrye Museum, London, 1990–; Imperial War Museum, 1991–; Exec. Dir, Mitchell Prize for the Hist. of Art, 1976–87; Vice-Pres., King's Lynn Fest., 1994–. Governor: Camberwell Coll. of Arts and Crafts, 1971–82; Bath Acad. of Art, Corsham, 1978–81. Curated: Critic's Choice, Tooth's, 1974; Painter as Photographer, touring exhibn, UK, 1982–85; Shining Through, Crafts Council, 1995. *Publications:* 100 Masterpieces of Art, 1979; Andrew Wyeth, 1980; The Artist as Photographer, 1982; Peter Blake, 1985; Christiane Kubrick, 1990; Christo, 1990; Sorensen, 1994. *Address:* 24 Heathfield Terrace, Chiswick, W4 4JE. *T:* 0181–994 7994, *Fax:* 0181–995 8057.

VAJPAYEE, Atal Bihari; Member, Lok Sabha, 1957–62, 1967–84 and since 1991; Leader, Bharatiya Janata Party Parliamentary Party, 1980–84 and 1986–91; *b* Gwalior, Madhya Pradesh, 25 Dec. 1926; *s* of Shri Krishna Bihari; unmarried. *Educ:* Victoria Coll., Gwalior; D.A.V. Coll., Kanpur (MA). Journalist and social worker. Arrested in freedom movement, 1942; Founder Mem., Jana Sangh, 1951–77; Leader, Jana Sangh Parly Party, 1957–77; Pres., Bharatiaya Jana Sangh, 1968–73; detained 26 June 1975, during Emergency; Founder Member: Janata Party, 1977–80; Bharatiya Janata Party, 1980– (Pres., 1980–86). Mem., Rajya Sabha, 1962–67 and 1986–91; Minister of External Affairs, 1977–79; Chairman: Cttee on Govt Assurances, 1966–67; Public Accounts Cttee, 1969–70, 1991–92; CTEE on Petitions, 1990–91. Member: Parly Goodwill Mission to E Africa, 1965; Parly Delegns to Australia, 1967, Eur. Parlt, 1983; Member: Indian Delegation: to CPA meetings in Canada, 1966, Zambia, 1980, IOM, 1984; to IPU Confs in Japan, 1974, Sri Lanka, 1975, Switzerland, 1984; to UN Gen. Assembly, 1988, 1989, 1990, 1991. Mem., Nat. Integration Council, 1958–62, 1967–73, 1986, 1991–. President: All India Station Masters and Asst Station Masters Assoc., 1965–70; Pandit Deen Dayal Upadhyay Smarak Samiti, 1968–84; Pandit Deen Dayal Upadhyaya Janma Bhumi Smarak Samiti, 1979–. Formerly Editor: Rashtra-dharma; Panchajanya; Veer Arjun. *Publications:* Lok Sabha Men Atalji (collection of speeches); Qaidi Kavirai ki Kundaliyan; New Dimensions of India's Foreign Policy; Sansad Men Teen Dashak (collection of speeches). *Address:* Shinde ki Chhawni, Gwalior, MP, India; 6 Raisina Road, New Delhi 110001, India. *T:* 385166.

VALDAR, Colin Gordon; Consultant Editor; *b* 18 Dec. 1918; 3rd *s* of Lionel and Mary Valdar; *m* 1st, 1940, Evelyn Margaret Barriff (marr. diss.); two *s*; 2nd, Jill, (*née* Davis). *Educ:* Haberdashers' Aske's Hampstead School. Free-lance journalist, 1936–39. Served War of 1939–45, Royal Engineers, 1939–42. Successively Production Editor, Features Editor, Asst Editor, Sunday Pictorial, 1942–46; Features Editor, Daily Express, 1946–51; Asst Editor, Daily Express, 1951–53; Editor, Sunday Pictorial, 1953–59; Editor, Daily Sketch, 1959–62. Director, Sunday Pictorial Newspapers Ltd, 1957–59; Director, Daily Sketch and Daily Graphic Ltd, 1959–62; Chm., Bouverie Publishing Co., 1964–83. Founded UK Press Gazette, 1965. *Address:* 2A Ratcliffe Wharf, 18–22 Narrow Street, E14 8DQ. *T:* 0171–791 2155.

VALDIVIESO-BELAUNDE, Felipe; Grand Cross, Order Al Merito por Servicios Distinguidos (Peru), 1980; Peruvian Ambassador to the Court of St James's, 1989–92; *b* 21 Nov. 1928; *s* of Francisco Valdivieso and Rosario Belaunde de Valdivieso; *m* 1973, Samija de Valdivieso-Belaunde. *Educ:* Pontificia Universidad Católica, Peru. Joined Foreign Ministry, 1947; served: Holy See, 1952–54; Argentina, 1954–56; Brasil, 1956; USA, Washington, 1957–59; OAS, Washington, 1960–61; Costa Rica, 1961–62; Head, Foreign Minister's Cabinet, 1962–63; Counsellor, France, 1963–67; Foreign Ministry: Chief, UN Dept, 1967–69; Minister, Dir of Inf. and Planning, 1969; Ambassador: Morocco, 1970–71; Egypt, 1971–75; Dir Gen., Protocol, Foreign Ministry, 1975; Ambassador, Argentina, 1975–79; Perm. Rep., UN Internat. Orgs, Geneva, 1979–82; Ambassador, Ecuador, 1982–87; Under Sec. for Bilateral Affairs, Foreign Ministry, 1987–88, Sec. Gen. and Vice-Minister of Foreign Affairs, 1988–89. Holds numerous foreign decorations. *Recreation:* tennis. *Address:* Parque Miguel Dammert Muelle, 125 San Isidro, Lima 27, Peru. *Clubs:* Nacional (Lima); Lima Golf.

VALE, Brian, CBE 1994 (OBE 1977); Regional Director for Middle East and North Africa, British Council, 1995; retired; *b* 26 May 1938; *s* of Leslie Vale and May (*née* Knowles); *m* 1966, Margaret Mary Cookson; two *s*. *Educ:* Sir Joseph Williamson's Mathematical Sch., Rochester; Keele Univ. (BA, DipEd); King's Coll., London (MPhil). HMOCS, N Rhodesia, 1960–63; Assistant to Comr for N Rhodesia, London, 1963–64; Educn Attaché, Zambia High Commn, London, 1964–65; British Council: Rio de Janeiro, 1965–68; Appts Div., 1968–72; Educn and Sci. Div., 1972–75; Rep., Saudi Arabia, 1975–78; Dep. Controller, Educn and Sci. Div., 1978–80; Dir Tech. Educn and Trng Orgn for Overseas Countries, 1980–81; Controller, Sci., Technol. and Educn Div., 1981–83; Rep. in Egypt, and Cultural Counsellor, British Embassy, Cairo, 1983–87; Asst Dir Gen., 1987–90; Dir, Spain, and Cultural Attaché, British Embassy, Madrid, 1991–95. FRSA. *Publications:* contribs to specialist jls on educnl subjects and naval hist. *Recreations:* reading, talking, naval history. *Address:* 40 Gloucester Circus, SE10 8RY. *T:* 0171–858 6233.

VALENTIA, 15th Viscount *cr* 1622 (Ireland); **Richard John Dighton Annesley;** Bt 1620; Baron Mountnorris 1628; farmer in Zimbabwe, since 1957; *b* 15 Aug. 1929; *s* of 14th Viscount Valentia, MC, MRCS, LRCP, and Joan Elizabeth (*d* 1986), *d* of late John Joseph Curtis; *S* father, 1983; *m* 1957, Anita Phyllis, *o d* of William Arthur Joy, Bristol; two *s* one *d* (and one *s* decd). *Educ:* Marlborough; RMA Sandhurst. BA Univ. of S Africa. Commnd RA, 1950; retd, rank of Captain, 1957. Schoolmaster, Ruzawi Prep. Sch., Marondera, Zimbabwe, 1977–83. *Recreations:* sport, shooting, fishing, leisure riding. *Heir: s* Hon. Francis William Dighton Annesley [*b* 29 Dec. 1959; *m* 1982, Shaneen Hobbs; two *d*]. *Address:* East Range Farm, PO Chinhoyi, Zimbabwe.

VALENTINE, Rt Rev. Barry, MA, BD, LTh, DD; Rector, Parish of Salt Spring Island, British Columbia, 1989–95; *b* 26 Sept. 1927; *s* of Harry John Valentine and Ethel Margaret Purkiss; *m* 1st, 1952, Mary Currell Hayes; three *s* one *d*; 2nd, 1984, Shirley Carolyn Shean Evans. *Educ:* Brentwood Sch.; St John's Coll., Cambridge; McGill Univ., Montreal. Curate, Christ Church Cath., Montreal, 1952; Incumbent, Chateauguay-Beauharnois, 1954; Dir, Religious Educn, Dio. Montreal, 1957; Rector of St Lambert, PQ, 1961; Exec. Officer, Dio. Montreal, 1965; Dean of Montreal, 1968; Bishop Coadjutor of Rupert's Land, 1969; Bishop of Rupert's Land, 1970–82; Chaplain, Univ. of British Columbia,

1984–85; Asst Bishop of Maryland, 1986–89. Chancellor, 1970, Res. Fellow, 1983, St John's Coll., Winnipeg. Hon. DD: St John's Coll., Winnipeg, 1969; Montreal Dio. Theol Coll., 1970. *Publication:* The Gift that is in you, 1984. *Recreations:* music, theatre, walking, reading. *Address:* 111 Carlin Avenue, Salt Spring Island, BC V8K 2J5, Canada.

VALENTINE, Caroline, (Mrs Malcolm Valentine); *see* Charles, Caroline.

VALIANT, Prof. Leslie Gabriel, FRS 1991; Gordon McKay Professor of Computer Science and Applied Mathematics, Harvard University, since 1982; *b* 28 March 1949; *s* of Leslie Valiant and Eva Julia (*née* Ujlaki); *m* 1977, Gayle Lynne Dyckoff; two *s*. *Educ:* Tynemouth High Sch.; Latymer Upper Sch.; King's Coll., Cambridge (MA); Imperial Coll., London (DIC); Warwick Univ. (PhD). Vis. Asst Prof., Carnegie Mellon Univ., Pittsburgh, 1973–74; Lecturer: Leeds Univ., 1974–76; Edinburgh Univ., 1977–81, Reader 1981–82. Vis. Prof., Harvard Univ., 1982; Vis. Fellow, Oxford Univ. Computing Lab. and Merton Coll., Oxford, 1987–88; Guggenheim Fellow, 1985–86. Fellow, Amer. Assoc. for Artificial Intelligence. Nevanlinna Prize, IMU, 1986. *Publications:* Circuits of the Mind, 1994; research papers in scientific jls. *Address:* Division of Applied Sciences, Harvard University, 33 Oxford Street, Cambridge, MA 02138, USA. *T:* (617) 4955817.

VALIN, Reginald Pierre; business consultant; *b* 8 March 1938; *s* of Pierre Louis Valin and Molly Doreen Valin; *m* 1960, Brigitte Karin Leister; one *d*. *Educ:* Emanuel School. Bank of America, 1959–60; Charles Barker & Sons Ltd, later Charles Barker City, 1960–79: Associate Dir, 1970–71; Dir, 1971–73; Man. Dir, 1973–76; Chief Exec., 1976–79; Founder Dir, Valin Pollen, 1979; Chm. and Chief Exec., 1984–89, Dep. Chm., 1989–90, Valin Pollen Internat., subseq. The VPI Gp. Dir, Lifeline, 1995–. Advr, Nat. Foundn for Teaching Entrepreneurship, 1994–; Trustee, MacIntyre Charitable Trust, 1994–. *Address:* 38 Monckton Court, Melbury Road, W14 8NF. *T:* 0171–371 1872.

VALIOS, Nicholas Paul; QC 1991; a Recorder of the Crown Court, since 1986; *b* 5 May 1943; *s* of Nicholas William and Elizabeth Joan Valios; *m* 1967, Cynthia Valerie Horton; one *s* one *d*. *Educ:* Stonyhurst Coll., Lancs. Called to the Bar, Inner Temple, 1964; Mem., SE Circuit. *Recreations:* windsurfing, golf, reading, computers. *Address:* Francis Taylor Building, Temple, EC4Y 7BY. *T:* 0171–353 7768.

VALLANCE, Dr Elizabeth Mary, (Lady Vallance); JP; Chairman, St George's Healthcare NHS Trust, since 1993; *b* 8 April 1945; *e d* of William Henderson McGonnigill and Hon. Jean, *d* of 1st Baron Kirkwood; *m* 1967, Sir Iain David Thomas Vallance, *qv*;; one *s* one *d*. *Educ:* Laurel Bank Sch., Glasgow; Univ. of St Andrews (MA); LSE (MSc); Univ. of London (PhD); London Business Sch. (Sloan Fellow). Queen Mary College, later Queen Mary and Westfield College, University of London: Asst Lectr, Lectr, Sen. Lectr, Reader in Govt and Politics, 1968–85; Head, Dept of Politics, 1985–88; Vis. Prof., 1990–. Director: HMV Group, 1990–; Norwich Union, 1995–. Chm. of Govs, James Allen's Girls' Sch., 1991–94. JP Inner London, 1993. *Publications:* (ed) The State, Society and Self-destruction, 1975; Women in the House, 1979; (with Davies) Women in Europe, 1982; (with Radice and Willis) MP: the job of a backbencher, 1988; (with Mahoney) Business Ethics in a New Europe, 1992; Business Ethics at Work, 1995; contribs to other books, academic acticles, journalism. *Recreations:* writing, reading novels, ski-ing, opera. *Address:* St George's Healthcare NHS Trust, Blackshaw Road, SW17 0QT. *T:* 0181–725 3323.

VALLANCE, Sir Iain (David Thomas), Kt 1994; Chairman, British Telecommunications plc, since 1987 (a Corporate Director, since 1981); Vice-Chairman, Royal Bank of Scotland, since 1994; *b* 20 May 1943; *s* of Edmund Thomas Vallance and Janet Wright Bell Ross Davidson; *m* 1967, Elizabeth Mary McGonnigill (*see* E. M. Vallance); one *s* one *d*. *Educ:* Edinburgh Acad.; Dulwich Coll.; Glasgow Acad.; Brasenose Coll., Oxford; London Graduate School of Business Studies (MSc). Joined Post Office, 1966; Director: Central Finance, 1976–78; Telecommunications Finance, 1978–79; Materials Dept, 1979–81; British Telecommunications: Board Mem. for Orgn and Business Systems, 1981–83; Man. Dir, Local Communications Services Div., 1983–85; Chief of Operations, 1985–86; Chief Exec., 1986–87. Dir, Royal Bank of Scotland, 1993–. Member, President's Committee: CBI, 1988–; (also Adv. Council), BITC, 1988–; Eur. Foundn for Quality Management, 1988–. Member: Listed Cos Adv. Cttee, London Stock Exchange, 1993–; Eur. Adv. Cttee, New York Stock Exchange, 1995–; Internat. Adv. Bd, British-American Chamber of Commerce, 1991–. Chm., Princess Royal Trust for Carers, 1991. Trustee: Police Foundn, 1989–; Monteverdi Trust. Hon. Gov., Glasgow Acad., 1993–. Fellow, London Business School, 1989. Hon. DSc: Ulster, 1992; Napier, 1994; Hon. DTech: Loughborough, 1992; Robert Gordon, 1994; Hon. DBA Kingston, 1993; Hon. DEng Heriot-Watt, 1995. Liveryman, Wheelwright's Co.; Freeman, City of London. *Recreations:* hill walking, music. *Address:* c/o 81 Newgate Street, EC1A 7AJ.

VALLANCE, Michael Wilson; Headmaster of Bloxham School 1982–91; *b* 9 Sept. 1933; *er s* of late Vivian Victor Wilson Vallance and Kate Vallance, Wandsworth and Helston; *m* 1970, Mary Winifred Ann, *d* of John Steele Garnett; one *s* two *d*. *Educ:* Brighton Coll.; St John's Coll., Cambridge (MA). On staff of United Steel Companies Ltd, 1952–53; awarded United Steel Companies Scholarship (held at Cambridge), 1953; Asst Master, Abingdon School, 1957–61; Asst Master, Harrow School, 1961–72; Headmaster, Durham Sch., 1972–82. Chairman: Cttee of Northern Isis, 1976–77; NE Div., HMC, 1981–82. World Challenge Expeditions Ltd: Consultant, 1991–; Dir, 1992–; Chm. Bd, 1995–. Chm., Council for the Registration of Schools Teaching Dyslexic Pupils, (formerly Nat. Registration Council), 1992–. Trustee, Bloxham Project, 1987–91. *Recreations:* reading, cricket, gardens (sitting in), the sea. *Address:* 22 Foxholes Hill, Exmouth, Devon EX8 2DQ. *T:* Exmouth (01395) 271633. *Clubs:* MCC, Jesters.

VALLANCE, Philip Ian Fergus; QC 1989; *b* 20 Dec. 1943; *o s* of Aylmer Vallance and Helen Gosse; *m* 1973, Wendy, *d* of J. D. Alston; one *s* one *d*. *Educ:* Bryanston; New Coll., Oxford (BA Mod. Hist). Called to the Bar, Inner Temple, 1968. *Recreations:* cooking, drystone walling. *Address:* (chambers) 1 Crown Office Row, Temple, EC4Y 7HH. *T:* 0171–797 7500. *Club:* Travellers'.

VALLANCE-OWEN, Prof. John, MA, MD, FRCP, FRCPI, FRCPath; Visiting Professor, Royal Postgraduate Medical School, Hammersmith Hospital; Consultant Physician, London Independent Hospital, since 1988; *b* 31 Oct. 1920; *s* of late Prof. E. A. Owen; *m* 1950, Renee Thornton; two *s* two *d*. *Educ:* Friar's Sch., Bangor; Epsom Coll.; St John's Coll., Cambridge (de Havilland Schol. from Epsom); London Hosp. (Schol.). BA 1943; MA, MB, BChir Cantab, 1946; MD Cantab 1951; FRCP 1962; Hon. FRCPI 1970; FRCPath 1971; FRCPI 1973. Various appts incl. Pathology Asst and Med. 1st Asst, London Hosp., 1946–51; Med. Tutor, Royal Postgrad. Med. Sch., Hammersmith Hosp., 1952–55 and 1956–58; Rockefeller Trav. Fellowship, at George S. Cox Med. Research Inst., Univ. of Pennsylvania, 1955–56; Cons. Phys. and Lectr in Medicine, Univ. of Durham, 1958–64; Cons. Phys., Royal Victoria Infirmary and Reader in Medicine, Univ. of Newcastle upon Tyne, 1964–66; Prof. of Medicine, QUB, 1966–82; Consultant Physician: Royal Victoria Hosp., Belfast, 1966–82 (Chm., Med. Div., 1979–81); Belfast City Hosp., 1966–82; Forster Green Hosp., Belfast, 1975–82 (Chm., Med. Staff Cttee, 1979–82); Dir of Med. Services, Maltese Is, 1981–82; Chinese University of Hong Kong: Foundation Prof. and Chm., Dept of Medicine, 1983–88; Associate Dean, Faculty of Medicine, 1984–88. Hon. Consultant in Medicine: to Hong Kong Govt, 1984–88; to the British Army in Hong Kong, 1985–88. Med. Advr on Clinical Complaints, NE Thames RHA, 1989–, S Thames RHA, 1995–. Member: Standing Med. Adv. Cttee, Min. of Health and Social Services, NI, 1970–73; Specialist Adv. Cttee (General Internal Medicine) to the Govt; Northern Health and Social Services Bd, Dept of Health and Soc. Services, NI; Mem., Exec. Cttee, Assoc. of Physicians of GB and Ireland, 1976–79; Regional Adviser for N Ire, to RCP, 1970–75 and Councillor, RCP, 1976–79 (Oliver-Sharpey Prize, RCP, 1976); Councillor, RCPI, 1978–82; Mem. Research Cttee, Brit. Diabetic Assoc.; Brit. Council Lectr, Dept Medicine, Zürich Univ., 1963; 1st Helen Martin Lectr, Diabetic Assoc. of S Calif, Wm H. Mulberg Lectr, Cincinnati Diabetes Assoc., and Lectr, Brookhaven Nat. Labs, NY, 1965; Brit. Council Lectr, Haile Selassie Univ., Makerere UC and S African Univs, 1966; Guest Lecturer: Japan Endocrinological Soc., 1968; Madrid Univ., 1969; Endocrine Soc. of Australia, 1970; Bologna Univ., 1976. *Publications:* Essentials of Cardiology, 1961 (2nd edn 1968); Diabetes: its physiological and biochemical basis, 1976; papers in biochem., med., and scientific jls on carbohydrate and fat metabolism and aetiology of diabetes mellitus and related conditions, with special reference to insulin antagonism. *Recreations:* tennis, golf, music. *Address:* 10 Spinney Drive, Great Shelford, Cambridge CB2 5LY. *T:* Cambridge (01223) 842767; 17 St Matthews Lodge, Oakley Square, NW1 1NB. *T:* 0171–388 3644. *Clubs:* East India, Royal Society of Medicine; Gog Magog Golf (Cambridge); United Services Recreation (Hong Kong).

VALLANCE WHITE, James Ashton; Principal Clerk, Judicial Office and Fourth Clerk at the Table, House of Lords, since 1983; *b* 25 Feb. 1938; *s* of Frank Ashton White and Dieudonnée Vallance; *m* 1987, Anne O'Donnell. *Educ:* Allhallows School; Albert Schweitzer College, Switzerland; St Peter's College, Oxford (MA). Clerk, House of Lords, 1961; Clerk of Committees, 1971–78; Chief Clerk, Public Bill Office, 1978–83. *Address:* 14 Gerald Road, SW1W 9EQ. *T:* 0171–730 7658; Biniparrell, San Luis, Menorca. *T:* (71) 151476. *Club:* Brooks's.

VALLAT, Prof. Sir Francis Aimé, GBE 1982; KCMG 1962 (CMG 1955); QC 1961; Barrister-at-Law; Emeritus Professor of International Law, University of London; *b* 25 May 1912; *s* of Col Frederick W. Vallat, OBE; *m* 1st, 1939, Mary Alison Cockell (marr. diss. 1973); one *s* one *d*; 2nd, 1988, Patricia Maria Morton Anderson (*d* 1995). *Educ:* University College, Toronto (BA Hons); Gonville and Caius Coll., Cambridge (LLB). Called to Bar, Gray's Inn, 1935, Bencher, 1971; Assistant Lecturer, Bristol Univ., 1935–36; practice at Bar, London, 1936–39; RAFVR (Flt Lieut), 1941–45; Asst Legal Adviser, Foreign Office, 1945–50; Legal Adviser, UK Permanent Deleg. to UN, 1950–54; Deputy Legal Adviser, FO, 1954–60, Legal Adviser, 1960–68. (On leave of absence) Actg Director, Inst. of Air and Space Law, and Vis. Prof. of Law, McGill Univ., 1965–66. Dir of International Law Studies, King's Coll. London, 1968–76 (Reader, 1969–70, Prof., 1970–76). Dir of Studies, Internat. Law Assoc., 1969–73. UK Mem., UN Fact Finding Panel, 1969–. Associate Mem., Institut de Droit International, 1965, elected Mem. 1977; Member: Internat. Law Commn, 1973–81 (Chm. 1977–78); Permanent Court of Arbitration, 1980–92; Curatorium, Hague Acad., 1982– (Vice-Pres., 1993–). Jt Vice-Pres., David Davies Meml Inst. of Internat. Relations Studies, 1982–. Expert Consultant, UN Conf. on Succession of States in respect of Treaties, 1977–78. Dr en dr. *hc*, Lausanne Univ., 1979. *Publications:* International Law and the Practitioner, 1966; Introduction to the Study of Human Rights, 1972; articles in British Year Book of International Law and other journals. *Recreations:* restoration of antiques, gardening. *Address:* 40 Paultons Square, SW3 5DT. *T:* 0171–352 7646. *Club:* Hurlingham.

VALLINGS, Vice-Adm. Sir George (Montague Francis), KCB 1986; Secretary, Chartered Institute of Management Accountants, 1987–95; *b* 31 May 1932; *s* of Robert Archibald Vallings and Alice Mary Joan Vallings (*née* Bramsden); *m* 1964, Tessa Julia Cousins; three *s*. *Educ:* Belhaven Hill, Dunbar; Royal Naval College, Dartmouth. Midshipman, HMS Theseus, 1950–51; HMS Scarborough, 1961–65; HMS Defender, 1967–68; HMS Bristol, 1970–73; Naval Adviser and RNLO Australia, 1974–76; Captain F2, HMS Apollo, 1977–78; Dir, Naval Ops and Trade, 1978–80; Commodore, Clyde, 1980–82; Flag Officer: Gibraltar, 1983–85; Scotland and NI, 1985–87. Chm., STA Race Cttee, 1988–. *Recreations:* family and sport. *Address:* c/o Midland Bank, Charing Cross Branch, 455 Strand, WC2R 0RH. *Clubs:* Royal Ocean Racing; Woking Golf.

VALLIS, Rear-Adm. Michael Anthony, CB 1986; FEng 1987; consultant engineer; *b* 30 June 1929; *s* of R. W. H. Vallis and S. J. Dewsnup; *m* 1959, Pauline Dorothy Abbott, Wymondham, Leics; three *s* one *d*. *Educ:* RN College, Dartmouth; RN Engineering College, Plymouth; RN College, Greenwich. MIMechE, FIMarE. RN Service, 1943–86. Mem., Engrg Council, 1993–. *Recreations:* fishing, gardening, walking, food and wine, theatre. *Address:* Holly Lodge, 54 Bloomfield Park, Bath, Avon BA2 2BX. *Club:* Royal Over-Seas League.

VALOIS, Dame Ninette de; *see* de Valois.

VAN ALLAN, Richard; principal bass; Director, National Opera Studio, since 1986; *b* 28 May 1935; *s* of Joseph Arthur and Irene Hannah Van Allan; *m* 1976, Elisabeth Rosemary (marr. diss. 1986); two *s* one *d*. *Educ:* Worcester College of Education (DipEd Science); Birmingham School of Music. Glyndebourne, 1964; Welsh National Opera, 1968; English National Opera, 1969 (Mem. Bd of Dirs, 1995–); Royal Opera House, Covent Garden, 1971; performances also: l'Opéra de Paris, Bordeaux, Nice, Toulouse, Rome, Brussels; USA: Boston, San Diego, Phoenix, Houston, Austin, San Antonio, New Orleans, NY; Argentina: Buenos Aires; Spain: Madrid and Barcelona; Hong Kong; Victoria State Opera, Melbourne. Recordings incl. Don Giovanni, Così fan tutte (Grammy Award), Luisa Miller, L'Oracolo, Britten's Gloriana. Hon. RAM 1987. FBSM 1991. *Recreations:* shooting, tennis, golf. *Address:* 18 Octavia Street, SW11 3DN.

VAN ALLEN, Prof. James Alfred; Professor of Physics and Head of Department of Physics (of Physics and Astronomy, 1959–85), 1951–85, Carver Professor of Physics, 1972–85, now Regent Distinguished Professor, University of Iowa, USA; *b* Iowa, 7 Sept. 1914; *s* of Alfred Morris and Alma Olney Van Allen; *m* 1945, Abigail Fithian Halsey II; two *s* three *d*. *Educ:* Public High School, and Iowa Wesleyan Coll., Mount Pleasant, Iowa (BSc); University of Iowa, Iowa City (MSc, PhD). Research Fellow, then Physicist, Carnegie Instn of Washington, 1939–42; Physicist, Applied Physics Lab., Johns Hopkins Univ., Md, 1942. Ordnance and Gunnery Officer and Combat Observer, USN, 1942–46, Lt-Comdr 1946. Supervisor of High-Altitude Research Group and of Proximity Fuze Unit, Johns Hopkins Univ., 1946–50. Leader, various scientific expeditions to Central and S Pacific, Arctic and Antarctic, for study of cosmic rays and earth's magnetic field, using Aerobee and balloon-launched rockets, 1949–57. Took part in promotion and planning of International Geophysical Year, 1957–58; developed radiation measuring equipment on first American satellite, Explorer I, and subseq. satellites (discoverer of Van Allen Radiation Belts of the earth, 1958); has continued study of earth's radiation belts, aurorae, cosmic rays, energetic particles in interplanetary space, planetary magnetospheres. Research Fellow, Guggenheim Memorial Foundation, 1951; Research Associate (controlled thermonuclear reactions), Princeton Univ., Project Matterhorn, 1953–54;

Regents' Fellow, Smithsonian Inst., 1981. Acting Ed., Jl of Geophysical Research—Space Physics, 1991–92. Mem., Space Science Bd of Nat. Acad. of Sciences, 1958–70, 1980–83; Fellow: American Phys. Society; Amer. Geophysical Union (Pres., 1982–84), etc; Member: Nat. Acad. of Sciences; RAS; Royal Swedish Acad. of Sciences; Founder Member, International Acad. of Astronautics, etc. Holds many awards and hon. doctorates; Gold Medal, RAS, 1978; US Nat. Medal of Sci., 1987; Crafoord Prize, Royal Swedish Acad. of Scis, 1989; Nansen Award and Prize, Norwegian Acad. of Sci. and Letters, 1990. *Publications:* (ed and contrib.) Scientific Uses of Earth Satellites, 1956, 2nd edn 1958; (jtly) Pioneer: first to Jupiter, Saturn and beyond, 1980; Origins of Magnetospheric Physics, 1983; (ed) Cosmic Rays, the Sun, and Geomagnetism: the works of Scott E. Forbush, 1993; 924 Elementary Problems and Answers in Solar System Astronomy, 1993; numerous articles in learned journals and contribs to scientific works. *Address:* Department of Physics and Astronomy, University of Iowa, Iowa City, IA 52242, USA; 5 Woodland Mounds Road, Iowa City, IA 52245, USA.

van ANDEL, Dr Katharine Bridget, (Mrs T. H. van Andel); *see* Pretty, Dr K. B.

VAN CAENEGEM, Prof. Raoul Charles Joseph; Ordinary Professor of Medieval History and of Legal History, University of Ghent, Belgium, 1964–92, now Emeritus; *b* 14 July 1927; *s* of Joseph Van Caenegem and Irma Barbaix; *m* 1954, Patricia Mary Carson; two *s* one *d*. *Educ:* Univ. of Ghent (LLD 1951; PhD 1953); Univ. of Paris; London Univ. Ghent University: Assistant to Prof. of Medieval Hist., 1954; Lectr, 1960. Vis. Fellow, UC, Cambridge, 1968; Arthur L. Goodhart Prof. in Legal Science, and Vis. Fellow of Peterhouse, Cambridge Univ., 1984–85; Erasmus Lectr on the History and Civilization of the Netherlands, Harvard Univ., 1991. Corresp. Fellow, Medieval Acad. of Amer., 1971; Corresp. FBA 1982; Sir Henry Savile Fellow, Merton Coll., Oxford, 1989. Mem. Acad. of Scis, Brussels, 1974; For. Mem., Acad. of Scis, Amsterdam, 1977. Hon. Dr: Tübingen, 1977; Catholic Univ., Louvain, 1984; Paris, 1988. Francqui Prize, Brussels, 1974; Solvay Prize, Brussels, 1990. *Publications:* Royal Writs in England from the Conquest to Glanvill: studies in the early history of the common law, 1959; The Birth of the English Common Law, 1973, 2nd edn 1988; Geschiedenis van Engeland: van Stonehenge tot het tijdperk der vakbonden (History of England: from Stonehenge to the era of the trade unions), 1982; Judges, Legislators and Professors: chapters in European legal history, 1987; An Historical Introduction to Private Law, 1992; An Historical Introduction to Western Constitutional Law, 1995; (contrib.) International Encyclopaedia of Comparative Law, 1973. *Recreations:* wine (Bordeaux, Alsace), swimming, classical music, bridge. *Address:* Veurestraat 47, 9051 Afsnee, Belgium. *T:* (9) 2226211. *Club:* Universitaire Stichting (Brussels).

VANCE, Charles Ivan; actor, director and theatrical producer; *b* 6 Dec. 1929; *s* of Eric Goldblatt and Sarah (*née* Freeman); *m* 1959, Hon. Imogen Moynihan; one *d*. *Educ:* Royal Sch., Dungannon; Queen's Univ., Belfast. FInstD 1972; FRSA 1975. Early career as broadcaster; acting debut with Anew MacMaster Co., Gaiety, Dublin, 1949; dir, first prodn, The Glass Menagerie, Arts, Cambridge, 1960; founded Civic Theatre, Chelmsford, 1962; i/c rep. cos, Tunbridge Wells, Torquay, Whitby and Hastings, 1962; as Dir of Charles Vance Prodns, created Eastbourne Theatre Co., 1969; dir. own adaptation of Wuthering Heights, 1972; wrote and staged four pantomimes, 1972–75; devised and dir. The Jolson Revue, 1974 (staged revival, Australia, 1978; world tour, 1981); played Sir Thomas More in A Man for All Seasons, and dir, Oh! What a Lovely War, Greenwood, 1975; purchased Leas Pavilion Theatre, Folkestone, 1976 (HQ of own theatre organisation until 1985); prod and dir. world tour of Paddington Bear, 1978; produced: Cinderella, Stafford, 1981; Aladdin, Bognor, 1981; (London and national tours): Stop the World—I Want to Get Off (revival), 1976; Salad Days (revival), 1977; (also dir.) In Praise of Love, 1977; Witness for the Prosecution, (revival), 1979, 1992; Hallo Paris, 1980; This Happy Breed (revival), 1980; Starlite Spectacular, 1981; The Kingfisher (revival), 1981; The Hollow (revival), 1982 (also dir.); The Little Hut, Australia (also dir.), 1982; Cinderella, 1982, 1992 (also dir.); Aladdin, 1982 (also wrote); Lady Chatterley's Lover, 1983; The Mating Game, 1983; Cinderella, The Sleeping Beauty, The Gingerbread Man, The Wizard of Oz, 1983; Dick Whittington, Jack and the Beanstalk, Cinderella, Pinocchio, Jesus Christ Superstar (revival), 1984; Mr Cinders (revival), 1985; Policy for Murder, 1984 (also dir.); Jane Eyre, 1985 (also wrote and dir.); Oh Calcutta! (revival), 1985–86; Wuthering Heights (own adaptation), 1987; The Creeper (revival tour), 1994; directed: Verdict (revival), 1984; Alice in Wonderland, 1985 (also wrote); Dick Whittington, Aladdin, Jack and the Beanstalk, Cinderella, 1986–87 (also wrote); Dénouement (also prod), 1988; Spiders Web (Agatha Christie Centenary Prodn) (also prod), 1990; The Mousetrap, USA (also prod), 1990; Daisy Pulls it Off (also prod), 1991; Gaslight (also prod), 1991; Time and Time Again (also prod), 1991; My Cousin Rachel (also prod), 1992; Godspell (also prod), 1993–94; Peter Pan, 1993; Dick Whittington, 1994; Brideshead Revisited (also prod), 1995. Controlled: Floral Hall Th., Scarborough, 1984–86; Beck Th., Hillingdon, 1986–90; Grand Opera House York, 1980–89; controls Summer Th., Manor Pavilion, Sidmouth, 1987–; rep. seasons: Harlow Playhouse, 1993–94; Grand Th., Wolverhampton, 1994; launched first UK Dinner Theatre, Imperial Hotel, Torquay, 1990. Theatrical Management Association: Mem. Council, 1969; Pres., 1971–73 and 1973–76; Exec. Vice-Pres., 1976– (also of Council of Reg. Theatre). Advisor to Govt of Ghana on bldg Nat. Theatre, 1969. Director: Theatres Investment Fund, 1975–83; Entertainment Investments Ltd, 1980–82; International Holiday Investments, 1980–87; Southern Counties Television, 1980–87; Channel Radio, 1981–86; Gateway Broadcasting Ltd, 1982; Prestige Plays Ltd, 1987–; Operations Dir, Contemporary Theatre Ltd, 1992–94; Trustee Dir, Folkestone Theatre Co., 1979–85. Chairman: Provincial Theatre Council, 1971–87; Standing Adv. Cttee on Local Authority and the Theatre, 1977–90 (Vice-Chm., 1975–77); Gala and Fund-raising Cttee, British Theatre Assoc., 1986–89; Standing Adv. Cttee on Local Authority and the Performing Arts, 1990–93. Vice-Chairman: Theatres Adv. Council, resp. for theatres threatened by devel t, 1974–; (also dir.) Festival of Brit. Theatre, 1975–. Member: Theatres Nat. Cttee, 1971–; Drama Adv. Panel, SE Arts Assoc., 1974–85; Prince of Wales' Jubilee Entertainments Cttee, 1977; Entertainment Exec. Cttee, Artists' Benev. Fund, 1980–; Variety Club of GB, 1984–; Rotary Internat., 1971–; Patron, Voluntary Arts Network, 1992–; Vice-Pres., E Sussex Br., RSPCA, 1975–; Rotary Club of London, 1986–. Founded Vance Offord (Publications) Ltd, publishers of British Theatre Directory, British Theatre Review, and Municipal Entertainment, 1971; Chm., Platform Publications Ltd, 1987–; Editor in Chief, Team Publishing, 1986–87; Editor, Amateur Stage, and Preview, 1987–. Chambellain, Ordre de Coteaux de Champagne, 1993. *Publications:* British Theatre Directory, 1972, 1973, 1974, 1975; (ed) Amateur Theatre Yearbook, 1989, 1991, and 1993; Agatha Christie, The Theatrical Celebration, 1990. *Recreations:* sailing (crossed Atlantic single-handed, 1956), cooking (Cordon Bleu, 1957), travelling, animals. *Address:* Oak Lodge, Perry Hill, Farway, near Colyton, East Devon EX13 6DH. *Clubs:* Hurlingham, Royal Automobile, Directors', Kennel (Mem. Cttee, 1989–), Dorchester, Groucho, Wig and Pen, Lord's Taverners.

VANCE, Cyrus Roberts, Hon. KBE 1994; Secretary of State, USA, 1977–80; barrister-at-law; *b* Clarksburg, W Va, 27 March 1917; *m* 1947, Grace Elsie Sloane; one *s* four *d*. *Educ:* Kent Sch.; Yale Univ. (BA 1939); Yale Univ. Law Sch. (LLB 1942). Served War, USNR, to Lieut (s.g.), 1942–46. Asst to Pres., The Mead Corp., 1946–47; admitted to New York Bar, 1947; Associate and Partner of Simpson Thacher & Bartlett, New York, 1947–60, Partner, Jan. 1956–60, 1967–77 and 1980–. Special Counsel, Preparedness Investigation Sub-cttee of Senate Armed Services Cttee, 1957–60; Consulting Counsel, Special Cttee on Space and Astronautics, US Senate, 1958; Gen. Counsel, Dept of Defense, 1961–62; Sec. of the Army, 1962–64; Dep. Sec. of Defense, 1964–67; Special Rep. of the President: in Civil Disturbances in Detroit, July-Aug. 1967 and in Washington, DC, April 1968; in Cyprus, Nov.-Dec. 1967; in Korea, Feb. 1968; one of two US Negotiators, Paris Peace Conf. on Vietnam, May 1968–Feb. 1969; Personal Envoy of UN Secretary-General: in Yugoslavia crisis, 1991–93; to Nagorno-Karabakh, 1992; to South Africa, 1992; Mem., Commn to Investigate Alleged Police Corruption in NYC, 1970–72. Mem., Bd of Govs, Federal Reserve Bank of NY (Chm., 1989–91). Pres., Assoc. of Bar of City of New York, 1974–76. Mem. Bd of Trustees: Rockefeller Foundn, 1970–77, 1980–82 (Chm., 1975–77); Yale Univ., 1968–78, 1980–87; Amer. Ditchley Foundn, 1980– (Chm., 1981–); Mayo Foundn, 1980–90. Hon. degrees: Marshall, 1963; Trinity Coll., 1966; Yale, 1968; West Virginia, Bowling Green, 1969; Salem Coll., 1970; Brandeis, 1971; Amherst, W Virginia Wesleyan, 1974; Harvard, Colgate, Gen. Theol Seminary, Williams Coll., 1981. Medal of Freedom (US), 1969. *Publications:* The Choice is Ours, 1983; Hard Choices, 1983. *Address:* Simpson Thacher & Bartlett, 425 Lexington Avenue, New York, NY 10017–3909, USA. *T:* (212) 4557190.

VANCOUVER, Archbishop of, (RC), since 1991; **Most Rev. Adam Exner;** *b* 24 Dec. 1928. *Educ:* St Joseph's Coll., Yorkton, Sask; Gregorian Univ., Rome (LPH 1954; STB 1956; STL 1958); Ottawa Univ. (STD). Entered novitiate, Oblates of Mary Immaculate, St Norbert, Manitoba, 1950; ordained Roviano, Rome, 1957; St Charles Scholasticate, Battleford, Saskatchewan: Prof., 1960–64 and 1971–72; Rector and Superior, 1965–71; Prof. of Moral Theology, Newman Theol Coll., Edmonton, Alberta, 1972–74; Bishop of Kamloops, BC, 1974–82; Archbishop of Winnipeg, 1982–91. Secretary: BC and Yukon Conf. of Bishops, 1974–79; Conf. of Catholic Bishops, 1974–80. Canadian Conference of Catholic Bishops: Mem., Admin. Bd, 1976–83; Rep. of Western Conf. of Bishops, 1981–83; Mem., Episcopal Commn for Christian Educn, 1983–88; Mem., Social Communications Commn, 1989–; Rep. of W Reg. of Bishops on Permanent Council, 1989–; Mem., Cttee on Sexual Abuse, 1990–. Chm., Conf. of Bishops of Manitoba, 1983; Member: Sacred Congregation for Bishops, 1984–90; Nat. Catholic-Lutheran Dialogue, 1987–89. Chaplain, Knight of Columbus, 1974–82; Liaison Bp and Chaplain, Catholic Sch. Trustees Assoc. of BC, 1974–82; Mem., St Paul's Coll. Bd, Univ. of Manitoba, 1982. *Publications:* contrib. to Catholic Press, 1960–82. *Recreations:* playing piano and accordian, golf, working out, cross country ski-ing, jogging. *Address:* 150 Robson Street, Vancouver, BC V6B 2A7, Canada.

VAN CULIN, Rev. Canon Samuel; Secretary General, Anglican Consultative Council, 1983–94; *b* 20 Sept. 1930; *s* of Samuel Van Culin and Susie (*née* Mossman). *Educ:* High School, Honolulu; Princeton University (AB); Virginia Theological Seminary (BD). Ordained 1955; Curate, St Andrew's Cathedral, Honolulu, 1955–56; Canon Precentor and Rector, Hawaiian Congregation, 1956–58; Asst Rector, St John, Washington DC, 1958–60; Gen. Sec., Laymen International, Washington, 1960–61; Asst Sec., Overseas Dept, Episcopal Church, USA, 1962–68; Sec. for Africa and Middle East, Episcopal Church, USA, 1968–76; Executive, World Mission, 1976–83. Hon. Canon: Canterbury Cathedral, 1983; Ibadan, Nigeria, 1983; Jerusalem, 1984; Southern Africa, 1989. Hon. DD: Virginia Seminary, 1977; Gen. Theol Seminary, 1983. *Recreations:* music, swimming. *Address:* 16A Burgate, Canterbury, Kent CT1 2HG. *Clubs:* Athenæum; Princeton, Huguenot Society (New York).

VANDEN-BEMPDE-JOHNSTONE; *see* Johnstone.

van den BERGH, Prof. Sidney, OC 1994; FRS 1988; FRSC 1970; Astronomer, Dominion Astrophysical Observatory, Victoria, British Columbia, since 1977; *b* 20 May 1929; *s* of S. J. van den Bergh and S. M. van den Berg; *m* 1st, 1957, Roswitha Koropp (marr. diss.); one *s* two *d*; 2nd, 1978, Gretchen Krause (*d* 1987); 3rd, 1990, Paulette Brown. *Educ:* Princeton Univ. (AB); Ohio State Univ. (MSc); Göttingen Univ. (Dr rer. nat.). Asst Prof., Ohio State Univ., 1956–58; progressively, Asst Prof., Associate Prof., Prof., Univ. of Toronto, 1958–77; Dir, Dominion Astrophys. Observatory, 1977–86. Res. Associate, Mt Wilson and Palomar Observatories, 1967–68. ARAS 1984. Hon. DSc 1995. NRCC President's Research Medal, 1988. *Publications:* approx. 510 articles in various scholarly jls. *Recreations:* photography, archaelogy. *Address:* Dominion Astrophysical Observatory, 5071 West Saanich Road, Victoria, BC V8X 4M6, Canada.

VAN DEN BOGAERDE, Sir Derek Niven, (Sir Dirk Bogarde), Kt 1992; actor; *b* 28 March 1921. *Educ:* University College School; Allan Glen's (Scotland). Served War of 1939–45: Queen's Royal Regt, 1940–46, Europe and Far East, and Air Photographic Intelligence. Reviewer, Daily Telegraph, 1988–95. Hon. DLitt: St Andrews, 1985; Sussex, 1993. Commandeur de l'Ordre des Arts et des Lettres, 1990 (Chevalier, 1982). Films include (since 1947): Hunted, Appointment in London, They Who Dare, The Sleeping Tiger, Doctor in the House, Doctor at Sea, Doctor at Large, Simba, The Spanish Gardener, Cast a Dark Shadow, Ill Met by Moonlight, The Blue Lamp, So Long at the Fair, Quartet, A Tale of Two Cities (Sidney Carton), The Wind Cannot Read, The Doctor's Dilemma, Libel, Song Without End, The Angel Wore Red, The Singer Not The Song, Victim, HMS Defiant, The Password is Courage, The Lonely Stage, The Mindbenders, The Servant, Doctor in Distress, Hot Enough for June, The High Bright Sun, King and Country, Darling . . ., Modesty Blaise, Accident, Our Mother's House, Mister Sebastian, The Fixer, Oh What A Lovely War, Götterdämmerung, Justine, Death in Venice, Upon This Rock, Le Serpent, The Night Porter, Permission To Kill, Providence, A Bridge Too Far, Despair, These Foolish Things; *television:* The Patricia Neal Story (USA), 1981 (film); May We Borrow Your Husband? (also adapted), 1986 (play); The Vision, 1987 (film); By Myself (series), 1992; *radio* includes Galsworthy in serial, The Forsyte Chronicles, 1990–91; No Man's Land, 1992. *Theatre:* Cliff, in Power Without Glory, 1947; Orpheus, in Point of Departure, 1950; Nicky, in The Vortex, 1953; Alberto, in Summertime, 1955–56; Jezebel, Oxford Playhouse, 1958, etc. *Publications: autobiography:* A Postillion Struck by Lightning, 1977; Snakes and Ladders, 1978; An Orderly Man, 1983; Backcloth, 1986; A Particular Friendship, 1989; The Great Meadow, 1992; A Short Walk From Harrods, 1993; Cleared for Take Off, 1995; *novels:* A Gentle Occupation, 1980; Voices in the Garden, 1981 (televised 1993); West of Sunset, 1984; Jericho, 1992; A Period of Adjustment, 1994. *Address:* c/o JAA, 2 Goodwins Court, WC2N 4LL.

van den BROEK, Hans, Grand Cross Order of Oranje Nassau; Hon. GCMG; Member, European Commission (formerly Commission of the European Communities), since 1993; *b* 11 Dec. 1936; *m* 1965, Josephine van Schendel; two *d*. *Educ:* Univ. of Utrecht (Law degree). Lawyer, Rotterdam, 1965–68; Enka Bv., Arnhem: Sec., Man. Bd, 1969–73; Commercial Manager, 1973–76. Member: Lower House of Parliament, Netherlands, 1976–78; Exec., Catholic People's Party, 1978–81; State Sec. for Foreign Affairs, 1981–82; Minister for Foreign Affairs, 1982–93. Grand Cross: Order of Merit (Italy); Order of Isabel la Católica (Spain); Nat. Order of Merit (France); Order of Merit (Germany); Order of the Rising Sun (Japan). *Address:* Square de Meeus 22A, 1040 Brussels, Belgium; Persijnlaan 17, 2245 CJ Wassenaar, Netherlands.

VAN DEN HOVEN, Helmert Frans; *see* Hoven.

VANDERFELT, Sir Robin (Victor), KBE 1973 (OBE 1954); Secretary-General, Commonwealth Parliamentary Association, 1961–86; *b* 24 July 1921; *y s* of late Sydney Gorton Vanderfelt, OBE, and Ethel Maude Vanderfelt (*née* Tremayne); *m* 1962, Jean Margaret Becker, *d* of John and Eve Steward; two *s* (and one step *s* one step *d*). *Educ:* Haileybury; Peterhouse, Cambridge. Served War in India and Burma, 1941–45. Asst Secretary, UK Branch, CPA, 1949–59; Secretary, 1960–61. Secretary, UK Delegn, Commonwealth Parly Conf., India, 1957; as Sec.-Gen., CPA, served as Secretary to Parliamentary Conferences throughout Commonwealth, 1961–85, also attended many area and regional confs and Confs of Commonwealth Speakers and Clerks. Mem. Internat. Services Bd, RIPA, 1986–89; Governor: Queen Elizabeth House, Oxford, 1980–87; E-SU, 1984–89. *Recreation:* gardening. *Address:* No 6 Saddler's Mead, Wilton, Salisbury, Wilts SP2 0DE. *T:* Salisbury (01722) 742637. *Clubs:* Royal Over-Seas League, English-Speaking Union.

VAN DER KISTE, Wing Commander Robert Edgar Guy, DSO 1941; OBE 1957; Royal Auxiliary Air Force, retired; Director, Plymouth Incorporated Chamber of Trade and Commerce, 1974–80 (Secretary, 1964–74); *b* 20 July 1912; *y s* of late Lt-Col F. W. Van der Kiste, DSO; *m* 1939, Nancy Kathleen, *er d* of Alec George Holman, MRCS, LRCP, and Grace Kathleen Brown; one *s* two *d* (and one *s* decd). *Educ:* Cheltenham College. Commissioned Royal Air Force, Nov. 1936. Served War of 1939–45 (despatches, DSO); retired, 1959. Commanded No 3 MHQ Unit, Royal Auxiliary Air Force. *Recreation:* caravanning. *Address:* Lavandou, Moorland Park, South Brent, Devon TQ10 9AR.

van der LOON, Prof. Piet; Professor of Chinese, University of Oxford, and Fellow of University College, Oxford, 1972–87, now Emeritus Professor and Emeritus Fellow; *b* 7 April 1920; *m* 1947, Minnie C. Snellen; two *d*. *Educ:* Univ. of Leiden. Litt. Drs Leiden, MA Cantab. Univ. Asst Lectr, Cambridge, 1948; Univ. Lectr, Cambridge, 1949. *Publications:* Taoist Books in the Libraries of the Sung Period, 1984; The Classical Theatre and Art Song of South Fukien, 1992; articles in Asia Major, T'oung Pao, Jl Asiatique. *Recreations:* travel, gardening. *Address:* Midhurst, Old Boars Hill, Oxford OX1 5JQ. *T:* Oxford (01865) 739318.

VANDERMEER, (Arnold) Roy; QC 1978; a Recorder of the Crown Court, since 1972; *b* London, 26 June 1931; *o s* of late William Arnold Vandermeer and Katherine Nora Vandermeer; *m* 1964, Caroline Veronica (*née* Christopher); one *s* two *d*. *Educ:* Dame Alice Owen's Sch., Islington; King's Coll., London (LLB). Called to Bar, Gray's Inn, 1955, Bencher, 1988. Flt-Lt, RAF, 1955–58. Chairman: Greater Manchester Structure Plan Examination in Public, 1978; County of Avon Structure Plan Examination in Public, 1983. *Recreations:* reading, cricket. *Address:* The Field House, Barnet Lane, Elstree, Herts WD6 3QU. *T:* 0181–953 2244. *Club:* MCC.

van der MEER, Dr Simon; Ridder Nederlandse Leeuw, 1985; Senior Engineer, CERN, Geneva (European Organisation for Nuclear Research), 1956–90; *b* 24 Nov. 1925; *s* of Pieter van der Meer and Jetske Groeneveld; *m* 1966, Catharina M. Koopman; one *s* one *d*. *Educ:* Technical University, Delft, Netherlands; physical engineer. Philips Research Laboratories, Eindhoven, 1952–56. Hon. degrees: Univ. of Geneva, 1983; Amsterdam, 1984; Genoa, 1985. Nobel Prize for Physics (jtly), 1984. *Recreation:* literature. *Address:* 4 chemin des Corbillettes, 1218 Grand-Saconnex, Switzerland. *T:* (22) 7984305.

van der POST, Sir Laurens (Jan), Kt 1981; CBE 1947; writer, farmer, soldier, explorer, conservationist; Trustee, World Wilderness Foundation, since 1974; *b* Philippolis, S Africa, 13 Dec. 1906; *s* of late C. W. H. Van Der Post, Chairman of Orange Free State Republic Volksraad, and late M. M. Lubbe, Boesmansfontein, Wolwekop, and Stilton; *m* 1928, Marjorie Wendt (*d* 1995); one *d* (one *s* decd); *m* 1949, Ingaret Giffard. Served War of 1939–45: Ethiopia; North Africa; Syria; Dutch East Indies; Java; commanded 43 Special Military Mission, Prisoner of War 1943–45, thereafter Lord Mountbatten's Military-Political Officer, attached to 15 Indian Army Corps, Java, and subseq. to British Minister, Batavia, until 1947. Since then has undertaken several missions for British Government and Colonial Development Corp. in Africa, including Government Mission to Kalahari, 1952. FRSL. Hon. DLitt: Univ. of Natal, 1964; Univ. of Liverpool, 1976; Rhodes Univ., 1978; St Andrews, 1980; DUniv Surrey, 1971; Hon. LLD Dundee, 1989. *Films:* Lost World of Kalahari, 1956; A Region of Shadow, 1971; The Story of Carl Gustav Jung, 1971; All Africa Within Us, 1975; Shakespeare in Perspective—The Tempest, 1976; Zulu Wilderness: Black Umfolozi Re-discovered, 1979. *Publications:* In a Province, 1934; Venture to the Interior, 1952 (Book Society choice and Amy Woolf Memorial Prize); A Bar of Shadow, 1952 (repr., 1972); The Face Beside the Fire, 1953; Flamingo Feather, 1955 (German Book Society choice); The Dark Eye in Africa, 1955; Creative Pattern in Primitive Man, 1956; The Lost World of the Kalahari, 1958 (American Literary Guild Choice), rev. edn with long epilogue, The Great and Little Memory, 1988; The Heart of the Hunter, 1961; The Seed and the Sower, 1963 (South African CNA Award for best work published in 1963; filmed, 1983, as Merry Christmas, Mr Lawrence); Journey into Russia, 1964; A Portrait of all The Russias, 1967; The Hunter and the Whale, 1967 (CNA and Yorkshire Post Fiction Awards); A Portrait of Japan, 1968; The Night of the New Moon, 1970; A Story like the Wind, 1972; A Far Off Place, 1974 (filmed, 1993); A Mantis Carol, 1975; Jung and the Story of Our Time, 1976; First Catch Your Eland: a taste of Africa, 1977; Yet Being Someone Other, 1982; (with Jane Taylor) Testament to the Bushmen, 1984; About Blady: a pattern out of time, 1991; The Voice of the Thunder, 1993; Feather Fall (anthology), 1994; *relevant publication:* A Walk with a White Bushman: Laurens van der Post in conversation with Jean-Marc Pottiez, 1986. *Recreations:* walking, climbing, ski-ing, tennis, studying grasses and cooking in winter. *Address:* lives in London.

van der WATEREN, Jan Floris; Keeper and Chief Librarian, National Art Library, since 1988; *b* 14 May 1940; *s* of late Jacob van der Wateren and of Wilhelmina (*née* Labuschagne). *Educ:* Potchefstroom Univ., S Africa (MA); University Coll. London (Postgrad. Dip. Librarianship). ALA 1971. Lectr in Philosophy, Potchefstroom Univ., 1962–64; Asst Librarian, Univ. of London Inst. of Educn, 1967–71; Dep. Librarian, Sir Banister Fletcher Liby, RIBA, 1971–78; British Architectural Library: Managing Librarian, 1978–83; Dir and Sir Banister Fletcher Librarian, 1983–88. Sec., British Architectural Liby Trust, 1983–88. Hon. FRIBA 1995. FRSA 1994. *Publications:* articles, reviews for librarianship jls. *Address:* 52 Blenheim Crescent, W11 1NY. *T:* 0171–221 6221. *Clubs:* Architecture; Grolier (New York).

van der WERFF, Jonathan Ervine; His Honour Judge van der Werff; a Circuit Judge, since 1986; Resident Judge, Inner London Crown Court, since 1993; *b* 23 June 1935; *s* of H. H. J. van der Werff; *m* 1968, Katharine Bridget, *d* of Major J. B. Colvin, Withypool, Som; two *d*. *Educ:* St Piran's Sch., Maidenhead; Harrow; RMA, Sandhurst. Commnd in Coldstream Guards, 1955; Adjt 1st Bn, 1962–63; Major 1967, retired 1968. Called to Bar, Inner Temple, 1969; a Recorder, 1986; Resident Judge, Croydon Law Courts, 1989–93; Sen. Circuit Judge, 1993. *Address:* The Crown Court, Inner London Sessions House, Newington Causeway, SE1 6AZ. *Clubs:* Pratt's, Something; Bembridge Sailing.

VANDER ZALM, Hon. William N.; Premier of the Province of British Columbia, 1986–91; MLA (Social Credit Party) for Richmond, British Columbia; *b* Noordwykerhout, Holland, 29 May 1934; *s* of Wilhelmus Nicholaas van der Zalm and Agatha C. Warmerdam; *m* 1956, Lillian Mahalick; two *s* two *d*. *Educ:* Phillip Sheffield Sen. Secondary Sch., Abbotsford, BC. Purchased Art Knapp Nurseries Ltd, and became Co. Pres., 1956. Alderman 1965, Mayor 1969, Surrey Municipal Council. Minister of Human Resources, BC, 1975; Minister of Municipal Affairs and Minister responsible for Urban Transit Authority, 1978; Minister of Educn and Minister responsible for BC Transit, 1982; Leader, BC Social Credit Party, 1986–. Established Fantasy Garden World, major tourist attraction in Richmond, BC, 1983–. *Publication:* The Northwest Gardener's Almanac, 1982. *Recreations:* gardening, fishing, soccer. *Address:* Normandy Manor, 3553 Arthur Drive, Ladner, BC V4K 3N2, Canada. *Clubs:* Union (Victoria, BC); Hon. Member: Victoria Golf, Royal Vancouver Yacht, Royal Victoria Yacht.

VANDORE, Peter Kerr; QC (Scot.) 1982; *b* 7 June 1943; *s* of James Vandore and Janet Kerr Fife; *m* 1970, Hilary Ann Davies; two *d*. *Educ:* Berwickshire High Sch., Duns; Edinburgh Univ. (MA Hons Hist.; LLB). Called to the Scottish Bar, 1968; Standing Counsel to Sec. of State for Scotland, for private legislation procedure, 1975–86. Mem., Legal Aid Central Cttee, 1972–85. *Publications:* contribs to Juridical Rev. *Recreation:* seeing Emma and Sara from time to time. *Address:* 17 King's Stables Lane, Edinburgh EH1 2LQ.

VANDYK, Neville David, PhD; Editor, Solicitors' Journal, 1968–88; *b* 6 Sept. 1923; *yr s* of late Arthur Vandyk, solicitor, and Constance Vandyk (*née* Berton); *m* 1956, Paula (*née* Borchert); one *d*. *Educ:* St Paul's Sch.; London School of Economics, Univ. of London (BCom 1947, PhD 1950). Admitted Solicitor, 1957. HM Forces, incl. service in India, Burma and Japan, 1942–46; research asst, LSE, 1951–52; with Herbert Oppenheimer, Nathan & Vandyk, Solicitors, 1953–58; Asst Editor, 1958, Managing Editor, 1963, Solicitors' Journal; Member for its duration, Law Society's Constitution Cttee prior to the adoption in 1969 of their revised Bye-Laws, 1966–68. Founder Mem., W London Law Soc. (Pres., 1970–71); Mem. Council, Medico-Legal Soc., 1963–66, Vice-Pres. 1966–67, and 1985–90, Hon. Treas. 1967–85; Founder Mem., Assoc. of Disabled Professionals, Vice-Chm. 1972–80; Mem. for its duration, Royal Bor. of Kensington and Chelsea's Working Gp on the Disabled and their Families, 1980–81. Governor (nominated by Univ. of London) William Blake County Secondary Sch., 1957–70. Freeman 1962, Liveryman 1963, Worshipful Co. of Solicitors of City of London. Founder's Meml Lecture, Brit. Council for Rehabilitation of the Disabled, 1971; Hon. Prof. of Legal Ethics, Univ. of Birmingham, 1981–83. Life Member: Burma Star Assoc., RAFA; Hon. Life Mem., British Legal Assoc., 1989. *Publications:* Tribunals and Inquiries, 1965; Accidents and the Law, 1975, 2nd edn 1979; (title) National Health Service, in Halsbury's Laws of England, 3rd edn 1959, 4th edn 1982. *Address:* c/o Law Society Records Office, Ipsley Court, Berrington Close, Redditch, Worcs B98 0TD.

VANE; *see* Fletcher-Vane, family name of Baron Inglewood.

VANE, family name of **Baron Barnard.**

VANE, Sir John (Robert), Kt 1984; FRS 1974; Chairman, William Harvey Research Institute, since 1990 (Director, 1986–90); Professor of Pharmacology and of Medicine, New York Medical College, since 1986; *b* 29 March 1927; *s* of Maurice Vane and Frances Florence Vane (*née* Fisher); *m* 1948, Elizabeth Daphne Page; two *d*. *Educ:* Birmingham Univ. (BSc Chemistry, 1946); St Catherine's Coll., Oxford (BSc Pharmacology, 1949; DPhil 1953; DSc 1970; Hon. Fellow, 1983). Stothert Research Fellow of Royal Soc., 1951–53; Asst Prof. of Pharmacology, Yale Univ., 1953–55; Sen. Lectr in Pharmacology, Inst. of Basic Medical Sciences, RCS, 1955–61; Reader in Pharmacology, RCS, Univ. of London, 1961–65; Prof. of Experimental Pharmacology, RCS, Univ. of London, 1966–73; Gp Res. and Devélt Dir, Wellcome Foundn, 1973–85. Visiting Professor: King's Coll., London, 1976; Charing Cross Hosp. Med. Sch., 1979; Harvard Univ., 1979; St Marianna Univ., Japan, 1993. British Pharmacological Soc.: Meetings Sec., 1967–70; Gen. Sec., 1970–73; For. Sec., 1979–85; Hon. Mem., 1985; a Vice Pres., Royal Soc., 1985–87. Mem., Royal Acad. of Medicine, Belgium, 1978 (Hon. Foreign Mem., 1983). Foreign Member: Royal Netherlands Acad. of Arts and Scis, 1979; Polish Acad. of Scis, 1980; For. Associate, US Nat. Acad. of Scis, 1983; For. Hon. Mem., Amer. Acad. of Arts and Scis, 1982; Hon. Member: Polish Pharmacological Soc., 1973; Japanese Pharm. Soc., 1990; Alpha Omega Alpha Honor Med. Soc., USA, 1990; Hon. FACP, 1978; Hon. FRCP, 1983; Hon. FRCPath, 1990; Hon. Fellow, Swedish Soc. of Medical Scis, 1982. Hon. DM: Krakow, 1977; Vienna, 1993; Hon. Dr René Descartes Univ., Paris, 1978; Hon. DSc: Mount Sinai Med. Sch., NY, 1980; Aberdeen, 1983; NY Med. Coll., 1984; Birmingham, 1984; Camerino, 1984; Catholic Univ., Louvain, 1986; London, 1995; DUniv Surrey, 1984; Dr *hc* Buenos Aires, 1986; Hon. DPharm Milan, 1993; Hon. Dr Med. Surg. Florence, 1991. (Jtly) Albert Lasker Basic Med. Res. Award, 1977; Baly Medal, RCP, 1977; (jtly) Peter Debye Prize, Univ. of Maastricht, 1980; Feldberg Foundn Prize, 1980; Ciba Geigy Drew Award, Drew Univ., 1980; Dale Medal, Soc. for Endocrinol., 1981; Nobel Prize for Physiology or Medicine (jtly), 1982; Galen Medal, Apothecaries' Soc., 1983; Biol Council Medal, 1983; Louis Pasteur Foundn Prize, Calif, 1984; Royal Medal, Royal Soc., 1989; Special Award, Tsukuba City, Japan, 1990; Meml Prize, Fernandez-Cruz Foundn, 1991; Golden Medal Medicus Magnus, Polish Acad. of Medicine, 1995. Freeman: Scranton, USA, 1988; Taipei, Taiwan, 1989; New Orleans, USA, 1995. *Publications:* (ed jtly) Adrenergic Mechanisms, 1960; (ed jtly) Prostaglandin Synthetase Inhibitors, 1974; (ed jtly) Metabolic Functions of the Lung, Vol. 4, 1977; (ed jtly) Handbook of Experimental Pharmacology, 1978; (ed jtly) Prostacyclin, 1979; (ed jtly) Interactions Between Platelets and Vessel Walls, 1981; (ed jtly) Endothelin, Vol. I, 1989, Vol. II, 1991, Vol. III, 1993, Vol. IV, 1995; (ed jtly) Aspirin and Other Salicylates, 1992; (ed jtly) Prostacyclin: new perspectives in basic research and novel therapeutic indications, 1992; (ed jtly) Therapeutic Applications of Prostaglandins, 1993; numerous papers in learned jls. *Recreations:* photography, travel, underwater swimming. *Address:* William Harvey Research Institute, St Bartholomew's Hospital Medical College, Charterhouse Square, EC1M 6BQ. *Clubs:* Athenæum, Garrick.

VANE-TEMPEST-STEWART, family name of **Marquess of Londonderry.**

van EYCK, Aldo Ernest; Officer, Order of House of Orange; architect in private practice; *b* 16 March 1918; *s* of Peter Nicolaas van Eyck and Nellie Estelle van Eyck-Benjamins; *m* 1943, Hannie van Roojen; one *s* one *d*. *Educ:* Federal Sch. of Technology, Zürich. Private practice, 1951–, with Theo Bosch, 1971–82, with wife Hannie, 1983–; Prof. of Architecture, Delft Univ. of Technology, 1966–85; Paul Philip Cret Prof. of Architecture, Pennsylvania Univ., Philadelphia, 1979–84. Hon. FAIA 1981; Hon. RIAS 1985; Hon. Fellow, Bund Deutscher Arch. 1983; Hon. FRIBA 1988; Hon. Fellow: Royal Acad., Belgium 1981; Royal Soc. of Architects in Holland, 1994. Hon. degrees from Dutch, Canadian and US Univs. Wihuri Internat. Culture Prize, Finland, 1982; Royal Gold Medal for Arch., RIBA, 1990; Medal for Science and Art, Austria, 1991; (jtly) Silver Cube, Royal Soc. of Architects in Holland, 1994. *Publications: essays:* Steps towards a configurative discipline, 1962; Miracles of moderation, 1968; Rats, Posts and other Pests,

1981 (RIBA annual discourse). *Recreations:* world-wide travel, lecturing. *Address:* Entrepotdok 23–24, 1018 AD Amsterdam, Holland. *T:* (20) 230947.

VANEZIS, Prof. Peter, MD; FRCPath; Regius Professor of Forensic Medicine and Science, University of Glasgow, since 1993; *b* 11 Dec. 1947; *s* of Savvas Vanezis and Efrosini Vanezis; *m* 1981, Maria Galatariotis; one *s* one *d*. *Educ:* Wanstead High Sch.; Bristol Univ. (MB ChB, MD, PhD); DMJ Path. Jun. appt, St Olave's Hosp. (Guy's), 1973–74; Jun. Lectr, Lectr and Sen. Lectr in Forensic Medicine, London Hosp. Med. Coll., 1974–90; Reader and Head of Dept of Forensic Medicine and Toxicology, Charing Cross and Westminster Med. Sch. and Hon. Consultant, Riverside AHA, 1990–93. Hon. Consultant: Tower Hamlets AHA, 1982–90; the Army, 1992–; Gtr Glasgow Health Bd, 1993–; Govt of Republic of Cyprus, 1984–93. Mem., numerous forensic science socs, UK and USA. Mem., Edtl Bd (Path), Science and Justice. *Publications:* Pathology of Neck Injury, 1989; Suspicious Death-Scene Investigation, 1995; articles on forensic medicine and science in learned jls. *Recreations:* painting, golf. *Address:* Department of Forensic Medicine and Science, The University, Glasgow G12 8QQ. *T:* 0141–330 4573.

van HASSELT, Marc; Headmaster, Cranleigh School, 1970–84; *b* 24 April 1924; *s* of Marc and Helen van Hasselt; *m* 1st, 1949, Geraldine Frances Sinclair (marr. diss. 1976); three *s* one *d*; 2nd, 1989, Tessa Carolyn, *d* of Mrs B. Gofton-Salmond. *Educ:* Sherborne; Selwyn Coll., Cambridge (MA); Corpus Christi Coll., Oxford (DipEd). Served War of 1939–45 (despatches): commissioned in Essex Yeomanry, RHA, 1944; served North-West Europe (D-day). Lecturer in Commonwealth Studies, RMA, Sandhurst, 1950–58; Asst Master, Oundle School, 1959–70 (Housemaster, Sanderson House, 1963–70). *Publications:* occasional articles in Yachting World. *Recreations:* cruising under sail, governing schools. *Address:* Blue Cedars, 12 Solent Avenue, Lymington, Hants SO41 3SD. *Clubs:* Royal Cruising; Royal Lymington Yacht.

van LENNEP, Jonkheer Emile; Commander, Order of the Netherlands Lion; Commander, Order of Orange Nassau; Minister of State, since 1986; Secretary-General, OECD, 1969–84; *b* 20 Jan. 1915; *s* of Louis Henri van Lennep and Catharina Hillegonda Enschede; *m* 1941, Alexa Alison Labberton; two *s* two *d*. *Educ:* Univ. of Amsterdam. Foreign Exchange Inst., 1940–45; Netherlands Bank, 1945–48; Financial Counsellor, High Representative of the Crown, Indonesia, 1948–50; Netherlands Bank, 1950–51. Treasurer-General, Ministry of Finance, The Netherlands, 1951–69. Chairman: Monetary Cttee, EEC, 1958–69; Working Party No 3, OECD, 1962–69; Mem., Board Directors, KLM (Airline), 1951–69. KStJ. Grand Cross or Grand Officer in various foreign orders. *Address:* Ruychrocklaan 444, 2597 EJ The Hague, Netherlands. *Club:* Haagsche (The Hague).

van MAURIK, Ernest Henry, OBE 1944; HM Diplomatic Service, retired; *b* 24 Aug. 1916; *s* of late Justus van Maurik and Sybil van Maurik (*née* Ebert), BEM; *m* 1945, Winifred Emery Ritchie Hay (*d* 1984); one *s* one *d*. *Educ:* Lancing Coll.; Ecole Sup. de Commerce, Neuchatel, Switzerland. Worked in Tea Export, Mincing Lane, 1936–39. Commnd as 2nd Lt, in Wiltshire Regt, 1939; seconded to Special Ops Exec., 1941–46; demob. with hon. rank of Lt-Col (subst. Major), 1946. Joined Foreign Office, 1946; Moscow, 1948–50; West Germany and West Berlin, 1952–56; Buenos Aires, 1958–62; Copenhagen, 1965–67; Rio de Janeiro, 1968–71; FCO, 1971–75. Officier de la Couronne (Belgium), 1944. *Recreations:* golf, gardening, languages. *Address:* Parkside, The Common, Sevenoaks, Kent TN13 1SQ. *T:* Sevenoaks (01732) 452173. *Club:* Special Forces.

VAN MIERT, Karel; Belgian Member of European Commission (formerly Commission of the European Communities), since 1989 (responsible for competition policy); *b* 17 Jan. 1942; *m* 1971, Annegret Sinner; one *s*. *Educ:* Univ. of Ghent; European Univ. Centre, Nancy. With Sicco Mansholt, 1968–70; Asst in Internat. Law, New Univ. of Brussels, 1971–73; Office of Vice-Pres. of EC, 1973–75; Head of Private Office of Minister of Economic Affairs, Belgium, 1977; part-time Lectr on European Instns, New Univ. of Brussels, 1978; Mem., European Parlt, 1979–85; Mem., Belgian Chamber of Reps, 1985–88. Vice-Chm., Socialist Internat., 1986. *Publications:* papers on European integration. *Address:* European Commission, rue de la Loi 200, B1049 Brussels, Belgium.

VANN, (William) Stanley, DMus(Lambeth); *b* 15 Feb. 1910; *s* of Frederick and Bertha Vann; *m* 1934, Frances Wilson; one *s* one *d*. *Educ:* privately. BMus London; FRCO; ARCM. Asst Organist, Leicester Cath., 1931–33; Chorus Master, Leicester Phil. Soc., 1931–36; Organist and Choirmaster, Gainsborough Parish Ch., Dir of Music, Queen Elizabeth Grammar Sch. and High Sch., Gainsborough, Conductor, Gainsborough Mus. and Orch. Socs, also Breckin Choir, Doncaster, 1933–39; Organist and Choirmaster, Holy Trinity PC, Leamington Spa, Founder-Conductor, Leamington Bach Choir and Warwicks Symph. Orch., and Dir of Music, Emscote Lawn Sch., Warwick, 1939–49. Served War of 1939–45, RA, final rank Captain. Master of Music, Chelmsford Cath., Conductor, Chelmsford Singers, Founder Conductor, Essex Symph Orch., Prof., Trinity Coll. of Music, London, 1949–53; Master of Music, Peterborough Cath., Conductor, Peterborough Phil. Choir and Orch., 1953–77, retired. Conductor, St Mary's Singers, 1984–. Examiner, TCL, 1953–77; Mem. Council and Examr RCO, 1972–; Mem., ISM; Adjudicator, Brit. Fed. of Festivals, Canadian Fed. Fest. and Hong Kong Fest., 1950–84; Chairman: Peterborough Music Fest., 1953–; Eastern Area Council, British Fedn of Music Festivals, 1982–; President: Essex Symph. Orch., 1990–; Peterborough Children's Choir, 1994–. Patron, Precincts Soc., 1985–. DMus Lambeth 1971 (for eminent services to church music); Hon. FTCL 1953. *Publications:* seven settings of Missa Brevis; three settings of Rite A Communion Service; two settings of Rite B Communion Service; Evening Services in E minor and C major and for Rochester, Gloucester, Hereford, Lincoln, Peterborough, Chester, Salisbury, York, Chichester and Worcester Cathedrals; over 100 anthems, motets, carols, organ works and choral arrangements of folk-songs and of Handel; five sets of Preces and Responses and a Collection of Anglican Chants. *Recreations:* railway modelling, painting, gardening. *Address:* Holly Tree Cottage, Wansford, Peterborough PE8 6PL. *T:* Stamford (01780) 782192.

VANNECK, family name of **Baron Huntingfield.**

VANNECK, Air Commodore Hon. Sir Peter Beckford Rutgers, GBE 1977 (OBE (mil.) 1963); CB 1973; AFC 1955; AE 1954; MA, DSc; JP; DL; *b* 7 Jan. 1922; *y s* of 5th Baron Huntingfield, KCMG and Margaret Eleanor, *d* of Judge Ernest Crosby, NY; *m* 1st, 1943, Cordelia (marr. diss. 1984), *y d* of Captain R. H. Errington, RN (retd); one *d* (and one *d* decd); 2nd, 1984, Mrs Elizabeth Forbes; one step *s* one step *d*. *Educ:* Geelong Grammar Sch.; Stowe Sch. (Scholar); Trinity Coll., Cambridge (MA); Harvard; IEng; MIAgrE. Cadet, RN, 1939; served in Nelson, King George V, Eskimo, 55th LCA Flot., Wren, MTB 696 (in comd), 771 Sqdn and 807 Sqdn FAA, resigned 1949; Cambridge Univ. Air Sqdn, 1949; 601 (Co. of London) Sqdn RAuxAF, 1950–57 (101 Sqdn Mass. Air Nat. Guard, 1953); 3619 (Co. of Suffolk) Fighter Control Unit, 1958–61 (in comd 1959–61); No 1 Maritime HQ Unit, 1961–63; Group Captain, 1963; Inspector RAuxAF, 1963–73, Hon. Inspector-General 1974–83; ADC to the Queen, 1963–73; Hon. Air Cdre, No 1 (Co. Hertford) Maritime HQ Unit, RAuxAF, 1973–87. Gentleman Usher to the Queen, 1967–79. Mem., Stock Exchange Council, 1968–79 (Dep. Chm., 1973–75). Mem. (C) Cleveland, 1979–84, Cleveland and Yorks N, 1984–89, contested (C) Cleveland and Yorks N, 1989, European Parliament; Mem., Energy, Res. and Technology Cttee, 1979–89; Vice-Chm., Political Affairs Cttee, 1984–89. Prime Warden, Fishmongers' Co., 1981–82; Past Master: Gunmakers' Co., 1977 and 1988; Guild of Air Pilots and Air Navigators, 1976–77; Freeman, Watermen's and Lightermen's Co., 1978; Alderman of Cordwainer Ward, City of London, 1969–79; Sheriff, City of London, 1974–75; Lord Mayor of London, 1977–78. Member: Ipswich Gp Hosps Bd, 1956–62; City and E London AHA, 1973–77; Gov. Body, Brit. Post Graduate Medical Fedn, Univ. of London, 1963–71; St Bartholomew's Hosp. Bd of Governors, 1971–73; Special Trustee, St Bartholomew's Hosp., 1974–82. Pres., Anglo-Netherlands Soc., 1989–. Trustee: RAF Museum, 1976–87; Royal Academy Trust, 1981–87; Governor, RSC, 1974–87. President: Gun Trades Assoc., 1976–87; Stock Exchange Ski Club, 1977–87. KStJ (former Mem., Chapter General). Hon. DSc City Univ. Supernumerary JP City of London; DL Greater London, 1970; High Sheriff, Suffolk, 1979. Churchwarden of St Mary-le-Bow, 1969–84. Commander, Legion of Honour (France), 1981; Grand Officer, Order of the Crown (Belgium), 1983. *Recreations:* sailing, shooting, bad bridge. *Address:* 10 Brompton Square, SW3 2AA; Red House, Sudbourne, Woodbridge, Suffolk IP12 2AT. *Clubs:* White's, Pratt's; Stock Exchange Ski; Royal Yacht Squadron, Royal London Yacht (Commodore, 1977–78); Bembridge Sailing, Island Sailing, Orford Sailing; Seawanhaka Corinthian Yacht (US).

See also H. D. Stevenson.

VANNI d'ARCHIRAFI, Raniero; Italian Ambassador to Spain, since 1995; *b* 1932; *m* 1956, Simonetta Fiocca; two *s*. *Educ:* Univ. of Rome (Degree in Law). Joined Italian Diplomatic Service; served on Permanent Representation of Italy to EC, Brussels, 1961–66; Counsellor, Directorate General for Econ. Affairs, 1969–73; 1st Counsellor, Madrid, 1973; Minister Plenipotentiary, EC Summit, Feb. 1980; Head, Cabinet of Minister of Foreign Affairs, 1980–83; Ambassador to: Spain, 1983–87; FRG, 1987–89; Director General for: Econ. Affairs, 1989–91; Political Affairs, 1991–93; Mem., CEC, later EC, 1993–95. Gran Cruz, Isabela la Católica (Spain), 1986; Cavaliere di Gran Croce della Rep. Italiana, 1990. *Address:* Calle Lagasca 98, 28006 Madrid, Spain.

van RIEMSDIJK, John Theodore, CIMechE; Keeper of Mechanical and Civil Engineering, Science Museum, 1976–84; author and broadcaster; *b* 13 Nov. 1924; *s* of late Adrianus Kors van Riemsdijk and Nora Phyllis van Riemsdijk (*née* James); *m* 1957, Jocelyn Kilma Arfon-Price. *Educ:* University College Sch.; Birkbeck Coll. (BA). Served SOE, 1943–46. Manufacturer of gearing, 1946–54; Science Museum: Asst, 1954; Lectr, 1961; Educn Officer, 1969. Engaged in setting up Nat. Railway Mus., York, 1973–75. *Publications:* Pregrouping Railways, 1972; Pictorial History of Steam Power, 1980; Compound Locomotives, 1982, 2nd edn 1994; Science Museum Books; contribs to: BBC Publications; Newcomen Soc. Trans, Procs of IMechE. *Recreations:* oil painting, making models. *Address:* Le Moulin du Gavot, St Maximin, 30700 Uzès, Gard, France. *T:* 66227378.

van ROIJEN, Jan Herman Robert Dudley; Knight, Order of the Netherlands Lion; Officer, Order of Orange Nassau; Netherlands Ambassador to the Court of St James's, since 1995, and concurrently to Iceland; *b* 17 Dec. 1936; *s* of late Dr Jan Herman van Roijen and Anne (*née* Jonkvrouw Snouck Hurgronje); *m* 1963, Jonkvrouw Caroline H. W. Reuchlin; one *s* two *d*. *Educ:* Groton Sch., Mass, USA; Univ. of Utrecht (LLM 1961). Mil. service, Platoon Comdr in New Guinea, 1962. Foreign Service, 1963–; served Jakarta, Paris (NATO), Brussels (NATO), Saigon; Counsellor and Dep. Chief of Mission: Athens, 1975; Ottawa, 1978; Minister and Dep. Chief of Mission, Jakarta, 1981; Dep. Dir-Gen., Internat. Co-operation, Min. of Foreign Affairs, 1983; Ambassador, Tel Aviv, 1986; Principal Dir of Personnel, Diplomatic Budget and Buildings, Min. of Foreign Affairs, 1990; Ambassador, Jakarta, 1992. *Recreations:* tennis, ski-ing. *Address:* 8 Palace Green, W8 4QA; 38 Hyde Park Gate, SW7 5DP. *T:* 0171–584 5040. *Clubs:* Athenæum; The Haagsche (The Hague).

van STRAUBENZEE, Sir William (Radcliffe), Kt 1981; MBE 1954; *b* 27 Jan. 1924; *o s* of late Brig. A. B. van Straubenzee, DSO, MC and late Margaret Joan, 3rd *d* of A. N. Radcliffe, Kensington Square, W8, and Bag Park, Widecombe-in-the-Moor, Newton Abbot, S Devon. *Educ:* Westminster. Served War of 1939–45: five years with Royal Artillery (Major); Regimental and Staff Appointments, including two years in Far East. Admitted a Solicitor, 1952. Chairman, Young Conservative Nat. Advisory Cttee, 1951–53. Contested Wandsworth (Clapham), 1955. MP (C) Wokingham, 1959–87. PPS to Minister of Educn (Sir David Eccles), 1960–62; Jt Parly Under-Sec. of State, Dept of Educn and Science, 1970–72; Minister of State, NI Office, 1972–74. Chairman: Select Cttee on Assistance to Private Members, 1975–77; Select Cttee on Educn and the Arts, 1984–87; Cons. Parly Educn Cttee, 1979–83. Mem. Exec. Cttee, 1922 Cttee, 1979–87. Member of Richmond (Surrey) Borough Council, 1955–58. Chairman: United and Cecil Club, 1965–68 (Hon. Sec., 1952–59); Westminster House Boys' Club, Camberwell, 1965–68 (Hon. Sec., 1952–65); Nat. Council for Drama Training, 1976–81. Hon. Sec., Fedn of Conservative Students, 1965–71, Vice-Pres., 1974. Mem. House of Laity, Church Assembly, 1965–70, Mem. General Synod, 1975–85; Chairman: Dioceses Commn, 1978–86; Commn on Sen. Church Appts, 1988–92; Second Church Estates Commissioner, 1979–87. Patron of Living of Rockbourne, Hants. Freeman: Wokingham, 1980; Bracknell, 1994. *Recreations:* walking, reading. *Address:* 199 Westminster Bridge Road, SE1 7UT. *T:* 0171–928 6855. *Clubs:* Carlton, Garrick.

van WACHEM, Lodewijk Christiaan; Knight, Order of the Netherlands Lion, 1981; Commander, Order of Orange-Nassau, 1990; Hon. KBE 1988 (Hon. CBE 1977); mechanical engineer, Netherlands; Chairman, Supervisory Board, Royal Dutch Petroleum Co., The Hague, since 1992 (Managing Director, 1976–82; President, 1982–92); *b* Pangkalan Brandan, Indonesia, 31 July 1931; *m* 1958, Elisabeth G. Cristofoli; two *s* one *d*. *Educ:* Technological Univ., Delft (mech. engr). Joined BPM, The Hague, 1953; Mech. Engr, Compania Shell de Venezuela, 1954–63; Shell-BP Petr. Develt Co. of Nigeria: Chief Engr, 1963–66; Engrg Manager, 1966–67; Brunei Shell Petr. Co. Ltd: Head of Techn. Admin., 1967–69; Techn. Dir, 1969–71; Head of Prod. Div., SIPM, The Hague, 1971–72; Chm. and Managing Dir, Shell-BP Petr. Develt Co. of Nigeria, 1972–76; Co-ordinator, Exploration and Prod., SIPM, The Hague, 1976–79; Mem. Presidium, Bd of Dirs, Shell Petroleum NV, 1976–92; Man. Dir, Shell Petroleum Co. Ltd, 1976–92; Chm., Cttee of Man. Dirs, Royal Dutch/Shell Gp of Cos, 1985–92. Chm., Shell Oil Co., USA, 1982–92; Dir, Shell Canada Ltd, 1982–92. *Address:* Carel van Bylandtlaan 30, 2596 HR The Hague, Holland. *T:* (70) 3772118.

VARAH, Rev. Dr (Edward) Chad, CBE 1995 (OBE 1969); Rector, Lord Mayor's Parish Church of St Stephen Walbrook, in the City of London, since 1953; a Prebendary of St Paul's Cathedral, since 1975; Founder, The Samaritans (to befriend the suicidal and despairing), 1953, President of London Branch, 1974–86 (Director, 1953–74); President, Befrienders International (Samaritans Worldwide), 1983–86 (Chairman 1974–83); *b* 12 Nov. 1911; *e s* of Canon William Edward Varah, Vicar of Barton-on-Humber, and Mary (*née* Atkinson); *m* 1940, Doris Susan Whanslaw, OBE (*d* 1993); four *s* (three of them triplets) one *d*. *Educ:* Worksop Coll., Notts; Keble Coll., Oxford (Hon. Fellow 1981); Lincoln Theol. Coll.; Exhibnr in Nat. Sci. (Keble); BA Oxon (Hons in PPE), 1933, MA

1943. Secretary: OU Russian Club, 1931; OU Slavonic Club, 1932; Founder Pres., OU Scandinavian Club, 1931–33. Deacon, 1935, Priest, 1936. Curate of: St Giles, Lincoln, 1935–38; Putney, 1938–40; Barrow-in-Furness, 1940–42; Vicar of: Holy Trinity, Blackburn, 1942–49; St Paul, Clapham Junction, 1949–53. Staff Scriptwriter-Visualiser for Eagle and Girl, 1950–61; Sec., Orthodox Churches Aid Fund, 1952–69; Pres., Cttee for Publishing Russian Orthodox Church Music, 1960–76; Chm., The Samaritans (Inc.), 1963–66; Pres., Internat. Fedn for Services of Emergency Telephonic Help, 1964–67. Consultant: Forum Magazine, 1967–87; Assoc. for Crisis Intervention, China, 1994. Patron, Outsiders' Club, 1984–; Terrence Higgins Trust, 1987–. Hon. Liveryman, Worshipful Co. of Carmen, 1977, Worshipful Co. of Grocers, 1994. Hon. LLD: Leicester, 1979; St Andrews, 1993; Leeds, 1995; Hon. DSc City, 1993. Roumanian Patriarchal Cross, 1968. Albert Schweitzer Gold Medal, 1972; Louis Dublin Award, Amer. Assoc. Suicidology, 1974; with Befrienders International, Prix de l'Institut de la Vie, 1978; Honra ao Mérito Medal, São Paulo TV, Brazil, 1982. *Publications:* Notny Sbornik Russkogo Pravoslavnogo Tserkovnogo Peniya, vol. 1 Bozhestveniya Liturgia, 1962, vol. 2 Pt 1 Vsenoshchnaya, 1975; (ed) The Samaritans, 1965; Samariter: Hilfe durchs Telefon, 1966; Vänskap som hjälp, 1971; (TV play) Nobody Understands Miranda, 1972; (ed) The Samaritans in the 70s, 1973, rev. edn 1977; Telephone Masturbators, 1976; (ed) The Samaritans in the 80s, 1980, rev. edn as The Samaritans: befriending the suicidal, 1984, 2nd edn 1988; Before I Die Again (autobiog.), 1992. *Recreations:* reading, listening to music, watching videos of nature programmes on television. *Address:* St Stephen's Church, 39 Walbrook, EC4N 8BN. *T:* 0171–283 4444, 0171–626 8242.

VARCOE, (Christopher) Stephen; baritone; *b* 19 May 1949; *s* of Philip William and Mary Northwood Varcoe; *m* 1972, Melinda Davies; two *s* two *d* (and one *s* decd). *Educ:* King's School, Canterbury; King's College, Cambridge (MA). Freelance concert and opera singer, 1970–; Calouste Gulbenkian Foundation Fellowship, 1977. *Recreations:* painting, gardening, building. *Address:* Ansells Farm, Alphamstone, Bures, Suffolk CO8 5HN. *T:* Twinstead (01787)269570.

VARCOE, Jeremy Richard Lovering Grosvenor, CMG 1989; HM Diplomatic Service, retired; Deputy Director, Development Office, Oxford University, since 1995; *b* 20 Sept. 1937; *s* of late Ronald A. G. Varcoe and Zoe E. Varcoe (*née* Lovering); *m* 1st, 1961, Wendy Anne Moss (*d* 1991); two *d*; 2nd, 1995, Ruth Murdoch (*née* Wallis). *Educ:* Charterhouse; Lincoln Coll., Oxford (MA). National Service, Royal Tank Regt, 2nd Lieut, 1956–58. HMOCS: District Officer, Swaziland, 1962–65. Called to the Bar, Gray's Inn, 1966; Lectr in Law, Univ. of Birmingham, 1967–70; resigned to enter HM Diplomatic Service, 1970; FCO, 1970–72; Dep. Secretary General, Pearce Commn on Rhodesian Opinion, 1972; First Sec. (Information), Ankara, 1972–74; First Sec. and Head of Chancery, Lusaka, 1974–78; FCO, 1978–79; Commercial Counsellor, Kuala Lumpur, 1979–82; Head of Southern African Dept, FCO, 1982–84; Counsellor, Ankara, 1984–85; on special leave with Standard Chartered Bank, Istanbul, 1985–87; Ambassador to Somalia, 1987–89; Minister/Dep. High Comr, Lagos, 1989–90; Asst Under-Sec. of State, FCO, 1990–92. Co-ordinator, London Economic Summit, 1991. Dir Gen., United World Colls, 1992–94. *Publication:* Legal Aid in Criminal Proceedings—a Regional Survey (Birmingham Univ.), 1970. *Recreations:* sailing, golf. *Address:* Cuddy Thorne, Berrick Salome, Wallingford, Oxon OX10 6JJ. *Club:* Commonwealth Trust.

VARCOE, Stephen; *see* Varcoe, C. S.

VAREY, Prof. John Earl, PhD, LittD; FBA 1985; Principal, Westfield College, 1984–89, and Professor of Spanish, 1963–89, now Emeritus, London University; *b* 26 Aug. 1922; *s* of Harold Varey and Dorothy Halstead Varey; *m* 1948, Cicely Rainford Virgo; two *s* one *d* (and one *s* decd). *Educ:* Blackburn Grammar Sch.; Emmanuel Coll., Cambridge. MA 1948; PhD 1951; LittD 1981. Navigator, Bomber and Transport Commands, RAF, 1942–45. Westfield College: Lectr in Spanish, 1952; Reader, 1957; Actg Principal, 1983. Leverhulme Trust Fellow, 1970–71 and 1976; Visiting Professor: Univ. of Indiana, 1970, 1971; Purdue Univ., 1977. Pres., Assoc. of Hispanists of GB and Ireland, 1979–81. Corresp. Mem., Spanish Royal Acad., 1981; Hon. Mem., Instituto de Estudios Madrileños, 1988. Hon. Fellow, QMW, 1989. Hijo ilustre de Madrid, 1980. Co-founder, Tamesis Books Ltd, 1963; Partner, Editorial Támesis SL, 1992; Gen. Editor, Colección Támesis, 1963– (Chm., 1992–95). Hon. Dr Univ. Valencia, 1989. *Publications:* Historia de los títeres en España, 1957; (with N. D. Shergold) Los autos sacramentales en Madrid en la época de Calderón: 1637–1681, 1961; (ed) Galdós Studies, 1970; (ed with N. D. Shergold and Jack Sage) Juan Vélez de Guevara: Los celos hacen estrellas, 1970; Pérez Galdós: Doña Perfecta, 1971, 2nd edn 1993 (Spanish trans., 1989); (with N. D. Shergold and others) Fuentes para la historia del teatro en España, 18 vols, 1971–; (with D. W. Cruickshank) The Comedias of Calderón, 19 vols, 1973; (ed with J. M. Ruano) Lope de Vega: Peribáñez y el Comendador de Ocaña, 1980; Cosmovisión y escenografía: el teatro español en el Siglo de Oro, 1988; contrib. Bull. of Hispanic Studies, etc. *Recreation:* travel. *Address:* 38 Platt's Lane, NW3 7NT. *T:* 0171–435 1764.

VARFIS, Grigoris; Member (Socialist), European Parliament, 1984–89; *b* 1927. *Educ:* Univ. of Athens; Univ. of Paris. Journalist, Paris, 1953–58; OECD, 1958–62; Econ. Adviser to permt Greek delegn to EEC, 1963–74; Dir-Gen., Econ. Min. of Co-ordination, 1974–77; Man. Dir in chemical industry, 1977–81; Vice-Minister of Foreign Affairs, 1981–84; Greek Comr to EC, 1985–88 (responsible for structural funds and consumer protection, 1986–88). *Address:* Kypseli, Aegina 18010, Greece.

VARGAS LLOSA, Mario; writer; *b* Arequipa, Peru, 28 March 1936; *m* 1st, 1955, Julia Urquidi; 2nd, 1965, Patricia Llosa; two *s* one *d*. *Educ:* Univ. Nacional Mayor de San Marcos, Lima (BA); Univ. of Madrid (PhD 1959). Journalist and broadcaster, Lima and Paris; Lecturer: Washington State Univ., 1968; KCL; Univ. of Puerto Rico; Cambridge Univ., 1977–78; Writer in Residence, Wilson Center, Smithsonian Instn, 1980; Vis. Fellow, Wissenschaftskolleg, Berlin, 1991–92; Visiting Professor: QMC, 1967; KCL, 1969; Columbia Univ., 1975; Syracuse Univ., 1988; Florida Internat. Univ., 1991; Harvard Univ., 1992–93; Princeton Univ., 1993; Georgetown Univ., 1994. Founder of political party, Movimiento Libertad, 1988; Presidential candidate, Peru, 1990. Pres., PEN Club Internat., 1976–79. Member: Acad. Peruana de la Lengua, 1976; Royal Spanish Acad., 1994. Biblioteca Breve prize, 1963; Rómulo Gallegos Internat. Literature prize (Venezuela), 1967; Ritz Paris Hemingway prize (France), 1985; Asturias prize (Spain), 1986; Planeta prize (Spain), 1993; Cervantes prize (Spain), 1994; Jerusalem prize (Israel), 1995. Congressional Medal of Honour (Peru), 1981; Légion d'honneur (France), 1985; Chevalier, Ordre des Arts et des Lettres (France), 1993. *Publications:* Los jefes (short stories), 1958; *novels:* La ciudad y los perros, 1962; La casa verde, 1965; Los cachorros, 1967; Conversación en la Catedral, 1969; Historia secreta de una novela, 1971; Pantaleón y las visitadoras, 1973; La tía Julia y el escribidor, 1977 (filmed as Tune in Tomorrow, 1990); La guerra del fin del mundo, 1981; La historia de Mayta, 1984; ¿Quién mató a Palomino Molero?, 1986; El hablador, 1987; Elogio de la madrastra, 1988; Lituma en los Andes, 1993; *plays:* La señorita de Tacna, 1981; Kathie y el hipopótamo, 1981; La Chunga, 1986; El loco de los balcones, 1993; *non-fiction:* Contra viento y marea (essays), vols I and II, 1986, vol. III, 1990; El pez en el agua (autobiog.), 1993; Desafíos a la libertad (essays), 1994. *Address:* (until July 1996) Avenida Angamos Oeste 1630, San Isidro, Lima 27, Peru. *Fax:* (1) 4216381; Malecón Paul Harris 194, Barranco, Lima 04, Peru. *Fax:* (1) 4773518; c/o Faber & Faber Ltd, 3 Queen Square, WC1N 3AU. *Fax:* 0171–465 0034.

VARLEY, family name of **Baron Varley.**

VARLEY, Baron *cr* 1990 (Life Peer), of Chesterfield in the County of Derbyshire; **Eric Graham Varley,** PC 1974; DL; Director: Ashgate Hospice Ltd, since 1987; Cathelco Ltd, since 1989; Laxgate Ltd, since 1991; *b* 11 Aug. 1932; *s* of Frank Varley, retired miner, and Eva Varley; *m* 1955, Marjorie Turner; one *s*. *Educ:* Secondary Modern and Technical Schools; Ruskin Coll., Oxford. Apprentice Engineer's Turner, 1947–52; Engineer's Turner, 1952–55; Mining Industry (Coal) Craftsman, 1955–64. National Union of Mineworkers: Branch Sec., 1955–64; Mem. Area Exec. Cttee, Derbyshire, 1956–64. Chm., and Chief Exec., Coalite Gp, 1984–89; N and E Midlands Regl Dir, 1987–89, Midlands and N Wales Regl Dir, 1989–91, Lloyds Bank PLC. MP (Lab) Chesterfield, 1964–84; Asst Govt Whip, 1967–68; PPS to the Prime Minister, 1968–69; Minister of State, Min. of Technology, 1969–70; Chm., Trade Union Gp of Labour MPs, 1971–74; Secretary of State: for Energy, 1974–75; for Industry, 1975–79; Principal Opposition Spokesman on employment, 1979–83; Treasurer, Labour Party, 1981–83. Mem., H of L European Communities Select Cttee, 1991–. Vis. Fellow, Nuffield Coll., 1977–81. DL Derbys, 1989. *Recreations:* reading, gardening, music, sport. *Address:* c/o House of Lords, SW1A 0PW.

VARLEY, Dame Joan (Fleetwood), DBE 1985 (CBE 1974); Director, Local Government Organisation, Conservative Central Office, 1976–84; *b* 22 Feb. 1920; *d* of late F. Ireton and Elizabeth Varley. *Educ:* Cheltenham Ladies' College; London School of Economics (BSc Econ). Section Officer, WAAF, 1944–46. Conservative Agent, Shrewsbury, 1952–56; Dep. Central Office Agent, NW Area, 1957–65; Dep. Dir Orgn, 1966–74, Dir, Central Admin, 1975–76, Cons. Central Office. Chm., Friends of St James Norlands Assoc., 1986–; Pro Chancellor, Univ. of Greenwich Court of Governors, 1992–94 (Vice-Chm., 1986–91, Chm., 1991–92, Thames Polytechnic Court of Governors); pt-time Mem., Panel of VAT Tribunals, 1986–94. *Recreations:* gardening, walking. *Address:* 9 Queensdale Walk, W11 4QQ. *T:* 0171–727 1292. *Club:* St Stephen's Constitutional.

VARMUS, Prof. Harold Eliot, MD; Director, National Institutes of Health, Bethesda, Maryland, since 1993; Professor of Microbiology and Immunology, since 1979, Department of Biochemistry and Biophysics, since 1982, University of California Medical Center, San Francisco (on leave of absence); *b* 18 Dec. 1939; *s* of Frank Varmus and Beatrice Barasch Varmus; *m* 1969, Constance Louise Casey; two *s*. *Educ:* Freeport High Sch., NY; Amherst Coll., Mass (BA 1961); Harvard Univ. (MA 1962); Columbia Univ., NY (MD 1966). Surgeon, US Public Health Service, 1968–70; Dept of Microbiology, Univ. of California Medical Center, San Francisco: Lectr, 1970–72; Asst Prof., 1972–74; Associate Prof., 1974–79; Amer. Cancer Soc. Prof. of Molecular Virology, 1984–. Scientific Consultant, Chiron Corp., 1982–87; Member, Scientific Adv. Bd: Merck Corp., 1985–88; Gilead Corp., 1988–. Associate Editor: Cell, 1974–78, 1979–; Virology, 1974–84; Genes and Devlt, 1986–; Editor, Molecular and Cellular Biol., 1984–88; Mem., Editl Bd, Trends in Genetics, 1989–. Member: Special Grants Cttee, Calif. Div., Amer. Cancer Soc., 1973–76; Breast Cancer Virus Wkg Gp, Virus Cancer Program, 1973–74. Bd of Scientific Counselors, Div. of Cancer Biol. and Diagnosis, 1983–87, Nat. Cancer Inst.; Virology Study Section, NIH, 1976–80. Member: AAAS; Amer. Soc. Microbiology; Amer. Soc. Biochem. and Molecular Biol; Amer. Soc. Virology; Nat. Acad. Scis, 1984; Amer. Acad. Arts and Scis, 1988. Hon. DSc: Amherst Coll., 1984; Columbia Univ., 1990. Numerous awards and prizes incl. (jtly) Nobel Prize for Physiology or Medicine, 1989. *Address:* National Institutes of Health, Rockville Pike, Building 1, Bethesda, MD 20892, USA; c/o Department of Microbiology and Immunology, University of California Medical Center, San Francisco, CA 94143, USA.

VARNAM, Ivor; Deputy Director, Royal Armament Research and Development Establishment, 1974–82, retired; *b* 12 Aug. 1922; *s* of Walter Varnam and Gertrude Susan Varnam (*née* Vincent); *m* 1942, Doris May Thomas; two *s* *Educ:* Alleyn's Coll., Dulwich; University Coll., Cardiff; Birkbeck Coll., London. BSc Wales 1944; BSc (Hons) London 1952. Served War, RAF, 1940–46 (commnd 1944). Joined Tannoy Products, 1946; Atomic Energy Research Estabt, 1947; Siemens Bros., 1948; Royal Armament Research and Development Estabt, 1953–60 and 1962–82 (Defence Research Staff, Washington, USA, 1960–62), as: Supt Mil. ADP Br., 1964; Supt GW Br., 1967; Prin. Supt Systems Div., 1969; Head, Applied Physics Dept, 1972. *Publications:* official reports. *Recreations:* gardening, photography, bridge, music.

VARNISH, Peter, OBE 1992; CEng, FIEE; Director of Science for Ballistic Missile Defence, Ministry of Defence, since 1993; *b* 30 May 1947; *s* of John Varnish and Ilma Varnish (*née* Godfrey); *m* 1968, Shirley-Anne Bendelow; two *s*. *Educ:* Warwick Sch.; UCNW, Bangor (BSc Hons 1968). Res., Services Electronics Res. Lab., Baldock, 1968–75; Scientific Advr to MoD, British Embassy, Washington, 1975–79; Res. Area Co-ordinator for Electrical Warfare in UK, ASWE Portsdown, 1979–81; Officer i/c, ASWE Funtington, 1981–84; Head: Radar Div., ASWE Portsdown, 1984–86; Signature Control, ARE Funtington, 1986–88; Electronic Warfare and Weapons Dept, ARE Portsdown, 1988–90; Dir, Above Water Weapons, DRA, 1990–92; RCDS 1992; Dir, SDI Participation Office, 1993. Chairman: Common Defence Forum, 1988; Military Microwaves, 1990; Stealth Conf., 1990. Sen. Mem., Inst. of Electrical and Electronic Engrg; MIMgt. Several patents on stealth technology. *Publications:* numerous papers on electron bombarded semiconductor devices, radar, electronic warfare, Stealth, SDI, ballistic missile defence and res. policy. *Recreations:* Rugby football, hi-fi, classical music, photography, furtherance of science in UK, travelling. *Address:* 1 Greatfield Way, Rowlands Castle, Hants PO9 6AG. *T:* Rowlands Castle (01705) 412440.

VASARY, Tamàs; pianist and conductor; Joint Musical Director, Northern Sinfonia Orchestra, since 1979; Musical Director: Bournemouth Sinfonietta, since 1990; Hungarian Radio Orchestra, since 1993; *b* 11 Aug. 1933; *s* of Jozsef Vàsàry and Elizabeth (*née* Baltazàr); *m* 1967, Ildiko (*née* Kovàcs). *Educ:* Franz Liszt Music Academ Budapest. First concert at age of 8 in Debrecen, Hungary; First Prize, Franz Liszt Competition, Budapest, 1947; prizes at internat. competitions in Warsaw, Paris, Brussels, Rio de Janeiro; Bach and Paderewski medals, London, 1961; début in London, 1961, in Carnegie Hall, NY, 1961; plays with major orchestras and at festivals in Europe, USA, Australasia and Far East; 3 world tours. Conducting debut, 1970; conducts in Europe and USA. Records Chopin, Debussy, Liszt, Rachmaninov (in Germany), Brahms, Mozart, Honnegger, Respighi, Martinu. *Recreations:* yoga, writing, sports. *Address:* c/o IMG Artists, Media House, 3 Burlington Lane, Chiswick, W4 2TH.

VASCONCELLOS, Josefina Alys Hermes de, MBE 1985; Hon. DLitt; FRBS; sculptor; Founder, The Harriet Trust, Beached Trawler adapted for Nature-observation Base for Young Disabled; *b* 26 Oct. 1904; *d* of late H. H. de Vasconcellos, Brazilian Consul-General in England, and Freda Coleman; *m* 1930, Delmar Banner (*d* 1983), painter. *Educ:* sculpture: London, Paris, Florence; Royal Academy Schools. Mem., IPI. Works: High Altar and Statue, Varengeville, Normandy, 1925; Bronze St Hubert, Nat. Gall. of Brazil, 1926; Music in Trees, in stone, Southampton Gall., 1933; Ducks, in marble, Glasgow Art

Gall., 1946; Refugees, in stone, Sheffield Art Gall., 1949; Episcopal Crozier, in perspex, for Bristol Cathedral, 1948. Exhibits RA, Leicester Galls. Exhibn with husband, of 46 sculptures in 20 materials at RWS Gall., 1947; Last Chimera, Canongate Kirk, Edinburgh; 8ft Christ (in Portland Stone), Nat. War Meml to Battle of Britain, Aldershot, 1950. Two works, Festival of Britain, Lambeth Palace, 1951; Sculpture Exhibn, with husband, RWS Galls, 1955; War Memorial, St Bees School, 1955; two figures, St Bees Priory, 1955; life-size Mary and Child and design group of 11 sculptures by 11 collaborators, for Nativity, St Paul's Cathedral, Christmas 1955; Mary and Child bought for St Paul's, 1956; life-size Resurrection for St Mary, Westfield, Workington, 1956–57; Madonna and Child, St James's, Piccadilly, (now in Burrswood, Dorothy Kerin Trust), 1957; Rising Christ in St Bartholomew the Great, Smithfield; Winter, carving in Perspex, Oldham Gallery, 1958; Nativity (for ruins of Coventry Cathedral), 1958; Flight into Egypt, for St Martin-in-the-Fields, 1958 (now in Cartmel Priory); War Memorial, Reredos of carved oak, Rossall School Chapel, 1959; Nativity Set, life-size figures, St Martin-in-the-Fields, annually in Trafalgar Sq.; Winged Victory Crucifix, Clewer Church, 1964, and Canongate Kirk, Edinburgh; life-size Holy Family, Liverpool Cathedral and Gloucester Cathedral, 1965; life-size Virgin and Child, Blackburn Cathedral, 1974; Reunion, Bradford Univ., 1977; Return of the Carpenter, group of 10 life-size children, Samlesbury Hall, 1978; life-size Holy Family, for St Martin-in-the-Fields, 1983, 1992; life-size Holy Family, in cold cast stone, Norwich Cathedral, 1985; Revelation XXI, 'and God shall wipe the tears from their eyes', life-size two figure group, in plaster, for Lake Artists Exhibn, Grasmere, 1986; life-size Virgin and Child, Ambleside Parish Church, 1988; Reredos, Wordsworth Chapel, 1988; life-size Mary and Babe, Carlisle Cathedral, 1989; Sea Legend, in bronze, Hutton in the Forest, 1990; Childline to God, life-size figures of Christ, angels and 4 children, the Fratery, Carlisle Cathedral, 1990; life-size Holy Family, Manchester Cathedral, 1992 (exhibited Lake Artists Exhibn); Father Forgive, Rydal Hall, 1993; St Michael, life-size bronze, Cartmel Priory, 1995; one man exhibn: A Christmas Exhibition of Sculpture, Painting and Poems, Manchester Cath., 1991–92, Rydal Hall, 1992; sculptures at Dallas, Tulsa, Chicago, USA; Portraits: bronze of Lord Denning, 1969; Bishop Fleming; Rev. Austen Williams; Mario Borelli; and Rev. Dr M. S. Israel. Documentary film Out of Nature (on her work), 1949; BBC programme, Viewpoint TV, 1968; film, Moments of Truth, Border TV, 1993. Pres., Guild of Lakeland Craftsmen, 1971–73; Brother, Art Workers Guild. Mem., Inst. of Patentees and Inventors; Hon. Member, Glider Pilots Regimental Assoc. Hon. DLitt Bradford, 1977. *Publications:* Woodcut illustrations for The Cup (Poems by F. Johnson), 1938; contrib. to They Became Christians (ed Dewi Morgan), 1966. *Recreation:* musical composition. *Address:* Old Wash House Studio, Peggy Hill, Ambleside, Cumbria LA22 9EG. *T:* Ambleside (015394) 33794. *Club:* Royal Over-Seas League.

VASQUEZ, Hon. Sir Alfred (Joseph), Kt 1988; CBE 1974; QC (Gibraltar) 1986; Speaker, Gibraltar House of Assembly, 1970–89; *b* 2 March 1923; *s* of Alfred Joseph Vasquez and Maria Josefa (*née* Rugeroni); *m* 1950, Carmen, *o d* of Lt-Col Robert Sheppard-Capurro, OBE, JP; three *s* one *d*. *Educ:* Mount St Mary's Sch., Millfield; Fitzwilliam Coll., Cambridge (MA). Gibraltar Defence Force, 1943–45; The Gibraltar Regt, 1957–64, Captain. Called to the Bar, Inner Temple, 1950; called to Gibraltar Bar, 1950. Consultant, Triay & Triay, barristers and solicitors. Mayor of Gibraltar, 1970–76. *Recreations:* golf, shooting, gardening, bridge. *Address:* St Vincent House, Rosia Parade, Gibraltar. *T:* Gibraltar 73710. *Clubs:* Royal Gibraltar Yacht; Sotogrande Golf (Spain).

VASSAR-SMITH, Sir John (Rathborne), 4th Bt *cr* 1917, of Charlton Park, Charlton Kings, Co. Gloucester; Headmaster, St Ronan's Preparatory School, since 1972; *b* 23 July 1936; *o s* of Major Sir Richard Rathborne Vassar-Smith, 3rd Bt and of Mary Dawn, *d* of Sir Raymond Woods, CBE; *S* father, 1995; *m* 1971, Roberta Elaine, *y d* of Wing Comdr N. Williamson; two *s*. *Educ:* Eton. *Heir: s* Richard Rathborne Vassar-Smith, *b* 29 Dec. 1975. *Address:* St Ronan's, Hawkhurst, Kent TN18 5DJ.

VASSILIOU, Dr George Vassos; President of Cyprus, 1988–93; Leader, The Free Democrats Movement, Cyprus, since 1993; *b* 20 May 1931; *s* of Vassos Vassiliou and Fofo Vassiliou; *m* Androulla Georgiades; one *s* two *d*. *Educ:* Univs of Geneva, Vienna and Budapest (DEcon). Market researcher, Reed Paper Group, UK; Founder: Middle East Marketing Research Bureau, 1962 (Chm. and Man. Dir); Middle East Centres for Management and Computing Studies, 1984; Cyprus Branch, Inst. of Directors (Hon. Sec.). Vis. Prof., Cranfield School of Management, 1985–. Member: Bd and Exec. Cttee, Bank of Cyprus, 1984–88; Econ. Adv. Council, Church of Cyprus, 1980–88; Educn Adv. Council, 1986–88; Inter Action Council, 1994–. Mem. Bd, World Inst. for Develt Econs Res. of UN Univ., Helsinki, 1995–. Trustee, Malaysian Commonwealth Studies Centre, 1995–. Dr *hc:* Univ. of Athens; Univ. of Econs, Budapest. Grand Cross: Legion of Honour (France); Order of the Saviour (Greece); Order of Republic of Italy; Standard (Flag) Order (Hungarian People's Republic); Grand Collar, Order of Austria. *Publications:* Marketing in the Middle East, 1976, etc. *Address:* 21 Academia Ave. Aglanja, PO Box 2098, Nicosia, Cyprus.

VAUGHAN, family name of **Earl of Lisburne.**

VAUGHAN, Viscount; David John Francis Malet Vaughan; artist; *b* 15 June 1945; *e s* of 8th Earl of Lisburne, *qv*; *m* 1973, Jennifer Jane Sheila Fraser Campbell, artist, *d* of James and Dorothy Campbell, Invergarry; one *s* one *d*. *Educ:* Ampleforth Coll.

VAUGHAN, Rt. Rev. Benjamin Noel Young; Hon. Assistant Bishop, Swansea and Brecon, since 1988; *b* 25 Dec. 1917; *s* of late Alderman and Mrs J. O. Vaughan, Newport, Pembs; *m* 1st, 1945, Nesta Lewis (*d* 1980); 2nd, 1987, Magdalene Reynolds. *Educ:* St David's Coll., Lampeter (BA; Hon. Fellow, 1990); St Edmund Hall, Oxford (MA); Westcott House, Cambridge. Deacon, 1943; Priest, 1944. Curate of: Llannon, 1943–45; St David's, Carmarthen, 1945–48; Tutor, Codrington Coll., Barbados, 1948–52; Lecturer in Theology, St David's Coll., Lampeter, and Public Preacher, Diocese of St David's, 1952–55; Rector, Holy Trinity Cathedral, Port of Spain, and Dean of Trinidad, 1955–61; Bishop Suffragan of Mandeville, 1961–67; Bishop of British Honduras, 1967–71; Assistant Bishop and Dean of Bangor, 1971–76; Bishop of Swansea and Brecon, 1976–87. Examining Chaplain to Bishop of Barbados, 1951–52, to Bishop of Trinidad, 1955–61; Commissary for Barbados, 1952–55. Formerly Chairman: Nat. Council for Educn in British Honduras; Govt Junior Secondary Sch.; Provincial Commn on Theological Educn in WI; Provincial Cttee on Reunion of Churches, Christian Social Council of British Honduras; Ecumenical Commn of British Honduras; Agric. Commn of Churches of British Honduras; Pres., Belize Church Assoc., 1974–. Chairman: Provincial Cttee on Missions, Church in Wales; Church and Society Dept, Council of Churches for Wales; Adv. Cttee on Church and Society, Church in Wales, 1977; Judge of Provincial Court, Church in Wales. Pres., Council of Churches for Wales, 1980–82. Member: Council, St David's Univ. Coll., Lampeter, 1976–89 (Sub-Visitor, 1987–); Council and Ct, Swansea Univ. Coll., 1976–89; Ct, Univ. of Wales, 1986–89. Chm. of Govs, Christ Coll., Brecon, 1976–87. Sub-Prelate, OStJ, 1977; Order of Druids, Gorsedd y Beirdd. *Publications:* Structures for Renewal, 1967; Wealth, Peace and Godliness, 1968; The Expectation of the Poor, 1972. *Address:* 4 Caswell Drive, Caswell, Swansea, West Glamorgan SA3 4RJ. *T:* Swansea (01792) 360646.

VAUGHAN, David Arthur John; QC 1981; QC (NI) 1981; a Recorder, since 1994; *b* 24 Aug. 1938; *s* of late Captain F. H. M. Vaughan, OBE, RN and J. M. Vaughan; *m* 1st, 1967, (marr. diss.); 2nd, 1985, Leslie Anne Fenwick Irwin; one *s* one *d*. *Educ:* Eton Coll.; Trinity Coll., Cambridge (MA). 2nd Lieut, 14th/20th King's Hussars, 1958–59. Called to the Bar, Inner Temple, 1962, Bencher, 1988. Vis. Prof. in Law, Durham Univ., 1989–. Member: Bar Council, 1968–72, 1984–86; Bar Cttee, 1987–88; International Relations Committee of Bar Council, 1968–86 (Chm., 1984–86); Bar/Law Soc. Working Party on EEC Competition Law, 1977– (Chm., 1978–88); UK Delegation to Consultative Committee of the Bars and Law Societies of the European Communities, 1978–81 (Chm., Special Cttee on EEC Competition Law, 1978–88); Law Adv. Cttee, British Council, 1982–85; Bar European Gp, 1978– (Founder and Chm., 1978–80, Hon. Vice-Pres., 1990–); EEC Section, Union Internationale des Avocats, 1987–91 (Chm., 1987–91); Adv. Bd, Centre for Europ. Legal Studies, Cambridge Univ., 1991–; Council of Management, British Inst. of Internat. and Comparative Law, 1992–. Consulting editor for numerous pubns on EC Law. Bronze Medal, Bar of Bordeaux, 1985. *Publications:* co-ordinating editor, vols on European Community Law, Halsbury's Laws of England, 1986; (ed) Vaughan on Law of the European Communities, 2 vols, 1986, 2nd edn 1993–94. *Recreations:* fishing, tennis. *Address:* 50 Oxford Gardens, W10 5UN. *T:* 0181–960 5865; 0181–969 0707; Brick Court Chambers, 15/19 Devereux Court, WC2R 3JJ. *T:* 0171–583 0777; 8 Avenue de la Joyeuse Entrée, B-1040 Brussels, Belgium. *T:* (2) 2303161. *Clubs:* Brooks's, Pratt's.

VAUGHAN, Elizabeth, (Mrs Ray Brown), FRAM; international operatic soprano; *b* Llanfyllin, Montgomeryshire; *m* 1968, Ray Brown (Gen. Manager, D'Oyly Carte Opera); one *s* one *d*. *Educ:* Llanfyllin Grammar Sch.; RAM (ARAM, LRAM); Kathleen Ferrier Prize. Joined Royal Opera House; rôles in: Benvenuto Cellini; La Bohème; Midsummer Night's Dream; Madame Butterfly; Rigoletto; Simon Boccanegra; La Traviata; Il Trovatore; Turandot; Don Giovanni; Un Ballo in Maschera; Ernani; Nabucco; Aida; Cassandra; La Forza del Destino; Tosca; Idomeneo; Macbeth; Gloriana; Herodias; Kabanicha. Frequent appearances with: ENO; WNO; Opera North; Scottish Opera; Vienna State Opera; Deutsche Oper, Berlin; Hamburg State Opera; Metropolitan Opera, NY; Paris Opera. Professor of Singing: Welsh Coll. of Music and Drama, 1987–94; Guildhall School of Music, 1989–; RNCM, 1994–. Has toured in: Europe; USA; Australia; Canada; Japan; S America. Hon. DMus Wales. *Recreations:* tapestry, antiques, cookery. *Address:* c/o IMG, Media House, Burlington Lane, W4 2TH.

VAUGHAN, Sir Gerard (Folliott), Kt 1984; FRCP; MP (C) Reading East, since 1983 (Reading, 1970–74; Reading South, 1974–83); *b* Xinavane, Portuguese E Africa, 11 June 1923; *s* of late Leonard Vaughan, DSO, DFC, and Joan Vaughan (*née* Folliott); *m* 1955, Joyce Thurle (*née* Laver); one *s* one *d*. *Educ:* privately in E Africa; London Univ.; Guy's Hosp. MB, BS 1947; MRCP 1949; Academic DPM London 1952; FRCP 1966; FRCPsych 1972. Consultant Staff, Guy's Hosp., 1958–79, now Consultant Emeritus. Contested (C) Poplar, 1955. Minister for Health, DHSS, 1979–82; Minister of State (Consumer Affairs), Dept of Trade, 1982–83. Member: Select Cttee on Educn, 1983–93; Select Cttee on Sci. and Technol., 1993–. Chm., Party and Scientific Cttee, 1991–94. Parly Mem., MRC, 1973–76. Alderman: LCC, 1955–61; LCC Streatham, 1961–64; GLC Lambeth, 1966–70; Alderman, GLC, 1970–72; Chm., Strategic Planning Cttee GLC, 1968–71; Mem., SE Economic Planning Council, 1968–71. Governor, UCL, 1959–68. Liveryman, Worshipful Co. of Barbers (Master, 1992–93). Hon. FASI (FFAS 1978); Hon. FRCS 1993. *Publications:* various professional and general literary publications. *Recreations:* painting, fishing. *Address:* House of Commons, SW1A 0AA. *Clubs:* Carlton, White's.

VAUGHAN, Prof. John Patrick, MD; FRCPE, FFPHM; Professor in Health Care Epidemiology, London School of Hygiene and Tropical Medicine, University of London, since 1987; *b* 27 Dec. 1937; *s* of Thomas Frances Gerald Vaughan and Ellalline (*neé* Norwood); *m* 1st, 1960, Patricia Elspeth Pooley; two *s*; 2nd, 1975, Pauline Winifred Macaulay; two step *s* one step *d*. *Educ:* Bishop Wordsworth GS, Salisbury (Holgate and Folliott Prizes); Guy's Hosp. Med. Sch. (MB BS 1961; MD 1978). FRCPE 1982; FFPHM 1988. Specialist physician, Papua New Guinea, 1966–68; Head, Dept of Epidemiology and Biostats, Univ. of Dar es Salaam, 1969–73; Sen. Lectr in Epidem. and Public Health, Med. Sch., Nottingham, 1973–75; London School of Hygiene and Tropical Medicine: Sen. Lectr, 1975–83; Dir, Trop. Epidem. Unit, 1975–79; Reader, 1983–87; Head of Dept of Public Health and Policy, 1989–93. Visiting Professor: Pelotas Fed. Univ., Brazil, 1986–90; Andalucian Sch. of Public Health, Spain, 1994. Specialist Advr in Public Health to World Bank, 1989; hon. consultancies include: NHS, 1975–; MRC; WHO, in foreign countries. Member: Amnesty Internat.; WWF; Dorset Trust for Nature Conservation. Founder and Editor, Health Policy and Planning Jl, 1985–93. Okeke and William Simpson Prizes for best student, LSHTM, 1969. *Publications:* (jtly) Community Health, 1981; (ed jtly and contrib.) Refugee Community Health Care, 1983; (jtly) Community Health Workers: the Tanzanian experience, 1987; (jtly) In the Shadow of the City: community health and the urban poor, 1988; (with R. Morrow) Manual of Epidemiology for District Health Management, 1989 (trans. French, Portuguese, Spanish, Turkish); (jtly) Health System Decentralization: concepts, issues and country experience, 1990 (trans. French, Spanish, Indonesian); (ed with C. Normand) Europe without Frontiers: the implications for health, 1993; (contrib.) Disease Control Priorities in Developing Countries, 1993; monographs on health and medicine; contrib. learned jls on health and epidemiology. *Recreations:* travel, yachting, reading, art history, wild life, natural history. *Address:* Department of Public Health and Policy, London School of Hygiene and Tropical Medicine, Keppel Street, WC1E 7HT. *T:* 0171–636 8636.

VAUGHAN, Prof. Leslie Clifford, FRCVS; Professor of Veterinary Surgery, 1974–91, now Emeritus, and Vice-Principal, 1982–91, Royal Veterinary College; *b* 9 Jan. 1927; *s* of Edwin Clifford and Elizabeth Louise Vaughan; *m* 1951, Margaret Joyce Lawson; one *s* one *d*. *Educ:* Bishop Gore Grammar School, Swansea; Royal Veterinary College, Univ. of London (DVR 1967, DSc 1970). FRCVS 1957. Lectr in Veterinary Surgery, RVC, 1951; Reader, London Univ., 1968; Prof. of Vet. Orthopaedics, 1972. Junior Vice-Pres., 1986, Pres., 1987–88, Senior Vice-Pres., 1988–89, 1989–90, RCVS. Francis Hogg Prize for contribs to small animal medicine and surgery, RCVS, 1962; Simon Award for small animal surgery, 1966, Bourgelat Prize, 1975, British Small Animal Vet. Assoc.; Victory Medal, Central Vet. Soc., 1982. *Publications:* papers in sci jls. *Recreations:* gardening, watching rugby football. *Address:* Royal Veterinary College, Hawkshead Lane, North Mymms, near Hatfield, Herts AL9 7TA. *T:* Potters Bar (01707) 666333.

VAUGHAN, Prof. Peter Rolfe, FEng 1991; FICE; Professor of Ground Engineering, Imperial College, London, since 1987; *b* 10 March 1935; *s* of Ernest Alfred Vaughan and Clarrice Marjorie Vaughan. *Educ:* Luton Grammar Sch.; Imperial Coll., London (BSc Eng, PhD, DSc). Industry; postgraduate studies; work on Kainji Dam, Nigeria, 1964–67; academic staff, Imperial Coll., 1969–. Dir, Geotechnical Consulting Group, 1982–. *Publications:* numerous technical papers. *Recreations:* fishing, eating and drinking. *Address:* Department of Civil Engineering, Imperial College, SW7 2AZ. *T:* 0171–589 5111.

VAUGHAN, Rt. Rev. Peter St George; *see* Ramsbury, Area Bishop of.

VAUGHAN, Prof. Robert Charles, FRS 1990; Professor of Pure Mathematics, Imperial College of Science, Technology and Medicine, since 1980; *b* 1945. Imperial College, 1972–; SERC Senior Fellow, 1992. *Publication:* The Hardy-Littlewood Method, 1981. *Address:* Department of Mathematics, Huxley Building, Imperial College, 180 Queen's Gate, SW7 2BZ. *T:* 0171–589 5111.

VAUGHAN, Roger, PhD; FEng; FRINA; engineering and management consultant, since 1993; *b* 14 June 1944; *s* of Benjamin Frederick Vaughan and Marjorie (*née* Wallace); *m* 1st, 1968 (marr. diss.); three *s* two *d*; 2nd, 1987, Valerie (*née* Truelove); two step *s*. *Educ:* Newcastle Univ. (BSc Hons Naval Architecture and Shipbuilding 1966, PhD 1971). Student apprentice, Vickers Gp, 1962; Shipbuilding Devell Engr, Swan Hunter Shipbuilders Ltd, 1970–71; Dir, 1971–81, Man. Dir, 1978–81, A&P Appledore Ltd; Dir, Performance Improvement and Productivity, British Shipbuilders, 1981–86; took part in privatisation of Swan Hunter, 1986; Joint Chief Exec., Swan Hunter, 1988–93. Member: Nat. Curriculum Council, 1992–94; Council, Newcastle Univ., 1992– (Chm., Engrg Design Centre, 1990–94). Pres., Shipbuilders and Shiprepairers Assoc., 1991–93. FRSA 1993. Shipbuilding Gold Medal, NECInst, 1969. *Recreations:* music, theatre, ballet, opera, sailing, walking, reading. *Address:* Correslaw, Netherwitton, Morpeth, Northumberland NE61 4NW.

VAUGHAN, Roger Davison, OBE 1986; FEng 1981; General Manager, Fast Reactor Projects, National Nuclear Corporation Ltd, 1977–88, retired; Director, Fast Reactor Technology Ltd, 1984–88; *b* 2 Oct. 1923; *s* of late David William and Olive Marion Vaughan; *m* 1951, Doreen Stewart; four *s*. *Educ:* University High Sch., Melbourne; Univ. of Melbourne, Aust. BMechE; FIMechE. Engineer Officer, RAAF, 1945–46. Chemical Engr, Commonwealth Serum Laboratories, 1946–47; Works apprenticeship, C. A. Parsons & Co., 1948–49; Chief Engr, C. A. Parsons Calcutta, 1950–53; AERE, Harwell, 1954; Chief Engineer: Nuclear Power Plant Co., 1955–59 (Director, 1958); The Nuclear Power Group, 1960–75; Manager, Technology Div., Nuclear Power Co., 1976–77. Chm., Gas-cooled Breeder Reactor Assoc., Brussels, 1970–; Member: Bd, BSI, 1989–92 (Chm., BSI Engineering Council, 1983–88); BSI Standards Bd, 1992–. Mem. Council, IMechE, 1977–81, 1985–89 (Chm., Power Industries Div., 1985–89). *Publications:* papers in jls of IMechE, Brit. Nuc. Energy Soc., World Energy Conf. *Recreations:* skiing, mountain walking; questionable performer on piano and clarinet. *Address:* Otterburn House, Manor Park South, Knutsford, Cheshire WA16 8AG. *T:* Knutsford (01565) 632514. *Clubs:* Ski of Great Britain; Himalayan (Bombay).

VAUGHAN, William Randal; Founder and Proprietor, W. R. Vaughan Associates Ltd (formerly W. R. Vaughan Ltd), since 1945; *b* 11 March 1912; *m* 1945, K. A. Headland; three *s* one *d*. *Educ:* Centaur Trade School, Coventry. FIProdE. Apprenticed, Alfred Herbert Ltd, 1926; Coventry Gauge & Tool Co. Ltd, 1933; A. C. Wickman Ltd, 1934; A. Pattison Ltd, 1942; C. G. Wade Ltd, London, 1943. Chairman, Machine Tool Industry Research Assoc., 1974–83 (Vice-Pres., 1983–); President, Machine Tool Trades Assoc., 1977–79. Member of Lloyd's. *Recreations:* squash, skiing, sailing, flying. *Address:* Rowley Bank, Rowley Lane, Arkley, Barnet, Herts EN5 3HS. *T:* 0181–441 4800. *Clubs:* Lansdowne, Royal Automobile.

VAUGHAN-JACKSON, Oliver James, VRD 1951; FRCS; Consulting Orthopaedic Surgeon to London Hospital, since 1971; *b* 6 July 1907; *e s* of Surgeon Captain P. Vaughan-Jackson, RN, Carramore, Ballina, County Mayo; *m* 1939, Joan Madeline, *er d* of E. A. Bowring, CBE, St Johns, Newfoundland; two *s*. *Educ:* Berkhamsted School; Balliol Coll., Oxford; The London Hospital. Kitchener Scholar; BA, BM, BCh Oxon, 1932; MRCS, LRCP, 1932; FRCS 1936. House Physician, Demonstrator of Pathology, House Surgeon, Resident Accoucheur, and Surgical Registrar at The London Hosp. Surgeon Lieut-Comdr RNVR, Retd, Surgical specialist, Roy. Naval Hosp., Sydney, Australia. Sen. Registrar (Orthopædic), The London Hosp.; Orthopaedic Surgeon to: The London Hosp., 1946–71; St Bartholomew's Hosp., Rochester, 1947–70; Medway Hosp., 1970–71; Claybury Mental Hosp., 1946–64; Halliwick Cripples Sch., 1946–71; Cons. In Orthopaedics to Royal Navy, 1956–71; Vis. Prof. of Orthopaedics, Memorial Univ. of Newfoundland, 1971–73; Senior Consultant in Orthopaedics at St John's Gen. Hosp., St Clare Mercy Hosp. and Janeway Child Health Centre, St John's, Newfoundland, 1971–73. Fellow: British Orthopædic Assoc.; RSM (Pres., Section of Orthopædics, 1968–69); Med. Soc. London; Member: Soc. Internat. de Chirurgie Orthopédique et de Traumatologie; British Soc. for Surgery of the Hand. Trustee, Meml Univ. of Newfoundland's Harlow Campus Trust, 1988–91. Former Mem., Editorial Board of Jl of Bone and Joint Surgery. Hon. DSc Memorial Univ. of Newfoundland, 1973. *Publications:* Sections on: Arthrodesis (Maingot's Techniques in British Surgery), 1950; Arthrodesis of the Hip, and Osteotomy of the Upper End of Femur (Operative Surgery, ed Rob and Smith), 1958; Surgery of the Hand; Orthopædic Surgery in Spastic conditions; Peripheral Nerve Injuries (Textbook of British Surgery, ed Sir Henry Souttar and Prof. J. C. Goligher), 1959; The Rheumatoid Hand; Carpal Tunnel Compression of the Median Nerve (Clinical Surgery, ed Rob and Smith), 1966; Surgery in Arthritis of the Hand, in Textbook of Rheumatic Diseases, 1968; The Rheumatoid Hand, in Operative Surgery, 2nd edn, 1971; contribs to Jl of Bone and Joint Surgery, etc. *Recreations:* gardening, photography. *Address:* 25 Barton Farm, Cerne Abbas, Dorchester, Dorset DT2 7LF.

VAUX OF HARROWDEN, 10th Baron *cr* 1523; **John Hugh Philip Gilbey;** *b* 4 Aug. 1915; 2nd *s* of William Gordon Gilbey (*d* 1965) and Grace Mary Eleanor, 8th Baroness Vaux of Harrowden (*d* 1958); *S* brother, 1977; *m* 1939, Maureen Pamela, *e d* of Hugh Gilbey; three *s* one *d*. *Educ:* Ampleforth College; Christ Church, Oxford (BA 1937). Formerly Major, Duke of Wellington's Regt; served War of 1939–45. *Heir:* *s* Hon. Anthony William Gilbey [*b* 25 May 1940; *m* 1964, Beverley Anne, *o d* of Charles Alexander Walton; two *s* two *d*]. *Address:* Cholmondeley Cottage, 2 Cholmondeley Walk, Richmond, Surrey TW9 1NS.

VAUX, Maj.-Gen. Nicholas Francis, CB 1989; DSO 1982; Consultant and Managing Director, UK-Russia Security Group, London and Moscow, since 1993; Major General Royal Marines Commando Forces, 1987–90, retired; *b* 15 April 1936; *s* of late Harry and of Penelope Vaux; *m* 1966, Zoya Hellings; one *s* two *d*. *Educ:* Stonyhurst College. Commissioned RM, 1954; served Suez, 1956; Far East, 1958–61; West Indies Frigate, 1962–64; Staff Coll., Camberley, 1969; MoD (Army), 1975–77; Special Advisor, USMC, 1979–81; CO 42 Commando RM, 1981–83; Falklands, 1982; RCDS, 1985. *Publication:* March to the South Atlantic, 1986. *Recreations:* field sports. *Address:* National Westminster Bank, Old Town Street, Plymouth PL1 1DG. *Clubs:* Farmers', Special Forces.

VAVASOUR, Comdr Sir Geoffrey William, 5th Bt *cr* 1828; DSC 1943; RN (retired); a Director of W. M. Still & Sons, 1962–80, retired; *b* 5 Sept. 1914; *s* of Captain Sir Leonard Vavasour, 4th Bt, RN, and Ellice Margaret Nelson; *S* father, 1961; *m* 1st, 1940, Joan Robb (marr. diss. 1947); two *d*; 2nd, 1971, Marcia Christine, *d* of late Marshall Lodge, Batley, Yorks. *Educ:* RNC Dartmouth. *Heir:* *kinsman* Eric Michael Joseph Marmaduke Vavasour [*b* 3 Jan 1953; *m* 1976, Isabelle, *d* of André van Hille; two *s* one *d*]. *Address:* 8 Bede House, Manor Fields, Putney, SW15 3LT. *Club:* All England Lawn Tennis.

VAZ, (Nigel) Keith (Anthony Standish); MP (Lab) Leicester East, since 1987; *b* Aden, 26 Nov. 1956; *m* 1993, Maria Fernandes; one *s*. *Educ:* St Joseph's Convent, Aden; Latymer Upper Sch., Hammersmith; Gonville and Caius Coll., Cambridge; Coll. of Law, Lancaster Gate. Senior Solicitor, Islington Borough Council, 1982–85; Solicitor, Highfields and Belgrave Law Centre, Leicester, 1985–87. Contested (Lab): Richmond and Barnes (gen. election), 1983; Surrey W (European Parlt election), 1984. Opposition front bench spokesman on inner cities and urban areas, 1992–. Mem., Home Affairs Select Cttee, H of C, 1987–92; Secretary: Indo-British Parly Gp; PLP Wool and Textiles Gp. Clothing and Footwear Inst., 1988–94. Chairman: All-Party Footwear & Leather Industries Gp; PLP Legal Services Gp; Unison Gp of MPs. Chm., City 2020, Urban Policy Commn, 1993–; Member: NUPE, 1985–; Nat. Adv. Cttee, Crime Concern, 1989–93; Adv. Bd, TV Asia, 1992–; Adv. Bd, Skillshare Africa. Vice Pres., Assoc. of Dist Councils, 1993–. Patron, Gingerbread, 1990–92; Jt Patron, UN Year of Tolerance, 1995; Pres., Leicester and S Leics RSPCA, 1988–. Chm., Adv. Bd, Asian Times, 1992–; Columnist: Tribune; Catholic Herald; New Life (Gujarat Samachar). President: Hillcroft FC; Thurnby Lodge Boys' Club FC. *Address:* 144 Uppingham Road, Leicester LE5 0QF. *T:* Leicester (0116) 276 8834. *Clubs:* Safari (Leicester); Scraptoft Valley Working Men's.

VEAL, Group Captain John Bartholomew, CBE 1956; AFC 1940; Civil Aviation Safety Adviser, Department of Trade and Industry, 1972–74, retired; *b* 28 September 1909; *er s* of John Henry and Sarah Grace Veal; *m* 1933, Enid Marjorie Hill (*d* 1987); two *s*. *Educ:* Christ's Hosp. Special trainee, Metropolitan-Vickers, 1926–27; commissioned in RAF as pilot officer, 1927; served in Nos 4 and 501 Squadrons and as flying Instructor at Central Flying School, transferring to RAFO, 1932; Flying-Instructor, Chief Flying Instructor, and Test Pilot, Air Service Training Ltd, 1932–39; recalled to regular RAF service, 1939; commanded navigation and flying training schools, 1939–43; Air Staff No. 46 Transport Group, 1944 and Transport Command, 1945–46 (despatches); released from RAF, 1946, to become Deputy Director of Training, Ministry of Civil Aviation; Director of Air Safety and Training, 1947; Director of Operations, Safety and Licensing, 1952; Deputy Director-General of Navigational Services, Ministry of Transport and Civil Aviation, 1958; Director-General of Navigational Services, Ministry of Aviation, 1959–62; Chief Inspector of Accidents, Civil Aviation Department, Board of Trade (formerly Min. of Aviation), 1963–68; Dir Gen. of Safety and Operations, DTI (formerly BOT), 1968–72. FRAeS 1967 (AFRAeS 1958). *Recreation:* trout fishing. *Address:* Woodacre, Horsham Road, Cranleigh, Surrey GU6 8DZ. *T:* Cranleigh (01483) 274490. *Club:* Royal Air Force.

VEAL, Kevin Anthony; Sheriff of Tayside Central and Fife, since 1993; *b* 16 Sept. 1946; *s* of George Algernon Veal and Pauline Grace Short; *m* 1969, Monica Flynn; two *s* two *d*. *Educ:* St Joseph's Primary Sch., Dundee; Lawside Acad., Dundee; Univ. of St Andrews (LLB 1966). Partner, Burns Veal & Gillan, Dundee, 1971–93; Temp. Sheriff, 1984–93. Dean, Faculty of Procurators and Solicitors in Dundee, 1991–93; part-time Tutor, Dept of Law, Univ. of Dundee, 1978–85. KHS 1989; KSG 1993. *Recreations:* choral music, organ playing, classical music, hill-walking. *Address:* Sheriff Court House, Market Street, Forfar, Angus DD8 3LA; Viewfield,70 Blackness Avenue, Dundee DD2 1JL. *T:* Dundee (01382)668633.

VEALE, Sir Alan (John Ralph), Kt 1984; FEng 1980; Chairman: Rossmore Warwick Ltd, 1986–88; RFS Industries Ltd, 1987–92; Exeter Enterprise Ltd, since 1990; *b* 2 Feb. 1920; *s* of Leslie H. Veale and Eleanor Veale; *m* 1946, Muriel Veale; two *s* (and one *s* decd). *Educ:* Exeter School; Manchester College of Technology. AMCT, FIMechE, FIEE. Manufacturing Dir, AEI Turbine Generators Ltd, 1963; Director and General Manager: Heavy Plant Div., AEI, 1966; Motor Control Group, AEI, 1967; Managing Director: GEC Diesels Ltd, 1969; GEC Power Engineering Ltd, 1970–85; Dir, GEC plc, 1973–85; Chm., Fairey Gp, 1987; Dir, Throgmorton Trust PLC, 1986–90. Pres., IProdE, 1985–86. CBIM. Hon. DSc Salford, 1984. *Recreations:* sailing, walking. *Address:* 41 Northumberland Road, Leamington Spa CV32 6HF. *T:* Leamington Spa (01926) 424349.

VEASEY, Josephine, CBE 1970; opera singer (mezzo soprano), retired; teaching privately, since 1982; vocal consultant to English National Opera, 1985–94; *b* London, 10 July 1930; *m* (marr. diss.); one *s* one *d*. Joined chorus of Royal Opera House, Covent Garden, 1949; a Principal there, 1955– (interval on tour, in opera, for Arts Council). Teacher of voice production, RAM, 1983–84. Has sung at Royal Opera House, Glyndebourne, Metropolitan (NY), La Scala, and in France, Germany, Spain, Switzerland, South America; operatic Roles include: Octavian in Der Rosenkavalier; Cherubino in Figaro; name role in Iphigenie; Dorabella in Cosi fan Tutte; Amneris in Aida, Fricka in Die Walküre; Fricka in Das Rheingold; name role in Carmen; Dido and Cassandra in the Trojans; Marguerite in The Damnation of Faust; Charlotte in The Sorrows of Werther; Eboli, Don Carlos; name role, Orfeo; Adalgesa in Norma; Rosina in The Barber of Seville; Kundry in Parsifal; Gertrude in Hamlet, 1980. Concerts, 1960–70 (Conductors included Giulini, Bernstein, Solti, Mehta, Sargent). Verdi's Requiem; Monteverdi's Combattimento di Tancredi e Clorinda, Aix Festival, 1967; various works of Mahler; two tours of Israel (Solti); subseq. sang in Los Angeles (Mehta); then Berlioz: Death of Cleopatra, Royal Festival Hall, and L'enfance du Christ, London and Paris; Rossini's Petite Messe Solennelle, London and Huddersfield (with late Sir Malcolm Sargent); Handel's Messiah, England, Munich, Oporto, Lisbon; Berlioz' Romeo and Juliette, London, and Bergen Festival; Rossini's Stabat Mater, Festival d'Angers and London, 1971; Berlioz' Beatrice and Benedict, NY, and London; Emperor in 1st perf. Henze's We Come to the River, Covent Garden, 1976. Has sung Elgar's Dream of Gerontius all over England. Frequently makes recordings. Hon. RAM, 1972. *Recreations:* reading, gardening. *Address:* 2 Pound Cottage, St Mary Bourne, Andover, Hants SP11 6EQ. *T:* St Mary Bourne (01264) 738282.

VEEDER, Van Vechten; QC 1986; *b* 14 Dec. 1948; *s* of John Van Vechten Veeder and Helen Letham Townley; *m* 1st, 1970; one *s* one *d*; 2nd, 1991, Marie Lombardi. *Educ:* Ecole Rue de la Ferme, Neuilly, Paris; Clifton College, Bristol; Jesus College, Cambridge. Called to the Bar, Inner Temple, 1971. *Recreations:* sailing, travelling, reading. *Address:* Essex Court Chambers, 24 Lincoln's Inn Fields, WC2A 3ED. *T:* 0171–813 8000, *Fax:* 0171–813 8080.

VEIL, Simone Annie, Chevalier de l'Ordre national du Mérite; Magistrate; Minister of Social Affairs, France, 1993–95; *b* Nice, 13 July 1927; *d* of André Jacob and Yvonne (*née* Steinmetz); *m* 1946, Antoine Veil, Inspecteur des Finances, President, A. V. Consultants; three *s*. *Educ:* Lycée de Nice; Lic. en droit, dipl. de l'Institut d'Etudes Politiques, Paris; qualified as Magistrate, 1956. Deported to Auschwitz and Bergen-Belsen, March 1944–May 1945. Ministry of Justice, 1957–69; Technical Advr to Office of Minister of Justice, 1969; Gen.-Sec., Conseil Supérieur de la magistrature, 1970–74. Minister of Health, France, 1974–76; Minister of Health and Social Security, France, 1976–79. European Parliament: Member, 1979–93; Pres., 1979–82; Chm., Liberal and Democratic Reformist Gp, 1984–89. Monismanie Prize, 1978; Onassis Foundn Prize, Athens, 1980; Charlemagne Prize, Prix Louise Weiss, 1981; Louise Michel Prize, 1983; Jabotinsky Prize, 1983; Prize for Everyday Courage, 1984; Special Freedom Prize, Eleanor and Franklin Roosevelt Foundn, 1984; Fiera di Messina Prize, 1984; Living Legacy Award, San Diego, Univ. d'Acadie, 1987; Johanna Lowenherz Prize, Neuwied, 1987; Thomas Dehler Prize, Munich, 1988. D*hc*: Princeton, 1975; Institut Weizmann, 1976; Yale, Cambridge,

Edinburgh, Jerusalem, 1980; Georgetown, Urbino, 1981; Yeschiva, Sussex, 1982; Free Univ., Brussels, 1984; Brandeis, 1989. *Publication:* (with Prof. Launay and Dr Soulé) les Données psycho-sociologiques de l'Adoption, 1969. *Address:* 11 place Vauban, 75007 Paris, France.

VENABLES, (Harold) David (Spenser), CB 1993; Official Solicitor to the Supreme Court, 1980–93; *b* 14 Oct. 1932; *s* of late Cedric Venables and Gladys Venables (*née* Hall); *m* 1964, Teresa Grace, *d* of late J. C. Watts; one *d* one *s*. *Educ:* Denstone College. Admitted Solicitor, 1956. Pilot Officer, Royal Air Force, 1957–58. Legal Assistant, Official Solicitor's Office, 1960; Secretary, Lord Chancellor's Cttee on the Age of Majority, 1965–67; Asst Official Solicitor, 1977–80. *Publications:* A Guide to the Law Affecting Mental Patients, 1975; The Racing Fifteen-Hundreds: a history of voiturette racing 1931–40, 1984; contributor, Halsbury's Laws of England, 4th edn. *Recreations:* vintage cars, motoring and military history. *Address:* 11 Onslow Road, Hove, Sussex BN3 6TA. *T:* Brighton (01273) 502374.

VENABLES, Richard William Ogilvie; Member of Council and Board, Direct Mail Services Standards Board, since 1983; *b* 23 Feb. 1928; *s* of late Canon and Mrs E. M. Venables; *m* 1952, Ann Richards; three *s* two *d*. *Educ:* Marlborough Coll.; Christ Church, Oxford (BA, MA). Joined former Mather and Crowther Ltd, as trainee, 1952; Account Group Director, 1965; Board Member, 1966; Mem. Executive Cttee, 1972; Managing Director, 1974; joined Board of Ogilvy and Mather International, 1975; Chm., Ogilvy Benson and Mather Ltd, 1978–81; retired early, 1981, to pursue new career in the making of violins, violas, lutes, harpsichords. Chm., Apple and Pear Develt Council, 1980–83; Council and Bd Mem., Direct Mail Services Standards Bd, 1983–95. *Recreations:* fly fishing, hill walking, cabinet making, golf. *Address:* First Field, Combe Hay, Bath, Avon BA2 8RD. *T:* Bath (01225) 833694.

VENABLES, Robert; QC 1990; *b* 1 Oct. 1947; *s* of Walter Edwin Venables, MM, and Mildred Daisy Robson Venables. *Educ:* Merton Coll., Oxford (MA); London School of Economics (LLM). FTII. Called to Bar, Middle Temple, 1973; private practice as barrister, 1976–. Lecturer: Merton Coll., Oxford, 1972–75; UCL, 1973–75; Official Fellow and Tutor in Jurisprudence, St Edmund Hall, Oxford, and CUF Lectr, Oxford Univ., 1975–80; Fellow, St Edmund Hall, Oxford, 1992–. Treasurer, CRUSAID, 1991–; Dir, Yves Guihannec Foundn, 1992–. *Publications:* Inheritance Tax Planning, 1986, 2nd edn 1988; Preserving the Family Farm, 1987, 2nd edn 1989; Non-Resident Trusts, 1988, 5th edn 1993; Tax Planning and Fundraising for Charities, 1989, 2nd edn 1994; Tax Planning Through Trusts—Inheritance Tax, 1990; National Insurance Contributions Planning, 1990; Hold-Over Relief, 1990; The Company Car, 1990; Capital Gains Tax Planning for Non-UK Residents, 1991. *Recreation:* music making. *Address:* 24 Old Buildings, Lincoln's Inn, WC2A 3UJ. *T:* 0171–242 2744, *Fax:* 0171–831 8095. *Club:* Travellers'.

VENABLES, Robert Michael Cochrane; Charity Commissioner, since 1989; *b* 8 Feb. 1939; *s* of late Cdre Gilbert Henry Venables, DSO, OBE, RN and Muriel Joan Haes; *m* 1972, Hazel Lesley Gowing, BSc; two *s* two *d*. *Educ:* Portsmouth Grammar Sch. Admitted solicitor, 1962; in private practice, London, Petersfield and Portsmouth, 1962–70; Treasury Solicitor's Department: Legal Asst, 1970; Sen. Legal Asst, 1973; Asst Treasury Solicitor, 1980. Mem. Council, Law Soc., 1993–. Chm., Legal Sect., FDA, 1981–83 (Mem. Exec. Cttee, 1981–83, 1987–92). FRSA. *Recreations:* opera, theatre, collecting domestic anachronisms. *Address:* St Albans House, 57–60 Haymarket, SW1Y 4QX. *T:* 0171–210 4410, *Fax:* 0171–210 4604.

VENABLES, Terence Frederick; Coach, England football team, since 1994; *b* 6 Jan. 1943; *m* Yvette; two *d*. *Educ:* Dagenham. Played at football clubs: Chelsea, 1958–66 (Captain, 1962); Tottenham Hotspur, 1966–68 (winners FA Cup 1967); Queen's Park Rangers, 1968–73; represented England at all levels; Club Manager: Crystal Palace, 1976–80 (took club from 3rd Div. to top of 1st Div.); QPR, 1980–84 (won 2nd Div. title, 1980); Barcelona, 1984–87 (won Spanish championship, 1984); Tottenham Hotspur, 1987–93 (won FA Cup, 1991; Chief Exec., 1991–93). *Publications:* They Used to Play on Grass, 1971; (with Gordon Williams) TV detective series Hazell: Hazell plays Solomon, 1974; Hazell and the Three Card Trick, 1975; Hazell and the Menacing Jester, 1976; (with Neil Hanson) Terry Venables: the Autobiography, 1994. *Address:* Terence Venables Holdings Ltd, 213 Putney Bridge Road, SW15 2NY. *T:* 0181–874 5001.

VENABLES-LLEWELYN, Sir John (Michael) Dillwyn-, 4th Bt *cr* 1890; farmer, since 1975; *b* 12 Aug. 1938; *s* of Sir Charles Michael Dillwyn-Venables-Llewelyn, 3rd Bt, MVO, and of Lady Delia Mary Dillwyn-Venables-Llewelyn, *g d* of 1st Earl St Aldwyn; *S* father, 1976; *m* 1st, 1963, Nina (marr. diss. 1972) (*d* 1995), *d* of late Lt J. S. Hallam; two *d*; 2nd, 1975, Nina Gay Richardson Oliver; one *d* decd. *Recreation:* racing vintage cars. *Address:* Llysdinam, Newbridge-on-Wye, Llandrindod Wells, Powys LD1 6NB.

VENKATARAMAN, Ramaswamy; President of India, 1987–92 (Vice-President, 1984–87); *b* 4 Dec. 1910; *s* of Ramaswami Iyer; *m* 1938, Janaki; three *d*. *Educ:* Madras Univ. (MA, LLB). Formerly in practice as a lawyer, Madras High Court and Supreme Court; prominent trade union leader, also political and social worker. Mem., Provisional Parlt, 1950; Mem., Lok Sabha, 1952–57 and (for Madras S), 1977–84; Leader of the House, Madras Legislative Council, and Minister of Industries, 1957–67; Mem., Planning Commn, Madras, 1967–71. Minister of: Finance and Industry, 1980–82; Defence, 1982–84. Sec., Madras Provincial Bar Fedn, 1947–50. Chm., Nat. Research and Develt Corp. Leader, Indian delegation to Internat. Labour Organisation, 1958, and delegate, UN Gen. Assembly, 1953–61. *Address:* c/o Rashtrapati Bhavan, New Delhi 110004, India.

VENNER, Rt. Rev. Stephen Squires; *see* Middleton, Bishop Suffragan of.

VENNING, Philip Duncombe Riley, FSA; Secretary, Society for the Protection of Ancient Buildings, since 1984; *b* 24 March 1947; *s* of late Roger Venning and of Rosemary (*née* Mann); *m* 1987, Elizabeth Frances Ann, *d* of M. A. R. Powers; two *d*. *Educ:* Sherborne Sch.; Trinity Hall, Cambridge (MA). Times Educational Supplement, 1970–81 (Asst Editor, 1978–81); freelance journalist and writer, 1981–84. Sec., William Morris Craft Fellowship Cttee, 1986–. Mem., Conf. on Training in Architectural Conservation, 1988–. Mem. Council, Nat. Trust, 1992–; Trustee, Historic Churches Preservation Trust, 1995–. FSA 1989; FRSA 1990. *Publications:* contribs to books and other pubns on educn and on historic buildings. *Recreations:* exploring Britain, book collecting. *Address:* c/o SPAB, 37 Spital Square, E1 6DY.

VENNING, Robert William Dawe; Principal Establishment and Finance Officer, Cabinet Office, since 1993; *b* 25 July 1946; *s* of Tom William Dawe and Elsie Lillian Venning; *m* 1969, Jennifer Mei-Ling Jackson; one *s* one *d*. *Educ:* Midhurst Sch.; Univ. of Birmingham (BA Special Hons Philosophy 1968). Tutor in Philosophy, Univ. of Birmingham, 1968; Lectr in Logic and Scientific Method, Lanchester Polytechnic, 1969; Department of Health and Social Security: Admin. Trainee, 1971; Private Sec. to Minister for Disabled, 1974; Principal, 1975; Private Sec. to Minister for Health, 1981; Asst Sec., 1983; Under Sec., HA Personnel Div., DoH, 1990–93. Non-Exec. Dir, Compel plc, 1990–93. *Recreations:* playing classical and flamenco guitar; electronics and computing. *Address:* c/o Cabinet Office, 70 Whitehall, SW1A 2AS.

VENTRY, 8th Baron *cr* 1800 (Ire.); **Andrew Wesley Daubeny de Moleyns;** Bt 1797; Director: Burgie Lodge Farms Ltd, since 1970; C. & R. Briggs Commercials Ltd, since 1986; Glenscott Motor Controls Inc., since 1987 (Vice-President); *b* 28 May 1943; *s* of Hon. Francis Alexander Innys Eveleigh Ross de Moleyns (*d* 1964) (2nd *s* of 6th Baron) and of Joan (now Joan Springett), *e d* of Harold Wesley; assumed by deed poll, 1966, surname of Daubeny de Moleyns; *S* uncle, 1987; *m* 1st, 1963, Nelly Renée (marr. diss. 1979), *d* of Abel Chaumillon; one *s* two *d*; 2nd, 1983, Jill Rosemary, *d* of C. W. Oramon; one *d*. *Educ:* Edge Grove; Aldenham. Farmer, 1961–; in electronics, 1986–. *Recreations:* shooting, stalking, photography, sailing, ski-ing. *Heir: s* Hon. Francis Wesley Daubeny de Moleyns, *b* 1 May 1965.

VENTURI, Robert; architect; Principal, Venturi, Scott Brown and Associates, Inc., since 1989 (Venturi, Rauch and Scott Brown, 1980–89); *b* 25 June 1925; *s* of Robert Charles Venturi and Vanna Venturi (*née* Lanzetta); *m* 1967, Denise Scott Brown; one *s*. *Educ:* Princeton Univ. (AB 1947, MFA 1950). Designer, Oskar Stonorov, 1950, Eero Saarinen & Assoc., 1950–53; Rome Prize Fellow, Amer. Acad. in Rome, 1954–56; designer, Louis I Kahn, 1957; Principal: Venturi, Cope and Lippincott, 1958–61; Venturi and Short, 1961–64; Venturi and Rauch, 1964–80. Associate Prof., Univ. of Pennsylvania, 1957–65; Charlotte Shepherd Davenport Prof. of Architecture, Yale, 1966–70. Works include: Vanna Venturi House, 1961, Guild House, 1961, Franklin Court, 1972, Inst. for Sci. Inf. Corp. HQ, 1978 (all Philadelphia); Allen Meml Art Museum Addition (Oberlin, Ohio), 1973; Gordon Wu Hall (Princeton), 1980; Seattle Art Mus., 1984; Sainsbury Wing, Nat. Gall., London, 1986; Fisher and Bendheim Halls, Princeton Univ., 1986; Gordon and Virginia MacDonald Med. Res. Labs (with Payette Associates), UCLA, 1986; Charles P. Stevenson Jr Library, Bard Coll., 1989; Regl Govt Bldg, Toulouse, France, 1992; Kirifuri resort facilities, Nikko, Japan, 1992. Fellow: Amer. Inst. of Architects; Amer. Acad. in Rome; Accad. Nazionale di San Luca; Amer. Acad. of Arts and Letters; Amer. Acad. of Arts and Scis; Hon. FFRIAS; Hon. RIBA. Hon. DFA: Oberlin Coll., 1977; Yale, 1979; Univ. of Pennsylvania, 1980; Princeton Univ., 1983; Philadelphia Coll. of Art, 1985; Hon. LHD NJ Inst. of Technology, 1984. James Madison Medal, Princeton Univ., 1985; Thomas Jefferson Meml Foundn Medal, Univ. of Virginia, 1983; Pritzker Architecture Prize, Hyatt Foundn, 1991; US Nat. Medal of Arts, 1992; Benjamin Franklin Medal, RSA, 1993. *Publications:* A View from the Campidoglio: selected essays, 1953–84 (with Denise Scott Brown), 1984; Complexity and Contradiction in Architecture, 1966, 2nd edn 1977; Learning from Las Vegas (with Denise Scott Brown and Steven Izenour), 1972, 2nd edn 1977; articles in periodicals. *Recreation:* travel. *Address:* Venturi, Scott Brown and Associates, Inc., 4236 Main Street, Philadelphia, PA 19127, USA. *T:* (215) 4870400.

VENUGOPAL, Dr Sriramashetty, OBE 1992; Principal in General Practice, Aston, Birmingham, since 1967; *b* 14 May 1933; *s* of Satyanarayan and Manikyamma Sriramashetty; *m* 1960, Subhadra Venugopal; one *s* one *d*. *Educ:* Osmania Univ., Hyderabad, India (BSc, MB BS); Madras Univ. (DMRD). Medical posts, Osmania Hosp., State Med. Services, Hyderabad, Singareni Collieries, 1959–65; Registrar, Radiology, Selly Oak Hosp., Birmingham, 1965–66; Registrar, Chest Medicine, Springfield Hosp., Grimsby, 1966–67; Hosp. Practitioner, Psychiatry, All Saints Hosp., Birmingham, 1972–94. Member: Working Group, DHSS, 1984–; Local Med. Cttee, 1975–; Dist. Med. Cttee, 1978–; GMC, 1984–; West Birmingham HA, 1982– (Chm., sub-cttee on needs of ethnic minorities, 1982–85); Birmingham FPC, 1984–; Birmingham Community Liaison Adv. Cttee, 1985. Vice-Chm., Birmingham Div., BMA, 1986–87 (Chm., 1985–86). Mem., Local Review Cttee for Winson Green Prison, 1981–83. Founder Mem., Overseas Doctors' Assoc., 1975–81 (Dep. Treasurer, 1975–81; Nat. Vice-Chm., 1981–87; Inf. and Adv. Service, 1981–; Nat. Chm., 1987–93; Pres., 1993–); Founder Mem. and Chm., Link House Council, 1975–. Founder Mem., Osmania Grad. Med. Assoc. in UK, 1984–. Vice-Chm., Hyderabad Charitable Trust, 1985–. FRSocMed 1986; FRIPHH 1988; MRCGP 1990. *Publications:* contribs to learned jls on medico-political topics. *Recreations:* medical politics, music, gardening. *Address:* Aston Health Centre, 175 Trinity Road, Aston, Birmingham B6 6JA. *T:* 0121–328 3597; 24 Melville Road, Edgbaston, Birmingham B16 9JT. *T:* 0121–454 1725. *Club:* Aston Rotary (Pres., 1984–85).

VERCO, Sir Walter (John George), KCVO 1981 (CVO 1970; MVO 1952); OStJ 1954; Secretary of the Order of the Garter, 1974–88; Secretary to the Earl Marshal, since 1961; Surrey Herald of Arms Extraordinary, since 1980; *b* 18 January 1907; *s* of late John Walter Verco, Chelsea; *m* 1929, Ada Rose (*d* 1989), *d* of late Bertram Leonard Bennett, Lymington, Hants; one *s* one *d*. Served War, 1940–45, with RAFVR, Flight Lt. Secretary to Garter King of Arms, 1949–60; Rouge Croix Pursuivant of Arms, 1954–60; Chester Herald, 1960–71; Norroy and Ulster King of Arms, 1971–80. Hon. Genealogist to Royal Victorian Order, 1968–88; Inspector, RAF Badges, 1970–, RAAF Badges, 1971–; Adviser on Naval Heraldry, 1970–. *Address:* College of Arms, Queen Victoria Street, EC4V 4BT. *T:* 0171–248 6185; 8 Park Court, Linkfield Lane, Redhill, Surrey RH1 1QT. *T:* Redhill (01737) 771794.

VERCOE, Rt. Rev. Whakahuihui; *see* Aotearoa, Bishop of.

VERE-HODGE, Michael John Davy; QC 1993; a Recorder, since 1989; *b* 2 July 1946; *s* of Nicholas and Anne Vere-Hodge; *m* 1978, Jane Gilmour Semple; one *s* one *d*. *Educ:* Winchester Coll.; Grenoble Univ. Called to the Bar, Gray's Inn, 1970. *Recreations:* clay shooting, fishing. *Address:* 2 King's Bench Walk, Temple, EC4Y 7DE. *T:* 0171–353 1746.

VEREKER, family name of **Viscount Gort.**

VEREKER, John Michael Medlicott, CB 1992; Permanent Secretary, Overseas Development Administration, since 1993; *b* 9 Aug. 1944; *s* of late Comdr C. W. M. Vereker and M. H. Vereker (*née* Whatley); *m* 1971, Judith Diane, *d* of Hobart and Alice Rowen, Washington, DC; one *s* one *d*. *Educ:* Marlborough Coll.; Keele Univ. (BA Hons 1967). Asst Principal, ODM, 1967–69; World Bank, Washington, 1970–72; Principal, ODM, 1972; Private Sec. to successive Ministers of Overseas Develt, 1977–78; Asst Sec., 1978; Prime Minister's Office, 1980–83; Under Sec., 1983–88, and Principal Finance Officer, 1986–88, ODA, FCO; Dep. Sec., DES, then DFE, 1988–93. Chm., Students Loans Co. Ltd, 1989–91. Mem. Council, Inst. of Manpower Studies, 1989–92; Member Board: British Council, 1994–; IDS, 1994–; VSO, 1994–. *Address:* c/o Overseas Development Administration, 94 Victoria Street, SW1E 5JL.
See also P. W. M. Vereker.

VEREKER, Peter William Medlicott; HM Diplomatic Service; Ambassador and UK Permanent Representative to OECD, Paris, since 1995; *b* 13 Oct. 1939; *s* of late Comdr Charles William Medlicott Vereker and Marjorie Hughes Whatley; *m* 1967, Susan Elizabeth, *d* of Maj.-Gen. A. J. Dyball, CBE, MC; three *s*. *Educ:* Elstree Sch.; Marlborough Coll.; Trinity Coll., Cambridge (MA); Harvard Univ. (Henry Fellow, 1962). CUAS (RAFVR), 1958–61. Assistant d'Anglais, Paris, 1963; joined FO, 1963; Bangkok, 1964; Chiang Mai, 1967; FCO, 1968; Canberra, 1971; Head of Chancery, Athens, 1975; Asst Head, W European Dept, FCO, 1978; RCDS, 1982; Counsellor and Consul-Gen.,

Bangkok, 1983 (acted as Chargé d'Affaires, 1984, 1986); Dep. Perm. Rep., UK Mission at Geneva, 1987; Head, Arms Control and Disarmament Dept, FCO, 1991; Sen. Civilian Dir, RCDS, 1994. *Recreations:* writing, sport. *Address:* c/o Foreign and Commonwealth Office, SW1A 2AH.

See also J. M. M. Vereker.

VEREY, David John; Chief Executive, since 1990, Chairman, since 1992, Lazard Brothers; *b* 8 Dec. 1950; *s* of Michael John Verey, *qv*; *m* 1st, 1974, Luise Jaschke (marr. diss. 1990); two *s* one *d*; 2nd, 1990, Emma Katharine Broadhead (*née* Laidlaw). *Educ:* Eton College; Trinity College, Cambridge (MA). Lazard Brothers: joined 1972; Dir, 1983; Dep. Chief Exec., 1985. Trustee, Tate Gall., 1992–. *Recreations:* stalking, bridge, gardening, travel. *Address:* Lazard Brothers & Co., 21 Moorfields, EC2P 2HT. *T:* 0171–588 2721.

VEREY, Michael John, TD 1945; *b* 12 Oct. 1912; *yr s* of late Henry Edward and late Lucy Alice Verey; *m* 1947, Sylvia Mary, *widow* of Charles Bartlet and *d* of Lt-Col Denis Wilson and Mary Henrietta Wilson; two *s* one *d. Educ:* Eton; Trinity College, Cambridge (MA). Joined Helbert, Wagg & Co. Ltd, 1934. Served War of 1939–45, Warwickshire Yeomanry; BEF Palestine; campaigns in Iraq, Syria, Persia, Western Desert, Italy; Lt Col comdg, 1944. Chairman: J. Henry Schroder Wagg & Co. Ltd, 1972–73 (Dep. Chm., 1966–72); Schroders Ltd, 1973–77; Accepting Houses Cttee, 1974–77; Broadstone Investment Trust Ltd, 1962–83; Brixton Estate Ltd 1971–83; Trustees, Charities Official Investment Fund, 1974–83; American Energy Investments Ltd, 1981–83; Director: British Petroleum Co. Ltd, 1974–82; The Boots Co. (Vice-Chm., 1978–83); Commercial Union Assurance Co. Ltd (Vice-Chm., 1975–78; Dep. Chm., 1978–82); BI International, and other cos; Mem., Covent Garden Market Authority, 1961–66. High Sheriff of Berkshire, 1968. Pres., Warwickshire Yeomanry Regtl Assoc., 1976–86. *Recreations:* gardening, travel. *Address:* The Lodge, Little Bowden, Pangbourne, Berks RG8 8JR. *T:* Pangbourne (01734) 842210. *Club:* Boodle's.

See also D. J. Verey.

VERITY, Anthony Courtenay Froude, MA; Master of Dulwich College, since 1986; *b* 25 Feb. 1939; *s* of Arthur and Alice Kathleen Verity; *m* 1962, Patricia Ann Siddall; one *s* one *d. Educ:* Queen Elizabeth's Hosp., Bristol; Pembroke Coll., Cambridge (MA). Assistant Master: Dulwich Coll., 1962–65; Manchester Grammar Sch., 1965–69; Head of Classics, Bristol Grammar Sch., 1969–76; Headmaster, Leeds Grammar Sch., 1976–86. Chm., Schools' Arabic Project, 1988–. Editor, Greece and Rome, 1971–76. *Publications:* Latin as Literature, 1971; contribs to Jl of Arabic Lit. *Recreations:* music, fell-walking, squash. *Address:* Elm Lawn, Dulwich Common, SE21 7EW. *Club:* Academy.

VERMES, Prof. Geza, FBA 1985; Professor of Jewish Studies, 1989–91, now Professor Emeritus, and Fellow of Wolfson College, 1965–91, now Fellow Emeritus, Oxford University; Director, Oxford Forum for Qumran Research, Oxford Centre for Hebrew and Jewish Studies (formerly for Postgraduate Hebrew Studies), since 1991; *b* 22 June 1924; *s* of late Ernö Vermes and Terézia Riesz; *m* 1958, Mrs Pamela Curle (*née* Hobson) (*d* 1993). *Educ:* Univ. of Budapest; Coll. St Albert de Louvain, Louvain Univ. Licencié en Histoire et Philologie Orientales (avec la plus grande distinction), 1952; DTheol 1953; MA Oxon 1965, DLitt 1988. Asst Editor, Cahiers Sioniens, Paris, 1953–55; research worker, CNRS, Paris, 1955–57; Lectr, later Sen. Lectr in Divinity, Newcastle Univ., 1957–65; Reader in Jewish Studies, Oxford Univ., 1965–89; Chm. of Curators of Oriental Inst., Oxford, 1971–74; Chm. Bd of Faculty of Oriental Studies, Oxford, 1978–80; Emeritus Governor, Oxford Centre for Postgrad. Hebrew Studies (Governor, 1972–92). Vis. Prof. in Religious Studies, Brown Univ., 1971; Rosenstiel Res. Fellow, Univ. of Notre Dame, 1972; Margaret Harris Lectr in Religion, Dundee Univ., 1977; Riddell Meml Lectr, Newcastle Univ., 1981; Dist. Vis. Prof. in Judeo-Christian Studies, Tulane Univ., 1982; Igor Kaplan Vis. Lectr, Toronto Sch. of Theology, 1985, 1987; Vis. Prof. of History, Univ. of Calif, San Diego, 1995. Pres., British Assoc. for Jewish Studies, 1975, 1988; Pres., European Assoc. for Jewish Studies, 1981–84. Editor, Jl of Jewish Studies, 1971–. Hon. DD: Edinburgh, 1989; Durham, 1990; Hon. DLitt Sheffield, 1994. *Publications:* Les manuscrits du désert de Juda, 1953; Discovery in the Judean Desert, 1956; Scripture and Tradition in Judaism, 1961; The Dead Sea Scrolls in English, 1962, 4th edn 1995 (trans. Portuguese); Jesus the Jew, 1973 (trans. Spanish, French, Japanese, Italian, Portuguese, German, Hungarian); Post-Biblical Jewish Studies, 1975; (with Pamela Vermes) The Dead Sea Scrolls: Qumran in perspective, 1977 (trans. Spanish), 3rd edn 1994; The Gospel of Jesus the Jew, 1981; (ed jtly) Essays in Honour of Y. Yadin, 1982; Jesus and the World of Judaism, 1983; (ed and rev., with F. G. B. Millar and M. D. Goodman) E. Schürer, The History of the Jewish People in the Age of Jesus Christ I–III, 1973–87 (trans. Spanish, Italian); (with M. D. Goodman) The Essenes according to the Classical Sources, 1989; The Religion of Jesus the Jew, 1993; (ed) Pamela Vermes, The Riddle of the Sparks, 1993. *Recreations:* watching wild life, correcting proofs. *Address:* Oriental Institute, Pusey Lane, Oxford OX1 2LE; West Wood Cottage, Foxcombe Lane, Boars Hill, Oxford OX1 5DH. *T:* Oxford (01865) 735384, *Fax:* (01865) 735034.

VERMEULE, Prof. Emily Dickinson Townsend, FSA; Zemurray-Stone-Radcliffe Professor, Harvard University, since 1970; Fellow for Research, Museum of Fine Arts, Boston, since 1963; *b* 11 Aug. 1928; *d* of Clinton Blake Townsend and Eleanor Mary Meneely; *m* 1957, Cornelius Clarkson Vermeule III; one *s* one *d. Educ:* The Brearley Sch.; Bryn Mawr Coll. (BA, PhD); Radcliffe Coll. (MA). FSA 1975. Instructor in Greek: Bryn Mawr, 1956–57; Wellesley Coll., 1957–58; Asst Prof. of Classics, 1958–61, Associate Prof. of Classics, 1961–64, Boston Univ.; Prof. of Greek and Fine Arts, Wellesley, 1965–70. James Loeb Vis. Prof. of Classical Philology, Harvard Univ., 1969; Sather Prof. of Classical Literature, Univ. of California, Berkeley, 1975; Geddes-Harrower Prof. of Greek Art and Archaeology, Univ. of Aberdeen, 1980–81; Bernhard Vis. Prof., Williams Coll., 1986. Corresp. Member: German Archaeological Inst., 1964; British Academy, 1982. Member: Archaeological Inst. of America, 1950; Soc. for Preservation of Hellenic Studies, 1954; Amer. Philosophical Soc., 1971; Amer. Acad. of Arts and Scis, 1970; Bd of Scholars, Library of Congress, 1982–87; Smithsonian Council, 1983–90. National Endowment for the Humanities Jefferson Lectr, 1981. Hon. degrees: DLitt: Douglass Coll., Rutgers, 1968; Smith Coll., 1971; Wheaton Coll., 1973; Tufts, 1980; Univ. of Pittsburgh, 1983; Bates Coll., 1983; DFA, Univ. of Massachusetts at Amherst, 1970; LLD: Regis Coll., 1970; LHD: Trinity Coll., Hartford, Conn., 1974; Emmanuel Coll., Boston, 1980; Princeton, 1989; Bard Coll., 1994. Gold Medal, Radcliffe Coll., 1968; Charles Goodwin Award of Merit, American Philological Assoc., 1980. *Publications:* Euripides' Electra, 1959; Greece in the Bronze Age, 1964, 7th edn 1980; The Trojan War in Greek Art, 1964; Götterkult, Archaeologia Homerica V, 1974; The Mound of Darkness, 1974; The Art of the Shaft Graves, 1975; Death in Early Greek Art and Poetry, 1979; (with V. Karageorghis) Mycenaean Pictorial Vase-Painting, 1982; Toumba tou Skourou, A Bronze Age Potters' Quarter on Morphou Bay in Cyprus, 1990; contribs to Jl of Hellenic Studies, American Jl of Archaeology, Jahrbuch des d.Arch. Insts, Classical Philology, etc. *Recreations:* dogs, gardening. *Address:* 47 Coolidge Hill Road, Cambridge, MA 02138, USA. *T:* (617) 8641879. *Club:* Cosmopolitan (New York City).

VERNEY, family name of **Baron Willoughby de Broke.**

VERNEY, (Sir) (John) Sebastian, (3rd Bt *cr* 1946, of Eaton Square, City of Westminster; *S* father, 1993, but does not use the title). *Heir: cousin* Christopher Ralph Evelyn Verney [*b* 4 Oct. 1948; *m* 1976, Madeliene Lindberg].

VERNEY, Sir Lawrence (John), Kt 1993; TD 1955; DL; **His Honour Judge Verney;** Recorder of London, since 1990; *b* 19 July 1924; *y s* of Sir Harry Verney, 4th Bt, DSO; *m* 1972, Zoë Auriel, *d* of Lt-Col P. G. Goodeve-Docker. *Educ:* Harrow; Oriel Coll., Oxford. Called to Bar, Inner Temple, 1952, Bencher, 1990. Dep. Chm., Bucks QS, 1962–71; Dep. Chm., Middlesex Sessions, then a Circuit Judge, 1971–90. Editor, Harrow School Register, 1948–; Governor, Harrow Sch., 1972–87. Master, Co. of Pattenmakers, 1988. DL Bucks 1967. OStJ 1992. *Address:* Central Criminal Court, EC4M 7EH.

See also Sir R. B. Verney, Bt, Rt Rev. S. E. Verney.

VERNEY, Sir Ralph (Bruce), 5th Bt *cr* 1818; KBE 1974; JP; Landowner; Vice Lord-Lieutenant (formerly Vice-Lieutenant) of Buckinghamshire, 1965–84; *b* 18 Jan. 1915; *e s* of Sir Harry Calvert Williams Verney, 4th Bt, DSO, and Lady Rachel Bruce (*d* 1964), *d* of 9th Earl of Elgin; *S* father, 1974; *m* 1948, Mary Vestey; one *s* three *d. Educ:* Canford; Balliol Coll., Oxford. 2nd Lieut Bucks Yeomanry, 1940; Major, Berks Yeomanry, 1945 and Bucks Yeomanry, 1946. Pres., Country Landowners' Assoc., 1961–63; Vice-President for Great Britain, Confédération Européenne de L'Agriculture, 1965–71, Counsellor, 1971–; Chairman, Forestry Commn Cttee for England, 1967–80; Member: Forestry Commn, 1968–80; Milton Keynes New Town Corporation, 1967–74; BBC Adv. Cttee on Agriculture, 1970–78; Royal Commn on Environmental Pollution, 1973–79; Chm., Nature Conservancy Council, 1980–83 (Mem., 1966–71); Chm., Sec. of State for the Environment's Adv. Cttee on Aggregates for Construction Industry, 1972–77. Trustee: Radcliffe Trust; Ernest Cook Trust; Chequers Trust; Sch. of Water Sciences, Cranfield, 1982–87. Member, Council: Buckingham Univ., 1983–87; Royal Soc. of Arts, 1983–87 (FRSA 1972). Buckinghamshire County Council: Member, 1951; Chairman, Finance Cttee, 1957; Planning Cttee, 1967; CA 1961; JP Bucks, 1954; High Sheriff of Buckinghamshire, 1957–58; DL Bucks, 1960; High Steward of Buckingham, 1966. Prime Warden, Worshipful Co. of Dyers, 1969–70. Hon. Fellow: RIBA, 1977; Green Coll., Oxford, 1980. DUniv Buckingham, 1991. Chevalier de Tastevin, Clos Vougeot, 1978. *Recreations:* trees, wine. *Heir: s* Edmund Ralph Verney [*b* 28 June 1950; *m* 1982, Daphne Fausset-Farquhar; one *s* one *d*]. *Address:* Ballams, Middle Claydon, Buckingham MK18 2ET. *T:* Aylesbury (01296) 730297; Plas Rhôscolyn, Holyhead LL65 2NZ. *T:* Trearddur Bay (01407) 860288. *Club:* Cavalry and Guards.

See also Sir L. J. Verney, Rt Rev. S. E. Verney.

VERNEY, Sir Sebastian; *see* Verney, Sir J. S.

VERNEY, Rt. Rev. Stephen Edmund, MBE 1945; Assistant Bishop, diocese of Oxford, since 1991; *b* 17 April 1919; 2nd *s* of late Sir Harry Verney, 4th Bt, DSO and Lady Rachel Verney (*née* Bruce); *m* 1st, 1947, Priscilla Avice Sophie Schwerdt (*d* 1974); one *s* three *d*; 2nd, 1981, Sandra Ann Bailey; (one *s* decd). *Educ:* Harrow School; Balliol College, Oxford (MA). Curate of Gedling, Nottingham, 1950; Priest-in-charge and then first Vicar, St Francis, Clifton, Nottingham, 1952; Vicar of Leamington Hastings and Diocesan Missioner, Dio. Coventry, 1958; Canon Residentiary, Coventry Cathedral, 1964; Canon of Windsor, 1970; Bishop Suffragan of Repton, 1977–85. *Publications:* Fire in Coventry, 1964; People and Cities, 1969; Into the New Age, 1976; Water into Wine, 1985; The Dance of Love, 1989. *Recreations:* conversation and aloneness; music, gardening, travel. *Address:* Charity School House, Church Road, Blewbury, Oxon OX11 9PY. *Club:* English-Speaking Union.

See also Sir L. J. Verney, Sir R. B. Verney, Bt.

VERNIER-PALLIEZ, Bernard Maurice Alexandre; Commandeur de la Légion d'Honneur; Croix de Guerre; Médaille de la Résistance; Ambassadeur de France, 1984; *b* 2 March 1918; *s* of Maurice Vernier and Marie-Thérèse Palliez; *m* 1952, Denise Silet-Pathe; one *s* three *d. Educ:* Ecole des Hautes Etudes Commerciales; Ecole Libre des Sciences Politiques. Licencié en Droit. Joined Régie Nationale des Usines, Renault, 1945 (dealing with personnel and trade unions); Sécretaire Général, RNUR, 1948–67; Directeur Général Adjoint, RNUR, 1967–71; Président Directeur Général, SAVIEM, 1967–74; Délégué Général aux Vehicules Industriels, Cars et Bus à la RNUR, Président du Directoire de Berliet, and Vice-Président du Conseil de Surveillance de SAVIEM, Jan.-Dec. 1975; Président Directeur Général, RNUR, Dec. 1975–1981; Ambassador to Washington, 1982–84. Dir, Public Affairs for Europe, International Distillers and Vintners, 1987–; Pres. Bd, Bureau d'Information et de prévisions économiques, 1989–; Member: American International Gp Adv. Bd, 1985–; Tenneco European Adv. Council, 1985–. *Address:* 25 Grande Rue, 78170 La Celle St-Cloud, France. *T:* (1) 39693011.

VERNON, family name of **Barons Lyveden** and **Vernon.**

VERNON, 10th Baron, *cr* 1762; **John Lawrance Vernon;** *b* 1 Feb. 1923; *s* of 9th Baron, and Violet (*d* 1978), *d* of Colonel Clay; *S* father, 1963; *m* 1st, 1955, Sheila Jean (marr. diss. 1982), *d* of W. Marshall Clark, Johannesburg; one *d* (and one *d* decd); 2nd, 1982, Sally, *d* of Robin Stratford, QC. *Educ:* Eton; Magdalen Coll., Oxford. Served in Scots Guards, 1942–46, retiring with rank of Captain. Called to Bar, Lincoln's Inn, 1949. Served in various Government Departments, 1950–61; attached to Colonial Office (for service in Kenya), 1957–58. Chm., Population Concern, 1984–89. JP Derbyshire, 1965–77. *Heir: kinsman* Col William Ronald Denis Vernon-Harcourt, OBE [*b* 4 May 1909; *m* 1937, Nancy Everil, *d* of Lt-Col Bertram Henry Leatham, DSO; one *s* one *d*]. *Address:* Sudbury House, Sudbury, Ashbourne, Derbyshire DE6 5HT. *Club:* Boodle's.

VERNON, David Bowater; Under Secretary, Inland Revenue, 1975–84; *b* 14 Nov. 1926; *s* of Lt-Col Herbert Bowater Vernon, MC, and Ivy Margaret Vernon; *m* 1954, Anne de Montmorency Fleming, *d* of late John and Margaret Fleming; three *s* three *d. Educ:* Marlborough Coll.; Oriel Coll., Oxford (MA). RA, 1945–48 (Lieut). Inland Revenue, 1951–84. *Recreation:* gardening. *Address:* The Oast, Gedges Farm, Matfield, Tonbridge, Kent TN12 7EJ. *T:* Brenchley (01892) 722400.

VERNON, Sir James, AC 1980; Kt 1965; CBE 1962 (OBE 1960); Director, O'Connell Street Associates Pty Ltd, since 1976; *b* 13 June 1910; *s* of Donald Vernon, Tamworth, New South Wales; *m* 1935, Mavis, *d* of C. Lonsdale Smith; two *d. Educ:* Sydney Univ. (BSc); University College, London (PhD). CSR Ltd: Chief Chemist, 1938–51; Senior Exec. Officer, 1951–56; Asst General Manager, 1956–57; Gen. Manager, 1958–72; Dir, 1958–82; Chm., 1978–80. Chairman: Commonwealth Cttee of Economic Enquiry, 1963–65; Australian Post Office Commn of Inquiry, 1973; Internat. Pres., Pacific Basin Econ. Council, 1980–82. FRACI; FAIM; FTS. Hon. DSc: Sydney, 1965; Newcastle, 1969. Leighton Medal, Royal Australian Chemical Inst., 1965; John Storey Medal, Aust. Inst. of Management, 1971. Order of Sacred Treasure, 1st cl. (Japan), 1983. *Address:* 27 Manning Road, Double Bay, NSW 2028, Australia. *Clubs:* Australian, Union (Sydney).

VERNON, James William, CMG 1964; retired; *b* 19 Nov. 1915; *s* of late John Alfred Vernon; *m* 1941, Betty Désirée, *d* of Gordon E. Nathan; one *s* one *d. Educ:* Wallasey Grammar Sch.; Emmanuel Coll., Cambridge (Scholar). BA 1937 (Senior Wrangler); MA 1940. Entered Civil Service, Ministry of Food, 1939; Flt Lieut, RAF, 1943; Wing Comdr (despatches), 1945; Principal Scientific Officer, Ministry of Works, 1945; Assistant Secretary, Colonial Office, 1954–64; Economic Adviser, British High Commission, Lusaka, 1966; Asst Under-Sec. of State, DEA, 1966–69; Under-Sec., Min. of Housing and Local Govt, later DoE, 1969–72. Called to Bar, Inner Temple, 1975. Queen's Commendation for Brave Conduct, 1955. *Recreations:* gardening, computer science, chaos. *Address:* 20 Grove Hill, Topsham, Devon EX3 0EG.

VERNON, Kenneth Robert, CBE 1978; Deputy Chairman and Chief Executive, North of Scotland Hydro-Electric Board, 1973–88; *b* 15 March 1923; *s* of late Cecil W. Vernon and Jessie McGaw, Dumfries; *m* 1946, Pamela Hands, Harrow; one *s* three *d* (and one *d* decd). *Educ:* Dumfries Academy; Glasgow University. BSc, FEng, FIEE, FIMechE. BTH Co., Edinburgh Corp., British Electricity Authority, 1948–55; South of Scotland Electricity Bd, 1955–56; North of Scotland Hydro-Electric Bd, 1956: Chief Electrical and Mech. Engr, 1964; Gen. Man., 1966; Bd Mem., 1970. Dir, British Electricity International Ltd, 1976–88; Mem. Bd, Northern Ireland Electricity Service, 1979–85. *Publications:* various papers to technical instns. *Recreations:* fishing, gardening. *Address:* 10 Keith Crescent, Edinburgh EH4 3NH. *T:* 0131–332 4610.

VERNON, Sir Michael; *see* Vernon, Sir William M.

VERNON, Sir Nigel (John Douglas), 4th Bt, *cr* 1914; Director, Bain Hogg Ltd UK Division; *b* 2 May 1924; *s* of Sir (William) Norman Vernon, 3rd Bt, and Janet Lady Vernon (*d* 1973); *S* father, 1967; *m* 1947, Margaret Ellen (*née* Dobell); one *s* one *d* (and one *s* decd). *Educ:* Charterhouse. Royal Naval Volunteer Reserve (Lieutenant), 1942–45. Spillers Ltd, 1945–65; Director: Castle Brick Co Ltd, 1965–71; Deeside Merchants Ltd, 1971–74; Travel Finance Ltd, 1971–87. *Recreations:* golf, shooting, gardening. *Heir: s* James William Vernon, FCA [*b* 2 April 1949; *m* 1981, Davinia, *er d* of Christopher David Howard, Ryton, Shrewsbury; two *s* one *d*]. *Address:* Top-y-Fron Hall, Kelsterton, near Flint, N Wales CH6 5TF. *T:* Deeside (01244) 830010. *Clubs:* Naval, Army and Navy.

VERNON, Sir (William) Michael, Kt 1995; Chairman, Royal National Lifeboat Institution, since 1989 (Deputy Chairman, 1980–89, and Vice-President, since 1975); *b* 17 April 1926; *o* surv. *s* of late Sir Wilfred Vernon; *m* 1st, 1952, Rosheen O'Meara; one *s*; 2nd, 1977, Mrs Jane Colston (*née* Kilham-Roberts). *Educ:* Marlborough Coll.; Trinity Coll., Cambridge. MA 1948. Lieut, Royal Marines, 1944–46. Joined Spillers Ltd, 1948: Dir 1960; Jt Man. Dir 1962; Chm. and Chief Exec., 1968–80; Chm., Granville Meat Co. Ltd, 1981–94. Director: EMI Ltd, 1973–80; Strong & Fisher (Hldgs) plc, 1980–90; Chm., Famous Names Ltd, 1981–85. Pres., Nat. Assoc. of British and Irish Millers, 1965; Vice-Chm., Millers' Mutual Assoc., 1968–80; Pres., British Food Export Council, 1977–80. CIMgt. Bronze Medal, RHS, 1956. *Recreations:* sailing, shooting, ski-ing. *Address:* Fyfield Manor, Andover, Hants SP11 8EN. *Clubs:* Royal Ocean Racing (Cdre 1964–68); Royal Yacht Squadron.

VERULAM, 7th Earl of, *cr* 1815; **John Duncan Grimston;** Bt 1629; Baron Forrester (Scot.), 1633; Baron Dunboyne and Viscount Grimston (Ire.), 1719; Baron Verulam (Gt. Brit.), 1790; Viscount Grimston (UK), 1815; *b* 21 April 1951; *s* of 6th Earl of Verulam and Marjorie Ray (*d* 1994), *d* of late Walter Atholl Duncan; *S* father, 1973; *m* 1976, Dione Angela, *e d* of Jeremy Smith, *qv*; three *s* one *d*. *Educ:* Eton; Christ Church, Oxford (MA 1976). Dir, Baring Brothers Ltd, 1987–. *Heir: s* Viscount Grimston, *qv*. *Address:* Gorhambury, St Albans, Herts AL3 6AH. *T:* St Albans (01727) 855000. *Clubs:* White's, Beefsteak.

VESEY, family name of **Viscount de Vesci.**

VESEY, Sir Henry; *see* Vesey, Sir N. H. P.

VESEY, Sir (Nathaniel) Henry (Peniston), Kt 1965; CBE 1953; Chairman, H. A. & E. Smith Ltd, since 1939; Chairman, Bank of N. T. Butterfield & Son Ltd, 1970–86; Member of House of Assembly, Bermuda, 1938–72; *b* 1 June 1901; *s* of late Hon. Nathaniel Vesey, Devonshire, Bermuda; *m* 1920, Louise Marie, *d* of late Captain J. A. Stubbs, Shelly Bay, Bermuda; two *s*. *Educ:* Saltus Grammar Sch. Chairman: Food and Supplies Control Board, 1941–42; Board of Trade, 1943; Finance Cttee of House of Assembly, 1943–44; Bermuda Trade Development Board, 1945–56, 1960–69; Board of Civil Aviation, 1957–59; Board of Agriculture, 1957–59. MEC, 1948–57, Mem. Executive Council for Tourism and Trade, 1968–69. *Recreations:* fishing, golf. *Address:* Windward, Shelly Bay, Bermuda FL BX. *T:* 930186. *Clubs:* Naval and Military; Royal Bermuda Yacht, Mid Ocean, Coral Beach (Bermuda).

VESSEY, Prof. Martin Paterson, CBE 1994; FRS 1991; Professor of Social and Community Medicine, University of Oxford, since 1974; Fellow of St Cross College, Oxford, since 1973; *b* 22 July 1936; *s* of Sidney J. Vessey and Catherine P. Vessey (*née* Thomson); *m* 1959, Anne Platt; two *s* one *d*. *Educ:* University College Sch., Hampstead; University Coll. London (Fellow, 1992); University Coll. Hosp. Med. Sch., London. MB, BS London 1959; MD London 1971; FFCM RCP 1972; MA Oxon 1974; MRCPE 1978; FRCPE 1979; FRCGP 1983; FRCP 1987; FRCOG 1989. Scientific Officer, Dept of Statistics, Rothamsted Exper. Stn, 1960–65; House Surg. and House Phys., Barnet Gen. Hosp., 1965–66; Mem. Sci. Staff, MRC Statistical Research Unit, 1966–69; Lectr in Epidemiology, Univ. of Oxford, 1969–74. Chm., Adv. Cttee on Breast Cancer Screening, DHSS, subseq. Dept of Health, 1987–; Member: Cttee on Safety of Medicines, 1980–92; Royal Commn on Environmental Pollution, 1984–89. *Publications:* many sci. articles in learned jls, notably on med. aspects of fertility control, safety of drugs, and epidemiology of cancer. *Recreations:* motoring, fine arts, conservation. *Address:* 8 Warnborough Road, Oxford OX2 6HZ. *T:* Oxford (01865) 52698.

VEST, Prof. Charles Marstiller, PhD; President, Massachusetts Institute of Technology, since 1990; *b* 9 Sept. 1941; *m* 1963, Rebecca McCue; one *s* one *d*. *Educ:* West Virginia Univ.; Univ. of Michigan (MSc 1964; PhD 1967). Asst Prof., then Associate Prof., 1968–77, Prof. of Mechl Engrg, 1977–90, Univ. of Michigan. *Publication:* Holographic Interferometry, 1979. *Address:* Office of the President, Massachusetts Institute of Technology, Cambridge, MA 02139, USA.

VESTEY, family name of **Baron Vestey.**

VESTEY, 3rd Baron, *cr* 1922, of Kingswood; **Samuel George Armstrong Vestey;** Bt, *cr* 1913; DL; *b* 19 March 1941; *s* of late Captain the Hon. William Howarth Vestey (killed in action in Italy, 1944; *o s* of 2nd Baron Vestey and Frances Sarah Howarth) and of Pamela Helen Fullerton, *d* of George Nesbitt Armstrong; *S* grandfather, 1954; *m* 1st, 1970, Kathryn Mary (marr. diss. 1981), *er d* of John Eccles, Moor Park, Herts; two *d*; 2nd, 1981, Celia Elizabeth, *d* of late Major Guy Knight, MC, Lockinge Manor, Wantage, Oxon; two *s* one *d*. *Educ:* Eton. Lieut, Scots Guards. Chm., Vestey Group Ltd. President: London Meat Trade and Drovers Benevolent Assoc., 1973; Inst. of Meat, 1978–83; Chm., Meat Training Council, 1991–95. President: Three Counties Agricl Soc., 1978; Royal Bath and W of England Soc., 1994; BHS, 1994–. Pres., Glos Assoc. of Boys' Clubs, 1979–. Liveryman, Butchers' Co. DL Glos, 1982. GCStJ 1987 (Chancellor of the Order, 1988–91, Lord Prior, 1991–). *Recreations:* racing, shooting. *Heir: s* Hon. William Guy Vestey, Page of Honour to the Queen, *b* 27 Aug. 1983. *Address:* Stowell Park, Northleach, Glos GL54 3LE. *Clubs:* White's; Jockey (Newmarket); Melbourne (Melbourne).

VESTEY, Edmund Hoyle, DL; Chairman: Blue Star Line, since 1971; Director, Vestey Group Ltd, since 1993; *b* 1932; *o s* of late Ronald Arthur Vestey and Florence Ellen McLean, *e d* of Col T. G. Luis, VD; *m* 1960, Anne Moubray, *yr d* of Gen. Sir Geoffry Scoones, KCB, KBE, CSI, DSO, MC; four *s*. *Educ:* Eton. 2nd Lieut Queen's Bays, 1951; Lieut, City of London Yeomanry. Chm., Associated Container Transportation (Australia), 1979–82, 1985–88. Pres., Gen. Council of British Shipping, later Chamber of Shipping, 1981–82, 1992–94. FRSA; FCIT 1982. Joint Master, Thurlow Foxhounds; Chm., Masters of Foxhounds Assoc., 1992–. President: Essex County Scout Council, 1979–87; E of England Agricl Soc., 1995–. High Sheriff, Essex, 1977; DL Essex, 1978; DL Suffolk, 1991. *Address:* Little Thurlow Hall, Haverhill, Suffolk CB9 7LQ; Iolaire Lodge, Lochinver, Sutherland IV27 4LU; Sunnyside Farmhouse, Hawick, Roxburghshire TD9 9SS. *Clubs:* Cavalry and Guards, Carlton.

VESTEY, Sir (John) Derek, 2nd Bt, *cr* 1921; *b* 4 June 1914; *s* of John Joseph Vestey (*d* 1932) and Dorothy Mary (*d* 1918), *d* of John Henry Beaver, Gawthorpe Hall, Bingley, Yorkshire; *g s* of Sir Edmund Vestey, 1st Bt; *S* grandfather 1953; *m* 1938, Phyllis Irene, *o d* of H. Brewer, Banstead, Surrey; one *s* one *d*. *Educ:* Leys Sch., Cambridge. Served War of 1939–45: Flt-Lieut, RAFVR, 1940–45. *Heir: s* Paul Edmund Vestey [*b* 15 Feb. 1944; *m* 1971, Victoria Anne Scudamore, *d* of John Salter, Tiverton, Devon; three *d*. *Educ:* Radley]. *Address:* Park Penthouse, 355 Kings Road, Chelsea, SW3 5ES. *T:* 0171–352 5940. *Clubs:* MCC, Royal Automobile.

VIAL, Sir Kenneth Harold, Kt 1978; CBE 1969; chartered accountant; retired; *b* 11 Aug. 1912; *s* of G. O. Vial, Melbourne; *m* 1937, Adele, *d* of R. G. R. Ball; one *s* two *d*. *Educ:* Scotch Coll., Melbourne. Served RAAF, 1941–46 (Flight Lieut). Partner, Arthur Andersen & Co. (formerly Fuller King & Co.), 1946–69; Chairman: Yarra Falls Ltd, 1969–74; Rocke Tompsitt & Co. Ltd, 1975–79; Director: Michaelis Bayley Ltd, 1969–81 (Chm., 1975–81); Mono Pumps (Aust.) Pty Ltd, 1969–81; F. H. Faulding & Co. Ltd, 1978–84; Hortico Ltd, 1981–84 (Chm., 1981–84). Member: Aust. Nat. Airlines Commn, 1956–79 (Chm., 1975–79); Aviation Industry Adv. Council, 1978–79; Council, Aust. Services Canteens Organisation, 1959–76 (Chm., Bd of Management, 1971–76); Council, La Trobe Univ., 1966–74 (Dep. Chancellor, 1970–72); Melbourne Underground Rail Loop Authority, 1971–81. *Address:* 1/70 Madeley Street, Ocean Grove, Vic 3226, Australia. *Clubs:* Athenæum, Naval and Military (Melbourne).

VICARY, Rev. Douglas Reginald; Canon Residentiary and Precentor of Wells Cathedral, 1975–88; *b* 24 Sept. 1916; *e s* of R. W. Vicary, Walthamstow; *m* 1947, Ruth, *y d* of late F. J. L. Hickinbotham, JP, and of Mrs Hickinbotham, Edgbaston; two *s* two *d*. *Educ:* Sir George Monoux Grammar Sch., Walthamstow; Trinity Coll., Oxford (Open Scholar), Wycliffe Hall, Oxford. 1st Class Nat. Sci. 1939; BSc 1939, MA 1942; Diploma in Theology with distinction, 1940; deacon, 1940; priest, 1941. Curate of St Peter and St Paul, Courteenhall, and Asst Chaplain and House Master, St Lawrence Coll., Ramsgate, while evacuated at Courteenhall, Northampton, 1940–44; Chaplain, Hertford Coll., Oxford, 1945–48; Tutor at Wycliffe Hall, 1945–47, Chaplain 1947–48; Dir of Religious Education, Rochester Diocese, 1948–57; Sec., CACTM Exams Cttee and GOE, 1952–57; Dir, Post-Ordination Training, 1952–57, Headmaster of King's School, Rochester, 1957–75; Chaplain to HM the Queen, 1977–86. Minor Canon, Rochester Cathedral, 1949–52; Canon Residentiary and Precentor, 1952–57; Hon. Canon, 1957–75. Exam. Chaplain to Bishop of Rochester, 1950–88, to Bishop of Bath and Wells, 1975–87. Mem. Court, Kent Univ., 1965–75. FRSA 1970. *Publication:* contrib. Canterbury Chapters, 1976. *Recreations:* music, architecture, hill-walking, reading. *Address:* 8 Tor Street, Wells, Somerset BA5 2US. *T:* Wells (01749) 679137.

VICK, Arnold Oughtred Russell; QC 1980; **His Honour Judge Russell Vick,** a Circuit Judge, since 1982; a Designated Family Judge, since 1991; *b* 14 Sept. 1933; *yr s* of late His Honour Judge Sir Godfrey Russell Vick, QC and late Lady Russell Vick, JP, *d* of J. A. Compston, KC; *m* 1959, Zinnia Mary, *e d* of Thomas Brown Yates, Godalming; two *s* one *d*. *Educ:* The Leys Sch., Cambridge; Jesus Coll., Cambridge (MA). Pilot, RAF, 1952–54. Called to Bar, Inner Temple, 1958; Mem. Gen. Council of the Bar, 1964–68; Prosecuting Counsel to the Post Office, 1964–69; Dep. Recorder, Rochester City QS, 1971; a Recorder of the Crown Court, 1972–82; Principal Judge for Civil Matters in Kent, 1990–. Mem., Lord Chancellor's County Court Rules Cttee, 1972–80; Recorder, SE Circuit Bar Mess, 1978–80. Gov., New Beacon Sch., Sevenoaks, 1982–. Master, Curriers' Co., 1976–77. *Publication:* A Hundred Years of Golf at Wildernesse, 1990. *Recreations:* golf, cricket. *Address:* The Law Courts, Barker Road, Maidstone ME16 8SF. *T:* Maidstone (01622) 754966. *Clubs:* MCC; Hawks (Cambridge); Wildernesse (Captain 1978) (Sevenoaks); Royal Worlington and Newmarket Golf.

VICK, Sir (Francis) Arthur, Kt 1973; OBE 1945; PhD; FIEE, FInstP; MRIA; President and Vice-Chancellor, Queen's University of Belfast, 1966–76; Pro-Chancellor, University of Warwick, 1977–92 (Chairman of Council, 1977–90); *b* 5 June 1911; *s* of late Wallace Devenport Vick and late Clara (*née* Taylor); *m* 1943, Elizabeth Dorothy Story (*d* 1989); one *d*. *Educ:* Waverley Grammar School, Birmingham; Birmingham Univ. Asst Lectr in Physics, University Coll., London, 1936–39, Lectr, 1939–44; Asst Dir of Scientific Research, Min. of Supply, 1939–44; Lectr in Physics, Manchester Univ., 1944–47, Sen. Lectr, 1947–50; Prof. of Physics, University Coll. of N Staffs, 1950–59 (Vice-Principal, 1950–54, Actg Principal, 1952–53); Dep. Dir, AERE, Harwell, 1959–60, Dir, 1960–64; Dir of Research Group, UKAEA, 1961–64; Mem. for Research, 1964–66. Institute of Physics: Mem. Bd, 1946–51; Chm., Manchester and District Branch, 1948–51; Vice-Pres., 1953–56; Hon. Sec., 1956–60. Chairman: Manchester Fedn of Scientific Societies, 1949–51; Naval Educn Adv. Cttee, 1964–70; Academic Adv. Council, MoD, 1969–76; Standing Conf. on Univ. Entrance, 1968–75. Pres., Assoc. of Teachers in Colls and Depts of Educn, 1964–72, Hon. Mem., 1972; Vice-Pres., Arts Council of NI, 1966–76. Member: Adv. Council on Bldg Research, Min. of Works, 1955–59; Scientific Adv. Council, Min. of Supply, 1956–59; UGC, 1959–66; Colonial Univ. Grants Adv. Cttee, 1960–65; Adv. Council on Research and Develt, Min. of Power, 1960–63; Nuclear Safety Adv. Cttee, Min. of Power, 1960–66; Governing Body, Nat. Inst. for Research in Nuclear Science, 1964–65. MRIA 1973. Hon. DSc: Keele, 1972; NUI, 1976; Birmingham, 1988; Warwick, 1993; Hon. LLD: Dublin, 1973; Belfast, 1977; Hon. DCL Kent, 1977. Kt Comdr, Liberian Humane Order of African Redemption, 1962. *Publications:* various scientific papers and contributions to books. *Recreations:* music, gardening, using tools. *Address:* Fieldhead Cottage, Fieldhead Lane, Myton Road, Warwick CV34 6QF. *T:* Warwick (01926) 491822. *Clubs:* Athenæum, Savile.

VICK, His Honour Richard (William); a Circuit Judge (formerly County Court Judge), 1969–89; Senior Circuit Judge in England and Wales, 1987–89; Judge, Wandsworth County Court, 1985–89; Honorary Recorder of Guildford, since 1973; *b* 9 Dec. 1917; *s* of late Richard William Vick, JP, and Hilda Josephine (*née* Carlton), Windsor, Berks; *m* 1st, 1947, Judith Jean Warren (*d* 1974); one *s* two *d*; 2nd, 1975, Mrs Joan Chesney Frost, BA (*d* 1994), *d* of Arthur Blaney Powe, MA, Sydney, Australia. *Educ:* Stowe; Jesus Coll.,

Cambridge (BA Hons). Served in RNVR, 1939–46: i/c Coastal Forces, Western Approaches, Mediterranean and N Sea. Called to Bar, Inner Temple, 1940. Partner, R. W. Vick Jr & Co., Lloyd's Insurance Brokers, 1944–46; Associate Mem. of Lloyd's, 1944–46; Deputy Chairman: W Kent QS, 1960–62; Kent QS, 1962–65; QS for Middx Area of Gtr London, 1965–69; Resident Judge, 1978–83, Liaison Judge for Magistrates, 1979–83, Kingston Gp of Courts. Chm., London Gp of County Court Judges, 1983–89. Vice-Chm., Surrey Magistrates Soc., 1972–83; Member: Magistrates' Courts Cttee; Probation Cttee, 1972–83; Circuit Adviser, Judicial Studies Bd, 1981–83. *Publication:* The Administration of Civil Justice in England and Wales, 1967. *Recreations:* sailing, swimming, bridge. *Address:* 18 Ibis Lane, Chiswick, W4 3UP. *Clubs:* Savage; Hawks (Cambridge); Bar Yacht; Royal Naval Sailing Association (Portsmouth).

VICKERMAN, Prof. Keith, FRS 1984; FRSE 1971; Regius Professor of Zoology, University of Glasgow, since 1984; *b* 21 March 1933; *s* of Jack Vickerman and Mabel Vickerman (*née* Dyson); *m* 1961, Moira Dutton, LLB; one *d*. *Educ:* King James' Grammar School, Almondbury; University College London (Fellow, 1985). BSc 1955; PhD 1960; DSc 1970. Wellcome Trust Lectr, Zoology Dept, UCL, 1958–63; Royal Soc. Tropical Res. Fellow, UCL, 1963–68; Glasgow University: Reader in Zoology, 1968–74; Prof., 1974–; Head of Dept of Zoology, 1979–85. Leeuwenhoek Lectr, Royal Soc., 1994. Mem., WHO Panel of Consultant Experts on Parasitic Diseases, 1973–. *Publications:* The Protozoa (with F. E. G. Cox), 1967; numerous papers on protozoa (esp. trypanosomes) in scientific and med. jls. *Recreations:* sketching, gardening. *Address:* Institute of Biomedical and Life Sciences, University of Glasgow, Glasgow G12 8QQ. *T:* 0141–330 4433, *Fax:* 0141–330 5973; 16 Mirrlees Drive, Glasgow G12 0SH. *T:* 0141–334 2794.

VICKERS, Eric, CB 1979; Director of Defence Services, Department of the Environment, 1972–81; *b* 25 April 1921; *s* of late Charles Vickers and late Ida Vickers; *m* 1945, Barbara Mary Jones; one *s* one *d*. *Educ:* King's School, Grantham. Joined India Office, 1938; RAF (Fl/Lt Coastal Command), 1941–46; Ministry of Works, 1948; Principal, 1950; Assistant Secretary, 1962; Imperial Defence College, 1969; Dir of Home Estate Management, DoE, 1970–72. *Recreation:* photography, caravanning, wine appreciation. *Address:* 46 Stamford Road, Oakham, Rutland, Leicestershire LE15 6JA. *T:* Oakham (01572) 724166.

VICKERS, James Oswald Noel, OBE 1977; General Secretary, Civil Service Union, 1963–77 (Deputy General Secretary, 1960–62); *b* 6 April 1916; *s* of Noel Muschamp and Linda Vickers; *m* 1940, Winifred Mary Lambert; one *s* one *d*. *Educ:* Stowe Sch.; Queens' Coll., Cambridge. Exhibnr, BA Hons Hist., MA. Served War, HM Forces, 1939–45. Warden, Wedgwood Memorial Coll., 1946–49; Educn Officer, ETU, and Head of Esher Coll., 1949–56. Member: Civil Service Nat. Whitley Council, 1962–77 (Chm. Staff Side, 1975–77); TUC Inter-Union Disputes Panel, 1970–77; TUC Non-Manual Workers Adv. Cttee, 1973–75; Fabian Soc. Trade Union and Industrial Relations Cttee, 1964–81 (Chm. 1973–78; Vice-Chm., 1978–79); UCL Coll. Cttee, 1974–79; Council, Tavistock Inst., 1976–80; Employment Appeal Tribunal, 1978–86; CS Appeal Bd, 1978–86. *Publications:* contrib. to Fabian pamphlets. *Recreations:* bird-watching, gardening, travel. *Address:* 5 The Butts, Brentford, Mddx TW8 8BJ. *T:* 0181–560 3482; Heber Vale Cottage, Timberscombe, near Minehead, Som TA24 7TX.

VICKERS, Prof. John Stuart; Drummond Professor of Political Economy, Oxford University, and Fellow of All Souls College, since 1991; *b* 7 July 1958; *s* of Aubrey and Kay Vickers; *m* 1991, Maureen Freed; one *s*. *Educ:* Eastbourne Grammar Sch.; Oriel Coll., Oxford (BA PPE 1979); MPhil Econs Oxon 1983; DPhil Econs Oxon 1985. Financial Analyst, Shell UK, 1979–81; Fellow, All Souls Coll., Oxford, 1979–84; Roy Harrod Fellow in Economics of Business and Public Policy, Nuffield Coll., Oxford, 1984–90. Vis. Fellow, Princeton, 1988; Vis. Lectr, Harvard, 1989, 1990. *Publications:* (jtly) Privatisation and the Natural Monopolies, 1985; (jtly) Privatization: an economic analysis, 1988; (jtly) Regulatory Reform, 1994; articles in econ. jls on industrial organisation, regulation, competition. *Address:* All Souls College, Oxford OX1 4AL. *T:* Oxford (01865) 279379.

VICKERS, Jon, CC (Canada) 1968; dramatic tenor; *b* Prince Albert, Saskatchewan, 1926; *m* 1953, Henrietta Outerbridge; three *s* two *d*. Studied under George Lambert, Royal Conservatory of Music, Toronto. Made debut with Toronto Opera Company, 1952; Stratford (Ontario) Festival, 1956. Joined Royal Opera House, Covent Garden, 1957. First sang at: Bayreuth Festival, 1958; Vienna State Opera, San Francisco Opera, and Chicago Lyric, 1959; Metropolitan, New York, and La Scala, Milan, 1960; Buenos Aires, 1962; Salzburg Festival, 1966; appeared in other opera houses of Argentina, Austria, Brazil, France, Germany, Greece, Mexico and USA. *Films:* Carmen; Pagliacci; Otello; Norma; Peter Grimes; Fidelio; Samson et Delilah. Has made many recordings. Presbyterian. Hon. Dr: University of Saskatchewan, 1963; Bishop's Univ., 1965; Univ. West Ontario, 1970; Brandon Univ., 1976; Laval Univ., 1977; Univ. of Guelph, 1978; Illinois, 1983; Queens, Canada, 1984; Toronto, 1987. RAM 1977. Canada Centennial Medal, 1967; Critics' Award, London, 1978; Grammy Award, 1979. *Address:* c/o John Coast Opera Management, 31 Sinclair Road, W14 0NS.

VICKERS, Prof. Michael Douglas Allen; Professor of Anaesthetics, University of Wales College of Medicine (formerly Welsh National School of Medicine), 1976–95, now Emeritus; Vice Provost, University of Wales College of Medicine, 1990–93; *b* 11 May 1929; *s* of George and Freda Vickers; *m* 1959, Ann Hazel Courtney; two *s* one *d*. *Educ:* Abingdon Sch.; Guy's Hosp. Med. Sch. MB, BS; FFARCS; FRSM. Lectr, RPMS, 1965–68; Consultant Anaesthetist, Birmingham AHA, 1968–76. Mem. Bd, Faculty of Anaesthetists, 1971–85; President: Assoc. of Anaesthetists of GB and Ireland, 1982–84 (Hon. Sec., 1974–76; John Snow Lectr, 1982); European Acad. of Anaesthesiology, 1988– (Sec., 1982–84, Pres., 1988–91); Sec. Gen., World Fedn of Socs of Anaesthesiologists, 1992–April 1996 (Chm., Exec. Cttee, 1988–92). Hon. FANZCA. Editor: European Journal of Anaesthesiology, 1983–94; Today's Anaesthetist, 1994–. *Publications:* (jtly) Principles of Measurement for Anaesthetists, 1970 (2nd edn, as Principles of Measurement, 1981, 3rd edn 1991); (jtly) Drugs in Anaesthetic Practice, 3rd edn 1968, to 7th edn 1991; Medicine for Anaesthetists, 1977, 3rd edn 1989; (jtly) Ethical Issues in Anaesthesia, 1994; (jtly) OSCEs for Anaesthetists, 1995. *Recreations:* music, theatre. *Address:* c/o Department of Anaesthetics, University of Wales College of Medicine, Heath Park, Cardiff CF4 4XN. *T:* Cardiff (01222) 743110.

VICKERS, Rt. Rev. Michael Edwin; Area Bishop of Colchester, 1988–94; Assistant Bishop, Diocese of Blackburn, since 1994; *b* 13 Jan. 1929; *s* of William Edwin and Florence Alice Vickers; *m* 1960, Janet Cynthia Croasdale; three *d*. *Educ:* St Lawrence Coll., Ramsgate; Worcester Coll., Oxford (BA Mod. History, 1952, MA 1956); Cranmer Hall, Durham (DipTheol with distinction, 1959). Company Secretary, Hoares (Ceylon) Ltd, 1952–56; Refugee Administrator for British Council for Aid to Refugees, 1956–57; Lay Worker, Diocese of Oklahoma, 1959; Curate of Christ Church, Bexleyheath, 1959–62; Sen. Chaplain, Lee Abbey Community, 1962–67; Vicar of St John's, Newland, Hull, 1967–81; Area Dean, Central and North Hull, 1972–81; Archdeacon of E Riding, 1981–88. Chm., York Diocesan House of Clergy, 1975–85; Canon and Prebendary of York, 1981–88. Mem., Gen. Synod, 1975–88 (Proctor in Convocation, 1975–85). *Recreations:* gardening, fell-walking, travel, drama. *Address:* 2 Collingham Park, Lancaster LA1 4PD. *T:* Lancaster (01524) 848492.

VICKERS, Lt-Gen. Sir Richard (Maurice Hilton), KCB 1983; LVO 1959; OBE 1970 (MBE 1964); a Gentleman Usher to the Queen, since 1986; *b* 21 Aug. 1928; *s* of Lt-Gen. W. G. H. Vickers, CB, OBE; *m* 1957, Gaie, *d* of Maj.-Gen. G. P. B. Roberts, *qv*; three *d*. *Educ:* Haileybury and Imperial Service Coll.; RMA. Commissioned Royal Tank Regt, 1948; 1st RTR, BAOR, Korea, Middle East, 1948–54; Equerry to HM The Queen, 1956–59; Brigade Major, 7 Armd Bde, 1962–64; 4th RTR, Borneo and Malaysia, 1964–66; CO The Royal Dragoons, 1967–68, The Blues and Royals, 1968–69; Comdr, 11th Armd Brigade, 1972–74; Dep. Dir of Army Training, 1975–77; GOC 4th Armoured Div., 1977–79; Comdt, RMA, 1979–82; Dir-Gen. of Army Training, 1982–83. Dir Gen., Winston Churchill Meml Trust, 1983–93. *Recreations:* squash, flyfishing. *Club:* Cavalry and Guards.

VICKERS, Roger Henry, FRCS; Orthopaedic Surgeon to HM the Queen, since 1992; Consultant Orthopaedic Surgeon: St George's Hospital, since 1980; King Edward VII Hospital for Officers, since 1992; Civilian Consultant Orthopaedic Surgeon to the Army, since 1992; *b* 26 July 1945; *s* of late Dr H. Renwick Vickers, FRCP and of Penelope Evelyn (*née* Peck); *m* 1972, Joanna, *d* of late John Francis Mordaunt; two *s* two *d*. *Educ:* Winchester Coll.; Magdalen Coll., Oxford (MA); St Thomas's Hosp. (BM, BCh 1970). FRCS 1975. Sen. Orthopaedic Registrar, Charing Cross, St Mary's and Royal Nat. Orthopaedic Hosps, 1977–80; Consultant Orthopaedic Surgeon, St James' Hosp., London, 1980–88. Mem. Council, Med. Defence Union, 1983–. *Recreations:* sailing, Real tennis. *Address:* 11 Edenhurst Avenue, SW6 3PD; 149 Harley Street, W1N 1HG. *Clubs:* Hurlingham; Seacourt; Hayling Island Sailing.

VICKERS, Thomas Douglas, CMG 1956; *b* 25 Sept. 1916; 2nd *s* of late Ronald Vickers, Scaitcliffe, Englefield Green, Surrey; *m* 1951, Margaret Awdry, *o c* of late E. A. Headley, Wagga, NSW; one *s* one *d*. *Educ:* Eton; King's Coll., Cambridge (MA Hons). Cadet, Colonial Administrative Service, 1938. Served War of 1939–45; Coldstream Guards, 1940–45. Colonial Office, 1938–40 and 1945–50; Gold Coast, 1950–53; Colonial Secretary, British Honduras, 1953–60; Chief Secretary, Mauritius, 1960–67, Dep. Governor, 1967–68; retired from HMOCS, Oct. 1968. Head of Personnel Services, Imperial Cancer Research Fund, 1969–81. *Address:* Wood End, Worplesdon, Surrey GU3 3RJ. *T:* Worplesdon (01483) 233468. *Club:* Army and Navy.

VICKERS, Dr Tony; Project Manager, UK Human Genome Mapping Project, 1990–92; *b* 6 July 1932; *s* of Harry and Frances Vickers; *m* 1964, Anne Dorothy Wallis (marr. diss. 1986); two *d*. *Educ:* Manchester Grammar Sch.; Sidney Sussex Coll., Cambridge (MA, PhD). University of Cambridge: Demonstrator, 1956; Lectr in Physiology, 1961–72; Fellow, Sidney Sussex Coll., 1956–70; Headquarters Office, MRC, 1972–84 (Head of Medical Div., 1980–84); UK Administrator, Ludwig Inst. for Cancer Res., 1985–89. Member of Council: BAAS, 1969–72, 1982–85 (Pres., Biomed. Scis Sect., 1977); Cancer Res. Campaign, 1980–85 (Mem., Scientific Cttee, 1979–85); Paterson Labs, Manchester, 1984–85. Chm., Tenovus Sci. Adv. Cttee, 1987–91; Mem. Res. Cttee, Clatterbridge Centre for Oncology and Cancer Res. Trust, 1994–. Governor, Beatson Inst., Glasgow, 1983–85. *Address:* 42 Bengeo Street, Hertford, Herts SG14 3ET.

VICKERY, Prof. Brian Campbell, FLA, FIInfSc; Professor of Library Studies and Director, School of Library Archive and Information Studies, University College London, 1973–83, now Professor Emeritus; *b* 11 Sept. 1918; *s* of Adam Cairns McCay and Violet Mary Watson; *m* 1st, 1945, Manuletta McMenamin; one *s* one *d*; 2nd, 1970, Alina Gralewska. *Educ:* King's Sch., Canterbury; Brasenose Coll., Oxford. MA. Chemist, Royal Ordnance Factory, Somerset, 1941–45; Librarian, ICI Ltd, Welwyn, 1946–60; Principal Scientific Officer, Nat. Lending Library for Sci. and Technology, 1960–64; Librarian, UMIST, 1964–66; Head of R&D, Aslib, 1966–73. *Publications:* Classification and Indexing in Science, 1958, 3rd edn 1975; On Retrieval System Theory, 1961, 2nd edn 1965; Techniques of Information Retrieval, 1970; Information Systems, 1973; Information Science, 1987, 2nd edn 1992; Online Search Interface Design, 1993; (ed) Fifty Years of Information Progress, 1994; articles in professional jls. *Recreations:* reading history, poetry, philosophy; music and theatre; personal computing. *Address:* 9 Clover Close, Cumnor Hill, Oxford OX2 9JH. *T:* Oxford (01865) 863306.

VICTOR, Ed; Chairman and Managing Director, Ed Victor Ltd, since 1977; *b* 9 Sept. 1939; *s* of Jack Victor and Lydia Victor; *m* 1st, 1963, Michelene Dinah Samuels (marr. diss.); two *s*; 2nd, 1980, Carol Lois Ryan; one *s*. *Educ:* Dartmouth Coll. USA (BA *summa cum laude* 1961); Pembroke Coll., Cambridge (MLitt 1963). Began as art books editor, later editorial Dir, Weidenfeld & Nicolson, 1964–67; editorial Dir, Jonathan Cape Ltd, 1967–71; Senior Editor, Alfred A. Knopf Inc., NY, 1972–73; literary agent and Dir, John Farquharson Ltd (lit. agents), 1974–76; founded Ed Victor Ltd (lit. agency), 1977. Council Mem., Aids Crisis Trust, 1986–. Dir, Almeida Theatre, 1993–. Trustee, The Arts Foundn, 1991–. *Recreations:* tennis, travel, opera. *Address:* 10 Cambridge Gate, Regent's Park, NW1 4JX. *T:* 0171–224 3030. *Club:* Groucho.

VICUÑA, Francisco O.; *see* Orrego-Vicuña.

VIDAL, Gore; author; *b* 3 Oct. 1925; *s* of Eugene and Nina Gore Vidal. *Educ:* Phillips Exeter Academy, New Hampshire, USA (grad. 1943). Army of the US, 1943–46: Private to Warrant Officer (jg) and First Mate, Army FS-35, Pacific Theatre Ops. Democratic-Liberal candidate for US Congress, 1960; candidate for Democratic nomination for election to US Senate from California, 1982. Apptd to President Kennedy's Adv. Council of the Arts, 1961–63. *Publications: novels:* Williwaw, 1946; In a Yellow Wood, 1947; The City and the Pillar, 1948; The Season of Comfort, 1949; A Search for the King, 1950; Dark Green, Bright Red, 1950; The Judgment of Paris, 1952; Messiah, 1954; Julian, 1964; Washington, DC, 1967; Myra Breckinridge, 1968 (filmed 1969); Two Sisters, 1970; Burr, 1973; Myron, 1975; 1876, 1976; Kalki, 1978; Creation, 1981; Duluth, 1983; Lincoln, 1984; Empire, 1987; Hollywood, 1989; Live from Golgotha, 1992; *essays:* Rocking the Boat, 1962; Reflections upon a Sinking Ship, 1969; Homage to Daniel Shays (collected essays 1952–72), 1972; Matters of Fact and of Fiction, 1977; The Second American Revolution (UK title, Pink Triangle and Yellow Star and other essays (1976–1982)), 1982; Armageddon?, 1987; At Home, 1988; A View from the Diner's Club, 1991; Screening History, 1992; United States: essays 1952–1992, 1993 (Nat. Book Award, 1994); *short stories:* A Thirsty Evil, 1956; *travel:* Vidal in Venice, 1987; *memoir:* Palimpsest, 1995; *plays:* Visit to a Small Planet (NY prod.), 1957; The Best Man (NY prod.), 1960; Romulus (adapted from F. Dürrenmatt) (NY prod.), 1962; Weekend (NY prod.), 1968; On the March to the Sea (German prod.), 1962; An Evening with Richard Nixon (NY prod.), 1972; *screenplays,* from 1955: Wedding Breakfast, 1957; Suddenly Last Summer, 1958; The Best Man, 1964, etc; *television plays:* 1954–56: The Death of Billy the Kid (translated to screen as The Lefthanded Gun, 1959, and as Gore Vidal's Billy the Kid, 1989), etc; *literary and political criticism for:* NY Review of Books, Esquire, Partisan Review, TLS, etc. *Recreations:* as noted above. *Address:* La Rondinaia, 84010 Ravello, (Salerno), Italy. *Club:* Athenæum.

VIELER, Geoffrey Herbert, FCA; Member of Board, Post Office Corporation, 1969–71; *b* 21 Aug. 1910; *s* of late Herbert Charles Stuart Vieler, Huddersfield, and Emily Mary; *m* 1934, Phyllis Violet (*d* 1993); one *d*. *Educ:* Fairway Sch., Bexhill-on-Sea. With Vale & West, Chartered Accountants, Reading, 1927–41 (qual. 1932); War Service, 1941–46: commnd RAOC, 1943, Major 1945; joined Binder Hamlyn, Chartered Accountants, 1946, Partner 1959–69; Managing Dir, Posts and National Giro, 1969–71. Member: Techn. Adv. Cttee, Inst. of Chartered Accountants in England and Wales, 1967–74; Special Cttee, Tax Law Consultative Bodies, 1986–91. Chm., London Chartered Accountants, 1976–77; Chm., Taxation Cttee, ABCC, 1985–91. *Address:* Robins Wood, Monks Drive, South Ascot, Berks SL5 9BB; Riversmeet, Mill Lane, Lower Shiplake RG9 3LY.

VIERTEL, Deborah Kerr; *see* Kerr, D. J.

VIGARS, Della, (Mrs Paul Vigars); *see* Jones, D.

VIGARS, Robert Lewis; *b* 26 May 1923; *s* of late Francis Henry Vigars and Susan Laurina May Vigars (*née* Lewis); *m* 1962, Margaret Ann Christine, *y d* of late Sir John Walton, KCIE, CB, MC, and Lady Walton; two *d*. *Educ:* Truro Cathedral Sch.; London Univ. (LLB (Hons)). Served War of 1939–45: RA and Royal Corps of Signals, 1942–47; attached Indian Army (Captain), 1944–47; Captain, Princess Louise's Kensington Regt, TA, 1951–54. Qualified as solicitor (Hons), 1948. Partner, Simmons & Simmons, London, EC2, 1951–75. Member: Kensington Borough Council, 1953–59; London and Home Counties Traffic Adv. Cttee, 1956–58; London Roads (Nugent) Cttee, 1958–59; LCC and GLC Kensington (formerly South Kensington), 1955–86; Environmental Planning Cttee, GLC, 1967–71 (Chm.); Strategic Planning Cttee, GLC, 1971–73 (Chm.); Leader of Opposition, ILEA, 1974–79; Chm. of the GLC, 1979–80; Mem., Standing Conf. on London and SE Regional Planning and SE Economic Planning Council, 1968–75. Gen. Comr of Income Tax (Highbury), 1988–; Mem., Central London Valuation Tribunal, 1989–. Dir, Heritage of London Trust, 1985–; Mem., Historic Buildings and Monuments Commn for England, 1986–88 (Mem., London Adv. Cttee, 1986–92 (Chm. 1986–88)); Trustee, Historic Chapels Trust, 1993–. Mem. Court, London Univ., 1977–82. *Recreation:* mountain walking. *Address:* 24 Cope Place, Kensington, W8 6AA. *Clubs:* Carlton, Hurlingham.

VIGGERS, Peter John; MP (C) Gosport, since Feb. 1974; *b* 13 March 1938; *s* of late J. S. Viggers and E. F. Viggers (later Mrs V. E. J. Neal), Gosport; *m* 1968, Jennifer Mary McMillan, MB, BS, LRCP, MRCS, DA, *d* of late Dr R. B. McMillan, MD, FRCP, Guildford, and late Mrs J. T. C. McMillan, MA, MIB; two *s* one *d*. *Educ:* Portsmouth Grammar Sch.; Trinity Hall, Cambridge (MA 1961). Chm., Cambridge Univ. Cons. Assoc., 1960. Solicitor 1967. Royal Canadian Air Force (pilot), 1956–58. PPS to Solicitor-General, 1979–83, to Chief Sec. of HM Treasury, 1983–85; Parly Under-Sec. of State (Industry Minister), NI Office, 1986–89. Chm., Select Cttee on Armed Forces Bill, 1986; Member: Select Cttee on Members' Interests, 1991–93; Select Cttee on Defence, 1992–; Chm., British-Japanese Parly Gp, 1992–; UK Delegate: Jt IPU and UN Conf. on Conventional Disarmament, Mexico City, 1985; N Atlantic Assembly, 1981–86, 1992–. Chm. and dir of public and private cos, 1972–; Dir, NYNEX Gp of Cos, 1991–. Underwriting Member of Lloyd's (Council Mem., 1992–). Mem., Management Cttee, RNLI, 1979–89, Vice-Pres., 1989–. Commnd 457 (Wessex) Regt, RA (TA), 1963. *Recreations:* beagling, opera, France. *Address:* House of Commons, SW1A 0AA.

VIGNOLES, Roger Hutton, ARCM; pianoforte accompanist and conductor; *b* 12 July 1945; *s* of late Keith Hutton Vignoles and of Phyllis Mary (*née* Pearson); *m* 1st, 1972, Teresa Ann Elizabeth Henderson (marr. diss. 1982); 2nd, 1982, Jessica Virginia, *d* of Prof. Boris Ford, *qv*; one *s* one *d*. *Educ:* Canterbury Cathedral Choir Sch.; Sedbergh Sch.; Magdalene Coll., Cambridge (BA, BMus); Royal College of Music, London (ARCM). Accompanist of national and internat. reputation, regularly appearing with the most distinguished internat. singers and instrumentalists, both in London and provinces and at major music festivals (*eg* Aldeburgh, Cheltenham, Edinburgh, Brighton, Bath, Salzburg, Prague, etc) and broadcasting for BBC Radio 3 and television. International tours incl. USA, Canada, Australia-New Zealand, Hong Kong, Scandinavia, and recitals at Opera Houses of Cologne, Brussels, Frankfurt, Lincoln Center, NY, San Francisco, Tokyo, Carnegie Hall, NY, Venice, Paris, Munich, Berlin, etc. Repetiteur: Royal Opera House, Covent Garden, 1969–71; English Opera Group, 1968–74; Australian Opera Company, 1976. Professor of Accompaniment, RCM, 1974–81; Consultant Prof. of Accompaniment, RAM, 1989–; Artistic Dir, Young Brahms Fest., QEH, 1992. Has conducted: Buxton Fest., 1992; Bath and Wessex Opera, 1993; Hallé Orch., 1993, etc. Gramophone recordings of extensive vocal and chamber music repertoire. Hon. RAM 1984. *Recreations:* drawing, painting, looking at pictures, swimming, sailing. *Address:* 1 Ascham Street, Kentish Town, NW5 2PB. *T:* 0171–267 3187.

VILE, Prof. Maurice John Crawley; Director of Research, Canterbury Christ Church College, since 1994; Professor Emeritus of Political Science, University of Kent at Canterbury; *b* 23 July 1927; *s* of Edward M. and Elsie M. Vile; two *s*. *Educ:* London Sch. of Economics. BSc (Econ) 1951; PhD London, 1954; MA Oxford, 1962. FRHistS 1989. Lectr in Politics, Univ. of Exeter, 1954–62; Fellow of Nuffield Coll., Oxford, 1962–65; Lectr in Politics, Magdalen Coll., Oxford, 1963–64; University of Kent: Reader in Politics and Govt, 1965–68; Prof. of Political Sci., 1968–84; Dir of Internat. Progs, 1984–87; Dean of Faculty of Social Scis, 1969–75; Pro-Vice-Chancellor, 1975–81; Dep. Vice-Chancellor, 1981–84; Dir of British Progs, Boston Univ., 1989–94. Visiting Professor: Univ. of Massachusetts, 1960; Smith College, Mass., 1961. Royer Lectr, Univ. of Calif., Berkeley, 1974. Hon. DCL Kent, 1993. *Publications:* The Structure of American Federalism, 1961; Constitutionalism and the Separation of Powers, 1967; Politics in the USA, 1970, 4th edn 1987; Federalism in the United States, Canada and Australia (Res. Paper No 2, Commn on the Constitution), 1973; The Presidency (Amer. Hist. Documents Vol. IV), 1974. *Address:* Little Cob, Garlinge Green, Petham, Canterbury, Kent CT4 5RT. *T:* Canterbury (01277) 700432.

VILIKOVSKÝ, Ján, PhD; Ambassador of the Slovak Republic to the Court of St James's, since 1993; *b* 13 July 1937; *s* of late Prof. Ján Vilikovský and Dr Julia Vilikovský (*née* Bárdošová); *m* 1st, 1962, Božica Štúrová (*d* 1985); two *d*; 2nd, 1992, Mária Horváthová. *Educ:* Comenius Univ., Bratislava (BA 1959; MA 1975; PhD 1982). Editor, Slovak Writers' Publishing House, 1959–70; Asst Prof., Inst. of Translators, 1970–74; Asst Prof., Dept of English and American Studies, Comenius Univ., 1974–90; Sec.-Gen., Slovak Translators' Assoc., 1986–90; Dir, Tatran Publishers, 1990–92; Ministry of Foreign Affairs, 1992; Ambassador of Czechoslavakia, 1992. Ján Hollý Prize for Translation, 1969, 1980. *Publications:* Slovak-English Dictionary, 1959, 5th edn 1992; Preklad ako tvorba (Translation as a creative process), 1984; contribs to learned jls; translations from English and American literature. *Recreations:* classical music, reading, talking. *Address:* Embassy of the Slovak Republic, 25 Kensington Palace Gardens, W8 2QY. *T:* 0171–727 9432.

VILJOEN, Marais, DMS 1976; State President of the Republic of South Africa, 1979–84; *b* 2 Dec. 1915; *s* of Gabriel François Viljoen and Magdalena Debora (*née* de Villiers); *m* 1940, Dorothea Maria Brink; one *d*. *Educ:* Jan van Riebeeck High Sch., Cape Town; Univ. of Cape Town. After leaving school, employed in Dept of Posts and Telegraphs, 1932–37; on editorial staff, Die Transvaler newspaper, 1937–40; manager, Transvaler book trade business, Potchefstroom, 1940; co-founder and provincial leader of Nat. Youth League, 1940–45; organiser of Transvaal National Party, 1945–49; Member, Provincial Council, Transvaal, 1949–53; Information Officer, Transvaal National Party, several years from 1951; Chairman, Inf. Service of Federal Council, National Party of S Africa, 1969–74; Dep. Chm., Nat. Party, Transvaal, 1966–75. MP Alberton, 1953–76; Dep. Minister of Labour and of Mines, 1958–61; various other ministerial offices, incl. Interior and Immigration, until 1966; Cabinet appointments, 1966–: Minister of Labour and of Coloured Affairs, 1966–69, also of Rehoboth Affairs, 1969–70; Minister of Labour and of Posts and Telecommunications, 1970–76. President of the Senate, 1976–79. Special Cl., Grand Collar, Order of Good Hope, Republic of S Africa, 1981. *Recreations:* golf, bowls, reading. *Address:* PO Box 5555, Pretoria, 0001, Republic of South Africa.

VILJOEN, Theo Leon; His Honour Judge Viljoen; a Circuit Judge, since 1992; *b* 25 Aug. 1937; *s* of Robert Bartlett Viljoen and Cecilia Jacoba Viljoen (*née* van der Walt); *m* 1967, Dorothy Nina Raybould, *d* of late Prof. S. G. Raybould; two *d*. *Educ:* Afrikaanse Hoer Seunskool; Univ. of Pretoria. Called to the Bar, Middle Temple, 1972; a Recorder, 1991–92. Mem., N Lambeth and Kennington Gardens Guild. *Recreations:* walking, gardening, wine. *Address:* 2 Harcourt Buildings, Temple, EC4Y 9DB. *T:* 0171–583 9020.

VILLIERS; *see* Child Villiers, family name of Earl of Jersey.

VILLIERS; *see* de Villiers.

VILLIERS, family name of **Earl of Clarendon.**

VILLIERS, Viscount; George Henry Child Villiers; guitarist and composer; *b* 29 Aug. 1948; *s* and *heir* of 9th Earl of Jersey, *qv*; *m* 1st, 1969, Verna (marr. diss. 1973), 2nd *d* of K. A. Stott, St Mary, Jersey; one *d*; 2nd, 1974, Sandra (marr. diss. 1988), step *d* of H. Briginshaw, Feremina, St Martin, Guernsey; one *s* two *d*; 3rd, 1992, Stephanie Louise, *d* of J. J. Penman; one *s*. *Educ:* Eton; Millfield. Late The Royal Hussars (PWO). Leader, George Villiers Express. Recordings: Magical Dance, 1988; Dawn, 1989; No Dog Required, 1995. *Publication:* (ed) Classic Duets for Guitar. *Heir:* *s* Hon. George Francis William Child Villiers, *b* 5 Feb. 1976.

VILLIERS, Charles Nigel, FCA; Managing Director of Corporate Development, Abbey National plc (formerly Abbey National Building Society), since 1988; *b* 25 Jan. 1941; *s* of Robert Alexander and Elizabeth Mary Villiers; *m* 1970, Sally Priscilla Magnay; one *s* one *d*. *Educ:* Winchester Coll.; New Coll., Oxford (MA German and Russian). Arthur Andersen & Co., 1963–67; ICFC, 1967–72; County Bank Ltd, 1972–86; Dir, 1974; Dep. Chief Exec., 1977; Chm. and Chief Exec., 1984–85; Exec. Chm., 1985–86; Exec. Dir, National Westminster Bank, 1985–88; Chief Exec., NatWest Investment Bank Ltd (estab. June 1986 incorporating the business of County Bank Ltd), 1986–88; Chm., County NatWest Ltd, 1986–88. *Recreations:* opera, squash, ski-ing, tennis. *Clubs:* Hurlingham, Institute of Directors.

VINCENT, Anthony Lionel; Legal Adviser, Department of Foreign Affairs and Trade, Canberra, since 1994; *b* 18 Oct. 1933; *s* of Harold Francis Vincent and Lesley Allison Vincent; *m* 1958, Helen Frances Beasley; one *s* one *d*. *Educ:* Univ. of Western Australia, Perth (LLB); Univ. of Oxford (BCL). Joined Dept of Foreign Affairs, Aust., 1958; served: Karachi, 1959–61; Hong Kong, 1963–66; Singapore, 1966–69; Belgrade, 1972–74; Paris, 1977–80; Australian Ambassador to: Iraq, 1981–83; GDR, 1984; Dep. High Comr in London, 1984–87; Asst Sec., Treaties and Sea Law Br., 1987–89, Intelligence and Defence Br., 1989–90, Dept of Foreign Affairs and Trade, Canberra; Ambassador to Czech and Slovak Federal Republic, subseq. to Czech and Slovak Republics, 1990–93; Asst Sec., Corporate Evaluation Br., Dept of Foreign Affairs and Trade, 1993–94. *Recreations:* walking, cycling, reading. *Address:* c/o Department of Foreign Affairs and Trade, Canberra, ACT 2600, Australia.

VINCENT, Maj.-Gen. Douglas, CB 1969; AM 1994; OBE 1954; Director, Alcatel Australia, 1973–93; *b* Australia, 10 March 1916; *s* of William Frederick Vincent, civil engineer, and Sarah Jane Vincent; *m* 1947, Margaret Ector, *d* of N. W. Persse, Melbourne; two *s* one *d*. *Educ:* Brisbane State High School; Royal Military Coll., Duntroon. Commissioned, Dec. 1938; Middle East (7 Div.), 1940–42; BLA, 1944; NW Europe (30 Corps); Borneo Campaign, 1945; Brit. Commonwealth Forces, Korea, 1954; Dir of Signals, 1954–58; Dir of Staff Duties, 1958–60; Chief of Staff, Eastern Command, 1960–62; Commander, Aust. Army Force, 1962–63 (Singapore, Malaya); idc 1964; Commander: 1 Task Force, 1965; 1st Div., 1966; Aust. Force, Vietnam, 1967–68; Head, Aust. Jt Services Staff, Washington, DC, USA, 1968–70; Adjutant General, Australian Army, 1970–73. Mem. Nat. Exec., RSL (Defence Adviser, 1975–). SMIREE(Aust). *Recreations:* golf, swimming. *Address:* 41 Hampton Circuit, Yarralumla, Canberra, ACT 2600, Australia.

VINCENT, Prof. Ewart Albert; Professor of Geology, and Fellow of University College, Oxford, 1967–86, now Emeritus; *b* 23 Aug. 1919; *o s* of Albert and Winifred Vincent, Aylesbury; *m* 1944, Myrtle Ablett; two *d*. *Educ:* Reading Sch.; Univ. of Reading. BSc (Reading) 1940; PhD 1951; MA (Oxon) 1952; MSc (Manch.) 1966. FGS. Chemist, Min. of Supply, 1940–45; Geologist, Anglo-Iranian Oil Co., 1945–46; Lectr in Mineralogy and Crystallography, Univ. of Durham, 1946–51; Lectr in Geology, Oxford Univ., 1951–56; Reader in Mineralogy, Oxford Univ., 1956–62; Prof. of Geology, Manchester Univ., 1962–66. Mem. NERC, 1975–78. Vice-Pres., Internat. Assoc. of Volcanology, 1968–71; Pres., Mineralogical Soc. of GB, 1974–76; Mem. Council, Geol Soc., 1973–76. Fellow, Mineralogical Soc. of Amer. Hon. Corresp. Mem., Soc. Géol. de Belgique. Awarded Wollaston Fund, Geol Soc. London, 1961. *Publications:* scientific papers in learned jls. *Recreations:* music, photography. *Address:* 2 Linch Farm, Wytham, Oxford OX2 8QP. *T:* Oxford (01865) 723170; Department of Earth Sciences, Parks Road, Oxford OX1 3PR. *T:* Oxford (01865) 272000.

VINCENT, Rev. Irvin James; Minister, Temple Methodist Church, Taunton, since 1986; *b* 22 July 1932; *s* of Amy Mary Catharine Vincent (*née* Nye) and Vince Thomas Vincent; *m* 1959, Stella Margaret (*née* Chaplin); one *s* two *d*. *Educ:* Mitcham Grammar School; Didsbury College (Methodist), Bristol. BA Open Univ. Accountancy, 1948; National Service, RAF, 1950–52; Local Govt, 1952–55; theological training, 1955–59; Methodist Circuit, Stonehouse and Dursley, 1959–61; entered RN as Chaplain, 1961; Malta, 1968–72; exchange with USN, 1976–78; Principal Chaplain, Church of Scotland and Free Churches (Navy), 1984–86; QHC, 1984–86. *Recreations:* soccer, cricket, drama, music, gardening. *Address:* Temple Methodist Church, Upper High Street, Taunton, Somerset TA1 3PY. *T:* Taunton (01823) 288662.

VINCENT, Rev. Dr John James; Methodist Minister; Superintendent, Sheffield Inner City Ecumenical Mission, and Director, Urban Theology Unit, since 1970; President of the Methodist Conference, 1989–90; *b* 29 Dec. 1929; *s* of late David Vincent and of Ethel Beatrice (*née* Gadd); *m* 1958, Grace Johnston, *d* of Rev. Wilfred Stafford, Bangor, Co. Down; two *s* one *d*. *Educ:* Manchester Grammar Sch.; Richmond Coll.; London Univ.

(BD 1954); Drew Univ., USA (STM 1955); Basel Univ., Switzerland (DTheol 1960). Sgt, RAMC, 1948–49. Minister, Manchester and Salford Mission, 1956–62; Supt, Rochdale Mission, 1962–69; Founder and Leader, The Ashram Community, 1967–. Visiting Professor of Theology: Boston Univ., and New York Theol Seminary, 1969–70; Drew Univ., 1977; Adjunct Prof. of Theol., New York Theol Seminary, 1979–88. Hon. Lectr in Biblical Studies, Sheffield Univ., 1990–. Chairman: NW Campaign for Nuclear Disarmament, 1957–63; Alliance of Radical Methodists, 1970–76; Urban Mission Trng Assoc., 1982–90; Trustee Savings Bank Depositors Assoc. (also litigant in High Court and H of L, TSB *v* Vincent), 1986; Director: British Liberation Theol. Inst., 1995–; Doctor of Ministry Programme of GB, 1988–; Member: Studiorum Novi Testamenti Societas, 1961–; Council, Christian Orgns for Social, Political and Econ. Change, 1981–91; Exec., Assoc. of Centres of Adult Theol. Educn, 1984–90. *Publications:* Christ in a Nuclear World, 1962; Christian Nuclear Perspective, 1964; Christ and Methodism, 1965; Here I Stand, 1967; Secular Christ, 1968; The Race Race, 1970; The Jesus Thing, 1973; Stirrings: essays Christian and Radical, 1975; Alternative Church, 1976; Disciple and Lord: discipleship in the Synoptic Gospels, 1976; Starting All Over Again, 1981; Into the City, 1982; OK, Let's Be Methodists, 1984; Radical Jesus, 1986; Mark at Work, 1986; Britain in the Nineties, 1989; Discipleship in the Nineties, 1991; A Petition of Distress from the Cities (to the Queen and Govt), 1993; A British Liberation Theology, 1994. *Recreations:* jogging, writing. *Address:* 178 Abbeyfield Road, Sheffield S4 7AY. *T:* Sheffield (0114) 243 6688, (Urban Theology Unit) Sheffield (0114) 243 5342.

VINCENT, Prof. John Joseph, MSc, MSc Tech., CText, FTI; Professor of Textile Technology, University of Manchester Institute of Science and Technology, 1957–74, now Emeritus; *b* 29 June 1907; 2nd *s* of J. H. Vincent, MA, DSc; *m* 1935, M. Monica Watson, MSc, PhD (*d* 1992), of Sheffield; one *s* one *d*. *Educ:* County Grammar Sch., Harrow; University Coll., London. Mathematics Dept, University Coll., London, 1927–29; Shirley Inst., Manchester, 1929–42 and 1945–57. Ministry of Aircraft Production, 1942–45. Hon. Life Mem., Textile Institute, 1976 (Mem. Council, 1959–74; Vice-Pres., 1971–74); Pres., British Assoc. of Managers of Textile Works, 1963–64; Mem., Cotton and Allied Textiles Industry Training Bd, 1966–74. Textile Inst. Medal, 1968; Leverhulme Emeritus Fellowship, 1976. *Publications:* Shuttleless Looms, 1980; papers on textile technology. *Recreations:* gardening, reading, listening to music. *Address:* The White House, Perranarworthal, Truro, Cornwall TR3 7QE. *T:* Truro (01872) 863504.

See also J. R. Vincent.

VINCENT, Prof. John Russell; Professor of History, University of Bristol, since 1984; *b* 20 Dec. 1937; *s* of Prof. J. J. Vincent, *qv*; *m* 1972, Nicolette Elizabeth Kenworthy; one *s* (and one *s* decd). *Educ:* Bedales Sch.; Christ's Coll., Cambridge. Lectr in Modern British History, Cambridge Univ., 1967–70; Prof. of Modern History, Univ. of Bristol, 1970–84. Chm., Bristol Br., NCCL, 1972–74. *Publications:* The Formation of the Liberal Party, 1966 (2nd edn as The Formation of the British Liberal Party 1857–68, 1980); Poll Books: How Victorians voted, 1967; (ed with A. B. Cooke) Lord Carlingford's Journal, 1971; (ed with M. Stenton) McCalmont's Parliamentary Poll Book 1832–1918, 1971; (with A. B. Cooke) The Governing Passion: Cabinet Government and party politics in Britain 1885–86, 1974; (ed) Disraeli, Derby and the Conservative Party: the political journals of Lord Stanley 1849–69, 1978; Gladstone and Ireland (Raleigh Lecture), 1979; (ed) The Crawford Papers: the journals of David Lindsay, Twenty-Seventh Earl of Crawford and Tenth Earl of Balcarres during the years 1892 to 1940, 1984; Disraeli, 1990; (ed) The Derby Diaries 1869–1878, 1995; What is History?, 1995; (contrib) Twentieth-Century Britain: an encyclopaedia, 1995. *Recreation:* journalism. *Address:* History Department, The University, Bristol BS8 1TH.

VINCENT, Leonard Grange, CBE 1960; FRIBA, FRTPI, Distinction Town Planning (RIBA); formerly architect and town planner, and Principal Partner, Vincent and Gorbing, Architects and Planning Consultants; *b* 13 April 1916; *s* of late Godfrey Grange Vincent; *m* 1942, Evelyn (*née* Gretton); twin *s* one *d*. *Educ:* Forest House School. Trained as architect in London, 1933, and subsequently as a town planner; experience in private practice and local government. Served War of 1939–45: Royal Engineers (Major); mostly overseas, in Western Desert, and Italian campaigns with 8th Army, 1940–45. Formerly Chief Architect and Planner, Stevenage Development Corporation. *Publications:* various technical and planning articles in technical press. *Recreations:* archaeology, painting. *Address:* Medbury, Rectory Lane, Stevenage, Hertfordshire SG1 4BX. *T:* Stevenage (01438) 351175.

VINCENT, Field Marshal Sir Richard (Frederick), GBE 1990; KCB 1984; DSO 1972; FIMechE; FRAeS; Chairman of Military Committee, NATO, 1993–Feb. 1996; *b* 23 Aug. 1931; *s* of late Frederick Vincent and Frances Elizabeth (*née* Coleshill); *m* 1955, Jean Paterson, *d* of Kenneth Stewart and Jane (*née* Banks); one *s* one *d* (and one *s* decd). *Educ:* Aldenham Sch.; RMCS. Commnd RA, National Service, 1951; Germany, 1951–55; Gunnery Staff, 1959; Radar Res. Estabt, Malvern, 1960–61; BAOR, 1962; Technical Staff Training, 1963–64; Staff Coll., 1965; Commonwealth Bde, Malaysia, 1966–68; MoD, 1968–70; Comd 12th Light Air Def. Regt, Germany, UK and NI, 1970–72; Instr, Staff Coll., 1972–73; Greenlands Staff Coll., Henley, 1974; Mil. Dir of Studies, RMCS, 1974–75; Comd 19 Airportable Bde, 1975–77; RCDS, 1978; Dep. Mil. Sec., 1979–80; Comdt, Royal Military College of Science, 1980–83; Master-Gen. of the Ordnance, MoD, 1983–87; VCDS, 1987–91; CDS, 1991–92. Col Commandant: REME, 1981–87; RA, 1983–; Hon. Colonel: 100 (Yeomanry) Field Regt RA, TA, 1982–91; 12th Air Defence Regt, 1987–91. President: Combined Services Winter Sports Assoc., 1983–90; Army Ski-ing Assoc., 1983–87. Kermit Rooosevelt Lectr, 1988; Vis. Fellow, Australian Coll. of Defence and Strategic Studies, 1995–. Member: Court, Cranfield Inst. of Technol., 1981–83; Adv. Council, RMCS, 1983–91; Gov., Aldenham Sch., 1987–. Freeman, City of London, 1992. FRAeS 1990; FIMechE 1990. Hon. DSc Cranfield, 1985. *Publications:* contrib. mil. jls and pubns. *Recreations:* contemplating a second career. *Address:* c/o Midland Bank, Shaftesbury, Dorset SP7 8JX.

VINCENT, Robin Anthony; Circuit Administrator, Northern Circuit, Court Service Agency (formerly Lord Chancellor's Department), since 1993; *b* 27 Feb. 1944; *s* of late John Kenneth Vincent and of Ivy Elizabeth Ann Vincent (*née* Grayer); *m* 1971, Hazel Ruth Perkins; two *s*. *Educ:* King's Sch., Worcester. Clerk, Worcs QS, 1962–70; Sen. Asst and Dep. Clerk, Worcs County Justices, 1970–72; Higher Executive Officer: Worcester Crown Court, 1972–76; Worcs County Court, 1976–77; Court Business Officer, 1977–79; Sen. Exec. Officer (Personnel), Circuit Administrator's Office, Birmingham, 1979–80; Chief Clerk, Worcester Crown Court, 1980–82; Principal Chief Clerk, Manchester Crown Court, 1982–86; Head of Division, Lord Chancellor's Department: Court Service Develt, London, 1986–91; Personnel Mgt, 1991–93; Judicial Appts, 1993. *Recreations:* cricket (playing), music, drinking red wine with Steve Baines. *Address:* The Moorings, 33 Grange Road, Bramhall, Stockport, Cheshire SK7 3BD. *T:* 0161–440 9526; Circuit Administrator's Office, 15 Quay Street, Manchester M60 9FD. *Clubs:* Old Vigornians (Worcester); Eggington Cricket (Leighton Buzzard); Stockport Georgians (Stockport).

VINCENT, Sir William (Percy Maxwell), 3rd Bt, *cr* 1936; Director, M & G (North America) Ltd, since 1992; *b* 1 February 1945; *o s* of Sir Lacey Vincent, 2nd Bt, and of Helen Millicent, *d* of Field Marshal Sir William Robert Robertson, 1st Bt, GCB, GCMG, GCVO, DSO; *S* father, 1963; *m* 1976, Christine Margaret, *d* of Rev. E. G. Walton; three *s*. *Educ:* Eton College. 2nd Lieutenant, Irish Guards, 1964–67. Jt Man. Dir, 1987–92, and Investment Dir, 1986–92, Touche Remnant & Co. and Touche Remnant Holdings; Dir, Touche Remnant & Co., 1985–92. Dir, Save and Prosper Investment Management, 1980–85. *Recreations:* water ski-ing, sailing. *Heir:* *s* Edward Mark William Vincent, *b* 6 March 1978. *Address:* Whistlers, Buriton, Petersfield, Hampshire GU31 5RU. *T:* Petersfield (01730) 63532.

VINCENT BROWN, Kenneth; *see* Brown.

VINE, David Martin; broadcaster and promotions consultant, since 1960; *b* 3 Jan. 1935; *s* of Dorothy and Harold Vine; *m* Mandy; two *s* two *d*. *Educ:* Barnstaple Grammar Sch. Journalist: North Devon Journal-Herald, 1953; Western Morning News, 1956; Westward Television, 1960; BBC TV, 1965–. *Publication:* The Superstars, 1984. *Recreation:* relaxing. *Club:* Leander.

VINE, Prof. Frederick John, FRS 1974; Professor, since 1974, Dean, 1977–80 and since 1993, School of Environmental Sciences, University of East Anglia; *b* 17 June 1939; *s* of Frederick Royston Vine and Ivy Grace Vine (*née* Bryant); *m* 1964, Susan Alice McCall; one *s* one *d*. *Educ:* Latymer Upper Sch., Hammersmith; St John's Coll., Cambridge (BA, PhD). Instructor, 1965–67, and Asst Professor, 1967–70, Dept of Geological and Geophysical Sciences, Princeton Univ., NJ, USA; Reader, School of Environmental Sciences, Univ. of E Anglia, 1970–74. *Publications:* (jtly) Global Tectonics, 1990; articles in Nature, Science, Phil. Trans Roy. Soc. London, etc. *Recreations:* walking, camping. *Address:* 144 Christchurch Road, Norwich NR2 3PG.

VINE, Col (Roland) Stephen, FRCPath, FZS; Chief Inspector, Cruelty to Animals Act (1876), Home Office, 1962–75; *b* 26 Dec. 1910; *s* of late Joseph Soutter Vine and of Josephine Vine (*née* Moylan); *m* 1935, Flora Betty, *d* of Charles Strutton Brookes, MBE, Dovercourt; three *d*. *Educ:* Southend-on-Sea High Sch.; Guy's Hosp. BSc; MRCS, LRCP, FRCPath, FZS(Scientific). Royal Army Medical Corps, 1934–60 (incl. War of 1939–45). Home Office, 1960–75. Former Mem., Council, Res. Defence Soc., 1977–85. *Publications:* chapter in: Biomedical Technology in Hospital Diagnosis, 1972; Animals in Scientific Research, 1983; articles in RAMC Jl. *Recreations:* gardening, bowling. *Address:* Shola, Fielden Road, Crowborough, Sussex TN6 1TR. *T:* Crowborough (01892) 661381. *Club:* Civil Service.

VINE, Roy; Director: First National Finance Corporation plc, 1984–93; First National Commercial Bank Ltd, 1990–93; *b* 1923; *m* 1945, Dorothy A. Yates; one *s* one *d*. *Educ:* Taunton's Sch., Southampton. Served RAF (Flt Lieut), 1942–46 and 1951–53. Vice-Chm., Barclays Bank UK Ltd, 1982–84; Dir, Barclays Bank plc, 1979–84 (Gen. Man., 1972; Senior Gen. Man., 1979–81). Dir, First National Bank Plc (formerly First National Securities Ltd), 1985–90. FCIB 1951. *Recreations:* golf, football, music. *Address:* Summerfold, Itchen Abbas, Winchester SO21 1AX.

VINELOTT, Sir John (Evelyn), Kt 1978; Judge of the High Court of Justice, Chancery Division, 1978–95; *b* 15 Oct. 1923; *s* of George Frederick Vine-Lott and Vera Lilian Vine-Lott (*née* Mockford); *m* 1956, Sally Elizabeth, *d* of His Honour Sir Walker Kelly Carter, QC; two *s* one *d*. *Educ:* Queen Elizabeth's Gram. Sch., Faversham, Kent; Queens' Coll., Cambridge (MA). War Service, Sub-Lieut RNVR, 1942–46. Called to Bar, Gray's Inn, 1953 (Atkin Scholar; Bencher, 1974; Treas., 1993); QC 1968; practised at the Chancery Bar. Chm., Insolvency Rules Adv. Cttee, 1984–92. Président, L'association de Bousquetara, 1989–. *Publications:* essays and articles on Revenue and Administration Law, in specialist periodicals. *Address:* 22 Portland Road, W11 4LG. *T:* 0171–727 4778. *Club:* Garrick.

VINEN, William Frank, (Joe), FRS 1973; Poynting Professor of Physics, University of Birmingham, since 1974 (Professor of Physics, 1962–74); *b* 15 Feb. 1930; *o s* of Gilbert Vinen and Olive Maud Vinen (*née* Roach); *m* 1960, Susan-Mary Audrey Master; one *s* one *d*. *Educ:* Watford Grammar Sch.; Clare College, Cambridge. Research Fellow, Clare College, 1955–58. Royal Air Force, 1948–49. Demonstrator in Physics, Univ. of Cambridge and Fellow of Pembroke Coll., 1958–62. Hon. Life Fellow, Coventry Univ. (formerly Poly.), 1989. Simon Meml Prize, Inst. of Physics, 1963; Holweck Medal and Prize, Inst. of Physics and French Physical Soc., 1978; Rumford Medal, Royal Soc., 1980. *Recreation:* good food. *Address:* 52 Middle Park Road, Birmingham B29 4BJ. *T:* 0121–475 1328.

VINER, Monique Sylvaine, (Mrs M. S. Gray), CBE 1994; QC 1979; **Her Honour Judge Viner;** a Circuit Judge, since 1990; *b* 3 Oct. 1926; *d* of late Hugh Viner and Eliane Viner; *m* 1958, Dr Pieter Francis Gray; one *s* three *d*. *Educ:* Convent of the Sacred Heart, Roehampton; St Hugh's Coll., Oxford (MA; Hon. Fellow, 1990). In teaching, publishing, factory and shop work, 1947–50. Called to the Bar, Gray's Inn, 1950, Bencher, 1988. A Recorder, 1986–90. Chm. of five Wages Councils, 1952–94; Mem., Industrial Court, 1976. *Recreations:* talking, reading, tennis, music, piano, walking, gardening, cooking, bird watching, history. *Address:* Old Glebe, Waldron, Heathfield, East Sussex TN21 0RB. *T:* Heathfield (01435) 863865.

VINES, David Anthony, PhD; Fellow and Tutor in Economics, Balliol College, Oxford, since 1992; Adjunct Professor of Economics, Research School of Pacific and Asian Studies, Australian National University, since 1991; *b* 8 May 1949; *s* of Robert Godfrey and Vera Frances Vines; *m* 1st, 1979, Susannah Lucy (marr. diss. 1992); three *s*; 2nd, 1995, Jane Elizabeth Bingham. *Educ:* Scotch Coll., Melbourne; Melbourne Univ. (BA 1971); Cambridge Univ. (BA 1974; MA 1977; PhD 1984). Cambridge University: Fellow, Pembroke Coll., 1976–85; Res. Officer and Sen. Res. Officer, Dept of Applied Econs, 1979–85; Adam Smith Prof. of Political Economy, Univ. of Glasgow, 1985–92; Res. Fellow, Centre for Econ. Policy Res., London, 1985–. Board Member: Channel 4 Television, 1987–92; Glasgow Develt Agency, 1990–92. Economic Consultant to Sec. of State for Scotland, 1987–92; Consultant, IMF, 1988–. Economic and Social Research Council: Member: Econ. Affairs Cttee, 1985–87; Res. Progs Bd, 1992–93; Dir, Res. Prog. on Global Econ. Instns, 1994–. Mem. Academic Panel, HM Treasury, 1986–. Mem. Council, Royal Economic Soc., 1988–92. Bd Mem., Analysys, 1989–. Comr, BFI Enquiry into the Future of the BBC, 1992. Bd Mem., Scottish Early Music Consort, 1990–. *Publications:* (with J. E. Meade and J. M. Maciejowski) Stagflation, Vol. II: Demand Management, 1983; (with D. A. Currie) Macroeconomic Interactions Between North and South, 1988; (jtly) Macroeconomic Policy: inflation, wealth and the exchange rate, 1989; (with G. Hughes) Deregulation and the Future of Commercial Television, 1989; (with A. Stevenson) Information, Strategy, and Public Policy, 1991; (with D. A. Currie) North South Interactions and International Macroeconomic Policy, 1995; papers on international macroeconomics, balance of payments and economic policy, in professional jls. *Recreations:* hillwalking, music. *Address:* Balliol College, Oxford OX1 3BJ. *T:* Oxford (01865) 277777, *Fax:* (01865) 277803.

VINES, Eric Victor, CMG 1984; OBE 1971; HM Diplomatic Service, retired; *b* 28 May 1929; *s* of late Henry E. Vines; *m* 1953, Ellen-Grethe Ella Küppers; one *s*. *Educ:* St

Dunstan's Coll., London; St Catharine's Coll., Cambridge (MA). Army service, 1947–49. Joined Commonwealth Relations Office, 1952; Colombo, 1954–55; 1st Sec., Singapore, 1958–61; Canberra, 1961–65; Diplomatic Service Administration Office, 1965–68; 1st Sec., Information, Mexico City, 1968–70; Counsellor, Exec. Sec.-Gen., SEATO Conf., London, 1971; Head, Cultural Exchange Dept, FCO, 1971–74; Counsellor (Commercial), Tel Aviv, 1974–77, Stockholm, 1977–80; Consul-Gen., Barcelona, 1980–83; Ambassador to Mozambique, 1984–85; Ambassador to Uruguay, 1986–89; Staff Assessor, FCO, 1991–94. Trustee: Centre for S African Studies, York Univ., 1989–94; Gemini Ethiopian Trust, 1990–. *Recreations:* opera, archaeology, Africa. *Address:* c/o Foreign and Commonwealth Office, King Charles Street, SW1A 2AH. *Club:* Commonwealth Trust.

VINES, Sir William (Joshua), AC 1987; Kt 1977; CMG 1969; FASA, ACIS; psc; Chairman, ANZ Banking Group, 1982–89 (Director, since 1976); Director, Dalgety Australia Ltd, 1980–91 (Chairman, 1970–80); grazier at Tara, Queensland, 1965–82 and Cliffdale, Currabubula, NSW, since 1982; *b* 27 May 1916; *s* of P. V. Vines, Canterbury, Victoria, Australia; *m* 1st, 1939, Thelma J. (*d* 1988), *d* of late F. J. Ogden; one *s* two *d*; 2nd, 1990, Judith Anne Ploeg, *d* of late T. E. Raynsford. *Educ:* Haileybury College, Brighton Beach, Victoria. Managing Director: Internat. Wool Secretariat, 1961–69 (Board Mem., 1969–79); Berger, Jenson & Nicholson Ltd, 1960 (Dir, 1961–69); Dalgety Australia Ltd, 1971–76 (Chm., 1970–80); Group Managing Director, Lewis Berger & Sons Ltd, 1955–61; Director: Lewis Berger & Sons (Aust.) Pty Ltd & Sherwin Williams Co. (Aust.) Pty Ltd, 1952–55; Goodlass Wall & Co. Pty Ltd, 1947–49; Dalgety Ltd; Dalgety New Zealand Ltd, 1969–80; Port Phillip Mills Pty Ltd, 1969–88; Wiggins Teape Ltd (UK), 1970–79; Tubemakers of Australia Ltd, 1970–86 (Dep. Chm., 1973–86); Associated Pulp & Paper Mills Ltd, 1971–83 (Dep. Chm. 1977, Chm. 1979–83); Conzinc Rio Tinto of Australia, 1977–84; Grindlays Hldgs, subseq. ANZ UK Hldgs, 1985–89; Grindlays Bank, 1987–89; Chm., Thorn Holdings Pty Ltd, 1969–74. Vice-President Melbourne Legacy, 1949–51; Pres. Building Industry Congress, Vic., 1954–55. Chm., Aust. Wool Commn, 1970–72; Mem. Exec., CSIRO, 1973–78; Chm. Council, Hawkesbury Agric. Coll., 1975–85. Mem., Australia New Zealand Foundn, 1979–84. Chm., The Sir Robert Menzies Meml Trust, 1978–92. Served War of 1939–45 (despatches, C-in-C's commendation for gallantry, El Alamein), 2nd AIF, 2/23 Aust. Inf. Bn, Middle East, New Guinea and Borneo, Capt. Hon. DSc Econ Sydney, 1993. *Address:* Cliffdale, Currabubula, NSW 2342, Australia. *T:* (67) 689109. *Club:* Union (Sydney).

VINEY, Hon. Anne Margaret, (Hon. Mrs Viney), JP; barrister; Part-time Chairman, Social Security Appeal Tribunals, since 1987; *b* 14 June 1926; *d* of late Baron Morton of Henryton, PC, MC, and Lady Morton of Henryton; *m* 1947, Peter Andrew Hopwood Viney; one *s* two *d*. *Educ:* Priorsfield, Godalming, Surrey. Called to the Bar, Lincoln's Inn, 1979. Councillor, Kensington and Chelsea BC, 1960–62. JP, 1961. Mem., Inner London Juvenile Court panel, 1961–87 (Chm. 1970). Helped to found London Adventure Playground Assoc., 1962 (Sec. 1962–69); Chm., Consumer Protection Adv. Cttee, 1973–82. *Recreations:* conversation, playing poetry game. *Address:* Worth House, Worth Matravers, near Swanage, Dorset BH19 3LQ.

VINEY, Elliott (Merriam), DSO 1945; MBE 1946; TD; JP; DL; FSA; Director: British Printing Corporation Ltd, 1964–75; Hazell, Watson & Viney Ltd, 1947–78; *b* 21 Aug. 1913; *s* of late Col. Oscar Viney, TD, DL, and Edith Merriam; *m* 1950, Rosamund Ann Pelly; two *d*. *Educ:* Oundle; Univ. Coll., Oxford. Bucks Bn, Oxford and Bucks Light Infantry (TA), 1932–46. Governor and Trustee, Museum of London, 1972–88. Pres., British Fedn of Master Printers, 1972–73. Master, Grocers' Company, 1970–71. County Dir, Bucks St John Amb. Assoc., 1953–55; Trustee, Bucks Historic Churches Trust, 1957; Pres., Bucks Archaeol. Soc., 1979 (Hon. Sec., 1954–79); Pres., CPRE (Bucks), 1990–93 (Chm., 1976–90); Chm., Bucks Record Soc., 1986. JP 1950, DL 1952, High Sheriff, 1964, Buckinghamshire. OStJ 1953. Editor: Oxford Mountaineering, 1935; Climbers' Club Jl, 1936–39; (jt) Records of Bucks, 1947–74. *Publications:* The Sheriffs of Buckinghamshire, 1965; (jtly) Old Aylesbury, 1976. *Recreations:* conservation, music, walking. *Address:* Cross Farmhouse, Quainton, Aylesbury, Bucks HP22 4AR. *Clubs:* Alpine; County Hall (Aylesbury).

VINING, Rowena Adelaide, OBE 1979 (MBE 1964); HM Diplomatic Service, retired; *b* 25 Sept. 1921; *er d* of late Col Percival Llewellyn Vining and Phyllis Servante Vining. *Educ:* privately, and at Chiddingstone Castle, Edenbridge, Kent. Foreign Office, 1941–52 (war service in Italy, Indonesia, 1943–45). Commonwealth Relations Office, 1952–55; Second Secretary: Karachi, 1955–58; Sydney, 1958–62; First Sec.: CRO, 1962–65; Canberra, 1965–67; Commonwealth Office (later Foreign and Commonwealth Office), 1967–71; Vienna, 1972–74; Consul, Florence and Consul-General, San Marino, 1974–78; Dep. UK Permanent Rep. to the Council of Europe, 1978–81; Consul-General, Strasbourg, 1979–80. Staff Assessor, FCO, 1983–86. *Recreations:* gardening, music. *Address:* Dorchester Cottage, Greywell, near Basingstoke RG25 1BT.

VINSON, family name of **Baron Vinson.**

VINSON, Baron *cr* 1985 (Life Peer), of Roddam Dene in the County of Northumberland; **Nigel Vinson,** LVO 1979; DL; Inventor; Deputy Chairman, Electra Investment Trust, since 1990 (Director, since 1975); Chairman of the Trustees, Institute of Economic Affairs, since 1989 (Trustee, since 1972); *b* Nettlestead Place, Kent, 27 Jan. 1931; *s* of late Ronald Vinson and Bettina Vinson (*née* Southwell-Sander); *m* 1972, Yvonne Ann Collin; three *d*. *Educ:* Pangbourne Naval Coll. Lieut, Queen's Royal Regt, 1949–51. Chm., 1952–72, and Founder, Plastic Coatings Ltd (started in a Nissen hut, 1952, flotation, 1969; Queen's Award to Industry, 1971). Member: Crafts Adv. Cttee, 1971–77; Design Council, 1973–80; Dep. Chm., CBI Smaller Firms Council, 1979–84; Chairman: CoSIRA, 1980–82; Rural Develt Commn, 1980–90 (Mem., 1978–90); Industry Year Steering Cttee, RSA, 1985–87; Pres., Industrial Participation Assoc., 1979–89 (Chm., 1971–78). Director: British Airports Authority, 1973–80; Centre for Policy Studies, 1974–80; Hon. Dir, Queen's Silver Jubilee Appeal, 1976–78; Dir, Fleming High Income Growth Trust (formerly Fleming Tech. Trust), 1972–; Dir, Barclays Bank UK, 1982–88. Member: Northumbrian Nat. Parks Countryside Cttee, 1977–89; Regional Cttee, Nat. Trust, 1977–84. Council Mem., St George's House, Windsor Castle, 1990–. FRSA, CIMgt. DL Northumberland, 1990. *Publications:* Personal and Portable Pensions for All, 1984; Owners All, 1985. *Recreations:* fine art and craftmanship, horses, farming. *Address:* 34 Kynance Mews, SW7 4QR. *T:* Wooperton (01668) 21230. *Club:* Boodle's.

VINTER, (Frederick Robert) Peter, CB 1965; *b* 27 March 1914; *e s* of P. J. Vinter (Headmaster, Archbishop Holgate's Grammar Sch., York, 1915–37) and Harriet Mary (*née* Cammack); *m* 1938, Margaret, *d* of S. I. Rake, Pembroke; two *s*. *Educ:* Haileybury Coll.; King's Coll., Cambridge (MA). Min. of Economic Warfare, 1939; Cabinet Office, 1943; HM Treasury, 1945–69, Third Sec., 1965–69; Dep. Sec., Min. of Technology and DTI, 1969–73. Overseas Adviser to CEGB, 1973–79; Dir (non-Exec.), Vickers Ltd, 1974–80. Nuffield Travelling Fellowship (in India), 1950–51.

VINTER, Peter; *see* Vinter, F. R. P.

VINTON, Alfred Merton; Chairman, Electra Kingsway Managers, since 1995; *b* 11 May 1938; *s* of Alfred Merton Vinton and Jean Rosalie Vinton (*née* Guiterman); *m* 1st, 1963, Mary Bedell Weber; two *s* one *d*; 2nd, 1983, Anna-Maria Hawser (*née* Dugan-Chapman); one *s* one *d*. *Educ:* Harvard College (AB Econs 1960). US Navy Lieut (JG), 1960–62. J. P. Morgan, 1962–88; Chief Operating Officer, N. M. Rothschild & Sons, 1988–92; Chief Exec. Officer, Enterprises Quilmes SA, 1992–94. *Recreations:* tennis, riding, music. *Address:* Stoke Albany House, Market Harborough, Leics LE16 8PT. *T:* Dingley (01858) 535227. *Clubs:* White's, Mark's; Queen's; Harvard (NY).

VIOT, Jacques Edmond; Commandeur de la Légion d'Honneur; Commandeur de l'Ordre National du Mérite; President: France-Great Britain Association, since 1987; French section, Franco-British Council, since 1992; Alliance Française de Paris, since 1994; *b* 25 Aug. 1921; *m* 1950, Jeanne de Martimprey de Romécourt. *Educ:* Bordeaux and Paris Lycées; Ecole Normale Supérieure; Ecole Nationale d'Administration. Foreign Office (European Dept), 1951–53; Second Sec., London, 1953–57; First Sec., Rabat, 1957–61; Tech. Advisor to Foreign Minister, 1961–62; Head of Technical Co-operation, FO, 1962–68; Dir for Personnel and Gen. Admin, 1968–72; Ambassador to Canada, 1972–77; Gen. Inspector for Foreign Affairs, 1977–78; Directeur de Cabinet to Foreign Minister, 1978–81; Gen. Inspector for Foreign Affairs, 1981–84; Ambassador to the Court of St James's, 1984–86; Ambassadeur de France, 1986; Chm., Review Cttee on Foreign Affairs, Paris, 1986–87. Chm. Entrance Examination Bd, Ecole Nat. d'Admin, 1987. Fellow, St Antony's College, Oxford. *Address:* 19 rue de Civry, 75016 Paris, France.

VIRANI, Nazmudin Gulamhusein; Chairman and Chief Executive, Control Securities PLC, property and leisure company, 1985–92; *b* 2 March 1948; *s* of Gulamhusein Virani and Fatma Virani; *m* 1970, Yasmin Abdul Rasul Ismail; two *s* one *d*. *Educ:* Aga Khan Sch., Kampala, Uganda. Left Uganda for UK, 1972; founded Virani gp of companies, 1972 (Chm. and Chief Exec.); Chm. and Chief Exec., Belhaven PLC, 1983–86. *Recreations:* cricket, travel, philanthropy.

VISHNEVSKAYA, Galina; soprano; *b* 25 Oct. 1926; *m* 1955, Mstislav Rostropovich, *qv*; two *d*. *Educ:* studied with Vera Garina. Toured with Leningrad Light Opera Co., 1944–48, with Leningrad Philharmonic Soc., 1948–52; joined Bolshoi Theatre, 1952. Concert appearances in Europe and USA, 1950–; first appeared at Metropolitan Opera, NY, 1961. Rôles include: Leonora in Fidelio, Tatiana in Eugene Onegin, Iolanta. Has sung in Britain at Festival Hall, Aldeburgh Festival, Edinburgh Festival, Covent Garden, Rostropovich Festival, Snape; Dir, Iolanta, Aldeburgh Fest., 1988. Makes concert tours with her husband. Has made many recordings. *Publication:* Galina (autobiog.), 1984. *Address:* c/o Victor Hochhauser, 4 Oak Hill Way, NW3 7LR.

VISSER, John Bancroft; Director of Administration, Science and Engineering Research Council (formerly Science Research Council), 1974–88; *b* 29 Jan. 1928; *o s* of late Gilbert and Ethel Visser; *m* 1955, Astrid Margareta Olson; two *s* one *d*. *Educ:* Mill Hill Sch.; New Coll., Oxford (Exhibnr). Entered Civil Service, Asst Principal, Min. of Supply, 1951; Principal, 1956; Min. of Aviation, 1959; Admin. Staff Coll., 1965; Asst Sec., 1965; Min. of Technology, 1967; Royal Coll. of Defence Studies, 1970; Civil Service Dept, 1971; Procurement Exec., MoD, 1971; Under-Sec., 1974; Sec. of Nat. Defence Industries Council, 1971–74. *Recreations:* sport, music, gardening, walking. *Address:* Rosslyn, 3 Berkeley Road, Cirencester, Glos GL7 1TY. *T:* Cirencester (01285) 652626. *Club:* Old Millhillians.

VIVIAN, family name of **Barons Swansea** and **Vivian.**

VIVIAN, 6th Baron *cr* 1841; **Nicholas Crespigny Laurence Vivian;** Bt 1828; *b* 11 Dec. 1935; *s* of 5th Baron Vivian and Victoria (*d* 1985), *er d* of late Captain H. G. L. Oliphant, DSO, MVO; *S* father, 1991; *m* 1st, 1960, Catherine Joyce (marr. diss. 1972), *y d* of late James Kenneth Hope, CBE; one *s* one *d*; 2nd, 1972, Carol, *e d* of F. Alan Martineau, MBE; two *d*. *Educ:* Eton; Madrid Univ. CO 16th/5th The Queen's Royal Lancers, 1976–79; Col, MoD, 1980–84; Dep. Comdr Land Forces and Chief of Staff, Cyprus, 1984–87; Brig., 1987; Comdr, British Communication Zone (Antwerp), 1987–90. Conservative; Hon. Sec., All-Party Defence Study Gp; Member: Defence Review Gp; IPU; CPA; Assoc. of Cons. Peers. *Recreation:* travel. *Heir: s* Hon. Charles Crespigny Hussey Vivian, *b* 20 Dec. 1966. *Address:* House of Lords, SW1A 0PW. *Clubs:* White's, Cavalry and Guards.

VIVIAN, Michael Hugh; Full-time Board Member, 1974–80, and Deputy Chairman, 1978–80, Civil Aviation Authority; *b* 15 Dec. 1919; *s* of Hugh Vivian and Mary (*née* Gilbertson); *m* 1st, 1951, June Stiven; one *s* one *d*; 2nd, Joy D. Maude. *Educ:* Uppingham; Oxford. Served War: RAF (139 Sqdn), Flying Instructor, Test Pilot, 1940–44. Min. of Civil Aviation, 1945; Private Sec. to Parly Sec. for Civil Aviation, 1945–46; various operational appts, 1947–61; Dep. Dir of Flight Safety, 1961–66; Dir of Flight Safety, 1966–67; Dir of Advanced Aircraft Ops, 1967–71; Civil Aviation Authority, 1972: Dir-Gen. Safety Ops, 1972–74; Gp Dir, Safety Services, 1974–78; Dir, CSE Aviation Ltd, 1980–82. *Recreations:* golf, vintage cars. *Address:* Willow Cottage, The Dickredge, Steeple Aston, Bicester, Oxfordshire OX6 3RS. *T:* Steeple Aston (01869) 347171. *Club:* Royal Air Force.

VOCKLER, Rt. Rev. John Charles, (Rt. Rev. Brother John-Charles); engaged in writing and research and active preaching and teaching ministry; Founder, and Superior, Franciscan Order of the Divine Compassion, since 1990; *b* 22 July 1924; *e s* of John Thomas Vockler and Mary Catherine Vockler (*née* Widerberg), Sydney, New South Wales. *Educ:* Sydney Boys' High Sch.; after studying accountancy, matriculated by private study and correspondence (Metropolitan Business Coll. and Internat. Correspondence Schs, Sydney) to the Univ. of Sydney; Moore Theol Coll.; St John's Theol College, Morpeth, NSW; Australian Coll. of Theology (LTh 1948; Hey Sharp Prize for NT Greek); Univ. of Queensland (BA (1st cl. Hons History) 1953; Univ. Gold Medal for outstanding achievement, 1953; Walter and Eliza Hall Foundn Travelling Scholarship, 1953); Fulbright Schol., 1953; BA Univ. of Adelaide, *aegr.*, 1961; Gen. Theol Seminary, NY (MDiv 1954; STM 1956). Junior Clerk, W. R. Carpenter & Co. Ltd, Sydney, NSW, 1939–43. Deacon, 1948; priest, 1948; Asst Deacon, Christ Church Cathedral, Newcastle, 1948; Asst Priest, 1948–50; Vice-Warden of St John's Coll., Univ. of Queensland, 1950–53; Acting Chaplain, C of E Grammar Sch. for Boys, Brisbane, 1953; Acting Vice-Warden, St John's Coll., Morpeth and Lectr in Old Testament, 1953; Asst Priest, Cathedral of S John the Divine, NY and Chaplain, St Luke's Home for Aged Women and the Home for Old Men and Aged Couples, 1953–54; Australian Delegate to Anglican Congress, 1954; Fellow and Tutor, GTS, 1954–56; Asst Priest, St Stephen's Church, West 69th Street, NY, 1955; Priest-in-charge, St Stephen's, New York, 1956; Asst Priest, parish of Singleton, NSW, 1956–59; Lecturer in Theology, St John's Theol Coll., Morpeth, NSW, 1956–59; Secretary, Newcastle Diocesan Board of Education, 1958–59; Titular Bishop of Mount Gambier and Assistant Bishop of Adelaide (Coadjutor, 1959; title changed to Assistant, 1961), until 1962; also Archdeacon of Eyre Peninsula, 1959–62; Vicar-General, Examining Chaplain to Bishop of Adelaide, 1960–62; Bishop of Polynesia, 1962–68. Society of St Francis: entered Soc., 1969; professed, 1972; Chaplain, Third Order, European Province, 1972–74; made life profession, 1975; Guardian, Friary of St Francis,

Brisbane, 1975–77, Islington, NSW, 1978–79; Minister Provincial, Pacific Province, 1976–81; Archivist, Amer. Province, 1985–89; left SSF, 1990; Vicar, Trinity Church, Monmouth, Ill, 1990–93; Adjunct Prof. of Ascetical Theology, Nashotah House Seminary, 1991–93; received into Anglican Catholic Church, USA, 1994; Asst Bp to the Metropolitan, Anglican Catholic Church, 1995–; Dean, Holyrood Seminary, Liberty, NY, 1995– (Sub-Dean for Acad. Affairs, 1994–95). Warden: Community of St Clare, Newcastle, NSW, 1975–80; Soc. of Sacred Advent, 1976–80; Poor Clares of Reparation, Mt Sinai, NY, 1982–83 (Bishop Protector, 1987–93); Spiritual Dir, Community of the Holy Spirit, NY, 1988–89; Bishop Visitor, Order of the Incarnation, NY, 1990–93 (Spiritual Advr, 1988–89); Spiritual Dir to Bishops and Priests of the Catholic and Apostolic Church of N America, 1988–; Confessor Extraordinary, Soc. of St John the Evangelist, Cambridge, Mass, 1987–89; Chaplain to Monmouth Community Hosp., 1990–93. Collegial Mem., House of Bishops, Episcopal Church, USA, 1983–93; Member: House of Bishops' Cttee on Religious Life, 1986–89; Episcopal Synod of America, 1989–93. President, Harry Charman's All Races Sports and Social Club, Suva, Fiji, 1962–68, Hon. Life Vice-Pres., 1968; Chairman: S Pacific Anglican Council, 1963–68; Council of Pacific Theol Coll., 1963–68; President: Fiji Council of Social Services, 1964–68; Fiji Branch, Royal Commonwealth Soc., 1966–68. Writing Grant, Literature Bd of Australia Council, 1979, 1981. Member: Soc. of Authors; Australian Soc. of Authors; PEN (International), Sydney Br. and New York Br.; Guild of Writers Inc., NY; Christian Writers' Fellowship (USA); Aust. Professional Writers' Services; Penman Club (UK); National Writers' Club (USA); Federated Clerks Union of Aust., 1978–81; Internat. Center for Integrative Studies, NY 1983–93; Internat. Ecumenical Fellowship; Guild of All Souls; Confraternity of the Blessed Sacrament; Soc. of Mary; Catholic and Evangelical Mission; Anglican Pacifist Fellowship; Fellowship of Reconciliation; Fellowship of S Alban and S Sergius; Anglican Fellowship of Prayer, USA; Fellowship of Three Kings, Haddington, Scotland; Amnesty Internat., USA (Mem., Urgent Action Gp); Soc. of the Holy Cross, 1992–94; The Living Rosary of Our Lady and St Dominic, 1992–. Priest Associate, Shrine of Our Lady, Walsingham and Priory of Our Lady of Pew, Westminster Abbey; Associate, Guild of St Vincent, 1985–; Priest Mem., OGS, 1952–75. Sec., Adv. Council for Religious Communities in Aust. and Pacific, 1976–80. Permission to officiate in various dioceses, UK, NZ, USA, Australia, 1969–93. Vice-Pres. and Mem. Council, USPG, 1973–74; Vice-Pres., Missions to Seamen, 1963–69; Hon. Asst Bp of Worcester, 1972–73; Assistant Bishop: Chelmsford, 1973–74; Southwark, 1974–75; Assisting Bishop, dio. of Quincy, USA, 1990–93; Hon. Canon of Southwark, 1975, Canon Emeritus 1975; Hon. Mission Chaplain, dio. Brisbane, 1975–79. Examnr for Aust. Coll. of Theology, 1975–76 and 1979. ThD (*jure dig.*) ACT, 1961; STD (*hc*) Gen. Theological Seminary, NY, 1961; BD (*ad eund.*) Melbourne College of Divinity, 1960. Bishop's Cross, dio. of Long Is, 1989. *Publications:* Can Anglicans Believe Anything—The Nature and Spirit of Anglicanism, 1961 (NSW); Forward Day by Day, 1962; (ed) Believing in God (by M. L. Yates), 1962 (Australian edn), revd edn 1983 (US). One Man's Journey, 1972; St Francis: Franciscanism and the Society of St Francis, 1980; contributions to: Preparatory Volume for Anglican Congress, Toronto, 1963; Anglican Mosaic, 1963; Mutual Responsibility: Questions and Answers, 1964; All One Body (ed T. Wilson), 1968; Australian Dictionary of Biography (4 articles); St Mark's Review, Australian Church Quarterly, The Anglican, The Young Anglican, Pacific Journal of Theology, New Zealand Theological Review, weekly feature, Newcastle Morning Herald, NSW; book reviews in Amer. theol jls; Aust. corresp. to New Fire, 1980–81; book review Editor, New York Episcopalians, 1986–91. *Recreations:* classical music, detective stories, theatre, films, prints and engravings. *Address:* The Friary of Our Lady of the Angels at Holyrood Seminary, PO Box 111, Liberty, NY 12754–0111, USA. *T:* (914) 2920149, *Fax:* (914) 2920162. *Clubs:* Tonga (Nukualofa); St John's Coll. (Brisbane) (Hon Mem., 1976–).

VOELCKER, Christopher David, TD 1967; Metropolitan Stipendiary Magistrate, since 1982; *b* 10 May 1933; *s* of Eric Voelcker and Carmen Muriel Lyon Voelcker (*née* Henstock); *m* 1st, 1964, Sybil Russell Stoneham (marr. diss. 1985); two *d*; 2nd, 1991, Petrina Alexandra Keany (*née* Holdsworth). *Educ:* Wellington Coll., Berks. Called to Bar, Middle Temple, 1955. National Service, 8th King's Royal Irish Hussars, 1952–53. 3/4 County of London Yeomanry (Sharpshooters) TA, 1953–60; Kent and County of London Yeomanry (Sharpshooters) TA, 1960–67. A Recorder, 1989–94. Member: Inner London Probation Cttee, 1986–92; Recruitment and Trng Cttee, Central Council of Probation for England and Wales, 1988–91. *Recreations:* military history, gardening. *Address:* 6 Pump Court, Temple, EC4Y 7AR. *T:* 0171–353 7242. *Club:* Cavalry and Guards.

VOGEL, Hans-Jochen, Hon. CBE; Dr jur; Chairman, Social Democratic Party (SPD), Federal Republic of Germany, 1987–91; Member, Bundestag, since 1972 (Social Democratic Party); Leader of the Opposition, 1983–91; *b* 3 Feb. 1926; *s* of Dr Hermann Vogel and Caroline (*née* Brinz); *m* 1st, 1951, Ilse Leisnering (marr. diss. 1970); one *s* two *d*; 2nd, 1972, Liselotte Sonnenholzer. *Educ:* Göttingen and Giessen; Univs of Marburg and Munich (Dr jur 1950). Army service, 1943–45 (PoW). Admitted Bavarian Bar, 1951; Legal Asst, Bavarian Min. of Justice, 1952–54; District Court Counsel, Traunstein, 1954–58; staff of Bavarian State Chancellery, 1955–58; Munich City Council, 1958, Oberbürgermeister (Chief Executive), Munich, 1960–72 (re-elected, 1966); Vice-Pres., Org. Cttee, Olympic Games, 1972. Chm., Bavarian SDP, 1972–77; Minister of regional planning, housing and urban develt, 1972–74; Minister of Justice, 1974–81; Mayor of West Berlin, Jan.–June 1981, leader of opposition, 1981–83. Bundesverdienstkreuz; Bavarian Verdienstorden. *Publications:* Städte im Wandel, 1971; Die Amtskette: Meine 12 Münchner Jahre, 1972; Reale Reformen, 1973. *Recreations:* mountaineering, swimming, reading history. *Address:* c/o Bundeshaus, 53113 Bonn, Germany.

VOGELPOEL, Pauline, (Mrs R. D. Mann), MBE 1962; Vice-President, Contemporary Art Society, since 1984; *d* of late Pieter Vogelpoel and Yvonne Vogelpoel, Mozambique; *m* 1975, Richard David Mann, *s* of F. A. Mann, CBE, FBA. *Educ:* Herschel School, Cape Town; University of Cape Town (BA). Joined Contemporary Art Society, 1954, as Organising Secretary; Director 1976–82. Zurich Editor, Harpers & Queen Magazine, 1982–86. Mem., Adv. Council, Victoria and Albert Museum, 1977–82. *Publications:* occasional journalism. *Recreations:* cooking, music, junkshops, pugs. *Address:* Hebelstrasse 15, 4056 Basle, Switzerland.

VOGT, Dr Marthe Louise, FRS 1952; Dr med Berlin, Dr phil Berlin; PhD Cantab; *b* 1903; *d* of Oskar Vogt and Cécile Vogt (*née* Mugnier). *Educ:* Auguste Viktoria-Schule, Berlin; University of Berlin. Research Assistant, Department of Pharmacology, Berlin Univ., 1930; Research Assistant and head of chemical division, Kaiser Wilhelm Institut für Hirnforschung, Berlin, 1931–35; Rockefeller Travelling Fellow, 1935–36; Research Worker, Dept of Pharmacology, Cambridge Univ., 1935–40; Alfred Yarrow Research Fellow of Girton Coll., 1937–40; Member Staff of College of Pharmaceutical Society, London, 1941–46; Lecturer, later Reader, in Pharmacology, University of Edinburgh, 1947–60; Head of Pharmacology Unit, Agricultural Research Council Institute of Animal Physiology, 1960–68. Vis. Associate Prof. in Pharmacology, Columbia Univ., New York, 1949; Vis. Prof., Sydney 1965, Montreal 1968. Life Fellow, Girton Coll., Cambridge, 1970. For. Hon. Mem., Amer. Acad. of Arts and Scis, 1977. Hon. Fellow RSM 1980. Corresp. Mem., Deutsche Physiologische Gesellschaft, 1976; Hon. Member: Physiological Soc., 1974; British Pharmacological Soc., 1971; Hungarian Acad. of Scis, 1981; British Assoc. for Psychopharmacol., 1983. Hon. DSc: Edinburgh, 1974; Cambridge, 1983. Royal Medal, Royal Soc., 1981. *Publications:* papers in neurological, physiological and pharmacological journals. *Address:* Chateau La Jolla Terrace, 7544 La Jolla Boulevard, La Jolla, CA 92037, USA.

VOLCKER, Paul A.; Chairman: James D. Wolfensohn Incorporated, since 1988; J. Rothschild, Wolfensohn & Co., since 1992; Frederick H. Schultz Professor of International Economic Policy, Princeton University, since 1988; *b* Cape May, New Jersey, 5 Sept. 1927; *s* of Paul A. Volcker and Alma Louise Klippel; *m* 1954, Barbara Marie Bahnson; one *s* one *d*. *Educ:* Princeton Univ. (AB *summa cum laude*); Harvard Univ. (MA); LSE. Special Asst, Securities Dept, Fed. Reserve Bank, NY, 1953–57; Financial Economist, Chase Manhattan Bank, NYC, 1957–62; Vice-Pres. and Dir of Forward Planning, 1965–69; Dir, Office of Financial Analysis, US Treasury Dept, 1962–63; Dep. Under-Sec. for Monetary Affairs, 1963–65; Under-Sec. for Monetary Affairs, 1969–74; Senior Fellow, Woodrow Wilson Sch. of Public and Internat. Affairs, Princeton Univ., 1974–75; Pres. NY Federal Reserve Bank, 1975–79; Chairman: American Federal Reserve Board, 1979–87; Trilateral Commn, 1992–; Group of Thirty, 1992–. *Address:* 151 E 79th Street, New York, NY 10021, USA.

VOLGER, Dr Hendrik Cornelis; Manager, Sittingbourne Research Centre, and Director, Shell Research Ltd, 1989–93; *b* 6 March 1932; *s* of Ferdinand Pieter and Marijtje Spaans Volger; *m* 1959, Aaltje Roorda; two *d*. *Educ:* Univ. of Groningen (PhD). Lieut, Special Branch, Royal Dutch Air Force, 1958–59; Shell Research BV, Amsterdam, 1960 and 1969–75; Shell Development Co., USA, 1968–69; Director: Shell Milstead Lab., 1975–77; Shell Biotech. Res., 1977–83; Product Res. Lab., Amsterdam, 1983–89. Mem., Royal Dutch Akademie of Science, 1987. AKZO Prize, 1972. *Publications:* Organic Chemistry, 1956; Organometal Complexes, 1961; Homogenous Catalysis, 1965. *Recreations:* tennis, gardening.

VOLLRATH, Prof. Lutz Ernst Wolf; Professor of Histology and Embryology, University of Mainz, Germany, since 1974; *b* 2 Sept. 1936; *s* of Pastor Richard Hermann Vollrath and Rita (*née* Brügmann); *m* 1963, Gisela (*née* Dialer); three *d*. *Educ:* Ulrich von Hutten-Schule, Berlin; Univs of Berlin, Kiel and Tübingen. Dr med Kiel, 1961. Wissenschaftlicher Assistent, Dept of Anatomy, Würzburg, Germany, 1963; Res. Fellow, Dept of Anatomy, Birmingham, 1964; Wissenschaftlicher Assistent, Dept of Anatomy, Würzburg, 1965–71 (Privatdozent, 1968; Oberassistent, 1969; Universitätsdozent, 1970); King's College London: Reader in Anatomy, 1971; Prof. of Anatomy, 1973–74. Editor: Cell & Tissue Research, 1978–; Annals of Anatomy, 1992–. *Publications:* (co-editor) Neurosecretion: the final neuroendocrine pathway, 1974; The Pineal Organ, 1981; (ed) Handbook of Microscopic Anatomy (formerly Handbuch der mikr. Anat. des Menschen) (series), 1978–; research publications on histochemistry and ultrastructure of organogenesis and various aspects of neuroendocrinology, in Annals of Anatomy, Z Zellforsch., Histochemie, Phil. Trans Royal Society B, Erg. Anat. Entw.gesch. *Recreations:* gardening, tennis. *Address:* c/o Anatomisches Institut, 55099 Mainz, Saarstr. 19/21, Germany.

von BITTENFELD; *see* Herwarth von Bittenfeld.

von CLEMM, Michael; Chairman and Chief Executive, Highmount Capital, since 1993; *b* 18 March 1935; *s* of Werner Conrad Clemm von Hohenberg and Veronica Rudge Green; *m* 1956, Louisa Bronson Hunnewell; two *d*. *Educ:* Harvard College (AB cum laude 1956); Harvard Graduate School of Arts and Sciences; Corpus Christi College, Oxford (MLitt 1959, DPhil 1962). Staff journalist, Boston Globe, 1959–60; First National City Bank, 1962–67; Faculty, Harvard Graduate Sch. of Business Administration, 1967–71; Pres., Roux Restaurants, 1990–93 (Chm., 1971–89); White Weld & Co.: Exec. Dir, 1971–75; Man. Dir, 1975–78; Dep. Chm., 1976; Chm., Credit Suisse First Boston Ltd, 1978–86; Exec. Vice Pres., Merrill Lynch & Co. Inc., 1986–93; Chm., Merrill Lynch Capital Markets, 1986–93; Director: The India Fund, 1987–; Merrill Lynch Capital Partners, 1989–; Liberty Mutual Insce Gp, 1993– (Mem., Exec. Cttee, 1993–); Liberty Financial Co., 1993–; Rust International, 1993–95 (Member: Compensation Cttee; Audit Cttee); Eastman Chemical (Chm., Finance Cttee); Hafslund Nycomed, 1994–; Member Advisory Board: E African Develt Bank, 1979–; Creditanstalt Bankverein, Vienna, 1986–93. President: Foundn for Preservation of the Archaeol Heritage, USA, 1979–87; ESU of US, 1991–94; Vice-Pres., City of London Archaeol Trust, 1979–; Member: Court of The Mary Rose, 1982–; Adv. Bd, Royal Acad. of Arts, 1986–; Council, Compton Verney Opera Project, 1986–; Corp., Massachusetts Gen. Hosp., 1980–; Nat. Tanglewood Cttee, 1986–91; US–Japan Business Council, 1982–; US–Korea Business Council, 1988– (Chm.); Vis. Cttee, Harvard Univ. Grad. Sch. of Design, 1983–89 (Co-Chm., Resources Council, 1985–89); Cttee on Univ. Resources, Harvard Univ., 1986–; Vis. Cttee, Harvard Univ. Sch. of Public Health, 1990–; Bd of Fellows, Harvard Med. Sch., 1990–; Trustee and Hon. Treasurer, British Museum Develt Trust, 1979–94; Trustee: Gen. Hosp. Corp., 1988–; NY Historical Soc., 1989–92. *Publications:* contribs to Economic Botany, 1963, Harvard Business Review, 1971, Public Utilities Fortnightly, Euromoney and Jl of Comparative Corporate Law and Securities. *Recreations:* collecting Michelin Guide stars (with Albert and Michel Roux), collecting airline boarding cards. *Address:* (office) 2 Drayson Mews, W8 4LY. *T:* 0171–499 7812. *Clubs:* White's, Boodle's; Porcellian (Trustee, 1988–) (Cambridge, Mass); Brook (NY).

von HASE, Karl-Günther, Hon. GCVO 1972; Hon. KCMG 1965; Hon. President, Deutsch-Englische Gesellschaft, Düsseldorf, since 1993 (Chairman, 1982–93); *b* 15 Dec. 1917; *m* 1945, Renate Stumpff; five *d*. *Educ:* German schools. Professional Soldier, 1936–45; War Academy, 1943–44; Training College for Diplomats, 1950–51; Georgetown Univ., Washington DC, 1952. German Foreign Service: German Embassy, Ottawa, 1953–56; Spokesman, Foreign Office Bonn, 1958–61; Head, West European Dept, 1961–62; Spokesman of German Federal Government, 1962–67; State Secretary, Min. of Defence, German Federal Govt, 1968–69; German Ambassador to the Court of St James's, 1970–77; Dir-Gen., Zweites Deutsches Fernsehen, 1977–82. Hon. LLD Manchester, 1987. Holds German and other foreign decorations. *Recreations:* shooting, music. *Address:* Am Stadtwald 60, 53177 Bonn, Germany.

von KLITZING, Prof. Klaus, PhD; Director, Max-Planck-Institut für Festkörperforschung, Stuttgart, since 1985; *b* 28 June 1943; *s* of Bogislav and Anny von Klitzing; *m* 1971, Renate Falkenberg; two *s* one *d*. *Educ:* Technische Univ., Braunschweig (Dipl Phys); Univ. of Würzburg (PhD; Habilitation (univ. teaching qual.). Prof., Technische Univ., München, 1980–84; Hon. Prof., Univ. of Stuttgart, 1985. Nobel Prize for Physics, 1985. *Address:* Max-Planck-Institut für Festkörperforschung, Heisenbergstrasse 1, 70569 Stuttgart, Federal Republic of Germany. *T:* (711) 6891570.

von KUENHEIM, Eberhard; Chairman: Executive Board, 1970–93, Supervisory Board, since 1993, BMW AG, Munich; *b* 2 Oct. 1928, E Prussia. *Educ:* Stuttgart Technical Univ. (Diplom-Ingenieur; MSc). Technical Dir, Machine tool factory, Hanover, 1954–65; joined QUANDT Gp, 1965; Dep. Chm., Exec. Bd., Industriewerke Karlsruhe Augsburg AG, 1968–70. Mem. Supervisory Board: Bayerische Vereinsbank, Munich; Royal Dutch Petroleum Co.; Münchner Rückversicherungsges; Delton AG. Mem. Senate, Max Planck

Soc. for Advancement of Scis. Hon. Senator, Munich Technical Univ. Hon. doctorates: Clausthal-Zellerfeld Technical Univ.; Munich Technical Univ. *Address:* 80788 Munich, Petuelring 130, Germany.

von MALLINCKRODT, Georg Wilhelm; President, Schroders plc, since 1995 (Chairman, 1984–95; Director, since 1977); Chairman and Chief Executive Officer, Schroders Incorporated, New York, since 1985; Chairman, J. Henry Schroder Bank AG, Zurich, since 1984; *b* 19 Aug. 1930; *s* of Arnold Wilhelm von Mallinckrodt and Valentine von Mallinckrodt (*née* von Joest); *m* 1958, Charmaine Brenda Schroder; two *s* two *d*. *Educ:* Salem, West Germany. Agfa AG Munich, 1948–51; Münchmeyer & Co., Hamburg, 1951–53; Kleinwort Sons & Co., London, 1953–54; J. Henry Schroder Banking Corp., New York, 1954–55; Union Bank of Switzerland, Geneva 1956; J. Henry Schroder Banking Corp., NY, 1957–60; J. Henry Schroder & Co., subseq. J. Henry Schroder Wagg & Co., London, 1960–85, Director, 1967–; Chm. and Chief Exec. Officer, J. Henry Schroder Bank & Trust Co., NY, 1984–86. Director: Schroder Asseily & Co., 1981–; Schroders Australia Hldgs Ltd, Sydney, 1984–; Wertheim Schroder Hldgs Inc., NY, 1986–; Wertheim Schroder & Co. Inc., NY, 1986–; NM UK, 1986–90; Euris SA, Paris, 1987–; Schroder Internat. Merchant Bankers, 1988–; Siemens plc, 1989–. Vice-Pres., German Chamber of Industry and Commerce in UK, 1971–92; Mem., Europ. Adv. Cttee, McGraw Hill Inc., USA, 1986–89; Dir, Europ. Arts Foundn, 1987–; Pres., German-British Chamber of Industry and Commerce, 1992–95. Member: British N American Cttee, 1988–; City Adv. Gp, CBI, 1990–. Pres., German YMCA, London, 1961–; Member: Ct of Benefactors, Oxford Univ., 1990–; Nat. Art Collection Develt Fund, 1995–; BM Develt Trust, 1995–; Trustee: Kurt Hahn Trust, 1991; Prague Heritage Fund, 1992. FRSA 1986; CIMgt (CBIM 1986). Hon. DCL Bishop's Univ., Canada, 1994. Verdienstkreuz am Bande des Verdienstordens (FRG), 1986; Verdienstkreuz 1 Klasse des Verdienstordens (FRG), 1990. *Recreations:* music, gardening, shooting, ski-ing. *Address:* 120 Cheapside, EC2V 6DS. *T:* 0171–382 6000.

VONNEGUT, Kurt, Jr; writer; *b* Indianapolis, 11 Nov. 1922; *m* 1st, 1945, Jane Marie Cox (marr. diss. 1979; decd); one *s* two *d*; 2nd, 1979, Jill Krementz. *Educ:* Cornell Univ.; Carnegie Inst. of Technol.; Univ. of Chicago. Served War, US Army, 1942–45 (POW). Reporter, Chicago City News Bureau, 1945–47; PRO, GEC, Schenectady, 1947–50; freelance writer, 1950–65; Lectr, Writers' Workshop, Univ. of Iowa, 1965–67; Guggenheim Fellow, 1967–68; Lectr in English, Harvard, 1970; Dist. Prof., City Coll., New York, 1973–74. Mem., National Inst. of Arts and Letters. *Publications:* Player Piano, 1951; The Sirens of Titan, 1959; Mother Night, 1961; Cat's Cradle, 1963; God Bless You, Mr Rosewater, 1964; Welcome to the Monkey House (short stories), 1968; Slaughterhouse-Five, 1969; Happy Birthday, Wanda June (play), 1970; Between Time and Timbuktu or Prometheus-5 (TV script), 1972; Breakfast of Champions, 1973; Wampeters, Foma and Granfalloons (essays), 1974; Slapstick, or Lonesome No More, 1976; Jailbird, 1979; (with Ivan Chermayeff) Sun Moon Star, 1980; Palm Sunday (autobiog.), 1981; Deadeye Dick, 1982; Galapagos, 1985; Bluebeard, 1988; Hocus Pocus, 1990; Fates Worse Than Death (essays and speeches), 1991. *Address:* c/o Donald C. Farber Esq., Tanner Propp & Farber, 99 Park Avenue, 25th Floor, New York, NY 10016, USA.

von OTTER, Anne Sofie; singer (mezzo-soprano); *b* Stockholm, 9 May 1955. *Educ:* Stockholm Acad. of Music; GSMD; vocal studies with Vera Rozsa, 1981–. With Basle Opera, 1983–85; freelance, 1985–; appearances at most major opera houses incl. Covent Garden, 1985–; Metropolitan Opera, 1985–; La Scala, Milan, 1987–; Geneva, Aix-en-Provence, Chicago, Berlin and Munich; has also given recitals in many European countries. Rôles include: Mozart: Cherubino, Sextus, Idamante, Dorabella, Ramiro; Strauss: Octavian, Clairon, Componist; Bellini: Romeo; Rossini: Tancredi, Cenerentola; Gluck: Orfeo. Major recordings include: Così fan tutte; Orfeo ed Euridice; Hansel and Gretel; Der Rosenkavalier; Le Nozze di Figaro; Idomeneo; Titus; Les Contes d'Hoffman; La Damnation de Faust; Nuits d'Eté, Mahler cycles, and lieder by Mahler, Brahms, Grieg, Wolf, etc. *Address:* c/o IMG, 3 Burlington Lane, Chiswick, W4 2TH. *T:* 0181–747 9977.

von REITZENSTEIN, Hans-Joachim Freiherr; *see* Leech, John.

von RICHTHOFEN, Baron Hermann, Hon. GCVO 1992; Permanent Representative of the Federal Republic of Germany to NATO, since 1993; *b* 20 Nov. 1933; *s* of Baron Herbert von Richthofen and Baroness Gisela von Richthofen (*née* Schöller); *m* 1966, Christa, Countess von Schwerin; one *s* two *d*. *Educ:* Univs of Heidelberg, Munich and Bonn; Dr in law Cologne Univ. 1963. Joined Diplomatic Service of FRG, 1963; served Boston, Mass, 1963–64; FO, 1964–66; Saigon, 1966–68; Jakarta, 1968–70; FO, 1970–74; Dep. Hd, Sect. for Internat. Law, FO, 1974; Hd, Sect. for For. Policy, Perm. Mission to GDR, 1975–78; Hd of Dept for German and Berlin Affairs, FO, 1978–80; seconded to Fed. Chancellery as Hd of Intra-German Policy Unit, 1980–86; Dir Gen. of Legal Div., 1986, of Political Div., and Political Dir, 1986–88, FO; Ambassador to UK, 1988–93. KStJ, ER 1961, RR 1985; Officer's Cross, Order of the Knights of Malta, 1967; Commander's Cross: Order of Merit (Italy), 1979; Legion of Honour (France), 1987; Grand Officer's Cross, Order of Infante D. Henrique (Portugal), 1988; Knight's Commander's Cross, Order of Merit (Luxembourg), 1988; Knight Commander's Cross, 2nd class (Austria), 1989. *Recreations:* ski-ing, swimming, gardening, reading history, arts. *Address:* NATO, Boulevard Léopold III, 1110 Brussels, Belgium. *T:* (2) 7277611.

von SCHRAMEK, Sir Eric (Emil), Kt 1982; FRIBA; Chairman, von Schramek and Dawes Pty Ltd, 1963–91; Consultant to Hames Sharley International, Architects and Planners, since 1989; *b* 4 April 1921; *s* of Emil and Annie von Schramek; *m* Edith, *d* of Dipl. Ing. W. Popper; one *s* two *d*. *Educ:* Stefans Gymnasium, Prague; Technical Univ., Prague. DiplIngArch; Life Fellow RAIA, FIArbA. Town Planner, Bavaria, 1946–48; Sen. Supervising Architect, Dept of Works and Housing, Darwin, NT, 1948–51; Evans, Bruer & Partners (later von Schramek and Dawes), 1951–91: work includes multi-storey office buildings in Adelaide (Nat. Mutual Centre; State Govt Insce Bldg; Wales House; Qantas Bldg, etc); Wesley House, Melbourne; Westpac House, Hobart; AMP Bldg and Qantas Bldg, Darwin; numerous churches throughout Australia and New Guinea. National Pres., Building Science Forum of Aust., 1970–72; President: RAIA (SA Chapter), 1974–76; Inst. of Arbitrators, Aust. (SA Chapter), 1977–80. Vis. Lectr, Univ. of Adelaide; Vis. Lectr, S Australian Inst. of Technol. Past National Dep. Chm., Austcare; past Councillor, Council of Professions; past Chm., Commn on Worship and other Depts, Lutheran Church of Australia. Hon. Associate (Arch.), SA Inst. of Technology, 1989. *Publications:* contribs and articles in architectural pubns. *Recreations:* music, reading, golf. *Address:* The Olives, PO Box 457, Yankalilla, SA 5203, Australia. *T:* (85) 583341.

von WECHMAR, Baron Rüdiger, Hon. GCVO 1986; Member (FDP) for Germany, European Parliament, 1989–94; *b* 15 Nov. 1923; *s* of Irnfried von Wechmar and Ilse (*née* von Binzer); *m* 1961, Dina-Susanne (Susie) (*née* Woldenga); one *d* (one *s* one *d* of previous marr.). *Educ:* Oberrealschule, Berlin; Univ. of Minnesota, USA (as prisoner of war). MA Journalism. Army, 3rd Reconnaissance Battalion, Western Desert and PoW Camp, 1941–46. Journalist, 1946–58; joined German Foreign Service as Consul, New York, 1958; Dir, German Inf. Centre, NY; Dep. Head, Govt Press and Inf. Office, Bonn, 1969; State Sec. and Chief Govt Spokesman, 1972; Perm. Rep. to UN, 1974–81; Pres., UN Security Council, 1977–78; Pres., 35th Gen. Assembly, UN, 1980–81; Ambassador to Italy, 1981–83; Ambassador to UK, 1983–88. Member: North-South Round Table, Deutsche Ges. für Auswärtige Politik. Commander's Cross, Order of Merit (FRG), 1980; decorations from UK, Sweden, Norway, Japan, Netherlands, Egypt, Mexico, Italy, Romania. Paul Klinger Award, DAG, 1973; UN Peace Gold Medal, 1980. *Address:* Hiltenspergerstrasse 15, 80798 München, Germany.

von WEIZSÄCKER, Freiherr Carl-Friedrich, Dr Phil; University Professor Emeritus; *b* Kiel, 28 June 1912; *m* 1937, Gundalena (*née* Wille); three *s* one *d*. *Educ:* Universities of Berlin, Leipzig, Göttingen, Copenhagen, 1929–33. Dr.phil 1933, Dr.phil.habil, 1936, Univ. Leipzig; Asst., Inst. of Theor. Physik, Univ. of Leipzig, 1934–36; Wissenschaftl. Mitarb., Kaiser Wilhelm Inst., Berlin, 1936–42; Dozent, Univ. of Berlin, 1937–42; pl. ao. Prof. Theor. Physik, Univ. of Strassburg, 1942–44; Kaiser-Wilhelm-Inst., Berlin and Hechingen, 1944–45; Hon. Prof., Univ. Göttingen and Abt. Leiter, Max Planck Inst. für Physik, Göttingen, 1946–57; Ord. Prof. of Philosophy, Univ. of Hamburg, 1957–69. Hon. Prof., Univ. of Munich, and Dir, Max-Planck-Institut on the preconditions of human life in the modern world, 1970–80. Gifford Lecturer, Glasgow Univ., 1959–61. Member: Deutsche Akademie der Naturforscher Leopoldina, Halle; Akademie der Wissenschaften, Göttingen; Joachim-Jungius-Gesellschaft der Wissenschaften, Hamburg; Bayerische Akademie der Wissenschaften, München; Österreichische Akademie der Wissenschaften, Wien; Sächsische Akademie der Wissenschaften zu Leipzig. Verdienstorden der Bundesrepublik Deutschland, 1959–73; Orden Pour le Mérite für Wissenschaften und Künste, 1961; Max Planck Medal, 1957; Goethe Prize (Frankfurt) 1958; Friedenspreis des deutschen Buchhandels, 1963; Erasmus Prize (with Gabriel Marcel), 1969; Templeton Prize for Progress in Religion (jtly), 1989. Hon. Dr theol: Univ. Tübingen, 1977; Univ. Basel, 1989; Hon. Dr iur Free Univ., Amsterdam, 1977; Hon. LLD: Alberta, Canada, 1981; Aberdeen, 1989; Hon. Dr rer. nat. Karl-Marx-Univ., Leipzig, 1987. Dr.phil *hc*: Technische Univ., Berlin, 1987; Aachen, 1988. *Publications:* Die Atomkerne, 1937; Zum Weltbild der Physik, 11th edn, 1970 (English, London, 1952); Die Geschichte der Natur, 7th edn, 1970 (English, Chicago, 1949); Physik der Gegenwart (with J. Juilfs), 2nd edn, 1958 (Engl., 1957); Die Verantwortung der Wissenschaft im Atomzeitalter, 5th edn, 1969; Atomenergie und Atomzeitalter, 3rd edn, 1958; Bedingungen des Friedens, 1963, 5th edn, 1970; Die Tragweite der Wissenschaft, 1964; Der ungesicherte Friede, 1969; Die Einheit der Natur, 1971, 3rd edn, 1972; (ed) Kriegsfolgen und Kriegsverhütung, 1970, 3rd edn, 1971; Voraussetzungen der naturwissenschaftlichen Denkens, 1972, 2nd edn, 1972; Fragen zur Weltpolitik, 1975; Wege in der Gefahr, 1976; Der Garten des Menschlichen, Beiträge zur geschichtlichen Anthropologie, 1977; Deutlichkeit, Beiträge zu politischen und religiösen Gegenwartsfragen, 1978; Der bedrohte Friede, 1981; Wahrnehmung der Neuzeit, 1983; Aufbau der Physik, 1985; Die Zeit drängt — Eine Weltversammlung der Christen für Gerechtigkeit, Frieden und die Bewahrung der Schöpfung, 1986; Bewusstseinswandel, 1988; Bedingungen der Freiheit, 1990; Der Mensch in seiner Geschichte, 1991; Zeit und Wissen, 1992; relevant publication: bibliography in Einheit und Vielheit, Festschrift…ed Scheibe and Süssmann, 1973. *Recreations:* hiking, chess. *Address:* 82319 Starnberg, Maximilianstrasse 14c, Germany.

See also R. von Weizsäcker.

von WEIZSÄCKER, Richard, Dr jur; President of the Federal Republic of Germany, 1984–94; *b* 15 April 1920; *s* of late Baron Ernst von Weizsäcker; *m* 1953, Marianne von Kretschmann; three *s* one *d*. *Educ:* Berlin and Bern; Univs of Oxford, Grenoble and Göttingen (Dr jur). Army service, 1938–45 (Captain, wounded). Formerly with Allianz Lebensversicherung, Stuttgart and Robeco-Gruppe, Amsterdam. Member: Robert Bosch Foundn, Stuttgart; Synod and Council, German Evangelical Church, 1969– (Pres., Congress). Joined Christian Democratic Union, 1954: Mem., Fed. Board; Chm., Gen. Policy Commn, 1971–74; Chm., Basic Prog. Commn, 1974–77; Dep. Chm., CDU/CSU Parlt Gp, 1972–79; Presidential candidate, 1974; First Chm., Berlin CDU, 1981–83. Mem., Bundestag, 1969–81, Vice-Pres., 1979–81; Governing Mayor of West Berlin, 1981–84. Royal Victorian Chain, 1992. *Address:* (office) Am Kupfergraben 7, 10117 Berlin, Germany.

See also Carl-Friedrich von Weizsäcker.

von WINTERFELDT, (Hans) Dominik, Member, Board of Directors, Cassella AG, since 1994; *b* 3 July 1937; *s* of late Curt von Winterfeldt and Anna Franziska Margaretha Luise (*née* Petersen); *m* 1966, Cornelia Waldthausen; one *s* one *d*. *Educ:* German schools; Stanford-INSEAD, Fontainebleau (Industriekaufmann). DipICC. Joined Hoechst AG, Frankfurt/Main, 1957; Asst Manager, Hoechst Colombiana Ltda, 1960; Commercial Manager, Pharmaceuticals, Hoechst Peruana SA, 1963; General Manager, Hoechst Dyechemie W. L. L., Iraq, 1965; Man. Dir, Hoechst Pakistan Ltd and Hoechst Pharmaceuticals Ltd, 1967; Hoechst UK Ltd: Dep. Man. Dir, 1972; Man. Dir and Chief Exec., 1975; Exec. Chm., 1984; Dir (Corporate PR and Communications), 1987–94. Member: Anglo-German Assoc., 1975–; British Deer Soc., 1979–; British Assoc. for Shooting and Conservation, 1979–. *Recreations:* music, deer stalking, golf. *Address:* Cassella AG, PO Box 61 01 44, 60343 Frankfurt (M), Germany. *T:* (69) 4109–01.

VOS, Geoffrey Charles; QC 1993; *b* 22 April 1955; *s* of Bernard Vos and Pamela Celeste Rose (*née* Heilbuth; now Craig); *m* 1984, Vivien Mary Fieldhouse (*née* Dowdeswell); one *d* and one step *s* two step *d*. *Educ:* University College Sch., London; Gonville and Caius Coll., Cambridge (BA, MA). Called to the Bar, Inner Temple, 1977; Mem., Lincoln's Inn. Hon. Sec., Chancery Bar Assoc., 1994–. *Recreations:* farming, wine, photography. *Address:* Netherley, Mathon, near Malvern, Worcs WR13 5LW; 46 Fordington Road, Highgate, N6 4TJ. *Clubs:* United Oxford & Cambridge University; Worcestershire Golf.

VOS, His Honour Geoffrey Michael; a Circuit Judge, 1978–94; *b* 18 Feb. 1927; *s* of Louis and Rachel Eva Vos; *m* 1955, Marcia Joan Goldstone (marr. diss. 1977); two *s* two *d*; *m* 1981, Mrs Anne Wilson. *Educ:* St Joseph's College, Blackpool; Gonville and Caius College, Cambridge. MA, LLB. Called to the Bar, Gray's Inn, 1950. A Recorder of the Crown Court, 1976–78. *Recreations:* swimming, walking. *Address:* c/o The Crown Court, The Law Courts, Quayside, Newcastle upon Tyne NE1 3LA. *T:* Newcastle upon Tyne (0191) 201 2000.

VOWLES, Paul Foster; Academic Registrar, University of London, 1973–82; *b* 12 June 1919; *s* of late E. F. Vowles and G. M. Vowles, Bristol; *m* 1948, Valerie Eleanor Hickman; one *s* two *d*. *Educ:* Bristol Grammar Sch.; Corpus Christi Coll., Oxford (schol.; MA). Served Gloucestershire Regt and King's African Rifles, 1939–46 (despatches, Major). Asst Secretary: Appts Bd, Univ. of Birmingham, 1947–48; Inter-University Council for Higher Educn Overseas, 1948–51; Registrar, Makerere University Coll., E Africa, 1951–63; Sen. Asst to Principal, Univ. of London, 1964–68; Warden, Lillian Penson Hall, 1965–69; External Registrar, 1968–73. Mem., 1983–89, Vice-Chm., 1986–89, Westfield Coll. Council. Fellow, Queen Mary and Westfield Coll., 1991. *Address:* 13 Dale Close, Oxford OX1 1TU. *T:* Oxford (01865) 244042. *Club:* Athenæum.

VRAALSEN, Tom; Commander, Royal Order of Saint Olav 1987; Norwegian Ambassador to the Court of St James's, since 1994; *b* 26 Jan. 1936; *m* 1977, Viebecke Strøm; two *d*. *Educ:* Arhus Sch. of Econs and Business Admin, Denmark (MEcon). Entered Norwegian

Foreign Service, 1960; served Peking, Cairo, Manila, 1960–71; Head of Div., Min. of Foreign Affairs, 1971–75; Minister-Counsellor, Perm. Mission of Norway to UN, NY, 1975–81; Dir-Gen., Min. of Foreign Affairs, 1981–82; Ambassador, Perm. Mission of Norway to UN, NY, 1982–89; Minister of Develt Assistance, 1989–90; Dir of Information, Saga Petroleum, 1991–92; Asst Sec. Gen., Min. of Foreign Affairs, 1992–94. *Address:* 10 Palace Green, W8 4QA.

VREDELING, Hendrikus, (Henk); Member of Supervisory Board, Weekbladpers, since 1983; *b* 20 Nov. 1924. *Educ:* Agricultural Univ., Wageningen. Member: Second Chamber of States-General, Netherlands, 1956–73; European Parliament, 1958–73; Socio-Economic Adviser to Agricultural Workers' Union, Netherlands, 1950–73; Minister of Defence, 1973–76; Mem. and Vice-Pres. of Commn of European Communities (for Employment and Social Affairs), 1977–80. Member: Dutch Emancipation Council, 1981–85; Dutch Council on Peace and Security, 1987–94. *Address:* Rembrandtlaan 13A, 3712 AJ Huis ter Heide, Netherlands.

VULLIAMY, Shirley, (Mrs J. S. P. Vulliamy); *see* Hughes, S.

VYVYAN, Maj.-Gen. Charles Gerard Courtenay, CBE 1990 (MBE 1974); Chief of Staff, HQ and Command (formerly UK Land Forces), since 1994; *b* 29 Sept. 1944; *er s* of John Michal Kenneth Vyvyan and Elizabeth Mary Lowder Vyvyan; *m* 1989, Elizabeth Frances, 3rd *d* of Sir John Paget, 3rd Bt, Haygrass, Taunton. *Educ:* Winchester Coll.; Balliol Coll., Oxford (BA Mod . Hist. 1966; MA 1991); Nat. Defence Coll., Pakistan (MSc, Defence and Strategic Studies). Commnd, Royal Green Jackets (Rifle Bde), 1967; Sultan of Oman's Armed Forces, 1975–76; Staff Coll., 1978; CO 1st Bn RGJ, 1984–86; Col GS Mil. Ops, 1986–87; Comdr 3 Inf. Bde, 1988–90; student, Nat. Defence Coll., Pakistan, 1990–91; DCS, HQ UKLF, 1991–94. Col Commandant, 1 RGJ, 1994–. *Recreations:* mountains, gardens, travel, fishing, Alexander the Great. *Address:* c/o Barclays Bank, PO Box 333, High Street, Oxford OX1 3HS. *Clubs:* Boodle's, Beefsteak.

VYVYAN, Sir John (Stanley), 12th Bt *cr* 1645; Owner of Trelowarren Estate, since 1950 (property acquired by marriage in 1427); *b* 20 Jan. 1916; *s* of Major-General Ralph Ernest Vyvyan, CBE, MC (*d* 1971) and Vera Grace (*d* 1956), *d* of Robert Arthur Alexander; *S* cousin, 1978; *m* 1958, Jonet Noël, *d* of Lt-Col Alexander Hubert Barclay, DSO, MC; one *s* one *d* (and one *d* (decd) of former marriage). *Educ:* Charterhouse; and British-American Tobacco Co. Ltd, who sent him to London School of Oriental Studies. With British-American Tobacco Co. Ltd in England and China until War. Commissioned RCS in India, 1940 and served, 1940–46, in Arakan, Bangalore, etc; Temp. Major; GSO II Signals, Southern Army, 1944. *Recreations:* gardening, photography and books; travel when possible. *Heir: s* Ralph Ferrers Alexander Vyvyan, [*b* 21 Aug. 1960; *m* 1986, Victoria, *y d* of M. B. Ogle, Skerraton, Buckfastleigh, Devon; four *s*]. *Address:* Trelowarren Mill, Mawgan, Helston, Cornwall TR12 6AE. *T:* Mawgan (01326) 221505. *Clubs:* Army and Navy; Royal Cornwall Yacht (Falmouth).

W

WADDELL, Sir Alexander (Nicol Anton), KCMG 1959 (CMG 1955); DSC 1944; HM Overseas Civil Service, retired; *b* 8 Nov. 1913; *yr s* of late Rev. Alexander Waddell, Eassie, Angus, Scotland, and late Effie Thompson Anton Waddell; *m* 1949, Jean Margot Lesbia, *d* of late W. E. Masters. *Educ:* Fettes Coll., Edinburgh; Edinburgh Univ. (MA); Gonville and Caius Coll., Cambridge. Colonial Administrative Service, 1937; British Solomon Islands Protectorate: Cadet, 1937; District Officer, 1938; District Commissioner, 1945; Acting Resident Commissioner, 1945; Malayan Civil Service, 1946; Principal Asst Secretary, North Borneo, 1947–52 (Acting Dep. Chief Secretary, periods, 1947–51). Colonial Secretary, Gambia, 1952–56; Colonial Secretary, Sierra Leone, 1956–58; Dep. Governor, Sierra Leone, 1958–60; Governor and Commander-in-Chief of Sarawak, 1960–63; UK Comr, British Phosphate Commissioners, 1965–77. Mem., Panel of Independent Inspectors, Dept of the Environment, 1979–85. On Naval Service (Coastwatcher), 1942–44. Lieut, RANVR; on Military Service, 1945–47, Lt-Col, Gen. List (British Mil. Administration). *Recreations:* hill walking, golf, gardening. *Address:* Pilgrim Cottage, Ashton Keynes, Wilts SN6 6PD. *Clubs:* Commonwealth Trust, East India, Devonshire, Sports and Public Schools.

WADDELL, Gordon Herbert; Chairman: Fairway Group plc (formerly Fairway (London)), since 1989; Shanks & McEwan, since 1992; *b* Glasgow, 12 April 1937; *s* of late Herbert Waddell; *m* 1st, 1965, Mary (marr. diss. 1971), *d* of H. F. Oppenheimer, *qv*; 2nd, 1973, Kathy May, *d* of W. S. Gallagher. *Educ:* St Mary's Sch., Melrose; Fettes Coll., Edinburgh; Cambridge Univ. (BA); Stanford Univ. (MBA). Rugby Blue, Cambridge Univ., 1958, 1959, 1961; Member, British Isles Rugby Touring Team: to Australia and NZ, 1959; to South Africa, 1962; eighteen rugby caps for Scotland. MP (Progressive Party) for Johannesburg North, April 1974–Nov. 1977. Dir, E. Oppenheimer & Son Ltd, 1965–87; Exec. Dir, Anglo American Corp. of South Africa Ltd, 1971–87; Chairman: Johannesburg Consolidated Investment Co. Ltd, 1981–87; Rustenburg Platinum Mines Ltd, 1981–87; South African Breweries Ltd, 1984–87; Ryan Gp (formerly Digger), 1991–95; Gartmore Scotland Investment Trust, 1991–; Tor Investment Trust, 1992–; Mersey Docks and Harbour Co., 1993–; Director: Cadbury Schweppes, 1988–; Scottish Nat. Trust, 1988–; London and Strathclyde Trust, 1989–. *Recreation:* golf. *Address:* 14 Thurloe Square, SW7 2TE; Corbet Tower, Morebattle, Kelso TD5 8AQ. *Clubs:* Hawks (Cambridge); Honourable Company of Edinburgh Golfers; Royal and Ancient (St Andrews).

WADDELL, Sir James (Henderson), Kt 1974; CB 1960; Deputy Chairman, Police Complaints Board, 1977–81; *b* 5 Oct. 1914; *s* of D. M. Waddell and J. C. Fleming; *m* 1940, Dorothy Abbie Wright; one *s* one *d*. *Educ:* George Heriot's Sch.; Edinburgh Univ. Assistance Board, 1936; Ministry of Information, 1940; Reconnaissance Corps, 1942; Ministry of Housing and Local Government, 1946; Under-Secretary, 1955; Under-Secretary, Cabinet Office, 1961–63; Dep.-Secretary, Min. of Housing and Local Government, 1963–66; Dep. Under-Sec., Home Office, 1966–75. *Address:* Long Meadow, East Lavant, Chichester, W Sussex PO18 0AH. *T:* Chichester (01243) 527129.

WADDELL, Rear-Adm. William Angus, CB 1981; OBE 1966; *b* 5 Nov. 1924; *s* of late James Whitefield Waddell and Christina Waddell (*née* Maclean); *m* 1950, Thelma Evelyn Tomlins; one *s* one *d*. *Educ:* Glasgow University. BSc (Hons) Maths and Nat. Phil.; Cleland Gold Medal. CEng; FIEE. Midshipman, Sub Lieut RNVR (Special Branch), HMS Ranee, HMS Collingwood, 1945–47; Instr Lieut, HMS Collingwood, HMS Glasgow, HMS Siskin, HMS Gambia, 1947–59 (RMCS 1956–57); Instr Comdr, HMS Albion, 1959–61; Staff of Dir, Naval Educn Service, 1961–63; Sen. British Naval Officer, Dam Neck, Virginia, 1963–66; Officer i/c RN Polaris Sch., 1966–68; Instr Captain, Staff of SACLANT (Dir, Inf. Systems Gp), 1969–72; Dean, RN Coll., Greenwich, 1973–75; Dir Naval Officer Appointments (Instr), 1975–78; Rear-Adm. 1979; Chief Naval Instructor Officer, 1978–81 and Flag Officer, Admiralty Interview Bd, 1979–81. ADC to HM the Queen, 1976–79. Assoc. Teacher, City Univ., 1973–75; Sec. and Chief Exec., RIPH & H, 1982–90. Hon. FRIPHH 1990. *Publication:* An Introduction to Servomechanisms (with F. L. Westwater), 1961, repr. 1968. *Address:* c/o National Westminster Bank, 1 Lee Road, Blackheath, SE3 9RM.

WADDILOVE, Lewis Edgar, CBE 1978 (OBE 1965); JP; Deputy Chairman, Housing Corporation, 1978–83 (Member since 1968); Director, Joseph Rowntree Memorial Trust, 1961–79 (Executive Officer of the Trust, 1946–61); *b* 5 Sept. 1914; *s* of Alfred and Edith Waddilove; *m* 1st, 1940, Louise Power (*d* 1967); one *s* one *d*; 2nd, 1969, Maureen Piper. *Educ:* Westcliff High Sch.; Univ. of London (DPA). Admin. Officer, LCC Educn Dept, 1936–38; Govt Evacuation Scheme, Min. of Health, 1938–43; Friends Ambulance Unit, Middle East, 1943–45 (Exec. Chm., 1946); Chairman, Friends Service Council, 1961–67. Chm., Nat. Fedn of Housing Assocs (formerly Socs), 1965–73 and 1977–79 (Vice-Pres., 1982–90); Member: Cttee on Housing in Greater London (Milner Holland), 1963–65; Nat. Cttee for Commonwealth Immigrants, 1966–68; Social Science Research Council, 1967–71; Public Schools Commn, 1968–70; Central Housing Advisory Cttee, 1960–75; Standing Cttee, Centre for Socio-Legal Studies at Oxford, 1972–75; Legal Aid Advisory Cttee, 1972–78; Adv. Cttee on Rent Rebates and Rent Allowances, 1975–81; Cttee on Voluntary Organisations, 1974–78; Working Party on Housing Cooperatives, 1974–76; Central Appeals Adv. Cttee (BBC and IBA), 1974–84 (Chm., 1978–84); Chairman: Advisory Cttee on Fair Rents, 1973–74; Advisory Cttee on Housing Cooperatives, 1976–79; York City Charities, 1957–65 and 1972–88; York Univ. Council, 1977–87; Personal Social Services Council, 1977–80; Coal Mining Subsidence Compensation Review Cttee, 1983–84; Trustee, Shelter, 1966–74 (Chm. 1970–72). Presiding Clerk, 4th World Conf. of Friends, in N Carolina, 1967. Governor, Co. of Merchant Adventurers, City of York, 1978–79. Governor: Leighton Park Sch., 1951–71; Bootham and The Mount Schs., 1972–81 (Chm. 1974–81). JP York, 1968. DUniv: Brunel, 1978; York, 1987. *Publications:* One Man's Vision, 1954; Housing Associations (PEP), 1962; Private Philanthropy and Public Welfare, 1983; various articles in technical jls. *Address:* Red Oaks, Hawthorn Terrace, New Earswick, York YO3 4AJ. *T:* York (01904) 768696.

WADDINGTON, family name of **Baron Waddington.**

WADDINGTON, Baron *cr* 1990 (Life Peer), of Read in the County of Lancashire; **David Charles Waddington,** GCVO 1994; PC 1987; DL; QC 1971; Governor and Commander-in-Chief of Bermuda, since 1992; a Recorder of the Crown Court, since 1972; *b* 2 Aug. 1929; *o s* of late Charles Waddington and of Mrs Minnie Hughan Waddington; *m* 1958, Gillian Rosemary, *d* of late Alan Green, CBE; three *s* two *d*. *Educ:* Sedbergh; Hertford Coll., Oxford. President, Oxford Univ. Conservative Assoc., 1950. 2nd Lieut, XII Royal Lancers, 1951–53. Called to Bar, Gray's Inn, 1951, Bencher, 1985. Contested (C): Farnworth Div., 1955; Nelson and Colne Div., 1964; Heywood and Royton Div., 1966; MP (C): Nelson and Colne, 1968–Sept. 1974; Clitheroe, March 1979–1983; Ribble Valley, 1983–90; a Lord Comr, HM Treasury, 1979–81; Parly Under-Sec. of State, Dept of Employment, 1981–83; Minister of State, Home Office, 1983–87; Parly Sec., HM Treasury and Govt Chief Whip, 1987–89; Sec. of State, Home Office, 1989–90; Lord Privy Seal and Leader of H of L, 1990–92. DL Lancs 1991. *Address:* Government House, Hamilton, Bermuda.

WADDINGTON, Prof. David James; Professor of Chemical Education, University of York, since 1978; *b* 27 May 1932; *s* of Eric James and Marjorie Edith Waddington; *m* 1957, Isobel Hesketh; two *s* one *d*. *Educ:* Marlborough College; Imperial College, Univ. of London (BSc, ARCS, DIC, PhD). Head of Chemistry Dept, 1959, Head of Science Dept, 1961, Wellington College; York University: Sen. Lectr, 1965; Head Chemistry Dept, 1983–92; Pro-Vice-Chancellor, 1985–91. Pres., Educn Div., Royal Soc. of Chem., 1981–83; Sec., 1977, Chm., 1981–86, Cttee on Teaching of Chemistry, IUPAC; Sec., 1986–89, Chm., 1990–94, Cttee on Teaching of Science, ICSU. Nyholm Medal, RSC, 1985; Brasted Award, ACS, 1988. *Publications:* Organic Chemistry, 1962; (with H. S. Finlay) Organic Chemistry Through Experiment, 1965; (with R. O. C. Norman) Modern Organic Chemistry, 1972; (with A. Kornhauser and C. N. R. Rao) Chemical Education in the 70s, 1980; (ed) Teaching School Chemistry, 1985; (ed) Education, Industry and Technology, 1987; (jtly) Introducing Chemistry: the Salters' approach, 1989; Chemistry: the Salters' approach, 1990; (jtly) Salters' Advanced Chemistry, 1994; (ed) Science for Understanding Tomorrow's World: global change, 1994. *Recreations:* golf, gardening. *Address:* Department of Chemistry, University of York, York YO1 5DD. *Club:* Tang Hall Horticultural Society (York).

WADDINGTON, Gerald Eugene, CBE 1975; QC (Cayman Islands) 1971; Attorney General of the Cayman Islands, 1970–April 1977; *b* 31 Jan. 1909; *o s* of Walter George Waddington and Una Blanche Waddington (*née* Hammond); *m* 1935, Hylda Kathleen (*née* Allen); one *s* one *d*. *Educ:* Jamaica Coll.; Wolmer's Schl., Jamaica. Solicitor, Supreme Court, Jamaica, 1932; LLB (London) 1949; Solicitor, Supreme Court, England, 1950; called to the Bar, Gray's Inn, 1957. Deputy Clerk of Courts, Jamaica, 1939; Asst Crown Solicitor, Jamaica, 1943–48; Resident Magistrate, 1948–58; Puisne Judge, 1959–64; Judge of the Court of Appeal, Jamaica, 1964–70, retired. Joint ed. West Indian Law Reports. Vice-Pres. Nat. Rifle Assoc. Chm. St John Council for Jamaica. CStJ 1962, KStJ 1970. *Recreation:* shooting (Member of Jamaica Rifle Team to Bisley, 1937, 1950, 1953, 1956, 1957, 1960, 1963, 1965, 1967, 1968; Captain, 1950, 1953, 1957, 1967; Captain, WI Rifle Team, 1960). *Address:* 41 Pretty Street, Stittsville, Ontario K2S 1N5, Canada.

WADDINGTON, Leslie; Managing Director, Waddington Galleries, since 1966; *b* Dublin, 9 Feb. 1934; *s* of late Victor and Zelda Waddington; *m* 1st, 1967, Ferriel Lyle (marr. diss. 1983); two *d*; 2nd, 1985, Clodagh Frances Fanshawe. *Educ:* Portora Royal School; Sorbonne; Ecole du Louvre (Diplômé). Formed Waddington Galleries with father, 1957. Sen. Fellow, RCA, 1993. *Recreations:* chess, backgammon, reading. *Address:* 11 Cork Street, W1X 1PD. *T:* 0171–437 8611.

WADDINGTON, Very Rev. Robert Murray; Dean of Manchester, 1984–93, now Emeritus; *b* 24 Oct. 1927; *s* of Percy Nevill and Dorothy Waddington. *Educ:* Dulwich Coll.; Selwyn Coll., Cambridge; Ely Theological Coll. MA (2nd cl. Theol.). Asst Curate St John's, Bethnal Green, 1953–55; Chaplain, Slade Sch., Warwick, Qld, Aust., 1955–59; Curate, St Luke's, Cambridge, 1959–61; Headmaster, St Barnabas Sch., Ravenshoe, N Qld, Aust., 1961–70; Oxford Univ. Dept of Education, 1971–72; Residentiary Canon, Carlisle Cathedral, and Bishop's Adviser for Education, 1972–77; Gen. Sec., C of E Bd of Education and Nat. Soc. for Promoting Religious Education, 1977–84. Superior, Oratory of the Good Shepherd, 1987–90. *Recreations:* cooking, films, sociology. *Address:* 6 Waverley Street, York YO3 7QZ. *T:* York (01904) 670200.

WADDINGTON, Susan Andrée; Member (Lab) Leicester, European Parliament, since 1994; *b* 23 Aug. 1944; *m* 1966, Ivan Waddington; one *s* one *d*. *Educ:* Blyth GS, Norwich; Leicester Univ. (BA; MEd). Mem. (Lab) Leics CC, 1973–91. Contested (Lab) Leics NW, 1987. *Address:* European Parliament, 97 Rue Belliard, 1040 Brussels, Belgium.

WADDS, Mrs Jean Casselman, OC 1982; Member, Royal Commission on Economic Union and Development Prospects for Canada, 1983–85; *b* 16 Sept. 1920; *d* of Hon. Earl Rowe and Treva Lennox Rowe; *m* 1st, 1946, Clair Casselman; one *s* one *d*; 2nd, 1964, Robert Wadds (marr. diss. 1977). *Educ:* Univ. of Toronto (BA); Weller Business Coll. First elected to Canadian House of Commons (Riding Grenville-Dundas), 1958; re-elected: 1962, 1963, 1965; defeated (Riding Grenville-Carlton), 1968. Member, Canada's Delegn to United Nations, 1961; Parliamentary Sec. to Minister of Health and Welfare, 1962. National Sec., Progressive Conservative Party, 1971–75; Member, Ontario Municipal Bd, 1975–79. Canadian High Comr to UK, 1980–83. Former Director: Bell

Canada; Royal Trustco Ltd; Air Canada. Adv. Bd, Norman Paterson Sch. of Internat. Affairs, Carleton Univ., Ont. Freeman, City of London, 1981. Hon. DCL Acadia Univ., NS, 1981; Hon. LLD St Thomas Univ., NB, 1983; hon. degrees: Univ. of Toronto, 1985; Dalhousie Univ., NS, 1985. Hon. Fellowship Award, Bretton Hall Coll., W Yorks, 1982; Hon. Patron, Grenville Christian Coll., Brockville, 1981. *Recreations:* walking, swimming. *Address:* PO Box 579, Prescott, Ont K0E 1T0, Canada. *Clubs:* Albany (Toronto); Rideau (Ottawa).

WADDY, Rev. Lawrence Heber; retired; Lecturer, University of California, San Diego, 1970–80; *b* 5 Oct. 1914; *s* of late Archdeacon Stacy Waddy, Secretary of SPG, and Etheldred (*née* Spittal). *Educ:* Marlborough Coll.; Balliol Coll., Oxford. Domus Exhibitioner in Classics, Balliol, 1933; 1st Class Hon. Mods., Oxford, 1935; de Paravicini Scholar, 1935; Craven Scholar, 1935; 2nd Class Lit. Hum., 1937; BA 1937; MA 1945; Asst Master: Marlborough Coll., 1937–38; Winchester Coll., 1938–42 and 1946–49 (Chaplain, 1946). Headmaster, Tonbridge Sch., 1949–62. Select Preacher, Cambridge Univ., 1951; Oxford Univ., 1954–56. Examining Chaplain to the Bishop of Rochester, 1959–63; Hon. Canon of Rochester, 1961–63; Hon. Chaplain to the Bishop of Rochester, 1963. Deacon, 1940; Priest, 1941; Chaplain, RNVR, 1942–46. Lecturer in Classics, University of California, 1961. Education Officer, School Broadcasting Council, 1962–63; Chaplain to The Bishop's School, La Jolla, California, 1963–67; Headmaster, Santa Maria Internat. Acad., Chula Vista, Calif, 1967–70; Vicar, Church of the Good Samaritan, University City, 1970–74; Hon. Asst, St James', La Jolla, 1974–94. *Publications:* Pax Romana and World Peace, 1950; The Prodigal Son (musical play), 1963; The Bible as Drama, 1974; Faith of Our Fathers, 1975; Symphony, 1977; Drama in Worship, 1978; Mayor's Race, 1980; A Parish by the Sea, 1988; First Bible Stories, 1994; Shakespeare Remembers, 1994; Florence Nightingale, 1995; Jonah, 1995. *Recreations:* cricket and other games. *Address:* 5910 Camino de la Costa, La Jolla, CA 92037, USA.

WADE, family name of **Baron Wade.**

WADE OF CHORLTON, Baron *cr* 1990 (Life Peer), of Chester in the County of Cheshire; **(William) Oulton Wade**, Kt 1982; JP; farmer and cheese master; company director; consultant; Chairman, NIMTECH; *b* 24 Dec. 1932; *s* of Samuel Norman Wade and Joan Ferris Wade (*née* Wild); *m* 1959 Gillian Margaret Leete, Buxton, Derbys; one *s* one *d. Educ:* Birkenhead Sch.; Queen's Univ., Belfast. Jt Treas., Cons. Party, 1982–90; Chm., Parly Rural Economy Gp. Director: Murray Vernon (Holdings) Ltd; John Wilman Ltd. President: Combined Heat and Power Assoc., Energy from Waste Assoc. JP Cheshire 1967. Freeman, City of London, 1980; Liveryman, Farmers' Co., 1980–. *Publications:* contribs to Dairy Industries Internat., Jl of Soc. of Dairy Technol. *Recreations:* politics, reading, shooting, food, travel. *Address:* Chorlton Lodge, Chorlton-by-Backford, Chester CH2 4DB. *T:* Chester (01244) 381451. *Clubs:* Carlton, Farmers'; Chester City (Chester); St James's (Manchester).

WADE, Maj.-Gen. (Douglas) Ashton (Lofft), CB 1946; OBE 1941; MC 1918; BA; CEng; MIEE; *b* 13 March 1898; 2nd *s* of C. S. D. Wade, Solicitor, Saffron Walden, Essex; *m* 1st, 1926, Heather Mary Patricia Bulmer (*d* 1968), Sowerby, Thirsk, Yorkshire; one *d*; 2nd, 1972, Cynthia Halliday (*née* Allen). *Educ:* St Lawrence Coll., Ramsgate; Royal Military Acad., Woolwich; Clare Coll., Cambridge. Commnd into Royal Artillery, 1916; served European War, France, Italy and S Russia; seconded RE 1918–21; transferred to Royal Signals, 1921; Staff Coll., Camberley, 1933–34; DAQMG India, 1937–40; GSO 1, GHQ, BEF and GHQ Home Forces, 1940–41; AA and QMG 2nd Division, 1941–42; Dep. Ajt.-General, India, 1942–44; Comdr, Madras Area, India, 1944–47; GOC Malaya District, 1947–48; Mem., Indian Armed Forces Nationalisation Cttee, 1947; Special Appointment War Office, 1948–49; retired, 1950; Telecommunications Attaché, British Embassy, Washington, 1951–54; Sen. Planning Engineer, Independent Television Authority, 1954–60; Regional Officer, East Anglia, Independent Television Authority, 1960–64. Technical Consultant: Inter-University Research Unit, Cambridge, 1965–69; WRVS Headquarters, 1970–75. Chm., South East Forum for closed circuit TV in educn, 1967–73. Chm., Royal Signals Institute, 1957–63; National Vice-Chairman Dunkirk Veterans' Association, 1962–67, National Chairman, 1967–74. *Publications:* A Life on the Line (autobiog.), 1988; contributed to various Services publications, including RUSI Journal, United Services Journal (India), and Brassey's Annual. *Recreations:* gardening, writing. *Address:* Phoenix Cottage, 6 Church Street, Old Catton, Norwich NR6 7DS. *T:* Norwich (01603) 425755.

WADE, Prof. Sir (Henry) William (Rawson), Kt 1985; QC 1968; FBA 1969; MA; LLD (Cantab); DCL (Oxon); Master of Gonville and Caius College, Cambridge, 1976–88; Barrister-at-Law; *b* 16 Jan. 1918; *s* of late Colonel H. O. Wade and of E. L. Rawson-Ackroyd; *m* 1st, 1943, Marie (*d* 1980), *d* of late G. E. Osland-Hill; two *s*; 2nd, 1982, Marjorie, *d* of late Surgeon-Capt. H. Hope-Gill, RN, and *widow* of B. C. Browne. *Educ:* Shrewsbury Sch. (Governor, 1977–85); Gonville and Caius Coll., Cambridge. Henry Fellow, Harvard Univ., 1939; temp. officer, Treasury, 1940–46. Called to the Bar, Lincoln's Inn, 1946; Hon. Bencher, 1964. Fellow of Trinity Coll., Cambridge, 1946–61, Hon. Fellow, 1991; University Lecturer, 1947; Reader, 1959; Prof. of English Law, Oxford Univ., 1961–76; Fellow, St John's College, Oxford, 1961–76, Hon. Fellow, 1976; Rouse Ball Prof. of English Law, Cambridge Univ., 1978–82. Lectr, Council of Legal Education, 1957; British Council Lectr in Scandinavia, 1958, and Turkey, 1959; Cooley Lectr, Michigan Univ., 1961; Vithalbai Patel Lectr, New Delhi, 1971; Chettyar Lectr, Madras, 1974; Chitaley Lectr, New Delhi, 1982; Cassel Lectr, Stockholm, 1987; Nambyar Lectr, India, 1992. Vice-Pres., British Acad., 1981–83. Member: Council on Tribunals, 1958–71; Relationships Commn, Uganda, 1961; Royal Commn on Tribunals of Inquiry, 1966. *Publications:* The Law of Real Property, 1957 (with Rt Hon. Sir Robert Megarry), 6th edn 1994; Administrative Law, 1961, 7th edn (with Dr C. F. Forsyth) 1994; Towards Administrative Justice, 1963; (with Prof. B. Schwartz) Legal Control of Government, 1972; Constitutional Fundamentals (Hamlyn Lectures), 1980, rev. edn 1989; articles in legal journals; broadcast talks. *Recreations:* climbing, gardening. *Address:* 1A Ludlow Lane, Fulbourn, Cambridge CB1 5BL. *T:* Cambridge (01223) 881745; Gonville and Caius College, Cambridge CB2 1TA. *T:* Cambridge (01223) 332400, *Fax:* (01223) 332456. *Club:* Alpine.

WADE, Joseph Frederick; General Secretary, National Graphical Association, 1976–84; Visiting Professor, University of Strathclyde, 1985–88; *b* 18 Dec. 1919; *s* of James and Ellen Wade; *m* Joan Ann; two *s. Educ:* elementary sch., Blackburn, Lancs. Trained as compositor, The Blackburn Times, 1934–40; served UK and overseas, East Lancs Regt and RAOC, 1940–46; newspaper compositor, 1946–56. Full-time Trade Union official, Typographical Assoc., 1956; Nat. Officer, NGA, 1964; Asst Gen. Sec., NGA, 1968; Gen. Sec., NGA, 1976, NGA '82 (after amalgamation) 1982. Member: Exec. Cttee, Printing and Kindred Trades Fedn, 1971–74; Exec. Cttee, Internat. Graphical Fedn, 1976–85 (Vice-Pres.); TUC Printing Industries Cttee, 1976–84; TUC Gen. Council, 1983–84; Printing and Publishing Industry Training Bd, 1977–82; Printing Industries EDC, 1979–84. Mem., Blackburn County Borough Council, 1952–56. *Recreations:* walking, Scrabble, gardening. *Address:* 10 Spring Vale, Swarthmoor, Ulverston, Cumbria LA12 0XA.

WADE, Prof. Kenneth, FRS 1989; CChem, FRSC; Professor of Chemistry, Durham University, since 1983; *b* Sleaford, Lincs, 13 Oct. 1932; 2nd *s* of Harry Kennington Wade and Anna Elizabeth (*née* Cartwright); *m* 1962, Gertrud Rosmarie Hetzel; one *s* two *d. Educ:* Carre's Grammar Sch., Sleaford; Nottingham Univ. (BSc, PhD; DSc 1970). Postdoctoral research assistant: Cambridge Univ., 1957–59; Cornell Univ., 1959–60; Lectr in Inorganic Chemistry, Derby Coll. of Technology, 1960–61; Durham University: Lectr 1961–71, Sen. Lectr 1971–77, Reader 1977–83, in Chemistry; Chm., Dept of Chemistry, 1986–89. Vis. Res. Fellow, Loker Hydrocarbon Res. Inst., USC, LA, 1979–. Visiting Professor: Technical Univ., Warsaw, 1974; Free Univ., Amsterdam, 1977–78; Univ. of S California, 1979 and 1984–85; Notre Dame Univ., 1983; McMaster Univ., 1984; Western Ontario Univ., 1991. Tilden Lectr, RSC, 1987–88; Emanuel Merck Lectr, Darmstadt, 1994. Pres., Dalton Div., RSC, 1995–. Main Gp Element Award, RSC, 1982. *Publications:* (jtly) Organometallic Compounds: the main group elements, 1967; (jtly) Principles of Organometallic Chemistry, 1968; Electron Deficient Compounds, 1971; (jtly) The Chemistry of Aluminium, Gallium, Indium and Thallium, 1973; (jtly) Organometallic Chemistry, 1976; Hypercarbon Chemistry, 1987; Electron Deficient Boron and Carbon Clusters, 1990; many papers (res. and rev. articles) in learned jls. *Recreations:* (a) musing, (b) musing, (c) walking. *Address:* Chemistry Department, Durham University Science Laboratories, South Road, Durham DH1 3LE. *T:* Durham (0191) 3743122.

WADE, Prof. Owen Lyndon, CBE 1983; MD; FRCP; FRCPI; FFPM; Professor of Therapeutics and Clinical Pharmacology, 1971–86, now Emeritus, and Pro-Vice-Chancellor and Vice-Principal, 1985–86, University of Birmingham; *b* 17 May 1921; *s* of J. O. D. Wade, MS, FRCS, and Kate Wade, Cardiff; *m* 1948, Margaret Burton, LDS; three *d. Educ:* Repton; Cambridge; University College Hospital, London. Senior Scholar, Emmanuel Coll., Cambridge, 1941; Achison and Atkinson Morley Schol., UCH, 1945; Resident Medical Officer, UCH, 1946; Clinical Assistant, Pneumoconiosis Research Unit of the Medical Research Council, 1948–51; Lecturer and Sen. Lecturer in Medicine, Dept of Medicine, University of Birmingham, 1951–57; Whitla Prof. of Therapeutics and Pharmacology, Queen's Univ., Belfast, 1957–71; Dean, Faculty of Medicine and Dentistry, Univ. of Birmingham, 1978–84. Rockefeller Travelling Fellowship in Medicine, 1954–55; Research Fellow, Columbia Univ. at Department of Medicine, Presbyterian Hospital, New York, 1954–55; Consultant, WHO. Chm., Cttee on the Review of Medicines, 1978–84; Chm., Jt Formulary Cttee for British Nat. Formulary, 1978–86. Mem. GMC, 1981–84. Hon. MD QUB, 1989. *Publications:* (with J. M. Bishop) The Cardiac Output and Regional Blood Flow, 1962; Adverse Reactions to Drugs, 1970, 2nd edn with L. Beeley, 1976; papers on cardiorespiratory research, adverse reactions to drugs and drug use in the community, in Jl Physiology, Clinical Science, Brit. Med. Bull., Jl Clin. Invest. *Recreations:* books, travel and sailing. *Address:* c/o The Medical School, Birmingham University. *Club:* Athenæum.

WADE, Richard Lawrence; Fellow and Director of Development, St Edmund Hall, Oxford, since 1993; *b* 5 July 1938; *s* of Wilfred George Wade and Frances Mary (*née* Smith); *m* 1962, Angela Lee Mikhelson (marr. diss. 1995); two *d. Educ:* Bedford Sch.; New Coll., Oxford (MA Oriental Studies). Management Trainee, Unilever Ltd, 1961–63; BBC: TV Dir and Producer, incl. Editor, Tomorrow's World, 1963–75; Chief Asst, Radio 4 and Hd of Radio 4, 1975–83; Chief Asst to Man. Dir, BBC Radio, 1983–86; Marketing Dir, BITC, 1986–88; Man. Dir, Business in the Cities, 1988–89; Dir Gen., Advertising Assoc., 1990–93. Mem., BAFTA, 1968–. Freeman, City of London, 1988. *Recreations:* ski-ing, conversation, photography. *Address:* 49 Park Town, Oxford OX2 6SL. *T:* Oxford (01865) 511984. *Club:* United Oxford & Cambridge University.

WADE, R(obert) Hunter; New Zealand diplomat, retired; *b* 14 June 1916; *s* of R. H. Wade, Balclutha, NZ; *m* 1941, Avelda Grace Petersen (*d* 1990); one *s* two *d* (and one *s* decd). *Educ:* Waitaki; Otago Univ. NZ Treasury and Marketing Depts, 1939; NZ Govt diplomatic appts, Delhi, Simla, Sydney, Canberra, 1941–49; Head of Eastern Political Div., Dept of External Affairs, Wellington, NZ, 1949; NZ Embassy, Washington, 1951; NZ High Commn, Ottawa, 1956; Director of Colombo Plan Bureau, Colombo, 1957; Dir, External Aid, Wellington, 1959; Comr for NZ in Singapore and British Borneo, 1962; High Comr in Malaya/Malaysia, 1963–67; Dep. High Comr in London, 1967–69; NZ Ambassador to Japan and Korea, 1969–71; Dep. Sec.-Gen. of the Commonwealth, 1972–75; NZ Ambassador to Federal Republic of Germany and to Switzerland, 1975–78. Represented New Zealand at Independence of: Uganda, 1962; Botswana, 1966; Lesotho, 1966. Pres., Asiatic Soc. of Japan, 1971. *Address:* 12 Pleasant Place, Howick, Auckland, New Zealand. *Club:* Northern (Auckland).

WADE, Major-General Ronald Eustace, CB 1961; CBE 1956; retired; *b* 28 Oct. 1905; *s* of late Rev. E. V. Wade and Marcia Wade; *m* 1933, Doris, *d* of late C. K. Ross, Kojonup, WA; one *s* one *d. Educ:* Melbourne Church of England Grammar Sch.; RMC, Duntroon. ACT. Commissioned, 1927; attached 4/7 DG (India), 1928–29; Adjutant 10 LH and 9 LH, 1930–38; Captain, 1935; Major, 1940; served War of 1939–45, Lieut-Colonel (CO 2/10 Aust. Armd Regt), 1942; Colonel (Colonel A, Adv. LHQ, Morotai), 1945; Colonel Q, AHQ, Melbourne, 1946; idc 1948; Director of Cadets, 1949; Director of Quartering, 1950–51; Director of Personal Services, 1951–52; Military Secretary, 1952–53; Comd 11 Inf. Bde (Brig.), 1953–55; Maj.-General (Head Aust. Joint Service Staff, Washington), 1956–57; Adjutant-General, 1957–60; GOC Northern Command, 1961–62, retired, 1962. *Address:* Windsor, 1/20 Comer Street, Como, WA 6152, Australia.

WADE, Air Chief Marshal Sir Ruthven (Lowry), KCB 1974 (CB 1970); DFC 1944; Chief of Personnel and Logistics, Ministry of Defence, 1976–78, retired 1978; Director, Acatos and Hutcheson, since 1979; *b* 1920. *Educ:* Cheltenham Coll.; RAF Coll., Cranwell. RAF, 1939; served War of 1939–45, UK and Mediterranean (DFC); psa, 1953; HQ 2nd Tactical Air Force, Germany; RAF Flying Coll.; Gp Captain 1960; Staff Officer, Air HQ, Malta; Comdr, Bomber Comd station, RAF Gaydon, 1962–65; Air Cdre, 1964; idc 1965; Air Exec. to Deputy for Nuclear Affairs, SHAPE, 1967–68; AOC No 1 (Bomber) Gp, Strike Comd, 1968–71; Air Vice-Marshal, 1968; Dep. Comdr, RAF Germany, 1971–72; ACAS (Ops), 1973; Vice Chief of Air Staff, 1973–76; Air Marshal, 1974; Air Chief Marshal, 1976. *Address:* White Gables, Westlington, Dinton, Aylesbury, Bucks HP17 8UR. *T:* Aylesbury (01296) 748884.

WADE, (Sarah) Virginia, OBE 1986 (MBE 1969); tennis player; commentator, BBC Television, since 1980; *b* 10 July 1945; *d* of late Eustace Holland Wade and of Joan Barbara Wade. *Educ:* Sussex Univ. (BSc). Won tennis championships: US Open, 1968; Italian, 1971; Australian, 1972; Wimbledon, 1977; played for GB in Wightman Cup and Federation Cup 20 times (record); Captain, GB team. Mem. Cttee, All England Lawn Tennis Club, 1983–91. Hon. LLD Sussex, 1985. Elected into Internat. Tennis Hall of Fame, 1989. *Publications:* Courting Triumph, 1978; Ladies of the Court, 1984. *Address:* c/o IMG, Pier House, Strand on the Green, W4 3NN. *T:* (office) 0181–994 1444.

WADE, Sir William; see Wade, Sir H. W. R.

WADE-GERY, Sir Robert (Lucian), KCMG 1983 (CMG 1979); KCVO 1983; Vice-Chairman, BZW, since 1994 (Executive Director, since 1987); *b* 22 April 1929; *o s* of late Prof. H. T. Wade-Gery; *m* 1962, Sarah, *er d* of A. D. Marris, CMG; one *s* one *d. Educ:*

Winchester; New Coll., Oxford. 1st cl. Hon. Mods 1949 and Lit. Hum. 1951; Hon. Fellow, 1985. Fellow, All Souls Coll., Oxford, 1951–73, 1987–89. Joined HM Foreign (now Diplomatic) Service, 1951; FO (Economic Relations Dept), 1951–54; Bonn, 1954–57; FO (Private Sec. to Perm. Under-Sec., later Southern Dept), 1957–60; Tel Aviv, 1961–64; FO (Planning Staff), 1964–67; Saigon, 1967–68; Cabinet Office (Sec. to Duncan Cttee), 1968–69; Counsellor 1969; on loan to Bank of England, 1969; Head of Financial Policy and Aid Dept, FCO, 1969–70; Under-Sec., Central Policy Review Staff, Cabinet Office, 1971–73; Minister, Madrid, 1973–77; Minister, Moscow, 1977–79; Dep. Sec. of the Cabinet, 1979–82; High Comr to India, 1982–87. Hon. Treas., IISS, 1991–. Chm., Anglo-Spanish Soc., 1995–. Chm. of Govs, SOAS, 1990–. *Recreations:* walking, sailing, travel, history. *Address:* BZW, Ebbgate House, Swan Lane, EC4R 3TS. *T:* 0171–956 4849, *Fax:* 0171–956 3006; 7 Rothwell Street, NW1 8YH. *T:* 0171–722 4754; Church Cottage, Cold Aston, Cheltenham GL54 3BN. *T:* Cotswold (01451) 21115. *Club:* Boodle's.

WADHAMS, Dr Peter, FRGS; Reader in Polar Studies, Cambridge University, since 1992; *b* 14 May 1948; *s* of late Frank Cecil Wadhams and of Winifred Grace Wadhams (*née* Smith); *m* 1980, Maria Pia Casarini. *Educ:* Palmer's Sch., Grays, Essex; Churchill Coll., Cambridge (BA Phys. 1969; MA 1972; ScD 1994); graduate res., Scott Polar Res. Inst. (PhD 1974). Res. Scientist, Bedford Inst. of Oceanography, Dartmouth, Canada, 1969–70 (asst to Sen. Scientist on Hudson '70 expedn, first circumnavigation of Americas); Fellow, NRC Canada, 1974–75 (Inst. Ocean Scis, Victoria, BC); Scott Polar Research Institute, 1976–: leader, Sea Ice Gp, 1976; Asst Dir of Res., 1981; Dep. Dir, 1983–88; Dir, 1988–92; Sen. Res. Fellow, Churchill Coll., Cambridge, 1983–93. Leader, 25 field ops in Arctic, 5 in Antarctic; UK Deleg., Arctic Ocean Scis Bd, 1984–; Member: IAPSO Commn on Sea Ice, 1987–; SCAR Gp of specialists in Antarctic Sea Ice, 1989–; IASC Wkg Gp on Global Change, 1992–. Vis. Prof., Naval Postgrad. Sch., Monterey, 1980–81; Green Schol Scripps Instn, 1987–88; Walker-Ames Vis. Prof., Univ. of Washington, WA, 1988. W. S. Bruce Prize, RSE 1977; Polar Medal, 1987; Italgas Prize for Envmtl Scis, 1990. *Publications:* (contrib.) The Nordic Seas, 1986; (contrib.) The Geophysics of Sea Ice, 1986; (ed) Ice Technology for Polar Operations, 1990; (contrib.) Microwave Remote Sensing of Sea Ice, 1992; (ed) Advances in Ice Technology, 1992; Marine, Offshore and Ice Technology, 1994; numerous sci. papers on glaciology and polar oceanography. *Recreations:* painting, music, sailing. *Address:* 40 Grafton Street, Cambridge CB1 1DS. *T:* Cambridge (01223) 359433. *Clubs:* Arctic, Antarctic.

WADIA, Jim, FCA; Managing Partner, United Kingdom, Arthur Andersen, since 1993; *b* 12 April 1948; *m* 1972, Joelle Garnier; one *s* one *d. Educ:* Le Rosey, Rolle, Switzerland; Inns of Court Sch. of Law. Called to the Bar, Inner Temple, 1969. Arthur Andersen: Partner, 1982–; Hd, London Tax, 1989–93. FRSA. *Recreations:* tennis, theatre. *Address:* 28 Eldon Road, W8 5PT. *T:* 0171–438 3501.

WADSWORTH, James Patrick, QC 1981; barrister; a Recorder of the Crown Court, since 1980; *b* 7 Sept. 1940; *s* of Francis Thomas Bernard Wadsworth, Newcastle, and Geraldine Rosa (*née* Brannan); *m* 1963, Judith Stuart Morrison, *e d* of Morrison Scott, Newport-on-Tay; one *s* one *d. Educ:* Stonyhurst; University Coll., Oxford (MA). Called to the Bar, Inner Temple, 1963, Bencher, 1988. Member: Bar Council, 1992–; Bar Professional Standards Cttee, 1993–. *Recreations:* eating, idling. *Address:* 4 Paper Buildings, Temple, EC4. *T:* 0171–353 3366.

WAGNER, Gerrit Abram, KBE (Hon.) 1977 (CBE (Hon.) 1964); Kt, Order of Netherlands Lion, 1969; Grand Officer, Order of Oranje Nassau, 1983 (Commander 1977); Chairman, Supervisory Board, Royal Dutch Petroleum Co., 1977–87 (President, 1971–77); *b* 21 Oct. 1916; *m* 1946, M. van der Heul; one *s* three *d. Educ:* Leyden Univ. LLM 1939. After a period in a bank in Rotterdam and in Civil Service in Rotterdam and The Hague, joined Royal Dutch Shell Group, 1946; assignments in The Hague, Curaçao, Venezuela, London and Indonesia; apptd Man. Dir, Royal Dutch Petroleum Co. and Shell Petroleum Co. Ltd; Mem. Presidium of Bd of Directors of Shell Petroleum NV, 1964; Dir, Shell Canada Ltd, 1971–77; Chm., Cttee of Man. Dirs, Royal Dutch/Shell Group, 1972–77; Chm., Shell Oil USA, 1972–77. Former Chairman, Supervisory Board: De Nederlandsche Bank NV; Gist-Brocades NV; KLM; Smit Internat.; Vice-Chm., Supervisory Bd, Hoogovens Gp BV, Beverwijk; Member, International Advisory Committee: Chase Manhattan Bank, NY; Robert Bosch, Stuttgart. Order of Francisco de Miranda, Grand Officer (Venezuela), 1965; Officier Légion d'Honneur (France), 1974. *Address:* 13 Teylingeshosstlaan 13, 2244 EJ Wassenaar, The Netherlands.

WAGNER, Dame Gillian (Mary Millicent), (Lady Wagner), DBE 1994 (OBE 1977); Chairman, Court of Governors, Thomas Coram Foundation for Children, 1990–95; *b* 25 Oct. 1927; *e d* of late Major Henry Archibald Roger Graham, and of Hon. Margaret Beatrix, *d* of 1st Baron Roborough; *m* 1953, Sir Anthony Wagner, KCB, KCVO; two *s* one *d. Educ:* Cheltenham Ladies' Coll.; Geneva Univ. (Licence ès Sciences Morales); London Sch. of Economics (Dip. Social Admin). PhD London 1977. Mem. Council, Dr Barnardo's, 1969– (Chm., Exec./Finance Cttee, 1973–78; Chm. Council, 1978–84); Chairman: Volunteer Centre, 1984–89 (Pres., 1990–); Review of Residential Care, 1986–88; The Leche Trust, 1992–; Chair, Community Care Inquiry for people with learning difficulties, Mental Health Foundn, 1995–; President: Skill: Nat. Bureau for Students with Disabilities, 1978–91; IAPS, 1985–90 (Gov., 1974–). Mem. Exec. Cttee, Georgian Gp, 1970–78. Chm. of Governors, Felixstowe Coll., 1980–87; Gov., Nat. Inst. for Social Work, 1988–. Trustee, Carnegie UK Trust, 1980– (Chm., 1995–). Governor, LSE, 1991–. Hon. DSc Bristol, 1989; Hon. LLD Liverpool, 1990. *Publications:* Barnardo, 1979; Children of the Empire, 1982; The Chocolate Conscience, 1987; various articles on residential care. *Recreations:* sailing, gardening, travelling. *Address:* 10 Physic Place, Royal Hospital Road, SW3 4HQ. *T:* 0171–352 0934; Wyndham Cottage, Crespigny Road, Aldeburgh, Suffolk IP15 5DL. *T:* Aldeburgh (01728) 452596. *Club:* Aldeburgh Yacht.

WAGNER, Prof. Leslie, MA; Principal and Chief Executive, and Professor, Leeds Metropolitan University, since 1994; *b* 21 Feb. 1943; *s* of Herman and Toby Wagner; *m* 1967, Jennifer Jean Fineberg; one *s* one *d. Educ:* Salford Grammar Sch.; Manchester Univ. (MAEcon). Economic Asst and Economic Advr, DEA, 1966–69; Economic Advr, Min. of Technology, 1969–70; Lectr in Econs, Open Univ., 1970–76; Hd of Social Sciences, 1976–82, Prof., 1980, Polytechnic of Central London; Asst Sec. (Academic), Nat. Adv. Body for Local Authy Higher Educn, 1982–85; Dep. Sec., Nat. Adv. Body for Public Sector Higher Educn, 1985–87; Dir, Poly. of N London, 1987–92, then Vice-Chancellor and Chief Exec., Univ. of N London, 1992–93. Member: Bd, Open Learning Foundn, 1990– (Chm., 1990–93); Bd, HEQC, 1992–; Council for Industry and Higher Educn, 1992–; Chairman: SRHE, 1994–; Higher Educn for Capability, 1994–. Councillor (Lab) London Bor. of Harrow, 1971–78, Chm., Educn Cttee, 1972–74. Contested (Lab) Harrow W, Feb. 1974. Vice-Pres., Utd Synagogue, 1992–93; Chm., Jewish Community Allocations Bd, 1994–. *Publications:* (ed) Readings in Applied Microeconomics, 1973, 2nd edn 1981; (ed) Agenda for Institutional Change in Higher Education, 1982; The Economics of Educational Media, 1982; (jtly) Choosing to Learn: a study of mature students, 1987. *Address:* Leeds Metropolitan University, Calverley Street, Leeds LS1 3HE. *T:* Leeds (0113) 283 2600. *Club:* Reform.

WAGSTAFF, Ven. Christopher John Harold; Archdeacon of Gloucester, since 1982; *b* 25 June 1936; *s* of Harold Maurice Wagstaff and Kathleen Mary Wagstaff (*née* Bean); *m* 1964, Margaret Louise (*née* Macdonald); two *s* one *d. Educ:* Bishop's Stortford College, Herts; Essex Inst. of Agriculture, Chelmsford (Dipl. in Horticulture 1959); St David's Coll., Lampeter (BA 1962, Dipl. in Theol. 1963). Deacon 1963, priest 1964; Curate, All Saints, Queensbury, 1963–68; Vicar, St Michael's, Tokyngton, Wembley, 1968–73; Vicar of Coleford with Staunton, 1973–83; RD, South Forest, 1975–82. Diocese of Gloucester: Chairman: House of Clergy, 1983–95; Bd of Social Responsibility, 1983–; Diocesan Trust, 1983–; Diocesan Assoc. for the Deaf, 1989–94; Diocesan Adv. Cttee, 1988–. Mem., General Synod, 1988–. Hon. Canon, St Andrew's Cathedral, Njombe, Tanzania, 1993–. Freeman, City of London; Liveryman, Worshipful Co. of Armourers and Brasiers. *Recreations:* gardening, walking, travel. *Address:* Christchurch Vicarage, Montpellier, Gloucester GL1 1LB. *T:* Gloucester (01452) 528500.

WAGSTAFF, David St John Rivers; a Recorder of the Crown Court, 1974–94; barrister, retired; *b* 22 June 1930; *s* of late Prof. John Edward Pretty Wagstaff and Dorothy Margaret (*née* McRobie); *m* 1970, Dorothy Elizabeth Starkie; two *d. Educ:* Winchester Coll. (Schol.); Trinity Coll., Cambridge (Schol., MA, LLB). Called to Bar, Lincoln's Inn, 1954. *Recreations:* mountaineering, fencing. *Address:* 8 Breary Lane East, Bramhope, Leeds LS16 9BJ. *Clubs:* Alpine; Fell and Rock Climbing (Lake District), Leeds (Leeds).

WAGSTAFF, Edward Malise Wynter; HM Diplomatic Service, retired; psychotherapist; *b* 27 June 1930; *s* of late Col Henry Wynter Wagstaff, CSI, MC, and Jean Mathieson, MB, BS; *m* 1957, Eva Margot, *d* of Erik Hedelius; one *s* two *d. Educ:* Wellington Coll.; RMA Sandhurst; Pembroke Coll., Cambridge (MA; Mech Scis Tripos); Staff Coll., Camberley; psc. Commissioned RE, 1949; served in UK, Germany and Gibraltar, 1950–62; seconded to Federal Regular Army, Fedn of S Arabia, 1963–65; Asst Mil. Attaché, Amman, 1967–69 (Major, 1962; GSM; South Arabia Radfan bar). Joined FCO, 1969; served Saigon, 1973, FCO, 1975, Oslo, 1976, Copenhagen, 1978, FCO, 1981; Counsellor, FCO, 1982–92; Advr, later Consultant FCO, 1992–95. Qualified as psychosynthesis psychotherapist, 1993. Kt, First Degree, Order of Dannebrog, 1979. *Recreations:* God, concern for the bewildered, plumbing. *Address:* c/o Lloyds Bank PLC, 32 Commercial Way, Woking, Surrey GU21 1ER.

WAHLSTRÖM, General Jarl Holger; International Leader of The Salvation Army, 1981–86; *b* 9 July 1918; *s* of Rafael Alexander Wahlström and Aina Maria Wahlström (*née* Dahlberg); *m* 1944, Maire Helfrid Nyberg; two *s* one *d. Educ:* Salvation Army International Training Coll. Salvation Army, Finland: Corps Officer, 1939–45; Scout Organizer, 1945–52; Private Sec. to Territorial Commander, 1952–54; Youth Sec., 1954–60; Divisional Comdr, 1960–63; Principal, Training Coll., 1963–68; Chief Secretary, 1968–72; Territorial Comdr, 1976–80; Salvation Army, Canada and Bermuda: Chief Secretary, 1972–76; Salvation Army, Sweden: Territorial Comdr, 1981. Hon. DHL Western Illinois, 1985. Cross of Liberty, IV cl., Finland, 1941; Knight, Order of Lion of Finland, 1964; Order of Civil Merit, Mugunghwa Medal, Republic of Korea, 1983; Comdr, Order of White Rose, Finland, 1989. *Publications:* (autobiog.) Matkalaulu (Finnish edn), En Vallfartssång (Swedish edn), 1989; contribs to Salvation Army papers and magazines, English, Finnish, Swedish. *Recreation:* music. *Address:* Borgströminkuja 1 A 10, 00840 Helsinki, Finland. *T:* (0) 6982413. *Club:* Rotary.

WAIAPU, Bishop of, since 1991; **Rt. Rev. Murray John Mills;** *b* 29 May 1936; *s* of Robert Claude Mills and Mabel Winifred Mills; *m* 1961, Judith Anne Cotton; two *s* three *d. Educ:* Auckland Univ. (BA, MA); St John's Theol Coll. (LTh (First Cl. Hons)). Ordained: Deacon, 1960; Priest, 1961 (dio. of Auckland); Assistant Curate: Papakura, 1960–63; Whangarei, 1963–65; Vicar: Bay of Islands, 1965–70; Matamata, 1970–75; Archdeacon of Waikato, 1976–81; Vicar-Gen., dio. of Waikato, 1978–84; Vicar: Tokoroa, 1981–84; St John's Cathedral, Napier (dio. of Waiapu) and Dean of Waiapu, 1984–91. Examining Chaplain to Bishop of Waikato, 1974–84, Advr in Christian Educn, 1976–81. *Publication:* History of Christ Church, Papakura, 1961. *Recreations:* tramping, gardening, drama, politics, music, reading. *Address:* (home) 8 Cameron Terrace, Napier, New Zealand. *T:* (6) 8357846; (office) Diocesan Office, PO Box 227, Napier, New Zealand. *T:* (6) 8358230.

WAIARU, Rt. Rev. Amos Stanley; Archbishop of Melanesia, and Bishop of Central Melanesia, 1988–93; *b* 19 April 1944; *s* of late Stanley Qagora and Emma Kaifo; *m* 1976, Mary Marjorie Waiaru (*née* Mwele); one *s* three *d. Educ:* Bishop Patteson Theol Coll., Kohimarama, Solomon Is; Pacific Theol Coll., Suva, Fiji Is (DipTh). Tutor, Torgil Training Centre, Vanuatu, 1976; Chaplain, Vureas High School, Vanuatu, 1977–78, Head Master 1979–80; Bishop of Temotu, Solomon Is, 1981–87. Chm., S Pacific Anglican Council, 1991–93. *Recreations:* gardening, fishing. *Address:* Ngafinuatoga Village, Santa Anna, Makira-Ulawa Province, Solomon Islands.

WAIDE, (Edward) Bevan, OBE 1988; Partner, Coopers & Lybrand, 1988–93; Chief Adviser, Privatisation, Tanzanian Government, since 1993; *b* 14 Sept. 1936; *s* of William Leathley Waide and Louisa Winifred Waide (*née* Evershed); *m* 1961, Pu-Chin (marr. diss. 1993); one *s* one *d. Educ:* Farnham Grammar Sch.; Emmanuel Coll., Cambridge (BA); Univ. of California, Berkeley (MA). Teaching Asst, Univ. of California, 1959–61; Sen. Economist, Asia, World Bank, 1962–69; Chief Advisor, Min. of Economic Affairs and Develt Planning, Govt of Tanzania, 1969–73; Dir, N Region Strategy Team, DoE, 1973–76; World Bank: Chief Economist, S Asia, 1976–79; Dir, Develt Policy, 1979–82; Dir, Country Policy Dept, 1982–84; Dir, New Delhi Office, 1984–88. Mem., Commonwealth Develt Corp., 1990–93. *Publications:* (jtly) India: an industrialising economy in transition, 1989; World Develt Reports, World Bank; articles on develt and regional planning issues; country reports. *Recreations:* tennis, car restoration. *Address:* Laburnum Cottage, The Butts, Napton-on-the-Hill, Southam, Warwicks CV23 8NW. *T:* Southam (01926) 817024. *Clubs:* Reform; Vintage Sports Car.

WAIGEL, Theodor; Minister of Finance, Germany, since 1989; *b* 22 April 1939; *s* of August Waigel and Genoveva Konrad; *m* 1st, 1966, Karin Hönig; one *s* one *d*; 2nd, 1994, Dr Irene Epple. *Educ:* Univ. of Munich; Univ. of Würzburg. Lawyer, 1967–69; posts in Min. of Finance, and Min. of Economy and Transport, Bavaria, 1969–72; Mem. of Bundestag, 1972–. Chm., CSU, 1988– (Chm., Bavarian CSU Parly Gp, 1982–89). *Address:* Ministry of Finance, 53117 Bonn, Graurheindorfer Strasse 108, Germany.

WAIKATO, Bishop of, since 1993; **Rt. Rev. David John Moxon;** *b* 6 Sept. 1951; *s* of John Rosher Moxon and Joan Moxon; *m*; two *s* two *d. Educ:* Freyberg High Sch., Palmerston North; Massey Univ. (MA Hons). MA Oxford Univ. Volunteer service abroad (school leaver scheme), 1970; Univ. Tutor, Educn Dept, Massey Univ., 1974–75; Curate, St Luke's, Havelock North, 1978–81; Vicar, St George's Gate, PA, 1981–87; Dir, Theol Educn by Extension Unit, Anglican Province of NZ, 1987–93. Hon. LTh Aotearoa. Gold Duke of Edinburgh Award, 1969. *Recreations:* playing flute, reading, tramping, swimming. *Address:* Bishop's House, 3 Lake Domain Drive, Hamilton, NZ. *T:* (7) 8395308; (office) Anglican Church House, 33 Victoria Street, Hamilton, NZ. *T:* (7) 8382309.

WAIN, Prof. (Ralph) Louis, CBE 1968; DSc, PhD; FRS 1960, FRSC; Hon. Professor of Chemistry, University of Kent, since 1977 and Emeritus Professor, University of London, since 1978; Professor of Agricultural Chemistry, University of London, 1950–78, and Head of Department of Physical Sciences at Wye College (University of London), 1945–78; Hon. Director, Agricultural Research Council Unit on Plant Growth Substances and Systemic Fungicides, 1953–78; Fellow of Wye College, since 1981; *b* 29 May 1911; 2nd *s* of late G. Wain, Hyde, Cheshire; *m* 1940, Joan Bowker; one *s* one *d*. *Educ:* County Grammar Sch., Hyde, Cheshire; University of Sheffield (First Class Hons Chemistry, 1932; MSc 1933; PhD 1935; Hon. DSc 1977); DSc London, 1949; Town Trustees Fellow, University of Sheffield, 1934; Research Assistant, University of Manchester, 1935–37; Lecturer in Chemistry, Wye Coll., 1937–39; Research Chemist, Long Ashton Research Station (University of Bristol), 1939–45; Rockefeller Fellow, 1950 and 1962. Vice-President, Royal Institute of Chemistry, 1961–64, 1975–78; Member: Governing Body, Glasshouse Crops Res. Inst., 1953–71; E African Natural Resources Res. Council, 1963–; Manager, Royal Instn, 1971–74. Chm., AFRC Wain Fellowships Cttee, 1976–. Nuffield Vis. Prof., Ibadan Univ., 1959; Vis. Prof., Cornell Univ., 1966; NZ Prestige Fellowship, 1973; Leverhulme Emeritus Fellowship, 1978–. Elected to Académie Internationale de Lutèce, 1980. Lectures: Sir Thomas Middleton Meml, London, 1955; Frankland Meml, Birmingham, 1965; Benjamin Minge Duggar Meml, Alabama, 1966; Amos Meml, E Malling, 1969; Masters Meml, London, 1973; Sir Jesse Boot Foundn, Nottingham, 1974; Ronald Slack Meml, London, 1975; Extramural Centenary, London Univ., 1976; Vis. Lectr, Pontifical Acad. Scis, 1976; Douglas Wills, Bristol, 1977; Gooding Meml, London, 1978; Drummond Meml, London, 1979; John Dalton, Manchester, 1979; Holden, Nottingham, 1984; Hannaford Meml, Adelaide, 1985. Royal Soc. Vis. Prof. to Jordan, 1960, Sudan, 1965, Czechoslovakia, 1968, Mexico, 1971, China, 1973 and 1982, Romania, 1974, Poland, 1976, Bulgaria, 1978, Israel, 1979, Hungary, 1980, West Indies and Philippines, 1981, Hong Kong, 1984, 1988, Indonesia, 1989, S Korea, 1990, Japan 1991, Australia 1992, Taiwan 1993. Pruthivi Gold Medal, 1957; RASE Research Medal, 1960; John Scott Award, 1963; Flintoff Medal, Chem. Soc., 1969; Internat. Award, Amer. Chem. Soc., 1972; Internat. Medal for Research on Plant Growth Substances, 1973; John Jeyes Gold Medal and Award, Chem. Soc., 1976; Royal Instn Actonian Award, 1977; Mullard Award and Medal, Royal Soc., 1988. Hon. DAgricSci, Ghent, 1963; Hon. DSc: Kent, 1976; Lausanne, 1977. *Publications:* numerous research publications in Annals of Applied Biology, Journal of Agric. Science, Journal of Chemical Society, Berichte der Deutschen Chemischen Gesellschaft, Proc. Royal Society, etc. *Recreations:* painting, travel. *Address:* Crown Point, Scotton Street, Wye, Ashford, Kent TN25 5BZ. *T:* Wye (01233) 812157.

WAINE, Dr Colin, OBE 1990; FRCGP, FRCPath; Director of Primary Care, Sunderland Health Commission, since 1993; Chairman, Council, Royal College of General Practitioners, 1990–93; *b* 12 March 1936; *m* 1959, Gwendoline Jameson; two *d*. *Educ:* King James I Grammar Sch., Bishop Auckland; Medical Sch., King's Coll., Univ. of Durham (MB BS Hons). MRCGP (dist.) 1975, FRCGP 1976, FRCPath 1993. Principal in general practice, Bishop Auckland, 1962–93; Hosp. Practitioner in Paediatrics, Bishop Auckland General Hosp., 1963–88; Gen. Manager, SW Durham HA, 1985–92. Course Organiser (Continuing Educn), Regional Post Grad. Inst., Newcastle upon Tyne, 1978–86. Consultant and UK Delegate, European Health Cttee, Primary Care and Prevention Gp, Council of Europe, Strasbourg, 1983–85. *Publications:* (contrib.) Handbook of Preventative Care for Pre-School Children, 1984; Organisation of Prevention in Primary Care, 1986; Why not care for your diabetic patients?, 1986; (contrib.) Chronic Disease in Medical Audit in General Practice, 1990; contrib. to reports of working parties and papers and articles on diabetes, health care for children, asthma, etc in BMJ, The Practitioner, Cardiology in Practice, Members Reference Books, RCGP. *Recreations:* reading, gardening, music, cricket. *Address:* 42 Etherley Lane, Bishop Auckland, Co. Durham DL14 7QZ. *T:* Bishop Auckland (01388) 604429.

WAINE, Rt. Rev. John; *see* Chelmsford, Bishop of.

WAINWRIGHT, Edwin, BEM 1957; *b* 12 Aug. 1908; *s* of John Wainwright and Ellen (*née* Hodgson); *m* 1938, Dorothy Metcalfe; two *s* two *d*. *Educ:* Darfield Council School; Wombwell and Barnsley Technical Colleges. WEA student for 20 years. Started work at 14, at Darfield Main Colliery; Nat. Union of Mineworkers: Member Branch Cttee, 1933–39; Delegate, 1939–48; Branch Sec., 1948–59; Member, Nat. Exec. Cttee, 1952–59. Member, Wombwell UDC, 1939–59. Sec./Agent, Dearne Valley Labour Party, 1951–59. MP (Lab) Dearne Valley, S Yorks, Oct. 1959–1983; Mem., Select Cttee on Energy, 1979–83. Secretary: PLP Trade Union Gp, 1966–83; Yorkshire Gp of PLP, 1966–83. *Recreations:* gardening, reading. *Address:* 20 Dovecliffe Road, Wombwell, near Barnsley, South Yorks S73 8UE. *T:* Barnsley (01226) 752153.

WAINWRIGHT, Geoffrey John, MBE 1991; PhD; FSA; Chief Archaeologist, English Heritage, since 1990; *b* 19 Sept. 1937; *s* of Frederick and Dorothy Wainwright; *m* 1977, Judith; one *s* two *d*. *Educ:* Pembroke Docks Sch.; Univ. of Wales (BA); Univ. of London (PhD). FSA 1967; MIFA 1984. Prof. of Archaeology, Univ. of Baroda, India, 1961–63; Inspectorate of Ancient Monuments, English Heritage (formerly part of DoE), 1963–; Principal Inspector, 1963–90. Dir, Soc. of Antiquaries, 1984–90. Mem., Royal Commn on Ancient and Historical Monuments in Wales, 1987–; President: Cornwall Archaeological Soc., 1980–84; Prehistoric Soc., 1982–86. Visiting Professor: Univ. of Southampton, 1991–; UCL, 1995–. Fellow, University Coll., Cardiff, 1985. FRSA 1991. *Publications:* Stone Age in North India, 1964; Coygan Camp, Carms, 1967; Durrington Walls, Wilts, 1971; Mount Pleasant, Dorset, 1979; Gussage All Saints, Dorset, 1979; The Henge Monuments, 1990; numerous articles in learned jls. *Recreations:* Rugby football, racing, food and drink. *Address:* 13 Park Cottages, Crown Road, Twickenham, TW1 3EQ. *T:* 0181–891 2429; March Pres, Pontfaen, Dyfed SA65 9TT.

WAINWRIGHT, Richard Scurrah; *b* 11 April 1918; *o s* of late Henry Scurrah and Emily Wainwright; *m* 1948, Joyce Mary Hollis; one *s* two *d* (and one *s* decd). *Educ:* Shrewsbury Sch.; Clare Coll., Cambridge (Open Scholar). BA Hons (History), 1939. Friends Ambulance Unit, NW Europe, 1939–46. Retired Partner, Peat Marwick Mitchell & Co., Chartered Accountants. Pres., Leeds/Bradford Society of Chartered Accountants, 1965–66. MP (L) Colne Valley, 1966–70 and Feb. 1974–87, retired. Chm., Liberal Party Research Dept, 1968–70; Chm., Liberal Party, 1970–72; Mem., Select Cttee on Treasury, 1979–87; Liberal spokesman on the economy, 1979–85, on employment, 1985–87. Dep. Chm., Wider Share Ownership Council, 1968–92. Pres., Yorks Fedn of Lib Dems, 1989–. *Recreations:* gardening, swimming. *Address:* 8 Dunstarn Lane, Leeds LS16 8EL. *T:* Leeds (0113) 267 3938.

WAINWRIGHT, Sam, CBE 1982; Member: Monopolies and Mergers Commission, 1985–91; Post Office Audit Committee, 1989–92; Director, BICC, 1985–90; *b* 2 Oct. 1924; *m* Ruth Strom; three *s* one *d*. *Educ:* Regent Street Polytechnic; LSE (MSc Econ). Financial journalist, Glasgow Herald, 1950; Deputy City Editor, 1952–55; Director: Rea Brothers Ltd (Merchant Bankers), 1960–77 (Managing Dir, 1965–77); Furness Withy & Co. Ltd, 1971–77; Stothert & Pitt Ltd, 1970–77 (Chm., 1975–77); Aeronautical & General Instruments Ltd, 1968–77; Lancashire & London Investment Trust Ltd, 1963–77; Scottish Cities Investment Trust Ltd, 1961–77; Scottish & Mercantile Investment Co. Ltd, 1964–77; AMDAHL (UK), 1987–93; Post Office Corporation: Mem. Bd, 1977–85; Dep. Chm., 1981–85; Man. Dir, Nat. Girobank, 1977–85; Dir Postel Investment Ltd, 1982–85; Dir, 1972–87, Dep. Chm., 1985–86, Chm., 1986–87, Manders (Hldgs). Mem. Council, Soc. of Investment Analysts, 1961–75, Fellow, 1980. Chm., Jigsaw Day Nurseries, 1991–95. Hon. Editor, The Investment Analyst, 1961–74. *Publications:* articles in various Bank Reviews. *Recreations:* reading, bridge, walking. *Address:* Flat 5, 29 Warrington Crescent, W9 1EJ. *T:* 0171–286 8050. *Club:* Reform.

WAITE, Rt. Hon. Sir John (Douglas), Kt 1982; PC 1993; **Rt. Hon. Lord Justice Waite;** a Lord Justice of Appeal, since 1993; *b* 3 July 1932; *s* of late Archibald Harvey Waite and Betty, *d* of late Ernest Bates; *m* 1966, Julia Mary, *er d* of late Joseph Tangye; three *s* two step *s*. *Educ:* Sherborne Sch.; Corpus Christi Coll., Cambridge (MA). President of Cambridge Union, 1955. Nat. Service, 2nd Lieut, RA, 1951–52. Called to Bar, Gray's Inn, 1956, Bencher, 1981; QC 1975; a Judge of the High Court of Justice, Family Div., 1982–93; Presiding Judge, North Eastern Circuit, 1990–93. Pres., Employment Appeal Tribunal, 1983–85. *Recreations:* reading (haphazardly), sailing (uncertainly), gardening (optimistically). *Address:* Royal Courts of Justice, Strand, WC2A 2LL.

WAITE, Terence Hardy, CBE 1992 (MBE 1982); writer and lecturer; Adviser to Archbishop of Canterbury on Anglican Communion Affairs, 1980–92; Fellow Commoner, Trinity Hall, Cambridge, 1992–93; *b* 31 May 1939; *s* of Thomas William Waite and Lena (*née* Hardy); *m* 1964, Helen Frances Watters; one *s* three *d*. *Educ:* Wilmslow and Stockton Heath, Cheshire; Church Army Coll., London; privately in USA and Europe. Lay training adviser to Bishop and Diocese of Bristol, 1964–68; Adviser to Archbishop of Uganda, Rwanda and Burundi, 1968–71; Internat. Consultant working with Roman Catholic Church, 1972–79. Member, National Assembly, Church of England, 1966–68 (resigned on moving to Africa); Co-ordinator, Southern Sudan Relief Project, 1969–71. Founder-Chm., Y Care International, 1985–. Mem., Royal Inst. of International Affairs, 1980–. Paul Harris Fellow, Internat. Rotarian Organisation, 1983–. Member: World Wildlife Council, 1985–; Council, Internat. Year of Shelter for the Homeless, 1987; Council, Uganda Soc. for Disabled Children; Central Cttee, Victim Support. Trustee, Butler Trust. Patron: Strode Park Foundn for the Disabled, Herne, Kent, 1985; Friends of the Commonwealth Inst.; Bunyan Church and Mus. Appeal, 1992; The Warrington Project; Bury St Edmunds Volunteer Centre; Wintercomfort (housing charity). Templeton UK Project Award, 1985. Hon. DCL: City, 1986; Kent at Canterbury, 1986; Durham, 1992; Hon. LLD: Liverpool, 1986; Sussex, 1992; Yale, 1992. Franklin D. Roosevelt Four Freedom Award, 1992. *Publication:* Taken on Trust, 1993. *Recreations:* music, walking, travel (esp. in remote parts of the world), Jungian studies, international affairs and politics, Left-Handed Society, preservation of old Blackheath. *Address:* Trinity Hall, Cambridge CB2 1TJ. *Clubs:* Travellers'; Empire (Canada).

WAJDA, Andrzej; Polish film and theatre director; Managing Director, Teatr Powszechny, Warsaw, 1989–90; Senator, Polish People's Republic, 1989–91; *b* 6 March 1926; *s* of Jakub Wajda and Aniela Wajda; *m* 1st, 1967, Beata Tyszkiewicz (marr. diss.); one *d*; 2nd, 1975, Krystyna Zachwatowicz. *Educ:* Acad. Fine Arts, Cracow; Film Acad., Łódź. Asst Stage Manager, 1953; film dir, 1954–; Stage Manager, Teatr Stary, Cracow, 1973. Pres., Polish Film Assoc., 1978–83. Hon. Mem., Union of Polish Artists and Designers, 1977. Dr *hc*: American, Washington, 1981; Bologna, 1988; Jagiellonian, Cracow, 1989. British Acad. Award for Services to Film, 1982; BAFTA Fellowship, 1982. Order of Banner of Labour, 1975; Officer's Cross of Polonia Restituta; Officier, Légion d'Honneur (France), 1982; Order of Kirill and Methodius (Bulgaria). *Films:* Generation, 1954; I'm Going to the Sun, 1955; Kanal, 1956 (Silver Palm, Cannes, 1957); Ashes and Diamonds, 1957; Lotna, 1959; Innocent Sorcerers, 1959; Samson, 1960; Serbian Lady Macbeth, 1961; Love at Twenty, 1961; Ashes, 1965; Gates of Paradise, 1967; Everything For Sale, 1968; Jigsaw Puzzle (for TV), 1969; Hunting Flies, 1969; Macbeth (TV), 1969; Landscape After Battle, 1970; The Birch Wood, 1970; Pilatus (TV), 1971; Master and Margaret (TV), 1972; The Wedding, 1972 (Silver Prize, San Sebastian, 1973); The Promised Land, 1974 (Grand Prix, Moscow Film Festival, 1975); The Shadow Line, 1976; A Dead Class (TV), 1976; Man of Marble, 1977; Rough Treatment, 1978; The Orchestral Conductor, 1979; The Maids of Wilko, 1979 (Oscar nomination, 1980); Man of Iron, 1981 (Palme D'Or, Cannes, 1981); Danton, 1982; Love in Germany, 1985; Chronicle of Love Affairs, 1986; The Possessed, 1987; Korczak, 1990; *plays:* Hatful of Rain, 1959; Hamlet, 1960, 1980, 1989; Two on the Seesaw, 1960, 1990; The Wedding, 1962; The Possessed, 1963, 1971, 1975; Play Strindberg, 1969; Idiot, 1971, 1975; Sticks and Bones, Moscow, 1972; Der Mittmacher, 1973; November Night, 1974; The Danton Case, 1975, 1978; When Reason is Asleep, 1976; Emigrés, 1976; Nastasia Philipovna (improvisation based on Dostoyevsky's The Idiot), 1977; Conversation with the Executioner, 1977; Gone with the Years, Gone with the Days . . ., 1978; Antygone, 1984; Crime and Punishment, 1984, 1986, 1987; Miss Julia, 1988; Dybuk, 1988; Lesson of Polish Language, 1988; Nastasya (adapted from The Idiot), 1989; Hamlet IV, 1989; Romeo and Juliet, 1990; The Wedding, 1991. *Publication:* My Life in Film (autobiog.), 1989. *Address:* Film Polski, ul. Mazowiecka 6/8, Warsaw, Poland.

WAKE, Sir Hereward, 14th Bt *cr* 1621; MC 1942; Vice Lord-Lieutenant of Northamptonshire, 1984–91; Major (retired) King's Royal Rifle Corps; *b* 7 Oct. 1916; *e s* of Maj. Gen. Sir Hereward Wake, 13th Bt, CB, CMG, DSO, and Margaret W. (*d* 1976), *er d* of R. H. Benson; *S* father, 1963; *m* 1952, Julia Rosemary, JP, *yr d* of late Capt. G. W. M. Lees, Falcutt House, Nr Brackley, Northants; one *s* three *d*. *Educ:* Eton; RMC, Sandhurst. Served War of 1939–45 (wounded, MC). Retired from 60th Rifles, 1947, and studied Estate Management and Agriculture. High Sheriff, 1955, DL 1969, Northants. *Heir: s* Hereward Charles Wake [*b* 22 Nov. 1952; *m* 1977, Lady Doune Ogilvy, *e d* of Earl of Airlie, *qv*; two *s* one *d* (and one *s* decd)]. *Address:* Courteenhall, Northampton NN7 2QD. *Club:* Brooks's.

WAKEFIELD, Bishop of, since 1992; **Rt. Rev. Nigel Simeon McCulloch;** *b* 17 Jan. 1942; *s* of late Pilot Officer Kenneth McCulloch, RAFVR, and of Audrey Muriel McCulloch; *m* 1974, Celia Hume Townshend, *d* of Canon H. L. H. Townshend; two *d*. *Educ:* Liverpool College; Selwyn Coll., Cambridge (Kitchener Schol., BA 1964, MA 1969); Cuddesdon Coll., Oxford. Ordained, 1966; Curate of Ellesmere Port, 1966–70; Chaplain of Christ's Coll., Cambridge, 1970–73; Director of Theological Studies, Christ's Coll., Cambridge, 1970–75; permission to officiate, dio. of Liverpool, 1970–73; Diocesan Missioner for Norwich Diocese, 1973–78; Rector of St Thomas' and St Edmund's, Salisbury, 1978–86; Archdeacon of Sarum, 1979–86; Bishop Suffragan of Taunton, 1986–92. Prebendary of Ogbourne, Salisbury Cathedral, 1979–86, of Wanstrow, Wells Cathedral, 1986–92; Canon Emeritus of Salisbury Cathedral, 1989. Mem., House of Bishops, Gen. Synod of C of E, 1990–. Chairman: Finance Cttee, ACCM, 1988–92; Decade of Evangelism Steering Gp, 1989–; C of E Communications Unit, 1993–. Pres., Somerset Rural Music Sch., 1986–92; Mem. Council, RSCM, 1984–. Chm., Somerset County Scout Assoc., 1988–92; Pres., Central Yorks Scouts, 1992–. *Publications:* A Gospel to Proclaim, 1992; Barriers to Belief, 1994. *Recreations:* music, walking in the Lake District. *Address:* Bishop's Lodge, Woodthorpe Lane, Wakefield, W Yorks WF2 6JL. *Club:* Commonwealth Trust.

WAKEFIELD, Provost of; *see* Allen, Very Rev. J. E.

WAKEFIELD, Derek John, CB 1982; Under Secretary, Government Communications Headquarters, 1978–82; *b* 21 Jan. 1922; *s* of Archibald John Thomas and Evelyn Bessie Wakefield; *m* 1951, Audrey Ellen Smith; one *d*. *Educ:* The Commonweal School. Air Ministry, 1939–42 and 1947–52. Served War, Lieut, Royal Pioneer Corps, 1942–47. Government Communications Headquarters, 1952–82. Mem., Airship Assoc. Governor, Barnwood House Trust, Gloucester, 1973–90. *Recreation:* airships. *Club:* Naval and Military.

WAKEFIELD, Sir (Edward) Humphry (Tyrrell), 2nd Bt *cr* 1962; *b* 11 July 1936; *s* of Sir Edward Birkbeck Wakefield, 1st Bt, CIE, and of Constance Lalage, *e d* of late Sir John Perronet Thompson, KCSI, KCIE; *S* father, 1969; *m* 1st, 1960, Priscilla (marr. diss. 1964), *e d* of O. R. Bagot; 2nd, 1966, Hon. Elizabeth Sophia (from whom he obt. a divorce, 1971), *e d* of 1st Viscount De L'Isle, VC, KG, PC, GCMG, GCVO, and former wife of G. S. O. A. Colthurst; one *s*; 3rd, 1974, Hon. Katharine Mary Alice Baring, *d* of 1st Baron Howick of Glendale, KG, GCMG, KCVO, and of Lady Mary Howick; one *s* one *d* (and one *s* decd). *Educ:* Gordonstoun; Trinity Coll., Cambridge (MA Hons). Formerly Captain, 10th Royal Hussars. Exec. Vice-Pres., Mallett, America Ltd, 1970–75; Chm., Tyrrell & Moore Ltd, 1978–92; Director: Mallett & Son (Antiques) Ltd, 1971–78; Tree of Life Foundn 1976–. Dir, Spoleto Fest. of Two Worlds, USA and Italy, 1973–80. President: Northumberland Nat. Park Search and Rescue Team; Avison Trust; Appeals Consultant, London Br., British Red Cross Soc. Mem., Standing Council of Baronetage. Fellow, Pierrepont Morgan Library. Mem., Norman Vaughan Antarctic Expedn, 1993. *Recreations:* riding, writing, music, shooting. *Heir: s* Maximilian Edward Vereker Wakefield [*b* 22 Feb. 1967; *m* 1994, Lucinda Katharine Elizabeth, *d* of Lt-Col and Mrs David Pipe. *Educ:* Milton Abbey; RMA Sandhurst]. *Address:* Chillingham Castle, Alnwick, Northumberland NE66 5NJ. *Clubs:* Cavalry and Guards, Turf; Harlequins Rugby Football (Twickenham).

WAKEFIELD, Rev. Gordon Stevens; Principal of the Queen's College, Birmingham, 1979–87; Director, Alister Hardy Research Centre, Oxford, 1989–92; *b* 15 Jan. 1921; *s* of Ernest and Lucy Wakefield; *m* 1949, Beryl Dimes; one *s* three *d*. *Educ:* Crewe County Sec. School; Univ. of Manchester; Fitzwilliam Coll. and Wesley House, Cambridge; St Catherine's Coll., Oxford. MA (Cantab); MLitt (Oxon). Methodist Circuit Minister in Edgware, Woodstock, Stockport, Newcastle upon Tyne, Bristol, 1944–63; Methodist Connexional Editor, 1963–72; Chairman, Manchester and Stockport Methodist District, 1971–79; Chaplain, Westminster Coll., Oxford, 1988–89. Fernley-Hartley Lectr, 1957; Select Preacher: Univ. of Oxford, 1971 and 1982; Cambridge, 1988. Recognized Lectr, Univ. of Birmingham, 1979–87. Member, Joint Liturgical Group (Chairman, 1978–84). DD Lambeth, 1986. *Publications:* Puritan Devotion, 1957; (with Hetley Price) Unity at the Local Level, 1965; Methodist Devotion, 1966; The Life of the Spirit in the World of Today, 1969; On the Edge of the Mystery, 1969; Robert Newton Flew, 1971; Fire of Love, 1976; (ed, with biographical introdns of E. C. Hoskyns and F. N. Davey) Crucifixion—Resurrection, 1981; (ed) Dictionary of Christian Spirituality, 1983; Kindly Light, 1984; The Liturgy of St John, 1985; John Wesley, 1990; Bunyan the Christian, 1992; contribs to theological jls and symposia. *Recreations:* watching and talking cricket; churches and cathedrals. *Address:* 56 Wissage Road, Lichfield WS13 6SW. *T:* Lichfield (01543) 414029.

WAKEFIELD, Sir Humphry; *see* Wakefield, Sir E. H. T.

WAKEFIELD, Sir Norman (Edward), Kt 1988; Chairman, Y. J. Lovell (Holdings) plc, 1987–90; *b* 30 Dec. 1929; *s* of Edward and Muriel Wakefield; *m* 1953, Denise Mary Bayliss; two *s* four *d*. *Educ:* Wallington County Sch.; Croydon and Brixton Technical Colls. Articled student, Wates Ltd, 1947; Man. Dir, Wates Construction Ltd, 1967; Pres., jt venture co., USA, between Wates and Rouse Co., 1970–73; Man. Dir, Holland, Hannen & Cubitts, 1973; Chief Exec., 1977–83, Chm. and Chief Exec., 1983–87, Y. J. Lovell (Holdings). Dep. Chm., Housing Corp., 1990–94. Director: Lloyds Abbey Life, 1986–93; English Estates, 1990–94. Pres., CIOB, 1985–86. *Recreations:* opera, walking, gardening. *Address:* Dovey End, Brownshill, Stroud, Glos GL6 8AS. *T:* Brimscombe (01453) 884366. *Club:* Arts.

WAKEFIELD, Sir Peter (George Arthur), KBE 1977; CMG 1973; HM Diplomatic Service, retired; art management consultant; Director, UK, Trust for Museum Exhibitions, since 1992; *b* 13 May 1922; *s* of John Bunting Wakefield and Dorothy Ina Stace; *m* 1951, Felicity Maurice-Jones; four *s* one *d*. *Educ:* Cranleigh Sch.; Corpus Christi Coll., Oxford. Army Service, 1942–47; Military Govt, Eritrea, 1946–47; Hulton Press, 1947–49; entered Diplomatic Service, 1949; Middle East Centre for Arab Studies, 1950; 2nd Sec., Amman, 1950–52; Foreign Office, 1953–55; 1st Sec., British Middle East Office, Nicosia, 1955–56; 1st Sec. (Commercial), Cairo, 1956; Administrative Staff Coll., Henley, 1957; 1st Sec. (Commercial), Vienna, 1957–60; 1st Sec. (Commercial), Tokyo, 1960–63; Foreign Office, 1964–66; Consul-General and Counsellor, Benghazi, 1966–69; Econ. and Commercial Counsellor, Tokyo, 1970–72; Econ. and Commercial Minister, Tokyo, 1973; seconded as Special Adviser on the Japanese Market, BOTB, 1973–75; Ambassador to the Lebanon, 1975–78, to Belgium, 1979–82. Dir, NACF, 1982–92. Chairman: Richmond Theatre Trust, 1989–; Heritage Co-ordination Gp, 1992–; Asia House, London, 1993–. *Recreations:* ceramics and restoring ruins. *Address:* Lincoln House, 28 Montpelier Row, Twickenham, Mddx TW1 2NQ. *T:* 0181–892 6390; La Molineta, Frigiliana, near Malaga, Spain. *T:* (52) 533175. *Clubs:* Travellers', Arts.

WAKEFIELD, William Barry, CB 1990; Deputy Director (Research), National Commission on Education, 1991–95; *b* 6 June 1930; *s* of Stanley Arthur and Evelyn Grace Wakefield; *m* 1953, Elizabeth Violet (*née* Alexander); three *s* one *d*. *Educ:* Harrow County Grammar Sch.; University Coll., London. BSc; FSS. Statistician, NCB, 1953–62; DES, 1962–67; Chief Statistician, MoD, 1967–72, CSO, 1972–75; Asst Dir, CSO, Cabinet Office, 1975–79; Dir of Statistics, DES, 1979–90. Member, United Reformed Church. *Recreations:* horse racing, gardening, family history. *Address:* Egg Hall Cottage, 14 Birch Street, Nayland, Colchester CO6 4JA.

WAKEFORD, Geoffrey Michael Montgomery, OBE 1995; Clerk to the Worshipful Company of Mercers, since 1974; Barrister-at-Law; *b* 10 Dec. 1937; *o s* of late Geoffrey and Helen Wakeford; *m* 1966, Diana Margaret Loy Cooper; two *s* two *d*. *Educ:* Downside; Clare Coll., Cambridge (Classical Schol., MA, LLB). Called to Bar, Gray's Inn and South Eastern Circuit, 1961; practised at Common Law Bar until 1971. Apptd Dep. Clerk to the Mercers Co., 1971. Clerk to: Governors St Paul's Schs; Joint Grand Gresham Cttee; City & Metropolitan Welfare Trustees; Collyers Foundn Trustees; Council of Gresham Coll., 1980–84 (Mem. Council, 1988–). Trustee, Lord Mayor's 800th Anniv. Awards Trust. Member: Small Business Cttee, London Enterprise Agency, 1986–; Council, City Technology Colls Trust, 1988–. Hon. Sec., GBA, 1991–. Governor: London Internat. Film Sch., 1981–85, 1990–; Molecule Theatre, 1986–; The Hall Sch., 1990–; Thomas Telford Sch., 1990–. *Address:* Mercers' Hall, Ironmonger Lane, EC2V 8HE. *T:* 0171–726 4991. *Club:* Travellers'.

WAKEFORD, Air Marshal Sir Richard (Gordon), KCB 1976; LVO 1961; OBE 1958; AFC 1952; Director, RAF Benevolent Fund, Scotland, 1978–89; *b* 20 April 1922; *s* of Charles Edward Augustus Wakeford; *m* 1948, Anne Butler; two *s* one *d* (and one *d* decd). *Educ:* Montpelier Sch., Paignton; Kelly Coll., Tavistock. Joined RAF, 1941; flying Catalina flying boats, Coastal Comd, operating out of India, Scotland, N Ireland, 1942–45; flying Liberator and York transport aircraft on overseas routes, 1945–47; CFS 1947; Flying Instructor, RAF Coll. Cranwell; CFS Examining Wing; ground appts, incl. 2‘ years on staff of Dir of Emergency Ops in Malaya, 1952–58; comdg Queen's Flight, 1958–61; Directing Staff, RAF Staff Coll., 1961–64; subseq.: comdg RAF Scampton; SASO, HQ 3 Group Bomber Comd; Asst Comdt (Cadets), RAF Coll. Cranwell; idc 1969; Comdr N Maritime Air Region, and Air Officer Scotland and N Ireland, 1970–72; Dir of Service Intelligence, MoD, 1972–73; ANZUK Force Comdr, Singapore, 1974–75; Dep. Chief of Defence Staff (Intell.), 1975–78; HM Comr, Queen Victoria Sch., Dunblane; Vice-Chm. (Air), Lowland T&AVR. Trustee, McRobert Trusts (Chm., 1982–94); Director: Thistle Foundn; Cromar Nominees. CStJ 1986. *Recreations:* golf, fishing. *Address:* Sweethome Cottage, Inchberry Road, Fochabers, Moray IV32 7QA. *T:* Fochabers (01343) 820436. *Clubs:* Flyfishers', Royal Air Force.

WAKEHAM, family name of **Baron Wakeham.**

WAKEHAM, Baron *cr* 1992 (Life Peer), of Maldon in the County of Essex; **John Wakeham;** PC 1983; JP; FCA; Chairman, Press Complaints Commission, since 1995; *b* 22 June 1932; *s* of late Major W. J. Wakeham and late Mrs E. R. Wakeham; *m* 1st, 1965, Anne Roberta Bailey (*d* 1984); two *s*; 2nd, 1985, Alison Bridget Ward, MBE, *d* of Ven. E. J. G. Ward, *qv*; one *s*. *Educ:* Charterhouse. Chartered Accountant. MP (C) Maldon, Feb. 1974–1983, Colchester South and Maldon, 1983–92; Asst Govt Whip, 1979–81; a Lord Comr of HM Treasury (Govt Whip), 1981; Parly Under-Sec. of State, DoI, 1981–82; Minister of State, HM Treasury, 1982–83; Parly Sec. to HM Treasury and Govt Chief Whip, 1983–87; Lord Privy Seal, 1987–88; Leader of the H of C, 1987–89; Lord Pres. of the Council, 1988–89; Sec. of State for Energy, 1989–92; Minister responsible for co-ordinating develt of presentation of govt policies, 1990–92; Lord Privy Seal and Leader of the H of L, 1992–94. Member: British Horseracing Bd, 1995–; Cttee of Mgt, RNLI, 1995–. JP Inner London 1972. *Recreations:* farming, sailing, racing, reading. *Address:* House of Lords, SW1A 0PW. *Clubs:* Carlton (Chm. 1992–), St Stephen's Constitutional, Buck's, Garrick; Royal Yacht Squadron.

WAKEHAM, Prof. William Arnot; Professor in Chemical Physics, since 1985, and Head of Department of Chemical Engineering and Chemical Technology, Imperial College, London; *b* 25 Sept. 1944; *s* of Stanley William Wakeham; *m* 1st, 1969, Christina Marjorie Stone (marr. diss. 1974); one *s*; 2nd, 1978, Sylvia Frances Tolley; two *s*. *Educ:* Univ. of Exeter (BSc 1966; PhD 1969; DSc 1985). Research Associate, Brown Univ., USA, 1969–71; Department of Chemical Engineering, Imperial College: Lectr in Transport Processes, 1971–78; Reader in Chemical Physics, 1978–85. Chm., Commn of IUPAC, 1993–. *Publications:* Intermolecular Forces: their origin and determination, 1981; Forces between Molecules, 1988; The Transport Properties of Fluids, 1987; International Thermodynamic Tables, vol. XI, 1989; Experimental Thermodynamics, vol. III, 1992; numerous articles in learned jls. *Recreations:* water ski-ing, cycling. *Address:* Department of Chemical Engineering, Imperial College, SW7 2BY. *T:* 0171–594 5556; 21 Lavender Gardens, SW11 1DH.

WAKEHURST, 3rd Baron *cr* 1934, of Ardingly; **(John) Christopher Loder;** Chairman: Anglo & Overseas Trust PLC (formerly Anglo-American Securities Corporation), since 1980 (Director, since 1968); The Overseas Investment Trust PLC (formerly North Atlantic Securities Corporation), since 1980; Morgan Grenfell Equity Income Trust PLC, since 1991; *b* 23 Sept. 1925; *s* of 2nd Baron Wakehurst, KG, KCMG, and Dowager Lady Wakehurst, (Dame Margaret Wakehurst), DBE (*d* 1994); *S* father, 1970; *m* 1956, Ingeborg Krumbholz-Hess (*d* 1977); one *s* one *d*; *m* 1983, Brigid, *yr d* of William Noble, Cirencester. *Educ:* Eton; King's School, nr Sydney, NSW; Trinity College, Cambridge (BA 1948, LLB 1949, MA 1953). Served War as Sub Lieut RANVR and RNVR; South West Pacific, 1943–45. Barrister, Inner Temple, 1950. Chm., Morgan Grenfell Trust Managers Ltd, 1991–94; Director: Mayfair & City Properties plc, 1984–87; The Nineteen Twenty-Eight Investment Trust plc, 1984–86; Morgan Grenfell Latin American Cos Trust, 1994–; Chm. and Dir, Hampton Gold Mining Areas, 1981–86; Chairman: Continental Illinois Ltd, 1973–84; Philadelphia National Ltd, 1985–90; Dep. Chm., London and Manchester Gp, 1970– (Dir, 1966–). Trustee: The Photographers' Gallery Ltd, 1979–90; Photographers' Trust Fund, 1986–91. CStJ. *Heir: s* Hon. Timothy Walter Loder, *b* 28 March 1958. *Address:* 26 Wakehurst Road, SW11 6BY. *T:* 0171–247 2000. *Clubs:* City of London, Chelsea Arts.

WAKELEY, Sir John (Cecil Nicholson), 2nd Bt *cr* 1952; FRCS; Consultant Surgeon, West Cheshire Group of Hospitals, 1961–88, retired; *b* 27 Aug. 1926; *s* of Sir Cecil Pembrey Grey Wakeley, 1st Bt, KBE, CB, MCh, FRCS, and Elizabeth Muriel (*d* 1985), *d* of James Nicholson-Smith; *S* father, 1979; *m* 1954, June Leney; two *s* one *d*. *Educ:* Canford School. MB, BS London 1950; LRCP 1950, FRCS 1955 (MRCS 1950), FACS 1973. Lectr in Anatomy, Univ. of London, 1951–52. Sqdn Ldr, RAF, 1953–54. Councillor, RCS, 1971–83; Member: Mersey Regional Health Authority, 1974–78; Editorial Bd, Health Trends, DHSS, 1968–71; Examiner for Gen. Nursing Council for England and Wales, 1954–59; Consultant Adviser in Surgery to RAF, 1981–89, Hon. Consultant Advr, 1990–. Liveryman: Worshipful Soc. of Apothecaries; Worshipful Co. of Barbers; Freeman of City of London. FACS 1973. CStJ 1959. *Publications:* papers on leading med. jls, incl. British Empire Cancer Campaign Scientific Report, Vol. II: Zinc 65 and the prostate, 1958; report on distribution and radiation dosimetry of Zinc 65 in the rat, 1959. *Recreations:* music, photography, bird-watching. *Heir: s* Nicholas Jeremy Wakeley [*b* 17 Oct. 1957; *m* 1991, Sarah Ann, *d* of Air Vice-Marshal B. L. Robinson, *qv*]. *Address:* Mickle Lodge, Mickle Trafford, Chester CH2 4EB. *T:* Mickle Trafford (01244) 300316. *Club:* Council Club of Royal College of Surgeons.

WAKELING, Rt Rev. John Denis, MC 1945; *b* 12 Dec. 1918; *s* of Rev. John Lucas Wakeling and Mary Louise (*née* Glover); *m* 1941, Josephine Margaret, *d* of Dr Benjamin Charles Broomhall and Marion (*née* Aldwinckle); two *s* (and one *s* decd). *Educ:* Dean Close Sch., Cheltenham; St Catharine's Coll., Cambridge. MA Cantab 1944. Commnd Officer in Royal Marines, 1939–45 (Actg Maj.). Ridley Hall, Cambridge, 1946–47. Deacon, 1947; Priest, 1948. Asst Curate, Barwell, Leics, 1947; Chaplain of Clare Coll., Cambridge, and Chaplain to the Cambridge Pastorate, 1950–52; Vicar of Emmanuel, Plymouth, 1952–59; Prebendary of Exeter Cathedral, 1957, Prebendary Emeritus, 1959; Vicar of Barking, Essex, 1959–65; Archdeacon of West Ham, 1965–70; Bishop of Southwell, 1970–85. Entered House of Lords, June 1974. Chairman: Archbishops' Council on Evangelism, 1976–79; Lee Abbey Council, 1976–84. Hon. DD Nottingham, 1985. *Recreations:* formerly cricket and hockey (Cambridge Univ. Hockey Club, 1938, 1939, 1945, 1946, English Trials Caps, 1939, 1946–49), gardening, water colours, fly fishing. *Address:* 50 St Ann Place, Salisbury, Wilts SP1 2SU. *T:* Salisbury (01722) 322016. *Club:* Hawks (Cambridge).

WAKELING, Richard Keith Arthur; Chief Executive, Johnson Matthey, 1991–94; *b* 19 Nov. 1946; *s* of late Eric George Wakeling and of Dorothy Ethel Wakeling; *m* 1971, Carmen; three *s*. *Educ:* Churchill Coll., Cambridge (MA). Called to the Bar, Inner Temple, 1971. Group Treasurer, BOC Group, 1973–83; Finance Dir, John Brown, 1983–86; Finance Dir, 1986–88, Acting Chief Exec., 1988–89, Charter Consolidated; Dep. Chief Exec., Johnson Matthey, 1990. Dep. Chm., Celtic Group Holdings Ltd, 1994–; Director: Costain, 1992–; Laura Ashley Holdings, 1994–; Logica, 1995–; Staveley Industries, 1995–; HTR Income and Growth Split Trust, 1995–. *Recreations:* mediaeval history and architecture, golf, music, gardening. *Address:* 46 The Bourne, Southgate, N14 6QS.

WAKEMAN, Sir Edward Offley Bertram, 6th Bt *cr* 1828, of Perdiswell Hall, Worcestershire; *b* 31 July 1934; *s* of Captain Sir Offley Wakeman, 4th Bt, CBE and of his 2nd wife, Josceline Ethelreda, *e d* of Maj.-Gen. Bertram Revely Mitford, CB, CMG, DSO; *S* half-brother, 1991. *Heir:* none.

WAKERLEY, Richard MacLennon; QC 1982; a Recorder of the Crown Court, since 1982; *b* 7 June 1942; *s* of late Charles William Wakerley and Gladys MacLennon Wakerley; *m* Marian Heather Dawson; two *s* two *d*. *Educ:* De Aston Sch., Market Rasen; Emmanuel Coll., Cambridge (MA), Called to the Bar, Gray's Inn, 1965, Bencher, 1991. Leader, Midland and Oxford Circuit, 1992– (Dep. Leader, 1989–92). *Recreations:* theatre, bridge, gardening. *Address:* Croft House, Grendon, Atherstone, Warwicks CV9 3DP. *T:* Atherstone (01827) 712329.

WAKLEY, His Honour Bertram Joseph, MBE 1945; a Circuit Judge, 1973–92; *b* 7 July 1917; *s* of Major Bertram Joseph Wakley and Hon. Mrs Dorothy Wakley (*née* Hamilton); *m* 1953, Alice Margaret Lorimer. *Educ:* Wellington Coll.; Christ Church, Oxford. BA 1939, MA 1943. Commnd S Lancs Regt, 1940; Captain 1941; Major 1943; served N Africa, Italy, Greece (despatches). Called to Bar, Gray's Inn, 1948. A Recorder of the Crown Court, 1972–73. Reader, Diocese of Southwark, 1977–. *Publications:* History of the Wimbledon Cricket Club, 1954; Bradman the Great, 1959; Classic Centuries, 1964. *Recreations:* cricket, golf. *Address:* 4 The Watergardens, Warren Road, Kingston Hill, Surrey KT2 7LF. *T:* 0181–546 7587. *Clubs:* Carlton, MCC, Roehampton.

WALBANK, Frank William, CBE 1993; FBA 1953; MA; Rathbone Professor of Ancient History and Classical Archæology in the University of Liverpool, 1951–77, now Professor Emeritus; Dean, Faculty of Arts, 1974–77; *b* 10 Dec. 1909; *s* of A. J. D. and C. Walbank, Bingley, Yorks; *m* 1935, Mary Woodward (*d* 1987), *e d* of O. C. A. and D. Fox, Shipley, Yorks; one *s* two *d*. *Educ:* Bradford Grammar School; Peterhouse, Cambridge (Hon. Fellow, 1984). Scholar of Peterhouse, 1928–31; First Class, Parts I and II Classical Tripos, 1930–31; Hugo de Balsham Research Student, Peterhouse, 1931–32; Senior Classics Master at North Manchester High School, 1932–33; Thirlwall Prize, 1933; Asst Lecturer, 1934–36, Lecturer, 1936–46, in Latin, Professor of Latin, 1946–51, University of Liverpool; Public Orator, 1956–60; Hare Prize, 1939. J. H. Gray Lectr, Univ. of Cambridge, 1957; Andrew Mellon Vis. Prof., Univ. Pittsburgh, 1964; Myres Memorial Lectr, Univ. of Oxford, 1964–65; Sather Prof., Univ. of Calif (Berkeley), 1971. Pres., Cambridge Phil Soc., 1982–84; Member Council: Classical Assoc., 1944–48, 1958–61 (Pres. 1969–70); Roman Soc., 1948–51 (Vice-Pres., 1953–; Pres., 1961–64); Hellenic Soc., 1951–54, 1955–56; Classical Journals Bd, 1948–66; British Acad., 1960–63; British Sch. at Rome, 1979–87. Mem., Inst. for Advanced Study, Princeton, 1970–71; Foreign Mem., Royal Netherlands Acad. of Arts and Sciences, 1981–; Corresp. Mem., German Archaeol Inst., 1987–. Hon. Mem., Israel Soc. for Promotion of Classical Studies, 1992–. Hon. DLitt Exeter, 1988. Kenyon Medal, British Acad., 1989; Steven Runciman Prize, Anglo-Hellenic Soc., 1989. *Publications:* Aratos of Sicyon, 1933; Philip V of Macedon, 1940; Latin Prose Versions contributed to Key to Bradley's Arnold, Latin Prose Composition, ed J. F. Mountford, 1940; The Decline of the Roman Empire in the West, 1946; A Historical Commentary on Polybius, Vol. i, 1957, Vol. ii, 1967, Vol. iii, 1979; The Awful Revolution, 1969; Polybius, 1972; The Hellenistic World, 1981; Selected Papers: Studies in Greek and Roman history and historiography, 1985; (with N. G. L. Hammond) A History of Macedonia, Vol. III: 336–167 BC, 1988; chapters in: The Cambridge Economic History of Europe, Vol. II, 1952, 2nd edn 1987; A Scientific Survey of Merseyside, 1953; (ed jtly and contrib.) Cambridge Ancient History, Vol. VII pt 1, 1984, pt 2, 1989, Vol VIII 1989; contribs to: the Oxford Classical Dictionary, 1949; Chambers' Encyclopædia, 1950; Encyclopædia Britannica, 1960 and 1974; English and foreign classical books and periodicals. *Address:* 64 Grantchester Meadows, Cambridge CB3 9JL. *T:* Cambridge (01223) 64350.

WALBY, Christine Mary; Director of Social Services, Staffordshire County Council, since 1991; *b* 9 Feb. 1940; *d* of Kathleen Walby (*née* Bradburn) and late James Walby. *Educ:* University College of Wales, Aberystwyth (BA, DipEd); Manchester Univ. (Dip. Social Admin and Social Work); University College Cardiff (MSc Econ). Youth Leader Trainer, 1961–64; Social Worker, Children's Dept, Cheshire, 1964–70; Training Officer, Salford; Tutor, Manchester Univ.; Area Officer, Salford Social Services, 1970–74; Principal Officer, S Glam Social Services, 1974–81; Divl Dir, Berks Social Services, 1981–87; Dir, Social Services, Solihull MDC, 1987–91. Sen. Vis. Res. Fellow, Keele Univ. Mem., Human Fertilization and Embryology Authy, 1991–93. Chm., Early Childhood Unit Adv. Gp, Nat. Children's Bureau; Mem. Council and Trustee, Children's Rights Develt Unit; Mem., Nat. Commn of Inquiry into Prevention of Child Abuse; Hon. Mem. Council, NSPCC. *Publications:* Who Am I?: identity, adoption and human fertilization (with Barbara Symons), 1990; contrib. professional jls. *Recreations:* mountain walking, bird watching, theatre, music. *Address:* Social Services Department, St Chad's Place, Stafford ST16 2LR. *T:* Stafford (01785) 277000.

WALCOTT, Sir Clyde (Leopold), KA 1993; GCM 1991; OBE 1966; Chairman, International Cricket Council, since 1993; *b* 17 Jan. 1926; *s* of late Frank Eyre Walcott and Ruth Walcott (*née* Morris); *m* 1951, Muriel Edith Ashby; two *s*. *Educ:* Harrison Coll., Barbados. Début for Barbados Cricket IX, 1942; played for Barbados, 1942–55, for British Guiana, 1955–64 (record highest score of 314 not out for Barbados *v* Trinidad, 1946); 44 caps for WI, 1947–60 (scored record 5 centuries in single Test series, *v* Australia, 1955). Chief Personnel Officer and Dir, Barbados Shipping and Trading Co. Ltd, 1980–91, retd. Mem., Barbados Public Service Commn, 1982–87. Barbados Employers' Confederation: Pres., 1978–81; Trustee, 1987–91; President: Guyana Cricket Bd of Control, 1968–70; WI Cricket Bd of Control, 1988–93 (Chm., Selection Cttee, 1973–88); Hon. Life Vice-Pres., Barbados Cricket Assoc. *Publication:* Island Cricketers, 1958. *Recreations:* cricket, football. *Address:* Wildey Heights, St Michael, Barbados, WI. *T:* 4294638. *Club:* MCC (Hon. Life Mem.).

WALCOTT, Derek Alton; poet and playwright; *b* Castries, St Lucia, 23 Jan. 1930; twin *s* of late Warwick and Alix Walcott; *m* 1954, Fay Moston (marr. diss. 1959); one *s*; *m* 1962, Margaret Ruth Maillard (marr. diss.); two *d*; *m* Norline Metivier (marr. diss.). *Educ:* St Mary's Coll., St Lucia; Univ. of WI (BA 1953). Formerly teacher at schs in St Lucia and Grenada, and at Kingston Coll., Jamaica. Founded Trinidad Theatre Workshop, 1958. Lecturer: Rutgers Univ.; Yale Univ. Visiting Professor: Columbia Univ., 1981; Harvard Univ., 1982; Boston Univ., 1985–. Hon. DLitt Univ. of WI, 1972. Heinemann Award, RSL, 1966, 1983; Cholmodeley Award, 1969; Queen's Gold Medal for Poetry, 1989; Nobel Prize for Literature, 1992. Order of the Hummingbird (Trinidad and Tobago), 1969. *Publications include:* In a Green Night, 1962; Selected Poems, 1964; Castaway, 1965; Gulf and other poems, 1969; Another Life, 1973; Sea Grapes, 1976; Joker of Seville, 1979; Remembrance, and Pantomime, 1980; The Star-Apple Kingdom, 1980; The Fortunate Traveller, 1982; Midsummer, 1984; Collected Poems 1948–84, 1986; The Arkansas Testament, 1988; Three Plays: The Last Carnival, Beef No Chicken, A Branch of the Blue Nile, 1988; Collected Poems, 1990; Poems 1965–80, 1992; Omeros, 1990 (W. H. Smith Literary Award, 1991); Selected Poetry, 1993; Odyssey, 1993. *Address:* c/o Faber & Faber, 3 Queen Square, WC1N 3AU; 71 St Mary's Street, Brookline, Mass 02215, USA.

WALCOTT, Prof. Richard Irving, PhD; FRS 1991; FRSNZ; Professor of Geology, Victoria University, Wellington, New Zealand, since 1985; *b* 14 May 1933; *s* of James Farrar Walcott and Lilian Stewart (*née* Irving); *m* 1960, Genevieve Rae Lovatt; one *s* two *d*. *Educ:* Victoria Univ., Wellington (BSc Hons 1962; PhD 1965). Meteorological Asst, Falkland Is Dependencies Survey, 1955–58; Post-doctoral Fellow, Geophysics Dept, Univ. of BC, 1966–67; Research Scientist: Earth Physics Br., Dept of Energy, Mines and Resources, Ottawa, 1967–74; Geophysics Div., Dept Sci. and Industrial Res., Wellington, NZ, 1975–84. FRSNZ 1982. *Recreations:* tramping, gardening. *Address:* 24 Mahoe Street, Eastbourne, Wellington, New Zealand. *T:* (4) 5628040.

WALD, Prof. George; Higgins Professor of Biology, Harvard University, 1968–77, now Emeritus Professor; *b* 18 Nov. 1906; *s* of Isaac Wald and Ernestine (*née* Rosenmann); *m* 1st, 1931, Frances Kingsley (marr. diss.); two *s*; 2nd, 1958, Ruth Hubbard; one *s* one *d*. *Educ:* Washington Square Coll. of New York Univ. (BS); Columbia Univ. (PhD). Nat. Research Coun. Fellowship, 1932–34. Harvard University: Instr and Tutor in Biology, 1934–39; Faculty Instr, 1939–44; Associate Prof., 1944–48; Prof. of Biology, 1948–77, Emeritus Prof., 1977–. Nobel Prize in Physiology and Medicine (jointly), 1967. Vice-Pres., People's Permanent Tribunal, Rome (Pres., internat. tribunals on El Salvador, Philippines, Afghanistan, Zaire, Guatemala). Writes and lectures on cold war, arms race, human rights, nuclear power and weapons; developed World-Third World relations. Has many hon. doctorates from univs in USA and abroad; Guest, China Assoc. for Friendship with Foreign Peoples, Jan.–Feb. 1972; US/Japan Distinguished Scientist Exchange, 1973. *Publications:* (co-author) General Education in a Free Society; (co-author) Twenty-six Afternoons of Biology. Many sci. papers (on the biochemistry and physiology of vision and on biochem. evolution) in: Jl of Gen. Physiology, Nature, Science, Jl of Opt. Soc. of Amer., etc. *Recreations:* art, archæology. *Address:* 21 Lakeview Avenue, Cambridge, MA 02138–3325, USA. *T:* (617) 8687748.

WALD, Prof. Nicholas John, FRCP, FFPHM, FRCOG; Professor and Head of Department of Environmental and Preventive Medicine, St Bartholomew's Hospital Medical College, since 1983; Hon. Consultant, St Bartholomew's Hospital, since 1983; *b* 31 May 1944; *s* of Adolf Max Wald and Frieda (*née* Shatsow); *m* 1966, Nancy Evelyn Miller; three *s* one *d*. *Educ:* Owen's Sch., EC1; University Coll. London; University Coll. Hosp. Med. Sch. (MB BS); DSc (Med) London 1987. FRCP 1986 (MRCP 1971); FFPHM (FFCM 1982; MFCM 1980); FRCOG 1992. VSO, India, 1966. Ho. appts, UCH and Barnet Gen. Hosp., 1968–69; Med. Registrar, UCH, 1970; Member: MRC Sci. Staff, MRC Epidemiology and Med. Care Unit, 1971; Sci. Staff, ICRF (formerly DHSS) Cancer Epidem. and Clin. Trials Unit, 1972–82, Dep. Dir, 1982–83; Wellcome Vis. Prof. in Basic Med. Scis, at Foundn for Blood Res., USA, 1980, then Hon. Sen. Res. Scientist. Chm., Wolfson Inst. of Preventive Medicine, St Bartholomew's Hosp. Med. Coll., 1991–95; Hon. Dir, CRC. Chairman: MRC Smoking Res. Rev. Cttee, 1986–89; MRC Study Monitoring Cttee of Randomised Trial of Colo-rectal Cancer Screening, 1986–; MRC Volatile Substance Abuse Wkg Party, 1985–87; NE Thames Reg. Breast Cancer Res. Cttee, 1988–; Nat. Inst. of Child Health and Human Develt Wkg Gp on Quality Control of Alpha-fetoprotein Measurement, 1978; Member: MRC Neurosciences Bd, 1962–86; MRC Steering Cttee of Randomised Trial of Multivitamins and Neural Tube Defects, 1983–; DHSS Adv. Cttee on Breast Cancer, 1988–; DHSS Cttee on Med. Aspects of Contamination of Air, Soil and Water, 1985–89; DHSS Cttee on Carcinogenicity of Chemicals in Food, Consumer Products and the Environment, 1984–89; DHSS Indep. Sci. Cttee on Smoking and Health, 1983–91; CMO's Health of the Nation Wkg Gp, 1991–; CMO's Scientific Cttee on Tobacco and Health, 1993–; ACOST Med. Res. and Health Cttee, 1991–92; RCP Cttee on Ethical Issues in Medicine, 1988–; RCP Computer Cttee, 1988–92, and special Adv. Gp to the RCP Med. IT Cttee, 1992–; Physiol. and Pharmacol. Panel, Wellcome Trust, 1995–; Cttee on Environmental Tobacco Smoke, Nat. Acad. of Sci., USA, 1985–86. William Julius Mickle Fellow, Univ. of London, 1990. Inaugural Ed., Jl of Medical Screening, 1994. *Publications:* (ed) Antenatal and Neonatal Screening, 1984; (ed with Sir Richard Doll) Interpretation of Negative Epidemiological Evidence for Carcinogenicity, 1985; (ed jtly) UK Smoking Statistics, 1988; (ed with Sir Peter Froggatt) Nicotine, Smoking and the Low Tar Programme, 1989; (ed with J. Baron) Smoking and Hormone Related Disorders, 1990; (jtly) International Smoking Statistics, 1993; articles in sci. jls on screening for neural tube defects, Down's Syndrome and other disorders, on health effects of tobacco, on the aetiology and prevention of cancer, cardiovascular disease and congenital malformations. *Recreations:* ski-ing, boating, economics. *Address:* Department of Environmental and Preventive Medicine, Wolfson Institute of Preventive Medicine, St Bartholomew's Hospital Medical College, Charterhouse Square, EC1M 6BQ; 9 Park Crescent Mews East, W1N 5HB. *T:* 0171–636 2721. *Club:* Athenæum.

WALDEGRAVE, family name of **Earl Waldegrave.**

WALDEGRAVE, 13th Earl, *cr* 1729; **James Sherbrooke Waldegrave;** Bt 1643; Baron Waldegrave 1685; Viscount Chewton 1729; *b* 8 Dec. 1940; *e s* of 12th Earl Waldegrave, KG, GCVO and of Mary Hermione, *d* of Lt-Col A. M. Grenfell, DSO; *S* father, 1995; *m* 1986, Mary Alison Anthea, *d* of late Sir Robert Furness, KBE, CMG, and of Lady Furness, 13 Emmanuel Road, Cambridge; two *s*. *Educ:* Eton Coll.; Trinity Coll., Cambridge. *Heir:* *s* Viscount Chewton, *qv*. *Address:* West End Farm, Chewton Mendip, Bath. *Club:* Beefsteak.

WALDEGRAVE, Rt. Hon. William (Arthur), PC 1990; MP (C) Bristol West, since 1979; Chief Secretary to HM Treasury, since 1995; *b* 15 Aug. 1946; *yr s* of 12th Earl Waldegrave, KG, GCVO; *m* 1977, Caroline, *y d* of Major and Mrs Richard Burrows, Tunbridge Wells, Kent; one *s* three *d*. *Educ:* Eton (Newcastle Schol.); Corpus Christi Coll., Oxford (Open Schol.; 1st Cl. Lit. Hum. 1969; Hon. Fellow, 1991) (President, Oxford Union and Oxford Univ. Conservative Assoc.); Harvard Univ. (Kennedy Fellow). Fellow, All Souls Coll., Oxford, 1971–86. Central Policy Review Staff, Cabinet Office, 1971–73; Political Staff, 10 Downing Street, 1973–74; Head of Leader of Opposition's Office, 1974–75. Parly Under-Sec. of State, DES, 1981–83, DoE, 1983–85. Minister of State for the Environment and Countryside, 1985–87, for Planning, 1986–88, and for Housing, 1987–88, DoE; Minister of State, FCO, 1988–90; Sec. of State for Health, 1990–92; Chancellor of the Duchy of Lancaster, 1992–94; Minister of Agric., Fisheries and Food, 1994–95. GEC Ltd, 1975–81. JP Inner London Juvenile Court, 1975–79.

Mem., IBA Adv. Council, 1980–81. *Publication:* The Binding of Leviathan, 1977. *Address:* House of Commons, SW1A 0AA. *T:* 0171–219 4574. *Clubs:* Beefsteak, Pratt's; Clifton (Bristol).

WALDEN, (Alastair) Brian; television presenter and journalist; *b* 8 July 1932; *s* of W. F. Walden; *m* Hazel Downes, *d* of William A. Downes; one *s* (and three *s* of former marriages). *Educ:* West Bromwich Grammar School; Queen's College and Nuffield College, Oxford; Pres., Oxford Union, 1957. University Lecturer. MP (Lab): Birmingham, All Saints, 1964–74; Birmingham, Ladywood, 1974–77. Mem., W Midland Bd, Central TV, 1981–84. Columnist: London Standard, 1983–86; Thomson Regional Newspapers, 1983–86; Sunday Times, 1986–90. Presenter: Weekend World, LWT, 1977–86; The Walden Interview, ITV, 1988 and 1989; Walden, LWT, 1990–94. Shell International Award, 1982; BAFTA Richard Dimbleby Award, 1985; Aims of Industry Special Free Enterprise Award, 1990; TV Times Favourite TV Current Affairs Personality, 1990; Television and Radio Industries Club ITV Personality of the Year, 1991. *Publication:* The Walden Interviews, 1990. *Recreations:* chess, reading. *Address:* Landfall, Fort Road, St Peter Port, Guernsey.

WALDEN, George Gordon Harvey, CMG 1981; MP (C) Buckingham, since 1983; *b* 15 Sept. 1939; *s* of G. G. Walden; *m* 1970, Sarah Nicolette Hunt; two *s* one *d*. *Educ:* Latymer Upper Sch.; Jesus Coll., Cambridge; Moscow Univ. (post-graduate). Research Dept, Foreign Office, 1962–65; Chinese Language Student, Hong Kong Univ., 1965–67; Second Secretary, Office of HM Chargé d'Affaires, Peking, 1967–70; First Sec., FCO (Soviet Desk), 1970–73; Ecole Nationale d'Administration, Paris, 1973–74; First Sec., HM Embassy, Paris, 1974–78; Principal Private Sec. to Foreign and Commonwealth Sec., 1978–81; sabbatical year, Harvard, 1981; Head of Planning Staff, FCO, 1982–83; retired from HM Diplomatic Service, 1983. PPS to Sec. of State for Educn and Science, 1984–85; Parly Under-Sec. of State, DES, 1985–87. Columnist, Daily Telegraph, 1987–. *Publications:* The Shoeblack and the Sovereign, 1988; Ethics and Foreign Policy, 1990. *Address:* House of Commons, SW1A 0AA.

WALDEN, Rt. Rev. Graham Howard; *see* Murray, Bishop of The.

WALDEN, Herbert Richard Charles, CBE 1986; part-time Member, Building Societies Commission, 1986–94; *b* 6 Oct. 1926; *s* of Reginald George Walden and Matilda Ethel Walden; *m* 1950, Margaret Walker (*d* 1995); two *d*. *Educ:* Westgate Sch., Warwick. FCIS; FCIB. War service, 1944–47, Royal Warwickshire Regt and Royal Leicestershire Regt (UK and Gold Coast) (Captain). Asst Sec., Warwick Building Soc., 1955, Gen. Manager 1962; Gen. Manager, Rugby and Warwick Building Soc. (on merger), 1967; Gen. Manager, Heart of England Building Soc. (on merger), 1974, Dir and Gen. Manager, 1974–86. Mem. Bd, Housing Corp., 1985–88. Chm., Midland Assoc. of Building Socs, 1972–73, Vice-Pres., 1986; Vice President: Building Societies Assoc., 1994– (Mem. Council, 1974–86, Dep. Chm. 1981–83, Chm., 1983–85); CBSI, 1988–93. Mem., Warwick BC, 1955–63; Chm., S Warwickshire HMC, 1964–72; Mem., Warwick Schs Foundn, 1962–90 (Chm., 1986–90); Trustee, various Warwick Charities; Founder Pres., Rotary Club of Warwick, 1965; Vice Pres., Warwickshire Scout Assoc., 1969– (Hon. Treas., 1958–68). Chm., Finance Cttee, Northgate Methodist Church, Warwick, 1965–82, 1986–. Chm., Warwicks Adv. Cttee, Tax Comrs, 1983– (Mem., 1969–). *Recreation:* watching cricket and soccer. *Address:* Fieldgate House, 24 Hill Wootton Road, Leek Wootton, Warwick CV35 7QL. *T:* Kenilworth (01926) 54291. *Club:* Naval and Military.

WALDER, Edwin James, CMG 1971; NSW Civil Service, retired; *b* 5 Aug. 1921; *s* of Edwin James Walder and Dulcie Muriel Walder (*née* Griffiths); *m* 1944, Norma Cheslin; two *d*. *Educ:* North Newtown High Sch.; Univ. of Sydney (BEc). FRAIPA 1983. Apptd NSW Civil Service, 1938; NSW State Treasury: 1945; Asst Under-Sec. (Finance), 1959–61; Dep. Under-Sec., 1961–63; Under-Sec. and Comptroller of Accounts, 1963–65; Pres., Metrop. Water, Sewerage and Drainage Bd, Sydney, 1965–81. Member: State Pollution Control Commn, 1971–81; Metropolitan Waste Disposal Authority (Sydney), 1971–81; management consultant and co. dir, 1981–92. *Recreations:* lawn bowls, fishing, swimming. *Address:* 44 Del Monte Place, Copacabana, NSW 2251, Australia. *Clubs:* City Tattersall's (Sydney); Central Coast League's (Gosford); Avoca Beach Bowling; Avoca Beach Probus.

WALDER, Ruth Christabel, (Mrs Wesierska), OBE 1956; *b* 15 Jan. 1906; *d* of Rev. Ernest Walder; *m* 1955, Maj.-Gen. George Wesierski (*d* 1967), formerly Judge Advocate General of the Polish Forces. *Educ:* Cheltenham Ladies' College. General Organiser, National Federation of Women's Institutes, 1934–40; Admiralty, 1940–41; Relief Department, Foreign Office, 1942–44; UNRRA, Sec. Food Cttee of Council for Europe, 1944–47; Secretary United Nations Appeal for Children (in the UK), 1948; National General Secretary, YWCA of Great Britain, 1949–67. Lectr for the European Community, 1970–. Defence Medal, 1946. Polish Gold Cross of Merit, 1969. *Publication:* (as Ruth Walder Wesierska) They built a Jolly Good Mess (memoirs, in Europe 1939–45), 1987. *Address:* Westhope, Langton Herring, Weymouth, Dorset DT3 4HZ. *T:* Abbotsbury (01305) 871233. *Clubs:* Naval and Military; Royal Dorset Yacht.

WALDHEIM, Dr Kurt; President of the Republic of Austria, 1986–92; *b* 21 Dec. 1918; *m* 1944, Elisabeth Ritschel Waldheim; one *s* two *d*. *Educ:* Consular Academy, Vienna; Univ. of Vienna (Dr Jr 1944). Entered Austrian foreign service, 1945; served in Min. for Foreign Affairs; Mem., Austrian Delegn to Paris, London and Moscow for negotiations on Austrian State Treaty, 1945–47; 1st Sec., Embassy, Paris, 1948–51; apptd Counsellor and Head of Personnel Div., Min. of Foreign Affairs, 1951–55; Permanent Austrian Observer to UN, 1955–56; Minister Plenipotentiary to Canada, 1956–58; Ambassador to Canada, 1958–60; Dir-Gen. for Political Affairs, Min. of Foreign Affairs, 1960–64; Permanent Rep. of Austria to UN, 1964–68 (Chm., Outer Space Cttee of UN 1965–68 and 1970–71); Federal Minister for Foreign Affairs, 1968–70; Candidate for the Presidency of Republic of Austria, 1971; Permanent Rep. of Austria to UN, 1970–Dec. 1971; Sec.-Gen. of UN, 1972–81. Guest Prof. of Diplomacy, Georgetown Univ., Washington DC, 1982–84. Chm., InterAction Council for Internat. Co-operation, 1983–85. Hon. LLD: Chile, Carleton, Rutgers, Fordham, 1972; Jawaharlal Nehru, Bucharest, 1973; Wagner Coll., NY, Catholic Univ. of America, Wilfrid Laurier, 1974; Catholic Univ. of Leuven, Charles Univ., Hamilton Coll., Clinton, NY, 1975; Denver, Philippines, Nice, 1976; American Univ., Kent State, Warsaw, Moscow State Univ., Mongolian State Univ., 1977; Atlanta Univ., Humboldt Univ., Univ. of S Carolina, 1979; Notre Dame, USA, 1980. George Marshall Peace Award, USA, 1977; Dr Karl Renner Prize, City of Vienna, 1978. *Publications:* The Austrian Example, 1971, English edn 1973; The Challenge of Peace, 1977, English edn 1980; Building the Future Order, 1980; In the Eye of the Storm, 1985. *Recreations:* sailing, swimming, skiing, horseback riding. *Address:* 1 Lobkowitz-Platz, 1010 Vienna, Austria.

WALDMANN, Prof. Herman, FRS 1990; Professor of Pathology, Oxford University, since 1994; Fellow of Lincoln College, Oxford, since 1994; *b* 27 Feb. 1945; *s* of Leon and Rene Ryfka Waldmann; *m* 1971, Judith Ruth Young. *Educ:* Sir George Monoux Grammar Sch., Walthamstow; Sidney Sussex Coll., Cambridge (BA); London Hosp. Med Coll. (MB BChir); PhD Cantab. MRCPath, MRCP. Cambridge University: Dept of Pathology, 1971–94; Fellow, King's Coll., 1985–94; Kay Kendall Prof. of Therapeutic Immunology, 1989–93. Graham Bull Prize for Clinical Res., RCP, 1991. *Publications:* Limiting Dilution Analysis (with Dr I. Lefkovits), 1977; The Immune System (with Dr I. McConnell and A. Munro), 1981; (ed) Monoclonal Antibodies, 1988; many scientific papers. *Recreations:* family, food, friends, travel, music. *Address:* Lincoln College, Oxford OX1 3DR.

WALDRON-RAMSEY, Waldo Emerson; Barrister and Attorney-at-Law; international consultant; *b* 1 Jan. 1930; *s* of Wyatt and Delcina Waldron-Ramsey; *m* 1954, Shiela Pamella Beresford, Georgetown, Guyana; one *s* two *d*. *Educ:* Barbados; Hague Academy; London Sch. of Economics; Yugoslavia. LLB Hons; BSc (Econ) Hons; PhD. Called to Bar, Middle Temple; practised London Bar and SW Circuit, 1957–60; Marketing Economist, Shell International, 1960–61; Tanzanian Foreign Service, 1961–70; High Comr for Barbados in UK, and Ambassador to France, Netherlands and Germany, 1970–71; Ambassador and Perm. Rep. for Barbados to UN, 1971–76. UN Legal Expert: in field of human rights, 1967–71; on Israel, 1968–71. Mem., National Exec., Barbados Labour Party, 1980–. Senator, Parlt of Barbados, 1983. Editor, Beacon Newspaper, 1982. Member: Amer. Acad. of Political and Social Sciences; Amer. Soc. of Internat. Law; Amer. Inst. of Petroleum (Marketing Div.). Hon. Fellow, Hebrew Univ. of Jerusalem, 1972. DSc (Pol. Econ.) Univ. of Phnom-Penh, 1973; Hon. LLD Chung-Ang Univ., Republic of Korea, 1975. Grand Officer (1st Class), Nat. Order of Honneur et Mérite, Republic of Haiti, 1968; Grand Officier, Ordre Nat. de l'Amitié et Mérite, Khymèr, 1973; Order of Distinguished Diplomatic Service Merit, Gwangwha (1st Class), Republic of Korea, 1974. *Recreations:* cricket, tennis, bridge, travel. *Address:* (chambers) 50 Swan Street, Bridgetown, Barbados. *T:* 4278280, 4242021; (chambers) 26 Court Street, Brooklyn, New York 11225, USA; The Monticello, 30 Park Avenue, Mount Vernon, New York 10550, USA. *T:* (London) 071–229 4870; (N Carolina) (919) 7650080. *Clubs:* Royal Automobile; Lincoln Lodge (Connecticut).

WALES, Archbishop of, since 1991; **Most Rev. Alwyn Rice Jones;** Bishop of St Asaph, since 1982; *b* 25 March 1934; *s* of John Griffith and Annie Jones, Capel Curig, Caernarvonshire; *m* 1968, Meriel Anne Thomas; one *d*. *Educ:* Llanrwst Grammar School, Denbighshire; St David's Coll., Lampeter (BA Hons Welsh 1955); Fitzwilliam House, Cambridge (BA 1957 Theology Tripos, MA 1961); St Michael's Coll., Llandaff. Deacon 1958, priest 1959, Bangor Cathedral; Asst Curate, Llanfairisgaer, 1958–62; Secretary for SCM in N Wales Colleges and SCM in schools, 1962–65; Director of Education, Diocese of Bangor, 1965–75; Chaplain, St Winifred's School Llanfairfechan, 1965–67; Diocesan Warden of Ordinands, 1970–75; Vicar of Porthmadog, dio. Bangor, 1975–79; Exam. Chaplain to Archbishop of Wales, 1970–79; Hon. Canon, Bangor Cathedrals, 1974–78, Preb. of Llanfair, 1978–79; Dean of Brecon Cathedral, 1979–82. Mem., IBA Panel of Religious Advisers and Welsh Cttee, IBA, 1972–76; Asst Tutor in Religious Education, UCNW, Bangor, 1973–76. Fellow, Trinity Coll., Carmarthen, 1993. *Recreations:* music and walking. *Address:* Esgobty, St Asaph, Clwyd LL17 0TW. *T:* St Asaph (01745) 583503.

WALES, Daphne Beatrice; Chairman, Board for Mission and Unity, General Synod of the Church of England, 1983–88; *b* 6 Dec. 1917; *d* of Frederick James Wales and Lilian Frederica (*née* Whitnall). Principal, Bank of England, retd. Mem., General Synod, 1975–90 (Mem., Panel of Chairmen, 1983); Chm., St Albans Diocese House of Laity, 1979–85. Chm., Highway Trust, 1992 (Vice-Chm., 1983–92); Governor: Partnership for World Mission, 1978–90; S American Missionary Soc., 1983– (Vice-Chm., 1989–). Mem. Council, Oak Hill Theol Coll., 1981–91. *Address:* 41 Park Road, Watford, Herts WD1 3QW. *T:* Watford (01923) 225643.

WAŁESA, Lech; Hon. GCB 1991; President of Poland, since 1990; *b* Popowo, 29 Sept. 1943; *s* of late Bolesław Wałesa and Feliksa Wałesa; *m* 1969, Danuta; four *s* four *d*. *Educ:* Lipno primary and tech. schools; trained as electrician. Lenin Shipyard, Gdańsk, 1966–76, 1980–90 (Chm., Strike Cttees, 1970, 1980); founder Chm., Nat. Co-ordinating Commn of Indep. Autonomous Trade Union Solidarity (NSZZ Solidarność), 1981–82; in custody, 1981–82; returned to Gdańsk Shipyard, 1983; Leader, (outlawed) Solidarity, 1983–88, (re-instated) Solidarity, 1988–90. Dr *hc*, including: Alliance Coll., Cambridge, Mass, 1981; Harvard, 1983; Gdańsk, 1990. Nobel Peace Prize, 1983. Presidential Medal of Freedom (USA); Grand Cross, Legion of Honour (France); Order of Merit (Italian Republic); Order of Pius, 1st Cl. (Holy See); Grand Ribbon, Order of Leopold (Belgium). *Publication:* A Path of Hope: An Autobiography, 1987. *Address:* Kancelaria Prezydenta RP, ul. Wiejska 10, 00–902 Warsaw, Poland; ul. Pilotow 17D/3, Gdańsk-Zaspa, Poland.

WALEY, Daniel Philip, FBA 1991; PhD; Keeper of Manuscripts, British Library, 1973–86 (Keeper of Manuscripts, British Museum, 1972–73); *b* 20 March 1921; *er s* of late Hubert David Waley and Margaret Hendelah Waley; *m* 1945, Pamela Joan Griffiths; one *s* two *d*. *Educ:* Dauntsey's Sch.; King's Coll., Cambridge (MA, PhD). Historical Tripos, Cambridge, 1939–40 and 1945–46 (cl. 1). Served War, 1940–45. Fellow of King's Coll., Cambridge, 1950–54. Asst Lectr in Medieval History, London School of Economics and Political Science, Univ. of London, 1949–51, Lectr, 1951–61, Reader in History, 1961–70, Prof. of History, 1970–72. Hon. Res. Fellow, Westfield Coll., London, 1986; Emer. Fellow, Leverhulme Trust, 1986–87. British Acad. Italian Lectr, 1975. Corresp. Fellow, Deputazione di Storia Patria per l'Umbria, 1991. Serena Medal, British Acad., 1990. *Publications:* Mediaeval Orvieto, 1952; The Papal State in the 13th Century, 1961; Later Medieval Europe, 1964 (2nd edn 1985); The Italian City Republics, 1969 (3rd edn 1988); British Public Opinion and the Abyssinian War, 1935–36, 1975; (ed) George Eliot's Blotter: A Commonplace-Book, 1980; (contrib.) Storia d'Italia, ed by G. Galasso, vol. 7, 1987; Siena and the Sienese in the Thirteenth Century, 1991; (ed) J. K. Hyde, Literacy and Its Uses: studies on late medieval Italy, 1993; contributor to: Dizionario Biografico degli Italiani, English Hist. Review, Trans Royal Hist. Soc., Papers of British Sch. at Rome, Jl of Ecclesiastical Hist., Jl of the History of Ideas, Rivista Storica Italiana, Rivista di Storia della Chiesa in Italia, Procs Brit. Acad., British Library Jl, Bull. of John Rylands Liby, Sussex Archaeol Collections, etc. *Recreation:* walking. *Address:* The Croft, 43 Southover High Street, Lewes, E Sussex BN7 1HX.

WALEY-COHEN, Hon. Joyce Constance Ina, MA; **(Joyce, Hon. Lady Waley-Cohen);** President, Independent Schools Information Service Council, 1981–85 (Member, 1972–80); *b* 20 Jan. 1920; *o d* of 1st Baron Nathan, PC, TD, and Eleanor Joan Clara, *d* of C. Stettauer; *m* 1943, Sir Bernard Nathaniel Waley-Cohen, 1st Bt, (*d* 1991); two *s* two *d*. *Educ:* St Felix Sch., Southwold; Girton Coll., Cambridge (MA). Member: Governing Body, St Felix Sch., 1945–83 (Chm., 1970–83); Westminster Hosp. Bd of Governors, 1952–68; Chairman: Westminster Children's Hosp., 1952–68; Gordon Hosp., 1961–68; Governing Bodies of Girls' Schools' Assoc., 1974–79 (Mem., 1963); Ind. Schs Jt Council, 1977–80. Governor: Taunton Sch., 1978–90; Wellington Coll., 1979–90. JP Mddx 1949–59, Somerset 1959–86. *Recreations:* hunting, spinning, family life. *Address:* Honeymead, Simonsbath, Minehead, Somerset TA24 7JX. *T:* Exford (01643) 831242.

WALEY-COHEN, Sir Stephen (Harry), 2nd Bt *cr* 1961, of Honeymead, Co. Somerset; Managing Director: Victoria Palace Theatre, since 1989; Mousetrap Productions, since 1993; *b* 22 June 1946; *s* of Sir Bernard Nathaniel Waley-Cohen, 1st Bt and Hon. Joyce

Constance Ina Waley-Cohen, *qv*; *S* father, 1991; *m* 1st, 1972, Pamela Elizabeth (marr. diss.), *yr d* of J. E. Doniger; two *s* one *d*; 2nd, 1986, Josephine Burnett, *yr d* of late Duncan M. Spencer; two *d*. *Educ:* Wellesley House Sch.; Eton (Oppidan Scholar); Magdalene Coll., Cambridge (MA Hons). Financial journalist, Daily Mail, 1968–73; Publisher, Euromoney, 1969–83; Chief Exec., Maybox Theatres, 1984–89; Chairman: Thorndike Holdings, management training, 1989–; Willis Faber & Dumas (Agencies), 1992– (Dir, 1988–); Policy Portfolio, 1993–; Director: Badgworthy Land Co., 1982–; St Martin's Theatre, 1989–; Theatresoft, 1992–; Theatre Investment Fund, 1992–; Exeter Preferred Capital Investment Trust, 1992–; Portsmouth & Sunderland Newspapers, 1994–. Mem., SOLT (formerly SWET), 1984– (Mem., Finance Cttee, 1989–). Mem. Council, JCA Charitable Foundn (formerly Jewish Colonisation Assoc.), 1985– (Pres., 1992–); Chm. Exec. Cttee, British American Project for Successor Generation, 1986–92. Member: Public Affairs Cttee, British Field Sports Soc., 1972–92; Cttee, Devon & Somerset Staghounds, 1974–. Mem., UCL Finance Cttee, 1984–89; Governor, Wellesley House Sch., 1974–. Contested (C) Manchester, Gorton, Feb. and Oct. 1974. *Recreations:* family, theatre, hunting. *Heir: s* Lionel Robert Waley-Cohen, *b* 7 Aug. 1974. *Address:* 1 Wallingford Avenue, W10 6QA. *T:* 0181–968 6268; Honeymead, Simonsbath, Minehead, Somerset TA24 7JX. *T:* Exford (01643) 831584. *Club:* Garrick.

WALFORD, Sir Christopher (Rupert), Kt 1995, TEM 1972; Lord Mayor of London, 1994–95; Partner, Allen & Overy, since 1970; *b* 15 Oct. 1935; *s* of John Rupert Charles Walford, MBE and Gladys Irene Walford (*née* Sperrin); *m* 1967, Anne Elizabeth Viggars; two *s* (and one *s* decd). *Educ:* Charterhouse; Oriel College, Oxford (MA). Solicitor (Hons). National Service, commissioned RA, 1954–56; HAC 1957–72 (to Warrant Officer). Allen & Overy, 1959–. Councillor, Kensington, 1962–65, Kensington & Chelsea, 1964–82, Dep. Mayor, 1974–75, Mayor, 1979–80; Alderman, Ward of Farringdon Within, 1982–; Sheriff, City of London, 1990–91. Member: Council, CGLI, 1984–; Council, and Policy and Exec. Cttees, Inst. of Directors, 1986–94; Court of Assistants and Finance Cttee, Corp. of Sons of the Clergy, 1989–; Trustee: St Paul's Cathedral Choir Sch. Foundn, 1985–; Guildhall Sch., Music and Drama Foundn, 1989–; Morden Coll., 1991–. Governor, Bridewell Royal Hosp., 1984–. Freeman, City of London, 1964; Liveryman: Makers of Playing Cards Co., 1978 (Master, 1987–88); City of London Solicitors Co., 1983– (Master, 1993). FRSA. Hon. DCL City, 1994. *Recreations:* listening to music (especially opera), kitchen bridge, watching Rugby football and cricket, horse racing, hill walking. *Address:* Allen & Overy, One New Change, EC4M 9QQ. *T:* 0171–330 3000. *Clubs:* MCC, City Livery, United Wards, Farringdon Ward (Patron); Berkhamsted Golf, Braemar Golf.

WALFORD, Dr Diana Marion; Director, Public Health Laboratory Service, since 1993; *b* 26 Feb. 1944; *d* of Lt-Col Joseph Norton, LLM, and Thelma Norton (*née* Nurick); *m* 1970, Arthur David Walford, LLB; one *s* one *d*. *Educ:* Calder High Sch. for Girls, Liverpool; Liverpool Univ. (George Holt Medal, Physiol.; J. H. Abram Prize, Pharmacol.; BSc (1st Cl. Hons Physiol.) 1965; MB ChB 1968; MD 1976); London Univ. (MSc (Epidemiology) 1987). FRCP 1990 (MRCP 1972); FRCPath 1986 (MRCPath 1974); MFPHM 1989, FFPHM 1994. Ho. Officer posts, Liverpool Royal Inf., 1968–69; Sen. Ho. Officer posts and Sen. Registrar, St Mary's Hosp., Paddington, and Northwick Park Hosp., Harrow, 1969–75; MRC Research (Training) Fellow, Clin. Res. Centre, 1975–76; Sen. MO 1976–79, PMO 1979–83, SPMO (Under Sec.), 1983–89, Dep. CMO, 1989–92, DHSS, subseq. Dept of Health. Hon. Consultant Haematologist, Central Middlesex Hosp., 1977–87. Mem., British Soc. for Haematology, 1978–; Founder Mem., British Blood Transfusion Soc., 1983–; Hon. Life Mem., British Assoc. of Med. Managers. FRSM. *Publications:* chapters on haematological side effects of drugs in: Meyler's Side Effects of Drugs, 9th edn 1980; Side Effects of Drugs Annual, 1980; Drug-Induced Emergencies, 1980; articles on alpha-thalassaemia. *Recreations:* theatre, painting, travel. *Address:* Public Health Laboratory Service, 61 Colindale Avenue, NW9 5DF. *T:* 0181–200 1295.

WALFORD, John de Guise; His Honour Judge Walford; a Circuit Judge, since 1993; *b* 23 Feb. 1948; *s* of late Edward Wynn Walford and of Dorothy Ann Walford; *m* 1977, Pamela Elizabeth Russell; one *s* one *d*. *Educ:* Sedbergh Sch.; Queens' Coll., Cambridge (MA). Called to the Bar, Middle Temple, 1971; practice on NE Circuit, 1974; Asst Recorder, 1985–89; Recorder, 1989–93. Standing Counsel (Criminal) to DHSS, NE Circuit, 1991–93. *Recreations:* cricket, tennis, opera, watching Middlesbrough FC. *Address:* Law Courts, Exchange Square, Drake Street, Bradford BD1 1JA. *T:* Bradford (01274) 840274. *Clubs:* Hawks (Cambridge); Free Foresters.

WALFORD, John Howard; President, Solicitors' Disciplinary Tribunal, 1979–88; Senior Legal Officer, Office of the Banking Ombudsman, since 1991; *b* 16 May 1927; *s* of Henry Howard Walford and Marjorie Josephine Solomon; *m* 1953, Peggy Ann Jessel; two *s* two *d*. *Educ:* Cheltenham College; Gonville and Caius College, Cambridge; MA (Hons). Solicitor, 1950; Senior Partner, 1979–88, Consultant, 1988–91, Bischoff & Co. Mem. Council, Law Society, 1961–69; Governor, College of Law, 1967–88; Senior Warden, City of London Solicitors' Co., 1980–81, Master, 1981–82. Governor, St John's Hosp. for Diseases of the Skin, 1960–82; Chm., Appeal Cttee, Skin Disease Research Fund, 1974–93; Mem., Bd of Management, Petworth Cottage Nursing and Convalescent Home (Chm., 1988–93). Mem., Arbitration Panel, The Securities and Futures Authority Consumer Arbitration Scheme, 1988–94. Hon. Mem., British Assoc. of Dermatologists, 1993. Commander, Order of Bernardo O'Higgins, Chile, 1972. *Address:* Pheasant Court, Northchapel, near Petworth, W Sussex GU28 9LJ. *Clubs:* Garrick, City Law; Leconfield Flyfishing.

WALFORD, John Thomas, OBE 1985; General Secretary, Multiple Sclerosis Society of Great Britain and Northern Ireland, 1977–95 (Deputy General Secretary, 1965–77); *b* 6 Feb. 1933; *s* of Frederick Thomas Walford and Rose Elizabeth Walford; *m* 1955, June Muriel Harding (marr. diss. 1970); two *s* one *d*. *Educ:* Richmond and East Sheen County Grammar Sch. Served RAF, 1951–53. C. C. Wakefield & Co. Ltd, 1949–51 and 1953–55; Stanley Eades & Co., 1955–60; Moo Cow Milk Bars Ltd, 1960–64. DL Greater London, 1988–95. Editor, MS News (qly jl of Multiple Sclerosis Soc.), 1977–95. *Recreation:* collecting Victorian fairings. *Address:* Rhoslyn, Talley, Llandeilo, Dyfed SA19 7AX. *T:* Llandeilo (01558) 685744. *Club:* Royal Society of Medicine.

WALFORD, Lionel Kingsley, PhD; FInstP; Head, Welsh Office Agriculture Department, since 1994; *b* 19 May 1939; *s* of late Edward Walford and of Muriel (*née* Davies); *m* 1963, Linda Jones; two *d*. *Educ:* Whitchurch Grammar Sch., Cardiff; Univ. of Wales (BSc 1st Cl. Hons Physics, 1960); St Catharine's Coll., Cambridge (PhD 1963). FInstP 1972. Southern Illinois University, USA: Asst Prof., 1963–67; Associate Prof., 1967–72; Prof. of Physics, 1972–78; Research Consultant, McDonnell Douglas Corp., 1964–72; joined Welsh Office, 1978: Principal, 1978–84; Sen. Principal seconded to WDA, 1984–85; Dir, Manpower Services in Wales, 1985–88; Asst Sec., Welsh Office Agriculture Dept, 1988–94; Under Sec., 1994. *Publications:* numerous articles in jls on applied physics; one US patent. *Address:* Agriculture Department, Welsh Office, Cathays Park, Cardiff CF1 3NQ. *T:* Cardiff (01222) 823114.

WALKER, family name of **Baron Walker of Worcester**.

WALKER OF WORCESTER, Baron *cr* 1992 (Life Peer), of Abbots Morton in the County of Hereford and Worcester; **Peter Edward Walker,** PC 1970; MBE 1960; *b* 25 March 1932; *s* of Sydney and Rose Walker; *m* 1969, Tessa, *d* of G. I. Pout; three *s* two *d*. *Educ:* Latymer Upper Sch. Member, National Executive of Conservative Party, 1956–70; Nat. Chairman, Young Conservatives, 1958–60; contested (C) Dartford, 1955 and 1959. MP (C) Worcester, March 1961–1992. PPS to Leader of House of Commons, 1963–64; Opposition Front Bench Spokesman: on Finance and Economics, 1964–66; on Transport, 1966–68; on Local Government, Housing, and Land, 1968–70; Minister of Housing and Local Govt, June-Oct. 1970; Secretary of State for: the Environment, 1970–72; Trade and Industry, 1972–74; Opposition Spokesman on Trade, Industry and Consumer Affairs, Feb.-June 1974, on Defence, June 1974–Feb. 1975; Minister of Agric., Fisheries and Food, 1979–83; Sec. of State for Energy, 1983–87, for Wales, 1987–90. Chairman: Thornton & Co., 1991–; Cornhill Insurance, 1992–; Non-Executive Director: British Gas, 1990–; Dalgety, 1990–; Smith New Court, 1990–; Tate & Lyle, 1990–. *Publications:* The Ascent of Britain, 1977; Trust The People, 1987; Staying Power (autobiog.), 1991. *Address:* Abbots Morton Manor, Gooms Hill, Abbots Morton, Worcester WR7 4LT. *Clubs:* Buck's, Carlton, Pratt's; Worcestershire County Cricket, Union and County (Worcester).

WALKER, Rev. Sir Alan, Kt 1981; OBE 1955; Principal, Pacific College for Evangelism, 1989–95; Principal Emeritus, Alan Walker College of Evangelism, since 1995; *b* 1911; *s* of Rev. Alfred Edgar Walker, former Pres., NSW Methodist Conf., and Violet Louise Walker; *m* 1938, Winifred Garrard Walker (*née* Channon); three *s* one *d*. *Educ:* Leigh Theological Coll., Sydney; Univ. of Sydney (BA, MA); Bethany Biblical Seminary, Chicago. Minister, Cessnock, NSW, 1939–44; Supt, Waverley Methodist Mission, 1944–54; Dir, Australian Mission to the Nation, 1953–56; Vis. Professor: of Evangelism, Boston Sch. of Theology, 1957; of Evangelism and Preaching, Claremont Sch. of Theol., USA, 1973; Supt, Central Methodist Mission, Sydney, 1958–78; Dir, World Evangelism, World Methodist Council, 1978–87. Deleg. to First Assembly of WCC, Amsterdam, 1948; Adviser to: Aust. Delegn at UN, 1949; Third Ass. of WCC, New Delhi, 1962; Fourth Ass., WCC, Uppsala, 1968; Missions to: Fiji, S Africa, S America, Singapore and Malaysia, Sri Lanka, 1962–75; Founder, Sydney Life Line Tel. Counselling Centre, 1963 (Pres., Life Line Internat., 1966–87); Sec., NSW Methodist Conf., 1970, Pres., 1971; lectures, various times, USA. Hon. DD Bethany Biblical Sem., 1954. Inst. de la Vie award, Paris, for services to humanity, 1978; (with Lady Walker) World Methodist Peace Award, 1986. *Publications include:* There is Always God, 1938; Everybody's Calvary, 1943; Coal Town, 1944; Heritage Without End, 1953; The Whole Gospel for the Whole World, 1957; The Many Sided Cross of Jesus, 1962; How Jesus Helped People, 1964; A Ringing Call to Mission, 1966; The Life Line Story, 1967 (USA, As Close as the Telephone); Breakthrough, 1969; God, the Disturber, 1973 (USA); Jesus, the Liberator, 1973 (USA); The New Evangelism, 1974 (USA); Love in Action, 1977; Life Grows with Christ, 1981; Life Ends in Christ, 1983; Standing Up To Preach, 1983; Your Life Can Be Changed, 1985; Life in the Holy Spirit, 1986; Try God, 1990; Herald of Hope, 1994. *Recreations:* swimming, tennis. *Address:* 14 Owen Stanley Avenue, Beacon Hill, NSW 2100, Australia. *T:* (2) 4513923.

WALKER, Alexander; Film Critic, London Evening Standard, since 1960; *b* Portadown, N Ireland, 22 March 1930; *s* of Alfred and Ethel Walker. *Educ:* Portadown Grammar Sch.; The Queen's Univ., Belfast (BA); Collège d'Europe, Bruges; Univ. of Michigan, Ann Arbor. Lecturer in political philosophy and comparative govt, Univ. of Michigan, 1952–54. Features editor, Birmingham Gazette, 1954–56; leader writer and film critic, The Birmingham Post, 1956–59; columnist, Vogue magazine, 1974–86. Frequent broadcaster on the arts on radio and television; author: TV series Moviemen; BBC Radio series Film Star; author and co-producer of TV programmes on History of Hollywood, Garbo and Chaplin. Member: British Screen Adv. Council (formerly Wilson Interim Action Cttee on the Film Industry), 1977–92; Bd of Govs, BFI, 1989–95. Chevalier de l'Ordre des Arts et des Lettres, 1981. Twice named Critic of the Year, in annual British Press awards, 1970, 1974, commended, 1985; Award of Golden Eagle, Philippines, for services to internat. cinema, 1982. *Publications:* The Celluloid Sacrifice: aspects of sex in the movies, 1966; Stardom: the Hollywood phenomenon, 1970; Stanley Kubrick Directs, 1971; Hollywood, England: the British film industry in the sixties, 1974; Rudolph Valentino, 1976; Double Takes: notes and afterthoughts on the movies 1956–76, 1977; Superstars, 1978; The Shattered Silents: how the talkies came to stay, 1978; Garbo, 1980; Peter Sellers: the authorized biography, 1981; Joan Crawford, 1983; Dietrich, 1984; (ed) No Bells on Sunday: journals of Rachel Roberts, 1984; National Heroes: British cinema industry in the seventies and eighties, 1985; Bette Davis, 1986; trans., Benayoun, Woody Allen: beyond words, 1986; Vivien: the life of Vivien Leigh, 1987; It's Only a Movie, Ingrid: encounters on and off screen, 1988; Elizabeth: the life of Elizabeth Taylor, 1990; (jtly) Zinnemann: an autobiography, 1992; Fatal Charm: the life of Rex Harrison, 1992; Audrey: her real story, 1994; contributor to many British and foreign publications. *Recreations:* ski-ing, persecuting smokers. *Address:* 1 Marlborough, 38–40 Maida Vale, W9 1RW. *T:* 0171–289 0985.

WALKER, Alexandra Margaret Jane; Assistant Under-Secretary of State (Service Personnel), Ministry of Defence, since 1993; *b* 31 Oct. 1945; *d* of late Frederic Douglas Walker and Hertha Julie (*née* Freiin Gemmingen von Massenbach); one *d*. *Educ:* Nikolaus Cusanus Gymnasium, Bonn; Lady Margaret Hall, Oxford (Schol.; BA Lit. Hum.). Joined MoD as admin. trainee, 1973; Principal, 1976; on secondment to: Plessey Co., 1979–81; LSE as Nancy Seear Fellow in Industrial Relns, 1981–82; Asst Sec. and Hd of Civilian Mgt (Industrial Relns), 1983–86; rcds 1987; Counsellor, British Embassy, Bonn, 1988–92. *Recreations:* children, animals, subsidence, theology. *Address:* c/o Ministry of Defence, Whitehall, SW1A 2HB.

WALKER, (Alfred) Cecil, JP; MP (OUP) Belfast North, since 1983 (resigned seat Dec. 1985 in protest against Anglo-Irish Agreement; re-elected Jan. 1986); *b* 17 Dec. 1924; *s* of Alfred George Walker and Margaret Lucinda Walker; *m* 1953, Ann May Joan Verrant; two *s*. *Educ:* Methodist College. Senior Certificate. In timber business with James P. Corry & Co. Ltd, Belfast, 1941–, Departmental Manager, 1952. JP Belfast, 1966. *Recreations:* sailing, sea angling. *Address:* 1 Wynnland Road, Newtownabbey, Northern Ireland. *T:* Glengormley (01232) 833463. *Club:* Down Cruising.

WALKER, Andrew John; Chief Executive, SWALEC, since 1993. *Educ:* Univ. of Cambridge (MA). MIMechE. *Address:* SWALEC, Newport Road, St Mellons, Cardiff CF3 9XW. *T:* Cardiff (01222) 792111.

WALKER, Angus Henry; Director, Genrho SA, since 1993; *b* 30 Aug. 1935; *s* of late Frederick William Walker and of Esther Victoria (*née* Wrangle); *m* 1st, 1968, Beverly Phillpotts (*see* B. J. Anderson) (marr. diss. 1976); 2nd, 1979, Ann (*née* Griffiths), *widow* of Richard Snow; two *d* and two step *d*. *Educ:* Erith Grammar Sch., Kent; Balliol Coll., Oxford (Domus Scholar; 1st Cl. Hons BA Mod. Hist. 1959; Stanhope Prize, 1958; MA 1968). Nat. Service, 1954–56 (Comdr RA). Senior Scholar, St Antony's Coll., Oxford,

1959–63; HM Diplomatic Service, 1963–68: FO, 1963–65; First Sec., Washington, 1965–68. Lectr, SSEES, London Univ., 1968–70; Univ. Lectr in Russian Social and Political Thought, Oxford, and Lectr, Balliol Coll., 1971–76; Fellow, Wolfson Coll., Oxford, 1971–76; Dir, SSEES, London Univ., 1976–79; British Petroleum Co. Plc, 1979–84; Dir, Corporate Strategy, British Telecom PLC, 1985–88; Managing Director: Strategic Planning Associates, 1988–91; A. T. Kearney, 1991–94. Co-opted Mem., Arts Sub-Cttee, UGC, for enquiry into Russian in British Univs, 1978–79; Governor, Centre for Economic Policy Res., 1986–89. CompIEE 1988. *Publications:* trans. from Polish: Political Economy, by Oskar Lange, vol. 1, 1963; Marx: His Theory in its Context, 1978, 2nd edn 1989. *Address:* 5 North Square, NW11 7AA. *Club:* Reform.

WALKER, Hon. Anna Elizabeth Blackstock (Hon. Mrs Walker); Deputy Director General, Office of Telecommunications, since 1994; *b* 5 May 1951; *d* of Baron Butterworth, *qv*; *m* 1983, Timothy Edward Hanson Walker, *qv*; three *d*. *Educ:* Benenden Sch., Kent; Bryn Mawr Coll., USA; Lady Margaret Hall, Oxford (MA History). British Council, 1972–73; CBI, 1973–74; joined Department of Trade, 1975: Commonwealth Relations and Exports Div. (ME), 1975; Post and Telecommunications Div., 1976; Private Sec. to Sec. of State for Industry, 1977–78; Shipping Policy Div. (Grade 7), 1979–82; Finance Div., 1983–84; Interdeptl Rev. of Budgetary Controls, 1985; Cabinet Office (on secondment), 1986; Personnel Div. (Grade 6), 1987–88; Competition Policy Div. (Grade 5), 1988–91; Dir, Competition Oftel, 1991–94. *Recreations:* travel, theatre, cycling. *Address:* c/o Office of Telecommunications, 50 Ludgate Hill, EC4M 7JJ. *T:* 0171–634 8804.

WALKER, Gen. Sir Antony (Kenneth Frederick), KCB 1987; Military Adviser, Porton International plc, since 1992; Senior Military Adviser, Electronic Data Systems Ltd, since 1994; *b* 16 May 1934; *o s* of late Kenneth Walker and Iris Walker; *m* 1961, Diana Merran Steward (marr. diss. 1983); one *s* one *d*; *m* 1991, Sqn Ldr Hannah Watts, WRAF. *Educ:* Merchant Taylors' School; RMA Sandhurst. Commissioned into Royal Tank Regt, 1954; served BAOR, Libya, Ghana, Northern Ireland, Hong Kong, Cyprus; Instructor, Staff Coll., 1971–73; CO 1st Royal Tank Regt, 1974–76 (despatches); Col GS HQ UK Land Forces, 1976–78; Comdr Task Force Golf (11 Armd Bde), 1978–80; Dep. Mil. Sec. (A), 1980–82; Comdr, 3rd Armoured Div., 1982–84; Chief of Staff, HQ UKLF, 1985–87; Dep. CDS (Commitments), MoD, 1987–89; Comdt, RCDS, 1990–92. Sec.-Gen., OPSIS (Nat. Assoc. for Educn, Trng and Support of Blind and Partially Sighted People), 1992–94. Col Comdt, Royal Tank Regt, 1983–94 (Rep., 1985–91). Mem. Council, RUSI, 1982–85 and 1990–94. Governor, Centre for Internat. Briefing, Farnham Castle, 1987–91. Chairman: Army Bobsleigh Assoc., 1983–92; British Bobsleigh Assoc., 1992– (Mem. Council, 1989–); President: Services' Dry Fly Fishing Assoc., 1988–92; Combined Services' Winter Sports Assoc., 1990–92. Mem., Council of Management, Salisbury Festival, 1988– (Vice-Chm., 1990–93; Chm., 1994–). Trustee, Tank Mus., 1994–. *Recreations:* bird watching, fly-fishing, music, practical study of wine. *Address:* c/o National Westminster Bank plc, PO Box 237, 72–74 High Street, Watford, Herts WD1 2BQ. *Club:* Royal Air Force (Associate).

WALKER, Arthur Geoffrey, FRS 1955; Professor of Pure Mathematics, Liverpool University, 1952–74, now Emeritus; *b* 17 July 1909; 2nd *s* of late A. J. Walker, Watford, Herts; *m* 1939, Phyllis Ashcroft, *d* of late Sterry B. Freeman, CBE. *Educ:* Watford Grammar Sch.; Balliol Coll., Oxford. MA (Oxon); PhD, DSc (Edinburgh); FRSE; Lectr at Imperial Coll. Science and Technology, 1935–36; at Liverpool Univ., 1936–47; Prof. of Mathematics in the Univ. of Sheffield, 1947–52. Mem. of Council, Royal Soc., 1962–63. Pres., London Mathematical Soc., 1963–65. Junior Berwick Prize of London Mathematical Soc., 1947; Keith Medal of Royal Society of Edinburgh, 1950. *Publication:* Harmonic Spaces (with H. S. Ruse and T. J. Willmore), 1962. *Address:* Beechcroft, Roundabout Lane, West Chiltington, Pulborough, W Sussex RH20 2RL. *T:* West Chiltington (01798) 812412.

WALKER, Sir Baldwin Patrick, 4th Bt, *cr* 1856; *b* 10 Sept. 1924; *s* of late Comdr Baldwin Charles Walker, *o s* of 3rd Bt and Mary, *d* of F. P. Barnett of Whalton, Northumberland; *S* grandfather, 1928; *m* 1948, Joy Yvonne (marr. diss., 1954); *m* 1954, Sandra Stewart; *m* 1966, Rosemary Ann, *d* of late Henry Hollingdrake; one *s* one *d*; *m* 1980, Vanessa Hilton. *Educ:* Gordonstoun. Served Royal Navy, Fleet Air Arm, 1943–58. Lieut, RN, retired. *Heir:* *s* Christopher Robert Baldwin Walker, *b* 25 Oct. 1969. *Address:* 8 Sweet Valley Road, Bergvliet, Cape Town, 7945, South Africa.

WALKER, Bill; *see* Walker, W. C.

WALKER, Bobby; *see* Walker, W. B. S.

WALKER, (Brian) Stuart, RDI 1989; freelance film production designer, since 1990; *b* 5 March 1932; *s* of William and Annie Walker; *m* 1961, Adrienne Elizabeth Atkinson (separated); two *d*. *Educ:* Blackpool Sch. of Art (Intermediate Exam. in Arts and Crafts; Nat. Diploma in Painting (1st cl. Hons)); RA Schs (RA Dip.). BBC Television, 1958–90: Design Assistant, 1958; Designer, 1961; Sen. Designer, 1970. BAFTA Award for TV Design, 1983, 1990; RTS Award for Production Design, 1988. *Address:* c/o Casarotto Marsh Ltd, National House, 60–66 Wardour Street, W1V 3HP. *T:* 0171–287 4450.

WALKER, Brian Wilson; consultant in ecology and development; Executive Director, Earthwatch Europe, 1989–95; *b* 31 Oct. 1930; *s* of Arthur Walker and Eleanor (*née* Wilson); *m* 1954, Nancy Margaret Gawith; one *s* five *d*. *Educ:* Heversham Sch., Westmorland; Leicester Coll. of Technology; Faculty Technology, Manchester Univ. Management Trainee, Sommerville Bros, Kendal, 1952–55; Personnel Man., Pye Radio, Larne, 1956–61; Bridgeport Brass Ltd, Lisburn: Personnel Man., 1961–66; Gen. Man. (Develt), 1966–69; Gen. Man. (Manufrg), 1969–74; Dir Gen., Oxfam, 1974–83; Dir, Independent Commn on Internat. Humanitarian Issues, 1983–85; Pres., Internat. Inst. for Envmt and Develt, 1985–89. Chairman: Band Aid—Live Aid Projects Cttee, 1985–90; SOS Sahel, 1988–95. Founder Chm., New Ulster Movt, 1969–74; Founder Pres., New Ulster Movt Ltd, 1974. Member: Standing Adv. Commn on Human Rights for NI, 1975–77; World Commn on Food and Peace, 1989–95. Mem., Editl Cttee, World Resources Report, 1985–95. Trustee: Cambodia Trust, 1989–95; Internat. Inst. for Environment and Develt, 1989–95; Artizan Trust, 1992–. Hon. MA Oxon, 1983. Kt, Sov. Order of St Thomas of Acre; Kentucky Colonel, 1966. *Publications:* Authentic Development—Africa, 1986; various political/religious papers on Northern Ireland problem and Third World subjects. *Recreations:* gardening, Irish politics, classical music, active Quaker. *Address:* 5 Colesbergh Court, Arnside, Cumbria LA5 0DA. *Club:* Athenæum.

WALKER, Carl, GC 1972; Police Inspector, 1976–82; *b* 31 March 1934; English; *m* 1955, Kathleen Barker; one *s*. *Educ:* Kendal Grammar Sch., Westmorland. RAF Police, 1952–54 (Corporal). Lancashire Police, Oct. 1954–March 1956, resigned; Blackpool Police, 1959–82 (amalgamated with Lancashire Constabulary, April 1968); Sergeant, 1971. Retired 1982, as a result of the injuries sustained from gunshot wounds on 23 Aug. 1971 during an armed raid by thieves on a jeweller's shop in Blackpool (GC). *Recreations:* Rugby; Cumberland and Westmorland wrestling, photography, walking. *Address:* 9 Lawnswood Avenue, Poulton-Le-Fylde, Blackpool FY6 7ED.

WALKER, Catherine Marguerite Marie-Therese; French couturier; Founder, The Chelsea Design Company Ltd, 1978; *b* Pas de Calais; *d* of Remy Baheux and Agnes (*née* Lefebvre); *m* John Walker (decd); two *d*. *Educ:* Univ. of Lille; Univ. of Aix-en-Provence. Dir, Film Dept, French Inst., London, 1970; Lecture Dept, French Embassy, London, 1971. Designer of the Year Award: for British Couture, 1990–91; for Glamour, 1991–92. *Address:* The Chelsea Design Co., 65 Sydney Street, Chelsea, SW3 6PX. *T:* 0171–352 4626.

WALKER, Cecil; *see* Walker, A. C.

WALKER, Sir (Charles) Michael, GCMG 1976 (KCMG 1963; CMG 1960); HM Diplomatic Service, retired; Chairman, Commonwealth Scholarship Commission in the UK, 1977–87; *b* 22 Nov. 1916; *s* of late Col C. W. G. Walker, CMG, DSO; *m* 1945, Enid Dorothy, *d* of late W. A. McAdam, CMG; one *s* one *d*. *Educ:* Charterhouse; New Coll., Oxford. Clerk of House of Lords, June 1939. Enlisted in Army, Oct. 1939, and served in RA until 1946 when released with rank of Lt-Col. Dominions Office, 1947; First Sec., British Embasssy, Washington, 1949–51; Office of United Kingdom High Comr in Calcutta and New Delhi, 1952–55; Establishment Officer, Commonwealth Relations Office, 1955–58. Imperial Defence Coll., 1958; Asst Under-Sec. of State and Dir of Establishment and Organisation, CRO, 1959–62; British High Commissioner in: Ceylon, 1962–65 (concurrently Ambassador to Maldive Islands, July–Nov. 1965), Malaysia, 1966–71; Sec., ODA, FCO, 1971–73; High Comr, India, 1974–76. Chm., Festival of India Trust, 1980–83. Hon. DCL City, 1980. *Recreations:* fishing, gardening, golf. *Address:* Herongate House, West Chiltington Common, Pulborough, Sussex RH20 2NL. *T:* West Chiltington (01798) 813473. *Club:* Oriental.

See also Sir R. N. O. Couper, Bt.

WALKER, Charls E., PhD; Consultant, Washington, DC, since 1973; *b* Graham, Texas, 24 Dec. 1923; *s* of Pinkney Clay and Sammye McCombs Walker; *m* 1949, Harmolyn Hart, Laurens, S Carolina; one *s* one *d*. *Educ:* Univ. of Texas (MBA); Wharton Sch. of Finance, Univ. of Pennsylvania (PhD). Instructor in Finance, 1947–48, and later Asst and Associate Prof., 1950–54, at Univ. of Texas, in the interim teaching at Wharton Sch. of Finance, Univ. of Pennsylvania; Associate Economist, Fed. Reserve Bank: of Philadelphia, 1953, of Dallas, 1954 (Vice-Pres. and Economic Advr, 1958–61); Economist and Special Asst to Pres. of Republic Nat. Bank of Dallas, 1955–56 (took leave to serve as Asst to Treasury Sec., Robert B. Anderson, April 1959–Jan. 1961); Exec. Vice-Pres., Amer. Bankers Assoc., 1961–69. Under-Sec. of the Treasury, 1969–72, Dep. Sec., 1972–73. Chm., American Council for Capital Formation; Mem. Council on Foreign Relations; Co-Chm., Bretton Woods Cttee. Adjunct Prof. of Finance and Public Affairs, Univ. of Texas at Austin, 1985–. Dist. Alumnus, Univ. of Texas, 1994. Hon. LLD Ashland Coll., 1970. Co-editor, The Banker's Handbook, 1988–. *Publications:* (ed) New Directions in Federal Tax Policy, 1983; (ed) The Consumption Tax, 1987; (ed) The US Savings Challenge, 1990; contribs to learned jls, periodicals. *Recreations:* golf, fishing, music. *Address:* 10120 Chapel Road, Potomac, MD 20854, USA. *T:* (301) 2995414. *Clubs:* Congressional Country, Burning Tree Golf (Bethesda, Md); Hills of Lakeway Golf and Tennis (Austin, Texas).

WALKER, (Christopher) Roy, CB 1992; Chief Officer, Joint Nature Conservation Committee, since 1993; *b* 5 Dec. 1934; *s* of Christopher Harry Walker and late Dorothy Jessica Walker; *m* 1961, Hilary Mary Biddiscombe; two *s*. *Educ:* Sir George Monoux Grammar Sch., E17; Sidney Sussex Coll., Cambridge (BA); Université Libre de Bruxelles. National Service, Essex Regt, 1952–54. BoT, 1958; CSD, 1968; Private Sec. to Lord Privy Seal, 1968–71; Treasury, 1973; DTI, 1973; Dept of Energy, 1974; Cabinet Office, 1974; Dept of Energy, 1975; Under Secretary: DES, 1977; Dept. of Employment, 1986; seconded as Dir, Business in the Cities, 1989; Dep. Head of Sci. and Technol. Secretariat, Cabinet Office, 1989–92. Associate Dir, RIPA, 1992. *Recreations:* hill walking, sailing. *Club:* Chipstead Sailing (Sevenoaks).

WALKER, Sir Colin (John Shedlock), Kt 1991; OBE 1981; Chairman, National Blood Authority, since 1993; *b* 7 Oct. 1934; *s* of Arthur John Walker and Olave Gertrude Walker; *m* 1963, Wendy Elizabeth Ellis; two *s*. *Educ:* St Edward's Sch., Oxford; Royal Agricultural Coll., Cirencester. Landowner, farmer and businessman. Chm., Harwich Haven Authority (formerly Harbour Bd), 1988–. Mem., 1985–88, Vice-Chm., 1991–93, Central Blood Labs Authority; Chairman: E Suffolk HA, 1986–87; E Anglian RHA, 1987–94 (Mem., 1983–86). Chm., All Party European Movement in Suffolk, 1979–81; various posts, incl. Chm., of Constituency Cons. Assoc., 1968–88. Mem., Suffolk CC, 1976–80. Chm. of Govs, Orwell Park Sch., 1991–. *Recreations:* shooting, gardening, reading, forestry, conservation. *Address:* Blomvyle Hall, Hacheston, Woodbridge, Suffolk IP13 0DY. *T:* Wickham Market (01728) 746756, *Fax:* (01278) 747737. *Club:* Royal Over-Seas League.

WALKER, Prof. David Alan, PhD, DSc; FRS 1979; Professor of Photosynthesis, University of Sheffield, 1988–93, now Emeritus; *b* 18 Aug. 1928; *s* of Cyril Walker and Dorothy Walker (*née* Dobson); *m* 1956, Shirley Wynne Walker (*née* Mason); one *s* one *d*. *Educ:* King's Coll., Univ. of Durham (BSc, PhD, DSc). Royal Naval Air Service, 1946–48. Lecturer, 1958–63, Reader, 1963–65, Queen Mary Coll., Univ. of London; Reader, Imperial Coll., Univ. of London, 1965–70; University of Sheffield: Prof. of Biology, 1970–84; Prof. and Dir, Res. Inst. for Photosynthesis, 1984–88. Leverhulme Emeritus Fellow, 1991–93. Corresp. Mem., Amer. Soc. Plant Physiol., 1979; MAE 1994. Alexander von Humboldt Prize, Alexander von Humboldt Foundn, Bonn, 1991. *Publications:* Energy Plants and Man, 1979, 2nd edn 1992; (with G. E. Edwards) C3, C4—Mechanisms, Cellular and Environmental Regulation of Photosynthesis, 1983; The Use of the Oxygen Electrode and Fluorescence Probes in Simple Measurements of Photosynthesis, 1987, 2nd edn 1990; papers, mostly in field of photosynthesis. *Recreations:* changing the Biddlestone landscape, singing the Sheffield Carols. *Address:* Department of Animal and Plant Sciences, University of Sheffield, Sheffield S10 2UQ. *T:* Sheffield (0114) 282 4779.

WALKER, Sir David (Alan), Kt 1991; Director, Morgan Stanley Inc., since 1994; Chairman, Morgan Stanley Group (Europe) plc, since 1994; *b* 31 Dec. 1939; *m* 1963, Isobel Cooper; one *s* two *d*. *Educ:* Chesterfield Sch.; Queens' Coll., Cambridge (MA; Hon. Fellow, 1989). Joined HM Treasury, 1961; Private Sec. to Joint Permanent Secretary, 1964–66; seconded to Staff of International Monetary Fund, Washington, 1970–73; Asst Secretary, HM Treasury, 1973–77; joined Bank of England as Chief Adviser, then Chief of Economic Intelligence Dept, 1977; a Dir, 1982–93 (non-exec., 1988–93); Chairman: Johnson Matthey Bankers, later Minories Finance, 1985–88; SIB, 1988–92; Agricl Mortgage Corp., 1993–94; Dep. Chm., Lloyds Bank plc, 1992–94. Chm., Steering Gp, Financial Markets Gp, LSE, 1987–94. Pt-time Mem. of Bd, CEGB, 1987–89; non-exec. Director: National Power, 1990, 1993–94; British Invisibles, 1993–; Reuters Holdings, 1994–. Mem., The Group of Thirty, 1993–. Nominated Mem., Council of Lloyd's, 1988–92 (Chm., Inquiry into LMX Spiral, 1992). Governor, Henley Management Coll., 1993–. FRSA 1987; CIMgt (CBIM 1986). *Recreations:* music, long-distance walking. *Address:* Morgan Stanley, 25 Cabot Square, Canary Wharf, E14 4QA. *Club:* Reform.

WALKER, David Bruce; Member (part-time), British Coal Corporation, 1988–95; *b* 30 Aug. 1934; *s* of Noel B. Walker and June R. Walker (*née* Sutherland); *m* 1961, Leonora C. Freeman; two *s*. *Educ:* Knox Grammar Sch., Wahroonga, NSW; Univ. of Sydney (BSc (Hons), MSc, Geology). Demonstrator in Geology: Univ. of Sydney, 1956–58; Bristol Univ., 1958–59; British Petroleum Co., 1959–85: worked as geologist in UK, Gambia, Algeria, Libya, Colombia, Kuwait, Iran and US; Vice-Pres., Production Planning, USA, 1974–77; Regional Coordinator, Western Hemisphere, 1977–79; Controller, BP Exploration, 1979–80; Chief Executive, BP Petroleum Development (UK), 1980–82; Dir, Resources Development, BP Australia, 1982–85; Chief Exec., Britoil plc, 1985–88. Chairman: Sun Internat. Exploration and Production Co., 1988–91; Sun Oil Britain, 1988–91. Distinguished Lectr, Soc. of Petroleum Engineers, 1976. President, UK Offshore Operators Assoc., 1982. *Recreations:* music, gardening. *Address:* Spring Cottage, Chetnole, Sherborne, Dorset DT9 6PF. *T:* Sherborne (01935) 872604.

WALKER, David Critchlow, CMG 1993; CVO 1988 (MVO 1976); HM Diplomatic Service; High Commissioner to Ghana, and Ambassador (non-resident) to Togo, since 1992; *b* 9 Jan. 1940; *s* of John Walker and Mary Walker (*née* Cross); *m* 1965, Tineke van der Leek; three *s*. *Educ:* Manchester Grammar Sch.; St Catharine's Coll., Cambridge (BA,MA,DipEd). Assistant Lecturer, Dept of Geography, Manchester Univ., 1962; Commonwealth Relations Office, 1963; Third Secretary, British Embassy, Mexico City, 1965; Second Secretary, Brussels, 1968; First Secretary: FCO, 1970; Washington, 1973; First Sec., later Counsellor, FCO, 1978–83; Consul General, São Paulo, 1983–86; Minister, Madrid, 1986–89; Counsellor, FCO, 1989–92. *Address:* c/o Foreign and Commonwealth Office, SW1A 2AH.

WALKER, Prof. David Maxwell, CBE 1986; QC (Scot.) 1958; FBA 1976; FRSE 1980; Regius Professor of Law, Glasgow University, 1958–90, now Professor Emeritus and Senior Research Fellow; Dean of the Faculty of Law, 1956–59; Senate Assessor on University Court, 1962–66; *b* 9 April 1920; *o s* of James Mitchell Walker, Branch Manager, Union Bank of Scotland, and Mary Paton Colquhoun Irvine; *m* 1954, Margaret Knox, OBE, MA, *yr d* of Robert Knox, yarn merchant, Brookfield, Renfrewshire. *Educ:* High School of Glasgow (Mackindlay Prizeman in Classics); Glasgow, Edinburgh and London Universities. MA (Glasgow) 1946; LLB (Distinction), Robertson Schol., 1948; Faulds Fellow in Law, 1949–52; PhD (Edinburgh), 1952; Blackwell Prize, Aberdeen Univ., 1955; LLB (London), 1957; LLD (Edinburgh), 1960; LLD (London), 1968; LLD (Glasgow), 1985. Served War of 1939–45, NCO Cameronians; commissioned HLI, 1940; seconded to RIASC, 1941; served with Indian Forces in India, 1942, Middle East, 1942–43, and Italy, 1943–46, in MT companies and as Brigade Supply and Transport Officer (Captain). HQ 21 Ind. Inf. Bde, 8 Ind. Div. Advocate of Scottish Bar, 1948; Barrister, Middle Temple, 1957; QC (Scotland) 1958; practised at Scottish Bar, 1948–53; studied at Inst. of Advanced Legal Studies, Univ. of London, 1953–54; Prof. of Jurisprudence, Glasgow Univ., 1954–58. Dir, Scottish Univs' Law Inst., 1974–80. Trustee, Hamlyn Trust, 1954–93. Vice-Pres., RSE, 1985–88. Governor: Scottish College of Commerce, 1957–64; High School of Glasgow (and Chm., Educational Trust), 1974–. Hon. Sheriff of Lanarkshire at Glasgow, 1966–82. FSAScot 1966; FRSA 1991. Hon. LLD Edinburgh, 1974. *Publications:* (ed) Faculty Digest of Decisions, 1940–50, Supplements, 1951 and 1952; Law of Damages in Scotland, 1955; The Scottish Legal System, 1959, 6th edn 1992; Law of Delict in Scotland, 1966, 2nd edn 1981; Scottish Courts and Tribunals, 1969, 5th edn 1985; Principles of Scottish Private Law (2 vols), 1970, 4th edn (4 vols), 1988–89; Law of Prescription and Limitation in Scotland, 1973, 4th edn 1990; Law of Civil Remedies in Scotland, 1974; Law of Contracts in Scotland, 1979, 3rd edn 1995; Oxford Companion to Law, 1980; (ed) Stair's Institutions (6th edn), 1981; (ed) Stair Tercentenary Studies, 1981; The Scottish Jurists, 1985; Legal History of Scotland, vol. I, 1988, vol. II, 1990, vol. III, 1995; Scottish Part of Topham and Ivamy's Company Law, 12th edn 1955, to 16th edn 1978; contribs to collaborative works; articles in legal periodicals; *festschrift:* Obligations in Context, ed A. J. Gamble, 1990. *Recreations:* motoring, book collecting, Scottish history. *Address:* 1 Beaumont Gate, Glasgow G12 9EE. *T:* 0141–339 2802. *Club:* Royal Scottish Automobile (Glasgow).

WALKER, Maj.-Gen. Derek William Rothwell; Manager, CBI Overseas Scholarships, 1980–89, retired; *b* 12 Dec. 1924; *s* of Frederick and Eileen Walker; *m* 1950, Florence Margaret Panting; two *s* (and one *s* decd). *Educ:* Mitcham County Grammar Sch.; Battersea Polytechnic. FIMechE 1970–89; FIEE 1971–89. Commissioned REME, 1946; served: Middle East, 1947–50 (despatches 1949); BAOR, 1951–53; Far East, 1954–56 (despatches 1957); Near East, 1960–62; Far East, 1964–67; psc 1957. Lt-Col 1964, Col 1970, Brig. 1973. Appts include: Comdr, REME Support Group, 1976–77; Dir, Equipment Engineering, 1977–79. Mem. Council, IEE, 1975–79; Pres., SEE, 1979–81. *Recreations:* fishing, sailing, wine-making. *Address:* 26 Cranford Drive, Holybourne, Alton, Hants GU34 4HJ. *T:* Alton (01420) 84737.

WALKER, Prof. Donald, FRS 1985; Professor of Biogeography, Institute of Advanced Studies, Australian National University, Canberra, 1969–88; *b* 14 May 1928; *s* of Arthur Walker and Eva (*née* Risdon); *m* 1959, Patricia Mary Smith; two *d*. *Educ:* Morecambe Grammar School; Sheffield Univ. (BSc); MA, PhD Cantab. Commission, RAF (Nat. Service), 1953–55. Research Scholar and Asst in Res., later Sen. Asst, Sub-Dept of Quaternary Res., Cambridge Univ., 1949–60; Fellow of Clare College, 1952–60 (Asst Tutor, 1955–60); Reader in Biogeography, ANU, 1960–68; Head of Dept of Biogeography and Geomorphology, ANU, 1969–88. Hon. Prof., Chinese Acad. of Science, 1986–. *Publications:* articles on plant ecology, palaeoecology and related topics in sci. jls. *Recreations:* pottery, architecture, prehistory. *Address:* 8 Galali Place, Aranda, ACT 2614, Australia. *T:* (6) 2513136.

WALKER, Prof. Frederick, MD; FRCPath; Regius Professor of Pathology, University of Aberdeen, since 1984; Consultant Pathologist, Grampian Health Board, since 1984; *b* 21 Dec. 1934; *s* of Frederick James Walker and Helen Stitt Halliday; *m* 1963, Cathleen Anne Gordon, BSc; two *d*. *Educ:* Kirkcudbright Academy; Univ. of Glasgow. MB ChB 1958; PhD 1964; MD 1971; MRCPath 1966, FRCPath 1978. Lectr in Pathology, Univ. of Glasgow, 1962–67; Vis. Asst Prof., Univ. of Minnesota, 1964–65; Sen. Lectr in Pathology, Univ. of Aberdeen, 1968–73; Foundation Prof. of Pathology, Univ. of Leicester, 1973–84. Chm., Nat. Quality Assurance Adv. Panel (Histopathology and Cytology), 1991–; Mem. Council, RCPath, 1990–93; Chm. and Gen. Sec., Pathol Soc. of GB and Ireland, 1992– (Mem. Cttee, 1990–92). Gen. Editor, Biopsy Pathology Series, 1978–; Editor, Jl of Pathology, 1983–93. *Publications:* papers in scientific and med. jls. *Recreations:* writing, walking. *Address:* Department of Pathology, University Medical Buildings, Foresterhill, Aberdeen AB9 2ZD. *T:* Aberdeen (01224) 681818.

WALKER, George Alfred; Chief Executive, Walkers International, 1992; *b* 14 April 1929; *s* of William James Walker and Ellen (*née* Page); *m* 1957, Jean Maureen Walker (*née* Hatton); one *s* two *d*. *Educ:* Jubilee Sch., Bedford, Essex. Formerly boxer and boxing manager; Amateur Boxing Champion, GB, 1951. *Recreations:* ski-ing, ocean racing, climbing. *Address:* Pell House, High Road, Fobbing, Essex SS17 9JJ.

WALKER, Dr George Patrick Leonard, FRS 1975; G. A. Macdonald Professor of Volcanology, University of Hawaii, 1981–95; *b* 2 March 1926; *s* of Leonard Richard Thomas Walker and Evelyn Frances Walker; *m* 1958, Hazel Rosemary (*née* Smith); one *s* one *d*. *Educ:* Wallace High Sch., Lisburn, N Ire.; Queen's Univ., Belfast (BSc, MSc); Univ. of Leeds (PhD 1956); Univ. of London (DSc 1982). Research, Univ. of Leeds, 1948–51; Asst Lectr and Lectr, Imperial Coll., 1951–64; Reader in Geology, Imperial Coll., 1964–79; Captain J. Cook Res. Fellow, Royal Soc. of NZ, 1978–80. Fellow: Geol Soc. of America, 1987; Amer. Geophysical Union, 1988. Awarded moiety of Lyell Fund of Geological Soc. of London, 1963, Lyell Medal, 1982; Wollaston Medal, 1995. Hon. Member: Vísindafjelag Íslendinga, (Iceland), 1968; Royal Soc. of NZ, 1987. Hon. DSc Iceland, 1988. McKay Hammer Award, Geol Soc. of NZ, 1982. Icelandic Order of the Falcon, Knight's Class, 1980. *Publications:* scientific papers on mineralogy, the geology of Iceland, and volcanology. *Recreation:* visiting volcanoes. *Address:* 1 Huntley Close, Abbey Mead, Gloucester, Glos GL4 7GU.

WALKER, Sir Gervas (George), Kt 1979; JP; DL; Chairman and Leader, Avon County Council, 1973–81; *b* 12 Sept. 1920; *yr s* of late Harry James Walker and Susanna Mary Walker; *m* 1944, Jessie Eileen (*née* Maxwell); two *s*. *Educ:* Monmouth Sch. Bristol City Council: Councillor, 1956–74; Alderman, 1970–74; Leader of Council, 1966–72; Leader of Opposition Party, 1972–74; Chm., Planning and Transportation Cttee, 1960–63 and 1966–72; Chm., Bristol Avon River Authority, 1963–66. Member: SW Regional Economic Planning Council, 1972–79; Local Authorities' Conditions of Service Adv. Bd, 1974–81; Severn Barrage Cttee, 1978–81; British Rail (Western) Bd, 1979–85. Chm., Assoc. of County Councils, 1979–81 (Vice-Chm., 1978–79). Chairman, Bristol Conservative Assoc., 1975–79. JP Bristol, 1969; DL Avon, 1982. *Recreation:* fly-fishing. *Address:* Bulverton Well Farm, Sidmouth, Devon EX10 9DW. *T:* Sidmouth (01395) 516902.

WALKER, Rt. Hon. Sir Harold, Kt 1992; PC 1979; MP (Lab) Doncaster Central, since 1983 (Doncaster, 1964–83); *b* 12 July 1927; *s* of Harold and Phyllis Walker; *m* 1984, Mary Griffin; one *d* by former marriage. *Educ:* Manchester College of Technology. Served RN, 1946–48. An Assistant Government Whip, 1967–68; Jt Parly Under-Sec. of State, Dept of Employment and Productivity, 1968–70; Opposition Front-Bench spokesman on Industrial Relations, 1970–74, on Employment, 1979–83; Parly Under-Sec. of State, Dept of Employment, 1974–76; Minister of State, Dept of Employment, 1976–79; Chm. of Ways and Means and Dep. Speaker, H of C, 1983–92. *Recreations:* reading, gardening. *Address:* House of Commons, SW1A 0AA. *Clubs:* Westminster, Clay Lane, Doncaster Trades, RN, Catholic (all Doncaster).

WALKER, Sir Harold (Berners), KCMG 1991 (CMG 1979); HM Diplomatic Service, retired; *b* 19 Oct. 1932; *s* of late Admiral Sir Harold Walker, KCB, RN, and Lady Walker (*née* Berners); *m* 1960, Jane, *d* of late Capt. C. J. L. Bittleston, CBE, DSC, RN; one *s* two *d*. *Educ:* Winchester; Worcester Coll., Oxford. BA 1955. 2nd Lieut RE, 1951–52. Foreign Office, 1955; MECAS, 1957; Asst Political Agent, Dubai, 1958; Foreign Office, 1960; Principal Instructor, MECAS, 1963; First Sec., Cairo, 1964; Head of Chancery and Consul, Damascus, 1966; Foreign Office (later FCO), 1967; First Sec. (Commercial), Washington, 1970; Counsellor, Jedda, 1973; Dep. Head, Personnel Operations Dept, FCO, 1975–76, Head of Dept, 1976–78; Corpus Christi Coll., Cambridge, 1978; Ambassador to Bahrein, 1979–81, to United Arab Emirates, 1981–86, to Ethiopia, 1986–90, to Iraq, 1990–91; retd 1992. Member: Commonwealth War Graves Commn, 1992–; Bd, CARE Britain, 1992– (Chm., 1994–). Pres., Friends of Imperial War Mus., 1992–. Chm., Bahrain Soc., 1993–. Associate Fellow, RUSI, 1992–. *Recreation:* tennis. *Address:* Turaco House, Hook Heath Avenue, Woking, Surrey GU22 0HX. *Club:* United Oxford & Cambridge University.

WALKER, His Honour Judge Harry; *see* Walker, P. H. C.

WALKER, Major Sir Hugh (Ronald), 4th Bt, *cr* 1906; *b* 13 Dec. 1925; *s* of Major Sir Cecil Edward Walker, 3rd Bt, DSO, MC, and Violet (*née* McMaster); *S* father, 1964; *m* 1971, Norna, *er d* of Lt-Cdr R. D. Baird, RNR; two *s*. *Educ:* Wellington Coll., Berks. Joined Royal Artillery, 1943; commissioned Sept. 1945; 2 iC, RA Range, Benbecula, Outer Hebrides, 1964–66; Commanding No 1 Army Information Team, in Aden and Hong Kong, 1966–68; Larkhill, 1969–73, retired. Mem., Assoc. of Supervisory and Executive Engineers. *Recreation:* horses. *Heir:* *s* Robert Cecil Walker, *b* 26 Sept. 1974. *Address:* Ballinamona, Hospital, Kilmallock, Co. Limerick, Ireland.

WALKER, Rev. Dr James Bernard; Chaplain, St Andrews University, since 1993; *b* 7 May 1946; *s* of Rev. Dr Robert B. W. Walker and Grace B. Walker; *m* 1972, Sheila Mary Easton; three *s*. *Educ:* Hamilton Academy, Lanarkshire; Edinburgh Univ. (MA 1st cl. Hons Mental Philosophy 1968; BD 1st cl. Hons Systematic Theol. 1971); Merton Coll., Oxford (DPhil 1981). Church of Scotland minister, ordained 1975, Dundee; Associate Minister, Mid Craigie Parish Church linked with Wallacetown Parish Church, Dundee, 1975–78; Minister, Old and St Paul's Parish Church, Galashiels, 1978–87; Principal, Queen's Coll., Birmingham, 1987–93. *Publications:* Israel—Covenant and Land, 1986; (contrib.) Politique et Théologie chez Athanase d' Alexandrie (ed C. Kannengiesser), 1974. *Recreations:* golf, tennis, swimming, hill walking. *Address:* The Chaplaincy Centre, University of St Andrews, 3a St Mary's Place, St Andrews, Fife KY16 9UY. *T:* St Andrews (01334) 462865.

WALKER, James Findlay, QPM 1964; Commandant, National Police College, 1973–76; *b* 20 May 1916; *m* 1941, Gertrude Eleanor Bell (*d* 1993); one *s*. *Educ:* Arbroath High Sch., Angus, Scotland. Joined Metropolitan Police, 1936. Served War, 1943–46: commissioned Black Watch; demobilised rank Captain. Served in Metropolitan Police through ranks to Chief Supt, 1963; Staff of Police Coll., 1963–65; Asst Chief Constable: W Riding Constabulary, 1965–68; W Yorks Constabulary, 1968–70; Dep. Chief Constable, W Yorks Constabulary, 1970–73. *Recreations:* gardening, golf. *Address:* 33 Cortachy Crescent, Kirriemuir, Angus DD8 4TP.

WALKER, Sir James (Graham), Kt 1972; MBE 1963; Part Owner of Cumberland Santa Gertrudis Stud and Camden Park, Greenwoods and Wakefield sheep properties; *b* Bellingen, NSW, 7 May 1913; *s* of late Albert Edward Walker and Adelaide Walker, Sydney, NSW; *m* 1939, Mary Vivienne Maude Poole; two *s* three *d*. *Educ:* New England Grammar Sch., Glen Innes, NSW. Councillor, Longreach Shire Council, 1953– (Chm., 1957–91); Vice-Pres., Local Authorities of Qld, 1966, Sen. Vice-Chm., 1972–89. Dep. Chm., Longreach Pastoral Coll., since inception, 1966–78, Chm. 1978–89. Exec. Mem., Central Western Queensland Local Authorities' Assoc. and Queensland Local Authorities' Assoc., 1964–79. Chm., Central Western Electricity Bd, 1966–76; Dep. Chm., Capricornia Electricity Bd, 1968–76, Chm., 1976–85; Dep. Chm., Longreach Printing Co. Chm., Santa Gertrudis Assoc., Australia, 1976–77. Past Asst Grand Master, United Grand Lodge of Qld, 1970. Session Clerk, St Andrews Church, Longreach, 1948–78. Nat. Chm., Stockman's Hall of Fame and Out Back Heritage Centre, 1983–90. Fellow, Internat. Inst. of Community Service, 1975; Paul Harris Rotary Fellow, Longreach Rotary Club, 1985. Freeman, City of London, 1990. Hon. LLD Queensland Univ., 1985. *Recreations:* bowls, golf, surfing, painting. *Address:* Camden Park, Longreach, Queensland 4730, Australia. *T:* Longreach (7) 4581331. *Clubs:* Queensland, Tattersall's (Brisbane); Longreach, Longreach Rotary, Diggers (Longreach).

WALKER, Sir James Heron, 5th Bt, *cr* 1868; *b* 7 April 1914; *s* of 4th Bt and Synolda, *y d* of late James Thursby-Pelham; *S* father, 1930; *m* 1st, 1939, Angela Margaret, *o d* of Victor Alexandre Beaufort; one *s* (one *d* decd); 2nd, 1972, Sharrone, *er d* of David Read; one *s*. *Educ:* Eton Coll.; Magdalene Coll., Cambridge. *Recreations:* long haired Dachshunds and music. *Heir: s* Victor Stewart Heron Walker [*b* 8 Oct. 1942; *m* 1st, 1969, Caroline Louise (marr. diss. 1982), *d* of late Lt-Col F. E. B. Wignall; two *s* one *d*; 2nd, 1982, Svea, *o d* of late Captain Ernst Hugo Gothard Knutson Borg and of Mary Hilary Borg]. *Address:* Oakhill, Port Soderick, Isle of Man.

See also Baron Cornwallis.

WALKER, John; Director, National Gallery of Art, Washington, DC, 1956–69, now Director Emeritus; *b* 24 Dec. 1906; *s* of Hay Walker and Rebekah Jane Friend; *m* 1937, Lady Margaret Gwendolen Mary Drummond (*d* 1987); one *d* (and one *s* decd). *Educ:* Harvard Univ. (AB). Associate in charge Dept Fine Arts American Acad., Rome, 1935–39 (now Trustee); Chief Curator, National Gall., Washington DC, 1939–56. Connected with protection and preservation of artistic and historic monuments; John Harvard Fellow, Harvard Univ., 1930–31; American Federation of Arts; Board of Advisers, Dumbarton Oaks; Trustee: Andrew W. Mellon Educational and Charitable Trust; American Federation of Arts; Wallace Foundation, NY; National Trust for Historic Preservation; Mem., Art Adv. Panel, National Trust (UK); Member Advisory Council: Univ. of Notre Dame; New York Univ.; Hon. Dr Fine Arts: Tufts Univ., 1958; Brown Univ., 1959; La Salle Coll., 1962; LittD: Notre Dame, 1959, Washington and Jefferson Univs, 1960; LHD: Catholic Univ. of America, 1964; Univ. of New York, 1965; Maryland Inst.; Georgetown Univ., 1966; William and Mary Univ., 1967. Holds foreign decorations. *Publications:* (with Macgill James) Great American Paintings from Smibert to Bellows, 1943; (with Huntington Cairns) Masterpieces of Painting from National Gallery of Art, 1944; Paintings from America, 1951; (with Huntington Cairns) Great Paintings from the National Gallery of Art, 1952; National Gallery of Art, Washington, 1956; Bellini and Titian at Ferrara, 1957; Treasures from the National Gallery of Art, 1963; The National Gallery of Art, Washington, DC, 1964; (with H. Cairns) Pageant of Painting, 1966; Self-Portrait with Donors, 1974; National Gallery of Art, 1976; Turner, 1976; Constable, 1978; Whistler, 1987. *Address:* Easter Barton, Amberley, near Arundel, Sussex BN18 9NE; 214 South Beach Road, Jupiter Island, Hobe Sound, FL 33435, USA. *Clubs:* Turf, Dilettanti, Pilgrims'; Century Association (New York City); Chevy Chase, Metropolitan (Washington, DC).

WALKER, John; Under Secretary, Scottish Development Department, 1985, retired; *b* 16 Dec. 1929; *s* of John Walker and Elizabeth Whyte Fish; *m* 1952, Rena Robertson McEwan; two *d*. *Educ:* Falkirk High School. Entered Civil Service, Min. of Labour, as clerical officer, 1946. National Service, RAF, 1948–50. Asst Principal, Dept of Health for Scotland, 1958; Scottish Home and Health Dept: Principal, 1960; Secretary, Cttee on General Medical Services in the Highlands and Islands, 1964–67; Asst Sec., 1969; Scottish Development Dept, 1975–78; Under Sec., Scottish Home and Health Dept, 1978–85. Asst Comr, Scottish Local Govt Boundary Commn, 1987–94. *Recreations:* grandparenthood, being looked after by Rena. *Address:* 8/1 Back Dean, Ravelston Terrace, Edinburgh EH4 3UA. *T:* 0131–343 3811.

WALKER, His Honour John David, DL; a Circuit Judge, 1972–89; *b* 13 March 1924; *y s* of late L. C. Walker, MA, MB (Cantab), BCh, and late Mrs J. Walker, Malton; *m* 1953, Elizabeth Mary Emma (*née* Owbridge); one *s* two *d*. *Educ:* Oundle (1937–42); Christ's Coll., Cambridge (1947–50); BA 1950, MA 1953. War of 1939–45: commissioned Frontier Force Rifles, Indian Army, 1943; demob., Captain, 1947. Called to the Bar, Middle Temple, 1951; a Recorder, 1972. A Pres., Mental Health Review Tribunals, 1986–. Mem., Parole Bd, 1992–. DL Humberside, 1985. *Recreations:* shooting, fishing. *Address:* Arden House, North Bar Without, Beverley, North Humberside HU17 7AG. *Club:* Lansdowne.

WALKER, John Eric A.; *see* Austin-Walker.

WALKER, John Ernest, DPhil; FRS 1995; Staff Scientist, Medical Research Council, Laboratory of Molecular Biology, Cambridge, since 1974; *b* 7 Jan. 1941; *s* of Thomas Ernest Walker and Elsie (*née* Lawton); *m* 1963, Christina Jane Westcott; two *d*. *Educ.* Rastrick Grammar Sch., W Yorks; St Catherine's Coll., Oxford (BA; DPhil). Vis. Research Fellow, Univ. of Wisconsin, 1969–71; NATO Res. Fellow, CNRS, Gif-sur-Yvette, France, 1971–72; EMBO Res. Fellow, Pasteur Inst., Paris, 1972–74. Mem., EMBO, 1983. Johnson Foundn Prize, Univ. of Pennsylvania, 1994. *Publications:* research papers and reviews in scientific jls. *Recreations:* cricket, opera music, walking. *Address:* MRC Laboratory of Molecular Biology, Hills Road, Cambridge CB2 2QH. *T:* Cambridge (01223) 402239.

WALKER, John Malcolm; Principal Assistant Director of Public Prosecutions (Grade 3), 1985–86, retired; *b* 25 Feb. 1930; *s* of James and Mary Walker; *m* 1955, Barbara Anne Fawcett (*d* 1989); two *d*. *Educ:* St Edward's Sch., Oxford; Leeds Univ. (LLB). Served Royal Artillery, 1948–50. Called to Bar, Gray's Inn, 1955, joined Director of Public Prosecutions as Temp. Legal Asst, 1956; Legal Asst, 1958; Sen. Legal Asst, 1964; Asst Solicitor, 1974, Asst Director, 1977. *Recreations:* music, painting. *Address:* 10 Second Cross Road, Twickenham, Middlesex TW2 5RF.

WALKER, Air Marshal Sir John (Robert), KCB 1992; CBE 1978; AFC; Ministry of Defence, 1989–95; *b* 26 May 1936. rcds; psc. SASO, Strike Comd, 1985–87; Dep. CoS (Ops), HQ AAFCE, 1987–89. Wing Comdr 1970; Gp Capt. 1975; Air Cdre 1980; Air Vice-Marshal 1986; Air Marshal 1991. *Address:* c/o Ministry of Defence, Main Building, Whitehall, SW1A 2HB.

WALKER, Julian Fortay, CMG 1981; MBE 1960; HM Diplomatic Service, retired; Special Adviser on Syria, 1987–93, and on Iraq, 1990–93, Research and Analysis Department, Foreign and Commonwealth Office; *b* 7 May 1929; *s* of Kenneth Macfarlane Walker, FRCS, and Eileen Marjorie Walker (*née* Wilson); *m* 1983, Virginia Anne Austin (*née* Stevens); three step *d*. *Educ:* Harvey Sch., Hawthorne, New York; Stowe; Bryanston; Cambridge Univ. (MA). National Service, RN, 1947–49; Cambridge, 1949–52; London Univ. Sch. of African and Oriental Studies, 1952. Foreign Service: MECAS, 1953; Asst Political Agent, Trucial States, 1953–55; 3rd and 2nd Sec., Bahrain Residency, 1955–57; FCO and Frontier Settlement, Oman, 1957–60; 2nd and 1st Sec., Oslo, 1960–63; FCO News Dept Spokesman, 1963–67; 1st Sec., Baghdad, 1967; 1st Sec., Morocco (Rabat), 1967–69; FCO, 1969–71; Political Agent, Dubai, Trucial States, 1971, Consul-Gen. and Counsellor, British Embassy, Dubai, United Arab Emirates, 1971–72; Cambridge Univ. on sabbatical leave, 1972–73; Political Advr and Head of Chancery, British Mil. Govt, Berlin, 1973–76; NI Office, Stormont Castle, 1976–77; Dir, MECAS, 1977–78; Ambassador to Yemen Arab Republic and Republic of Jibuti, 1979–84; Ambassador to Qatar, 1984–87. *Publication:* (ed) The UAE Internal Boundaries and Boundaries with Oman, 8 vols, 1994. *Recreations:* skiing, sailing, tennis, music, cooking.

WALKER, Julian Guy Hudsmith, CB 1991; independent consultant; Director General, Policy and Special Projects, Ministry of Defence, 1992–94, retired; *b* 2 Oct. 1936; *s* of Nathanial and Frieda Walker; *m* 1960, Margaret Burns (*née* Jamieson). *Educ:* Winchester College; Southampton Univ. (BSc Mech Eng). CEng, FIMechE. Hawker Aircraft Co., 1958–61; Logistic Vehicles, FVRDE, WO, subseq. MoD, 1961–69; Ministry of Defence: Special Projects, MVEE, 1970–80; Head, Vehicle Engrg Dept, 1980–84; Scientific Adviser (Land), 1984–87; Dir, Estabts and Research (B), 1987–89; Head, RARDE, Chertsey, 1989–92. *Recreations:* vintage cars, photography, wood-turning, Wombling, solving practical problems.

WALKER, Linda, (Mrs P. B. Walker); *see* Sutcliffe, L.

WALKER, Lorna Margaret S.; *see* Secker-Walker.

WALKER, Malcolm Conrad, CBE 1995; Chairman and Chief Executive, Iceland Group plc (formerly Iceland Frozen Foods plc), since 1973; *b* 11 Feb. 1946; *s* of Willie Walker and Ethel Mary Walker; *m* 1969, Nest Rhianydd; one *s* two *d*. *Educ:* Mirfield Grammar Sch. Trainee Manager, F. W. Woolworth & Co., 1964–71; Jt Founder, Iceland Frozen Foods, 1970. Non-exec. Dir, DFS Furniture Co. plc. *Recreations:* ski-ing, shooting, stalking, business, home and family. *Address:* Iceland Group plc, Second Avenue, Deeside Industrial Park, Deeside, Clwyd CH5 2NW. *T:* Deeside (01244) 830100.

WALKER, Sir Michael; *see* Walker, Sir C. M.

WALKER, Michael; His Honour Judge Michael Walker; a Circuit Judge, since 1978; *b* 13 April 1931; *m* 1959, Elizabeth Mary Currie; two *s*. *Educ:* Chadderton Grammar Sch.; Sheffield Univ. (LLM). Called to the Bar, Gray's Inn, 1956. Joined North Eastern Circuit, 1958. A Recorder of the Crown Court, 1972–78.

WALKER, Lt-Gen. Sir Michael John Dawson, KCB 1995; CBE 1990 (OBE 1982); Commander, Ace Rapid Reaction Corps, since 1994; *b* 7 July 1944; *s* of William Hampden Dawson Walker and Dorothy Helena Walker (*née* Shiach); *m* 1973, Victoria Margaret Holme; two *s* one *d*. *Educ:* Milton Sch., Bulawayo; Woodhouse Grove Sch., Yorks; RMA Sandhurst. Commissioned Royal Anglian Regt, 1966; Regtl and Staff duties, 1966–82; Staff Coll., 1976–77; MA to CGS, 1982–85; CO 1 Royal Anglian Regt, 1985–87; Comdr, 20th Armoured Brigade, 1987–89; COS, 1 (Br) Corps, 1989–91; GOC NE District and Comdr, 2nd Inf. Div., 1991–92; GOC Eastern District, 1992; ACGS, MoD, 1992–94. Colonel Commandant: Queen's Div., 1991–; AAC, 1994–; Dep. Col, Royal Anglian Regt, 1991–. *Recreations:* ski-ing, sailing, shooting, golf, family. *Address:* c/o C. Hoare & Co., 37 Fleet Street, EC4P 4DQ.

WALKER, Sir Michael Leolin F.; *see* Forestier-Walker.

WALKER, Miles Rawstron, CBE 1991; Chief Minister, Isle of Man, since 1986; *b* 13 Nov. 1940; *s* of George Denis Walker and Alice (*née* Whittaker); *m* 1966, Mary Lilian Cowell; one *s* one *d*. *Educ:* Arbory Primary Sch.; Castle Rushen High Sch.; Shropshire Coll. of Agric. Company Dir, farming and retail dairy trade, 1960–. Mem. and Chm., Arbory Parish Comrs, 1970–76; Mem., House of Keys for Rushen, 1976–. Hon. LLD. *Address:* Chief Minister's Office, Government Offices, Buck's Road, Douglas, Isle of Man. *T:* Douglas (01624) 685702; Magher Feailley, Main Road, Colby, Isle of Man. *T:* Douglas (01624) 833728.

WALKER, Prof. Nigel David, CBE 1979; MA Oxon, PhD Edinburgh, DLitt Oxon; Wolfson Professor of Criminology and Fellow of King's College, Cambridge, 1973–84 (Director, Institute of Criminology, 1973–81); *b* 6 Aug. 1917; *s* of David B. Walker and Violet Walker (*née* Johnson); *m* 1939, Sheila Margaret Johnston; one *d*. *Educ:* Tientsin Grammar Sch.; Edinburgh Academy; Christ Church, Oxford (Hon. Scholar). Served War, Infantry officer (Camerons and Lovat Scouts), 1940–46. Scottish Office, 1946–61; Gwilym Gibbon Fellow, Nuffield Coll., 1958–59; University Reader in Criminology and Fellow of Nuffield Coll., Oxford, 1961–73. Visiting Professor: Berkeley, 1965; Yale, 1973; Stockholm, 1978; Cape Town, 1984. Chairman: Home Secretary's Adv. Council on Probation and After-care, 1972–76; Study Gp on Legal Training of Social Workers, 1972–73; President: Nat. Assoc. of Probation Officers, 1980–84; British Soc. of Criminology, 1984–87; Member: Home Sec.'s TV Research Cttee, 1963–69; Adv. Council on Penal System, 1969–73; Cttee on Mentally Abnormal Offenders, 1972–75; Working Party on Judicial Training and Information, 1975–78; Floud Cttee on Dangerous Offenders; Hodgson Cttee on Profits of Crime; Parole Bd, 1986–89. Hon. LLD: Leicester, 1976, Edinburgh 1985. Hon. FRCPsych 1987. *Publications:* Delphi, 1936 (Chancellor's Prize Latin Poem); A Short History of Psychotherapy, 1957 (various trans); Morale in the Civil Service, 1961; Crime and Punishment in Britain, 1965; Crime and Insanity in England, 2 vols, 1968 and 1972; Sentencing in a Rational Society, 1969 (various trans.); Crimes, Courts and Figures, 1971; Explaining Misbehaviour (inaug. lecture), 1974; Treatment and Justice (Sandoz lecture), 1976; Behaviour and Misbehaviour, 1977; Punishment, Danger and Stigma, 1980; Sentencing Theory Law and Practice, 1985; Crime and Criminology, 1987; (jtly) Public Attitudes to Sentencing, 1988; Why Punish?, 1991 (Italian trans.); reports, articles, etc. *Recreations:* chess, hill-climbing. *Address:* King's College, Cambridge CB2 1ST. *Club:* Royal Society of Medicine.

WALKER, Noel John; Chief Executive, Commission for the New Towns, since 1992; *b* 18 Dec. 1948; *s* of Robert and Nora Walker; *m* 1979, Pamela Gordon; two *s*. *Educ:* Liverpool Univ. (BSc 1970); Trent Polytechnic (DipTP 1972). Planning Officer, Hartlepool BC, 1972–74; Sen. Planner, Cleveland CC, 1974; travelled abroad, 1974–75; Milton Keynes Development Corporation: Employment Planner, 1975–76; Head of Policy Evaluation, 1976–78; Dep. Planning Manager, 1978–79; Planning Manager, 1979–80; Dir of Planning, 1980–87; Dep. Gen. Manager, 1987–92. Chm., Bucks Manpower Cttee, 1982–83. Founder Mem., Nat. Energy Foundn, 1988–. Board Member: Milton Keynes Marketing, 1992–93; Telford Develt Agency, 1992–; Peterborough Develt Agency, 1992–94. *Recreations:* squash, gardening, travelling. *Address:* Fullers Barn, The Green, Loughton, Milton Keynes MK5 8AW.

WALKER, Patricia Kathleen Randall; *see* Mann, P. K. R.

WALKER, Sir Patrick (Jeremy), KCB 1990; *b* 25 Feb. 1932; *s* of late Reginald Plumer Walker, sometime Chief Accountant, East African Railways, and Gladys Walker; *m* 1955, Susan Mary Hastings; two *s* one *d*. *Educ:* King's Sch., Canterbury; Trinity Coll., Oxford (MA). Uganda Admin, 1956–62; Ministry of Defence, Security Service, 1963–92, Dir Gen., 1988–92. Chm., Internat. Cttee, Leonard Cheshire Foundn, 1995. *Recreations:* music, African history, art. *Club:* United Oxford & Cambridge University.

WALKER, Dr Paul Crawford; Senior Partner, Independent Public Health, since 1994; *b* 9 Dec. 1940; *s* of Joseph Viccars Walker and Mary Tilley (*née* Crawford); *m* 1963, Barbara Georgina Bliss; three *d*. *Educ:* Queen Elizabeth Grammar Sch., Darlington; Downing Coll., Cambridge (MA); University College Hospital Med. Sch. (MB, BChir); Edinburgh Univ. (DipSocMed); Harvard Bus. Sch. (Program for Health Systems Management, 1980). FFPHM (FFCM 1980). Asst Senior Medical Officer, Birmingham Regional Hosp. Bd, 1969–72; Dep. Medical Officer of Health and Dep. Principal Sch. MO, Wolverhampton County Borough Council, 1972–74; District Community Physician, Staffordshire AHA, 1974–76; Area MO, Wakefield AHA, 1976–77; Regional MO, NE Thames RHA, 1978–85; Dist Gen. Manager, Frenchay HA, 1985–88; Hon. Consultant in Community

Medicine, Bristol and Weston HA, 1988–89; Dir of Public Health, Norwich HA, 1989–93; Sen. Lectr in Applied Epidemiology, Univ. of Wales Coll. of Medicine, 1993–94. Hon. Sen. Lectr, Dept of Community Medicine, LSHTM, 1983–85; Co-Dir, Centre for Health Policy Res., UEA, 1990–93; Vis. Prof., QMC, London Univ., 1985. Governor, Moorfields Eye Hosp., 1981–82; Vice-Chm., Professional Adv. Gp, NHS Trng Authy, 1986–88; Member: Bd of Management, LSHTM, 1983–85; Adv. Cttee on Drug Misuse, 1983–87; Exec. Cttee, Greater London Alcohol Adv. Service, 1978–85; NHS Computer Policy Cttee, 1984–85; Editl Bd, Jl of Management in Medicine, 1985–; Norwich HA, 1989–93; Frenchay Mental Handicap Trust, 1986–88; Frenchay Mental Health Trust, 1986–88; Norwich and Norfolk Care Trust, 1991–; Frenchay Community Care Trust, 1994–; Peckham Pioneer Health Centre Ltd, 1994–. Chm., Stoke Bishop and Sea Mills Br., Labour Party. JP Epping and Ongar, 1980–85. Captain, RAMC (V). FIMgt (FBIM 1988). *Publications:* Healthy Norfolk People, 1990; (ed) Helping People with Disabilities in East Anglia, 1991; contribs to medical and health service jls. *Recreations:* music, natural history, railway history. *Address:* Chagford, 8 Church Avenue, Sneyd Park, Bristol BS9 1LD. *Club:* Athenæum.

WALKER, Paul Francis; Marketing Consultant, Royal College of Pathologists, since 1991; *b* 22 April 1932; *s* of Robert Philip Sebastian Walker and Nora (*née* Parsons); *m* 1961, Sally Jonquil Taylor; three *s*. *Educ:* Stonyhurst Coll.; London Univ. BBC studio manager and announcer, 1953–55; TV producer and Internat. Exec., J. Walter Thompson, 1955–72; Educn Dir, Help The Aged, 1972–73; Exec. Dir, Muscular Dystrophy Gp of GB and NI, 1973–91. Mem., English Cttee, Internat. Year of Disabled People, 1981. Founder Trustee, Stackpole Trust, 1981–; Trustee: Child Rescue International, 1986–; Patrick Foundn, 1987–. Pres., Neuromuscular Centre, 1992–95. *Recreations:* bridge, snooker. *Address:* The Quarry, Quarry Road, Oxted, Surrey RH8 9HF. *T:* Oxted (01883) 712834.

WALKER, Pauline Ann, (Mrs D. D. Walker); *see* Oliver, P. A.

WALKER, Rt. Rev. Peter Knight, MA, DD; Bishop of Ely, 1977–89; an Hon. Assistant Bishop, diocese of Oxford, since 1989; *b* 6 Dec. 1919; *s* of late George Walker and Eva Muriel (*née* Knight); *m* 1973, Mary Jean, JP 1976, *yr d* of late Lt-Col J. A. Ferguson, OBE. *Educ:* Leeds Grammar Sch. (Schol.); The Queen's Coll., Oxford (Hastings schol.; Cl. 2 Classical Hon. Mods. 1940, Cl. 1 Lit. Hum. 1947; MA Oxon 1947; Hon. Fellow, 1981); Westcott House, Cambridge. MA Cantab by incorporation, 1958; Hon. DD Cantab, 1978. Served in RN (Lieut, RNVR), 1940–45. Asst Master: King's Sch., Peterborough, 1947–50; Merchant Taylors' Sch., 1950–56. Ordained, 1954; Curate of Hemel Hempstead, 1956–58; Fellow, Dean of Chapel and Lectr in Theology, Corpus Christi Coll., Cambridge, 1958–62 (Asst Tutor, 1959–62), Hon. Fellow, 1978; Principal of Westcott House, Cambridge, 1962–72; Commissary to Bishop of Delhi, 1962–66; Hon. Canon of Ely Cathedral, 1966–72; Bishop Suffragan of Dorchester, and Canon of Christ Church, Oxford, 1972–77. Select Preacher: Univ. of Cambridge, 1962, 1967 (Hulsean), 1986; Univ. of Oxford, 1975, 1980, 1990; Examining Chaplain to Bishop of Portsmouth, 1962–72. Chm., Hosp. Chaplaincies Council, 1982–86. Pres., British Sect., Internat. Bonhoeffer Soc., 1987–. A Governor, St Edward's Sch., Oxford. Hon. Fellow: St John's Coll., Cambridge, 1989; St Edmund's Coll., Cambridge, 1989. *Publications:* The Anglican Church Today: rediscovering the middle way, 1988; contrib. to: Classical Quarterly; Theology, etc. *Address:* Anchorage House, The Lanes, Bampton, Oxon OX18 2LA. *T:* Bampton Castle (01993) 850943. *Club:* Cambridge County.

WALKER, Prof. Peter Martin Brabazon, CBE 1976; FRSE; Honorary Professor and Director, MRC Mammalian Genome Unit, 1973–80; *b* 1 May 1922; *e s* of Major Ernest Walker and Mildred Walker (*née* Heaton-Ellis), Kenya; *m* 1st, 1943, Violet Norah Wright (*d* 1985); one *s* three *d*; 2nd, 1986, Joan Patricia Taylor; one *d*. *Educ:* Haileybury Coll.; Trinity Coll., Cambridge, 1945. BA, PhD. Tool and instrument maker, 1939 (during War); Scientific Staff, MRC Biophysics Research Unit, King's Coll., London, 1948; Royal Society Research Fellow, Edinburgh, 1958; Univ. of Edinburgh: Lectr in Zoology, 1962; Reader in Zoology, 1963; Professor of Natural History, 1966–73. Member: Biological Research Bd, MRC, 1967 (Chm., 1970–72); MRC, 1970–72; Ext. Scientific Staff, MRC, 1980–84; Chief Scientist Cttee, Scottish Home and Health Dept, 1973–85; Chm., Equipment Res. Cttee, Scottish Home and Health Dept, 1973–79; Mem. Council, Imp. Cancer Res. Fund, 1971–; Chm., Imp. Cancer Res. Fund Scientific Adv. Cttee, 1975–85; Mem., Scientific Adv. Cttee of European Molecular Biology Lab., 1976–81. General Editor: Chambers Science & Technology Dictionary, 1985–; Chambers Biology Dictionary, 1989; Chambers Air and Space Dictionary, 1990; Chambers Earth Sciences Dictionary, 1991. *Publications:* contribs to the molecular biology of the genetic material of mammals in: Nature; Jl of Molecular Biology, etc. *Recreations:* gardening, design of scientific instruments, railway history. *Address:* Drumlaggan, The Ross, Comrie, Perthshire. *T:* Comrie (01764) 70303.

WALKER, Philip Andrew Geoffrey; Editor, Daily Star, since 1994; *b* 28 July 1944; *m* 1st, 1965, Stella Kaspar; one *s* three *d*; 2nd, 1987, Sharon Ring. *Educ:* Howardian High Sch., Cardiff. South Wales Echo, 1962–64; Daily Sketch, 1964–65; Evening Post, Reading, 1966–68; Daily Mail, 1968–69; Asst Editor, Daily Mirror, 1969–80; Associate Editor, Daily Express, 1980–83; Dep. Editor, Daily Mirror, 1983–88; freelance journalist, 1988–90; Dep. Editor, Daily Star, 1990–94. *Recreation:* twitching. *Address:* Daily Star, Express Newspapers, Ludgate House, 245 Blackfriars Road, SE1 9UX. *T:* 0171–928 8000.

WALKER, Philip Gordon, FCA; Chairman: Chapman Industries PLC, 1968–83; *b* 9 June 1912; *s* of late William and Kate Blanche Walker; *m* 1st, 1938, Anne May (marr. diss.); one *s* two *d*; 2nd, 1962, Elizabeth Oliver. *Educ:* Epworth Coll., Rhyl, North Wales. Bourner, Bullock & Co., Chartered Accountants, 1929–35; Walkers (Century Oils) Ltd, 1935–40; Layton Bennett, Billingham & Co., Chartered Accountants, 1940, Partner, 1944–51 (now Arthur Young McLelland Moore); Albert E. Reed & Co Ltd (now Reed International), Man. Dir, 1951–63; Chm. and Man. Dir, Philblack Ltd, 1963–71; Chm., Sun Life Assurance Soc. Ltd, 1971–82 (Exec. Chm. 1976–82). Part-time Mem. Monopolies Commn, 1963–65; Member: Performing Right Tribunal, 1971–83; Restrictive Practices Court, 1973–83. *Recreation:* golf. *Address:* The Garden Flat, Scotswood, Devenish Road, Sunningdale, Berks SL5 9QP. *Clubs:* Brooks's; Wildernesse (Sevenoaks); Rye; Berkshire.

WALKER, Philip Henry Conyers; His Honour Judge Harry Walker; a Circuit Judge, since 1979; *b* 22 Dec. 1926; *o c* of Philip Howard and Kathleen Walker; *m* 1953, Mary Elizabeth Ross; two *s* two *d*. *Educ:* Marlborough; Oriel Coll., Oxford. MA, BCL (Oxon); DipTh (London). Army (6 AB Sigs), 1944–48 (despatches, 1948). Solicitor in private practice, 1954–79; a Recorder of the Crown Court, 1972–79. Mem., Church Assembly, Nat. Synod of C of E, 1960–80. Chm., Agricultural Land Tribunal (Yorks & Lancs), 1977–79; Dep. Chm., Agricultural Land Tribunal (Western), 1989–; Mem., Criminal Law Revision Cttee, 1981–. *Recreations:* fishing, shooting, sailing, walking. *Address:* Pond House, Askwith, Otley, West Yorks LS21 2JN. *T:* Otley (01943) 463196.

WALKER, Raymond Augustus; QC 1988; a Recorder, since 1993; *b* 26 Aug. 1943; *s* of Air Chief Marshal Sir Augustus Walker, GCB, CBE, DSO, DFC, AFC and Lady Walker; *m* 1976, June Rose Tunesi; one *s*. *Educ:* Radley; Trinity Hall, Cambridge (BA). Called to the Bar, Middle Temple, 1966. *Recreations:* golf, tennis, ski-ing, sailing, opera. *Address:* 1 Harcourt Buildings, Temple, EC4. *T:* 0171–353 0375. *Clubs:* Garrick; Royal Dornoch Golf, Royal West Norfolk Golf, Huntercombe Golf, Sunningdale Golf.

WALKER, Raymond James, OBE 1991; Chief Executive, Simpler Trade Procedures Board (formerly Simplification of International Trade Procedures Board), since 1983; *b* 13 April 1943; *s* of Cyril James Walker and Louie Walker; *m* 1969, Mary Eastwood Whittaker; one *d*. *Educ:* St Audreys', Hatfield; University of Lancaster. BA (Hons). Personnel Director, Saracen Ltd, 1971–73; Jt Man. Dir, Carrington Viyella Exports Ltd, 1973–78; Export Dir, Carrington Viyella Home Furnishings (DORMA), 1978–83. Co-Chm., Jt Electronic Data Interchange Cttee, UN Econ. Commn for Europe, 1985–87; Rapporteur for Western Europe, UN-Electronic Data Interchange for Admin, Commerce and Transport, 1987–. Amer. Nat. Standards Inst. Award, 1986; Electronic Data Interchange Award, Internat. Data Exchange Assoc., 1988. *Recreations:* collecting wine labels, a fascination for maps, growing clematis. *Clubs:* Royal Automobile; Belle Toute (Lancaster).

WALKER, Richard; His Honour Judge Richard Walker; a Circuit Judge, since 1989; *b* 9 March 1942; *s* of Edwin Roland Walker and Barbara Joan (*née* Swann); *m* 1969, Angela Joan Hodgkinson; two *d*. *Educ:* Epsom Coll.; Worcester Coll., Oxford (MA). Called to the Bar, Inner Temple, 1966; in practise at the Bar, 1966–89; Asst Boundary Comr, 1979–88; a Recorder, 1989. Judicial Mem., Mental Health Review Tribunal, 1991–. Commissary Gen., City and Dio. of Canterbury, 1995–. *Publication:* (ed jtly) Carter-Ruck on Libel and Slander, 3rd edn 1985, 4th edn 1992. *Address:* c/o 1 Brick Court, Temple, EC4Y 9BY. *T:* 0171–353 8845.

WALKER, Richard Alwyne F.; *see* Fyjis-Walker.

WALKER, Richard John Boileau, MA; FSA; picture cataloguer; *b* 4 June 1916; *s* of Comdr Kenneth Walker and Caroline Livingstone-Learmonth; *m* 1946, Margaret, *d* of Brig. Roy Firebrace, CBE; one *s* two *d*. *Educ:* Harrow; Magdalene Coll., Cambridge (MA); Courtauld Institute of Art. Active service, RNVR, 1939–45. British Council, 1946; Tate Gallery, 1947–48; Min. of Works Picture Adviser, 1949–76; Curator of the Palace of Westminster, 1950–76; Nat. Portrait Gallery Cataloguer, 1976–85; Royal Collection Cataloguer, 1985–91; Nat. Trust Cataloguer, 1990–. Trustee: Nat. Maritime Museum, 1977–84; Army Museums Ogilby Trust, 1979–90. *Publications:* Catalogue of Pictures at Audley End, 1950 and 1973; Old Westminster Bridge, 1979; Regency Portraits, 1985; Palace of Westminster: a catalogue, 4 vols, 1988; Royal Collection: the 18th century miniatures, 1992. *Recreations:* looking at pictures and finding quotations. *Address:* 31 Cadogan Place, SW1X 9RX. *T:* 0171–235 1801. *Clubs:* Athenæum, United Oxford & Cambridge University.

WALKER, Robert; HM Diplomatic Service, retired; *b* 1 May 1924; *s* of Young and Gladys Walker, Luddendenfoot, Yorks; *m* 1949, Rita Thomas; one *s* one *d*. *Educ:* Sowerby Bridge Grammar Sch.; Peterhouse, Cambridge. Commissioned RNVR 1944; served in minesweepers in home waters. Cambridge, 1942–43 and 1946–48; BA Hons History, 1948; MA 1963. Joined CRO, 1948; served Peshawar and Karachi, 1949–51; New Delhi, 1955–59; Sen. First Sec., Accra, 1962–64; Dep. British High Comr, in Ghana, 1964–65; FCO, 1965–68. IDC, 1969; Commercial Counsellor, Ankara, 1970–71; Dep. High Comr, Nairobi, 1971–72. Dep. Registrar, Hull Univ., 1972–79. Mem., Craven DC, 1984– (Chm., 1991–92). Contested (L): Haltemprice, Feb. and Oct. 1974, 1979; Humberside, European election, 1979; South Ribble, 1983. Mem., Liberal Party Council, 1976–87; Chm., Yorkshire Liberal Fedn, 1977–81. Mem. Council, Lancaster Univ., 1986–94. Founder Mem. and first Chm., Ribblesdale Trust, 1987–94. Mem. Cttee, Yorkshire Dales Nat. Park, 1992–. *Recreations:* golf, country wine making. *Address:* Manor Farm, Langcliffe, North Yorks BD24 9NQ. *T:* Settle (01729) 823205.

WALKER, Hon. Sir Robert, Kt 1994; **Hon. Mr Justice Walker;** a Judge of the High Court of Justice, Chancery Division, since 1994; *b* 17 March 1938; *s* of Ronald Robert Antony Walker and Mary Helen Walker (*née* Welsh); *m* 1962, Suzanne Diana Leggi; one *s* three *d*. *Educ:* Downside Sch.; Trinity Coll., Cambridge (BA). Called to Bar, Lincoln's Inn, 1960, Bencher 1990; QC 1982; in practice at Chancery Bar, 1961–94. *Address:* c/o Royal Courts of Justice, Strand, WC2A 2LL.

WALKER, Rodney Myerscough; Chairman: Sports Council of Great Britain, 1994–Apr. 1996; English Sports Council, from April 1996; Rugby Football League, since 1993; *b* 10 April 1943; *s* of Norman and Lucy Walker; *m* 1974, Anne Margaret Aspinall; two *s*. *Educ:* Thornes House Grammar Sch. CEng. Founder Chm., Myerscough Holdings, 1976; activities incl. grass concrete, civil engrg, motor retail, and develt. Mem., Wakefield HA, 1982–90; Chairman: Bradford Hosps NHS Trust; NHS Trust Fedn; W Yorks Broadcasting; Chm., Wakefield Theatre Trust; Vice Chm., Yorks Sculpture Park. FInstD; FRSA. *Recreations:* golf, theatre, travel. *Address:* Walker House, Bond Street, Wakefield WF1 2QP. *T:* Wakefield (01924) 379443; Pine Lodge, Home Farm, Woolley, Wakefield WF4 2JS. *T:* Barnsley (01226) 384089. *Club:* Lansdowne.

WALKER, Comdr Roger Antony Martineau-, RN; Private Secretary to the Duke and Duchess of Kent, 1990–93; Extra Equerry to the Duke of Kent, since 1992; *b* 15 Oct. 1940; *s* of Antony Philip Martineau-Walker and Sheila Hazeal Mayoh Wilson; *m* Inger Lene Brag-Nielsen; two *s*. *Educ:* Haileybury and Imperial Service College, Hertford; BRNC Dartmouth. Commissioned RN, 1962; served Malta, Singapore and Sarawak, 1962–65; Torpedo and Antisubmarine Course, HMS Vernon, 1968; HMS Galatea, 1973–76; NDC Latimer, 1977–78; Naval and Defence Staff, MoD, 1978–83; Naval Manpower Planning, with special responsibility for introd. of longer career for ratings (2nd Open Engagement), 1983–85; operational staff (UK commitments), 1985–87; Head, Naval Sec's Policy Staff, 1987–90; Promotion System Study, 1990. *Recreations:* fishing, photography, music. *Address:* 13 The Peak, Rowlands Castle, Hants PO9 6AH. *Club:* Army and Navy.

WALKER, Ronald Jack; QC 1983; a Recorder, since 1986; *b* 24 June 1940; *s* of Jack Harris Walker and Ann Frances Walker; *m* 1964, Caroline Fox; two *s*. *Educ:* Owen's School, London; University College London. LLB (Hons). Called to the Bar, Gray's Inn, 1962, Bencher, 1993. Mem. Gen. Council of the Bar, 1993– (Chm. Professional Conduct Cttee, 1993–94). *Publications:* English Legal System (with M. G. Walker), 1967, 7th edn 1994; contributing ed., Bullen & Leake & Jacob's Precedents of Pleadings, 13th edn 1990. *Address:* 12 King's Bench Walk, Temple, EC4Y 7EL. *T:* 0171–583 0811.

WALKER, Roy; *see* Walker, C. R.

WALKER, Sarah Elizabeth Royle, (Mrs R. G. Allum), CBE 1991; mezzo-soprano; *d* of Elizabeth Brownrigg and Alan Royle Walker; *m* 1972, Graham Allum. *Educ:* Pate's Grammar School for Girls, Cheltenham; Royal College of Music. FRCM 1987; LRAM. Prince Consort Prof. of Singing, RCM, 1993–. Pres., Cheltenham Bach Choir, 1986–. Major appearances at concerts and in recital in Britain, America, Australia, New Zealand, Europe; operatic débuts include: Coronation of Poppea, Kent Opera, 1969, San Francisco Opera, 1981; La Calisto, Glyndebourne, 1970; Les Troyens, Scottish Opera, 1972, Wien

Staatsoper, 1980; Principal Mezzo Soprano, ENO, 1972–77; Die Meistersinger, Chicago Lyric Opera, 1977; Werther, Covent Garden, 1979; Giulio Caesare, Le Grand Théâtre, Genêve, 1983; Capriccio, Brussels, 1983; Teseo, Sienna, 1985; Samson, NY Metropolitan Opera, 1986; numerous recordings and video recordings, incl. title rôle in Britten's Gloriana. Hon. GSM 1988. *Recreations:* interior design, encouraging her husband with the gardening. *Address:* 152 Inchmery Road, SE6 1DF. *T:* 0181–697 6152.

WALKER, Sheila Mosley, (Mrs Owen Walker), CBE 1981; JP; Chief Commissioner, Girl Guides Association, 1975–80; *b* 11 Dec. 1917; *yr d* of late Charles Eric Mosley Mayne, Indian Cavalry, and Evelyn Mary, *d* of Sir Thomas Skewes-Cox, MP; *m* 1st, 1940, Major Bruce Dawson, MC, Royal Berkshire Regt (killed, Arnhem, 1944); one *s* one *d*; 2nd, 1955, Henry William Owen, *s* of late Sir Henry Walker, CBE; one step *s* one step *d*. *Educ:* St Mary's Hall, Brighton; St James' Secretarial Coll., London. Midlands Regional Chief Comr, 1970–75, Vice-Pres., 1988–, Girl Guides Assoc. Vice-Chm., CPRE, 1988–. JP Nottingham City, 1970. *Recreations:* children, animals, all country and nature conservation. *Address:* Dingley Hall, near Market Harborough, Leics LE16 8PJ. *T:* Market Harborough (01858) 535388. *Club:* New Cavendish (Chm. Bd, 1983–93).

WALKER, Stuart; *see* Walker, B. S.

WALKER, Terence William, (Terry Walker); *b* 26 Oct. 1935; *s* of William Edwin and Lilian Grace Walker; *m* 1959, Priscilla Dart (marr. diss. 1983); two *s* one *d*; *m* 1983, Rosalie Fripp. *Educ:* Grammar Sch. and Coll. of Further Educn, Bristol. Employed by Courage (Western) Ltd at Bristol for 23 yrs, Mem. Chief Accountant's Dept. MP (Lab) Kingswood, Feb. 1974–1979; Second Church Estates Comr, 1974–79. Contested (Lab): Kingswood, 1983; Bristol NW, 1987. Mem., Avon CC, 1981– (Vice-Chm., 1992–93; Chm., 1993–94); Chm., Avon Public Protection Cttee, 1981–86. *Recreations:* cricket, football. *Address:* 28 Cherington Road, Westbury-on-Trym, Bristol BS10 5BJ. *T:* Bristol (0117) 962 3027.

WALKER, Ven. Thomas Overington; Archdeacon of Nottingham, since 1991; *b* 7 Dec. 1933; *m* 1957, Molly Anne Gilmour; one *s* two *d*. *Educ:* Keble Coll., Oxford (BA 1958; MA 1961); Oak Hill Theol Coll. Ordained 1960. Curate: St Paul, Woking, dio. of Guildford, 1960–62; St Leon, St Leonards, dio. of Chichester, 1962–64; Travelling Sec., Inter-Varsity Fellowship, 1964–67; Succentor, Birmingham Cathedral, 1967–70; Vicar, Harborne Heath, 1970–91; Priest-in-charge, St Germain, Edgbaston, 1983–91; Rural Dean, Edgbaston, 1989–91; Hon. Canon, Birmingham Cathedral, 1980–91. Proctor in Convocation, 1985–92. *Publications:* Renew Us By Your Spirit, 1982; The Occult Web, 1987, 3rd edn 1989; From Here to Heaven, 1987; Small Streams Big Rivers, 1991. *Recreations:* sport, music, reading, dry stone walling. *Address:* 16 Woodthorpe Avenue, Woodthorpe, Nottingham NG5 4FD. *T:* Nottingham (0115) 926 7349.

WALKER, Prof. Thomas William, ARCS; DSc; DIC; Professor of Soil Science, Lincoln College, New Zealand, 1961–79, now Emeritus; *b* 22 July 1916; *m* 1940, Edith Edna Bott; four *d*. *Educ:* Loughborough Grammar School; Royal College of Science. Royal Scholar and Kitchener Scholar, 1935–39; Salter's Fellow, 1939–41; Lecturer and Adviser in Agricultural Chemistry, Univ. of Manchester, 1941–46. Provincial Advisory Soil Chemist, NAAS, 1946–51; Prof. of Soil Science, Canterbury Agric. Coll., New Zealand, 1952–58; Prof. of Agric., King's Coll., Newcastle upon Tyne, 1958–61. *Publications:* Vegetable Growers Handbook for New Zealanders, 1992; numerous research. *Recreations:* fishing, gardening. *Address:* 843 Cashmere Road, Christchurch 3, New Zealand.

WALKER, Timothy Edward; QC 1985; a Recorder of the Crown Court, since 1986; *b* 13 May 1946; *s* of George Edward Walker, solicitor, and Muriel Edith Walker; *m* 1968, Mary (*née* Tyndall); two *d*. *Educ:* Harrow Sch.; University Coll., Oxford (MA; Plumptre Schol., 1965; 1st Cl. Hons Jurisprudence). Asst Lectr in Law, King's Coll., London, 1967–68; called to the Bar, Inner Temple, 1968; Eldon Law schol., 1969. *Address:* Fountain Court, Temple EC4Y 9DH. *T:* 0171–583 3335; (home) 58 Lamont Road, SW10 0HX; Eastcourt House, Ham, Wilts SN8 3RB.

WALKER, Timothy Edward Hanson; Deputy Secretary, Home Office, since 1995; *b* 27 July 1945; *s* of late Harris and of Elizabeth Walker; *m* 1st, 1969, Judith Mann (*d* 1976); one *d*; 2nd, 1983, Hon. Anna Butterworth (*see* Hon. A. E. B. Walker); two *d*. *Educ:* Tonbridge Sch.; Brasenose Coll., Oxford (BA Chemistry, 1967; MA, DPhil 1969). Weir Jun. Res. Fellow, University Coll., Oxford, and Exhibnr of Royal Commn of 1851, Oxford and Paris, 1969; Harkness Fellow, Commonwealth Fund of New York, 1971, Univ. of Virginia, 1971 and Northwestern Univ., 1972; Strategic Planner, GLC, 1974; Principal, Dept of Trade, 1977; Sloan Fellow, London Business Sch., 1983; Department of Trade and Industry: Asst Sec., 1983; Dir (Admin), Alvey Programme, 1983; Head, Policy Planning Unit, 1985; Principal Private Sec. to successive Secs of State for Trade and Industry, 1986; Under Sec., 1987; Dir, Inf. Engrg Directorate, 1987; Head, Atomic Energy Div., Dept of Energy, then DTI, 1989–95. Non-exec. Dir, ICI Chemicals and Polymers Ltd, 1988–89. UK Gov., IAEA, 1989–94; non exec. Dir, Govt Div., UKAEA, 1994–95. Chm., Assembly of Donors, Nuclear Safety Account, EBRD, 1993–95. Governor, St Anne's Sch., Wandsworth, 1977–82. *Publications:* contribs to scientific jls. *Recreations:* cookery, gardening, collecting modern prints. *Address:* c/o Home Office, 50 Queen Anne's Gate, SW1H 9AT.

WALKER, Victoria Patricia Ann, (Mrs F. A. Woods Walker); *see* Woods, V. P. A.

WALKER, Walter Basil Scarlett, (Bobby Walker), MA; FCA; Deputy UK Senior Partner, Peat, Marwick, Mitchell & Co., 1979–82; *b* 19 Dec. 1915; *s* of James and Hilda Walker, Southport; *m* 1945, Teresa Mary Louise John; one *d* (and one *s* decd). *Educ:* Rugby Sch.; Clare Coll., Cambridge (MA). Joined Peat, Marwick, Mitchell & Co., 1937, leaving temporarily, 1939, to join RNVR; service in Home Fleet, incl. convoys to Russia and Malta, 1940–42; finally, Asst Sec. to British Naval C-in-C in Germany; Lt-Comdr. Returned to Peat, Marwick, Mitchell & Co., 1946, becoming a partner, 1956. Mem. (part-time), UKAEA, 1972–81. Governor, Royal Ballet, Covent Garden, 1980–90. *Recreations:* ballet, gardening, golf. *Address:* 11 Sloane Avenue, SW3 3JD. *T:* 0171–589 4133; Coles, Privett, near Alton, Hants GU34 3PH. *T:* Privett (01730) 828223. *Club:* Royal Automobile

WALKER, Gen. Sir Walter (Colyear), KCB 1968 (CB 1964); CBE 1959 (OBE 1949); DSO 1946 and Bars, 1953 and 1965; Commander-in-Chief, Allied Forces Northern Europe, 1969–72, retired; *b* 11 Nov. 1912; *s* of late Arthur Colyear Walker; *m* 1938, Beryl (*d* 1990), *d* of late E.N.W. Johnston; two *s* one *d*. *Educ:* Blundell's; RMC, Sandhurst. Waziristan, 1939–41 (despatches twice); Burma, 1942, 1944–46 (despatches, DSO); Malaya, 1949–59 (despatches twice, OBE, Bar to DSO, CBE); Bt Lieut Col, 1952; Atomic Trials, Maralinga, SA, 1956; Dir of Operations, Borneo, 1962–65 (CB, Bar to DSO); Deputy Chief of Staff, HQ ALFCE, 1965; Acting Chief of Staff, 1966–67; GOC-in-C, Northern Command, 1967–69. psc† 1942; jssc 1950; idc 1960. Col, 7th Duke of Edinburgh's Own Gurkha Rifles, 1964–75. Dato Seri Setia, Order of Paduka Stia Negara, Brunei, 1964; Hon. Panglima Mangku Negara, Malaysia, 1965. *Publications:* The Bear at the Back Door, 1978; The Next Domino, 1980. *Recreations:* normal. *Address:* Haydon Farmhouse, Sherborne, Dorset DT9 5JB.

WALKER, William Connoll, (Bill Walker), FIPM; MP (C) Tayside North, since 1983 (Perth and East Perthshire, 1979–83); Chairman, Walker Associates, since 1975; *b* 20 Feb. 1929; *s* of Charles and Williamina Walker; *m* 1956, Mavis Evelyn Lambert; three *d*. *Educ:* Logie Sch., Dundee; Trades Coll., Dundee; College for Distributive Trades. FIPM 1968; FIMgt. Message boy, 1943–44; office boy, 1944–46. Commissioned RAF, 1946–49; Sqdn Leader, RAFVR, 1949–. Salesman, public service vehicle driver, general manager, 1949–59; RAF, 1959–65; training and education officer, furnishing industry, 1965–67; company director, 1967–79; pt-time presenter, TV progs, 1969–75. Director: Stagecoach Malaŵi, 1989–; Stagecoach Internat. Services, 1989–. FRSA 1970. *Recreations:* RAFVR, gliding, caravanning, walking, youth work. *Address:* Candletrees, Golf Course Road, Rosemount, Blairgowrie, Perthshire PH10 6LQ. *T:* Blairgowrie (01250) 2660. *Club:* Royal Air Force.

WALKER, William MacLelland, QC (Scot.) 1971; Social Security Commissioner, since 1988; a Child Support Commissioner, since 1993; *b* 19 May 1933; *s* of late Hon. Lord Walker; *m* 1957, Joan Margaret, *d* of late Charles Hutchison Wood, headmaster, Dundee; one *d*. *Educ:* Edinburgh Academy; Edinburgh Univ. (MA, LLB). Advocate, 1957; Flying Officer, RAF, 1957–59; Standing Junior Counsel: Min. of Aviation, 1963–68; BoT (Aviation), 1968–71; Min. of Technology, 1968–70; Dept of Trade and Industry (Power), 1971; Min. of Aviation Supply, 1971. Chairman: Industrial Tribunals in Scotland, 1972–88; VAT Tribunals, 1985–88. *Recreations:* shooting, travel, photography. *Address:* 58B Manor Place, Edinburgh EH3 7EH; Edenside, Gordon, Berwickshire TD3 6LB. *Clubs:* Royal Air Force; New (Edinburgh).

WALKER-ARNOTT, Edward Ian; Senior Partner, Herbert Smith, since 1992; *b* 18 Sept. 1939; *s* of late Charles Douglas Walker-Arnott and of Kathleen Margaret (*née* Brittain); *m* 1971, (Phyllis) Jane Ricketts; one *s* two *d*. *Educ:* Haileybury Coll.; London Univ. (LLB ext.); University Coll. London (LLM). Admitted solicitor, 1963; Partner, Herbert Smith, 1968–. Dir, Sturge Hldgs, 1989–95. Member: Cork Cttee on Review of Insolvency Law, 1977–82; Insolvency Practitioners Tribunal, 1987–. Mem. Council of Lloyds, 1983–88. Member, Governing Body: Haileybury Coll., 1967–; Benenden Sch., 1987–93. *Recreations:* reading, gardening, cycling, watching sport. *Address:* Manuden Hall, Manuden, near Bishop's Stortford, Herts CM23 1DY. *Club:* City of London.

WALKER-HAWORTH, John Liegh; Director, S. G. Warburg & Co., since 1981; *b* 25 Oct. 1944; *s* of William and Julia Walker-Haworth; *m* 1976, Caroline Mary Blair Purves; two *s*. *Educ:* Charterhouse; Pembroke College, Oxford. Called to the Bar, Inner Temple, 1967. Dir-Gen., City Panel on Take-overs and Mergers, 1985–87. Chm., Charities Effectiveness Review Trust, 1991–93. *Address:* 23 Eldon Road, W8 5PT. *T:* 0171–937 3883.

WALKER-OKEOVER, Sir Peter (Ralph Leopold), 4th Bt *cr* 1886; DL; *b* 22 July 1947; *s* of Colonel Sir Ian Peter Andrew Monro Walker-Okeover, 3rd Bt, DSO, TD, and of Dorothy Elizabeth, *yr d* of Captain Josceline Heber-Percy; *S* father, 1982; *m* 1972, Catherine Mary Maule (marr. diss. 1991), *d* of Colonel George Maule Ramsay; two *s* one *d*. *Educ:* Eton; RMA Sandhurst. Captain, Blues and Royals, retired. DL Staffs, 1992. *Heir:* *s* Andrew Peter Monro Walker-Okeover, *b* 22 May 1978. *Address:* Okeover Hall, Ashbourne, Derbyshire DE6 2DE; House of Glenmuick, Ballater, Aberdeenshire.

WALKER-SMITH, Sir (John) Jonah, 2nd Bt *cr* 1960, of Broxbourne, Co. Herts; a Recorder of the Crown Court, since 1980; *b* 6 Sept. 1939; *s* of Baron Broxbourne (Life Peer), QC, TD and of Dorothy, *d* of late L. J. W. Etherton; *S* to baronetcy of father, 1992; *m* 1974, Aileen Marie Smith; one *s* one *d*. *Educ:* Westminster School; Christ Church, Oxford. Called to Bar, Middle Temple, 1963. *Heir:* *s* Daniel Derek Walker-Smith, *b* 26 March 1980. *Address:* 11 Doughty Street, WC1N 2PG. *Club:* Garrick.

WALKINE, Herbert Cleveland, CMG 1990; CVO 1994; OBE 1985; Secretary to the Cabinet, Bahamas, 1987–94; *b* 28 Nov. 1929; *s* of late Herbert Granville Walkine and Rebecca Walkine; *m* 1966, Julliette Pam Maria Sherman; three *d*. *Educ:* Government High Sch., Nassau; Bahamas Teachers' Coll.; Univ. of Manchester. Started career as teacher; served as District Commissioner, 1958–68; Asst Sec., 1968, First Asst Sec., 1969, Dep. Perm. Sec., 1970, Under Sec., 1972, Perm. Sec., 1974–87, Bahamas. *Recreations:* fishing, reading, watching boxing matches. *Address:* PO Box CB 13333, Nassau, Bahamas. *T:* 3222805.

WALL, Alfreda, (Mrs D. R. Wall); *see* Thorogood, A.

WALL, (Alice) Anne, (Mrs Michael Wall), DCVO 1982 (CVO 1972; MVO 1964); Extra Woman of the Bedchamber to HM the Queen, since 1981; *b* 1928; *d* of late Admiral Sir Geoffrey Hawkins, KBE, CB, MVO, DSC and late Lady Margaret Montagu-Douglas-Scott, *d* of 7th Duke of Buccleuch; *m* 1975, Commander Michael E. St Q. Wall, Royal Navy. *Educ:* Miss Faunce's PNEU School. Asst Press Sec. to the Queen, 1958–81. *Address:* Ivy House, Lambourn, Hungerford, Berks RG17 8PB. *T:* Lambourn (01488) 72348; 6 Chester Way, Kennington, SE11 4UT. *T:* 0171–582 0692.

WALL, Brian Owen, CEng, FRINA; RCNC; Chief Naval Architect, Ministry of Defence, 1985–90; *b* 17 June 1933; *s* of Maurice Stanley Wall and Ruby Wall; *m* 1960, Patricia Thora Hughes; one *s*. *Educ:* Newport High School, Mon; Imperial Coll. of Science and Technology; RN Coll., Greenwich. BSc Eng. ACGI. MoD Bath: Ship Vulnerability, 1958–61; Submarine Design, 1961–66; Head of Propeller Design, Admiralty Experiment Works, Haslar, 1966–71; Staff of C-in-C Fleet, Portsmouth, 1971–73; Submarine Support and Modernisation Group, MoD Bath, 1973–77; RCDS 1977; MoD Bath: Ship Production Div., 1978–79; Project Director, Vanguard Class, 1979–84; Dir, Cost Estimating and Analysis, 1985. *Recreations:* photography, chess, music, walking, golf. *Address:* Wychwood, 39 High Bannerdown, Batheaston, Bath BA1 7JZ.

WALL, Prof. Charles Terence Clegg, FRS 1969; Professor of Pure Mathematics, Liverpool University, since 1965; *b* 14 Dec. 1936; *s* of late Charles Wall, schoolteacher; *m* 1959, Alexandra Joy, *d* of late Prof. Leslie Spencer Hearnshaw; two *s* two *d*. *Educ:* Marlborough Coll.; Trinity Coll., Cambridge. PhD Cantab 1960. Fellow, Trinity Coll., 1959–64; Harkness Fellow, Princeton, 1960–61; Univ. Lectr, Cambridge, 1961–64; Reader in Mathematics, and Fellow of St Catherine's Coll., Oxford, 1964–65. SERC Sen. Fellowship, 1983–88. Royal Soc. Leverhulme Vis. Prof., CIEA, Mexico, 1967. Pres., London Mathematical Soc., 1978–80 (Mem. Council, 1973–80 and 1992–). Fellow, Royal Danish Academy, 1990. Sylvester Medal, Royal Soc., 1988. *Publications:* Surgery on Compact Manifolds, 1970; A Geometric Introduction to Topology, 1972; (with A. A. du Plessis) The Geometry of Topological Stability, 1995; papers on various problems in geometric topology, and related algebra. *Recreations:* gardening, home winemaking. *Address:* 5 Kirby Park, West Kirby, Wirral, Merseyside L48 2HA. *T:* 0151–625 5063.

WALL, David (Richard), CBE 1985; Dance Consultant, Remedial Dance Clinic, since 1991; Director of graduate boys, London Studio Centre, since 1992; *b* 15 March 1946; *s* of Charles and Dorothy Wall; *m* 1967, Alfreda Thorogood, *qv*; one *s* one *d*. *Educ:* Royal Ballet Sch. Joined Royal Ballet Co., Aug. 1964. Promotion to: Soloist, Aug. 1966; Junior Principal Dancer, Aug. 1967; Senior Principal Dancer, Aug. 1968; during period of employment danced all major roles and had many ballets created for him; retired from dancing, 1984. Assoc. Dir, 1984–87, Dir, 1987–91, Royal Acad. of Dancing. Guest repetiteur, London City Ballet, 1993–. Evening Standard Award for Ballet, 1977. *Recreations:* music, theatre. *Address:* 34 Croham Manor Road, South Croydon, Surrey CR2 7BE.

WALL, Rt. Rev. Eric St Quintin; *b* 19 April 1915; *s* of Rev. Sydney Herbert Wall, MA, and Ethel Marion Wall (*née* Wilkins); *m* 1942, Doreen Clare (*née* Loveley); one *s* one *d*. *Educ:* Clifton; Brasenose Coll., Oxford (MA); Wells Theol. College. Deacon, 1938; Priest, 1939; Curate of Boston, 1938–41; Chaplain, RAFVR, 1941–45; Vicar of Sherston Magna, 1944–53; Rural Dean of Malmesbury, 1951–53; Vicar of Cricklade with Latton, 1953–60; Hon. Chaplain to Bp of Bristol, 1960–66; Hon. Canon, Bristol, 1960–72; Diocesan Adviser on Christian Stewardship, Dio. Bristol, 1960–66; Proc. Conv., 1964–69; Vicar, St Alban's, Westbury Park, Bristol, 1966–72; Rural Dean of Clifton, 1967–72; Canon Residentiary of Ely, 1972–80; Bishop Suffragan of Huntingdon, 1972–80. *Recreation:* golf. *Address:* 7 Peregrine Close, Diss, Norfolk IP22 3PG. *T:* Diss (01379) 644331.

WALL, John Anthony, CBE 1994; Chairman, Royal National Institute for the Blind, since 1990; Consultant, Lawrence Graham, solicitors, since 1993 (Partner, 1977–93); *b* 4 June 1930; *s* of George and Edith Wall; *m* 1956, Joan Reeve (*d* 1991); four *s*. *Educ:* Worcester Coll. for the Blind; Balliol Coll., Oxford (MA). Legal Officer, NALGO, 1956–74; Partner, Middleton Lewis, 1974–77; Dep. Master of High Court, Chancery Div., 1990–. Mem., Supreme Ct Rule Cttee, 1993. Sec.-Gen., European Blind Union, 1992– (Mem. Bd, 1990–); Hon. Sec., Soc. of Blind Lawyers, 1993–. Vice-Pres., British Chess Fedn, 1991–. Gold Medal, IBCA Correspondence Chess Olympiad, 1987. *Publications:* articles in learned periodicals. *Recreation:* chess (Oxford *v* Cambridge 1949 and 1951). *Address:* 20 Cleveland Road, Worcester Park, Surrey KT4 7JH. *T:* 0181–330 1290. *Club:* Reform.

WALL, (John) Stephen, CMG 1990; LVO 1983; HM Diplomatic Service; Ambassador and UK Permanent Representative to the European Union, Brussels, since 1995; *b* 10 Jan. 1947; *s* of John Derwent Wall and Maria Laetitia Wall (*née* Whitmarsh); *m* 1975, Catharine Jane Reddaway; one *s*. *Educ:* Douai Sch.; Selwyn Coll., Cambridge (BA). FCO 1968; Addis Ababa, 1969–72; Private Sec. to HM Ambassador, Paris, 1972–74; First Sec., FCO, 1974–76; Press Officer, No 10 Downing Street, 1976–77; Asst Private Sec. to Sec. of State for Foreign and Commonwealth Affairs, 1977–79; First Sec., Washington, 1979–83; Asst Head, later Head, European Community Dept, FCO, 1983–88; Private Secretary: to Foreign and Commonwealth Sec., 1988–90; to the Prime Minister, 1991–93; Ambassador to Portugal, 1993–95. *Recreations:* walking, photography. *Address:* c/o Foreign and Commonwealth Office, King Charles Street, SW1A 2AH.

See also G. F. N. Reddaway.

WALL, Mrs Michael; *see* Wall, A. A.

WALL, Hon. Sir Nicholas (Peter Rathbone), Kt 1993; **Hon. Mr Justice Wall;** a Judge of the High Court of Justice, Family Division, since 1993; *b* 14 March 1945; *s* of late Frederick Stanley Wall and of Margaret Helen Wall; *m* 1973, Margaret Sydee, JP; four *c*. *Educ:* Dulwich College; Trinity Coll., Cambridge (Scholar; MA). Pres., Cambridge Union Soc., 1967; Mem., combined univs debating tour, USA, 1968. Called to the Bar, Gray's Inn, 1969, Bencher, 1993; QC 1988; Asst Recorder, 1988–90; a Recorder, 1990–93. *Publications:* (ed jtly) Supplements to Rayden and Jackson on Divorce, 15th edn, 1988–91; (ed jtly) Rayden and Jackson on Divorce, 16th edn, 1991–. *Recreations:* collecting, binding and restoring books, theatre, opera, walking, composing clerihews. *Address:* Royal Courts of Justice, Strand, WC2A 2LL.

WALL, Prof. Patrick David, MA, DM; FRCP; FRS 1989; Professor of Anatomy and Director, Cerebral Functions Research Group, University College, London, 1967–90, Professor Emeritus, 1990; *b* 5 April 1925; *s* of T. Wall, MC, and R. Wall (*née* Cresswell). *Educ:* St Paul's; Christ Church, Oxford. MA 1947; BM, BCh 1948; DM 1960. Instructor, Yale School of Medicine, 1948–50; Asst Prof., Univ. of Chicago, 1950–53; Instructor, Harvard Univ., 1953–55; Assoc. Prof., 1957–60, Professor 1960–67, MIT. Vis. Prof., Hebrew Univ., Jerusalem, 1973–. Founding Chm., Brain Research Assoc. Hon. FRCA 1992. Hon. MD: Sienna, 1987; Debrecen, 1994. Bonica Award, Internat. Assoc. Study of Pain, 1987; Sherrington Medal, RSM, 1988; Wakeman Award, Duke Univ., 1988; Research on Pain Award, Bristol-Myers, 1988. First Editor in Chief, Pain. *Publications:* Trio, The Revolting Intellectuals' Organizations (novel), 1966 (US 1965); (with R. Melzack) The Challenge of Pain, 1982, 2nd edn 1989; The Textbook of Pain, 1983, 3rd edn 1993; many papers on anat. and physiol. of nervous system. *Recreation:* kibbitzing. *Address:* 141 Gray's Inn Road, WC1X 8UB.

WALL, Major Sir Patrick (Henry Bligh), Kt 1981; MC 1945; VRD 1957; RM (retd); *b* 19 Oct. 1916; *s* of Henry Benedict Wall and Gladys Eleanor Finney; *m* 1953, Sheila Elizabeth Putnam (*d* 1983); one *d*. *Educ:* Downside. Commissioned in RM 1935 (specialised in naval gunnery). Served in HM Ships, support craft, with RM Commandos and US Navy. Actg Major, 1943; RN Staff Coll., 1945; Joint Services Staff Coll., 1947; Major, 1949. CO 47 Commando RMFVR, 1951–57; Comr for Sea Scouts in London, 1950–66. Westminster City Council, 1953–62. Contested Cleveland Division (Yorks), 1951 and 1952. MP (C): Haltemprice Div. of Hull, Feb. 1954–55; Haltemprice Div. of E Yorks, 1955–83; Beverley, 1983–87, retd. Parliamentary Private Secretary to: Minister of Agriculture, Fisheries and Food, 1955–57; Chancellor of the Exchequer, 1958–59. Mem., Select Cttee on Defence, 1980–83. Chm. Mediterranean Group of Conservative Commonwealth Council, 1954–67; Chm. Cons. Parly East and Central Africa Cttee, 1956–59; Vice-Chairman: Conservative Commonwealth Affairs Cttee, 1960–68; Cons. Overseas Bureau, 1963–73; Cons. Defence Cttee, 1965–77; Vice-Chm. or Treasurer, IPU, 1974–82 (Chairman: British-Maltese, Anglo-Bahrain, Anglo-South African, Anglo-Taiwan Groups; Vice-Chm., Anglo-Portuguese, Treasurer, Anglo-Korean Groups). North Atlantic Assembly: Leader, British Delegn, 1979–87; Pres., 1983–85; Chm., Mil. Cttee, 1978–81; Chm., Cons./Christian Democrat Gp, 1977–87. Mem. Defence Cttee, WEU and Council of Europe, 1972–75. Chairman: Cons. Fisheries Sub-Cttee, 1962–83; Africa Centre, 1961–65; Joint East and Central Africa Board, 1965–75; Cons. Southern Africa Group, 1970–78; Cons. Africa Sub-Cttee, 1979–83; RM Parly Group, 1956–87; British Rep. at 17th General Assembly of UN, 1962. Chm., Monday Club, 1978–80. Pres., Yorks Area Young Conservatives, 1955–60. Pres., British UFO Res. Assoc.; Vice-Pres., British Sub-Aqua Club, 1955–87. FIJ 1989. Freeman of Beverley, 1989. Kt, SMO Malta; USA Legion of Merit, 1945; Gold Star of Taiwan, 1988. *Publications:* Royal Marine Pocket Book, 1944; Student Power, 1968; Defence Policy, 1969; Overseas Aid, 1969; The Soviet Maritime Threat, 1973; The Indian Ocean and the Threat to the West, 1975; Prelude to Detente, 1975; Southern Oceans and the Security of the Free World, 1977; co-author of a number of political pamphlets. *Recreation:* ship and aircraft models. *Address:* Lordington Park, Lordington, near Chichester, West Sussex PO18 9DX. *T:* Emsworth (01243) 370989. *Club:* Royal Naval Sailing Association.

WALL, Maj.-Gen. Robert Percival Walter, CB 1978; Member, North East Thames Regional Health Authority, 1990–94; Chairman, Essex Family Health Services Authority, since 1990; *b* 23 Aug. 1927; *s* of Frank Ernest and Ethel Elizabeth Wall; *m* 1st, 1953 (marr. diss. 1985); two *s* one *d*; 2nd, 1986, Jennifer Hilary Anning. Joined Royal Marines, 1945; regimental soldiering in Commandos, followed by service at sea and on staff of HQ 3 Commando Bde RM, 1945–58; psc(M) 1959; jssc 1961; Asst Sec., Chiefs of Staff Secretariat, 1962–65; 43 Commando RM, 1965–66; Naval Staff, 1966–68; Directing Staff, JSS Coll., 1969–71; Col GS Commando Forces and Dept of Commandant General RM, 1971–74; course at RCDS, 1975; Chief of Staff to Commandant General, RM, 1976–79. Dir, Land Decade Educnl Council, 1982–90. Chm., Essex FPC, 1985–90. Vice-Pres., River Thames Soc., 1983– (Chm., 1978–83); Mem. Council, Thames Heritage Trust, 1980–83; Pres., Blackheath Football Club (RFU), 1983–85; Council, Officers' Pension Soc., 1980–91. Freeman of City of London, 1977; Freeman, Co. of Watermen and Lightermen of River Thames, 1979. FIMgt; FRSA 1985. JP: City of London, 1982–92; Essex, 1992. *Recreations:* cricket, rugby, walking, reading. *Address:* c/o Barclays Bank, 116 Goodmayes Road, Goodmayes, Ilford, Essex IG3 9XB. *Clubs:* Army and Navy, MCC.

WALL, Sir Robert (William), Kt 1987; OBE 1980; Pro-Chancellor, University of Bristol, since 1990; Leader, Conservative Group, Bristol City Council, since 1974; *b* 27 Sept. 1929; *s* of William George and Gladys Perina Wall; *m* 1968, Jean Ashworth; one *d* (and one *s* decd). *Educ:* Monmouth School; Bristol Coll. of Technology. HND MechEng; AMRAeS, TechEng. Student apprentice, Bristol Aeroplane Co., 1947–52; commissioned RAF Eng. Branch, and Mountain Rescue Service, 1955–57; management posts with British Aircraft Corp., 1957–67, Chief Ratefixer, 1969–75, Manager, Cost Control, 1975–88. Bristol City Council: Councillor 1959; Alderman 1971; re-elected Councillor 1974; Chm., Public Works Cttee, 1968–72; Dep. Leader, 1971–72, Council Leader, 1983–84. Mem., Bristol Develt Corp., 1993–. Chairman: Bristol Cons. Assoc., 1979–88; Western Area Provincial Council, Nat. Union of Cons. and Unionist Assocs, 1988–91. Mem. Council, Univ. of Bristol, 1974– (Chairman: GP Cttee, 1979–87; Buildings Cttee, 1987–91; Audit Cttee, 1991–); Governor, Bristol Old Vic Theatre Trust, 1974–87, and 1988–93; Mem. Council, SS Great Britain Project, 1975–; Chm., Transport Users' Cons. Cttee for W England, 1982–. Mem., Audit Commn, 1986–94. Pres., Bristol Soc. of Model and Experimental Engrs, 1972–. FCIT. FRSA. Freeman, Co. of Watermen and Lightermen. Hon. MA Bristol, 1982. *Publications:* Bristol Channel Pleasure Steamers, 1973; Ocean Liners, 1978 (trans. German, French, Dutch), 2nd edn 1984; Air Liners, 1980; Bristol: maritime city, 1981; The Story of HMS Bristol, 1986; Quayside Bristol, 1992. *Recreations:* writing maritime history, collecting postcards, hill walking. *Address:* 1 Ormerod Road, Stoke Bishop, Bristol BS9 1BA. *T:* Bristol (0117) 968 2910; The Glebe, Winsford, Somerset TA24 7BJ. *Clubs:* Bristol Savages, Clifton (Bristol).

WALL, Stephen; *see* Wall, J. S.

WALL, Prof. William Douglas, PhD, DLit; CPsychol, FBPsS; Professor of Educational Psychology, Institute of Education, University of London, 1973–78, now Professor Emeritus; *b* 22 Aug. 1913; *s* of late John Henry Wall and Ann McCulloch Wall, Wallington, Surrey; *m* 1st, 1936, Doris Margaret (*née* Satchel) (marr. diss. 1960); two *s* one *d*; 2nd, 1960, Ursula Maria (*née* Gallusser); one *s*. *Educ:* Univ. Coll. London, 1931–34 (BA Hons); Univ. Coll. London/Univ. of Birmingham, 1944–48 (PhD (Psychol.)); DLit (London) 1979. Mem., Social Psych. Sect., Child and Educnl Psych. Sect., BPsS. Univ. of Birmingham Educn Dept, 1945–53; Reader, 1948–53; Head, Educn and Child Develt Unit, UNESCO, Paris, 1951–56; Dir, Nat. Foundn for Educnl Res. in England and Wales, 1956–68; Dean, Inst. of Educn, Univ. of London, 1968–73; Scientific Advr, Bernard van Leer Foundn, 1978–82. Visiting Professor: Univ. of Michigan, 1957; Univ. of Jerusalem, 1962; Univ. of Tel Aviv, 1967. Chm., Internat. Project Evaluation of Educnl Attainment, 1958–62; Mem., Police Trng Council, 1970–78; Co-Dir, 1958–75, and Chm., Nat. Child Develt Study, 1958–78; Mem. Council, Internat. Children's Centre, Paris, 1970–78. *Publications:* (many trans. various langs): Adolescent Child, 1948 (2nd edn, 1952); Education and Mental Health, 1955; Psychological Services for Schools, 1956; Child of our Times, 1959; Failure in School, 1962; Adolescents in School and Society, 1968; Longitudinal Studies and the Social Sciences, 1970; Constructive Education for Children, 1975; Constructive Education for Adolescents, 1977; Constructive Education for Handicapped, 1979; contrib: British Jl Educnl Psych.; British Jl Psych., Educnl Res. (Editor, 1958–68), Educnl Rev., Enfance, Human Develt, Internat. Rev. Educn. *Recreations:* painting (one-man exhibitions: Windsor, 1986, 1988; London, 1987; Open Studio, Visual Images Gp, 1993), gardening. *Address:* La Geneste, Rose Hill, Burnham, Bucks SL1 8LW.

WALLACE, family name of **Barons Wallace of Campsie** and **Wallace of Coslany.**

WALLACE OF CAMPSIE, Baron *cr* 1974 (Life Peer), of Newlands, Glasgow; **George Wallace,** JP; DL; Life President, Wallace, Cameron (Holdings) Ltd, since 1981 (President, 1977–81); Director, Smith & Nephew Associated Companies Ltd, 1973–77; *b* 13 Feb. 1915; *s* of John Wallace and Mary Pollock; *m* 1977, Irene Alice Langdon Phipps, *er d* of Ernest Phipps, Glasgow. *Educ:* Queen's Park Secondary Sch., Glasgow; Glasgow Univ. Estd Wallace, Cameron & Co. Ltd, 1948, Chm., 1950–77. Solicitor before the Supreme Courts, 1950–; Hon. Sheriff at Hamilton, 1971–. Chm., E Kilbride and Stonehouse Develt Corp., 1969–75; Mem. Bd, S of Scotland Electricity Bd, 1966–68; founder Mem. Bd, Scottish Develt Agency, 1975–78; Chm., E Kilbride Business Centre, 1984–89. Pres., Glasgow Chamber of Commerce, 1974–76; Vice-Pres., Scottish Assoc. of Youth Clubs, 1971–; Chm., Adv. Bd (Strathclyde) Salvation Army, 1972–90; Mem. Court, Univ. of Strathclyde, 1973–74; Hon. Pres., Town and Country Planning Assoc. (Scottish Sect.), 1969–; Chm., Scottish Exec. Cttee, Brit. Heart Foundn, 1973–76; Chm., Britannia Cttee, British Sailors' Soc., 1967–77; Vice-Chm., Scottish Retirement Council, 1975–; Hon. Pres., Lanarkshire Samaritans, 1984–. FRSA 1970; FSAScot 1990; FCIM (FInstM 1968); FIMgt (FBIM 1990). JP 1968, DL 1971, Glasgow. KStJ 1976. *Recreation:* reading. *Address:* 14 Fernleigh Road, Newlands, Glasgow G43 2UE. *T:* 0141–637 3337. *Club:* Royal Scottish Automobile (Glasgow).

WALLACE OF COSLANY, Baron *cr* 1974 (Life Peer), of Coslany in the City of Norwich; **George Douglas Wallace;** *b* 18 April 1906; *e s* of late George Wallace, Cheltenham Spa, Gloucestershire; *m* 1932, Vera Randall, Guildford, Surrey; one *s* one *d*. *Educ:* Central School, Cheltenham Spa. Mem. of Management Cttee, in early years, of YMCA at East Bristol and Guildford; Mem. Chislehurst-Sidcup UDC, 1937–46; has been Divisional Sec. and also Chm., Chislehurst Labour Party; also Chm. of Parks and Cemeteries Cttee of UDC, Schools Manager and Member of Chislehurst, Sidcup and Orpington Divisional Education Executive; Mem., Cray Valley and Sevenoaks Hosp. Management Cttee; Chm., House Cttee, Queen Mary's Hosp.; Vice-Chm., Greenwich and Bexley AHA, 1974–77. Joined Royal Air Force, reaching rank of Sergeant. Served in No 11 Group Fighter Command, 1941–45. MP (Lab) Chislehurst Div. of Kent, 1945–50; Junior Govt Whip, 1947–50; MP (Lab) Norwich North, Oct. 1964–Feb. 1974; PPS: to Lord President of the Council, Nov. 1964–65; to Sec. of State for Commonwealth Affairs, 1965; to Minister of State, Min. of Housing and Local Govt, 1967–68; Mem. Speaker's Panel of Chairmen, 1970–74; a Lord in Waiting (Govt Whip), 1977–79; opposition spokesman and Whip, H of L, 1979–84. Delegate to Council of Europe and WEU, 1975–77.

Member: Commonwealth Parly Assoc.; Commonwealth War Graves Commn, 1970–86; Kent CC, 1952–57. *Recreations:* interested in Youth Movements and social welfare schemes. *Address:* 44 Shuttle Close, Sidcup, Kent DA15 8EP. *T:* 0181–300 3634.

WALLACE, Albert Frederick, CBE 1963 (OBE 1955); DFC 1943; Controller of Manpower, Greater London Council, 1978–82; *b* 22 Aug. 1921; *s* of Major Frederick Wallace and Ada Wallace; *m* 1940, Evelyn M. White; one *s* one *d. Educ:* Roan School, Blackheath, SE3. MIPM, MBIM, MILGA. Regular Officer, Royal Air Force, 1939–69; retired in rank of Group Captain. Regional Advisory Officer, Local Authorities Management Services and Computer Cttee, 1969–71; Asst Clerk of the Council, Warwickshire CC, 1971–73; County Personnel Officer, W Midlands CC, 1973–78. *Recreations:* golf, bridge. *Address:* Rochester Close, Eastbourne BN20 7TW. *T:* Eastbourne (01323) 730668. *Club:* Royal Air Force.

WALLACE, Charles William, CMG 1983; CVO 1975; HM Diplomatic Service, retired; *b* 19 Jan. 1926; *s* of Percival Francis and Julia Wallace; *m* 1957, Gloria Regina de Ros Ribas (*née* Sanz-Agero). *Educ:* privately and abroad. HM Foreign (later Diplomatic) Service, 1949; served: Asuncion; Barcelona; Bari; Bahrain; Tegucigalpa; Guatemala; Panama; Foreign Office; Baghdad; Buenos Aires; Montevideo; FO, later FCO, Asst Head of American Dept; Counsellor 1969; Rome and Milan; Mexico City; Ambassador: Paraguay, 1976–79; Peru, 1979–83; Uruguay, 1983–86. Freeman, City of London, 1981. *Publication:* The Valedictory, 1992. *Recreations:* sailing, fishing. *Address:* c/o Lloyds Private Banking, 50 Grosvenor Street, W1X 9FH; Calle del Sol 5, 17121 Corsa, Girona, Spain. *Club:* Travellers.

WALLACE, Prof. David James, FRS 1986; FRSE; Vice-Chancellor, Loughborough University of Technology, since 1994; *b* 7 Oct. 1945; *s* of Robert Elder Wallace and Jane McConnell Wallace (*née* Elliot); *m* 1970, Elizabeth Anne Yeats; one *d. Educ:* Hawick High Sch.; Univ. of Edinburgh (BSc, PhD). FRSE 1982; FInstP 1991. Harkness Fellow, Princeton Univ., 1970–72; Lecturer in Physics, 1972–78, Reader in Physics, 1978–79, Southampton Univ.; Tait Prof. of Mathematical Physics, 1979–93, Hd of Physics, 1984–87, Edinburgh Univ. Assoc. Dir, Res. Inst. on Pattern Recognition, RSRE, Malvern, 1986–90. Director: Edinburgh Concurrent Supercomputer, 1987–89; Edinburgh Parallel Computing Centre, 1990–93. Science and Engineering Research Council, subseq. Engineering and Physical Sciences Research Council: Chm., Physics Cttee, 1987–90; Chm., Science Bd, 1990–94; Mem. Council, 1990–. European Commission: Mem., High Performance Computing and Networking Adv. Cttee, 1991–92; Physics Panel, Human Capital and Mobility Prog., 1991–; Member: Royal Soc. sci. and industl award Cttees, 1990–; SHEFC, 1993–. Pres., Physics Sect., BAAS, 1994. Frequent visiting scientist abroad, incl. Europe, Israel, North and South America. Maxwell Medal of Inst. of Physics, 1980. *Publications:* in research and review jls, in a number of areas of theoretical physics. *Recreations:* running, eating at La Potinière, mycophagy. *Address:* Loughborough University of Technology, Loughborough LE11 3TU. *T:* Loughborough (01509) 222001.

WALLACE, (Dorothy) Jacqueline H.; *see* Hope-Wallace.

WALLACE, Fleming; *see* Wallace, J. F.

WALLACE, Ian Alexander; JP; Headmaster, Canford School, 1961–76; *b* 5 Oct. 1917; *s* of late Very Rev. A. R. Wallace and Winifred, *d* of late Rev. H. C. Sturges; *m* 1947, Janet Glossop; two *s* two *d. Educ:* Clifton; Corpus Christi College, Cambridge (open scholar). Classical Tripos, Part I, 1st Cl.; Theological Tripos Part I, 2nd Cl. Div. One. Served War of 1939–45, Mountain Artillery, NW Frontier, India, 1941; School of Artillery, India, 1942–43; Arakan, 1944; Mandalay, 1945 (despatches). Rossall School: Assistant Master, 1946; Housemaster, 1951–61. SW Regional Sec., Independent Schools Careers Organisation, 1976–84; Project Manager for India, GAP Activity Projects, 1984–89; Wilts Regional Dir, HOST, 1992–95. Governor: Portsmouth Grammar Sch., 1977–89; King's Sch., Bruton, 1977–92. JP Poole Borough, 1966. *Address:* Steeple Close, Hindon, Salisbury, Wilts SP1 6DJ.

WALLACE, Ian Bryce, OBE 1983; Hon. RAM; Hon. RCM; singer, actor and broadcaster; *b* London, 10 July 1919; *o s* of late Sir John Wallace, Kirkcaldy, Fife (one-time MP for Dunfermline), and Mary Bryce Wallace (*née* Temple), Glasgow; *m* 1948, Patricia Gordon Black, Edenwood, Cupar, Fife; one *s* one *d. Educ:* Charterhouse; Trinity Hall, Cambridge (MA). Served War of 1939–45, (invalided from) RA, 1944. London stage debut in The Forrigan Reel, Sadler's Wells, 1945. Opera debut, as Schaunard, in La Bohème, with New London Opera Co., Cambridge Theatre, London, 1946. Sang principal roles for NLOC, 1946–49, incl. Dr Bartolo in Il Barbiere di Siviglia. Glyndebourne debut, Masetto, Don Giovanni, Edin. Fest., 1948. Regular appearances as principal *buffo* for Glyndebourne, both in Sussex and at Edin. Fest., 1948–61, incl. perfs as Don Magnifico in La Cenerentola, at Berlin Festwoche, 1954. Italian debut: Masetto, Don Giovanni, at Parma, 1950; also Don Magnifico, La Cenerentola, Rome, 1955, Dr Bartolo, Il Barbiere di Siviglia, Venice, 1956, and Bregenz Fest., 1964–65. Regular appearances for Scottish Opera, 1965–, incl. Leporello in Don Giovanni, Pistola in Falstaff, Duke of Plaza Toro in The Gondoliers. Don Pasquale, Welsh Nat. Opera, 1967, Dr Dulcamara, L'Elisir d'Amore, Glyndebourne Touring Opera, 1968. Devised, wrote and presented three series of adult education programmes on opera, entitled Singing For Your Supper, for Scottish Television (ITV), 1967–70. Recordings include: Gilbert and Sullivan Operas with Sir Malcolm Sargent, and humorous songs by Flanders and Swann. Theatrical career includes: a Royal Command Variety Perf., London Palladium, 1952; Cesar in Fanny, Theatre Royal, Drury Lane, 1956; 4 to the Bar, Criterion, 1960; Toad in Toad of Toad Hall, Queen's, 1964. Regular broadcaster, 1944–: radio and TV, as singer, actor and compere; a regular panellist on radio musical quiz game, My Music; acted in series, Porterhouse Blue, Channel 4 TV, 1987. President: ISM, 1979–80; Council for Music in Hosps, 1988–. Hon. DMus St Andrews, 1991. Sir Charles Santley Meml Award, Musicians' Co., 1984. *Publications:* Promise Me You'll Sing Mud (autobiog.), 1975; Nothing Quite Like It (autobiog.), 1982; Reflections on Scotland, 1988. *Recreations:* walking, reading, sport watching, photography; singing a song about a hippopotamus to children of all ages. *Address:* c/o Peters, Fraser & Dunlop, 5th floor, The Chambers, Chelsea Harbour, Lots Road, SW10 0XF. *T:* 0171–344 1010. *Clubs:* Garrick, MCC; Stage Golfing Society.

WALLACE, Sir Ian (James), Kt 1982; CBE 1971 (OBE (mil.) 1942); Director, Coventry Motor and Sundries Co. Ltd, 1986–92; Chairman, SNR Bearings (UK) Ltd, 1975–85; *b* 25 Feb. 1916; *s* of John Madder Wallace, CBE; *m* 1942, Catherine Frost Mitchell, *e d* of Cleveland S. Mitchell; one *s* one *d. Educ:* Uppingham Sch.; Jesus Coll., Cambridge (BA). Underwriting at Lloyd's, 1935–39. War Service, Fleet Air Arm: Cmdr (A) RNVR, 1939–46. Harry Ferguson Ltd from 1947: Dir 1950; later Massey Ferguson Ltd, Dir Holdings Board until 1970. Coventry Conservative Association: Treas., 1956–68; Chm., 1968–88; Pres., 1988–92; Pres., S Worcs Cons. Assoc., 1992–; Chm., W Midlands Cons. Council, 1967–70 (Treas., 1962–67); Pres., W Midlands Area Cons. Council. Member: Severn-Trent Water Authority, 1974–82; W Midlands Econ. Planning Council, 1965–75; Vice-Chm., Midland Regional Council, CBI, 1964, Chm., 1967–69; President: Coventry Chamber of Commerce, 1972–74; Birmingham and Midland Inst., 1992–93. Pres., Hereford and Worcester (formerly Worcs County) Rifle Assoc., 1983–. *Recreations:* rifle shooting, horology. *Address:* Little House, 156 High Street, Broadway, Worcs WR12 7AJ. *T:* Broadway (01386) 852414. *Clubs:* Carlton, Naval and Military, North London Rifle.

WALLACE, Ian Norman Duncan, QC 1973; *b* 21 April 1922; *s* of late Duncan Gardner Wallace, HBM Crown Advocate in Egypt, Paymaster-Comdr RNR and Eileen Agnes Wallace. *Educ:* Loretto; Oriel Coll., Oxford (MA). Served War of 1939–45: Ordinary Seaman RN, 1940; Lieut RNVR, 1941–46. Called to Bar, Middle Temple, 1948; Western Circuit, 1949. Vis. Scholar, Berkeley Univ., Calif, 1977–; Vis. Prof., Centre of Construction Law, KCL, 1987–. Mem. Editl Bd, Construction Law Jl, 1984–. *Publications:* (ed) Hudson on Building and Civil Engineering Contracts, 8th edn 1959, to 11th edn 1995; Building and Civil Engineering Standard Forms, 1969; Further Building and Engineering Standard Forms, 1973; The International Civil Engineering Contract, 1974, supplement 1980; The ICE Conditions (5th edn), 1978; Construction Contracts: principles and policies in Tort and Contract, 1986; contrib. Law Qly Review, Jl of Internat. Law and Commerce, Construction Law Jl, Internat. Construction Law Rev., Arbitration Internat. *Recreations:* shooting, keeping fit, foreign travel. *Address:* 53 Holland Park, W11 3RS. *T:* 0171–727 7640. *Clubs:* Lansdowne, Hurlingham.

WALLACE, Ivan Harold Nutt, CB 1991; Senior Chief Inspector, Department of Education, Northern Ireland, 1979–95; *b* 20 Feb. 1935; *s* of late Harold Wallace and Annie McClure Wallace; *m* 1962, Winifred Ervine Armstrong; two *d. Educ:* Grosvenor High Sch., Belfast; QUB (BSc 1957). MRSC 1963. School Teacher: Leeds Central High Sch., 1957–60; Foyle Coll., Londonderry, 1960–69; Inspector of Schools, NI, 1969–75; Sen. Inspector, 1975–77; Staff Inspector, 1977–78; Chief Inspector, 1978–79. *Recreations:* music, walking. *Address:* 25 Tudor Oaks, Holywood, Co. Down, N Ireland.

WALLACE, (James) Fleming; QC (Scot) 1985; Counsel to Scottish Law Commission, 1979–93; *b* 19 March 1931; *s* of James F. B. Wallace, SSC and Margaret B. Gray, MA; *m* 1st, 1964, Valerie Mary (*d* 1986), *d* of Leslie Lawrence, solicitor, and Madge Lawrence, Ramsbury, Wilts; two *d*; 2nd, 1990, Linda Ann, solicitor, *d* of Robert Grant, civil engineer, and Alice Grant. *Educ:* Edinburgh Academy; Edinburgh University (MA 1951; LLB 1954). Served RA, 1954–56 (2nd Lieut); TA 1956–60. Admitted Faculty of Advocates, 1957; practised at Scottish Bar until 1960; Parly Draftsman and Legal Secretary, Lord Advocate's Dept, London, 1960–79. Part-time Chm., Industrial Tribunals, Scotland, 1993–. *Publication:* The Businessman's Lawyer (Scottish Section), 1965, 2nd edn 1973. *Recreations:* hill walking, choral singing, golf, badminton. *Address:* 24 Corrennie Gardens, Edinburgh EH10 6DB.

WALLACE, James Robert; MP Orkney and Shetland, since 1983 (L 1983–88, Lib Dem since 1988); *b* 25 Aug. 1954; *s* of John F. T. Wallace and Grace Hannah Wallace (*née* Maxwell); *m* 1983, Rosemary Janet Fraser; two *d. Educ:* Annan Academy; Downing College, Cambridge (BA 1975, MA 1979); Edinburgh University (LLB 1977). Chm., Edinburgh Univ. Liberal Club, 1976–77. Called to the Scots Bar, 1979; practised as Advocate, 1979–83. Contested Dumfriesshire (L), 1979; contested South of Scotland (L), European Parlt election, 1979. Mem., Scottish Liberal Exec., 1976–85; Vice-Chm. (Policy), Scottish Liberal Party, 1982–85; Hon. Pres., Scottish Young Liberals, 1984–85; Leader, Scottish Liberal Democrats, 1992–. Liberal spokesman on defence, 1985–87; Deputy Whip, 1985–87, Chief Whip, 1987–88; first Lib Dem Chief Whip, 1988–92; Alliance spokesman on Transport, 1987; Lib Dem spokesman on employment and training, 1988–92, on fisheries, 1988–, on Scottish affairs, 1992–, on maritime affairs, 1994–. *Recreations:* golf, music, travel. *Address:* Northwood House, Tankerness, Orkney KW17 2QS. *T:* Tankerness (01856) 861383. *Clubs:* Caledonian; Scottish Liberal (Edinburgh).

WALLACE, John Malcolm Agnew; JP; Vice Lord-Lieutenant, Dumfries and Galloway (District of Wigtown), since 1990; *b* 30 Jan. 1928; *s* of John Alexander Agnew Wallace and Marjory Murray Wallace; *m* 1955, Louise Haworth-Booth; one *s* two *d. Educ:* Harrow; West of Scotland Agricultural College. Farmer. JP Stranraer, 1970; DL Dumfries and Galloway, 1971. *Address:* Lochryan, Stranraer DG9 8QY. *T:* Cairnryan (01581) 200284.

WALLACE, John Williamson, OBE 1995; Principal Trumpet: Philharmonia Orchestra, since 1976; London Sinfonietta, since 1987; freelance soloist, composer, conductor; *b* 14 April 1949; *s* of Christopher Kidd Wallace and Ann Drummond Allan; *m* 1971, Elizabeth Jane Hartwell; one *s* one *d. Educ:* Buckhaven High Sch.; King's Coll., Cambridge (MA); York Univ.; Royal Acad. of Music (ARAM 1983; FRAM 1990). ARCM 1968; Hon. RCM 1985. Asst Principal Trumpet, LSO, 1974–76; founded The Wallace Collection (brass-interest music gp), 1986. Trumpet solo recordings. *Publications:* Five Easy Pieces, 1984; First Book of Trumpet Solos, 1985; Second Book of Trumpet Solos, 1985, 2nd edn 1987; Grieg's Seven Lyric Pieces, 1985, Kornukopia, 1986; Prime Number, 1990. *Recreations:* family life, worrying, holidaying in France. *Address:* 16 Woodstock Road, Croydon CR0 1JR. *T:* 0181–688 1170.

WALLACE, Lawrence James, OC 1972; CVO 1983; Deputy Minister to the Premier of British Columbia, 1980–81; *b* Victoria, BC, Canada, 24 April 1913; *s* of John Wallace and Mary Wallace (*née* Parker); *m* 1942, Lois Leeming; three *d. Educ:* Univ. of British Columbia (BA); Univ. of Washington, USA (MEd). Served War, Lt-Comdr, Royal Canadian Navy Voluntary Reserve, 1941–45. Joined British Columbia Govt, as Dir of Community Programmes and Adult Educn, 1953; Dep. Provincial Sec., 1959–77, Dep. to Premier, 1969–72; Agent-General for British Columbia in UK and Europe, 1977–80. General Chairman: four centennial celebrations, marking founding of Crown Colony of British Columbia in 1858, union of Crown Colonies of Vancouver Is. and British Columbia, 1866, Canadian Confedn, 1867, and joining into confedn by British Columbia in 1871. Former Dir, Provincial Capital Commn; Vice Chm., BC Press Council; Past Chm., Inter-Provincial Lottery Corp., Queen Elizabeth II Schol. Cttee, and Nancy Green Schol. Cttee; Hon. Trustee, British Columbia Sports Hall of Fame. Director: Sen. Citizens Lottery; BC Forest Museum; Adv. Bd, Salvation Army; Canadian Council of Christians and Jews; President: Duke of Edinburgh Awards Cttee, BC; McPherson Playhouse Foundn; Hon. Pres., Univ of Victoria Alumni; Hon. Co-Chm., Operation Eye Sight, BC; Chm., Historic Royal Theatre Renovations and Restoration; Hon. Member: BC High Sch. Basketball Assoc.; BC Recreation Assoc.; Hon. Life Mem., BC Legislative Press Gallery, 1984. Freeman of City of London, 1978. Hon. LLD: British Columbia, 1978; Royal Roads Military Coll., 1994. Named British Columbia Man of the Year, 1958, and Greater Vancouver Man of the Year, 1967; Canadian Centennial Medal, 1967; Comdr Brother, OStJ, 1969; City of Victoria Citizenship Award, 1971; Silver Jubilee Medal, 1977; 125 Confederation Medal; Good Servant Award, Canadian Council of Christians and Jews, 1980; Pearkes Meml Citizenship Award, 1991. Hon. Chief: Alberni, Gilford and Southern Vancouver Is Indian Bands. *Recreations:* gardening, community activities. *Address:* 1345 Fairfield Road, Victoria, BC V8S 1E4, Canada.

WALLACE, Major Malcolm Charles Robarts; Director of Regulation, Jockey Club, since 1994; *b* 12 June 1947; *s* of Lionel John Wallace and Maureen Winefride (*née* Robarts); *m* 1st, 1974, Caroline Anne Doyne-Ditmas (marr. diss. 1990); one *s* one *d*; 2nd, 1991, Mrs Jane Thelwall; one *s. Educ:* Blackrock College, Co. Dublin. Student pupil with

Lt-Col J. Hume-Dudgeon at Burton Hall, Co. Dublin, 1965–67; Mons Officer Cadet Sch.; commissioned RA, 1967; gun line officer, 18 Light Regt, Hong Kong; 3rd Regt RHA, 1969; King's Troop RHA, 1970 (long equitation course, RAVC Melton Mowbray); Troop Comdr, 19 Field Regt, 1974; Adjutant 101 Northumbrian Field Artillery, 1976; Staff Officer, HQ UKLF, 1978–82; Comd King's Troop RHA, 1982–85, retired. Dir Gen., BEF, 1985–94. Chef d'Equipe to British Internat. and Olympic Three Day Event Teams, 1979–84; Chef de Mission, Equestrian Team, Olympic Games, Seoul, 1988 and Barcelona, 1992. Freeman, Saddlers' Co., 1985. *Publication:* The King's Troop Royal Horse Artillery, 1984. *Recreations:* field sports, cricket, racing. *Address:* The Manor House, Stoke Albany, Market Harborough, LE16 8PT. *T:* Dingley (01858) 535250, *Fax:* (01858) 535499. *Club:* Cavalry and Guards.

WALLACE, Marjorie Shiona, MBE 1994; Chief Executive, SANE, mental health charity, since 1989; author, journalist; *d* of William Wallace and Doris Tulloch; *m* Count Andrzej Skarbek; three *s* one *d*. *Educ:* Rodeane; Johannesburg; Parsons' Mead, Ashtead; University College London (BA Hons Psych and Phil). Television: The Frost Programme, 1966–68; ITV religious programmes, 1966–68; LWT current affairs, 1968–69; Dir/reporter, current affairs, BBC TV, 1969–72; Insight team (thalidomide campaign), feature writer, Sunday Times, 1972–89, incl. Forgotten Illness (Schizophrenia) campaign, The Times, 1985–89; Guardian Res. Fellow, Nuffield Coll., Oxford, 1989–91. Institute of Psychiatry: Member: Cttee of Management, 1989–; Ethics Cttee (Res.), 1991–; Schiz. Adv. Panel, 1991–; Adv. Panel, Sainsbury Centre, 1992–. Chm., Friends of Open Air Theatre, 1991–. Campaigning Journalist of the Year, British Press Awards, 1982, 1986; John Pringle Meml Award, 1986; Oddfellows Book Trust Prize, 1987; Snowdon Special Award, 1988; Medical Journalist of the Year, 1988; Evian Health Award, 1991. *Publications:* (jtly) On Giant's Shoulders, 1976 (also original TV screenplay (Internat. Emmy award), 1979); (jtly) Suffer the Children: the story of Thalidomide, 1978; (jtly) The Superpoison, The Dioxin Disaster, 1980; The Silent Twins, 1986 (also TV screenplay); Campaign and Be Damned, 1991. *Recreations:* poetry, music, piano, Victorian ballads, opera, dining out. *Address:* 26 Bisham Gardens, N6 6DD. *T:* 0181–341 0435. *Club:* Groucho.

WALLACE, Reginald James, CMG 1979; OBE 1961; fiscal adviser; Chairman: Norwich Union Fire Insurance Society (Gibraltar) Ltd, since 1984; Abbey National Gibraltar Ltd, since 1987; *b* 16 Aug. 1919; *s* of James Wallace and Doris (*née* Welch); *m* 1st, 1943, Doris Barbara Brown, MD, FRCS, MRCOG (decd); one *d*; 2nd, 1973, Maureen Coady (*d* 1983); 3rd, 1983, Marilyn Ryan (*née* Gareze); one *d*. *Educ:* John Gulson Sch., Coventry; Tatterford Sch., Norfolk; Leeds Univ. (BA); Queen's Coll., Oxford. Served War, 1939–46, 7th Rajput Regt, Indian Army (Major). Gold Coast/Ghana Admin. Service, 1947–58; Sen. District Comr, 1955; Asst Chief Regional Officer, Northern Region, 1957; Regional Sec., 1958; Financial Sec., British Somaliland, 1958–60; War Office, 1961–66; HM Treasury, 1966–78; seconded to Solomon Is, as Financial Sec. (later Financial Adviser), 1973–76; seconded, as British Mem., Anglo/French Mission on Admin. Reform in the Condominium of the New Hebrides, 1977; Governor of Gilbert Is, 1978 to Independence, July 1979; Financial and Develt Sec., Gibraltar, 1979–83. *Recreations:* walking, music. *Club:* Commonwealth Trust.

WALLACE, Richard Alexander; Principal Finance Officer, Welsh Office, since 1990; *b* 24 Nov. 1946; *s* of Lawrence Mervyn and Norah Wallace; *m* 1970, Teresa Caroline Harington Smith; three *c* (and one *c* decd). *Educ:* Bembridge and Sandown C of E Primary Schools; Clifton Coll. Prep. Sch.; Clifton Coll.; King's Coll., Cambridge (MA). Asst Master, Woking County GS for Boys, 1967; Min. of Social Security, 1968; Principal, DHSS, 1972, Asst Sec., 1981; transf. to Welsh Office, 1986; Under Sec., 1988. *Recreation:* not working. *Address:* Welsh Office, Cathays Park, Cardiff CF1 3NQ.

WALLACE, Walter Wilkinson, CVO 1977; CBE 1973 (OBE 1964); DSC 1944; Foreign and Commonwealth Office; *b* 23 Sept. 1923; *s* of late Walter Wallace and Helen Wallace (*née* Douglas); *m* 1955, Susan Blanche, *d* of Brig. F. W. B. Parry, CBE; one *s* one *d*. *Educ:* George Heriot's, Edinburgh. Served War, Royal Marines, 1942–46 (Captain). Joined Colonial Service, 1946; Asst Dist Comr, Sierra Leone, 1948; Dist Comr, 1954; seconded to Colonial Office, 1955–57; Sen. Dist Comr, 1961; Provincial Comr, 1961; Develt Sec., 1962–64; Estabt Sec., Bahamas, 1964–67; Sec. to Cabinet, Bermuda, 1968–73; HM Commissioner, Anguilla, 1973; Governor, British Virgin Islands, 1974–78. Constitutional Comr, St Helena, 1987, Cayman Islands, 1991, Turks and Caicos Is, 1992, British Virgin Islands, 1993, Falkland Islands, 1995. *Recreation:* golf. *Address:* Becketts, Itchenor, Sussex PO20 7DE. *T:* Birdham (01243) 512438. *Club:* Army and Navy.

WALLACE, Wellesley Theodore Octavius; Chairman, VAT and Duties (formerly VAT) Tribunal, since 1989 (part-time, 1989–92); Special Commissioner of Income Tax, since 1992; *b* 10 April 1938; *s* of late Dr Caleb Paul Wallace and Dr Lucy Elizabeth Rainsford (*née* Pigott); *m* 1988, Maria Amelia Abercromby, *d* of Sir Ian Abercromby, Bt, *qv*; one *s* one *d*. *Educ:* Charterhouse; Christ Church, Oxford. 2nd Lt, RA, 1958; Lt, Surrey Yeomanry, TA, 1959–62. Called to the Bar, Inner Temple, 1963. Hon. Sec., Taxation of Sub-cttee, Soc. of Cons. Lawyers, 1974–92. Contested (C): Pontypool, Feb. 1974; S Battersea, Oct. 1974, 1979. *Publication:* (jtly with John Wakeham) The Case Against Wealth Tax, 1968. *Recreation:* lawn tennis. *Address:* 46 Belleville Road, SW11 4QT. *T:* 0171–228 7740; Whitecroft, W Clandon, Surrey GU4 7TD. *T:* Guildford (01483) 222574.

WALLACE, William John Lawrence; Professor of International Studies, Central European University, Prague, since 1994; Reader in International Relations, London School of Economics, since 1995; *b* 12 March 1941; *s* of William E. Wallace and Mary A. Tricks; *m* 1968, Helen Sarah Rushworth; one *s* one *d*. *Educ:* Westminster Abbey Choir School (Sen. Chorister, 1954); St Edward's Sch., Oxford; King's Coll., Cambridge (Exhibnr, 1959; BA Hist 1962); Nuffield Coll., Oxford; Cornell Univ. (PhD Govt 1968). Lectr in Govt, Univ. of Manchester, 1967–77; Dep. Dir, RIIA, 1978–90; Sen. Res. Fellow in European Studies, St Antony's Coll., Oxford, 1990–95. Contested (L): Huddersfield West, 1970; Manchester Moss Side, Feb. and Oct. 1974; Shipley, 1983 and 1987. Vice-Chm., Liberal Party Policy Cttee, 1980–87. Editor, Jl of Common Market Studies, 1974–78. Hon. Dr, Free Univ. of Brussels, 1993. *Publications:* Foreign Policy and the Political Process, 1972; The Foreign Policy Process in Britain, 1977; (with Christopher Tugendhat) Options for British Foreign Policy in the 1990s, 1988; The Transformation of Western Europe, 1990; Regional Integration: the West European Experience, 1994. *Address:* Department of International Relations, London School of Economics, Houghton Street, WC2A 2AD.

WALLACE-HADRILL, Prof. Andrew Frederic, DPhil; Director, British School at Rome, since 1995; Professor of Classics, Unviersity of Reading, since 1987 (on leave of absence); *b* 29 July 1951; *s* of John Michael Wallace-Hadrill and Anne (*née* Wakefield); *m* 1976, Josephine Claire Braddock; one *s* one *d*. *Educ:* Rugby Sch.; Corpus Christi Coll., Oxford (MA); St John's Coll., Oxford (DPhil). Fellow and Dir of Studies in Classics, Magdalene Coll., Cambridge, 1976–83; Lectr in Ancient History, Univ. of Leicester, 1983–87; Head, Dept of Classics, Reading Univ., 1988–94. Editor, Jl of Roman Studies, 1991–95. *Publications:* Suetonius: the scholar and his Caesars, 1983, 2nd edn 1995; (ed) Patronage in Ancient Society, 1989; (ed with J. W. Rich) City and Country in the Ancient World, 1991; Augustan Rome, 1993; Houses and Society in Pompeii and Herculaneum, 1994. *Address:* The British School at Rome, piazzale Winston Churchill 5, già via Gramsci 61, Rome, Italy.

WALLEN, Ella Kathleen, MA (Oxon); Headmistress, St Mary's School, Wantage, 1977–80; *b* 15 Feb. 1914. *Educ:* Camden School for Girls; St Hugh's College, Oxford. History Mistress, Queen Victoria High School, Stockton-on-Tees, 1937–41; Senior History Mistress, High School for Girls, Gloucester, 1942–59; Headmistress: Queen Victoria High School, Stockton-on Tees, 1959–65; Bedford High Sch., 1965–76. *Address:* 10 Dove House Close, Upper Wolvercote, Oxford OX2 8BG.

WALLENBERG, Peter, Order of Wasa, 1974; King's Medal 12th Class, 1983; Hon. KBE 1989; First Vice Chairman, Skandinaviska Enskilda Banken, since 1984 (Vice Chairman, 1980–84); Chairman: Atlas Copco AB, since 1974; Investor AB, since 1982; Wallenberg Foundation, since 1982; ASEA AB, since 1991; *b* Stockholm, 26 May 1926; *s* of Marcus Wallenberg and Dorothy (*née* Mackay); *m* (marr. diss.); two *s* one *d*. *Educ:* Stockholm Univ. (LLB 1953). Various positions within Atlas Copco Gp, 1953–68; Man. Dir, Atlas Copco MCT AB, 1968–70; Dep. Man. Dir, Atlas Copco AB, 1970–74; Industrial Advr to Skandinaviska Enskilda Banken, 1974–80. Co-Chm., ASEA Brown Boveri Ltd (ABB) (Zürich), 1991–; Vice Chm., Telefonaktiebolaget LM Ericsson, 1976–; Member: Internat. Adv. Bd, National Westminster Bank; Council of Internat. Advrs, Swiss Bank Corp.; European Adv. Council, General Motors. Member of Board: Fedn of Swedish Industries, 1975–; Stockholm Sch. of Econs, 1976–; Per Jacobson Foundn (USA), 1983–; Joseph H. Lauder Inst. (USA), 1983–; Nobel Foundn, 1986–. Adv. Bd, Wharton Sch., Univ. of Pennsylvania. Pres., ICC, 1989–90. Hon. Dr: Stockholm Sch. of Econ., 1984; Augustana Coll., Ill, 1985; Upsala Coll., NJ, 1989; Georgetown, Wash, 1990. Orden de Isabel la Católica (Spain), 1979; Comdr, Légion d'Honneur (France), 1987; Comdr 1st Cl. Order of Lion of Finland, 1988; Comdr l'Ordre de Léopold (Belgium), 1989; Grand Cross, Ordem do Merito e Industrial (Portugal), 1990; Grand Cross, Order of Gregorius the Great (Vatican), 1991; Comdr 1st Cl., Royal Norwegian Order of Merit, 1992. *Recreations:* hunting, sailing, tennis. *Address:* Skandinaviska Enskilda Banken, 106 40 Stockholm, Sweden. *T:* (8) 221900.

WALLER, Gary Peter Anthony; MP (C) Keighley, since 1983 (Brighouse and Spenborough, 1979–83); *b* 24 June 1945; *s* of late John Waller and of Elizabeth Waller. *Educ:* Rugby Sch.; Univ. of Lancaster (BA Hons). Chairman: Lancaster Univ. Conservative Assoc., 1965; Spen Valley Civic Soc., 1978–80; Vice-Chm., Nat. Assoc. of Cons. Graduates, 1970–73 and 1976–77. Member: Exec. Cttee, Cons. Nat. Union, 1976–77; Management Cttee, Bradford and Dist Housing Assoc., 1976–90. Exec. Sec., Wider Share Ownership Council, 1973–76. Contested (C): Kensington, Bor. Council elecns, 1971, 1974; Leyton, GLC elecn, 1973; Rother Valley, parly elecn, Feb. and Oct. 1974. PPS to Sec. of State for Transport, 1982–83. Chm., Select Cttee on Information, 1992– (Mem., 1991–); Member: H of C Select Cttee on Transport, 1979–82; Jt Cttee on Consolidation Bills, 1982–92; Select Cttee on Finance and Services, 1992–; Chm., All Party Wool Textile Gp, 1984–89 (Sec., 1979–83); Vice-Chairman: Parly Food and Health Forum, 1985–; Parly IT Cttee, 1987– (Treas., 1981–87); Cons. Parly Transport Cttee, 1992–94 (Sec., 1985–87, 1988–92); Secretary: Cons. Parly Sport and Recreation Cttee, 1979–81; Yorkshire Cons. Members, 1979–83; All-Party Rugby League Gp, 1989–; Hon. Sec., Parly and Scientific Cttee, 1988–91. Mem. Council, Consumers' Assoc., 1995–; Pres., Brighouse Citizens Advice Bureau, 1979–83; Vice-President: Newham S Cons. Assoc., 1979– (Chm., 1971–74); Bethnal Green and Bow Cons. Assoc., 1982–83. Vice-President: Inst. of Trading Standards Admin, 1988–; Keighley Sea Cadets, 1984–; Friends of the Settle–Carlisle Railway, 1987–; AMA, 1992–. Governor: George Green's Sch., Tower Hamlets, 1968–70; Isaac Newton Sch., N Kensington, 1971–73; Manager, Moorend C of E Primary Sch., Cleckheaton, 1977–80. *Recreations:* music, photography, sport. *Address:* House of Commons, SW1A 0AA. *T:* 0171–219 4010, *Fax:* 0171–219 4935. *Clubs:* Keighley Conservative, Haworth Conservative, Silsden Conservative, Ilkley Constitutional.

WALLER, Hon. Sir (George) Mark, Kt 1989; **Hon. Mr Justice Waller;** a Judge of the High Court of Justice, Queen's Bench Division, since 1989; Presiding Judge, North-East Circuit, since 1992; *b* 13 Oct. 1940; *s* of Rt Hon. Sir George Waller, *qv*; *m* 1967, Rachel Elizabeth, *d* of His Honour Judge Beaumont, *qv*; three *s*. *Educ:* Oundle Sch.; Durham Univ. (LLB). Called to the Bar, Gray's Inn, 1964, Bencher, 1988; QC 1979; a Recorder, 1986–89. *Recreations:* tennis, golf. *Address:* Royal Courts of Justice, Strand, WC2A 2LL. *Clubs:* Garrick, MCC.

WALLER, Rt. Hon. Sir George (Stanley), Kt 1965; OBE 1945; PC 1976; a Lord Justice of Appeal, 1976–84; *b* 3 Aug. 1911; *s* of late James Stanley and late Ann Waller; *m* 1936, Elizabeth Margery, *d* of 1st Baron Hacking; two *s* one *d*. *Educ:* Oundle; Queens' Coll., Cambridge (Hon. Fellow 1974). Called to the Bar, Gray's Inn, 1934, Bencher, 1961, Treasurer, 1978. RAFO, 1931–36; served War of 1939–45, in RAFVR, Coastal Command; 502 Sqdn, 1940–41; Wing Comdr, 1943 (despatches). Chm., Northern Dist Valuation Bd, 1948–55; QC 1954; Recorder of Doncaster, 1953–54, of Sunderland, 1954–55, of Bradford, 1955–57, of Sheffield, 1957–61, and of Leeds, 1961–65; a Judge of the High Court, Queen's Bench Div., 1965–76; Presiding Judge, NE Circuit, 1973–76. Solicitor-General of the County Palatine of Durham, 1957–61; Attorney-General of the County Palatine of Durham, 1961–65; Member: Criminal Injuries Compensation Board, 1964–65; General Council of the Bar, 1958–62 and 1963–65; Parole Bd, 1969–72 (Vice-Chm., 1971–72); Adv. Council on the Penal System, 1970–73 and 1974–78; Criminal Law Revision Cttee, 1977–85; Chm., Policy Adv. Cttee on Sexual Offences, 1977–85. President: Inns of Court and Bar, 1979–80; British Acad. of Forensic Sciences, 1983–84. *Address:* Hatchway, Hatch Lane, Kingsley Green, Haslemere, Surrey GU27 3LJ. *T:* Haslemere (01428) 644629. *Clubs:* Army and Navy; Hawks (Cambridge).

See also G. M. Waller.

WALLER, Rt. Rev. John Stevens; an Assistant Bishop, diocese of Bath and Wells, since 1987; *b* 18 April 1924; *m* 1951, Pamela Peregrine; two *s* three *d*. *Educ:* St Edward's School, Oxford; Peterhouse, Cambridge (MA); Wells Theol Coll. War service with RNVR, 1942–46. Deacon 1950, priest 1951, London; Leader, Strood Gp of Parishes, 1967–72, Team Rector of Strood 1972–73; Rector of St Nicholas, Harpenden, Herts, 1973–79; Bishop Suffragan of Stafford, 1979–87; Team Vicar, Long Sutton and Long Load, Som, 1987–89. *Address:* 102 Harnham Road, Salisbury, Wilts SP2 8JW. *T:* Salisbury (01722) 329739.

WALLER, Hon. Sir Mark; *see* Waller, Hon. Sir G. M.

WALLER, Philip Anthony; District Judge, Principal Registry of the Family Division, since 1994; *b* 12 Oct. 1952; *s* of Robert Waller and Olive (*née* Deakin); *m* 1978, Linda Andrews; two *d*. *Educ:* Whitgift Sch.; Univ. of Exeter (LLB Hons 1974); Inns of Court Sch. of Law. Called to the Bar, Inner Temple, 1975; with Reed, Smith, Shaw & McClay, Attorneys, Pittsburgh, USA, 1976; practised London, 1977–93. Mem., Ecclesiastical Law Soc., 1988–. *Recreations:* choral singing, early music, historic houses and gardens, wine,

France. *Address:* Principal Registry, Family Division, Somerset House, Strand, WC2R 1LP.

WALLER, Sir Robert William, 9th Bt, *cr* 1780, of Newport, Co. Tipperary; employed by the General Electric Co. of America as an Industrial Engineer, 1957–91; *b* 16 June 1934; *s* of Sir Roland Edgar Waller, 8th Bt, and Helen Madeline, *d* of Joseph Radl, Matawan, New Jersey, USA; *S* father 1958; is a citizen of the United States; *m* 1960 (marr. diss.); two *s* two *d* (and one *s* decd). *Educ:* St Peter's Prep. Sch.; Newark Coll. of Engrg; Fairleigh Dickinson University. *Heir: s* John Michael Waller [*b* 14 May 1962; *m* 1986, Maria Renee Gonzalez; two *s* two *d*]. *Address:* 5 Lookout Terrace, Lynnfield, MA 01940, USA.

WALLEY, Dr Francis, CB 1978; FEng 1985; consulting engineer; Consultant to the Ove Arup Partnership; *b* 30 Dec. 1918; *s* of late Reginald M. Walley and Maria M. Walley; *m* 1946, Margaret, *yr d* of late Rev. Thomas and Margaret J. Probert; two *d*. *Educ:* Cheltenham Grammar Sch.; Bristol Univ. MSc, PhD; FICE (Mem. Council, 1978–81); FIStructE (Vice-Pres., 1982–83; Hon. Treasurer, 1981; Hon. Sec., 1979–81); Lewis Kent Award, IStructE, 1985. Entered Min. of Home Security as Engr, 1941: reported to CIGS on allied bombing of Pantellaria, 1943; Member: British Bombing Survey Unit, France, 1944–45; Jt UK/USA Survey Unit of Nagasaki and Hiroshima, 1945. Min. of Works, 1945; Suptg Civil Engr, 1963; Dep. Dir of Building Develt, 1965; Dir of Estate Management Overseas, 1969; Dir of Post Office Services, 1971; Under-Sec., Dir of Civil Engineering Services, DoE, 1973–78. I/c of Civil Defence Structures, British Atomic Trials, Aust., 1954; Mem., British Govt team looking at building construction in USSR, 1966. Mem., Standing Cttee on Structural Safety, 1977–88; Chairman: BSI Code Cttee for Structural Use of Concrete, 1987–; ISO Cttee of Design of Concrete Structures, 1989–. *Publications:* Prestressed Concrete Design and Construction, 1954; (with Dr S. C. C. Bate) A Guide to the Code of Practice CP 115, 1960; several papers to ICE and techn. jls. *Recreations:* gardening, furniture-making. *Address:* 13 Julien Road, Coulsdon, Surrey CR5 2DN. *T:* 0181–660 3290.

See also Sir John Walley.

WALLEY, Joan Lorraine; MP (Lab) Stoke-on-Trent North, since 1987; *b* 23 Jan. 1949; *d* of late Arthur Walley and Mary Walley; *m* 1980, Jan Ostrowski; two *s*. *Educ:* Biddulph Grammar School; Hull Univ. (BA); University Coll. Swansea (Dip. Community Work). Alcoholics Recovery Project, 1970–73; Swansea City Council, 1974–78; Wandsworth Borough Council, 1978–79; NACRO, 1979–82. Mem., Lambeth Borough Council, 1982–86 (Chair: Health and Consumer Services Cttee; Assoc. of London Authorities Public Protection Cttee). Opposition front-bench spokesman on envmtl protection, 1988–90, on transport, 1990–. Sponsored by UNISON. Pres., West Midlands Home and Water Safety Council, 1990–. Vice-Pres., Inst. of Environmental Health Officers, 1987–. *Address:* House of Commons, SW1A 0AA. *Clubs:* Newchapel Sports and Social Inst.; Fegg Hayes Sports and Social.

WALLEY, Sir John, KBE 1965; CB 1950; retired as Deputy Secretary, Ministry of Social Security, 1966 (Ministry of Pensions and National Insurance, 1958–66); *b* Barnstaple, Devon, 3 April 1906; *e s* of late R. M. Walley; *m* 1934, Elisabeth Mary, *e d* of late R. H. Pinhorn, OBE; two *s* two *d*. *Educ:* Hereford High Sch.; Hereford Cathedral Sch.; Merton Coll., Oxford; Postmaster, 1924–28; Hons Maths and Dip., Pol. and Econ. Sci. Ministry of Labour: Asst Principal, 1929; Sec., Cabinet Cttee on Unemployment, 1932; Principal, 1934; Asst Sec., Min. of National Service, 1941; promoted Under-Sec. to take charge of legislation and other preparations for Beveridge Nat. Insce Scheme, in new Min. of National Insurance, 1945; Chm., Dental Benefit Council, 1945–48. Chm., Hampstead Centre, National Trust, 1969–79, Pres., 1980–90. *Publications:* Social Security-Another British Failure?, 1972; contribs: to The Future of the Social Services, ed Robson and Crick, 1970; on Children's Allowances, in Family Poverty, ed David Bull, 1971; vol. in British Oral Archive of Political and Administrative History, 1980; articles in journals and the press on Social Security matters. *Address:* Brookland House, 24 High Street, Cottenham, Cambs CB4 4SA. *T:* Cottenham (01954) 250931.

See also F. Walley.

WALLEY, Keith Henry, FEng 1981; FIChemE; Managing Director, Shell Chemicals UK Ltd, 1978–84; *b* 26 June 1928; *s* of Eric Henry James Walley and Rose Walley; *m* 1950, Betty Warner; one *s* one *d*. *Educ:* Hinckley Grammar School; Loughborough College (Dip. Chem. 1949, Dip. Chem. Eng. 1952); FIChemE 1972. Commissioned RAOC 1949–51. Joined Royal Dutch/Shell Group, 1952; served in Holland, 1952–69; Works Manager, Shell Chemicals, Carrington, 1970–71; Head, Manufacturing Economic and Ops, The Hague, 1972–73; Gen. Man., Base Chemicals Shell International Chemicals, 1974–77; Jt Man. Dir, Shell UK Ltd, 1978–84; Chm., International Military Services, 1985–91 (Dir, 1984–91); Dep. Chm., Johnson Matthey, 1986–91 (Dir, 1985–91). Non-executive Director: John Brown plc, 1984–86; Reckitt & Colman plc, 1986–90. Vis. Prof., UCL, 1986–. Pres., Soc. of Chemical Industry, 1984–86 (Vice-Pres., 1981–84); Member Council: Chem. Ind. Assoc., 1978–84 (Chm., Educn and Sci. Policy Cttee, 1980–84); IChemE, 1983– (Vice-Pres., 1985; Pres., 1987); Royal Acad. (formerly Fellowship) of Engineering, 1984–. CIMgt (CBIM 1982). Hon. DSc Loughborough, 1989. *Publications:* papers in chem. jls and planning jls. *Recreations:* the Pyrenees, opera, tennis, ski-ing. *Club:* Athenæum.

WALLFISCH, Raphael; 'cellist; *b* 15 June 1953; *s* of Peter Wallfisch, pianist; *m*; one *s*. *Educ:* Univ. of Southern California; studies with Amaryllis Fleming, Amadeo Baldovino, Derek Simpson and Gregor Piatigorsky. London début, QEH, 1974. 1st recordings of compositions by Bax, Strauss and others; numerous other recordings. Won Gaspar Cassado Internat. Cello competition, 1977. *Address:* c/o Clarion/Seven Muses, 47 Whitehall Park, N19 3TW; 24 Versailles Road, SE20 8AX.

WALLINGTON, Jeremy Francis; publisher and television producer; Director, Wallington, Irving, Jackson Ltd, since 1990; Publishing Director, Headwater Communications, since 1994; *b* 7 July 1935; *s* of Ernest Francis Wallington and Nell (*née* Howe); *m* 1955, Margaret Ivy Willment; three *s* one *d*. *Educ:* Royal Grammar Sch., High Wycombe, Bucks. Reporter on several Fleet Street newspapers, 1956–62; Managing Editor, Topic Magazine, 1962; Co-Founder of Insight, Sunday Times, 1963; Assistant Editor: Sunday Times, 1963–65; Daily Mail, 1965–67; Editor, Investigations Bureau, World in Action, Granada Television, 1967–68; Jt Editor, then Editor, World in Action, 1968–72; Head of Documentaries, Granada Television, 1972–77 (prod Burgess, Philby and Maclean, 1977); Dir of Progs, Southern TV, 1977–81; Chief Exec., Limehouse Prodns, 1982–86. *Publication:* (jtly) Scandal '63, 1963. *Recreations:* choral singing, old cars. *Address:* 28 Merrick Square, SE1 4JB. *T:* 0171–403 0570.

WALLIS, (Diana) Lynn; Artistic Director, Royal Academy of Dancing, since 1994; *b* 11 Dec. 1946; *d* of Dennis Blackwell Wallis and Joan Wallis. *Educ:* Tonbridge Grammar Sch. for Girls; Royal Ballet Upper Sch. FISTD. Royal Ballet Touring Co., 1965–68; Royal Ballet School: Ballet Mistress, 1969–81; Dep. Principal, 1981–84; National Ballet of Canada: Artistic Co-ordinator, 1984–86; Associate Artistic Dir, 1986–87; Co-Artistic Dir, 1987–89; Dep. Artistic Dir, English National Ballet, 1990–94. *Recreations:* music, theatre, cinema. *Address:* 41 Musard Road, W6 8NR. *T:* 0171–385 8618.

WALLIS, Edmund Arthur, CEng; Chief Executive, PowerGen, since 1988; *b* 3 July 1939; *s* of Reuben Wallis and Iris Mary Cliff; *m* 1964, Gillian Joan Mitchell; two *s*. CEng 1978; MIEE 1971; MIMechE 1972. Central Electricity Generating Board: Stn Manager, Oldbury Power Stn, 1977–79; Dir of System Op., 1981–86; Divl Dir of Ops, 1986–88. Non-executive Director: BSI, 1992–; Lucas Industries, 1995–; Indep. non-exec. Dir, Mercury European Privatisation Trust plc, 1994–; Mem. Econ. Adv. Bd, RWE Energie Aktienges., 1991–. Lay Mem. Council, Aston Univ., 1992–. CIMgt (CBIM 1991; AMBIM 1973). *Address:* PowerGen, Westwood Way, Westwood Business Park, Coventry CV4 8LG.

WALLIS, Frederick Alfred John E.; *see* Emery-Wallis.

WALLIS, Jeffrey Joseph; retail consultant; *b* 25 Nov. 1923; *s* of Nathaniel and Rebecca Wallis; *m* 1948, Barbara Brickman; one *s* one *d*. *Educ:* Owen's; Coll. Aeronautical Engrg. Man. Dir, Wallis Fashion Group, 1948–80. Mem., Monopolies and Mergers Commn, 1981–85. Formerly Member: CNAA; Clothing Export Council; NEDC (Textiles). Involved in art educn throughout career; various governorships. *Recreations:* motor racing, motor boating, industrial design. *Address:* 37 Avenue Close, NW8 6DA. *T:* 0171–722 8665.

WALLIS, Prof. Kenneth Frank, FBA 1994; Professor of Econometrics, University of Warwick, since 1977; *b* 26 March 1938; *s* of late Leslie Wallis and Vera Daisy Wallis (*née* Stone); *m* 1963, Margaret Sheila Campbell. *Educ:* Wath-on-Dearne GS; Manchester Univ. (BSc, MScTech); Stanford Univ. (PhD). Mem. Exec., NUS, 1961–63. Lectr, then Reader, in Stats, LSE, 1966–77; Dir, ESRC Macroeconomic Modelling Bureau, 1983–. Mem., HM Treasury Academic Panel, 1980– (Chm., 1987–91). Member Council: Royal Stat. Soc., 1972–76; Royal Econ. Soc., 1989–94; Econometric Soc., 1995– (Fellow, 1975). *Publications:* Introductory Econometrics, 1972; Topics in Applied Econometrics, 1973; (ed with D. F. Hendry) Econometrics and Quantitative Economics, 1984; Models of the UK Economy 1–4, 1984–87; (ed) Macroeconometric Modelling, 1994; Time Series Analysis and Macroeconometric Modelling, 1995; articles in learned jls. *Recreations:* travel, music, gardening, swimming. *Address:* Department of Economics, University of Warwick, Coventry CV4 7AL. *T:* Coventry (01203) 523468; 4 Walkers Orchard, Stoneleigh, Warwicks CV8 3JG. *T:* Coventry (01203) 414271.

WALLIS, Lynn; *see* Wallis, D. L.

WALLIS, Sir Peter (Gordon), KCVO 1992; CMG 1990; HM Diplomatic Service, retired; High Commissioner to Malta, 1991–94; *b* 2 Aug. 1935; *s* of Arthur Gordon Wallis, DFC, BScEcon, and late Winifred Florence Maud Wallis; *m* 1965, Delysia Elizabeth (*née* Leonard); three *s* one *d*. *Educ:* Taunton and Whitgift Schools; Pembroke Coll., Oxford (MA). Ministry of Labour and National Service, 1958; HM Customs and Excise, 1959 (Private Sec., 1961–64); HM Diplomatic Service, 1968; Tel Aviv, 1970; Nairobi, 1974; Counsellor (Econ. and Comm.), Ankara, 1977; RCDS, 1981; Cabinet Office, 1982; Hd, Perm. Under-Sec.'s Dept, FCO, 1983; Minister, Pretoria, 1987; Minister, British Liaison Office, 1989, and subseq. Acting High Comr, 1990, Windhoek, Namibia; Political Advr to Jt Comdr, British Forces in the Gulf, Jan.–April 1991, to Comdr, British Forces, SE Turkey and N Iraq, May–July 1991. *Recreations:* reading, writing, music, children. *Address:* c/o Foreign and Commonwealth Office, SW1A 2AH.

WALLIS, Peter Ralph; Deputy Controller, Aircraft Weapons and Electronics, Ministry of Defence, 1980–84; *b* 17 Aug. 1924; *s* of Leonard Francis Wallis and Molly McCulloch Wallis (*née* Jones); *m* 1949, Frances Jean Patricia Cowie; three *s* one *d*. *Educ:* University College Sch., Hampstead; Imperial Coll. of Science and Technology, London (BSc(Eng)). Henrici and Siemens Medals of the College, 1944. Joined Royal Naval Scientific Service 1944; work at Admty Signal and Radar Estab. till 1959, Admty Underwater Weapons Estab. till 1968; Asst Chief Scientific Advr (Research), MoD, 1968–71, Dir Gen. Research Weapons, 1971–75, Dir Gen. Guided Weapons and Electronics, 1975–78, Dir Gen. Research A (Electronics) and Dep. Chief Scientist (Navy), 1978–80. Marconi Award, IERE, 1964; FCGI. *Publications:* articles in Jl of IEE, IERE and Op. Res. Quarterly. *Recreations:* skiing, mountain walking, archæology, sailing, Hampstead Scientific Soc. *Address:* 22 Flask Walk, Hampstead, NW3 1HE. *Clubs:* Alpine Ski, Eagle Ski.

WALLIS, Peter Spencer; a Metropolitan Stipendiary Magistrate, since 1993; *b* 31 March 1945; *s* of Philip Wallis and Winifred Wallis; *m* 1970, Ann Margaret Bentham; one *s* one *d*. *Educ:* Maidstone Grammar Sch.; Lincoln Coll., Oxford (MA). Pilot, RAF, 1967–72. Admitted solicitor, 1976. Clerk to: Tonbridge and Malling Justices, 1977–88; Dover and Ashford Justices, 1988–93; Folkestone and Hythe Justices, 1990–93. Mem. Council, Justices' Clerks' Soc., 1983–93 (Pres., 1993). *Publications:* The Transport Acts 1981 and 1982, 1982, 2nd edn 1985; Road Traffic: guide to Part I of the 1991 Act, 1991; General Editor, Wilkinson's Road Traffic Offences, 16th edn 1993, 17th edn 1995. *Recreations:* flying, cricket, choral singing. *Address:* c/o Greenwich Magistrates' Court, 9 Blackheath Road, SE10 8PG. *Tel:* 0181–694 0033. *Club:* Royal Air Force.

WALLIS, Stuart Michael; Chief Executive, Fisons plc, since 1994; *b* 8 Oct. 1945; *s* of Stanley Oswald Wallis and Margaret Ethel Wallis; *m* 1971; Eileen; one *s*. *Educ:* Hawesdown Sch., West Wickham, Kent. FCA, ATII. Roland Goodman & Co., 1962–68; Chrysler, 1968–71; Shipton Automation, 1971–73; Star Computer Services, 1973–74; Hestair Gp, 1974–85 (Main Board, 1977); Exec. Dir, Octopus, 1985–87; Main Board Dir, Bowater plc, 1988–94. Non-exec. Dir, Boddington Gp, 1993–. *Recreations:* golf, squash, ski-ing. *Address:* Fisons, 85 London Wall, EC2M 7AD. *Clubs:* Royal Anglo-Belgian; Ashridge Golf.

WALLIS, Sir Timothy (William), Kt 1994; Managing Director, Alpine Deer Group; *b* 9 Sept. 1938; *s* of Arthur Wallis and Janice Blunden; *m* 1974, Prudence Ann Hazledine; four *s*. *Educ:* Christ's Coll., Christchurch; Canterbury Univ. Director: The Helicopter Line; Altyn Keri; joint venture deer farm, Russia/NZ. Mem. Council, NZ Deer Farmers' Assoc., 1977–84 (Hon. Life Mem.); founding Chm. and Hon. Life Mem., NZ Wapiti Soc.; Mem., Waihi Trust Bd. E. A. Gibson Award, 1980, for contribs to NZ aviation; Sir Arthur Ward Award, 1985, for contribs to agric.; Commem. Medal for services to deer industry, 1990. *Recreations:* scuba diving, hunting, fly fishing; represented West Coast-Buller 1958, S Canterbury 1959, at Rugby. *Address:* Benfiddich, Mount Barker, Wanaka, New Zealand.

WALLIS, Victor Harry; Assistant Under Secretary of State, Police and Fire Department, Home Office, 1980–82; *b* 21 Dec. 1922; *s* of Harry Stewart Wallis, MBE, and Ada Elizabeth (*née* Jarratt); *m* 1948, Margaret Teresa (*née* Meadowcroft); one *s* three *d*. *Educ:* Wilson's Grammar School. Served Royal Scots and Indian Army (Major), 1941–47 (War, Burma and Defence medals); RARO, 1947–48; Territorial Army and TARO (Int. Corps), 1948–77. Entered Home Office, Immigration Service, 1947; Regional Officer, 1952; Policy Div., 1958; Chief Trng Officer, 1967; Establishments, 1968. Chm., various cttees, Fire Brigades Adv. Council, 1980–82; Chm., Residents' Assoc., 1989–. *Recreations:*

philately, military history, painting. *Clubs:* Civil Service, St Stephen's Constitutional, Royal British Legion.

WALLIS-JONES, His Honour Ewan Perrins; a Circuit Judge (formerly County Court Judge), 1964–84; *b* 22 June 1913; *s* of late William James Wallis-Jones, MBE, and late Ethel Perrins Wallis-Jones; *m* 1940, Veronica Mary (*née* Fowler); one *s* two *d.* *Educ:* Mill Hill Sch.; University Coll. of Wales, Aberystwyth; Balliol Coll., Oxford. LLB Hons Wales, 1934; BA Oxon 1936; MA Oxon 1941. Qualified Solicitor, 1935; called to Bar, Gray's Inn, 1938. Chm., Carmarthenshire QS, 1966–71 (Dep. Chm., 1965–66); Jt Pres., Council of Circuit Judges, 1982. ARPS. *Recreations:* music, reading and photography. *Address:* 25 Cotham Grove, Bristol BS6 6AN. *T:* Bristol (0117) 924 8908. *Club:* Royal Photographic Society.

WALLIS-KING, Maj.-Gen. Colin Sainthill, CBE 1975 (OBE 1971); retired; *b* 13 Sept. 1926; *s* of late Lt-Col Frank King, DSO, OBE, 4th Hussars, and Colline Ammabel, *d* of late Lt-Col C. G. H. St Hill; *m* 1962, Lisabeth, *d* of late Swan Swanstrøm, Oslo, Norway; two *d.* *Educ:* Stowe. Commissioned Coldstream Guards, 1945; Liaison Officer with Fleet Air Arm, 1954; Staff Coll., 1960; Regtl Adjutant, Coldstream Guards, 1961; seconded to Para. Regt, 1963; ACOS HQ Land Norway, 1965; Comdr 2nd Bn Coldstream Guards, 1969; Dep. Comdr 8 Inf. Brigade, 1972; Comdr 3 Inf. Brigade, 1973; BGS Intell., MoD, 1975; Dir of Service Intelligence, 1977–80. Dir, Kongsberg Ltd, 1982–87; UK Agent for Norsk Forsvarsteknologi A/S, 1987–93. *Recreations:* equitation, sailing, music, cross-country skiing, fishing. *Address:* c/o Royal Bank of Scotland, Lawrie House, Victoria Road, Farnborough, Hants GU14 7NR. *Club:* Cavalry and Guards.

WALLOP, family name of **Earl of Portsmouth.**

WALLROCK, John; Chairman, Conocean International Consultants Group, Hong Kong, 1984–92; *b* 14 Nov. 1922; *s* of Samuel and Marie Kate Wallrock; *m* 1967, Audrey Louise Ariow; one *s* two *d.* *Educ:* Bradfield Coll., Berks. Cadet, Merchant Navy, 1939; Lieut RNR, 1943; Master Mariner, 1949; J. H. Minet & Co. Ltd, 1950, Dir, 1955–79, Chm., 1972–79; Chairman: Minet Holdings, 1972–82; St Katherine Insurance Co. Ltd, London, 1972–82; Dir, Tugu Insce Co. Ltd, Hong Kong, 1976–84. Underwriting Mem. of Lloyd's, 1951–86. Mem., Council of Management, White Ensign Assoc. Ltd, 1974–83. Liveryman, Master Mariners' Co., 1954–; Freeman, City of London, 1965. FCIB, MNI. *Recreations:* yachting, shooting. *Address:* 14 Lowndes Square, SW1X 9HB; Kits Croft, Up Green, Eversley, Hants RG27 0PE. *Clubs:* East India, Naval; Royal London Yacht, Royal Southern Yacht.

WALLS, Prof. Daniel Frank, FRS 1992; FRSNZ; Professor of Physics, University of Auckland, since 1987; *b* 13 Sept. 1942; *s* of James Reginald Walls and Barbara Gertrude Walls (*née* Leddra); *m* 1968, Fari Khoy (marr. diss. 1986); one *s.* *Educ:* Univ. of Auckland (MSc); Harvard Univ. (PhD). Asst Prof., Univ. of Stuttgart, 1970; Postdoctoral Fellow, Univ. of Auckland, 1971; University of Waikato: Sen. Lectr, 1972; Reader, 1976; Prof., 1980. FAPS; Fellow, Optical Soc. of America. Paul Dirac Medal, Inst. of Physics, 1995. *Publications:* numerous papers on quantum optics in learned jls. *Recreations:* ski-ing, swimming, tramping. *Address:* 75A Selwyn Avenue, Mission Bay, Auckland, New Zealand.

WALLS, Prof. Eldred Wright; Emeritus Professor of Anatomy in the University of London at Middlesex Hospital Medical School (Dean, Medical School, 1967–74); Hon. Consultant Anatomist, St Mark's Hospital; *b* 17 Aug. 1912; 2nd *s* of late J. T. Walls, Glasgow; *m* 1939, Jessie Vivien Mary Robb, MB, ChB, DPH, *o d* of late R. F. Robb and late M. T. Robb; one *s* one *d.* *Educ:* Hillhead High Sch.; Glasgow Univ. BSc, 1931; MB, ChB (Hons), 1934; MD (Hons), 1947, FRSE, FRCS, FRCSE; Struthers Medal and Prize, 1942. Demonstrator and Lectr in Anatomy, Glasgow Univ., 1935–41; Senior Lectr in Anatomy, University Coll. of S Wales and Monmouthshire, 1941–47; Reader in Anatomy, Middlesex Hospital Medical Sch. 1947–49, S. A. Courtauld Prof. of Anatomy, 1949–74; Lectr in Anatomy, Edinburgh Univ., 1975–82. Past President: Anatomical Soc. of GB and Ireland; Chartered Soc. of Physiotherapy. Lectures: West., UC Cardiff, 1965; Osler, Soc. of Apothecaries, 1967; Astor, Mddx Hosp., 1975; Gordon Taylor, RCS, 1976; Struthers, RCSE, 1983. Farquharson Award, RCSE, 1988. *Publications:* (co-editor) Rest and Pain (by John Hilton) (6th edn), 1950; (co-author) Sir Charles Bell, His Life and Times, 1958; contrib. Blood-vascular and Lymphatic Systems, to Cunningham's Textbook Anat., 1981; contrib. to Journal of Anatomy, Lancet, etc. *Recreation:* annual visit to Lord's. *Address:* 19 Dean Park Crescent, Edinburgh EH4 1PH. *T:* 0131–332 7164. *Clubs:* MCC; New (Edinburgh).

WALLS, Geoffrey Nowell; Agent General for South Australia, since 1986; *b* 17 Feb. 1945; *s* of late Andrew Nowell Walls and of Hilda Margaret Thompson; *m* 1975, Vanessa Bodger; one *s* three *d.* *Educ:* Trinity Grammar Sch., Melbourne; Univ. of Melbourne (BComm 1965). Australian Regular Army, 2nd Lieut RAAOC, 1966–69; Australian Trade Comr Service, 1970–79; served Jakarta, Singapore, Cairo, Beirut, Bahrain, Manila, Baghdad; Regional Dir, Adelaide, Commonwealth Dept of Trade, 1980–83; Gen. Manager, ATCO Industries (Aust) Pty Ltd, 1983–86. *Recreations:* golf, tennis, gardening. *Address:* South Australia House, 115 Strand, WC2R 0AJ. *Clubs:* Royal Automobile, East India.

WALLS, Rev. Brother Roland Charles; Member, Community of the Transfiguration, since 1965; *b* 7 June 1917; *s* of late Roland William Walls and late Tina Josephine Hayward. *Educ:* Sandown Grammar Sch.; Corpus Christi Coll., Cambridge; Kelham Theological Coll. Curate of St James', Crossgates, Leeds, 1940–42; Curate of St Cecilia's, Parson Cross, Sheffield, 1942–45; Licensed preacher, Diocese of Ely, 1945–48; Fellow of Corpus Christi Coll., Cambridge, 1948–62; Lecturer in Theology, Kelham Theological Coll., 1948–51; Chaplain and Dean of Chapel, Corpus Christi Coll., Cambridge, 1952–58; Canon Residentiary, Sheffield Cathedral, 1958–62; Chaplain of Rosslyn Chapel, Midlothian, 1962–68. Examining Chaplain to Bishop of Edinburgh. Lecturer at Coates Hall Theological Coll.; Lecturer in Dogmatics Dept, New Coll., Edinburgh, 1963–74. Received into RC Church, ordained priest, 1983. *Publications:* (contrib.) Theological Word Book (ed A. Richardson), 1950; Law and Gospel, 1980; (contrib.) Dictionary of Christian Spirituality, 1983; (contrib.) Dictionary of Pastoral Counsel, 1984; The Royal Mysteries, 1990. *Recreations:* botany, music, etc. *Address:* The Monastery, 23 Manse Road, Roslin, Midlothian EH25 9LF.

WALLS, Stephen Roderick; Chairman, The Albert Fisher Group PLC, since 1992 (Director, 1991–92); *b* 8 Aug. 1947; *s* of late R. W. Walls and of D. M. Walls; *m*; one *s.* Chartered Accountant. Senior Auditor, Deloitte & Co., 1969; Group Chief Accountant, Lindustries, 1971; Financial Planning Exec., Vernons, 1974; Chesebrough Ponds: Finance Dir, UK and Geneva, 1975; Internat. Finance Dir, Geneva, 1981; Vice-Pres., Finance, 1981–87; Dir of Finance, 1987, Man. Dir, 1988–89, Plessey Co.; Chm., 1990–91, Chief Exec., 1990–92, Wiggins Teape Appleton, later Arjo Wiggins Appleton; non-executive Director: Lonrho, 1993–; Servisair, 1994–. Mem., Financial Reporting Council, 1990–. *Recreations:* running, tennis, music, theatre. *Address:* c/o The Albert Fisher Group PLC, Sefton Park, Bells Hill, Stoke Poges, Bucks SL2 4HS. *Club:* Royal Automobile.

WALLWORK, John, FRCSE; Consultant Cardiothoracic Surgeon, since 1981, and Director of Transplantation, since 1989, Papworth Hospital; *b* 8 July 1946; *s* of Thomas and Vera Wallwork; *m* 1973, Elizabeth Ann Medley; one *s* two *d.* *Educ:* Accrington Grammar Sch.; Edinburgh Univ. (BSc Hons Pharm. 1966; MB ChB 1970); MA Cantab 1986. FRCSE 1974. Surgical Registrar, Royal Infirmary, Edinburgh, 1975–76; Senior Registrar: Adelaide Hosp., SA, 1977–78; Royal Infirmary, Glasgow, 1978–79; St Bartholomew's Hosp., 1979–81; Chief Resident in Cardiovascular and Cardiac Transplant Surgery, Stanford Univ. Med. Sch., 1980–81. Lister Prof., RCSE, 1985–86. *Publications:* (with R. Stepney) Heart Disease: what it is and how it is treated, 1987; (ed) Heart and Heart-Lung Transplantation, 1989; numerous papers on cardiothoracic and cardiopulmonary topics. *Recreations:* tennis, conversation, making phone calls from the bath. *Address:* 3 Latham Road, Cambridge CB2 2EG. *T:* Cambridge (01223) 352827. *Club:* Caledonian.

WALLWORK, John Sackfield, CBE 1982; Director, Daily Mail and General Trust PLC, 1982–91; Managing Director, Northcliffe Newspapers Group Ltd, 1972–82 (General Manager, 1967–71); *b* 2 Nov. 1918; *s* of Peter Wallwork and Clara Cawthorne Wallwork; *m* 1945, Bessie Bray; one *s* one *d.* *Educ:* Leigh Grammar Sch., Leigh, Lancs. FCIS. General Manager, Scottish Daily Mail, Edinburgh, 1959–62; Asst Gen. Man., Associated Newspapers Gp Ltd, London, 1962–66, Dir, 1973–82. Chm., Press Association Ltd, 1973–74 (Dir, 1969–76); Director: Reuters Ltd, 1973–76; Reuters Founders Share Co. Ltd, 1984–87; Reuters Trustee, 1978–84; Member Press Council, 1974–75; Newspaper Society: Mem. Council, 1967–85; Jun. Vice-Pres. 1975; Sen. Vice-Pres., 1976, Pres., 1977–78. Commander, Order of Merit, Republic of Italy, 1973. *Recreations:* golf, travel. *Address:* Greenfield, Manor Road, Sidmouth, Devon EX10 8RR. *T:* Sidmouth (01395) 513489.

WALLWORTH, Cyril; Assistant Under-Secretary of State, Ministry of Defence, 1964–76; Gwilym Gibbon Fellow, Nuffield College, Oxford, 1975–76; *b* 6 June 1916; *s* of Albert A. Wallworth and Eva (*née* Taylor); unmarried. *Educ:* Oldham High Sch.; Manchester Univ. BA (Hons) History, 1937. Asst Principal, Admiralty, 1939; Asst Private Secretary to First Lord, 1941–45, Principal, 1943; Asst Secretary, 1951; IDC 1960; Under-Secretary, 1964. Liveryman: Basketmakers' Co., 1990; Upholders' Co., 1991. *Recreations:* music, wine, cooking, photography. *Address:* 5 Leinster Mews, W2 3EY. *Clubs:* Hurlingham, Lansdowne, United Wards, City Livery.

WALMSLEY, Arnold Robert, CMG 1963; MBE 1946; HM Diplomatic Service, retired; *b* 29 Aug. 1912; *s* of late Rev. Canon A. M. Walmsley; *m* 1944, Frances Councell de Mouilpied. *Educ:* Rossall Sch.; Hertford Coll., Oxford. 1st Class Maths Mods, 1st Class Modern Greats. Private Sec. to Julius Meinl, Vienna, 1935–38; Foreign Office, 1939–45; established in Foreign Service, 1946; Foreign Office, 1946–50; British Consul in Jerusalem, 1950–54; Foreign Office, 1954–63; Head of Arabian Dept, 1961; Counsellor, Khartoum, 1963–65; Dir, Middle East Centre of Arab Studies, Lebanon, 1965–69. Order of the Two Niles (Sudan), 1965. *Publications:* (as Nicholas Roland) The Great One, 1967; Natural Causes, 1969; Who Came by Night, 1971. *Address:* 10 Park Lane, Saffron Walden, Essex CB10 1DA. *Club:* Travellers'.

WALMSLEY, Brian; Under Secretary, Social Security Policy Group, Department of Social Security, 1990–94; *b* 22 April 1936; *s* of late Albert Edward Walmsley and Ivy Doreen Walmsley (*née* Black); *m* 1st, 1956, Sheila Maybury (marr. diss. 1993); two *d*; 2nd, 1994, Margaret Wilson. *Educ:* Prescot Grammar School. National Service, RAF, 1955–57. Joined Min. of Pensions and Nat. Insurance, 1957, later Min. of Social Security and DHSS; Sec. to Industrial Injuries Adv. Council, 1978–79; Asst Sec., 1979; Under Sec., 1985; Civil Service Comr, OMCS, Cabinet Office (on secondment), 1988–90. *Recreations:* following cricket, playing golf, reading, gardening. *Address:* 1 Malthouse Lane, West End, Woking, Surrey GU24 9JF. *Club:* MCC.

WALMSLEY, Rt. Rev. Francis Joseph, CBE 1979; Roman Catholic Bishop of the Forces, since 1979; Titular Bishop of Tamalluma; *b* 9 Nov. 1926; *s* of Edwin Walmsley and Mary Walmsley (*née* Hall). *Educ:* St Joseph's Coll., Mark Cross, Tunbridge Wells; St John's Seminary, Wonersh, Guildford. Ordained, 1953; Asst Priest, Woolwich, 1953; Shoreham-by-Sea, Sussex, 1958; Chaplain, Royal Navy, 1960; Principal RC Chaplain, RN, 1975; retired from RN, 1979. Prelate of Honour to HH Pope Paul VI, 1975; ordained Bishop, 1979. *Recreations:* photography, gardening.

WALMSLEY, Nigel Norman; Chairman: Carlton UK Television, since 1994 (Chief Executive, 1991–94); GMTV, 1994–April 1996; Director: (non-executive), Central Independent Television, since 1991; Carlton Communications plc, since 1994; General Cable plc, since 1994; *b* 26 Jan. 1942; *s* of Norman and Ida Walmsley; *m* 1969, Jane Walmsley, broadcaster and author; one *d.* *Educ:* William Hulme's Sch.; Brasenose Coll., Oxford (BA English). Joined the Post Office, 1964; Asst Private Secretary to Postmaster General, 1967; Asst Director of Marketing, Post Office, 1973–75; Asst Sec., Industrial Planning Division of Dept of Industry, 1975–76; Director of Marketing, Post Office, 1977–81, Board Mem. for Marketing 1981–82; Man. Dir, Capital Radio, 1982–91. Board Member: Ind. Radio News, 1983–91; South Bank Centre, 1985–92; Dir, The Builder Gp, 1986–92. Chm., GLAA, 1985–86; Vice Chm., Advertising Assoc., 1992–. *Recreation:* intensive inactivity. *Address:* 26 Belsize Road, NW6 4RD. *T:* 0171–586 1950.

WALMSLEY, Peter James, MBE 1975; Director-General (formerly Director) of Petroleum Engineering Division, Department of Energy, 1981–89; *b* 29 April 1929; *s* of George Stanley and Elizabeth Martin Walmsley; *m* 1970, Edna Fisher; three *s* one *d.* *Educ:* Caterham Sch., Surrey; Imperial Coll., London (BSc; ARSM). Geologist: Iraq Petroleum Co., 1951–59; BP Trinidad, 1959–65; BP London, 1965–72; Exploration Manager, BP Aberdeen, 1972–78; Dep. Chief Geologist, BP London, 1978–79; Regional Exploration Manager, BP London, 1979–81. Chairman, Petroleum Exploration Soc. of Gt Britain, 1971–72; Pres., RSM Assoc., 1995–June 1996. *Publications:* contribs to various learned jls on North Sea geology. *Recreations:* home and garden. *Address:* Elm Tree Cottage, 10 Great Austins, Farnham, Surrey GU9 8JG.

WALMSLEY, Prof. Robert, TD 1984; MD; DSc; FRCPE, FRCSE, FRSE; formerly Bute Professor of Anatomy, University of St Andrews, 1946–73; *b* 24 Aug. 1906; *s* of late Thomas Walmsley, Supt Marine Engr; *m* 1939, Isabel Mary, *e d* of James Mathieson, Aberdeen; two *s.* *Educ:* Greenock Acad.; Univ. of Edinburgh; Carnegie Inst. of Embryology, Baltimore, USA. MB, ChB (Edinburgh); MD (Edinburgh) with Gold Medal, 1937. Demonstrator, Lectr and Senior Lectr on Anatomy, Univ. of Edinburgh, 1931–46; Goodsir Fellowship in Anatomy, 1933; Rockefeller Fellowship, 1935–36; served as Pathologist in RAMC in UK and MEF, 1939–44. Struthers Lectr, Royal Coll. of Surgeons, Edinburgh, 1952; Fulbright Advanced Scholarship, 1960; Pres., Edinburgh Harveian Soc., 1963–64. Vis. Prof. of Anatomy: George Washington Univ., USA, 1960; Auckland, NZ, 1967. Formerly: Master, St Salvator's Coll.; Chm., Council St Leonards and St Katherines Schs; Hon. Pres., British Medical Students Assoc.; External Examiner in Anatomy, Cambridge, Edinburgh, Durham, Glasgow, Aberdeen, Liverpool, Singapore, Kingston (WI), Accra, etc. Life Mem. Anatomical Soc. Hon. Fellow, British Assoc. of Clinical Anatomists, 1980. Hon. DSc St Andrews, 1972. First Farquharson Award,

RCSEd, 1974. *Publications:* Co-author Manual of Surgical Anatomy, 1964; (jtly) Clinical Anatomy of the Heart, 1978; co-reviser, Jamieson's Illustrations Regional Anatomy, 1981; contribs to various jls, on Heart, Bone and Joints, and on Whales. *Recreation:* gardening. *Address:* 45 Kilrymont Road, St Andrews, Fife KY16 8DE. *T:* St Andrews (01334) 72879.
See also Vice-Adm. Sir R. Walmsley.

WALMSLEY, Vice-Adm. Sir Robert, KCB 1995; FIEE; Controller of the Navy, since 1994; *b* Aberdeen, 1 Feb. 1941; *s* of Robert Walmsley, *qv*; *m* 1967, Christina Veronica Melvill; one *s* two *d*. *Educ:* Fettes Coll.; RN Coll., Dartmouth; Queens' Coll., Cambridge (MA MechScis); RN Coll., Greenwich (MSc Nuclear Sci.). FIEE 1994. HMS Ark Royal, 1962–63; HMS Otus, 1964–66; HMS Churchill, 1968–72; Ship Dept, MoD, 1973–74; HM Dockyard, Chatham, 1975–78; MoD, PE, 1979–80; Chm., Naval Nuclear Technical Safety Panel, 1981–83; Naval Staff, 1984; MoD, PE, 1985–86; Dir Operational Requirements (Sea), 1987–89; ACDS (Communications, Command, Control and Information Systems), 1990–93; Dir Gen. Submarines, Chief Naval Engr Officer and Sen. Naval Rep. in Bath, 1993–94. *Recreations:* fly fishing, West Ham United FC, Scotland. *Address:* Ministry of Defence, Main Building, Whitehall, SW1A 2HB. *Club:* Army and Navy.

WALPOLE, family name of **Baron Walpole.**

WALPOLE, 10th Baron *cr* 1723, of Walpole; **Robert Horatio Walpole;** Baron Walpole of Wolterton, 1756; *b* 8 Dec. 1938; *s* of 9th Baron Walpole, TD and of Nancy Louisa, OBE, *y d* of late Frank Harding Jones; *S* father, 1989; *m* 1st, 1962, S. Judith Schofield (later S. J. Chaplin, OBE, MP; marr. diss. 1979; she *d* 1993); two *s* two *d*; 2nd, 1980, Laurel Celia, *o d* of S. T. Ball; two *s* one *d*. *Educ:* Eton; King's College, Cambridge (MA, Dip Agric). Member, Norfolk CC, 1970–81 (Chm. of various cttees). Chairman: Area Museums Service for South East England, 1976–79; Norwich School of Art, 1977–87; Textile Conservation Centre, 1981–88 (Pres. 1988); East Anglian Tourist Board, 1982–88. JP Norfolk, 1972. *Heir: s* Hon. Jonathan Robert Hugh Walpole, *b* 16 Nov. 1967. *Address:* Mannington Hall, Norwich NR11 7BB. *T:* Saxthorpe (01263) 587763. *Clubs:* none on principle.

WALSH, Sir Alan, Kt 1977; DSc; FRS 1969; Consultant Spectroscopist; *b* 19 Dec. 1916; *s* of late Thomas Haworth and Betsy Alice Walsh, Hoddlesden, Lancs; *m* 1949, Audrey Dale Hutchinson; two *s*. *Educ:* Darwen Grammar Sch.; Manchester Univ. BSc 1938; MSc (Tech.) 1946; DSc 1960. FAA 1958. British Non-Ferrous Metals Research Assoc., 1939–42 and 1944–46; Min. of Aircraft Production, 1943; Div. of Chemical Physics, CSIRO, Melbourne, 1946–77 (Asst Chief of Div., 1961–77). Einstein Memorial Lectr, Australian Inst. of Physics, 1967; Pres., Australian Inst. of Physics, 1967–69. Hon. Member: Soc. of Analytical Chemistry, 1969; Royal Soc. NZ, 1975. Foreign Mem., Royal Acad. of Sciences, Stockholm, 1969. FTS 1982. Hon. FCS, 1973; Hon. FAIP, 1981; Hon. Mem., Japan Soc. of Analytical Chemistry, 1981. Hon. DSc: Monash, 1970; Manchester, 1984, Britannica Australia Science Award, 1966; Research Medal, Royal Soc. of Victoria, 1968; Talanta Gold Medal, 1969; Maurice Hasler Award, Soc. of Applied Spectroscopy, USA, 1972; James Cook Medal, Royal Soc. of NSW, 1975; Torbern Bergman Medal, Swedish Chem. Soc., 1976; Royal Medal, Royal Soc., 1976; John Scott Award, City of Philadelphia, 1977; Matthew Flinders Medal, Aust. Acad. of Science, 1980; Robert Boyle Medal, RSC, 1982; K. L. Sutherland Medal, Aust. Acad. of Technol Sciences, 1982; Inaugural CSI Award, Colloquium Spectroscopicum Internationale, 1991. *Publications:* papers in learned jls. *Address:* 43A Carpenter Street, Brighton, Vic 3186, Australia. *T:* (3) 95924897. *Club:* Metropolitan Golf (Melbourne).

WALSH, Arthur Stephen, CBE 1979; FEng 1980; FIEE; Chairman: National Transcommunications Ltd, since 1991; Telemetrix Plc, since 1991; *b* 16 Aug. 1926; *s* of Wilfred and Doris Walsh; *m* 2nd, 1985, Judith Martha Westenborg. *Educ:* Selwyn Coll., Cambridge (MA). FIEE 1974. GEC Group, 1952–79: various sen. appts within the Group; Managing Director: Marconi Space and Defence Systems, 1969–86; Marconi Co., 1982–85; Dir, GEC, 1983; Chief Exec., 1985–91, Chm., 1989–91, STC. Chm., GTI Inc., 1991–; Dir, FKI plc, 1991–. Hon. DSc: Ulster, 1988; Southampton, 1993. *Recreations:* ski-ing, golf. *Address:* Aiglemont, Trout Rise, Loudwater, Rickmansworth, Herts WD3 4JS. *T:* Rickmansworth (01923) 770883.

WALSH, Brian, QC 1977; a Recorder of the Crown Court, since 1972; *b* 17 June 1935; *er s* of late Percy Walsh and Sheila (*née* Frais), Leeds; *m* 1964, Susan Margaret, *d* of late Eli (Kay) Frieze and of Doris Frieze; two *d*. *Educ:* Sheikh Bagh Sch., Srinagar, Kashmir; Leeds Grammar Sch. (Head Boy, 1954); Gonville and Caius Coll., Cambridge (BA, LLB; MA 1992). Pres., Cambridge Union Soc., 1959. Served RAF (Pilot Officer), 1954–56. Called to the Bar, Middle Temple, 1961 (Blackstone Scholar, Harmsworth Scholar); Bencher, 1986. Joined North Eastern Circuit, 1961; Leader, 1990–94. Member: Circuit Exec. Cttee, 1980–; Gen. Council of the Bar, 1982–84, and 1990–; Mental Health Review Tribunal, 1986–. Mem. Court, Leeds Univ., 1988–; Vice-Pres., Yorks CCC, 1993– (Mem. Cttee, 1984–93, Chm., 1986–91); Governor: Leeds Grammar Sch., 1977–; Leeds Girls' High Sch., 1978–; Pres., Old Leodiensian Assoc., 1983–85. *Recreations:* golf, cricket, eating. *Address:* Park Court Chambers, 40 Park Cross Street, Leeds LS1 2QH. *T:* Leeds (0113) 243 3277.

WALSH, Colin Stephen, FRCO; Organist and Master of the Choristers, Lincoln Cathedral, since 1988; *b* 26 Jan. 1955. *Educ:* Portsmouth Grammar Sch.; St George's Chapel, Windsor Castle (Organ Scholar); Christ Church, Oxford (Organ Scholar; MA 1980). DipEd 1978. ARCM 1973; FRCO 1976. Asst Organist, Salisbury Cathedral, 1978–85; Master of the Music, St Alban's Cathedral, 1985–88. Recitals in UK (incl. Royal Festival Hall), France, Scandinavia, Czechoslovakia and USA. Recordings incl. French organ music, esp. by Vierne. *Recreations:* walking, dining out, theatre, travel. *Address:* 12 Minster Yard, Lincoln LN2 1PJ. *T:* Lincoln (01522) 532877.

WALSH, Lt-Gen. Geoffrey, CBE 1944; DSO 1943; CD; *b* 1909; *s* of late H. L. Walsh; *m* 1935, Gwynn Abigail Currie; one *s*. *Educ:* Royal Military Coll., Kingston; McGill Univ. (BEngEE). DSc(Mil) RMC, Kingston, 1971. Chief Engineer, 1st Canadian Army, 1944–45 (mentioned in despatches (twice) 1945); DQMG, 1945–46; Comdr Northwest Highway System, 1946–48; Comdr Eastern Ontario Area, 1948–51; Comdr 27 Bde (Europe), 1951–52; DGMT 1953–55; QMG 1955–58; GOC, Western Command, 1958–61; Chief of the General Staff, Canada, 1961–64; Vice Chief of the Defence Staff, Canada, 1964–65. Col Comdt, Royal Canadian Army Cadets and Cadet Services of Canada, 1970–73. Legion of Merit (US); Comdr of Orange Order of Nassau (Netherlands). *Recreations:* golf, fishing, philately. *Address:* 201 Northcote Place, Rockcliffe Park, Ottawa, Ont K1M 0Y7, Canada. *Clubs:* RMC, Royal Ottawa Golf (Ottawa); USI (Ottawa and Edmonton).

WALSH, Rt Rev. (Geoffrey David) Jeremy; Bishop Suffragan of Tewkesbury, 1986–95; *b* 7 Dec. 1929; *s* of late Howard Wilton Walsh, OBE and Helen Maud Walsh (*née* Lovell); *m* 1961, Cynthia Helen, *d* of late F. P. Knight, FLS, VMH, and H. I. C. Knight, OBE; two *s* one *d*. *Educ:* Felsted Sch., Essex; Pembroke Coll., Cambridge (MA Econ.); Lincoln Theological Coll. Curate, Christ Church, Southgate, London, 1955–58; Staff Sec., SCM, and Curate, St Mary the Great, Cambridge, 1958–61; Vicar, St Matthew, Moorfields, Bristol, 1961–66; Rector of Marlborough, Wilts, 1966–76; Rector of Elmsett with Aldham, 1976–80; Archdeacon of Ipswich, 1976–86. Hon. Canon, Salisbury Cathedral, 1973–76. *Recreations:* gardening, golf, bird-watching. *Address:* 6 Warren Lane, Martlesham Heath, Ipswich IP5 7SH. *T:* Ipswich (01473) 620797.

WALSH, Graham Robert, FCA; company director; Director: Moss Bros Group plc, since 1988; Rodamco UK BV, since 1992; *b* 30 July 1989; *s* of Robert Arthur Walsh and Ella Marian (*née* Jacks); *m* 1967, Margaret Ann Alexander; one *s* one *d*. *Educ:* Hurstpierpoint Coll., Sussex. Qualified as chartered accountant, 1962; joined Philip Hill Higginson Erlangers (now Hill Samuel & Co. Ltd), 1964; Director, Hill Samuel, 1970, resigned 1973; Dir, 1973–87, Head of Corporate Finance Div., and Mem. Management Cttee, 1981–87, Morgan Grenfell & Co. Ltd; Man. Dir, Bankers Trust Co., 1988–91; Director: Morgan Grenfell Group plc (formerly Morgan Grenfell Holdings), 1985–87; Armitage Shanks Group Ltd, 1973–80; Phoenix Opera Ltd, 1970–87; Ward White Group plc, 1981–89; Rush & Tompkins Gp plc, 1988–90; Haslemere Estates, 1989–92. Dir Gen., Panel on Takeovers and Mergers, 1979–81; Chm., Issuing Houses Assoc., 1985–87 (Dep. Chm., 1979 and 1983–85). Gov., Dulwich Coll. Pres. Sch., 1995–. *Recreations:* opera, theatre, music, gardening. *Address:* 19 Alleyn Park, Dulwich, SE21 8AU. *T:* 0181–670 0676.

WALSH, Henry George; Deputy Chairman, Building Societies Commission, since 1991; *b* 28 Sept. 1939; *s* of James Isidore Walsh and Sybil Bertha Bazeley; *m* 1968, Janet Ann Grainger; three *d*. *Educ:* West Hill High Sch., Montreal; McGill Univ.; Churchill Coll., Cambridge. HM Treasury, 1966–74; Private Secretary to Chancellor of the Duchy of Lancaster, 1974–76; HM Treasury, 1976–78; Cabinet Office Secretariat, 1978–80; Counsellor (Economic), Washington, 1980–85; HM Treasury: Hd of Monetary Policy Div., 1985–86; Hd of IMF and Debt Div., 1986–89; Hd of Financial Instns and Markets Gp, 1989–91. *Recreations:* golf, reading philosophical works, being taken for walks by Labrador retrievers. *Address:* 16 Crowborough Road, SW17 9QQ. *Club:* Dulwich and Sydenham Hill Golf.

WALSH, James Mark, CMG 1956; OBE 1948; HM Diplomatic Service; Consul-General, Zürich, 1962–68; *b* 18 Aug. 1909; *s* of Mark Walsh and Emily (*née* Porter); *m* 1st, 1937, Mireille Loir (*d* 1966); one *s*; 2nd, 1967, Bertha Hoch. *Educ:* Mayfield Coll., Sussex; King's Coll., London; Lincoln's Inn, London. BA (Hons), 1929; LLB, 1932; Barrister, 1932; passed an examination and appointed to Foreign Service, 1932; Vice-Consul: Paris, 1932–33, Rotterdam, 1933–34; Judge of HBM Provincial Court, Alexandria, Egypt, 1934–38; Acting Consul-General, Barcelona, 1939; Vice-Consul, Philadelphia, 1939–44; Consul, Antwerp, 1944–45. First Secretary, British Legation: Helsinki, 1945–46, Budapest, 1946–48; Dep. Consul-General, New York, 1948–50; Counsellor (Commercial), Ankara, 1950–54, and Berne, 1954–59; Consul-General, Jerusalem, 1959–62. *Recreations:* painting, golf. *Address:* Fairfield, The Paddock, Haslemere, Surrey GU27 1HB. *T:* Haslemere (01428) 652089.

WALSH, Rt Rev. Jeremy; *see* Walsh, Rt Rev. G. D. J.

WALSH, Jill P.; *see* Paton Walsh.

WALSH, John; Director, J. Paul Getty Museum, since 1983; *b* 9 Dec. 1937; *s* of John J. Walsh and Eleanor Walsh (*née* Wilson); *m* 1961, Virginia Alys Galston; two *s* one *d*. *Educ:* Yale Univ. (BA 1961); Univ. of Leyden, Netherlands; Columbia Univ. (MA 1965; PhD 1971). Lectr, Research Asst, Frick Collection, NY, 1966–68; Metropolitan Museum of Art, NY: Associate for Higher Educn, 1968–71; Associate Curator and Curator, 1970–75, Vice-Chm., 1974–75, Dept of European Paintings; Columbia University: Adjunct Associate Prof., 1972–75; Prof. of Art History, Barnard Coll., 1975–77; Mrs Russell W. Baker Curator of Paintings, Museum of Fine Arts, Boston, 1977–83. Vis Prof. of Fine Arts, Harvard, 1979. Member: Governing Bd, Yale Univ. Art Gallery, 1975–; Bd of Fellows, Claremont Grad. Sch. and Univ. Center, 1988–; Assoc. of Art Museum Dirs, 1983– (Trustee, 1986 ; Pres., 1989); Amer. Antiquarian Soc., 1984–. *Publications:* exhibition catalogues, art bulletins, guides; numerous contribs to learned jls. *Address:* J. Paul Getty Museum, PO Box 2112, Santa Monica, CA 90406, USA. *T:* (310) 4597611. *Club:* Century Association (NY).

WALSH, John Henry Martin; Literary Editor, Independent, since 1995; *b* 24 Oct. 1953; *s* of Martin Walsh and Anne Walsh (*née* Durkin); partner, Carolyn Clare Hart; one *s* two *d*. *Educ:* Wimbledon Coll.; Exeter Coll., Oxford (BA Hons); University Coll., Dublin (MA). Advertisement Dept, Tablet Magazine, 1977; Publicity Dept, Victor Gollancz, 1978–79; Associate Editor, The Director, 1979–83; freelance writer, 1983–87; Literary Editor, 1987, Features and Literary Editor, 1988, Evening Standard; Literary Editor, Sunday Times, 1988–92; Editor, Independent Magazine, 1993–95. Presenter, Books and Company, BBC Radio 4, 1995–. *Publication:* Growing Up Catholic, 1989. *Recreations:* drinking, talking, music. *Address:* 119 Knatchbull Road, SE5. *T:* 0171–274 1268. *Club:* Groucho.

WALSH, John P.; *see* Pakenham-Walsh.

WALSH, Sir John (Patrick), KBE 1960; Professor of Dentistry and Dean and Director, University of Otago Dental School, 1946–72; *b* 5 July 1911; *s* of John Patrick Walsh and Lillian Jane (*née* Burbidge), Vic, Australia; *m* 1934, Enid Morris; one *s* three *d*. *Educ:* Ormond Coll.; Melbourne Univ. BDSc 1st Cl. Hons Melbourne; LDS Victoria, 1936; MB, BS Melbourne, 1943; DDSc Melbourne, 1950; FDSRCS 1950; FDSRCS Edinburgh, 1951; MDS NUI, 1952; FRSNZ 1961; FACD 1962; Hon. FACDS, 1967; Hon. DSc Otago, 1975. Hosp. and teaching appointments in Melbourne till 1946. MO, RAAF, 1945–46. Consultant, WHO Dental Health Seminars: Wellington, 1954; Adelaide, 1959. Speaker: 11th and 12th Internat. Dental Congresses, London and Rome; Centennial Congress of Amer. Dental Assoc., New York, 1959; 12th, 14th and 15th Australian Dental Congresses. Chairman: Dental Council of NZ, 1956–72; Mental Health Assoc. of Otago, 1960. Dominion Pres., UNA, 1960–64. Member: MRC of NZ, 1950–72 (Chm. Dental Cttee, 1947–60); Scientific Commn; Fedn Dentaire Internat., 1954–61; Council, Univ. of Otago, 1958–63; Nat. Commn for UNESCO, 1961–69; Educn Commn, 1961–; Expert Panel on Dental Health, WHO, 1962; Nat. Council, Duke of Edinburgh's Award, 1963–68. CC, Dunedin, 1968–73. Pres., Dunedin Rotary Club, 1960, Governor Dist 298, 1966–67. Paul Harris Fellow, 1981. Hon. Mem., American Dental Assoc., 1969–; List of Honour, FDI, 1969–. Holds hon. degrees. *Publications:* A Manual of Stomatology, 1957; Living with Uncertainty, 1968; Psychiatry and Dentistry, 1976; numerous articles in scientific literature. *Recreation:* retirement. *Address:* Unit 29, Hillsborough Heights Village, Dominion Road, Auckland 4, New Zealand. *T:* (9) 676583.

WALSH, Dr Julia M.; Chief Executive, Agricultural Development and Advisory Service, since 1991. *Address:* ADAS Headquarters, Oxford Spires Business Park, The Boulevard, Kidlington, Oxon OX5 1NZ. *T:* Oxford (01865) 845002.

WALSH, (Mary) Noëlle; Editor, The Good Deal Directory, since 1992; Director, The Value for Money Company Ltd, since 1992; *b* 26 Dec. 1954; *d* of late Thomas Walsh and of Mary Kate Ferguson; *m* 1988, David Heslam; one *s* one *d*. *Educ:* Univ. of East Anglia

(BA Hons European Studies (History and German)). Editorial Asst, PR Dept, St Dunstan's Orgn for the War-Blinded, 1977–79; News Editor, Cosmopolitan, 1979–85; Editor, London Week newspaper, 1985–86; freelance writer, 1986; Dep. Editor, 1986–87, Editor, 1987–91, Good Housekeeping; Dep. Editor, You and Your Family, Daily Telegraph, 1992. Member: Network; 300 Group; Forum UK. Presenter, Recession Beaters, GMTV, 1993–. Editor, The Good Deal Directory monthly newsletter, 1992–. *Publications:* Hot Lips, the Ultimate Kiss and Tell Guide, 1985; (co-ed) Ragtime to Wartime: the best of Good Housekeeping 1922–39, 1986; (co-ed) The Home Front: the best of Good Housekeeping 1939–1945, 1987; (co-ed) The Christmas Book: the best of Good Housekeeping at Christmas 1922–1962, 1988; (ed jtly) Food Glorious Food: eating and drinking with Good Housekeeping 1922–1942, 1990; Things my Mother Should Have Told Me, 1991; Childhood Memories, 1991; (ed) The Good Deal Directory, annually, 1994–; (ed) The Good Deal Directory Food Guide, 1993; (ed) The Home Shopping Handbook, 1994; Baby on a Budget, 1995; The Factory Shopping and Sightseeing Guide, 1995; The Good Mail Order Guide, 1996. *Recreations:* unofficial agony aunt, medieval Irish history. *Address:* Pip Cottage, Filkins, near Lechlade, Glos GL7 3JJ. *Club:* Groucho.

WALSH, Maj.-Gen. Michael John Hatley, CB 1980; DSO 1968; DL; Director of Overseas Relations, St John's Ambulance, 1989–95; *b* 10 June 1927; *s* of Captain Victor Michael Walsh, late Royal Sussex, and Audrey Walsh; *m* 1952, Angela, *d* of Col Leonard Beswick; two *d*. *Educ:* Sedbergh Sch. Commnd, KRRC, 1946; served in Malaya, Germany, Cyprus, Suez, Aden, Australia and Singapore; Bde Maj. 44 Parachute Bde, 1960–61; GSO1 Defence Planning Staff, 1966; CO 1 Para Bn, 1967–69; Col AQ 1 Div., 1969–71; Comdr, 28 Commonwealth Bde, 1971–73; BGS HQ BAOR, 1973–76; GOC 3rd Armoured Div., 1976–79; Dir of Army Training, MoD, 1979–81. Hon. Col, 1st Bn Wessex Regt, TA, 1981–89. Chief Scout of the UK and Dependent Territories, 1982–88. Council Mem., Operation Raleigh, 1984; Royal National Life-boat Institution: Member: Cttee of Management, 1988–; Search and Rescue Sub-cttee, 1989–; Fund Raising Sub-cttee, 1991–. Kt Pres., Hon. Soc. of Knights of the Round Table, 1988– (Kt 1986–); Mem., St John Council, Wilts, 1989–. DL Greater London, 1986. Freeman, City of London, 1987. CStJ 1990. *Recreations:* athletics, boxing (Life Pres., Army Boxing Assoc., 1986), parachuting (Pres., Army Parachute Assoc., 1979–81), sailing, Australian Rules football. *Address:* c/o Barclays Bank, James Street, Harrogate. *Club:* Royal Yacht Squadron (Cowes).

WALSH, Michael Thomas; Head, International Department, Trades Union Congress, since 1980; *b* 22 Oct. 1943; *s* of Michael Walsh and late Bridget (*née* O'Sullivan); *m* 1972, Margaret Patricia Blaxhall; two *s* two *d*. *Educ:* Gunnersbury Grammar Sch.; Exeter Coll., Oxford (Hons degree PPE). International Dept, TUC, 1966; Deputy Overseas Labour Adviser, FCO, 1977–79. Member: Economic and Social Committee of the European Community, 1976–77 and 1979–80; World of Work Cttee, Catholic Bishops' Conf. of England and Wales, 1992–. Member: Wilton Park Academic Council, 1994–; Governing Body, Plater Coll., Oxford, 1995–. *Recreations:* cricket, historical research, music. *Address:* 77 Uvedale Road, Enfield EN2 6HD.

WALSH, Lt-Col Noel Perrings; Under Secretary, and Director of Home Regional Services, Department of the Environment, 1976–79; *b* 25 Dec. 1919; *s* of late John and Nancy Walsh; *m* 1st, 1945, Olive Mary (*d* 1987), *y d* of late Thomas Walsh, Waterford; three *s* one *d*; 2nd, 1988, Mary Ruth, *d* of late Rev. R. D. M. Hughes. *Educ:* Purbrook Park Grammar Sch.; Open Univ.; Birmingham Univ. (MSocSc). Served Army, 1939–66; India, 1941–44; Arakan Campaign, 1944–45; DAQMG, 52 (L) Div., 1951–53; GSO2 RA, HQ BAOR, 1955–57; GSO1 PR, MoD Army, 1964–66; retired Lt-Col, RA, 1966. Entered Home Civil Service as Principal, MPBW, 1966; Regional Director: Far East, 1969–70; Midland Region, 1970–75. Vice-Chm., Midland Study Centre for Building Team, 1982–90; Regional Chm., W Midlands Council, CIOB, 1988–90. Vice-Pres., W Midlands Central SSAFA, 1995– (Chm., 1991–95). FCIOB 1972; FIMgt (FBIM 1978); FRSA 1987. *Recreations:* gardening, economic history, gauge O railway modelling. *Address:* 25 Oakfield Road, Selly Park, Birmingham B29 7HH. *T:* 0121–472 2031. *Clubs:* Naval and Military; Birmingham.

WALSH, Most Rev. Patrick Joseph; *see* Down and Connor, Bishop of.

WALSH, Robin; Controller, BBC Northern Ireland, 1991–94; *b* 6 Feb. 1940; *s* of Charles and Ellen Walsh; *m* 1964, Dorothy Beattie; two *d*. *Educ:* Foyle College, Londonderry; Royal Belfast Academical Inst. Reporter, Belfast Telegraph, 1958–65; Reporter/News Editor, Ulster TV, 1965–74; BBC: News Editor, NI, 1974–81; Dep. Editor, TV News, 1982–85; Managing Editor, News and Current Affairs—TV, 1985–88; Asst Controller, News and Current Affairs, Regions, 1988–90. *Recreations:* cricket, walking. *Address:* Holly Lodge, 3A Ballymullan Road, Crawfordsburn, Co. Down, NI. *T:* Holywood (01247) 852709.

WALSH, Prof. William; Professor of Commonwealth Literature, 1972–84, now Emeritus, and Acting Vice-Chancellor, 1981–83, University of Leeds; Douglas Grant Fellow in Commonwealth Literature in the School of English, since 1969; Chairman, School of English, 1973–78; *b* 23 Feb. 1916; *e s* of William and Elizabeth Walsh; *m* 1945, May Watson; one *s* one *d*. *Educ:* Downing Coll., Cambridge; University of London. Schoolmaster, 1943–51; Senior English Master, Raynes Park County Grammar Sch., 1945–51; Lecturer in Education, University Coll. of N Staffordshire, 1951–53; Lecturer in Education, Univ. of Edinburgh, 1953–57; Prof. of Education, and Head of Dept. of Education, Univ. of Leeds, 1957–72; Chm., Sch. of Education, 1969–72; Chm., Bd of combined Faculties of Arts, Economics, Social Studies and Law, Univ. of Leeds, 1964–66; Pro-Vice-Chancellor, Univ. of Leeds, 1965–67; Chm. Bd of Adult Educn, 1969–77; Member: IBA Adult Educn Cttee, 1974–76; IBA Educn Adv. Cttee, 1976–81; Bd of Foundn for Canadian Studies in UK, 1981–. Dir, Yorkshire TV, 1967–86; Trustee, Edward Boyle Meml Trust, 1981–. Vis. Prof., ANU, 1968; Australian Commonwealth Vis. Fellow, 1970; Vis. Prof., Canadian Univs, 1973; Leverhulme Emeritus Fellow, 1986–88. Hon. LLD Leeds, 1984. *Publications:* Use of Imagination, 1959; A Human Idiom, 1964; Coleridge: The Work and the Relevance, 1967; A Manifold Voice, 1970; R. K. Narayan, 1972; V. S. Naipaul, 1972; Commonwealth Literature, 1973; Readings in Commonwealth Literature, 1973; D. J. Enright: poet of humanism, 1974; Patrick White: Voss, 1976; Patrick White's Fiction, 1977; F. R. Leavis, 1981; Introduction to Keats, 1981; R. K. Narayan, 1982; Indian Literature in English, 1990; contributions to: From Blake to Byron, 1957; Young Writers, Young Readers, 1960; Speaking of the Famous, 1962; F. R. Leavis-Some Aspects of his Work, 1963; The Teaching of English Literature Overseas, 1963; Higher Education: patterns of change in the 1970s, 1972; Literatures of the World in English, 1974; Considerations, 1977; Indo-English Literature, 1977; Perspectives on Mulk Raj Anand, 1978; Awakened Conscience, 1978; The Study of Education, vol. 1, 1980; The Twofold Voice: essays in honour of Ramesh Mohan, 1982; Life by Other Means: essays on D. J. Enright, 1990; Edward Boyle: his life by his friends, 1991; papers and essays on literary and educational topics in British and American journals. *Address:* 27 Moor Drive, Headingley, Leeds LS6 4BY. *T:* Leeds (0113) 275 5705.

WALSH-ATKINS, Leonard Brian, CMG 1962; CVO 1961; Assistant Under-Secretary of State, Commonwealth Relations Office, 1962; retired 1970; *b* 15 March 1915; *o c* of late Leonard and Gladys Atkins; step *s* of late Geoffrey Walsh, CMG, CBE; *m* 1st, 1940, Marguerite Black (marr. diss. 1968); three *s*; 2nd, 1969, Margaret Lady Runcorn. *Educ:* Charterhouse (Scholar); Hertford Coll., Oxford (Scholar; BA 1937). Asst Principal, India Office, 1937. Fleet Air Arm, 1940–45; Lieut-Comdr (A), RNVR (despatches). Burma Office, 1945–47; Commonwealth Relations Office, 1947; Counsellor, Dublin, 1953–56; idc 1957; Dep. High Comr, Pakistan, 1959–61. The Abbeyfield Society, 1971–89 (Nat. Vice Chm., 1984–88); Dep. Chm., Nat. Fedn of Housing Assocs, 1984–86. *Address:* Berkeley Cottage, Mayfield, E Sussex TN20 6AU.

WALSHAM, Sir Timothy (John), 5th Bt *cr* 1831, of Knill Court, Herefordshire; horticulturalist; *b* 26 April 1939; *o s* of Rear Adm. Sir John Walsham, 4th Bt, CB, OBE and of Sheila Christina, *o d* of Comdr B. Bannerman, DSO; *S* father, 1992. *Educ:* Sherborne. Peninsular & Oriental Shipping Company, 1960–67; Royal Fleet Auxiliary Service, 1968–72. *Recreation:* horticulture. *Heir: cousin* Percy Robert Stewart Walsham [*b* 6 April 1904; *m* 1937, Tamara Ellis (*d* 1981); one *s* one *d*]. *Address:* 19 Beckford Close, Tisbury, Wiltshire SP3 6QT.

WALSINGHAM, 9th Baron, *cr* 1780; **John de Grey,** MC 1952; Lieut-Colonel, Royal Artillery, retired, 1968; *b* 21 Feb. 1925; *s* of 8th Baron Walsingham, DSO, OBE, and Hyacinth (*d* 1968), *o d* of late Lt-Col Lambart Henry Bouwens, RA; *S* father, 1965; *m* 1963, Wendy, *er d* of E. Hoare, Southwick, Sussex; one *s* two *d*. *Educ:* Wellington Coll.; Aberdeen Univ.; Magdalen Coll., Oxford; RMCS. BA Oxon, 1950; MA 1959. Army in India, 1945–47; Palestine, 1947; Oxford Univ., 1947–50; Foreign Office, 1950; Army in Korea, 1951–52; Hong Kong, 1952–54; Malaya, 1954–56; Cyprus, Suez, 1956; Aden, 1957–58; Royal Military Coll. of Science, 1958–60; Aden, 1961–63; Malaysia, 1963–65. *Heir: s* Hon. Robert de Grey [*b* 21 June 1969; *m* 1995, Josephine Elizabeth, *d* of Richard Haryott]. *Address:* Merton Hall, Thetford, Norfolk IP25 6QJ. *T:* Watton (Norfolk) (01953) 881226. *Clubs:* Army and Navy, Special Forces; Norfolk County (Norwich).

WALTER, Hon. Sir Harold (Edward), Kt 1972; QC (Mauritius) 1985; Barrister-at-Law; MLA 1959–82, Minister of External Affairs, Tourism and Emigration, 1976–82, Mauritius; *b* 17 April 1920; *e s* of Rev. Edward Walter and Marie Augusta Donat; *m* 1942, Yvette Nidza, MBE, *d* of James Toolsy; no *c*. *Educ:* Royal Coll., Mauritius. Served in HM Forces, 1940–48, Mauritius Sub-Area; E Africa Comd, GHQ MELF. Called to Bar, Lincoln's Inn, 1951. Village Councillor, 1952; Municipal Councillor, Port Louis, 1956. Minister: of Works and Internal Communications, 1959–65; of Health, 1965–67 and 1971–76; of Labour, 1967–71; mem. numerous ministerial delegns. Chm., Commonwealth Med. Conf., 1972–74; Dep. Leader, UN General Assembly, NY, 1973, 1974, 1975; Pres., Security Council, UN, 1979; Mem. Exec. Bd, WHO, 1973–75, Pres., 1975–76. Chm., Council of Ministers, Organisation of African Unity, 1976–77; Vice Pres., Internat. Cttee for the Communities of Democracy (Washington), 1985. Trustee, Child Alive Program (Geneva), 1984–. Hon. DCL Univ. of Mauritius, 1984. Commandeur de l'Ordre National Français des Palmes Académiques, 1974; Comdr de la Légion d'Honneur (France), 1980; Diplomatic Order of Merit (Korea), 1981. *Recreations:* shooting, fishing, swimming, gardening. *Address:* La Rocca, Eau Coulée, Mauritius. *T:* 860300. *Clubs:* Wings, Racing (Mauritius).

WALTER, Harriet Mary; actress; *b* 24 Sept. 1950; *d* of Roderick Walter and Xandra Carandini (*née* Lee). *Educ:* Cranborne Chase Sch.; LAMDA. Associate Artist, RSC, 1987–; Associate Artistic Dir, Royal Exchange Theatre, Manchester, 1992–. *Theatre:* Ragged Trousered Philanthropists, Joint Stock Co., 1978; Hamlet, Cloud Nine, Royal Court, 1980; Nicholas Nickleby, RSC, 1980; Seagull, Royal Court, 1981; RSC seasons, 1981–83: Midsummer Night's Dream; All's Well That Ends Well (also on Broadway, 1983); The Lucky Chance, Royal Court, 1984; The Castle, RSC, 1985; Merchant of Venice, Royal Exchange, Manchester, 1987; RSC seasons, 1987–89: Cymbeline; Twelfth Night; Three Sisters; Question of Geography (Best Actress, Olivier Awards, 1988); Duchess of Malfi, RSC, 1989–90; Three Birds Alighting on a Field, Royal Court, 1991–92, NY, 1994; Arcadia, 1993, The Children's Hour, 1994, National; Old Times, Wyndham's, 1995; *television:* The Imitation Game, 1980; Cherry Orchard, 1981; The Price, 1985; Lord Peter Wimsey, 1987; Benefactors, 1989; They Never Slept, 1990; The Men's Room, 1991; Ashenden, 1991; Inspector Morse, 1992; The Maitlands, 1993; Hard Times, 1994; many radio performances (Sony Award, Best Actress, 1988 and 1992); *films:* Reflections, 1983; Turtle Diary, 1985; The Good Father, 1986; Milou en Mai, 1990; The Hour of the Pig, 1993; Sense and Sensibility, 1995. *Publications:* contribs to: Clamorous Voices, 1988; Players of Shakespeare, Vol. III, 1993; Mothers, Reflections by Daughters, 1995. *Address:* c/o Conway van Gelder, 18–21 Jermyn Street, SW1Y 6HP. *T:* 0171–287 0077.

WALTER, Kenneth Burwood, CVO 1978; Full-time Member, British Airports Authority, 1975–77; *b* 16 Oct. 1918; *s* of late Leonard James Walter and Jesse Florence Walter; *m* 1940, Elsie Marjorie Collett; two *s*. *Educ:* St Dunstan's Coll., SE6. Dept of Civil Aviation, Air Ministry, 1936. Served War, Royal Artillery (Anti Aircraft and Field), home and Far East, 1940–46. Ministries of: Civil Aviation; Transport and Civil Aviation; Aviation, 1946–66; British Airports Authority: Dep. Dir Planning, 1966; Dir Planning, 1972; Airport Dir, Heathrow, 1973–77. MCIT, ARAeS. *Publications:* various papers on airports. *Recreations:* music, swimming, fishing, gardening. *Address:* 7 Willersley Avenue, Orpington, Kent BR6 9RT.

WALTER, Neil Douglas; Deputy Secretary, Ministry of Foreign Affairs and Trade, New Zealand, since 1994; *b* 11 Dec. 1942; *s* of Ernest Edward Walter and Anita Walter (*née* Frethey); *m* 1966, Berys Anne (*née* Robertson); one *s* two *d*. *Educ:* New Plymouth Boys' High School; Auckland University (MA). Second Sec., Bangkok, 1966–70; First Sec., NZ Mission to UN, NY, 1972–76; Official Sec., Tokelau Public Service, Apia, 1976–78; Minister, Paris and NZ Permt Deleg. to Unesco, 1981–85; Dep. High Comr for NZ in London, 1985–87; Asst Sec., Ministry of External Relations, NZ, 1987–90; NZ Ambassador to Indonesia, 1990–94. *Recreations:* sport, reading. *Address:* Ministry of Foreign Affairs and Trade, Private Bag, Wellington, New Zealand.

WALTERS, Sir Alan (Arthur), Kt 1983; Vice-Chairman and Director, AIG Trading Group, Inc., since 1991; Professor of Economics, Johns Hopkins University, Maryland, 1976–91; *b* 17 June 1926; *s* of James Arthur Walters and Claribel Walters (*née* Heywood); *m* 1975, Margaret Patricia (Paddie) Wilson; one *d* of former marr. *Educ:* Alderman Newton's Sch., Leicester; University Coll., Leicester (BSc (Econ) London); Nuffield Coll., Oxford (MA). Lectr in Econometrics, Univ. of Birmingham, 1951; Visiting Prof. of Economics, Northwestern Univ., Evanston, Ill, USA, 1958–59; Prof. of Econometrics and Social Statistics, Univ. of Birmingham, 1961; Cassel Prof. of Economics, LSE, 1968–76. Vis. Prof. of Econs, MIT, 1966–67; Vis. Fellow, Nuffield Coll., Oxford, 1982–84; Sen. Fellow, Amer. Enterprise Inst., 1983– (Boyer Lectr, 1983). Economic Adviser to World Bank, 1976–80, 1984–88; Personal Econ. Advr to the Prime Minister (on secondment), 1981–84, 1989. Mem. Commission on Third London Airport (the Roskill Commission), 1968–70. Fellow, Econometric Soc., 1971. Hon. DLitt Leicester, 1981; Hon. DSocSc: Birmingham, 1984; Francisco Marroquin Univ., 1994. *Publications:* Growth Without Development (with R. Clower and G. Dalton), 1966 (USA); Economics of Road User Charges, 1968; An Introduction to Econometrics, 1969 (2nd edn 1971);

Economics of Ocean Freight Rates (with E. Bennathan), 1969 (USA); Money in Boom and Slump, 1970 (3rd edn 1971); Noise and Prices, 1974; (with R. G. Layard) Microeconomic Theory, 1977; (with Esra Bennathan) Port Pricing and Investment Policy for Developing Countries, 1979; Britain's Economic Renaissance, 1986; Sterling in Danger, 1990. *Recreations:* music, Thai porcelain, tennis. *Address:* 2820 P Street NW, Washington, DC 20007, USA. *Club:* Political Economy.

WALTERS, Sir Dennis, Kt 1988; MBE 1960; *b* 28 Nov. 1928; *s* of late Douglas L. Walters and Clara Walters (*née* Pomello); *m* 1st, 1955, Vanora McIndoe (marr. diss. 1969); one *s* one *d*; 2nd, 1970, Hon. Celia (*née* Sandys) (marr. diss. 1979); one *s*; 3rd, 1981, Bridgett, *d* of J. Francis Shearer; one *s* one *d*. *Educ:* Downside; St Catharine's College (Exhibitioner), Cambridge (MA). War of 1939–45: interned in Italy; served with Italian Resistance Movement behind German lines after Armistice; repatriated and continued normal educn, 1944. Chm., Fedn of Univ. Conservative and Unionist Assocs, 1950; Personal Asst to Lord Hailsham throughout his Chairmanship of Conservative Party; Chm., Coningsby Club, 1959. Contested (C) Blyth, 1959 and Nov. 1960; MP (C) Westbury Div. of Wilts, 1964–92. Jt Hon. Sec., Conservative Parly Foreign Affairs Cttee, 1965–71, Jt Vice-Chm., 1974–78; Jt Chm., Euro-Arab Parly Assoc., 1978–81; Mem., UK Parly Delegn to UN, 1966; UK Deleg. to Council of Europe and Assembly of WEU, 1970–73. Introduced Children and Young Persons (Amendment) Bill, 1985 (Royal Assent, 1986). Pres., Cons. ME Council, 1992– (Chm., 1980–92). Director: Cluff Oil Inc.; The Spectator, 1983–84; Middle East Internat., 1971–90 (Chm., 1990–). Chm., Asthma Research Council, 1968–88; Vice Pres., Nat. Asthma Campaign, 1989–. Chm., UK/Saudi Jt Cultural Cttee, 1988–; Jt Chm., Council for Advancement of Arab British Understanding, 1970–82 (Jt Vice-Chm., 1967–70); Mem., Kuwait Investment Adv. Cttee, 1969–. Governor, British Inst. of Florence, 1965–. Comdr, Order of Cedar of Lebanon, 1969. *Publication:* Not Always with the Pack (autobiographical memoirs), 1989 (trans. Italian, rev. edn, as Benedetti Inglesi Benedetti Italiani, 1991). *Address:* 43 Royal Avenue, SW3 4QE. *T:* 0171–730 9431; Orchardleigh, Corton, Warminster, Wilts BA12 0SZ. *T:* Warminster (01985) 850369. *Club:* Boodle's.

WALTERS, Very Rev. Derrick; *see* Walters, Very Rev. R. D. C.

WALTERS, Sir Donald, Kt 1983; Chairman, Llandongh Hospital NHS Trust, since 1992; *b* 5 Oct. 1925; *s* of Percival Donald and Irene Walters; *m* 1950, Adelaide Jean McQuistin; one *s*. *Educ:* Howardian High Sch., Cardiff; London School of Economics and Political Science (LLB). Called to Bar, Inner Temple, 1946; practised at Bar, Wales and Chester circuit, 1948–59. Dir, 1959–85, Dep. Man. Dir, 1975–85, Chartered Trust plc. Member: Welsh Develt Agency, 1980–93 (Dep. Chm., 1984–92); Develt Bd for Rural Wales, 1984–; Dir, WNO, 1985–(Vice-Chm., 1990); Chairman: Wales Council for Voluntary Action, 1987–93; Council, Univ. of Wales Coll. of Cardiff, 1988–. High Sheriff, S Glamorgan, 1987–88. Hon. LLD Wales, 1990. *Recreations:* politics, gardening, walking. *Address:* 120 Cyncoed Road, Cardiff CF2 6BL. *T:* Cardiff (01222) 753166.

WALTERS, Geraint Gwynn, CBE 1958; Director for Wales, Ministry of Public Building and Works and Department of the Environment, 1966–72, retired; *b* in the Welsh Colony in Patagonia, 6 June 1910; *s* of Rev. D. D. Walters; *m* 1st, 1942, Doreena Owen (*d* 1959); 2nd, 1968, Sarah Ann Ruth Price; no *c*. *Educ:* various schools in Argentina and Wales; University Coll., Bangor (BA). Gladstone Prizeman, Foyle Prizeman. Schoolmaster, 1933–35; political organizer on staff of Rt Hon. David Lloyd George, 1935–40; Min. of Information, 1940–45; Dep. Regional Dir of Inf., Bristol and Plymouth, 1942–45; Principal, Min. of Works HQ, 1945–48; Dir for Wales, Min. of Works, 1948–63; Dir, Far East Region, Min. of Public Building and Works, 1963–66. Chm., Royal Inst. of Public Admin (S Wales Br.), 1960–61; Hon. Mem. of Gorsedd, 1961; Pres., St David's Soc. of Singapore, 1965; Leader of Welsh Overseas, at Nat. Eisteddfod of Wales, 1965; Chm., Argentine Welsh Soc., 1976–78, Pres., 1979–82. Chm., Civil Service Sports Council for Wales, 1970–72. Govt Housing Comr for Merthyr Tydfil, 1972–73; Member: Welsh Bd for Industry, 1948–62; Housing Production Bd for Wales; Cttee of Inquiry on Welsh Television, 1963. Mem. Council, Univ. of Wales Inst. of Science and Technology, 1970–87 (Vice-Chm., 1980–83); Mem. Court, Univ. of Wales, 1982–88; Life Mem. Court, Univ. of Wales Coll. of Cardiff, 1989–. *Recreations:* reading Talking Books, radio, travel. *Address:* 1 The Mount, Cardiff Road, Llandaff, Cardiff CF5 2AR. *T:* Cardiff (01222) 568739. *Clubs:* Civil Service; Cardiff and County (Cardiff).

WALTERS, Rear-Adm. John William Townshend, CB 1984; Chairman, Industrial Tribunals, Southampton, since 1987 (London Central, 1984–87); Deputy Chairman, Data Protection Tribunal, since 1985; *b* 23 April 1926; *s* of William Bernard Walters and Lilian Martha Walters (*née* Hartridge); *m* 1949, Margaret Sarah Patricia Jeffkins; two *s* one *d*. *Educ:* John Fisher Sch., Purley, Surrey. Called to Bar, Middle Temple, 1956. Special Entry to RN, 1944; HMS King George V, 1944–46; HMS London, 1946–49; RN Air Station, Arbroath, 1949–51; Staff of C-in-C Mediterranean, 1951–53; Office of Vice Chief of Naval Staff, 1954–56; Sqdn Supply Officer, 8th Destroyer Sqdn, 1957–59; Staff of C-in-C Mediterranean, 1959–62; Secretary: to Flag Officer Middle East, 1962–64; to Naval Secretary, 1964–66; jssc 1967; Supply Officer, HMS Albion, 1967–69; Secretary to Chief of Fleet Support, 1969–72; Chief Naval Judge Advocate, 1972–75; Captain Naval Drafting, 1975–78; Director Naval Administrative Planning, 1978–80; UN Law of the Sea Conf., 1980–81; ACDS (Personnel and Logistics), 1981–84, retired. *Address:* Good Holding, 5 Hollycombe Close, Liphook, Hants GU30 7HR. *T:* Liphook (01428) 723222. *Clubs:* Army and Navy, Royal Naval Sailing Association.

WALTERS, Joyce Dora; Headmistress, Clifton High School, Bristol, 1985–95; *m* 1979, Lt-Col Howard C. Walters (*d* 1983); one *s*. *Educ:* St Anne's College, Oxford. Headmistress, St Mary's, Calne, 1972–85. *Recreations:* travelling, reading, cooking. *Address:* 4 Longwood House, Failand, Bristol BS8 3TL. *T:* Bristol (0117) 939 2092.

WALTERS, Julie; actress; *b* 22 Feb. 1950; *d* of late Thomas and Mary Walters; one *d*. *Educ:* Holly Lodge Grammar Sch., Smethwick; Manchester Polytechnic (Teaching Certificate). *Theatre:* Educating Rita, 1980 (Drama Critics' Most Promising Newcomer Award; Variety Club Best Newcomer); Having a Ball, Lyric, Hammersmith, 1981; Fool for Love, NT, 1984; Macbeth, Leicester Haymarket, 1985; When I was a Girl I used to Scream and Shout, Whitehall, 1986; Frankie and Johnny in the Clair de Lune, Comedy, 1989; The Rose Tattoo, Playhouse, 1991. *Films:* Educating Rita, 1983 (Variety Club of GB's Award for best film actress; BAFTA Award for best actress; Hollywood Golden Globe Award); She'll be Wearing Pink Pyjamas, 1985; Car Trouble, 1986; Personal Services, 1987 (British Video Award, Best Actress); Prick Up Your Ears, 1987; Buster, 1988; Killing Dad, 1989; Stepping Out (Variety Club Best Film Actress), 1991; Just Like a Woman, 1992; Clothes in the Wardrobe, 1992; Wide Eyed and Legless, 1993; Bambino Mio, 1994; Pat and Margaret, 1994; Sister My Sister, 1995; *Television:* series include: Wood and Walters, 1981–82; Victoria Wood as Seen on TV, 1984, 2nd series, 1986; The Secret Diary of Adrian Mole, 1985; Victoria Wood Series, 1989; GBH, 1991; Jake's Progress, 1995; film: Little Red Riding Hood, 1995; also television plays, incl. monologue in series, Talking Heads, 1988. *Publication:* Baby Talk, 1990. *Recreations:* reading, television, travel. *Address:* ICM, 76 Oxford Street, W1R 1RB.

WALTERS, Prof. Kenneth, PhD, DSc; FRS 1991; Professor of Applied Mathematics, University of Wales, Aberystwyth, since 1973; *b* 14 Sept. 1934; *s* of late Trevor Walters and of Lilian (*née* Price); *m* 1963, Mary Ross Eccles; two *s* one *d*. *Educ:* University Coll. of Swansea (BSc 1956; MSc 1957; PhD 1959; DSc 1984; Hon. Fellow, 1992). Dept of Mathematics, University Coll. of Wales, Aberystwyth: Lectr, 1960–65; Sen. Lectr, 1965–70; Reader, 1970–73. Church Warden, St Michael's, Aberystwyth, 1993–. For. Associate, NAE, USA, 1995. Gold Medal, British Soc. of Rheology, 1984. *Publications:* Rheometry, 1975; (ed) Rheometry: industrial applications, 1980; (with M. J. Crochet and A. R. Davies) Numerical Simulation of non-Newtonian Flow, 1984; (with H. A. Barnes amd J. F. Hutton) An Introduction to Rheology, 1989; (with D. V. Boger) Rheological Phenomena in Focus, 1993. *Recreation:* golf. *Address:* Department of Mathematics, University of Wales, Penglais, Aberystwyth, Dyfed SY23 3BZ. *T:* Aberystwyth (01970) 622750; 8 Pen y Graig, Aberystwyth, Dyfed SY23 2JA. *T:* Aberystwyth (01970) 615276.

WALTERS, Max; *see* Walters, S. M.

WALTERS, Michael Quentin; Senior Partner, Theodore Goddard, Solicitors, 1983–89; *b* 14 Oct. 1927; *s* of Leslie Walters and Helen Marie Walters; *m* 1954, Lysbeth Ann Falconer. *Educ:* Merchant Taylors' School; Worcester College, Oxford. MA. Served Army, 1946–48, 2nd Lieut. Joined Theodore Goddard, 1951; admitted Solicitor, 1954. Chm., EIS Group plc, 1977–94; Deputy Chairman: Martonair International plc, 1980–86; Tilbury Douglas plc, 1991–; Dir, Delta plc, 1980–95. Mem., Management Cttee, Inst. of Neurology, 1986–91. *Recreations:* fishing, gardening, reading. *Address:* Derryfield Cottage, Ashton Keynes, Swindon, Wilts SN6 6PA. *T:* Cirencester (01285) 861362.

WALTERS, Peter Ernest, CMG 1965; Group Staff Manager, Courage Ltd, 1967–78; Member, London (South) Industrial Tribunal, 1978–82; *b* 9 Oct. 1913; *s* of Ernest Helm Walters and Kathleen Walters (*née* Farrer-Baynes); *m* 1943, Ayesha Margaret, *d* of Alfred and Winifred Bunker; three *d*. *Educ:* Windlesham House Sch. Emigrated to Kenya, 1931. Army Service, 1939–45; commissioned KAR, 1940; Major 1944. Cadet, Colonial Admin. Service, Kenya, 1945; Dist Comr, 1948; Provincial Comr, Northern Prov., 1959; Civil Sec., Eastern Region, Kenya, 1963–65; retd from Colonial Service, 1965. Principal, Min. of Aviation (London), 1965–67. Staff Manager, Courage, Barclay and Simonds Ltd, 1967. Member Management Committee: Southern Housing Gp, 1983–; Coastal Counties Housing Assoc., 1983–; CAB, Dorking, 1986–. *Address:* Cherry Orchard, Ockley, near Dorking, Surrey RH5 5NS. *T:* Dorking (01306) 711119. *Club:* Nairobi (Kenya).

WALTERS, Sir Peter (Ingram), Kt 1984; Chairman: Blue Circle Industries PLC, since 1990; SmithKline Beecham, since 1994 (Director, since 1989); Director, since 1989, and Deputy Chairman, since 1990, Thorn EMI; Deputy Chairman, HSBC Holdings, since 1992; *b* 11 March 1931; *s* of late Stephen Walters and of Edna Walters (*née* Redgate); *m* 1st, 1960, Patricia Anne (*née* Tulloch) (marr. diss. 1991); two *s* one *d*; 2nd, 1992, Meryl Marshall. *Educ:* King Edward's Sch., Birmingham; Birmingham Univ. (BCom). NS Commn; RASC, 1952–54; British Petroleum Co., 1954–90: Man. Dir, 1973–90; Chm., 1981–90; Vice-Pres., BP North America, 1965–67; Chairman: BP Chemicals, 1976–81; BP Chemicals Internat., 1981. Dir, 1981–89, Dep. Chm., 1988–89, Nat. Westminster Bank; Chm., Midland Bank, 1991–94. Member: Indust. Soc. Council, 1975–90; Post Office Bd, 1978–79; Coal Industry Adv. Bd, 1981–85; Inst. of Manpower Studies, 1986–88 (Vice-Pres., 1977–80; Pres., 1980–86); Gen. Cttee, Lloyds Register of Shipping, 1976–90; President's Cttee, CBI, 1982–90; President: Soc. of Chem. Industry, 1978–80; Gen. Council of British Shipping, 1977–78; Inst. of Directors, 1986–92. Chm. Governors, London Business Sch., 1987–91 (Governor, 1981–91); Governor Nat. Inst. of Economic and Social Affairs, 1981–90; Mem. Foundn Bd, 1982–83, Chm., 1984–86, Internat. Management Inst.; Trustee: Nat. Maritime Museum, 1983–90; E Malling Res. Station, 1983–; Police Foundn, 1985–; Inst. of Economic Affairs, 1986–. Hon. DSocSc Birmingham, 1986; DUniv Stirling, 1987. Comdr, Order of Leopold (Belgium), 1984. *Recreations:* golf, gardening, sailing. *Address:* 84 Eccleston Square, SW1V 1PX. *Club.* Athenæum.

WALTERS, Very Rev. (Rhys) Derrick (Chamberlain), OBE 1994; Dean of Liverpool, since 1983; *b* 10 March 1932; *s* of Ivor Chamberlain Walters and Rosamund Grace Walters (*née* Jackson); 1959, Joan Trollope (*née* Fisher); two *s*. *Educ:* Gowerton Boys' Grammar School; London School of Economics; Ripon Hall, Oxford. BSc(Soc) Lond, 1955. Curate, Manselton, Swansea, 1957–58; Anglican Chaplain, University College, Swansea and Curate, St Mary's, 1958–62; Vicar of All Saints, Totley, 1962–67; Vicar of St Mary's, Boulton by Derby, 1967–74; Diocesan Missioner, Diocese of Salisbury, 1974–82; Vicar of Burcombe, 1974–79; Non-residentiary Canon of Salisbury, 1978; Residentiary Canon and Treasurer of Salisbury Cathedral, 1979–82. Hon. Fellow, Liverpool John Moores Univ. (formerly Liverpool Poly.), 1988. *Recreations:* escapist literature, croquet, classical music. *Address:* Liverpool Cathedral, L1 7AZ. *T:* 0151–709 6271.

WALTERS, Sir Roger (Talbot), KBE 1971 (CBE 1965); FRIBA, FIStructE; architect in private practice, 1984–87; *b* 31 March 1917; 3rd *s* of Alfred Bernard Walters, Sudbury, Suffolk; *m* 1976, Claire Myfanwy Chappell. *Educ:* Oundle; Architectural Association School of Architecture; Liverpool University. Diploma in Architecture, 1939. Served in Royal Engineers, 1943–46. Office of Sir E. Owen Williams, KBE, 1936; Directorate of Constructional Design, Min. of Works, 1941–43; Architect to Timber Development Assoc., 1946–49; Principal Asst Architect, Eastern Region, British Railways, 1949–59; Chief Architect (Development), Directorate of Works, War Office, 1959–62; Dep. Dir-Gen., R&D, MPBW, 1962–67; Dir-Gen., Production, 1967–69; Controller General, 1969–71; Architect and Controller of Construction Services, GLC, 1971–78; Birkbeck Coll., 1978–80 (BA 1980); Principal, The Self-Employed Agency, 1981–83. Hon. FAIA. *Address:* 46 Princess Road, NW1 8JL. *T:* 0171–722 3740. *Club:* Reform.

WALTERS, S(tuart) Max, ScD; VMH; Director, University Botanic Garden, Cambridge, 1973–83, retired; *b* 23 May 1920; *s* of Bernard Walters and Ivy Dane; *m* 1948, Lorna Mary Strutt; two *s* one *d*. *Educ:* Penistone Grammar Sch.; St John's Coll., Cambridge. 1st cl. hons Pt I Nat. Scis Tripos 1940 and Pt II Botany 1946; PhD 1949. Research Fellow, St John's Coll., 1947–50; Curator of Herbarium, Botany Sch., Cambridge, 1948–73; Lectr in Botany 1962–73; Fellow of King's Coll., Cambridge, 1964–84. VMH 1984; Linnean Medal for Botany, 1995. *Publications:* (with J. S. L. Gilmour) Wild Flowers, 1954; (with J. Raven) Mountain Flowers, 1956; (ed, with F. H. Perring) Atlas of the British Flora, 1962; (with F. H. Perring, P. D. Sell and H. L. K. Whitehouse) A Flora of Cambridgeshire, 1964; (with D. Briggs) Plant Variation and Evolution, 1969, 2nd edn 1984; The Shaping of Cambridge Botany, 1981; Wild and Garden Plants, 1993. *Address:* 1 Symonds Lane, Grantchester, Cambridge CB3 9NU. *T:* Cambridge (01223) 841295.

WALTHER, Robert Philippe, FIA; Group Chief Executive, Clerical Medical Investment Group, since 1995; *b* 31 July 1943; *s* of Prof. D. P. Walther and Barbara (*née* Brook); *m* 1969, Anne Wigglesworth. *Educ:* Charterhouse; Christ Church, Oxford (MA). FIA 1970. Clerical Medical Investment Group: Investment Manager, 1974–85; Investment Dir, 1985–94; Dep. Man. Dir, 1994–95. *Recreations:* hockey, golf, sailing, bridge. *Address:* Ashwells Barn, Chesham Lane, Chalfont St Giles, Bucks HP8 4AS. *T:* Chalfont St Giles (01494) 875575. *Club:* United Oxford & Cambridge University.

WALTON, family name of **Baron Walton of Detchant.**

WALTON OF DETCHANT, Baron *cr* 1989 (Life Peer), of Detchant in the County of Northumberland; **John Nicholas Walton;** Kt 1979; TD 1962; FRCP; Warden, Green College, University of Oxford, 1983–89; *b* 16 Sept. 1922; *s* of Herbert Walton and Eleanor Watson Walton; *m* 1946, Mary Elizabeth Harrison; one *s* two *d. Educ:* Alderman Wraith Grammar Sch., Spennymoor, Co. Durham; Med. Sch., King's Coll., Univ. of Durham. MB, BS (1st Cl. Hons) 1945; MD (Durham) 1952; DSc (Newcastle) 1972; MA(Oxon) 1983; FRCP 1963 (MRCP 1950). Ho. Phys., Royal Victoria Inf., Newcastle, 1946–47; service in RAMC, 1947–49; Med. Registrar, Royal Vic. Inf., 1949–51; Research Asst, Univ. of Durham, 1951–56; Nuffield Foundn Fellow, Mass. Gen. Hosp. and Harvard Univ., 1953–54; King's Coll. Fellow, Neurological Res. Unit, Nat. Hosp., Queen Square, 1954–55; First Asst in Neurology, Newcastle upon Tyne, 1956–58; Cons. Neurologist, Newcastle Univ. Hosps, 1958–83; Prof. of Neurology, 1968–83, and Dean of Medicine, 1971–81, Univ. of Newcastle upon Tyne. Numerous named lectureships and overseas visiting professorships. Member: MRC, 1974–78; GMC, 1971–89 (Chm. Educn Cttee, 1975–82; Pres., 1982–89); President: BMA, 1980–82; Royal Soc. of Medicine, 1984–86 (Hon. Fellow, 1988); ASME 1982–94; Assoc. of British Neurologists, 1987–88; World Fedn Neurol., 1989– (First Vice-Pres., 1981–89; Chm., Res. Cttee); Chm., Hamlyn Nat. Commn on Educn, 1991–95; UK Rep., EEC Adv. Cttee, Med. Educn, 1975–83; Editor-in-Chief, Jl of Neurological Sciences, 1966–77; Chm., Muscular Dystrophy Gp of GB, 1970–95, etc. Chm., H of L Select Cttee on Med. Ethics, 1993–94; Mem., H of L Select Cttee on Sci. and Technol. (Chm., Sub-Cttee 1). Col (late RAMC) and OC 1 (N) Gen. Hosp. (TA), 1963–66; Hon. Col 201(N) Gen. Hosp. (T&AVR), 1971–77. Freeman, City of London, 1978. Foreign Member: Norwegian Acad. of Sci. and Letters, 1987; Venezuelan Acad. of Medicine, 1992; Russian Acad. of Med. Scis, 1993; Hon. Mem., Osler Soc. of London; Hon. Foreign Member: Amer. Neurological Assoc., Amer. Acad. of Neurology, Assoc. Amer. Phys., Amer. Osler Soc., Japan Osler Soc., and of Canadian, French, German, Australian, Austrian, Spanish, Polish, Venezuelan, Thai, Japanese, Russian and Brazilian Neurological Assocs. Hon. FACP 1980; Hon. FRCPE 1981; Hon. FRCP (Can) 1984; Hon. FRCPath 1993; Hon. FRCPsych 1993; Hon. Fellow, Inst. of Educn, Univ. of London, 1994. Dr de l'Univ. (Hon.) Aix-Marseille, 1975; Hon. DSc: Leeds, 1979; Leicester, 1980; Hull, 1988; Oxford Brookes, 1994; Hon. MD Sheffield, 1987; Hon. DCL Newcastle, 1988; Laurea *hc* Genoa, 1992. Hon. Freeman, Newcastle upon Tyne, 1980. *Publications:* Subarachnoid Haemorrhage, 1956; (with R. D. Adams) Polymyositis, 1958; Essentials of Neurology, 1961, 6th edn 1989; Disorders of Voluntary Muscle, 1964, 6th edn 1994; Brain's Diseases of the Nervous System, 7th edn 1969, 10th edn 1993; (with F. L. Mastaglia) Skeletal Muscle Pathology, 1982, 2nd edn 1991, etc; (ed jtly) The Oxford Companion to Medicine, 1986; The Spice of Life (autobiog.), 1993; (ed jtly) The Oxford Medical Companion, 1994; numerous chapters in books and papers in sci. jls. *Recreations:* cricket, golf and other sports, reading, music. *Address:* 13 Norham Gardens, Oxford OX2 6PS. *T:* Oxford (01865) 512492. *Clubs:* Athenæum, United Oxford & Cambridge University.

WALTON, Anthony Michael, QC 1970; *b* 4 May 1925; *y s* of Henry Herbert Walton and Clara Martha Walton, Dulwich; *m* 1955, Jean Frederica, *o d* of William Montague Hey, Bedford; one *s. Educ:* Dulwich College (sometime Scholar); Hertford College, Oxford (sometime Scholar); pupil to W. L. Ferrar (maths) and C. H. S. Fifoot (law). BA 1946; BCL 1950; MA 1950. Pres., Oxford Union Society, Trinity Term 1945. Nat. Service as physicist. Called to the Bar, Middle Temple, 1950; Bencher, 1978; pupil to Lord Justice Winn. Interested in education. Liveryman, Worshipful Co. of Gunmakers. Freeman, City of London, 1968. *Publications:* (ed) (Asst to Hon. H. Fletcher-Moulton) Digest of the Patent, Design, Trade Mark and Other Cases, 1959; (ed) Russell on Arbitration, 17th edn, 1963–20th edn, 1982; (with Hugh Laddie) Patent Law of Europe and the United Kingdom, 1978. *Address:* 62 Kingsmead Road, SW2 3JG.

WALTON, Arthur Halsall, FCA; Partner in Lysons, Haworth & Sankey, 1949–85; *b* 13 July 1916; *s* of Arthur Walton and Elizabeth Leeming (*née* Halsall); *m* 1958, Kathleen Elsie Abram; three *s. Educ:* The Leys School. Articled in Lysons & Talbot, 1934; ACA 1940. Military Service, 1939–48: commnd Lancs Fusiliers, 1940. Inst. of Chartered Accountants: Mem. Council 1959; Vice-Pres., 1969; Dep. Pres. 1970; Pres. 1971. *Recreation:* reading. *Address:* 19 Cavendish Mews, Wilmslow SK9 1PW. *Club:* St James's (Manchester).

WALTON, Ven. Geoffrey Elmer; Archdeacon of Dorset, since 1982; *b* 19 Feb. 1934; *s* of Harold and Edith Margaret Walton; *m* 1961, Edith Mollie O'Connor; one *s. Educ:* St John's Coll., Univ. of Durham (BA); Queen's Coll., Birmingham (DipTh). Asst Curate, Warsop with Sookholme, 1961–65; Vicar of Norwell, Notts, 1965–69; Recruitment and Selection Sec., ACCM, 1969–75; Vicar of Holy Trinity, Weymouth, 1975–82; RD of Weymouth, 1980–82; Non-Residentiary Canon of Salisbury, 1981–. *Recreations:* conjuring, religious drama. *Address:* The Vicarage, Witchampton, Wimborne, Dorset BH21 5AP. *T:* Witchampton (01258) 840422.

WALTON, Sir John Robert, Kt 1971; retired; Director, Waltons Ltd Group, Australia (Managing Director, 1951–72, Chairman, 1961–72); Chairman, FNCB-Waltons Corp. Ltd, Australia, 1966–75; *b* 7 Feb. 1904; *s* of John Thomas Walton; *m* 1938, Peggy Everley Gamble; one *s* one *d. Educ:* Scots Coll., Sydney. National Cash Register Co. Pty Ltd, 1930: NSW Manager, 1934, Managing Director in Australia, 1946–51. *Recreations:* gardening, swimming, golf, reading. *Address:* 9A Longwood, 5 Thornton Street, Darling Point, NSW 2027, Australia. *Clubs:* Rotary, Royal Sydney Golf, American National, Tattersall's (all in Sydney).

WALTON, John William Scott; Director of Statistics, Board of Inland Revenue, 1977–85; *b* 25 Sept. 1925; *s* of late Sir John Charles Walton, KCIE, CB, MC, and late Nelly Margaret, Lady Walton, *d* of late Prof. W. R. Scott. *Educ:* Marlborough; Brasenose Coll., Oxford. Army (RA), 1943–47. Mutual Security Agency, Paris, 1952; Inland Revenue, 1954; Central Statistical Office, 1958, Chief Statistician, 1967, Asst Dir, 1972. *Publications:* (contrib. jtly) M. Perlman, The Organization and Retrieval of Economic Knowledge, 1977; articles in The Review of Income and Wealth, Economic Trends, Business Economist, Statistical News. *Club:* United Oxford & Cambridge University.

WALTON, William Stephen; Chief Education Officer, Sheffield, 1985–90; *b* 28 March 1933; *s* of Thomas Leslie Walton and Ena Walton (*née* Naylor); *m* 1964, Lois Elicia Petts; three *d* (incl. twins). *Educ:* King's School, Pontefract; Univ. of Birmingham (BA). RAF, gen. duties (flying), 1951–55. Production Management, Dunlop Rubber Co., 1958–61; Derbyshire Local Educn Authy School Teacher, 1961–67; Educational Administration: Hull, 1967–70; Newcastle upon Tyne, 1970–79; Sheffield 1979–90. Visiting Professor: Univ. of Simon Fraser, BC, 1990–91; Univ. of Portland, Oregon, 1990–91. Pres., Soc. of Educn Officers, 1989–90; Chm., Sch. Curriculum Industry Partnership/Mini Enterprise Schs Project, 1990–95. Dir, Outward Bound, 1989–95. Registered Inspector of Schools, 1993–. Hon. Fellow, Sheffield City Polytechnic, 1990. *Recreation:* travel. *Address:* 3 Bentham Road, Chesterfield, Derbyshire S40 4EZ. *T:* Chesterfield (01246) 203769. *Club:* Royal Air Force.

WALWYN, Peter Tyndall; racehorse trainer, since 1960; *b* 1 July 1933; *s* of late Lt-Col Charles Lawrence Tyndall Walwyn, DSO, OBE, MC, Moreton in Marsh, Glos; *m* 1960, Virginia Gaselee, *d* of A. S. Gaselee, MFH; one *s* one *d. Educ:* Amesbury Sch., Hindhead, Surrey; Charterhouse. Leading trainer on the flat, 1974, 1975; leading trainer, Ireland, 1974, 1975; a new record in earnings (£373,563), 1975. Major races won include: One Thousand Guineas, 1970, Humble Duty; Oaks Stakes, 1974, Polygamy; Irish Derby, 1974, English Prince, and 1975, Grundy; King George VI and Queen Elizabeth Stakes, Ascot, 1975, Grundy; Epsom Derby, 1975, Grundy. Chm., Lambourn Trainers' Assoc., 1989–. *Recreations:* foxhunting, shooting. *Address:* Windsor House, Lambourn, Berks RG16 7NR. *T:* Lambourn (01488) 71347. *Clubs:* Turf; Jockey Club Rooms (Newmarket).

WANAMAKER, Zoë; actor; *b* 13 May; *d* of late Sam Wanamaker, Hon. CBE, and of Charlotte (*née* Holland); *m* 1994, Gawn Grainger. *Stage includes:* A Midsummer Night's Dream, 69 Theatre Co., 1970; repertory at Royal Lyceum, 1971–72, Oxford Playhouse, 1974–75 and Nottingham, 1975–76; Royal Shakespeare Company: The Devil's Disciple, Ivanov, Wild Oats, 1976; Captain Swing, The Taming of the Shrew, Piaf, 1978 (NY, 1980); Once in a Lifetime, 1979; Comedy of Errors, Twelfth Night, The Time of your Life, 1983; Mother Courage (Drama magazine award), 1984; Othello, 1989; National Theatre: The Importance of Being Earnest, 1982; The Bay at Nice, Wrecked Eggs, 1986; Mrs Klein, 1988, transf. Apollo, 1989; The Crucible, 1990; New York: Loot, 1986; The Last Yankee, 1993; Dead Funny, 1994; *films include:* Inside the Third Reich, The Hunger, 1982; The Raggedy Rawney, 1987; *television includes:* Strike, 1981; Richard III, 1982; Enemies of the State, 1982; The Edge of Darkness, 1985; Paradise Postponed, 1985; Once in a Lifetime, 1987; The Dog it was that died, 1988; Prime Suspect, 1991; Love Hurts, 1992, 1993, 1994; The Blackheath Poisonings, 1992; Momento Mori, 1992; The Countess Alice, 1992; The Widowing of Mrs Holroyd, 1995; has also appeared in radio plays. *Address:* c/o Peggy Thompson, 7 High Park Road, Kew, Richmond, Surrey TW9 4BL.

WANDSWORTH, Archdeacon of; *see* Gerrard, Ven. D. K. R.

WANG Gungwu, Prof., CBE 1991; FAHA; Chairman, Institute of East Asian Political Economy, since 1996; Vice-Chancellor, University of Hong Kong, 1986–95; *b* 9 Oct. 1930; *s* of Wang Fo Wen and Ting Yien; *m* 1955, Margaret Lim Ping-Ting; one *s* two *d. Educ:* Anderson Sch., Ipoh, Malaya; Nat. Central Univ., Nanking, China; Univ. of Malaya, Singapore (BA Hons, MA); Univ. of London (PhD 1957). University of Malaya, Singapore: Asst Lectr, 1957–59; Lectr, 1959; University of Malaya, Kuala Lumpur: Lectr, 1959–61; Sen. Lectr, 1961–63; Dean of Arts, 1962–63; Prof. of History, 1963–68; Australian National University: Prof. of Far Eastern History, 1968–86, Emeritus Prof., 1988; Dir, Res. Sch. of Pacific Studies, 1975–80; Univ. Fellow, 1996–. Rockefeller Fellow, 1961–62, Sen. Vis. Fellow, 1972, Univ. of London; Vis. Fellow, All Souls Coll., Oxford, 1974–75; John A. Burns Distinguished Vis. Prof. of History, Univ. of Hawaii, 1979; Rose Morgan Vis. Prof. of History, Univ. of Kansas, 1983. Dir, East Asian History of Science Foundation Ltd, 1987–. MEC, Hong Kong, 1990–92. Chairman: Australia-China Council, 1984–86; Envmt Pollution Cttee, HK, 1988–93; Adv. Council on the Envmt, 1993–95; Council for the Performing Arts, HK, 1989–94; Member: Commn of Inquiry on Singapore Riots, 1964–65; Internat. Adv. Panel, E-W Center, Honolulu, 1979–91; Cttee on Aust.-Japan Relations, 1980–81; Regional Council, Inst. of SE Asian Studies, Singapore, 1982–; Admin. Bd, Assoc. of SE Asian Instns of Higher Learning, 1986–92; Council, Chinese Univ. of Hong Kong, 1986–95; Exec. Council, WWF, HK, 1987–; Council, Asia-Aust. Inst., Sydney, 1991–95; Council, Asia Soc., HK, 1991–95; Council, IISS, 1992–; President: Internat. Assoc. of Historians of Asia, 1964–68, 1988–91; Asian Studies Assoc. of Aust., 1979–80; Australian Acad. of the Humanities, 1980–83 (Fellow 1970); Hon. Corresp. Mem. for Hong Kong, RSA, 1987 (Fellow 1987; Chm., Hong Kong Chapter, 1992–95). Mem., Academia Sinica, 1992. For. Hon. Mem., Amer. Acad. of Arts and Scis., 1995. Editor: (also Councillor), Jl of Nanyang Hsueh-hui, Singapore, 1958–68; (also Vice-Pres.), Jl of RAS, Malaysian Br., 1962–68; Gen. Editor, East Asian Historical Monographs series for OUP, 1968–. Hon. DLitt Sydney, 1992; Hon. LLD Monash, 1992; DUniv: Soka, 1993; Griffith, 1995. *Publications:* The Nanhai Trade: a study of the early history of Chinese trade in the South China Sea, 1958; A Short History of the Nanyang Chinese, 1959; Latar Belakang Kebudayaan Pendudok di-Tanah Melayu: Bahagian Kebudayaan China (The Cultural Background of the Peoples of Malaysia: Chinese culture), 1962; The Structure of Power in North China during the Five Dynasties, 1963; (ed) Malaysia: a survey, 1964; (ed jtly) Essays on the Sources for Chinese History, 1974; (ed) Self and Biography: essays on the individual and society in Asia, 1975; China and the World since 1949: the impact of independence, modernity and revolution, 1977; (ed jtly) Hong Kong: dilemmas of growth, 1980; Community and Nation: essays on Southeast Asia and the Chinese, 1981; (ed jtly) Society and the Writer: essays on literature in modern Asia, 1981; Dongnanya yu Huaren (Southeast Asia and the Chinese), 1987; Nanhai Maoyi yu Nanyang Huaren (Chinese Trade and Southeast Asia), 1988; (ed with J. Cushman) Changing Indentities of Southeast Asian Chinese since World War II, 1988; Lishi di Gongneng (The Functions of History), 1990; China and the Chinese Overseas, 1991; The Chineseness of China: selected essays, 1991; Community and Nation: China, Australia and Southeast Asia, 1992; Zhongguo yu Haiwai Huaren (China and the Chinese Overseas), 1994; contribs to collected vols on Asian history; articles on Chinese and Southeast Asian history in internat. jls. *Recreations:* music, reading, walking. *Address:* Institute of East Asian Political Economy, Arts and Social Sciences Faculty, National University of Singapore, Kent Ridge, Singapore 0511. *T:* 7791037, *Fax:* 7793409.

WANGARATTA, Bishop of, since 1995; **Rt Rev. Paul Richardson;** *b* 16 Jan. 1947; *s* of William and Ilene Richardson. *Educ:* Keswick Sch.; The Queen's Coll., Oxford (BA (Mod. History) 1968, (Theol.) 1970; MA 1975); Harvard Divinity Sch.; Cuddesdon Theol Coll. Ordained deacon, 1972, priest, 1973; Asst Curate, St John's, Earlsfield, 1972–75; Asst Chaplain, Oslo, Norway, 1975–77; Mission Priest, Nambaiyufa, PNG, 1977–79; Lectr, 1979–81, Principal, 1981–85, Newton Theol Coll.; Dean, St John's Cathedral, Port Moresby, 1985–86; Bishop of Aipo Rongo, PNG, 1987–95. *Recreations:* reading, walking, travel. *Address:* PO Box 457, Wangaratta, Vic 3677, Australia. *T:* (57) 213643.

WANI, Most Rev. Silvanus; *b* July 1916; *s* of late Mana Ada Wani and late Daa Miriam; *m* 1936, Penina Yopa Wani; six *s* two *d* (and two *s* decd). *Educ:* Kampala Normal School, Makerere (Teacher's Cert.). Teaching, Arua Primary School, 1936–39; student, Buwalasi Theol. Coll., 1940–42; ordained as one of first two priests in West Nile District, 1943; Chaplain, King's African Rifles, 1944–46; Parish Priest: Arua, 1947–50; Koboko, 1951–60; Canon and Rural Dean, Koboko, 1953–60; attended Oak Hill Theological Coll., 1955–56; Diocesan Secretary/Treasurer, N Uganda Diocese, 1961–64; student (Christianity and Islam), St George's Coll., Jerusalem, 1963–64; Asst Bishop, later full Bishop, N Uganda, 1964; Bishop of Madi/West Nile Diocese, 1969; Dean, Province of Church of Uganda, Rwanda, Burundi and Boga Zaire, 1974–77; Archbishop of Uganda (also of Rwanda, Burundi and Boga Zaire, 1977–80) and Bishop of Kampala, 1977–83; retd, on health and age grounds, to home area, 1983. Chaplain Gen. to Uganda Armed Forces, 1964–78. *Recreations:* reading, walking, gardening. *Address:* c/o PO Box 370, Arua, Uganda.

WANLESS, Derek, FCIB; Group Chief Executive, National Westminster Bank plc, since 1992; *b* 29 Sept. 1947; *s* of Norman Wanless and Edna (*née* Charlton); *m* 1971, Vera West;

one *s* four *d*. *Educ:* Royal Grammar Sch., Newcastle upon Tyne; King's Coll., Cambridge (BA 1st cl. Hons Maths, MA). MIS 1973. Joined National Westminster Bank, 1970; appts include: Area Dir, NE Area, 1982–85, W Yorks, 1985–86; Dir of Personal Banking, 1986–88; Gen. Manager, UK Branch Business, 1989–90; Chief Exec., UK Financial Services, 1990–92; Dir, 1991–; Dep. Gp Chief Exec., Feb.–March 1992. Chm., Adv. Cttee on Business and Envmt set up by Secs of State for Envmt and Trade and Ind., 1993– (Mem., 1991–93); Member: Envmtl Management Wkg Gp, 1991–93; Financial Sector Wkg Gp, 1993– (Chm., 1991–93); Business in the Envmt, 1992–; EC Consultative Forum, on the Envmt, 1994–; WBCSD (formerly WICE), 1993–. FRSA 1991; CIMgt (CBIM 1992). Freeman, City of London, 1992. *Recreations:* all sports, chess, music, walking, gardening. *Address:* National Westminster Bank plc, 41 Lothbury, EC2P 2BP. *T:* 0171–726 1212.

WANSTALL, Hon. Sir Charles Gray, Kt 1974; Chief Justice of Queensland, Australia, 1977–82; *b* 17 Feb. 1912; *m* 1938, Olwyn Mabel, *d* of C. O. John; one *d*. *Educ:* Roma and Gympie State Schs; Gympie High Sch., Queensland, Australia. Called to Queensland Bar, 1933. High Court, 1942. MLA (Liberal) for Toowong, 1944–50; Pres., Liberal Party of Australia (Qld Div.), 1950–53. QC 1956; Judge, Supreme Court, Qld, 1958; Sen. Puisne Judge, 1971. *Recreations:* reading, photography. *Address:* 26/36 Jerdanefield Road, St Lucia, Brisbane, Queensland 4067, Australia. *Clubs:* Queensland (Brisbane); St Lucia Bowling.

WAPSHOTT, Nicholas Henry; Editor, The Times Magazine, since 1992; *b* 13 Jan. 1952; *s* of Raymond Gibson Wapshott and Olivia Beryl Darch; *m* 1980, Louise Nicholson; two *s*. *Educ:* Dursley County Primary Sch.; Rendcomb Coll., Cirencester; Univ. of York (BA Hons). The Scotsman, 1973–76; The Times, 1976–84; The Observer, 1984–92, Political Editor, 1988–92. *Publications:* Peter O'Toole, 1982; (with George Brock) Thatcher, 1983; The Man Between: a biography of Carol Reed, 1990; Rex Harrison, 1991. *Recreations:* cinema, music, elephants. *Address:* The Times, 1 Pennington Street, E1 9XN. *T:* 0171–782 5937; 35 Cross Street, Islington, N1 2BH. *T:* 0171–226 5278. *Clubs:* Reform, Morton's.

WARBURTON, Col Alfred Arthur, CBE 1961; DSO 1945; DL; JP; Chairman, SHEF Engineering Ltd, 1970–75; Company Director since 1953; *b* 12 April 1913; *s* of late A. V. Warburton. *Educ:* Sedbergh. Served War of 1939–45, with Essex Yeomanry; Lt-Col comdg South Notts Hussars Yeomanry, 1953–58; Hon. Col 1966–76; Col DCRA 49th Inf. Div. TA, 1958–60; ADC to the Queen, 1961–66; Chm., Notts Cttee TA&VR Assoc. for E Midlands, 1970–78. Director, John Shaw Ltd, Worksop, 1953–66. President: East Midlands Area, Royal British Legion, 1976–77, 1981–82, 1986–87, 1991–92; Notts County Royal British Legion, 1979–95. DL 1966, High Sheriff 1968, JP 1968, Notts. *Recreations:* shooting, fishing, gardening. *Address:* Wigthorpe House, Wigthorpe, Worksop, Notts S81 8BT. *T:* Worksop (01909) 730357. *Club:* Cavalry and Guards.

WARBURTON, Dame Anne (Marion), DCVO 1979 (CVO 1965); CMG 1977; HM Diplomatic Service, 1957–85; President, Lucy Cavendish College, Cambridge, 1985–94; *b* 8 June 1927; *d* of Captain Eliot Warburton, MC and Mary Louise (*née* Thompson), US. *Educ:* Barnard Coll., Columbia Univ. (BA); Somerville Coll., Oxford (BA, MA); Hon. Fellow, 1977. Economic Cooperation Administration, London, 1949–52; NATO Secretariat, Paris, 1952–54; Lazard Bros, London, 1955–57; entered Diplomatic Service, Nov. 1957; 2nd Sec., FO, 1957–59; 2nd, then 1st Sec., UK Mission to UN, NY, 1959–62; 1st Sec., Bonn, 1962–65; 1st Sec., DSAO, London, 1965–67; 1st Sec., FO, then FCO, 1967–70; Counsellor, UK Mission to UN, Geneva, 1970–75; Head of Guidance and Information Policy Dept, FCO, 1975–76; Ambassador to Denmark, 1976–83; Ambassador and UK Permanent Rep. to UN and other internat. organisations, Geneva, 1983–85. Dep. Leader, UK Delegn to UN Women's Conf., Nairobi, 1985; Leader, EC Investigative Mission: Abuse of Bosnian Muslim Women, 1992–93; Mem., Cttee on Standards in Public Life, 1994–. Member: Equal Opportunities Commn, 1986–88; British Library Bd, 1989–95; Council, UEA, 1991–. Governor, ESU, 1992–. Hon. LLD Arkansas, 1994. Verdienstkreuz, 1st Class (West Germany), 1965; Grand Cross, Order of Dannebrog, 1979; Lazo de Dama, Order of Isabel la Católica (Spain), 1988. *Recreations:* travel, walking, the arts. *Address:* Ansted, Thornham Magna, Eye, Suffolk IP23 8HB. *Clubs:* United Oxford & Cambridge University, English-Speaking Union.

WARBURTON, David; Senior National Officer: GMB (formerly General, Municipal, Boilermakers and Allied Trades Union), since 1973; APEX (white collar section of GMB), since 1990; *b* 10 Jan. 1942; *s* of Harold and Ada Warburton; *m* 1966, Carole Anne Susan Tomney; two *d*. *Educ:* Cottingley Manor Sch., Bingley, Yorks; Coleg Harlech, Merioneth, N Wales. Campaign Officer, Labour Party, 1964; Educn Officer, G&MWU, 1965–66, Reg. Officer, 1966–73. Secretary: Chemical Unions Council; Rubber Industry Jt Unions, 1980–86; Health Care Textile Unions, 1988–; Chm., Paper and Packaging Industry Unions, 1988–. Mem., Europ. Co-ord. Cttee, Chem., Rubber and Glass Unions, 1975–. Chm., Chem. and Allied Industries Jt Indust. Council, 1973–86; Mem., Govt Industrial Workers Jt Consultative Cttee, 1988–; Sec., Home Office Jt Indust. Council, 1989–; Treas., Electricity Supply Nat. Jt Council, 1990–. Vice-Pres., Internat. Fedn of Chemical, Energy and Gen. Workers, 1986–. Member: NEDC, 1973–86; Commonwealth Develt Corp., 1979–87; TUC Energy Cttee, 1978–92; Nat. Jt Council for Civil Air Transport, 1992–; Chm., TUC Gen. Purposes Cttee, 1984–. Nat. Sec., UK Friends of Palestine, 1983–. *Publications:* Pharmaceuticals for the People, 1973; Drug Industry: which way to control, 1975; UK Chemicals: The Way Forward, 1977; Economic Detente, 1980; The Case for Voters Tax Credits, 1983; Forward Labour, 1985; Facts, Figures and Damned Statistics, 1987. *Recreations:* music, American politics, flicking through reference books, films of the thirties and forties. *Address:* 47 Hill Rise, Chorleywood, Rickmansworth, Herts WD3 2NY. *T:* Rickmansworth (01923) 778726.

WARBURTON, Prof. Geoffrey Barratt, FEng 1985; Hives Professor of Mechanical Engineering, University of Nottingham, 1982–89; *b* 9 June 1924; *s* of Ernest McPherson and Beatrice Warburton; *m* 1952, Margaret Coan; three *d*. *Educ:* William Hulme's Grammar School, Manchester; Peterhouse, Cambridge (Open Exhibition in Mathematics, 1942; 1st cl. Hons in Mechanical Sciences Tripos, 1944; BA 1945; MA 1949); PhD Edinburgh, 1949. Junior Demonstrator, Cambridge Univ., 1944–46; Asst Lecturer in Engineering, Univ. Coll. of Swansea, 1946–47; Dept of Engineering, Univ. of Edinburgh: Assistant, 1947–48, Lecturer, 1948–50 and 1953–56; ICI Research Fellow, 1950–53; Head of Post-graduate School of Applied Dynamics, 1956–61; Nottingham University: Prof. of Applied Mechanics, 1961–82; a Pro-Vice-Chancellor, 1984–88. Vis. Prof., Dept of Civil Engrg, Imperial Coll., 1990–95. FRSE 1960; FIMechE 1968. Rayleigh Medal, Inst. of Acoustics, 1982. Editor, Earthquake Engineering and Structural Dynamics, 1988– (Associate Editor, 1972–88); Member, Editorial Boards: Internat. Jl of Mechanical Sciences, 1967–92; Internat. Jl for Numerical Methods in Engineering, 1969–; Jl of Sound and Vibration, 1971–; Communications in Applied Numerical Methods, 1985–. *Publications:* The Dynamical Behaviour of Structures, 1964, 2nd edn 1976; research on mechanical vibrations, in several scientific journals. *Address:* 18 Grangewood Road, Wollaton, Nottingham NG8 2SH.

WARBURTON, Ivor William; Managing Director, British Rail InterCity West Coast Ltd, since 1992; *b* 13 Aug. 1946; *s* of late Dennis and of Edna Margaret Warburton; *m* 1969, Carole-Ann (*née* Ashton) (marr. diss. 1982); three *d*. *Educ:* Dulwich Coll.; Queens' Coll., Cambridge (MA); Univ. of Warwick (MSc). FCIT 1989; MCIM. British Railways, 1968–: graduate trainee, 1968–70; local ops posts, London Midland Region, 1970–73; Divl Passenger Manager, Bristol, 1974–78; Overseas Tourist Manager, 1978–82; Regional Passenger Manager, York, 1982–83; Dir, Passenger Marketing Services, 1984–85; Asst Gen. Manager, London Midland Region, 1985–87; Employee Relations Manager, 1987–88; Dir of Operations, 1988–90; Gen. Manager, London Midland Region, 1990–92. Pres., Railway Study Assoc., 1993–94. *Recreations:* cooking Chinese style, music, opera, handicapped scouting, Marketors' Livery Company. *Address:* 34 St Clair's Road, Croydon CR0 5NE. *T:* 0181–688 2742.

WARBURTON, John Kenneth, CBE 1983; Director General, Birmingham Chamber of Commerce and Industry, 1994 (Chief Executive, 1978–94); *b* 7 May 1932; *s* of Frederick and Eva Warburton; *m* 1960, Patricia Gordon; one *d*. *Educ:* Newcastle-under-Lyme High Sch.; Keble Coll., Oxford (MA Jurisprudence). Called to Bar, Gray's Inn, 1977. London Chamber of Commerce, 1956–59; Birmingham Chamber of Commerce and Industry, 1959–94. President, British Chambers of Commerce Executives, 1979–81; Member: Steering Cttee, Internat. Bureau of Chambers of Commerce, 1976–94; Nat. Council, Assoc. of British Chambers of Commerce, 1978–94; European Trade Cttee and Business Link Gp, BOTB, 1979–87; E European Trade Council, BOTB, 1984–93; Review Body on Doctors' and Dentists' Remuneration, 1982–92; MSC Task Gp on Employment Trng, 1987; Disciplinary Panels, FIMBRA, 1989–93; Lord Chancellor's Birmingham Adv. Cttee, 1993–; Chm., Adv. Council, W Midlands Industrial Develt Assoc., 1983–86. Mediator, Centre for Dispute Resolution, 1994. Director: National Garden Festival 1986 Ltd, 1983–87; National Exhibition Centre Ltd, 1989–. Chm., Birmingham Macmillan Nurses Appeal, 1994–. Companion, BITC, 1992–. Trustee, Holy Child Sch., Edgbaston, 1992–; Governor: Univ. of Birmingham, 1982–; Newman Coll., 1993–. FRSA. *Address:* 35 Hampshire Drive, Edgbaston, Birmingham B15 3NY. *T:* 0121–454 6764.

WARBURTON, Richard Maurice, OBE 1987; Director General, Royal Society for the Prevention of Accidents, 1979–90; *b* 14 June 1928; *s* of Richard and Phylis Agnes Warburton; *m* 1952, Lois May Green; two *s*. *Educ:* Wigan Grammar Sch.; Birmingham Univ. (BA 1st Cl. Hons). Flying Officer, RAF, 1950–52. HM Inspector of Factories, 1952–79; Head of Accident Prevention Advisory Unit, Health and Safety Executive, 1972–79. *Recreations:* golf, gardening, fell walking. *Address:* Cornaa, Wyfordby Avenue, Blackburn, Lancs BB2 7AR. *T:* Blackburn (01254) 56824.

WARD, family name of **Earl of Dudley** and of **Viscount Bangor.**

WARD, Prof. Alan Gordon, CBE 1972 (OBE 1959); Procter Professor of Food and Leather Science, Leeds University, 1961–77, now Emeritus; *b* 18 April 1914; *s* of Lionel Howell Ward and Lily Maud Ward (*née* Morgan); *m* 1938, Cicely Jean Chapman; one *s* two *d*. *Educ:* Queen Elizabeth's Grammar Sch., Wimborne; Trinity Coll., Cambridge (schol.). BA (Cantab) 1935; MA (Cantab) 1940; FInstP 1946; FIFST 1966; CPhys; FSLTC 1986. Lectr in Physics and Mathematics, N Staffs Technical Coll., 1937–40; Experimental Officer, Min. of Supply, 1940–46; Sen. Scientific Officer, Building Research Station, 1946–48; Principal Scientific Officer, 1948–49; Dir of Research, The British Gelatine and Glue Research Assoc., 1949–59; Prof. of Leather Industries, Leeds Univ., 1959–61. Chm., Food Standards Cttee set up by Minister of Agriculture, 1965–79. Hon. FIFST 1979; Hon. FAIFST 1979. *Publications:* Nature of Crystals, 1938; Colloids, Their Properties and Applications, 1945; The Science and Technology of Gelatin, 1977; papers in Trans. Far. Soc., Jl Sci. Instr, Biochem. Jl, etc. *Recreation:* music. *Address:* 35 Templar Gardens, Wetherby, West Yorkshire LS22 7TG. *T:* Wetherby (01937) 584177.

WARD, Rt Hon. Sir Alan Hylton, Kt 1988; PC 1995; **Rt Hon. Lord Justice Ward;** a Lord Justice of Appeal, since 1995; *b* 15 Feb. 1938; *s* of late Stanley Victor Ward and of Mary Ward; *m* 1st, 1963 (marr. diss. 1982); one *s* two *d*, 2nd, 1983, Helen (*née* Gilbert); twin *d*. *Educ:* Christian Brothers Coll., Pretoria; Univ. of Pretoria (BA, LLB); Pembroke Coll., Cambridge (MA, LLB). Called to the Bar, Gray's Inn, 1964, Bencher, 1988; QC 1984; a Recorder, 1985–88; a Judge of the High Court, Family Div., 1988–95; Family Div. Liaison Judge, Midland and Oxford Circuit, 1990–95. Formerly an Attorney of Supreme Court of South Africa. Mem., Matrimonial Causes Procedure Cttee, 1982–85. Consulting Editor, Children Law and Practice, 1991–. *Recreation:* mowing the lawn but dreaming of my cover drive. *Address:* Royal Courts of Justice, Strand, WC2A 2LL. *Club:* MCC.

WARD, (Albert Joseph) Reginald; Chief Executive, ISLEF, Danish property company, 1989–92; Visiting Professor, Leeds Business School; *b* 5 Oct. 1927; *s* of Albert E. and Gwendolene M. E. Ward, Lydbook, Glos; *m* 1954, Betty Anne Tooze; one *s* one *d*. *Educ:* East Dean Grammar Sch., Cinderford, Glos; Univ. of Manchester (BA Hons History). HM Inspector of Taxes, 1952–65; Chief Administrator, County Architects Dept, Lancashire CC, 1965–68; Business Manager, Shankland Cox & Associates, 1968–69; Corporation Secretary, Irvine New Town Development Corporation, 1969–72; Chief Executive: Coatbridge Borough Council, 1972–74; London Borough of Hammersmith, 1974–76; Hereford and Worcester CC, 1976–80; LDDC, 1981–88. Mem., Duke of Edinburgh's Commn into Housing, 1986–87. Hon. Fellow, QMC, 1987; Fellow, Univ. of London. FRSA. *Recreations:* walking, tennis, music, architecture and urban design. *Address:* Field House, Awre, near Newnham on Severn, Glos GL14 1EH. *T:* Blakeney (01594) 517298.

WARD, Mrs Ann Sarita; non-executive Director, Lambeth, Southwark, Lewisham Family Health Services Authority, since 1991; *b* 4 Aug. 1923; *d* of Denis Godfrey and Marion Phyllis Godfrey; *m* Frank Ward (*d* 1991); one *s*. *Educ:* St Paul's Girls' Sch., Hammersmith. Professional photographer; photo journalist, Daily Mail, 1962–67, Daily Mirror, 1967–70; award winner, British Press Photographs of Year, 1967. Councillor, London Bor. of Southwark, 1971–86 (Dep. Leader, 1978–83); Chm., ILEA, 1981–82. Contested (Lab) Streatham, Gen. Election, 1970. Associate Mem., Camberwell HA, 1990–93 (Mem., 1982–90). Special Trustee, KCH, 1983–88. Mem., Internat. Shakespeare Globe Centre, 1988–92; Hon. Vice Pres., Friends of Shakespeare's Globe, 1992– (Chm., 1987–92). Co-ordinator, Emily's List UK, 1992–. *Recreations:* theatre, gardening. *Address:* 204 Peckham Rye, SE22 0LU. *T:* 0181–693 4251.

WARD, Ven. Arthur Frederick, BA; Archdeacon of Exeter, 1970–81, Archdeacon Emeritus since 1981; Canon Residentiary of Exeter Cathedral, 1970–81, Precentor, 1972–81; *b* 23 April 1912; *s* of William Thomas and Annie Florence Ward, Corbridge, Northumberland; *m* 1937, Margaret Melrose, Tynemouth, Northumberland; two *d*. *Educ:* Durham Choir School; Newcastle upon Tyne Royal Grammar School; Durham University; Ridley Hall, Cambridge. Curate, Byker Parish Church, Newcastle, 1935–40; Rector of Harpurhey, North Manchester, 1940–44; Vicar of Nelson, 1944–55; Vicar of Christ Church, Paignton, 1955–62; Archdeacon of Barnstaple and Rector of Shirwell with Loxhore, Devon, 1962–70. *Recreations:* gardening, cricket, touring. *Address:* Melrose, Christow, Devon EX6 7LY. *T:* Christow (01647) 52498.

WARD, Cecil, CBE 1989; JP; Town Clerk, Belfast City Council, 1979–89; *b* 26 Oct. 1929; *s* of William and Mary Caroline Ward. *Educ:* Technical High Sch., Belfast; College of Technology, Belfast. Employed by Belfast City Council (formerly Belfast County Borough Council), 1947–89; Asst Town Clerk (Administration), 1977–79. Mem., Local Govt Staff Commn, 1983–89. Member: Arts Council NI, 1980–85, 1987–89; Bd, Ulster Mus., 1989–; Dir, Ulster Orchestra Soc., 1980–94 (Chm., 1990–94). Mem., Senate, QUB, 1990–. Mem., Bd, Mater Hosp., 1994–. JP Belfast, 1988. Hon. MA QUB, 1988. *Recreations:* music, reading, hill walking. *Address:* 24 Thornhill, Malone, Belfast, Northern Ireland BT9 6SS. *T:* Belfast (01232) 668950; Hatter's Field, Drumawier, Greencastle, Co. Donegal, Ireland.

WARD, Christopher John; Editorial Director and Joint Founder, Redwood Publishing, since 1983; Director, Acorn Computer plc, since 1983; *b* 25 Aug. 1942; *s* of John Stanley Ward and Jacqueline Law-Hume Costin; *m* 1st, 1971 (marr. diss.); one *s* two *d*; 2nd, 1990, Nonie Niesewand (*née* Fogarty). *Educ:* King's Coll. Sch., Wimbledon. Successively on staff of Driffield Times, 1959, and Newcastle Evening Chronicle, 1960–63; reporter, sub-editor, then feature writer and columnist, 1963–76, Daily Mirror; Assistant Editor: Sunday Mirror, 1976–79; Daily Mirror, 1979–81; Editor, Daily Express, 1981–83. Trustee, WWF, 1994–. *Publications:* How to Complain, 1974; Our Cheque is in the Post, 1980. *Recreations:* shooting, walking in the Cheviots. *Address:* 7 Rochester Road, NW1 9JH. *T:* 0171–267 9070, *Fax:* 0171–267 9022. *Club:* Savile.

WARD, Christopher John Ferguson; solicitor; Senior Partner, Clarks, Reading, since 1993; *b* 26 Dec. 1942; *m* Janet Ward, JP, LLB; one *s* one *d* and two *s* one *d* by former marr. *Educ:* Magdalen College Sch.; Law Society Sch. of Law. Partner, Clark & Son, subseq. Clarks, Reading, 1965–. MP (C) Swindon, Oct. 1969–June 1970; contested (C) Eton and Slough, 1979. Mem., Berks CC, 1965–81 (Leader of the Council and Chm., Policy Cttee, 1979–81). Gov., Chiltern Nursery Trng Coll., 1975– (Chm., 1988–91). Treas., United & Cecil Club, 1993 (Hon. Sec., 1982–87). *Address:* Ramblings, Maidenhead Thicket, Berks SL6 3QE. *T:* (office) Reading (01734) 604687.

WARD, (Christopher) John (William); Director of Corporate Affairs, West Yorkshire Playhouse, since 1994; *b* 21 June 1942; *s* of late Thomas Maxfield and of Peggy Ward; *m* 1970, Diane Lelliott (marr. diss. 1988). *Educ:* Oundle Sch.; Corpus Christi Coll., Oxford (BA LitHum); Univ. of East Anglia (Graduate DipEcon). Overseas and Economic Intelligence Depts, Bank of England, 1965; General Secretary, Bank of England Staff Organisation, 1973; Gen. Sec., Assoc. of First Div. Civil Servants, 1980; Head of Development, Opera North, 1988–94. *Recreations:* opera, theatre, football. *Address:* West Yorkshire Playhouse, Playhouse Square, Leeds LS2 7UP. *T:* Leeds (0113) 244 2141. *Club:* Swindon Town Supporters.

WARD, David; Partner, Atkinson Ritson (formerly Atkinson & North), Solicitors, Carlisle, since 1964; President, The Law Society, 1989–90; *b* 23 Feb. 1937; *s* of Rev. Frank Ward, Darfield, Yorks, and Elizabeth Ward (*née* Pattinson), Appleby, Westmorland; *m* 1978, Antoinette, *d* of Maj.-Gen. D. A. B. Clarke, CB, CBE; two *s* one *d*. *Educ:* Dame Allan's Sch., Newcastle upon Tyne; Queen Elizabeth Grammar Sch., Penrith; St Edmund Hall, Oxford (BA). Admitted solicitor, 1962. Articled Clerk, 1959, Assistant, 1962, Atkinson & North. Mem., Lord Chancellor's Adv. Cttee on Legal Educn and Conduct, 1991–. Mem. Council, 1972–91, Vice-Pres., 1988–89, Law Soc.; Pres., Carlisle and District Law Soc., 1985–86. Pres., Carlisle Mountaineering Club, 1985–88. Methodist local preacher, 1955–. *Recreations:* mountaineering, choral and church music. *Address:* The Green, Caldbeck, Wigton, Cumbria CA7 8ER. *T:* Caldbeck (016974) 78220.

WARD, Rev. David Conisbee; Non-stipendiary Minister, St George's, Tolworth, since 1995; Councillor (Lib Dem) Kingston-upon-Thames, since 1994; *b* 7 Jan. 1933; *s* of late Sydney L. Ward and Ivy A. Ward; *m* 1958, Patricia Jeanette (*née* Nobes); one *s* one *d*. *Educ:* Kingston Grammar Sch.; St John's Coll., Cambridge (Scholar, MA). Asst Principal, Nat. Assistance Bd, 1956, Principal, 1961; Asst Sec., DHSS, 1970, Under Sec., 1976–83. Southwark Ordination Course, 1977–80; Deacon, 1980; Priest, 1981; Non-Stipendiary Curate, St Matthew, Surbiton, 1980–83; Curate, Immanuel Church, Streatham Common, 1983–84, parish priest, 1984–87; Vicar, St Paul's, Hook, Surrey, 1987–93; NSM, All Saints, Kingston, 1993–95. Governor, Kingston GS, 1988–. *Recreations:* member Chelsea FC; Pitcairn Islands Study Group (philately) (Dir-at-Large). *Address:* 50 Elgar Avenue, Tolworth, Surbiton, Surrey KT5 9JN. *T:* 0181–399 9679. *Clubs:* Civil Service, Sion College.

WARD, Donald Albert; *b* 30 March 1920; *s* of Albert and Rosie Ward; *m* 1948, Maureen Molloy; five *s*. *Educ:* Brewery Road Elementary Sch.; Southend-on-Sea High Sch.; The Queen's Coll., Oxford. BA(Hons)(Maths); MA. Served War, Indian Army (RIASC), 10th Indian Div., Middle East and Italy, 1940–45 (despatches). Min. of Food, 1946–53; Export Credits Guarantee Dept, 1953–74 (Under-Sec., 1971–74); Sec. Gen., Internat. Union of Credit and Investment Insurers (Berne Union), 1974–86. *Address:* Lindisfarne, St Nicholas Hill, Leatherhead, Surrey KT22 8NE. *Club:* United Oxford & Cambridge University.

WARD, Edmund Fisher, CBE 1972; Architect; Member, Royal Fine Art Commission, 1974–83; Consultant (formerly Partner), Gollins Melvin Ward Partnership. *Address:* White Cottage, The Street, Chipperfield, near King's Langley, Hertfordshire WD4 9BH.

WARD, Ven. Edwin James Greenfield, LVO 1963; Archdeacon of Sherborne, 1968–84; Archdeacon Emeritus and Canon Emeritus of Salisbury Cathedral, since 1985; Extra Chaplain to the Queen, since 1989 (Chaplain, 1955–89); *b* 26 Oct. 1919; *er s* of Canon F. G. Ward, MC, lately of Canberra, Australia; *m* 1946, Grizell Evelyn Buxton (*d* 1985); one *s* two *d*. *Educ:* St John's, Leatherhead; Christ's Coll., Cambridge (MA). Served King's Dragoon Guards, 1940; Reserve, 1946. Ordained 1948; Vicar of North Elmham, Norfolk, 1950–55; Chaplain, Royal Chapel, Windsor Great Park, 1955–67; Rector of West Stafford, 1967–84. Mem. of Council, Marlborough Coll., 1969–88; Visitor, Milton Abbey School, 1991–94 (Mem., Bd of Govs, 1983–91). *Recreation:* fishing. *Address:* 14 Arle Close, Alresford, Hants SO14 9BG. *T:* Alresford (01962) 735501.
See also Baron Wakeham.

WARD, Frank Dixon; *see* Dixon Ward.

WARD, Hubert, MA; Principal, English College, Prague, since 1992; *b* 26 Sept. 1931; *s* of Allan Miles Ward and Joan Mary Ward; *m* 1958, Elizabeth Cynthia Fearn Bechervaise; one *s* two *d*. *Educ:* Westminster Sch.; Trinity Coll., Cambridge. Asst Master (Maths), Geelong C of E Grammar Sch., Victoria, 1955–66; Asst Master (Maths), Westminster Sch., London, 1966–69; Headmaster, King's Sch., Ely, 1970–92. Mem. (L) Cambs CC, 1985–89. JP Cambs, 1976–92. *Publication:* (with K. Lewis) Starting Statistics, 1969. *Recreations:* rowing, sailing, bird-watching. *Address:* 1 The Green, Mistley, Manningtree, Essex CO11 1EU; 1067/33 Střešovická, 16200 Prague 6, Czech Republic.

WARD, Prof. Ian Macmillan, FRS 1983; FInstP; Research Professor and Technical Director, Centre for Industrial Polymers, University of Leeds, since 1994 (Professor of Physics, 1970–94, and Cavendish Professor, 1987–94); *b* 9 April 1928; *s* of Harry Ward and Joan Moodie (*née* Burt); *m* 1960, Margaret (*née* Linley); two *s* one *d*. *Educ:* Royal Grammar Sch., Newcastle upon Tyne; Magdalen Coll., Oxford (MA, DPhil). FInstP 1965; FPRI 1974. Technical Officer, ICI Fibres, 1954–61; seconded to Division of Applied Mathematics, Brown Univ., USA, 1961–62; Head of Basic Physics Section, ICI Fibres, 1962–65, ICI Research Associate, 1964; Sen. Lectr in Physics of Materials, Univ. of Bristol, 1965–69; Chm., Dept of Polymer Physics, Univ. of Leeds, 1975–78, 1987–89; Dir, Interdisciplinary Res. Centre in Polymer Sci. and Technol., Univs of Leeds, Bradford and Durham, 1989–94. Secretary, Polymer Physics Gp, Inst. of Physics, 1964–71, Chm. 1971–75; Chairman, Macromolecular Physics Gp, European Physical Soc., 1976–81; Pres., British Soc. of Rheology, 1984–86. Hon. DSc Bradford, 1993. A. A. Griffith Medal, 1982; S. G. Smith Meml Medal, Textile Inst., 1984; Swinburne Medal, Plastics and Rubber Inst., 1988; Charles Vernon Boys Medal, Inst. of Physics, 1993. *Publications:* Mechanical Properties of Solid Polymers, 1971, 2nd edn 1983; (ed) Structure and Properties of Oriented Polymers, 1975; (ed jtly) Ultra High Modulus Polymers, 1979; (with D. Hadley) An Introduction to the Mechanical Properties of Solid Polymers, 1993; contribs to Polymer, Jl of Polymer Science, Jl of Materials Science, Proc. Royal Soc., etc. *Recreations:* music, walking. *Address:* Kirskill, 2 Creskeld Drive, Bramhope, Leeds LS16 9EL. *T:* Leeds (0113) 267 3637.

WARD, Ivor William, (Bill), OBE 1968; independent televison producer and director, since 1982; Deputy Managing Director, Associated Television (Network) Ltd, 1974–77; *b* 19 Jan. 1916; *s* of Stanley James Ward and Emily Ward; *m* 1st, 1940, Patricia Aston; two *s* one *d*; 2nd, 1970, Betty Nichols; one step *s*; 3rd, 1988, Sandra Calkins Hastie. *Educ:* Hoe Grammar Sch., Plymouth. Asst Engr, BBC Radio Plymouth, 1932; Technical Asst, BBC Experimental TV Service, Alexandra Palace, 1936; Maintenance Engr, BBC TV London, 1937. Instructor Radar, REME and Military Coll. of Science, 1939–45. Studio Manager, BBC TV, 1946; Producer, BBC TV, 1947–55; Head of Light Entertainment, ATV (Network) ITV, 1955–61; Production Controller, ATV, 1961–63; Executive Controller and Production Controller, ATV, 1963–67; Director of Programmes, ATV, 1968–76. Chm., ITV Network Sports Cttee, 1972–77; Head of Ops Gp, EBU: World Cup 1978, 1977–78; Moscow Olympics 1980, 1978–82; Exec. producer, Highway series, ITV, 1983. FRTS 1989; FRSA. *Recreations:* sport, golf, fishing, motor sport and motor cars, photography, music. *Address:* 50 Frith Street, W1V 5TE.

WARD, John; *see* Ward, C. J. W.

WARD, Most Rev. John Aloysius; *see* Cardiff, Archbishop of, (RC).

WARD, Prof. John Clive, FRS 1965; Professor, Macquarie University, Sydney, NSW, 1967–84, now Emeritus; *b* 1 Aug. 1924; *s* of Joseph William Ward and Winifred Palmer. *Educ:* Bishops Stortford Coll.; Merton Coll., Oxford (Hon. Fellow, 1995). Member, Inst. for Advanced Study, Princeton, 1951–52, 1955–56, 1960–61; Professor of Physics, Carnegie Inst. of Technology, Pittsburgh, 1959–60; The Johns Hopkins University, Baltimore, 1961–66. Hughes Medal, Royal Soc., 1983. *Publications:* various articles on particle theory and statistical mechanics. *Recreations:* travel, music. *Address:* 3477 Arbutus Drive South, Cobble Hill, British Columbia V0R 1L1, Canada.

WARD, John Devereux, CBE 1973; BSc; CEng, FICE, FIStructE; MP (C) Poole, since 1979; *b* 8 March 1925; *s* of late Thomas Edward and Evelyn Victoria Ward; *m* 1955, Jean Miller Aitken; one *s* one *d*. *Educ:* Romford County Technical Sch.; Univ. of St Andrews (BSc). Navigator, RAF, 1943–47; student, 1949–53. Employed, Consulting Engineers, 1953–58, Taylor Woodrow Ltd, 1958–79; Man. Dir, Taylor Woodrow Arcon, Arcon Building Exports, 1976–78. PPS to: Financial Sec. to Treasury, 1984–86; Sec. of State for Social Security, 1987–89; Prime Minister, 1994–. UK Rep. to Council of Europe and WEU, 1983–87, 1989–94. Chm., British Gp, IPU, 1993–94 (Mem., Exec. Cttee, 1982–94). Chm., Wessex Area Conservatives, 1966–69; Conservative Party: Mem., Nat. Union Exec., 1965–78 (Mem., Gen. Purposes Cttee, 1966–72, 1975–78); Mem., Central Bd of Finance, 1969–78; Vice-Chm., Cons. Trade and Industry Cttee, 1983–84. *Address:* House of Commons, SW1A 0AA. *T:* 0171–219 3000.

WARD, John Stanton, CBE 1985; RA 1965 (ARA 1956); RP 1952; *b* 10 Oct. 1917; *s* of Russell Stanton and Jessie Elizabeth Ward; *m* 1950, Alison Christine Mary Williams; four *s* twin *d*. *Educ:* St Owen's School, Hereford; Royal College of Art. Royal Engineers, 1939–46. Vogue Magazine, 1948–52. Former Vice-Pres., Royal Soc. of Portrait Painters. Mem. Exec., Nat. Art-Collections Fund, 1976–87. Trustee, Royal Acad. Has held exhibitions at Agnews Gallery and Maas Gallery. Freeman, City of Hereford, 1991. Hon. DLitt. *Recreation:* book illustration. *Address:* Bilting Court, Bilting, Ashford, Kent TN25 4HF. *T:* Wye (01233) 812478. *Clubs:* Athenæum, Buck's, Harry's Bar.

WARD, Rev. Prof. (John Stephen) Keith; Regius Professor of Divinity, University of Oxford, since 1991; Canon of Christ Church, Oxford, since 1991; *b* 22 Aug. 1938; *s* of John George Ward and Evelyn (*née* Simpson); *m* 1963, Marian Trotman; one *s* one *d*. *Educ:* Universities of Wales and Oxford. BA Wales, BLitt Oxon; MA Cantab. Ordained priest of Church of England, 1972. Lecturer in Logic, Univ. of Glasgow, 1964–69; Lectr in Philosophy, Univ. of St Andrews, 1969–71; Lectr in Philosophy of Religion, Univ. of London, 1971–75; Dean of Trinity Hall, Cambridge, 1975–82. F. D. Maurice Prof. of Moral and Social Theology, Univ. of London, 1982–85; Prof. of History and Phil. of Religion, King's Coll. London, 1985–91. Jt Editor, Religious Studies, 1990–. Jt Pres., World Congress of Faiths, 1992–. *Publications:* Ethics and Christianity, 1970; Kant's View of Ethics, 1972; The Divine Image, 1976; The Concept of God, 1977; The Promise, 1981; Rational Theology and the Creativity of God, 1982; Holding Fast to God, 1982; The Living God, 1984; Battle for the Soul, 1985; Images of Eternity, 1987; The Rule of Love, 1989; Divine Action, 1990; A Vision to Pursue, 1991; Religion and Revelation, 1994; Religion and Creation, 1996. *Recreations:* music, walking. *Address:* Christ Church, Oxford OX1 1DP. *T:* Oxford (01865) 276246.

WARD, Joseph Haggitt; *b* 7 July 1926; *s* of Joseph G. and Gladys Ward; *m* 1961, Anthea Clemo; one *s* one *d*. *Educ:* St Olave's Grammar School; Sidney Sussex College, Cambridge. Asst Principal, Min. of National Insurance, 1951; Private Sec. to Minister of Social Security, 1966–68; Asst Sec., 1968; Min. of Housing, later DoE, 1969–72; DHSS, 1972; Under-Sec. (pensions and nat. insce contributions), DHSS, 1976–86. *Recreations:* music, history of music. *Address:* 34 Uffington Road, SE27 0ND. *T:* 0181–670 1732.

WARD, Sir Joseph James Laffey, 4th Bt *cr* 1911; *b* 11 Nov. 1946; *s* of Sir Joseph George Davidson Ward, 3rd Bt, and of Joan Mary Haden, *d* of Major Thomas J. Laffey, NZSC; *S* father, 1970; *m* 1968, Robyn Allison, *d* of William Maitland Martin, Rotorua, NZ; one *s* one *d*. *Heir:* *s* Joseph James Martin Ward, *b* 20 Feb. 1971.

WARD, Keith; *see* Ward, J. S. K.

WARD, Malcolm Beverley; His Honour Judge Malcolm Ward; a Circuit Judge, Midland and Oxford Circuit, since 1979; *b* 3 May 1931; *s* of Edgar and Dora Mary Ward; *m* 1958, Muriel Winifred, *d* of Dr E. D. M. Wallace, Perth; two *s* two *d*. *Educ:* Wolverhampton Grammar Sch.; St John's Coll., Cambridge (Open Mathematical Schol.; MA, LLM). Called to the Bar, Inner Temple, 1956; practised Oxford (later Midland and Oxford) Circuit; a Recorder of the Crown Court, 1974–79. Governor, Wolverhampton

Grammar Sch., 1972– (Chm., 1981–). *Recreations:* golf, music, (in theory) horticulture. *Address:* 1 Fountain Court, Birmingham B4 6DR.

WARD, Malcolm Stanley; Editor, Evening News, Worcester, since 1992; *b* 24 Sept. 1951; *s* of Hugh Ward and Rebecca Ward (*née* Rogerson). *Educ:* Gilberd School, Colchester. Dep. Editor, Gulf News, Dubai, 1978–79; Editor, Woodham and Wickford Chronicle, Essex, 1979–81; Dep. Editor, Gulf Times, Qatar, 1981–84; Dep. Editor, 1984–86, Dir and Editor, 1986–91, Daily News, Birmingham; Editor, Metro News, Birmingham, 1991–92. *Recreations:* writing, travel, soccer, driving, tennis. *Address:* 3 Rectory Park Avenue, Sutton Coldfield, West Midlands B75 7BL. *T:* 0121–329 2589.

WARD, Michael Jackson, CBE 1980; British Council Director, Germany, 1990–91, retired; *b* 16 Sept. 1931; *s* of late Harry Ward, CBE, and Dorothy Julia Ward (*née* Clutterbuck); *m* 1955, Eileen Patricia Foster; one *s* one *d. Educ:* Drayton Manor Grammar Sch.; University Coll. London (BA); Univ. of Freiburg; Corpus Christi Coll., Oxford. HM Forces, 1953–55; 2nd Lieut Royal Signals. Admin. Officer, HMOCS, serving as Dist Comr and Asst Sec. to Govt, Gilbert and Ellice Is; British Council, 1961–91: Schs Recruitment Dept, 1961–64; Regional Rep., Sarawak, 1964–68; Dep. Rep., Pakistan, 1968–70; Dir, Appointments Services Dept, 1970–72; Dir, Personnel Dept, 1972–75; Controller, Personnel and Appts Div., 1975–77; Representative, Italy, 1977–81; Controller, Home Div., 1981–85; Asst Dir-Gen., 1985–90. Hon. Mem., British Council, 1991. *Recreations:* music, golf. *Address:* 1 Knapp Rise, Haslingfield, Cambridge CB3 7LO. *Club:* Gog Magog Golf.

WARD, Michael John; Assistant General Secretary, Public Relations, Association of Chief Officers of Probation, 1989–95; *b* 7 April 1931; *s* of late Stanley William Ward and Margaret Annie Ward; *m* 1953, Lilian Lomas; two *d. Educ:* Mawney Road Jun. Mixed Sch., Romford; Royal Liberty Sch., Romford; Bungay Grammar Sch.; Univ. of Manchester. BA (Admin). FIPR. Education Officer, RAF, 1953–57; Registrar, Chartered Inst. of Secretaries, 1958–60; S. J. Noel-Brown & Co. Ltd: O&M consultant to local authorities, 1960–61; Local Govt Officer to Labour Party, 1961–65; Public Relns consultant to local authorities, 1965–70; Press Officer, ILEA, 1970–74 and 1979–80; Public Relns Officer, London Borough of Lewisham, 1980–84; Dir of Information, ILEA, 1984–86; Public Affairs Officer, Gas Consumers Council, 1986–88; Exec. Officer to Rt Hon. Paddy Ashdown, MP, 1988–89. Contested: (Lab) Peterborough, 1966, 1970, Feb. 1974; (SDP/Alliance) Tonbridge and Malling, 1987. MP (Lab) Peterborough, Oct. 1974–1979; PPS to Sec. of State for Educn and Science, 1975–76, to Minister for Overseas Develt, 1976, to Minister of State, FCO, 1976–79. Sponsored Unfair Contract Terms Act, 1977. Councillor, Borough of Romford, 1958–65; London Borough of Havering: Councillor, 1964–78; Alderman, 1971–78; Leader of Council, 1971–74. Labour Chief Whip, London Boroughs Assoc., 1968–71; Member: Essex River Authority, 1964–71; Greenwich DHA, 1982–85; Greenwich and Bexley FPC, 1982–85. Mem. Council, Inst. of Public Relns, 1992–95 (Chm., Professional Practices Cttee, 1993–95). FRSA 1992. *Recreations:* gardens, music, reading, travel. *Address:* 5 The Lane, Blackheath Park, SE3 9SL. *Club:* National Liberal.

WARD, Michael Phelps, CBE 1983; FRCS; FRGS; Consultant Surgeon: City and East London Area Health Authority (Teaching), 1964–93; St Andrew's Hospital, Bow, 1964–93; Newham Hospital, 1983–93; Lecturer in Clinical Surgery, London Hospital Medical College, 1975–93; *b* 26 March 1925; *s* of late Wilfrid Arthur Ward, CMG, MC and Norah Anne Phelps; *m* 1957, Felicity Jane Ewbank; one *s. Educ:* Marlborough Coll., Wilts; Peterhouse, Cambridge (Ironmongers' Co. Exhibn); London Hosp. Med. Coll. BA Hons Cantab 1945, MA 1961; MB BChir 1949, MD 1968. FRCS 1955. Ho. Surg., Surgical Registrar, Sen. Surgical Registrar, London Hosp.; Asst Resident, Royal Victoria Hosp., Montreal, Canada; Consultant Surg., Poplar Hosp., E14, 1964–75; Hunterian Prof., RCS, 1954. Served RAMC, Captain, 1950–52. Fellow, Assoc. of Surgs of Gt Britain; FRSM. Master, Soc. of Apothecaries, 1993–94 (Mem., Court of Assts, 1986). Mount Everest Reconnaissance Expedn, 1951; Mount Everest Expedn, 1953 (1st Ascent); Scientific Expedn to Everest Region, 1960–61 (Leader, 1st Winter Ascents of Amadablam and other peaks); Scientific Expedns to Bhutan Himal, 1964 and 1965; scientific and mountaineering expedn to West Kun Lun, China, 1980–81; Royal Soc./Chinese Acad. of Sciences Tibet Geotraverse, 1985. FRGS 1961. Dickson Asia Lectr, RGS, 1966, 1985; Monkton Copeman Lectr, Soc. of Apothecaries, 1994. Cuthbert Peek Award, RGS, 1973, Founder's (Royal) Medal, RGS, 1982; Cullum Medal, Amer. Geog. Soc., 1954. Chm., Mount Everest Foundn, 1978–80. *Publications:* Mountaineers' Companion, 1966; In this Short Span, 1972; Mountain Medicine, 1975; (jtly) High Altitude Medicine and Physiology, 1989, 2nd edn 1994; many scientific and medical papers on the effects of great altitude, exposure to cold, and on exercise; also on exploratory journeys to Nepal, Bhutan, Chinese Central Asia and Tibet. *Recreations:* mountaineering, ski-ing. *Clubs:* Alpine (Vice-Pres., 1968–69; Hon. Mem., 1993); Cambridge Alpine (Pres., 1986–95).

WARD, Air Vice-Marshal Peter Alexander; *b* 26 Jan. 1930; *s* of Arthur Charles Ward and Laura Mary (*née* Squires); *m* 1963, Patricia Louise (*née* Robertson); two *s. Educ:* Woking Grammar School. Joined RAF, 1947; Flying and Staff appointments; OC 511 Sqdn, 1968–70; jssc 1970; ndc 1971; Station Comdr, RAF Brize Norton, 1974–75; Senior Air Staff Officer, HQ 38 Group, 1976–79; rcds 1979; Dir Gen., RAF Training, 1980–82; Dep. COS (Ops), HQ Allied Air Forces Central Europe, 1982–84. Gen. Manager, Bromley HA, 1985–87. Director: Corps of Commissionaires Management; OEF Management Services; Vice-Chm., Regular Forces Employment Assoc.; Mem., Royal Patriotic Fund Corp. Chm., St Barbe Foundn; Trustee, Lymington Mus. Trust. Gov., Bromley Coll. *Address:* Swiss Cottage, Lower Buckland Road, Lymington, Hampshire SO41 9DU.

WARD, Peter Simms; Provincial Stipendiary Magistrate for Merseyside, since 1994; *b* 20 June 1943; *s* of Norman and Marie Ward; *m* 1974, Monica Stalker; three *s. Educ:* Bolton Sch.; Bristol Univ. (LLB). Articled to J. J. Rothwell, Solicitor, Salford; admitted Solicitor, 1969; Partner, Rothwell & Evans, Solicitors, Salford, Gtr Manchester, 1969–94. *Recreations:* reading, walking, swimming. *Address:* Liverpool Magistrates' Court, 107 Dale Street, Liverpool L2 2JQ. *T:* 0151–243 5554.

WARD, Maj.-Gen. Sir Philip (John Newling), KCVO 1976; CBE 1972; Lord-Lieutenant for West Sussex, since 1994 (Vice Lord-Lieutenant, 1990–94); *b* 10 July 1924; *s* of George William Newling Ward and Mary Florence Ward; *m* 1948, Pamela Ann Glennie; two *s* two *d.* Commnd Welsh Guards, 1943; Adjt, RMA Sandhurst, 1960–62; Bde Major, Household Bde, 1962–65; Comdg 1st Bn Welsh Guards, 1965–67; Comdr Land Forces, Gulf, 1969–71; GOC London Dist and Maj.-Gen. comdg Household Div., 1973–76; Comdt, RMA, 1976–79. Communar of Chichester Cathedral, 1980–83. Dir, Public Affairs, Internat. Distillers and Vintners (UK), 1980–89; Chm., Peter Hamilton Security Consultants, 1986–90; Director: W & A Gilbey (formerly Gilbey Vintners), 1983–89; Morgan Furze, 1983–89; Justerini & Brooks, 1987–89; Southern Reg., Lloyds Bank, 1983–90. Pres., S of England Agricl Soc., 1994–95; Chairman: Queen Alexandra Hosp. Home; Royal Soldiers Daughters School, 1980–83; Governor and Comdt, Church Lads and Church Girls Bde., 1980–86. Patron, Chichester Cathedral Trust, 1995. Freeman, City of London, 1976. DL West Sussex, 1981, High Sheriff, 1985–86. *Recreation:* gardening. *Address:* 15 Tarrant Wharf, Arundel, W Sussex BN18 9NY. *Clubs:* Cavalry and Guards (Chm., 1987–90), Buck's.

WARD, Reginald; *see* Ward, A. J. R.

WARD, Reginald George; Director, Statistics and Economic Office, Inland Revenue, since 1994; *b* 6 July 1942; *s* of Thomas George and Ada May Ward; *m* 1964, Chandan Mistry; two *s* one *d. Educ:* Leicester, Aberdeen and Oxford Universities; London Business Sch. Lectr in Economics, St Andrews Univ., 1965; Analyst, National Cash Register, 1969; Economist, ICL, 1970; DTI, 1971; Chief Statistician: HM Treasury, 1978; Cabinet Office, 1982; Dir, Business Statistics Office, DTI, 1986; Asst Dir, CSO, 1989–94. *Recreation:* sailing. *Address:* Room F3, Somerset House, WC2R 1LB.

WARD, Maj.-Gen. Robert William, CB 1989; MBE 1972; plantsman, landscape and garden design consultant, since 1992; *b* 17 Oct. 1935; *s* of late Lt-Col William Denby Ward and Monica Thérèse Ward (*née* Collett-White); *m* 1966, Lavinia Dorothy Cramsie; two *s* one *d. Educ:* Rugby School; RMA Sandhurst. Commissioned Queen's Bays (later 1st Queen's Dragoon Guards), 1955; served Jordan, Libya, BAOR, Borneo and Persian Gulf; MA to C-in-C BAOR, 1973–75; CO 1st Queen's Dragoon Guards, 1975–77; Col GS Staff Coll., 1977–79; Comdr 22 Armd Brigade, 1979–82; RCDS Canada, 1982–83; Asst Chief of Staff, Northern Army Group, 1983–86; GOC Western Dist, 1986–89, retd. Col, 1st Queen's Dragoon Guards, 1991–. Sec., Game Conservancy, Shropshire, 1993–. Pres., SSAFA, Shropshire, 1994–. *Recreations:* gardening, outdoor sports, country pursuits, travel, food, wine. *Clubs:* Cavalry and Guards, MCC, I Zingari.

WARD, Robin William; Director-General, West Yorkshire Passenger Transport Executive, 1976–82; *b* 14 Jan. 1931; *s* of William Frederick and Elsie Gertrude Ward; *m* 1974, Jean Catherine Laird; three *s. Educ:* Colston's Sch., Bristol; University Coll. London. BScEcon, 1st Cl. Hons. Pilot Officer/Flying Officer, RAF Educn Br., 1954–55. Various posts, London Transport Exec., 1955–67; seconded to Brit. Transport Staff Coll. as mem. staff and latterly Asst Principal (incl. course at Harvard Business Sch.), 1967–70; Industrial Relations Officer, London Transport Exec., 1970–74; Dir of Personnel, W Yorks Passenger Transport Exec., 1974–76. *Recreations:* Scottish country dancing; trying to learn the piano. *Address:* 29 Stanley Street, Palmwoods, Qld 4555, Australia.

WARD, His Honour Roy Livingstone, QC 1972; a Circuit Judge, 1979–94; *b* 31 Aug. 1925; *m* 1972, Barbara Anne (*née* Brockbank) (marr. diss); one *s* one *d. Educ:* Taunton Sch.; Pembroke Coll., Cambridge. BA(Hons). Served RAF, 1943–47 (commnd 1945). Called to Bar, Middle Temple, 1950. A Recorder of the Crown Court, 1972–79. *Address:* Tethers End, Shelsley Drive, Colwall, Worcs WR13 6PS. *Club:* United Oxford & Cambridge University.

WARD, Rt. Rev. Simon B.; *see* Barrington-Ward.

WARD, Thomas William, ARCA 1949; RE 1955; RWS 1957; sometime Course Director, Illustration, Harrow College of Technology and Art; painter in water colour and oil colour, draughtsman, engraver, illustrator; *b* 8 Nov. 1918; *s* of John B. Ward, Master Stationer, and Lilly B. Ward (*née* Hunt), Sheffield; *m* Joan Palmer, ARCA, *d* of F. N. Palmer, Blackheath; one *s* one *d. Educ:* Nether Edge Grammar Sch., Sheffield; Sheffield Coll. of Art (part-time); Royal Coll. of Art, 1946–49, Silver Medal, 1949, Postgrad. Scholarship, 1949–50. Cadet, Merchant Service, 1935–36; stationer, 1936–39; Military service, 1939–46: commissioned N Staffs Regt, 1942; GSO3 1944–46. *One Man Exhibitions include:* Walker Gall., 1957, 1960; Wakefield City Art Gall., 1962; Shipley Art Gall., 1962; Middlesbrough Art Gall., 1963; St John's Coll., York, 1965; Bohun Gall., Henley, 1974; Digby Gall., Colchester, 1981; Coach House Gall., CI, 1987; Wherry Quay Gall., Ipswich, 1992; Grove House, Ipswich, 1993. *Group Exhibitions include:* Leicester Gall.; Kensington Gall.; Zwemmer Gall.; Bohun Gall; Bankside Gall., 1987; Chappel Gall., Essex, 1995. *Open Exhibitions include:* RA, RSA, NEAC, London Group, RSMA, and in Japan, USA, S Africa, NZ. *Important purchases include:* S London Art Gall.; V&A; Nat. Gall. of NZ; Leicester, Oxford and Durham Univs; Arts Council; Contemp. Art Soc.; Bowes Mus.; Graves Art Gall.; Rochdale Art Gall.; Lord Clark. *Illustrations include:* Colman Prentis Varley; Shell Mex; Editions Lausanne; books for Country Life, Conway Maritime Press, MAP. Designer of theatre properties, Tom Arnold Ice Show. *Recreation:* sailing. *Address:* Hollydene, Ipswich Road, Holbrook, Ipswich IP9 2QT.

WARD, Tony; Commissioner, since 1990, Deputy Chairman, since 1993, Commission for Racial Equality; Director of Human Resources, Kingfisher plc, since 1992; *b* 20 Feb. 1950; *s* of Kenneth H. Ward and Elsie M. Ward; *m* 1972, Margaret Harrison; one *d. Educ:* Univ. of Leeds (BSc 1st Class Hons 1972). Personnel Manager, Stone Platt Industries, 1972–81; Personnel Director (Divisional), GrandMet, 1981–91. Chm., Equal Opportunities Panel, CBI. *Recreations:* golf, CRE work. *Address:* Kingfisher PLC, 119 Marylebone Road, NW1 5PX. *T:* 0171–724 7749; 57 Gregories Road, Beaconsfield, Bucks HP9 1HL. *Club:* Lambourne Golf.

WARD, William Alan H.; *see* Heaton-Ward.

WARD, William Alec; HM Diplomatic Service, retired; *b* 27 Nov. 1928; *s* of William Leslie Ward and Gladys Ward; *m* 1955, Sheila Joan Hawking; two *s* two *d. Educ:* King's Coll. Sch., Wimbledon; Christ Church, Oxford. HM Forces, 1947–49. Colonial Office, 1952; Private Sec. to Permanent Under-Sec., 1955–57; Singapore, 1960–64; seconded to CRO, 1963; Karachi, 1964–66; Islamabad, 1966–68; joined HM Diplomatic Service, 1968; FCO, 1968–71; Salisbury, 1971–72; Dep. High Comr, Colombo, 1973–76; High Comr, Mauritius, 1977–81. *Recreations:* music, walking. *Address:* The Grange, Ellesmere, Shropshire SY12 9DE.

WARD, William Kenneth, CMG 1977; Under-Secretary, Department of Trade, retired; *b* 20 Jan. 1918; *e s* of late Harold and Emily Ward; *m* 1949, Victoria Emily, *d* of late Ralph Perkins, Carcavelos, Portugal; three *s* one *d. Educ:* Queen Elizabeth's Grammar Sch., Ashbourne; Trinity Coll., Cambridge. 1st class Hons Modern and Medieval Langs Tripos. Entered Ministry of Supply, 1939; Board of Trade, 1955; HM Principal Trade Commissioner, Vancouver, BC, 1959–63; Under-Sec., BoT, 1966–69, Min. of Technology, later DTI and Dept of Trade, 1969–78; Sec., BOTB, 1973. *Recreation:* gardening. *Address:* 31 Plough Lane, Purley, Surrey CR8 3QG. *T:* 0181–660 2462.

WARD-BOOTH, Maj.-Gen. John Antony, OBE 1971; DL; Consultant, Francis Graves and Partners, since 1989; *b* 18 July 1927; *s* of Rev. J. Ward-Booth and Mrs E. M. Ward-Booth; *m* 1952, Margaret Joan Hooper; one *s* two *d* (and one *s* decd). *Educ:* Worksop College, Notts. Joined Army, 1945; commnd into Worcestershire Regt in India, 1946; served India and Middle East, 1946–48; regular commn Bedfordshire and Hertfordshire Regt, 1948; served BAOR, Far East, Nigeria and Congo, 1950–63, trans. to Parachute Regt, 1963; commanded 3rd Bn, Parachute Regt, 1967–69; Hong Kong, 1969–70; Comdr, 16 Parachute Bde, 1970–73; Nat. Defence Coll., Canada, 1973–74; DAG, HQ BAOR, 1974–75; Dir, Army Air Corps, 1976–79; GOC Western District, 1979–82. Dep. Col, Royal Anglian Regt, 1982–87. Sec., Eastern Wessex TAVRA, 1982–89. Governor:

Enham Village Centre, 1982–; Clayesmore Sch., Dorset, 1985– (Chm., 1989–94). DL Hants, 1988. *Recreations:* sailing, golf, cricket. *Address:* 22 Winchester Gardens, Andover, Hants SP10 2EH. *T:* Andover (01264) 354317. *Clubs:* Army and Navy, MCC.

WARD-JACKSON, Mrs (Audrey) Muriel; *b* 30 Oct. 1914; *d* of late William James Jenkins and Alice Jenkins (*née* Glyde); *m* 1946, George Ralph Norman Ward-Jackson (*d* 1982); no *c. Educ:* Queenswood, Hatfield, Herts; Lady Margaret Hall, Oxford (MA). Home Civil Service (Ministries of Works, Town and Country Planning, Housing and Local Government, and Central Econ. Planning Staff, HM Treasury): Asst Principal, 1937; Principal, 1942; Asst Sec., 1946–55. A Director (concerned mainly with Finance), John Lewis Partnership, 1955–74; John Lewis Partnership Ltd: Dir, 1957–74; Dir, John Lewis Properties Ltd, 1969–74; Chm., John Lewis Partnership Pensions Trust, 1964–74. On Civil Service Arbitration Tribunal, 1959–64; Chm., Consumers Cttees (Agric. Marketing), 1971–75; Member: Nat. Savings Review Cttee, 1971–73; Royal Commn on Standards of Conduct in Public Life, 1974–76. A Governor, British Film Inst., 1962–65; Mem. Council, Bedford Coll., London Univ., 1967–72. *Recreation:* swimming. *Address:* The Grange, Grange Close, Goring-on-Thames, Oxon RG8 9DY. *T:* Goring-on-Thames (01491) 872843. *Club:* Lansdowne.

WARD-JONES, Norman Arthur, CBE 1990; VRD 1959; Chairman, Gaming Board for Great Britain, 1986–92 (Member, 1984–92); *b* 19 Sept. 1922; *s* of Alfred Thomas Ward-Jones and Claire Mayall Lees; *m* 1962, Pamela Catherine Ainslie (*née* Glessing). *Educ:* Oundle Sch.; Brasenose Coll., Oxford. Solicitor 1950. War service, Royal Marines (Captain), 1941–46; RM Reserve, 1948–64, Lt-Col and CO RMR (City of London), 1961–64; Hon. Col 1968–74. Solicitor, Lawrance Messer & Co., Sen. Partner, 1981–85, retired 1989. Hon. Solicitor, Magistrates' Assoc., 1960–85. Chm., East Anglian Real Property Co. Ltd, 1970–80, non-exec. Dir, 1980–89. Pres., Brasenose Soc., 1991–92. JP N Westminster PSD, 1966–92. *Recreation:* wine drinking. *Address:* The Cottage, Barnhorne Manor, 75 Barnhorn Road, Little Common, Bexhill-on-Sea, East Sussex TN39 4QB; 19 Irving Street, WC2. *Club:* East India.

WARD-THOMAS, Evelyn, (Mrs Michael Ward-Thomas); *see* Anthony, Evelyn.

WARD THOMAS, Gwyn Edward, CBE 1973; DFC; Chairman and Chief Executive, Yorkshire–Tyne Tees Television Holdings plc; Director: Tyne Tees Television; Boardwalk Entertainment (USA); *b* 1 Aug. 1923; *o s* of William J. and Constance Thomas; *m* 1st, 1945, Patricia Cornelius (marr. diss. 1989); one *d*; 2nd, 1991, Janice Thomas; one *s. Educ:* Bloxham Sch.; The Lycée, Rouen. Served RAF, 1 Group Bomber Command and 229 Group Transport Command, 1941–46. Granada Television, 1955–61; Man. Dir, Grampian Television, 1961–67; Man. Dir, 1967–73, Dep. Chm., 1973–81, Yorkshire Television; Man. Dir, 1970–84, Chm., 1976–84, Trident Television. Chairman: Castlewood Investments Ltd, 1969–83; Don Robinson Holdings Ltd, 1969–83; Watts & Corry Ltd, 1969–83; Trident Casinos, 1982–84. British Bureau of Television Advertising: Dir, 1966; Chm., 1968–70; Mem. Council, Independent Television Companies Assoc., 1961–76 (Chairman: Labour Relations Cttee, 1967; Network Programme Cttee, 1971). Croix de Guerre, 1945. *Recreations:* ski-ing, boats, photography. *Address:* La Gamberge, Les Hauts de St Paul 06570, France; Pipers Lodge, Wentworth, Surrey GU25 4AW.

WARDALE, Sir Geoffrey (Charles), KCB 1979 (CB 1974); Second Permanent Secretary, Department of the Environment, 1978–80; *b* 29 Nov. 1919; *m* 1944, Rosemary Octavia Dyer; one *s* one *d. Educ:* Altrincham Grammar Sch.; Queens' Coll., Cambridge (Schol.). Army Service, 1940–41. Joined Ministry of War Transport as Temp. Asst Princ., 1942; Private Sec. to Perm. Sec., 1946; Princ., 1948; Asst Sec., 1957; Under-Sec., Min. of Transport, later DoE, 1966; Dep. Sec., 1972. Led inquiry: into the Open Structure in the Civil Service (The Wardale Report), 1981; into cases of fraud and corruption in PSA, 1982–83. Mem. Council, Univ. of Sussex, 1986–92; Chm., Brighton Coll. Council, 1985–90. President: Friends of Lewes Soc., 1993–; Lewes Area CABx, 1989–. *Recreations:* transport history, painting, listening to music. *Address:* 89 Paddock Lane, Lewes, East Sussex BN7 1TW. *T:* Lewes (01273) 473468. *Club:* United Oxford & Cambridge University.

WARDE, His Honour John Robins; a Circuit Judge, 1977–90; *b* 25 April 1920; (Guardian) A. W. Ormond, CBE, FRCS; *m* 1941, Edna Holliday Gipson; three *s. Educ:* Radley Coll., Abingdon, Berks; Corpus Christi Coll., Oxford (MA). Served War, 1940–45: Lieut, RA; awarded C-in-C's cert. for outstanding good service in the campaign in NW Europe. Member: Devon CC, 1946–49; Devon Agricl Exec. Cttee, 1948–53; West Regional Advisory Council of BBC, 1950–53. Admitted a solicitor, 1950; Partner in Waugh and Co., Solicitors, Haywards Heath and East Grinstead, Sussex, 1960–70. A Recorder of the Crown Court, 1972–77. Registrar of Clerkenwell County Court, 1970–77. Liveryman, Gardeners' Co., 1983–. *Recreations:* mountaineering, watching cricket, listening to music. *Address:* 20 Clifton Terrace, Brighton, East Sussex BN1 3HA. *T:* Brighton (01273) 326642. *Clubs:* Law Society, MCC; Forty.

WARDELL, Gareth Lodwig; MP (Lab) Gower, since Sept. 1982; *b* 29 Nov. 1944; *s* of John Thomas Wardell and Jenny Ceridwen Wardell; *m* 1967, Jennifer Dawn Evans; one *s. Educ:* London Sch. of Econs and Pol. Science (BScEcon, MSc). Geography Master, Chislehurst and Sidcup Technical High Sch., 1967–68; Head of Econs Dept, St Clement Danes Grammar Sch., 1968–70; Sixth Form Econs Master, Haberdashers' Aske's Sch., Elstree, 1970–72; Educn Lectr, Bedford Coll. of Physical Educn, 1972–73; Sen. Lectr in Geography, Trinity Coll., Carmarthen, 1973–82. *Publications:* articles on regional issues in British Econ. Survey. *Recreations:* cycling, cross-country running. *Address:* House of Commons, SW1A 0AA.

WARDINGTON, 2nd Baron, *cr* 1936, of Alnmouth in the County of Northumberland; **Christopher Henry Beaumont Pease;** *b* 22 Jan. 1924; *s* of 1st Baron and Hon. Dorothy Charlotte (*d* 1983), *er d* of 1st Baron Forster; *S* father, 1950; *m* 1964, Margaret Audrey Dunfee, *d* of John and Eva White; one *s* two *d* (adopted). *Educ:* Eton. Served War of 1939–45, in Scots Guards, 1942–47, Captain. Partner in Stockbroking firm of Hoare Govett Ltd, 1947–86. Alderman of Broad Street Ward, City of London, 1960–63. Mem., Council of Foreign Bondholders, 1967–. Comr, Public Works Loan Bd, 1969–73. Trustee, Royal Jubilee Trusts; Chm., Athlone Trust, 1983–. Chm., Friends of the British Library, 1988–94. *Recreations:* cricket, golf, book collecting. *Heir: b* Hon. William Simon Pease [*b* 15 Oct. 1925; *m* 1962, Hon. Elizabeth Jane Ormsby-Gore, *d* of 4th Baron Harlech, KG, PC, GCMG]. *Address:* Wardington Manor, Banbury, Oxon OX17 1SW. *T:* Banbury (01295) 750202; 29 Moore Street, SW3. *T:* 0171–584 5245. *Clubs:* Royal Automobile, Garrick, Roxburghe; All England Lawn Tennis.

WARDLAW, Sir Henry (John), 21st Bt *cr* 1631, of Pitreavie; *b* 30 Nov. 1930; *s* of Sir Henry Wardlaw, 20th Bt, and Ellen (decd), *d* of John Francis Brady; *S* father, 1983; *m* 1962, Julie-Ann, *d* of late Edward Patrick Kirwan; five *s* two *d. Educ:* Melbourne Univ. (MB, BS). *Heir: s* (Henry) Justin Wardlaw, *b* 10 Aug. 1963. *Address:* Mandalay, 75–77 Two Bays Road, Mount Eliza, Vic 3930, Australia.

WARDLE, Charles Frederick; MP (C) Bexhill and Battle, since 1983; *b* 23 Aug. 1939; *s* of late Frederick Maclean Wardle; *m* 1964, Lesley Ann, *d* of Sidney Wells; one *d. Educ:* Tonbridge Sch.; Lincoln Coll., Oxford; Harvard Business Sch. MA Oxon 1968; MBA Harvard. Asst to Pres., American Express Co., NY, 1966–69; Merchant Banking, London, 1969–72; Chairman: Benjamin Priest Gp plc, 1977–84 (Dir, 1972–74, Man. Dir, 1974–77); Warne, Wright and Rowland, 1978–84; Dir, Asset Special Situations Trust plc, 1982–84. CBI: Mem. Council, 1980–84; Mem., W Midlands Regional Council, 1980–84. PPS: to Minister of State (Health), 1984; to Sec. of State for Social Services, 1984–87; to Sec. of State for Scotland, 1990–92; Parly Under-Sec. of State, Home Office, 1992–94, DTI, 1994–95. Member Select Committee: on Trade and Industry, 1983–84; on Treasury and Civil Service, 1990–91. Chm., Cons. One Nation Forum, 1989–90. Member: Commercial and Econ. Cttee, EEF, 1981–83; Midlands Cttee, InstD, 1981–83. FRGS 1977. *Recreations:* books, sport, travel. *Address:* House of Commons, SW1A 0AA. *T:* 0171–219 3000.

WARDLE, (John) Irving; Drama Critic, The Independent on Sunday, since 1990; *b* 20 July 1929; *s* of John Wardle and Nellie Partington; *m* 1958, Joan Notkin (marr. diss.); *m* 1963, Fay Crowder (marr. diss.); two *s*; *m* 1975, Elizabeth Grist; one *s* one *d. Educ:* Bolton Sch.; Wadham Coll., Oxford (BA); Royal Coll. of Music (ARCM). Joined Times Educational Supplement as sub-editor, 1956; Dep. Theatre Critic, The Observer, 1960; Drama Critic, The Times, 1963–89. Editor, Gambit, 1973–75. Play: The Houseboy, prod Open Space Theatre, 1974, ITV, 1982. *Publications:* The Theatres of George Devine (biog.), 1978; Theatre Criticism, 1992. *Recreation:* piano playing. *Address:* 51 Richmond Road, New Barnet, Herts EN5 1SF. *T:* 0181–440 3671.

WARDLE, Sir Thomas (Edward Jewell), Kt 1970; Lord Mayor of Perth, Western Australia, 1967–72; *b* 18 Aug. 1912; *s* of Walter Wardle and Lily Wardle (*née* Jewell); *m* 1940, Hulda May Olson; one *s* one *d. Educ:* Perth Boys' Sch., Western Australia. Member: King's Park Bd, 1970–81; Bd, Churchland Teachers Coll., 1973–78; Chairman: Trustees, WA Museum, 1973–82; Aboriginal Loans Commn, 1974–80; Pres., Nat. Trust of WA, 1971–82. Hon. LLD Univ. of WA, 1973. Commendatore, Order of Merit (Italy), 1970. *Recreations:* boating, fishing. *Address:* 3 Kent Street, Bicton, WA 6157, Australia. *Club:* Returned Services League (Western Australia).

WARE, Anna, (Mrs T. D. O. Ware); *see* Pavord, A.

WARE, Cyril George, CB 1981; Under-Secretary, Inland Revenue, 1974–82; *b* 25 May 1922; *s* of Frederick George Ware and Elizabeth Mary Ware; *m* 1946, Gwennie (*née* Wooding); two *s* one *d. Educ:* Leyton County High Sch. Entered Inland Revenue as Tax Officer, 1939; Inspector of Taxes, 1949; Sen. Principal Inspector, 1969. *Recreations:* music, woodwork, gardening, swimming. *Address:* 86 Tycehurst Hill, Loughton, Essex IG10 1DA. *T:* 0181–508 3588.

WARE, Martin, FRCP; Editor, British Medical Journal, 1966–75; *b* 1 Aug. 1915; *o s* of late Canon Martin Stewart Ware and late Margaret Isabel (*née* Baker, later Baker Wilbraham); *m* 1938, Winifred Elsie Boyce; two *s* three *d. Educ:* Eton; St Bartholomew's Hospital. MB, BS (London) 1939; MRCP 1945; FRCP 1967; MSc (Wales) 1978; BA (Open) 1989. House-surgeon, St Bartholomew's Hosp., 1939; served with RAMC, attached to Royal W African Frontier Force, 1940–45; HQ staff, Medical Research Council, 1946–50; editorial staff, British Medical Jl, 1950–75; research in micropalaeontology, UCW, Aberystwyth, 1975–84. Vice-President: BMA; Internat. Union of Med. Press, 1966–75. *Recreations:* bird watching, reading, Alpines. *Address:* 4 Ellis Close, Cottenham, Cambs CB4 4UN. *T:* Cottenham (01954) 251428.

WARE, Michael John, CB 1985; QC 1988; barrister-at-law; Solicitor and Legal Adviser, Department of the Environment, 1982–92; *b* 7 May 1932; *s* of Kenneth George Ware and Phyllis Matilda (*née* Joynes); *m* 1966, Susan Ann Maitland three *d. Educ:* Cheltenham Grammar Sch.; Trinity Hall, Cambridge (BA(Law), LLB). Called to Bar, Middle Temple. Nat. Service, 2/Lieut RASC, 1954–56. Board of Trade (later Dept of Trade and Industry): Legal Asst, 1957–64; Sen. Legal Asst, 1964–72; Asst Solicitor, 1972–73; Dir, Legal Dept, Office of Fair Trading, 1973–77; Under Secretary: Dept of Trade, 1977–81; DoE, 1982. Chm., Meat Hygiene Appeals Tribunals for England and Wales and for Scotland, 1993–. *Address:* 12 Hill Road, Haslemere, Surrey GU27 2JN.

WAREING, Prof. Philip Frank, OBE 1986; PhD, DSc London; FRS 1969; Professor of Botany, University College of Wales, Aberystwyth, 1958–81, now Emeritus; *b* 27 April 1914; *e s* of late Frank Wareing; *m* 1939, Helen Clark; one *s* one *d* (and one *d* decd). *Educ:* Watford Grammar School; Birkbeck Coll., Univ. of London. Exec. Officer, Inland Revenue, 1931–41. Captain, REME, 1942–46. Lectr, Bedford Coll., Univ. of London, 1947–50; Lectr, then Sen. Lectr, Univ. of Manchester, 1950–58. Man. Dir, Hortotec Ltd, 1985–91. Member: Nature Conservancy, 1965–68; Water Resources Board, 1968–71; Chm. Res. Adv. Cttee, Forestry Commn, 1972–86. President: Sect. K, British Assoc., 1970; Internat. Plant Growth Substances Assoc., 1982–85; Mem. Council, Royal Soc., 1972. Mem., Leopoldina Acad. of Science, 1971. *Publications:* (with I. D. J. Phillips) Control of Growth and Differentiation in Plants, 1970, 3rd edn as Growth and Differentiation in Plants, 1981; (ed with C. F. Graham) Development Control of Animals and Plants, 1976, 2nd edn 1984; various papers on plant physiology in scientific journals. *Recreation:* gardening. *Address:* Brynrhedyn, Cae Melyn, Aberystwyth, Dyfed SY23 2HA. *T:* Aberystwyth (01970) 623910.

WAREING, Robert Nelson; MP (Lab) Liverpool, West Derby, since 1983; *b* 20 Aug. 1930; *s* of late Robert Wareing and late Florence Wareing (*née* Mallon); *m* 1962, Betty Coward (decd). *Educ:* Ranworth Square Sch., Liverpool; Alsop High Sch., Liverpool; Bolton Coll. of Educn. BSc (Econ) London Univ., 1956. RAF, 1948–50. Administrative Asst, Liverpool City Bldg Surveyor's Dept, 1946–56; Lecturer: Brooklyn Technical Coll., Birmingham, 1957–59; Wigan and Dist Mining and Technical Coll., 1959–63; Liverpool Coll. of Commerce, 1963–64; Liverpool City Inst. of Further Educn, 1964–72; Central Liverpool Coll. of Further Educn, 1972–83. Merseyside County Council: Mem., 1981–86; Chief Whip, Labour Gp, 1981–83; Chm., Economic Develt Cttee, 1981–83; Chm., Merseyside Economic Develt Co. Ltd, 1981–86. A Vice-Pres., AMA, 1984–. Joined Labour Party, 1947: Pres., Liverpool Dist Labour Party, 1974–81; Mem., MSF. Introduced Chronically Sick and Disabled Persons Bill, 1983; Asst Labour Whip, 1987–92, with responsibility for health and social security, employment, sport, environment and foreign affairs. Mem., Select Cttee on Foreign Affairs, 1992–. Vice-Chairman: British–Yugoslav Parly Gp, 1985–94; British–Russian Parly Gp, 1992–. *Recreations:* watching soccer (especially Everton FC), concert-going and ballet, motoring and travel. *Address:* House of Commons, SW1A 0AA. *Club:* Pirrie Ward Labour (Liverpool).

WARHURST, Alan, CBE 1990; Director, Manchester Museum, 1977–93; *b* 6 Feb. 1927; *s* of W. Warhurst; *m* 1953, Sheila Lilian Bradbury; one *s* two *d. Educ:* Canon Slade Sch., Bolton; Manchester Univ. (BA Hons History 1950). FSA 1958; FMA 1958. Commnd Lancashire Fusiliers, 1947. Asst, Grosvenor Museum, Chester, 1950–51; Asst Curator, Maidstone Museum and Art Gallery, 1951–55; Curator, Northampton Museum and Art Gallery, 1955–60; Director: City Museum, Bristol, 1960–70; Ulster Museum, 1970–77. Chm., NW Museum and Art Gallery Service, subseq. NW Museums Service, 1992– (Dep. Chm., 1987–92). Mem., Museums and Galls Commn, 1994–. Chm., Irish Nat. Cttee, ICOM, 1973–75; President: S Western Fedn Museums and Galls, 1966–68;

Museums Assoc., 1975–76; N Western Fedn of Museums and Art Galls, 1979–80; Hon. Sec., Univ. Museums Gp, 1987–93. Trustee, Boat Mus., Ellesmere Port, 1990–92. Chm., Hulme Hall Cttee, Univ. of Manchester, 1986–93; Gov., Hulme Hall Trust Foundn, 1994–. Hon. MA Belfast, 1982. *Publications:* various archaeological and museum contribs to learned jls. *Address:* Calabar Cottage, Woodville Road, Altrincham, Cheshire WA14 2AL.

WARING, Sir (Alfred) Holburt, 3rd Bt *cr* 1935; *b* 2 Aug. 1933; *s* of Sir Alfred Harold Waring, 2nd Bt, and Winifred (*d* 1992), *d* of late Albert Boston, Stockton-on-Tees; *S* father, 1981; *m* 1958, Anita, *d* of late Valentin Medinilla, Madrid; one *s* two *d*. *Educ:* Rossall School; Leeds College of Commerce. Director: SRM Plastics Ltd; Waring Investments Ltd; Property Realisation Co. Ltd. Governor, Med. Coll. of St Bartholomew's Hosp. *Recreations:* tennis, golf, squash, swimming. *Heir: s* Michael Holburt Waring, *b* 3 Jan. 1964. *Address:* Earls Croft, 30 Russell Road, Moor Park, Northwood, Middlesex HA6 2LR. *T:* Northwood (01923) 824570. *Club:* Moor Park Golf (Rickmansworth).

WARKE, Rt. Rev. Robert Alexander; *see* Cork, Cloyne and Ross, Bishop of.

WARMAN, Oliver Byrne, RBA 1984; ROI 1989; Chief Executive, Federation of British Artists, 1984–92; *b* 10 June 1932. *Educ:* Stowe; Exeter Univ.; Balliol Coll., Oxford. Commissioned Welsh Guards, 1952; GSO3 Cabinet Office; Instructor, Intelligence Centre; Staff College; RMCS; retired 1970. Dir, Public Relations, Ship and Boat Builders Fedn, 1970; Director: Ashlyns, 1978; Tulsemead, 1983. First exhibited RA, 1980; exhib. at RBA, RWA, NEAC, RSMA, ROI; work in public collections, incl. US Embassy, Sultanate of Oman and Crown Commn. *Publications:* Arnhem 1944, 1970; articles on wine and military history, 1968–. *Recreations:* France, food, wine, sailing, painting, mongrel dogs. *Address:* 8 Church Street, Bridgnorth, Shropshire WV16 4DU; Le Moulin de la Roque, 50210 Montpinchon, Manche, France. *Clubs:* Cavalry and Guards, Arts, Chelsea Arts; Royal Cornwall Yacht.

WARMINGTON, Sir (Marshall Denham) Malcolm, 4th Bt *cr* 1908, of Pembridge Square, Royal Borough of Kensington; *b* 5 Jan. 1934; *s* of Sir Marshall George Clitheroe Warmington, 3rd Bt and his 1st wife Mollie Warmington (*née* Kennard); *S* father, 1995. *Educ:* privately. *Heir: half-b* David Marshall Warmington [*b* 14 Feb. 1944; *m* 1st, 1966, Susan Mary Chapman; two *s*; 2nd, 1981, Eileen Victoria Johnston]. *Address:* c/o D. M. Warmington, 139 Highlands Heath, Putney, SW15 3TZ.

WARNE, Maj.-Gen. Antony M.; *see* Makepeace-Warne.

WARNE, (Ernest) John (David), CB 1982; Secretary, Institute of Chartered Accountants in England and Wales, 1982–90; *b* 4 Dec. 1926; *m* 1953, Rena Wolfe; three *s*. *Educ:* Univ. of London (BA(Hons)). Civil Service Commission, 1953; Asst Comr and Principal, Civil Service Commn, 1958; BoT, later DTI and Dept of Industry: Principal, 1962; Asst Sec., 1967; Under-Sec., 1972; Dir for Scotland, 1972–75; Under-Secretary: Personnel Div., 1975–77; Industrial and Commercial Policy Div., 1977–79; Dep. Sec., Dep. Dir-Gen., OFT, 1979–82. *Recreations:* reading, collecting prints, languages. *Address:* 29 Tower Park, Fowey, Cornwall PL23 1JD. *T:* Fowey (01726) 832589.

WARNER, Prof. Anne Elizabeth, FRS 1985; Royal Society Foulerton Research Professor, and Professor of Developmental Biology, University College London, since 1986; *b* 25 Aug. 1940; *d* of James Frederick Crompton Brooks and Elizabeth Marshall; *m* 1963, Michael Henry Warner. *Educ:* Pate's Grammar School for Girls, Cheltenham; University College London (BSc); Nat. Inst. for Med. Res. (PhD). Res. Associate, Middlesex Hosp. Med. Sch., 1968–71, Lectr in Physiology 1971–75, Sen. Lectr 1975–76, Royal Free Hosp Sch. of Medicine; Sen. Lectr in Anatomy, 1976–80, Reader in Anatomy, 1980–86, Fellow, 1993, UCL. *Publications:* papers in Jl of Physiology and other learned jls. *Address:* University College London, Gower Street, WC1E 6BT.

WARNER, Deborah; free-lance theatre director, since 1980; *b* 12 May 1959; *d* of Ruth and Roger Warner. *Educ:* Sidcot Sch., Avon; St Clare's Coll., Oxford; Central Sch. of Speech and Drama. Founder, 1980, and Artistic Dir, 1980–86, Kick Theatre Co.; Resident Dir, RSC, 1987–89; Associate Dir, Royal Nat. Theatre, 1989 . *Productions:* Kick Theatre Co.: The Good Person of Szechwan, 1980; Woyzeck, 1981, 1982, The Tempest, 1983; Measure for Measure, 1984; King Lear, 1985; Coriolanus, 1986; Royal Shakespeare Co.: Titus Andronicus, 1987 (Laurence Olivier and Evening Standard Awards for Best Dir); King John, Electra, 1988; Electra (also in Paris), 1991; Royal National Theatre: The Good Person of Sichuan, 1989; King Lear, 1990; Richard II, 1995; other productions: Wozzeck, Opera North, 1993; Coriolanus, Salzburg Fest., 1993; Hedda Gabler, Abbey Theatre, Dublin, and Playhouse, 1991 (Laurence Olivier Award for Best Dir and Best Prodn); Don Giovanni, Glyndebourne, 1994; Footfalls, Garrick, 1994. Chevalier de l'Ordre des Arts et des Lettres (France), 1992. *Recreation:* travelling. *Address:* c/o Jeremy Conway, 18–21 Jermyn Street, SW1Y 6HP. *T:* 0171–287 0077.

WARNER, Sir (Edward Courtenay) Henry, 3rd Bt, *cr* 1910; *m*; three *s*. *Heir: s* Philip Courtenay Thomas Warner, *b* 3 April 1951.

WARNER, Sir Edward (Redston), KCMG 1965 (CMG 1955); OBE 1948; HM Diplomatic Service, retired; *b* 23 March 1911; *s* of late Sir George Redston Warner, KCVO, CMG, and Margery Catherine (*née* Nicol); *m* 1943, Grizel Margaret Clerk Rattray; three *s* one *d*. *Educ:* Oundle; King's College, Cambridge. Entered Foreign Office and Diplomatic Service, 1935; UK Delegation to OEEC, Paris, 1956–59; Minister at HM Embassy, Tokyo, 1959–62; Ambassador to Cameroon, 1963–66; UK Rep., Econ. and Social Council of UN, 1966–67; Ambassador to Tunisia, 1968–70. *Address:* The Old Royal Oak, High Street, Blockley, Glos GL56 9EX. *Club:* United Oxford & Cambridge University.

WARNER, Francis (Robert Le Plastrier); poet and dramatist; Lord White Fellow in English Literature and Senior English Tutor, St Peter's College, Oxford; *b* Bishopthorpe, Yorks, 21 Oct. 1937; *s* of Rev. Hugh Compton Warner and Nancy Le Plastrier (*née* Owen); *m* 1st, 1958, Mary Hall (marr. diss. 1972); two *d*; 2nd, 1983, Penelope Anne Davis; one *s* one *d*. *Educ:* Christ's Hosp., London Coll. of Music; St Catharine's Coll., Cambridge (BA, MA). Supervisor, St Catharine's Coll., Cambridge, 1959–63; Staff Tutor in English, Cambridge Univ. Bd of Extra-Mural Studies, 1963–65; Oxford University: Fellow and Tutor, 1965–, Fellow Librarian, 1966–76, Dean of Degrees, 1984–, and Vice-Master, 1987–89, St Peter's Coll.; University Lectr (CUF), 1965–; Pro Sen. Proctor, 1989–90; Chm., Examiners, English Hon. Mods, 1993. Foreign Academician, Acad. de Letras e Artes, Portugal, 1993. Messing Internat. Award for distinguished contribs to Literature, 1972. Benemerenti Silver Medal, Kts of St George, Constantinian Order (Italy), 1990. *Publications: poetry:* Perennia, 1962; Early Poems, 1964; Experimental Sonnets, 1965; Madrigals, 1967; The Poetry of Francis Warner, USA 1970; Lucca Quartet, 1975; Morning Vespers, 1980; Spring Harvest, 1981; Epithalamium, 1983; Collected Poems 1960–84, 1985; Nightingales, 1995; *plays:* Maquettes, a trilogy of one-act plays, 1972; Requiem: Pt 1, Lying Figures, 1972, Pt 2, Killing Time, 1976, Pt 3, Meeting Ends, 1974; A Conception of Love, 1978; Light Shadows, 1980; Moving Reflections, 1983; Living Creation, 1985; Healing Nature: the Athens of Pericles, 1988; Byzantium, 1990; Virgil and Caesar, 1993; Agora: an epic, 1994; King Francis 1st, 1995; *edited:* Eleven Poems by Edmund Blunden, 1965; Garland, 1968; Studies in the Arts, 1968; *relevant publications:* by G. Pursglove: Francis Warner and Tradition, 1981; Francis Warner's Poetry: a critical assessment, 1988. *Recreations:* children, cathedral music, travel. *Address:* St Peter's College, Oxford OX1 2DL. *T:* Oxford (01865) 278900. *Club:* Athenæum.

WARNER, Prof. Sir Frederick (Edward), Kt 1968; FRS 1976; FEng 1977; Visiting Professor, Essex University, since 1983; *b* 31 March 1910; *s* of Frederick Warner; *m* 1st, Margaret Anderson McCrea; two *s* two *d*; 2nd, Barbara Ivy Reynolds. *Educ:* Bancrofts Sch.; University Coll., London. Pres., Univ. of London Union, 1933. Chemical Engr with various cos, 1934–56; self-employed, 1956–. Joined Cremer and Warner, 1956, Senior Partner 1963–80. Inst. of Chemical Engrs: Hon. Sec., 1953; Pres., 1966; Mem. Council, Engrg Instns, 1962; President: Fedn Européenne d'Assocs nationales d'Ingénieurs, 1968–71 (European Engr, 1987); Brit. Assoc. for Commercial and Industrial Educn, 1977–89; Inst. of Quality Assurance, 1987–90; Vice- Pres., BSI, 1976–80 and 1983–89 (Chm., Exec. Bd, 1973–76; Pres., 1980–83). Missions and Consultations in India, Russia, Iran, Egypt, Greece, France. Assessor, Windscale Inquiry, 1977. Chairman: Cttee on Detergents, 1970–74; Process Plant Working Party, 1971–77; Sch. of Pharmacy, Univ. of London, 1971–79; CSTI, 1987–90; Member: Royal Commn on Environmental Pollution, 1973–76; Adv. Council for Energy Conservation, 1974–79; Treasurer, SCOPE (Scientific Cttee on Problems of Environment), 1982–88 (Chm., Environmental Consequences of Nuclear Warfare, 1983–88). Vis. Professor: Imperial Coll., 1970–78 and 1993–; UCL, 1970–86; Pro-Chancellor, Open Univ., 1974–79; Member Court: Cranfield Inst. of Technology; Essex Univ.; Fellow UCL, 1967. Hon. FRSC 1991; Hon. Fellow: UMIST, 1986; Sch. of Pharmacy, 1979. Ordinario, Accademia Tiberina, 1969. Hon. DTech, Bradford, 1969; Hon. DSc: Aston, 1970; Cranfield, 1978; Heriot-Watt, 1978; Newcastle, 1979; DUniv: Open, 1980; Essex, 1992. Gold Medal, Czecho-Slovak Soc. for Internat. Relations, 1969; Medal, Insinöö-riliitto, Finland, 1969; Leverhulme Medal, Royal Soc., 1978; Buchanan Medal, 1982; Environment Medal, Technical Inspectorate of the Rheinland, 1984; Gerard Piel Award, 1991; World Fedn of Engrg Organs Medal for World Engrg Excellence, 1993. Hon. Mem., Koninklijk Instituut van Ingenieurs, 1972; Academico Correspondiente, AI Mexico, 1972. *Publications:* Problem in Chemical Engineering Design (with J. M. Coulson), 1949; Technology Today (ed de Bono), 1971; Standards in the Engineering Industries, NEDO, 1977; Risk Assessment, Royal Soc., 1982; (ed jtly) Treatment and Handling of Wastes, 1992; (ed jtly) Radioecology since Chernobyl, 1992; (ed) Risk Analysis, Perception and Assessment, 1992; (ed) Quality 2000, 1992; papers on Kuwait oil fires, nuclear winter, underground gasification of coal, air and water pollution, contracts, planning, safety, professional and continuous education. *Recreations:* monumental brasses, ceramics, gardens. *Address:* Essex University, Colchester CO4 3SQ. *T:* Colchester (01206) 873370. *Club:* Athenæum.

WARNER, Sir Gerald Chierici, KCMG 1995 (CMG 1984); Deputy Secretary, Cabinet Office, 1991; *b* 27 Sept. 1931; *s* of Howard Warner and Elizabeth (*née* Chierici-Kendall); *m* 1956, Mary Wynne Davies, DMath, Reader, City Univ.; one *s* two *d*. *Educ:* Univ. of Oxford (BA). Joined HM Diplomatic Service, 1954; 3rd Sec., Peking, 1956–58; 2nd Sec., Rangoon, 1960–61; 1st Sec., Warsaw, 1964–66, Geneva, 1966–68; Counsellor, Kuala Lumpur, 1974–76; FCO, 1976–90, retd. Mem., Police Complaints Authy, 1990. *Address:* c/o Coutts & Co., 440 Strand, WC2R 0QS.

WARNER, Graeme Christopher; Sheriff of Grampian, Highland and Islands, since 1992; *b* 20 Oct. 1948; *s* of Richard James Lewis Warner and Jean McDonald McIntyre or Warner; *m* 1976, Rachel Kidd Gear (marr. diss. 1994); one *s* one *d*. *Educ:* Belmont House, Glasgow; Strathallan, by Perth; Edinburgh Univ. (LLB). NP, WS. Law Apprentice, 1969–71; Law Assistant, 1971–72; Partner: Boyd, Janson & Young, WS, Leith, 1972–76; Ross Harper & Murphy, WS, Edinburgh, 1976–88; Macbeth, Currie & Co., WS, Edinburgh, 1989–91. *Recreation:* staying alive! *Address:* Parliament House, 8 Springdale Place, Bieldside, Aberdeen AB1 9FD; Sheriff Court House, Exchequer Road, Aberdeen. *T:* Aberdeen (01224) 648316. *Club:* Royal Northern and University (Aberdeen).

WARNER, Sir Henry, *see* Warner, Sir E. C. H.

WARNER, Sir Jean-Pierre (Frank Eugene), Kt 1981; Judge of the High Court of Justice, Chancery Division, 1981–94; a Judge of the Restrictive Practices Court, 1982–94; *b* 24 Sept. 1924; *s* of late Frank Cloudesley ffolliot Warner and of Louise Marie Blanche Warner (*née* Gouet); *m* 1950, Sylvia Frances, *d* of Sir Ernest Goodale, CBE, MC; two *d*. *Educ:* Sainte Croix de Neuilly; Ecole des Roches; Harrow; Trinity Coll., Cambridge (MA). Served in Rifle Bde, 1943–47, Actg Major, GSO2 (Ops) GHQ Far East. Called to Bar, Lincoln's Inn, 1950 (Cassel Schol.), Bencher 1966, Treasurer 1985; Mem. Gen. Council of Bar, 1969–72. Junior Counsel: to Registrar of Restrictive Trading Agreements, 1961–64; to Treasury (Chancery), 1964–72; QC 1972; Advocate-Gen., Ct of Justice of European Communities, 1973–81. Councillor: Royal Borough of Kensington, 1959–65 (Chm., Gen. Purposes Cttee, 1963–65); Royal Borough of Kensington and Chelsea, 1964–68. Dir, Warner & Sons Ltd and subsids, 1952–70. Pres., UK Assoc. for European Law, 1983–89 (Vice-Pres., 1975–83). Hon. Mem., Soc. of Public Teachers of Law, 1982. Hon. LLD: Exeter, 1983; Leicester, 1984; Edinburgh, 1987. Liveryman, Worshipful Co. of Weavers, 1957. Chevalier du Tastevin, 1952, Commandeur 1960; Mem., Confrérie St Etienne d'Alsace, 1981. *Recreation:* sitting in the sun with a cool drink. *Address:* 32 Abingdon Villas, W8 6BX. *T:* 0171–937 7023.

WARNER, Marina Sarah, FRSL; writer and critic; *b* 9 Nov. 1946; *d* of Esmond Pelham Warner and Emilia (*née* Terzulli); *m* 1st, 1971, Hon. William Shawcross, *qv*; one *s*; 2nd, 1981, John Dewe Mathews. *Educ:* Lady Margaret Hall, Oxford (MA Mod. Langs, French and Italian). FRSL 1985. Getty Schol., Getty Centre for Hist. of Art and Humanities, Calif, 1987–88; Vis. Fellow, BFI, 1992; Tinbergen Prof., Erasmus Univ., Rotterdam, 1991; Visiting Professor: Univ. of Ulster, 1995; QMW, 1995–. Reith Lectr, 1994. Mem. Adv. Bd, Royal Mint, 1986–93. Member: Council, Charter 88, 1990–; Cttee of Management, Nat. Council for One-Parent Families, 1990–; Adv. Council, British Liby, 1992–; Literature Panel, Arts Council, 1992–. Hon. DLitt: Exeter, 1995; Sheffield Hallam, 1995. Libretti: The Legs of the Queen of Sheba, 1991; Then Suddenly . . ., 1996. *Publications:* The Dragon Empress, 1972; Alone of All Her Sex: the myth and the cult of the Virgin Mary, 1976; Queen Victoria's Sketchbook, 1980; Joan of Arc: the image of female heroism, 1981; Monuments and Maidens: the allegory of the female form, 1985; L'Atalante, 1993; Managing Monsters: six myths of our time (Reith Lectures), 1994; From the Beast to the Blonde: on fairy tales and their tellers, 1994; *fiction:* In a Dark Wood, 1977; The Skating Party, 1983; The Lost Father, 1988; Indigo, 1992; The Mermaids in the Basement, 1993; (ed) Wonder Tales, 1994; *children's books:* The Impossible Day, 1981; The Impossible Night, 1981; The Impossible Bath, 1982; The Impossible Rocket, 1982; The Wobbly Tooth, 1984; *juvenile:* The Crack in the Teacup, 1979; pamphlet in Counterblasts series; short stories, arts criticism, radio and television broadcasting. *Recreations:* friends, travels, reading. *Address:* c/o Rogers, Coleridge & White, 20 Powis Mews, W11 1NJ.

WARNER, Norman Reginald; Managing Director, Warner Consultancy and Training Services Ltd, since 1991; Chairman, City and East London Family Health Services

Authority, 1991–94; *b* 8 Sept. 1940; *s* of Albert Henry Edwin Warner and Laura Warner; *m* 1961, Anne Lesley Lawrence; one *s* one *d* (marr. diss. 1981); *m* 1990, Suzanne Elizabeth Reeve (*see* S. E. Warner); one *s*. *Educ:* Dulwich College; University of California, Berkeley (MPH). Min. of Health, 1959; Asst Private Sec. to Minister of Health, 1967–68, to Sec. of State for Social Services, 1968–69; Executive Councils Div., DHSS, 1969–71; Harkness Fellowship, USA, 1971–73; NHS Reorganisation, DHSS, 1973–74; Principal Private Sec. to Sec. of State for Social Services, 1974–76; Supplementary Benefits Div., 1976–78; Management Services, DHSS, 1979–81; Regional Controller, Wales and S Western Region, DHSS, 1981–83; Gwilym Gibbon Fellow, Nuffield Coll., Oxford, 1983–84; Under Sec., Supplementary Benefits Div., DHSS, 1984–85; Dir of Social Services, Kent CC, 1985–91. Sen. Fellow in European Social Welfare and Chm., European Inst. of Social Services, Univ. of Kent, 1991–. Chm., Expert Panel for UK Harkness Fellowships, 1994–. Chairman: Nat. Inquiry into Selection, Develt and Management of Staff in Children's Homes, 1991–92 (report, Choosing with Care, 1992); Inquiry on Learning Disability Services in Thameside Trust, 1994 (report, Learning from the Past, 1994). Adviser to: Price Waterhouse, 1991–; Assoc. of Dist Councils, 1994–; Member, National Management Committee: Royal Philanthropic Soc., 1991– (Chm., 1993–); Carers Nat. Assoc., 1991–94. Trustee: Leonard Cheshire Foundn, 1994–; MacIntyre Care, 1994–; Chm., Residential Forum, in Assoc, with Nat. Inst. for Social Work, 1994–. *Publications:* (ed) Commissioning Community Alternatives in European Social and Health Care, 1993; res. reports; articles in Jl of Public Admin., Community Care, The Guardian, Local Govt Chronicle, etc. *Recreations:* reading, cinema, theatre, exercise. *Address:* 8 College Gardens, Dulwich SE21 7BE. *T:* 0181–693 8083.

WARNER, Suzanne Elizabeth, (Mrs Norman Warner); Head of Group Government Relations, Cable and Wireless plc, since 1993; Director, Warner Consultancy and Training Services, since 1991; *b* 12 Aug. 1942; *d* of Charles Clifford Reeder and Elizabeth Joan Armstrong Reeder; *m* 1st, 1967, Jonathan Reeve (marr. diss. 1980); one *s*; 2nd, 1990, Norman Reginald Warner, *qv*; one *s*. *Educ:* Badminton Sch., Bristol; Univ. of Sussex (BA Hons History); Univ. of Cambridge (Dip. Criminology). Home Office Res. Unit, 1966–67; Personal Assistant to Sec. of State for Social Services, DHSS, 1968–70; Principal, DHSS, 1970–73; Central Policy Review Staff, 1973–74; Asst Sec., DHSS, 1979–85; Sec., 1985–88, Actg Chm., 1987–88, ESRC; Exec. Dir, Food from Britain, 1988–90; Chief Exec., Foundn for Educn Business Partnerships, 1990–91; Personal Advr to Dep. Chm., BT plc, 1991–93. Member: Management Bd, Sci. Policy Support Unit, Royal Soc., 1991–93; Technology Foresight Steering Gp, OST, 1994–; Council, Industry and Parlt Trust, 1994–. Non-executive Director: SE Thames RHA, 1993–; S Thames RHA, 1994–. *Recreations:* family life, cooking, gardening, reading, films. *Address:* 8 College Gardens, Dulwich, SE21 7BE.

WARNOCK, family name of **Baroness Warnock.**

WARNOCK, Baroness *cr* 1985 (Life Peer), of Weeke in the City of Winchester; **Helen Mary Warnock,** DBE 1984; Mistress of Girton College, Cambridge, 1985–91; *b* 14 April 1924; *d* of late Archibald Edward Wilson, Winchester; *m* 1949, Sir Geoffrey Warnock, *qv*; two *s* three *d*. *Educ:* St Swithun's, Winchester; Lady Margaret Hall, Oxford (Hon. Fellow 1984). Fellow and Tutor in Philosophy, St Hugh's Coll., Oxford, 1949–66; Headmistress, Oxford High Sch., GPDST, 1966–72; Talbot Res. Fellow, Lady Margaret Hall, Oxford, 1972–76; Sen. Res. Fellow, St Hugh's Coll., Oxford, 1976–84 (Hon. Fellow, 1985). Member: IBA, 1973–81; Cttee of Inquiry into Special Educn, 1974–78 (Chm.); Royal Commn on Environmental Pollution, 1979–84; Adv. Cttee on Animal Experiments, 1979–85 (Chm.); SSRC, 1981–85; UK Nat. Commn for Unesco, 1981–84; Cttee of Inquiry into Human Fertilization, 1982–84 (Chm.); Cttee of Inquiry into Validation of Public Sector Higher Educn, 1984; Ctttee on Teaching Quality, PCFC, 1990 (Chm.); European Adv. Gp on Bioethics, 1992–94; Archbishop of Canterbury's Adv. Gp on Medical Ethics, 1992–; Chm., Educn Cttee, GPDST, 1994–. Gifford Lectr, Univ. of Glasgow, 1991–92; Reed Tuckwell Lectr, Univ. of Bristol, 1992. Leverhulme Emeritus Fellow, 1992–94. FRCP 1979; FRSM 1989; Hon. FIC 1986. Hon. degrees: Open, Essex, Melbourne, Manchester, Bath, Exeter, Glasgow, York, Nottingham, Warwick, Liverpool, London and St Andrews Univs.; Leeds Polytechnic; Leicester Polytechnic. *Publications:* Ethics since 1900, 1960, 3rd edn 1978; J.-P. Sartre, 1963; Existentialist Ethics, 1966; Existentialism, 1970; Imagination, 1976; Schools of Thought, 1977; (with T. Devlin) What Must We Teach?, 1977; Education: a way forward, 1979; A Question of Life, 1985; Teacher Teach Thyself (Dimbleby Lect.), 1985; Memory, 1987; A Common Policy for Education, 1988; Universities: knowing our minds, 1989; The Uses of Philosophy, 1992; Imagination and Time, 1994; (ed) Women Philosophers, 1995. *Recreations:* music, gardening. *Address:* Brick House, Axford SN8 2EX. *T:* Marlborough (01672) 514686.

WARNOCK, Sir Geoffrey (James), Kt 1986; Principal, Hertford College, Oxford, 1971–88, Hon. Fellow, 1988; Vice-Chancellor, University of Oxford, 1981–85; *b* 16 Aug. 1923; *s* of James Warnock, OBE, MD; *m* 1949, Helen Mary Wilson (*see* Baroness Warnock); two *s* three *d*. *Educ:* Winchester Coll.; New Coll., Oxford (Hon. Fellow, 1973). Served War of 1939–45: Irish Guards, 1942–45 (Captain). Fellow by Examination, Magdalen Coll., 1949; Fellow and Tutor, Brasenose Coll., 1950–53; Fellow and Tutor in Philosophy, Magdalen Coll., 1953–71, Emeritus Fellow, 1972, Hon. Fellow, 1980. Visiting Lectr, Univ. of Illinois, 1957; Visiting Professor: Princeton Univ., 1962; Univ. of Wisconsin, 1966. Hon. DH Univ. of Hartford, 1986. *Publications:* Berkeley, 1953; English Philosophy since 1900, 1958, 2nd edn 1969; Contemporary Moral Philosophy, 1967; (ed with J. O. Urmson) J. L. Austin: Philosophical Papers, 2nd edn, 1970; The Object of Morality, 1971; Morality and Language, 1983; J. L. Austin, 1989; articles in: Mind, Proc. Aristotelian Soc., etc. *Address:* Brick House, Axford, Marlborough, Wilts SN8 2EX.

WARR, John James; Deputy Chairman, Clive Discount Co. Ltd, 1973–87, retired; President of the MCC, 1987–88; *b* 16 July 1927; *s* of late George and Florence May Warr; *m* 1957, Valerie Powell (*née* Peter); two *d*. *Educ:* Ealing County Grammar Sch.; Emmanuel Coll., Cambridge (BA Hons 1952). Served RN, 1945–48. Man. Dir, Union Discount Co., 1952–73. Chm., Racecourse Assoc., 1989–93. Mem., Jockey Club, 1977–. Pres., Berks CCC, 1990–. *Recreations:* racing, cricket, golf, good music. *Address:* Orchard Farm, Touchen End, Maidenhead, Berks SL6 3TA. *T:* Maidenhead (01628) 22994. *Clubs:* Saints and Sinners (Chm., 1991–92), MCC, XL, Lord's Taverners; Temple Golf, Berkshire Golf.

WARRELL, Prof. David Alan, DM; DSc; FRCP; Professor of Tropical Medicine and Infectious Diseases, since 1987, and Director, Centre for Tropical Medicine, since 1991, University of Oxford; Fellow, St Cross College, Oxford, since 1977; *b* 6 Oct. 1939; *s* of Alan and Mildred Warrell; *m* 1975, Dr Mary Jean Prentice; two *d*. *Educ:* Portsmouth Grammar Sch.; Christ Church, Oxford (MA, BCh 1964; DM 1970; DSc 1990). MRCS 1965; FRCP 1977. Oxford Univ. Radcliffe Travelling Fellow, Univ. of Calif at San Diego, 1969–70; Sen. Lectr, Ahmadu Bello Univ., Zaria, Nigeria, 1970–74; Lectr, RPMS, London, 1974–75; Consultant Physician, Radcliffe Infirmary, Oxford, 1975–79; Founding Dir, Wellcome-Mahidol Univ. Oxford Tropical Medicine Research Programme in Bangkok, 1979–86. WHO Consultant on malaria and snake bite, 1979–. Chm., MRC's AIDS Therapeutic Trials Cttee, 1987–93; Mem., MRC's Tropical Medicine Res. Bd, 1986–89. Hon. Consultant Malariologist to the Army, 1989–; Hon. Med. Advr, RGS, 1993–. Vice President: Internat. Fedn for Tropical Medicine, 1992–; RSTM&H, 1995–. Lectures: Marc Daniels, RCP, 1977; Bradshaw, RCP, 1989; Croonian, RCP, 1996. Scientific FZS 1976; FRGS 1989. Hon. Fellow, Ceylon Coll. of Physicians, 1985. Chalmers Medal, RSTM&H, 1981; Ambuj Nath Bose Prize, RCP, 1994. *Publications:* Rabies—the Facts, 1977, 2nd edn 1986; (ed) Oxford Textbook of Medicine, 1983, 3rd edn 1995; (ed) Bruce-Chwatt's Essential Malariology, 3rd edn 1993; chapters in textbooks of tropical medicine; papers in learned jls (Lancet, New England Jl of Medicine, etc) on respiratory physiology, malaria, rabies, infectious diseases and snake bite. *Recreations:* book collecting, music, bird watching, hill walking. *Address:* University of Oxford, Nuffield Department of Clinical Medicine, John Radcliffe Hospital, Headington, Oxford OX3 9DU. *T:* Oxford (01865) 220968 and 221332, *Fax:* (01865) 220984. *Club:* Royal Society of Medicine.

WARRELL, David Watson, MD; FRCOG; urological gynaecologist, since 1969; Chairman, Mid-Cheshire Hospitals NHS Trust, since 1994; *b* 20 June 1929; *s* of Charles Warrell and Sarah (*née* Gill); *m* 1955, Valerie Jean Fairclough; one *s* one *d*. *Educ:* Sheffield Univ. MB ChB 1953; MD 1964; FRCOG 1970. Sen. Lectr and Hon. Consultant Obstetrician and Gynaecologist, Jessop Hosp. for Women, 1965–69; St Mary's Hosp., Manchester, 1969–: established Dept of Urological Gynaecology; Med. Dir, 1991–92, Chief Exec., 1992–94, Central Manchester Health Care Trust. Blair Bell Travelling Fellowship, 1967. *Publications:* chapters and papers on urinary control in women. *Recreations:* farming, hill-walking. *Address:* Upper Water Meetings Farm, Water Meetings Lane, Romiley, Stockport, Cheshire SK6 4HJ.

WARRELL, Ernest Herbert, MBE 1991; Organist, King's College, London, 1980–91 (Lecturer in Music, KCL, 1953–80); *b* 23 June 1915; *er s* of Herbert Henry Warrell and Edith Peacock; *m* 1952, Jean Denton Denton; two *s* one *d*. *Educ:* Loughborough School. Articled pupil (Dr E. T. Cook), Southwark Cath., 1938; Asst Organist, Southwark Cath., 1946–54; Organist, St Mary's, Primrose Hill, 1954–57; Lectr in Plainsong, RSCM, 1954–59; Organist, St John the Divine, Kennington, SW9, 1961–68; Organist and Dir of Music, Southwark Cathedral, 1968–76; Musical Dir, Gregorian Assoc., 1969–82. Chief Examiner in Music, Internat. Baccalaureate, 1984–89. Hon. FCTL 1977; FKC 1979; Hon. FGCM 1988. *Publications:* Accompaniments to the Psalm Tones, 1942; Plainsong and the Anglican Organist, 1943. *Recreation:* sailing. *Address:* 41 Beechhill Road, Eltham, SE9 1HJ. *T:* 0181–850 7800. *Clubs:* Special Forces, Little Ship; Royal Scots (Edinburgh).

WARREN, Very Rev. Alan Christopher; Provost of Leicester, 1978–92, now Provost Emeritus; *b* 27 June 1932; *s* of Arthur Henry and Gwendoline Catherine Warren; *m* 1957, Sylvia Mary (*née* Matthews); three *d*. *Educ:* Dulwich College; Corpus Christi Coll., Cambridge (Exhibnr, MA); Ridley Hall, Cambridge. Curate, St Paul's, Margate, 1957–59; Curate, St Andrew, Plymouth, 1959–62; Chaplain of Kelly College, Tavistock, 1962–64; Vicar of Holy Apostles, Leicester, 1964–72; Coventry Diocesan Missioner, 1972–78; Hon. Canon, Coventry Cathedral, 1972–78; Proctor in Convocation, 1977–78, 1980–85. Mem., Cathedral Statutes Commn, 1981–85. Trustee, St Martin's, Birmingham, 1979–. Chm., Leicester Council of Christians and Jews, 1985–92; President: Leicester Council of Churches, 1985–92; Leicester Civic Soc., 1983–92. Tutor, Adult Educn, Norfolk, 1993–; Dir of Music, W Norfolk Choral Soc., 1993–. Mem., MCC, 1960–76. Pres., Alleyn Club, 1991–92 (Vice-Pres., 1990–91). *Publications:* Putting it Across, 1975; The Miserable Warren, 1991; articles on church music, evangelism and sport in Church Times and other journals. *Recreations:* music, golf, steam trains. *Address:* 9 Queens Drive, Hunstanton, Norfolk PE36 6EY. *T:* Hunstanton (01485) 534533. *Clubs:* Free Foresters; Hunstanton Golf.

WARREN, Alastair Kennedy, TD 1953; Editor, Dumfries and Galloway Standard, 1976–86; *b* 17 July 1922; *s* of John Russell Warren, MC, and Jean Cousin Warren; *m* 1952, Ann Lindsay Maclean; two *s*. *Educ:* Glasgow Acad.; Loretto; Glasgow Univ. (MA Hons). Served War of 1939–45; HLI, 1940–46; Major, 1946. Served 5/6th Bn HLI (TA) 1947–63. Sales Clerk, Stewarts & Lloyds Ltd, 1950–53; joined editorial staff of The Glasgow Herald as Sub-Editor, 1954; Leader Writer, 1955–58; Features Editor, 1958–59; Commercial Editor, 1960–64; City Editor, 1964–65; Editor, 1965–74; Regional Editor, Scottish and Universal Newspapers Ltd, 1974–76. Provost of New Galloway and Kells Community Council, 1978–81; Chairman: Loch Arthur Village Community (Camphill Movt), 1985–92; Nithsdale Council of Voluntary Service, 1988–91 (Pres., 1992–). *Publications:* contribs to various periodicals. *Recreations:* swimming, hill walking, marathon running. *Address:* Rathan, New Galloway, Castle Douglas DG7 3RN. *T:* New Galloway (01644) 420257.

WARREN, Dame (Alice) Josephine (Mary Taylor); *see* Barnes, Dame A. J. M. T.

WARREN, Sir Brian; *see* Warren, Sir H. B. S.

WARREN, Sir Brian Charles Pennefather, 9th Bt *cr* 1784; *b* 4 June 1923; *o s* of Sir Thomas Richard Pennefather Warren, 8th Bt, CBE; *S* father, 1961; *m* 1976, Cola, *d* of Captain E. L. Cazenove, Great Dalby, Leics. *Educ:* Wellington College. Served War of 1939–45; Lt, 1943–45, 2nd Bn Irish Guards. *Recreations:* hunting, squash. *Heir: cousin* Michael Blackley Warren [*b* 12 Nov. 1918; *m* 1941, Marie Noelle, *e d* of Ernest Marcel Laffaille; one *d*]. *Address:* The Wilderness, Castle Oliver, Kilmallock, Co. Limerick. *Club:* Cavalry and Guards.

WARREN, Rt. Rev. Cecil Allan; Rector, Old Brampton and Loundsley Green, 1983–88; Assistant Bishop, Diocese of Derby, 1983–88; *b* 25 Feb. 1924; *s* of Charles Henry and Eliza Warren; *m* 1947, Doreen Muriel Burrows. *Educ:* Sydney Univ. (BA 1950); Queen's Coll., Oxford (MA 1959). Deacon 1950, Priest 1951, Dio. of Canberra and Goulburn; appointments in Diocese of Oxford, 1953–57; Canberra, 1957–63; Organising Sec. Church Society, and Director of Forward in Faith Movement, Dio. of Canberra and Goulburn, 1963–65; Asst Bishop of Canberra and Goulburn, 1965–72; Bishop of Canberra and Goulburn, 1972–83. *Publication:* A Little Foolishness: an autobiographical history, 1993. *Address:* 2/19 Sidney Street, Toowoomba, Qld 4350, Australia.

WARREN, Frederick Lloyd, MA, BSc (Oxon), PhD, DSc (London); Professor of Biochemistry, London Hospital Medical College, 1952–78, now Emeritus; *b* 2 Oct. 1911; *s* of Frederick James and Edith Agnes Warren; *m* 1st, 1949, Natalia Vera Peierls (*née* Ladan) (marr. diss., 1958); two *s* one *d*; 2nd, 1961, Ruth Natallé Jacobs. *Educ:* Bristol Grammar Sch.; Exeter Coll., Oxford. Demonstrator, Biochem. Dept, Oxford, 1932–34; Sir Halley Stewart Res. Fellow, Chester Beatty Research Institute, Royal Cancer Hospital, 1934–46; Laura de Saliceto Student, University of London, 1937–42; Anna Fuller Research Student, 1942–46; Senior Lecturer in Biochemistry, St Mary's Hospital Medical School, 1946–48; Reader in Biochemistry, University College, London, 1948–52. *Publications:* papers and articles in scientific journals. *Address:* 5 River View, Enfield, Mddx EN2 6PX. *T:* 0181–366 0674.

WARREN, Sir Frederick Miles, ONZ 1995; KBE 1985 (CBE 1974); FNZIA; ARIBA; Senior Partner, Warren & Mahoney, Architects Ltd, since 1958; *b* Christchurch, 10 May 1929. *Educ:* Christ's Coll., Christchurch; Auckland Univ. DipArch; ARIBA 1952; FNZIA 1965. Founded Warren & Mahoney, 1958. Award-winning designs include: Christchurch

Town Hall and Civic Centre; NZ Chancery, Washington; Canterbury Public Library; Michael Fowler Centre, Wellington; St Patrick's Church, Napier; Ohinetahi, Governors Bay; Rotorua Dist Council Civic Offices; Mulholland Hse, Wanganui; Parkroyal Hotel, Christchurch. Pres., Canterbury Soc. of Arts, 1972–76. Gold Medal, NZIA, 1960, 1964, 1969, 1973; Nat. Awards, NZIA, 1980, 1981, 1983–86, 1988, 1989, 1990, 1991. *Publication:* Warren & Mahoney Architects, 1990. *Recreation:* making a garden. *Address:* 65 Cambridge Terrace, Christchurch 1, New Zealand.

WARREN, Dr Graham Barry; Principal Scientist, Imperial Cancer Research Fund, since 1989; *b* 25 Feb. 1948; *s* of Joyce Thelma and Charles Graham Thomas Warren; *m* 1966, Philippa Mary Adeline (*née* Temple-Cole); four *d.* *Educ:* Willesden County Grammar Sch.; Pembroke Coll., Cambridge (MA, PhD). MRC Fellow, Nat. Inst. for Med. Research, 1972–75; Royal Soc. Stothert Research Fellow, Dept of Biochemistry, Cambridge, 1975–77; Research Fellow, Gonville & Caius Coll., Cambridge, 1975–77; Group Leader then Senior Scientist, European Molecular Biology Lab., Heidelberg, 1977–85; Prof. and Hd of Dept of Biochemistry, Dundee Univ., 1985–88. Mem., EMBO, 1986–. *Publications:* papers in learned jls on cell biology. *Recreation:* woodworking. *Address:* 17 Grosvenor Road, N10 2DR. *T:* 0181–444 5808.

WARREN, Sir (Harold) Brian (Seymour), Kt 1974; physician; *b* 19 Dec. 1914; *er s* of late Harold Warren, St Ives, Hunts and Marian Jessie Emlyn; *m* 1st, 1942, Dame Alice Josephine Mary Taylor Barnes, *qv* (marr. diss. 1964); one *s* two *d*; 2nd, 1964, Elizabeth Anne (*d* 1983), *y d* of late Walter William Marsh, Wordsley, Staffs; two *s.* *Educ:* Bishop's Stortford Coll.; University Coll. London; University Coll. Hosp. MRCS, LRCP. Pres., Univ. of London Union, 1937–38. House Phys. and House Surg., UCH, 1942. War service with RAMC, RMO 1st Bn Gren. Gds and DADMS Gds Div., 1942–46 (despatches). Mem., Westminster City Council, 1955–64 and 1968–78; rep. West Woolwich on LCC, 1955–58, County Alderman 1961–62. Contested (C) Brixton Div. of Lambeth, 1959. Personal Phys. to Prime Minister, 1970–74. Mem., Westminster, Chelsea and Kensington AHA, 1975–77. Visitor and Mem. Emergency Bed Service Cttee, King Edward's Hosp. Fund for London, 1966–72; Mem. Governing Body, Westminster Hosp., 1970–74; Mem. Council, King Edward VII's Hosp. for Officers (Surg.-Apothecary, 1952–80). Pres., Chelsea Clinical Soc., 1955–56. Mem., Develt Cttee, BTA, 1978–87. Liveryman, Apothecaries' Soc., 1950; Freeman, City of London. *Publications:* contrib. Encycl. Gen. Practice. *Recreations:* reading, gardening, travel, listening to music. *Address:* 94 Oakley Street, SW3 5NR. *T:* 0171–351 6462. *Club:* Pratt's.
See also A. I. Holden, M. G. J. Neary.

WARREN, Ian Scott; Senior Master of the Supreme Court (Queen's Bench Division) and Queen's Remembrancer, 1988–90 (Master, 1970–90); *b* 30 March 1917; *er s* of Arthur Owen Warren and Margaret Cromarty Warren (*née* Macnaughton); *m* 1st, 1943, Barbara (marr. diss.), *er d* of Walter Myrick, Tillsonburg, Ont.; four *s* one *d*; 2nd, Jeanne Hicklin (marr. diss.), *d* of late Frederick and Lydia Shaw, Crosland Moor; 3rd, 1987, Olive Sybil, *d* of late James Charles Montgomerie Wilson. *Educ:* Charterhouse (Exhbnr); Magdalene Coll., Cambridge (Exhbnr); BA 1938, MA 1950. Colonial Administrative Service, 1938–41, serving Gold Coast (Asst DC, 1940); RAF, 1942–46; Flying Badge and commissioned, 1943; Flt Lieut, 1944. Called to Bar, Lincoln's Inn, 1947, Bencher 1967; practised at Common Law Bar, London, 1947–70. *Publications:* Verses from Lincoln's Inn (jtly), 1975; Aesop's Fables: a selection, 1982. *Recreations:* ski-ing, walking, poetry. *Clubs:* Garrick, MCC.

WARREN, Jack Hamilton, OC 1982; principal trade policy advisor, Government of Quebec, 1986–94; *b* 10 April 1921; *s* of Tom Hamilton Warren and Olive Sykes (*née* Horsfall); *m* 1953, Hilary Joan Titterington; two *s* two *d.* *Educ:* Queen's Univ., Kingston, (BA). Served War, with Royal Canadian Navy. Public Service, 1945–57: Dept of External Affairs; Dept of Finance; diplomatic postings in Ottawa, London, Washington, Paris and Geneva; Asst Dep. Minister of Trade and Commerce, 1958; Chm., Council of Representatives, 1960, and Chm., Contracting Parties, 1962 and 1964, GATT; Dep. Minister: Dept of Trade and Commerce, 1964; Dept of Industry, Trade and Commerce, 1969; High Comr for Canada in London, 1971–74; Ambassador to USA, 1975–77; Ambassador, and Canadian Co-ordinator for the Multilateral Trade Negotiations, 1977–79; Vice-Chm., Bank of Montreal, 1979–86; Director: Roins Holdings Ltd, 1980–91; Royal Insurance Co. of Canada, 1980–91; Western Assurance Co., 1980–91; Pratt and Whitney, Canada, 1983–91; PACCAR of Canada Ltd, 1984–91. Dep. Chm. (N America), Trilateral Commn, 1985–91. Hon. LLD Queen's, Ont, 1974. Outstanding Achievement Award, Public Service of Canada, 1975. *Recreations:* fishing, gardening, golf, ski-ing. *Address:* PO Box 282 RR1, Chelsea, Que J0X IN0, Canada. *Clubs:* Rideau (Ottawa); White Pine Fishing, Larrimac Golf (Canada).

WARREN, John; QC 1994; a Recorder, Midland and Oxford Circuit, since 1993; *b* 25 Aug. 1945; *s* of Frank Warren and Dora Warren (*née* Thomas); *m* 1968, Anne Marlor; one *s* one *d* (twins). *Educ:* Chadderton Grammar Sch., near Oldham; Univ. of Nottingham (LLB). Called to the Bar, Gray's Inn, 1968. *Recreations:* opera and classical music, supporting Nottingham Forest FC, doing The Times crossword in bed with my wife. *Address:* 1 High Pavement, Nottingham NG1 1HF. *T:* Nottingham (0115) 941 8218. *Clubs:* Nottingham and Notts United Services, Keyworth and Ruddington Rotary (Nottingham).

WARREN, Dame Josephine; *see* Barnes, Dame A. J. M. T.

WARREN, Sir Kenneth (Robin), Kt 1994; Eur Ing, CEng, FRAeS; FCIT; FRSA; consultant in engineering; director of a number of companies; *b* 15 Aug. 1926; *s* of Edward Charles Warren and Ella Mary Warren (*née* Adams); *m* 1962, Elizabeth Anne Chamberlain, MA Cantab and MA Lond; one *s* two *d.* *Educ:* Midsomer Norton; Aldenham; London Univ.; De Havilland Aeronautical Technical Sch. Fulbright Scholar, USA, 1949; Research Engineer, BOAC, 1951–57; Personal Asst to Gen. Manager, Smiths Aircraft Instruments Ltd, 1957–60; Elliott Automation Ltd, 1960–69; Military Flight Systems: Manager, 1960–63; Divisional Manager, 1963–66; Marketing Manager, 1966–69. MP (C) Hastings, 1970–83, Hastings and Rye, 1983–92. Mem., Select Cttee on Science and Technology, 1970–79 (Chm., Offshore Engrg Sub-Cttee, 1975–76); Mem., Council of Europe, 1973–80; Chm., WEU, Science, Technology and Aerospace Cttee, 1976–79; Chm., Cons. Party Aviation Cttee, 1975–77; PPS to Sec. of State for Industry, 1979–81, to Sec. of State for Educn and Sci., 1981–83; Chairman: Select Cttee on Trade and Industry, 1983–92; British Soviet Party Gp, 1986–92. Former branch officer, G&MWU. Pres., British Resorts Assoc., 1987–92. Liveryman: Coachmakers' Co.; GAPAN; Freeman, City of London. Hon. Fellow, Exeter Univ., 1994. *Publications:* various papers to technical confs on aeronautical engineering and management, in USA, UK, Hungary, Netherlands and Japan. *Recreations:* mountaineering, flying, gardening. *Address:* Woodfield House, Goudhurst, Kent TN17 2NN. *T:* Goudhurst (01580) 211590, *Fax:* (01580) 212152.

WARREN, Maurice Eric; Chairman: Dalgety PLC, since 1993 (Chief Executive, 1989–93; Director, since 1982); South Western Electricity plc, since 1993; CAMAS, since 1994; *b* 21 June 1933; *s* of Frederick Leonard and Winifred Warren; *m* 1954, Molly Warren; one *s* one *d.* *Educ:* St Brendan's Coll., Bristol. Certified Accountant, FCCA. Crosfield & Calthrop, 1958–74 (Dir, 1970–74); Managing Director: Dalgety Crosfields, 1974–76; Dalgety Agriculture Ltd, 1976–81; Dalgety UK Ltd, 1981–87; Dalgety plc, 1987–89. *Recreation:* golf. *Address:* Dalgety PLC, 100 George Street, W1H 5RH. *T:* 0171–486 0200.

WARREN, Prof. Michael Donald, MD, FRCP, FFPHM; Emeritus Professor of Social Medicine, University of Kent, since 1983; *b* 19 Dec. 1923; *s* of late Charles Warren and Dorothy Gladys Thornton Reeks; *m* 1946, Joan Lavina Peacock; one *s* two *d.* *Educ:* Bedford Sch.; Guy's Hosp.; London Sch. of Hygiene and Tropical Medicine. MB 1946, MD 1952; DPH 1952, DIH 1952; MRCP 1969, FRCP 1975; FFCM 1972; Hon. FFPHM 1991. Sqdn Ldr RAF, Med. Branch, 1947–51; Dep. MOH, Metropolitan Borough of Hampstead, 1952–54; Asst Principal MO, LCC, 1954–58; Sen. Lectr and Hon. Consultant in Social Medicine, Royal Free Hosp. Sch., Royal Free Hosp. and London Sch. of Hygiene and Tropical Medicine, 1958–64; Sen. Lectr in Social Medicine, LSHTM, 1964–67; Reader in Public Health, Univ. of London, 1967–71; Prof. of Community Health, Univ. of London, 1978–80; Dir, Health Services Res. Unit, and Prof. of Social Medicine, Univ. of Kent, 1971–83, jtly with Specialist in Community Medicine (Epidemiology and Health Services Res.), SE Thames RHA, 1980–83. Chm., Soc. of Social Medicine, 1982–83. Academic Registrar, Faculty of Community Medicine, Royal Colls of Physicians, 1972–77. Jt Editor, British Jl of Preventive and Social Medicine, 1969–72. *Publications:* (jtly) Public Health and Social Services, 4th edn 1957, 6th edn 1965; (ed jtly) Management and the Health Services, 1971; (jtly) Physiotherapy in the Community, 1977; (jtly) Physically Disabled People Living at Home, 1978; (ed jtly) Recalling the Medical Officer of Health, 1987; (jtly) Health Services for Adults with Physical Disabilities, 1990; contribs to BMJ, Lancet, Internat. Jl of Epidemiology. *Recreations:* enjoying gardens, genealogy, reading, listening to music. *Address:* 2 Bridge Down, Bridge, Canterbury, Kent CT4 5AZ. *T:* Canterbury (01227) 830233. *Clubs:* Royal Society of Medicine; Kent County Cricket.

WARREN, Nicholas Roger; QC 1993; *b* 20 May 1949; *s* of Roger Warren and Muriel (*née* Reeves); *m* 1st, 1978 (marr. diss. 1989); two *s* one *d*; 2nd, 1994, Catherine Graham-Harrison. *Educ:* Bryanston Sch.; University Coll., Oxford. Called to the Bar, Middle Temple, 1972. *Recreations:* music, sailing. *Address:* Wilberforce Chambers, 8 New Square, Lincoln's Inn, WC2A 3QP.

WARREN, Ven. Norman Leonard; Archdeacon of Rochester, since 1989; *b* 19 July 1934; *s* of Arthur Henry Warren and Gwendoline Catharine Warren; *m* 1961, Yvonne Sheather; three *s* two *d.* *Educ:* Dulwich College; Corpus Christi Coll., Cambridge (MA). Asst Curate, Bedworth, 1960–63; Vicar, St Paul's, Leamington Priors, 1963–77; Rector of Morden, 1977–89; RD of Merton, 1984–88. Musical Editor: Hymns for Today's Church, 1982; Jesus Praise, 1982. *Publications:* Journey into Life, 1964; The Way Ahead, 1965; Directions, 1969; What's the Point?, 1986; The Path of Peace, 1988; A Certain Faith, 1988; Is God there?, 1990; Why Believe?, 1993; Responsorial Psalms of the Alternative Services Book. *Recreations:* cricket, soccer and Rugby, walking, music. *Address:* The Archdeaconry, Rochester, Kent ME1 1SX. *T:* Medway (01634) 842527.

WARREN, Peter Francis; Director, Abbott Mead Vickers plc, since 1992; *b* 2 Dec. 1940; *s* of Francis Joseph Warren and Freda Ruth Hunter; *m* 1962, Susan Poole; two *s* one *d.* *Educ:* Finchley Grammar School. Deputy Managing Director, Ogilvy Benson & Mather Ltd, 1977; Director, Ogilvy & Mather International Inc., 1978; Man. Dir, Ogilvy Benson & Mather Ltd, 1978; Chairman: Ogilvy & Mather (Hldgs), subseq. The Ogilvy Gp (Hldgs) Ltd, 1981–90; Ogilvy & Mather Europe, 1988–90; Consultant, Ogilvy & Mather Worldwide, 1991 (Dir, 1985–90). *Address:* Abbott Mead Vickers, 191 Old Marylebone Road, NW1 5DW. *T:* 0171–402 4100.

WARREN, Prof. Peter Michael, PhD; FSA; Professor of Ancient History and Classical Archaeology, since 1977 and University Fellow, 1995–July 1996, University of Bristol; *b* 23 June 1938; *s* of Arthur George Warren and Alison Joan Warren (*née* White); *m* 1966, Elizabeth Margaret Halliday; one *s* one *d.* *Educ:* Sandbach Sch.; Llandovery Coll.; University College of N Wales, Bangor (Ellen Thomas Stanford Schol.; BA 1st Cl. Hons Greek and Latin); Corpus Christi Coll., Cambridge (Exhibnr; BA Classical Tripos Pt II 1962; MA 1966; PhD 1966; Fellow, 1965–68); student, British Sch. at Athens, 1963–65. FSA 1973. Research Fellow in Arts, Univ. of Durham, 1968–70; Asst Director, British Sch. at Athens, 1970–72; University of Birmingham: Lectr in Aegean Archaeol., 1972–74; Sen. Lectr, 1974–76; Reader, 1976; Bristol University: Dean, Faculty of Arts, 1988–90; Pro-Vice-Chancellor, 1991–95. Vis. Prof., Univ. of Minnesota, 1981; Geddes-Harrower Prof. of Greek Art and Archaeol., Univ. of Aberdeen, 1986–87; Neubergh Lectr, Univ. of Göteborg, 1986. Dir of excavations, Myrtos, Crete, 1967–68; Debla, Crete, 1971; Knossos, 1971–73, 1978–82. Member: Managing Cttee, British Sch. at Athens, 1973–77, 1978–79, 1986–90, 1994– (Chm., 1979–83); Council, Soc. for Promotion of Hellenic Studies, 1978–81; Vice-Chm. Council, Bristol and Glos Archaeol Soc., 1980–81, Chm., 1981–84, Vice-Pres., 1989–93. Hon. Fellow, Archaeol Soc. of Athens, 1987; Corresp. Fellow, Soc. for Cretan Historical Studies, 1992. *Publications:* Minoan Stone Vases, 1969; Myrtos, an Early Bronze Age Settlement in Crete, 1972; The Aegean Civilizations, 1975, 2nd edn 1989; Minoan Religion as Ritual Action, 1988; (with V. Hankey) Aegean Bronze Age Chronology, 1989; articles on Aegean Bronze Age, particularly Minoan archaeology, in archaeol and classical jls. *Recreations:* contemporary British politics, history of Greek botany. *Address:* Claremont House, Merlin Haven, Wotton-under-Edge, Glos GL12 7BA. *T:* Dursley (01453) 842290.

WARREN, Peter Tolman, PhD; Executive Secretary, The Royal Society, since 1985; *b* 20 Dec. 1937; *s* of late Hugh Alan Warren and Florence Christine Warren (*née* Tolman); *m* 1961, Angela Mary (*née* Curtis); two *s* one *d.* *Educ:* Whitgift Sch., Croydon; Queens' Coll., Cambridge (MA, PhD); CGeol. Geological Survey of GB, 1962; Chief Scientific Adviser's Staff, Cabinet Office, 1972; Private Sec. to Lord Zuckerman, 1973–76; Science and Technology Secretariat, Cabinet Office, 1974–76; Safety Adviser, NERC, 1976–77; Dep. Exec. Sec., Royal Soc., 1977–85. Mem. Council, Parly and Scientific Cttee, 1992– (Vice-Pres., 1995–). Mem. Council, GPDST, 1989–. Vice-Pres., Geol Soc., 1992–95. Editor, Monographs of Palaeontographical Soc., 1968–77. *Publications:* (ed) Geological Aspects of Development and Planning in Northern England, 1970; (co-author) Geology of the Country around Rhyl and Denbigh, 1984; papers on geology in learned jls. *Recreations:* geology, gardening. *Address:* Flat One, 6 Carlton House Terrace, SW1Y 5AG. *T:* 0171–839 5260. *Club:* Athenæum.

WARREN, Prof. Raymond Henry Charles, MusD; Stanley Hugh Badock Professor of Music, University of Bristol, 1972–94; *b* 7 Nov. 1928; *m* 1953, Roberta Lydia Alice Smith; three *s* one *d.* *Educ:* Bancroft's Sch.; Corpus Christi Coll., Cambridge (MA, MusD). Music Master, Wolverstone Hall Sch., 1952–55; Queen's University Belfast: Lectr in Music, 1955–66; Prof. of Composition, 1966–72; Resident Composer, Ulster Orchestra, 1967–72. Compositions incl. 2 symphonies, 3 string quartets and 6 operas. *Publications:* *compositions:* The Passion, 1963; String Quartet No 1, 1967; Violin Concerto, 1967; Songs of Old Age, 1971; Continuing Cities (oratorio), 1989. *Recreation:* walking. *Address:* 9 Cabot Rise, Portishead, Bristol BS20 9NX. *T:* Portishead (01275) 844289.

WARREN, Stanley Anthony Treleaven, CB 1984; CEng, FRINA, FIMechE; RCNC; Director General Submarines, Ministry of Defence (Procurement Executive), 1979–85, retired; *b* 26 Sept. 1925; *s* of Stanley Howard Warren and Mabel Harriett (*née* Ham); *m* 1950, Sheila Glo May (*née* Rowe); two *s* one *d*. *Educ:* King's Coll., Univ. of London (BSc 1st Cl. Hons Engrg); RNC, Greenwich (1st Cl. Naval Architecture). FRINA 1967; FIMechE 1970. Sub-Lieut, RN, 1945–47; Constructor Lieut, RCNC, 1947–51; Royal Yacht Britannia design, 1951–54; frigate modernisations, 1954–57; Constructor, HM Dockyard, Malta, 1957–60; Admiralty Constructor Overseer, John Brown and Yarrow, 1960–64; Polaris Submarine design, 1964–67; Chief Constructor and Principal Naval Overseer, Birkenhead, 1967–72; Asst Dir and Invincible Class Proj. Manager, 1972–76; Dep. Dir of Submarines (Polaris), MoD (PE), 1976–79. *Publications:* contribs to learned societies. *Recreations:* golf, motoring, gardening.

WARREN EVANS, (John) Roger, FCIOB; Managing Director, First Lexikon Ltd, since 1994; Property Director, Estates & Agency Holdings plc, since 1995; *b* 11 Dec. 1935; *s* of Thomas and Mary Warren Evans; *m* 1966, Elizabeth M. James; one *s* one *d*. *Educ:* Leighton Park Sch., Reading; Trinity Coll., Cambridge (BA History, 1st Cl.); London Sch. of Economics. Called to Bar, Gray's Inn, 1962. Television Interviewer, Anglia Television, 1960–61; Research Officer, Centre for Urban Studies, London, 1961; practice at Bar, 1962–69; Legal Correspondent, New Society, 1964–68; general management functions with Bovis Gp, in construction and develt, 1969–74, incl. Man. Dir, Bovis Homes Southern Ltd, 1971–74; Under-Secretary, DoE, 1975; Industrial Advr on Construction, DoE, 1975–76; Man. Dir, Barratt Develts (London), Ltd, 1977–79; Dir, Swansea Centre for Trade and Industry, 1979–85; Man. Dir, Demos Ltd, 1985–87; SavaCentre Property Develt Manager, 1987–88; Regl Property Dir, J. Sainsbury plc, 1988–94. Member: Welsh Consumer Council, 1992–95; Cttee, Community Selfbuild Agency, 1995–. Mem. Bd, Assoc. of Self Employed, 1995–. Gov., Gillespie Primary Sch., Islington, 1993–. Trustee, Inst. of Community Studies, 1975–. London Borough Councillor (Hackney), 1971–73. FCIOB 1976. *Recreations:* tennis, talking, playing the guitar. *Address:* 23 St Peter's Road, Newton, Swansea SA3 4SB. *T:* Swansea (01792) 368003.

WARRENDER, family name of **Baron Bruntisfield.**

WARRENDER, Hon. Robin Hugh; Non-executive Director, Bain Hogg Ltd; *b* 24 Dec. 1927; 3rd *s* of 1st Baron Bruntisfield, MC; *m* 1951, Gillian, *d* of Leonard Rossiter; one *s* two *d*. *Educ:* Eton; Trinity Coll., Oxford. Underwriting Member of Lloyd's, 1953; Tudor & Co. (Insurance) Ltd, 1958–62; Managing Director, Fenchurch Insurance Holdings Ltd, 1963–69; Dep. Chm., A. W. Bain & Sons Ltd, 1970; Chairman: Bain Dawes PLC and other group companies, 1973–85; London Wall Hldgs Ltd, 1986–94. Director: Comindus S. A. (France), 1980–; Worms & Co., 1981–; Varity Corporation (Canada), 1982–; Varity Holdings Ltd, 1982–; Heritable Group Holdings Ltd, 1983–; Société Centrale Préservatrice Foncière Assurances, 1986–89; Gp Athena, 1989–93. Mem. Council and Cttee of Lloyd's, 1983–86. Mem. Council, Bath Univ., 1979–; Hon. Treas., Governing Cttee, Royal Choral Soc., 1979–. *Recreations:* shooting, gardening, bridge. *Address:* Capps Lodge House, Fulbrook, Burford, Oxon OX18 4DB. *T:* Burford (01993) 822262. *Club:* White's.
See also Baron Colgrain.

WARRINGTON, Bishop Suffragan of, since 1976; **Rt. Rev. Michael Henshall;** *b* 29 Feb. 1928; *m* Ann Elizabeth (*née* Stephenson); two *s* one *d*. *Educ:* Manchester Grammar Sch.; St Chad's Coll., Durham (BA 1954, DipTh 1956). Deacon 1956, priest 1957, dio. York; Curate of Holy Trinity, Bridlington and of Sewerby, 1956–59; Priest-in-charge, All Saints, Conventional District of Micklehurst, 1959–62; Vicar, 1962–63; Vicar of Altrincham, 1963–75; Proctor in Convocation, 1964–75; Mem., Terms of Ministry Cttee, General Synod, 1970–75; Hon. Canon of Chester, 1972–75; Secretary, Chester Diocesan Advisory Board for Ministry, 1968–75; Canon Emeritus of Chester Cathedral, 1979. Chairman: Northern Ordination Course Council, 1985–; Churches Gp NW, Industry Year, 1985–. Editor for 12 years of local newspaper, Spearhead. *Recreations:* military history, old battlefields, etc. *Address:* Martinsfield, Elm Avenue, Great Crosby, Liverpool, Merseyside L23 2SX. *T:* 0151–924 7004; (office) 0151–709 9722.

WARRINGTON, Archdeacon of; *see* Woodhouse, Ven. C. D. S.

WARRINGTON, Prof. Elizabeth Kerr, FRS 1986; Professor of Clinical Neuropsychology, National Hospital for Neurology and Neurosurgery, since 1982; *d* of late Prof. John Alfred Valentine Butler, FRS and Margaret Lois Butler; one *d*. *Educ:* University College London (BSc 1954; PhD 1960; DSc 1975; Fellow 1994). Research Fellow, Inst. of Neurology, 1956; National Hospital: Senior Clinical Psychologist, 1960; Principal Psychologist, 1962; Top Grade Clinical Psychologist, 1972–82. *Publications:* (with R. A. McCarthy) Cognitive Neuropsychology, 1990; numerous papers in neurological and psychological jls. *Recreations:* gardening, entertaining grandchildren. *Address:* National Hospital for Neurology and Neurosurgery, Queen Square, WC1N 3BG. *T:* 0171–837 3611.

WARTNABY, Dr John; Keeper, Department of Earth and Space Sciences, Science Museum, South Kensington, 1969–82; *b* 6 Jan. 1926; *o s* of Ernest John and Beatrice Hilda Wartnaby; *m* 1962, Kathleen Mary Barber, MD, MRCP, DPM; one *s* one *d*. *Educ:* Chiswick Grammar Sch.; Chelsea Coll. (BSc 1946); Imperial Coll. of Science and Technology (DIC 1950); University Coll., London (MSc 1967; PhD 1972). FInstP 1971. Asst Keeper, Dept of Astronomy and Geophysics, Science Museum, 1951; Deputy Keeper, 1960. *Publications:* Seismology, 1957; The International Geophysical Year, 1957; Surveying, 1968; papers in learned jls. *Recreations:* country walking, Zen. *Address:* 11 Greenhurst Lane, Oxted, Surrey RH8 0LD. *T:* Oxted (01883) 714461.

WARWICK; *see* Turner-Warwick.

WARWICK, 8th Earl of, *cr* 1759; **David Robin Francis Guy Greville;** Baron Brooke 1621; Earl Brooke 1746; *b* 15 May 1934; *s* of 7th Earl of Warwick, and Rose, *d* of late D. C. Bingham; *S* father, 1984; *m* 1956, Sarah Anne (marr. diss. 1967), *d* of late Alfred Chester Beatty and Mrs Pamela Neilson; one *s* one *d*. *Educ:* Eton. Life Guards, 1952; Warwicks Yeo. (TA), 1954. *Heir:* *s* Lord Brooke, *qv*. *Clubs:* White's; The Brook (NY); Eagle Ski (Gstaad).

WARWICK, Bishop Suffragan of, since 1990; **Rt. Rev. (George) Clive Handford;** *b* 17 April 1937; *s* of Cyril Percy Dawson Handford and Alice Ethel Handford; *m* 1962, Anne Elizabeth Jane Atherley; one *d*. *Educ:* Hatfield Coll., Durham (BA); Queen's Coll., Birmingham and Univ. of Birmingham (DipTh). Curate, Mansfield Parish Church, 1963–66; Chaplain: Baghdad, 1967; Beirut, 1967–73; Dean, St George's Cathedral, Jerusalem, 1974–78; Archdeacon in the Gulf and Chaplain in Abu Dhabi and Qatar, 1978–83; Vicar of Kneesall with Laxton, and Wellow and Rufford, 1983–84; RD of Tuxford and Norwell, 1983–84; Archdeacon of Nottingham, 1984–90. ChStJ 1976. *Address:* Warwick House, 139 Kenilworth Road, Coventry CV4 7AF. *T:* Coventry (01203) 416200.

WARWICK, Archdeacon of; *see* Paget-Wilkes, Ven. M. J. J.

WARWICK, Diana; Chief Executive, Committee of Vice Chancellors and Principals, since 1995; *b* 16 July 1945; *d* of Jack and Olive Warwick; *m* 1969. *Educ:* St Joseph's Coll., Bradford; Bedford Coll., Univ. of London (BA Hons). Technical Asst to the Gen. Sec., NUT, 1969–72; Asst Sec., CPSA, 1972–83; Gen. Sec., AUT, 1983–92; Chief Exec., Westminster Foundn for Democracy, 1992–95. Mem., Cttee on Standards in Public Life, 1994–. Member: Bd, British Council, 1985–; Employment Appeal Tribunal, 1987–; Exec. and Council, Industrial Soc., 1987–; TUC Gen. Council, 1989–92; Council, Duke of Edinburgh's Seventh Commonwealth Study Conf., 1991. Gov., Commonwealth Inst., 1988–. Trustee, Royal Anniversary Trust, 1991–93. FRSA 1984. Hon. DLitt Bradford, 1993. *Recreations:* reading, riding, looking at pictures. *Address:* Committee of Vice Chancellors and Principals, 29 Tavistock Square, WC1H 9EZ. *T:* 0171–387 9231.

WARWICK, Hannah Cambell Grant; *see* Gordon, H. C. G.

WARWICK, Judith Caroline Anne, (Mrs M. G. Warwick); *see* Hughes, J. C. A.

WARWICK, Captain William Eldon, CBE 1971; RD; RNR retired; Commodore, Cunard Line Ltd, 1970–75; First Master, RMS Queen Elizabeth 2, 1966–72; *b* 12 Nov. 1912; *e s* of Eldon Warwick, architect and Gertrude Florence Gent; *m* 1939, Evelyn King (*née* Williams); three *s*. *Educ:* Birkenhead Sch.; HMTS Conway. Joined Merchant Service, 1928, serving in Indian Ocean and Red Sea; awarded Master Mariner's Certificate, 1936; joined Cunard White Star as Jun. Officer (Lancastria), 1937; commissioned in RNR, 1937. Mobilized in RN War Service, 1939, in Coastal Forces and Corvettes in North Atlantic, Russian Convoys and Normandy Landings, 1939–46 (despatches, 1946). First cargo command, Alsatia, 1954; first passenger command, Carinthia, 1958; followed by command of almost all the passenger liners in Cunard fleet. Promoted Captain RNR, 1960; retd RNR, 1965. Treas., Internat. Fedn of Shipmasters' Assocs., 1973–92. Younger Brother of Trinity House; Liveryman, Hon. Co. of Master Mariners (Master, 1976–77); Freeman of City of London. *Recreations:* reading, music, walking. *Address:* 50 Algarth Road, Pocklington, York YO4 2HJ. *T:* Pocklington (01759) 306534. *Club:* Naval.

WASS, Sir Douglas (William Gretton), GCB 1980 (KCB 1975; CB 1971); Chairman: Axa Equity & Law (formerly Equity & Law) Life Assurance Society plc, since 1986 (Director, since 1984); Nomura International plc, since 1986; Permanent Secretary to HM Treasury, 1974–83, and Joint Head of the Home Civil Service, 1981–83; *b* 15 April 1923; *s* of late Arthur W. and late Elsie W. Wass; *m* 1954, Dr Milica Pavičić; one *s* one *d*. *Educ:* Nottingham High Sch.; St John's Coll., Cambridge (MA; Hon. Fellow, 1982). Served War, 1943–46: Scientific Research with Admiralty, at home and in Far East. Entered HM Treasury as Asst Principal, 1946; Principal, 1951; Commonwealth Fund Fellow in USA, 1958–59; Vis. Fellow, Brookings Instn, Washington, DC, 1959; Private Sec.: to Chancellor of the Exchequer, 1959–61; to Chief Sec. to Treasury, 1961–62; Asst Sec., 1962; Alternate Exec. Dir, Internat. Monetary Fund, and Financial Counsellor, British Embassy, Washington, DC, 1965–67; HM Treasury: Under-Sec., 1968; Dep. Sec., 1970–73; Second Permanent Sec., 1973–74. Chm., NCM (Credit Insce), 1991–95; Director: Barclays Bank, 1984–87; De La Rue Company plc, 1984–93; Equitable Cos Inc., 1992–; Equitable Life Assurance Soc., USA, 1992–93; NCM (NV), Amsterdam, 1992–95; Administrateur, Axa SA (formerly Cie du Midi), 1987–; Consultant to Coopers & Lybrand, 1984–86. Chairman: British Selection Cttee of Harkness Fellowships, 1981–84; UN Adv. Gp on Financial Flows for Africa, 1987–88; SIB Adv. Cttee on Pension Transfers, 1993–94; Syndicate on the Government of Univ. of Cambridge, 1988–89. Pres., Market Res. Soc., 1987–91. Dep. Chm., Council of Policy Studies Inst, 1981–85; Vice-Pres., 1984–91, and Mem. Adv. Bd, Constitutional Reform Centre; Vice Chm., Africa Capacity Building Foundn, 1991–; Governor, Ditchley Foundn, 1981–; Member, Council: Centre for Econ. Policy Res., 1983–90; Employment Inst., 1985–92; Univ. of Bath, 1985–91; British Heart Foundn, 1990–; ODI, 1991–. Lectures: Reith, BBC, 1983; Shell, St Andrews Univ., 1985; Harry Street Meml, Univ. of Manchester, 1987. Hon. DLitt Bath, 1985. *Publications:* Government and the Governed, 1984; articles in newspapers and jls. *Address:* 6 Dora Road, SW19 7HH. *T:* 0181–946 5556. *Club:* Reform.

WASSALL, Philip Hugh; Provincial Stipendiary Magistrate, Devonshire, since 1994; *b* 11 March 1950; *s* of Derek William Wassall and Avril Mary Holden Wassall; *m* 1991, Julia Lesley; one *d*. *Educ:* Aldridge Grammar Sch.; Chelmsford Coll. (LLB Hons ext. London). Criminal Law Clerk, 1969–75; Articled Clerk, 1976–78; Solicitor, 1979–94. *Recreations:* golf, fishing, winter sports, cooking, music, walking. *Address:* Plymouth Magistrates' Court, St Andrew Street, Plymouth PL1 2DP. *T:* Plymouth (01752) 220471.

WASSERMAN, Gordon Joshua; Assistant Under Secretary of State, Home Office, since 1983; *b* Montreal, 26 July 1938; *s* of late John J. Wasserman, QC, and Prof. Rachel Chait Wasserman, Montreal; *m* 1964, Cressida Frances, *yr d* of late Rt Hon. Hugh Gaitskell, PC, CBE, MP, and Baroness Gaitskell; two *d*. *Educ:* Westmount High Sch., Montreal; McGill Univ. (BA); New Coll., Oxford (MA). Rhodes Scholar (Quebec and New Coll.), 1959; Sen. Research Scholar, St Antony's Coll., Oxford, 1961–64; Lectr in Economics, Merton Coll., Oxford, 1963–64; Research Fellow, New Coll., Oxford, 1964–67; joined Home Office as Economic Adviser, 1967, Sen. Econ. Adviser, 1972, Asst Sec., 1977–81; Head, Urban Deprivation Unit, 1973–77; Civil Service Travelling Fellowship in USA, 1977–78; Under Sec., Central Policy Review Staff, Cabinet Office, 1981–83. Vice-Pres., English Basket Ball Assoc., 1983–86. *Recreations:* gardening, walking, theatre, music. *Address:* c/o Home Office, SW1V 1PU. *Clubs:* Reform, Beefsteak.

WASTELL, Cyril Gordon, CBE 1975; Secretary General of Lloyd's, 1967–76, retired; *b* 10 Jan. 1916; *s* of Arthur Edward Wastell and Lilian Wastell; *m* 1947, Margaret Lilian (*née* Moore); one *d*. *Educ:* Brentwood Sch., Essex. Joined Staff of Corporation of Lloyd's, 1932; apart from war service (Lieut Royal Corps of Signals), 1939–46, progressed through various depts and positions at Lloyd's, until retirement. *Recreations:* reading, gardening under duress, golf, various trivial pursuits. *Address:* Candys, Burgmann's Hill, Lympstone, Devon EX8 5HP.

WASTIE, Winston Victor, CB 1962; OBE 1946 (MBE 1937); Under-Secretary, Ministry of Public Building and Works, Scotland, 1959–62, retired; *b* 5 March 1900; *s* of H. Wastie; *m* 1924, Charmbury Billows (*d* 1986); one *d*. *Educ:* Greenwich Secondary Sch. Civil Service, New Scotland Yard, 1915–42; Chief Licensing Officer, Civil Building Control, Ministry of Works, 1942–46; Assistant Secretary, Scottish HQ, Ministry of Works, 1946–59; Under-Secretary, 1959. *Recreations:* bridge, gardening and sport. *Address:* North Hill, 9 Clifford Avenue, Ilkley, West Yorks LS29 0AS.

WATERFIELD, Giles Adrian, FSA; Director, Dulwich Picture Gallery, since 1979; *b* 24 July 1949; *s* of late Anthony and Honor Waterfield. *Educ:* Eton College; Magdalen College, Oxford (BA); Courtauld Institute (MA). FSA 1991. Education Officer, Royal Pavilion, Art Gallery and Museums, Brighton, 1976–79. Jt Dir, Attingham Summer Sch., 1994–. *Publications:* Faces, 1983; Collection for a King (catalogue), 1985; Soane and After, 1987; Rich Summer of Art, 1988; Palaces of Art, 1991; Art for the People, 1994; articles in Apollo, Connoisseur, Country Life, TLS, Turner Studies. *Recreation:* sightseeing. *Address:* c/o Dulwich Picture Gallery, College Road, SE21 7AD. *Club:* Travellers'.

WATERFIELD, John Percival; *b* Dublin, 5 Oct. 1921; *er s* of late Sir Percival Waterfield, KBE, CB; *m* 1st, 1950, Margaret Lee Thomas (*d* 1990); two *s* one *d*; 2nd, 1991, Tilla Hevesi Vahanian. *Educ:* Dragon Sch.; Charterhouse (schol.); Christ Church, Oxford (schol.). Served War of 1939–45: 1st Bn, The King's Royal Rifle Corps (60th Rifles), Western Desert, Tunisia, Italy and Austria (despatches). Entered HM Foreign (subseq. Diplomatic) Service, 1946; Third Secretary, Moscow, 1947; Second Secretary, Tokyo, 1950; Foreign Office, 1952; First Secretary, Santiago, Chile, 1954; HM Consul (Commercial), New York, 1957; FO, 1960; Ambassador to Mali Republic, 1964–65, concurrently to Guinea, 1965; duties connected with NATO, 1966; Counsellor and Head of Chancery, New Delhi, 1966–68; Head of Western Organizations Dept, FCO, 1969; Man. Dir, BEAMA, 1971; Principal Estabs and Finance Officer, NI Office, 1973–79; on secondment to Internat. Military Services Ltd, 1979–80; retired from public service, 1980; company dir and consultant, 1980–84. *Address:* 5 North Street, Somerton, Somerset TA11 7NY. *T:* Somerton (01458) 72389.

WATERFIELD, Prof. Michael Derek, PhD; FRCPath; FRS 1991; Director of Research, Ludwig Institute for Cancer Research, since 1986 and Courtauld Professor of Biochemistry and Head of Department of Biochemistry and Molecular Biology, since 1991, University College London; *b* 14 May 1941; *s* of Leslie N. Waterfield and Kathleen A. (*née* Marshall); *m* 1982, Sally E. James, MB BS, PhD; two *d*. *Educ:* Brunel Univ. (BSc 1963); Univ. of London (PhD 1967). FRCPath 1994. Res. Fellow, Harvard Univ. Med. Sch., 1967–70; Sen. Res. Fellow, CIT, 1970–72; Hd, Protein Chem. Lab., ICRF Labs, 1972–86. Hon. MD Ferrara, Italy, 1991. *Publications:* numerous articles in scientific jls on biochem. and molecular biol. as applied to cancer research. *Recreation:* gardening. *Address:* Chantemerle, Speen Lane, Newbury, Berks RG13 1RN.

WATERFORD, 8th Marquess of, *cr* 1789; **John Hubert de la Poer Beresford;** Baron Le Poer, 1375; Baronet, 1668; Viscount Tyrone, Baron Beresford, 1720; Earl of Tyrone, 1746; Baron Tyrone (Great Britain), 1786; *b* 14 July 1933; *er s* of 7th Marquess and Juliet Mary (who *m* 2nd, 1946, Lieut-Colonel John Silcock), 2nd *d* of late David Lindsay; *S* father, 1934; *m* 1957, Lady Caroline Wyndham-Quin, *yr d* of 6th Earl of Dunraven and Mount-Earl, CB, CBE, MC; three *s* one *d*. *Educ:* Eton. Lieut, RHG Reserve. *Heir: s* Earl of Tyrone, *qv*. *Address:* Curraghmore, Portlaw, Co. Waterford. *T:* Waterford (51) 387102, *Fax:* Waterford (51) 387481. *Club:* White's.

WATERHOUSE, David Martin; Regional Director for South Asia and Pacific, British Council, since 1994; *b* 23 July 1937; *s* of Rev. John W. Waterhouse and Dr Esther Waterhouse; *m* 1966, Verena Johnson; one *s* two *d*. *Educ:* Kingswood Sch., Bath; Merton Coll., Oxford (MA). Joined British Council, 1961; Enugu, Nigeria, 1962–65; Glasgow, 1965–68; Ndola, Zambia, 1968–71; Inst. of Educn, London Univ., 1971–72; Representative: Nepal, 1972–77; Thailand, 1977–80; Dir, Personnel Management Dept, 1980–85; Rep., Nigeria, 1985–89; Controller, Home Div., subseq. Dir, Exchanges and Training Div., British Council, 1989–91; Dir, Germany, 1991–93. *Recreations:* walking, music. *Address:* c/o The British Council, 10 Spring Gardens, SW1A 2BN. *T:* 0171–930 8466.

WATERHOUSE, Dr Douglas Frew, AO 1980; CMG 1970; FRS 1967; FAA 1954; FRACI 1948; Chief of Division of Entomology, Commonwealth Scientific and Industrial Research Organization, 1960–81, Honorary Research Fellow, since 1981; *b* 3 June 1916; *s* of late Prof. E. G. Waterhouse, CMG, OBE, and Janet Frew Kellie, MA; *m* 1944, Allison D., *d* of J. H. Calthorpe; three *s* one *d*. *Educ:* Sydney C of E Grammar Sch.; Universities of Sydney and Cambridge. BSc Hons, University Medal, MSc, DSc, Sydney. Served War of 1939–45, Captain, AAMC Medical Entomology. Joined Research Staff, CSIRO, 1938; Asst Chief, Div. of Entomology, 1953–60. Biological Secretary, Australian Acad. of Science, 1961–66; Chairman: Council, Canberra Coll. of Advanced Educn, 1969–84; Council for Internat. Congresses of Entomology, 1980–84 (Hon. mem., 1984); Nat. Sci. Summer Sch., Aust. Industry Develt Corp., 1985–88; Pres., ACT Br., Nat. Trust of Australia, 1984–88. Corresp. Mem., Brazilian Acad. of Sciences, 1974. Hon. For. Mem., All-Union Entomological Soc. of USSR, 1979; For. Mem., Russian (formerly USSR) Acad. of Science, 1982; Foreign Assoc., US Nat. Acad. of Scis, 1983. Hon. FRES 1972. Hon. DSc ANU, 1978. David Syme Research Prize, 1953; Mueller Medal, ANZAAS, 1972; Farrer Medal, Farrer Meml Trust, 1973; Medal, 10th Internat. Congress of Plant Protection, 1983; Principal Bicentennial Contrib. to Agriculture Award, 1988. *Publications:* (jtly) Butterflies of Australia, 1972, rev. edn 1981; (jtly) Biological Control: Pacific prospects, 1987; Supplement 1 (jtly), 1989, Suppl. 2, 1993; Major Pests and Weeds of Southeast Asia, 1993; Biological Control of Weeds: Southeast Asian prospects, 1994; numerous articles on insect physiology, biochemistry, ecology and biological control of insects. *Recreations:* gardening, fishing, gyotaku. *Address:* 60 National Circuit, Deakin, ACT 2600, Australia. *T:* (6) 2731772. *Club:* Commonwealth (Canberra).

WATERHOUSE, Frederick Harry; Freshwater House Antiques, since 1994; *b* 3 June 1932; *m* 1954, Olive Carter; two *d*. *Educ:* King Edward's, Aston, Birmingham; London Univ. (BScEcon). Associate Mem. Inst. of Cost and Management Accountants. Chief Accountant, Copper Div., Imperial Metal Industries, 1967–70; Asst Chief Accountant, Agricl Div., ICI, 1970–72; Chief Accountant, Plant Protection Div., ICI, 1972–78; Dir, Société pour la Protection d'Agriculture (SOPRA), France, 1976–78; Dir, Solplant SA, Italy, 1976–78; Bd Member, Finance and Corporate Planning, The Post Office, 1978–79; Treasurer's Dept, ICI Ltd, Millbank, 1979–82. Partner, Bognor Antiques, 1984–87; Chief Accountant, Jelkeep Ltd, Deerhyde Ltd and Thawscroft Ltd, Selsey, 1988–94. *Recreations:* golf, gardening, sailing. *Address:* Little Halt, Pound Green, Freshwater, Isle of Wight PO40 9HQ.

WATERHOUSE, Keith Spencer, CBE 1991; FRSL; writer; *b* 6 Feb. 1929; 4th *s* of Ernest and Elsie Edith Waterhouse; *m* 1984, Stella Bingham (marr. diss. 1989); one *s* two *d* by previous *m*. *Educ:* Leeds. Journalist in Leeds and London, 1950–; Columnist with: Daily Mirror, 1970–86; Daily Mail, 1986–; Contributor to various periodicals; Mem. Punch Table, 1979. Mem., Kingman Cttee on Teaching of English Language, 1987–88. Hon. Fellow, Leeds Metropolitan Univ. (formerly Poly.), 1991. Granada Columnist of the Year Award, 1970; IPC Descriptive Writer of the Year Award, 1970; IPC Columnist of the Year Award, 1973; British Press Awards Columnist of the Year, 1978, 1991; Granada Special Quarter Century Award, 1982. Films (with Willis Hall) include: Billy Liar; Whistle Down the Wind; A Kind of Loving; Lock Up Your Daughters. Plays: Mr and Mrs Nobody, 1986; Jeffrey Bernard is Unwell, 1989 (Evening Standard Best Comedy Award, 1990); Bookends, 1990; Our Song, 1992; plays with Willis Hall include: Billy Liar, 1960 (from which musical Billy was adapted, 1974); Celebration, 1961; All Things Bright and Beautiful, 1963; Say Who You Are, 1965; Whoops-a-Daisy, 1968; Children's Day, 1969; Who's Who, 1972; The Card (musical), 1973; Saturday, Sunday, Monday (adaptation from de Filippo), 1973; Filumena (adaptation from de Filippo), 1977; Worzel Gummidge, 1981; Budgie (musical), 1988. TV series: Budgie, Queenie's Castle, The Upper Crusts, Billy Liar, The Upchat Line, The Upchat Connection, Worzel Gummidge, West End Tales, The Happy Apple, Charters and Caldicott, Andy Capp; TV films: Charlie Muffin, 1983; This Office Life, 1985; The Great Paper Chase, 1988. *Publications: novels:* There is a Happy Land, 1957; Billy Liar, 1959; Jubb, 1963; The Bucket Shop, 1968; Billy Liar on the Moon, 1975; Office Life, 1978; Maggie Muggins, 1981; In the Mood, 1983; Thinks, 1984; Our Song, 1988; Bimbo, 1990; Unsweet Charity, 1992; *plays:* Jeffrey Bernard Is Unwell and other plays, 1991; (with Willis Hall) include: Billy Liar, 1960; Celebration, 1961; All Things Bright and Beautiful, 1963; Say Who You Are, 1965; Who's Who, 1974; Saturday, Sunday, Monday (adaptation from de Filippo), 1974; Filumena (adaptation from de Filippo), 1977; *general:* (with Guy Deghy) Café Royal, 1956; (ed) Writers' Theatre, 1967; The Passing of The Third-floor Buck, 1974; Mondays, Thursdays, 1976; Rhubarb, Rhubarb, 1979; Daily Mirror Style, 1980, rev. and expanded edn, Newspaper Style, 1989; Fanny Peculiar, 1983; Mrs Pooter's Diary, 1983; Waterhouse At Large, 1985; Collected Letters of a Nobody, 1986; The Theory and Practice of Lunch, 1986; The Theory and Practice of Travel, 1989; English Our English, 1991; Sharon & Tracy & The Rest, 1992; City Lights, 1994. *Recreation:* lunch. *Address:* 29 Kenway Road, SW5 0RP. *Club:* Garrick.

WATERHOUSE, Dame Rachel (Elizabeth), DBE 1990 (CBE 1980); PhD; Chairman, Consumers' Association, 1982–90 (Member Council, since 1966, Deputy Chairman, 1979–82); *b* 2 Jan. 1923; *d* of Percival John Franklin and Ruby Susanna Franklin; *m* 1947, John A. H. Waterhouse; two *s* two *d*. *Educ:* King Edward's High Sch., Birmingham; St Hugh's Coll., Oxford (BA 1944, MA 1948); Univ. of Birmingham (PhD 1950). WEA and Extra-mural tutor, 1944–47. Birmingham Consumer Group: Sec., 1964–65, Chm. 1966–68, Mem. Cttee, 1968–; Member: Nat. Consumer Council, 1975–86; Consumers' Consultative Cttee of EEC Commn, 1977–84; Price Commn, 1977–79; Council, Advertising Standards Authority, 1980–85; NEDC, 1981–91; BBC Consultative Gp on Industrial and Business Affairs, 1984–89; Richmond Cttee on Microbiol Safety of Food, 1989–90; HSC, 1990–95; Adv. Cttee on Microbiological Safety of Food, 1991–95. Ministerial nominee to Potato Marketing Bd, 1969–81; Chm., Council for Licensed Conveyancers, 1986–89; Member: Home Office Working Party on Internal Shop Security, 1971–73; Adv. Cttee on Asbestos, 1976–79; Council for the Securities Industry, 1983–85; Securities and Investments Board, 1985–92; Organising Cttee, Marketing of Investments Bd, 1985–86; Council, Office of the Banking Ombudsman, 1985–95; Duke of Edinburgh's Inquiry into British Housing, 1984–85; Adv. Bd, Inst. of Food Res., 1988–93. Pres., Inst. of Consumer Ergonomics, Univ. of Loughborough, 1980– (Chm., 1970–80); Vice-Pres., Nat. Fedn of Consumer Gps, 1980–; Member: Council, Birmingham and Midland Inst., 1993 (Pres., 1992); Court of Govs, Univ. of Birmingham, 1992–. Chairman: Birmingham Gp, Victorian Soc., 1966–67, 1972–74; Lunar Soc., 1990–. Trustee, Joseph Rowntree Foundn, 1990–. Hon. FGIA (Hon. CGIA 1988). Hon. DLitt Univ. of Technology, Loughborough, 1978; Hon. DSocSc Birmingham, 1990. *Publications:* The Birmingham and Midland Institute 1854–1954, 1954; A Hundred Years of Engineering Craftsmanship, 1957; Children in Hospital: a hundred years of child care in Birmingham, 1962; (with John Whybrow) How Birmingham became a Great City, 1976; King Edward VI High School for Girls 1883–1983, 1983. *Address:* 252 Bristol Road, Birmingham B5 7SL. *T:* 0121–472 0427.

WATERHOUSE, Roger William; Vice-Chancellor, University of Derby, since 1992; *b* 29 April 1940; *s* of Ronald Waterhouse and Dorthy May Waterhouse (*née* Holmes); *m* 1st, 1962, Mania Jevinsky (marr. diss.); one *s* two *d*; 2nd, 1979, Jacqueline Mary Dymond; one *s* one *d*. *Educ:* Corpus Christi Coll., Oxford (BA, MA Phil. & Psychol.). Lectr, Shoreditch Coll., 1961–62; Teacher, Kibbutz Ma'abarot, Israel, 1962–64; Hd of Econs, Myers Grove Comprehensive Sch., Sheffield, 1966–68; Asst Lectr, Lectr, Sen. Lectr and Principal Lectr, Hendon Coll. of Technol., 1968–73; Hd, Dept of Humanities and Dean of Humanities, Middx Poly., 1973–86; Dep. Dir (Acad. Planning), Wolverhampton Poly., 1986–89; Dir, Derbys Coll. of Higher Educn, 1989–92. Chm., Derbyshire Careers Service Ltd, 1995–. FRSA 1993. *Publications:* A Heidegger Critique, 1981; jl articles on modern European philosophy, higher educn, credit accumulation and transfer. *Recreation:* wood-turning. *Address:* University of Derby, Kedleston Road, Derby DE22 1GB. *T:* Derby (01332) 622200.

WATERHOUSE, Hon. Sir Ronald (Gough), Kt 1978; **Hon. Mr Justice Waterhouse;** Judge of the High Court of Justice, Family Division, 1978–88, Queen's Bench Division, since 1988; *b* Holywell, Flintshire, 8 May 1926; *s* of late Thomas Waterhouse, CBE, and Doris Helena Waterhouse (*née* Gough); *m* 1960, Sarah Selina, *d* of late Captain E. A. Ingram and Diana Mary Ingram (*née* Leigh-Bennett); one *s* two *d*. *Educ:* Holywell Grammar Sch.; St John's Coll., Cambridge. RAFVR, 1944–48. McMahon Schol., St John's Coll., 1949; Pres., Cambridge Union Soc., 1950; MA, LLM; called to Bar, Middle Temple, 1952 (Harmsworth Schol.), Bencher, 1977, Treas., 1985; Wales and Chester Circuit, Leader, 1978; QC 1969; a Recorder of the Crown Court, 1972–77; Presiding Judge, Wales and Chester Circuit, 1980–84; a Judge, Employment Appeal Tribunal, 1979–87. Mem. Bar Council, 1961–65. Deputy Chairman: Cheshire QS, 1964–71; Flintshire QS, 1966–71. Contested (Lab) West Flintshire, 1959. Chairman: Inter-departmental Cttee of Inquiry on Rabies, 1970; Cttees of Investigation for GB and England and Wales, under Agricultural Mkting Act, 1971–78; Local Govt Boundary Commn for Wales, 1974–78. Pres., CAB, Royal Courts of Justice, 1992– (Chm., 1981–92). A Vice-Pres., Zoological Soc. of London, 1981–84 and 1992–93 (Mem. Council, 1972–89, 1991–93). President: Llangollen Internat. Musical Eisteddfod, 1994–; St John's Wood Soc., 1994–. Hon. LLD Wales, 1986. *Recreations:* music, golf. *Address:* Royal Courts of Justice, Strand, WC2A 2LL. *Clubs:* Garrick, Pilgrims, MCC; Cardiff and County (Cardiff).

See also J. B. Thompson.

WATERLOW, Anthony John; Chairman and Managing Director, Kodak, since 1992; *b* 14 July 1938; *s* of George Joseph Waterlow and Sylvia Netta Waterlow; *m* 1st, 1962, Sheila; three *s*; 2nd, 1992, Ann. *Educ:* Harrow County Grammar Sch.; Ealing College; Chartered Inst. of Management Accountants. Joined Kodak as accountant trainee, 1954. *Recreation:* bridge. *Address:* Kodak Ltd, Kodak House, Hemel Hempstead, Herts HP1 1JU. *T:* Hemel Hempstead (01442) 61122.

WATERLOW, Sir Christopher Rupert, 5th Bt *cr* 1873; musician; *b* 12 Aug. 1959; *s* of (Peter) Rupert Waterlow (*d* 1969) and Jill Elizabeth (*d* 1961), *e d* of E. T. Gourlay; *S* grandfather 1973; *m* 1986, Sally-Ann, *o d* of Maurice and Betty Bitten. *Educ:* Stonyhurst Coll., Lancs. *Recreations:* pistol shooting, squash, listening to music, supporting Wasps RFC. *Heir: cousin* Nicholas Anthony Waterlow [*b* 30 Aug. 1941; *m* 1965, Rosemary, *o d* of W. J. O'Brien; two *s* one *d*]. *Address:* 26 Barfield Road, Bickley, Kent BR1 2HS. *Clubs:* Stonyhurst Association; Wasps Rugby Football.

WATERLOW, Sir (James) Gerard, 4th Bt *cr* 1930; management consultant; *b* 3 Sept. 1939; *s* of Sir Thomas Gordon Waterlow, 3rd Bt, CBE and Helen Elizabeth (*d* 1970), *yr d* of Gerard A. H. Robinson; *S* father, 1982; *m* 1965, Diana Suzanne, *yr d* of Sir Thomas Skyrme, *qv*; one *s* one *d*. *Educ:* Marlborough; Trinity College, Cambridge. *Recreations:* tennis, bridge. *Heir: s* (Thomas) James Waterlow, *b* 20 March 1970. *Address:* River House, Remenham, Henley-on-Thames RG9 3DD. *T:* Henley-on-Thames (01491) 576306. *Club:* Lansdowne.

WATERLOW, Prof. John Conrad, CMG 1970; MD, ScD; FRCP; FRS 1982; FRGS; Professor of Human Nutrition, London School of Hygiene and Tropical Medicine, 1970–82, now Emeritus; *b* 13 June 1916; *o s* of Sir Sydney Waterlow, KCMG, CBE, HM Diplomatic Service; *m* 1939, Angela Pauline Cecil Gray; two *s* one *d*. *Educ:* Eton Coll.;

Trinity Coll., Cambridge (MD, ScD); London Hosp. Med. College. Mem., Scientific Staff, MRC, 1942; Dir, MRC Tropical Metabolism Research Unit, Univ. of the West Indies, 1954–70. For. Associate Mem., Nat. Acad. of Scis, USA, 1992. *Publications:* numerous papers on protein malnutrition and protein metabolism. *Recreation:* mountain walking. *Address:* 15 Hillgate Street, W8 7SP; Oare, Marlborough, Wilts SN8 4JA. *Club:* Savile.

WATERMAN, Fanny, OBE 1971; FRCM; Chairman, Leeds International Pianoforte Competition, since 1963 (in association with Harveys of Bristol, since 1985), also Chairman of Jury, since 1981; *b* 22 March 1920; *d* of Myer Waterman and Mary Waterman (*née* Behrmann); *m* 1944, Dr Geoffrey de Keyser; two *s*. *Educ:* Allerton High Sch., Leeds; Tobias Matthay, Cyril Smith, Royal College of Music, London (FRCM 1972). Concert pianist, teacher of international reputation. Vice-President: European Piano-Teachers Assoc., 1975–; World Fedn of Internat. Music Competitions, 1992–; Trustee, Edward Boyle Meml Trust, 1981–. Governor, Harrogate Fest., 1983. Founded (with Marion Harewood) Leeds International Pianoforte Competition, 1961. Member of International Juries: Beethoven, Vienna, 1977, 1993; Casagrande, Terni, 1978; Munich, 1979, 1986; Bach, Leipzig, 1980, 1984, 1988; Calgary, 1982; Gina Bachauer, Salt Lake City, 1982, 1984; Viña del Mar (Chm.), 1982, 1987, 1992; Maryland, 1983; Cologne, 1983, 1986, 1989; Pretoria, 1984, 1992; Santander, 1984; Rubinstein, Israel (Vice-Pres.), 1986, 1989; Tchaikowsky, Moscow, 1986; Vladigerov, Bulgaria, 1986; Lisbon, 1987, 1991; Canadian Broadcasting Corp., Toronto, 1989; first Internat. Pianoforte Competitions, China and Korea. Piano Progress series on ITV Channel 4. Hon. MA 1966, Hon. DMus 1992, Leeds; DUniv York, 1995. *Publications:* (with Marion Harewood): series of Piano Tutors, 1967–: 1st Year Piano lessons: 1st Year Repertoire; 2nd Year Piano lessons: 2nd Year Repertoire; 3rd Year Piano lessons: 3rd Year Repertoire; Duets and Piano Playtime, 1978; Recital Book for pianists, Book 1, 1981; Sonatina and Sonata Book, 1982; Four Study Books for Piano (Playtime Studies and Progress Studies), 1986; (with Paul de Keyser) Young Violinists Repertoire books, 1–4; Fanny Waterman on Piano Playing and Performing, 1983; Music Lovers Diary, 1984–86; Merry Christmas Carols, 1986; Christmas Carol Time, 1986; Nursery Rhyme Time, 1987; Piano for Pleasure, Bks 1 and 2, 1988; Me and my Piano, 1988, Book 2, 1989; Animal Magic, 1989; Monkey Puzzles, Books 1 and 2, 1990; (with Wendy Thompson) Piano Competition: the story of the Leeds, 1990; Me and my Piano: repertoire and duets, Bks 1 and 2, 1992; Young Pianist's Dictionary, 1992. *Recreations:* travel, reading, voluntary work, cooking. *Address:* Woodgarth, Oakwood Grove, Leeds LS8 2PA. *T:* Leeds (0113) 265 5771.

WATERPARK, 7th Baron *cr* 1792; **Frederick Caryll Philip Cavendish,** Bt 1755; Managing Director, CSE International Ltd, since 1985; Director, Airborn Group plc, since 1990; *b* 6 Oct. 1926; *s* of Brig.-General Frederick William Laurence Sheppard Hart Cavendish, CMG, DSO (*d* 1931) and Enid, Countess of Kenmare (she *m* 3rd, 1933, as his 3rd wife, 1st Viscount Furness, who *d* 1940; 4th, as his 2nd wife, 6th Earl of Kenmare), *d* of Charles Lindeman, Sydney, New South Wales, and *widow* of Roderick Cameron, New York; *S* uncle 1948; *m* 1951, Daniele, *e d* of Roger Guirche, Paris; one *s* two *d*. *Educ:* Eton. Lieut, 4th and 1st Bn Grenadier Guards, 1944–46. Served as Assistant District Commandant Kenya Police Reserve, 1952–55, during Mau Mau Rebellion. Man. Dir, Spartan Air Services, 1955–60; Dep. Chm., 1984–90, Chief Exec., 1990, CSE Aviation Ltd; Dir, Handley Page Ltd, 1968–70. *Heir:* *s* Hon. Roderick Alexander Cavendish [*b* 10 Oct. 1959; *m* 1989, Anne, *d* of Hon. Luke Asquith; one *s*]. *Address:* (home) 74 Elm Park Road, SW3. *Club:* Cavalry and Guards.

WATERS, Gen. Sir (Charles) John, GCB 1995 (KCB 1988); CBE 1981 (OBE 1977); Deputy Supreme Allied Commander, Europe, 1993–94; Aide-de-Camp General to The Queen, 1992–95; *b* 2 Sept. 1935; *s* of Patrick George Waters and Margaret Ronaldson Waters (*née* Clark); *m* 1962, Hilary Doyle Nettleton; three *s*. *Educ:* Oundle; Royal Military Academy, Sandhurst. Commissioned, The Gloucestershire Regt, 1955; GSO2, MO1 (MoD), 1970–72; Instructor, GSO1 (DS), Staff Coll., Camberley, 1973–74; Commanding Officer, 1st Bn, Gloucestershire Regt, 1975–77; Colonel General Staff, 1st Armoured Div., 1977–79; Comdr 3 Infantry Bde, 1979–81; RCDS 1982; Dep. Comdr, Land Forces, Falkland Islands, May–July 1982; Comdr 4th Armoured Div., 1983–85; Comdt, Staff Coll., Camberley, 1986–88; GOC and Dir of Ops, NI, 1988–90; C-in-C, UKLF, 1990–93. Col, The Gloucestershire Regt, 1985–91; Col Comdt, POW Div., 1988–91; Hon. Colonel: Royal Wessex Yeomanry, 1991–; Royal Devonshire Yeomanry, 1991–. Mem. Adv. Council, Victory Meml Mus., Arlon, Belgium; Mem. Council, Cheltenham Coll. Admiral: Army Sailing Assoc., 1990–93; Infantry Sailing Assoc. Kermit Roosevelt Lectr, USA, 1992. FRSA 1993. *Recreations:* sailing, skiing, painting. *Address:* c/o Lloyds Bank, Colyton, Devon EX13 6DY. *Clubs:* Army and Navy; British Keil Yacht, Axe Yacht.

WATERS, David Ebsworth Benjamin; Senior Treasury Counsel at Central Criminal Court, since 1994; a Recorder, since 1990; *b* 24 April 1945; *s* of William Thomas Ebsworth Waters and Esther Jane Waters; *m* 1971, Susan Jennifer Bulmer (marr. diss. 1986); two *d*. *Educ:* Greenhill Grammar Sch., Tenby. Admitted Solicitor, 1969; called to the Bar, Middle Temple, 1973; Junior Treasury Counsel, CCC, 1989–94. *Recreations:* golf, fishing. *Address:* 1 Hare Court, Temple, EC4Y 7BE. *T:* 0171–353 3982. *Clubs:* MCC; Royal Wimbledon Golf.

WATERS, David Watkin, Lt-Comdr RN; *b* 2 Aug. 1911; *s* of Eng. Lt William Waters, RN, and Jessie Rhena (*née* Whitemore); *m* 1946, Hope Waters (*née* Pritchard); one step *s* one step *d*. *Educ:* RN Coll., Dartmouth. Joined RN, 1925; Cadet and Midshipman, HMS Barham, 1929; specialised in Aviation (Pilot), 1935. Served War of 1939–45: Fleet Air Arm, Malta (PoW, Italy, Germany, 1940–45). Admlty, 1946–50; retd, 1950. Admlty Historian (Defence of Shipping), 1946–60; Head of Dept of Navigation and Astronomy, Nat. Maritime Museum, 1960–76, and Sec. of Museum, 1968–71; Dep. Dir, 1971–78. Pres., British Soc. for Hist. of Sci., 1976–78 (Vice-Pres., 1972–74, 1978–81). Vis. Prof. of History, Simon Fraser Univ., Burnaby, BC, 1978; Regents' Prof., UCLA, 1979; Caird Res. Fellow, Nat. Maritime Museum, 1979–83; Alexander O. Victor Res. Fellow, John Carter Brown Library, Brown Univ., Providence, RI, 1990. Chm., Japan Animal Welfare Soc., 1972–80. Gold Medal, Admiralty Naval History, 1936, and Special Award, 1946; FRHistS 1951; Fellow, Inst. Internac. da Cultura Portuguesa, 1966; FSA 1970. Hon. Member: Royal Inst. of Navigation, 1989 (Fellow 1959); Scientific Instrument Soc., 1989; Acad. de Marinha Portuguesa, 1989. *Publications:* The True and Perfect Newes of Syr Francis Drake, 1955; (with F. Barley) Naval Staff History, Second World War, Defeat of the Enemy attack on Shipping, 1939–1945, 1957; The Art of Navigation in England in Elizabethan and Early Stuart Times, 1958, 2nd edn 1978; The Sea—or Mariner's Astrolabe, 1966; The Rutter of the Sea, 1967; (with Hope Waters) The Saluki in History, Art, and Sport, 1969, 2nd edn 1984; (with G. P. B. Naish) The Elizabethan Navy and the Armada of Spain, 1975; Science and the Techniques of Navigation in the Renaissance, 1976; (with Thomas R. Adams) English Maritime Books relating to ships and their construction and operation at sea printed before 1801, 1995; contrib.: Jl RIN; RUSI; Mariners' Mirror; American Neptune; Jl RN Scientific Service; Jl British Soc. of History of Science; Navy International; Revista da Universidade de Coímbra. *Recreations:* maritime history, history of technology (medieval, Renaissance and Scientific Revolution, and Chinese sailing craft). *Address:* c/o Cobwebs, Graffham, Petworth, West Sussex GU28 0PY. *Club:* English-Speaking Union.

WATERS, Donald Henry, OBE 1994; Chief Executive, since 1987, and Deputy Chairman, since 1993, Grampian Television PLC; *b* 17 Dec. 1937; *s* of late Henry Lethbridge Waters, WS, and Jean Manson Baxter; *m* 1962, June Leslie, *d* of late Andrew Hutchison; one *s* two *d*. *Educ:* George Watson's, Edinburgh; Inverness Royal Acad. Mem. ICA(Scot.) 1961. Dir, John M. Henderson and Co. Ltd, 1969–74; Grampian Television: Company Sec., 1975; Dir of Finance, 1979. Chm., Glenburnie Properties, 1993–; Director: Blenheim Travel, 1981–91; Moray Firth Radio, 1982–; Independent Television Publications Ltd, 1988–90; Cablevision (Scotland) PLC, 1988–91; Central Scotland Radio, 1994–; GRT Bus Group, 1994–; British Linen Bank Gp, 1995–. Vis. Prof. of Film and Media Studies, Stirling Univ., 1992–. Scottish Vice Chm., BAFTA, 1992–; Chm., Celtic Film and Television Assoc., 1994– (Trustee for Scotland, 1991–94). Chm., Police Dependent Trust, Aberdeen, 1991–. FRTS 1992; FRSA. *Recreations:* gardening, travel. *Address:* Balquhidder, Milltimber, Aberdeen AB1 0JS. *T:* Aberdeen (01224) 867131. *Club:* Royal Northern (Chm., 1987–88) (Aberdeen).

WATERS, Mrs Frank; *see* Brown, D. L.

WATERS, Gen. Sir John; *see* Waters, Gen. Sir C. J.

WATERS, Montague, QC 1968; *b* 28 Feb. 1917; *s* of Elias Wasserman, BSc, and Rose Waters; *m* 1st, 1940, Jessica Freedman (*d* 1988); three *s*; 2nd, 1991, Georgia Heather Schaverien. *Educ:* Central Foundation Sch., City of London; London University. LLB (Hons) London, 1938. Solicitor of the Supreme Court, 1939. Military Service, KRRC, Intelligence Corps and Dept of HM Judge Advocate General, 1940–46 (Defence and Victory Medals, 1939–45 Star). Called to the Bar, Inner Temple, 1946; released from HM Forces with rank of Major (Legal Staff), 1946. Governor, Central Foundation Schools, 1968. Freeman, City of London, 1962. *Recreations:* theatre, sport. *Address:* 1 Fineshade, Martello Park, Canford Cliffs, Poole, Dorset BH13 7BA. *T:* Bournemouth (01202) 701170.

WATERSON, Nigel Christopher; MP (C) Eastbourne, since 1992; *b* 12 Oct. 1950; *s* of James Waterson and Katherine (*née* Mahon); *m* 1st, 1979, Gisela Guettler (marr. diss. 1989); 2nd, 1989, Bernadette Ann O'Halloran. *Educ:* Leeds Grammar Sch.; Queen's Coll., Oxford (MA Jurisprudence); College of Law. Called to the Bar, Gray's Inn, 1973; admitted solicitor, 1979. Pres., Oxford Univ. Cons. Assoc., 1970. Res. Asst to Sally Oppenheim, MP, 1972–73. Cllr, London Borough of Hammersmith, 1974–78. Chairman: Bow Gp, 1986–87 (Hon. Patron, 1993–95); Hammersmith Cons. Assoc., 1987–90; Hammersmith and Fulham Jt Management Cttee, 1988–90; Member: Cons. Gtr London Area Exec. Cttee, 1990–91; Soc. of Cons. Lawyers Exec. Cttee, 1993–; Conservative Political Centre: Mem., Adv. Cttee, 1986–90; Mem., Gtr London Gen. Purposes Cttee, 1990–91. Pres., SE Area Cons. Educn Adv. Cttee, 1993–. Mem., Select Cttee on Nat. Heritage; Vice Chairman: Cons. Backbench Tourism Cttee; Cons. Backbench Transport Cttee; Sec., Cons. Backbench Shipping and Shipbuilding Cttee, 1992–; Vice Chairman: All-Party Daylight Extra Gp, 1993–; All-Party British Greek Gp, 1993–; Sec., British Cyprus Gp, CPA, 1992–. Member: London West European Constituency Council, 1987–91; Management Cttee, Stonham Housing Assoc. Hostel for Ex-Offenders, 1988–90. *Publications:* papers on an Alternative Manifesto, 1973, the future of Hong Kong, and on shipping. *Recreations:* sailing, polo, shooting, reading, music. *Address:* House of Commons, SW1A 0AA. *Clubs:* Carlton, Coningsby; Eastbourne Constitutional; Guards' Polo; Sussex CC.

WATERSTON, Dr Charles Dewar, FRSE, FGS; formerly Keeper of Geology, Royal Scottish Museum; *b* 15 Feb. 1925; *s* of Allan Waterston and Martha Dewar (*née* Robertson); *m* 1965, Marjory Home Douglas. *Educ:* Highgate Sch., London; Univ. of Edinburgh (BSc 1st Cl. Hons 1947; Vans Dunlop Scholar, PhD 1949; DSc 1980). FRSE 1958; FGS 1949. Asst Keeper, Royal Scottish Museum, 1950–63, Keeper, 1963–85. Member: Scottish Cttee, Nature Conservancy, 1969–73; Adv. Cttee for Scotland, Nature Conservancy Council, 1974–82; Chairman's Cttee, 1978–80, Exec. Cttee, 1980–82, Council for Museums and Galleries in Scotland; Adv. Cttee on Sites of Special Scientific Interest, 1992–95; Gen. Sec., RSE, 1986–91 (Mem. Council, 1967–70; Vice-Pres., 1980–83; Sec., 1985–86); Hon. Sec., Edinburgh Geol Soc., 1953–58 (Pres., 1969–71). Keith Prize, 1969–71, Bicentenary Medal, 1992, RSE; Clough Medal, Edinburgh Geol Soc., 1984–85; (first) A. G. Brighton Medal, Geol Curators' Gp, 1992. *Publications:* (with G. Y. Craig and D. B. McIntyre) James Hutton's Theory of the Earth: the lost drawings, 1978; (with H. E. Stace and C. W. A. Pettitt) Natural Science Collections in Scotland, 1987; technical papers in scientific jls, chiefly relating to extinct arthropods and the history of geology. *Address:* 30 Boswall Road, Edinburgh EH5 3RN.

WATERSTONE, David George Stuart, CBE 1991; UK Chairman, Ansaldo Ltd, since 1995; *b* 9 Aug. 1935; *s* of Malcolm Waterstone and Sylvia Sawday; *m* 1st, 1960, Dominique Viriot (marr. diss.); one *s* two *d*; 2nd, 1988, Sandra Packer (*née* Willey). *Educ:* Tonbridge; St Catharine's Coll., Cambridge (MA). HM Diplomatic Service, 1959–70; Sen. Exec., IRC, 1970–71; BSC, 1971–81: Board Mem., 1976–81; Man. Dir, Commercial, 1972–77; subseq. Executive Chairman, BSC Chemicals, 1977–81, and Redpath Dorman Long, 1977–81; Chief Exec., Welsh Develt Agency, 1983–90; Chief Exec., Energy and Technical Services Gp plc, 1990–95. Director: Portsmouth and Sunderland Newspapers, 1983–; Hunting, 1995–; Precoat Internat., 1995–. Chm., Combined Heat and Power Assoc., 1993–95. *Recreations:* sailing, walking, painting, furniture making. *Address:* (office) 93–95 Gresham Street, EC2V 7NB. *T:* 0171–600 4797; (home) 1 Prior Park Buildings, Prior Park Road, Bath BA2 4NP. *T:* Bath (01225) 427346. *Club:* Reform.

See also T. J. S. Waterstone.

WATERSTONE, Timothy John Stuart; Founder, Chairman and Chief Executive, Waterstone's Booksellers Ltd (formerly Waterstone & Co.), 1982–93; *b* 30 May 1939; *s* of Malcolm Waterstone and Sylvia Sawday; *m* 1st, Patricia Harcourt-Poole (marr. diss.); two *s* one *d*; 2nd, Clare Perkins (marr. diss.); one *s* two *d*; 3rd, Mary Rose Alison; two *d*. *Educ:* Tonbridge; St Catharine's College, Cambridge (MA). Carritt Moran, Calcutta, 1962–64; Allied Breweries, 1964–73; W. H. Smith, 1973–81; Chairman: Priory Investments Ltd, 1990–95; Golden Rose Radio (London Jazz FM), 1992–93; Dep. Chm., Sinclair-Stevenson Ltd, 1989–92; Member of Board: Yale Univ. Press, 1992–; Future Start, 1992–; Virago Press., 1995–. Chm., Shelter 25th Anniversary Appeal Cttee, 1991–92. Member: Bd of Trustees, English International (Internat. House), 1987–92; Bd, London Philharmonic Orch., 1990– (Trustee, 1995–); Chairman: Acad. of Ancient Music, 1990–95; London Internat. Festival of Theatre, 1991–92; Elgar Foundn, 1992–. Co-Founder BOOKAID, 1992–93. Adv. Mem., Booker Prize Management Cttee, 1986–93; Chm. of Judges, Prince's Youth Business Trust Awards, 1990. *Publications:* novels: Lilley & Chase, 1994; An Imperfect Marriage, 1995; A Token for Good, 1996. *Recreations:* books, music. *Address:* 1/11 Hay Hill, W1X 7LF. *T:* 0171–409 7339. *Club:* Garrick.

See also D. G. S. Waterstone.

WATERTON, Sqdn Leader William Arthur, GM 1952; AFC 1942, Bar 1946; *b* Edmonton, Canada, 18 March 1916. *Educ:* Royal Military College of Canada; University of Alberta. Cadet Royal Military College of Canada, 1934–37; Subaltern and Lieut, 19th Alberta Dragoons, Canadian Cavalry, 1937–39; served RAF, 1939–46: Fighter Squadrons; Training Command; Transatlantic Ferrying Command; Fighter Command; Meteorological Flight; Fighter Experimental Unit; CFE High Speed Flight World Speed Record. Joined Gloster Aircraft Co. Ltd, 1946. 100 km closed circuit record, 1947; Paris/London record (618.5 mph), 1947; "Hare and Tortoise" Helicopter and jet aircraft Centre of London to Centre of Paris (47 mins), 1948. Chief Test Pilot Gloster Aircraft Co. Ltd, 1946–54. Prototype trials on first Canadian jet fighter, Canuck and British first operational delta wing fighter, the Javelin. *Publications:* The Comet Riddle, 1956; The Quick and The Dead, 1956; aeronautical and meteorological articles. *Recreations:* sailing, riding, photography, motoring, shooting. *Address:* c/o Royal Bank of Scotland, 49 Charing Cross, SW1A 2DZ. *Club:* Royal Military College of Canada (Kingston, Ont.).

WATERWORTH, Alan William, JP; Lord-Lieutenant of Merseyside, since 1993 (Vice Lord-Lieutenant, 1989–93); *b* 22 Sept. 1931; *s* of late James and Alice Waterworth, Liverpool; *m* 1955, Myriam, *d* of late Edouard Baete and Magdelaine Baete, formerly of Brussels; three *s* one *d*. *Educ:* Uppingham Sch.; Trinity Coll., Cambridge (MA). National Service, commnd King's Regt, 1950. Waterworth Bros Ltd: progressively, Dir, Man. Dir, Chm., 1954–69. Gen Comr, Inland Revenue, 1965–72. Dir, NHS Hosp. Trust, Liverpool, 1992–93. Member: Skelmersdale Develt Corp., 1971–85 (Dep. Chm., 1979–85); Merseyside Police Authority, 1984–92; Cttee, Merseyside Br., Inst. of Dirs, 1965–77 (Chm., 1974–77). Chm., IBA Adv. Cttee for Radio on Merseyside, 1975–78. Chairman: Liverpool Boys' Assoc., 1967–75; Merseyside Youth Assoc., 1971–75; Everton FC, 1973–76 (Dir, 1970–93). Mem. Council, Liverpool Univ., 1993–. Trustee, Nat. Museums and Galls on Merseyside, 1994–. JP Liverpool 1961 (Chm., Juvenile Panel, 1974–83; Chm. of Bench, 1985–89); DL Co. Merseyside 1986, High Sheriff, Co. Merseyside, 1992. Hon. Col, Merseyside Cadet Force, 1994–. KStJ 1994. *Recreations:* local history, bibliomania, shooting. *Address:* Crewood Hall, Kingsley, Cheshire WA6 8HR. *T:* Kingsley (01928) 788316. *Clubs:* Army and Navy; Athenæum (Liverpool).

WATES, Sir Christopher (Stephen), Kt 1989; BA; FCA; Chief Executive, Wates Building Group, since 1984; Chairman: Criterion Holdings, since 1981; Wates Built Homes Ltd, since 1984; *b* 25 Dec. 1939; *s* of Norman Edward Wates and Margot Irene Sidwell; *m* 1965, Sandra Mouroutsos (marr. diss. 1975); three *d*; *m* 1992, Georgina Ferris McCallum. *Educ:* Stowe School; Brasenose College, Oxford (BA 1962; Rugby blue, 1961; Hon. Fellow, 1993). FCA 1975 (ACA 1965). Financial Director, Wates Ltd, 1970–76. Director: Electra Investment Trust, 1980–93; Equitable Life Assurance Society, 1983–94; Scottish Ontario Investment Co. Ltd, 1978–83; NB Smaller Companies Trust plc (formerly North British Canadian Investment Co.), 1983–; Wates City of London Properties plc, 1984–; Mem., 1980–89, Chm., 1983–89, English Industrial Estates Corp.; Chm., Keymer Brick & Tile Co. Ltd, 1985–89. A Church Comr, 1992–. Governor of Council, 1984–, Dep. Chm., 1989–, London Goodenough Trust (formerly London House for Overseas Graduates); Trustee: Chatham Historic Dockyard Trust, 1984–87; Science Museum, 1987–; Lambeth Palace Library, 1990–. FRSA 1988. Hon. Mem., RICS, 1990. *Address:* Tufton Place, Northiam, near Rye, East Sussex TN31 6HL. *T:* Northiam (01797) 252125.

WATES, Michael Edward, Chairman, Wates Group, since 1974; *b* 19 June 1935; 2nd *s* of Sir Ronald Wallace Wates and of Phyllis Mary Wates (*née* Trace); *m* 1959, Caroline Josephine Connolly; four *s* one *d*. *Educ:* Oundle School; Emmanuel College, Cambridge (MA); Harvard Business Sch. (PMD 1963). Served RM, 1953–55. Joined Wates 1959; Director: Wates Construction, 1963; Wates Built Homes, 1966. Mem., Nat. Housebuilding Council, 1974–80. Chm., British Bloodstock Agency plc, 1986–92; Member: Council, Thoroughbred Breeders Assoc., 1978–82 (Chm., 1980–82); Horserace Betting Levy Bd, 1987–90. King's College Hospital: Deleg., Sch. of Medicine and Dentistry, 1983–; Chm., Equipment Cttee, 1983–91; Special Trustee, 1985 (Chm., Trustees, 1985). Hon. FRIBA. *Address:* Manor House, Langton Long, Blandford Forum, Dorset DT11 9HS. *T:* Blandford (01258) 455241.

WATHEN, Julian Philip Gerard; Chairman, Hall School Charitable Trust, since 1972; *b* 21 May 1923; *s* of late Gerard Anstruther Wathen, CIE, and Melicent Louis (*née* Buxton); *m* 1948 Priscilla Florence Wilson; one *s* two *d*. *Educ:* Harrow. Served War, 60th Rifles, 1942–46. Third Secretary, HBM Embassy, Athens, 1946–47. Barclays Bank DCO, 1948; Ghana Director, 1961–65; General Manager, 1966; Sen. Gen. Manager, Barclays Bank International, 1974; Vice Chm., 1976; Vice Chairman: Barclays Bank, 1979–84; Banque du Caire, Barclays International, 1976–83; Dep. Chm., Allied Arab Bank, 1977–84; Director: Barclays Australia International, 1973–84; Barclays Bank of Kenya, 1975–84; Mercantile & General Reinsurance Co., 1977–91. Pres., Royal African Soc., 1984–89 (Chm., 1978–84); Chm., City of London Endowment Trust for St Paul's Cathedral, 1983–; Member Council: London Goodenough Trust (formerly London House for Overseas Graduates), 1971– (Vice-Chm., 1984–89); Book Aid Internat., 1988–; Governor: St Paul's Schs, 1981–; SOAS, 1983–92; Overseas Develt Inst., 1984–; Dauntsey's Sch., 1985–; Abingdon Sch., 1985–; Thomas Telford Sch., 1990–. Mem. Cttee, GBA, 1986–94. Master, Mercers' Co., 1984–85. *Address:* Woodcock House, Owlpen, Dursley, Glos GL11 5BY. *T:* Dursley (01453) 860214; 1 Montagu Place, Marylebone, W1H 1RG. *T:* 0171–935 8569. *Club:* Travellers'.

WATKIN, Rt. Rev. Abbot (Christopher) Aelred (Paul); titular Abbot of Glastonbury; Headmaster of Downside School, 1962–75; *b* 23 Feb. 1918; *s* of late Edward Ingram Watkin and Helena Watkin (*née* Shepheard). *Educ:* Blackfriars Sch., Laxton; Christ's Coll., Cambridge (1st class Parts I and II, historical Tripos). Ordained Priest, 1943. Housemaster at Downside Sch., 1948–62. Mayor of Beccles, 1979. FRHistS, 1946; FSA, 1950; FRSA, 1969. *Publications:* Wells Cathedral Miscellany, 1943; (ed) Great Chartulary of Glastonbury, 3 vols, 1946–58; (ed) Registrum Archidiaconatus Norwyci, 2 vols, 1946–48; Heart of the World, 1954; The Enemies of Love, 1958; Resurrection is Now, 1975; Through the Church's Year, 1991; articles in Eng. Hist. Rev., Cambridge Hist. Journal, Victoria County History of Wilts, etc. *Address:* Downside Abbey, Stratton-on-the-Fosse, Bath BA3 4RH. *T:* Stratton-on-the-Fosse (01761) 232295.

WATKIN, David John, MA, PhD, LittD; FSA; Fellow of Peterhouse, Cambridge, since 1970; Reader in History of Architecture, Cambridge University, since 1993; *b* 7 April 1941; *o s* of Thomas Charles and Vera Mary Watkin. *Educ:* Farnham Grammar Sch.; Trinity Hall, Cambridge (Exhibnr; BA (1st Cl. Hons Fine Arts Tripos); PhD; LittD 1993). University of Cambridge: Librarian, Fine Arts Faculty, 1967–72; University Lectr in History of Art, 1972–93; Head, Dept of History of Art, 1989–92. Mem., Historic Bldgs Council for England, then Historic Bldgs Adv. Cttee, Historic Bldgs and Monuments Commn for England, 1980–95. *Publications:* Thomas Hope (1769–1831) and the Neo-Classical Idea, 1968; (ed) Sale Catalogues of Libraries of Eminent Persons, vol. 4, Architects, 1970; The Life and Work of C. R. Cockerell, RA, 1974 (Alice Davis Hitchcock medallion, 1975); The Triumph of the Classical, Cambridge Architecture 1804–34, 1977; Morality and Architecture, 1977; The Rise of Architectural History, 1980; English Architecture, a Concise History, 1980; (with Hugh Montgomery-Massingberd) The London Ritz, a Social and Architectural History, 1980; (with Robin Middleton) Neo-Classical and Nineteenth-century Architecture, 1980; (jtly) Burke's and Savills Guide to Country Houses, vol. 3, East Anglia, 1981; The Buildings of Britain, Regency: a Guide and Gazetteer, 1982; Athenian Stuart, Pioneer of the Greek Revival, 1982; The English Vision: The Picturesque in Architecture, Landscape and Garden Design, 1982; (contrib.) John Soane, 1983; The Royal Interiors of Regency England, 1984; Peterhouse: an architectural record 1284–1984, 1984; (contrib.) Grand Hotel: the golden age of palace hotels, an architectural and social history, 1984; (contrib.) A House in Town: 22 Arlington Street, its owners and builders, 1984; A History of Western Architecture, 1986; (with Tilman Mellinghoff) German Architecture and the Classical Ideal: 1740–1840, 1987; (contrib.) The Legacy of Rome: a new appraisal, 1992; Sir John Soane: Enlightenment Thought and the Royal Academy Lectures, 1996. *Address:* Peterhouse, Cambridge CB2 1RD. *Clubs:* Travellers', Beefsteak; University Pitt (Cambridge).

WATKIN WILLIAMS, Sir Peter, Kt 1963; *b* 8 July 1911; *s* of late Robert Thesiger Watkin Williams, late Master of the Supreme Court, and Mary Watkin Williams; *m* 1938, Jane Dickinson (*née* Wilkin); two *d*. *Educ:* Sherborne; Pembroke Coll., Cambridge. Partner in Hansons, legal practitioners, Shanghai, 1937–40; served War of 1939–45, Rhodesia and Middle East, 1940–46. Resident Magistrate, Uganda, 1946–55; Puisne Judge, Trinidad and Tobago, 1955–58; Puisne Judge, Sierra Leone, 1958–61; Plebiscite Judge, Cameroons, 1961; Chief Justice of Basutoland, Bechuanaland and Swaziland, and President of the Court of Appeal, 1961–65; High Court Judge, Malawi, 1967–69; Chief Justice of Malawi, 1969–70. *Recreation:* fishing. *Address:* Lower East Horner, Stockland, Honiton, Devon EX14 9EY.

WATKINS, Dr Alan Keith; Deputy Chairman, Senior Engineering Group, since 1995 (Director, since 1994); *b* 9 Oct. 1938; *s* of late Wilfred Victor Watkins and Dorothy Hilda Watkins; *m* 1963, Diana Edith Wynne (*née* Hughes); two *s*. *Educ:* Moseley Grammar School, Birmingham; Univ. of Birmingham (BSc Hons, PhD). FIM (Mem. Council, 1990–); CEng; FIMfgE (Vice-Pres., 1991); FIEE (Mem. Council, 1991–92). Lucas Research Centre, 1962; Lucas Batteries, 1969, subseq. Manufacturing Dir; Lucas Aerospace, 1975; Man. Dir, Aerospace Lucas Industries, 1987–89; Man. Dir and Chief Exec., Hawker Siddeley Gp, 1989–91; London Transport: Chief Exec., 1992–94; Vice-Chm., 1992–93; Dep. Chm., 1993–94. Director: Dobson Park Industries plc, 1992–; Hepworth plc, 1995–. Member: DTI Aviation Cttee, 1985–89; Review Bd for Govt Contracts, 1993–. Member Council: SBAC, 1982–89 (Vice-Pres., 1988–89); CBI, 1992–94. Vice-Pres., EEF, 1989–91. *Recreations:* tennis, golf, hot-air ballooning, photography. *Club:* Olton Golf.

WATKINS, Alan (Rhun); journalist; Political Columnist, Independent on Sunday, since 1993; *b* 3 April 1933; *o c* of late D. J. Watkins, schoolmaster, Tycroes, Carmarthenshire, and Violet Harris; *m* 1955, Ruth Howard (*d* 1982); one *s* one *d* (and one *d* decd). *Educ:* Amman Valley Grammar Sch., Ammanford; Queens' Coll., Cambridge (MA, LLM). Chm., Cambridge Univ. Labour Club, 1954. National Service, FO, Educn Br., RAF, 1955–57. Called to Bar, Lincoln's Inn, 1957. Research Asst to W. A. Robson, LSE, 1958–59; Editorial Staff, Sunday Express, 1959–64 (New York Corresp., 1961; Actg Political Corresp., 1963; Crossbencher Columnist, 1963–64); Political Correspondent: Spectator, 1964–67; New Statesman, 1967–76; Political Columnist: Sunday Mirror, 1968–69; Observer, 1976–93; Columnist, Evening Standard, 1974–75; Rugby Columnist: Field, 1984–86; Independent, 1986–; Drink Columnist, Observer Magazine, 1992–93. Mem. (Lab) Fulham Bor. Council, 1959–62. Dir, The Statesman and Nation Publishing Co. Ltd, 1973–76. Chm., Political Adv. Gp, British Youth Council, 1978–81. Awards: Granada, Political Columnist, 1973; British Press, Columnist, 1982, commended 1984. *Publications:* The Liberal Dilemma, 1966; (contrib.) The Left, 1966; (with A. Alexander) The Making of the Prime Minister 1970, 1970; Brief Lives with some memoirs, 1982; (contrib.) The Queen Observed, 1986, Sportswriter's Eye, 1989; A Slight Case of Libel: Meacher *v* Trelford and others, 1990; A Conservative Coup: the fall of Margaret Thatcher, 1991, 2nd edn 1992. *Recreations:* reading, walking. *Address:* 54 Barnsbury Street, N1 1ER. *T:* 0171–607 0812. *Clubs:* Garrick, Beefsteak.

WATKINS, Brian, CMG 1993; HM Diplomatic Service, retired; Immigration Adjudicator (part time), since 1993; *b* 26 July 1933; *s* of late James Edward Watkins and late Gladys Anne Watkins (*née* Fletcher); *m* 1st, 1957 (marr. diss. 1978); one *s*; 2nd, 1982, Elisabeth, *d* of A. and M. Arfon-Jones; one *d*. *Educ:* London School of Economics (BSc Econ); Worcester College, Oxford. Solicitor. Flying Officer, RAF, 1955–58. HMOCS, Sierra Leone, 1959–63; Local Govt, 1963–66; Administrator, Tristan da Cunha, 1966–69; Lectr, Univ. of Manchester, 1969–71, HM Diplomatic Service, 1971; FCO, 1971–73; New York, 1973–75; seconded to N Ireland Office, 1976–78; FCO, 1978–81; Counsellor, 1981; Dep. Governor, Bermuda, 1981–83; Consul General and Counsellor (Economic, Commercial, Aid), Islamabad, 1983–86; Consul Gen., Vancouver, 1986–90; High Comr to Swaziland, 1990–93. Swazi Rep. on Council, British Commonwealth Ex-Services League, 1993–. OStJ 1994 (Mem., Gwent Council, 1994–). *Recreations:* reading history and spy stories, watching theatre, watching TV, dancing. *Address:* c/o Royal Bank of Scotland, Drummonds Branch, Charing Cross, SW1A 2DX. *Clubs:* St James's, Commonwealth Trust.

WATKINS, David John; Director, Council for the Advancement of Arab-British Understanding, 1983–90 (Joint Chairman, 1979–83); company director and consultant; *b* 27 Aug. 1925; *s* of Thomas George Watkins and Alice Elizabeth (*née* Allen); unmarried. *Educ:* Bristol. Member: Bristol City Council, 1954–57; Bristol Educn Cttee, 1958–66; Labour Party, 1950–; Amalgamated Engineering Union, 1942–; Sec., AEU Gp of MPs, 1968–77. Contested Bristol NW, 1964. MP (Lab) Consett, 1966–83; Mem., House of Commons Chairmen's Panel, 1978–83. Sponsored Employers Liability (Compulsory Insurance) Act, 1969, and Industrial Common Ownership Act, 1976 as Private Member's Bills; introd Drained Weight Bill, 1973, and Consett Steel Works Common Ownership Bill, 1980. Chm., Labour Middle East Council, 1974–83; Treas., Internat. Co-ord Cttee, UN Meeting of Non-Governmental Organisations on Question of Palestine, 1985–90. Dir, 1987–, Chm., 1990–, Courtlands Estate (Richmond) Ltd (Vice Chm., 1988–90). *Publications:* Labour and Palestine, 1975; Industrial Common Ownership, 1978; The World and Palestine, 1980; The Exceptional Conflict, 1984; Palestine: an inescapable duty, 1992. *Recreations:* reading, listening to music, swimming. *Address:* 1 Carisbrooke House, Courtlands, Sheen Road, Richmond, Surrey TW10 5AZ. *Club:* Commonwealth Trust.

WATKINS, Gerwyn Rhidian; Stipendiary Magistrate for South Glamorgan, since 1993; *b* 22 Jan. 1943; *s* of late William Watkins and Margaret Watkins (*née* Evans); *m* 1966, Eleanor Margaret Hemingway; two *s*. *Educ:* Ardwyn Grammar Sch., Aberystwyth; University Coll. of Wales, Aberystwyth (LLB). Articled to Thomas Andrews, Bracknell, 1966–68; Court Clerk, Cardiff Magistrates' Court, 1968–71; Justices' Clerk: Bromsgrove and Redditch, 1971–74; Vale of Glamorgan, 1974–93. Pres., Barry Rotary Club, 1990–91. *Address:* Magistrates' Court, Fitzalan Place, Cardiff CF2 1RZ. *T:* Cardiff (01222) 463040.

WATKINS, Rev. Gordon Derek; Secretary, London Diocesan Advisory Committee, 1984–94; *b* 16 July 1929; *s* of Clifford and Margaret Watkins; *m* 1957, Beryl Evelyn Whitaker. *Educ:* St Brendan's College, Clifton. Nat. Service, RAOC, 1947–49. Staff of W. D. & H. O. Wills, 1944–51; deacon 1953, priest 1954; Curate, Grafton Cathedral, NSW, 1953–56; Vicar of Texas, Qld, 1957–61; Curate, St Wilfrid's, Harrogate, 1961–63; Vicar of Upton Park, 1963–67; Rector: Great and Little Bentley, 1967–73; Great Canfield, 1973–78; Pastoral Sec., Dio. London, 1978–84; Vicar, St Martin-within-Ludgate, City and Dio. of London, 1984–89; Priest Vicar, Westminster Abbey, 1984–90; Priest in Ordinary to the Queen, 1984–. Freeman, City of London, 1984. *Recreations:* reading, music, country life. *Club:* Athenæum.

WATKINS, Maj.-Gen. Guy Hansard, CB 1986; OBE 1974; Chief Executive, Royal Hong Kong Jockey Club, since 1986; *b* 30 Nov. 1933; *s* of Col A. N. M. Watkins and Mrs S. C. Watkins; *m* 1958, Sylvia Margaret Grant; two *s* two *d*. *Educ:* The King's Sch., Canterbury; Royal Military Academy, Sandhurst. Commissioned into Royal Artillery, 1953; CO 39 Medium Regt RA, 1973; Comd Task Force 'B'/Dep. Comd 1 Armd Div., 1977; Director, Public Relations (Army), 1980; Maj. Gen. RA and GOC Artillery Div., 1982; Dir Gen., Army Manning and Recruiting, 1985; retd 1986. *Recreations:* riding, fly fishing, skiing. *Address:* The Royal Hong Kong Jockey Club, Happy Valley, Hong Kong. *Clubs:* Army and Navy; Shek O (Hong Kong); Littlehampton Golf.

WATKINS, Prof. Jeffrey Clifton, PhD; FRS 1988; Hon. Professor of Pharmacology, Department of Pharmacology, School of Medical Sciences (formerly The Medical School), Bristol, since 1989 (Senior Research Fellow, 1983–89); *b* 20 Dec. 1929; *s* of Colin Hereward and Amelia Miriam Watkins; *m* 1973, Beatrice Joan Thacher; one *s* one *d*. *Educ:* Univ. of Western Australia (MSc 1954); Univ. of Cambridge (PhD 1954). Research Fellow, Chemistry Department: Univ. of Cambridge, 1954–55; Univ. of Yale, 1955–57; Res. Fellow, 1958–61, Fellow, 1961–65, Physiology Dept, ANU; Scientific Officer, ARC Inst. of Animal Physiology, Babraham, Cambridge, 1965–67; Res. Scientist, MRC Neuropsychiatry Unit, Carshalton, Surrey, 1967–73; Senior Research Fellow, Dept of Physiology, The Med. Sch., Bristol, 1973–83 (Leader of Excitatory Amino Acid Gp). *Publications:* The NMDA Receptor, 1989, 2nd edn 1995; approx. 250 pubns in learned jls, eg Jl of Physiol., Brit. Jl of Pharmacol., Nature, Brain Res., Exptl Brain Res., Eur. Jl of Pharmacol., Neuroscience, Neuroscience Letters, Jl of Neuroscience. *Address:* 8 Lower Court Road, Lower Almondsbury, Bristol, Avon BS12 4DX. *T:* Almondsbury (01454) 613829.

WATKINS, Peter Rodney; Office for Standards in Education Inspector, since 1993; education consultant, since 1993; *b* 8 Oct. 1931; *s* of late Frank Arthur Watkins and of Mary Gwyneth Watkins (neé Price); *m* 1971, Jillian Ann Burge; two *d*. *Educ:* Solihull Sch.; Emmanuel Coll., Cambridge (Exhibnr; Hist. Tripos Pts I and II 1952, 1953; Cert. in Educn 1954; MA 1957). Flying Officer, RAF, 1954–56; History Master, East Ham Grammar Sch., 1956–59; Sixth Form Hist. Master, Brentwood Sch., 1959–64; Sen. Hist. Master, Bristol Grammar Sch., 1964–69; Headmaster, King Edward's Five Ways Sch., Birmingham, 1969–74; Headmaster, Chichester High Sch. for Boys, 1974–79; Principal, Price's Sixth Form Coll., Fareham, 1980–84; Dep. Chief Exec., Sch. Curriculum Develt Cttee, 1984–88, Nat. Curricululm Council, 1988–91. Exec., SHA, 1980–84. Chm., Christian Educn Movement, 1980–87. Reader, St Peter's, Bishop's Waltham, dio. of Portsmouth, 1989–. *Publications:* The Sixth Form College in Practice, 1982; Modular Approaches to the Secondary Curriculum, 1986. *Recreations:* fell walking, local history, theology. *Address:* 7 Crofton Way, Swanmore, near Southampton SO32 2RF. *T:* Bishop's Waltham (01489) 894789.

WATKINS, Rt. Hon. Sir Tasker, VC 1944; GBE 1990; Kt 1971; PC 1980; DL; a Lord Justice of Appeal, 1980–93; Deputy Chief Justice of England, 1988–93; *b* 18 Nov. 1918; *s* of late Bertram and Jane Watkins, Nelson, Glam; *m* 1941, Eirwen Evans; one *d* (one *s* decd). *Educ:* Pontypridd Grammar Sch. Served War, 1939–45 (Major, the Welch Regiment). Called to Bar, Middle Temple, 1948, Bencher 1970; QC 1965; Deputy Chairman: Radnor QS, 1962–71; Carmarthenshire QS, 1966–71. Recorder: Merthyr Tydfil, 1968–70, Swansea, 1970–71; Leader, Wales and Chester Circuit, 1970–71; Judge of the High Court of Justice, Family Div., 1971–74, QBD, 1974–80; Presiding Judge, Wales and Chester Circuit, 1975–80; Sen. Presiding Judge for England and Wales, 1983–91. Counsel (as Deputy to Attorney-General) to Inquiry into Aberfan Disaster, 1966. Chairman: Mental Health Review Tribunal, Wales Region, 1960–71; Judicial Studies Bd, 1979–80. Pres., Univ. of Wales Coll. of Medicine, 1987–. Pres., British Legion, Wales, 1947–68; Mem., TA Assoc., Glamorgan and Wales, 1947–. Chm., Welsh RU Charitable Trust, 1975–; Pres., Welsh RU, 1993–. DL Glamorgan, 1956. Hon. FRCS 1992. Hon. LLD Wales, 1979. *Address:* Fairwater Lodge, Fairwater Road, Llandaff, Glamorgan CF5 2LE. *T:* Cardiff (01222) 563558; 5 Pump Court, Middle Temple, EC4Y 7AP. *T:* 0171–353 1993. *Clubs:* Army and Navy; Cardiff and County (Cardiff); Glamorgan Wanderers Rugby Football (Pres., 1968–).

See also J. G. Williams.

WATKINS, Thomas Frederick; Director, Chemical Defence Establishment, Porton, 1972–74; *b* 19 Feb. 1914; *s* of late Edward and late Louisa Watkins; *m* 1939, Jeannie Blodwen Roberts; two *d*. *Educ:* Cowbridge Grammar Sch.; Univ. of Wales, Cardiff. BSc Hons Wales 1935; MSc Wales 1936; FRIC 1947. Joined Scientific Staff of War Dept, 1936; seconded to Govt of India, 1939–44; seconded to Dept of Nat. Defence, Canada, 1947–49; Head of Research Section, CDRE, Sutton Oak and Min. of Supply CDE, Nancekuke, 1949–56; Supt Chemistry Research Div., CDE, Porton, 1956; Asst Dir Chemical Research, CDE, Porton, 1963; Dep. Dir, CDE, Porton, 1966. *Publications:* various papers on organic chemistry. *Recreation:* gardening. *Address:* 34 Harnwood Road, Salisbury, Wilts SP2 8DB. *T:* Salisbury (01722) 335135.

WATKINS, Dr Winifred May, FRS 1969; Visiting Professor and Senior Research Fellow, Royal Postgraduate Medical School, University of London, since 1990; Head of Division of Immunochemical Genetics, Clinical Research Centre, Medical Research Council, 1976–89; *b* 6 Aug. 1924; *d* of Albert E. and Annie B. Watkins. *Educ:* Godolphin and Latymer Sch., London; Univ. of London. PhD 1950; DSc 1963. Research Asst in Biochemistry, St Bartholomew's Hosp. Med. Sch., 1948–50; Beit Memorial Research Fellow, 1952–55; Mem. of Staff of Lister Inst. of Preventive Medicine, 1955–75; Wellcome Travelling Research Fellow, Univ. of California, 1960–61; Reader in Biochemistry, 1965; Prof. of Biochemistry, Univ. of London, 1968–75; William Julius Mickle Fellow, London Univ., 1971. Mem. Council, Royal Soc., 1984–86. Hon. Mem., Internat. Soc. of Blood Transfusion, 1982; Foreign Mem., Polish Acad. of Sciences, 1988. Hon. Mem., Japanese Biochemical Soc., 1990. FRCPath 1983. Hon. FRCP 1990. Hon. DSc Utrecht, 1990. Landsteiner Memorial Award (jtly), 1967; Paul Ehrlich-Ludwig Darmstädter Prize (jtly), 1969; Kenneth Goldsmith Award, British Blood Transfusion Soc., 1986; Royal Medal, Royal Soc., 1988; Franz Oehlecker Medal, German Soc. of Transfusion Medicine and Immunohaematology, 1989; (jtly) Philip Levine Award, Amer. Soc. of Clin. Pathologists, 1990. *Publications:* various papers in biochemical and immunological jls. *Address:* Department of Haematology, Royal Postgraduate Medical School, Hammersmith Hospital, Du Cane Road, W12 0NN. *T:* 0181–743 2030, ext. 2171.

WATKINSON, family name of **Viscount Watkinson.**

WATKINSON, 1st Viscount *cr* 1964, of Woking; **Harold Arthur Watkinson,** PC 1955; CH 1962; President, Confederation of British Industry, 1976–77; Chairman of Cadbury Schweppes Ltd, 1969–74 (Group Managing Director, Schweppes Ltd, 1963–68); Director: British Insulated Callender's Cables, 1968–77; Midland Bank Ltd, 1970–83; *b* 25 Jan. 1910; *e s* of A. G. Watkinson, Walton-on-Thames; *m* 1939, Vera, *y d* of John Langmead, West Sussex; two *d*. *Educ:* Queen's College, Taunton; King's College, London. Family business, 1929–35; technical and engineering journalism, 1935–39. Served War of 1939–45, active service, Lieut-Comdr RNVR. Chairman Production Efficiency Panel for S England, Machine Tool Trades Association, 1948; Chairman (first) Dorking Div. Conservative Assoc., 1948–49. MP (C) Woking Division of Surrey, 1950–64; Parliamentary Private Secretary to the Minister of Transport and Civil Aviation, 1951–52; Parliamentary Secretary to Ministry of Labour and National Service, 1952–55; Minister of Transport and Civil Aviation, Dec. 1955–59; Minister of Defence, 1959–62; Cabinet Minister, 1957–62. Mem., Brit. Nat. Export Council 1964–70; Chairman: Cttee for Exports to the United States, 1964–67; Nat. Advisory Cttee on the Employment of Older Men and Women, 1952–55; Companies Cttee, CBI, 1972–; a Vice-Pres., Council, BIM, 1970–73, Pres., 1973–78 (Chm., 1968–70). President: Grocers' Inst., 1970–71; Inst. of Grocery Distribution, 1972–73; Member: Council, RSA, 1972–77; NEDC, 1976–77; Falkland Islands Review Cttee, 1982–83. President: RNVR Officers' Assoc., 1973–76; Weald and Downland Museum, 1982–88. Chairman: Council, Cranleigh and Bramley Schools, 1973–87; Recruitment Working Party, Duke of Edinburgh's 1974 Study Conf., 1972–74. *Publications:* Blueprint for Industrial Survival, 1976; Turning Points, 1986; The Mountain, 1988; Jewels and Old Shoes, 1990. *Recreations:* mountaineering, walking, sailing. *Heir:* none. *Address:* Tyma House, Bosham, near Chichester, Sussex PO18 8HZ. *Clubs:* Naval; Royal Southern Yacht (Southampton).

WATKINSON, John Taylor; solicitor; Principal, Watkinson & Co., since 1989; *b* 25 Jan. 1941; *s* of William Forshaw Watkinson; *m* 1969, Jane Elizabeth Miller; two *s* two *d*. *Educ:* Bristol Grammar Sch.; Worcester Coll., Oxford. Schoolmaster, Rugby Sch., Warwicks, 1964–71. Called to the Bar, Middle Temple, 1971; practised, Midland Circuit, 1972–74, South East Circuit, 1978–79; Solicitor of the Supreme Ct, 1986–. MP (Lab) Gloucestershire West, Oct. 1974–1979; PPS to Sec. of State, Home Office, 1975–79; Member: Public Accounts Cttee, 1976–79; Expenditure Cttee, 1978–79; Speakers' Conf. on Northern Ireland, 1979; Hon. Sec., Anglo-Swiss Parly Gp, 1977–79; Mem. and Rapporteur, Council of Europe and WEU, 1976–79; Rapporteur, first Europ. Declaration on the Police. Contested: (Lab) Warwick and Leamington, 1970; (SDP) Glos West, 1983, 1987. Financial Reporter, BBC TV, 1979–82; Director: Interconnect Communications Ltd, 1986–; Wyedean Review Ltd, 1987–. Advr to Polish, Macedonian, Bulgarian and Latvian Govts on telecommunications laws and regulatory regimes, 1992–93. Visitor, Onley Borstal, Warwicks, 1970–71. Mem., NUJ. Amateur Rugby Fives Champion (Singles 3 times, Doubles 4 times), 1964–70. *Publications:* (jtly) UK Telecommunications Approval Manual, 1987; Telecommunications Approval Report, 1987; European Telecommunications Manual, 1990. *Recreations:* rackets, cricket, golf. *Address:* Clanna Lodge, Alvington, Lydney, Glos GL15 6AJ.

WATLING, (David) Brian, QC 1979; **His Honour Judge Watling;** a Circuit Judge, since 1981; *b* 18 June 1935; *o s* of late Russell and Stella Watling; *m* 1964, Noelle Louise Bugden. *Educ:* Charterhouse; King's Coll., London (LLB). Sub-Lieut RNR. Called to Bar, Middle Temple, 1957; Advocate, Gibraltar, 1980. Various Crown appts, 1969–72; Treasury Counsel, Central Criminal Court, 1972–79; a Recorder of the Crown Court, 1979–81. Vis. Lectr, 1978–80, Vis. Prof. in Criminal Law, 1980–84, University Coll. at Buckingham (now Univ. of Buckingham). Diocese of St Edmundsbury and Ipswich: Reader 1985; Deacon 1987; Priest 1988. Chm., Mistley Bk Club, 1989–; Pres., Dedham Vale Soc., 1994–. *Publication:* (contrib.) Serving Two Masters, 1988. *Recreations:* sailing, langlauf, hill walking, theatre and ballet, fireside reading, the company of old friends. *Address:* The Crown Court, PO Box 9, Chelmsford CM1 1EL. *Club:* Garrick.

WATSON, family name of **Baron Manton.**

WATSON, Adam; *see* Watson, John Hugh A.

WATSON, Alan; *see* Watson, W. A. J.

WATSON, Prof. Alan Albert, JP; FRCPath; Regius Professor of Forensic Medicine, University of Glasgow, 1985–92, now Emeritus; *b* 20 Feb. 1929; *s* of Wilfrid Roy Watson and Gladys Cusden or Watson; *m* 1955, Jeannette Anne Pitts or Watson; three *s*. Educ: Reading Sch.; St Mary's Hosp. Med. Sch., Univ. of London (MB BS); MA Cantab; FRCPGlas; DMJ; DTM&H (Antwerp); BD Glasgow. Director, Ntondo Hosp., Zaire, 1958; Lectr in Pathology, Glasgow Univ., 1964; Asst Pathologist, Cambridge Univ., 1969, Fellow, Queens' Coll., Cambridge, 1970; Sen. Lectr, Forensic Medicine, Glasgow, 1971. District Court Judge, 1982; JP Glasgow, 1982–93, Kilmarnock and Loudoun Dist, 1993–. Fellow, Royal Belgian Acad. of Medicine, 1983. *Publications:* Legal Aspects of Dental Practice, 1975; Forensic Medicine, 1989; Lecture Notes on Forensic Medicine, 1989; contribs to Jls of Forensic Medicine, and Pathology. *Address:* Cessnock Castle, Galston, KA4 8LJ. *T:* Galston (01563) 820980.

WATSON, Prof. Alan Andrew, FRAS; Professor of Physics, University of Leeds, since 1984; *b* 26 Sept. 1938; *s* of William John Watson and Elsie Robinson; *m* 1973, Susan Lorraine Cartman; one *s* one *d*. *Educ:* Daniel Stewart's College, Edinburgh; Edinburgh Univ. (BSc 1st cl. hons Physics 1960; PhD 1964). Asst Lectr, Univ. of Edinburgh, 1962–64; University of Leeds: Lectr, 1964–76; Reader in Particle Cosmic Physics, 1976–84; Chm., Physics Dept, 1989–93; Pro Vice-Chancellor, 1994–96. Science and Engineering Research Council: Member: Astronomy and Planetary Science Bd, 1986–90; Nuclear Physics Bd, 1987–90; Space Science Program Bd, 1990–92; Astronomy and Astrophysics Cttee, 1992–93. Mem., Cosmic Ray Commn, IUPAP, 1991–95. Member, Editorial Board: Astroparticle Physics, 1992–; Nuclear Instruments and Methods, 1993–. *Publications:* contribs to Physical Review Letters, Astrophysical Jl, Jl of Physics, Nuclear Instruments and Methods, Nature. *Recreations:* malt whisky tasting, tennis, watching Scotland win Grand Slams, theatre. *Address:* Department of Physics, University of Leeds, Leeds LS2 9JT. *T:* Leeds (0113) 233 3888.

WATSON, Rear-Adm. Alan George, CB 1975. Served Royal Navy, 1941–77; Asst Chief of Naval Staff, 1974–77, retired. Chairman: Church of England Soldiers', Sailors' and Airmen's Clubs, 1979–; Church of England Soldiers', Sailors' and Airmen's Housing Assoc., 1979–.

WATSON, Alan John, CBE 1985; Chairman: Corporate Vision Ltd, since 1989; Corporate Television Networks, since 1992; Burston-Marstellar UK, since 1994; Director, Burson-Marsteller Worldwide, since 1992; *b* 3 Feb. 1941; *s* of Rev. John William Watson and Edna Mary (*née* Peters); *m* 1965, Karen Lederer; two *s*. *Educ:* Diocesan Coll., Cape Town,

SA; Kingswood Sch., Bath, Somerset; Jesus Coll., Cambridge (Open Schol. in History 1959, State Schol. 1959) (MA Hons). Vice-Pres., Cambridge Union; Pres., Cambridge Univ. Liberal Club. Research Asst to Cambridge Prof. of Modern History on post-war history of Unilever, 1962–64. General trainee, BBC, 1965–66; Reporter, BBC TV, The Money Programme, 1966–68; Chief Public Affairs Commentator, London Weekend Television, 1969–70; Reporter, Panorama, BBC TV, 1971–74; Presenter, The Money Programme, 1974–75; Head of TV, Radio, Audio-Visual Div., EEC, and Editor, European Community Newsreel Service to Lomé Convention Countries, 1975–79; Dir, Charles Barker City Ltd, 1980–85 (Chief Exec., 1980–83); Chairman: City and Corporate Counsel Ltd, 1987–94; Threadneedle Publishing Gp, 1987–94. Pres., Liberal Party, 1984–85. Vice Chm., European Movt, 1995–. Presenter: You and 1992, BBC 1 series, 1990; The Germans, Channel 4, 1992. Vis. Fellow, Louvanium Internat. Business Centre, Brussels, 1990–; Vis. Erasmus Prof. in European Studies, Louvain Univ., 1990–. Chm., RTS, 1992–94 (Mem. Council, 1989–). Chm., Anglo-German Assoc., 1992–95. Pres., Heathrow Assoc. for Control of Aircraft Noise, 1992–. Chm. of Governors, Westminster Coll., Oxford, 1989–94; Gov., ESU, 1993– (Internat. Dep. Chm., 1995–). Hon. DHL St Lawrence Univ., 1992. Grand Prix Eurodiaporama of European Community for Common Market Coverage, 1974. Order of Merit (Germany), 1995. *Publications:* Europe at Risk, 1972; The Germans: who are they now?, 1992 (German, US and Japanese edns). *Recreation:* historical biography. *Address:* Cholmondeley House, 3 Cholmondeley Walk, Richmond upon Thames, Surrey TW9 1NS; Somerset Lodge, Nunney, Somerset BA11 4NP. *Clubs:* Brooks's, United Oxford & Cambridge University, Royal Automobile, Kennel.

WATSON, Sir Andrew; *see* Watson, Sir J. A.

WATSON, Maj.-Gen. Andrew Linton, CB 1981; Lieutenant Governor and Secretary, Royal Hospital, Chelsea, 1984–92; *b* 9 April 1927; *s* of Col W. L. Watson, OBE, and Mrs D. E. Watson (*née* Lea); *m* 1952, Mary Elizabeth, *d* of Mr and Mrs A. S. Rigby, Warrenpoint, Co. Down; two *s* one *d. Educ:* Wellington Coll., Berks. psc, jssc, rcds. Commnd The Black Watch, 1946; served, 1946–66: with 1st and 2nd Bns, Black Watch, in UK, Germany, Cyprus and British Guiana; with UN Force, Cyprus; as GSO 2 and 3 on Staff, UK and Germany; GSO 1 HQ 17 Div./Malaya Dist, 1966–68; CO 1st Bn The Black Watch, UK, Gibraltar and NI, 1969–71; Comdr 19 Airportable Bde, Colchester, 1972–73; RCDS, 1974; Comdr British Army Staff, and Military Attaché, Washington, DC, 1975–77; GOC Eastern District, 1977–80; COS, Allied Forces, Northern Europe, 1980–82. Col, The Black Watch, 1981–92. *Recreations:* tennis, walking, classical music. *Address:* c/o Royal Bank of Scotland, 12 Dunkeld Road, Perth PH1 5RB. *T:* Perth (01738) 21777. *Clubs:* Army and Navy, Pitt.

WATSON, (Angus) Gavin; Under Secretary, since 1986, and Head, Cities, Countryside and Private Finance Directorate, since 1994, Department of the Environment; Head of Government Office Central Unit; *b* 14 April 1944; *s* of late H. E. and M. Watson; *m* 1967, Susan Naomi Beal (marr. diss. 1991); two *s* (and one *d* decd). *Educ:* Carlisle Grammar School; Merton College, Oxford. MA. Joined Dept of the Environment, 1971; Private Office, Secretary of State, 1975–77; Asst Sec., 1980–86; Under Sec., Housing Policy, 1986–91; Hd, Water Directorate, Jun.–July 1991; Directorate of Envmtl Policy and Analysis, 1991–94. *Recreations:* looking at buildings, industrial archaeology, fell walking. *Address:* c/o Department of the Environment, 2 Marsham Street, SW1P 3EP. *T:* 0171–276 4209.

WATSON, Anthony Gerard; Editor, Yorkshire Post, since 1989; *b* 28 May 1955; *s* of George Maurice Watson and Ann (*née* McDonnell); *m* 1982, Susan Ann Gutteridge (separated 1991); two *s* two *d. Educ:* St John Fisher Sch., Peterborough. N Staffs Polytechnic (BA Pol. and Internat. Relns). Journalist with E Midlands Allied Press, Peterborough, 1977–79; joined Westminster Press—Evening Despatch, Darlington, 1979, News Editor, 1983–84; Yorkshire Post, 1984–86; Researcher, World in Action, Granada TV, 1986–88; Dep. Editor, Yorkshire Post, 1988–89. Provincial Journalist of the Year, British Press Awards, 1987. *Address:* Yorkshire Post, Wellington Street, Leeds LS1 1RF. *T:* Leeds (0113) 275 1477.

WATSON, Anthony Heriot, CBE 1965; *b* 13 April 1912; *s* of William Watson and Dora Isabel Watson (*née* Fisher); *m* 1946, Hilary Margaret Fyfe. *Educ:* St Paul's Sch.; Christ Church, Oxford; University Coll., London. Statistical Officer, British Cotton Industry Research Assoc., 1936. Min. of Supply, 1940: Statistician; Asst Dir of Statistics; Min. of Aircraft Production, 1942; Statistician, Dept of Civil Aviation, Air Ministry, 1945; Chief Statistician: Min. of Civil Aviation, 1951; Min. of Transport and Civil Aviation, 1954; Min. of Aviation, 1959; Min. of Transport, 1964, Dir of Statistics, 1966; DoE, 1970; retired 1973. *Recreations:* music, garden. *Address:* 9 Kirk Park, Edinburgh EH16 6HZ. *T:* 0131–664 7428.

WATSON, Antony Edward Douglas; QC 1986; *b* 6 March 1945; *s* of William Edward Watson and Margaret Watson (*née* Douglas); *m* 1972, Gillian Mary Bevan-Arthur; two *d. Educ:* Sedbergh School; Sidney Sussex College, Cambridge (MA). Called to the Bar, Inner Temple, 1968. Dep. Chm., Copyright Tribunal, 1994. *Publication:* (jtly) Terrell on Patents (1884), 13th edn 1982, 14th edn 1994. *Recreations:* wine, opera, country pursuits. *Address:* The Old Rectory, Milden, Suffolk IP7 7AF. *T:* Bildeston (01449) 740227.

WATSON, Arthur Christopher, CMG 1977; HM Diplomatic Service, retired; Governor of Montserrat, West Indies, 1985–87; *b* 2 Jan. 1927; *s* of late Dr A. J. Watson and Dr Mary Watson, Kunming, China, and Chinnor; *m* 1956, Mary Cecil Candler (*née* Earl); one *d*; and one step *s* one step *d. Educ:* Norwich Sch.; St Catharine's Coll., Cambridge. Naval Service, 1945–48 (commissioned RNVR, 1946). Colonial Administrative Service, Uganda, 1951; District Commissioner, 1959; Principal Asst Sec., 1960; Principal, Commonwealth Relations Office, 1963; HM Diplomatic Service, 1965; Karachi, 1964–67; Lahore, 1967; FCO, 1967–71; HM Comr in Anguilla, 1971–74; Governor, Turks and Caicos Islands, 1975–78; High Comr in Brunei, 1978–83; FCO, 1983–84. *Address:* Old School House, Newport Road, Whitwell, Isle of Wight PO38 2QW. *Club:* Commonwealth Trust.

WATSON, Sir Bruce (Dunstan), Kt 1985; Chairman, M.I.M. Holdings Limited, 1983–90 (Chief Executive Officer, 1981–90); *b* 1 Aug. 1928; *s* of James Harvey and Edith Mary (Crawford); *m* 1952, June Kilgour; one *s* two *d. Educ:* University of Queensland (BE (Elec) 1949, BCom 1957). Engineer, Tasmanian Hydro Elecricity Commn, 1950–54, Townsville Regional Electricity Board, 1954–56; MIM Group of Companies: Engineer, Copper Refineries Pty Ltd, Townsville, 1956–69; Mount Isa Mines Ltd, 1970–73; Group Industrial Relations Manager, MIM Group, Brisbane, 1973–75; First Gen. Man., Agnew Mining Co., WA, 1975–77; M.I.M. Holdings Ltd, Brisbane: Director, 1977; Man. Dir. 1980; Man. Dir and Chief Exec. Officer, 1981. Director: Asarco Inc., 1985–90; National Australia Bank, 1984–91, 1992–; Boral, 1990–; Mem., Supervisory Bd, Metallgesellschaft AG, 1988–93. Member: Business Council of Australia, 1983–90; Exec. Cttee, Australian Mining Industry Council, 1980–90. Bd Mem., Australian Management Coll., Mt Eliza. Hon. DEng Queensland, 1989. *Recreation:* golf. *Address:* M.I.M. Holdings Limited, 410 Ann Street, Brisbane, Qld 4000, Australia. *T:* (7) 38338000.

WATSON, (Daniel) Stewart, CB 1967; OBE 1958; *b* 30 Dec. 1911; *s* of Reverend Dr William Watson, DD, DLitt, and Mary Mackintosh Watson; *m* 1939, Isabel (*née* Gibson) (*d* 1991); one *s. Educ:* Robert Gordon's Coll.; Aberdeen University. Student Apprentice, British Thomson Houston, Rugby, 1933, Research Engr, 1936. Scientific Officer, Admiralty, 1938–; Dir, Admiralty Surface Weapons Establishment, 1961–68; Dep. Chief Scientist (Naval), MoD, 1968–72; Dir Gen. Establishments, Resources Programme A, MoD, 1972–73. *Publications:* contribs to IEEJ. *Recreations:* thoroughbred cars; caravanning. *Address:* 28 Longhope Drive, Wrecclesham, Farnham, Surrey GU10 4SN. *T:* Farnham (01252) 733126.

WATSON, Prof. David John; Director, University of Brighton (formerly Brighton Polytechnic), since 1990; *b* 22 March 1949; *s* of late Lewis James Watson and of Berenice Nichols; *m* 1975, Betty Pinto Skolnick; one *d* one *s. Educ:* Cheshunt Grammar School; Eton College; Clare College, Cambridge (MA); Univ. of Pennsylvania (PhD). Sen. Lectr, Principal Lectr in Humanities, Crewe and Alsager Coll. of Higher Educn, 1975–81; Dean, Modular Course, Asst Dir, Dep. Dir, Oxford Polytechnic, 1981–90. Member: Council, CNAA, 1989–93 (Mem., 1977–93); PCFC, 1988–93; HEFCE, 1992–; Paul Hamlyn Foundn Nat. Commn on Educn, 1991–93; Open Univ. Validation Bd, 1992–; Chm., Univs Assoc. for Contg Educn, 1994–. *Publications:* Margaret Fuller, 1988; Managing the Modular Course, 1989; (jtly) Developing Professional Education, 1992; Arendt, 1992; (jtly) Managing the University Curriculum, 1994; papers on history of American and British ideas, higher education policy. *Recreations:* family, music (piano and saxophone), cricket. *Address:* University of Brighton, Mithras House, Lewes Road, Brighton BN2 4AT. *T:* Brighton (01273) 642001.

WATSON, Sir Duncan; *see* Watson, Sir N. D.

WATSON, Sir Duncan (Amos), Kt 1993; CBE 1986; Principal Assistant Treasury Solicitor, Common Law, 1978–86; Chairman, Executive Council, Royal National Institute for the Blind, 1975–90; *b* 10 May 1926; *m* 1954, Mercia Casey, Auckland, NZ. *Educ:* Worcester College for the Blind; St Edmund Hall, Oxford (BA). Solicitor. Chm., Access Cttee for England, 1989–93; Pres., World Blind Union, 1988–92. *Address:* 19 Great Russell Mansions, WC1B 3BE. *Club:* MCC.

WATSON, Gavin; *see* Watson, A. G.

WATSON, Gerald Walter; Partner, Financial Services Group, Ernst & Young (formerly Arthur Young), since 1989; *b* 13 Dec. 1934; *s* of Reginald Harold Watson and Gertrude Hilda Watson (*née* Ruffell); *m* 1961, Janet Rosemary (*née* Hovey); one *s* two *d. Educ:* King Edward VI, Norwich School; Corpus Christi Coll., Cambridge (MA). National Service, RAF Regt, 1953–55. War Office, 1958–64; MoD, 1964–69; Civil Service Dept, 1969–73; Northern Ireland Office, 1973–75; CSD, 1975–81; HM Treasury, 1981–86; Dir, Central Computer and Telecommunications Agency, 1978–82. Dep. Chm., Building Socs Commn, 1986–88. *Recreations:* opera and theatre going, equestrian sports. *Address:* c/o Drummonds Branch, Royal Bank of Scotland, 49 Charing Cross, SW1A 2DX.

WATSON, Graham Robert; Member (Lib Dem) Somerset and North Devon, European Parliament, since 1994; *b* 23 March 1956; *s* of late Gordon Graham Watson and of Stephanie Revill-Johnson; *m* 1987, Rita Giannini; one *d. Educ:* City of Bath Boys' Sch.; Heriot-Watt Univ. (BA Hons Mod. Langs). Freelance interpreter and translator, 1979–80; Administrator, Paisley Coll. of Tech., 1980–83; Head, Private Office of Rt Hon. David Steel, MP, 1983–87; Sen. Press Officer, TSB Group, 1987–88; HSBC Holdings: Public Affairs Manager, 1988–91; Govt Affairs Manager, 1992–94. *Publications:* (ed) The Liberals in the North-South Dialogue, 1980; articles on politics in magazines and nat. newspapers. *Recreations:* writing, choir singing, walking the dog. *Address:* European Parliament, 1040 Brussels, Belgium. *T:* (2) 2842111; Liberal Democrat Office, 10 Belvedere Road, Taunton, Som TA1 1BW. *Club:* National Liberal.

WATSON, Henry, CBE 1969; QPM 1963; Chief Constable of Cheshire, 1963–74; *b* 16 Oct. 1910; *s* of John and Ann Watson, Preston, Lancs; *m* 1933, Nellie Greenhalgh; two *d. Educ:* Preston Victoria Junior Technical Coll. Admitted to Inst. of Chartered Accountants, 1934; joined Ashton-under-Lyne Borough Police, 1934; King's Lynn Borough Police, 1942; Norfolk County Constabulary, 1947; Asst Chief Constable, Cumberland and Westmorland, 1955, Chief Constable, 1959. CStJ 1973. *Recreation:* golf. *Address:* Gorgate Road, Hoe, Dereham, Norfolk NR20 4BG.

WATSON, Maj.-Gen. (Henry) Stuart (Ramsay), CBE 1973 (MBE 1954); *b* 9 July 1922; *yr s* of Major H. A. Watson, CBE, MVO and Mrs Dorothy Bannerman Watson, OBE; *m* 1965, Susan, *o d* of Col W. H. Jackson, CBE, DL; two *s* one *d. Educ:* Winchester College. Commnd 2nd Lieut 13th/18th Royal Hussars, 1942; Lieut 1943; Captain 1945; Adjt 13/18 H, 1945–46 and 1948–50; psc 1951; GSO2, HQ 1st Corps, 1952–53; Instr RMA Sandhurst, 1955–57; Instr Staff Coll. Camberley, 1960–62; CO 13/18 H, 1962–64; GSO1, MoD, 1964–65; Col GS, SHAPE, 1965–68; Col, Defence Policy Staff. MoD, 1968; idc 1969; BGS HQ BAOR, 1970–73; Dir Defence Policy, MoD, 1973–74; Sen. Army Directing Staff, RCDS, 1974–76. Col, 13th/18th Royal Hussars, 1979–90. Exec. Dir, 1977–85, Dep. Dir Gen., 1985–88, Inst. of Dirs; Dir, Treasurers' Dept, Cons. Central Office, 1992–94. *Recreations:* golf, gardening. *Address:* The Glebe House, Little Kimble, Aylesbury, Bucks HP17 0UE. *T:* Stoke Mandeville (01296) 612200. *Clubs:* Cavalry and Guards; Huntercombe Golf.

WATSON, Sir (James) Andrew, 5th Bt, *cr* 1866; a Recorder, since 1989; *b* 30 Dec. 1937; *s* of 4th Bt and Ella Marguerite, *y d* of late Sir George Farrar, 1st Bt; *S* father, 1941; *m* 1965, Christabel Mary, *e d* of K. R. M. Carlisle and Hon. Mrs Carlisle; two *s* one *d. Educ:* Eton. Barrister-at-law. *Heir: s* Roland Victor Watson, *b* 4 March 1966. *Address:* Talton House, Newbold on Stour, Stratford-upon-Avon, Warwickshire CV37 8UD. *T:* Alderminster (01789) 450212.

WATSON, Prof. James Dewey; President, Cold Spring Harbor Laboratory, since 1994 (Director, 1968–94); *b* 6 April 1928; *s* of James D. and Jean Mitchell Watson; *m* 1968, Elizabeth Lewis; two *s. Educ:* Univ. of Chicago (BS); Indiana Univ. (PhD); Clare Coll., Cambridge. Senior Res. Fellow in Biology, California Inst. of Technology, 1953–55; Harvard University: Asst Prof. of Biology, 1955–57; Associate Prof., 1958–61; Prof. of Molecular Biology, 1961–76. Dir, Nat. Center for Human Genome Res., NIH, 1989–92. Newton-Abraham Vis. Prof., Oxford, 1994. Member: US National Acad. Sciences, 1962–; Amer Acad. of Arts and Sciences, 1957; Royal Danish Acad. 1962; Amer. Philosophical Soc., 1976; Foreign Member: Royal Soc., 1981; Acad. of Scis, Russia (formerly USSR), 1989. Hon. DSc: Chicago, 1961; Indiana, 1963; Long Island, 1970; Adelphi, 1972; Brandeis, 1973; Albert Einstein Coll. of Medicine, 1974; Hofstra, 1976; Harvard, 1978; Rockefeller, 1980; Clarkson Coll., 1981; SUNY, 1983; Rutgers, 1988; Bard Coll., 1991; Univ. of Stellenbosch, S Africa, 1993; Fairfield Univ., Conn, 1993; Univ. of Cambridge, 1993; Hon. MD Buenos Aires, 1986; Hon. LLD Notre Dame, 1965. Hon. Fellow, Clare Coll., Camb., 1967. Nobel Award in Medicine and Physiology (jointly), 1962; Carty Medal, US National Acad. of Sciences, 1971; Kaul Foundn Award for Excellence, 1992; Copley Medal, Royal Soc., 1993; Nat. Biotechnol. Venture Award, 1993. US Presidential Medal of Freedom, 1977. *Publications:* (jtly) Molecular Biology of the Gene, 1965, 4th edn 1986; The Double Helix, 1968; (with John Tooze) The DNA Story, 1981; (with others) The Molecular Biology of the Cell, 1983, 3rd edn 1994; (with John Tooze and David T. Kurtz) Recombinant DNA: a short course, 1984, 2nd edn (with others) 1992; scientific papers on the mechanism of heredity. *Recreation:* tennis. *Address:* Bungtown Road, Cold Spring Harbor, NY 11724, USA. *Clubs:* Century, Piping Rock (New York).

WATSON, James Kay Graham, PhD; FRS 1987; FRSC 1990; Principal Research Officer, National Research Council of Canada, since 1987 (Senior Research Officer, 1982–87); *b* Denny, Stirlingshire, 20 April 1936; *s* of Thomas Watson and Mary Catherine (*née* Miller); *m* 1981, Carolyn Margaret Landon Kerr, *e d* of Robert Reid Kerr, *qv*. *Educ:* Denny High Sch.; High School of Stirling; Univ. of Glasgow (BScChem, PhD). Postdoctoral Fellow: UCL, 1961–63; Nat. Res. Council, Ottawa, 1963–65; Univ. of Reading, 1965–66; Lectr in Chem. Physics, Univ. of Reading, 1966–71; Vis. Associate Prof. of Physics, Ohio State Univ., Columbus, 1971–75; SRC Sen. Res. Fellow in Chemistry, Univ. of Southampton, 1975–82. Fellow, American Physical Soc., 1990. Award for Theoretical Chemistry and Spectroscopy, Chemical Soc., 1974; Plyler Prize, Amer. Phys. Soc., 1986. *Publications:* 110 articles on molecular physics and spectroscopy in learned jls. *Recreations:* music, golf, tree-watching. *Address:* 183 Stanley Avenue, Ottawa, Ontario K1M 1P2, Canada. *T:* (613) 7457928; (business) Steacie Institute for Molecular Sciences, National Research Council of Canada, Ottawa, Ontario K1A OR6, Canada.

WATSON, James Kenneth, FCA; Chairman: Watson & Philip plc, since 1994; NFC plc (formerly National Freight Consortium), 1991–94 (Finance Director, 1982–84; Deputy Chairman, 1985–90); *b* 16 Jan. 1935; *s* of James and Helen Watson; *m* 1959, Eileen Fay Waller; two *s* one *d*. *Educ:* Watford Grammar Sch.; Stanford Univ., California, USA. Baker Sutton & Co., Chartered Accountants, 1964; Financial Controller, Times Group, 1968; Finance Director: British Road Services Ltd, 1970–76; Nat. Freight Corp., later Nat. Freight Co., 1977–82. Non-executive Director: Gartmore, 1993–; Henlys Group, 1994–; National Express, 1994–. Chm., Inst. of Management, 1993–. *Publications:* contribs to transport, management and financial press. *Recreations:* cricket, theatre, history. *Address:* Benton Potts, Hawridge Common, near Chesham, Bucks HP5 2UH. *Clubs:* Royal Automobile, MCC.

WATSON, Prof. James Patrick; Professor of Psychiatry, United Medical and Dental Schools of Guy's and St Thomas' Hospitals (formerly Guy's Hospital Medical School), since 1974; *b* 14 May 1936; *e s* of Hubert Timothy Watson and Grace Emily (*née* Mizen); *m* 1962, Dr Christine Mary Colley; four *s*. *Educ:* Roan Sch. for Boys, Greenwich; Trinity Coll., Cambridge; King's Coll. Hosp. Med. Sch., London. MA, MD; FRCP, FRCPsych, DPM, DCH. Qualified, 1960. Hosp. appts in Medicine, Paediatrics, Pathology, Neurosurgery, at King's Coll. Hosp. and elsewhere, 1960–64; Registrar and Sen. Registrar, Bethlem Royal and Maudsley Hosps, 1964–71; Sen. Lectr in Psychiatry, St George's Hosp. Med. Sch., and Hon. Consultant Psychiatrist, St George's Hosp., 1971–74. Member: British Assoc. for Behavioural Psychotherapy; British Psychological Soc.; Soc. for Psychotherapy Res.; Assoc. of Sexual and Marital Therapists. Mem., various bodies concerned with interfaces between counselling and psychotherapy, religion and medicine. *Publications:* (ed jtly) Personal Meanings, 1982; papers on gp, family, marital and behavioural psychotherapy, treatment of phobias, hospital ward environmental effects on patients, postnatal depression, community psychiatry, in BMJ, Lancet, British Jl of Psychiatry, British Jl of Med. Psychology, British Jl of Clin. Psychology, Behaviour Research and Therapy. *Recreations:* mountains; music, especially opera, especially Mozart. *Address:* 36 Alleyn Road, SE21 8AL. *T:* 0181–670 0444.

WATSON, Ven. Jeffrey John Seagrief; Archdeacon of Ely, since 1993; *b* 29 April 1939; *s* of late John Cole Watson and of Marguerite Freda Rose Watson; *m* 1969, Rosemary Grace Lea; one *s* one *d*. *Educ:* University College Sch., Hampstead; Emmanuel Coll., Cambridge (MA Hons Classics); Clifton Theol Coll., Bristol. Curate: Christ Church, Beckenham, 1965–69; St Jude, Southsea, 1969–71; Vicar: Christ Church, Winchester, 1971–81; Holy Saviour, Bitterne, 1981–93; Examining Chaplain to Bishop of Winchester, 1976–93; RD of Southampton, 1983–93; Hon. Canon: Winchester Cathedral, 1991–93; Ely Cathedral, 1993–. Mem., Gen. Synod, 1985–; Chm., C of E Vocations Adv. Sub-Cttee, 1991–. *Recreations:* photography, barbershop singing, walking, travel (when I have time and money!). *Address:* St Botolph's Rectory, 1a Summerfield, Cambridge CB3 9HE.

WATSON, John, FRCS, FRCSE; Consultant Plastic Surgeon to: Queen Victoria Hospital, East Grinstead, 1950–77, now Hon. Consultant; King Edward VII Hospital for Officers, 1963–87; London Hospital, 1963–82; *b* 10 Sept. 1914; *s* of late John Watson; *m* 1941, June Christine Stiles; one *s* three *d*. *Educ:* Leighton Park, Reading; Jesus Coll., Cambridge; Guy's Hospital. MRCS, LRCP 1938; MA, MB, BChir (Cantab) 1939; FRCS(Ed.) 1946; FRCS 1963. Served as Sqdn Ldr (temp.) RAF, 1940–46 (despatches twice). Marks Fellow in Plastic Surgery, Queen Victoria Hosp., E Grinstead, 1947–50; Consultant Plastic Surgeon, Queen Victoria Hospital, East Grinstead, and Tunbridge Wells Gp of Hospitals, 1950–77. Gen. Sec., Internat. Confedn for Plastic and Reconstructive Surgery, 1971–75; Hon. Mem. Brit. Assoc. of Plastic Surgeons, 1979– (Hon. Sec., 1960–62, Pres., 1969); Hon. FRSM. *Publications:* numerous articles on plastic surgery in techn. jls and scientific periodicals. Chapters in: Textbook of Surgery, Plastic Surgery for Nurses, Modern Trends in Plastic Surgery, Clinical Surgery. *Recreations:* fishing, astronomy. *Address:* Iddons, Henley's Down, Catsfield, Battle, East Sussex TN33 9BN. *T:* Crowhurst (01424) 830226.

WATSON, Sir John Forbes I.; *see* Inglefield-Watson.

WATSON, John Grenville Bernard; Chief Executive, Bradford City Challenge Ltd, since 1992; *b* 21 Feb. 1943; *s* of Norman V. Watson and Ruby E. Watson; *m* 1965, Deanna Wood; one *s* two *d*. *Educ:* Moorlands Sch., Leeds; Bootham Sch., York; College of Law, Guildford. Articled, 1962, qualified as solicitor, 1967; joined John Waddington Ltd as managerial trainee, 1968; Export Director, Plastona John Waddington Ltd, 1972; Marketing Dir, 1975, Man. Dir, 1977, Waddington Games Ltd, responsible for Security Printing Div., 1984–89, for Johnsen & Jorgensen, 1988–89; Director: John Waddington PLC, 1979–89; Goddard Kay Rogers (Northern) Ltd, 1989–; Chm., Murray Luckett Communications Ltd, 1989–90. Mem., Leeds Develt Corp., 1988–92. Joined Young Conservatives, 1965; Chairman, Yorkshire YC, 1969; Personal Asst to Rt Hon. Edward Heath, 1970; Chm., Nat. YC, 1971; contested (C) York, general elections, Feb. and Oct. 1974. MP (C): Skipton, 1979–83; Skipton and Ripon, 1983–87. Chm., Conservative Candidates Assoc., 1975–79. Mem., Parly Select Cttee on Energy, 1980–82; PPS, NI Office, 1982–83; PPS, Dept of Energy, 1983–85. Chm., British Atlantic Gp of Young Political Leaders, 1982–84; Nat. Vice Pres., Young Conservative Orgn, 1984–86. Pres., British Youth Council, 1980–83. *Recreations:* train spotting, bungee jumping, impersonating Elvis Presley. *Address:* Bay Horse Corner, Ling Lane, Scarcroft, Leeds LS14 3HY. *T:* Leeds (0113) 289 2209.

See also V. H. Watson.

WATSON, (John Hugh) Adam, CMG 1958; Professor, Center for Advanced Studies, University of Virginia, 1980–95; *b* 10 Aug. 1914; *er s* of Joseph Charlton Watson and Alice (*née* Tate); *m* 1950, Katharine Anne Campbell; two *s* one *d*. *Educ:* Rugby; King's Coll., Camb. Entered the Diplomatic Service, 1937; Brit. Legation, Bucharest, 1939; Brit. Embassy, Cairo, 1940; Brit. Embassy, Moscow, 1944; FO, 1947; Brit. Embassy, Washington, 1950; Head of African Dept, Foreign Office, 1956–59; appointed British Consul-General at Dakar, 1959; British Ambassador: to the Federation of Mali, 1960–61; to Senegal, Mauritania and Togo, 1960–62; to Cuba, 1963–66; Under-Secretary, Foreign Office, 1966–68; Diplomatic Adviser, British Leyland Motor Corp., 1968–73. Gwilym Gibbon Fellow, Nuffield Coll., Oxford, Oct. 1962–Oct. 1963. Vis. Fellow, ANU, 1973; Vis. Prof., Univ. of Virginia, 1978. Dir Gen., Internat. Assoc. for Cultural Freedom, 1974. *Publications:* The War of the Goldsmith's Daughter, 1964; Nature and Problems of Third World, 1968; (ed) The Origins of History, 1981; Diplomacy: the dialogue between States, 1982; (with Hedley Bull) The Expansion of International Society, 1984; The Evolution of International Society, 1992; various plays broadcast by BBC. *Address:* Sharnden Old Manor, Mayfield, East Sussex TN20 6QA. *T:* Mayfield (01435) 872441; 1871 Field Road, Charlottesville, VA 22903, USA. *T:* (804) 2958295. *Club:* Brooks's.

WATSON, (Leslie) Michael (Macdonald) S.; *see* Saunders Watson.

WATSON, Michael Goodall; MP (Lab) Glasgow Central, since 1989; *b* 1 May 1949; *s* of late Clarke Watson and Senga (*née* Goodall); *m* 1986, Lorraine Therese, *d* of late William McManus and of Mary McManus. *Educ:* Invergowrie Primary Sch., Dundee; Dundee High Sch.; Heriot-Watt Univ., Edinburgh (BA 2nd Cl. Hons Econs and Industrial Relns). Development Officer, WEA, E Midlands Dist, 1974–77; full-time official, ASTMS, then MSF, 1977–89. Mem., Scottish Exec. Cttee, Labour Party, 1987–90; Chm., PLP Overseas Develt Aid Cttee, 1991–. *Publications:* Rags to Riches: the official history of Dundee United Football Club, 1985. *Recreations:* supporting Dundee United FC, reading, especially political biographies, running. *Address:* Room 537, 7 Millbank, SW1P 3JA.

WATSON, Sir Michael M.; *see* Milne-Watson.

WATSON, Prof. Newton Frank, RIBA; Haden/Pilkington Professor of Environmental Design and Engineering, and Head, Bartlett School of Architecture and Planning, University College London, 1985–88, now Emeritus Professor; Dean of the Faculty of Environmental Studies, 1986–88; *b* 29 July 1923; *s* of Frank Watson and Amy Watson (*née* Cole); *m* 1944, Bridget Williams; two *d*. *Educ:* Holywell Grammar Sch.; King's Coll., Univ. of Durham. BArch. Wartime service, RWF (Lieut). Asst architect in practice, 1951–55; Res. Fellow, Nuffield Foundn Div. for Architectural Studies, 1955–57; Lectr in Arch., Poly. of N London, 1957–60; Lectr/Sen. Lectr in Arch., UCL, 1960–69; Bartlett Prof. of Architecture, UCL, 1969–85. Vis. Prof., Dept. of Arch., Univ. of California at Berkeley, 1965–66; Vis. Scholar, Sch. of Design, N Carolina State Univ., 1989. Awards (jtly) by Illuminating Soc. of Amer. for lighting design of London Stock Exchange, 1974, and Tate Gall., 1980. *Publications:* (jtly) in Design for Research, 1986; contribs to professional jls on lighting design (CIBSE medal (jtly) 1982, for contrib. Preferred Lighting Levels for Viewing Works of Art. *Recreations:* etching, France. *Address:* 1b Oval Road, NW1 7EA. *T:* 0171–485 4796. *Club:* Athenæum.

WATSON, Sir (Noel) Duncan, KCMG 1967 (CMG 1960); HM Diplomatic Service, retired; *b* 16 Dec. 1915; *s* of late Harry and Mary Noel Watson, Bradford, Yorks; *m* 1951, Aileen Bryans (*d* 1980), *d* of late Charles Bell, Dublin. *Educ:* Bradford Grammar School; New College, Oxford. Colonial Administrative Service: Admin. Officer, Cyprus, 1938–43; Assistant Colonial Secretary, Trinidad, 1943–45; Principal, Colonial Office (secondment), 1946; transferred to Home Civil Service, 1947; Principal Private Sec. to Sec. of State for the Colonies, 1947–50; Asst Sec.: CO, 1950–62, Cent. Af. Office, 1962–63; Under-Secretary, 1963; Asst Under-Sec. of State, CO and CRO, 1964–67; Political Adviser to C-in-C Far East, 1967–70; High Comr in Malta, 1970–72; Dep. Under-Sec. of State, FCO, 1972–75. Mem., Central Council, Royal Commonwealth Soc., 1975– (Dep. Chm., 1983–87). *Address:* Sconce, Steels Lane, Oxshott, Surrey KT22 0QH. *Clubs:* Travellers', Commonwealth Trust; Leander.

WATSON, Dr Peter, OBE 1988; Chief Executive, AEA Technology, since 1994; *b* 9 Jan. 1944; *m* 1966, Elizabeth Buttery; two *s*. *Educ:* Univ. of Leeds (BSc 1966); Univ. of Waterloo, Canada (MSc 1968; PhD 1971). PSO, British Railways Res., 1971–76; GKN Technology Ltd, 1976–89 (Chm., 1982–89); Chm., GKN Axles Ltd, 1986–91; Technical Dir, British Railways, 1991–94. Pres., Engrg Integrity Soc., 1988–. FRSA 1988. *Publications:* numerous articles on metal fatigue and management. *Address:* 49 Suckling Green Lane, Codsall, Wolverhampton, W Midlands WV8 2BT. *T:* Codsall (01902) 845252.

WATSON, Rt Rev. Peter Robert; an Assistant Bishop of Sydney, since 1989 (Bishop of Parramatta, 1989–93, of South Sydney, since 1993); *b* 1 Jan. 1936; *s* of Noel Frederick and Helen Elizabeth Watson; *m* 1962, Margo Eleanor Deans; three *d*. *Educ:* Canterbury Boys' High Sch., Sydney; Sydney Univ. (BEc); Moore Theological Coll., Sydney (ThL). Asst Priest, St Paul's, Chatswood, 1961–63; Curate-in-Charge, Lalor Park and Seven Hills, 1963–73; Rector, Lalor Park and Seven Hills, 1973–74; RD of Prospect, 1968–74; Canon, Prov. Cathedral of St John, Parramatta, 1969–74; Rector: St Luke's, Miranda, 1974–84; St Thomas, North Sydney, 1984–89; Area Dean, North Sydney, 1986–89. *Recreations:* caravanning, squash, swimming. *Address:* St Andrew's House, Sydney Square, Sydney, NSW 2000, Australia. *T:* (2) 2651523, *Fax:* (2) 2651543. *Clubs:* Sydney City Tattersalls; NSW Leagues.

WATSON, Vice-Adm. Sir Philip (Alexander), KBE 1976; LVO 1960; *b* 7 Oct. 1919; *yr s* of A. H. St C. Watson; *m* 1948, Jennifer Beatrice Tanner; one *s* two *d*. *Educ:* St Albans School. FIEE 1963; CBIM 1973. Sub-Lt RNVR, 1940; qual. Torpedo Specialist, 1943; transf. to RN, 1946; Comdr 1955; HM Yacht Britannia, 1957–59; Captain 1963; MoD (Ship Dept), 1963; Senior Officers' War Course, 1966; comd HMS Collingwood, 1967; Dep. Dir of Engrg (Ship Dept), MoD, 1969; Dir Gen. Weapons (Naval), MoD, 1970–77; Chief Naval Engineer Officer, 1974–77. Rear-Adm. 1970; Vice-Adm. 1974. Director: Marconi International Marine Co. Ltd, 1977–86; Marconi Radar Systems Ltd, 1981–86 (Chm., 1981–85); Consultant, GEC–Marconi Ltd, 1986–87. Mem. Council, IEE, 1975–78, 1982–91, Chm. South East Centre, 1982–83. Adm. Pres., Midland Naval Officers Assoc., 1979–85, Vice Pres., 1985–. *Address:* The Hermitage, Bodicote, Banbury, Oxon OX15 4BZ. *T:* Banbury (01295) 263300. *Club:* Army and Navy.

WATSON, Dr Reginald Gordon Harry, (Rex), CB 1987; CChem, FRSC; Director, Building Research Establishment, Department of the Environment, 1983–88; *b* 3 Nov. 1928; *s* of Gordon Henry and Winifred Catherine Watson; *m* 1951, Molly Joyce Groom (*d* 1989); one *s* two *d*. *Educ:* Chislehurst and Sidcup Grammar Sch.; Imperial Coll., London (Royal Schol.). BSc (1st cl. Hons Chem.), PhD; DIC; ARCS. Res. Worker (Fuel Cells), Dept of Chemical Engrg, Univ. of Cambridge, 1951–56; joined Royal Naval Scientific Service, 1956, as Sen. Scientific Officer, Admty Materials Lab.; Head of Chemical Engrg Div., 1958–66; Naval Staff Course, 1962; Individual Merit Sen. Principal Scientific Officer, 1965; Director: Naval R&D Admin, 1967–69; Admty Materials Lab., 1969–74; Chemical Defence Estab., Porton Down, 1974–83. *Publications:* papers on electrochemistry, chemical engineering and materials science. *Recreations:* photography, natural history, sailing. *Address:* 20 Merriefield Drive, Broadstone, Dorset BH18 8BP. *T:* Broadstone (01202) 692128. *Club:* Civil Service.

WATSON, Rt. Rev. Richard Charles Challinor; Hon. Assistant Bishop, Diocese of Oxford, since 1988; *b* 16 Feb. 1923; *o s* of Col Francis W. Watson, CB, MC, DL, The Glebe House, Dinton, Aylesbury, Bucks; *m* 1955, Anna, *er d* of Rt Rev. C. M. Chavasse, OBE, MC, MA, DD, then Bishop of Rochester; one *s* one *d*. *Educ:* Rugby; New Coll., Oxford; Westcott House, Cambridge. Served Indian Artillery, Lt and Capt. RA, 1942–45. Oxford Hon. Sch. Lang. and Lit., 1948, Theology 1949; Westcott House, Cambridge, 1950–51. Curate of Stratford, London E, 1952–53; Tutor and Chaplain, Wycliffe Hall, Oxford, 1954–57; Chaplain of Wadham Coll. and Chaplain of Oxford Pastorate, 1957–61; Vicar of Hornchurch, 1962–70; Asst Rural Dean of Havering, 1967–70; Rector of Burnley, 1970–77; Bishop Suffragan of Burnley, 1970–87; Hon. Canon of Blackburn Cathedral, 1970–87. Examining Chaplain to Bishop Rochester, 1956–61, to Bishop of Chelmsford, 1962–70. *Recreations:* reading, gardening. *Address:* 6 Church Road, Thame, Oxon OX9 3AJ. *T:* Thame (0184421) 3853.

WATSON, Richard (Eagleson Gordon) Burges, CMG 1985; HM Diplomatic Service, retired; Ambassador to Nepal, 1987–90; *b* 23 Sept. 1930; *er s* of late Harold Burges Watson and Marjorie Eleanor (*née* Gordon); *m* 1966, Ann Rosamund Clarke; two *s* three *d*. *Educ:* King Edward VI Sch., Bury St Edmunds; St John's Coll., Cambridge. RA, 1948–50. Joined HM Foreign (subseq. Diplomatic) Service, 1954; Tokyo, 1954–60; FO, 1960–63; Bamako (Mali), 1963–66; British Delegn to OECD, 1966–69; FCO, 1969–71; Vis. Student, Woodrow Wilson Sch., Princeton, 1971–72; Tokyo, 1972–76; Brussels, 1976–78; FCO, 1978–81; Foundn for Internat. Research and Studies, Florence, 1981–82; FCO, 1982–83; Minister (Commercial) and Consul-Gen., Milan, 1983–86. *Recreations:* ski-ing, swimming, walking. *Address:* 101 Howards Lane, Putney, SW15 6NZ. *T:* 0181–785 9053. *Clubs:* Travellers'; Hurlingham.

WATSON, Roy William, CBE 1983; Director General, National Farmers' Union, 1979–85, retired; *b* 7 Feb. 1926; *s* of William and Eleanor Maud Watson; *m* 1st, 1947, Margaret Peasey; two *s*; 2nd, 1977, Phyllis Frances Brotherwood (*née* Farrer). *Educ:* Alleyn's Sch., Dulwich. Intelligence Corps, 1945–48. National Farmers' Union, 1948–85: Asst Dir General, 1973–78; Dep. Dir General, 1978. Mem., UK Employer Delegn to ILO, 1961–76; formerly Mem., ILO Permanent Agric. Cttee and Cttee on Rural Develt; Employer Deleg. to World Employment Conf., 1976. *Recreations:* music, military history, golf, gardening. *Address:* Avalon, Exeter Road, Honiton, Devon EX14 8AU. *T:* Honiton (01404) 42586.

WATSON, Prof. Stephen Roger; Dean, Lancaster University Management School, since 1994; Fellow of Emmanuel College, Cambridge, since 1968; *b* 29 Aug. 1943; *s* of John C. Watson and Marguerite F. R. Watson; *m* 1969, Rosemary Victoria Tucker; one *s* one *d*. *Educ:* University College Sch., Hampstead; Emmanuel Coll., Cambridge (BA 1964, MA 1968, PhD 1969). Research Fellow, Emmanuel Coll., Cambridge, 1968–70; Shell International, 1970–71; Cambridge University: Univ. Lectr in Operational Research, Engineering Dept, 1971–86; Tutor, Emmanuel Coll., 1973–85; Dir, Judge Inst. of Management Studies, 1990–94. Peat, Marwick Prof. of Management Studies, 1986–94; Director: Cambridge Decision Analysts Ltd, 1984–; Environmental Resources Management, 1989–. *Publications:* Decision Synthesis (with D. M. Buede), 1987; papers in learned jls. *Recreations:* singing, development issues. *Address:* 8 Castle Park, Lancaster LA1 1YQ. *T:* Lancaster (01524) 64755.

WATSON, Stewart; *see* Watson, D. S.

WATSON, Maj.-Gen. Stuart; *see* Watson, Maj.-Gen. H. S. R.

WATSON, Thomas Sturges; professional golfer, since 1971; *b* 4 Sept. 1949; *s* of Raymond Etheridge Watson and Sarah Elizabeth Watson (*née* Ridge); *m* 1973, Linda Tova Rubin; one *s* one *d*. *Educ:* Stanford Univ. (BS 1971). Championships include: Open, 1975, 1977, 1980, 1982, 1983; US Open, 1982; Masters, 1977, 1981; Mem., Ryder Cup team, 1977, 1981, 1983, 1989, Captain, 1993. *Address:* 1901 W 47th Place, Suite 200, Shawnee Mission, KS 66205, USA.

WATSON, Thomas Yirrell, CMG 1955; MBE 1943; *b* 27 May 1906; *s* of William Scott Watson and Edith Rose Watson (*née* Yirrell); *m* 1st, 1935, Margaret Alice (*d* 1978), *d* of late J. J. Watson; one *d*; 2nd, 1984, Katharine Margaret, *widow* of W. J. Mill Irving, OBE and *d* of late James Kay. *Educ:* Aberdeen Grammar Sch.; Aberdeen Univ. (BSc); Cambridge Univ. (Diploma in Agricultural Science); Pretoria Univ., South Africa. Colonial Agricultural Scholar, 1929–31; Agricultural Officer, Kenya, 1931–43; Senior Agricultural Officer, Kenya, 1943–48; Dep. Director of Agriculture, Uganda, 1948–51; Director of Agriculture, Uganda, 1951–53; Secretary for Agriculture and Natural Resources, Uganda, 1954–55; Minister of Natural Resources, 1955–56. General Manager, Uganda Lint Cotton Marketing Board, 1951–53; MEC and MLC, Uganda, 1951–56. Member: Commission of Inquiry into Land and Population Problems, Fiji, 1959–60; Economic Development Commn, Zanzibar, 1961; Commission of Inquiry into Cotton Ginning Industry, Uganda, 1962; Commissioner, Burley Tobacco Industry Inquiry, Malawi, 1964. Coronation Medal, 1953. *Address:* 2 Lennox Milne Court, Haddington, East Lothian EH41 4DF. *T:* Haddington (01620) 824490.

WATSON, Victor Hugo, CBE 1987; DL; *b* 26 Sept. 1928; *s* of Norman Victor and Ruby Ernestine Watson; *m* 1952, Sheila May Bryan; two *d*. *Educ:* Clare Coll., Cambridge (MA). Served Royal Engineers (2nd Lieut), 1946–48. Joined John Waddington Ltd, 1951; Chm., 1977–93, retired. Director: John Foster & Son PLC, 1985– (Chm., 1985–92); Leeds & Holbeck Building Soc., 1986– (Pres., 1989–91); Leeds TEC Ltd, 1990–; Yorkshire-Tyne Tees Television, 1992–; Stylo PLC, 1993–. Pres., Inst. of Packaging, 1984–. DL West Yorks, 1991. *Recreations:* music, golf, sailing. *Address:* Moat Field, Moor Lane, East Keswick, Leeds LS17 9ET.

WATSON, Prof. William, CBE 1982; MA; FBA 1972; FSA; Professor of Chinese Art and Archaeology in University of London, at the School of Oriental and African Studies, 1966–83, now Emeritus, and Head of the Percival David Foundation of Chinese Art, 1966–83; *b* 9 Dec. 1917; *s* of Robert Scoular Watson and Lily Waterfield; *m* 1940, Katherine Sylvia Mary, *d* of Mr and Mrs J. H. Armfield, Ringwood, Hants; four *s*. *Educ:* Glasgow High Sch.; Herbert Strutt Sch.; Gonville and Caius Coll., Cantab (Scholar; tripos in Modern and Medieval Langs). Served Intelligence Corps, 1940–46, Egypt, N Africa, Italy, India, ending as Major. Asst Keeper, British Museum, first in Dept of British and Medieval Antiquities, then in Dept of Oriental Antiquities, 1947–66. Slade Prof. of Fine Art, Cambridge University, 1975–76. Trustee, BM, 1980–90. Pres., Oriental Ceramic Soc., 1981–84. Hon. DLitt Chinese Univ. of Hong Kong, 1984. Sir Percy Sykes Meml Medal, 1973. *Publications:* The Sculpture of Japan, 1959; Archaeology in China, 1960; China before the Han Dynasty, 1961; Ancient Chinese Bronzes, 1961; Jade Books in the Chester Beatty Library, 1963; Cultural Frontiers in Ancient East Asia, 1971; The Genius of China (catalogue of Burlington House exhibn), 1973; Style in the Arts of China, 1974; L'Art de l'Ancienne Chine, 1980; (ed) Catalogue of the Great Japan Exhibition (at Burlington House 1981–82); Tang and Liao Ceramics, 1984; Pre-Tang Ceramics of China, 1991. *Recreation:* exploring N Wales, Romanesque France and Spain. *Address:* Cefn y Maes, Parc, Bala, Gwynedd LL23 7YS. *T:* Bala (01678) 4302.

WATSON, William Albert, CB 1989; PhD; FRCVS; Director, Veterinary Laboratories, Ministry of Agriculture, Fisheries and Food, 1986–90; *b* 8 March 1930; *s* of Henry Watson and Mary Emily Watson; *m* 1956, Wilma, *d* of Rev. Theodorus Johannas Henricus Steenbeck; one *s* one *d*. *Educ:* Preston Grammar School; University of Bristol (PhD, BVSc). Private practice, Garstang, Lancs, 1954–55; Asst Vet. Investigation Officer, Weybridge, 1954–56, Leeds, 1956–66; Animal Health Expert, FAO, Turkey, 1966–67; Vet. Investigation Officer, Penrith, 1967–71; Dep. Regional Vet. Officer, Nottingham, 1971–75; Regional Vet. Officer, Edinburgh, 1975–77; Asst Chief Vet. Officer, Tolworth, 1977–84; Dep. Dir, Vet. Labs, Weybridge, 1984–86. External Examr, London, Liverpool, Dublin and Edinburgh Univs. *Publications:* contribs to vet. jls and textbooks. *Recreations:* fishing, gardening, restoration of listed property, farming.

WATSON, Prof. William Alexander Jardine; Ernest P. Rogers Professor of Law, University of Georgia, since 1989; *b* 27 Oct. 1933; *s* of James W. and Janet J. Watson; *m* 1st, 1958, Cynthia Betty Balls, MA, MLitt (marr. diss.); one *s* one *d*; 2nd, 1986, Harriett Camilla Emanuel, BA, MS, JD, LLM; one *d*. *Educ:* Univ. of Glasgow (MA 1954, LLB 1957); Univ. of Oxford (BA (by decree) 1957, MA 1958, DPhil 1960, DCL 1973). Lectr, Wadham Coll., Oxford, 1957–59; Lectr, 1959–60, Fellow, 1960–65, Oriel Coll., Oxford; Pro-Proctor, Oxford Univ., 1962–63; Douglas Prof. of Civil Law, Univ. of Glasgow, 1965–68; Prof. of Civil Law, Univ. of Edinburgh, 1968–79; University of Pennsylvania: Prof. of Law and Classical Studies, 1979–84; Dir, Center for Advanced Studies in Legal Hist., 1980–89; Nicholas F. Gallichio Prof. of Law, 1984–86; Univ. Prof. of Law, 1986–89. Visiting Professor of Law: Tulane Univ., 1967; Univ. of Virginia, 1970 and 1974; Univ. of Cape Town, 1974 and 1975; Univ. of Michigan, 1977. Mem. Council, Stair Soc., 1970–; Hon. Mem., Speculative Soc., 1975. Hon. LLD Glasgow, 1993. *Publications:* (as Alan Watson): Contract of Mandate in Roman Law, 1961; Law of Obligations in Later Roman Republic, 1965; Law of Persons in Later Roman Republic, 1967; Law of Property in Later Roman Republic, 1968; Law of the Ancient Romans, 1970; Roman Private Law Around 200 BC, 1971; Law of Succession in Later Roman Republic, 1971; Law Making in Later Roman Republic, 1974; Legal Transplants, An Approach to Comparative Law, 1974, 2nd edn 1993; (ed) Daube Noster, 1974; Rome of the Twelve Tables, 1975; Society and Legal Change, 1977; The Nature of Law, 1977; The Making of the Civil Law, 1981; Sources of Law, Legal Change, and Ambiguity, 1984; The Evolution of Law, 1985; (ed) The Digest of Justinian (4 vols), 1986; Failures of the Legal Imagination, 1988; Slave Law of the Americas, 1989; Roman Law and Comparative Law, 1991; The State, Law and Religion: pagan Rome, 1991; Studies in Roman Private Law, 1991; Legal Origins and Legal Change, 1991; The State, Law and Religion: archaic Rome, 1992; Joseph Story and the Comity of Errors, 1993; International Law in Archaic Rome, 1993; The Spirit of Roman Law, 1995; Jesus and the Jews, 1995; The Trial of Jesus, 1995; various articles. *Recreations:* Roman numismatics, shooting. *Address:* Law School, University of Georgia, Herty Drive, Athens, GA 30602, USA.

WATT; *see* Gibson-Watt.

WATT, Very Rev. Alfred Ian; Dean of the United Diocese of St Andrews, Dunkeld and Dunblane, since 1989; *b* 1934. *Educ:* Edinburgh Theological College. Deacon, 1960, priest 1961, Diocese of Brechin; Curate, St Paul's Cathedral, Dundee, 1960–63; Precentor, 1963–66; Rector of Arbroath, 1966–69; Provost of St Ninian's Cathedral, Perth, 1969–82; Canon, 1982–89; Rector, St Paul's, Kinross, 1982–95. Convenor, Mission Bd of General Synod, 1982–87. *Address:* 33 Stirling Road, Milnathort, Kinross KY13 7XS.

WATT, Andrew, CBE 1963; Forestry Commissioner, 1965–69; *b* 10 Nov. 1909; 2nd surv. *s* of late James Watt, LLD, WS, and late Menie Watt; *m* 1943, Helen McGuffog (*d* 1969); two *s* one *d*. *Educ:* Winchester; Magdalen Coll., Oxford, BA 1931. District Officer, Forestry Commn, 1934; Divisional Officer, 1940; Conservator, 1946; Director of Forestry for Scotland, 1957–63; Director of Forest Research, 1963–65. *Address:* 7A Ravelston Park, Edinburgh EH4 3DX. *T:* 0131–332 1084.

WATT, Charlotte Joanne, (Mrs G. L. Watt); *see* Erickson, Prof. C. J.

WATT, Prof. Donald Cameron; *see* Cameron Watt.

WATT, Hamish; writer, politician, farmer; Rector of Aberdeen University, 1985–88; *b* 27 Dec. 1925; *s* of Wm Watt and Caroline C. Allan; *m* 1948, Mary Helen Grant (marr. diss. 1989); one *s* two *d*. *Educ:* Keith Grammar Sch.; St Andrews Univ. Engaged in farming (dairy and sheep). Subseq. company director, quarries. Contested (C), Caithness, 1966; contested (SNP): Banff, 1970; Moray, 1983. MP (SNP) Banff, Feb. 1974–1979. Regional and Dist Councillor (SNP), Moray, 1985–90 (Chm., Educn Cttee, 1986–90). Columnist, after-dinner speaker, story writer. JP Moray, 1984. Hon. LLD Aberdeen, 1988. *Address:* Mill of Buckie, Buckie, Banffshire AB5 2AA. *T:* Buckie (01542) 32591. *Clubs:* Farmers', Whitehall Court.

WATT, Surgeon Vice-Adm. Sir James, KBE 1975; MS, FRCS; Medical Director-General (Navy), 1972–77; *b* 19 Aug. 1914; *s* of Thomas Watt and Sarah Alice Clarkson. *Educ:* King Edward VI Sch., Morpeth; Univ. of Durham. MB, BS 1938; MS 1949; FRCS 1955; MD 1972; FRCP 1975. Served War, RN, FE and N Atlantic, 1941–46 (despatches, 1945). Surgical Registrar, Royal Vic. Infirm., Newcastle upon Tyne, 1947; Surgical Specialist: N Ire., 1949; RN Hosp., Hong Kong, 1954; Consultant in Surgery, RN Hospitals: Plymouth, 1956; Haslar, 1959; Malta, 1961; Haslar, 1963; Jt Prof. of Naval Surgery, RCS and RN Hosp., Haslar, 1965–69; Dean of Naval Medicine and MO i/c, Inst. of Naval Medicine, 1969–72. Chm., RN Clin. Research Working Party, 1969–77; Chm. Bd of Trustees, Naval Christian Fellowship, 1968–75; President: Royal Naval Lay Readers Soc., 1973–83; Inst. of Religion and Medicine, 1989–91. QHS 1969–77. Surg. Comdr 1956; Surg. Captain 1965; Surg. Rear-Adm. 1969; Surg. Vice-Adm. 1972. Mem., Environmental Medicine Res. Policy Cttee, MRC, 1974–77. Thomas Vicary Lectr, RCS, 1974; University House Vis. Fellow, ANU, 1986. FICS 1964; Fellow: Assoc. of Surgeons of GB and Ire.; Med. Soc. of London (Mem. Council, 1976; Lettsomian Lectr, 1979; Pres., 1980–81; Vice-Pres., 1981–83); FRSM (Pres., 1982–84); FSA 1991; Hon. FRCSE; Member: Brit. Soc. for Surgery of the Hand; Internat. Soc. for Burns Injuries; Corr. Mem., Surgical Research Soc., 1966–77; Mem. Editorial Bd, Brit. Jl of Surgery, 1966–77. FRGS 1982; Mem. Council, RGS, 1985–88. Pres., ECHO, 1989–; Vice-Pres., Churches' Council for Health and Healing, 1987–. Trustee: Marylebone Centre Trust, 1989–93; Medical Soc. of London, 1986–. Gov., Epsom Coll., 1990–. Hon. Mem., Smeatonian Soc. of Civil Engineers, 1978–. Hon. Freeman, Co. of Barbers, 1978. Hon. DCh Newcastle, 1978. Errol-Eldridge Prize, 1968; Gilbert Blane Medal, 1971. CStJ 1972. *Publications:* edited: Starving Sailors, 1981; Talking Health, 1988; What is Wrong with Christian Healing?, 1993; papers on: burns, cancer chemotherapy, peptic ulceration, hyberbaric oxygen therapy, naval medical history. *Recreations:* mountain walking, music. *Address:* 7 Cambisgate, Church Road, Wimbledon, SW19 5AL. *Club:* Royal Over-Seas League.

WATT, Sir James H.; *see* Harvie-Watt.

WATT, James Wilfrid; HM Diplomatic Service; Deputy Head of Mission and Consul General, Amman, since 1992; *b* 5 Nov. 1951; *s* of late Anthony James MacDonald Watt and Sona Elvey (*née* White); *m* 1980, Elizabeth Ghislaine Villeneuve, *d* of Marcel Villeneuve and Lorna Oliver Tudsbery; one *s* one *d*. *Educ:* Ampleforth Coll., York; Queen's Coll., Oxford (MA Mod. Langs 1974). Kleinwort Benson, 1974–75; freelance broadcaster and interpreter, Madrid, 1975–77; entered HM Diplomatic Service, 1977; MECAS, 1978; FCO, 1979–80; Abu Dhabi, 1980–83; FCO, 1983–85; UK Permanent Mission to UN, NY, 1985–89; Dep. Hd, UN Dept and Hd, Human Rights Unit, FCO, 1989–92. *Recreations:* good company, landscapes, tea. *Address:* c/o Foreign and Commonwealth Office, King Charles Street, SW1A 2AH.

WATT, John Gillies McArthur; QC (Scot.) 1992; *b* 14 Oct. 1949; *s* of Peter Julius Watt and Nancy (*née* McArthur); *m* 1st, 1972, Catherine (marr. diss. 1988), *d* of Robert Russell, Toronto, Canada; two *d*; 2nd, 1988, Susan, *d* of Dr Tom C. Sparks, Ardmore, Oklahoma, USA. *Educ:* Clydebank High Sch.; Glasgow Univ.; Edinburgh Univ. (LLB 1971). Solicitor, 1974–78; Advocate at Scottish Bar, 1979; Advocate Depute *ad hoc*, 1990; Temporary Sheriff, 1991; called to the Bar, Middle Temple, 1992. *Recreations:* shooting, ski-ing, sailing, opera. *Address:* 6511 Devinney Court, Arvada, CO 80004, USA. *T:* and *Fax:* (303) 4568416. *Clubs:* Lansdowne; Royal Western Yacht (Glasgow).

WATT, Robert; His Honour Judge Watt; County Court Judge since 1971; *b* 10 March 1923; *s* of John Watt, schoolmaster, Ballymena, Co. Antrim; *m* 1951, Edna Rea; one *d*. *Educ:* Ballymena Academy; Queen's Univ., Belfast (LLB). Called to Bar, Gray's Inn, 1946; called to Bar of Northern Ireland, 1946; QC (NI) 1964; subseq. Sen. Crown Prosecutor Counties Fermanagh and Tyrone. *Recreation:* sailing. *Address:* 12 Deramore Drive, Belfast BT9 5JQ. *Club:* Royal North of Ireland Yacht.

WATT, Prof. W(illiam) Montgomery; Professor of Arabic and Islamic Studies, University of Edinburgh, 1964–79; *b* Ceres, Fife, 14 March 1909; *o c* of late Rev. Andrew Watt; *m* 1943, Jean Macdonald, *er d* of late Prof. Robert Donaldson; one *s* four *d*. *Educ:* George Watson's Coll., Edinburgh; University of Edinburgh; Balliol Coll., Oxford; University of Jena; Cuddesdon Coll. Warner Exhibition (Balliol), 1930; Ferguson Schol. in Classics, 1931; MA, PhD (Edinburgh); MA, BLitt (Oxon). Asst Lecturer, Moral Philosophy, University of Edinburgh, 1934–38; Curate, St Mary Boltons, London, 1939–41; Curate, Old St Paul's, Edinburgh, 1941–43; Arabic specialist to Bishop in Jerusalem, 1943–46; Lecturer, Ancient Philosophy, University of Edinburgh, 1946–47; Lectr, Sen. Lectr and Reader in Arabic, Univ. of Edinburgh, 1947–64. Visiting Professor: of Islamic Studies, University of Toronto, 1963; Collège de France, Paris, 1970; of Religious Studies, Univ. of Toronto, 1978; of Arab Studies, Georgetown Univ., 1978–79. Chairman, Assoc. of British Orientalists, 1964–65. Editor, series, Islamic Surveys. Hon. DD Aberdeen, 1966. Levi Della Vida Medal, Los Angeles, 1981. *Publications:* Free Will and Predestination in Early Islam, 1949; The Faith and Practice of al-Ghazali, 1953; Muhammad at Mecca, 1953; Muhammad at Medina, 1956; The Reality of God, 1958; The Cure for Human Troubles, 1959; Islam and the Integration of Society, 1961; Muhammad Prophet and Statesman, 1961; Islamic Philosophy and Theology, 1962, new enlarged edn, 1986; Muslim Intellectual, 1963; Truth in the Religions, 1963; Islamic Spain, 1965; Islam (in Propyläen Weltgeschichte, XI), 1965; A Companion to the Qur'an, 1967; What is Islam?, 1968; Islamic Political Thought, 1968; Islamic Revelation and the Modern World, 1970; Bell's Introduction to the Qur'an, 1970; The Influence of Islam on Medieval Europe, 1972; The Formative Period of Islamic Thought, 1973; The Majesty that was Islam, 1974; Der Islam, i, 1980, ii, 1985; Islam and Christianity Today, 1984; Muhammad's Mecca, 1988; Islamic Fundamentalism and Modernity, 1988; Early Islam, 1991; Muslim-Christian Encounters, 1991; Islamic Creeds: a selection, 1994; Religious Truth for Our Time, 1995; contribs learned journals. *Address:* 2 Bridgend, Dalkeith, Midlothian EH22 1JT. *T:* 0131–663 3197.

WATT, Emeritus Prof. William Smith, MA (Glasgow and Oxon); FBA 1989; Regius Professor of Humanity in the University of Aberdeen, 1952–79, Vice-Principal, 1969–72; *b* 20 June 1913; *s* of John Watt and Agnes Smith; *m* 1944, Dorothea, *e d* of R. J. Codrington Smith; one *s*. *Educ:* University of Glasgow; Balliol Coll., Oxford (Snell Exhibitioner and Hon. Scholar). First Class Hons in Classics, Glasgow Univ., 1933; Ferguson Schol., 1934; Craven Schol., 1934; First Class, Classical Moderations, 1935; Hertford Schol., 1935; Ireland Schol., 1935; First Class, Lit. Hum., 1937. Lecturer in Greek and Greek History, University of Glasgow, 1937–38; Fellow and Tutor in Classics, Balliol Coll., Oxford, 1938–52. Civilian Officer, Admiralty (Naval Intelligence Div.), 1941–45. Convener, Scottish Univs Council on Entrance, 1973–77. Governor, Aberdeen Coll. of Educn, 1958–75 (Chm. of Governors 1971–75). Pres., Classical Assoc. of Scotland, 1983–88. *Publications:* (ed) Ciceronis Epistulae ad Quintum fratrem, etc, 1958, 1965; (ed) Ciceronis Epistularum ad Atticum Libri I-VIII, 1965; (ed) Ciceronis Epistulae ad familiares, 1982; (ed with P. J. Ford) George Buchanan's Miscellaneorum Liber, 1982; (ed) Vellei Paterculi Historiae, 1988; many articles in classical periodicals. *Address:* 38 Woodburn Gardens, Aberdeen AB1 8JA. *T:* Aberdeen (01224) 314369. *Club:* Business and Professional (Aberdeen).

WATTERS, David George; JP; General Secretary, Primary Immunodeficiency Association, since 1994; *b* 14 Jan. 1945. *Educ:* Stromness Acad., Orkney Is. Church of Scotland lay worker, 1964–68; Social Worker, St Martin-in-the-Fields, 1968–73; Director: Threshold Centre, 1973–78; Alone In London Service, 1978–81; Gen. Sec., Haemophilia Soc., 1981–93. JP 1980. *Recreations:* music, photography, birdwatching, travel, reading. *Address:* 81c Trinity Road, SW17 7SQ. *T:* 0181–672 3888.

WATTLEY, Graham Richard; Director, Driver and Vehicle Licensing Directorate, Department of Transport, 1985–90, retired; *b* 12 March 1930; *s* of R. C. H. Wattley and Sylvia Joyce Wattley (*née* Orman); *m* 1953, Yvonne Heale (*d* 1990); one *s* two *d*. *Educ:* Devonport High School. Pilot Officer, RAF, 1949–50. Min. of Works, 1950–71; Dept of the Environment, 1971–73; Department of Transport, 1973–90: Asst Sec., DVLC Computer Div., 1978–85; Under Sec., 1986. Treas., Dewi Sant Housing Assoc., 1991–95. Mem., Governing Body, Church in Wales, 1992–94. Warden, St Paul's Church, Sketty, 1991–. Walk Leader, HF Holidays, 1994–. *Recreations:* walking, cooking, bird-watching. *Address:* 36 The Ridge, Derwen Fawr, Swansea SA2 8AG. *T:* Swansea (01792) 290408. *Club:* Civil Service.

WATTON, Rt Rev. James Augustus, BA, DD; *b* 23 Oct. 1915; *s* of Geo. A. Watton and Ada Wynn; *m* 1st, 1941, Irene A. Foster; one *s* two *d*; 2nd 1986, Janet Miller. *Educ:* Univ. of Western Ontario (BA); Huron Coll. (STh); Post graduate Univ. of Michigan. Deacon 1938; Priest 1939. Bishop of Moosonee, 1963–80; Archbishop of Moosonee and Metropolitan of Ontario, 1974–79; retired 1980. DD (*jure dig.*), 1955. *Address:* 124 Meadow Heights Drive, Bracebridge, Ontario P1L 1A3, Canada.

WATTS, Prof. Anthony Brian, PhD; Professor of Marine Geology and Geophysics, University of Oxford, since 1990; *b* 23 July 1945; *s* of Dennis Granville Watts and of late Vera (*née* Fisher); *m* 1970, Mary Tarbit; two *d*. *Educ:* University Coll. London (BSc); Univ. of Durham (PhD). Post-Doctoral Fellow, Nat. Res. Council of Canada, 1970–71; Res. Scientist, Lamont-Doherty Geol Observatory, Palisades, NY, 1971–81; Arthur D. Storke Meml Prof. of Geol Scis, Columbia Univ., NY, 1981–90. Fellow, Amer. Geophysical Union, 1986. A. I. Levorsen Meml Award, Amer. Assoc. Petroleum Geologists, 1981; Rosenstiel Award, Univ. of Miami, 1982; Murchison Medal, Geol Soc., 1993. *Publications:* numerous articles in scientific jls. *Recreations:* cricket, carpentry. *Address:* Department of Earth Sciences, University of Oxford, Parks Road, Oxford OX2 3PR. *T:* Oxford (01865) 272032. *Club:* Geological Society.

WATTS, Sir Arthur (Desmond), KCMG 1989 (CMG 1977); QC 1988; barrister; *b* 14 Nov. 1931; *o s* of Col A. E. Watts, MA (Cantab); *m* 1957, Iris Ann Collier, MA (Cantab); one *s* one *d*. *Educ:* Haileybury and Imperial Service College; Royal Military Academy, Sandhurst; Downing Coll., Cambridge (Schol.). BA 1954; LLM (First Cl.) 1955; Whewell Schol. in Internat. Law, 1955; called to Bar, Gray's Inn, 1957; MA. Legal Asst, Foreign Office, 1956–59; Legal Adviser, British Property Commn (later British Embassy), Cairo, 1959–62; Asst Legal Adviser, FO, 1962–67; Legal Adviser, British Embassy, Bonn, 1967–69; Asst Solicitor, Law Officers Dept, 1969–70; Legal Counsellor, FCO, 1970–73; Counsellor (Legal Advr), Office of UK Permanent Rep. to EEC, 1973–77; Legal Counsellor, 1977–82, Dep. Legal Advr, 1982–87, Legal Advr, 1987–91, FCO. Member: Bd of Management, British Inst. of Internat. and Comparative Law, 1987–; Bd, Inst. of Advanced Legal Studies, 1988–91; Adv. Bd, Inst für Internationales Recht, Kiel Univ., 1989–; Associate Mem., Inst de Droit Internat., 1991–. Pres., British Br., Internat. Law Assoc., 1992–. Mem. Editl Cttee, British Year Book of International Law, 1991–. *Publications:* Legal Effects of War, 4th edn (with Lord McNair), 1966; (with C. and A. Parry and J. Grant) Encyclopaedic Dictionary of International Law, 1986; (with Sir Robert Jennings) Oppenheim's International Law, vol. 1, 9th edn 1992; International Law and the Antarctic Treaty System, 1992; contribs to: British Year Book of Internat. Law; Internat. and Comparative Law Quarterly, and other internat. law publications. *Recreation:* cricket (County Cap, Shropshire, 1955; in Antarctica, 1985). *Address:* 20 Essex Street, WC2R 3AL.

WATTS, Donald Walter, PhD; FTS; FRACI; FACE; FAIM; Executive Chairman, Northern Territory, Trade Development Zone Authority, since 1993; Chairman, Australian Space Council, Canberra, since 1993; *b* 1 April 1934; *s* of late Horace Frederick Watts and Esme Anne Watts; *m* 1960, Michelle Rose Yeomans; two *s*. *Educ:* Hale Sch., Perth; University of Western Australia (BSc Hons, PhD); University College London. FRACI 1967. Post-Doctoral Fellow, UCL, 1959–61; University of Western Australia: Sen. Lectr, 1962; Reader, 1969; Associate Prof., 1971; Personal Chair in Physical and Inorganic Chemistry, 1977–79; Dir, W Australian Inst. of Tech., 1980–86, renamed Vice-Chancellor, Curtin Univ. of Tech., Jan.–June 1987; Pres. and Vice-Chancellor, Bond Univ., Australia, 1987–90, now Emeritus. Vis. Scientist, Univ. of S California, 1967; Visiting Professor: Australian National Univ., 1973; Univ. of Toronto, 1974; Japan Foundn Vis. Fellow, 1984. Chairman: Aust. Cttee of Dirs and Principals in Advanced Education Ltd, 1986–87; NT Employment and Trng Authy, 1991–93; Member: Aust. Science and Technol. Council, 1984–90; Technology Develt Authority of WA, 1984–87. Hon. Fellow, Marketing Inst. of Singapore, 1987. Hon. DTech Curtin, 1987. *Publications:* Chemical Properties and Reactions (jtly) (Univ. of W Aust.), 1978 (trans. Japanese, 1987); (jtly) Chemistry for Australian Secondary School Students (Aust. Acad. of Sci.), 1979; (jtly) The School Chemistry Project—a secondary school chemistry syllabus for comment, 1984; Earth, Air, Fire and Water, and associated manuals (Aust. Acad. of Sci. Sch. Chem. Project), 1984; numerous papers on phys. and inorganic chemistry in internat. jls; several papers presented at nat. and internat. confs. *Recreations:* tennis (Mem. Interstate Tennis Team, 1952–53), squash (Mem. Interstate Squash Team, 1957–66), golf. *Address:* Trade Development Zone Authority, Berrimah Road, East Arm, Darwin, NT 0828, Australia. *Clubs:* Brisbane (Brisbane); Royal Kings Park Tennis (Perth); Nedlands Tennis (Nedlands); Lake Karrinyup Golf (Karrinyup); Darwin Golf; Vines Resort (Swan Valley).

WATTS, Edward, (Ted), FRICS; Chairman, Watts & Partners, since 1976; *b* 19 March 1940; *s* of Edward Samuel Window Watts and Louise Coffey; *m* 1960, Iris Josephine Frost; two *s* (one *d* decd). *Educ:* SW Essex Technical Coll. FRICS 1971 (ARICS 1962). Established own practice, 1967 (surveyors, architects and engineers). Founder Chm., Hyde Housing Assoc., 1967–70 (Mem., 1967–85). Director: Surveyors Hldgs, 1983–88; People Need Homes, 1991–; WASP, 1994–; Buildingcare, 1994–; non-executive Director: WSP Gp, 1993–; Thamesmead Town, 1994–; Mem. Adv. Bd, Property Hldgs, 1992–. Chm., Technical Cttee, Bldg Conservation Trust, 1984–86. Member: ARCUK, 1991–; Urban Villages Gp, 1992–; Bd, Coll. of Estate Management, 1994–. Royal Institution of Chartered Surveyors: Pres., 1991–92; Mem., Gen. Council, 1982–; Dir, RICS Journals Ltd, 1982–88 (Chm., 1986–88). FIMgt (FBIM 1982). Freeman, City of London, 1985; Liveryman, Chartered Surveyors' Co., 1985–. Hon. DSc South Bank, 1992. *Recreations:* sailing, cruising, racing offshore. *Address:* 11 Haymarket, SW1Y 4BP. *T:* 0171–930 6652. *Clubs:* Royal Automobile, Royal Ocean Racing; Royal Lymington Yacht (Hants); Island Sailing (Cowes, IoW).

WATTS, Helen Josephine, (Mrs Michael Mitchell), CBE 1978; Hon. FRAM; concert, lieder and opera singer (contralto), retired 1985; *b* 7 Dec. 1927; *d* of Thomas Watts and Winifred (*née* Morgan); *m* 1980, Michael Mitchell. *Educ:* St Mary and St Anne's Sch., Abbots Bromley; Royal Academy of Music (LRAM). Hon. FRAM 1961 (Hon. ARAM 1955); FRSA 1982. *Recreation:* gardening.

WATTS, John Arthur, FCA; MP (C) Slough, since 1983; Minister of State, Department of Transport, since 1994; *b* 19 April 1947; *s* of late Arthur and Ivy Watts; *m* 1974, Susan Jennifer Swan; one *s* three *d*. *Educ:* Bishopshalt Grammar Sch., Hillingdon; Gonville and Caius Coll., Cambridge (MA). Qual. as chartered accountant, 1972; FCA 1979. Chairman: Cambridge Univ. Cons. Assoc., 1968; Uxbridge Cons. Assoc., 1973–76; Mem., Hillingdon Bor. Council, 1973–86 (Leader, 1978–84). PPS: to Minister for Housing and Construction, 1984–85; to Minister of State, Treasury, 1985. Chm., Treasury and CS Select Cttee, 1992–94 (Mem., 1986–94). *Recreation:* reading. *Address:* House of Commons, SW1A 0AA. *T:* 0171–219 3589.

WATTS, Colonel John Cadman, OBE 1959; MC 1946; FRCS 1949; first Professor of Military Surgery, Royal College of Surgeons, 1960–64; *b* 13 April 1913; *s* of John Nixon Watts, solicitor, and Amy Bettina (*née* Cadman); *m* 1938, Joan Lilian (*née* Inwood); three *s* one *d*. *Educ:* Merchant Taylors' Sch.; St Thomas's Hospital. MRCS, LRCP, 1936; MB, BS, 1938. Casualty Officer, Resident Anæsthetist, House Surgeon, St Thomas's Hospital, 1937; Surgical Specialist, RAMC, 1938–60, serving in Palestine, Egypt, Libya, Syria, Tunisia, Italy, France, Holland, Germany, Malaya, Java, Japan, and Cyprus. Hunterian Professor, RCS, 1960; Conslt Surgeon, Bedford Gen. Hosp., 1966–76. Co. Comr, St John Ambulance Brigade, 1970. British Medical Association: Chm., N Beds Div., 1971; Mem. Council, 1972–74; Chm., Armed Forces Cttee, 1978–82; Pres., Ipswich Div., 1982–83. OStJ 1970. *Publications:* Surgeon at War, 1955; Clinical Surgery, 1964; Exploration Medicine, 1964. *Recreations:* sailing, gardening. *Address:* Lowood Lodge, Hasketon, near Woodbridge, Suffolk IP13 6JL. *T:* Grundisburgh (01473) 735326. *Clubs:* Deben Yacht (Woodbridge); United Hospitals Sailing (Burnham-on-Crouch).

WATTS, John Francis, BA; educational writer; Principal, Countesthorpe College, Leicestershire, 1972–81; *b* 18 Oct. 1926; *s* of John Weldon Watts and Norah K. Watts; *m*

1st, 1950, Elizabeth Hamilton (marr. diss.); four *s* one *d*; 2nd, 1985, Madeleine Marshall. *Educ:* West Buckland Sch.; Univ. of Bristol (BA). First Headmaster, Les Quennevais Sch., Jersey, CI, 1964–69; Lectr, Univ. of London, 1969–72. Chm., Nat. Assoc. for Teaching of English (NATE), 1974–76. *Publications:* Encounters, 1965, 2nd edn 1983; Contact, 1970 (Australia); Interplay, 1972; Teaching, 1974; The Countesthorpe Experience, 1977; Towards an Open School, 1980; Hearings, 1994; contrib. to various publications. *Address:* Kingfisher Barn, Kings Lane, Weston, Beccles, Suffolk NR34 8TX.

WATTS, Lt-Gen. Sir John Peter Barry Condliffe, KBE 1988 (CBE 1979; OBE 1972); CB 1985; MC 1960; Chief of Defence Staff, Sultan of Oman's Armed Forces, 1984–87; *b* 27 Aug. 1930; *m*; seven *c*. *Educ:* Westminster Sch.; Phillips Acad., Andover, USA; RMA Sandhurst. Commissioned, RUR, 1951 (Royal Irish Rangers, 1968); served Hong Kong, Malaya (despatches), Cyprus, Oman (MC), BAOR, Borneo and South Arabia; 48 Gurkha Inf. Bde, 1967–69; CO 22 SAS Regt, 1970–72; Directing Staff, Staff Coll., 1972–74; MoD, 1974; Comdr, SAS Gp, 1975–78; Comdr, Sultan of Oman's Land Forces, 1979–84.

WATTS, Mark Francis; Member (Lab) Kent East, European Parliament, since 1994; *b* 11 June 1964; *s* of Albert Charles Watts and Carole Emmah Watts (*née* Fleischman); *m* 1988, Kim McEachan; two *s*. *Educ:* Maidstone Grammar Sch.; LSE (BSc Econ; MSc Econ). Planning Officer, Royal Borough of Kingston-upon-Thames, 1988–94. Maidstone Borough Council: Councillor, 1986–; Leader, Lab. Gp, 1990–94. *Recreations:* walking, enjoying the countryside, spending time with my family, swimming. *Address:* Transport House, Apsley Street, Ashford, Kent TN23 1LF. *T:* Ashford (01233) 663668, *Fax:* (01233) 663510.

WATTS, Rachel Mary; *see* Rosser, R. M.

WATTS, Thomas Rowland, (Tom), CBE 1978; Chartered Accountant; *b* 1 Jan. 1917; *s* of late Thomas William Watts and late Daisy Maud Watts (*née* Bultitude); *m* 1955, Hester Zoë Armitstead; one *s* two *d*. *Educ:* Gresham's Sch., Holt. Served War, TA, 1939–41, Royal Marines (Captain), 1941–46. Articled to Price Waterhouse & Co., 1934–39, Partner, 1963–82. Dir, Jarrold & Sons Ltd, Norwich, 1982–87. Chm., Accounting Standards Cttee (UK and Ireland), 1978–82; Mem. Council, Inst. of Chartered Accountants in England and Wales, 1974–82; Mem. City EEC Cttee, 1974–82; Adviser to Dept of Trade on EEC company law, 1974–83; Vice-Pres. d'honneur, Groupe d'Etudes des experts comptables de la CEE, 1979–88 (Vice-Pres., 1975–79); Chm., EEC Liaison Cttee of UK Accountancy Bodies, 1986–88; Chm., Dental Rates Study Gp, 1982–85. A Gen. Comr of Income Tax, 1986–92. Hon. Vis. Prof., City of London Polytech., 1983–86. Liveryman, Chartered Accountants' Co., 1977–. Chartered Accountants Founding Socs' Centenary Award, 1982. *Publications:* editor, various professional books; papers in professional jls. *Recreations:* travel, music, opera costume designs. *Address:* 13 Fitzwalter Road, Colchester, Essex CO3 3SY. *T:* Colchester (01206) 573520.

WATTS, Victor Brian; His Honour Judge Watts; a Circuit Judge, since 1980; *b* 7 Jan. 1927; *o s* of Percy William King Watts and Doris Millicent Watts; *m* 1965, Patricia Eileen (*née* Steer); one *s* one *d*. *Educ:* Colfe's Grammar Sch.; University Coll., Oxford. MA(Oxon): BCL. Called to the Bar, Middle Temple, 1950; subseq. Western Circuit; a Recorder of the Crown Court, 1972–80. Flying Officer, Royal Air Force, 1950–52. Churchwarden, St Peter's Church, Hammersmith, 1984–90. *Publications:* Landlord and Tenant Act, 1954; Leading Cases on the Law of Contract, 1955; occasional articles of a legal nature. *Recreations:* the arts, walking, tennis, riding. *Address:* 28 Abinger Road, W4 1EL. *T:* 0181–994 4435. *Club:* Hurlingham.

WATTS, William Arthur, MA, ScD; Provost, Trinity College, Dublin, 1981–91; *b* 26 May 1930; *s* of William Low Watts and Bessie (*née* Dickinson); *m* 1954, Geraldine Mary Magrath; two *s* one *d*. *Educ:* Trinity Coll., Dublin (MA, ScD). Lecturer in Botany, Univ. of Hull, 1953–55; Trinity College, Dublin: Lectr in Botany, 1955–65; Fellow, 1970; Professor of Botany, 1965–80; Prof. of Quaternary Ecology, 1980–81. Adjunct Prof. of Geology, Univ. of Minnesota, 1975–. Pres., RIA, 1982–85; Governor: National Gallery of Ireland, 1982–85; Marsh's Library, 1981–; Member: Dublin Inst. for Advanced Studies, 1981–; Scholarship Exchange Bd, Ireland, 1982–. Chairman: Federated Dublin Voluntary Hosps, 1983–; Mercer's Hosp., 1975–83; Mercer's Hosp. Foundn, 1983–; Health Res. Bd, Ireland, 1987–89. Hon. LLD QUB, 1990; Hon. DSc NUI, 1991. *Publications:* numerous articles on aspects of quaternary ecology. *Recreations:* walking, conservation studies, music. *Address:* Room 24.02, Trinity College, Dublin 2. *T:* 772941. *Club:* Kildare Street and University (Dublin).

WAUCHOPE, Sir Roger (Hamilton) Don-, 11th Bt *cr* 1667 (NS), of Newton Don; chartered accountant, South Africa; Partner, Deloitte & Touche, since 1972; *b* 16 Oct. 1938; *s* of Sir Patrick George Don-Wauchope, 10th Bt and Ismay Lilian Ursula (who later *m* George William Shipman), *d* of Sidney Richard Hodges; *S* father, 1989; *m* 1963, Sallee, *yr d* of Lt-Col Harold Mill-Colman, OBE, AMICE, Durban; two *s* one *d*. *Educ:* Hilton Coll., Natal; Univ. of Natal, Durban; Univ. of Natal, Pietermaritzburg (Higher Diploma in Taxation). *Heir: s* Dr Andrew Craig Don-Wauchope, *b* 18 May 1966. *Address:* Newton, 53 Montrose Drive, Pietermaritzburg 3201, Natal, South Africa. *T:* (331) 471107; PO Box 365, Pietermaritzburg 3200, Natal, South Africa. *Clubs:* Victoria (Chm., 1993–95), Maritzburg Country (Pietermaritzburg); Durban Country (Durban); Old Hiltonian (Chm., 1992–).

WAUGH, Auberon Alexander; Editor, The Literary Review, since 1986; Columnist: The Spectator, since 1976; The Daily Telegraph, since 1990; *b* 17 Nov. 1939; *e s* of late Evelyn Waugh, writer, and late Laura Waugh, Combe Florey House, Somerset; *m* 1961, Teresa, *o d* of 6th Earl of Onslow, KBE, MC, and *sister* of 7th Earl of Onslow, *qv*; two *s* two *d*. *Educ:* Downside (schol. in Classics); Christ Church, Oxford (exhibn in English, read PPE). Editorial staff, Daily Telgraph, 1960–63. Commissioned Royal Horse Guards, 1957; served Cyprus; retd with wounds, 1958. Weekly Columnist, Catholic Herald, 1963–64; special writer, Mirror group, 1964–67; Political Correspondent: Spectator, 1967–70; Private Eye, 1970–86; Weekly Columnist: The Times, 1970–71; New Statesman, 1973–76; Sunday Telegraph, 1981–90; Chief Fiction Reviewer: Spectator, 1970–73; Evening Standard, 1973–80; Daily Mail, 1981–86; Chief Book Reviewer, The Independent, 1986–89; monthly contributor, Books and Bookmen, 1973–80. Contested (Dog Lovers' Party) Devon North, 1979. Pres., British Croatian Soc., 1973–92. Nat. Press 'Critic of the Year' commendations, 1976, 1978; 'What the Papers Say' Columnist of the Year, Granada TV, 1979, 1988. *Publications: novels:* The Foxglove Saga, 1960; Path of Dalliance, 1963; Who are the Violets Now?, 1966; Consider the Lilies, 1968; A Bed of Flowers, 1971; *non-fiction:* (with S. Cronje) Biafra: Britain's Shame, 1969; Four Crowded Years: the Diaries of Auberon Waugh, 1976; The Last Word: an Eyewitness Account of the Thorpe Trial, 1980; Auberon Waugh's Yearbook, 1981; The Diaries of Auberon Waugh: a turbulent decade 1976–85, 1985; Waugh on Wine, 1986; Will This Do? the first fifty years of Auberon Waugh (autobiog.), 1991; Way of the World, 1994; *essays:* Country Topics, 1974; In The Lion's Den, 1978; Another Voice, 1986; *anthology:* (ed) The Literary Review Anthology of Real Poetry, 1991. *Recreation:* gossip. *Address:* Combe Florey House, near Taunton, Somerset TA4 3JD; 7 Phoenix Lodge Mansions, Brook Green, W6 7BG. *Clubs:* Beefsteak, Academy.

WAUGH, Rev. Eric Alexander; Missioner, Kingdom Communications Trust, Southern Africa, since 1992; *b* 9 May 1933; *s* of Hugh Waugh and Marion Waugh (*née* McLay); *m* 1955, Agnes-Jean (Sheena) Saunders; two *s*. *Educ:* Glasgow Univ.; Edinburgh Univ. (LTh). Local government officer, 1948–64. Assistant Minister, High Church, Bathgate, 1969–70; Missionary, Kenya Highlands, 1970–73; Minister, Mowbray Presbyterian Church, Cape Town, 1973–78; Missioner, Presbyterian Church of Southern Africa, 1978–85; Minister, City Temple, URC, 1986–91. *Recreations:* hill walking, gardening. *Address:* Flat 1202, Salwood Court, Arbor Road, Rondebosch, Cape Town, 7700, South Africa.

WAVERLEY, 3rd Viscount *cr* 1952, of Westdean; **John Desmond Forbes Anderson;** *b* 31 Oct. 1949; *s* of 2nd Viscount Waverley and of Myrtle Ledgerwood; *S* father, 1990. *Educ:* Malvern. *Address:* c/o Chanders, Aldworth, Berks RG8 9RU.

WAY, Col Anthony Gerald, MC 1944; Member, HM Body Guard of the Honourable Corps of Gentlemen at Arms, 1972–90 (Standard Bearer, 1988–90); *b* 5 Nov. 1920; *s* of Roger Hill Way and Brenda Lathbury; *m* 1st, 1946, Elizabeth Leslie Richmond (*d* 1986); one *s* one *d*; 2nd, 1989, Mrs Anthea Methven, St Martin's Abbey, by Perth. *Educ:* Stowe Sch.; RMC Sandhurst. Joined Grenadier Guards, 1939, 2nd Lieut; served in N Africa and Italy; CO, 3rd Bn, 1960–61; Lt-Col comdg Grenadier Guards, 1961–64. *Recreations:* shooting, gardening. *Address:* Kincairney, Dunkeld, Perthshire PH8 0RE. *T:* Caputh (01738) 710304. *Club:* Pratt's.

WAY, Sir Richard (George Kitchener), KCB 1961 (CB 1957); CBE 1952; Principal, King's College London, 1975–80; *b* 15 Sept. 1914; *s* of Frederick and Clara Way; *m* 1947, Ursula Joan Starr; one *s* two *d*. *Educ:* Polytechnic Secondary Sch., London. Joined Civil Service as Exec. Officer, 1933; Higher Executive Officer, 1940; Principal, 1942; Asst Secretary, 1946; Asst Under-Secretary of State, 1954; Deputy Under-Secretary of State, War Office, 1955–57; Dep. Secretary, Ministry of Defence, 1957–58; Dep. Secretary, Ministry of Supply, 1958–59; Permanent Under-Secretary of State, War Office, 1960–63; Permanent Secretary, Ministry of Aviation, 1963–66. Dep. Chm., Lansing Bagnall Ltd, 1966–67, Chm. 1967–69; Chm., LTE, 1970–74. Chairman, EDC Machine Tool Industry, 1967–70; Member (part-time) Board of: BOAC, 1967–73; Dobson Park Industries Ltd, 1975–85. Chm., Council of Roedean Sch., 1969–74; Chm., Royal Commn for the Exhibn of 1851, 1978–87. London Zoological Society: Mem. Council 1977–82 and 1984–87; Vice-Pres., 1979–82 and 1984–87; Treasurer, 1983–84. CSTJ 1974. FKC 1975. Hon. DSc Loughborough, 1986. Coronation Medal, 1953. American Medal of Freedom (with bronze palm), 1946. *Address:* The Old Forge, Shalden, Alton, Hants GU34 4DX. *T:* Alton (01420) 82383. *Club:* Brooks's.

WAYMOUTH, Charity, BSc (London), PhD (Aberdeen); Senior Staff Scientist, The Jackson Laboratory, Bar Harbor, Maine, 1963–81, now Emeritus; *b* 29 April 1915; *o d* of Charles Sydney Herbert Waymouth, Major, The Dorsetshire Regt, and Ada Curror Scott Dalgleish; unmarried. *Educ:* Royal School for Daughters of Officers of the Army, Bath; University of London; University of Aberdeen. Biochemist, City of Manchester General Hospitals, 1938–41; Research Fellow, University of Aberdeen, 1944; Beit Memorial Fellow for Medical Research, 1944–46; Member of scientific staff and head of tissue culture dept, Chester Beatty Research Institute for Cancer Research (University of London), 1947–52; British Empire Cancer Campaign-American Cancer Society Exchange Fellow, 1952–53; The Jackson Laboratory: Staff Scientist, 1952–63; Asst Dir (Training), 1969–72; Asst Dir (Research), 1976–77; Associate Dir (Scientific Affairs), 1977–80; Dir *ad interim*, 1980–81. Mem. Bd of Dirs, W. Alton Jones Cell Sci. Center, 1979–82. Rose Morgan Vis. Prof., Univ. of Kansas, 1971. Member: Tissue Culture Association (President, 1960–62, Editor-in-Chief 1968–75; Mem. Council, 1980–84); various British and American professional and learned societies. Hon. Life member and Hon. Director, Psora Society (Canada); Episcopal Church of the USA: Vice-Chm., Clergy Deployment Bd, 1971–79, and Exec. Council, 1967–70; Deputy, Gen. Convention, 1970, 1973, 1976, 1979, 1982, 1985, 1988; Member, Diocesan Council, 1962–70, 1971–76, and Standing Cttee, 1984–87, Dio. of Maine; Chm., Cttee on the State of the Church, 1976–79; Mem., Standing Commn on Health, 1988–91. DD *hc* Gen. Theol Seminary, NY, 1979; Hon. ScD Bowdoin College, 1982. *Publications:* numerous papers in scientific journals, on nucleic acids and on tissue culture and cell nutrition. *Recreations:* reading, gardening. *Address:* 16 Atlantic Avenue, Bar Harbor, ME 04609, USA. *T:* (207) 2884008.

WAYWELL, Prof. Geoffrey Bryan, FSA 1979; Professor of Classical Archaeology, King's College, University of London, since 1987; *b* 16 Jan. 1944; *s* of Francis Marsh Waywell and Jenny Waywell; *m* 1970, Elisabeth Ramsden; two *s*. *Educ:* Eltham Coll.; St John's Coll., Cambridge (BA, MA, PhD). Walston Student, Cambridge Univ., 1965–67; School Student, British Sch. at Athens, 1966–67; King's College, London: Asst Lectr in Classics, 1968; Lectr in Classics, 1970; Reader in Classical Archaeology, 1982; Hon. Curator, Ashmole Archive, 1985. Dir of excavations at ancient Sparta, 1989–. *Publications:* The Free-Standing Sculptures of the Mausoleum at Halicarnassus in the British Museum, 1978; The Lever and Hope Sculptures, 1986; numerous articles and reviews in archaeol and classical jls. *Recreations:* music, excavating. *Address:* Department of Classics, King's College London, Strand, WC2R 2LS. *T:* 0171–836 5454.

WEARE, Trevor John, OBE 1990; PhD; Managing Director, HR Wallingford (formerly Hydraulics Research) Ltd, since 1982; *b* 31 Dec. 1943; *s* of Trevor Leslie Weare and Edna Margaret (*née* Roberts); *m* 1964, Margaret Ann Wright; two *s*. *Educ:* Aston Technical Coll.; Imperial College of Science and Technology (BSc Physics, PhD). Post-doctoral Research Fellow: Dept of Mathematical Physics, McGill Univ., Montreal, 1968–70; Dept of Theoretical Physics, Univ. of Oxford, 1970–72; Sen. Scientific Officer, Hydraulics Res. Station, 1972; Principal Scientific Officer, 1975; Sen. Principal Scientific Officer, Head of Estuaries Div., 1978; Chief Scientific Officer, DoE, 1981. *Publications:* numerous contribs to scientific jls on theoretical High Energy Nuclear Physics, and on computational modelling in Civil Engineering Hydraulics; archaeological paper in Oxoniensia. *Recreations:* music, walking, archaeology. *Address:* Rose Cottage, Dunsomer Hill, North Moreton, Oxon OX11 9AR. *T:* Didcot (01235) 818544.

WEATHERALL, Sir David (John), Kt 1987; MD, FRCP; FRCPE 1983; FRS 1977; Regius Professor of Medicine, University of Oxford, since 1992; Student of Christ Church, Oxford, since 1992; Hon. Director: Molecular Haematology Unit, Medical Research Council, since 1980; Institute for Molecular Medicine, University of Oxford, since 1988; *b* 9 March 1933; *s* of late Harry and Gwendoline Weatherall; *m* 1962, Stella Mayorga Nestler; one *s*. *Educ:* Calday Grange Grammar Sch.; Univ. of Liverpool. MB, ChB 1956; MD 1962; FRCP 1967; FRCPath 1969; MA Oxon 1974. Ho. Officer in Med. and Surg., United Liverpool Hosps, 1956–58; Captain, RAMC, Jun. Med. Specialist, BMH, Singapore, and BMH, Kamunting, Malaya, 1958–60; Research Fellow in Genetics, Johns Hopkins Hosp., Baltimore, USA, 1960–62; Sen. Med. Registrar, Liverpool Royal Infirmary, 1962–63; Research Fellow in Haematology, Johns Hopkins Hosp., 1963–65; Consultant, WHO, 1966–70; Univ. of Liverpool: Lectr in Med., 1965–66; Sen. Lectr in Med., 1966–69; Reader in Med., 1969–71; Prof. of Haematology, 1971–74; Consultant Physician, United Liverpool Hosps, 1966–74; Nuffield Prof. of Clinical Medicine, Univ.

of Oxford, 1974–92; Fellow, Magdalen Coll., Oxford, 1974–92, Emeritus 1992–. Mem. Soc. of Scholars, and Centennial Schol., Johns Hopkins Univ., 1976; Physician-in-Chief *pro tem.*, Peter Bent Brigham Hosp., Harvard Med. Sch., 1980. RSocMed Foundn Vis. Prof., 1981; Sims Commonwealth Vis. Prof., 1982; Phillip K. Bondy Prof., Yale, 1982. K. Diamond Prof., Univ. of Calif in San Francisco, 1986; HM Queen Elizabeth the Queen Mother Fellow, Nuffield Prov. Hosps Trust, 1982. Lectures: Watson Smith, RCP, 1974; Foundn, RCPath, 1979; Darwin, Eugenics Soc., 1979; Croonian, RCP, 1984; Fink Meml, Yale, 1984; Sir Francis Frazer, Univ. of London, 1985; Roy Cameron, RCPath, 1986; Hamm Meml, Amer. Soc. of Haematology, 1986; Still Meml, BPA, 1987; Harveian, RCP, 1992. President: British Soc. for Haematology, 1980–; Internat. Soc. of Haematology, 1992; BAAS, 1992–93; Chm., Med. and Scientific Adv. Panel, Leukaemia Res. Fund, 1985–89; Mem. Council, Royal Soc., 1989– (Vice Pres., 1990–91); Mem., MRC, 1992–; Trustee, Wellcome Trust, 1990–. Foreign Member: Nat. Acad. of Scis, USA, 1990; Inst. of Medicine, Nat. Acad. of Scis, USA, 1991; Hon. Member: Assoc. of Physicians of GB and Ireland, 1968 (Pres., 1989); Assoc. of Amer. Physicians, 1976; Amer. Soc. of Haematology, 1982; Eur. Molecular Biology Orgn, 1983; Amer. Acad. of Arts and Scis, 1988; Alpha Omega Alpha Honor Med. Soc., USA, 1988. Hon. FRACP 1986; Hon. FRCOG 1988; Hon. FIC 1989; Hon. FACP 1991; Hon. Fellow, Green Coll., Oxford, 1993. Hon. DSc: Manchester, 1988; Edinburgh, 1989; Leicester, 1991; Aberdeen, 1991; London, 1993; Keele, 1993; Hon. MD: Leeds, 1988; Sheffield, 1989; Nottingham, 1993; Hon. DHL Johns Hopkins, 1990; Hon. LLD: Liverpool, 1992; Bristol, 1994. Ambuj Nath Bose Prize, RCP, 1980; Ballantyne Prize, RCPE, 1982; Stratton Prize, Internat. Soc. Haematology, 1982; Feldberg Prize, 1984; Royal Medal, Royal Soc., 1989; Gold Medal, RSM, 1992; Conway Evans Prize, RCP and Royal Soc., 1992; Buchanan Medal, Royal Soc., 1994. *Publications:* (with J. B. Clegg) The Thalassaemia Syndromes, 1965, 3rd edn 1981; (with R. M. Hardisty) Blood and its Disorders, 1973, 2nd edn 1981; The New Genetics and Clinical Practice, 1982, 3rd edn 1991; (ed, with J. G. G. Ledingham and D. A. Warrell) Oxford Textbook of Medicine, 1983, 3rd edn 1995; many papers on Abnormal Haemoglobin Synthesis and related disorders. *Recreations:* music, oriental food. *Address:* 8 Cumnor Rise Road, Cumnor Hill, Oxford OX2 9HD. *T:* Oxford (01865) 862467.

WEATHERALL, Vice-Adm. Sir James (Lamb), KBE 1989; HM Marshal of the Diplomatic Corps, since 1992; *b* 28 Feb. 1936; *s* of Alwyn Thomas Hirst Weatherall and Olive Catherine Joan Weatherall (*née* Cuthbert); *m* 1962, Hon. Jean Stewart Macpherson, *d* of 1st Baron Drumalbyn, KBE, PC; two *s* three *d. Educ:* Glasgow Academy; Gordonstoun School. Joined RN 1954; commanded HM Ships: Soberton, 1966–67; Ulster, 1970–72; Tartar, 1975–76; Andromeda, 1982–84 (incl. Falklands conflict); Ark Royal, 1985–87; with SACEUR, 1987–89; Dep. Supreme Allied Comdr Atlantic, 1989–91. Chairman: Sea Cadet Council, 1992–; Sea Cadet Assoc., 1992–. Trustee, Marwell Preservation Trust, 1992–. Chm. Bd of Govs, Box Hill Sch., 1993– (Trustee, 1992–); Gov., Gordonstoun Sch., 1993–. Mem., Ct of Assts, Shipwrights' Co., 1989–; Younger Brother, Corp. of Trinity House, 1986. *Recreations:* stamp collecting, fishing. *Club:* Royal Navy of 1765 and 1785.

WEATHERALL, Miles, MA, DM, DSc; FIBiol; *b* 14 Oct. 1920; *s* of Rev. J. H. and Mary Weatherall; *m* 1944, Josephine A. C. Ogston; three *d. Educ:* Dragon School and St Edward's School, Oxford; Oriel College, Oxford. BA, BSc 1941; BM 1943; MA 1945; DM 1951; DSc 1966. Open Schol. in Nat. Sci., Oriel Coll., 1938. Lecturer in Pharmacology, Edinburgh University, 1945; Head of Dept of Pharmacology, London Hosp. Med. Coll., 1949–66; Prof. of Pharmacology, Univ. of London, 1958–66; Wellcome Research Laboratories: Head, Therapeutic Res. Div., 1967–75; Dep. Dir, 1969–74; Dir of Estblt, 1974–79. Member: Adv. Cttee on Pesticides and other Toxic Chemicals, 1964–66; Council, Pharmaceutical Soc., 1966–70; Council, Roy. Soc. Med., 1972–82 (Hon. Sec. 1974–82); Comr, Medicines Commn, 1979–81. Chm., Sci. Co-ord. Cttee, Arthritis and Rheumatism Council, 1983–88. Chm., Council, Chelsea Coll., Univ. of London, 1970–83. Hon. Lecturer: UCL, 1968–89; KCL, 1979–82, Hon. Fellow: Chelsea Coll., London, 1984; KCL, 1985. Mem. Cttee, Wine Soc., 1964–72. *Publications:* Statistics for Medical Students (jointly with L. Bernstein), 1952; Scientific Method, 1968; (ed jtly) Safety Testing of New Drugs, 1984; In Search of a Cure, 1990; papers in scientific and medical journals. *Recreations:* writing, gardening, cooking. *Address:* Willows, Charlbury, Oxford OX7 3PX. *Club:* Royal Society of Medicine.

WEATHERBY, Jonathan Roger; Chairman, Weatherbys Group Ltd, since 1993; *b* 30 Nov. 1959; *s* of Christopher Nicholas Weatherby and Alison Beatrix (*née* Pease); *m* 1993, Sophie Frances Cliffe-Jones; one *d. Educ:* Eton Coll. Joined Weatherbys, 1979; Dir, 1988–. *Recreations:* horse-racing, soccer, hunting. *Address:* Weatherbys Group Ltd, Sanders Road, Wellingborough, Northants NN8 4BX. *T:* Wellingborough (01933) 440077. *Clubs:* White's, Turf.

WEATHERHEAD, Alexander Stewart, OBE 1985; TD; solicitor; Partner in Tindal Oatts (formerly Tindal Oatts & Rodger, then Tindal Oatts Buchanan and McIlwraith), Solicitors, Glasgow, since 1960; *b* Edinburgh, 3 Aug. 1931; *er s* of Kenneth Kilpatrick Weatherhead and Katharine Weatherhead (*née* Stewart); *m* 1972, Harriett Foye, *d* of Rev. Dr Arthur Organ, Toronto, Canada; two *d. Educ:* Glasgow Acad.; Glasgow Univ. MA 1955, LLB 1958. Served in RA, 1950–52, 2nd Lieut, 1950. Solicitor, 1958; Temp. Sheriff, 1985–92. Hon. Vice-Pres., Law Society of Scotland, 1983–84 (Mem. Council, 1971–84); Member: Royal Faculty of Procurators in Glasgow, 1960– (Dean, 1992–95); Council, Soc. for Computers and Law, 1973–86 (Vice-Chm., 1973–82; Chm., 1982–84; Hon. Mem., 1986); Mem., Royal Commn on Legal Services in Scotland, 1976–80. Trustee, Nat. Technol. and Law Trust (formerly Nat. Law Library Trust), 1979–86; Mem., Internat. Bar Assoc.; Examr in Conveyancing, Univ. of Aberdeen, 1984–86. Dir, Glasgow Chamber of Commerce, 1992–95. Joined TA, 1952; Lt Col Comdg 277 (A&SH) Field Regt, RA (TA), 1965–67; The Lowland Regt (RA(T)), 1967 and Glasgow & Strathclyde Univs OTC, 1971–73; Col 1974; TAVR Col Lowlands (West), 1974–76; ADC (TAVR) to the Queen, 1977–81; Member: TAVR Assoc. Lowlands, 1967– (Vice-Chm., 1987–90; Chm., 1990–93); RA Council for Scotland, 1972–. Hon. Col, Glasgow and Strathclyde Univs OTC, 1982–. Commodore, Royal Western Yacht Club, 1995– (Vice Cdre, 1991–95; Hon. Sec., 1981–84). *Recreations:* sailing, reading, music, tennis. *Address:* 52 Partickhill Road, Glasgow G11 5AB. *T:* 0141–334 6277. *Clubs:* New (Edinburgh); Royal Highland Yacht (Oban); Royal Western Yacht, Clyde Cruising (Glasgow).

WEATHERHEAD, Very Rev. James Leslie; Principal Clerk of the General Assembly of the Church of Scotland, 1985–93 and 1994–Sept. 1996 (Moderator, 1993–94); Chaplain to the Queen in Scotland, since 1991; *b* 29 March 1931; *s* of Leslie Binnie Weatherhead, MBE, MM and Janet Hood Arnot Smith or Weatherhead; *m* 1962, Dr Anne Elizabeth Shepherd; two *s. Educ:* High Sch., Dundee; Univ. of Edinburgh (MA, LLB; Senior Pres., Students' Repr. Council, 1953–54); New Coll., Univ. of Edinburgh (Pres., Univ. Union, 1959–60). Temp. Acting Sub-Lieut RNVR (Nat. Service), 1955–56. Licensed by Presb. of Dundee, 1960; ordained by Presb. of Ayr, 1960; Asst Minister, Auld Kirk of Ayr, 1960–62; Minister, Trinity Church, Rothesay, 1962–69; Minister, Old Church, Montrose, 1969–85. Convener, Business Cttee of Gen. Assembly, 1981–84. Mem., Broadcasting Council for Scotland, BBC, 1978–82. Hon. DD Edinburgh, 1993. *Recreations:* sailing, music. *Address:* (home) 28 Castle Terrace, Edinburgh EH1 2EL. *T:* 0131–228 6460; (until Sept. 1996) Church of Scotland Offices, 121 George Street, Edinburgh EH2 4YN. *T:* 0131–225 5722. *Clubs:* Victory Services; RNVR Yacht.

WEATHERILL, family name of **Baron Weatherill.**

WEATHERILL, Baron *cr* 1992 (Life Peer), of North East Croydon in the London Borough of Croydon; **Bruce Bernard Weatherill;** PC 1980; DL; *b* 25 Nov. 1920; *s* of late Bernard Weatherill, Spring Hill, Guildford, and Annie Gertrude (*née* Creak); *m* 1949, Lyn, *d* of late H. T. Eatwell; two *s* one *d. Educ:* Malvern College. Served War of 1939–45; commissioned 4/7th Royal Dragoon Guards, 1940; transferred to Indian Army, 1941 and served with 19th King George V's Own Lancers, 1941–45 (Captain). Man. Dir, Bernard Weatherill Ltd, 1957–70. First Chm., Guildford Young Conservatives, 1946–49; Chm., Guildford Cons. Assoc., 1959–63; Vice-Chm., SE Area Prov. Council, 1962–64; Member National Union of Cons. Party, 1963–64. MP (C) Croydon NE, 1964–83 (when elected Speaker); MP Croydon NE and Speaker of The House of Commons, 1983–92; an Opposition Whip, 1967; a Lord Comr of HM Treasury, 1970–71; Vice-Chamberlain, HM Household, 1971–72; Comptroller of HM Household, 1972–73; Treasurer of HM Household and Dep. Chief Govt Whip, 1973–74; Opposition Dep. Chief Whip, 1974–79; Chm. of Ways and Means and Dep. Speaker, 1979–83. Convenor, Cross Bench Peers, 1995–. Chairman: Commonwealth Speakers and Presiding Officers, 1986–88; Industry and Parlt Trust, 1994–. Pres., CPA, 1986. High Bailiff of Westminster Abbey, 1989–. Freeman of City of London, 1949; Freeman of Borough of Croydon, 1983. Hon. Bencher, Lincoln's Inn, 1988. DL Kent, 1992. Hon. LLD Coll. of William and Mary, Va, 1989; Hon. DCL: Kent, 1990; Denver, 1992; DUniv Open, 1993. KStJ 1992; Vice-Chancellor, Order of St John of Jerusalem, 1992. Hilal-e-Pakistan 1993. *Recreation:* playing with grandchildren. *Address:* Emmetts House, Ide Hill, Kent TN14 6BA.

WEATHERLEY, Prof. Paul Egerton, FRS 1973; Regius Professor of Botany in the University of Aberdeen, 1959–81, now Emeritus; *b* 6 May 1917; *o s* of late Leonard Roger Weatherley and late Ethel Maude (*née* Collin), Leicester; *m* 1942, Margaret Logan, *o d* of late John Pirie, JP, Castle of Auchry, Aberdeenshire; one *s* three *d. Educ:* Wyggeston School; Keble College (Open Schol.), Oxford. Final Sch. of Nat. Sci. (Hons Botany) 1939; Keble Research Schol., 1939–40, elected to Colonial Agric. Schol., 1940. Trained in RE, then Colonial Office cadet at Imperial Coll. of Tropical Agric. Trinidad, 1940–42. Govt Botanist in Dept of Agriculture, Uganda Protectorate, 1942–47; Asst Lectr, Univ. of Manchester, 1947–49; Lecturer in Botany, 1949–59 (Sen. Lectr 1956), Univ. of Nottingham. *Publications:* papers in (mainly) botanical journals. *Recreations:* music, sketching. *Address:* Greystones, Torphins, Aberdeenshire AB31 4HP.

WEATHERSTON, (William) Alastair (Paterson), CB 1993; Under Secretary, Scottish Office Education Department, 1989–95; *b* 20 Nov. 1935; *s* of William Robert Weatherston and Isabella (*née* Paterson); *m* 1961, Margaret Jardine; two *s* one *d. Educ:* Peebles High Sch.; Edinburgh Univ. (MA Hons History). Asst Principal, Dept of Health for Scotland and Scottish Educn Dept, 1959–63; Private Sec. to Permanent Under Sec. of State, Scottish Office, 1963–64; Principal, Scottish Educn Dept, 1964–72, Cabinet Office, 1972–74; Assistant Secretary: SHHD, 1974–77; Scottish Educn Dept, 1977–79; Central Services, Scottish Office, 1979–82; Dir, Scottish Courts Admin, 1982–86; Fisheries Sec., Dept of Agric. and Fisheries for Scotland, 1986–89. FRSA. *Recreations:* reading, music. *Address:* 1 Coltbridge Terrace, Edinburgh EH12 6AB. *T:* 0131–337 3339.

WEATHERSTONE, Sir Dennis, KBE 1990; Director, J. P. Morgan & Co., New York; *b* 29 Nov. 1930; *s* of Henry and Gladys Weatherstone; *m* 1959, Marion Blunsum; one *s* three *d. Educ:* Northwestern Polytechnic, London. Morgan Guaranty Trust Co., subseq. J. P. Morgan & Co.: Sen. Vice-Pres., 1972–77; Exec. Vice-Pres., 1977–79; Treas., 1977–79; Vice-Chm., 1979–80; Chm., Exec. Cttee, 1980–86; Pres., 1987–89; Chm. and Chief Exec., 1990–94. *Address:* J. P. Morgan & Co., 60 Wall Street, New York, NY 10015, USA.

WEATHERSTONE, Robert Bruce, TD 1962; CA; Chairman, Lothian Health Board, 1986–90; *b* 14 May 1926; *s* of Sir Duncan Mackay Weatherstone, MC, TD, and late Janet Pringle; *m* 1954, Agnes Elaine Jean Fisher; one *s* one *d. Educ:* Edinburgh and Dollar Academies. CA 1951. Served Royal Marines, 44 Commando, 1944–47. Dir/Sec., J. T. Salvesen Ltd, 1954–62; Dir and Mem., Management Cttee, Christian Salvesen Ltd, 1962–83; Dir, Lothian Region Transport plc, 1986–92. Chm., Leith Enterprise Trust, 1983–88; Trustee, Leonard Cheshire Foundn, 1973–. *Recreations:* hill-walking, ornithology. *Address:* 27 Ravelston Garden, Edinburgh EH4 3LE. *T:* 0131–337 4035. *Clubs:* Army and Navy; New (Edinburgh).

WEAVER, Leonard John, CBE 1990; Chairman: Jones & Shipman, since 1988; Eutech Engineering Services, since 1995; *b* 10 June 1936; *s* of late A. W. Weaver and of B. I. M. Weaver (*née* Geleyns); *m* 1963, Penelope Ann Sturge-Young; five *s* one *d. Educ:* St Mary's Sch.; Battersea Coll. of Advanced Technology (Surrey Univ.). CEng, FIEE, FIM, FIMfgE, FIMC. Served Kenya Regt, 1955–57. AEI, 1962–64; PYE-TMC, 1964–66; Consultant, Dir and Man. Dir, P-E Internat., 1966–82; Chairman: Polymark Internat., 1982–92; Manifold Industries, 1982–95; Pearson Engineering, 1985–88. Member: Council, BIM, 1978–83; Council, Inst. of Management Consultants, 1978–86 (Pres., 1983–84); Council, IProdE, 1980–91 (Pres., 1990–91); NEDO Prod. Control Adv. Gp (Chm., 1980–82); NEDO Advanced Manfg Systems Gp, 1983–86; SERC Teaching Co. Mangt Cttee, 1983–86; Jt DTI/SERC Advanced Manfg Tech. Cttee, 1983–91 (Chm., 1987–91); SERC Engrg Bd, 1987–91; Indust. Develt Adv. Bd, 1989–95; Innovation Adv. Bd, 1991–93; Steering Bd, NPL, 1993–; Council, IEE, 1991–. Hon. Mem., Soc. of Manfg Engrs, USA, 1990. Freeman, City of London, 1984; Mem., Court of Assts, Co. of Engrs, 1991–. CIMgt (Vice-Chm., Council, 1993–); FRSA, FSME. DUniv Surrey, 1991. Sandforth Smith Award, Inst. of Management Consultants, 1984; Internat. Engineer of the Year, San Fernando Valley Engrs Council, 1985; Calif. State Legis. Commend., 1985. *Publications:* contribs to professional jls. *Recreations:* book collecting, cricket. *Address:* Crab Apple Court, Oxshott Road, Leatherhead, Surrey KT22 0DQ. *T:* Leatherhead (01372) 843637. *Clubs:* Reform, City Livery, MCC.

WEAVER, Oliver; QC 1985; *b* 27 March 1942; *s* of Denis Weaver and Kathleen (*née* Lynch); *m* 1964, Julia (*née* MacClymont); one *s* two *d. Educ:* Friends' Sch., Saffron Walden; Trinity Coll., Cambridge (MA, LLM). President, Cambridge Union Society, 1963. Called to the Bar, Middle Temple, 1965; Lincoln's Inn, 1969. Mem. Bar Council, 1981–84; Vice-Chm., Bar Law Reform Cttee, 1987–89; Member: Incorporated Council of Law Reporting, 1987–93; Panel of Chairmen of Authorisation and Disciplinary Tribunals, Securities and Futures Authy (formerly Securities Assoc., then Securities and Futures Assoc.), 1988–93. *Recreations:* fishing, racing, gun dogs. *Address:* Kennel Farm, Albury End, Ware, Herts SG11 2HS. *T:* Albury (01279) 771331.

WEAVER, Sir Tobias Rushton, (Sir Toby Weaver), Kt 1973; CB 1962; *b* 19 July 1911; *s* of late Sir Lawrence Weaver, KBE, and late Lady Weaver (*née* Kathleen Purcell); *m* 1941, Marjorie, *d* of Rt Hon. Sir Charles Trevelyan, 3rd Bt, PC; one *s* three *d. Educ:* Clifton

College; Corpus Christi College, Cambridge. Bank clerk, Toronto, 1932; teaching at Barking, 1935, Eton, 1936; Asst Director of Education: Wilts CC 1936, Essex CC 1939. Admiralty, 1941; War Office, 1942; Dept of Education and Science, 1946–73; Under-Secretary, 1956; Deputy Secretary, 1962. Visiting Professor of Education: Univ. of Southampton, 1973; Univ. of London Inst. of Educn, 1974; Open Univ., 1976–78. FIC 1986; Hon. Fellow: Manchester Poly., 1970; Huddersfield Poly., 1972; Hatfield Poly., 1973; NE London Poly., 1985. Hon. LLD CNAA, 1972. *Address:* 14 Marston Close, NW6 4EU. *T:* 0171–624 4263.

WEBB, Prof. Adrian Leonard, DLitt; Vice-Chancellor, University of Glamorgan, since 1993; *b* 19 July 1943; *s* of Leonard and Rosina Webb; *m* 1966, Caroline Williams; two *s*. *Educ:* Birmingham Univ. (1st cl. Hons BSocSci 1965); LSE (MSc (Econ) 1966); DLitt Loughborough 1993. Lectr, LSE, 1966–74; Res. Dir, Personal Social Services Council, 1974–76; Loughborough University: Prof. of Social Policy, 1976–93; Dir, Centre for Res. in Social Policy, 1983–90; Dean, then Pro-Chancellor, subseq. Sen. Pro Vice-Chancellor, 1986–93. FRSA. *Publications:* Change, Choice and Conflict in Social Policy, 1975; Planning Need and Scarcity: essays on the personal social services, 1986; The Economic Approach to Social Policy, 1986; Social Work, Social Care and Social Planning, 1987; Joint Approaches to Social Policy: rationality and practice, 1988; contribs on social policy to professional periodicals. *Recreations:* walking, painting (water colour), ornithology. *Address:* University of Glamorgan, Pontypridd, Mid Glam CF37 1DL. *T:* Pontypridd (01443) 480480. *Clubs:* Athenæum, National Liberal.

WEBB, Anthony Michael Francis, CMG 1963; QC (Kenya) 1961; JP; *b* 27 Dec. 1914; *s* of late Sir (Ambrose) Henry Webb; *m* 1948, Diana Mary, *e d* of late Capt. Graham Farley, Indian Army, and Mrs Herbert Browne (*née* Pyper); one *s* one *d*. *Educ:* Ampleforth; Magdalen Coll., Oxford (MA). Barrister-at-Law, Gray's Inn, 1939. Served War, 1939–46, Maj. GSO2, The Queen's Bays. Colonial Legal Service (HMOCS), 1947–64 (Malaya; Kenya; MLC 1958–63; Attorney-General and Minister for Legal Affairs, 1961–63); Sec., Nat. Adv. Council on Trng of Magistrates, and Trng Officer, 1964–73, Dep. Sec. of Commns, 1969–75, Head of Court Business, 1975–77, Lord Chancellor's Office; retd 1977. A Chm. of Indust. Tribunals, 1978–87. Member of Council of Kenya Lawn Tennis Association, 1957–63. JP, Kent, 1966. *Publication:* The Natzweiler Trial (ed). *Address:* 19 Crittle's Court, Wadhurst, E Sussex TN5 6BY. *T:* Wadhurst (01892) 782399. *Club:* Special Forces.

WEBB, Rear-Adm. Arthur Brooke, CB 1975; retired; *b* 13 June 1918; *m* 1949, Rachel Marian Gerrish; three *d*. Joined Royal Navy, 1936. Comdr 1954, Captain 1963, Rear-Adm. 1973. *Recreations:* gardening, walking, survival. *Address:* Shearwater, Downderry, Torpoint, Cornwall PL11 3LL.

WEBB, Prof. Colin Edward, DPhil; FRS 1991; FInstP; Professor, Department of Physics, University of Oxford, since 1992; Senior Research Fellow, Jesus College, Oxford, since 1988; Founder and Chairman, Oxford Lasers Ltd, since 1977; *b* 9 Dec. 1937; *s* of Alfred Edward Webb and Doris (*née* Collins); *m* 1964, Pamela Mabel Cooper White (*d* 1992); two *d*. *Educ:* Univ. of Nottingham (BSc 1960); Oriel Coll., Oxford (DPhil 1964). FInstP 1985. Mem., Technical Staff, Bell Labs, Murray Hill, NJ, 1964–68; University of Oxford: AEI Res. Fellow in Physics, Clarendon Lab., 1968–71; Univ. Lectr, 1971–90; Tutorial Fellow, Jesus Coll., 1973–88; Reader, Dept of Physics, 1990–92. Vis. Prof., Dept of Pure and Applied Physics, Univ. of Salford, 1987–. Fellow, Optical Soc. of America, 1988. Duddell Medal and Prize, Inst. of Physics, 1985. *Publications:* contribs on lasers, laser mechanisms and applications to learned jls. *Recreations:* travel, photography, music, reading. *Address:* Clarendon Laboratory, Parks Road, Oxford OX1 3PU. *T:* Oxford (01865) 272210.

WEBB, Colin Thomas; General Manager, Press Association, since 1994 (Director, since 1989); *b* 26 March 1939; *e s* of late William Thomas and Ada Alexandra Webb; *m* 1970, Margaret Frances, *y d* of late Maurice George and Joan Rowden Cheshire; two *s* one *d*. *Educ:* Portsmouth Grammar School. Reporter, Portsmouth Evening News, Surrey Mirror, Press Assoc., Daily Telegraph, The Times; Royal Army Pay Corps Short Service Commission (to Captain), 1960–64; Home News Editor, The Times, 1969–74; Editor, Cambridge Evening News, 1974–82; Dep. Editor, The Times, 1982–86; Journalist Dir, Times Newspaper Holdings, 1983–86. Ed.-in-Chief, Press Assoc., 1986–94. Member: Core Cttee, British Executive Internat. Press Inst., 1984–; Council, Commonwealth Press Union, 1985–. Hon. Fellow, Univ. of Portsmouth (formerly Portsmouth Polytechnic), 1991. *Publication:* (co-author with The Times News Team) Black Man in Search of Power, 1968. *Recreations:* family, walking, history books. *Address:* 49 Winterbrook Road, SE24 9HZ. *T:* 0171–274 4533. *Club:* Garrick.

WEBB, Prof. Edwin Clifford; Emeritus Professor, University of Queensland; Vice-Chancellor, Macquarie University, 1976–86; *b* 21 May 1921; *s* of William Webb and Nellie Webb; *m* 1st, 1942, Violet Sheila Joan (*née* Tucker) (marr. diss. 1987); one *s* four *d* (and one *s* decd); 2nd, 1988, Miriam Margaret Therese (*née* Armstrong). *Educ:* Poole Grammar Sch.; Cambridge Univ. (BA, MA, PhD). FRACI 1968. Cambridge University: Beit Meml Res. Fellow, 1944–46; Univ. Demonstrator in Biochem., 1946–50; Univ. Lectr in Biochem., 1950–62; University of Queensland: Foundn Prof. of Biochem. and Head of Dept, 1962–70; Dep. Vice-Chancellor (Academic), 1970–76. Pres., Australasian Council on Chiropractic and Osteopathic Educn, 1991–. Hon. DSc: Queensland, 1978; Macquarie, 1988. *Publications:* Enzymes, 1959, 3rd edn 1979; 56 scientific papers. *Recreations:* photography, music, motoring, coin collecting. *Address:* 1/221 King's Road, Mundingburra, Townsville, Qld 4812, Australia.

WEBB, George Hannam, CMG 1984; OBE 1974; *b* 24 Dec. 1929; *s* of late George Ernest Webb, HM Colonial Service, Kenya, and Mary Hannam (*née* Stephens); *m* 1956, Josephine (later MA Cantab; JP Surrey), *d* of late Richard Chatterton, Horncastle; two *s* two *d*. *Educ:* Malvern Coll.; King's Coll., Cambridge (MA). Served 14/20th King's Hussars, 1948–49; Parachute Regt (TA), 1950–53. Joined Colonial Administration, Kenya, 1953: District Officer, Central Nyanza, 1954–56; N Nyanza, 1956–57; District Commissioner, Moyale, 1958–60; Secretariat, Nairobi, 1960–62; retired 1963 and joined HM Diplomatic Service; First Sec., Bangkok, 1964–67; Accra, 1969–73; Counsellor, Tehran, 1977–79, Washington, 1980–82; retd 1985. Dir, Management Develt, 1985–89, Sen. Fellow, 1989–93, City Univ. Member Council: Royal Soc. for Asian Affairs, 1984–91; Friends of Nat. Army Museum, 1988–; Gresham Coll., 1988–; Horatian Soc., 1991–; Trustee: Hakluyt Soc., 1986–; Encounter, 1989–91. FRSA. Liveryman, Scriveners' Co., 1989–. Editor, *Kipling Journal*, 1980–. *Publications:* The Bigger Bang: growth of a financial revolution, 1987; (ed with Sir Hugh Cortazzi) Kipling's Japan, 1988; contribs to learned jls. *Recreations:* books, travel. *Address:* Weavers, Danes Hill, Woking GU22 7HQ. *T:* Woking (01483) 761989. *Clubs:* Travellers' (Chm., 1987–91), Beefsteak.

WEBB, Prof. John Stuart, FEng; Professor of Applied Geochemistry in the University of London, 1961–79, now Emeritus, and Senior Research Fellow, 1979–89, Imperial College of Science and Technology; *b* 28 Aug. 1920; *s* of Stuart George Webb and Caroline Rabjohns Webb (*née* Pengelly); *m* 1946, Jean Millicent Dyer; one *s*. *Educ:* Westminster City School; Royal School of Mines, Imperial College of Science and Technology, BSc, ARSM, 1941. Served War of 1939–45, Royal Engineers, 1941–43. Geological Survey of Nigeria, 1943–44; Royal School of Mines, Imperial Coll., 1945–; Beit Scientific Research Fellow, 1945–47; PhD, DIC, in Mining Geology, 1947; Lecturer in Mining Geology, 1947–55; Reader in Applied Geochemistry, 1955–61. DSc, 1967. Mem., Home Office Forensic Science Cttee, 1969–75. Mem. Council, Instn of Mining and Metallurgy, 1964–71, and 1974–83, Vice Pres., 1971–73, Pres., 1973–74; Mem. Bd, Council Engineering Instns, 1973–74; Reg. Vice-Pres. (Europe), Soc. of Econ. Geologists, USA, 1979–81. Mem., Royal Soc. Wkg Pty on Environmental Geochem. and Health, 1979–83. Hon. Mem., Assoc. Exploration Geochemists, USA, 1977; Hon. FIMM 1980. Consolidated Goldfields of SA Gold Medal, IMM, 1953; William Smith Medal, Geol Soc. of London, 1981. *Publications:* (with H. E. Hawkes) Geochemistry in Mineral Exploration, 1962, 2nd edn (with A. W. Rose) 1979; (jtly) Geochemical Atlas of Northern Ireland, 1973; (jtly) Wolfson Geochemical Atlas of England and Wales, 1978; contrib. to scientific and technical jls. *Recreations:* fishing, wild life photography, amateur radio. *Address:* Stone Cottage, Lyons Road, Slinfold, Horsham, Sussex RH13 7QT. *T:* Slinfold (01403) 790243.

WEBB, Prof. Joseph Ernest, PhD (London) 1944, DSc (London) 1949; CBiol, FIBiol; FLS; FZS; Professor of Zoology, 1960–80, and Vice-Principal, 1976–80, Westfield College, University of London, now Emeritus Professor; *b* 22 March 1915; *s* of Joseph Webb and Constance Inman Webb (*née* Hickox); *m* 1940, Gwenlilian Clara Coldwell (*d* 1994); three *s*. *Educ:* Rutlish School; Birkbeck College, London (BSc 1940). FZS 1943; CBiol, FIBiol 1963; FLS 1972. Research Entomologist and Parasitologist at The Cooper Technical Bureau, Berkhamsted, Herts, 1940–46; Lecturer, Univ. of Aberdeen, 1946–48; Senior Lecturer, 1948–50, Professor of Zoology, 1950–60, University Coll., Ibadan, Nigeria. Hon. Fellow, QMW (formerly Westfield Coll.), 1986. *Publications:* (jointly): Guide to Invertebrate Animals, 1975, 2nd edn 1978; Guide to Living Mammals, 1977, 2nd edn 1979; Guide to Living Reptiles, 1978; Guide to Living Birds, 1979; Guide to Living Fishes, 1981; Guide to Living Amphibians, 1981; various on insect physiology, insecticides, systematics, populations, tropical ecology, marine biology and sedimentology. *Recreations:* art, music, photography, gardening. *Address:* 43 Hill Top, NW11 6EA. *T:* 0181–458 2571. *Club:* Athenæum.

WEBB, Kaye, MBE 1974; Chairman and Founder of Puffin Club (for children), since 1967; Director, Unicorn Children's Theatre, since 1972; Managing Director, Kaye Webb Ltd, since 1973; *b* 26 Jan. 1914; *d* of Arthur Webb and Kathleen Stevens, journalists; *m* 1st, Christopher Brierley; 2nd, Andrew Hunter; 3rd, 1946, Ronald Searle, *qv*; one *s* one *d*. Entered journalism via Picturegoer, 1931; joined Picture Post, 1938; Asst Editor, Lilliput, 1941–47; Theatre Corresp., The Leader, 1947–49; Feature Writer, News Chronicle, 1949–55; Editor of children's magazine Elizabethan, 1955–58; Theatre Critic to National Review, 1957–58; Children's Editor, Puffin Books, and Publishing Dir, Children's Div., Penguin Books Ltd, 1961–79; Editor, Puffin Post, 1967–81. Children's Advisor, Goldcrest TV, 1978–84; Mem. UK Branch, UNICEF. Eleanor Farjeon Award for services to Children's Literature, 1969. *Publications:* (ed) C. Fry: Experience of Critics; (ed) Penguin Patrick Campbell; (ed) The Friday Miracle; (ed) The St Trinian's Story; (with Ronald Searle): Looking at London; Paris Sketchbook; Refugees 1960; (with Treld Bicknell) 1st and 2nd Puffin Annuals; Puffins Pleasure; (ed) I Like This Poem, 1979; (ed) Lilliput Goes to War, 1985; (ed) I Like This Story, 1986; Round About Six, 1991; Meet my Friends, 1991; Family Tree, 1994. *Recreations:* children and their interests, theatre. *Address:* 8 Lampard House, Maida Avenue, W2 1SS. *T:* 0171–262 4695.

WEBB, Prof. Leslie Roy; Vice-Chancellor, Griffith University, since 1985; *b* 18 July 1935; *s* of Leslie Hugh Charles Webb and Alice Myra Webb; *m* 1966, Heather, *d* of late H. Brown; one *s* one *d*. *Educ:* Wesley College, Univ. of Melbourne (BCom 1957); Univ. of London (PhD 1962). FASSA 1986; FAIM 1989; MACE 1991. Sen. Lectr in Economics, Univ. of Melbourne, 1964–68; Reader in Economics, La Trobe Univ., 1968–72; University of Melbourne: Truby Williams Prof. of Economics, 1973–84, Prof. Emeritus, 1984; Pro-Vice-Chancellor, 1982–84; Chm., Academic Bd, 1983–84. Vis. Prof., Cornell, 1967–68. Chairman: Bd, Qld Tertiary Admissions Centre, 1986, 1991, 1992 (Mem., 1985–); Australian-Amer. Educnl Foundn (Fulbright Program), 1986–90 (Mem., 1985–89); Member: Conf. of Qld Vice-Chancellors, 1985– (Chm., 1988); Cttee, Sir Robert Menzies Australian Studies Centre, Univ. of London, 1990–92; Bd of Govs, Foundn for Develt Co-operation, 1990–. Consultant, UN Conf. on Trade and Develt, 1974–75; Chm., Cttee of Inquiry into S Australian Dairy Industry, 1977; Mem., Council of Advice, Bureau of Industry Economics, 1982–84; Pres., Victoria Branch, Econ. Soc. of Aust. and NZ, 1976. Award for outstanding achievement, US Inf. Agency, 1987. Joint Editor, The Economic Record, 1973–77. *Publication:* (ed jtly) Industrial Economics: Australian studies, 1982. *Recreations:* music, art. *Address:* Griffith University, Kessels Road, Nathan, Qld 4111, Australia. *T:* (7) 38757340.

WEBB, Margaret Elizabeth Barbieri; *see* Barbieri, M. E.

WEBB, Maysie (Florence), CBE 1979; BSc; Deputy Director, British Museum, 1971–83 (Assistant Director 1968–71); *b* 1 May 1923; *d* of Charles and Florence Webb. *Educ:* Kingsbury County School; Northern Polytechnic. Southwark Public Libraries, 1940–45; A. C. Cossor Ltd, 1945–50; British Non-Ferrous Metals Research Assoc., 1950–52; Mullard Equipment Ltd, 1952–55; Morgan Crucible Co. Ltd, 1955–60; Patent Office Library, 1960–66; Keeper, National Reference Library of Science and Invention, 1966–68. General Comr in England and Wales, 1976–. Trustee of the Royal Armouries, 1984–90. *Recreations:* family and friends, homes and gardens, thinking.

WEBB, Pauline Mary, FKC; retired; author and broadcaster; *b* 28 June 1927; *d* of Rev. Leonard F. Webb. *Educ:* King's Coll., London Univ. (BA, AKC, FKC 1985); Union Theological Seminary, New York (STM). BA English Hons (King's), 1948; Teacher's Diploma, London Inst. of Educn, 1949. Asst Mistress, Thames Valley Grammar Sch., 1949–52; Editor, Methodist Missionary Soc., 1955–66; Vice-Pres., Methodist Conf., 1965–66; Dir, Lay Training, Methodist Church, 1967–73; Area Sec., Methodist Missionary Soc., 1973–79; Chm., Community and Race Relns Unit, BCC, 1976–79; Organiser, Religious Broadcasting, BBC World Service, 1979–87. Vice-Chm., Central Cttee, WCC, 1968–75; Jt Chm., World Conf. on Religion and Peace, 1989–93. Hon. Dr: in Protestant Theology, Univ. of Brussels, 1984; of Sacred Letters, Victoria Univ., Toronto, Canada, 1985; of Humane Letters, Mt St Vincent Univ., Nova Scotia, 1987. *Publications:* Women of Our Company, 1958; Women of Our Time, 1960; Operation-Healing, 1964; All God's Children, 1964; Are We Yet Alive?, 1966; Agenda for the Churches, 1968; Salvation Today, 1974; Eventful Worship, 1975; Where are the Women?, 1979; Faith and Faithfulness, 1985; Celebrating Friendship, 1986; Evidence for the Power of Prayer, 1987; Candles for Advent, 1989; (ed jtly) Dictionary of the Ecumenical Movement, 1991; She Flies Beyond, 1993; (ed) The Long Struggle: the World Council of Churches' involvement with South Africa, 1994. *Address:* 14 Paddocks Green, Salmon Street, NW9 8NH. *Club:* BBC.

WEBB, Richard Murton Lumley; Chairman, Morgan Grenfell & Co. Ltd, since 1989; *b* 7 March 1939; *s* of Richard Henry Lumley Webb and Elizabeth Martin (*née* Munro Kerr); *m* 1966, Juliet Wendy English Devenish; one *s* one *d*. *Educ:* Winchester Coll.; New Coll.,

Oxford (BA Modern Hist.). Mem., Inst. Chartered Accountants of Scotland, 1965. Brown Fleming & Murray, 1961–68; Morgan Grenfell & Co. Ltd, 1968–; Morgan Grenfell Gp PLC, 1988–. *Address:* (office) 23 Great Winchester Street, EC2P 2AX. *T:* 0171–588 4545. *Club:* Hurlingham.

WEBB, Robert Stopford; QC 1988; a Recorder, since 1993; *b* 4 Oct. 1948; *s* of late Robert Victor Bertram Webb, MC and of Isabella Raine Webb (*née* Hinks); *m* 1975, Angela Mary Freshwater; two *s*. *Educ:* Wycliffe Coll.; Exeter Univ. (LLB 1970). Called to the Bar, Inner Temple, 1971; Western Circuit. Chm., Air Law Gp, RAeS, 1988–93 (FRAeS 1992); Vice Chm., Air Law Cttee, 1990–93, English Bar Rep., 1994–, Internat. Bar Assoc.; Member: Commn d'Arbitrage Aerien et Spatial, Paris, 1994–; Bd, Internat. Acad. of Trial Lawyers, 1994– (Fellow, 1990). Mem., Chancellor's Adv. Council, Exeter Univ., 1994–. *Recreations:* fly-fishing, golf. *Address:* 5 Bell Yard, WC2A 2JR. *T:* 0171–333 8811, *Fax:* 0171–333 8831. *Clubs:* Royal Automobile; Royal Wimbledon Golf, Royal Lytham St Anne's Golf, Prestbury Golf.

WEBB, Sir Thomas (Langley), Kt 1975; *b* 25 April 1908; *s* of Robert Langley Webb and Alice Mary Webb; *m* 1942, Jeannette Alison Lang; one *s* one *d*. *Educ:* Melbourne Church of England Grammar Sch. Joined Huddart Parker Ltd, 1926 (Man. Dir, 1955–61). Served War, AIF, 1940–45. Dir, Commercial Bank of Aust., 1960–78 (Chm., 1970–78); Dir and Vice-Chm., McIlwraith McEacharn Ltd, 1961–92. *Recreations:* golf, tennis. *Address:* 6 Yarradale Road, Toorak, Victoria 3142, Australia. *T:* Melbourne (3) 98275259. *Clubs:* MCC; Australian, Melbourne, Royal Melbourne Golf, Royal South Yarra Tennis (all Melbourne).

WEBB, William Grierson; Artistic Director, London College of Music, since 1991; freelance conductor; Associate Artistic Director, The Rehearsal Orchestra, since 1994; *b* 16 Oct. 1947; *s* of Horace James Harry Webb and Marjorie Cairns (*née* Grierson); *m* 1984, Elizabeth Jean Shannon; two *s*. *Educ:* Rugby School; Merton Coll., Oxford (MA); Salzburg Mozarteum (Dip.). Hon. FLCM. Conductor, Trier Opera House, Germany, 1973–76; Asst General Administrator, Scottish Nat. Orchestra, 1976–78; Founder Administrator, Nat. Youth Orchestra of Scotland, 1978–87; Dep. Dir, London Coll. of Music, 1987–90. Musical Dir, Aberdeen Internat. Youth Festival, 1989–91. Chm., Mendelssohn and Boise Scholarship Foundns, 1992–94. *Publication:* (trans.) Tyrol through the Ages, 1973. *Address:* c/o London College of Music, Thames Valley University, St Mary's Road, Ealing, W5 5RF. *T:* 0181–231 2304.

WEBBER; *see* Lloyd Webber.

WEBBER, Rev. Canon Lionel Frank; Rector of Basildon, since 1976; Chaplain to the Queen, since 1994; *b* 12 July 1935; *s* of Nellie and Sydney Webber; *m* 1961, Jean Thomas; one *d*. *Educ:* Danetree Road Co. Secondary Sch., Ewell; Kelham Theol Coll.; St Michael's Theol Coll., Llandaff. Ordained deacon, 1960, priest, 1961; Curate: The Saviour, Bolton, 1960–63; Holy Trinity, Aberavon, 1963–65; Rector, Stowell Meml Parish Ch., Salford, 1965–69; Vicar, Holy Trinity, Aberavon, 1969–74; Team Vicar, Stantonbury, Milton Keynes, 1974–76. Hon. Canon, Chelmsford Cathedral, 1984–. *Recreations:* motor racing, sailing. *Address:* St Martin's Rectory, Town Centre, Basildon, Essex SS14 1DX. *T:* Basildon (01268) 522455.

WEBBER, Roy Seymour, IPFA, FCCA; Town Clerk and Chief Executive, Royal Borough of Kensington and Chelsea, 1979–90; *b* 8 April 1933; *s* of A. E. and A. M. Webber; *m* 1960, Barbara Ann (*née* Harries); one *s* three *d*. *Educ:* Ipswich School. Ipswich CBC, 1949–55; Coventry CBC, 1955–58; St Pancras BC, 1958–61; IBM (UK) Ltd, 1961–62; Woolwich BC, 1962–65; Greenwich LBC, 1965–68; Royal Borough of Kensington and Chelsea: Dep. Borough Treasurer, 1968–73; Director of Finance, 1973–79. *Recreation:* walking. *Address:* 11 River Park, Marlborough, Wilts SN8 1NH. *T:* Marlborough (01672) 511426.

WEBER, Catherine Elisabeth Dorcas; *see* Bell, C. E. D.

WEBER, (Edmund) Derek (Craig); Editor, The Geographical Magazine, 1967–81; *b* 29 April 1921; 3rd *s* of late R. J. C. and B. M. Weber; *m* 1953, Molly Patricia (*d* 1994), *d* of the late R. O. and Ellen Podger; one *s* four *d*. *Educ:* Bristol Grammar School. Journalist on newspapers in Swindon, Bristol and Bath, and on magazines in London from 1937 until 1953, except for War Service in RAF, 1940–46. The Geographical Magazine: Art Editor, 1953; Assoc. Editor, 1965. Hon. FRGS 1980. Hon. Life Member: IBG, 1981; NUJ, 1981. Hon. MA Open, 1982. *Address:* 32 London Road, Maldon, Essex CM9 6HD. *T:* Maldon (01621) 852871. *Club:* Savage.

WEBER, Jürgen; Chairman, Executive Board, Lufthansa German Airlines, since 1991; *b* 17 Oct. 1941; *m* 1965, Sabine Rossberg; one *s* one *d*. *Educ:* Stuttgart Tech. Univ. (Dipl. Ing. Aeronautical Engrg 1965); MIT (Sen. Mgt Trng 1980). Joined Lufthansa, 1967: Engrg Div., 1967–74; Director: Line Maintenance Dept, 1974–78; Aircraft Engrg Subdiv., 1978–87; Chief Operating Officer (Tech.), 1987–89; Dep. Mem., Exec. Bd, 1989–90; Chief Exec., Tech., 1990–91. *Recreations:* jogging, ski-ing. *Address:* Deutsche Lufthansa AG, Lufthansa Basis, 60546 Frankfurt, Germany. *T:* (69) 6962200.

WEBER, Prof. Richard Robert, Jr, PhD; Churchill Professor of the Mathematics for Operational Research, Cambridge University, since 1994; Fellow of Queens' College, Cambridge, since 1978; *b* 25 Feb. 1953; *s* of Richard Robert Weber and Elizabeth Bray. *Educ:* Walnut Hills High Sch., USA; Solihull Sch.; Downing Coll., Cambridge (BA 1974; MA 1978; PhD 1980). Cambridge University: Asst Lectr and Lectr in Engrg, 1978–92; Reader in Management Sci., Engrg, 1992–94; Queens' College: Res. Fellow, 1977–78; Tutor, 1979–92; Dir of Studies (Maths), 1985–94. *Publications:* numerous articles on stochastic systems, scheduling and queueing theory. *Recreations:* hiking, travel. *Address:* Queens' College, Cambridge CB3 9ET; Statistical Laboratory, 16 Mill Lane, Cambridge CB2 1SB. *T:* Cambridge (01223) 335570, 337953.

WEBLIN, Harold; Chairman, Liberty's, 1984–95 (Chief Executive, 1984–93); *b* 10 April 1930; *s* of E. W. Weblin and B. Weblin; *m* 1954, June Weblin (decd); two *s*. *Educ:* Walpole Grammar School, London. General Manager, Way-In, Harrods, 1948–71; General Manager, Liberty's, 1971–84. *Recreation:* gardening. *Address:* 84 The Uplands, Gerrards Cross, Bucks SL9 7JG. *T:* Gerrards Cross (01753) 887280.

WEBSTER, Very Rev. Alan Brunskill, KCVO 1988; Dean of St Paul's, 1978–87; *b* 1918; *s* of Rev. J. Webster; *m* 1951, M. C. F. Falconer; two *s* two *d*. *Educ:* Shrewsbury School; Queen's College, Oxford. MA, BD. Ordained, 1942; Curate of Attercliffe Parishes, Sheffield, 1942; Curate of St Paul's, Arbourthorne, Sheffield, 1944; Westcott House, 1946; Vicar of Barnard Castle, 1953; Warden, Lincoln Theol Coll., 1959–70; Dean of Norwich, 1970–78. Pres., Cathedral Camps, 1981–. Hon. DD City Univ., 1983. *Publications:* Joshua Watson, 1954; Broken Bones May Joy, 1968; Julian of Norwich, 1974 (rev. edn 1980). Contributor to The Historic Episcopate, 1954; Living the Faith, 1980; Strategist for the Spirit, 1985. *Recreation:* writing. *Address:* 20 Beechbank, Norwich, Norfolk NR2 2AL. *T:* Norwich (01603) 455833.

WEBSTER, Alec, FCCA; CIGasE; Regional Chairman, British Gas Wales, 1989–92; *b* 22 March 1934; *s* of Clifford Webster and Rose Webster (*née* Proctor); *m* 1958, Jean Thompson; one *s* two *d*. *Educ:* Hull Univ. (BScEcon Hons). Chief Accountant, British Gas Southern, 1974; Controller of Audit and Investigations, British Gas, 1979; Treas., British Gas, 1981; Reg. Dep. Chm., British Gas Southern, 1984. Pres., Chartered Assoc. of Certified Accountants, 1989–90. Chairman: Hendref Building Preservation Trust, 1992–; Darwin Centre for Biology and Medicine, 1993–. FRSA 1990. *Recreations:* sailing, mountaineering, wood carving. *Address:* Tŷ Carreg, 2 Maillards Haven, Penarth, S Glam CF64 5RF.

WEBSTER, Alistair Stevenson; QC 1995; an Assistant Recorder, since 1992; *b* 28 April 1953; *s* of His Honour I. S. Webster, *qv*; *m* 1977, Barbara Anne Longbottom; two *d*. *Educ:* Hulme Grammar Sch., Oldham; Brasenose Coll., Oxford (BA Hons Jurisp.). Called to the Bar, Middle Temple, 1976; practice on Northern Circuit, 1976–. Hon. Sec., Northern Circuit, 1988–93; Mem., Bar Council, 1995–. *Recreations:* cricket, tennis, ski-ing, football. *Address:* Lincoln House Chambers, 1 Brazennose Street, Manchester M2 5EL. *T:* 0161–832 5701. *Clubs:* Manchester Racquets; Rochdale Racquets; I Volenti CC.

WEBSTER, Maj.-Gen. Bryan Courtney, CB 1986; CBE 1981; Director of Army Quartering, 1982–86; *b* 2 Feb. 1931; *s* of Captain H. J. Webster, Royal Fusiliers (killed in action, 1940) and late M. J. Webster; *m* 1957, Elizabeth Rowland Waldron Smithers, *d* of Prof. Sir David Smithers; two *s* one *d*. *Educ:* Haileybury College; RMA Sandhurst. Commissioned Royal Fusiliers, 1951; ADC to GOC, 16 Airborne Div., 1953–55; served BAOR, Korea, Egypt, Malta, Gibraltar, Hong Kong; Directing Staff, Staff Coll., 1969–70; Comd 1st Bn Royal Regt of Fusiliers, 1971–73; Comd 8th Inf. Brigade, 1975–77 (Despatches); Dep. Col, Royal Regt of Fusiliers (City of London), 1976–89; Nat. Defence Coll., India, 1979; Staff appts, Far East, MoD, incl. Dir of Admin Planning (Army), 1980–82. Chm., Army Benevolent Fund, Surrey, 1988–. Mem. Council, Wine Guild of UK, 1991–. FIMgt. Freeman, City of London, 1984. *Recreations:* ornithology, shooting, wine. *Address:* c/o Midland Bank, Sevenoaks, Kent TN13 1LB.

WEBSTER, Charles, DSc; FBA 1982; Senior Research Fellow, All Souls College, Oxford, since 1988. University Reader in the History of Medicine, University of Oxford, 1972–88; Director, Wellcome Unit for the History of Medicine, 1972–88; Fellow of Corpus Christi College, Oxford, 1972–88. *Publications:* The Great Instauration, 1975; From Paracelsus to Newton, 1982; Problems of Health Care: the British National Health Service before 1957, 1988; (ed) Aneurin Bevan on the National Health Service, 1991; (ed) Caring for Health, History and Diversity, 1993. *Address:* All Souls College, Oxford OX1 4AL. *T:* Oxford (01865) 279379.

WEBSTER, Dr Cyril Charles, CMG 1966; Chief Scientific Officer, Agricultural Research Council, 1971–75 (Scientific Adviser, 1965–71); *b* 28 Dec. 1909; *s* of Ernest Webster; *m* 1947, Mary, *d* of H. R. Wimhurst; one *s* one *d*. *Educ:* Beckenham County Sch.; Wye Coll.; Selwyn Coll., Cambridge; Imperial Coll. of Tropical Agriculture, Trinidad. Colonial Agricultural Service, 1936–57: Nigeria, 1936–38; Nyasaland, 1938–50; Kenya (Chief Research Officer), 1950–55; Malaya (Dep. Dir of Agriculture), 1956–57; Prof. of Agriculture, Imperial Coll. of Tropical Agriculture, Univ. of W Indies, 1957–60; Dir, Rubber Research Inst. of Malaya, subseq. of Malaysia, 1961–65; Dir-Gen., Palm Oil Research Inst. of Malaysia, 1978–80. JMN, 1965. *Publications:* (with P. N. Wilson) Agriculture in the Tropics, 1966; (with W. J. Baulkwill) Rubber, 1989; scientific papers in agricultural jls. *Address:* 5 Shenden Way, Sevenoaks, Kent TN13 1SE. *T:* Sevenoaks (01732) 453984.

WEBSTER, David; Chairman, Trans-Atlantic Dialogue on European Broadcasting, since 1988; President, RadioSar International, since 1991; consultant to international companies and institutions; *b* 11 Jan. 1931; *s* of Alec Webster and Clare Webster; *m* 1st, 1955, Lucy Law (marr. diss.), Princeton, NJ; two *s*; 2nd, 1981, Elizabeth Drew, author, Washington, DC. *Educ:* Taunton Sch.; Ruskin Coll., Oxford. British Broadcasting Corporation: Sub-Editor, External Services News Dept, 1953–59; Producer, Panorama, 1959–64; Exec. Producer, Enquiry, and Encounter, BBC-2, 1964–66; Dep. Editor, Panorama, 1966, Editor, 1967–69; Exec. Editor, Current Affairs Group, 1969, Asst Head, 1970; BBC Rep. in USA, 1971–76; Controller, Information Services, 1976–77; Dir, Public Affairs, 1977–80; Dir, US, BBC, 1981–85. Mem., Bd of Management, BBC, 1977–85. Resident Associate, Carnegie Endowment, 1985–87; Sen. Fellow, Annenberg Washington Program on Communications Policy Studies, 1987–92. Special Adviser, Communications Studies and Planning Internat., 1987–88; Chm., Internat. Disaster Communications Project, 1987–91. Mem., Twentieth Century Fund Task Force on the Flow of the News, 1978. Mem. Adv. Council, Ditchley Foundn of US, 1981–; Mem., Nat. Adv. Cttee for the William Benton Fellowship Prog., Univ. of Chicago, 1983–89. Fellow, Internat. Council, National Acad. of Television Arts and Sciences, USA, 1980– (Chm., Internat. Council, 1974 and 1975). *Recreation:* coarse tennis. *Address:* 3000 Woodland Drive, Washington, DC 20008, USA. *T:* (202) 3427131, *Fax:* (202) 3422518. *Club:* Century Association (NY).

See also S. H. E. Kitzinger.

WEBSTER, David MacLaren, QC 1980; **His Honour Judge MacLaren Webster;** a Circuit Judge, since 1987; *b* 21 Dec. 1937; *s* of late John MacLaren Webster and Winning McGregor Webster (*née* Rough); *m* 1964, Frances Sally McLaren, RE, *o d* of late Lt-Col J. A. McLaren and of Mrs H. S. Scammell; three *s*. *Educ:* Hutchesons', Glasgow; Christ Church, Oxford (MA (Eng Lang. and Lit.)); Conservatoire d'Art Dramatique and Sorbonne (French Govt Schol. 1960–61). Radio and television work in drama and current affairs, Scotland, 1949–64; called to the Bar, Gray's Inn, 1964; joined Western Circuit; a Dep. Circuit Judge, 1976–79; a Recorder, 1979–87. Member: Bar Council, 1972–74; Senate of Inns of Court and Bar, 1974–79, 1982–85 (Senate Representative, Commonwealth Law Conf., Edinburgh, 1977); Matrimonial Causes Rules Cttee, 1976–79; Crown Court Rules Cttee, 1983–87; Western Circuit Univs Liaison Cttee, 1978–84. Gold Medal, LAMDA, 1954; LRAM 1955. President, Oxford Univ. Experimental Theatre Club, 1958–59; Secretary, Mermaid's, 1958; Chm., Bar Theatrical Soc., 1976–86. Governor, Port Regis Sch., 1983–. *Recreations:* theatre, sailing, cricket, Scottish literature. *Address:* c/o The Law Courts, Winchester, Hants SO23 9EL. *Clubs:* Garrick, MCC; Hampshire (Winchester); Bar Yacht.

WEBSTER, Derek Adrian, CBE 1979; Chairman and Editorial Director, Scottish Daily Record and Sunday Mail Ltd, 1974–86; *b* 24 March 1927; *s* of James Tulloch Webster and Isobel Webster; *m* 1966, Dorothy Frances Johnson; two *s* one *d*. *Educ:* St Peter's, Bournemouth. Served RN, 1944–48. Reporter, Western Morning News, 1943; Staff Journalist, Daily Mail, 1949–51; joined Mirror Group, 1952; Northern Editor, Daily Mirror, 1964–67; Editor, Daily Record, 1967–72; Director: Mirror Gp Newspapers, 1974–86; Clyde Cable Vision, 1983–87. Mem., Press Council, 1981–84 (Jt Vice-Chm., 1982–83). Vice-Chm., Age Concern (Scotland), 1977–83; Hon. Vice-Pres., Newspaper Press Fund, 1983–; Mem. Council, CPU, 1984–86. *Recreations:* travel, photography. *Address:* 32 Athole Gardens, Dowanhill, Glasgow G12 9BD. *T:* Glasgow 0141–339 6239.

WEBSTER, Henry George, CBE 1974; FSAE; Chairman, SKF Steel UK, 1982–87; retired; *b* Coventry, 27 May 1917; *s* of William George Webster; *m* 1943, Margaret, *d* of

H. C. Sharp; one *d* decd. *Educ:* Welshpool County Sch.; Coventry Technical Coll. Standard Motor Co. Ltd: apprenticed, 1932; Asst Technl Engr, 1938–40; Dep. Chief Inspector, 1940–46; Asst Technl Engr, 1946–48; Chief Chassis Engr, 1948–55; Chief Engr, 1955–57; Dir and Chief Engr, Standard-Triumph Internat., 1957–68; Technical Dir, Austin Morris Div., British Leyland UK Ltd, 1968–74; Group Engineering Dir, Automotive Products, 1974–83. Joined original Instn of Automobile Engrs, as a grad., 1937 (Sec. of Grad. Section, Coventry Br. of Instn, 1941–45); transf. to Associate Mem., 1946, Mem., 1964. MSAE, 1958; FSAE, 1976; FRSA. Freeman, City of Coventry. *Recreation:* golf. *Address:* The Old School House, Barrowfield Lane, Kenilworth, Warwickshire CV8 1EP. *T:* Kenilworth (01926) 53363.

WEBSTER, His Honour Ian Stevenson; a Circuit Judge, 1981–95; *b* 20 March 1925; *s* of late Harvey Webster and Annabella Stevenson Webster (*née* McBain); *m* 1951, Margaret (*née* Sharples); two *s*. *Educ:* Rochdale Grammar Sch.; Manchester Univ. Sub. Lieut (A), RNVR, 1944. Called to the Bar, Middle Temple, 1948. Asst Recorder: of Oldham, 1970; of Salford, 1971; a Recorder of the Crown Court, 1972–76, 1981; Chm., Industrial Tribunals for Manchester, 1976–81; Liaison Judge: for Burnley, Reedley and Accrington Benches, 1981–86; for Rochdale, Middleton and Heywood Benches, 1987–95. Hon. Recorder, Burnley, 1991. *Recreations:* gardening, sailing, golf. *Address:* 1 Higher Lodge, Norden, Rochdale OL11 5TZ. *Club:* Rochdale Golf.

See also A. S. Webster.

WEBSTER, Janice Helen, WS; Consultant, Bell & Scott, WS, Edinburgh, since 1994; *b* 2 April 1944; *d* of James Bell Reid and Janet (*née* Johnston); *m* 1968, Hon. R. M. Webster; two *d*. *Educ:* Edinburgh Univ. (LLB 1964). Solicitor and Notary Public. Apprenticeship, Cochran Sayers and Cook, Glasgow, 1964–67; Legal Asst, then Sen. Solicitor, Falkirk Town Council, 1967–71; in private practice, Alston Nairn & Hogg, Edinburgh, 1971–74; Dep. Sec., Law Soc. of Scotland, 1974–80; Crown Counsel, then Magistrate, Govt of Seychelles, 1980–82; Law Society of Scotland, 1982–90 (Dep. Sec., Dir, European Affairs and Sec., Scottish Lawyers' European Gp); Dir Gen., CCBE, 1991–93. Mem., Scottish Records Adv. Council, 1995–. *Publications:* (with R. M. Webster) Professional Ethics and Practice for Scottish Solicitors, 2nd edn 1984; numerous articles in professional jls incl. Jl Law Soc. Scotland. *Recreations:* singing, walking, gardening. *Address:* Bell & Scott, WS, 16 Hill Street, Edinburgh EH2 3LD. *Club:* New (Edinburgh).

WEBSTER, John Alexander R.; *see* Riddell-Webster.

WEBSTER, John Lawrence Harvey, CMG 1963; *b* 10 March 1913; *s* of late Sydney Webster, Hindhead, and Elsie Gwendoline Webster (*née* Harvey); *m* 1st, 1940, Elizabeth Marshall Gilbertson (marr. diss., 1959); two *d*; 2nd, 1960, Jessie Lillian Royston-Smith. *Educ:* Rugby Sch.; Balliol College, Oxford (MA). District Officer, Colonial Administrative Service, Kenya, 1935–49; Secretary for Development, 1949–54; Administrative Sec., 1954–56; Sec. to Cabinet, 1956–58; Permanent Sec., Kenya, 1958–63; on retirement from HMOCS, with the British Council, 1964–80, in Thailand, Sri Lanka, Hong Kong, Istanbul and London. *Recreations:* travel, reading, swimming. *Address:* Timbercroft, 11 Pevensey Road, West Worthing, Sussex BN11 5NP. *T:* Worthing (01903) 248617. *Clubs:* Commonwealth Trust; Leander; Nairobi (Kenya).

WEBSTER, Vice-Adm. Sir John (Morrison), KCB 1986; retired 1990; painter; President, Royal Naval Benevolent Trust, since 1991; *b* 3 Nov. 1932; *s* of late Frank Martin Webster and Kathleen Mary (*née* Morrison) *m* 1962, Valerie Anne Villiers; two *d* (one *s* decd). *Educ:* Pangbourne College. Joined RN, 1951; specialised navigation, 1959; RAN, 1959–61; HMS Lowestoft, 1961–63; BRNC Dartmouth, 1963–65; HMS Dido, 1965–67; RN Tactical Sch., 1967–69; in command HMS Argonaut, 1969–71; MoD Navy, 1971–73; RNLO Ottawa, 1974–76; in command HMS Cleopatra and 4th Frigate Sqdn, 1976–78; MoD, Director Naval Warfare, 1980–82; Flag Officer Sea Trng, 1982–84; C of S to C-in-C Fleet, 1984–86; Flag Officer Plymouth, Naval Base Comdr Devonport, Comdr Central Sub Area Eastern Atlantic and Comdr Plymouth Sub Area Channel, 1987–90. Lt-Comdr 1963, Comdr 1967, Captain 1973, Rear-Adm. 1982, Vice-Adm. 1985. Younger Brother of Trinity House, 1970–. Mem., Armed Forces Art Soc., 1967 (Chm., 1990–). One-man exhibitions of paintings: Canada, 1976; Winchester, 1980; London, 1982, 1984, 1986, 1988, 1991, 1993. Governor: Canford Sch., 1984–; Pangbourne College, 1990– (Chm., 1992–). *Recreations:* painting, sailing. *Address:* c/o Royal Bank of Scotland, 62 Threadneedle Street, EC2. *Clubs:* Royal Naval Sailing Association, Royal Cruising; Royal Western Yacht (Plymouth).

WEBSTER, Prof. John Paul Garrett, PhD; Professor of Agricultural Business Management, Wye College, University of London, since 1991; *b* 16 July 1942; *s* of Leonard Garrett Webster and Dorothy Agnes Webster (*née* White); *m* 1972, Dr Amanda Jane Hetigin; one *s* one *d*. *Educ:* Reading Univ. (BSc); Wye Coll., London Univ. (PhD). Lecturer: in Agricl Econs, Wye Coll., 1967–. Visiting appointments: Makerere Univ., Uganda, 1970–71; Drapers Lectr, Univ. of New England, Australia, 1974–75; Economist, Internat. Rice Res. Inst., Philippines, 1980–81. FIMgt (FBIM 1985); FRSA 1987. *Publications:* articles in Jl Agricl Econs, Amer. Jl Agricl Econs, Farm Mgt, etc. *Recreation:* water polo. *Address:* c/o Wye College, Ashford, Kent TN25 5AH. *T:* Ashford (01233) 812401. *Club:* Farmers'.

WEBSTER, Prof. Keith Edward, PhD; Professor of Anatomy and Human Biology (formerly Professor of Anatomy), King's College, University of London, since 1975; *b* 18 June 1935; *e s* of Thomas Brotherwick Webster and Edna Pyzer; 1st marr. diss. 1983; two *s*; 2nd marr. diss. 1990. *Educ:* UCL (BSc 1957, PhD 1960); UCH Med. Sch. (MB, BS 1962). University Coll. London: Lectr in Anatomy, 1962–66; Sen. Lectr in Anat., 1966–74; Reader in Anat., 1974–75. Symington Prize, British Anatomical Soc., 1966. *Publications:* A Manual of Human Anatomy, Vol. 5: The Central Nervous System (with J. T. Aitken and J. Z. Young), 1967; papers on the nervous system in Brain Res., Jl of Comp. Neurol., Neuroscience and Neurocytology. *Recreation:* Mozart, Wagner and language: the deification of the unspeakable. *Address:* Department of Anatomy and Human Biology, King's College London, Strand, WC2R 2LS. *T:* 0171–836 5454.

WEBSTER, Maj. Michael; *see* Webster, R. M. O.

WEBSTER, Michael George Thomas; Chairman, DRG plc (formerly Dickinson Robinson Group), 1985–87 (Director, since 1976–87; Deputy Chairman, 1983–85); *b* 27 May 1920; *s* of late J. A. Webster, CB, DSO, and late Constance A. Webster, 2nd *d* of late Richard and Lady Constance Combe; *m* 1947, Mrs Isabel Margaret Bucknill, *d* of late Major J. L. Dent, DSO, MC; three *d*. *Educ:* Stowe; Magdalen Coll., Oxford (MA). Commnd Grenadier Guards, 1940–46: NW Europe Campaign, 1944–45 (despatches). Joined Watney Combe Reid & Co. Ltd, 1946; Chm., Watney Combe Reid, 1963–68; Watney Mann Ltd: Vice-Chm., 1965–70; Chm., 1970–72; Deputy Chm., 1972–74; Chm., Watney Mann & Truman Holdings, 1974; Director: Grand Metropolitan Ltd, 1972–74; National Provident Instn, 1973–85; Chm., Fitch Lovell PLC, 1977–83. Master of Brewers' Co., 1964–65; a Vice-Pres., The Brewers' Soc., 1975–. Gov., Gabbitas Truman & Thring, 1986–90 (Chm., Truman and Knightley Educnl Trust, 1985–87; Gov., Gabbitas Thring, 1986–87). Chm., Aldenham Sch. Governing Body, 1977–84. High Sheriff, Berks, 1971; DL Berks, 1975–90. *Recreations:* fishing, golf. *Address:* Little Manor Farm, Dummer, Basingstoke, Hants RG25 2AD. *Clubs:* Cavalry and Guards, MCC.

See also Viscount Torrington.

WEBSTER, Patrick; Barrister-at-Law; part-time Chairman, Industrial Tribunals, Cardiff Region, 1965–75, and since 1993 (a full-time Chairman, 1976–93); a Recorder, 1972–93; *b* 6 January 1928; *s* of Francis Glyn Webster and late Ann Webster; *m* 1955, Elizabeth Knight; two *s* four *d*. *Educ:* Swansea Grammar Sch.; Rockwell Coll., Eire; St Edmund's Coll., Ware; Downing Coll., Cambridge (BA). Called to Bar, Gray's Inn, 1950. Practised at bar, in Swansea, 1950–75; Chm., Medical Appeals Tribunal (part-time), 1971–75. *Recreations:* listening to music, watching rowing and sailing. *Address:* Langland, 24 Maillard's Haven, Penarth, South Glam CF64 5RF. *T:* Penarth (01222) 704758. *Clubs:* Penarth Yacht; Beechwood (Swansea).

WEBSTER, Hon. Sir Peter (Edlin), Kt 1980; a Judge of the High Court of Justice, Queen's Bench Division, 1980–92; *b* 16 Feb. 1924; *s* of Herbert Edlin Webster and Florence Helen Webster; *m* 1955, Susan Elizabeth Richards (marr. diss.); one *s* two *d*; *m* 1968, Avril Carolyn Simpson, *d* of Dr John Ernest McCrae Harrisson. *Educ:* Haileybury; Merton Coll., Oxford (MA). RNVR, 1943–46 and 1950, Lieut (A). Imperial Tobacco Co., 1949; Lectr in Law, Lincoln Coll., Oxford, 1950–52; called to Bar, Middle Temple, 1952; Bencher, 1972; Standing Jun. Counsel to Min. of Labour, 1964–67; QC 1967; a Recorder of the Crown Court, 1972–80. Mem., Council of Justice, 1955–60, 1965–70; Mem., General Council of the Bar, 1967–74, and of Senate of the Inns of Court and the Bar, 1974–81 (Vice-Chm. 1975–76; Chm., 1976–77); Chairman: London Common Law Bar Assoc., 1975–79; Judicial Studies Bd, 1981–83 (Mem., 1979–83); Review Bd for Govt Contracts, 1993–; Mem., City Disputes Panel, 1994–. Dir, Booker McConnell, 1978–79. FCIArb 1993. *Address:* 9 Cranbourne Court, Albert Bridge Road, SW11 4PE.

WEBSTER, Maj. (Richard) Michael (Otley); Clerk of the Course: Kempton Park, since 1980; Epsom, since 1988; one of HM Body Guard, Honourable Corps of Gentlemen-at-Arms, since 1993; *b* 11 Aug. 1942; *s* of Brig. Frederick Richard Webster and Beryl Helena Sellars (*née* Otley): *m* 1971, Joanna Gay Enid Simpson, *d* of Lt-Col R. H. O. Simpson, DSO; two *s*. *Educ:* Charterhouse; RMA, Sandhurst. Commnd RA, 1962; Army Staff Coll., 1975; CO, King's Troop, RHA, 1976–78. United Racecourses, 1979–; Clerk of the Course, Lingfield Park, 1986–87. Mem., Horseracing Adv. Council, 1987–90. *Recreations:* cricket, racing, shooting, walking. *Address:* Coopers Farm, Hartley Wespall, Hook, Hants RG27 0BQ. *Club:* Cavalry and Guards.

WEBSTER, Prof. Robert Gordon, FRS 1989; Head of Department and Rose Marie Thomas Professor of Virology and Molecular Biology, St Jude Children's Research Hospital, Memphis, USA, since 1988; *b* 5 July 1932; *s* of Robert Duncan Webster and Mollie Sherriffs; *m* 1957, Marjorie Freegard; two *s* one *d*. *Educ:* Otago Univ., NZ (BSc, MSc); Australian Nat. Univ., Canberra (PhD). Virologist, NZ Dept of Agric., 1958–59; Postdoctoral Fellow, Sch. of Public Health, Univ. of Michigan, Ann Arbor (Fullbright Schol.), 1962–63; Res. Fellow, then Fellow, Dept of Microbiology, John Curtin Med. Sch., ANU, 1964–67; Associate Mem., then Mem., Dept of Virology and Molecular Biol., St Jude Children's Res. Hosp., 1968–88. Fogarty Internat. Sen. Fellow, Nat. Inst. for Med. Res., MRC, London, 1978–79. *Publications:* contribs on influenza viruses etc. to learned jls, incl. Virology, Nature, and Cell. *Recreations:* gardening, sea-fishing, walking. *Address:* Department of Virology and Molecular Biology, St Jude Children's Research Hospital, 332 N Lauderdale, PO Box 318, Memphis, TN 38101, USA. *T:* (901) 5220403. *Club:* Royal Society of Medicine.

WECHSLER, David Keith; Chief Executive, London Borough of Croydon, since 1993; *b* 17 June 1946; *s* of Bernard James Victor Wechsler and Kathleen Nora Wechsler (*née* Ramm); *m* 1968, Muriel-Anne (Polly) Stuart; one *s* one *d*. *Educ:* Sloane Sch., Chelsea; Leicester Univ. (BA Social Sci.). London Borough of Croydon: grad. trainee, 1970–72; Corporate Planner, 1972–79; Hd, Exec. Office, 1979–87; Dep. Chief Exec., 1987–91; Dir, Econ. and Strategic Develt, 1991–93. Director: S London TEC, 1993–; Croydon Business Venture, 1993–. *Publications:* articles on corporate planning and local govt mgt in specialist jls. *Recreations:* sailing, music, swimming, making ice cream. *Address:* London Borough of Croydon, Taberner House, Park Lane, Croydon, Surrey CR9 3JS. *T:* 0181–686 4433.

WEDD, George Morton, CB 1989; consultant; South-West Regional Director, Departments of the Environment and Transport, Bristol, 1983–90; *b* 30 March 1930; *s* of Albert Wedd and Dora Wedd; *m* 1953, Kate Pullin; two *s* one *d*. *Educ:* various schs in Derbyshire; St John's Coll., Cambridge (BA 1951). Joined Min. of Housing and Local Govt (later DoE), 1951; Principal, 1957; Asst Sec., 1966; Under Sec., 1976. *Address:* The Lodge, High Littleton, Avon BS18 5HG.

WEDDERBURN, family name of **Baron Wedderburn of Charlton.**

WEDDERBURN OF CHARLTON, Baron *cr* 1977 (Life Peer), of Highgate; **(Kenneth) William Wedderburn,** FBA 1981; QC 1990; Cassel Professor of Commercial Law, London School of Economics, University of London, 1964–92, now Professor Emeritus; *b* 13 April 1927; *o s* of Herbert J. and Mabel Wedderburn, Deptford; *m* 1st, 1951, Nina Salaman; one *s* two *d*; 2nd 1962, Dorothy E. Cole; 3rd, 1969, Frances Ann Knight; one *s*. *Educ:* Aske's Hatcham School; Whitgift School; Queens' College, Cambridge (MA 1951; LLB 1949). Royal Air Force, 1949–51. Called to the Bar, Middle Temple, 1953. Fellow, 1952–64, Tutor, 1957–60, Clare College, Cambridge; Asst Lectr, 1953–55, Lectr 1955–64, Faculty of Law, Cambridge University. Visiting Professor: UCLA Law Sch., 1967; Harvard Law Sch., 1969–70. Staff Panel Mem., Civil Service Arbitration Tribunal; Chm., Independent Review Cttee, 1976–; Mem., Cttee on Industrial Democracy, 1976–77. Pres., Inst of Employment Rights, 1989–. Independent Chm., London and Provincial Theatre Councils, 1973–93. Hon. Doctor of Jurisprudence, Pavia, 1987; Hon. Doctor of Econs, Siena, 1991. Gen. Editor, Modern Law Review, 1971–88. *Publications:* The Worker and the Law, 1965, 3rd edn 1986; Cases and Materials on Labour Law, 1967; (with P. Davies) Employment Grievances and Disputes Procedures in Britain, 1969; (ed) Contracts, Sutton and Shannon, 1956, 1963; (Asst Editor) Torts, Clerk and Lindsell, 1969, 1975, 1982, 1989; (ed with B. Aaron) Industrial Conflict, 1972; (with S. Sciarra *et al*) Democrazia Politica e Democrazia Industriale, 1978; (ed with Folke Schmidt) Discrimination in Employment, 1978; (with R. Lewis and J. Clark) Labour Law and Industrial Relations, 1983; (ed with W. T. Murphy) Labour, Law and the Community, 1983; (with S. Ghimpu and B. Veneziani) Diritto del Lavoro in Europa, 1987; Social Charter, European Company and Employment Rights, 1990; Employment Rights in Britain and Europe, 1991; Labour Law and Freedom, 1995; articles in legal and other jls. *Recreation:* Charlton Athletic Football Club. *Address:* London School of Economics, Aldwych, WC2A 2AE. *T:* 0171–405 7686.

WEDDERBURN, Sir Andrew John Alexander O.; *see* Ogilvy-Wedderburn.

WEDDERBURN, Prof. Dorothy Enid Cole; Senior Research Fellow, Imperial College, London, since 1981; Principal, Royal Holloway and Bedford New College, 1985–90, and a Pro-Vice-Chancellor, 1986–88, University of London; *b* 18 Sept. 1925; *d* of Frederick

C. Barnard and Ethel C. Barnard. *Educ:* Walthamstow High Sch. for Girls; Girton Coll., Cambridge (MA). Research Officer, subseq. Sen. Res. Officer, Dept of Applied Economics, Cambridge, 1950–65; Imperial College of Science and Technology: Lectr in Industrial Sociology, 1965–70, Reader, 1970–77, Prof., 1977–81; Dir, Industrial Sociol. Unit, 1973–81; Head, Dept of Social and Economic Studies, 1978–81; Principal, Bedford Coll., 1981–85. Mem. Court, Univ. of London, 1981–Aug. 1990. Vis. Prof., Sloan Sch. of Management, MIT, 1969–70. Mem. SSRC, 1976–82; Chm., SERC/SSRC Jt Cttee, 1980–82. Member: Govt Cttee on the Pay and Condition of Nurses, 1974–75; (part-time), Royal Commn on the Distribution of Income and Wealth, 1974–78; Council, Advisory Conciliation and Arbitration Service, 1976–82; Cttee of Vice-Chancellors and Principals, 1988–90; Bd, Anglo-German Foundn, 1987–; Bd of Governors, London Guildhall Univ. (formerly City of London Polytechnic), 1989–; Council, Loughborough Univ., 1990–93; Court, City Univ., 1992–; Council, Goldsmiths' Coll., London Univ., 1993–. Mem., Kensington, Chelsea and Westminster DHA, 1993–. Hon. Pres., Fawcett Soc., 1986–. Hon. Fellow: Ealing Coll. of Higher Educn, 1985; RHBNC, 1991; Hon. FIC 1986. Hon. DLitt: Warwick, 1984; Loughborough, 1989; DUniv Brunel, 1990; Hon. LLD Cambridge, 1991. Hon. DSc City, 1991. *Publications:* White Collar Redundancy, 1964; Redundancy and the Railwayman, 1964; Enterprise Planning for Change, 1968; (with J. E. G. Utting) The Economic Circumstances of Old People, 1962; (with Peter Townsend) The Aged in the Welfare State, 1965; (jtly) Old Age in Three Industrial Societies, 1968; (with Rosemary Crompton) Workers' Attitudes and Technology, 1972; (ed) Poverty, Inequality and Class Structure, 1974; contrib. Jl of Royal Statistical Soc.; Sociological Review; New Society, etc. *Recreations:* politics, walking, cooking. *Address:* Management School, Imperial College of Science, Technology and Medicine, 52/53 Princes Gate, Exhibition Road, SW7 2AZ; Flat 5, 65 Ladbroke Grove, W11 2PD.

See also Professor G. A. Barnard.

WEDDERSPOON, Very Rev. Alexander Gillan; Dean of Guildford, since 1987; *b* 3 April 1931; *s* of Rev. Robert John Wedderspoon and Amy Beatrice Woolley; *m* 1968, Judith Joyce Wynne Plumptre; one *s* one *d. Educ:* Westminster School; Jesus Coll., Oxford (MA, BD); Cuddesdon Theological Coll. Nat. Service, 1949–51; commnd, RA. Ordained 1961; Curate, Kingston Parish Church, 1961–63; Lectr in Religious Education, Univ. of London, 1963–66; Education Adviser, C of E Schools Council, 1966–69; Sec. of Commn on Religious Education, 1966–69; Priest in charge, St Margaret's, Westminster, 1969–70; Canon Residentiary, Winchester Cathedral, 1970–87. *Recreations:* walking, travel. *Address:* The Deanery, 1 Cathedral Close, Guildford GU2 5TL. *T:* Guildford (01483) 60328.

WEDELL, Prof. (Eberhard Arthur Otto) George; Professor of Communications Policy, University of Manchester, 1983–92, Professor Emeritus since 1992; Vice President, European Institute for the Media, 1993–95 (Director, 1983–90; Director-General, 1991–93); *b* 4 April 1927; *er s* of late Rev. Dr H. Wedell and Gertrude (*née* Bonhoeffer); *m* 1948, Rosemarie (*née* Winckler); three *s* one *d. Educ:* Cranbrook; London School of Economics (BSc Econ., 1947). Ministry of Education, 1950–58; Sec., Bd for Social Responsibility, Nat. Assembly of Church of England, 1958–60; Dep. Sec., ITA, 1960–61, Secretary, 1961–64; Prof. of Adult Educn and Dir of Extra-Mural Studies, Manchester Univ., 1964–75, Vis. Prof. of Employment Policy, 1975–83; Senior Official, European Commn, 1973–82. Emeritus Fellow, Leverhulme Trust, 1994–June 1996. Contested (L) Greater Manchester West, 1979, (L-SDP Alliance) Greater Manchester Central, 1984, European Parly elections; Chm., British Liberals in EEC, 1980–82; Vice-President: Greater Manchester Liberal Party, 1984–88; EC-ACP Cultural Foundn, 1992–. Chairman: Wyndham Place Trust, 1983–; Beatrice Hankey Foundn, 1984–. Director, Royal Exchange Theatre Company, 1968–89, Hon. Mem., 1989. FRSA; FRTS. Hon. MEd Manchester, 1968; Dr *hc* Kazakstan, 1994. Lord of the Manor of Clotton Hoofield in the County Palatine of Chester. Chevalier de l'Ordre des Arts et des Lettres (France), 1989; Verdienstkreuz (1 Klasse) des Verdienstordens (Germany), 1991; Comdr, Order of Merit (Portugal), 1993. *Publications:* The Use of Television in Education, 1963; Broadcasting and Public Policy, 1968; (with H. D. Perraton) Teaching at a Distance, 1968; (ed) Structures of Broadcasting, 1970; (with R. Glatter) Study by Correspondence, 1971; Correspondence Education in Europe, 1971; Teachers and Educational Development in Cyprus, 1971; (ed) Education and the Development of Malawi, 1973; (with E. Katz) Broadcasting in the Third World, 1977 (Nat. Assoc. of Educational Broadcasters of USA Book Award, 1978); (with G. M. Luyken and R. Leonard) Mass Communications in Western Europe, 1985; (ed) Making Broadcasting Useful, 1986; (with G. M. Luyken) Media in Competition, 1986; (ed and contrib.) Europe 2000: what kind of television?, 1988; (with P. Crookes) Radio 2000, 1991; (with R. Rocholl) Vom Segen des Glaubens, 1995; general editor, Media Monographs, 1985–93. *Recreations:* gardening, theatre, reading. *Address:* 18 Cranmer Road, Manchester M20 6AW. *T:* 0161–445 5106; Vigneau, Lachapelle, 47350 Seyches, France. *T:* 53838871. *Clubs:* Athenæum; St James's (Manchester); Fondation Universitaire (Brussels).

See also Ven. H. Lockley.

WEDGWOOD, family name of **Baron Wedgwood.**

WEDGWOOD, 4th Baron *cr* 1942, of Barlaston; **Piers Anthony Weymouth Wedgwood;** *b* 20 Sept. 1954; *s* of 3rd Baron Wedgwood and of Lady Wedgwood (Jane Weymouth, *d* of W. J. Poulton, Kenjockety, Molo, Kenya); *S* father, 1970; *m* 1985, Mary Regina Margaret Kavanagh Quinn, *d* of late Judge Edward Thomas Quinn and of Helen Marie Buchanan Quinn of Philadelphia; one *d. Educ:* Marlborough College; RMA Sandhurst. Royal Scots, 1973–80. GSM for N Ireland, 1976. *Heir: cousin* John Wedgwood, CBE, MD, FRCP [*b* 28 Sept. 1919; *m* 1st, 1943, Margaret (marr. diss. 1971), *d* of A. S. Mason; three *s* two *d*; 2nd, 1972, Joan, *d* of J. Ripsher]. *Address:* House of Lords, SW1A 0PW.

WEDGWOOD, Dame (Cicely) Veronica, OM 1969; DBE 1968 (CBE 1956); FRHistS; FBA 1975; Hon. LLD Glasgow; Hon. LittD Sheffield; Hon. DLitt: Smith College; Harvard; Oxford; Keele; Sussex; Liverpool; Historian; *b* 20 July 1910; *d* of Sir Ralph Wedgwood, 1st Bt, CB, CMG. *Educ:* privately; Lady Margaret Hall, Oxford. 1st Class Mod. Hist. 1931. Mem., Royal Commn on Historical MSS, 1953–78. President: English Assoc., 1955–56; English Centre of Internat. Pen Club, 1951–57; Society of Authors, 1972–77; Member: Arts Council, 1958–61; Arts Council Literature Panel, 1965–67; Institute for Advanced Study, Princeton, USA, 1953–68; Adv. Council, V&A Museum, 1960–69; Trustee, Nat. Gall., 1962–68, 1969–76; Hon. Member: American Academy of Arts and Letters, 1966; American Acad. of Arts and Scis, 1973; Amer. Philosophical Soc., 1973. Special Lecturer, UCL, 1962–91. Hon. Fellow: Lady Margaret Hall, Oxford, 1962; UCL, 1965; LSE 1975. Hon. Bencher, Middle Temple, 1978. Officer, Order of Orange-Nassau, 1946; Goethe Medal, 1958. *Publications:* Strafford, 1935 (revd edn, as Thomas Wentworth, 1961); The Thirty Years' War, 1938; Oliver Cromwell 1939, rev. edn 1973; Charles V by Carl Brandi (trans.), 1939; William the Silent, 1944 (James Tait Black Prize for 1944); Auto da Fé by Elias Canetti (translation), 1946; Velvet Studies, 1946; Richelieu and the French Monarchy, 1949; Seventeenth Century Literature, 1950; Montrose, 1952; The King's Peace, 1955; The King's War, 1958; Truth and Opinion, 1960; Poetry and Politics, 1960; The Trial of Charles I, 1964 (in USA as A Coffin for King Charles, 1964); Milton and his World, 1969; The Political Career of Rubens, 1975; The Spoils of Time, vol. 1, 1984; History and Hope: collected essays, 1987. *Address:* Whitegate, Alciston, Polegate, E Sussex BN26 6UN.

WEDGWOOD, Sir (Hugo) Martin, 3rd Bt *cr* 1942, of Etruria, Co. Stafford; *b* 27 Dec. 1933; *s* of Sir John Hamilton Wedgwood, 2nd Bt, TD and Diana Mildred (*d* 1976), *d* of late Col Oliver Hawkshaw, TD; *S* father, 1989; *m* 1963, Alexandra Mary Gordon Clark, *er d* of late Judge Alfred Gordon Clark; one *s* two *d. Educ:* Eton; Trinity Coll., Oxford. Mem., Stock Exchange, 1973–91; Partner, Laurence, Prust and Co., 1973–84; Dir, Smith New Court Far East Ltd, 1986–91. *Heir: s* Ralph Nicholas Wedgwood, *b* 10 Dec. 1964. *Recreation:* ceramics. *Club:* Oriental.

See also Dame C. V. Wedgwood.

WEDGWOOD, John Alleyne, CBE 1984; MA, FCIS; Chairman, Southern Electricity Board, 1977–84; *b* 26 Jan. 1920; *s* of Rev. Charles Henry Wedgwood and Myrtle Winifred Perry; *m* 1st, 1942, Freda Mary Lambert (*d* 1963); one *s*; 2nd, 1974, Lilian Nora Forey (*d* 1992); 3rd, 1992, Jeanette May England. *Educ:* Monkton Combe Sch.; Queens' Coll., Cambridge (MA Hons Hist. Tripos). FCIS, CompIEE. Served War, Lincs Regt and Durham LI, 1940–46 (Actg Major). Asst Principal, Min. of Fuel and Power, 1946–48; Admin. Officer, British Electricity Authority, 1948–55; Dep. Sec., London Electricity Bd, 1955–58; Dep. Sec., Electricity Council, 1958–65, Sec., 1965–74; Dep. Chm., S Eastern Elec. Bd, 1974–77. President: Inst. of Chartered Secs and Administrators, 1976; Electric Vehicle Assoc., 1983–86; Chm. Bd of Management, Electrical and Electronics Industries Benevolent Assoc., 1977–83. Member: Worshipful Co. of Scriveners, 1973–; SE Econ. Planning Council, 1975–79. Founder Master, Worshipful Co. of Chartered Secs and Administrators, 1978. Freeman, City of London, 1973. *Recreations:* gardening, music, railways, ornithology. *Address:* Bexington, 9 Roberts Grove, Wokingham, Berks RG41 4WR. *T:* Wokingham (01734) 785901. *Club:* Phyllis Court (Henley).

WEDGWOOD, Dame Veronica; *see* Wedgwood, Dame C. V.

WEE CHONG JIN, Hon.; Chief Justice of the Supreme Court, Singapore, 1963–90; *b* 28 Sept. 1917; *s* of late Wee Gim Puay and Lim Paik Yew; *m* 1955, Cecilia Mary Henderson; three *s* one *d. Educ:* Penang Free Sch.; St John's Coll., Cambridge. Called to Bar, Middle Temple, 1938; admitted Advocate and Solicitor of Straits Settlement, 1940; practised in Penang and Singapore, 1940–57; Puisne Judge, Singapore, 1957. Hon. DCL Oxon, 1987. *Recreation:* golf. *Address:* 1 Colombo Court #09–05, Singapore 0617.

WEE KIM WEE, Hon. GCB 1989; President of Singapore, 1985–93; *b* 4 Nov. 1915; *m* 1936, Koh Sok Hiong; one *s* six *d. Educ:* Pearl's Hill School; Raffles Instn. Joined Straits Times, 1930; United Press Assoc., 1941 and 1945–59; Straits Times, 1959–73 (Dep. Editor, Singapore); High Comr to Malaysia, 1973–80; Ambassador to Japan, 1980–84 and to Republic of Korea, 1981–84; Chm., Singapore Broadcasting Corp., 1984–85. Formerly Member: Rent Control Bd, Film Appeal Cttee; Land Acquisition Bd; Bd of Visiting Justices; Nat. Theatre Trust; former Chm., Singapore Anti-Tuberculosis Assoc.; former Pres., Singapore Badminton Assoc. and Vice-Pres., Badminton Assoc. of Malaya. JP 1966. DLitt Nat. Univ. of Singapore, 1994. Public Service Star, 1963; Meritorious Service Medal, 1979. Order of Temasek, 1st cl. (Singapore), 1993; Most Esteemed Family Order Laila Utama (Brunei), 1990. *Address:* 25 Siglap Plain, Singapore 1545.

WEEDON, Prof. Basil Charles Leicester, CBE 1974; DSc; PhD; FRS 1971; FRSC; Vice-Chancellor, Nottingham University, 1976–88; *b* 18 July 1923; *s* of late Charles William Weedon; *m* 1959, Barbara Mary Dawe; one *s* one *d. Educ:* Wandsworth Sch.; Imperial Coll. of Science and Technology (ARCS; DIC). Research Chemist, ICI Ltd (Dyestuffs Div.), 1943–47; Lecturer in Organic Chemistry, Imperial Coll., 1947–55, Reader, 1955–60; Prof. of Organic Chemistry, QMC, 1960–76, Fellow, 1984; Hon. Prof., Nottingham Univ., 1988–. Chm., Food Additives and Contaminants Cttee, 1968–83; Mem., EEC Scientific Cttee for Food, 1974–81; Scientific Editor, Pure and Applied Chemistry, 1960–75. Member: UGC, 1974–76; Council, National Stone Centre, 1985–93 (Chm. Council, 1985–91). Chm., E Midlands Reg., Electricity Consumers' Cttee, 1990–94. Tilden Lecturer, Chemical Society, 1966. Hon. DTech Brunel Univ., 1975; Hon. LLD Nottingham, 1988. Meldola Medal, Roy. Inst. of Chemistry, 1952. *Publications:* A Guide to Qualitative Organic Chemical Analysis (with Sir Patrick Linstead), 1956; scientific papers, mainly in Jl Chem. Soc. *Address:* Sheepwash Grange, Heighington Road, Canwick, Lincoln LN4 2RJ. *T:* Lincoln (01522) 522488.

WEEDON, Dudley William, BSc(Eng), CEng, FIEE; retired; *b* 25 June 1920; *s* of Reginald Percy and Ada Kate Weedon; *m* 1951, Monica Rose Smith; two *s* one *d. Educ:* Colchester Royal Grammar Sch.; Northampton Polytechnic. Marconi's Wireless Telegraph Co., 1937–48; Cable & Wireless Ltd, 1949–82 (Dir, 1979–82); Chm., Energy Communications Ltd, 1980–82. *Recreation:* sailing. *Address:* 103 Lexden Road, Colchester, Essex CO3 3RB.

WEEKES, Rt. Rev. Ambrose Walter Marcus, CB 1970; FKC; Auxiliary Bishop, Diocese in Europe, since 1988; *b* 25 April 1919; *s* of Lt-Comdr William Charles Tinnoth Weekes, DSO, RNVR, and Ethel Sarah Weekes, JP. *Educ:* Cathedral Choir Sch., Rochester; Sir Joseph Williamson's Sch., Rochester; King's Coll., London; AKC 1941, FKC 1972; Scholae Cancellarii, Lincoln. Asst Curate, St Luke's, Gillingham, Kent, 1942–44; Chaplain, RNVR, 1944–46, RN 1946–72; HMS: Ganges, 1946–48; Ulster, 1948–49; Triumph, 1949–51; Royal Marines, Deal, 1951–53; 3 Commando Bde, RM, 1953–55; HMS: Ganges, 1955–56; St Vincent, 1956–58; Tyne, 1958–60; Ganges, 1960–62; 40 Commando, RM, 1962–63; MoD, 1963–65; HMS: Eagle, 1965–66; Vernon, 1966–67; Terror, and Staff of Comdr Far East Fleet, 1967–68; HMS Mercury, 1968–69; Chaplain of the Fleet and Archdeacon for the Royal Navy, 1969–72; QHC, 1969–72; Chaplain of St Andrew, Tangier, 1972–73; Dean of Gibraltar, 1973–77; Assistant Bishop, Diocese of Gibraltar, 1977, until creation of new diocese, 1980; Suffragan Bishop of Gibraltar in Europe, 1980–86; Dean, Pro-Cathedral of the Holy Trinity, Brussels, 1980–86; Hon. Asst Bishop of Rochester, 1986–88; Hon. Canon of Rochester Cathedral, 1986–88; Chaplain at Montreux, Switzerland, 1988–92. *Recreations:* yachting, music. *Address:* 7 Margaret Street, W1N 8JQ. *Club:* MCC.

WEEKES, Mark K.; *see* Kinkead-Weekes.

WEEKES, Philip Gordon, CBE 1993 (OBE 1977); CEng, FIMinE; Chairman: S. V. Waste Services Ltd, since 1992; Tower Goitre Anthracite Ltd, since 1994; *b* 12 June 1920; *s* of Albert Edwin and Gwladys Magdaline Weekes; *m* 1944, Branwen Mair Jones; two *s* two *d. Educ:* Tredegar Sch.; University Coll., Cardiff (BSc Hons; Fellow, 1982). Jun. official, Tredegar Iron & Coal Co., 1939. Served War, RAF, 1942–44. Manager: Wyllie Colliery, Tredegar (Southern) Colliery Co., 1946; Oakdale Colliery, 1948; seconded to Colonial Office, 1950; Colliery Agent, S Wales, 1951; HQ Work Study Engr, 1952; Gp Manager, Dep. Prod. Manager, Area Prod. Manager, in various areas in S Wales, 1954; Dir of Studies, NCB Staff Coll., 1964; Dep. Dir (Mining), S Midlands Area, 1967; Chief Mining Engr, Nat. HQ, 1970; Dir-Gen. of Mining, Nat. HQ, 1971; Area Dir, S Wales Coalfield, 1973–85; part-time Mem., NCB, 1977–84. Chairman: 1992 Garden Fest. Wales Ltd, 1987–94; Flectalon Ltd, 1988–95; Dir, B.W. Aviation Ltd, 1986–93. Dir, Civic Trust for Wales, 1983–94; Member: Prince of Wales' Cttee, 1978–89; IBA Wales

Adv. Cttee, 1983–90. Gov., United World Coll. of the Atlantic, 1981–95. OStJ 1977. *Publications:* articles in professional and techn. jls and transactions. *Address:* Hillbrow, Llantwit Major, South Glamorgan CF61 1RE. *T:* Llantwit Major (01446) 792125. *Club:* Cardiff and County; Cardiff Aero (Rhoose).

WEEKS, Alan Frederick; Governor, Sports Aid Foundation, since 1983; *b* 8 Sept. 1923; *s* of late Captain Frederick Charles Weeks, MN, and Ada Frances Weeks; *m* 1947, Barbara Jane (*née* Huckle); one *s* (and one *s* one *d* decd). *Educ:* Brighton, Hove and Sussex Grammar School. Served: MN, Cadet, 1939–41; RNR, Midshipman to Lieut, 1941–46. PRO, Sports Stadium, Brighton, 1946–65; Sec., Brighton Tigers Ice Hockey Club, 1946–65; Dir, London Lions Ice Hockey Club, 1973–74; first Director, Sports Aid Foundn, 1976–83. BBC Commentator: Ice Hockey, 1951–88; Football, 1956–78; Ice Skating, 1958–; Gymnastics, 1962–89; Swimming, 1971–90; Presenter: Summer Grandstand, 1959–62; Olympics, 1960, 1964; BBC Commentator: Winter Olympics: 1964, 1968, 1972, 1976, 1980, 1984, 1988, 1992, 1994; Olympics: 1968, 1972, 1976, 1980, 1984, 1988; World Cup: 1966, 1970, 1974, 1978; Commonwealth Games: 1970, 1974, 1978, 1982, 1986; Presenter, Pot Black, 1970–84. Life Mem., Nat. Skating Assoc. of GB, 1984 (Chm. Trustees, 1993–); Mem. Council, British Ice Hockey Assoc., 1983–; inducted British Ice Hockey Hall of Fame, 1988. Life Pres., Brighton and Hove Entertainment Managers' Assoc., 1985. Hon. Mem., Amateur Swimming Assoc., 1990. *Recreation:* swimming. *Address:* c/o B.H.O., 141–143 Drury Lane, WC2B 5TB. *Club:* Lord's Taverners.

WEEKS, John Henry, QC 1983; **His Honour Judge Weeks;** a Circuit Judge, since 1991; *b* 11 May 1938; *s* of Henry James and Ada Weeks; *m* 1970, Caroline Mary, *d* of Lt Col J. F. Ross; one *s* two *d.* *Educ:* Cheltenham Coll.; Worcester Coll., Oxford (MA). Called to Bar, Inner Temple, 1963; in practice in Chancery, 1963–91. *Publication:* Limitation of Actions, 1989. *Recreation:* walking the dog. *Address:* Brympton d'Evercy, Yeovil, Somerset BA22 8TD. *T:* West Coker (01935) 862528.

WEEPLE, Edward John; Under Secretary, Scottish Office Industry Department, since 1990; *b* 15 May 1945; *s* of Edward Weeple and Mary Catherine (*née* McGrath); *m* 1970, Joan (*née* Shaw); three *s* one *d.* *Educ:* St Aloysius' Coll., Glasgow; Glasgow Univ. (MA). Asst Principal, Min. of Health, 1968–71; Private Sec. to Minister of Health, 1971–73; Principal: DHSS, 1973–78; Scottish Econ. Planning Dept, 1978–80; Assistant Secretary: SHHD, 1980–85; Dept of Agriculture and Fisheries for Scotland, 1985–90. *Address:* (office) New St Andrew's House, Edinburgh EH1 3TD. *T:* 0131–244 4605; 19 Lauder Road, Edinburgh EH9 2JG. *T:* 0131–668 1150.

WEETCH, Kenneth Thomas; *b* 17 Sept. 1933; *s* of Kenneth George and Charlotte Irene Weetch; *m* 1961, Audrey Wilson; two *d.* *Educ:* Newbridge Grammar Sch., Mon; London School of Economics. MSc(Econ), DipEd (London Inst. of Educn). National Service: Sgt, RAEC, Hong Kong, 1955–57; Walthamstow and Ilford Educn Authorities and Research at LSE, 1957–64; Head of History Dept, Hockerill Coll. of Educn, Bishop's Stortford, 1964–74. Contested (Lab): Saffron Walden, 1970; Ipswich, 1987. MP (Lab) Ipswich, Oct. 1974–1987. PPS to Sec. of State for Transport, 1976–79. Member: Lab Select Cttee on Home Affairs, 1981–83; Select Cttee on Parly Comr for Administration, 1983–87. *Recreations:* walking, reading, watching Association football, playing the piano in pubs, eating junk food. *Address:* 4 Appleby Close, Ipswich, Suffolk IP2 9XS. *Club:* Silent Street Labour (Ipswich).

WEIDENBAUM, Murray Lew, PhD; Chairman, Center for the Study of American Business, Washington University (Director, 1975–81 and since 1983); Mallinckrodt Distinguished University Professor, Washington University, 1971–81 and since 1982; *b* 10 Feb. 1927; *m* 1954, Phyllis Green; one *s* two *d.* *Educ:* City Coll., NY; Columbia Univ. (MA); Princeton Univ. (PhD 1958). Fiscal Economist, Budget Bureau, Washington, 1949–57; Corp. Economist, Boeing Co., Seattle, 1958–63; Sen. Economist, Stanford Res. Inst., 1963–64; Washington Univ., St Louis, 1964–81, 1982–, Prof. and Chm. of Dept of Econs, 1966–69; Asst Sec., Treasury Dept, Washington, 1969–71 (on secondment); Chairman, Council of Economic Advisers, USA, 1981–82. Hon. LLD: Baruch Coll., 1981; Evansville, 1983. Mem., Free Market Hall of Fame, 1983. Nat. Order of Merit, Republic of France, 1985. *Publications:* Federal Budgeting, 1964; Economic Impact of the Vietnam War, 1967; Modern Public Sector, 1969; Economics of Peacetime Defense, 1974; Government-Mandated Price Increases, 1975; Business, Government, and the Public, 1977, 5th edn (as Business and Goverment in the Global Marketplace), 1995; The Future of Business Regulation, 1980; Rendezvous with Reality: the American economy after Reagan, 1988; Small Wars, Big Defense, 1992. *Address:* Center for the Study of American Business, Washington University, Campus Box 1208, St Louis, MO 63130–4899, USA.

WEIDENFELD, family name of **Baron Weidenfeld.**

WEIDENFELD, Baron *cr* 1976 (Life Peer), of Chelsea; **Arthur George Weidenfeld,** Kt 1969; Chairman, Weidenfeld & Nicolson Ltd since 1948, and associated companies; *b* 13 Sept. 1919; *o s* of late Max and Rosa Weidenfeld; *m* 1st, 1952, Jane Sieff; one *d*; 2nd, 1956, Barbara Connolly (*née* Skelton) (marr. diss. 1961); 3rd, 1966, Sandra Payson Meyer (marr. diss. 1976); 4th, 1992, Annabelle Whitestone. *Educ:* Piaristen Gymnasium, Vienna; University of Vienna (Law); Konsular Akademie (Diplomatic College). BBC Monitoring Service, 1939–42; BBC News Commentator on European Affairs on BBC Empire & North American service, 1942–46. Wrote weekly foreign affairs column, News Chronicle, 1943–44; Founder: Contact Magazine and Books, 1945; Weidenfeld & Nicolson Ltd, 1948. One year's leave as Political Adviser and Chief of Cabinet of President Weizmann of Israel. Jt Vice-Pres., Campaign for Oxford, 1992–95; Vice-Chm., Oxford Develt Prog., 1995–. Vice-Chm., Bd of Governors, Ben Gurion Univ. of the Negev, Beer-Sheva, 1976–; Governor: Univ. of Tel Aviv, 1980–; Weizmann Inst. of Science, 1964–; Bezalel Acad. of Arts, Jerusalem, 1985 ; Member: South Bank Bd, 1986–; ENO Bd, 1988–; Trustee, Nat. Portrait Gall., 1988–. Hon. Fellow: St Peter's Coll., Oxford, 1992; St Anne's Coll., Oxford, 1994. Hon. PhD Ben Gurion Univ. of the Negev, 1984; Hon. MA Oxon. Golden Kt's Cross with Star, Order of Merit (Austria), 1989; Chevalier, Légion d'Honneur (France), 1990; Kt Comdr, Order of Merit (Germany), 1991. *Publications:* The Goebbels Experiment, 1943 (also publ. USA); Remembering My Good Friends (autobiog.), 1994. *Recreations:* travel, opera. *Address:* 9 Chelsea Embankment, SW3 4LE. *Club:* Garrick.

See also C. A. Barnett.

WEIGALL, Peter Raymond; Managing Director, P. R. Weigall & Co. Ltd, 1976–84; *b* 24 Feb. 1922; *s* of Henry Stuart Brome Weigall and Madeleine Bezard; *m* 1950, Nancy, *d* of Alexander Webster, CIE, and Margaret Webster; one *s* one *d.* *Educ:* Lycée Janson, Paris; Edinburgh Univ. (BSc). Served War, Captain, RE, 1942–46. Henry Wiggin & Co. Ltd, Birmingham, 1949–51; Petrochemicals Ltd, London, 1951–54; Chemical Industry Admin, Shell Petroleum Co., London, 1954–58; Chemicals Manager, Shell Sekiyu, Tokyo, 1958–63; Shell Internat. Chemical Co., London, 1964–69; Managing Dir, Monteshell, Milan, 1970–73; Industrial Advr to HM Govt, DTI, 1973–75. Member: Movement of Exports EDC, 1974–75; Chemicals EDC, 1974–75; Motor Vehicle Distribution and Repair EDC, 1974–75; Mergers Panel, Office of Fair Trading, 1974–75. *Recreations:* sailing, skiing. *Club:* Royal Engineer Yacht.

WEIGH, Brian, CBE 1982; QPM 1976; HM Inspector of Constabulary for South-West England and part of East Anglia, 1983–88; *b* 22 Sept. 1926; *s* of late Edwin Walter Weigh and Ellen Weigh; *m* 1952, Audrey; one *d.* *Educ:* St Joseph's Coll., Blackpool, Lancs; Queen's Univ., Belfast. All ranks to Supt, Metrop. Police, 1948–67; Asst Chief Constable, 1967–69, Dep. Chief Constable, 1969–74, Somerset and Bath Constab.; Chief Constable: Gloucestershire Constab., 1975–79; Avon and Somerset Constab., 1979–83 (Dep. Chief Constable, 1974–75). Pres., County of Avon Special Olympics, 1982–; Mem., Royal Life Saving Soc. (UK Pres., 1989–92). *Recreations:* walking, gardening, golf. *Address:* c/o Bridge House, Sion Place, Clifton Down, Bristol BS8 4XA.

WEIGHELL, Sidney; General Secretary, National Union of Railwaymen, 1975–Jan. 1983; Member, Trades Union General Council, 1975–83; *b* 31 March 1922; *s* of John Thomas and Rose Lena Weighell; *m* 1st, 1949, Margaret Alison Hunter (killed, 1956); one *s* (one *d*, killed, 1956); 2nd, 1959, Joan Sheila Willetts. *Educ:* Church of England Sch., Northallerton, Yorks. Joined LNER, Motive Power Dept, 1938. Elected to: NUR Exec., 1953; full-time NUR Official, 1954; Asst Gen. Sec., 1965. Labour Party Agent, 1947–52; Mem., Labour Party Exec., 1972–75. Non-exec. Dir, BAA plc (formerly BAA), 1987–88 (pt-time Bd Mem., 1983–87); Mem., Programme Consultative Panel, Tyne Tees TV Ltd, 1984–87. Pres., Great Yorks Rly Preservation Soc., 1986–; Mem., Ditchley Foundn, 1983–89 (Gov., 1983–92). *Publications:* On the Rails, 1983; A Hundred Years of Railway Weighells (autobiog.), 1984. *Recreations:* trout fishing, swimming, gardening; professional footballer, Sunderland FC, 1945–47. *Address:* Blenheim, 2 Moor Park Close, Beckwithshaw, near Harrogate, North Yorkshire HG3 1TR.

WEIGHILL, Air Cdre Robert Harold George, CBE 1973; DFC 1944; Secretary, Rugby Football Union, 1973–86; *b* 9 Sept. 1920; *s* of late Harold James and Elsie Weighill, Heswall, Cheshire; *m* 1946, Beryl (*d* 1981), *d* of late W. Y. Hodgson, Bromborough, Cheshire; two *s* (one *d* decd). *Educ:* Wirral Grammar Sch., Bebington, Cheshire. Served War: RAF, 1941; No 2 F R Sqdn, 1942–44; No 19 F Sqdn, 1944–45. Sqdn Comdr, RAF Coll., Cranwell, 1948–52; Student, RAF Staff Coll., 1952; CO, No 2 FR Sqdn and 138 F Wing, 1953–57; Student, JSSC, 1959; Directing Staff, Imperial Defence Coll., 1959–61; CO, RAF, Cottesmore, 1961–64; Gp Captain Ops, RAF Germany, 1964–67; Asst Comdt, RAF Coll. of Air Warfare, 1967–68; Comdt, RAF Halton, 1968–73. ADC to the Queen, 1968–73. Hon. Secretary: Internat. Rugby Football Bd, 1986–88; Five Nation Rugby Cttee, 1986–. *Recreations:* Rugby (Harlequins, Barbarians, Cheshire, RAF, Combined Services, England), squash, swimming. *Address:* 3 Bridle Manor, Halton, Aylesbury, Bucks HP22 5PQ. *T:* Wendover (01296) 625172. *Clubs:* Royal Air Force, East India, Devonshire, Sports and Public Schools.

WEIGHT, Prof. Carel Victor Morlais, CH 1995; CBE 1961; RA 1965 (ARA 1955); Hon. RBA 1972 (RBA 1934); Hon. RWS 1985; practising artist (painter); Professor Emeritus, since 1973, Senior Fellow, since 1984, Royal College of Art; *b* London, 10 Sept. 1908; *s* of Sidney Louis and Blanche H. C. Weight; British. *Educ:* Sloane School; Goldsmiths' Coll., Univ. of London (Sen. County Scholarship, 1933; Hon. Fellow, 1990). First exhibited at Royal Acad., 1931; first one-man show, Cooling Galls, 1934; 2nd and 3rd exhibns, Picture Hire Ltd, 1936 and 1938. Official War Artist, 1945. Royal College of Art: Teacher of Painting, 1947; Fellow, 1956; Prof. of Painting, 1957–73. One-man Shows: Leicester Galls, 1946, 1952, 1968; Zwemmer Gall., 1956, 1959, 1961, 1965; Agnew's, 1959; Russell Cotes Gall., Bournemouth, 1962; Fieldbourne Galleries, 1972; New Grafton Gall., 1974, 1976; exhibited in: 60 Paintings for 1951; (by invitation) exhibns of Contemporary British Art in provinces and overseas, incl. USSR, 1957; Retrospective exhibitions: Reading Museum and Art Gallery, 1970; RCA, 1973; Royal Acad., 1982; Bernard Jacobson Gall., 1988; exhibn, Tate Gall., 1992–93; travelling exhibn, Newport, Llandudno, London (Christie's), 1993. Work purchased by: Chantry Bequest for Tate Gall., 1955, 1956, 1957, 1963, 1968; Walker Art Gall., Liverpool; Southampton, Hastings and Oldham Art Galls, etc; Art Gall., Melbourne; Nat. Gall., Adelaide; Arts Council; New Coll., Oxford; Contemporary Art Soc.; V & A Museum. Mural for: Festival of Britain, 1951; Manchester Cathedral, 1963. Picture, Transfiguration, presented by Roman Catholics to the Pope. Member: London Group, 1950; West of England Acad.; Fine Arts Panel, Arts Council, 1951–57; Rome Faculty of Art, 1960. Mem., Cttee of Enquiry into the Economic Situation of the Visual Artist (Gulbenkian Foundn), 1978. Vice Pres., Artists' Gen. Benevolent Inst., 1980. Trustee, RA, 1975–84. DUniv Heriot-Watt, 1983; Dr *hc* Edinburgh, 1983. *Recreations:* music, reading. *Address:* 33 Spencer Road, SW18 2SP. *T:* 0171–228 6928. *Club:* Chelsea Arts.

WEILER, Terence Gerard, OBE 1993; *b* 12 Oct. 1919; *s* of Charles and Clare Weiler; *m* 1952, Truda, *d* of Wilfrid and Mary Woollen; two *s* two *d.* *Educ:* Wimbledon College; University College, London. Army (RA and Queen's Royal Regiment), 1940–45; UCL, 1937–39 and 1946–47; Home Office: Asst Principal, 1947; Principal, 1948; Asst Sec., 1958; Asst Under-Sec. of State, 1967–80; Mem., Prisons Board, 1962–66, 1971–80; Chm., Working Party: on Habitual Drunken Offenders, 1967–70; on Adjudication Procedures in Prisons, 1975. *Recreations:* cinema, crime fiction. *Address:* 4 Vincent Road, Isleworth, Mddx TW7 4LT. *T:* 0181–560 7822.

WEILL, Michel Alexandre D.; *see* David-Weill.

WEINBERG, Prof. Felix Jiri, FRS 1983; CPhys, FInstP; Emeritus Professor of Combustion Physics, University of London, since 1993; Senior Research Fellow, Imperial College, University of London, since 1993 (Professor of Combustion Physics, 1967–93); consultant to numerous industrial and government research organisations in UK and USA; *b* 2 April 1928; *s* of Victor Weinberg and Nelly Marie (*née* Altschul); *m* 1954, Jill Nesta (*née* Piggott); three *s.* *Educ:* Univ. of London (BSc, PhD, DIC, DSc). Lecturer 1956–60, Sen. Lectr 1960–64, Reader in Combustion, 1964–67, Dept of Chemical Engrg and Chem. Technology, Imperial Coll. Director, Combustion Inst., 1978–88 (Chm. British Sect., 1975–80); Founder and first Chm., Combustion Physics Gp, Inst. of Physics, 1974–77, and Rep. on Watt Cttee on Energy, 1979–85; Mem. Council, Inst. of Energy, 1976–79; Mem., Royal Institution. Leverhulme Emeritus Fellow, 1994. DSc *hc* Israel Inst. of Technol., Haifa, 1990. Combustion Inst. Silver Combustion Medal 1972, Bernard Lewis Gold Medal 1980; Rumford Medal, Royal Soc., 1988; ItalGas Prize for Res. and Innovation in Energy Scis, Turin Acad., 1991. *Publications:* Optics of Flames, 1963; Electrical Aspects of Combustion, 1969; (ed) Combustion Institute European Symposium, 1973; Advanced Combustion Methods, 1986; over 170 papers in Proc., jls and symposia of learned socs. *Recreations:* Eastern philosophies, motor cycling, travel. *Address:* Imperial College, SW7 2BY. *T:* 0171–594 5580; 59 Vicarage Road, SW14 8RY. *T:* 0181–876 1540.

WEINBERG, Sir Mark (Aubrey), Kt 1987; Chairman: J Rothschild Assurance, since 1991; Life Assurance Holding Corporation, since 1994; Joint Chairman, St James's Place Capital, since 1991; *b* 9 Aug. 1931; *s* of Philip and Eva Weinberg; *m* 1st, 1961, Sandra Le Roith (*d* 1978); three *d*; 2nd, 1980, Anouska Hempel; one *s.* *Educ:* King Edward VII Sch., Johannesburg; Univ. of the Witwatersrand (BCom, LLB); London Sch. of Econs (LLM).

Called to the Bar, South Africa, 1955. Barrister, S Africa, 1955–61; Man. Dir, Abbey Life Assurance Co., 1961–70; Hambro Life Assurance, subseq. Allied Dunbar Assurance: Man. Dir, 1971–83; Chm., 1984–90. Chm., Organizing Cttee, Marketing of Investments Bd, 1985–86; Dep. Chm., Securities and Investment Bd, 1986–90 (Mem., 1985–90); Trustee, Tate Gall., 1985–92. Hon. Treas., NSPCC, 1983–91. *Publication:* Take-overs and Mergers, 1962, 5th edn 1989. *Recreations:* ski-ing, tennis. *Address:* Spencer House, 27 St James's Place, SW1A 1NR. *T:* 0171–493 8111.

WEINBERG, Prof. Steven, PhD; Josey Regental Professor of Science, University of Texas, since 1982; *b* 3 May 1933; *s* of Fred and Eva Weinberg; *m* 1954, Louise Goldwasser; one *d.* *Educ:* Cornell Univ. (AB); Copenhagen Institute for Theoretical Physics; Princeton Univ. (PhD). Instructor, Columbia Univ., 1957–59; Research Associate, Lawrence Berkeley Laboratory, 1959–60; Faculty, Univ. of California at Berkeley, 1960–69; full prof., 1964; on leave: Imperial Coll., London, 1961–62; Loeb Lectr, Harvard, 1966–67; Vis. Prof., MIT, 1967–69; Prof., MIT, 1969–73; Higgins Prof. of Physics, Harvard Univ., and concurrently Senior Scientist, Smithsonian Astrophysical Observatory, 1973–83 (Sen. Consultant, 1983–). Morris Loeb Vis. Prof., Harvard Univ., 1983–; Dir, Jerusalem Winter Sch. of Theoretical Physics, 1983–94. Lectures: Richtmeyer, Amer. Assoc. of Physics Teachers, 1974; Scott, Cavendish Lab., 1975; Silliman, Yale Univ., 1977; Lauritsen, Calif. Inst. of Technol., 1979; Bethe, Cornell, 1979; Schild, Texas, 1979; de Shalit, Weizmann Inst., 1979; Henry, Princeton, 1981; Harris, Northwestern, 1981; Cherwell-Simon, Oxford, 1983; Bampton, Columbia, 1983; Einstein, Israel Acad. of Arts and Sciences, 1984; Hilldale, Wisconsin, 1985; Dirac, Cambridge, 1986; Klein, Stockholm, 1989; Brittin, Colorado, 1992; Gibbs, Amer. Math. Soc., 1996. Mem., Science Policy Cttee, Superconducting Supercollider Lab., 1989–93. Fellow, Amer. Acad. of Arts and Scis; Member: US Nat. Acad. of Scis; Amer. Philosophical Soc.; Phil Soc. of Texas (Pres., 1994); IAU; Amer. Medieval Acad.; Amer. Historical Assoc.; Texas Inst. of Letters; For. Mem., Royal Soc.; Hon. ScD: Knox Coll. 1978; Chicago, 1978; Rochester, 1979; Yale, 1979; City Univ. of New York, 1980; Clark, 1982; Dartmouth Coll., 1984; Columbia, 1990; Salamanca, 1992; Padua, 1992; Hon. PhD Weizmann Inst., 1985; Hon. DLitt, Washington Coll., 1985. J. R. Oppenheimer Prize, 1973; Heinemann Prize in Mathematical Physics, 1977; Amer. Inst. of Physics—US Steel Foundn Science Writing Award, 1977; Elliott Cresson Medal of Franklin Inst., 1979; (jtly) Nobel Prize in Physics, 1979; Madison Medal, Princeton, 1991; US Nat. Medal of Sci., 1991. Co-editor, CUP Monographs on Mathematical Physics; Mem., Bd of Dirs, Daedalus, 1990–. *Publications:* Gravitation and Cosmology: principles and applications of the general theory of relativity, 1972; The First Three Minutes: a modern view of the origin of the universe, 1977; The Discovery of the Subatomic Particles, 1982; (jtly) Elementary Particles and the Laws of Physics, 1988; Dreams of a Final Theory, 1993; The Quantum Theory of Fields, vol. I, 1995; numerous articles in learned jls. *Recreation:* reading history. *Address:* Physics Department, University of Texas, Austin, TX 78712, USA. *T:* (512) 4714394. *Clubs:* Saturday (Boston, Mass); Cambridge Scientific (Cambridge, Mass); Headliners, Tuesday (Austin, Texas).

WEINBERGER, Caspar Willard, Hon. GBE 1988; Secretary of Defense, United States of America, 1981–87; Chairman, Forbes Magazine, since 1993; *b* San Francisco, Calif, 18 Aug. 1917; *s* of Herman and Cerise Carpenter (Hampson) Weinberger; *m* 1942, Jane Dalton; one *s* one *d.* *Educ:* Harvard Coll. (AB *magna cum laude*); Harvard Law Sch. (LLB). Member: Phi Beta Kappa; Amer. Bar Assoc.; State Bar of Calif; Dist of Columbia Bar. Served in Infantry, Private to Captain, AUS, 1941–45 (Bronze Star). Law Clerk to US Ct of Appeals Judge William E. Orr, 1945–47; with law firm Heller, Ehrman, White & McAuliffe, 1947–69, partner, 1959–69. Member, Calif Legislature from 21st Dist, 1952–58; Vice-Chm., Calif Republican Central Cttee, 1960–62, Chm. 1962–64; Chm., Commn on Calif State Govt Organization and Economy, 1967–68; Dir of Finance, Calif, 1968–69; Chm., Fed. Trade Commn, 1970; Dep. Dir, 1970–72, Dir 1972–73, Office of Management and Budget; Counsellor to the President, 1973; Sec., HEW, 1973–75. Gen. Counsel, Vice-Pres., Dir, Bechtel gp of companies, 1975–81; Counsel, Rogers & Wells Internat. Law Firm, 1988–94; former Dir, Pepsi Co. Inc., Quaker Oats Co. Distinguished Vis. Prof., Edinburgh Univ., 1988. Formerly staff book reviewer, San Francisco Chronicle; moderator weekly TV prog., Profile, Bay area, station KQED, San Francisco, 1959–68. Frank Nelson Doubleday (Smithsonian) Lectr, 1974; Chm., Pres.'s Commn on Mental Retardation, 1973–75; Chm., USA–Republic of China Economic Council, 1991–; Member: Nat. Econ. Commn, 1988–89; Pres's For. Intelligence Adv. Bd, 1988–; former Member: Trilateral Commn; Adv. Council, Amer. Ditchley Foundn; Bd of Trustees, St Luke's Hosp., San Francisco; former Nat. Trustee, Nat. Symphony, Washington, DC. Hon. LLD Leeds, 1989; Hon. DLitt Buckingham, 1995. Medal of Freedom, with Distinction (USA), 1987; Grand Cordon, Order of Rising Sun (Japan), 1988; Order of Brilliant Star, with Grand Cordon (China), 1988; Hilal-i-Pakistan (Pakistan), 1989. *Publications:* Fighting for Peace: seven critical years in the Pentagon, 1990; contributed a semi-weekly column for a number of Calif newspapers. *Address:* 1901 L Street NW, Suite 711, Washington, DC 20036, USA. *T:* (202) 3317760; Forbes Magazine, 60–5th Avenue, New York, NY 10011, USA. *Clubs:* Century (NY); Bohemian and Pacific-Union (San Francisco); Harvard (San Francisco/Washington DC).

WEINER, Edmund Simon Christopher; Deputy Chief Editor, Oxford English Dictionary, since 1993 (Co-Editor, 1984–93); Supernumerary Fellow, Kellogg College (formerly Rewley House), Oxford, since 1991; *b* 27 Aug. 1950; *s* of Prof. Joseph Sidney Weiner and Marjorie Winifred (*née* Daw); *m* 1973, Christine Mary Wheeler; two *s* one *d.* *Educ:* Westminster; Christ Church, Oxford (BA Eng. Lang. and Lit.; MA). Lectr, Christ Church, Oxford, 1974–77; Mem. Staff, A Supplement to The Oxford English Dictionary, 1977–84. *Publications:* Oxford Guide to English Usage, 1983, 2nd edn (with A. Delahunty) 1993; (ed jtly) The Oxford English Dictionary, 2nd edn, 1989; (with Sylvia Chalker) The Oxford Dictionary of English Grammar, 1994. *Recreations:* language, music, family life, the Church, history. *Address:* Oxford University Press, Walton Street, Oxford OX2 6DP. *T:* Oxford (01865) 56767.

WEINSTOCK, family name of **Baron Weinstock.**

WEINSTOCK, Baron *cr* 1980 (Life Peer), of Bowden in the County of Wiltshire; **Arnold Weinstock;** Kt 1970; BSc (Econ), FSS; Managing Director, General Electric Co. plc, since 1963; *b* 29 July 1924; *s* of Simon and Golda Weinstock; *m* 1949, Netta, *d* of Sir Michael Sobell; one *s* one *d.* *Educ:* University of London. Degree in Statistics. Junior administrative officer, Admiralty, 1944–47; engaged in finance and property development, group of private companies, 1947–54; Radio & Allied Industries Ltd (later Radio & Allied Holdings Ltd), 1954–63 (Managing Director); General Electric Co. Ltd, Director 1961. Dir, Rolls-Royce (1971) Ltd, 1971–73. Dir, Friends ofthe Ravenna Fest., 1993–; Trustee: British Museum, 1985–; Royal Philharmonic Soc., Foundn. Fund, 1984–92. Mem., Jockey Club. Hon. FRCR 1975. Hon. Fellow: Peterhouse, Cambridge, 1982; LSE, 1985. Hon. Bencher, Gray's Inn, 1982. Hon. DSc: Salford, 1975; Aston, 1976; Bath, 1978; Reading, 1978; Ulster, 1987; Hon. LLD: Leeds, 1978; Wales, 1985; Hon. DTech Loughborough, 1981; DUniv Anglia Poly. Univ., 1994. Commendatore nell' Ordine al Merito (Italy), 1991; Officier, Légion d'Honneur (France), 1992. *Recreations:* racing and music. *Address:* 7 Grosvenor Square, W1X 9LA.

WEIR, family name of **Baron Inverforth** and **Viscount Weir.**

WEIR, 3rd Viscount *cr* 1938; **William Kenneth James Weir;** Chairman, The Weir Group PLC; Vice Chairman, St James's Place Capital (formerly J. Rothschild Holdings) plc, since 1985; Deputy Chairman, BICC Ltd, since 1991 (Director, 1977–91); Director, Canadian Pacific Ltd, since 1989; *b* 9 Nov 1933; *e s* of 2nd Viscount Weir, CBE, and Lucy (*d* 1972), *d* of late James F. Crowdy, MVO; *S* father, 1975; *m* 1st, 1964, Diana (marr. diss.), *o d* of Peter L. MacDougall; one *s* one *d*; 2nd, 1976, Mrs Jacqueline Mary Marr (marr. diss.), *er d* of late Baron Louis de Chollet; 3rd, 1989, Marina, *d* of late Marc Sevastopoulo; one *s.* *Educ:* Eton; Trinity Coll., Cambridge (BA). Dir, BSC, 1972–76. Dir, 1970, Chm., 1975–82, Great Northern Investment Trust Ltd; Co-Chm., RIT and Northern plc, 1982–83. Member: London Adv. Cttee, Hongkong & Shanghai Banking Corp., 1980–92; Court, Bank of England, 1972–84; Export Guarantees Adv. Council, 1992–. Chm., Engrg Design Res. Centre, 1989–91; Pres., BEAMA, 1988–89, 1994–95; Vice Pres., China-Britain Trade Gp. Chm., Patrons of Nat. Galls of Scotland, 1985–. Mem., Queen's Body Guard for Scotland (Royal Co. of Archers). FRSA. Hon. FEng, 1993. Hon. DEng Glasgow, 1993. *Recreations:* shooting, golf, fishing. *Heir: s* Hon. James William Hartland Weir, *b* 6 June 1965. *Address:* Rodinghead, Mauchline, Ayrshire KA5 5TR. *T:* Fiveways (01563) 884233. *Club:* White's.

WEIR, Hon. Lord; David Bruce Weir; a Senator of the College of Justice in Scotland, since 1985; *b* 19 Dec. 1931; *yr s* of late James Douglas Weir and Kathleen Maxwell Weir (*née* Auld); *m* 1964, Katharine Lindsay, *yr d* of Hon. Lord Cameron, *qv*; three *s.* *Educ:* Kelvinside Academy; Glasgow Academy; The Leys Sch., Cambridge; Glasgow Univ. (MA, LLB). Royal Naval Reserve, 1955–64, Lieut RNR. Admitted to Faculty of Advocates, 1959; Advocate Depute for Sheriff Court, 1964; Standing Junior Counsel: to MPBW, 1969; to DoE, 1970; QC (Scot.) 1971; Advocate Depute, 1979–82. Chairman: Medical Appeal Tribunal, 1972–77; Pensions Appeal Tribunal for Scotland, 1978–84 (Pres., 1984–85); NHS Tribunal, Scotland, 1983–85; Member: Criminal Injuries Compensation Bd, 1974–79 and 1984–85; Transport Tribunal, 1979–85; Parole Bd, Scotland, 1989–92. Mem., Law Adv. Cttee, 1988–95, Chm., Scottish Law Cttee, 1994–95, British Council. Governor, Fettes Coll., 1986– (Chm., 1989–). *Publication:* (contrib.) The Laws of Scotland: Stair Memorial Encyclopaedia, 1990. *Recreations:* sailing, music. *Address:* Parliament House, Edinburgh EH1 1RQ. *T:* 0131–225 2595. *Clubs:* New (Edinburgh); Royal Highland Yacht.

WEIR, Rear-Adm. Alexander Fortune Rose, CB 1981; JP; DL; Senior Associate, McMullen Associates (formerly Captain Colin McMullen and Associates), Marine Consultants, since 1982; *b* 17 June 1928; *s* of late Comdr Patrick Wylie Rose Weir and Minna Ranken Forrester Weir (*née* Fortune); *m* 1953, Ann Ross Hamilton Crawford, Ardmore, Co. Londonderry; four *d.* *Educ:* Royal Naval Coll., Dartmouth. FBIM 1979; AVCM 1982. Cadet, 1945–46; Midshipman, 1946–47; Actg Sub-Lieut under trng, HMS Zephyr, Portland, 1947; Sub-Lieut professional courses, 1947–48; Sub-Lieut and Lieut, HMS Loch Arkaig, Londonderry Sqdn, 1949–51; ADC to Governor of Victoria, Aust., 1951–53; HMS Mariner, Fishery Protection Sqdn, Home waters and Arctic, 1953–54; qual. as Navigating Officer, 1954; HMS St Austell Bay, WI, Navigating Officer, 1955–56; HMS Wave, Fishery Protection Sqdn, Home, Arctic and Iceland, 1956–58; Lt-Comdr, advanced navigation course, 1958; Staff ND Officer, Flag Officer Sea Trng at Portland, Dorset, 1958–61; HMS Plymouth, Staff Officer Ops, 4th Frigate Sqdn, Far East Station, 1961–62; Comdr 1962; Trng Comdr, BRNC Dartmouth, 1962–64; Comd, HMS Rothesay, WI Station, 1965–66; Staff of C-in-C Portsmouth, Staff Officer Ops, 1966–68; 2nd in Comd and Exec. Officer, HMS Eagle, 1968–69; Captain 1969; jssc 1969–70; Pres., Far East Comd Midshipman's Bd, 1970; Asst Dir Naval Operational Requirements, MoD(N), 1970–72; Captain (F) 6th Frigate Sqdn (8 ships) and HMS Andromeda, 1972–74; NATO Def. Coll., Rome, 1974–75; ACOS Strategic Policy Requirements and Long Range Objectives, SACLANT, 1975–77; Captain HMS Bristol, 1977–78; Rear-Adm. 1978; Dep. Asst Chief of Staff (Ops) to SACEUR, 1978–81. FBIM. Associate, Victoria Coll. of Music. Member: Nautical Inst.; Royal Inst. of Navigation. Licenced Royal Naval Lay Reader, 1981; Licensed Lay Reader, St Kew Parish, Dio. Truro, 1984–. JP: Chichester, 1982–84; Bodmin, 1985–; DL Cornwall, 1993. *Recreations:* sailing, shooting, golf. *Address:* Tipton, St Kew, Bodmin, Cornwall PL30 3ET. *T:* St Mabyn (01208) 841289, *Fax:* (01208) 841675; Yeoman House, Penge, SE20 7TP. *T:* 0181–663 6565. *Clubs:* Naval, Royal Navy 1765 and 1785, Institute of Directors; Royal Yacht Squadron, Royal Yachting Association, Royal Naval Sailing Association.

WEIR, Very Rev. Andrew John, MSc; Clerk of Assembly and General Secretary, The Presbyterian Church in Ireland, 1964–85, Emeritus since 1985; *b* 24 March 1919; *s* of Rev. Andrew Weir and Margaret Weir, Missionaries to Manchuria of the Presbyterian Church in Ireland. *Educ:* Campbell Coll., Belfast; Queen's Univ., Belfast (BD, MSc); New Coll., Edinburgh; Presbyterian Coll., Belfast. Ordained, 1944; Missionary to China, 1945–51; Minister, Trinity Presbyterian Church, Letterkenny, Co. Donegal, 1952–62; Asst Clerk of Assembly and Home Mission Convener, The Presbyterian Church in Ireland, 1962–64. Moderator of the General Assembly, The Presbyterian Church in Ireland, 1976–77. Hon. DD: Presbyterian Theol Faculty, Ireland, 1972; QUB, 1990. *Address:* 18 Cyprus Park, Belfast BT5 6EA. *T:* Belfast (01232) 651276.

WEIR, David Bruce; *see* Weir, Hon. Lord.

WEIR, Prof. David Thomas Henderson; Director, Bradford University Management Centre and Professsor of Management, Bradford University, since 1989; *b* 10 April 1939; *s* of late Johnstone Mather Weir and Irene Florence Brooks; *m* 1st, 1959, Janeen Elizabeth Whitson Fletcher; one *s* one *d*; 2nd, 1967, Mary Willows; one *s.* *Educ:* Ilkley Grammar Sch.; Bradford Grammar Sch.; Queen's Coll., Oxford (Hastings Scholar, Sir William Akroyd's Scholar, MA, Dip PSA), Research and lecturing, Univs of Aberdeen, Leeds, Hull, Manchester, 1961–72; Sen. Lectr, Manchester Business Sch., 1972–74; University of Glasgow: Prof. of Organizational Behaviour, 1974–89; Head, Dept of Management Studies, 1981–89; Dean, Scottish Business Sch., 1977–79; Chm., Glasgow Business Sch., 1985–89. Visiting Professor: Bolton Inst., 1993; Southampton Inst., 1994. Dir, Gulliver Foods, 1980–81; Arbitrator, Dairy Industry, Scotland, 1985–89. Consultant, World Bank, Unesco, SDA and many companies. Member: Cttee of Inquiry, Engrg Profession (Finniston Cttee), 1977–79; CNAA, 1986–89; Incorp. of Gardeners of Glasgow, 1985; Conseil Scient. de l'Univ. des eaux de vies, Segonzac, 1989. Chm., Assoc. of Business Schs, 1994–; Mem. Council, Nat. Forum for Management Educn and Develt, 1994–. Member Council: Prague Internat. Business Sch., 1992; Cyprus Internat. Business Sch., 1990. CIMgt (FBIM 1984); FRSA. Burgess, City of Glasgow, 1985. *Publications:* with Eric Butterworth: Sociology of Modern Britain, 1970, 3rd edn 1980; Social Problems of Modern Britain, 1972; New Sociology of Modern Britain, 1984; Men and Work in Modern Britain, 1973; (with Camilla Lambert) Cities in Modern Britain, 1974; (jtly) Computer Programs for Social Scientists, 1972. *Recreations:* playing cricket, supporting Leeds United FC, listening to music, fell walking, wine appreciation. *Address:* Rockbanks, Wheatley Lane, Ben Rhydding, Ilkley, West Yorks LS29 8SF. *T:* Ilkley (01943) 816222; Smorthwaite Hill, Garsdale, Cumbria LA10 5PG. *Clubs:* Athenæum, Groucho; Ilkley Cricket.

WEIR, Gillian Constance, CBE 1989; concert organist; President, Royal College of Organists, 1994–Oct. 1996; *b* 17 Jan. 1941; *d* of Cecil Alexander Weir and Clarice M. Foy Weir. *Educ:* Royal College of Music, London. LRSM, LRAM, LTCL; Hon. FRCO. Winner of St Albans Internat. Organ Competition, 1964; Début, 1965: Royal Festival Hall, solo recital; Royal Albert Hall, concerto soloist, opening night of Promenade Concerts; since then, worldwide career solely as touring concert organist; concerto appearances with all major British orchestras, also with Boston Symphony, Seattle Symphony, Württemberg Chamber Orch., and others; solo appearances at leading internat. Festivals, incl. Bath, Aldeburgh, Edinburgh, English Bach, Europalia, Europe and USA (AGO Nat. Conventions, RCCO Diamond Jubilee Nat. Convention, etc). Frequent radio and television appearances: BBC Third Prog., USA, Australasia, Europe; TV film, Toccata: two weeks in the life of Gillian Weir, 1981 (shown NZ TV 1982); presenter and performer, The King of Instruments, TV series BBC2 and Europe, Australia etc, 1989; many first performances, incl. major works by Fricker, Connolly, Camilleri, Messiaen. Master-classes, adjudicator internat. competitions, UK, France, N America, Japan. Organ consultant, Symphony Hall, Birmingham, St Martin-in-the-Fields, London, etc. Hon. FRCO and Mem. Council, RCO, 1977–; President: Incorp. Assoc. of Organists, 1981–83; ISM, 1992–93; Hon. RAM, 1989. Internat. Performer of the Year Award, NY Amer. Guild of Organists, 1981; Internat. Music Guide's Musician of the Year Award, 1982; Turnovsky Prize for outstanding achievement in the arts, Turnovsky Foundn for the Arts, NZ, 1985. Hon. Fellow, Royal Canadian Coll. of Organists, 1983; Hon. DMus, Victoria Univ. of Wellington, NZ, 1983. Recordings include complete organ works of Messiaen, 1994. *Publications:* contributor to: Grove's Internat. Dictionary of Music and Musicians, 1980; musical jls and periodicals. *Recreation:* theatre. *Address:* 78 Robin Way, Tilehurst, Berks RG3 5SW.

See also Sir R. B. Weir.

WEIR, Judith, CBE 1995; composer; *b* 11 May 1954; *d* of Jack and Ishbel Weir. *Educ:* King's Coll., Cambridge (MA). Cramb Fellow, Glasgow Univ., 1979–82; Fellow-Commoner, Trinity Coll., Cambridge, 1983–85; Composer-in-Residence, RSAMD, Glasgow, 1988–91; Jt Artistic Dir, Spitalfields Fest., 1994–; Fairbairn Composer in assoc. with CBSO, 1995–. Critics' Circle Award for outstanding contrib. to British musical life, 1994. *Publications include: compositions:* King Harald's Saga, 1979; The Consolations of Scholarship, 1985; Missa Del Cid, 1988; Heaven Ablaze In His Breast, 1989; Music Untangled, 1991–92; Heroic Strokes of the Bow, 1992; Moon and Star, 1995; *operas:* A Night at the Chinese Opera, 1987; The Vanishing Bridegroom, 1990; Blond Eckbert, 1994. *Address:* c/o Chester Music, 8/9 Frith Street, W1V 5TZ. *T:* 0171–434 0066.

WEIR, Sir Michael (Scott), KCMG 1980 (CMG 1974); HM Diplomatic Service, retired; Director, 21st Century Trust, since 1990; *b* 28 Jan. 1925; *s* of Archibald and Agnes Weir; *m* 1953, Alison Walker; two *s* two *d*; *m* 1976, Hilary Reid; two *s*. *Educ:* Dunfermline High School; Balliol College, Oxford. Served RAF (Flt Lt), 1944–47; subseq. HM Diplomatic Service; Foreign Office, 1950; Political Agent, Trucial States, 1952–54; FO, 1954–56; Consul, San Francisco, 1956–58; 1st Secretary: Washington, 1958–61; Cairo, 1961–63; FO, 1963–68; Counsellor, Head of Arabian Dept, 1966; Dep. Political Resident, Persian Gulf, Bahrain, 1968–71; Head of Chancery, UK Mission to UN, NY, 1971–73; Asst Under-Sec. of State, FCO, 1974–79; Ambassador, Cairo, 1979–85. Pres., Egypt Exploration Soc., 1988–; Chm., British Egyptian Soc., 1990–. *Recreations:* golf, music. *Address:* 37 Lansdowne Gardens, SW8 2EL. *Clubs:* Rye Golf, Royal Wimbledon Golf.

WEIR, Peter Lindsay, AM 1982; film director, since 1969; *b* 21 Aug. 1944; *s* of Lindsay Weir and Peggy Barnsley Weir; *m* 1966, Wendy Stites; one *s* one *d*. *Educ:* Scots Coll., Sydney; Vaucluse High Sch.; Sydney Univ. Short Film: Homesdale, 1971; Feature Films: The Cars That Ate Paris, 1973; Picnic at Hanging Rock, 1975; Last Wave, 1977; The Plumber (for TV), 1979; Gallipoli, 1980; The Year of Living Dangerously, 1982; Witness, 1985; The Mosquito Coast, 1986; Dead Poets Society, 1989; Green Card, 1991; Fearless, 1994. *Address:* c/o Australian Film Commission, 8 West Street, North Sydney, NSW 2060, Australia.

WEIR, Richard Stanton; Director-General, Institutional Fund Managers' Association, 1989–95; *b* 5 Jan. 1933; *o s* of Brig. R. A. Weir, OBE and Dr M. L. Cowan; *m* 1961, Helen Eugenie Guthrie; one *d*. *Educ:* Repton Sch., Derbys; Christ Church, Oxford (MA). Called to the Bar, Inner Temple, 1957. Commnd 3rd Carabiniers (Prince of Wales' Dragoon Guards), 1952. Head of Legal Dept, Soc. of Motor Mfrs and Traders Ltd, 1958–61; Exec., British Motor Corp. Ltd, 1961–64; Dep. Co. Sec., Rank Organisation Ltd, 1964–67; Head of Admin, Rank Leisure Services, 1967–69; Sec., CWS Ltd, 1969–74; Dir, 1975–81, Dir-Gen., 1987–89, Retail Consortium; Sec. Gen. (Chief Exec.), BSA, 1981–86; Dir, British Retailers' Assoc., 1987–89. Mem., Consumer Protection Adv. Cttee set up under Fair Trading Act, 1973, 1973–76. *Recreations:* reading, walking, shooting. *Address:* PO Box 427, Umhlali, Kwazulu, Natal 4390, Republic of South Africa. *T:* (322) 5773. *Club:* United Oxford & Cambridge University.

WEIR, Sir Roderick (Bignell), Kt 1984; JP; Chairman, McKechnie Pacific Ltd, since 1983; *b* 14 July 1927; *s* of Cecil Alexander Weir and Clarice Mildred Foy; *m* 1952, Loys Agnes Wilson (*d* 1984); one *d*; *m* 1986, Anna Jane Mcfarlane. *Educ:* Wanganui Boys' Coll., NZ. Various positions to regional manager, Dalgety NZ Ltd, Wanganui, 1943–63; formed stock and station co., Rod Weir & Co. Ltd, 1963; formed Crown Consolidated Ltd, 1976; Chairman: Amuri Corp. Ltd; NZ Casing Co. Ltd; Crown Meats Ltd; Danaflex Packaging Corp. Ltd; Dep. Chm., Rangatira; Director: Sun Alliance Insurance Ltd; Sun Alliance Life Assurance Co.; Fluid Control; Westrays Ltd. Chm., Massey Coll. Business & Property Trust. Past President: NZ Stock and Station Agents' Assoc.; Asean Business Council. Mem., NZ Inst. of Econ. Res. Inc.; Board Member and Patron: Massey Univ. Foundn; Medic Alert; Wellington Sch. of Medicine; Wellington Med. Res. Foundn; Mem., Adv. Bd, Salvation Army; Director: NZ Symphony Orchestra Ltd; Winston Churchill Meml Trust; Trustee: Wanganui Old Boys' Assoc.; Waitangi Foundn (UK). JP NZ 1972. Hon. DSc Massey, 1993. *Recreations:* fishing, shooting, boxing. *Address:* Jellicoe Towers, 5/189 The Terrace, Wellington, New Zealand. *T:* (4) 4724033; The Grove, Main Road, Waikanae, New Zealand. *T:* (4) 2936373. *Clubs:* Wellington (Wellington); Heretaunga (Lower Hutt); Levin (Levin).

See also Gillian Weir.

WEIR, Stuart Peter; Director and Joint Editor, Democratic Audit of the United Kingdom, and Senior Research Fellow, Human Rights Centre, Essex University, since 1991; *b* 13 Oct. 1938; *e s* of Robert Hendry Weir, CB and Edna Frances (*née* Lewis); *m* 1st, 1963, Doffy Burnham; two *s*; 2nd, 1987, Elizabeth Ellen Bisset; one *s* two *d*. *Educ:* Peter Symonds Sch., Winchester; Brasenose Coll., Oxford (BA Hons Modern History). Feature writer, Oxford Mail, 1964–67; diarist, The Times, 1967–71; Dir, Citizens Rights Office, CPAG, 1971–75; Founding Editor, Roof magazine, 1975–77; Dep. Editor, New Society, 1977–84; Editor: New Socialist, 1984–87; New Statesman, 1987–88, New Statesman and Society, 1988–90. WEA and Adult Educn lectr, 1969–73. Founder Chair, Family Rights Gp, 1975; Founder and Exec. Mem., Charter 88, 1988–95; Chm., Charter 88 Trust, 1991–92. Member: Exec., CPAG and Finer Jt Action Cttee, 1970–84; (Founding), Labour Co-ordinating Cttee, 1979. Active in anti-racist and community groups, Oxford and Hackney, 1964–72; Mem. (Lab), London Bor. of Hackney Council, 1972–76. Mem., Human Rights Commn, Helsinki Citizens Assembly, 1990–92; Sen. Internat. Facilitator, EU Democracy and Governance Project, Namibia, 1994–95; Trustee, Civil Liberties Trust, 1990–. Columnist: Community Care, 1973–75; London Daily News, 1987; script consultant: Spongers, BBC TV, 1977; United Kingdom, BBC TV, 1980–81; editorial consultant, The People's Parliament, 1994–95; C4 Dispatches, Behind Closed Doors, 1995. *Publications:* (contrib.) Towards Better Social Services, 1973; Social Insecurity, 1974; Supplementary Benefits: a social worker's guide, 1975; (ed and contrib.) Manifesto, 1981; (contrib.) The Other Britain, 1982; (contrib.) Consuming Secrets, 1982; (with W. Hall) EGO-TRIP, 1994; (with W. Hall) Behind Closed Doors, 1995. *Recreations:* cooking, gardening, being with my children. *Address:* 15 Grazebrook Road, N16 0HU.

WEISKRANTZ, Lawrence, FRS 1980; Professor of Psychology, Oxford University, 1967–93; Fellow, Magdalen College, Oxford, since 1967; *b* 28 March 1926; *s* of Dr Benjamin Weiskrantz and Rose (*née* Rifkin); *m* 1954, Barbara Collins; one *s* one *d*. *Educ:* Girard College; Swarthmore; Univs of Oxford and Harvard. Part-time Lectr, Tufts University, 1952; Research Assoc., Inst. of Living, 1952–55; Sen. Postdoctoral Fellow, US Nat. Res. Coun., 1955–56; Research Assoc., Cambridge Univ., 1956–61; Asst Dir of Research, Cambridge Univ., 1961–66; Reader in Physiological Psychology, Cambridge Univ., 1966–67. Member, US Nat. Acad. of Scis, 1987. Ferrier Lectr, Royal Soc., 1989; Hughlings Jackson Lectr/Medallist, RSM, 1990. Kenneth Craik Research Award, St John's Coll., Cambridge, 1975–76; Williams James Award, Amer. Psychol Soc., 1992. Dep. Editor, Brain, 1981–; Co-Editor, Oxford Psychology Series, 1979–. *Publications:* (jtly) Analysis of Behavioural Change, 1967; The Neuropsychology of Cognitive Function, 1982; Animal Intelligence, 1985; Blindsight, 1986; Thought Without Language, 1988; articles in Science, Nature, Quarterly Jl of Experimental Psychology, Jl of Comparative and Physiological Psychology, Animal Behaviour. *Recreations:* music, walking. *Address:* Department of Experimental Psychology, South Parks Road, Oxford OX1 3UD.

WEISMAN, Malcolm; Barrister-at-law; a Recorder of the Crown Court, since 1980; *s* of David and Jeanie Pearl Weisman; *m* 1958, Rosalie, *d* of Dr and Mrs A. Spiro; two *s*. *Educ:* Harrogate Grammar Sch.; Parmiter's Sch.; London School of Economics; St Catherine's Coll., Oxford (MA). Blackstone Pupillage Prize. Chaplain (Sqdn Ldr), Royal Air Force, 1956; called to Bar, Middle Temple, 1961; Head of Chambers, 1982–90. Senior Jewish Chaplain, HM Forces, 1972; Religious advisor to small congregations, and Hon. Chaplain, Oxford, Cambridge and new universities, 1963–; Chm. and Sec.-Gen., 1981–92, Pres., 1993–94, Allied Air Forces in Europe Chief of Chaplains Cttee; Sec., Former Chiefs of Chaplains Assoc., 1994; Mem. Exec., USA Jewish Chaplains Assoc., 1992–; Hon. Vice-Pres., Monash Br., RBL, 1992–. Mem., Cabinet of the Chief Rabbi, 1967–; Hon. Chaplain to: Lord Mayor of Westminster, 1992–93; Mayor of Barnet, 1994–95. Asst Comr of Parly Boundaries, 1976–85. Mem., Senior Common Room, Essex, Kent and Lancaster Univs, 1964–; Fellow, Inst. of Theology, Univ. of Essex, 1992–. Member of Court: Univ. of Lancaster, 1970–; Warwick Univ., 1983–; Univ. of East Anglia, 1985–; Essex Univ., 1990–; Mem. Council, Selly Oak Coll., Birmingham, 1992–. Gov., 1980–, Trustee, 1994–, Parmiter's Sch. Trustee, B'nai B'rith Music Fest., 1995–. Patron, Holy Land Trust, 1993–. Chief Rabbi's Award for Excellence, 1993. Editor, Menorah Jl, 1972–. *Recreations:* travelling, reading, doing nothing. *Address:* 1 Gray's Inn Square, WC1R 5AA. *T:* 0171–405 8946.

WEISS, Mrs Althea McNish; *see* McNish, A. M.

WEISS, John Roger; Director, Asset Management Group, Export Credits Guarantee Department, since 1990; *b* 27 Dec. 1944; *s* of Ernst and Betsy Weiss; *m* 1967, Hazel Kay Lang. *Educ:* St Helen's Coll., Thames Ditton. Tax Officer, Inland Revenue, 1961–64; ECGD, 1964–. *Recreations:* music, walking. *Address:* Export Credits Guarantee Department, 2 Exchange Tower, Harbour Exchange Square, E14 9GS. *T:* 0171–512 7376.

WEISS, Prof. Nigel Oscar, FRS 1992; Professor of Mathematical Astrophysics, since 1987, and Chairman, School of Physical Sciences, since 1993, Cambridge University; Fellow of Clare College, Cambridge, since 1965; *b* 16 Dec. 1936; *s* of Oscar and Molly Weiss; *m* 1968, Judith Elizabeth Martin; one *s* two *d*. *Educ:* Hilton College, Natal; Rugby School; Clare College, Cambridge (BA 1957; PhD 1962; ScD 1993). Research Associate, UKAEA Culham Lab., 1962–65; Lectr, Dept of Applied Maths and Theoretical Physics, Cambridge, 1965–79; Reader in Astrophysics, 1979–87; Sen. Fellow, SERC, 1987–92. Vis. Prof., Sch. of Math. Scis, QMC, then QMW, London, 1986–; temporary appointments: MIT; Max Planck Inst. für Astrophysik, Munich; Nat. Solar Observatory, New Mexico; Harvard-Smithsonian Center for Astrophysics. *Publications:* papers on solar and stellar magnetic fields, astrophysical and geophysical fluid dynamics and nonlinear systems. *Recreation:* travel. *Address:* Department of Applied Mathematics and Theoretical Physics, Silver Street, Cambridge CB3 9EW. *T:* Cambridge (01223) 337910; 10 Lansdowne Road, Cambridge CB3 0EU. *T:* Cambridge (01223) 355032.

WEISS, Prof. Robert Anthony, (Robin), PhD; FRCPath; Director of Research, Institute of Cancer Research, since 1990; *b* 20 Feb. 1940; *s* of Hans Weiss and Stefanie Löwensohn; *m* 1964, Margaret Rose D'Costa; two *d*. *Educ:* University College London (BSc, PhD). Lecturer in Embryology, University Coll. London, 1963–70; Eleanor Roosevelt Internat. Cancer Research Fellow, Univ. of Washington, Seattle, 1970–71; Visiting Associate Prof., Microbiology, Univ. of Southern California, 1971–72; Staff Scientist, Imperial Cancer Research Fund Laboratories, 1972–80, Gustav Stern Award in Virology, 1973; Dir, Inst. of Cancer Res., 1980–89. Researching into retroviruses causing leukaemia and AIDS. Hon. MRCP. *Publications:* RNA Tumour Viruses, 1982, 2nd edn (2 vols) 1985; various articles on cell biology, virology and genetics. *Recreations:* music, natural history. *Address:* Institute of Cancer Research, Chester Beatty Laboratories, Fulham Road, SW3 6JB. *T:* 0171–352 8133, *Fax:* 0171–352 3299.

WEISSKOPF, Prof. Victor Frederick; Professor of Physics at Massachusetts Institute of Technology, Cambridge, Mass, USA, since 1946 (on leave, 1961–65); Chairman, Department of Physics, MIT, 1967–73; *b* 19 Sept. 1908; *m* 1st, 1934, Ellen Margrete Tvede (*d* 1989); one *s* one *d*; 2nd, 1991, Duscha Schmid. *Educ:* Göttingen, Germany. PhD 1931. Research Associate: Berlin Univ., 1932; Eidgenossiche Technische Hochschule (Swiss Federal Institute of Technology), Zürich, 1933–35; Inst. for Theoretical Physics, Copenhagen, 1936; Asst Professor of Physics, Univ. of Rochester, NY, USA, 1937–43; Dep. Division Leader, Manhattan Project, Los Alamos, USA, 1943–45; Director-Gen., CERN, Geneva, 1961–65. Chm., High Energy Physics Adv. Panel, AEC, 1967–75. Mem., Nat. Acad. of Sciences, Washington, 1954; Pres., Amer. Acad. of Arts and Sciences, 1976–79; Corresp. Member: French Acad. of Sciences, 1957; Scottish Acad. of Scis, 1959; Royal Danish Scientific Soc., 1961; Bavarian Acad. of Scis, 1962; Austrian Acad. of Scis, 1963; Spanish Acad. of Scis, 1964; Soviet Acad. of Scis, 1976; Pontifical Acad. of Scis, 1976. Hon. Fellow: Weizmann Inst., Rehovot, Israel, 1962; Inst. of Physics, France, 1980. Hon. PhD: Manchester, 1961; Uppsala, 1964; Yale, 1964; Chicago, 1967; Hon. DSc: Montreal, 1959; Sussex, 1961; Lyon, 1962; Basle, 1962; Bonn, 1963; Genève, 1964; Oxford, 1965; Vienna, 1965; Paris, 1966; Copenhagen, 1966; Torino, 1968; Yale, 1968; Upsala, 1969; Harvard, 1984; Graz, 1985. Cherwell-Simon Memorial Lecturer, Oxford,

1963–64. Planck Medal, 1956; Gamov Award, 1969; Prix Mondial Del Duca, 1972; Killian Award, 1973; Smoluchovski Medal, Polish Physical Soc., 1979; Nat. Medal of Science, 1979; Wolf Prize (Israel), 1981; Enrico Fermi Award, 1989; Nat. Acad. Public Welfare Medal, 1991; Compton Award, 1992. Légion d'Honneur (France), 1959; Pour le Mérite Order, Germany, 1978. *Publications:* Theoretical Nuclear Physics, 1952; Knowledge and Wonder, 1962; Physics in the XX Century, 1972; Concepts of Particle Physics, 1984; The Privilege of Being a Physicist, 1989; The Joy of Insight, 1991; papers on theoretical physics in various journals. *Address:* 20 Bartlett Terrace, Newton, MA 02159, USA.

WEISSMÜLLER, Alberto Augusto, FCIB; President and Chief Executive Officer, A. A. Weissmüller Ltd, since 1992; General Partner, The Stillwaters Group, Washington, since 1992; *b* 2 March 1927; *s* of late Carlos Weissmüller and Michela Cottura; *m* 1976, Joan Ann Freifrau von Süsskind-Schwendi (*née* Smithson); one *s* one *d* by previous *m.* *Educ:* Univ. of Buenos Aires, Argentina; Illinois Inst. of Technol., Chicago, USA. Civil Engr, 1952; FCIB (FIB 1977). The Lummus Co., New York, 1958–59; Office of Graham Parker, NY, 1960–62; Bankers Trust Co., NY, 1962–71: Edge Act subsid., 1962–64; Asst Treasurer, and Mem., Bd of Corporation Financiera Nacional, Colombia, 1964–65; Asst Vice-Pres., 1965–67; Vice-Pres., 1967–71; Rome Rep., 1968–71; Man. Dir, Bankers Trust Finanziaria, SpA, Rome, 1970–71; Crocker National Bank, San Francisco, seconded to United Internat. Bank (now Unibank Ltd), London, as Chief Exec., 1971–79; Chief Adviser, Bank of England, 1979–81; Chief Exec. (UK), Banca Commerciale Italiana, 1981–82; Chm., BCI Ltd, London, 1981–83; Dir, N American Bancorp Inc. (a subsid. of Banca Commerciale Italiana), 1982–87; Rep. of Banca Commerciale Italiana in Washington, 1983–92 and in Mexico City, 1987–92. *Publication:* Castles from the Heart of Spain, 1977. *Recreations:* medieval fortified architecture, photography (architectural). *Address:* A. A. Weissmüller Ltd, 13801 Deakins Lane, Germantown, MD 20874, USA. *Club:* Board Room (New York).

WEITZ, Dr Bernard George Felix, OBE 1965; DSc; MRCVS; FIBiol; Chief Scientist, Ministry of Agriculture, Fisheries and Food, 1977–81; *b* London, 14 Aug. 1919; *m* 1945, Elizabeth Shine; one *s* one *d.* *Educ:* St Andrew, Bruges, Belgium; Royal Veterinary College, London. MRCVS 1942; DSc London 1961. Temp. Research Worker, ARC Field Station, Compton, Berks, 1942; Research Officer, Veterinary Laboratory, Min. of Agric. and Fisheries, 1942–47; Asst Bacteriologist, Lister Inst. of Preventive Medicine, Elstree, Herts, 1947; Head of Serum Dept, 1952; Dir, Nat. Inst. for Res. in Dairying, Univ. of Reading, Shinfield, Berks, 1967–77. Vis. Prof., Dept of Agriculture and Horticulture, Univ. of Reading, 1980–88. Member: ARC, 1978–81; NERC, 1978–81. Hon. FRASE, 1977. *Publications:* many contribs to scientific journals on Immunology and Tropical Medicine. *Recreations:* music, croquet. *Address:* 21 Hartley Close, Charlton Kings, Cheltenham, Glos GL53 9DN.

WEITZMAN, Peter, QC 1973; a Recorder of the Crown Court, since 1974; *b* 20 June 1926; *s* of late David Weitzman, QC, and Fanny Weitzman; *m* 1954, Anne Mary Larkam; two *s* two *d.* *Educ:* Cheltenham Coll.; Christ Church, Oxford (MA). Royal Artillery, 1945–48. Called to Bar, Gray's Inn, 1952; Bencher, 1981; Leader, Midland and Oxford Circuit, 1988–92 (Dep. Leader, 1985–88). Mem., Senate of Inns of Court, 1980–81, 1984–92. Member: Criminal Injuries Compensation Bd, 1986–; Mental Health Review Tribunal, 1986–. *Recreations:* hedging and ditching. *Address:* 21 St James's Gardens, W11 4RE; Little Leigh, Kingsbridge, Devon TQ7 4AG.

WEIZMAN, Maj.-Gen. Ezer; President of Israel, since 1993; *b* Tel Aviv, 15 June 1924; *s* of Yechiel Weizman and Yehudit Weizman; *m* 1950, Reuma Schwartz; one *d* (one *s* decd). Joined RAF, 1942; fighter pilot, 1944; served ME and FE; co-founder, Israeli Air Force, 1947; fighter pilot, War of Independence, 1948–49; Comdr, first Israeli fighter sqdn, 1949; RAF Staff Coll., 1952; Air Base Comdr, 1953–57; Maj.-Gen. and Comdr, Israeli Air Force, 1958–66; Dep. COS, Israel Defence Forces, 1966–69; retd, 1969. Israeli Government: Mem., Knesset, 1977–92; Minister: of Tspt, 1969–70; of Defence, 1977–80; for Arab Affairs, 1984–88; of Sci. and Technol., 1988–90. *Publications:* On Eagles' Wings, 1974; The Battle for Peace, 1981. *Address:* The President's Residence, Jerusalem, Israel.

WELANDER, Rev. Canon David Charles St Vincent; Canon Residentiary and Librarian, Gloucester Cathedral, 1975–91, now Emeritus; *b* 22 Jan. 1925; *s* of late Ernest Sven Alexis Welander, Orebro and Uppsala, Sweden, and Louisa Georgina Downes Welander (*née* Panter) *m* 1952, Nancy O'Rorke Stanley; two *s* three *d.* *Educ:* Unthank Coll., Norwich: London Univ. (BD 1947, Rubie Hebrew Prize 1947); ALCD (1st Cl.) 1947; Toronto Univ., 1947–48 (Hon. Mem. Alumni, Wycliffe Coll., 1948). FSA 1981. Deacon 1948, Priest 1949; Asst Curate, Holy Trinity, Norwich, 1948–51; Chaplain and Tutor, London Coll. of Divinity, 1952–56; Vicar: of Iver, Bucks, 1956–62; of Christ Church, Cheltenham, 1963–75; Rural Dean of Cheltenham, 1973–75. Member: Council, St Paul's and St Mary's Colls of Educn, Cheltenham, 1963–78; Council, Malvern Girls' Coll., 1982–91; Bishops' Cttee on Inspections of Theol Colls, 1967–81; Sen. Inspector of Theol Colls, 1970–84; Mem., Gen. Synod of C of E, 1970–85. Mem., Cathedrals Cttee, English Heritage, 1990–94. Trustee: Church Patronage Trust, 1969–78; Stained Glass Mus., 1986–. *Publications:* History of Iver, 1954; Gloucester Cathedral, 1979; The Stained Glass of Gloucester Cathedral, 1984; Gloucester Cathedral: its history, art and architecture, 1990; Gloucester Cathedral, 1995; contrib. Expository Times, etc. *Recreations:* walking, church architecture, music. *Address:* 1 Sandpits Lane, Sherston Magna, near Malmesbury, Wilts SN16 0NN. *T:* Malmesbury (01666) 840180.

WELBOURN, Prof. Richard Burkewood, MA, MD, FRCS; Professor of Surgical Endocrinology, Royal Postgraduate Medical School, University of London, 1979–82, now Emeritus Professor; *b* 1919; *y s* of late Burkewood Welbourn, MEng, MIEE, and Edith Welbourn, Rainhill, Lancs; *m* 1944, Rachel Mary Haighton, BDS, Nantwich, Cheshire; one *s* four *d.* *Educ:* Rugby School; Emmanuel College, Cambridge; Liverpool University. MB, BChir 1942; FRCS 1948; MA, MD Cambridge, 1953. War of 1939–45: RAMC. Senior Registrar, Liverpool Royal Infirmary, 1948; Research Asst, Dept of Surgery, Liverpool Univ., 1949. Fellow in Surgical Research, Mayo Foundation, Rochester, Minn., 1951. Professor of Surgical Science, Queen's University of Belfast, 1958–63; Surgeon, Royal Victoria Hospital, Belfast, 1951–63 and Belfast City Hosp., 1962–63; Prof. of Surgery, Univ. of London and Dir, Dept of Surgery, RPMS and Hammersmith Hosp., 1963–79; Hon. Consultant Surgeon, Hammersmith Hosp., 1979–82. Consultant Adviser in Surgery to Dept of Health and Social Security, 1971–79; Consultant (Vis. Schol., res. in hist. of Endocrine Surgery), Dept of Surgery, UCLA, 1983–89. Member: Council, MRC, 1971–75; Council, Royal Postgraduate Med. Sch, 1963–82. Hunterian Professor, RCS of England, 1958 (James Berry Prize, 1970); Harvey Lectr, Yale Univ., 1995. Member: Society of Sigma XI; British Medical Association; Internat. Assoc. of Endocrine Surgeons, 1979– (Peter Heimann Lectr, 1989; Distinguished Service Award, 1991); Internat. Surgical Soc., 1979–; British Soc. of Gastro-enterology and Assoc. of Surgeons; 58th Member King James IV Surgical Association Inc.; Fellow, West African Coll. of Surgeons; FRSM (Former Mem. Council, Section of Endocrinology, former Vice-Pres., Section of Surgery); Hon. Fellow Amer. Surgical Assoc.; Hon. Mem., Soc. for Surgery of the Alimentary Tract; formerly: Pres., Surgical Res. Soc. (Hon. Mem.); British Assoc. of Endocrine Surgeons (Hon. Mem.); Chm., Assoc. of Profs of Surgery; Mem., Jt Cttee for Higher Surgical Training; formerly Examr in Surgery, Univs of Manchester, Glasgow, Oxford, Sheffield, Edinburgh, QUB, and Liverpool; formerly Examr in Applied Physiology, RCS. Chm., Editorial Cttee, Journal of Medical Ethics, 1974–81; former Member: Editorial Cttee, Gut; Exec. Cttee, British Jl of Surgery. Formerly: Pres., Internat. Surgical Gp; Chm. Governing Body, Inst. of Medical Ethics; Pres., Prout Club. Hon. Mem., Roy. Coll. of Surgeons of Univs of Denmark, 1978; Hon. FACS 1984. Hon. MD Karolinska Inst., Stockholm, 1974; Hon. DSc QUB, 1985. Biennial Medal and Prize, Internat. Surgical Soc., 1995. *Publications:* (with D. A. D. Montgomery): Clinical Endocrinology for Surgeons, 1963, rev. edn, Medical and Surgical Endocrinology, 1975; (with A. S. Duncan and G. R. Dunstan) Dictionary of Medical Ethics, 1977, 2nd edn 1980, American edn 1981; The History of Endocrine Surgery, 1990; chapters in books and papers, mainly on gastro-intestinal and endocrine surgery and physiology, and history of endocrinology, in med. and surg. jls. *Recreations:* reading, writing, gardening, music. *Address:* 2 The Beeches, Tilehurst, Reading RG3 6RQ; 102 Gloucester Court, Kew Road, Kew, Richmond, Surrey TW9 3DZ.

WELBY, Sir (Richard) Bruno (Gregory), 7th Bt *cr* 1801; *b* 11 March 1928; *s* of Sir Oliver Charles Earle Welby, 6th Bt, TD, and Barbara Angela Mary Lind (*d* 1983), *d* of late John Duncan Gregory, CB, CMG; *S* father, 1977; *m* 1952, Jane Biddulph, *y d* of late Ralph Wilfred Hodder-Williams, MC; three *s* one *d.* *Educ:* Eton; Christ Church, Oxford (BA 1950). *Heir: s* Charles William Hodder Welby [*b* 6 May 1953; *m* 1978, Suzanna, *o d* of Major Ian Stuart-Routledge, Harston Hall, Grantham; three *d*]. *Address:* Denton Manor, Grantham, Lincs NG32 1JX.

WELBY-EVERARD, Maj.-Gen. Sir Christopher Earle, KBE 1965 (OBE 1945); CB 1961; DL; *b* 9 Aug. 1909; *s* of late E. E. E. Welby-Everard, Gosberton House, near Spalding, Lincolnshire; *m* 1938, Sybil Juliet Wake Shorrock (*d* 1994); two *s.* *Educ:* Charterhouse; CCC, Oxford. Gazetted The Lincolnshire Regt, 1930; OC 2 Lincolns, 1944; GSO1, 49 (WR) Inf. Div., 1944–46; GSO1 GHQ, MELF, 1946–48; OC 1 Royal Lincolnshire Regt, 1949–51; Comd 264 Scottish Beach Bde and 157 (L) Inf. Bde, 1954–57. BGS (Ops), HQ, BAOR, and HQ Northern Army Group, 1957–59; Chief of Staff, HQ Allied Forces, Northern Europe, 1959–61; GOC Nigerian Army, 1962–65; retd. DL Lincolnshire, 1966; High Sheriff of Lincolnshire, 1974. *Recreations:* shooting, cricket. *Address:* The Manor House, Sapperton, Sleaford, Lincolnshire NG34 0TB. *T:* Ingoldsby (01476) 585273. *Clubs:* Army and Navy; Free Foresters.

WELCH, Colin; *see* Welch, J. C. R.

WELCH, David; Chief Executive, The Royal Parks, since 1992; *s* of late Thomas Welch and Eleanor (*née* Foster); *m* 1960, Eva Doring; three *s* one *d.* Horticultural Officer, Blackpool CB, 1959–63; Hd, Parks and Recreation Dept, Borough of Bebington, Cheshire, 1963–67; Dir, Leisure and Recreation, City of Aberdeen, 1967–89; Consultant, 1989–92. President: Inst. Parks and Recreation, 1977–78; Inst. Leisure and Amenity Mgt, 1992–93; Inst. Hort., 1992–94; RHS of Aberdeen, 1987–94. Associate of Honour, RHS, 1990. Hon. LLD Aberdeen, 1990. Scottish Horticultural Medal, Royal Caledonian Horticultural Soc., 1973. *Publications:* Roses, 1988; Managing Urban Parks, 1990; Managing the Public Use of Open Space, 1995. *Recreations:* walking, theatre, after dinner speaking, horticultural writing. *Address:* The Old Police House, Hyde Park, W2 2UH. *T:* 0171–298 2000. *Club:* Royal Northern and University (Aberdeen).

WELCH, (James) Colin (Ross); freelance columnist and book critic; *b* 23 April 1924; *s* of James William Welch and Irene Margherita (*née* Paton), Ickleton Abbey, Cambridgeshire; *m* 1950, Sybil Russell; one *s* one *d.* *Educ:* Stowe Sch. (schol.); Peterhouse, Cambridge (major schol., BA Hons). Commissioned Royal Warwickshire Regt, 1942; served NW Europe, twice wounded. Glasgow Herald, 1948; Colonial Office, 1949; Daily Telegraph: leader writer, columnist (Peter Simple, with Michael Wharton), parliamentary sketch-writer, 1950–64; Dep. Editor, 1964–80; regular column, 1981–83; Editor-in-Chief, Chief Executive magazine, 1980–82; parly sketch-writer, Daily Mail, 1984–92; columnist and critic for The Times (formerly for The Independent, Spectator, American Spectator, National Review). Granada Journalist of the Year, 1974; Specialist Writer, British Press Awards, 1986. Knight's Cross, Order of Polonia Restituta, 1972. *Publications:* (ed) Sir Frederick Ponsonby: Recollections of Three Reigns, 1951; (trans. with Sybil Welch) Nestroy: Liberty Comes to Krähwinkel, 1954 (BBC); articles in Encounter, Spectator, New Statesman, American Spectator, etc; contribs to symposia, incl. The Future that Doesn't Work, 1977 (New York). *Address:* 4 Goddard's Lane, Aldbourne, Wilts SN8 2DL. *T:* Marlborough (01672) 40010.

WELCH, John K.; *see* Kemp-Welch.

WELCH, Sir John (Reader), 2nd Bt *cr* 1957; Partner, Wedlake Bell, since 1972; Chairman, John Fairfax (UK) Ltd, 1977–90; *b* 26 July 1933; *s* of Sir (George James) Cullum Welch, 1st Bt, OBE, MC, and Gertrude Evelyn Sladin Welch (*d* 1966); *S* father, 1980; *m* 1962, Margaret Kerry, *o d* of K. Douglass, Killara, NSW; one *s* twin *d.* *Educ:* Marlborough College; Hertford Coll., Oxford (MA). National service in RCS, 1952–54. Admitted a solicitor, 1960. Partner, Bell Brodrick & Gray, 1961–71. Ward Clerk of Walbrook Ward, City of London, 1961–74, Common Councilman, 1975–86 (Chm., Planning and Communications Cttee, 1981, 1982); Registrar of Archdeaconry of London. FRSA. Liveryman, Haberdashers' Co., 1955 (Court of Assistants, 1973; Master, 1990–91); Freeman, Parish Clerks' Co. (Master, 1967). Chm., Cttee of Management, London Homes for the Elderly, 1980–90; Pres., Grand Charity of Freemasons, 1985–95. CStJ 1981. *Recreation:* piano. *Heir: s* James Douglass Cullum Welch, *b* 10 Nov. 1973. *Address:* 28 Rivermead Court, Ranelagh Gardens, SW6 3RU; 16 Bedford Street, Covent Garden, WC2E 9HF. *T:* 0171–379 7266. *Clubs:* City Livery (Hon. Solicitor, 1983–90, Pres., 1986–87), Walbrook Ward (Chm., 1978–79), Hurlingham, Surrey County Cricket.

WELCH, Rt Rev. Neville; *see* Welch, Rt Rev. W. N.

WELCH, Robert Radford, MBE 1979; RDI 1965; FCSD (FSIAD 1962); designer and silversmith; *b* 21 May 1929; *m* 1959, Patricia Marguerite Hinksman; two *s* one *d.* *Educ:* Hanley Castle Grammar Sch.; Malvern Sch. of Art; Birmingham Coll. of Art; Royal Coll. of Art (DesRCA). FRSA 1967. Hon. Fellow RCA, 1972. Started own workshop in Chipping Campden, 1955; Design Consultant to Old Hall Tableware, 1955–83; opened Robert Welch Studio Shop, Chipping Campden, 1969, and second Studio Shop, Warwick, 1991. Major retrospective exhibn for 40th anniv. of workshop and design studio, Cheltenham, Manchester and Birmingham Art Galls, 1995–96. Visiting Lecturer: Central Sch. of Art and Design, 1957–63; RCA, 1963–71; visited India by invitation of All India Handicraft Bd, 1975. Silver commns for various clients, incl. civic plate, university colls, Goldsmiths' Hall, Canterbury Cathedral, V&A Museum, and British Govt Gift to St Lucia; tableware for British Ambassador's residence, Manila; British Museum; Silver Trust for No 10 Downing St; design commns in Denmark, Germany, USA, Japan and Korea. Liveryman, Goldsmiths' Co., 1982. *Publications:* Design in a Cotswold Workshop (with Alan Crawford), 1973; Hand and Machine, 1986. *Recreations:* drawing, painting. *Address:* Lower High Street, Chipping Campden, Glos GL55 6DU. *T:* Evesham (01386) 840522.

WELCH, Rt. Rev. (William) Neville, MA; *b* 30 April 1906; *s* of Thomas William and Agnes Maud Welch; *m* 1935, Kathleen Margaret Beattie; two *s* two *d*. *Educ:* Dean Close Sch., Cheltenham; Keble Coll., Oxford; Wycliffe Hall, Oxford. Asst Curate: Kidderminster, 1929–32; St Michael's, St Albans, 1932–34; Organising Sec., Missions to Seamen, 1934–39; Vicar of Grays, 1939–43; Officiating Chaplain, Training Ship Exmouth, 1939–40; Vicar of Ilford, 1943–53; Rural Dean of Barking, 1948–53; Vicar of Great Burstead, 1953–56; Archdeacon of Southend, 1953–72; Bishop Suffragan of Bradwell, 1968–73. Proctor in Convocation, 1945 and 1950; Hon. Canon of Chelmsford, 1951–53. *Address:* 112 Earlham Road, Norwich NR2 3HE. *T:* Norwich (01603) 618192.

WELD FORESTER, family name of **Baron Forester.**

WELDON, Sir Anthony (William), 9th Bt *cr* 1723; *b* 11 May 1947; *s* of Sir Thomas Brian Weldon, 8th Bt, and of Marie Isobel (now Countess Cathcart), *d* of Hon. William Joseph French; *S* father, 1979; *m* 1980, Mrs Amanda Wigan, *d* of Major Geoffrey and Hon. Mrs North; two *d*. *Educ:* Sherborne. Formerly Lieutenant, Irish Guards. *Recreations:* stalking, fishing, antiquarian books, champagne. *Heir: cousin* Kevin Nicholas Weldon [*b* 19 April 1951; *m* 1973, Catherine Main; one *s*]. *Clubs:* White's, Stranded Whales.

WELDON, Duncan Clark; theatrical producer; Chairman and Managing Director, Duncan C. Weldon Productions Ltd; *b* 19 March 1941; *s* of Clarence Weldon and Margaret Mary Andrew; *m* 1974, Janet Mahoney; one *d*. *Educ:* King George V School, Southport. Formerly a photographer; first stage production, A Funny Kind of Evening, with David Kossoff, Theatre Royal, Bath, 1965; co-founder, Triumph Theatre Productions, 1970; Director: Theatre Royal Haymarket Ltd; Strand Theatre; Triumph Proscenium Productions Ltd; Chichester Festival Theatre, 1994–. First London production, Tons of Money, Mayfair Theatre, 1968; 163 productions in the West End: When We are Married, 1970; The Chalk Garden, Big Bad Mouse, The Wizard of Oz, 1971; Lord Arthur Savile's Crime, Bunny, The Wizard of Oz, 1972; Mother Adam, Grease, The King and I, 1973; Dead Easy, 1974; The Case in Question, Hedda Gabler, Dad's Army, Betzi, On Approval, 1975; 13 Rue de l'Amour, A Bedful of Foreigners, Three Sisters, The Seagull, Fringe Benefits, The Circle, 1976; Separate Tables, Stevie, Hedda Gabler, On Approval, The Good Woman of Setzuan, Rosmersholm, Laburnum Grove, The Apple Cart, 1977; Waters of the Moon, Kings and Clowns, The Travelling Music Show, A Family, Look After Lulu, The Millionairess, 1978; The Crucifer of Blood, 1979; Reflections, Rattle of a Simple Man, The Last of Mrs Cheyney, Early Days, 1980; Virginia, Overheard, Dave Allen, Worzel Gummidge, 1981; Murder In Mind, Hobson's Choice, A Coat of Varnish, Captain Brassbound's Conversion, Design for Living, Uncle Vanya, Key for Two, The Rules of the Game, Man and Superman, 1982; The School for Scandal, DASH, Heartbreak House, Call Me Madam, Romantic Comedy, Liza Minnelli, Beethoven's Tenth, Edmund Kean, Fiddler on the Roof, A Patriot for Me, Cowardice, Great and Small, The Cherry Orchard, Dial 'M' for Murder, Dear Anyone, The Sleeping Prince, Hi-De-Hi!, 1983; Hello, Dolly!, The Aspern Papers, Strange Interlude, Serjeant Musgrave's Dance, Aren't We All?, American Buffalo, The Way of the World, Extremities, 1984; The Wind in the Willows, The Lonely Road, The Caine Mutiny Court-Martial, Other Places, Old Times, The Corn is Green, Waste, Strippers, Guys and Dolls, Sweet Bird of Youth, Interpreters, Fatal Attraction, The Scarlet Pimpernel, 1985; The Apple Cart, Across From the Garden of Allah, Antony and Cleopatra, The Taming of the Shrew, Circe & Bravo, Annie Get Your Gun, Long Day's Journey Into Night, Rookery Nook, Breaking the Code, Mr and Mrs Nobody, 1986; A Piece of My Mind, Court in the Act!, Canaries Sometimes Sing, Kiss Me Kate, Melon, Portraits, Groucho: a Life In Review, A Man for All Seasons, You Never Can Tell, Babes in the Wood, 1987; A Touch of the Poet, The Deep Blue Sea, The Admirable Crichton, The Secret of Sherlock Holmes, A Walk in the Woods, Richard II, Orpheus Descending, 1988; Richard III, The Royal Baccarat Scandal, Ivanov, Much Ado About Nothing, The Merchant of Venice, Veterans Day, Another Time, The Baker's Wife, London Assurance, 1989; Salome, Bent, An Evening with Peter Ustinov, The Wild Duck, Henry IV, Kean, Love Letters, Time and the Conways, 1990; The Homecoming, The Philanthropist, The Caretaker, Becket, Tovarich, The Cabinet Minister, 1991; Talking Heads, A Woman of No Importance, Lost in Yonkers, Trelawny of the "Wells", Cyrano de Bergerac, 1992; Relative Values, Two Gentlemen of Verona, Macbeth, 1993; Travesties, A Month in the Country, Rope, An Evening with Peter Ustinov, Arcadia, Home, Saint Joan, Lady Windermere's Fan, The Rivals, 1994; presented on Broadway: Brief Lives, 1974; Edmund Kean, Heartbreak House, 1983; Beethoven's Tenth, 1984; Strange Interlude, Aren't We All?, 1985; Wild Honey, 1986; Blithe Spirit, Pygmalion, Breaking the Code, 1987; Orpheus Descending, The Merchant of Venice, 1989; has also presented in Europe, Australia, Canada and Hong Kong. *Address:* Suite 4, Waldorf Chambers, 11 Aldwych, WC2B 4DA. *T:* 0171–836 0186.

WELDON, Fay; writer; *b* 22 Sept. 1931; *d* of Frank Birkinshaw and Margaret Jepson; *m* 1962, Ron Weldon (*d* 1994); four *s*; *m* 1995, Nick Fox. *Educ:* Hampstead Girls' High Sch.; St Andrews Univ. (DLitt). Has written or adapted numerous television and radio plays, dramatizations, and series, and nine stage plays. Chm. of Judges, Booker McConnell Prize, 1983. *Libretto:* A Small Green Space, 1989. *Publications:* The Fat Woman's Joke, 1967; Down Among the Women, 1972; Female Friends, 1975; Remember Me, 1976; Little Sisters, 1977 (as Words of Advice, NY, 1977); Praxis, 1978 (Booker Prize Nomination); Puffball, 1980; Watching Me, Watching You (short stories), 1981; The President's Child, 1982; The Life and Loves of a She-Devil, 1984 (televised, 1986; filmed as She-Devil, 1990); Letters to Alice—on First Reading Jane Austen, 1984; Polaris and other Stories, 1985; Rebecca West, 1985; The Shrapnel Academy, 1986; Heart of the Country, 1987 (televised, 1987); The Hearts and Lives of Men, 1987; The Rules of Life, 1987; Leader of the Band, 1988; (for children) Wolf the Mechanical Dog, 1989; The Cloning of Joanna May, 1989 (televised, 1992); (for children) Party Puddle, 1989; Darcy's Utopia, 1990; (contrib.) Storia 4: Green, 1990; Moon over Minneapolis or Why She Couldn't Stay (short stories), 1991; Life Force, 1992; Growing Rich, 1992; Affliction, 1994, Splitting, 1995; (with David Bailey) The Lady is a Tramp: portraits of Catherine Bailey, 1995. *Address:* c/o Casarotto Co. Ltd, National House, 62/66 Wardour Street, W1V 3HP.

WELEMINSKY, Judith Ruth; Associate, Centre for Voluntary Sector and Not for Profit Management, City University Business School, since 1994; Consultant, Compass Partnership, since 1994; *b* 25 Oct. 1950; *d* of Dr Anton Weleminsky and Gerda Weleminsky (*née* Loewenstamm); partner, Robert James Armstrong Smith; two *d*. *Educ:* Birmingham Univ. (BSc Hons Psych); Lancaster Univ. (MA Organisational Psych). Personnel and Training Officer, Lowfield (Storage and Distbn), 1973–75; Community Relations Officer, Lambeth, 1975–78; Equal Opportunities Officer, Wandsworth, 1978–80; Employment Development Officer, NACRO, 1980–82; Dir, Nat. Fedn of Community Orgns, 1982–85; Dir, Nat. Schizophrenia Fellowship, 1985–90; Dir, NCVO, 1991–94. FRSA. *Recreations:* family, friends, food. *Address:* Compass Partnership, 10 Barley Mow Passage, W4 4PH. *T:* 0181–994 6477.

WELLAND, Colin, (Colin Williams); actor, playwright; *b* 4 July 1934; *s* of John Arthur Williams and Norah Williams; *m* 1962, Patricia Sweeney; one *s* three *d*. *Educ:* Newton-le-Willows Grammar Sch.; Bretton Hall Coll.; Goldsmiths' Coll., London (Teacher's Dip. in Art and Drama). Art teacher, 1958–62; entered theatre, 1962; Library Theatre, Manchester, 1962–64; television, films, theatre, 1962–. Films (actor): Kes; Villain; Straw Dogs; Sweeney; Dancing through the Dark; (original screenplay): Yanks, 1978; Chariots of Fire, 1980 (won Oscar, Evening Standard and Broadcasting Press Guild Awards, 1982); Twice in a Lifetime, 1986; A Dry White Season, 1989; War of the Buttons, 1994. Plays (author): Say Goodnight to Grandma, St Martin's, 1973; Roll on Four O'clock, Palace, 1981. Award winning TV plays include: Roll on Four O'clock, Kisses at 50, Leeds United, Jack Point, Your Man from Six Counties, Bambino Mio. Best TV Playwright, Writers Guild, 1970, 1973 and 1974; Best TV Writer, and Best Supporting Film Actor, BAFTA Awards, 1970; Broadcasting Press Guild Award (for writing), 1973. *Publications:* Northern Humour, 1982; plays: Roomful of Holes, 1972; Say Goodnight to Grandma, 1973. *Recreations:* sport, theatre, cinema, politics, dining out. *Address:* c/o Peters, Fraser & Dunlop, 5th Floor, The Chambers, Chelsea Harbour, Lots Road, SW10 0XF.

WELLBELOVED, James; commercial consultant; writer and broadcaster on foreign and domestic affairs; Director General, National Kidney Research Fund, 1985–93; *b* 29 July 1926; *s* of Wilfred Henry Wellbeloved, Sydenham and Brockley (London), and Paddock Wood, Kent; *m* 1948, Mavis Beryl Ratcliff; two *s* one *d*. *Educ:* South East London Technical College. Boy seaman, 1942–46. Contested (SDP/Alliance) Erith and Crayford, 1987. MP (Lab 1965–81, SDP 1981–83) Erith and Crayford, Nov. 1965–1983; Parly Private Secretary: Minister of Defence (Admin), 1967–69; Sec. of State for Foreign and Commonwealth Affairs, 1969–70; an Opposition Whip, 1972–74; Parly Under-Sec. of State for Defence (RAF), MoD, 1976–79. UK Rep., North Atlantic Assembly, 1972–76, 1979–82. Dep. Chm., London MPs Parly Gp, 1970–81; Chairman: River Thames Gp; All Party Parly Camping and Caravanning Gp, 1967–74; Nat. Whitley Council, MoD, 1976–79; Member: Ecclesiastical Cttee, 1971–76; RACS Political Purposes Cttee, 1973–83; PLP Liaison Cttee, 1974–78; Defence Council, 1976–79; Unrelated Live Transplant Regulatory Authority, 1990–; Vice Chm., Labour Party Defence Gp, 1970–81. Contested, 1983, Prospective Parly Cand., 1985 (SDP) Erith and Crayford. Dir, Assoc. of Former MPs, 1983–. Pres., British Transplant Organ Donor Soc., 1992–. Nat. Vice-Pres., Camping and Caravanning Club, 1974–. Former Governor, Greenwich Hosp. Sch. *Publication:* Local Government, 1971. *Recreations:* camping, travel. *Address:* 9 Woodstock Close, Bexley, Kent DA5 3JT.

WELLBY, Rear-Adm. Roger Stanley, CB 1958; DSO 1940; DL; Retired; lately Head of UK Services Liaison Staff in Australia and Senior Naval Adviser to UK High Commissioner, 1956–59; *b* 28 Apr. 1906; *o s* of Dr Stanley Wellby and Marian Schwann; *m* 1936, Elaine, *d* of late Sir Clifford Heathcote-Smith; three *s*. *Educ:* RNC, Dartmouth. Qualified as Torpedo Officer, 1931; Commander, 1939; Special Service in France, 1940 (DSO, Croix de Guerre); Captain, 1947; Imperial Defence College; Rear-Adm. 1956. Dep. Comr-in-Chief, St John Ambulance Brigade, 1963–71; Comr, St John Ambulance Brigade, Bucks, 1971–75. DL Bucks 1972. KStJ 1966. *Recreation:* hockey, for Navy. *Address:* Oakengrove, Hastoe, Tring HP23 6LY. *T:* Tring (01442) 823233.

WELLER, Dr Thomas Huckle; Richard Pearson Strong Professor of Tropical Public Health, Harvard University, 1954–85, Emeritus 1985 (Head, Department of Tropical Public Health, 1954–81); Director Center for Prevention of Infectious Diseases, Harvard School of Public Health, 1966–81; *b* 15 June 1915; *s* of Carl V. and Elsie H. Weller; *m* 1945, Kathleen R. Fahey; two *s* two *d*. *Educ:* University of Michigan (AB, MS); Harvard (MD). Fellow, Departments of Comparative Pathology and Tropical Medicine and Bacteriology, Harvard Medical School, 1940–41; Intern, Children's Hosp., Boston, 1941–42. Served War, 1942–45: 1st Lieut to Major, Medical Corps, US Army. Asst Resident in Medicine, Children's Hosp., 1946; Fellow, Pediatrics, Harvard Medical School, 1947; Instructor, Dept Tropical Public Health, Harvard School of Public Health, 1948; Assistant Professor, 1949; Associate Professor, 1950. Asst Director, Research Div. of Infectious Diseases, Children's Medical Center, Boston, 1949–55; Dir, Commission on Parasitic Diseases, Armed Forces Epidemiological Bd, 1953–59, Mem. 1959–72; Mem. Trop. Med. and parasitology study sect., US Public Health Service, 1953–56. Diplomate, American Board of Pediatrics, 1948; Amer. Acad. of Arts and Sciences, 1955; National Academy of Sciences, USA. Consultant on tropical medicine and infectious diseases to foundations and industries, 1985–. Hon. FRSTM&H, 1987. Hon. LLD Michigan, 1956; Hon. DSc: Gustavus Adolphus Coll., 1975; Univ. of Mass Med. Sch., 1986; Hon. LHD Lowell, 1977. Mead Johnson Award of Amer. Acad. of Pediatrics (jointly), 1954; Kimble Methodology Award (jointly), 1954; Nobel Prize Physiology or Medicine (jointly), 1954; Ledlie Prize, 1963; United Cerebral Palsy Weinstein-Goldenson Award, 1974; Bristol Award, Infectious Diseases Soc. of America, 1980; First Scientific Achievement Award, VZV Res. Foundn, 1993. *Publications:* numerous scientific papers on *in vitro* cultivation of viruses and on helminth infections of man. *Recreations:* gardening, photography. *Address:* 56 Winding River Road, Needham, MA 02192, USA. *Club:* Harvard (Boston).

WELLER, Walter; Principal Conductor and Music Director, Royal Scottish National Orchestra, since 1992; Principal Guest Conductor, National Orchestra of Spain, since 1987; *b* 30 Nov. 1939; *s* of Walter and Anna Weller; *m* 1966, Elisabeth Samohyl; one *s*. *Educ:* Realgymnasium, Vienna; Akademie für Musik, Vienna (degree for violin and piano). Founder of Weller Quartet, 1958–69; Member, Vienna Philharmonic, 1958–69. First Leader, 1960–69; Conductor, Vienna State Opera, 1969–75; Guest Conductor with all main European and American Orchestras, also in Japan and Israel, 1973–; Principal Conductor and Artistic Adviser, Royal Liverpool Philharmonic Orch., 1977–80, Guest Conductor Laureate, 1980–; Principal Conductor, RPO, 1980–85. Artistic Dir, Allgemeine Musikges. Basel, 1994–95. Many recordings (Grand Prix du disque Charles Cros). Medal of Arts and Sciences, Austria, 1968. *Recreations:* magic, model railway, sailing, swimming, stamp-collecting, ski-ing. *Address:* c/o Harrison-Parrott Ltd, 12 Penzance Place, W11 4PA.

WELLESLEY, family name of **Earl Cowley** and of **Duke of Wellington.**

WELLESLEY, Julian Valerian; Chairman, East Sussex Health Authority, since 1993; *b* 9 Aug. 1933; *s* of late Gerald Valerian Wellesley, MC, and Elizabeth Thornton Harvey; *m* 1965, Elizabeth Joan Hall; one *s* one *d*; three step *d*. *Educ:* Royal Naval Colleges, Dartmouth (schol.) and Greenwich. Royal Navy, 1947–61: America and West Indies, 1955–56; Far East, 1957–58; Navigation Specialist, 1959. Joined Charles Barker, 1961: a Dir, 1963; Dep. Chm., 1975; Chm., Charles Barker Group, 1978–83; Consultant, TSB Gp, 1984; Director: Horizon Travel, 1984–87; Chatsworth Food Ltd, 1986–90; E. & R. Garrould Ltd, 1988–90. Dir, Assoc. of Lloyd's Mems, 1985–91. Mem., 1986–90, Chm., 1990–93, Eastbourne HA. Vice-Chm., Wealden Cons. Assoc., 1988–91. Chm. Govs, Uplands Community Coll., 1994– (Gov., 1991–). FIPA 1976; FRSA 1991. *Recreations:* family, gardening, opera, playing tennis and bridge, watching cricket. *Address:* Tidebrook Manor, Wadhurst, Sussex TN5 6PD. *Clubs:* Brooks's, MCC; Sussex.

WELLINGS, David Gordon; Group Chief Executive, Cadbury Schweppes plc, since 1993; *b* 13 Dec. 1940; *s* of Gordon Henry and Muriel Wellings; *m* 1962, Jennifer Christine Simpson; one *s* one *d*. *Educ:* Manchester Grammar Sch.; Oriel Coll., Oxford (MA Mod.

Langs). Joined Cadbury Bros Ltd, 1962; Marketing Dir, Associated Fisheries & Food, 1970–73; Man. Dir, Northray Foods Ltd, 1973–78; Dir, Fish Ops, Ross Foods Ltd, 1978–82; Chm. and Chief Exec., Golden Wonder/HP Foods, 1982–86; Managing Director: Cadbury Ltd, 1986–89; Gp Confectionery, Cadbury Schweppes plc, 1989–93. *Recreations:* ornithology, golf. *Address:* Cadbury Schweppes plc, 25 Berkeley Square, W1X 6HT. *T:* 0171–409 1313.

WELLINGS, Sir Jack (Alfred), Kt 1975; CBE 1970; Chairman, 1968–87, Managing Director, 1963–84, The 600 Group Ltd; *b* 16 Aug. 1917; *s* of Edward Josiah and Selina Wellings; *m* 1946, Greta, *d* of late George Tidey; one *s* two *d*. *Educ:* Selhurst Grammar Sch.; London Polytechnic. Vice-Pres., Hawker Siddeley (Canada) Ltd, 1954–62; Dep. Man. Dir, 600 Group Ltd, 1962. Member: NCB, 1971–77; NEB, 1977–79; part-time Mem., British Aerospace, 1980–87; non-exec. Dir, Clausing Corp., USA, 1982–84. *Address:* Boundary Meadow, Collum Green Road, Stoke Poges, Bucks SL2 4BB. *T:* Fulmer (01753) 662978.

WELLINGS, Victor Gordon, QC 1973; President of the Lands Tribunal, 1989–92 (Member, 1973–88); Deputy Judge of the High Court, 1975–92; *b* 19 July 1919; *e s* of late Gordon Arthur Wellings, solicitor, and Alice Adelaide Wellings (later Poole); *m* 1948, Helen Margaret Jill Lovell; three *s*. *Educ:* Reading Sch.; Exeter Coll., Oxford (MA). Called to Bar, Gray's Inn, 1949; practised 1949–73. War service, 1940–46; Captain Indian Army, 17th Dogra Regt; Intell. Corps, India; Captain, TARO, 1949–. Hon. ARICS 1993. *Publications:* Editor, Woodfall, The Law of Landlord and Tenant, 28th edn, 1978 (Jt Editor 26th and 27th edns, 1963 and 1968), and other works on same subject. *Recreations:* golf, fishing. *Address:* Cherry Tree Cottage, Whitchurch Hill, Pangbourne, Berks RG8 7PT. *T:* Pangbourne (01734) 842918. *Club:* United Oxford & Cambridge University.

WELLINGTON, 8th Duke of, *cr* 1814; **Arthur Valerian Wellesley,** KG 1990; LVO 1952; OBE 1957; MC 1941; DL; Baron Mornington, 1746; Earl of Mornington, Viscount Wellesley, 1760; Viscount Wellington of Talavera and Wellington, Somersetshire, Baron Douro, 1809; Earl of Wellington, Feb. 1812; Marquess of Wellington, Oct. 1812; Marquess Douro, 1814; Prince of Waterloo, 1815, Netherlands; Count of Vimeiro, Marquess of Torres Vedras and Duke of Victoria in Portugal; Duke of Ciudad Rodrigo and a Grandee of Spain, 1st class; *b* 2 July 1915; *s* of 7th Duke of Wellington, KG, and Dorothy Violet (*d* 1956), *d* of Robert Ashton, Croughton, Cheshire; *S* father, 1972; *m* 1944, Diana Ruth, *o d* of Maj.-Gen. D. F. McConnel; four *s* one *d*. *Educ:* Eton; New Coll., Oxford. Served War of 1939–45 in Middle East (MC), CMF and BLA. Lt-Col Comdg Royal Horse Guards, 1954–58; Silver Stick-in-Waiting and Lt-Col Comdg the Household Cavalry, 1959–60; Comdr 22nd Armoured Bde, 1960–61; Comdr RAC 1st (Br.) Corps, 1962–64; Defence Attaché, Madrid, 1964–67, retired; Col-in-Chief, The Duke of Wellington's Regt, 1974–; Hon. Col 2nd Bn, The Wessex Regt, 1974–80. Director: Massey Ferguson Holdings Ltd, 1967–89; Massey Ferguson Ltd, 1973–84. President: Game Conservancy, 1976–81 (Dep. Pres., 1981–87); SE Branch, Royal British Legion, 1978; BSJA, 1980–82; Rare Breeds Survival Trust, 1984–87; Council for Environmental Conservation, 1983–87; Atlantic Salmon Trust, 1983–. Vice-Pres., Zool Soc. of London, 1983–89; Mem. Council, RASE, 1976– (Dep. Pres., 1993). HM's Rep. Trustee, Bd of Royal Armouries, 1983–95; Trustee, WWF (UK), 1985–90. Hampshire CC 1967–74; DL Hants, 1975. Governor of Wellington Coll., 1964–; Chm., Pitt Club. OStJ. Officier, Légion d'Honneur (France); Kt Grand Cross: Order of St Michael of the Wing (Portugal), 1984; Order of Isabel the Catholic (Spain), 1986. *Heir: s* Marquess of Douro, *qv*. *Address:* Stratfield Saye House, Basingstoke, Hants RG27 0AS; Apsley House, 149 Piccadilly, W1V 9FA. *Club:* Buck's.

WELLINGTON (NZ), Archbishop of, (RC), since 1979; **His Eminence Cardinal Thomas Stafford Williams,** DD; Metropolitan of New Zealand; *b* 20 March 1930; *s* of Thomas Stafford Williams and Lillian Maude Kelly. *Educ:* Holy Cross Primary School, Miramar; SS Peter and Paul Primary School, Lower Hutt; St Patrick's Coll., Wellington; Victoria University Coll., Wellington; St Kevin's Coll., Oamaru; Holy Cross Coll., Mosgiel; Collegio Urbano de Propaganda Fide, Rome (STL); University Coll., Dublin (BSocSc); Hon. DD. Assistant Priest, St Patrick's Parish, Palmerston North, 1963–64; Director of Studies, Catholic Enquiry Centre, Wellington, 1965–70; Parish Priest: St Anne's Parish, Leulumoega, W Samoa, 1971–75; Holy Family Parish, Porirua, NZ, 1976–79. Cardinal, 1983. *Address:* Viard, 21 Eccleston Hill, Wellington 1, New Zealand. *T:* (4) 4961795.

WELLINGTON (NZ), Bishop of; *see* New Zealand, Primate and Archbishop of.

WELLINGTON, Peter Scott, CBE 1981; DSC; PhD; ARCS; FLS; FIBiol; FRAgS; Director, National Institute of Agricultural Botany, 1970–81; *b* 20 March 1919; *er s* of late Robert Wellington, MBE, MC; *m* 1947, Kathleen Joyce, *widow* of E. H. Coombe; one *s* one *d*. *Educ:* Kelly Coll.; Imperial Coll. of Science. BSc 1946. Observer, Fleet Air Arm, 1940–45 (Lt-Comdr (A) RNVR). Research Asst 1948–52, Chief Officer 1953–61, Official Seed Testing Stn for England and Wales; Asst Dir 1961–68, Dep. Dir 1968–69, Nat. Inst. of Agricultural Botany. Vice-Pres., Internat. Seed Testing Assoc., 1953–56 (Chm. Germination Cttee, 1956–70); Chief Officer, UK Variety Classification Unit, 1965–70; Chm., Technical Working Group, Internat. Convention for Protection of Plant Varieties, 1966–68; Mem., Governing Body, Nat. Seed Develt Orgn Ltd, 1982–87. *Publications:* papers on germination of cereals and weeds, seed-testing and seed legislation. *Recreations:* gardening, walking, reading. *Address:* Colescus, Gorran Haven, St Austell, Cornwall PL26 6JJ. *T:* Mevagissey (01726) 842065.

WELLS, Dean of; *see* Lewis, Very Rev. R.

WELLS, Archdeacon of; *see* Acworth, Ven. R. F.

WELLS, Dr Alan Arthur, OBE 1982; FRS 1977; FEng 1978; Director-General, The Welding Institute, 1977–88; *s* of Arthur John Wells and Lydia Wells; *m* 1950, Rosemary Edith Alice Mitchell; four *s* one *d*. *Educ:* City of London Sch.; Univ. of Nottingham (BScEng); Clare Coll., Cambridge (PhD). MIMechE, Hon. FWeldI. British Welding Res. Association: Asst Dir, 1956; Dep. Dir (Scientific), 1963; Queen's University of Belfast: Prof. of Struct. Science, 1964; Head of Civil Engrg Dept, 1970–77; Dean, Faculty of Applied Science and Technol., 1973–76; Professorial Fellow, 1990. Hon. Dr, Faculty of Engrg, Univ. of Gent, 1972; Hon. DSc Glasgow, 1982; Hon. DScEng QUB, 1986. *Publications:* Brittle Fracture of Welded Plate (jtly), 1967; res. papers on welding technol. and fracture mechanics. *Recreation:* handyman about the house and garden. *Address:* The Welding Institute, Abington Hall, Abington, Cambs CB1 6AL. *T:* Cambridge (01223) 891162. *Club:* Athenæum.

WELLS, Bowen; MP (C) Hertford and Stortford, since 1983 (Hertford and Stevenage, 1979–83); a Lord Commissioner of HM Treasury (Government Whip), since 1995; *b* 4 Aug. 1935; *s* of late Reginald Laird Wells and of Agnes Mary Wells (*née* Hunter); 1975, Rennie Heyde; two *s*. *Educ:* St Paul's School; Univ. of Exeter (BA Hons); Regent St Polytechnic School of Management (Dip. Business Management). National Service, RN (promoted to Sub Lt), 1954–56. Schoolmaster, Colet Court, 1956–57; sales trainee, British Aluminium, 1957–58; Univ. of Exeter, 1958–61; Commonwealth Development Corporation, 1961–73; Owner Manager, Substation Group Services Ltd, 1973–79. Parliamentary Private Secretary: to Minister of State for Employment, 1982–83; to Minister of State at Dept of Transport, 1992–94; an Asst Govt Whip, 1994–95. Member: For. Affairs Select Cttee, 1981–92; European Legislation Select Cttee, 1983–92; Chairman: UN Parly Gp, 1983–92; British-Caribbean Gp; Jt Hon. Sec., Parly Cons. Trade and Industry Gp, 1984–91 (Vice-Chm., 1983–84); Sec., All Party Overseas Develt Gp., 1984–94; Sec., Cons. Envmt Cttee, 1991–92; Mem., British-American Gp, 1985. Mem., UK Br. Exec., CPA, 1984–; Regl Rep., Internat. CPA. Trustee, Industry and Parlt Trust, 1985–. Gov., Inst. of Development Studies, 1980–94. *Recreations:* music, walking, gardening cooking, sailing. *Address:* House of Commons, SW1A 0AA. *T:* 0171–219 5154.

WELLS, Brigid; *see* Wells, J. B. E.

WELLS, Sir Charles Maltby, 2nd Bt *cr* 1944; TD 1960; *b* 24 July 1908; *e s* of 1st Bt, and Mary Dorothy Maltby (*d* 1956); *S* father, 1956; *m* 1935, Katharine Boulton, *d* of Frank Boteler Kenrick, Toronto; two *s*. *Educ:* Bedford School; Pembroke College, Cambridge. Joined RE (TA), 1933; Capt. 1939; served War of 1939–45: 54th (EA) Div., 1939–41; Lt-Col 1941; 76th Div., 1941–43; British Army Staff, Washington, 1943–45. *Heir: s* Christopher Charles Wells [*b* 12 Aug. 1936; *m* 1st, 1960, Elizabeth Florence Vaughan (marr. diss. 1983), *d* of I. F. Griffiths, Outremont, Quebec; two *s* two *d*; 2nd, 1985, Lynda Anne Cormack; one *s*]. *Address:* 41 Sherwood Avenue, Toronto, Ont M4P 2A6, Canada.

WELLS, Hon. Clyde Kirby; QC (Can.) 1977; MHA (Liberal) Bay of Islands, since 1989; Premier of Newfoundland and Labrador, since 1989; *b* 9 Nov. 1937; *s* of Ralph Pennell Wells and Maude Wells (*née* Kirby); *m* 1962, Eleanor, *d* of Arthur and Daisy Bishop; two *s* one *d*. *Educ:* All Saints Sch., Stephenville Crossing; Memorial Univ., Newfoundland (BA 1959); Dalhousie Univ. Law Sch. (LLB 1962). Served with Canadian Army, JAG's Office, 1962–64; called to the Bar, Nova Scotia, 1963, Newfoundland, 1964; private practice, 1964, later Senior Partner, Wells & Co. MHA Humber East, 1966, Windsor-Buchans, 1987; Minister of Labour, 1966; Leader of Liberal Party, 1987. *Address:* Confederation Building, St John's, Newfoundland A1B 4J6, Canada; 3 Glenridge Crescent, St John's, Newfoundland.

WELLS, Prof. David Arthur; Professor of German, Birbeck College, University of London, since 1987; *b* 26 April 1941; *s* of Arthur William Wells and Rosina Elizabeth (*née* Jones). *Educ:* Christ's Hosp., Horsham; Gonville and Caius Coll., Cambridge; Univs of Strasbourg, Vienna and Münster. Mod. and Med. Langs Tripos, BA 1963, Tiarks Studentship 1963–64, MA, PhD Cantab 1967. Asst Lectr 1966–67, Lectr 1967–69, in German, Univ. of Southampton; Lectr in German, Bedford Coll., Univ. of London, 1969–74; Sec., London Univ. Bd of Staff Examiners in German, 1973–74; Tutor, Nat. Extension Coll., Cambridge, 1966–74; Prof. of German, QUB, 1974–87. Lecture tour of NZ univs, 1975. Mem., Managing Body, Oakington Manor Jun. Mixed and Infant Sch., London Bor. of Brent, 1972–74; Hon. Sec., Mod. Humanities Res. Assoc., 1969–; Hon. Treas., Assoc. for Literary and Linguistic Computing, 1973–78; Sec.-Gen., Internat. Fedn for Modern Langs and Lits, 1981–. Editor, MHRA Ann. Bull. of Modern Humanities Research Assoc., 1969–; Jt Editor, The Year's Work in Modern Language Studies, 1976– (Editor, 1982). FRSA 1983. *Publications:* The Vorau Moses and Balaam: a study of their relationship to exegetical tradition, 1970; The Wild Man from the Epic of Gilgamesh to Hartmann von Aue's Iwein, 1975; A Complete Concordance to the Vorauer Bücher Moses (Concordances to the Early Middle High German Biblical Epic), 1976; contribs to MHRA Style Book: Notes for Authors and Editors, 1971, 4th edn 1991; articles, monographs and reviews in learned jls. *Recreations:* travel, theatre, music. *Address:* Department of German, Birkbeck College, 43 Gordon Square, WC1H 0PD. *T:* 0171–631 6103; 128 Belgrave Road, SW1V 2BL. *T:* 0171–834 6558.

WELLS, David George; Managing Director, Service (formerly Servicing and Installation), British Gas plc, since 1993; *b* 6 Aug. 1941; *s* of George Henry Wells and Marian (*née* Trolley); *m* 1967, Patricia Ann Fenwick; two *s*. Educ: Market Harborough Grammar Sch.; Reading Univ. (BA). FCA 1966. Hancock, Gilbert & Morris, 1962–67; Esso Chemical Ltd, 1967–69; joined Gas Council, 1969; Investment Accountant (Investment Appraisal), 1970–73; British Gas Corporation: Chief Accountant, Admin, 1973–76; Chief Investment Accountant, 1976; Dir of Finance, SE Reg., 1976–83; Dep. Chm., W Midlands Reg., 1983–88; Regl Chm., S Eastern, 1988–93; Man. Dir, Regl Services, 1993. Director: Metrogas Bldg Soc., 1978–86 (Dep. Chm., 1979–83); Port Greenwich Ltd, 1989–. Chm., S London Trng and Enterprise Council, 1989–93. CIGasE 1988; CIMgt (CBIM 1990); FRSA 1991. *Recreations:* walking, reading, photography, gardening. *Address:* British Gas plc, 30 The Causeway, Staines, Mddx TW18 3BY. *T:* Staines (01784) 874000.

WELLS, Doreen Patricia, (Marchioness of Londonderry); dancer and actress; Ballerina of the Royal Ballet, 1955–74; *m* 9th Marquess of Londonderry, *qv*; two *s*. *Educ:* Walthamstow; Bush Davies School; Royal Ballet School. Engaged in Pantomime, 1952 and 1953. Joined Royal Ballet, 1955; became Principal Dancer, 1960; has danced leading roles in Noctambules, Harlequin in April, Dance Concertante, Sleeping Beauty, Coppelia, Swan Lake, Sylvia, La Fille mal Gardée, Two Pigeons, Giselle, Invitation, Rendezvous, Blood Wedding, Raymonda, Concerto, Nutcracker, Romeo and Juliet, Concerto No 2 (Ballet Imperial); has created leading roles in Toccata, La Création du Monde, Sinfonietta, Prometheus, Grand Tour; now playing leading roles in musical shows. Adeline Genée Gold Medal, 1954. *Recreations:* classical music, reading, theatre-going, aikido.

WELLS, Prof. George Albert, MA, BSc, PhD; Professor of German, Birkbeck College, University of London, 1968–88, now Emeritus; *b* 22 May 1926; *s* of George John and Lilian Maud Wells; *m* 1969, Elisabeth Delhey. *Educ:* University College London (BA, MA German; PhD Philosophy; BSc Geology). Lecturer in German, 1949–64, Reader in German, 1964–68, University Coll. London. Hon. Associate, Rationalist Press Assoc., 1989 (Dir, 1974–89). Mem., Acad. of Humanism, 1983– (Humanist Laureate, 1983). *Publications:* Herder and After, 1959; The Plays of Grillparzer, 1969; The Jesus of the Early Christians, 1971; Did Jesus Exist?, 1975, 2nd edn 1986; Goethe and the Development of Science 1750–1900, 1978; The Historical Evidence for Jesus, 1982; The Origin of Language: aspects of the discussion from Condillac to Wundt, 1987; (ed and contrib.) J. M. Robertson (1856–1933), Liberal, Rationalist and Scholar, 1987; Religious Postures, 1988; Who Was Jesus? a critique of the New Testament record, 1989; Belief and Make Believe: critical reflections on the sources of credulity, 1991; What's in a Name?: reflections on language, magic and religion, 1993; articles in Jl of History of Ideas, Jl of English and Germanic Philology, German Life and Letters, Question, Trivium, Wirkendes Wort. *Recreation:* walking. *Address:* 35 St Stephen's Avenue, St Albans, Herts AL3 4AA. *T:* St Albans (01727) 851347.

WELLS, Jack Dennis; Executive Director, Aircraft Owners and Pilots Association, since 1991; Assistant Director, Central Statistical Office, 1979–88; *b* 8 April 1928; *s* of late C. W. Wells and H. M. Wells (*née* Clark); *m* 1st, 1953, Jean Allison; one *s* one *d*; 2nd, 1987, Cynthia Palmer. *Educ:* Hampton Grammar Sch.; Polytechnic of Central London. AIS 1955. Ministry of Fuel and Power, 1947; Royal Air Force, 1947–49; Min. of (Fuel and) Power, 1949–69; Private Secretary to Paymaster General, 1957–59; Chief Statistician, Dept of Economic Affairs, 1969; Min. of Technology, 1969; HM Treasury, 1970; Dept of (Trade and) Industry, 1971–79. Pres., CS Aviation Assoc., 1988–. Past Chairman, Old Hamptonians Assoc. *Publications:* contribs to Long Range Planning, Economic Trends, Statistical News, Review of Income and Wealth, Jl of Banking and Finance, BIEC Yearbook. *Recreations:* flying, cricket, jazz, travel. *Clubs:* Civil Service, MCC.

WELLS, (Jennifer) Brigid (Ellen), (Mrs Ian Wells); JP; Chairman Assessor, Civil Service Selection Board, 1989–95; *b* 18 Feb. 1928; *d* of Dr Leonard John Haydon, TD, MA Cantab, MB BCh and Susan Eleanor Haydon (*née* Richmond), actress; *m* 1962, Ian Vane Wells; three *d*. *Educ:* schools in UK, USA, Canada; Edinburgh Univ.; Lady Margaret Hall, Oxford (scholar; BA Mod. Hist.; MA). Commonwealth Relations Office, 1949; UK High Commn, NZ, 1952–54; Private Sec. to Parly Under-Sec. of State, CRO, 1954–56; MAFF, 1956–62; teaching: LCC, 1962–63; Haringey, 1967; Camden Sch. for Girls, 1969–75 (to Head of Dept); Head of Dept, St David's and St Katharine's, Hornsey, 1975–77; Headmistress, Brighton and Hove High Sch., GPDST, 1978–88. Chm. designate, W Sussex Ambulance NHS Trust, 1992–93. Member: Local Radio Council, 1980–82; Broadcasting Complaints Commn, 1986–93 (Chm., Jan.–June 1992); Chairman: Educn Cttee, GSA, 1987–88; SE Region, GSA, 1984–86. Project Manager (USA), GAP, 1989–91; Mem., British Atlantic Council, 1988–93; Governor, Woldingham Sch., 1989–; Comr, Duke of York's Royal Mil. Sch., Dover, 1993–. Chm., Friends of GPDST, 1991– (Dep. Chm., 1989–91). JP Inner London, 1972–77, Brighton and Hove, 1980. *Publications:* articles in learned jls. *Recreations:* decorating, dressmaking, travel. *Address:* 2 Elm Cottage, Roud, Ventnor, Isle of Wight PO38 3LH. *T:* Godshill (01983) 840422.

WELLS, John Campbell; writer, actor and director; *b* 17 Nov. 1936; *s* of Eric George Wells and Dorothy Amy Thompson; *m* 1982, Teresa (*née* Chancellor). *Educ:* Eastbourne Coll.; St Edmund Hall, Oxford. Taught: English at Landerziehungsheim Schondorf am Ammersee, 1958–59; French and German at Eton, 1961–63; Co-Editor, Private Eye, 1964–67; Afterthought column, The Spectator, 1966–68. *Author of: revues, etc (also performer):* Never Too Late, 1960, Late Night Final, 1961 (both jtly), Edinburgh Fest.; A Man Apart (jtly), 1968, Changing Scenes, 1969, BBC Radio; Charlie's Grants (jtly), 1970, Up Sunday, 1973–74, The End of the Pier Show (jtly), 1975, BBC TV; Return to Leeds (jtly), Yorkshire TV, 1974; In the Looking Glass (jtly), 1976; Frontiers—East/West Germany (documentary), BBC TV, 1990; *plays:* (with Claud Cockburn) Listen to the Knocking Bird, Nottingham Playhouse, 1965; (with Richard Ingrams) Mrs Wilson's Diary, Th. Royal, Stratford East, transf. Criterion, 1968; The Projector, 1970, and Cranford, 1970, Th. Royal, Stratford East; (with Barry Fantoni) Lionel, New London, 1977; (with Julius Gellner) The Immortal Haydon, Mermaid, 1978; The Peace, Scottish Opera Go Round, 1978; (with Robert Morley) A Picture of Innocence, Brighton, 1979; Anyone for Denis?, Whitehall, 1981–82 (also title rôle); Alice in Wonderland, Lyric, Hammersmith, 1986; A Brand from the Burning (also dir.), RSC, 1995; *television plays:* The Scriblerus Club, 1967; Voltaire in England, 1968; Orpheus in the Underground, 1977; The Arnolfini Marriage, 1978; *film:* (jtly) Princess Caraboo (also acted), 1994; *radio play adaptations:* Alice in Wonderland, 1978; Alice Through the Looking Glass, 1980; *translations:* Danton's Death, 1971, The Marriage of Figaro, 1974, NT; The Barber of Seville, and A Mother's Guilt, 1984, BBC Radio; Women All Over, Edinburgh, 1984; La Vie Parisienne, Scottish Opera, 1986 (also dir, Glasgow, 1987); The Magic Flute, City of Birmingham Touring Opera, 1988; The Merry Widow, Scottish Opera, 1989; Cyrano de Bergerac, Theatre Royal, Haymarket, 1992; La Belle Hélène, Scottish Opera, 1995. *Actor:* An Italian Straw Hat, Lyric, Hammersmith, 1961; Murderous Angels, Paris, 1971; Private Lives, Newcastle, 1972; Jumpers, 1973, Design for Living, 1974, Nottingham Playhouse; Bartholomew Fair, Round House, 1978; Greystoke (film), 1984; The Philanthropist, Chichester Fest., 1985; Rude Health, Channel Four, 1985–86; Bartholomew Fair, NT, 1988; Dunrulin', BBC TV, 1990; The Philanthropist, Wyndham's, 1991; Travels With My Aunt, Wyndham's, 1992, Sydney Fest., 1994; Beatrice and Benedict (narrator), Glyndebourne Opera, RFH, 1993; *director:* (with Jonathan Miller) Candide, Glasgow, 1988; The Mikado, D'Oyly Carte tour, 1989; The Bold Fisherman, TVS, 1991. *Publications:* (with Richard Ingrams) Mrs Wilson's Diary, 1964–70 and 1974–76; The Exploding Present, 1971; (with John Fortune) A Melon for Ecstacy, 1971; (with Richard Ingrams) The Dear Bill Letters, 1980–; Anyone for Denis?, 1982; Masterpieces, 1982; Fifty Glorious Years, 1984; Rude Words: a history of the London Library, 1991; Princess Caraboo: her true story, 1994. *Recreations:* walking, talking. *Address:* 1A Scarsdale Villas, W8 6PT. *T:* 0171–937 0534.

WELLS, Prof. John Christopher, PhD; FIL, Professor of Phonetics, since 1988 and Head of Department of Phonetics and Linguistics, since 1990, University College London; *b* 11 March 1939; *s* of Rev. Philip Cuthbert Wells and Winifred May (*née* Peaker). *Educ:* St John's Sch., Leatherhead; Trinity Coll., Cambridge (BA 1960; MA 1964); University Coll., London (MA 1962; PhD 1971). FIL 1982. University College London: Asst Lectr in Phonetics, 1962–65; Lectr, 1965–82; Reader, 1982–88. Sec., Internat. Phonetic Assoc., 1973–86; Pres., World Esperanto Assoc., 1989–; Mem., Esperanto Acad., 1971–. Editor, Jl Internat. Phonetic Assoc., 1971–87. Contribs to radio and TV programmes. *Publications:* Concise Esperanto and English Dictionary, 1969; (with G. Colson) Practical Phonetics, 1971; Jamaican Pronunciation in London, 1973; (jtly) Jen Nia Mondo 1, 1974 (trans. Italian, Icelandic, Swedish, Finnish; (jtly) Jen Nia Mondo 2, 1977; Lingvistikaj aspektoj de Esperanto, 1978, 2nd edn 1989 (trans. Danish; Accents of English (three vols and cassette), 1982; Geiriadur Esperanto/Kimra vortaro, 1985; (pronunciation editor) Universal Dictionary, 1987; (pronunciation editor) Hutchinson Encyclopedia, 8th edn 1988, 9th edn 1990; Longman Pronunciation Dictionary, 1990; articles in learned jls and collective works. *Recreations:* reading, walking, running. *Address:* Department of Phonetics and Linguistics, University College London, Gower Street, WC1E 6BT. *T:* 0171–380 7175; 5 Poplar Road, SW19 3JR. *T:* 0181–542 0302. *Club:* Esperanto.

WELLS, Sir John (Julius), Kt 1984; DL; *b* 30 March 1925; *s* of A. Reginald K. Wells, Marlands, Sampford Arundel, Som; *m* 1948, Lucinda Meath-Baker; two *s* two *d*. *Educ:* Eton; Corpus Christi College, Oxford (MA). War of 1939–45: joined RN as ordinary seaman, 1942; commissioned, 1943, served in submarines until 1946. Contested (C) Smethwick Division, General Election, 1955. MP (C) Maidstone, 1959–87. Chairman: Cons. Party Horticulture Cttee, 1965–71, 1973–87; Horticultural sub-Cttee, Select Cttee on Agriculture, 1968; Parly Waterways Group, 1974–80; Vice-Chm., Cons. Party Agriculture Cttee, 1970; Mem., Mr Speaker's Panel of Chairmen, 1974. Hon. Freeman, Borough of Maidstone, 1979. DL Kent, 1992. Kt Comdr, Order of Civil Merit (Spain), 1972; Comdr, Order of Lion of Finland, 1984. *Recreations:* country pursuits. *Address:* Mere House Barn, Mereworth, Kent ME18 5NB; Acheillie, Rogart, Sutherland IV28 3UB.

WELLS, Malcolm Henry Weston, FCA; Director, Carclo Engineering Group PLC, since 1982 (Deputy Chairman, 1987–93); *b* 26 July 1927; *s* of late Lt-Comdr Geoffrey Weston Wells; *m* 1952, Elizabeth A. Harland, *d* of late Rt Rev. M. H. Harland, DD; one *s* one *d*. *Educ:* Eton Coll. ACA 1951, FCA 1961. Served RNVR, 1945–48. Peat, Marwick Mitchell, 1948–58; Siebe Gorman and Co. Ltd, 1958–63; Charterhouse Japhet, 1963–80 (Chm., 1973–80); Dir, Charterhouse Gp, 1971–80; Chairman: Charterhouse Petroleum PLC, 1977–82; Granville Business Expansion Funds, 1983–93; BWD Securities, 1987–95; London rep., Bank in Liechtenstein, 1981–85; Director: Bank in Liechtenstein (UK) Ltd, 1985–90; Nat. Home Loans Corp., 1989–93. Mem., CAA, 1974–77. Mem. Solicitors' Disciplinary Tribunal, 1975–81. *Recreation:* sailing. *Address:* Holmbush House, Findon, West Sussex BN14 0SY. *T:* Findon (01903) 873630. *Clubs:* City of London, Hurlingham; West Wittering Sailing.

WELLS, Petrie Bowen; *see* Wells, B.

WELLS, Richard Burton, QPM 1987; Chief Constable, South Yorkshire Police, since 1990; *b* 10 Aug. 1940; *s* of Walter Percival Wells and Daphne Joan Wells (*née* Harris); *m* 1970, Patricia Ann Smith; one *s* one *d*. *Educ:* Sir Roger Manwood's Grammar Sch., Sandwich; Priory Sch. for Boys, Shrewsbury; St Peter's Coll., Oxford (Open Exhibnr 1959; BA 1962; MA 1965); principal educn, 28 yrs with the Metropolitan Police. Constable, Bow Street, 1962–66; Sergeant, Notting Hill, 1966–68; Special Course, Police Staff Coll., 1966–67; Inspector, Leman St and Hendon, 1968–73; Chief Inspector, Notting Hill, 1973–76; Supt, Hampstead, 1976–79; Chief Supt, Hammersmith and New Scotland Yard, 1979–82; Sen. Command Course, Police Staff Coll., 1981; Comdt, Hendon Training Sch., 1982–83; Dep. Asst Comr, Dir of Public Affairs, New Scotland Yard, 1983–86; Dep. Asst Commissioner, OC NW London, 1986–90. Chairman: Media Adv. Gp, ACPO, 1992–; Nat. Conf. of Police Press and PROs, 1994–; Sec., Personnel and Trng Cttee, ACPO, 1993–. Sec., Provincial Police Award Selection Cttee, 1990–. Member: Rathbone Corporate Partnership Gp, 1993–; Selection Cttee, Fulbright Fellowship in Police Studies, 1991–; Forensic Psychotherapy Course Adv. Gp, 1990–; Barnsley City Challenge Bd, 1992–; Sheffield Common Purpose Adv. Gp and Council, 1993–. President: Young Enterprise Bd for S Yorks and S Humberside, 1993–; Deepcar Brass Band, 1992–; Patron: S Yorks Br., RLSS, 1990–; Weston Park Hosp. Cancer Care Appeal, 1993–. Pres., St Peter's Soc., Oxford Univ., 1989–; Vice Pres., Police Athletics Assoc. Men's Hockey, 1989–. Mem., St John Council for S and W Yorks, 1990–. Freeman, City of London, 1992. CIMgt (CBIM 1991). Chm. Editl Bd, Policing Today, 1994–. *Publications:* (contrib.) The Roots of Urban Unrest, ed Benyon and Solomos, 1987; (contrib.) Perspectives on Violence, 1994; contrib. Cropwood Conf., and Die Streife Jl. *Recreations:* hockey, walking, painting (watercolour, gloss and emulsion), photography, philately. *Address:* South Yorkshire Police HQ, Snig Hill, Sheffield S3 8LY. *T:* Sheffield (0114) 276 8522.

WELLS, Ven. Roderick John; Archdeacon of Stow, since 1989, and of Lindsey, since 1994; *b* 17 Nov. 1936; *s* of Leonard Arthur and Dorothy Alice Wells; *m* 1969, Alice Louise Scholl; one *s* two *d*. *Educ:* Durham Univ. (BA Hons Theol.); Hull Univ. (MA). Insurance clerk, 1953–55 and 1957–58. RAF, 1955–57 (Radar Mechanic). Asst Master, Chester Choir School, 1958–59; Asst Curate, St Mary at Lambeth, 1965–68, Priest-in-Charge 1968–71; Rector of Skegness, 1971–78; Team Rector, West Grimsby Team Ministry (Parish of Great and Little Coates with Bradley), 1978–89; Area Dean of Grimsby and Cleethorpes, 1983–89. *Recreations:* music (pianist and organist), walking, geology. *Address:* The Vicarage, Hackthorn, Lincoln LN2 3PF. *T:* Welton (01673) 860382.

WELLS, Ronald Alfred, OBE 1965; BSc, FRSC, FIMM; retired; *b* 11 February 1920; *s* of Alfred John Wells and Winifred Jessie (*née* Lambert); *m* 1953, Anne Brebner Lanshe; two *s*. *Educ:* Birkbeck College, London; Newport Technical College. Service with Government Chemist, 1939–40; Royal Naval Scientific Service, 1940–47; Joined Nat. Chemical Laboratory, 1947; Mem. UK Scientific Mission, Washington, 1951–52; Head of Radio-chemical Group, 1956; Head of Div. of Inorganic and Mineral Chemistry, 1963; Deputy Director, Nov. 1963; Director of National Chemical Laboratory, 1964; Dir of Research, TBA Industrial Products Ltd, 1965–70, Jt Man. Dir, 1970–77; Man. Dir, AMFU Ltd (Turner & Newall), 1977–81; Gp Scientist, Turner & Newall, 1981–83; industrial consultant, 1983–87. Director: Salford Univ. Industrial Centre Ltd, 1981–82; Rochdale Private Surgical Unit, 1975–81; non-exec. Dir, Eversave (UK) Ltd, 1984–85. Mem. Council, Royal Inst. Chemistry, 1965–68. *Publications:* numerous contribs to Inorganic Chromatography and Extractive Metallurgy. *Recreations:* gardening, golf, mineralogy. *Address:* Westbury, 19 First Avenue, Charmandean, Worthing, Sussex BN14 9NJ. *T:* Worthing (01903) 233844.

WELLS, Mrs Stanley; *see* Hill, S. E.

WELLS, Prof. Stanley William; Professor of Shakespeare Studies, and Director of the Shakespeare Institute, University of Birmingham, since 1988; General Editor of the Oxford Shakespeare since 1978; *b* 21 May 1930; *s* of Stanley Cecil Wells and Doris Wells; *m* 1975, Susan Elizabeth Hill, *qv*; two *d* (and one *d* decd). *Educ:* Kingston High Sch., Hull; University Coll., London (BA; Fellow, 1995); Shakespeare Inst., Univ. of Birmingham (PhD). Fellow, Shakespeare Inst., 1962–77: Lectr, 1962; Sen. Lectr, 1971; Reader, 1973–77; Hon. Fellow, 1979–88; Head of Shakespeare Dept, OUP, 1978–88. Sen. Res. Fellow, Balliol Coll., Oxford, 1980–88. Consultant in English, Wroxton Coll., 1964–80. Chm., Membership Cttee, 1991–, Collections Cttee, 1992–, RSC; Mem., Exec. Council, 1976–, Exec. (formerly F and GP) Cttee, 1991–, Royal Shakespeare Theatre (Gov., 1974–, Vice Chm. of Govs, 1991–); Dir, Royal Shakespeare Theatre Summer Sch., 1971–. Pres., Shakespeare Club of Stratford-upon-Avon, 1972–73; Vice-Chm., Internat. Shakespeare Assoc., 1991–; Member: Council, Malone Soc., 1967–90; Exec. Cttee, Shakespeare's Birthplace, 1976–78, 1988– (Trustee, 1975–81, 1984–; Chm. Trustees, 1991–); Trustee, Rose Theatre, 1991–; Pres., Wolverhampton Shakespeare Soc., 1992–93. Governor, King Edward VI Grammar Sch. for Boys, Stratford-upon-Avon, 1973–77. Guest lectr, British and overseas univs; Lectures: British Acad. Annual Shakespeare, 1987; Hilda Hulme Meml, 1987; first annual Globe, 1990; Melchiori, Rome, 1991. Hon. DLitt Furman Univ., SC, 1978. Walcott Award, LA, 1995. Associate Editor, New Penguin Shakespeare, 1967–77; Editor, Shakespeare Survey, 1980–. *Publications:* (ed) Thomas Nashe, Selected Writings, 1964; (ed, New Penguin Shakespeare): A Midsummer Night's Dream, 1967, Richard II, 1969, The Comedy of Errors, 1972; Shakespeare, A Reading Guide, 1969 (2nd edn 1970); Literature and Drama, 1970; (ed, Select Bibliographical Guides): Shakespeare, 1973 (new edn 1990), English Drama excluding Shakespeare, 1975; Royal Shakespeare, 1977, 2nd edn 1978; (compiled) Nineteenth-Century Shakespeare Burlesques (5 vols), 1977; Shakespeare: an illustrated dictionary, 1978, 2nd edn 1985; Shakespeare: the writer and his work, 1978; (ed with R. L. Smallwood) Thomas Dekker, The Shoemaker's Holiday, 1979; (with Gary Taylor) Modernizing Shakespeare's Spelling, with three studies in the text of Henry V, 1979; Re-Editing Shakespeare for the Modern Reader, 1984; (ed) Shakespeare's Sonnets, 1985; (ed with Gary Taylor *et al*) The Complete Oxford Shakespeare, 1986; (ed) The Cambridge Companion to Shakespeare Studies, 1986; (with Gary Taylor *et al*) William Shakespeare: a textual companion, 1987; An Oxford Anthology of Shakespeare, 1987; Shakespeare: a dramatic life, 1994; contrib. Shak. Survey, Shak. Qly, Shak. Jahrbuch, Theatre Notebook, Stratford-upon-Avon Studies, TLS, etc. *Recreations:* music, theatre, the countryside. *Address:* Longmoor Farmhouse, Ebrington, Glos GL55 6NW. *T:* Paxford (01386) 593352.

WELLS, Thomas Leonard; President, TLW Consulting, since 1993; *b* 2 May 1930; *s* of Leonard Wells and Lilian May Butler; *m* 1954, Audrey Alice Richardson; one *s* two *d*. *Educ:* University of Toronto. Advertising Manager: Canadian Hosp. Jl, 1951–61; Canadian Med. Assoc. Jl, 1961–67; Chm., Scarborough, Ont Bd of Educn, 1961, 1962; MLA

(Progressive C) for Scarborough N, Ontario, 1963–85; Minister: without Portfolio (responsible for Youth Affairs), 1966–69; of Health, 1969–71; of Social and Family Services, 1971–72; of Education, 1972–78; of Intergovtl Affairs, 1978–85; Govt House Leader, Ont, 1980–85; Agent Gen. for Ont in UK, 1985–91; Comr, Expo 98 Canada Corp., 1991–92. Vice Chm., Bd, N York Performing Arts Centre; Mem., Bd of Dirs, Metro Toronto Convention Centre. Hon. Fellow, Ont Teachers' Fedn, 1976. Hon. DLitt Univ. of Windsor, Ont, 1985. Freeman, City of London, 1985; Mem., Guild of Freemen of the City of London, 1987–. CLJ 1984. Confederation Medal, Canada, 1967; Silver Jubilee Medal, 1977; Confederation 125 Medal, 1992. *Recreations:* photography, walking, theatre, cinema. *Address:* 808–65 Spring Garden Avenue, Willowdale, Ont M2N 6H9, Canada. *T:* (416) 2228914. *Clubs:* Royal Over-Seas League, Commonwealth Trust; Albany, Empire (Toronto).

WELLS, Thomas Umfrey, MA; Headmaster, Wanganui Collegiate School, New Zealand, 1960–80; *b* 6 Feb. 1927; *s* of Athol Umfrey and Gladys Colebrook Wells; *m* 1953, Valerie Esther Brewis; two *s* one *d*. *Educ:* King's College, Auckland, New Zealand; Auckland University (BA); (Orford Studentship to) King's College, Cambridge. BA 1951; MA 1954. Assistant Master, Clifton College, 1952–60 (Senior English Master, 1957–60). Pres., NZ Assoc. of Heads of Independent Secondary Schs, 1972–75. Member: Univs Entrance Bd, 1972–80; HMC; Tongariro Forest Park Promotion Cttee, 1984–87; Taumarunui and Dist Promotion and Develt Council, 1985–; Executive Member: CKC Visual Arts Trust, 1986– (Chm., 1986–91); Wanganui River Floats Coalition, 1987–; Taumarunui Community Arts Council, 1987–; Trustee: Avonlea, 1984–; Outdoor Pursuits Centre, Tawhiti-kuri, 1985–90; Taumarunui Museum Trust, 1987–. Synodsman, 1985–, Mem. Standing Cttee, 1989–, Waikato Dio.; Mem. of Vestry, Taumarunui Anglican Church, 1981–. Pres., Taumarunui Cricket Club Assoc., 1984–86, Patron, 1986–; Mem., Rotary Club of Wanganui, 1961–80 (Pres., 1979–80), of Taumarunui, 1980–95, of Te Awamutu, 1995–; Chm., Dist 993 Rotaract Cttee, 1983–85. *Recreations:* reading, theatre, cricket (NZU Blue, 1948–49 (Capt., 1949); Cambridge Blue, 1950), tennis, fishing; formerly Rugby football (Cambridge Blue, 1951; England Final Trial, 1951; Trial, 1954; Bristol, 1952–56; Glos, 1953–56). *Address:* c/o Windsor Court Rest Home, Sandes Street, Ohaupo, New Zealand. *Clubs:* MCC; Hawks (Cambridge); Wanganui, Rotary of Taumarunui (NZ).

WELLS, William Henry Weston, FRICS; Chairman, Chesterton, London, since 1984 (Partner, since 1965); Chairman, South Thames Regional Health Authority, since 1994; *b* 3 May 1940; *s* of Sir Henry Wells, CBE, and Lady Wells; *m* 1966, Penelope Jean Broadbent; two *s* (and one *s* decd). *Educ:* Radley Coll.; Magdalene Coll., Cambridge (BA). Joined Chestertons, 1959; Chairman: Land and House Property Corporation, 1977; Frincon Holdings Ltd, 1977–87. Director: London Life Assoc., 1984–; AMP UK, 1994–; Pearl Assurance, 1994–; Norwich and Peterborough Bldg Soc., 1994–. Dir, NHS Policy Bd, 1994–; Mem. Council, NHS Trust Fedn, 1991–93 (Vice Chm., 1992–93). Chairman: Hampstead HA, 1982–90; Royal Free Hampstead NHS Trust, 1990–94. Mem., Gen. Council and Management Cttee, King Edward's Hosp. Fund for London, 1995–. Member: Board of Governors, Royal Free Hosp., 1968–74; Camden and Islington AHA, 1974–82; Chm., Special Trustees of Royal Free Hosp., 1979–; Member, Council: Royal Free Hosp. Sch. of Medicine, 1977–91; UMDS, Guy's and St Thomas' Hosps, 1994–; Mem., Delegacy, King's Coll. Sch. of Medicine and Dentistry, 1995–. Hon. Treasurer: RCN, 1988–; Nat. Assoc. of Leagues of Hosp. Friends, 1992–. *Recreations:* family, philately, gardening. *Club:* Boodle's.

WELMAN, Douglas Pole, CBE 1966; *b* 22 June 1902; *s* of late Col Arthur Pole Welman and late Lady Scott; *m* 1st, 1929, Denise, *d* of Charles Steers Peel; one *d*; 2nd, 1946, Betty Marjorie, *d* of late Henry Huth. *Educ:* Tonbridge Sch.; Faraday House Engineering Coll. DFH, CEng, FIMechE, FIEE, CIGasE. Asst Engr, Preece Cardew & Ryder, 1926–28; Resident Engr, Grenada, 1928–29, Grenada and St Vincent, 1930; Chief Engr, Windward Islands, 1930–32; consulting practice, London, 1932–37; Man. Dir of Foster, Yates and Thom Limited, Heavy Precision Engineers, 1937–50; Chairman of number of wartime committees in Lancashire including Armaments Production, Emergency Services Organisation, and Ministry of Production; went to Ministry of Aircraft Production at request of Minister as Director of Engine Production, 1942; Deputy Director-General, 1943; Control of Directorate-Gen. including Propeller and Accessory Production, 1944; Part Time Member North Western Gas Board, 1949, Chairman, 1950–64; Chairman, Southern Gas Board, 1964–67; Member, Gas Council, 1950–67; Chm. and Man. Dir, Allspeeds Holdings Ltd, 1967–72. Member, Ct of Govs, Univ. of Manchester Inst. of Sci. and Techn., 1956–64, 1968–72 (Mem. Coun., 1960–64, 1968–72). CStJ 1968 (OStJ 1964). FRSA. *Publications:* articles and papers on company management. *Recreations:* sailing, fishing. *Address:* 11 St Michael's Gardens, St Cross, Winchester SO23 9JD. *T:* Winchester (01962) 868091. *Club:* Royal Thames Yacht.

WELSBY, John Kay, CBE 1990; Chairman, since 1995, Chief Executive, since 1990, British Railways Board (Board Member, since 1987); *b* 26 May 1938; *s* of late Samuel and Sarah Ellen Welsby; *m* 1964, Jill Carole Richards; one *s* one *d*. *Educ:* Heywood Grammar Sch.; Univ. of Exeter (BA); Univ. of London (MSc). FCIT 1990. Govt Economic Service, 1966–81; British Railways Board: Dir, Provincial Services, 1982–84; Managing Dir, Procurement, 1985–87. Mem., Business Adv. Council, Northwestern Univ., Evanston, Ill. Trustee, Industry in Educn. CIMgt 1991. Freeman, City of London, 1992; Liveryman, Carmen's Co., 1992. *Publications:* articles on economic matters. *Recreations:* walking, music, swimming. *Address:* British Railways Board, Euston House, 24 Eversholt Street, NW1 1DZ.

WELSBY, Rev. Canon Paul Antony; Canon Residentiary and Vice-Dean of Rochester Cathedral, 1966–88, Canon Emeritus since 1988; Chaplain to the Queen, 1980–90; *b* 18 Aug. 1920; *m* 1948, Cynthia Mary Hosmer; one *d*. *Educ:* Alcester Grammar Sch.; University Coll., Durham (MA); Lincoln Theological Coll.; Univ. of Sheffield (PhD). Curate at Boxley, Kent, 1944–47; Curate, St Mary-le-Tower, Ipswich, 1947–52; Rector of Copdock with Washbrook, 1952–66; Rural Dean of Samford, 1964–66. Director of Post-Ordination Training for Dio. of Rochester, 1966–88; Examining Chaplain to Bp of Rochester, 1966–88, Personal Chaplain 1988–90. Member, Church Assembly, 1964–70, General Synod, 1970–80; Chm., House of Clergy at Gen. Synod and Prolocutor of Convocation of Canterbury, 1974–80. *Publications:* A Modern Catechism, 1956; Lancelot Andrewes, 1958; How the Church of England Works, 1960, new edn, 1985; The Unwanted Archbishop, 1962; The Bond of Church and State, 1962; Sermons and Society, 1970; A History of the Church of England 1945–80, 1984; contrib. Theology. *Recreations:* reading detective fiction, visiting National Trust properties. *Address:* 20 Knights Ridge, Pembury, Kent TN2 4HP. *T:* Pembury (01892) 823053.

WELSH, Andrew Paton; MP (SNP) Angus East, since 1987; *b* 19 April 1944; *s* of William and Agnes Welsh; *m* 1971, Sheena Margaret Cannon; one *d*. *Educ:* Univ. of Glasgow. MA (Hons) History and Politics; DipEd, 1980. Teacher of History, 1972–74; Lectr in Public Admin and Economics, Dundee Coll. of Commerce, 1979–83; Sen. Lectr in Business and Admin. Studies, Angus Technical Coll., 1983–87. MP (SNP) South Angus, Oct. 1974–1979; SNP Parly Chief Whip, 1978–79, 1987–; SNP Spokesman on: Housing, 1974–78; Self Employed Affairs and Small Businesses, 1975–79, 1987–; Agriculture, 1976–79, 1987–; Local Govt, 1987–; SNP Exec. Vice Chm. for Admin, 1979–87; SNP Vice-Pres., 1987–. Contested (SNP) Angus E, 1983. Mem., Angus District Council, 1984–87; Provost of Angus, 1984–87. *Recreations:* music, horse riding, languages. *Address:* Community Centre, Marketgate, Arbroath, Angus DD11 1HR. *T:* Arbroath (01241) 874522. *Club:* Glasgow University Union.

WELSH, Prof. Dominic; *see* Welsh, J. A. D.

WELSH, Frank Reeson; writer; Director, Grindlays Bank, 1971–85; *b* 16 Aug. 1931; *s* of F. C. Welsh and D. M. Welsh; *m* 1954, Agnes Cowley; two *s* two *d*. *Educ:* Gateshead and Blaydon Grammar Schools; Magdalene Coll., Cambridge (schol.; MA). With John Lewis Partnership, 1954–1958; CAS Group, 1958–64; Man. Dir, William Brandt's Sons & Co. Ltd, 1965–72; Chairman: Hadfields Ltd, 1967–79; Jensen Motors Ltd, 1968–72; Cox & Kings, 1972–76; Dir, Henry Ansbacher & Co., 1976–82. Member: British Waterways Board, 1975–81; Gen. Adv. Council, IBA, 1976–80; Royal Commn on Nat. Health Service, 1976–79; Health Educn Council, 1978–80. Dir, Trireme Trust, 1983–. Vis. Lectr and Alcoa Schol., Graduate Sch. of Business Studies, Univ. of Tennessee, Knoxville, 1979–85. CIMgt. *Publications:* The Profit of the State, 1982; (contrib.) Judging People, 1982; The Afflicted State, 1983; First Blood, 1985; (with George Ridley) Bend'Or, Duke of Westminster, 1985; Uneasy City, 1986; Building the Trireme, 1988; Companion Guide to the Lake District, 1989; Hong Kong: a history (US edn as A Borrowed Place), 1993. *Recreation:* sailing. *Clubs:* United Oxford & Cambridge University, Savile.

WELSH, Prof. (James Anthony) Dominic, DPhil; Professor of Mathematics, Oxford University, since 1992; Fellow of Merton College, Oxford, since 1966; *b* 29 Aug. 1938; *s* of late James Welsh and Teresa Welsh (*née* O'Callaghan); *m* 1966, Bridget Elizabeth Pratt; two *s* (and one *s* decd). *Educ:* Bishop Gore Grammar Sch., Swansea; Merton Coll., Oxford (MA DPhil); Carnegie Mellon Univ. (Fulbright Scholar). Bell Telephone Labs, Murray Hill, 1961; Oxford University: Jun. Lectr, Mathematical Inst., 1963–66; Tutor in Maths, Merton Coll., 1966–90; Reader in Maths, 1990–92. Vis. appts, Univs of Michigan, Waterloo, Calgary, Stockholm, North Carolina; John von Neumann Prof., Univ. of Bonn, 1990–91. Chm., British Combinatorial Cttee, 1983–87. *Publications:* (ed) Combinatorial Mathematics and its Applications, 1971; (ed jtly) Combinatorics, 1973; Matroid Theory, 1976; (with G. R. Grimmett) Probability: an introduction, 1986; Codes and Cryptography, 1988, German edn, 1991; (ed jtly) Disorder in Physical Systems, 1990; Complexity: knots, colourings and counting, 1993; articles in math. jls. *Recreations:* real tennis, rugby, walking. *Address:* Merton College, Oxford OX1 4JD; South Lodge, Rose Lane, Oxford OX1 4DT. *T:* Oxford (01865) 247449.

WELSH, Michael Collins; *b* 23 Nov. 1926; *s* of Danny and Winnie Welsh; *m* 1950, Brenda Nicholson; two *s*. *Educ:* Sheffield Univ. (Dept of Extramural Studies, Day Release Course, three years); Ruskin Coll., Oxford. Miner from age of 14 years. Member, Doncaster Local Authority, 1962–69. MP (Lab) Don Valley, 1979–83, Doncaster North, 1983–92. *Club:* Carcroft Village Workingmen's (Carcroft, near Doncaster).

WELSH, Michael John; Chairman, Chorley and South Ribble NHS Trust; Chief Executive, Action Centre for Europe Ltd; *b* 22 May 1942; *s* of Comdr David Welsh, RN, and Una Mary (*née* Willmore); *m* 1963, Jennifer Caroline Pollitt; one *s* one *d*. *Educ:* Dover Coll.; Lincoln Coll., Oxford (BA (Hons) Jurisprudence). Proprietors of Hays Wharf Ltd, 1963–69; Levi Strauss & Co. Europe Ltd, 1969–79 (Dir of Market Development, 1976). MEP (C) Lancashire Central, 1979–94; contested (C) Lancashire Central, Eur. Parly elecns, 1994; Chm., Cttee for Social Affairs and Employment, Eur. Parlt, 1984–87. Chm., Positive Europe Gp, 1988–94. Res. Associate, Univ. of Central Lancs. *Recreations:* amateur drama, sailing, rough walking. *Address:* Watercrook, 181 Town Lane, Whittle le Woods, Chorley, Lancs PR6 8AG. *T:* Chorley (012572) 76992. *Club:* Carlton.

WELSH, Maj.-Gen. Peter Miles, OBE 1983; MC 1967; President, Regular Commissions Board, 1983–85; *b* 23 Dec. 1930; *s* of William Miles Moss O'Donnel Welsh and Mary Edith Margaret Gertrude Louise Welsh (*née* Hearn); *m* 1974, June Patricia McCausland (*née* Macadam); two step *s* one step *d*. *Educ:* Winchester College; RMA Sandhurst. Commissioned, KRRC, 1951; Kenya Regt, 1958–60; student, Staff Coll., 1961; Malaya and Borneo, 1965–66; Royal Green Jackets, 1966; JSSC, 1967; Instructor, Staff Coll., 1968–71; CO 2 RGJ, 1971–73; Comd 5 Inf. Bde, 1974–76; RCDS, 1977; HQ BAOR, 1978–80; Brig., Light Div., 1980–83. *Recreations:* shooting, fishing, vegetable gardening, cooking, golf. *Clubs:* MCC, Free Foresters, I Zingari, Jesters; Berks Golf.

WELTY, Eudora; Gold Medal for the Novel, Amer. Acad. and Inst. of Arts and Letters, 1972; National Medal for Literature, 1980; Presidential Medal of Freedom, 1980. *Publications:* A Curtain of Green, 1943; The Robber Bridegroom, 1944; The Wide Net, 1945; Delta Wedding, 1947; Golden Apples, 1950; The Ponder Heart, 1954; The Bride of Innisfallen, 1955; The Shoe Bird, 1964; Losing Battles, US 1970, UK 1982; One Time, One Place, 1971; The Optimist's Daughter, 1972 (Pulitzer Prize, 1973); The Eye of the Story, 1979; The Collected Stories of Eudora Welty, 1980; One Writer's Beginnings, 1984; Eudora Welty Photographs, 1989; A Writer's Eye: collected book reviews, 1994; Monuments to Interruption: collected book reviews, 1994. *Address:* 1119 Pinehurst Street, Jackson, MS 39202–1812, USA.

WEMYSS, 12th Earl of *cr* 1633, **AND MARCH,** 8th Earl of *cr* 1697; **Francis David Charteris,** KT 1966; Lord Wemyss of Elcho, 1628; Lord Elcho and Methil, 1633; Viscount Peebles, Baron Douglas of Neidpath, Lyne and Munard, 1697; Baron Wemyss of Wemyss (UK), 1821; President, The National Trust for Scotland, 1967–91, now President Emeritus (Chairman of Council, 1946–69); Lord Clerk Register of Scotland and Keeper of the Signet, since 1974; *b* 19 Jan. 1912; *s* of late Lord Elcho (killed in action, 1916) and Lady Violet Manners (she *m* 2nd, 1921, Guy Holford Benson (decd), and *d* 1971), 2nd *d* of 8th Duke of Rutland; *S* grandfather, 1937; *m* 1st, 1940, Mavis Lynette Gordon, BA (*d* 1988), *er d* of late E. E. Murray, Hermanus, Cape Province; one *s* one *d* (and one *s* and one *d* decd); 2nd, 1995, Shelagh Kathleen Kennedy, *d* of George Ernest Thrift, Vancouver. *Educ:* Eton; Balliol College, Oxford. Assistant District Commissioner, Basutoland, 1937–44. Served with Basuto Troops in Middle East, 1941–44. Lieut, Queen's Body Guard for Scotland, Royal Company of Archers; Lord High Comr to Gen. Assembly of Church of Scotland, 1959, 1960, 1977; Chairman: Scottish Cttee, Marie Curie Meml Foundn, 1952–86; Royal Commn on Ancient and Historical Monuments, Scotland, 1949–84; Scottish Churches Council, 1964–71; Hon. Pres., The Thistle Foundn; Mem., Central Cttee, WCC, 1961–75; Mem., Royal Commn on Historical Manuscripts, 1975–85. Consultant, Wemyss and March Estates Management Co. Ltd; formerly Director: Standard Life Assurance Co. Ltd; Scottish Television Ltd. Lord-Lieut, E Lothian, 1967–87. Hon. LLD St Andrews, 1953; DUniv Edinburgh, 1983. *Heir:* *s* Lord Neidpath, *qv*. *Address:* Gosford House, Longniddry, East Lothian EH32 0PX. *Club:* New (Edinburgh).

See also D. H. Benson, Baron Charteris of Amisfield.

WEMYSS, Rear-Adm. Martin La Touche, CB 1981; *b* 5 Dec. 1927; *s* of late Comdr David Edward Gillespie Wemyss, DSO, DSC, RN, and Edith Mary Digges La Touche; *m* 1st, 1951, Ann Hall (marr. diss. 1973); one *s* one *d*; 2nd, 1973, Elizabeth Loveday

Alexander; one *s* one *d*. *Educ:* Shrewsbury School. CO HMS Sentinel, 1956–57; Naval Intell. Div., 1957–59; CO HMS Alliance, 1959–60; CO Commanding Officers' Qualifying Course, 1961–63; Naval Staff, 1963–65; CO HMS Cleopatra, 1965–67; Naval Asst to First Sea Lord, 1967–70; CO 3rd Submarine Sqdn, 1970–73; CO HMS Norfolk, 1973–74; Dir of Naval Warfare, 1974–76; Rear-Adm., 1977; Flag Officer, Second Flotilla, 1977–78; Asst Chief of Naval Staff (Ops), 1979–81. Clerk to Brewers' Co., 1981–91. *Recreations:* sailing, shooting. *Address:* The Old Post House, Emberton, near Olney, Bucks MK46 5BX. *T:* Bedford (01234) 713838. *Clubs:* White's, Army and Navy.

WEN, Eric Lewis; freelance writer and music producer; Director, Biddulph Recordings, since 1989; *b* 18 May 1953; *s* of Adam and Mimi Wen; *m* 1989, Louise Anne, *d* of Sir Brian Barder, *qv*; two *d*. *Educ:* Columbia Univ. (BA); Yale Univ. (MPhil); Cambridge Univ. Lecturer: Guildhall Sch. of Music, 1978–84; Goldsmiths' Coll., Univ. of London, 1980–84; Mannes Coll. of Music, NY, 1984–86; Editor: The Strad, 1986–89; The Musical Times, 1988–90. *Publications:* (contrib.) Schenker Studies, 1989; (contrib.) Trends in Schenkerian Research, 1990; (ed) The Fritz Kreisler Collection, 1990; (contrib.) Cambridge Companion to the Violin, 1992; (ed) The Heifetz Collection, 1995; contrib. various music jls. *Recreations:* music, chess, cooking. *Address:* 18 Beech Croft Road, Summertown, Oxford OX2 7AZ. *T:* Oxford (01865) 512847.

WENBAN-SMITH, Nigel; *see* Wenban-Smith, W. N.

WENBAN-SMITH, William, CMG 1960; CBE 1957; *b* 8 June 1908; *o s* of late Frederick Wenban-Smith, Worthing; *m* 1935, Ruth Orme, *e d* of late S. B. B. McElderry, CMG; three *s* two *d*. *Educ:* Bradfield; King's Coll., Cambridge (MA). Colonial Administrative Service, 1931–61: Cadet, Zanzibar, 1931; Administrative Officer, Grade II, 1933; Asst DO, Tanganyika, 1935; DO, 1943; Sen. DO, 1951 (acted on various occasions as Resident Magistrate, Comr for Co-op. Development, Provincial Comr, and Sec. for Finance); Dir of Establishments, 1953; Minister for Social Services, 1958; Minister for Education and Labour, 1959–61. Chairman, Public Service Commission and Speaker, Legislative Council, Nyasaland, 1961–63. HM Diplomatic Service, Kuala Lumpur, 1964–69. *Publication:* Walks in the New Forest, 1975. *Recreation:* music. *Address:* Lane End, School Lane, Lymington, Hants SO41 9EJ. *T:* Lymington (01590) 679343. *Club:* Commonwealth Trust.
See also W. N. Wenban-Smith.

WENBAN-SMITH, (William) Nigel, CMG 1991; HM Diplomatic Service, retired; Secretary General, Commonwealth Magistrates' and Judges' Association, 1993–94; *b* 1 Sept. 1936; *s* of William Wenban-Smith, *qv*; *m* 1st, 1961, Charlotte Chapman-Andrews (marr. diss 1975; she *m* 2nd, Sir Peter Leslie, *qv*); two *s* two *d*; 2nd, 1976, Charlotte Susanna Rycroft (*d* 1990); two *s*; 3rd, 1993, Frances Catharine Barlow; two step *d*. *Educ:* King's Sch., Canterbury; King's Coll., Cambridge (BA). National Service, RN. Plebiscite Supervisory Officer, Southern Cameroons, 1960–61; Asst Principal, CRO, 1961–65 (Private Sec. to Parly Under Sec., 1963–64); Second Sec., Leopoldville, 1965–67; First Sec. and (1968) Head of Chancery, Kampala, 1967–70; FCO, 1970–74; Dublin, 1975; Commercial Sec., Brussels, 1976–78; Commercial Counsellor, Brussels, 1978–80; on loan to Cabinet Office, 1980–82; Hd of E Africa Dept and Comr, British Indian Ocean Territory, FCO, 1982–85; National Defence Coll. of Canada, 1985–86; Deputy High Comr, Ottawa, 1986–89; High Comr, Malaŵi, 1990–93. *Recreations:* walking, gardening. *Address:* Hawkley Hurst, near Liss, Hants GU33 6NS.

WENDT, Henry, Hon. CBE 1995; Chairman: SmithKline Beecham, 1989–94; The Finisterre Fund; *b* 19 July 1933; *s* of Henry Wendt and Rachel L. (*née* Wood); *m* 1956, Holly Peterson; one *s* one *d*. *Educ:* Princeton Univ. (AB 1955). Joined SmithKline & French Labs, 1955: various positions in Internat. Div.; Pres., 1976–82; Chief Exec. Officer, 1982–87; Chm., 1987–89 (merger of SmithKline Beckman and Beecham, 1989). Director: Arjo Wiggins Appleton plc, 1990–92; Allergan Inc., 1989–; Beckman Instruments Inc., 1989–; Atlantic Richfield Co., 1987–. Trustee: Amer. Enterprises Inst.; Philadelphia Museum of Art; HFT Develt Trust. Order of the Rising Sun with Gold and Silver Star (Japan), 1994. *Publication:* Global Embrace, 1993. *Recreations:* sailing, flyfishing, tennis, viticulture. *Address:* Quivira Vineyard, 4900 West Dry Creek Road, Healdsburg, CA 95448, USA. *Clubs:* Reform, Flyfishers'; Links (NYC).

WENDT, Robin Glover; DL; Secretary, Association of County Councils, since 1989; *b* 7 Jan. 1941; *er s* of late William Romilly Wendt and Doris May (*née* Glover), Preston, Lancs; *m* 1965, Prudence Ann Dalby; two *d*. *Educ:* Hutton GS, Preston; Wadham Coll., Oxford Univ. (BA 1962; MA 1992). Asst Principal 1962, Principal 1966, Min. of Pensions and Nat. Insurance; Principal Private Sec. to Sec. of State for Social Services, 1970; Asst Sec., DHSS, 1972; Dep. Sec., 1975, Chief Exec., 1979–89, Cheshire CC; Clerk of Cheshire Lieutenancy, 1979–90. Member: Social Security Adv. Cttee, 1982–; PCFC, 1989–93; Council, RIPA, 1989–92; Council for Charitable Support, 1991–; DoH Wider Health Working Gp, 1991–; Adv. Bd, Fire Service Coll., 1992–; Citizenship Foundn Adv. Council, 1993–; Joseph Rowntree Foundn Income and Wealth Inquiry, 1993–95. Trustee, Indep. Living Funds, 1993–. DL Cheshire, 1990. *Publications:* various articles and reviews on public service issues. *Recreations:* music, swimming, following sport, travel. *Address:* 28 Church Lane, Upton, Chester CH2 1DJ; Flat 6, 5 Old Pye Street, SW1P 2LD.

WENHAM, Brian George; media consultant and journalist; *b* 9 Feb. 1937; *s* of late George Frederick Wenham and of Harriet Wenham, London; *m* 1966, Elisabeth Downing, *d* of Keith and Margery Woolley; two *d*. *Educ:* Royal Masonic Sch., Bushey; St John's Coll., Oxon. Television journalist, Independent Television News, 1962–69; Editor, Panorama, BBC, 1969–71; Head of Current Affairs Gp, 1971–78; Controller, BBC 2, 1978–82; Dir of Programmes, BBC TV, 1983–85; Man. Dir, BBC Radio, 1985–87; Chm, UK Radio Developments, 1993–; Director: Renaissance Films, 1990–; Carlton Television, 1991–; English Touring Opera, 1991–. FRTS 1986. *Publication:* (ed) The Third Age of Broadcasting, 1982. *Address:* Red Cottage, Wey Road, Weybridge, Surrey KT13 8HW. *T:* Weybridge (01932) 843313.

WENNER, Michael Alfred; HM Diplomatic Service, retired; President, Wenner Communications Co. (formerly Wenner Trading Co.), since 1982; *b* 17 March 1921; *s* of Alfred E. Wenner and of Simone Roussel; *m* 1st, 1950, Gunilla Cecilia Ståhle (*d* 1986), *d* of Envoyé Nils K. Ståhle, CBE, and Birgit Olsson; four *s*; 2nd, 1990, Holly (Raven) Adrianne Johnson, *d* of Adrian W. Johnson and Ophelia A. Matley. *Educ:* Stonyhurst; Oriel College, Oxford (Scholar). Served E Yorks Regt, 1940; Lancs Fusiliers and 151 Parachute Bn, India, 1941–42; 156 Bn, N Africa, 1943; No 9 Commando, Italy and Greece, 1944–45. Entered HM Foreign Service, 1947; 3rd Sec., Stockholm, 1948–51; 2nd Sec., Washington, 1951–53; Foreign Office, 1953–55; 1st Sec., Tel Aviv, 1956–59; Head of Chancery, La Paz, 1959–61, and at Vienna, 1961–63; Inspector of Diplomatic Establishments, 1964–67; Ambassador to El Salvador, 1967–70. Commercial Advr, Consulate-Gen. of Switzerland in Houston, 1974–91. Hon. Mem., Consular Corps of Houston, 1992–. *Publications:* Advances in Controlled Droplet Application, Agrichemical Age, 1979; So It Was (memoirs), 1993; Telephone Tales, 1996. *Recreations:* fly-fishing, old maps, choral singing, elocution. *Address:* 7917 Westwood Drive, Houston, TX 77055, USA. *T* and *Fax:* (713) 4659169; Laythams Farm, Slaidburn, Clitheroe, Lancs BB7 3AJ. *T:* Slaidburn (012006) 446677.

WENT, David; Chief Executive, Coutts & Co. Group, since 1994; *b* 25 March 1947; *s* of Arthur Edward James Went and Phyllis (*née* Howell); *m* 1972, Mary Christine Milligan; one *s* one *d*. *Educ:* High Sch., Dublin; Trinity Coll., Dublin (BA Mod; LLB). Called to the Bar, King's Inns, Dublin, 1970. Graduate Trainee, Citibank, Dublin, 1970; Gen. Manager, Citibank, Jeddah, 1975–76; Dir 1976, Chief Exec. 1982, Ulster Investment Bank; Ulster Bank: Dep. Chief Exec., 1987; Chief Exec., 1988–94. Chm., NI Bankers' Assoc., 1988–89; President: Irish Bankers' Fedn, 1991–92; Inst. of Bankers in Ireland, 1993–94. *Recreations:* tennis, reading, theatre. *Address:* Coutts & Co. Group, 27 Bush Lane, Cannon Street, EC4R 0AA. *T:* 0171–203 4770. *Clubs:* Kildare Street and University (Dublin); Fitzwilliam Lawn Tennis; Royal Belfast Golf; Royal North of Ireland Yacht.

WENT, Rt Rev. John Stewart; *see* Tewkesbury, Bishop Suffragan of.

WENTWORTH, Maurice Frank Gerard, CMG 1957; OBE 1946; *b* 5 Nov. 1908; *s* of F. B. Wentworth, Finchley, N3; *m* 1962, Belinda Margaret, *d* of late B. S. Tatham and Mrs Tatham, Mickleham, Surrey; one *s* one *d*. *Educ:* Haileybury; University Coll., London (BA). Military Service, 1939–46, Lieutenant-Colonel. Gold Coast: Inspector of Schools, 1930; Sen. Education Officer, 1945; Principal, Teacher Training Coll., Tamale, 1946; Administrative Officer Class I, 1951; Permanent Secretary, 1953; Establishment Secretary, 1954–57 (Ghana Civil Service); Chairman: Public Service Commission: Sierra Leone, 1958–61; E African High Commn, 1961–64; Appointments Officer, ODM, 1964–73. *Address:* Quarry Hill, Todber, Sturminster Newton, Dorset DT10 1HY.

WENTWORTH, Stephen; Under Secretary and Fisheries Secretary, Ministry of Agriculture, Fisheries and Food, since 1993; *b* 23 Aug. 1943; *s* of Ronald Wentworth, OBE and Elizabeth Mary Wentworth (*née* Collins); *m* 1970, Katharine Laura Hopkinson; three *d*. *Educ:* King's College Sch., Wimbledon; Merton Coll., Oxford (MA, MSc). Ministry of Agriculture, Fisheries and Food, 1967–; seconded: to CSSB, 1974; to FCO, as First Sec., UK Perm. Repn to EEC, Brussels, 1976; Head of Beef Div., 1978; to Cabinet Office, 1980; Head of: Milk Div., 1982; European Communities Div., 1985; Under-Sec. and Head of Meat Gp, 1986; Head of Livestock Products Gp, 1989; Head of EC and External Trade Policy Gp, 1991. *Address:* Ministry of Agriculture, Fisheries and Food, Nobel House, Smith Square, SW1P 3JR.

WERNER, Alfred Emil Anthony; Chairman, Pacific Regional Conservation Center, 1975–82, retired; *b* 18 June 1911; *o s* of late Professor Emil Alphonse Werner, Dublin; *m* 1939, Marion Jane Davies; two *d*. *Educ:* St Gerard's School, Bray; Trinity College, Dublin. MSc (Dublin Univ.) and ARIC 1936; MA (Dublin) and DPhil (Univ. of Freiburg im Breisgau) 1937; Hon. ScD (Dublin) 1971. Lecturer in Chemistry, TCD, 1937; Reader in Organic Chemistry, TCD, 1946; Research Chemist, National Gallery, 1948; Principal Scientific Officer, British Museum Research Laboratory, 1954, Keeper, 1959–75. Prof. of Chemistry, Royal Acad., 1962–75. FSA 1958; FMA 1959 (President, 1967); MRIA 1963. Pres., International Institute for the Conservation of Artistic and Historic Works, 1971 (Hon. Treasurer, 1962). *Publications:* The Scientific Examination of Paintings, 1952; (with H. Roosen-Runge) Codex Lindisfarnensis, Part V, 1961; (with H. J. Plenderleith) The Conservation of Antiquities and Works of Art, 1972; Dufy, 1987; articles in scientific and museum journals. *Recreations:* chess, travelling. *Address:* Smalls Farm, Groton, Sudbury, Suffolk CO10 5EG. *T:* Boxford (01787) 210231; 11/73 South Street, Bellerive, Tas 7018, Australia. *T:* (02) 446959. *Clubs:* Athenæum; Tasmanian (Hobart).

WERNER, Ronald Louis, AM 1980; MSc, PhD; company director; President, New South Wales Institute of Technology, 1974–86; Emeritus Professor, University of Technology, Sydney, since 1988; *b* 12 Sept. 1924; *s* of Frank Werner and Olive Maude Werner; *m* 1948, Valerie Irene (*née* Bean); two *s* one *d*. *Educ:* Univ. of New South Wales (BSc (1st Cl. Hons; Univ. Medal); MSc, PhD). FRACI. Sen. Lectr, 1954–60, Associate Prof., 1961–67, Head of Dept of Phys. Chemistry, 1964–67, Univ. of New South Wales; Dep. Dir, 1967–68, Director, 1968–73, NSW Inst. of Technology. Chm., NSW Advanced Educn Bd, 1969–71; Trustee, Mus. of Applied Arts and Scis, 1973–86 (Pres., Bd of Trustees, 1976–84); Chairman: Conf. of Dirs of Central Insts of Technology, 1975; ACDP, 1982–83; Member: Science and Industry Forum, Aust. Acad. of Science, 1971–76; Council for Tech. and Further Educn, 1970–85; Hong Kong UPGC, 1972–90; NSW Bicentennial Exhibition Cttee, 1985–88; Adv. Council, Univ. of Western Sydney, 1986–88; Governor, College of Law, 1972–76. Director: NRMA Ltd, 1977–; NRMA Life Ltd, 1985–; NRMA Travel Ltd, 1986–; Open Road Publishing Co., 1986–; NRMA Sales & Service, 1986–; NRMA Finance Ltd, 1992–. Councillor, Nat. Roads and Motorists Assoc., 1977–. DUniv Univ. of Tech., Sydney, 1988. *Publications:* numerous papers in scientific jls. *Recreations:* yachting, golf. *Address:* 13 Capri Close, Clareville, NSW 2107, Australia.

WERNHAM, Prof. Richard Bruce, MA Oxon; FBA 1995; Professor of Modern History, Oxford University, 1951–72; Fellow of Worcester College, Oxford, 1951–72; now Professor and Fellow Emeritus; *b* 11 Oct. 1906; *o s* of Richard George and Eleanor Mary Wernham; *m* 1939, Isobel Hendry Macmillan (*d* 1987), Vancouver BC; one *d*. *Educ:* Newbury Grammar School; Exeter College, Oxford. Research Asst, Inst. of Historical Research, London Univ., 1929–30; Temp. Asst, Public Record Office, 1930–32; Editor, PRO, State Papers, Foreign Series, 1932–; Lecturer in Modern History, University Coll., London, 1933–34; Fellow of Trinity College, Oxford, 1934–51, Senior Tutor, 1940–41 and 1948–51; University Lecturer in Modern History, Oxford, 1941–51; Examiner in Final Honour School of Modern History, Oxford, 1946–48. Vis. Professor: Univ. of S Carolina, 1958; Univ. of California, Berkeley, 1965–66; Una's Lectr, Berkeley, 1978. Served in RAF, 1941–45. *Publications:* Before the Armada: the Growth of English Foreign Policy 1485–1588, 1966; The Making of Elizabethan Policy, 1980; After the Armada: Elizabethan England and the Struggle for Western Europe 1588–95, 1984; The Return of the Armadas: the last years of the Elizabethan war with Spain, 1994; Calendars of State Papers, Foreign Series, Elizabeth; (ed) Vol III, New Cambridge Modern History: The Counter-Reformation and Price Revolution, 1559–1610, 1968; (ed) Expedition of Sir John Norris and Sir Francis Drake to Spain and Portugal, 1589, 1988; articles in English Hist. Review, History, Trans Royal Hist. Soc., Encyclopædia Britannica. *Address:* 63 Hill Head Road, Hill Head, Fareham, Hants PO14 3JL.

WESIERSKA, Mrs George; *see* Walder, Ruth C.

WESIL, Dennis; Senior Director, Posts, 1971–75, and Member, 1975, Post Office Management Board; *b* 18 Feb. 1915; *e s* of Jack and Polly Wesil, London; *m* 1941, Kathleen, *d* of H. S. McAlpine; two *d*. *Educ:* Central Foundation Sch.; University Coll., London. Entered London telephone service as Asst Supt of Traffic, 1937; PO Investigation Branch, 1941; Asst Postal Controller, 1947; Principal, GPO Headqrtrs, 1953; Dep. Chief Inspector of Postal Services, 1961; Asst Sec. in charge of Postal Mechanisation Branch, 1963; Dep. Dir, NE Region (GPO), 1966; Director: NE Postal Region, 1967; London Postal Region, 1970–71. *Recreations:* reading, golf. *Address:* 2 Stoneleigh, Martello Road South, Poole, Dorset BH13 7HQ. *T:* Canford Cliffs (01202) 707304.

WESKER, Arnold, FRSL 1985; playwright; director; Founder Director of Centre Fortytwo, 1961 (dissolved 1970); Chairman, British Centre of International Theatre

Institute, 1978–82; President, International Playwrights' Committee, 1979–83; *b* 24 May 1932; *s* of Joseph Wesker and Leah Perlmutter; *m* 1958, Dusty Bicker; two *s* two *d*. *Educ:* Upton House School, Hackney. Furniture Maker's Apprentice, Carpenter's Mate, 1948; Bookseller's Asst, 1949 and 1952; Royal Air Force, 1950–52; Plumber's Mate, 1952; Farm Labourer, Seed Sorter, 1953; Kitchen Porter, 1953–54; Pastry Cook, 1954–58. Former Mem., Youth Service Council. Hon. Fellow, QMW, 1995. Hon. LittD UEA, 1989. Author of plays: The Kitchen, produced at Royal Court Theatre, 1959, 1961, 1994 (filmed, 1961); Trilogy of plays (Chicken Soup with Barley, Roots, I'm Talking about Jerusalem) produced Belgrade Theatre (Coventry), 1958–60, Royal Court Theatre, 1960; Chips with Everything, Royal Court, 1962, Vaudeville, 1962 and Plymouth Theatre, Broadway, 1963; The Four Seasons, Belgrade Theatre (Coventry) and Saville, 1965; Their Very Own and Golden City, Brussels and Royal Court, 1966 (Marzotto Drama Prize, 1964); The Friends, Stockholm and London, 1970 (also dir); The Old Ones, Royal Court, 1972; The Wedding Feast, Stockholm, 1974, Leeds 1977; The Journalists, Coventry (amateur), 1977, Yugoslav TV, 1978, Germany, 1981; The Merchant, subseq. entitled Shylock, Stockholm and Aarhus, 1976, Broadway, 1977, Birmingham, 1978; Love Letters on Blue Paper, Nat. Theatre, 1978 (also dir); Fatlips (for young people), 1978; Caritas (Scandinavian Project commission), 1980, Nat. Theatre, 1981, adapted as opera libretto (music by Robert Saxton), 1991; Sullied Hand, 1981, Edinburgh Festival and Finnish TV, 1984; Four Portraits (Japanese commn), Tokyo, 1982, Edinburgh Festival, 1984; Annie Wobbler, Suddeutscher Rundfunk, Germany, Birmingham and New End Theatre, 1983, Fortune Theatre, 1984, New York, 1986; One More Ride on the Merry-Go-Round, Leicester, 1985; Yardsale, Edinburgh Fest. and Stratford-on-Avon (RSC Actors' Fest.), 1985 (also dir); When God Wanted A Son, 1986; Whatever Happened to Betty Lemon (double-bill with Yardsale), Lyric Studio, 1987 (also dir); Little Old Lady (for young people), Sigtuna, Sweden, 1988; The Mistress, 1988, Rome (also dir); Beorhtel's Hill, Towngate, Basildon, 1989; Three Women Talking, 1990, Chicago, 1992; Letter to a Daughter, 1990; Blood Libel, 1991; Wild Spring, 1992, Tokyo, 1994. *Film scripts:* Lady Othello, 1980; Homage to Catalonia, 1990; Maudie, 1995 (adapted from Diary of Jane Somers, by Doris Lessing). *Television:* (first play) Menace, 1963; Breakfast, 1981; (adapted) Thieves in the Night, by A. Koestler, 1984; (adapted) Diary of Jane Somers, by Doris Lessing, 1989. *Radio:* Yardsale, 1984; Bluey (Eur. Radio Commn), Cologne Radio 1984, BBC Radio 3, 1985 (adapted as stage play, 1993). *Publications:* Chicken Soup with Barley, 1959; Roots, 1959; I'm Talking about Jerusalem, 1960; The Wesker Trilogy, 1960; The Kitchen, 1961; Chips with Everything, 1962; The Four Seasons, 1966; Their Very Own and Golden City, 1966; The Friends, 1970; Fears of Fragmentation (essays), 1971; Six Sundays in January, 1971; The Old Ones, 1972; The Journalists, 1974 (in Dialog; repr. 1975); Love Letters on Blue Paper (stories), 1974, 2nd edn 1990; (with John Allin) Say Goodbye! You May Never See Them Again, 1974; Words—as definitions of experience, 1976; The Wedding Feast, 1977; Journey Into Journalism, 1977; Said the Old Man to the Young Man (stories), 1978; The Merchant, 1978; Fatlips (for young people), 1978; The Journalists, a triptych (with Journey into Journalism and A Diary of the Writing of The Journalists), 1979; Caritas, 1981; The Merchant, 1983; Distinctions, 1985; Yardsale, 1987; Whatever Happened to Betty Lemon, 1987; Little Old Lady, 1988; Shoeshine, 1989; Collected Plays: vols 1 and 5, 1989, vols 2, 3, 4 and 6, 1990, vol. 7, 1994; As Much As I Dare (autobiog.), 1994. *Address:* 37 Ashley Road, N19 3AG.

WESLEY, Mary; *see* Siepmann, M. A.

WEST; *see* Sackville-West, family name of Baron Sackville.

WEST, Rear-Adm. Alan William John, DSC 1982; Naval Secretary, 1994–Jan. 1996; Commander, UK Task Group, and Commander, Anti-Submarine Warfare Striking Force, from Feb. 1996; *b* 21 April 1948; *m* 1973, Rosemary Anne Linington Childs; two *s* one *d*. *Educ:* Windsor Grammar Sch.; Clydebank High Sch. Joined RN 1965; seagoing appts, 1966–73; CO HMS Yarnton, 1973; qualified Principal Warfare Officer, 1975; HMS Juno, 1976; HMS Ambuscade, 1977; RN Staff Course, 1978; qualified Advanced Warfare Officer, 1978; HMS Norfolk, 1979; CO HMS Ardent, 1980; Naval Staff, 1982; CO HMS Bristol, 1987; Naval Staff, 1988; RCDS 1992; Higher Comd and Staff Course, Camberley, 1993; Dir, Naval Staff Duties, 1993. *Recreations:* keelboat racing, swimming. *Address:* c/o Naval Secretary, Victory Building, HM Naval Base, Portsmouth, Hants PO1 3LS. *Club:* Royal Yacht Squadron.

WEST, Brian John; media consultant; Director and Chief Executive, Association of Independent Radio Companies, 1983–95; *b* 4 Aug. 1935; *s* of Herbert Frank West and Nellie (*née* Painter); *m* 1st, 1960, Patricia Ivy White (marr. diss. 1986); 2nd, 1987, Gillian Bond. *Educ:* Tiffin Sch., Kingston upon Thames. Sub-Lt (O), Fleet Air Arm, RN, 1956–58. Journalist, Richmond Herald, Surrey Comet and Western Morning News, 1952–60; Surrey Comet: Asst Editor, 1960–64; Editor, 1964–70; Editor, Leicester Mercury, 1970–74; Head of Advertising and PR, Littlewoods Orgn Plc, 1974–83. Founder Pres., Assoc. of European Radios, 1992–93; Council Mem., Advertising Assoc., 1987–95; Dir, Radio Jt Audience Res. Ltd, 1992–94. *Recreations:* music, riding, walking, gardening, photography, cherishing my wife. *Address:* West Media, Hapusrwydd, 21 Old London Road, Flint CH6 5EY. *T:* Flint (01352) 732552.

WEST, Christopher John; Solicitor to HM Land Registry, since 1991; *b* 4 May 1941; *s* of George William West and Kathleen Mary West; *m* 1978, Susan Elizabeth Kirkby; one *d*. *Educ:* Raynes Park County Grammar Sch.; Inns of Court Sch. of Law. Called to the Bar, Lincoln's Inn, 1966. Exec. Officer, Charity Commn, 1961; HM Land Registry, 1969–; Sen. Land Registrar, 1983; Dist Land Registrar, Tunbridge Wells Dist land Registry, 1987. *Publications:* (contrib.) Land Registration (jtly) and Land Charges, to Halsbury's Laws of England, 4th edn, 1977; (contrib.) Atkin's Court Forms, 1978, 1987; (with T. B. F. Ruoff) Concise Land Registration Practice and Land Registration Forms, 1982; (ed jtly) Ruoff and Roper's Registered Conveyancing, 5th edn 1986, 6th edn 1991. *Recreations:* theatre, jazz, watching cricket. *Address:* 32 Lincoln's Inn Fields, WC2A 3PH. *T:* 0171–917 8888.

WEST, David Arthur James; Assistant Under Secretary of State (Naval Personnel), Ministry of Defence, 1981–84, retired; *b* 10 Dec. 1927; *s* of Wilfred West and Edith West (*née* Jones). *Educ:* Cotham Grammar Sch., Bristol. Executive Officer, Air Ministry, 1946; Higher Executive Officer, 1955; Principal, 1961; Assistant Secretary, 1972; Asst Under Sec. of State, 1979. *Address:* 66 Denton Road, East Twickenham TW1 2HQ. *T:* 0181–892 6890.

WEST, David Thomson, CBE 1982; *b* 10 March 1923; *m* 1958, Marie Sellar; one *s* one *d*. *Educ:* Malvern Coll.; St John's Coll., Oxford. Served in RNVR, 1942–45; HM Diplomatic Service, 1946–76; served in Foreign Office, Office of Comr General for UK in SE Asia, HM Embassies, Paris, Lima, and Tunis; Counsellor, 1964; Commercial Inspector, 1965–68; Counsellor (Commercial) Berne, 1968–71; Head of Export Promotion Dept, FCO, 1971–72; seconded to Civil Service Dept as Head of Manpower Div., 1972–76; transf. to Home Civil Service, 1976, retired 1983. *Address:* The Manor House, Great Sampford, Essex CB10 2RL. *T:* Great Sampford (01799) 586305. *Club:* Garrick.

WEST, Prof. Donald James; Professor of Clinical Criminology 1979–84, now Emeritus, and Director 1981–84, University of Cambridge Institute of Criminology; Fellow of Darwin College, Cambridge, 1967–91, now Emeritus; Hon. Consultant Psychiatrist, National Health Service, 1961–86, retired; *b* 9 June 1924; *s* of John Charles and Jessie Mercedes West. *Educ:* Merchant Taylors' Sch., Crosby; Liverpool Univ. (MD). LittD Cambridge. FRCPsych. Research Officer, Soc. for Psychical Research, London, and pt-time graduate student in psychiatry, 1947–50; in hospital practice in psychiatry, 1951–59; Sen. Registrar, Forensic Psychiatry Unit, Maudsley Hosp., 1957–59; Inst. of Criminology, Cambridge, 1960–. Leverhulme Emeritus Fellow, 1988–89. Mental Health Act Comr, 1989–. Vice Pres., 1981–, and former Pres., British Soc. of Criminology; Pres., Soc. for Psychical Research, 1963–65, 1984–87; Chm., Forensic Section, World Psychiatric Assoc., 1983–89; Chm., Streetwise Youth, 1986–92. *Publications:* Psychical Research Today, 1954 (revd edn 1962); Eleven Lourdes Miracles (med. inquiry under Parapsych. Foundn Grant), 1957; The Habitual Prisoner (for Inst. of Criminology), 1963; Murder followed by Suicide (for Inst. of Criminology), 1965; The Young Offender, 1967; Homosexuality, 1968; Present Conduct and Future Delinquency, 1969; (ed) The Future of Parole, 1972; (jtly) Who Becomes Delinquent?, 1973; (jtly) The Delinquent Way of Life, 1977; Homosexuality Re-examined, 1977; (ed, jtly) Daniel McNaughton: his trial and the aftermath, 1977; (jtly) Understanding Sexual Attacks, 1978; Delinquency: its roots, careers and prospects, 1982; Sexual Victimisation, 1985; Sexual Crimes and Confrontations, 1987; (jtly) Children's Sexual Encounters with Adults, 1990; Male Prostitution, 1992; (ed) Sex Crimes, 1994; various contribs to British Jl of Criminology, Jl of Adolescence. *Recreations:* travel, parapsychology. *Address:* 32 Fen Road, Milton, Cambridge CB4 6AD. *T:* Cambridge (01223) 860308.

WEST, Edward Mark, CMG 1987; *b* 11 March 1923; *m* 1948, Lydia Hollander; three *s*. *Educ:* Hendon County Sch.; University Coll., Oxford (MA). Served RA (W/Lieut), 1943; ICU BAOR (A/Captain), 1945. Asst Principal, Colonial Office, 1947; Private Sec., PUS, Colonial Office, 1950–51, Principal, 1951–58; Head of Chancery, UK Commn, Singapore, 1958–61; Private Secretary to Secretary of State, Colonial Affairs, 1961–62; Private Secretary to Secretary of State for Commonwealth and Colonial Affairs, 1963; Asst Sec., ODM, 1964–70; Food and Agriculture Organization: Director, Programme and Budget Formulation, 1970; Asst Dir-Gen., Administration and Finance Dept, 1974; Asst Dir-Gen., Programme and Budget Formulation, 1976; Dep, Dir-Gen. of Orgn, 1982–86; Special Rep., Internat. Conf. on Nutrition, 1992. Mem. Corp., Trinity Coll. of Music, 1992–95. *Address:* 10 Warwick Mansions, Cromwell Crescent, SW5 9QR.

WEST, Rt. Rev. Francis Horner, MA; *b* 9 Jan. 1909; *o s* of Sydney Hague and Mary West, St Albans, Herts; *m* 1947, Beryl Elaine, 2nd *d* of late Rev. W. A. Renwick, Smallbridge, Rochdale; one *s* one *d*. *Educ:* Berkhamsted School; Magdalene Coll. and Ridley Hall, Cambridge. Exhibitioner, Magdalene, Cambridge; MA 1934; Curate St Agnes, Leeds, 1933–36; Chaplain, Ridley Hall, Cambridge, 1936–38; Vicar of Starbeck, Yorks, 1938–42. Served War of 1939–45, as CF with BEF, MEF, CMF and SEAC, 1939–46 (despatches, 1945); Director of Service Ordination Candidates, 1946–47; Vicar of Upton, Notts, 1947–51; Archdeacon of Newark, 1947–62; Vicar of East Retford, 1951–55; Bishop Suffragan of Taunton, 1962–77; Prebendary of Wells, 1962–77; Rector of Dinder, Somerset, 1962–71. Select Preacher, Cambridge Univ., 1962. Visitor, Croft House School, 1968–79. *Publications:* Rude Forefathers, The Story of an English Village, 1600–1666, 1949, reprinted 1989; The Great North Road in Nottinghamshire, 1956; Sparrows of the Spirit, 1957; The Country Parish Today and Tomorrow, 1960; F. R. B.: a portrait of Bishop F. R. Barry, 1980; The Story of a Wiltshire Country Church, 1987. *Recreation:* gardening. *Address:* 11 Castle Street, Aldbourne, Marlborough, Wilts SN8 2DA. *T:* Marlborough (01672) 40630.

WEST, Lt-Col George Arthur Alston-Roberts-, CVO 1988; DL; Comptroller, Lord Chamberlain's Office, 1987–90 (Assistant Comptroller, 1981–87); an Extra Equerry to the Queen, since 1982; Director, Care Ltd, since 1991; *b* 1937; *s* of Major W. R. J. Alston-Roberts-West, Grenadier Guards (killed in action 1940) and late Mrs W. R. J. Alston-Roberts-West; *m* 1970, Hazel, *d* of late Sir Thomas Cook and of Lady Cook. *Educ:* Eton Coll.; RMA, Sandhurst. Commissioned into Grenadier Guards, Dec. 1957; served in England, Northern Ireland, Germany and Cyprus; retired, 1980. DL Warwicks, 1988. *Address:* Atherstone Hill Farm, Stratford-on-Avon, Warwicks CV37 8NF. *Clubs:* Boodle's, Pratt's.

WEST, Rt. Hon. Henry William, PC (N Ire) 1960; Leader, Ulster Unionist Party, 1974–79; *b* 27 March 1917; *s* of late W. H. West, JP; *m* 1956, Maureen Elizabeth Hall; four *s* three *d*. *Educ:* Enniskillen Model School; Portora Royal School. Farmer. MP for Enniskillen, NI Parlt, 1954–72; Mem. (U), Fermanagh and S Tyrone, NI Assembly, 1973–75; Parly Sec. to Minister of Agriculture, 1958; Minister of Agriculture, 1960–67, and 1971–72; MP (UUUC) Fermanagh and South Tyrone, Feb.-Sept. 1974; Mem. (UUUC), for Fermanagh and South Tyrone, NI Constitutional Convention, 1975–76. N Ireland representative on British Wool Marketing Board, 1950–58; President, Ulster Farmers' Union, 1955–56. High Sheriff, Co. Fermanagh, 1954. *Address:* Rossahilly House, Enniskillen, Northern Ireland. *T:* Enniskillen (01365) 3060.

WEST, Prof. John Clifford, CBE 1977; PhD, DSc; FEng; FIEE; FRGS; Vice-Chancellor and Principal, University of Bradford, 1979–89; *b* 4 June 1922; *s* of J. H. West and Mrs West (*née* Ascroft); *m* 1946, Winefride Mary Turner; three *d*. *Educ:* Hindley and Abram Grammar School; Victoria Univ., Manchester. PhD 1953, DSc 1957. Matthew Kirtley Entrance Schol., Manchester Univ., 1940. Electrical Lieutenant, RNVR, 1943–46. Lecturer, University of Manchester, 1946–57; Professor of Electrical Engineering, The Queen's University of Belfast, 1958–65; University of Sussex: Prof. of Electrical and Control Engineering, 1965–78; Founder Dean, Sch. of Applied Scis, 1965–73, Pro-Vice-Chancellor, 1967–71; Dir, Phillips' Philatelic Unit, 1970–78. Director, A. C. E. Machinery Ltd, 1966–79. Member: UGC, 1973–78 (Chm., Technology Sub-Cttee, 1973–78); Science Res. Council Cttee on Systems and Electrical Engineering, 1963–67; Science Res. Council Engrg Bd, 1976–79; Vis. Cttee, Dept of Educn and Science, Cranfield; Civil Service Commn Special Merit Promotions Panel, 1966–72; Naval Educn Adv. Cttee, 1965–72; Crawford Cttee on Broadcasting Coverage, 1973–74; Inter-Univ. Inst. of Engrg Control, 1967–83 (Dir, 1967–70); Chairman: Council for Educnl Technology, 1980–85; Educn Task Gp, IStructE, 1988–89. Pres., IEE, 1984–85 (Dep. Pres. 1982–84); Chm., Automation and Control Div., IEE, 1970–71. Treasurer, Yorkshire Cancer Res. Campaign, 1989–. Chm., Internat. Commn on Higher Educn, Botswana, 1990; UK deleg., Conf. on Higher Educn, Madagascar, 1992. Member: Royal Philatelic Soc., 1960–; Sociedad Filatélica de Chile, 1970–; Chm., British Philatelic Council, 1980–81; Trustee, Nat. Philatelic Trust, 1989–; Keeper of the Roll of Distinguished Philatelists, 1992–. FRPSL 1970–; Fellow, Inst. of Paper Conservation, 1980. Hon. FInstMC 1984; Hon. FIEE 1992. Hon. DSc Sussex, 1988; DUniv Bradford, 1990. Hartley Medal, Inst. Measurement and Control, 1979. *Publications:* Textbook of Servomechanisms, 1953; Analytical Techniques for Non-Linear Control Systems, 1960; papers in Proc. IEE, Trans Amer. IEE, Brit. Jl of Applied Physics, Jl of Scientific Instruments, Proc. Inst. Measurement and Control. *Recreations:* philately, postal history. *Address:* 6 Park Crescent, Guiseley, Leeds

LS20 8EL. *T:* Guiseley (01943) 872605, *Fax:* 879910. *Clubs:* Athenæum, Commonwealth Trust.

WEST, Kenneth, CChem, FRSC; Deputy Chairman, ICI Fibres Division, 1980–84 (Technical Director, 1977–80); *b* 1 Sept. 1930; *s* of Albert West and Ethel Kirby (*née* Kendall); *m* 1980, Elizabeth Ann Borland (*née* Campbell); one step *s*, and three *d* by a previous marriage. *Educ:* Archbishop Holgate's Grammar Sch., York; University Coll., Oxford (BA). Customer Service Manager, ICI Fibres, 1960; Res. and Engrg Manager, FII, 1967; Director: South African Nylon Spinners, Cape Town, 1970; Fibre Industries Inc., N Carolina, 1974; Man. Dir, TWA, 1984–85; Dir, Water Res. Council, 1984–85. Dir, Seahorse Internat. Ltd, 1987–89. FRSA. *Recreations:* sailing, flying, music, whisky. *Address:* Stone Ridge, Niton Undercliff, Ventnor, Isle of Wight PO38 2LY. *T:* Isle of Wight (01983) 730846. *Clubs:* Yorkshire Aeroplane; Lymington Town Sailing.

WEST, Martin Litchfield, DPhil, DLitt; FBA 1973; Senior Research Fellow, All Souls College, University of Oxford, since 1991; *b* 23 Sept. 1937; *s* of Maurice Charles West and Catherine Baker West (*née* Stainthorpe); *m* 1960, Stephanie Roberta Pickard (*see* S. R. West); one *s* one *d*. *Educ:* St Paul's Sch.; Balliol Coll., Oxford (MA 1962; DPhil 1963; DLitt 1994). Chancellor's Prizes for Latin Prose and Verse, 1957; Hertford and de Paravicini Schols, 1957; Ireland Schol., 1957; Conington Prize, 1965. Woodhouse Jun. Research Fellow, St John's Coll., Oxford, 1960–63; Fellow and Praelector in Classics, University Coll., Oxford, 1963–74; Prof. of Greek, Bedford Coll., then at RHBNC, London Univ., 1974–91. Corresp. Mem., Akademie der Wissenschaften zu Göttingen, 1991. Editor of Liddell and Scott's Greek-English Lexicon, 1965–81. *Publications:* Hesiod, Theogony (ed), 1966; Fragmenta Hesiodea (ed with R. Merkelbach), 1967; Early Greek Philosophy and the Orient, 1971; Sing Me, Goddess, 1971; Iambi et Elegi Graeci (ed), 1971–72; Textual Criticism and Editorial Technique, 1973; Studies in Greek Elegy and Iambus, 1974; Hesiod, Works and Days (ed), 1978; Theognidis et Phocylidis fragmenta, 1978; Delectus ex Iambis et Elegis Graecis, 1980; Greek Metre, 1982; The Orphic Poems, 1983; Carmina Anacreontea, 1984; The Hesiodic Catalogue of Women, 1985; Euripides, Orestes (ed), 1987; Introduction to Greek Metre, 1987; Hesiod (trans.), 1988; Aeschyli Tragoediae, 1990; Studies in Aeschylus, 1990; Ancient Greek Music, 1992; Greek Lyric Poetry (trans.), 1993; articles in classical periodicals. *Recreation:* strong music. *Address:* All Souls College, Oxford OX1 4AL.

WEST, Michael Charles B.; *see* Beresford-West.

WEST, Morris (Langlo), AM 1985; novelist; *b* Melbourne, 26 April 1916; *s* of Charles Langlo West and Florence Guilfoyle Hanlon; *m* Joyce Lawford; three *s* one *d*. *Educ:* Melbourne Univ. (BA 1937). Taught modern langs and maths, NSW and Tas, 1933–39. Served, Lieutenant, AIF, South Pacific, 1939–43. Sec. to William Morris Hughes, former PM of Australia, 1943. FRSL; Fellow World Acad. of Art and Science. Hon. DLitt, Univ. of Santa Clara, 1969; Hon. DLitt: Mercy Coll., NY, 1982; Univ. of Western Sydney, 1993; ANU, Canberra, 1995. Internat. Dag Hammarskjold Prize (Grand Collar of Merit), 1978. *Publications:* Gallows on the Sand, 1955; Kundu, 1956; Children of the Sun, 1957; The Crooked Road, 1957 (Eng.: The Big Story); The Concubine, 1958; Backlash, 1958 (Eng.: The Second Victory); The Devil's Advocate, 1959 (National Brotherhood Award, National Council of Christians and Jews 1960; James Tait Black Memorial Prize, 1960; RSL Heinemann Award, 1960; filmed 1977); The Naked Country, 1960; Daughter of Silence (novel), 1961, (play), 1961; The Shoes of the Fisherman, 1963; The Ambassador, 1965; The Tower of Babel, 1968; The Heretic, a Play in Three Acts, 1970; (with R. Francis) Scandal in the Assembly, 1970; Summer of the Red Wolf, 1971; The Salamander, 1973; Harlequin, 1974; The Navigator, 1976; Proteus, 1979; The Clowns of God, 1981 (Universe Literary Prize, 1981); The World is Made of Glass, 1983 (play 1984); Cassidy, 1986; Masterclass, 1988; Lazarus, 1990; The Ringmaster, 1991; The Lovers, 1993. *Address:* PO Box 102, Avalon, NSW 2107, Australia. *Clubs:* Australian, Royal Prince Alfred Yacht (Sydney).

WEST, Nigel; *see* Allason, R. W. S.

WEST, Norman; Member (Lab) Yorkshire South, European Parliament, since 1984; *b* 26 Nov. 1935; *m*; two *s*. *Educ:* Barnsley; Sheffield Univ. Miner. Mem., South Yorks CC (Chm., Highways Cttee; Mem., anti-nuclear working party). Member: NUM; CND. Mem., Energy, Research and Technology Cttee, European Parlt, 1984–. *Address:* 43 Coronation Drive, Birdwell, Barnsley, South Yorks S10 5RJ.

WEST, Peter; BBC television commentator/anchorman, 1950–86; commentaries for radio, 1947–85; Chairman, West Nally Group (sports marketing), 1971–83; *b* 12 Aug. 1920; *s* of Harold William and Dorcas Anne West; *m* 1946, Pauline Mary Pike; two *s* one *d*. *Educ:* Cranbrook Sch.; RMC, Sandhurst. Served War of 1939–45: Duke of Wellington's Regt. TV/Radio commentaries every year: on Test matches, 1952–86; on Wimbledon, 1955–82; on Rugby Union, 1950–85; Olympics, 1948–60–64–68–72–76. Rugby Football Correspondent of The Times, 1971–82. TV shows: Chairman of: Why?, 1953; Guess my Story, 1953–54–55. Introduced: At Home, 1955; First Hand and It's Up to You, 1956–57; Box Office, 1957; Come Dancing, 1957–72 (incl.); Be Your Own Boss and Wish You Were Here, 1958; Get Ahead, 1958–62; Good Companions, 1958–62; First Years at Work (Schs TV), 1958–69 (incl.); Miss World, 1961–66 (incl.); Facing West (HTV, Bristol), 1986–88. Children's TV: introd.: Question Marks, 1957; Ask Your Dad, 1958; What's New?, 1962–63–64. Radio: introd.: What Shall We Call It?, 1955; Sound Idea, 1958; Morning Call, 1960–61; Treble Chance, 1962; Sporting Chance, 1964; Games People Play, 1985. Pres., Cheltenham Cricket Soc., 1984–. *Publications:* The Fight for the Ashes, 1953; The Fight for the Ashes, 1956; Flannelled Fool and Muddied Oaf (autobiog.), 1986; Clean Sweep, 1987; Denis Compton—Cricketing Genius, 1989. *Recreations:* gardening, rubber bridge. *Address:* The Paddock, Duntisbourne Abbotts, Cirencester, Glos GL7 7JW. *T:* Cirencester (01285) 821380.

WEST, Prunella Margaret Rumney, (Mrs T. L. West); *see* Scales, Prunella.

WEST, Prof. Richard Gilbert, FRS 1968; FSA; FGS; Fellow of Clare College, Cambridge, since 1954; Professor of Botany, University of Cambridge, 1977–91; *b* 31 May 1926; *m* 1st, 1958; one *s*; 2nd, 1973, Hazel Gristwood; two *d*. *Educ:* King's School, Canterbury; Univ. of Cambridge. Cambridge University: Demonstrator in Botany, 1957–60; Lecturer in Botany, 1960–67; Dir, Subdept of Quaternary Research, 1966–87; Reader in Quaternary Research, 1967–75; Prof. of Palaeoecology, 1975–77. Member: Council for Scientific Policy, 1971–73; NERC, 1973–76; Ancient Monuments Bd for England, 1980–84. Darwin Lecturer to the British Association, 1959; Lyell Fund, 1961, Bigsby Medal, 1969, Lyell Medal, 1988, Geological Society of London. Hon. MRIA. *Publications:* Pleistocene Geology and Biology, 1968, 2nd edn 1977; (jtly) The Ice Age in Britain, 1972, 2nd edn 1981; The Pre-glacial Pleistocene of the Norfolk and Suffolk coasts, 1980; Pleistocene Palaeoecology of Central Norfolk, 1991. *Address:* 3A Woollards Lane, Great Shelford, Cambs CB2 5LZ. *T:* Cambridge (01223) 842578; Clare College, Cambridge CB2 1TL.

WEST, Prof. Richard John, FRCP; Medical Postgraduate Dean to South Western Region, and Hon. Professor, University of Bristol, since 1991; *b* 8 May 1939; *s* of late Cecil J. West and of Alice B. West (*née* Court); *m* 1962, Jenny Winn Hawkins; one *s* two *d*. *Educ:* Tiffin Boys' Sch.; Middlesex Hospital Medical School (MB, BS, MD, DCH, DObstRCOG). FRCP 1979. Research Fellow, Inst. of Child Health, London, 1971–73; Sen. Registrar, Hosp. for Sick Children, London, 1973–74; Lectr, Inst. of Child Health, 1974–75; Sen. Lectr, 1975–91, Dean, 1982–87, St George's Hosp. Med. Sch.; Consultant Paediatrician, St George's Hosp., 1975–91; Hon. Consultant Paediatrician, Royal Hosp. for Sick Children Bristol. Member: Wandsworth HA, 1981–82, 1989–90; SW Thames RHA, 1982–88. Member: DoH Clinical Outcomes Gp, 1991–; Steering Gp on Undergraduate Med. and Dental Educn and Res., 1992–. Member: Governing Body: Inst. of Med. Ethics, 1985– (Gen. Sec., 1989–); Tiffin Boys' Sch., 1983–86; Wimbledon High Sch., 1988–91. *Publications:* Family Guide to Children's Ailments, 1983; Royal Society of Medicine Child Health Guide, 1992; research papers on metabolic diseases, incl. lipid disorders. *Recreations:* windmills, medical history, travel. *Address:* University of Bristol Medical Postgraduate Department, Academic Centre, Frenchay Hospital, Bristol BS16 1LE. *T:* Bristol (0117) 975 7050.

WEST, Dr Stephanie Roberta, FBA 1990; Senior Research Fellow in Classics and Librarian, Hertford College, Oxford, since 1990; *b* 1 Dec. 1937; *d* of Robert Enoch Pickard and Ruth (*née* Batters); *m* 1960, Martin Litchfield West, *qv*; one *s* one *d*. *Educ:* Nottingham High Sch. for Girls; Somerville Coll., Oxford (1st cl. Classics Mods 1958, 1st cl. Lit. Hum. 1960; Gaisford Prize for Greek Verse Composition 1959; Ireland Scholar 1959, Derby Scholar 1960); MA 1963, DPhil 1964, Oxon. Oxford University: Mary Ewart Res. Fellow, Somerville Coll., 1965–67; Lecturer: in Classics, Hertford Coll., 1966–90; in Greek, Keble Coll., 1981–. Mem. Council, GPDST, 1974–87. *Publications:* The Ptolemaic Papyri of Homer, 1967; Omero, Odissea 1 (libri I–IV), 1981; (with A. Heubeck and J. B. Hainsworth) A commentary on Homer's Odyssey 1, 1988; articles and reviews in learned jls. *Recreations:* opera, curious information. *Address:* 42 Portland Road, Oxford OX2 7EY. *T:* Oxford (01865) 56060.

WEST, Dr Stephen Craig, FRS 1995; Principal Scientist, Imperial Cancer Research Fund, since 1989; *b* 11 April 1952; *s* of Joseph and Louise West; *m* 1985, Phyllis Fraenza. *Educ:* Univ. of Newcastle upon Tyne (BSc 1974; PhD 1977). Post-doctoral Research Associate: Univ. of Newcastle upon Tyne, 1977–78; Dept of Molecular Biophysics and Biochemistry, and Therapeutic Radiology, Yale Univ., 1978–83 (Res. Scientist, Dept of Therapeutic Radiology, 1983–85); Sen. Scientist, ICRF, 1985–89. Mem., EMBO, 1994–. *Publications:* numerous res. papers in biochem. and molecular biol. *Recreations:* squash, skiing, music. *Address:* Imperial Cancer Research Fund, Clare Hall Laboratories, South Mimms, Potters Bar, Herts EN6 3LD.

WEST, Prof. Thomas Summers, CBE 1988; FRS 1989; FRSE, FRSC; Director, Macaulay Institute for Soil Research, Aberdeen, 1975–87; Honorary Research Professor, University of Aberdeen, 1983–87, now Emeritus; *b* 18 Nov. 1927; *s* of late Thomas West and Mary Ann Summers; *m* 1952, Margaret Officer Lawson, MA; one *s* two *d*. *Educ:* Tarbat Old Public Sch., Portmahomack; Royal Acad., Tain; Aberdeen Univ. (BSc 1st Cl. Hons Chemistry, 1949); Univ. of Birmingham (PhD 1952, DSc 1962). FRSC (FRIC 1962); FRSE 1979. Univ. of Birmingham: Sen. DSIR Fellow, 1952–55; Lectr in Chem., 1955–63; Imperial Coll., London: Reader in Analytical Chem., 1963–65; Prof. of Analytical Chem., 1965–75. Royal Society: Mem., British National Cttee for Chem., and Chm., Analytical Sub-cttee, 1965–82; Mem., Internat. Cttee, 1990–92; Mem., Internat. Exchanges Cttee, 1992–95 (Chm. Panel, I(c)). Sec. Gen., IUPAC, 1983–91 (Pres., Analytical Div., 1977–79); Pres., Soc. for Analytical Chem., 1969–71; Chm., Finance Cttee, ICSU, 1990–92; Mem., British Nat. Cttee for IUPAC, RSC, 1990–; Hon. Sec., Chemical Soc., 1972–75 (Redwood Lectr, 1974); Hon. Member: Bunseki Kagakukai (Japan), 1981; Fondation de la Maison de la Chimie (Paris), 1985. Meldola Medal, RIC, 1956; Instrumentation Medal, 1976, and Gold Medal, 1977, Chemical Soc.; Johannes Marcus Medal for Spectroscopy, Spectroscopic Soc. of Bohemia, 1977. *Publications:* Analytical Applications of Diamino ethane tetra acetic acid, 1958, 2nd edn 1961; New Methods of Analytical Chemistry, 1964; Complexometry with EDTA and Related Reagents, 1969. *Recreations:* gardening, motoring, reading, music, family history research. *Address:* 31 Baillieswells Drive, Bieldside, Aberdeen AB1 9AT. *T:* Aberdeen (01224) 868294.

WEST, Timothy Lancaster, CBE 1984; actor and director; *b* 20 Oct. 1934; *s* of late Harry Lockwood West and Olive Carleton-Crowe; *m* 1st, 1956, Jacqueline Boyer (marr. diss.); one *d*; 2nd, 1963, Prunella Scales, *qv*; two *s*. *Educ:* John Lyon Sch., Harrow; Regent Street Polytechnic. Entered profession as asst stage manager, Wimbledon, 1956; first London appearance, Caught Napping, Piccadilly, 1959; Mem., RSC, 1964–66; Prospect Theatre Co., 1966–72: Dr Samuel Johnson, Prospero, Bolingbroke, young Mortimer in Edward II, King Lear, Emerson in A Room with a View, Alderman Smuggler in The Constant Couple, and Holofernes in Love's Labour's Lost; Otto in The Italian Girl, 1968; Gilles in Abelard and Heloise, 1970; Robert Hand in Exiles, 1970; Gilbert in The Critic as Artist, 1971; Sir William Gower in Trelawny (musical), Bristol, 1972; Falstaff in Henry IV Pts I and II, Bristol, 1973; Shpigelsky in A Month in the Country, Chichester, 1974 (London, 1975); Brack in Hedda Gabler, RSC, 1975; Iago in Othello, Nottingham, 1976; with Prospect Co.: Harry in Staircase, 1976, Claudius in Hamlet, storyteller in War Music, and Enobarbus in Antony and Cleopatra, 1977; Ivan and Gottlieb in Laughter, and Max in The Homecoming, 1978; with Old Vic Co.: Narrator in Lancelot and Guinevere, Shylock in The Merchant of Venice, 1980; Beecham, Apollo, 1980, NZ, 1983, Dublin, 1986; Uncle Vanya, Australia, 1982; Stalin in Master Class, Leicester, 1983, Old Vic, 1984; Charlie Mucklebrass in Big in Brazil, 1984; The War at Home, Hampstead, 1984; When We Are Married, Whitehall, 1986; The Sneeze, Aldwych, 1988; Bristol Old Vic: The Master Builder, 1989; The Clandestine Marriage, Uncle Vanya, 1990; James Tyrone, in Long Day's Journey into Night, 1991, also at NT; Andrew in It's Ralph, Comedy, 1991; King Lear, Dublin, 1992, Willie Loman in Death of a Salesman, Theatr Clwyd, 1993; Christopher Cameron in Himself, Salisbury, 1993; Sir Anthony Absolute in The Rivals, Chichester, 1994; Macbeth, Theatr Clwyd, 1994; Mail Order Bride, 1994, Getting On, 1995, W Yorks Playhouse. *Directed:* plays for Prospect Co., Open Space, Gardner Centre, Brighton, and rep. at Salisbury, Bristol, Northampton and Cheltenham; own season, The Forum, Billingham, 1973; Artistic Dir, Old Vic Co., 1980–81. *Television includes:* Edward VII, 1973; Hard Times, 1977; Crime and Punishment, 1979; Brass, 1982–84, 1990; The Last Bastion, 1984; The Nightingale Saga, Tender is the Night, 1985; The Monocled Mutineer, 1986; The Train, 1987; A Shadow on the Sun, 1988; The Gospels, Framed, 1992; *plays:* Richard II, 1969; Edward II, The Boswell and Johnson Show, 1970; Horatio Bottomley, 1972; Churchill and the Generals, 1979 (RTS Award); The Good Doctor Bodkin Adams, 1986; What the Butler Saw, Harry's Kingdom, When We Are Married, Breakthrough at Reykjavik, 1987; Strife, The Contractor, 1988; Blore, MP, Beecham, 1989; Survival of the Fittest, 1990; Bye Bye Columbus, 1991; Framed, 1992; Reith to the Nation, Smokescreen, 1993; Hiroshima, 1995. *Films:* The Looking-Glass War, 1968; Nicholas and Alexandra, 1970; The Day of the Jackal, 1972; Hedda, 1975; Joseph Andrews, and The Devil's Advocate, 1976; William Morris, 1977; Agatha, and The 39 Steps, 1978; The Antagonists, 1980; Murder is Easy, and Oliver Twist, 1981; Cry Freedom, 1986; Consuming Passions, 1987. Compiles and dir. recital progs; sound broadcaster. Chairman: All Change Arts Ltd, 1986–; LAMDA, 1992–. FRSA 1992. DUniv Bradford, 1993; Hon. DLitt West of England, 1994. *Recreations:* theatre history, travel, music, old railways. *Address:* c/o James Sharkey Associates Ltd, 21 Golden Square, W1R 3PA. *Clubs:* Garrick, Groucho.

WEST CUMBERLAND, Archdeacon of; *see* Packer, Ven. J. R.

WEST HAM, Archdeacon of; *no new appointment at time of going to press.*

WEST INDIES, Archbishop of, since 1986; **Most Rev. Orland Ugham Lindsay;** Bishop of the North-Eastern Caribbean and Aruba (formerly Antigua), since 1970; *b* 24 March 1928; *s* of Hubert and Ida Lindsay; *m* 1959, Olga Daphne (*née* Wright); three *s*. *Educ:* Culham Coll., Oxon (Teachers' Cert.); St Peter's Coll., Jamaica; McGill Univ. BD (London) 1957. RAF, 1944–47. Teacher, Franklyn Town Govt School, Jamaica, 1949–52; Asst Master, Kingston College, 1952–53. Deacon 1956, priest 1957; Asst Curate, St Peter's Vere, Jamaica, 1956–57; Asst Master, Kingston Coll., 1958–67, Chaplain 1962–63; Priest-in-Charge, Manchioneal Cure, Jamaica, 1960; Chaplain, Jamaica Defence Force, 1963–67; Principal, Church Teachers' Coll., Mandeville, 1967–70. Sec. to Jamaica Synod, 1962–70. Hon. DD Berkeley Divinity School at Yale, 1978. *Recreations:* jazz music, photography. *Address:* Bishop's Lodge, PO Box 23, St John's, Antigua. *T:* (office and home) 4620151, (direct line) 4622091, *Fax:* 4622090.

WEST-RUSSELL, His Honour Sir David (Sturrock), Kt 1986; President of Industrial Tribunals for England and Wales, 1984–91; *b* 17 July 1921; *o s* of late Sir Alexander West-Russell and late Agnes West-Russell (*née* Sturrock); *m* Christine (*née* Tyler); one *s* two *d*. *Educ:* Rugby; Pembroke Coll., Cambridge. Served war: Buffs, 1940; commissioned Queen's Own Cameron Highlanders, 1941; Parachute Regt, 1942–46; N Africa, Italy, France, Greece, Norway and Palestine (despatches, Major). Management Trainee, Guest Keen and Nettlefold, 1948–50; Harmsworth Law Scholar, 1952; called to Bar, Middle Temple, 1953, Bencher, 1986; SE Circuit; Dep. Chm., Inner London Quarter Sessions, 1966–72; Circuit Judge, 1972; Sen. Circuit Judge, Inner London Crown Court, 1979–82, Southwark Crown Court, 1983–84. Mem., Departmental Cttee on Legal Aid in Criminal Proceedings, 1964–65. Comr (NI Emergency Provisions Act), 1974–80; Chairman: Lord Chancellor's Adv. Cttee on Appts of Magistrates for Inner London, 1976–87; Home Sec's Adv. Bd on Restricted Patients, 1985–91; Inner London Probation Cttee, 1988–89 (Mem., 1979–89); Member: Lord Chancellor's Adv. Cttee on the Trng of Magistrates, 1980–85; Judicial Studies Bd, 1980–84, 1987–90; Parole Bd, 1980–82; Parole Review Cttee, 1987–88; Criminal Injuries Compensation Bd, 1991–95. Pres., Inner London Magistrates' Assoc., 1979–85; Jt Pres., Council of HM Circuit Judges, 1985. *Address:* Old Sarum Cottage, Teffont Magna, Salisbury, Wilts SP3 5QX. *Club:* Garrick.

WESTBROOK, Eric Ernest, CB 1981; painter and writer; Chairman, Deakin University Art Museum Committee, 1994; *b* 29 Sept. 1915; *s* of Ernest James and Helen Westbrook; *m* 1st, 1942, Ingrid Nyström; one *d*; 2nd, 1964, Dawn Sime. *Educ:* Alleyn's Sch., Dulwich; various schools of art. Lecturer for Arts Council of Gt Britain, 1943; Director, Wakefield City Art Gallery, Yorks, 1946; Chief Exhibitions Officer, British Council, 1949; Director: Auckland City Art Gallery, NZ, 1952–55; National Gallery of Victoria, Melbourne, Aust., 1956–73; Director (Permanent Head), Ministry for the Arts, Victoria, 1973–80, retired. Hon. LLD Monash, 1974. Chevalier de l'Ordre des Arts et Lettres (France), 1972; Palmes Académiques, 1989. *Publications:* Birth of a Gallery, 1968; various articles and reviews in arts and museum pubns. *Recreations:* music, gardening. *Address:* Houghton Park, Odgers Road, Castlemaine, Vic 3450, Australia. *T:* (054) 724171.

WESTBROOK, Michael John David, OBE 1988; composer, pianist and band-leader; *b* 21 March 1936; *s* of Philip Beckford Westbrook and Vera Agnes (*née* Butler); *m* 1976, Katherine Jane (*née* Duckham), singer, songwriter and painter; one *s* one *d* of previous marriage. *Educ:* Kelly Coll., Tavistock; Plymouth Coll. of Art (NDD); Hornsey Coll. of Art (ATD). Formed first band at Plymouth Art Sch., 1958; moved to London, 1962, and has since led a succession of groups incl. The Mike Westbrook Brass Band, formed with Phil Minton in 1973, The Mike Westbrook Orch., 1974–, and Westbrook Trio (with Kate Westbrook and Chris Biscoe), formed in 1982. Has toured extensively in Britain and Europe, and performed in Australia, Canada, NY, Singapore and Hong Kong. Has written commissioned works for fests in Britain, France and other European countries, composed music for theatre, radio, TV and films, and made numerous LPs. Principal compositions/recordings include: Marching Song, 1967; Metropolis, 1969; Tyger: a celebration of William Blake (with Adrian Mitchell), 1971; Citadel/Room 315, 1974; On Duke's Birthday (dedicated to the memory of Duke Ellington), 1984; Bean Rows and Blues Shots (saxophone concerto), 1991; Coming Through Slaughter (opera), 1994; TV scores incl. Caught on a Train, 1983; film score: Moulin Rouge, 1990; with Kate Westbrook: concert works incorporating European poetry and folk song, notably The Cortège, for voices and jazz orch., 1979, and London Bridge is Broken Down, for voice, jazz orch. and chamber orch., 1987; also a succession of music-theatre pieces, including: Mama Chicago, 1978; Westbrook-Rossini, 1984; The Ass (based on poem by D. H. Lawrence), 1985; Pier Rides, 1986; Quichotte (opera), 1989; Goodbye Peter Lorre, 1991; Measure for Measure, 1992; Good Friday 1663 (TV opera), 1994. *Recreation:* walking by the Erme Estuary. *Address:* Brent House, Holbeton, near Plymouth, Devon PL8 1LX; Flat 17, Tamar House, 12 Tavistock Place, WC1H 9RA.

WESTBROOK, Sir Neil (Gowanloch), Kt 1988; CBE 1981; Chairman, Trafford Park Estates PLC; *b* 21 Jan. 1917; *s* of Frank and Dorothy Westbrook; *m* 1945, Hon. Mary Joan Fraser, *o d* of 1st Baron Strathalmond, CBE; one *s* one *d*. *Educ:* Oundle Sch.; Clare Coll., Cambridge (MA). FRICS. Served War of 1939–45: Sapper, 1939; Actg Lt-Col 1945 (despatches). Chm., NW Industrial Council, 1982–87; Member: Council, CBI North West Region, 1982–88 (Chairman: NW Inner Cities Studies Gp, 1985; NW Working Party on Derelict Land Clearance, 1986); Inst. of Directors Greater Manchester Branch Cttee, 1972–86. Treas., Manchester Conservative Assoc., 1964–73, Dep. Chm., 1973–74, Chm., 1974–83; Chairman: Greater Manchester Co-ordinating Cttee, NW Area Cons. Assoc., 1977–86; Exchange Div. Cons. Assoc., 1973; Manchester Euro South Cons. Assoc., 1978–84; Member: NW Area F and GP Cttee, Cons. Party, 1974–87; Nat. Union Exec. Cttee, 1975–81; Cons. Bd of Finance, 1984–87. Mem., Manchester City Council, 1949–71; Dep. Leader 1967–69; Lord Mayor 1969–70. Chm., North Western Art Galleries and Museums Service, 1965–68; Mem., Exec. Cttee, Museums Assoc., 1965–69. Pres., Central Manchester Br., Arthritis and Rheumatism Council, 1970. Member: Duke of Edinburgh's Award Scheme Cttee, Manchester Area, 1972–75; Bd, Manchester YMCA, 1960–73. Mem., Chartered Auctioneers & Estate Agents Agricl Cttee, 1949–70; Mem., ABCC Rating Cttee, 1971–74. *Recreations:* football, fishing, horse racing. *Address:* c/o Trafford Park Estates PLC, Estate Office, Trafford Park, Manchester M17 1AU. *Clubs:* Carlton; Manchester Tennis and Racquets.

WESTBROOK, Roger, CMG 1990; HM Diplomatic Service; Ambassador to Portugal, since 1995; *b* 26 May 1941; *e s* of Edward George Westbrook and Beatrice Minnie Westbrook (*née* Marshall). *Educ:* Dulwich Coll.; Hertford Coll., Oxford (MA Modern History). Foreign Office, 1964; Asst Private Sec. to Chancellor of Duchy of Lancaster and Minister of State, FO, 1965; Yaoundé, 1967; Rio de Janeiro, 1971; Brasilia, 1972; Private Sec. to Minister of State, FCO, 1975; Head of Chancery, Lisbon, 1977; Dep. Head, News Dept, FCO, 1980; Dep. Head, Falkland Is Dept, FCO, 1982; Overseas Inspectorate, FCO, 1984; High Comr, Negara Brunei Darussalam, 1986–91; Ambassador to Zaire, 1991–92; High Comr, Tanzania, 1992–95. *Recreations:* doodling, sightseeing, theatre, reading, dining. *Address:* c/o Foreign and Commonwealth Office, SW1A 2AH. *Club:* Travellers'.

WESTBURY, 5th Baron, *cr* 1861; **David Alan Bethell,** CBE 1994; MC 1942; DL; *b* 16 July 1922; *s* of Captain The Hon. Richard Bethell (*d* 1929; *o c* of 3rd Baron); *S* brother, 1961; *m* 1947, Ursula Mary Rose James, CBE; two *s* one *d*. *Educ:* Harrow. 2nd Lieut 1940, Capt. 1944, Scots Guards. Equerry to the Duke of Gloucester, 1946–49. DL N Yorks, formerly NR Yorks, 1973. GCStJ 1988 (KStJ 1977). *Heir: s* Hon. Richard Nicholas Bethell, MBE 1979 [*b* 29 May 1950; *m* 1st, 1975; one *s* two *d*; 2nd, 1993, Charlotte Sarah-Jane, *d* of Jack Gore. *Educ:* Harrow; RMA Sandhurst. Major Scots Guards, retired]. *Address:* Barton Cottage, Malton, North Yorkshire YO17 0AT. *T:* Malton (01653) 692293.

WESTBURY, Prof. Gerald, OBE 1990; FRCP, FRCS; Professor of Surgery, 1982–89, now Professor Emeritus, and Dean, 1986–92, Institute of Cancer Research; Hon. Consultant Surgeon, Royal Marsden Hospital, 1982–89; *b* 29 July 1927; *s* of Lew and Celia Westbury; *m* 1965, Hazel Frame; three *d*. *Educ:* St Marylebone Grammar Sch.; Westminster Med. Sch., Univ. of London (MB, BS (Hons) 1949); FRCS 1952; FRCP 1976. House Surg., Westminster and Royal Northern Hosps, 1949–50; RAF Med. Service, 1950–52; RSO, Brompton Hosp., 1952–53; Registrar and Sen. Registrar, Westminster Hosp., 1953–60; Fellow in Surgery, Harvard Med. Sch., 1957; Cons. Surg., Westminster Hosp., 1960–82 (Hon. Cons. Surgeon, 1982–89); Hon. Cons. in Surgery to the Army, 1980–89. Pres., British Assoc. of Surgical Oncology, 1989–92. Examiner, Univs of London, Edinburgh, Cambridge, Hong Kong; Hunterian Prof., RCS, 1963; Honyman Gillespie Lectr, Univ. of Edinburgh, 1965; Semon Lectr and Haddow Lectr, RSM, 1982; Gordon-Taylor Lectr, RCS, 1989. Hon. FRCSE, 1993. Walker Prize, RCS, 1990. *Publications:* medical articles and contribs to text books. *Recreations:* music, bird watching. *Club:* Athenæum.

WESTCOTT, Prof. John Hugh, DSc(Eng), PhD, DIC; FRS 1983; FEng, FCGI, FInstD; Emeritus Professor of Control Systems, and Senior Research Fellow, Imperial College of Science and Technology; Chairman: Feedback plc; Churchill Controls Ltd; *b* 3 Nov. 1920; *s* of John Stanley Westcott and Margaret Elisabeth Westcott (*née* Bass); *m* 1950, Helen Fay Morgan; two *s* one *d*. *Educ:* Wandsworth Sch.; City and Guilds Coll., London; Massachusetts Inst. of Technology. Royal Commission for the Exhibition of 1851 Senior Studentship; Apprenticeship BTH Co., Rugby. Radar Research and Develt Estabt, 1941–45; Lectr, Imperial Coll., 1950; Reader, 1956; Prof., 1961; Head of Computing and Control Dept, 1970–79. Control Commn for Germany, 1945–46. Consultant to: Bataafsche Petroleum Maatschappij (Shell), The Hague, Holland, 1953–58; AEI, 1955–69; ICI, 1965–69; George Wimpey & Son, 1975–80; Westland plc, 1983–85. Chm., Control and Automation Div., Instn of Electrical Engrs, 1968–69. Mem., Exec. Council of Internat. Fedn of Automatic Control, 1969–75; Chm., United Kingdom Automation Council, 1973–79; Pres., Inst. of Measurement and Control, 1979–80. Mem., Adv. Council, RMCS, 1986–; Governor, Kingston Polytechnic, 1974–80. Hon. FIEE; Hon. FInstMC. *Publications:* An Exposition of Adaptive Control, 1962; monographs and papers, mainly on Control Systems and related topics. *Recreations:* gardening, reading. *Address:* (home) 8 Fernhill, Oxshott, Surrey KT22 0JH; Department of Electrical Engineering, Imperial College, SW7 2BT. *T:* 0171–594 6240.

WESTENRA, family name of **Baron Rossmore.**

WESTERMAN, Sir (Wilfred) Alan, Kt 1963; CBE 1962 (OBE 1957); EdD; MAEcon; Chairman, Australian Industry Development Corporation, 1971–83; *b* NZ, 25 March 1913; *s* of W. J. Westerman, Sydney, NSW; *m* 1969, Margaret, *d* of late B. H. White. *Educ:* Knox Grammar School; Universities of Tasmania, Melbourne and Columbia. Chairman, Commonwealth Tariff Board, 1958–60; Sec., Dept of Trade and Industry, Canberra, 1960–71. Director: Ampol Ltd; Philips Industries Holdings Ltd; Oak Systems of Australia Pty Limited; Chm., Stevedoring Industry Consultative Council, 1978–. *Recreation:* tennis. *Address:* 47 Tasmania Circle, Forrest, ACT 2603, Australia. *Clubs:* Commonwealth (Canberra); Athenæum (Melbourne); Union (Sydney).

WESTHEIMER, Prof. Gerald, FRS 1985; Professor of Neurobiology, University of California, Berkeley, since 1989 (Professor of Physiology, 1967–89; Head of Division of Neurobiology, 1989–92); *b* Berlin, 13 May 1924; *s* of late Isaac Westheimer and Ilse Westheimer (*née* Cohn). *Educ:* Sydney Tech. Coll. (Optometry dip. 1943, Fellowship dip. 1949); Univ. of Sydney (BSc 1947); Ohio State Univ. (PhD 1953); postdoctoral training at Marine Biol. Lab., Woods Hole, 1957 and at Physiolog. Lab., Cambridge, 1958–59. Australian citizen, 1945; practising optometrist, Sydney, 1945–51; faculties of Optometry Schools: Univ. of Houston, 1953–54; Ohio State Univ., 1954–60; Univ. of California, Berkeley, 1960–67. Associate: Bosch Vision Res. Center, Salk Inst., 1984–92; Neurosciences Res. Program, NY, 1985–95; Chairman: Visual Scis Study Sect., NIH, 1977–79; Bd of Scientific Counsellors, Nat. Eye Inst., 1981–83; Bd of Editors, Vision Research, 1986–91; service on numerous professional cttees. Adjunct Prof., Rockefeller Univ., NY, 1992–. Fellow or Member, scientific socs, UK and overseas; Fellow, Amer. Acad. of Arts and Scis. Lectures: Sackler, in Med. Sci., Tel Aviv Univ., 1989; Perception, Eur. Conf. on Visual Perception, 1989; D. O. Hebb, McGill Univ., Canada, 1991; Ferrier, Royal Soc., 1992. Hon. DSc: New South Wales, 1988; SUNY, 1990. Tillyer Medal, Optical Soc. of America, 1978; Proctor Medal, Assoc. for Res. in Vision and Ophthalmology, 1979; von Sallmann Prize, Coll. of Physicians and Surgeons, Columbia Univ., 1986; Prentice Medal, Amer. Acad. of Optometry, 1986; Bicentennial Medal, Aust. Optometric Assoc., 1988. *Publications:* research articles in sci. and professional optometric and ophth. jls; edtl work for sci. jls. *Recreations:* chamber music (violin), foundation and history of sensory physiology. *Address:* 582 Santa Barbara Road, Berkeley, CA 94707, USA. *Club:* Cosmos (Washington).

WESTLAKE, Peter Alan Grant, CMG 1972; MC 1943; *b* 2 Feb. 1919; *s* of A. R. C. Westlake, CSI, CIE, and late Dorothy Louise (*née* Turner) *m* 1943, Katherine Spackman (*d* 1990); two *s*. *Educ:* Sherborne; Corpus Christi Coll., Oxford; Military College of Science. Served with 1st Regt RHA (Adjt 1942), and on the staff (despatches). HM Foreign Service (now Diplomatic Service), 1946–76: served in Japan and at Foreign Office; Joint Services Staff College, 1954; Israel, 1955; Japan, 1957; Administrative Staff Coll., 1961; Counsellor: Foreign Office, 1961; Washington, 1965; British High Commn, Canberra, 1967–71; Minister, Tokyo, 1971–76. Pres., Asiatic Soc. of Japan, 1972–74. UK Comr-General, Internat. Ocean Expo, Okinawa, 1975. BD Wales 1981, MSc Wales, 1981; Deacon, Church in Wales, 1981, Priest 1982. FRAS. Order of the Rising Sun, Japan. *Publications:* The Proud Walkers, 1992; Holy Island, 1992; Equations of motion for the Earth's crust, 1993. *Address:* 53 Church Street, Beaumaris, Anglesey LL58 8AB.

WESTMACOTT, Peter John, LVO 1993; HM Diplomatic Service; Counsellor, Washington, since 1993; *b* 23 Dec. 1950; *s* of Prebendary Ian Field Westmacott and

Rosemary Patricia Spencer Westmacott; *m* 1972, Angela Margaret Lugg; two *s* one *d*. *Educ:* Taunton Sch.; New Coll., Oxford (MA). Entered FCO 1972; served Tehran 1974, Brussels, 1978; First Sec., Paris, 1980; Private Sec. to Minister of State, FCO, 1984; Head of Chancery, Ankara, 1987; Dep. Private Sec. to Prince of Wales, 1990. *Recreations:* tennis, ski-ing, squash. *Address:* c/o Foreign and Commonwealth Office, SW1A 2AH. *Club:* University (Washington).

WESTMACOTT, Richard Kelso; Chairman: R. G. B. Capital Holdings Ltd, since 1994; Deputy Chairman, Maritime Trust, since 1992; *b* 20 Feb. 1934; *s* of Comdr John Rowe Westmacott, RN and Ruth Pharazyn; *m* 1965, Karen Husbands; one *s* one *d*. *Educ:* Eton College. Royal Navy, 1952–54. Hoare & Co., 1955; Mem., Stock Exchange, 1960; Chairman: Hoare Govett Ltd, 1975–90; Security Pacific Hoare Govett (Holdings) Ltd, 1985–90. Director: General Consolidated Investment Trust Ltd, 1992–; Citadel Reinsurance Co., 1992–; H. W. (Park Place) Ltd, 1993–; Advanced Fluid Systems Ltd, 1994–. *Recreations:* sailing, shooting. *Address:* 9 Alexander Square, SW3 2AY. *Clubs:* White's; Royal Yacht Squadron.

WESTMEATH, 13th Earl of, *cr* 1621; **William Anthony Nugent;** Baron Delvin, by tenure temp. Henry II; by summons, 1486; Senior Master, St Andrew's School, Pangbourne, 1980–88; *b* 21 Nov. 1928; *s* of 12th Earl of Westmeath and Doris (*d* 1968), 2nd *d* of C. Imlach, Liverpool; *S* father, 1971; *m* 1963, Susanna Margaret, *o d* of J. C. B. W. Leonard, *qv*; two *s*. *Educ:* Marlborough Coll. Captain, RA, retired. Staff of St Andrew's Sch., Pangbourne, 1961–88. *Heir:* *s* Hon. Sean Charles Weston Nugent, *b* 16 Feb. 1965. *Address:* Farthings, Rotten Row Hill, Bradfield, Berks RG7 6LL. *T:* Bradfield (01734) 744426.

WESTMINSTER, 6th Duke of, *cr* 1874; **Gerald Cavendish Grosvenor;** OBE 1995; TD 1994; DL; Bt 1622; Baron Grosvenor, 1761; Earl Grosvenor and Viscount Belgrave, 1784; Marquess of Westminster, 1831; *b* 22 Dec. 1951; *s* of 5th Duke of Westminster, TD, and Viola Maud (*d* 1987), *d* of 9th Viscount Cobham, KCB, TD; *S* father, 1979; *m* 1978, Natalia, *d* of Lt-Col H. P. J. Phillips; one *s* three *d*. *Educ:* Harrow. Commnd Queen's Own Yeomanry, RAC, TA, 1973; Captain, 1979; Major, 1985; Lt-Col, 1992; Comd, 1993–95; Col, 1995. Director: Internat. Students Trust, 1976–93; Claridges Hotel Ltd, 1981–93; Marcher Sound Ltd, 1982–; Grosvenor Estate Hldgs, 1989–; Westminster Christmas Appeal Trust Ltd, 1989–94; NW Business Leadership Team Ltd, 1990–; BITC, 1991–95; Manchester Olympic Games Co-ordinating Cttee Ltd, 1991–94. Governor: Royal Agricl Soc. of England; Chester Teacher Training Coll., 1979; Pro-Chancellor, Univ. of Keele, 1986–93; Chancellor, Manchester Metropolitan Univ., 1993–. President: NW Industrialists' Council, 1979–93; Chester City Conservative Assoc., 1977–93; RNIB, 1986–; Arthritis Care, 1987–; Spastics Soc., 1985–; Game Conservancy; London Fedn of Boys' Clubs; Abbeyfield Soc., 1989–; Nat. Kidney Res. Fund; Drug and Alcohol Foundn. Member, Committee: Rural Target Team, Business in the Community; N Amer. Adv. Gp, BOTB; Nat. Army Mus.; Prince's Youth Business Trust; US Inf. Agency; Winston Churchill Meml Trust. Patron: Worcs CCC (Pres., 1984–86); British Holstein Soc.; British Kidney Patients Assoc.; Dyslexia Inst., 1989–. Trustee: TSB Foundn for England and Wales; Grosvenor Estate; Westminster Abbey Trust; Westminster Foundn; Westminster Housing Trust. Freeman: Chester, 1973; England, 1979; City of London, 1980. Liveryman: GAPAN; Gunmakers' Co.; Weavers' Co.; Armourers and Braziers' Co.; Marketors' Co.; Goldsmiths' Co.; Fishmongers' Co. FRSA; FRAS; FCIM; FCIOB. Hon. MRICS. KStJ 1991. DL Cheshire, 1982. *Recreations:* shooting, fishing, scuba diving. *Heir:* *s* Earl Grosvenor, *qv*. *Address:* Eaton Hall, Chester, Cheshire CH4 9EJ. *Clubs:* Brooks's, Cavalry, MCC; Royal Yacht Squadron.

WESTMINSTER, Archbishop of, (RC), since 1976; **His Eminence Cardinal (George) Basil Hume;** *b* 2 March 1923; *s* of Sir William Hume, CMG, FRCP. *Educ:* Ampleforth Coll.; St Benet's Hall, Oxford; Fribourg Univ., Switzerland. Ordained priest 1950. Ampleforth College: Senior Modern Language Master, 1952–63; Housemaster, 1955–63; Prof. of Dogmatic Theology, 1955–63; Magister Scholarum of the English Benedictine Congregation, 1957–63; Abbot of Ampleforth, 1963–76. Cardinal, 1976. President: RC Bishops' Conf. of England and Wales, 1979–; Council of European Bishops' Confs, 1979–86; (jtly) Churches Together in England, 1990–; Member: Council for Secretariat of Internat. Synod of Bishops, 1978–87; Congregation for Eastern Churches, 1994. Hon. Bencher, Inner Temple, 1976. Hon. DD: Cantab, 1979; Newcastle upon Tyne, 1979; London, 1980; Oxon, 1981; York, 1982; Kent, 1983; Durham, 1987; Collegio S Anselmo, Rome, 1987; Hull, 1989; Hon. DHL: Manhattan Coll., NY, 1980; Catholic Univ. of America, 1980; Hon. LLD Newcastle upon Tyne Polytechnic, 1992; DUniv Surrey, 1992. *Publications:* Searching for God, 1977; In Praise of Benedict, 1981; To Be a Pilgrim, 1984; Towards a Civilisation of Love, 1988; Light in the Lord, 1991; Remaking Europe: the gospel in a divided continent, 1994. *Address:* Archbishop's House, Westminster, SW1P 1QJ.

WESTMINSTER, Auxiliary Bishops of, (RC); *see* Guazzelli, Rt Rev. V.; Nichols, Rt Rev. V. G.; O'Brien, Rt Rev. J. J., and O'Donoghue, Rt Rev. P.

WESTMINSTER, Dean of; *see* Mayne, Very Rev. M. C. O.

WESTMORLAND, 16th Earl of *cr* 1624; **Anthony David Francis Henry Fane;** Baron Burghersh, 1624; *b* 1 Aug. 1951; *s* of 15th Earl of Westmorland, GCVO and of Jane, *d* of Lt-Col Sir Roland Lewis Findlay, 3rd Bt; *S* father, 1993; *m* 1985, Caroline Eldred, *d* of Keon Hughes; one *d*. *Educ:* Eton. Mem., Orbitex North Pole Expedn, 1990. Life Pres., St Moritz Sporting Club. Governor, Guild of Veteran Pilots and Racing Drivers. *Heir:* *b* Hon. Harry St Clair Fane [*b* 19 March 1953; *m* 1984, Tessa, *d* of Captain Michael Philip Forsyth-Forrest; one *s* one *d*]. *Address:* London SW10. *Club:* Turf.

WESTMORLAND AND FURNESS, Archdeacon of; *see* Jenkins, Ven. D. T. I.

WESTOLL, James, DL; *b* 26 July 1918, *s* of late James Westoll, Glingerbank, Longtown; *m* 1946, Sylvia Jane Luxmoore, MBE, *d* of late Lord Justice Luxmoore, Bilsington, Kent; two *s* two *d*. *Educ:* Eton; Trinity College, Cambridge (MA). Served War of 1939–45: Major, The Border Regiment (despatches). Called to Bar, Lincoln's Inn, 1952. Member, NW Electricity Board, 1959–66; Deputy Chm., Cumberland Quarter Sessions, 1960–71; Cumberland County Council: CC 1947; CA 1959–74; Chm., 1958–74; Chm., Cumbria Local Govt Reorganisation Jt Cttee, 1973; Chm., Cumbria CC, 1973–76. DL 1963, High Sheriff 1964, Cumberland. Warden, 1973–75, Master, 1983–84, Clothworkers' Company. Hon. LLD Leeds, 1984. KStJ 1983. *Recreations:* gardening, shooting. *Address:* Dykeside, Longtown, Carlisle, Cumbria CA6 5ND. *T:* Longtown (01228) 791235. *Clubs:* Boodle's, Farmers'; County and Border (Carlisle).

WESTON, Bertram John, CMG 1960; OBE 1957; retired from the public service; Estate Factor to British Union Trust Ltd, 1964–81; *b* 30 March 1907; *o s* of late J. G. Weston, Kennington, Kent; *m* 1932, Irene Carey; two *d*. *Educ:* Ashford Grammar School; Sidney Sussex College, Cambridge (MA); Pretoria University, SA (MSc, Agric); Cornell University, USA (Post Grad.). Horticulturist, Cyprus, 1931; Asst Comr, Nicosia (on secondment), 1937; Administrative Officer, 1939. War Service, 1940–43 (Major). Commissioner for development and post-war construction, Cyprus, 1943; Commissioner, 1946; Administrative Officer Class I, 1951; Senior Administrative Officer, 1954; Senior Commissioner, 1958; Government Sec., St Helena, 1960–63; acted as Governor and C-in-C, St Helena, at various times during this period. *Recreations:* lawn tennis, gardening, watching cricket and other sports. *Address:* 10 Westfield Close, Uphill, Weston-super-Mare BS23 4XQ. *Club:* Commonwealth Trust.

WESTON, Bryan Henry; Chairman: Manweb plc (formerly Merseyside and North Wales Electricity Board), 1985–94; The National Grid Holding, 1991–93; *b* 9 April 1930; *s* of Henry James Weston and Rose Grace Weston; *m* 1956, Heather West; two *s* two *d*. *Educ:* St George Grammar School, Bristol; Bristol, Rutherford and Oxford Technical Colleges. CEng, FIEE; CIMgt. South Western Electricity Board: Commercial Manager, 1973–75; Bd Mem., 1975; Exec. Mem., 1975–77; Dep. Chm., Yorkshire Electricity Bd, 1977–85. *Recreations:* caravanning, walking, gardening. *Address:* Fountainhead Cottage, Brassey Green, near Tarporley, Cheshire CW6 9UG. *T:* Tarporley (01829) 733523.

WESTON, Rear-Adm. Charles Arthur Winfield, CB 1978; Admiral President, RN College, Greenwich, 1976–78; Appeals Secretary, King Edward VII's Hospital for Officers, 1979–87; *b* 12 July 1922; *s* of late Charles Winfield Weston and of Edith Alice Weston; *m* 1946, Jeanie Findlay Miller; one *s* one *d*. *Educ:* Merchant Taylors' Sch. Entered RN as Special Entry Cadet, 1940; HM Ships: Glasgow, 1940; Durban, 1942; Staff of C-in-C Mediterranean, as Sec. to Captain of the Fleet, 1944–45 (despatches 1945); Sec. to Cdre in Charge Sheerness, 1946–47, to Flag Captain Home Fleet, HMS Duke of York, 1947–48; Loan Service, RAN, 1948–50; HM Ships: St Vincent, 1952–53; Ceres, 1954–55; Decoy, 1956; Sec. to DCNP (Trng and Manning), 1957–58, to DG Trng, 1959; CO HMS Jufair, 1960; Supply Officer, St Vincent, 1961–62; Sec. to Fleet Comdr Far East Fleet, 1963–64, to Second Sea Lord, 1965–67; sowc 1968; Chief Staff Officer (Q) to C-in-C Naval Home Comd, 1969–70; DNPTS, 1971; Director Defence Admin Planning Staff, 1972–74; Dir of Quartering (Navy), 1975. ADC to the Queen, 1976. Rear-Adm. 1976. Liveryman, 1979–93, Freeman, 1993, Shipwrights' Co. *Recreations:* golf, gardening, music, watching cricket. *Address:* Flinten Barn, Little Thornage, Holt, Norfolk NR25 7JD. *T:* Holt (01263) 713523. *Clubs:* MCC; Norfolk (Norwich); Sheringham Golf.

WESTON, Christopher John; Chairman and Chief Executive: Phillips Son & Neale, since 1972; Glendining & Co., and subsidiaries, since 1972; *b* 3 March 1937; *s* of Eric Tudor Weston and Evelyn Nellie Weston; *m* 1969, Josephine Annabel Moir; one *d*. *Educ:* Lancing Coll. FIA (Scot.). Director: Phillips, 1964–; Foreign and Colonial Pacific Investment Trust, 1984–; Hodder Headline Plc (formerly Headline Book Publishing PLC), 1986–; Foreign & Colonial Enterprise Trust plc, 1987–; Oxford Molecular Group plc, 1994–; Chm., Bradford Peters (Holdings) Ltd, 1977–. Chm., Council, Quit-Soc. of Non Smokers, 1993–. Chm. Council, Parnham Trust, 1992–. Pres., Soc. of Fine Art Auctioneers, 1987– (Chm., 1973–87). Liveryman, Painters-Stainers' Co. FRSA (Mem. Council, 1985). *Recreations:* theatre, music. *Address:* 101 New Bond Street, W1Y 0AS. *T:* 0171–629 6602. *Club:* Oriental.

WESTON, Rev. Canon David Wilfrid Valentine, PhD; Residentiary Canon of Carlisle Cathedral, since 1994; Canon Librarian, since 1995; *b* 8 Dec. 1937; *s* of late Rev. William Valentine Weston and late Mrs Gertrude Hamilton Weston; *m* 1984, Helen Strachan Macdonald, *d* of James and Barbara Macdonald; two *s*. *Educ:* St Edmund's Sch., Canterbury; Lancaster Univ. (PhD 1993). Entered Nashdom Abbey, 1960; deacon, 1967, priest, 1968; Novice Master, 1969–74; Prior, 1971–74; Abbot, 1974–84; Curate, St Peter's, Chorley, 1984–85; Vicar, St John the Baptist, Pilling, 1985–89; Domestic Chaplain to Bishop of Carlisle, 1989–94. Freeman, City of London; Liveryman of Salters' Co. *Address:* 3 The Abbey, Carlisle, Cumbria CA3 8TZ.

See also Ven. F. V. Weston.

WESTON, Ven. Frank Valentine; Archdeacon of Oxford and a Canon of Christ Church, Oxford, since 1982; *b* 16 Sept. 1935; *s* of William Valentine Weston and Gertrude Hamilton Weston; *m* 1963, Penelope Brighid, *d* of Marmaduke Carver Middleton Athorpe, formerly of Dinnington, Yorks and Hilda Bridget (*née* Waterfall); one *s* two *d*. *Educ:* Christ's Hospital; Queen's Coll., Oxford; Lichfield Theological Coll. BA 1960, MA 1964. Curate, St John the Baptist, Atherton, Lancs, 1961–65; Chaplain, 1965–69, Principal, 1969–76, College of the Ascension, Selly Oak, Birmingham; Vice-Pres., Selly Oak Colls, 1973–76; Principal and Pantonian Prof., Edinburgh Theological Coll., 1976–82. Court of Assistants, Salters' Co., 1984– (Master, 1992–93). Governor: St Augustine's Upper Sch., Oxford, 1983–; Christ's Hosp., 1988–; Tudor Hall Sch., 1988–. *Publications:* (contrib.) Quel Missionnaire, 1971; (contrib.) Gestalten der Kirchengeschichte, 1984. *Recreations:* wine, persons and song; exploring the countryside. *Address:* Archdeacon's Lodging, Christ Church, Oxford OX1 1DP. *T:* Oxford (01865) 276185.

See also Rev. D. W. V. Weston.

WESTON, Galen; *see* Weston, W. G.

WESTON, Garfield Howard, (Garry); Chairman: Associated British Foods plc, since 1967; Fortnum and Mason, since 1978; British Sugar PLC, since 1991; *b* 28 April 1927; *s* of late Willard Garfield Weston and Reta Lila Howard; *m* 1959, Mary Ruth, *d* of late Major-Gen. Sir Howard Kippenberger; three *s* three *d*. *Educ:* Sir William Borlase School, Marlow; New College, Oxford; Harvard University (Economics). Man. Dir, Weston Biscuit Co., Aust., 1954; Vice-Chairman, Associated British Foods Ltd, 1960; Chm., George Weston Holdings Ltd, 1978. *Recreations:* gardening, tennis, walking. *Address:* Weston Centre, Bowater House, 68 Knightsbridge, SW1X 7LR. *T:* 0171–589 6363.

WESTON, Geoffrey Harold, CBE 1975; FHSM; retired; Deputy Health Service Commissioner for England, Scotland and for Wales, 1977–82; *b* 11 Sept. 1920; *s* of George and Florence Mary Weston; *m* 1953, Monica Mary Grace Comyns; three *d*. *Educ:* Wolverhampton Sch. War Service, 1940–46. Gp Sec., Reading and Dist Hosp Management Cttee, 1955–65; Board Sec., NW Metropolitan Regional Hosp. Bd, 1965–73; Regional Administrator, NW Thames RHA, 1973–76. Member: Salmon Cttee, 1963–65; Whitley Councils: Mem. Management side of Optical Council, 1955–65, and of Nurses and Midwives Council, 1966–76; Mem., Working Party on Collab. between Local Govt and Nat. Health Service, 1973–74. Inst. of Health Service Administrators: Mem., Nat. and Reg. Councils, 1959–78 (Vice-Chm. of Council, 1968, Chm. 1969, Pres. of Inst., 1970). Bd Mem., London and Provincial Nursing Services Ltd, 1973–90; Member: Mental Health Review Tribunal, 1982–93; Oxford RHA, 1983–89; Trustee, Goring Day Centre, 1978–89. Vice-Chm., Goring Decorative and Fine Arts Soc., 1990–93 (Treas., 1987–89). Parish Councillor, Goring, 1979–87. *Recreations:* travel, dining with friends. *Address:* 15 Hill Gardens, Streatley, near Reading, Berks RG8 9QF. *T:* Goring on Thames (01491) 872881. *Club:* Royal Air Force.

WESTON, Sir John; *see* Weston, Sir P. J.

WESTON, Dr John Carruthers; General Manager, Northampton Development Corporation, 1969–77. *Educ:* Univ. of Nottingham. Admiralty Research, 1940–46; Plessey Co., 1946–47; Building Research Station, 1947–64; Chief Exec. Operational Div., Nat. Building Agency, 1964–65; Dir, Building Research Station, MPBW, 1966–69. *Recreations:* gardening, music, walking, reading and living.

WESTON, John Pix, BSc(Eng), BSc(Econ); CEng, FIEE; investment consultant, since 1984; *b* 3 Jan. 1920; *s* of John Pix Weston and Margaret Elizabeth (*née* Cox); *m* 1948, Ivy (*née* Glover); three *s*. *Educ:* King Edward's Sch., Birmingham, 1931–36; Univ. of Aston, 1946–50 (BSc(Eng), Hons); Univ. of London (LSE), 1954–57 (BSc(Econ), Hons). CEng 1953, FIEE 1966; FSS 1958; FREconS 1958; FIMgt (FBIM 1977). City of Birmingham: Police Dept, 1936–39; Electricity Supply Dept, 1939–48; Midlands Electricity Bd, 1948–50; English Electricity Co., 1950–51; NW Elec. Bd, 1951–58; Eastern Elec. Bd, 1958–60; Dep. Operating Man., Jamaica Public Services Co., 1960–61; Principal Asst Engr, Midlands Elec. Bd, 1961–64; Asst Ch. Commercial Officer, S of Scotland Elec. Bd, 1964–66; Sen. Econ. Adviser to Mrs Barbara Castle, MoT, 1966–69; Sen. Econ. and Chartered Engr, IBRD, 1968–70; Michelin Tyre Co., France, 1970–72; Dir of Post Experience Courses, Open Univ., 1972–75; Dir Gen., RoSPA, 1975–77; Gen. Sec., Birmingham Anglers' Assoc., 1977; Industrial Develt Officer, Argyll and Bute, 1977–79; Health, Safety and Welfare Officer, Newcastle Polytechnic, and Central Safety Advr, Northants CC, 1979; Chief Admin. Officer and Clerk to Governors, W Bromwich Coll. of Comm. and Tech., 1979–85. Hon. Sec. and Treasurer, Assoc. of Coll. Registrars and Administrators (W Midlands), 1982–85. Council Mem., Midlands Counties Photographic Fedn, 1984–86; Hon. Prog., Competition and Outings Sec. and Council Mem., Birmingham Photographic Soc., 1981–86; MIES 1963; Mem., Assoc. of Public Lighting Engrs, 1962. Chm., Upper Marlbrook Residents' Assoc., 1982–87; Treasurer, Laugharne Cons. Assoc., 1991–94 (Asst Treasurer, 1990–91). Member: Narbeth and Dist Probus Club, 1988–; St Clears Probus Club, 1989– (Pres., 1990–91); Tenby Probus Club, 1990–. Page Prize, IEE, 1950; Rosebery Prize, Univ. of London, 1957. SBStJ 1962. *Publications:* papers, reports and other contribs on electricity, highways, educn (espec. function and progress of the Open University), safety, etc, to public bodies, congresses and conferences, UK and abroad. *Recreations:* cine photography, gardening, swimming, fell walking. *Address:* Brook Mill & Woodside, Brook, Pendine, Dyfed SA33 4NX. *T:* Laugharne (01994) 427477. *Clubs:* Farmers', St John House; Birmingham Press.

See also J. P. Weston.

WESTON, John Pix, CBE 1994; CEng, FRAeS; Chairman and Managing Director, British Aerospace Defence Ltd, since 1992; Director, British Aerospace plc, since 1994; *b* 16 Aug. 1951; *s* of John Pix Weston, *qv* and Ivy (*née* Glover); *m* 1974, Susan West; one *s* one *d*. *Educ:* King's Sch., Worcester; Trinity Hall., Cambridge (MA Eng.). CEng 1992; FRAeS 1992. British Aerospace: undergrad. apprenticeship, 1970–74; sales appts on Jaguar and Tornado projects, 1974–82; on secondment to MoD Sales Orgn, 1982–85; Military Aircraft Division, Warton: ME Sales Manager, Project Manager, Al Yamamah Project and Exec. Dir, Saudi Ops, 1985–89; Dir, 1989–92; Man. Dir, 1990–92. *Recreations:* ski-ing, photography, hill-walking. *Address:* British Aerospace Defence Ltd, Lancaster House, Farnborough Aerospace Centre, Farnborough, Hants GU14 6YU. *T:* Farnborough (01252) 384820.

WESTON, John William, CB 1979; Principal Assistant Solicitor, Board of Inland Revenue, 1967–80; *b* 3 Feb. 1915; *s* of Herbert Edward Weston, MA, and Emma Gertrude Weston; *m* 1943, Frances Winifred (*née* Johnson); two *s* one *d*. *Educ:* Berkhamsted Sch., Herts. Solicitor, 1937. Joined Inland Revenue, 1940; Sen. Legal Asst, 1948; Asst Solicitor, 1954. *Recreation:* golf. *Address:* 5 Dickerage Road, Kingston Hill, Surrey KT1 3SP. *T:* 0181–942 8130.

WESTON, Dame Margaret (Kate), DBE 1979; BScEng (London); CEng, MIEE, FINucE; FMA; Director of the Science Museum, 1973–86; *b* 7 March 1926; *o c* of late Charles Edward and Margaret Weston. *Educ:* Stroud High School; College of Technology, Birmingham (now Univ. of Aston). Engineering apprenticeship with General Electric Co. Ltd, followed in 1949 by development work, very largely on high voltage insulation problems. Joined Science Museum as an Assistant Keeper, Dept of Electrical Engineering and Communications, 1955; Deputy Keeper, 1962; Keeper, Dept of Museum Services, 1967–72. Member: Ancient Monuments Bd for England, 1977–84; 1851 Commission, 1987–; Museums and Galleries Commission, 1988–; Steering Gp, Museum in Docklands, 1986–90. Member: SE Elec. Bd, 1981–90; BBC Sci. Consultative Gp, 1986–89. Chm., Horniman Public Mus. and Public Park Trust, 1990–; Trustee: Hunterian Collection, 1981–; Brooklands, 1987–; Fleet Air Arm Mus., 1992–. Governor, Imperial Coll., 1974–90 (FIC 1975); Governor and Mem. Management Cttee, Ditchley Foundn, 1984–. Pres., Assoc. of Railway Preservation Socs, 1985–. FMA 1976; Sen. Fellow, RCA, 1986; FRSA (Mem. Council, 1985–90); CIMgt. Hon. Fellow, Newnham Coll., Cambridge, 1986. Hon. DEng Bradford, 1984; Hon. DSc: Aston, 1974; Salford, 1984; Leeds, 1987; Loughborough, 1988; DUniv Open, 1987. *Address:* 7 Shawley Way, Epsom, Surrey KT18 5NZ. *T:* Burgh Heath (01737) 355885.

WESTON, Sir Michael (Charles Swift), KCMG 1991; CVO 1979; HM Diplomatic Service; UK Permanent Representative to Conference on Disarmament, Geneva (with personal rank of Ambassador), since 1992; *b* 4 Aug. 1937; *s* of late Edward Charles Swift Weston and of Kathleen Mary Weston (*née* Mockett); *m* 1st, 1959, Veronica Anne Tickner (marr. diss. 1990); two *s* one *d*; 2nd, 1990, Christine Julia Ferguson; one *s*. *Educ:* Dover Coll.; St Catharine's Coll., Cambridge (Exhibitioner). BA, MA. Joined HM Diplomatic Service, 1961; 3rd Sec., Kuwait, 1962; 2nd Sec., FCO, 1965; 1st Secretary: Tehran, 1968; UK Mission, New York, 1970; FCO, 1974; Counsellor, Jedda, 1977; RCDS, 1980; Counsellor (Information), Paris, 1981; Counsellor, Cairo, 1984; Head of Southern European Dept, FCO, 1987; Ambassador to Kuwait, 1990–92. *Recreations:* tennis, squash, walking. *Address:* c/o Foreign and Commonwealth Office, SW1A 2AH. *Club:* United Oxford & Cambridge University.

WESTON, Sir (Philip) John, KCMG 1992 (CMG 1985); HM Diplomatic Service; British Permanent Representative to the United Nations, since 1995; *b* 13 April 1938; *s* of late Philip George Weston and Edith Alice Bray (*née* Ansell); *m* 1967, Margaret Sally Ehlers; two *s* one *d*. *Educ:* Sherborne; Worcester Coll., Oxford. 1st Cl. Hons, Honour Mods Classics and Lit. Hum. Served with Royal Marines, 1956–58. Entered Diplomatic Service, 1962; FO, 1962–63; Treasury Centre for Admin. Studies, 1964; Chinese Language student, Hong Kong, 1964–66; Peking, 1967–68; FO, 1969–71; Office of UK Permanent Representative to EEC, 1972–74; Asst Private Sec. to Sec. of State for Foreign and Commonwealth Affairs (Rt Hon. James Callaghan, Rt Hon. Anthony Crosland), 1974–76; Counsellor, Head of EEC Presidency Secretariat, FCO, 1976–77; Vis. Fellow, All Souls Coll., Oxford, 1977–78; Counsellor, Washington, 1978–81; Hd Defence Dept, FCO, 1981–84; Asst Under-Sec. of State, FCO, 1984–85; Minister, Paris, 1985–88; Dep. Sec. to Cabinet, Cabinet Office, 1988–89 (on secondment); Dep. Under-Sec. of State (Defence), FCO, 1989–90; Political Dir, FCO, 1990–91; Ambassador and UK Perm. Rep. to N Atlantic Council (NATO), 1991–95, to Perm. Council of WEU, 1992–95. *Recreations:* fly-fishing, birds, running. *Address:* c/o Foreign and Commonwealth Office, SW1A 2AH. *Clubs:* Garrick, Flyfishers', United Oxford & Cambridge University.

WESTON, W(illard) Galen, OC 1990; President, since 1974 and Chairman, since 1978, George Weston Ltd, Toronto; *b* England, 29 Oct. 1940; *s* of W. Garfield Weston and Reta Lila (*née* Howard); *m* 1966, Hilary Mary Frayne; one *s* one *d*. Chairman: Loblaw Companies Ltd; Holt Renfrew & Co. Ltd; Weston Foods Ltd; Weston Resources Ltd; Wittington Investments Ltd; Vice-Chm., Fortnum & Mason plc (UK); Director: Canadian Imperial Bank of Commerce; Associated British Foods plc (UK); Brown Thomas Group Ltd (Eire). Pres. and Trustee, W. Garfield Weston Foundation, Canada; Chairman and Trustee: Lester B. Pearson Coll. of Pacific; United World Colls of Canada Inc. Hon. LLD Univ. of Western Ont. *Recreations:* polo, tennis. *Address:* Suite 2001, George Weston Ltd, 22 St Clair Avenue East, Toronto, Ont M4T 2S3, Canada. *T:* (416) 922500, *Fax:* (416) 9224394. *Clubs:* Guards' Polo; Toronto, York (Toronto); Lyford Cay (Bahamas); Windsor (Florida).

WESTWELL, Alan Reynolds, PhD, MSc; CEng, MIMechE, MIEE; FCIT; Managing Director and Chief Executive, Greater Manchester Buses North Ltd, since 1993 (Managing Director and Chief Executive, Greater Manchester Buses Ltd, 1990–93); *b* 11 April 1940; *s* of Stanley Westwell and Margaret (*née* Reynolds); *m* 1967, Elizabeth Aileen Birrell; two *s* one *d*. *Educ:* Old Swan Coll.; Liverpool Polytechnic (ACT Hons); Salford Univ. (MSc 1983); Keele Univ. (PhD 1991). Liverpool City Transport Dept: progressively, student apprentice, Technical Asst, Asst Works Manager, 1956–67; Chief Engineer: Southport Corporation Transport Dept, 1967–69; Coventry Corp. Transport Dept, 1969–72; Glasgow Corp. Transport Dept, 1972–74; Director of Public Transport (responsible for bus/rail, airport, harbours), Tayside Regional Council, 1974–79; Dir Gen., Strathclyde PTE, 1979–86; Chm., Man. Dir and Chief Exec., 1987–90, Strathclyde Buses Ltd. Professional Advr, COSLA, 1976–86. President: Scottish Council of Confedn of British Road Passenger Transport, 1982–83 (Vice-Pres., 1981–82); Bus and Coach Council, UK, 1989–90 (Vice Pres., 1985–88; Sen. Vice-Pres., 1988–89). Mem., Parly Road Transport Cttee, 1986–. Chm., IMechE, Automobile Div., Scottish Centre, 1982–84; Mem. Council, CIT, UK, 1986–89 (Chm. Scottish Centre, 1983–84); Mem. Management Cttee, UITP, 1991– (Mem. Internat. Metropolitan Railway Cttee, 1979–86; Mem. Internat. Commn, Traffic and Urban Planning, 1986–; Mem., European Action Cttee, 1988–). *Publications:* various papers. *Recreations:* golf, swimming, tennis, music, model making, reading. *Address:* 6 Amberley Drive, Hale Barns, Cheshire WA15 0DT. *T:* 0161–980 3551.

WESTWOOD, family name of **Baron Westwood.**

WESTWOOD, 3rd Baron *cr* 1944, of Gosforth; **William Gavin Westwood;** *b* 30 Jan. 1944; *s* of 2nd Baron and of Marjorie, *o c* of Arthur Bonwick; *S* father, 1991; *m* 1969, Penelope, *e d* of Dr C. E. Shafto; two *s*. *Educ:* Fettes. *Recreations:* golf, squash, music, reading. *Heir:* *s* Hon. (William) Fergus Westwood, *b* 24 Nov. 1972. *Address:* Ferndale, Clayton Road, Newcastle upon Tyne NE2 1TL. *T:* 0191–212 0567.

WESTWOOD, Vivienne Isabel, OBE 1992; fashion designer; *b* 8 April 1941; two *s*. In partnership with Malcolm McLaren 1970–83, designed a series of influential avant-garde collections shown at World's End, Chelsea; fashion shows included: Savage, 1981, Pirate and Buffalo, 1982, London; Punkature, 1982, Witches, 1983, Paris; Hypnos, Paris and Tokyo, 1983; solo career, 1984–: opened shop in Mayfair, 1990; shows include: Clint Eastwood, Paris, 1984; Mini Crini, Paris and NY, 1985; London: Harris Tweed, 1987; Pagan 1, 1987; Time Machine, and Civilizade, 1988; Voyage to Cythera, and Pagan V, 1989; Portrait, and Cut, Slash & Pull, 1990; Dressing Up, and Salon, 1991; Paris: Always on Camera, 1992; Grand Hotel, and Anglomania, 1993; Café Society, and On Liberty, 1994; Erotic Zones, and Vive La Cocotte, 1995. Professor of Fashion: Acad. of Applied Arts, Vienna, 1989–91; Hochschule der Künste, Berlin, 1993–. Sen. FRCA 1992. British Designer of the Year, 1990, 1991. *Address:* Laburnum House, Lantern Business Centre, Bridge Lane, SW11 3AD.

WESTWOOD, Rt Rev. William John; Bishop of Peterborough, 1984–95; *b* 28 Dec. 1925; *s* of Ernest and Charlotte Westwood; *m* 1954, Shirley Ann, *yr d* of Dr Norman Jennings; one *s* one *d*. *Educ:* Grove Park Grammar Sch., Wrexham; Emmanuel Coll. (Exhibnr 1944; Hon. Fellow 1989) and Westcott House, Cambridge. MA. Soldier, 1944–47. Curate of Hull, 1952–57; Rector of Lowestoft, 1957–65; Vicar of S Peter Mancroft, Norwich, 1965–75; Hon. Canon, Norwich Cathedral, 1969–75; Rural Dean of Norwich, 1966–70, City Dean, 1970–73; Area Bishop of Edmonton, 1975–84. Member: General Synod, 1970–75 and 1977–95; Archbishop's Commission on Church and State, 1966–70; Press Council, 1975–81; Church Commissioner, 1973–78 and 1985–92; Chm., C of E Cttee for Communications, 1979–86; Member: IBA Panel of Religious Advisers, 1983–87; Video Consultative Council, 1985–89; Broadcasting Standards Council, 1988–92; HEA, 1992–; Volunteering Partnership, 1995–. President: Nat. Deaf-Blind League, 1991–95; E of England Agricl Soc., 1994. Chm., Emmanuel Soc., 1989–. Chm. Governors, Coll. of All Saints, Tottenham, 1976–78; Mem. Court, Nene Coll., Northampton, 1990–95. Trustee: Oakham Sch., 1984–94; Uppingham Sch., 1984–95 (Chm., Trustees, 1994–95); Brooke Weston City Technol. Coll., Corby, 1992–95. Pres., English Churches Housing (formerly Church Housing Assoc.), 1985–95; Chairman: Lowestoft Church and Town Charities, 1957–65; Norwich Housing Soc., 1969–74; Cotman Housing Assoc., Norwich, 1972–75. Freeman, City of London, 1977. Hon. LLD Leicester, 1991. *Recreations:* the countryside, art galleries, wine bars. *Address:* 102 Thwaite Street, Cottingham, Yorks HU16 4RQ.

WETHERED, Joyce, (Lady Heathcoat Amory); *b* 17 Nov. 1901; *o d* of Newton and Marian Wethered of Brook, Surrey; *m* 1937, Major Sir John Heathcoat Amory, 3rd Bt (*d* 1972). *Educ:* privately. Learned golf playing with brother Roger, during holidays at Dornoch; Ladies Open Amateur Golf Champion 1922, 1924, 1925, 1929, runner-up 1921; English Ladies' Golf Champion, 1920–24; runner-up French Ladies' Championship, 1921; English International (golf), 1921–25 and 1929; First Curtis Cup, 1929 (Captain); GB *v* France, 1931; GB *v* USA, 1932 (Captain); won Worplesdon Mixed Foursomes 8 times between 1922 and 1936 with 7 diff. partners, and with husband runners-up, 1948; professional golf adviser to Fortnum & Mason, 1933–37; tour of USA, exhibn matches, 1935; reinstated as amateur, 1946; 1st Pres., English Ladies' Golf Assoc., 1951; Pres. and Hon. Life Mem., Worplesden Golf; Hall of Fame, USA. With husband, created gardens at Knightshayes Court (now Nat. Trust). VMH. *Publications:* Golf from Two Sides (with Roger Wethered), 1922; 3 chapters in The Game of Golf (Lonsdale Library), 1931; Golfing Memories and Methods, 1933; contribs to numerous books and jls. *Recreations:* gardening, reading, needlework. *Address:* Knightshayes House, Tiverton, Devon EX16 7RQ.

WETHERED, Julian Frank Baldwin; consultant; Director, International Division, United States Banknote Corporation, 1992–94; *b* 9 Nov. 1929; *s* of late Comdr Owen Francis McTier Wethered, RN retd and Betty (*née* Baldwin); *m* 1st, 1952, Britt Eva Hindmarsh (marr. diss. 1971); one *s* one *d*; 2nd, 1973, Antonia Mary Ettrick Roberts; two *s*. *Educ:* Eton Col.; Jesus Coll., Cambridge (BA Hons Hist. 1952; MA). National Service, RM, HMS Diadem, 1948–49. Trainee, Expandite Ltd, 1952–54; Sales Rep., Remington Rand, 1955–56; Thomas De La Rue and Co.: trainee, 1956; Mem., PA Study Team, 1957; Printing Preliminaries Manager, Currency Div., 1958–62; Special Rep., Africa, 1963–67; Manager, Banknote Printing Co., 1968–69; Regl Manager, FE, 1970–75; Associate Dir of Sales, Africa and FE, 1976–83; Regl Dir, FE, De La Rue Co. plc, 1984–88; Associate Dir of Sales, Thomas De La Rue & Co., 1989. Dir Gen., RoSPA, 1990–91. Chm.,

Riding for the Disabled Assoc. of Singapore, 1987–88. Pres., British Business Assoc. of Singapore, 1988. FInstD; FRSA. *Recreations:* sailing, riding, the arts. *Address:* Cadley House, near Marlborough, Wilts SN8 4NE. *T:* Marlborough (01672) 513407. *Club:* Travellers'

WETHERELL, Alan Marmaduke, PhD; FRS 1971; Senior Physicist, CERN (European Organisation for Nuclear Research), Geneva, since 1963 (Division Leader, Experimental Physics Division, 1981–84); *b* 31 Dec. 1932; *s* of Marmaduke and Margaret Edna Wetherell; *m* 1957, Alison Morag Dunn (*d* 1974); one *s*. *Educ:* Univ. of Liverpool (BSc, PhD). Demonstrator in Physics, Univ. of Liverpool, 1956–57; Commonwealth Fund Fellow, California Inst. of Technology, Pasadena, Calif., 1957–59; Physicist, CERN, 1959–63. Vis. Prof., Dept of Physics, Univ. of Liverpool, 1981–. *Publications:* scientific papers in: Proc. Phys. Soc. (London), Proc. Roy. Soc. (London), Physical Review, Physical Review Letters, Physics Letters, Nuovo Cimento, Nuclear Physics, Nuclear Instruments and Methods, Yadernaya Fizika, Uspekhi Fizicheski Nauk. *Recreations:* skiing, water skiing. *Address:* Experimental Physics Division, CERN, 1211 Geneva 23, Switzerland; 27 Chemin de la Vendee, 1213 Petit Lancy, Geneva, Switzerland. *T:* (22) 928742.

WETHERELL, Gordon Geoffrey; HM Diplomatic Service; Head, Personnel Services Department, Foreign and Commonwealth Office, since 1994; *b* 11 Nov. 1948; *s* of Geoffrey and Georgette Maria Wetherell; *m* 1981, Rosemary Anne Myles; four *d*. *Educ:* Bradfield Coll., Berks; New Coll., Oxford (BA 1969; MA 1975); Univ. of Chicago (MA 1971). Joined HM Diplomatic Service, 1973; FCO, 1973–74; E Berlin, 1974–77; First Sec., FCO, 1977; UK Delegn to Comprehensive Test Ban Negotiations, Geneva, 1977–80; New Delhi, 1980–83; FCO, 1983–85; on secondment to HM Treasury, 1986–87; Asst Head, European Communities Dept (External), FCO, 1987–88; Counsellor and Dep. Head of Mission, Warsaw, 1988–92; Counsellor (Politico-Military), Bonn, 1992–94. *Recreations:* reading, travel, Manchester United Football Club. *Address:* c/o Foreign and Commonwealth Office, King Charles Street, SW1A 2AH. *Club:* United Oxford & Cambridge University.

WETTON, Hilary John D.; *see* Davan Wetton.

WETTON, Philip Henry Davan, CMG 1993; HM Diplomatic Service; Consul-General, Milan, since 1990; *b* 21 Sept. 1937; *s* of late Eric Davan Wetton, CBE and Kathleen Valerie Davan Wetton; *m* 1983, Roswitha Kortner. *Educ:* Westminster; Christ Church, Oxford (MA). Unilever Ltd, 1958–65; FCO, 1965–68; served Tokyo, Osaka and FCO, 1968–73; Head of Division, later Director, Secretariat of Council of Ministers of European Communities, 1973–83; Counsellor, Seoul, 1983–87; FCO, 1987–90. *Recreations:* rowing, music, astronomy. *Address:* c/o Foreign and Commonwealth Office, SW1A 2AH.

WETZEL, Dave; Proprietor, Granny's Attic Antique Shop, since 1994; *b* 9 Oct. 1942; *s* of Fred Wetzel and Ivy Donaldson; *m* 1973, Heather Allman; two *d*. *Educ:* Spring Grove Grammar Sch.; Southall Technical Coll., Ealing Coll., and the Henry George Sch. of Social Sciences (part-time courses). Student apprentice, 1959–62; Bus Conductor/Driver, 1962–65, Bus Official, 1965–69, London Transport; Br. Manager, Initial Services, 1969–70; Pilot Roster Officer, British Airways, 1970–74 (ASTMS Shop Steward); Political Organiser, Co-operative Soc., 1974–81; Member (Lab) for Hammersmith N, GLC, 1981–86 (Transport Cttee Chair, 1981–86); Mem. (Lab) Hounslow Borough Council, 1964–68, 1986–94 (Dep. Leader and Chair, Environmental Planning, 1986–87; Leader, 1987–91). Contested (Lab) Richmond upon Thames, 1979. Vice-Chm., Public Transport Cttee, AMA, 1993–94; Mem. Management Cttee, Hounslow Community Transport and Central London Dial-a-Ride, 1991–94. Dir, DaRT (Dial-a-Ride and Taxicard Users), 1989–94. Pres., W London Peace Council, 1982–; Chair, Labour Land Campaign, 1982–. Mem. Bd, Riverside Studios, Hammersmith, 1983–86. Founder and co-ordinator, Trade Union and Co-op Esperanto Gp, 1976–80. President: Thames Valley Esperanto Soc., 1982–; Transport Studies Soc., 1991–92. Mem. Editl Bd, Voice of the Unions, 1975–79; Editor, Civil Aviation News, 1978–81. *Recreations:* politics, Esperanto, boating. *Address:* Granny's Attic, 18 Church Street, Mevagissey, Cornwall PL26 6SP. *T:* Mevagissey (01726) 843818. *Clubs:* Feltham Labour; Mevagissey Social.

WEYLAND, Joseph; Ambassador of Luxembourg to the Court of St James's, since 1993; *b* 24 April 1943; *s* of Adolphe Weyland and Marie Kox; *m* 1st, 1969, France Munhowen; two *s*; 2nd, 1993, Bénédicte Boucqueau. *Educ:* LLD, and Dip. of Inst. d'Etudes Politiques, Univ. of Paris. Foreign Ministry, Luxembourg, 1968; served Bonn and EEC, Brussels; Ambassador to UN, NY, 1982; Perm. Rep. to EEC, Brussels, 1985 (Mem., Intergovt. Conf. leading to Single European Act, 1985, later Chm., Intergovt Conf. on Political Union leading to Treaty of Maastricht, 1991; Sec.-Gen., Foreign Ministry, Luxembourg, 1992. *Publication:* (jtly) Le Traité de Maastricht, 1993. *Recreations:* art, sports, music. *Address:* 27 Wilton Crescent, SW1X 8SD. *T:* 0171–235 6961. *Club:* Rotary.

WEYMES, John Barnard, OBE 1975; HM Diplomatic Service, retired; Managing Director, Cayman Islands News Bureau, Grand Cayman, 1981–83; *b* 18 Oct. 1927; *s* of William Stanley Weymes and Irene Innes Weymes; *m* 1978, Beverley Pauline Gliddon; three *c* (by a previous marr.). *Educ:* Dame Allan's Sch., Newcastle upon Tyne; King's Coll., Durham Univ., Newcastle upon Tyne. Served HM Forces, 1945–48. Foreign Office, 1949–52; 3rd Sec., Panama City, 1952–56; 2nd Sec., Bogotá, 1957–60; Vice-Consul, Berlin, 1960–63; Dep-Consul, Tamsui, Taiwan, 1963–65; 1st Sec., FCO, 1965–68; Prime Minister's Office, 1968–70; Consul, Guatemala City, 1970–74; 1st Sec., FCO, 1974–77; Consul-Gen., Vancouver, 1977–78; Ambassador to Honduras, 1978–81. *Recreations:* outdoor sport, partic. cricket; chess, reading. *Address:* Nuthatches, Balcombe Green, Sedlescombe, Battle, E Sussex TN33 0QL. *T:* Sedlescombe (01424) 870455. *Clubs:* MCC, Middlesex County Cricket; Sedlescombe Cricket.

WEYMOUTH, Viscount; Ceawlin Henry Laszlo Thynn; *b* 6 June 1974; *s* and heir of Marquess of Bath, *qv*.

WHADDON, Baron *cr* 1978 (Life Peer), of Whaddon in the County of Cambridgeshire; **(John) Derek Page;** Chairman: Cambridge Chemical Co. Ltd, since 1991 (Director, since 1962); Daltrade, since 1983; Skorimpex-Rind, since 1985; *b* 14 Aug. 1927; *s* of John Page and Clare Page (*née* Maher); *m* 1st, 1948, Catherine Audrey Halls (*d* 1979); one *s* one *d*; 2nd, 1981, Angela Rixson. *Educ:* St Bede's College, Manchester; London University. External BSc (Soc.). MP (Lab) King's Lynn, 1964–70; contested (Lab) Norfolk NW, Feb. 1974. Mem., Council of Management, CoSIRA, 1975–82; Mem., E Anglia Economic Planning Council, 1975–80. Golden Insignia of Order of Merit (Poland), 1989. *Recreation:* private pilot. *Club:* Reform.

WHALE, John Hilary; journalist; Editor, Church Times, 1989–95; *b* 19 Dec. 1931; *s* of Rev. Dr John Seldon Whale, *qv*; *m* 1957, Judith Laurie Hackett; one *s*. *Educ:* Winchester; Corpus Christi College, Oxford. BA Lit Hum 1955, MA 1958. Lieut, Intelligence Corps, 1950–51 (Nat. Service). Writing, acting and teaching, 1954–58; Section Anglaise, French radio, Paris, 1958–59; ITN, 1960–69: Political Corresp., 1963–67; US Corresp., Washington, 1967–69; Sunday Times, 1969–84: political staff, 1969–79; Religious Affairs Corresp., 1979–84; Asst Editor, 1981–84; leader-writer throughout; Head of Religious Programmes, BBC TV, 1984–89. Dir, London programme, Univ. of Missouri Sch. of Journalism, 1980–83. Churchwarden, St. Mary's, Barnes, 1976–81. *Publications:* The Half-Shut Eye, 1969; Journalism and Government, 1972; The Politics of the Media, 1977; One Church, One Lord, 1979 (Winifred Mary Stanford Prize, 1980); (ed) The Pope from Poland, 1980; Put it in Writing, 1984; (contrib.) Why I am Still an Anglican, 1986; The Future of Anglicanism, 1988; contribs to books, quarterlies, weeklies. *Address:* 45 Shakespeare Road, W3 6SE. *T:* 0181–993 7952.

WHALE, Rev. John Seldon, MA (Oxon); DD (Glasgow); *b* 19 Dec. 1896; *s* of Rev. John Whale and Alice Emily Seldon; *m* Mary, *d* of Rev. H. C. Carter, MA; two *s* one *d* (and one *s* one *d* decd). *Educ:* Caterham School, Surrey; St Catherine's Society and Mansfield College, Oxford; 1st Class Hons Sch. of Mod. Hist. 1922; Magdalene College, Cambridge, 1933. Minister of Bowdon Downs Congregational Church, Manchester, 1925–29; Mackennal Professor of Ecclesiastical History, Mansfield College, Oxford, and Tutor in Modern History, St Catherine's, 1929–33; President of Cheshunt College, Cambridge, 1933–44; Headmaster of Mill Hill School, 1944–51; Visiting Professor of Christian Theology, Drew Univ., Madison, NJ, USA, 1951–53. Moderator of Free Church Federal Council, 1942–43; Select Preacher, Univ. of Cambridge, 1943, 1957; Warrack Lecturer, 1944; Russell Lecturer (Auburn and New York), 1936 and 1948; Alden Tuthill Lecturer, Chicago, 1952; Greene Lecturer, Andover, 1952; Currie Lecturer, Austin, Texas, 1953; Hill Lectr, St Olaf Coll., Minnesota, 1954; Visiting Lecturer, Univ. of Toronto, 1957; Danforth Scholar, USA, 1958; Sir D. Owen Evans Lectures, Aberystwyth, 1958. Visiting Professor, Univ. of Chicago, 1959; Senior Fellow of Council of Humanities, Princeton Univ., 1960. *Publications:* The Christian Answer to the Problem of Evil, 1936; What is a Living Church?, 1937; This Christian Faith, 1938; Facing the Facts, 1940; Christian Doctrine, 1941; The Protestant Tradition, 1955; Victor and Victim: the Christian doctrine of Redemption, 1960; Christian Reunion: historic divisions reconsidered, 1971; The Coming Dark Age, 1973 (Eng. trans. of Roberto Vacca's Il Medioevo Prossimo Venturo, 1972). *Address:* Wild Goose, Widecombe-in-the-Moor, Newton Abbot, S Devon TQ13 7TY. *T:* Widecombe-in-the-Moor (013642) 260.

See also J. H. Whale.

WHALEN, Sir Geoffrey Henry, Kt 1995; CBE 1989; FIMI, FIPD; Deputy Chairman, Peugeot Talbot Motor Co. Ltd, since 1990 (Managing Director, 1984–94); *b* 8 Jan. 1936; *s* of Henry and Mabel Whalen; *m* 1961, Elizabeth Charlotte; two *s* three *d*. *Educ:* Magdalen College, Oxford. MA Hons Modern History. National Coal Board, Scotland (industrial relations), 1959–66; Divl Personnel Manager, A. C. Delco Div., General Motors, Dunstable, 1966–70; British Leyland, 1970–78; Personnel Dir, Leyland Cars, 1975–78; Personnel Dir, Rank Hovis McDougall Bakeries Div., 1978–80; Personnel and Indust. Rel. Dir, Talbot Motor Co., 1980–81, Asst Man. Dir, 1981–84. Director: Coventry Building Soc., 1992–; T & N plc, 1995–; Lombard North Central plc, 1995–; Chm., Hills Precision Components Ltd, 1990–. Pres., SMMT, 1988–90 and 1993– (Dep. Pres., 1990–91 and 1992–93; Vice Pres., 1991–92); Vice Pres., Inst. of Motor Industry, 1986–; Chm., Coventry and Warwicks TEC, 1990–94. FIPD (FIPM 1974); FIMI 1986; FCGI 1989; CIMgt (CBIM 1987). Midlander of the Year Award, Bass Mitchells & Butlers Ltd, 1988; Midlands Businessman of the Year, 1992. Chevalier de la Légion d'Honneur (France), 1990. *Address:* Victoria Lodge, 8 Park Crescent, Abingdon, Oxon OX14 1DF. *Club:* United Oxford & Cambridge University.

WHALLEY, Jeffrey; Chairman, FKI, since 1991; *b* 20 Nov. 1942; *s* of William Henry and Elsie Whalley; *m* 1965, Maureen Ann Ivers; three *s*. *Educ:* Grammar School and Polytechnic. Managing Director: Dynamo Electrical Services, 1970–75; Whipp & Bourne Switchgear, 1975–80; FKI Electricals, 1980–87; Man. Dir and Dep. Chm., FKI Babcock, 1987–89; Jt Dep. Chm., Babcock International, 1989–95; Man. Dir, Gartland & Whalley Securities, later Gartland Whalley & Barker Ltd, 1989–95. FRSA; FIMgt; FInstD. *Recreations:* tennis, fishing, football. *Address:* Broncroft Castle, Craven Arms, Shropshire SY7 9HL. *Club:* Royal Automobile.

WHALLEY, John Mayson, FRTPI; FRIBA; PPLI; Consultant, Derek Lovejoy Partnership, since 1993; *b* 14 Sept. 1932; *s* of George Mayson Whalley and Ada Florence Cairns; *m* 1966, Elizabeth Gillian Hide; one *s* two *d*. *Educ:* Grammar Sch., Preston; Univ. of Liverpool (BArch, 1st Cl. Hons, MCivic Des.); Univ. of Pennsylvania (MLandscape Arch). Sir Charles Reilly Medal and Prize for thesis design, 1956; Leverhulme and Italian Govt Fellowships for study in Scandinavia and Univ. of Rome, 1957; Fulbright Schol., 1958; Manchester Soc. of Architects Winstanley Fellowship, 1965. Asst architect to Sir Frederick Gibberd, Harlow, 1956; architect/landscape architect: Oskar Stonorov, Philadelphia, 1958–60; Grenfell Baines and Hargreaves Building Design Partnership, Preston, 1960–62; Associate, 1963–68, Sen. Partner, 1968–93, Derek Lovejoy & Associates. Chm., NW Region, RIBA, 1984–85; President: Manchester Soc. of Architects, 1980–81; Landscape Inst., 1985–87; Mem. Council, National Trust, 1989–. Civic Trust awards: W Burton Power Stn, 1968; Cheshire Constabulary HQ, 1969; Rochdale Canal, 1973; Royal Life, Peterborough, 1992; design competitions 1st prizes: Cergy-Pontoise, 1970; La Courneuve, Paris, 1972; Liverpool Anglican Cathedral precinct, 1982; Urban Park, Vitoria-Gasteiz, 1991; Regional Park, Mito City, Japan, 1992; Garden Festivals: Liverpool, 1982; Stoke-on-Trent, 1983; Glasgow, 1985. Civic Trust awards assessor, 1970–; UN Tech. Expert, Riyadh, 1975. Mem., Order of Architectes de France; FRSA. Contribs to radio and TV. *Publications:* Selected Architects Details, 1958; articles in professional jls. *Recreations:* jazz, salmon fishing, photography, cricket, good wine and food. *Address:* Derek Lovejoy Partnership, Arkwright House, Parsonage Gardens, Manchester M3 2LE. *T:* 0161–834 8825; Dilworth House, Longridge, Preston, Lancs PR3 3ST. *T:* Longridge (01772) 783262. *Clubs:* Landsdowne; St James's (Manchester).

WHALLEY, Richard Carlton; Chairman, Ewden Associates Ltd, since 1981; *b* Quetta, India, 4 July 1922; *s* of Frederick Seymour Whalley, MC, FCGI, MIMechE, and Gwendolen, *d* of Sir William Collingwood; *m* 1945, Mary Christian Bradley; two *s* twin *d*. *Educ:* Shrewsbury Sch.; 151 OCTU, Aldershot. Served War: Private, Royal Berkshire Regt, 1940; commissioned 2nd Lieut, Royal Corps of Signals, 1942; Captain and Adjt, 2nd Div. Signals, India, Assam, Burma, 1942–45 (despatches). War Office, AG II (O), 1945–48; GHQ Singapore, 1948–51. Vulcan Foundry Ltd: Asst Sec., 1952–58; Commercial Manager, 1958–60; Dep. Gen. Manager, 1960–65; Manager, English Electric Diesel Engine Div., 1965–67; Dir and Gen. Manager, Glacier Metal Co., 1968–70. 1970–78: Dep. Chm. and Managing Dir, Millspaugh Ltd; Chm. and Managing Dir, C. A. Harnden Ltd, Westbury Engrg Ltd, Hargreaves & Jennings Ltd, and T. Rowbottom Ltd; Director: Bertram-Scott Ltd; Sulzer Bros (UK) Ltd; Mem., Bd of British Shipbuilders (with special responsibility for personnel, indust. relations, and trng), 1978–80. Chairman: F. & M. Ducker Ltd, 1981–84; A. Spafford & Co. Ltd, 1981–82; Pennine Plastics Ltd, 1981–82; Eaton and Booth Ltd, 1984–87; (also Chief Exec.) Eaton and Booth Rolling Mills Ltd, 1984–87; John King and Co. Ltd, 1985–87; Director: Estridge & Ropner Ltd, 1981–84; Sheffield Photoco, 1983–84; Dep. Chm., Malacarp Group, 1982–84. Freeman, Co. of Cutlers in Hallamshire, 1986. *Recreations:* rowing, walking. *Address:* Sunnybank Farm, Bolsterstone, Sheffield S30 5ZL. *T:* Sheffield (0114) 288 3116. *Clubs:* National Liberal; Sheffield (Sheffield); London Rowing.

WHALLEY, Prof. William Basil; Professor of Chemistry and Head of Department of Pharmaceutical Chemistry, School of Pharmacy, 1961–82, now Emeritus Professor of Chemistry, University of London; *b* 17 Dec. 1916; *s* of William and Catherine Lucy Whalley; *m* 1945, Marie Agnes Alston; four *s* one *d*. *Educ:* St Edward's College, Liverpool; Liverpool University. BSc Hons 1938; PhD 1940; DSc 1952; FRIC 1950. MOS and ICI 1940–45. Lecturer, 1946–55, Sen. Lectr, 1955–57, Reader, 1957–61, in Organic Chemistry, at Liverpool University. *Publications:* contrib. on organic chemistry to several books: *eg* Heterocyclic Compounds, Vol. 7, Edited R. C. Elderfield, Wiley (New York); many pubns in Jl of Chem. Soc., Jl Amer. Chem. Soc., etc. *Recreations:* music and mountaineering. *Address:* 9 Peaks Hill, Purley, Surrey CR8 3JG. *T:* 0181–668 2244.

WHALLEY, Maj.-Gen. William Leonard, CB 1985; *b* 19 March 1930; *m* 1955, Honor Mary (*née* Golden); one *d*. *Educ:* Sir William Turner's Sch., Coatham. Joined Army (Nat. Service), 1948; sc 1962; Commander, RAOC, 1st Div., 1968–71; Dir of Ordnance Services, BAOR, 1980–83; Dir Gen. of Ordnance Services, MoD, 1983–85. Colonel Commandant: RAOC, 1986–93; RLC, 1993. Life Vice-Pres., Army Boxing Assoc. (Chm., 1983–85). Chm., Little Aston Br., Conservative Assoc., 1987–. Chm. of Govs, Brooke Weston (formerly Corby) City Technol. Coll., 1991– (Project Dir, 1989–91). *Recreations:* bridge, computers, cabinet making. *Address:* Midland Bank, 8 High Street, Sutton Coldfield, West Midlands B72 1XB.

WHARNCLIFFE, 5th Earl of, *cr* 1876; **Richard Alan Montagu Stuart Wortley;** Baron Wharncliffe 1826; Viscount Carlton 1876; *b* 26 May 1953; *s* of Alan Ralph Montagu-Stuart-Wortley (*d* 1986) and Virginia Anne (*d* 1993), *d* of W. Martin Claybaugh; *S* cousin, 1987; *m* 1979, Mary Elizabeth Reed; three *s*. *Heir: s* Viscount Carlton, *qv*. *Address:* 270 Main Street, Cumberland, ME 04021, USA.

WHARTON, Baroness, 11th in line, *cr* 1544–5; **Myrtle Olive Felix Robertson, (Ziki);** *b* 20 Feb. 1934; *d* of David George Arbuthnot (*d* 1985) and Baroness Wharton, 10th in line (*d* 1974); *S* to Barony of mother (called out of abeyance, 1990); *m* 1958, Henry McLeod Robertson; three *s* one *d*. *Recreations:* animal welfare, photography, skiing, opera. *Heir: s* Hon. Myles Christopher David Robertson, *b* 1 Oct. 1964. *Address:* c/o House of Lords, SW1A 0PW.

WHARTON, Rt. Rev. John Martin; *see* Kingston-Upon-Thames, Area Bishop of.

WHARTON, Michael Bernard; author and journalist; 'Peter Simple' Columnist, Daily and Sunday Telegraph, since 1957; *b* 19 April 1913; *s* of Paul Nathan and Bertha Wharton; *m* 1st, 1936, Joan Atkey (marr. diss. 1947); one *s*; 2nd 1952, Catherine Mary Derrington (marr. diss. 1972; she *d* 1992); one *d*; 3rd, 1974, Susan Moller. *Educ:* Bradford Grammar Sch.; Lincoln Coll., Oxford. Army service, Royal Artillery and General Staff, 1940–46. Scriptwriter and Producer, BBC, 1946–56; (with Colin Welch) writer of Peter Simple column, Daily Telegraph, 1957–60. *Publications: as Michael Wharton:* (ed) A Nation's Security, 1955; Sheldrake (novel), 1958; The Missing Will (autobiog.), 1984; A Dubious Codicil (autobiog.), 1991; editor and mainly writer of anthologies of Peter Simple column, 1963, 1965, 1969, 1971, 1973, 1975, 1978, 1980, 1984, 1987; *under pseudonym Simon Crabtree:* Forgotten Memories, 1941; Hector Tumbler Investigates, 1943. *Recreations:* walking, gardening, Celtic studies. *Address:* Forge Cottage, Naphill Common, High Wycombe, Bucks HP14 4SU. *T:* Naphill (01494) 563454.

WHATLEY, Prof. Frederick Robert, FRS 1975; Sherardian Professor of Botany, Oxford University, 1971–91; Fellow of Magdalen College, Oxford, since 1971; *b* 26 Jan. 1924; *s* of Frederick Norman Whatley and Maud Louise (*née* Hare); *m* 1951, Jean Margaret Smith Bowie; two *d*. *Educ:* Bishop Wordsworth's Sch., Salisbury; (Scholar) Selwyn Coll., Cambridge University (BA, PhD). Benn W. Levy Student, Cambridge, 1947. Sen. Lectr. in Biochemistry, Univ. of Sydney, 1950–53; Asst Biochemist, Univ. of California at Berkeley, 1954–58; Associate Biochemist, 1959–64; Guggenheim Fellowship (Oxford and Stockholm), 1960; Prof. of Botany, King's Coll., London, 1964–71. Vis. Fellow, ANU, 1979. *Publications:* articles and reviews in scientific jls. *Address:* Magdalen College, Oxford OX1 4AU.

WHATLEY, William Henry Potts, OBE 1986; General Secretary, Union of Shop Distributive and Allied Workers, 1979–85; *b* 16 Dec. 1922; *s* of Arthur John and Ethel Whatley; *m* 1946, Margaret Ann Harrison. *Educ:* Gosforth Secondary School. Clerk, CWS, Newcastle upon Tyne, 1938; War Service, RAF, War of 1939–45; Area Organiser, USDAW, Bristol, 1948; National Officer, 1966; Chief Organising Officer, 1976; Member: TUC General Council, 1979–85; TUC Economic Cttee, 1979; Pres., EURO-FIET, 1982–87. *Recreations:* gardening, reading. *Address:* 72 St Martin's Road, Ashton-on-Mersey, Sale, Cheshire M33 5PZ. *T:* 0161–973 3772.

WHATMOUGH, Rev. Michael Anthony; Vicar, St Mary Redcliffe, Bristol, since 1993; *b* 14 Oct. 1950; *s* of Derrick and Molly Whatmough; *m* 1975, Jean Macdonald Watt; two *s* two *d*. *Educ:* Exeter Univ. (BA 1972); Edinburgh Univ. (BD 1981). ARCO 1972. Teacher of music, Forrester High Sch., Edinburgh, 1973–74; Sub-Organist, Old St Paul's Church, Edinburgh, 1973–78; Music Master, George Watson's Coll., Edinburgh, 1974–78; ordained deacon, 1981, priest, 1982; Curate, St Hilda and St Fillan, Edinburgh, 1981–84; Vis. Lectr in Music, Faculty of Divinity, Edinburgh Univ., 1981–84; Curate and Rector, Salisbury St Thomas, 1984–93; Rural Dean, Salisbury, 1990–93. *Recreations:* harpsichord playing, walking the Yorkshire Dales with family, drinking wine in France. *Address:* The Vicarage, 10 Redcliffe Parade West, Bristol BS1 6SP. *T:* Bristol (0117) 929 1487.

WHEADON, Richard Anthony; Principal, Elizabeth College, Guernsey, 1972–88, retired; *b* 31 Aug. 1933; *s* of Ivor Cecil Newman Wheadon and Margarita Augusta (*née* Cash); *m* 1961, Ann Mary (*née* Richardson); three *s*. *Educ:* Cranleigh Sch. Balliol Coll., Oxford. MA (Physics). Commissioned RAF, 1955 (Sword of Honour); Air Radar Officer, 1955–57; Asst Master, Eton Coll., 1957–66; Dep. Head Master and Head of Science Dept, Dauntsey's Sch., 1966–71. Mem., Wilts Educn Cttee's Science Adv. Panel, 1967–71. Rowed bow for Oxford, 1954, for GB in European Championships and Olympic Games, 1956; Captain RAF VIII, 1956 and 1957; Olympic Selector and Nat. Coach, 1964–66. Contingent Comdr, Dauntsey's Sch. CCF, 1969–70. Reader, C of E, dio. of Winchester, 1995–. *Publication:* The Principles of Light and Optics, 1968. *Recreations:* French horn, photography, electronics, singing, sailing, words. *Address:* L'Enclos Gallienne, Rue du Court Laurent, Torteval, Guernsey, Channel Islands GY8 0LH. *T:* Guernsey (0481) 64988.

WHEARE, Thomas David, MA; Headmaster of Bryanston School, since 1983; *b* 11 Oct. 1944; *s* of late Sir Kenneth Wheare, CMG, FBA, and of Lady (Joan) Wheare; *m* 1977, Rosalind Clare Spice; two *d*. *Educ:* Dragon Sch.; Magdalen College Sch., Oxford; King's Coll., Cambridge (BA, MA); Christ Church, Oxford (DipEd). Assistant Master, Eton College, 1967–76; Housemaster of School House, Shrewsbury School, 1976–83. Hon. Treas., HMC, 1993–. FRSA 1989. *Recreations:* music, reading. *Address:* Bryanston School, Blandford, Dorset DT11 0PX. *T:* Blandford (01258) 452728.

WHEAT, Rev. Fr Charles Donald Edmund, SSM; Vicar, All Saints', Middlesbrough, 1988–95; *b* 17 May 1937; *s* of Charles and Alice Wheat. *Educ:* Kelham Theol Coll.; Nottingham Univ. (BA); Sheffield Univ. (MA). Curate, St Paul's, Arbourthorne, Sheffield, 1962–67; licensed, Dio. Southwell, 1967–70; Mem., SSM, 1969–; Chaplain, St Martin's Coll., Lancaster, 1970–73; Prior, SSM Priory, Sheffield, 1973–75; Curate, St John, Ranmoor and Asst Chaplain, Sheffield Univ., 1975–77, Chaplain 1977–80; Provincial, English Province, 1981–91, Dir, 1982–89, SSM. Mem., Gen. Synod, 1975–80. *Recreations:* reading, watching soap operas. *Address:* SSM Priory, 96 Vassall Road, Kennington, SW9 6IA. *T:* 0171–582 2162.

WHEATCROFT, Stephen Frederick, OBE 1974; Director, Aviation and Tourism International Ltd, since 1983; Economic Adviser, World Travel and Tourism Council, since 1991; *b* 11 Sept. 1921; *s* of late Percy and Fanny Wheatcroft; *m* 1st, 1943, Joy (*d* 1974), *d* of late Cecil Reed; two *s* one *d*; 2nd, 1974, Alison, *d* of late Arnold Dessau; two *s*. *Educ:* Latymer Sch., N9; London Sch. of Economics. BSc(Econ) 1942. Served War, Pilot in Fleet Air Arm, 1942–45. Commercial Planning Manager, BEA, 1946–53; Simon Research Fellow, Manchester Univ., 1953–55; private practice as Aviation Consultant, 1956–72; retained as Economic Adviser to BEA. Commns for Govts of: Canada, India, W Indies, E African Community, Afghanistan; Consultant to World Bank; Assessor to Edwards Cttee on British Air Transport in the Seventies; Mem. Bd, British Airways (Dir of Economic Devolt), 1972–82. Governor, London Sch. of Economics. FRAeS, FCIT (Pres., 1978–79); FAIAA. *Publications:* Economics of European Air Transport, 1956; Airline Competition in Canada, 1958; Air Transport Policy, 1966; Air Transport in a Competitive European Market, 1986; European Liberalisation and World Air Transport, 1990; Europe's Senior Travel Market, 1993; Aviation and Tourism Policies, 1994; Europe's Youth Travel Market, 1995; articles in professional jls. *Recreation:* travel. *Address:* (office) 33 Park Walk, SW10 0AJ. *T:* 0171–352 4150. *Club:* Reform.

WHEATLEY, Alan Edward, FCA; *b* 23 May 1938; *s* of late Edward and of Margaret Wheatley (*née* Turner); *m* 1962, Marion Frances (*née* Wilson); two *s* one *d*. *Educ:* Ilford Grammar School. Chartered Accountant. Norton Slade, 1954–60, qualified 1960; joined Price Waterhouse, 1960; admitted to partnership, 1970; Mem., Policy Cttee, 1981–92; Sen. Partner (London Office), 1985–92; Chm., 3i Gp, 1992–93; Dep Chm., Ashtead Gp, 1994–. Non-exec. Director: EBS Investments (Bank of England sub.), 1977–90; British Steel plc (formerly BSC), 1984–94; Babcock International Gp, 1993–; Legal & General Gp, 1993–; Forte, 1993–; N M Rothschild & Sons, 1993–; Govt Dir, Cable & Wireless, 1981–84, non-exec. Dep. Chm., 1984–85. Mem., Ind. Develt Adv. Bd, 1985–92. Governor, Solefield School, 1985–. *Recreations:* golf, tennis, bridge. *Address:* Highcroft, Kippington Road, Sevenoaks, Kent TN13 2LN. *T:* Sevenoaks (01732) 453088. *Club:* Wildernesse (Seal, Kent).

WHEATLEY, Rear-Adm. Anthony, CB 1988; General Manager, National Hospital for Neurology and Neurosurgery, Queen Square, since 1988; *b* 3 Oct. 1933; *yr s* of Edgar C. Wheatley and late Audrey G. Barton Hall; *m* 1962, Iona Sheila Haig; one *d*. *Educ:* Berkhamsted School. Entered RN Coll., Dartmouth, 1950; RNEC, Manadon, 1953–57; HMS Ceylon, 1958–60; HMS Ganges, 1960–61; HMS Cambrian, 1962–64; Staff of RNEC, Manadon, 1964–67; Staff of Comdr British Navy Staff, Washington, 1967–69; HMS Diomede, 1970–72; Staff of C-in-C Fleet, 1972–74; Exec. Officer, RNEC Manadon, 1975–76; MoD Procurement Exec., 1977–79; British Naval Attaché, Brasilia, 1979–81; RCDS course 1982; HMS Collingwood (in Command), 1982–85; Flag Officer, Portsmouth, Naval Base Comdr and Head of Establishment of Fleet Maintenance and Repair Orgn, Portsmouth, 1985–87. *Recreations:* cricket, golf, music. *Address:* 2 Claridge Court, Munster Road, SW6 4EY. *Clubs:* Army and Navy; Free Foresters, Incogniti.

WHEATLEY, Rev. Canon Arthur; Priest in Charge of St Columba's, Grantown-on-Spey and St John's, Rothiemurchus, 1983–95; *b* 4 March 1931; *s* of George and Elizabeth Wheatley; *m* 1959, Sheena Morag Wilde; two *s* two *d*. *Educ:* Alloa Academy; Coates Hall Theol Coll., Edinburgh. Deacon 1970, priest 1970, Dio. Brechin; 1st Curate's title, St Salvador's with St Martin's, Dundee, 1970–71; Curate in Charge, St Ninian's Mission, Dundee, 1971–76; Rector of Holy Trinity, Elgin with St Margaret's Church, Lossiemouth, Dio. Moray, Ross and Caithness, 1976–80; Canon of St Andrew's Cathedral, 1978–80; Provost, 1980–83; Canon of Inverness Cathedral, 1985–. Episcopalian Chaplain to HM Prison, Porterfield, 1980–; Anglican Chaplain to RAF Unit, Grantown-on-Spey, 1984–. *Recreations:* fishing, bee keeping. *Address:* Wester Curr Cottage, Dulnain Bridge, near Grantown-on-Spey, Moray PH26 3LX. *T:* Dulnain Bridge (01479) 851273.

WHEATLEY, Derek Peter Francis, QC 1981; Barrister-at-Law; banking consultant; Member, Joint Law Society/Bar Council Working Party on Banking Law, since 1976; *b* 18 Dec. 1925; 3rd *s* of late Edward Pearse Wheatley, company director, and Gladys Wheatley; *m* 1955, Elizabeth Pamela, *d* of John and Gertrude Reynolds; two *s* one *d*. *Educ:* The Leys Sch., Cambridge; University Coll., Oxford (MA). Served War of 1939–45, Army, 1944–47: (short univ. course, Oxford, 1944); commissioned into 8th King's Royal Irish Hussars, 1945, Lieut. University Coll., Oxford, 1947–49; called to the Bar, Middle Temple, 1951; Deputy Coroner: to the Royal Household, 1959–64; for London, 1959–64; Recorder of the Crown Court, 1972–74. Chief Legal Advr to Lloyds Bank, 1976–89. Member: Commercial Court Cttee, 1976–90; Senate of Inns of Court and the Bar, 1975–78, 1982–85; Exec. Cttee, Bar Council, 1982–85; Bar Council, 1986–90 (Member: Professional Standards Cttee, 1986–88; F and GP Cttee, 1988–); Vice-Pres., Bar Assoc. for Commerce, Finance and Industry, 1986– (Chm., 1982–83). Chm., Legal Cttee, Cttee of London and Scottish Bankers, 1985–87. FRSA 1994. *Publications:* articles in legal jls and The Times, etc. *Recreation:* sailing. *Address:* 3 Gray's Inn Place, Gray's Inn, WC1R 5EA. *T:* 0171–831 8441, *Fax:* 0171–831 8479. *Clubs:* Roehampton; Bar Yacht.

WHEATLEY, John Derek, CBE 1993; Member, National Rivers Authority, since 1989 (Chief Executive, 1991–92); *b* 24 July 1927; *s* of Leslie Sydney and Lydia Florence Wheatley; *m* 1956, Marie Gowers; one *s* one *d*. *Educ:* Sir Thomas Rich's Sch., Gloucester; Loughborough Coll., 1944–46 (Teacher's Cert.); Carnegie College of Physical Educn, 1952–53 (DipPE). Served RAF, 1946–52; Surrey Education Authority, 1953–54; Central Council of Physical Recreation: London and SE, 1954–58; Secretary, Northern Ireland, 1959–69; Principal Regional Officer, SW, 1970–72; Sports Council: Regional Director, SW, 1972–80; Director of Administrative Services, Headquarters, 1980–83; Dir Gen., 1983–88. Chm., Nat. Small-Bore Rifle Assoc., 1989–95. *Recreation:* gardening.

WHEATLEY, Hon. John Francis; QC (Scot.) 1993; Sheriff of Tayside Central and Fife at Perth, since 1980 (at Dunfermline, 1979–80); *b* 9 May 1941; *s* of Rt Hon. John Thomas Wheatley (Baron Wheatley) and late Agnes Nichol; *m* 1970, Bronwen Catherine Fraser; two *s*. *Educ:* Mount St Mary's Coll., Derbyshire; Edinburgh Univ. (BL). Called to the Scottish Bar, 1966; Standing Counsel to Scottish Develt Dept, 1971; Advocate Depute, 1975. *Recreations:* gardening, music. *Address:* Braefoot Farmhouse, Crook of Devon, Fossoway, Kinross-shire KY13 7UL. *T:* Fossoway (01577) 840212.

WHEATLEY, Oswald Stephen, (Ossie); Chairman, Sports Council for Wales, since 1990; company director; *b* 28 May 1935; *s* of late Harold Wheatley and Laura Wheatley (*née* Owens); *m* 1964, Christine Mary Godwin; one *s* (two *d* decd). *Educ:* King Edward's

Sch., Birmingham; Caius Coll., Cambridge (MA Econs and Law). 2nd Lieut, RA, 1954. Cambridge Cricket Blue, 1957–58; played for Warwicks CCC, 1957–1960; Glamorgan CCC, 1961–69 (Captain, 1961–66); Chm., Glamorgan CCC, 1977–84. Test and County Cricket Board: Test Selector, 1972–74; Chairman: Discipline Cttee, 1978–83; Cricket Cttee, 1987–95; Mem., England Cttee, 1989–93. Mem., Sports Council of GB, 1984–88 and 1990–. Chm., Nat. Sports Medicine Inst., St Bartholomew's Hosp., 1991–. Freeman, City of Newcastle-upon-Tyne, 1976. *Recreations:* sport, art. *Address:* Sports Council for Wales, Sophia Gardens, Cardiff CF1 9SW. *T:* Cardiff (01222) 397571. *Clubs:* MCC, Free Foresters, Cardiff and County; Glamorgan CC.

WHEATLEY, Ven. Paul Charles; Archdeacon of Sherborne and Priest in Charge of West Stafford with Frome Billet, since 1991; *b* 27 May 1938; *s* of Charles Lewis and Doris Amy Wheatley; *m* 1963, Iris Mary Lacey; two *s* one *d*. *Educ:* Wycliffe Coll.; St John's Coll., Durham (BA 1961); Lincoln Theol Coll. Ordained deacon 1963, priest 1964; Curate, Bishopston, Bristol, 1963–68; Youth Chaplain, dio. of Bristol, 1968–73; Team Rector, Dorcan, Swindon, 1973–79; Rector, Ross, Hereford, 1979–81; Team Rector, Ross with Brampton Abbots, Bridstow, Peterstow, 1979–91; Prebendary, Hereford Cathedral, 1987–91; Ecumenical Officer, Hereford, 1987–91; Hon. Canon, Salisbury Cathedral, 1991–. *Recreations:* travel, gardening, opera, model railways. *Address:* The Rectory, West Stafford, Dorchester, Dorset DT2 8AB. *T:* Dorchester (01305) 264637.

WHEATLEY, Ven. Peter William; Archdeacon of Hampstead, since 1995; *b* 7 Sept. 1947; *er s* of late William Nobes Wheatley and Muriel (*née* Ounsted). *Educ:* Ipswich Sch. (Queen's and Foundn Schol.); Queen's Coll., Oxford (Styring Schol., MA); Pembroke Coll., Cambridge (MA); Coll. of the Resurrection, Mirfield; Ripon Hall, Oxford. Deacon 1973, priest 1974; Asst Curate, All Saints, Fulham, 1973–78; Vicar: Holy Cross with St Jude and St Peter, St Pancras, 1978–82; St James, W Hampstead, 1982–95; Priest-in-charge: St Mary, Kilburn, 1982–90; St Mary with All Souls, Kilburn, 1990–95; Curate-in-charge, All Souls, S Hampstead, 1982–90. Proctor in Convocation and Mem. Gen. Synod, C of E, 1975–95. *Recreation:* music. *Address:* 27 Thurlow Road, NW3 5PP. *T:* 0171–435 5890.

WHEATON, Rev. Canon David Harry; Vicar of Christ Church, Ware, since 1986; Chaplain to The Queen, since 1990; *b* 2 June 1930; *s* of Harry Wheaton, MBE, and Kathleen Mary (*née* Frost); m 1956, Helen Joy Forrer; one *s* two *d*. *Educ:* Abingdon Sch.; St John's Coll., Oxford (Exhibnr; MA); London Univ. (BD (London Bible Coll.)); Oak Hill Theol Coll. NCO, Wiltshire Regt, 1948–49. Deacon, 1959; priest, 1960; Tutor, Oak Hill Coll., 1954–62; Rector of Ludgershall, Bucks, 1962–66; Vicar of St Paul, Onslow Square, S Kensington, 1966–71; Chaplain, Brompton Chest Hosp., 1969–71; Principal Oak Hill Theol Coll., 1971–86; RD of Hertford, 1988–91. Hon. Canon, Cathedral and Abbey Church of St Alban, 1976. *Publications: contributed to:* Baker's Dictionary of Theology, 1960; New Bible Dictionary, 1962; New Bible Commentary (rev.), 1970, 21st century edn 1994; Evangelical Dictionary of Theology, 1984; Here We Stand, 1986; Restoring the Vision, 1990. *Recreations:* walking, carpentry and do-it-yourself. *Address:* Christ Church Vicarage, 15 Hanbury Close, Ware, Herts SG12 7BZ. *T:* Ware (01920) 463165.

WHEELER, Sir Anthony; *see* Wheeler, Sir H. A.

WHEELER, Captain Arthur Walter, RN retd; CEng; Keeper, HMS Belfast, 1983–88; *b* 18 Oct. 1927; *s* of Walter Sidney Wheeler and Annie Ethel Marsh; *m* 1st, 1957, Elizabeth Jane Glendinning Bowman (marr. diss. 1968); two *s*; 2nd, 1968, Mary Elvis Findon; one *s*. *Educ:* Woodhouse Sch., Finchley; HMS Fisgard, Torpoint; RN Engineering Coll., Manadon. FIMechE, MIMarE. Joined Royal Navy as artificer apprentice, 1943; served in cruiser Birmingham, 1947–50. Progressively, Sub Lieut 1950 to Captain 1974. Served in frigate Palliser and aircraft carriers Bulwark, Hermes and Ark Royal 1954–74; Sea Trng Staff at Portland, 1961–63; MoD, Ship Dept, 1966–70 and 1975–78; CSO(Engrg) to Flag Officer Third Flotilla, 1979–80; HMS Daedalus in comd, 1980–82, retired. Received into RC Church, 1987. *Recreations:* painting and drawing, music and opera, English history.

WHEELER, Arthur William Edge, CBE 1979 (OBE 1967); Chairman, Foreign Compensation Commission, since 1983; a Social Security Commissioner, since 1992; a Child Support Commissioner, since 1993; *b* 1 Aug. 1930; *e s* of Arthur William Wheeler and Rowena (*née* Edge); *m* 1956, Gay; two *s* one *d*. *Educ:* Mountjoy Sch.; Trinity Coll., Dublin (Reid Prof.'s Prize, MA, LLB). Called to the Irish Bar, King's Inns, 1953; called to the Bar, Gray's Inn, 1960. Crown Counsel, Nigeria, 1955; Legal Sec. (Actg), Southern Cameroons, and Mem. Exec. Council and House of Assembly, 1958; Principal Crown Counsel, Fedn of Nigeria, 1961; Northern Nigeria: Dep. Solicitor Gen., 1964; Dir of Public Prosecutions, 1966; High Court Judge, 1967; Chief Judge (formerly Chief Justice), Kaduna State of Nigeria, 1975; Comr for Law Revision, northern states of Nigeria, 1980. Mem., Body of Benchers, Nigeria, 1975; Associate Mem., Commonwealth Parly Assoc. *Recreations:* sport (university colours for hockey and assoc. football; Nigerian hockey internat.), music. *Address:* c/o Foreign Compensation Commission, Room 3/56, Old Admiralty Building, Whitehall, SW1A 2AF. *Club:* Commonwealth Trust.

WHEELER, Charles (Cornelius-); journalist and broadcaster, since 1940; *b* 26 March 1923; *s* of late Wing-Comdr Charles Cornelius-Wheeler, RFC and RAFVR, and Winifred (*née* Rees); *m* 1962, Dip Singh; two *d*. *Educ:* Cranbrook School. Began journalism as tape-boy, Daily Sketch, 1940. Served War, Royal Marines, 1942–46; Captain 1944 (despatches NW Europe). Sub-editor, BBC Latin American Service, 1947–49; German Service Correspondent in Berlin, 1950–53; Talks writer, European Service, 1954–56; Producer, Panorama, 1956–58; S Asia Correspondent, 1958–62; Berlin Corresp., 1962–65; Washington Corresp., 1965–68; Chief Correspondent: USA, 1969–73; Europe, 1973–76; BBC Television News, 1977; Panorama, 1977–79; Newsnight, 1980–. Documentaries include: The Kennedy Legacy, 1970; Battle for Berlin, 1985; The Road to War (series), 1989; Bloody Sunday in Tbilisi, 1989; Beyond Reasonable Doubt, 1990; The Legacy of Martin Luther King, 1993; D-Day: the Battle of Normandy, 1994; Burma: the forgotten war, 1995; America (series), 1996. DUniv Open, 1992. TV Journalist of the Year, RTS, 1988; Internat. Documentary Award, RTS, 1989; James Cameron Meml Award, City Univ., 1990; RTS Special Commendation, 1992; Cyril Bennett Award, RTS, 1993. *Publication:* The East German Rising (with Stefan Brant), 1955. *Recreations:* gardening, travel. *Address:* 10A Portland Road, W11 4LA.

WHEELER, Prof. David John, FRS 1981; Professor of Computer Science, Cambridge University, 1978–94, now Emeritus; Fellow of Darwin College, Cambridge, 1967–94, now Emeritus; *b* 9 Feb. 1927; *s* of Arthur William Wheeler and Agnes Marjorie (*née* Gudgeon); *m* 1957, Joyce Margaret Blackler. *Educ:* Camp Hill Grammar Sch., Birmingham; Hanley High Sch., Stoke on Trent; Trinity Coll., Cambridge. Research Fellow, Trinity Coll., Cambridge, 1951–57; Visiting Asst Prof., Univ. of Illinois, USA, 1951–53; Asst Director of Research, Cambridge Univ., 1956–66; Reader in Computer Science, Cambridge Univ., 1966–78. Fellow, Assoc. of Computing Machinery, 1994. *Publication:* The Preparation of Programs for an Electronic Digital Computer, 1951. *Address:* 131 Richmond Road, Cambridge CB4 3PS. *T:* Cambridge (01223) 351319.

WHEELER, Frank Basil, CMG 1990; HM Diplomatic Service; Ambassador to Chile, since 1993; *b* 24 April 1937; *s* of late Harold Gifford Wheeler and Winifred Lucy Wheeler (*née* Childs); *m* 1st, 1959, Catherine Saunders Campbell (*d* 1979); one *s*; 2nd, 1984, Alyson Ruth Lund (*née* Powell) (marr. diss. 1989); 3rd, 1991, Susana Plaza Larrea. *Educ:* Mill Hill Sch. HM Forces, 1956–58. HM Foreign Service, 1958–: Foreign Office, 1958–61; Third Sec. (Commercial), Moscow, 1961–63; Asst Private Sec. to Minister of State, FO, 1963–65; Second Sec. (Commercial), Berne, 1965–67; First Sec., FO (later FCO), 1967–72; Wellington, 1972–75; FCO, 1975–77; Counsellor and Head of Chancery, Prague, 1977–79; Inspector, 1979–82; Head of Personnel Policy Dept, FCO, 1982–84; Counsellor and Head of Chancery, UK Delegn to NATO, Brussels, 1984–86; Counsellor, on loan to DTI, 1986–89; Ambassador to Ecuador, 1989–93. *Recreations:* music, tennis. *Address:* c/o Foreign and Commonwealth Office, SW1A 2AH.

WHEELER, Sir Frederick (Henry), AC 1979; Kt 1967; CBE 1962 (OBE 1952); Secretary to the Treasury, Australia, 1971–79; *b* 9 Jan. 1914; *s* of late A. H. Wheeler; *m* 1939, Peggy Hilda (*d* 1975), *d* of Basil P. Bell; one *s* two *d*. *Educ:* Scotch College; Melbourne University (BCom). State Savings Bank of Victoria, 1929–39; Treasury: Research Officer, 1939; Economist, 1944; Asst Sec., 1946; First Asst Sec., 1949–52; Treasurer Comptroller, ILO, Geneva, 1952–60; Chm., Commonwealth Public Service Bd, Canberra, 1961–71; Member: Aust. delegn to various British Commonwealth Finance Ministers' Conferences; Austr. Delegn Bretton Woods Monetary Conf.; UN Civil Service Adv. Bd, 1969–72; Commonwealth Govt Defence Review Cttee, 1981–82. Director: Amatil Ltd, 1979–84; Alliance Holdings Ltd, 1979–86. Dir, Winston Churchill Meml Trust (Aust.), 1965– (Nat. Pres., 1992–). *Address:* 9 Charlotte Street, Red Hill, ACT 2603, Australia. *T:* (6) 2959888. *Clubs:* (Pres. 1966–69) Commonwealth (Canberra); Royal Canberra Golf.

WHEELER, Rt. Rev. Monsignor Gordon; *see* Wheeler, W. G.

WHEELER, Sir (Harry) Anthony, Kt 1988; OBE 1973; RSA, FRIBA, FRIAS; President, Royal Scottish Academy, 1983–90; Consultant, Wheeler & Sproson, Architects and Planning Consultants, Edinburgh and Kirkcaldy, since 1986 (Senior Partner, 1954–86); *b* 7 Nov. 1919; *s* of Herbert George Wheeler and Laura Emma Groom; *m* 1944, Dorothy Jean Campbell; one *d*. *Educ:* Stranraer High Sch.; Royal Technical Coll., Glasgow; Glasgow School of Art; Univ. of Strathclyde (BArch). RIBA, DipTP, MRTPI. Glasgow Sch. of Architecture, 1937–48 (war service, Royal Artillery, 1939–46); John Keppie Scholar and Sir Rowand Anderson Studentship, 1948; RIBA Grissell Gold Medallist, 1948, and Neale Bursar, 1949. Assistant: to City Architect, Oxford, 1948; to Sir Herbert Baker & Scott, London, 1949; Sen. Architect, Glenrothes New Town, 1949–51; Sen. Lectr, Dundee Sch. of Arch., 1952–58; commenced private practice in Fife, 1952. Principal works include: Woodside Shopping Centre and St Columba's Parish Church, Glenrothes; Reconstruction of Giles Pittenweem; Redevelopment of Dysart and of Old Buckhaven; Town Centre Renewal, Grangemouth; Students' Union, Univ. of St Andrews; Hunter Building, Edinburgh Coll. of Art; St Peter's Episcopal Ch., Kirkcaldy. Member: Royal Fine Art Commn for Scotland, 1967–86; Scottish Housing Adv. Cttee, 1971–75; Trustee, Scottish Civic Trust, 1970–83; Pres., Royal Incorpn of Architects in Scotland, 1973–75; Vice-Pres., RIBA, 1973–75. FRSA; RSA 1975 (ARSA 1963; Treasurer, 1978–80; Sec., 1980–83); Hon. RA 1983; Hon. RHA 1983; Hon. RGI 1987. Hon. DDes Robert Gordon's Inst. of Technology, 1991. 22 Saltire Awards and Commendations for Housing and Reconstruction; 12 Civic Trust Awards and Commendations. *Publications:* articles on civic design and housing in technical jls. *Recreations:* making gardens, sketching and water colours, fishing, music and drama. *Address:* Hawthornbank House, Dean Village, Edinburgh EH4 3BH. *T:* 0131–225 2334. *Clubs:* New, Scottish Arts (Edinburgh).

WHEELER, Air Chief Marshal Sir (Henry) Neil (George), GCB 1975 (KCB 1969; CB 1967); CBE 1957 (OBE 1949); DSO 1943; DFC 1941 (Bar 1943); AFC 1954; *b* 8 July 1917; *s* of late T. H. Wheeler, South African Police; *m* 1942, Elizabeth, *d* of late W. H. Weightman, CMG; two *s* one *d*. *Educ:* St Helen's College, Southsea, Hants. Entered Royal Air Force College, Cranwell, 1935; Bomber Comd, 1937–40; Fighter and Coastal Comds, 1940–45; RAF and US Army Staff Colls, 1943–44; Cabinet Office, 1944–45; Directing Staff, RAF Staff Coll., 1945–46; FEAF, 1947–49; Directing Staff, JSSC, 1949–51; Bomber Comd, 1951–53; Air Min., 1953–57. Asst Comdt, RAF Coll., 1957–59; OC, RAF Laarbruch, 1959–60; IDC, 1961; Min. of Defence, 1961–63; Senior Air Staff Officer, HQ, RAF Germany (2nd TAF), Sept. 1963–66; Asst Chief of Defence Staff (Operational Requirements), MoD, 1966–67, Deputy Chief of Defence Staff, 1967–68; Commander, FEAF, 1969–70; Air Mem. for Supply and Organisation, MoD, 1970–73; Controller, Aircraft, MoD Procurement Exec., 1973–75. ADC to the Queen, 1957–61. Director: Rolls-Royce Ltd, 1977–82; Flight Refuelling (Holdings) Ltd, 1977–85. Chm., Anglo-Ecuadorian Soc., 1986–88. Vice-Pres., Air League; Liveryman, GAPAN, 1980, Master, 1986–87. FRAeS; CIMgt. *Address:* Boundary Hall, Cooksbridge, Lewes, East Sussex BN8 4PT. *Clubs:* Royal Air Force, Flyfishers'.

WHEELER, Rt. Hon. Sir John (Daniel), Kt 1990; PC 1993; JP; DL; MP (C) Westminster North, since 1983 (City of Westminster, Paddington Division, 1979–83); Minister of State, Northern Ireland Office, since 1993; *b* 1 May 1940; *s* of late Frederick Harry Wheeler and of Constance Elsie (*née* Foreman); *m* 1967, Laura Margaret Langley; one *s* one *d*. *Educ:* county sch., Suffolk; Staff Coll., Wakefield. Home Office: Asst Prison Governor, 1967–74; Res. Officer (looking into causes of crime and delinquency and treatment of offenders), 1974–76; Dir-Gen., BSIA, 1976–88 (Hon. Mem., 1990). Dir, National Supervisory Council for Intruder Alarms, 1977–88. Chairman: Nat. Inspectorate of Security Guard Patrol and Transport Services, 1982–92; Security Systems Inspectorate, 1987–90; Inspectorate of the Security Industry, 1992–93. Chm., HunterPrint Group PLC, 1992. Member: Home Office Crime Prevention Cttee, 1976–92; Cons. Party National Adv. CPC Cttee, 1978–80; Home Affairs Select Cttee, 1979–92 (Chm., 1987–92); Chairman: Home Affairs Sub-Cttee, Race Relations and Immigration, 1980–87; All Party Penal Affairs Gp, 1986–93 (Vice-Chm., 1979–86); Vice-Chairman: Cons. Home Affairs Cttee, 1987–92 (Jt Sec., 1980–87); British Pakistan Parly Gp, 1987–93; Chm., Cons. Greater London Area Members' Cttee, 1983–90 (Jt Sec., 1980–83). Mem., Lloyd's, 1986–. Mem. Council, Order of St John for London, 1990–; Vice Pres., Paddington Div., St John Ambulance, 1990–. OStJ 1991. JP Inner London, 1978; DL Greater London, 1989. Freeman, City of London, 1987. James Smart Lecture, SHHD, 1991 (Silver Medal). CStJ 1992 (Mem., Chapter Gen., 1993–). Hilal-i-Quaid-i-Azam (Pakistan), 1991. *Publications:* Who Prevents Crime?, 1980; (jtly) The Standard Catalogue of the Coins of the British Commonwealth, 1642 to present day, 1986. *Recreation:* enjoying life. *Address:* House of Commons, SW1A 0AA. *T:* 0171–219 6427.

WHEELER, Sir John (Hieron), 3rd Bt *cr* 1920; formerly Chairman, Raithby, Lawrence & Co. Ltd, retired 1973; *b* 22 July 1905; 2nd *s* of Sir Arthur Wheeler, 1st Bt; *S* brother, Sir Arthur (Frederick Pullman) Wheeler, 1964; *m* 1929, Gwendolen Alice (*née* Oram); two *s*. *Educ:* Charterhouse. Engaged in Print. Served War of 1939–45, Trooper, RTR, 1941–45. After the war, returned to printing. *Recreations:* whittling, dry stone walling. *Heir:* *s* John Frederick Wheeler [*b* 3 May 1933; *m* 1963, Barbara Mary, *d* of Raymond

Flint, Leicester; two *s* one *d*]. *Address:* 39 Morland Avenue, Leicester LE2 2PF. *Club:* Wig and Pen.

WHEELER, Hon. Sir Kenneth (Henry), Kt 1976; JP; Speaker of the Victorian Parliament, Australia, 1973–79; *b* 7 Sept. 1912; *s* of William Henry Wheeler and Alma Nellie Wheeler; *m* 1934, Hazel Jean Collins; one *s* one *d*. *Educ:* Mernda State Sch., Vic. Grazier and retail dairyman for 19 years. Municipal Councillor, 1950–59; Mayor, City of Coburg, Vic., 1955–56; elected to Parliament of Victoria for Essendon, 1958. Member: CPA; Victorian Parly Former Mems Assoc.; Life Mem., Coburg FC. Life Governor: Essendon Hosp.; Essendon Lions Club. *Recreations:* golf, football, exhibition of horses. *Clubs:* Essendon; Coburg Rotary; Royal-Park Golf; Royal Automobile of Victoria.

WHEELER, Air Vice-Marshal Leslie William Frederick; Independent Inspector for Public Inquiries and Chairman of Appointments Boards for Civil Service Commissioners and Ministry of Defence, 1984–94; *b* 4 July 1930; *s* of late George Douglas Wheeler and of Susan Wheeler; *m* 1960, Joan, *d* of late Harry Carpenter and of Evelyn Carpenter; two *d*. *Educ:* Creighton School, Carlisle. Commnd, 1952; Egypt and Cyprus, 1954–56; Specialist in Signals, 1958; Aden, 1958–60; V-force (Valiants), 1961–65; India (Staff Coll.), 1965–66; Headquarters Signals Command, 1966–69; OC 360 Sqdn, 1970–72; Dir, RAF Staff Coll., 1972–74; Electronic Warfare and Recce Operations, MoD, 1975–77; Stn Comdr, RAF Finningley, 1977–79; Air Cdre Policy & Plans, Headquarters RAF Support Comd, 1979–83; Dir-Gen., Personal Services (RAF), MoD, 1983–84, retired. *Recreations:* walking, golf, philately, painting and drawing. *Address:* c/o Midland Bank, Brampton, Cumbria CA8 1NQ. *Club:* Royal Air Force.

WHEELER, Sir Neil; *see* Wheeler, Sir H. N. G.

WHEELER, Lt-Gen. Sir Roger (Neil), KCB 1993; CBE 1983; General Officer Commanding and Director of Military Operations, Northern Ireland, since 1993; *b* 16 Dec. 1941; *s* of Maj.-Gen. T. N. S. Wheeler, CB, CBE; *m* 1980, Felicity Hares; three *s* one *d* by former marriage. *Educ:* All Hallows Sch., Devon. Early Army service in Borneo and ME, 1964–70; Bde Major, Cyprus Emergency, 1974; Mem., Lord Carver's Staff, Rhodesia talks, 1977; Bn Comd, Belize, Gibraltar, Berlin and Canada, 1979–82; COS, Falkland Is, June–Dec. 1982; Bde Comd, BAOR, 1985–86; Dir, Army Plans, 1987–89; Comdr, 1st Armoured Div., BAOR, 1989–90; ACGS, MoD, 1990–92. President: Army RFU; Army Rifle Assoc. *Recreations:* fly-fishing, cricket, shooting, ornithology. *Clubs:* Army and Navy; Stragglers of Asia CC, Devon Dumplings CC.

WHEELER, (Selwyn) Charles (Cornelius-); *see* Wheeler, C. C.

WHEELER, Rt. Rev. (William) Gordon, MA Oxon; Hon. DD Leeds; Bishop Emeritus of Leeds; *b* 5 May 1910; *o s* of late Frederick Wheeler and Marjorie (*née* Upjohn). *Educ:* Manchester Gram. Sch.; University Coll. and St Stephen's House, Oxford; Beda Coll., Rome. Curate, St Bartholomew's, Brighton, 1933; Curate, St Mary and All Saints, Chesterfield, 1934; Asst Chaplain, Lancing Coll., 1935. Received into Roman Catholic Church at Downside, 1936; Beda Coll., Rome, 1936–40; ordained priest, 1940; Asst St Edmund's, Lower Edmonton, 1940–44; Chaplain of Westminster Cathedral and Editor of Westminster Cathedral Chronicle, 1944–50; Chaplain to the Catholics in the University, London, 1950–54, and Ecclesiastical Adviser to the Union of Catholic Students, 1953–60; Privy Chamberlain to HH The Pope, 1952; Hon. Canon of Westminster, 1954, Administrator of Cathedral, 1954–65; Created Domestic Prelate to HH Pope Pius XII, 1955; Grand Cross Conventual Chaplain to the British Association of the Sovereign and Military Order of Malta, 1986; Coadjutor Bishop of Middlesbrough, 1964–66; present at 2nd Vatican Council, Rome, 1964 and 1965; Bishop of Leeds, 1966–85. *Publications:* In Truth and Love (memoirs), 1990; edited and contributed to Homage to Newman, 1945; Richard Challoner, 1947; The English Catholics, etc.; contribs to Dublin Review, The Tablet, Clergy Review, etc. *Address:* College of the Blessed Virgin, 62 Headingley Lane, Leeds, W Yorks LS6 2BX.

WHEELER, William Henry, CMG 1959; PhD (London); Chairman, Mark Laboratories Ltd, since 1960; *b* Petersfield, Hants, 5 March 1907; *s* of John William and Ellen Wheeler; *m* 1937, Mary Inkpen; no *c*. *Educ:* St Catharine's Coll., Cambridge (BA); Imperial Coll. of Science (DIC). Beit Memorial Research Fellow, Imperial Coll., 1931. Man. British Automatic Refrigerators, London, 1935; Government Scientific Service, 1937; Dir, Guided Weapons Research & Development, 1950; Head of UK Ministry of Supply Staff and Scientific Adviser to UK High Commission, Australia, 1955; Director of Explosives Research, Waltham Abbey, 1959. Man. Dir, 1961–82, and Dep. Chm., 1968–82, Urquhart Engineering Co. Ltd; Chairman: Urquhart Engineering Co. (Pty) Ltd, 1971–82; Urquhart Engineering GmbH, 1973–82; Dep. Chm., Steam and Combustion Engineering Ltd, 1973–82; Chm., Process Combustion Corp., USA, 1970–82. *Publications:* papers on Combustion and Detonation in Proc. and Trans. Royal Society, and on Rocket Propellants in Nature, Proc. of Inst. of Fuel and Instn of Chemical Engineers; papers on the Mechanism of Cavitation Erosion for DSIR and American Soc. of Mechanical Engineers. *Recreation:* private research laboratory. *Address:* 9 Bulstrode Court, Oxford Road, Gerrards Cross, Bucks SL9 7RR.

WHEELER-BENNETT, Richard Clement; Chairman, Marie Curie Memorial Foundation, since 1990 (Chairman, Executive Committee, since 1978); *b* 14 June 1927; *s* of Dr Clement Wheeler-Bennett and Enid Lucy (*née* Boosey); *m* 1954, Joan Ellen Havelock; two *d* (one *s* decd). *Educ:* Radley; Christ Church, Oxford (MA); Harvard Business Sch. Served Royal Marines, 1944–48. First Nat. City Bank of NY, 1951–66, Manager 1960–66; Australia and New Zealand Banking Group, 1966–80; Exec. Dir, 1967–78; Gen. Manager Europe, 1978–80; Chm., Thomas Borthwick & Sons Ltd, 1980–85; Director: Fleming Technology Trust, 1983–90; Fleming Internat. High Income Investment Trust, 1990–92; ANZ Grindlays Bank, 1993–. Pres. Dir Gen., Boucheries Bernard SA, Paris, 1980–85. Chm., British Overseas and Commonwealth Banks Assoc., 1980. Founder Chm., Prospect Housing Assoc., 1965–77. Chm. of Govs, Springfields Sch., Calne, 1991–. Chm., Roehampton Club Ltd, 1988–92. Freeman, City of London; Liveryman, Butchers' Co. *Recreations:* flyfishing, golf, shooting, viticulture. *Address:* 94 Rosebank, SW6 6LJ. *T:* 0171–385 4970; The Mill House, Calstone Wellington, near Calne, Wilts SN11 8QF. *T:* Calne (01249) 813241. *Clubs:* Brooks's, Pratt's, MCC.

WHEELER-BOOTH, Sir Michael (Addison John), KCB 1994; Clerk of the Parliaments, since 1991; *b* 25 Feb. 1934; *s* of Addison James Wheeler and Mary Angela Wheeler-Booth (*née* Blakeney-Booth); *m* 1982, Emily Frances Smith; one *s* two *d*. *Educ:* Leighton Park Sch.; Magdalen Coll., Oxford (Exhibnr; MA). Nat. Service, Midshipman (Sp.) RNVR, 1952–54. A Clerk, House of Lords, 1960–; seconded as Private Secretary to Leader of House and Government Chief Whip, 1965; seconded as Jt Sec., Inter-Party Conference on House of Lords Reform, 1967; Clerk of the Journals, 1970–74, 1983–90; Chief Clerk, Overseas and European Office, 1972, Principal Clerk, 1978; Reading Clerk, 1983; Clerk Asst, 1988. Trustee, Industry and Parliament Trust. *Publications:* (contrib.) Griffith and Ryle, Parliament, 1989; contribs to parly jls. *Address:* Northfields, Sandford St Martin, Chipping Norton, Oxon OX7 7AG. *T:* Great Tew (01608) 683632; 11 Dewhurst Road, W14 0ET. *T:* 0171–602 0838. *Clubs:* Brooks's, Garrick.

WHEEN, Natalie Kathleen; broadcaster and writer; *b* Shanghai, China, 29 July 1947; *d* of late Edward Leslie Lee Wheen and Galina (*née* Youriеff). *Educ:* Downe House, Newbury; London Univ. (BMus 1967); Royal Coll. of Music (ARCM). BBC, 1968–80: radio studio manager; attachments as Asst Producer, BBC TV Music and Arts, 1970; Radio 3 Music Producer, Manchester and London, 1971–72; Asst Producer, Music Now, Radio 3, 1972–73; Producer, Music Now, Talking About Music and various documentaries, 1973–80 (Best Music Documentary, Imperial Tobacco Soc. Authors Awards for Radio, 1978); London Arts Corresp., Canadian Broadcasting; freelance broadcaster, 1980–; Presenter: Kaleidoscope, Radio 4; Mainly for Pleasure, subseq. In Tune, Radio 3; Music Now, World Service; interviews, Third Ear, etc; documentaries on arts subjects. Partner, Worsley Wheen prodns, 1983–88. Contributing Editor, 3 mag., 1983–86. Lectr and Workshop Leader in presentation and communication skills; Consultant, GSMD, 1991–; Presenter, British Airways In-flight Light Classics Channel, 1991–. Governor, Downe House Sch., 1986–. *Publications:* (jtly) A Life on the Fiddle: Max Jaffa's Autobiography, 1991; publications on trng and employment for Careers and Occupational Information Centre, and Dept of Employment. *Recreations:* windsurfing, women's issues, whisky, laughter, anarchy. *Address:* c/o David Higham Associates Ltd, 5–8 Lower Street, Golden Square, W1R 4HA. *T:* 0171–437 7888. *Clubs:* Chelsea Arts, Groucho.

WHELAN, Michael George; Chief Executive, Parkinson's Disease Society, since 1992; *b* 13 Oct. 1947; *s* of George Henry Whelan and Vera Frances Whelan (*née* Davies); *m* 1st, 1968, Veronica Gemma Merron (marr. diss. 1986); one *s* one *d*; 2nd, 1987, Anne Vivien Williams; one *s*. *Educ:* LSE (BSc(Econ) Hons, MSc(Econ)). Operational Manager, Walton Hosp., Liverpool, then Good Hope Hosp., Sutton Coldfield, and Hope Hosp., Salford, 1964–72; Tutor in Management, and Principal Trng Officer, N Western RHA, 1972–74; Deputy Chief Officer: Tameside and Glossop HA, 1974–78; Surrey AHA, 1978–80; Chief Officer, SW Surrey HA, 1980–85; Gp Manager, Healthcare, KPMG Management Consultants,1985–90; Partner, Pannell Kerr Forster, 1990–92. AIPM 1975; FHSM 1980. *Recreations:* music, entertaining, family. *Address:* (office) 22 Upper Woburn Place, WC1H 0RA. *T:* 0171–383 3513.

WHELAN, Prof. Michael John, MA, PhD, DPhil; FRS 1976; FInstP; Professor of Microscopy of Materials, Department of Materials, University of Oxford, since 1992; Fellow of Linacre College, Oxford, since 1967; *b* 2 Nov. 1931; *s* of William Whelan and Ellen Pound. *Educ:* Farnborough Grammar Sch.; Gonville and Caius Coll., Cambridge. FInstP 1976. Fellow of Gonville and Caius Coll., 1958–66; Demonstrator in Physics, Univ. of Cambridge, 1961–65; Asst Dir of Research in Physics, Univ. of Cambridge, 1965–66; Reader, Dept of Materials, Univ. of Oxford, 1966–92. *Publications:* (co-author) Electron Microscopy of Thin Crystals, 1965; Worked Examples in Dislocations, 1990; numerous papers in learned jls. *Recreation:* gardening. *Address:* 18 Salford Road, Old Marston, Oxford OX3 0RX. *T:* Oxford (01865) 244556.

WHELAN, Terence Leonard; Editor, Ideal Home Magazine, since 1977; *b* 5 Dec. 1936; *s* of Thomas James and Gertrude Beatrice Whelan; *m* 1972, Margaret Elizabeth Bowen; two *s* one *d*. *Educ:* Oakfield Secondary School. NDD 1955; MSTD 1972. Studied Graphic Design at Beckenham College of Art, 1953–56. Art Editor, Publishers, Condé Nast, working on Vogue Pattern Book, Vogue South Africa and British Vogue, 1959–68; gained a number of Design and Art Direction awards during this period; Art Editor, 1968–74, Asst Editor/Art Director, 1974–77, Ideal Home magazine. FRSA 1993. Editor of the Year, Special Interest Section, British Soc. of Magazine Editors, 1988. *Publications:* writer and broadcaster on home improvements. *Address:* Ideal Home Magazine, King's Reach Tower, Stamford Street, SE1 9LS. *T:* 0171–261 6474.

WHELAN, Prof. William Joseph, PhD, DSc; FRS 1992; Professor of Biochemistry and Molecular Biology, University of Miami School of Medicine, since 1967 (Chairman of Department, 1967–91); *b* 14 Nov. 1924; *s* of William Joseph Whelan and Jane Antoinette Whelan (*née* Bertram); *m* 1951, Margaret Miller Birnie (*d* 1993). *Educ:* Univ. of Birmingham, England (BSc Hons 1944; PhD 1948; DSc 1955). Asst Lectr, Univ. of Birmingham, 1947–48; Asst Lectr, Lectr and Sen. Lectr, UCNW, Bangor, 1948–55; Sen. Mem., Lister Inst. of Preventive Medicine, Univ. of London, 1956–64; Prof. and Head, Dept of Biochemistry, Royal Free Hosp. Sch. of Medicine, Univ. of London, 1964–67. FAAAS 1989. Hon. MRCP 1985; Hon. Mem., Biochemical Soc., 1993. Alsberg Medal, 1967; Ciba Medal, 1968; Saare Medal, 1979. Editor-in-Chief: Trends in Biochemical Sciences, 1975–78; BioEssays, 1984–89; Fedn Procs, 1986–87; FASEB Jl, 1987–. *Recreations:* publishing, travel. *Address:* Department of Biochemistry and Molecular Biology, University of Miami School of Medicine (M823), PO Box 016129, Miami, FL 33101–6129, USA. *T:* (305) 2436267, *Fax:* (305) 3245665. *Club:* Athenæum.

WHELDON, Juliet Louise, CB 1994; Legal Secretary to the Law Officers, since 1989; *b* 26 March 1950; *d* of John Wheldon and Ursula Mabel Caillard. *Educ:* Sherborne School for Girls; Lady Margaret Hall, Oxford (1st Cl. Hons Mod. Hist.). Called to the Bar, Gray's Inn, 1975. Treasury Solicitor's Dept, 1976–83; Law Officers Dept, 1983–84; Treasury Solicitor's Dept, 1984–86; Asst Legal Sec. to the Law Officers, 1986–87; Hd of Central Adv. Div., Treasury Solicitor's Dept (Under-Sec.), 1987–89. *Address:* c/o Legal Secretariat to the Law Officers, Attorney General's Chambers, 9 Buckingham Gate, SW1E 6JP.

WHELER, Sir Edward (Woodford), 14th Bt *cr* 1660, of City of Westminster; Company Secretary, Robert Lewis (St James's) Ltd, 1981–90; *b* 13 June 1920; *s* of Sir Trevor Wood Wheler, 13th Bt, and Margaret Idris (*d* 1987), *y d* of late Sir Ernest Birch, KCMG; *S* father, 1986; *m* 1945, Molly Ashworth, *e d* of Thomas Lever, Devon; one *s* one *d*. *Educ:* Radley College. Joined Army (RA), 1940; commnd Royal Sussex Regt, 1941; attached 15 Punjab Regt, IA, 1941–45; BAOR, 1945–47. Oversea Audit Service, Uganda and Ghana, 1948–58; Automobile Association of East Africa, Kenya, 1958–70; Benson & Hedges Ltd, 1971–81, Director 1979–81. Liveryman, Co. of Pipe Makers and Tobacco Blenders, 1980; Freeman, City of London, 1980. *Heir: s* Trevor Woodford Wheler [*b* 11 April 1946; *m* 1974, Rosalie Margaret, *d* of late Ronald Thomas Stunt; two *s*].

WHELON, Charles Patrick Clavell; a Recorder of the Crown Court, since 1978; *b* 18 Jan. 1930; *s* of Charles Eric Whelon and Margaret Whelon; *m* 1968, Prudence Mary (*née* Potter); one *s* one *d*. *Educ:* Wellington Coll.; Pembroke Coll., Cambridge (MA Hons). Called to Bar, Middle Temple, 1954. Liveryman of Vintners' Co., 1952–. *Recreations:* gardening, cartooning. *Address:* 2 Harcourt Buildings, Temple, EC4. *T:* 0171–353 2112; Russets, Pyott's Hill, Old Basing, Hants RG24 0AP. *T:* Basingstoke (01256) 469964.

WHENT, Sir Gerald Arthur, Kt 1995; CBE 1989; Chief Executive: Racal Telecom plc, since 1988; Vodafone Group PLC, since 1991; *b* 1 March 1927; *m* 1st, Coris Dorothy (*née* Bellman-Thomas); one *s* one *d*; 2nd, Sarah Louise (*née* Donaldson); two step *s* one step *d*. *Educ:* St Mary's College, Southampton. Dent Allcroft & Co.: Management Trainee, 1952; Asst Div. Manager, 1957; Div. Manager, 1959–62; Plessey Co.: Dept Manager, 1962; Div. Gen. Manager, 1966–69; Dir, Racal Recorders, 1970–72; Man. Dir, Racal Comsec, 1973–76; Man. Dir, Racal-Tacticom, 1977–80; Chm. and Man. Dir, Racal Radio Group, 1980–85; Dir, Racal Electronics plc, 1982–; Chm. and Chief Exec., Racal Telecommunications Group, 1983–88. *Recreations:* golf, ski-ing, horse riding, chess, bridge.

Address: The Bothy, Horris Bank, Horris Hill, Newtown Common, Newbury, Berks RG15 9DF. *T:* Newbury (01635) 42855.

WHETNALL, Andrew Donard; Head, Machinery of Government Division, since 1989, Under Secretary, since 1993, Cabinet Office; *b* 18 May 1948; *s* of late Donard and of Joan Whetnall (*née* Mummery); *m* 1972, Jane Lepel Glass; two *s* two *d*. *Educ:* King's Norton Grammar Sch.; Univ. of Sussex (MA). Joined DoE, 1975; Principal, Dept of Transport, 1980–83; Department of the Environment: Principal, 1983–87, Asst Sec., 1987–88, Inner Cities; Water Legislation, 1988–89. *Recreations:* reading, music. *Address:* Cabinet Office, 70 Whitehall, SW1A 2AS. *T:* 0171–270 0067.

WHETSTONE, Rear-Adm. Anthony John, CB 1982; Director, DESC Ltd, since 1991; Chairman of Trustees, Royal Navy Submarine Museum, since 1990; *b* 12 June 1927; *s* of Albert Whetstone; *m* 1951, Elizabeth Stewart Georgeson; one *s* two *d*. *Educ:* King Henry VIII School, Coventry. Joined RN, 1945; specialised in submarines, 1949; Commanded: HMS Sea Scout, 1956–57; HMS Artful, 1959–61; HMS Repulse, 1968–70; HMS Juno, 1972–73; HMS Norfolk, 1977–78; Flag Officer Sea Training, 1978–80; Asst Chief of Naval Staff (Operations), 1981–83. Director-General: Cable TV Assoc., 1983–86; Nat. Television Rental Assoc., 1983–87. Dep. Sec., Defence Press and Broadcasting Cttee, 1987–92. Nat. Pres., Submarine Old Comrades Assoc., 1988–. FIMgt (FBIM 1979). *Recreations:* hill walking, fishing, amateur dramatics (Chm., Civil Service Drama Fedn, 1985–92). *Address:* 17 Anglesey Road, Alverstoke, Hants PO12 2EG. *Clubs:* Army and Navy, Naval.

See also N. K. Whetstone.

WHETSTONE, (Norman) Keith, OBE 1983; VRD; journalist and editorial consultant; *b* 17 June 1930; *yr s* of Albert and Anne Whetstone; *m* 1952, Monica Joan Clayton, Leamington Spa; three *s*. *Educ:* King Henry VIII Sch., Coventry. Served Royal Navy, 1949–50, 1951–52; Lt Comdr (S) RNVR, retired, 1965. Coventry Evening Telegraph, 1950–51; Western Morning News, 1952–55; Birmingham Post, 1955–58; Coventry Evening Telegraph, 1958–63; Editor, Cambridge Evening News, 1964–70; Editor, Coventry Evening Telegraph, 1970–80; Editor-in-Chief: Birmingham Evening Mail series, 1980–84; Birmingham Post and Birmingham Evening Mail series, 1984–86; Dir, Birmingham Post & Mail Ltd, 1980–86. Nat. Pres., Guild of British Newspaper Editors, 1976–77. Mem. Press Council, 1980–86. *Recreations:* theatre, Rugby football, golf. *Address:* 4 The Green, Meriden, Coventry CV7 7LN. *T:* Meriden (01676) 522654; Niaudon, 46220 Prayssac, Lot, France. *T:* 65224661.

See also A. J. Whetstone.

WHEWAY, Albert James; Director, Hogg Robinson Travel Ltd, since 1976; *b* 6 April 1922; *s* of Albert and Alice Wheway; *m* 1st, 1946, Joan Simpson; 2nd, 1984, Susannah Mary Gray (*née* Luesby). *Educ:* Kimberworth School, Rotherham. Cooper Bros (later Cooper Lybrand), 1946–53; S. G. Warburg, 1953–57; industry, 1957–63; Ionian Bank, 1963–70; internat. industry and commerce, 1970–; Chm., Hogg Robinson Group plc, 1983–87. *Recreations:* art collecting, music. *Address:* Beaumont, Duddington, near Stamford, Lincs PE9 3QE. *T:* Duddington (01780) 444237; Bilancia, Cappella Alta, Lucca, Italy. *T:* (583) 394473.

WHICHER, Peter George, CEng; FRAeS; MIEE; Principal, INECO, since 1994; *b* 10 March 1929; *o s* of late Reginald George Whicher and Suzanne (*née* Dexter); *m* 1st, 1962, Susan Rosemary Strong (*d* 1989); one *s* one *d*; 2nd, 1992, Margaret Rosemary (*née* Rickman). *Educ:* Chichester High School. BSc(Eng) London 1948; CEng, MIEE 1957. STC, 1948–51; Flying Officer, RAF, 1951–53; Min. of Aviation, 1953; Principal Expert in Telecommunications, Eurocontrol Agency, Paris, 1962–64; Cabinet Office, 1964–66; Asst Dir, Telecommunications R & D, and Manager, Skynet Satellite Communications Project, Min. of Technology, 1967–71; Superintendent, Communications Div., RAE, 1971–73; Dir, Air Radio, MoD(PE), 1973–76; RCDS, 1977; Dir, Defence Sci. (Electronics), MoD, 1978–81; Dep. Dir, RAE, 1981–84. Consultant, Logica, 1985–94. FRAeS 1985. *Publications:* reports and papers for professional instns. *Recreations:* sailing, innovation, arts. *Address:* Widgers Wood, Sheets Health, Brookwood, Woking, Surrey GU23 0EJ. *Club:* Royal Ocean Racing.

WHICKER, Alan Donald; television broadcaster (Whicker's World); writer; *b* 2 Aug. 1925; *o s* of late Charles Henry Whicker and late Anne Jane Cross. *Educ:* Haberdashers' Aske's Sch. Capt., Devonshire Regt; Dir, Army Film and Photo Section, with 8th Army and US 5th Army. War Corresp. in Korea, Foreign Corresp., novelist, writer and radio Broadcaster. Joined BBC TV, 1957; Tonight programme (appeared nightly in filmed reports from around the world, studio interviews, outside broadcasts, Eurovision, and Telstar, incl. first Telstar two-way transmission at opening of UN Assembly, NY, 1962); TV Series: Whicker's World, 1959–60; Whicker Down Under, 1961; Whicker on Top of the World!, 1962; Whicker in Sweden, Whicker in the Heart of Texas, Whicker Down Mexico Way, 1963; Alan Whicker Report series: The Solitary Billionaire (J. Paul Getty), etc; wrote and appeared in own series of monthly documentaries on BBC 2, subseq. repeated on BBC 1, under series title, Whicker's World, 1965–67 (31 programmes later shown around the world); BBC radio programmes and articles for The Listener, etc; left BBC, 1968. Various cinema films, incl. The Angry Silence. Mem., successful consortium for Yorkshire Television, 1967. Completed 16 Documentaries for Yorkshire TV during its first year of operation, incl. Whicker's New World series, and Specials on Gen. Stroessner of Paraguay, Count von Rosen, and Pres. Duvalier of Haiti; Whicker in Europe; Whicker's Walkabout; Broken Hill—Walled City; Gairy's Grenada; documentary series, World of Whicker; Whicker's Orient; Whicker within a Woman's World, 1972; Whicker's South Seas, Whicker way out West, 1973; Whicker's World, series on cities, 1974–77; Whicker's World—Down Under, 1976; Whicker's World: US, 1977 (4 progs); India, 1978 (7 progs); Indonesia, 1979; California, 1980 (6 progs); Peter Sellers Meml programme, 1980; Whicker's World Aboard the Orient Express, 1982; Around Whicker's World in 25 Years (3 YTV retrospect. progs), 1982; BBC TV, 1982–92; Whicker's World—the First Million Miles (6 retrospect. progs), 1982; Whicker's World—a Fast Boat to China (4 QE2 progs), 1984; Whicker! (10 talk shows), 1984; Whicker's World—Living with Uncle Sam (10 progs), 1985; Whicker's World—Living with Waltzing Matilda (10 progs), 1987–88; Whicker's World—Hong Kong (8 progs), 1990; Whicker's World—a Taste of Spain (8 progs), 1992; returned to ITV for: Around Whicker's World—the Ultimate Package! (4 progs), 1992; Whicker's World—The Absolute Monarch (the Sultan of Brunei), 1992; South Africa: Whicker's Miss World, and Whicker's World—The Sun King, 1993; South-East Asia: Whicker's World Aboard the real Orient Express; Whicker—the Mahatir Interview (Dr Mahatir Mohammed, PM of Malaysia); Pavarotti in Paradise, 1994. BBC Radio: Chm., Start the Week; Whicker's Wireless World (3 series), 1983; Various awards, 1963–, incl. Screenwriters' Guild, best Documentary Script, 1963; Guild of Television Producers and Directors Personality of the Year, 1964; Silver Medal, Royal Television Soc., 1968; Dumont Award, Univ. of California, 1970; Best Interview Prog. Award, Hollywood Festival of TV, 1973; Dimbleby Award, BAFTA, 1978; TV Times Special Award, 1978; first to be named in RTS Hall of Fame for outstanding creative contribution to British TV, 1993. FRSA 1970. *Publications:* Some Rise by Sin, 1949; Away—with Alan Whicker, 1963; Best of Everything, 1980; Within Whicker's World: an autobiography, 1982; Whicker's Business Traveller's Guide (with BAA), 1983; Whicker's New World, 1985; Whicker's World Down Under, 1988; Sunday newspaper columns; contrib. various internat. pubns. *Recreations:* people, photography, writing, travel, and reading (usually airline timetables). *Address:* Le Gallais Chambers, St Helier, Jersey.

WHIFFEN, David Hardy, MA, DPhil (Oxon), DSc (Birmingham); FRS 1966; FRSC; Professor of Physical Chemistry, 1968–85, Head of School of Chemistry, 1978–85, Pro-Vice-Chancellor, 1980–83, University of Newcastle upon Tyne (Dean of Science, 1974–77); *s* of late Noël H. and Mary Whiffen; *m* Jean P. Bell; four *s*. *Educ:* Oundle School; St John's College, Oxford (Scholar). Sometime Commonwealth Fund Fellow, Sen. Student of Commn for 1851 Exhibition. Formerly: Lectr in Chemistry, Univ. of Birmingham; Supt, Molecular Science Div., NPL. Vice-Chm., Newcastle HA, 1983–85 (Mem., Newcastle AHA, 1978–82, Newcastle HA, 1982–85). Pres., Faraday Div., RSC, 1981–83. *Publications:* Spectroscopy, 1966; The Royal Society of Chemistry: the first 150 years, 1991; papers in scientific jls.

WHINNEY, Rt Rev. Michael Humphrey Dickens; Hon. Assistant Bishop, Diocese of Birmingham, since 1996 (Assistant Bishop, 1988–95); Canon Residentiary, Birmingham Cathedral, 1992–95; *b* 8 July 1930; *s* of late Humphrey Charles Dickens Whinney and Evelyn Lawrence Revell Whinney (*née* Low); great-great-grandson of Charles Dickens; *m* 1958, Veronica (*née* Webster); two *s* one *d*. *Educ:* Charterhouse; Pembroke Coll., Cambridge (BA 1955, MA 1958); Ridley Hall, Cambridge; General Theological Seminary, NY (STM 1990). National Service commission, RA, 1949 (served in 5th Regt, RHA and Surrey Yeo. Queen Mary's Regt). Articled clerk to Chartered Accountants, Whinney Smith & Whinney (now Ernst Young), 1950–52. Curate, Rainham Parish Church, Essex, 1957–60; Head, Cambridge University Mission Settlement, Bermondsey, 1960–67, Chaplain, 1967–72; Vicar, St James' with Christ Church, Bermondsey, 1967–73; Archdeacon and Borough Dean of Southwark, 1973–82; Bishop Suffragan of Aston, 1982–85; Bishop of Southwell, 1985–88. *Address:* Moorcroft, 3 Moor Green Lane, Moseley, Birmingham B13 8NE.

WHIPPLE, Prof. Fred Lawrence; Senior Scientist, Smithsonian Astrophysical Observatory, since 1973; Director, Smithsonian Institution Astrophysical Observatory, 1955–73; Phillips Professor of Astronomy, Harvard University, 1968–77; *b* 5 Nov. 1906; *s* of Harry Lawrence Whipple and Celestia Whipple (*née* MacFarland); *m* 1st, 1928, Dorothy Woods (divorced 1935); one *s*; 2nd, 1946, Babette Frances Samelson; two *d*. *Educ:* Long Beach High School, Calif; UCLA; Univ. of California, Berkeley. Lick Observatory Fellow, 1930–31; Staff Member, Harvard Univ., 1931–; Instructor, 1932–38; Lecturer, 1938–45; Assoc. Prof., 1945–50; Professor, 1950–77; Chm. Dept of Astronomy, 1949–56. US Nat. Cttee of Internat. Geophysical Year: Chm. Techn. Panel on Rocketry, 1955–59; Member: Techn. Panel on Earth Satellite Program, 1955–59; Working Group on Satellite Tracking and Computation, 1955–58; Scientific Advisory Bd to USAF, 1953–62; Cttee on Meteorology, Nat. Acad. of Sciences, Nat. Research Coun., 1958–61; Special Cttees on Space Techn., Nat. Advisory Cttee for Aeronautics, 1958–63 (now NASA), US; Space Sciences Working Group on Orbiting Astronomical Observatories, Nat. Acad. of Sciences (Mem. Nat. Acad. of Sciences, 1959–); Advisory Panel to Cttee on Sci. and Astronautics of US House of Representatives, 1960–73; Amer. Philosophical Soc., Philadelphia; Amer. Acad. of Arts and Sciences, Boston; New York Acad. of Science, NY; several technical societies. Associate, Royal Astronomical Soc., 1970–. Benjamin Franklin Fellow, RSA, 1968–. Editor: Smithsonian Contributions to Astrophysics, 1956–73; Planetary and Space Science, 1958–. Hon. degrees: MA, Harvard Univ., 1945; DSc, Amer. Internat. Coll., 1958; DLitt, North-eastern Univ., 1961; DS: Temple Univ., 1961; Arizona, 1979; LLD, CW Post Coll. of Long Island Univ., 1962. J. Lawrence Smith Medal of Nat. Acad. of Sciences, 1949; Donohue Medals, 1932, 1933, 1937, 1940, 1942 (received two medals that year); Presidential Certificate of Merit, 1948; Exceptional Service Award, US Air Force Scientific Adv. Bd, 1960; Space Flight Award, Amer. Astron. Soc., 1961; President's Award for Distinguished Federal Civilian Service, 1963; Space Pioneers Medallion, 1968; NASA Public Services Award, 1969; Kepler Medal, AAAS, 1971; Nat. Civil Service League's Civil Service Award, 1972; Henry Medal, Smithsonian Instn, 1973; Alumnus of the Year Award, UCLA, 1976; Gold Medal, Royal Astronomical Soc., 1983; Bruce Gold Medal, Astronomical Soc. of Pacific, 1986; other foreign awards. Depicted on postal stamp, Mauritania, 1986 (in recognition of contribn to understanding of comets, and to commemorate Halley's Comet) and on stamp of St Vincent, 1994. *Publications:* Earth, Moon and Planets, 1942, 3rd edn 1968; Orbiting the Sun, 1981; The Mystery of Comets, 1985; many technical papers in various astronomical and geophysical journals and books; popular articles in magazines and in Encyclopædia Britannica. *Recreation:* cultivation of roses. *Address:* Smithsonian Astrophysical Observatory, 60 Garden Street, Cambridge, MA 02138, USA. *T:* (617) 8647383.

WHIPPMAN, Michael Lewis, PhD; Under Secretary, Social Security Policy Division B, Department of Social Security, since 1994; *b* 20 Sept. 1938; *s* of Matthew Whippman and Adelina Whippman (*née* Abrahams); *m* 1967, Constance Baskett; two *d*. *Educ:* King Edward VII Sch.; Univ. of the Witwatersrand; Clare Coll., Cambridge (PhD). Res. Fellow 1963–65, Asst Prof. 1965–71, Univ. of Pennsylvania; Sen. Res. Fellow, Univ. of Helsinki, 1971–73; Principal 1973, Asst Sec. 1980, Under Sec., 1988, DHSS; Under Sec., Home and Educn Gp, HM Treasury, 1990–94. Fellow, Amer. Phys. Soc., 1971. *Publications:* papers in Phys. Rev., Annals of Physics, Il Nuovo Cimento, etc. *Recreations:* opera, arguing. *Address:* Department of Social Security, The Adelphi, 1–11 John Adam Street, WC2N 6HT.

WHISH, Prof. Richard Peter; Professor of Law, King's College London, since 1991; Partner, Watson, Farley and Williams (Solicitors), London, since 1989; *b* 23 March 1953; *s* of Thomas Stanton Whish and Avis Mary Whish (*née* Sullivan). *Educ:* Clifton Coll., Bristol; Worcester Coll., Oxford (BA 1st Cl. Hons 1974; BCL 1st Cl. Hons 1978). Qualified as solicitor, 1977; University of Bristol: Lectr in Law, 1978–88; Reader in Commercial Law, 1988–90. Mem., Exec. Council, Centre for European Law, KCL, 1991–. Member: Adv. Cttee, Centre for Study of Regulated Industries, 1991–; Bd, European Maritime Law Orgn, 1993–; Editl Bd, European Business Law Review, 1994–. FRSA 1995. *Publications:* (jtly) Conveyancing Solutions, 1987; (Gen. Ed.) Butterworth's Competition Law, 1991; Competition Law, 3rd edn 1993; (jtly) Merger Cases in the Real World: a study of merger control procedures, 1994; (ed) Halsbury's Laws of England, Vol. 47, 4th edn 1994; numerous articles, case-notes and book reviews in legal periodicals and books. *Recreations:* opera and music, travelling (in particular in the sub-continent), gardening, conservation, Bristol Rovers FC. *Address:* 4 Glebe House, 15 Fitzroy Mews, W1P 5DQ.

WHISHAW, Anthony Popham Law, RA 1989 (ARA 1980); RWA 1992; *b* 22 May 1930; *s* of Robert Whishaw and Joyce (*née* Wheeler); *m* 1957, Jean Gibson; two *d*. *Educ:* Tonbridge Sch.; Chelsea Sch. of Art (Higher Cert); Royal College of Art (ARCA). Travelling Schol., RCA; Abbey Minor Schol.; Spanish Govt Schol.; Abbey Premier Schol., 1982; Lorne Schol., 1982–83. John Moores Minor Painting Prize, 1982; (jtly) 1st Prize, Hunting Group Art Awards, 1986. *One-Man Exhibitions:* Libreria Abril, Madrid, 1957; Rowland Browse and Delbranco, London, 1960, 1961, 1963, 1965, 1968; ICA,

1971; New Art Centre, 1972; Folkestone Arts Centre, 1973; Hoya Gall., London, 1974; Oxford Gall., Oxford, 1974; ACME, London, 1978; Newcastle upon Tyne Polytech. Gall., 1979; (with Martin Froy) New Ashgate Gall., Farnham, 1979; Nicola Jacobs Gall., London 1981; From Landscape, Kettle's Yard, Cambridge, Ferens Gall., Hull, Bede Gall., Jarrow, 1982–84; Works on Paper, Nicola Jacobs Gall., 1983; Paintings, Nicola Jacobs Gall., 1984; Mappin Art Gall., Sheffield, 1985; Large Paintings, RA 1986; Reflections after Las Meninas (touring): Royal Acad., and Hatton Gall., Newcastle upon Tyne, 1987; Mead Gall., Warwick Univ., John Hansard Gall., Southampton Univ., and Spacex Gall., Exeter, 1988; Infaust Gall., Shanghai and Hamburg, 1989; Blason Gall., London, 1991; artspace, London, 1992 and 1995; RWA Bristol, 1993; Barbican, 1994 and tour, Mappin Gall., Sheffield, 1994, Newport Mus. and Art Gall., Bolton Metropolitan Mus. and Art Gall., 1995; Maclaurin Gall., Ayr, Huddersfield Gall., Royal Hibernian Acad. of Arts, Gallagher Gall., Dublin, Hatton Gall., Newcastle, 1994. *Group Exhibitions:* Gimpel Fils, AIA Gall., Café Royal Centen., Towards Art (RCA), Camden Arts Centre, London, Ashmoleum Mus., Oxford, 1957–72; Brit. Drawing Biennale, Teesside, 1973; British Landscape, Graves Art Gall., Sheffield, Chichester Nat. Art, 1975; Summer Exhibn, RA, 1974–81; British Painting, 1952–77, RA, 1977; London Group, Whitechapel Open, 1978, A Free Hand, Arts Council (touring show), 1978; The British Art Show, Arts Council (touring), Recent Arts Council Purchases and Awards, Serpentine Gall., First Exhibition, Nicola Jacobs Gall., Tolly Cobbold (touring), 55 Wapping Artists, London, 1979; Four Artists, Nicola Jacobs Gall., Sculpture and Works on Paper, Nicola Jacobs, Wapping Open Studios, Hayward Annual, Hayward Gall., Whitechapel Open, Whitechapel Gall., John Moore's Liverpool Exhibn 12, 1980, Exhibn 13, 1982, Walker Art Gall., Liverpool; London Gp, S London Art Gall., Wapping Artists, 1981; Images for Today, Graves Art Gall., Sheffield, 1982; Nine Artists (touring), Helsinki, 1983; Tolly Cobbold/Eastern Arts Fourth (touring), 1983; Three Decades 1953–83, RA, 1983; Romantic Tradition in Contemporary British Painting (touring), Murcia and Madrid, Spain, and Ikon Gall., Birmingham, 1988. *Works in Collections:* Arts Council of GB, Tate Gall., Coventry Art Gall., Leicester Art Gall., Nat. Gall. of Wales, Sheffield City Art Galls, Financial Times, Shell-BP, Museo de Bahia, Brazil, Nat. Gall. of Victoria, Melb., Seattle Mus. of Art, Bank of Boston, Chantrey Bequest, W Australia Art Gall., Bayer Pharmaceuticals, DoE, Nat. Westminster Bank, Power Art Gall., Aust. European Parlt, Ferens Art Gall, Museum, Murcia, Spain, Alliance & Leicester, Rosehaven PLC, Royal Academy, Linklater and Baines, Mus. of Contemp. Art, Helsinki, Christchurch, Kensington, Long Term Credit Bank of Japan, Andersen Consulting, Ashikaga Bank of Tokyo, Tetrapak, Zeneca, RWA. *Recreations:* chess, badminton. *Address:* 7a Albert Place, Victoria Road, W8 5PD. *T:* 0171–937 5197.

WHISHAW, Sir Charles (Percival Law), Kt 1969; solicitor (retired); *b* 29 October 1909; 2nd *s* of late Montague Law Whishaw and Erna Louise (*née* Spies); *m* 1936, Margaret Joan (*d* 1989), *e d* of late Col T. H. Hawkins, CMG, RMLI; one *s* two *d*. *Educ:* Charterhouse; Worcester College, Oxford. Called to Bar, Inner Temple, 1932; Solicitor, 1938; Partner in Freshfields, 1943–74. Trustee, Calouste Gulbenkian Foundn, 1956–81. Member: Iron and Steel Holding and Realisation Agency, 1953–67; Council, Law Soc., 1967–76. Comdr, Order of Prince Henry (Portugal), 1981. *Address:* Clare Park, near Farnham, Surrey GU10 5DT. *T:* Aldershot (01252) 851333, 850681.

WHISTLER, Laurence, CBE 1973 (OBE 1955); engraver on glass; writer; *b* 21 Jan. 1912; *s* of Henry Whistler and Helen (*née* Ward); *yr b* of late Rex Whistler; *m* 1st, 1939, Jill (*d* 1944), *d* of Sir Ralph Furse, KCMG, DSO; one *s* one *d*; 2nd, 1950, Theresa (marr. diss.), *yr sister* of Jill Furse; one *s* one *d*; 3rd, 1987, Carol Dawson (marr. diss. 1991), *d* of John Dudley Groves, *qv*. *Educ:* Stowe; Balliol College, Oxford (Hon. Fellow 1974). BA Oxon (MA 1985). Chancellor's Essay Prize, 1934. Served War of 1939–45: private soldier, 1940; commissioned in The Rifle Brigade, 1941; Captain 1942. King's Gold Medal for Poetry, 1935 (first award); Atlantic Award for Literature, 1945. First Pres., Guild of Glass Engravers, 1975–80. Hon. DLitt Oxon, 1993. *Work on glass includes:* goblets, etc, in point-engraving and drill, and engraved church windows and panels at: Sherborne Abbey; Moreton, Dorset; Checkendon, Oxon; Ilton, Som; Eastbury, Berks (window to Edward and Helen Thomas); Guards' Chapel, London; Stowe, Bucks; St Hugh's Coll., Oxford; Ashmansworth, Berks; Steep, Hants (windows to Edward Thomas); Hannington, Hants; Yalding, Kent (windows to Edmund Blunden); Thornham Parva, Suffolk; Salisbury Cathedral; Curry Rivel, Som; Wootton St Lawrence, Hants. *Exhibitions:* Agnews, Bond Street, 1969; Marble Hill, Twickenham, 1972; Corning Museum, USA, 1974; Ashmolean, 1976, 1985; Sotheby's, 1992; (with Simon Whistler) S Wilts Mus., Salisbury, 1993. *Publications include:* Sir John Vanbrugh (biography), 1938; The English Festivals, 1947; Rex Whistler, His Life and His Drawings, 1948; The World's Room (Collected Poems), 1949; The Engraved Glass of Laurence Whistler, 1952; Rex Whistler: The Königsmark Drawings, 1952; The Imagination of Vanbrugh and his Fellow Artists, 1954; The View From This Window (poems), 1956; Engraved Glass, 1952–58; The Work of Rex Whistler (with Ronald Fuller), 1960; Audible Silence (poems), 1961; The Initials in the Heart: the story of a marriage, 1964, rev. edn 1975; To Celebrate Her Living (poems), 1967; Pictures on Glass, 1972; The Image on the Glass, 1975; Scenes and Signs on Glass, 1985; The Laughter and the Urn: the life of Rex Whistler, 1985; Enter (poems), 1987; Point Engraving on Glass, 1992. *Address:* Watlington, Oxford OX9 5PZ.

WHISTON, Peter Rice, RSA 1977; ARIBA; FRIAS; Consultant Architect, since 1977; *b* 19 Oct. 1912; *s* of Thomas Whiston and Marie Barrett; *m* 1947, Kathleen Anne Parker (*d* 1983); one *s* four *d*. *Educ:* Holy Cross Acad.; Sch. of Architecture, Edinburgh Coll. of Art. RIBA Silver Medallist for Recognised Schs, 1937. Served War, Staff Captain RE, 1940–45. Articled, City Architect, Edinburgh, 1930–35; Partner, Dick Peddie McKay & Jamieson, 1937–38; Chief Architect, SSHA, 1946–49; Sen. Lectr, Sch. of Architecture, ECA, 1950–69; Dir, Arch. Conservation Studies, at Heriot Watt Univ., 1969–77. Visiting Lectr at Internat. Centre for Conservation, Rome, 1971; Ecclesiological Practice, 1950–77. *Works include:* Cistercian Abbey at Nunraw; St Margaret's, St Mark's and St Paul's, Edin.; St Columba, Cupar; St Mary Magdalene's, Perth; St Ninian's and St Leonard's, Dundee; Our Lady, Mother of the Church, Edin.; Corpus Christi, Glasgow; St Mark's, Rutherglen; St Bernadette's, Tullibody. Awarded Papal Knighthood of St Gregory for Services to Architecture, (KSG), 1969. *Recreations:* travel, sketching, painting. *Address:* Grange Lodge, Grange Road, North Berwick, East Lothian EH39 4QT.

WHITAKER, Benjamin Charles George; author; Director, Gulbenkian Foundation (UK), since 1988; *b* 15 Sept. 1934; 3rd *s* of late Maj.-Gen. Sir John Whitaker, 2nd Bt, CB, CBE, and late Lady Whitaker (*née* Snowden), Babworth, Retford, Notts; *m* 1964, Janet Alison Stewart; two *s* one *d*. *Educ:* Eton; New Coll., Oxford. BA (Modern History). Called to Bar, Inner Temple, 1959 (Yarborough-Anderson Scholar). Practised as Barrister, 1959–67. Extra-mural Lectr in Law, London Univ., 1963–64. MP (Lab) Hampstead, 1966–70; PPS to Minister of: Overseas Development, 1966; Housing and Local Govt, 1966–67; Parly Sec., ODM, 1969–70. Exec. Dir, Minority Rights Group, 1971–88. Member: UN Human Rights Sub-Commn, 1975–88 (Vice-Chm., 1979); Goodman Cttee on Charity Law Reform, 1974–76; UK Nat. Commn for UNESCO, 1978–85; Speaker's Commn on Citizenship, 1989–90; Chairman: UN Working Gp on Slavery, 1976–78; Defence of Literature and Arts Soc., 1976–82; City Poverty Cttee, 1971–83; Friends of Regent's Park, 1991–93. Judge: NCR Book Award, 1990; RIBA Architecture Awards, 1992. Lieut, Order of Merit (Portugal), 1993. *Publications:* The Police, 1964; (ed) A Radical Future, 1967; Crime and Society, 1967; Participation and Poverty, 1968; Parks for People, 1971; (ed) The Fourth World, 1972; The Foundations, 1974; The Police in Society, 1979; (contrib.) Human Rights and American Foreign Policy, 1979; UN Report on Slavery, 1982; (ed) Teaching about Prejudice, 1983; A Bridge of People, 1983; (ed) Minorities: a question of human rights?, 1984; UN Report on Genocide, 1985; The Global Connection, 1987; (contrib.) The United Kingdom—The United Nations, 1990; Gen. Editor, Sources for Contemporary Issues series (7 vols), 1973–75. *Address:* 13 Elsworthy Road, NW3 3DS.

See also Sir James Whitaker, Bt.

WHITAKER, David Haddon, OBE 1991; Chairman, J. Whitaker & Sons, Ltd, since 1982 (Editorial Director, 1980–91); Director, since 1966, and Chairman, since 1982, Standard Book Numbering Agency; Director, Imperial Cancer Research Fund Trading Ltd, since 1993; *b* 6 March 1931; *s* of late Edgar Haddon Whitaker, OBE and of Mollie Marian, *y d* of George and Louisa Seely; *m* 1st, 1959, Veronica Wallace (decd); two *s* two *d*; 2nd, 1976, Audrey Miller (marr. diss.). *Educ:* Boscastle Infants' Sch.; Marlborough; St John's Coll., Cambridge. Joined family firm of publishers, J. Whitaker & Sons, Ltd, 1955; Dir, 1966; Editor, The Bookseller, 1977–79. Member: Adv. Panel, Internat. Standard Book Numbering Agency (Berlin), 1979– (Chm., 1990–); Adv. Panel, Registrar for Public Lending Right, 1983–93 (Chm., 1989–93); Standing Cttee on Technology, Booksellers' Assoc., 1984–89; Library and Information Services Council, 1985–89; Chairman: Information and Library Services Lead Body for Nat. Vocational Qualifications, 1992–95; British Nat. Bibliography Res. Fund, 1992–. Chairman: Soc. of Bookmen, 1984–86; Book Trade Electronic Data Interchange Standards Cttee, 1987–90. Hon. Vice-Pres., LA, 1990. *Recreations:* reading, walking. *Address:* 5 Queen's Mansions, 59 Queen's Avenue, N10 3PA. *T:* 0181–883 9710. *Clubs:* Garrick, Thames Rowing; Leander (Henley-on-Thames).

WHITAKER, (Edwin) John, MBE 1991; show-jumper; *b* 5 Aug. 1955; *er s* of Donald Whitaker and Enid (*née* Lockwood); *m* Claire Barr; one *s* two *d*. British champion, 1992, 1993; other European championship wins: team and individual silver medals, 1983 (Ryan's Son); team gold and individual bronze, 1985 (Hopscotch); team gold and individual silver, 1987 (Milton); individual and team gold, 1989 (Milton); World Cup gold medals, 1990, 1991 (Milton); Olympic individual and team silver medals, 1980 (Ryan's Son); jumping Derby, 1983 (Ryan's Son); King George V Gold Cup, 1986 (Ryan's Son), and 1990 (Milton). Leading Jumper of the Year, Horse of the Year Show, 1993; numerous other wins and awards. *Address:* c/o British Show Jumping Association, Stoneleigh, Warwicks CV8 2LR.

See also M. Whitaker.

WHITAKER, Sir James Herbert Ingham, 3rd Bt, *cr* 1936; Vice-Chairman, Halifax Building Society, 1973–94; *b* 27 July 1925; *s* of late Maj.-Gen. Sir John Whitaker, 2nd Bt, CB, CBE, and Lady Whitaker (*née* Snowden); *S* father 1957; *m* 1948, Mary Elisabeth Lander Urling Clark (*née* Johnston), *widow* of Captain D. Urling Clark, MC; one *s* one *d*. *Educ:* Eton. Coldstream Guards, 1944. Served in North West Europe. Retired, 1947. Dir, Governing Body, Atlantic College. High Sheriff of Notts, 1969–70. *Recreation:* shooting. *Heir: s* John James Ingham Whitaker, BSc, FCA, AMIEE [*b* 23 October 1952; *m* 1981, Janey, *d* of L. J. R. Starke, New Zealand; one *s* three *d*]. *Address:* Babworth Hall, Retford, Notts DN22 8EP. *T:* Retford (01777) 703454; Auchnafree, Dunkeld, Perthshire PH8 0EH. *Club:* Boodle's.

See also B. C. G. Whitaker.

WHITAKER, John; *see* Whitaker, E. J.

WHITAKER, Michael; show-jumper; *b* 17 March 1960; *yr s* of Donald Whitaker and Enid (*née* Lockwood); *m* 1980, Veronique Dalems, *d* of Dino Vastapane. British champion, 1984, 1989; other European championship wins: Junior, 1978; team gold medal, 1985 (Warren Point); team gold, 1987 (Amanda); team gold and individual silver, 1989 (Monsanta); Olympic silver medal, 1984 (Amanda); Jumping Derby: 1980 (Owen Gregory); 1991 and 1992 (Monsanta); 1993 (My Messieur); King George V Gold Cup: 1982 (Disney Way); 1989 (Didi); 1992 (Midnight Madness); bareback high jump record, Dublin, 1980. *Address:* c/o British Show Jumping Association, Stoneleigh, Warwicks CV8 2LR.

See also E. J. Whitaker.

WHITAKER, Sheila; Director, London Film Festival, since 1987; *b* 1 April 1936; *d* of Hilda and Charles Whitaker. *Educ:* Cathays High Sch. for Girls, Cardiff; Kings Norton Grammar Sch. for Girls, Birmingham; Univ. of Warwick (BA Hons). Secretarial and admin. posts in commerce and industry, 1956–68; Chief Stills Officer, National Film Archive, 1968–74; Univ. of Warwick, 1975–78; Dir, Tyneside Cinema, Tyneside Film Festival, Newcastle upon Tyne, 1979–84; Head, Programming, NFT, 1984–90. Mem. Jury, Venice Internat. Film Festival, 1992. Founder and Co-Editor, Writing Women, 1981–84; Gen. Editor, Tyneside Publications, 1984. *Publications:* contribs to Framework, Screen, Sight and Sound. *Recreations:* reading, pottering in the garden. *Address:* 9 Buckingham Road, N1 4DG. *Club:* Groucho.

WHITAKER, Thomas Kenneth; Chancellor, National University of Ireland, since 1976; Member, Council of State, Ireland, since 1991; Chairman, Constitution Review Group, 1995; President, Royal Irish Academy, 1985–87; *b* 8 Dec. 1916; *s* of Edward Whitaker and Jane O'Connor; *m* 1941, Nora Fogarty; five *s* one *d*. *Educ:* Christian Brothers' Sch., Drogheda; London Univ. (External Student; BScEcon, MScEcon). Irish CS, 1934–69 (Sec., Dept of Finance, 1956–69); Governor, Central Bank of Ireland, 1969–76; Dir, Bank of Ireland, 1976–85. Dir, Arthur Guinness Son & Co. Ltd, 1976–84. Chairman: Bord na Gaeilge, 1975–78; Agency for Personal Service Overseas, 1973–78; Mem., Seanad Éireann, 1977–82. Jt Chm., Anglo-Irish Encounter, 1983–89. Former Pres., Econ. and Social Res. Inst.; Chm. Council, Dublin Inst. for Advanced Studies. Hon. DEconSc National Univ. of Ireland, 1962; Hon. LLD: Univ. of Dublin, 1976; Queen's Univ. of Belfast, 1980; Hon. DSc NUU, 1984. Commandeur de la Légion d'Honneur, France, 1976. *Publications:* Financing by Credit Creation, 1947; Economic Development, 1958; Interests, 1983. *Recreations:* fishing, golf, music. *Address:* 148 Stillorgan Road, Donnybrook, Dublin 4, Ireland. *T:* Dublin 2693474.

WHITBREAD, Samuel Charles, JP; Director, Whitbread plc, since 1972 (Chairman, 1984–92); Lord-Lieutenant of Bedfordshire, since 1991; *b* 22 Feb. 1937; *s* of late Major Simon Whitbread and of Helen Beatrice Margaret (*née* Trefusis); *m* 1961, Jane Mary Hayter; three *s* one *d*. *Educ:* Eton College. Beds and Herts Regt, 1955–57. Joined Board, Whitbread & Co., 1972, Dep. Chm., Jan. 1984. Director: Whitbread Investment Co., 1977–93; Sun Alliance Gp, 1989–92. Chm., Mid-Beds Conservative Assoc., 1969–72 (Pres., 1986–91). President: Shire Horse Soc., 1990–92; E of England Agricl Soc., 1991–92; St John Council for Beds, 1991–; Beds TA&VRA, 1991–; Vice-Pres., E Anglia TA&VRA, 1991–. Bedfordshire: JP, 1969–83, 1991; High Sheriff, 1973–74; DL, 1974; County Councillor, 1974–82. KStJ 1992. *Recreations:* shooting, travel, photography, music.

Address: Southill Park, Biggleswade, Beds SG18 9LL. *T:* Hitchin (01462) 813272. *Club:* Brooks's.

WHITBY, Bishop Suffragan of, since 1983; **Rt. Rev. Gordon Bates;** *b* 16 March 1934; *s* of Ernest and Kathleen Bates; *m* 1960, Betty (*née* Vaux); two *d. Educ:* Kelham Theological Coll. (SSM). Curate of All Saints, New Eltham, 1958–62; Youth Chaplain in Gloucester Diocese, 1962–64; Diocesan Youth Officer and Chaplain of Liverpool Cathedral, 1965–69; Vicar of Huyton, 1969–73; Canon Residentiary and Precentor of Liverpool Cathedral and Diocesan Director of Ordinands, 1973–83. Mem., House of Bishops, Gen. Synod, 1988–. Mem., Central Religious Adv. Council to BBC and ITV, 1990–93. Trustee, Sandford St Martin Trust, 1990–93. *Recreations:* golf, music, writing. *Address:* Handyside, 60 West Green, Stokesley, Cleveland TS9 5BD. *T:* Stokesley (01642) 710390. *Club:* Royal Over-Seas League.

WHITBY, Charles Harley, QC 1970; a Recorder of the Crown Court, Western Circuit, since 1972; *b* 2 April 1926; *s* of late Arthur William Whitby and Florence Whitby; *m* 1981, Eileen Scott. *Educ:* St John's, Leatherhead; Peterhouse, Cambridge. Open Schol., Peterhouse, 1943; served RAFVR, 1944–48; BA (History) 1st cl. 1949, MA 1951. Called to Bar, Middle Temple, 1952; Bencher, 1977; Mem. Bar Council, 1969–71, 1972–78. Mem., Criminal Injuries Compensation Bd, 1975–. Chm. Council, St John's Sch., Leatherhead, 1985– (Mem., 1977–). *Publications:* contrib. to Master and Servant in Halsbury's Laws of England, 3rd edn, Vol. 25, 1959 and Master and Servant in Atkin's Encyclopaedia of Court Forms, 2nd edn, Vol. 25, 1962. *Recreations:* golf, watching soccer, boating, fishing, swimming, theatre, cinema. *Address:* 12 King's Bench Walk, Temple, EC4Y 7EL. *T:* 0171–583 0811. *Clubs:* United Oxford & Cambridge University, Royal Automobile (Steward, 1985–), Garrick; Woking Golf.

WHITBY, Mrs Joy; Director, Grasshopper Productions Ltd; *b* 27 July 1930; *d* of James and Esther Field; *m* 1954, Anthony Charles Whitby (*d* 1975); three *s. Educ:* St Anne's Coll., Oxford. Schools Producer, BBC Radio, 1956–62; Children's Producer, BBC Television, 1962–67; Executive Producer, Children's Programmes, London Weekend Television, 1967–70; freelance producer and writer, 1970–76; Head of Children's Programmes, Yorkshire TV, 1976–85. Dir, Bd of Channel 4, 1980–84; Member: Adv. Panel for Youth, Nat. Trust, 1985–89; Bd, Unicorn Theatre, 1987–92. Devised for television: Play School, 1964; Jackanory, 1965; The Book Tower, 1979; Under the Same Sky (EBU Drama Exchange), 1984. Independent film productions: Grasshopper Island, 1971; A Pattern of Roses, 1983; Emma and Grandpa, 1984; East of the Moon, 1988; The Angel and the Soldier Boy, 1989 (ACE Award, 1991); On Christmas Eve, 1992; The Mousehole Cat, 1993. BAFTA Award and Prix Jeunesse: for Play School, 1965; for The Book Tower, 1980 (also BAFTA Award, 1983); Eleanor Farjeon Award for Services to Children's Books, 1979. *Publications:* Grasshopper Island, 1971; Emma and Grandpa (4 vols), 1984.

WHITBY, Professor Lionel Gordon, FRSE, FRCP, FRCPE, FRCPath, FIBiol; Professor of Clinical Chemistry, University of Edinburgh, 1963–91, Emeritus Professor since 1991; Biochemist-in-charge, Royal Infirmary of Edinburgh, 1963–91; *b* London, 18 July 1926; *s* of late Sir Lionel Whitby, CVO, MC, MD, FRCP, Regius Prof. of Physic and Master of Downing Coll., Cambridge; *m* 1949, Joan Hunter Sanderson; one *s* two *d. Educ:* Eton; King's Coll., Cambridge; Middlesex Hosp. MA, PhD, MD, BChir. Fellow of King's College, Cambridge, 1951–55; W. A. Meek Schol., Univ. of Cambridge, 1951; Murchison Schol., RCP, 1958; Rockefeller Trav. Res. Fellow, Nat. Insts of Health Bethesda, Md, USA, 1959. Registrar and Asst Lectr in Chem. Path., Hammersmith Hosp. and Postgrad. Med. Sch. of London, 1958–60; Univ. Biochemist to Addenbrooke's Hosp., 1960–63, and Fellow of Peterhouse, 1961–62, Cambridge; University of Edinburgh: Dean of Faculty of Medicine, 1969–72 and 1983–86; Curator of Patronage, 1978–91; Vice-Principal, 1979–83. Chm., Scottish sub-Cttee, Adv. Cttee on Distinction Awards, 1991–92 and 1993– (Mem., 1989–92); Member: Standing Adv. Cttee, Lab. Services, SHHD, 1965–72; Laboratory Develt Adv. Group, DHSS, 1972–76; Scientific Services Adv. Gp, SHHD, 1974–77; Screening Sub-Cttee of Standing Medical Adv. Cttee, 1975–81; Training Cttee, RCPath, 1977–79; Med. Lab. Technicians Bd, 1978–94; GMC, 1986–91; Adv. Council, British Library, 1986–91. Guest Lectr, Amer. Chem. Soc., 1966; Vis. Prof. of Chemical Pathology, RPMS, 1974. Vice-Pres., RSE, 1983–86. Trustee, Nat. Library of Scotland, 1982–91. *Publications:* (ed jointly) Principles and Practice of Medical Computing, 1971; (jointly) Lecture Notes on Clinical Chemistry, 1975, 5th edn 1993, as Lecture Notes on Clinical Biochemistry; (jtly) Multiple Choice Questions on Clinical Chemistry, 1981; scientific papers on flavinglucosides, catecholamines and metabolites, several aspects of clin. chem., and early detection of disease by chemical tests. *Recreations:* gardening, photography. *Address:* 51 Dick Place, Edinburgh EH9 2JA. *T:* 0131–667 4358.

WHITE, family name of **Baron Annaly** and **Baronesses James of Holland Park** and **White.**

WHITE, Baroness *cr* 1970 (Life Peer), of Rhymney, Monmouth; **Eirene Lloyd White;** a Deputy Speaker, House of Lords, 1979–89; *b* 7 Nov. 1909; *d* of late Dr Thomas Jones, CH; *m* 1948, John Cameron White (*d* 1968). *Educ:* St Paul's Girls' Sch.; Somerville Coll., Oxford. Ministry of Labour officer, 1933–37 and 1941–45; Political Correspondent, Manchester Evening News, 1945–49; contested (Lab) Flintshire, 1945; MP (Lab) East Flint, 1950–70. Nat. Exec. Cttee of the Labour Party, 1947–53, 1958–72, Chm. 1968–69; Parly Secretary, Colonial Office, 1964–66; Minister of State for Foreign Affairs, 1966–67; Minister of State, Welsh Office, 1967–70; Chm., Select Cttee on Eur. Communities, and Principal Dep. Chm. of Cttees, H of L, 1979–82; Dep. Chm., Parly Scientific Cttee, 1986–89. Member: Royal Commn on Environmental Pollution, 1974–81; British Waterways Bd, 1974–80. Governor: National Library of Wales, 1950–70; Brit. Film Inst. and National Film Theatre, 1959–64; Indep. Mem. Cinematograph Films Council, 1946–64. Chairman, Fabian Society, 1958–59; President. Nursery School Assoc., 1964–66; Council for Protection of Rural Wales, 1974–89; former Pres., Nat. Council of Women (Wales); Lord President's nominee, Council, UCW, Aberystwyth, 1973–77, Court (elected), 1977–85; Member: UGC, 1977–80; Council, UCNW Bangor, 1977–80; Council, Univ. of Wales Coll. of Cardiff (formerly UWIST), 1981–93 (Chm., 1983–88; Pres., 1987–88; Vice-Pres., 1988–93); Chairman: Internat. Cttee, Nat. Council of Social Service, 1973–77; Coleg Harlech, 1974–84; Adv. Cttee on Oil Pollution at sea, 1974–78; Land Authority for Wales, 1975–80; Dep. Chm., Metrication Bd, 1972–76; Vice-President: Commonwealth Countries League; Commonwealth Youth Exchange Council, 1976–79; Council for National Parks, 1985–; TCPA, 1983–91. Hon. Mem., RTPI, 1987; Hon. Fellow: Somerville College, Oxford, 1966; Univ. of Wales, Cardiff, 1989. Hon. LLD: Wales, 1979; Queen's Univ., Belfast, 1981; Bath, 1983. *Publication:* The Ladies of Gregynog, 1985. *Address:* 64 Vandon Court, Petty France, SW1H 9HF. *T:* 0171–222 5107; Treberfydd, Bwlch, Powys LD3 7PX. *T:* Brecon (01874) 730911. *Club:* Commonwealth Trust.

WHITE, Aidan Patrick; General Secretary, International Federation of Journalists, since 1987; *b* 2 March 1951; *s* of Thomas White and Kathleen Ann McLaughlin. *Educ:* King's Sch., Peterborough. Dep. Gp Editor, Stratford Express, 1977–79; journalist, The Guardian, 1980–87. Mem., Press Council, 1978–80. National Union of Journalists: Mem. Exec. Council, 1974, 1976, 1977; Treasurer, 1984–86; Chm., National Newspapers Council, 1981. Vice-Chm., Campaign for Press and Broadcasting Freedom, 1983–84. *Address:* 92 Quilter Street, E2 7BT. *T:* 0171–739 3598.

WHITE, Alan, CMG 1985; OBE 1973; HM Diplomatic Service, retired; Ambassador to Chile, 1987–90; *b* 13 Aug. 1930; *s* of William White and Ida (*née* Hall); *m* 1st, 1954, Cynthia Maidwell; two *s* one *d*; 2nd, 1980, Clare Corley Smith. SSC Army 1954 (Capt.); Hong Kong, 1959–63; MoD (Central), 1965; First Sec., FO (later FCO), 1966; Mexico City, 1969; First Sec., UK Disarmament Delegn, Geneva, 1974; Counsellor (Commercial), Madrid, 1976; Counsellor and Head of Chancery, Kuala Lumpur, 1980–83; Hd, Trade Relns and Exports Dept, FCO, 1983–85; Ambassador to Bolivia, 1985–87. *Recreations:* reading, travel. *Address:* c/o Foreign and Commonwealth Office, SW1A 2AH.

WHITE, Rev. Barrington Raymond; Senior Research Fellow, Regent's Park College, Oxford, since 1989 (Principal, 1972–89; Tutor in Ecclesiastical History, 1989–91); *b* 28 Jan. 1934; *s* of Raymond Gerard and Lucy Mildred White; *m* 1957, Margaret Muriel Hooper; two *d. Educ:* Chislehurst and Sidcup Grammar Sch.; Queens' Coll., Cambridge (BA Theol, MA); Regent's Park Coll., Oxford (DPhil). Ordained, 1959; Minister, Andover Baptist Church, 1959–63; Lectr in Ecclesiastical History, Regent's Park Coll., Oxford, 1963–72. First Breman Prof. of Social Relations, Univ. of N Carolina at Asheville, 1976. FRHistS 1973. *Publications:* The English Separatist Tradition, 1971; Association Records of the Particular Baptists to 1660, Part I, 1971, Part II, 1973, Part III, 1974; Authority: a Baptist view, 1976; Hanserd Knollys and Radical Dissent, 1977; contrib. Reformation, Conformity and Dissent, ed R. Buick Knox, 1977; The English Puritan Tradition, 1980; contrib. Biographical Dictionary of British Radicals in the Seventeenth Century, ed Greaves and Zaller, 1982–84; The English Baptists of the Seventeenth Century, 1983; contribs to Baptist Qly, Jl of Theological Studies, Jl of Ecclesiastical History, Welsh Baptist Studies. *Recreation:* recorded music. *Address:* Regent's Park College, Oxford OX1 2LB.

WHITE, Bryan Oliver; HM Diplomatic Service, retired; consultant on Latin American affairs; *b* 3 Oct. 1929; *s* of Thomas Frederick White and Olive May Turvey; *m* 1958, Helen McLeod Jenkins; one *s* two *d. Educ:* The Perse Sch.; Wadham Coll., Oxford (Lit.Hum.). HM Forces, 1948–49; FO, 1953; Kabul, Vienna, Conakry, Rio de Janeiro, the Cabinet Office, and Havana, 1953–79; Counsellor, Paris, 1980–82; Head of Mexico and Central America Dept, FCO, 1982–84; Ambassador to Honduras and (non-resident) to El Salvador, 1984–87; Consul-Gen., Lyon, 1987–89. *Recreation:* the Romance languages. *Address:* 45 Westminster Palace Gardens, SW1P 1RR.

WHITE, Hon. Byron R(aymond); Associate Justice of the Supreme Court of the United States, 1962–93; *b* Fort Collins, Colorado, 8 June 1917; *s* of Alpha White, Wellington, Colorado; *m* 1946, Marion Lloyd Stearns, *d* of Dr Robert L. Stearns; one *s* one *d. Educ:* Wellington High Sch.; Univ. of Colorado; Oxford Univ. (Rhodes Scholar); Yale Univ. Law Sch (before and after War). Served War of 1939–45: USNR, Naval Intell., Pacific (two Bronze Stars). Law Clerk to Chief Justice of the United States, 1946–47; law practice in Denver, Colorado, 1947–60, with firm of Lewis, Grant, Newton, Davis and Henry (later Lewis, Grant and Davis). Dep. Attorney-Gen., 1961–62. Phi Beta Kappa, Phi Gamma Delta. As a Democrat, he was a prominent supporter of John F. Kennedy in the Presidential campaign of 1960. *Recreations:* ski-ing, paddle tennis, fishing. *Address:* c/o US Supreme Court, 1 First Street NE, Washington, DC 20543, USA.

WHITE, (Charles) John (Branford); HM Diplomatic Service; Deputy Head of Mission and Consul-General, Tel Aviv, since 1993; *b* 24 Sept. 1946; *s* of Frederick Bernard White and Violet Phyllis White (*née* Palmer); *m* 1975, Judith Margaret Lewis. *Educ:* Taunton Sch.; Brentwood Sch.; Pembroke Coll., Cambridge (Trevelyan Schol., MA); University Coll. London (MSc 1983). ODI Fellow, Govt of Botswana, 1968–71; ODA, 1971–77; Economic Advr, E Africa Develt Div., ODM, 1977–82; ODA, 1983–86; Asst Head, Economic Relations Dept, FCO, 1986–90; First Sec., Lagos, 1990–93. *Recreations:* golf, ski-ing. *Address:* c/o Foreign and Commonwealth Office, King Charles Street, SW1A 2AH. *Clubs:* Ski Club of Great Britain; Royal Mid-Surrey Golf; Nairobi (Kenya); Caesarea Country (Israel).

WHITE, Prof. Christopher John, CVO 1995; PhD; FBA 1989; Director, Ashmolean Museum, Oxford, since 1985; Fellow of Worcester College, since 1985, and Professor of the Art of the Netherlands, since 1992, Oxford University; *b* 19 Sept. 1930; *s* of late Gabriel Ernest Edward Francis White, CBE and Elizabeth Grace Ardizzone; *m* 1957, Rosemary Katharine Desages; one *s* two *d. Educ:* Downside Sch.; Courtauld Institute of Art, London Univ. BA (Hons) 1954, PhD 1970. Served Army, 1949–50; commnd, RA, 1949. Asst Keeper, Dept of Prints and Drawings, British Museum, 1954–65; Director, P. and D. Colnaghi, 1965–71; Curator of Graphic Arts, Nat. Gall. of Art, Washington, 1971–73; Dir of Studies, Paul Mellon Centre for Studies in British Art, 1973–85; Adjunct Prof. of History of Art, 1976–85; Associate Dir, Yale Center for British Art, 1976–85. Dutch Govt Schol., 1956; Hermione Lectr, Alexandra Coll., Dublin, 1959; Adjunct Prof., Inst. of Fine Arts, New York Univ., 1973 and 1976; Conference Dir, European-Amer. Assembly on Art Museums, Ditchley Park, 1975; Visiting Prof., Dept of History of Art, Yale Univ., 1976. Dir, Burlington Magazine, 1981–. Reviews Editor, Master Drawings, 1967–80. *Publications:* Rembrandt and his World, 1964; The Flower Drawings of Jan van Huysum, 1965; Rubens and his World, 1968; Rembrandt as an Etcher, 1969; (jtly) Rembrandt's Etchings: a catalogue raisonné, 1970; Dürer: the artist and his drawings, 1972; English Landscape 1630–1850, 1977; The Dutch Paintings in the Collection of HM The Queen, 1982; (ed) Rembrandt in Eighteenth Century England, 1983; Rembrandt, 1984; Peter Paul Rubens: man and artist, 1987 (Eugène Baie Prize, 1983–87); (jtly) Drawing in England from Hilliard to Hogarth, 1987; (jtly) Rubens in Oxford, 1988; (jtly) One Hundred Old Master Drawings from the Ashmolean Museum, 1991; (jtly) The Dutch and Flemish Drawings at Windsor Castle, 1994; Anthony van Dyck: Thomas Howard, the Earl of Arundel, 1995; film (script and commentary), Rembrandt's Three Crosses, 1969; various exhibn catalogues; contribs to Burlington Mag., Master Drawings, etc. *Recreation:* husbandry. *Address:* 39 St Giles, Oxford OX1 3LW. *T:* Oxford (01865) 512289; 14 South Villas, NW1 9BS. *T:* 0171–485 9148; Shingle House, St Cross, Harleston, Norfolk IP20 0NT. *T:* St Cross (01986) 782264.

WHITE, Sir Christopher (Robert Meadows), 3rd Bt *cr* 1937, of Boulge Hall, Suffolk; *b* 26 Aug. 1940; *s* of Sir (Eric) Richard Meadows White, 2nd Bt, and Lady Elizabeth Mary Gladys (*d* 1950), *o d* of 6th Marquess Townshend; *S* father, 1972; *m* 1st, 1962, Anne Marie Ghislaine (marr. diss. 1968), *yr d* of Major Tom Brown, OBE; 2nd, 1968, Dinah Mary Sutton (marr. diss. 1972), Orange House, Heacham, Norfolk; 3rd, 1976, Ingrid Carolyn Jowett, *e d* of Eric Jowett, Great Baddow; two step *s. Educ:* Bradfield Coll., Berks. Imperial Russian Ballet School, Cannes, France, 1961; schoolmaster, 1961–72; Professore, Istituto Shenker, Rome, and Scuola Specialisti Aeronauta, Macerata, 1962–63; Housemaster, St Michael's Sch., Ingoldisthorpe, Norfolk, 1963–69. Hon. Pres., Warnborough House, Oxford, 1973–. Lieutenant, TA, Norfolk, 1969. *Recreations:* dogs, vintage cars, antiques.

WHITE, Christopher Stuart Stuart-; *see* Stuart-White.

WHITE, Sir David Harry, Kt 1992; DL; Chairman: Nottingham Health Authority, since 1986; Mansfield Brewing, since 1993; Coal Authority, since 1994; Director, 1970–88, a Deputy Chairman, 1988–90, Chairman of Trustees, since 1986, National Freight Consortium; *b* 12 Oct. 1929; *s* of late Harry White, OBE, FCA, and Kathleen White; *m* 1971, Valerie Jeanne White; one *s* four *d*. *Educ:* Nottingham High Sch.; HMS Conway. Master Mariner's F. G. Certificate. Sea career, apprentice to Master Mariner, 1946–56; Terminal Manager, Texaco (UK) Ltd, 1956–64; Operations Manager, Gulf Oil (GB) Ltd, 1964–68; Asst Man. Dir, Samuel Williams Dagenham, 1968–70; Trainee to Gp Managing Director, British Road Services Ltd, 1970–76; Group Managing Director: British Road Services, 1976–82; Pickfords, 1982–84; NFC Property Gp, 1984–87; Director (non-executive): BR Property Bd, 1985–87; Y. J. Lovell Ltd, 1987–94; European Leisure PLC, 1991–. Mem., British Coal Corp., 1993–94. Chairman: Nottingham Develt Enterprise, 1987–93; Bd of Governors, Nottingham Trent Univ. (formerly Nottingham Poly.), 1989–. Trustee, Djanogly City Technology Coll., 1989–. Hon-Pres., Notts County Branch, RSPCA, 1987–. Governor, Nottingham High Sch., 1987–. DL Notts, 1989. *Recreations:* football supporter (Nottingham Forest), walking. *Address:* Whitehaven, 6 Croft Road, Edwalton, Nottingham NG12 4BW. *Club:* Royal Automobile.

WHITE, David Thomas, (Tom), CBE 1990; Principal and Chief Executive, NCH Action for Children (formerly National Children's Home), since 1990; *b* 10 Oct. 1931; *s* of Walter Henry White and Annie White; *m* 1956, Eileen May Moore; two *d* (and one *s* decd). *Educ:* Council Primary and Maesydderwen Grammar Sch., Ystradgynlais, Swansea Valley; University Coll., Swansea (Social Sci.); London School of Economics (Social Work). Clerical Officer, CS, 1947–54; National Service, RAF, 1951–53. Social work and management posts, Devon CC, 1957–61; Dep. Children's Officer, Monmouthshire, 1961–65; Dep. County Children's Officer, Lancs, 1965–70; Dir of Social Services, Coventry, 1970–85; Dir of Social Work, Nat. Children's Home, 1985–90. Past President: Assoc. of Child Care Officers; Assoc. of Directors of Social Services; Gov., Nat. Inst. of Social Work, 1973–. *Publication:* (contrib.) Social Work, the Media and Public Relations, 1991. *Recreations:* gardening, golf, walking. *Address:* (home) 102 Kenilworth Road, Coventry CV4 7AH. *T:* Coventry (01203) 419949; (office) 85 Highbury Park, N5 1UD. *T:* 0171–226 2033. *Club:* Coventry Golf (Finham, Coventry).

WHITE, Derek Leslie; HM Diplomatic Service, retired; *b* 18 April 1933; *s* of John William and Hilda White; *m* 1989, Elisabeth Denise Marcelle Lemoine; one *d* from previous marr. *Educ:* Catshill Secondary Sch., Bromsgrove; RAF Apprentice Sch. Served RAF, 1950–63. For. Office (later HM Diplomatic Service), 1963; served Helsinki, Sofia, Algiers; Vice Consul, Tripoli, 1970; FCO, 1972; Commercial Officer, Baghdad, 1975, Second Sec., 1977; Port Louis, 1979; Antananarivo, 1983; FCO, 1984, First Sec., 1985; Consul, Marseilles and Principality of Monaco, 1986; FCO, 1989; High Comr to Kiribati, 1990–93, and concurrently Ambassador to Federated States of Micronesia and to Marshall Is, 1992–93. *Recreations:* sailing, cooking, music. *Address:* Cansargue, 83470 Pourcieux, France. *T:* 94597879.

WHITE, Edward George, OBE 1976; HM Diplomatic Service, retired; *b* 30 June 1923; *s* of late George Johnson White, OBE, ISO, and Edith (*née* Birch); *m* 1st, 1945, Sylvia Shears; two *d*; 2nd, 1966, Veronica Pauline Crosling. *Educ:* Bec Secondary Sch., London SW. Served RAF, 1941–47. Various consular and diplomatic appts in Guatemala, USA, Madagascar, Burma, Thailand and India; Dep. Head of Finance Dept, FCO, 1976–78; Counsellor (Admin), Bonn, 1978–79. Specialist Adviser, Foreign Affairs Cttee, H of C, 1980–87. *Publication:* Nightfighter Navigator, 1994. *Address:* 7 Crosslands, Thurlestone, Kingsbridge, Devon TQ7 3TF. *T:* Kingsbridge (01548) 560236.

WHITE, (Edward) Martin (Everatt); Chairman, The Curlew Partnership Ltd, since 1990; *b* 22 Feb. 1938; *s* of Frank and Norah White; *m* 1969, Jean Catherine Armour; one *s* one *d*. *Educ:* Priory Boys' Grammar Sch., Shrewsbury; King's Coll., Cambridge (MA). Solicitor. Asst Solicitor, Lancs County Council, 1962–65; Sen. Asst Solicitor, then Asst Clerk, then Principal Asst Clerk, Kent County Council, 1965–72; Dep. Chief Exec., Somerset County Council, 1972–74; Chief Executive: Winchester City Council, 1974–80; Bucks County Council, 1980–88; Nat. Assoc. of Citizens Advice Bureaux, 1988–90. *Recreations:* gardening, walking, other outdoor pursuits. *Address:* The Spinney, Sevenacres, Chilton Road, Long Crendon, Bucks HP18 9DU. *T:* Long Crendon (01844) 208914.

WHITE, Frank John; His Honour Judge White; a Senior Circuit Judge, since 1994 (a Circuit Judge, 1974–94); *b* 12 March 1927; *s* of late Frank Byron White and Marie-Thérèse Renée White; *m* 1953, Anne Rowlandson, MBE, *d* of late Sir Harold Gibson Howitt, GBE, DSO, MC; two *s* two *d*. *Educ:* Reading Sch.; King's Coll., London. LLB, LLM (London). Sub-Lt, RNVR, 1945–47; called to the Bar, Gray's Inn, 1951; Mem., General Council of the Bar, 1969–73; Dep. Chm., Berkshire QS, 1970–72; a Recorder of the Crown Court, 1972–74. Pres., Council of HM Circuit Judges, 1990–91. Member: Lord Chancellor's Adv. Cttee on Legal Aid, 1977–83; Judicial Studies Bd, 1985–89; County Court Rule Cttee, 1991– (Chm., 1993–). *Publication:* Bench Notes and Exercises for Assistant Recorders, 1988. *Recreations:* walking, photography. *Address:* 8 Queen's Ride, SW13 0JB. *T:* 0181–788 8903; Blauvac, Vaucluse, France. *Clubs:* Athenæum, Roehampton.

WHITE, Frank Richard, JP; executive director and industrial relations adviser; Director, National Training College, GMB (formerly General, Municipal, Boilermakers and Allied Trades Union), since 1988; *b* Nov. 1939; *m*; three *c*. *Educ:* Bolton Tech. Coll. Member: Bolton CC, 1963–74; Greater Manchester CC, 1973–75; Bolton DC, 1986–. Member: GMB; IPM; Inst. of Management Services. Contested (Lab): Bury and Radcliffe, Feb. 1974; Bury North, 1983; Bolton NE, 1987. MP (Lab) Bury and Radcliffe, Oct. 1974–1983; PPS to Minister of State, Dept of Industry, 1975–76; Asst Govt Whip, 1976–78; Opposition Whip, 1980–82; opposition spokesman on church affairs, 1980–83. Chairman: All Party Paper Industry Gp, 1979–83; NW Lab Gp, 1979–83; Mem., NW Regional Exec., Labour Party, 1986–88. President: Bolton United Services Veterans' Assoc., 1988–; Bolton Male Voice Choir, 1992–; Vice-Pres., E Lancs Railway Preservation Soc., 1983–. JP Bolton, 1968 (Chm. Bench, 1993). Hon. Fellow, Bolton Inst., 1993. *Address:* 4 Ashdown Drive, Firwood Fold, Bolton, Lancs BL2 3AX.

WHITE, Air Vice-Marshal George Alan, CB 1984; AFC 1973; FRAeS; Commandant, Royal Air Force Staff College, 1984–87; *b* 11 March 1932; *s* of James Magee White and Evangeline (*née* Henderson); *m* 1955, Mary Esmé (*née* Magowan); two *d*. *Educ:* Queen's Univ., Belfast; University of London (LLB). Pilot, 1956; served in RAF Squadrons and OCUs, 1956–64; RAF Staff College, 1964; HQ Middle East Command, 1966–67; 11 Sqn, 1968–70; 5 Sqn, 1970–72; Nat. Defence Coll., 1972–73; in command, RAF Leuchars, 1973–75; Royal Coll. of Defence Studies, 1976; Dir of Ops (Air Defence and Overseas), 1977–78; SASO No 11 Group, 1979–80; Air Cdre Plans, HQ Strike Comd, 1981–82; Dep. Comdr, RAF Germany, 1982–84. FRAeS 1985. *Recreations:* sailing, hill walking, bridge. *Address:* PO Box 2048, Paphos, Cyprus. *Club:* Royal Air Force.

WHITE, Sir George (Stanley James), 4th Bt *cr* 1904, of Cotham House, Bristol; JP; FSA; clockmaker and horological consultant; Keeper of the Collection of the Worshipful Company of Clockmakers, since 1988; *b* 4 Nov. 1948; *s* of Sir George Stanley Midelton White, 3rd Bt, and of Diane Eleanor, *d* of late Bernard Abdy Collins, CIE; *S* father, 1983; *m* 1st, 1974; one *d*; 2nd, 1979, Elizabeth Jane, *d* of Sir Reginald Verdon-Smith and of Jane Margaret, *d* of V. W. J. Hobbs; one *s* one *d*. *Educ:* Harrow School. Pres., Gloucestershire Soc., 1993; Member: Gloucester Diocesan Adv. Cttee for Care of Churches, 1985– (Clocks Advr, 1986–); Council, Bristol and Glos Archaeological Soc., 1987– (Chm., 1992–). Pres., Bristol Br., British Horological Inst., 1993. Liveryman, 1986, Asst, 1994, Co. of Clockmakers. High Sheriff, Avon, 1989; JP Bristol, 1991. FSA 1988. *Publications:* (with E. J. White) St Mary's Church, Hawkesbury, 1980; English Lantern Clocks, 1989; contrib. Antiquaries' Jl, Antiquarian Horology, etc. *Heir:* *s* George Philip James White, *b* 19 Dec. 1987.

WHITE, Maj.-Gen. Gilbert Anthony, MBE 1944; *b* 10 June 1916; *s* of Cecil James Lawrence White and Muriel (*née* Collins); *m* 1939, Margaret Isabel Duncan Wallet; two *d*. *Educ:* Christ's Hosp., Horsham. Member of Lloyd's, 1938. Joined TA Artists Rifles, 1937; TA Commn, E Surrey Regt, 1939; served BEF, 1940, N Africa, 1943–44, Italy, 1944–45; Staff Coll., 1944; Instructor, Staff Coll., Haifa, 1946; with UK Delegn to UN, 1946–48; served on Lord Mountbatten's personal staff in MoD, 1960–61; idc 1965; BAOR, 1966–69; Chief, Jt Services Liaison Orgn, Bonn, 1969–71; retd 1971. Mem. Council, Guide Dogs for the Blind, 1971–92. *Recreations:* golf, racing. *Address:* Speedwell, Tekels Avenue, Camberley, Surrey GU15 2LB. *T:* Camberley (01276) 23812.

WHITE, Harold Clare, MBE 1967; HM Diplomatic Service, retired; Consul-General, Seattle, 1976–79; *b* 26 Oct. 1919; *s* of Alfred John White and Nora White; *m* 1951, Marie Elizabeth Richardson; two *d*. *Educ:* Grammar Sch., Warrington. Served War, Royal Signals, 1939–45. GPO, 1937–39 and 1946; FO, 1947; Third Sec., Djakarta, 1951; FO, 1955; Vice-Consul, Piraeus, Kirkuk, San Francisco, and Durban, 1957–64; 1st Secretary: Kinshasa, 1964; Kuala Lumpur, 1968; FCO, 1972; Dep. Consul-Gen., Chicago, 1974. *Recreations:* cricket, golf. *Address:* 31 Stuart Avenue, Eastbourne, East Sussex BN21 1UR. *T:* Eastbourne (01323) 31148. *Club:* Civil Service.

WHITE, Harvey, DM; FRCS; Consulting Surgeon: Royal Marsden Hospital, since 1976; King Edward VII Hospital for Officers, since 1983; *b* 10 March 1936; *s* of Arthur White and Doris (*née* Dunstan); *m* 1965, Diana Mary Bannister; one *s* one *d*. *Educ:* Winchester Coll.; Magdalen Coll., Oxford (DM, MCh); St Bartholomew's Hosp. FRCS 1970. St Bartholomew's Hospital: Lectr in Physiol., 1966–71; Sen. Surgical Registrar, 1971–76; Chm., Div. of Surgery, Royal Marsden Hosp., 1987–89. Editor: Oxford Med. Gazette, 1956–57; St Bartholomew's Hosp. Jl, 1960–61; Clinical Oncology, 1983–84; European Jl of Surgical Oncology, 1985–87. Hunterian Prof., RCS, 1988; Hunterian Oration, 1993. Vice-Pres., Brit. Assoc. of Surgical Oncology, 1984; Pres., Med. Soc. of London, 1995–Oct. 1996. Mem. Council, Cancer Relief Macmillan Fund, 1991–. Chm., Brendoncare Foundn of Elderly, 1986–; Trustee, Duchess of Somerset's Almshouses, 1992–. Ernest Miles Medal, Brit. Assoc. of Surgical Oncology, 1989. *Publications:* (jtly) The Greater Omentum, 1983, Russian edn 1989; (jtly) The Omentum and Malignant Diseases, 1984; An Atlas of Omental Transposition, 1987; contrib. to: History of Surgery, 1974; Royal Hospital St Bartholomew, 1974; Surgical Oncology for Nurses, 1978; The Laser in General Surgery, 1979; Oxford Companion to Medicine, 1986; European Handbook of Oncology, 1989; Aird's Companion to Surgery, 1992; contrib. various learned surgical and cancer jls. *Recreations:* dog-walking, rackets and Real tennis, sailing, fishing. *Address:* (office) 149 Harley Street, W1N 2DE. *T:* 0171–935 4444; 7 Arlington Square, N1 7DS. *T:* 0171–226 4628; Lakelands, Goleen, W Cork, Republic of Ireland. *T:* Skibbereen (028) 35232. *Clubs:* Garrick, Royal Society of Medicine.

WHITE, Sir Henry Arthur Dalrymple D.; *see* Dalrymple-White.

WHITE, Adm. Sir Hugo (Moresby), GCB 1995 (KCB 1991); CBE 1985; Commander-in-Chief, Fleet, Allied Commander-in-Chief, Eastern Atlantic, 1992–95 (also Allied Commander-in-Chief, Channel, 1991–94); Naval Commander, North West Command, 1994–95; *b* 22 Oct. 1939; *s* of late Hugh Fortescue Moresby White, CMG and Betty Sophia Pennington White; *m* 1966 Josephine Mary Lorimer Pedler; two *s*. *Educ:* Dragon School; Nautical Coll., Pangbourne; Britannia RN Coll., Dartmouth. HMS Blackpool, 1960; submarine training, 1961; HM Submarines Tabard, Tiptoe, Odin, 1961–65; Long Navigation Course, HMS Dryad, 1966; Navigator, HMS Warspite, 1967; First Lieut, HMS Osiris, 1968–69; in Comd, HMS Oracle, 1969–70; Staff, BRNC Dartmouth, 1971–72; Submarine Sea Training, 1973–74; in Comd, HMS Salisbury (cod war), 1975–76; Naval Sec.'s Dept, 1976–78; Naval Plans, 1978–80; in Comd, HMS Avenger (Falklands) and 4th Frigate Sqn, 1980–82; Principal Staff Officer to Chief of Defence Staff, 1982–85; in Comd, HMS Bristol and Flag Captain, 1985–87; Flag Officer Third Flotilla, and Comdr Anti-Submarine Warfare Striking Force, 1987–88; ACNS, 1988–91; Flag Officer Scotland and NI, 1991–92. *Recreations:* sailing, travelling, gardening, reading. *Address:* c/o Naval Secretary, Victory Building, HM Naval Base, Portsmouth PO1 3LS. *Club:* Army and Navy.

WHITE, Ian; Member (Lab) Bristol, European Parliament, since 1989; former Partner, McCarthy and White, solicitors. *Address:* (office) 138 Gloucester Road North, Filton, Bristol BS12 7BQ.

WHITE, James; Managing Director, Glasgow Car Collection Ltd, since 1959; *m*; one *s* two *d*. *Educ:* Knightswood Secondary School. Served Eighth Army, War of 1939–45 (African and Italian Stars; Defence Medal). MP (Lab) Glasgow (Pollok), 1970–87. Mem. Commonwealth Parly Assoc. Delegns, Bangladesh, 1973, Nepal, 1981. *Address:* 23 Alder Road, Glasgow G43 2UU.

WHITE, James; author and art historian; Professor of History of Painting, Royal Hibernian Academy, since 1968; *b* 16 Sept. 1913; *s* of Thomas John White and Florence Coffey; *m* 1941, Agnes Bowe; three *s* two *d*. *Educ:* Belvedere Coll., Dublin; privately in European museums and collections. Art Critic: Standard, 1940–50; Irish Press, 1950–59; Irish Times, 1959–62. Curator, Municipal Gallery of Modern Art, Dublin, 1960–64; Director, Nat. Gallery of Ireland, 1964–80. Chm., Irish Arts Council, 1978–84; Hon. Sec., Royal Dublin Soc., 1986–. Ext. Lectr in History of Art, University Coll., Dublin, 1955–77; Visiting Lectr in Univs and Socs in GB, Italy, USA, Canada. Trustee, Chester Beatty Library of Oriental Art, Dublin. Radio and Television contribs: BBC, RTE, and in the USA. Irish Comr to Biennale at Venice and at Paris on various occasions; Organiser of Exhibns in Dublin, London, Paris, etc., incl. Paintings from Irish Collections, 1957. Corresp. Mem., Real Academia de Bellas Artes de San Fernando, 1975. Hon. LLD NUI, 1970. Arnold K. Henry Medal of RCS of Ireland. Chevalier, Légion d'Honneur, 1974; Order of Merit, Govt of Italy, 1977; Commander of the Order of Merit, Federal Republic of Germany, 1983. *Publications:* Irish Stained Glass (with Michael Wynne), 1963; The National Gallery of Ireland, 1968; Jack B. Yeats, 1971; John Butler Yeats and the Irish Renaissance, 1972; Masterpieces of the National Gallery of Ireland, 1978; Pauline Bewick: painting a life, 1985; Gerard Dillon, a Biography, 1993; monographs on Louis Le Brocquy, George Campbell, Brian Bourke; contributor to: Apollo, Art News, Studio, Connoisseur, Blackfriars, Manchester Guardian, The Furrow, Doctrine and Life, Art Notes, Merian, Werk, Das Munster, Hollandsche Art, La Biennale, La Revue Française, Il Milione, Encyclopaedia of Art, etc. *Recreations:* golf, swimming, gardening, bridge. *Address:* 15

Herbert Park, Ballsbridge, Dublin 4. *T:* 6683723. *Club:* Kildare Street and University (Dublin).

WHITE, James Ashton V.; *see* Vallance White.

WHITE, Jeremy Nigel; Deputy Chairman, Youthnet UK, since 1995; *b* 20 Jan. 1955; *s* of Colin Lawrence White and Drusilla Marie Goodman; *m* 1989, Kim-Marie Klinger; one *s* three *d*. *Educ:* Leeds Grammar Sch.; Leeds Polytechnic (Dip. Management, Accounting and Finance, Marketing); City Univ. (MBA); Pepperdine Univ. (MA Educn and Psychology; Dist Alumni 1995). Man. Dir, RSS Gp, 1975–79; Chm., White Gp Electronics, 1979–85; Britannia Group: Jt Man. Dir, 1985–86; Pres., 1986–88; Chm., Data Safe Inc., 1988–94; Chief Exec. and Dep. Chm., Prince's Youth Business Trust, 1994–95. Mem., Bd, British-Amer. Chamber of Commerce, S Calif., 1993–94, and other LA orgns, 1992–94. Mem., Youth Enterprise Nat. Council, 1987–; Trustee, Prince of Wales Award for Innovation. Gov., Pepperdine Univ., 1993–; Mem. Council, City Univ. Business Sch., 1995–. Mem., BSES exp. to W Himalayas, 1989; flying records: Lisbon to LA, 1990; LA to Albuquerque, 1990; Buenos Aires to LA, 1991; La Paz to LA, 1991. FRGS. *Publication:* The Retail Financial Services Sector, 1985. *Recreations:* private flying, collecting. *Clubs:* Brooks's, Pilgrims', Carlton, Royal Geographical.

WHITE, Jeremy Richard, (Jerry); Commissioner for Local Administration in England (Local Government Ombudsman), since 1995; *b* 23 March 1949; *s* of John Robert White and Molly Loiseau; *m* 1st, 1981, Sandra Margaret Smith (marr. diss. 1995); two *s* one *d*; 2nd, 1995, Rosie Cooper; one *d*. *Educ:* Swanage Grammar Sch.; Cosham and Hackney Technical Colls. Sen. Public Health Inspector, Islington, 1970–81; Asst Borough Housing Officer, Haringey, 1981–84; London Borough of Hackney: Head, Environmental Health, 1984–87; Dir, Environmental Health and Consumer Protection, 1987–89; Chief Exec. and Town Clerk, 1989–95. *Publications:* Rothschild Buildings: life in an East End tenement block 1887–1920, 1980; The Worst Street in North London: Campbell Road, Islington, between the wars, 1986; Fear of Voting: local democracy and its enemies 1894–1994, 1994. *Recreations:* reading, music, London. *Address:* Commission for Local Administration, 2 The Oaks, Westwood Way, Coventry CV4 8JB. *T:* Coventry (01203) 695999.

WHITE, John; *see* White, C. J. B.

WHITE, Rev. Canon John Austin; Canon of Windsor, since 1982; *b* 27 June 1942; *s* of Charles White and Alice Emily (*née* Precious). *Educ:* The Grammar Sch., Batley, W Yorkshire; Univ. of Hull (BA Hons); College of the Resurrection, Mirfield. Assistant Curate, St Aidan's Church, Leeds, 1966–69; Asst Chaplain, Univ. of Leeds, 1969–73; Asst Director, post ordination training, Dio. of Ripon, 1970–73; Chaplain, Northern Ordination Course, 1973–82. *Publications:* (with Julia Neuberger) A Necessary End: attitudes to death, 1991; various articles. *Recreations:* medieval iconography, drama, Italy, cooking. *Address:* 8 The Cloisters, Windsor Castle SL4 1NJ. *T:* Windsor (01753) 860409.

WHITE, Hon. Sir John (Charles), Kt 1982; MBE (mil.) 1942; Judge of High Court of New Zealand, retired 1981, sat as retired Judge, 1982–84; *b* 1 Nov. 1911; *s* of Charles Gilbert White and Nora Addison Scott White; *m* 1st, 1943, Dora Eyre Wild (*d* 1982); one *s* three *d*; 2nd, 1987, Margaret Elspeth Maxwell Fletcher. *Educ:* Wellesley Coll., Wellington; John McGlashan Coll., Dunedin; Victoria University Coll., Wellington; Univ. of New Zealand (LLM Hons). Barrister and Solicitor of Supreme Court of New Zealand. Judge's Associate, 1937–38; served War, Middle East, Greece, Crete, N Africa, Italy, 1940–45, final rank Major; formerly Dominion Vice-Pres., New Zealand Returned Services Assoc.; Private practice as barrister and solicitor, Wellington, 1945–66; Pres., Wellington Law Soc., Vice-Pres., NZ Law Soc., 1966; QC and Solicitor General of New Zealand, 1966; Judge of the Supreme Court (now High Court), 1970, retd 1981; Judge Advocate General of Defence Forces, 1966–87. Actg Chief Justice, Solomon Islands, 1984. Pres., Solomon Is Court of Appeal, 1985–87. Royal Comr, Inquiry into 1982 Fiji Gen. Election, 1983. Asst Editor, Sim's Practice & Procedure, 9th edn, 1955, and 10th edn 1966. *Recreations:* formerly Rugby, cricket, tennis, golf, bowls. *Address:* 23 Selwyn Terrace, Wellington 1, New Zealand. *T:* (4) 4725502. *Clubs:* Wellington; Dunedin; Melbourne.

WHITE, Prof. John Edward Clement Twarowski, CBE 1983; FSA; Durning-Lawrence Professor of the History of Art, University College London, 1971–90 (Vice-Provost, 1984–88; Pro Provost, 1990–95); *b* 4 Oct. 1924; *s* of Brigadier A. E. White and Suzanne Twarowska; *m* 1950, Xenia Joannides (*d* 1991). *Educ:* Ampleforth College; Trinity College, Oxford; Courtauld Institute of Art, University of London. Served in RAF, 1943–47. BA London 1950; Junior Research Fellow, Warburg Inst., 1950–52; PhD Lond. 1952; MA Manchester 1963. Lectr in History of Art, Courtauld Inst., 1952–58; Alexander White Vis. Prof., Univ. of Chicago, 1958; Reader in History of Art, Courtauld Inst., 1958–59; Pilkington Prof. of the History of Art and Dir of The Whitworth Art Gallery, Univ. of Manchester, 1959–66; Vis. Ferens Prof. of Fine Art, Univ. of Hull, 1961–62; Prof. of the History of Art and Chm., Dept of History of Art, Johns Hopkins Univ., USA, 1966–71. Member: Adv. Council of V&A, 1973–76; Exec. Cttee, Assoc. of Art Historians, 1974–81 (Chm., 1976–80); Art Panel, Arts Council, 1974–78; Vis. Cttee of RCA, 1977–86; Armed Forces Pay Review Body, 1986–92; Chm., Reviewing Cttee on Export of Works of Art, 1976–82 (Mem., 1975–82). Trustee, Whitechapel Art Gall., 1976–93 (Vice-Chm., 1985–93). Membre Titulaire, 1983–95, Membre du Bureau, 1986–92, Comité International d'Histoire de l'Art. *Publications:* Perspective in Ancient Drawing and Painting, 1956; The Birth and Rebirth of Pictorial Space, 1957, 3rd edn 1987 (Italian trans. 1971; French trans. 1992; Spanish trans. 1994); Art and Architecture in Italy, 1250–1400, 1966, 3rd edn 1993 (Spanish trans. 1989); Duccio: Tuscan Art and the Medieval Workshop, 1979; Studies in Renaissance Art, 1983; Studies in Late Medieval Italian Art, 1984; Poems Poèmes Poesie, 1992; Quartet Quartetto Quatuor, 1993; Trinity Trinita Trinité, 1994; articles in Art History, Art Bulletin, Burlington Magazine, Jl of Warburg and Courtauld Institutes. *Address:* 25 Cadogan Place, SW1X 9SA. *Club:* Athenæum.

WHITE, John Sampson, AO 1982; CMG 1970; Secretary to the Governor, South Australia, 1976–82; *b* 9 June 1916; *s* of late W. J. White; *m* 1941, Dorothy G., *d* of late E. J. Griffin; one *s* one *d*. *Educ:* Black Forest Primary and Adelaide High Schs. AASA. Attorney-General's Dept, 1933–61. Served War, 2nd AIF, 1941–45, Captain. Asst Sec., Industries Develt Cttee, 1950, Sec., 1951–61; Sec., Land Agents' Bd, 1951–61; Sec. to Premier, SA, 1961–65; Mem., SA Superannuation Fund Bd, 1961–74; Sec., Premier's Dept, SA, 1965–74; Agent-Gen. for SA, 1974–76; Comr of Charitable Funds, 1964–74. Member: State Exec. Cttee, Meals on Wheels Inc., 1982–89 (Vice Pres., 1989–91; Pres., 1991–); Exec. Cttee, SA Br., Victoria League for Commonwealth Friendship, 1982–; Bd of Dirs, Service to Youth Council, 1982–84; Casino Supervisory Authy, 1983–86. Mem., Council of Governors, Presb. Girls' Coll., 1958–73. Freeman, City of London. *Recreations:* swimming, tennis. *Address:* 4 Evans Avenue, Mitcham, SA 5062, Australia. *Clubs:* Adelaide, Naval, Military and Air Force, Sturt (Adelaide).

WHITE, John William, CMG 1981; DPhil; FRS 1993; FRSC; FAA; Professor of Physical and Theoretical Chemistry, since 1985, Pro Vice-Chancellor and Chairman, Board of Institute of Advanced Studies, since 1992, Dean, Research School of Chemistry, 1995, Australian National University, Canberra; *b* Newcastle, Australia, 25 April 1937; *s* of late George John White and of Jean Florence White; *m* 1966, Ailsa Barbara, *d* of A. A. and S. Vise, Southport, Qld; one *s* three *d*. *Educ:* Newcastle High Sch.; Sydney Univ. (MSc); Lincoln Coll., Oxford (1851 Schol., 1959; MA, DPhil). ICI Fellow, Oxford Univ.; Research Fellow, Lincoln Coll., 1962; University Lectr, Oxford, 1963–85, Assessor, 1981–82; Fellow, St John's Coll., Oxford, 1963–85 (Vice-Pres. 1973). Neutron Beam Coordinator, AERE, Harwell, 1974; Asst Director, 1975, Director 1977–80, Institut Laue-Langevin, Grenoble. Argonne Fellow, Argonne Nat. Lab. and Univ. of Chicago, 1985; Christensen Fellow, St Catherine's Coll., Oxford, 1991. Pres., Soc. of Crystallographers, Aust., 1989–92; Chm., Nat. Cttee for Crystallography, Aust., 1992–. Chm., Dirs' Adv. Council, Intense Pulsed Neutron Source, Argonne Nat. Lab., and Univ of Chicago, 1989–. Lectures: Tilden, Chemical Soc., 1975; Liversidge, Sydney Univ., 1985; Hinshelwood, Oxford Univ., 1991; Foundn, Assoc. of Asian Chemical Socs, 1991. Member of Council: Epsom Coll., 1981–85; Wycliffe Hall, Oxford, 1983–85. FRSC 1982; FRACI 1985; FAIP 1986; FAA 1991. Marlow Medal, Faraday Soc., 1969. *Publications:* various contribs to scientific jls. *Recreations:* family, squash, skiing. *Address:* 2 Spencer Street, Turner, ACT 2601, Australia. *T:* Canberra (6) 62486836.

WHITE, Sir John (Woolmer), 4th Bt *cr* 1922; *b* 4 Feb. 1947; *s* of Sir Headley Dymoke White, 3rd Bt and of Elizabeth Victoria Mary, *er d* of late Wilfrid Ingram Wrightson; *S* father, 1971; *m* 1987, Joan Borland; one *s*. *Educ:* Hurst Court, Hastings; Cheltenham College; RAC, Cirencester. *Heir:* *s* Kyle Dymoke Wilfrid White, *b* 16 March 1988. *Address:* Salle Park, Norwich, Norfolk NR10 4SG. *Club:* Athenæum.

WHITE, Kenneth James; District Judge, Principal Registry of Family Division, since 1991; *b* 24 March 1948; *s* of Kenneth William John White and Pamela Blanche Emily White (*née* Seth); *m* 1971, Anne Christine Butcher; one *s* one *d*. *Educ:* Gosport County Grammar Sch., Hants; QMC, Univ. of London (LLB Hons 1969). Qualified as Solicitor, 1972; Partner, R. V. Stokes & Co., Solicitors, Portsmouth, 1974, Sen. Partner, 1991. Mem., Portsmouth & Southsea Voluntary Lifeguards, 1968– (Pres. 1985–); Chm. Nat. Lifeguard Cttee, RLSS, 1992– (Pres., Wessex Br., 1981). *Publication:* (consulting editor) Family Court Reporter, 1992. *Recreations:* swimming, reading, travel, lifesaving, bowls. *Address:* Somerset House, Strand, WC2R 1LP. *T:* 0171–936 6000.

WHITE, Lawrence John, CMG 1972; formerly Assistant Secretary, Board of Customs and Excise, 1961–75, retired; *b* 23 Feb. 1915; *s* of Arthur Yirrell White and Helen Christina White; *m* 1936, Ivy Margaret Coates; one *s*. *Educ:* Banbury Grammar Sch. Joined Customs and Excise, 1933; Commonwealth Relations Office, 1948–50; Customs and Excise, 1951–75. *Recreations:* reading, walking. *Address:* Peach Tree Cottage, Fifield, Oxon OX7 6HL. *T:* Shipton under Wychwood (01993) 830806.

WHITE, Sir Lynton (Stuart), Kt 1985; MBE (mil.) 1943; TD 1950; DL; Chairman, Hampshire County Council, 1977–85; *b* 11 Aug. 1916; 2nd *s* of Sir Dymoke White, 2nd Bt, JP, DL; *m* 1945, Phyllis Marie Rochfort Worley, *er d* of Sir Newnham Arthur Worley, KBE; four *s* one *d*. *Educ:* Harrow; Trinity College, Cambridge (MA 1938). Associate RIBA, 1947–82. TA 1939, as 2nd Lieut RA; served War of 1939–45: UK, 1939–40; Far East, 1940–45 (despatches, 1943); Hon. Lieut-Col RA, TA, 1946; TARO, 1948–71. Member Hampshire CC, 1970; Vice-Chm., 1976. DL Hants 1977.

WHITE, Martin; *see* White, E. M. E.

WHITE, Martin Andrew C.; *see* Campbell-White.

WHITE, Maj.-Gen. Martin Spencer, CBE 1991; FCIT; FILog; Director-General, Logistic Support (Army), since 1995; *b* 25 March 1944; *s* of Harold Spencer White and Mary Elizabeth White; *m* 1966, Fiona Margaret MacFarlane; three *s* one *d*. *Educ:* Sandown GS, IoW; Welbeck Coll.; RMA Sandhurst. FCIT 1992; FILog 1993. Commnd, RASC/RCT, 1966; Staff Coll., Camberley, 1977–78; Comd 4 Div., Transport Regt, 1983–85; Directing Staff, Army Staff Coll., 1985–87; Command: Logistic Support Gp, 1987–89; Force Maintenance Area (Gulf), 1990–91; Transport 1(BR) Corps, 1991–92; RCDS, 1993; Dir of Support, HQ Allied Land Forces Central Europe, 1993–95. *Publication:* Gulf Logistics: Black Adder's war, 1995. *Recreations:* cricket, off-shore sailing. *Address:* RHQ, Royal Logistic Corps, Deepcut, Hants GU16 6RW. *Clubs:* Army and Navy; Seaview Yacht.

WHITE, Michael Charles; Associate Editor, since 1989, Political Editor, since 1990, The Guardian; *b* 21 Oct. 1945; *y s* of Henry Wallis White, master mariner of St Just in Penwith, Cornwall and of Kay (*née* Wood); *m* 1973, Patricia Vivienne Gaudin; three *s*. *Educ:* Bodmin Grammar Sch.; University Coll. London (BA Hist. 1966). Reporter: Reading Evening Post, 1966–70; London Evening Standard, 1970–71; The Guardian, 1971–: Parly Sketchwriter, 1977–84; Washington Corresp., 1984–88; Columnist, The Listener, 1989–90; Co-presenter, Week in Westminster, Radio 4, 1989–. Vis. Fellow, Woodrow Wilson Foundn, Princeton, NJ, 1990–. What the Papers Say Sketchwriter of the Year Award, 1982. *Recreation:* dashing about. *Address:* Press Gallery, House of Commons, SW1A 0AA. *T:* 0171–219 4700; 7 The Avenue, Chiswick, W4 1HA. *T:* 0181–995 5055. *Club:* Beefsteak.

WHITE, Michael Simon; theatre and film producer; *b* 16 Jan. 1936; *s* of Victor R. and Doris G. White; *m* 1965, Sarah Hillsdon (marr. diss. 1973); two *s* one *d*; 2nd, 1985, Louise M. Moores, *d* of late Nigel Moores; one *s*. *Educ:* Lyceum Alpinum, Zuoz, Switzerland; Pisa University; Sorbonne, Paris. Asst to Sir Peter Daubeny, 1956–61; *stage:* London productions include: Rocky Horror Show; Sleuth; America Hurrah; Oh, Calcutta!; The Connection; Joseph and the Amazing Technicolor Dreamcoat; Loot; The Blood Knot; A Chorus Line; Deathtrap; Annie; Pirates of Penzance; On Your Toes; The Mystery of Edwin Drood; Metropolis; Bus Stop; Crazy for You; Looking Through a Glass Onion; Me and Mamie O'Rourke; She Loves Me; Fame; *films:* include: Monty Python and the Holy Grail; Rocky Horror Picture Show; My Dinner with André; Ploughman's Lunch; Moonlighting; Strangers's Kiss; The Comic Strip Presents; The Supergrass; High Season; Eat the Rich; White Mischief; The Deceivers; Nuns on the Run; Robert's Movie; The Pope Must Die; Widow's Peak. *Publication:* Empty Seats, 1984. *Recreations:* art, ski-ing, racing. *Address:* 13 Duke Street, St James's, SW1Y 6DB. *T:* 0171–839 3971.

WHITE, Neville Helme; Stipendiary Magistrate for Humberside, since 1985; *b* 12 April 1931; *s* of Noel Walter White and Irene Helme White; *m* 1958, Margaret Jennifer Catlin; two *s* one *d*. *Educ:* Newcastle-under-Lyme High School. RAF, 1949–51. Partner, Grindey & Co., Solicitors, Stoke-on-Trent, 1960–85. Pres., N Staffs Law Soc., 1980–81. Pres., Hull Boys' Club. *Recreations:* music, walking, gardening, reading, all sports, paintings. *Address:* 20 Waltham Lane, Beverley, North Humberside HU17 8HB.

WHITE, Norman Arthur, PhD; CEng, FIMechE; Eur Ing; corporate executive, international consultant and management academic; *b* Hetton-le-Hole, Durham, 11 April 1922; *s* of late Charles Brewster White and Lillian Sarah (*née* Finch); *m* 1st 1944, Joyce Marjorie Rogers (*d* 1982); one *s* one *d*; 2nd, 1983, Marjorie Iris Rushton. *Educ:* Luton Tech. Coll. (HNC); Manchester Inst. of Sci. and Technol. (AMCT Hons); London Univ. (BSc Eng (Hons)); Univ. of Philippines (MSc); London Polytechnic (DMS); Harvard

Business Sch. (grad. AMP 1968); LSE (PhD 1973). CEng; MRAeS; FInstPet; FInstE; FIMechE; FIMM. Industrial apprentice, George Kent, and D. Napier & Son; Flight Test Engr, Mil. Aircraft develt, 1943–45. Royal Dutch/Shell Gp, 1945–72: Petroleum Res. Engr, Thornton Res. Centre, 1945–51; Tech. Manager, Shell Co. of Philippines, 1951–55; Shell International Petroleum: Div. Hd, later Dep. Manager, Product Develt Dept, 1955–61; special assignments in various countries, 1961–63; Gen. Manager, Lubricants, Bitumen and LPG Divs, 1963–66; Dir of Marketing Develt, 1966–68; Chief Exec., New Enterprises Div., London and The Hague, 1968–72; Chm. and Dir, Shell oil and mining cos, UK and overseas, 1963–72. Established Norman White Associates (specialists in technology based enterprises and international resources), 1972, Director and Principal Executive, 1972–94; Energy Adviser: Hambros Bank, 1972–76; Tanks Consolidated Investments, Nassau, 1974–85; Chm./Dir, various petroleum exploration and prodn cos in UK, Netherlands, Canada and USA, 1974–92; Chairman: KBC Advanced Technologies, 1979–90; Tesel plc, 1983–85 (Dir, 1980–85); Ocean Thermal Energy Conversion Systems, 1982–; Process Automation and Computer Systems, 1985–94; Andaman Resources plc, 1986–90; Technology Transfer Centre Surrey Ltd, 1990–; Delta Media Solutions Ltd, 1990–93; Transnational Satellite Educn Centre, 1991–94; Director: Environmental Resources, 1973–87; Henley Centre for Forecasting, 1974–92 (Dep. Chm., 1974–87); Proscyon Partners, 1992–; Corporate Adviser: Placer Dome, Vancouver, 1973–78; Kennedy & Donkin Gp, 1986–94; Alcatel-Alsthom, Paris, 1993–. Mem., Parly and Scientific Cttee, House of Commons, 1977–83, 1987–92. World Energy Council, Member: British Nat. Cttee, 1977–88; Conservation Commn, 1979–87; Internat. Exec. Assembly, 1987–94; World Petroleum Congress: Chm., British Nat. Cttee, 1987–94 (Dep. Chm., 1977–87); Permanent Council, 1979–; Treasurer, 1983–91; Chm., Develt Cttee, 1989–94; Vice-Pres., 1991–94; Member: Bd and World Council, Internat. Road Fedn, Geneva and Washington, 1964–72; UK CAA Cttee of Enquiry on Flight Time Limitations (Bader Cttee), 1972–73; Internat. Energy/Petroleum Delegn to Russia, Rumania, E Germany, Hungary, Venezuela, Japan, Korea, People's Republic of China, Indonesia, India, Mexico, Argentina, Brazil, Iran and Southern Africa, 1979–; Royal Soc./Inst. of Petroleum Delegn to People's Republic of China, 1985; Chm., China Technical Exchange Cttee, 1985–89. Visiting Professor: Arthur D. Little Management Educn Inst., Boston, USA, 1977–79; Henley Management Coll., 1979–89 (Vis. Fellow 1976–79); Manchester Business Sch., 1981–90 (Vis. Industrial Dir 1971–81); City Univ., 1990– (ext. examnr, 1983–89); Vis. Lectr, RCDS, 1981–85. London University: Member: Senate, 1974–87; External Council, 1974–84; Governing Bd, Commerce Degree Bureau, 1975–84; Academic Adv. Bd in Engrg, 1976–85; Collegiate Council, 1984–87; Cttee of Mangt, Inst. of US Studies, 1984–92; Mem., Council of Mining and Metallurgical Instns, 1981–87; Member Council: Inst. of Petroleum, 1975–81 (Vice-Pres., 1978–81); IMechE, 1980–85, 1987–91 (Chm., Engrg Management Div., 1980–85, Southern Br., 1987–89; Presidential Award for Meritorious Service, 1994); Founder Chm., Jt Bd for Engrg Management, 1990–93 (Chm. Academic Bd, 1994–). FRSA 1944; FIMgt; MRI; Mem., RIIA; Founder Mem., British Inst. of Energy Econs. Associate, St George's House, Windsor Castle, 1972. Governor: King Edward VI Royal Grammar Sch., Guildford, 1976–; Reigate Grammar Sch., 1976–93. Freeman, City of London, 1983; Liveryman: Worshipful Co. of Engineers, 1984; Co. of Spectacle Makers, 1986; Member: Guild of Freemen, 1986; Co. of World Traders, 1989. *Publications:* Financing the International Petroleum Industry, 1978; The International Outlook for Oil Substitution to 2020, 1983; (contrib.) Handbook of Engineering Management, 1988; contribs to professional jls in UK, Philippines and Canada, on fluid mechanics, petroleum utilization, energy resources, R&D management, project financing and engrg management. *Recreations:* family and various others in moderation, country and coastal walking, wild life, browsing, international affairs, comparative religions, domestic odd-jobbing. *Address:* 9 Park House, 123–125 Harley Street, W1N 1HE. *T:* 0171–935 7387; Green Ridges, Downside Road, Guildford, Surrey GU4 8PH. *T:* Guildford (01483) 67523, *Fax:* (01483) 504314. *Clubs:* Athenæum, City Livery, Inst. of Directors, LSE; County (Guildford); Harvard Business (USA).

WHITE, Adm. Sir Peter, GBE 1977 (KBE 1976; CBE 1960; MBE 1944); Associate Director, Business in the Community, since 1988; *b* 25 Jan. 1919; *s* of William White, Amersham, Bucks; *m* 1947, Audrey Eileen (*d* 1991), *d* of Ernest Wallin, Northampton; two *s*. *Educ:* Dover College. Secretary: to Chief of Staff, Home Fleet, 1942–43; to Flag Officer Comdg 4th Cruiser Sqdn, 1944–45; to Asst Chief of Naval Personnel, 1946–47; to Flag Officer, Destroyers, Mediterranean, 1948–49; to Controller of the Navy, 1949–53; to C-in-C Home Fleet and C-in-C Eastern Atlantic, 1954–55; Naval Asst to Chm. BJSM, Washington, and UK Rep. of Standing Group, NATO, 1956–59; Supply Officer, HMS Adamant, 1960–61; Dep. Dir of Service Conditions and Fleet Supply Duties, Admty, 1961–63; idc 1964; CO HMS Raleigh, 1965–66; Principal Staff Officer to Chief of Defence Staff, 1967–69; Dir-Gen. Fleet Services, 1969–71; Port Admiral, Rosyth, 1972–74; Chief of Fleet Support, 1974–77. Consultant, Wilkinson Match Ltd, 1978–79; Associate Dir, The Industrial Soc., 1980–88. Underwriting Member of Lloyd's, 1979–. Chm., Officers Pension Society, 1982–90. Mem. Foundn Cttee, Gordon Boys' Sch., 1979–89.

WHITE, Peter Richard; Group Chief Executive and Managing Director, Alliance & Leicester Building Society, since 1991; *b* 11 Feb. 1942; *m* 1968, Mary Angela Bowyer; one *s* one *d*. *Educ:* St Paul's School. FCA; FCT. Price Waterhouse, 1965–69; Management Accountant, Chief Internal Auditor, Financial Controller, Abbey National Building Soc., 1970–82; Gen. Manager (Finance and Management Services), Alliance Building Soc., 1982–85; Alliance & Leicester Building Society: Gen. Manager (Admin. and Treasury), 1985–87; Dir and Gen. Manager (Develt), 1987–89; Dep. Group Chief Exec. and Man. Dir, 1989–91. MInstD. *Recreations:* golf, opera. *Address:* Alliance & Leicester Building Society, 49 Park Lane, W1Y 4EQ.

WHITE, Raymond Walter Ralph, CMG 1982; Chairman, NZ Advisory Board, Westpac Banking Corporation, 1991–95; *b* 23 June 1923; *s* of Henry Underhill White and Ethel Annie White; *m* 1946, Nola Colleen Adin; one *s* two *d*. *Educ:* Palmerston North Technical High Sch.; Victoria Univ. FCA 1981; FCIS 1968; FBINZ 1982. Dep. Governor, 1967–77, Governor, 1977–82, Reserve Bank of NZ. Chairman: BP New Zealand, 1984–92; Australian Guarantee Corp (NZ) Ltd, 1991–93; Director: NZ Guardian Trust Co., 1983–91; Alcan Australia Ltd, 1988–95; NZ Adv. Bd, ICI, 1990–93. *Recreations:* golf, tennis, gardening. *Address:* 63 Chatsworth Road, Silverstream, New Zealand. *T:* Wellington (4) 282084. *Club:* Wellington (NZ).

WHITE, Richard Hamilton Hayden; Legal Adviser to the Lord Chancellor's Department, since 1995; *b* 9 Aug. 1939; *s* of late Charles Henry Hayden White and of Helen Margherita Hamilton White. *Educ:* Sutton Valence Sch.; Trinity Coll., Oxford (MA). Admitted solicitor, 1963. Asst Solicitor, Freshfields, 1963–67; Lectr in Law, later Sen. Lectr, Univ. of Birmingham, 1967–74; Lord Chancellor's Department, 1974–: Temp. Legal Advr, then Sen. Legal Advr; Asst Solicitor, 1981; Under Sec. and Head of Legal Gp, 1992. Secretary: Rev. Body on Chancery Div., report pubd 1981; Civil Justice Rev., report pubd 1988. *Publications:* (contributed): Social Needs and Legal Action, 1973; Legal Services in Birmingham, 1975; Lawyers in their Social Setting, 1976; Rechtsbedürfnis und Rechtshilfe, 1978; EEC Conventions on Jurisdiction and Enforcement of Judgments, 1992. *Recreations:* rural pursuits, Sicily. *Address:* Lord Chancellor's Department, Southside, 105 Victoria Street, SW1E 6QT. *T:* 0171–210 3530.

WHITE, Prof. Robert Stephen, FRS 1994; FGS; Professor of Geophysics, Cambridge University, since 1989; Fellow of St Edmund's College, Cambridge, since 1988; *b* 12 Dec. 1952; 2nd *s* of James Henry White and Ethel Gladys (*née* Cornick); *m* 1976, Helen Elizabeth (*née* Pearce); one *s* one *d*. *Educ:* Market Harborough and West Bridgford Comprehensive Schs; Emmanuel Coll., Cambridge (Sen. Schol., 1972–74; Bachelor Schol., 1974–77; BA, MA, PhD). FRAS 1979; FGS 1989. Research Assistant: Berkeley Nuclear Labs, CEGB, 1970–71; Dept of Geodesy and Geophysics, Cambridge, 1978; postdoctoral schol., Woods Hole Oceanographic Instn, USA, 1978–79; Res. Fellow, Emmanuel Coll., Cambridge, 1979–82; Sen. Asst in Res., 1981–85, Asst Dir of Res., 1985–89, Dept of Earth Scis, Cambridge Univ. Cecil and Ida H. Green Schol., Scripps Instn of Oceanography, UCSD, USA, 1987; Guest Investigator, Woods Hole Oceanographic Instn, 1988. Bigsby Medal, Geol Soc., 1991. *Publications:* papers in many internat. jls. *Recreations:* building and flying radio-controlled model gliders, walking. *Address:* Bullard Laboratories, Madingley Road, Cambridge CB3 0EZ. *T:* Cambridge (01223) 840582.

WHITE, Robin Bernard G.; *see* Grove-White.

WHITE, Roger, FSA 1986; Executive Secretary, Garden History Society, since 1992; *b* 1 Sept. 1950; *s* of Geoffrey and Zoë White. *Educ:* Ifield Grammar School; Christ's College, Cambridge (1st class Hons, Hist. of Art Tripos); Wadham College, Oxford. GLC Historic Buildings Div., 1979–83; Sec., Georgian Gp, 1984–91; Mem., Chiswick House Adv. Panel, 1991–. Trustee, Pell Wall Preservation Trust, 1994–. Contributing Ed., House and Garden, 1994–. *Publications:* John Vardy, 1985; Georgian Arcadia: architecture for the park and garden, 1987; The Architectural Evolution of Magdalen College, Oxford, 1993; contribs to Architectural Hist., Jl of Garden Hist., Country Life. *Recreation:* visiting and writing about historic buildings. *Address:* 76 Clapham Common North Side, SW4 9SD.

WHITE, Roger Lowrey, JP; Managing Director, Research Information Services (Westminster) Ltd, 1975–93; Associate Director, Cargill Attwood International, since 1971; *b* 1 June 1928; *o s* of late George Frederick White and Dorothy Jeanette White; *m* 1962, Angela Mary (*née* Orman), company director. *Educ:* St Joseph's Coll., Beulah Hill. National Vice-Chm., Young Conservatives, 1958–59; Founder Mem., Conservative Commonwealth Council; Mem. Council, London Borough of Bromley, 1964–68. MP (C) Gravesend, 1970–Feb. 1974. Gen. Comr of Taxes, 1991–. Member: National Asthma Campaign (formerly Asthma Research) Council, 1973–; London Crime Stoppers Bd, 1989– (Dep. Chm., 1992–). Freeman, City of London, 1953; Liveryman, Worshipful Co. of Makers of Playing Cards, 1975–; JP Inner London Area, 1965; Chm., E Central Div. of Inner London Magistrates, 1989–91 (Dep. Chm., 1986–89). *Recreations:* golf, fishing. *Address:* 9 Dartmoor Drive, Huntingdon, Cambs PE18 8XT. *Clubs:* Carlton, English-Speaking Union.

WHITE, Stephen Fraser; consulting engineer; *b* 13 May 1922; *s* of Robert and Iola White; *m* 1953, Judith Hamilton Cox; two *s* one *d*. *Educ:* Friars, Bangor; Nottingham Univ. BSc; FICE, MIWEM. War Service in Indian Electrical and Mechanical Engineers, discharged 1947. G. H. Hill and Sons, Consulting Civil Engineers, 1947–59; Cardiff Corporation, 1959–62; Engineering Inspector, Min. of Housing and Local Govt, 1962–70; Dir of Water Engineering, Dept of the Environment, 1970–77; Sen. Technical Advr to Nat. Water Council, 1977–83. *Recreations:* golf, bridge. *Address:* Rosehill, 4 Goodens Lane, Great Doddington, Northants NN9 7TY.

WHITE, Air Vice-Marshal Terence Philip, CB 1987; DL; CEng, FIEE; at leisure; *b* 1 May 1932; *s* of Horace Arthur White and Evelyn Annie White (*née* Simpson); *m* 1956, Sheila Mary (*née* Taylor); three *d*. *Educ:* Wellingborough Technical Inst,; Rugby Coll. of Technology and Arts; RAF Engineering College. Electrical engineering apprentice, 1948–53; Junior Design Engineer, BTH Co., 1953; commissioned RAF Signals Officer, 1954–56; RAF Permt commn, Elect. Engr, 1957; attached RAAF, 1958–60; RAF weapons, communications and radar appts, 1963–67; OC Wing, RAF, Fylingdales, 1967–70; RAF Staff Coll., 1971; commanded RAF N Luffenham, 1972–74; Mem., RCDS, 1975; Senior Elect. Engr, HQ RAF Strike Command, 1976–77; Dir, Engineering Policy MoD (Air), 1978–80; Air Officer, Engrg and Supply, HQ RAF Germany, 1981–82; AOC Maintenance Units and AO Maintenance, RAF Support Comd, 1983–87. Vice Chm. (Air), E Midlands TAVRA, 1988–. Hon. Air Cdre, Lincoln RAuxAF Sqn, 1992–. DL Lincoln, 1994. *Publications:* contribs to RAF and professional jls. *Recreations:* rough shooting, antique and house restoration. *Address:* c/o Midland Bank, Grantham, Lincs NG31 6LF. *Club:* Royal Air Force.

WHITE, Thomas Anthony B.; *see* Blanco White.

WHITE, Sir Thomas Astley Woollaston, 5th Bt, *cr* 1802; JP; Hon. Sheriff for Wigtownshire, since 1963; *b* 13 May 1904; *s* of Sir Archibald Woollaston White, 4th Bt, and late Gladys Becher Love, *d* of Rev. E. A. B. Pitman; *S* father, 1945; *m* 1935, Daphne Margaret, *er d* of late Lt-Col F. R. I. Athill, CMG, OBE; one *d*. *Educ:* Wellington College. FRICS. JP Wigtownshire, 1952. *Heir: nephew* Nicholas Peter Archibald White [*b* 2 March 1939; *m* 1970, Susan Irene, *d* of G. W. B. Pollock; two *s* one *d*]. *Address:* Ha Hill, Torhousemuir, Wigtown, Newton Stewart DG8 9DJ. *T:* Wigtown (019884) 2238.

WHITE, Tom; *see* White, D. T.

WHITE, Willard Wentworth, CBE 1995; singer, actor; *b* 10 Oct. 1946; *s* of Egbert and Gertrude White; *m* 1972, Gillian Jackson; three *s* one *d*. *Educ:* Excelsior High Sch., Kingston, Jamaica; Juilliard Sch. of Music. BM. Guest singer, recitalist and recording artist, UK and overseas; singing rôles include Sarastro, Osmin, Sprecher, Leporello, Banquo, King Philip, Grand Inquisitor, Ferrando, Wotan, Klingsor, Hunding, Fafner, King Henry, Orestes, Porgy, Golaud, Pizarro, Prince Khovansky, Mephistopheles (Gounod's Faust); *stage:* title rôle, Othello, RSC, 1989. Prime Minister of Jamaica's Medal of Appreciation, 1987. *Address:* c/o IMG Artists Europe, Media House, 3 Burlington Lane, W4 2TH.

WHITE, William Kelvin Kennedy, CMG 1983; HM Diplomatic Service, retired; *b* 10 July 1930; *y s* of late Kennedy White, JP, Caldy, Cheshire, and Violet White; *m* 1957, Susan Margaret, *y d* of late R. T. Colthurst, JP, Malvern, Worcs; three *s*. *Educ:* Birkenhead Sch.; Merton Coll., Oxford. 2nd Lieut Manchester Regt, 1949–50; Lieut 13th (Lancs) Bn, Parachute Regt, TA, 1950–54. Entered HM Foreign (later Diplomatic) Service, 1954; Foreign Office, 1954–56, attending UN Gen. Assemblies, 1954 and 1955; 3rd Sec., Helsinki, 1956–57; 2nd Sec., Commissioner-General's Office, Singapore, 1957–61; 2nd Sec., then 1st Sec., FO, 1961–66; 1st Sec. (Commercial), Stockholm, 1966–69; 1st Sec., then Counsellor and Head of Republic of Ireland Dept, FCO, 1969–74; Counsellor, New Delhi, 1974–77; Head of South Asian Dept, FCO, 1978–80; Minister, Canberra, 1980–81; Dep. Chief Clerk and Chief Inspector, FCO, 1982–84; High Comr to Zambia, 1984–87; Ambassador to Indonesia, 1988–90. Mem. Council, Univ. of Surrey, 1991–. *Address:* Church Farm House, North Moreton, near Didcot, Oxon OX11 9BA. *Club:* Moreton CC.

WHITE-THOMSON, Very Rev. Ian Hugh; Dean of Canterbury, 1963–76; *b* 18 December 1904; *m* 1954, Wendy Ernesta Woolliams; two *s* two *d*. *Educ:* Harrow; Oxford. Deacon, 1929; Priest, 1930; Curacy, St Mary's, Ashford, Kent, 1929–34; Rector of S Martin's with St Paul's, Canterbury, 1934–39; Chaplain to Archbishops of Canterbury, 1939–47; Vicar of Folkestone, 1947–54; Archdeacon of Northumberland and Canon of Newcastle, 1955–63; Chaplain to King George VI, 1947–52, to the Queen, 1952–63; Examining Chaplain to Bishop of Newcastle, 1955–63. Hon. Canon of Canterbury Cathedral, 1950. Governor, Harrow School, 1947–62, 1965–70. Freeman, City of Canterbury, 1976. Hon. DCL Univ. of Kent at Canterbury, 1971. *Address:* Camphill, Harville Road, Wye, Ashford, Kent TN25 5EY. *T:* Wye (01233) 812210.

WHITEHEAD, Edward Anthony, (Ted); playwright; *b* 3 April 1933; *s* of Edward Whitehead and Catherine Curran; *m* 1st, 1958, Kathleen Horton (marr. diss. 1976); two *d*; 2nd, 1976, Gwenda Bagshaw. *Educ:* Christ's Coll., Cambridge (MA). Military Service, King's Regt (Infantry), 1955–57. *TV plays:* Under the Age; The Peddler; The Proofing Session; *TV adaptations:* The Detective; Jumping the Queue; The Life and Loves of a She-Devil; Firstborn; The Free Frenchman; Murder East, Murder West; The Cloning of Joanna May; A Question of Guilt; *stage adaptation:* The Dance of Death. Evening Standard Award, and George Devine Award, 1971; BAFTA Award, 1986; American Cable Entertainments Award, 1987. *Publications:* The Foursome, 1972; Alpha Beta, 1972; The Sea Anchor, 1975; Old Flames, 1976; The Punishment, 1976; Mecca, 1977; World's End, 1981; The Man Who Fell in Love with his Wife, 1984. *Recreations:* soccer, pubs, music. *Address:* c/o Jenne Casarotto, 2nd Floor, National House, 60–66 Wardour Street, W1V 3HP. *T:* 0171–287 4450.

WHITEHEAD, Frank Ernest; Deputy Director (Statistics), Office of Population Censuses and Surveys, 1987–89; *b* 21 Jan. 1930; *s* of Ernest Edward Whitehead and Isabel Leslie; *m* 1961, Anne Gillian Marston; three *s*. *Educ:* Leyton County High School; London School of Economics. BSc (Econ). National Service, RAF, 1948–49. Rio Tinto Co. Ltd, 1952–54; Professional Officer, Central Statistical Office, Fedn of Rhodesia and Nyasaland, 1955–64; Statistician, General Register Office, 1964–68; Chief Statistician, Min. of Social Security, later DHSS, 1968–77; Head of Social Survey Div., Office of Population Censuses and Surveys, 1977–82; Under Secretary, 1982; Dep. Dir, OPCS, 1982–87. Vice-Pres., Royal Statistical Soc., 1988–89 (Council, 1987–92). *Publications:* Social Security Statistics: Reviews of United Kingdom Statistical Sources, Vol. II (ed W. F. Maunder), 1974; contribs to Statistical News, Population Trends. *Recreations:* family history, unskilled garden labour. *Address:* Bryaton, Morwenstow, N Cornwall EX23 9SU.

WHITEHEAD, His Honour (Garnet) George (Archie), DFC 1944; a Circuit Judge, 1977–89; *b* 22 July 1916; *s* of late Archibald Payne Whitehead and Margaret Elizabeth Whitehead; *m* 1946, Monica (*née* Watson); two *d*. *Educ:* Wisbech. Admitted Solicitor, 1949. Served War, 1939–45, RAF, Pilot, Bomber Comd and Transport Comd; demob. as Flt Lt, 1 Jan. 1947. Articled to Edmund W. Roythorne, MBE, Solicitor, Spalding. Formerly Senior Partner, Roythorne & Co., Solicitor, Boston, Lincs (Partner, 1950–77); a Recorder of the Crown Court, 1972–77. Formerly Alderman, Boston Borough Council; Mayor of Boston, 1969–70. Reader, Diocese of Lincoln. *Recreations:* photography, walking. *Address:* 15 Burton Close, Boston, Lincs PE21 9QW. *T:* Boston (01205) 364977.

WHITEHEAD, George Sydney, CMG 1966; LVO 1961; HM Diplomatic Service, retired; re-employed in Foreign and Commonwealth Office (Security Department), 1976–81; *b* 15 Nov. 1915; *s* of William George and Annie Sabina Whitehead; *m* 1948, Constance Mary Hart (*née* Vale); one *d* (and one step *d*). Educ: Harrow County Sch.; London Sch. of Economics. India Office, 1934. Armed Forces (Royal Artillery), 1940–45. Private Sec. to Parly Under-Sec. of State for India and Burma, 1945–46; British Embassy, Rangoon, 1947; CRO 1948–52; British High Commn, Canberra, 1952–55; Counsellor, British High Commn, Calcutta, 1958–61; Inspector, Commonwealth Service, 1961–64; Inspector, Diplomatic Service, 1965; Head of Asia Economic Dept, CO, 1966–67; Head of Commonwealth Trade Dept, CO, 1967–68; Head of Commodities Dept, FCO, 1968–69; Dep. High Comr and Minister (Commercial), Ottawa, 1970 72; Asst Under-Sec. of State, 1972–75, Dep. Chief Clerk, 1973–75, FCO. Vice-Pres., RIPA, 1985– (Mem. Council, 1977–84). *Recreations:* gardening, reading, walking. *Address:* Victoria House, Victoria Road, Aldeburgh, Suffolk IP15 5ED. *T:* Aldeburgh (01728) 453671. *Clubs:* Civil Service, Victory Services, Middlesex County Cricket.

WHITEHEAD, Godfrey Oliver, CBE 1987; FICE; Chief Executive, Alfred McAlpine PLC, since 1993; *b* 9 Aug. 1941; *s* of late Clarence Whitehead and Mary Whitehead (*née* Gartside); *m* 1965, Stephanie McAllister; three *s* one *d*. *Educ:* Hulme Grammar Sch., Oldham; Univ. of Bradford (BSc Civil Engrg). FICE 1992. John Laing Plc, 1963–86: Man. Dir, John Laing Construction Ltd, 1982–86; Exec. Dir, John Laing Plc 1983–86; Chm., Jt Venture (Laing-Mowlem-ARC) which built Mt Pleasant Airport, Falkland Is, 1983–86; Chm., John Laing Internat., 1986; Exec. Dir, AMEC Plc, 1986–89; Gp Chief Exec., Babcock Internat. Gp PLC, 1989–93. Non-Exec. Dir, PSA, 1989–91. Manchester Ringway Developments PLC: Chm., 1987–89; Pres., 1989–. Lt-Col, Engr and Tspt Staff Corps, TA, 1989 (Major, 1984; Chm., Liaison Cttee, 1991–). Liveryman, Paviors' Co., 1986–. *Recreations:* gardening, shooting, opera. *Address:* Alfred McAlpine PLC, 8 Suffolk Street, SW1Y 4HG; 55 Copperkins Lane, Amersham, Bucks HP6 5RA.

WHITEHEAD, Graham Wright, CBE 1977; President, Jaguar Cars Inc., 1983–90; Chairman, Jaguar Canada Inc., Ontario, 1983–90; Director: Jaguar Cars Ltd, 1982–90; Jaguar plc, 1984–90; *m* Gabrielle Whitehead, OBE; one *s* one *d*. Joined Wolseley Motors, 1945; moved to US, 1959; Pres., BL Motors Inc., later Jaguar Rover Triumph Inc., NJ, 1968–83; Chm., Jaguar Rover Triumph Canada Inc., Ont, 1977–83. President: British-American Chamber of Commerce, NY, 1976–78; British Automobile Manufacturers Assoc., NY; St George's Soc. of NY; Governor, Nat. Assoc. of Securities Dealers, 1987–90. *Address:* 20 Meadow Place, Old Greenwich, CT 06870, USA. *Club:* Riverside Yacht (Conn).

WHITEHEAD, Dr John Ernest Michael, FRCPath; Director of Public Health Laboratory Service, 1981–85; *b* 7 Aug. 1920; *s* of Dr Charles Ernest Whitehead and Bertha Whitehead; *m* 1946, Elizabeth Bacchus (*née* Cochran); one *s* one *d*. *Educ:* Merchant Taylors' Sch.; Gonville and Caius Coll., Cambridge (MA); St Thomas's Hosp. Med. Sch. (MB BChir, DipBact). Jun. Ho. appts, St Thomas' Hosp., 1944–47; Lectr in Bacteriology, St Thomas's Hosp. Med. Sch., 1948–51; Travelling Fellowship, State Serum Inst., Copenhagen, 1949–50; Asst Bacteriologist, Central Public Health Laboratory, 1952–53; Dep. Dir, Public Health Lab., Sheffield, 1953–58; Dir, Public Health Lab., Coventry, 1958–75; Cons. Microbiologist, Coventry Hosps, 1958–75; Dep. Dir, Public Health Laboratory Service, 1975–81. Hon. Lecturer: Univ. of Sheffield, 1954–58; Univ. of Birmingham, 1962–75. Vice-Pres., RCPath, 1983–86; Member: Adv. Cttee on Dangerous Pathogens, 1981–85; Adv. Cttee on Irradiated and Novel Foods, 1982–86; Expert Adv. Gp on AIDS, 1985; Consultant Advr in Microbiol., DHSS, 1982–85; Specialist Advr to H of C Agric. Cttee, 1988–91, to H of C Social Services Cttee, 1989–90; Temporary Adviser and Chm., Working Gp on Safety Measures in Microbiology, WHO, 1976–82; Chm., Working Gp on Organisation and Administration of Public Health Laboratory Services, Council of Europe, 1977–79. *Publications:* chapters in The Pathological Basis of Medicine, ed R. C. Curran and D. G. Harnden, 1974; papers and reviews in med. microbiology in various med. and scientific jls. *Recreations:* house and garden maintenance, skiing, modern languages. *Address:* Martins, Churchend, Slimbridge, Gloucester GL2 7BL. *T:* Dursley (01453) 890726. *Club:* Athenæum.

WHITEHEAD, Sir John (Stainton), GCMG 1992 (KCMG 1986; CMG 1976); CVO 1978; HM Diplomatic Service, retired; *b* 20 Sept. 1932; *s* of late John William and Kathleen Whitehead; *m* 1964, Carolyn (*née* Hilton); two *s* two *d*. *Educ:* Christ's Hospital; Hertford Coll., Oxford (MA; Hon. Fellow 1991). HM Forces, 1950–52; Oxford, 1952–55; FO, 1955–56; Tokyo, 1956–61; FO, 1961–64; 1st Sec., Washington, 1964–67; 1st Sec. (Economic), Tokyo, 1968–71; FCO, 1971–76, Head of Personnel Services Dept, 1973–76; Counsellor, Bonn, 1976–80; Minister, Tokyo, 1980–84; Dep. Under-Sec. of State (Chief Clerk), FCO, 1984–86; Ambassador to Japan, 1986–92. Non-exec. Director: Cadbury Schweppes, 1993–; Serco Group, 1994–; BPB, 1995–; Sen. Advr, Morgan Grenfell Gp, 1992–; Advr to Pres. of BoT, 1992–; advr or consultant to various cos and organisations. Member: UK–Japan 2000 Gp, 1992– (Dir, 1995–); Council, Japan Soc., 1992–; Management Council, GB Sasakawa Foundn, 1993–. Trustee, Monteverdi Choir and Orchestra, 1991–; Member: Royal Opera House Trust, 1992–93; Council, Buckingham Univ., 1992–. Pres., Hertford Soc., 1991–. *Recreations:* new challenges, music, travel, golf, tree-felling. *Address:* Bracken Edge, High Pitfold, Hindhead, Surrey GU26 6BN. *Clubs:* Beefsteak, United Oxford & Cambridge University, MCC; Liphook Golf (Hants).

WHITEHEAD, Phillip; writer and television producer; Member (Lab) Staffordshire East and Derby, European Parliament, since 1994; *b* 30 May 1937; adopted *s* of late Harold and Frances Whitehead; *m* 1967, Christine, *d* of T. G. Usborne; two *s* one *d*. *Educ:* Lady Manners' Grammar Sch., Bakewell; Exeter Coll., Oxford. President, Oxford Union, 1961. BBC Producer, 1961–67, and WEA Lecturer, 1961–65; Editor of This Week, Thames TV, 1967–70. Guild of TV Producers Award for Factual Programmes, 1969; BPG Best Documentary Award and Emmy Award for Best Script, for the Kennedys, 1993. Vice-Chm., Young Fabian Group, 1965; Chm., Fabian Soc., 1978–79 (Centenary Dir, 1983–84). Chairman: New Society Ltd, 1986; Statesman and Nation Publications Ltd, 1985–90; Director: Goldcrest Film and Television Hldgs Ltd, 1984–87; Brook Productions, 1986–. Member: Annan Cttee on Future of Broadcasting, 1974–77; Council, Consumers' Assoc., 1982– (Chm., 1990–94). Vis. Fellow, Goldsmiths' Coll., Univ. of London, 1985–; MacTaggart Lectr, Edinburgh Internat. Television Festival, 1987. MP (Lab) Derby N, 1970–83; Front bench spokesman on higher educn, 1980–83 and on the arts, 1982–83; Member: Procedure Cttee, 1977–79; Select Cttee on Home Affairs, 1979–81; PLP Liaison Cttee, 1975–79; Council of Europe Assembly, 1975–80. Chm., Intergroup on Consumer Affairs, European Parlt, 1994–. Contested (Lab): W Derbys, 1966, Derby N, 1983, 1987. Member: NUJ; NUR. Times columnist, 1983–85; Presenter, Credo series, LWT, 1983–84. FRSA 1983. *Publications:* (jtly) Electoral Reform: time for change, 1982; (contrib.) Fabian Essays in Socialist Thought, 1984; The Writing on the Wall, 1985; (jtly) Stalin, a time for judgment, 1990; (jtly) The Windsors, a Dynasty Revealed, 1994. *Recreations:* walking, cinema, old model railways. *Address:* Mill House, Rowsley, Matlock, Derbys DE4 2EB. *T:* Matlock (01629) 732659.

WHITEHEAD, Dr Roger George, CBE 1992; Director, Dunn Nutrition Centre, Medical Research Council, Cambridge and Keneba, The Gambia, since 1973; Fellow of Darwin College, Cambridge, since 1973; *b* 7 Oct. 1933; *s* of late Arthur Charles Sanders Whitehead and Eleanor Jane Whitehead (*née* Farrer); *m* 1958, Jennifer Mary Lees; two *s* one *d*. *Educ:* Ulverston Grammar Sch.; Univ. of Leeds (BSc 1956; PhD 1959); MA Cantab 1973. FIBiol 1973; Hon. MRCP 1986, Hon. FRCP 1993. Scientific Staff, MRC, 1959–; Dir, Child Nutrition Unit, Kampala, 1968–73; Vice Master, Darwin Coll., Cambridge, 1989. Vis. Prof., KCL, 1992–; Hon. Prof., Shenyang Univ., China, 1995–. Committee on Medical Aspects of Food Policy: Mem., 1975–91; Chm., Dietary Reference Panel, 1987–91; Mem., MAFF Food Adv. Cttee, 1988–. Pres., Nutrition Soc., 1989–92; Chm., British Nutrition Foundn, 1994– (Vice-Chm., 1993–94). Drummond Prize, Nutrition Soc., 1968; Unesco Science Prize, 1983; British Nutrition Foundn Prize, 1990; Nutricia Internat. Award for Nutritional Sci., 1994. *Publications:* (jtly) Protein-Energy Malnutrition, 1977; (ed) Maternal Nutrition during Pregnancy and Lactation, 1980; (ed) New Techniques in Nutritional Research, 1991; contribs to learned jls. *Recreations:* photography, licensed amateur radio operator, G3ZUK, 5X5NA, C53U. *Address:* Church End, Weston Colville, Cambridge CB1 5PE. *T:* Cambridge (01223) 290524.

WHITEHEAD, Sir Rowland (John Rathbone), 5th Bt, *cr* 1889; *b* 24 June 1930; *s* of Major Sir Philip Henry Rathbone Whitehead, 4th Bt, and 1st wife Gertrude, *d* of J. C. Palmer, West Virginia, USA; *S* father, 1953; *m* 1954, Marie-Louise, *d* of Arnold Christian Gausel, Stavanger, Norway; one *s* one *d*. *Educ:* Radley; Trinity Hall, Cambridge (BA). Late 2nd Lieutenant RA. Chairman: Trustees, Rowland Hill Benevolent Fund, 1982–; Exec. Cttee, Standing Council of the Baronetage, 1984–; Brogdale Trust Appeal, 1995–; Trustee: Baronets' Trust, 1984– (founder Chm., 1984–89); Brogdale Horticultural Trust, 1994–. Governor, Appleby Grammar Sch., 1964–. Master, Co. of Fruiterers', 1994–95. Freeman, City of London. *Recreations:* poetry and rural indolence. *Heir:* *s* Philip Henry Rathbone Whitehead [*b* 13 Oct. 1957; *m* 1987, Emma, *d* of Captain A. M. D. Milne Home; one *s*. Late Welsh Guards]. *Address:* Sutton House, Chiswick Mall, W4 2PR. *T:* 0171–994 2710; Walnut Tree Cottage, Fyfield, Lechlade, Glos GL7 3NT. *Club:* Arts.

WHITEHEAD, Ted; *see* Whitehead, E. A.

WHITEHEAD, Prof. Thomas Patterson, CBE 1985; MCB, FRCPath, FRSC; Professor of Clinical Chemistry, University of Birmingham, 1968–87, retired; Consultant Biochemist, Queen Elizabeth Medical Centre, 1960–87; *b* 7 May 1923; *m* 1947, Doreen Grace Whitton, JP; two *s* one *d*. *Educ:* Salford Royal Technical Coll.; Univ. of Birmingham (PhD). Biochemist to S Warwickshire Hospital Gp, 1950–60. Dean, Faculty of Medicine and Dentistry, Birmingham Univ., 1984–87. Dir, Wolfson Research Laboratories, 1972–84. Council Mem., Med. Research Council, 1972–76; Mem., Health Service Research Bd, 1973–75; Chairman: Div. of Path. Studies, Birmingham, 1974–80; Board of Undergraduate Med. Educn, Birmingham, 1982–84; W Midlands RHA Res. Cttee, 1982–86; DHSS Adv. Cttee on Assessment of Laboratory Standards, 1969–84; W Midlands RHA Scientific Services Cttee, 1984–86; Member: Adv. Bd, CS Occupational Health Service, 1988–; Med. Adv. Panel on Driving and Alcohol and Substance Abuse, Dept of Transport, 1989–. Chief Scientific Advr, BUPA Med. Res., London, 1987–91; Consultant to: BUPA Medical Centre, London, 1969–91; BUPA Hosps, London, 1983–91; BUPA Med. R&D, 1991–95; Centro Diagnostico Italiano, Milan, 1972–92; WHO, Geneva, 1974–86; JS Pathology Services, London, 1983–. Pres., Assoc. of Clinical Biochemists, 1981–83; Mem. Council, RCPath, 1982–84. Hon. MRCP 1985. Kone Award Lectr, 1983. Wellcome Prize, 1972; Dade Award, Geneva, 1975; Disting. Internat. Services Award, Internat. Fedn of Clinical Chemistry, 1987; Rank Prize for Opto-Electronics, 1991. *Publications:* Quality Control in Clinical Chemistry, 1976; papers in med. and scientific jls. *Recreation:* growing and exhibiting sweet peas. *Address:* 70 Northumberland Road, Leamington Spa CV32 6HB. *T:* Leamington Spa (01926) 421974. *Club:* Athenæum.

WHITEHORN, John Roland Malcolm, CMG 1974; a Deputy Director-General, Confederation of British Industries, 1966–78; *b* 19 May 1924; *s* of late Alan and Edith Whitehorn; *m* 1st, 1951, Josephine (*née* Plummer) (marr. diss. 1973; she *d* 1990); no *c*; 2nd, 1973, Marion FitzGibbon (*née* Gutmann). *Educ:* Rugby Sch. (Exhbnr); Trinity Coll., Cambridge (Exhbnr). Served War, 1943–46, RAFVR (Flying Officer). Joined FBI, 1947; Dep. Overseas Dir, 1960; Overseas Dir, 1963; Overseas Dir, CBI, 1965–68; Dir, Mitchell Cotts plc, 1978–86; Consultant Dir, Lilly Industries, 1978–89. Member: BOTB, 1975–78; Bd, British Council, 1968–82; Gen. Adv. Council, BBC, 1976–82. *Address:* Casters Brook, Cocking, near Midhurst, W Sussex GU29 0HJ. *T:* Midhurst (01730) 813537. *Club:* Reform.

See also Katharine Whitehorn.

WHITEHORN, Katharine Elizabeth, (Mrs Gavin Lyall); Columnist, The Observer, since 1960 (Associate Editor, 1980–88); *b* London; *d* of late A. D. and E. M. Whitehorn; *m* 1958, Gavin Lyall, *qv*; two *s*. *Educ:* Blunt House; Roedean; Glasgow High School for Girls, and others; Newnham Coll., Cambridge. Publisher's Reader, 1950–53; Teacher-Secretary in Finland, 1953–54; Grad. Asst, Cornell Univ., USA, 1954–55; Picture Post, 1956–57; Woman's Own, 1958; Spectator, 1959–61. Member: Latey Cttee on Age of Majority, 1965–67; BBC Adv. Gp on Social Effects of Television, 1971–72; Board, British Airports Authority, 1972–77; Council, RSocMed, 1982–85. Director: Nationwide Building Soc., 1983–91; Nationwide Anglia Estate Agents, 1987–90. Vice-Pres., Patients Assoc., 1983–. Rector, St Andrews Univ., 1982–85. Hon. LLD St Andrews, 1985. *Publications:* Cooking in a Bedsitter, 1960; Roundabout, 1961; Only on Sundays, 1966; Whitehorn's Social Survival, 1968; Observations, 1970; How to Survive in Hospital, 1972; How to Survive Children, 1975; Sunday Best, 1976; How to Survive in the Kitchen, 1979; View from a Column, 1981; How to Survive your Money Problems, 1983. *Recreation:* river boat. *Address:* c/o The Observer, 119 Farringdon Road, EC1R 3ER. *T:* 0171–713 4314.

See also J. R. M. Whitehorn.

WHITEHOUSE, Dr David Bryn; Director and Trustee, The Corning Museum of Glass, Corning, USA, since 1992 (Chief Curator, 1984–88; Deputy Director, 1988–92); Trustee, The Rockwell Museum, since 1992; *b* 15 Oct. 1941; *s* of Brindley Charles Whitehouse and Alice Margaret Whitehouse; *m* 1st, 1963, Ruth Delamain Ainger; one *s* two *d*; 2nd, 1975, Elizabeth-Anne Ollemans; one *s* two *d*. *Educ:* King Edward's Sch., Birmingham; St John's Coll., Cambridge. MA, PhD; FSA; FRGS. Scholar, British Sch. at Rome, 1963–65; Wainwright Fellow in Near Eastern Archaeology, Univ. of Oxford, 1966–73; Dir, Sīrāf Expedn, 1966–73; Dir, British Inst. of Afghan Studies, 1973–74; Dir, British Sch. at Rome, 1974–84. President: Internat. Union of Institutes, 1980–81; Internat. Assoc. for Hist. of Glass, 1991– (Mem. Management Cttee, 1988–); Mem. Council, Internat. Assoc. for Classical Archaeology, 1974–84. Corresp. Mem., German Archaeological Inst.; Academician, Accademia Fiorentina dell'Arte del Disegno; Fellow: Pontificia Accademia Romana di Archeologia; Accademia di Archeologia, Lettere e Belle Arti, Naples. Ed., Jl of Glass Studies, 1988–. *Publications:* (jtly) Background to Archaeology, 1973; (jtly) The Origins of Europe, 1974; (with Ruth Whitehouse) Archaeological Atlas of the World, 1975; (ed jtly) Papers in Italian Archaeology I, 1978; Siraf III: The Congregational Mosque, 1980; (with David Andrews and John Osborne) Papers in Italian Archaeology III, 1981; (with Richard Hodges) Mohammed, Charlemagne and the Origins of Europe, 1983; (jtly) Glass of the Caesars, 1987; Glass of the Roman Empire, 1988; (jtly) Treasures from The Corning Museum of Glass, 1992; Glass: a pocket dictionary, 1993; English Cameo Glass, 1994; The Medieval Pottery of Central and Southern Italy, 1996; many papers in Iran, Antiquity, Med. Archaeol., Papers of Brit. Sch. at Rome, Jl of Glass Studies, etc. *Address:* The Corning Museum of Glass, One Museum Way, Corning, NY 14830–2253, USA. *T:* (607) 9375371. *Club:* Athenæum.

WHITEHOUSE, David Rae Beckwith; QC 1990; a Recorder, since 1987; *b* 5 Sept. 1945; *s* of David Barry Beckwith Whitehouse, MA, MD, FRCS, FRCOG and late Mary Beckwith Whitehouse, JP; *m* 1971, Linda Jane, *d* of Eric Vickers, CB and Barbara Mary Vickers; one *s*. *Educ:* Ellesmere College; Choate Sch., Wallingford, Conn., USA; Trinity College, Cambridge (MA). English-Speaking Union Scholarship, 1964. Called to the Bar, Gray's Inn, 1969; practice, SE Circuit. Member: Criminal Bar Assoc., 1969–; Central Criminal Court Bar Mess, 1970– (Cttee, 1981–84); Internat. Bar Assoc. (Business Crime section), 1990–. *Recreations:* the arts, esp. architecture, music and cinema; walking. *Address:* 3 Raymond Buildings, Gray's Inn, WC1R 5BH. *T:* 0171–831 3833, *Fax:* 0171–242 4221.

WHITEHOUSE, Mary, CBE 1980; Founder and President Emeritus, National Viewers' and Listeners' Association (Hon. General Secretary, 1965–80; President, 1980–93); freelance journalist, broadcaster; *b* 13 June 1910; *d* of James and Beatrice Hutcheson; *m* 1940, Ernest R. Whitehouse; three *s*. *Educ:* Chester City Grammar Sch.; Cheshire County Training Coll. Art Specialist: Wednesfield Sch., Wolverhampton, 1932–40; Brewood Grammar Sch., Staffs, 1943; Sen. Mistress, and Sen. Art Mistress, Madeley Sch., Shropshire, 1960–64. Co-founder, "Clean up TV campaign", 1964. *Publications:* Cleaning Up TV, 1966; "Who Does She Think She Is?", 1971; Whatever Happened to Sex?, 1977; A Most Dangerous Woman?, 1982; Mightier than the Sword, 1985; Quite Contrary (autobiog.), 1993. *Recreations:* reading, gardening, walking. *Address:* Ardleigh, Colchester, Essex CO7 7RH. *T:* Colchester (01206) 230123.

WHITEHOUSE, Prof. Norman Harold; Professor of Dental Public Health, and Dean, Dental School, University of Wales College of Medicine, since 1993; Chief Executive, University Dental Hospital NHS Trust, since 1995 (Chief Executive, Cardiff Dental Hospital, 1993–94); *b* 22 April 1938; *y s* of late Norman Lester Whitehouse, builder and Maud Whitehouse, Bloxwich, Walsall, Staffs; *m* 1963, Barbara Palmer; one *s* one *d*. *Educ:* Univ. of Leeds (LDS 1961; BChD 1962); Univ. of Birmingham (DDH 1970); DDPH RCS 1970; FDSRCSE (*ad hominem*) 1995; FDSRCS (by election), 1995. Chief Admin. Dental Officer and Specialist in Community Dental Health, S Glam and E Dyfed HAs, 1974–86; British Dental Association: Sec., 1986–91; Chief Exec. and Sec., 1991–93; Chief Admin. Dental Officer and Dir, Dental Public Health, Mid Glam HA, 1993–; Hon. Consultant in Dental Public Health, S and Mid Glam HAs, 1993–. *Publications:* contrib. articles in jls. *Recreations:* hill-walking, cross-country ski-ing. *Address:* University of Wales College of Medicine, Dental School, Heath Park, Cardiff CF4 4XY. *T:* Cardiff (01222) 742470.

WHITEHOUSE, Paul Chapple, QPM 1993; Chief Constable, Sussex Police, since 1993; *b* 26 Sept. 1944; *s* of Beatrice and Jack Whitehouse, Cambs; *m* 1970, Elizabeth Dinsmore; one *s* one *d*. *Educ:* Ipswich Sch.; Emmanuel Coll., Cambridge (BA 1967; MA 1969). VSO, Starehe Boys' Centre, Nairobi, 1963; Durham Constabulary, 1967; Northumbria Police, 1974; Asst Chief Constable, Greater Manchester Police, 1983; Dep. Chief Constable, W Yorkshire Police, 1987. Association of Chief Police Officers: Chm., Quality of Service Cttee, 1994; Vice-Chm., Media Adv. Group, 1994. Member: Nat. Adv. Council, Common Purpose, 1989; Council, Victim Support, 1993; Council, NACRO, 1994. Chm., Starehe Endowment Fund (UK), 1994. *Recreations:* collecting people, IT, steam, disputation, keeping the peace. *Address:* (office) Malling House, Lewes, E Sussex BN7 2DZ. *T:* Lewes (01273) 404001, *Fax:* (01273) 404263. *Club:* Royal Over-Seas League.

WHITEHOUSE, Walter Alexander; Professor of Theology, University of Kent, 1965–77; Master of Eliot College, University of Kent, 1965–69, and 1973–75; *b* 27 Feb. 1915; *e s* of Walter and Clara Whitehouse, Shelley, near Huddersfield; *m* 1st, 1946, Beatrice Mary Kent Smith (*d* 1971); 2nd, 1974, Audrey Ethel Lemmon. *Educ:* Penistone Gram. Sch.; St John's Coll., Cambridge; Mansfield Coll., Oxford. Minister of Elland Congregational Church, 1940–44; Chaplain at Mansfield College, Oxford, 1944–47; Reader in Divinity, Univ. of Durham, 1947–65. Principal of St Cuthbert's Soc., Univ. of Durham, 1955–60; Pro-Vice-Chancellor of Univ., and Sub-Warden, 1961–64. Minister at High Chapel, Ravenstonedale, 1977–82. Mem. (Lab), Glos CC, 1989–93. Hon. DD Edinburgh, 1960. *Publications:* Christian Faith and the Scientific Attitude, 1952; Order, Goodness, Glory (Riddell Memorial Lectures), 1959; The Authority of Grace, 1981. *Address:* 37 Cotswold Green, Stonehouse, Glos GL10 2ET.

WHITELAW, family name of **Viscount Whitelaw.**

WHITELAW, 1st Viscount *cr* 1983, of Penrith in the County of Cumbria; **William Stephen Ian Whitelaw,** KT 1990; CH 1974; MC; PC 1967; DL; farmer and landowner; *b* 28 June 1918; *s* of late W. A. Whitelaw and Mrs W. A. Whitelaw, Monkland, Nairn; *m* 1943, Cecilia Doriel, 2nd *d* of late Major Mark Sprot, Riddell, Melrose, Roxburghshire; four *d*. *Educ:* Winchester Coll.; Trinity Coll., Camb. Reg. Officer, Scots Guards; Emergency Commn, 1939; resigned Commn, 1947. MP (C) Penrith and the Border Div. of Cumberland, 1955–83; PPS to Chancellor of the Exchequer, 1957–58 (to Pres. of BOT, 1956); Asst Govt Whip, 1959–61; a Lord Comr of the Treasury, 1961–62; Parly Sec., Min. of Labour, July 1962–Oct. 1964; Chief Opposition Whip, 1964–70; Lord Pres. of Council and Leader, House of Commons, 1970–72; Secretary of State for: N Ireland, 1972–73; Employment, 1973–74; Chm., Conservative Party, 1974–75; Dep. Leader of the Opposition and spokesman on home affairs, 1975–79; Home Secretary, 1979–83; Lord President of the Council and Leader, H of L, 1983–88. Visiting Fellow, Nuffield Coll., Oxford, 1970–. DL Dunbartonshire, 1952–66; DL Cumbria, formerly Cumberland, 1967. *Publication:* The Whitelaw Memoirs, 1989. *Recreations:* golf, shooting. *Heir:* none. *Address:* Ennim, Penrith, Cumbria. *Clubs:* White's, Carlton (Chm., 1986–92); Royal and Ancient (Captain 1969–70).

See also Earl of Swinton.

WHITELAW, Billie, CBE 1991; actress; *b* 6 June 1932; *d* of Perceval and Frances Whitelaw; *m* Robert Muller, writer; one *s*. *Educ:* Thornton Grammar Sch., Bradford. Appeared in: *plays:* Hotel Paradiso, Winter Garden, 1954 and Oxford Playhouse, 1956; Progress to the Park, Theatre Workshop and Saville, 1961; England our England, Prince's, 1962; Touch of the Poet, Venice and Dublin, 1962; National Theatre, 1963–65: Othello, London and Moscow; Hobson's Choice; Beckett's Play; Trelawny of the Wells; The Dutch Courtesan; After Haggerty, Criterion, 1971; Not I, Royal Court, 1973 and 1975; Alphabetical Order, Mayfair, 1975; Footfalls, Royal Court, 1976; Molly, Comedy, 1978; Happy Days, Royal Court, 1979; The Greeks, Aldwych, 1980; Passion Play, Aldwych, 1981; Rockaby and Enough, NY, 1981, with Footfalls, 1984, NT 1982, Riverside, 1986, Adelaide Fest., 1986, Purchase Fest., NY, 1986; Tales from Hollywood, NT, 1983; Who's Afraid of Virginia Woolf?, Young Vic, 1987; *films:* No Love for Johnny; Charlie Bubbles; Twisted Nerve; The Adding Machine; Start the Revolution Without Me; Leo the Last; Eagle in a Cage; Gumshoe; Frenzy; Night Watch; The Omen; Leopard in the Snow; The Water Babies; An Unsuitable Job for a Woman; Slayground; Shadey; The Chain; The Dressmaker; Maurice; Joyriders; The Krays; Deadly Advice; Jane Eyre; *television:* No Trams to Lime Street; Lena Oh My Lena; Resurrection; The Skin Game; Beyond the Horizon; Anna Christie; Lady of the Camellias; The Pity of it all; Love on the Dole; A World of Time; You and Me; Poet Game; Sextet (8 plays); Napoleon and Love (9 plays: Josephine); The Fifty Pound Note (Ten from the Twenties); The Withered Arm (Wessex Tales); The Werewolf Reunion (2 plays); Ghost Trio, and But the Clouds, by Samuel Beckett; Not I; Eustace and Hilda (2 plays); The Serpent Son; Happy Days (dir. by Beckett); Private Schulz; Last Summer's Child; A Tale of Two Cities; Jamaica Inn; Camille; Old Girlfriends; The Secret Garden; Imaginary Friends (mini-series); The Picnic; Three Beckett plays; The 15 Streets; Lorna Doone; The Entertainer; A Murder of Quality; The Cloning of Joanna May; Firm Friends I and II (mini-series); *radio plays:* The Master Builder; Hindle Wakes; Jane Eyre; The Female Messiah; Alpha Beta; The Cherry Orchard; Vassa Zhelyezhova; Filumena. Lectr on Beckett at univs of Santa Barbara, Stanford and Denver, 1985; at Balliol Coll., Oxford, 1986; at Smith, Dartmouth, 1992, and Franklyn and Marshall Colls, 1993, USA; An Informal Evening with Samuel Beckett and lecture tours, USA, 1992–95. Annenberg/Beckett Fellow, Reading Univ., 1993. Silver Heart Variety Club Award, 1961; TV Actress of Year, 1961, 1972; British Academy Award, 1968; US Film Critics Award, 1968; Variety Club of GB Best Film Actress Award, 1977; Evening News Film Award as Best Actress, 1977; Sony Best Radio Actress Award, 1987; Evening Standard Film Award for Best Actress, 1988. Hon. DLitt Bradford 1981. *Publication:* Billie Whitelaw: who he? (autobiog.), 1995. *Recreation:* pottering about the house. *Address:* c/o Michael Foster, ICM, Oxford House, 76 Oxford Street, W1R 1RB.

WHITELAW, Prof. James Hunter, FEng 1991; FIMechE; Professor of Convective Heat Transfer, Imperial College, London, since 1974; *b* 28 Jan. 1936; *s* of James Whitelaw and Jean Ross Whitelaw (*née* Scott); *m* 1959, Elizabeth Shields; three *s*. *Educ:* Univ. of Glasgow (BSc 1957; PhD 1961); DSc London 1981. Res. Associate, Brown Univ., 1961–63; Lectr, Imperial Coll., 1963–69; Reader, Imperial Coll., 1969–74. Editor, Experiments in Fluids, 1983–. DSc *hc* Lisbon, 1980. *Publications:* (jtly) Data and Formulae Handbook, 1967, 2nd edn 1976; (jtly) Principles and Practice of Laser-Doppler Anemometry, 1976, 2nd edn 1981; (jtly) Engineering Calculation Methods for Turbulent Flow, 1981; ed. 25 vols proc., and published over 300 papers in learned jls, incl. Jl of Fluid Mechanics, Experiments in Fluids, proc. of learned socs. *Recreations:* gardening, music. *Address:* 149a Coombe Lane West, Kingston-upon-Thames, KT2 7DH. *T:* 0181–942 1836.

WHITELEY, family name of **Baron Marchamley.**

WHITELEY, Maj.-Gen. Gerald Abson, CB 1969; OBE 1952; *b* 4 March 1915; *s* of late Harry Whiteley, Walton Park, Bexhill; *m* 1943, Ellen Hanna (*d* 1973). *Educ:* Worksop Coll.; Emmanuel Coll., Cambridge (MA). Solicitor, 1938. Commissioned, RA, 1940; Maj., DJAG's Staff, ME, 1942–45. AAG, Mil. Dept, JAG's Office, WO, 1945–48; Asst Dir of Army Legal Services: FARELF, 1948–51; WO, 1952–53; Northern Army Gp, 1953–54; MELF, 1954–57; BAOR, 1957–60; Dep. Dir of Army Legal Services, BAOR, 1960–62; Col, Legal Staff, WO, 1962–64; Dir of Army Legal Services, MoD, 1964–69. *Recreations:* photography, walking. *Address:* 8 Kemnal Park, Haslemere, Surrey GU27 2LF. *T:* Haslemere (01428) 642803. *Club:* Army and Navy.

WHITELEY, Sir Hugo Baldwin H.; *see* Huntington-Whiteley.

WHITELEY, Dame Jane; *see* Gow, Dame J. E.

WHITELEY, Gen. Sir Peter (John Frederick), GCB 1979 (KCB 1976); OBE 1960; DL; Lieutenant-Governor and Commander-in-Chief, Jersey, 1979–84; *b* 13 Dec. 1920; *s* of late John George Whiteley; *m* 1948, Nancy Vivian, *d* of late W. Carter Clayden; two *s* two *d*. *Educ:* Bishop's Stortford Coll.; Bembridge Sch.; Ecole des Roches. Joined Royal Marines, 1940; 101 Bde, 1941; HMS: Resolution, 1941; Renown, 1942; HMNZS Gambia, 1942; seconded to Fleet Air Arm, 1946–50; Adjt 40 Commando, 1951; Staff Coll., Camberley, 1954; Bde Major 3rd Commando Bde, 1957; Instructor, Staff Coll., Camberley, 1960–63; CO 42 Commando, 1965–66 (despatches, Malaysia, 1966); Col GS Dept of CGRM, 1966–68; Nato Defence Coll., 1968; Comdr 3rd Commando Bde, 1968–70; Maj.-Gen. Commando Forces, 1970–72; C of S, HQ Allied Forces Northern Europe, 1972–75; Commandant General, Royal Marines, 1975–77; C-in-C Allied Forces Northern Europe, 1977–79. Col Comdt, RM, 1985–87; Hon. Col, 211 (Wessex) Field Hosp. RAMC (Volunteers), TA, 1985–90. Mem., Council, Union Jack Club, 1985–91; Vice Chm., Theatre Royal, Plymouth, 1991–; Pres., W Devon Area, 1985–87, Pres., Devon, 1987–, St John's Ambulance Bde. Trustee, Jersey Wildlife Preservation Trust. Governor: Bembridge Sch., 1981–; Kelly Coll., 1985–94; St Michael's Sch., Tavistock, 1985–89. Member: Royal Commonwealth Soc., 1981–; Anglo Norse Soc., 1980–; Anglo Danish Soc., 1980–; Jersey Soc. in London, 1984–. Liveryman, Fletchers' Co., 1982; Guild of Freemen of City of London: Mem. Ct of Assistants, 1980–; Master, 1987–88. DL Devon, 1987. CIMgt. KStJ 1980; Chevalier, Ordre de la Pléaiade, Assoc. of French Speaking Parliaments, 1984. *Publications:* contribs to Jane's Annual, NATO's Fifteen Nations, RUSI Jl, Nauticus. *Recreations:* music, photography, painting, wood carving, sailing, dogs. *Clubs:* Anchorites; Royal Marines Sailing, Royal Naval Sailing Assoc.

WHITELEY, Samuel Lloyd; Deputy Chief Land Registrar, 1967–73; Legal Assistant to the Clerk to the Haberdashers' Company 1973–78, Freeman, 1978; *b* 30 April 1913; *s* of Rev. Charles Whiteley and Ann Letitia Whiteley; *m* 1939, Kathleen Jones (*d* 1988); two *d*. *Educ:* George Dixon Sch.; Birmingham Univ. LLB (Hons) 1933. Admitted Solicitor, 1935; HM Land Registry, 1936; seconded Official Solicitor's Dept, 1939; RAF, 1940–46; HM Land Registry, 1946–73. *Recreation:* sport, as a reminiscent spectator. *Address:* 8 Stonehaven Court, Knole Road, Bexhill, Sussex TN40 1LW. *T:* Bexhill (01424) 213191.

WHITEMAN, Elizabeth Anne Osborn, DPhil; FRHistS, FSA; JP; Tutor in Modern History 1946–85, Fellow 1948–85, and Vice-Principal 1971–81, Lady Margaret Hall, Oxford; *b* 10 Feb. 1918; *d* of Harry Whitmore Whiteman and Dorothy May (*née* Austin). *Educ:* St Albans High Sch.; Somerville Coll., Oxford (MA 1945, DPhil 1951). FRHistS 1954; FSA 1958. Served War, WAAF, 1940–45: served in N Africa and Italy (mentioned in despatches, 1943). Rep. of Women's Colls, Oxford Univ., 1960–61. Member: Hebdomadal Council, Oxford Univ., 1968–85; Academic Planning Bd, Univ. of Warwick, 1961–65; UGC, 1976–83. Trustee, Ruskin Sch. of Drawing, 1974–77. JP City of Oxford, 1962. *Publications:* (contrib.) Victoria County History, Wilts, Vol. III, 1956; (contrib.) New Cambridge Modern History, Vol. V, 1961; (contrib.) From Uniformity to Unity, ed Chadwick and Nuttall, 1962; (ed with J. S. Bromley and P. G. M. Dickson, and contrib.) Statesmen, Scholars and Merchants: Essays in eighteenth-century History presented to Dame Lucy Sutherland, 1973; (ed with Mary Clapinson) The Compton Census of 1676, 1986; contrib. hist. jls. *Address:* 5 Observatory Street, Oxford OX2 6EW. *T:* Oxford (01865) 511009.

WHITEMAN, Prof. John Robert, PhD; CMath, FIMA; Vice Principal, since 1991, and Professor of Numerical Analysis, since 1981, Brunel University; Director, Brunel Institute of Computational Mathematics, since 1976; *b* 7 Dec. 1938; *s* of Robert Whiteman and Rita (*née* Neale); *m* 1964, Caroline Mary Leigh; two *s* (one *d* decd). *Educ:* Bromsgrove Sch.; Univ. of St Andrews (BSc); Worcester Coll., Oxford (DipEd); Univ. of London (PhD). FIMA 1970. Sen. Lectr, RMCS, Shrivenham, 1963–67; Assistant Professor: Univ. of Wisconsin, 1967–68; Univ. of Texas, Austin, 1968–70; Reader in Numerical Analysis, Brunel Univ., 1970–76; Richard Merton Gästprofessor, Univ. of Münster, 1975–76; Hd of Dept of Maths and Statistics, Brunel Univ., 1982–90. Visiting Professor: Univ. of Pisa, 1975; Univ. of Kuwait, 1986; Texas A & M Univ., 1986, 1988, 1989, 1990, 1992; Univ. of Stuttgart, 1989, 1992; Lectures: Geary, City Univ., 1986; Robert Todd Gregory, Univ. of Texas, Austin, 1990; Collatz Gedenkkolloquium, Hamburg Univ, 1991; Univ. of Stuttgart, 1995. Mem., SERC Maths Cttee, 1981–86 and Science Bd, 1989–91. FRSA. Hon. DSc West Bohemia Univ., 1995. Editor, Numerical Methods for Partial Differential Equations, 1985–; Member, Editorial Board: Computer Methods in Applied Mechanics and Engrg; Communications in Applied Numerical Methods; Internat. Jl for Numerical Methods in Fluids; Jl of Mathematical Engrg in Industry; Jl of Engrg Analysis. *Publications:* (ed) The Mathematics of Finite Elements and Applications, vols 1–8, 1973, 1976, 1979, 1982, 1985, 1988, 1991, 1994; numerous works on numerical solution of partial differential equations, particularly finite element methods for singularities in elliptic problems and for problems of linear and non linear solid mechanics. *Recreations:* walking, swimming, golf, orchestral and choral music. *Address:* Institute of Computational Mathematics, Brunel University, Uxbridge, Middx UB8 3PH. *T:* Uxbridge (01895) 203270.

WHITEMAN, Peter George; QC 1977; barrister-at-law; a Recorder, since 1989; Attorney and Counselor at Law, State of New York; Professor of Law, University of Virginia, since 1980; Member, Faculty of Laws, Florida University, since 1977; *b* 8 Aug. 1942; *s* of David Whiteman and Betsy Bessie Coster; *m* 1971, Katherine Ruth (*née* Ellenbogen); two *d*. *Educ:* Warwick Secondary Modern Sch.; Leyton County High Sch.; LSE (LLB, LLM with Distinction). Called to the Bar, Lincoln's Inn, 1967, Bencher, 1985; *ad eundem* Middle Temple, 1977. Lectr, London Univ., 1966–70. Visiting Professor: Virginia Univ., 1978; Univ. of California at Berkeley, 1980. Mem. Cttee, Unitary Tax Campaign (UK), 1982–. Pres., Dulwich Village Preservation Soc., 1987–; Chairman: Dulwich against the Rail Link, 1988–; Dulwich Jt Residents' Cttee, 1991–. Member: Cttee Dulwich Picture Gall., 1989–; Adv. Cttee, Dulwich Estate Govs' Scheme of Management, 1988–. FRSA. Mem. Bd, Univ. of Virginia Jl of Internat. Law, 1981–. *Publications:* Whiteman on Capital Gains Tax, 1967, 4th edn 1988; Whiteman on Income Tax, 1971, 3rd edn 1988; contrib. British Tax Encyc. *Recreations:* tennis, squash, mountain-walking, jogging, croquet. *Address:* University of Virginia School of Law, Charlottesville, VA 22901, USA. *T:* (804) 9243996; Hollis Whiteman Chambers, Queen Elizabeth Building, Temple, EC4Y 9BS. *T:* 0171–936 3131.

WHITEMAN, Ven. Rodney David Carter; Archdeacon of Bodmin, since 1989; *b* Par, Cornwall, 6 Oct. 1940; *s* of Leonard Archibald Whiteman and Sybil Mary (*née* Morshead); *m* 1969, Christine Anne Chelton; one *s* one *d*. *Educ:* St Austell Grammar School; Pershore Coll. of Horticulture; Ely Theological Coll. Deacon 1964, priest 1965; Curate of Kings Heath, Birmingham, 1964–70; Vicar: St Stephen, Rednal, Birmingham, 1970–79; St Barnabas, Erdington, 1979–89; RD of Aston, 1981–89; Hon. Canon of Birmingham Cathedral, 1985–89; Priest-in-charge of Cardinham with Helland, 1989–94; Hon. Canon of Truro Cathedral, 1989–. *Recreations:* gardening, music, historic buildings and monuments, walking. *Address:* The Rectory, Cardinham, Bodmin, Cornwall PL30 4BL. *T:* Cardinham (01208) 821614.

WHITEMORE, Hugh John; dramatist; *b* 16 June 1936; *s* of Samuel George Whitemore and Kathleen Alma Whitemore (*née* Fletcher); *m* 1st, Jill Brooke (marr. diss.); 2nd, 1976, Sheila Lemon (marr. diss.); one *s*. *Educ:* King Edward VI School, Southampton; RADA. *Stage:* Stevie, Vaudeville, 1977; Pack of Lies, Lyric, 1983; Breaking the Code, Haymarket, 1986, transf. Comedy, 1987 (Amer. Math. Soc. Communications Award, 1990); The Best of Friends, Apollo, 1988; It's Ralph, Comedy, 1991; *television:* plays and dramatisations include: Elizabeth R (Emmy award, 1970); Cider with Rosie (Writer's Guild award, 1971); Country Matters (Writer's Guild award, 1972); Dummy (RAI Prize, Prix Italia, 1979); Concealed Enemies (Emmy award, Neil Simon Jury award, 1984); The Final Days, 1989; *films:* Stevie, 1980; The Return of the Soldier, 1982; 84 Charing Cross Road, 1986 (Scriptor Award, Los Angeles, 1988); Utz, 1992; Jane Eyre, 1995. *Publications:* (contrib) Elizabeth R, 1972; Stevie, 1977, new edn 1984; (contrib.) My Drama School, 1978; (contrib.) Ah, Mischief!, 1982; Pack of Lies, 1983; Breaking the Code, 1986; The Best of Friends, 1988; It's Ralph, 1991. *Recreations:* music, movies, reading. *Address:* c/o Judy Daish Associates, 2 St Charles Place, W10 6EG. *T:* 0181–964 8811. *Club:* Garrick.

WHITEOAK, John Edward Harrison, MA, CIPFA; Group Director, Resources, since 1994, and County Treasurer, since 1981, Cheshire County Council; *b* 5 July 1947; *s* of Frank Whiteoak, farmer, and Marion Whiteoak; *m* 1st, 1969, Margaret Elizabeth Blakey (decd); one *s* two *d*; 2nd, 1983, Karen Lynne Wallace Stevenson, MB ChB, BSc; two *d*. *Educ:* Sheffield Univ. (MA). CIPFA 1971. Various positions in local govt, 1966–79 (Skipton RDC and UDC, Solihull CBC and MBC, Cleveland CC); Dep. County Treasurer, Cheshire CC, 1979–81. Financial Advr, ACC, 1984–. Lead negotiator on local govt finance for local authorities in England, 1994–. Member: Soc. of County Treasurers, 1981–; Accounting Standards Cttee, 1984–87. Chartered Institute of Public Finance and Accountancy: Mem., Technical Cttee, 1986–87 and 1991–; Mem., Accounting Panel, 1984–87 (Chm., 1987); Chm., Financial Reporting Panel, 1991–94; Chm., Corporate Governance Working Party, 1994; Pres., NW Region, 1994–95. *Publications:* (jtly) Public Sector Accounting and Financial Control, 1992; contrib. various professional and management journals. *Recreations:* social golf, tennis, snooker. *Address:* Huntington Hall, Chester CH3 6EA. *T:* (home) Chester (01244) 312901; (business) Chester (01244) 602000. *Clubs:* Royal Automobile; City (Chester); Eaton Golf.

WHITESIDE, Prof. Derek Thomas, PhD; FBA 1975; University Professor of History of Mathematics and Exact Sciences, Cambridge, since 1987; *b* 23 July 1932; *s* of Ernest Whiteside and Edith (*née* Watts); *m* 1962, Ruth Isabel Robinson; one *s* one *d*. *Educ:* Blackpool Grammar Sch.; Bristol Univ. (BA); Cambridge Univ. (PhD). Leverhulme Research Fellow, 1959–61; DSIR Research Fellow, 1961–63; Research Asst, 1963–72, Asst Dir of Research, 1972–76, University Reader in History of Mathematics, 1976–87, Univ. of Cambridge. Hon. DLitt Lancaster, 1987. Médaille Koyré, Académie Internat. d'Histoire des Sciences, 1968; Sarton Medal, Amer. History of Sci. Soc., 1977. *Publications:* Patterns of Mathematical Thought in the later Seventeenth Century, 1961; (ed) The Mathematical Papers of Isaac Newton, 1967–; (ed) The Preliminary Manuscripts for Isaac Newton's 1687 Principia: 1684–1685 (in facsimile), 1989; articles in Brit. Jl Hist. Science, Jl for Hist. of Astronomy, Physis, etc.; *Festschrift:* The Investigation of Difficult Things, 1992. *Recreation:* looking into space creatively. *Address:* Department of Pure Mathematics and Mathematical Statistics, 16 Mill Lane, Cambridge CB2 1SB.

WHITFIELD, family name of **Baron Kenswood.**

WHITFIELD, Adrian; QC 1983; a Recorder of the Crown Court since 1981; *b* 10 July 1937; *s* of Peter Henry Whitfield and Margaret Mary Burns; *m* 1st, 1962, Lucy Caroline Beckett (marr. diss.); two *d*; 2nd, 1971, Niamh O'Kelly; one *s* one *d*. *Educ:* Ampleforth Coll.; Magdalen Coll., Oxford (Demy; MA). 2nd Lieut, KOYLI (Nat. Service), 1956–58. Called to the Bar, Middle Temple, 1964, Bencher 1990; Member of Western Circuit. Chm., NHS Tribunal, 1993–. Vis. Fellow, Centre of Law and Med. Ethics, KCL, 1993–. *Publications:* contribs on legal matters in medical and dental pubns. *Recreations:* reading, visual arts, travel. *Address:* 47 Faroe Road, W14 0EL. *T:* 0171–603 8982; 3 Serjeants' Inn, EC4Y 1BQ *T:* 0171–353 5537.

WHITFIELD, Alan; Chief Highways Engineer, Ove Arup & Partners, since 1995; *b* 19 April 1939; *s* of John J. Whitfield and Annie Fothergill-Rawe; *m* 1964, Sheila Carr; two *s*. *Educ:* Consett Grammar Sch., Durham; Sunderland and Newcastle Colls of Advanced Technology. MICE 1968; MIMunE 1969; FIHT 1984. Surveyor/Engr, NCB, 1956–62; Engrg Asst, Northumberland CC, 1962–70; Department of Transport: Main Grade Engr, 1970–73; Prin. Professional, 1973–76; Suptg Engr, 1976–80; Dep. Dir, Midlands Road Construction Unit, 1980–83; Dir (Transport), W Midlands Reg. Office, 1983–89; Regl Dir, Eastern Region, DoE and Dept of Transport, 1989; Road Prog. Div., Dept of Transport, 1989–94, Highways Agency, 1994–95. *Publications:* papers on cost benefit analysis, centrifugal testing soils, road design and construction, etc. to IHT, ICE, Inst. Geo. Sci., etc. *Recreations:* bridge, golf, music. *Address:* Ove Arup & Partners, The Oaks, Westwood Way, Coventry CV4 8JB. *Club:* Royal Automobile.

WHITFIELD, Prof. Charles Richard, MD; FRCOG; FRCPGlas; Regius Professor of Midwifery in the University of Glasgow, 1976–92, now Emeritus; *b* 21 Oct. 1927; *s* of Charles Alexander and Aileen Muriel Whitfield; *m* 1953, Marion Douglas McKinney; one *s* two *d*. *Educ:* Campbell Coll., Belfast; Queen's Univ., Belfast (MD). House Surg. and Ho. Phys. appts in Belfast teaching hospitals, 1951–53; Specialist in Obstetrics and Gynaecology, RAMC (Lt-Col retd), 1953–64; Sen. Lectr/Hon. Reader in Dept of Midwifery and Gynaecology, Queen's Univ., Belfast, 1964–74; Consultant to Belfast teaching hosps, 1964–74; Prof. of Obstetrics and Gynaecology, Univ. of Manchester, 1974–76. Mem. Council, RCOG, 1985–91 (Chairman: Subspecialty Bd, 1984–89; Scottish Exec. Cttee, 1985–91; Higher Trng Cttee, 1989–92). *Publications:* (ed) Dewhurst's Obstetrics and Gynaecology for Postgraduates, 4th edn 1985, 5th edn 1995; papers on perinatal medicine, pregnancy anaemia and other obstetric and gynaec. topics in med. and scientific jls. *Recreations:* food, travel, sun-worship. *Address:* Redlands, 23 Thorn Road, Bearsden, Glasgow G61 4BS.

WHITFIELD, Rev. George Joshua Newbold; General Secretary, Church of England Board of Education, 1969–74; *b* 2 June 1909; *s* of late Joshua Newbold and Eva Whitfield; *m* 1937, Dr Audrey Priscilla Dence, *d* of late Rev. A. T. Dence; two *s* two *d*. *Educ:* Bede Gram. Sch., Sunderland; King's Coll., Univ. of London; Bishops' Coll., Cheshunt. BA 1st cl. Hons, Engl. and AKC, 1930 (Barry Prizeman); MA 1935. Asst Master, Trin. Sch., Croydon, 1931–34; Sen. Engl. Master: Doncaster Gram. Sch., 1934–36; Hymers Coll., Hull, 1937–43; Headmaster: Tavistock Gram. Sch., 1943–46; Stockport Sch., 1946–50; Hampton Sch., 1950–68 (Whitfield Building opened 1990). Chief Examr in Engl., Univ. of Durham Sch. Exams Bd, 1940–43. Deacon, 1962; Priest, 1963. Member: Duke of Edinburgh's Award Adv. Cttee, 1960–66; Headmasters' Conf., 1964–68; Corporation of Church House, 1974–; Pres., Headmasters' Assoc., 1967; Chm., Exeter Diocesan Educn Cttee, 1981–88. *Publications:* (ed) Teaching Poetry, 1937; An Introduction to Drama, 1938; God and Man in the Old Testament, 1949; (ed) Poetry in the Sixth Form, 1950; Philosophy and Religion, 1955; (jtly) Christliche Erziehung in Europa, Band I, England, 1975. *Recreations:* gardening, photography. *Address:* Bede Lodge, 31A Rolle Road, Exmouth, Devon EX8 2AW. *T:* Exmouth (01395) 274162.

WHITFIELD, John; Solicitor, family firm of Whitfield Hallam Goodall (formerly Whitfield Son and Hallam), of Batley, Dewsbury and Mirfield, since 1965; *b* 31 Oct. 1941; *s* of Sydney Richard Whitfield and Mary Rishworth Whitfield; *m*; three *s*. *Educ:* Sedbergh

Sch.; Leeds Univ. (LLB). MP (C) Dewsbury, 1983–87. Contested (C) Dewsbury, 1987 and 1992. Dir, Thomas Carr Ltd. *Recreations:* fishing, shooting, fighting socialism in all its manifestations. *Address:* Haughtop Farm, Krumlin, Barkisland, Halifax HX4 0EL. *T:* Halifax (01422) 822994. *Clubs:* Flyfishers'; Mirfield Constitutional; Tanfield Angling.

WHITFIELD, John Flett, JP, DL; Chairman, Surrey Police Authority, 1985–89; Chairman of Police Committee, Association of County Councils, 1985–88; *b* 1 June 1922; *s* of John and Bertha Whitfield; *m* 1946, Rosemary Elisabeth Joan Hartman; two *d. Educ:* Epsom Coll., Surrey. Served War, King's Royal Rifle Corps, 1939–46. HM Foreign Service, 1946–57; Director, Materials Handling Equipment (GB) Ltd, 1957–61; London Director, Hunslet Holdings Ltd, 1961–64. Director, Sunningdale Golf Club, 1973–77. Councillor: Berkshire CC, 1961–70; Surrey CC, 1970–89 (Chm., 1981–84). Contested (C) Pontefract, General Election, 1964. JP Berkshire 1971–, Chm. Windsor County Bench, 1978–80; DL Surrey 1982, High Sheriff, 1985–86. Chm., Surrey Univ. Council, 1986–88 (Vice-Chm., 1983–86). *Recreations:* golf, foreign languages, bookbinding. *Address:* Moor Cottage, Chobham Road, Sunningdale, Berks SL5 0HU. *T:* Ascot (01344) 20997. *Clubs:* Royal and Ancient Golf of St Andrews; Royal Cinque Ports Golf; Sunningdale Golf; Rye Golf.

WHITFIELD, June Rosemary, (Mrs T. J. Aitchison), OBE 1985; actress; *b* 11 Nov. 1925; *d* of John Herbert Whitfield and Bertha Georgina Whitfield; *m* 1955, Timothy John Aitchison; one *d. Educ:* Streatham Hill High School; RADA (Diploma 1944). Revue, musicals, pantomime, TV and radio; worked with Arthur Askey, Benny Hill, Frankie Howerd, Dick Emery, Bob Monkhouse, Leslie Crowther, Ronnie Barker; first worked with Terry Scott in 1969; *radio:* series include: Take It From Here (with Dick Bentley and Jimmy Edwards, 1953–60; The News Huddlines (with Roy Hudd and Chris Emmett), 1984–95; JW Radio Special, 1992; serials (as Miss Marple): Murder at the Vicarage, 1993; A Pocketful of Rye, 1994; At Bertram's Hotel, 1995; *films:* Carry on Nurse, 1959; Carry on Abroad, 1972; Bless This House, 1972; Carry on Girls, 1973; Carry On Columbus, 1992; *television:* This Is Your Life, 1976 and 1985; series include: Fast and Loose (with Bob Monkhouse), 1954; Faces of Jim (with Jimmy Edwards), 1962, 1963; Beggar My Neighbour, 1966, 1967; Scott On . . . (with Terry Scott), 1969–73; Happy Ever After, 1974; Terry and June, 1979–87; Cluedo, 1990; Absolutely Fabulous, 1993, 1994 and 1995; What's My Line?, 1994, 1995; *stage:* An Ideal Husband, Chichester, 1987; Ring Round the Moon, Chichester, 1988; Over My Dead Body, Savoy, 1989; Babes in the Wood, Croydon, 1990, Plymouth, 1991, Cardiff, 1992; Cinderella, Wimbledon, 1994. Freeman, City of London, 1982. Lifetime Achievement Award, British Comedy Awards, 1994. *Address:* c/o April Young, 11 Woodlands Road, Barnes, SW13 0JZ. *T:* 0181–876 7030.

WHITFIELD, Dr Michael, CChem, FRSC; FIBiol; Director and Secretary, Marine Biological Association, since 1987; Director, Plymouth Marine Laboratory, since 1994 (Deputy Director, 1988–94); *b* 15 June 1940; *s* of Arthur and Ethel Whitfield; *m* 1961, Jean Ann Rowe (*d* 1984); one *s* three *d. Educ:* Univ. of Leeds (BSc 1st cl. Hons Chem.; PhD Chem.). FRSC 1980; FIBiol 1994. Research Scientist, CSIRO Div. of Fisheries and Oceanography, Cronulla, NSW, 1964–69; Vis. Res. Fellow, KTH Stockholm, 1969, Univ. of Liverpool, 1970; Res. Scientist, Marine Biolog. Assoc., 1970–87. Vice Pres., Sir Alister Hardy Foundn for Ocean Science, 1991–. FRSA 1992. Dr (*hc*) Univ. of Göteborg, 1991. *Publications:* Ion-selective electrodes for the analysis of natural waters, 1970; Marine Electrochemistry, 1981; Tracers in the Ocean, 1988; Light and Life in the Sea, 1990; numerous papers in professional jls. *Recreations:* hill walking, bird watching, photography. *Address:* The Laboratory, Citadel Hill, Plymouth PL1 2PB. *T:* Plymouth (01752) 669762.

WHITFIELD, Prof. Roderick; Percival David Professor of Chinese and East Asian Art, University of London, since 1993 (Professor of Chinese and East Asian Art, and Head of Percival David Foundation of Chinese Art, 1984–93); *b* 20 July 1937; *s* of late John Humphreys Whitfield and Joan Herrin, ARCA; *m* 1st, 1963, Frances Elizabeth Oldfield, PhD (marr. diss 1983), *e d* of late Prof. R. C. Oldfield and Lady Kathleen Oldfield; one *s* two *d*; 2nd, 1983, Youngsook Pak, PhD, art historian, *e d* of late Pak Sang-Jon, Seoul. *Educ:* Woodbourne Acad.; King Edward's Sch., Birmingham; Sch. of Oriental and African Studies (Civil Service Interpreter, 2nd cl.); St John's Coll., Cambridge (BA Hons 1960, Oriental Studies Tripos); Princeton Univ. (MA 1963, PhD 1965). Research Associate and Lectr, Princeton, 1965–66; Research Fellow, St John's Coll., Cambridge, 1966–68; Asst Keeper I, Dept of Oriental Antiquities, British Museum, 1968–84. Trustee, Inst. of Buddhist Studies, 1987–. Mem. Editl Bd, Artibus Asiae, 1992–. *Publications:* In Pursuit of Antiquity: Chinese paintings of Ming and Ch'ing dynasties in collection of Mr and Mrs Earl Morse, 1969; The Art of Central Asia: the Stein collection at the British Museum, 3 vols, 1983–85; (ed) Treasures from Korea, 1984; (ed) Korean Art Treasures, 1986; (ed) Early Chinese Glass, 1988; Caves of the Thousand Buddhas, 1990; (ed) Problems in Meaning in Early Chinese Ritual Bronzes, 1993; Fascination of Nature: plants and insects in Chinese paintings and ceramics of the Yuan dynasty, 1993; Dunhuang, Caves of the Singing Sands: Buddhist Art from the Silk Road, 2 vols, 1995; articles in Asiatische Studien, Buddhica Britannica, Orientations, Burlington Magazine and other jls. *Address:* 7 St Paul's Crescent, NW1 9XN. *T:* 0171–267 2888.

WHITFIELD, Sir William, Kt 1993; CBE 1976; RIBA; Senior Partner, Whitfield Partners, architects. DipArch; DipTP. Prof. of Architecture, Victoria Univ. of Manchester, 1981. Surveyor to the Fabric, St Paul's Cathedral, 1985–90. Mem., Royal Fine Art Commn. Trustee, British Museum. *Address:* Whitfield Partners, 63–67 Carter Lane, EC4V 5HE. *T:* 0171–332 0324.

WHITFIELD LEWIS, Herbert John; *see* Lewis, H. J. W.

WHITFORD, Hon. Sir John (Norman Keates), Kt 1970; Judge of the High Court, Chancery Division, 1970–88; *b* 24 June 1913; *s* of Harry Whitford and Ella Mary Keates; *m* 1946, Rosemary, *d* of John Barcham Green and Emily Paillard; four *d. Educ:* University College School; Munich University; Peterhouse, Cambridge. President, ADC. Called to the Bar: Inner Temple, 1935; Middle Temple, 1946 (Bencher 1970). Served with RAFVR, 1939–44: Wing Comdr, 1942; Chief Radar Officer and Dep. Chief Signals Officer, Air Headquarters Eastern Mediterranean; Advisor on patents and information exchanged for war purposes, HM Embassy, Washington, 1944–45. QC 1965. Member of Bar Council, 1968–70. Chm., Departmental Cttee on Law Relating to Copyright and Designs, 1974–76. *Address:* 140 High Street, West Malling, Kent ME19 6NE.

WHITHAM, Prof. Gerald Beresford, FRS 1965; Charles Lee Powell Professor of Applied Mathematics, at the California Institute of Technology, Pasadena, Calif, since 1983; *b* 13 Dec. 1927; *s* of Harry and Elizabeth Ellen Whitham; *m* 1951, Nancy (*née* Lord); one *s* two *d. Educ:* Elland Gram. Sch., Elland, Yorks; Manchester University. PhD Maths, Manchester, 1953. Lectr in Applied Mathematics, Manchester Univ., 1953–56; Assoc. Prof., Applied Mathematics, New York Univ., 1956–59; Prof., Mathematics, MIT, 1959–62; Prof. of Aeronautics and Maths, 1962–67, Prof. of Applied Maths, 1967–83, CIT. FAAAS 1959. Wiener Prize in Applied Mathematics, 1980. *Publications:* Linear and Nonlinear Waves, 1974; Lectures on Wave Propagation, 1979; research papers in Proc. Roy. Soc., Jl Fluid Mechanics, Communications on Pure and Applied Maths. *Address:* Applied Mathematics 217–50, California Institute of Technology, Pasadena, CA 91125, USA.

WHITING, Alan; Under Secretary, Financial Regulation (formerly Securities and Investment Services), HM Treasury, since 1992; *b* 14 Jan. 1946; *s* of Albert Edward and Marjorie Irene Whiting; *m* 1968, Annette Frances Pocknee; two *s* two *d. Educ:* Acklam Hall Grammar Sch., Middlesbrough; Univ. of East Anglia (BA Hons); University College London (MSc Econ). Research Associate and Asst Lectr, Univ. of East Anglia, 1967; Cadet Economist, HM Treasury, 1968; Economic Asst, DEA, and Min. of Technology, 1969; Economist, EFTA, Geneva, 1970; Economist, CBI, 1972; Economic Adviser, DTI, 1974; Sen. Econ. Adviser, 1979; Industrial Policy Div., Dept of Industry, 1983–85; Under Sec., Economics Div., 1985; Finance and Resource Management Div., DTI, 1989–92. *Publications:* (jtly) The Trade Effects of EFTA and the EEC 1959–1967, 1972; (ed) The Economics of Industrial Subsidies, 1975; articles in economic jls. *Recreations:* building, gardening, music, sailing. *Address:* HM Treasury, Parliament Street, SW1P 3AG. *Club:* Littleton Sailing.

WHITING, Rev. Peter Graham, CBE 1984; Minister, Beechen Grove Baptist Church, since 1985; *b* 7 Nov. 1930; *s* of late Rev. Arthur Whiting and Olive Whiting; *m* 1960, Lorena Inns; two *s* three *d. Educ:* Yeovil Grammar Sch.; Irish Baptist Theol Coll., Dublin. Ordained into Baptist Ministry, 1956. Minister, King's Heath, Northampton, 1956–62; commnd RAChD, 1962; Regtl Chaplain, 1962–69 (Chaplain to 1st Bn The Parachutte Regt, 1964–66); Sen. Chaplain, 20 Armd Bde and Lippe Garrison, BAOR, 1969–72; Staff Chaplain, HQ BAOR, 1973–74; Sen. Chaplain, 24 Airportable Bde, 1974–75; Dep. Asst Chaplain Gen., W Midland Dist, Shrewsbury, 1975–78 (Sen. Chaplain, Young Entry Units, 1976–78); Asst Chaplain Gen., 1st British Corps, BAOR, 1978–81; Dep. Chaplain Gen. to the Forces (Army), 1981–84. QHC 1981–85. *Address:* 264 Hempstead Road, Watford, Herts WD1 3LY. *T:* (office) Watford (01923) 241858; (home) Watford (01923) 253197.

WHITLAM, Hon. (Edward) Gough, AC 1978; QC 1962; Member: Executive Board of Unesco, 1985–89 (Australian Ambassador to Unesco, 1983–86); Constitutional Commission, 1986–88; Prime Minister of Australia, 1972–75; *b* 11 July 1916; *s* of late H. F. E. Whitlam, Australian Crown Solicitor and Aust. rep. on UN Human Rights Commission; *m* 1942, Margaret Elaine, AO, *d* of late Mr Justice Dovey, NSW Supreme Court; three *s* one *d. Educ:* University of Sydney. BA 1938; LLB 1946. RAAF Flight Lieut, 1941–45. Barrister, 1947; MP for Werriwa, NSW, 1952–78; Mem., Jt Parly Cttee on Constitutional Rev., 1956–59; Leader, 1973 and 1975, Dep. Leader, 1977, Constnl Conventions; Deputy Leader, Aust. Labor Party, 1960, Leader, 1967–77; Leader of the Opposition, 1967–72 and 1976–77; Minister for Foreign Affairs, 1972–73. Vis. Fellow, 1978–79, First Nat. Fellow, 1980–81, ANU; Fellow, Univ. of Sydney Senate, 1981–83, 1986–89; Vis. Prof., Harvard Univ., 1979. Chairman: Australia–China Council, 1986–91; Australian Nat. Gall., 1987–90. Pres., Australian Sect., Internat. Commn of Jurists, 1982–83. Founder, Hanoi Architectural Foundn, 1993. FAHA 1993. Corresp. Mem., Acad. of Athens, 1992. Hon. DLitt: Sydney, 1981; Wollongong, 1989; La Trobe, Wodonga, 1992; Hon. LLD Philippines, 1974. Silver Plate of Honour, Socialist Internat., 1976; Mem. of Honour, IUCN, 1988; Redmond Barry Award, 1994. *Publications:* The Constitution *versus* Labor, 1957; Australian Foreign Policy, 1963; Socialism within the Constitution, 1965; Australia, Base or Bridge?, 1966; Beyond Vietnam: Australia's Regional Responsibility, 1968; An Urban Nation, 1969; A New Federalism, 1971; Urbanised Australia, 1972; Australian Public Administration and the Labor Government, 1973; Australia's Foreign Policy: New Directions, New Definitions, 1973; Road to Reform: Labor in Government, 1975; The New Federalism: Labor's Programs and Policies, 1975; Government of the People, for the People—by the People's House, 1975; On Australia's Constitution, 1977; Reform During Recession, 1978; The Truth of the Matter, 1979, 2nd edn 1983; The Italian Inspiration in English Literature, 1980; A Pacific Community, 1981; The Cost of Federalism, 1983; The Whitlam Government 1972–75, 1985; International Law-Making, 1989; Australia's Administrative Amnesia, 1990; Living with the United States: British Dominions and New Pacific States, 1990; National and International Maturity, 1991; Human Rights in One Nation, 1992. *Address:* 100 William Street, Sydney, NSW 2011, Australia.

See also N. R. Whitlam.

WHITLAM, Michael Richard; Director-General, The British Red Cross Society, since 1991; *b* 25 March 1947; *s* of late Richard William Whitlam and Mary Elizabeth Whitlam (*née* Land); *m* 1968, Anne Jane McCurley; two *d. Educ:* Morley Grammar Sch.; Tadcaster Grammar Sch.; Coventry Coll. of Educn, Univ. of Warwick (Cert. of Educn); Home Office Prison Dept Staff Coll. (Qual. Asst Governor Prison Dept); Cranfield Coll. of Technology (MPhil 1988). Biology teacher, Ripon, 1968–69; Asst Governor, HM Borstal, Hollesley Bay and HM Prison, Brixton, 1969–74; Dir, Hammersmith Teenage Project, NACRO, 1974–78; Dep. Dir/Dir, UK ops, Save the Children Fund, 1978–86; Chief Exec., RNID, 1986–90. Board Member: Britcross Ltd, 1991–; British Red Cross Events Ltd, 1991–; British Red Cross Trading, 1991–; Chm., Sound Advantage plc, 1988–90. Member: Exec. Council, Howard League, 1974–84; Community Alternative Young Offenders Cttee, NACRO, 1979–82; Exec. Council, Nat. Children's Bureau, 1980–86; Bd, City Literary Inst., 1989–90; Bd, Charity Appointments Ltd, 1990–; Chairman: London Intermediate Treatment Assoc., 1980–83; Assoc. of Chief Execs of Nat. Voluntary Orgns, 1988– (Mem. Policy and Res. Gp, 1994–). FRSA. *Publications:* numerous papers on juvenile delinquency and charity management. *Recreations:* painting, walking, family activities, voluntary organisations, politics, visiting France, cooking. *Address:* (office) 9 Grosvenor Crescent, SW1X 7EJ. *Club:* New Cavendish.

WHITLAM, Nicholas Richard; Chief Executive, Whitlam & Co., since 1990; Adviser, Asian Capital Partners, since 1993; *b* 6 Dec. 1945; *s* of Hon. (Edward) Gough Whitlam, *qv*; *m* 1973, Sandra Judith Frye; two *s* one *d. Educ:* Sydney High Sch.; Harvard Coll. (AB Hons); London Business Sch. (MBA). Morgan Guaranty Trust Co., 1969–75; American Express Co., 1975–78; Banque Paribas, 1978–80; Comr, Rural Bank of New South Wales, 1980–81, then Man. Dir, State Bank of New South Wales, 1981–87; Man. Dir, Whitlam Turnbull & Co. Ltd, 1987–90. Dep. Chm., Export Finance and Insurance Corp., 1991–94. Board Member: Aust. Graduate Sch. of Management, 1982– (Chm., 1988–); Aust. Trade Commn, 1985–91; Aust. Sports Foundn, 1986–; Sydney Symphony Orch., 1991– (Chm.); Trustee, Sydney Cricket and Sports Ground, 1984–88. *Recreations:* swimming, cycling. *Address:* Level 3, 6–10 O'Connell Street, Sydney, NSW 2000, Australia. *T:* (2) 2337300. *Clubs:* Hong Kong; Tattersall's (Chm., 1993–), Whale Beach Surf (Sydney).

WHITLEY, Elizabeth Young, (Mrs H. C. Whitley); social worker and journalist; *b* 28 Dec. 1915; *d* of Robert Thom and Mary Muir Wilson; *m* 1939, Henry Charles Whitley (Very Rev. Dr H. C. Whitley, CVO; *d* 1976); two *s* two *d* (and one *s* decd). *Educ:* Laurelbank School, Glasgow; Glasgow University. MA 1936; courses: in Italian at Perugia Univ., 1935, in Social Science at London School of Economics and Glasgow School of Social Science, 1938–39. Ran Girls' Clubs in Govan and Plantation, Glasgow, and Young Mothers' Clubs in Partick and Port Glasgow; Vice-Chm. Scottish Association of Girls'

Clubs and Mixed Clubs, 1957–61, and Chm. of Advisory Cttee, 1958–59. Broadcast regular programme with BBC (Scottish Home Service), 1953. Member: Faversham Committee on AID, 1958–60; Pilkington Committee on Broadcasting, 1960–62. Columnist, Scottish Daily Express. Adopted as Parly candidate for SNP by West Perth and Kinross, 1968. *Publications:* Plain Mr Knox, 1960; The Two Kingdoms: the story of the Scottish covenanters, 1977; descriptive and centenary articles for Scottish papers, particularly Glasgow Herald and Scotland's Magazine. *Recreations:* reading, gardening. *Address:* The Glebe, Southwick, by Dumfries DG2 8AR. *T:* Southwick (01387) 780276.

WHITLEY, John Reginald; His Honour Judge Whitley; a Circuit Judge, since 1986; *b* 22 March 1926; *o s* of late Reginald Whitley and of Marjorie Whitley (*née* Orton); *m* 1966, Susan Helen Kennaway; one *d*. *Educ:* Sherborne Sch.; Corpus Christi Coll., Cambridge. Served War, Army, Egypt, Palestine, 1944–48; commissioned, KRRC, 1945. Called to the Bar, Gray's Inn, 1953; Western Circuit, 1953; a Recorder, 1978–86. *Recreation:* golf. *Address:* Kingsrod, Friday's Hill, Kingsley Green, near Haslemere, Surrey GU27 3LL.

WHITLEY, Air Marshal Sir John (René), KBE 1956 (CBE 1945); CB 1946; DSO 1943; AFC 1937, Bar, 1956; *b* 7 September 1905; *s* of late A. Whitley, Condette, Pas de Calais, France; *m* 1st, 1932, Barbara Liscombe (*d* 1965); three *s* (and one *s* decd); 2nd, 1967, Alison (*d* 1986), *d* of Sir Nigel Campbell and *widow* of John Howard Russell; three step *s*. *Educ:* Haileybury. Entered Royal Air Force with a short-service commission, 1926; Permanent Commission, 1931; served in India, 1932–37; served in Bomber Command, 1937–45, as a Squadron Comdr, Station Comdr, Base Comdr and AOC 4 Group; HQ ACSEA Singapore, 1945; HQ India and Base Comdr, Karachi, 1946–47; Director of Organisation (Establishments), Air Ministry, 1948 and 1949; Imperial Defence College, 1950; AOA, 2nd Tactical Air Force, 1951 and 1952; AOC No 1 (Bomber) Group, 1953–56; Air Member for Personnel, 1957–59; Inspector-General, RAF, 1959–62; Controller, RAF Benevolent Fund, 1962–68, retd. *Address:* 2 Woodside Close, Woodside Avenue, Lymington SO41 8FH. *T:* Lymington (01590) 676920. *Clubs:* Royal Air Force; Royal Lymington Yacht.

WHITLEY, Oliver John; Managing Director, External Broadcasting, British Broadcasting Corporation, 1969–72, retired; *b* 12 Feb. 1912; *s* of Rt Hon. J. H. Whitley, and Marguerite (*née* Marchetti); *m* 1939, Elspeth Catherine (*née* Forrester-Paton); four *s* one *d*. *Educ:* Clifton Coll.; New Coll., Oxford. Barrister-at-Law, 1935; BBC, 1935–41. Served in RNVR, 1942–46; Coastal Forces and Combined Ops. BBC 1946–: seconded to Colonial Office, 1946–49; Head of General Overseas Service, 1950–54; Assistant Controller, Overseas Services, 1955–57; Appointments Officer, 1957–60; Controller, Staff Training and Appointments, 1960–64; Chief Assistant to Dir-Gen., 1964–68. Valiant for Truth Award, Order of Christian Unity, 1974. *Recreations:* reading and gardening. *Address:* Greenacre, Ganavan Road, Oban, Argyll PA34 5TU. *T:* Oban (01631) 62555.

WHITLOCK, William Charles; *b* 20 June 1918; *s* of late George Whitlock and Sarah Whitlock, Sholing, Southampton; *m* 1943, Jessie Hilda, *d* of George Reardon of Armagh; five *s*. *Educ:* Itchen Gram. Sch.; Southampton Univ. Army Service, 1939–46. Apptd full-time Trade Union Officer, Area Organiser of Union of Shop, Distributive and Allied Workers, 1946. President, Leicester and District Trades Council, 1955–56; President, Leicester City Labour Party, 1956–57; President, North-East Leicester Labour Party, 1955–56, and 1958–59. Member East Midlands Regional Council of Labour Party, 1955–67, Vice-Chairman 1961–62, Chairman 1962–63. MP (Lab) Nottingham N, Oct. 1959–1983; Opposition Whip, House of Commons, 1962–64; Vice-Chamberlain of the Household, 1964–66; Lord Comr of Treasury, March 1966–July 1966; Comptroller of HM Household, July 1966–March 1967; Dep. Chief Whip and Lord Comr of the Treasury, March–July 1967; Under Sec. of State for Commonwealth Affairs, 1967–68; Parly Under-Sec. of State, FCO, 1968–69. Contested (Lab) Nottingham N, 1983. DPhil *hc* Ukranian Free Univ., 1986. *Address:* 51 Stoughton Road, Stoneygate, Leicester LE2 2EF.

WHITMORE, Sir Clive (Anthony), GCB 1988 (KCB 1983); CVO 1983; Director, since 1994: Morgan Crucible Co. PLC; Boots Co. PLC; N. M. Rothschild & Sons Ltd; Racal Electronics PLC; *b* 18 Jan. 1935; *s* of Charles Arthur Whitmore and Louisa Lilian Whitmore; *m* 1961, Jennifer Mary Thorpe; one *s* two *d*. *Educ:* Sutton Grammar Sch., Surrey; Christ's Coll., Cambridge (BA). Asst Principal, WO, 1959; Private Sec. to Permanent Under-Sec. of State, WO, 1961; Asst Private Sec. to Sec. of State for War, 1962; Principal, 1964; Private Sec. to Permanent Under-Sec. of State, MoD, 1969; Asst Sec., 1971; Asst Under-Sec. of State (Defence Staff), MoD, 1975; Under Sec., Cabinet Office, 1977; Principal Private Sec. to the Prime Minister, 1979–82; Dep. Sec., 1981; Permanent Under-Secretary of State: MoD, 1983–88; Home Office, 1988–94. Chancellor, De Montfort Univ., 1995; Chm. Council, Inst. of Educn, Univ. of London, 1995. *Recreations:* gardening, listening to music. *Address:* c/o N. M. Rothschild & Sons Ltd, 19 St Swithin's Lane, EC4P 4DU.

WHITMORE, Sir John (Henry Douglas), 2nd Bt *cr* 1954; *b* 16 Oct. 1937; *s* of Col Sir Francis Henry Douglas Charlton Whitmore, 1st Bt, KCB, CMG, DSO, TD, and of Lady Whitmore (*née* Ellis Johnsen); *S* father 1961; *m* 1st, 1962, Gunilla (marr. diss. 1969), *e d* of Sven A. Hansson, OV, KLH, Danderyd, and *o d* of Mrs Ella Hansson, Stockholm, Sweden; one *d*; 2nd, 1977, Diana Elaine, *e d* of Fred A. Becchetti, California, USA; one *s*. *Educ:* Stone House, Kent; Eton; Sandhurst; Cirencester. Active in personal development and social change; retired professional racing driver; business trainer and sports psychologist. *Publications:* The Winning Mind, 1987; Superdriver, 1988; Coaching for Performance, 1992. *Recreations:* ski-ing, squash. *Heir:* *s* Jason Whitmore, *b* 26 Jan. 1983. *Address:* Southfield, Leigh, near Tonbridge TN11 8PJ. *Club:* British Racing Drivers.

WHITNEY, John Norton Braithwaite; Director, The Really Useful Group Ltd, since 1990 (Managing Director, 1989–90; Chairman, 1990–95); *b* 20 Dec. 1930; *s* of Dr Willis Bevan Whitney and Dorothy Anne Whitney; *m* 1956, Roma Elizabeth Hodgson; one *s* one *d*. *Educ:* Leighton Park Friends' Sch. Radio producer, 1951–64; formed Ross Radio Productions, 1951, and Autocue, 1955; founded Radio Antilles, 1963; Founder Dir, Sagitta Prodns, 1968–82; Man. Dir, Capital Radio, 1973–82; Dir Gen., IBA, 1982–89; Chm., Trans World Communications plc, 1992–94. Dir, Duke of York's Theatre, 1979–82. Chm., Friends' Provident Ethical Investment Trust plc, 1992–; Dir, Friends' Provident Life Office, 1982– (Chm., Friends' Provident Stewardship Cttee of Reference, 1985–); Chairman: Radio Joint Audience Research Ltd, 1992–; Sony Music Pace Partnership (National Bowl), 1992–95; Enterprise Radio Hldgs Ltd, 1994–; Dir, VCI plc, 1995–. Chm., Assoc. of Indep. Local Radio Contractors, 1973, 1974, 1975 and 1980. Wrote, edited and devised numerous television series, 1956–82. Chm., Sony Radio Awards Cttee, 1991–; Vice Pres., Japan Festival 1991, 1991–92 (Chm., Festival Media Cttee, 1991); Trustee, Japan Educn Trust, 1993–; Member: Bd, NT, later RNT, 1977–94; Films, TV and Video Adv. Cttee, British Council, 1983–89; RCM Centenary Develt Fund (formerly Appeals Cttee), 1982– (Chm., Media and Events Cttee, 1982–94); Bd, City of London Sinfonietta, 1994–; Exec. Cttee, Musicians Benevolent Fund, 1995–; Council: Royal London Aid Society, 1966–90; TRIC, 1979–89 (Pres., 1985–86; Companion, 1989–); Fairbridge Drake Soc. (formerly Drake Fellowship), 1981–; Council for Charitable Support, 1989–92; Bd, Open Coll., 1987–89; Chm., British Amer. Arts Assoc., 1992–. Pres., London Marriage Guidance Council, 1983–90; Vice President: Commonwealth Youth Exchange Council, 1982–83; RNID, 1988–; Chm., Trustees, Soundaround (National Sound Magazine for the Blind), 1981–; Chm., Artsline, 1983–; Trustee: Venture Trust, 1982–86; Hosp. Broadcasting Assoc. Patron, MusicSpace Trust, 1990–; Governor: English Nat. Ballet (formerly London Festival Ballet), 1989–91; Bd, Performing Arts and Technol. Sch., 1992–; Chm., Theatre Investment Fund, 1990–. Fellow and Vice Pres., RTS, 1986–89; Mem., BAFTA. FRSA; Hon. FRCM. *Recreations:* chess, photography, sculpture. *Address:* 4 Clifford Street, W1X 1RB. *Clubs:* Garrick, Pilgrims.

WHITNEY, Raymond William, OBE 1968; MP (C) Wycombe, Bucks, since April 1978; *b* 28 Nov. 1930; *o s* of late George Whitney, Northampton; *m* 1956, Sheila Margot Beswick Prince; two *s*. *Educ:* Wellingborough Sch.; RMA, Sandhurst; London Univ. (BA (Hons) Oriental Studies). Commnd Northamptonshire Regt, 1951; served in Trieste, Korea, Hong Kong, Germany; seconded to Australian Army HQ, 1960–63; resigned and entered HM Diplomatic Service, 1964; First Sec., Peking, 1966–68; Head of Chancery, Buenos Aires, 1969–72; FCO, 1972–73; Dep. High Comr, Dacca, 1973–76; FCO, 1976–78, Hd of Information Res. Dept and Hd of Overseas Inf. Dept, 1976–78. PPS to Treasury Ministers, 1979–80; Parly Under-Sec. of State, FCO, 1983–84, DHSS, 1984–86. Vice-Chm., Cons. Employment Cttee, 1980–83; Chm., Cons. For. Affairs Cttee, 1981–83; Mem., Public Accounts Cttee, 1981–83; Chairman: Parly Latin-America Cttee, 1987–; Council for Defence Information, 1987–; Positive European Gp, 1993–. Chairman: Mountbatten Community Trust (formerly Mountbatten Training), 1987–; The Cable Corp., 1989–. *Publications:* National Health Crisis—a modern solution, 1988; articles on Chinese and Asian affairs in professional jls. *Recreations:* theatricals, golf, tennis, bridge, walking, wind-surfing. *Address:* The Dial House, Sunninghill, Berks SL5 0AG. *T:* Ascot (01344) 23164.

WHITSEY, Fred; Gardening Correspondent, Daily Telegraph, since 1971; *b* 18 July 1919; *m* 1947, Patricia Searle. *Educ:* outside school hours, and continuously since then. Assistant Editor, Popular Gardening, 1948–64, Associate Editor, 1964–67, Editor, 1967–82. Gardening correspondent, Sunday Telegraph, 1961–71. Gold Veitch Meml Medal, RHS, 1979; VMH 1986; Lifetime Achievement Award, Garden Writers' Guild, 1994. *Publications:* Sunday Telegraph Gardening Book, 1966; Fred Whitsey's Garden Calendar, 1985; Garden for All Seasons, 1986; contribs to Country Life and The Garden. *Recreations:* gardening, music. *Address:* Avens Mead, 20 Oast Road, Oxted, Surrey RH8 9DU.

WHITSON, Keith Roderick; Chief Executive, Midland Bank, since 1994 (Deputy Chief Executive, 1992–94); *b* 25 March 1943; *m* 1968, Sabine Wiechert; one *s* two *d*. *Educ:* Alleyn's Sch., Dulwich. FCIB. Hong Kong and Shanghai Banking Corporation: Manager, Frankfurt, 1978; Manager, Indonesia, 1981; Gen. Manager and Chief Exec. Officer, UK, 1987; Exec. Dir, Marine Midland Bank, NY, 1990. *Address:* Midland Bank, 27–32 Poultry, EC2P 2BX.

WHITSON, Thomas Jackson, OBE 1985; Commandant, Scottish Police College, 1987–91; Director, Glenbervie Golf Club, 1995; *b* 5 Sept. 1930; *s* of Thomas and Susan Whitson; *m* 1953, Patricia Marion Bugden; two *s*. *Educ:* Knox Acad., Haddington. RN, 1949–56. Lothian and Peebles Police, 1956–75: Police Constable, 1956; Detective Constable, 1959; Detective Sergeant, 1966; Inspector, 1969; Chief Inspector, 1972; Superintendent, 1974; Lothian and Borders Police, 1975–80: Chief Superintendent, 1976; Dep. Chief Constable, Central Scotland Police, 1980–87. *Recreations:* golf, curling, angling. *Address:* 12 Plewlandcroft, South Queensferry EH30 9RG.

WHITTAKER, Air Vice-Marshal David, CB 1988; MBE 1967; Air Officer Administration and Air Officer Commanding Directly Administered Units, RAF Support Command, 1986–89, retired; *b* 25 June 1933; *s* of Lawson and Irene Whittaker; *m* 1956, Joyce Ann Noble; two *s*. *Educ:* Hutton Grammar School. Joined RAF, 1951; commissioned 1952; served No 222, No 3, No 26 and No 1 Squadrons, 1953–62; HQ 38 Group, 1962–63; HQ 24 Bde, 1963–65; Comd Metropolitan Comms Sqdn, 1966–68; RAF Staff Coll., 1968; Asst Air Adviser, New Delhi, 1969–70; RAF Leeming, 1971–73; Coll. of Air Warfare, 1973; Directing Staff, RNSC Greenwich, 1973–75; Staff of CDS, 1975–76; DACOS (Ops), AFCENT, 1977–80; RCDS 1980; Defence and Air Adviser, Ottawa, 1983–86. *Recreations:* fishing, gardening, travel. *Address:* Seronera, Copgrove, Harrogate, North Yorks HG3 3SZ. *T:* Boroughbridge (01423) 340459. *Club:* Royal Air Force.

WHITTAKER, Geoffrey Owen, OBE 1974 (MBE 1962); Governor of Anguilla, 1987–89; retired 1990; *b* 10 Jan. 1932; *s* of late Alfred James Whittaker and Gertrude (*née* Holvey); *m* 1959, Annette Faith Harris; one *s* and one *d*. *Educ:* Nottingham High Sch.; Bristol Univ. (BA). Auditor: Tanganyika, 1956–58; Dominica, 1958–60; Principal Auditor, Windward Is, 1960–64; Dir of Audit, Grenada, 1964–67; Audit Adviser, British Honduras, 1967–69; Colonial Treas., St Helena, 1970–75; Financial Sec. and Actg Governor, Montserrat, 1975–78; Financial Sec., British Virgin Is, 1978–80; Admin Officer, Hong Kong, 1980–87; Finance Br., 1980–83; Principal Asst Sec., Lands and Works Br., 1983–85; Gen. Man., Hong Kong Industrial Estates Corp., 1985–87. *Recreations:* music, Rugby football, heraldry. *Address:* Palmer's Piece, Hall Lane, Ashley, near Market Harborough, Leics LE16 8HE. *T:* Medbourne Green (01858) 565312.

WHITTAKER, Prof. John Brian, PhD, DSc; FRES; Professor of Ecology, University of Lancaster, since 1987; *b* 26 July 1939; *s* of Roland Whittaker and Freda (*née* Lord); *m* 1964, Helen May Thorley; two *s*. *Educ:* Bacup and Rawtenstall Grammar Sch.; Univ. of Durham (BSc, PhD, DSc). FRES 1979. Res. Officer, Univ. of Oxford, 1963–66; University of Lancaster: Lectr, then Sen. Lectr, 1966–87; Hd, Dept of Biol Scis, 1983–86 and 1991–94. Mem., Adv. Cttee on Sci., NCC, 1978–81; Chm., Terrestrial Life Scis Cttee, NERC, 1991–95. Member of Council: British Ecol Soc., 1970–75 and 1984–86 (Vice-Pres., 1987–89); Freshwater Biol Assoc., 1988–91. *Publications:* Practical Demonstration of Ecological Concepts, 1988; (ed jtly) Toward a More Exact Ecology, 1989; contribs to books and jls in insect ecology. *Recreations:* 18th century English furniture, fell-walking, family. *Address:* Division of Biological Sciences, Institute of Environmental and Biological Sciences, Lancaster University, Lancaster LA1 4YQ. *T:* Lancaster (01524) 65201.

WHITTAKER, Nigel; Executive Director, Kingfisher plc (formerly Woolworth Holdings), 1983–95; *b* 7 Nov. 1948; *s* of late Phillip Whittaker and Joan Whittaker; *m* 1972, Joyce Cadman; three *s*. *Educ:* Caterham Sch.; Clare Coll., Cambridge (MA); Yale Law Sch. (JD). Called to the Bar, Middle Temple, 1974. Roche Products, 1974–77; British Sugar, 1977–82; Woolworth Holdings, subseq. Kingfisher, 1982–95. Chm., CBI Distributive Trades Survey, 1986–94; Chm., British Retail Consortium (formerly Retail Consortium), 1995–; Mem., UK Ecolabelling Bd (formerly Nat. Adv. Gp on Environmental Labelling), 1993–. *Recreations:* cricket, aerobics, ski-ing, drums, running.

WHITTAKER, Stanley Henry, FCA; Consultant, Transmark, since 1992; Director of Finance and Planning, British Railways Board, 1988–91; *b* 14 Sept. 1935; *s* of Frederick

Whittaker and Gladys Margaret (*née* Thatcher); *m* 1959, Freda Smith; two *s*. *Educ:* Bec School. ACA 1958, FCA 1969; ACMA 1971. Articled clerk, G. H. Attenborough & Co., Chartered Accountants, 1953–57; Sen. Assistant, Slater, Chapman & Cooke, 1960–62; Partner, Tiplady, Brailsford & Co., 1962–65; Finance Manager, NCB, 1965–68; British Railways: Finance Manager, 1968–74; Corporate Budgets Manager, 1974–78; Sen. Finance Manager, 1978–80; Chief Finance Officer, Western Reg., 1980–82; Director: Budgetary Control, 1982–86; Finance Develt, 1986–87; Group Finance, 1987–88. *Recreations:* flying, ski-ing, industrial archaeology, travel. *Address:* 12 Kennylands Road, Sonning Common, Reading, Berks RG4 9JT. *T:* Reading (01734) 722951.

WHITTALL, (Harold) Astley, CBE 1978; CEng; Chairman: B.S.G. International Ltd, 1981–94; Ransomes plc (formerly Ransome, Sims & Jefferies Ltd), 1983–93 (Director 1979–93; Deputy Chairman, 1981–83); *b* 8 Sept. 1925; *s* of Harold and Margaret Whittall; *m* 1952, Diana Margharita Berner. *Educ:* Handsworth Grammar Sch., Birmingham; Handsworth and Birmingham Technical Colls. Gen. Manager, Belliss & Morcom, 1962; Managing Dir, Amalgamated Power Engineering, 1968, Chm., 1977–81; Director: LRC Internat., 1982–85; APV (formerly APV Baker and APV plc), 1982–95; R. Platnauer Ltd, 1984–; Sykes Pickervant, 1987–94; Inchcape Insurance Hldgs, 1988–90. Pres., Engineering Employers' Fedn, 1976–78; Chairman: Engrg ITB, 1985–91; ETA, 1990–94; British Iron and Steel Consumers Council, 1987–91. *Address:* Brook Farmhouse, Whelford, near Fairford, Glos GL7 4DY. *T:* Cirencester (01285) 712393. *Clubs:* Royal Automobile, St James'.

WHITTALL, Michael Charlton, CMG 1980; OBE 1963; HM Diplomatic Service; Counsellor, Foreign and Commonwealth Office, 1973–91; *b* 9 January 1926; *s* of Kenneth Edwin Whittall and Edna Ruth (*née* Lawson); *m* 1953, Susan Olivia La Fontaine one *d*. *Educ:* Rottingdean; Rugby; Trinity Hall, Cambridge. Served RAF, 1944–48. Foreign Office, 1949; Salonika, 1949; British Middle East Office, 1952; Vice-Consul, Basra, 1953; FO, 1955; Second Secretary, Beirut, 1956; FO, 1958; First Secretary, Amman, 1959. *Recreations:* railways (GWR), birdwatching, photography.

WHITTAM, Prof. Ronald, FRS 1973; Emeritus Professor, Leicester University, since 1983 (Professor of Physiology, 1966–83); *b* 21 March 1925; *e s* of Edward Whittam and May Whittam (*née* Butterworth), Oldham, Lancs; *m* 1957, Christine Patricia Margaret, 2nd *d* of Canon J. W. Lamb; one *s* one *d*. *Educ:* Council and Technical Schools, Oldham; Univs of Manchester and Sheffield and King's College, Cambridge. BSc 1st Class Hons (Manchester); PhD (Sheffield and Cambridge); MA (Oxon). Served RAF, 1943–47. John Stokes Fellow, Dept of Biochem., Univ. of Sheffield, 1953–55; Beit Memorial Fellow, Physiological Lab., Cambridge, 1955–58; Mem. Scientific Staff, MRC Cell Metabolism Research Unit, Oxford, 1958–60; Univ. Lectr in Biochemistry, Oxford, 1960–66; Bruno Mendel Fellow of Royal Society, 1965–66; Dean of Fac. of Science, Leicester Univ., 1979–82. Mem. Editorial Bd of Biochem. Jl, 1963–67; Hon. Sec., 1969–74, Hon. Mem., 1986, Physiological Soc.; Mem. Biological Research Bd of MRC, 1971–74, Co-Chm., 1973–74; Member: Biological Sciences Cttee, UGC, 1974–82; Educn Cttee, Royal Soc., 1979–83; Chm., Biological Educn Cttee, Royal Soc. and Inst Biol., 1974–77. Foundn Governor, St Thomas More Sch., Leicester, 1989–93. *Publications:* Transport and Diffusion in Red Blood Cells, 1964; scientific papers dealing with cell membranes. *Recreation:* walking. *Address:* 9 Guilford Road, Leicester LE2 2RD. *T:* Leicester (0116) 270 7132.

WHITTAM SMITH, Andreas; Chairman: Newspaper Publishing plc, since 1994 (Chief Executive, 1987–93; Director, since 1986); Notting Hill Publishing Ltd, since 1995; *b* 13 June 1937; *s* of Canon J. E. Smith and Mrs Smith (*née* Barlow); *m* 1964, Valerie Catherine, *d* of late Wing Comdr J. A. Sherry and of Mrs N. W. H. Wyllys; two *s*. *Educ:* Birkenhead Sch., Cheshire; Keble Coll., Oxford (BA) (Hon. Fellow, 1990). With N. M. Rothschild, 1960–62; Stock Exchange Gazette, 1962–63; Financial Times, 1963–64; The Times, 1964–66; Dep. City Editor, Daily Telegraph, 1966–69; City Editor, The Guardian, 1969–70; Editor, Investors Chronicle and Stock Exchange Gazette, and Dir, Throgmorton Publications, 1970–77; City Editor, Daily Telegraph, 1977–85; Editor, The Independent, 1986–94; Editor-in-Chief, Independent on Sunday, 1991–94. Dir, Editoriale la Repubblica SpA, 1992–95. Vice Pres., Nat. Council for One Parent Families, 1991– (Hon. Treas., 1982–86). Chm., Sir Winston Churchill Archive Trust, 1995–. Trustee, Architecture Foundn, 1994–. Hon. Fellow, UMIST, 1989. Hon. DLitt: St Andrews; Salford; City; Liverpool, 1992; Hon. LLD Bath. Wincott award, 1975; Marketing Man of the Year, Inst. of Marketing, 1987; Journalist of the Year, British Press Awards, 1987; Hemingway Europa Prize, 1988; Editor of the Year, Granada TV What the Papers Say award, 1989. *Recreations:* music, history, walking. *Address:* 31 Brunswick Gardens, W8 4AW. *Club:* Garrick.

WHITTELL, James Michael Scott, OBE 1984; Regional Director, European Union (formerly Community), British Council, since 1993; *b* 17 Feb. 1939; *s* of late Edward Arthur Whittell and Helen Elizabeth Whittell (*née* Scott); *m* 1962, Eleanor Jane Carling; three *s*. *Educ:* Gresham's School, Holt; Magdalen College, Oxford (MA, BSc); Manchester Univ. Teaching, Sherborne School, 1962–68, Nairobi School, 1968–72; British Council: Ibadan, Nigeria, 1973–76; Enugu, Nigeria, 1976–78; Director General's Dept, 1978–81; Rep., Algiers, 1981–85; Sec. to the British Council and Head of Dir Gen's Dept, 1985–88; seconded to PM's Efficiency Unit, 1988; Rep., subseq. Dir, Nigeria, 1989–92; Dir, Africa and ME Div., 1992. *Recreations:* walking, mountaineering, books, music. *Address:* British Council, 10 Spring Gardens, SW1A 2BN. *Club:* Alpine.

WHITTEMORE, Prof. Colin Trengove; Professor of Agriculture and Rural Economy, and Head, Institute of Ecology and Resource Management, University of Edinburgh, since 1990; *b* 16 July 1942; *s* of Hugh Ashcroft Whittemore and Dorothea Whittemore (*née* Nance); *m* 1966, Mary Christine Fenwick; one *s* three *d*. *Educ:* Rydal Sch.; Harper Adams Agricl Coll. (NDA); Univ. of Newcastle upon Tyne (BSc, PhD, DSc). FIBiol 1989; FRSE 1994. Lectr, Univ. of Edinburgh, 1970–79; Head, Animal Production Adv. and Develt, E of Scotland Coll. of Agric., 1979–84; Prof. of Animal Prodn, 1984–90, Head, Dept of Agric., 1989–90, Univ. of Edinburgh. Consultant, Cotswold Pig Develt Co., 1975–. Sir John Hammond Award, British Soc. of Animal Prodn, 1983; Res. Gold Medal, RASE, 1984; Oscar della Suinicoltura, Assoc. Mignini, 1987; David Black Award, Meat and Livestock Commn, 1990. *Publications:* Practical Pig Nutrition (with F. W. H. Elsley), 1976; Lactation, 1980; Pig Production, 1980; Elements of Pig Science, 1987; The Science and Practice of Pig Production, 1993. *Recreations:* ski-ing, horses, the pursuit of science. *Address:* Institute of Ecology and Resource Management, University of Edinburgh, School of Agriculture Building, West Mains Road, Edinburgh EH9 3JG. *T:* 0131–667 1041; Rowancroft, 17 Fergusson View, West Linton, Peeblesshire EH46 7DJ. *Club:* Farmers'.

WHITTEMORE, Ernest William, MM 1944 and Bar 1945; Under-Secretary, Department of Health and Social Security, 1973–76; *b* 31 Aug. 1916; *s* of late Ernest William Whittemore and Hilda Whittemore; *m* 1942, Irene Mollie Hudson; two *d*. *Educ:* Raine's Sch., Stepney; King's Coll., London. BA Hons English. Receiver's Office, New Scotland Yard, 1934–35; Min. of Health, 1935–45; Royal Artillery, 1942–46; Min. of Nat. Insce (and successor depts), 1945–76. *Recreations:* bibliomania, travel, sweet peas. *Address:* 39 Montalt Road, Woodford Green, Essex IG8 9RS. *T:* 0181–504 7028.

WHITTICK, Richard James; Assistant Under-Secretary of State, Home Office, 1967–72; *b* 21 August 1912; *s* of Ernest G. Whittick and Grace M. Shaw; *m* 1938, Elizabeth Mason; two *s*. *Educ:* George Heriot's School; Edinburgh University. British Museum (Natural History), 1936; Home Office, 1940; Principal Private Secretary to Home Secretary, 1952–53; Assistant Secretary, 1953. *Recreations:* gardening, photography (FRPS 1988). *Address:* Coombe Cottage, Coombe, Sherborne, Dorset DT9 4BX. *T:* Sherborne (01935) 814488.

WHITTINGDALE, John Flasby Lawrance, OBE 1990; MP (C) Colchester South and Maldon, since 1992; *b* 16 Oct. 1959; *s* of John Whittingdale and Margaret Esmé Scott Napier; *m* 1990, Ancilla Campbell Murfitt; one *s*. *Educ:* Sandroyd Sch.; Winchester Coll.; University Coll. London (BScEcon). Head of Political Section, Conservative Research Dept, 1982–84; Special Adviser to Sec. of State for Trade and Industry, 1984–87; Manager, N. M. Rothschild & Sons, 1987; Political Sec. to the Prime Minister, 1988–90; Private Sec. to Rt Hon. Margaret Thatcher, 1990–92. PPS to Min. of State for Educn, 1994–95, for Educn and Employment, 1995–. Mem., Select Cttee on Health, 1993–; Sec., Conservative Parly Home Affairs Cttee, 1992–94. *Recreations:* cinema, music. *Address:* c/o House of Commons, SW1A 0AA. *Clubs:* Reform; Essex.

WHITTINGHAM, Charles Percival, BA, PhD Cantab; Head of Department of Botany, Rothamsted Experimental Station, 1971–82; *b* 1922; *m* 1946, Alison Phillips; two *d*. *Educ:* St John's College, Cambridge. Professor of Botany, London University, at Queen Mary College, 1958–64; Head of Dept of Botany, 1967–71, and Prof. of Plant Physiology, 1964–71, Imperial Coll., Univ of London; Dean, Royal Coll. of Science, 1969–71; Hon. Dir, ARC Unit for Plant Physiology, 1964–71. Vis. Prof., Univ. of Nottingham, 1978. *Publications:* Chemistry of Plant Processes, 1964; (with R. Hill) Photosynthesis, 1955; The Mechanism of Photosynthesis, 1974; contrib. to scientific journals. *Recreations:* music, travel. *Address:* Red Cottage, The Green, Brisley, Dereham, Norfolk NR20 5LN.

WHITTINGTON, Prof. Geoffrey; Price Waterhouse Professor of Financial Accounting, since 1988, Fellow of Fitzwilliam College, 1966–72 and since 1988, Cambridge University; *b* 21 Sept. 1938; *s* of Bruce Whittington and Dorothy Gwendoline Whittington (*née* Gent); *m* 1963, Joyce Enid Smith; two *s*. *Educ:* Dudley Grammar Sch.; LSE (Leverhulme Schol.; BSc Econ); MA, PhD Cantab. FCA. Chartered Accountancy training, 1959–62; research posts, Dept of Applied Econ., Cambridge, 1962–72; Dir of Studies in Econs, Fitzwilliam Coll., Cambridge, 1967–72; Prof. of Accountancy and Finance, Edinburgh Univ., 1972–75; University of Bristol: Prof. of Accounting and Finance, 1975–88; Head of Dept of Econs, 1981–84; Dean, Faculty of Social Scis, 1985–87. Part-time Econ. Adviser, OFT, 1977–83; part-time Mem., Monopolies and Mergers Commn, 1987–; Academic Advr, 1990–94, Mem., 1994–, Accounting Standards Bd. *Publications:* Growth, Profitability and Valuation (with A. Singh), 1968; The Prediction of Profitability, 1971; Inflation Accounting, 1983; (with D. P. Tweedie) The Debate on Inflation Accounting, 1984; (ed jtly) Readings in the Concept and Measurement of Income, 1986; The Elements of Accounting, 1992; contribs to jls and books in accounting, economics and finance. *Recreations:* music, squash, badminton, walking, usual academic pursuits of reading my own books and laughing at my own jokes. *Address:* Faculty of Economics and Politics, Sidgwick Avenue, Cambridge CB3 9DD. *T:* Cambridge (01223) 335200.

WHITTINGTON, Prof. Harry Blackmore, FRS 1971; Woodwardian Professor of Geology, Cambridge University, 1966–83; *b* 24 March 1916; *s* of Harry Whittington and Edith M. (*née* Blackmore); *m* 1940, Dorothy E. Arnold; no *c*. *Educ:* Handsworth Gram. Sch.; Birmingham University. Commonwealth Fund Fellow, Yale Univ., 1938–40; Lectr in Geology, Judson Coll., Rangoon, 1940–42; Prof. of Geography, Ginling Coll., Chengtu, W China, 1943–45; Lectr in Geology, Birmingham Univ., 1945–49; Harvard Univ.: Vis. Lectr, 1949–50; Assoc. Prof. of Geology, 1950–58; Prof. of Geology, 1958–66. Trustee: British Museum (Nat. History), 1980–89; Uppingham Sch., 1983–91. Hon. Fellow, Geol Soc. of America, 1983. Hon. AM, Harvard Univ., 1950. Medal, Paleontol Soc., USA, 1983; Lyell Medal, Geological Soc., 1986; Mary Clark Thompson Medal, US Nat. Acad of Scis, 1990. *Publications:* The Burgess Shale, 1985; Trilobites, 1992; articles in Jl of Paleontology, Bulletin Geol. Soc. of Amer., Quarterly Jl Geol. Soc. London, Phil. Trans. Royal Soc., etc. *Address:* 20 Rutherford Road, Cambridge CB2 2HH. *Club:* Geological.

WHITTINGTON, Thomas Alan, CB 1977; TD 1986; Circuit Administrator, North Eastern Circuit, 1974–81; *b* 15 May 1916; *o s* of late George Whittington, JP and Mary Elizabeth Whittington; *m* 1939, Audrey Elizabeth, *y d* of late Craven Gilpin, Leeds; four *s*. *Educ:* Uppingham Sch.; Leeds Univ. (LLB). Commnd W Yorks Regt (Leeds Rifles) TA, 1937, serving War of 1939–45 in UK and 14th Army in India (Major). Solicitor of Supreme Court, 1945; Clerk of the Peace, Leeds, 1952–70; Senior Partner, Marklands, Solicitors, Leeds, 1967–70, Consultant, 1981–; Under-Sec., Lord Chancellor's Office, 1970; Circuit Administrator, Northern Circuit, 1970–74. *Recreations:* fishing, gardening. *Address:* The Cottage, School Lane, Collingham, Wetherby LS22 5BQ. *T:* Collingham Bridge (01937) 573881.

WHITTINGTON-SMITH, Marianne Christine, (Mrs C. A. Whittington-Smith); *see* Lutz, M. C.

WHITTLE, Air Cdre Sir Frank, OM 1986; KBE 1948 (CBE 1944); CB 1947; Comdr, US Legion of Merit, 1946; RDI 1985; FRS 1947; FEng; MA Cantab; RAF, retired; *b* 1 June 1907; *s* of M. Whittle; *m* 1930, Dorothy Mary Lee (marr. diss. 1976); two *s*; *m* 1976, Hazel S. Hall. *Educ:* Leamington Coll.; No 4 Apprentices' Wing, RAF Cranwell; RAF Coll., Cranwell; Peterhouse, Cambridge (Mechanical Sciences Tripos, BA 1st Cl. Hons). No 4 Apprentices' Wing, RAF Cranwell, 1923–26; Flight Cadet, RAF Coll., Cranwell, 1926–28 (Abdy-Gerrard-Fellowes Memorial Prize); Pilot Officer, 111 (Fighter) Sqdn, 1928–29; Flying Instructors' Course, Central Flying Sch., 1929; Flying Instructor, No 2 Flying Training Sch., RAF Digby, 1930; Test Pilot, Marine Aircraft Experimental Estab., RAF Felixstowe, 1931–32; RAF Sch. of Aeronautical Engrg, Henlow, 1932–34; Officer i/c Engine Test, Engine Repair Section, Henlow, 1934 (6 mths); Cambridge Univ., 1934–37 (Post-Graduate year, 1936–37); Special Duty List, attached Power Jets Ltd for develt of aircraft gas turbine for jet propulsion, 1937–46; War Course, RAF Staff Coll., 1943; Technical Adviser to Controller of Supplies (Air), Min. of Supply, 1946–48; retd RAF, 1948. Hon. Technical Adviser: Jet Aircraft, BOAC, 1948–52; Shell Gp, 1953–57; Consultant, Bristol Siddeley Engines/Rolls Royce on turbo drill project, 1961–70. Mem. Faculty, US Naval Acad., Annapolis, Maryland, 1977–. Partnered late Flt-Lt G. E. Campbell in Crazy Flying RAF Display, Hendon, 1930; 1st flights of Gloster jet-propelled aeroplane with Whittle engine, May 1941. Freeman of Royal Leamington Spa, 1944. Hon. FRAeS; Hon. FAeSI; Hon. FIMechE; Founder Fellow, Fellowship of Engineering, 1976. Hon. Mem., Franklin Inst.; Hon. FAIAA; Hon. Mem., Société Royale Belge des Ingénieurs; Hon. Foreign Mem., Amer. Acad. Arts and Scis, 1976; For. Assoc., US Nat. Acad. of Engrg, 1978; Hon. Fellow, Soc. of Experimental Test Pilots, USA; Hon. MEIC. Hon. Fellow, Peterhouse. Hon. DSc: Oxon; Manchester; Leicester; Bath; Warwick;

Exeter; Cranfield Inst. of Technology, 1987; Hon. LLD Edinburgh; Hon. ScD Cantab; Hon. DTech: Trondheim; Loughborough, 1987. James Alfred Ewing Medal, ICE, 1944; Gold Medal, RAeS, 1944; James Clayton Prize, IMechE, 1946; Daniel Guggenheim Medal, USA, 1946; Kelvin Gold Medal, 1947; Melchett Medal, 1949; Rumford Medal, Royal Soc., 1950; Gold Medal, Fedn Aeronautique Internat., 1951; Churchill Gold Medal, Soc. of Engineers, 1952; Albert Gold Medal, Soc. of Arts, 1952; Franklin Medal, USA, 1956; John Scott Award, 1957; Goddard Award, USA, 1965; Coventry Award of Merit, 1966; International Communications (Christopher Columbus) Prize, City of Genoa, 1966; Tony Jannus Award, Greater Tampa Chamber of Commerce, 1969; James Watt Internat. Gold Medal, IMechE, 1977; Nat. Air and Space Mus. Trophy, 1986; (first) Prince Philip Medal, Fellowship of Engrg, 1991; Charles Stark Draper Prize, Nat. Acad. of Engrng, 1991. *Publications:* Jet, 1953; Gas Turbine Aero-Thermodynamics, 1981. *Clubs:* Royal Air Force; Wings (New York).

WHITTLE, Kenneth Francis, CBE 1987; Chairman, South Western Electricity Board, 1977–87; *b* 28 April 1922; *s* of Thomas Whittle and May Whittle; *m* 1945, Dorothy Inskip; one *s* one *d*. *Educ:* Kingswood Sch., Bath; Faculty of Technol., Manchester Univ. (BScTech). Served War, Electrical Lieut, RNVR, 1943–46. Metropolitan Vickers Elec. Co. Ltd, 1946–48; NW Div., CEGB, 1948–55; North West Electricity Board: various posts, 1955–64; Area Commercial Officer, Blackburn, 1964–69; Manager, Peak Area, 1969–71; Manager, Manchester Area, 1971–74; Chief Commercial Officer, 1974–75; Dep. Chm., Yorks Elec. Bd, 1975–77. Chairman: British Electrotechnical Approvals Bd, 1985–; British Approvals Bd for Telecommunications, 1985–. *Recreation:* golf. *Address:* 8 Cambridge Road, Clevedon, Avon BS21 7HX. *T:* Clevedon (01275) 874017.

WHITTLE, Prof. Peter, FRS 1978; Churchill Professor of Mathematics for Operational Research, University of Cambridge, 1967–94, now Professor Emeritus; Fellow of Churchill College, Cambridge, since 1967; *b* 27 Feb. 1927; *s* of Percy Whittle and Elsie Tregurtha; *m* 1951, Käthe Hildegard Blomquist; three *s* three *d*. *Educ:* Wellington Coll., New Zealand. Docent, Uppsala Univ., 1951–53; employed New Zealand DSIR, 1953–59, rising to Senior Principal Scientifc Officer; Lectr, Univ. of Cambridge, 1959–61; Prof. of Mathematical Statistics, Univ. of Manchester, 1961–67. Sen. Fellow, SERC, 1988–91. Mem., Royal Soc. of NZ, 1981–. Hon. DSc Victoria Univ. of Wellington, NZ, 1987. *Publications:* Hypothesis Testing in Time Series Analysis, 1951; Prediction and Regulation, 1963; Probability, 1970; Optimisation under Constraints, 1971; Optimisation over Time, 1982; Systems in Stochastic Equilibrium, 1986; Risk-sensitive Optimal Control, 1990; Probability via Expectation, 1992; contribs to Jl Roy. Statistical Soc., Proc. Roy. Soc., Jl Stat. Phys, Systems and Control Letters. *Recreation:* the contemplation of lost Anglo-Celtic nationhood. *Address:* 268 Queen Edith's Way, Cambridge CB1 4NL; Statistical Laboratory, University of Cambridge CB2 1SB.

WHITTLE, Stephen Charles; Chief Adviser, Editorial Policy, Planning and Policy Directorate, BBC, since 1993; *b* 26 July 1945; *s* of Charles William Whittle and Vera Lillian Whittle (*née* Moss); *m* 1988, Claire Walmsley. *Educ:* St Ignatius College, Stamford Hill; University College London (LLB Hons). Asst Editor, New Christian, 1968–70; Communications Officer, World Council of Churches, Geneva, 1970–73; Editor, One World, WCC, 1973–77; Asst Head, Communications Dept, WCC, 1975–77; BBC: Sen. Producer, Religious Programmes, Manchester, 1977–82; Producer, Newsnight, 1982; Editor, Songs of Praise and Worship, 1983–89; Hd of Religious Progs, 1989–93. Freeman, City of London, 1990. Sandford St Martin Award for contrib. to religious broadcasting, 1993. *Publications:* Tickling Mrs Smith, 1970; contribs to One World and The Tablet. *Recreations:* cinema, theatre, music, reading, exercise. *Address:* BBC, Broadcasting House, W1A 1AA. *T:* 0171–765 5685.

WHITTOME, Sir (Leslie) Alan, Kt 1991; *b* 18 Jan. 1926; *s* of Leslie Whittome and Beryl Treherne-Thomas; *m* 1984, Eleanor Duncan Wood Moose, *o d* of James Moose, US Ambassador, two *d* by previous marr. *Educ:* Marlborough Coll.; Pembroke Coll., Cambridge (MA). Capt., RAC, 1944–48. Bank of England, 1951–64, Dep. Chief Cashier; International Monetary Fund: Dir, European Dept, 1964–86; Dir, ETR, 1986–90; Special Advr to Man. Dir, 1990–91. *Address:* 12653 Furnace Mountain Road, Lovettsville, VA 22080, USA. *T:* (703) 8229030.

WHITTON, Prof. Peter William; Deputy Vice-Chancellor, University of Melbourne, 1979–84, retired; *b* 2 Sept. 1925; *s* of William Whitton and Rosa Bungay; *m* 1950, Mary Katharine White; two *s* three *d*. *Educ:* Latymer Upper Sch., London; Southampton Univ. (BScEng); Imperial College of Science and Technology, London (DIC, PhD); ME Melbourne 1965. FIE(Aust). Engineering Cadet, English Electric Co., Preston, 1942–46; Wireless Officer, Royal Signals, Catterick and Singapore, 1946–48; Sen. Lectr in Mech. Engrg, Univ. of Melbourne, 1953–56; Head, Engrg Sect., ICI Metals Div. Research Dept, Birmingham, 1956–60; Foundation Prof. and Dean, Faculty of Engrg, Univ. of the West Indies, 1960–64; University of Melbourne: Prof. of Mech. Engrg, 1965–77, Emeritus Prof., 1977–; Dean, Faculty of Engrg, 1966; Principal, Royal Melbourne Inst. of Technology, 1977–78. *Publications:* various papers on metal forming, in Proc. IMechE, London, and Jl of Inst. of Metals, London. *Recreations:* reading, golf. *Address:* 425 Beach Road, Beaumaris, Victoria 3193, Australia.

WHITTUCK, Gerald Saumarez, CB 1959; *b* 13 Oct. 1912; *s* of late Francis Gerald Whittuck; *m* 1938, Catherine McCrea (*d* 1992); two *s*. *Educ:* Cheltenham; Clare Coll., Cambridge. Air Ministry, 1935; Private Secretary to Secretary of State, 1944–46; Asst Under-Secretary of State: Air Ministry, 1955–63; War Office, 1963–64; MoD, 1964–71; Dir, Greenwich Hosp., 1971–74. Mem., Royal Patriotic Fund Corp., 1971–74. *Address:* 15A Greenaway Gardens, NW3 7DH. *T:* 0171–435 3742.

WHITTY, John Lawrence, (Larry); European Co-ordinator, Labour Party, since 1994 (General Secretary, 1985–94); *b* 15 June 1943; *s* of Frederick James and Kathleen May Whitty; *m* 1969, Tanya Margaret (marr. diss. 1986); two *s*; *m* 1993, Angela Forrester. *Educ:* Latymer Upper School; St John's College, Cambridge (BA Hons Economics). Hawker Siddeley Aviation, 1960–62; Min. of Aviation Technology, 1965–70; Trades Union Congress, 1970–73; General, Municipal, Boilermakers and Allied Trade Union (formerly GMWU), 1973–85. *Recreations:* theatre, cinema, swimming. *Address:* 33 Gilbert House, Churchill Gardens, SW1V 3HN. *T:* 0171–834 8890.

WHITWAM, Derek Firth, CEng, FRINA; RCNC; quality engineering consultant, since 1988; *b* 7 Dec. 1932; *s* of Hilton and Marion Whitwam; *m* 1954, Pamela May (*née* Lander); one *s* one *d*. *Educ:* Royds Hall Sch., Huddersfield; Royal Naval Coll., Dartmouth; Royal Naval Engineering Coll., Manadon; Royal Naval Coll., Greenwich. Work on ship design, MoD (N) Bath, 1957–65; Rosyth Dockyard, 1965–68; Singapore Dockyard, 1968–70; DG Ships Bath, 1970–77; RCDS 1978; Production Manager, Rosyth Dockyard, 1979–80; Gen. Manager, Portsmouth Dockyard, 1981–84; Principal Dir of Planning and Policy, Chief Exec. Royal Dockyards, 1984–85; Dir of Quality Assurance, MoD, 1985–88. *Publications:* papers for Trans Royal Inst. of Naval Architects. *Recreations:* golf, music, walking.

WHITWELL, Stephen John, CMG 1969; MC; HM Diplomatic Service, retired; *b* 30 July 1920; *s* of Arthur Percy Whitwell and Marion Whitwell (*née* Greenwood). *Educ:* Stowe; Christ Church, Oxford. Coldstream Guards, 1941–47; joined HM Foreign Service (now Diplomatic Service), 1947; served: Tehran, 1947; FO, 1949; Belgrade, 1952; New Delhi, 1954; FO, 1958; Seoul, 1961. Polit. Adv. to C-in-C Middle East, Aden, 1964; Counsellor, Belgrade, 1965; Ambassador to Somalia, 1968–70; Head of East-West Contacts Dept, FCO, 1970–71. *Recreations:* reading, painting, looking at buildings. *Club:* Travellers'.

WHITWORTH, Francis John, OBE 1994; Member, Economic and Social Committee of the European Communities, since 1986; *b* 1 May 1925; *s* of late Captain Herbert Francis Whitworth, OBE, RNVR, and Helen Marguerite Whitworth (*née* Tait); *m* 1956, Auriol Myfanwy Medwyn Hughes; one *s* one *d*. *Educ:* Charterhouse (Jun. Schol.); Pembroke Coll., Oxford (Holford Schol.; MA Jurisprudence 1949). FIMgt (FBIM 1980; MBIM 1967). Served War, Royal Marines, 1943–46. Called to Bar, Middle Temple, 1950. Joined Cunard Steam-Ship Co., 1950; Personnel Director, 1965, Managing Dir Cunard Line, 1968, Group Admin Dir, 1969; joined British Shipping Fedn as Dep. Dir, Industrial Relations, 1972; Dep. Dir-Gen., Gen. Council of British Shipping, 1980–87; Dir, Internat. Shipping Fedn, 1980–88; Mem., Nat. Maritime Bd, 1962–87. Chairman: Internat. Cttee of Passenger Lines, 1968–71; Atlantic Passenger Steamship Conf., 1970–71; Employers' Gp, Jt Maritime Commn of ILO, 1980–88; Employers' Gp, Internat. Maritime (Labour) Conf. of ILO, 1986–87; Social Affairs Cttee, Comité des Assocs d'Armateurs des Communautés Européennes, 1983–88; Nat. Sea Training Schs, 1980–87; Merchant Navy Officers' Pension Fund Trustees, 1987–93; Member: Industrial Tribunals for England and Wales, 1978–94; Council, Marine Soc., 1988–; Council, Missions to Seamen, 1988–. *Recreations:* racing, opera, music, cricket. *Address:* The Old School House, Farley Chamberlayne, Romsey, Hants SO51 0QR. *Club:* United Oxford & Cambridge University.

WHITWORTH, Hugh Hope Aston, MBE 1945; Lay Assistant to the Archbishop of Canterbury, 1969–78; *b* 21 May 1914; *s* of Sidney Alexander Whitworth and Elsie Hope Aston; *m* 1st, 1944, Elizabeth Jean Boyes (*d* 1961); two *s* one *d*; 2nd, 1961, Catherine Helen Bell (*d* 1986). *Educ:* Bromsgrove Sch.; Pembroke Coll., Cambridge (BA). Indian Civil Service, Bombay Province, 1937–47; Administrator, Ahmedabad Municipality, 1942–44; Collector and District Magistrate, Nasik, 1945–46; Board of Trade, 1947–55; Scottish Home Dept, 1955; Asst Sec., 1957; Under-Sec., Scottish Home and Health Dept, 1968–69. *Recreations:* travel, gardening. *Address:* 7 Walpole Gardens, Strawberry Hill, Twickenham TW2 5SL. *T:* 0181–894 4590. *Club:* Commonwealth Trust.

WHITWORTH, Maj.-Gen. Reginald Henry, CB 1969; CBE 1963; MA; *b* 27 Aug. 1916; 2nd *s* of late Aymer William Whitworth and late Alice (*née* Hervey), Eton College; *m* 1946, June Rachel (*d* 1994), *o d* of late Sir Bartle Edwards, CVO, MC, and of Daphne, MBE, *d* of late Sir Cyril Kendall Butler, KBE; two *s* one *d*. *Educ:* Eton; Balliol College, Oxford, 1st cl. Hons, Modern History, 1938; Laming Travelling Fellow, Queen's Coll., Oxford, 1938–39. 2nd Lt Grenadier Guards, 1940; War Service in N Africa and Italy, 1943–45; GSO2, 78 Division, 1944; Bde Major, 24 Guards Brigade, 1945–46; GSO2, Staff College, Camberley, 1953–55; comdg 1st Bn Grenadier Guards, 1956–57; GSO1, SHAPE, 1958–59; Sen. Army Instructor, JSSC, 1959–61; Comdr Berlin Infantry Bde, 1961–63; DMS 1, Ministry of Defence, 1964–66; GOC: Yorkshire District, 1966–67; Northumbrian District, 1967–68; Chief of Staff, Southern Command, 1968–70. Bursar and Official Fellow, Exeter College, Oxford, 1970–81. Gov., St Mary's, Wantage (Chm.). Trustee, Historic Churches Preservation Trust. Bronze Star, USA, 1945. *Publications:* Field Marshal Earl Ligonier, 1958; Famous Regiments: the Grenadier Guards, 1974; Gunner at Large, 1988; William Augustus, Duke of Cumberland, 1992. *Recreations:* fishing, military history. *Address:* Abbey Farm, Goosey, Faringdon, Oxon SN7 8PA. *T:* Faringdon (01367) 710252. *Club:* Army and Navy.

WHITWORTH-JONES, Anthony; General Director (formerly General Administrator), Glyndebourne Festival Opera, since 1989; *b* 1 Sept. 1945; *s* of Henry Whitworth-Jones and Patience Martin; *m* 1974, Camilla (*née* Barlow); one *d*. *Educ:* Wellington College. Mem., Inst. of Chartered Accountants of Scotland. Thomson McLintock & Co., 1970–72, Administrative Dir, London Sinfonietta, 1972–81; Administrator, Glyndebourne Touring Opera and Opera Manager, Glyndebourne Festival Opera, 1981–89. Dir, SE Arts Bd. *Recreations:* enjoying the spirit and countryside of Wales, listening to music other than opera, contemporary art, golf. *Address:* 81 St Augustine's Road, NW1 9RR. *T:* 0171–284 0908.

WHYBREW, Edward Graham, (Ted); Certification Officer for Trade Unions and Employers' Associations, since 1992; Associate Partner, Jamieson Scott (Executive Search), since 1993; *b* 25 Sept. 1938; *s* of Ernest Whybrew and Winifred (*née* Castle); *m* 1967, Julia Helen Baird; one *s* two *d*. *Educ:* Hertford Grammar Sch.; Balliol Coll., Oxford (BA 1961); Nuffield Coll., Oxford. Economist: NEDO, 1963; DEA, 1964–69; Dept of Employment, subseq. EDG, 1969–92; Asst Sec., Employment, Trng and Industrial Relations, 1977–85; Under Sec., Industrial Relations Div., 1985–89; Dir, Personnel and Staff Develt, 1989–92. *Publication:* Overtime Working in Great Britain, 1968. *Recreations:* cricket, horse riding, gardening.

WHYBROW, Christopher John; QC 1992; *b* 7 Aug. 1942; *s* of Herbert William Whybrow, OBE and Ruby Kathleen Whybrow (*née* Watson); *m* 1st, 1969, Marion Janet Macaulay (marr. diss. 1976); 2nd, 1979, Susan Younge (marr. diss. 1990). *Educ:* Colchester Royal Grammar Sch.; King's Coll., London (LLB). Called to the Bar, Inner Temple, 1965. *Publications:* (contrib.) Atkins Court Forms; contribs to Jl of Planning and Environment Law. *Recreations:* cricket, tennis, gardening, country life. *Address:* 1 Serjeant's Inn, EC4Y 1NH. *Clubs:* Lansdowne, MCC; Leavenheath Cricket.

WHYBROW, John William; President and Chief Executive Officer, Phillips Lighting Holding BV, since 1995; *b* 11 March 1947; *s* of Charles Ernest James Whybrow and Doris Beatrice Whybrow (*née* Abbott); *m* 1968, Paula Miriam Hobart; one *s* one *d*. *Educ:* Hatfield Tech. GS; Imperial Coll., London (BSc Hons Mech. Engrg); Manchester Business Sch. (MBA); ACGI. English Electric, Rugby, 1968–70; Philips Electronics: Northern Operational Res. Gp, 1970–78; Ind. Engrg Head, Mullard Simonstone, 1979–82; Div. Manager, 1982–83, Plant Dir, 1983–87, Mullard Blackburn; Plant Dir, Hazel Grove, 1987–88; Man. Dir, TDS Circuits plc, 1988–90; Tech. Dir, Philips Components, 1990–91; Industrial Dir, 1991–93, Chm. and Man. Dir, 1993–95, Philips Electronics UK. Dir, Teletext Hldgs, 1993–. MInstD 1993. *Recreations:* sailing, squash. *Address:* Philips Lighting Holding BV, Building ED-5, PO Box 80020, 5600 JM Eindhoven, Netherlands. *Club:* East India.

WHYTE, Very Rev. James Aitken; Moderator of the General Assembly of the Church of Scotland, 1988–89; Professor of Practical Theology and Christian Ethics, University of St Andrews, 1958–87; *b* 28 Jan. 1920; 2nd *s* of late Andrew Whyte, Leith, and late Barbara Janet Pittillo Aitken; *m* 1st, 1942, Elisabeth (*d* 1988), *er d* of Rev. G. S. Mill, MA, BSc, Kalimpong, India; two *s* one *d*; 2nd, 1993, Ishbel Christina Rathie (*née* Macaulay); *widow* of William Rathie, MA. *Educ:* Daniel Stewart's Coll., Edinburgh; University of Edinburgh

(Arts and Divinity), MA 1st Cl. Hons Phil., 1942. Ordained, 1945; Chaplain to the Forces, 1945–48; Minister of: Dunollie Road, Oban, 1948–54; Mayfield, Edinburgh, 1954–58. St Andrews University: Dean, Faculty of Divinity, 1968–72; Principal, St Mary's Coll., 1978–82. Guest Lectr, Inst. for the Study of Worship and Religious Architecture, Birmingham, 1965–66; Lectures: Kerr, Univ. of Glasgow, 1969–72; Croall, Univ. of Edinburgh, 1972–73; Margaret Harris, Univ. of Dundee, 1990. Pres., Soc. for Study of Theol., 1983–84. Hon. LLD Dundee, 1981; Hon. DD St Andrews, 1989; DUniv Stirling, 1994. *Publications:* (ed jtly) Worship Now: Vol. 1, 1972, Vol. 2, 1989; Laughter and Tears, 1993; contributor to various dictionaries, composite volumes, journals, etc. *Address:* 13 Hope Street, St Andrews, Fife KY16 9HJ. *Club:* New (Edinburgh).

WHYTE, John Stuart, CBE 1976; MSc(Eng); FEng 1980; FIEE; Chairman, GPT (International) Ltd, 1988–90; *b* High Wycombe, 20 July 1923; *s* of late William W. Whyte and Ethel K. Whyte; *m* 1951, E. Joan M. (*née* Budd); one *s* one *d*. *Educ:* The John Lyon Sch., Harrow; Northampton Polytechnic, London Univ. BSc(Eng) (Hons), MSc(Eng). Post Office Radio Laboratory, Castleton, Cardiff, 1949–57; PO Research Station, Dollis Hill: Sen. Exec. Engr, 1957–61; Asst Staff Engr, 1961–65. Asst Sec., HM Treasury, 1965–68; Dep. Dir of Engrg, PO, 1968–71; Dir, Operational Programming, PO, 1971–75; Dir of Purchasing and Supply, 1975–76, Sen. Dir of Develt, 1977–79, Dep. Man. Dir, 1979–81, PO Telecommunications; Engr-in-Chief, Man. Dir (major systems), and Mem. Main Bd, British Telecom, 1981–83; Dir, British Telecommunications Systems Ltd, 1979–83; Chm., Astronet Corp., 1984–85; Pres., 1984–85, Chm., 1985–86, Stromberg Carlson Corp; Chm., Plessey Telecommunications (Internat.) Ltd, 1983–85; Dep. Chm., Plessey Telecommunications and Office Systems Ltd, 1985–88. Manager, Royal Instn, 1971–74 (Vice-Pres., 1972, 1973, 1974), Mem. Cttee of Visitors, 1975–78 (Chm., 1977–78), Chm., Membership Cttee, 1975–77. Mem., Nat. Electronics Council, 1977– (Mem. Exec. Cttee, 1977–; Dep. Chm., 1980–); Mem. Council, ERA, 1977–83. President: Instn of PO Electrical Engrs, 1977–82; Instn of British Telecommunications Engrs, 1982–83 (Hon. Mem., 1984); Mem. Council, IEE, 1980–84 (Vice-Pres., 1981–84; Chm. Professional Bd, 1981–84). Governor, Internat. Council for Computer Communication, 1985–91. Liveryman, Scientific Instrument Makers' Co. Freeman, City of London, 1979. Leader, British Hinku Expedn, 1979; Pres., Assoc. of British Members of Swiss Alpine Club, 1988–90. *Publications:* various articles and papers in professional telecommunications jls. *Recreations:* mountaineering, photography, opera. *Address:* Wild Hatch, Coleshill Lane, Winchmore Hill, Amersham, Bucks HP7 0NT. *T:* Amersham (01494) 722663. *Clubs:* Alpine; Cambridge Alpine (Hon.).

WHYTE, (John) Stuart Scott, CB 1986; Under Secretary, Department of Health and Social Security, 1978–86; *b* 1 April 1926; *er s* of late Thomas and Mysie Scott Whyte, Sandycove, Co. Dublin; *m* 1950, Jocelyn Margaret, *o d* of late George Hawley, CBE, Edinburgh; two *s* one *d*. *Educ:* St Andrew's Coll., Dublin; Trinity Coll., Univ. of Dublin. BA 1947; LLB 1948. Asst Principal, Dept of Health for Scotland, 1948; Principal, 1955; Principal Private Sec. to Sec. of State for Scotland, 1959; Asst Sec., Scottish Develt Dept, 1962; Asst Sec., Cabinet Office, 1969; Asst Under-Sec. of State, Scottish Office, 1969–74; Under Sec., Cabinet Office, 1974–78. *Address:* 27 The Circus, Bath, Avon BA1 2EU. *T:* Bath (01225) 339612; La Bâtisse, Bonin, 47120 Duras, France. *T:* 53837031.

WHYTE, Stuart Scott; *see* Whyte, J. S. S.

WIBLIN, Derek John, CB 1992; Under Secretary, Principal Establishment and Finance Officer, Crown Prosecution Service, 1988–93; *b* 18 March 1933; *s* of late Cyril G. H. Wiblin and of Winifred F. Wiblin (*née* Sandford); *m* 1960, Pamela Jeanne Hamshere; one *s* one *d*. *Educ:* Bishopshalt School, Hillingdon; Birmingham University (BSc Hons Chem 1954). RAF, 1954–57. Courtaulds Ltd, 1957–58; joined DSIR Building Research Station, 1958; Civil Service Commission, 1967–71; DoE, 1971–79; Ports Div., Dept of Transport, 1979–81; Estabs Div., DoE, 1981–83; Under Sec., Principal Estabt and Finance Officer, Lord Chancellor's Dept, 1984–88. Chm., First Division Pensioners' Gp, 1993–. *Recreations:* making violins, collecting books. *Address:* 19 Woodwaye, Oxhey, Watford, Herts WD1 4NN. *T:* Watford (01923) 228615. *Clubs:* Athenæum, Royal Air Force.

WICKBERG, Gen. Erik E.; Comdr of the Order of Vasa (Sweden), 1970; General of the Salvation Army, 1969–74; *b* 6 July 1904; *s* of David Wickberg, Commissioner, Salvation Army, and Betty (*née* Lundblad); *m* 1929, Ens. Frieda de Groot (*d* 1930); *m* 1932, Captain Margarete Dietrich (*d* 1976); two *s* two *d*; *m* 1977, Major Eivor Lindberg. *Educ:* Uppsala; Berlin; Stockholm. Salvation Army Internat. Training Coll., 1924–25, and Staff Coll., 1926; commissioned, 1925; appts in Scotland, Berlin, London; Divisional Commander, Uppsala, 1946–48; Chief Secretary, Switzerland, 1948–53; Chief Secretary, Sweden, 1953–57; Territorial Commander, Germany, 1957–61; Chief of the Staff, Internat. HQ, London, 1961–69; elected General of the Salvation Army, July 1969; assumed international leadership, Sept. 1969. Hon. LLD Choong Ang Univ., Seoul, 1970. Order of Moo-Koong-Wha, Korea, 1970; Grosses Verdienstkreuz, Germany, 1971; The King's golden medal (Sweden), 1980. *Publications:* In Darkest England Now, 1974; Inkallad (autobiography, in Swedish), 1978; Uppdraget (The Charge: my way to preaching, in Swedish), 1990; articles in Salvation Army periodicals and Year Book. *Recreations:* reading, fishing, chess. *Address:* c/o The Salvation Army, Box 5090, 10242 Stockholm, Sweden.

WICKENS, Prof. Alan Herbert, OBE 1980; FEng, FIMechE; Industrial Professor, Department of Mechanical Engineering, Loughborough University of Technology, since 1993; *b* 29 March 1929; *s* of late Herbert Leslie Wickens and of Sylvia Wickens; *m* 1st, 1953, Eleanor Joyce Waggott (*d* 1984); one *d*; 2nd, 1987, Patricia Anne McNeil. *Educ:* Ashville Coll., Harrogate; Loughborough Univ. of Technol. (DLC Eng, BScEng London, 1951; DSc Loughborough, 1978). CEng, FIMechE 1971; MRAeS. Res. Engr, Sir W. G. Armstrong Whitworth Aircraft Ltd, Coventry, 1951–55; Gp Leader, Dynamics Analysis, Canadair Ltd, Montreal, 1955–59; Head of Aeroelastics Section, Weapons Res. Div., A. V. Roe & Co., Ltd, Woodford, 1959–62; British Rail: Supt, Res. Dept, 1962–67; Advanced Projs Engr, 1967–68; Dir of Advanced Projs, 1968–71; Dir of Labs, 1971–78; Dir of Research, 1978–84; Dir of Engrg Develt and Research, 1984–89. Loughborough University of Technology: Industrial Prof. of Transport Technol., 1972–76; Prof. of Dynamics, Dept of Mechanical Engrg, 1989–92. Pres., Internat. Assoc. of Vehicle System Dynamics, 1981–86; Chm., Office of Res. and Experiments, Union Internationale de Chemins de fer, 1988–90. Mem., Amer. Inst. Aeronautics and Astronautics, 1958. FBIS; FRSA. Hon. Fellow, Derbyshire Coll. of Higher Educn, 1984. Hon. DTech CNAA, 1978; Hon. Dr Open Univ, 1980. George Stephenson Res. Prize, IMechE, 1966; (jtly) MacRobert Award, 1975. *Publications:* papers on dynamics of railway vehicles, high speed trains and future railway technology, publ. by IMechE, Amer. Soc. of Mech. Engrs, Internat. Jl of Solids and Structures, and Jl of Vehicle System Dynamics. *Recreations:* gardening, travel, music. *Address:* Ecclesbourne Farmhouse, Ecclesbourne Lane, Idridgehay, Derbys DE56 2SB. *T:* Cowers Lane (01773) 550368. *Club:* Royal Air Force.

WICKERSON, Sir John (Michael), Kt 1987; Partner, Ormerod Wilkinson Marshall (formerly Ormerod, Morris & Dumont), since 1962; President, Law Society, 1986–87; Chairman, Croydon Community NHS Trust, since 1991; *b* 22 Sept. 1937; *s* of Walter and Ruth Wickerson; *m* 1963, Shirley Maud Best; one *s*. *Educ:* Christ's Hospital; London University (LLB). Admitted solicitor, 1960; Mem. Council, Law Society, 1969 (Chm., Contentious Business Cttee; Vice-Pres., 1985–86). Member: Matrimonial Causes Rules Cttee, 1982–86; Royal Commn on Criminal Justice, 1991–93. Pres., London Criminal Courts Solicitors Assoc., 1980–81. Chm., R. Mansell Ltd, 1994–. Hon. Member: Amer. Bar Assoc., 1986; Canadian Bar Assoc., 1986; NZ Law Soc., 1987. *Publication:* Motorist and the Law, 1975, 2nd edn 1982. *Recreation:* golf. *Address:* c/o Ormerod Wilkinson Marshall, 10 High Street, Croydon, Surrey CR9 2BH. *T:* 0181–686 3841.

WICKES, Charles G.; *see* Goodson-Wickes.

WICKHAM, Daphne Elizabeth, (Mrs J. K. A. Alderson); a Metropolitan Stipendiary Magistrate, since 1989; *b* 31 Aug. 1946; *d* of late Major Harry Temple Wickham and of Phyllis Wickham (*née* Roycroft); *m* 1983, John Keith Ameers Alderson. *Educ:* Sydenham High Sch.; Chislehurst and Sidcup Girls' Grammar School. Called to the Bar, Inner Temple, 1967. *Recreation:* laughter. *Address:* 3 Temple Gardens, Temple, EC4Y 9AU. *T:* 071–353 3102.

WICKHAM, Glynne William Gladstone; Professor of Drama, University of Bristol, 1960–82, now Emeritus, and Senior Research Fellow, since 1995; *b* 15 May 1922; *s* of W. G. and Catherine Wickham; *m* 1954, Marjorie Heseltine (*née* Mudford); two *s* one *d*. *Educ:* Winchester College; New College, Oxford. Entered RAF, 1942; commissioned as Navigator, 1943; discharged as Flt Lt, 1946. BA, 1947; DPhil, 1951 (Oxon); President of OUDS, 1946–47. Bristol University: Asst Lectr, Drama Dept, 1948; Sen. Lectr and Head of Dept, 1955; Dean, Faculty of Arts, 1970–72. Worked sporadically as actor, script-writer and critic for BBC, from 1946; attended General Course in Broadcasting, BBC Staff Trg Sch., 1953. Travelled in America on Rockefeller Award, 1953. Visiting Prof., Drama Dept, State Univ. of Iowa, 1960; Ferens Vis. Prof. of Drama, Hull Univ., 1969; Vis. Prof. of Theatre History, Yale Univ., 1970; Killam Res. Prof., Dalhousie Univ., 1976–77; S. W. Brooks Vis. Prof., Univ. of Qld, 1983; Vis. Prof. in British Studies (Drama), Univ. of the South, Sewanee, 1984; Adjunct Prof. (Arts and Letters), Univ. of Notre Dame (London Campus), 1987–; Hon. Prof., Univ. of Warwick, 1990–95. Lectures: G. F. Reynolds Meml, Univ. of Colorado, 1960; Judith E. Wilson, in Poetry and Drama, Cambridge, 1960–61; Festvortrag, Deutsche Shakespeare Gesellschaft, 1973; Shakespeare, British Acad., 1984; British Council, in Europe, annually 1969–79. Directed: Amer. première, The Birthday Party, for Actors' Workshop, San Francisco, 1960; world première, Wole Soyinka's Brother Jero's Metamorphosis, 1974. Consultant to Finnish National Theatre and Theatre School on establishment of Drama Department in Univ. of Helsinki, 1963. Governor of Bristol Old Vic Trust, 1963–83; Vandyck Theatre, Bristol Univ., renamed Glynne Wickham Studio Theatre, 1983. Consultant to Univ. of E Africa on establishment of a Sch. of Drama in University Coll., Dar-es-Salaam, Tanzania, 1965; Dir, Theatre Seminar, for Summer Univ., Vaasa, Finland, 1965; External Examr to Sch. of Drama in Univ. of Ibadan, Nigeria, 1965–68. Chm., Nat. Drama Conf., Nat. Council of Social Service, 1970–76; Chm., and Chief Exec., Radio West plc (ILR Bristol), 1979–83; Pres., Soc. for Theatre Research, 1976–; Member: Adv. Cttee, British Theatre Museum, 1974–77; Culture Adv. Panel, UK Nat. Commn to UNESCO, 1984–86. Mem., Edit. Cttee, Shakespeare Survey, 1974–; Chairman: Adv. Bd, Theatre Research International, 1975–; Gen. Edit. Bd, Theatre in Europe: documents and sources, 1979–. Trustee, St Deiniol's Residential Library, Hawarden, 1985–; Dir, Bd of Internat. Shakespeare Globe Centre, 1986–91. Mem., Polish Acad. of Arts and Letters, 1991. Hon. DLitt: Loughborough, 1984; Univ. of the South, Sewanee, 1984. *Publications:* Early English Stages 1300–1660, Vol. I (1300–1576), 1959, 2nd edn 1980; Vol. II (1576–1660, Pt 1), 1962; Vol. II (Pt 2), 1972; Vol. III, 1981; Editor: The Relationship between Universities and Radio, Film and Television, 1954; Drama in a World of Science, 1962; Gen. Introd. to the London Shakespeare, 6 vols (ed J. Munro), 1958; Shakespeare's Dramatic Heritage, 1969; The Medieval Theatre, 1974, 3rd edn 1987; English Moral Interludes, 1975, 2nd edn 1985; A History of the Theatre, 1985, 2nd edn 1992. *Recreations:* gardening and travel. *Address:* 6 College Road, Clifton, Bristol BS8 3JB. *T:* Bristol (0117) 973 4918. *Clubs:* Garrick, National Liberal.

WICKHAM, John Ewart Alfred, FRCS; specialist in minimally invasive surgery and urology; Director, Academic Unit, Institute of Urology, University of London, since 1979; Surgeon: St Peter's Hospital, since 1967; King Edward VII Hospital, since 1972; Middlesex Hospital, since 1973; Surgeon and Senior Research Fellow, Guy's Hospital, since 1993; *b* 10 Dec. 1927; *s* of Alfred James Wickham and Hilda May Wickham (*née* Cummins); *m* 1961, (Gwendoline) Ann Loney; three *d*. *Educ:* Chichester Grammar Sch.; London Univ.; St Bartholomew's Hosp. Med. Coll. (BSc Hons 1953; MB BS 1955; MS 1966). FRCS 1959. Nat. Service, RAF, 1947–49. St Bartholomew's Hosp. and RPMS, 1955–66; Sen. Consultant Urological Surgeon, St Barts, 1966; Sen. Lectr, Inst of Urology, 1967–; Civilian Consultant Urologist, RAF, 1973–. Director: Lithotripter Units of London Clinic, 1984–, and of NE Thames Region, 1987–; Minimally Invasive Therapy, London Clinic, 1989–. First Pres., Internat. Soc. of Urological Endoscopy, 1982; President: Urological Sect., RSM, 1984–; Internat. Soc. of Minimally Invasive Therapy, 1989–; Founder Mem., Europ. Soc. of Urology, 1969; Member: Internat. Soc. of Urology, 1970; Italian-Belgian Soc. of Urology, 1980. Hon. FRCP 1993; Hon. FRCR 1993. Freeman, City of London; Liveryman, Barber Surgeon's Co., 1971. Hon. MD Gothenburg, 1994. Hunterian Prof. and Medal, RCS, 1967; Cutlers Prize and Medal, Assoc. of Surgeons, 1984; James Berry Medal, RCS, 1985; St Peter's Medal, British Assoc. of Urological Surgeons, 1985; J. K. Latimer Medal, Amer. Urological Assoc., 1990; Cecil Joll Prize, RCS, 1993; Rovsing Medal, Danish Soc. of Surgery, 1993. Editor, Jl of Minimally Invasive Therapy, 1990–. *Publications:* Urinary Calculus Disease, 1979; Percutaneous Renal Surgery, 1983; Intrarenal Surgery, 1984; Lithotripsy II, 1987; Urinary Stone Metabolic Basis and Clinical Practice, 1989; over 100 papers on urology and minimally invasive surgery. *Recreations:* mechanical engineering, tennis. *Address:* 29 Devonshire Place, W1N 1PE. *T:* 0171–935 2232; Stowe Maries, Balchins Lane, Westcott, Surrey RH4 3LR. *T:* Dorking (01306) 885557. *Clubs:* Athenæum, Royal Automobile.

WICKHAM, William Rayley; His Honour Judge Wickham; a Circuit Judge, since 1975; Hon. Recorder of Liverpool and Senior Circuit Judge, Liverpool, since 1992; *b* 22 Sept. 1926; *s* of late Rayley Esmond Wickham and late Mary Joyce Wickham; *m* 1957, Elizabeth Mary (*née* Thompson); one *s* two *d*. *Educ:* Sedbergh Sch.; Brasenose Coll., Oxford (MA, BCL). Served War of 1939–45, Army, 1944–48. Called to Bar, Inner Temple, 1951. Magistrate, Aden, 1953; Chief Magistrate, Aden, 1958; Crown Counsel, Tanganyika, 1959; Asst to Law Officers, Tanganyika, 1961–63; practised on Northern Circuit, 1963–75; a Recorder of the Crown Court, 1972–75. *Recreations:* fell walking, music, amateur dramatics. *Address:* Queen Elizabeth II Law Courts, Liverpool L2 1XA.

WICKINS, David Allen; Founder and Chairman, Southern Counties Car Auctions, later The British Car Auction Group, 1946–1989; *b* 15 Feb. 1920; *s* of Samuel Wickins and Edith Hannah Robinson; *m* 1969, Karen Esther Young; one *s* five *d*. *Educ:* St George's College, Weybridge. Trained as chartered accountant with Deloitte & Co., attached to Johannesburg Consolidated Investment Co. and moved to S Africa, 1938, to work on audits for Rhodesian copper mines and sawmills. War of 1939–45: S African Naval Forces (18 months with Eastern Fleet); seconded to RN; served with UK Coastal Forces. Former

Chairman: Attwoods plc; Group Lotus plc; Expedier Leisure plc. *Recreations:* tennis, golf, sailing. *Clubs:* St James's, Royal Thames Yacht; Sunningdale Golf; Wentworth Golf.

WICKRAMASINGHE, Prof. Nalin Chandra, PhD, ScD; Professor of Applied Mathematics and Astronomy in the School of Mathematics, University of Wales College of Cardiff, since 1988 (Professor and Head of Department of Applied Mathematics and Astronomy, University College, Cardiff, 1973–88); *b* 20 Jan. 1939; *s* of Percival Herbert Wickramasinghe and Theresa Elizabeth Wickramasinghe; *m* 1966, Nelum Priyadarshini Pereira; one *s* two *d*. *Educ:* Royal Coll., Colombo, Sri Lanka; Univ. of Ceylon (BSc); Univ. of Cambridge (MA, PhD, ScD). Commonwealth Scholar, Trinity Coll., Cambridge, 1960; Powell Prize for English Verse, 1961; Jesus College, Cambridge: Research Fellow, 1963–66; Fellow, 1967–73; Tutor, 1970–73; Staff Mem., Inst. of Theoretical Astronomy, Univ. of Cambridge, 1968–73. Visiting Professor: Vidyodaya Univ. of Ceylon, Univ. of Maryland, USA, Univ. of Arizona, USA, Univ. of Kyoto, Japan, 1966–70; Univ. of W Ontario, 1974, 1976; Inst. of Space and Astronautical Studies, Japan, 1993; UNDP Cons. and Scientific Advisor to President of Sri Lanka, 1970–81; Dir, Inst. of Fundamental Studies, Sri Lanka, 1982–83. Collaborator with Prof. Sir Fred Hoyle, and propounder with Hoyle of the theory of the space origin of life and of microorganisms. Dag Hammarskjöld Gold Medal in science, Académie Diplomatique de la Paix, 1986; Scholarly Achievement Award, Inst. of Oriental Philosophy, Japan, 1989; Internat. Peace and Culture Award, Soka Gakkai, 1993. Vidya Jyothi (Sri Lanka), 1992. *Publications:* Interstellar Grains, 1967; (with F. D. Kahn and P. G. Mezger) Interstellar Matter, 1972; Light Scattering Functions for Small Particles with Applications in Astronomy, 1973; The Cosmic Laboratory, 1975; (with D. J. Morgan) Solid State Astrophysics, 1976; Fundamental Studies and the Future of Science, 1984; (with F. Hoyle and J. Watkins) Viruses from Space, 1986; (with Daisaku Ikeda) Emergent Perspectives for 2000 AD, 1992; (with D. Ikeda) The Wonders of Life and the Universe, 1993; Glimpses of Life, Time and Space: an anthology of poetry, 1994; (with F. Hoyle): Lifecloud: the origin of life in the universe, 1978; Diseases From Space, 1979; The Origin of Life, 1980; Evolution From Space, 1981; Space Travellers, the Bringers of Life, 1981; From Grains to Bacteria, 1984; Living Comets, 1985; Archaeopteryx, the Primordial Bird: a case of fossil forgery, 1986; Cosmic Life Force, 1987; Theory of Cosmic Grains, 1991; Our Place in the Cosmos: the unfinished revolution, 1993; over 250 articles and papers in astronomical and scientific jls; contributor to anthologies of Commonwealth Poetry, incl. Young Commonwealth Poets '65, ed P. L. Brent, 1965. *Recreations:* photography, poetry—both writing and reading, history and philosophy of science. *Address:* School of Mathematics, University of Wales College of Cardiff, Senghenydd Road, Cardiff CF2 4AG. *T:* Cardiff (01222) 752146, *Fax:* Cardiff (01222) 753173. *Club:* Icosahedron Dining (Cardiff).

WICKREMESINGHE, Sarath Kusum; High Commissioner for Sri Lanka in London, since 1995; *b* 26 Jan. 1928; *m* 1953, Damayantha Hulugalle. *Educ:* St Thomas' Coll., Mt Lavinia; Univ. of Ceylon (BSc Hons Physics). Exec. in ICI (Export) Ltd, Colombo, 1951–66; Chief Exec., 1966–80, Chm., 1966–94, ICI associate co. in Sri Lanka; Chm., subsid. and associate cos, Coates Internat., 1982–84, BAT, 1985–91, and Standard Chartered Bank, 1989–94. *Address:* Sri Lanka High Commission, 13 Hyde Park Gardens, W2 2LU. *T:* 0171–262 1841. *Clubs:* Royal Over-Seas League; Royal Colombo Golf; Ceylon Rugby Football.

WICKREMESINGHE, Dr Walter Gerald, CMG 1954; OBE 1949; *b* 13 Feb. 1897; *s* of Peter Edwin Wickremesinghe and Charlotte Catherine Goonetilleka; *m* 1931, Irene Amelia Goontilleka; two *s* two *d*. *Educ:* Royal College, Colombo; Ceylon Medical College; London University (the London Hospital); Harvard University (School of Public Health). Licentiate in Medicine and Surgery (Ceylon), 1921; MRCS, LRCP, 1923; Master of Public Health (Harvard), 1926; Dr of Public Health (Harvard), 1927. Director of Medical and Sanitary Services, Ceylon, 1948–53. Chief Delegate from Ceylon at WHO Assembly and Executive board, Geneva, 1952; Mem. UN Health Planning Mission to Korea, 1952; WHO Consultant, Manila, 1965; Chairman, Committee of Inquiry into Mental Health Services, Ceylon, 1966. (Hon.) FAPHA 1952. OStJ. *Publications:* contributions to Brit. Med. Jl; Ceylon Med. Jl; Trans. Soc. of Med. Officers of Health, Ceylon; Amer. Jl of Public Health. *Recreations:* golf, tennis, riding, swimming. *Address:* 48 Buller's Lane, Colombo 7, Sri Lanka. *T:* Colombo (1) 581374. *Clubs:* Otter Aquatic, Royal Colombo Golf (Colombo); Nuwara Eliya Golf, Nuwara Eliya Hill; (Life Mem.) Health Dept Sports.

WICKS, Allan, CBE 1988; Organist, Canterbury Cathedral, 1961–88; *b* 6 June 1923; *s* of late Edward Kemble Wicks, priest, and Nancie (*née* Murgatroyd); *m* 1955, Elizabeth Kay Butcher; two *d*. *Educ:* Leatherhead; Christ Church, Oxford. Sub-organist, York Minster, 1947; Organist, Manchester Cathedral, 1954. MusDoc Lambeth, 1974; Hon. DMus Kent, 1985. *Address:* The Old Farm House, Lower Hardres, Canterbury, Kent CT4 5NR. *T:* Canterbury (01227) 700253.

WICKS, David Vaughan, RE 1961 (ARE 1950); Technical Artist, Bank of England Printing Works, 1954–79, retired, Consultant, 1979–85; *b* 20 Dec. 1918; British; *m* 1948, Margaret Gwyneth Downs (*d* 1990); one *s* one *d* (and one *s* decd). *Educ:* Wychwood, Bournemouth; Cranleigh School, Surrey. Polytechnic School of Art, 1936, silver medal for figure composition, 1938, 1939. Radio Officer, Merchant Navy, 1940–46. Royal College of Art, Engraving School, 1946–49, Diploma, ARCA Engraving. Taught Processes of Engraving at RCA, 1949–54. *Recreations:* gardening, bowls. *Address:* Flat 92, Orchard Court, The Avenue, Egham, Surrey TW20 9HA.

WICKS, Geoffrey Leonard; Metropolitan Stipendiary Magistrate, since 1987; *b* 23 July 1934; *s* of late Leonard James Wicks and Winifred Ellen Wicks; *m* 1st, 1959, Catherine Margaret Shanks (marr. diss. 1977); one *s* one *d*; 2nd, 1978, Maureen Evelyn Neville. *Educ:* Tollington Sch., N10; Law Society's Sch. of Law, London. Admitted Solicitor, 1957. National Service, RASC, 1957–59. Asst Solicitor, LCC, 1959–60, Asst Solicitor, 1960–61, Partner, 1961–79 (Abu Dhabi office, 1978), Oswald Hickson, Collier & Co., Solicitors, London, Chesham, Amersham, Slough; Principal, Geoffrey Wicks & Co., Solicitors, Chesham, Hemel Hempstead, 1979–82; Partner, Iliffes, Solicitors, London, Chesham, 1982–87. Member: Chesham Round Table, 1962–75 (Chm. 1968–69, Area Chm. Area 42, 1972–73); Chesham Rotary Club, 1974–77. *Recreations:* walking, sheep rearing, opera, ballet. *Address:* c/o Inner London Magistrates Court Service, 65 Romney Street, SW1P 3RD. *T:* 0171–799 3332.

WICKS, Sir James (Albert), Kt 1978; JP; Wanganui Computer Centre Privacy Commissioner, 1978–83; Acting District Court Judge, 1980–81; *b* 14 June 1910; *s* of Henry James Wilmont Wicks and Melanie de Rohan Wicks (*née* Staunton); *m* 1942 Lorna Margaret de la Cour; one *s* one *d*. *Educ:* Christchurch Boys' High Sch.; Canterbury Univ., NZ. LLM (Hons) Univ. of New Zealand. Admitted Barrister and Solicitor of Supreme Court of NZ, 1932; Notary Public, 1951; Lectr in Trustee Law, Canterbury Univ., 1946–55; in practice as barrister and solicitor (in Christchurch), 1945–61; Mem. Council, Canterbury Dist Law Soc., 1954–61. Stipendiary Magistrate, 1961–78. JP 1963; Chairman: Magistrates' Courts' Rules Cttee, 1967–78; NZ Magistrates' Exec., 1973–78; Dept of Justice's Editorial Bd, 1968–78; Chairman: various Appeal Boards and Statutory Cttees, 1965–78; Teachers' Disciplinary Bd, 1978–82; Cttee of Inquiry into the Administration of the Electoral Act, 1979; Public Service Appeal Bd, 1982; conducted inquiry into alleged improper political interference in administration of the State Services Commn, 1986; Mem. Bd of Dirs, Nat. Soc. on Alcoholism and Drug Dependence, NZ Inc., 1985–88. Consultant to Govt of Niue on legal, judicial and law enforcement systems and policies, 1983. *Publications:* papers to Australian Inst. of Criminology, Feb. 1974, and Commonwealth Magistrates' Conf., Kuala Lumpur, Aug. 1975; contribs to NZ Law Jl, Commonwealth Judicial Jl. *Address:* 29 Glen Road, Kelburn, Wellington 5, New Zealand. *T:* (4) 4759204. *Club:* Canterbury (Christchurch, NZ).

WICKS, Malcolm Hunt; MP (Lab) Croydon North West, since 1992; *b* 1 July 1947; *s* of Arthur Wicks and Daisy (*née* Hunt); *m* 1968, Margaret Baron; one *s* two *d*. *Educ:* Norfolk House; Elizabeth Coll., Guernsey; NW London Poly.; LSE (BSc Hons Sociology). Fellow, Dept of Social Admin, York Univ., 1968–70; res. worker, Centre for Envmtl Studies, 1970–72; Lectr in Social Admin, Dept of Govt Studies, Brunel Univ., 1970–74; Social Policy Analyst, Urban Deprivation Unit, Home Office, 1974–77; Lectr in Social Policy, Civil Service Coll., 1977–78; Res. Dir and Sec., Study Commn on the Family, 1978–83; Dir, Family Policy Studies Centre, 1983–92; Co-Dir, European Family and Social Policy Unit, 1992. Sec., PLP Social Security Cttee, 1994–. Mem., Family Policy Observatory, Eur. Commn, 1987–92. Chm., Winter Action on Cold Homes, 1986–92. Trustee, Nat. Energy Foundn, 1987–. *Publications:* Old and Cold: hypothermia and social policy, 1978; (jtly) Government and Urban Policy, 1983; A Future for All: do we need a welfare state?, 1987; (jtly) Family Change and Future Policy, 1990; contribs to books and periodicals. *Recreations:* walking, music, writing. *Address:* House of Commons, SW1A 0AA. *T:* 0171–219 3000. *Club:* Ruskin House Labour (Croydon).

WICKS, Sir Nigel (Leonard), KCB 1992; CVO 1989; CBE 1979; Second Permanent Secretary (Finance), HM Treasury, since 1989; *b* 16 June 1940; *s* of late Leonard Charles and Beatrice Irene Wicks; *m* 1969, Jennifer Mary (*née* Coveney) three *s*. *Educ:* Beckenham and Penge Grammar Sch.; Portsmouth Coll. of Technology; Univ. of Cambridge (MA); Univ. of London (MA). The British Petroleum Co. Ltd, 1958–68; HM Treasury, 1968–75; Private Sec. to the Prime Minister, 1975–78; HM Treasury, 1978–83; Economic Minister, British Embassy, Washington, and UK Exec. Dir, IMF and IBRD, 1983–85; Principal Private Sec. to the Prime Minister, 1985–88. Mem. Bd, BNOC, 1980–82. *Address:* HM Treasury, Parliament Street, SW1P 3AG.

WICKS, Rt. Rev. Ralph Edwin, OBE 1982; ED 1964; Bishop of the Southern Region, Diocese of Brisbane, 1985–88; *b* 16 Aug. 1921; *s* of Charles Thomas Wicks and Florence Maud Wicks (*née* White); *m* 1st, 1946, Gladys Hawgood (*d* 1981); one *s* one *d*; 2nd, 1988, Patricia Henderson. *Educ:* East State Sch. and State High Sch., Toowoomba, Qld; St Francis Theological Coll., Brisbane, Qld (LTh). Mem., Qld Public Service (Educn Dept), 1936–41; Theological Student, 1941–44; Asst Curate: Holy Trinity Ch., Fortitude Valley, Brisbane, 1944–47; St James' Ch., Toowoomba, Qld, 1947–48; Rector: Holy Trinity Ch., Goondiwindi, Qld, 1949–54; Holy Trinity Ch., Fortitude Valley, Brisbane, 1954–63; St James' Church, Toowoomba, Qld, 1963–72; Asst Bishop of Brisbane, 1973; Rector of St Andrew's Parish, Caloundra, and Commissary to Archbishop of Brisbane, 1983–85. Hon. Canon of St John's Cath., Brisbane, 1968; Archdeacon of Darling Downs, Qld, 1973. Chaplain to the Australian Army, 1949–70. *Recreations:* reading, gardening, music. *Address:* 1/9 The Esplanade, Mudjimba, Qld 4564, Australia.

WICKSTEAD, Cyril; Chairman, Eastern Electricity Board, 1978–82; Member, Electricity Council, 1978–82; *b* 27 Sept. 1922; *s* of John William and Mary Caroline Wickstead; *m* 1948, Freda May Hill; two *s*. *Educ:* Rowley Regis Central Sch.; City of Birmingham Commercial Coll. FCIS. Served War, Royal Navy (Lieut RNVR), 1942–46. Midland Electric Corporation for Power Distribution Ltd: various positions, 1937–42; Asst Sec., 1946–48; Midlands Electricity Board: Sec., S Staffs and N Worcs Sub-Area, 1948–59; Dep. Sec. of Bd, 1959–63; Sec., 1964–72; Dep. Chm., 1972–77. Freeman, City of London, 1979. *Recreations:* walking, music, gardening, sport. *Address:* Ryton, Brook Street, Dedham, Colchester, Essex CO7 6AD.

WIDDAS, Prof. Wilfred Faraday, MB, BS; BSc, PhD; DSc; Professor of Physiology in the University of London, and Head of the Department of Physiology, Bedford College, 1960–81, now Professor Emeritus; *b* 2 May 1916; *s* of late Percy Widdas, BSc, mining engineer, and Annie Maude (*née* Snowdon); *m* 1940, Gladys Green (*d* 1983); one *s* two *d*. *Educ:* Durham School; University of Durham College of Medicine and Royal Victoria Infirmary, Newcastle upon Tyne. MB, BS 1938; BSc 1947; PhD 1953; DSc 1958. Assistant in General Practice, 1938–39. Served in RAMC, 1939–47; Deputy Assistant Director-General Army Medical Services, War Office (Major), 1942–47. Research Fellow, St Mary's Hospital Medical School, 1947–49; Lecturer and Sen. Lecturer in Physiology, St Mary's Hospital Medical School, 1949–55; Senior Lecturer in Physiology, King's College, 1955–56; University Reader in Physiology at King's College, 1956–60. FRSocMed. Mem., Royal Institution of Gt Britain; Hon. Mem., Physiological Society. *Publications:* Membrane Transport of Sugars, chapter in Carbohydrate Metabolism and its Disorders; Permeability, chapter in Recent Advances in Physiology; also papers on similar topics in (chiefly) Jl of Physiology. *Recreations:* tennis, golf. *Address:* 67 Marksbury Avenue, Kew Gardens, Richmond, Surrey TW9 4JE. *T:* 0181–876 6374.

WIDDECOMBE, Ann Noreen; MP (C) Maidstone, since 1987; Minister of State, Home Office, since 1995; *b* 4 Oct. 1947; *d* of James Murray Widdecombe, *qv*. *Educ:* La Sainte Union Convent, Bath; Univ. of Birmingham; Lady Margaret Hall, Oxford (BA Hons, MA). Marketing, Unilever, 1973–75; Senior Administrator, Univ. of London, 1975–87. Contested (C): Burnley, 1979; Plymouth, Devonport, 1983. PPS to Tristan Garel-Jones, MP, Nov. 1990; Parly Under-Sec. of State, DSS, 1990–93, Dept of Employment, 1993–94; Minister of State, Dept of Employment, 1994–95. *Publication:* Layman's Guide to Defence, 1984. *Recreations:* reading, researching Charles II's escape. *Address:* 9 Tamar House, Kennington Lane, SE11 4XA. *T:* 0171–735 5192; Kloof Cottage, Sutton Valence, Maidstone, Kent. *T:* Maidstone (01622) 843868.

WIDDECOMBE, James Murray, CB 1968; OBE 1959; Director-General, Supplies and Transport (Naval), Ministry of Defence, 1968–70, retired; *b* 7 Jan. 1910; *s* of late Charles Frederick Widdecombe and late Alice Widdecombe; *m* 1936, Rita Noreen Plummer; one *s* one *d*. *Educ:* Devonport High Sch. Asst Naval Armament Supply Officer, Portsmouth, Holton Heath and Chatham, 1929–35; Dep. Naval Armt Supply Officer, Chatham, 1936; OC, RN Armt Depot, Gibraltar, 1936–40; Naval Armt Supply Officer: Admty, 1940–43; Levant, 1943–44. Capt. (SP) RNVR. Sen. Armt Supply Officer: Staff of C-in-C, Med., 1944–46; Admty, 1946–50; Asst Dir of Armt Supply, Admty, 1950–51, and 1956–59; Suptg Naval Armt Supply Officer, Portsmouth, 1951–53; Prin. Naval Armt Supply Officer, Staff of C-in-C, Far East, 1953–56; Dep. Dir of Armt Supply, Admiralty, 1959–61; Dir of Victualling, Admty, 1961–66; Head of RN Supply and Transport Service, MoD, 1966–68; special duties, Management Services, MoD, 1970–73. Gen. Sec., CS Retirement Fellowship, 1973–79. FIMgt; FCIPS. *Recreations:* golf, gardening, amateur dramatics. *Address:* 1 Manor Close, Haslemere, Surrey GU27 1PP. *T:* Haslemere (01428) 642899. *Club:* Navy Department Golfing Society (Pres.).

See also A. N. Widdecombe.

WIDDICOMBE, David Graham; QC 1965; a Recorder, since 1985; a Deputy High Court Judge, since 1983; *b* 7 Jan. 1924; *s* of Aubrey Guy Widdicombe and Margaret (*née* Puddy); *m* 1961, Anastasia Cecilia (*née* Leech) (marr. diss. 1983); two *s* one *d*. *Educ:* St Albans Sch.; Queen's Coll., Cambridge (BA 1st cl. Hons; LLB 1st cl. Hons; MA). Called to the Bar, Inner Temple, 1950, Bencher, 1973; Attorney at Law, State Bar of California, 1986. Mem., Cttee on Local Govt Rules of Conduct, 1973–74; Chairman: Oxfordshire Structure Plan Examination in Public, 1977; Cttee of Inquiry into Conduct of Local Authority Business, 1985–86. *Publication:* (ed) Ryde on Rating, 1968–83. *Address:* 2 Mitre Court Buildings, Temple, EC4Y 7BX. *T:* 0171–583 1380; 5 Albert Terrace, NW1 7SU. *T:* 0171–586 5209. *Clubs:* Athenæum, Garrick.

WIDDOWS, Air Commodore Charles; *see* Widdows, Air Commodore S. C.

WIDDOWS, Roland Hewlett, CB 1989; a Deputy Special Commissioner of Income Tax and Chairman (part-time) of Value Added Tax Tribunals, 1990–94; *b* 14 Aug. 1921; *s* of late A. E. Widdows, CB; *m* 1945, Diana Gweneth, *d* of late E. A. Dickson, Malayan Civil Service; two *s* one *d*. *Educ:* Stowe Sch.; Hertford Coll., Oxford (MA). Served in Royal Navy, Coastal Forces, 1941–45. Called to Bar, Middle Temple, 1948; entered Inland Revenue Solicitor's Office, 1951; Asst Solicitor, 1963; on staff of Law Commission, 1965–70; Lord Chancellor's Office, 1970–77; Under Secretary, 1972; Special Comr of Income Tax, 1977–90, Presiding Comr, 1984–90. *Recreation:* sailing. *Address:* 1 Chaucer Drive, Milford-on-Sea, Hants SO41 0SS. *T:* Lymington (01590) 644661. *Clubs:* United Oxford & Cambridge University; Royal Lymington Yacht.

WIDDOWS, Air Commodore (Stanley) Charles, CB 1959; DFC 1941 (despatches); RAF retired; People's Deputy, States of Guernsey, 1973–79; *b* 4 Oct. 1909; *s* of P. L. Widdows, Southend, Bradfield, Berkshire; *m* 1939, Irene Ethel, *d* of S. H. Rawlings, Ugley, Essex; two *s*. *Educ:* St Bartolomew's School, Newbury; No 1 School of Technical Training, RAF, Halton; Royal Air Force College, Cranwell. Commissioned, 1931; Fighting Area, RAF, 1931–32; RAF Middle East, Sudan and Palestine, 1933–37; Aeroplane and Armament Experimental Estab., 1937–40; OC 29 (Fighter) Sqdn, 1940–41; OC RAF West Malling, 1941–42; Gp Capt., Night Ops, HQ 11 and 12 Gp, 1942; SASO, No 85 (Base Defence) Gp, 1943–44, for Operation Overlord; Gp Capt. Organisation, HQ, Allied Expeditionary Air Force, 1944; OC, RAF Wahn, Germany, 1944–46; RAF Directing Staff, Sen. Officers War Course, RNC, Greenwich, 1946–48; Fighter Command, 1948–54: SASO HQ No 12 Gp; Chief Instructor, Air Defence Wing, School of Land/Air Warfare; Sector Commander, Eastern Sector. Imperial Defence College, 1955; Director of Operations (Air Defence), Air Ministry, 1956–58. Baulwick Rep., RAF Benevolent Fund, 1973–93. Vice-Pres., Guernsey Scout Assoc., 1990– (Chm., 1974–90). *Address:* Les Granges de Beauvoir, Rohais, St Peter Port, Guernsey GY1 1QT. *T:* Guernsey (01481) 720219. *Club:* Royal Channel Islands Yacht.

WIDDOWSON, Dr Elsie May, CH 1993; CBE 1979; FRS 1976; Department of Medicine, Addenbrooke's Hospital, Cambridge, 1972–88; *b* 21 Oct. 1906; *d* of Thomas Henry Widdowson and Rose Widdowson. *Educ:* Imperial Coll., London (BSc, PhD; FIC 1994); DSc London 1948. Courtauld Inst. of Biochemistry, Mddx Hosp., 1931–33; KCH, London, 1933–38; Cambridge University: Dept of Exper. Medicine, 1938–66; Infant Nutrition Res. Div., 1966–72. President: Nutrition Soc., 1977–80; Neonatal Soc., 1978–81; British Nutrition Foundn, 1986–. Hon. FRCP 1994; Hon. Fellow, Amer. Inst. of Nutrition, 1995. Hon. DSc: Manchester, 1974; Salford, 1995. James Spence Medal, British Paediatric Assoc., 1981; 2nd Bristol-Myers Award for Distinguished Achievement in Nutrition Res., 1982; 1st European Nutrition Award, Fedn of European Nutrition Socs, 1983; Rank Prize Funds Prize for Nutrition, 1984; McCollum Award, E. V. McCollum Commemorative Cttee, USA, 1985; Atwater Award, USA Agricl Res. Service, 1986; Nutritia Internat. Award, Nutricia Res. Foundn, 1988; 1st Edna and Robert Langholz Internat. Nutrition Award, 1992. *Publications:* (with R. A. McCance) The Composition of Foods, 1940 (2nd edn 1967); (with R. A. McCance) Breads White and Brown: Their Place in Thought and Social History, 1956; contrib. Proc. Royal Soc., Jl Physiol., Biochem. Jl, Brit. Jl Nut., Arch. Dis. Child., Lancet, BMJ, Nature, Biol. Neonate, Nut. Metabol., and Ped. Res. *Address:* Orchard House, 9 Boot Lane, Barrington, Cambridge CB2 5RA. *T:* Cambridge (01223) 870219.

WIDDOWSON, Prof. Henry George; Professor of Education, University of London, at Institute of Education, since 1977; Professor of Applied Linguistics, University of Essex, since 1993; *b* 28 May 1935; *s* of George Percival Widdowson and Edna Widdowson; *m* 1966, Dominique Dixmier (marr. diss.); two *s*. *Educ:* Alderman Newton's Sch., Leicester; King's Coll., Cambridge (MA); Univ. of Edinburgh (PhD). Lectr, Univ. of Indonesia, 1958–61; British Council Educn Officer, Sri Lanka, 1962–63; British Council English Language Officer, Bangladesh, 1963–64, 1965–68; Lectr, Dept of Linguistics, Univ. of Edinburgh, 1968–77. Chm., English Teaching Adv. Cttee, British Council, 1982–91; Mem., Kingman Cttee of Inquiry into Teaching of English Language, 1986–88. Editor, Jl of Applied Linguistics, 1980–85. *Publications:* Stylistics and the Teaching of Literature, 1975, Japanese edn 1989; Teaching Language as Communication, 1978, French edn 1981, Ital. edn 1982, Japanese edn 1991; Explorations in Applied Linguistics I, 1979; Learning Purpose and Language Use, 1983, Italian edn 1986; Explorations in Applied Linguistics II, 1984; (with Randolph Quirk) English in the World, 1985; Aspects of Language Teaching, 1990; Practical Stylistics, 1992; editor of series: English in Focus; Communicative Grammar; Language Teaching: a scheme for teacher education; papers in various jls. *Recreations:* poetry, rumination, walking. *Address:* Institute of Education, University of London, 20 Bedford Way, WC1H 0AL. *T:* 0171–612 6526.

WIDDUP, Malcolm, CB 1979; retired 1981; Under-Secretary, HM Treasury, 1971–80; *b* 9 May 1920; *s* of John and Frances Ellen Widdup; *m* 1947, Margaret Ruth Anderson; one *s* one *d*. *Educ:* Giggleswick Sch.; Trinity Coll., Oxford (MA). Served War, Army, RA and Staff, 1940–45. Ministry of Food, 1946–53; HM Treasury, 1953–55; Cabinet Office, 1955–57; HM Treasury, 1957–60; Min. of Health, 1960–62; HM Treasury, 1962–66; UK Delegn to OECD, 1966–68; HM Treasury, 1968–80; Sen. Clerk, House of Lords, 1980–81. *Recreations:* gardening, bridge, bowling.

WIDE, Charles Thomas; QC 1995; a Recorder, since 1995; *b* 16 April 1951; *s* of Nicholas Scott Wide, MC, and Ruth Mildred Norton Wide; *m* 1979, Ursula Margaret Bridget, *d* of Hon. William Buchan; one *s* one *d*. *Educ:* The Leys Sch., Cambridge; Exeter Univ. (LLB). Called to the Bar, Inner Temple, 1974; Midland and Oxford Circuit Junior, 1983; Standing Counsel to: HM Customs and Excise (Crime), 1989–95; Inland Revenue (Crime), 1991–95; Asst Recorder, 1991–95. *Recreation:* fell walking. *Address:* 9 Bedford Row, WC1R 4AZ. *T:* 0171–242 3555.

WIESEL, Prof. Elie; Andrew W. Mellon Professor in the Humanities, Boston University, since 1976; *b* 30 Sept. 1928; naturalised US citizen, 1963; *m* 1969, Marion Erster; one *s* one *d*. *Educ:* The Sorbonne, Univ. of Paris. Distinguished Prof. of Judaic Studies, City Coll., City Univ. of New York, 1972–76; Dist. Vis. Prof. of Literature and Philosophy, Florida Internat. Univ., 1982; Henry Luce Vis. Scholar in the Humanities and Social Thought, Whitney Humanities Center, Yale Univ., 1982–83. Founder, Elie Wiesel Foundn for Humanity, 1987. Chairman: US Holocaust Meml Council, 1980–86; US President's Commn on the Holocaust, 1979–80; Adv. Bd, World Union of Jewish Students, 1985–; Member, Board of Directors: Nat. Cttee on Amer. Foreign Policy, 1983– (Special Award, 1987); Internat. Rescue Cttee, 1985–; Hebrew Arts Sch.; HUMANITAS; Member, Board of Trustees: Amer. Jewish World Service, 1985–; Yeshiva Univ., 1977; Member, Board of Governors: Tel-Aviv Univ., 1976–; Haifa Univ., 1977–; Oxford Centre for Postgrad. Hebrew Studies, 1978–; Mem. Adv. Bd, Andrei Sakharov Inst.; Fellow: Jewish Acad. of Arts and Sciences; Amer. Acad. of Arts and Sciences, 1986; Member: Amnesty Internat.; Writers Guild of America (East); Authors' Guild; Writers and Artists for Peace in ME; Royal Norwegian Soc. of Sciences and Letters, 1987; Hon. Life Mem., Foreign Press Assoc., 1985. Holds hon. degrees from univs and colls. Elie Wiesel Chair in Judaic Studies endowed at Connecticut Coll., 1990. Nobel Peace Prize, 1986; other awards include: Anatoly Shcharansky Humanitarian Award, 1983; Congressional Gold Medal of Achievement, 1984; Achievement Award, Israel, 1987. Grand Officier de la Légion d'Honneur, France, 1990 (Commandeur, 1984); Grand Cross, Order of the Southern Cross, Brazil, 1987. *Publications:* Night (memoir), 1960; The Jews of Silence (personal testimony), 1966; Legends of Our Time, 1968; One Generation After, 1971; Souls on Fire: portraits and legends of the Hasidic masters, 1972; Messengers of God: portraits and legends of Biblical heroes, 1976; A Jew Today, 1978; Four Hasidic Masters, 1978; Images from the Bible, 1980; Le Testament d'un Poète Juif Assassiné, 1980 (Prix Livre-Inter, and Bourse Goncourt, France, 1980; Prix des Bibliothèquaires, France, 1981); Five Biblical Portraits, 1981; Paroles d'étranger, 1982; Somewhere a Master, 1982; The Golem, 1983; Signes d'Exode, 1985; Against Silence: the voice and vision of Elie Wiesel (collected shorter writings, ed Irving Abrahamson), 3 vols, 1985; Job ou Dieu dans la Tempête (dialogue and commentary with Josy Eisenberg), 1986; The Nobel Address, 1987; (jtly) The Six Days of Destruction, 1988; Silences et Mémoire d'hommes, 1989; From the Kingdom of Memory (reminiscences), 1990; Evil and Exile (dialogues with Philippe-Michael de Saint-Chéron), 1990; (with John Cardinal O'Connor) A Journey of Faith, 1990; Sages and Dreamers, 1991; *novels:* Dawn, 1961; The Accident, 1962; The Town beyond the Wall, 1964; The Gates of the Forest, 1966; A Beggar in Jerusalem, 1970; The Oath, 1973; The Testament, 1980; The Fifth Son, 1985 (Grand Prix de la Littérature, Paris); Twilight, 1988; L'Oublié, 1989 (The Forgotten, 1992); *cantatas:* Ani Maamin, 1973; A Song for Hope, 1987; *plays:* Zalmen, or the Madness of God, 1975; The Trial of God, 1979. *Address:* Boston University, 745 Commonwealth Avenue, Boston, MA 02215, USA. *Club:* PEN.

WIESEL, Prof. Torsten Nils, MD; Head of Laboratory of Neurobiology, since 1983, and President, since 1992, Rockefeller University; *b* 3 June 1924; *s* of Fritz S. Wiesel and Anna-Lisa Wiesel (*née* Bentzer); *m* 1st, 1956, Teeri Stenhammar (marr. diss. 1970); 2nd, 1973, Ann Yee (marr. diss. 1981); one *d*. *Educ:* Karolinska Inst., Stockholm (MD 1954). Instructor, Dept of Physiol., Karolinska Inst., 1954–55; Asst, Dept of Child Psychiatry, Karolinska Hosp., Stockholm, 1954–55; Fellow in Ophthalmol., 1955–58, Asst Prof. of Ophthalmic Physiol., 1958–59, Johns Hopkins Univ. Med. Sch., Baltimore; Harvard Medical School: Associate in Neurophysiol. and Neuropharmacol., 1959–60; Asst Prof., 1960–67; Prof. of Physiol., 1967–68; Prof. of Neurobiol., 1968–74; Chm., Dept of Neurobiol., 1973–82; Robert Winthrop Prof. of Neurobiol., 1974–83. Lectures: Ferrier, Royal Soc., 1972; Grass, Soc. for Neurosci., 1976. Member: Amer. Physiol Soc.; AAAS; Amer. Acad. of Arts and Scis; Amer. Philosophical Soc.; Soc. for Neurosci. (Pres. 1978–79); Nat. Acad. of Scis; Swedish Physiol Soc.; Foreign Mem., Royal Soc., 1982; Hon. Mem., Physiolog. Soc., 1982. Hon. AM Harvard Univ., 1967; Hon. MD Linköping, 1982; Hon. Dr of Med. and Surg. Ancona Univ., 1982; Hon. DSc Pennsylvania, 1982. Awards and Prizes: Dr Jules C. Stein, Trustees for Research to Prevent Blindness, 1971; Lewis S. Rosenstiel, Brandeis Univ., 1972; Friedenwald, Assoc. for Res. in Vision and Ophthalmology, 1975; Karl Spencer Lashley, Amer. Phil. Soc., 1977; Louisa Gross Horwitz, Columbia Univ., 1978; Dickson, Pittsburgh Univ., 1979; Ledlie, Harvard Univ., 1980; Soc. for Scholars, Johns Hopkins Univ., 1980; Nobel Prize in Physiology or Medicine, 1981. *Publications:* (contrib.) Physiological and Biochemical Aspects of Nervous Integration, 1968; (contrib.) The Organization of the Cerebral Cortex, 1981; contribs to professional jls, symposia and trans of learned socs. *Address:* Rockefeller University, 1230 York Avenue, New York, NY 10021–6399, USA. *T:* (212) 5707661. *Club:* Harvard (Boston).

WIGAN, Sir Alan (Lewis), 5th Bt *cr* 1898; *b* 19 Nov. 1913; second *s* of Sir Roderick Grey Wigan, 3rd Bt, and Ina (*d* 1977), *o c* of Lewis D. Wigan, Brandon Park, Suffolk; *S* brother, 1979; *m* 1950, Robina, *d* of Sir Iain Colquhoun, 7th Bt, KT, DSO; one *s* one *d*. *Educ:* Eton; Magdalen College, Oxford. Commissioned Suppl. Reserve, KRRC, 1936; served with KRRC, 1939–46; wounded and taken prisoner, Calais, 1940. Director, Charrington & Co. (Brewers), 1939–70. Master, Brewers' Co., 1958–59. *Recreations:* shooting, fishing, golf. *Heir: s* Michael Iain Wigan [*b* 3 Oct. 1951; *m* 1st, 1984, Frances (marr. diss. 1985), *d* of late Flt-Lt Angus Barr Faucett and of Mrs Antony Reid; 2nd, 1989, Julia, *d* of John de Courcy Ling, *qv*; two *s* one *d*]. *Address:* Badingham House, Badingham, Woodbridge, Suffolk IP13 8JP. *T:* Badingham (01728) 638664; Moorburn, The Lake, Kirkcudbright DG6 4XL. *T:* Kirkcudbright (01557) 30623. *Club:* Army and Navy.

WIGDOR, Lucien Simon, CEng, MRAeS; President, L. S. Wigdor Inc., New Hampshire, since 1984; Managing Director, L. S. Wigdor Ltd, since 1976; *b* Oct. 1919; *s* of William and Adèle Wigdor; *m* 1951, Marion Louise, *d* of Henry Risner; one *s* one *d*. *Educ:* Highgate Sch.; College of Aeronautical Engineering. Served War, RAF, early helicopter pilot, 1940–46 (Sqn Ldr); Operational Research, BEA: Research Engr, 1947–51; Manager, Industrial and Corporate Develt, Boeing Vertol Corp., USA, 1951–55; Managing Dir, Tunnel Refineries Ltd, 1955–69, Vice-Chm., 1969–72; Corporate Consultant, The Boeing Company, 1960–72; Dep. Dir-Gen., CBI, 1972–76; Chief Exec., Leslie & Godwin (Holdings) Ltd, 1977–78, Dir 1977–81; Chm., Weir Pumps Ltd, 1978–81; Director: The Weir Group, 1978–81; Rothschild Investment Trust, 1977–82; Zambian Engineering Services Ltd, 1979–84; Rothschild Internat. Investments SA, 1981–82. Special Adviser on Internat. Affairs, Bayerische Hypotheken-SPTund Wechsel-SPTBank AG, 1981–83; Consultant: Lazard Bros, 1982–84; Manufacturing and Financial Services Industries (L. S. Wigdor Inc.), 1984–. *Publications:* papers to Royal Aeronautical Soc., American Helicopter Soc. *Recreations:* ski-ing, experimental engineering. *Address:* Indian Point, Little Sunapee Road, PO Box 1035, New London, NH 03257, USA. *T:* (603) 5264456, *Fax:* (603) 5264963. *Club:* Royal Air Force.

WIGGHAM, Hon. (Edward) Barrie, CBE 1991; JP; Hong Kong Commissioner, USA, since 1993; *b* 1 March 1937; *s* of Edward and Agnes Wiggham; *m* 1961, Mavis Mitson; two *d* (one *s* decd). *Educ:* Woking Grammar Sch.; Queen's Coll., Oxford (MA Mod. Langs). Hong Kong Government: Admin. Officer, 1961–63; Dist Officer, New Territories, 1963–71; postings in finance, econ., security and information branches, 1971–79; Comr for Recreation and Culture, 1979–83; Regl Sec., 1983–86; seconded to British Embassy, Peking, 1986; Sec., General Duties, 1986–90; Mem. Gov's Exec. Council, 1989–92; Sec. for CS, 1990–93. JP Hong Kong, 1973. *Recreations:* music, people. *Address:* Hong Kong Economic and Trade Office, 1150 18th Street NW, Washington, DC 20036, USA; Government Secretariat, Lower Albert Road, Hong Kong. *Clubs:* Commonwealth Trust; Hong Kong, Foreign Correspondents, United Services (Hong Kong); George Town, National Press (Washington).

WIGGIN, Sir Alfred William, (Sir Jerry Wiggin), Kt 1993; TD 1970; MP (C) Weston-super-Mare since 1969; *b* 24 Feb. 1937; *e s* of late Col Sir William H. Wiggin, KCB, DSO, TD, DL, JP, and late Lady Wiggin, Worcestershire; *m* 1st, 1964, Rosemary Janet (marr. diss. 1982), *d* of David L. D. Orr; two *s* one *d*; 2nd, 1991, Morella Bulmer (*née* Kearton). *Educ:* Eton; Trinity Coll., Cambridge. 2nd Lieut, Queen's Own Warwickshire and Worcestershire Yeomanry (TA), 1959; Major, Royal Yeomanry, 1975–78. Contested (C), Montgomeryshire, 1964 and 1966. PPS to Lord Balniel, at MoD, later FCO, 1970–74, and to Ian Gilmour, MoD, 1971–72; Parly Sec., MAFF, 1979–81; Parly Under-Sec. of State for Armed Forces, MoD, 1981–83. Chm., Select Cttee on Agriculture, 1987–. Jt Hon. Sec., Conservative Defence Cttee, 1974–75; Vice-Chm., Conservative Agricultural Cttee, 1975–79; Chm., West Country Cons. Gp, 1978–79. Promoted Hallmarking Act, 1973. Chm., Economic Cttee, North Atlantic Assembly, 1990–94. Hon. Col, Warwickshire and Worcs Yeomanry (A) Sqn, Royal Mercian and Lancastrian Yeomanry, 1992–. *Address:* House of Commons, SW1A 0AA. *T:* 0171–219 4466; The Court, Axbridge, Somerset BS26 2BN. *T:* Axbridge (01934) 732527. *Clubs:* Beefsteak, Pratt's; Royal Yacht Squadron.

WIGGIN, Maj. Sir Charles Rupert John, 5th Bt *cr* 1892, of Metchley Grange, Harborne, Staffs; *b* 2 July 1949; *s* of Sir John Wiggin, 4th Bt, MC and his 1st wife, Lady Cecilia Evelyn Anson (*d* 1963), *yr d* of 4th Earl of Lichfield; *S* father, 1992; *m* 1979, Mrs Mary Burnett-Hitchcock; one *s* one *d*. *Educ:* Eton. Major, Grenadier Guards. *Heir: s* Richard Edward John Wiggin, *b* 1 July 1980. *Address:* c/o Child & Co., 1 Fleet Street, EC4Y 1BD.

WIGGIN, Sir Jerry; *see* Wiggin, Sir A. W.

WIGGINS, (Anthony) John; Member, Court of Auditors of the European Communities, since 1993; *b* 8 July 1938; *s* of late Rev. Arthur Wiggins and of Mavis Wiggins (*née* Brown); *m* 1962, Jennifer Anne Walkden; one *s* one *d*. *Educ:* Highgate Sch.; The Hotchkiss Sch., Lakeville, Conn, USA; Oriel Coll., Oxford (MA). Assistant Principal, HM Treasury, 1961; Private Sec. to Permanent Under Sec., Dept of Economic Affairs, 1964–66; Principal: Dept of Economic Affairs, 1966–67; HM Treasury, 1967–69; Harkness Fellow, Harvard Univ., 1969–71 (MPA 1970); Asst Sec., HM Treasury 1972–79; Principal Private Sec. to Chancellor of the Exchequer, 1980–81; Under Sec., Dept of Energy, 1981–84 (Mem. of BNOC, 1982–84); Under Sec., Cabinet Office, 1985–87; Under Sec., 1987–88, Dep. Sec., 1988–92, DES, subseq. DFE, on secondment to HM Treasury, 1992. Sec. to Royal Opera House Develt Bd, 1987–93 (Sec. to cttees, 1982–87). *Recreations:* mountaineering, skiing, opera. *Address:* 12 rue Alcide de Gasperi, 1615 Luxembourg. *Club:* Alpine.

WIGGINS, Prof. David, FBA 1978; Wykeham Professor of Logic, and Fellow of New College, Oxford University, since 1994; *b* 8 March 1933; *s* of late Norman Wiggins and Diana Wiggins (*née* Priestley); *m* 1979, Jennifer Hornsby. *Educ:* St Paul's Sch.; Brasenose Coll., Oxford. BA 1955; MA 1958. Asst Principal, Colonial Office, London 1957–58. Jane Eliza Procter Vis. Fellow, Princeton Univ., 1958–59; Lectr, 1959, then Fellow and Lecturer, 1960–67, New College, Oxford; Prof. of Philosophy, Bedford Coll., Univ. of London, 1967–80; Fellow and Praelector in Philosophy, University Coll., Oxford, 1981–89; Prof. of Philosophy, Birkbeck Coll., Univ. of London, 1989–94. Visiting appointments: Stanford, 1964 and 1965; Harvard, 1968 and 1972; All Souls College, 1973; Princeton, 1980; New York Univ., 1988; Fellow, Center for Advanced Study in the Behavioral Sciences, Stanford, 1985–86. Mem., Indep. Commn on Transport, 1973–74; Chm., Transport Users' Consultative Cttee for the South East, 1977–79. Mem., Institut International de Philosophie. For. Hon. Mem., Amer. Acad. of Arts and Scis, 1992. *Publications:* Identity and Spatio-Temporal Continuity, 1967; Truth, Invention and the Meaning of Life, 1978; Sameness and Substance, 1980; Needs, Values, Truth: essays in the philosophy of value, 1986; philosophical articles in Philosophical Review, Analysis, Philosophy, Synthèse, Phil Qly, Ratio; articles on environmental and transport subjects in Spectator, Times, Tribune.

WIGGINS, John; *see* Wiggins, A. J.

WIGGINS, Rt Rev. Maxwell Lester; Bishop of Victoria Nyanza, 1963–76; retired; *b* 5 Feb. 1915; *s* of Herbert Lester and Isobel Jane Wiggins; *m* 1941, Margaret Agnes Evans (decd); one *s* two *d*. *Educ:* Christchurch Boys' High Sch., NZ; Canterbury University College, NZ (BA). Asst Curate, St Mary's, Merivale, NZ, 1938; Vicar of Oxford, NZ, 1941; CMS Missionary, Diocese Central Tanganyika, 1945; Head Master, Alliance Secondary Sch., Dodoma, 1948; Provost, Cathedral of Holy Spirit, Dodoma, 1949; Principal, St Philip's Theological Coll., and Canon of Cathedral of Holy Spirit, Dodoma, 1954; Archdeacon of Lake Province, 1956; Asst Bishop of Central Tanganyika, 1959; Asst Bishop of Wellington, 1976–81; Pres., NZ CMS, 1986– (Gen. Sec., 1982–83). Sen. ChLJ, 1982–. *Address:* 42 Otara Street, Christchurch 5, New Zealand.

WIGGLESWORTH, Gordon Hardy, RIBA; Consultant, Alan Turner Associates, architects, planning and development consultants, 1988–92 (Director, 1984–88); *b* 27 June 1920; *m* 1952, Cherry Diana Heath; three *d*. *Educ:* Highgate; University Coll., London; Architectural Association. AADipl; RIBA 1948. Served War of 1939–45: Royal Engineers, 1941–46. Architectural Assoc., 1946–48; private practice and Univ. of Hong Kong, 1948–52; private practice: London, 1952–54; Hong Kong, 1954–56; London, 1956–57. Asst Chief Architect, Dept of Education and Science, 1957–67; Dir of Building Develt, MPBW, later DoE, 1967–72; Principal Architect, Educn, GLC (ILEA), 1972–74; Housing Architect, GLC, 1974–80. FRSA. *Address:* 53 Canonbury Park South, N1 2JL. *T:* 0171–226 7734.

WIGGLESWORTH, Mark Harmon; orchestral conductor; Music Director, BBC National Orchestra of Wales, since 1996; *b* 19 July 1964; *s* of Martin Wigglesworth and Angela (*née* Field). *Educ:* Bryanston Sch.; Manchester Univ. (BMus); Royal Acad. of Music. Winner, Kondrashin Comp., 1989. Founder and Music Dir, Première Ensemble, 1989–; Associate Conductor, BBC SO, 1991–93; Music Dir, Opera Factory, 1991–94. *Address:* c/o Harold Holt Ltd, 31 Sinclair Road, W14 0NS. *T:* 0171–603 4600.

WIGGLESWORTH, William Robert Brian; Director, Redheath Ltd; Joint Director, International Institute for Regulations in Telecommunications, City University; *b* 8 Aug. 1937; *s* of Sir Vincent Wigglesworth, CBE, FRS; *m* 1969, Susan Mary, *d* of late Arthur Baker, JP, Lavenham; one *s* one *d*. *Educ:* Marlborough; Magdalen College, Oxford (BA). Nat. Service, 2nd Lieut, Royal Signals, 1956–58. Ranks, Hovis McDougall Ltd, 1961–70: trainee; Gen. Manager, Mother's Pride Bakery, Cheltenham; PA to Group Chief Exec.; Gen. Manager, Baughans of Colchester; Board of Trade, 1970; Fair Trading Div., Dept of Prices and Consumer Protection, 1975; Posts and Telecommunications Div., 1978, Inf. Tech. Div., 1982, Dept of Industry; Dep. Dir Gen. of Telecommunications, 1984–94, Actg Dir, 1992–93. Prin. Advr, Telecoms Forum, Internat. Inst. of Communications; Mem. Bd, UKERNA. *Recreations:* fishing, gardening, history. *Address:* Millfield House, Heath Road, Polstead, Colchester CO6 5AN. *T:* Boxford (01787) 210590, *Fax:* (01787) 210592.

WIGHT, Robin; Chairman, WCRS, since 1987; *b* 6 July 1944; *s* of late Brig. I. L. Wight and of C. P. Wight; *m* 1st (marr. diss.); two *s* one *d*; 2nd, 1991, Anastasia Alexander; one *d*. *Educ:* Wellington Coll.; St Catharine's Coll., Cambridge. Copywriter: Robert Sharp and Partners, 1966; CDP and Partners, 1967; Creative Director: Richard Cope and Partners, 1968; Euro Advertising, 1968; Creative Partner, Wight, Collins, Rutherford, Scott, 1979. Marketing Adviser to Rt Hon. Peter Walker, 1982–84. Chm., Duke of Edinburgh Award Charter for Business, 1992. Mem. Council, ABSA, 1994–. Contested (C) Bishop Auckland, 1987. *Publication:* The Day the Pigs Refused to be Driven to Market, 1972. *Recreations:* horseriding, oenology. *Address:* Tally Ho Barns, Cloud Hill, near Guiting Power, Glos.

WIGHTMAN, Very Rev. William David; Provost of St Andrew's Cathedral, Aberdeen, since 1991; Priest in charge of St Ninian, Aberdeen, since 1991; *b* 29 Jan. 1939; *s* of William Osborne Wightman and Madge Wightman; *m* 1963, Karen Elizabeth Harker; two *s* two *d*. *Educ:* Alderman Newton's GS, Leicester; George Dixon GS, Birmingham; Univ. of Birmingham (BA Hons Theol.); Wells Theol Coll. Ordained deacon, 1963; priest, 1964; Curate: St Mary and All Saints, Rotherham, 1963–67; St Mary, Castlechurch, Stafford, 1967–70; Vicar: St Aidan, Buttershaw, Bradford, 1970–76; St John the Evangelist, Cullingworth, Bradford, 1976–83; Rector: St Peter, Peterhead, 1983–91; St John Longside, St Drostan, Old Deer and All Saints, Strichen, 1990–91; Chaplain, HM Prison, Peterhead, 1989–91; Dir, Training for Ministry, Dio. of Aberdeen and Orkney, 1989–94. Hon. Canon, Christ Church Cathedral, Hartford, Conn, USA, 1991. *Recreations:* fishing, choral music, swimming, gardening. *Address:* 15 Morningfield Road, Aberdeen AB2 4AP. *T:* Aberdeen (01224) 314765.

WIGHTWICK, Charles Christopher Brooke, MA; educational consultant, since 1991; *b* 16 Aug. 1931; *s* of Charles Frederick Wightwick and Marion Frances Wightwick (*née* Smith); *m* 1st, 1955, Pamela Layzell (marr. diss. 1986); one *s* two *d*; 2nd, 1986, Gillian Rosemary Anderson (*née* Dalziel). *Educ:* St Michael's, Otford Court; Lancing Coll.; St Edmund Hall, Oxford. BA 1954, MA 1958. Asst Master, Hurstpierpoint Coll., 1954–59; Head of German, Denstone Coll., 1959–65; Head of Languages, then Director of Studies, Westminster Sch., 1965–75; Head Master, King's College Sch., Wimbledon, 1975–80; HM Inspector of Schs, 1980–91; Staff Inspector for Mod. Langs, 1988–91. Series Editor, Berlitz Language Reference Handbooks, 1992–; Gen. Editor, Cambridge French Programme, 1993–. *Publications:* (co-author) Longman Audio-Lingual German, 3 vols., 1974–78; German Grammar Handbook, 1993. *Recreations:* photography, computer programming, running, judo, language. *Address:* 19 Nottingham Road, SW17 7EA. *T:* 0181–767 6161.

WIGLEY, Dafydd; MP (Plaid Cymru) Caernarfon since Feb. 1974; President, Plaid Cymru, 1981–84, and since 1991; industrial economist; *b* April 1943; *s* of Elfyn Edward Wigley, former County Treasurer, Caernarfonshire CC; *m* Elinor Bennett (*née* Owen), *d* of late Emrys Bennett Owen, Dolgellau; one *s* one *d* (and two *s* decd). *Educ:* Caernarfon Grammar Sch.; Rydal Sch., Colwyn Bay; Manchester Univ. Ford Motor Co., 1964–67; Chief Cost Accountant and Financial Planning Manager, Mars Ltd, 1967–71; Financial Controller, Hoover Ltd, Merthyr Tydfil, 1971–74. Mem., Merthyr Tydfil Borough Council, 1972–74. Mem., Select Cttee on Welsh Affairs, 1983–87. Vice-Chairman: Parly Social Services Gp, 1985–88; All-Party Disablement Gp, 1992–; British-Slovene Parly Gp, 1993–; Mem., Standing Cttee on Eur. Legislation, 1991–. Sponsor, Disabled Persons Act, 1981. Contested (Plaid Cymru), N Wales, Eur. Parly elecns, 1994. Vice-Pres., Nat. Fedn of Industrial Develt Authorities, 1981–. Mem., Nat. Cttee for Electoral Reform. Pres., Spastic Soc. of Wales, 1985–90. Pres. (unpaid), S Caernarfonshire Creamery. Fellow, UCNW, Bangor, 1994. *Publications:* An Economic Plan for Wales, 1970; O Ddifri, 1992; Dal Ati, 1993. *Address:* House of Commons, SW1A 0AA.

WIGMORE, James Arthur Joseph; His Honour Judge Wigmore; a Circuit Judge, since 1990; *b* 7 Aug. 1928; *s* of Sqdn-Ldr Arthur J. O. Wigmore, MB, and Kathleen (*née* Jowett); *m* 1966, Diana, *d* of Comdr H. J. Holemans, RN; three *d*. *Educ:* Downside Sch.; Royal Military Acad., Sandhurst; English Coll., Rome. BSc London; PhL, STL, Gregorian Univ., Rome. Served Royal Signals, 1946–52, commnd 1948. Lectured in Philosophy: Downside Abbey, 1960–63; Oscott Coll., 1963–66. Called to the Bar, Inner Temple, 1971; Dep. Coroner, Bristol, 1976–88; a Recorder, 1989. *Club:* Naval and Military.

WIGODER, family name of **Baron Wigoder.**

WIGODER, Baron *cr* 1974 (Life Peer), of Cheetham in the City of Manchester; **Basil Thomas Wigoder,** QC 1966; Vice-President, British United Provident Association, since 1992 (Chairman, 1981–92); *b* 12 Feb. 1921; *s* of late Dr P. I. Wigoder and Mrs R. R. Wigoder, JP, Manchester; *m* 1948, Yoland Levinson; three *s* one *d* (of whom one *s* one *d* are twins). *Educ:* Manchester Gram. Sch.; Oriel Coll., Oxford (Open Scholar, Mod. Hist.; MA 1946). Served RA, 1942–45. Pres. Oxford Union, 1946. Called to Bar, Gray's Inn, 1946, Master of the Bench, 1972, Vice-Treas., 1988, Treas., 1989. A Recorder of the Crown Court, 1972–84. BoT Inspector, Pinnock Finance (GB) Ltd, 1967. Member: Council of Justice, 1960–; Gen. Council of the Bar, 1970–74; Crown Court Rules Cttee, 1971–77; Council on Tribunals, 1980–86; Home Office Adv. Cttee on Service Candidates, 1984–; Chm., Health Services Bd, 1977–80; a Tribunal Chm., Securities Assoc., 1988–92. Chm., Liberal Party Exec., 1963–65; Chm., Liberal Party Organising Cttee, 1965–66; Liberal Chief Whip, House of Lords, 1977–84 (Dep. Whip, 1976–77). Contested (L): Bournemouth, 1945 and by-election, Oct. 1945; Westbury, 1959 and 1964. Vice-President: Nuffield Hosps, 1981–92; Statute Law Soc., 1984–90; Mem. Court, Nene Coll., 1982–90; Trustee, Oxford Union Soc., 1982–92. *Recreations:* cricket, music. *Address:* House of Lords, SW1A 0PW. *Clubs:* National Liberal, MCC.

WIGRAM, family name of **Baron Wigram.**

WIGRAM, 2nd Baron, *cr* 1935, of Clewer; **George Neville Clive Wigram,** MC 1945; JP; DL; *b* 2 Aug. 1915; *s* of Clive, 1st Baron Wigram, PC, GCB, GCVO, CSI, and Nora Mary (*d* 1956), *d* of Sir Neville Chamberlain, KCB, KCVO; *S* father 1960; *m* 1941, Margaret Helen (*d* 1986), *yr d* of late General Sir Andrew Thorne, KCB, CMG, DSO; one *s* two *d*. *Educ:* Winchester and Magdalen College, Oxford. Page of Honour to HM King George V, 1925–32; served in Grenadier Guards, 1937–57: Military Secretary and Comptroller to Governor-General of New Zealand, 1946–49; commanded 1st Bn Grenadier Guards, 1955–56. Governor of Westminster Hospital, 1967–74. JP Gloucestershire, 1959, DL 1969. *Heir: s* Major Hon. Andrew (Francis Clive) Wigram, MVO, late Grenadier Guards [*b* 18 March 1949; *m* 1974, Gabrielle Diana, *y d* of late R. D. Moore; three *s* one *d*]. *Address:* Poulton Fields, Cirencester, Gloucestershire GL7 5SS. *T:* Cirencester (01285) 851250. *Club:* Cavalry and Guards.

WIGRAM, Rev. Canon Sir Clifford Woolmore, 7th Bt, *cr* 1805; Vicar of Marston St Lawrence with Warkworth, near Banbury, 1945–83, also of Thenford, 1975–83; Non-Residentiary Canon of Peterborough Cathedral, 1973–83, Canon Emeritus since 1983; *b* 24 Jan. 1911; *er s* of late Robert Ainger Wigram and Evelyn Dorothy, *d* of C. W. E. Henslowe; *S* uncle, 1935; *m* 1948, Christobel Joan Marriott (*d* 1983), *d* of late William Winter Goode. *Educ:* Winchester; Trinity Coll., Cambridge. Asst Priest at St Ann's,

Brondesbury, 1934–37; Chaplain Ely Theological College, 1937. *Heir: b* Maj. Edward Robert Woolmore Wigram, Indian Army [*b* 19 July 1913; *m* 1944, Viva Ann, *d* of late Douglas Bailey, Laughton Lodge, near Lewes, Sussex; one *d. Educ:* Winchester; Trinity Coll., Cambridge. Attached 2nd Batt. South Staffordshire Regt, Bangalore, 1935; Major, 19th KGO Lancers, Lahore, 1938]. *Address:* 2 Mold Cottages, Marston St Lawrence, Banbury, Oxon OX17 2DB.

WIGRAM, Derek Roland, MA, BSc (Econ.); Headmaster of Monkton Combe School, near Bath, 1946–68; *b* 18 Mar. 1908; *er s* of late Roland Lewis Wigram and of Mildred (*née* Willock); *m* 1944, Catharine Mary, *d* of late Very Rev. W. R. Inge, KCVO, DD, former Dean of St Paul's; one *s* one *d. Educ:* Marlborough Coll.; Peterhouse, Cambridge (Scholar). 1st Class Hons Classical Tripos, 1929; 2nd Class Hons Economics and Political Science, London, 1943; Assistant Master and Careers Master, Whitgift School, Croydon, 1929–36; House Master and Careers Master, Bryanston School, 1936–46. Hon. Associate Mem., Headmasters' Conf. (Chm., 1963–64); Vice-Pres., CMS (Chm., Exec. Cttee, 1956–58, 1969–72); Patron, Oxford Conf. in Education; Vice Pres. and Trustee of Lee Abbey; Founder Mem., Coll. of Preachers, 1962. Bishops' Inspector of Theological Colls (Mem. Archbishops' Commn, 1970–71). *Publication:* (Jt Editor) Hymns for Church and School, 1964. *Address:* The Old Schoolhouse, The Common, Swardeston, Norwich NR14 8EB. *T:* Mulbarton (01508) 578060.

WIIN-NIELSEN, Aksel Christopher, Fil.Dr; Professor, Geophysical Institute, University of Copenhagen, 1988–94, now Emeritus; *b* 17 Dec. 1924; *s* of Aage Nielsen and Marie Petre (*née* Kristoffersen); *m* 1953, Bente Havsteen (*née* Zimsen); three *d. Educ:* Univ of Copenhagen (MSc 1950); Univ. of Stockholm (Fil.Lic. 1957; Fil.Dr 1960). Danish Meteorol Inst., 1952–55; Staff Member: Internat. Meteorol Inst., Stockholm, 1955–58; Jt Numerical Weather Prediction Unit, Suitland, Md, USA, 1959–61; Asst Dir, Nat. Center for Atmospherical Research, Boulder, Colorado, 1961–63; Prof., Dept of Atmospheric and Oceanic Sci., Univ. of Michigan, 1963–73; Dir, European Centre for Medium-Range Weather Forecasts, Reading, 1974–79; Sec.-Gen., WMO, 1980–83; Dir, Danish Meteorol Office, 1984–87. Pres., European Geophysical Soc., 1988–90; Vice-Pres., Danish Acad. of Technical Scis, 1989–92 (Mem., 1984–); Member: Finnish Acad. of Arts and Scis; Royal Swedish Acad. of Sci.; Danish Royal Soc., 1986–; Hon. Member: RMetS; Amer. Meteorol Soc., 1994. Hon. DSc: Reading, 1982; Copenhagen, 1986. Buys Ballot Medal, Royal Netherlands Acad., 1982; Wihuri Internat. Prize, Finland, 1983; Rossby Prize, Sweden, 1987; Friedman Rescue Award, 1993. *Publications:* Dynamic Meteorology, 1970; Predictability, 1987; Fundamentals of Atmospheric Energetics, 1993; over 100 scientific publications. *Recreation:* tennis. *Address:* Solbakken 6, 3230 Graested, Denmark.

WILBERFORCE, family name of **Baron Wilberforce.**

WILBERFORCE, Baron, *cr* 1964 (Life Peer); **Richard Orme Wilberforce,** PC 1964; Kt 1961; CMG 1956; OBE 1944; a Lord of Appeal in Ordinary, 1964–82; Fellow, All Souls College, Oxford, since 1932; *b* 11 Mar. 1907; *s* of late S. Wilberforce; *m* 1947, Yvette, *d* of Roger Lenoan, Judge of Court of Cassation, France; one *s* one *d. Educ:* Winchester; New College, Oxford. Called to the Bar, 1932; served War, 1939–46 (Hon. Brig.); Under Sec., Control Office Germany and Austria, 1946–47; returned to Bar, 1947; QC 1954; Judge of the High Court of Justice (Chancery Division), 1961–64; Bencher, Middle Temple, 1961. Chm. Exec. Council, Internat. Law Assoc., 1966–88; Mem., Permanent Court of Arbitration; President: Fédération Internationale du Droit Européen, 1978; Appeal Tribunal, Lloyd's of London, 1983–87. Jt Pres., Anti-Slavery Soc.; Vice-President: (jt) RCM; David Davies Meml Inst. Chancellor, Univ. of Hull, 1978–94; University of Oxford: High Steward, 1967–90; Visitor: Wolfson Coll., 1974–90; Linacre Coll., 1983–90; Hon. Fellow: New Coll., 1965; Wolfson Coll., 1991. Hon. FRCM. Hon. Comp. Royal Aeronautical Society. Hon. Mem., Scottish Faculty of Advocates, 1978. Hon. DCL Oxon, 1968; Hon. LLD: London, 1972; Hull, 1973; Bristol, 1983. Diplôme d'Honneur, Corp. des Vignerons de Champagne. US Bronze Star, 1944. *Publications:* The Law of Restrictive Trade Practices, 1956; articles and pamphlets on Air Law and International Law. *Recreations:* the turf, travel, opera. *Address:* House of Lords, SW1A 0PW. *Club:* Athenæum.

WILBERFORCE, William John Antony, CMG 1981; HM Diplomatic Service, retired; *b* 3 Jan. 1930; *s* of late Lt-Col W. B. Wilberforce and Cecilia (*née* Dormer); *m* 1953, Laura Lyon, *d* of late Howard Sykes, Englewood, NJ; one *s* two *d. Educ:* Ampleforth; Christ Church, Oxford. Army National Service, 2nd Lieut KOYLI, 1948–49. HM Foreign Service, 1953; served: Oslo, 1955–57; Berlin, 1957–59; Ankara, 1962–64; Abidjan, 1964–67; Asst Head of UN (Econ. and Social) Dept, 1967–70, and of Southern European Dept, 1970–72; Counsellor, 1972–74, and Head of Chancery, 1974–75, Washington; Hd of Defence Dept, FCO, 1975–78; Asst Under-Sec., RCDS, 1979; Leader of UK Delegn to Madrid Conf. on Security and Cooperation in Europe Review Meeting, with rank of Ambassador, 1980–82; High Comr in Cyprus, 1982–88. Hon. DHum Wilberforce, 1973. *Recreations:* the turf, travel, gardening. *Address:* Markington Hall, Harrogate HG3 3PQ. *T:* Ripon (01765) 677356. *Club:* Athenæum.

WILBRAHAM; *see* Bootle-Wilbraham, family name of Baron Skelmersdale.

WILBRAHAM, Sir Richard B.; *see* Baker Wilbraham.

WILBY, Peter John; Editor, Independent on Sunday, since 1995; *b* 7 Nov. 1944; *s* of Lawrence Edward Wilby and Emily Lavinia Wilby; *m* 1967, Sandra James; two *s. Educ:* Kibworth Beauchamp Grammar Sch., Leics; Univ. of Sussex (BA Hons). Reporter, Observer, 1968–72; Education Correspondent: Observer, 1972–75; New Statesman, 1975–77; Sunday Times, 1977–86; Educn Editor, Independent, 1986–89; Independent on Sunday: Home Editor, 1990–91; Dep. Editor, 1991–95. *Publications:* Parent's Rights, 1983; Sunday Times Good University Guide, 1984; Sunday Times Good Careers Guide, 1985; (ed with Henry Pluckrose): The Condition of English Schooling, 1981; Education 2000, 1982. *Recreations:* reading, cooking, lunching. *Address:* Independent on Sunday, One Canada Square, Canary Wharf, E14 5DL. *T:* 0171–293 2490.

WILCOCK, Christopher Camplin; Head of Nuclear Power Privatization Team, Department of Trade and Industry, since 1995; *b* 13 Sept. 1939; *s* of Arthur Camplin Wilcock and Dorothy (*née* Haigh); *m* 1965, Evelyn Clare Gollin; two *d. Educ:* Berkhamsted and Ipswich Schs; Trinity Hall, Cambridge (BA 1st Cl. Hons; MA). FO, 1962–63; MECAS, 1963–64; 3rd Sec., Khartoum, 1964–66; FO, 1966–68; 2nd Sec., UK Delegn to NATO, 1968–70; FO, 1970–72; Hosp. Bldg Div., DHSS, 1972–74; Petroleum Prodn, subseq. Continental Shelf Policy Div., Dept of Energy, 1974–78, Asst Sec. 1976; Electricity Div., 1978–81; on secondment to Shell UK Ltd, 1982–83; Department of Energy, subseq. of Trade and Industry: Hd of Finance Br., 1984–86; Dir of Resource Management (Grade 4), 1986–88; Grade 3, 1988; Hd of Electricity Div. A, 1988–91; Hd of Electricity Div., 1991–94; Hd of Electricity and Nuclear Fuels Div., 1994–95. Order of the Two Niles, Fifth Cl. (Sudan), 1965. *Recreations:* reading, history, cinema. *Address:* Department of Trade and Industry, 1 Palace Street, SW1E 5HE.

WILCOCK, Prof. William Leslie; consultant in industrial instrumentation; Professor of Physics, University College of North Wales, Bangor, 1965–82, now Emeritus; *b* 7 July 1922. *Educ:* Manchester Univ. (BSc, PhD). Instrument Dept, RAE, 1943–45. Asst Lectr in Physics, 1945–48, Lectr, 1950–56, Manchester Univ.; DSIR Res. Fellow, St Andrews Univ., 1948–50; Reader in Instrument Technol., 1956–61, in Applied Physics, 1961–65, Imperial Coll. of Science and Technology, London. Arnold O. Beckman Award, Instrument Soc. of Amer., 1977. Mem., SERC, 1981–85. *Publications:* (contrib.) Principles of Optics, 1959; Advances in Electronics and Electron Physics, vols 12–16 (ed jtly), 1960–61; numerous papers in scientific jls. *Address:* Fferm Felin Hen, Y Felin Hen, Bangor, Gwynedd LL57 4BB.

WILCOX, Albert Frederick, CBE 1967; QPM 1957; Chief Constable of Hertfordshire, 1947–69, retired; *b* 18 April 1909; *s* of late Albert Clement Wilcox, Ashley Hill, Bristol; *m* 1939, Ethel, *d* of late E. H. W. Wilmott, Manor House, Whitchurch, Bristol; one *s* two *d. Educ:* Fairfield Grammar School, Bristol. Joined Bristol City Police, 1929; Hendon Police Coll., 1934; Metropolitan Police, 1934–43. Served Allied Mil. Govt, Italy and Austria (Lt-Col), 1943–46. Asst Chief Constable of Buckinghamshire, 1946. Cropwood Fellowship, Inst. of Criminology, Cambridge, 1969. Pres. Assoc. of Chief Police Officers, Eng. and Wales, 1966–67; Chm. of Management Cttee, Police Dependents' Trust, 1967–69. Regional Police Commander (designate), 1962–69. Member, Parole Board, 1970–73. Criminological Res. Fellowship, Council of Europe, 1974–76. Barrister-at-Law, Gray's Inn, 1941. *Publication:* The Decision to Prosecute, 1972. *Address:* 34 Roundwood Park, Harpenden, Herts AL5 3AF.

WILCOX, David John Reed; His Honour Judge David Wilcox; a Circuit Judge, since 1985; *b* 8 March 1939; *s* of Leslie Leonard Kennedy Wilcox and Margaret Ada Reed Wilcox (*née* Rapson); *m* 1962, Wendy Feay Christine Whiteley; one *s* one *d. Educ:* Wednesbury Boys' High Sch.; King's Coll., London (LLB Hons). Called to the Bar, Gray's Inn, 1962. Directorate, Army Legal Services (Captain): Legal Staff, 1962–63; Legal Aid, Far East Land Forces, Singapore, 1963–65. Crown Counsel, Hong Kong, 1965–68; Member, Hong Kong Bar, 1968; in practice, Midland and Midland and Oxford Circuits, 1968–85; a Recorder of the Crown Court, 1979–85. Resident Judge, Great Grimsby Combined Court Centre, 1989–94; County Court Judge: Lincs and S Humberside, 1989–94; Birmingham, 1994–; Care Judge, Birmingham, 1994–. Lord Chancellor's Rep., Humberside Probation Cttee, 1989–94. Chm., Nottingham Friendship Housing Assoc., 1970–75. *Recreations:* reading, gardening, travel. *Address:* c/o Birmingham County Court, 2 Newton Street, Birmingham B4 7LU.

WILCOX, Rt Rev. David Peter; Bishop Suffragan of Dorking, 1986–95; an Assistant Bishop, diocese of Chichester, since 1995; *b* 29 June 1930; *s* of John Wilcox and Stella Wilcox (*née* Bower); *m* 1956, Pamela Ann Hedges; two *s* two *d. Educ:* Northampton Grammar School; St John's Coll., Oxford (2nd cl. Hons Theol., MA); Lincoln Theological Coll. Deacon 1954, priest 1955; Asst Curate, St Peter's, St Helier, Morden, Surrey, 1954–56; Asst Curate, University Church, Oxford and SCM Staff Secretary in Oxford, 1956–59; on staff of Lincoln Theological Coll., 1959–64; USPG Missionary on staff of United Theological Coll., Bangalore, and Presbyter in Church of S India, 1964–70; Vicar of Great Gransden with Little Gransden, dio. Ely, 1970–72; Canon Residentiary, Derby Cathedral and Warden, E Midlands Joint Ordination Training Scheme, 1972–77; Proctor in Convocation, 1973–77; Principal of Ripon College, Cuddesdon and Vicar of All Saints', Cuddesdon, 1977–85. *Recreations:* walking, music, art. *Address:* 4 The Court, Hoo Gardens, Willingdon, Eastbourne BN20 9AX.

WILCOX, Desmond John; independent television producer/reporter; journalist and author; *b* 21 May 1931; *e s* of late John Wallace Wilcox and Alice May Wilcox; *m* 1st (marr. diss.); one *s* two *d*; 2nd, 1977, Esther Rantzen, *qv*; one *s* two *d. Educ:* Cheltenham Grammar Sch.; Christ's Coll., London; Outward Bound Sea Sch. Sail training apprentice, 1947; Deckhand, Merchant Marine, 1948; Reporter, weekly papers, 1949; commissioned Army, National Service, 1949–51; News Agency reporter, 1951–52; Reporter and Foreign Correspondent, Daily Mirror, incl. New York Bureau and UN, 1952–60; Reporter, This Week, ITV, 1960–65; joined BBC 1965: Co-Editor/Presenter, Man Alive, 1965; formed Man Alive Unit, 1968; Head of General Features, BBC TV, 1972–80; Writer/Presenter, Americans, TV documentary, 1979; Presenter/Chm., Where it Matters, ITV discussion series, 1981; Producer/Presenter TV series: The Visit, BBC, 1982–91 (TV Radio Industries Club Award for Best Documentary, 1984, 1986), ITV, 1993; The Marriage, BBC, 1986; Black in Blue, BBC, 1990, 1992; A Day in the Life, ITV, 1993; Presenter, 60 Minutes, BBC TV, 1983–84. Man. Dir, Desmond Wilcox Productions Ltd, 1994–; Chm., Man Alive Gp, 1994–. Trustee: Conservation Foundn, 1982–; The Walk Fund (Walk Again Limb Kinetics), 1984–; Mem. of Bd, Disfigurement Guidance Centre, 1988–; Patron: Wessex Heartbeat (Wessex Cardiac Trust); All Hear Cochlear Implant Charity; CHIT (Children's Head Injury Trust); Headway; Harefield Hosp. Fund; British Deaf Assoc.; TIME (Transplants in Mind). SFTA Award for best factual programme series, 1967; Richard Dimbleby Award, SFTA, for most important personal contrib. in factual television, 1971. *Publications:* (jtly) Explorers, 1975; Americans, 1978; (with Esther Rantzen) Kill the Chocolate Biscuit: or Behind the Screen, 1981; (with Esther Rantzen) Baby Love, 1985; Return Visit, 1991. *Recreations:* riding, gardening, television. *Address:* Desmond Wilcox Productions, Westpoint, 33–34 Warple Way, W3 0RG; (agents) Noel Gay Artists, 76 Oxford Street, W1N 0AT. *T:* 0171–412 0300. *Clubs:* Arts, Groucho.

WILCOX, Esther Louise, (Mrs Desmond Wilcox); *see* Rantzen, E. L.

WILCOX, Judith Ann, (Lady Wilcox); Chairman, National Consumer Council, since 1990; *d* of John and Elsie Freeman; *m* 1st, 1961, Keith Davenport; one *s*; 2nd, 1986, Sir Malcolm George Wilcox, CBE (*d* 1986). *Educ:* St Dunstan's Abbey, Devon; St Mary's Convent, Wantage; Plymouth Polytechnic. Management of family business, High Street trading, Devon, 1960–70; Financial Director: Capstan Foods, Devon, 1970–78; Channel Foods, Cornwall, 1980–88; Pres. Dir Gen., Pêcheries de la Morinie, France, 1988–90; Partner, Morinie et Cie, France, 1990–. Member: (non-exec.), Inland Revenue Bd, 1992–; PLA, 1993–; Prime Minister's Adv. Panel to Citizen's Charter Unit, 1992–; Chm., Citizen's Charter Complaints Task Force, 1993–. Member: Nat. Cttee for Develt of Nat. Curriculum in England and Wales; Money Advice Trust, FHA; Adv. Gp on Eco-labelling, DoE; Gen. Adv. Council, BBC; former Member: Electricity Consumers Council; Area Manpower Boards for Devon and Cornwall; ITEC in Cornwall; Cornwall Cttee for Disabled. Mem. Council, Inst. of Dirs, 1991–. Governor: Ashridge Management Coll., 1992–; Plymouth Univ. FIMgt. FRSA. *Recreations:* sailing, birdwatching, flyfishing, calligraphy. *Address:* 17 Great College Street, SW1P 3RX. *Clubs:* Reform; St Mawes Sailing.

WILD, Dr David; Director of Public Health, South West Thames Regional Health Authority, 1989–90, retired; *b* 27 Jan. 1930; *s* of Frederick and Lena Wild; *m* 1954, Dr Sheila Wightman; one *s* one *d. Educ:* Manchester Grammar Sch.; Univ. of Manchester (MB, ChB); Univ. of Liverpool (DPH; FFCM, DMA). Deputy County Medical Officer, 1962, Area Medical Officer, 1974, West Sussex; Regional MO, 1982–86, Dir of Prof. Services, 1986–89, SW Thames RHA. Non-exec. Dir, Worthing DHA, 1990–95. Dir, Inf. Unit for Conf. of Med. Royal Colls and their Faculties in UK, 1991–93. Editor (with Dr Brian Williams), Community Medicine, 1978–84. *Publications:* contribs Jl Central Council of Health Educn, Medical Officer, Archives of Disease in Childhood. *Recreation:*

conversation. *Address:* 16 Brandy Hole Lane, Chichester, Sussex PO19 4RY. *T:* Chichester (01243) 527125; 13 Surrendale Place, W9. *T:* 0171–289 7257.

WILD, His Honour David Humphrey; a Circuit Judge, 1972–92; *b* 24 May 1927; *s* of John S. Wild and Edith Lemarchand; *m* 1963, Estelle Grace Prowett, *d* of James Marshall, Aberdeen and Malaya; one *s*. *Educ:* Whitgift Middle Sch., Croydon. Served War of 1939–45, Royal Navy, 1944–48. Called to Bar, Middle Temple, 1951. Practised, London and SE Circuit, 1951–58, Midland Circuit, 1958–72; resident judge, Cambridge Crown Court, 1973–84. Councillor, Oundle and Thrapston RDC, 1968–72. Mem., St Catharine's Coll., Cambridge, 1973. *Publication:* The Law of Hire Purchase, 1960 (2nd edn, 1964). *Clubs:* Naval and Military, Savile, Sette of Odd Volumes.

WILD, Major Hon. Gerald Percy, AM 1980; MBE 1941; Company Director; Agent-General for Western Australia in London, 1965–71; *b* 2 Jan. 1908; *m* 1944, Virginia Mary Baxter; two *s* one *d*. *Educ:* Shoreham Gram. Sch., Sussex; Chivers Acad., Portsmouth, Hants. Served War of 1939–45 (despatches, MBE): Middle East, Greece, Crete, Syria, New Guinea and Moratai, Netherlands East Indies (Major). Elected MLA for Western Australia, 1947; Minister for Housing and Forests, 1950–53; Minister for Works and Water Supplies and Labour (WA), 1959–65. JP Perth (WA), 1953. *Recreations:* golf, tennis, cricket, football. *Address:* 80 Culeenup Road, North Yunderup, WA 6208, Australia. *T:* (95) 376191. *Clubs:* East India, Devonshire, Sports and Public Schools; West Australian Turf (WA).

WILD, Dr (John) Paul, AC 1986; CBE 1978; FRS 1970; FAA 1962; FTS 1978; Chairman and Chief Executive, Commonwealth Scientific and Industrial Research Organization, 1978–85 (Associate Member of Executive, 1977; Chief, Division of Radiophysics, 1971); *b* 1923; *s* of late Alwyn Howard Wild and late Bessie Delafield (*née* Arnold); *m* 1st, 1948, Elaine Poole Hull (*d* 1991); two *s* one *d*, 2nd, 1991, Margaret Lyndon. *Educ:* Whitgift Sch.; Peterhouse, Cambridge (Hon. Fellow 1982). ScD 1962. Radar Officer in Royal Navy, 1943–47; joined Research Staff of Div. of Radiophysics, 1947, working on problems in radio astronomy, esp. of the sun, later also radio navigation (Interscan aircraft landing system). Dep. Chm., 1973–75, 1980–82, Chm., 1975–80, Anglo-Australian Telescope Bd; Mem. Bd, Interscan (Australia) Pty Ltd, 1978–84. For. Hon. Mem., Amer. Acad. of Arts and Scis, 1961; For. Mem., Amer. Philos. Soc., 1962; Corresp. Mem., Royal Soc. of Scis, Liège, 1969; For. Sec., Australian Acad. of Science, 1973–77. Hon. FIE(Aust), 1991; Hon. FRSA 1991. Hon. DSc: ANU, 1979; Newcastle (NSW), 1982. Edgeworth David Medal, 1958; Hendryk Arctowski Gold Medal, US Nat. Acad. of Scis, 1969; Balthasar van der Pol Gold Medal, Internat. Union of Radio Science, 1969; 1st Herschel Medal, RAS, 1974; Thomas Ranken Lyle Medal, Aust. Acad. of Science, 1975; Royal Medal, Royal Soc., 1980; Hale Medal, Amer. Astronomical Soc., 1980; ANZAAS Medal, 1984; Hartnett Medal, RSA, 1988. *Publications:* numerous research papers and reviews on radio astronomy in scientific jls. *Address:* 4/1 Grant Crescent, Griffith, ACT 2603, Australia; 800 Avon Road, Ann Arbor, MI 48104, USA.

WILD, John Vernon, CMG 1960; OBE 1955; Colonial Administrative Service, retired; *b* 26 April 1915; *m* 1st, 1942, Margaret Patricia Rendell (*d* 1975); one *d* (one *s* decd); 2nd, 1976, Marjorie Mary Lovatt Robertson. *Educ:* Taunton School; King's College, Cambridge. Senior Optime, Cambridge Univ., 1937; Cricket Blue, 1938. Colonial Administrative Service, Uganda: Assistant District Officer, 1938; Assistant Chief Secretary, 1950; Establishment Secretary, 1951; Administrative Secretary, 1955–60; Chairman, Constitutional Committee, 1959. Teacher and Lectr in Mathematics, 1960–76. *Publications:* The Story of the Uganda Agreement; The Uganda Mutiny; Early Travellers in Acholi. *Recreations:* golf, gardening. *Address:* Maplestone Farm, Brede, near Rye, East Sussex TN31 6EP. *T:* Brede (01424) 882261. *Club:* Rye Golf.

WILD, Paul; *see* Wild, J. P.

WILD, Prof. Raymond, DSc, PhD; CEng, FIMechE, FIEE; Principal, Henley Management College, since 1990; *b* 24 Dec. 1940; *s* of Alice Wild and Frank Wild; *m* 1965, Carol Ann Mellor; one *s* one *d*. *Educ:* Stockport College; Bradford University (PhD (Management), MSc (Eng), MSc (Management)). DSc Brunel, 1988; WhF. Engineering apprentice, Crossley Bros, 1957–62, design engineer, 1962–63, research engineer, 1963–65; postgrad. student, Bradford Univ., 1965–66; production engineer, English Electric, 1966–67; Res. Fellow then Senior Res. Fellow, Bradford Univ., 1967–73; Dir of Grad. Studies, Admin. Staff Coll., Henley, 1973–77, Mem., Senior Staff, Henley Management Coll., 1973–; Brunel University: Dir, Special Engineering Programme, 1977–84; Hd, Dept of Engrg and Management Systems, 1977–86; Hd, Dept of Prodn Technology, 1984–86; Hd, Dept of Manufacturing and Engrg Systems, 1986–89; Pro-Vice-Chancellor, 1988–89. CIMgt; FRSA. Editor-in-Chief, Internat. Jl of Computer Integrated Manufacturing Systems, 1988–91. *Publications:* The Techniques of Production Management, 1971; Management and Production, 1972, trans. Greek 1984; (with A. B. Hill and C. C. Ridgeway) Women in the Factory, 1972; Mass Production Management, 1972; (with B. Lowes) Principles of Modern Management, 1972; Work Organization, 1975; Concepts for Operations Management, 1977; Production and Operations Management, 1979, 5th edn 1994; Operations Management: a policy framework, 1980; Essentials of Production and Operations Management, 1980, 4th edn 1995; (ed) Management and Production Readings, 1981; Read and Explain (4 children's books on technology), 1982 and 1983, trans. French, Swedish, German, Danish; How to Manage, 1983, 2nd edn 1995; (ed) International Handbook of Production and Operations Management, 1989; (ed) Technology and Management, 1990; papers in learned jls. *Recreations:* writing, restoring houses, travel, painting. *Address:* Broomfield, New Road, Shiplake, Henley on Thames, Oxon RG9 3LA. *T:* Wargrave (01734) 404102.

WILD, Robert; Director, Project Underwriting Group, Export Credits Guarantee Department, 1989–92; *b* 19 April 1932, *s* of Thomas Egan Wild and Janet Wild; *m* 1955, Irene Whitton Martin; two *d*. *Educ:* King Edward VII Sch., Lytham. Board of Trade, 1950; Export Credits Guarantee Dept, 1959. *Recreations:* bird watching, archaeology, reading.

WILDE, Peter Appleton; HM Diplomatic Service, retired; *b* 5 April 1925; *m* 1950, Frances Elisabeth Candida Bayliss; two *s*. *Educ:* Chesterfield Grammar Sch.; St Edmund Hall, Oxford. Army (National Service), 1943–47; Temp. Asst Lectr, Southampton, 1950; FO, 1950; 3rd Sec., Bangkok, 1951–53; Vice-Consul, Zürich, 1953–54; FO, 1954–57; 2nd Sec., Baghdad, 1957–58; 1st Sec., UK Delegn to OEEC (later OECD), Paris, 1958–61; 1st Sec., Katmandu, 1961–64; FO (later FCO), 1964–69; Consul-Gen., Lourenço Marques, 1969–71; Dep. High Comr, Colombo, 1971–73. Mem., Llanfihangel Rhosycorn Community Council, 1974–83. Member: Management Cttee, Carmarthenshire Pest Control Soc. Ltd, 1974–82; Council, Royal Forestry Soc., 1977–86; Regional Adv. Cttee, Wales Conservancy, Forestry Commn, 1985–87 (Mem., Regional Adv. Cttee, S Wales Conservancy, 1983–85). *Recreation:* forestry. *Address:* Nantyperchyll, Gwernogle, Carmarthen, Dyfed SA32 7RR. *T:* Brechfa (01267) 223181.

WILDENSTEIN, Daniel Leopold; art historian; President, Wildenstein Institute Inc., since 1964; Chairman, Wildenstein & Co Inc., New York, since 1968 (Vice-President, 1943–59, President, 1959–68); Vice-President, Florence Gould Foundation, since 1983; *b* Verrières-le-Buisson, France, 11 Sept. 1917; *s* of Georges Wildenstein; *m* 1939, Martine Kapferer (marr. diss. 1968); two *s*; *m* 1978, Sylvia Roth. *Educ:* Cours Hattemer; Sorbonne (LèsL 1938). Gp Sec., French Pavilion, World's Fair, 1937; went to US, 1940; with Wildenstein & Co. Inc., New York, 1940–; Director: Wildenstein & Co. Inc., London, 1963–; Wildenstein Arte, Buenos Aires, 1963–. Dir, Gazette des Beaux Arts, 1963–; Dir of Activities, Musée Jacquemart-André, Paris, 1956–62; Musée Chaalis, Institut de France, Paris, 1956–62; organiser of art competitions (Hallmark art award). Mem., French Chamber of Commerce in US (Conseiller), 1942–; Founder (1947) and Mem., Amer. Inst. of France (Sec.). Mem., Institut de France (Académie des Beaux-Arts), 1971; Membre du Haut Comité du Musée de Monaco. *Publications:* Claude Monet, vol. 1, 1975, vols 2 and 3, 1979, vol. 4, 1985, vol. 5, 1992; Edouard Manet, vol. 1, 1976, vol. 2, 1977; Gustave Courbet, vol. 1, 1977, vol. 2, 1978. *Recreation:* horse racing (leading owner, 1977). *Address:* Seidenstrasse 6, 8853 Lachen, Switzerland; (office) 57 rue La Boétie, 75008 Paris, France. *T:* 45616161. *Clubs:* Brooks's; Turf and Field, Madison Square Garden (New York); Cercle de Deauville, Tir au Pigeon (Paris); Jockey (Buenos Aires).

WILDING, Richard William Longworth, CB 1979; Head of Office of Arts and Libraries, Cabinet Office, 1984–88; *b* 22 April 1929; *er s* of late L. A. Wilding; *m* 1954, Mary Rosamund de Villiers; one *s* two *d*. *Educ:* Dragon Sch., Oxford; Winchester Coll.; New Coll., Oxford (MA). HM Foreign Service, 1953–59; transf. to Home Civil Service, 1959; Principal, HM Treasury, 1959–67; Sec., Fulton Cttee on Civil Service, 1966–68; Asst Sec., Civil Service Dept, 1968–70; Asst Sec., Supplementary Benefits Commn, DHSS, 1970–72; Under-Sec., Management Services, 1972–76, Pay, 1976, CSD; Deputy Secretary: CSD, 1976–81; HM Treasury, 1981–83. Review of Structure of Arts Funding in England, 1989; Review of Redundant Churches Fund, 1990. Trustee, Nat. Museums and Galleries on Merseyside, 1989–. *Publications:* (with L. A. Wilding) A Classical Anthology, 1954; Key to Latin Course for Schools, 1966; The Care of Redundant Churches, 1990; articles in Jl Public Administration, Social Work Today, Studies. *Recreations:* music, gardening. *Address:* 14 The Lodge, Kensington Park Gardens, W11 3HA. *T:* 0171–727 6880. *Club:* Athenæum.

WILDISH, Vice-Adm. Denis Bryan Harvey, CB 1968; *b* 24 Dec. 1914; *s* of late Engr Rear-Adm. Sir Henry William Wildish, KBE, CB; *m* 1941, Leslie Henrietta Jacob; two *d*. *Educ:* RNC Dartmouth; RNEC. Entered Royal Navy, 1928; sea service HM Ships Ramillies, Revenge, Nelson, 1932–39; War service, Atlantic, Mediterranean, FE, HM Ships Prince of Wales, Kedah and Isis (despatches); subseq. various Admiralty appts; HMS Implacable, 1946–48; Planning Staff, Exercise Trident, 1948–49; Asst Naval Attaché, Rome, Berne, 1951–53; HMS Eagle, 1953–56; Asst Dir, then Dir, Fleet Maintenance, 1960–64; Commodore Naval Drafting and i/c HMS Centurion, 1964–66; Adm. Supt, HM Dockyard, Devonport, 1966–70; Dir Gen. of Personal Services and Trng (Navy) and Dep. Second Sea Lord, 1970–72; retired. Rep. RN at cricket, also RN, Combined Services, Devon, and W of England at hockey. *Recreations:* walking, cricket, painting (Mem., Armed Forces Art Soc.). *Address:* 78 Grenehurst Way, Petersfield, Hants GU31 4AZ. *Clubs:* Army and Navy, MCC; I Zingari, XL, Incogniti, Devon Dumplings, Royal Navy Cricket.

WILDSMITH, Brian Lawrence; artist and maker of picture books for young children; *b* 22 Jan. 1930; *s* of Paul Wildsmith and Annie Elizabeth Oxley; *m* 1955, Aurelie Janet Craigie Ithurbide; one *s* three *d*. *Educ:* de la Salle Coll.; Barnsley Sch. of Art; Slade Sch. of Fine Arts. Art Master, Selhurst Grammar School for Boys, 1954–57; freelance artist, 1975–; one-man shows, Tokyo, Kyoto, Osaka and Shimonoseki, 1995. Production design, illustrations, titles and graphics for first USA-USSR Leningrad film co-production of the Blue Bird. Brian Wildsmith Museum opened Izu, Japan, 1994. Kate Greenaway Medal, 1962; Soka Gakkai Japan Educn Medal, 1988. *Publications:* ABC, 1962; The Lion and the Rat, 1963; The North Wind and the Sun, 1964; Mother Goose, 1964; 1; 2; 3;, 1965; The Rich Man and the Shoemaker, 1965; The Hare and the Tortoise, 1966; Birds, 1967; Animals, 1967; Fish, 1968; The Miller the Boy and the Donkey, 1969; The Circus, 1970; Puzzles, 1970; The Owl and the Woodpecker, 1971; The Twelve Days of Christmas, 1972; The Little Wood Duck, 1972; The Lazy Bear, 1973; Squirrels, 1974; Pythons Party, 1974; The Blue Bird, 1976; The True Cross, 1977; What the Moon Saw, 1978; Hunter and his Dog, 1979; Animal Shapes, 1980; Animal Homes, 1980; Animal Games, 1980; Animal Tricks, 1980; The Seasons, 1980; Professor Noah's Spaceship, 1980; Bears Adventure, 1981; The Trunk, 1982; Cat on the Mat, 1982; Pelican, 1982; The Apple Bird, 1983; The Island, 1983; All Fall Down, 1983; The Nest, 1983; Daisy, 1984; Who's Shoes, 1984; Toot Toot, 1984; Give a Dog a Bone, 1985; Goats Trail, 1986; My Dream, 1986; What a Tail, 1986; If I Were You, 1987; Giddy Up . . ., 1987; Carousel, 1988; The Christmas Story, 1989; The Snow Country Prince, 1990; The Cherry Tree, 1991; The Princess and the Moon, 1991; Over the Deep Blue Sea, 1992; The Easter Story, 1993; Noah's Ark Pop Up, 1994; Saint Francis, 1995; The Creation (pop up), 1995; with Rebecca Wildsmith: Wake Up Wake Up, 1993; Whose Hat Was That?, 1993; Look Closer, 1993; What Did I Find?, 1993; Jack and the Meanstalk, 1995. *Recreations:* squash, tennis, music (piano). *Address:* 11 Castellaras, 06370 Mouans-Sartoux, France. *T:* 93752411. *Club:* Reform.

WILEMAN, Margaret Annie, MA; Honorary Fellow, Hughes Hall, Cambridge, since 1973 (President (formerly Principal), 1953–73); *b* 19 July 1908; *e d* of Clement Wileman and Alice (*née* Brinson). *Educ:* Lady Margaret Hall, Oxford, and the University of Paris. Scholar of Lady Margaret Hall, Oxford, 1927; First in Hons School of Mod. Langs, 1930; Zaharoff Travelling Scholar, 1931; Assistant, Abbey School, Reading, 1934; Senior Tutor, Queen's College, Harley Street, 1937; Lecturer, St Katherine's Coll., Liverpool, 1940; Resident Tutor, Bedford College, Univ. of London, 1944–53; Univ. Lectr, and Dir of Women Students, Dept of Educn, Cambridge Univ., 1953–73. *Address:* 5 Drosier Road, Cambridge CB1 2EY. *T:* Cambridge (01223) 351846. *Club:* University Women's.

WILES, Prof. Andrew John, PhD; FRS 1989; Professor of Mathematics, Princeton University, 1980–88 and since 1990. *Educ:* Clare Coll., Cambridge (MA 1977; PhD 1980); MA Oxon 1988. Sometime Fellow, Clare Coll., Cambridge; Royal Society Research Professor in Maths and Professorial Fellow of Merton Coll., Oxford University, 1988–90. (Jtly) Jun. Whitehead Prize, London Math. Soc., 1988. *Address:* Department of Mathematics, Princeton University, Fine Hall, Washington Hall, Princeton, NJ 08544, USA.

WILES, Sir Donald (Alonzo), KA 1984; CMG 1965; OBE 1960; Consultant to Barbados National Trust, since 1985; *b* 8 Jan. 1912; *s* of Donald Alonzo Wiles and Millicent Wiles; *m* 1938, Amelia Elsie Pemberton; two *d*. *Educ:* Harrison Coll., Barbados; Univs of London, Toronto, Oxford. Member of Staff of Harrison College, Barbados, 1931–45; Public Librarian, Barbados, 1945–50; Asst Colonial Secretary, Barbados, 1950–54; Permanent Secretary, Barbados, 1954–60; Administrator, Montserrat, 1960–64; Administrative Sec., Da Costa & Musson Ltd, 1965–79. Exec. Dir, Barbados Nat. Trust, 1980–84. *Recreations:* swimming, hiking, tennis. *Address:* Casa Loma, Sunrise Drive, Pine Gardens, St Michael, Barbados. *T:* 4266875.

WILES, Rev. Prof. Maurice Frank, FBA 1981; Canon of Christ Church, Oxford, and Regius Professor of Divinity, 1970–91; *b* 17 Oct. 1923; *s* of late Sir Harold Wiles, KBE, CB, and Lady Wiles; *m* 1950, Patricia Margaret (*née* Mowll); two *s* one *d*. *Educ:* Tonbridge School; Christ's College, Cambridge. Curate, St George's, Stockport, 1950–52; Chaplain, Ridley Hall, Cambridge, 1952–55; Lectr in New Testament Studies, Ibadan, Nigeria, 1955–59; Lectr in Divinity, Univ. of Cambridge, and Dean of Clare College, 1959–67; Prof. of Christian Doctrine, King's Coll., Univ. of London, 1967–70; Bampton Lectr, Univ. of Oxford, 1986. FKC 1972. *Publications:* The Spiritual Gospel, 1960; The Christian Fathers, 1966; The Divine Apostle, 1967; The Making of Christian Doctrine, 1967; The Remaking of Christian Doctrine, 1974; (with M. Santer) Documents in Early Christian Thought, 1975; Working Papers in Doctrine, 1976; What is Theology?, 1976; Explorations in Theology 4, 1979; Faith and the Mystery of God, 1982 (Collins Biennial Religious Book Award, 1983); God's Action in the World, 1986; Christian Theology and Interreligious Dialogue, 1992; A Shared Search, 1994. *Address:* Christ Church, Oxford OX1 1DP.

WILES, Prof. Peter John de la Fosse, FBA 1990; Professor of Russian Social and Economic Studies, University of London, 1965–85, now Emeritus Professor of Sovietological Economics; *b* 25 Nov. 1919; *m* 1st, 1945, Elizabeth Coppin (marr. diss., 1960); one *s* two *d*; 2nd, 1960, Carolyn Stedman. *Educ:* Lambrook Sch.; Winchester Coll.; New Coll., Oxford. Royal Artillery, 1940–45 (despatches twice; mainly attached Intelligence Corps). Fellow, All Souls Coll., Oxford, 1947–48; Fellow, New Coll., Oxford, 1948–60; Prof., Brandeis Univ., USA, 1960–63; Research Associate, Institutet för Internationell Ekonomi, Stockholm, 1963–64. Visiting Professor: Columbia Univ., USA, 1958; City Coll. of New York, 1964 and 1967; Collège de France, 1972; Ecole des Sciences Politiques, 1979; Univ. of Windsor, Ont., 1986. *Publications:* The Political Economy of Communism, 1962; Price, Cost and Output (2nd edn), 1962; Communist International Economics, 1968; Economic Institutions Compared, 1977; Die Parallelwirtschaft, 1981; The Black Market; (ed) The New Communist Third World, 1981; (ed with Guy Routh) Economics in Disarray, 1985; article, Cost Inflation and the State of Economic Theory, Econ. Jl, 1973. *Recreations:* simple. *Address:* 23 Ridgmount Gardens, WC1E 7AR.

WILFORD, Sir (Kenneth) Michael, GCMG 1980 (KCMG 1976; CMG 1967); HM Diplomatic Service, retired; *b* Wellington, New Zealand, 31 Jan. 1922; *yr s* of late George McLean Wilford and late Dorothy Veronica (*née* Wilson); *m* 1944, Joan Mary, *d* of Captain E. F. B. Law, RN; three *d*. *Educ:* Wrekin College; Pembroke College, Cambridge. Served in Royal Engineers, 1940–46 (despatches). Entered HM Foreign (subseq. Diplomatic) Service, 1947; Third Sec., Berlin, 1947; Asst Private Secretary to Secretary of State, Foreign Office, 1949; Paris, 1952; Singapore, 1955; Asst Private Sec. to Sec. of State, Foreign Office, 1959; Private Sec. to the Lord Privy Seal, 1960; served Rabat, 1962; Counsellor (Office of British Chargé d'Affaires) also Consul-General, Peking, 1964–66; Visiting Fellow of All Souls, Oxford, 1966–67; Counsellor, Washington, 1967–69; Asst Under Sec. of State, FCO, 1969–73; Dep. Under Sec. of State, FCO, 1973–75; Ambassador to Japan, 1975–80. Director: Lloyds Bank Internat., 1982–85; Lloyds Merchant Bank Ltd, 1986–87; Adviser, Baring Internat. Investment Management, 1982–90. Chm., Royal Soc. for Asian Affairs, 1984–94 (Hon. Vice Pres., 1994–); Hon. Pres., Japan Assoc., 1981–. Pres., Old Wrekinian Assoc., 1995–. *Recreations:* golf, gardening. *Address:* Brook Cottage, Abbotts Ann, Andover, Hants SP11 7DS. *T:* Andover (01264) 710509.

WILHELM, Most Rev. Joseph Lawrence, DD, JCD; former Archbishop of Kingston, Ontario, (RC); *b* Walkerton, Ontario, 16 Nov. 1909. *Educ:* St Augustine's Seminary, Toronto; Ottawa Univ., Ottawa, Ont. Ordained priest, Toronto, 1934. Mil. Chaplain to Canadian Forces, 1940–46 (MC, Sicily, 1943). Auxiliary Bishop, Calgary, Alberta, 1963–66; Archbishop of Kingston, Ont, 1967–82. Hon. DD Queen's Univ., Kingston, Ont, 1970. *Address:* The Anchorage, Belleville, Ont K8N 5K7, Canada.

WILKES, Prof. Eric, OBE (civil) 1974 (MBE (mil.) 1943); DL; FRCP, FRCGP, FRCPsych; Professor of Community Care and General Practice, Sheffield University, 1973–83, now Emeritus; *b* 12 Jan. 1920; *s* of George and Doris Wilkes; *m* 1953, Jessica Mary Grant; two *s* one *d*. *Educ:* Royal Grammar Sch., Newcastle upon Tyne; King's Coll., Cambridge (MA); St Thomas' Hosp., SE1 (MB, BChir). Lt-Col, Royal Signals, 1944. General Medical Practitioner, Derbyshire, 1954–73. High Sheriff of S Yorkshire, 1977–78. Med. Director, St Luke's Nursing Home, later St Luke's Hospice, Sheffield, 1971–86; Emeritus Consultant, Centre for Palliative and Continuing Care, Trent RHA, 1993. Chairman: Sheffield and Rotherham Assoc. for the Care and Resettlement of Offenders, 1976–83; Sheffield Council on Alcoholism, 1976–83; Prevention Cttee, Nat. Council on Alcoholism, 1980–83; Trinity Day Care Trust, 1979–83; Sheffield Victim Support Scheme, 1983–84; Mem., Nat. Cancer sub cttee, 1979–88; President: Inst. of Religion and Medicine, 1982–83; High Peak Hospice, Chapel and Thornhill House, Great Longstone, Derbyshire, 1992–; Co-Pres., St Luke's Hospice, Sheffield, 1986–; Vice-Pres., Ashgate Hospice, Chesterfield, 1990–; Hon. Vice-Pres., Nat. Hospice Council, 1992–; Trustee, Help the Hospices, 1984– (Vice-Chm., 1993–; Co-Chm., 1984–93). DL Derbys, 1984. Hon. Fellow, Sheffield City Polytechnic, 1985. Hon. MD Sheffield, 1986. *Publications:* The Dying Patient, 1982; Long-Term Prescribing, 1982; various chapters and papers, mainly on chronic and incurable illness. *Recreations:* gardening, walking, natural history. *Address:* Curbar View Farm, Calver, Sheffield S30 1XR. *T:* Hope Valley (01433) 631291.

WILKES, Prof. John Joseph, FSA; FBA 1986; Yates Professor of Greek and Roman Archaeology, University College London, since 1992; *b* 12 July 1936; *s* of Arthur Cyril Wilkes and Enid Cecilia Eustance; *m* 1980, Dr Susan Walker; one *s*. *Educ:* King Henry VIII Grammar Sch., Coventry; Harrow County Grammar Sch.; University Coll. London (BA); Univ. of Durham (St Cuthbert's Society) (PhD). FSA 1969. Research Fellow, Univ. of Birmingham, 1961–63; Asst Lectr in History and Archaeology, Univ. of Manchester, 1963–64; Lectr in Roman History, 1964–71, Sen. Lectr 1971–74, Univ. of Birmingham; Prof. of Archaeology of the Roman Provinces, Univ. of London, 1974–92. Chm., Faculty of Archaeology, Hist. and Letters, British Sch. at Rome, 1979–83. Vis. Fellow, Inst. of Humanistic Studies, Pennsylvania State Univ., 1971. Mem., Ancient Monuments Bd for Scotland, 1981–91. Vice-Pres., Soc. for Promotion of Roman Studies, 1978; Pres., London and Middx Archaeological Soc., 1982–85. Corresp. Mem., German Archaeol Inst., 1976. Governor, Mus. of London, 1981–95. Member: Council, British Sch. at Rome, 1988–; Man. Cttee, British Sch. at Athens, 1990–. Editor, Britannia, 1980–84. *Publications:* Dalmatia (Provinces of Roman Empire series), 1969; (jtly) Diocletian's Palace: joint excavations in the southeast quarter, Pt 1, Split, 1972; (ed jtly) Victoria County History of Cambridgeshire, vol. VII, Roman Cambridgeshire, 1978; Rhind Lectures (Edinburgh), 1984; Diocletian's Palace, Split (2nd Ian Saunders Meml Lecture, expanded), 1986; (jtly) Strageath: excavations within the Roman Fort 1973–1986, 1989; The Illyrians, 1992; papers, excavation reports and reviews in learned jls of Britain, Amer., and Europe. *Recreations:* listening to music, watching Association football. *Address:* Institute of Archaeology, University College London, 31–34 Gordon Square, WC1H 0PY. *T:* 0171–380 7489.

WILKES, Maurice Vincent, MA, PhD; FRS 1956; FEng 1976; FIEE; FBCS; Consultant on Research Strategy, Olivetti Research Directorate, since 1990 (Member for Research Strategy, Olivetti Research Board, 1980–86); Head of the Computer Laboratory, Cambridge (formerly Mathematical Laboratory), 1970–80; Professor of Computer Technology, 1965–80, now Emeritus Professor; Fellow of St John's College, since 1950; *b* 26 June 1913; *s* of late Vincent J. Wilkes, OBE; *m* 1947, Nina Twyman; one *s* two *d*. *Educ:* King Edward's School, Stourbridge; St John's College, Cambridge. Mathematical Tripos (Wrangler). Research in physics at Cavendish Lab.; Univ. Demonstrator, 1937. Served War of 1939–45, Radar and Operational Research. Univ. Lecturer and Acting Dir of Mathematical Laboratory, Cambridge, 1945; Dir of Mathematical Laboratory, 1946–70. Computer Engr, Digital Equipment Corp., USA, 1980–86; Adjunct Prof. of Computer Sci. and Elect. Engrg, MIT, 1981–85. Member: Measurement and Control Section Committee, IEE, 1956–59; Council, IEE, 1973–76; First President British Computer Soc., 1957–60, Distinguished Fellow 1973. Mem. Council, IFIP, 1960–63; Chm. IEE E Anglia Sub-Centre, 1969–70; Turing Lectr Assoc. for Computing Machinery, 1967. Foreign Hon. Mem., Amer. Acad. of Arts and Sciences, 1974; Foreign Corresponding Mem., Royal Spanish Acad. of Sciences, 1979; Foreign Associate: US Nat. Acad. of Engrg, 1977; US Nat. Acad. of Scis, 1980. Hon. DSc: Newcastle upon Tyne, 1972; Hull, 1974; Kent, 1975; City, 1975; Amsterdam, 1978; Munich, 1978; Bath, 1987; Cambridge, 1993; Hon. DTech Linköping, 1975. Harry Goode Award, Amer. Fedn of Inf. Processing Socs, 1968; Eckert-Mauchly Award, Assoc. for Computing Machinery and IEEE Computer Soc., 1980; McDowell Award, IEEE Computer Soc., 1981; Faraday Medal, IEE, 1981; Pender Award, Univ. of Pennsylvania, 1982; C & C Prize, Foundn for C & C Promotions, Tokyo, 1988; Italgas Prize for Computer Science, 1991; Kyoto Prize, Cambridge Univ., 1992. *Publications:* Oscillations of the Earth's Atmosphere, 1949; (joint) Preparations of Programs for an Electronic Digital Computer, Addison-Wesley (Cambridge, Mass), 1951, 2nd edn 1958; Automatic Digital Computers, 1956; A Short Introduction to Numerical Analysis, 1966; Time-sharing Computer System, 1968, 3rd edn 1975; (jtly) The Cambridge CAP Computer and its Operating System, 1979; Memoirs of a Computer Pioneer, 1985; Computing Perspectives, 1995; papers in scientific jls. *Address:* Olivetti Research Ltd, 24a Trumpington Street, Cambridge CB2 3NJ. *T:* Cambridge (01223) 343300. *Club:* Athenæum.

WILKES, Ven. Michael Jocelyn James P.; *see* Paget-Wilkes.

WILKES, Gen. Sir Michael (John), KCB 1991; CBE 1988 (OBE 1980); Lieutenant-Governor and Commander-in-Chief, Jersey, since 1995; *b* 11 June 1940; *s* of late Lt-Col Jack Wilkes, OBE, MC and of Phyllis Wilkes; *m* 1966, Anne Jacqueline Huelin; two *s*. *Educ:* King's Sch., Rochester; RMA Sandhurst. Commnd RA, 1960; joined 7 Para Regt, RHA, 1961; served ME Troop, Comdr Special Forces, 1964–67, Radfan, S Arabia, Borneo; Staff Coll., 1971–72; Bde Major RA, HQ3 Armd Div., 1973–74; Battery Comdr Chestnut Troop, 1 RHA (BAOR), 1975–76, CO, 1977–79; Mil. Asst to CGS, 1980–81; COS, 3 Armd Div., 1982–83; Comdr, 22 Armd Bde, 1984–85; Arms Dir, MoD, 1986–88; GOC 3 Armd Div., 1988–90; Comdr UK Field Army and Inspector Gen., TA, 1990–93; Adjutant Gen., 1993–95. ME Advr to MoD, 1992–95. Order of Mil. Merit, 1st class (Jordan), 1994. *Recreations:* golf, sailing, ski-ing, military history. *Clubs:* Naval and Military, Special Forces, Royal Thames Yacht.

WILKES, Richard Geoffrey, CBE 1990 (OBE (mil.) 1969); TD 1959; DL; FCA; Director, Cassidy, Davis Insurance Group Ltd, since 1989, and other companies; Partner, Price Waterhouse, Chartered Accountants, 1969–90; *b* 12 June 1928; *s* of Geoffrey W. Wilkes and Kathleen (*née* Quinn); *m* 1953, Wendy Elaine, *d* of Rev. C. Ward; one *s* three *d*. *Educ:* Repton (Exhibnr). ACA 1952; FCA 1957. Partner, Bolton Bullivant, Chartered Accountants, Leicester, 1953–69. Pres., Leics and Northants Soc. of Chartered Accountants, 1967–68; Mem. Council, Inst. of Chartered Accountants in England and Wales, 1969–90 (Dep. Pres., 1979–80; Pres., 1980–81); Chairman: UK Auditing Practices Cttee, 1976–78; CA Compensation Scheme, 1990–; International Federation of Accountants: UK Rep; Mem. Council, 1983–87; Dep. Pres., 1985–87; Pres., 1987–90; Mem., Internat. Auditing Practices Cttee, 1978–79; Adviser on self-regulation, Lloyd's of London, 1983–85. Governor, CARE for the Mentally Handicapped, 1972– (Chm., 1995–). Commnd RHA, 1947; served TA, RA and Royal Leics Regt, 1948–69; CO 4/5th Bn Royal Leics Regt (TA), 1966–69; Col TAVR E Midlands Dist, 1969–73; ADC (TAVR) to the Queen, 1972–77. Dep. Hon. Col, Royal Anglian Regt (Leics), 1981–88; Vice Chm., E Midlands TA&VRA, 1980–89 (Chm., Leics Co. Cttee, 1980–89); Chm., E Midlands TAVRA Employers Liaison Cttee, 1990–. Comdt, Leics Special Constab., 1972–79. Chm., Leics SSAFA, 1991– (Treas., 1969–91). Mem., Court, Worshipful Co. of Chartered Accountants in England and Wales, 1977– (Master, 1991–92). DL Leics, 1967. Internat. Award, ICA, 1990. *Recreations:* shooting, sailing. *Address:* The Hermitage, Swingbridge Street, Foxton, Market Harborough, Leics LE16 7RH. *T:* East Langton (01858) 545213. *Club:* Army and Navy.

WILKIE, Alan Fraser; QC 1992; a Recorder, since 1995; *b* 26 Dec. 1947; *s* of James and Helen Wilkie; *m* 1972, Susan Elizabeth Musgrave; one *s* one *d*. *Educ:* Hutcheson's Grammar Sch., Glasgow; Manchester Grammar Sch.; Balliol Coll., Oxford (BA, BCL). Lecturer in Law: Exeter Coll., Oxford, 1971–72; Southampton Univ., 1972–74; called to the Bar, Inner Temple, 1974; an Asst Recorder, 1992–95. *Recreations:* music, films, watching football, playing tennis, cycling. *Address:* 11 King's Bench Walk, Temple, EC4Y 7EQ. *T:* 0171–583 0610.

WILKIE, Prof. Douglas Robert, FRS 1971; Jodrell Research Professor of Physiology, in the University of London, 1979–88, now Emeritus Research Professor of Experimental Physiology; *b* 2 Oct. 1922; *m* 1949, June Rosalind Hill (marr. diss. 1982); one *s*. *Educ:* Medical Student, University Coll. London, 1940–42 (Fellow, 1972); Yale Univ. (MD), 1942–43; University Coll. Hosp., MB, BS, 1944, MRCP 1945; FRCP 1972. Lectr, Dept of Physiology, UCL, 1948; Inst. of Aviation Medicine, Farnborough (Mil. Service), 1948–50; London University: Locke Research Fellowship (Royal Soc.), UCL, 1951–54; Readership in Experimental Physiology, UCL, 1954–65; Prof. of Experimental Physiology, 1965–69; Jodrell Prof., and Head of Physiology Dept, UCL, 1969–79. SRC Sen. Res. Fellowship, 1978. *Publications:* Muscle, 1968; 130 contribs to learned jls, etc, mainly research on energetics of muscular contraction, and attempts to explain thermodynamics simply, recently, application of nuclear magnetic resonance in medicine. *Recreations:* sailing, friends, photography. *Address:* 2 Wychwood End, Stanhope Road, N6 5ND. *T:* 0171–272 4024.

WILKIN, (Frederick) John, CBE 1978 (OBE 1968); DFM 1943; President, National Incorporated Beneficent Society (Member of Council, since 1973); Chairman, The Wickenby Register (12 and 626 Squadrons Association), since 1983; *b* 15 Aug. 1916; *s* of late George Wilkin and Rosetta Christina Wilkin; *m* 1st, 1943, Marjorie Joan Wilson (*d* 1972); one *d*; 2nd, 1975, Laura Elizabeth Eason (*d* 1993); one *s* one *d*. *Educ:* Southwark Central Sch.; Morley Coll., London. Served RAF, 1940–46: Navigator (12, 101 and 156 Sqdns); Permanent Award Pathfinder Badge. Asst Accountant, House of Commons, 1955, Chief Accountant, 1962–80; Secretary: House of Commons Members' Fund, 1962–81; Parliamentary Contributory Pensions Fund, 1965–80; Head of Admin Dept, House of

Commons, 1980–81. Associate Mem. of Special Trustees, Charing Cross and Westminster Hosps, 1979–91; Vice-Chm., Hammersmith and Fulham DHA, 1982–83. Mem., Guild of Freemen of City of London. *Recreations:* gardening, watching sport; formerly cricket, cycling, table tennis. *Address:* 14 Forest Ridge, Beckenham, Kent BR3 3NH. *T:* 0181–650 5261. *Club:* Royal Air Force.

WILKINS, Sir Graham John, (Bob), Kt 1980; Director, Eastern Electricity, since 1989; Chairman, THORN EMI, 1985–89, retired (Chief Executive, 1985–87); President, Beecham Group Ltd, 1984–89 (Chairman and Chief Executive, 1975–84); *b* 22 Jan. 1924; *s* of George William and Anne May Wilkins; *m* 1st, 1945, Daphne Mildred Haynes; 2nd, 1990, Helen Catherine McGregor. *Educ:* Yeovil Sch.; University Coll., South West of England, Exeter (BSc). Dir and Vice-Pres., Beecham (Canada) Ltd, 1954–59; C. L. Bencard Ltd, and Beecham Research Labs Ltd: Asst Man. Dir, 1959; Man. Dir, 1960; Dir, Beecham Pharmaceutical Div., 1962–64; Beecham Group Ltd: Dir and Chm., Pharmaceutical Div., 1964–72; Man. Dir (Pharmaceuticals), 1972; Exec. Vice-Chm., 1974; Chm., ICC UK, 1985–89 (Vice Chm., 1984–85); Director: Beecham Inc., 1967–86; Hill Samuel Gp Ltd, 1977–87; THORN EMI (formerly Thorn Electrical Industries) Ltd, 1978–89; Rowntree, 1985–88 (Dep. Chm., 1988); Courage Pensions, 1989–. Mem., Doctors' and Dentists' Remuneration Rev. Bd, 1980–90 (Chm., 1986–90). Vice-Chm., Proprietary Assoc. of GB, 1966–68; President: Assoc. of Brit. Pharmaceutical Industry, 1969–71 (Vice-Pres., 1968–69); European Fedn of Pharmaceutical Industries Assoc., 1978–82; Chm., Medico-Pharmaceutical Forum, 1971–73 (Vice-Chm., 1969–70). Mem., BOTB, 1977–80. Pres., Advertising Assoc., 1983–89. Mem. Council, Sch. of Pharmacy, London Univ., 1984– (Chm., 1987–). Hon. FRCP 1984. *Publications:* various papers on pharmaceutical industry. *Recreations:* golf, theatre-going. *Address:* Alceda, Walton Lane, Shepperton-on-Thames, Mddx TW17 8LQ.

WILKINS, John Anthony Francis; Editor of The Tablet, since 1982; *b* 20 Dec. 1936; *s* of Edward Manwaring Wilkins and Ena Gwendolen Francis. *Educ:* Clifton Coll., Bristol (Scholar); Clare Coll., Cambridge (State Scholar, 1954; Major Scholar and Foundn Scholar; Classical Tripos 1959, Theol Tripos 1961; BA 1961). Served 1st Bn Glos Regt, 1955–57 (2nd Lieut). Planning Div., Marine Dept, Head Office of Esso Petroleum, London, 1962–63; Asst Editor: Frontier, 1964–67; The Tablet, 1967–72; features writer, BBC External Services, 1972–81; Producer, Radio 4, 1978. Ondas Radio Prize, 1973. *Publications:* (ed) How I Pray, 1993; (ed) Understanding Veritatis Splendor, 1994. *Recreation:* ornithology. *Address:* The Tablet, 1 King Street Cloisters, Clifton Walk, W6 0QZ. *T:* 0181–748 8484.

WILKINS, Prof. Malcolm Barrett, FRSE 1972; Regius Professor of Botany, University of Glasgow, since 1970; *b* 27 Feb. 1933; *s* of Barrett Charles Wilkins and Eleanor Mary Wilkins (*née* Jenkins); *m* 1959, Mary Patricia Maltby; one *s* (one *d* decd). *Educ:* Monkton House Sch., Cardiff; King's Coll., London. BSc 1955; PhD London 1958; AKC 1958; DSc 1972. Lectr in Botany, King's Coll., London, 1958–64; Rockefeller Foundn Fellow, Yale Univ., 1961–62; Research Fellow, Harvard Univ., 1962–63; Lectr in Biology, Univ. of East Anglia, 1964–65; Prof. of Biology, Univ. of East Anglia, 1965–67; Prof. of Plant Physiology, Univ. of Nottingham, 1967–70; Glasgow University: Dean, Faculty of Science, 1984–87; Chm., Sch. of Biol Scis, 1988–92. Darwin Lectr, British Assoc. for Advancement of Science, 1967. Member: Biol. Sci. Cttee of SRC, 1971–74; Governing Body: Hill Farming Res. Orgn, 1971–80; Scottish Crops Research Inst, 1974–89; Glasshouse Crops Res. Inst., 1979–88; W of Scotland Agricl Coll., 1983–92; Exec. Cttee, Scottish Field Studies Assoc.; British Nat. Cttee for Biology, 1977–82; Life Science Working Gp, ESA, 1983–89 (Chm., 1987–89); Microgravity Adv. Cttee, ESA, 1985–89; NASA Lifesat Science Cttee, 1986–91; Court, Glasgow Univ., 1993–. Vice-Pres., RSE, 1994– (Mem. Council, 1989–92). Trustee, Royal Botanic Gdn, Edinburgh, 1990– (Chm., 1994–); Adv. Council, Scottish Agricl Coll. Corresp. Mem., Amer. Soc. of Plant Physiologists, 1985. Dir, West of Scotland Sch. Co.; Chm., Laurel Bank Sch. Co. Ltd. Cons. Editor in Plant Biology, McGraw-Hill Publishing Co., 1968–80; Managing Editor, Planta, 1977–. *Publications:* (ed) The Physiology of Plant Growth and Development, 1969; (ed) Advanced Plant Physiology, 1984; Plantwatching, 1988; papers in Jl of Experimental Botany, Plant Physiology, Planta, Nature, Proc. Royal Soc. *Recreations:* sailing, fishing, model engineering. *Address:* Institute of Biomedical and Life Science, Bower Building, The University, Glasgow G12 8QQ. *T:* 0141–330 4450. *Clubs:* Caledonian; New (Edinburgh).

WILKINS, Maurice Hugh Frederick, CBE 1963; MA, PhD; FRS 1959; Professor of Bio-physics, 1970–81, Emeritus Professor of Biophysics since 1981, and Fellow, since 1973, King's College, University of London; Director, Medical Research Council Cell Biophysics Unit, 1974–80 (Deputy Director, 1955–70, Director, 1970–72, Biophysics Unit; Director Neurobiology Unit, 1972–74); *b* 15 Dec. 1916; *s* of late Edgar Henry Wilkins and of Eveline Constance Jane (*née* Whittaker), both of Dublin; *m* 1959, Patricia Ann Chidgey; two *s* two *d*. *Educ:* King Edward's Sch., Birmingham: St John's College, Cambridge (Hon. Fellow, 1972). Research on luminescence of solids at Physics Department, Birmingham University, with Ministry of Home Security and Aircraft Production, 1938; PhD 1940; Manhattan Project (Ministry of Supply), Univ. of California (research on separation of uranium isotopes by mass spectrograph), 1944; Lectr in Physics, St Andrews Univ., 1945; MRC Biophysics Unit in Physics Department, King's College, London, 1946; Hon. Lecturer in the sub-department of Biophysics, 1958; Prof. of Molecular Biology, King's Coll., 1963–70. President: British Soc. for Social Responsibility in Science, 1969–91; Food and Disarmament Internat., 1984–. Hon. Mem., Amer. Soc. of Biological Chemists, 1964; For. Hon. Mem., Amer. Acad. of Arts and Scis, 1970. Albert Lasker Award, Amer. Public Health Assoc., 1960. Hon. LLD Glasgow, 1972; Hon. ScD: TCD, 1992; Birmingham, 1992. (Jt) Nobel Prize for Medicine, 1962. *Publications:* papers in scientific journals on luminescence and topics in bio-physics, *eg* molecular structure of nucleic acids and structure of nerve membranes. *Address:* 30 St John's Park, SE3 7JH. *T:* 0181–858 1817.

WILKINS, Nancy; barrister-at-law; *b* 16 June 1932; three *s* one *d*. *Educ:* School of St Helen and St Katharine, Abingdon, Berkshire. Called to the Bar, Gray's Inn, Nov. 1962; in practice, Midland Circuit, 1962–85; Dep. Circuit Judge, 1974–78; a Recorder, 1978–85; practised in solicitors' office, 1986–90; retired. *Publication:* An Outline of the Law of Evidence (with late Prof. Sir Rupert Cross), 1964, 5th edn 1980. *Recreation:* writing my memoirs. *Address:* Santa Marta 77, Marchuquera Baixa, Gandia 46700, Spain.

WILKINSON; *see* Browne-Wilkinson.

WILKINSON, Rev. Canon Alan Bassindale, PhD; lecturer, writer and Open University tutor; honorary priest, Portsmouth Cathedral, since 1988, and diocesan theologian, since 1993; *b* 26 Jan. 1931; *s* of late Rev. J. T. Wilkinson, DD; *m* 1975, Fenella Holland; two *s* one *d* of first marriage. *Educ:* William Hulme's Grammar Sch., Manchester; St Catharine's Coll., Cambridge; College of the Resurrection, Mirfield. MA 1958, PhD 1959 (Cambridge). Deacon, 1959; Priest, 1960; Asst Curate, St Augustine's, Kilburn, 1959–61; Chaplain, St Catharine's Coll., Cambridge, 1961–67; Vicar of Barrow Gurney and Lecturer in Theology, College of St Matthias, Bristol, 1967–70; Principal, Chichester Theol. Coll., 1970–74; Canon and Prebendary of Thorney, 1970–74, Canon Emeritus, 1975; Warden of Verulam House, Dir of Training for Auxiliary Ministry, dio. of St Albans, 1974–75; Lectr in Theology and Ethics, Crewe and Alsager Coll. of Higher Educn, 1975–78; Dir of Training, Diocese of Ripon, 1978–84; Hon. Canon, Ripon Cathedral, 1984; Priest-in-Charge, Darley with Thruscross and Thornthwaite, 1984–88. Vis. Fellow, Chichester Inst. of Higher Educn, 1995–. Hulsean Preacher, 1967–68; Select Preacher, Oxford Univ., 1982. Mem., Bd of Educn, Gen. Synod, 1981–85; Vice-Chm., Leeds Marriage and Personal Counselling Service, 1981–83. Governor: SPCK, 1982–91; Coll. of Ripon and York St John, 1985–88. Scott Holland Trustee, 1993–95. *Publications:* The Church of England and the First World War, 1978; Would You Believe It?, 1980; More Ready to Hear, 1983; Christian Choices, 1983; Dissent or Conform?, 1986; The Community of the Resurrection: a centenary history, 1992; contributor to: Cambridge Sermons on Christian Unity, 1966; Catholic Anglicans Today, 1968; A Work Book in Popular Religion, 1986; Chesterton and the Modernist Crisis, 1990; Britain and the Threat to Stability in Europe, 1993; Forever Building, 1995; also to: Faith and Unity, Sobornost, Preacher's Quarterly, London Quarterly Holborn Review, Theology, Clergy Review, New Fire, Church Times, Chesterton Review, Internat. Christian Digest, Modern Hist. Rev. *Recreations:* gardening, walking, cinema, Victorian architecture. *Address:* Hope Cottage, 27 Great Southsea Street, Portsmouth PO5 3BY. *T:* Portsmouth (01705) 825788.

WILKINSON, Alexander Birrell; QC (Scot.) 1993; Sheriff of Glasgow and Strathkelvin, since 1991; *b* 2 Feb. 1932; *o s* of late Captain Alexander Wilkinson, MBE, The Black Watch and Isabella Bell Birrell; *m* 1965, Wendy Imogen, *d* of late Ernest Albert Barrett and R. V. H. Barrett; one *s* one *d*. *Educ:* Perth Academy; Univs of St Andrews and Edinburgh. Walker Trust Scholar 1950, Grieve Prizeman in Moral Philosophy 1952, MA(Hons Classics) 1954, Univ. of St Andrews. National Service, RAEC, 1954–56. Balfour Keith Prizeman in Constitutional Law 1957, LLB (with distinction) 1959, Univ. of Edinburgh. Admitted to Faculty of Advocates, 1959; in practice at Scottish bar, 1959–69; Lecturer in Scots Law, Univ. of Edinburgh, 1965–69; Sheriff of Stirling, Dunbarton and Clackmannan at Stirling and Alloa, 1969–72; Prof. of Private Law, 1972–86, and Dean of Faculty of Law, 1974–76 and 1986, Univ. of Dundee; Sheriff of Tayside, Central and Fife at Falkirk, 1986–91. Chancellor: Dio. of Brechin, 1982–; Dio. of Argyll and the Isles, 1985–. Chairman: Central Scotland Marriage Guidance Council, 1970–72; Scottish Marriage Guidance Council, 1974–77; Legal Services Gp, Scottish Assoc. of CAB, 1979–83. Vice-Pres., Sheriffs' Assoc., 1995–. *Publications:* (ed jtly) Gloag and Henderson's Introduction to the Law of Scotland, 8th edn 1980, 9th edn 1987; The Scottish Law of Evidence, 1986; (jtly) The Law of Parent and Child in Scotland, 1993; articles in legal periodicals. *Recreations:* collecting books and pictures, reading, travel. *Address:* 25 Glencairn Crescent, Edinburgh EH12 5BT. *T:* 0131–346 1797. *Club:* New (Edinburgh).

WILKINSON, Prof. Christopher David Wicks, PhD; FRSE; James Watt Professor of Electrical Engineering, Glasgow University, since 1992; *b* 1 Sept. 1940; *s* of Charles Norman Wilkinson and Doris Margaret (*née* Wicks); *m* 1963, Dr Judith Anne Hughes; one *s* two *d*. *Educ:* Balliol Coll., Oxford (BA Physics; MA); Stanford Univ. (PhD Applied Physics). FRSE 1987. Engr, English Electric Valve Co., Chelmsford, 1968; Department of Electronics and Electrical Engineering, Glasgow University: Lectr, 1969–75; Sen. Lectr, 1975–79; Reader, 1979–82; Titular Prof., 1982–92. Vis. Scientist, IBM Res. Centre, Yorktown Heights, USA, 1975–76; Vis. Prof., NTT Labs, Tokyo, 1982. *Publications:* 150 papers on nanoelectronics, optoelectronics and bioelectronics, in learned jls. *Recreations:* hill walker, allotment holder, cooking, theatre. *Address:* 31 Hyndland Road, Glasgow G12 9UY. *T:* 0141–357 0204.

WILKINSON, Christopher Richard; Adviser, Directorate General, Telecommunications Information Market and Exploitation of Research (DG XIII), Commission of the European Communities, since 1993; *b* 3 July 1941; *s* of Rev. Thomas Richard Wilkinson and Winifred Frances Wilkinson (*née* Steel). *Educ:* Hymers Coll., Kingston upon Hull; Heath Grammar Sch., Halifax; Selwyn Coll., Cambridge (MA). Commonwealth Economic Cttee, 1963–65; OECD, Paris and Madrid, 1965–66; World Bank, Washington DC and Lagos, 1966–73; EEC: Head of Division: Directorate Gen. for Regional Policy, 1973–78; Directorate Gen. for Internal Market and Industrial Affairs, 1978–82; Directorate Gen. for Telecommunications, Information Industries and Innovation, 1983–93. Vis. Fellow, Center for Internat. Affairs, Harvard Univ., 1982–83. Vice-Pres., European School Parents Assoc., Brussels, 1974, 1976–77. *Recreations:* mountain walking, gardening, cooking. *Address:* rue Charles Quint 55, 1040 Brussels, Belgium.

WILKINSON, Clive Victor; Chairman, Wolverhampton Health Care NHS Trust, since 1995; *b* 26 May 1938; *s* of Mrs Winifred Jobson; *m* 1961, Elizabeth Ann Pugh; two *d*. *Educ:* Four Dwellings Secondary Sch., Quinton; Birmingham Modern Sch. Birmingham City Council: Member, 1970–84; Leader, 1973–76 and 1980–82; Leader of Opposition, 1976–80, 1982–84. Dir, Nat. Exhibn Centre, 1973–84; Financial and Commercial Dir, Birmingham Rep. Theatre, 1983–87. Chm., CoSIRA, 1977–80; Dep. Chairman: AMA, 1974–76; Redditch Develt Corp., 1977–81. Chm., Sandwell DHA, 1986–94. Member: Develt Commn, 1977–86; Electricity Consumers Council, 1977–80; Audit Commn, 1987–; Black Country Develt Corp., 1989–92; Local Govt Commn, 1992–95; Midlands Industrial Assoc., 1978– (Chm., 1980–88). Chairman: Birmingham Civil Housing Assoc., 1979–; Customer Services Cttee, Severn Trent Region, Office of Water Services, 1990–. Mem. Council, Univ. of Birmingham, 1974–84. Trustee, Bournville Village Trust, 1982–. Hon. Alderman, City of Birmingham, 1984. *Recreations:* watching Birmingham City Football Club, playing squash. *Address:* 53 Middle Park Road, Birmingham B29 4BH. *T:* 0121–475 1829.

WILKINSON, David Anthony, CB 1994; Under Secretary, Office of Public Service and Science, since 1992; *b* 27 Nov. 1947; *s* of Ambrose Wilkinson and Doreen (*née* Durden); *m* 1973, Meryl, *d* of Edison and Margaret Pugh; three *d*. *Educ:* Boteler Grammar Sch., Warrington; Wigan and District Mining and Technical Coll.; Bedford Coll., Univ. of London (BA History); London School of Economics; Moscow State Univ. Department of Education and Science, 1974–92: Hd of Inf. Br., 1987–88; Dep. Dir of Establishments, 1988–89; Under Sec., 1989–92; Hd of Sci. Br., 1989–92, RCDS, 1995. *Address:* Government Offices, Great George Street, SW1P 3AT. *Club:* Wimbledon Squash and Badminton.

WILKINSON, Sir D. G. B.; *see* Wilkinson, Sir Graham.

WILKINSON, Prof. David Gregor, (Greg), FRCPE; FRCPsych; Professor of Liaison Psychiatry, Liverpool University, since 1994; *b* 17 May 1951; *s* of David Pryde Wilkinson and Joan (*née* McCabe); *m* 1984, Christine Mary Lewis; three *s* one *d*. *Educ:* Lawside Acad., Dundee; Edinburgh Univ. (BSc, MB ChB); MPhil London. FRCPE 1989; FRCPsych 1991. House Physician and Surgeon, Royal Infirmary, Edinburgh, 1975–76; Sen. House Physician, Leith Hosp., 1976–78; Registrar, Maudsley Hosp., 1978–81; Sen. Registrar, Maudsley Hosp. and KCH, 1981–83; Res. Worker and Lectr, then Sen. Lectr, Inst. of Psychiatry, Univ. of London, 1983–89; Sen. Lectr and Reader, Academic Sub-dept of Psychol Medicine in N Wales, 1989–91; Prof. of Psychiatry, London Hosp. Med. Coll., London Univ., 1992–94. Editor, Brit. Jl of Psychiatry, 1993–. *Publications:* Mental Health Practices in Primary Care Settings, 1985; (jtly) Mental Illness in Primary Care Settings, 1986; (jtly) The Provision of Mental Health Services in Britain, 1986; Coping with Stress, 1987, 2nd edn as Understanding Stress, 1993; Depression, 1989; Recognising and Treating Depression in General Practice, 1989; (jtly) The Scope of Epidemiological Psychiatry, 1989; Recognising and Treating Anxiety in General Practice, 1992; Talking About Psychiatry, 1993; (jtly) Psychiatry and General Practice Today, 1994; articles in general and specialist med. jls. *Recreations:* family, rural pursuits, being a pimp of discourse. *Address:* The Courtyard, Gwaenynog, Denbigh, Clwyd LL16 5NU. *T:* Denbigh (01745) 816795. *Club:* Athenæum.

WILKINSON, David Lloyd; Chief Executive and General Secretary, Cooperative Union, since 1975; *b* 28 May 1937; *m* 1960; one *s* one *d*. *Educ:* Royds Hall Grammar Sch. ACIS; CSD. *Address:* 2 Old House, Marsden, Huddersfield HD7 6AS. *T:* Huddersfield (01484) 844580.

WILKINSON, Sir Denys (Haigh), Kt 1974; FRS 1956; Vice-Chancellor, University of Sussex, 1976–87 (Emeritus Professor of Physics, 1987); *b* Leeds, Yorks, 5 September 1922; *o s* of late Charles Wilkinson and Hilda Wilkinson (*née* Haigh); *m* 1st, 1947, Christiane Andrée Clavier (marriage dissolved, 1967); three *d*; 2nd, 1967, Helen Sellschop; two step *d*. *Educ:* Loughborough Gram. Sch.; Jesus Coll. Cambridge (Fellow, 1944–59, Hon. Fellow 1961). BA 1943, MA, PhD 1947, ScD 1961. British and Canadian Atomic Energy Projects, 1943–46; Univ. Demonstrator, Cambridge, 1947–51; Univ. Lecturer, 1951–56; Reader in Nuclear Physics, Univ. of Cambridge, 1956–57; Professor of Nuclear Physics, Univ. of Oxford, 1957–59; Prof. of Experimental Physics, Univ. of Oxford, 1959–76, Head of Dept of Nuclear Physics, 1962–76; Student, Christ Church, Oxford, 1957–76, Emeritus Student, 1976, Hon. Student, 1979. Dir, Internat. Sch. of Nuclear Physics, Erice, Sicily, 1975–83. Mem. Governing Board of National Institute for Research in Nuclear Science, 1957–63 and 1964–65; Member: SRC, 1967–70; Wilton Park Acad. Council, 1979–83; Council, ACU, 1980–87; Royal Commn for the Exhibn of 1851, 1983–90 (Chm., Science Scholarships Cttee, 1983–90); British Council, 1987– (Chm., Sci. Adv. Panel and Cttee, 1977–86); Chairman: Nuclear Physics Board of SRC, 1968–70; Physics III Cttee, CERN, Geneva, 1971–75; Radioactive Waste Management Adv. Cttee, 1978–83; Pres., Inst. of Physics, 1980–82; Vice-Pres., IUPAP, 1985–93. Lectures: Welch, Houston, 1957; Scott, Cambridge Univ., 1961; Rutherford Meml, Brit. Physical Soc., 1962; Graham Young, Glasgow Univ., 1964; Queen's, Berlin, 1966; Silliman, Yale Univ., 1966; Cherwell-Simon, Oxford Univ., 1970; Distinguished, Utah State Univ., 1971, 1983, 1988; Goodspeed-Richard, Pennsylvania Univ., 1973 and 1986; Welsh, Toronto Univ., 1975; Tizard Meml, Westminster Sch., 1975; Lauritsen Meml, Cal. Tech., 1976; Herbert Spencer, Oxford Univ., 1976; Schiff Meml, Stanford Univ., 1977; Racah Meml, Hebrew Univ. Jerusalem, 1977; Cecil Green, Univ. of BC, 1978; Distinguished, Univ. of Alberta, 1979; Wolfson, Oxford Univ., 1980; Waterloo-Guelph Distinguished, Guelph Univ., 1981; Herzberg, Ottawa, 1984; Solly Cohen Meml, Hebrew Univ., Jerusalem, 1985; Peter Axel Meml, Univ. of Illinois, 1985; Breit Meml, Yale Univ., 1987; Moon, Birmingham Univ., 1987; Rochester, Durham Univ., 1988; Pegram, Brookhaven Nat. Lab., 1989; W. B. Lewis Meml, Chalk River, Ont, 1989; Humphry Davy, Académie des Sciences, Paris, 1990; Rutherford Meml, Royal Soc., 1991; W. V. Houston Meml, Rice Univ., 1994; Hudspeth, Univ. of Texas at Austin, 1994; Anna McPherson, McGill Univ., 1995. Walker Ames Prof., Univ. of Washington, 1968; Battelle Distinguished Prof., Univ. of Washington, 1970–71; Vis. Prof., Tokyo Univ., 1995. For. Mem., Royal Swedish Acad. of Scis, 1980; Mem. Acad. Europaea, 1990. Holweck Medal, British and French Physical Socs, 1957; Rutherford Prize, British Physical Soc., 1962; Hughes Medal, Royal Society, 1965; Bruce-Preller Prize, RSE, 1969; Bonner Prize, American Physical Soc., 1974; Royal Medal, Royal Soc., 1980; Guthrie Medal and Prize, Inst. of Physics, 1986; Gold Medal, Centro Cultura Scientifica Ettore Majorana, Sicily, 1988. Hon. Mem., Mark Twain Soc, 1978. Hon. DSc: Saskatchewan, 1964; Utah State, 1975; Guelph, 1981; Queen's, Kingston, 1987; William and Mary, Va, 1989; Hon. FilDr Uppsala, 1980; Hon. LLD Sussex, 1987. Comm. Bontemps Médoc et Graves, 1973. *Publications:* Ionization Chambers and Counters, 1951; (ed) Isospin in Nuclear Physics, 1969; (ed) Progress in Particle and Nuclear Physics, 1978–84; (ed jtly) Mesons in Nuclei, 1979; Our Universes, 1991; papers on nuclear physics and bird navigation. *Recreations:* mediæval church architecture and watching birds. *Address:* Gayles Orchard, Friston, Eastbourne, East Sussex BN20 0BA. *T:* East Dean (01323) 423333, *Fax:* (01323) 423329.

WILKINSON, Elizabeth Mary, PhD; FBA 1972; Professor of German, University College London, 1960–76, now Emeritus; *b* 17 Sept. 1909; *d* of Frank Wilkinson and Martha E. Gilleard, Keighley, Yorks. *Educ:* Whalley Range High Sch., Manchester; Bedford Coll., London (BA, PhD; Hon. Fellow 1985); DipEd Oxford. Vis. Prof., Univ. of Chicago, 1955; first Virginia C. Gildersleeve Prof., Barnard Coll., Columbia Univ., 1958; Prof.-at-Large of Cornell Univ., 1967–. President: English Goethe Soc., 1974–86; Modern Language Assoc., GB, 1964; Hon. Mem., Modern Language Assoc. of America, 1965. Former Governor, Bedford Coll., London. Korresp. Mitglied, Akademie der Wissenschaften zu Göttingen, 1973; Deutsche Akad. für Sprache und Dichtung, 1976. Hon. LLD Smith Coll., Mass, 1966; Hon. DLitt Kent, 1971. Medaille in Gold des Goethe-Instituts, 1965; Preis für Germanistik im Ausland der Deutschen Akad. für Sprache und Dichtung, 1974. German Editor, Notebooks of Samuel Taylor Coleridge, 1950–62 (vols 1 and 2); Editor, publications of the English Goethe Soc., 1951–70. *Publications:* Thomas Mann's Tonio Kröger, 1943; (with L. A. Willoughby) Schiller's Kabale und Liebe, 1944; J. E. Schlegel: A German Pioneer in Aesthetics, 1945, German edn 1973 (Wissenschaftliche Buchges.) (J. G. Robertson Prize); Edward Bullough's Aesthetics, 1957; (with L. A. Willoughby) Goethe: Poet and Thinker, 1962 (German edn 1974); (with L. A. Willoughby) Schiller: On the Aesthetic Education of Man, 1967 (German edn 1977); Goethe Revisited, 1983; contrib. on Goethe to Encyclopædia Britannica, 1963 and subsq. edns. *Address:* 33 Queen Court, Queen Square, WC1N 3BB.

WILKINSON, Prof. Sir Geoffrey, Kt 1976; FRS 1965; Sir Edward Frankland Professor of Inorganic Chemistry, University of London, 1956–88, now Emeritus; Senior Research Fellow, Imperial College, since 1988; *b* 14 July 1921; *s* of Henry and Ruth Wilkinson; *m* 1951, Lise Sølver, *o d* of Rektor Prof. Svend Aa. Schou, Copenhagen; two *d*. *Educ:* Todmorden Secondary Sch (Royal Scholar, 1939); Imperial Coll., London; USA. Junior Scientific Officer, Nat. Res. Council, Atomic Energy Div., Canada, 1943–46; Research Fellow: Radiation Lab., Univ. of Calif, Berkeley, Calif, USA, 1946–50; Chemistry Dept, Mass Inst. of Technology, Cambridge, Mass, USA, 1950–51; Asst Prof. of Chemistry, Harvard Univ., Cambridge, Mass, 1951–56; Prof. of Inorganic Chemistry at Imperial Coll., Univ. of London, 1956, Sir Edward Frankland Prof. 1978. Arthur D. Little Visiting Prof., MIT, 1967; Lectures: William Draper Harkins' Meml, Univ. of Chicago, 1968; Leermakers, Wesleyan Univ., 1975; First Mond, Chem. Soc., 1980; First Sir Edward Frankland, RSC, 1983; Tovborg Jensen, Univ. of Copenhagen, 1992. John Simon Guggenheim Fellow, 1954. Foreign Member: Roy. Danish Acad. of Science and Arts (math.-phys section), 1968; Amer. Acad. of Arts and Sciences, 1970; Foreign Assoc., Nat. Acad. of Scis, 1975; Centennial Foreign Fellow, Amer. Chem. Soc., 1976. Hon. Fellow: Lady Margaret Hall, Oxford, 1984; UMIST, 1989. Hon. DSc: Edinburgh, 1975; Granada, 1976; Columbia, 1978; Bath, 1980; Essex, 1989. American Chem. Soc. Award in Inorganic Chemistry, 1965; Lavoisier Medal, Société Chimique de France, 1968; Chem. Soc. Award for Transition Metal Chemistry, 1972; (jtly) Nobel Prize for Chemistry, 1973; Consejero de Honor, Spanish Council for Scientific Res., 1974; Hiroshima Univ. Medal, 1978; Royal Medal, Royal Soc., 1981; Galileo Medal, Univ. of Pisa, 1983; Longstaff Medal, RSC, 1987; Medal, Univ. of Camerino, Italy, 1989; Messel Medal, SCI, 1990. Hon. Citizen Award, Todmorden Town Council, 1990. *Publications:* (jtly) Advanced Inorganic Chemistry: a Comprehensive Text, 1962, 5th edn 1988; Basic Inorganic Chemistry, 1976, 3rd edn 1995; numerous in Physical Review, Journal of the American Chemical Society, etc. *Address:* Chemistry Department, Imperial College, SW7 2AY. *T:* 0171–594 5764.

WILKINSON, Geoffrey Crichton, CBE 1986; AFC; Chief Inspector of Accidents (Aircraft), 1981–86; *b* 7 Nov. 1926; *s* of Col W. E. D. Wilkinson and Mrs E. K. Wilkinson; *m* 1958, Virginia Mary Broom; two *d*. *Educ:* Bedford Sch. Graduate, Empire Test Pilots Sch.; FRAES. Royal Indian Mil. Coll., 1943–44; served RN, 1944–47; aeronautical engrg course, 1948; served RAF, 1949–59 (Air Force Cross, 1956); Turner and Newall, 1959–61; Mercury Airlines, 1961–65; Accidents Investigation Br., 1965–86. Air Medal, USA, 1953. *Recreations:* sailing, skiing, music. *Address:* Buckingham House, 50 Hyde Street, Winchester, Hants SO23 7DY. *T:* Winchester (01962) 865823. *Club:* Royal Air Force.

WILKINSON, Sir Graham, 3rd Bt *cr* 1941; Managing Director, S.E.I.C. Services (UK) Ltd, 1985–89; *b* 18 May 1947; *s* of Sir David Wilkinson, 2nd Bt, DSC, and of Sylvia Anne, *d* of late Professor Bosley Alan Rex Gater; *S* father, 1972; *m* 1977, Sandra Caroline, *d* of Dr Richard Rossdale; two *d*. *Educ:* Millfield; Christ Church, Oxford. Orion Royal Bank Ltd, 1971–85 (Dir 1979–85); Non-Exec. Dir, Galveston-Houston Co., USA, 1986–89. CStJ 1995. *Club:* Royal Yacht Squadron.

WILKINSON, Greg; *see* Wilkinson, David Gregor.

WILKINSON, Heather Carol, (Mrs Nigel Wilkinson); *see* Hallett, H. C.

WILKINSON, Jeffrey Vernon; Director, since 1986, and Partner, since 1988, Apax Partners & Co. (formerly Alan Patricof Associates); Chairman of several private companies, since 1985; Chairman and Chief Executive Officer, Spear & Jackson, since 1992; *b* 21 Aug. 1930; *s* of late Arthur Wilkinson and Winifred May Allison; *m* 1955, Jean Vera Nurse; two *d*. *Educ:* Mathew Humberstone Foundation Sch.; King's Coll., Cambridge (MA); Sorbonne. FBCS, CIMgt. Joined Joseph Lucas as graduate apprentice, 1954; Director, CAV, 1963; Director and General Manager, Diesel Equipment, CAV, 1967; Director: Simon Engineering, 1968; Joseph Lucas, 1974; Gen. Manager, Lucas Electrical, 1974; Divisional Man. Dir, Joseph Lucas Ltd, 1978; Jt Gp Man. Dir, Lucas Industries plc, 1979–84. Chairman: Automotive Components Manufacturers, 1979–84; Plastics Processing EDC, 1985–87; Mem. Council and Exec., SMMT, 1979–84. Liveryman, Wheelwrights Company, 1971–. *Recreations:* water-skiing, swimming, reading, theatre, art. *Address:* Hillcroft, 15 Mearse Lane, Barnt Green, Birmingham B45 8HG. *T:* 0121–447 7750.

WILKINSON, John Arbuthnot Du Cane; MP (C) Ruislip Northwood, since 1979; *b* 23 Sept. 1940; 2nd *s* of late Denys Wilkinson and Gillian Wilkinson, Eton College; *m* 1st, 1969 (marr. diss. 1987); one *d*; 2nd, 1987, Cecilia Cienfuegos, *d* of Raul Cienfuegos Lyon, Santiago, Chile; one *s*. *Educ:* Eton (King's Scholar); RAF Coll., Cranwell; Churchill Coll., Cambridge (2nd cl. Hons Mod. Hist.; MA). Flight Cadet, RAF Coll., Cranwell, 1959–61 (Philip Sassoon Meml Prize, qualified French Interpreter); commnd 1961; Flying Instructor, No 8 FTS, Swinderby, 1962. Churchill Coll., Cambridge, Oct. 1962–65. Trooper, 21st Special Air Service Regt (Artists'), TA, 1963–65; rejoined RAF 1965; Flying Instructor, RAF Coll., Cranwell, 1966–67; Tutor, Stanford Univ.'s British Campus, 1967; ADC to Comdr 2nd Allied Tactical Air Force, Germany, 1967; resigned RAF, 1967. Head of Universities' Dept, Conservative Central Office, 1967–68; Aviation Specialist, Cons. Research Dept, 1969; Senior Administration Officer (Anglo-French Jaguar Project), Preston Div., British Aircraft Corp., 1969–70; Tutor, Open Univ., 1970–71; Vis. Lectr, OCTU RAF Henlow, 1971–75; Chief Flying Instructor, Skywork Ltd, Stansted, 1974–75; Gen. Manager, General Aviation Div., Brooklands Aviation Ltd, 1975–76; PA to Chm., BAC, 1975–77; Senior Sales Executive, Eagle Aircraft Services Ltd, 1977–78; Sales Manager, Klingair Ltd, 1978–79. MP (C) Bradford W, 1970–Feb. 1974; Chairman: Cons. Parly Aviation Cttee, 1983–85, and 1992–93 (Jt Sec., 1972–74; Vice-Chm., 1979); Cons. Parly Defence Cttee, 1993–94 (Vice-Chm., 1983–85, 1990–91, 1992–93; Sec., 1972–74 and 1980–81); Member Select Committee on: Race Relations and Immigration, 1972–74; Sci. and Technol., 1972–74; Defence, 1987–90; contested (C) Bradford W, Feb. and Oct. 1974; PPS to Minister of State for Industry, 1979–80, to Sec. of State for Defence, 1981–82; Chairman: Anglo-Asian Cons. Soc., 1979–82; European Freedom Council, 1982–90; Cons. Space Sub Cttee, 1986–90 (Vice-Chm., 1983–85). Chm., Horn of Africa Council, 1984–88. Delegate to Council of Europe (Chm., Space Sub-Cttee, 1984–88) and WEU (Chm., Cttee on Scientific, Technological and Aerospace Questions, 1986–89), 1979–90. Chm., EMC Communications Ltd, 1984–. Parly Industrial Fellow, GKN plc, 1989–90; Postgrad. Fellow, TI plc, 1993; Parly Armed Forces Scheme attachment, RM, 1993–94. HQA Pakistan, 1989. *Publications:* (jtly) The Uncertain Ally, 1982; British Defence: a blueprint for reform, 1987; pamphlets and articles on defence and politics. *Recreation:* flying. *Address:* c/o House of Commons, SW1A 0AA.

See also R. D. Wilkinson, Sir W. H. N. Wilkinson.

WILKINSON, John Francis; Director of Public Affairs, BBC, 1980–85; *b* 2 Oct. 1926; *s* of late Col W. T. Wilkinson, DSO, and Evelyn S. Wilkinson (*née* Ward); *m* 1951, Alison, *d* of late Hugh and Marian Malcolm; two *s* one *d*. *Educ:* Wellington Coll.; Edinburgh Univ. Naval Short Course, 1944–45; Cambridge and London Univs Colonial Course, 1947–48. Served Royal Navy (Fleet Air Arm trainee pilot, 1945), 1945–47; HM Colonial Service, N Nigeria, 1949; Asst District Officer, Bida, 1949; Asst Sec., Lands and Mines, Kaduna, 1950; Private Sec. to Chief Comr, N Nigeria, 1951; transf. to Nigerian Broadcasting Corp., 1952; Controller: Northern Region, 1952–56; National Programme, Lagos, 1956–58; joined BBC African Service as African Programme Organiser, 1958; East and Central African Programme Organiser, 1961; BBC TV Production Trng Course and attachment to Panorama, 1963; Asst Head, 1964, Head, 1969, BBC African Service; attachment to Horizon, 1972; Head of Production and Planning, BBC World Service, 1976; Secretary of the BBC, 1977–80. Dir, 1986–90, Trustee, 1990–, The One World Broadcasting Trust. Chm. of Governors, Centre for Internat. Briefing, Farnham Castle, 1977–87, Vice-Pres., 1987–. Vice-Pres., Royal African Soc., 1978–82. MUniv Open, 1989. *Publications:* Broadcasting in Africa, in African Affairs (Jl of Royal African Soc.), 1972; contrib. to Broadcasting in Africa, a continental survey of radio and television, 1974. *Recreations:* sailing, occasional golf. *Address:* Compass Cottage, Box, Minchinhampton, near Stroud, Glos GL6 9HD. *T:* Stroud (01453) 833072. *Club:* Commonwealth Trust.

WILKINSON, Dr John Frederick, FRCP, MD (Gold Medal), ChB, BSc (1st Cl. Hons Chem.), MSc, PhD Manchester, DSc (Hon.) Bradford; CChem, FRSC; author; Consulting Physician; Consulting Haematologist, United Manchester Hospitals; late Director of

Department of Hæmatology, University and Royal Infirmary of Manchester; late Reader in Hæmatology, and Lecturer in Systematic Medicine, Univ. of Manchester; late Hon. Consulting Hæmatologist, The Christie Cancer Hospital, Holt Radium Institute and The Duchess of York Hospital for Babies, Manchester; Hon. Fellow and Editor, Manchester Medical Society; formerly President, European Hæmatological Soc.; Life Councillor, International Hæmatological Soc.; *b* Oldham, 10 June 1897; *s* of John Frederick Wilkinson, Oldham and Stockport, and Annie, *d* of late Reverend E. Wareham, DD, Rector of Heaton Mersey. *Educ:* Arnold School, Blackpool; University of Manchester; Manchester Royal Infirmary. Served European War, 1916–19, RNAS, RN, and later attached Tank Corps, France; also served on Vindictive at Zeebrugge, 1918, and ballotted for Victoria Cross award; Chemical Research Manchester University, 1919–28; Medical Research since 1929; Regional Transfusion Officer, and Regional Adviser on Resuscitation, Ministry of Health, NW Region, 1940–46. Graduate Scholarship (Chemistry), 1920; Dalton Research Scholarship; Sir Clement Royds Research Fellowship; Medical (Graduate) Scholarship, 1923; Hon. Demonstrator in Crystallography; Research Asst in Physiology; Sidney Renshaw Physiology Prizeman; Gold Medal for Dissertation in Med., 1931, University of Manchester. RCP Lectures: Oliver Sharpey, 1948; Samuel Gee, 1977. Worshipful Society of Apothecaries, London: Liveryman, 1948; Osler Lectr, 1981; Hon. Fellow 1982 (Faculty of History and Philosophy of Medicine and Pharmacy). Freeman City of London, 1949. Hon. DSc Bradford, 1976. *Publications:* scientific and medical publications since 1920 in English and foreign journals, etc. Sections on Blood Diseases, Anæmias and Leukæmias in British Encyclopædia of Medical Practice, 1936, 1950 and yearly supplements since 1951, and in Encyclopædia of General Practice, 1964; Section on Emergencies in Blood Diseases, in Medical Emergencies, 1948 to date; ed Modern Trends in Diseases of the Blood, 1955, 1975; The Diagnosis and Treatment of Blood Diseases, 1973; ed, Section in Clinical Surgery, 1967; articles on antiques, Old English and continental apothecaries' drug jars, etc, in miscellaneous medical and art jls, 1970–. *Recreations:* motoring, antiques, travel, zoos, tropical fish keeping, lecturing, scouting since 1908. *Address:* 1 Old Hall Cottage, Hall Lane, Mobberley, Knutsford, Cheshire WA16 7JF. *T:* Mobberley (01565) 872111.

WILKINSON, Rev. Keith Howard; Headmaster, Berkhamsted School, 1989–Aug. 1996; Headmaster, King's School, Canterbury, from Sept. 1996; *b* 25 June 1948; *s* of Kenneth John Wilkinson and Grace Winifred (*née* Bowler); *m* 1972, Carolyn Gilbert; two *d*. *Educ:* Beaumont Leys Coll.; Gateway Sch., Leicester; Univ. of Hull (BA Hons); Emmanuel Coll., Cambridge (Lady Romney Exhibnr, MA status); Westcott House, Cambridge. Hd of Religious Studies, Bricknell High Sch., 1970–72; Hd of Faculty (Humanities), Kelvin Hall Comprehensive Sch., Kingston upon Hull, 1972–74; Deacon 1976; Priest 1977; Asst Priest, St Jude, Westwood, Peterborough, 1977; Asst Master and Chaplain, Eton Coll., Windsor, 1979–84; Sen. Chaplain and Hd of Religious Studies, Malvern Coll., 1984–89; Sen. Tutor, Malvern Coll., 1988–89. *Publications:* various articles and reviews. *Recreations:* films, drama, music, walking, buildings and building, ecology. *Address:* (until Aug. 1996) Wilson House, The School, Castle Street, Berkhamsted, Herts HP4 2BE. *T:* Berkhamsted (01442) 864827; (from Sept. 1996) The King's School, Canterbury, Kent CT1 2ES. *Club:* East India.

WILKINSON, Leon Guy, FCIB; a General Commissioner of Income Tax, City of London, since 1989; part-time Member, VAT Tribunal, since 1989; *b* 6 Nov. 1928; *s* of Thomas Guy and Olive May Wilkinson; *m* 1953, Joan Margaret; one *s* one *d*. *Educ:* Bude Grammar Sch. CMS Oxon. Lloyds Bank: Regional Gen. Man., N and E Midlands, 1976–79; Asst Gen. Man., 1979–83; Gen. Man. (Finance), 1984–86; Chief Financial Officer, 1986–88. *Recreation:* sports. *Address:* Astons, Bishops Down Park Road, Tunbridge Wells, Kent TN4 8XR. *T:* Tunbridge Wells (01892) 541184. *Clubs:* MCC, Royal Over-Seas League; Nevill Golf (Tunbridge Wells).

WILKINSON, Rear-Adm. Nicholas John, CB 1994; Commandant, Joint Service Defence College, since 1994, and Chief Naval Supply and Secretariat Officer, since 1993; *b* 14 April 1941; *s* of Lt-Col Michael Douglas Wilkinson, RE and Joan Mary Wilkinson (*née* Cosens); *m* 1969, Penelope Ann Stephenson; three *s* one *d*. *Educ:* English School, Cairo; Cheltenham College; BRNC Dartmouth. Served HM Ships Venus, Vidal and Hermes, 1960–64; RN Air Station, Arbroath, 1964–65; HMS Fife, 1965–67; Asst Sec. to Vice-Chief of Naval Staff, 1968–70; HMS Endurance, 1970–72; Army Staff Course, 1973 (Mitchell Prizewinner); Clyde Submarine Base, 1974–75; Sec. to ACNS (Policy), 1975–77; HMS London, 1977–78; Asst Dir, Naval Officer Appts (SW), 1978–80; Trng Comdr, HMS Pembroke, 1980–82; NATO Defence Coll., Rome, 1982–83; MA to Dir, NATO Internat. Mil. Staff, 1983–85; RCDS, 1986; Dir, Defence Logistics, 1986; Sec. to First Sea Lord, 1989–90; Sen. Mil. Mem., Defence Organisation Study and Project Team, 1991–92; Dir Gen. of Naval Manpower and Trng, 1992–94. *Publications:* articles in The Naval Review. *Recreations:* RN Volunteer Bands, swimming, cricket, opera, jazz, cuisine périgourdine. *Address:* c/o Naval Secretary, Victory Building, HM Naval Base, Portsmouth PO1 3LS. *Club:* MCC.

WILKINSON, Nigel Vivian Marshall; QC 1990; a Recorder, since 1992; *b* 18 Nov. 1949; *s* of late John Marshall Wilkinson and of Vivien Wilkinson; *m* 1974, Heather Carol Hallett, *qv*; two *s*. *Educ:* Charterhouse; Christ Church, Oxford (Holford exhibnr; MA). Called to the Bar, Middle Temple, 1972; Astbury Scholar, 1972; Midland and Oxford Circuit, 1972–; an Asst Recorder, 1988–92. Dep. Chm., Appeals Cttee, Cricket Council, 1991–. Gov., Brambletye Sch., 1992–. *Recreations:* cricket, golf, theatre. *Address:* 2 Crown Office Row, Temple, EC4Y 7HJ. *T:* 0171–353 9337. *Clubs:* MCC; Vincent's (Oxford); Roehampton, I Zingari, Butterflies CC, Invalids CC, Armadillos CC, Rye Golf, Woking Golf, Royal Wimbledon Golf.

WILKINSON, Prof. Paul; Professor of International Relations, University of St Andrews, since 1990; *b* 9 May 1937; *s* of late Walter Ross Wilkinson and of Joan Rosemary (*née* Paul); 1960, Susan; two *s* one *d*. *Educ:* Lower School of John Lyon; University Coll., Swansea, Univ. of Wales (BA (jt Hons Mod. Hist. and Politics), MA; Hon. Fellow, 1986). Royal Air Force regular officer, 1959–65. Asst Lecturer in Politics, 1966–68, Lectr in Politics, 1968–75, Sen. Lectr in Politics, 1975–77, University Coll., Cardiff; Reader, Univ. of Wales, 1978–79; Prof., Internat. Relations, 1979–89, Hd, Dept of Politics and Internat. Relations, 1985–89, Univ. of Aberdeen; Dir, Res. Inst. for Study of Conflict and Terrorism, 1989–94. Member: IBA Scottish Adv. Cttee, 1982–85; Academic Adv. Bd, Hughenden Foundn, 1986–. Special Consultant, CBS Broadcasting Co., USA, 1986–91; Security Advr, Internat. Foundn of Airline Passengers Assocs, 1988–. Editorial Adviser, Contemporary Review, 1980–; Gen. Editor, Key Concepts in International Relations, 1980–; Jt Editor, Terrorism and Political Violence Jl, 1988–; Emeritus Editor, Handbook of Security, 1991–. *Publications:* Social Movement, 1971; Political Terrorism, 1974; Terrorism versus Liberal Democracy, 1976; Terrorism and the Liberal State, 1977, rev. edn 1986; (jtly) Terrorism: theory and practice, 1978; (ed) British Perspectives on Terrorism, 1981; The New Fascists, 1981, rev. edn 1983; Defence of the West, 1983; (jtly) Contemporary Research on Terrorism, 1987; Lessons of Lockerbie, 1989; Terrorist Targets and Tactics: new risks to world order, 1990; Northern Ireland: reappraising Republican violence, 1991; (ed) Technology and Terrorism, 1993; (ed) Terrorism: British perspectives, 1993; contribs to wide range of jls in Britain, USA and Canada. *Recreations:* modern art, poetry, walking. *Address:* Department of International Relations, North Street, St Andrews, Fife KY16 9AL. *T:* St Andrews (01334) 462900. *Club:* Savile.

WILKINSON, Sir Peter (Allix), KCMG 1970 (CMG 1960); DSO 1944; OBE 1944; HM Diplomatic Service, retired; *b* 15 April 1914; *s* of late Captain Osborn Cecil Wilkinson (killed in action, 1915) and Esmé, *d* of late Sir Alexander Wilson; *m* 1945, Mary Theresa (*d* 1984), *d* of late Algernon Villiers; two *d*. *Educ:* Rugby; Corpus Christi Coll., Cambridge. Commissioned in 2nd Bn Royal Fusiliers, 1935; active service in Poland (despatches), France, ME, Italy, Balkans and Central Europe; commanded No 6 Special Force (SOE), 1943–45; retired with rank of Lieut-Colonel, 1947. Entered HM Foreign Service, appointed 1st Secretary at British Legation, Vienna, 1947; 1st Secretary at British Embassy, Washington, 1952; Secretary-General of Heads of Government Meeting at Geneva, 1955; Counsellor, HM Embassy, Bonn, 1955; Counsellor, Foreign Office, 1960–63; Under-Secretary, Cabinet Office, 1963–64; Senior Civilian Instructor at the Imperial Defence Coll., 1964–66; Ambassador to Vietnam, 1966–67; Under-Secretary, Foreign Office, 1967–68; Chief of Administration, HM Diplomatic Service, 1968–70; Ambassador to Vienna, 1970–71; Co-ordinator of intelligence, Cabinet Office, 1972–73. Cross of Valour (Poland), 1940; Order of White Lion (IV Class) (Czechoslovakia), 1945; Order of Jugoslav Banner (Hon.), 1984. *Recreations:* gardening, sailing, fishing. *Address:* 28 High Street, Charing, Kent TN27 0HX. *T:* Charing (01233) 712306. *Clubs:* White's, Army and Navy.

WILKINSON, Sir Philip (William), Kt 1988; FCIB; Director: National Westminster Bank PLC, 1979–90 (Deputy Chairman, 1987–90); HandelsBank NatWest, 1983–90 (Deputy Chairman, 1987–90); *b* 8 May 1927; *m* 1951, Eileen Patricia (*née* Malkin) (*d* 1991); one *s* two d. *Educ:* Leyton County High School. With Westminster Bank, later National Westminster Bank, 1943–90; Chief Executive, Lombard North Central Ltd, 1975; General Manager, Related Banking Services Division, 1978; Dir, 1979–90; Dep. Group Chief Executive, 1980; Group Chief Executive, 1983–87; Chm., NatWest Investment Bank, 1987–89; Director: Internat. Westminster Bank, 1982–90; Nat. Westminster Bank, USA, 1987–90. Director: BAe, 1987–91; Nat. Power, 1990–93. Former Mem., Bd of Banking Supervision, Bank of England; a Vice-Pres., Chartered Inst. of Bankers, 1989–. Dir, ENO, 1987–93. Mem. Council, Imperial Cancer Res. Fund, 1990–; Chm., Wishbone Trust, 1994–. Trustee, Baptist Building Fund, 1987–. Freeman, City of London, 1969. *Recreations:* theatre, golf, watching sport. *Address:* Pine Court, Whichert Close, Knotty Green, Beaconsfield, Bucks HP9 2TP. *Club:* Royal Automobile.

WILKINSON, Rev. Canon Raymond Stewart; Rector of Solihull, 1971–87; Chaplain to the Queen, 1982–89; Hon. Canon of Birmingham, since 1976; *b* 5 June 1919; *s* of Sidney Ewart and Florence Miriam Wilkinson; *m* 1945, Dorothy Elinor Church; four *s*. *Educ:* Luton Grammar Sch.; King's Coll., London (AKC); Bishop's Coll., Cheshunt. Curate of Croxley Green, 1943–45; Vicar: S Oswald's, Croxley Green, 1945–50; Abbot's Langley, 1950–61; Rector of Woodchurch, 1961–71; Proctor in Convocation and Mem., Church Assembly, 1964–71. Member, various educnl governing bodies. *Publications:* To the More Edifying, 1952; The Church and Parish of Abbot's Langley, 1955; My Confirmation Search Book, 1962, 10th edn 1982; An Adult Confirmation Candidate's Handbook, 1964, 6th edn 1984; Gospel Sermons for Alternative Service Book, 1983; Learning about Vestments and Altar Serving, 1984; A Pocket Guide for Servers, 1985; The Essence of Anglicanism, 1986. *Recreations:* producing, acting in and conducting Gilbert and Sullivan operas; church architecture, organising youth holidays. *Address:* 42 Coten End, Warwick, CV34 4NP. *T:* Warwick (01926) 493510. *Clubs:* Commonwealth Trust, Royal Society of Arts.

WILKINSON, Richard Denys, CVO 1992; HM Diplomatic Service; Head of Eastern Department, Foreign and Commonwealth Office, since 1994; *b* 11 May 1946; *y s* of late Denys and Gillian Wilkinson; *m* 1982, Maria Angela Morris; two *s* one *d*. *Educ:* Eton Coll. (King's Schol.); Trinity Coll., Cambridge (MA, MLitt, Wace Medallist); Ecole Nat. des Langues Orientales Vivantes, Univ. de Paris; Ecole des Langues Orientales Anciennes, Inst. Catholique de Paris. Hayter Postdoctoral Fellow in Soviet Studies, SSEES, London, 1971; joined Diplomatic Service, 1972: Madrid, 1973; FCO, 1977; Vis. Prof., Univ. of Michigan, Ann Arbor, 1980; FCO, 1980; Ankara, 1983; Mexico City, 1985; Counsellor (Information), Paris, 1988; Head of Policy Planning Staff, FCO, 1993–94. *Publications:* articles and reviews in learned jls. *Recreations:* sightseeing, oriental studies. *Address:* c/o Foreign and Commonwealth Office, SW1A 2AH. *Club:* United Oxford & Cambridge University.

See also J. A. D. Wilkinson, Sir W. H. N. Wilkinson.

WILKINSON, Robert Purdy, OBE 1990; Director of Surveillance, The Stock Exchange, 1984–90; Director of Enforcement and Deputy Chief Executive, The Securities Association, 1987–90; *b* 23 Aug. 1933; *s* of Robert Purdy and Lily Ingham Wilkinson; *m* 1957, June (*née* Palmer); two *d*. *Educ:* Univ. of Durham (BA). Kleinwort Sons & Co., 1958–62; Estabrook & Co., 1962–64; Partner, W. I. Carr Sons & Co., 1966–81. Stock Exchange: Mem. Council, 1978–81; Cttee Chm., 1980–81; Stock Exchange Inspector, 1981–84. Director: Invesco Gp, 1994–; Tradepoint, 1994–. Consultant: Morgan Grenfell Internat., 1991; S Africa Financial Markets Bd, 1991; Johannesburg Stock Exchange, 1991; DTI Inspector, 1987, 1989, 1991. Mem., Financial Services Tribunal, 1991–94; Special Advisor: Assoc. of Swiss Stock Exchanges, 1991; Czech Ministry of Finance, 1995–. Testified US Congress Cttee, 1988. Chm. of Govs, Sevenoaks Sch., 1992–. *Publications:* contrib. to French Society of Investment Jl; various articles on securities regulation and insider dealing. *Recreations:* walking, ski-ing, schools' sport. *Address:* Bessels House, Bessels Green, Sevenoaks, Kent TN13 2PS. *T:* Sevenoaks (01732) 457782.

WILKINSON, Sir William (Henry Nairn), Kt 1989; Chairman, Nature Conservancy Council, 1983–91; *b* 22 July 1932; *e s* of late Denys and Gillian Wilkinson, of Eton College; *m* 1964, Katharine Louise Frederica, *er d* of late F. W. H. Loudon and of Lady Prudence Loudon; one *s* two *d*. *Educ:* Eton Coll. (King's Schol.); Trinity Coll., Cambridge (Major Scholar; MA). President: London Wildlife Trust, 1992–; British Trust for Ornithology, 1993–; Vice-President: RSPB, 1991–; Plantlife, 1991–; Kent Trust for Nature Conservation, 1991–; British Butterfly Conservation Soc., 1993–; Chm., West Palaearctic Birds Ltd, 1987–; Member of Council: Wildfowl and Wetlands Trust, 1991–; Game Conservancy, 1993–. Chm., TSL Thermal Syndicate plc, 1984–88 (Dir, 1976–88); Director: Kleinwort Benson Ltd, 1973–85; John Mowlem and Co. plc, 1977–87; Mem., CEGB, 1986–89. Mem. Council, Winston Churchill Meml Trust, 1985–93. FRSA. *Publications:* papers for ornithological conferences. *Recreations:* ornithology, opera and music, archaeology. *Address:* 119 Castelnau, Barnes, SW13 9EL; Pill House, Llanmadoc, Gower, West Glamorgan SA3 1DB. *Club:* Brooks's.

See also J. A. D. Wilkinson, R. D. Wilkinson.

WILKINSON, Dr William Lionel, CBE 1987; FRS 1990; FEng 1980; Deputy Chairman, Allied Colloids plc, since 1992 (Director, since 1990); *b* 16 Feb. 1931; *s* of Lionel and Dorothy Wilkinson; *m* 1955, Josephine Anne Pilgrim; five *s*. *Educ:* Christ's Coll., Cambridge. MA, PhD, ScD; FIChemE. Salters' Res. Schol., Christ's Coll., Cambridge, 1953–56; Lectr in Chem. Engrg, UC Swansea, 1956–59; UKAEA Production Gp,

1959–67; Prof. of Chem. Engrg, Univ. of Bradford, 1967–79; British Nuclear Fuels Ltd: Dep. Dir, 1979–84; Technical Dir, 1984–86; Dep. Chief Exec., 1986–92; Non.-exec. Dir, 1992–. Vis. Prof. of Chemical Engrg, Imperial Coll., London, 1980–. Chm., British Nuclear Industry Forum, 1992–; Pres., Eur. Atomic Forum, 1994–. Member: SERC, 1981–85; ACOST, 1990–. Pres., IChemE, 1980. Liveryman, Salters' Co., 1985. Hon. DEng Bradford, 1989. *Publications:* Non-Newtonian Flow, 1960; contribs to sci. and engrg jls on heat transfer, fluid mechanics, polymer processing and process dynamics. *Recreations:* sailing, fell-walking. *Address:* Tree Tops, Legh Road, Knutsford, Cheshire WA16 8LP. *T:* Knutsford (01565) 653344. *Club:* Athenæum.

WILKS, Jean Ruth Fraser, CBE 1977; Chairman of Council and Pro-Chancellor, Birmingham University, 1985–89; *b* 14 April 1917; *d* of Mark Wilks. *Educ:* North London Collegiate Sch.; Somerville Coll., Oxford (MA; Hon. Fellow, 1985). Assistant Mistress: Truro High Sch., 1940–43; James Allen's Girls' Sch., Dulwich, 1943–51; Head Mistress, Hertfordshire and Essex High Sch., Bishop's Stortford, Hertfordshire, 1951–64; Head Mistress, King Edward VI High Sch. for Girls, Birmingham, 1965–77. Pres., Assoc. of Head Mistresses, 1972–74; Member: Public Schools Commn, 1968–70; Governing Council of Schools Council, 1972–75; Adv. Council on Supply and Trng of Teachers, 1973–78; Educn Cttee, Royal Coll. of Nursing, 1973–79; University Authorities Panel, 1982–89. University of Birmingham: Mem. Council, 1971–89; Life Mem. Court, 1977; Chm., Academic Staffing Cttee, 1978–85; Dep. Pro-Chancellor, 1979–85. Pres., ASM, Somerville Coll., Oxford, 1982–85. Chm. Governors, Ellerslie, Malvern, 1982–89; Mem. Council, Malvern Coll., 1992–93. FCP 1978. Hon. LLD Birmingham, 1986. *Address:* 4 Hayward Road, Oxford OX2 8LW.

WILKS, Jim; *see* Wilks, Stanley David.

WILKS, Stanley David, (Jim Wilks), CB 1979; MIEx; Consultant Director, Strategy International, since 1992; *b* 1 Aug. 1920; *m* 1947, Dorothy Irene Adamthwaite; one *s* one *d. Educ:* Polytechnic Sch., London. Royal Armoured Corps, 1939–46; service with 48th Bn, Royal Tank Regt; 3rd Carabiniers, Imphal, 1944. Home Office, 1946–50; Board of Trade, later Dept of Trade and Industry, 1950–80: posts included 1st Sec., British Embassy, Washington, 1950–53; GATT, non-ferrous metals, ECGD, airports policy; Chief Exec., BOTB, 1975–80. Deputy Chairman, Technology Transfer Gp, 1981–89; Trade Network Internat., 1989 (Chm., Export Network, 1986–89); Director: Matthew Hall Internat. Devclt, subseq. Matthew Hall Business Develt, 1981–89; Hadson Petroleum Internat., 1981–91; Hadson Corp., 1985–93; Associated Gas Supplies, 1988–90; Regl Dir, James Hallam, 1984–. Vice-Chm., Internat. Tin Council, 1968–69; Chm., Tech. Help for Exporters Management Cttee, BSI, 1982–88. Commodore, UK Wayfarer Assoc., 1993– (Chm., 1982–89). MIEx 1981. *Recreation:* dinghy racing. *Address:* 6 Foxgrove Avenue, Beckenham, Kent BR3 2BA. *Clubs:* Civil Service; Medway Yacht (Rochester).

WILL, Ronald Kerr; Deputy Keeper of Her Majesty's Signet, 1975–83; formerly Senior Partner, Dundas & Wilson, CS, Edinburgh; *b* 22 March 1918; 3rd *s* of late James Alexander Will, WS and late Bessie Kennedy Salmon, Dumfries; *m* 1953, Margaret Joyce, *d* of late D. Alan Stevenson, BSc, FRSE; two *s. Educ:* Merchiston Castle Sch.; Edinburgh Univ. Commnd King's Own Scottish Borderers, 1940; served with 1st Bn and in Staff appts (despatches); psc; GSO2. Writer to the Signet, 1950. Director: Scottish Equitable Life Assce Soc., 1965–88 (Chm., 1980–84); Scottish Investment Trust PLC, 1963–88; Standard Property Investment PLC, 1972–87. Mem. Council on Tribunals, 1971–76 and Chm. of Scottish Cttee, 1972–76. Governor, Merchiston Castle Sch., 1953–76. *Recreations:* fishing, gardening. *Address:* Chapelhill Cottage, Dirleton, East Lothian EH39 5HG. *T:* Dirleton (01620) 850338. *Club:* New (Edinburgh).

WILLACY, Michael James Ormerod, CBE 1989; Managing Partner, Michael Willacy Associates, since 1990; *b* 7 June 1933; *s* of James and Marjorie Willacy (*née* Sanders); *m* 1st, 1961, Merle Louise de Lange; two *s* one *d*; 2nd, 1985, Victoria Stuart John; three *s* one *d. Educ:* Taunton Sch., Somerset. FCIPS. Purchasing Agent, Shell Venezuela, 1964–73; Procurement Advr, Shell Internat., The Hague, 1974–77; Supt., Shell Stanlow, 1978–80; Manager, Shell Wilmslow, 1981–83; Gen. Man., Shell Materials Services, 1983–85; Dir, Central Unit on Purchasing, 1985–90, Procurement Advr, 1991–92, HM Treasury. Chairman: Macclesfield Chamber of Commerce, 1981–83; Macclesfield Business Ventures, 1982–83. Old Tauntonian Association: Gen. Sec., 1978–91; Pres., 1988–89; Vice-Pres., 1990–; Mem. Council, Taunton Sch., 1993–. *Recreations:* golf, travel, gardening. *Address:* Furzefield, Rattery, South Brent, Devon TQ10 9LF. *T:* and *Fax:* Modbury (01548) 830591. *Clubs:* Commonwealth Trust; Old Tauntonian Association (Taunton).

WILLAN, Edward Gervase, CMG 1964; HM Diplomatic Service, retired; Ambassador to Czechoslovakia, 1974–77; *b* 17 May 1917; *er s* of late Captain F. G. L. Willan, RNR; *m* 1944, Mary Bickley Joy (*d* 1992), *d* of late Lieut-Colonel H. A. Joy, IAOC. *Educ:* Radley; Pembroke Coll., Cambridge (Exhibitioner, MA). Indian Civil Service, 1939–47; 2nd Secretary (from 1948, 1st Secretary) on staff of UK High Commissioner, New Delhi, 1947–49; appointed to HM Diplomatic Service, 1948; Foreign Office, 1949–52; 1st Secretary, HM Embassy, The Hague, 1953–55; 1st Secretary, HM Legation, Bucharest, 1956–58 (Chargé d'Affaires, 1956, 1957 and 1958); Head of Communications Dept, FO, 1958–62; Political Adviser to Hong Kong Government, 1962–65; Head of Scientific Relations Dept, FO, 1966–68; Minister, Lagos, 1968–70; Ambassador at Rangoon, 1970–74. *Recreations:* walking, gardening. *Address:* Cherry Tree Cottage, Shappen Hill, Burley, Hants BH24 4AH.

WILLATT, Sir Hugh, Kt 1972; Secretary General of the Arts Council of Great Britain, 1968–75 (Member, 1958–68); *b* 25 April 1909; *m* 1945, Evelyn Gibbs (*d* 1991), ARE, ARCA, (Rome Scholar); no *c. Educ:* Repton; Pembroke Coll., Oxford (MA). Admitted a Solicitor, 1934; Partner, Hunt, Dickins and Willatt, Nottingham, and later Partner in Lewis, Silkin & Partners, Westminster. Served War of 1939–45, in RAF. Member BBC Midland Regional Adv. Council, 1953–58; Member Arts Council Drama Panel, 1955–68 (Chairman, 1960–68). Pres., Riverside Studios, Hammersmith, 1983– (Chm., 1976–82); Vice-Pres., English Stage Co. (Royal Court Theatre), 1993– (Mem., 1976–92); Chm. Bd, Nat. Opera Studio, 1977–93; Member Board: National Theatre, 1964–68; Mercury Trust Ltd (Ballet Rambert) (Chm.), 1961–67; Nottingham Theatre Trust Ltd, 1949–60; Visiting Arts Unit (Chm., 1977–83). Trustee, Shakespeare's Birthplace, 1968–94. FRSA 1974. Hon. MA, University of Nottingham. *Address:* 4 St Peter's Wharf, Hammersmith Terrace, W6 9UD. *Clubs:* Garrick, Arts.

WILLCOCK, His Honour Kenneth Milner, QC 1972; a Circuit Judge, 1972–94. MA; BCL. Called to Bar, Inner Temple, 1950. Dep. Chm., Somerset QS, 1969–71; a Recorder of the Crown Court, 1972. *Address:* c/o Queen Elizabeth Building, Temple, EC4Y 9BS.

WILLCOCK, Prof. Malcolm Maurice; Professor of Latin, 1980–91, now Emeritus, and Vice-Provost, 1988–91, University College London; *b* 1 Oct. 1925; *s* of late Dr Maurice Excel Willcock and Evelyn Clarice Willcock (*née* Brooks); *m* 1957, Sheena Gourlay; four *d. Educ:* Fettes Coll.; Pembroke Coll., Cambridge (MA). Served Royal Air Force, 1944–47. Research Fellow, Pembroke Coll., Cambridge, 1951–52; Sidney Sussex College: Fellow, 1952–65; Sen. Tutor, 1962–65; University of Lancaster: first Professor of Classics, 1965–79; Principal, Bowland Coll., 1966–79; Pro-Vice-Chancellor, 1975–79. *Publications:* ed, Plautus, Casina, 1976; Companion to the Iliad, 1976; ed, Iliad of Homer, vol. 1 (Books I–XII) 1978, vol. 2 (Books XIII–XXIV) 1984; ed, Plautus, Pseudolus, 1987. *Recreation:* bridge. *Address:* 1 Lancaster Avenue, SE27. *T:* 0181–761 5615.

WILLCOCKS, Sir David (Valentine), Kt 1977; CBE 1971; MC 1944; Musical Director of the Bach Choir since 1960; General Editor, OUP Church Music, since 1961; *b* 30 Dec. 1919; *s* of late T. H. Willcocks; *m* 1947, Rachel Gordon, *d* of late Rev. A. C. Blyth, Fellow of Selwyn Coll., Cambridge; one *s* two *d* (and one *s* decd). *Educ:* Clifton Coll.; King's Coll., Cambridge (MA; MusB). Chorister, Westminster Abbey, 1929–33; Scholar, Clifton Coll., 1934–38; FRCO, 1938; Scholar at College of St Nicolas (RSCM), 1938–39; Organ Scholar, King's Coll., Cambridge, 1939–40; Open Foundation Scholarship, King's Coll., Cambridge, 1940; Stewart of Rannoch Scholarship, 1940. Served War of 1939–45, 5th Bn DCLI, 1940–45. Organ Scholar, King's Coll., Cambridge, 1945–47; Fellow of King's Coll., Cambridge, 1947–51, Hon. Fellow, 1979–; Organist of Salisbury Cathedral, 1947–50; Master of the Choristers and Organist, Worcester Cathedral, 1950–57; Fellow and Organist, King's Coll., Cambridge, 1957–73; Univ. Lectr in Music, Cambridge Univ., 1957–74; Univ. Organist, Cambridge Univ., 1958–74; Dir, RCM, 1974–84. Conductor: Cambridge Philharmonic Soc., 1947; City of Birmingham Choir, 1950–57; Bradford Festival Choral Soc., 1957–74; Cambridge Univ. Musical Soc., 1958–73. President: RCO, 1966–68; ISM, 1978–79; Old Cliftonian Soc., 1979–81; Nat. Fedn of Music Socs, 1980–89; Assoc. of British Choral Dirs, 1993–. Mem. Council, Winston Churchill Trust, 1980–90. Freeman, City of London, 1981. FRSCM 1965; FRCM 1971; FRNCM 1977; FRSAMD 1982; Hon. RAM 1965; Hon. FTCL 1976; Hon. GSM 1980; Hon. FRCCO 1967. Hon. MA Bradford, 1973; Hon. DMus: Exeter, 1976; Leicester, 1977; Westminster Choir Coll., Princeton, 1980; Bristol, 1981; St Olaf Coll., Minnesota, 1991; Hon. DLitt Sussex, 1982; Hon. Dr of Sacred Letters, Trinity Coll., Toronto, 1985. *Publications:* miscellaneous choral and instrumental works. *Address:* 13 Grange Road, Cambridge CB3 9AS. *T:* Cambridge (01223) 359559. *Clubs:* Athenæum, Arts.

WILLCOCKS, Maj.-Gen. Michael Alan; Chief of Staff Allied Command Europe Rapid Reaction Corps, since 1994; *b* 27 July 1944; *s* of Henry Willcocks and late Georgina Willcocks (*née* Lawton); *m* 1966, Jean Paton Weir; one *s* two *d. Educ:* St John's Coll.; RMA Sandhurst; London Univ. (BSc Hons). Commnd RA, 1964; served Malaya, Borneo, UK, Germany, 1965–72; Instructor, RMA Sandhurst, 1972–74; MoD, 1977–79; Comd M Battery, RHA, 1979–80; Directing Staff, Staff Coll., 1981–83; CO, 1st Regt, RHA, 1983–85; Dep. ACOS, HQ UKLF, 1985–87; ACOS, Intelligence/Ops, HQ UKLF, 1988; CRA, 4th Armd Div., 1989–90; rcds 1991; ACOS, Land Ops, Joint War HQ, Gulf War, 1991; Dir Army Plans and Programme, 1991–93; Dir Gen. Land Warfare, 1993–94. *Publications:* Airmobility and the Armoured Experience, 1989. *Recreations:* books, music, tennis, fishing, sailing. *Club:* National Liberal.

WILLCOX, James Henry, CB 1988; Clerk of Public Bills, House of Commons, 1982–88, retired; *b* 31 March 1923; *s* of George Henry and Annie Elizabeth Willcox; *m* 1st, 1950, Winsome Rosemarie Adèle Dallas Ross (*d* 1984); one *s* one *d*; 2nd, 1985, Pamela, *widow* of Col John Lefroy Knyvett. *Educ:* St George's Coll., Weybridge; St John's Coll., Oxford (Schol.; MA). Served RNVR, 1942–45. Assistant Clerk, House of Commons, 1947; Sen. Clerk, 1951; Clerk of Standing Committees, 1975–76; Clerk of Overseas Office, 1976–77; Clerk of Private Bills, Examiner of Petitions for Private Bills and Taxing Officer, 1977–82. *Recreations:* walking, gardening. *Address:* Ibthorpe Farm House, Ibthorpe, near Andover, Hants SP11 0BN. *T:* Hurstbourne Tarrant (01264) 736575. *Club:* Garrick.

WILLEBRANDS, His Eminence Cardinal Johannes Gerardus Maria; President, Vatican Secretariat for Promoting Christian Unity, 1969–89, now President Emeritus; Archbishop of Utrecht and Primate of Holland, 1975–83; *b* Netherlands, 4 Sept. 1909. *Educ:* Warmond Seminary, Holland; Angelicum, Rome (Dr Phil.). Priest, 1934; Chaplain, Begijnhof Church, Amsterdam, 1937–40; Prof. of Philosophy, Warmond, 1940; Director, 1945; Pres., St Willibrord Assoc., 1946; organised Catholic Conf. on Ecumenical Questions, 1951; Sec., Vatican Secretariat for Promoting Christian Unity, 1960; Titular Bishop of Mauriana, 1964; Cardinal, 1969; Cardinal with the Title of St Sebastian, Martyr, 1975. Hon. Dr of Letters: Notre Dame Univ.; St Louis Univ.; St Olaf Coll., USA; St Thomas' Coll., St Paul's, Minn, 1979; Assumption Coll., Worcester, Mass, 1980; Hon. Dr of Theology: Catholic Univ. of Louvain, 1971; Leningrad Theological Acad, 1973; Catholic Univ., Lublin, Poland, 1985; Hon. DD Oxon, 1987; Hon. DTheol Catholic Univ., München, 1987; Hon. DH Hellenic Coll./Holy Cross Orthodox Sch. of Theol., Brookline, Mass, 1989; Hon. DTheol St Michael's Univ. Coll., Toronto, 1990. *Publications:* Oecuménisme et Problèmes Actuels, 1969; Mandatum Unitatis: Beiträge zur Oekumene, 1989; Church and Jewish People, 1992; reports on the ecumenical situation and articles on inter-church relationships. *Address:* Via dell'Erba 1, 00193 Rome, Italy.

WILLESDEN, Area Bishop of, since 1992; **Rt. Rev. Geoffrey Graham Dow;** *b* 4 July 1942; *s* of Ronald Graham Dow and Dorothy May Dow (*née* Christie); *m* 1966, Molly Patricia (*née* Sturges); three *s* one *d. Educ:* St Alban's Sch.; Queen's Coll., Oxford (BA 1963; BSc 1965; MA 1968); Clifton Theol Coll.; Birmingham Univ. (Dip. Pastoral Studies 1974); Nottingham Univ. (MPhil 1982). Ordained: deacon, 1967; priest, 1968; Asst Curate, Tonbridge Parish Church, 1967–72; Chaplain-Student, St John's Coll., Oxford, 1972–75; Lectr in Christian Doctrine, St John's Coll., Nottingham, 1975–81; Vicar, Holy Trinity, Coventry, 1981–92. Canon Theologian, Coventry Cathedral, 1989–. *Publications:* Dark Satanic Mills? Shaftesbury Project, 1979; The Local Church's Political Responsibility, 1980; St John's College Extension Studies B1—God and the World, 1980; Whose Hand on the Tiller?, 1983; Those Tiresome Intruders, 1990; Explaining Deliverance, 1991; Christian Renewal in Europe, 1992; A Christian Understanding of Daily Work, 1994. *Recreations:* steam and narrow gauge railways, model railways, travel, music. *Address:* 173 Willesden Lane, NW6 7YN. *T:* 0181–451 0189.

WILLESEE, Hon. Donald Robert; Member of Senate for Western Australia, 1949–75; *b* 14 April 1916; *m*; four *s* two *d. Educ:* Carnarvon, Western Australia. Special Minister of State, Minister assisting Prime Minister, Minister assisting Minister for Foreign Affairs and Vice-Pres. of Exec. Council, 1972–73; Minister for Foreign Affairs, 1973–75; Leader of Opposition in the Senate, 1966–67; Deputy Leader of Opposition in Senate, 1969–72; Deputy Leader of Govt in Senate, 1972. *Recreation:* swimming. *Address:* 5 Walton Place, Quinns Rock, WA 6030, Australia.

WILLETT, Prof. Frank, CBE 1985; FRSE 1979; Emeritus Professor and Hon. Senior Research Fellow, Hunterian Museum, University of Glasgow, since 1990; *b* 18 Aug. 1925; *s* of Thomas Willett and Frances (*née* Latham); *m* 1950, Mary Constance Hewitt; one *s* three *d. Educ:* Bolton Municipal Secondary Sch.; University Coll., Oxford. MA (Oxon); Dip. Anthropology (Oxon). War damage clerk, Inland Revenue, 1940; RAF Linguist, Japanese, 1943–44. Keeper, Dept of Ethnology and Gen. Archaeology, Manchester Museum, 1950–58; Hon. Surveyor of Antiquities, Nigerian Federal Govt, 1956–57, 1957–58; Archaeologist and Curator, Mus. of Ife Antiquities, Nigerian Fed. Govt, 1958–63; Supply Teacher, Bolton Educn Cttee, 1963–64; Leverhulme Research Fellow, 1964; Research Fellow, Nuffield Coll., Oxford, 1964–66; Prof. of Art History,

African and Interdisciplinary Studies, Northwestern Univ., Evanston, Ill, USA, 1966–76; Dir and Titular Prof., Hunterian Mus. and Art Gall., Glasgow, 1976–90. Research Collaborator, Smithsonian Instn, 1992–. Vis. Fellow, Clare Hall, Cambridge, 1970–71. Curator, RSE, 1992–. Hon. Corresp. Member, Manchester Literary and Philosophical Soc., 1958–. *Publications:* Ife in the History of West African Sculpture, 1967, rev. edn, Ife: une Civilisation Africaine, 1971; African Art: An Introduction, 1971, rev. edn 1993; (with Ekpo Eyo) Treasures of Ancient Nigeria, 1980; articles in Encyc. Britannica, Man, Jl of Afr. Hist., Afr. Arts, Africa, Jl of Nigerian Historical Soc., Odu, SA Archaeol Bull., Archæometry; many conf. reports and chapters in several books. *Recreations:* relaxing, baiting architects. *Address:* Hunterian Museum, University of Glasgow, Glasgow G12 8QQ. *T:* 0141–330 4221. *Club:* Commonwealth Trust.

WILLETT, Michael John, FRAeS; Board Member, Civil Aviation Authority and Group Director, Safety Regulation, since 1992; *b* 2 Oct. 1944; *s* of Reginald John Willett and Nora Else Willett; *m* 1967, Gillian Margaret Pope (separated 1993); two *s* one *d. Educ:* Grammar Sch., Tottenham; Open Univ. (BA Hons); Open Business Sch. (MBA). RAF, 1963–71; Airline Captain, Laker Airways, 1973–82; Flight Ops Inspectorate, CAA, 1982–92. Liveryman, GAPAN, 1991–. *Recreation:* horse riding. *Address:* Civil Aviation Authority, Aviation House, South Area, Gatwick Airport, West Sussex RH6 0YR. *T:* Gatwick (01293) 573078.

WILLETTS, David Lindsay; MP (C) Havant, since 1992; a Lord Commissioner of HM Treasury (Government Whip), since 1995; *b* 9 March 1956; *s* of John Roland Willetts and Hilary Sheila Willetts; *m* 1986, Hon. Sarah Harriet Ann, *d* of Lord Butterfield, *qv*; one *s* one *d. Educ:* King Edward's Sch., Birmingham; Christ Church, Oxford (BA 1st cl. Hons PPE). Res. Asst to Nigel Lawson, MP, 1978; HM Treasury, 1978–84: Pvte Sec. to Financial Sec., 1981–82; Principal Monetary Policy Div., 1982–84; Prime Minister's Downing Street Policy Unit, 1984–86; Dir of Studies, Centre for Policy Studies, 1987–92. PPS to Chm. of Cons. Party, 1993–94; an Asst Govt Whip, 1994–95. Consultant Dir, Cons. Res. Dept, 1987–92. Director: Retirement Security Ltd, 1988–94; Electra Corporate Ventures Ltd, 1988–94. Mem., Social Security Adv. Cttee, 1989–92. Member: Parkside HA, 1988–90; Lambeth, Lewisham and Southwark FPC, 1987–90. *Publications:* Modern Conservatism, 1992; Civic Conservatism, 1994; paper, The Role of the Prime Minister's Policy Unit, 1987 (Haldane Medal, RIPA); various pamphlets. *Recreations:* swimming, reading. *Address:* c/o House of Commons, SW1A 0AA. *T:* 0171–219 3000.

WILLIAMS; *see* Rees-Williams, family name of Baron Ogmore.

WILLIAMS, family name of **Barons Williams of Elvel** and **Williams of Mostyn** and **Baroness Williams of Crosby.**

WILLIAMS OF CROSBY, Baroness *cr* 1993 (Life Peer), of Stevenage in the County of Hertfordshire; **Shirley Vivien Teresa Brittain Williams;** PC 1974; Co-founder, Social Democratic Party, 1981, President, 1982–88; Professor of Elective Politics, John F. Kennedy School of Government, Harvard University, since 1988; Director, Project Liberty, since 1990; *b* 27 July 1930; *d* of late Prof. Sir George Catlin, and late Mrs Catlin, (Vera Brittain); *m* 1st, 1955, Prof. Bernard Arthur Owen Williams (marr. diss. 1974), *qv*; one *d*; 2nd, 1987, Prof. Richard Elliott Neustadt. *Educ:* eight schools in UK and USA; Somerville Coll., Oxford (scholar; MA, Hon. Fellow, 1970); Columbia Univ., New York (Smith-Mundt Scholar). General Secretary, Fabian Soc., 1960–64 (Chm., 1980–81). Contested: (Lab) Harwich, Essex, 1954 and 1955, and Southampton Test, 1959; (SDP) Crosby, 1983; (SDP/Alliance) Cambridge, 1987. MP: (Lab) Hitchin, 1964–74; (Lab) Hertford and Stevenage, 1974–79; (first-elected SDP MP) Crosby, Nov. 1981–1983; PPS, Minister of Health, 1964–66; Parly Sec., Min. of Labour, 1966–67; Minister of State: Education and Science, 1967–69; Home Office, 1969–70; Opposition spokesman on: Social Services, 1970–71, on Home Affairs, 1971–73; Prices and Consumer Protection, 1973–74; Sec. of State for Prices and Consumer Protection, 1974–76; Sec. of State for Educn and Science, 1976–79; Paymaster General, 1976–79. Chm., OECD study on youth employment, 1979; Mem., Council of Advrs to Praesidium, Ukraine, 1991–. Mem., Labour Party Nat. Exec. Cttee, 1970–81. Visiting Fellow, Nuffield College, Oxford, 1967–75; Res. Fellow, PSI, 1979–85; Visiting Faculty, Internat. Management Inst., Geneva, 1979–88; Fellow, Inst. of Politics, Harvard, 1979–80 (Mem., Sen. Adv. Council, 1986–; Acting Dir, 1989–90); Director: Turing Inst., Glasgow, 1985–90; Learning by Experience Trust, 1986–94. Lectures: Godkin, Harvard, 1980; Rede, Cambridge, 1980; Janeway, Princeton, 1981; Regents', Univ. of Calif., Berkeley, 1991. Hon. Fellow, Newnham Coll., Cambridge, 1977. Hon. DEd CNAA, 1969; Hon. Dr Pol. Econ.: Univ. of Leuven, 1976; Radcliffe Coll., Harvard, 1978; Leeds, 1980; Bath, 1980; Hon. LLD: Sheffield, 1980; Southampton, 1981; Hon. DLitt Heriot-Watt, 1980; Hon. DSc Aston, 1981. *Publications:* Politics is for People, 1981; Jobs for the 1980s; Youth Without Work, 1981; (jtly) Unemployment and Growth in the Western Economies, 1984; A Job to Live, 1985. *Recreations:* music, hill walking.

WILLIAMS OF ELVEL, Baron *cr* 1985 (Life Peer), of Llansantffraed in Elvel in the County of Powys; **Charles Cuthbert Powell Williams,** CBE 1980; Opposition spokesman on Defence, since 1990 and on Environment, since 1992, House of Lords; *b* 9 Feb. 1933; *s* of late Dr Norman Powell Williams, DD, and Mrs Muriel de Lérisson Williams (*née* Cazenove); *m* 1975, Jane Gillian (*née* Portal), DL, JP; one step *s. Educ:* Westminster Sch.; Christ Church, Oxford (MA); LSE. British Petroleum Co. Ltd, 1958–64; Bank of London and Montreal, 1964–66; Eurofinance SA, Paris, 1966–70; Baring Brothers and Co. Ltd, 1970–77 (Man. Dir, 1971–77); Chm., Price Commn, 1977–79; Man. Dir 1980–82, Chm. 1982–85, Henry Ansbacher & Co. Ltd; Chief Exec., Henry Ansbacher Holdings PLC, 1982–85. Parly Candidate (Lab), Colchester, 1964. House of Lords: Dep. Leader of Opposition, 1989–92; Opposition spokesman on Trade and Industry, 1986–92, on Energy, 1988–90. Founder Mem, Labour Econ. Finance and Taxation Assoc. (Vice-Chm., 1975–77, 1979–83). Director: Pergamon Holdings Ltd, 1985–91; Mirror Group Newspapers Ltd, 1985–91, Mirror Group Newspapers PLC, 1991–92; Chm., Acoustigride UK Ltd, 1989–. President: Campaign for Protection of Rural Wales, 1989–; Fedn of Economic Develt Authorities, 1990–. *Publication:* The Last Great Frenchman: a life of General de Gaulle, 1993. *Recreations:* cricket (Oxford Univ. CC, 1953–55, Captain 1955; Essex CCC, 1953–59); music, real tennis. *Address:* 48 Thurloe Square, SW7 2SX. *T:* 0171–581 1783; Pant-y-Rhiw, Llansantffraed in Elvel, Powys LD1 5RH. *Clubs:* Reform, MCC.

WILLIAMS OF MOSTYN, Baron *cr* 1992 (Life Peer), of Great Tew in the County of Oxfordshire; **Gareth Wyn Williams;** QC 1978; a Recorder of the Crown Court, since 1978; *b* 5 Feb. 1941; *s* of Albert Thomas Williams and Selina Williams; *m* 1962, Pauline Clarke (marr. diss.); one *s* two *d*; *m* 1994, V. M. Russell; one *d. Educ:* Rhyl Grammar Sch.; Queens' Coll., Cambridge (Open Schol. (History) 1958; Univ. Prize, Jurisprudence 1962; Foundn Schol. 1964; LLB (1st Cl.) 1964; MA 1965). Called to the Bar, Gray's Inn, 1965, Bencher, 1991; Leader, Wales and Chester Circuit, 1987–89. Member: Bar Council, 1986–92 (Chm., 1992); Council of Justice, 1993–. Opposition front bench spokesman on NI, home and legal affairs, H of L, 1992–. President: Prisoners Advice Service, 1992–; Commonwealth and Ethnic Bar Assoc., 1993–. Trustee, NSPCC, 1993–; Patron, Redress Trust, 1993–. Pro-Chancellor, Univ. of Wales, 1994–. Fellow, Univ. of Wales, Aberystwyth, 1993. *Address:* Farrars Building, Temple, EC4Y 7BD. *T:* 0171–583 9241.

WILLIAMS, Prof. Alan Harold; Professor in the Department of Economics, University of York, since 1968; *b* 9 June 1927; *s* of Harold George Williams and Gladys May Williams (*née* Clark); *m* 1953, June Frances Porter; two *s* one *d. Educ:* King Edward's, Birmingham; Univ. of Birmingham (BCom). Lecturer, Exeter Univ., 1954–63; Sen. Lectr and Reader, Univ. of York, 1964–68. Visiting Lecturer: MIT, 1957–58; Princeton, 1963–64; Director of Economic Studies, HM Treasury Centre for Administrative Studies, 1966–68. Member: Yorkshire Water Authority, 1973–76; DHSS Chief Scientists Research Cttee, 1973–78; Royal Commission on the NHS, 1976–78; various SSRC Cttees and Panels, 1973–; Nat. Water Council, 1980–83. Hon. DPhil Lund, 1977. *Publications:* Public Finance and Budgetary Policy, 1963; (with Robert Anderson) Efficiency in the Social Services, 1975; (with Robert Sugden) Principles of Practical Cost-Benefit Analysis, 1978; articles in Economica, Jl of Political Econ., Jl of Public Econs, Nat. Tax Jl, Jl of Health Econ., BMJ and elsewhere; numerous conf. papers on various aspects of public expenditure appraisal, esp. health and health care. *Recreations:* music, walking, teasing.

WILLIAMS, Rt Hon. Alan John, PC 1977; MP (Lab) Swansea West since 1964; *b* 14 Oct. 1930; *m* 1957, Mary Patricia Rees, Blackwood, Mon; two *s* one *d. Educ:* Cardiff High Sch.; Cardiff College of Technology; University College, Oxford. BSc (London); BA (Oxon). Lecturer in economics, Welsh College of Advanced Technology; Free-lance Journalist. Joined Labour Party, 1950. Member: NATFHE (formerly of ATTI), 1958–; Fabian Society; Co-operative Party; National Union of Students delegation to Russia, 1954. Advr, Assoc. of First Div. Civil Servants, 1982–. Contested (Lab) Poole, 1959. PPS to Postmaster General, 1966–67; Parly Under-Sec., DEA, 1967–69; Parly Sec., Min. of Technology, 1969–70; Opposition Spokesman on Consumer Protection, Small Businesses, Minerals, 1970–74; Minister of State: Dept of Prices and Consumer Protection, 1974–76; DoI, 1976–79; Opposition spokesman on Wales, 1979–80; Shadow Minister for CS, 1980–83; opposition spokesman on: trade and industry, 1983–87; Wales, 1987–89; Dep. Shadow Leader of the House, 1983–89 and 1988–89; Shadow Sec. of State for Wales, 1987–88. Member: Public Accts Cttee, 1966–67, 1990–; Privileges Cttee, 1994–; Jt Chm., All-Party Minerals Cttee, 1979–86; Chairman, Welsh PLP, 1966–67; Delegate, Council of Europe and WEU, 1966–67. Sponsored by TSSA (Mem., 1984–). *Address:* House of Commons, SW1A 0AA. *Club:* Clyne Golf.

WILLIAMS, Alan Lee, OBE 1973; Director, Atlantic Council, since 1993 (Director, 1972–74 and 1992–93, Chairman, 1980–83, British Atlantic Committee); *b* 29 Nov. 1930; *m* 1974, Jennifer Ford. *Educ:* Roan Sch., Greenwich; Ruskin Coll., Oxford. National Service, RAF, 1951–53; Oxford, 1954–56; National Youth Officer, Labour Party, 1956–62. Dir-Gen., E-SU, 1979–86; Warden and Chief Exec., Toynbee Hall, 1987–92. MP (Lab) Hornchurch, 1966–70, Havering, Hornchurch, Feb. 1974–1979; PPS to Sec. of State for Defence, 1969–70, 1976; PPS to Sec. of State for NI, 1976–78; Chm., Parly Lab. Party Defence Cttee, 1976–79. Member: FO Adv. Cttee on Disarmament and Arms Control, 1975–79; Adv. Council on Public Records, 1977–84; Chm., Delegn to 4th Cttee of UN, NY, 1969; Chm., Transport on Water Assoc.; Deputy Director, European Movement, 1970–71, Treasurer, 1972–79; Vice Pres., European-Atlantic Gp, 1983–; Chm., European Working Gp of Internat. Centre for Strategic and Internat. Studies, Washington DC, 1987– (Mem., 1974–); Member: RUSI, 1968–; Trilateral Commn, 1976–. Chairman: Cedar Centre, Isle of Dogs, 1991–; Toynbee Housing Assoc., 1993–. Chm. of Govs, City Coll., 1990–. Freeman: City of London, 1969; Co. of Watermen and Lightermen, 1952–. Fellow, QMW, 1993. DLitt (*hc*) Schiller Internat. Univ., 1987. FRSA. *Publications:* Radical Essays, 1966; Europe or the Open Sea?, 1971; Crisis in European Defence, 1973; The European Defence Initiative: Europe's bid for equality, 1985; The Decline of Labour and the Fall of the SDP, 1989; Islamic Resurgence, 1991; Prospects for a Common European Foreign and Security Policy, 1995; NATO's Future in the Balance: time for a rethink, 1995. *Recreations:* reading, history, walking. *Address:* 6 North Several, Blackheath, SE3 0QR. *Clubs:* Reform, Pilgrims.

WILLIAMS, Dr Alan Wynne; MP (Lab) Carmarthen, since 1987; *b* 21 Dec. 1945; *s* of Tom and Mary Hannah Williams; *m* 1973, Marian Williams. *Educ:* Carmarthen Grammar School; Jesus College, Oxford. BA Chem. 1st cl. hons; DPhil. Senior Lecturer in Environmental Science, Trinity College, Carmarthen, 1971–87. *Recreations:* reading, watching sport. *Address:* Gwendraeth, 79 Parklands Road, Penybanc, Ammanford, Dyfed SA18 3TD. *T:* Ammanford (01269) 594710.

WILLIAMS, Sir Alastair Edgcumbe James D., *see* Dudley-Williams.

WILLIAMS, Albert; General Secretary, Union of Construction, Allied Trades and Technicians, 1985–92; President, European Federation of Building and Woodworkers, 1988–92; *b* 12 Feb 1927; *s* of William Arthur Williams and Phyllis Williams (*née* Barnes); *m* 1954, Edna Bradley; two *s. Educ:* Houldsworth School, Reddish; Manchester School of Building (1st and 2nd year Union of Lancs and Cheshire Insts Certs of Training). Apprentice bricklayer, Manchester City Corp., 1941; Armed Forces, 1944–48; bricklaying for various contractors; Member: Exec., Amalgamated Union of Building Trade Workers, 1958; Exec., Council of UCATT, 1971–92; Construction Ind. Trng Bd, 1979–92; Gen. Council, TUC, 1986–92; Dir, Bldg and Civil Engrg Holidays Scheme Management Ltd, 1979–92; Operatives' Side Sec., Nat. Jt Council for Building Industry, 1984–. Director: Builders Trng Assoc., 1992–; Operative Sub Contractors Assoc., 1992–; Labour Train Contract Services, 1994–. Chm. of Trustees, Working Class Liby, Salford, 1971–. *Recreations:* poetry and work. *Address:* 3 Cornflower Lane, Shirley, Croydon, Surrey CR0 8XJ.

WILLIAMS, (Albert) Trevor; management scientist; *b* 7 April 1938; *s* of Ben and Minnie Williams; *m* 1st, 1970, Mary Lynn Lyster; three *s*; 2nd, 1978, Deborah Sarah Fraser Duncan (*née* Milne); one *s*, and one step *s* two step *d. Educ:* King George V Sch., Southport; Queens' Coll., Cambridge (MA); Cranfield Institute of Technology (MSc). Rotary Foundation Fellow, Univ. of Ghana, 1961–62; Business Operations Research Ltd: Director, 1965–68; various academic appointments, 1968–82, including: Sen. Lectr and Vis. Professor, Graduate School of Business, Cape Town Univ.; Sen. Research Fellow, Sussex Univ.; Vis. Associate Prof., Wisconsin Univ.; Vis. Prof., INSEAD; taught corporate strategy at Hong Kong Univ., 1989 (Hon. Prof.), at LSE, 1990–91, at Cape Town Univ., 1992–95 (Vis. Prof.). Dir, Novy Eddison and Partners, 1971–74; Dep.-Dir for Futures Research, Univ. of Stellenbosch, 1974–78; Dep. Chief Scientific Officer, Price Commission, 1978–79; Advisor on Technology Projects, Scottish Development Agency, 1979; Dir, Henley Centre for Forecasting, 1980–81. Consultant, Sen. Industrial Advr and Team Manager, Monopolies and Mergers Commn, 1982–90. *Publications:* A Guide to Futures Studies, 1976; comtrib. Futures. *Recreations:* walking, reading. *Address:* Bodenham House, Dinedor, Hereford HR2 6LQ. *T:* Holme Lacy (01432) 870243; 13 Highcroft, 170 Highgate Road, NW5 1EJ. *Clubs:* Athenæum, Institute of Directors.

WILLIAMS, Alexander, CB 1991; FInstP; Government Chemist, 1987–91; *b* 30 March 1931; *s* of Henry and Dorothy Williams; *m* 1957, Beryl Wynne Williams (*née* Williams); one *s. Educ:* Grove Park Grammar Sch., Wrexham; University College of North Wales,

Bangor (BSc). National Service, REME, 1953–55; Monsanto Chemicals, 1955–56; Southern Instruments, Camberley, 1956–59; National Physical Laboratory: Div. of Radiation Science, 1959–78; Head, Div. of Mechanical and Optical Metrology, 1978–81; Under Sec., Res. and Technology Policy Div., DTI 1981–87. Dir, Assoc. of Official Analytical Chemists, 1989–93. Pres., British Measurement and Testing Assoc., 1995–. *Publications:* A Code of Practice for the Detailed Statement of Accuracy (with P. J. Campion and J. E. Burns), 1973; numerous papers on measurements of radio-activity etc, to Internat. Jl of Applied Radiation and Isotopes, Nucl. Instruments and Methods, etc. *Recreations:* bell-ringing, music, opera, walking.

WILLIAMS, Sir Alwyn, Kt 1983; PhD; FRS 1967; FRSE, MRIA, FGS; Principal and Vice-Chancellor of University of Glasgow, 1976–88, Hon. Senior Research Fellow in Geology, since 1988; *b* 8 June 1921; *s* of D. Daniel Williams and E. May (*née* Rogers); *m* 1949, E. Joan Bevan; one *s* one *d*. *Educ:* Aberdare Boys' Grammar Sch.; University College of Wales, Aberystwyth (Hon. Fellow, 1990). PhD Wales. Fellow, Univ. of Wales, 1946–48. Harkness Fund Fellow at US National Museum, Washington, DC, 1948–50; Lecturer in Geology in University of Glasgow, 1950–54; Prof. of Geology, 1954–74, Pro-Vice-Chancellor, 1967–74, Queen's Univ. of Belfast; Lapworth Prof. of Geology, and Head of Dept, Univ. of Birmingham, 1974–76. Pres., Palaeontological Assoc., 1968–70. Trustee, British Museum (Nat. History), 1971–79, Chm. of Trustees, 1974–79. Member: Equip. and Phys. Sci. sub-cttees, UGC, 1974–76; NERC, 1974–76; Adv. Council, British Library, 1975–77; Scottish Tertiary Educn Adv. Council, 1983–87; Adv. Bd for the Res. Councils, 1985–88; Chairman: Cttee on Nat. Museums and Galls in Scotland, 1979–81; Cttee on Scottish Agricl Colls, 1989; Scottish Hospitals Endowment Res. Trust, 1989–; Vice-Chm., Cttee of Vice-Chancellors and Principals, 1979–81. Dir, Scottish Daily Record & Sunday Mail Ltd, 1984–90. Pres., Royal Soc. of Edinburgh, 1985–88. Hon. FRSAMD 1988; Hon. Fellow, Geol Soc. of America, 1970–; For. Mem., Polish Academy of Sciences, 1979–; Hon. Associate, BM (Nat. Hist.), 1981–; Hon. FRCPS; Hon. FDS RCPS; Hon. DSc: Wales, 1974; Belfast, 1975; Edinburgh, 1979; Hon. LLD: Strathclyde, 1982; Glasgow, 1988; Hon. DCL Oxford, 1987; DUniv Paisley, 1993. Bigsby Medal, 1961, Murchison Medal, 1973, Geol Soc.; Clough Medal, Edin. Geol. Soc., 1976; T. Neville George Medal, Glasgow Geol. Soc., 1984. *Publications:* contrib. to Trans Royal Socs of London and Edinburgh, Jl Geological Society; Geological Magazine; Washington Acad. of Sciences; Geological Societies of London and America; Palaeontology; Journal of Paleontology, etc. *Address:* Department of Geology and Applied Geology, The University, Glasgow G12 8QQ; 25 Sutherland Avenue, Pollokshields, Glasgow G41 4HG. *T:* 0141–427 0589.

WILLIAMS, Anna Maureen, (Mrs G. H. G. Williams); *see* Worrall, A. M.

WILLIAMS, Sir Arthur (Dennis Pitt), Kt 1991; Chairman, Williams Holdings Ltd, since 1965; *b* 15 Oct. 1928; *s* of Arthur Henry Williams and Dora Ruth Williams; *m* 1st, 1951, Ngaire Garbett; three *s* two *d*; 2nd, 1989, Jeanne Brinkworth; one *s*. *Educ:* Salmerston; Margate College. Served RN, 1944–46. Apprentice carpenter, 1942–44 and 1946–47; carpenter, NZ, 1951–53; builder, 1953–, and property owner. Govt Appointee, Govt Property Services Ltd, 1991. Fellow: NZ Inst. of Builders; Aust. Inst. of Builders; NZ Inst. of Management. NZ Commemorative Medal, 1990. *Recreations:* horse breeding and racing. *Address:* Cranbrook, Cranbrook Grove, Waikanae, New Zealand. *T:* (business) (63) 647739, *Fax:* (63) 647605. *Club:* Wellesley (Wellington, NZ).

WILLIAMS, Hon. Atanda F.; *see* Fatayi-Williams.

WILLIAMS, Rev. Austen; *see* Williams, Rev. S. A.

WILLIAMS, Prof. Bernard Arthur Owen, FBA 1971; White's Professor of Moral Philosophy, and Fellow of Corpus Christi College, University of Oxford, 1990–Oct. 1996; Monroe Deutsch Professor of Philosophy, University of California, Berkeley, since 1988; *b* 21 Sept. 1929; *s* of late O. P. D. Williams, OBE and H. A. Williams; *m* 1955, Shirley Vivienne Teresa Brittain Catlin (*see* Baroness Williams of Crosby) (marr. diss. 1974); one *d*; *m* 1974, Patricia Law Skinner; two *s*. *Educ:* Chigwell Sch., Essex; Balliol Coll., Oxford (Hon. Fellow 1984). BA (Oxon) 1951; MA 1954. Fellow of All Souls Coll., Oxford, 1951–54; RAF (Gen. Duties Br.), 1951–53; Fellow of New Coll., Oxford, 1954–59; Vis. Lectr, Univ. Coll. of Ghana, 1958–59; Lectr in Philosophy, Univ. Coll., London, 1959–64; Professor of Philosophy, Bedford College, London, 1964–67 (Hon. Fellow 1985); Knightbridge Prof. of Philosophy, Cambridge, 1967–79; Fellow, 1967–79 and 1988, Provost, 1979–87, King's Coll., Cambridge. Visiting Professor: Princeton Univ., USA, 1963; Harvard Univ., 1973; Univ. of California, Berkeley, 1986; Sather Prof. of Classics, Univ. of Calif, Berkeley, 1989; Vis. Fellow, Inst. of Advanced Studies, ANU, 1969; Sen. Vis. Fellow, Princeton, 1978, 1991; Gauss Seminar in Criticism, Princeton, 1992. Member: Public Schools Commn, 1965–70; Royal Commn on Gambling, 1976–78; Commn on Social Justice, 1993–94; Chairman: Cttee on Obscenity and Film Censorship, 1977–79; Fitzwilliam Mus. Syndicate, 1984–87. Dir, English Nat. Opera (formerly Sadler's Wells Opera), 1968–86. Foreign Hon. Mem., Amer. Acad. of Arts and Sciences, 1983. FRSA 1993. Hon. LittD Dublin, 1981; Hon. DLitt: Aberdeen, 1987; Keele, 1995. Author and presenter, What is Truth? series, Channel 4, 1988. *Publications:* (ed with A. C. Montefiore) British Analytical Philosophy, 1966; Morality, 1972; Problems of the Self, 1973; A Critique of Utilitarianism, 1973; Descartes: The Project of Pure Enquiry, 1978; Moral Luck, 1981; (ed with A. K. Sen) Utilitarianism and Beyond, 1982; Ethics and the Limits of Philosophy, 1985; Shame and Necessity, 1993; Making Sense of Humanity, 1995; articles in philosophical jls, etc. *Recreation:* music, particularly opera. *Address:* (until Oct. 1996) Corpus Christi College, Oxford OX1 4JF; 18 Farndon Road, Oxford OX2 6RT; Department of Philosophy, University of California, Berkeley, CA 94720, USA.

WILLIAMS, Betty; *see* Williams, Elizabeth.

WILLIAMS, Prof. Sir Bruce (Rodda), KBE 1980; Professor of the University of Sydney, since 1967, and Fellow of the Senate, since 1994 (Vice-Chancellor and Principal, 1967–81); *b* 10 January 1919; *s* of late Reverend W. J. Williams and Helen Baud; *m* 1942, Roma Olive Hotten (*d* 1991); five *d*. *Educ:* Wesley College; Queen's College, University of Melbourne (BA 1939). MA Adelaide 1942; MA(Econ) Manchester, 1963. FASSA 1968. Lecturer in Economics, University of Adelaide, 1939–46 and at Queen's University of Belfast, 1946–50; Professor of Economics, University College of North Staffordshire, 1950–59; Robert Otley Prof., 1959–63, and Stanley Jevons Prof., 1963–67, Univ. of Manchester; Dir, Technical Change Centre and Vis. Prof., Imperial Coll., London, 1981–86. Vis. Fellow, ANU, 1987, 1988, 1990, 1992–94. Secretary and Joint Director of Research, Science and Industry Committee, 1952–59. Member, National Board for Prices and Incomes, 1966–67; Econ. Adviser to Minister of Technology, 1966–67; Member: Central Advisory Council on Science and Technology, 1967; Reserve Bank Board, 1969–81; Chairman: NSW State Cancer Council, 1967–81; Australian Vice Chancellors Cttee, 1972–74; Aust. Govt Cttee of Inquiry into Educn and Trng, 1976–79; (Australian) Review of Discipline of Engrg, 1987–88; Dep. Chm., Parramatta Hosps Bd, 1979–81. Pres., Sydney Conservatorium of Music Foundn; Chm., Internat. Piano Comp. of Australia. Editor, The Sociological Review, 1953–59, and The Manchester Sch., 1959–67. President Economics Section of British Assoc., 1964. Hon. FIE(Aust) 1989. Hon. DLitt: Keele, 1973; Sydney, 1982; Hon. DEcon Qld, 1980; Hon. LLD: Melbourne, 1981; Manchester, 1982; Hon. DSc Aston, 1982. Kirby Meml Award, IProdE, 1988. *Publications:* The Socialist Order and Freedom, 1942; (with C. F. Carter): Industry and Technical Progress, 1957, Investment in Innovation, 1958, and Science in Industry, 1959; Investment Behaviour, 1962; Investment Proposals and Decisions, 1965; Investment, Technology and Growth, 1967; (ed) Science and Technology in Economic Growth, 1973; Systems of Higher Education: Australia, 1978; Education, Training and Employment, 1979; Living with Technology, 1982; (ed) Knowns and Unknowns in Technical Change, 1985; Attitudes to New Technologies and Economic Growth, 1986; Review of the Discipline of Engineering, 1988; University Responses to Research Selectivity, 1991; Higher Education and Employment, 1994. *Address:* 55 McIntyre Place, Canberra, ACT 2604, Australia; 106 Grange Road, W5 3PJ. *Club:* Athenæum.

WILLIAMS, Catrin Mary, FRCS; Consultant Ear, Nose and Throat Surgeon, Clwyd Health Authority (North), 1956–86; Chairman, Wales Council for the Deaf, 1986–88; *b* 19 May 1922; *d* of late Alderman Richard Williams, JP, Pwllheli, and Mrs Margaret Williams; unmarried. *Educ:* Pwllheli Grammar Sch.; Welsh National Sch. of Medicine (BSc 1942, MB, BCh 1945). FRCS 1948. Co-Chm., Women's National Commn, 1981–83; Chm., Wales Womens' European Network. Pres., Medical Women's Fedn, 1973–74; Founding Vice-Pres., Gymdeithas Feddygol Gymraeg (Welsh Med. Soc.), 1975–79; Vice-Chm., Meniere's Soc., 1986–90, Chm., 1990–; Member: Exec. Cttee, Wales Council for the Disabled, 1988–; Regl Vice-Pres., Med. Women's Internat. Assoc., 1992– (Procedure Advr, 1984–92); Trustee, RNID, 1992– (Mem. Council and Exec. Cttee, 1986–92). *Recreations:* reading, embroidery. *Address:* Gwrych House, Abergele, Clwyd LL22 8EU. *T:* Abergele (01745) 832256.

WILLIAMS, Cecil Beaumont, CHB 1980; OBE 1963; retired; Executive Director, Da Costa & Musson Ltd, Barbados, 1980–91; *b* 8 March 1926; *s* of George Cuthbert and Violet Irene Williams; *m* 1952, Dorothy Marshall; two *s* one *d*. *Educ:* Harrison Coll., Barbados; Durham Univ. (BA, DipEd); Oxford Univ. Asst Master, Harrison Coll., 1948–54. Asst Sec., Govt Personnel Dept, and Min. of Trade, Industry and Labour (Barbados), 1954–56; Permanent Secretary: Min. of Educn, 1958; Min. of Trade, Industry and Labour, 1958–63; Dir, Economic Planning Unit, 1964–65; Manager, Industrial Devel Corp., 1966–67; High Comr to Canada, 1967–70; Permanent Sec., Min. of External Affairs, 1971–74; Ambassador to USA and Perm. Rep. to OAS, 1974–75; High Comr in UK, 1976–79. *Recreations:* music, tennis, reading, gardening. *Address:* Moonshine Hall, St George, Barbados.

WILLIAMS, Rear-Adm. Charles Bernard, CB 1980; OBE 1967; Flag Officer Medway and Port Admiral Chatham, 1978–80, retired; *b* 19 Feb. 1925; *s* of Charles Williams and Elizabeth (*née* Malherbe); *m* 1946, Patricia Mary, *d* of Henry Brownlow Thorp and Ellen Thorp; one *s* one *d*. *Educ:* Graeme Coll., Grahamstown, SA; Royal Naval Engineering Coll., Plymouth. Served in HM Ships Nigeria, Hornet, Triumph, 1946–53; in charge: Flight deck trials unit, 1953; Naval Wing, Nat. Gas Turbine Estabt, 1956; Sen. Engr, HMS Cumberland, 1958; in charge Admiralty Fuel Experimental Station, 1960; Comdr 1960; Engineer Officer, HMS London, 1962; Staff Engr, Flag Officer ME, 1964; Duty Comdr, Naval Ops MoD (N), 1967; Captain 1969; Dep. Manager, Portsmouth Dockyard, 1969; Supt, Clyde Submarine Base, 1972; Captain, HMS Sultan, 1975; Rear-Adm. 1978. *Recreations:* sailing (Chm., Whitbread Round the World Race, 1981–90), walking, music. *Address:* Green Shutters, Montserrat Road, Lee-on-Solent PO13 9LT. *T:* Lee-on-Solent (01705) 550816. *Clubs:* Royal Yacht Squadron; Royal Ocean Racing; Royal Naval Sailing Association (Life Vice Cdre); Lee-on-Solent Sailing; Royal London Yacht (Hon. Mem.); Royal Southern Yacht (Hon. Mem.); Royal Southampton Yacht (Hon. Mem.); Cruising Association of South Africa (Life Mem.).

WILLIAMS, Rt. Rev. Christopher; *see* Williams, Rt Rev. J. C. R., Bishop of The Arctic.

WILLIAMS, Dr Christopher John Hacon, FRCP; Senior Lecturer and Hon. Consultant Physician in Medical Oncology, Southampton Univesity, since 1980; *b* 3 Aug. 1946; *s* of Owen Henry Williams and Joyce May Hacon Deavin; *m* 1970, Susan Tennant (marr. diss. 1995); two *d*. *Educ:* Reed's Sch., Surrey; London Univ., St Mary's Hosp. (MBBS); DM Southampton 1980. Jun. posts, London Hosps, 1971–74; Jun. Registrar, Med. Oncology, St Bartholomew's, 1974–75; Postdoctoral Res. Fellow, Stanford Univ., 1975–77; Res. Fellow, Southampton Univ., 1977–80. Chairman: MRC Gynaecol Cancer Working Party, 1989–93; MRC Cancer Therapy Cttee, 1994–; Co-ordinator: ICON trials for ovarian carcinoma, 1991; Cochrane Cancer Network, 1995–. *Publications:* Recent Advances in Clinical Oncology, 1982; All About Cancer, 1983; Lung Cancer: the facts, 1984; Cancer Investigations and Management, 1985; Cancer: a guide for patients and family, 1986; (with R. B. Buchanan) Medical Management of Breast Cancer, 1987; Textbook of Uncommon Cancer, 1988; Cancer Biology and Management, 1989; (with J. S. Tobias) Cancer: a colour atlas, 1991; Introducing New Treatments for Cancer, 1992 (Medical Textbook of the Year, 1993); papers on new therapies for cancer, esp. clinical trials. *Recreations:* active participation in painting and sculpture, writing, gentle walking; passive participation in theatre, music, films, books; gathering art objects. *Address:* 4 Bassett Wood Mews, 35 Bassett Crescent West, Southampton SO16 7DW. *T:* Southampton (01703) 781258.

WILLIAMS, Clifford; Associate Director, Royal Shakespeare Company, 1963–91, Hon. Associate Artist, since 1991; *b* 30 Dec. 1926; *s* of George Frederick Williams and Florence Maud Williams (*née* Gapper); *m* 1st, 1952, Joanna Douglas (marr. diss. 1959); no *c*; 2nd, 1962, Josiane Eugenie Peset; two *d*. *Educ:* Highbury County Grammar Sch. Acted in London (These Mortals, Larissa, Wolves and Sheep, Great Catherine), and repertory theatres, 1945–48; founded and directed Mime Theatre Company, 1950–53; Dir of Productions: at Marlowe Theatre, Canterbury, 1955–56; at Queen's Theatre, Hornchurch, 1957. Directed at Arts Theatre, London: Yerma, 1957; Radio Rescue, 1958; Dark Halo, Quartet for Five, The Marriage of Mr Mississippi (all in 1959); Moon for the Misbegotten, The Shepherd's Chameleon, Victims of Duty (all in 1960); The Race of Adam, Llandaff Festival, 1961. Joined Royal Shakespeare Company, 1961; Directed: Afore Night Come, 1962; The Comedy of Errors, 1963. Productions for RSC in Stratford and London: The Tempest, The Representative, The Comedy of Errors (revival), 1963; Richard II, Henry IV Pts I and II (co-dir), Afore Night Come (revival), The Jew of Malta, 1964; The Merchant of Venice, The Jew of Malta (revival), The Comedy of Errors (revival), 1965; The Meteor, Twelfth Night, Henry IV Pts I and II (co-dir, revivals), 1966; Doctor Faustus, 1968; Major Barbara, 1970; The Duchess of Malfi, 1971; The Comedy of Errors (revival), 1972; The Taming of the Shrew, A Lesson in Blood and Roses, 1973; Cymbeline (co-dir), 1974; The Mouth Organ, Too True to be Good, 1975; Wild Oats, 1976, 1979; Man and Superman, 1977; The Tempest, 1978; The Love-Girl and the Innocent, 1981; The Happiest Days of Your Life, 1984; Il Candelaio, 1986; The Beaux' Stratagem, 1988. Other productions include: Our Man Crichton, 1964, and the Flying Dutchman, 1966, in London; The Gardener's Dog, 1965, and The Merry Wives of Windsor, 1967, for the Finnish National Theatre; Volpone at Yale Univ., 1967; Othello, for Bulgarian Nat. Theatre, Soldiers, New York and London, 1968; Dido and Aeneas, Windsor Festival,

Famine, English Stage Soc., 1969; As You Like It, 1967, and Back to Methuselah, 1969, both for the Nat. Theatre of GB; The Winter's Tale, 1969, for Yugoslav Nat. Theatre; Sleuth, London, NY and Paris, 1970; Oh! Calcutta!, London and Paris, 1970; Emperor Henry IV, New York, 1973; As You Like It (revival), New York, What Every Woman Knows, London, Emperor Henry IV, London, 1974; Murderer, London, 1975; Mardi-Gras, London, Carte Blanche, London, 1976; Stevie, The Old Country, Rosmerholm, London, 1977; The Passion of Dracula, London, 1978; Richard III, Mexican Nat. Theatre, 1979; Threepenny Opera, 1979, and The Love-Girl and the Innocent, 1980, Aalborg; Born in the Gardens, London, 1980; Overheard, London, To Grandmother's House We Go, NY, The Carmelites, Aalborg, 1981; Othello, Bad Hersfeld, Chapter 17, London, 1982; Richard III, Madrid, Merry Wives of Windsor, USA, Scheherazade, Festival Ballet, 1983; Pack of Lies, London, 1983, NY, 1985; A Child's Christmas in Wales (revival), USA, 1983; Rise and Fall of the City of Mahagonny, Aalborg, 1984; Aren't We All?, London, 1984, NY, 1985; The Cherry Orchard, Tokyo, 1984; Measure for Measure, Norrköping, St Joan, British tour, 1985; Legends, USA, 1986; Breaking the Code, London, 1986, NY, 1987; Aren't We All?, Australia, 1986; The Importance of Being Earnest, Copenhagen, 1987; A Chorus of Disapproval, British tour, Richard II, London, 1988; Richard III, London, Song at Nightfall, Dorset Music Fest., Wheel of Fire, Mérida Fest., Spain, 1989; Bellman's Opera, Stockholm, 1990; A Slight Hangover, British tour, Painting Churches, Southampton, It's Ralph, London, 1991; Pygmalion, Denmark, Breaking the Code, British tour, Bellman's Opera, London, 1992; A Murder of No Importance, Matters Matrimonial, British tours, 1993; Arsenic and Old Lace, British tour, 1994; Harvey, London, 1995. Also directed plays for the Arena Theatre, Triumph Theatre Co., Theatre Workshop, Guildford, Oxford, Coventry, Windsor, Toronto, Los Angeles, Washington, Houston, Johannesburg, Edinburgh Festival; Malvern Festival; Dir, Man and Superman (film), 1986. Mem. Welsh Arts Council, 1963–72; Chairman: Welsh Nat. Theatre Co., 1968–72; British Theatre Assoc., 1977–90; Chm., British Children's Theatre Assoc., 1968–71; Governor, Welsh Coll. of Music and Drama, 1981–90. Associate Artist of Yugoslav Nat. Theatre, 1969; FTCL 1960; FWCMD 1994. *Publications:* (ed) John O'Keeffe, Wild Oats, 1977; *plays:* The Disguises of Arlecchino, 1951; The Sleeping Princess, 1953; The Goose Girl, 1954; The Secret Garden, 1955; (with Donald Jonson) Stephen Dedalus, 1956; Matters Matrimonial, 1993; (with Daphne du Maurier) Rebecca, 1994; *translations:* Ionesco, The Duel, Double Act, 1979; Pirandello, As You Desire Me, 1981; Chekhov, The Cherry Orchard, 1981. *Recreations:* motor boating, water-ski-ing. *Address:* 62 Maltings Place, Bagleys Lane, SW6 2BY; 12 Chemin Cambarnier Nord, 06560 Opio, Valbonne, France.

WILLIAMS, Colin; *see* Welland, C.

WILLIAMS, Colin Hartley; Partner, Williams & Williams, PR consultants, since 1992; *b* 7 Dec. 1938; *s* of late Gwilym Robert Williams and Margaret (*née* Hartley); *m* 1964, Carolyn (*née* Bulman) (*d* 1993); one *s* two *d*. *Educ:* Grangefield Grammar Sch., Stockton-on-Tees; University College of Wales, Aberystwyth (BA). Journalist: Evening Gazette, Middlesbrough, 1960–63; Today Magazine, Odhams Press, 1964; Daily Sketch, 1964–66; Senior Lecturer, International Press Inst., Nairobi, 1967–68; Corporate and Public Relations Executive, 1969–74; Press Officer, Corporation of City of London, 1975–76; Asst Dir, City Communications Centre, 1977, Exec. Dir, 1979–83; Exec. Dir, Cttee on Invisible Exports, 1982–83; Chief Press Relations Manager, 1983–90, Hd of Corporate Communications, 1990–91, Hd of PR Gp, 1991–92, Nat. Westminster Bank. *Recreations:* writing, wine, golf. *Address:* Croesor, 84 Clare Road, Prestwood, near Great Missenden, Bucks HP16 0NU. *T:* Great Missenden (01494) 864464.

WILLIAMS, Dafydd Wyn J.; *see* Jones-Williams.

WILLIAMS, Prof. David, FRS 1984; Professor of Mathematical Sciences, Bath University, since 1992; *b* 9 April 1938; *s* of Gwyn Williams and Margaret Elizabeth Williams; *m* 1966, Sheila Margaret Harrison; two *d*. *Educ:* Jesus College, Oxford (DPhil); Grey College, Durham. Instructor, Stanford Univ., 1962; Lectr, Durham Univ., 1963; Shell Research Lectr, Statistical Lab., and Res. Fellow, Clare Coll., Cambridge, 1966; Lectr, 1969, Prof. of Maths, 1972, University Coll., Swansea; Prof. of Mathematical Stats and Professorial Fellow, Clare Coll., Cambridge Univ., 1985–92. Vis. Fellow, Bath Univ., 1991–92. Hon. Fellow, UC, Swansea, 1991–. *Publications:* Diffusions, Markov processes, and martingales, vol. 1, Foundations, 1979, vol. 2 (with L. C. G. Rogers), Itô calculus, 1987; papers in Séminaire de probabilités and other jls. *Recreations:* music, cycling, walking. *Address:* Mathematical Sciences Department, University of Bath, Claverton Down, Bath BA2 7AY.

WILLIAMS, Adm. Sir David, GCB 1977 (KCB 1975); DL; Governor and Commander-in-Chief, Gibraltar, 1982–85; a Gentleman Usher to The Queen, 1979–82, an Extra Gentleman Usher, since 1982; *b* 22 Oct. 1921; 3rd *s* of A. E. Williams, Ashford, Kent; *m* 1947, Philippa Beatrice Stevens; two *s*. *Educ:* Yardley Court Sch., Tonbridge; RN College, Dartmouth. Cadet, Dartmouth, 1935. Graduate, US Naval War Coll., Newport, RI. Served War of 1939–45 at sea in RN. Qual. in Gunnery, 1946; Comdr, 1952; Captain, 1960; Naval Asst to First Sea Lord, 1961–64; HMS Devonshire, 1964–66; Dir of Naval Plans, 1966–68; Captain, BRNC, Dartmouth, 1968–70; Rear-Adm. 1970; Flag Officer, Second in Command Far East Fleet, 1970–72; Vice-Adm. 1973; Dir-Gen. Naval Manpower and Training, 1972–74; Adm. 1974; Chief of Naval Personnel and Second Sea Lord, 1974–77; C-in-C Naval Home Comd, and ADC to the Queen, 1977–79, retired. Pres., Ex Services Mental Welfare Soc., 1979–91; Chm. of Council, Missions to Seamen, 1989–93. Member: Commonwealth War Graves Commn, 1980–89 (Vice Chm., 1985–89); Museums and Galleries Commn, 1987–93. Hon. Liveryman, Fruiterers' Co.; KStJ 1982. DL Devon, 1981. *Recreations:* sailing, gardening. *Address:* Brockholt, Strete, Dartmouth, Devon TQ6 0RR. *Clubs:* Army and Navy; Royal Dart Yacht; RN Sailing Association; Royal Yacht Squadron.

WILLIAMS, Prof. David Arnold, PhD, DSc; CPhys, FInstP; FRAS; Perren Professor of Astronomy, University College London, since 1994; *b* 9 Sept. 1937; *s* of James Arnold Williams and Frances Barbara Williams (*née* Begg); *m* 1964, Doreen Jane Bell; two *s*. *Educ:* Larne Grammar Sch.; Queen's Univ., Belfast (BSc, PhD, DSc). CPhys 1968; FInstP 1994; FRAS 1967. Maths Dept, Manchester Coll. of Sci. and Technol., 1963–65; NASA Goddard Space Flight Centre, Md, USA, 1965–67; Lectr, Sen. Lectr, Reader, Maths Dept, 1967–84, Prof. of Theoretical Astrophysics, 1984–94, UMIST. *Publications:* (with J. E. Dyson) The Physics of the Interstellar Medium, 1980; (with W. W. Duley) Interstellar Chemistry, 1984; (with T. W. Hartquist) The Chemically Controlled Cosmos, 1994; contrib. numerous articles in learned jls. *Recreations:* hill-walking, choral singing, beer and wine. *Address:* Department of Physics and Astronomy, University College London, Gower Street, WC1E 6BT.

WILLIAMS, David Claverly, CVO 1970; CBE 1977; *b* 31 July 1917; *s* of late Rev. Canon Henry Williams, OBE, and late Ethel Florence Williams; *m* 1944, Elizabeth Anne Fraser; three *d*. *Educ:* Christ's Coll., Christchurch, NZ; Victoria Univ. of Wellington. Professional Exam. in Public Administration. Inland Revenue Dept, 1936–39. Served War, 2NZEF, Pacific and Middle East, 1939–46. NZ Forest Service, 1946–60; Official Sec. to the Governor-General of NZ, 1960–77; Sec./Manager, The Wellington Club (Inc.), 1978–82. *Address:* 443 Muritai Road, Eastbourne, New Zealand. *Clubs:* Wellington (Wellington).

WILLIAMS, Sir David (Glyndwr Tudor), Kt 1991; DL; Vice-Chancellor, Cambridge University, 1989–Sept. 1996; Professor of Law, Cambridge University, from Oct. 1996; President, Wolfson College, University of Cambridge, 1980–92, Hon. Fellow, 1993; Rouse Ball Professor of English Law, Cambridge University, 1983–92; *b* 22 Oct. 1930; *s* of late Tudor Williams, OBE (Headmaster of Queen Elizabeth Grammar Sch., Carmarthen, 1929–55), and late Anne Williams; *m* 1959, Sally Gillian Mary Cole; one *s* two *d*. *Educ:* Queen Elizabeth Grammar Sch., Carmarthen; Emmanuel Coll., Cambridge (MA, LLB, Hon. Fellow 1984). LLM Calif. Nat. Service, RAF, 1949–50. Called to the Bar, Lincoln's Inn, 1956, Hon. Bencher, 1985. Commonwealth Fund Fellow of Harkness Foundn, Berkeley and Harvard, 1956–58; Lecturer: Univ. of Nottingham, 1958–63; Univ. of Oxford, 1963–67 (Fellow of Keble Coll.); Emmanuel College, Cambridge: Fellow, 1967–80; Sen. Tutor and Tutor for Admissions, 1970–76; Reader in Public Law, Cambridge Univ., 1976–83. Vis. Fellow, ANU, Canberra, 1974; Allen, Allen and Hemsley Vis. Fellow, Law Dept, Univ. of Sydney, 1985. Lectures: Martland, Alberta and Calgary, 1988; Read, Dalhousie, 1989; Fuchs, Indiana, 1993; Laskin, Osgoode Hall, 1993; Samuel Gee, RCP, 1993; Morris of Borth-y-Gest, Bangor, 1993; Wynne Baxter Godfree, Sussex, 1994; Spencer Mason, Auckland, 1994. Pres., Nat. Soc. for Clean Air, 1983–85; Chm., Animal Procedures Cttee, 1987–90. Member: Clean Air Council, 1971–79; Royal Commn on Environmental Pollution, 1976–83; Commn on Energy and the Environment, 1978–81; Council on Tribunals, 1972–82; Justice/All Souls Cttee on Adminstrative Law, 1978–88; Berrill Cttee of Investigation, SSRC, 1982–83; Marre Cttee on Future of Legal Profession, 1986–88; Univ. Comr, 1988–. Mem., Amer. Law Inst., 1986; For. Hon. Mem., Amer. Acad. of Arts and Scis, 1994. Mem., Internat. Jury, Indira Gandhi Prize, 1992–. DL Cambs, 1995. Hon. Fellow: Keble Coll., Oxford, 1992; Pembroke Coll., Cambridge, 1993; Hon. QC 1994. Hon. DLitt: William Jewell Coll., 1984; Loughborough Univ. of Technology, 1988; Davidson Coll., 1992; Hon. LLD: Hull, 1989; Sydney 1990; Nottingham, 1991; Liverpool, 1994; McGill, De Montfort, 1995. *Publications:* Not in the Public Interest, 1965; Keeping the Peace, 1967; articles in legal jls. *Address:* The Old Schools, Trinity Lane, Cambridge CB2 1TN. *T:* Cambridge (01223) 332291.

WILLIAMS, Sir David Innes, Kt 1985; MD, MChir Cambridge, FRCS; Consulting Urologist: Hospital for Sick Children, Great Ormond Street (Urologist, 1952–78); St Peter's Hospital, London (Surgeon, 1950–78); *b* 12 June 1919; *s* of late Gwynne E. O. Williams, MS, FRCS; *m* 1944, Margaret Eileen Harding; two *s*. *Educ:* Sherborne Sch.; Trinity Hall, Cambridge; Univ. College Hospital (Hon. Fellow, 1986). RAMC, 1945–48 (Major, Surg. Specialist). Urologist, Royal Masonic Hosp., 1963–72; Civilian Consultant Urologist to RN, 1974–84; Dir, BPMF, 1978–86, Pro-Vice-Chancellor, 1985–87, Univ. of London. Mem., 1975–91, Chm., 1982–91, Council, ICRF; Chm., Council for Postgrad. Med. Educn in England and Wales, 1985–88. Mem., Home Sec's Adv. Cttee on Cruelty to Animals, 1975–79. Mem., GMC, 1979–89 (Chm., Overseas Cttee, 1981–88); Vice-Pres., RCS, 1983–85 (Mem. Council, 1974–86; Mem. Jt Consultants Cttee, 1983–85; Hon. Medal, 1987); President: BMA, 1988–89; RSocMed, 1990–92 (Past Pres., Urology Sect.). Hon. Member: British Assoc. Paediatric Surgeons (Denis Browne Medal, 1977); British Assoc. Urological Surgeons (Past Pres.; St Peter's Medal, 1967); Assoc. Française d'Urologie; Amer. Surgical Assoc.; British Paediatric Assoc.; Amer. Acad. Pediatrics (Urology Medal, 1986). Hon. FACS 1983; Hon. FRCSI 1984; Hon. FDSRCS; Hon. FRSM 1993. *Publications:* Urology of Childhood, 1958; Paediatric Urology, 1968, 2nd edn 1982; Scientific Foundations of Urology, 1976, 2nd edn 1982; various contributions to medical journals. *Address:* 66 Murray Road, SW19 4PE. *T:* 0181–879 1042; The Old Rectory, East Knoyle, Salisbury, Wilts SP3 6AQ. *T:* East Knoyle (01747) 830255.

See also J. M. Williams, Sir R. E. O. Williams.

WILLIAMS, David John; *b* 10 July 1914; *s* of late James Herbert Williams and late Ethel (*née* Redman); unmarried. *Educ:* Lancing College; Christ Church, Oxford (MA). Called to Bar, Inner Temple, 1939. Postgrad. Dip. in Social Anthropology, LSE, 1965. Served War of 1939–45, Royal Artillery. Practised as Barrister, Norwich, 1946–51; Resident Magistrate, Tanganyika, 1951–56; Senior Resident Magistrate, 1956–60; Judge of High Court of Tanganyika, 1960–62; Lord Chancellor's Office, 1966–79. *Recreations:* the arts and travelling. *Address:* 10e Thorney Crescent, Morgan's Walk, SW11 3TR. *Clubs:* Travellers', Hurlingham.

WILLIAMS, David John, QPM 1992; Chief Constable, Surrey Police, since 1991 (Deputy Chief Constable, 1989–91); *b* 7 April 1941; *s* of late John Isaac Williams and of Edith (*née* Stoneham); *m* 1962, Johanna Murphy; two *s*. *Educ:* Ystalyfera Grammar Sch.; University Coll. London (LLB Hons). Called to the Bar, Middle Temple, 1977. Metropolitan Police, 1960–84; FBI Nat. Acad., 1982; on secondment to Home Office Inspectorate, 1983; Herts Constabulary, 1984–89; Nat. Exec. Inst., USA, 1994. Sec., Traffic Cttee, ACPO, 1992–. OStJ 1995. Queen's Commendation for Bravery, 1976; Police Long Service and Good Conduct Medal, 1982. *Recreations:* music, Rugby football, countryside walking, keeping fit. *Address:* Surrey Police HQ, Mount Browne, Sandy Lane, Guildford, Surrey GU3 1HG. *T:* Guildford (01483) 571212.

WILLIAMS, (David John) Delwyn; solicitor and company director; *b* 1 Nov. 1938; *s* of David Lewis Williams and Irena Violet Gwendoline Williams; *m* 1963, Olive Elizabeth Jerman; one *s* one *d*. *Educ:* Welshpool High School; University College of Wales, Aberystwyth. LLB. Solicitor and company director. MP (C) Montgomery, 1979–83; former Member: Select Cttee on Wales; Statutory Instruments Cttee; Jt Sec., All-Party Leisure and Recreation Industry Cttee. Contested (C) Montgomery, 1983. Mem., British Field Sports Soc. *Recreations:* race horse owner; cricket, golf, small bore shooting. *Address:* Frondeg, Guilsfield, Welshpool, Powys SY21 9NQ. *T:* Welshpool (01938) 3400.

WILLIAMS, David Lincoln; Chairman and Managing Director, Costa Rica Coffee Co. Ltd, since 1988; Chairman, Allied Profiles Ltd, since 1981; *b* 10 Feb. 1937; *s* of Lewis Bernard Williams and Eileen Elizabeth Cadogan; *m* 1959, Gillian Elisabeth, *d* of Dr William Phillips; one *s* one *d*. *Educ:* Cheltenham College. Served RA Gibraltar, 1955–57. Chairman: Allied Windows (S Wales) Ltd, 1971–85; Cardiff Broadcasting PLC, 1979–84; Chm. and Man. Dir, John Williams of Cardiff PLC, 1983–88 (Dir, 1968–88). Chm., Cox (Penarth), 1987–94. President, Aluminium Window Assoc., 1971–72. Member: CBI Welsh Council, 1986–89; Welsh Arts Council, 1987–94 (Chm., Music Cttee, 1988–94). Chm., Vale of Glamorgan Festival, 1978–; Director: Cardiff Bay Opera House Trust, 1994–; WNO, 1994– (Nat. Chm., Friends of WNO, 1980–). FInstD. Freeman, City of London, 1986; Liveryman, Founders' Co., 1986. *Recreations:* opera, gardening, fine weather sailing. *Address:* Rose Revived, Llantrithyd, Cowbridge, S Glam CF7 7UB. *T:* Bonvilston (01446) 781357. *Club:* Cardiff and County (Cardiff).

WILLIAMS, David Oliver; General Secretary, Confederation of Health Service Employees, 1983–87; *b* 12 March 1926; *m* 1949, Kathleen Eleanor Jones, Dinorwic; two *s* five *d* (and one *s* decd). *Educ:* Brynrefail Grammar Sch.; North Wales Hospital, Denbigh (RMN

1951). COHSE: full-time officer, Regional Secretary, Yorkshire Region, 1955; National Officer, Head Office, 1962; Sen. National Officer, 1969; Asst General Secretary, 1974. Chairman: Nurses and Midwives Whitley Council Staff Side, 1977–87; General Whitley Council Staff Side, 1974–87. Jubilee Medal, 1977. *Recreations:* walking, birdwatching, swimming, music. *Address:* 1 King's Court, Beddington Gardens, Wallington, Surrey SM6 0HR. *T:* 0181–647 6412.

WILLIAMS, Air Vice-Marshal David Owen C.; *see* Crwys-Williams.

WILLIAMS, Prof. David Raymond, OBE 1993; Professor of Speciation and Analytical Chemistry (formerly Applied Chemistry), University of Wales, Cardiff, since 1977; *b* 20 March 1941; *s* of Eric Thomas and Amy Gwendoline Williams; *m* 1964, Gillian Kirkpatrick Murray; two *d*. *Educ:* Grove Park Grammar Sch., Wrexham, Clwyd; Univ. of Wales, Bangor (BSc (1st Cl. Hons Chemistry); PhD); DSc St Andrews. CChem, FRSC, 1976; EurChem 1992. NATO Postdoctoral Fellowship, Univ. of Lund, 1965–66; Lectr in Chemistry, Univ. of St Andrews, 1966–77. Chm., Sci. Adv. Cttee, British Council, 1986–94; Member: Radioactive Waste Management Adv. Cttee, DoE, 1980–; Cttee on Medical Aspects of Radiation in the Environment, DHSS, later Dept of Health, 1985–89. FRSA 1978. Jeyes Silver Medal, RSC, 1987; Wolfson Foundn Res. Award, 1988. *Publications:* The Metals of Life, 1970; An Introduction to Bioinorganic Chemistry, 1976; The Principles of Bioinorganic Chemistry, 1977; Laboratory Introduction to Bioinorganic Chemistry, 1979; Analysis Using Glass Electrodes, 1984; Trace Metals in Medicine and Chelation Therapy, 1995; 400 res. papers. *Recreations:* cycling, swimming, other outdoor pursuits, public speaking. *Address:* Department of Chemistry, University of Wales, Cardiff, PO Box 912, Cardiff CF1 3TB. *T:* Cardiff (01222) 874778.

WILLIAMS, David Wakelin, (Lyn), MSc, PhD; CBiol, FIBiol; retired as Director, Department of Agriculture and Fisheries for Scotland, Agricultural Scientific Services, 1963–73; *b* 2 Oct. 1913; *e s* of John Thomas Williams and Ethel (*née* Lock); *m* 1948, Margaret Mary Wills, BSc (*d* 1993), *d* of late Rev. R. H. Wills; one *s*. *Educ:* Rhondda Grammar School, Porth; University College, Cardiff. Demonstrator, Zoology Dept, Univ. Coll., Cardiff, 1937–38; Lectr in Zoology and Botany, Tech. Coll., Crumlin, Mon., 1938–39; research work on nematode physiology, etc. (MSc, PhD), 1937–41; biochemical work on enzymes (Industrial Estate, Treforest), 1942–43. Food Infestation Control Inspector (Min. of Food), Glasgow; Sen. Inspector, W Scotland, 1945; Scotland and N Ireland, 1946. Prin. Scientific Officer, Dept Agriculture for Scotland, 1948; Sen. Prin. Scientific Officer, 1961; Dep. Chief Scientific Officer (Director), 1963. Chairman, Potato Trials Advisory Cttee, 1963–; FIBiol 1966 (Council Mem. Scottish Br., 1966–69). MBIM, 1970–76. *Publications:* various papers, especially for the intelligent layman, on the environment, and on pest control and its side effects. *Recreations:* writing, music, Hi-Fi, photography, natural history. *Address:* 8 Hillview Road, Edinburgh EH12 8QN. *T:* 0131–334 1108.

WILLIAMS, Delwyn; *see* Williams, D. J. D.

WILLIAMS, Sir Denys (Ambrose), KCMG 1993; Kt 1987; Gold Crown of Merit, Barbados, 1981; Chief Justice of Barbados, since 1987; *b* 12 Oct. 1929; *s* of George Cuthbert and Violet Irene Williams; *m* 1954, Carmel Mary Coleman; two *s* four *d*. *Educ:* Combermere and Harrison College, Barbados; Worcester College, Oxford (BCL, MA). Called to the Bar, Middle Temple, 1954. Asst Legal Draftsman, Barbados, 1957; Asst to Attorney General, 1959; Asst Legal Draftsman, Fedn of West Indies, 1959; Senior Parly Counsel, Barbados, 1963; Judge of the Supreme Court, 1967. *Recreations:* horse racing, tennis, walking. *Address:* No 9, Garrison, St Michael, Barbados. *T:* 4271164. *Clubs:* Carlton, Barbados Turf (Barbados).

WILLIAMS, Derek Alfred H.; *see* Hutton-Williams.

WILLIAMS, Derrick; *see* Williams, R. D.

WILLIAMS, Sir Dillwyn; *see* Williams, Sir E. D.

WILLIAMS, Rev. Doiran George; Chairman of Medical Appeal Tribunals, since 1987; Non-Stipendiary Minister, Greater Whitbourne, since 1993; *b* 27 June 1926; *s* of Rev. Dr Robert Richard Williams and Dilys Rachel Williams; *m* 1st, 1949, Flora Samitz (decd); one *s* one *d*; 2nd, 1977, Maureen Dorothy Baker; one *d*. *Educ:* Hereford Cathedral Sch.; Colwyn Bay Grammar Sch.; Liverpool Coll.; John F. Hughes Sch., Utica, NY. Served Army (Infantry), 1944–47. Called to the Bar, Gray's Inn, 1952; practised in Liverpool, 1952–58; Dept of Dir of Public Prosecutions, 1959, Asst Dir, 1977–82, Principal Asst Dir of Public Prosecutions, 1982–86. Sec., Liverpool Fabian Soc., 1956–58. Reader: Liverpool Dio., 1953–58; London Dio., 1959–63; Southwark Dio., 1963–88; Hereford Dio., 1988–93; Member: Southwark Dio. Synod, 1971–73; Southwark Readers' Bd, 1977–88. Ordained deacon, 1993, priest, 1994. *Recreations:* arts, mountains, sport, wine. *Address:* Howberry, Whitbourne, Worcester WR6 5RZ.

WILLIAMS, Sir Donald Mark, 10th Bt *cr* 1866; *b* 7 Nov. 1954; *s* of Sir Robert Ernest Williams, 9th Bt, and of Ruth Margaret, *d* of Charles Edwin Butcher, Hudson Bay, Saskatchewan, Canada; *S* father, 1976; *m* 1982, Denise, *o d* of Royston H. Cory; one *d* (one *s* decd). *Educ:* West Buckland School, Devon. *Heir:* *b* Barton Matthew Williams, *b* 21 Nov. 1956. *Address:* Upcott House, Barnstaple, N Devon EX31 4DR.

WILLIAMS, Douglas, CB 1977; CVO 1966; Deputy Secretary, Ministry of Overseas Development (later Overseas Development Administration), 1973–77, retired; *b* 14 May 1917; *s* of late James E. Williams and Elsie Williams; *m* 1948, Marie Jacquot; no *c*. *Educ:* Wolverhampton Sch.; Exeter Coll., Oxford. Served War, 1939–46 (despatches): Major, RA. Colonial Office, 1947; Principal, 1949; Colonial Attaché, Washington, 1956–60; Asst Sec., Colonial Office, 1961; transferred to ODM (later ODA), 1967, Under-Sec., 1968–73. Member: Bd, Crown Agents, 1978–84; EEC Econ. and Social Cttee, 1978–82; Governing Council, ODI, 1979–85. Trustee, Help the Aged and associated charities, 1984–92 (Chm. of Exec. Cttee, 1985–87, Chm., Overseas Cttee, 1987–88); Mem. Exec. Cttee, David Davies Meml Inst. of Internat. Studies, 1986–. *Publications:* The Specialized Agencies and the United Nations: the system in crisis, 1987; contrib. to United Kingdom—United Nations, 1990; articles on human rights and economic development, British colonial history. *Address:* 14 Gomshall Road, Cheam, Sutton, Surrey SM2 7JZ. *T:* 0181–393 7306. *Clubs:* Commonwealth Trust, United Oxford & Cambridge University.

WILLIAMS, Dudley Howard, PhD, ScD; FRS 1983; Reader in Organic Chemistry, University of Cambridge, since 1974; Extraordinary Fellow of Churchill College, since 1989; *b* 25 May 1937; *s* of Lawrence Williams and Evelyn (*née* Hudson); *m* 1963, Lorna Patricia Phyllis, *d* of Anthony and Lorna Bedford; two *s*. *Educ:* Grammar Sch., Pudsey, Yorks; Univ. of Leeds (state schol.; BSc, PhD); MA, ScD Cantab. Post-doctoral Fellow and Research Associate, Stanford Univ., Calif, 1961–64; University of Cambridge: Fellow of Churchill Coll., 1964–; Sen. Asst in Research, 1964–66; Asst Dir of Research, 1966–74. Nuffield Vis. Lectr, Sydney Univ., 1973; Dist. Vis. Lectr, Texas A & M Univ., 1986; Visiting Professor: Univ. of California, Irvine, 1967, 1986 and 1989; Univ. of Cape Town, 1972; Univ. of Wisconsin, 1975; Univ. of Copenhagen, 1976; ANU, 1980. Lectures: Arun Guthikonda Meml Award, Columbia Univ., 1985; Rohrer, Ohio State Univ., 1989; Foundn, Univ. of Auckland, 1991; Pacific Coast, Syntex Corp., 1991; Steel, Univ. of Queensland, 1994. Mem. Acad. Europaea. Meldola Medal, RIC, 1966; Corday-Morgan Medal, 1968; Tilden Medal and Lectr, 1983; Structural Chemistry Award, 1984, Bader Award, 1991, RSC. *Publications:* Applications of NMR in Organic Chemistry, 1964; Spectroscopic Methods in Organic Chemistry, 1966, 5th edn 1995; Mass Spectrometry of Organic Compounds, 1967; Mass Spectrometry—Principles and Applications, 1981; papers in chemical and biochemical jls. *Recreations:* music, squash. *Address:* 7 Balsham Road, Fulbourn, Cambridge CB1 5BZ. *T:* Cambridge (01223) 880592.

WILLIAMS, Dr Dyfri John Roderick, FSA; Keeper, Department of Greek and Roman Antiquities, British Museum, since 1993; *b* 8 Feb. 1952; *s* of Roderick Trevor Williams and Eira Williams (*née* Evans); *m* 1980, Korinna Pilafidis; one *s* one *d*. *Educ:* Repton Sch.; University Coll. London (BA); Lincoln Coll., Oxford (DPhil). FSA 1987. Shuffrey Jun. Res. Fellow, Lincoln Coll., Oxford, 1976–79; Department of Greek and Roman Antiquities, British Museum, 1979–: Res. Asst, 1979–83; Asst Keeper, 1983–93. Corresp. Mem., German Archaeol Inst., 1984. *Publications:* Greek Vases, 1985; Corpus Vasorum Antiquorum, BM fasc. 9, 1993; Greek Gold: jewellery of the classical world, 1994. *Recreations:* family, reading, music. *Address:* Department of Greek and Roman Antiquities, British Museum, Great Russell Street, WC1B 3DG. *T:* 0171–323 8411.

WILLIAMS, Prof. Sir (Edward) Dillwyn, Kt 1990; FRCP; FRCPath; Professor of Histopathology, University of Cambridge, since 1992; *b* 1 April 1929; *s* of Edward Williams and Ceinwen Williams (*née* James); *m* 1st, 1954, Ruth Hill; one *s* two *d* (and one *s* decd); 2nd, 1976, Olwen Williams; one *s* one *d*. *Educ:* Christ's Coll., Cambridge (MA, MD; Hon. Fellow, 1991); London Hospital Med. Coll. Jun. appts, London Hosp. and RPMS; successively Lectr, Sen. Lectr, Reader, in Morbid Anatomy, RPMS; Prof. of Pathology, 1969–92, Vice-Provost, 1982–84, Univ. of Wales Coll. of Medicine. Consultant Pathologist, Cardiff, 1969–92. Res. Fellowship, Harvard Univ., 1962–63. Pres., RCPath, 1987–90; Hd and Prin. Investigator of WHO's Internat. Reference Centre for Endocrine Tumours, 1972–; Chm., Welsh Sci. Adv. Cttee, 1985–92; Mem., GMC, 1987–90. Corresp. Mem., Amer. Thyroid Assoc.; President: Thyroid Club of GB, 1987–90; European Thyroid Assoc., 1993–. *Publications:* International Histological Classification of Tumours: histological typing of endocrine tumours, 1980; Pathology and Management of Thyroid Disease, 1981; Current Endocrine Concepts, 1982; numerous contribs to learned jls in field of endocrine pathology and carcinogenesis. *Recreations:* natural history in general, birdwatching in particular, mountain walking. *Address:* Burford House, Hildersham, Cambs CB1 6BU. *T:* Cambridge (01223) 893316. *Club:* Reform.

WILLIAMS, Air Cdre Edward Stanley, CBE 1975 (OBE 1968); defence consultant; *b* 27 Sept. 1924; *s* of late William Stanley Williams and Ethel Williams; *m* 1947, Maureen Donovan; two *d*. *Educ:* Wallasey Central Sch.; London Univ. Sch. of Slavonic and E European Studies; St John's Coll., Cambridge (MPhil (Internat. Relations), 1982). Joined RAF, 1942; trained in Canada; service in flying boats, 1944; seconded BOAC, 1944–48; 18 Sqdn, Transport Comd, 1949; Instr, Central Navigation Sch., RAF Shawbury, 1950–52; Russian Language Study, 1952–54; Flying Appts MEAF, A&AEE, 216 Sqdn Transport Comd, 1954–61; OC RAF Element, Army Intell. Centre, 1961–64; Asst Air Attaché, Moscow, 1964–67; first RAF Defence Fellow, UCL, 1967–68; comd Jt Wing, Sch. of Service Intell., 1968–71; Chief, Target Plans, HQ Second ATAF, 1971–73; Chief Intell. Officer, HQ British Forces Near East, 1973–75; comd Jt Air Reconn. Intell. Centre, 1976–77; Defence and Air Attaché, Moscow, 1978–81, retired RAF, 1981. Vice-Chm. (Air), NW Area, TAVRA, 1988–93. *Publications:* The Soviet Military, 1986; Soviet Air Power: prospects for the future, 1990; various articles in professional jls. *Recreations:* Russian studies, walking, photography. *Address:* c/o Midland Bank, 2 Liscard Way, Wallasey, Merseyside L44 5TR. *Club:* Royal Air Force.

WILLIAMS, Hon. Sir Edward (Stratten), KCMG 1983; KBE 1981; QC (Australia) 1965; *b* 29 Dec. 1921; *s* of Edward Stratten and Zilla Claudia Williams; *m* 1949, Dorothy May Murray; three *s* four *d* (and one *s* decd). *Educ:* Yungaburra State Sch., Qld; Mt Carmel Coll., Charters Towers, Qld; Univ. of London (LLB Hons). Served RAAF, UK and Aust., 1942–46. Barrister-at-Law, 1946; Justice of Supreme Court of Qld, 1971–84. Judge, Fiji Court of Appeal, 1993–. Chairman: Parole Board of Qld, 1976–83; Qld Corrective Services Commn Bd, 1989–90; Royal Commissioner, Aust. Royal Commn of Inquiry into Drugs, 1977–80; Member, Internat. Narcotics Control Board (UN), 1982–87. Comr-Gen., Expo 88, Brisbane, 1984–88; Director: Elders IXL Ltd, then Fosters Brewing Gp, 1984–91; Aust. Hydrocarbons NL, 1985–94. Chairman, Commonwealth Games Foundn Brisbane (1982), 1976–83. Pres., Playground and Recreation Assoc. of Qld, 1971–94. Mem., Anti-Cancer Council, 1983–95, Trustee, 1987–95, Queensland Cancer Fund. Australian of the Year, 1982; Queenslander of the Year, 1983. *Publications:* Report of Australian Royal Commission of Inquiry into Drugs and associated reports. *Recreations:* horse racing, gardening, golf. *Address:* 150 Adelaide Street East, Clayfield, Queensland 4011, Australia. *T:* (7) 32624802, *Fax:* (7) 32627610. *Clubs:* Brisbane, United Services, Queensland Turf (Chairman, 1980–91), Rugby Union, BATC, Tattersall's, Albion Park Trotting, Far North Queensland Amateur Turf (all Queensland).

See also Sir H. S. Williams.

WILLIAMS, Edward Taylor, CMG 1962; MICE; retired as General Manager, Malayan Railway; civil engineering railway consultant with Kennedy Henderson Ltd (formerly Henderson, Busby partnership), consulting engineers and economists, since 1965; *b* Bolton, Lancashire, 15 October 1911; *s* of Edward and Harriet Williams; *m* 1940, Ethel Gertrude Bradley (*d* 1983); one step *s* one step *d*. *Educ:* Accrington Grammar School; Manchester College of Technology. LMS Rly, pupil engineer, 1929–36; Sudan Rly, Asst Civil Engr, 1936–38; Metropolitan Water Board, Civil Engr, 1939–41; Malayan Rly, 1941–62 (Gen. Man. 1959–62); Rly Advr, Saudi Govt Railroad, 1963–65. Interned in Singapore, in Changi and Sime Road, 1941–45. *Recreation:* travel. *Address:* 8 Cromartie Point, Livermead, Torquay, Devon TQ2 6QY. *T:* Torquay (01803) 606393.

WILLIAMS, Elizabeth, (Betty), (Mrs J. T. Perkins); working for peace, since 1976; *b* 22 May 1943; *m* 1st, 1961, Ralph Williams (marr. diss.); one *s* one *d*; 2nd, 1982, James T. Perkins. *Educ:* St Dominic's Grammar School. Office Receptionist. Leader, NI Peace Movement, 1976–78. Hon. LLD, Yale Univ., 1977; Hon. HLD, Coll. of Sienna Heights, Michigan, 1977. Nobel Peace Prize (jtly), 1976; Carl-von-Ossietsky Medal for Courage, 1976. *Recreation:* gardening. *Address:* PO Box 725, Valparaiso, FL 32580–0725, USA.

WILLIAMS, Evelyn Faithfull M.; *see* Monier-Williams.

WILLIAMS, Francis Julian, CBE 1986; JP; DL; Member of Prince of Wales' Council, Duchy of Cornwall, 1969–85; *b* 16 April 1927; 2nd *s* of late Alfred Martyn Williams, CBE, DSC; *m* Delia Fearne Marshall, *e d* of Captain and Mrs Campbell Marshall, St Mawes; two *s*. *Educ:* Eton; Trinity Coll., Cambridge (BA). RAF, 1945–48. Chm., Cambridge Univ. Conservative Assoc;, 1950; Pres., Cambridge Union, 1951. Contested (C) All Saints Div. of Birmingham, 1955. Mem., Devon and Cornwall Bd, Lloyds Bank, 1971–90. Succeeded to Caerhays, 1955. Pres., Cornwall Cricket Club. Mem., Cornwall CC, 1967–89 (Vice-Chm., 1974; Chm., 1980–89). JP 1970, DL 1977, Cornwall.

Recreation: gardening. *Address:* Caerhays Castle, Gorran, St Austell, Cornwall PL26 6LY. *T:* Truro (01872) 501250. *Clubs:* Brooks's, White's.

WILLIAMS, Francis Owen Garbett, (Frank Williams), CBE 1987; Managing Director, Williams Grand Prix Engineering Ltd; *b* 16 April 1942; *s* of Owen Garbett Williams; *m* 1974, Virginia Jane, *d* of Raymond Berry; three *c. Educ:* St Joseph's Coll., Dumfries. Racing driver to 1966, competing first in Austin A40; grand prix team management, 1969–; Formula One with Brabham BT 26A; founded Frank Williams Racing Cars, 1975; first Grand Prix race, with FW07, Silverstone, 1979; won Constructors' Cup, 1980, 1981, 1986, 1987, 1992, 1993, 1994; introduced active ride system, 1988, semi-automatic 6-speed gear box, 1991. *Address:* Williams Grand Prix Engineering, Basil Hill Road, Didcot, Oxon OX11 7HW.

WILLIAMS, Frank Denry Clement, CMG 1956; *b* 3 May 1913; *s* of Frank Norris Williams and Joanna Esther Williams; *m* 1941, Traute Kahn; no *c. Educ:* Leighton Park School, Reading; London School of Economics (BSc Econ.). Cadet, Colonial Administrative Service, 1946; Asst Financial Sec., Nigeria, 1952; Financial Secretary: Jamaica, 1954; Federation of Nigeria, 1956; Economic Adviser, Federation of Nigeria, 1957–58; Permanent Secretary, Prime Minister's Dept, Fedn of The W Indies, 1958–62; Financial Sec., The Gambia, 1962–65. *Recreations:* walking, languages. *Address:* 51 The Priory, London Road, Brighton, Sussex BN1 8QT.

WILLIAMS, Prof. Gareth Howel; Professor of Chemistry, University of London, 1967–84 (Head of Department of Chemistry, Bedford College, 1967–84), now Emeritus Professor; *b* 17 June 1925; *s* of Morgan John and Miriam Williams, Treherbert, Glam; *m* 1955, Marie, BA, *yr d* of William and Jessie Mary Mitchell, Wanlockhead, Dumfriesshire; one *s* one *d. Educ:* Pentre Grammar Sch.; University Coll., London. BSc, PhD, DSc London; FRSC. Asst Lectr, then Lectr in Chemistry, King's Coll., Univ of London, 1947–60; Research Fellow, Univ. of Chicago, 1953–54; Reader in Organic Chemistry, Birkbeck Coll., Univ. of London, 1960–67. Vis. Lectr, Univ. of Ife, Nigeria, 1965; Rose Morgan Vis. Prof., Univ. of Kansas, 1969–70; Vis. Prof., Univ. of Auckland, NZ, 1977. External Examr: Univ. of Rhodesia, 1967–70; Univ. of Khartoum, 1967–73, 1976–80; City Univ., 1968–74; Univ. of Surrey, 1974–76; Brunel Univ., 1980–85. Chm., London Welsh Assoc., 1987–90. JP Brent, 1979–95 (Dep. Chm., 1989–91). *Publications:* Homolytic Aromatic Substitution, 1960; Organic Chemistry: a conceptual approach, 1977; (Editor) Advances in Free-Radical Chemistry, Vol. I, 1965, Vol. II, 1967, Vol. III, 1969, Vol. IV, 1972, Vol. V, 1975, Vol. VI, 1980; numerous papers in Jl Chem. Soc. and other scientific jls. *Recreation:* music. *Address:* Hillside, 22 Watford Road, Northwood, Mddx HA6 3NT. *T:* Northwood (01923) 825297. *Club:* Athenæum.

WILLIAMS, Prof. Gareth Lloyd; Professor of Educational Administration, Institute of Education, University of London, since 1984; *b* 19 Oct. 1935; *s* of Lloyd and Katherine Enid Williams; *m* 1960, Elizabeth Ann Peck; two *s* one *d. Educ:* Creeting St Mary; Framlingham; Cambridge Univ. (MA). Res. Officer, Agricl Econs Res. Inst., Oxford Univ., 1959–62; Res. Fellow, OECD, Athens, 1962–64; Principal Administrator, OECD, Paris, 1964–68; Associate Dir, Higher Educn Res. Unit, LSE, 1968–73; Prof. of Educnl Planning, Univ. of Lancaster, 1973–84. Visiting Professor: Melbourne Univ., 1981–82; Coll. of Europe, 1994–. Specialist Adviser to Arts and Educn Sub-Cttee to House of Commons Cttee on Expenditure, 1972–76; Consultant to OECD, ILO, UNESCO, and World Bank. Member: Council, Policy Studies Inst., 1979–85; Governing Council for Soc. for Res. into Higher Educn, 1970– (Chm., 1978–80, 1986–88). Mem. Bd, Red Rose Radio PLC, 1981–92. FRSA 1982. *Publications:* (with Greenaway) Patterns of Change in Graduate Employment, 1973; (with Blackstone and Metcalf) The Academic Labour Market in Britain, 1974; Towards Lifelong Learning, 1978; (with Zabalza and Turnbull) The Economics of Teacher Supply, 1979; (with Woodhall) Independent Further Education, 1979; (with Blackstone) Response to Adversity, 1983; Higher Education in Ireland, 1985; (with Woodhall and O'Brien) Overseas Students and their Place of Study, 1986; Changing Patterns of Finance in Higher Education, 1992. *Address:* 11 Thornfield, Ashton Road, Lancaster LA1 5AG. *T:* Lancaster (01524) 66002.

WILLIAMS, Sir Gareth R.; *see* Rhys Williams, Sir A. G. L. E.

WILLIAMS, Geoffrey Guy; Public Works Loan Commissioner, since 1990; *b* 12 July 1930; *s* of late Captain Guy Williams, OBE, and Mrs Margaret Williams (*née* Thomas). *Educ:* Blundell's Sch.; Christ's Coll., Cambridge (MA, LLM). Slaughter and May, Solicitors, 1952–66, Partner 1961; Dir, J. Henry Schroder Wagg & Co. Ltd, 1966–90, Vice-Chm. 1974, Dep. Chm., 1977–90. Chm., National Film Finance Corp., 1976–85 (Dir, 1970). Director: Bass plc, 1971–91; Schroders plc, 1976–90; John Brown plc, 1977–85; Standard Chartered plc, 1990–94. Chm., Issuing Houses Assoc., 1979–81. *Recreations:* reading, theatre, cinema. *Address:* 18G Eaton Square, SW1W 9DD. *T:* 0171–235 5212. *Club:* Brooks's.

WILLIAMS, (George Haigh) Graeme; QC 1983; barrister; a Recorder of the Crown Court, since 1981; *b* 5 July 1935; *s* of Dr Leslie Graeme Williams and Joan Haigh Williams (*née* Iago); *m* 1963, Anna Maureen Worrall, *qv*; two *d. Educ:* Tonbridge Sch. (Scholar); Brasenose Coll., Oxford (MA). Nat. Service, RA, England and Hong Kong, 1953–55. Called to the Bar, Inner Temple, 1959. Mem., No 3 Legal Aid Area Cttee, 1980–. *Address:* 13 King's Bench Walk, Temple, EC4Y 7EN. *T:* 0171–353 7204.

WILLIAMS, George Mervyn, CBE 1977; MC 1944; TD; Vice Lord-Lieutenant of Mid Glamorgan, 1986–94; *b* 30 Oct. 1918; *yr s* of late Owain Williams and late Mrs Williams; *m* 1st, 1940, Penelope (marr. diss. 1946), *d* of late Sir Frank Mitchell, KCVO; 2nd, 1950, Grizel Margaretta Cochrane, DStJ, *d* of late Major Walter Stewart, DSO; one *s. Educ:* Radley Coll. Served Royal Fusiliers, N Africa and Italy, 1939–46; Major, British Military Mission to Greece, 1945. Great Universal Stores, 1946–49; Christie-Tyler PLC: Sales Dir, 1949; Man. Dir, 1950–80; Chm., 1959–85; Director: Lloyds Bank plc, 1972–77; Lloyds Bank UK Management Ltd, 1975–85; Chm., S Wales Regl Bd, Lloyds Bank, 1977–87. Governor, United World Coll. of Atlantic, 1980–88. JP 1965–70, High Sheriff 1966, DL 1967–86, Glamorgan. CStJ. *Address:* 27 Broad Street, Ludlow, Shropshire SY8 1NJ. *T:* Ludlow (01584) 872877; Llanharan House, Llanharan, Mid Glamorgan CF7 9A. *T:* Llantrisant (01443) 226253. *Clubs:* Brooks's; Cardiff and County (Cardiff).

WILLIAMS, Sir Glanmor, Kt 1995; CBE 1981; FBA 1986; Professor of History, University College of Swansea, 1957–82; Chairman, Ancient Monuments Board (Wales), 1983–95; *b* 5 May 1920; *s* of Daniel and Ceinwen Williams, Dowlais, Glam; *m* 1946, Margaret Fay Davies; one *s* one *d. Educ:* Cyfarthfa Grammar Sch., Merthyr Tydfil; Univ. Coll. of Wales, Aberystwyth. MA 1947; DLitt 1962. University College of Swansea: Asst Lectr in History, 1945; Sen. Lectr, 1952; a Vice-Principal, 1975–78; Hon. Fellow, 1988. Nat. Governor, BBC, for Wales, 1965–71; Chm., Royal Commn on Ancient and Historical Monuments in Wales, 1986–90 (Mem., 1962–90); Member: Historic Bldgs Council for Wales, 1962–; British Library Bd, 1973–80 (Chm., Adv. Council, 1981–85); Adv. Council on Public Records, 1974–82; Welsh Arts Council, 1978–81; Council, Nat. Museum of Wales, 1983–90; Chm., Welsh Folk-Museum Cttee, 1987–90. Vice-Pres., Univ. of Wales, Aberystwyth, 1986–, and Hon. Fellow, 1993. Chm., Pantyfedwen Foundations, 1973–79; Pres., Cambrian Arch. Assoc., 1980. FRHistS 1954 (Vice-Pres., 1979–83); FSA 1978. Medal of Hon. Soc. of Cymmrodorion, 1991. *Publications:* Yr Esgob Richard Davies, 1953; The Welsh Church, 1962; Owen Glendower, 1966; Welsh Reformation Essays, 1967; (ed) Glamorgan County History, vol II 1984, vol. III 1971, vol. IV 1974, vol. V 1980, vol. VI 1988; Religion, Language and Nationality in Wales, 1979; Grym Tafodau Tân, 1984; Henry Tudor and Wales, 1985; Wales 1415–1642, 1987; (ed) Swansea: an illustrated history, 1990; (ed) The Celts and the Renaissance, 1990; The Welsh and their Religion, 1991; (ed) Social Policy, Crime and Punishment, 1994; contrib. to: History, Welsh History Review, etc. *Recreations:* music, camera. *Address:* 11 Grosvenor Road, Swansea SA2 0SP. *T:* Swansea (01792) 204113.

WILLIAMS, Glanville Llewelyn, QC 1968; FBA 1957; Fellow of Jesus College, Cambridge, 1955–78, Hon. Fellow, 1978, and Rouse Ball Professor of English Law in the University of Cambridge, 1968–78 (Reader, 1957–65; Professor, 1966); *b* 15 Feb. 1911; *s* of late B. E. Williams, Bridgend, Glam; *m* 1939, Lorna Margaret, *d* of late F. W. Lawfield, Cambridge; one *s. Educ:* Cowbridge; University College of Wales, Aberystwyth; St John's Coll., Cambridge. Called to the Bar, 1935; PhD (Cantab), 1936; Research Fellow of St John's Coll., 1936–42; LLD (Cantab), 1946; Reader in English Law and successively Professor of Public Law and Quain Professor of Jurisprudence, University of London, 1945–55. Carpentier Lecturer in Columbia Univ., 1956; Cohen Lecturer in Hebrew University of Jerusalem, 1957; first Walter E. Meyer Visiting Research Professor, New York Univ., 1959–60; Charles Inglis Thompson Guest Professor, University of Colorado, 1965; Vis. Prof., Univ. of Washington, 1969. Special Consultant for the American Law Institute's Model Penal Code, 1956–58; Member: Standing Cttee on Criminal Law Revision, 1959–80; Law Commn's Working Party on Codification of Criminal Law, 1967; Cttee on Mentally Abnormal Offenders, 1972. Pres., Abortion Law Reform Assoc., 1962–; Vice-Pres., Voluntary Euthanasia, 1985–. Hon. Bencher, Middle Temple, 1966. Fellow, Galton Inst.; For. Hon. Mem., Amer. Acad. of Arts and Sci., 1985; Hon. Life Mem., Soc. for Reform of Criminal Law, 1992. Ames Prize, Harvard, 1963; (joint) Swiney Prize, RSA, 1964. Hon. LLD: Nottingham, 1963; Wales, 1974; Glasgow, 1980; Sussex, 1987; Hon. DCL Durham, 1984; Hon. LittD Cantab, 1995. *Publications:* Liability for Animals, 1939; chapters in McElroy's Impossibility of Performance, 1941; The Law Reform (Frustrated Contracts) Act (1943), 1944; Learning the Law, 1st edn 1945, 11th edn 1982; Crown Proceedings, 1948; Joint Obligations, 1949; Joint Torts and Contributory Negligence, 1950; Speedhand Shorthand, 1952, 8th edn 1980; Criminal Law; The General Part, 1st edn 1953, 2nd edn 1961; The Proof of Guilt, 1st edn 1955, 3rd edn 1963; The Sanctity of Life and the Criminal Law, American edn 1956, English edn 1958; The Mental Element in Crime, 1965; (with B. A. Hepple) Foundations of the Law of Tort, 1976, 2nd edn 1984; Textbook of Criminal Law, 1978, 3rd edn 1995; articles in legal periodicals. *Address:* Merrion Gate, Gazeley Lane, Cambridge CB2 2HB. *T:* Cambridge (01223) 841175.

WILLIAMS, Glynn Anthony, FRBS, FRCA; sculptor; Professor of Sculpture, Royal College of Art, since 1990; *b* 30 March 1939; *s* of Idris Merion Williams and Muriel Elizabeth Purslow; *m* 1963, Heather Woodhall; two *d. Educ:* Wolverhampton Grammar Sch.; Wolverhampton Coll. of Art (NDD Sculpture Special Level); British Sch. in Rome (Rome Scholar). Head of Sculpture Departments: Leeds Coll. of Art, later Leeds Polytechnic, 1968–75; Wimbledon Sch. of Art, 1976–90. 21 one-man exhibns incl. retrospective, Margam Park, S Wales, 1992; numerous group exhibns incl. British Sculpture of 20th Century, Whitechapel Gall., 1981; rep. GB, Kotara Takamura Grand Prize Exhibn, Japan, 1984; work in collections: Arts Council of GB; Bottisham Village Coll., Cambridge; Bradford City Art Gall.; British Sch. in Rome; Grisedale Theatre in the Forest, Cumbria; Hakone Open Air Mus., Japan; Hampshire Sculpture Trust; Haroldwood Hosp., Essex; Hemel Hempstead Arts Trust; Henry Moore Centre for Sculpture, Leeds; Hove Mus. and Art Gall.; Hull City Art Gall.; Leeds City Council; Lincoln City Council; London Borough of Hounslow; Middlesbrough Council; Milton Keynes Develt Corp.; Newport (Gwent) Educn Cttee; Northern Arts Assoc.; Peterborough Develt Corp.; Southern Arts Assoc.; Tate Gall.; V & A; Welsh Arts Council; Welsh Sculpture Trust; Wolverhampton Educn Cttee; Yorkshire Arts Assoc. FRCA 1991; FRBS 1992. Hon. Fellow, Wolverhampton Polytechnic, 1989. *Publications:* contribs to arts magazines, jls, TLS. *Recreations:* cooking, crosswords, music, annoying the enemy. *Address:* c/o Bernard Jacobson Gallery, 14A Clifford Street, W1X 1RF. *Club:* Chelsea Arts.

WILLIAMS, Graeme; *see* Williams, George H. G.

WILLIAMS, Air Vice-Marshal Graham Charles, AFC 1970 and Bar 1975; FRAeS; Marketing Advisor, Loral International Inc., since 1993; Commandant General, RAF Regiment and Director General of Security (RAF), 1990–91; *b* 4 June 1937; *s* of Charles Francis Williams and Molly (*née* Chapman); *m* 1962, Judith Teresa Ann Walker; one *s* one *d. Educ:* Marlborough College; RAF College, Cranwell. FRAeS 1984. 54 Sqn, 229 OCU, 8 Sqn, Empire Test Pilots' School, A Sqn, A&AEE, 1958–70; RAF Staff Coll., 1971; OC 3 Sqn, Wildenrath, 1972–74; Junior Directing Staff (Air), RCDS, 1975–77; OC RAF Brüggen, 1978–79; Group Captain Ops, HQ RAF Germany, 1980–82; CO Experimental Flying Dept, RAE, 1983; Comdt, Aeroplane and Armament Exptl Estabt, 1983–85; Dir, Operational Requirements, MoD, 1986; ACDS, Operational Requirements (Air), 1986–89. Harmon Internat. Trophy for Aviators, USA, 1970. *Recreations:* old cars, golf. *Address:* The Garden Cottage, Brookside Lane, Little Kimble, Bucks HP17 0JF. *Club:* Royal Air Force.

WILLIAMS, Harri Llwyd H.; *see* Hudson-Williams.

WILLIAMS, Rev. Harry Abbott; Community of the Resurrection, since 1969; *b* 10 May 1919; *s* of late Captain Harry Williams, RN, and Annie Williams. *Educ:* Cranleigh Sch.; Trinity Coll., Cambridge; Cuddesdon Coll., Oxford. BA 1941; MA 1945. Deacon, 1943; Priest, 1944. Curate of St Barnabas, Pimlico, 1943–45; Curate of All Saints, Margaret Street, 1945–48; Chaplain and Tutor of Westcott House, Cambridge, 1948–51; Fellow of Trinity Coll., Cambridge, 1951–69; Dean of Chapel, 1958–69, and Tutor, 1958–68; Exam. Chaplain to Bishop of London, 1948–69. Mem., Anglican delegation to Russian Orthodox Church, Moscow, 1956; Select Preacher, Univ. of Cambridge, 1950, 1958, 1975; Hulsean Preacher, 1962, 1975; Select Preacher, Univ. of Oxford, 1974. Licensed to officiate in Dio. of Ely, 1948–, Dio. of Wakefield, 1979–. *Publications:* Jesus and the Resurrection, 1951; God's Wisdom in Christ's Cross, 1960; The Four Last Things, 1960; The True Wilderness, 1965; True Resurrection, 1972; Poverty, Chastity and Obedience: the true virtues, 1975; Tensions, 1976; Becoming What I Am, 1977; The Joy of God, 1979; Some Day I'll Find You (autobiog.), 1982; contribs to: Soundings, 1962; Objections to Christian Belief, 1963; The God I Want, 1967. *Recreations:* idleness and religion. *Address:* House of the Resurrection, Mirfield, West Yorks WF14 0BN.

WILLIAMS, Helen Elizabeth Webber, MA; Principal, RNIB New College, Worcester, since 1995; *b* 28 April 1938; *o d* of Alwyn and Eleanor Thomas; *m* 1962, Dr Peter Williams (marr. diss. 1974); one *s* one *d. Educ:* Redland High Sch., Bristol; Girton Coll., Cambridge (MA; DipEd). Assistant English Mistress: St Paul's Girls' Sch., 1962–63; St George's Sch., Edinburgh, 1963–64; Edinburgh University: Asst Lectr, Dept of English, 1964–67; Lectr

in English and Dir of Studies, Faculty of Arts, 1967–78; Headmistress, Blackheath High Sch., 1978–89; High Mistress, St Paul's Girls' Sch., 1989–92; Trevelyan Fellow, Trevelyan Coll., Univ. of Durham, 1993; English teacher, The Brearley Sch., NY, 1993–94. Member: HMC, 1994–; Governing Body, SOAS, 1988–; Council, City Univ., 1990–92; Governing Body, Stowe Sch., 1992–. *Publication:* (ed) T. S. Eliot: The Wasteland, 1968. *Recreations:* music, drama, cookery, gardening. *Address:* The Principal's House, RNIB New College, Worcester, Whittington Road, Worcester WR5 2JX; 4/2 Advocates Close, The Royal Mile, Edinburgh EH1 1PS.

WILLIAMS, Helen Mary, (Mrs D. M. Forrester); Under Secretary, Office of Science and Technology, Department of Trade and Industry (formerly Cabinet Office), since 1993; *b* 30 June 1950; *d* of Graham Myatt and Mary (*née* Harrison); *m* 1st, 1975, Ian Vaughan Williams (marr. diss. 1982); 2nd, 1993, David Michael Forrester, *qv*; one *s* one *d*. *Educ:* Allerton High Sch., Leeds; St Hilda's Coll., Oxford (BA Hons Mod. Hist.). Joined DES, 1972; Private Sec. to Joan Lester and to Margaret Jackson, 1975–76; Asst Sec., DES, subseq. DFE, 1984–93. *Recreations:* family life, walking, bell-ringing. *Address:* Office of Public Service and Science, Cabinet Office, Albany House, 84–86 Petty France, SW1H 9ST. *T:* 0171–271 2020.

WILLIAMS, Ven. Henry Leslie; Archdeacon of Chester, 1975–88; *b* 26 Dec. 1919; *m* 1949, Elsie Marie; one *s*. *Educ:* Bethesda Gram. Sch.; St David's Coll., Lampeter (BA); St Michael's Coll., Llandaff. Deacon 1943, priest 1944, Bangor; Curate of Aberdovey, 1943–45; St Mary's, Bangor, 1945–48; Chaplain, HMS Conway, 1948–49; Curate, St Mary-without-the-Walls, Chester, 1949–53; Vicar of Barnston, Wirral, 1953–84. RD of Wirral North, 1967–75; Hon. Canon of Chester Cathedral, 1972–75. Mem., General Synod, 1978–80, 1985–88. CF (TA), 1953–62. *Recreations:* fly-fishing, bee-keeping, grandparenthood. *Address:* 1 Bartholomew Way, Westminster Park, Chester CH4 7RJ. *T:* Chester (01244) 675296.

WILLIAMS, Sir (Henry) Sydney, Kt 1983; OBE 1978; company director; *b* 10 Jan. 1920; *s* of Edward Stratten Williams and Zilla Williams (*née* McHugh); *m* 1940, Joyce Veronica Meldon; four *s*. *Educ:* Mt Carmel Coll., Charters Towers, Qld, Aust. Served 7th Aust. Div. Cavalry Regt, ME and PNG, 1940–45; 51st Inf. Bn (Far North Qld Regt), 1947–57, Lt-Col Comd 1954–57. Chm., Air Queensland Ltd (formerly Bush Pilots Airways Ltd), 1960–86; Chairman: Willtrac Pty Ltd, 1964–; Lizard Island Pty Ltd, 1970–86; Director: Carlton & United Breweries (NQ) Ltd, 1964–90; Placer Pacific Ltd, 1986–90. Member: Queensland Art Gall., 1981–; Cairns Port Authority, 1982–; Life Mem., Cairns RSSAILA; Trustee, WWF, 1981–; Councillor, Enterprise Australia, 1980–; Pres., Far North Queensland Amateur Turf Club, 1959–; past Dep. Chm., Australian Tourist Commn; past Pres., Cairns Legacy Club. Hon. Col, 51st Infantry Bn (Far North Qld Regt), 1987–; Patron, Light Horse Assoc. Ltd, Qld, 1989–93. *Recreations:* fishing, bowls, golf. *Address:* 14 Bellevue Crescent, Edge Hill, Cairns, Qld 4870, Australia. *T:* (70) 531489. *Clubs:* North Queensland (Townsville), United Services, Brisbane (Brisbane).

See also Hon. Sir Edward Williams.

WILLIAMS, Hilary a'Beckett E.; *see* Eccles-Williams.

WILLIAMS, Hubert Glyn, AE 1944; a Recorder of the Crown Court, 1974–77; Senior Partner, Blake, Lapthorn, Rea & Williams, Solicitors, Portsmouth and District, 1973–83; *b* 18 Dec. 1912; *s* of John Christmas Williams and Florence Jane Williams (*née* Jones); *m* 1952, Audrey Elizabeth Righton; one *s* one *d*. *Educ:* Ruthin. Admitted solicitor, 1934 (2nd cl. Hons). Served War of 1939–45 (Sqdn Ldr; AE): AAF, 1939–41; RAFVR, 1941–45; UK, Egypt, E Africa, Palestine. Pres., Hampshire Inc. Law Soc., 1977–78. *Recreation:* cricket. *Address:* 29 The Avenue, Alverstoke, Gosport, Hants PO12 2JS. *T:* Gosport (01705) 583058. *Club:* MCC.

WILLIAMS, Hugo Mordaunt; writer; *b* 20 Feb. 1942; *s* of Hugh Williams, actor and playwright, and late Margaret Vyner; *m* 1965, Hermine Demoriane; one *d*. *Educ:* Eton College. Asst Editor, London Magazine, 1961–70; television critic, 1983–88, and poetry editor, 1984–93, New Statesman; theatre critic, The Sunday Correspondent, 1989–91; columnist, TLS, 1988–; film critic, Harpers & Queen, 1993–. Henfield Writer's Fellowship, Univ. of East Anglia, 1981. Awards (for poetry): Eric Gregory, 1965; Cholmondeley, 1970; Geoffrey Faber Memorial Prize, 1979. *Publications: poems:* Symptoms of Loss, 1965; Sugar Daddy, 1970; Some Sweet Day, 1975; Love-Life, 1979; Writing Home, 1985; Selected Poems, 1989; Self-Portrait With A Slide, 1990; Dock Leaves, 1994; *travel:* All the Time in the World, 1966; No Particular Place to Go, 1981; *journalism:* Freelancing, 1995. *Address:* 3 Raleigh Street, N1 8NW. *T:* 0171–226 1655.

WILLIAMS, Ian Malcolm Gordon, CBE 1960 (OBE 1954; MBE 1945); *b* 7 May 1914; *s* of late Thomas and Mabel Williams. *Educ:* Tatterford Sch., Norfolk; Leeds Univ.; Gonville and Caius Coll., Cambridge. President, Leeds University Students' Union, 1939. Volunteered Military Service, Sept. 1939; Officer Cadet, 123 OCTU; Commnd Royal Regt of Artillery, March 1940; NW Frontier of India and Burma, 1940–45, as Major, RA, and Mountain Artillery, Indian Army (despatches, MBE). Staff Officer, Hong Kong Planning Unit, 1946; Adjutant, Hong Kong Defence Force, 1946. Entered Colonial Administrative Service, 1946; was District Officer and Asst Colonial Secretary, Hong Kong, 1946–49; at Colonial Office, 1949–51; Senior Asst Secretary, Secretariat, Cyprus, 1951–53; Commissioner: of Paphos, 1953–55, of Larnaca, 1955–57, of Limassol, 1957–60; Chief Officer, Sovereign Base Areas of Akrotiri and Dhekelia, 1960–64; Member Administrator's Advisory Board; UK Chairman, Joint Consultative Board, 1960–64; Min. of Technology, 1965–67; DoE, 1967–71; Programme Dir, UN/Thai Programme for Drug Abuse Control in Thailand, 1972–79. Comdr, Most Noble Order of the Crown of Thailand, 1981. *Recreations:* art, Cypriot archæology, swimming. *Address:* White House, Adderbury, near Banbury, Oxfordshire OX17 3NL. *Club:* East India, Devonshire, Sports and Public Schools.

WILLIAMS, Prof. James Gordon, FRS 1994; FEng 1982; Professor and Head of Department of Mechanical Engineering, Imperial College, London, since 1990; *b* 13 June 1938; *s* of John William and Eira Williams; *m* 1960, Ann Marie Joscelyne; two *s* one *d*. *Educ:* Imperial Coll. (BScEng, PhD, DScEng); FCGI. RAE, Farnborough, 1956–61; Imperial College: Asst Lectr, 1962–64; Lectr, 1964–70; Reader, 1970–75; Prof. of Polymer Engrg, 1975–90. *Publications:* Stress Analysis of Polymers, 1973, 2nd edn 1981; Fracture Mechanics of Polymers, 1984. *Recreations:* gardening, mountains (walking and ski-ing), golf. *Address:* Mechanical Engineering Department, Imperial College, Exhibition Road, South Kensington, SW7 2BX. *T:* 0171–594 7000.

WILLIAMS, Jennifer Mary; Head, Railways Privatisation Directorate, since 1993; *b* 26 Sept. 1948; *d* of Baron Donaldson of Lymington, *qv* and Dame Mary Donaldson, *qv*; *m* 1970, Michael Lodwig Williams, *qv*; three *s*. *Educ:* New Hall, Cambridge (BA 1953; MA 1970). Joined Home Office, 1973; Dir, PSA Privatisation and Strategy, 1990–93. Non-exec. Dir, Morley Coll. *Address:* Department of Transport, 76 Marsham Street, SW1P 4DR.

WILLIAMS, John, AO 1987; OBE 1980; guitarist; *b* Melbourne, 24 April 1941. Studied with father, Segovia and at the Accademia Musicale Chigiana, Siena and RCM, London; since when has given many recitals, concerts, made TV and radio appearances worldwide, and recordings of both solo guitar, and chamber and orchestral music. Mem., Sky, 1979–84. Artistic Dir, South Bank Summer Music, 1984 and 1985; Artistic Dir, Melbourne Arts Fest., 1987; formed ATTACCA, for performance of specially commissioned contemp. music, tour of UK and Australia, 1992. Recordings include Vivaldi concerts, Iberia, and The Seville Concert. Hon. FRCM; Hon. FRNCM. *Recreations:* people, living, chess, table-tennis, music. *Address:* c/o Harold Holt Ltd, 31 Sinclair Road, W14 0NS.

WILLIAMS, John Brinley, OBE 1988; FCIT; Managing Director, Associated British Ports (formerly British Transport Docks Board), 1985–89 (Board Member, 1980–89; Joint Managing Director, 1982–85); *b* 18 Aug. 1927; *s* of late Leslie Williams and Alice Maud Williams; *m* 1951, Eileen (*née* Court) one *s* one *d*. *Educ:* Eveswell Sch., Newport. Asst Manager, Cardiff Docks, 1963–65; Commercial and Development Asst to Chief Docks Manager, South Wales Ports, 1965–67; Docks Manager: Cardiff and Penarth Docks, 1968–72; Hull Docks, 1972–75; Port Director: South Wales Ports, 1976–78; Southampton, 1978–82. *Recreations:* Rugby, open air pursuits. *Address:* 34 Marine Drive, Barry, S Glamorgan CF6 6QP. *T:* Barry (01446) 737477.

WILLIAMS, (John Bucknall) Kingsley; solicitor; *b* 28 July 1927; *s* of Charles Kingsley Williams and Margaret Elizabeth (*née* Bucknall); *m* 1961, Brenda (*née* Baldwin); two *s*. *Educ:* Kingswood Sch., Bath; Trinity Hall, Cambridge (MA, LLB). Partner, Dutton Gregory & Williams, Solicitors, Winchester, 1956–91. Chm., Wessex RHA, 1975–82. Member: Winchester City Council, 1966–73; Hampshire CC, 1973–75; Assoc. of County Councils, 1973–75. Chairman: Exec. Cttee, NHS Supply Council, 1980–82; Adv. Cttee, Wessex Inst. of Public Health Medicine, 1991–. Vice-Chm., Council, Southampton Univ., 1976–87, Chm., 1987–; Chm. of Governors, Winchester Sch. of Art, 1986–. *Address:* Danesacre, Worthy Road, Winchester, Hants SO23 7AD. *T:* Winchester (01962) 852594, *Fax:* Winchester (01962) 869883.

WILLIAMS, Ven. John Charles; Archdeacon of Worcester, 1975–80, now Archdeacon Emeritus; Residentiary Canon of Worcester Cathedral, 1975–80; *b* 17 July 1912; *s* of William and Edith Williams; *m* 1940, Agnes Mildred Hutchings, MA; one *s* one *d*. *Educ:* Cowbridge Sch.; St David's University Coll., Lampeter; University College, Oxford. Asst Curate, Christ Church, Summerfield, Birmingham, 1937–39; Asst Curate, Hales Owen, in charge of St Margaret's, Hasbury, 1939–43; Vicar: Cradley Heath, Staffs, 1943–48; Redditch, Worcs, 1948–59. Surrogate, 1951–71; Rural Dean of Bromsgrove, 1958–59; Rector, Hales Owen, 1959–70; Archdeacon of Dudley, 1968–75; Vicar of Dodderhill, 1970–75. Hon. Canon, Worcester Cathedral, 1965–75; Examng Chaplain to Bishop of Worcester, 1969–80; Dir, Worcester Diocesan Central Services, 1974–75; Director of Ordination Candidates, 1975–79. Substitute Chaplain, HM Prison Long Lartin, Evesham, 1982–87. *Publication:* One Hundred Years, 1847–1947; A History of Cradley Heath Parish. *Recreations:* history of architecture, sailing. *Address:* The Old Vicarage, Norton with Lenchwick, Evesham, Worcs WR11 4TL. *Clubs:* Oxford University Occasionals, United Oxford & Cambridge University.

WILLIAMS, John Charles, PhD; FEng 1990; FIEE; Secretary and Chief Executive, Institution of Electrical Engineers, since 1989; *b* 17 July 1938; *s* of Frank and Miriam Williams; *m* 1968, Susan Winifred Ellis; one *s* one *d*. *Educ:* High Wycombe Royal GS; Queen Mary Coll. (BScEng (1st Cl. Hons), 1960; PhD 1964; Fellow, 1995). Philips Research Labs, 1964–78; GEC Marconi Space and Defence Systems, Stanmore, 1978–80; GEC Central Res. Labs, Wembley, 1980–82; GEC Marconi Res. Centre, Gt Baddow, 1982–88. *Recreations:* traditional jazz, contract bridge, walking his dog, gardening, listening to his family play classical music. *Address:* c/o Institution of Electrical Engineers, Savoy Place, WC2R 0BL. *T:* 0171–240 1871.

WILLIAMS, John Eirwyn F.; *see* Ffowcs Williams.

WILLIAMS, Prof. John Ellis Caerwyn, FBA 1978; FSA; Professor of Irish, University College of Wales, Aberystwyth, 1965–79, now Professor Emeritus; Director of Centre for Advanced Welsh and Celtic Studies, Aberystwyth, 1978–85; *b* 17 Jan. 1912; *s* of John R. Williams and Maria Williams; *m* 1946, Gwen Watkins. *Educ:* Ystalyfera Int. County Sch.; University Coll. of N Wales, Bangor (BA Hons: Latin 1933, Welsh 1934; MA); Nat. Univ. of Ireland, Dublin; TCD; United Theol Coll., Aberystwyth (BD 1944); Theol Coll., Bala. Research Lectr, UC of N Wales, Bangor, 1937–39; Fellow, Univ. of Wales, 1939–41; Lectr, 1945–51, Sen. Lectr, 1951–53, Prof. of Welsh, 1953–65, UC of N Wales. Leverhulme Fellow, 1963–64; Vis. Prof. Celtic, UCLA, 1968; Summer Sch., Harvard, 1968; Lectures: O'Donnell, in Celtic Studies, Oxford Univ., 1979–80; Dr Daniel Williams, Aberystwyth, 1983; Sir John Morris Jones, Oxford, 1983; R. T. Jenkins, Bangor, 1983. Pres., Welsh Acad., 1989– (Chm., 1965–75); Mem., Council for Name Studies in GB and Ireland, 1965–. Cons. Editor, Univ. of Wales Welsh Dict. Fasc. xxiii–; Chm., Editorial Cttee, Welsh Acad. Dict., 1976–; Editor: Y Traethodydd, 1965–; Ysgrifau Beirniadol, i–xix; Studia Celtica, i–xxvii; Llên y Llenor, 1983–; Llyfryddiaeth yr Iaith Gymraeg, 1988; Cerddi Waldo Williams, 1992. FSA 1975; Hon. MRIA 1990; Hon. DLitt: Celt., Univ. of Ireland, 1967; Univ. of Wales, 1983. Derek Allen Prize, British Acad., 1985. *Publications:* trans., Ystoriau ac Ysgrifau Pádraic Ó Conaire, 1947; trans., Yr Ebol Glas, 1954; Traddodiad Llenyddol Iwerddon, 1958; trans., Aderyn y Gwirionedd, 1961; Edward Jones, Maes-y-Plwm, 1963; ed, Llên a Llafar Môn, 1963; trans., I. Williams, Canu Taliesin (Poems of Taliesin), 1968; The Court Poet in Medieval Ireland, 1972; Y Storïwr Gwyddeleg a'i Chwedlau, 1972; Beirdd y Tywysogion—Arolwg 1970, in Llên Cymru, and separately 1972; ed, Literature in Celtic Countries, 1971; trans. Jakez Riou, An Ti Satanazet (Diawl yn y Tŷ), 1972; Canu Crefyddol y Gogynfeirdd (Darlith Goffa Henry Lewis), 1976; The Poets of the Welsh Princes, 1978, 2nd edn 1994; Cerddi'r Gogynfeirdd i Wragedd a Merched, 1979; (with Máirín Ní Mhuiríosa) Traidisiún Liteartha Na nGael, 1979; Geiriadurwyr y Gymraeg yng nghyfnod y Dadeni, 1983; Y Bardd Celtaidd, 1991; (with Patrick Ford) The Irish Literary Tradition, 1992; contribs to Encyclopaedia Britannica, Princeton Encyclopedia of Poetry and Poetics, Bull. Bd of Celt. Studies, Celtica, Études Celt., Llên Cymru, Proc. of British Acad., etc. *Recreation:* walking. *Address:* Centre for Advanced Welsh and Celtic Studies, National Library of Wales, Aberystwyth SY23 3HH. *T:* Aberystwyth (01970) 626717; Iwerydd, 6 Pant-y-Rhos, Aberystwyth, Dyfed SY23 3QE. *T:* Aberystwyth (01970) 612959.

WILLIAMS, Prof. John Eryl Hall; Professor Emeritus of Criminology with Special Reference to Penology, London School of Economics, University of London; *b* 21 Sept. 1921; *s* of late Edward Hall Williams and Kitty Hall Williams; *m* 1951, Constance Mary Evans. *Educ:* Barry County Sch.; University Coll. of Wales, Aberystwyth (LLB 1942, LLM 1953). Called to the Bar, Middle Temple, 1949. Lectr, Dept of Law, University Coll. of Hull, 1946–50; LSE: Lectr, Law Dept, 1950–59; Reader in Criminology, 1959; Prof. of Criminology with Special Reference to Penology, 1984–86. Vis. Associate Prof., NY Univ. Sch. of Law, 1955–56; Senior Fellow and Vis. Lectr, Yale Law Sch., 1965–66. Mem., Parole Bd, 1970–72, 1976–78. Pres., British Soc. of Criminology, 1970–72; Sec.-Gen., Internat. Soc. for Criminology, 1974–79, Vice-Pres., 1985–94; Mem., Criminological Scientific Council, Council of Europe, 1985–89. Hon. LLD JFK Univ., Calif., 1981. Jt Editor, British Jl of Criminology, 1966–79. *Publications:* The English Penal

System in Transition, 1970; Changing Prisons, 1975; (with L. H. Leigh) The Management of the Prosecution Process in Denmark, Sweden and The Netherlands, 1981; Criminology and Criminal Justice, 1982; (ed) The Role of the Prosecutor, 1988; (ed jtly) Punishment, Custody and the Community: reflections and comments on the Green Paper, 1989; A Page of History in Relief, 1993. *Recreations:* landscape painting, foreign travel. *Address:* Law Department, London School of Economics and Political Science, Houghton Street, Aldwych, WC2A 2AE. *T:* 0171–405 7686.

See also R. H. Williams.

WILLIAMS, John Griffith; QC 1985; a Recorder of the Crown Court, since 1984; *b* 20 Dec. 1944; *s* of Griffith John Williams, TD and Alison Williams; *m* 1971, Mair Tasker Watkins, *d* of Rt Hon. Sir Tasker Watkins, *qv;* two *d. Educ:* King's School, Bruton; The Queen's College, Oxford (MA). Served 4th Bn, RWF (TA), 1965–68; Welsh Volunteers (TAVR), 1968–71 (Lieut). Called to the Bar, Gray's Inn, 1968, Bencher, 1994. Mem., Bar Council, 1990–93; Treas., Wales and Chester Circuit, 1993–. Asst Comr, Boundary Commn for Wales, 1994–. *Recreation:* golf. *Address:* 144 Pencisely Road, Llandaff, Cardiff CF5 1DR. *T:* Cardiff (01222) 562981. *Clubs:* Army and Navy; Cardiff and County (Cardiff); Royal Porthcawl Golf.

WILLIAMS, Rev. John Herbert, LVO 1989; Chaplain to the Royal Victorian Order and Chaplain of the Queen's Chapel of the Savoy, 1983–89; Chaplain to the Queen, 1988–89; *b* 15 Aug. 1919; *s* of Thomas and Mary Williams; *m* 1948, Joan Elizabeth (*née* Morgan); one *s Educ:* St David's Coll., Lampeter (BA Hons); Salisbury Theological Coll. Deacon 1943; priest 1944; Curate: Blaenavon (Gwent), 1943–46; Llanishen, Cardiff, 1946–48; Priest in Charge, Rogerstone (Gwent), 1948–51; Asst Chaplain, HM Prison, Manchester, 1951; Chaplain, HM Prison: Holloway, 1952; Birmingham, 1957; Wormwood Scrubs, 1964; South East Regional Chaplain, 1971; Deputy Chaplain General, Home Office Prison Dept, 1974–83; Priest-in-Ordinary to the Queen, 1980–83. *Recreations:* Rugby, classical music/opera, Francophile. *Address:* 75 Monks Drive, W3 0ED. *T:* 0181–992 5206. *Clubs:* Sion College, City Livery.

WILLIAMS, (John) Kyffin, OBE 1982; DL; RA 1974 (ARA 1970); *b* 9 May 1918; *s* of Henry Inglis Wynne Williams and Essyllt Mary Williams (*née* Williams). *Educ:* Shrewsbury Sch.; Slade Sch. of Art. Sen. Art Master, Highgate Sch., 1944–73. One-man shows: Leicester Galleries, 1951, 1953, 1956, 1960, 1966, 1970; Colnaghi Galleries, 1948, 1949, 1965, 1970; Thackeray Gall., biennially 1975–. Retrospective exhibn, Nat. Mus. of Wales, Mostyn Art Gall., Llandudno and Glynn Vivian Art Gall., Swansea, 1987. Pres., Royal Cambrian Acad., 1969–76 and 1992–. Winston Churchill Fellow, 1968; Hon. Fellow: University Coll. of Swansea, 1989; UCNW, 1991; UCW, Aberystwyth, 1992. DL Gwynedd 1985. Hon. MA Wales, 1973; Hon. DLitt Wales, 1993. Medal, Hon. Soc. of Cymmrodorion, 1991. *Publications:* Across the Straits (autobiog.), 1973; A Wider Sky (autobiog.), 1991. *Recreations:* the countryside, sport. *Address:* Pwllfanogl, Llanfairpwll, Gwynedd LL61 6PD. *T:* Llanfairpwll (01248) 714693.

WILLIAMS, John Leighton; QC 1986; a Recorder of the Crown Court, since 1985; *b* 15 Aug. 1941; *s* of Reginald John Williams and Beatrice Beynon; *m* 1969, Sally Elizabeth Williams; two *s. Educ:* Neath Boys' Grammar School; King's College London (LLB); Trinity Hall, Cambridge (MA). Called to the Bar, Gray's Inn, 1964. Mem., Criminal Injuries Compensation Bd, 1987–. *Address:* Farrar's Building, Temple, EC4Y 7BD. *T:* 0171–583 9241.

WILLIAMS, John Melville; QC 1977; a Recorder, 1986–94; *b* 20 June 1931; *o s* of late Baron Francis-Williams and late Lady (Jessie Melville) Francis-Williams; *m* 1955, Jean Margaret, *d* of Harold and Hilda Lucas, Huddersfield; three *s* one *d. Educ:* St Christopher Sch., Letchworth; St John's Coll., Cambridge (BA). Called to the Bar, Inner Temple, 1955, Bencher, 1985. A legal assessor to GMC; first Pres., Assoc. of Personal Injury Lawyers, 1990–94; Co-Chm., Internat. Practice Sect., Assoc. of Trial Lawyers of Amer., 1991–92; Mem., Indep. Review Body Under New Colliery Review Procedure, 1985–. *Recreations:* mountain scrambling and walking (including climbing Munros), mountain and bird photography. *Address:* Deers Hill, Sutton Abinger, near Dorking, Surrey RH5 6PS. *T:* Dorking (01306) 730331, *Fax:* (01306) 730913; Cnoclochan, Scourie, by Lairg, Sutherland IV27 4TF; Old Square Chambers, 1 Verulam Buildings, Gray's Inn, WC1R 5LQ. *T:* 0171–831 0801, *Fax:* 0171–405 1387. *Club:* Holmbury St Mary Village.

WILLIAMS, John M(eredith), CBE 1988; Chairman, Welsh Development Agency, 1982–88; *b* 20 Oct. 1926; *s* of Gwynne Evan Owen Williams and Cicely Mary Innes; *m* 1953, Jean Constance (*née* Emerson); two *d. Educ:* Sherborne Sch., Dorset; Trinity Hall, Cambridge. Dir, BOC Gp, 1969–78; Chm., Newman Industries Ltd, 1980–82; Director: Stone-Platt Industries Ltd, 1981–82; Harland and Wolff Ltd, 1982–89. Mem., Milk Marketing Bd, 1984–94. *Address:* 95 Hurlingham Court, Ranelagh Gardens, SW6 3UR. *T:* 0171–731 0686; Victuals Grove, St Briavels, Lydney, Glos GL15 6RW. *T:* Dean (01594) 530494. *Clubs:* Hurlingham, Himalayan.

See also Sir D. I. Williams, Sir R. E. O. Williams.

WILLIAMS, Rt. Rev. Monsignor John Noctor, CBE 1989; Prelate of Honour, 1985; Principal Roman Catholic Chaplain (Army), 1985–89, retired; Vicar General, 1986; *b* 9 Aug. 1931; *s* of Thomas Williams and Anne Williams (*née* Noctor). *Educ:* St Anselm's Grammar School, Birkenhead; Ushaw College, Durham. Curate: St Laurence's, Birkenhead, 1956; St Joseph's, Sale, 1958; Sacred Heart, Moreton, 1958; Our Lady's, Birkenhead, 1959–66. Army, Chaplains' Dept, 1966; 7 Armd Bde, 1966; Singapore, 1969; 6 Armd Bde, 1971; UN, Cyprus, 1972; Senior Chaplain: Hong Kong, 1976; 1 Div., 1978; N Ireland, 1980; HQ BAOR, 1982; SE District, 1984. *Recreations:* bridge, golf, motoring. *Address:* St Michaels, Scotland Street, Ellesmere, Shropshire SY12 0ED. *Clubs:* Sandiway Golf, Worplesdon Golf, Delamere Forest Golf.

WILLIAMS, John Peter Rhys, MBE 1977; FRCSEd; Consultant in Trauma and Orthopaedic Surgery, Princess of Wales Hospital, Bridgend, since 1986; *b* 2 March 1949; *s* of Peter Williams, MB, BCh and Margaret Williams, MB, BCh; *m* 1973, Priscilla Parkin, MB, BS, DObst, RCOG, DA; one *s*; three *d. Educ:* Bridgend Grammar School; Millfield; St Mary's Hosp. Med. School. MB, BS London 1973; LRCP, MRCS, 1973; Primary FRCS 1976; FRCSEd 1980. University Hosp., Cardiff, Battle Hosp., Reading, St Mary's Hosp., London, 1973–78; Surgical Registrar, 1978–80, Orthopaedic Registrar, 1980–82, Cardiff Gp of Hosps; Sen. Orthopaedic Registrar, St Mary's Hosp., London, 1982–86. Played Rugby for Bridgend, 1967–68, 1976–79 (Captain, 1978–79), 1980–81, for London Welsh, 1968–76; 1st cap for Wales, 1969 (Captain, 1978); British Lions tours, 1971, 1974; a record 55 caps for Wales, to 1981; won Wimbledon Lawn Tennis Junior Championship, 1966. *Publication:* JPR (autobiog.), 1979. *Recreations:* sport and music. *Address:* Llansannor Lodge, Llansannor, near Cowbridge, South Glamorgan CF7 7RX. *Clubs:* Wig and Pen; Lord's Taverners.

WILLIAMS, Sir John (Robert), KCMG 1982 (CMG 1973); HM Diplomatic Service, retired; Chairman, Board of Governors, Commonwealth Institute, 1984–87; *b* 15 Sept. 1922; *s* of late Sydney James Williams, Salisbury; *m* 1958, Helga Elizabeth, *d* of Frederick Konow Lund, Bergen; two *s* two *d. Educ:* Sheen County School; Fitzwilliam House, Cambridge (Hon. Fellow 1984). Served War of 1939–45, with 1st Bn King's African Rifles in East Africa and Burma Campaign (Captain). Joined Colonial Office as Asst Principal, 1949; First Secretary, UK High Commission, New Delhi, 1956; Commonwealth Relations Office, 1958; Deputy High Commissioner in North Malaya, 1959–63; Counsellor, New Delhi, 1963–66; Commonwealth Office, 1966; Private Sec. to Commonwealth Secretary, 1967; Diplomatic Service Inspectorate, 1968; High Comr, Suva, 1970–74; Minister, Lagos, 1974–79 and concurrently Ambassador (non-resident) to Benin, 1976–79; Asst. Under-Sec. of State, FCO, 1979; High Comr in Kenya, 1979–82; Perm. British Rep. to UN Environment Prog. and to UN Centre for Human Settlements, 1979–82. Mem. Gen. Council, Royal Over-Seas League, 1983–87 (Vice Pres., 1995). Chm., Salisbury and S Wilts Museum, 1989–95. *Recreations:* music, gardening. *Address:* Eton House, Hanging Langford, Salisbury SP3 4NN. *Club:* United Oxford & Cambridge University.

WILLIAMS, John Towner; composer of film scores; *b* 8 Feb. 1932. *Educ:* Juilliard Sch., NY. Conductor, Boston Pops Orchestra, 1980–84. Hon. DMus: Berklee Coll. of Music, Boston, 1980; St Anselm Coll., Manchester, NH, 1981; Boston Conservatory of Music, 1982; Hon. DHL S Carolina, 1981; Hon. Dr of Fine Arts Northeastern Univ. (Boston), 1981; Hon. DMus, William Woods Coll., USA, 1982. Awards include Oscars for: Fiddler on the Roof (filmscore arrangement), 1971; Jaws, 1976; Star Wars, 1978; E.T., 1983; 14 Grammies, 2 Emmys and many other awards; 16 Academy Award nominations. *Composer of film scores:* The Secret Ways, 1961; Diamond Head, 1962; None but the Brave, 1965; How to Steal a Million, 1966; Valley of the Dolls, 1967; The Cowboys, 1972; The Poseidon Adventure, 1972; Tom Sawyer, 1973; Earthquake, 1974; The Towering Inferno, 1974; Jaws, 1975; Jaws 2, 1976; The Eiger Sanction, 1975; Family Plot, 1976; Midway, 1976; The Missouri Breaks, 1976; Raggedy Ann and Andy, 1977; Black Sunday, 1977; Star Wars, 1977; Close Encounters of the 3rd Kind, 1977; The Fury, 1978; Superman, 1978; Dracula, 1979; The Empire Strikes Back, 1980; Raiders of the Lost Ark, 1981; E. T. (The Extra Terrestial), 1982; Return of the Jedi, 1983; Indiana Jones and the Temple of Doom, 1984; Empire of the Sun, 1988; Jurassic Park, 1993; Schindler's List, 1994; many TV films. *Address:* 20th Century Fox, Music Department, PO Box 900, Beverly Hills, CA 90213, USA.

WILLIAMS, Rev. John Tudno, PhD; Professor of Biblical Studies, United Theological College, Aberystwyth, since 1973; Moderator of the Free Church Federal Council, March 1990–91; *b* 31 Dec. 1938; *s* of late Rev. Arthur Tudno Williams and Primrose (*née* Hughes Parry); *m* 1964, Ina Lloyd-Evans; one *s* one *d. Educ:* Liverpool Inst. High School; Colfe's GS, Lewisham; Jesus Coll., Oxford (MA); UCW, Aberystwyth (PhD); United Theol Coll., Aberystwyth. Ordained as Welsh Presbyterian Minister, 1963; Minister in Borth, Cards, 1963–73; Part-time Lecturer: United Theol Coll., 1966–73; UCW (Religious Studies), 1976–87; Tutor responsible for Religious Studies, external degree through medium of Welsh, UCW, 1984–; Dean, Aberystwyth and Lampeter Sch. of Theology, 1985–87, 1994–. Secretary: Theology Section, Univ. of Wales Guild of Graduates, 1967–; Educn Cttee, Gen. Assembly of Presbyterian Church of Wales, 1979–; Bd of Trustees, Davies Lecture, 1983– (Lectr, 1993). External examnr, QUB; examiner in religious studies and member of various educn cttees. Mem., Aberystwyth Town Council, 1979–87. *Publications:* Cewri'r Ffydd (Heroes of the Faith), 1974, 2nd edn 1979; Problem Dioddefaint a Llyfr Job (The Problem of Suffering and the Book of Job), 1980; Yr Epistol Cyntaf at y Corinthiaid (Commentary on I Corinthians), 1991; contrib. to: Studia Biblica, 1978, Vol. ii 1980; C. H. Dodd, The Centenary Lectures, 1985; articles in Welsh jls. *Recreations:* music (singing), Welsh language and culture. *Address:* United Theological College, Aberystwyth, Dyfed SY23 2LT. *T:* Aberystwyth (01970) 624574. *Club:* Penn.

WILLIAMS, Jonathan R.; *see* Rees-Williams.

WILLIAMS, Dame Judi; *see* Dench, Dame J. O.

WILLIAMS, Kevin Raymond; Managing Director, Parcelforce, since 1993; *b* 14 May 1948; *s* of Kenneth Williams and Betty (*née* Haskell); *m* 1972, Shionagh Mary Gee; two *s* one *d. Educ:* St Bartholomew's Grammar Sch., Newbury; Exeter Univ. (BA Hons). Head Postmaster: Aldershot, 1982–85; Portsmouth, 1985–86; Dist Head Postmaster, City of London, 1986–88; Royal Mail: Dir, Employee Relns, 1988–90; Dir, Business Develt, 1990–92; Ops Dir, 1992–93. *Recreations:* cricket, travel, gardening, European twinning movement, supporting Aldershot Town FC. *Club:* Headley Cricket.

WILLIAMS, Kingsley; *see* Williams, J. B. K.

WILLIAMS, Kyffin; *see* Williams, John K.

WILLIAMS, Sir Lawrence (Hugh), 9th Bt *cr* 1798, of Bodelwyddan, Flintshire; farmer; *b* 25 Aug. 1929; *s* of Col Lawrence Williams, OBE, DL (*d* 1958) (*gs* of 1st Bt), and his 2nd wife, Elinor Henrietta (*d* 1980), *d* of Sir William Williams, 4th Bt of Bodelwyddan; *S* half-brother, 1995; *m* 1952, Sara Margaret Helen, 3rd *d* of Sir Harry Platt, 1st Bt; two *d. Educ:* Royal Naval Coll., Dartmouth. Commnd Royal Marines, 1947; served Korea 1951, Cyprus 1955, Near East 1956; Captain, 1959, retired 1964. Chm., Parciau Caravans Ltd, 1964–. Underwriting Mem., Lloyds, 1977–. Lieut Comdr, RNXS, 1965–87. High Sheriff, Anglesey, 1970. *Recreations:* enjoying all aspects of country life, gentle sailing. *Heir:* none. *Address:* Old Parciau, Marianglas, Anglesey LL73 8PH. *Clubs:* Army and Navy; Royal Naval Sailing Association.

WILLIAMS, Sir Leonard, KBE 1981; CB 1975; Director-General for Energy, Commission of the European Communities, 1976–81; *b* 19 Sept. 1919; *m* Anne Taylor Witherley; three *d. Educ:* St Olave's Grammar Sch.; King's Coll., London. Inland Revenue, 1938. War Service (RA), 1940–47. Ministry of Defence, 1948; NATO, 1951–54; Min. of Supply (later Aviation), 1954; Min. of Technology (later DTI), 1964; IDC 1966; Dep. Sec., 1973; Dept of Energy, 1974–76. *Address:* Blue Vines, Bramshott Vale, Liphook, Hants GU30 7PZ.

WILLIAMS, Leonard Edmund Henry, CBE 1981; DFC 1944; President, Nationwide Anglia Building Society, 1989–92 (Chairman, 1987–88); *b* 6 Dec. 1919; *s* of William Edmund Williams; *m* 1946, Marie Harries-Jones; four *s* one *d. Educ:* Acton County Grammar School. FCA, FCIB, IPFA; FRSA; CIMgt. RAF, 1939–46. Acton Borough Council, 1935–39, Chief Internal Auditor 1946–49; Asst Accountant, Gas Council, 1949–53; Nationwide Building Society: Finance Officer, 1954–61; Dep. Gen. Man., 1961–67; Chief Exec., 1967–81; Dir, 1975–87; Chm., 1982–87. Director: Y. J. Lovell (Hldgs) plc, 1982–89; Peachey Property Corp. plc, 1982–88; Dep. Chm., BUPA Ltd, 1988–90 (Governor, 1982–88); Mem., Housing Corp., 1976–82. Chm., Building Socs Assoc., 1979–81 (Dep. Chm., 1977–79); Pres., Metrop. Assoc. of Building Socs, 1989–92 (Chm., 1972–73). Pres., Chartered Building Socs Inst., 1969–70. Hon. Life Mem., Internat. Union of Housing Finance Instns. *Publication:* Building Society Accounts, 1966. *Recreation:* reading. *Address:* The Romanys, Albury Road, Burwood Park, Walton-on-Thames, Surrey KT12 5DY. *T:* Walton-on-Thames (01932) 242758. *Clubs:* Royal Air Force, City Livery.

WILLIAMS, Ven. Leslie Arthur, MA; Archdeacon of Bristol, 1967–79; *b* 14 May 1909; *s* of Arthur and Susan Williams; *m* 1937, Margaret Mary, *d* of Richard Crocker; one *s* one *d*. *Educ:* Knutsford; Downing Coll., Cambridge. Curate of Holy Trinity, Bristol, 1934–37; Licensed to officiate, St Andrew the Great, Cambridge, 1937–40; Curate in Charge, St Peter, Lowden, Chippenham, 1940–42; Chaplain, RAFVR, 1942–46; Curate, Stoke Bishop, 1946–47; Vicar: Corsham, Wilts, 1947–53; Bishopston, Bristol, 1953–60; Stoke Bishop, Bristol, 1960–67. Rural Dean of Clifton, 1966–67; Hon. Canon of Bristol, 1958. *Recreation:* gardening. *Address:* St Monica Home, Westbury on Trym, Bristol BS9 3UN. *Clubs:* Hawks (Cambridge); Savage (Bristol).

WILLIAMS, Lyn; *see* Williams, D. W.

WILLIAMS, Martin John, CVO 1983; OBE 1979; HM Diplomatic Service; on secondment to Northern Ireland Office, since 1993; *b* 3 Nov. 1941; *s* of John Henry Stroud Williams and Barbara (*née* Benington); *m* 1964, Susan Dent; two *s*. *Educ:* Manchester Grammar Sch.; Corpus Christi Coll., Oxford (BA). Joined Commonwealth Relations Office, 1963; Private Sec. to Permanent Under Secretary, 1964; Manila, 1966; Milan, 1970; Civil Service College, 1972; FCO, 1973; Tehran, 1977; FCO, 1980; New Delhi, 1982; Rome, 1986; Hd of S Asian Dept, FCO, 1990. *Recreations:* music, gardening. *Address:* c/o Northern Ireland Office, Stormont House, Belfast BT4 3ST. *Club:* Commonwealth Trust.

WILLIAMS, Sir Max; *see* Williams, Sir W. M. H.

WILLIAMS, Dr Michael, FBA 1989; Reader in Geography, since 1990, Sir Walter Raleigh Fellow of Oriel College and Lecturer, St Anne's College, since 1978, Director, MSc course, Environmental Change Unit, since 1994, University of Oxford; *b* 24 June 1935; *s* of Benjamin Williams and Ethel (*née* Marshell); *m* 1955, Eleanore Lerch; two *d*. *Educ:* Emmanuel Grammar Sch.; Dynevor Grammar Sch., Swansea; Swansea UC (BA 1956; PhD 1960; DLitt 1991); St Catharine's Coll., Cambridge (DipEd 1960). Deptl Demonstrator in Geography, Swansea, 1957–60; University of Adelaide: Lectr in Geog., 1960–66; Sen. Lectr, 1966–69; Reader, 1970–77; Lectr in Geog., Oxford Univ., 1978–89. Visiting Professor: Univ. of Wisconsin-Madison, 1973 and 1994; Univ. of Chicago, 1989; UCLA, 1994; Vis. Lectr, UCL, 1966, 1973. Mem., State Commn on Uniform Regl Boundaries, SA, 1974–75; Chm., Histl Geog. Res. Gp, Inst. of British Geographers, 1983–86; Sec., Inst. of Aust. Geographers, 1969–72; Pres., SA Br., RGS, 1975–76 (Ed. of Procs, 1962–70). Mem. Council, British Acad., 1993– (Chm., Sect. N, Geog. and Social Anthropology, 1994–). Editor: Trans of Inst. of British Geographers, 1983–88; Progress in Human Geography, 1991–; Global Environmental Change, 1993–. John Lewis Gold Medal, RGS, SA, 1979; Lit. Prize, Adelaide Fest. of Arts, 1976; Hidy Award, Forest Hist. Soc., Durham, NC, 1987 (Hon. Fellow, 1990). *Publications:* South Australia from the Air, 1969; The Draining of the Somerset Levels, 1970; The Making of the South Australian Landscape, 1974; (ed jtly) Australian Space, Australian Time, 1975; The Changing Rural Landscape of South Australia, 1977, 2nd edn 1992; Americans and their Forests, 1989; (ed) Wetlands: a threatened landscape, 1991; (ed) Planet Management, 1992; edited vols of essays; contribs to geogl and histl jls. *Recreations:* walking, music. *Address:* Westgates, Vernon Avenue, Harcourt Hill, Oxford OX2 9AU. *T:* Oxford (01865) 243725.

WILLIAMS, Michael Edward John; Golf Correspondent, Daily Telegraph, since 1971; *b* 19 Oct. 1933; *s* of Edward Williams and Norah Marguerite Williams (*née* Skinner); *m* 1959, Judith Ann Sanderson; one *s* three *d*. *Educ:* Ipswich Sch. Sports reporter, E Anglian Daily Times, 1950–57; sports sub-ed., Evening Standard, 1957–59; news ed., Stratford Express (London), 1959–60; Sports sub-ed., Daily Telegraph, 1960–63; sports columnist, Sunday Telegraph, 1963–71. Chm., Assoc. of Golf Writers, 1987–92. Chelmsford Golf Club: Capt., 1968; Centenary Capt., 1993. Ed., Royal & Ancient Golfers' Handbook, 1993–. *Publications:* History of Golf, 1985; Grand Slam Golf, 1988; Official History of the Ryder Cup, 1989. *Recreations:* golf, snooker, bowls. *Address:* Fairlight, 45 Birch Lane, Stock, Ingatestone, Essex CM4 9NB. *Clubs:* Royal & Ancient (St Andrews), Chelmsford Golf; Old Ipswichians (Pres., 1991).

WILLIAMS, Rev. Canon Michael Joseph; Principal of the Northern Ordination Course, since 1989; *b* 26 Feb. 1942; *s* of James and Edith Williams; *m* 1971, Mary Miranda Bayley; one *s* one *d*. *Educ:* St John's College, Durham (BA in Philosophy 1968). Apprentice Mechanical Engineer, then Engineer, with W & T Avery, Birmingham, 1958–63 (HNC in Mech. Eng 1962). Deacon 1970, priest 1971; Curate, then Team Vicar, St Philemon, Toxteth, 1970–78; Director of Pastoral Studies, St John's Coll., Durham, 1978–88. Hon. Tutor in Pastoral Theology, Univ. of Manchester, 1990–. Hon. Canon, Liverpool Cathedral, 1992–. Pres., Northern Fedn for Trng in Ministry, 1991–93. *Publications:* The Power and the Kingdom, 1989; regular contribs to Anvil. *Address:* Luther King House, Brighton Grove, Rusholme, Manchester M14 5JP.

WILLIAMS, Michael Leonard; actor; Associate Artist, Royal Shakespeare Company, since 1966; *b* 9 July 1935; *s* of Michael Leonard Williams and Elizabeth (*née* Mulligan); *m* 1971, Judith Olivia Dench (*see* Dame Judi Dench); one *d*. *Educ:* St Edward's Coll., Liverpool; RADA (Coronation Scholar). Début, Nottingham Playhouse, 1959; London début, Celebration, Duchess Theatre, 1961; joined RSC, 1963; rôles include: Puck in A Midsummer Night Dream, Filch in The Beggar's Opera, Eichmann in The Representative, 1963; Oswald in King Lear (also NY), Pinch in The Comedy of Errors, Kokol in Marat/Sade, Lodowick in The Jew of Malta, 1964; Dromio of Syracuse in The Comedy of Errors, Guildenstern in Hamlet, Herald in Marat/Sade (also NY), 1965; Arthur in Tango, 1966; Petruchio in The Taming of the Shrew, Orlando in As You Like It, 1967; Fool in King Lear, Troilus in Troilus and Cressida, 1968; Charles Courtly in London Assurance, 1970; Bassanio in The Merchant of Venice, Ferdinand in The Duchess of Malfi, title rôle in Henry V, 1971; Mole in Toad of Toad Hall, 1972; Stellio in Content to Whisper, 1973; Private Meek in Too True to be Good, 1975; title rôle in Schweyk in the Second World War, Dromio in The Comedy of Errors (musical version), Autolycus in The Winter's Tale, Fool in King Lear, 1976; title rôle in national tour, Quartermaine's Terms, 1982; Bob in Pack of Lies, Lyric, 1983; George in Two Into One, Shaftesbury, 1984; Charles Pooter in Mr and Mrs Nobody, Garrick, 1986; George in Out of Order, Shaftesbury, 1990; *films* include: The Marat/Sade, 1966; Eagle in a Cage, 1969; Dead Cert, 1974; In Search of Alexander the Great, 1980; Enigma, 1981; Educating Rita, 1982; Henry V, 1990; *television* includes: Elizabeth R, 1971; A Raging Calm, The Hanged Man, 1974; My Son, My Son, 1978; Love in a Cold Climate, 1980; Quest of Eagles, 1980; A Fine Romance, 1980–81, 1982; Blunt, 1986; Double First, 1988; Angel Voices, 1989; Can you hear me thinking?, 1990; September Song, 1992–94; Conjugal Rites, 1993–94. Chm., Catholic Stage Guild, 1977–87. *Recreations:* family, pottering, gardening. *Address:* c/o Julian Belfrage Associates, 68 St James's Street, SW1A 1PH. *T:* 0171–491 4400. *Club:* Garrick.

WILLIAMS, Michael Lodwig; Deputy Director, Industry, HM Treasury; *b* 22 Jan. 1948; *s* of John and Eileen Williams; *m* 1970, Jennifer Mary Donaldson (*see* J. M. Williams); three *s*. *Educ:* Wycliffe Coll., Stonehouse, Glos; Trinity Hall, Cambridge (BA 1969; MA); Nuffield Coll., Oxford. Min. of Finance, Lusaka, Zambia, 1969–71; HM Treasury, 1973–: on secondment to Price Waterhouse, 1980–81; Under Sec., 1992. *Address:* HM Treasury, Parliament Street, SW1P 3AG. *T:* 0171–270 4449.

WILLIAMS, Prof. Michael Maurice Rudolph; consultant engineer; Professor of Nuclear Engineering, University of Michigan, 1987–89; Professor of Nuclear Engineering, 1970–86, now Emeritus, and Head of Department, 1980–86, Queen Mary College, London University; *b* 1 Dec. 1935; *s* of late M. F. Williams and G. M. A. Denton; *m* 1958, Ann Doreen Betty; one *s* one *d*. *Educ:* Ewell Castle Sch.; Croydon Polytechnic; King's Coll., London; Queen Mary Coll., London. BSc, PhD, DSc; CEng; Fellow, Instn Nuclear Engrs (Vice-Pres., 1971); FInstP. Engr with Central Electricity Generating Board, 1962; Research Associate at Brookhaven Nat. Lab., USA, 1962–63; Lectr, Dept of Physics, Univ. of Birmingham, 1963–65; Reader in Nuclear Engrg, Queen Mary Coll., London Univ., 1965–70. Mem., Adv. Cttee on Safety of Nuclear Installations, 1983–86. UN Advr on Engrg Educn in Argentina, 1979–89. Mem., Electrical Engrg Coll., EPSRC, 1995–. Chm. of Governors, Ewell Castle Sch., 1976–79; Mem., Academic Bd, RNC, Greenwich, 1975–86. Exec. Editor, Annals of Nuclear Energy. Fellow American Nuclear Soc. (Arthur Holly Compton Award, 1994). *Publications:* The Slowing Down and Thermalization of Neutrons, 1966; Mathematical Methods in Particle Transport Theory, 1971; Random Processes in Nuclear Reactors, 1974; Aerosol Science, 1991; contribs to Proc. Camb. Phil. Soc., Nucl. Science and Engrg, Jl Nuclear Energy, Jl Physics. *Address:* 2A Lytchgate Close, South Croydon, Surrey CR2 0DX.

WILLIAMS, Sir Michael O.; *see* Williams, Sir Osmond.

WILLIAMS, Nicholas James Donald; *b* 21 Oct. 1925; *s* of late Nicholas Thomas Williams and Daisy Eustace (*née* Hollow); *m* 1st, 1947, Dawn Vyvyan (*née* Hill); one *s* one *d*; 2nd, 1955, Sheila Mary (*née* Dalgety); two *s* one *d*. *Educ:* St Erbyn's Sch., Penzance; Rugby Sch. (Scholar). Admitted Solicitor 1949. Served Royal Marines, 1943–47 (Captain). Partner, Nicholas Williams & Co., Solicitors, London, 1950; Senior Partner, Surridge & Beecheno, Solicitors, Karachi, 1955; Burmah Oil Co. Ltd: Legal Adviser, 1961; Co-ordinator for Eastern ops, 1963; Dir, 1965; Asst Man. Dir, 1967; Man. Dir and Chief Exec., 1969–75; Man. Dir and Chief Exec., Don Engineering, 1977–84. Director: Flarebay Ltd, 1978–85; EBC Gp PLC, 1986–90; Ranvet Ltd, 1986–92. *Recreation:* sailing. *Address:* Purlieus Farmhouse, Ewen, Cirencester, Glos GL7 6BY. *Clubs:* Royal Ocean Racing; Royal Cornwall Yacht.

WILLIAMS, Nicholas John S.; *see* Sims-Williams.

WILLIAMS, Nigel Christopher Ransome, CMG 1985; HM Diplomatic Service; UK Permanent Representative to the Office of the United Nations and other international organisations, Geneva, since 1993; *b* 29 April 1937; *s* of Cecil Gwynne Ransome Williams and Corinne Belden (*née* Rudd). *Educ:* Merchant Taylors' Sch.; St John's Coll., Oxford. Joined Foreign Service and posted to Tokyo, 1961; FO, 1966; Private Secretary: to Minister of State, 1968; to Chancellor of Duchy of Lancaster, 1969; UK Mission to UN, New York, 1970; FCO, 1973; Counsellor (Economic), Tokyo, 1976; Cabinet Office, 1980; Hd of UN Dept, FCO, 1980–84; Minister, Bonn, 1985–88; Ambassador to Denmark, 1989–93. *Address:* c/o Foreign and Commonwealth Office, SW1A 2AH.

WILLIAMS, Noel Ignace B.; *see* Bond-Williams.

WILLIAMS, Norman; *see* Williams, R. N.

WILLIAMS, Sir Osmond, 2nd Bt, *cr* 1909; MC 1944; JP; *b* 22 April 1914; *s* of late Captain Osmond T. D. Williams, DSO, 2nd *s* of 1st Bt, and Lady Gladys Margaret Finch Hatton, *o d* of 13th Earl of Winchilsea; *S* grandfather, 1927; *m* 1947, Benita Mary, *yr d* of late G. Henry Booker, and late Mrs Michael Burn; two *d*. *Educ:* Eton; Freiburg Univ. Royal Scots Greys, 1935–37, and 1939–45; served Palestine, Africa, Italy and NW Europe. Chm., Quarry Tours Ltd (Llechwedd Slate Caverns), 1973–77. Vice-Chm., Amnesty Internat. (British Sect.), 1971–74. Trustee: Internat. Prisoners of Conscience Fund; Festiniog Rly Trust; Mem., Merioneth Park Planning Cttee, 1971–74. Governor, Rainer Foundn Outdoor Pursuits Centre, 1964–76. JP 1960 (Chairman of the Bench, Ardudwy-uwch-Artro, Gwynedd, 1974–84). Chevalier, Order of Leopold II with Palm; Croix de Guerre with Palm (Belgium), 1940. *Recreations:* music, travelling. *Heir:* none. *Address:* Borthwen, Penrhyndeudraeth, Gwynedd LL48 6EN. *Club:* Travellers'.

WILLIAMS, Owen Lenn; retired; Regional Financial and Development Adviser, St Vincent, West Indies, 1976–78; *b* 4 March 1914; *s* of Richard Owen Williams and Frances Daisy Williams (*née* Lenn); *m* 1959, Gisela Frucht (*d* 1991). *Educ:* St Albans Sch.; London University. Asst Principal, Export Credit Guarantee Dept, 1938; Asst Principal, Treasury, 1939; UK High Commn, Ottawa, 1941; Principal, Treasury, 1945; Asst Treasury Representative, UK High Commn, New Delhi, 1953; Treasury Rep., UK High Commn, Karachi, 1955; Economic and Financial Adviser, Leeward Islands, 1957; Perm. Sec., Min. of Finance, Eastern Nigeria, 1959; Asst Sec., Treasury, 1962; Counsellor, UK Delegn to OECD, 1968–73; Gen. Fiscal Adviser to Minister of Finance, Sierra Leone, 1974–75. *Recreations:* music, travel. *Address:* c/o National Westminster Bank, Stag Place, Victoria, SW1E 5NW. *Club:* Reform.

WILLIAMS, Paul Glyn; consultant, Hogg Robinson Career Services, since 1991; *b* 14 Nov. 1922; *s* of late Samuel O. Williams and Esmée I. Williams (*née* Cail); *m* 1947, Barbara Joan Hardy (marr. diss. 1964); two *d*; *m* 1964, Gillian Foote, *e d* of A. G. Howland Jackson, Elstead, Surrey, and of Mrs E. J. Foote and step *d* of late E. J. Foote, Estoril, Portugal; one *d*. *Educ:* Marlborough; Trinity Hall, Cambridge (MA). MP (C) Sunderland South, (C 1953–57, Ind. C 1957–58, C 1958–64). Chairman, Monday Club, 1964–69. Chm. and Man. Dir, Mount Charlotte Investments, 1966–77; Chm., Backer Electric Co., 1978–87. Director: First South African Cordage, 1947–54; Transair, 1955–62; Hodgkinson Partners Ltd, PR consultants, 1956–64; Minster Executive, 1977–83; Henry Sykes, 1980–83; consultant, P-E Internat. plc, 1983–91. FInstD; FIMgt. *Address:* 54 Bovingdon Road, SW6 2AP. *T:* 0171–731 2040. *Clubs:* Boodle's, Institute of Directors.

WILLIAMS, Paul H.; *see* Hodder-Williams.

WILLIAMS, Dr Paul Randall, FInstP; Chairman and Chief Executive, CCL, since 1995; *b* 21 March 1934; *s* of Fred and Eileen Westbrook Williams; *m* 1957, Marion Frances Lewis; one *s* one *d*. *Educ:* Baines' Grammar School; Loughborough College (BSc London external); Liverpool Univ. (PhD). DLC. ICI Research Fellow, Liverpool Univ., 1957; Research Physicist, British Nat. Bubble Chamber, 1958–62; Rutherford Lab., SRC, 1962–79 (Dep. Div. Head, Laser Div., 1976–79); Science and Engineering Research Council: Head, Astronomy, Space and Radio Div., 1979–81; Head, Engineering Div., 1981–83; Dep. Dir, 1983–87, Dir, 1987–94, Rutherford Appleton Lab.; Dir, Daresbury and Rutherford Appleton Lab., EPSRC, 1994–95. Chm., Abingdon Coll. Corp., 1993–. Local Preacher, Methodist Church. Glazebrook Medal, Inst. of Physics, 1994. *Recreations:* sailing, choral singing, ski-ing. *Address:* 5 Tatham Road, Abingdon, Oxon OX14 1QB. *T:* Abingdon (01235) 524654.

WILLIAMS, Penry Herbert; Fellow and Tutor in Modern History, New College, Oxford, 1964–92, now Emeritus Fellow; *b* 25 Feb. 1925; *s* of late Douglas Williams and Dorothy

Williams (*née* Murray); *m* 1952, June Carey Hobson (*d* 1991), *d* of late George and Kathleene Hobson; one *s* one *d*. *Educ:* Marlborough Coll.; New Coll., Oxford, 1947–50; St Antony's Coll., Oxford, 1950–51. MA, DPhil Oxon. Served Royal Artillery, 1943–45, Royal Indian Artillery, 1945–47. Asst Lecturer in History, 1951–54, Lectr, 1954–63, Sen. Lectr, 1963–64, Univ. of Manchester. Sexual Harrassment Officer and Dir, Graduate Studies, Faculty of Modern History, Univ. of Oxford, 1989–90. Fellow of Winchester Coll., 1978–93. Chairman: New Coll. Develt Cttee, 1992–; Thomas Wall Trust, 1995–. Jt Editor, English Historical Review, 1982–90. *Publications:* The Council in the Marches of Wales under Elizabeth I, 1958; Life in Tudor England, 1963; The Tudor Regime, 1979; (ed with John Buxton) New College, Oxford 1379–1979, 1979; The Later Tudors: England 1547–1603, 1995; contribs to learned jls. *Recreations:* hill-walking, travel, theatre. *Address:* New College, Oxford OX1 3BN; Green Corner, Wood Green, Witney, Oxon OX8 6DQ. *T:* Witney (01993) 702545.

WILLIAMS, Peter F.; *see* Firmston-Williams.

WILLIAMS, Peter Keegan, CMG 1992; HM Diplomatic Service; Ambassador to Socialist Republic of Vietnam, since 1990; *b* 3 April 1938; *s* of William Edward Williams and Lilian (*née* Spright); *m* 1969, Rosamund Mary de Worms; two *d*. *Educ:* Calday Grange Grammar Sch.; Collège de Marcq-en-Baroeul (Nord); Univ. de Lille; Pembroke Coll., Oxford (MA). Joined Diplomatic Service, 1962; language student, MECAS, Lebanon, 1962; Second Sec., Beirut, 1963, Jedda, 1964; Commonwealth Office, 1967; First Sec., FCO, 1969; Director, Policy and Reference Div., British Information Services, New York, 1970; First Sec., FCO, 1973; First Sec., Head of Chancery and Consul, Rabat, 1976 (Chargé d'Affaires, 1978 and 1979); Counsellor, GATT, UK Mission, Geneva, 1979–83 (Chm. Panel, USA/Canada, 1980–81; Chm., Cttee on Finance, 1981–83); Ambassador, People's Democratic Republic of Yemen, 1983–85; Hd of UN Dept, FCO, 1986–89; RCDS, 1989. *Recreations:* wine, walking. *Address:* c/o Foreign and Commonwealth Office, SW1A 2AH. *Clubs:* Travellers', United Oxford & Cambridge University.

WILLIAMS, Peter Michael, CBE 1992; PhD; Chief Executive, since 1985, Chairman, since 1991, Oxford Instruments Group plc (Managing Director, 1983–85); Chairman, Particle Physics and Astronomy Research Council, since 1994; *b* 22 March 1945; *s* of Cyril Lewis and Gladys Williams; *m* 1970, Jennifer Margaret Cox; one *s*. *Educ:* Hymers College, Hull; Trinity College, Cambridge. MA, PhD. Mullard Research Fellow, Selwyn College, Cambridge, 1969–70; Lectr, Dept of Chemical Engineering and Chemical Technology, Imperial College, 1970–75; VG Instruments Group, 1975–82 (Dep. Man. Dir, 1979–82); Oxford Instruments Group plc, 1982–. Mem., Council for Sci. and Technology, 1993–. Supernumerary Fellow, St John's Coll., Oxford, 1988–. Guardian Young Business Man of the Year, 1986. *Publications:* numerous contribs to jls relating to solid state physics. *Recreations:* ski-ing, gardening. *Address:* Yew Cottage, Old Boars Hill, Oxford OX1 5JJ. *T:* Oxford (01865) 739470.

WILLIAMS, Dr Peter Orchard, CBE 1991; FRCP; Director: The Wellcome Trust, 1965–91; Wellcome Institute for the History of Medicine, 1981–83; *b* 23 Sept. 1925; *s* of Robert Orchard Williams, CBE, and Agnes Annie Birkinshaw; *m* 1949, Billie Innes Brown; two *d*. *Educ:* Caterham Sch.; Queen's Royal College, Trinidad; St John's Coll., Cambridge (MA); St Mary's Hospital Medical School. MB, BChir 1950; MRCP 1952; FRCP 1970. House Physician, St Mary's Hospital, 1950–51; Registrar, Royal Free Hospital, 1951–52; Medical Specialist, RAMC, BMH Iserlohn, 1954; Medical Officer, Headquarters, MRC, 1955–60; Wellcome Trust: Asst and Dep. Scientific Secretary, 1960–64; Scientific Secretary, 1964–65. Vice-Pres., Royal Soc. of Tropical Med. and Hygiene, 1975–77, Pres., 1991–93; Member: Nat. Council of Soc. Services Cttee of Enquiry into Charity Law and Practice, 1974–76; BBC, IBA Central Appeals Adv. Cttee, 1978–83; DHSS Jt Planning Adv. Cttee, 1986–; Chairman: Foundations Forum, 1977–79; Assoc. of Med. Res. Charities, 1974–76, 1979–83; Hague Club (European Foundns), 1981–83. Hon. Vis. Fellow, Green Coll., Oxford, 1993. Hon. Fellow, LSHTM, 1986. Hon. DSc: Birmingham, 1989; West Indies, 1991; Glasgow, 1992; Hon. DM: Nottingham, 1990; Oxford, 1993. Mary Kingsley Medal for Services to Tropical Medicine, Liverpool Sch. of Trop. Med., 1983. *Publications:* Careers in Medicine, 1952; papers in scientific journals. *Recreations:* gardening, travel, golf. *Address:* 18 Beaufort Close, Lynden Gate, Putney, SW15 3TL.

WILLIAMS, Sir Peter W.; *see* Watkin Williams.

WILLIAMS, Sir Philip; *see* Williams, Sir R. P. N.

WILLIAMS, Raymond Lloyd, CBE 1987; DPhil, DSc; CChem, FRSC; Director, Metropolitan Police Laboratory, 1968–87; Visiting Professor in Chemistry, University of East Anglia, since 1968; *b* Bournemouth, 27 Feb. 1927; *s* of late Walter Raymond Williams and Vera Mary Williams; *m* 1956, Sylvia Mary Lawson Whitaker; one *s* one *d*. *Educ:* Bournemouth Sch.; St John's Coll., Oxford (schol.). Gibbs Univ. Schol. 1948, BA 1st Cl. Hons Nat Sci-Chem, MA, DPhil, DSc Oxon. Research Fellow, Pressed Steel Co., 1951–53; Commonwealth Fund Fellow, Univ. of California, Berkeley, 1953–54; progressively, Sen. Res. Fellow, Sen. Scientific Officer, Principal Sci. Officer, Explosives R&D Estab., 1955–60; PSO, Admiralty Materials Lab., 1960–62; Explosives R&D Establishment: SPSO, 1962; Supt, Analytical Services Gp, 1962–65; Supt, Non-metallic Materials Gp, 1965–68. External Examiner: Univ. of Strathclyde, 1983–85; KCL, 1986–88. Vis. Lectr, Univ. of Lausanne, 1989; Lectures: Theophilus Redwood, RSC, 1984; Schools, RSC, 1988; Public, RSC, 1990; Dalton, RSC, 1995. Jt Editor: Forensic Science International, 1978–; Forensic Science Progress, 1984–92. Pres., Forensic Science Soc., 1983–85; Hon. Mem., Assoc. of Police Surgeons of GB, 1980. Adelaide Medal, Internat. Assoc. of Forensic Scis, 1993. *Publications:* papers in scientific jls on spectroscopy, analytical chemistry, and forensic science. *Recreations:* lawn tennis (played for Civil Service and Oxfordshire: representative colours), squash rackets, carpentry. *Address:* 9 Meon Road, Bournemouth, Dorset BH7 6PN. *T:* Bournemouth (01202) 423446.

WILLIAMS, (Reginald) Norman, CB 1982; Assistant Registrar of Friendly Societies, 1984–93; *b* 23 Oct. 1917; *s* of Reginald Gardnar Williams and Janet Mary Williams; *m* 1956, Hilary Frances West; two *s*. *Educ:* Neath Grammar Sch.; Swansea Univ. Served War: Captain RA and later Staff Captain HQ 30 Corps, 1940–46. Solicitor in private practice, 1947–48. Dept of Health and Social Security (formerly Min. of Nat. Insurance): Legal Asst, 1948; Sen. Legal Asst, 1959; Asst Solicitor, 1966; Principal Asst Solicitor, 1974; Under Sec., 1977–82. Member of Law Society. *Recreations:* golf, photography, reading. *Address:* Brecon, 23 Castle Hill Avenue, Berkhamsted, Herts HP4 1HJ. *T:* Berkhamsted (01442) 865291.

WILLIAMS, (Richard) Derrick, MA (Cantab); Principal, Gloucestershire College of Arts and Technology, 1981–89; *b* 30 March 1926; *s* of Richard Leslie Williams and Lizzie Paddington; *m* 1949, Beryl Newbury Stonebanks; four *s*. *Educ:* St John's Coll., Cambridge. Asst Master, Lawrence Sherrif Sch., Rugby, 1950–51; Lectr, University Coll., Ibadan, Nigeria, 1951–52; Adult Tutor, Ashby-de-la-Zouch Community Coll., Leicestershire, 1952–54; Further Educn Organising Tutor, Oxfordshire, 1954–60; Asst Educn Officer: West Suffolk, 1960–65; Bristol, 1965–67; Dep. Chief Educn Officer, Bristol, 1967–73; Chief Educn Officer, County of Avon, 1973–76; Dir, Glos Inst. of Higher Educn, 1977–80. *Recreations:* cricket, music. *Address:* Glan y Nant, Bryniau, Brithdir, Dolgellau, Gwynedd LL40 2TY.

WILLIAMS, Richard Hall; Under Secretary, Agriculture Department, Welsh Office, Cardiff, 1981–86; Deputy Chairman, Local Government Boundary Commission for Wales, since 1989; *b* 21 Oct. 1926; *s* of late Edward Hall Williams and Kitty Hall Williams; *m* 1949, Nia Wynn (*née* Jones); two *s* two *d*. *Educ:* Barry Grammar Sch., Glamorgan; University College of Wales, Aberystwyth (BScEcon Hons). Career within Welsh Office included service in Health and Economic Planning Groups before entering Agriculture Dept, 1978. Treasurer, Ministerial Bd, Presbyterian Church of Wales, 1986–95. Vice Chm., Age Concern Wales, 1990–93. *Recreation:* enjoying all things Welsh. *Address:* Argoed, 17 West Orchard Crescent, Llandaff, Cardiff CF5 1AR. *T:* Cardiff (01222) 562472.

See also J. E. H. Williams.

WILLIAMS, Sir Robert (Evan Owen), Kt 1976; MD, FRCP, FRCPath; FFPHM; Director, Public Health Laboratory Service, 1973–81; Chairman, Advisory Committee on Genetic Manipulation, Health and Safety Executive, 1984–86 (Chairman, Genetic Manipulation Advisory Group, 1981–84); *b* 30 June 1916; *s* of Gwynne Evan Owen Williams and Cicely Mary (*née* Innes); *m* 1944, Margaret (*née* Lumsden) (*d* 1990); one *s* two *d*. *Educ:* Sherborne Sch., Dorset; University College, London and University College Hospital. Assistant Pathologist, EMS, 1941–42; Pathologist, Medical Research Council Unit, Birmingham Accident Hospital, 1942–46; on staff Public Health Laboratory Service, 1946–60 (Director, Streptococcus, Staphylococcus and Air Hygiene Laboratory, 1949–60); Prof. of Bacteriology, Univ. of London, at St Mary's Hosp. Med. Sch., 1960–73, Dean 1967–73. Mem. MRC, 1969–73. Pres., RCPath, 1975–78. Fellow, UCL, 1968. Hon. FRCPA, 1977; Hon. MD Uppsala, 1972; Hon. DSc Bath, 1977; Dr *hc* Lisbon, 1992. *Publications:* (jt author) Hospital Infection, 1966; Microbiology for the Public Health, 1985; numerous publications in journals on bacteriological and epidemiological subjects. *Recreation:* horticulture. *Address:* Little Platt, Plush, Dorchester, Dorset DT2 7RQ. *T:* Piddletrenthide (01300) 348320. *Club:* Athenæum.

See also Sir D. I. Williams, J. M. Williams.

WILLIAMS, Prof. Robert Hughes, (Robin), FRS 1990; CPhys, FInstP; Vice-Chancellor and Principal, University of Wales, Swansea, since 1994; *b* 22 Dec. 1941; *s* of Emrys and Catherine Williams; *m* 1967, Gillian Mary Harrison; one *s* one *d*. *Educ:* Bala Boys' Grammar Sch.; University College of North Wales, Bangor (BSc, PhD, DSc). Res. Fellow, Univ. of Wales, 1966–68; Lectr, then Reader and Prof., New University of Ulster, 1968–83; Prof. and Hd of Dept of Physics, late Physics and Astronomy, 1984–94, Dep. Principal, 1993–94, Univ. of Wales Coll. of Cardiff. Visiting Professor: Max Planck Inst., Stuttgart, 1975; Xerox Res. Labs, Palo Alto, USA, 1979; IBM Res. Labs, Yorktown Heights, USA, 1982. Mott Lectr, Inst. of Physics, 1992. Silver Medal, British Vacuum Council, 1988; Max Born Medal and Prize, German Physics Soc. and Inst. of Physics, 1989. *Publications:* Metal-Semiconductor Contacts (with E. H. Rhoderick), 1988; over 250 pubns in field of solid state physics and semiconductor devices. *Recreations:* walking, fishing, soccer. *Address:* Dolwerdd, Trerhyngyll, Cowbridge, S Glamorgan CF7 7TN. *T:* Cowbridge (01446) 773402; Danver House, 236 Gower Road, Sketty, Swansea, W Glam.

WILLIAMS, Prof. Robert Joseph Paton, DPhil; FRS 1972; Senior Research Fellow, Wadham College, Oxford, since 1991 (Fellow, since 1955); Royal Society Napier Research Professor at Oxford, 1974–91; *b* 25 Feb. 1926; *m* 1952, Jelly Klara (*née* Büchli); two *s*. *Educ:* Wallasey Grammar Sch.; Merton Coll., Oxford (MA, DPhil). FRSC. Rotary Foundn Fellow, Uppsala, 1950–51; Jun. Res. Fellow, Merton Coll., Oxford, 1951–55; Lectr, 1955–72, Reader in Inorganic Chemistry, 1972–74, Univ. of Oxford. Associate, Peter Bent Brigham Hosp., Boston, USA; Commonwealth Fellow, Mass, 1965–66; Vis. Prof., Royal Free Hosp., London Univ., 1991–. Liversidge Lectr, Chem. Soc., 1979; Commem. Lectr, Biochem. Inst., Univ. of Zurich, 1981; Bakerian Lectr, Royal Soc., 1981. President: Chem. Sect., BAAS, 1985–86; Dalton Div., RSC, 1991–93. Foreign Member: Acad. of Science, Portugal, 1981; Royal Soc. of Science, Liège, 1981; Royal Swedish Acad. of Sciences, 1983; Czechoslovak Acad. of Science, 1989. Hon. DSc: Liège, 1980; Leicester, 1985; East Anglia, 1992; Keele, 1993. Tilden Medal, Chem. Soc., 1970; Keilin Medal, Biochem. Soc., 1972; Hughes Medal, Royal Soc., 1979; Claire Bruylants Medal, Louvain, 1980; Krebs Medal, Europ. Biochem. Soc., 1985; Linderstrøm-Lang Medal, Carlsberg Foundn, Copenhagen, 1986; Sigillum Magnum (Medal), Univ. of Bologna, 1987; Heyrovsky Medal, Internat. Union of Biochem., 1988; Frederick Gowland Hopkins Medal, Biochem. Soc., 1989. *Publications:* (with C. S. G. Phillips) Inorganic Chemistry, 1965; (jtly) Nuclear Magnetic Resonance in Biology, 1977; (ed jtly) New Trends in Bio-Inorganic Chemistry, 1978; (with S. Mann and J. Webb) Biomineralization, 1989; (with J. J. R. Frausto da Silva) The Biological Chemistry of the Elements, 1991; papers in Jl Chem. Soc., biochemical jls, etc. *Recreation:* walking in the country. *Address:* Wadham College, Oxford OX1 3QR. *T:* Oxford (01865) 242564.

WILLIAMS, Robert Martin, CB 1981; CBE 1973; retired; Chairman, State Services Commission, New Zealand, 1975–81; *b* 30 March 1919; *s* of late Canon Henry Williams; *m* 1944, Mary Constance, *d* of late Rev. Francis H. Thorpe; one *s* two *d*. *Educ:* Christ's Coll., NZ; Canterbury University College, NZ; St John's Coll., Cambridge. MA. 1st Class Hons Mathematics, Univ. Sen. Schol., Shirtcliffe Fellow, NZ, 1940; BA, 1st Class Hons Mathematics Tripos, Cantab, 1947; PhD Math. Statistics, Cantab, 1949. Mathematician at Radar Development Laboratory, DSIR, NZ, 1941–44; Member UK Atomic Group in US, 1944–45; Member, 1949–53, Director, 1953–62, Applied Mathematics Laboratory, DSIR, NZ; Harkness Commonwealth Fellow and Vis. Fellow, at Princeton Univ., 1957–58; State Services Commissioner, NZ Public Service, 1963–67; Vice-Chancellor: Univ. of Otago, Dunedin, 1967–73; ANU, 1973–75. Mem., NZ Metric Adv. Bd, 1969–73. Mem., Internat. Statistical Inst., 1961–. Chairman: Cttee of Inquiry into Educnl TV, 1970–72; Policy Cttee, Dictionary of NZ Biography, 1983–90. Pres., NZ Book Council, 1989–. Carnegie Travel Award, 1969. Hon. LLD Otago, 1972. *Publications:* papers mainly on mathematical statistics and related topics. *Address:* 21 Wadestown Road, Wellington, New Zealand. *Club:* Wellington (Wellington, NZ).

WILLIAMS, Sir (Robert) Philip (Nathaniel), 4th Bt *cr* 1915; JP; DL; *b* 3 May 1950; *s* of Sir David Philip Williams, 3rd Bt and of Elizabeth Mary Garneys, *d* of late William Ralph Garneys Bond; *S* father, 1970; *m* 1979, Catherine Margaret Godwin, *d* of Canon Cosmo Pouncey, Tewkesbury; one *s* three *d*. *Educ:* Marlborough; St Andrews Univ. MA Hons. JP W Dorset PSD (formerly Dorchester), 1992; DL Dorset, 1995. *Heir:* *s* David Robert Mark Williams, *b* 31 Oct. 1980. *Address:* Bridehead, Littlebredy, Dorchester, Dorset DT2 9JA. *T:* Long Bredy (01308) 482232. *Club:* MCC.

WILLIAMS, Robin; *see* Williams, Robert H.

WILLIAMS, Maj.-Gen. Robin Guy, CB 1983; MBE 1969; retired; Chief Executive Officer, Auckland Regional Trust Board, Order of St John, since 1993; *b* 14 Aug. 1930; *s* of John Upham and Margaret Joan Williams; *m* 1953, Jill Rollo Tyrie; one *s* two *d*. *Educ:* Nelson Coll., New Zealand. psc(UK) 1963, jssc(AS) 1972, rcds(UK) 1976. Commissioned

RMC, Duntroon, 1952; 1 Fiji Inf. Regt Malaya, 1953–54; Adjt/Coy Comd 2 NZ Regt Malaya, 1959–61 Chief Instructor Sch. of Inf. (NZ), 1964–65; BM 28 Comwel Inf. Bde, Malaysia, 1965–68; CO 1 Bn Depot (NZ), 1969; CO 1 RNZIR (Singapore), 1969–71; GSO1 Field Force Comd (NZ), 1972–73; CofS Field Force Comd (NZ), 1973–74; Col SD, Army GS, 1974–75; Comd Field Force, 1977–79; ACDS (Ops/Plans), 1979–81; DCGS 1981; CGS, 1981–84. Hon. Col 1 RNZIR, 1986–88; Col, RNZIR, 1988–90. Chm., Bell Helicopter (BH) Pacific, 1988–90. Vice-Chm., 1985–86, Chm., 1986–88, Operation Raleigh, NZ; Chief Executive: Order of St John (NZ), 1986–87; Auckland Div., Cancer Soc. of NZ, 1988–93. *Recreations:* golf, swimming, walking. *Address:* 14 Walton Street, Remuera, Auckland 5, New Zealand. *T:* (9) 5201547. *Clubs:* Northern (Auckland); Auckland Golf (Middlemore, NZ).

WILLIAMS, Sir Robin (Philip), 2nd Bt, *cr* 1953; Insurance Broker, 1952–91; Lloyd's Underwriter, 1961; 2nd Lieut, retired, RA; *b* 27 May 1928; *s* of Sir Herbert Geraint Williams, 1st Bt, MP, MSc, MEngAssoc, MInstCE; *S* father 1954; *m* 1955, Wendy Adèle Marguerite, *o d* of late Felix Joseph Alexander, London and Hong Kong; two *s*. *Educ:* Eton Coll.; St John's Coll., Cambridge (MA). 2nd Lieut, Royal Artillery, 1947. Vice-Chairman, Federation of Univ. Conservative and Unionist Assocs, 1951–52; Acting Chairman, 1952; Chairman of Bow Group (Conservative Research Society), 1954. Called to Bar, Middle Temple, 1954; Chm., Anti-Common Market League, 1969–84; Dir, Common Market Safeguards Campaign, 1973–76; Hon. Secretary: Safeguard Britain Campaign, 1978–89; Campaign for an Independent Britain, 1989–. Councillor, Haringey, 1968–74. *Publication:* Whose Public Schools?, 1957. *Heir:* *s* Anthony Geraint Williams [*b* 22 Dec. 1958; *m* 1990, Rachel Jane, *e d* of Norman Jennings; two *s*]. *Address:* 1 Broadlands Close, Highgate, N6 4AF.

WILLIAMS, Prof. Roger; Vice-Chancellor of The University of Reading, since 1993; *b* 21 March 1942; *s* of late M. O. Williams, MBE and W. Williams; *m* 1967, Rae Kirkbright; two *d*. *Educ:* Tredegar Grammar Sch.; Worcester Coll., Oxford (BA Nat. Scis (Physics)); Univ. of Manchester (MA). Nat. Coal Bd, 1963–64; Department of Government, University of Manchester: Res. Student, 1964–66; Asst Lectr, Lectr, Sen. Lectr, 1966–78; Prof. of Govt and Sci. Policy, 1979–93; Dean of Economic and Social Studies, 1989–92. NATO Envtl Fellowship, 1977–79; Aust. Univs Fellowship, 1984; Vis. Prof., Univ. of Montreal, 1981. Sci. Advr, Sci. Council of Canada (on secondment), 1974–75; Specialist Advr, H of L Select Cttees on Sci. and Technology, 1986–92, on European Communities, 1990. Chm., Jt SERC-ESRC Cttee, 1991–93; Mem., ESRC Cttees. British Council Delegn to China, 1985. *Publications:* Politics and Technology, 1972; European Technology, 1973; The Nuclear Power Decisions, 1980; Public Acceptability of New Technology, 1986. *Address:* The University of Reading, Whiteknights, Reading, Berks RG6 2AH. *T:* Reading (01734) 875123. *Club:* Athenæum.

WILLIAMS, Prof. Roger Stanley, CBE 1993; MD; FRCP, FRCS; Consultant Physician, King's College Hospital, since 1966; Director, Institute of Liver Studies (formerly Liver Research Unit), since 1966, and Professor of Hepatology, since 1994, King's College School of Medicine and Dentistry (formerly King's College Hospital and Medical School); Consultant, Liver Research Unit Trust, since 1974; Hon. Consultant in medicine to the Army, since 1988; *b* 28 Aug. 1931; *s* of Stanley George Williams and Doris Dagmar Clatworthy; *m* 1st, 1954, Lindsay Mary Elliott (marr. diss. 1977); two *s* three *d*; 2nd, 1978, Stephanie Gay de Laszlo; one *s* two *d*. *Educ:* St Mary's Coll., Southampton; London Hosp. Med. Coll., Univ. of London. MB, BS (Hons), MD; LRCP, MRCP, FRCP 1966; MRCS, FRCS 1988; FRCPE 1990; FRACP 1991. House appointments and Pathology Asst, London Hospital, 1953–56; Jun. Med. Specialist, Queen Alexandra Hospital, Millbank, 1956–58; Medical Registrar and Tutor, Royal Postgrad. Med. Sch., 1958–59; Lectr in Medicine, Royal Free Hospital, 1959–65; Consultant Physician, Royal South Hants and Southampton General Hospital, 1965–66. Member: Clinical Standards Adv. Gp, 1994–; Adv. Gp on Hepatitis, DHSS, 1980–; Transplant Adv. Panel, DHSS, 1974–83; WHO Scientific Gp on Viral Hepatitis, Geneva, 1972. Rockefeller Travelling Fellowship in Medicine, 1962; Legg Award, Royal Free Hosp. Med. Sch., 1964; Sir Ernest Finch Vis. Prof., Sheffield, 1974; Lectures: Melrose Meml, Glasgow, 1970; Goulstonian, RCP, 1970; Searle, Amer. Assoc. for the Study of Liver Diseases, 1972; Fleming, Glasgow Coll. of Physicians and Surgeons, 1975; Sir Arthur Hurst Meml, British Soc. of Gastroenterology, 1975; Skinner, Royal Coll. of Radiologists, 1978; Albert M. Snell Meml, Palo Alto Med. Foundn, 1981; Milford Rouse, Baylor Med. Center, Dallas, 1989; Norman Tanner Meml, St George's Hosp., 1992; Searle Special, St Bartholomew's Hosp., 1992; Datta Meml Oration, India, 1984; Quadrennial Review, World Congress of Gastroenterol., Sydney, 1990; Sir Jules Thorn, RCP, 1994. Vice-Pres., RCP, 1991–93; Pres., Internat. Med. Club, 1989–; Member: European Assoc. for the Study of the Liver, 1966– (Cttee Mem., 1966–70; Pres., 1983); Harveian Soc. of London (Sec., Councillor and Vice-Pres., 1963–70, Pres., 1974–75); British Assoc. for Study of Liver (formerly Liver Club) (Sec. and Treasurer, 1968–71; Pres., 1984–86); Royal Soc. of Medicine (Sec. of Section, 1969–71); British Soc. of Gastroenterology (Pres., 1989). FKC 1992. Hon. FACP 1992. Gold Medal, Canadian Liver Foundn, 1992. *Publications:* (ed) Fifth Symposium on Advanced Medicine, 1969; edited jointly: Immunology of the Liver, 1971; Artificial Liver Support, 1975; Immune Reactions in Liver Disease, 1978; Drug Reactions and the Liver, 1981; Variceal Bleeding, 1982; Antiviral Agents in Chronic Hepatitis B Virus Infection, 1985; The Practice of Liver Transplantation, 1995; International Developments in Health Care, 1995; author of over 2000 scientific papers, review articles and book chapters. *Recreations:* tennis, sailing, opera. *Address:* Reed House, Satchell Lane, Hamble, Hants SO3 5HL. *T:* Southampton (01703) 453747; 8 Eldon Road, W8 5PU. *T:* 0171–937 5301. *Clubs:* Carlton, Saints and Sinners, Royal Ocean Racing; Royal Yacht Squadron (Cowes).

WILLIAMS, Rt. Rev. Ronald John Chantler; Bishop of the Southern Region, and an Assistant Bishop, Diocese of Brisbane, since 1993; *b* 19 July 1938; *s* of Walter Chantler Williams and Constance Bertha Williams (*née* Pool); *m* 1963, Kathryn Rohrsheim; two *s* one *d*. *Educ:* Prince Alfred Coll., Adelaide; St John's Coll., Morpeth (ThL); St Mark's Coll., Adelaide Univ. (BA); Bristol Univ. (MSc 1974); Australian Management Coll., Mt Eliza (AMP). Ordained deacon, 1963, priest, 1964; Curate, Toorak Gardens, 1963–64; Australian Bd of Missions, Sydney, 1965; Domestic Chaplain, Bishop of Polynesia, 1966–67; Priest, Labasa, Fiji, 1967–71; Hon. Priest, Bedminster, Bristol, 1972–74; Dean of Suva, Fiji, 1974–79; Rector, Campbelltown, Adelaide, 1979–84; Priest to City of Adelaide and founding Dir, St Paul's Centre, 1984–93; Hon. Canon, St Peter's Cathedral, Adelaide, 1986–93. *Recreation:* jazz musician—double bass. *Address:* GPO Box 421, Brisbane, Qld 4001, Australia. *T:* (office) (7) 38352213, (home) (7) 38431546.

WILLIAMS, Ronald Millward, CBE 1990; DL; Member, Essex County Council, 1970–93 (Chairman, 1983–86); *b* 9 Dec. 1922; *s* of George and Gladys Williams; *m* 1943, Joyce; one *s* two *d*. *Educ:* Leeds College of Technology. Electrical Engineer, then Industrial Eng Superintendent, Mobil Oil Co. Ltd, 1954–82. Member: Benfleet Urban Dist Council, 1960–74 (Chm. 1963–66, 1972–74); Castle Point Dist Council, 1974–87 (Chm. 1980–81; Leader, 1981–87); Essex County Council: Leader Cons. Gp, 1977–83, 1986–87; Chairman: County Planning Cttee, 1981–83; County Highways Cttee, 1989–93. Chm., Southend Health Authority, 1982–90, Southend Health Care Services, NHS Trust, 1990–. Chm., SE Essex Abbeyfield Soc., 1983–88. DL Essex 1983. *Recreations:* supporter, football, cricket, bowls, tennis; video filming of countryside. *Address:* 41 Poors Lane, Hadleigh, Benfleet, Essex SS7 2LA. *T:* Southend on Sea (01702) 559565.

WILLIAMS, Ronald William; Director, Office of Manpower Economics, 1980–86 (on secondment); *b* 19 Dec. 1926; *yr s* of late Albert Williams and Katherine Teresa Williams (*née* Chilver). *Educ:* City of London Sch.; Downing Coll., Cambridge (BA, LLB). RN, 1945–48. Iraq Petroleum Co. Ltd, 1956–58; Philips Electrical Industries Ltd, 1958–64; Consultant, later Sen. Consultant, PA Management Consultants Ltd, 1964–69; Asst Sec., NBPI, 1969–71; Sen. Consultant, Office of Manpower Economics, 1971–73; Asst Sec., CSD, 1973–80 (UK Govt rep., ILO Tripartite Conf. on Public Servs, 1975); Under Sec. 1980; HM Treasury, 1982; Dept of Employment, 1986. Sen. Advr, Coopers & Lybrand, 1986–93. *Recreations:* music, visual arts. *Address:* 126 Defoe House, Barbican, EC2Y 8ND. *T:* 0171–638 5456.

WILLIAMS, Rt. Rev. Rowan Douglas; *see* Monmouth, Bishop of.

WILLIAMS, Roy, CB 1989; Deputy Secretary, Department of Trade and Industry, 1984–94; *b* 31 Dec. 1934; *s* of Eric Williams and Ellen Williams; *m* 1959, Shirley, *d* of Captain and Mrs O. Warwick; one *s* one *d*. *Educ:* Liverpool Univ. (1st Cl. BA Econs). Asst Principal, Min. of Power, 1956; Principal, 1961; Harkness Commonwealth Fellow, Univs of Chicago and Berkeley, 1963–64; Principal Private Sec., Minister of Power and subseq. Paymaster Gen., 1969; Asst Sec., DTI, 1971; Principal Private Sec., Sec. of State for Industry, 1974; Under-Sec., DoI, later DTI, 1976–84. UK Mem., EU High Level Gp on Eureka prog., 1995–; Mem., Design Council, 1995–. Mem. Management Cttee, St Pier's Sch., Lingfield, 1995–. *Address:* Darl Oast, The Street, Ightham, Sevenoaks, Kent TN15 9HH. *T:* Borough Green (01732) 883944.

WILLIAMS, Rev. Samuel Lewis; Minister, St Columba's United Reformed Church, Gosport, since 1991; *b* 8 Jan. 1934; *s* of Thomas John Williams and Miriam Mary Williams (*née* West); *m* 1958, Mary Sansom (*née* Benjamin); one *s* one *d*. *Educ:* Pagefield College Public Day School, Newport, Gwent; Memorial Coll. (Congregational), Brecon. Local government officer, 1950–52; RAF, 1952–55; theol. training, 1955–58. Ordained Congregational (URC) Minister, 1958; Mill Street Congregational Church, Newport, Gwent, 1958–63; Bettws Congregational Church, 1963–68; Llanvaches Congregational Church, 1966–68; Free Churches Chaplain, St Woolas Hosp., Newport, 1964–68. Entered RN as Chaplain, 1968; served HMS: Seahawk, 1968–69; Hermes, 1969–70; Raleigh, 1970–71; Seahawk, 1971–73; Daedalus, 1973–74; served Malta, 1974–76; C-in-C Naval Home Comd staff, 1977–81; HMS Sultan, 1981–84; Flag Officer Scotland and NI staff, 1984–86; HMS Heron, 1986; Prin. Chaplain (Navy), Ch. of Scotland and Free Churches, 1986–91; RN retired, 1991. QHC, 1986–91. *Recreations:* oil painting, golf, hill walking, music, gardening, Rugby. *Address:* 18 Brodrick Avenue, Gosport, Hants PO12 2EN. *T:* Gosport (01705) 581114.

WILLIAMS, Rev. (Sidney) Austen, CVO 1980; Vicar of St Martin-in-the-Fields, 1956–84; Chaplain to the Queen's Household, 1961–82, Extra Chaplain since 1982; a Prebendary of St Paul's Cathedral, since 1973; *b* 23 Feb. 1912; *s* of Sidney Herbert and Dorothy Williams; *m* 1945, Daphne Joan McWilliam; one *s* one *d*. *Educ:* Bromsgrove School; St Catharine's College, Cambridge (MA); Westcott House, Cambridge. Curate of St Paul, Harringay, 1937–40. Chaplain, Toc H, France and Germany, 1940–48 (POW, 1940–44). Curate of: All Hallows, Barking by the Tower, 1945–46; St Martin-in-the-Fields, 1946–51; Vicar of St Albans, Westbury Park, Clifton, Bristol, 1951–56. Freeman of the City of London, 1977. *Recreations:* photography, ornithology. *Address:* 37 Tulsemere Road, SE27 9EH. *T:* 0181–670 7945.

WILLIAMS, Susan Elizabeth; Director of Nursing, Greater Glasgow Community and Mental Health NHS Trust, since 1994; *b* 30 Oct. 1942; *d* of late Ernest George Fost and of Kathleen Beatrice Maud Fost; *m* 1st, 1964, Dennis Norman Carnevale (decd); one *s* one *d*; 2nd, 1977, Keith Edward Williams. *Educ:* Grammar School for Girls, Weston-super-Mare; Wolverhampton Polytechnic (Post-grad. DipPsych); Bristol Royal Hosps (RSCN, RGN, RNT); BEd (Hons), DipN London. Ward Sister, Royal Hosp. for Sick Children, Bristol, 1972–76; Nurse Tutor, Salop Area Sch. of Nursing, 1976–80; Sen. Tutor, Dudley AHA, 1980–83; Reg. Nurse (Educn and Res.), W Midlands RHA, 1983–87; Chief Nurse Advr/Dir of Nurse Educn, Bromsgrove and Redditch HA, 1987–88; Regl Dir of Nursing and Quality Assurance, W Midlands RHA, 1988–93; Dep. Dir of Nursing Management Exec., DoH, 1993–94. *Recreations:* hill walking, photography, reading, listening to music, foreign travel. *Address:* Greater Glasgow Community and Mental Health NHS Trust, Gartnavel Royal Hospital, Great Western Road, Glasgow G12 0XH. *T:* 0141–211 3647.

WILLIAMS, Mrs Susan Eva, MBE 1959; Lord-Lieutenant of South Glamorgan, 1985–90; *b* 17 Aug. 1915; *d* of Robert Henry Williams and Dorothy Marie Williams; *m* 1950, Charles Crofts Llewellyn Williams (*d* 1952). *Educ:* St James's, West Malvern. WAAF, 1939–45. JP 1961, High Sheriff 1968, DL 1973, Glamorgan; Lieut, S Glam, 1981–85. DStJ 1990. *Recreation:* National Hunt racing. *Address:* Caercady, Welsh St Donats, Cowbridge, S Glamorgan CF7 7ST. *T:* Cowbridge (01446) 772346.

WILLIAMS, Sir Sydney; *see* Williams, Sir Henry S.

WILLIAMS, Prof. Thomas Eifion Hopkins, CBE 1980; CEng; Research Professor of Civil Engineering, University of Southampton, 1983–93, now Emeritus Professor (Professor of Civil Engineering, 1967–83); *b* 14 June 1923; *s* of David Garfield Williams and Annie Mary Williams (*née* Hopkins), Cwmtwrch, Brecon; *m* 1947, Elizabeth Lois Davies; one *s* two *d*. *Educ:* Ystradgynlais Grammar Sch.; Univ. of Wales (BSc, MSc); Univ. of Durham (PhD). FICE, MIStructE, FIHT, FCIT. Research Stressman, Sir W. G. Armstrong-Whitworth Aircraft, 1945; Asst Engr, Trunk Roads, Glam CC, 1946; Asst Lectr Civil Engrg, UC Swansea, 1947; Lectr in Civil Engrg, King's Coll., Univ. of Durham, 1948; Resident Site Engr, R. T. James & Partners, 1952; Post-doctoral Visitor, Univ. of California at Berkeley, 1955; Vis. Prof., Civil Engrg, Northwestern Univ., 1957; Sen. Lectr, Reader and Prof. of Civil and Transport Engrg, King's Coll., Univ. of Durham (subseq. Univ. of Newcastle upon Tyne), 1958–67. Chairman: Civil Engrg EDC, 1976–78; Standing Adv. Cttee on Trunk Rd Assessment, Dept of Transport, 1980–87 (Mem., Adv. Cttee, 1977–80); Member: EDC Civil Engrg, 1967–76; Transport Cttee, SRC; Roads Engrg Bd, ICE; British Nat. Cttee, PIARC; Council and Transp. Engrg Bd, Inst. Highway Engrs (Pres. 1979–80); Public Policy Cttee, RAC, 1981–. Visitor, TRRL, 1982–88 (Mem., Adv. Cttee on Traffic and Safety, 1977–80); Special Advisor, H of L Select Cttee on European Transport, 1989. Mem. Council, Church Schools Co., 1982–90. *Publications:* (Editor) Urban Survival and Traffic, 1961; Capacity, in Traffic Engineering Practice, 1963; Prediction of Traffic in Industrial Areas, 1966; Autostrade: Strategia, di sviluppo industriale e la vitalita delle nostre citta, 1965; Inter-City VTOL: Potential Traffic and Sites, 1969; Mobility and the Environment, 1971; (ed) Transportation and Environment: policies, plans and practice, 1973; Integrated Transport: developments and trends, 1976; Air, Rail and Road Inter-City Transport Systems, 1976; Land Use, Highways and Traffic, 1977; Motor Vehicles in a Changing World, 1978; Traffic Engineering

Recreations: reading, sport. *Address:* Murdoch Research Institute, Royal Children's Hospital, Flemington Road, Parkville, Melbourne, Vic 3052, Australia. *T:* (3) 93455045.

WILLIAMSON, (Robert) Brian, CBE 1989; Chairman, Gerrard & National Holdings PLC, since 1989 (Managing Director, 1978–89); *b* 16 Feb. 1945; *m* 1986, Diane Marie Christine de Jacquier de Rosée. *Educ:* Trinity College, Dublin (MA). Personal Asst to Rt Hon. Maurice Macmillan (later Viscount Macmillan), 1967–71; Editor, International Currency Review, 1971; Chairman: LIFFE, 1985–88 (Dir, 1982–89); GNI Ltd, 1985–89; Director: Fleming Internat. High Income Investment Trust plc, 1990–; Court, Bank of Ireland, 1990–; Electra Investment Trust plc, 1994–; Member: Bd, Bank of Ireland Britain Hldgs, 1986–90; Council, 1985–88, Council, Eur. Cttee, 1988–90, British Invisible Exports Council; Securities and Investments Bd, 1986–. Gov. at Large, Nat. Assoc. of Securities Dealers, USA, 1995–. Mem. HAC, commissioned 1975. Dir, Rowing Mus., Henley Foundn, 1992–94. Contested (C) Sheffield Hillsborough, Feb. and Oct. 1974; prosp. parly cand., Truro, 1976–77. FRSA 1991. *Address:* 23 Paultons Square, SW3 5AP. *Clubs:* Pratt's; Kildare and University (Dublin).

WILLIAMSON, Rt. Rev. Robert Kerr; *see* Southwark, Bishop of.

WILLIAMSON, Prof. Robin Charles Noel, FRCS; Professor and Director of Surgery, Royal Postgraduate Medical School, University of London and Hammersmith Hospital, since 1987; *b* 19 Dec. 1942; *s* of James Charles Frederick Lloyd Williamson and Helena Frances Williamson (*née* Madden); *m* 1967, Judith Marjorie (*née* Bull); three *s*. *Educ:* Rugby School; Emmanuel College, Cambridge; St Bartholomew's Hosp. Med. Coll. MA, MD, MChir (Cantab). Surgical Registrar, Reading, 1971–73; Sen. Surgical Registrar, Bristol, 1973–75; Res. Fellow, Harvard, 1975–76; Consultant Sen. Lectr, Bristol, 1977–79; Prof. of Surgery, Univ. of Bristol, 1979–87. Mem., Cell Biology and Disorders Bd, MRC, 1987–91. Fulbright-Hays Sen. Res. Scholar, USA, 1975; Sen. Penman Vis. Fellow, South Africa, 1985; Paul Grange Vis. Fellow, Univ. of Monash, 1986; Hunterian Prof., RCS, 1981–82; Raine Vis. Prof., Univ. of Western Australia, 1983; Richardson Prof., Mass Gen. Hosp., 1985; Visiting Professor: Univ. of Lund, Sweden, 1985; Univ. of Hong Kong, 1987; Johnson and Johnson Vis. Prof., Univ. of Calif, San Francisco, 1989; Edwin Tooth Guest Prof., Royal Brisbane Hosp., Qld, 1989; Totalisator Bd Vis. Prof., Nat. Univ. of Singapore, 1994. Lectures: Arris and Gale, RCS, 1977–78; Finlayson Meml, RCPSG, 1985; Sir Gordon Bell Meml, RACS, NZ, 1988. Moynihan Fellow, Assoc. of Surgeons, 1979. Pres., Pancreatic Soc. of GB and Ireland, 1984–85; Chm., Educn Cttee, British Soc. of Gastroenterology, 1981–87; Mem., Med. Adv. Cttee, British Council, 1988–94; Secretary General: World Assoc. of Hepatopancreatobiliary Surgery, 1990–94 (Treas., 1986–90); Internat. Hepatopancreatobiliary Assoc., 1994–; Mem. Council, Assoc. of Surgeons of GB and Ireland, 1993–. Examiner, Primary FRCS, 1981–87. Hon. FRCS Thailand, 1992. Hon. PhD Mahidol Univ., Thailand, 1994. Hallett Prize, RCS, 1970; Research Medal, British Soc. of Gastroenterology, 1982. Sen. Ed., British Jl of Surgery, 1991– (Co. Sec., 1983–91). *Publications:* edited jointly: Colonic Carcinogenesis, 1982; General Surgical Operations, 2nd edn 1987; Emergency Abdominal Surgery, 1990; Surgical Management, 2nd edn 1991; Clinical Gastroenterology: gastrointestinal emergencies, 1991; Scott, An Aid to Clinical Surgery, 5th edn 1994; Hepatobiliary and Pancreatic Tumours, 1994; numerous papers in surgical and med. jls. *Recreations:* travel, military uniforms and history. *Address:* The Barn, 88 Lower Road, Gerrards Cross, Bucks SL9 8LB. *T:* Gerrards Cross (01753) 889816. *Club:* United Oxford & Cambridge University.

WILLIAMSON, Rt. Rev. Roy; *see* Williamson, Rt Rev. Robert K.

WILLIAMSON, Prof. Stephen; Professor of Engineering, Cambridge, since 1989; Fellow, St John's College, Cambridge, since 1990; *b* 15 Dec. 1948; *s* of Donald Williamson and Patricia K. M. Williamson (*née* Leyland); *m* 1970, Zita Mellor; one *s* two *d*. *Educ:* Burnage Grammar Sch., Manchester; Imperial Coll. of Science and Technology (BScEng, ACGI, PhD, DIC; DScEng 1989). Lectr in Engineering, Univ. of Aberdeen, 1973–81; Sen. Lectr, 1981–85, Reader, 1985–89, Dept of Electrical Engineering, Imperial College. FCGI 1989. Institution of Electrical Engineers: John Hopkinson Premium, 1981; Crompton Premium, 1987; Swan Premium, 1989; SET Divl Premium, 1991. *Publications:* papers relating to induction machines. *Recreations:* reading, walking, gardening. *Address:* Cambridge University Engineering Department, Trumpington Street, Cambridge CB2 1PZ. *T:* Cambridge (01223) 332664.

WILLING, Maria Paula Figueiroa, (Mrs Victor Willing); *see* Rego, Paula.

WILLINK, Sir Charles (William), 2nd Bt *cr* 1957; *b* 10 Sept. 1929; *s* of Rt Hon. Sir Henry Urmston Willink, 1st Bt, MC, QC (*d* 1973), and Cynthia Frances (*d* 1959), *d* of H. Morley Fletcher, MD, FRCP; *S* father, 1973; *m* 1954, Elizabeth, *d* of Humfrey Andrewes, Highgate, London; one *s* one *d*. *Educ:* Eton College (scholar); Trinity College, Cambridge (scholar; MA, PhD). Assistant Master: Marlborough College, 1952–54; Eton College, 1954–85 (Housemaster, 1964–77). FRSA. *Publications:* (ed) Euripides' Orestes, 1986; articles in Classical Quarterly. *Recreations:* bridge, field botany, music (bassoon). *Heir:* *s* Edward Daniel Willink, *b* 18 Feb. 1957. *Address:* 22 North Grove, Highgate, N6 4SL. *T:* 0181–340 3996.

WILLIS, Charles Reginald; Director, Tiverton Gazette & Associated Papers Ltd, since 1971; Member, Press Council, 1967; *b* 11 June 1906; *s* of Charles and Marie Willis, Tiverton, Devon; *m* 1929, Violet Stubbs; one *d*. *Educ:* Tiverton Grammar Sch. Tiverton Gazette, 1922–27; North Western Daily Mail, 1927–29; Evening Chronicle, Newcastle upon Tyne, 1929–1935; Evening Chronicle, Manchester, 1935–42; Empire News, London, 1942–43; The Evening News, London, 1943 (Editor, 1954–66); Dir, Associated Newspapers Ltd, 1961–71; Editorial Dir, Harmsworth Publications, 1967–70. *Recreation:* cricket. *Address:* Howden Heyes, Ashley, Tiverton, Devon EX16 5PB. *T:* Tiverton (01884) 254829.

WILLIS, Hon. Sir Eric (Archibald), KBE 1975; CMG 1974; *b* 15 Jan. 1922; *s* of Archibald Clarence Willis and Vida Mabel Willis (*née* Buttenshaw); *m* 1st, 1951, Norma Dorothy Thompson (*née* Knight) (marr. diss.); two *s* one *d*; 2nd, 1982, Lynn Anitra Ward (*née* Roberts) (marr. diss.). *Educ:* Murwillumbah High Sch., NSW; Univ. of Sydney (BA Hons). MLA (Liberal) for Earlwood, NSW, 1950–78; Dep. Leader, NSW Parly Liberal Party, 1959–75, Leader, 1976–77; Minister for Labour and Industry, Chief Secretary and Minister for Tourism, 1965–71; Chief Sec. and Minister for Tourism and Sport, 1971–72; Minister for Education, 1972–76; Premier and Treasurer, 1976; Leader of the Opposition, NSW Parlt, 1976–77. Exec. Sec., Royal Australian Coll. of Ophthalmologists, 1978–83; Exec. Dir, Arthritis Foundn of NSW, 1984–91. *Recreation:* reading. *Address:* 5/94 Kurraba Road, Neutral Bay, NSW 2089, Australia. *T:* (2) 99093432.

WILLIS, Frank William; Director of Advertising and Sponsorship, Independent Television Commission, since 1991; *b* 6 April 1947; *s* of late Prof. F. M. Willis and of J. C. Willis; *m* 1972, Jennifer Carol Arnold; two *d*. *Educ:* Bradford Grammar School; Magdalen Coll., Oxford (BA, BPhil). HM Diplomatic Service, 1971; Moscow, 1972–74; Ecole Nationale d'Administration, 1974–75; First Sec., FCO, 1975–79; Dept of Trade, later DTI, 1980; Asst Sec., Consumer Affairs Div., DTI, 1984; Controller of Advertising, IBA, 1987–90. *Recreations:* shopping in Muswell Hill, moors and mountains, wine. *Address:* ITC, 33 Foley Street, W1P 7LB.

WILLIS, Gaspard; *see* Willis, R. W. G.

WILLIS, Vice-Adm. Sir (Guido) James, KBE 1981; AO 1976; Chief of Naval Staff, Australia, 1979–82, retired; *b* 18 Oct. 1923; *s* of late Jack Rupert Law Willis and Théa Willis; *m* 1976, Marjorie J. Rogers. *Educ:* Wesley Coll., Melbourne; Royal Australian Naval Coll. Imperial Defence Coll., 1967; Director General Operations and Plans, 1968–71; CO HMAS Melbourne, 1971–72; DDL Project Director, 1972–73; Chief of Naval Personnel, 1973–75; Chief of Naval Material, 1975–76; Asst Chief of Defence Force Staff, 1976–78; Flag Officer Commanding HMA Fleet, 1978–79. Commander 1956, Captain 1962, Rear-Adm. 1973, Vice-Adm. 1979. *Address:* Lynmere, 32 Charlotte Street, Bowral, NSW 2576, Australia.

WILLIS, Sir James; *see* Willis, Sir G. J.

WILLIS, His Honour John Brooke; a Circuit Judge (formerly County Court Judge), 1965–80; Barrister-at-Law; *b* 3 July 1906; *yr s* of William Brooke Willis and Maud Mary Willis, Rotherham; *m* 1929, Mary Margaret Coward (marr. diss., 1946); one *s* one *d*; *m* 1964, Terena Ann Steel (formerly Hood); two *d*. *Educ:* Bedford Modern Sch.; Sheffield Univ. Called to the Bar, Middle Temple, 1938, North Eastern Circuit. Served War of 1939–45. RAFVR, 1940–45, Sqdn Leader. Recorder, Rotherham, 1955–59, Huddersfield, 1959–65; Dep. Chm., W Riding of Yorks QS, 1958–71. Chairman, Medical Appeal Tribunal under the National Insurance (Industrial Injuries) Acts, 1953–65. *Address:* 14 Larchwood, Woodlands Drive, Rawdon, Leeds LS19 6JZ.

WILLIS, Maj.-Gen. John Brooker, CB 1981; independent defence and marketing consultant; *b* 28 July 1926; *s* of late William Noel Willis and of Elaine Willis; *m* 1959, Yda Belinda Jane Firbank; two *s* two *d*. *Educ:* privately, until 1941; Redhill Technical Coll. ptsc, jssc. Enlisted in Royal Navy (Fleet Air Arm) as Trainee Pilot; basic training in USA, 1944; returned to UK, transf. to Indian Army, attended Armoured OTS Ahmed Nagar, 1945; commnd 1947, joined 10th Royal Hussars; attended 13 Technical Staff Course, RMCS, 1958–60; Bt Lt-Col 1965, in comd 10th Hussars Aden and BAOR; GSO1 (Armour) DS RMCS, 1968–69; Col GS MGO Secretariat, MoD, 1969–71; Dep. Comdt, RAC Centre, 1971–74; Sen. Officers' War Course, Greenwich, 1974; Dir, Projects (Fighting Vehicles), 1974–77; Dir Gen., Fighting Vehicles and Engr Equipment, 1977–81, retd. *Recreations:* golf, gardening, aviation, amateur dramatics. *Address:* c/o Lloyds Bank, 26 Hammersmith Broadway, W6 7AH. *Club:* Army and Navy.

WILLIS, John Edward; Director of Programmes, Channel Four Television, since 1993; *b* 4 April 1946; *s* of late Lord Willis and of Lady (Audrey Mary) Willis (*née* Hale); *m* 1972, Janet Ann Sperrin; one *s* one *d*. *Educ:* Eltham Coll.; Fitzwilliam Coll., Cambridge (MA); Bristol Univ. (PG Cert. in Film and TV). Yorkshire Television: journalist, 1970–75; Documentary Dir, 1975–82; Controller of Documentaries and Current Affairs, 1982–88; Channel Four Television: Controller of Factual Progs, 1988–89; Dep. Dir of Progs, 1990–92. FRTS, 1993. Numerous prizes and awards. *Publications:* Johnny Go Home, 1976; Churchill's Few: the Battle of Britain remembered, 1985. *Recreations:* cycling, soccer, cinema, theatre. *Address:* Channel Four Television, 124 Horseferry Road, SW1P 2TX. *T:* 0171–306 8400.

WILLIS, Air Chief Marshal Sir John (Frederick), KCB 1993 (CB 1991); CBE 1988; Vice Chief of the Defence Staff, since 1995; *b* 27 Oct. 1937; *s* of F. A. and K. E. Willis; *m* 1959, Merrill Thewliss; three *s* two *d*. *Educ:* Dulwich Coll.; RAF Coll., Cranwell. Entered RAF, 1955; comnd, 1958; Pilot, 83/44/9/Sqdns (Vulcan), 1958–64; Flying Instr, 1964–67; Officer and Aircrew Selection Centre, 1967–69; Staff Coll., 1970; Chief Flying Instr, Vulcan OCU, Flt Comdr/Sqdn Comdr, 27 Sqdn, 1971–77; Policy Div., Air Force Dept, MoD, 1977 82; Stn Comdr, Akrotiri, Cyprus, 1982–84; Briefing Officer to CAS, 1984–85; SHAPE, 1985–88; ACDS (Policy and Nuclear), 1989–90; Dir Gen. of Trng, RAF, 1991–92; AOC-in-C, RAF Support Comd, 1992–94; COS, RAF Logistics Comd, 1994–95. *Recreation:* making things. *Address:* Ministry of Defence, Main Building, Whitehall, SW1A 2HB. *Club:* Royal Air Force.

WILLIS, Prof. John Raymond, PhD; FRS 1992; FIMA; Professor of Theoretical Solid Mechanics, Cambridge University, since 1994; Fellow of Fitzwilliam College, Cambridge, 1966–72 and since 1994; *b* 27 March 1940; *s* of John V. G. and L. Gwendoline Willis; *m* 1964, Juliette Louise Ireland; three *d*. *Educ:* Imperial Coll., London (BSc, PhD). MA Cantab 1966. ARCS, DIC; FIMA 1966. Asst Lectr, Imperial Coll., 1962–64; Res. Associate, NY Univ., 1964–65; Cambridge University: Sen. Asst in Research, 1965–67; Asst Dir of Research, 1968–72; Dir of Studies in Maths, Fitzwilliam Coll., 1966–72; Prof. of Applied Maths, Bath Univ., 1972–94. Editor-in-Chief, 1982–92, Jt Editor, 1992–, Jl Mechanics and Physics of Solids. *Publications:* papers on mechanics of solids in learned jls. *Recreations:* swimming, hiking, music. *Address:* Department of Applied Mathematics and Theoretical Physics, Silver Street, Cambridge CB3 9EW. *T:* Cambridge (01223) 339251.

WILLIS, John Trueman, DFM 1942; housing consultant; *b* 27 Oct. 1918; *s* of Gordon and Ethel Willis, Headington, Oxford; *m* 1947, Audrey Joan, *d* of Aubrey and Gertrude Gurden, Headington, Oxford; one *s* one *d*. *Educ:* Oxford High Sch., Oxford. Estates Management, Magdalen Coll., Oxford, 1935–36; Industrial Trng, Lockheed Hydraulic Brake Co., Leamington Spa, 1937–38. Served War of 1939–45: Pilot on 14 Sqdn RAF Middle East, 1940–42; PoW Stalag Luft III, Germany, 1943–45. Estates Management, 1946–64, Estates Sec., 1953–65, Magdalen Coll., Oxford; Rent Officer for Oxford, 1965–67; Sec. Housing Societies Charitable Trust, 1968–69; Director: Shelter, 1971–72 (Housing Dir, 1969–70); Liverpool Housing Trust, 1973–75; Castle Rock Housing Assoc., 1976–78. Director: Kingdomwide Ltd, 1981–92; Kingdomwide Housing Trust, 1982; Kingdomwide Develt Ltd, 1982. Member: NEDO Housing Strategy Cttee, 1975–78; Management Cttees, North British (formerly Kingdomwide) Housing Assoc., S Yorks Reg., 1986–, W Yorks Reg., 1992–. Promoted housing conf., Planning for Home Work, 1984. ICSA. *Publication:* Housing and Poverty Report, 1970. *Recreations:* diminishing. *Address:* 36 Kings Court, The Kings Gap, Hoylake, Wirral, Merseyside L47 1JE. *T:* 0151–632 3873.

WILLIS, Joseph Robert McKenzie, CB 1952; CMG 1946; Deputy Chairman, Board of Inland Revenue, 1957–71; *b* 18 March 1909; 2nd *s* of Charles Frederick Willis and Lucy Alice McKenzie; *m* 1945, Elizabeth Browning, *er d* of James Ewing; one *s* one *d*. *Educ:* Eton; Christ Church, Oxford. Entered Inland Revenue Dept, 1932; Under Secretary, Central Economic Planning Staff, Treasury, 1948–49; Commissioner of Inland Revenue, 1949; Student of Imperial Defence Coll., 1948. Professorial Res. Fellow and Vis. Prof., Bath Univ., 1972–79. Specialist advr to Select Cttee on Wealth Tax, 1975. *Publications:* (with C. T. Sandford and D. J. Ironside): An Accessions Tax, 1973; An Annual Wealth Tax, 1975; (with P. J. W. Hardwick) Tax Expenditures in the United Kingdom, 1978. *Address:* Bunbury, Lower Shiplake, Henley-on-Thames, Oxon RG9 3PD. *T:* Wargrave (01734) 402726.

WILLIS, Rear-Adm. Kenneth Henry George, CB 1981; Director General, Home Farm Trust Ltd, Bristol, 1982–88, retired; *m*; three *d*. *Educ:* Royal Naval Engineering Coll.; Royal Naval Coll.; Jesus Coll., Cambridge (BA 1949). Joined RN 1944; served at sea and in shore weapons depts; Resident Officer, Polaris Executive, Clyde Submarine Base, 1965–68; i/c training, HMS Collingwood, 1969–70; Asst Dir, Underwater Weapon Dept, 1970; sowc 1974; Dep. Dir, RN Staff Coll., Greenwich, 1975–76, Dir, 1976; CO HMS Collingwood, 1976–79; C of S to C-in-C, Naval Home Command, 1979–81, retired. Trustee, Foundn Trust for Mentally Handicapped, 1987–. MInstD. FRSA. *Address:* c/o Barclays Bank, 1 Manvers Street, Bath, Avon. *Club:* Bath and County (Bath).

WILLIS, Norman David; General Secretary, Trades Union Congress, 1984–93; *b* 21 Jan. 1933; *s* of Victor J. M. and Kate E. Willis; *m* 1963, Maureen Kenning; one *s* one *d*. *Educ:* Ashford County Grammar Sch.; Ruskin and Oriel Colls, Oxford, 1955–59 (Hon. Fellow, Oriel Coll., 1984). Employed by TGWU, 1949; Nat. Service, 1951–53; PA to Gen. Sec., TGWU, 1959–70; Nat. Sec., Research and Educn, TGWU, 1970–74; TUC: Asst Gen. Sec., 1974–77, Dep. Gen. Sec., 1977–84. Councillor (Lab) Staines UDC, 1971–74. Member: NEDC, 1984–92; Council, ODI, 1985–93; Council, Motability, 1985–93; Employment Appeal Tribunal, 1995–; Chm., Nat. Pensioners' Convention Steering Cttee, 1979–93; Vice-President: IMS, 1985–93; ICFTU, 1984–93; WEA, 1985–93; Trades Union Adv. Cttee to OECD, 1986–93; Pres., ETUC, 1991–93 (Vice-Pres., 1984–91). Member: Exec. Bd, UNICEF, 1986–90; Council for Charitable Support, 1988–93; Trustee: Duke of Edinburgh's Commonwealth Study Conf., 1986–93; Anglo-German Foundn for the Study of Industrial Soc., 1986–95; Council, Prince of Wales Youth Business Trust, 1986–93; Patron, West Indian Welfare (UK) Trust, 1986–93. Vice-Pres., Poetry Soc.; Member: Norfolk Naturalist Trust; Northumberland Naturalist Trust; Wildfowl and Wetlands Trust; Nat. Trust; English Heritage; Arthur Ransome Soc.; Betjeman Soc.; Embroiderers' Guild. Hon. Mem., Writers' Guild of GB. Fellow, RSPB. *Recreations:* painting, poetry, embroidery, birdwatching, canals. *Address:* c/o Trades Union Congress, Congress House, Great Russell Street, WC1B 3LS.

WILLIS, Hon. Ralph; Treasurer of Australia, Dec. 1990, and since 1993; MHR (Lab) for Gellibrand, Victoria, since 1972; *b* 14 April 1938; *s* of S. Willis; *m* 1970, Carol Dawson; one *s* two *d*. *Educ:* Footscray Central Sch.; University High Sch.; Melbourne Univ. (BCom). Australian Council of Trade Unions: Research Officer, 1960–70; Industrial Advocate, 1970–72. Instrumental in developing econ., finance and ind. relns policies for Opposition, 1976–83; Opposition spokesperson on: Ind. Relns, 1976–77; Econ. Affairs, 1977–83; Econ. Develt, Jan.–March 1983; Minister for Employment and Ind. Relns and Minister Assisting the Prime Minister for Public Service Matters, 1983–88; Minister for Transport and Communications, 1988–90; Minister of Finance, 1990–93. *Recreations:* tennis, reading, football. *Address:* Parliament House, Canberra, ACT 2600, Australia; 4 Treasury Place, Melbourne, Vic 3000, Australia.

WILLIS, Very Rev. Robert Andrew; Dean of Hereford, since 1992; *b* 17 May 1947; *s* of Thomas Willis and Vera Rosina Willis (*née* Britton). *Educ:* Kingswood Grammar Sch.; Warwick Univ. (BA); Worcester Coll., Oxford (DipTheol); Cuddesdon Coll., Oxford. Ordained deacon, 1972, priest, 1973; Curate, St Chad's, Shrewsbury, 1972–75; Vicar Choral, Salisbury Cathedral and Chaplain to Cathedral Sch., 1975–78; Team Rector, Tisbury, Wilts, 1978–87; Chaplain, Cranborne Chase Sch. and RAF Chilmark, 1978–87; RD, Chalke, 1982–87; Vicar, Sherborne with Castleton and Lillington, 1987–92; Chaplain, Sherborne Sch. for Girls, 1987–92; RD, Sherborne, 1991–92; Priest-in-charge, St John the Baptist, Hereford, 1992–. Canon and Prebendary of Salisbury Cathedral, 1988–92; Proctor in Convocation, 1985–92. Member: Council, Partnership for World Mission, 1990–; Cathedrals' Fabric Commn for England, 1994–. Governor: Cranborne Chase Sch., 1985–87; Sherborne Sch., 1987–92; Chm. of Govs, Hereford Cathedral Sch., 1993–. FRSA 1993. Sub ChStJ, 1991. *Publications:* (contrib.) Hymns Ancient and Modern, New Standard edn, 1983; (jtly) The Chorister's Companion, 1989. *Recreations:* music, literature, travel. *Address:* The Deanery, Hereford HR1 2NG. *T:* Hereford (01432) 359880. *Club:* United Oxford & Cambridge University.

WILLIS, (Robert William) Gaspard, MA; Founder and Headmaster of Copford Glebe School, 1958–69, Principal, 1969–72, retired; *b* 22 Nov. 1905; *s* of Rev. W. N. Willis, founder and Headmaster for 38 years of Ascham St Vincent's, Eastbourne, and Sophia Caroline Baker; *m* 1930, Ernestine Ruth Kimber; two *s* two *d*. *Educ:* Ascham St Vincent's, Eastbourne; Eton Coll. (Foundation Scholar); Corpus Christi Coll., Cambridge (Scholar). Assistant Master at Malvern Coll., Worcs, 1927–39 (Mathematics and Classics); Senior Mathematical Master at The King's School, Macclesfield, Cheshire, 1939–41; Headmaster of Sir William Turner's School (Coatham School), Redcar, 1941–53; Headmaster of English High School for Boys, Istanbul, Turkey, 1953–57. Hon. Fellow, Huguenot Soc. of London. Hon. Life Mem., Gainsborough's House Soc., Sudbury. Reader, 1935–92. *Publication:* A Centenary History of Ascham 1889–1989, 1989. *Recreation:* golf. *Address:* 24 St Peter's Court, Petersfield, Hants GU32 3JH. *Clubs:* Royal Over-Seas League; Newton Green Golf.

WILLIS, His Honour Roger Blenkiron, TD; a Circuit Judge (formerly County Court Judge), 1959–81; *b* 22 June 1906; *s* of late William Outhwaite Willis, KC, and Margaret Alice (*née* Blenkiron); *m* 1933, Joan Eleanor Amy Good (*d* 1990); two *d*. *Educ:* Charterhouse School; Emmanuel Coll., Cambridge. Barrister, Inner Temple, Nov. 1930. Joined Middlesex Yeomanry (TA), 1938. Served War of 1939–45. *Address:* 18 Turners Reach House, 9 Chelsea Embankment, SW3. *Clubs:* Garrick, MCC.

WILLIS, His Honour Stephen Murrell; a Circuit Judge, 1986–95; *b* 21 June 1929; *s* of late John Henry Willis and late Eileen Marian (*née* Heard), Hadleigh, Suffolk; *m* 1st, 1953, Jean Irene Eve; one *s* three *d*; 2nd, 1975, Doris Florence Davies (*née* Redding); two step *d*. *Educ:* (chorister) Christ Church Cathedral, Oxford; Bloxham Sch. (scholar). Admitted solicitor, 1955; Partner: Chamberlin Talbot & Bracey, Lowestoft and Beccles, Suffolk, 1955–63; Pearless, de Rougemont & Co., East Grinstead, Sussex, 1964–85; a Recorder, 1980–85. Chm., Lord Chancellor's Adv. Cttee for SE London, 1987–95. Founded The Suffolk Singers, 1960; Founder and Director, The Prodigal Singers and Gallery Band, 1964–. *Compositions:* mediaeval song settings for radio and theatre plays. *Recording:* (with The Prodigal Singers) Christmas Tree Carols. *Recreations:* performing early music, sailing, travel. *Address:* Villa Callisto, PO Box 1040, 8130, Paphos, Cyprus. *Club:* Noblemen and Gentlemen's Catch.

WILLISON, Lt-Gen. Sir David (John), KCB 1973; OBE 1958; MC 1945; Director General of Intelligence (Deputy Under-Secretary of State), Ministry of Defence, 1975–78; Chief Royal Engineer, 1977–82; *b* 25 Dec. 1919; *s* of Brig. A. C. Willison, DSO, MC; *m* 1st, 1941, Betty Vernon Bates (*d* 1989); one *s* two *d*; 2nd, 1994, Trisha Clitherow. *Educ:* Wellington; RMA Woolwich. 2/Lt RE, 1939; First Instructor, Bailey Bridge SME Ripon, 1942–43; OC 17 and 246 Field Cos, 1944–45; Staff Coll., Camberley 1945; Brigade Major, Indian Inf. Brigade, Java, 1946; Malaya, 1947; WO, 1948–50; OC 16 Field Co., Egypt, 1950–52; GHQ MELF, 1952–53; OC, RE Troops, Berlin, 1953–55; Directing Staff, Staff Coll., Camberley, 1955–58; AQMG (Ops), HQ British Forces Aden, 1958–60; CO, 38 Engr Regt, 1960–63; Col GS MI/DI4, MoD, 1963–66; idc 1966; BGS (Intell.), MoD, 1967–70; BGS (Intell. and Security)/ACOS, G2, HQ NORTHAG, 1970–71; Dir of Service Intelligence, MoD, 1971–72; Dep. Chief Defence Staff (Int.), 1972–75. Col Comdt RE, 1973–82. Chm., RE Widows Soc., 1987–91. Consultant on Internat. Affairs, Nat. Westminster Bank Gp, 1980–84; Consultant: County Natwest Investment Bank, 1985–91; Pareto Partners, 1991–95. Pres., Western Area, Hants, St John's Ambulance, 1987–94; Freeman, City of London, 1981. *Recreations:* sailing, shooting, gardening. *Address:* The Old Coach House, 14 Fairfield Close, Lymington, Hants SO41 3NP. *Clubs:* Naval and Military; Royal Lymington Yacht.

WILLISON, Sir John (Alexander), Kt 1970; OBE 1964; QPM 1968; DL; *b* 3 Jan. 1914; *s* of John Willison Gow Willison and Mabel Willison, Dalry, Ayrshire; *m* 1947, Jess Morris Bruce. *Educ:* Sedbergh School. Joined City of London Police, 1933; served with RNVR, 1943–46; Chief Constable: Berwick, Roxburgh and Selkirk, 1952–58; Worcestershire Constabulary, 1958–67; West Mercia Constabulary, 1967–74. DL Worcs 1968. KStJ 1973. *Address:* Ravenhills Green, Lulsley, near Worcester.

WILLMAN, John; Features Editor, Financial Times, since 1994 (Public Policy Editor, 1991–94); *b* 27 May 1949; *s* of late John Willman and of Kate Willman (*née* Thornton); *m* 1978, Margaret Shanahan; one *s* two *d*. *Educ:* Bolton Sch.; Jesus Coll., Cambridge (MA); Westminster Coll., Oxford (CertEd). Teacher, Brentford Sch. for Girls, Brentford, Mddx, 1972–76; Financial Researcher, Money Which?, 1976–79; Editor, Taxes and Assessment (Inland Revenue Staff Fedn pubn), 1979–83; Pubns Manager, Peat, Marwick, Mitchell & Co., 1983–85; Gen. Sec., Fabian Soc., 1985–89; Jt Editor, New Socialist, 1989; Editor, Consumer Policy Review, 1990–91. *Publications:* Lloyds Bank Tax Guide, annually, 1987–; Make Your Will, 1989; Labour's Electoral Challenge, 1989; Sorting Out Someone's Will, 1990; The Which? Guide to Planning and Conservation, 1990; Work for Yourself, 1991. *Address:* 143 Jerningham Road, SE14 5NJ. *T:* 0171–639 3826.

WILLMER, Prof. (Edward) Nevill, ScD; FRS 1960; Emeritus Professor of Histology, University of Cambridge, since 1969; Fellow of Clare College since 1936; *b* 15 Aug. 1902; 5th *s* of Arthur W. Willmer, Birkenhead; *m* 1939, Henrietta Noreen (Penny), 2nd *d* of H. Napier Rowlatt; two *s* two *d*. *Educ:* Birkenhead Sch.; Corpus Christi Coll., Oxford (Hon. Fellow, 1983). BA (Oxon) 1924; MA (Oxon) 1965; MSc (Manchester) 1927; ScD (Cambridge) 1944. Demonstrator and Assistant Lecturer in Physiology, Manchester, 1924–29; Lecturer in Histology, Cambridge, 1930–48; Reader, 1948–65, Prof., 1966–69. Editor, Biological Reviews, 1969–80. *Publications:* Tissue Culture, 1934; Retinal Structure and Colour Vision, 1946; Cytology and Evolution, 1960, 2nd edn 1970; (ed) Cells and Tissues in Culture, vols 1 and 2, 1965, vol. 3, 1966; Old Grantchester, 1976; The River Cam, 1979; Waen and the Willmers, 1988; What the Poet Saw, 1994; contrib. physiological and biological journals. *Recreations:* painting, gardening, walking. *Address:* Yew Garth, Grantchester, Cambridge CB3 9ND. *T:* Cambridge (01223) 840360.

See also B. J. Davenport.

WILLMER, John Franklin, QC 1967; Lloyd's Appeal Arbitrator in Salvage Cases, since 1991; *b* 30 May 1930; *s* of Rt Hon. Sir (Henry) Gordon Willmer, OBE, TD and of Barbara, *d* of Sir Archibald Hurd; *m* 1st, 1958, Nicola Ann Dickinson (marr. diss. 1979); one *s* three *d*; 2nd, 1979, Margaret Lilian, *d* of Chester B. Berryman. *Educ:* Winchester; Corpus Christi Coll., Oxford. National Service, 2nd Lieut, Cheshire Regt, 1949–50; TA Cheshire Regt, 1950–51; Middlesex Regt, 1951–57 (Captain). Called to Bar, Inner Temple, 1955, Bencher, 1975. A Gen. Comr of Income Tax for Inner Temple, 1982. Member: panel of Lloyd's Arbitrators in Salvage Cases, 1967–91; panel from which Wreck Commissioners appointed, 1967–79, reapptd 1987–. Leader, Admiralty Bar, 1992–. Freeman, Arbitrators' Co., 1992. *Recreations:* walking, visiting ancient sites and buildings. *Address:* Flat 4, 23 Lymington Road, NW6 1HZ. *T:* 0171–435 9245. *Club:* United Oxford & Cambridge University.

WILLMER, Nevill; *see* Willmer, E. N.

WILLMORE, Prof. (Albert) Peter, FRAS; Professor of Space Research, University of Birmingham, since 1972; *b* 28 April 1930; *s* of Albert Mervyn Willmore and Kathleen Helen Willmore; *m* 1st, 1963, Geraldine Anne Smith; two *s*; 2nd, 1972, Stephanie Ruth Alden; one *s* one *d*. *Educ:* Holloway Sch.; University Coll. London (BSc, PhD). Research interests: fusion res., AERE, 1954–57; upper atmosphere, using sounding rockets and satellites, esp. Ariel I (launched 1962), UCL, 1957–70; X-ray astromony, using sounding rockets and satellites, UCL, 1970–72, Univ. of Birmingham, 1972–. Tsiolkowski Medal, USSR, 1987. *Publications:* approx. 150 papers in learned jls, together with many other articles and reviews. *Recreations:* music, playing the violin (though this may not be music), literature, Bronze Age history, travel, sailing. *Address:* 38 Grove Avenue, Moseley, Birmingham B13 9RY. *T:* 0121–449 2616.

WILLMOTT, Dennis James, CBE 1988; QFSM 1981; Group Contingency Manager, 1988–93, and Fire Safety Consultant, since 1993, Avon Rubber plc; *b* 10 July 1932; *s* of James Arthur Willmott and Esther Winifred Maude Willmott (*née* Styles); *m* 1958, Mary Patricia Currey; three *s*. *Educ:* St Albans County Grammar School. MIFireE. Regular Army Service, East Surrey Regt, 1950–51, Royal Norfolk Regt, 1951–57. London, Bucks, Hants and Isle of Wight Fire Brigades, 1957–74; Dep. Chief Officer, Wilts Fire Brigade, 1974–76; Chief Staff Officer, 1976–81, Dep. Chief Officer, 1981–83, London Fire Brigade; Chief Fire Officer, Merseyside Fire Brigade, 1983–88. Member: Kennet DC, 1991–; (C) Wilts CC, 1993–. *Recreation:* walking. *Address:* 27 Highlands, Potterne, Devizes, Wilts SN10 5NS. *T:* Devizes (01380) 725672. *Clubs:* Conservative (Devizes); Royal British Legion (Potterne).

WILLMOTT, Maj.-Gen. Edward George, CB 1990; OBE 1979; CEng, FICE; Chief Executive, Construction Industry Training Board, since 1991; *b* 18 Feb. 1936; *s* of late T. E. Willmott and E. R. Willmott (*née* Murphy); *m* 1960, Sally Penelope (*née* Banyard); two *s* one *d*. *Educ:* Gonville and Caius Coll., Cambridge (MA). FICE 1989; CEng 1990. Commissioned RE 1956; psc 1968; active service, N Borneo 1963, N Ireland 1971, 1972, 1977; comd 8 Field Sqdn, 1971–73; 23 Engr Regt, 1976; 2 Armd Div. Engr Regt, 1977–78; 30 Engr Bde, 1981–82; RCDS 1983; Dep. Comdt RMCS, 1984–85; Vice-Pres. (Army), Ordnance Bd, 1985–86; Pres., Ordnance Bd, 1986–88; Dir Gen., Weapons (Army), 1988–90. Col Comdt, RE, 1987–95. Hon. Col 101 (London) Engr Regt (V), 1990–. Pres., Instn of Royal Engrs, 1987–90. Mem., Court of Assistants, Engineers' Co., 1994–. Mem. Council, Roedean Sch., 1994–. *Recreation:* gardening. *Club:* Institute of Directors.

WILLMOTT, Prof. John Charles, CBE 1983; PhD; Professor of Physics, University of Manchester, 1964–89 (Director of the Physical Laboratories, 1967–89; a Pro-Vice-Chancellor, 1982–85; Adviser to Vice-Chancellor on Research Exploitation, 1988–93); *b* 1 April 1922; *s* of Arthur George Willmott and Annie Elizabeth Willmott; *m* 1952, Sheila Madeleine Dumbell; two *s* one *d*. *Educ:* Bancroft's Sch., Woodford; Imperial Coll. of Science and Technol. (BSc, PhD). ARCS. Lectr in Physics, Liverpool Univ., 1948–58, Sen. Lectr, 1958–63, Reader, 1963–64. Member: SERC (formerly SRC), 1978–82; Science for Stability Cttee, NATO, 1981–. *Publications:* Tables of Coefficients for the Analysis of Triple Angular Correlations of Gamma-rays from Aligned Nuclei, 1968;

Atomic Physics, 1975; articles on nuclear structure in learned jls. *Address:* 37 Hall Moss Lane, Bramhall, Cheshire SK7 1RB. *T:* 0161–439 4169.

WILLMOTT, Peter; Senior Fellow, Policy Studies Institute, since 1983; *b* 18 Sept. 1923; *s* of Benjamin Merriman Willmott and Dorothy Willmott (*née* Waymouth); *m* 1948, Phyllis Mary Noble; two *s*. *Educ:* Tollington Sch., London; Ruskin Coll., Oxford. BSc (Soc) (external) London. Research Asst, Labour Party, 1948–54; Institute of Community Studies: Res. Officer, 1954–60; Dep. Dir, 1960–64; Co-Dir, 1964–78; Chm., 1978–. Dir, Centre for Environmental Studies, 1978–80; Head of Central Policy Unit, GLC, 1981–83; Vis. Prof., Bartlett Sch. of Architecture and Planning, UCL, 1972–83. Visiting Professor: Ecole Pratique des Hautes Etudes, Paris, 1972; LSE, 1983–88; Regents' Lectr, Univ. of California, 1982. Hon. LitD Univ. of Orleans, 1990. Editor, Policy Studies, 1988–. *Publications:* (with Michael Young) Family and Kinship in East London, 1957; (with Michael Young) Family and Class in a London Suburb, 1960; The Evolution of a Community, 1963; Adolescent Boys of East London, 1966; (with Michael Young) The Symmetrical Family, 1973; (ed) Sharing Inflation? Poverty Report, 1976; (with Graeme Shankland and David Jordan) Inner London: policies for dispersal and balance, 1977; (with Charles Madge) Inner City Poverty in Paris and London, 1981; (with Roger Mitton and Phyllis Willmott) Unemployment, Poverty and Social Policy in Europe, 1983; Community in Social Policy, 1984; Social Networks, Informal Care and Public Policy, 1986; Friendship Networks and Social Support, 1987; (with Alan Murie) Polarisation and Social Housing, 1988; Community Initiatives: patterns and prospects, 1989; (ed) Urban Trends 1, 1992; (ed) Urban Trends 2, 1994. *Address:* 27 Kingsley Place, N6 5EA. *T:* 0181–348 3958.

WILLOCHRA, Bishop of, since 1987; **Rt. Rev. William David Hair McCall;** *b* 29 Feb. 1940; *s* of late Rt Rev. Theodore Bruce McCall, ThD, Bishop of Wangaratta, and Helen Christie McCall; *m* 1969, Marion Carmel le Breton; two *s* three *d*. *Educ:* Launceston and Sydney Grammar Schools; Saint Michael's House, Crafers. Deacon 1963, priest 1964, dio. Riverina; Assistant Curate: St Alban's, Griffith, 1963–64; St Peter's, Broken Hill, 1965–67; Priest-in-charge, Barellan-Weethalle, 1967–73; Rector: St John's, Corowa, 1973–78; St George's, Goodwood, 1978–87; Pastoral Chaplain, St Barnabas' Theol Coll., 1980–87. *Recreations:* reading, walking. *Address:* Bishop's House, Gladstone, SA 5473, Australia. *T:* (86) 622057.

WILLOTT, Brian; *see* Willott, W. B.

WILLOTT, (William) Brian, PhD; Chief Executive, Export Credits Guarantee Department, since 1992; *b* 14 May 1940; *s* of late Dr William Harford Willott and Dr Beryl P. M. Willott; *m* 1970, Alison Leyland Pyke-Lees; two *s* two *d*. *Educ:* Trinity Coll., Cambridge (MA, PhD). Research Associate, Univ. of Maryland, USA, 1965–67; Asst Principal, Board of Trade, 1967–69; Principal: BoT, 1969–73; HM Treasury, 1973–75; Asst Sec., Dept of Industry, 1975–78; Secretary: Industrial Development Unit, DoI, 1978–80; NEB, 1980–81; Chief Exec., British Technology Gp (NEB and NRDC), 1981–84; Head of IT Div., DTI, 1984–87; Hd of Financial Services Div., DTI, 1987–92. *Recreations:* music, reading, ancient history, gardening. *Address:* Export Credits Guarantee Department, 2 Exchange Tower, Harbour Exchange Square, E14 9GS.

WILLOUGHBY, family name of **Baron Middleton.**

WILLOUGHBY DE BROKE, 21st Baron *cr* 1491; **Leopold David Verney;** *b* 14 Sept. 1938; *s* of 20th Baron Willoughby de Broke, MC, AFC, AE and Rachel (*d* 1991), *d* of Sir Bourchier Wrey, 11th Bt; *S* father, 1986; *m* 1965, Petra, 2nd *d* of Sir John Aird, 3rd Bt, MVO, MC; three *s*. *Educ:* Le Rosey; New College, Oxford. *Heir: s* Hon. Rupert Greville Verney, *b* 4 March 1966. *Address:* Ditchford Farm, Moreton-in-Marsh, Glos GL56 9RD.

WILLOUGHBY DE ERESBY, Baroness (27th in line), *cr* 1313; **Nancy Jane Marie Heathcote-Drummond-Willoughby;** DL; *b* 1 Dec. 1934; *d* of 3rd Earl of Ancaster, KCVO, TD, and Hon. Nancy Phyllis Louise Astor (*d* 1975), *d* of 2nd Viscount Astor; *S* to barony of father, 1983. DL Lincs, 1993. *Heir: co heiresses:* Lady Catherine Mary Clementina Hume [*b* 25 Sept. 1906; *m* 1st, 1935, John St Maur Ramsden (marr. diss. 1947), *s* of Sir John Frecheville Ramsden 6th Bt; one *d*; 2nd, 1948, Charles Wedderburn Hume (*d* 1974)]; Lady Priscilla Aird [*b* 29 Oct. 1909; *m* 1939, Col Sir John Renton Aird, 3rd Bt, MVO, MC; one *s* three *d*]. *Address:* Grimsthorpe, Bourne, Lincs PE10 0LZ. *T:* Edenham (01778) 591222.

WILLOUGHBY, Ven. David Albert; Archdeacon of the Isle of Man, 1982–Feb. 1996; Vicar of St George's with All Saints, Douglas, 1980–Feb. 1996; *b* 8 Feb. 1931; *s* of John Robert and Jane May Willoughby; *m* 1959, Brenda Mary (*née* Watson); two *s*. *Educ:* Bradford Grammar School; St John's Coll., Univ. of Durham (BA, Dip. Theol.). Assistant Curate: St Peter's, Shipley, 1957–60; Barnoldswick with Bracewell, 1960–62; Rector of St Chad's, New Moston, Manchester, 1962–72; Vicar of Marown, Isle of Man, 1972–80; Rural Dean of Douglas, 1980–82. Chaplain, Noble's Hospital, Douglas, 1980–96; Mem. Gen. Synod, 1982–96; Church Commissioner for IOM, 1982–96. *Recreations:* motor cycling, competition singing and involvement in light entertainment. *Address:* (until Feb. 1996) St George's with All Saints Vicarage, 16 Devonshire Road, Douglas, Isle of Man IM2 3RB. *T:* Douglas (01624) 675430; (from Feb. 1996) 19 Glen Vine Park, Glen Vine, Isle of Man IM4 4EZ. *T:* Douglas (01624) 852493.

WILLOUGHBY, Kenneth James; *b* 6 Nov. 1922; *y s* of late Frank Albert Willoughby and late Florence Rose (*née* Darbyshire); *m* 1943, Vera May Dickerson; one *s* one *d*. *Educ:* Hackney Downs (Grocers') Sch.; Selwyn Coll., Cambridge. Tax Officer, Inland Revenue, 1939; Royal Engineers, UK, Egypt, Italy, Austria, Greece, 1941–47 (despatches, Captain); Asst Auditor, Exchequer and Audit Dept, 1947; Asst Prin., Min. of Civil Aviation, 1949; Asst Private Sec. to Minister of Civil Aviation, 1950; Private Sec. to Perm. Sec., 1951; Principal, Min. of Transport (and later, Civil Aviation), 1951; Sec., Air Transport Adv. Council, 1957–61; Asst Sec., Min. of Aviation, 1962; Under-Secretary: Min. of Technology, 1968–70; DTI, 1970–74. *Recreations:* music, reading. *Address:* 84 Douglas Avenue, Exmouth, Devon EX8 2HG. *T:* Exmouth (01395) 271175.

WILLOUGHBY, Rt. Rev. Noel Vincent; *see* Cashel and Ossory, Bishop of.

WILLOUGHBY, Roger James; Clerk of Private Bills, since 1988, Registrar of Members' Interests, since 1994, House of Commons; *b* 30 Sept. 1939; *s* of late Hugh Lloyd Willoughby and Gerd Willoughby; *m* 1970, Veronica, *d* of Frank and Elisabeth Lepper. *Educ:* Shrewsbury Sch.; Balliol Coll., Oxford (BA). A Clerk in the House of Commons, 1962–; Dep. Principal Clerk, 1975; Sec. to UK Delegn to European Parlt, 1976; Clerk of Home Affairs Cttee, 1979; Clerk of Supply, Public Bill Office, 1984. *Recreations:* literature, cricket, walking in solitary places, bonfires. *Address:* 35 Defoe Avenue, Kew, Richmond, Surrey TW9 4DS. *T:* 0181–876 1718.

WILLS, family name of **Baron Dulverton.**

WILLS, Arthur William, OBE 1990; DMus (Dunelm), FRCO (CHM), ADCM; composer; Organist, Ely Cathedral, 1958–90; *b* 19 Sept. 1926; *s* of Violet Elizabeth and Archibald Wills; *m* 1953, Mary Elizabeth Titterton; one *s* one *d*. *Educ:* St John's Sch., Coventry. Sub. Organist, Ely Cathedral, 1949; Director of Music, King's School, Ely, 1953–65; Prof., Royal Academy of Music, 1964–92. Mem. Council, RCO, 1966–; Examr to Royal Schs of Music, 1966–. Recital tours in Canada, Europe, USA, Australia and New Zealand; recording artist. Hon. RAM, Hon. FLCM, FRSCM. *Publications:* (contrib.) English Church Music, 1978; Organ, 1984, 2nd edn 1993; numerous musical compositions include: *organ:* Sonata, Trio Sonata, Christmas Meditations, Prelude and Fugue (Alkmaar), Tongues of Fire, Variations on Amazing Grace, Symphonia Eliensis, Concerto (organ, strings and timpani), The Fenlands (symphonic suite for brass band and organ), Etheldreda Rag (organ or piano); *brass band:* Overture: A Muse of Fire; *guitar:* Sonata, Pavane and Galliard, Hommage à Ravel, Four Elizabethan Love Songs (alto and guitar), Moods and Diversions, The Year of the Tiger, Suite Africana, Concerto Lirico for Guitar Quartet; Concerto for guitar and organ; *chamber:* Sacrae Symphoniae: Veni Creator Spiritus; A Toccata of Galuppi's (counter-tenor and string quartet); *piano:* Sonata; *choral:* Missa Eliensis, The Child for Today (carol sequence), The Light Invisible (double choir, organ and percussion), Missa in Memoriam Benjamin Britten, An English Requiem, Jerusalem Luminosa (choir and organ), Ely (part-song for treble voices), Caedmon: a children's cantata, The Gods of Music (choral concerto); *vocal:* When the Spirit Comes (four poems of Emily Brontë), The Dark Lady (eight Shakespeare Sonnets); Eternity's Sunrise (three poems of William Blake); *opera:* '1984'; *orchestra:* Symphony No 1 in A minor. *Recreations:* travel, antique collecting, Eastern philosophy. *Address:* Paradise House, 26 New Barns Road, Ely, Cambs CB7 4PN. *T:* Ely (01353) 662084.

WILLS, Brian Alan, PhD; FPS, CChem, FRSC; Chief Pharmacist, Department of Health (formerly of Health and Social Security), 1978–89, retired; *b* 17 Feb. 1927; *s* of late William Wills and Emily (*née* Hibbert); *m* 1955, Barbara Joan Oggelsby; one *d*. *Educ:* Univ. of Nottingham (BPharm); PhD (London). FPS 1972 (MPS 1949); FRSC (FRIC 1967, ARIC 1957); CChem 1975. Lecturer in Pharmaceutics, Sch. of Pharmacy, Univ. of London, 1951–57; Head of Research and Control Dept, Allen & Hanburys (Africa) Ltd, Durban, S Africa, 1957–62; Head of Control Div., Allen & Hanburys Ltd, London, E2, 1962–78. Member: British Pharmacopoeia Commn, 1973–94; UK delegn to European Pharmacopoeia Commn, 1975–94; UK delegn to Council of Europe Public Health Cttee (Partial Agreement) on Pharmaceutical Questions, 1979–89; WHO Expert Adv. Panel on Internat. Pharmacopoeia and Pharmaceutical Preparations, 1979–89. Vis. Professor: Univ. of Bath, 1979–83; Univ. of Bradford, 1984–. Member: Jt Formulary Cttee for British Nat. Formulary, 1979–89; Pharmacy Working Party, Nat. Adv. Body for Local Authy Higher Educn, 1982–89; Bd of Studies in Pharmacy, London Univ., 1979–87; Council, Sch. of Pharmacy, London Univ., 1981–89. Hon. Auditor, RPSGB, 1990–. Mem. Ct of Assts, Soc. of Apothecaries of London, 1987–. *Publications:* papers on sterilisation and disinfection and on the preservation, stability and quality control of pharmaceutical preparations. *Address:* 41 King's Mead, Ripon, N Yorks HG4 1EJ. *T:* Ripon (01765) 601589.

WILLS, Colin Spencer, FCA; Chairman, Visiting Arts Office of Great Britain and Northern Ireland, since 1990; Director: Breadwinners (London) Ltd, since 1987; Rhinegold Publishing Ltd, since 1991; *b* 25 June 1937; *s* of Sir John Spencer Wills and late Elizabeth Garcke. *Educ:* Eton; Queens' Coll., Cambridge (MA). FCA 1967. Qualified, 1962; worked in USA, 1963–64; Rediffusion Television, 1964–68; Dep. Gen. Man., ATV Network, Birmingham, 1968–69; employed by British Electric Traction, 1970–88 as Managing Director: Humphries Holdings plc, 1977–85; A-R Television, 1972–88; Director: Thames Television, 1970–91; Euston Films, 1972–91; Wembley Stadium, 1974–84; BAFTA, 1980–94. Gov., English Nat. Ballet, 1988–94. *Recreations:* music, opera, travel, country pursuits. *Address:* 12 Campden Hill Square, W8 7LB. *T:* 0171–727 0534; Old Brick Farm, Burwash, East Sussex. *T:* Burwash (01435) 882234. *Club:* White's.
See also N. K. S. Wills.

WILLS, Sir David; *see* Wills, Sir H. D. H.

WILLS, Sir (David) Seton, 5th Bt *cr* 1904, of Hazelwood and Clapton-in-Gordano; FRICS; *b* 29 Dec. 1939; *s* of Major George Seton Wills (*d* 1979) (*yr s* of 3rd Bt) and Lilah Mary, *y d* of Captain Percy Richard Hare; *S* uncle, 1983; *m* 1968, Gillian, twin *d* of A. P. Eastoe; one *s* three *d*. *Educ:* Eton. *Heir: s* James Seton Wills, *b* 24 Nov. 1970. *Address:* Eastridge House, Ramsbury, Marlborough, Wilts SN8 2HJ.

WILLS, Dean Robert, AO 1994 (AM 1986); Chairman, Coca-Cola Amatil Ltd (formerly Amatil Ltd), since 1984 (Director, since 1975; Deputy Chairman, 1983–84; Managing Director, 1984–94); *b* 10 July 1933; *s* of Walter William Wills and Violet Wills (*née* Kent); *m* 1955, Margaret Florence Williams, *d* of E. G. Williams; one *s* two *d*. *Educ:* Sacred Heart Coll., S. Aust.; SA Inst. of Technology. AASA. Dir, 1974, Man. Dir, 1977, Chm., 1983–89, W. D. & H. O. Wills (Australia) Ltd; Chm., Australian Eagle Insurance Co., 1986–89. Director: Nat. Mutual Life Assoc., 1991– (Vice Chm., 1992–); Australian Grand Prix Corp., 1994– (Dep. Chm.); Westfield Hldgs, 1994–; John Fairfax Hldgs, 1994–. Member: Business Council of Aust., 1984–94 (Vice Pres., 1987–88, Pres., 1988–90); Bd of Aust. Graduate Sch. of Management, Univ. of NSW, 1985–. Pres., 1991, Gov., 1992–94, Med. Foundn; Trustee, Mus. of Applied Arts and Sciences (Powerhouse Mus.), NSW, 1986–90. *Recreations:* tennis, classic cars. *Address:* Coc-Cola Amatil Ltd, GPO Box 145, Sydney, NSW 2001, Australia.

WILLS, Helen; *see* Roark, H. W.

WILLS, Sir (Hugh) David (Hamilton), Kt 1980; CBE 1971 (MBE 1946); TD 1964; DL; *b* 19 June 1917; 2nd *s* of late Frederick Noel Hamilton Wills and of Margery Hamilton Sinclair; *m* 1949, Eva Helen, JP, *d* of late Major A. T. McMorrough Kavanagh, MC; one *s* one *d*. *Educ:* Eton; Magdalen Coll., Oxford. Served War of 1939–45 with Queen's Own Cameron Highlanders (TA): France 1940, Aruba 1941; GSO 3 (Ops) GHQ Home Forces, 1942–43; GSO 2 (Ops) Southern Command, 1943–44. Chairman of Trustees, Rendcomb Coll., 1955–83; Chm., Ditchley Foundation, 1972–83; Mem. Governing Body, Atlantic Coll., 1963–73, 1980–. High Sheriff Oxfordshire 1961, DL 1967. *Recreations:* fishing, sailing. *Address:* Sandford Park, Sandford St Martin, Oxford OX7 7AJ. *T:* Great Tew (01608) 683238. *Clubs:* Boodle's, Ends of the Earth.

WILLS, Sir John Vernon, 4th Bt, *cr* 1923; TD; FRICS; JP; Lord-Lieutenant and Custos Rotulorum of Avon, 1974–April 1996; Lord-Lieutenant of Somerset, since 1994; President, Bristol and West Building Society, since 1993 (Director, 1969–93; Vice-Chairman, 1982–88; Chairman, 1988–93); Chairman, Bristol Waterworks Co., since 1986 (Director, 1964–73; Deputy Chairman, 1983–86); Director, Bristol Evening Post, since 1973 (Deputy Chairman, since 1978); Deputy Chairman, Bristol United Press, since 1980; *b* 3 July 1928; *s* of Sir George Vernon Proctor Wills, 2nd Bt, and Lady Nellie Jeannie, ARRC, JP, *y d* of late J. T. Rutherford, Abergavenny; *S* brother 1945; *m* 1953, Diana Veronica Cecil (Jane), *o d* of Douglas R. M. Baker, Winsford, Somerset; four *s*. *Educ:* Eton. Served Coldstream Guards, 1946–49; Lt-Col Comdg N Somerset and Bristol Yeomanry, 1965–67; Bt Col 1967; now TARO. Hon. Col, 37th (Wessex and Welsh) Signal Regt, T&AVR, 1975–87; Hon. Capt., RNR, 1988. Chm., Wessex Water Auth., 1973–82; Mem., Nat. Water Council, 1973–82; Chm., Bristol Marketing Bd, 1984–86. Local Dir, Barclays Bank, 1981–87. Pro-Chancellor, Univ. of Bath, 1979–. Pres., Royal Bath and West Southern Counties Soc., 1980. Member of Somerset CC. JP 1962, DL 1968, High Sheriff, 1968, Somerset. KStJ 1978. Hon. LLD Bristol, 1986; Hon. DLitt

Bath, 1993. *Heir:* s David James Vernon Wills, *b* 2 Jan. 1955. *Address:* Langford Court, near Bristol BS18 7DA. *T:* Wrington (01934) 862338. *Club:* Cavalry and Guards.

WILLS, Nicholas Kenneth Spencer, FCA; international consultant; Chairman, The Eclectic American Catalogue Co. Ltd, since 1992; *b* 18 May 1941; *s* of Sir John Spencer Wills, and late Elizabeth Drusilla Alice Clare Garcke; *m* 1st, 1973, Hilary Ann (marr. diss. 1983); two *s* two *d*; 2nd, 1985, Philippa Trench Casson, *d* of Rev. D. Casson; one *d*. *Educ:* Rugby Sch.; Queens' Coll., Cambridge (MA; Hon. Fellow, 1990). Binder Hamlyn & Co., 1963–67; Morgan Grenfell, 1967–70; BET plc, 1970–92 (Director, 1975–92; Man. Dir, 1982–91; Chief Exec., 1985–91; Chm., 1991–92). Managing Director: Birmingham & Dist Investment Trust, 1970–91; Electrical & Industrial Investment, 1970–91; National Electric Construction, 1971–91; Chairman: Argus Press Hldgs, 1974–83; Electrical Press, 1974–83; Boulton & Paul plc, 1979–84; Initial plc, 1979–87; BET Building Services Ltd, 1984–87; Dep. Chm., Nat. Mutual Home Loans, 1994–; Director: Bradbury, Agnew & Co. Ltd, 1974–83; National Mutual Life Assce Soc., 1974–85, 1991– (Dep. Chm., 1992–); St George Assce Co. Ltd, 1974–81; Colonial Securities Trust Co. Ltd, 1976–82; Cable Trust Ltd, 1976–77; Globe Investment Trust plc, 1977–90; Drayton Consolidated, 1982–92; Barings Tribune Investment Trust, 1992–; Hitchin Priory Ltd, 1992– (Dep. Chm., 1994–); Onslow Trading and Commercial, 1994–; American Chamber of Commerce (UK), 1985– (Vice-Pres., 1988–); United World Colls (Internat.) Ltd, 1987–; Advr, City and West End, National Westminster Bank, 1982–91; Adv. Bd, Charterhouse Buy-Out Funds, 1990–. Member: Council, CBI, 1987–92 (Member: Overseas Cttee, 1987–90; Public Expenditure Task Force, 1988; Economic Affairs Cttee, 1991–); Council, Business in the Community, 1987–92; Adv. Bd, Fishman-Davidson Center for Study of Service Sector, Wharton Sch., Univ. of Pennsylvania, 1988–92. Mem. Adv. Council, Prince's Youth Business Trust, 1988– (Hon. Treas., 1989–92; Mem., Investment Cttee, 1992–); Chm., Internat. Trustees, Internat. Fedn of Keystone Youth Orgns, 1990–. Treasurer and Churchwarden, Church of St Bride, Fleet Street, 1978–; Asst, Worshipful Co. of Haberdashers', 1981–; Gov., Haberdashers' Aske's Schs, Elstree, 1989– (Chm., Girls' Sch. Cttee, 1994–). CIMgt; FCIM; FCT; FRSA. *Recreations:* shooting, trying to farm in the Highlands. *Address:* 75 Brook Street, W1Y 2EB. *T:* 0171–495 8919. *Clubs:* White's, Royal Automobile, City Livery; Clyde Cruising.
See also C. S. Wills.

WILLS, Peter Gordon Bethune, TD 1967; Director: Hambro Clearing Ltd (formerly Sheppards and Chase Options Ltd), 1977–93 (Chairman, 1977–92); BCW Stock Lending Consultants Ltd, 1992–93; *b* 25 Oct. 1931; *s* of P. L. B. Wills and E. W. Wills (*née* Stapleton); *m* 1st, Linda Hutton; two *s* one *d*; 2nd, Gloria Hart; 3rd, Faith Hines. *Educ:* Malvern Coll.; Corpus Christi Coll., Cambridge, 1952–55 (MA). National Service with Royal Inniskilling Fusiliers, N Ireland and Korea, 1950–52; TA, London Irish Rifles, 1952–67. Joined Sheppards & Co. (later Sheppards and Chase), 1955, Partner, 1960–85; Chairman, Sheppards Moneybrokers Ltd, 1985–89. Member, Stock Exchange Council, 1973–87 (Dep. Chm., 1979–82; Chm., Money Brokers' Cttee, 1985–89). Director: Wills Group plc, 1969–87 (Vice Chm.); LIFFE, 1982; BAII Holding, 1986–89; The Securities Assoc., 1986–89 (Chm., Membership Cttee); London Clear, 1986–89; The Securities Inst., 1992–93 (Chm., Membership Cttee; Fellow, 1993). Specialist Advr to Social Security Cttee, H of C, 1993. *Recreation:* collecting mangles. *Address:* Far Horizons, Haytor, Newton Abbot, Devon TQ13 9XU. *Club:* Brooks's.

WILLS, Sir Seton; *see* Wills, Sir D. S.

WILLSON, Prof. (Francis Michael) Glenn; Vice-Chancellor, 1978–84, Emeritus Professor, since 1985, Murdoch University, Western Australia; *b* 29 Sept. 1924; *s* of late Christopher Glenn Willson and late Elsie Katrine (*née* Mattick); *m* 1945, Jean (*née* Carlyle); two *d*. *Educ:* Carlisle Grammar Sch.; Manchester Univ. (BA Admin); Balliol and Nuffield Colls, Oxford (DPhil, MA). Merchant Navy, 1941–42; RAF, 1943–46; BOAC 1946–47. Research Officer, Royal Inst. of Public Admin, 1953–60; Res. Fellow, Nuffield Coll., Oxford, 1955–60; Lectr in Politics, St Edmund Hall, Oxford, 1958–60; Prof. of Govt, UC Rhodesia and Nyasaland, 1960–64; Dean, Faculty of Social Studies, UC Rhodesia and Nyasaland, 1962–64; University of California, Santa Cruz: Prof. of Govt/Politics, 1965–74; Provost of Stevenson Coll., 1967–74; Vice-Chancellor, College and Student Affairs, 1973–74; Vis. Prof., 1985–92; Warden, Goldsmiths' Coll., London, 1974–75; Principal of Univ. of London, 1975–78. *Publications:* (with D.N. Chester) The Organization of British Central Government 1914–56, 2nd edn 1914–64, 1968; Administrators in Action, 1961; A Strong Supporting Cast: the Shaw Lefevres 1789–1936, 1993; Our Minerva: the men and politics of the University of London 1836–1858, 1995; contrib. Public Admin, Polit. Studies, Parly Affairs, etc. *Address:* 32 Digby Mansions, Hammersmith Bridge Road, W6 9DF.

WILLSON, John Michael, CMG 1988; HM Diplomatic Service, retired; High Commissioner in Zambia, 1988–90; *b* 15 July 1931; *e s* of late Richard and Kathleen Willson; *m* 1954, Phyllis Marian Dawn, *o c* of late William and Phyllis Holman Richards, OBE; two *s* two *d*. *Educ:* Wimbledon Coll.; University Coll., Oxford (MA); Trinity Hall, Cambridge. National Service, 1949–51. HM Colonial Service, N Rhodesia, 1955–64; Min. of Overseas Development, 1965–70 (seconded to British High Commn, Malta, 1967–70); joined HM Diplomatic Service, 1970; British Consulate-General, Johannesburg, 1972–75; FCO (W Indian and N American Depts), 1975–78; Special Counsellor for African Affairs, 1978; Secretary-General, Rhodesian Independence Conf., 1979; Salisbury (on staff of Governor of Rhodesia), 1979–80; Counsellor, Bucharest, 1980–82; Ambassador to Ivory Coast, Burkina (formerly Upper Volta) and Niger, 1983–87; seconded to RCDS, 1987. *Recreations:* gardening, photography, music. *Address:* c/o C. Hoare & Co., 37 Fleet Street, EC4P 4DQ; La Boussaque, 83830 Claviers, France. *Club:* Commonwealth Trust.

WILMINGTON, Joseph (Robert); JP; Chairman and Managing Director, Wilmington Employment Agencies Ltd, since 1966; *b* 21 April 1932; *s* of Joseph R. Wilmington and Magtilda Susanna Wilmington; *m* Anne; two *s*. *Educ:* Alsop High Sch., Liverpool; London Sch. of Economics. Mem., Liverpool City Council, 1962; Past Chm., Liverpool Liberal Party, 1965–67; Chairman: Personnel Cttee, Liverpool City Council; Markets Cttee, Liverpool City Council; Chief Whip; Lord Mayor of Liverpool, 1974–75. Chm., NW Fedn of Employment Consultants; Mem. Nat. Exec., Fedn of Employment Consultants; Mem. Inst. Employment Consultants. JP Liverpool, 1976. *Recreations:* koi keeping, music and the arts. *Address:* Jordaan, New Mill Stile, Church Road, Woolton, Liverpool L25 6DA. *T:* 0151–428 5817.

WILMOT, David, QPM 1989; Chief Constable, Greater Manchester Police, since 1991; *b* 12 March 1943; *m* Ann Marilyn (*née* Doyle). *Educ:* Southampton Univ. (BSc). Lancashire Constabulary, 1962; Merseyside Police, 1974; W Yorkshire Police, 1983; Deputy Chief Constable, Greater Manchester Police, 1987. *Address:* Greater Manchester Police, PO Box 22 (S West PDO), Chester House, Boyer Street, Manchester M16 0RE. *T:* 0161–872 5050.

WILMOT, Sir Henry Robert, 9th Bt *cr* 1759; *b* 10 April 1967; *s* of Sir Robert Arthur Wilmot, 8th Bt, and of Juliet Elvira, *e d* of Captain M. N. Tufnell, RN; *S* father, 1974; *m* 1995, Susan Clare, *er d* of John Malvern. *Heir: kinsman* Martyn Sacheverel Wilmot [*b* 2 Sept. 1914; *m* 1948, Mona Elizabeth, *yr d* of Stanley David Milnes Horner; two *s* one *d*]. *Address:* The Garden Lodge, Chittoe, Chippenham, Wilts SN15 2EW. *Clubs:* Buck's, Boodle's.

WILMOT, Sir John Assheton E.; *see* Eardley-Wilmot.

WILMOT, Robert William, (Robb Wilmot), CBE 1985; Founder and Chairman: Wilmot Consulting Inc., since 1994; WAM Communications Inc., since 1994; Poqet Computer Inc., since 1987; Voicewaves Inc., since 1993; *b* 2 Jan. 1945; *s* of Thomas Arthur William Wilmot and Frances Mary Hull; *m* 1969, Mary Josephine Sharkey; two *s*. *Educ:* Royal Grammar Sch., Worcester; Nottingham Univ. BSc (1st cl. Hons) Electrical Engrg. Texas Instruments, 1966–81: European Technical Dir, France, 1973–74; Div. Dir, USA, 1974–78; Man. Dir, 1978–81; Asst Vice Pres., 1980; International Computers (ICL): Man. Dir, 1981–83; Chief Exec., 1983–84; Chm., 1985. Chairman: Virtual Vineyards Inc., 1995–; Euroventures BV, 1993–; Founder Dir, Movid Technology Inc., 1986–; Director: Sequent Inc., 1990–; Com 21 Inc., 1995–. Hon. DSc: Nottingham, 1983; City, 1984; Cranfield, 1988. *Recreations:* music, theatre, walking, vintage boats. *Address:* 13,333 La Cresta Drive, Los Altos Hills, CA 94022, USA.

WILMOT-SITWELL, Peter Sacheverell; Director, S. G. Warburg (formerly S. G. Warburg, Akroyd, Rowe & Pitman, Mullens) Securities Ltd (Joint Chairman, 1986–90; Chairman, 1990–94); *b* 28 March 1935; *s* of late Robert Bradshaw Wilmot-Sitwell and Barbara Elizabeth Fisher; *m* 1960, Clare Veronica Cobbold (LVO 1991); two *s* one *d*. *Educ:* Eton Coll.; Oxford Univ., 1955–58 (BA, MA). Commnd Coldstream Guards, 1953–55. Trainee, Hambros Bank Ltd, 1958–59; Partner 1959–82, Sen. Partner 1982–86, Rowe & Pitman. Chm., Mercury World Mining Trust, 1993–; Director (non-executive): W. H. Smith Ltd, 1987–; Stock Exchange Bd, 1991–94. *Recreations:* shooting, golf, tennis. *Address:* Portman House, Dummer, near Basingstoke, Hants RG25 2AD. *Clubs:* White's; Swinley Forest (Ascot).

WILMOT-SMITH, Richard James Crosbie; QC 1994; *b* 12 May 1952; *s* of late John Patrick Wilmot-Smith and of Rosalys Wilmot-Smith (*née* Massy); *m* 1978, Jenny, *d* of late R. W. Castle and L. M. Castle; one *s* two *d*. *Educ:* Charterhouse; Univ. of N Carolina (Morehead Schol.; AB 1975). Called to the Bar, Middle Temple, 1978 (Benefactors Law Schol.). *Publications:* Encyclopedia of Forms and Precedents, 5th edn: (contrib. and ed) Vol. 5, Building and Engineering Contracts, 1986; (contrib.) Vol. 12, Contracts for Services, 1994. *Recreations:* music, theatre, cinema, playing cricket with my children. *Address:* 39 Essex Street, WC2A 3AT. *T:* 0171–583 1111. *Club:* Kent CC.

WILMOTT, Peter Graham; Director-General (Customs and Indirect Taxation), Commission of the European Communities, since 1990; *b* 6 Jan. 1947; *s* of John Joseph Wilmott and Violet Ena Wilmott; *m* 1969, Jennifer Carolyn Plummer; two *d*. *Educ:* Hove Grammar Sch.; Trinity Coll., Cambridge (MA). Asst Principal, Customs and Excise, 1968; Second Sec., UK Delegn to EEC, Brussels, 1971; Principal, Customs and Excise, 1973; First Sec., UK Perm. Rep's Office to EEC, Brussels, 1977; Asst to UK Mem., European Ct of Auditors, Luxembourg, 1980; Asst Sec., Customs and Excise, 1983; a Comr of Customs and Excise, 1988. *Recreations:* travelling, building and mending things.

WILMSHURST, Jon Barry; Under Secretary, Economic and Social Division, and Chief Economist, Overseas Development Administration, since 1990; *b* 25 Oct. 1936; *s* of Edwin and Sylvia Wilmshurst (*née* Munson); *m* 1960, June Taylor; four *d*. *Educ:* Beckenham and Penge Grammar Sch.; Manchester Univ. (BA Econ.). Statistician, Fedn of Rhodesia and Nyasaland, 1960–63; Inst. of Economic and Social Research, 1964; Statistician and Economic Adviser, ODA, 1964–71; Senior Economic Adviser: ODA, 1971–79; Dept of Transport, 1979–83; Monopolies and Mergers Commn, 1983–85; ODA, 1985–90. *Recreations:* golf, gardening. *Address:* Overseas Development Administration, 94 Victoria Street, SW1E 5JL. *Club:* Langley Park Golf.

WILMSHURST, Michael Joseph; HM Diplomatic Service, retired; *b* 14 Sept. 1934; *s* of Mr and Mrs E. J. Wilmshurst; *m* 1958, Mary Elizabeth Kemp; one *s* one *d*. *Educ:* Latymer Upper Sch.; Christ's Coll., Cambridge. BA 1959. Entered Foreign Service, 1953. 2nd Lieut, Royal Signals, 1953–55. Asst Private Sec. to Foreign Secretary, 1960–62; 2nd Sec., The Hague, 1962–65; 1st Sec. (Commercial), Bogota, 1965–67; Western European Dept, FCO, 1968–70; 1st Sec. (Commercial), Cairo, 1970–73; Asst Head of Energy Dept, FCO, 1974–75; Asst Head of Energy and Arms Control and Disarmament Depts, 1975–77; Counsellor and Head of Joint Nuclear Unit, FCO, 1977–78; Consul, Guatemala City, 1978–81; Sabbatical, Stiftung Wissenschaft und Politik, Ebenhausen, 1982; UK Permanent Rep. to IAEA, UNIDO and UN, Vienna, 1982–87; seconded to IAEA, Vienna as Dir of External Relns, 1987; retd from HM Diplomatic Service, 1989, from IAEA, 1991. *Publications:* Nuclear Non-Proliferation: can the policies of the Eighties prove more successful than those of the Seventies?, 1982; (contrib.) The International Nuclear Non-Proliferation System: challenges and choices, 1984. *Recreations:* reading, bird-watching. *Address:* 7 East Street, Southwold, Suffolk IP18 6EH.

WILSEY, Gen. Sir John (Finlay Willasey), KCB 1991; CBE 1985 (OBE 1982); Commander-in-Chief, Land Command (formerly United Kingdom Land Forces), since 1993; Joint Commander, British Forces in the Former Republic of Yugoslavia, since 1993; Aide de Camp General to the Queen, since 1994; *b* 18 Feb. 1939; *s* of Maj.-Gen. John Harold Owen Wilsey, CB, CBE, DSO and of Beatrice Sarah Finlay Wilsey; *m* 1975, Elizabeth Patricia Nottingham; one *s* one *d*. *Educ:* Sherborne Sch.; RMA Sandhurst. Commissioned, Devonshire and Dorset Regt, 1959; regtl service in Cyprus, Libya, British Guyana, Germany, Malta, UK; Instructor, RMA, 1967–68; Great Abbai (Blue Nile) Expedition, 1968; Staff Coll., 1973, Defence Policy Staff, MoD, 1974–75; Co. Comdr, 1976–77, BAOR and NI (despatches 1976); Directing Staff, Staff Coll., 1978–79; Comd 1st Bn Devonshire and Dorset Regt, 1979–82 (despatches 1981); COS, HQ NI, 1982–84; Comdr 1st Inf. Brigade, 1984–86; RCDS 1987; COS, HQ UKLF, 1988–90; GOC NI, 1990–93. Col Comdt, RLC, 1992–; Col, Devonshire and Dorset Regt, 1990–. Gov., Sherborne Sch., 1994–. Mem., Scientific Exploration Soc. *Publication:* Service for the Nation: Seaford papers, 1987. *Recreations:* ski-ing, fishing, expeditions and collecting water colours. *Address:* c/o Lloyds Bank, 9 Broad Street, St Helier, Jersey, CI. *Clubs:* Army and Navy; St Moritz Tobogganing.

WILSHIRE, David; MP (C) Spelthorne, since 1987; *b* 16 Sept. 1943; *m* 1967, Margaret Weeks; one *s* (and one *d* decd). *Educ:* Kingswood School, Bath; Fitzwilliam College, Cambridge. Partner, Western Political Research Services, 1979–; Co-Director, Political Management Programme, Brunel Univ., 1986–91. Mem., Avon CC, 1977–81; Leader, Wansdyke DC, 1981–87. Parliamentary Private Secretary: to Minister for Defence Procurement, 1991–92; to Minister of State, Home Office, 1992–94. *Recreations:* gardening, grape growing, wine making. *Address:* 55 Cherry Orchard, Staines, Middx. *T:* Staines (01784) 450822.

WILSON, family name of **Barons Moran, Nunburnholme, Wilson, Wilson of Langside** and **Wilson of Tillyorn.**

WILSON, 2nd Baron, *cr* 1946, of Libya and of Stowlangtoft; **Patrick Maitland Wilson;** *b* 14 Sept. 1915; *s* of Field-Marshal 1st Baron Wilson, GCB, GBE, DSO, and Hester Mary (*d* 1979), *d* of Philip James Digby Wykeham, Tythrop House, Oxon; *S* father 1964; *m* 1945, Violet Storeen (*d* 1990), *d* of late Major James Hamilton Douglas Campbell, OBE. *Educ:* Eton; King's College, Cambridge. Served War of 1939–45 (despatches). *Heir:* none. *Address:* c/o Barclays Bank, Cambridge CB2 3PZ.

WILSON OF LANGSIDE, Baron *cr* 1969 (Life Peer); **Henry Stephen Wilson,** PC 1967; QC (Scot.) 1965; *b* 21 March 1916; *s* of James Wilson, Solicitor, Glasgow, and Margaret Wilson (*née* Young); *m* 1942, Jessie Forrester Waters; no *c. Educ:* High School, Glasgow; Univ. of Glasgow (MA, LLB). Joined Army, 1939; Commd 1940; Regl Officer, HLI and RAC, 1940–46. Called to Scottish Bar, 1946; Advocate-Depute, 1948–51. Sheriff-Substitute: Greenock, 1955–56; Glasgow, 1956–65; Solicitor-General for Scotland, 1965–67; Lord Advocate, 1967–70; Dir, Scottish Courts Administration, 1971–74; Sheriff Principal of Glasgow and Strathkelvin, 1975–77. Contested (Lab) Dumfriesshire, 1950, 1955, W Edinburgh, 1951; Mem. SDP, 1981–92. Cross-bencher. *Recreations:* hill walking, gardening. *Address:* Dunallan, Kippen, Stirlingshire FK8 3HL. *T:* Kippen (01786) 870210. *Club:* Western (Glasgow).

WILSON OF TILLYORN, Baron *cr* 1992 (Life Peer), of Finzean in the District of Kincardine and Deeside and of Fanling in Hong Kong; **David Clive Wilson,** GCMG 1991 (KCMG 1987; CMG 1985); PhD; Chairman, Scottish Hydro-Electric plc, since 1993; *b* 14 Feb. 1935; *s* of Rev. William Skinner Wilson and Enid Wilson; *m* 1967, Natasha Helen Mary Alexander; two *s. Educ:* Trinity Coll., Glenalmond; Keble Coll., Oxford (schol., MA); PhD London 1973. National Service, The Black Watch, 1953–55; entered Foreign Service, 1958; Third Secretary, Vientiane, 1959–60; Language Student, Hong Kong, 1960–62; Second, later First Secretary, Peking, 1963–65; FCO, 1965–68; resigned, 1968; Editor, China Quarterly, 1968–74; Vis. Scholar, Columbia Univ., New York, 1972; rejoined Diplomatic Service, 1974; Cabinet Office, 1974–77; Political Adviser, Hong Kong, 1977–81; Hd, S European Dept, FCO, 1981–84; Asst Under-Sec. of State, FCO, 1984–87; Governor and C-in-C, Hong Kong, 1987–92. Dir, Martin Currie Pacific Trust plc, 1993–. Mem. Board, British Council, 1993– (Chm., Scottish Cttee, 1993–). Chancellor's Assessor, Court, Univ. of Aberdeen, 1993–; Mem., Governing Body, SOAS, 1992–. Oxford Univ. Somaliland Expedn, 1957; British Mt Kongur Expedn (NW China), 1981. President: Bhutan Soc. of UK, 1993–; Hong Kong Assoc. and Hong Kong Soc., 1994–. Hon. LLD Aberdeen 1990; Hon. DLitt: Sydney, 1991; Abertay Dundee, 1994. KStJ 1987. *Recreations:* mountaineering, ski-ing, reading. *Address:* c/o House of Lords, SW1A 0PW; Scottish Hydro-Electric plc, 10 Dunkeld Road, Perth PH1 5WA. *T:* Perth (01738) 455040. *Clubs:* Alpine; New (Edinburgh).

WILSON, Prof. Alan Geoffrey, FBA 1994; Professor of Urban and Regional Geography, since 1970, Vice-Chancellor, since 1991, University of Leeds (Pro-Vice-Chancellor, 1989–91); *b* 8 Jan. 1939; *s* of Harry Wilson and Gladys (*née* Naylor); *m* 1987, Sarah Caroline Fildes. *Educ:* Corpus Christi Coll., Cambridge (MA). Scientific Officer, Rutherford High Energy Lab., 1961–64; Res. Officer, Inst. of Econs and Statistics, Univ. of Oxford, 1964–66; Math. Adviser, MoT, 1966–68; Asst Dir, Centre for Environmental Studies, London, 1968–70. Mem., Kirklees AHA, 1979–82; Vice-Chm., Dewsbury HA, 1982–85; non-exec. Mem., Northern and Yorks RHA, 1994–March 1996. Vice-Chm. Environment and Planning Cttee, ESRC, 1986–88. Mem., Academia Europaea, 1991. Gill Meml Award, RGS, 1978; Honours Award, Assoc. of Amer. Geographers, 1987; Founder's Medal, RGS, 1992. *Publications:* Entropy in Urban and Regional Modelling, 1970; Papers in Urban and Regional Analysis, 1972; Urban and Regional Models in Geography and Planning, 1974; (with M. J. Kirkby) Mathematics for Geographers and Planners, 1975, 2nd edn 1980; (with P. H. Rees) Spatial Population Analysis, 1977; (ed with P. H. Rees and C. M. Leigh) Models of Cities and Regions, 1977; Catastrophe Theory and Bifurcation: applications to urban and regional systems, 1981; (jtly) Optimization in Locational and Transport Analysis, 1981; Geography and the Environment: Systems Analytical Methods, 1981; (with R. J. Bennett) Mathematical Methods in Geography and Planning, 1985; (ed jtly) Urban Systems, 1987; (ed jtly) Urban Dynamics, 1990; (ed jtly) Modelling the City, 1994; (jtly) Intelligent Geographical Information Systems, 1995. *Recreations:* writing, miscellaneous fads. *Address:* Vice-Chancellor's Office, University of Leeds, Leeds LS2 9JT. *T:* Leeds (0113) 233 3000. *Club:* Athenæum.

WILSON, Alan Martin; QC 1982; a Recorder of the Crown Court, since 1979; *b* 12 Feb. 1940; *s* of late Joseph Norris Wilson and Kate Wilson; *m* 1st, 1966, Pauline Frances Kibart (marr. diss. 1975); two *d;* 2nd, 1976, Julia Mary Carter; one *d. Educ:* Kilburn Grammar Sch.; Nottingham Univ. (LLB Hons). Called to the Bar, Gray's Inn, 1963. Occasional Mem., Hong Kong Bar, 1988–. *Recreations:* shooting, sailing, poetry. *Address:* 1 Serjeant's Inn, EC4Y 1LL. *Clubs:* Sloane; Bar Yacht.

WILSON, Alastair James Drysdale; QC 1987; *b* 26 May 1946; *s* of A. Robin Wilson and Mary Damaris Wilson; *m* (marr. diss.); one *s* two *d. Educ:* Wellington College; Pembroke College, Cambridge. Called to the Bar, Middle Temple, 1968. *Recreations:* gardening, restoring old buildings. *Address:* 19 Old Buildings, Lincoln's Inn, WC2A 3UP. *T:* 0171–405 2001, *Fax:* 0171–405 0001; Rainthorpe Hall, Tasburgh, Norfolk NR15 1RQ.

WILSON, Alexander, CBE 1986; FLA; Director General, British Library Reference Division, 1980–86; *b* 12 Feb. 1921; *s* of late William Wilson and Amelia Wilson; *m* 1949, Mary Catherin Traynor; two *s. Educ:* Bolton County Grammar Sch. FLA 1950; Hon. FLA 1984. Served War, RAF, 1941–46. Librarian at Bolton, Harrogate, Taunton, and Swindon, 1946–52; Dir of Library and Cultural Services, Dudley and later Coventry, 1952–72; Dir, Cheshire Libraries and Museums Service, 1972–79. Member: Library Adv. Council (England), 1971–74; British Library Bd, 1974–86. Pres., LA, 1986. Fellow, Birmingham Polytechnic, 1989. Hon. DLit Sheffield, 1989. *Publications:* contrib. books and periodicals on libraries and other cultural services. *Recreations:* walking, listening to music. *Address:* 1 Brockway West, Tattenhall, Chester CH3 9EZ.

WILSON, Lt-Gen. Sir (Alexander) James, KBE 1974 (CBE 1966; MBE 1948); MC 1945; DL; adviser in politics and economics, Standard Commercial Corporation, since 1992; Chief Executive, Tobacco Advisory Council, 1983–85 (Chairman, 1977–83); *b* 13 April 1921; *s* of Maj.-Gen. Bevil Thomson Wilson, CB, DSO, and of Florence Erica, *d* of Sir John Starkey, 1st Bt; *m* 1958, Hon. Jean Margaret Paul, 2nd *d* of 2nd Baron Rankeillour; two *s. Educ:* Winchester Coll.; New Coll., Oxford (BA Law, MA). Served War of 1939–45, North Africa and Italy, Rifle Bde (despatches); Adjt, IMA Dehra Dun, 1945–47; PS to C-in-C Pakistan, 1948–49; Co. Comdr, 1st Bn Rifle Bde, BAOR 1949 and 1951–52, Kenya 1954–55 (despatches); psc 1950; Bde Major 11th Armd Div., BAOR, 1952–54; Instr, Staff Coll. Camberley, 1955–58; 2nd in comd 3rd Green Jackets, BAOR, 1959–60; GSO1 Sandhurst, 1960–62; CO 1st Bn XX Lancs Fus, 1962–64; Chief of Staff, UN Force in Cyprus, 1964–66 (Actg Force Comdr, 1965–66); Comdr, 147 Inf. Bde TA, 1966–67; Dir of Army Recruiting, MoD, 1967–70; GOC NW District, 1970–72; Vice Adjutant General, MoD, 1972–74; GOC SE District, 1974–77. Dep. Col (Lancashire), RRF, 1973–77, Col, 1977–82; Hon. Col, Oxford Univ. OTC, 1978–82. Col Commandant: Queen's Division, 1974–77; RAEC, 1975–79; Royal Green Jackets, 1977–81. Director: Standard Commercial Corp., 1983–92; Standard Wool, 1987–92; Mem., Marketing Council, 1990–92, and Adv. Consultant, 1992–94, Drake Beam Morin (UK). Chm., Council, RUSI, 1973–75. Member: Sports Council, 1973–82; Council, CBI, 1977–85; Pres., Army Cricket Assoc., 1973–76; Vice-Pres., Army Football Assoc., 1973–76, Chm., 1976–77, Pres., 1977–82; Hon. Vice-Pres., FA, 1976–82. Chm., Crown and Manor Club, Hoxton, 1977–; Vice Pres., NABC, 1990– (Vice Chm., 1977–90); President: Notts Assoc. of Boys and Keystone Clubs, 1986–; Broadway Lodge (formerly Broadway Foundn), 1989–. Association Football Correspondent, Sunday Times, 1957–90; Review Editor, Army Quarterly, 1985–. DL Notts, 1993. *Publications:* articles and book reviews on mil. subjects. *Recreations:* cricket, Association football. *Address:* 151 Rivermead Court, SW6 3SF. *T:* 0171–736 7228. *Clubs:* Travellers, MCC; Notts CC.

WILSON, Air Chief Marshal Sir Andrew; *see* Wilson, Air Chief Marshal Sir R. A. F.

WILSON, Andrew James; *see* Wilson, Snoo.

WILSON, Andrew N.; author; Literary Editor, Evening Standard, since 1990; *b* 27 Oct. 1950; *s* of late N. Wilson and of Jean Dorothy Wilson (*née* Crowder); *m* Katherine Duncan-Jones; two *d; m* 1991, Ruth Alexandra Guilding. *Educ:* Rugby; New College, Oxford (MA). Chancellor's Essay Prize, 1971, and Ellerton Theological Prize, 1975. Asst Master, Merchant Taylors' Sch., 1975–76; Lectr, St Hugh's Coll. and New Coll., Oxford, 1976–81; Literary Ed., Spectator, 1981–83. Mem., AAIL, 1988. FRSL 1981. *Publications: novels:* The Sweets of Pimlico, 1977 (John Llewellyn Rhys Memorial Prize, 1978); Unguarded Hours, 1978; Kindly Light, 1979; The Healing Art, 1980 (Somerset Maugham Award, 1981; Arts Council National Book Award, 1981; Southern Arts Prize, 1981); Who was Oswald Fish?, 1981; Wise Virgin, 1982 (W. H. Smith Literary Award, 1983); Scandal, 1983; Gentlemen in England, 1985; Love Unknown, 1986; Stray, 1987; Incline Our Hearts, 1988; A Bottle in the Smoke, 1990; Daughters of Albion, 1991; The Vicar of Sorrows, 1993; Hearing Voices, 1995; *non fiction:* The Laird of Abbotsford, 1980 (John Llewellyn Rhys Memorial Prize, 1981); A Life of John Milton, 1983; Hilaire Belloc, 1984; How Can We Know?, 1985; (jtly) The Church in Crisis, 1986; The Lion and the Honeycomb, 1987; Penfriends from Porlock, 1988; Tolstoy, 1988 (Whitbread Biography Award); Eminent Victorians, 1989; C. S. Lewis, a biography, 1990; Against Religion, 1991; Jesus, 1992; (ed) The Faber Book of Church and Clergy, 1992; The Rise and Fall of the House of Windsor, 1993; (ed) The Faber Book of London, 1993. *Address:* 91 Albert Street, NW1 7LX. *Club:* Travellers'.

WILSON, Andrew Thomas, CMG 1982; Chief Natural Resources Adviser, Overseas Development Administration, 1983–87, retired; *b* 21 June 1926; *s* of John Wilson, farmer, and Gertrude (*née* Lucas); *m* 1954, Hilda Mary (*née* Williams); two *d. Educ:* Cowley Sch.; Leeds Univ. (BSc); St John's Coll., Cambridge (DipAg); Imperial College of Tropical Agriculture (DTA). Colonial Service/HMOCS, Northern Rhodesia/Zambia, 1949–66: Agricultural Officer, 1949; Chief Agricl Officer, 1959; Chief Agricl Research Officer, 1961; Dep. Director of Agriculture, 1963; ODM/ODA: Agricl Adviser, British Development Div. in the Caribbean, 1967; FCO: Agricl Adviser, Nairobi and Kampala, 1969; ODM/ODA: Agricl Adviser, E Africa Development Div., 1974; Agricl Adviser, Middle East Development Div., 1976; Head of British Develt Div. in S Africa, 1979. *Recreations:* sport, gardening. *Address:* Beechwood House, Great Hockham, Thetford, Norfolk IP24 1NY. *Clubs:* Farmers'; Nairobi (Kenya).

WILSON, Sir Anthony, Kt 1988; FCA; Member, Review Body on Top Salaries, since 1989; Head of Government Accountancy Service and Accounting Adviser to HM Treasury, 1984–88; *b* 17 Feb. 1928; *s* of late Charles Ernest Wilson and Martha Clarice Wilson (*née* Mee); *m* 1955, Margaret Josephine Hudson; two *s* one *d. Educ:* Giggleswick School. Royal Navy, 1946–49. John Gordon Walton & Co., 1945–46 and 1949–52; Price Waterhouse, 1952, Partner, 1961–84; HM Treasury, 1984–88. Non-exec. Dir, Capita Gp plc, 1989–92. Chm., Jt Disciplinary Scheme of UK Accountancy Profession, 1990–93; Member: UK Govt Production Statistics Adv. Cttee, 1972–84; Accounting Standards Cttee, 1981–88; Auditing Practices Cttee, 1987–88; Council, Inst. of Chartered Accountants in England and Wales, 1985–88. Mem. Management Cttee, SW Regl Arts Assoc., 1983–91 (Chm., 1988–91); Member: English Ceramic Circle, 1983–; Northern Ceramic Soc., 1976–89. Pres., Chandos Chamber Choir, 1986–88; Chairman: Dorset Opera, 1988–93; Dorset Musical Instruments Trust, 1994–; Dir, Opera-80 Ltd, 1989–91. Court, Needlemakers' Co.; Liveryman, Chartered Accountants' Co. FRSA 1983. *Recreations:* fishing, gardening, golf, collecting pottery. *Address:* The Barn House, 89 Newland, Sherborne, Dorset DT9 3AG. *T:* Sherborne (01935) 815674. *Club:* Reform.

WILSON, Anthony Joseph, (Joe); Member (Lab) North Wales, European Parliament, since 1989; *b* 6 July 1937; *s* of Joseph Samuel Wilson and Eleanor Annie (*née* Jones); *m* 1959, June Mary Sockett; one *s* two *d. Educ:* Birkenhead Sch.; Loughborough Coll. (DLC); Univ. of Wales (BEd Hons). National Service, RAPC, 1955–57. Teacher: Vauvert Sec. Mod. Sch., Guernsey, 1960–64; Les Beaucamps Sec. Mod. Sch., Guernsey, 1964–66; Man., St Mary's Bay Sch. Journey Centre, Kent, 1966–69; Lectr in PE, Wrexham Tech. Coll., subseq. NE Wales Inst. of Higher Educn, 1969–89. *Recreations:* basketball, camping. *Address:* 79 Ruabon Road, Wrexham, North Wales LL13 7PU. *T:* Wrexham (01978) 352808.

WILSON, Anthony Keith; Chief Executive of the Press, University Printer and Secretary, Press Syndicate, Cambridge University Press, since 1992; Fellow of Wolfson College, Cambridge, since 1994; *b* 28 Sept. 1939; *s* of late Sidney Walter Wilson and Doris Jessie Wilson (*née* Garlick), Streatham; *m* 1963, Christina Helen, *d* of late Ivor Gray Nixon and of Margaret Joan Nixon; two *s* one *d. Educ:* Lexden House Sch.; Dulwich Coll.; Corpus Christi Coll., Cambridge (Maj. Scholar; BA Hons Modern and Medieval Langs 1961; MA 1966). Longmans Green & Co. Ltd, 1961–64; Thomas Nelson & Sons Ltd, 1964–68; George Allen & Unwin Ltd, 1968–72; Cambridge University Press, 1972–: Sen. Editor, R&D, 1972–73; Publishing Ops Dir, 1973–82, Dep. Sec., Press Syndicate, 1979–92; Actg Man. Dir, 1982–83, Man. Dir, 1983–92, Publishing Div.; Dep. Chief Exec., 1991–92. Royal Shakespeare Company: Gov., 1983–; Mem. Council, 1991–; Mem., Exec. Cttee, 1991–; Chm., Budget Cttee, 1991–. Gov., Perse Sch. for Girls, Cambridge, 1979– (Chm. Govs, 1988–). FInstD 1978 (Life-Mem.); FRSA 1985. *Recreations:* walking, talking, walking and talking. *Address:* Cambridge University Press, The Edinburgh Building, Shaftesbury Road, Cambridge CB2 2RU.

WILSON, Arthur Andrew; Chief Executive, Plymouth Hospitals NHS Trust, since 1993; *b* 23 July 1946; *s* of Arthur James Wilson and Hilda Mellor Wilson (*née* Kennedy); *m* 1968, Susan Ann Faulkner; one *s* one *d. Educ:* Moulton Sch., Northampton. CIPFA; IHSM. W. H. Grigg & Co., 1963; Calne and Chippenham RDC, 1963–66; Berkshire CC, 1966–67; Bath City Council, 1967–73; Chief Accountant, Avon CC, 1973–76; Principal Asst Regl Treasurer, SW RHA, 1976–82; Dist Treasurer, Plymouth HA, 1982–84; South Western RHA: Regl Treasurer, 1984–91; Dep. Regl Gen. Manager, 1991–93. *Recreations:* squash, reading, listening to music, musical theatre, first editions of modern novels. *Address:* Plymouth Hospitals NHS Trust, Derriford Hospital, Plymouth PL6 8DH. *T:* Plymouth (01752) 777111; Heathfield, Sowton Road, Yelverton, Plymouth PL20 6DD. *T:* Yelverton (01822) 853309.

WILSON, Austin Peter; Assistant Under Secretary of State, since 1981; Fire and Emergency Planning Department, Home Office, since 1994; *b* 31 March 1938; *s* of Joseph and Irene Wilson; *m* 1962, Norma Louise, *y d* of D. R. Mill; one *s* two *d. Educ:* Leeds Grammar Sch.; St Edmund Hall, Oxford (BA). Entered Home Office, 1961; Private Secretary to Minister of State, 1964–66; Principal, 1966; Secretary, Deptl Cttee on Death Certification and Coroners (Brodrick Cttee), 1968–71; Asst Sec., 1974, Prison Dept; seconded to N Ireland Office, 1977–80; Asst Under Secretary of State, Criminal Justice Dept, 1981; Hd of Community Progs and Equal Opportunities Dept, 1982–86, Equal Opportunities and Gen. Dept, 1986–87, Police Dept, 1987–88, Home Office; NI Office, 1988–92; Criminal Policy Dept, Home Office, 1992–94. *Recreations:* theatre, walking, travel. *Address:* Home Office, Horseferry House, Dean Ryle Street, SW1P 2AW. *T:* 0171–217 8209.

WILSON, Vice-Adm. Sir Barry (Nigel), KCB 1990; Deputy Chief of Defence Staff (Programmes and Personnel), 1989–92; *b* 5 June 1936; *s* of Rear-Adm. G. A. M. Wilson, CB, and of Dorothy Wilson; *m* 1961, Elizabeth Ann (*née* Hardy); one *s* one *d. Educ:* St Edward's Sch., Oxford; Britannia Royal Naval Coll. Commanded: HMS Mohawk, 1973–74; HMS Cardiff, 1978–80; RCDS 1982; Dir Navy Plans, 1983–85; Flag Officer Sea Training, 1986–87; ACDS (Progs), 1987–89. Chairman: Bede House, Bermondsey, 1990–; SSAFA, 1994–; Trustees, Royal Naval Mus., Portsmouth, 1994–. Mem. Bd of Visitors, Guys Marsh YOI, 1994–. *Recreations:* campanology, gardening. *Address:* Green Bough, Child Okeford, Blandford Forum, Dorset DT11 8HD.

WILSON, Lt-Col Sir Blair Aubyn S.; *see* Stewart-Wilson.

WILSON, Brian David Henderson; MP (Lab) Cunninghame North, since 1987; *b* 13 Dec. 1948; *s* of late John Forrest Wilson and of Marion MacIntyre; *m* 1981, Joni Buchanan; one *s* one *d. Educ:* Dunoon Grammar School; Dundee Univ. (MA Hons); University College Cardiff (Dip. Journalism Studies). Publisher and founding editor, West Highland Free Press, 1972–. Front bench spokesman on Scottish Affairs, 1988–92, on Transport, 1992–94, on Trade and Industry, 1994–. First winner, Nicholas Tomalin Meml Award, 1975. *Publications:* Celtic: a century with honour, 1988; contribs to Guardian, Glasgow Herald, New Statesman, etc. *Address:* House of Commons, SW1A 0AA; 37 Main Street, Kilbirnie, Ayrshire. *T:* (office) Kilbirnie (01505) 682847; 219 Queen Victoria Drive, Glasgow G13 1UU. *T:* 0141–959 1758; Miavaig House, Isle of Lewis. *T:* Timsgarry (01851) 672357. *Clubs:* Garnock Labour; Kilbirnie Place Golf.

WILSON, Prof. Brian Graham, AO 1995; Vice-Chancellor, University of Queensland, since 1979; *b* 9 April 1930; *s* of Charles Wesley Wilson and Isobel Christie (*née* Ferguson); *m* 1st, 1959, Barbara Elizabeth Wilkie; two *s* one *d*; 2nd, 1978, Margaret Jeanne Henry; 3rd, 1988, Joan Patricia Opdebeeck; three *s. Educ:* Queen's Univ., Belfast (BSc Hons); National Univ. of Ireland (PhD Cosmic Radiation). Post-doctoral Fellow, National Research Council, Canada, 1955–57; Officer in Charge, Sulphur Mt Lab., Banff, 1957–60, Associate Res. Officer, 1959–60; Associate Prof. of Physics, Univ. of Calgary, 1960–65, Prof., 1965–70, Dean of Arts and Science, 1967–70; Prof. of Astronomy and Academic Vice-Pres., Simon Fraser Univ., 1970–78. Pres., Internat. Develt Program of Australian Univs and Colls, 1991–93 (Dep. Chm., 1987–88); Chairman: Australian Vice-Chancellors' Cttee, 1989–90; Quality Assurance in Higher Educn, 1993–. Member: Council, Northern Territory Univ., 1988–93; Council, Univ. of South Pacific, 1991–. FTS 1990. Hon. LLD Calgary, 1984. *Publications:* numerous, on astrophysics, in learned jls. *Recreations:* golf, swimming. *Address:* 55 Walcott Street, St Lucia, Queensland 4067, Australia. *T:* (7) 38708757. *Club:* Brisbane (Brisbane).

WILSON, Brian Harvey, CBE 1972 (MBE 1944); solicitor, retired; Town Clerk and Chief Executive, London Borough of Camden, 1965–77; *b* 4 Sept. 1915; *o s* of Sydney John Wilson, MC, and Bessie Mildred (*née* Scott); *m* 1941, Constance Jane (*née* Gee); one *s. Educ:* Manchester Grammar Sch.; (Exhibitioner) Corpus Christi Coll., Cambridge (MA, LLB). Chief Asst Solicitor, Warrington, 1946–48; Dep. Town Clerk: Grimsby, 1948–53; Ilford, 1953–56; Town Clerk, Hampstead, 1956–65 (now Camden). Hon. Clerk to Housing and Works Cttee, London Boroughs Assoc., 1965–79; Chm., Metropolitan Housing Trust, 1978–85. Chm., Royal Inst. of Public Administration, 1973–75. Member: Uganda Resettlement Board, 1972–73; DoE Study Gp on Agrément, 1978. Chairman: Public Examn, Glos Structure Plan, 1980; Indep. Inquiry into death of Maria Mehmedagi, 1981; GLC Independent Inquiry into financial terms of GLC housing transferred to London Boroughs and Districts, 1984–85. *Address:* Victoria House, Church Path, Shipton-under-Wychwood, Oxon OX7 6BQ. *T:* Shipton-under-Wychwood (01993) 830695.

WILSON, Brian William John Gregg, MA; Deputy Head, St Mary's School, Wantage, since 1989; *b* 16 June 1937; *s* of late Cecil S. and Margaret D. Wilson; *m* 1969, Sara Remington (*née* Hollins); two *d. Educ:* Sedbergh Sch., Yorks; Christ's Coll., Cambridge (MA). NI short service commn, RIrF, 1955–57. Asst Master, Radley Coll., 1960–65; Housemaster, King's Sch., Canterbury, 1965–73; Dir of Studies, Eastbourne Coll., 1973–76; Headmaster, Campbell Coll., Belfast, 1977–87. Project Manager, Navan Fort Initative Gp, 1987–88. Member: Central Religious Adv. Cttee, BBC/ITV, 1982–86; Management Cttee, NISTRO, 1980–87. Hon. Sec., Ancient History Cttee, JACT, 1967–77. *Publications:* (with W. K. Lacey) Res Publica, 1970; (with D. J. Miller) Stories from Herodotus, 1973. *Recreations:* fives, squash, golf, cricket, hockey, etc; translating, theology, stock market, drama. *Address:* 60 Alfredston Place, Wantage, Oxon OX12 8DL.

WILSON, Rt. Rev. Bruce Winston; *see* Bathurst (NSW), Bishop of.

WILSON, Bryan Ronald, PhD, DLitt; FBA 1994; Reader in Sociology, University of Oxford, 1962–93; Fellow, 1963–93, and Domestic Bursar, 1989–93, All Souls College, Oxford (Sub-Warden, 1988–90); *b* 25 June 1926. *Educ:* University Coll., Leicester (BSc Econ London); London Sch. of Economics (PhD); MA, DLitt Oxon. Lectr in Sociology, Univ. of Leeds, 1955–62. Commonwealth Fund Fellow (Harkness), 1957–58; Fellow, Amer. Council of Learned Socs, 1966–67; Visiting Professor or Fellow, Universities of: Louvain, 1976,1982, 1986, 1993; Toronto, 1978; Melbourne (Ormond Coll.), 1981; Queensland, 1986; California, Santa Barbara, 1987. Pres., Conf. Internat. de sociologie religieuse, 1971–75. Sen. Treasurer, Oxford Union Soc., 1983–91. Hon. DLitt Soka Univ., Japan, 1985; Dr *hc* Louvain, 1992. *Publications:* Sects and Society, 1961; Religion in Secular Society, 1966; (ed) Patterns of Sectarianism, 1967; The Youth Culture and the Universities, 1970; (ed) Rationality, 1970; Religious Sects, 1970; Magic and the Millenium, 1973; (ed) Education, Equality and Society, 1975; The Noble Savages, 1975; Contemporary Transformations of Religion, 1976; (ed) The Social Impact of New Religious Movements, 1981; Religion in Sociological Perspective, 1982; (with Daisaku Ikeda) Human Values in a Changing World, 1984; (ed with Brenda Almond) Values: a symposium, 1988; The Social Dimensions of Sectarianism, 1990; (ed) Religion: contemporary issues, 1992; (with K. Dobbelaere) A Time to Chant, 1994; contribs to learned jls. *Address:* 12 Victoria Court, London Road, Headington, Oxford OX3 7SP.

WILSON, Catherine Mary, (Mrs P. J. Wilson), FMA, FSA; Director, Norfolk Museums Service, since 1991; *b* 10 April 1945; *d* of Arthur Thomas Bowyer and Kathleen May (*née* Hawes); *m* 1968, Peter John Wilson. *Educ:* Windsor County Grammar Sch. FMA 1984 (AMA 1972); FSA 1990. Museum Asst, Lincoln City Museums, 1964; Curator, Museum of Lincolnshire Life, 1972; Asst Dir (Museums), Lincs CC, 1983. *Recreations:* industrial archaeology, vernacular architecture, all local history. *Address:* Castle Museum, Norwich, Norfolk NR1 3JU. *Club:* Norfolk (Norwich).

WILSON, Brig. Charles Edward T.; *see* Tryon-Wilson.

WILSON, Sir Charles Haynes, Kt 1965; MA Glasgow and Oxon; Principal and Vice-Chancellor of University of Glasgow, 1961–76; *b* 16 May 1909; 2nd *s* of late George Wilson and Florence Margaret Hannay; *m* 1935, Jessie Gilmour Wilson; one *s* two *d. Educ:* Hillhead High School; Glasgow Univ.; Oxford Univ. Glasgow University Faulds Fellow in Political Philosophy, 1932–34. Lecturer in Political Science, London School of Economics, 1934–39; Fellow and Tutor in Modern History, Corpus Christi College, Oxford, 1939–52. Junior Proctor, 1945; Faculty Fellow, Nuffield College. Visiting Professor in Comparative Government at Ohio State Univ., 1950; Principal, The University College of Leicester, 1952–57; Vice-Chancellor, Univ. of Leicester, 1957–61. Chairman: Commn on Fourah Bay Coll., Sierra Leone, 1957; Miners' Welfare Nat. Schol. Scheme Selec. Cttee, 1959–64; Acad. Planning Bd for Univ. of E Anglia, 1960; Member: Academic Planning Cttee and Council of UC of Sussex, 1958; Acad. Adv. Cttee, Royal Coll. of Science and Technology, Glasgow (now Univ. of Strathclyde), 1962; British Cttee of Selection for Harkness Fellowships of Commonwealth Fund, 1962–67; Heyworth Cttee on Social Studies, 1962; Acad. Planning Bd, Univ. of Stirling, 1964; Chairman, Cttee of Vice-Chancellors and Principals, 1964–67; Chm., Assoc. of Commonwealth Univs, 1966–67 and 1972–74. Mem., Museums and Galleries Commn (formerly Standing Commn on Museums and Galleries), 1976–83. Hon. Fellow: Corpus Christi Coll., Oxford, 1963; LSE, 1965. Hon. LLD: Glasgow, 1957; Leicester, 1961; Rhodes Univ., 1964; Queen's Univ., Kingston, Ont, 1967; Ohio State Univ., 1969; Pennsylvania, 1975; Hon. DLitt: Strathclyde, 1966; NUU, 1976; Heriot-Watt, 1977; Hon. DCL East Anglia, 1966. Comdr, St Olav (Norway), 1966; Chevalier, Legion of Honour, 1976. *Address:* Whinnymuir, Dalry, Castle Douglas DG7 3TT. *T:* Dalry (016443) 218. *Club:* Royal Scottish Automobile.

WILSON, Charles Martin; Managing Director, Mirror Group (formerly Mirror Group Newspapers) plc, since 1992 (Editorial Director, 1991–92); Managing Director and Editor-in-chief, The Sporting Life, since 1990; *b* 18 Aug. 1935; *s* of Adam and Ruth Wilson; *m* 1st, 1968, Anne Robinson, *qv* (marr. diss. 1973); one *d*; 2nd, 1980, Sally Angela O'Sullivan, *qv*; one *s* one *d. Educ:* Eastbank Academy, Glasgow. News Chronicle, 1959–60; Daily Mail, 1960–71; Dep. Northern Editor, Daily Mail, 1971–74; Asst Editor, London Evening News, 1974–76; Editor, Glasgow Evening Times, Glasgow Herald, Scottish Sunday Standard, 1976–82; The Times: Exec. Editor, 1982; Dep. Editor, 1983; Editor, 1985–90; Internat. Develts Dir, News Internat. plc, 1990. Mem., Jockey Club, 1993–. *Recreations:* reading, horse racing. *Address:* Mirror Group plc, 1 Canada Square, Canary Wharf, E14 5AP. *Club:* Reform.

WILSON, (Christopher) David, CBE 1968; MC 1945; Chairman: Southern Television Ltd, 1976–81 (Managing Director, 1959–76); Southstar Television International, 1976–81; Beaumont (UK) Ltd, 1979–81; *b* 17 Dec. 1916; *s* of late James Anthony Wilson, Highclere, Worplesdon, Surrey; *m* 1947, Jean Barbara Morton Smith; no *c. Educ:* St George's Sch., Windsor; Aldenham. Served War of 1939–45: Captain RA, in India, Middle East and Italy. Business Manager, Associated Newspapers Ltd, 1955–57; Dir, Associated Rediffusion Ltd, 1956–57; Gen. Manager, Southern Television Ltd, 1957–59; Chm., ITN Ltd, 1969–71. Mem. Council, Southampton Univ., 1980–89; Trustee, Chichester Festival Theatre Trust Ltd. FCA 1947. *Recreations:* sailing, music. *Address:* Little Croft, Upham, Hants SO3 1JH. *T:* Durley (01489) 860204. *Clubs:* MCC; Royal Southern Yacht.

WILSON, Christopher Maynard, DIC, PhD; Chairman, LCE (Holdings) Ltd (formerly LCE Computer Maintenance Ltd), since 1987; Director, Inspec Group Ltd, since 1992; *b* 19 Dec. 1928; *s* of late George Henry Cyril Wilson and of Adelaide Flora Marie Wilson; *m* 1953, Elizabeth Ursula Canning; one *s* two *d. Educ:* King Edward VII Sch., Sheffield; Worksop Coll., Notts; Imperial Coll., London Univ. (BSc, ARCS, DIC, PhD). National Service, RAF, 1947–49. Ferranti Computers, 1953–63; Ferranti merged with ICT, 1963, ICT merged with English Electric Computers to become ICL, 1968; Manager, UK Sales, 1968–70; Director: Marketing and Product Strategy, 1970–72; Internat. Div., 1972–77; Man. Dir, International Computers Ltd, 1977–81; Chm., Exxel Consultants Ltd, 1982–86; Man. Dir, Ansafone Corp., 1984–86. *Recreations:* squash, tennis, gardening, golf. *Address:* Tiles Cottage, Forest Road, Winkfield Row, near Bracknell, Berks RG42 7NR.

WILSON, Clifford; Professor of Medicine, University of London, at the London Hospital and Director, Medical Unit, The London Hospital, 1946–71, now Emeritus Professor; *b* 27 Jan. 1906; *m* 1936, Kathleen Hebden; one *s* one *d. Educ:* Balliol College, Oxford. Brackenbury Scholar, Balliol Coll., Oxford, 1924; 1st Class Oxford Final Hons School of Nat. Sciences, 1928; BM BCh 1933; DM 1936. MRCS 1931; FRCP 1951 (MRCP 1946). House Physician, etc., London Hospital, 1931–34; Rockefeller Travelling Fellow, 1934–35; Research Fellow, Harvard Univ.; Asst Director, Medical Unit, London Hosp., 1938; Univ. Reader in Medicine, London Hosp., 1940; Major RAMC, Medical Research Section, 1942–45. President Renal Association, 1963–64. Examiner MRCP, 1960–; Censor, RCP, 1964–66; Senior Censor and Senior Vice-Pres., 1967–68. Dean, Faculty of Medicine, Univ. of London, 1968–71. Hon. Fellow, London Hosp. Medical Coll., 1986. *Publications:* sections on renal diseases and diseases of the arteries in Price's Text Book of Medicine; papers on renal disease, hypertension, arterial disease and other medical subjects, 1930–70. *Address:* The White Cottage, Woodgreen, Fordingbridge, Hants SP6 2BD.

WILSON, Clive Hebden; Director, Office of the Health Service Commissioner, since 1995; on secondment from Department of Health; *b* 1 Feb. 1940; *s* of Joseph and Irene Wilson; *m* 1976, Jill Garland Evans; two *d. Educ:* Leeds Grammar Sch.; Corpus Christi Coll., Oxford. Joined Civil Service, 1962; Ministry of Health: Asst Principal, 1962–67; Asst Private Sec. to Minister of Health, 1965–66; Principal, 1967–73; Assistant Secretary: DHSS, 1973–77; Cabinet Office, 1977–79; DHSS, 1979–82; Under Sec., DHSS, later DoH, 1982–; Dir of Estabs (HQ), 1982–84; Child Care Div., 1984–86; Children, Maternity, Prevention Div., 1986–87; Medicines Div., 1987–90; Priority Health Services Div., subseq. Health Care (A) Div., 1990–92; Hd of Health and Community Care Gp, NCVO, 1992–95. *Recreations:* walking, gardening, tennis.

WILSON, Colin Alexander Megaw; Scottish Parliamentary Counsel, since 1993; Assistant Legal Secretary to Lord Advocate, since 1979; *b* 4 Jan. 1952; *s* of James Thompson Wilson and Sarah Elizabeth Howard Wilson (*née* Megaw); *m* 1987, Mandy Esca Clay; one *s* one *d. Educ:* Glasgow High Sch.; Edinburgh Univ. (LLB Hons 1973). Admitted solicitor, Scotland, 1975; Asst Solicitor, then Partner, Archibald Campbell & Harley, WS, Edinburgh, 1975–79; Asst, later Depute, Parly Draftsman for Scotland, 1979–93. *Recreations:* choral singing, walking, reading. *Address:* Lord Advocate's Chambers, 2 Carlton Gardens, SW1Y 5AA. *T:* 0171–210 1022.

WILSON, Prof. Colin Alexander St John, RA 1991 (ARA 1990); FRIBA; Professor of Architecture, Cambridge University, 1975–89, now Emeritus Professor; Fellow, Pembroke College, Cambridge, since 1977; Architect (own private practice); *b* 14 March 1922; *yr s* of late Rt Rev. Henry A. Wilson, CBE, DD; *m* 1st, 1955, Muriel Lavender (marr. diss. 1971); 2nd, 1972, Mary Jane Long; one *s* one *d*. *Educ:* Felsted Sch.; Corpus Christi Coll., Cambridge, 1940–42 (MA); Sch. of Architecture, London Univ., 1946–49 (Dip. Lond.). Served War, RNVR, 1942–46. Asst in Housing Div., Architects Dept, LCC, 1950–55; Lectr at Sch. of Architecture, Univ. of Cambridge, 1955–69; Fellow, Churchill Coll., Cambridge, 1962–71. Practised in assoc. with Sir Leslie Martin, 1955–64: on bldgs in Cambridge (Harvey Court, Gonville and Caius Coll.; Stone Building, Peterhouse); Univ. of Oxford, Law Library; Univ. of Leicester, Science Campus; Univ. of London, Royal Holloway Coll. In own practice Buildings include: Extension to Sch. of Architecture, Cambridge; Research Laboratory, Babraham; Extension to British Museum; Library for QMC, Univ. of London (SCONUL award for design excellence); Meml Library for Bishop Wilson Sch., Spring Field; The British Library, St Pancras (commenced construction, 1982); various residences; Projects for Liverpool Civic and Social Centre, and Group Headquarters and Research Campus for Lucas Industries Ltd. Vis. Critic to Yale Sch. of Architecture, USA, 1960, 1964 and 1983; Bemis Prof. of Architecture, MIT, USA, 1970–72. Consultant, Chicago City Library. Member: Fitzwilliam Mus. Syndicate, 1985–89; Arts Council of GB, 1990–94 (Chair, Architecture Unit, 1992–94). Trustee: Tate Gall., 1973–80; Nat. Gall., 1977–80. FRSA. Commander, Order of the Lion (Finland), 1992. *Publications:* Architectural Reflections, 1992; articles in: The Observer; professional jls in UK, USA, France, Spain, Japan, Germany, Norway, Italy, Switzerland, Finland, etc. *Address:* 31A Grove End Road, NW8. *T:* 0171–286 8306; (office) Colin St John Wilson & Partners, Highbury Crescent Rooms, 70 Ronalds Road, N5 1XW. *T:* 0171–354 2030.

WILSON, Colin Henry; author; *b* Leicester, 26 June 1931; *s* of Arthur Wilson and Annetta Jones; *m* Dorothy Betty Troop; one *s*; *m* Joy Stewart; two *s* one *d*. *Educ:* The Gateway Secondary Technical School, Leicester. Left school at 16. Laboratory Asst (Gateway School), 1948–49; Civil Servant (collector of taxes), Leicester and Rugby, 1949–50; national service with RAF, AC2, 1949–50. Various jobs, and a period spent in Paris and Strasbourg, 1950; came to London, 1951; various labouring jobs, long period in plastic factory; returned to Paris, 1953; labouring jobs in London until Dec. 1954, when began writing The Outsider: has since made a living at writing. Visiting Professor: Hollins Coll., Va, 1966–67; Univ. of Washington, Seattle, 1967; Dowling Coll., Majorca, 1969; Rutgers Univ., NJ, 1974. Plays produced: Viennese Interlude; The Metal Flower Blossom; Strindberg. *Publications:* The Outsider, 1956; Religion and the Rebel, 1957; The Age of Defeat, 1959; Ritual in the Dark, 1960; Adrift in Soho, 1961; An Encyclopædia of Murder, 1961; The Strength to Dream, 1962; Origins of the Sexual Impulse, 1963; The Man without a Shadow, 1963; The World of Violence, 1963; Rasputin and the Fall of the Romanovs, 1964; The Brandy of the Damned (musical essays), 1964; Necessary Doubt, 1964; Beyond the Outsider, 1965; Eagle and Earwig, 1965; The Mind Parasites, 1966; Introduction to The New Existentialism, 1966; The Glass Cage, 1966; Sex and the Intelligent Teenager, 1966; The Philosopher's Stone, 1968; Strindberg (play), 1968; Bernard Shaw: A Reassessment, 1969; Voyage to a Beginning, 1969; Poetry and Mysticism, 1970; The Black Room, 1970; A Casebook of Murder, 1970; The God of the Labyrinth, 1970; Lingard, 1970; (jtly) The Strange Genius of David Lindsay, 1970; The Occult, 1971; New Pathways in Psychology, 1972; Order of Assassins, 1971; Tree by Tolkien, 1973; Hermann Hesse, 1973; Strange Powers, 1973; The Schoolgirl Murder Case, 1974; Return of the Lloigor, 1974; A Book of Booze, 1974; The Craft of the Novel, 1975; The Space Vampires, 1976 (filmed as Lifeforce, 1985); Men of Strange Powers, 1976; Enigmas and Mysteries, 1977; The Geller Phenomenon, 1977; Mysteries, 1978; Mysteries (play), 1979; The Quest for Wilhelm Reich, 1979; The War Against Sleep: the philosophy of Gurdjieff, 1980; Starseekers, 1980; Frankenstein's Castle, 1981; (ed with John Grant) The Directory of Possibilities, 1981; Poltergeist!, 1981; Access to Inner Worlds, 1982; The Criminal History of Mankind, 1983; (with Donald Seaman) Encyclopaedia of Modern Murder, 1983; Psychic Detectives, 1983; The Janus Murder Case, 1984; The Essential Colin Wilson, 1984; The Personality Surgeon, 1985; Spider World: the tower, 1987; (with Damon Wilson) Encyclopedia of Unsolved Mysteries, 1987; Spider World: the delta, 1987; (ed with Ronald Duncan) Marx Refuted, 1987; Aleister Crowley: the nature of the beast, 1987; (with Robin Odell) Jack the Ripper: summing up and verdict, 1987; The Magician from Siberia, 1988; The Misfits: a study of sexual outsiders, 1988; Beyond the Occult, 1988; Written in Blood, 1989; (with Donald Seaman) The Serial Killers, 1990; Mozart's Journey to Prague (play), 1991; Spider World: the magician, 1992; The Strange Life of P. D. Ouspensky, 1993; contribs to: The Times, Literary Review, Audio, etc. *Recreations:* collecting gramophone records, mainly opera; mathematics. *Address:* Tetherdown, Trewallock Lane, Gorran Haven, Cornwall PL26 6NT. *Club:* Savage.

WILSON, Maj.-Gen. Dare; *see* Wilson, Maj.-Gen. R. D.

WILSON, David; *see* Wilson, C. D.

WILSON, Sir David, 3rd Bt *cr* 1920; solicitor; *b* 30 Oct. 1928; *s* of Sir John Mitchell Harvey Wilson, 2nd Bt, KCVO, and Mary Elizabeth (*d* 1979), *d* of late William Richards, CBE; *S* father, 1975; *m* 1955, Eva Margareta, *e d* of Tore Lindell, Malmö, Sweden; two *s* one *d*. *Educ:* Deerfield Acad., Mass., USA; Harrow School; Oriel Coll., Oxford (Brisco Owen Schol.). Barrister, Lincoln's Inn, 1954–61; admitted Solicitor, 1962; Partner, Simmons & Simmons, EC2, 1963–92. *Heir: s* Thomas David Wilson [*b* 6 Jan. 1959; *m* 1984, Valerie, *er d* of Vivian Stogdale, Shotover, Oxford; two *s*]. *Address:* Tandem House, Queen's Drive, Oxshott, Leatherhead, Surrey KT22 0PH. *Clubs:* Arts; Royal Southern Yacht.

WILSON, Sir David (Mackenzie), Kt 1984; FBA 1981; Director of the British Museum, 1977–92; *b* 30 Oct. 1931; *e s* of Rev. Joseph Wilson; *m* 1955, Eva, *o d* of Dr Gunnar Sjögren, Stockholm; one *s* one *d*. *Educ:* Kingswood Sch.; St John's Coll., Cambridge (LittD; Hon. Fellow, 1985); Lund Univ., Sweden. Research Asst, Cambridge Univ., 1954; Asst Keeper, British Museum, 1954–64; Reader in Archaeology of Anglo-Saxon Period, London Univ., 1964–71; Prof. of Medieval Archaeology, Univ. of London, 1971–76; Jt Head of Dept of Scandinavian Studies, UCL, 1973–76 (Hon. Fellow, 1988). Slade Prof., Cambridge, 1985–86. Member: Ancient Monuments Bd for England, 1976–84; Historic Bldgs and Monuments Commn, 1990–. Governor, Museum of London, 1976–81; Trustee: Nat. Museums of Scotland, 1985–87; Nat. Museums of Merseyside, 1986–. Crabtree Orator 1966. Member: Royal Swedish Acad. of Sci.; Royal Acad. of Letters, History and Antiquities, Sweden; Norwegian Acad. of Science and Letters; German Archaeological Inst.; Royal Gustav Adolf's Acad. of Sweden; Royal Soc. of Letters of Lund; Vetenskapssocieteten, Lund; Royal Soc. of Sci. and Letters, Gothenburg; Royal Soc. of Sci., Uppsala; Royal Norwegian Soc. of Sci. and Letters; FSA; Hon. MRIA; Hon. Mem., Polish Archaeological and Numismatic Soc.; Hon. FMA. Sec., Soc. for Medieval Archaeology, 1957–77; Pres., Viking Soc., 1968–70; Pres., Brit. Archaeological Assoc., 1962–68. Mem. Council, Nottingham Univ., 1988–94. Hon. Fil.Dr Stockholm; Hon. Dr Phil: Aarhus; Oslo; Hon. DLitt: Liverpool; Birmingham; Nottingham; Leicester; Hon LLD Pennsylvania. Félix Neuburgh Prize, Gothenburg Univ., 1978; Gold Medal, Soc. of Antiquaries, 1995. Order of Polar Star, 1st cl. (Sweden), 1977. *Publications:* The Anglo-Saxons, 1960, 3rd edn 1981; Anglo-Saxon Metalwork 700–1100 in British Museum, 1964; (with O. Klindt-Jensen) Viking Art, 1966; (with G. Bersu) Three Viking Graves in the Isle of Man, 1969; The Vikings and their Origins, 1970, 2nd edn 1980; (with P. G. Foote) The Viking Achievement, 1970; (with A. Small and C. Thomas) St Ninian's Isle and its Treasure, 1973; The Viking Age in the Isle of Man, 1974; (ed) Anglo-Saxon Archaeology, 1976; (ed) The Northern World, 1980; The Forgotten Collector, 1984; Anglo-Saxon Art, 1984; The Bayeux Tapestry, 1985; The British Museum: purpose and politics, 1989; Awful Ends, 1992; Showing the Flag, 1992; Vikingatidens Konst, 1995. *Address:* The Lifeboat House, Castletown, Isle of Man IM9 1LD. *T:* Castletown (0624) 822800. *Clubs:* Athenæum, Brooks's.

WILSON, David William; Chairman, Wilson Bowden PLC, since 1987; *b* 5 Dec. 1941; *s* of Albert Henry Wilson and Kathleen May Wilson; *m* 1st, 1964, Ann Taberner; one *s* one *d*; 2nd, 1985, Laura Isobel Knifton; two *s*. *Educ:* Ashby Boys' Grammar Sch.; Leicester Polytechnic. Created from scratch what is now Wilson Bowden PLC. Non-exec. Dir, Equitable Life Assce Soc., 1994–. *Recreation:* farming. *Address:* Lowesby Hall, Lowesby, Leics LE7 9DD. *T:* Leicester (0116) 259 5321.

WILSON, Des; Director of Corporate and Public Affairs, BAA plc, since 1994; *b* 5 March 1941; *s* of Albert H. Wilson, Oamaru, New Zealand; *m* 1985, Jane Dunmore; one *s* one *d* by a previous marriage. *Educ:* Waitaki Boys' High Sch., New Zealand. Journalist-Broadcaster, 1957–67; Director, Shelter, Nat. Campaign for the Homeless, 1967–71; Head of Public Affairs, RSC, 1974–76; Editor, Social Work Today, 1976–79; Dep. Editor, Illustrated London News, 1979–81; Chm., 1981–85, Project Advr, 1985–89, CLEAR (Campaign for Lead-Free Air); Gen. Election Campaign Dir, Lib Dems, 1990–92; Dir of Public Affairs, 1993–94, World Wide Vice Chm., Public Affairs, 1994, Burson-Marsteller. Chairman: Friends of the Earth (UK), 1982–86; Campaign for Freedom of Information, 1984–91; Citizen Action, 1983–91; Parents Against Tobacco, 1990. Member: Nat. Exec., Nat. Council for Civil Liberties, 1971–73; Cttee for City Poverty, 1972–73; Bd, Shelter, 1982– (Trustee, 1982–86); Trustee, Internat. Year of Shelter for the Homeless (UK), 1985–87. Columnist, The Guardian, 1968–70; Columnist, The Observer, 1971–75; regular contributor, Illustrated London News, 1972–85. Contested (L) Hove, 1973, 1974; Liberal Party: Mem. Council, 1973–74 and 1984–85; Mem., Nat. Exec., 1984–85; Pres., 1986–87; Pres., NLYL, 1984–85; Mem. Federal Exec., SLD, 1988. *Publications:* I Know It Was the Place's Fault, 1970; Des Wilson's Minority Report (a diary of protest), 1973; So you want to be Prime Minister: a personal view of British politics, 1979; The Lead Scandal, 1982; Pressure, the A to Z of Campaigning in Britain, 1984; (ed) The Environmental Crisis, 1984; (ed) The Secrets File, 1984; The Citizen Action Handbook, 1986; Battle for Power — Inside the Alliance General Election Campaign, 1987; Costa Del Sol (novel), 1990; Campaign (novel), 1992; Campaigning, 1993. *Address:* Milestone House, 39 Main Road, Long Bennington, near Newark, Notts NG23 5DJ.

WILSON, Sir Donald; *see* Wilson, Sir R. D.

WILSON, Prof. Edward Osborne, PhD; Curator in Entomology, since 1972, and Pellegrino University Professor, since 1994, Harvard University; *b* 10 June 1929; *s* of Edward O. Wilson, Sen. and Inez Freeman (*née* Huddleston); *m* 1955, Irene Kelley; one *d*. *Educ:* Univ. of Alabama (BS 1949; MS 1950); Harvard Univ. (PhD 1955). Harvard University: Jun. Fellow, Soc. of Fellows, 1953–56; Prof. of Zoology, 1964–76; Baird Prof. of Sci., 1976–94; Mellon Prof. of the Scis, 1990–93. Hon. DSc Oxon, 1993; 15 other hon. doctorates. Nat. Medal of Sci., USA, 1978; Pulitzer Prize for General Non-Fiction, 1978 and 1991; Tyler Prize for Envmtl Achievement, 1984; Crafoord Prize, Swedish Royal Acad. of Sci., 1990; Internat. Prize for Biol., Japan, 1994. *Publications:* The Insect Societies, 1971; Sociobiology: the new synthesis, 1975; On Human Nature, 1978; Biophilia, 1985; (with B. Holldohler) The Ants, 1990; The Diversity of Life, 1992; Naturalist (autobiog.), 1995. *Address:* Museum of Comparative Zoology, Harvard University, Cambridge, MA 02138, USA. *T:* (617) 4952315.

WILSON, Lt-Col Eric Charles Twelves, VC 1940; retired; *b* 2 October 1912; *s* of Rev. C. C. C. Wilson; *m* 1943, Ann (from whom he obtained a divorce, 1953), *d* of Major Humphrey Pleydell-Bouverie, MBE; two *s*; *m* 1953, Angela Joy, *d* of Lt-Col J. McK. Gordon, MC; one *s*. *Educ:* Marlborough; RMC, Sandhurst. Commissioned in East Surrey Regt, 1933; seconded to King's African Rifles, 1937; seconded to Somaliland Camel Corps, 1939; Long Range Desert Gp, 1941–42, Burma, 1944; seconded to N Rhodesia Regt, 1946; retd from Regular Army, 1949; Admin Officer, HM Overseas Civil Service, Tanganyika, 1949–61; Dep. Warden, London House, 1962, Warden, 1966–77. Hon. Sec., Anglo-Somali Soc., 1972–77 and 1988–90. *Publication:* Stowell in the Blackmore Vale, 1986. *Recreation:* country life. *T:* Templecombe (01963) 370264.

WILSON, Frank Richard, CMG 1963; OBE 1946; Controller of Administration, Commonwealth Development Corporation, 1976–80; retired HMOCS Oct. 1963; *b* 26 Oct. 1920; *er s* of late Sir Leonard Wilson, KCIE and the late Muriel Wilson; *m* 1947, Alexandra Dorothy Mary (*née* Haigh); two *s*. *Educ:* Oundle Sch.; Trinity Hall, Cambridge (1939–40 only). Commnd Indian Army, 1941; retired as Lieut-Col, 1946. Joined Colonial Administrative Service (later HMOCS) in Kenya, 1947; District Comr, 1950–56; Private Sec. to the Governor, 1956–59; Provincial Comr, Central Province, 1959–63; Civil Sec., Central Region, 1963. With Commonwealth Develt Corp., 1964–80. *Address:* Chelsea House, Mickleton, Chipping Campden, Glos GL55 6SD.

WILSON, Geoffrey; Chairman, Wells, O'Brien & Co., since 1972; *b* 11 July 1929; *m* 1962, Philomena Mary Kavanagh; one *s* one *d*. *Educ:* Bolton County Grammar Sch.; Univ. of Birmingham; Linacre Coll., Oxford. PE Consulting Group, 1958–63; British Railways, 1963–71; Mem., BR Bd, 1968–71, Chief Exec. (Railways), 1971. Member: Council, Royal Inst. of Public Admin, 1970–71; Council, Inst. of Transport, 1970–71. *Recreations:* golf, gardening, painting. *Address:* 10 Montpellier Grove, Cheltenham, Glos GL50 2XB.

WILSON, Geoffrey Alan; Chairman, Equity Land Ltd, since 1994; *b* 19 Feb. 1934; *s* of Lewis Wilson and Doris Wilson (*née* Shrier); *m* 1963, Marilyn Helen Freedman; one *s* two *d*. *Educ:* Haberdashers' Aske's School; College of Estate Management. FRICS. 2nd Lieut RA, 1955–56. Private practice, 1957–60; Director: Amalgamated Investment & Property Co., 1961–70; Sterling Land Co., 1971–73 (and co-founder); Greycoat, 1976–94 (Chm., 1985–94, and co-founder); Perspectives on Architecture (formerly Perfect Harmony) Ltd, 1993–. Member: W Metropolitan Conciliation Cttee, Race Relations Bd, 1969–71; Council, Central British Fund for World Jewish Relief, 1993–. Trustee: ORT Trust, 1980–; Public Art Develt Trust, 1990–95. Comr, English Heritage, 1992– (Chm., London Adv. Cttee, 1995–).. Mem., Governing Council, UCS, 1991–. Hon. FRIBA 1995. *Recreations:* reading, architecture, art, film. *Address:* Equity Land Ltd, 7 Cavendish Square, W1M 9HA. *T:* 0171–636 7078. *Clubs:* Reform, Royal Automobile.

WILSON, Hon. Geoffrey Hazlitt, CVO 1989; FCA, FCMA; Chairman, Southern Electric plc, since 1993 (Director, since 1989); *b* 28 Dec. 1929; *yr s* of 1st Baron Moran, MC, MD, FRCP, and Lady Moran, MBE; *m* 1955, Barbara Jane Hebblethwaite; two *s* two *d*. *Educ:* Eton; King's Coll., Cambridge (BA Hons). JDipMA. Articled to Barton Mayhew (now Ernst & Whinney), 1952; Chartered Accountant 1955; joined English

Electric, 1956; Dep. Comptroller, 1965; Financial Controller (Overseas), GEC, 1968; joined Delta Group as Financial Dir, Cables Div., 1969; elected to Main Board as Gp Financial Dir, 1972; Jt Man. Dir, 1977; Dep. Chief Executive, 1980; Chief Exec., 1981–88; Chm., 1982–94. Director: Blue Circle Industries plc, 1980–; Drayton English & International Trust, 1978–; W Midlands and Wales Regl Bd, Nat. Westminster Bank PLC, 1985–92 (Chm., 1990–92); Johnson Matthey plc, 1990– (Dep. Chm., 1994–); UK Adv. Bd, National Westminster Bank, 1990–92. Member: Council, Inst. of Cost and Management Accountants, 1972–78; Accounting Standards Cttee, 1978–79; Financial Reporting Council, 1990–93; London Metal Exchange, 1982–; Chm., 100 Gp of Chartered Accountants, 1979–80 (Hon. Mem., 1985). Mem. Management Bd, Engineering Employers Fedn, 1979–83 (Vice-Pres., 1983–86 and 1990–94; Dep. Pres., 1986–90); Chm., EEF Cttee on Future of Wage Bargaining, 1980; Dep. Pres., 1986–87, Pres., 1987–88, Counsellor, 1989–, BEAMA; Member: Administrative Council, Royal Jubilee Trusts, 1979–88, Hon. Treas., 1980–89; Council, Winchester Cathedral Trust, 1985–93; Council, St Mary's Hosp. Med. Sch., 1985–88. CIMgt. Mem. Ct of Assistants, Chartered Accountants' Co., 1982–, Master, 1988–89. *Recreations:* family, reading, walking, ski-ing, vintage cars. *Address:* Southern Electric plc, Westacott Way, Littlewick Green, Maidenhead, Berks SL6 3QB. *T:* Littlewick Green (01628) 822166. *Clubs:* Boodle's, Royal Automobile.

WILSON, Sir Geoffrey Masterman, KCB 1969 (CB 1968); CMG 1962; Chairman, Oxfam, 1977–83; *b* 7 April 1910; 3rd *s* of late Alexander Cowan Wilson and Edith Jane Brayshaw; *m* 1st, 1946, Julie Stafford Trowbridge (marr. diss. 1979); two *s* two *d*; 2nd, 1989, Stephanie Stainsby (*née* Ross). *Educ:* Manchester Grammar School; Oriel College, Oxford. Chairman, Oxford Univ. Labour Club, 1930; Pres., Oxford Union, 1931. Harmsworth Law Scholar, Middle Temple, 1931; called to Bar, Middle Temple, 1934. Served in HM Embassy, Moscow, and Russian Dept of Foreign Office, 1940–45. Cabinet Office, 1947; Treasury, 1948; Director, Colombo Plan Technical Co-operation Bureau, 1951–53; Under-Secretary, Treasury, 1956–58; Deputy Head of UK Treasury Delegn and Alternate Exec. Dir for UK, Internat. Bank, Washington, 1958; Vice-President, International Bank, Washington, 1961–66; Deputy Secretary, ODM, 1966–68, Permanent Secretary, 1968–70; Dep. Sec.-Gen. (Economic), Commonwealth Secretariat, 1971. Chm., Race Relations Bd, 1971–77. Hon. Fellow: Wolfson Coll., Cambridge, 1971; Inst. of Develt Studies, Brighton, 1981; Oriel Coll., Oxford, 1992. *Address:* 4 Polstead Road, Oxford OX2 6TN.

See also Prof. J. E. Meade.

WILSON, Geoffrey Studholme, CMG 1961; Commissioner of Police, Tanganyika Police Force, 1958–62; *b* 5 June 1913; *s* of late J. E. S. Wilson; *m* 1936, Joy Noel, *d* of Capt. C. St G. Harris-Walker; two *s*. *Educ:* Radley College. Joined Hong Kong Police, 1933; Commissioner of Police, Sarawak Constabulary, 1953–58. King's Police Medal, 1950. OStJ 1961. *Recreations:* golf, fishing, sailing. *Address:* British Bank of the Middle East, Falcon House, Curzon Street, W1Y 8AA. *Club:* Hong Kong (Hong Kong).

WILSON, George; *see* Wilson, W. G.

WILSON, George Pritchard Harvey, CMG 1966; JP; Chairman, Victorian Inland Meat Authority, 1973–77 (Deputy Chairman, 1970–73); *b* 10 March 1918; *s* of late G. L. Wilson; *m* 1945, Fay Hobart Duff; two *s* one *d*. *Educ:* Geelong Grammar School. Nuffield Scholar (Farming), 1952. Council Member, Monash University, 1961–69; Royal Agricultural Society of Victoria: Councillor, 1950; President, 1964–73; Trustee, 1968–. Member: Victoria Promotion Cttee, 1968–81; Victoria Economic Develt Corp., 1981–82. Chm., Australian Nuffield Farming Scholars Assoc., 1973–89; Hon. Trustee, UK Nuffield Farming Scholarship Trust, 1989–. JP 1957. *Recreation:* fishing. *Address:* Wilson House, Berwick, Victoria 3806, Australia. *T:* Berwick 7071271. *Clubs:* Melbourne, Royal Automobile of Victoria (Melbourne); Melbourne Cricket.

WILSON, Gerald Robertson, CB 1991; Secretary, The Scottish Office Education and Industry Department, since 1995; *b* 7 Sept. 1939; *s* of Charles Robertson Wilson and Margaret Wilson (*née* Early); *m* 1963, Margaret Anne, *d* of late John S. and Agnes Wight; one *s* one *d*. *Educ:* Holy Cross Academy, Edinburgh; University of Edinburgh. MA. Asst Principal, Scottish Home and Health Dept, 1961–65; Private Sec. to Minister of State for Scotland, 1965–66; Principal, Scottish Home and Health Dept, 1966–72; Private Sec. to Lord Privy Seal, 1972–74, to Minister of State, Civil Service Dept, 1974; Asst Sec., Scottish Economic Planning Dept, 1974–77; Counsellor, Office of the UK Perm. Rep. to the European Communities, Brussels, 1977–82; Asst Sec., Scottish Office, 1982–84; Under Sec., Industry Dept for Scotland, 1984–88; Sec., Scottish Office Educn Dept, 1988–95. Chm., E Scotland, RIPA, 1990–92. *Recreation:* music. *Address:* c/o The Scottish Office Education and Industry Department, Victoria Quay, Edinburgh EH6 6QQ. *Club:* New (Edinburgh).

WILSON, (Gerald) Roy; Under Secretary and Deputy Director of Savings, Department for National Savings, 1986–89, retired; *b* 11 Jan. 1930; *s* of late Fred Wilson and Elsie Wilson (*née* Morrison); *m* 1st, 1965, Doreen Chadderton (*d* 1990); one *s* one *d*; 2nd, 1990, Patricia Henderson (*née* Ive). *Educ:* High School, Oldham. Min. of Works, 1947; HM Stationery Office, 1949; Post Office Savings Dept, 1957; PO HQ, 1963; National Girobank, 1966; Dept for National Savings, 1969–89; Controller, Savings Certificate and SAYE Office, Durham, 1978–86. FIMgt; Mensa. *Recreations:* swimming, reading, drawing, photography, travel. *Address:* 6 West Farm Court, Broompark, Durham DH7 7RN. *Clubs:* Civil Service; Rotary, Probus (Durham); Durham City Swimming, Durham City Cricket.

WILSON, Gillian Brenda, (Mrs Kenneth Wilson); *see* Babington-Browne, G. B.

WILSON, Gordon; *see* Wilson, Robert G.

WILSON, Gordon Wallace, CB 1986; Under Secretary, Ministry of Agriculture, Fisheries and Food, 1975–86, retired; *b* 14 July 1926; *s* of late John Wallace Wilson and of Mrs Joyce Elizabeth Grace Sherwood-Smith; *m* 1951, Gillian Maxwell (*née* Wood); three *s*. *Educ:* King's Sch., Bruton; Queen's Coll., Oxford (BA PPE). Entered Civil Service (War Office), 1950; Principal Private Sec. to Sec. of State for War, 1962; Asst Sec., MoD, 1964; Dir, Centre of Admin Studies, HM Treasury, 1965; Asst Sec., DEA, 1968; HM Treasury, 1969. *Recreations:* tennis, gardening, sketching, recording vernacular architecture.

WILSON, Guy Murray, MA; FSA; Master of the Armouries, since 1988; *b* 18 Feb. 1950; *s* of late Rowland George Wilson and Mollie (*née* Munson; later Mrs Youngs); *m* 1972, Pamela Ruth McCredie; two *s* two *d*. *Educ:* New Coll., Oxford (MA); Manchester Univ. (Dip. Art, Gallery and Museum Studies). FSA 1984. Joined Royal Armouries, 1972; Keeper of Edged Weapons, 1978; Dep. Master of the Armouries, 1981. Member: British Commn for Military History, 1978–; Adv. Cttee on History Wreck Sites, 1981–; Arms and Armour Soc. of GB, 1973–; Arms and Armour Soc. of Denmark, 1978–; Meyrick Soc., 1980–. FRSA 1992. *Publications:* Treasures of the Tower: Crossbows, 1975; (with A. V. B. Norman) Treasures from the Tower of London, 1982; contribs to museum and exhibn catalogues and to Jl of Arms and Armour Soc., Internat. Jl of Nautical Archaeol., Connoisseur, Burlington, Country Life, Museums Jl, Guns Rev., etc. *Recreations:* theatre, music, reading, walking. *Address:* Tang Croft, Tang Road, High Birstwith, Harrogate, North Yorks HG3 2JU; 8 Tower Green, HM Tower of London, EC3N 4AB.

WILSON, Harold; His Honour Judge Harold Wilson; a Circuit Judge, since 1981 (Midland and Oxford Circuit); *b* 19 Sept. 1931; *s* of late Edward Simpson Wilson; *m* 1st, Diana Marion (marr. diss.), *d* of late (Philip) Guy (Dudley) Sixsmith; three *s* one *d*; 2nd, Jill Ginever, *d* of late Charles Edward Walter Barlow; one step *s* one step *d*. *Educ:* St Albans Sch.; Sidney Sussex Coll., Cambridge (State Scholar; MA). Commnd service, RAF, RAFVR, RAuxAF, 1950–disbandment. Administrative Trainee, KCH, 1954–56; Schoolmaster, 1957–59. Called to the Bar, Gray's Inn, 1958 (Holker Exhbr; runner-up, Lee Essay Prize, 1959); Oxford Circuit, 1960–70 (Circuit Junior, 1964–65); Midland and Oxford Circuit, 1971–75; Dep. Chm., Monmouthshire Quarter Sessions, 1970; a Recorder, Midland and Oxford Circuit, 1971–75; Chm. of Industrial Tribunals, Birmingham, 1976–81; Resident Judge, Coventry Crown Ct, 1983–92; Liaison Judge, 1986–92; Hon. Recorder of Coventry, 1986–93; designated Care Centre Judge, Coventry, 1991–92, Oxford, 1993–; Resident Judge, Oxford Crown Ct, 1993–; Liaison Judge to Oxfordshire Magistrates, 1993–. Pres., Transport Tribunal, 1991–; Chm., Coventry Reparation Unit Adv. Cttee, 1991–92. Member: Matrimonial Causes Rules Cttee, 1984–88; W Midlands Probation Cttee, 1985–92. *Recreations:* watching rugby football, reading and listening to music. *Address:* 2 Harcourt Buildings, Temple, EC4Y 9DB. *T:* 0171–353 6961; Judges' Chambers, Oxford Crown and County Court, St Aldates, Oxford OX1 1TL. *T:* Oxford (01865) 264200. *Club:* Royal Air Force.

WILSON, Harold Arthur Cooper B.; *see* Bird-Wilson.

WILSON, Harry; *see* Wilson of Langside, Baron.

WILSON, Henry Braithwaite; Assistant Under-Secretary of State, Home Office, 1963–71; *b* 6 Aug. 1911; *s* of Charles Braithwaite Wilson and Ellen Blanche Hargrove; *m* 1936, Margaret Bodden; two *s* two *d*. *Educ:* Leighton Park School; Lincoln College, Oxford. Editorial work for Joseph Rowntree Social Service Trust, 1933–40; Sub-Warden, Toynbee Hall, 1940–41; Home Office: Temp. Administrative Asst, 1941–44; Sec., Departmental Cttee on War Damaged Licensed Premises and Reconstruction, 1942–44; Principal, 1944 (estab. 1946); Asst Sec., 1956. *Address:* 14 Lawn Terrace, Silloth, Cumbria CA5 4AH.

WILSON, Prof. Henry Wallace, PhD; CPhys, FInstP; FRSE; physicist; Director, Scottish Universities' Research and Reactor Centre, 1962–85; Personal Professor of Physics, Strathclyde University, 1966–85, now Emeritus; *b* 30 Aug. 1923; *s* of Frank Binnington Wilson and Janet (*née* Wilson); *m* 1955, Fiona McPherson Martin, *d* of Alfred Charles Steinmetz Martin and Agnes Mary (*née* McPherson); three *s*. *Educ:* Allan Glen's Sch., Glasgow; Glasgow Univ. (BSc, PhD Physics). AInstP 1949, FInstP 1962; FRSE 1963. Wartime work as Physicist, Explosives Res. Div., ICI, Ardeer. Asst Lectr, Natural Philosophy Dept, Glasgow Univ., 1947–51; post-doctoral Res. Fellow, Univ. of Calif, Berkeley, 1951–52; Lectr, Nat. Phil. Dept, Glasgow Univ., 1952–55; Leader of Physical Measurements Gp, UKAEA, Aldermaston, 1955–62 (Sen. Principal Scientific Officer, 1958). Hon. Scientific Advr, Nat. Mus. of Antiquities of Scotland, 1969. Mem., Nuclear Safety Cttee, 1964–89, and Consultant, SSEB; Mem., Radioactive Substances Adv. Cttee, 1966–70. Inst. of Physics: Mem. Council, 1970–71; Chm., Scottish Br., 1969–71; mem. several cttees; Royal Soc. of Edinburgh: Mem. Council, 1966–69, 1976–79; Vice Pres., 1979–81. Member: Brit. Nuclear Energy Soc.; British Mass Spectrometry Soc. (Chm., 1977–79). *Publications:* contributions to: Alpha, Beta and Gamma-ray Spectroscopy, ed K. Siegbahn, 1965; Activation Analysis, ed Lenihan and Thomson, 1965; Modern Aspects of Mass Spectrometry, ed R. I. Reed, 1968; Encyclopaedic Dictionary of Physics, ed J. Thewlis, 1973; (ed) Nuclear Engineering sect., Chambers' Science and Technology Dictionary, gen. ed. P. M. B. Walker, 1988; papers on radioactivity, low energy nuclear physics, meson physics, mass spectrometry, isotope separation, effects of radiation, and reactor physics, in Phil. Mag., Nature, Phys. Rev., Proc. Phys. Soc., etc. *Recreations:* sailing, hill-walking, industrial archaeology, photography. *Address:* Ashgrove, The Crescent, Busby, Glasgow G76 8HT. *T:* 0141–644 3107. *Club:* Caledonian (Edinburgh).

WILSON, Ian D.; *see* Douglas-Wilson.

WILSON, Ian Matthew, CB 1985; *b* 12 Dec. 1926; *s* of Matthew Thomson Wilson and Mary Lily Barnett; *m* 1953, Anne Chalmers (*d* 1991); three *s*. *Educ:* George Watson's Coll.; Edinburgh Univ. (MA). Asst Principal, Scottish Home Dept, 1950; Private Sec. to Perm. Under-Sec. of State, Scottish Office, 1953–55; Principal, Scottish Home Dept, 1955; Asst Secretary: Scottish Educn Dept, 1963; SHHD, 1971; Asst Under-Sec. of State, Scottish Office, 1974–77; Under Sec., Scottish Educn Dept, 1977–86. Sec. of Commns for Scotland, 1987–92. Mem., Bd of Govs, RSAMD, 1992–. Pres., Univ. of Edinburgh Graduates' Assoc., 1995–. *Address:* 1 Bonaly Drive, Edinburgh EH13 0EJ. *T:* 0131–441 2541. *Clubs:* New, University (Edinburgh).

WILSON, Ivan Patrick; Under Secretary, Public Enterprises Group, HM Treasury, since 1993; *b* 24 Aug. 1941; *s* of William Wilson and Jessie (*née* Bateson); *m* 1966, Kathleen Mary Price; three *s*. *Educ:* Royal Sch., Dungannon; Academy, Omagh; Queen's Univ., Belfast. HM Treasury, 1965–; Private Sec. to Perm. Sec., Overseas Finance, 1971–73; Press Office, 1973–76; Defence Policy and Budget Div., 1981–84; RCDS 1985; Information Systems, 1986–89; Under-Sec., Industry and Employment Gp, 1989–90; Dir, Govt Centre for Information Systems, 1990–93. *Recreations:* foreign travel, sport, walking. *Address:* HM Treasury, Parliament Street, SW1P 3AG. *T:* 0171–270 4440.

WILSON, Sir James; *see* Wilson, Sir A. J.

WILSON, Brig. James, CBE 1986; Director, Edinburgh Old Town Trust, 1987–90; Chief Executive, Livingston Development Corporation, 1977–87; *b* 12 March 1922; *s* of late Alexander Robertson Wilson and Elizabeth Wylie Wilson (*née* Murray); *m* 1949, Audrie Veronica, *er d* of late A. W. and O. V. Haines; three *d*. *Educ:* Irvine Royal Academy; Edinburgh Academy; Aberdeen Univ. Commissioned RA, 1941; served War with 71 (West Riding) Field Regt, N Africa and Italy, 1941–45; Instructor, Sch. of Artillery, India, 1945–47; Adjt, Sussex Yeo., 1948–49; active service in Malaya and ME, 1950–53; psc 1954; DAQMG, War Office, 1955–57; Instructor, Staff Coll., 1959–61; CO, 439 (Tyne) Light Air Defence Regt, 1964–67; AQMG, Northern Comd, 1967–68; Col GS SD, HQ BAOR, 1969–71; AMA and DCBAS, Washington, 1972–73; DQMG, HQ UKLF, 1974–77. Member: Executive Council, TCPA (Scotland), 1977–87; Edin. Univ. Careers Adv. Cttee, 1982–86; Scottish Cttee, Inst. of Dirs, 1983–86; Dir, Edinburgh Chamber of Commerce, 1979–82. Mem., Royal Artillery Council for Scotland, 1979–93; Chairman: W Lothian SSAFA, 1983–93; E Scotland SSAFA Cttee, 1986–93; (also Pres.) RA Assoc. (Scotland), 1987–94. FIMgt (FBIM 1980). *Recreations:* golf, sailing, bridge. *Address:* 2 The Gardens, Aberlady, East Lothian EH32 0SF. *T:* Aberlady (01875) 870583. *Clubs:* New (Edinburgh); Hon. Co. of Edinburgh Golfers.

WILSON, Dr James Maxwell Glover, FRCP, FRCPE, FFPHM; Senior Principal Medical Officer, Department of Health and Social Security, 1972–76; *b* 31 Aug. 1913; *s* of late James Thomas Wilson and Mabel Salomons; *m* Lallie Methley; three *s*. *Educ:* King's College Choir Sch., Cambridge; Oundle Sch.; St John's Coll., Cambridge; University

College Hosp., London. MA, MB, BChir (Cantab). Clinical appts, London and Cambridge, 1937–39. Served War, RAMC (Major, 6th Airborne Div.), 1939–45. Hospital appts, London and Edinburgh, 1945–54; medical work on tea estates in India, 1954–57; Medical Staff, Min. of Health (later DHSS), concerned with the centrally financed research programme, 1957–76; Sen. Res. Fellow, Inf. Services Div., Common Services Agency, Scottish Health Service, 1976–81. Lectr (part-time), Public Health Dept, London Sch. of Hygiene and Tropical Med., 1968–72. *Publications:* (with G. Jungner) Principles and Practice of Screening for Disease (WHO), 1968; contribs to med. jls, mainly on screening for disease. *Recreations:* reading, walking, conservation. *Address:* Millhill House, 77 Millhill, Musselburgh, Midlothian EH21 7RP. *T:* 0131–665 5829.

WILSON, James Noel, ChM, FRCS; retired; Consultant Orthopædic Surgeon: Royal National Orthopædic Hospital, London (Surgeon i/c Accident Unit, RNOH Stanmore), 1955–84; National Hospitals for Nervous Diseases, Queen Square and Maida Vale, 1962–84; Teacher of Orthopædics, Institute of Orthopædics, University of London; retired; *b* Coventry, 25 Dec. 1919; *s* of Alexander Wilson and Isobel Barbara Wilson (*née* Fairweather); *m* 1945, Patricia Norah McCullough; two *s* two *d*. *Educ:* King Henry VIII Sch., Coventry; University of Birmingham. Peter Thompson Prize in Anatomy, 1940; Sen. Surgical Prize, 1942; Arthur Foxwell Prize in Clinical Medicine, 1943; MB, ChB 1943; MRCS, LRCP, 1943; FRCS 1948; ChM (Birmingham) 1949; House Surgeon, Birmingham General Hospital, 1943; Heaton Award as Best Resident for 1943. Service in RAMC, Nov. 1943–Oct. 1946, discharged as Captain; qualified as Parachutist and served with 1st Airborne Division. Resident surgical posts, Birmingham General Hospital and Coventry and Warwickshire Hospital, 1947–49; Resident Surgical Officer, Robert Jones and Agnes Hunt Orthopædic Hospital, Oswestry, 1949–52; Consultant Orthopædic Surgeon to Cardiff Royal Infirmary and Welsh Regional Hospital Board, 1952–55. Prof. of Orthopaedics, Addis Ababa Univ., 1989. Watson-Jones Lectr, RCS, 1988; Duraiswami Meml Oration, Delhi Orthopaedic Assoc., 1989; Jackson Burrows Medal Lectr, Inst. of Orthopaedics, 1991. World Orthopaedic Concern: Pres., 1979–84; Chm., UK Region, 1984–90; Editor, News-Letter, 1988–. Vice-Chm., Impact (UK) Foundn; Pres., Orthopaedic Section, RSocMed, 1982–83; former Mem. Brit. Editorial Bd, Jl of Bone and Joint Surgery; Sen. Fellow, and formerly Editorial Sec., British Orthopædic Assoc. (BOA Travelling Fellowship to USA, 1954); FRSocMed. Life Mem., Bangladesh Orthopaedic Soc.; Hon. Mem., Egyptian Orthopaedic Assoc. *Publications:* (ed) Watson Jones Fractures and Joint Injuries, 6th edn 1982; former contributor, Butterworth's Operative Surgery; chapters and articles on orthopædic subjects to various books and journals. *Recreations:* golf, reluctant gardening, photography. *Address:* The Chequers, Waterdell, near Watford, Herts WD2 7LP. *T:* Garston (01923) 672364. *Club:* Royal Society of Medicine.

WILSON, Sir James (William Douglas), 5th Bt *cr* 1906; farmer; *b* 8 Oct. 1960; *s* of Captain Sir Thomas Douglas Wilson, 4th Bt, MC, and of Pamela Aileen, *d* of Sir Edward Hanmer, 7th Bt; *S* father, 1984; *m* 1985, Julia Margaret Louise, fourth *d* of J. C. F. Mutty, Mulberry Hall, Melbourn, Cambs; one *s* two *d*. *Educ:* London Univ. (BA Hons French). *Heir:* *s* Thomas Edward Douglas Wilson, *b* 15 April 1990. *Address:* Lillingstone Lovell Manor, Buckingham MK18 5BQ. *T:* Buckingham (01280) 860643.

WILSON, Joe; *see* Wilson, A. J.

WILSON, Sir John (Foster), Kt 1975; CBE 1965 (OBE 1955); Director, Royal Commonwealth Society for the Blind, 1950–83, Vice-President 1983; Senior Consultant, United Nations Development Programme, since 1983; President, International Agency for the Prevention of Blindness, 1974–83; *b* 20 Jan. 1919; *s* of late Rev. George Henry Wilson, Buxton, Derbys; *m* 1944, Chloe Jean McDermid, OBE 1981; two *d*. *Educ:* Worcester College for the Blind; St Catherine's, Oxford (MA Jurisprudence, Dipl. Public and Social Administration; Hon. Fellow, 1984). Asst Secretary, Royal National Inst. for the Blind, 1941–49; Member, Colonial Office Delegation investigating blindness in Africa, 1946–47. Proposed formation of Royal Commonwealth Society for Blind; became its first Director, 1950; extensive tours in Africa, Asia, Near and Far East, Caribbean and N America, 1952–67; formulated Asian plan for the Blind 1963, and African Plan for the Blind, 1966. Pres., Internat. Agency for the Prevention of Blindness, 1974–83; established UN Initiative Against Avoidable Disability IMPACT, 1983 (Chm., Internat. Council, 1991–). Hon. DCL Oxford, 1995. Helen Keller International Award, 1970; Lions Internat. Humanitarian Award, 1978; World Humanity Award, 1979; Albert Lasker Award, 1979; Richard T. Hewitt Award, RSM, 1991; Albert Schweitzer Internat. Prize, 1993. *Publications:* Blindness in African and Middle East Territories, 1948; Ghana's Handicapped Citizens, 1961; Travelling Blind, 1963; (ed) World Blindness and its Prevention, 1980; Disability Prevention—the Global Challenge, 1980, 2nd edn 1984; various on Commonwealth affairs and disability. *Recreations:* current affairs, travel, writing, tape-recording, wine-making. *Address:* 22 The Cliff, Roedean, Brighton, East Sussex BN2 5RE. *T:* Brighton (01273) 607667, *Fax:* (01273) 679624.

WILSON, Prof. John Graham; Cavendish Professor of Physics, 1963–76 (Professor, 1952–63), Pro-Vice-Chancellor, 1969–71, University of Leeds; now Emeritus Professor; *b* 28 April 1911; *er s* of J. E. Wilson, Hartlepool, Co. Durham; *m*; one *s* one *d*. *Educ:* West Hartlepool Secondary Sch.; Sidney Sussex Coll., Cambridge. Member of teaching staff, University of Manchester, 1938–52; Reader in Physics, 1951. University of York: Member, Academic Planning Board, 1960–63; Member of Council, 1964–84; Chairman, Joint Matriculation Board, 1964–67. DUniv York, 1975; Hon. DSc Durham, 1977. *Publications:* The Principles of Cloud Chamber Technique, 1951. Editor of Progress in Cosmic Ray Physics, 1952–71; (with G. D. Rochester), Cloud Chamber Photographs of the Cosmic Radiation, 1952. Papers on cosmic ray physics, articles in jls. *Recreation:* gardening. *Address:* 23 Newall Hall Park, Otley, West Yorks LS21 2RD. *T:* Otley (01943) 465184.

WILSON, Ven. John Hewitt, CB 1977; Canon Emeritus of Lincoln Cathedral, since 1980; Rector of The Heyfords with Rousham and Somerton, diocese of Oxford, 1981–93; *b* 14 Feb. 1924; 2nd *s* of John Joseph and Marion Wilson; *m* 1951, Gertrude Elsie Joan Weir; three *s* two *d*. *Educ:* Kilkenny Coll., Kilkenny; Mountjoy Sch., Dublin; Trinity Coll., Dublin. BA 1946, MA 1956. Curate, St George's Church, Dublin, 1947–50. Entered RAF, 1950: RAF Coll., Cranwell, 1950–52; Aden, 1952–55; RAF Wittering, 1955–57; RAF Cottesmore, 1957–58; RAF Germany, 1958–61; Staff Chaplain, Air Ministry, 1961–63; RAF Coll., Cranwell, 1963–66; Asst Chaplain-in-Chief: Far East Air Force, 1966–69; Strike command, 1969–73; Chaplain-in-Chief, RAF, 1973–80. QHC 1972–80. Liveryman, Coachmakers' and Coach-Harness Makers' Co., 1994– (Hon. Chaplain, 1977–). *Recreations:* Rugby football, golf, tennis, gardening, theatre. *Address:* Glencree, Philcote Street, Deddington, Banbury, Oxon OX15 0TB. *T:* Deddington (01869) 338903. *Club:* Royal Air Force.

WILSON, John James, FIEE; CIMgt; Chairman, London Electricity plc (formerly London Electricity Board), 1986–94; *b* 16 Feb. 1932; *s* of Norval John Wilson and Edna May (*née* Smith); *m* 1961, Connie Catherina Boldt Salomonsson; one *s*. *Educ:* Royal Grammar Sch., Worcester; College of Technology, Birmingham (BSc). Successive engineering appts, Midlands Electricity Bd, Southern Electricity Bd, 1955–68; Southern Electricity Board: Dist Manager, Swindon, 1968–69; Dist Manager, Reading, 1969–72; Area Manager, Portsmouth, 1972–77; Midlands Electricity Board: Chief Engineer, 1977–79; Dep. Chairman, 1979–82; Chairman, 1982–86. *Recreations:* golf, gardening.

WILSON, Dr John Murray, MBE 1964; Controller, Home Division, British Council, 1985–86; *b* 25 July 1926; *s* of Maurice John and Mary Ellen Wilson (*née* Murray); *m* 1957, Audrey Miriam Simmons; one *s* one *d*. *Educ:* Selwyn Avenue Junior, Highams Park; Bancroft's School, Essex; St John's College, Oxford (MA Botany 1952; DPhil 1957; *prox. acc.* Christopher Welch Scholarship 1951). Served RAF, 1945–48. British Council, 1955–86: Science Dept, 1955–58; Chile, 1958–62; Brazil, 1962–66; India, 1966–71; Dep. Rep./Sci. Officer, Italy, 1971–74; Sci. Officer, Germany, 1974–79; Dep. Rep., Germany, 1979–81; Dep. Controller, Home Div., 1981–85. *Publications:* (with J. L. Harley) papers in New Phytologist. *Recreations:* gardening, photography, messing about.

WILSON, Prof. John Stuart Gladstone, MA, DipCom; Professor of Economics and Commerce in the University of Hull, 1959–82, now Emeritus Professor; Head of Department, 1959–71, and 1974–77; *b* 18 Aug. 1916; *s* of Herbert Gladstone Wilson and Mary Buchanan Wilson (*née* Wylie); *m* 1943, Beryl Margaret Gibson, *d* of Alexander Millar Gibson and Bertha Noble Gibson; no *c*. *Educ:* University of Western Australia (1st Cl. Hons Econs, 1941). Lecturer in Economics: University of Tasmania, 1941–43; Sydney, 1944–45; Canberra, 1946–47; LSE, 1948–49. Reader in Economics, with special reference to Money and Banking, Univ. of London, 1950–59; Dean, Faculty of Social Sciences and Law, Univ. of Hull, 1962–65; Chairman, Centre for S-E Asian Studies, Univ. of Hull, 1963–66. Hackett Research Student, 1947; Leverhulme Research Award, 1955. Economic Survey of New Hebrides on behalf of Colonial Office, 1958–59; Consultant, Trade and Payments Dept, OECD, 1965–66; Consultant with Harvard Advisory Development Service in Liberia, 1967; headed Enquiry into Sources of Capital and Credit to UK Agriculture, 1970–73; Consultant, Directorate Gen. for Agric., EEC, 1974–75; Specialist Adviser, H of C Select Cttee on Nationalised Industries, 1976; Consultant, Cttee on Financial Markets, OECD, 1979–81; Dir, Centre for Jt Study of Economics, Politics and Sociology, 1980–82; SSRC Grant for comparative study of banking policy and structure, 1977–81; Leverhulme Emeritus Fellow, 1983–84. Mem. Cttee of Management, Inst. of Commonwealth Studies, London, 1960–77, Hon. Life Mem., 1980; Governor, SOAS, London, 1963–92. Member: Yorkshire Council for Further Education, 1963–67; Nat. Advisory Council on Education for Industry and Commerce, 1964–66; Languages Bd, CNAA, 1978–83. Société Universitaire Européenne de Recherches Financières: Mem., Steering Cttee, 1964–69; Sec.-Gen., 1968–72; Mem. Council, 1970–91; Pres., 1973–75; Vice-Pres., 1977–83. Editor, Yorkshire Bulletin of Economic and Social Research, 1964–67; Mem., Editorial Adv. Bd, Modern Asian Studies, 1966–89. *Publications:* French Banking Structure and Credit Policy, 1957; Economic Environment and Development Programmes, 1960; Monetary Policy and the Development of Money Markets, 1966; Economic Survey of the New Hebrides, 1966; (ed with C. R. Whittlesey) Essays in Money and Banking in Honour of R. S. Sayers, 1968, repr. 1970; Availability of Capital and Credit to United Kingdom Agriculture, 1973; (ed with C. F. Scheffer) Multinational Enterprises—Financial and Monetary Aspects, 1974; Credit to Agriculture—United Kingdom, 1975; The London Money Markets, 1976, 2nd edn 1989; (ed with J. E. Wadsworth and H. Fournier) The Development of Financial Institutions in Europe, 1956–1976, 1977; Industrial Banking: a comparative survey, 1978; Banking Policy and Structure: a comparative analysis, 1986; (ed) Managing Bank Assets and Liabilities, 1988; Money Markets: the international perspective, 1993; contributions to: Banking in the British Commonwealth (ed R. S. Sayers), 1952; Banking in Western Europe (ed R. S. Sayers), 1962; A Decade of the Commonwealth, 1955–64, ed W. B. Hamilton and others, 1966; International Encyclopaedia of the Social Sciences, 1968; Encyclopaedia Britannica, 15th edn, 1974; New Palgrave Dictionary of Money and Finance, 1992; Economica, Economic Journal, Journal of Political Econ., Economic Record, Banca Nazionale del Lavoro Quarterly Rev. *Recreations:* gardening, theatre, art galleries, travel, photography. *Address:* Department of Economics, The University, Hull, North Humberside HU6 7RX. *Club:* Reform.

WILSON, John Veitch D.; *see* Drysdale Wilson.

WILSON, John Warley; His Honour Judge John Wilson; a Circuit Judge, since 1982; *b* 13 April 1936; *s* of late John Pearson Wilson and of Nancy Wade Wilson (*née* Harston); *m* 1962, Rosalind Mary Pulford. *Educ:* Warwick Sch.; St Catharine's Coll., Cambridge (MA). Called to the Bar, Lincoln's Inn, 1960, in practice, 1960–82; a Recorder of the Crown Court, 1979–82. Dep. Chairman, West Midlands Agricultural Land Tribunal, 1978–82. *Recreations:* gardening, National Hunt racing. *Address:* Victoria House, Farm Street, Harbury, Leamington Spa CV33 9LR. *T:* Harbury (01926) 612572.

WILSON, Rt. Rev. John Warwick; Bishop of the Southern Region (Assistant Bishop, Diocese of Melbourne), since 1985; *b* 12 July 1937; *s* of Walter and Norma Wilson; *m* 1963, Jill Brady; two *d*. *Educ:* Bathurst Coll., NSW; Ridley Coll., Parkville, Victoria (ThL, ThSchol); London Univ. (BD (Hons)); Yale Univ. (STM); Duke Univ. (PhD). Educn Officer, Papua New Guinea, 1957–59. Ordained deacon and priest, 1964; Asst, St Cyprian's, Narrabri, 1964–67; Vicar, St Andrew, Tingha, 1967–68; Priest in charge, St John's Henderson, North Carolina, USA, 1969–72; Lectr in OT, Ridley Coll., 1973–85. *Publications:* The Old Testament and Christian Living, 1981, 2nd edn 1985; Ezekiel: God's Communicator, 1990. *Recreations:* reading, music, cinema. *Address:* St Paul's Cathedral Buildings, 209 Flinders Lane, Melbourne, Vic 3000, Australia. *T:* (3) 96534220.

WILSON, Joseph Albert; Secretary to the Cabinet, Sierra Leone Government, 1968–69; Barrister-at-Law; Solicitor of High Court of Sierra Leone; Notary Public; *b* 22 Jan. 1922; *e s* of late George Wilson; *m* 1947, Esther Massaquoi; two *s* four *d* (and one *s* decd). *Educ:* St Edward's Secondary Sch., Freetown, Sierra Leone; University of Exeter, (DPA); Middle Temple. Graded Clerical Service, Sierra Leone Government, 1941–47; family business, 1948–51; Secretary, Bonthe District Council, 1951–59; Administrative Officer, Sierra Leone Government, rising to rank of Cabinet Secretary, 1959; High Comr from Sierra Leone to UK, 1967–68. Manager (Special Duties), SLST Ltd, 1959. Comdr of the Republic, CR. *Recreations:* tennis, golf. *Address:* 9 Prince Williams Street, PO Box 64, Bo, Sierra Leone. *T:* (32) 310.

WILSON, Julian David Bonhôte; Racing Correspondent, BBC Television, since 1966; *s* of Peter Jardine Bonhôte Wilson, OBE and Helen Angela Josephine Mann; *m* 1st, 1970, Carolyn Anne Michael (marr. diss. 1980); one *s*; 2nd, 1981, Alison Christian Findlay Ramsay. *Educ:* Harrow. Writer and reporter, Mirror Group Newspapers, 1958–64; Editor, Tote Racing Annual, 1965. *Publications:* Lester Piggott: the pictorial biography, 1985; 100 Greatest Racehorses, 1987; The Racing World, 1991. *Recreation:* cricket. *Address:* 45 Old Church Street, SW3 5BS; Home Farm Cottage, Burrough Green, Newmarket, Suffolk CB8 9LY. *Club:* St Moritz Tobagganing.

WILSON, Mrs (Katherine) Muriel (Irwin), OBE 1985; Chairman and Chief Executive, Equal Opportunities Commission for Northern Ireland, 1981–84; *b* 3 Dec. 1920; *d* of Francis Hosford and Martha Evelyn (*née* Irwin); *m* 1949, William George Wilson; one *s*.

Educ: Methodist Coll., Belfast; The Queen's University of Belfast (DPA); MIMgt. Northern Ireland Civil Service, 1939–49; N Ireland Health Service, 1949–73: Eastern Special Care Management Cttee (Services for the Mentally Handicapped): Asst Sec., 1963–71; Gp Sec. and Chief Admin. Officer, 1971–73; Asst Chief Admin. Officer (Personnel and Management Services), Northern Health and Social Services Board, 1973–81. Chm. NI Div., 1977–79, National Vice-Pres. 1979–81, United Kingdom Fedn of Business and Professional Women; Member: Bd, Labour Relations Agency (NI), 1976–81; Fair Employment Agency for NI, 1981–84; NI Adv. Cttee, IBA, 1978–83; NI Council, RIPA, 1985–88; Women's Forum, NI, 1990–. Dir, Ulster Telethon Trust, 1989–. Chairman, Board of Governors: Glenravel Special Sch., Belfast, 1987–93; Hill Croft Sch., Newtownabbey, 1987–89; Glenveagh Sch., Belfast, 1993–; Chm., Whiteabbey Hosp. League of Friends, 1989–92. *Recreations:* swimming, reading.

WILSON, Rev. Dr Kenneth Brian, OBE 1993; Principal, Westminster College, Oxford, since 1981; *b* 10 April 1937; *s* of Norman Harold Wilson and Violet Frances Sarah Wilson; *m* 1962, Jennifer Rosemary Floyd; one *s* two *d. Educ:* Kingswood Sch., Bath; Univ. of Cambridge (MA); Univ. of Bristol (MLitt; PhD); Univ. of Oxford (MA). Ordained Minister in Methodist Church; Asst Minister, Hinde St Methodist Church, London, 1964–66; Asst Chaplain, 1966–69, Chaplain, 1969–73, Kingswood Sch., Bath; Rowbotham Prof. of Philosophy and Ethics, Wesley Coll., Bristol, 1973–80. FRSA. Hon. DTh Lycoming, 1994. *Publications:* Making Sense of It, 1973; Living it Out, 1975; (ed) Experience of Ordination, 1979; (with F. Young) Focus on God, 1986. *Recreations:* books, poetry, art, religion. *Address:* Field End, Harcourt Hill, Oxford OX2 9AS. *Club:* United Oxford & Cambridge University.

WILSON, Prof. Kenneth Geddes, PhD; Professor of Physics, Ohio State University, since 1988; *b* 8 June 1936; *s* of Edgar Bright Wilson and Emily Fisher Buckingham; *m* 1982, Alison Brown. *Educ:* Harvard Univ. (AB); Calif Inst. of Technol. (PhD). Cornell University: Asst Prof. of Physics, 1963; Prof. of Physics, 1963–88; Dir, Center for Theory and Simulation in Sci. and Engrg, 1985–88. Co-Prin. Investigator, Nat. Sci. Foundn Statewide Systematic Initiative, Project Discovery, Ohio, to reform sci. and math. educn, 1991–. Hon. PhD: Harvard, 1981; Chicago, 1976. Nobel Prize for Physics, 1982. *Publications:* (ed jtly) Broken Scale Invariance and the Light Cone, 1971; Quarks and Strings on a Lattice, 1975; (contrib.) New Pathways in High Energy Physics, Vol. II 1976; (contrib.) New Developments in Quantum Field Theory and Statistical Mechanics, 1977; (contrib.) Recent Developments in Gauge Theories, 1980; contrib. Jl of Math. Phys, Nuovo Cimento, Acta Phys. Austriaca, Phys Rev., Jl of Chem. Phys, Comm. Math. Phys, Phys Reports, Advances in Maths, Rev. of Mod. Phys, Scientific American; symposia and conf. papers. *Address:* Department of Physics, Ohio State University, 174 West 18th Avenue, Columbus, OH 43210–1106, USA. *T:* (614) 2929396.

WILSON, Leslie William, JP; Director-General, Association of Special Libraries and Information Bureaux (Aslib), 1950–78, retired; *b* 26 Sept. 1918; *s* of Harry Wilson and Ada Jane Wilson; *m* 1942, Valerie Jones; one *s* two *d. Educ:* Cambridgeshire High Sch.; Trinity Hall, Cambridge (Open Scholar, MA Mod. Langs). Army Service, India, 1940–46. Foreign Editor, Times Educnl Supplement, 1946–50. Mem., Parly and Scientific Cttee, 1965–78. Hon. Fellow, Internat. Fedn for Documentation, 1978; Hon. Member: Inst. of Information Scientists, 1977; US Special Libraries Assoc., 1978; Aslib, 1978. JP Mddx, 1971. *Address:* 6 Queensberry House, Friars Lane, Richmond, Surrey TW9 1NT. *T:* 0181–948 0421.

WILSON, Lynn Anthony; Chairman, Wilson (Connolly) Holdings PLC, since 1982; Director of 24 subsidiary companies; *b* 8 Dec. 1939; *s* of Connolly Thomas Wilson and Frances (*née* Chapman); *m* 1964, Judith Helen Mann; two *s. Educ:* Oakham Sch., Rutland. FCIOB; CBIM. Wilson Builders (N'pton) Ltd, 1957; Man. Dir, Wilson (Connolly) Holdings, on flotation, 1966. Nat. Pres., House Builders Fedn, 1981. Pres., Old Oakhamian Club, 1988; Trustee, Oakham Sch., 1983–. Chm., Northants CCC, 1990– (Mem. Cttee, 1971–80; Treas., 1974–79). *Recreations:* cricket, golf, horseracing, shooting. *Address:* c/o Wilson (Connolly) Holdings PLC, Thomas Wilson House, Tenter Road, Moulton Park, Northampton NN3 6QJ. *T:* Northampton (01604) 790909. *Clubs:* Farmers', MCC; Northants CC.

WILSON, Sir Mathew John Anthony, 6th Bt *cr* 1874, of Eshton Hall, Co. York; OBE 1979 (MBE 1971); MC 1972; *b* 2 Oct. 1935; *s* of Anthony Thomas Wilson (*d* 1979; 2nd *s* of Sir Mathew Richard Henry Wilson, 4th Bt) and Margaret (*d* 1980), *d* of late Alfred Holden; *S* uncle, 1991; *m* 1962, Janet Mary, *e d* of late E. W. Mowll, JP; one *s* one *d. Educ:* Trinity Coll. Sch., Ontario. Brig. KOYLI, retired 1983. Exec. Dir, Wilderness Foundn (UK), 1983–85. Former Vice-Pres., Internat. Wilderness Leadership Foundn. *Heir: s* Mathew Edward Amcotts Wilson, *b* 13 Oct. 1966.

WILSON, Michael Anthony, FRCGP; Principal in general practice, Strensall, since 1961; *b* 2 June 1936; *s* of late Charles Kenneth Wilson and Bertha Wilson; *m* 1959, Marlene (*née* Wilson); two *s. Educ:* Roundhay Grammar Sch., Leeds; Medical Sch., Univ. of Leeds (MB ChB 1958). DObst RCOG 1961; MRCGP 1965, FRCGP 1980. British Medical Association: Chm., Gen. Med. Services Cttee, 1984–90 (Dep. Chm., 1979–84); Pres., Yorkshire Regional Council, 1975–79; Mem. Council, 1977–90, 1992–; Fellow, 1979. Member: GMC, 1989–; Standing Med. Adv. Cttee to DHSS, 1967–69, 1978–90 (Dep. Chm., 1986–90); NHS Clinical Standards Adv. Gp, 1990–93; Med. Protection Soc. Adv. Bd, 1990–; Code of Practice Authy, Assoc. of British Pharmaceutical Industry, 1990–; Jt Consultants Cttee, 1991–. *Recreations:* golf, Rotary. *Address:* Longueville, Mill Hill, Huntington, York YO3 9PY. *T:* York (01904) 768861. *Clubs:* East India, Royal Society of Medicine.

WILSON, Michael Anthony; Chief Executive, Waltham Forest Housing Action Trust, since 1992; *b* 19 Feb. 1948; *s* of Alan Wilson and Christina Wilson (*née* McFarlane); *m* 1972, Aileen Athey (marr. diss. 1991); one *s* two *d. Educ:* Aston Univ. (BSc Hons Behavioural Sci. 1972); DipTP 1977. MRTPI 1979; AIH 1984. Planning Asst, London Borough of Barnet, 1972–74; Res. and Inf. Officer, Harlow Develt Corp., 1974–80; Housing Manager, City of Glasgow, 1980–84; Dir of Housing and Envmtl Services, London Borough of Brent, 1984–92. MIMgt 1978. *Recreations:* watching football (Spurs), cinema, theatre, good food and wine, the children. *Address:* 112 Mandeville Court, Lowerhall Lane, Chingford, E4 8JD. *Club:* Tottenham Hotspur Football.

WILSON, Maj.-Gen. Michael Peter Bruce Grant; Director-General, Military Survey and Chief Executive, Military Survey Defence Agency, since 1993; *b* 19 Aug. 1943; *s* of Ian Henry Wilson and Catherine Collingwood Wilson; *m* 1967, Margaret Ritchie; two *s* one *d. Educ:* Duke of York's Sch., Nairobi; Dip. Photogrammetry, UCL. ARICS 1988; FRGS 1990. Commnd RE, 1966; served UK, Kenya, Uganda, Nigeria, BAOR, MoD; UK Exchange Officer, US Defense Mapping Agency, 1978; Sen. Instructor in Air Survey and Cartography, Sch. of Mil. Survey, 1981; Asst Dir, Mil. Survey Systems and Techniques Unit, 1983; CO 512 Special Team RE and Comdr, Geographic Staff, Washington, 1986; Comdr, 42 Survey Engr Gp, 1987; Dir, Geographic Ops, MoD, 1990. FIMgt. *Recreations:* mountaineering, rock climbing, shooting, stalking, fishing, golf, cricket. *Address:* Directorate of Military Survey, Elmwood Avenue, Feltham, Middx TW13 7AH. *T:* 0181–218 2174. *Clubs:* Geographical; Pyrford Cricket.

WILSON, Michael Sumner; Chief Executive, J Rothschild Assurance, since 1992; *b* 5 Dec. 1943; *s* of late Peter and of Margaret Wilson; *m* 1975, Mary Drysdale; one *d. Educ:* St Edward's School, Oxford. Equity & Law, 1963–68; Abbey Life, 1968–71; Allied Dunbar (Hambro Life until 1985, when name was changed), 1971–91: Exec. Dir, 1973; Board Dir, 1976; Dep. Man. Dir, 1982; Man. Dir, 1984; Gp Chief Exec., 1988–91. Director: BAT Industries, 1989–91; Vendôme Luxury Gp, 1993–. *Recreations:* tennis, racing. *Club:* Raffles.

WILSON, Mrs Muriel; *see* Wilson, K. M. I.

WILSON, Prof. Nairn Hutchison Fulton, PhD; FDS; Professor of Restorative Dentistry and Head, Unit of Conservative Dentistry, University Dental Hospital, Manchester, since 1986; Dean, Faculty of Dental Surgery, Royal College of Surgeons of Edinburgh, since 1995; *b* 26 April 1950; *s* of William Fulton Wilson and Anne Wilson (*née* Hutchison); *m* 1st, 1971, Madeleine Christina Munro (marr. diss. 1981); two *d*; 2nd, 1982, Margaret Alexandra Jones; one *s* one *d. Educ:* Strathallan Sch.; Univ. of Edinburgh (BDS 1973); Univ. of Manchester (MSc 1979; PhD 1985); Royal Coll. of Surgeons of Edinburgh (FDS 1977; DRD 1980). FACD 1990; FADM 1991; FDS RCS (*ad eundem*), 1994. Lectr in Restorative Dentistry (Prosthetics), Univ. of Edinburgh, 1974–75; University of Manchester: Lectr in Conservative Dentistry, 1975–81; Sen. Lectr, 1981–86; Head, Dept of Conservative Dentistry, 1986–88, Dept of Restorative Dentistry, 1988–92; Dep. Dean, 1991–92, Dean and Clin. Dir, 1992–95, Univ. Dental Hosp. Hon. Consultant in Restorative Dentistry, Central Manchester Healthcare NHS Trust (formerly Central Manchester HA), 1982–. President: British Assoc. of Teachers of Conservative Dentistry, 1992; Sect. of Odontology, Manchester Med. Soc., 1993–94; British Soc. for Restorative Dentistry, 1994–95. Editor, Jl of Dentistry, 1986–. *Publications:* contrib. chaps in contemporary texts and numerous papers in jls. *Recreations:* D-I-Y, gardening, ski-ing. *Address:* Turner Dental School, University Dental Hospital of Manchester, Higher Cambridge Street, Manchester M15 6FH. *T:* 0161–275 6660. *Club:* Strathallan.

WILSON, Hon. Sir Nicholas (Allan Roy), Kt 1993; **Hon. Mr Justice Wilson;** a Judge of the High Court of Justice, Family Division, since 1993; *b* 9 May 1945; *s* of late Roderick Peter Garratt Wilson and of Dorothy Anne Wilson (*née* Chenevix-Trench); *m* 1974, Margaret (*née* Higgins); one *s* one *d. Educ:* Bryanston School; Worcester College, Oxford (BA 1st cl. hons Jurisp. 1966). Eldon Scholar, 1967. Called to the Bar, Inner Temple, 1967, Bencher, 1993; QC 1987; a Recorder, 1987–93. *Address:* Royal Courts of Justice, Strand, WC2A 2LL.

WILSON, Nigel Guy, FBA 1980; Fellow and Tutor in Classics, Lincoln College, Oxford, since 1962; *b* 23 July 1935; *s* of Noel Wilson and Joan Lovibond. *Educ:* University Coll. Sch.; Corpus Christi Coll., Oxford (1st Cl. Classics (Mods) 1955; 1st Cl. Lit. Hum. 1957; Hertford Scholar 1955; Ireland and Craven Scholar 1955; Derby Scholar 1957). Lectr, Merton Coll., Oxford, 1957–62. Jt Editor, Classical Rev., 1975–87. Ospite Linceo, Scuola normale superiore, Pisa, 1977; Visiting Professor: Univ. of Padua, 1985; Ecole Normale Supérieure, Paris, 1986. Gaisford Lectr, 1983. Gordon Duff Prize, 1968. *Publications:* (with L. D. Reynolds) Scribes and Scholars, 1968, 3rd edn 1991; An Anthology of Byzantine Prose, 1971; Medieval Greek Bookhands, 1973; St Basil on the Value of Greek Literature, 1975; Scholia in Aristophanis Acharnenses, 1975; (with D. A. Russell) Menander Rhetor, 1981; Scholars of Byzantium, 1983; (with Sir Hugh Lloyd-Jones) Sophoclea, 1990; (ed with Sir Hugh Lloyd-Jones) Sophocles: Fabulae, 1990; From Byzantium to Italy, 1992; Photius: the Bibliotheca, 1994; articles and reviews in various learned jls. *Recreations:* bridge, real tennis. *Address:* Lincoln College, Oxford OX1 3DR. *T:* Oxford (01865) 279794, *Fax:* 279802.

WILSON, Sir Patrick Michael Ernest David McN.; *see* McNair-Wilson.

WILSON, Pete; Governor of California, since 1991; *b* 23 Aug. 1933; *m* Betty Robertson (marr. diss.); *m* 1983, Gayle Edlund. *Educ:* Yale Univ. (BA); Univ. of California at Berkeley (JD). Admitted to California Bar, 1962. Mayor of San Diego, 1971–73; US Senator (Republican) from California, 1983–91. *Address:* Office of the Governor, Sacramento, CA 95814, USA.

WILSON, Prof. Peter Northcote, CBE 1987; FRSE; Scientific Director, Edinburgh Centre for Rural Research, since 1990; *b* 4 April 1928; *s* of Llewellyn W. C. M. Wilson and F. Louise Wilson; *m* 1950, Maud Ethel (*née* Bunn); two *s* one *d. Educ:* Whitgift School; Wye College, Univ. of London (BSc (Agric), MSc, PhD); Univ. of Edinburgh (Dip. Animal Genetics). CBiol, FIBiol; FRSE 1987. Lectr in Agriculture, Makerere Coll., UC of E Africa, 1951–57; Sen. Lectr in Animal Production, Imperial Coll. of Tropical Agriculture, 1957–61; Prof. of Agriculture, Univ. of W Indies, 1961–64; Senior Scientist, Unilever Res. Lab., 1964–68; Agricl Dir, SLF Ltd (Unilever), 1968–71; Chief Agricl Advr, BOCM Silcock Ltd (Unilever), 1971–83; Prof. of Agric. and Rural Economy and Hd of Sch. of Agric., Univ. of Edinburgh, 1984–90; Principal, East of Scotland Coll. of Agric., 1984–90. Vis. Prof. Univ. of Reading, 1975–83. President: Brit. Soc. of Animal Production, 1977; Edin. Agricl Soc., 1992–93 (Vice-Pres., 1991–92); Scotia Club, 1992–93 (Vice Pres., 1990–92); Hon. Sec., Inst. of Biol., 1992– (Vice-Pres., 1977–79, 1991–92); Mem. Council, Scottish Agricl Colls, 1995– (Sec.-Gen. Council, 1985–86; Mem. Exec. Bd, 1987–90). Chm., Frank Parkinson Agricl Trust, 1980–; Trustee, Frank Parkinson Yorks Trust, 1992–. FRSA. *Publications:* Agriculture in the Tropics, 1965, 3rd edn 1995; Improved Feeding of Cattle and Sheep, 1981; numerous papers in learned jls. *Recreations:* hill walking, photography, foreign travel, philately. *Address:* 8 St Thomas' Road, Edinburgh EH9 2LQ. *T:* 0131–667 3182. *Club:* Farmers'.

WILSON, Philip Alexander P.; *see* Poole-Wilson.

WILSON, Quintin Campbell, OBE 1975; HM Inspector of Constabulary for Scotland, 1975–79; *b* 19 Nov. 1913; *s* of William Wilson and Mary (*née* Cowan); *m* 1939, Adelia Campbell Scott; two *s. Educ:* Barr Primary Sch.; Girvan High Sch. Halifax Borough Police, April 1936; Ayrshire Constabulary, Nov. 1936; Chief Supt, Police Research and Planning Branch, Home Office, London, 1965; Dep. Chief Constable, Ayrshire, 1966; Chief Constable, Ayrshire, 1968–75. *Recreation:* golf. *Address:* 15 Portmark Avenue, Alloway, Ayr KA7 4DN. *T:* Alloway (01292) 43034.

WILSON, Sir Reginald (Holmes), Kt 1951; BCom; FCIT; CIMgt; Scottish Chartered Accountant; Director of business and finance companies; *b* 1905; *o s* of Alexander Wilson and Emily Holmes Wilson; *m* 1st, 1930, Rose Marie von Arnim; one *s* one *d*; 2nd, 1938, Sonia Havell. *Educ:* St Peter's Sch., Panchgani; St Lawrence, Ramsgate; London Univ. BCom. Partner in Whinney Murray & Co., 1937–72; HM Treasury, 1940; Principal Assistant Secretary, Ministry of Shipping, 1941; Director of Finance, Ministry of War Transport, 1941; Under-Secretary, Ministry of Transport, 1945; returned to City, 1946; Joint Financial Adviser, Ministry of Transport, 1946; Member of Royal Commission on Press, 1946; Vice-Chairman, Hemel Hempstead Development Corporation, 1946–56; Adviser on Special Matters, CCG, 1947. Comptroller BTC, 1947, Member BTC, 1953,

Chm. E Area Board, 1955–60, Chm. London Midland Area Board, 1960–62; Dep. Chm. and Man. Dir, Transport Holding Co., 1962–67; Chairman: Transport Holding Co., 1967–70; Nat. Freight Corp., 1969–70; Transport Develt Gp, 1971–74 (Dep. Chm., 1970–71); Thos Cook & Son Ltd, 1967–76. Mem., Cttee of Enquiry into Civil Air Transport, 1967–69. Chm., Bd for Simplification of Internat. Trade Procedures, 1976–79. Award of Merit, Inst. Transport, 1953; President, Inst. Transport, 1957–58. Governor, LSE, 1954–58; Chairman, Board of Governors: Hospitals for Diseases of the Chest, 1960–71; National Heart Hospital, 1968–71; National Heart and Chest Hospitals, 1971–80; Chm., Cardiothoracic Inst., 1960–80; UK Rep., Council of Management, Internat. Hosp. Fedn, 1973–79. *Publications:* various papers on transport matters. *Recreations:* music, walking. *Address:* 49 Gloucester Square, W2 2TQ. *Club:* Athenæum.

WILSON, Richard, OBE 1994; actor and director; *b* 9 July 1936; *s* of John Boyd Wilson and Euphemia (*née* Colquhoun). *Educ:* Greenock High Sch.; Royal Acad. of Dramatic Art. *Theatre* includes: Normal Service, Hampstead, 1979; Operation Bad Apple, 1982, An Honourable Trade, 1984, May Days, 1990, Royal Court; The Weekend, Strand, 1994; *plays directed:* Heaven and Hell, 1981, Other Worlds, 1983, Royal Court; An Inspector Calls, Manchester Royal Exchange, 1986; A Wholly Healthy Glasgow, Manchester Royal Exchange, Royal Court and Edinburgh Fest., 1987, 1988; Prin, Lyric, Hammersmith, 1989; Imagine Drowning, Hampstead, 1991; Women Laughing, Manchester Royal Exchange, transf. Royal Court, 1992; *television series* include: My Good Woman, 1972; Crown Court, 1973–84; A Sharp Intake of Breath, 1979–81; Only When I Laugh, 1979–82; High and Dry, 1987; Tutti Frutti, 1987; One Foot in the Grave, five series, 1989–; *films* include: A Passage to India, 1984; Whoops Apocalypse, 1986; Prick Up Your Ears, 1987; How to Get Ahead in Advertising, 1989; Fellow Traveller, 1990; Carry on Columbus, 1992. Hon. DLitt Glasgow Caledonian, 1995. Top TV Comedy Actor, British Comedy Awards, 1991; Light Entertainment Award, BAFTA, 1992. *Recreations:* squash, collecting work of living Scottish painters. *Address:* c/o Conway van Gelder Robinson Ltd, 18–21 Jermyn Street, SW1Y 6HP. *T:* 0171–287 0077. *Clubs:* Royal Automobile, Groucho.

WILSON, Prof. Richard Middlewood; Professor of English Language, University of Sheffield, 1955–73; *b* 20 Sept. 1908; *e s* of late R. L. Wilson, The Grange, Kilham, Driffield, E Yorks; *m* 1938, Dorothy Muriel, *y d* of late C. E. Leeson, Eastgate House, Kilham, Driffield; one *d. Educ:* Woodhouse Grove School; Leeds University. Asst Lecturer, Leeds Univ., 1931, Lecturer, 1936; Senior Lecturer and Head of Dept of English Language, Sheffield Univ., 1946. *Publications:* Sawles Warde, 1939; Early Middle English Literature, 1939; (with B. Dickins) Early Middle English Texts, 1951; The Lost Literature of Medieval England, 1952; (with D. J. Price) The Equatorie of the Planetis, 1955; (contrib.) A Dictionary of English Surnames, 2nd edn 1976, 3rd edn 1991; articles and reviews. *Recreation:* cricket.

WILSON, Richard Thomas James, CB 1991; Permanent Secretary, Home Office, since 1994; *b* 11 Oct. 1942; *s* of late Richard Ridley Wilson and Frieda Bell Wilson (*née* Finlay); *m* 1972, Caroline Margaret, *y d* of Rt Hon. Sir Frank Lee, GCMG, KCB and of Lady Lee; one *s* one *d. Educ:* Radley Coll.; Clare Coll., Cambridge (Exhibnr; BA 1964, LLB 1965). Called to the Bar, Middle Temple, 1965. Joined BoT as Asst Principal, 1966; Private Sec. to Minister of State, BoT, 1969–71; Principal: Cabinet Office, 1971–73; Dept of Energy, 1974; Asst Sec., 1977–82; Under Sec., 1982; Prin. Estabt and Finance Officer, Dept of Energy, 1982–86; on loan to Cabinet Office (MPO), 1986–87; Dep. Sec., Cabinet Office, 1987–90; Dep. Sec. (Industry), HM Treasury, 1990–92; Permanent Sec., DoE, 1992–94. *Address:* c/o Home Office, Queen Anne's Gate, SW1H 9AT.

WILSON, Sir Robert, Kt 1989; CBE 1978; FRS 1975; Perren Professor of Astronomy, University College London, 1972–94, now Emeritus; *b* 16 April 1927; *s* of Robert Graham Wilson and Anne Wilson; *m* 1986, Fiona (*née* Nicholson). *Educ:* King's Coll., Univ. of Durham; Univ. of Edinburgh. BSc (Physics) Dunelm, 1948; PhD (Astrophysics), Edin., 1952. SSO, Royal Observatory, Edinburgh, 1952–57; Research Fellow, Dominion Astrophysical Observatory, Canada, 1957–58; Leader of Plasma Spectroscopy Gp, CTR Div., Harwell, 1959–61; Head of Spectroscopy Div., Culham Laboratory, 1962–68; Dir, Science Research Council's Astrophysics Research Unit, Culham, 1968–72; Dean, Faculty Sci., 1982–85, Head, Dept of Physics and Astronomy, 1987–93, UCL. Member: SERC, 1985–89; NERC, 1985–88; Chairman: British National Cttee for Space Res., 1983–88; Anglo-Australian Telescope Bd, 1986–89; James Clerk Maxwell Telescope Bd, 1987–91; Council, Royal Instn, 1992–93. Foreign Mem., Société Royale des Sciences, Liège; Vice-Pres., Internat. Astronomical Union, 1979–85; Trustee, Internat. Acad. of Astronautics, 1985; Mem., COSPAR Bureau, 1986–90. Hon. Fellow, UCL, 1990. Hon. DSc QUB, 1995. (Jtly) Herschel Medal, RAS, 1986; Science Award, Internat. Acad. of Astronautics, 1987; President Reagan's Award for design excellence (on behalf of UK team on the Internat. Ultraviolet Explorer), 1988; Royal Soc./COSPAR Massey Award, 1994. *Publications:* papers in many jls on: optical astronomy, plasma spectroscopy, solar physics, ultraviolet astronomy. *Address:* Department of Physics and Astronomy, University College London, Gower Street, WC1E 6BT. *T:* 0171–380 7154.

WILSON, Sir (Robert) Donald, KBE 1995; Kt 1987; DL; farmer; Chairman: North West Regional Health Authority, since 1994; Electricity Consultative Council (North West), since 1981; *b* 6 June 1922; *s* of John and Kate Wilson; *m* 1946, E. Elizabeth Ellis. *Educ:* Grove Park Sch., Wrexham, Clwyd. Served RAF, 1940–46. Tyre industry, 1946–60; farming, 1954–; Director of various farming and property companies; Board Mem. (part-time), North West Electricity Bd (NORWEB), 1981–87. Chairman: Mersey RHA, 1982–93, 1993–94; West Midlands RHA, 1993. Mem., School Teachers' Review Body, 1991–92. Chairman: Ayrshire Cattle Soc., 1966–67; Cheshire Br., CLA, 1980–82; Nat. Staff Cttee, Admin, Catering and Other Services, 1983–85. Vice-Chm. Governors, Cheshire Coll. of Agric., 1980–84. High Sheriff, Cheshire, 1985–86, DL, 1987. FRSA 1986. Hon. Fellow, Liverpool John Moores, 1994. Hon. LLD Liverpool, 1991. *Recreation:* fishing. *Address:* The Oldfields, Pulford, Chester, Cheshire CH4 9EJ. *T:* Rossett (01244) 570207. *Clubs:* Farmers'; City (Chester).

WILSON, (Robert) Gordon; solicitor in private practice, with Wilson & Duncan; *b* 16 April 1938; *s* of R. G. Wilson; *m* 1965, Edith M. Hassall; two *d. Educ:* Douglas High Sch.; Edinburgh Univ. (BL). Scottish National Party: Nat. Sec., 1963–71; Exec. Vice-Chm., 1972–73; Sen. Vice-Chm., 1973–74; Dep Leader, 1974–79; Nat. Convener (formerly Chm.), 1979–90; Vice-Pres., 1992–. Contested (SNP) Dundee E, 1987. MP (SNP) Dundee E, Feb. 1974–1987. Parly Spokesman: on Energy, 1974–79; on Home Affairs, 1975–76; on Devolution (jt responsibility), 1976–79; SNP spokesman: on energy, 1992–93; on Treasury affairs, 1993–94. Rector, Dundee Univ., 1983–86. Chm., Marriage Counselling (Tayside) (formerly Dundee Marriage Guidance Council), 1989–92. Gov., Dundee Inst. of Technology, subseq. Univ. of Abertay, 1991–. Hon. LLD Dundee, 1986. *Recreations:* reading, walking, photography, sailing. *Address:* 48 Monifieth Road, Broughty Ferry, Dundee DD5 2RX. *T:* Dundee (01382) 79009; Wilson & Duncan, 26 Castle Street, Dundee DD1 3AF.

WILSON, Robert Julian, (Robin), MA; Headmaster, Trinity School of John Whitgift, Croydon, 1972–94; *b* 6 July 1933; *s* of late Prof. Frank Percy Wilson, FBA, and Joanna Wilson (*née* Perry-Keene); *m* 1957, Caroline Anne (*née* Maher); two *d* (and one *s* one *d* decd). *Educ:* St Edward's Sch., Oxford; Trinity Coll., Cambridge (MA). Lektor, Univ. of Münster, Westphalia, 1955–58; Assistant Master: St Peter's, York, 1958–62; Nottingham High Sch. (Hd of English), 1962–72. Mem. Cttee, HMC, 1987–94 (Chm., 1993); Vice-Chm., Academic Policy Cttee, 1990–92; Mem. Council, GPDST, 1994–. Gov., Brentwood Sch. FRSA 1982. *Publications:* Bertelsmann Sprachkursus English (jtly), 1959; (ed) The Merchant of Venice, 1971; articles on the teaching of English. *Recreations:* drama, travel, ski-ing, golf. *Address:* 22 Beech House Road, Croydon, Surrey CR0 1JP. *T:* 0181–686 1915. *Clubs:* East India, Devonshire, Sports and Public Schools; Addington Golf.

WILSON, Prof. Robert McLachlan, FBA 1977; Professor of Biblical Criticism, University of St Andrews, 1978–83; *b* 13 Feb. 1916; *er s* of Hugh McL. Wilson and Janet N. (*née* Struthers); *m* 1945, Enid Mary, *d* of Rev. and Mrs F. J. Bomford, Bournemouth, Hants; two *s. Educ:* Greenock Acad.; Royal High Sch., Edinburgh; Univ. of Edinburgh (MA 1939, BD 1942); Univ. of Cambridge (PhD 1945). Minister of Rankin Church, Strathaven, Lanarkshire, 1946–54; Lectr in New Testament Language and Literature, St Mary's Coll., Univ. of St Andrews, 1954, Sen. Lectr, 1964, Prof., 1969–78. Vis. Prof., Vanderbilt Divinity Sch., Nashville, Tenn, 1964–65. Pres., Studiorum Novi Testamenti Societas, 1981–82. Hon. Mem., Soc. of Biblical Literature, 1972–. Associate Editor, New Testament Studies, 1967–77, Editor 1977–83; Mem., Internat. Cttee for publication of Nag Hammadi Codices, and of Editorial Bd of Nag Hammadi Studies monograph series. Hon. DD Aberdeen, 1982. Burkitt Medal for Biblical Studies, British Academy, 1990. *Publications:* The Gnostic Problem, 1958; Studies in the Gospel of Thomas, 1960; The Gospel of Philip, 1962; Gnosis and the New Testament, 1968; (ed) English trans., Hennecke-Schneemelcher, NT Apocrypha: vol. 1, 1963 (3rd edn, completely revised, 1991); vol. 2, 1965 (3rd edn 1993); (ed) English trans., Haenchen, The Acts of the Apostles, 1971; (ed) English trans., Foerster, Gnosis: vol. 1, 1972; vol. 2, 1974; (ed and trans., jtly) Jung Codex treatises: De Resurrectione, 1963, Epistula Jacobi Apocrypha, 1968, Tractatus Tripartitus, pars I, 1973, partes II et III, 1975; (ed) Nag Hammadi and Gnosis, 1978; (ed) The Future of Coptology, 1978; (ed jtly) Text and Interpretation, 1979; (ed) English trans., Rudolph, Gnosis, 1983; Commentary on Hebrews, 1987; articles in British, Amer. and continental jls. *Recreation:* golf. *Address:* 10 Murrayfield Road, St Andrews, Fife KY16 9NB. *T:* St Andrews (01334) 474331.

WILSON, Robert Peter; Chief Executive, RTZ Corporation plc, since 1991; *b* 2 Sept. 1943; *s* of late Alfred Wilson and Dorothy (*née* Mathews); *m* 1975, Shirley Elisabeth Robson; one *s* one *d. Educ:* Epsom Coll.; Sussex Univ. (BA); Harvard Business Sch. (AMP). With Dunlop Ltd, 1966–67; Mobil Oil Co. Ltd, 1967–70; RTZ Corporation plc, 1970–, Dir, Main Bd, 1987–. Non-Executive Director: CRA Ltd (Australia), 1990–; The Boots Co. PLC, 1991–. Trustee, Camborne Sch. of Mines. Hon. DSc Exeter, 1993. *Recreations:* theatre, opera, tennis. *Address:* 6 St James's Square, SW1Y 4LD. *T:* 0171–930 2399.

WILSON, Dr Robert Woodrow; Senior Scientist, Harvard Smithsonian Center for Astrophysics, since 1994; *b* 10 Jan. 1936; *s* of Ralph Woodrow Wilson and Fannie May Willis; *m* 1958, Elizabeth Rhoads Sawin; two *s* one *d. Educ:* Rice Univ. (BA Physics, 1957); Calif Inst. of Technol. (PhD 1962). Post-doctoral Fellowship, Calif Inst. of Technol., 1962–63; Mem. Technical Staff, Bell Labs, Holmdel, NJ, 1963–76; Head, Radio Physics Res. Dept, AT&T Bell Labs, 1976–94. Adjunct Prof. of Astrophysics, Princeton Univ., 1984–. Member: Phi Beta Kappa; Amer. Acad. of Arts and Sciences, 1978; US Nat. Acad. of Science, 1979. Hon. degrees: Monmouth Coll., 1979; Jersey City State Coll., 1979; Thiel Coll., 1980. Henry Draper Award, 1977; Herschel Award, RAS, 1977; (jtly) Nobel Prize for Physics, 1978. *Publications:* contrib. to Astrophys. Jl. *Recreations:* running, skiing. *Address:* 9 Valley Point Drive, Holmdel, NJ 07733–1320, USA. *T:* (201) 6717807.

WILSON, Robin; *see* Wilson, R. J.

WILSON, Robin Lee, CBE 1992; FEng 1986; consulting engineer; Chairman: Construction Industry Council, since 1994; Board for Engineers' Registration, since 1994; *b* 4 March 1933; *s* of late Henry Eric Wilson, OBE and Catherine Margaret Wilson; *m* 1956, Gillian Margaret, *d* of late L. J. N. Kirkby and Margaret Kirkby; one *s* two *d. Educ:* Glenalmond College; Univ. of Glasgow (BSc Eng. 1955). FICE 1966; FIHT 1966; MConsE 1966; FCIT 1992. Joined R. Travers Morgan & Partners, 1956, Partner, 1966, Sen. Partner, 1985; Dir and Gp Chm., Travers Morgan Ltd, Consulting Engineers, 1988–91; Chairman: New Builder Publications Ltd, 1989–94; Thomas Telford Ltd, publishers, 1990–94. Dir, Mid Kent Hldgs, 1994–. Member Council: ICE, 1977–80, 1983–86, 1987–93 (Pres., 1991–92); ACE, 1985–88; Construction Industry Council, 1990–; Engrg Council, 1991–; Glenalmond Coll., 1985–. Minister's nominee, SE Council for Sport and Recreation, 1987–90. DSc *hc* City Univ., 1991. Coopers Hill Meml Prize, ICE, 1989; Instn of Highways and Transportation Award, 1990. *Publications:* papers in learned jls on highway engineering and related subjects. *Recreations:* sailing, golf. *Address:* The Grove House, Little Bognor, Pulborough, Sussex RH20 1JT. *T:* Fittleworth (01798) 865569. *Clubs:* Royal Thames Yacht; Itchenor Sailing, West Sussex Golf.

WILSON, Rodney Herbert William; Director, Department of Film, Video and Broadcasting, Arts Council of England, since 1986; *b* 21 June 1942; *s* of Herbert Herman Wilson and Vera Anne Faulkner. *Educ:* Windsor Grammar Sch. for Boys; Berkshire Coll. of Art (Intermediate Diploma); Camberwell Sch. of Art (NDD); Hornsey Coll. of Art (ATD). Asst Lectr, Loughborough Coll. of Art, 1965–69; Film Officer, 1970, Head of Film Section, 1980, Arts Council of GB. Member: Film, Video and Television Adv. Cttee, British Council, 1983–; Council, Edinburgh Film Festival, 1984–94; Festival Council, Art Film Fest., Slovakia, 1995–; RTS, 1994. Exec. Producer for Arts Council Films, 1970–, including: Lautrec (Palm d'Or, Cannes, 1975); Monet in London (BAFTA Best Factual Film, 1975); Tom Philips (Grierson Award, 1977); Ubu (Golden Bear, Berlin, 1979); Give Us This Day (Grierson Award, 1983); Shadows from Light (Best Film, Montreal, 1984); Steve Reich: a new musical language (Best TV Arts Film, Rio de Janeiro, 1987); Jacob Epstein: rebel angel (Best TV Arts Film, Montreal, 1988); Dance (for Camera series, and Sound on Film series). BFI Award for Ind. Film, 1984. *Recreations:* walking, doodling, photography. *Address:* The Arts Council of England, 14 Great Peter Street, SW1P 3NQ.

WILSON, Rt Rev. Roger Plumpton, KCVO 1974; DD (Lambeth), 1949; Clerk of the Closet to the Queen, 1963–75; Hon. Assistant Bishop, Diocese of Bath and Wells, since 1974; *b* 3 Aug. 1905; *s* of Canon Clifford Plumpton Wilson, Bristol, and Hester Marion Wansey; *m* 1935, Mabel Joyce Avery (*d* 1995), Leigh Woods, Bristol; two *s* one *d. Educ:* Winchester Coll. (Exhibitioner); Keble Coll., Oxford (Classical Scholar). Hon. Mods in Classics 1st Class, Lit. Hum. 2nd Class, BA 1928; MA 1932. Classical Master, Shrewsbury Sch., 1928–30, 1932–34; Classical Master, St Andrew's Coll., Grahamstown, S Africa, 1930–32. Deacon, 1935; Priest, 1936; Curacies: St Paul's, Prince's Park, Liverpool, 1935–38; St John's, Smith Square, SW1, 1938–39; Vicar of South Shore, Blackpool, 1939–45; Archdeacon of Nottingham and Vicar of Radcliffe on Trent, 1945–49; also

Vicar of Shelford (in plurality), 1946–49; Bishop of Wakefield, 1949–58; Bishop of Chichester, 1958–74. Chm., Church of England Schools Council, 1957–71; Mem., Presidium, Conf. of European Churches, 1967–74. *Recreations:* Oxford University Authentics Cricket Club, Oxford University Centaurs Football Club, golf. *Address:* Kingsett, Wrington, Bristol BS18 7NH. *T:* Wrington (01934) 862464. *Club:* Commonwealth Trust.

WILSON, Sir Roland, KBE 1965 (CBE 1941); Kt 1955; Chairman: Commonwealth Banking Corporation, 1966–75; Qantas Airways Ltd, 1966–73; Wentworth Hotel, 1966–73; Director: The MLC Ltd, 1969–79; ICI Australia, 1967–74; economic and financial consultant; *b* Ulverstone, Tasmania, 7 April 1904; *s* of Thomas Wilson; *m* 1930, Valeska (*d* 1971), *d* of William Thompson; *m* 1975, Joyce, *d* of Clarence Henry Chivers. *Educ:* Devonport High School; Univ. of Tasmania; Oriel College, Oxford; Chicago University. Rhodes Scholar for Tasmania, 1925; BCom 1926, Univ. of Tasmania; Dipl. in Economics and Political Science 1926, and DPhil 1929, Oxon; Commonwealth Fund Fellow, 1928, and PhD 1930, Chicago. Pitt Cobbett Lecturer in Economics, Univ. of Tasmania, 1930–32; Director of Tutorial Classes, Univ. of Tasmania, 1931–32; Asst Commonwealth Statistician and Economist, 1932; Economist, Statistician's Branch, Commonwealth Treasury, 1933; Commonwealth Statistician and Economic Adviser to the Treasury, Commonwealth of Australia, 1936–40 and 1946–51; Sec. to Dept Labour and Nat. Service, 1941–46; Chairman Economic and Employment Commission, United Nations, 1948–49. Secretary to Treasury, Commonwealth of Australia, 1951–66; Member Bd: Commonwealth Bank of Australia, 1951–59; Reserve Bank of Australia, 1960–66; Qantas Empire Airways, 1954–66; Commonwealth Banking Corp., 1960–75. Hon. Fellow, Acad. of Social Scis in Australia, 1972. Hon. LLD Tasmania, 1969. Distinguished Fellow Award, Econ. Soc. of Australia, 1988. *Publications:* Capital Imports and the Terms of Trade, 1931; Public and Private Investment in Australia, 1939; Facts and Fancies of Productivity, 1946. *Address:* 64 Empire Circuit, Forrest, Canberra, ACT 2603, Australia. *T:* (6) 2952560. *Club:* Commonwealth (Canberra).

WILSON, Air Chief Marshal Sir (Ronald) Andrew (Fellowes), (Sir Sandy), KCB 1991 (CB 1990); AFC 1978; Air Member for Personnel and Air Aide-de-Camp to the Queen, 1993–95; *b* 27 Feb. 1941; *s* of late Ronald Denis Wilson and Gladys Vera Groombridge; *m* 1979, Mary Christine Anderson; one *d* and one step *s* one step *d. Educ:* Tonbridge Sch.; RAF Coll., Cranwell. Flying Instr, 1963–65; No 2 Sqn, 1966–68; ADC to C-in-C, RAF Germany, 1967–68; Flt Comdr No 2 Sqn, 1968–72; RAF Staff Coll., 1973; HQ STC, 1974–75; CO No 2 Sqn, 1975–77; Air Plans, MoD, 1977–79; CO RAF Lossiemouth, 1980–82; Air Cdre Falkland Islands, 1982–83; Central Staff, MoD, 1983–85; Dir Ops Strike, MoD, 1985; Dir Air Offensive, MoD, 1986–87; SASO, HQ, RAF Strike Comd, 1987–89; AOC No 1 Group, 1989–91; Comdr, British Forces during Op. Granby, ME, Aug.–Dec. 1990; C-in-C, RAF Germany and Comdr Second ATAF, 1991–93. Freeman, City of London, 1966; Liveryman, 1970, Mem. Court, 1984–87, 1994–, Worshipful Co. of Skinners. CIMgt 1993; FRAeS 1994. *Recreations:* painting, antique restoration, genealogy, golf. *Address:* c/o MoD Innsworth, Gloucester GL3 1EZ. *Club:* Royal Air Force.

WILSON, Maj.-Gen. (Ronald) Dare, CBE 1968 (MBE 1949); MC 1945; MA Cantab; DL; retired; current interests farming and forestry; *b* 3 Aug. 1919; *s* of Sydney E. D. Wilson and Dorothea, *d* of George Burgess; *m* 1973, Sarah, *d* of Sir Peter Stallard, *qv*; two *s. Educ:* Shrewsbury Sch.; St John's Coll. Cambridge. Commissioned into Royal Northumberland Fusiliers, 1939; served War, 1939–45: BEF 1940, ME and NW Europe (MC, despatches 1946); 6th Airborne Div., 1945–48; 1st Bn Parachute Regt, 1949; MoD, 1950; Royal Northumberland Fusiliers: Korea, 1951; Kenya, 1953; GSO2, Staff Coll., Camberley, 1954–56; AA&QMG, 3rd Div., 1958–59; comd 22 Special Air Service Regt, 1960–62; Canadian Nat. Defence Coll., 1962–63; Col GS 1(BR) Corps BAOR, 1963–65; comd 149 Infantry Bde (TA), 1966–67; Brig. 1966; Brig., AQ ME Comd, 1967; Maj.-Gen. 1968; Dir, Land/Air Warfare, MoD, 1968–69; Dir, Army Aviation, MoD, 1970–71. Exmoor Nat. Park Officer, 1974–78. Formerly Consultant to Fedn of Nature and Nat. Parks of Europe. Speaker for E-SU in USA. Church Warden, Church of St George, Morebath, Devon. Helicopter and light aircraft pilot; Mem., Army Cresta Run Team and Army Rifle VIII; captained British Free-Fall Parachute Team, 1962–65; Chm., British Parachute Assoc., 1962–65. Mem. Council, Cambridge Soc., 1989–. FRGS. DL Somerset, 1979. Royal Humane Soc. Award, 1953; Royal Aero Club Silver Medal, 1967. *Publications:* Cordon and Search, 1948, reissued USA, 1984; contribs to military jls. *Recreations:* country pursuits, travelling, winter sports. *Address:* Combeland, Dulverton, Somerset TA22 9LJ. *Club:* Flyfishers'.

WILSON, Hon. Sir Ronald (Darling), AC 1988; KBE 1979; CMG 1978; Justice of the High Court of Australia, 1979–89; President: Uniting Church in Australia, 1988–91; Human Rights and Equal Opportunity Commission, since 1990; *b* 23 Aug. 1922; *s* of Harold Wilson and Jean Ferguson Wilson (*née* Darling); *m* 1950, Leila Amy Gibson Smith; three *s* two *d. Educ:* Geraldton State School; Univ. of Western Australia (LLB Hons; Hon. LLD 1980); Univ. of Pennsylvania (LLM). Assistant Crown Prosecutor, Western Australia, 1954–59; Chief Crown Prosecutor, WA, 1959–61; Crown Counsel, WA, 1961–69; QC 1963; Solicitor General, WA, 1969–79. Moderator, Presbyterian Church in Western Australia, 1965; Moderator, WA Synod, Uniting Church in Australia, 1977–79. Chancellor, Murdoch Univ., 1980–95. Hon. DEd Keimyung Univ., Korea, 1989; DUniv Murdoch, 1995. *Address:* 6B Atkins Road, Applecross, WA 6153, Australia.

WILSON, Ronald Marshall, CBE 1982; sole proprietor, Ronnie Wilson, Chartered Surveyors, since 1983; Chairman, Nightingale Secretariat PLC, 1985–92; *b* 6 March 1923; *s* of Marshall Lang Wilson and Margaret Wilson Wilson; *m* 1948, Marion Robertson Scobie (marr. diss. 1985); two *s. Educ:* Sedbergh; London Univ. (BSc Estate Management 1950). Served War of 1939–45; North Irish Horse; Court Orderly Officer, Wüppertal War Crimes Trial, 1946. Partner, Bell-Ingram, Chartered Surveyors, 1957–83. Director: Central Farmers Ltd, 1972–86; Control Securities plc, 1986–92. Royal Institution of Chartered Surveyors: Mem. General Council, 1973–; President, 1979–80; Mem. Land Agency and Agricl Divisional Council, 1970–77 (Chm., 1974–75); Chm., Internat. Cttee, 1976–78. *Publications:* articles on technical and professional subjects, incl. Planning in the Countryside. *Recreations:* golf, fishing, shooting. *Address:* 9 The Forty, Cholsey, Wallingford, Oxon OX10 9LH. *T:* (01491) 651200. *Club:* Farmers'.

WILSON, Roy; *see* Wilson, G. R.

WILSON, Roy Vernon, CEng, MICE; Director, Eastern Region, Property Services Agency, Department of the Environment, 1980–82; *b* 23 July 1922; *s* of late Alfred Vincent Wilson and Theresa Elsie Wilson; *m* 1951, Elsie Hannah Barrett; three *s. Educ:* Cheadle Hulme Sch.; Manchester Univ. (BScTech Hons). Served Royal Engineers, 1942–44. Civil Engineer, local govt, 1945–51; Harlow Develt Corp., 1951–54; Air Ministry Works Directorate: Warrington, 1954–59; Newmarket, 1959–62; Germany, 1962–65; District Works Officer: Wethersfield, 1965–67; Mildenhall, 1967–72; Area Officer, Letchworth (PSA), 1972–76; Regional Director, Cyprus (PSA), 1976–79; Chief Works Officer, Ruislip, 1979. *Recreations:* lacrosse (earlier years), golf, tennis. *Address:* 12 Diomed Drive, Great Barton, Bury St Edmunds, Suffolk IP31 2TD. *Club:* Civil Service.

WILSON, Sally Angela, (Mrs Charles Wilson); *see* O'Sullivan, S. A.

WILSON, Samuel; Lord Mayor of Belfast, June 1986–87; *b* 4 April 1953; *s* of Alexander and Mary Wilson. *Educ:* Methodist Coll., Belfast; The Queen's Univ., Belfast (BScEcon; PGCE). Teacher of Economics, 1975–83; Researcher in N Ireland Assembly, 1983–86. Councillor, Belfast CC, 1981–; Press Officer for Democratic Unionist Party, 1982–. *Publications:* The Carson Trail, 1982; The Unionist Case—The Forum Report Answered, 1984; Data Response Questions in Economics, 1995. *Recreations:* reading, motor cycling, windsurfing. *Address:* 19 Jocelyn Gardens, Belfast. *T:* Belfast (01232) 59934.

WILSON, Air Chief Marshal Sir Sandy; *see* Wilson, Air Chief Marshal Sir R. A. F.

WILSON, Sandy; composer, lyric writer, playwright; *b* 19 May 1924; *s* of George Walter Wilson and Caroline Elsie (*née* Humphrey). *Educ:* Elstree Preparatory School; Harrow School; Oriel College, Oxford (BA Eng. Lit.). Contributed material to Oranges and Lemons, Slings and Arrows, 1948; wrote lyrics for touring musical play Caprice, 1950; words and music for two revues at Watergate Theatre, 1951 and 1952; (musical comedy) The Boy Friend for Players' Theatre, 1953, later produced in West End and on Broadway, 1954, revival, Comedy, 1967 (also directed), revival, Old Vic, 1984, 40th anniv. production, Players' Theatre, 1994; (musical play) The Buccaneer, 1955; Valmouth (musical play, based on Firbank's novel), Lyric, Hammersmith and Savile Theatre, 1959, New York, 1960, revival, Chichester, 1982; songs for Call It Love, Wyndham's Theatre, 1960; Divorce Me, Darling! (musical comedy), Players' Theatre, 1964, Globe, 1965; music for TV series, The World of Wooster, 1965–66; music for As Dorothy Parker Once Said, Fortune, 1969; songs for Danny la Rue's Charley's Aunt (TV), 1969; wrote and performed in Sandy Wilson Thanks the Ladies, Hampstead Theatre Club, 1971; His Monkey Wife, Hampstead, 1971; The Clapham Wonder, Canterbury, 1978; Aladdin, Lyric, Hammersmith, 1979. *Publications:* This is Sylvia (with own illustrs), 1954; The Boy Friend (with own illustrs), 1955; Who's Who for Beginners (with photographs by Jon Rose), 1957; Prince What Shall I Do (illustrations, with Rhoda Levine), 1961; The Poodle from Rome, 1962; I Could Be Happy (autobiog.), 1975; Ivor, 1975; Caught in the Act, 1976; The Roaring Twenties, 1977. *Recreations:* visiting the National Film Theatre and writing musicals. *Address:* 2 Southwell Gardens, SW7 4SB. *T:* 0171–373 6172. *Club:* Players' Theatre.

WILSON, Snoo; writer, since 1969; *b* 2 Aug. 1948; *s* of Leslie Wilson and Pamela Mary Wilson; *m* 1976, Ann McFerran; two *s* one *d. Educ:* Bradfield Coll.; Univ. of East Anglia (BA English and American Studies). Associate Director, Portable Theatre, 1970–75; Dramaturge, Royal Shakespeare Co., 1975–76; Script Editor, Play for Today, 1976; Associate Prof. of Theatre, Univ. of Calif at San Diego, 1987. Henfield Fellow, Univ. of E Anglia, 1978; US Bicentennial Fellow in Playwriting, 1981–82. Hon. Texan, 1992. *Filmscripts:* Shadey, 1986; The Touch, 1989; *opera:* (adapted) Gounod's La Colombe, 1983; *radio plays:* Poonsh, 1993; The Good Doctor, 1994; Johnson's Xmas Interlude, 1994. *Publications: plays:* Layby (jtly), 1972; Pignight, 1972; The Pleasure Principle, 1973; Blowjob, 1974; Soul of the White Ant, 1976; England England, 1978; Vampire, 1978; The Glad Hand, 1978; A Greenish Man, 1978; The Number of the Beast, 1982; Flaming Bodies, 1982; Grass Widow, 1983; Loving Reno, 1983; Hamlyn, 1984; More Light, 1987; Lynchville, 1989; Callas, 1990; Erofeyev's Walpurgis Night (adaptation), 1991; HRH, 1994; Darwin's Flood, 1994; Bedbug (adaptation), 1995, etc; *novels:* Spaceache, 1984 (adapted for radio, 1990); Inside Babel, 1985; *opera:* Orpheus in the Underworld (new version), 1984; *musical:* 80 Days, 1988. *Recreations:* beekeeping, space travel. *Address:* 41 The Chase, SW4 0NP.

WILSON, Stanley John, CBE 1981; FCIS; Chairman, Burmah Oil (South Africa) (Pty) Ltd, since 1982; Managing Director, 1975–82 and Chief Executive, 1980–82, The Burmah Oil Co. Ltd; *b* 23 Oct. 1921; *s* of Joseph Wilson and Jessie Cormack; *m* 1952, Molly Ann (*née* Clarkson); two *s. Educ:* King Edward VII Sch., Johannesburg Witwatersrand Univ. CA (SA); ASAA, ACMA; FCIS 1945; CIMgt; FInst Pet. 1945–73: Chartered Accountant, Savory & Dickinson; Sec. and Sales Man., Rhodesian Timber Hldgs; Chm. and Chief Exec. for S Africa, Vacuum Oil Co.; Reg. Vice Pres. for S and E Asia, Mobil Petroleum; Pres., Mobil Sekiyu; Pres., subseq. Reg. Vice Pres. for Europe, Mobil Europe Inc.; Pres., Mobil East Inc., and Reg. Vice Pres. for Far East, S and SE Asia, Australia, Indian Sub-Continent, etc, 1973–75. Underwriting Mem. of Lloyd's. Freeman, City of London; Liveryman, Basketmakers' Co. FRSA. *Recreations:* golf, shooting, fishing. *Address:* The Jetty, PO Box 751, Plettenberg Bay, Cape Province, 6600, South Africa. *T:* Plettenberg Bay 9624. *Clubs:* City of London, Royal Automobile; Royal & Ancient Golf; Tidworth Garrison Golf; City (Cape Town); Rand (Johannesburg); Heresewentien (SA).

WILSON, Prof. Thomas, OBE 1945; FBA 1976; FRSE 1980; Adam Smith Professor of Political Economy, University of Glasgow, 1958–82; Hon. Fellow, London School of Economics, 1979; *b* 23 June 1916; *s* of late John Bright and Margaret G. Wilson, Belfast; *m* 1943, Dorothy Joan Parry, MVO 1945; one *s* two *d. Educ:* Methodist College and Queen's University, Belfast; London School of Economics. Mins of Economic Warfare and Aircraft Production, 1940–42; Prime Minister's Statistical Branch, 1942–45. Fellow of University College, Oxford, 1946–58; Faculty Fellow of Nuffield College, Oxford, 1950–58; Vis. Fellow, All Souls Coll., Oxford, 1974–75; Editor, Oxford Economic Papers, 1948–58. Vice-Chm., Scottish Council's Cttee of Inquiry into the Scottish Economy, 1960–61; Nuffield Foundation Visiting Prof., Univ. of Ibadan, 1962. Economic Consultant to Govt of N Ireland, 1964–65, 1968–70; to Sec. of State for Scotland, 1963–64 and 1970–83; Shipbuilding Industry Cttee, 1965; Assessor, DoE, 1984–85. Dir, Scottish Mutual Assce Soc., 1966–87 (Chm., 1978–81). FRSA 1992. DUniv Stirling, 1982. *Publications:* Fluctuations in Income and Employment, 1941; (ed) Ulster under Home Rule, 1955; Inflation, 1960; Planning and Growth, 1964; (ed) Pensions, Inflation and Growth, 1974; (ed with A. S. Skinner) Essays on Adam Smith, 1975; (ed with A. S. Skinner) The Market and the State, 1976; The Political Economy of Inflation (British Acad. Keynes Lecture), 1976; (with D. J. Wilson) The Political Economy of the Welfare State, 1982; Inflation, Unemployment and the Market, 1985; Ulster—Conflict and Consent, 1989; (ed with D. J. Wilson) The State and Social Welfare, 1991; Churchill and the Prof, 1995. *Recreations:* sailing, hill walking. *Address:* 1 Chatford House, The Promenade, Clifton, Bristol BS8 3NG. *T:* Bristol (0117) 973 0741. *Club:* Athenæum.

WILSON, Thomas Marcus; Assistant Under-Secretary, Ministry of Defence (Procurement Executive), 1971–73; retired; *b* 15 April 1913; *s* of Reverend C. Wilson; *m* 1939, Norah Boyes (*née* Sinclair) (*d* 1984); no *c. Educ:* Manchester Grammar School; Jesus College, Cambridge. Asst Principal, Customs and Excise, 1936; Private Secretary: to Board of Customs and Excise, 1939; to Chm. Bd, 1940; Principal, 1941; lent to Treasury, 1942; lent to Office of Lord President of Council, 1946; Asst Sec., 1947; seconded: Min. of Food, 1949; Min. of Supply, 1953, Under-Sec., 1962, and Prin. Scientific and Civil Aviation Adv. to Brit. High Comr in Australia, also Head of Defence Research and Supply Staff, 1962–64; Under-Secretary: Min. of Aviation, 1964–67; Min. of Technology, 1967–70; Min. of Aviation Supply, 1970–71; MoD, 1971–73. *Recreations:* reading, music, painting and travel, especially in France. *Address:* Flat 6, 21 Queen Square, Bath BA1 2HX.

WILSON, Timothy Hugh, FSA; Keeper of Western Art, Ashmolean Museum, Oxford, since 1990; Professorial Fellow, Balliol College, Oxford, since 1990; *b* 8 April 1950; *s* of late Col Hugh Walker Wilson and of Lilian Rosemary (*née* Kirke); *m* 1984, Jane Lott; two *s* one *d*. *Educ:* Winchester Coll.; Mercersburg Acad., USA; Corpus Christi Coll., Oxford (BA 1973; MA); Warburg Inst., London Univ. (MPhil 1976); Dept of Museum Studies, Leicester Univ. FSA 1989. Res. Asst, Dept of Weapons and Antiquities, Nat. Maritime Mus., Greenwich, 1977–79; Asst Keeper (Renaissance collections), Dept of Medieval and Later Antiquities, BM, 1979–90. Trustee, Ruskin Foundn, 1994–. Fellow, Harvard Univ. Center for Renaissance Studies, Villa I Tatti, Florence, 1984; Hon. Fellow, Royal Soc. Painter-Printmakers, 1991. *Publications:* (jtly) The Art of the Jeweller, 1984; Flags at Sea, 1986; Ceramic Art of the Italian Renaissance, 1987; Maiolica, 1989; (ed) Italian Renaissance Pottery, 1991; (jtly) Systematic Catalogue of the National Gallery of Art: Western Decorative Arts, Part 1, 1993; articles in Apollo, Burlington Mag., Faenza, Jl Warburg and Courtauld Insts, etc; contribs exhibition catalogues. *Recreations:* cycling, second-hand bookshops. *Address:* Balliol College, Oxford OX1 3BJ; 6 Longworth Road, Oxford OX2 6RA. *T:* Oxford (01865) 511029.

WILSON, William; DL; *b* 28 June 1913; *s* of Charles and Charlotte Wilson; *m* 1939, Bernice Wilson; one *s*. *Educ:* Wheatley St Sch.; Cheylesmore Sch.; Coventry Jun. Technical School. Qual. as Solicitor, 1939. Entered Army, 1941; served in N Africa, Italy and Greece; demobilised, 1946 (Sergeant). Contested (Lab) Warwick and Leamington, 1951, 1955, March 1957, 1959. MP (Lab) Coventry S, 1964–74, Coventry SE, 1974–83; Mem., Commons Select Cttee on Race Relations and Immigration, 1970–79. Mem., Warwicks CC, 1958–70 (Leader Labour Group), 1972–93. DL County of Warwick, 1967. *Recreations:* gardening, theatre, watching Association football. *Address:* Avonside House, High Street, Barford, Warwickshire CV35 8BU. *T:* Barford (01926) 624278.

WILSON, William Desmond, OBE 1964 (MBE 1954); MC 1945; DSC (USA) 1945; HM Diplomatic Service, retired; Deputy High Commissioner, Kaduna, Nigeria, 1975–81; *b* 2 Jan. 1922; *s* of late Crozier Irvine Wilson and Mabel Evelyn (*née* Richardson); *m* 1949, Lucy Bride; two *s*. *Educ:* Royal Belfast Acad. Instn; QUB; Trinity Coll., Cambridge. Joined Indian Army, 1941; served with 10 Gurkha Rifles, India and Italy, 1942–46 (Major). Colonial Admin. Service: Northern Nigeria, 1948–63 (MBE for Gallantry, 1954); retd as Permanent Sec.; joined Foreign (subseq. Diplomatic) Service, 1963; First Sec., Ankara, 1963–67; UN (Polit.) Dept, FO, 1967; First Sec. and Head of Chancery, Kathmandu, 1969–74; Counsellor, 1975; Sen. Officers' War Course, RNC Greenwich, 1975. *Recreations:* shooting, riding. *Address:* The Spinney, Forge Hill, Pluckley, Kent TN27 0SJ. *T:* Pluckley (01233) 840300. *Club:* East India.

WILSON, (William) George, OBE 1960; Associate Director, PA Consulting Group, 1989–92; *b* 19 Feb. 1921; *s* of late William James Wilson and late Susannah Wilson; *m* 1948, Freda Huddleston; three *s*. Min. of Health, 1939. Served War, Army, in India and Ceylon, 1940–46. Min. of Nat. Insurance, 1947; Asst Principal, Colonial Office, 1947; Principal, CO, 1950–57 (Adviser, UK Delegn to UN Gen. Assembly, 1951); Financial Sec., Mauritius, 1957–60; Asst Sec., MoH, 1962; Consultant, Hosp. Design and Construction, Middle East and Africa, 1968–70; Asst Sec., DHSS, 1971; Under-Sec., DHSS, 1972–81. Chm., Paul James & George Wilson Ltd, Health Service Devel Advrs, 1986–89 (Dir, 1983–86). *Recreations:* Border history and genealogy. *Address:* Clarghyll Hall, Alston, Cumbria CA9 3NF. *Club:* Commonwealth Trust.

WILSON, Rt. Rev. William Gilbert, BD, PhD; Bishop of Kilmore, Elphin and Ardagh, 1981–93; *b* 23 Jan. 1918; *s* of Adam and Rebecca R. Wilson; *m* 1944, Peggy Muriel Busby; three *s* three *d*. *Educ:* Belfast Royal Academy; Trinity Coll., Dublin. BA 1939; MA, BD 1944; PhD 1949. Curate Assistant, St Mary Magdalene, Belfast, 1941–44; St Comgall's, Bangor, 1944–47; Rector of Armoy with Loughguile, 1947–76; Prebendary of Cairncastle in Chapter of St Saviour's, Connor, 1964–76; Dean of Connor, 1976–81; Rector of Lisburn Cathedral, 1976–81; Clerical Hon. Sec. of Connor Synod and Council, 1956–81. *Publications:* A Guild of Youth Handbook, 1944; Church Teaching, A Church of Ireland Handbook, 1954, revised edn 1970; How the Church of Ireland is Governed, 1964; (jtly) Anglican Teaching—An Exposition of the Thirty-nine Articles, 1964; The Church of Ireland after 1970—Advance or Retreat?, 1968; The Church of Ireland—Why Conservative?, 1970; Is there a Life after Death?, 1974; A Critique of 'Authority in the Church', 1977; Irish Churchwardens' Handbook, 1979 (expanded, revised and rewritten edn of 1901 pubn); The Faith of an Anglican, 1980; The Way of the Church, 1982; Should we have Women Deacons?, 1984; Why no Women Priests?, 1988; Towards Accepting Women Priests, 1989; contribs to Jl of Theol Studies and The Church Qly Review. *Recreations:* gardening, woodworking. *Address:* 24 Pennington Park, Cairnshill Road, Belfast BT8 4GJ. *T:* Belfast (01232) 701742.

WILSON, William Napier M.; *see* Menzies-Wilson.

WILSON-BARNETT, Prof. Jenifer, (Mrs M. R. Trimble); Professor of Nursing and Midwifery, and Head of Department of Nursing Studies, King's College, London, since 1986 (Head of Department and Division of Nursing and Midwifery, since 1994); *b* 10 Aug. 1944; adopted by Edith M. Barnett and Barbara M. Wilson; *m* 1975, Michael Robert Trimble. *Educ:* Chichester High School for Girls; St George's Hosp., London (student nurse), 1963–66; Univ. of Leicester, 1967–70 (BA Politics); Edinburgh Univ., 1970–72 (MSc); Guy's Hosp. Med. Sch., London (PhD 1977). FRCN 1984; FKC 1995. Staff Nurse, 1966, Nursing Sister, 1972–74, St George's Hosp.; Researcher, Guy's Hosp., 1974–77; Chelsea College: Lectr in Nursing, 1977; Sen. Lectr, 1983; Reader and Hd of Dept, 1984. *Publications:* Stress in Hospital: patients' psychological reactions to illness and health care, 1979; (with Morva Fordham) Recovery from Illness, 1982; Patient Teaching, 1983; Nursing Research: ten studies in patient care, 1983; Nursing Issues and Research in Terminal Care, 1988; Patient Problems: a research base for nursing care, 1988; (with Sarah Robinson) Direction in Nursing Research, 1989; (with Jill Macleod Clark) Health Promotion and Nursing Research, 1993. *Recreations:* ski-ing, music, clothes-shopping, writing, 'singing'. *Address:* Department of Nursing Studies, Cornwall House Annexe, Waterloo Road, SE1 8TX. *Clubs:* Royal Automobile, Royal College of Nursing, Royal Society of Medicine.

WILSON-JOHNSON, David Robert; baritone; *b* 16 Nov. 1950; *s* of Sylvia Constance Wilson and Harry Kenneth Johnson. *Educ:* Wellingborough School; British Institute, Florence; St Catharine's College, Cambridge (BA Hons 1973); Royal Acad. of Music. NFMS Award, 1977; Gulbenkian Fellowship, 1978–81. Royal Opera House, Covent Garden: We Come to the River (début), 1976; Billy Budd, 1982; L'Enfant et les Sortilèges, 1983; Le Rossignol, 1983; Les Noces, Boris Godunov, 1984; Die Zauberflöte, 1985; Werther, Turandot, 1987; Madam Butterfly, 1988; title rôle, St François d'Assise (Messiaen), 1988–89; Wigmore Hall recital début, 1977; BBC Proms début, 1981; Paris Opera début (Die Meistersinger), 1989; US début, Cleveland Orch., 1990; appearances at Netherlands Opera, Geneva, Houston, New York, Turin, etc; numerous recordings, including works by Bach, Schönberg and Schubert. FRAM 1988 (ARAM 1982). *Recreations:* swimming, slimming, gardening and growing walnuts at Dordogne house. *Address:* 28 Englefield Road, N1 4ET. *T:* 0171–254 0941.

WILSON JONES, Prof. Edward, FRCP, FRCPath; Professor of Dermatopathology, Institute of Dermatology, University of London, 1974–91, now Emeritus (Dean, 1980–89); *b* 26 July 1926; *s* of Percy George Jones and Margaret Louisa Wilson; *m* 1952, Hilda Mary Rees; one *s* one *d*. *Educ:* Oundle Sch.; Trinity Hall, Cambridge (MB, BChir 1951); St Thomas' Hosp., London. FRCP 1970; FRCPath 1975. National Service, Army, 1953–54. House Surgeon (Ophthalmic), St Thomas' Hosp., 1951; House Physician (Gen. Medicine), St Helier Hosp., Carshalton, 1951–52; House Physician (Neurology and Chest Diseases), St Thomas' Hosp., 1955; Registrar (Gen. Medicine), Watford Peace Meml Hosp., 1955–57; Registrar (Derm.), St Thomas' Hosp., 1957–60; Inst. of Dermatology, St John's Hosp. for Diseases of the Skin: Sen. Registrar (Derm.), 1960–62; Sen. Registrar (Dermatopath.), 1962–63; Sen. Lectr (Dermatopath.), 1963–74; Hon. Consultant, St John's Hosp. for Diseases of Skin, 1974–. *Publications:* (contrib.) Textbook of Dermatology, ed Rook, Wilkinson and Ebling, 3rd edn 1979; articles on dermatopath. subjects in British Jl of Derm., Arch. of Derm., Acta Dermatovenereologica, Dermatologica, Clin. and Exptl Derm., Histopath., and in Human Path. *Recreation:* art history. *Address:* 80 Harley Street, W1N 1AE. *T:* 0171–580 8356.

WILTON, 7th Earl of, *cr* 1801; **Seymour William Arthur John Egerton;** Viscount Grey de Wilton, 1801; *b* 29 May 1921; *s* of 6th Earl and Brenda (*d* 1930), *d* of late Sir William Petersen, KBE; *S* father, 1927; *m* 1962, Mrs Diana Naylor Leyland. *Heir:* (by special remainder) *kinsman* Baron Ebury, *qv*. *Address:* The Old Vicarage, Castle Hedingham, Halstead, Essex CO9 3EZ. *Club:* White's.

WILTON, Andrew; *see* Wilton, J. A. R.

WILTON, Sir (Arthur) John, KCMG 1979 (CMG 1967); KCVO 1979; MC 1945; MA; HM Diplomatic Service, retired; *b* 21 Oct. 1921; *s* of Walter Wilton and Annetta Irene Wilton (*née* Perman); *m* 1950, Maureen Elizabeth Alison Meaker; four *s* one *d*. *Educ:* Wanstead High School; Open Schol., St John's Coll., Oxford, 1940. Commissioned, Royal Ulster Rifles, 1942; served with Irish Brigade, N Africa, Italy and Austria, 1943–46. Entered HM Diplomatic Service, 1947; served Lebanon, Egypt, Gulf Shaikhdoms, Roumania, Aden, and Yugoslavia; Dir, Middle East Centre for Arabic Studies, Shemlan, 1960–65; Ambassador to Kuwait, 1970–74; Asst Under-Sec. of State, FCO, 1974–76; Ambassador to Saudi Arabia, 1976–79. Dir, London House for Overseas Graduates, 1979–86. Chm., Arab-British Centre, 1981–86; Pres., Plymouth Br., ESU, 1991– (Vice-Pres., 1988–91); Trustee, Arab-British Chamber Charitable Foundn, 1989–. Gov., Hele Sch., Plympton, 1988–92. Hon. LLD New England Coll., NH, 1986. *Recreations:* reading, gardening. *Address:* Legassick House, 69 Fore Street, Plympton St Maurice, Plymouth PL7 3NA.

See also C. E. J. Wilton.

WILTON, Christopher Edward John; HM Diplomatic Service; Consul General, Dubai, since 1994; *b* 16 Dec. 1951; *s* of Sir (Arthur) John Wilton, *qv*; *m* 1975, Dianne Hodgkinson; one *s* one *d*. *Educ:* Tonbridge Sch.; Manchester Univ. (Hons Near Eastern Studies). Production Supervisor, Esso Petroleum, 1975–77; FCO, 1977; Bahrain, 1978–81; FCO, 1981–84; Tokyo, 1984–88; on loan to Cabinet Office, 1988–90; Commercial Counsellor, Riyadh, 1990–94. *Recreations:* squash, tennis, golf, piano. *Address:* c/o Foreign and Commonwealth Office, SW1A 2AH.

WILTON, (James) Andrew (Rutley); Keeper of British Art, Tate Gallery, since 1989; *b* 7 Feb. 1942; *s* of Herbert Rutley Wilton and Mary Cecilia Morris (*née* Buckerfield); *m* 1976, Christina Frances Benn (marr. diss.); one *s*. *Educ:* Dulwich Coll.; Trinity Coll., Cambridge (MA). Assistant Keeper: Walker Art Gallery, Liverpool, 1965; Dept of Prints and Drawings, BM, 1967; Curator of Prints and Drawings, Yale Center for British Art, 1976; Asst Keeper, Turner Collection, BM, 1981; Curator, Turner Collection, Tate Gallery, 1985. *Publications:* Turner in Switzerland (with John Russell), 1976; British Watercolours 1750–1850, 1977; The Wood Engravings of William Blake, 1977; The Life and Work of J. M. W. Turner, 1979; The Art of Alexander and John Robert Cozens, 1979; William Pars: journey through the Alps, 1979; Turner and the Sublime, 1980; Turner Abroad, 1982; Turner in his Time, 1987; Painting and Poetry, 1990; The Swagger Portrait, 1992; The Great Age of British Watercolour, 1992; contribs to arts magazines. *Recreations:* people, nature, the arts. *Address:* Tate Gallery, SW1P 4RG. *Club:* Athenæum.

WILTON, Sir John; *see* Wilton, Sir A. J.

WILTS, Archdeacon of; *see* Smith, Ven. B. J.

WILTSHAW, Dr Eve, OBE 1992; FRCP, FRCOG; Medical Director, Royal Marsden Hospital, 1986–94; *b* 23 Jan. 1927. *Educ:* Univ. of Wales Med. Sch. (MB BCh, MD). Jun. med. posts, 1951–52; jun. post in clin. haematol., Tufts Med. Sch., Boston, 1953–55; Inst. of Cancer Res., 1955–74; Consultant in Cancer Medicine, Royal Marsden Hosp., 1974–92. *Address:* 38A Kelso Place, W8 5QP. *T:* 0171–937 8497.

WILTSHIRE, Earl of; Christopher John Hilton Paulet; *b* 30 July 1969; *s* and *heir* of Marquess of Winchester, *qv*; *m*; one *d*.

WILTSHIRE, Edward Parr, CBE 1965; HM Diplomatic Service, retired; *b* 18 Feb. 1910; 2nd *s* of late Major Percy Wiltshire and Kathleen Olivier Lefroy Parr Wiltshire, Great Yarmouth; *m* 1942, Gladys Mabel Stevens; one *d*. *Educ:* Cheltenham College; Jesus College, Cambridge. Entered Foreign Service, 1932. Served in: Beirut, Mosul, Baghdad, Tehran, Basra, New York (one of HM Vice-Consuls, 1944); promoted Consul, 1945; transf. Cairo, 1946 (Actg Consul-Gen., 1947, 1948); transf. Shiraz (having qual. in Arabic, and subseq. in Persian); Consul, Port Said, 1952; 1st Sec. and Consul: Baghdad, 1952, Rio de Janeiro, 1957; promoted Counsellor, 1959; Political Agent, Bahrain, 1959–63, Consul-General, Geneva, 1963–67; Dir, Diplomatic Service Language Centre, London, 1967–68; worked for Council for Nature (Editor, Habitat), 1968–69; Consul, Le Havre, 1969–75. Hon. Associate, BM (Nat. Hist.), 1980. *Publications:* The Lepidoptera of Iraq, 1957; A Revision of the Armadini, 1979. *Recreations:* music, entomology. *Address:* Wychwood, High Road, Cookham, Berks SL6 9JS.

WILTSHIRE, Sir Frederick Munro, Kt 1976; CBE 1970 (OBE 1966); FTS 1976; Managing Director: Wiltshire File Co. Pty Ltd, Australia, 1938–77; Wiltshire Cutlery Co. Pty Ltd, 1959–77; Director: Repco Ltd, 1966–81; Australian Paper Manufacturers Ltd, 1966–83; *b* 1911; *m* 1938, Jennie L., *d* of F. M. Frencham; one *d*. Chm., Dept of Trade and Industry Adv. Cttee on Small Businesses, 1968; Chm., Cttees of Inquiry, etc. Mem., Executive, CSIRO, 1974–78. Past Pres., Aust. Industries Develt Assoc.; Member, Manufacturing Industries Adv. Council, 1957–77 (Vice-Pres. 1972); Industrial Member, Science and Industry Forum of Aust. Acad. of Science, 1967–80; FAIM (Councillor, 1955–59). *Address:* 38 Rockley Road, South Yarra, Vic 3141, Australia. *Clubs:* Athenæum (Melbourne); Kingston Heath Golf (Aust.).

WIMBORNE, 4th Viscount *cr* 1918; **Ivor Mervyn Vigors Guest;** Baron Wimborne 1880; Baron Ashby St Ledgers 1910; Bt 1838; *b* 19 Sept. 1968; *o s* of 3rd Viscount

Wimborne and of his 1st wife, Victoria Ann, *o d* of Col Mervyn Vigors, DSO, MC; *S* father, 1993. *Educ:* Eton. *Heir: uncle* Hon. Julian John Guest [*b* 12 Oct. 1945; *m* 1st, 1970, Emma Jane Arlette (marr. diss. 1978), *e d* of Cdre Archibald Gray, RN; 2nd, 1983, Jillian, *d* of late N. S. G. Bannatine]. *Address:* House of Lords, SW1A 0PW.

WINCH, Prof. Donald Norman, FBA 1986; FRHistS; Professor of History of Economics, University of Sussex, since 1969; *b* 15 April 1935; *s* of Sidney and Iris Winch; *m* 1983, Doreen Lidster. *Educ:* Sutton Grammar Sch.; LSE (BSc Econ 1956); Princeton Univ. (PhD 1960). Vis. Lectr, Univ. of California, 1959–60; Lectr in Economics, Univ. of Edinburgh, 1960–63; University of Sussex: Lectr, 1963–66; Reader, 1966–69; Dean, Sch. of Social Scis, 1968–74; Pro-Vice-Chancellor (Arts and Social Studies), 1986–89. Visiting Fellow: Sch. of Social Sci., Inst. for Advanced Study, Princeton, 1974–75; King's Coll., Cambridge, 1983; History of Ideas Unit, ANU, 1983; St Catharine's Coll., Cambridge, 1989; All Souls Coll., Oxford, 1994; British Council Distinguished Vis. Fellow, Kyoto Univ., 1992. Carlyle Lectr, Oxford Univ., 1995. Vice-Pres., British Acad., 1993–94. Publications Sec., Royal Economic Soc., 1971–; Review Editor, Economic Jl, 1976–83. *Publications:* Classical Political Economy and Colonies, 1965; James Mill: selected economic writings, 1966; Economics and Policy, 1969; (with S. K. Howson) The Economic Advisory Council 1930–1939, 1976; Adam Smith's Politics, 1978; (with S. Collini and J. W. Burrow) That Noble Science of Politics, 1983; Malthus, 1987; Riches and Poverty, 1996. *Address:* Arts E, University of Sussex, Brighton BN1 9QN. *T:* Brighton (01273) 678037.

WINCHESTER, 18th Marquess of, *cr* 1551; **Nigel George Paulet;** Baron St John of Basing, 1539; Earl of Wiltshire, 1550; Premier Marquess of England; *b* 23 Dec. 1941; *s* of George Cecil Paulet (*g g g s* of 13th Marquess) (*d* 1961), and Hazel Margaret (*d* 1976), *o d* of late Major Danvers Wheeler, RA, Salisbury, Rhodesia; *S* kinsman, 1968; *m* 1967, Rosemary Anne, *d* of Major Aubrey John Hilton; two *s* one *d*. *Heir: s* Earl of Wiltshire, *qv*. *Address:* 6A Main Road, Irene 1675, Transvaal, South Africa.

WINCHESTER, Bishop of, since 1995; **Rt Rev. Michael Charles Scott-Joynt;** *b* 1943; *m* 1965, Louise White; two *s* one *d*. *Educ:* King's College, Cambridge (BA 1965, MA 1968); Cuddesdon Theological College. Deacon 1967, priest 1968; Curate, Cuddesdon, 1967–70; Tutor, Cuddesdon Coll., 1967–71, Chaplain 1971–72; Team Vicar, Newbury, 1972–75; Priest-in-charge: Caversfield, 1975–79; Bicester, 1975–79; Bucknell, 1976–79; Rector, Bicester Area Team Ministry, 1979–81; RD of Bicester and Islip, 1976–81; Canon Residentiary of St Albans, 1982–87; Dir of Ordinands and In-Service Training, Diocese of St Albans, 1982–87; Suffragan Bishop of Stafford, 1987–95. *Address:* Wolvesey, Winchester, Hants SO23 9ND. *T:* Winchester (01962) 854050.

WINCHESTER, Dean of; *see* Beeson, Very Rev. T. R.

WINCHESTER, Archdeacon of; *see* Clarkson, Ven. A. G.

WINCHILSEA, 16th Earl of, *cr* 1628, **AND NOTTINGHAM,** 11th Earl of, *cr* 1681; **Christopher Denys Stormont Finch Hatton,** Bart 1611; Viscount Maidstone, 1623; Bart English, 1660; Baron Finch, 1674; Custodian of Royal Manor of Wye; *b* 17 Nov. 1936; *er s* of 15th Earl and Countess Gladys Széchényi (*d* 1978) (who obtained a divorce, 1946; she *m* 1954, Arthur Talbot Peterson), 3rd *d* of Count László Széchényi; *S* father, 1950; *m* 1962, Shirley, *e d* of late Bernard Hatfield, Wylde Green, Sutton Coldfield; one *s* one *d*. *Heir: s* Viscount Maidstone, *qv*. *Address:* South Cadbury House, Yeovil, Somerset.

WINCKLES, Kenneth, MBE 1945; business consultant; Director, Dowson-Shurman Associates Ltd, since 1988; *b* 17 June 1918; *s* of Frank and Emily Winckles; *m* 1941, Peggy Joan Hodges; one *s* one *d*. *Educ:* Lower School of John Lyon, Harrow. FCA. Served War, Army, 1939–46, demobilised Lt-Col. Company Secretary, Scribbans-Kemp Ltd, 1947–48; Rank Organisation, 1948–67: Director and Gp Asst Managing Dir; Managing Dir, Theatre Div.; Dir, Southern Television Ltd; Dir, Rank-Xerox Ltd; Chm., Odeon Theatres (Canada) Ltd; Chm., Visnews Ltd. Chm. and Man. Dir, United Artists Corp, 1967–69; Man. Dir, Cunard Line Ltd, 1969–70; Dir, Hill Samuel Gp Ltd, 1971–80; Dep. Chm., ITL Information Technology plc, 1981–89. Director: Horserace Totalisator Bd, 1974–76; CAA, 1978–80. *Publications:* The Practice of Successful Business Management, 1986; Funding Your Business, 1988. *Recreations:* swimming, gardening, music. *Address:* Moor House, Fishers Wood, Sunningdale, Ascot, Berks SL5 0JF. *T:* Ascot (01344) 24800.

WINDER, Robert James; Literary Editor, Independent, 1989–95; *b* 26 Sept. 1959; *s* of Herbert James Winder and Mary Nina (*née* Dalby); *m* 1989, Hermione Davies; one *s*. *Educ:* Bradfield Coll.; St Catherine's Coll., Oxford (BA English). Euromoney Publications, 1982–86; Dep. Lit. Ed., The Independent, 1986–89. *Publications:* No Admission, 1988; The Marriage of Time and Convenience, 1994. *Recreations:* reading, writing, walking, talking, etc. *Address:* c/o Independent, No 1 Canada Square, Canary Wharf, E14 5AP. *T:* 0171–293 3000.

WINDHAM, William Ashe Dymoke; Chairman, Skelmersdale Development Corporation, 1979–85; (Deputy Chairman, 1977); *b* 2 April 1926; *s* of late Lt-Col Henry Steuart Windham and Marjory Russell Dymock; *m* 1956, Alison Audrey, *d* of late Maj. P. P. Curtis, MC and Ellinor Kidston; two *s* one *d*. *Educ:* Bedford; Christ's Coll., Cambridge (schol.; University prize; MA). Gen. Manager, Runcorn Div., Arthur Guinness Son & Co. (GB), 1972–84. Mem., Runcorn Develt Corp., 1975–77. Steward, Henley Royal Regatta, 1953– (Mem. Cttee of Mgt, 1972–94); rowed for: Cambridge, 1947 and 1951; England, Empire Games, 1950; GB, European Championships, 1950 and 1951 (Gold Medal); Olympic Games, 1952. *Recreations:* shooting, fishing. *Address:* Parc Gwynne, Glasbury-on-Wye, via Hereford HR3 5LL. *T:* Glasbury (01497) 847289. *Clubs:* Hawks (Cambridge); Leander (Henley) (Pres., 1993–).

WINDLE, Prof. Alan Hardwick; PhD; FIM; Professor of Materials Science, University of Cambridge, since 1992; Fellow, Trinity College, Cambridge, since 1978; *b* 20 June 1942; *s* of Stuart George Windle and Myrtle Lillian (*née* Povey); *m* 1968, Janet Susan Carr; one *s* three *d*. *Educ:* Whitgift Sch.; Imperial Coll., London (BSc Eng. 1963; ARSM 1963); Trinity Coll., Cambridge (PhD 1966). MInstP. Imperial College, University of London: ICI Res. Fellow, 1966–67; Lectr in Metallurgy, 1967–75; Lectr in Metallurgy and Materials Sci., Cambridge Univ., 1975–92; Trinity College, Cambridge: Lectr and Dir of Studies in Natural Scis, 1978–92; Tutor, 1983–91. Vis. Prof., N Carolina State Univ., 1980. Bessemer Medal, Imperial Coll., 1963; Silver Medal, RSA, 1963; Rosenhain Medal and Prize, Inst. Metals, 1987; Swinburne Medal and Prize, PRI, 1992. *Publications:* A First Course in Crystallography, 1978; (with A. M. Donald) Liquid Crystalline Polymers, 1992; contribs to learned jls mainly on polymer morphology, polymer glasses, polymer diffusion, liquid crystalline polymers and polymer modelling. *Recreation:* flying light aircraft. *Address:* Department of Materials Science and Metallurgy, Pembroke Street, Cambridge CB2 3QZ. *T:* Cambridge (01223) 334321.

WINDLE, Terence Leslie William, CBE 1991; Director, Directorate General for Agriculture, European Commission, 1980–91; *b* 15 Jan. 1926; *s* of Joseph William Windle and Dorothy Windle (*née* Haigh); *m* 1957, Joy Winifred Shield; one *s* two *d*. *Educ:* Gonville and Caius College, Cambridge (MA); London University (Colonial Course). Colonial/HMOCS: Nigeria, 1951–59; Zambia, 1959–69 (Under Sec., Min. of Natural Resources and Tourism); Home Civil Service, MAFF, 1969–73; Commn of EC, 1973–91. *Address:* rue du Fond Agny 20, 1380 Lasne, Belgium. *T:* (2) 6334410.

WINDLESHAM, 3rd Baron, *cr* 1937; **David James George Hennessy,** CVO 1981; PC 1973; Bt 1927; Principal, Brasenose College, Oxford, since 1989; Chairman, Trustees of the British Museum, since 1986 (Trustee, since 1981); *b* 28 Jan. 1932; *s* of 2nd Baron Windlesham; *S* father, 1962; *m* 1965, Prudence Glynn (*d* 1986); one *s* one *d*. *Educ:* Ampleforth; Trinity Coll., Oxford (MA; Hon. Fellow 1982). Chairman, Bow Group, 1959–60, 1962–63; Member, Westminster City Council, 1958–62. Minister of State, Home Office, 1970–72; Minister of State for Northern Ireland, 1972–73; Lord Privy Seal and Leader of the House of Lords, 1973–74. Mem., Cttee of Privy Counsellors on Ministerial Memoirs, 1975. Man. Dir, Grampian Television, 1967–70; Jt Man. Dir, 1974–75, Man. Dir, 1975–81, Chm., 1981, ATV Network; Director: The Observer, 1981–89; W. H. Smith Gp plc, 1986–. Vis. Fellow, All Souls Coll., Oxford, 1986. Chm., The Parole Bd, 1982–88. Pres., Victim Support, 1992–; Vice-Pres., Royal Television Soc., 1977–82; Jt Dep. Chm., Queen's Silver Jubilee Appeal, 1977; Dep. Chm., The Royal Jubilee Trusts, 1977–80; Chairman: Oxford Preservation Trust, 1979–89; Oxford Society, 1985–88; Mem, Museums and Galleries Commn, 1984–86. Ditchley Foundation: Governor and Mem., Council of Management, 1983–; Vice-Chm., 1987–; Trustee: Charities Aid Foundn, 1977–81; Community Service Volunteers, 1981–; Royal Collection Trust, 1993–. *Publications:* Communication and Political Power, 1966; Politics in Practice, 1975; Broadcasting in a Free Society, 1980; Responses to Crime, Vol. 1 1987, Vol. 2 1993; (with Richard Rampton) The Windlesham/Rampton Report on Death on the Rock, 1989. *Heir: s* Hon. James Hennessy, *b* 9 Nov. 1968. *Address:* Brasenose College, Oxford OX1 4AJ.

WINDSOR, Viscount; Ivor Edward Other Windsor-Clive; *b* 19 Nov. 1951; *s* and *heir* of 3rd Earl of Plymouth, *qv*; *m* 1979, Caroline, *d* of Frederick Nettlefold and Hon. Mrs Juliana Roberts; three *s* one *d*. *Educ:* Harrow; Royal Agricl Coll., Cirencester. Co-founder, and Dir, Centre for the Study of Modern Art, 1973. *Recreation:* cricket. *Heir: s* Hon. Robert Other Ivor Windsor-Clive, *b* 25 March 1981. *Address:* Oakly Park, Ludlow, Shropshire SY8 2JW; 6 Oakley Street, SW3 5NN.

WINDSOR, Dean of; *see* Mitchell, Very Rev. P. R.

WINDSOR, Dr Colin George, FRS 1995; FInstP; Senior Scientist, National Non-Destructive Testing Centre, AEA Technology (formerly United Kingdom Atomic Energy Authority), since 1988; *b* 28 June 1938; *s* of late George Thomas Macdonald Windsor and of Mabel (*née* Rayment); *m* 1963, Margaret Lee; one *s* two *d*. *Educ:* Beckenham Grammar Sch.; Magdalen Coll., Oxford (BA 1st Cl. Hons Physics; DPhil 1963). FInstP 1975; FInstNDT 1993. Magnetic resonance research, Clarendon Lab., Oxford, 1963; Res. Fellow, Yale Univ., 1964; Neutron scattering research, Harwell, 1964–. Fellow: Japanese Soc. for Promotion of Sci., 1980; Neural Network Applications, 1987. Hon. Prof. of Physics, Birmingham Univ., 1990. *Publications:* Pulsed Neutron Scattering, 1981; Four Computer Models, 1982; (ed jtly) Solid State Science, Past, Present and Predicted, 1987; contrib. to learned jls. *Recreations:* cycling to work, tennis, sketching, singing, piano, composing. *Address:* B 521, Harwell Laboratory, Oxon OX11 0RA. *T:* Didcot (01235) 435101.

WINDSOR-CLIVE, family name of **Earl of Plymouth.**

WINDWARD ISLANDS, Bishop of, since 1994; **Rt. Rev. Sehon Sylvester Goodridge;** *b* Barbados, 9 Oct. 1937; *s* of Simeon Goodridge and late Vernese (*née* Burrows); *m* 1966, Janet Rosalind Thomas; one *s* two *d*. *Educ:* Harrison Coll., Barbados; Codrington Coll., Barbados; King's Coll. London (BD 1966, AKC 1991). Asst Master, Grenada Boys' Sec. Sch., 1957–58. Deacon 1963, priest 1964, Windward Is; Curate, Holy Trinity, St Lucia, 1964–66; Anglican Chaplain, Univ. of W Indies and part-time Teacher, Kingston Coll., 1967–69; Anglican Tutor, United Theol Coll. of W Indies, Mona, Jamaica, 1969–71; Principal, Codrington Coll., Barbados, 1971–82; Warden/Student Counsellor, Univ. of W Indies, Cave Hill Campus, Barbados, 1983–89; Mem., Synod Council, Dio. Barbados, 1973–87; Hon. Canon, Dio. Barbados, 1976–; Principal, Simon of Cyrene Theol Inst., 1989–94. Chaplain to the Queen, 1993–94. Member: Inter-Anglican Theol and Doctrinal Commn, 1981–85; Bd of Govs, Coll. of Ascension, Birmingham, 1989–94; Standing Cttee on Theol Educn, CCBI, 1989–94; Bd for Social Responsibility, Gen. Synod, C of E, 1990–94; Council of Southwark Ordination Course, 1990–94; Partnership Adv. Gp, USPG, 1990–94; URC Trng Cttee, 1991–94; Initial Ministerial Educn Cttee, ABM, 1991–94; Gov. Body, SPCK, 1991–94; Bd, William Temple Foundn, 1992–94. Exam. Chaplain to Bishop of Southwark, 1990–94. Vis. Prof., Gen. Theol Seminary, NY, 1986. Hon. DD: Huron Coll., Univ. of W Ont, 1977; Gen. Theol Seminary, Episcopal Church, NY, 1995. Mem. of Privy Council, Barbados, 1986–91. *Publications:* St Mary's: 1827–1977, 1977; Facing the Challenge of Emancipation, 1981; A Companion to Liberation Theology, 1984; *monographs:* Politics and the Caribbean Church, 1971; The Church Amidst Politics and Revolution, 1977; The Abortion Question, 1977; articles in Bull. E Caribbean Affairs, The Bajan, Caribbean Contact, Christian Action Jl, The Month, Crucible. *Recreations:* reading, cricket, gardening. *Address:* PO Box 128, Bishop's House, Kingstown, St Vincent, WI.

WINEGARTEN, Jonathan Isaac; Master of the Supreme Court, Chancery Division, since 1991; *b* 10 Dec. 1944; *s* of Moshe Winegarten and Hannah Deborah Winegarten (*née* Cohen). *Educ:* Hasmonean Grammar Sch., Hendon (Head Boy 1962); Gateshead Yeshiva; University Coll. London (LLB Hons 1967); Slabodka Yeshiva, Israel. Chm., Yavneh, 1966. Winston Churchill Award and called to the Bar, Middle Temple, 1969, *ad eundem* Lincoln's Inn, 1972; in practice, Chancery Bar, 1970–91. Member: Chancery Bar Assoc. Cttee, 1982, 1983; Supreme Court Procedure Cttee, 1992–. Member: Bd of Deputies, 1973–79; Council, Jews Coll., 1989–; Vice Pres., Fedn of Synagogues, 1989–. Pres., Shomrei Hadath Synagogue, 1988–. Freeman, City of London, 1992. Adv. Editor, Atkin's Court Forms, 1993–; Editor, Tristram and Coote's Probate Practice, 1995–. *Publications:* (ed) Collected works of Rabbi Z. H. Ferber (11 vols), 1983–92. *Recreations:* violin playing, painting, esp. glass painting and etching, music, reading, publishing. *Address:* Thomas More Building, Royal Courts of Justice, Strand, WC2A 2LL.

WINFIELD, Dr Graham, CBE 1991; Chairman: Booker Tate Ltd, since 1993; Retail and Distribution Panel, Technology Foresight, Cabinet Office, since 1994; *b* 28 May 1931; *s* of Josiah and Gladys Winfield; *m* 1959, Olive Johnson; three *s* one *d*. *Educ:* Univ. of Liverpool (BSc, PhD Chemistry). Chemist, Min. of Supply, 1956–57; Lectr, Univ. of Liverpool, 1957–58; Chief Chemist, later Develt Manager, Ciba ARL, 1958–62; Develt Manager, MaxMeyer Co., Milan, 1962–63; BOC Group, 1963–89: R&D, marketing, gen. management; Chief Executive: Metals Div. UK, 1969–74; Gases Div. UK, 1974–79; Overseas Gp, 1979–89. Non-exec. Dir., Baker Perkins Group, 1984–87. Mem., ESRC, 1985–90; Chm., Post Grad. Trng Bd, 1987–90. Dir, Newton Abbot CAB, 1993–. *Publications:* numerous papers in pure and applied chemistry. *Recreations:* golf, bridge, music, reading. *Address:* Carmel, 18 Coach Place, Newton Abbot, Devon TQ12 1ES. *T:* Newton Abbot (01626) 336638.

WINFIELD, Peter Stevens, FRICS; Senior Partner, Healey & Baker, London, Amsterdam, Brussels, New York, Paris, St Helier, Jersey, 1975–88, Consultant, since 1988; *b* 24 March 1927; *s* of late Harold Stevens Winfield and Susan Cooper; *m* 1955, Mary Gabrielle Kenrick; four *s* two *d. Educ:* Sloane Sch., Chelsea; West London College of Commerce. Served Royal Artillery, 1944–48. Joined Healey & Baker, 1951. Governor, Guy's Hospital, 1973–74, Special Trustee, 1974–; Chairman: London Auction Mart Ltd, 1980–92 (Dir, 1970–92); Letinvest plc, 1987–94; Director: Manders (formerly Manders (Holdings)) plc, 1987–; Golden Square Properties Ltd, 1990–. Member: Lloyd's of London, 1978–; Property Investment Cttee of Save & Prosper Gp Ltd, 1980–; Horserace Totalisator Bd, 1981–92. Dir, Kingston Theatre Trust, 1990–. Liveryman: Worshipful Company of Farriers, 1967–; Worshipful Company of Feltmakers, 1972–, Asst to the Court, 1979–, Master, 1990–91. *Recreations:* horseracing, cricket. *Address:* 29 St George Street, W1A 3BG. *T:* 0171–629 9292. *Clubs:* Buck's, Royal Automobile, United & Cecil, MCC.

WING, Prof. John Kenneth, CBE 1990; MD, PhD; DPM; FRCPsych; Director of Research Unit, Royal College of Psychiatrists, since 1989; Professor of Social Psychiatry, Institute of Psychiatry and London School of Hygiene and Tropical Medicine, 1970–89, now Emeritus Professor, University of London; *b* 22 Oct. 1923. *Educ:* Strand Sch.; University College London (MB, BS, MD, PhD). Served RNVR, 1942–46, Lieut (A). Dir, MRC Social Psychiatry Unit, 1965–89. Mem., MRC, 1985–89 (Chm., Neurosciences Bd, 1985–87; Chm., Health Services Res. Cttee, 1987–89). Hon. Consultant Psychiatrist, Maudsley and Bethlem Royal Hosp., 1960–89. Advr to H of C Social Services Cttee, 1984–85 and 1990. Hon. MD Heidelberg, 1977. *Publications:* (ed) Early Childhood Autism, 1966, 2nd edn 1975 (trans. Italian 1970, German 1973); (with G. W. Brown) Institutionalism and Schizophrenia, 1970; (with J. E. Cooper and N. Sartorius) Description and Classification of Psychiatric Symptoms, 1974 (trans. German 1978, French 1980, Japanese 1981); Reasoning about Madness, 1978 (trans. Portuguese 1978, German 1982, Italian 1983); ed, Schizophrenia: towards a new synthesis, 1978; ed (with R. Olsen), Community Care for the Mentally Disabled, 1979; (with J. Leach) Helping Destitute Men, 1979; (ed jtly) What is a Case?, 1981; (ed jtly) Handbook of Psychiatric Rehabilitation, 1981; (with L. G. Wing) Psychoses of Uncertain Aetiology, vol. III of Cambridge Handbook of Psychiatry, 1982; (ed) Contributions to Health Services Planning and Research, 1989; (ed) Measurement for Mental Health, 1995; (jtly) Diagnosis and Clinical Measurement in Psychiatry, 1995. *Address:* Royal College of Psychiatrists Research Unit, 11 Grosvenor Crescent, SW1X 7EE. *T:* 0171–235 2351, ext. 282.

WINGATE, Captain Sir Miles (Buckley), KCVO 1982; FNI; Deputy Master and Chairman of the Board of Trinity House, London, 1976–88, retired; *b* 17 May 1923; *s* of Terrence Wingate and Edith Wingate; *m* 1947, Alicia Forbes Philip; three *d. Educ:* Taunton Grammar Sch.; Southampton and Prior Park Coll., Somerset. Master Mariner. Apprenticed to Royal Mail Lines Ltd, 1939; first Comd, 1957; elected to Bd of Trinity House, 1968. Commonwealth War Graves Comr, 1986–91. Vice-President: Seamen's Hosp. Soc., 1980–; Royal Alfred Seafarers Soc., 1980–; British Maritime Charitable Foundn, 1983–; Pres., Internat. Assoc. of Lighthouse Authorities, 1985–88 (Vice-Pres., 1980–85); Dep. Chm., Gen. Council, King George's Fund for Sailors, 1983–93; Mem., Cttee of Management, RNLI, 1976–; Council, Missions to Seamen, 1982–93. Liveryman: Hon. Co. of Master Mariners, 1970–; Shipwrights' Co., 1977–90; Freeman, Watermen and Lightermen's Co.. 1984. Governor, Pangbourne Coll., 1982–91. *Recreation:* golf. *Address:* Trinity House, Tower Hill, EC3N 4DH. *T:* 0171–480 6601.

WINGFIELD, family name of **Viscount Powerscourt.**

WINGFIELD DIGBY; *see* Digby.

WINGFIELD DIGBY, Very Rev. Richard Shuttleworth, MA; Dean of Peterborough, 1966–80, Dean Emeritus since 1980; *b* 19 Aug. 1911; *s* of late Everard George Wingfield Digby and Dorothy (*née* Loughnan); *m* 1936, Rosamond Frances, *d* of late Col W. T. Digby, RE; two *s* one *d. Educ:* Nautical Coll., Pangbourne; Royal Navy; Christ's Coll., Cambridge; Westcott House, Cambridge. BA 1935; MA 1939. Asst Curate of St Andrew's, Rugby, 1936–46. Chaplain to the Forces (4th Cl. Emergency Commn), 1940–45; POW, 1940–45. Vicar of All Saints, Newmarket, 1946–53; Rector of Bury, Lancs, 1953–66; Rural Dean of Bury, 1962–66. Pres. and Chm., Bury Trustee Savings Bank, 1953–66; Dep. Chm., Trustee Savings Bank Assoc., North-West Area, 1965–66. Hon. Canon of Manchester Cathedral, 1965; Hon. Chaplain to Regt XX, The Lancs Fusiliers, 1965. Chm. C of E Council for Places of Worship, 1976–81. *Recreations:* walking, dry stone walling. *Address:* Byways, Higher Holton, near Wincanton, Somerset BA9 8AP. *T:* Wincanton (01963) 32137. *Club:* Army and Navy.

WINGFIELD DIGBY, Ven. Stephen Basil, MBE 1944; Archdeacon of Sarum, 1968–79; Canon Residentiary, 1968–79, and Treasurer, 1971–79, Salisbury Cathedral; *b* 10 Nov. 1910; *m* 1940, Barbara Hatton Budge (*d* 1987); three *s* one *d. Educ:* Marlborough Coll.; Christ Church, Oxford; Wycliffe Hall, Oxford. Asst Master, Kenton Coll., Kenya, 1933–36; Curate, St Paul's, Salisbury, 1936–38; Priest-in-Charge, St George's, Oakdale, Poole, 1938–47. CF (temp.), 1939–45; SCF, 7th Armoured Div., 1943–45. Vicar of Sherborne with Castleton and Lillington, 1947–68. RD of Sherborne and Canon of Salisbury Cathedral, 1954–68. *Recreations:* fishing, gardening. *Address:* Eastbury House, Long Street, Sherborne, Dorset DT9 3BZ. *T:* Sherborne (01935) 812876.

WINKELMAN, Joseph William, RE 1982 (ARE 1979); RWA 1990 (ARWA 1983); free-lance painter-printmaker, since 1971; President, Royal Society of Painter-Printmakers (formerly Royal Society of Painter-Etchers and Engravers), 1989–95; *b* 20 Sept. 1941; *s* of George William Winkelman and Cleo Lucretia (*née* Harness); *m* 1969, Harriet Lowell Belin; two *d. Educ:* Univ. of the South, Sewanee, Tenn (BA English 1964); Wharton School of Finance, Univ. of Pennsylvania; Univ. of Oxford (Cert. of Fine Art 1971). Royal Society of Painter Etchers and Engravers: Hon. Sec., 1982; Vice-Pres., 1986; Fellow, Printmakers' Council of GB, 1978 (Hon. Fellow, 1988). Former tutor for: Sch. of Architecture, Oxford Polytechnic; Ruskin Sch. of Drawing, Oxford Univ.; Dept for External Studies, Oxford Univ. Chm., Oxford Art Soc., 1987–93 (Vice Pres., 1994–). Chm., Nat. Assoc. of Blood Donors. Gov., Windmill First Sch., Headington, Oxford. *Recreations:* gardening, hill walking. *Address:* The Hermitage, 69 Old High Street, Headington, Oxford OX3 9HT. *T:* Oxford (01865) 62839. *Club:* Arts.

WINKLEY, Dr Stephen Charles, MA; Headmaster, Uppingham School, since 1991; *b* 9 July 1944; *e s* of late George Winkley and Eunice Winkley (*née* Golding); *m* 1st, 1968, Georgina Smart; two *s*; 2nd, 1983, Jennifer Burt; two *d. Educ:* St Edward's School, Oxford; Brasenose College, Oxford (MA 1967; DPhil 1973). Asst Master, Cranleigh Sch., 1969–85; Second Master, Winchester College, 1985–91. *Recreations:* music, water colours. *Address:* Headmaster's House, Spring Back Way, Uppingham, Rutland LE15 9QE. *T:* Uppingham (01572) 822688.

WINKS, Prof. Robin W(illiam Evert), MA, PhD; Randolph W. Townsend Professor of History, Yale University, since 1957; *b* 5 Dec. 1930; *s* of Evert McKinley Winks and Jewell Sampson; *m* 1952, Avril Flockton, Wellington, NZ; one *s* one *d. Educ:* Univ. of Colorado (BA Hons 1952, MA 1953); Victoria Univ., NZ (Cert. 1952); Johns Hopkins Univ. (PhD 1957). Yale University: Dir, Office of Special Projects and Foundns, 1974–76; Master of Berkeley Coll., 1977–90; Chairman: Council of Masters, 1978–84, 1986–88; Studies in the Envmt, 1993–. Smith-Mundt Prof., Univ. of Malaya, 1962; Vis. Prof., Univ. of Sydney, 1963; Vis. Fellow, Inst. of Commonwealth Studies, 1966–67; Guggenheim Fellow, 1976–77; Vis. Prof. of Economics, Univ. of Stellenbosch, 1983; Fellow, Amer. Sch. for Research, 1985 and 1991; George Eastman Vis. Prof., Oxford Univ., 1992–93. Cultural Attaché, Amer. Embassy, London, 1969–71; Advisor to Dept of State, 1971–. Chm., Nat. Park Service Adv. Bd, 1981–83; Trustee, Nat. Parks and Conservation Assoc., 1985–. Mem. Council on For. Relations. FRHistS; Fellow, Explorers' Club, 1986. Hon. MA: Yale 1967; Oxon, 1992; Hon. DLitt: Nebraska, 1976; Colorado, 1987; Westminster Coll., 1995. *Publications:* Canada and the United States, 1960, 3rd edn 1988; The Cold War, 1964, 2nd edn 1977; Historiography of the British Empire-Commonwealth, 1966; Malaysia, 1966, 2nd edn 1979; Age of Imperialism, 1969; Pastmasters, 1969; The Historian as Detective, 1969; The Blacks in Canada, 1971; Slavery, 1972; An American's Guide to Britain, 1977, 3rd edn 1987; Other Voices, Other Views, 1978; The Relevance of Canadian History, 1979, 2nd edn 1988; World Civilization, 1979, 3rd edn 1993; Detective Fiction, 1980; The British Empire, 1981; Modus Operandi, 1982; History of Civilization, 1984, 9th edn 1995; Cloak and Gown, 1987; Asia in Western Language Fiction, 1990; Frederick Billings: a life, 1991; articles in Amer. Hist. Rev. *Recreations:* travel, conservation, detective fiction. *Address:* Box 208324 Yale Station, New Haven, CT 06520, USA. *Clubs:* Athenæum, Commonwealth Trust; Yale, Explorers' (NY).

WINKWORTH-SMITH, (Michael) John; Regional Managing Partner, Leeds Office, Dibb Lupton Broomhead, since 1995; *b* 4 May 1944; *s* of late Frank Winkworth-Smith and of Marjorie Beaumont Winkworth-Smith (*née* Smith); *m* 1974, Sarah Elisabeth Jackson; two *s* (one *d* decd). *Educ:* Ermysted's Grammar Sch., Skipton. Admitted solicitor, 1970; Partner, Broomhead Wightman & Reed, later Dibb Lupton Broomhead, 1972–. Treas., Royal Sheffield Instn for the Blind, 1972–78; Mem., Sheffield CVS, 1978–90; Dir, Broomgrove Trust, 1980–; Chairman: Taptonholme Ltd, 1984–; Champion Hse, Derby Diocesan Youth Centre, 1988–93. Director: European Dispute Resolution Ltd, 1991–; Japan Adv. Services Ltd, 1991–. *Recreations:* family, farming. *Address:* Churchdale Farm, Ashford-in-the-Water, Bakewell, Derbys DE45 1NX. *T:* Bakewell (01629) 640269.

WINN, family name of **Baron St Oswald.**

WINN, Allan Kendal, FCIT; Editor, Flight International, since 1989; *b* 19 March 1950; *s* of Atkinson Winn and Janet Winn; *m* 1994, Jacqueline Christina Worsley; one step *s* one step *d. Educ:* Nelson Coll., NZ; Univ. of Canterbury, Christchurch, NZ (BEng, Diploma in Journalism). FCIT 1992. Technical Editor, Consulting Engineer, 1975–77; Technical Editor, Editor, Man. Editor, Engineering Today, later New Technology, 1977–85; Editor, Commercial Motor, 1985–88. Chm., Assoc. of Friends of Brooklands Mus., 1995–. *Recreation:* vintage motor vehicles. *Address:* Flight International, Quadrant House, The Quadrant, Sutton, Surrey SM2 5AS. *T:* 0181–652 3882; 39 Heathcote, Tadworth, Surrey KT20 5TH. *T:* Tadworth (01737) 362760. *Clubs:* Aviation of Great Britain (Chm., 1991–), Vintage Sports Car (Dir), Bentley Drivers'.

WINNER, Michael Robert; Chairman: Scimitar Films Ltd, Michael Winner Ltd, Motion Picture and Theatrical Investments Ltd, since 1957; *b* 30 Oct. 1935; *s* of late George Joseph and Helen Winner. *Educ:* St Christopher's Sch., Letchworth; Downing Coll., Cambridge Univ. (MA). Film critic and Fleet Street journalist and contributor to: The Spectator, Daily Express, London Evening Standard, etc; columnist, Sunday Times and News of the World. Panellist, Any Questions, BBC radio; presenter, Michael Winner's True Crimes, LWT. Entered Motion Pictures, 1956, as Screen Writer, Asst Director, Editor. Sen. Mem. Council, Directors' Guild of Great Britain, 1991– (Mem. Council, Chief Censorship Officer, and Trustee, 1983–). Films include: Play It Cool (Dir), 1962; The Cool Mikado (Dir and Writer), 1962; West Eleven (Dir), 1963; The System (Prod. and Dir), 1963; You Must Be Joking (Prod., Dir, Writer), 1965; The Jokers (Prod., Dir, Writer), 1966; I'll Never Forget What's 'isname (Prod. and Dir), 1967; Hannibal Brooks (Prod., Dir, Writer), 1968; The Games (Prod. and Dir), 1969; Lawman (Prod. and Dir), 1970; The Nightcomers (Prod. and Dir), 1971; Chato's Land (Prod. and Dir), 1971; The Mechanic (Dir), 1972; Scorpio (Prod. and Dir), 1972; The Stone Killer (Prod. and Dir), 1973; Death Wish (Prod. and Dir), 1974; Won Ton Ton The Dog That Saved Hollywood (Prod. and Dir), 1975; The Sentinel (Prod., Dir, Writer), 1976; The Big Sleep (Prod., Dir, Writer), 1977; Firepower (Prod., Dir), 1978; Death Wish Two (Prod., Dir, Writer), 1981; The Wicked Lady (Prod., Dir, Writer), 1982; Scream for Help (Prod., Dir), 1984; Death Wish Three (Prod. and Dir), 1985; Appointment with Death (Prod., Dir, Writer), 1988; A Chorus of Disapproval (Prod., Dir, Jt screenplay writer), 1989; Bullseye! (Prod., Dir, jt screenplay writer), 1990; Dirty Weekend (Prod., Dir, jt screenplay writer), 1993. Theatre productions: The Tempest, Wyndhams, 1974; A Day in Hollywood A Night in the Ukraine, 1978. Founder and Chm., Police Meml Trust, 1984–. *Recreations:* walking around art galleries, museums, antique shops, eating, being difficult. *Address:* 6/8 Sackville Street, W1X 1DD. *T:* 0171–734 8385.

WINNICK, David Julian; MP (Lab) Walsall North, since 1979; *b* Brighton, 26 June 1933; *s* of late Eugene and Rose Winnick; one *s*; *m* 1968, Bengi Rona (marr. diss.), *d* of Tarik and Zeynep Rona. *Educ:* secondary school; London Sch. of Economics (Dip. in Social Admin). Army National Service, 1951–53. Branch Secretary, Clerical and Administrative Workers' Union, 1956–62 (now APEX GMB; Mem. Exec. Council, 1978–88, Vice-Pres., 1983–88); Advertisement Manager, Tribune, 1963–66; employed by UKIAS, 1970–79 (Chm., 1984–90). Member: Willesden Borough Council, 1959–64; London Borough of Brent Council, 1964–66 (Chairman, Children Cttee, 1965–66). Contested (Lab) Harwich, 1964; MP (Lab) Croydon South, 1966–70; contested (Lab): Croydon Central, Oct. 1974; Walsall N, Nov. 1976. Member: Select Cttee on the Environment, 1979–83; Home Affairs Cttee, 1983–87; Select Cttee on Procedure, 1989–; Vice-Chm., British-Irish Inter-Parly Body, 1993–. *Recreations:* walking, cinema, theatre, reading. *Address:* House of Commons, SW1A 0AA.

WINNIFRITH, Charles Boniface; Clerk of Committees, House of Commons, since 1995; *b* 12 May 1936; *s* of Sir John Winnifrith, KCB and late Lesbia Margaret Winnifrith; *m* 1st, 1962, Josephine Poile, MBE (*d* 1991); one *s* two *d*; 2nd, 1993, Sandra (*née* Stewart). *Educ:* Tonbridge Sch.; Christ Church, Oxford (MA). 2nd Lieut, RAEC, 1958–60. Joined Dept of the Clerk of the House of Commons, 1960; Second Clerk of Select Cttees, 1983; Clerk of Select Cttees, 1987; Principal Clerk of the Table Office, 1989. Mem., General Synod of C of E, 1970–90. Governor, Ashford Sch., Kent, 1973–93. *Recreations:* cricket, American soap opera. *Address:* Gale Lodge Farm, Long Buckby, Northants NN6 7PH. *T:* Northampton (01604) 770396; Cliffe Cottage, St Margaret's-at-Cliffe, Kent CT15 6BJ. *T:* Dover (01304) 853280. *Club:* MCC.

WINNING, His Eminence Cardinal Thomas J.; *see* Glasgow, Archbishop of, (RC).

WINNINGTON, Sir Francis Salwey William, 6th Bt, *cr* 1755; Lieut, late Welsh Guards; *b* 24 June 1907; *er s* of late Francis Salwey Winnington, *e s* of 5th Bt and Blanch, *d* of Commander William John Casberd-Boteler, RN; *S* grandfather, 1931; *m* 1944, Anne, *o d* of late Captain Lawrence Drury-Lowe; one *d*. *Educ:* Eton. Served War of 1939–45 (wounded, prisoner). Owns 4700 acres. *Heir: b* Colonel Thomas Foley Churchill Winnington, MBE, Grenadier Guards [*b* 16 Aug. 1910; *m* 1944, Lady Betty Marjorie Anson, *er d* of 4th Earl of Lichfield; two *s* two *d*]. *Address:* Brockhill Court, Shelsley Beauchamp, Worcs. *Club:* Cavalry and Guards.

See also Viscount Campden.

WINNINGTON-INGRAM, Edward John; Managing Director, Mail Newspapers Plc (formerly Associated Newspapers Group), 1986–89, retired; *b* 20 April 1926; *s* of Rev. Preb. Edward Francis and Gladys Winnington-Ingram; *m* 1st, 1953, Shirley Lamotte (marr. diss. 1968); two *s*; 2nd, 1973, Elizabeth Linda Few Brown. *Educ:* Shrewsbury; Keble Coll., Oxford (BA). Served RN (Sub-Lieut), 1944–47. Joined Associated Newspapers, 1949; Circulation Manager, Daily Mail, 1960–65; Gen. Manager, Daily Mail Manchester, 1965–70; helped create Northprint Manchester Ltd, a jt printing consortium with Manchester Guardian and Evening News and Associated, 1969; Dir, Associated Newspapers, 1971; Managing Director: Harmsworth Publishing, 1973; Mail on Sunday, 1982; Dir, Associated Newspapers Holdings, 1983; non-executive Director: NAAFI, 1987–93; Burlington Gp, 1988–92. *Recreations:* tennis, shooting, beagling, gardening, music, defending the 1662 Prayer Book. *Address:* Old Manor Farm, Cottisford, Brackley, Northants NN13 5SW. *T:* Finmere (01280) 848367. *Clubs:* Buck's, Roehampton.

WINSHIP, Peter James Joseph, QPM 1990; HM Inspector of Constabulary, since 1995; *b* 21 July 1943; *s* of late Francis Edward Winship and Iris May (*née* Adams); *m* 1st, 1963, Carol Ann McNaughton; two *s* one *d*; 2nd, 1989, Janet Mary Bird; one *d*. *Educ:* Bicester Grammar Sch.; St John's Coll., Oxford (BA Eng. Lang. and Lit.; MA). Oxfordshire Constabulary, 1962; Sergeant to Supt, Thames Valley Police, 1968–79; Graduate, FBI Acad., 1980; Chief Supt, Metropolitan Police, 1982; Asst Chief Constable, Thames Valley Police, 1984; Metropolitan Police: Dep. Asst Comr, Policy & Planning, 1987, No 1 Area HQ, 1988; Asst Comr, 1989–95; Management Support and Strategy Dept, 1989–91; Inspection and Review Dept, 1992–95. Dir, Police Extended Interviews, 1993–95. Chm., Technical and Res. Cttee, ACPO, 1992–95. Member: Exec. Council, London Fedn of Boys' Clubs, 1988–95; Exec. Cttee, Royal Humane Soc., 1989–95; Governing Bd, Revolving Doors Agency, 1993–95. Chairman: Met. Police Shooting Club, 1987–95; Met. Police Flying Club, 1988–95. FIMgt. *Publications:* articles in police jls and other periodicals on professionally related subjects, travel, and treatment of police in literature; essay on delinquency and social policy (Queen's Police Gold Medal, Essay Competition, 1969). *Recreations:* reading, riding, gardening, music. *Address:* (office) White Rose Court, Oriental Road, Woking, Surrey GU22 7LG.

WINSKILL, Air Commodore Sir Archibald (Little), KCVO 1980 (CVO 1973); CBE 1960; DFC 1941 and Bar 1943; AE 1944; Extra Equerry to The Queen; *b* 24 Jan. 1917; *s* of late James Winskill; *m* 1947, Christiane Amilie Pauline, *d* of M. Bailleux, Calais, France; one *d* (one *s* decd). War of 1939–45: Fighter Pilot: Battle of Britain; European and North African Theatres; evaded capture in enemy territory, occupied France, 1941, Tunisia, 1943. Post-war: Air Adviser to Belgian Govt; Station Cmdr, RAF Turnhouse and Duxford; Gp Capt. Ops Germany; Air Attaché, Paris; Dir of Public Relations, MoD (RAF); Captain of the Queen's Flight, 1968–82. Life Vice Pres., Queen's Flight Assoc. Freedom of City of London, 1978. *Recreation:* golf. *Address:* Anchors, Coastal Road, West Kingston Estate, East Preston, West Sussex BN16 1SN. *T:* Rustington (01903) 775439. *Club:* Royal Air Force.

See also C. J. R. Meyer.

WINSTANLEY, Rt. Rev. Alan Leslie; Vicar of Eastham, and Assistant Bishop, diocese of Chester, since 1994; *b* 7 May 1949; *s* of John Leslie Winstanley and Eva Winstanley; *m* 1972, Vivien Mary Parkinson; two *s* one *d*. *Educ:* St John's College, Nottingham (BTh, ALCD). Deacon 1972, priest 1973, Blackburn; Curate: St Andrew's, Livesey, Blackburn, 1972–75; St Mary's, Great Sankey, dio. Liverpool, with responsibility for St Paul's, Penketh, 1975–77; Vicar of Penketh, 1978–81; SAMS Missionary in Peru: Lima, 1981–85; Arequipa, 1986–87; Bishop of Peru and Bolivia, 1988–93. *Recreations:* caravanning, steam locomotives. *Address:* The Vicarage, Ferry Road, Eastham, Wirral, Merseyside L62 0AJ. *T:* 0151–327 2182.

WINSTANLEY, John, MC 1944; TD 1951; FRCS, FRCOphth; Hon. Consultant Ophthalmic Surgeon, St Thomas' Hospital, since 1983 (Ophthalmic Surgeon, 1960–83); *b* 11 May 1919; 3rd *s* of late Captain Bernard Joseph Winstanley and Grace Taunton; *m* 1959, Jane Frost; one *s* two *d*. *Educ:* Wellington Coll., Berks; St Thomas's Hosp. Med. Sch. (MB, BS 1951). FRCS 1957; FRCOphth (FCOphth 1988). Served 4th Bn Queen's Own Royal West Kent Regt, 1937–46 (despatches BEF, 1940). Resident med. appts, St Thomas' and Moorfields Eye Hosps, 1951–56; Chief Clin. Asst, Moorfields Eye Hosp., 1956–60; Sen. Registrar, St Thomas' Hosp., 1956–60; recog. teacher of ophthalmol., St Thomas' Hosp., 1960–83; Ophth. Surg., Lewisham and Greenwich Health Dists, 1959–70; Hon. Ophthalmic Surgeon: Royal Hosp., Chelsea, 1963–85; Queen Alexandra's Mil. Hosp., Millbank,1966–72; Queen Elizabeth Mil. Hosp., Woolwich, 1972–83. Hon. Civilian Consultant in Ophthalmol. to MOD (Army), 1971–83. Examiner in Ophthalmology (DipOphth of Examining Bd of RCP and RCS, 1968–72; Mem. Court of Examiners, RCS, 1972–78). FRSM 1963 (Vice-Pres., Sect. of Ophth., 1979); Member: Ophthal. Soc. UK, 1958–88 (Hon. Sec. 1966–68, Vice-Pres. 1980–83); Faculty of Ophthalmologists, 1958–88, Mem. Council, 1973–85, Vice-Pres., 1979–85; Mem. Council, Medical Protection Soc., 1979–90. Liveryman, Soc. of Apothecaries, 1965 (Mem. Livery Cttee, 1982). *Publications:* chapter, Rose's Medical Ophthalmology, 1983; papers on ophthalmic topics and med. hist. in med. jls. *Recreations:* shooting, fishing, medical history. *Address:* The Churchill Clinic, 80 Lambeth Road, SE1 7PW. *T:* 0181–928 5633; 10 Pembroke Villas, The Green, Richmond, Surrey TW9 1QF. *T:* 0181–940 6247. *Clubs:* Army and Navy, Flyfishers'.

WINSTON, Clive Noel; Assistant Director, Federation Against Copyright Theft Ltd, 1985–88; *b* 20 April 1925; *s* of George and Alida Winston; *m* 1952, Beatrice Jeanette; two *d*. *Educ:* Highgate Sch.; Trinity Hall, Cambridge (BA). Admitted solicitor, 1951. Joined Metropolitan Police, 1951; Dep. Solicitor, Metropolitan Police, 1982–85. Chairman, Union of Liberal and Progressive Synagogues, 1981–85 (Vice-Pres., 1985–); Treas., Eur. Bd, World Union of Progressive Judaism, 1990–. *Recreations:* golf, gardening.

WINSTON, Prof. Robert Maurice Lipson, FRCOG; Professor of Fertility Studies, University of London at the Institute of Obstetrics and Gynaecology, Royal Postgraduate Medical School, since 1987; Consultant Obstetrician and Gynaecologist: Hammersmith Hospital, since 1978; Royal Masonic Hospital, since 1988; *b* 15 July 1940; *s* of late Laurence Winston and of Ruth Winston-Fox, *qv*; *m* 1973, Lira Helen Feigenbaum; two *s* one *d*. *Educ:* St Paul's Sch., London; London Hosp. Med. Coll., London Univ. (MB, BS 1964). MRCS, LRCP 1964; FRCOG 1983 (MRCOG 1971). Jun. posts, London Hosp., 1964–66; Registrar and Sen. Registrar, Hammersmith Hosp., 1970–74; Wellcome Res. Sen. Lectr, Inst. of Obs and Gyn., 1974–78; Sen. Lectr, Hammersmith Hosp., 1978–81; Reader in Fertility Studies, RPMS, 1982–86. Vis. Prof., Univ. of Leuven, Belgium. 1976–77; Prof. of Gyn., Univ. of Texas at San Antonio, 1980–81; Clyman Vis. Prof., Mt Sinai Hosp., New York, 1985. Member, Steering Cttee, WHO: on Tubal Occlusion, 1975–77; on Ovum Transport, 1977–78. Pres., Internat. Fallopius Soc., 1987–. Vice Pres., Progress (all-party parly campaign for res. into human reprodn), 1992– (Chm., 1988–91). Founder Mem., British Fertility Soc., 1975–; Hon. Member: Georgian Obs Soc., 1983–; Pacific Fertility Soc., 1983–; Spanish Fertility Soc., 1985–. Mem. Council, RPMS, 1992–. Presenter, Your Life in their Hands, BBC TV, 1979–87; Member, Editorial Board: Internat. Jl of Microsurgery, 1981–; Clinical Reproduction and Fertility, 1985–. Chief Rabbinate Award for Contribn to Society, 1992–93; Victor Bonney Prize, RCS, 1991–93; Cedric Carter Medal, Clinical Genetics Soc., 1993. *Publications:* Reversibility of Sterilization, 1978; (jtly) Tubal Infertility, 1981; Infertility, a Sympathetic Approach, 1987; scientific pubns on human and experimental reproduction. *Recreations:* theatre (directed award-winning Pirandello production, Each in his Own Way, Edinburgh Fest., 1969), broadcasting, music, wine. *Address:* 11 Denman Drive, NW11 6RE. *T:* 0181–455 7475.

WINSTON-FOX, Mrs Ruth, JP; Co-Chairman, Women's National Commission, 1979–81 (Member, since 1971); *b* 12 Sept. 1912; *d* of Major the Rev. Solomon Lipson, Hon. SCF, and Tilly Lipson (*née* Shandel); *m* 1st, 1938, Laurence Winston (*d* 1949); two *s* one *d*; 2nd, 1960, Goodwin Fox (*d* 1974). *Educ:* St Paul's Girls' Sch.; London Univ. BSc Household and Social Sci.; Home Office Child Care Cert. Mental Hosps Dept and Child Care Dept, LCC, 1936–39; Dep. Centre Organiser, WVS, Southgate, 1941–45; Southgate Borough Council: Member, 1945–65; Alderman, 1955–65; Mayor of Southgate, 1958–59, Dep. Mayor, 1959–61; Sen. Officer, Adoptions Consultant, Social Services Dept, Herts CC, 1949–77. Member: London Rent Assessment Panel and Tribunals, 1975–; Review Cttee for Secure Accommodation, London Borough of Enfield, 1982–; Bd of Deputies of British Jews, 1960– (Chm. Educn Cttee, 1974–80; voluntary nat. organiser, exhibn Jewish Way of Life, 1978–, which visited 44 communities in Britain); Vice-Pres., Internat. Council of Jewish Women, 1974– (Chairman: Status of Women Cttee, 1966–75; Inter-Affiliate Travel Cttee, 1975–81); Mem. Governing Body, World Jewish Congress, 1981–; Co-Chm., Jewish Community Exhibn Centre, 1984–. Founder, one of first Day Centres for the Elderly in GB, Ruth Winston House, Southgate Old People's Centre, opened by Princess Alexandra, 1961, and again, 1972; Vice-President: Southgate Old People's Welfare Cttee, 1974–; Southgate Horticultural Soc.; President: League of Jewish Women, 1969–72; First Women's Lodge, England, 1972–74; Enfield Relate (formerly Enfield Marriage Guidance Council), 1984–. JP Mddx Area GLC, 1954–. *Publications:* articles only. *Recreations:* five grandchildren, travel, voluntary service. *Address:* 4 Morton Crescent, Southgate, N14 7AH. *T:* 0181–886 5056. *Clubs:* University Women's, Bnai Brith.

See also R. M. L. Winston.

WINSTONE, Dame Dorothy (Gertrude), DBE 1990; CMG 1976; *b* 23 Jan. 1919; *d* of Stanley Fowler and Constance May Fowler (*née* Sherwin); *m* 1941, Wilfrid Frank Winstone; three *s* one *d*. *Educ:* Auckland Girls' Grammar Sch.; Auckland Teachers' Coll.; Auckland University Coll. (BA, DipEd 1940). Primary School Teacher, 1938; Asst Mistress, Seddon Memorial Tech. Coll., 1939–45; voluntary community worker, 1945–. Dir, Virginia Gildersleeve Fund, Internat. Fedn of Univ. Women, 1993–. Member Emerita, NZ Fedn of Univ. Women, 1973; Life Mem., Nat. Council of Women of NZ, 1980. Hon. LLD Univ. of Auckland, 1983. Adelaide Ristori Medal, Centro Culturale Italiano, 1975; New Zealand Suffrage Centennial Medal, 1993. *Recreations:* reading, gardening, 13 grandchildren. *Address:* 17 Tuhaere Street, Auckland 5, New Zealand. *T:* (9) 5203407.

WINTER, Rt. Rev. Allen Ernest; *b* 8 Dec. 1903; *o s* of Ernest Thomas and Margaret Winter, Malvern, Vic; *m* 1939, Eunice Eleanor, 3rd *d* of Albert and Eleanor Sambell; three *s* two *d*. *Educ:* Melbourne C of E Grammar School; Trinity Coll., Univ. of Melbourne (BA 1926, MA 1928); University Coll., Oxford (BA 1932, MA 1951); Australian College of Theology (ThL 1927, ThD 1951 iur. dig.). Deacon, 1927, priest, 1928, Melbourne; Curate, Christ Church, S Yarra, 1927–29; on leave, Oxford, 1929–32; Curate, St James', Ivanhoe, 1932–35; Minister of Sunshine, 1935–39; Incumbent of St Luke's, Brighton, Melb., 1939–48; Chaplain, AIF, 1942–46; Incumbent of Christ Church, Essendon, 1948–49; Canon-Residentiary and Rector of All Saints' Cathedral, Bathurst, 1949–51; Bishop of St Arnaud, 1951–73; Chaplain, St John's Coll., Morpeth, NSW, 1974. *Address:* Wynnstay Nursing Home, 21 Wynnstay Street, Armadale, Vic 3143, Australia.

WINTER, Charles Milne, CBE 1990; FIBScot; a Vice-Chairman, Royal Bank of Scotland Group plc, 1992–93 (Director, 1981–93); *b* 21 July 1933; *s* of David and Annie Winter; *m* 1957, Audrey Hynd; one *s* one *d*. *Educ:* Harris Acad., Dundee. FIBScot 1979. Served RAF, 1951–53. Joined The Royal Bank of Scotland, 1949; Exec. Dir, 1981–86; Man. Dir, 1982–85; Dep. Gp Chief Exec., 1985; Gp Chief Exec., 1985. Dir, Williams & Glyn's Bank, 1982–85 (Man. Dir, March–Oct. 1985). President: Inst. of Bankers in Scotland, 1981–83; Edinburgh Chamber of Commerce and Manufactures, 1992–94; Chm., Cttee of Scottish Clearing Bankers, 1983–85, 1989–91; Dir-Gen., The Scottish Chamber of Commerce, 1995. *Recreations:* golf, choral music. *Club:* Royal and Ancient Golf (St Andrews).

WINTER, Rev. Canon David Brian; Hon. Curate, Hermitage Team Ministry, since 1995; Hon. Canon, Christ Church Cathedral, Oxford, since 1995; *b* 19 Nov. 1929; *s* of Walter George Winter and Winifred Ella Winter; *m* 1961, Christine Ellen Martin; two *s* one *d*. *Educ:* Machynlleth County Sch.; Trinity County Grammar Sch., Wood Green; King's Coll., Univ. of London (BA, PGCE). Nat. Service, RAF, 1948–50. Teacher: Ware CE Secondary Sch., 1954–58; Tottenham County Grammar Sch., 1958–59; Editor, Crusade, 1959–70; freelance writer and broadcaster, 1970–71; BBC: Producer, Religious Broadcasting, 1971–75, Sen. Producer, 1975–82; Hd of Religious Progs, Radio, and Dep. Hd, Religious Broadcasting, 1982–87; Hd of Religious Broadcasting, 1987–89. Chm., Arts Centre Gp, 1976–82. Oak Hill Ministerial Trng Course, 1985–87. Deacon, 1987, priest, 1988. Hon. Asst Curate, St Paul and St Luke, Finchley, 1987–89; Priest-in-Charge, Ducklington, 1989–95; Bishop's Officer for Evangelism, Dio. of Oxford, 1989–95. *Publications:* Ground of Truth, 1964; New Singer, New Song (biog. of Cliff Richard), 1967; (with S. Linden) Two a Penny, 1968; Closer than a Brother, 1971; Hereafter, 1972; (ed) Matthew Henry's Commentary on the New Testament, 1974; After the Gospels, 1977; But this I can believe, 1980; The Search for the Real Jesus, 1982; Truth in the Son, 1985; Living through Loss, 1985; Walking in the Light (confessions of St Augustine), 1986; Believing the Bible, 1987; Battered Bride, 1988; What happens after Death?, 1992; You Can Pray, 1993; What's in a Word, 1994; Mark for Starters, 1995. *Recreations:* watching cricket and writing about it, fish-keeping, talking. *Address:* St Mark's Vicarage, Cold Ash, Thatcham, Berks RG18 9PT. *T:* Newbury (01635) 864395.

WINTER, Frederick Thomas, CBE 1963; racehorse trainer, 1964–87, retired; *b* 20 Sept. 1926; *s* of late Frederick Neville Winter and Ann (*née* Flanagan); *m* 1956, Diana Pearson; three *d* (incl. twins). *Educ:* Ewell Castle. Served as Lieut, 6th Bn Para. Regt, 1944–47. Jockey, Flat, 1939–42; National Hunt jockey, 1947–64. *Recreations:* golf, gardening. *Address:* Montague House, Eastbury, Newbury, Berks RG16 7JL.

WINTER, Prof. Gerald Bernard, FDSRCS; Professor and Head of Department of Children's Dentistry, 1966–94, now Emeritus Professor, Dean and Director of Studies,

1983–93, Institute of Dental Surgery, University of London; *b* 24 Nov. 1928; *s* of Morris Winter and Edith (*née* Malter); *m* 1960, Brigitte Eva Fleischhacker; one *s* one *d*. *Educ:* Coopers' Company's Sch.; London Hospital Med. Coll. (BDS, MB BS); DCH London. Ho. Surg./Ho. Phys., London Hosp. Med. Coll., 1955–59; Lectr in Children's Dentistry, Royal Dental Hosp., London, 1959–62; Cons. Dent. Surg., Eastman Dental Hosp., 1962–94 (Hon. Cons. Dent. Surg., 1994–). Hon. Sec. 1962–65, Pres. 1970–71 and 1993–94, Brit. Paedodontic Soc., subseq. British Soc. for Paediatric Dentistry; Hon. Gen. Sec., Internat. Assoc. of Dentistry for Children, 1971–79; Founder Chm., Brit. Soc. of Dentistry for the Handicapped, 1976–77. *Publications:* A Colour Atlas of Clinical Conditions in Paedodontics (with R. Rapp), 1979; many chapters and sci. papers. *Recreations:* theatre, music, gardening. *Address:* Eastman Dental Institute, Eastman Dental Hospital, Gray's Inn Road, WC1X 8LD. *T:* 0171–915 1000; (private) 1 Hartfield Close, Elstree, Herts WD6 3JD. *T:* 0181–953 3403.

WINTER, Gregory Paul, FRS 1990; Joint Head, Division of Protein and Nucleic Acid Chemistry, Medical Research Council Laboratory of Molecular Biology, since 1994 and Deputy Director, Centre for Protein Engineering, since 1990; Senior Research Fellow, Trinity College, Cambridge, since 1991; *b* 14 April 1951; *m* Fiona Jane Winter. *Educ:* Royal Grammar Sch., Newcastle-upon-Tyne; Trinity College, Cambridge (BA Natural Scis 1973; MA; PhD 1976). Postgrad. studies in protein chem., Cambridge, 1973–76; Fellow, Trinity College, Cambridge (structure of genes and influenza virus), 1976–80; MRC–LMB (protein and antibody engineering), 1981–. Novo Biotechnology Award, Denmark, 1986; Colworth Medal, Biochem. Soc., 1986; Behring Prize, FRG, 1989; Louis Jeantet Foundn for Medicine, Switzerland, 1989; Pfizer Award, 1989; Milano Award, Italy, 1990; Scheele Award, Swedish Acad. of Pharmaceutical Scis, 1994; Biochemical Analysis Prize, German Soc. for Clin. Chem., 1995; King Faisal Internat. Prize in Medicine, 1995. *Publications:* articles in learned jls on protein and gene structure, enzymes, viral proteins and antibodies. *Address:* Medical Research Council Laboratory of Molecular Biology, Hills Road, Cambridge CB2 2QH.

WINTERBOTTOM, Prof. Michael, MA, DPhil; FBA 1978; Corpus Christi Professor of Latin, University of Oxford and Fellow, Corpus Christi College, Oxford, since 1993; *b* 22 Sept. 1934; *s* of Allan Winterbottom and Kathleen Mary (*née* Wallis); *m* 1st, 1963, Helen Spencer (marr. diss. 1983); two *s*; 2nd, 1986, Nicolette Janet Streatfeild Bergel. *Educ:* Dulwich Coll.; Pembroke Coll., Oxford. 1st Cl. Hon. Mods and Craven Schol., 1954; 1st Cl. Lit. Hum. and Derby Schol., 1956; Domus Sen. Schol., Merton Coll., 1958–59; Research Lectr, Christ Church, 1959–62. MA 1959, DPhil 1964 (Oxon). Lectr in Latin and Greek, University Coll. London, 1962–67; Fellow and Tutor in Classics, Worcester Coll., Oxford, 1967–92; Reader in Classical Langs, Univ. of Oxford, 1990–92. D*hc* Besançon, 1985. *Publications:* (ed) Quintilian, 1970; (with D. A. Russell) Ancient Literary Criticism, 1972; Three Lives of English Saints, 1972; (ed and trans.) The Elder Seneca, 1974; (ed with R. M. Ogilvie) Tacitus, *Opera Minora*, 1975; (ed and trans.) Gildas, 1978; Roman Declamation, 1980; (ed with commentary) The Minor Declamations ascribed to Quintilian, 1984; (with D. C. Innes) Sopatros the Rhetor, 1988; (with M. Brett and C. N. L. Brooke) rev. edn of Charles Johnson (ed), Hugh the Chanter, 1990; (ed) Cicero, *De Officiis*, 1994; articles and reviews in jls. *Recreations:* travel and plans for travel, hill walking, under-gardening. *Address:* 53 Thorncliffe Road, Oxford OX2 7BA. *T:* Oxford (01865) 513066.

WINTERBOTTOM, Sir Walter, Kt 1978; CBE 1972 (OBE 1963); retired; *b* 31 March 1913; *s* of James Winterbottom and Frances Holt; *m* 1942, Ann Richards; one *s* two *d*. *Educ:* Chester Coll. of Educn; Carnegie Coll. of Physical Educn. Schoolmaster, Oldham; Lectr, Carnegie Coll. of Phys. Educn; Wing Comdr, RAF, 1939–45; Dir of Coaching and Manager of England Team, Football Assoc., 1946–62; Gen. Sec., Central Council of Physical Recreation, 1963–72; Dir, The Sports Council, 1965–78. *Publications:* technical, on association football. *Recreations:* golf, bowls. *Address:* 15 Orchard Gardens, Cranleigh, Surrey GU6 7LG. *T:* Cranleigh (01483) 271593.

WINTERFLOOD, Brian Martin; Managing Director: Winterflood Securities Ltd, since 1988; Winterflood Gilts, since 1994; *b* 31 Jan. 1937; *s* of Thomas G. Winterflood and Doris M. Winterflood; *m* 1966, Doreen Stella McCartney; two *s* one *d*. *Educ:* Fray's Coll., Uxbridge. Greener Dreyfus & Co., 1953–55. National Service, 1955–57. Bisgood Bishop & Co. Ltd, 1957–85: Partner, 1967–71; Dir, 1971–81; Man. Dir, 1981–85, Man. Dir, County Bisgood, 1985–86; County NatWest Securities Ltd: Dir, 1986–87; Exec. Dir, 1987–88, resigned, 1988. Director: Union Discount Co. of London, 1991–93; Close Group, 1993–. Vice Pres., Rehabilitation and Med. Res. Trust, 1989–; Jt Chm., Cttee of USM Initiative, Prince's Youth Bus. Trust, 1989–. *Recreations:* family, travel. *Address:* Walbrook House, 23–29 Walbrook, EC4N 8LA. *T:* 0171–621 0004. *Club:* City of London.

WINTERSGILL, Dr William, FFPHM; Examining Medical Officer (part-time), Department of Health, since 1989; Member, Research and Advisory Committee, Cambridge Applied Nutrition, Toxicology and Biosciences Ltd, since 1984; *b* 20 Dec. 1922; *s* of Fred Wintersgill and May Wintersgill; *m* 1952, Iris May Holland; three *d*. *Educ:* Barnsley Holgate Grammar Sch.; Leeds Medical Sch., Univ. of Leeds (MB, ChB). MRCGP, MFCM; FFCM 1983. House Surgeon, 1948, and Registrar, 1948–49, Pontefract Infirmary; Principal, Gen. Practice, Snaith, Yorks, 1950–66; Dept of Health and Social Security (formerly Min. of Health): Reg. MO, 1967–70; SMO, 1970–72; PMO, 1972–76; SPMO, 1976–83. Specialist in Community Medicine, York HA, 1983–89. Pt-time MO, Cttee on Safety of Medicines, 1987–; Mem., Health Adv. Service Vis. Team, 1987–90; Dist Med. Advr, 1987–88. Chm., British Assoc. of Community Physicians, 1985–89. *Recreations:* gardening, antique collecting, playing the piano, choral singing, painting, old buildings. *Address:* 2 The Old Orchard, Easingwold, York YO6 3HE. *T:* Easingwold (01347) 821561.

WINTERSON, Jeanette; writer; *b* 27 Aug. 1959; partner, Dr M. Reynolds. *Educ:* St Catherine's Coll., Oxford (BA Hons English). Screenplay, Great Moments in Aviation, 1994. *Publications:* Oranges are not the only fruit, 1985 (Whitbread Prize, 1st Novel; numerous awards for 1990 adaptation, BBC TV 1990); The Passion, 1987 (John Llewellyn Rhys Prize); Sexing the Cherry, 1989 (E. M. Forster Award, Amer. Acad. and Inst. of Arts and Letters); Written on the Body, 1992; Art and Lies, 1994; Art Objects: essays on ecstasy and effrontery, 1995. *Recreations:* opera, ballet, champagne. *Address:* c/o Jonathan Cape, 20 Vauxhall Bridge Road, SW1V 2SA.

WINTERTON, 8th Earl *cr* 1766 (Ire.); **Donald David Turnour;** Baron Winterton 1761 (Ire.); Viscount Turnour 1766 (Ire.); *b* 13 Oct. 1943; *s* of Cecil Noel Turnour, DFM, CD (*d* 1987), *yr b* of 7th Earl Winterton and of Evelyn Isabel, *d* of Dr C. A. Oulton; *S* uncle, 1991; *m* 1968, Jill Pauline, *d* of late John Geddes Esplen; two *d*. *Educ:* Waterloo Lutheran Univ., Ontario (BA). *Heir: b* Robert Charles Turnour [*b* 1950; *m* 1st, 1974, Sheila (marr. diss. 1976), *d* of G. H. Stocking; 2nd, 1983, Patricia Ann, *d* of William Avery; one *d*].

WINTERTON, (Jane) Ann; MP (C) Congleton, since 1983; *b* 6 March 1941; *d* of Joseph Robert Hodgson and Ellen Jane Hodgson; *m* 1960, Nicholas R. Winterton, *qv*; two *s* one *d*. *Educ:* Erdington Grammar Sch. for Girls. Mem., Chairmen's Panel, 1992–; Mem., Agric. Select Cttee, 1987–; Chm., All Party Parly Pro-Life Gp, 1992–. *Recreations:* music, theatre, tennis, ski-ing. *Address:* House of Commons, SW1A 0AA.

WINTERTON, Nicholas Raymond; MP (C) Macclesfield since Sept. 1971; *b* 31 March 1938; *o s* of late N. H. Winterton, Lysways House, Longdon Green, near Rugeley, Staffs; *m* 1960, Jane Ann Hodgson (*see* J. A. Winterton); two *s* one *d*. *Educ:* Bilton Grange Prep. Sch.; Rugby Sch. Commnd 14th/20th King's Hussars, 1957–59. Sales Exec. Trainee, Shell-Mex and BP Ltd, 1959–60; Sales and Gen. Manager, Stevens and Hodgson Ltd, Birmingham (Co. engaged in sale and hire of construction equipment), 1960–71. Chairman: CPC Cttee, Meriden Cons. Assoc., 1966–68; Midland Branch, Contractors Mech. Plant Engrs Assoc., 1968–69. Member: W Midlands Cons. Council, 1966–69, 1971–72; Central Council, Nat. Union of Cons. and Unionist Assocs, 1971–72. Contested (C) Newcastle-under-Lyme, Oct. 1969, 1970. Chm., Select Cttee on Health, 1991–92. Treasurer: All Party Parly British Bahamas Gp; All Party Parly British Taiwan Gp; Chairman: All Party Parly Textile Gp; All Party Parly Gp for Paper and Board Industry; Anglo Danish Parly Gp; Vice Chairman: All Party Parly British Swedish Gp; British South Africa Parly Gp, 1983–89; UK Falkland Is Gp; Cons. Parly Sports and Recreation Cttee, 1979–84; Mem., H of C Chairmen's Panel, 1987–. Member: Exec. Cttee, Anglo-Austrian Soc., 1987–; Nat. Adv. Cttee, Duke of Edinburgh Award Scheme. County Councillor, Atherstone Div. Warwickshire CC, 1967–72. President: Macclesfield Fermain Club; Poynton Community Centre; Keele Univ. Conservative Assoc.; Upton Priory Youth Club, Macclesfield; Vice-President: NW Area Young Conservative Assoc.; Macclesfield and Congleton District Scout Council; Cheshire Scout Assoc.; E Cheshire Hospice. Hon. Mem., Macclesfield Lions Club; Hon. Life Mem., Macclesfield Rugby Union Football Club; Pres., Macclesfield Hockey Club; Patron: Macclesfield and District Sheep Dog Trials Assoc; Internat. Centre for Child Studies. President, Macclesfield Branch: Riding for the Disabled; Multiple Sclerosis Soc.; Trustee, NW Liver Res. Fund. Pres., Bollington Light Opera Gp; Life Mem., Poynton Gilbert and Sullivan Soc. Liveryman and Mem. of Court, Weavers' Co.; Freeman of the City of London. *Recreations:* Rugby football, squash, hockey, tennis, swimming, horse riding. *Address:* Whitehall Farm, Mow Lane, Newbold Astbury, Congleton, Cheshire CW12 3NH. *Clubs:* Cavalry and Guards, Lighthouse.

WINTLE, Rev. Canon Ruth Elizabeth; Bishop's Adviser on Women's Ministry, Worcester, since 1995; *b* 30 Sept. 1931; *d* of John Wintle and Vera (*née* Lane). *Educ:* Clarendon Sch., Malvern, and Abergele, Wales; Westfield Coll., London (BA Hons French 1953); St Hugh's Coll., Oxford (MA Theol. 1972); St Michael's House, Oxford (IDC 1966). Teacher, St Hilda's Sch., Jamaica, 1953–60; Travelling Sec., Inter-Varsity Fellowship and Technical Colls Christian Fellowship, 1960–63; Accredited Lay Worker, St Andrew's Church, N Oxford, 1967–69; Tutor, St John's Coll., Durham, 1969–74; Deaconess (C of E), 1972; Selection Sec., ACCM, 1974–83; Organiser, Internat. Diakonia Conf., Coventry, 1983; Diocesan Dir of Ordinands, Worcester, 1984–92; ordained Deacon, 1987, priest 1994; Parish Deacon, St John-in-Bedwardine, 1984–94. Mem., Bishop's Staff Meeting, Worcs, 1993–. Hon. Canon, Worcester Cathedral, 1987. Member: Church Army Bd, 1985–; Crown Appointments Commn, 1990–; Gen. Synod of C of E, 1990–. Mem. Council, Malvern Coll., 1991–. Chm., Li Tim-Oi Foundn, 1993–. *Recreations:* reading, driving, ornithology. *Address:* 72 Henwick Road, Worcester WR2 5NT. *T:* Worcester (01905) 422841.

WINTON, Alexander, CBE 1993; QFSM 1987; HM Chief Inspector of Fire Services for Scotland, 1990–93; *b* 13 July 1932; *s* of Alexander and Jean Winton; *m* 1957, Jean Dowie; two *s*. MIFireE. Fireman, Perth, 1958–64; Station Officer: Perth, 1964–67; Lancashire, 1967–69; Assistant Divisional Officer: E Riding, 1969–72; Angus, 1972–73; Divisional Officer III: Angus, 1973–75; Tayside, 1975–76; Divl Comdr (DOI), Tayside, 1976–80; Temp. Sen. Divl Officer, 1980–81; Dep. Firemaster, 1981–85; Firemaster, Tayside Fire Bde, 1985–89. *Recreations:* golf, curling, reading. *Address:* 5 Ferndale Drive, Broughty Ferry, Dundee DD5 3DB. *T:* Dundee (01382) 778156.

WINTON, Walter; Keeper, Department of Electrical Engineering, Telecommunications and Loan Circulation, Science Museum, 1976–80; *b* 15 May 1917; *m* 1942, Dorothy Rickard; two *s* one *d*. *Educ:* Glossop Grammar Sch.; Manchester Univ. (BSc and Teacher's Diploma). Royal Ordnance Factories, Chemist, 1940–45. Taught Science, Harrow County and Greenford, 1945–50; Assistant and Deputy Keeper, Science Museum, 1950–67, Keeper. Dept of Loan Circulation, Mining and Marine Technol., 1968–73; Dept of Museum Services, 1973; Dept of Mechanical and Civil Engrg and Loan Circulation, 1973–76. *Publications:* contrib. to journals. *Recreations:* Scottish dancing, sailing, fell-walking. *Address:* Lantern Lodge, Village Road, Denham, Bucks UB9 5BN. *T:* Denham (01895) 832692.

WINTOUR, Anna, (Mrs David Shaffer); Editor, US Vogue, since 1988; *b* 3 Nov. 1949; *d* of Charles Wintour, *qv*; *m* 1984, Dr David Shaffer; one *s* one *d*. *Educ:* Queen's College Sch., London; North London Collegiate Sch. Dep. Fashion Editor, Harpers and Queen Magazine, 1970–76; Fashion Editor, Harpers Bazaar, NY, 1976–77; Fashion and Beauty Editor, Viva Mag., 1977–78; Contributing Editor for Fashion and Style, Savvy Mag., 1980–81; Sen. Editor, New York Mag., NY, 1981–83; Creative Dir, US Vogue, 1983–86; Editor-in-Chief, Vogue, 1986–87; Editor, House and Garden, New York, 1987–88. *Address:* Condé Nast Publications Inc., 632 Broadway, New York, NY 10012, USA.

WINTOUR, Audrey Cecelia; *see* Slaughter, A. C.

WINTOUR, Charles Vere, CBE 1978 (MBE (mil.) 1945); journalist; *b* 18 May 1917; *s* of late Maj.-Gen. F. Wintour, CB, CBE; *m* 1st, 1940, Eleanor Trego Baker (marr. diss. 1979), *er d* of Prof. R. J. Baker, Harvard Univ.; two *s* two *d* (and one *s* decd); 2nd 1979, Mrs Audrey Slaughter, *qv*. *Educ:* Oundle Sch.; Peterhouse, Cambridge. BA 1939; MA 1946. Royal Norfolk Regt, 1940; GSO2 Headquarters of Chief of Staff to the Supreme Allied Commander (Designate) and SHAEF, 1943–45 (despatches). Joined Evening Standard, 1946: Dep. Editor, 1954–57; Editor, 1959–76 and 1978–80; Managing Dir, 1978–79; Chm., 1968–80; Asst Editor, Sunday Express, 1952–54; Managing Editor, Daily Express, 1957–59, Managing Dir, 1977–78; Editor: Sunday Express Magazine, 1981–82; UK Press Gazette, 1985–86; Editorial Consultant, London Daily News, 1986–87; Ombudsman, Sunday Times, 1990–95. Director: Evening Standard Co. Ltd, 1959–82; Express (formerly Beaverbrook) Newspapers Ltd, 1964–82; TV-am (News) Ltd, 1982–84; Wintour Publications, 1984–85. Mem., Press Council, 1979–81; Pres., Media Soc., 1989–91. Wilts Rep., NACF, 1995–. Croix de Guerre (France) 1945; Bronze Star (US) 1945. *Publications:* Pressures on the Press, 1972; The Rise and Fall of Fleet Street, 1989. *Recreations:* theatre-going, reading newspapers. *Address:* 60 East Hatch, Tisbury, Wilts SP3 6PH. *T:* Tisbury (01747) 870880. *Club:* Garrick.

See also A. Wintour.

WINYARD, Dr Graham Peter Arthur, FRCP; FFPHM; Deputy Chief Medical Officer, Medical Director NHS Management Executive, since 1993; *b* 19 Jan. 1947; *s* of Lyonel Arthur Winyard and Dorothy Elizabeth Payne; *m* 1979, Sandra Catherine Bent; one *s* two *d*. *Educ:* Southend High Sch.; Hertford Coll., Oxford (MA); Middlesex Hosp. (BM, BCh). Ho. Phys., Middlesex Hosp., Ho. Surg., Ipswich Hosp., 1972; Sen. House Officer, United Oxford Hosps, 1973–75; Registrar in Community Medicine, 1975–77; Provincial Health

Officer, Madang, PNG, 1977–79; Sen. Registrar in Community Medicine, Oxford RHA, and Lectr, LSHTM, 1979–82; Dist MO, Lewisham and N Southwark HA, 1982–87; SPMO, DHSS, later Dept of Health, 1987–90; Regl Med. Dir and Dir of Public Health, Wessex RHA, 1990–93. *Publications:* various on med. care in med. jls. *Recreations:* gardening, DIY, music.

WISBECH, Archdeacon of; *see* Rone, Ven. J.

WISDOM, Norman, OBE 1995; actor/comedian; *b* 4 Feb. 1915. Has starred regularly on stage and screen, since 1952. First film Trouble in Store, in 1953 (winning an Academy Award) since which has starred in 19 major films in both England and America; two Broadway awards for stage musical, Walking Happy; numerous Royal Performances, both film and stage. Freeman: Tirana, Albania, 1995; City of London, 1995. Lifetime Achievement Award for Comedy, British Comedy Awards, 1991. *Publication:* (with William Hall) Don't Laugh at Me, 1992. *Recreations:* all sports. *Address:* c/o Johnny Mans, Johnny Mans Productions Ltd, The Maltings, Brewery Road, Hoddesdon, Herts EN11 8HF.

WISE, family name of **Baron Wise.**

WISE, 2nd Baron, *cr* 1951, of King's Lynn; **John Clayton Wise;** farmer; *b* 11 June 1923; *s* of 1st Baron Wise and of Kate Elizabeth (*d* 1987), *e d* of late John Michael Sturgeon; *S* father, 1968; *m* 1st, 1946, Margaret Annie (marr. diss. 1986), *d* of Frederick Victor Snead, Banbury; two *s*; 2nd, 1993, Janice Harman Thompson. *Heir: s* Hon. Christopher John Clayton Wise, PhD, BSc Hons [*b* 19 March 1949. *Educ:* Norwich School; Univ. of Southampton. Plant Scientist].

WISE, Mrs Audrey; MP (Lab) Preston, since 1987; *d* of George and Elsie Crawford Brown; *m* John Wise; one *s* one *d*. Shorthand typist. MP (Lab) Coventry South West, Feb. 1974–1979. Contested (Lab) Woolwich, 1983. Mem., Labour Party NEC, 1982–87. Pres., USDAW, 1991–. *Publications:* Women and the Struggle for Workers' Control, 1973; Eyewitness in Revolutionary Portugal, 1975. *Recreations:* family life, gardening. *Address:* House of Commons, SW1A 0AA.

WISE, Derek; *see* Wise, R. D.

WISE, Prof. Douglass, OBE 1980; FRIBA; Principal, Douglass Wise & Partners, Architects, since 1959; Director, Institute of Advanced Architectural Studies, University of York, 1975–92; *b* 6 Nov. 1927; *s* of Horace Watson Wise and Doris Wise; *m* 1958, Yvonne Jeannine Czeiler; one *s* one *d*. *Educ:* King's Coll., Newcastle, Durham Univ. (BArch; DipTP). Lecturer in Architecture, 1959–65, Prof. of Architecture, 1965–69, Head of Dept of Architecture, 1969–75, Newcastle Univ. RIBA: Chm., Moderators, 1969–75; Chm., Examinations Cttee, 1969–75; Mem. Council, 1976–79; Chm., Heads of Schools Cttee, 1971–73; Mem. Bd of Management, North Eastern Housing Assoc., 1967–76 (Vice-Chm., 1974–76); Mem. Council, Newcastle Polytechnic, 1974–77; past Mem. Council, Senate and Court, Newcastle Univ.; Governor, Building Centre Trust, London, 1976–92; Chairman: NE Civic Trust, 1993–; Northern Regl Centre for the Built Envmt, 1994–. Hon. LittD Sheffield, 1992. *Publications:* contribs to various technical jls on housing, continuing educn and architectural theory. *Recreations:* painting, natural history. *Address:* Welburn, Kirkwhelpington, Newcastle upon Tyne NE19 2SA. *T:* Otterburn (01830) 540219.

WISE, Ernie; *see* Wiseman, Ernest.

WISE, Prof. Michael John, CBE 1979; MC 1945; PhD; FRGS; Emeritus Professor of Geography, University of London; *b* Stafford, 17 August 1918; *s* of Harry Cuthbert and Sarah Evelyn Wise; *m* 1942, Barbara Mary, *d* of C. L. Hodgetts, Wolverhampton; one *d* one *s*. *Educ:* Saltley Grammar School, Birmingham; University of Birmingham. BA (Hons Geography) Birmingham, and Mercator Prize in Geography, 1939; PhD Birmingham, 1951. Served War, Royal Artillery, 80th LAA Regt, 1941–44, 5th Bn The Northamptonshire Regt, 1944–46, in Middle East and Italy; commissioned, 1941, Major, 1944. Assistant Lecturer, Univ. of Birmingham, 1946–48, Lecturer in Geography, 1948–51; London School of Economics: Lecturer in Geography, 1951–54; Sir Ernest Cassel Reader in Economic Geography, 1954–58; Prof. of Geography, 1958–83; Pro-Director, 1983–85; Hon. Fellow, 1988. Chm., Departmental Cttee of Inquiry into Statutory Smallholdings, 1963–67; Mem., Dept of Transport Adv. Cttee on Landscape Treatment of Trunk Roads, 1971–90 (Chm., 1981–90). Mem., UGC for Hong Kong, 1966–73. Recorder, Sect. E, Brit. Assoc. for Advancement of Science, 1955–60 (Pres., 1965); President: Inst. of British Geographers, 1974 (Hon. Mem., 1989); IGU, 1976–80 (Vice-Pres., 1968–76); Geographical Assoc., 1976–77 (Hon. Treasurer, 1967–76, Hon. Mem., 1983); Vice-Pres., Nat. Assoc. for Envmtl Educn, 1977–; Mem., SSRC, 1976–82; Chm., Council for Extra-Mural Studies, Univ. of London, 1976–83; Chm., Exec. Cttee, Assoc. of Agriculture, 1972–83 (Vice-Pres., 1983–); Mem. Adv. Cttees, UN Univ., 1976–82; Hon. Sec., RGS, 1963–73, Vice-Pres., 1975–78, Hon. Vice-Pres., 1978–80, 1983–, Pres., 1980–82. Chm., Birkbeck Coll., 1983–89 (Governor, 1968–89; Fellow, 1989); Mem. Delegacy, Goldsmiths' Coll., 1984–88. Chm., Dudley Stamp Meml Trust, 1988– (Hon. Sec., 1966–88). Erskine Fellow, Univ. of Canterbury, NZ, 1970. Hon. Life Mem., Univ. of London Union, 1977. Hon. Member: Geog. Soc. of Russia, 1975; Assoc. of Japanese Geographers, 1980; Geog. Soc. of Mexico, 1984; Geog. Soc. of Poland, 1986; Membre d'Honneur, Société de Géographie, 1983. FRSA. Hon. FLI 1991. DUniv Open, 1978; Hon. DSc Birmingham, 1982. Received Gill Memorial award of RGS, 1958; RGS Founder's Medal, 1977; Alexander Körösi Csoma Medal, Hungarian Geographical Soc., 1980; Tokyo Geographical Soc. Medal, 1981; Lauréat d'Honneur, IGU, 1984. *Publications:* Hon. Editor, Birmingham and its Regional Setting, 1951; A Pictorial Geography of the West Midlands, 1958; General Consultant, An Atlas of Earth Resources, 1979; General Consultant, The Great Geographical Atlas, 1982; (consultant and contrib.) The Ordnance Survey Atlas of Great Britain, 1982; numerous articles on economic and urban geography. *Recreations:* music, gardening. *Address:* 45 Oakleigh Avenue, N20 9JE. *T:* 0181–445 6057. *Clubs:* Athenæum, Geographical.

WISE, Peter Anthony Surtees, MBE 1993; Director, Wise Consultancy Ltd; *b* 26 June 1934; *s* of late J. A. S. (Tony) Wise and Lenore Dugdale; *m* 1956, Elizabeth Muirhead Odhams; two *s*. *Educ:* Royal Naval College, Dartmouth. Served Royal Navy, 1948–56 (invalided). Marconi Instruments Ltd, 1956–60; Vickers Ltd, 1961–74; First Secretary, later Counsellor (Hong Kong Affairs), UK Mission, Geneva, 1974–78; Head of Commercial Div. (formerly Asst Comr (Commercial)), Hong Kong Govt Office, London, 1978–93; also Rep. for Commercial Relns with Austria and the Nordic Countries, 1980–93 (formerly non-resident Counsellor (HK Trade Affairs), Helsinki, Oslo, Stockholm, Vienna). *Address:* Field House, Westbrook, Berks RG16 8DN. *T:* Boxford (01488) 608302. *Club:* Hong Kong (Hong Kong).

WISE, Very Rev. Randolph George, VRD 1964; Dean of Peterborough, 1981–92; *b* 20 Jan. 1925; *s* of George and Agnes Lucy Wise; *m* 1951, Hazel Hebe Simpson; four *d*. *Educ:* St Olave's and St Saviour's Grammar School; Queen's Coll., Oxford (MA); Lincoln Theological Coll.; Ealing Technical Coll. (DMS). Served RNVR, 1943–47. Assistant Curate: Lady Margaret, Walworth, 1951–53; Stocksbridge, Sheffield, 1953–55; Vicar of Lady Margaret, Walworth, 1955–60; Vicar of Stocksbridge, 1960–66; Bishop of London's Industrial Chaplaincy, 1966–76; Guild Vicar, St Botolph, Aldersgate, 1972–76; Rector of Notting Hill, 1976–81. Member of Plaisterers' Company. *Recreations:* music, sculling. *Address:* 2 Derwent Drive, Oakham, Leics LE15 6SA. *T:* Oakham (01572) 756263. *Club:* Naval.

WISE, (Reginald) Derek, CBE 1977; Partner, Wise & Mercer, Paris, since 1983; *b* 29 July 1917; *s* of Reginald and Rita Wise; *m* 1957, Nancy Brenta Scialoya; two *s* one *d*. *Educ:* St Paul's Sch. Admitted solicitor, 1947. Served War of 1939–45, RA and Intell. Partner, Theodore Goddard, Paris, 1957–82. Legal Adviser, British Embassy, Paris, 1962–. *Address:* 203 bis Boulevard St Germain, 75007 Paris, France. *T:* 42220794. *Club:* Travellers' (Paris).

WISEMAN, Prof. Donald John, OBE 1943; DLit; FBA 1966; FSA; Professor of Assyriology in the University of London, 1961–82, Emeritus 1982; *b* 25 Oct. 1918; *s* of Air Cdre Percy John Wiseman, CBE, RAF; *m* 1948, Mary Catherine, *d* of P. O. Ruoff; three *d*. *Educ:* Dulwich College; King's College, London. BA (London); AKC, McCaul Hebrew Prize, 1939; FKC 1982. Served War of 1939–45, in RAFVR. Ops, 11 Fighter Group, 1939–41; Chief Intelligence Officer, Mediterranean Allied Tactical Air Forces with Rank of Group Capt., 1942–45. Heap Exhibitioner in Oriental Languages, Wadham Coll., Oxford, 1945–47; MA 1949. Asst Keeper, Dept of Egyptian and Assyrian, later Western Asiatic, Antiquities, British Museum, 1948–61. Epigraphist on archæological excavations at Nimrud, Harran, Rimah; Jt Dir of British School of Archæology in Iraq, 1961–65, Chm. 1970–88, Vice-Pres., 1988–93, Pres., 1993–. Trustee, British Sch. of Archaeology in Jerusalem, 1984–. Pres., Soc. for Old Testament Studies, 1980; Chm., Tyndale House for Biblical Research, Cambridge, 1957–86. Corresp. Mem., German Archæological Inst., 1961. Editor, Journal IRAQ, 1953–78; Joint Editor, Reallexion der Assyriologie, 1959–83. Bronze Star (USA), 1944. *Publications:* The Alalakh Tablets, 1953; Chronicles of Chaldaean Kings, 1956; Cuneiform Texts from Cappadocian Tablets in the British Museum, V, 1956; Cylinder-Seals of Western Asia, 1958; Vassal-Treaties of Esarhaddon, 1958; Illustrations from Biblical Archæology, 1958; Catalogue of Western Asiatic Seals in the British Museum, 1963; Peoples of Old Testament Times, 1973; Archaeology and the Bible, 1979; Essays on the Patriarchal Narratives, 1980; Nebuchadrezzar and Babylon, 1985; I and II Kings (commentary), 1993; contrib. to journals. *Address:* Low Barn, 26 Downs Way, Tadworth, Surrey KT20 5DZ. *T:* Tadworth (01737) 813536.

WISEMAN, Ernest, (Ernie Wise), OBE 1976; *b* 27 Nov. 1925; *s* of Harry and Connie Wiseman; *m* 1953, Doreen Blyth. *Educ:* Council School. Career in show business: radio, variety, TV, films. First double act (with E. Morecambe), at Empire Theatre, Liverpool, 1941; first radio broadcast, 1943; *television:* BBC and ITV series, 1955–84 (SFTA Best Light Entertainment Award, 1973); series sold to Time Life, USA, 1980; Morecambe and Wise Tribute Show, Bring Me Sunshine, 1984; The Best of Morecambe and Wise, BBC, 1984; What's My Line, 1985; Too Close for Comfort, 1985; Los Angilla's, 1985; The Importance of Being Ernie, 1993; *stage:* The Mystery of Edwin Drood, Savoy, 1987; Run for Your Wife, Criterion, 1988; Sleeping Beauty, Theatre Royal, Windsor, 1992; *films:* The Intelligence Men, 1964; That Riviera Touch, 1965; The Magnificent Two, 1966; (for TV) Night Train to Murder, 1983. *Awards:* BAFTA (formerly SFTA), 1963, 1971, 1972, 1973, 1977; Silver Heart, 1964; Water Rats, 1970; Radio Industries, 1971, 1972; Sun Newspaper, 1973; Sun, 1974; Water Rats Distinguished Services, 1974; TV Times Hall of Fame Award, 1980–81; Commendation, 1981, Special Mention, 1982, HM Queen Mother's Award, Keep Britain Tidy; Best Dressed Man Award, 1983; Variety Club of GB award for work for deprived children, 1983; TV Times Award, 1985. Telethon for Children's Charity, NZ, 1985. Freeman, City of London, 1976. *Publications:* (with E. Morecambe): Eric and Ernie: an autobiography of Morecambe and Wise, 1973; Scripts of Morecambe and Wise, 1974; Morecambe and Wise Special, 1977; There's No Answer to That, 1981; Still on My Way to Hollywood (autobiog.), 1990. *Recreations:* boating, tennis, swimming, jogging. *Address:* c/o Ian Kennedy, 19 Denmark Street, WC2H 8NA.

WISEMAN, Sir John William, 11th Bt, *cr* 1628; *b* 16 March 1957; *o s* of Sir William George Eden Wiseman, 10th Bt, and Joan Mary, *d* of late Arthur Phelps, Harrow; *S* father, 1962; *m* 1980, Nancy, *d* of Casimer Zyla, New Britain, Conn; two *d*. *Educ:* Millfield Sch.; Univ. of Hartford, Conn, USA. *Heir: kinsman* Thomas Alan Wiseman [*b* 8 July 1921; *m* 1946, Hildemarie Domnik (*d* 1991); (one *s* one *d* decd)]. *Address:* 395 North Road, Sudbury, MA 01776, USA.

WISEMAN, Prof. Timothy Peter, DPhil; FSA; FBA 1986; Professor of Classics, University of Exeter, since 1977; *b* 3 Feb. 1940; *s* of Stephen Wiseman and Winifred Agnes Wiseman (*née* Rigby); *m* 1962, Doreen Anne Williams. *Educ:* Manchester Grammar Sch.; Balliol Coll., Oxford (MA 1964; DPhil 1967). FSA 1977. Rome Schol. in Classical Studies, British Sch. at Rome, 1962–63; University of Leicester: Asst Lectr in Classics, 1963–65; Lectr, 1965–73; Reader in Roman History, 1973–76. Vice-Pres., British Acad., 1992–94; Pres., Roman Soc., 1992–95. Vis. Associate Prof., Univ. of Toronto, 1970–71; Lansdowne Lectr, Univ. of Victoria (BC), 1987; Whitney J. Oates Fellow, Princeton, 1988; Webster Lectr, Stanford, 1993. Hon. DLitt Durham, 1988. *Publications:* Catullan Questions, 1969; New Men in the Roman Senate, 1971; Cinna the Poet, 1974; Clio's Cosmetics, 1979; (with Anne Wiseman) Julius Caesar: The Battle for Gaul, 1980; (ed) Roman Political Life, 1985; Catullus and his World, 1985; Roman Studies Literary and Historical, 1987; trans., Flavius Josephus, Death of an Emperor, 1991; Talking to Virgil, 1992; Historiography and Imagination, 1994; Remus: a Roman myth, 1995. *Address:* Classics Department, The University, Exeter EX4 4QH. *T:* Exeter (01392) 264201.

WISHART, Maureen; *see* Lehane, M.

WISTRICH, Enid Barbara, PhD; Reader in Politics and Public Administration, Middlesex University (formerly Middlesex Polytechnic), since 1991 (Principal Lecturer, 1979–91); *b* 4 Sept. 1928; *d* of Zadik Heiber and Bertha Brown; *m* 1950, Ernest Wistrich, *qv*; two *c* (and one *c* decd). *Educ:* Froebel Institute Sch.; Brackley High Sch.; St Paul's Girls' Sch.; London School of Economics (BScEcon, PhD). Research Asst, LSE, 1950–52; Instructor, Mt Holyoke Coll., Mass, USA, 1952–53; Research Officer, Royal Inst. of Public Administration, 1954–56; Sen. Res. Officer, LSE, 1969–72; NEDO, 1977–79. Vis. Lectr, Univ. of Waikato, NZ, 1989. Councillor (Lab): Hampstead Metropolitan Bor. Council, 1962–65; London Bor. of Camden, 1964–68 and 1971–74; GLC, ILEA, 1973–77. Mem., Hampstead Community Health Council, 1984–92 (Chm., 1986–88). Governor: British Film Inst., 1974–81 (also Actg Chm., 1977–78); National Film Sch., 1978–82. Chm. of Governors, Heathlands Sch. for Autistic Children, 1976–86. *Publications:* Local Government Reorganisation: the first years of Camden, 1972; I Don't Mind the Sex, It's the Violence: film censorship explored, 1978; The Politics of Transport, 1983; articles in various jls. *Recreations:* experiencing the arts, admiring nature, fussing round the family. *Address:* 37B Gayton Road, NW3 1UB. *T:* 0171–435 8796.

WISTRICH, Ernest, CBE 1973; Director, European Movement (British Council), 1969–86; *b* 22 May 1923; *s* of Dr Arthur and Mrs Eva Wistrich; *m* 1950, Enid Barbara (*née*

Heiber), *qv*; two *c* (and one *c* decd). *Educ:* Poland; University Tutorial Coll., London. Served in RAF, 1942–46; Timber Merchant, 1946–67; Dir, Britain in Europe, 1967–69; Councillor, Hampstead Borough Council, 1959–65; Camden Borough Council, Alderman 1964–71, Councillor 1971–74; Chm., Camden Cttee for Community Relations, 1964–68; Mem., Skeffington Cttee on Public Participation in Planning, 1968–69. Contested (Lab): Isle of Thanet, 1964; Hendon North, 1966; Cleveland, 1979; contested (SDP) London Central, 1984, European Parly elections. Editor of various jls, incl. The European, 1986–88. *Publications:* After 1992, 1989; The United States of Europe, 1994; contrib. Into Europe, Facts, New Europe and other jls. *Recreations:* music, walking. *Address:* 37B Gayton Road, NW3 1UB. *T:* 0171–435 8796.

WITHALL, Maj.-Gen. William Nigel James, CB 1982; Marketing Director, and Member, Board of Directors, Link-Miles Ltd, 1985–93 (Consultant, 1984); *b* 14 Oct. 1928; *s* of late Bernard Withall and Enid (*née* Hill); *m* 1952, Pamela Hickman; one *s* one *d*. *Educ:* St Benedict's; Birmingham Univ. (Civil Engrg degree). Commnd RE, 1950; served in Hong Kong, Gulf States, Aden, Germany and India; Staff Coll., 1961; Sqdn Comd, 73 Fd Sqdn, 1964–66; Jt Services Staff Coll., Latimer, 1967; Mil. Asst to MGO, 1968–70; CO 26 Engr Regt, BAOR, 1970–72; Bde Comd, 11 Engr Bde, 1974–76; NDC, India, 1977; No 259 Army Pilots Course, 1978; Dir, Army Air Corps, 1979–83. Col Comdt RE, 1984–. Chm., Army Football Assoc., 1980–81; Pres., Army Cricket Assoc., 1981–83; Hon. Life Vice Pres., Aircrew Assoc., 1986; Chm., RE Assoc., 1993–. Freeman, City of London, 1981; Liveryman, GAPAN, 1981. *Recreations:* cricket, squash, all games, reading, walking. *Address:* c/o Barclays Bank, High Street, Andover, Hants SP10 1LN. *Clubs:* City Livery, MCC.

WITHERINGTON, Giles Somerville Gwynne; Member of Assembly, Save the Children Fund, since 1991 (Member of Council, 1980–91; Chairman, 1982–87); *b* 7 June 1919; *s* of Iltid Gwynne Witherington and Alice Isabel Gage Spicer; *m* 1951, Rowena Ann Spencer Lynch; one *s* three *d*. *Educ:* Charterhouse; University Coll., Oxford (MA). War Service, Royal Artillery, UK, N Africa, Italy, 1939–46 (despatches). Joined Spicers Ltd, 1946, Jt Managing Director, 1960; joined Reed International Ltd: Director, 1963; Dep. Chm., 1976; retired, 1982. Mem. Council, Textile Conservation Centre, 1984–92 (Chm. of Trustees of the Friends, 1984–91). Hon. LLD Birmingham, 1983. *Recreations:* shooting, gardening, modern art, travel. *Address:* Bishops, Widdington, Saffron Walden, Essex CB11 3SQ; Flat 2, 11 Netherton Grove, SW10 9TQ. *Club:* Arts.

WITHEROW, David Michael Lindley; Policy Consultant, BBC World Service, since 1994; Project Director, BBC DAB Services, since 1994; freelance writer; *b* 19 July 1937; *s* of Dr James Witherow and Greta (*née* Roberts); *m* 1st, 1960, Ragnhild Kadow (marr. diss. 1994); two *d*; 2nd, 1994, Elizabeth Anne Wright. *Educ:* King Edward's Sch., Birmingham (Foundn Schol.); Pembroke Coll., Cambridge (BA Hons 1960). Nat. service, RCS, 1955–57. Press Assoc., 1960–63; BBC, 1963–94: Ext. Services News, 1963–77, Editor, 1973–77; Editor, Weekly Progs, TV News, 1977–79; Chief Assistant, Regions, 1980; Head, then Gen. Manager, Monitoring Service, Caversham, 1980–85; Controller, Resources and Admin, Ext. Services, 1985–89; Dep. Man. Dir, BBC World Service, 1989–94. FRSA 1992. *Recreations:* travel, music, crime fiction. *Address:* 115 Mercers Road, N19 4PY.

WITHEROW, John Moore; Editor, The Sunday Times, since 1995; *b* Johannesburg, 20 Jan. 1952; *s* of Cecil and Millicent Witherow; *m* 1985, Sarah Jane Linton; two *s*. *Educ:* Bedford Sch.; York Univ. (BA Hons Hist.). Reuters trainee, London and Madrid, 1977–80; home and foreign corresp., The Times, 1980–83; Sunday Times: Defence corresp., 1984–85; Diplomatic Corresp., 1985–87; Focus Ed., 1987–89; Foreign Ed., 1989–92; Man. Ed. (News), 1992–94; Actg Ed., 1994. *Publications:* (with Patrick Bishop) The Winter War: the Falklands, 1982; The Gulf War, 1993. *Recreations:* ski-ing, sailing. *Address:* The Sunday Times, 1 Pennington Street, E1 9XW. *T:* 0171–782 5640. *Club:* Royal Automobile.

WITHERS, Googie, (Mrs John McCallum), AO 1980; Actress since 1932; *b* Karachi, India, 12 March 1917; *d* of late Captain E. C. Withers, CBE, CIE, RIM, and late Lizette Catherine Wilhelmina van Wageningen; *m* 1948, John Neil McCallum, *qv*; one *s* two *d*. *Educ:* Fredville Park, Nonnington, Kent; Convent of the Holy Family, Kensington. Started as dancer in Musical Comedy. First film contract at age of 17; has acted in over 50 pictures, starring in 30. *Films include:* One of our Aircraft is Missing; The Silver Fleet; On Approval; Loves of Joanna Godden; It Always Rains on Sunday; White Corridors; Nickel Queen; Country Life, 1994. *Plays include:* They Came to a City; Private Lives; Winter Journey; The Deep Blue Sea; Waiting for Gillian; Janus; Stratford on Avon Season, 1958: Beatrice in Much Ado About Nothing; Gertrude in Hamlet; The Complaisant Lover, New York, 1962; Exit the King, London, 1963; Getting Married, Strand, 1967; Madame Renevsky in The Cherry Orchard, Mrs Cheveley in An Ideal Husband, 1972; Lady Kitty in The Circle, Chichester Festival Theatre, 1976, Haymarket, 1977 (nominated for SWET best actress award), Toronto, 1978; Lady Bracknell in The Importance of Being Earnest, Chichester, 1979; Time and the Conways, Chichester, 1983; Lady Sneerwell in The School for Scandal, Duke of York's, 1984 (also European tour); The Chalk Garden, Chichester, 1986; Hay Fever, Ring Round the Moon, Chichester, 1988. Tours: Roar Like a Dove, The Constant Wife and Woman in a Dressing Gown, Australia and NZ, 1959; excerpts Shakespeare (Kate, Margaret of Anjou, Beatrice, Portia, Rosalind, Cleopatra), 1964; Beekman Place, Australia and NZ, 1965; Relatively Speaking, Australia, 1968; Plaza Suite, Australia and NZ, 1969–70; The Kingfisher, Australia, NZ and Far East, 1978–80, FE, ME and Gulf, 1987; The Cherry Orchard, The Skin Game, Dandy Dick, UK, 1981; Stardust, UK and Australia, 1984–85; The Cocktail Hour, Australia and UK, 1989–90; High Spirits, Australia, 1991, 1993; On Golden Pond, UK, 1992; The Chalk Garden, Australia, 1995. *Television* appearances in drama including The Public Prosecutor; Amphitryon 38; The Deep Blue Sea (Best Actress, 1954); Last Year's Confetti, Court Circular, 1971; Knightsbridge, 1972; The Cherry Orchard, 1973; series Within These Walls, 1974–76 (Best Actress of the Year, 1974); Time after Time (TV film), 1985 (Best Actress ACE Award, USA, 1988); Hotel du Lac (TV film), 1985; Northanger Abbey (TV film), 1986; Ending Up, 1989. *Recreations:* music, travel, reading, interior decorating. *Address:* 1740 Pittwater Road, Bay View, NSW 2104, Australia; c/o Coutts & Co., 440 Strand, WC2R 0QS.

WITHERS, John Keppel Ingold D.; *see* Douglas-Withers.

WITHERS, Rt. Hon. Reginald (Greive), PC 1977; Senator (L) for Western Australia, 1966–87; Lord Mayor of Perth, Western Australia, 1991–93; *b* 26 Oct. 1924; *s* of late F. J. Withers and I. L. Greive; *m* 1953, Shirley Lloyd-Jones; two *s* one *d*. *Educ:* Bunbury; Univ. of WA (LLB). Barrister-at-law 1953. Served War, RAN, 1942–46. Councillor, Bunbury Municipal Council, 1954–56; Mem., Bunbury Diocesan Council, 1958–59, Treasurer, 1961–68. State Vice-Pres., Liberal and Country League of WA, 1958–61, State Pres., 1961–65; Mem., Federal Exec. of Liberal Party, 1961–65; Fed. Vice-Pres., Liberal Party, 1962–65. Govt Whip in Senate, 1969–71; Leader of Opposition in Senate, 1972–75; Special Minister of State, Minister for Capital Territory, Minister for Media, and Minister for Tourism and Recreation, Nov.-Dec. 1975; Vice-Pres. of Exec. Council, Leader of Govt in Senate, and Minister for Admin. Services, 1975–78. Sec., SW Law Soc., 1955–68. *Recreations:* swimming, reading, painting. *Address:* 23 Malcolm Street, West Perth, WA 6005, Australia. *T:* (9) 3241322, *Fax:* (9) 3241426.

WITHERS, Roy Joseph, CBE 1983; FEng 1983; Chairman, Transmark, 1987–95 (Director, 1978–95); *b* 18 June 1924; *s* of Joseph Withers and Irene Ada Withers (*née* Jones); *m* 1947, Pauline M. G. Johnston; four *s*. *Educ:* Tiffin School, Kingston upon Thames; Trinity College, Cambridge (1st. cl. Hons Mech. Scis Tripos). ICI, 1948–55; Humphreys & Glasgow, 1955–63; Engineering Dir, then Man. Dir, Power-Gas Corp. (subsid. of Davy Corp.), 1963–71; Chief Exec., Davy Powergas International, 1972–73; Man. Dir, Davy Corp., 1973–83; Vice-Chm., Davy Corp, 1983–91. Director: A. Monk & Co., 1983–88; Vosper Thornycroft (Hldgs), 1985– (Chm., 1985–90). Mem., BOTB, 1983–86; Chm., Overseas Projects Board, 1983–86. FIMechE. Hon. FIChemE. *Recreations:* painting, golf, walking. *Address:* Wheelwrights Cottage, Bramshaw, Lyndhurst, Hants SO4 7JB. *T:* Lyndhurst (01703) 812543. *Clubs:* Carlton; Hampstead Golf, Bramshaw Golf.

WITHERS, Rupert Alfred; Director, Dalgety Ltd, 1969–83 (Deputy Chairman and Managing Director, 1969–71; Chairman, 1972–77); *b* 29 Oct. 1913; *o s* of late Herbert Withers, FRAM and Marguerite (*née* Elzy); *m*; three *d*. *Educ:* University College School. Fellow Institute of Chartered Accountants, 1938. Secretary and Chief Accountant, Gloster Aircraft Co. Ltd, 1940–44; a Senior Partner of Urwick Orr & Partners Ltd until 1959; Man. Dir, Ilford Ltd, 1959–64; Chm. and Chief Executive, 1964–68. *Recreations:* music, books, theatre. *Address:* 11K Stuart Tower, Maida Vale, W9 1UH. *T:* 0171–286 8706. *Clubs:* Savile, Buck's.

WITHY, George; retired journalist; Assistant Editor (night), Liverpool Echo, 1972–89; *b* Birkenhead, 15 May 1924; *er s* of George Withy and Alma Elizabeth Withy (*née* Stankley); *m* 1950, Dorothy Betty, *e c* of Bertram Allen and Dorothy Gray, Northfield, Birmingham; two *d*. *Educ:* Birkenhead Park High Sch. Served War, Royal Artillery, Britain and NW Europe, 1942–47. Trainee and Reporter, Birkenhead News, 1940; Chief Reporter, Redditch Indicator, 1948; District Reporter, Birmingham Post and Mail, 1950; Editor, Redditch Indicator, 1952. Joined Liverpool Daily Post 1960: successively Sub-Editor, Dep. Chief Sub-Editor, Asst News Editor, Chief Sub-Editor. Chief Sub-Editor, Liverpool Echo, 1970. Inst. of Journalists, 1962: successively Sec. and Chm., Liverpool District; Convenor, NW Region; Chm., Salaries and Conditions Bd, 1973–89; Vice-Pres. and then Pres., 1975; Fellow 1975. Chm., Nat. Council for the Trng of Journalists, 1974, 1982 (Mem., 1970; Vice-Chm., 1973, 1981; Chm., North-West Adv. Trng Cttee, 1974–76, 1983–85); Mem., Newspaper Trng Cttee, Printing and Publishing Industry Trng Bd; Mem., Press Council, 1973–79. *Recreations:* gardening, reading, philately. *Address:* 3 Woodside Road, Irby, Wirral, Merseyside L61 4UL. *T:* 0151–648 2809.

WITNEY, Kenneth Percy, CVO; *b* 19 March 1916; *s* of late Rev. Thomas and of Dr Myfanwy Witney, S India; *m* 1947, Joan Tait; one *s* one *d*. *Educ:* Eltham Coll.; Wadham Coll., Oxford (Schol.; BA Hons Mod. History, 1938; MA 1975); Univ. of Kent (DipArch 1990). Min. of Home Security, 1940; Private Sec. to Parly Under-Sec., 1942–44; Home Office, 1945; Asst Private Sec. to Home Sec., 1945–47; Colonial Office (Police Div.), 1955–57; Asst Sec., Home Office, 1957; Asst Under-Sec. of State, Home Office, 1969–76. Special Consultant to Royal Commn on Gambling, 1976–78. Chm., Kent Fedn of Amenity Socs, 1982–85. *Publications:* The Jutish Forest, 1976; The Kingdom of Kent, 1982; contribs to Econ. Hist. Rev., Archaeologia Cantiana, Agricl Hist. Rev. *Recreations:* local history, gardening. *Address:* 1 Loampits Close, Tonbridge, Kent TN9 1PX. *T:* Tonbridge (01732) 352971.

WITT, Rt. Rev. Howell Arthur John; Bishop of Bathurst, 1981–89; *b* 12 July 1920; *s* of Thomas Leyshon Witt and Harriet Jane Witt; *m* 1949, Gertrude Doreen Edwards; three *s* two *d*. *Educ:* Newport Sec. Sch.; Leeds Univ.; Coll. of the Resurrection, Mirfield. Deacon 1944; Priest 1945. Asst Curate of: Usk, Mon, 1944–47; St George's, Camberwell, 1948–49; Chaplain, Woomera, S Australia, 1949–54; Rector, St Mary Magdalene's, Adelaide, 1954–57; Priest in charge of Elizabeth, 1957–65; Missioner of St Peter's Coll. Mission, 1954–65; Bishop of North-West Australia, 1965–81. *Publication:* Bush Bishop (autobiography), 1980. *Recreation:* script writing. *Address:* Unit 20, DGV, 99 McCabe Street, Mosman Park, WA 6012, Australia. *Club:* Public Schools (Adelaide).

WITTEVEEN, Dr (Hendrikus) Johannes, Commander, Order of Netherlands Lion, Commander, Order of Orange Nassau; Chairman, Internationale Nederlanden Group, 1991–93 (Mem. Supervisory Board, 1979–90); Board Member: Royal Dutch Petroleum Co., 1971–73 and 1978–89; Robeco, 1971–73 and 1979–91 (Adviser, 1971–73); *b* Zeist, Netherlands, 12 June 1921; *m* 1949, Liesbeth de Vries Feyens; two *s* one *d*. *Educ:* Univ. Rotterdam (DrEcons). Central Planning Bureau, 1947–48; Prof., Univ. Rotterdam, 1948–63; Mem. Netherlands Parlt, First Chamber, 1959–63 and 1971–73, and Second Chamber, 1965–67; Minister of Finance, Netherlands, 1963–65 and 1967–71; First Deputy Prime Minister, 1967–71; Managing Director, IMF, 1973–78. Chm., Group of Thirty, 1979–85, Hon. Chm., 1985–; Member: Internat. Council, Morgan Guaranty Trust Co. of NY, 1978–85; European Adv. Council, General Motors, 1978–91; Bd Mem., Thyssen-Bornemisza NV, 1978–86; Advr for Internat. Affairs, Amro Bank, Amsterdam, 1979–90. Grand Cross, Order of Crown (Belgium); Order of Oak Wreath (Luxemburg); Order of Merit (Fed. Republic Germany). *Publications:* Loonshoogte en Werkgelegenheid, 1947; Growth and Business Cycles, 1954; articles in Economische Statistische Berichten, Euromoney. *Recreation:* hiking. *Address:* 2243 HL Wassenaar, Waldeck Pyrmontlaan 15, The Netherlands.

WITTY, (John) David, CBE 1985; Director, Great Portland Estates PLC, since 1987; *b* 1 Oct. 1924; *s* of late Harold Witty and Olive Witty, Beverley; *m* 1955, Doreen Hanlan; one *s*. *Educ:* Beverley Grammar Sch.; Balliol Coll., Oxford (MA). Served War, RN, 1943–46. Asst Town Clerk, Beverley, 1951–53; Asst Solicitor: Essex CC, 1953–54; Hornsey, 1954–60; Dep. Town Clerk: Kingston upon Thames, 1960–65; Merton, 1965–67; Asst Chief Exec., Westminster, 1967–77, Chief Exec., 1977–84. Hon. Sec., London Boroughs Assoc., 1978–84. Chm., London Enterprise Property Co., 1984–85. Lawyer Mem., London Rent Assessment Panel, 1984–92. Order of Infante D. Henrique (Portugal), 1978; Order of Right Hand (Nepal), 1980; Order of King Abdul Aziz (Saudi Arabia), 1981; Order of Oman, 1982; Order of Orange-Nassau, 1982. *Recreation:* golf. *Address:* 14 River House, 23–24 The Terrace, Barnes, SW13 0NR.

WIX, Ethel Rose; Special Commissioner of Income Tax, 1977–86; *b* 1 Nov. 1921; *d* of Michael Wix and Anna Wix (*née* Snyder). *Educ:* Henrietta Barnett Sch.; Cheltenham Ladies' Coll.; University Coll. London (BA Hons 1942); Hull University Coll. (Cert Ed 1943). Special Operations Executive, 1944–45; lived in S Africa, 1948–54; work for S African Inst. of Race Relations, 1950–54; Africa Bureau, London, 1955–56; Solicitor of Supreme Court, 1960; Partner, Herbert Oppenheimer, Nathan & Vandyk, 1960–75; General Commissioner of Income Tax, 1976–78. Mem., Arbitrators Panel, The Securities and Futures Authy Consumer Arbitration Scheme, 1988–94. Member: Exec. Cttee, Jewish Mus., 1987–93 (Hon. Treas., 1987–89); Exec. Cttee, Inst. of Jewish Affairs, 1990–92; Liby Cttee, Oxford Centre for Postgrad. Hebrew Studies, 1990–94. Mem. Council: Richmond Fellowship, 1975–85; Trinity Hospice, Clapham, 1981–90;

Cheltenham Ladies' Coll., 1983–93 (Vice-Chm., 1990–92); St Christopher's Hospice, 1985–; Clifton Coll., 1987–91; Governor, Warwick Schs Foundn, 1988–90, and 1992– (Vice-Chm., 1994–). *Publications:* papers on Cost of Living, 1951, and Industrial Feeding Facilities, 1953, for S African Inst. of Race Relations; summary of Royal Commn Report on E Africa, 1956, for Africa Bureau. *Recreations:* reading, cooking, theatre. *Address:* 5 Phillimore Gardens, W8 7QG. *T:* 0171–937 8899. *Clubs:* Reform, University Women's, Special Forces.

WODEHOUSE, family name of **Earl of Kimberley.**

WODEHOUSE, Lord; John Armine Wodehouse, CEng; Principal Systems Programmer, Glaxo Wellcome (formerly Glaxo), since 1987 (Systems Programmer, since 1979); *b* 15 Jan. 1951; *s* and *heir* of 4th Earl of Kimberley, *qv*; *m* 1973, Hon. Carol Palmer, (Rev. Lady Wodehouse), MA (Oxon), PGCE, *er d* of 3rd Baron Palmer, OBE; one *s* one *d*. *Educ:* Eton; Univ. of East Anglia. BSc (Chemistry) 1973; MSc (Physical Organic Chemistry) 1974. CEng 1993. FRSA. Research Chemist, Glaxo, 1974–79. Chm., UK Info Users Gp, 1981–83. Fellow, British Interplanetary Soc., 1984 (Associate Fellow, 1981–83). MBCS 1988. *Recreations:* interest in spaceflight, photography, computing, fantasy role playing games. *Heir: s* David Simon John Wodehouse, *b* 10 Oct. 1978. *Address:* Glendalough, Innings Road, Frieth, Henley-on-Thames, Oxon RG9 6NU.

WOGAN, Michael Terence, (Terry); jobbing broadcaster; *b* 3 Aug. 1938; *s* of late Michael Thomas and Rose Wogan; *m* 1965, Helen Joyce; two *s* one *d*. *Educ:* Crescent Coll., Limerick, Ireland; Belvedere Coll., Dublin. Joined RTE as Announcer, 1963, Sen. Announcer, 1964–66; various programmes for BBC Radio, 1965–67; Late Night Extra, BBC Radio, 1967–69; The Terry Wogan Show, BBC Radio One, 1969–72, BBC Radio Two, 1972–84 and 1993–95; television shows include: Lunchtime with Wogan, ATV; BBC: Come Dancing; Song for Europe; The Eurovision Song Contest; Children in Need; Wogan's Guide to the BBC; Blankety-Blank; Wogan; Terry Wogan's Friday Night; Auntie's Bloomers; Do the Right Thing; Auntie's Sporting Bloomers; Wogan's Island; Awards include: Pye Radio Award, 1980; Radio Industries Award (Radio Personality 3 times; TV Personality, 1982, 1984, 1985, 1987); TV Times TV Personality of the Year (10 times); Daily Express Award (twice); Carl Alan Award (3 times); Variety Club of GB: Special Award, 1982; Showbusiness Personality, 1984; Radio Personality of last 21 yrs, Daily Mail Nat. Radio Awards, 1988. *Publications:* Banjaxed, 1979; The Day Job, 1981; To Horse, To Horse, 1982; Wogan on Wogan, 1987; Wogan's Ireland, 1988. *Recreations:* tennis, golf, swimming, reading, writing. *Address:* c/o Jo Gurnett, 2 New Kings Road, SW6 4SA. *Clubs:* Garrick, Lord's Taverners; London Irish Rugby Football; Temple Golf (Henley-on-Thames).

WOGAN, Patrick Francis Michael, CMG 1991; HM Diplomatic Service; Ambassador and Consul-General, Qatar, since 1993. Joined FO, subseq. FCO, 1959; Second Sec., Bahrain, 1970; Second, then First, Sec., FCO, 1972; Brussels, 1976; FCO, 1981; Counsellor, FCO, 1983, Tehran, 1984; RCDS, 1987; Consul-Gen., Karachi, 1988; Ambassador to Iceland, 1991–93. *Address:* c/o Foreign and Commonwealth Office, SW1A 2AH.

WOLEDGE, Brian, FBA 1989; Emeritus Professor of French Language and Literature, University of London; Fielden Professor of French, University College, London, 1939–71; Hon. Research Fellow, University College London; *b* 16 Aug. 1904; *m* 1933, Christine Mary Craven; one *s* one *d*. *Educ:* Leeds Boys' Modern School; University of Leeds. BA (Leeds) 1926; MA (Leeds) 1928; Docteur de l'Université de Paris, 1930; Asst Lecturer in French, University College, Hull, 1930–32; Lecturer in French, University of Aberdeen, 1932–39. Visiting Andrew Mellon Professor of French, University of Pittsburg, 1967. Docteur *hc* de l'Université d'Aix-Marseille, 1970. *Publications:* L'Atre périlleux; études sur les manuscrits, la langue et l'importance littéraire du poème, 1930; L'Atre périlleux, roman de la Table ronde (Les Classiques français du moyen âge 76), 1935; Bibliographie des romans et nouvelles en prose française antérieurs à 1500, 1954, repr. 1975, Supplement 1975; The Penguin Book of French Verse, Vol. 1, To the Fifteenth Century, 1961; Répertoire des premiers textes en prose française, 842–1210 (with H. P. Clive), 1964; La Syntaxe des substantifs chez Chrétien de Troyes, 1979; Commentaire sur Yvain (Le Chevalier au Lion) de Chrétien de Troyes, Vol. 1, 1986, Vol. 2, 1988. *Address:* 28a Dobbins Lane, Wendover, Aylesbury, Bucks HP22 6DH. *T:* Wendover (01296) 622188.

WOLF, Prof. Peter Otto, FEng; FICE; FCIWEM; FRMetS; FASCE; consultant; Director, Pell Frischmann Consulting Engineers Ltd, since 1993; Professor and Head of Department of Civil Engineering, 1966–82, The City University, London, now Professor Emeritus; *b* 9 May 1918; *s* of Richard Wolf and Dora (*née* Bondy); *m* 1st, 1944, Jennie Robinson; two *s* one *d*; 2nd, 1977, Janet Elizabeth Robertson. *Educ:* University of London (BScEng). Assistant under agreement to C. E. Farren, Cons. Engr, 1941–44; Civilian Asst, a Dept of the War Office, 1944–45; Engineer (Chief Designer, Loch Sloy Project), under James Williamson, Cons. Engr, 1945–47; Engineer for Mullardoch Dam (Affric Project), John Cochrane & Sons Ltd, 1947–49; Imperial College of Science and Technology: Lectr in Fluid Mechanics and Hydraulic Engrg, 1949–55; Reader in Hydrology in Univ. of London, 1955–66. Private consultancy, London, 1950–. Chairman: Cttee on Flood Protection Res., MAFF, 1984–85; Standing Cttee on Natural Hazards, Hazards Forum, 1991–94; Mem., UK Co-ordination Cttee, UN Internat. Decade of Natural Disaster Reduction. Visiting Professor: Stanford Univ., Calif, 1959–60, 1961–64; Cornell Univ., 1963. Hon. Member: BHRA, 1984–; British Hydrol Soc., 1994– (Pres., 1987–89). Hon. DrIng Technological Univ. of Dresden, 1986. *Publications:* trans. and ed, Engineering Fluid Mechanics, by Charles Jaeger, 1956; papers in Proc. ICE, Jl IWE, UNESCO Reports, UNESCO Nature and Resources, Proc. Internat. Water Resources Assoc., etc. *Recreations:* classical music, reading, ski-ing, walking. *Address:* 69 Shepherds Hill, N6 5RE. *T:* and *Fax:* 0181–340 6638. *Club:* Athenæum.

WOLFE, Thomas Kennerly, PhD; author and journalist; *b* 2 March 1931; *m* Sheila; one *s* one *d*. *Educ:* Washington and Lee Univ.; Yale Univ. (PhD 1957). Reporter, Springfield (Mass) Union, 1956–59; Reporter and Latin America correspondent, Washington Post, 1959–62; Reporter and magazine writer, New York Herald Tribune, 1962–66; magazine writer, New York World Journal Tribune, 1966–67; Contributing Editor: New York, magazine, 1968–76; Esquire, 1977–. Contributing artist, Harper's, 1978–81; one-man exhibns of drawings, Maynard Walker Gall., NY, 1965, Tunnel Gall., NY, 1974. *Publications:* The Kandy-Kolored Tangerine-Flake Streamline Baby, 1965; The Electric Kool-Aid Acid Test, 1968; The Pump House Gang, 1968; Radical Chic and Mau-mauing the Flak Catchers, 1970; The New Journalism, 1973; The Painted Word, 1975; Mauve Gloves and Madmen, Clutter and Vine, 1976; The Right Stuff, 1979; In Our Time, 1980; From Bauhaus to Our House, 1981; Bonfire of the Vanities, 1987; The New America, 1989. *Address:* c/o Farrar, Straus and Giroux, 19 Union Square West, New York, NY 10003, USA.

WOLFE, William Cuthbertson; Member, SNP National Council, since 1991; *b* 22 Feb. 1924; *s* of late Major Tom Wolfe, TD, and Katie Cuthbertson; *m* 1st, 1953, Arna Mary (marr. diss. 1989), *d* of late Dr Melville Dinwiddie, CBE, DSO, MC; two *s* two *d*; 2nd, 1993, Catherine Margaret, *d* of late James Parker, *widow* of John McAteer. *Educ:* Bathgate Academy; George Watson's Coll., Edinburgh. CA. Army service, 1942–47, NW Europe and Far East; Air OP Pilot. Hon. Publications Treas., Saltire Society, 1953–60; Scout County Comr, West Lothian, 1960–64; Hon. Pres. (Rector), Students' Assoc., Heriot-Watt Univ., 1966–69. Contested (SNP): West Lothian, 1962, 1964, 1966, 1970, Feb. and Oct. 1974, 1979; North Edinburgh, Nov. 1973; Chm., SNP, 1969–79, Pres., 1980–82. Treas., Scottish CND, 1982–85; Sec., Scottish Poetry Liby, 1985–91. Mem., Forestry Commn Nat. Cttee for Scotland, 1974–87. *Publication:* Scotland Lives, 1973. *Address:* Burnside Forge, Burnside Road, Bathgate, W Lothian EH48 4PU. *T:* Bathgate (01506) 54785.

WOLFENDALE, Sir Arnold (Whittaker), Kt 1995; PhD, DSc; FRS 1977; FInstP, FRAS; Professor of Physics, University of Durham, 1965–92, now Emeritus; Astronomer Royal, 1991–95; *b* 25 June 1927; *s* of Arnold Wolfendale and Doris Wolfendale; *m* 1951, Audrey Darby; twin *s*. *Educ:* Univ. of Manchester (BSc Physics 1st Cl. Hons 1948, PhD 1953, DSc 1970). FInstP 1958; FRAS 1973. Asst Lectr, Univ. of Manchester, 1951, Lectr, 1954; Univ. of Durham: Lectr, 1956; Sen. Lectr, 1959; Reader in Physics, 1963; Head of Dept, 1973–77, 1980–83, 1986–89. Vis. Lectr, Univ. of Ceylon, 1952; Vis. Prof., Univ. of Hong Kong, 1977–78; Kan Tong Po Vis. Prof. of Physics, City Univ. of Hong Kong, 1995. Lectures: H. C. Bhuyan Meml, Gauhati Univ., 1978 and 1993; B. B. Roy Meml, Calcutta Univ., 1978; Norman Lockyer, Exeter Univ., 1978; E. A. Milne, Oxford Univ., 1982; Rochester, Durham Univ., 1990; A. W. Mailvaganam Meml, Colombo Univ., 1990; Perren, QMW, 1991; O'Neill, Glasgow, 1991; Durham Observatory Anniversary, 1992; Cormack, RSE, 1992; Robinson, Armagh, 1992; David Martin, Royal Soc./British Acad., 1992; Preston Guild, Univ. of Central Lancs, 1992; J. H. Holmes Meml, Newcastle Univ., 1993; Irvine Meml, Stirling, 1993; Tompion, Clockmakers' Co., 1993; Courtauld, Manchester Lit. and Phil., 1993; Minerva, Scientific Instrument Makers' Co., 1993; Hess, IUPAP Cosmis Ray Commn, 1993; Poynting, Univ. of Birmingham, 1994; Mme Curie, Inst. of Physics, 1995; Dee, Glasgow Univ., 1995. Home Office, Civil Defence, later Regl Scientific Advr, 1956–84. Chm., Northern Reg. Action Cttee, Manpower Services Commn's Job Creation Prog., 1975–78; Mem., SERC, 1988–94 (Chm., Astronomy and Planetary Sci. Bd, 1988–93; Chm., Particles, Space and Astronomy Bd, 1993–94). Chm., Cosmic Ray Commn, IUPAP, 1982–84. President: RAS, 1981–83; Antiquarian Horological Soc., 1993–; Inst. of Physics, 1994–Sept. 1996. Pres., Durham Univ. Soc. of Fellows, 1988–94. Freeman: Clockmakers' Co., 1991; Sci. Instrument Makers' Co., 1993. Foreign Fellow: INSA, 1990; Indian Nat. Acad. Scis; Hon. Fellow, Lancashire Poly., 1991; Hon. Professor: Univ. of Yunnan, China, 1995; Univ. of Sci. and Technology, Hefei, China, 1995. Hon. DSc: Univ. of Potchefstroom for Christian Higher Educn, 1989; Lodz, 1989; Teeside, 1993; Newcastle upon Tyne, 1994; DUniv Open, 1995. Univ. of Turku Medal, 1987; Armagh Observatory Medal, 1992; Marian Smoluchowski Medal, Polish Phys. Soc., 1993. Silver Jubilee Medal, 1977. *Publications:* Cosmic Rays, 1963; (ed) Cosmic Rays at Ground Level, 1973; (ed) Origin of Cosmic Rays, 1974; (ed jtly and contrib.) Origin of Cosmic Rays, 1981; (ed) Gamma Ray Astronomy, 1981; (ed) Progress in Cosmology, 1982; (with P. V. Ramana Murthy) Gamma Ray Astronomy, 1986, 2nd edn 1993; (with F. R. Stephenson) Secular Solar and Geomagnetic Variations in the last 1,000 years, 1988; (ed jtly) Observational Tests of Cosmological Inflation, 1991; original papers on studies of cosmic radiation and aspects of astrophysics. *Recreations:* walking, gardening, foreign travel. *Address:* Ansford, Potters Bank, Durham DH1 3RR. *T:* Durham (0191) 3845642.

WOLFF, Prof. Heinz Siegfried, FIBiol; FIEE; Director, Brunel Institute for Bioengineering, Brunel University, since 1983; *b* 29 April 1928; *s* of Oswald Wolff and Margot (*née* Saalfeld); *m* 1953, Joan Eleanor Stephenson; two *s*. *Educ:* City of Oxford Sch.; University Coll. London (BSc(Hons)Physiology) (Fellow, 1987). FBES. National Institute for Medical Research: Div. of Human Physiology, 1954–62; Hd, Div. of Biomedical Engrg, 1962–70; Hd, Bioengrg Div., Clinical Res. Centre of MRC, 1970–83. European Space Agency: Chm., Life Science Working Gp, 1976–82; Mem., Sci. Adv. Cttee, 1978–82; Chm., Microgravity Adv. Cttee, 1982–91. Chm., Microgravity Panel, Brit. Nat. Space Centre, 1986–87. Vice-Pres., Coll. of Occupational Therapy, 1990–. Pres., Sch. Natural Sci. Soc., 1988–. FRSA; Hon. Fellow, Ergonomics Soc., 1991. *Television series:* BBC TV Young Scientist of the Year (contributor), 1968–81; BBC2: Royal Instn Christmas Lectures, 1975; Great Egg Race, 1978–; Great Experiments, 1985–86. DUniv: Open, 1993; De Montfort, 1995. Harding Award, Action Res. for the Crippled Child/ RADAR, 1989; Edinburgh Medal, Edinburgh Internat. Sci. Fest., 1992; Donald Julius Groen Prize, IMechE, 1994. *Publications:* Biomedical Engineering, 1969 (German, French, Japanese and Spanish trans, 1970–72); about 120 papers in sci. jls and contribs to books. *Recreations:* working, lecturing to children, dignified practical joking. *Address:* Brunel Institute for Bioengineering, Brunel University, Uxbridge, Mddx UB8 3PH.

WOLFF, Michael, PPCSD; FRSA; President, Newhouse Associates, since 1993; Member, Board of Trustees, the Hunger Project, since 1979; *b* 12 Nov. 1933; *s* of Serge Wolff and Mary (*née* Gordon); *m* 1st, 1976, Susan Kent (marr. diss.); one *d*; 2nd, 1989, Martha Newhouse. *Educ:* Gresham's Sch., Holt, Norfolk; Architectural Association Sch. of Architecture. Designer: Sir William Crawford & Partners, 1957–61; BBC Television, 1961–62; Main Wolff & Partners, 1964–65; with Wolff Olins Ltd as a founder and Creative Director, 1965–83; Chm., Addison Design Consultants, 1987–92. Design Consultant, W H Smith Gp, 1990–. President: D & AD, 1971; SIAD, then CSD, 1985–87. *Recreations:* enjoying a family, seeing. *Address:* 9 Cumberland Gardens, WC1X 9AG. *T:* 0171–833 0007; (office) 0171–722 1113.

WOLFF, Prof. Otto Herbert, CBE 1985; MD, FRCP; Nuffield Professor of Child Health, University of London, 1965–85, now Emeritus Professor; Dean of the Institute of Child Health, 1982–85; *b* 10 Jan. 1920; *s* of Dr H. A. J. Wolff; *m* 1952, Dr Jill Freeborough; one *s* one *d*. *Educ:* Peterhouse, Cambridge; University College Hospital, London. Lieut and Capt. RAMC, 1944–47. Resident Medical Officer, Registrar and Sen. Med. Registrar, Birmingham Children's Hospital, 1948–51; Lecturer, Sen. Lectr, Reader, Dept of Pædiatrics and Child Health, Univ. of Birmingham, 1951–64. Senator, London Univ.; Representative of London Univ. on GMC. Past Pres., British Pædiatric Assoc.; Member: Royal Society of Medicine; American Pædiatric Society; New York Academy of Sciences; Amer. Academy of Pediatrics; European Soc. for Paediatric Research; European Soc. for Paediatric Gastroenterology; Deutsche Akad. der Naturforscher Leopoldina. Corresp. Member: Société Française de Pédiatrie; Société Suisse de Pédiatrie; Osterreichische Gesellschaft für Kinderheilkunde; Società Italiana di Pediatria; Deutsche Gesellschaft für Kinderheilkunde; Fellow, Indian Acad. of Pediatrics. Chm. of Trustees, Child-to-Child Charity, 1989–93. Dawson Williams Meml Prize, BMA, 1984; Medal, Assoc. Française pour le Dépistage et la Prévention des Maladies Métaboliques et des Handicaps de l'Enfant, 1986; Harding Award, Action Res. for Crippled Child, 1987; James Spence Medal, BPA, 1988. *Publications:* chapter on Disturbances of Serum Lipoproteins in Endocrine and Genetic Diseases of Childhood (ed L. I. Gardner); chapter on Obesity in Recent Advances in Paediatrics (ed David Hull); articles in Lancet, British Medical Journal, Archives of Disease in Childhood, Quarterly Jl of Medicine, etc. *Recreation:* music. *Address:* 53 Danbury Street, N1 8LE. *T:* 0171–226 0748.

WOLFF, Rosemary Langley; Member, Police Complaints Authority, 1985–92 (Member, Police Complaints Board, 1977–85); *b* 10 July 1926; *er d* of late A. C. V. Clarkson; *m*

1956, Michael Wolff, JP (*d* 1976); two *d.* *Educ:* Haberdashers' Aske's Sch. Mem., Community Relations Commn, 1973–77. Manager of various primary schs in North Kensington and Tower Hamlets, 1963–; Governor, City College; Chm., Conservative Contact Group, 1973–77; Mem., Managing Cttee, Working Ladies' Guild. Assoc. Mem., Kensington, Chelsea and Westminster FHSA, 1994. *Address:* 13 Holland Park, W11 3TH. *T:* 0171–727 9051.

WOLFSON, family name of **Barons Wolfson** and **Wolfson of Sunningdale.**

WOLFSON, Baron *cr* 1985 (Life Peer), of Marylebone in the City of Westminster; **Leonard Gordon Wolfson,** Bt 1962; Kt 1977; Chairman, since 1972, and Founder Trustee, since 1955, Wolfson Foundation; Chairman: Great Universal Stores, since 1981 (Managing Director, 1962–81; Director, 1952); Burberrys Ltd, since 1978; *b* 11 Nov. 1927; *s* of Sir Isaac Wolfson, 1st Bt, FRS (*d* 1991) and Edith Wolfson (*d* 1981); *m* 1st, 1949 (marr. diss. 1991); four *d;* 2nd, 1991, Estelle (*née* Feldman), *widow* of Michael Jackson, FCA; one step *s* one step *d.* *Educ:* King's School, Worcester. Hon. Fellow: St Catherine's Coll., Oxford; Wolfson Coll., Cambridge; Wolfson Coll., Oxford; Worcester Coll., Oxford; UCL; LSHTM 1985; QMC 1985; Poly. of Central London, 1991; Imperial Coll., 1991. Pres., Jewish Welfare Bd, 1972–82. Trustee, Imperial War Mus., 1988–94. Patron, Royal College of Surgeons, 1976; Hon. FRCP 1977; Hon. FRCS 1988; Hon. FBA 1986. Hon. DCL: Oxon, 1972; East Anglia, 1986; Hon. LLD: Strathclyde, 1972; Dundee, 1979; Cantab, 1982; London, 1982; Hon. DSc: Hull, 1977; Wales, 1984; Hon. PhD: Tel Aviv, 1971; Hebrew Univ., 1978; Weizmann Inst., 1988; Hon. DHL Bar Ilan Univ., 1983; DUniv Surrey, 1990; Hon. MD Birmingham, 1992. Winston Churchill Award, British Technion Soc., 1989. *Address:* 18–22 Haymarket, SW1Y 4DQ.

WOLFSON OF SUNNINGDALE, Baron *cr* 1991 (Life Peer), of Trevose in the County of Cornwall; **David Wolfson,** Kt 1984; Chairman, Next plc, since 1990; *b* 9 Nov. 1935; *s* of Charles Wolfson and Hylda Wolfson; *m* 1st, 1962, Patricia E. Rawlings (*see* Baroness Rawlings) (marr. diss. 1967); 2nd, 1967, Susan E. Davis; two *s* one *d.* *Educ:* Clifton Coll.; Trinity Coll., Cambridge (MA); Stanford Univ., California (MBA). Great Universal Stores, 1960–78, 1993–, Director, 1973–78 and 1993–; Secretary to Shadow Cabinet, 1978–79; Chief of Staff, Political Office, 10 Downing Street, 1979–85. Chm., Alexon Group PLC (formerly Steinberg Group PLC), 1982–86; non-executive Director: Stewart Wrightson Holdings PLC, 1985–87; Next, 1989–90. Hon. Fellow, Hughes Hall, Cambridge, 1989. Hon. FRCR 1978; Hon. FRCOG 1989. *Recreations:* golf, bridge. *Clubs:* Portland; Sunningdale; Woburn Golf.

WOLFSON, Sir Brian (Gordon), Kt 1990; Chairman: Wembley Stadium Ltd, 1986–95; National Training Task Force (formerly Training Commission, then Training Agency), 1988–92; *b* 2 Aug. 1935; *s* of Gabriel and Eve Wolfson; *m* 1958, Helen, *d* of late Lewis Grodner; one *s* one *d.* *Educ:* Liverpool Coll.; Liverpool Univ. Joined Granada Group, 1961, Jt Man. Dir, 1967–70; Chm., Anglo Nordic Holdings, 1976–87; Director: Kepner Tregoe Inc., USA, 1980–; Charles Ede Ltd, London, 1971–; Fruit of the Loom Inc., Chicago, 1992–. Chm., Investors in People (UK), 1992–. First non-North American World Pres., Young Presidents' Orgn, 1979–80; Mem., NEDC, 1989–92 (Chm., Cttee on leisure, 1987). University of Pennsylvania: Mem. Adv. Bd, Wharton Center for Internat. Management Studies, 1980–; Bd, Joseph H. Lauder Inst., 1983–. Governor: Ashridge Management Coll., 1991– (Chm., Ashridge MBA Prog., 1988–); NIESR, 1993–. CIMgt (FBIM 1969, CBIM 1970; Chm., 1986–88; Vice-Pres., 1988); Fellow, Inst BE. Hon. DBA, Liverpool Poly., 1989. *Recreations:* archaeological digs, making wildlife films.

WOLFSON, (Geoffrey) Mark; MP (C) Sevenoaks, since 1979; *b* 7 April 1934; *s* of late Captain V. Wolfson, OBE, VRD, RNR, and Dorothy Mary Wolfson; *m* 1965, Edna Webb (*née* Hardman); two *s.* *Educ:* Eton Coll.; Pembroke Coll., Cambridge (MA). Served Royal Navy, 1952–54; Cambridge, 1954–57; Teacher in Canada, 1958–59; Warden, Brathay Hall Centre, Westmorland, 1962–66; Head of Youth Services, Industrial Soc., 1966–69; Hd of Personnel, 1970–85, Dir, 1973–88, Hambros Bank. PPS to Minister of State for NI, 1983–84, to Minister of State for Defence Procurement, 1984–85, to Minister of State for Armed Forces, 1987–88. Mem., NI Select Cttee, 1994–. Officer, Cons. Backbench Employment Cttee, 1981–83. Mem., Parly Human Rights Delegn to Nicaragua, 1982, El Salvador and Baltic States, 1990. Chm., Brathay Hall Trust, 1991–. *Address:* House of Commons, SW1A 0AA.

WOLFSON, Mark; *see* Wolfson, G. M.

WOLKIND, Jack, CBE 1978; Chairman, World Trade Centre in London Ltd, 1991–93; *b* 16 Feb. 1920; *s* of Samuel and Golda Wolkind; *m* 1945, Bena Sternfeld; two *s* one *d.* *Educ:* Mile End Central Sch.; King's Coll., London. LLB Hons, LLM (London). Admitted Solicitor, 1953. Army service to 1945. Dep. Town Clerk and Solicitor, Stepney Borough Council, 1952–65; Chief Exec. (formerly Town Clerk), Tower Hamlets, 1964–85; Chief Exec., St Katharine by the Tower Ltd, 1990–91 (Dir, 1985–93). Mem., London Residuary Body. Chm., Claredale Housing Assoc. Ltd, 1987–. Governor: Toynbee Hall, 1981–; QMC, Univ. of London, 1981–90 (Fellow, 1985). FRSA 1980; Fellow, Guildhall Univ. (formerly City of London Poly.), 1985. *Recreations:* reading, music.

WOLLHEIM, Prof. Richard Arthur, FBA 1972; Professor of Philosophy, University of California, Berkeley, since 1985, and University of California, Davis, since 1989; Emeritus Grote Professor in the University of London; *b* 5 May 1923; *s* of Eric Wollheim; *m* 1st, 1950, Anne, *yr d* of Lieutenant-Colonel E. G. H. Powell (marr. diss. 1967); two *s;* 2nd, 1969, Mary Day, *er d* of Robert S. Lanier, NYC; one *d.* *Educ:* Westminster School; Balliol College, Oxford (MA). Served in the Army, N Europe, 1942–45 (POW during Aug. 1944). University College London: Asst Lectr in Philosophy, 1949; Lectr, 1951; Reader, 1960; Hon. Fellow, 1994; Grote Prof. of Philosophy of Mind and Logic in Univ. of London, 1963–82; Prof. of Philosophy, Columbia Univ., 1982–85. Visiting Professor: Columbia Univ., 1959–60, 1970; Visva-Bharati Univ., Santiniketan, India, 1968; Univ. of Minnesota, 1972; Graduate Centre, City Univ. of NY, 1975; Univ. of California, Berkeley, 1981; Harvard Univ., 1982; Sarah Lawrence Coll., 1987; Univ. of Guelph, 1988; Washington Univ., St Louis, 1989. Lectures: Ernest Jones, 1969; British Psychoanalytical Soc.; Power, Univ. of Sydney, 1972; Leslie Stephen, Univ. of Cambridge, 1979; William James, Harvard Univ., 1982; Andrew W. Mellon, Nat. Gall., Washington, 1984; Lewin, Washington Univ., 1989; Tamblyn, Univ. of W Ontario, 1989; Cassirer, Yale Univ., 1991; Hoffmann, Dallas Mus., 1992; David A. Jones, Claremont Coll., 1995. President: Aristotelian Soc., 1967–68; British Soc. of Aesthetics, 1993– (Vice-Pres., 1969–93). Mem., American Acad. of Arts and Scis, 1986. Hon. Affiliate, British Psychoanalytical Soc., 1982; Hon. Mem., San Francisco Psychoanalytic Inst., 1994. Award for Dist. Services to Psychoanalysis, Internat. Psychoanalytic Soc., 1991. *Publications:* F. H. Bradley, 1959, rev. edn 1969; Socialism and Culture, 1961; On Drawing an Object (Inaugural Lecture), 1965; Art and its Objects, 1968, 2nd edn with suppl. essays, 1980; A Family Romance (fiction), 1969; Freud, 1971; On Art and the Mind (essays and lectures), 1973; The Good Self and the Bad Self (Dawes Hicks lecture), 1976; The Sheep and the Ceremony (Leslie Stephen lecture), 1979; The Thread of Life, 1984; Painting as an Art, 1987; The Mind and its Depths (essays and lectures), 1993; edited: F. H. Bradley, Ethical Studies, 1961; Hume on Religion, 1963; F. H. Bradley, Appearance and Reality, 1968; Adrian Stokes, selected writings, 1972; Freud, a collection of critical essays, 1974; J. S. Mill, Three Essays, 1975; (with Jim Hopkins) Philosophical Essays on Freud, 1982; articles in anthologies, philosophical and literary jls. *Address:* 20 Ashchurch Park Villas, W12 9SP; 1814 Marin Avenue, Berkeley, CA 94707, USA.

WOLLONGONG, Bishop of; *see* Piper, Rt Rev. R. J.

WOLMER, Viscount; William Lewis Palmer; *b* 1 Sept. 1971; *s* and *heir* of 4th Earl of Selborne, *qv.* *Educ:* Eton Coll.; Christ Church, Oxford. *Address:* Temple Manor, Selborne, Alton, Hants GU34 3LR.

WOLPERT, Prof. Lewis, CBE 1990; DIC, PhD; FRS 1980; Professor of Biology as Applied to Medicine, London University, at University College London Medical School (formerly at Middlesex Hospital Medical School), since 1966; *b* 19 Oct. 1929; *s* of William and Sarah Wolpert; *m* 1961; two *s* two *d.* *Educ:* King Edward's Sch., Johannesburg; Univ. of Witwatersrand (BScEng); Imperial Coll., London (DIC); King's Coll., London (PhD). Personal Asst to Director of Building Research Inst., S African Council for Scientific and Industrial Research, 1951–52; Engineer, Israel Water Planning Dept, 1953–54; King's College, London: Asst Lectr in Zoology, 1958–60; Lectr in Zoology, 1960–64; Reader in Zoology, 1964–66; Hd of Dept of Biology as Applied to Medicine, later Dept of Anatomy and Biology as Applied to Medicine, Middlesex Hosp. Med. Sch., 1966–87. MRC: Mem. Council, 1984–88; Mem., 1982–88, Chm., 1984–88, Cell Bd; Chairman: Scientific Inf. Cttee, Royal Soc., 1983–88; COPUS, 1994–; Biology Concerted Action Cttee, EEC, 1988–91. President: British Soc. for Cell Biology, 1985–91; Inst. of Information Scientists, 1986–87. Lectures: Steinhaus, Univ. of California at Irvine, 1980; van der Horst, Univ. of Witwatersrand, Johannesburg, 1981; Bidder, Soc. for Experimental Biology, Leicester, 1982; Swirling, Dana-Faber, Boston, 1985; Lloyd-Roberts, RCP, 1986; Royal Instn Christmas Lectures, 1986; R. G. Williams, Univ. of Pennsylvania, 1988; Bernal, Birkbeck Coll., 1989; Radcliffe, Warwick Univ., 1990; Redfearn, Leicester, 1991; Wade, Southampton, 1991; Robb, Univ. of Auckland. Presenter, Antenna, BBC2, 1987–88; interviews with scientists, Radio 3, 1981–; radio documentaries: The Dark Lady of DNA, 1989; The Virgin Fathers of the Calculus, 1991. Hon. MRCP, 1986. Hon. DSc CNAA, 1992. Scientific Medal, Zoological Soc., 1968. *Publications:* A Passion for Science (with A. Richards), 1988; Triumph of the Embryo, 1991; The Unnatural Nature of Science, 1992; articles on cell and developmental biology in scientific jls. *Recreation:* tennis. *Address:* Department of Anatomy and Developmental Biology, University College London Medical School, Cleveland Street, W1P 6DB.

WOLRIGE-GORDON, Patrick; *b* 10 Aug. 1935; *s* of late Captain Robert Wolrige-Gordon, MC and Joan Wolrige-Gordon; *m* 1962, Anne, *o d* of late Peter D. Howard and Mrs Howard; one *s* two *d.* *Educ:* Eton; New College, Oxford. MP (C) Aberdeenshire East, Nov. 1958–Feb. 1974. Liveryman Worshipful Company of Wheelwrights, 1966. *Recreations:* reading, golf, music. *Address:* Ythan Lodge, Newburgh, Aberdeenshire. *Club:* Royal Over-Seas League.

See also John MacLeod of MacLeod.

WOLSELEY, Sir Charles Garnet Richard Mark, 11th Bt, *cr* 1628; Consultant, Smiths Gore, Chartered Surveyors, since 1987 (Associate Partner, 1974; Partner, 1979–87); *b* 16 June 1944; *s* of Capt. Stephen Garnet Hubert Francis Wolseley, Royal Artillery (*d* 1944, of wounds received in action), and of Pamela, *yr d* of late Capt. F. Barry and Mrs Lavinia Power, Wolseley Park, Rugeley, Staffs; *S* grandfather, Sir Edric Charles Joseph Wolseley, 10th Bt, 1954; *m* 1st, 1968, Anita Maria (marr. diss. 1984), *er d* of late H. J. Fried, Epsom, Surrey; one *s* three *d;* 2nd, 1984, Mrs Imogene Brown. *Educ:* St Bede's School, near Stafford; Ampleforth College, York. FRICS. *Recreations:* shooting, fishing, gardening. *Heir: s* Stephen Garnet Hugo Charles Wolseley, *b* 2 May 1980. *Address:* Wolseley Park, Rugeley, Staffs WS15 2TU. *T:* Rugeley (01889) 582346. *Clubs:* Farmers', Shikar.

WOLSELEY, Sir James Douglas, 13th Bt *cr* 1745 (Ire.), of Mount Wolseley, Co. Carlow; *b* 17 Sept. 1937; *s* of James Douglas Wolseley (*d* 1960), and of Olive, *d* of Carroll Walter Wofford; *S* kinsman, Sir Garnet Wolseley, 12th Bt, 1991; *m* 1st, 1965, Patricia Lynn (marr. diss. 1971), *d* of William R. Hunter; 2nd, 1984, Mary Anne, *d* of Thomas G. Brown. *Heir: kinsman* John Walter Wolseley [*b* 21 April 1938; *m* 1964, Patricia Ann Newland (marr. diss. 1978); two *s*]. *Address:* 4317 Clay Street, Fort Worth, TX, USA.

WOLSTENCROFT, Alan, CB 1961; Director, 1974–87, and Chairman, 1979–84, National Counties Building Society; *b* 18 Oct. 1914; *yr s* of late Walter and Bertha Wolstencroft; *m* 1951, Ellen, *d* of late W. Tomlinson. *Educ:* Lancaster Royal Grammar Sch.; Caius Coll., Cambridge (MA 1st Cl. Classical Tripos). Assistant Principal, GPO, 1936. Served War of 1939–45: Royal Engineers (Postal Section), France and Middle East. Principal GPO, 1945; Assistant Secretary, GPO, 1949; Secretary, Independent Television Authority, 1954; General Post Office: Director of Personnel, 1955; Director of Postal Services, 1957; Director of Radio Services, 1960–64; Deputy Director General, 1964–67; Man. Dir Posts, 1967, Posts and GIRO, 1968; Adviser on Special Projects to Chm. of Post Office Corporation, 1969–70; Sec. to Post Office, 1970–73; retired. *Address:* Green Court, 161 Long Lane, Tilehurst, Reading RG3 6YW.

WOLSTENHOLME, Sir Gordon (Ethelbert Ward), Kt 1976; OBE (mil.) 1944; MA, MB, BChir; MRCS, FRCP, FIBiol; Founder and Chairman, Action in International Medicine, since 1988; *b* Sheffield, 28 May 1913; *m* 1st; one *s* two *d;* 2nd; two *d.* *Educ:* Repton; Corpus Christi Coll., Cambridge; Middlesex Hosp. Med. Sch. Served with RAMC, 1940–47 (OBE); France, UK, ME and Central Mediterranean; specialist and advr in transfusion and resuscitation; OC Gen. Hosp. in Udine and Trieste; Dir, Ciba Foundn, 1949–78; Harveian Librarian, RCP, 1979–89; Fellow, Green Coll., Oxford, 1986–90. Mem., GMC, 1973–83; Chm., Genetic Manipulation Adv. Gp, 1976–78. Founder Mem. 1954, Treasurer 1955–61, Mem. Exec. Bd 1961–70, UK Cttee for WHO; Organizer and Advr, Haile Selassie I Prize Trust, 1963–74; Advr, La Trinidad Med. Centre, Caracas, 1969–78. Royal Society of Medicine: Hon. Sec. 1964–70; Pres. Library (Sci. Res) Sect., 1968–70; Chm. Working Party on Soc's Future, 1972–73; Pres., 1975–77, 1978; Zoological Society: Scientific Fellow and Vice-Pres.; Member: Finance Cttee, 1962–69; Council, 1962–66, 1967–70, 1976–80; Chm., Nuffield Inst. for Comparative Medicine, 1969–70; Chm. Governors, Inst. for Res. into Mental and Multiple Handicap, 1973–77. Founder Mem. 1950, Hon. Treasurer 1956–69, Renal Assoc. of GB; Chm. Congress Prog. Cttee, 1962–64, Mem. Finance Cttee 1968–72, Internat. Soc. for Endocrinology; Trustee and Mem. Res. Bd, Spastics' Soc., 1963–67; Founder Chm., European Soc. for Clinical Investigation, 1966–67 (Boerhaave Lectr, 1976); Mem. Council 1969–75, Sponsor 1976–, Inst. for Study of Drug Dependence; Dir, Nuffield Foundn Inquiry into Dental Educn, 1978–80; Chairman: Dental Res. Strategy Gp, 1986–89; Oral and Dental Res. Trust, 1989–. Member: Council, Westfield Coll., London Univ., 1965–73; Planning Bd, University College at Buckingham, 1969. Chm., Anglo-Ethiopian Soc., 1967–70. Emeritus Mem. Ct of Assistants, Soc. of Apothecaries, 1988– (Mem., 1969–88; Master, 1979–80; Chm., Faculty of Hist. and Philosophy of Med. and Pharmacy, 1973–75; Visitor, 1975–78); Chm., Skin Diseases Res. Fund, 1980–85. Vis. Prof., UCSD, 1982, 1983, 1984. Dir, IRL Press Ltd, 1980–88. Trustee, Foulkes Foundn; Trustee,

1978–90, Chm. Acad. Bd, 1978–88, St George's Univ. Sch. of Med., Grenada. Mem. Bd, Dahlem Konferenzen, 1978–90. Vice-Pres., ASLIB, 1979–82. Pres., Brit. Soc. Hist. Medicine, 1983–85. Patron, FRAME, 1977–. Hon. Life Governor, Middlesex Hosp., 1938. Fellow UCL, 1991; FRSA 1979. Hon. FACP, 1975; Hon. FDSRCS 1991; Hon. Fellow: Hunterian Soc., 1975 (Orator 1976); Royal Acad. of Med. in Ireland, 1976; European Soc. for Clinical Investigation, 1979; RSocMed, 1982; Faculty of Hist. Med. Pharm., 1982. Hon. Member: Swedish Soc. of Endocrinology, 1955; Soc. of Endocrinology, 1959; Swiss Acad. of Med. Sciences, 1975; Assoc. Med. Argentina, 1977; Internat. Assoc. for Dental Res., 1984; Osler Club, 1986 (Orator, 1986); Foreign Mem., Swedish Med. Soc., 1959; Hon. For. Mem., Amer. Acad. of Arts and Scis, 1981. Hon. LLD Cambridge, 1968; Hon. DTech Brunel, 1981; Hon. MD Grenada, 1982. Linnaeus Medal, Royal Swedish Acad. Sci., 1977; Pasteur Medal, Paris, 1982; Gold Medal: Perugia Univ., 1961; (class 1A) Italian Min. of Educn, 1961. Tito Lik, 1945; Chevalier, Légion d'Honneur, 1959; Star of Ethiopia, 1966. *Publications:* (ed) Ciba Foundation vols, 1950–78; Royal College of Physicians: Portraits, vol. I (ed with David Piper), 1964, vol. II (ed with John Kerslake), 1977; (ed with Valerie Luniewska) Munk's Roll, vol. VI, 1982, vol. VII, 1984, vol. VIII, 1989; (jtly) Portrait of Irish Medicine, 1984. *Recreations:* walking, photography. *Address:* 10 Wimpole Mews, W1M 7TF. *T:* 0171–486 3884.

WOLSTENHOLME, John Scott; His Honour Judge Wolstenholme; a Circuit Judge, since 1995; *b* 28 Nov. 1947; *s* of Donald Arthur Wolstenholme and Kaye (*née* Humphrys); *m* 1972, Lynne Harrison; three *s* one *d*. *Educ:* Roundhay Sch., Leeds; University Coll., Oxford (MA). Called to the Bar, Middle Temple, 1971; practised North Eastern Circuit, 1971–92; Chm., Industrial Tribunals, Leeds Region, 1992–95; a Recorder, 1992–95. *Recreations:* playing the drums, walking, photography. *Address:* Leeds Combined Court Centre, Oxford Row, Leeds LS1 3BG.

WOLSTENHOLME, Roy; County Treasurer, Surrey County Council, 1988–94; *b* 1 Jan. 1936; *m* 1959, Mary R. Wolstenholme; one *s* two *d*. *Educ:* Stretford Grammar Sch.; Manchester College of Commerce. Stretford Bor. Council, 1952–61; Worcs CC, 1961–63; Worthing Bor. Council, 1963–65; Glos CC, 1965–68; Holland (Lincs) CC, 1968–74; Lincs CC, 1974–77; County Treas., Northumberland CC, 1977–88. *Recreations:* music, walking, gardening, *Address:* 39 Foxhill Crescent, Camberley, Surrey GU15 1PR. *Club:* Royal Over-Seas League.

WOLTERS, Gwyneth Eleanor Mary; a Commissioner of Inland Revenue, 1971–78; *b* 21 Nov. 1918; *d* of late Prof. and Mrs A. W. Wolters. *Educ:* Abbey Sch., Reading; Reading Univ.; Newnham Coll., Cambridge (Class. Tripos; Hilda Richardson Prize). Temp. Admin. Asst, Min. of Works, 1941–47; Asst Principal, 1947–49, Principal, 1949–57, Asst Sec., 1957–71, Inland Revenue. *Address:* 45 Albert Road, Caversham, Reading RG4 7AW. *T:* Reading (01734) 472605.

WOLTON, Harry; QC 1982; a Recorder, since 1985; a Deputy High Court Judge, since 1990; *b* 1 Jan. 1938; *s* of late Harry William Wolton and Dorothy Beatrice Wolton; *m* 1971, Julie Rosina Josephine Lovell (*née* Mason); three *s*. *Educ:* King Edward's Sch., Birmingham; Univ. of Birmingham. Called to the Bar, Gray's Inn, 1969. *Recreations:* cattle breeding, dendrology. *Address:* The Black Venn, Edwyn Ralph, Bromyard, Herefordshire HR7 4LU; 3 Redcliffe Mews, SW10 9JT. *T:* 0171–370 3940.

WOLTZ, Alan Edward; Chairman, London International Group, 1985–93 (Chief Executive, 1985–91); *b* 29 Feb. 1932; *s* of Robert Woltz and Rose Woltz Katz; *m* 1977, Barbara Howell; three *s* one *d*. *Educ:* Dwight Morrow High Sch., Eaglewood, NJ; Wagner Coll., Staten Is, NY. Served US Army, Korea, 1952–54. Schmid Laboratories Inc.: Exec. Vice-Pres., 1971–74; Pres., 1974–78; Pres., LRC N America, 1978–79; Man. Dir and Chief Exec., London Internat. Gp, 1979–85. *Recreations:* golf, swimming. *Address:* c/o London International Group, 35 New Bridge Street, EC4V 6BJ. *T:* 0171–489 1977. *Clubs:* Wentworth Golf; Metropolitan (NY).

WOLVERHAMPTON, Bishop Suffragan of, since 1993; **Rt. Rev. Michael Bourke;** *b* 28 Nov. 1941; *s* of Gordon and Hilda Bourke; *m* 1968, Elizabeth Bieler; one *s* one *d*. *Educ:* Hamond's Grammar Sch., Swaffham, Norfolk; Corpus Christi Coll., Cambridge (Mod. Langs, MA); Univ. of Tübingen (Theology); Cuddesdon Theological Coll. Curate, St James', Grimsby, 1967–71; Priest-in-charge, Panshanger Conventional Dist (Local Ecumenical Project), Welwyn Garden City, 1971–78; Vicar, All Saints', Southill, Beds, 1978–86; Archdeacon of Bedford, 1986–93. Course Dir, St Albans Diocese Ministerial Trng Scheme, 1975–87. Hon. Canon, Lichfield Cathedral, 1993–. *Recreations:* astronomy, railways, European history. *Address:* 61 Richmond Road, Merridale, Wolverhampton WV3 9JH. *T:* Wolverhampton (01902) 23008.

WOLVERSON COPE, F(rederick); *see* Cope.

WOLVERTON, 7th Baron *cr* 1869; **Christopher Richard Glyn,** FRICS; *b* 5 Oct. 1938; *s* of 6th Baron Wolverton, CBE and of Audrey Margaret, *d* of late Richard Stubbs; *S* father, 1988; *m* 1st, 1961, Carolyn Jane (marr. diss. 1967), *yr d* of late Antony N. Hunter; two *d*; 2nd, 1975, Mrs Frances S. E. Stuart Black (marr. diss. 1989). *Educ:* Eton. Mem., Jockey Club. *Heir:* *b* Hon. Andrew John Glyn [*b* 30 June 1943; *m* 1st, 1965, Celia Laws (marr. diss. 1986); one *s* one *d*; 2nd, 1986, Wendy Carlin; one *d*]. *Address:* 97 Hurlingham Road, SW6 3NL.

WOMACK, Joanna Mary; Treasurer, Cambridge University, since 1993; Fellow, Trinity Hall, Cambridge, since 1990; *b* 12 Sept. 1947; *d* of Laurence Paul Hodges and Mary Elizabeth Hodges (*née* Lyon); *m* 1971, Michael Thomas Womack; three *s*. *Educ:* James Allen's Girls' Sch., Dulwich; New Hall, Cambridge (MA 1st Cl. Hons Law). Admitted solicitor, 1972; solicitor, Herbert Smith & Co., 1972–75; New Hall, Cambridge: Coll. Lectr in Law, 1975–83; Fellow, 1975–90; Bursar, 1983–90; Bursar and Steward, Trinity Hall, Cambridge, 1990–93. Gen. Comr of Tax, 1987–. Dir, Cambridge Building Soc., 1994–. Gov., Long Road VI Form Coll., Cambridge, 1992–. *Recreations:* family life, photography, music, hill-walking. *Address:* The Old Schools, Cambridge CB2 1TS. *T:* Cambridge (01223) 332209.

WOMBWELL, Sir George (Philip Frederick), 7th Bt *cr* 1778; *b* 21 May 1949; *s* of Sir (Frederick) Philip (Alfred William) Wombwell, 6th Bt, MBE, and late Ida Elizabeth, *er d* of Frederick J. Leitch; *S* father, 1977; *m* 1974, (Hermione) Jane, *e d* of T. S. Wrightson; one *s* one *d*. *Educ:* Repton. *Heir:* *s* Stephen Philip Henry Wombwell, *b* 12 May 1977. *Address:* Newburgh Priory, Coxwold, York YO6 4AS.

WOMERSLEY, (Denis) Keith, CBE 1974; HM Diplomatic Service, retired; *b* 21 March 1920; *s* of late Alfred Womersley, Bradford, Yorks, and late Agnes (*née* Keighley); *m* 1st, 1955, Eileen Georgina (*d* 1990), *d* of late George and Margaret Howe; 2nd, 1992, Gillian Anne, *widow* of Dr Gerard O'Donnell; three step *s* one step *d*. *Educ:* Christ's Hospital; Caius Coll., Cambridge (Hons, MA). Served War, HM Forces, 1940–46. Entered Foreign (later Diplomatic) Service, 1946; Foreign Office, 1948, Control Commn Germany, 1952; Vienna, 1955; Hong Kong, 1957, FO, 1960; Baghdad, 1962; FO, 1963; Aden, 1966; Beirut, 1967; FCO, 1969–71; Bonn, 1971–74; Counsellor, FCO, 1974–77. FRSA 1976. Gov., Christ's Hosp., 1991–. *Recreations:* violin-playing, Abbeyfield Soc. work. *Club:* Christ's Hospital (Horsham).

See also J. A. O'Donnell.

WOMERSLEY, Keith; *see* Womersley, D. K.

WOMERSLEY, Sir Peter (John Walter), 2nd Bt *cr* 1945; JP; Human Resources (formerly Personnel) Manager, SmithKline Beecham, since 1972; *b* 10 November 1941; *s* of Capt. John Womersley (*o s* of 1st Bt; killed in action in Italy, 1944), and of Betty, *d* of Cyril Williams, Elstead, Surrey; *S* grandfather, 1961; *m* 1968, Janet Margaret Grant; two *s* two *d*. *Educ:* Aldro; Charterhouse; RMA, Sandhurst. Entered Royal Military Academy (Regular Army), 1960; Lt, King's Own Royal Border Regt, 1964, retd 1968. JP Steyning, 1991. *Publication:* (with Neil Grant) Collecting Stamps, 1980. *Heir:* *s* John Gavin Grant Womersley, *b* 7 Dec. 1971. *Address:* Broomfields, Goring Road, Steyning, W Sussex BN44 3GF.

WONFOR, Andrea Jean; Joint Managing Director, Granada Television, since 1994 (Director of Programmes, 1993–94); *b* 31 July 1944; *d* of George Duncan and Audrey Joan Player; *m* 1st, 1967, Patrick Masefield (marr. diss. 1973); one *d*; 2nd, 1974, Geoffrey Wonfor; one *d*. *Educ:* Simon Langton Girls School, Canterbury; New Hall, Cambridge (BA). Graduate trainee, Granada Television, 1966–67; Tyne Tees Television: Researcher, 1969; Director, 1973; Head of Children's and Young People's Programmes, 1976; Dir of Progs, 1983–87; Channel Four Television: Controller, Arts and Entertainment, 1990–93; Dep. Dir of Progs, 1993. Man. Dir, Zenith North, 1988–90. Mem., Bd of Govs, BFI, 1989–94. FRTS 1991. *Recreations:* reading, music. *Address:* Fell Pasture, Ingoe, Matfen, Northumberland NE20 0SP. *T:* Stamfordham (01661) 886487.

WONG Kin Chow, Michael; Hon. Mr Justice Wong; Judge of the High Court, Hong Kong, since 1985; *b* 16 Aug. 1936; *s* of late Wong Chong and Au Ting; *m* 1963, Mae (*née* Fong); two *s* two *d*. *Educ:* Univ. of Liverpool (LLB Hons 1961). Called to the Bar, Middle Temple, 1962; private practice, Hong Kong, 1962–65; Hong Kong Government: Crown Counsel, Legal Dept, 1966–69; Senior Crown Counsel, 1969–72; Asst Principal Crown Counsel, 1973; Presiding Officer, Labour Tribunal, 1973–75; Asst Registrar, Supreme Court, 1975–77; District Judge, 1977. Chm., Release Under Supervision Bd, 1988–94. *Address:* Supreme Court, Hong Kong. *T:* 8254429. *Clubs:* Chinese, Royal Hong Kong Jockey, Kowloon Cricket (Hong Kong).

WOO, Kwok-Hing; Hon. Mr Justice Woo; High Court Judge, Hong Kong, since 1992; Chairman, Boundary and Election Commission, Hong Kong, since 1993; *b* 13 Jan. 1946; *s* of late Woo Leung and Leung Yuk-Ling; *m* 1973, Rowena Tang; two *s* two *d*. *Educ:* Univ. of Birmingham (LLB); University College, London (LLM). Called to the Bar, Gray's Inn, 1969; QC (Hong Kong), 1987; in private practice, Hong Kong, 1970–92. *Address:* Supreme Court, 38 Queensway, Hong Kong. *Clubs:* Royal Hong Kong Jockey, Hong Kong, Hong Kong Country.

WOO, Sir Leo (Joseph), Kt 1993; MBE 1984; Chairman and Chief Executive, Woo Holdings Group, since 1984; *b* 17 Oct. 1952; *s* of Gabriel Bernard Woo and Molly Woo; *m* 1973, Emilyn Cha; one *s* two *d*. *Educ:* De La Salle Oakhill Coll., Sydney. *Address:* PO Box 659, Boroko, NCD, Papua New Guinea. *T:* 201183, *Fax:* 201162.

WOOD, family name of **Earl of Halifax** and **Baron Holderness.**

WOOD, Alan John, CBE 1971; Tan Sri (Malaysia) 1972; Executive Vice President, Malwood Global, Inc., Aiken, since 1993; *b* 16 Feb. 1925; *s* of late Lt-Col Maurice Taylor Wood, MBE; *m* 1950 (marr. diss.); one *s* one *d*; *m* 1978, Marjorie Anne (*née* Bennett). *Educ:* King Edward VI Royal Grammar Sch., Guildford, Surrey, UK. Served Army, 1943–47; demobilised rank Captain. Various exec. and managerial positions with Borneo Motors Ltd, Singapore and Malaya, 1947–64 (Dir, 1964); Dir, Inchcape Bhd, 1968–73, Exec. Dep. Chm. 1973–74; Exec. Vice Pres., Sowers, Lewis, Wood Inc., Old Greenwich, Conn, 1975–78; Gen. Man., India, Singer Sewing Machine Co., 1979–82; Asst Dir, Delaware River Port Authority, World Trade Div., then World Trade and Econ. Devlt Div., 1983–93. Pres., Malaysian Internat. Chamber of Commerce, 1968–72; Chairman: Nat. Chambers of Commerce of Malaysia, 1968 and 1972; Internat. Trade Cttee, Chamber of Commerce of Southern NJ, 1990–93. Panglima Setia Mahkota (Hon.), 1972. *Recreation:* tennis. *Address:* 806 Oak Place, Aiken, SC 29801, USA. *Clubs:* Oriental; Lake (Kuala Lumpur); Penang (Penang); Houndslake (Aiken).

WOOD, Sir Alan Marshall M.; *see* Muir Wood.

WOOD, Alfred Arden, CBE 1988; TD 1960; FRIBA, FRTPI; architect and town planner; *b* 8 Sept. 1926; *s* of late Henry Arden Wood, AMIMechE, and Victoria Wood (*née* Holt); *m* 1957, Dorinda Rae (*née* Hartley) (*d* 1990); one *s* one *d*. *Educ:* Ashville Coll., Harrogate; Harrogate Grammar Sch.; Hertford Coll., Oxford; Leeds Schs of Architecture and Town Planning. Dip. and Dip. with Dist. Served 8th Royal Tank Regt, Leeds Rifles TA and Westminster Dragoons TA, 1944–62. Architect, Stockholm CC, Harlow New Town, W Riding CC, Leeds CC, Glasgow Corp., partner in private practice, 1951–65; City Planning Officer, Norwich, 1965–72; County Planner, Hereford and Worcester CC, 1972–73; County Architect and Planner, W Midlands CC, 1973–84; Head of Area Conservation, English Heritage, 1984–87. Buildings and other works include: housing in Harlow, Leeds and Glasgow, 1953–65; conservation, 1965–72, and first pedestrianisation in UK, Norwich, 1967; conservation, Jewellry Quarter, Birmingham, 1980–84; Birmingham Internat. Airport, 1984. Member: Historic Buildings Council for England, 1969–84; RTPI Council, 1969–75; UK Exec. European Architectural Heritage Year, 1975 (Chm., Heritage Grants Cttee); Preservation Policy Gp, 1967–70; Environmental Bd, 1975–78; Bd, Sheffield Develt Corp., 1990–94 (Chm., Design Panel, 1989–94); Comr, Indep. Transport Commn, 1972–74. Prof., Centre for the Conservation of Historic Towns and Bldgs, Katholieke Univ., Leuven, Belgium, ex Coll. of Europe, Bruges, 1976–86; External Examiner at several univs; adviser, at various times, Council of Europe, Strasbourg, and OECD, Paris; various lecture tours and conf. addresses in Europe and N America. Civic Trust awards, 1969, 1971. *Publications:* contributions to jls of learned societies. *Recreations:* cities, buildings, travel, trams, trains, music, many wines. *Address:* The Hall Barn, Dunley, near Stourport-on-Severn, Worcestershire DY13 0TX.

WOOD, Sir Andrew Marley, KCMG 1995 (CMG 1986); HM Diplomatic Service; Ambassador to the Russian Federation and to Moldova, since 1995; *b* 2 Jan. 1940; *s* of Robert George Wood; *m* 1st, 1972, Melanie LeRoy Masset (*d* 1977); one *s*; 2nd, 1978, Stephanie Lee Masset; one *s* one *d*. *Educ:* Ardingly Coll.; King's Coll., Cambridge (MA 1965). Foreign Office, 1961; Moscow, 1964; Washington, 1967; FCO, 1970; seconded to Cabinet Office, 1971; First Sec., FCO, 1973; First Sec. and Hd of Chancery, Belgrade, 1976; Counsellor, 1978; Hd of Chancery, Moscow, 1979; Hd of W European Dept, 1982, Hd of Personnel Operations Dept, 1983, FCO; Ambassador to Yugoslavia, 1985–89; Minister, Washington, 1989–92; Chief Clerk, FCO, 1992–95. *Address:* c/o Foreign and Commonwealth Office, SW1A 2AH.

WOOD, Sir Anthony John P.; *see* Page Wood.

WOOD, Anthony Richard; HM Diplomatic Service, retired; *b* 13 Feb. 1932; *s* of late Rev. T. J. Wood and of Phyllis Margaret (*née* Bold); *m* 1966, Sarah Drew (marr. diss. 1973); one *s* one *d*. *Educ:* St Edward's Sch.; Worcester Coll., Oxford (BA). HM Forces, 1950–52. British Sch. of Archaeology in Iraq, Nimrud, 1956; joined HM Foreign Service, 1957; served: Beirut, 1957; Bahrain, 1958; Paris, 1959; Benghazi, 1962; Aden, 1963; Basra, 1966; Tehran, 1970; Muscat, 1980; Counsellor, FCO, 1984–87. *Recreations:* walking, singing. *Clubs:* Army and Navy, Royal Green Jackets.

WOOD, Ven. Arnold; Warden, Community of the Epiphany, since 1985; Archdeacon of Cornwall and Canon Residentiary (Librarian), Truro Cathedral, 1981–88; Archdeacon and Canon Emeritus, 1988; *b* 24 Oct. 1918; *s* of Harry and Annie Wood; *m* 1945, Dorothy Charlotte Tapper; two *d*. *Educ:* Holy Trinity School, Halifax; London Univ. (Dip. Economics). Commissioned, RASC, 1939–49. Legal Adviser and Man. Director, CMI Engineering Co. Ltd, 1949–63; student, Clifton Theological Coll., 1963–65; Curate, Kirkheaton, W Yorks, 1965–67; Vicar, Mount Pellon, W Yorks, 1967–73; Rector of Lanreath and Vicar of Pelynt, 1973–81; Rural Dean, West Wivelshire, dio. Truro, 1976–81. Mem., General Synod, 1985–88. Gen. Comr of Income Tax, 1977–93. *Recreations:* walking, bowls, music. *Address:* Cobblers, Quethiock, Liskeard, Cornwall PL14 3SQ. *T:* Liskeard (01579) 344788. *Club:* Commonwealth Trust.

WOOD, Charles; Chief Executive, London Borough of Brent, since 1986; *b* 16 May 1950; *s* of Sir Frank Wood, KBE, CB and Lady (Olive May) Wood (*née* Wilson); *m* Carolyn Hall; three *s* two *d*. *Educ:* King's College London (BSc Hons); Polytechnic of Central London (DipTP). Engineer, GLC, 1971–76; Planner, and Dep. Dir of Housing, London Borough of Hammersmith and Fulham, 1976–82; Dir of Develt, London Borough of Brent, 1982–86. *Recreations:* walking, tennis. *Address:* Brent Town Hall, Forty Lane, Wembley, HA9 9HX.

WOOD, Charles Gerald, FRSL 1984; writer for films, television and the theatre, since 1962; *b* 6 Aug. 1932; *s* of John Edward Wood, actor and Catherine Mae (*née* Harris), actress; *m* 1954, Valerie Elizabeth Newman, actress; one *s* one *d*. *Educ:* King Charles I Sch., Kidderminster; Birmingham Coll. of Art. Corp., 17/21st Lancers, 1950–55; Factory worker, 1955–57; Stage Manager, advertising artist, cartoonist, scenic artist, 1957–59; Bristol Evening Post, 1959–62. Member: Drama Adv. Panel, South Western Arts, 1972–73; Council, BAFTA, 1991–93. Consultant to Nat. Film Develt Fund, 1980–82. *Wrote plays:* Prisoner and Escort, John Thomas, Spare, (Cockade), Arts Theatre, 1963; Meals on Wheels, Royal Court, 1965; Don't Make Me Laugh, Aldwych, 1966; Fill the Stage with Happy Hours, Nottingham Playhouse, Vaudeville Theatre, 1967; Dingo, Bristol Arts Centre, Royal Court, 1967; H, National Theatre, 1969; Welfare, Liverpool Everyman, 1971; Veterans, Lyceum, Edinburgh, Royal Court, 1972; Jingo, RSC, 1975; Has 'Washington' Legs?, Nat. Theatre, 1978; Red Star, RSC, 1984; Across from the Garden of Allah, Comedy, 1986; adapted Pirandello's Man, Beast and Virtue, Nat. Theatre, 1989 and The Mountain Giants, Nat. Theatre, 1993. *Screenplays include:* The Knack, 1965 (Grand Prix, Cannes; Writers Guild Award for Best Comedy); Help!, 1965; How I Won the War, 1967; The Charge of the Light Brigade, 1968; The Long Day's Dying, 1969; Cuba, 1980; Wagner, 1983; Red Monarch, 1983; Puccini, 1984; Tumbledown, 1988 (Prix Italia, RAI Prize, 1988; BAFTA, Broadcasting Press Guild and RTS awards, 1989); Shooting the Hero, 1991; An Awfully Big Adventure, 1993; Rakewell, 1993; *adapted:* Bed Sitting Room, 1973. Numerous television plays incl. Prisoner and Escort, Drums Along the Avon, Drill Pig, A Bit of a Holiday, A Bit of an Adventure, Do As I Say, Love Lies Bleeding, Dust to Dust; creator of Gordon Maple in series, Don't Forget to Write; Company of Adventurers (series for CBC), 1986; My Family and Other Animals (series for BBC), 1987; The Settling of the Sun, 1987; Sharpe's Company, 1994; A Breed of Heroes, 1994. Evening Standard Awards, 1963, 1973. *Publications:* plays: Cockade, 1965; Fill the Stage with Happy Hours, 1967; Dingo, 1967; H, 1970; Veterans, 1972; Has 'Washington' Legs?, 1978; Tumbledown, 1987; Man, Beast and Virtue, 1990; The Mountain Giants, 1993. *Recreations:* military and theatrical studies; gardening. *Address:* c/o Jane Annakin, William Morris (UK) Ltd, 31/32 Soho Square, W1V 5DG. *T:* 0171–434 2191. *Clubs:* Royal Over-Seas League, British Playwrights' Mafia.

WOOD, Rear Adm. Christopher Lainson, CB 1991; Director, Association of Leading Visitor Attractions, since 1992; *b* 9 Feb. 1936; *s* of Gordon and Eileen Wood; *m* 1962, Margot Price; two *s* one *d*. *Educ:* Pangbourne College. FBIM; MNI. Seaman Officer, RN, 1954; joined submarine service, 1958; CO's qualifying course, 1966; in comd, HMS Ambush, 1966–68; JSSC, 1970; nuclear submarine training, 1971; in comd, HMS Warspite, 1971–73; Staff of FO Submarines, 1973–75; Staff of Dir, Naval Op. Requirements, 1975–77; Underwater Weapons Acceptance, 1978–81; Dep. Dir, Naval Op. Requirements, 1981–83; Dir Gen., Underwater Weapons, 1983–85; Dir Gen., Fleet Support, 1986–88; ACDS, Operational Requirements (Sea Systems), 1988–91. *Recreations:* reading, outdoor pursuits, sailing, fishing, sporting interests, community and church work. *Clubs:* Institute of Directors, Royal Over-Seas League.

WOOD, Rt. Rev. Clyde Maurice, BA, ThL; Bishop of the Western Region, and an Assistant Bishop, Diocese of Brisbane, since 1992; *b* 7 Jan. 1936; *s* of Maurice O. Wood and Helen M. Wood; *m* 1957, Margaret Joan Burls; two *s* one *d*. *Educ:* Perry Hall, Melbourne (ThL 1964); Monash Univ. (BA 1974). Deacon 1965, priest 1965; Curate: St John's, Bentleigh, 1965–66; St Paul's, Ringwood, 1966–67; in Dept of Evangelism and Extension, 1967–70; Curate-in-Charge: St Philip's, Mount Waverley, 1967–70; Armadale/Hawksburn, 1970–73; Rector and Canon Res., Christ Church Cathedral, Darwin, 1974, Dean 1978–83; on leave, Rector St Timothy's Episcopal Church, Indianapolis, USA, 1981; Bishop of the Northern Territory, 1983–92. OStJ 1980; ChStJ 1985. *Recreations:* golf, sailing. *Address:* PO Box 2600, Toowoomba, Qld 4350, Australia; 19 East Street, Toowoomba, Qld 4350, Australia. *T:* (76) 327240, (office) (76) 391875.

WOOD, David; actor, playwright, composer, theatrical producer and director; *b* 21 Feb. 1944; *s* of Richard Edwin Wood and Audrey Adele Wood (*née* Fincham) *m* 1975, Jacqueline Stanbury; two *d*. *Educ:* Chichester High Sch. for Boys; Worcester Coll., Oxford. BA (Hons). Acted with OUDS and ETC at Oxford; first London appearance in ETC prodn, Hang Down Your Head and Die (also co-writer), Comedy, 1964; later performances include: A Spring Song, Mermaid, 1964; Dr Faustus (OUDS), 1966; Four Degrees Over, Edinburgh Festival and Fortune, 1966 (also contrib. lyrics and sketches); repertory, 1966–69; RSC's After Haggerty, Aldwych 1970, and Criterion 1971; A Voyage Round My Father, Greenwich, 1970, Toronto, 1972; Me Times Me, tour, 1971; Mrs Warren's Profession, 1972, and revue Just the Ticket, 1973, Thorndike, Leatherhead; The Provok'd Wife, Greenwich, 1973; Jeeves, Her Majesty's, 1975; Terra Nova, Chichester, 1980. *Films include:* If . . . , 1968; Aces High, 1975; Sweet William, 1978; North Sea Hijack, 1979. *TV plays and series include:* Mad Jack, Fathers and Sons, Cheri, The Vamp, Sporting Scenes, Disraeli, The Avengers, Van der Valk, Danger UXB, Huntingtower, Enemy at the Door, Jackanory, Jim'll Fix It, When the Boat Comes In, The Brack Report, Tricky Business, Watch. Various revues in collaboration with John Gould; music and lyrics, The Stiffkey Scandals of 1932, Queen's, 1967; with John Gould formed Whirligig Theatre, touring children's theatre company, 1979; has directed one of own plays on tour and at Sadler's Wells Theatre, annually 1979–; has performed David Wood Magic and Music Show in theatres all over UK, incl. Polka Theatre, Arts Theatre and Purcell Room, 1983–. Formed, jointly: Verronmead Ltd, indep. TV producing co., 1983; Westwood Theatrical Productions Ltd, 1986; W2 Productions Ltd, 1995. *TV series scripts:* Chips' Comic; Chish 'n' Fips; Seeing and Doing; The Gingerbread Man; *screenplays:* Swallows and Amazons, 1974; Back Home, 1989; Tide Race, 1989. *Publications: musical plays for children:* (with Sheila Ruskin) The Owl and the Pussycat went to see . . . , 1968; (with Sheila Ruskin) Larry the Lamb in Toytown, 1969; The Plotters of Cabbage Patch Corner, 1970; Flibberty and the Penguin, 1971; The Papertown Paperchase, 1972; Hijack over Hygenia, 1973; Old Mother Hubbard, 1975; The Gingerbread Man, 1976; Old Father Time, 1976; (with Tony Hatch and Jackie Trent) Rock Nativity, 1976; Nutcracker Sweet, 1977; Mother Goose's Golden Christmas, 1977; Tickle, 1978; Babes in the Magic Wood, 1978; There Was an Old Woman . . . , 1979; Cinderella, 1979; Aladdin, 1981; (with Dave and Toni Arthur) Robin Hood, 1981; Dick Whittington and Wondercat, 1981; Meg and Mog Show, 1981; The Ideal Gnome Expedition, 1982; Jack and the Giant, 1982; The Selfish Shellfish, 1983; (with ABBA and Don Black) Abbacadabra, 1984; (with Dave and Toni Arthur) Jack the Lad, 1984; (with Peter Pontzen) Dinosaurs and all that Rubbish, 1985; The Seesaw Tree, 1986; The Old Man of Lochnagar (based on book by HRH the Prince of Wales), 1986; (with Dave and Toni Arthur) The Pied Piper, 1988; Save the Human, 1990; The BFG (based on book by Roald Dahl), 1991; The Witches (based on book by Roald Dahl), 1992; Rupert and the Green Dragon, 1993; Noddy (based on books by Enid Blyton), 1994; *books for children:* The Gingerbread Man, 1985; (with Geoffrey Beitz) The Operats of Rodent Garden, 1984; (with Geoffrey Beitz) The Discorats, 1985; Chish 'n' Fips, 1987; Sidney the Monster, 1988; Save the Human, 1991; The BFG: plays for children, 1993; Meg and Mog: plays for children, 1994; with Richard Fowler: Play-Theatres, 1987; Happy Birthday, Mouse, 1991 (USA 1990); Baby Bear's Buggy Ride, 1993; Pop-up Theatre (Cinderella), 1994; Bedtime Story, 1995; The Magic Show, 1995; articles in Drama, London Drama. *Recreations:* writing, conjuring, collecting old books. *Address:* c/o Casarotto Ramsay Ltd, National House, 60 Wardour Street, W1V 3HP. *T:* 0171–287 4450, *Fax:* 0171–287 9128. *Club:* Green Room.

WOOD, Sir David (Basil) H.; *see* Hill-Wood.

WOOD, Rear-Adm. David John, CEng, FRAeS; Director General Aircraft (Navy), Ministry of Defence, since 1995; *b* 12 June 1942; *s* of John Herbert Wood and Nesta (*née* Jones); *m* 1966, Hilary Jolly; two *s* one *d*. *Educ:* St Paul's Sch.; BRNC Dartmouth; RNEC Manadon (BScEng 1965). Joined BRNC 1960; service in 892, 846, 707 Sqdns and HMS Ark Royal, 1967–73; Aircraft Dept (Navy), 1973–76; Air Engineer Officer, Lynx IFTU, 1976–77; Army Staff Course, 1978; Helicopter Procurement, MoD (PE), 1979–81; Naval Sec's Dept, MoD, 1981–84; Staff of FONAC, 1984–86; NATO Defence Coll., 1986–87; Asst Dir, EH101, MoD (PE), 1987–89; Dir, Aircraft Support Policy (Navy), 1989–91; Dir, Maritime Projects, MoD (PE), 1991–95. *Recreations:* cross-country and long distance running, choral singing. *Address:* Directorate General Aircraft (Navy), Ministry of Defence, Whitehall, SW1A 2HB. *Club:* Army and Navy.

WOOD, David Russell; His Honour Judge David Wood; a Circuit Judge, since 1995; *b* 13 Dec. 1948; *s* of Christopher Russell Wood and Muriel Wynn Wood (*née* Richardson); *m* 1979, Georgina Susan Buckle; two *s* one *d*. *Educ:* Sedbergh Sch.; Univ. of East Anglia (BA). Called to the Bar, Gray's Inn, 1973; Recorder, 1989–95. *Recreations:* shooting, fishing, farming, piano. *Address:* Newcastle upon Tyne Crown Court, Quayside, Newcastle upon Tyne. *Club:* Northern Counties (Newcastle upon Tyne).

WOOD, Maj.-Gen. Denys Broomfield, CB 1978; Independent Inquiry Inspector, 1984–93; General Commissioner for Taxes, since 1986; *b* 2 Nov. 1923; *s* of late Percy Neville Wood and Meryl Broomfield; *m* 1948, Jennifer Nora Page, *d* of late Air Cdre William Morton Page, CBE; one *s* two *d*. *Educ:* Radley; Pembroke Coll., Cambridge. MA: CEng, FIMechE. Commissioned into REME, 1944; war service in UK and Far East, 1944–47; Staff Captain, WO, 1948–49; Instructor, RMA, Sandhurst, 1949–52; Staff Coll., 1953; DAA&QMG, 11 Infantry Bde, 1955–57; OC, 10 Infantry Workshop, Malaya, 1958–60; jssc 1960; Directing Staff, Staff Coll., 1961–63; Comdr, REME, 3rd Div., 1963–65; Operational Observer, Viet Nam, 1966–67; Col GS, Staff Coll., 1967–69; idc 1970; Dir, Administrative Planning, 1971–73; Dep. Military Sec. (2), 1973–75; Dir of Army Quartering, 1975–78. Exec. Sec., 1978–82, Sec., 1982–84, CEI. Col Comdt, REME, 1978–84. Lay Mem., Law Soc. Adjudication Cttee, 1986–92. FRSA. *Recreations:* walking, gardening, reading. *Address:* Elmtree House, Hurtmore, Godalming, Surrey GU7 2RA. *T:* Godalming (01483) 416936. *Club:* Army and Navy.

WOOD, Derek Alexander, CBE 1995; QC 1978; a Recorder, since 1985; Principal, St Hugh's College, Oxford, since 1991; *b* 14 Oct. 1937; *s* of Alexander Cecil Wood and Rosetta (*née* Lelyveld); *m* 1961, Sally Teresa Clarke, *d* of Lady Elliott and step *d* of Sir Norman Elliott, CBE; two *d*. *Educ:* Tiffin Boys' Sch., Kingston-upon-Thames; University Coll., Oxford (MA, BCL). Called to the Bar, Middle Temple, 1964, Bencher, 1986. Department of the Environment: Mem., Adv. Gp on Commercial Property Develt, 1975–78; Mem., Property Adv. Gp, 1978–; Mem., Working Party on New Forms of Social Ownership and Tenure in Housing, 1976; Chm., Review of Rating of Plant and Machinery, 1991; Chm., Standing Adv. Cttee on Trunk Road Assessment, Dept of Transport, 1987–. Dep. Chm., Soc. of Labour Lawyers, 1978–90. Chm., Chislehurst Constituency Labour Party, 1972–76, 1979–84. Mem. Council, London Bor. of Bromley, 1975–78. Fellow, CAAV, 1988; FCIArb 1993. FRSA 1992. Hon. ARICS 1991. *Publication:* (with R. H. Bernstein) Handbook of Arbitration Practice, 1993. *Recreation:* music. *Address:* St Hugh's College, Oxford OX2 6LE. *Clubs:* Athenæum, Royal Automobile, Architecture; Kent Valuers' (Hon. Mem.).

WOOD, Prof. Derek Rawlins, FIBiol; Dean of Faculty of Medicine and Professor of Applied Pharmacology, University of Leeds, 1969–86, now Professor Emeritus; *b* 16 May 1921; *s* of Frederick Charles Wood and Ruth Dorothy (*née* Rawlins); *m* 1945, Mary Elizabeth Caldwell; two *s* two *d* (and one *s* decd). *Educ:* Wm Hulme's Grammar Sch., Manchester; Brasenose Coll. and Radcliffe Infirmary, Oxford. BM BCh, BSc, MA Oxford. House Physician, Radcliffe Inf., 1945; Demonstrator, Pharmacology, Oxford, 1945–46; Lectr 1946, Sen. Lectr 1952–57, Pharmacology, Univ. of Sheffield; J. H. Hunt Travelling Schol., 1949; J. H. Brown Fellow, Pharmacol., Yale, 1955–56; Associate Prof., Pharmacol., McGill Univ., 1957–60; Prof. and Head of Dept of Pharmacol., Univ. of Leeds, 1960–69. Hon. Sec., 1952–57, Hon. Treas., 1964–70, Hon. Mem., 1994, Brit. Pharmacol. Soc.; Member: Stag Jt Commn on Classification of Proprietary Remedies, 1964–69; British Nat. Formulary Cttee, 1967–74; Adv. Commn on Pesticides, 1968–70; Brit. Pharmacopoeia Commn, 1969–79; GMC, 1969–86; Gen. Dental Council, 1971–86; Leeds Reg. Hosp. Bd, 1969–74; Bd of Governors, United Leeds Hosps, 1969–74; Leeds AHA (T), 1974–82; Leeds DHA, West and East, 1982–84. Exec. Sec., University Hosps Assoc., 1988–91 (Chm., 1978–81). Mem. Court, Univs of Bradford, 1970–91, and Sheffield, 1966–79. Hon. MPS. *Publications:* Dental Pharmacology and Therapeutics (with L. E. Francis), 1961; contribs to Brit. Jl Pharmacol., Jl Physiol., and others. *Recreations:* gardening, music. *Address:* 5 Spring Terrace, Lothersdale, Keighley, W Yorks BD20 8HA. *T:* Cross Hills (01535) 632593.

WOOD, Dudley Ernest, CBE 1995; Secretary, Rugby Football Union, 1986–95; *b* 18 May 1930; *s* of Ernest Edward and Ethel Louise Wood; *m* 1955, Mary Christina Blake; two *s*. *Educ:* Luton Grammar School; St Edmund Hall, Oxford (BA Modern Languages). ICI 1954; Petrochemicals and Plastics Division, ICI: Overseas Manager, 1977–82; Sales and Marketing Manager, 1982–86. Rugby Football: Oxford Blue, 1952, 1953; played for Bedford, Rosslyn Park, Waterloo, Streatham-Croydon, East Midlands; Hon. Life Mem., Squash Rackets Assoc., 1984. *Recreations:* Rugby Football, squash, dog breeding (golden retriever), travel, Middle East affairs. *Address:* Mead Hall, Little Walden, Saffron Walden, Essex CB10 1UX. *Club:* East India.

WOOD, Eric; Finance Director (formerly Finance Officer), University of Bristol, 1979–91; *b* 22 Sept. 1931; *s* of Herbert Francis and Eva Wood; *m* 1955, Erica Twist; three *d*. *Educ:* West Hartlepool Grammar Sch.; Blandford Grammar Sch.; St Peter's Coll., Oxford (MA). IPFA. National Service, Army, 1950–51. Finance Depts, Cheshire, Durham and Notts County Councils, 1954–65; Finance Dept, London Transport, 1965–67; Asst Treasurer, GLC, 1967–73; Dir, CIPFA, 1973–79. *Publications:* articles in prof. accountancy press. *Recreations:* skiing, squash, hill-walking, bridge. *Address:* 14 Alexandra Road, Clifton, Bristol BS8 2DD. *T:* Bristol (0117) 973 0881.

WOOD, Francis Gordon, FIA; Deputy Chief General Manager, Prudential Assurance Co. Ltd, 1982–85; non-Executive Director, Prudential Corporation, 1985–90 (Director, 1984); *b* 30 Oct. 1924; *s* of Francis R. and Florence A. Wood; *m* 1950, Margaret Parr; two *d*. *Educ:* Alleyne's Grammar School, Stone, Staffs. ACII. Prudential Assurance Co. Ltd, 1941–85; Dir, 1981. *Recreation:* golf. *Address:* 6 Matching Lane, Bishop's Stortford, Herts CM23 2PP. *T:* Bishop's Stortford (01279) 652197.

WOOD, Frank; His Honour Judge Wood; Resident Judge, Sovereign Base Areas of Akrotiri and Dhekelia, since 1986; *b* 10 June 1929; *s* of late Robert Wood and Marjorie Edith Park Wood (*née* Senior); *m* 1951, Diana Mae Shenton; two *s* one *d*. *Educ:* Berkhamsted; RMA Sandhurst. Called to the Bar, Lincoln's Inn, 1969. Commissioned RASC, 1949–52. Bechuanaland Protectorate Police, 1953–65 (Supt 1965), Acting Dist Comr, 1957–58, 1959–60; Crown Counsel, Bechuanaland, 1965–66, State Counsel, 1966–67; Magistrate, Seychelles, 1970, Sen. Magistrate, 1974; Puisne Judge and Justice of Appeal, Seychelles, 1977–85, Acting Chief Justice, 1982–84; Chief Justice and Justice of Appeal, Solomon Islands, 1985–86; Justice of Appeal, Vanuatu, 1985–87. Chancellor, Dio. of Seychelles, 1973–84. Mem. Council, Commonwealth Magistrates' Assoc., 1973–77. *Publication:* Sovereign Base Areas Law Reports 1960–87, 1988. *Recreations:* reading, philately. *Address:* Judge's Chambers, HM Court, Episkopi, BFPO 53; The Barn, Ewyas Harold, Hereford HR2 0JF. *Clubs:* Royal Over-Seas League, Commonwealth Trust, Civil Service.

WOOD, Sir Frederick (Ambrose Stuart), Kt 1977; Hon. Life President, Croda International Ltd, since 1987 (Managing Director, 1953–85, Executive Chairman, 1960–85, non-executive Chairman, 1985–86); *b* 30 May 1926; *s* of Alfred Phillip Wood, Goole, Yorkshire, and Patras, Greece, and Charlotte Wood (*née* Barnes), Goole, Yorkshire, and Athens, Greece; *m* 1947, J. R. (Su) King; two *s* one *d*. *Educ:* Felsted Sch., Essex; Clare Coll., Cambridge. Served War, Sub-Lt (A) Observer, Fleet Air Arm, 1944–47. Trainee Manager, Croda Ltd, 1947–50; Pres., Croda Inc., New York, 1950–53. Chm., Nat. Bus Co., 1972–78. Mem., 1973–78, Chm., 1979–83, NRDC; Chm. NEB, 1981–83; Chm., British Technology Gp, 1981–83. Mem., Nationalised Industries Chms' Gp, 1975–78. Chm. British Sect., Centre Européen d'Entreprise Publique, 1976–78. Hon. LLD Hull, 1983. *Address:* Hearn Wood, The Mount, Headley, Hants GU35 8AG. *T:* Headley Down (01428) 712134.

WOOD, Gillian, (Mrs R. Wood); *see* Tishler, G.

WOOD, Maj.-Gen. Harry Stewart, CB 1967; TD 1950; *b* 16 Sept. 1913; *e s* of late Roland and Eva M. Wood; *m* 1939, Joan Gordon, *d* of Gordon S. King; two *s* (and one *s* decd). *Educ:* Nautical Coll., Pangbourne. Civil Engineer (inc. articled trg), 1931–39. Commnd RA (TA), 1937. Served War of 1939–45: Regimental Service, Sept. 1939–June 1944; subseq. Technical Staff. Dep. Dir of Artillery, Min. of Supply (Col), 1958–60; Dep. Dir, Inspectorate of Armaments (Brig.), 1960–62; Sen. Mil. Officer, Royal Armament Research and Development Estab. (Brig.), 1962–64; Vice-President, Ordnance Board, 1964–66, President, 1966–67. Maj.-Gen. 1964; retd, 1967. Legion of Merit, degree of Legionnaire (USA), 1947. *Recreations:* home and garden, motor sport. *Address:* Brook House, Faygate, near Horsham, Sussex RH12 4SS. *T:* Faygate (01293) 851342.

WOOD, Hugh Bradshaw; composer; University Lecturer in Music, Cambridge University, and Fellow of Churchill College, Cambridge, since 1977; *b* 27 June 1932; *s* of James Bonar Wood and Winifred Bradshaw Wood; *m* 1960, Susan McGaw; one *s* one *d* (and one *d* decd). *Educ:* Oundle Sch.; New Coll., Oxford (Major Scholar; 2nd Cl. Hons Modern History, 1954). ARCM (private study with Dr W. S. Lloyd Webber), 1955. Studied: composition with Iain Hamilton, and harmony and counterpoint with Anthony Milner, 1956–58; composition with Mátyás Seiber, 1958–60; taught at: Morley Coll., 1958–67; Royal Acad. of Music, 1962–65; Univ. of Glasgow (Cramb Res. Fellow), 1966–70; Univ. of Liverpool, 1971–75; Univ. of Leeds, 1975–76; teacher, Dartington Summer Sch. of Music, 1959–74. *Main compositions: for orchestra:* Scenes from Comus (with soprano and tenor), 1965; Concerto for Cello, 1969; Chamber Concerto, 1971; Concerto for Violin, 1972; Symphony, 1982; Concerto for Piano, 1991; *chamber music:* Variations for Viola and Piano, 1958; String Quartet No 1, 1962, No 2, 1970, No 3, 1976, No 4, 1993; Piano Trio, 1984; Horn Trio, 1989; *for voice(s) and ensembles:* Logue Songs, 1961; Song Cycle to Poems of Pablo Neruda, 1974; Cantata, 1989; *songs:* Robert Graves Songs, set no 1, 1976, set no 2, 1983, set no 3, 1985. *Recreation:* thinking about going to Greece. *Address:* Churchill College, Cambridge CB3 0DS. *T:* Cambridge (01223) 336215; 32 Woodsome Road, NW5 1RZ. *T:* 0171–267 0318.

WOOD, Humphrey; *see* Wood, J. H. A.

WOOD, Sir Ian (Clark), Kt 1994; CBE 1982; Chairman since 1981, and Managing Director since 1967, John Wood Group plc; Chairman, J. W. Holdings Ltd, since 1981; *b* 21 July 1942; *s* of John Wood and Margaret (*née* Clark); *m* 1970, Helen Macrae; three *s*. *Educ:* Aberdeen Univ. (BSc Psychology, First Cl. Hons 1964). Joined John Wood Group, 1964. Dir, Royal Bank of Scotland, 1988–. Chairman: Aberdeen Beyond 2000, 1986–90; Grampian Enterprise, 1990–95. Member: Aberdeen Harbour Bd, 1972–90; Sea Fish Industry Authority, 1981–87; Offshore Industry Adv. Bd, 1988–93; Offshore Industry Export Adv. Gp, 1989–93; Bd, Scottish Develt Agency, 1984–90; Scottish Econ. Council, 1987–; Scottish Sub-Cttee, UGC, subseq. UFC, 1988–91; SHEFC, 1992–; Nat. Trng Task Force, 1988–92. CIMgt (CBIM 1983). Hon. LLD Aberdeen, 1984. Scottish Free Enterprise Award, 1985; (jtly) Scottish Business Achievement Award Trust Award, 1992; Corporate Elite Leadership Award, 1992. Silver Jubilee Medal, 1977. *Recreations:* family, squash, hill walking, reading, art. *Address:* Marchmont, 42 Rubislaw Den South, Aberdeen AB2 6BB. *T:* Aberdeen (01224) 313625.

WOOD, John; actor. *Educ:* Bedford Sch.; Jesus Coll., Oxford (Pres. OUDS). Old Vic Co., 1954–56; Camino Real, Phoenix, 1957; The Making of Moo, Royal Court, 1957; Brouhaha, Aldwych, 1958; The Fantasticks, Apollo, 1961; Rosencrantz and Guildenstern are Dead, NY, 1967; Exiles, Mermaid, 1970; joined Royal Shakespeare Company, 1971; Enemies, The Man of Mode, Exiles, The Balcony, Aldwych, 1971; The Comedy of Errors, Stratford, 1972; Julius Caesar, Titus Andronicus, Stratford, 1972, Aldwych, 1973; Collaborators, Duchess, 1973; A Lesson in Blood and Roses, The Place, 1973; Sherlock Holmes, Travesties (Evening Standard Best Actor Award, 1974; Tony Award, 1976), Aldwych, 1974, NY, 1974; The Devil's Disciple, Ivanov, Aldwych, 1976; Death Trap, NY, 1978; Undiscovered Country, Richard III, Nat. Theatre, 1979; Piaf, Wyndham's, 1980; The Provok'd Wife, Nat. Theatre, 1980; Royal Shakespeare Co.: The Tempest, 1988; The Man Who Came to Dinner, The Master Builder, 1989; King Lear, 1990 (Evening Standard Best Actor Award, 1991); Love's Labours Lost, 1990. *Television:* A Tale of Two Cities, Barnaby Rudge, 1964–65; The Victorians, 1965; The Duel, 1966. *Films:* Nicholas and Alexandra, 1971; Slaughterhouse Five, 1972; War Games, 1983; The Madness of King George, 1994. *Address:* c/o Royal Shakespeare Company, Barbican Centre, Silk Street, EC2Y 8DS.

WOOD, John, CB 1989; Director of Public Prosecutions, Hong Kong, 1990–94; *b* 11 Jan. 1931; *s* of Thomas John Wood and Rebecca Grand; *m* 1958, Jean Iris Wood; two *s*. *Educ:* King's College Sch., Wimbledon. Admitted Solicitor, 1955. Director of Public Prosecutions: Legal Assistant, 1958; Sen. Legal Asst, 1963; Asst Solicitor, 1971; Asst Director, 1977; Principal Asst Dir, 1981; Dep. Dir., 1985–87; Head of Legal Services, Crown Prosecution Service, 1986–87; Dir of Serious Fraud Office, 1987–90. *Recreations:* cricket, Rugby football, badminton, music, theatre.

WOOD, John Edwin, PhD; consultant in underwater technology, since 1990; *b* 24 July 1928; *s* of late John Stanley Wood and Alice (*née* Hardy); *m* 1953, Patricia Edith Wilson Sheppard (marr. diss. 1978); two *s* two *d*. *Educ:* Darlington Grammar Sch.; Univ. of Leeds (BSc, PhD). Joined Royal Naval Scientific Service at HM Underwater Countermeasures and Weapons Estabt, 1951; Admiralty Underwater Weapons Estabt, 1959; Head of Acoustic Research Div., 1968; Head of Sonar Dept, 1972; Admiralty Surface Weapons Establishment: Head of Weapons Dept, 1976; Head of Communications, Command and Control Dept, 1979; Chief Scientist (Royal Navy), and Director General Research (A), 1980; joined Sperry Gyroscope (subseq. British Aerospace), Bracknell, 1981; Exec. Dir, BAe, Bristol, 1984–88; Dir of Underwater Engrg, BAe Dynamics Div., 1988–90. Pres., Gp 12, Council of British Archaeology, 1984–93. *Publications:* Sun, Moon and Standing Stones, 1978, 2nd edn 1980; papers and book reviews in technical and archaeological jls. *Recreations:* archaeology, fell-walking. *Address:* 7 Pennant Hills, Bedhampton, Havant, Hants PO9 3JZ. *T:* Havant (01705) 471411.

WOOD, (John) Humphrey (Askey); a Managing Director, Consolidated Gold Fields plc, 1979–89; Chairman, Vinten Group plc, since 1991; non-executive director of cos; *b* 26 Nov. 1932; *s* of late Lt-Col Edward Askey Wood and Irene Jeanne Askey Wood; *m* 1st, 1965, Jane Holland; one *s*; 2nd, 1981, Katherine Ruth Stewart Reardon (*née* Peverley); one step *s* one step *d*. *Educ:* Abberley Hall; Winchester College; Corpus Christi College, Cambridge. MA (Mech. Scis). De Havilland Aircraft Co. Ltd, 1956; Hawker Siddeley Aviation Ltd, 1964, Dir and Gen. Manager, Manchester, 1969–76; Man. Dir, Industrial and Marine Div., Rolls-Royce Ltd, 1976–79; Chm., Amey Roadstone Corp., 1979–86. Director: Gold Fields of South Africa Ltd, 1986–89; Blue Tee Corp., 1986–89; Non-Exec. Director: Birse Gp plc, 1989–; Albrighton plc, 1990– (Chm., 1993–). Butten Trustee, PA Consulting Gp, 1991–. Vice-Pres., Nat. Council of Building Material Producers, 1985–89. Mem. Council, CBI, 1983–89. *Recreations:* fly fishing, sailing, painting. *Address:* Albyn House, 239 New King's Road, SW6 4XG. *T:* 0171–731 5092.

WOOD, Sir John (Kember), Kt 1977; MC 1944; a Judge of the High Court of Justice, Family Division, 1977–93; President, Employment Appeal Tribunal, 1988–93 (Judge, 1985–88); *b* Hong Kong, 8 Aug. 1922; *s* of John Roskruge Wood and Gladys Frances (*née* Kember); *m* 1952, Kathleen Ann Lowe; one *s* one *d*. *Educ:* Shrewsbury Sch.; Magdalene Coll., Cambridge. Served War of 1939–45: Rifle Brigade, 1941–46; ME and Italy; PoW, 1944. Magdalene Coll., 1946–48. Barrister (Lincoln's Inn), 1949, Bencher, 1977; QC 1969; a Recorder of the Crown Court, 1975–77. Vice-Chm., Parole Bd, 1987–89 (Mem. 1986–89). *Recreations:* sport, travel. *Address:* 2 Lansdowne Road, Holland Park W11 3LW. *Clubs:* Garrick, MCC; Hawks (Cambridge).

WOOD, J(ohn) Laurence; Keeper, Department of Printed Books, British Library, 1966–76; retired; *b* 27 Nov. 1911; *s* of J. A. Wood and Clara Josephine (*née* Ryan); *m* 1947, Rowena Beatrice Ross; one *s* one *d*. *Educ:* Bishop Auckland; Merton Coll., Oxford (BA); Besançon; Paris. Lecteur, Univ. of Besançon, 1934; Asst Cataloguer, British Museum, 1936; seconded to Foreign Office, 1941; Asst Keeper, British Museum, 1946; Deputy Keeper, 1959. Editor, Factotum, 1978–. *Publications:* (trans.) The French Prisoner, Garneray, 1957; (trans.) Contours of the Middle Ages, Genicot, 1967. *Recreation:* bookbinding. *Address:* 88 Hampstead Way, NW11 7XY. *T:* 0181–455 4395.

WOOD, John Peter; freelance gardening journalist and broadcaster; *b* 27 March 1925; *s* of Walter Ralph Wood and Henrietta Martin; *m* 1956, Susan Maye White; one *s* one *d*. *Educ:* Grove Park Grammar Sch.; Seale Hayne Agricultural Coll. (NDH and Dip. in Hort., of College). FIHort 1986. Served War, 1943–46. Horticultural studies, 1946–52; Amateur Gardening: Asst Editor, 1952–66; Dep. Editor, 1966–71; Editor, 1971–86; Cons. Editor, 1986–89. *Publications:* Amateur Gardening Handbook—Bulbs, 1957; Amateur Gardening Picture Book—Greenhouse Management, 1959; (jtly) The Complete Book of Roses, 1993. *Recreations:* gardening, choral singing. *Address:* 1 Charlton House Court, Charlton Marshall, Blandford, Dorset DT11 9NT. *T:* Blandford (01258) 454653.

WOOD, Joseph Neville, (Johnnie), CBE 1978; Director General, The General Council of British Shipping, 1975–78; *b* 25 October 1916; *o s* of late Robert Hind Wood and Emily Wood, Durham; *m* 1st, 1944, Elizabeth May (*d* 1959); three *d*; 2nd, 1965, Josephine Samuel (*née* Dane) (*d* 1985); 3rd, 1986, Frances Howarth (*née* Skeer). *Educ:* Johnston School, Durham; London School of Economics. Entered Civil Service (Board of Trade), 1935; Ministry of War Transport, 1940; jssc 1950; Ministry of Transport: Asst Sec., 1951; Far East Representative, 1952–55; Under-Sec., 1961; Chief of Highway Administration, 1967–68. Joined Chamber of Shipping of the UK, 1968, Dep. Dir, 1970, Dir, 1972–78. Mem., Baltic Exchange, 1968–; Director: Finance for Shipping Ltd, 1978–82; Ship Mortgage Finance Co. Ltd, 1978–83. Mem. Chichester DC, 1979–91. Vice Pres., Shipwrecked Fishermen and Mariners Royal Benevolent Soc., 1989– (Dep. Chm., 1983–89). FCIT 1976. Freeman, City of London, 1978. Officier, Ordre de Mérite Maritime, 1950. *Recreation:* gardening. *Address:* Barbers Cottage, Heyshott, Midhurst, Sussex GU29 0DE. *T:* Midhurst (01730) 814282.

WOOD, Kenneth Maynard; consultant; *b* 4 Oct. 1916; *s* of late Frederick Cavendish Wood and Agnes Maynard; *m* Patricia Rose; two *s* two *d* (by previous marriage), and three step *s*. *Educ:* Bromley County School. Cadet, Merchant Navy, 1930–34; electrical and mechanical engineering, 1934–37; started own company radio, television and radar development, 1937–39; sold business and joined RAF, transferred for development of electronic equipment, 1939–46; started Kenwood Manufacturing Co. Ltd, 1946; Managing Director, 1946 until take-over by Thorn Electrical Industries Ltd, 1968; Chm. and Man.

Dir, Dawson-Keith Group of Companies, 1972–80; Chm, Hydrotech Systems Ltd, 1984–87. Fellow, Inst. of Ophthalmology. *Recreation:* golf. *Address:* Dellwood Cottage, Wheatsheaf Enclosure, Liphook, Hants GU30 7EH. *T:* Liphook (01428) 723108.

WOOD, Leonard George, CBE 1978; Director of Parent Board, 1965–80, and Group Director, Music, 1966–78, EMI Ltd; *s* of Leonard George Wood and Miriam (*née* Barnes); *m* 1936, Christine Florence Reason (*d* 1978). *Educ:* Bishopshalt Sch., Hillingdon, Mddx; London Univ. (BCom). Served War, RAF: Sgt, Airfield Controller, 1943; commnd Flying Control Officer, 1944–46. Asst Record Sales Manager, UK, EMI Ltd, 1939, Record Sales Man., 1947; EMI Records Ltd: Gen. Man., 1957; Man. Dir, 1959–66; Chm., 1966–78; EMI Ltd: Gp Divl Dir, 1961; Gp Asst Man. Dir, 1973–77. Internat. Fedn of Producers of Phonograms and Videograms: Chm. Council, 1968–73; Pres., 1973–76; Vice Pres. and Mem. Bd, 1967–81, Emeritus Vice-Pres., 1981–82; Mem. Bd, IFPI (Secretariat) Ltd, 1979–81. Chm., Record Merchandisers Ltd, 1975–81; Dep. Chm., Phonographic Performance Ltd, 1967–80; Hon. Pres., Brit. Phonographic Industry, 1980– (Chm., 1973–80); Governor, Brit. Inst. of Recorded Sound, 1974–78; Trustee, British Record Industry Trust, 1989–94. FRSA 1971–85. *Publication:* paper to RSA on growth and develt of recording industry. *Address:* Lark Rise, 39 Howards Thicket, Gerrards Cross, Bucks SL9 7NT. *T:* Gerrards Cross (01753) 884233.

WOOD, Leslie Walter; General Secretary, Union of Construction, Allied Trades and Technicians, 1978–85, retired; Member, TUC General Council, 1979–85; *b* 27 Nov. 1920; *s* of Walter William Wood and Alice Bertha Wood (*née* Clark); *m* 1945 Irene Gladys Emery; two *d*. *Educ:* Birmingham Central Technical Coll.; Ruskin Coll., Oxford. Apprenticed carpenter and joiner, 1935; RAF, 1939–45; Asst Workers' Sec., Cadbury's Works Council, 1948–49; full time employment in Union, 1953–85; Asst Gen. Sec., Amalgamated Soc. of Woodworkers, 1962. Mem. Council, ACAS, 1980–85. *Publication:* A Union to Build (history of Building Trades Unionism), 1979. *Recreations:* golf, swimming, bridge. *Address:* 67 Chestnut Grove, South Croydon, Surrey CR2 7LL. *T:* 0181–657 7852.

WOOD, Rt. Rev. Mark; *see* Wood, Rt Rev. S. M.

WOOD, Mark William; Editor-in-Chief, Reuters, since 1989; *b* 28 March 1952; *s* of Joseph Hatton Drew Wood and Joyce Wood; *m* 1986, Helen Lanzer; one *s* one *d*. *Educ:* Univs of Leeds (BA Hons), Warwick (MA) and Oxford. Joined Reuters, 1976; corresp. in Vienna, 1977–78, East Berlin, 1978–81, Moscow, 1981–85; Chief Corresp., West Germany, 1985–87; Editor, Europe, 1987–89. Director: Reuters Hldgs, 1990–; ITN, 1993–; Chm., Reuters Television, 1992–. *Recreations:* German literature, ski-ing. *Address:* c/o Reuters, 85 Fleet Street, EC4P 4AJ. *T:* 0171–250 1122.

WOOD, Sir Martin (Francis), Kt 1986; OBE 1982; FRS 1987; DL; Deputy Chairman, Oxford Instruments plc (Founder, 1959, Chairman, until 1983); Fellow, Wolfson College, Oxford, 1967–94, Hon. Fellow, 1994; *b* 1927; *s* of Arthur Henry Wood and Katharine Mary Altham (*née* Cumberlege); *m* 1955, Audrey Buxton (*née* Stanfield); one *s* one *d* and one step *s* one step *d*. *Educ:* Gresham's; Trinity Coll., Cambridge (MA); Imperial Coll. (RSM) (BSc); Christ Church, Oxford (MA). Nat. Service, Bevin Boy, S Wales and Derbyshire coalfields, 1945–48. NCB, 1953–55; Sen. Res. Officer, Clarendon Lab., Oxford Univ., 1956–69. Chm., Nat. Cttee for Superconductivity, SERC/DTI, 1987–92; Member: ABRC, 1983–89; ACOST, 1990–93; NRPB, 1991–; Council, Central Lab. of the Res. Councils, 1995–. Co-Founder and Chm., CONECTUS, 1994–. Director: ISIS Innovation Ltd, 1989–; Newport Technology Group Ltd, 1989–, and other cos. Vice-Chm. Council, FARM/AFRICA Ltd, 1985–. Founder: Northmoor Trust (for nature conservation); Oxford Trust (for encouragement of study and application of science and technol.). Trustee, Oxfordshire Council for Voluntary Action, 1994–. Hon. FEng 1994. Hon. Fellow UMIST, 1989. Hon. DSc Cranfield Inst. of Technol., 1983, Hon. DTech Loughborough Univ. of Technol., 1985. Mullard Medal, Royal Soc., 1982. DL 1985. *Address:* c/o Oxford Instruments plc, Old Station Way, Eynsham, Witney, Oxon OX8 1TL.

WOOD, Rt Rev. Maurice Arthur Ponsonby, DSC 1944; MA; RNR; an Hon. Assistant Bishop, Diocese of London, since 1985; *b* 26 Aug. 1916; *o s* of late Arthur Sheppard Wood and of Jane Elspeth Dalzell Wood (*née* Piper); *m* 1st, 1947, Marjorie (*née* Pennell) (*d* 1954); two *s* one *d*; 2nd, 1955, M. Margaret (*née* Sandford); two *s* one *d*. *Educ:* Monkton Combe Sch.; Queens' Coll., Cambridge (MA); Ridley Hall, Cambridge. Deacon, 1940; priest, 1941; Curate, St Paul's, Portman Square, 1940–43. Royal Naval Chaplain, 1943–47 (still Chap. to Commando Assoc.); attached RM Commandos, 1944–46 (landed on D-Day, June 1944); Chaplain, RNR, 1971–. Rector, St Ebbe's, Oxford, 1947–52; Vicar and RD of Islington, and Pres. Islington Clerical Conf., 1952–61; Principal, Oak Hill Theological Coll., Southgate, N14, 1961–71; Prebendary of St Paul's Cathedral, 1969–71; Bishop of Norwich, 1971–85; introduced to House of Lords, 1975; Abbot of St Benet's, 1971–85; Resident Priest of Englefield, 1987–94; Hon. Asst Bishop, dio. of Oxford, 1989–95. Proctor in Convocation of Canterbury and Mem. House of Clergy and Gen. Synod of Church of England (formerly Church Assembly), 1954–85 (House of Bishops, 1971–85); Member: Archbishops' Council on Evangelism, 1972–85; Church Comrs' Houses Cttee, 1980–85; Lords and Commons Family and Child Protection Gp, 1980–. Chairman: Theological Colls Principals' Conf., 1970–71; Norfolk Water Safety Assoc, 1966–71; Norwich RSPCA, 1971–85; The Manson Trust (India), 1984– (and Trustee); Order of Christian Unity, 1986–; Pres., Hildenborough Hall Christian Conf. Centre, 1970–85; Vice-President: Crosslinks Soc.; Boys' Brigade, 1986– (Chm., Anglican Council); Trustee: Mary Whitehouse Trust, 1986–90; Riding Lights Theatre Co., 1986–; Parly Christian Fellowship Trust, 1989–; Council Member: Wycliffe Hall, Oxford, 1981–94; British Atlantic Council, 1985–88; Commonwealth Human Ecology Council, 1986–. Patron, Friends of St Catherine's Church, Ludham, 1994–. Governor: Monkton Combe Sch., Bath; Gresham's Sch., Holt, 1971–85; St Helen's Sch., Abingdon, 1989–; Visitor: Langley Sch., Norfolk, 1980–89; Luckley-Oakfield Sch., 1990–. Chaplain, Weavers' Co., 1986–93, Hon. Freeman, 1993. Mission work with Dr Billy Graham in Tokyo, Toronto, Virginia, Osaka, Boston, Amsterdam. Mem., House of Lords, 1975–85. *Publications:* Like a Mighty Army, 1956; Comfort in Sorrow, 1957; Your Suffering, 1959; Christian Stability, 1968; To Everyman's Door, 1968; Into the Way of Peace, 1982; This is our Faith, 1985. *Recreations:* swimming, painting, (still) supporting Norwich City FC. *Address:* 41 Fir Tree Walk, Enfield EN1 3TZ. *T:* 0181–363 4491; Abbot's Cottage, Horning, Norfolk NR12 8NE. *Club:* Commonwealth Trust.

WOOD, Michael Charles, CMG 1995; HM Diplomatic Service; Legal Counsellor, Foreign and Commonwealth Office, since 1994; *b* 5 Feb. 1947; *s* of Walter Wood, *qv*. *Educ:* Solihull Sch.; Trinity Hall, Cambridge (MA, LLB); Free Univ., Brussels. Called to the Bar, Gray's Inn, 1968. HM Diplomatic Service, 1970; Asst Legal Advr, FCO, 1970–81; Legal Advr, Bonn, 1981–84; Legal Counsellor, FCO, 1986–91; Counsellor (Legal Advr), UK Mission to UN, NY, 1991–94. *Publications:* The Legal Status of Berlin, 1987; articles on internat. law. *Recreations:* walking, music, travel. *Address:* c/o Foreign and Commonwealth Office, King Charles Street, SW1A 2AH. *T:* 0171–270 3061.

WOOD, Norman, CBE 1965; Director: Co-operative Wholesale Society Ltd, 1942–64; Manchester Ship Canal Co., 1954–64; Associated British Foods Ltd, 1964–75, retired; *b* 2 Oct. 1905; *m* 1st, 1933, Ada Entwisle (*d* 1974); two *s* one *d*; 2nd, 1976, Nita Miller. *Educ:* Bolton Co. Grammar Sch.; Co-operative Coll. Nat. Exec. Co-operative Party, and Central Board of Co-operative Union, 1934; Ministry of Information, 1939; Chocolate and Sugar Confectionery War-time Assoc., 1942; British Tourist and Holidays Board (later BTA), 1947–70 (Dep. Chm., 1964–67); Plunkett Foundation, 1948– (Vice-Pres. 1972–; Hon. Life Mem., 1994); Cake and Biscuit Alliance, 1948; Wheat Commission, 1950; Domestic Coal Consumers Council, 1950; Coronation Accommodation Cttee, 1952. Member: British and Irish Millers, 1950–64; White Fish Authority, 1959–63; Food Res. Adv. Cttee, 1961–65; DTI Japan Trade Adv. Cttee, 1971–; Exec. Mem., British Food Export Council, 1970–75. Chairman: Food and Drink Cttee, British Week, Toronto, 1967, Tokyo, 1969; Chm., ten Food and Drink Missions to Hong Kong and Japan, 1968–76; Dir, Fedn of Agricl Co-ops (UK) Ltd, 1975–; Mem., Lab Party Study Gp on Export Services and Organisation, 1974; Founder Mem., SDP, 1981; Chm., SDP Surrey Forum, 1988–92 (the last expression of the SDP). *Recreations:* walking, music. *Address:* 17 Wallace Fields, Epsom, Surrey KT17 3AX. *T:* 0181–393 9052. *Club:* Oriental.

WOOD, Peter Anthony; Finance Director, Standard Chartered Bank, since 1993; *b* 4 Feb. 1943; *s* of Roger Sydney Wood and Winifred May (*née* Hine); *m* 1965, Janet Catherine Brown; one *s* one *d*. *Educ:* Oldershaw Grammar Sch.; Manchester Univ. (BSc Hons Maths); Birkbeck Coll., London Univ. (MSc Stats). ACIB; FCT; FSS. NCB, 1964–66; Barclays Bank, 1966–93: Treas., 1985–91; Finance Dir, 1991–93. *Recreations:* golf, birdwatching. *Address:* Standard Chartered Bank, 1 Aldermanbury Square, EC2V 7SB. *T:* 0171–280 7500. *Club:* Wildernesse (Sevenoaks).

WOOD, Peter Edric, OBE 1994; Chairman (part-time), West Yorkshire (formerly Huddersfield), Health Authority, since 1982; Member, Audit Commission, since 1990; *b* 17 July 1929; *s* of Edric Wood and Ruby (*née* Revill); *m* 1952, Barbara Evans; one *s* three *d*. *Educ:* RAF Coll.; Bradford Univ. (MSc); Open Univ. (BA). DipEE. RAF, 1946–61. With ICI, 1961–82; Lectr (part-time), Manchester Univ., 1982–84; Sen. Teaching Fellow (part-time), Leeds Univ., 1984–89. *Recreations:* reading, walking, golf. *Address:* 9 Abbey Close, Hade Edge, Holmfirth, Huddersfield HD7 1RT. *T:* Holmfirth (01484) 686977.

WOOD, Peter John; Founder and Chief Executive, Direct Line Insurance, since 1985; *m*; five *d*. Formerly with Alexander Howden, insce brokers. *Address:* Direct Line House, 3 Edridge Road, Croydon CR9 1AG.

WOOD, Peter (Lawrence); theatrical and television director; *b* 8 Oct. 1928; *s* of Frank Wood and Lucy Eleanor (*née* Meeson). *Educ:* Taunton School; Downing College, Cambridge. Resident Director, Arts Theatre, 1956–57; Associate Dir, NT, 1978–89. Director: The Iceman Cometh, Arts, 1958; The Birthday Party, Lyric, Hammersmith, 1958; Maria Stuart, Old Vic, 1958; As You Like It, Stratford, Canada, 1959; The Private Ear and The Public Eye, Globe, 1962, Morosco, New York, 1963; Carving a Statue, Haymarket, 1964; Poor Richard, Helen Hayes Theatre, New York, 1964; Incident at Vichy, Phœnix, 1966; The Prime of Miss Jean Brodie, Wyndham's, 1966; White Liars, and Black Comedy, 1968; In Search of Gregory (film), 1968–69; Design for Living, Los Angeles, 1971; Jumpers, Burgtheater, Vienna, 1973, Billy Rose Theatre, NY, 1974; Dear Love, Comedy, 1973; Macbeth, LA, 1975; The Mother of Us All (opera), Santa Fé, 1976; Long Day's Journey into Night, LA, 1977; Cosi Fan Tutte, Santa Fé, 1977; She Stoops to Conquer, Burgtheater, Vienna, 1978; Night and Day, Phoenix, 1978, NY, 1979; Il Seraglio, Glyndebourne, 1980, 1988; Don Giovanni, Covent Garden, 1981; Macbeth, Staatsoper, Vienna, 1982; The Real Thing, Strand, 1982; Orione (opera), Santa Fé, 1983; Orion, King's Theatre, Edinburgh, 1984; Jumpers, Aldwych, 1985; Wildfire, Phoenix, 1986; Otello, Staatsoper, Vienna, 1987; Les Liaisons Dangereuses, LA, 1988; Hapgood, Aldwych, 1988, LA, 1989; Map of the Heart, Globe, 1991; Midsummer Night's Dream, Zurich, 1992, Arcadia, Zurich, 1993; The Bed Before Yesterday, Almeida, 1994; Indian Ink, Aldwych, 1995; *Chichester:* The Silver King, 1990; Preserving Mr Panmure, 1991; She Stoops to Conquer, 1992; *Royal Shakespeare Company.* Winter's Tale, 1960; The Devils, 1961; Hamlet, 1961; The Beggar's Opera, 1963; Co-Dir, History Cycle, 1964; Travesties, 1974 (NY, 1975); Dr Jekyll and Mr Hyde, 1991; *National Theatre:* The Master Builder, 1964; Love for Love, 1965 (also Moscow); Jumpers, 1972; The Guardsman, The Double Dealer, 1978; Undiscovered Country, 1979; The Provok'd Wife, 1980; On the Razzle, 1981; The Rivals, 1983; Rough Crossing, 1984; Love for Love, 1985; Dalliance, 1986; The Threepenny Opera, 1986; The American Clock, 1986; The Beaux Strategem, 1989; The School for Scandal, 1990; *television:* Hamlet, USA, 1970; Long Day's Journey Into Night, USA, 1973; Shakespeare, episode I, 1976; Double Dealer, 1980; The Dog it was that Died, 1988. *Recreation:* gastronomic pursuits. *Address:* The Old Barn, Batcombe, Somerset BA4 6HD.

WOOD, Philip, OBE 1979; Under Secretary, Department of Transport, since 1986; *b* 30 June 1946; *s* of late Frank and Eleanor Wood; *m* 1971, Dilys Traylen Smith; one *s*. *Educ:* Queen Elizabeth Grammar Sch., Wakefield; Queen's Coll., Oxford. Entered Civil Service, 1967; Min. of Transport, 1967–70; DoE, 1970–75; a Private Sec. to the Prime Minister, 1975–79; Dept of Transport, 1979–: Sec. to Armitage Inquiry into Lorries and the Envmt, 1980; seconded to BRB, 1986–88. *Address:* Department of Transport, 2 Marsham Street, SW1P 3EB.

WOOD, (René) Victor; Director: Sun Life Corp. plc, since 1986; Wemyss Development Co. Ltd, since 1982; *b* 4 Oct. 1925; *e s* of late Frederick Wood and Jeanne Wood (*née* Raskin); *m* 1950, Helen Morag, *o d* of late Dr David S. Stewart. *Educ:* Jesus Coll., Oxford (BA). FFA. Chief Exec., 1969–79, Chm. 1974–79, Hill Samuel Insurance and Shipping Holdings Ltd; Chm., Lifeguard Assurance, 1976–84. Director: Haslemere Estates, 1976–86; Coalite Gp, 1977–89; Chandros Insce Co., 1979–89; Colbourne Insce Co., 1980–90; Criterion Insce Co., 1984–90, Scottinvest SA, 1985–; Wemyss Hotels France SA, 1985–; Les Résidences du Colombier SA, 1985–93; Domaine de Rimauresq SARL, 1985–; Worldwide and General Investment Co., 1992–. Vice-Pres., British Insurance Brokers' Assoc., 1981–84. *Publications:* (with Michael Pilch): Pension Schemes, 1960; New Trends in Pensions, 1964; Pension Scheme Practice, 1967; Company Pension Schemes, 1971; Managing Pension Schemes, 1974; Pension Schemes, 1979. *Address:* Little Woodbury, Newchapel, near Lingfield, Surrey RH7 6HR. *T:* Lingfield (01342) 832054.

WOOD, Prof. Richard Frederick Marshall, RD 1976; MD; FRCSG, FRCS; Professor of Surgery, University of Sheffield, and Hon. Consultant Surgeon, Northern General Hospital NHS Trust, since 1994; *b* 6 Jan. 1943; *s* of Sir Henry Peart Wood, CBE; *m* 1968, Christine Crawford Smith Jamieson; two *s*. *Educ:* Glasgow Acad.; Univ. of Glasgow (MB ChB 1967; MD 1976); MA Oxon 1981. FRCS 1972; FRCSG 1972. Surgeon Lt-Comdr, RNR, 1973–87. Jun. surgical appts at Western Infirmary, Glasgow, 1967–74; Lectr and Sen. Lectr in Surgery, Univ. of Leicester, 1974–81; Hon. Consultant Surgeon, Leics AHA, 1977–81; Clinical Reader in Surgery and Fellow of Green Coll., Oxford Univ., and Hon. Consultant Surgeon, Oxford AHA, 1981–84; Prof. of Surgery, St Bartholomew's Hosp. Med. Coll., Univ. of London, and Hon. Consultant Surgeon, City and Hackney Health Dist, 1984–94. Vis. Fellow, Peter Bent Brigham Hosp., Boston, 1980; Hunterian Prof.,

RCS, 1985. Mem., Management Cttee, UK Transplant Service, 1980–89. Sec., Surgical Res. Soc., 1987–90; Cllr, Transplantation Soc., 1992–. Fellow, Assoc. of Surgeons of GB; Member Editorial Board: British Jl of Surgery; Transplantation. *Publications:* Renal Transplantation: a clinical handbook, 1983; Surgical Aspects of Haemodialysis, 1983; Fundamental Anatomy for Operative General Surgery, 1989; (jtly) Small Bowel Transplantation, 1994; papers and chapters in textbooks on transplantation, and surgical topics. *Recreations:* music, sailing.

WOOD, Rt. Rev. Richard James; Hon. Assistant Bishop of York, since 1985; *b* 25 Aug. 1920; *s* of Alexander and Irene Wood; *m* 1st, 1946, Elsa Magdalena de Beer (*d* 1969); one *s* one *d* (twins); 2nd, 1972, Cathleen Anne Roark; two *d*. *Educ:* Oldham Hulme Grammar School; Regent St Polytechnic; Wells Theological Coll. Electrical Officer, RAF, then with Ceylon Fire Insurance Assoc. Curate, St Mary's, Calne, 1952–55; Curate, St Mark's Cathedral, George, S Africa, 1955–58; Rector, Christ Church, Beaufort West, 1958–62; Vicar of St Andrew's, Riversdale, 1962–65; Chaplain, S African Defence Force, 1965–68; Asst, St Alban's, E London, 1968; Rector of St John's, Fort Beaufort, 1969–71; Rector of Keetmanshoop, dio. Damaraland, 1971; Priest-in-Charge of Grace Church and St Michael's, Windhoek and Canon of St George's Cathedral, 1972; Vicar Gen. and Suffragan Bishop of Damaraland, 1973–75; expelled by S Africa, 1975; Hon. Asst Bishop of Damaraland, 1976–; Sec. to The Africa Bureau, 1977; Priest-in-Charge of St Mary, Lowgate, Hull, Chaplain to Hull Coll. of Higher Education and Hon. Asst Bishop of York, 1978–79; at St Mark's Theolog. Coll., Dar es Salaam, 1979–83; Interim Rector: St Matthew's, Wheeling, W Virginia, 1983–84; Trinity, Martinsburg, W Virginia, 1984–85. Hon. Life Mem., Hull Univ. Student Union. *Recreations:* general home interests.

WOOD, Prof. Robert Anderson, FRCSE, FRCPE; Postgraduate Dean, and Professor in Clinical Medicine, University of Aberdeen Medical School, since 1992; *b* 26 May 1939; *s* of late Dr John Fraser Anderson Wood and Janet Meikle Wood (*née* Hall); *m* 1966, Dr Sheila Margaret Pirie; one *s* three *d*. *Educ:* Edinburgh Academy; Univ. of Edinburgh (BSc Hons, MB ChB). House Officer, Royal Infirmary, Edinburgh, 1963–64, Asst Lectr, Univ. of Edinburgh, 1964–65; Registrar and Sen. Registrar in Medicine, Dundee Teaching Hosps, 1965–69; Lectr in Therapeutics, Univ. of Aberdeen, 1969–72; Sen. Lectr in Therapeutics, 1972–92, Dep. Dir, Postgrad. Med. Educn, 1986–92, Univ. of Dundee; Consultant Physician, Perth Royal Infirmary, 1972–92. Mem. Council, 1990–92, Dean, 1992–95, RCPE. *Publications:* papers on clinical pharmacology and medical education. *Recreations:* golf, gardening. *Address:* Ballomill House, Abernethy, Perthshire PH2 9LD. *T:* Abernethy (01738) 850201. *Club:* Royal & Ancient Golf (St Andrews).

WOOD, Air Vice-Marshal Robert Henry, OBE 1977; Director, British Red Cross, Leicestershire; *b* 24 Jan. 1936; *s* of Jack Cyril Wood and May Doris Wood; *m* 1957, Amy Cameron Wright; one *s* two *d*. *Educ:* Maldon Grammar School; cfs, psc, ndc, rcds. Commnd RAF, 1956; served Nos 617 and 88 Sqns, 1957–63; CFS, 1965–67; No 44 Sqn, 1967–69; attended Indian Staff Coll., 1970; MA to COS Far East Command, Singapore, 1970–71; PSO to Air Sec., 1972; NDC, Latimer, 1973; OC 51 Sqn, 1974; MoD Policy and Plans Dept, 1977; OC RAF Cranwell, 1978; OC RAF Linton-on-Ouse, 1979; Gp Capt. Flying Trng, HQ RAFSC, 1981–83; Dir Personal Services 1 (RAF), 1983–85; RCDS, 1985; Dep. Comdt, RAF Staff Coll., Bracknell, 1986; AOC and Comdt, RAF Coll., Cranwell, 1987–89; retd 1990. *Recreations:* golf, riding. *Club:* Royal Air Force.

WOOD, Robert Noel; psychotherapist; *b* 24 Dec. 1934; *s* of Ernest Clement Wood, CIE and Lucy Eileen Wood; *m* 1962, Sarah Child (marr. diss. 1981); one *s* one *d*. *Educ:* Sherborne Sch.; New Coll., Oxford (BA Hons PPE); LSE (Rockefeller Student; Certif. in Internat. Studies). Nat. Service Commn, RHA, 1953–55. Dep. Res. Dir, Internat. Div., Economist Intelligence Unit Ltd, 1959–65; Inst. of Econs and Statistics, Oxford, 1965–70; Sen. Economist, Min. of Econ. Affairs and Develt Planning, Tanzania, 1966–69; Econ. Advr, ODM, 1970; Dir of Studies, Overseas Develt Inst., 1970–74; Adviser to House of Commons Select Cttee on Overseas Develt, 1973–74; Dir, Overseas Develt Inst., 1974–82. Jungian analysis, 1982–90; full Mem., Inst. of Psychotherapy and Counselling. Chm., Friends of the Union Chapel, 1983–87; Mem., Religious Soc. of Friends (Quakers), 1982–. Gov., Quintin Kynaston Sch., 1974–86. *Publications:* contrib. Bull. Oxford Inst. of Econs and Statistics, ODI Rev. *Recreations:* Victorian artists, listening to music, singing, swimming, walking, Arsenal football club, poetry, Jung. *Address:* 19 Baalbec Road, N5 1QN. *T:* 0171–226 4775.

WOOD, Roderic Lionel James; QC 1993; *b* 8 March 1951; *s* of Lionel James Wood and Marjorie Wood (*née* Thompson). *Educ:* Nottingham High Sch.; Lincoln Coll., Oxford. Called to the Bar, Middle Temple, 1974. Member: Cttee, Family Law Bar Assoc., 1988–; Supreme Court Procedure Cttee, 1990–; Family Div. Sub-Cttee; Bar Council, 1993–; Professional Conduct Cttee of the Bar, 1993–; Legal Aid and Fees Cttee, 1995–. Jt Chm., Barristers/Clerks Liaison Cttee, 1994–. Mem., Editl Bd, Longman Practitioner's Child Law Bull., 1993–94. *Recreations:* music, theatre, travel. *Address:* 1 King's Bench Walk, Temple, EC4Y 7DB. *T:* 0171–583 6266.

WOOD, Rt. Rev. Roland Arthur; Rector, St James' Cathedral, and Dean of the Diocese of Athabasca, since 1993; Bishop of Saskatoon, 1981–93; *b* 1 Jan. 1933; *s* of Cyril Arthur Wood and Evelyn Mae Wood (*née* Cave); *m* 1959, Elizabeth Nora (*née* Deacon); one *s* two *d*. *Educ:* Bishop's Univ., Lennoxville, Quebec (BA 1956, LST 1958). Deacon, May 1958, priest. Dec. 1958; Asst Curate, St Matthew's, Winnipeg, 1958–60; Rector, Christ Church, Selkirk, 1960–64; Assistant Priest, St John's Cathedral, Saskatoon, 1964–67; Rector, Holy Trinity Church, Yorkton, 1967–71; Dean, St John's Cathedral, Saskatoon, 1971–81. Hon. DD, Coll. of Emmanuel and St Chad, Saskatoon, 1979. *Recreations:* model railroading, camping, painting, refurbishing old furniture. *Address:* St James' Cathedral, 9715 98th Avenue, Peace River, Alberta T8S 1J3, Canada.

WOOD, Prof. Ronald Karslake Starr, FRS; Professor of Plant Pathology, Imperial College, University of London, since 1964; *s* of Percival Thomas Evans Wood and Florence Dix Starr; *m* 1947, Marjorie Schofield; one *s* one *d*. *Educ:* Ferndale Grammar Sch.; Imperial College. Royal Scholar, 1937; Forbes Medal, 1941; Huxley Medal, 1950. Research Asst to Prof. W. Brown, 1941; Directorate of Aircraft Equipment, Min. of Aircraft Production, 1942; London University: Lectr, Imperial Coll., 1947; Reader in Plant Pathology, 1955; Prof. of Plant Pathology, 1964; Head of Dept of Pure and Applied Biol., Imperial Coll., 1981–84. Commonwealth Fund Fellow, 1950; Research Fellow, Connecticut Agric. Experiment Stn, 1957. Mem. Council, British Mycological Soc., 1948; Sec., Assoc. of Applied Biologists; Mem., 1949, Chm., 1987–91, Biological Council; Mem., Parly and Scientific Cttee; Consultant, Nat. Fedn of Fruit and Potato Trades, 1955; Mem. Council, Inst. of Biology, 1956 (Vice-Pres., 1991–); Chm., Plant Pathology Cttee, British Mycological Soc.; Mem. Governing Body, Nat. Fruit and Cider Inst., Barnes Memorial Lectr, 1962; Sec., First Internat. Congress of Plant Pathology, 1965; Mem. Governing Body: East Malling Research Stn, 1966 (Vice-Chm.); Inst. for Horticultural Res., 1987; Pres., Internat. Soc. for Plant Pathology, 1968 (Hon. Mem., 1988); Mem., Nat. Cttee for Biology, 1978; Chm., British Nat. Sub-Cttee for Botany, 1978; Dean, RCS, 1975–78; Founder Pres. and Hon. Mem., British Soc. for Plant Pathol., 1987. Scientific Dir, NATO Advanced Study Institute, Pugnochiuso, 1970, Sardinia, 1975, Cape Sounion, 1980; Consultant, FAO/UNDP, India, 1976. Fellow, Amer. Phytopathological Soc., 1972; Corres. Mem., Deutsche Phytomedizinische Gesellschaft, 1973. Otto-Appel-Denkmünster, 1978. Thurburn Fellow, Univ. of Sydney, 1979; Sir C. V. Raman Prof., Univ. of Madras, 1980; Regents' Lectr, Univ. of California, 1981. *Publications:* Physiological Plant Pathology, 1967; (ed) Phytotoxins in Plant Diseases, 1972; (ed) Specifity in Plant Diseases, 1976; (ed) Active Defence Mechanisms in Plants, 1981; (ed) Plant Diseases: infection, damage and loss, 1984; numerous papers in Annals of Applied Biology, Annals of Botany, Phytopathology, Trans British Mycological Soc. *Recreation:* gardening. *Address:* Pyrford Woods, Pyrford, near Woking, Surrey GU22 8QL. *T:* Byfleet (01932) 343827.

WOOD, Maj.-Gen. Roy; Director General of Military Survey, Ministry of Defence, 1990–94; *b* 14 May 1940; *s* of Alec and Lucy Maud Wood; *m* 1963, Susan Margaret Croxford; two *s*. *Educ:* Farnham Grammar Sch.; Welbeck College; RMA; Cambridge Univ. (MA); University College London (MSc 1971). FRICS; FRGS. Commissioned RE 1960; Mapping Surveys, Sarawak, Sierra Leone and Sabah, 1964–70; Instructor, Sch. of Military Survey, 1972–75; MoD, 1975–77; OC 14 Topo. Sqn, BAOR, 1977–79; CO Mapping and Charting Estabt, 1979–81; Defense Mapping Agency, USA, 1981–83; MoD, 1984; Comdr, 42 Survey Engr Gp, 1985–87; Dir, Military Survey, 1987–90. FIMgt. *Publications:* articles on surveying and mapping in professional and technical jls. *Recreations:* orienteering, hill walking, travel. *Club:* Geographical.

WOOD, Sir Russell (Dillon), KCVO 1985 (CVO 1979; MVO 1975); VRD 1964; Lt-Comdr, RNR; Deputy Treasurer to the Queen, 1969–85; an Extra Gentleman Usher to the Queen, since 1986; *b* 16 May 1922; *s* of William G. S. Wood, Whitstable, Kent, and Alice Wood; *m* 1948, Jean Violet Yelwa Davidson, *d* of late Alan S. Davidson, Lenham, Kent; one *s* three *d*. *Educ:* King's Sch., Canterbury. Fleet Air Arm Pilot, 1940–46 (despatches twice). Qual. as Chartered Accountant, 1951; financial management career with major public companies, 1951–68. *Recreations:* private flying, sailing, shooting. *Address:* The Old Forge, Dunwich, Suffolk IP17 3DU. *T:* Westleton (01728) 648595. *Clubs:* Army and Navy; East Anglian Flying, Aldeburgh Yacht.

WOOD, Rt. Rev. (Stanley) Mark; *b* 21 May 1919; *s* of Arthur Mark and Jane Wood; *m* 1947, Winifred Ruth, *d* of Edward James Toase; three *s* two *d*. *Educ:* Pontypridd County School; University College, Cardiff; College of the Resurrection, Mirfield. BA (2nd cl. Greek and Latin), Wales. Curate at St Mary's, Cardiff Docks, 1942–45; Curate, Sophiatown Mission, Johannesburg, 1945–47; Rector of Bloemhof, Transvaal, 1947–50; Priest in charge of St Cyprian's Mission, Johannesburg, 1950–55; Rector of Marandellas, Rhodesia, 1955–65; Dean of Salisbury, Rhodesia, 1965–70; Bishop of Matabeleland, 1971–77; Asst Bishop of Hereford, 1977–81; Archdeacon of Ludlow, 1982–83; Bishop Suffragan of Ludlow, 1981–87. *Address:* 13 Bruton Place, Llandaff, Cardiff CF5 2ER. *T:* Cardiff (01222) 560632.

WOOD, Terence Courtney, CMG 1989; HM Diplomatic Service; Ambassador to Austria, since 1992; *b* 6 Sept. 1936; *s* of Courtney and Alice Wood; *m* 1st, 1962, Kathleen Mary Jones (marr. diss. 1981); one *s* one *d*; 2nd, 1982, Diana Humphreys-Roberts. *Educ:* King Edward VI Sch., Chelmsford; Trinity Coll., Cambridge. BA Hons 1960. RA, 1955–57 (2nd Lieut). Information Officer, FBI (later CBI), 1963–67; entered HM Diplomatic Service, 1968; Foreign Office, 1968–69; 1st Sec., Rome, 1969–73; FCO, 1973–77; Counsellor (Economic and Commercial), New Delhi, 1977–81; Political Advr and Hd of Chancery, Brit. Mil. Govt, Berlin, 1981–84; Hd of S Asian Dept, FCO, 1984–86; Vis. Fellow, Center for Internat. Affairs, Harvard Univ., 1986–87; Minister, Rome, 1987–92; Head, UK Delegn to Negotiations on Conventional Arms Control in Europe, Vienna, 1992–93. sowc, Royal Naval Coll., Greenwich, 1977. *Recreations:* music, painting. *Address:* c/o Foreign and Commonwealth Office, SW1A 2AH. *Club:* Travellers'.

WOOD, Timothy John Rogerson; MP (C) Stevenage, since 1983; Comptroller of HM Household, since 1995; *b* 13 Aug. 1940; *s* of Thomas Geoffrey Wood and Norah Margaret Annie (*née* Rogerson); *m* 1969, Elizabeth Mary Spencer; one *s* one *d*. *Educ:* King James's Grammar Sch., Knaresborough, Yorks; Manchester Univ. (BSc Maths). Joined Ferranti Ltd as Lectr in Computer Programming, 1962; joined ICT Ltd (later ICL), 1963; subseq. involved in develt of ICL systems software; Sen. Proj. Management Consultant advising on introdn of large computer systems, 1977; Sen. Proj. Manager on application systems, 1981; resigned from ICL, 1983. PPS to: Minister for Armed Forces, 1986–87; Minister of State, 1987–89, Sec. of State, 1989–90, Northern Ireland; Asst Govt Whip, 1990–92; Lord Comr of HM Treasury (Govt Whip), 1992–95. Chm., Wokingham Cons. Assoc., 1980–83; Vice Chairman: National Assoc. of Cons. Graduates, 1975–76; Thames Valley Euro Constituency Council, 1979–83; Member: Bow Gp, 1962– (Mem. Council, 1968–71); Bracknell DC, 1975–83 (Leader, 1976–78); Bd, Bracknell Develt Corp., 1977–82. *Publications:* Bow Group pamphlets on educn, computers in Britain, and the Post Office. *Recreations:* gardening, chess, reading. *Address:* House of Commons, SW1A 0AA. *T:* 0171–219 3601.

WOOD, Victor; *see* Wood, R. V.

WOOD, Victoria; writer and comedienne; *b* 19 May 1953; *d* of Stanley and Helen Wood; *m* 1980, Geoffrey Durham; one *s* one *d*. *Educ:* Bury Grammar School for Girls; Univ. of Birmingham (BA Drama, Theatre Arts). Performed regularly on television and radio as singer/songwriter, 1974–78. First stage play, Talent, performed at Crucible Th., Sheffield, 1978; TV production of this, broadcast, 1979 (3 National Drama awards, 1980); wrote Good Fun, stage musical, 1980; wrote and performed, TV comedy series: Wood and Walters, 1981–82; Victoria Wood As Seen On TV, 1st series 1985 (Broadcasting Press Guilds Award; BAFTA Awards, Best Light Entertainment Prog., Best Light Entertainment Perf.), 2nd series 1986 (BAFTA Award, Best Light Entertainment Prog.), Special, 1987 (BAFTA Best Light Entertainment Prog.); An Audience with Victoria Wood, 1988 (BAFTA Best Light Entertainment Prog., BAFTA Best Light Entertainment Perf.); Victoria Wood, 1989; Victoria Wood's All Day Breakfast, 1992 (Writers' Guild Award); Victoria Wood Live in Your Own Home, 1994. Appeared in stage revues, Funny Turns, Duchess Th., 1982, Lucky Bag, Ambassadors, 1984; Victoria Wood, Palladium, 1987; Victoria Wood Up West, 1990. Variety Club BBC Personality of the Year, 1987. Hon. DLitt: Lancaster, 1989; Sunderland, 1994. *Screenplay:* Pat and Margaret, 1994 (BPG Award, Best Single Drama Critic's Award, Monte Carlo, and Nymphe d'Or). *Publications:* Victoria Wood Song Book, 1984; Up to you, Porky, 1985; Barmy, 1987; Mens Sana in Thingummy Doodah, 1990. *Recreations:* walking and talking. *Address:* c/o Richard Stone, 25 Whitehall, SW1A 2BS. *T:* 0171–839 6421.

WOOD, Walter; Town Clerk, City of Birmingham, 1972–74; *b* Bolton, 11 Jan. 1914; *s* of Walter Scott Wood; *m* 1939, Hilda Maude, *d* of Albert Forrester; two *s*. *Educ:* Canon Slade Sch., Bolton; Victoria Univ., Manchester (LLB). Served with RAF, 1940–45. Admitted solicitor, 1937 (Daniel Reardon and Clabon prizeman); legal associate member, RTPI, 1948; Asst Solicitor, Bradford, 1937. Swansea, 1939; Dep. Town Clerk, Grimsby, 1947; Principal Asst Solicitor, Sheffield, 1948; Asst Town Clerk, Birmingham, 1952; Dep. Town Clerk, Birmingham, 1960. Panel Inspector, DoE, 1974–85. Governor, Solihull Sch., 1974–84. Pres., Birmingham Law Soc., 1976. Pres., West Midland Rent Assessment

Panel, 1980–84. *Recreations:* swimming, philately. *Address:* 43 Sandgate Road, Hall Green, Birmingham B28 0UN. *T:* 0121–744 1195.
See also M. C. Wood.

WOOD, Rt. Rev. Wilfred Denniston; *see* Croydon, Bishop Suffragan of.

WOOD, Sir William (Alan), KCVO 1978; CB 1970; Second Crown Estate Commissioner, 1968–78; Ombudsman, Mirror Group Newspapers, 1985–89; Chairman, London and Quadrant Housing Trust, 1980–89; *b* 8 Dec. 1916; *m* 1st, 1943, Zoë (*d* 1985), *d* of Rev. Dr D. Frazer-Hurst; two *s* two *d*; 2nd, 1985, Mrs Mary Hall (*née* Cowper). *Educ:* Dulwich Coll.; Corpus Christi Coll., Cambridge (Scholar). Ministry of Home Affairs, N. Ireland, 1939. Lieut, RNVR, 1942–46. Ministry of Town and Country Planning, 1946; Minister's Private Secretary, 1951; Principal Regional Officer (West Midlands), Ministry of Housing and Local Government, 1954; Asst Secretary, 1956; Under-Secretary, 1964–68. Chm. Council, King Alfred Sch., 1966–78, Pres. 1978–. *Address:* Maplewood, 40 Picklers Hill, Abingdon, Oxon OX14 2BB. *T:* Abingdon (01235) 520515. *Club:* Athenæum.

WOODALL, Alec; *b* 20 Sept. 1918; *m* 1950; one *s* one *d*. *Educ:* South Road Elementary School. Colliery official. MP (Lab) Hemsworth, Feb. 1974–1987. PPS to Sec. of State for Trade, 1976–78. Mem. Nat. Council, 1975–87, case worker, 1987–95, SSAFA. *Address:* 2 Grove Terrace, Hemsworth, West Yorkshire WF9 4BQ. *T:* Hemsworth (01977) 613897.

WOODARD, Rear-Adm. Sir Robert (Nathaniel), KCVO 1995; Flag Officer Royal Yachts, 1990–95; an Extra Equerry to the Queen, since 1992; *b* 13 Jan. 1939; *s* of Francis Alwyne Woodard and Catherine Mary Woodard (*née* Hayes); *m* 1963, Rosamund Lucia, *d* of Lt-Col D. L. A. Gibbs, DSO and Lady Hilaria Gibbs (*née* Edgcumbe); two *s* one *d*. *Educ:* Lancing College. Joined Royal Navy as Cadet, 1958; specialised in flying; served HM Ships Ark Royal, Eagle, Victorious, Bulwark in 800, 801, 845, 846 and 848 Sqns (active service Malaya, Borneo); Commands: 771 Sqn, 1973–74; 848 Sqn, 1974–75; HMS Amazon, 1978–80; HMS Glasgow, 1983–84; HMS Osprey, 1984–86; MoD Op. Requirements, 1986–88; comd. Clyde Submarine Base, 1989–90. Dir, Woodard (Western Div.) plc; Fellow Western Div., Woodard Corp. Vice-Pres., Falmouth Br., Royal Naval Assoc. Pres., SSAFA, Cornwall, 1995. Governor: King's Coll., Taunton; King's Hall, Pyrland. Younger Brother, Trinity House, 1994–. FIMgt (FBIM 1979); MInstD 1995. *Recreations:* shooting, fishing, painting, sailing. *Clubs:* Navy and Military; Royal Yacht Squadron, Royal Cornwall Yacht, Port Navas Yacht.

WOODBINE PARISH, Sir David (Elmer), Kt 1980; CBE 1964; Chairman, City and Guilds of London Institute, 1967–79 (Council Member, since 1954, Life Vice-President, 1979); *b* 29 June 1911; *o s* of late Walter Woodbine Parish and Audrey Makins; *m* 1939, Mona Blair McGarel, BA (Arch), ARIBA (*d* 1991), *o d* of late Charles McGarel Johnston, Glynn, Co. Antrim; two *d*. *Educ:* Sandroyd; Eton; Lausanne, Switzerland. Chm. and Man. Dir, Holliday and Greenwood Ltd, 1953–59 (Dir., 1937–59); Chm., Bovis Ltd, 1959–66; Dep. Chm., Marine and General Mutual Life Assurance Soc., 1976–86 (Dir, 1971–86). Chm., Jt Mission Hosp. Equip. Bd (ECHO), 1973–78. President: London Master Builders Assoc., 1952; Nat. Fedn of Building Trades Employers, 1960; Vice-Pres., Internat. Fedn of European Contractors of Building and Public Works, 1967–71; Member: Regional Adv. Council for Technological Educn, London and Home Counties, 1952–69; Architects Registration Council, 1952–72; Nat. Adv. Council for Educn in Industry and Commerce, 1953–78; BIM Council, 1953–62, Bd of Fellows, 1966–72; Nat. Council for Technological Awards, 1955–61; Bd of Building Educn, 1955–66; Building Res. Bd, 1957–60; Industrial Training Council, 1958–64; Council, British Employers' Confedn, 1959–65; Council Foundn for Management Educn, 1959–65; British Productivity Council, 1961–70 (Chm., Educn and Trng Cttee, 1963–70); Human Sciences Cttee (SRC), 1963–66; Construction Industry Training Bd, 1964–70. Chairman: UK Nat. Cttee, Internat. Apprentice Competition, 1962–70; MPBW Working Party on Res. and Information, 1963; Nat. Examinations Bd for Supervisory Studies, 1964–73; Mem., Nat. Jt Consult. Cttee of Architects, Quantity Surveyors and Builders, 1958–70 (Chm. 1966–68); Chm., Dept of Health and Social Security Cttee of Inquiry on Hosp. Building Maintenance and Minor Capital Works, 1968–70; Member: Court, Russia Co., 1937–84; Court, City Univ., 1967–72; Bd of Governors, The Polytechnic, Regent Street, 1967–70; Court, Polytechnic of Central London, 1970–76; Governing Body, Imperial Coll. of Science and Technology, 1971–81. Vice-Chm., Bd of Governors, St Thomas' Hosp., 1967–74 (Chm., Rebuilding Cttee, 1968–76); Chairman: Council, St Thomas's Hosp. Med. Sch., 1970–82; St Thomas' Dist Educn Adv. Council, 1974–81; Florence Nightingale Museum Trust, 1982–86; Member: Nightingale Fund Council, 1974–84; Bd of Governors, Bethlem Royal Hosp. and Maudsley Hosp., 1975–78; Council of Governors, Utd Medical and Dental Schs of Guy's and St Thomas's Hosps, 1982–85. Chm., Sussex Area, Royal Sch. of Church Music, 1981–85. Master, Clothworkers' Co., 1974–75 (Warden, 1962–64; Chm., Angel Court Develt, 1969–80). Mem. Bd of Governors, Clothworkers' Foundation, 1977–. FCIOB (FIOB 1940); FRSA 1953; CIMgt (FBIM 1957). Fellow, Imperial Coll., 1976; Hon. FCGI 1979. Hon. LLD Leeds, 1975. *Publications:* contribs to technical jls concerned with construction. *Recreations:* garden, music. *Address:* The Glebe Barn, Pulborough, West Sussex RH20 2AF. *T:* Pulborough (01798) 872613. *Club:* Boodle's.

WOODCOCK, Gordon, FCA, CIPFA; County Treasurer of Staffordshire, 1973–83. Served War, Royal Navy, 1942–46. City Treasurer's Dept: Birmingham, 1937–42 and 1946–54; Stoke-on-Trent, 1954–73; City Treasurer of Stoke-on-Trent, 1971–73.

WOODCOCK, Sir John, Kt 1989; CBE 1983; QPM 1976; HM Chief Inspector of Constabulary, 1990–93; *b* 14 Jan. 1932; *s* of late Joseph Woodcock and of Elizabeth May Woodcock (*née* Whiteside); *m* 1953, Kathleen Margaret Abbott; two *s* one *d*. *Educ:* Preston, Lancs, elementary schs; Preston Technical Coll. Police cadet, Lancashire Constabulary, 1947–50; Army Special Investigation Branch, 1950–52; Constable to Chief Inspector, Lancashire Constabulary, 1952–65; Supt and Chief Supt, Bedfordshire and Luton Constabulary, 1965–68; Asst Chief Constable, 1968–70, Dep. Chief Constable, 1970–74, Gwent Constabulary; Dep. Chief Constable, Devon and Cornwall Constabulary, 1974–78; Chief Constable: N Yorkshire Police, 1978–79; S Wales Constabulary, 1979–83; HM Inspector of Constabulary, Wales and Midlands, 1983–90. Intermed. Comd Course, Police Coll., 1965, Sen. Comd Course, 1968; Study, Bavarian Police, 1977; European Discussion Centre, 1977; Internat. Police Course (Lectr), Sicily, Rome, 1978; FBI, Nat. Exec., Washington, 1981; Lectr, Denmark, 1983, Holland, 1990; Study, Royal Hong Kong Police, 1989. Vice-Pres., Welsh Assoc. of Youth Clubs, 1981–87; Chm., South Wales Cttee, Royal Jubilee and Prince's Trusts, 1983–85; Member: Admin. Council, Royal Jubilee Trusts, 1981–85; Prince's Trust Cttee for Wales, 1981–85; Mem., Governing Body, World College of the Atlantic, 1980–85. Pres., Police Mutual Assurance Soc., 1990–94. St John Council, N Yorks, S Glam, Mid Glam (Chm.), Hereford and Worcs, 1979–90. CStJ 1992; KSG 1984. *Recreations:* squash, badminton, walking, golf. *Address:* c/o Home Office, Queen Anne's Gate, SW1H 9AT. *Clubs:* St John's; Hon. Member, Swansea Lions.

WOODCOCK, John Charles; cricket writer; *b* 7 Aug. 1926; *s* of late Rev. Parry John Woodcock and Norah Mabel Woodcock (*née* Hutchinson). *Educ:* Dragon Sch.; St Edward's Sch., Oxford; Trinity Coll., Oxford (MA; OUHC *v* Cambridge, 1946, 1947). Manchester Guardian, 1952–54; Cricket Correspondent to The Times, 1954–, and to Country Life, 1962–91; Editor, Wisden Cricketers' Almanack, 1980–86; has covered over 40 Test tours, 1950–95, to Australia, 18 times, S Africa, W Indies, New Zealand, India and Pakistan. Mem., MCC Cttee, 1988–91 and 1992–95. Pres., Cricket Writers' Club, 1986–. Patron of the living of Longparish. Sports Journalist of the Year, British Press Awards, 1987. *Publications:* The Ashes, 1956; (with E. W. Swanton) Barclay's World of Cricket, 1980 (Associate Editor, 2nd edn 1986, Consultant Editor, 3rd edn, 1986). *Recreations:* the countryside, golf. *Address:* The Curacy, Longparish, near Andover, Hants SP11 6PB. *T:* Longparish (01264) 720259. *Clubs:* MCC, Flyfishers'; Vincent's (Oxford); St Enodoc Golf.

WOODCOCK, Michael, (Mike), JP; company director, consultant, researcher and writer; Visiting Professor, University of Lancaster Management School, since 1992; *b* 10 April 1943; *s* of Herbert Eric Woodcock and Violet Irene Woodcock; *m* 1969, Carole Ann (*née* Berry); one *s* one *d*. *Educ:* Queen Elizabeth's Grammar Sch., Mansfield, Notts; DLitt IMCB, 1988. Successively: Accountant, Personnel Officer, Management Development Adviser, Head of Small Business Development Unit, Consultant, Vice-Pres. of US Corp., Founder of four UK companies. Underwriting Mem. of Lloyd's, 1984–. MP (C) Ellesmere Port and Neston, 1983–92. Member: Trade and Industry Select Cttee, 1984–87; Home Affairs Select Cttee, 1987–92; Secretary: Cons. Smaller Business Cttee, 1990–92; All Party Transpennine Gp of MPs, 1990–92. Parly Advr, Chamber of Coal Traders, 1985–93. Nat. Vice Pres., Ramblers' Assoc., 1993–. Vis. Fellow, Leeds Business Sch., 1994–. Companion, IMCB, 1990. JP Mansfield, Notts, 1971. *Publications:* People at Work, 1975; Unblocking Your Organisation, 1978 (UK, USA and Holland); Team Development Manual, 1979 (UK, USA and Indonesia); Organisation Development Through Teambuilding, 1981 (UK and USA); The Unblocked Manager, 1982 (UK, USA and four foreign edns); 50 Activities for Self Development, 1982 (UK, USA and eight foreign edns); Manual of Management Development, 1985; 50 Activities for Teambuilding, 1989 (UK, USA and 11 foreign edns); (jtly) Clarifying Organisational Values, 1989 (UK and Sweden); 50 Activities for Unblocking Your Organisation, vol. 1, 1990, vol. 2, 1991; The Self Made Leader, 1990; Unblocking Organisational Values, 1990; Change: a collection of activities and exercises, 1992; The Woodcock Francis series of Management Audits, 1994; Teambuilding Strategy, 1994 (UK and India); The Teambuilders Toolkit, 1995; The Problem Sales Tookit, 1995. *Recreation:* walking. *Address:* 13 Denny Street, SE11 4UX. *Clubs:* Carlton, Farmers'.

WOODCOCK, Thomas, FSA; Somerset Herald, since 1982; *b* 20 May 1951; *s* of Thomas Woodcock, Hurst Green, Lancs, and Mary, *d* of William Woodcock, Holcombe, Lancs. *Educ:* Eton; University Coll., Durham (BA); Darwin Coll., Cambridge (LLB). FSA 1990. Called to Bar, Inner Temple, 1975. Research Assistant to Sir Anthony Wagner, Garter King of Arms, 1975–78; Rouge Croix Pursuivant, 1978–82. *Publications:* (with John Martin Robinson) The Oxford Guide to Heraldry, 1988; (ed with D. H. B. Chesshyre) Dictionary of British Arms: Medieval Ordinary, vol. 1, 1992. *Address:* 47 Regents Park Road, NW1 7SY. *T:* 0171–722 5166; College of Arms, Queen Victoria Street, EC4V 4BT. *T:* 0171–236 3634. *Club:* Travellers'.

WOODFIELD, Sir Philip (John), KCB 1983 (CB 1974); CBE 1963; Member, Royal Commission on Criminal Justice, 1991–93; Chairman, Irish Soldiers and Sailors Land Trust, since 1986; Staff Counsellor for the Security and Intelligence Services, 1987–95; *b* 30 Aug. 1923; *s* of late Ralph and Ruth Woodfield; *m* 1958, Diana Margaret, *d* of late Sydney and of Margaret Herington; three *d*. *Educ:* Alleyn's Sch., Dulwich; King's Coll., London. Served War of 1939–45: Royal Artillery, 1942–47 (Captain). Entered Home Office, 1950; Asst Private Secretary to Home Secretary, 1952; Federal Government of Nigeria, 1955–57; Home Office, 1957–60; Private Secretary to the Prime Minister, 1961–65; Asst Sec. 1965–67, Asst Under-Sec. of State, 1967–72, Home Office; Deputy Sec., NI Office, 1972–74, Home Office, 1974–81; Perm. Under-Sec. of State, NI Office, 1981–83. Secretary to: Commonwealth Immigration Mission, 1965; Lord Mountbatten's inquiry into prison security, Nov.-Dec. 1966; Chairman: Scrutiny of Supervision of Charities, 1987; Review of British Transport Police, 1987–88; Review of WRVS, 1991. Chm., London and Metropolitan Govt Staff Commn, 1984–91. *Recreation:* music. *Address:* c/o Lloyds Bank, 7 Pall Mall, SW1Y 5NA. *Clubs:* Garrick, Beefsteak.

WOODFORD, Air Vice-Marshal Anthony Arthur George, CB 1989; Home Bursar and Fellow, Magdalen College, Oxford, since 1992; *b* 6 Jan. 1939; *s* of Arthur and May Woodford; *m* 1965, Christine Barbara Tripp; one *s* two *d*. *Educ:* Haberdashers' Aske's Hampstead School; RAF College, Cranwell. BA Hons Open Univ. 1978; MA Oxon 1992. Commissioned pilot, 1959; served Nos 12, 44, 53, 101 Sqns and 4017th CCTS USAF; Asst Air Attaché, British Embassy, Washington, 1978–81; Comdr RAF St Mawgan, 1982–83; Comdr British Forces Ascension Island, 1982; ADC to the Queen, 1982–83; RCDS 1984; HQ Strike Command: Air Cdre Plans, 1985–87; AOA, 1987–89; ACOS Policy, SHAPE, 1989–92, retd. *Address:* Magdalen College, Oxford OX1 4AU. *Club:* Royal Air Force.

WOODFORD, Maj.-Gen. David Milner, CBE 1975; retired; Member, Lord Chancellor's Panel of Independent Inspectors, since 1988; *b* 26 May 1930; *s* of late Major R. M. Woodford, MC, and Marion Rosa Woodford (*née* Gregory); *m* 1959, Mary E. Jones (marr. diss. 1987); *m* 1995, Carole M. Westoby. *Educ:* Prince of Wales Sch., Nairobi; Wadham Coll., Oxford. psc, jsdc, rcds. National Service, then Regular, 1st Royal Fusiliers, Korea, 1953, then Regtl service, Egypt, Sudan, UK, 1953–55; ADC/GOC Berlin, 1956–58; Adjt and Co. Comd 1RF, Gulf, Kenya, Malta, Cyprus, Libya, UK, 1958–61; GSO3 Div./Dist, UK, 1962; sc Camberley, 1963; GSO2 MO 1, then MA/VCGS, 1964–66; Co. Comd 1RF, BAOR, UK, Gulf and Oman, 1966–68; GSO1 (DS) Staff Coll., 1968–70; CO 3 RRF, Gibraltar, UK, N Ireland, 1970–72; Col GS NEARELF (Cyprus), 1972–75; Comd 3 Inf. Bde (N Ireland), 1976–77; Dep. Col, RRF, 1976–81; RCDS 1978; D Comd and COS SE Dist, UK, 1979–80; Dir Army Training, 1981–82; Sen. Army Mem., RCDS, 1982–84; Comdt, JSDC, 1984–86. Col RRF, 1982–86. *Recreations:* literary, historical; passionate golfer. *Address:* c/o Regimental Headquarters, The Royal Regiment of Fusiliers, HM Tower of London, EC3N 4AB. *Clubs:* Army and Navy, New Zealand Golf.

WOODFORD, (Frederick) Peter, PhD; FRCPath; CChem, FRSC; FBES; Chief Scientific Officer, Department of Health (formerly of Health and Social Security), 1984–93; *b* 8 Nov. 1930; *s* of Wilfrid Charles Woodford and Mabel Rose (*née* Scarff); *m* 1964, Susan Silberman, NY; one *d*. *Educ:* Lewis Sch., Pengam, Glam; Balliol Coll., Oxford (Domus Exhibnr; BA (Hons Chem.) 1952; MA 1955); PhD Leeds 1955. FRCPath 1984; CChem, FRSC 1990; MBES 1991, FBES 1993. Res. Fellow, Leiden Univ., 1958–62; Vis. Scientist/Lectr, Univ. of Tennessee Med. Sch. and NIH, USA, 1962–63; Guest Investigator, Rockefeller Univ., NY, 1963–71; Scientific Historian, Ciba Foundn, and Scientific Associate, Wellcome Trust, 1971–74; Exec. Dir, Inst. for Res. into Mental and Multiple Handicap, 1974–77; PSO (Clin. Chem.), DHSS, 1977–84. Distinguished Visitor, Royal Free Hosp. Sch. of Med., 1994–. Consultant, Inst. of Pharmacology, Milan Univ. Managing/Executive Editor: Jl of Atherosclerosis Res., 1960–62; Jl of Lipid Res., 1963–69; Procs of Nat. Acad. of Scis, USA, 1970–71; Editor, Camden History Review,

1995–; Editl Consultant, King's Fund Centre for Health Service Develt, 1990–93. Hon. DSc Salford, 1993. Waverley Gold Medal for scientific writing, 1955; Meritorious Award, Council of Biology Editors, USA, 1984. *Publications:* Scientific Writing for Graduate Students, 1969, 4th edn 1986; Medical Research Systems in Europe, 1973; The Ciba Foundation: an analytic history 1949–1974, 1974; Writing Scientific Papers in English, 1975; From Primrose Hill to Euston Road; Atherosclerosis X; In-Service Training series: of Physiological Measurement Technicians, 1988; of Medical Physics Technicians, 1989; of Medical Laboratory Assistants, 1991; of Rehabilitation Engineering Technicians, 1992; articles on scientific writing, lipids of the arterial wall, editing of biomed. jls, prevention and treatment of handicapping disorders, screening for spina bifida, quality in pathology labs, costing and ethics in clin. chem. *Recreations:* chamber music (pianist), gardening, opera. *Address:* 1 Akenside Road, NW3 5BS.

WOODGATE, Joan Mary, CBE 1964; RRC 1959; Matron-in-Chief, Queen Alexandra's RN Nursing Service, 1962–66, retired; *b* 30 Aug. 1912; *d* of Sir Alfred Woodgate, CBE, and Louisa Alice (*née* Digby). *Educ:* Surbiton High Sch., Surrey. Trained at St George's Hospital, 1932–36, Sister, 1937–38; Queen Charlotte's Hospital, 1936. Joined QARNNS, 1938; served Middle East and Far East; HM Hospital Ship, Empire Clyde, 1945–47; HM Hospital Ship, Maine, 1953–54; Principal Matron: RNH Haslar, 1959–61; RNH Malta, 1961–62. OStJ 1959; QHNS, 1962–64. Member, Commonwealth War Graves Commn, 1966–83. *Recreations:* gardening, country pursuits. *Address:* Tiptoe, near Lymington, Hants SO41 6FS. *Club:* English-Speaking Union.

WOODHALL, David Massey, CBE 1992; Chief Executive, Commission for New Towns, 1982–92; *b* 25 Aug. 1934; *s* of Douglas J. D. and Esme Dorothy Woodhall; *m* 1954, Margaret A. Howarth; two *s*. *Educ:* Bishop Holgate's Sch., Barnsley; Royds Hall, Huddersfield; Henley Administrative Staff Coll. Dip. Leeds Sch. of Architecture and Town Planning. West Riding CC, 1951–60; Cumberland CC, 1960–63; Northamptonshire CC, 1963–82: County Planning Officer, 1971–80; Asst Chief Executive, 1980–82. *Recreations:* National Hunt racing, landscape, food and wine. *Address:* 5 Kylestrome House, Cundy Street, SW1W 9JT. *T:* 0171–730 0989.

WOODHAM, Professor Ronald Ernest; Professor of Music, Reading University, 1951–77; *b* 8 Feb. 1912; *s* of Ernest Victor Woodham, Beckenham, Kent; *m* 1949, Kathleen Isabel, *e d* of P. J. Malone; three *s*. *Educ:* Sherborne Sch.; Royal College of Music, London; Christ Church, Oxford. BA, DMus; FRCO, ARCM. Assistant Director of Music, Bradfield Coll., 1936. Served in RASC, in Middle East and Italy, 1939–45 (despatches). Acting Director of Music, Bradfield Coll., 1946; Director of Music, Sherborne Sch., 1946; Cramb Lecturer in Music, Glasgow Univ., 1947–51. *Address:* 8 Sutton Gardens, St Peter Street, Winchester, Hants SO23 8HP.

WOODHEAD, Vice-Adm. Sir (Anthony) Peter, KCB 1992; Prisons' Ombudsman, since 1994; *b* 30 July 1939; *s* of Leslie and Nancy Woodhead; *m* 1964, Carol; one *s* one *d*. *Educ:* Leeds Grammar Sch.; Conway; BRNC Dartmouth. Seaman Officer; Pilot, 1962; Aircraft Carriers, Borneo Campaign; CO, HM Ships Jupiter, 1974, Rhyl, 1975; NDC 1976; Naval Plans Div., MoD, 1977; CSO to Flag Officer, Third Flotilla, 1980; COS to FO Comdg Falklands Task Force, 1982; Captain, Fourth Frigate Sqdn, 1983; RCDS 1984; Dir, Naval Ops, 1985; CO HMS Illustrious, 1986; Flag Officer: Flotilla Two, 1988; Flotilla One, 1989. Dep. SACLANT, 1991–93. Lay Reader, Guildford, 1991. Pres., Marriage Resource, 1995. *Recreations:* ball games, antique restoration. *Club:* Royal Navy of 1765 and 1785.

WOODHEAD, Christopher Anthony; HM Chief Inspector of Schools, since 1994; *b* 20 Oct. 1946. *Educ:* Bristol Univ. (BA Sp. Hons English, PGCE); Univ. of Keele (MA). English Teacher, Priory Sch., Shrewsbury, 1969–72; Dep. Head of English, Newent Sch., Gloucester, 1972–74; Head of English, Gordano Sch., Avon, 1974–76; Tutor for English, Oxford Univ., 1976–82; English Advr, 1982–84, Chief Advr, 1984–88, Shropshire LEA; Dep. Chief Educn Officer, Devon LEA, 1988–90, Cornwall LEA, 1990–91; Dep. Chief Exec., 1991, Chief Exec., 1991–93, Nat. Curriculum Council; Chief Exec., SCAA, 1993–94. Special Prof., Univ. of Nottingham, 1993–. *Recreations:* rock climbing, running. *Address:* Office for Standards in Education, Alexandra House, 29–33 Kingsway, WC2B 6SE.

WOODHEAD, David James; National Director, Independent Schools Information Service, since 1985; *b* 9 Nov. 1943; *s* of Frank and Polly Woodhead; *m* 1974, Carole Underwood; two *s*. *Educ:* Queen Elizabeth Grammar Sch., Wakefield; Univ. of Leicester (BA Hons history, politics and English; Chm., Univ. Conservative Assoc., 1964–65). Journalist: Cambridge Evening News (educn corresp.), 1965; Sunday Telegraph, 1968; ILEA Press Office: Press Officer, 1975; Chief Press Officer, 1978. Editor, ISIS News, 1985–89; Editl Dir, The ISIS Magazine, 1990–. Trustee, Jt Educnl Trust, 1988–. Governor: Battle Abbey Sch., 1988–91; St John's Sch., Leatherhead, 1995–. FRSA 1990. *Publications:* Choosing Your Independent School, annually, 1985–; (ed) Good Communications Guide, 1986, 2nd edn 1989; numerous newspaper and magazine articles. *Recreations:* family, opera, classical music, enjoying being a Wagner fanatic, travel. *Address:* Independent Schools Information Service, 56 Buckingham Gate, SW1E 6AG. *T:* 0171–630 8796.

WOODHEAD, Vice-Adm. Sir Peter; *see* Woodhead, Vice-Adm. Sir A. P.

WOODHOUSE, family name of **Baron Terrington.**

WOODHOUSE, Ven. Andrew Henry, DSC 1945; MA; Archdeacon of Hereford and Canon Residentiary, Hereford Cathedral, 1982–91, now Archdeacon Emeritus; *b* 30 Jan. 1923; *s* of H. A. Woodhouse, Dental Surgeon, Hanover Square, W1, and Woking, Surrey, and Mrs P. Woodhouse; unmarried. *Educ:* Lancing Coll.; The Queen's Coll., Oxford. MA 1949. Served War, RNVR, 1942–46 (Lieut). Oxford, 1941–42 and 1946–47; Lincoln Theological Coll., 1948–50. Deacon, 1950; Priest, 1951; Curate of All Saints, Poplar, 1950–56; Vicar of St Martin, West Drayton, 1956–70; Rural Dean of Hillingdon, 1967–70; Archdeacon of Ludlow and Rector of Wistanstow, 1970–82. *Recreations:* photography, walking. *Address:* Orchard Cottage, Bracken Close, Woking, Surrey GU22 7HD. *T:* Guildford (01483) 760671. *Club:* Naval.
See also R. M. Woodhouse.

WOODHOUSE, Rt. Hon. Sir (Arthur) Owen, KBE 1981; Kt 1974; DSC 1944; PC 1974; Founding President, Law Commission, New Zealand, 1986–91; a Judge of the Supreme Court, New Zealand, 1961–86; a Judge of the Court of Appeal, 1974–86, President of the Court of Appeal, 1981–86; *b* Napier, 18 July 1916; *s* of A. J. Woodhouse and W. J. C. Woodhouse (*née* Allen); *m* 1940, Margaret Leah Thorp; four *s* two *d*. *Educ:* Napier Boys' High Sch.; Auckland Univ. (LLB). Served War of 1939–45, Lt-Comdr in RNZNVR on secondment to RN; service in MTBs; liaison officer with Yugoslav Partisans, 1943; Asst to Naval Attaché, HM Embassy Belgrade, 1945. Joined Lusk, Willis & Sproule, barristers and solicitors, 1946; Crown Solicitor, Napier, 1953; appointed Judge of Supreme Court, 1961. Chm., Royal Commn on Compensation and Rehabilitation in respect of Personal Injury in NZ, 1966–67, and of inquiry into similar questions in Australia, 1973–74. Hon. LLD: Victoria Univ. of Wellington, 1978; Univ. of York, Toronto, 1981. *Recreations:* music, golf. *Address:* 244 Remuera Road, Auckland 1005, New Zealand. *Clubs:* Northern (Auckland); Hawkes Bay (Napier); Wellesley, Wellington (Wellington).

WOODHOUSE, Ven. (Charles) David (Stewart); Archdeacon of Warrington, since 1981; Vicar of St Peter's, Hindley, 1981–92; *b* 23 Dec. 1934; *s* of Rev. Hector and Elsie Woodhouse. *Educ:* Silcoates School, Wakefield; Kelham Theological College. Curate of St Wilfrid's, Halton, Leeds, 1959–63; Youth Chaplain, Kirkby Team Ministry, Diocese of Liverpool, 1963–66; Curate of St John's, Pembroke, Bermuda, 1966–69; Asst Gen. Secretary, CEMS, 1969–70; Gen. Sec., 1970–76; Rector of Ideford, Ashcombe and Luton and Domestic Chaplain to Bishop of Exeter, 1976–81. Hon. Canon, Liverpool Cathedral, 1983. *Address:* 22 Rob Lane, Newton-le-Willows WA12 0DR. *T:* Newton-le-Willows (01925) 229247, *Fax:* (01925) 220423.

WOODHOUSE, Hon. (Christopher) Montague, DSO 1943; OBE 1944; MA (Oxon); *b* 11 May 1917; 2nd *s* of 3rd Baron Terrington, KBE; *b* and *heir-pres.* to 4th Baron Terrington, *qv*; *m* 1945, Lady Davina (*d* 1995), *d* of 2nd Earl of Lytton, KG, PC, GCSI, GCIE, and *widow* of 5th Earl of Erne; two *s* one *d*. *Educ:* Winchester; New Coll., Oxford (Craven and Hertford Schols, Gaisford Prizeman; Hon. Fellow, 1982). First Cl. Hon. Mods, 1937; First Class Lit. Hum., 1939; MA 1947; Lord Justice Holker Schol. Gray's Inn, 1939; enlisted RA, 1939, commissioned 1940; Colonel, Aug. 1943, in command of Allied Military Mission to Greek Guerillas in German-occupied Greece (despatches twice, DSO, OBE, Officer of Legion of Merit (USA), Commander of Order of the Phoenix, with Swords (Greece)). Served in HM Embassy, Athens, 1945, Tehran, 1951; Secretary-General, Allied Mission for Observing Greek Elections, 1946; worked in industry 1946–48; Asst Secretary, Nuffield Foundation, 1948–50; Foreign Office, 1952; Director-General, RIIA, and Dir. of Studies, 1955–59; MP (C) Oxford, 1959–66 and 1970–Sept. 1974; Parliamentary Secretary, Ministry of Aviation, 1961–62; Joint Under-Secretary of State, Home Office, July 1962–Oct. 1964. Dir, Educn and Training, CBI, 1966–70. President, Classical Assoc., 1968; Chm. Council, RSL, 1977–86. Fellow of Trinity Hall, Cambridge, 1950; Visiting Fellow, Nuffield Coll., Oxford, 1956; Vis. Prof., King's Coll., London, 1978. FRSL 1951. Special Mem., Acad. of Athens, 1980. *Publications:* Apple of Discord, 1948; One Omen, 1950; Dostoievsky, 1951; The Greek War of Independence, 1952; Britain and the Middle East, 1959; British Foreign Policy since the Second World War, 1961; Rhodes (with late J. G. Lockhart), 1963; The New Concert of Nations, 1964; The Battle of Navarino, 1965; Post-War Britain, 1966; The Story of Modern Greece, 1968, retitled Modern Greece, 5th edn 1991; The Philhellenes, 1969; Capodistria: the founder of Greek independence, 1973; The Struggle for Greece (1941–1949), 1976; Something Ventured, 1982; Karamanlis: the restorer of Greek democracy, 1982; The Rise and Fall of the Greek Colonels, 1985; Gemistos Plethon: the last of the Hellenes, 1986; Rhigas Velestinlis, 1995; numerous articles, translations, broadcasts. *Address:* Willow Cottage, Latimer, Bucks HP5 1TW. *T:* Little Chalfont (01494) 762627.

WOODHOUSE, Ven. David; *see* Woodhouse, Ven. C. D. S.

WOODHOUSE, Dr Frank; Director, British Institute of Florence, since 1988; *b* 29 April 1943; *s* of Samuel Woodhouse and Clarice (*née* Bache); *m* 1966, Melba Sterry; two *s*. *Educ:* King Edward VI Grammar Sch., Stourbridge; Birmingham Univ. (BCom); Trinity Hall, Cambridge (MA, PhD). Asst Lectr, later Lectr in Italian, Hull Univ., 1972–81; Lectr in Italian, Cambridge Univ., 1981–92; Fellow, 1983–92, Associate Dean, 1986–87, Darwin Coll., Cambridge. *Publications:* Language and Style in a Renaissance Epic, 1982; articles on Italian subjects. *Recreations:* reading, travel, Italy. *Address:* c/o British Institute of Florence, Palazzo Lanfredini, Lungarno Guicciardini 9, 50125 Firenze, Italy. *T:* (55) 284031. *Club:* Circolo dell'Unione (Florence).

WOODHOUSE, James Stephen; Director, ISIS East, since 1994; *b* 21 May 1933; *s* of late Rt Rev. J. W. Woodhouse, sometime Bishop of Thetford, and late Mrs K. M. Woodhouse; *m* 1957, Sarah, *d* of late Col Hubert Blount, Cley, Norfolk; three *s* one *d*. *Educ:* St Edward's Sch.; St Catharine's Coll., Cambridge. BA (English) Cantab, 1957; MA 1961. Nat. Service, 14th Field Regt RA, 1953. Asst Master, Westminster Sch., 1957; Under Master and Master of the Queen's Scholars, 1963; Headmaster, Rugby Sch., 1967–81; Headmaster, Lancing Coll., 1981–93. Chairman: NABC Religious Adv. Cttee, 1971–93; Bloxham Project, 1972–77; Head Masters' Conf., 1979; Joint Standing Cttee of HMC, IAPS and GSA, 1981–86; Vice-Chm., E-SU Schoolboy Scholarship Cttee, 1973–77. Director: The Norfolk Boat, 1993–; Holkham Pageant, 1994. *Recreations:* sailing, music, hill walking. *Address:* Welcome Cottage, Wiveton, Holt, Norfolk NR25 7TH.

WOODHOUSE, Prof. John Henry, PhD; Professor of Geophysics, and Fellow of Worcester College, Oxford, since 1989; *b* 15 April 1949; *s* of G. B. Woodhouse. *Educ:* Southall Grammar Sch.; Bristol Univ. (BSc 1970); King's Coll., Cambridge (MA, PhD 1975). Fellow, King's Coll., Cambridge, 1974–78; Vis. Asst Res. Geophysicist, Inst. of Geophysics and Planetary Physics, Univ. of Calif., San Diego, 1976–77; Asst Prof., 1978–80, Associate Prof., 1980–83, Prof. of Geophysics, 1983–89, Harvard Univ. Chm., Commn on Seismological Theory, Internat. Assoc. of Seismol. and Physics of Earth's Interior, 1983–87. Fellow, Amer. Geophys. Union (McElwane Award, 1984). Associate Ed., Jl of Geophysical Res., 1979–81. *Publications:* many contribs to learned jls. *Address:* Worcester College, Oxford OX1 2HB.

WOODHOUSE, Prof. John Robert, FBA 1995; Fiat Serena Professor of Italian Studies, Oxford, and Fellow, Magdalen College, since 1990; *b* 17 June 1937; *s* of Horace Woodhouse and Iris Evelyn Pewton; *m* 1967, Gaynor Mathias. *Educ:* King Edward VI Grammar School, Stourbridge; Hertford College, Oxford (MA, DLitt); Univ. of Pisa; PhD Wales. Asst Lectr in Italian, Univ. of Aberdeen, 1961–62; British Council Scholar, Scuola Normale Superiore, Pisa, 1962–63; Asst Lectr and Lectr, UCNW, Bangor, 1963–66; Lectr and Sen. Lectr, Univ. of Hull, 1966–73; Oxford University: Univ. Lectr in Italian and Fellow of St Cross Coll., 1973–84; Lectr at Jesus Coll., 1973, St Edmund Hall, 1975, Brasenose Coll., 1976; Fellow, 1984–89, Supernumerary Fellow, 1991, Pembroke Coll. Mem., Exec. Cttee, Soc. for Italian Studies, 1979–85. Harvard Old Dominion Foundn Fellow, Villa I Tatti, 1969; Founding Mem., Centro Studi Dannunziani, Pescara, 1979; Fellow: Accad. lett. ital. dell'Arcadia, 1980; Accademia della Crusca, 1991; Corresp. Fellow, Commissione per i Testi di Lingua, Bologna, 1993; Sen. Res. Fellow, Center for Medieval and Renaissance Studies, UCLA, 1985; Fellow: Huntington Liby, Calif., 1986; Newberry Liby, Chicago, 1988. Editor (Italian), Modern Language Review, 1984–94; Mem., Editl Bd, Italian Studies, 1987–91. Cavaliere Ufficiale, Order of Merit (Italy), 1991. *Publications:* Italo Calvino: a reappraisal and an appreciation of the trilogy, 1968; (ed) Italo Calvino, Il barone rampante, 1970; (ed) V. Borghini, Scritti inediti o rari sulla lingua, 1971; (ed) V. Borghini, Storia della nobiltà fiorentina, 1974; Baldesar Castiglione, a reassessment of the Cortegiano, 1978; (ed) G. d'Annunzio, Alcyone, 1978; (ed with P. R. Horne) G. Rossetti, Lettere familiari, 1983; (ed jtly) G. Rossetti, Carteggi, I, 1984, II, 1988, III, 1992; (ed jtly) The Languages of Literature in Renaissance Italy, 1988; From Castiglione to Chesterfield: the decline in the courtier's manual, 1991; articles in learned jls. *Recreations:* gardening, hill walking. *Address:* Magdalen College, Oxford OX1 4AU.

WOODHOUSE, Michael; *see* Woodhouse, R. M.

WOODHOUSE, Hon. Montague; *see* Woodhouse, Hon. C. M.

WOODHOUSE, Rt. Hon. Sir Owen; *see* Woodhouse, Rt Hon. Sir A. O.

WOODHOUSE, (Ronald) Michael; Chairman, Rexam PLC (formerly Bowater), since 1993 (Director, since 1988); Chairman, Prince's Trust Volunteers, since 1991; *b* 19 Aug. 1927; *s* of Henry Alfred Woodhouse and Phyllis Woodhouse (*née* Gemmell); *m* 1955, Quenilda Mary, *d* of Rt Rev. Neville Vincent Gorton; one *s* three *d*. *Educ:* Lancing Coll.; Queen's Coll., Oxford (BA Mod. History). Courtaulds plc, 1951–91: Dir, 1976–91; Dep. Chm., 1986–91. Director: RSA Exam. Board, 1991–; London Mozart Players, 1991–. *Recreations:* walking in Lake District, watching Rugby and cricket, listening to music, gardening, art. *Address:* Tankards, Wonersh, Guildford, Surrey GU5 0PF. *T:* Guildford (01483) 892078; Dalehead, Hartsop, Patterdale, Cumbria CA11 0NZ. *Club:* Carlton.
See also Ven. A. H. Woodhouse.

WOODHOUSE, Ven. Samuel Mostyn Forbes; Archdeacon of London and Canon Residentiary of St Paul's, 1967–78, Archdeacon Emeritus and Canon Emeritus, 1978; Archdeacon to: Retired Clergy, Bath and Wells, since 1978; Retired Clergy Association, since 1980; *b* 28 April 1912; *s* of Rev. Major James D. F. Woodhouse, DSO, and Elsie Noel Woodhouse, Water, Manaton, Devon; *m* 1939, Patricia Daniel; two *s* one *d*. *Educ:* Shrewsbury; Christ Church, Oxford; Wells Theological Coll. BA 1934; MA 1942. Deacon, 1936, Priest, 1937, Diocese of Blackburn; Curate, Lancaster Priory, 1936–39. Chaplain to the Forces (Army), 1939–45 (despatches thrice). Vicar, Holy Trinity, South Shore, Blackpool, 1945–49; Vicar of Leominster, 1949–57; Rural Dean of Leominster, 1956–57; Rector of Bristol City Parish Church (St Stephen's), 1957–67. *Recreations:* painting, architecture. *Address:* Under Copse Cottage, Redhill, Wrington, Bristol BS18 7SH. *T:* Wrington (01934) 862711. *Clubs:* Leander; Vincent's (Oxford).

WOODING, Sir Norman (Samuel), Kt 1992; CBE 1986; PhD; Chairman, East European Trade Council, since 1990; *b* 20 April 1927; *s* of Samuel and Nellie Gertrude Wooding; *m* 1949, Dorothy Elizabeth Smith; one *s* two *d*. *Educ:* Lawrence Sheriff Sch., Rugby; Univ. of London (BSc); Univ. of Leeds (PhD); Univ. of Manchester. Joined Courtaulds, 1944; Main Board Dir, 1973; Dep. Chm., 1976–87; retd. Earlys of Witney: Dir, 1971–84; Chm., 1978–83. Chairman: Agricl Genetics Co. Ltd, 1988–93; British Textile Technol. Gp, 1991–94; EIS Gp, 1994–; Dep. Chm. (non-Exec.), Royal London Mutual Insce Soc. Ltd, 1988–; Dir (non-Exec.), British Nuclear Fuels plc, 1987–. Pres., Brit. Soviet Chamber of Commerce, 1988–; Chm. Council, SSEES, Univ. of London, 1992–; Mem. Governing Body, Brit. Assoc. for Central and Eastern Europe, 1988–. Sen. Associate Mem., St Antony's Coll., Oxford, 1987–. CIMgt (CBIM 1983); FRSA 1992. *Publications:* papers in scientific journals, E European trade jls, etc. *Recreations:* mountain walking, gardening, fast cars. *Address:* East European Trade Council, Westminster Palace Gardens, SW1P 1RL. *Club:* Reform.

WOODLEY, Keith Spencer, FCA; in practice as chartered accountant, since 1990; President, Institute of Chartered Accountants in England and Wales, 1995–June 1996; *b* 23 Oct. 1939; *s* of Charles Spencer Woodley and Hilda Mary Woodley (*née* Brown); *m* 1962, Joyce Madeleine Toon; one *s* two *d*. *Educ:* Stationers' Co. Sch. Articled Clerk, Senior Deloitte Plender Griffiths & Co., 1959–69; Partner, Deloitte Haskins & Sells, 1969–90: Nat. Personnel Partner, 1978–82; Mem., Partnership Bd, 1985–90. Complaints Commissioner: SIB, 1990–94; SFA, 1990–; FIMBRA, 1990–; PIA, 1994 –; Indep. Investigator, Investors' Compensation Scheme, 1991–. Director: Royscot Trust, 1990–; National & Provincial Building Soc., 1991–. Mem. Council, ICAEW, 1988–. Hon. Treas., NACAB, 1991–94. *Recreations:* theatre, music, hill walking. *Address:* 11 Sion Hill, Bath BA1 2UH; (office) 24 Gay Street, Bath BA1 2PL.

WOODLEY, Ven. Ronald John; Archdeacon of Cleveland, 1985–91, Emeritus, since 1991; *b* 28 Dec. 1925; *s* of John Owen Woodley and Maggie Woodley; *m* 1959, Patricia Kneeshaw; one *s* two *d*. *Educ:* Montagu Road School, Edmonton; St Augustine's Coll., Canterbury; Bishops' Coll., Cheshunt. Deacon 1953, priest 1954; Curate: St Martin, Middlesbrough, 1953–58; Whitby, 1958–61; Curate in Charge 1961–66, and Vicar 1966–71, The Ascension, Middlesbrough; Rector of Stokesley, 1971–85; RD of Stokesley, 1977–84. Canon of York, 1982–. *Recreations:* gardening, walking. *Address:* Brierton House, 52 South Parade, Northallerton, N Yorks DL7 8SL. *T:* Northallerton (01609) 778818.

WOODLOCK, Jack Terence; Under-Secretary, Department of Health and Social Security, 1969–79, retired; *b* 10 July 1919; *s* of late James Patrick and Florence Woodlock; *m* 1941, Joan Mary Taylor; three *s* one *d*. *Educ:* Bromley Grammar School. Entered Civil Service, 1936; served in Royal Artillery, 1939–45; Ministry of Health, 1945; Asst Principal 1946; Principal 1950; Principal Private Sec. to Minister, 1958–59; Asst Sec. 1959. *Recreation:* historical studies. *Address:* 6 The King's Peace, Crossways Road, Grayshott, Hindhead, Surrey GU26 6HS.

WOODROFFE, Most Rev. George Cuthbert Manning, KBE 1980 (CBE 1973); MA, LTh; Archbishop of West Indies, 1980–86; Bishop of Windward Islands, 1969–86, retired; *b* 17 May 1918; *s* of James Manning Woodroffe and Evelyn Agatha (*née* Norton); *m* 1947, Aileen Alice Connell; one *s* one *d* (and one *s* decd). *Educ:* Grenada Boys' Secondary School; Codrington Coll., Barbados. Clerk in Civil Service, Grenada, 1936–41; Codrington Coll. (Univ. of Durham), 1941–44; Deacon 1944; Priest 1945; Asst Priest, St George's Cath., St Vincent, 1944–47; Vicar of St Simon's, Barbados, 1947–50; Rector: St Andrew, 1950–57; St Joseph, 1957–62; St John, 1962–67; Rural Dean of St John, Barbados, 1965–67; Sub-Dean and Rector of St George's Cathedral, St Vincent, Windward Islands, 1967–69. Vice-Chm., Anglican Consultative Council, 1974. Chm., Vis. Justices St Vincent Prisons, 1968–76. Mem., Prerogative of Mercy Cttee, St Vincent, 1969–86. Member: Bd of Educn, Barbados, 1964–67; National Trust of St Vincent, 1967– (Chm., 1972–82); Council, Univ. of the West Indies, 1980–83; Chm., Bd of Governors, Alleyne Sch., Barbados, 1951–57. Hon. DD Nashotah House, USA, 1980; Hon. LLD Univ. of the West Indies, 1981. *Recreations:* music, driving, detective tales and novels, military band music. *Address:* PO Box 919, Murray Road, St Vincent and the Grenadines, West Indies. *T:* 4561277. *Club:* Commonwealth Trust.

WOODROFFE, Jean Frances, (Mrs J. W. R. Woodroffe), CVO 1953; *b* 22 Feb. 1923; *d* of late Capt. A. V. Hambro; *m* 1st, 1942, Capt. Hon. Vicary Paul Gibbs, Grenadier Guards (killed in action, 1944), *er s* of 4th Baron Aldenham; one *d* (and one *d* decd); 2nd, 1946, Rev. Hon. Andrew Charles Victor Elphinstone (*d* 1975), 2nd *s* of 16th Lord Elphinstone, KT; one *d* (one *s* decd); 3rd, 1980, Lt-Col John William Richard Woodroffe (*d* 1990). Lady-in-Waiting to the Queen as Princess Elizabeth, 1945; Extra Woman of the Bedchamber to the Queen, 1952–. *Address:* Maryland, Worplesdon, Guildford, Surrey GU3 3RB. *T:* Worplesdon (01483) 232629.

WOODROOFE, Sir Ernest (George), Kt 1973; PhD, FInstP, FIChemE; *b* 6 Jan. 1912; *s* of late Ernest George Woodroofe and Ada (*née* Dickinson); *m* 1st, 1938, Margaret Downes (*d* 1961); one *d*; 2nd, 1962, Enid Grace Hutchinson Arnold. *Educ:* Cockburn High Sch.; Leeds Univ. Staff of Loders & Nucoline Ltd, 1935–44; Staff of British Oil & Cake Mills Ltd, 1944–50; Mem., Oil Mills Executive of Unilever Ltd, 1951–55; Director of British Oil & Cake Mills Ltd, 1951–55; Head of Research Division of Unilever Ltd, 1955–61; Director: United Africa Co. Ltd, 1961–63; Unilever NV, 1956–74; Chm., Unilever Ltd, 1970–74 (Dir, 1956–74; Vice-Chm., 1961–70); Trustee, Leverhulme Trust, 1962–82 (Chm., 1974–82). President, International Society for Fat Research, 1962. Member Cttee of Enquiry into the Organisation of Civil Science, 1962–63; A Vice-Pres., Soc. of Chemical Industry, 1963–66; Member: Tropical Products Inst. Cttee, 1964–69; Council for Nat. Academic Awards, 1964–67; Cttee of Award of the Commonwealth Fund, 1965–70; Royal Commn for the Exhibn of 1851, 1968–84; British Gas Corp., 1973–81. Director: Schroders Ltd, 1974–89; Burton Group Ltd, 1974–83; Guthrie Corp. Ltd, 1974–82. Chairman: Review Body on Doctors' and Dentists' Remuneration, 1975–79; CBI Research Cttee, 1966–69. Governor, London Business Sch., 1970–75 (Dep. Chm., 1973–75). Hon. ACT Liverpool, 1963; Hon. Fellow, University of Manchester Inst. of Science and Technology, 1968; Hon. LLD Leeds, 1968; DUniv Surrey, 1970; Hon. DSc: Cranfield, 1974; Liverpool, 1980. Vis. Fellow, Nuffield Coll., Oxford, 1972–80. Comdr, Order of Orange Nassau (Netherlands), 1972. *Recreation:* fishing. *Address:* 44 The Street, Puttenham, Surrey GU3 1AR. *T:* Guildford (01483) 810977.

WOODROW, David, CBE 1979; retired solicitor; *b* 16 March 1920; *s* of late Sydney Melson Woodrow and late Edith Constance (*née* Farmer); *m* 1st, 1950, Marie-Armande (marr. diss.; she *d* 1989), *d* of late Benjamin Barrios, KBE, and late Lady Ovey; two *d*; 2nd, 1983, Mary Miley, *d* of late Rupert Alexander Whitamore and Sally Whitamore. *Educ:* Shrewsbury; Trinity Coll., Oxford (MA). Commnd Royal Artillery, 1940; served SE Asia; POW Java and Japan, 1942–45. Admitted Solicitor, 1949. Chairman: Reading and District HMC, 1966–72; Oxford Regional Hosp. Bd, 1972–74; RHA, 1973–78; NHS Nat. Staff Cttee, Administrative and Clerical Staff, 1975–79. *Recreations:* painting and looking at pictures. *Address:* Dobsons, Brightwell-cum-Sotwell, Wallingford, Oxon OX10 0RH. *T:* Wallingford (01491) 36170. *Club:* Leander (Henley-on-Thames).

WOODROW, Gayford William; HM Diplomatic Service, retired; Consul, Algeciras, 1982–85; *b* 21 Feb. 1922; *s* of William Alexander Woodrow and Charlotte Louise (*née* Ellis); *m* 1946, Janine Suzanne Marcelle Jannot; one *s*. *Educ:* Brockley County School. Served War, RAF, 1941–46. Foreign Office, 1946; Caracas, 1949; Vice Consul: Barcelona, 1952; Panama, 1954; Consul: Cairo, 1960; Alexandria, 1961; First Sec. and Consul, Warsaw, 1962; Consul: Valencia, 1965; Jerusalem, 1969; First Sec., Ottawa, 1976; Consul General, Tangier, 1978–80; Asst, Consular Dept, FCO, 1980–81. *Recreations:* walking, swimming, history. *Address:* Apartment 3, Pitt House, Chudleigh, Devon TQ13 0EL.

WOODRUFF, Harry Wells, CMG 1966; retired, 1972; *b* 31 Oct. 1912; *s* of Leonard Wells Woodruff and Rosina Woodruff; *m* 1938, Margaret Bradley; one *d*. *Educ:* Reigate Grammar Sch.; London Univ. Trade Comr, Johannesburg, 1946–51; Trade Comr and Economic Adviser to High Commissioner: Salisbury, 1951–55; Kuala Lumpur, 1957–61; Commercial Counsellor, Canberra, 1962–66; Economic Adviser to Foreign Office, 1966–68; Asst Sec., Dept of Trade and Industry (formerly Bd of Trade), 1968–72. *Publication:* (jointly) Economic Development in Rhodesia and Nyasaland, 1955. *Recreation:* painting. *Address:* 387 Sandbanks Road, Poole, Dorset.

WOODRUFF, Prof. Sir Michael (Francis Addison), Kt 1969; FRS 1968; FRCS; DSc, MS (Melbourne); Emeritus Professor of Surgery, University of Edinburgh, and Surgeon, Edinburgh Royal Infirmary, 1957–76; Director, Nuffield Transplantation Surgery Unit, Edinburgh, 1968–76; *b* 3 April 1911; *s* of late Prof. Harold Addison Woodruff and Margaret Ada (*née* Cooper); *m* 1946, Hazel Gwenyth Ashby; two *s* one *d*. *Educ:* Wesley Coll., Melbourne; Queen's Coll., University of Melbourne. MB, BS (Melbourne) 1937, MD 1940, MS 1941; FRCS 1946. Captain, Australian Army Medical Corps, 1940–46. Tutor in Surgery, Univ. of Sheffield, 1946–48; Lecturer in Surgery, Univ. of Aberdeen, 1948–52; Hunterian Prof., RCS, 1952; Travelling Fellow, WHO, 1949; Prof. of Surgery, Univ. of Otago, Dunedin, NZ, 1953–56; Prof. of Surgery, Univ. of Edinburgh, 1957–76. Pres., Transplantation Soc., 1972–74. A Vice-Pres., Royal Soc., 1979. Associé Etranger, Académie de Chirurgie, 1964; Hon. Fellow American Surgical Assoc., 1965; Korrespondierenden Mitglied, Deutsche Gesellschaft für Chirurgie; Hon. FACS 1975; Hon. FRCPE 1982. Lister Medal, 1969; Gold Medal, Soc. of Apothecaries, 1974. *Publications:* (jtly) Deficiency Diseases in Japanese Prison Camps, 1951; Surgery for Dental Students, 1954; Transplantation of Tissues and Organs, 1960; (essays) On Science and Surgery, 1977; The Interaction of Cancer and Host, 1980; Cellular Variation and Adaptation in Cancer, 1990; contrib. Encyclopedia of Human Biology, 1991; articles on surgical topics and on experimental tissue transplantation. *Recreations:* music, sailing. *Address:* The Bield, 506 Lanark Road, Juniper Green, Edinburgh EH14 5DH. *Clubs:* Athenæum; New (Edinburgh).

WOODRUFF, Philip; *see* Mason, Philip.

WOODRUFF, William Charles, CBE 1985; FRAeS; *b* 14 Aug. 1921; *s* of late Thomas and Caroline Woodruff; *m* 1st, 1946, Ethel May Miles (*d* 1981); one *s* one *d*; 2nd, 1987, Olivia Minerva Henson. *Educ:* St George's, Ramsgate. RAF, 1941–46: Navigator/Observer, 1409 Flight; POW Germany, 1943–45. Seconded Air Min., 1945, and later Min. of Civil Aviation for Air Traffic Control planning; various air traffic control appts at Hurn, Northolt, Southern Centre, Heston and MTCA Hdqrs, 1946–56; Air Traffic Control Officer i/c Heathrow, 1956–62; Sec. of Patch Long-term Air Traffic Control Planning Group, 1960–61; Dep. Dir, 1962–67, Dir, 1967–69, Civil Air Traffic Ops; National Air Traffic Services: Jt Field Comdr, 1969–74; Dep. Controller, 1974–77; Controller, 1977–81. Assessor, Stanstead/Heathrow Airports Public Inquiries, 1981–84; Specialist Advr, H of C Transport Select Cttee on Air Safety, 1988–89. Guild of Air Traffic Control Officers: Clerk, 1952–56; Master, 1956. *Publications:* articles on aviation subjects. *Address:* Great Oaks, 36 Court Road, Ickenham, Uxbridge, Middx UB10 8TF. *T:* Ruislip (01895) 639134.

WOODS, His Honour Brian; DL; a Circuit Judge, 1975–94; *b* 5 Nov. 1928; *yr s* of late E. P. Woods, Woodmancote, Cheltenham; *m* 1957, Margaret, *d* of late F. J. Griffiths, Parkgate, Wirral; three *d*. *Educ:* City of Leicester Boys' Sch.; Nottingham Univ. (LLB 1952). National Service, RAF, 1947–49. Called to the Bar, Gray's Inn, 1955; Midland Circuit; Dep. Chm., Lincs (Lindsey) QS, 1968. Chancellor, Diocese of Leicester, 1977–79; Reader, dio. of Leicester, 1970–79, dio. of Lichfield, 1978–. Member Council: S Mary and S Anne's Sch., Abbots Bromley, 1977–92; Ellesmere Coll., 1983–84. Mem., Law Adv. Cttee, Nottingham Univ., 1979–94; a Legal Mem., Trent Region Mental Health Review Tribunal, 1983–. Fellow, Midland Div., Woodard Corp., 1979–92. DL Derbys, 1994. *Recreations:* daughters, musical music, taking photographs. *Address:* c/o Circuit Administrator, 2 Newton Street, Birmingham B4 7LU.

WOODS, Maj.-Gen. Charles William, CB 1970; MBE 1952; MC 1944; Chairman, Douglas Haig Memorial Homes, 1975–87; *b* 21 March 1917; *s* of late Captain F. W. U. Woods and of Mrs M. E. Woods, Gosbrook House, Binfield Heath, Henley-on-Thames; *m* 1940, Angela Helen Clay; one *d* (one *s* decd). *Educ:* Uppingham Sch.; Trinity Coll., Cambridge (MA). Commnd into Corps of Royal Engineers, 1938; served War of 1939–45,

N Africa, Sicily, Italy, NW Europe (D Landings with 50th Div.); Staff Coll., Camberley, 1946; served in Korea, 1951–52; comd 35 Corps Engineer Regt, BAOR, 1959–60; Dep. Military Secretary, 1964–67; Dir of Manning (Army), 1967–70. Col Comdt, RE, 1973–78. Chm., RE Assoc., 1971–77. *Recreations:* sailing, ski-ing. *Address:* 6 Grove Pastures, Lymington, Hants SO41 9RG. *T:* Lymington (01590) 673445. *Clubs:* Royal Ocean Racing, Royal Cruising, Ski Club of Great Britain; Royal Lymington Yacht, Royal Engineer Yacht, Island Sailing (Cowes).

WOODS, Christopher Matthew, CMG 1979; MC 1945; HM Diplomatic Service, retired; Special Operations Executive Adviser, Foreign and Commonwealth Office, 1982–88; *b* 26 May 1923; *s* of Matthew Grosvenor Woods; *m* 1st, 1954, Gillian Sara Rudd (*d* 1985); four *s* one *d*; 2nd, 1992, Mrs Patricia Temple Muir. *Educ:* Bradfield Coll.; Trinity Coll., Cambridge. HM Forces, KRRC and SOE, 1942–47; Foreign Office, 1948; served Cairo, Tehran, Milan, Warsaw, Rome; FO, later FCO, 1967. *Recreations:* birds, churches, music, books. *Address:* Bildeston Hall, Bildeston, Ipswich IP7 7EP. *T:* Bildeston (01449) 741525. *Club:* Special Forces.

WOODS, Sir Colin (Philip Joseph), KCVO 1977; CBE 1973; QPM 1980; Director, Caravan Club and Touring Club of Great Britain, since 1986; *b* London, 20 April 1920; *s* of late Michael Woods, Sub-divisional Inspector, Metropolitan Police; *m* 1941, Gladys Ella May (*née* Howell); one *d*. *Educ:* LCC Primary and Secondary Schs; Finchley Grammar Sch. Served War, in 60th Rifles and RUR, 1939–46. Metropolitan Police: Constable, through ranks, to Dep. Comdr; Commander, Traffic Dept, 1966–67; Head of Management Services, 1968; Comdt, National Police Coll., 1969–70; Asst Comr (Traffic Dept), 1970; Asst Comr (Crime), 1972; Dep. Comr, 1975–77; HM Chief Inspector of Constabulary, 1977–79; Comr, Australian Federal Police, 1979–82. Chm. Council, BSIA, 1987–92. *Recreations:* walking, gardening, caravanning. *Address:* Doversmead, Littleworth Road, The Sands, Farnham, Surrey GU10 1JW. *T:* Runfold (0125278) 2514.

WOODS, Elisabeth Ann; Director, VAT Control, and a Commissioner, HM Customs and Excise, since 1991; *b* 27 Oct. 1940; *d* of Norman Singleton, *qv*; *m* 1976, James Maurice Woods. *Educ:* South Hampstead High Sch.; Girton Coll., Cambridge (BA Hons Cl. 1 Modern Languages, 1963). Asst Principal, Min. of Pensions and Nat. Insurance, 1963–69 (Asst Private Sec. to the Minister, and Private Sec. to Permanent Sec.); Principal, DHSS, 1969–76 (Sec. to Cttees on Nursing and on Allocation of Resources to Health Authorities); Asst Sec., DHSS, 1976–88 (responsible for mental handicap policy, later for liaison with RHAs, finally for aspects of supplementary benefit); seconded to HM Treasury, 1980–82; Grade 3, DHSS Central Resource Management, 1988; Hd of Finance, DSS, 1988–91. *Recreations:* cycling, reading, cooking. *Address:* Wilberforce House, 25 The Strand, Liverpool L2 7QA. *T:* 0151–707 1234.

WOODS, Maj.-Gen. Henry Gabriel, CB 1979; MBE 1965; MC 1945; General Officer Commanding North East District, 1976–80, retired; Vice Lord-Lieutenant, North Yorkshire, since 1985; Secretary, then Director, St William's Foundation, since 1984; *b* 7 May 1924; *s* of late G. S. Woods and F. C. F. Woods (*née* McNevin); *m* 1953, Imogen Elizabeth Birchenough Dodd; two *d*. *Educ:* Highgate Sch.; Trinity Coll., Oxford (MA 1st Cl. Hons Mod. History). FIMgt. psc, jssc, rcds. Commnd 5th Royal Inniskilling Dragoon Guards, 1944; served NW Europe, 1944–45; Korea, 1951–52; Adjt, 1952–53; Sqdn Leader, 1954–55 and 1960–62; Army Staff Coll., 1956; Jt Services Staff Coll., 1960; Mil. Asst to Vice CDS, MoD, 1962–64; comd 5th Royal Inniskilling Dragoon Gds, 1965–67; Asst Mil. Sec. to C-in-C BAOR, 1968–69; Comdt, RAC Centre, 1969–71; RCDS, 1972; Mil. Attaché, Brit. Embassy, Washington, 1973–75. Head, Centre for Industrial and Educnl Liaison (W and N Yorks), 1980–87. Chairman: SATRO Panel, 1982–83; W and N Yorks Regl Microelectronics Educn Programme, 1982–86; Yorks and Humberside Industry/Educn Council, 1982–87; Bradford and W Yorks Br., BIM, 1982–84; N Yorks Scouts, 1982–; Yorks Region, Royal Soc. of Arts, 1982–92; Vice Chm., W Yorks Br. Exec. Cttee, Inst. of Dirs, 1985–91; Mem., Yorks Br. Exec. Cttee, BAAS, 1982–87. Mem. Council, Univ. of Leeds, 1980–91. Chm., 5th Royal Inniskilling Dragoon Guards Regtl Assoc., 1979–92. Pres. York and Humberside Br., Royal Soc. of St George, 1986–88. FRSA. Hon. Mem., Yorks Reg., RIBA, 1994. Mayor, Co. of Merchants of Staple of England, 1991–92; Mem., Merchant Adventurers of the City of York. DL N Yorks, 1984. Hon. DLitt Bradford, 1988. Officier, Ordre de Léopold, Belgium, 1965. *Publication:* Change and Challenge: the story of 5th Royal Inniskilling Dragon Guards, 1978. *Recreations:* hunting, fencing, sailing, military history. *Address:* Grafton House, Tockwith, York YO5 8PY. *T:* Tockwith (01423) 358735. *Clubs:* Cavalry and Guards; Ends of the Earth (UK section); Trinity Society, Oxford Society.

WOODS, Prof. Hubert Frank, FRCP, FRCPE; Sir George Franklin Professor of Medicine, since 1990, and Dean of Faculty of Medicine, since 1989, University of Sheffield; *b* 18 Nov. 1937; *s* of Hubert George Woods and Julia Augusta Woods; *m* 1966, Hilary Sheila Cox; one *s* two *d*. *Educ:* St Bees Sch., Cumbria; Leeds Univ. (BSc 1962); Pembroke Coll., Oxford (BM BCh 1965; DPhil 1970). FRCP 1978; FFPM 1989; FRCPE 1991. House appts, Radcliffe Infirmary and Hammersmith Hosp., 1965–67; Lectr in Medicine, Oxford Univ., 1967–72; Mem., MRC Ext. Clinical Scientific Staff and Hon. Sen. Registrar, MRC Clinical Pharmacology Unit, Radcliffe Infirmary, 1972–76; Prof. of Clinical Pharmacology and Therapeutics, Univ. of Sheffield, 1976–90; Consultant Physician, 1976–. Non-Exec. Mem., Sheffield HA, 1990–. Chm., Adv. Cttee on Toxicity of Food, Consumer Products and the Environment, DoH, 1992–; Member: Adv. Cttee on novel foods and processes, MAFF, 1992–; Food Adv. Cttee, MAFF, 1992–. Mem., GMC, 1994– (Mem., Health Cttee., 1994–). Hon. FFOM 1995. *Publications:* (with R. D. Cohen) Lactic Acidosis, 1976; papers in med. and sci. jls. *Recreations:* gardening, fly fishing, works of Raymond Chandler. *Address:* 68 Ivy Park Road, Sheffield SD10 3LD. *T:* Sheffield (0114) 272 9358. *Club:* Athenæum.

WOODS, Ivan; *see* Woods, W. I.

WOODS, Prof. John David, CBE 1991; PhD; Dean of Graduate School of the Environment, Professor of Oceanography, and Head of Department of Earth Resources Engineering, Imperial College, University of London, since 1994; Adjunct Fellow, Linacre College, Oxford, since 1991; *b* 26 Oct. 1939; *s* of late Ronald Ernest Goff Woods and of Ethel Marjorie Woods; *m* 1971, Irina, *y d* of Bernd von Arnim and Elizabeth Gräfin Platen-Hallermund; one *s* one *d*. *Educ:* Imperial College, Univ. of London. BSc Physics 1961, PhD 1965. Research Asst, Imperial Coll., 1964–66; Sen., later Principal, Research Fellow, Meteorol Office, 1966–72; Prof. of Physical Oceanography, Southampton Univ., 1972–77; Ordinarius für Ozeanographie, Christian Albrechts Universität und Direktor Regionale Ozeanographie, Kiel Institut für Meereskunde, Beamter auf Lebenzeit Schleswig-Holstein, 1977–86; Dir, Marine and Atmospheric Sci., NERC, 1986–94. Vis. Prof. Atmospheric Scis, Miami Univ., 1969; Hon. Prof. of Oceanography, Southampton Univ., 1994–. Member: NERC, 1979–82; Meteorol Res. Cttee, Meteorol Office, 1976–77, 1987–. Council Member: Underwater Assoc., 1967–72 (Hon. life mem., 1987); RMetS, 1972–75; RGS, 1975–77, 1987–92 (Vice-Pres., 1989–91); Member, international scientific committees for: Global Atmospheric Research Prog., 1976–79; Climate Change and the Ocean, 1979–84; World Climate Research Prog., 1980–86; World Ocean Circulation Experiment, 1983–89 (Chm., 1984–86); Internat. Geosphere Biosphere Prog., 1987–91; Global Ocean Observing System, 1994–. Mem., Academia Europaea, 1988. Lectures: Iselin, Harvard, 1989; Linacre, Oxford, 1991; Adye, Fellowship of Engrg, 1991; European Geophys. Soc., Edinburgh, 1992; Bruun, Unesco, 1993. Hon. DSc: Liège, 1980; Plymouth, 1991. L. G. Groves Prize, MoD, 1968; Medal of Helsinki Univ., 1982. *Publications:* (with J. Lythgoe) Underwater Science, 1971; (with E. Drew and J. Lythgoe) Underwater Research, 1976; papers on atmospheric physics and oceanography in learned jls. *Recreations:* underwater swimming, history. *Address:* Graduate School of the Environment, Imperial College, SW7 2AZ. *T:* 0171–594 7400. *Club:* Athenæum.

WOODS, Rev. Canon John Mawhinney; *b* 16 Dec. 1919; *s* of Robert and Sarah Hannah Woods. *Educ:* Edinburgh Theological College. Deacon 1958, for St Peter's, Kirkcaldy, Fife; priest, 1959; Rector of Walpole St Peter, Norfolk, 1960–75; Provost, St Andrew's Cathedral, Inverness, 1975–80; Rector of The Suttons with Tydd, 1980–85; Canon of Inverness, 1980–. *Address:* 4 Trenowath Place, King Street, King's Lynn, Norfolk PE30 1EN.

WOODS, Prof. Leslie Colin, BE, MA, DPhil, DSc; Professor of Mathematics (Theory of Plasma), University of Oxford, 1970–90, now Emeritus Professor; Fellow of Balliol College, Oxford, 1970–90, Emeritus Fellow, since 1991; *b* Reporoa, NZ, 6 Dec. 1922; *s* of A. B. Woodhead, Sandringham, NZ; *m* 1st, 1943; five *d*; 2nd, 1977; 3rd, 1990, Suzanne Griffiths. *Educ:* Auckland Univ. Coll.; Merton Coll., Oxford. Fighter pilot, RNZAF, Pacific Area, 1942–45. Rhodes Schol., Merton Coll., Oxford, 1948–51; Scientist (NZ Scientific Defense Corps) with Aerodynamics Div., NPL Mddx, 1951–54; Senior Lectr in Applied Maths, Sydney Univ., 1954–56; Nuffield Research Prof. of Engineering, Univ. of New South Wales, 1956–60; Fellow and Tutor in Engrg Science, Balliol Coll., Oxford, 1960–70; Reader in Applied Maths, Oxford, 1964–70. Chm., Mathematical Inst., Oxford, 1984–89. Hon. DSc Auckland, 1983. *Publications:* The Theory of Subsonic Plane Flow, 1961; Introduction to Neutron Distribution Theory, 1964; The Thermodynamics of Fluid Systems, 1975; Principles of Magnetoplasma Dynamics, 1987; Kinetic Theory of Gases and Magnetoplasmas, 1993; many research papers in aerodynamics and plasma physics in Proc. Royal Soc., Physics of Fluids, etc. *Recreations:* music, gardening. *Address:* Balliol College, Oxford OX1 3BJ.

WOODS, Maurice Eric; Regional Chairman, Industrial Tribunals (Bristol), since 1990; *b* 28 June 1933; *s* of late Leslie Eric Woods and of Winifred Rose Woods (*née* Boniface); *m* 1956, Freda Pauline Schlosser; two *s* two *d*. *Educ:* Moulsham Secondary Modern Sch., Chelmsford. LLB London. National Service (Army), 1951–53. Clerk with Essex CC, 1948–51; Police Constable, Essex Police Force, 1954–59; Claims Assistant, Cornhill Insce, 1959–61; Solicitors' Clerk and Articled Clerk, Barlow Lyde and Gilbert, 1961–65; admitted Solicitor, 1965; private practice, 1965–84; Dep. County Court Registrar, 1977–84; Chairman: Suppl. Benefit Appeal Tribunals and Social Security Appeal Tribunals, 1981–84; Industrial Tribunals, Bristol, 1984–90. *Recreations:* music, travel. *Address:* Regional Office of Industrial Tribunals, 1st Floor, The Crescent Centre, Temple Back, Bristol BS1 6EZ. *T:* Bristol (0117) 929 8261.

WOODS, Rt. Rev. Robert Wilmer, KCMG 1989; KCVO 1971; MA; Assistant Bishop, Diocese of Gloucester, since 1982; Prelate of the Most Distinguished Order of St Michael and St George, 1971–89; *b* 15 Feb. 1914; *s* of late Edward Woods, Bishop of Lichfield, and Clemence (*née* Barclay); *m* 1942, Henrietta Marion (JP 1966), *d* of late K. H. Wilson; two *s* three *d*. *Educ:* Gresham's Sch., Holt; Trinity Coll., Cambridge. Asst Sec., Student Christian Movement, 1937–42; Chaplain to the Forces, 1942–46 (despatches, 1944); Vicar of South Wigston, Leicester, 1946–51; Archdeacon of Singapore and Vicar of St Andrew's Cathedral, 1951–58; Archdeacon of Sheffield and Rector of Tankersley, 1958–62; Dean of Windsor, 1962–70; Domestic Chaplain to the Queen, 1962–70; Register of the Most Noble Order of the Garter, 1962–70; Bishop of Worcester, 1970–81. Secretary, Anglican/Methodist Commn for Unity, 1965–74; Member: Council, Duke of Edinburgh's Award Scheme, 1968; Public Schools Commn, 1968–70; Governor, Haileybury Coll.; Pres, Queen's Coll., Birmingham, and Chm. Council, 1970–85; Chairman: Windsor Festival Co., 1969–71; Churches Television Centre, 1969–79; Dir, Christian Aid, 1969. Chm., Birmingham and Hereford and Worcester Bd, MSC, 1976–83. Visitor, Malvern Coll., 1970–81. *Publication:* Robin Woods: an autobiography, 1986. *Recreations:* shooting, painting. *Address:* Torse End, Tirley, Gloucester GL19 4EU. *T:* Gloucester (01452) 780327.

WOODS, Ronald Earl; Executive Director, World Affairs Council, since 1993; *b* 10 Oct. 1938; *s* of Earl L. Woods and Marie C. Woods; *m* 1959, Judith M. Wishner; two *d*. *Educ:* Georgetown Univ.; School of Foreign Service (BSFS 1961). Joined US Foreign Service, 1961; served: Cairo, 1962; Washington, 1963; Rome, 1966; Paris, 1969; Strasbourg, 1971; Washington, 1974; Madrid, 1979; Oslo, 1982; Brussels, 1985; Minister, London, 1989–93. *Recreations:* tennis, ski-ing, walking. *Address:* 4527 52 Avenue South, Seattle, WA 98118, USA.

WOODS, Timothy Phillips, MA, DPhil; Head of History, Trent College, since 1985; *b* 24 Dec. 1943; *s* of late Arthur Phillips Woods and of Katherine Isabella Woods; *m* 1969, Erica Lobb. *Educ:* Cordwalles Prep. Sch., Natal; Michaelhouse Sch., Natal; Rhodes Univ. (BA Hons, MA; UED); Oxford Univ. (DPhil). Cape Province Rhodes Scholar, 1968; Felsted School: Asst Master, 1971; Head of History, 1975; Headmaster, Gresham's Sch. 1982–85. *Recreations:* cricket, hockey, squash, gardening, music, history and architecture of cathedrals. *Address:* 63 Curzon Street, Long Eaton, Nottingham NG10 4FG. *T:* Nottingham (0115) 972 0927. *Club:* Vincent's (Oxford).

WOODS, Victoria Patricia Ann, (Vicki), (Mrs F. A. Woods Walker); Contributing Editor, Vogue (USA), since 1994; *b* 25 Sept. 1947; *d* of Frederick Woods and Barbara Joan (*née* Hinchliffe); *m* 1980, Frank A. Walker; one *s* one *d*. *Educ:* Lancaster Girls' Grammar Sch.; Univ. of Lancaster (BA). Sub-editor, Harpers & Queen, 1970–73; Chief sub-editor, Radio Times, 1973–75; Exec. Editor, Harpers & Queen, 1975–79; Associate Editor, then Dep. Editor, Tatler, 1982–87; Femail Editor, Daily Mail, 1987–89; Contributing Editor, Vogue (USA) and Associate Editor, Spectator, 1989–91; Editor, Harpers & Queen, 1991–94. *Address:* Rogers, Coleridge, White, 20 Powys Mews, W11. *Club:* Academy.

WOODS, (William) Ivan; 3rd *s* of late William and Anna Woods, Annaghmore, Co. Armagh; *m* (1st wife *d* 1965); one *s* one *d*; 2nd, 1966, Florence Margaret, *o d* of late William and Florence Sloan, Ach-na-mara, Donaghadee, Co. Down; one *s* two *d*. *Educ:* Ranelagh Sch., Athlone; Mountjoy Sch., Dublin. Accountant, Min. of Finance for N Ire., 1962; N Ire. Govt Liaison Officer in London, 1963; Dir of Office of Parliamentary Commissioner for Administration, NI, 1969; Dir of Office of Commissioner for Complaints, NI, 1969; Dep. Sec., Dept of Finance for NI, 1973–76. Sec., Milibern Trust, 1976–79. *Recreations:* golf, sailing. *Address:* 112 Warren Road, Donaghadee, Co. Down BT21 0PQ. *T:* Donaghadee (01247) 883568. *Clubs:* Portaferry Sailing, Mitchels GA (Co. Down).

WOODS WALKER, Victoria Patricia Ann, (Mrs F. A. Woods Walker); *see* Woods, V. P. A.

WOODSTOCK, Viscount; Timothy Charles Robert Noel Bentinck; Count of the Holy Roman Empire; actor; *b* 1 June 1953; *s* and *heir* of Earl of Portland, *qv*; *m* 1979, Judith Ann, *d* of John Robert Emerson; two *s*. *Educ:* Harrow; Univ. of East Anglia (BA Hons). Trained Bristol Old Vic Theatre Sch. Winner BBC Drama Schs Radio Competition, 1978. London theatre appearances include: Pirates of Penzance, Theatre Royal, Drury Lane, 1982; Reluctant Heroes, Theatre of Comedy, 1984; Hedda Gabler, King's Head Theatre, 1990; A Doll's House, Bridge Lane Theatre, London, 1992; Arcadia, Haymarket, 1994; *radio:* David Archer in The Archers; over 75 plays; *films:* North Sea Hijack, 1979; Pirates of Penzance, 1981; Winter Flight, 1985; Year of the Comet, 1992; *television* includes: By the Sword Divided, 1983; Square Deal, 1989; Made in Heaven, 1990; Sharpe, 1993; Grange Hill, 1994; Strike Command, 1995; composer of theme music for Easy Money, BBC TV, 1984. Inventor of The Hippo (child-carrying device). HGV licence. *Recreations:* songwriting, ski-ing, swimming, house renovation, computer programming. *Heir: s* Hon. William Jack Henry Bentinck, *b* 19 May 1984.

WOODWARD, Hon. Sir (Albert) Edward, Kt 1982; OBE 1969; Chancellor, University of Melbourne, since 1990; *b* 6 Aug. 1928; *s* of Lt-Gen. Sir Eric Winslow Woodward, KCMG, KCVO, CB, CBE, DSO, and Amy Freame Woodward (*née* Weller); *m* 1950, Lois Thorpe; one *s* six *d*. *Educ:* Melbourne C of E Grammar Sch.; Melbourne Univ. (LLM). Practising barrister, 1953–72; QC 1965; Judge: Australian Industrial Court and Supreme Court of Australian Capital Territory, 1972–90; Federal Ct of Australia, 1977–90. Chairman, Armed Services Pay Inquiry, 1972; Royal Commissioner: Aboriginal Land Rights, 1973–75; into Australian Meat Industry, 1981–82; into Tricontinental Gp Cos, 1991–92; President: Trade Practices Tribunal, 1974–76; Defence Force Discipline Appeal Tribunal, 1988–90; Director-General of Security, 1976–81. Chairman: Victorian Dried Fruits Bd, 1963–72; Nat. Stevedoring Industry Conf. and Stevedoring Industry Council, 1965–72; Australian Defence Force Academy Council, 1985–; Schizophrenia Australia Foundn, 1985–. Mem. Council, Melbourne Univ., 1973–76, 1986–; Chm. Council, Camberwell Grammar Sch., 1983–87. Hon. LLD New South Wales, 1986. *Address:* 63 Tivoli Road, South Yarra, Victoria 3141, Australia. *T:* (3) 98268404.

WOODWARD, Barry; His Honour Judge Woodward; a Circuit Judge, since 1990; *s* of Wilfred and Mary Hannah Woodward; *m* 1963, Patricia Holland; two *d*. *Educ:* Sheffield Univ. (LLM). Called to the Bar, Gray's Inn, 1970. Teaching positions, 1961–70; practice on Northern Circuit, 1970–84; Chm., Industrial Tribunals, Manchester Region, 1984; a Recorder, 1988. *Recreations:* ski-ing, windsurfing, any other sporting activity that time and fitness permits, messing with classic motor cars. *Address:* Courts of Justice, Crown Square, Manchester M60 9DJ. *T:* 0161–832 8393.

WOODWARD, Prof. C. Vann; Sterling Professor of History, Yale University, 1961–77, now Emeritus Professor; *b* 13 Nov. 1908; *s* of Hugh Allison Woodward and Bess (*née* Vann); *m* 1937, Glenn Boyd MacLeod; one *s*. *Educ:* Emory Univ. (PhB); Universities of Columbia (MA), North Carolina (PhD). Asst Professor of History, University of Florida, 1937–39; Visiting Asst Professor of History, University of Virginia, 1939–40; Assoc. Professor of History, Scripps Coll., 1940–43; Assoc. Professor of History, Johns Hopkins University, 1946; Professor of American History, Johns Hopkins Univ., 1947–61. Served with US Naval Reserve, 1943–46. Commonwealth Lecturer, UCL, 1954; Harold Vyvyan Harmsworth Professor of American History, University of Oxford, 1954–55. Corresp. Fellow: British Academy, 1972, RHistS, 1978. Member: American Academy of Arts and Sciences (Vice-Pres., 1988–89); American Philosophical Society; Amer. Acad. of Arts and Letters; American Historical Assoc. (President, 1969); Orgn of American Historians (President, 1968–69). Hon. MA Oxon, 1954; hon. doctoral degrees from univs of Arkansas, Brandeis, Cambridge, Colgate, Columbia, Dartmouth, Emory, Henderson, Johns Hopkins, Michigan, N Carolina, Northwestern, Pennsylvania, Princeton, Rutgers, Tulane, Washington and Lee, William and Mary, and Rhodes Coll. Literary Award, Amer. Acad. and Inst. of Arts and Letters, 1954; Gold Medal for History, 1990. *Publications:* Tom Watson: Agrarian Rebel, 1938; The Battle for Leyte Gulf, 1947; Origins of the New South (1877–1913), 1951 (Bancroft Prize, 1952); Reunion and Reaction, 1951; The Strange Career of Jim Crow, 1955; The Burden of Southern History, 1960; American Counterpoint, 1971; Thinking Back, 1986; The Future of the Past, 1989; The Old World's New World, 1991; (ed) The Comparative Approach to American History, 1968; (ed) Mary Chesnut's Civil War, 1981 (Pulitzer Prize, 1982). *Address:* 83 Rogers Road, Hamden, CT 06517, USA.

WOODWARD, Hon. Sir Edward; *see* Woodward, Hon. Sir A. E.

WOODWARD, Edward, OBE 1978; actor and singer, since 1946; *b* 1 June 1930; *s* of Edward Oliver Woodward and Violet Edith Woodward; *m* 1st, 1952, Venetia Mary Collett; two *s* one *d*; 2nd, 1987, Michele Dotrice; one *d*. *Educ:* Kingston Coll.; RADA. *Stage:* Castle Theatre, Farnham, 1946; appeared for some years in rep. cos throughout England and Scotland; first appearance on London stage, Where There's a Will, Garrick, 1955; Mercutio in Romeo and Juliet, and Laertes in Hamlet, Stratford, 1958; Rattle of a Simple Man, Garrick, 1962; Two Cities (musical), 1968; Cyrano in Cyrano de Bergerac, and Flamineo in The White Devil, Nat. Theatre Co., 1971; The Wolf, Apollo, 1973; Male of the Species, Piccadilly, 1975; On Approval, Theatre Royal Haymarket, 1976; The Dark Horse, Comedy, 1978; starred in and directed Beggar's Opera, 1980; Private Lives, Australia, 1980; The Assassin, Greenwich, 1982; Richard III, Ludlow Fest., 1982; The Dead Secret, Plymouth and Richmond, 1992; has appeared in 3 prodns in NY; *films:* Becket, 1966; File on the Golden Goose, 1968; Hunted, 1973; Sitting Target, Young Winston, The Wicker Man, 1974; Stand Up Virgin Soldiers, 1977; Breaker Morant, 1980; The Appointment, 1981; Who Dares Wins, Forever Love, Merlin and the Sword, 1982; Champions, 1983; Christmas Carol, 1984; King David, Uncle Tom's Cabin, 1986; Mister Johnson, 1990; Deadly Advice, 1993; A Christmas Reunion, 1994; Gulliver's Travels, 1995; *television:* over 2000 prodns, inc. Callan (series and film, and in Wet Job, 1981); The Trial of Lady Chatterley, Blunt Instrument, 1980; Churchill: The Wilderness Years, 1981; The Equalizer (series), 1985–89; Codename Kyril, 1987; Hunted, 1988; The Man in the Brown Suit, 1988; Hands of a Murderer, or The Napoleon of Crime, 1990; Over My Dead Body (series), 1990; In Suspicious Circumstances (series), 1991–95; In My Defence, 1991; America at Risk (series), 1991–92; Harrison, 1994; Common as Muck (series), 1994; Cry of the City, 1995; 12 long-playing records (singing), 3 records (poetry) and 14 talking book recordings. Over 20 national and internat. acting awards incl. BAFTA best actor award and an Emmy. *Recreations:* boating, geology. *Address:* c/o Ginette Chalmers, Peters, Fraser and Dunlop, 503/4 The Chambers, Chelsea Harbour, SW10 0XF. *T:* 0171–344 1000, *Fax:* 0171–352 8135. *Clubs:* Garrick, Green Room.

WOODWARD, Geoffrey Frederick, RIBA; jssc; Assistant Director General of Design Services, Property Services Agency, Department of the Environment, 1983–84; *b* 29 June 1924; *s* of Joseph Frederick and Edith Mary Woodward; *m* 1953, Elizabeth Marjory McCubbin; four *s*. *Educ:* Wirral Grammar School for Boys; Trinity College, Cambridge Univ.; School of Architecture, Liverpool Univ. (BArch). Architects' Dept: Hertfordshire CC, 1952–56; British Transport Commn, 1956–60; Directorate of Army Works, 1960–63; Directorate of Research & Development, Min. of Public Building and Works, 1963–67; Directorate of Works (Married Quarters), MPBW, 1967–70; Directorate of Works (Navy Home), PSA, 1970–71; Director of Works (Navy Home), PSA, 1971–75; Director, Directorate General of Design Services, Design Office, 1975–78; Under Sec., PSA, DoE, 1978; Dir of Architectural Services, 1978–81; Dir, Diplomatic and Post Office Services, 1981–83. jssc 1963. *Recreations:* motoring, walking. *Address:* Little Orchard, Cuddington Way, Cheam, Sutton, Surrey SM2 7JA. *T:* 0181–643 1964.

WOODWARD, Adm. Sir John (Forster), GBE 1989; KCB 1982; Director, Offshore Command Training Organisation, since 1992; Independent Inspector, Lord Chancellor's Panel, since 1994; management consultant; *b* Penzance, Cornwall, 1 May 1932; *s* of late T. Woodward and M. B. M. Woodward; *m* 1960, Charlotte Mary McMurtrie; one *s* one *d*. *Educ:* Royal Naval College, Dartmouth. Under training, Home Fleet, until 1953; Submarine Specialist, serving in HMS Sanguine, Porpoise, Valiant, and commanding HMS Tireless, Grampus and Warspite, from 1953; Min. of Defence and senior training posts, from 1971, plus comd HMS Sheffield, 1976–77; Director of Naval Plans, 1978–81; Flag Officer, First Flotilla, 1981–83, Sen. Task Gp Comdr, S Atlantic, during Falklands Campaign, Apr.–July 1982; Flag Officer, Submarines, and Comdr, Submarines Eastern Atlantic, 1983–84; Dep. Chief of Defence Staff (Commitments), 1985–87; C-in-C, Naval Home Command, 1987–89; Flag ADC to the Queen, 1987–89. Hon. Liveryman, Glass Sellers' Co., 1982. *Publication:* One Hundred Days: the memoirs of the Falklands Battle Group Commander, 1992. *Recreations:* sailing, philately, skiing. *Address:* c/o The Naval Secretary, Victory Building, HM Naval Base, Portsmouth PO1 3LS. *Club:* Royal Naval Sailing Association.

WOODWARD, Rev. Max Wakerley; Methodist Minister, retired 1973; *b* 29 Jan. 1908; *s* of Alfred Woodward, Methodist Minister, and Mabel (*née* Wakerley); *m* 1934, Kathleen May Beaty; three *s* one *d*. *Educ:* Orme Sch., Newcastle; Kingswood Sch., Bath; Handsworth Coll., Birmingham. Missionary to Ceylon, 1929–42; Chaplain, Royal Navy, 1942–46; Minister: Leamington Spa, 1946–50; Finsbury Park, 1950–54; Harrow, 1954–58; Wesley's Chapel, London, 1958–64; Secretary, World Methodist Council, 1964–69; Minister, Bromley, Kent, 1969–73. Exchange Preacher, Univ. Methodist Church, Baton Rouge, La, 1957. Dir, Methodist Newspaper Co. Ltd, 1962–84. *Publication:* One At London, 1966. *Recreations:* gardening, stamp collecting. *Address:* 6a Field End Road, Pinner, Mddx HA5 2QL. *T:* 0181–429 0608.

WOODWARD, Shaun Anthony; Visiting Professorial Fellow, Queen Mary and Westfield College, University of London, since 1992; *b* 26 Oct. 1958; *s* of Dennis George Woodward and Joan Lillian (*née* Nunn); *m* 1987, Camilla Davan, *e d* of Rt Hon. Sir Timothy Sainsbury, *qv*; one *s* two *d*. *Educ:* Bristol Grammar Sch.; Jesus Coll., Cambridge (MA). Parly Lobbyist, Nat. Consumer Council, 1981–82; BBC TV: Researcher, That's Life!, 1982–85; Producer: Newsnight, 1985–87; Panorama, 1988–89; Editor, That's Life!, 1989–91; Researcher, Lost Babies, 1983; Producer: Drugwatch, 1985; The Gift of Life!, 1987; Dir of Communications, Cons. Party, 1991–92. Fellow, Inst. of Politics at Kennedy Sch., Harvard Univ., 1994–95. Dir and Chm., Redevelt Campaign, ENO; Dir, Jerusalem Productions. Chm., Ben Hardwick Meml Fund, 1984–95; Trustee: Understanding Industry; Childline (Dep. Chm.). *Publications:* (with Ron Lacey) Tranquillisers, 1983; (with Esther Rantzen) Ben: the story of Ben Hardwick, 1985; (with Sarah Caplin) Drugwatch, 1986. *Recreations:* opera, tennis, reading, gardening, family. *Address:* Sarsden House, Sarsden, Chipping Norton, Oxon OX7 6PW.

WOODWARD, Thomas Jones, (Tom Jones); entertainer; *b* 7 June 1940; *s* of Thomas Woodward and Freda (*née* Jones); *m* 1956, Melinda Trenchard; one *s*. Singing début at age of 3; sang in clubs and dance halls; first hit record, It's Not Unusual, 1964; toured US, 1965; many internat. hit records; radio and TV appearances, incl. series, This is Tom Jones, 1969–71; has toured worldwide. Score for musical play, Matador, 1987. MTV Video Award, 1988. *Recreations:* music, history. *Address:* Tom Jones Enterprises, 10100 Santa Monica Boulevard, Suite 205, Los Angeles, CA 90067, USA. *T:* (310) 5520044. *Club:* Friars (Los Angeles and New York).

WOODWARD, William Charles; QC 1985; a Recorder, since 1989; *b* 27 May 1940; *s* of Wilfred Charles Woodward and Annie Stewart Woodward (*née* Young); *m* 1965, Carolyn Edna Johns; two *s* one *d*. *Educ:* South County Junior Sch.; Nottingham High Sch.; St John's Coll., Oxford (BA Jurisp). Marshall to Sir Donald Finnemore, Michaelmas 1962. Called to the Bar, Inner Temple, 1964; pupillage with Brian J. Appleby, QC; Midland and Oxford Circuit, 1964–; Head of Chambers, 24 The Ropewalk, Nottingham, 1986–94. Mem., E Midlands Area Cttee, Law Soc.; Founder Mem., Notts Medico-Legal Soc. *Recreations:* family, friends, holidays. *Address:* (chambers): 24 The Ropewalk, Nottingham NG1 5EF. *T:* Nottingham (0115) 947 2581, *Fax:* Nottingham (0115) 947 6532; 22 Old Buildings, Lincoln's Inn, WC2A 3UR. *Clubs:* Pre War Austin Seven; Nottingham and Notts United Services.

WOOF, Robert Edward; Member and former official, National Union of Mineworkers; *b* 24 Oct. 1911; *m* Mary Bell (*d* 1971); one *d*. *Educ:* Elementary School. Began work in the mines at an early age, subsequently coal face worker. Member of the Labour Party, 1937–; MP (Lab) Blaydon, Co. Durham, Feb. 1956–1979. Member Durham County Council, 1947–56. *Address:* 10 Ramsay Road, Chopwell, Newcastle upon Tyne NE17 7AG.

WOOF, Robert Samuel, PhD; Director, Wordsworth Trust, Dove Cottage, Grasmere, since 1989; *b* 20 April 1931; *s* of late William Woof and Annie (*née* Mason); *m* 1958, Pamela Shirley Moore; two *s* two *d*. *Educ:* Lancaster Royal Grammar School; Pembroke College, Oxford (MA); University of Toronto (PhD). Goldsmith Travelling Fellow, 1953–55; Lectr, Univ. of Toronto, 1958–61; University of Newcastle: Lord Adams of Ennerdale Fellow, 1961–62; Lectr, 1962; Reader in Eng. Lit., 1971–92; Leverhulme Fellow, 1983–84. Vice-Chm., Northern Arts Assoc., 1974–81; Hon. Keeper of Collections, Trustees of Dove Cottage, Grasmere, 1974–89, Hon. Sec. and Treasurer, 1978–95. Mem., 1982–88, Rep., 1988–, Arts Council: Vice-Chm., 1982–88, acting Chm, 1985–86, Drama Panel; Chm., Literature Panel, 1984–88 (Vice-Chm., 1983–84). *Publications:* (ed) T. W. Thompson, Wordsworth's Hawkshead, 1970; The Wordsworth Circle, 1979; (with Peter Bicknell) The Discovery of the Lake District 1750–1810, 1982; (with Peter Bicknell) The Lake District Discovered 1810–50, 1983; Thomas De Quincey: an English opium-eater 1785–1859, 1985; (with David Thomason) Derwentwater, the Vale of Elysium, 1986; The Artist as Evacuee, 1987; (with Jonathan Wordsworth and Michael C. Jaye) William Wordsworth and the Age of English Romanticism, 1987; Matthew Arnold, a Centennial Exhibition, 1988; Byron: a dangerous romantic?, 1989; Tennyson: a bicentenary tribute, 1992; Shelley: an ineffectual angel?, 1992. *Recreations:* the arts, the Lake District. *Address:* 4 Burdon Terrace, Jesmond, Newcastle upon Tyne NE2 3AE. *T:* 0191–281 2680; The Wordsworth Trust, Dove Cottage, Grasmere, Cumbria LA22 9SH. *T:* Grasmere (015394) 35580/35544.

WOOL, Dr Rosemary Jane, CB 1995; FRCPsych; Director of Health Care, Prison Service (formerly Prison Medical Service), since 1989. *Educ:* University of London

(Charing Cross Hospital Medical School). MB BS, DPM, DRCOG. *Address:* Home Office Prison Service, Cleland House, Page Street, SW1P 4LN.

WOOLARD, Edgar Smith; Chairman and Chief Executive Officer, Du Pont, since 1989; *b* 15 April 1934; *s* of Edgar S. Woolard and Mamie (Boone) Woolard; *m* 1956, Peggy Harrell; two *d*. *Educ:* North Carolina State Univ. (BSc Indust. Eng. 1956). Joined Du Pont 1957; industrial engineer, Kinston, NC, 1957–59; group supervisor, industrial engrg, 1959–62; supervisor, manufg sect., 1962–64; planning supervisor, 1964–65; staff asst to Prodn Manager, Wilmington, 1965–66; product supt, Old Hickory, Tenn, 1966–69; engrg supt, 1969–70; Asst Plant Manager, Camden, SC, 1970–71; Plant Manager, 1971–73; Dir of products marketing div., Wilmington, 1973–75; Man. Dir, textile marketing div., 1975–76; Manager, corp. plans dept, 1976–77; Gen. Dir, products and planning div., 1977–78; Gen. Manager, textile fibers, 1978–81; Vice-Pres., textile fibers, 1981–83; Exec. Vice President, 1983–85; Vice Chm., 1985–87; Pres. and Chief Operating Officer, 1987–89. Director: Citicorp; N Carolina Textile Foundn; Member: Bd of Trustees, Winterthur Mus.; Bd of Trustees, N Carolina State Univ.; Med. Center of Delaware; Protestant Episcopal Theol Seminary, Virginia; Exec. Cttee, Delaware Roundtable; Bretton Woods Cttee; World Affairs Council; Business Roundtable. *Address:* Du Pont, 1007 Market Street, Wilmington, DE 19898, USA.

WOOLDRIDGE, Ian Edmund, OBE 1991; Sports Columnist, Daily Mail, since 1972; BBC Television documentary reporter and writer; *b* 14 Jan. 1932; *s* of late Edmund and Bertha Wooldridge; *m* 1st, Veronica Ann Churcher; three *s*; 2nd, Sarah Margaret Chappell Lourenço. *Educ:* Brockenhurst Grammar School. New Milton Advertiser, 1948; Bournemouth Times, 1953; News Chronicle, 1956; Sunday Dispatch, 1960; Daily Mail, 1961. Columnist of Year, 1975 and 1976; Sportswriter of Year, 1972, 1974, 1981, 1989, in British Press Awards; Sports Council Awards: Sportswriter of the Year, 1987, 1988; Sports Feature Writer of the Year, 1991. *Publications:* Cricket, Lovely Cricket, 1963; (with Mary Peters) Mary P, 1974; (with Colin Cowdrey) MCC: The Autobiography of a Cricketer, 1976; The Best of Wooldridge, 1978; Travelling Reserve, 1982; Sport in the Eighties, 1989. *Recreations:* travel, golf, Beethoven and dry Martinis. *Address:* 11 Collingham Gardens, SW5 0HS. *Club:* Reform.

WOOLF, family name of **Baron Woolf.**

WOOLF, Baron *cr* 1992 (Life Peer), of Barnes in the London Borough of Richmond; **Harry Kenneth Woolf,** Kt 1979; PC 1986; a Lord of Appeal in Ordinary, since 1992; *b* 2 May 1933; *s* of late Alexander Woolf and Leah Woolf (*née* Cussins); *m* 1961, Marguerite Sassoon, *d* of late George Sassoon; three *s*. *Educ:* Fettes Coll.; University Coll., London (LLB; Fellow, 1981). Called to Bar, Inner Temple, 1954; Bencher, 1976. Commnd (Nat. Service), 15/19th Royal Hussars, 1954; seconded Army Legal Services, 1955; Captain 1955. Started practice at Bar, 1956. A Recorder of the Crown Court, 1972–79; Jun. Counsel, Inland Revenue, 1973–74; First Treasury Junior Counsel (Common Law), 1974–79; a Judge of the High Court of Justice, Queen's Bench Div., 1979–86; Presiding Judge, SE Circuit, 1981–84; a Lord Justice of Appeal, 1986–92. Held inquiry into prison disturbances, 1990, Part II with Judge Tumin, report 1991; conducted inquiry, Access to Justice, 1994–96. Member: Senate, Inns of Court and Bar, 1981–85 (Chm., Accommodation Cttee, 1982–85); Bd of Management, Inst. of Advanced Legal Studies, 1985–94 (Chm., 1986–94); Chairman: Lord Chancellor's Adv. Cttee on Legal Educn., 1986–91; Mddx Adv. Cttee on Justices of the Peace, 1986–90; President: Assoc. of Law Teachers, 1985–89; Central Council of Jewish Social Services, 1987–; SW London Magistrates Assoc., 1987–93; Assoc. of Mems of Bds of Visitors, 1994–. Pro-Chancellor, London Univ., 1994–. Chairman: Trustees, Butler Trust, 1992– (Trustee, 1991–); Special Trustees, St Mary's Hosp., Paddington, 1993–. Gov. Emeritus, Oxford Centre for Postgrad. Hebrew Studies, 1989–93. Hon. Mem., SPTL, 1988. Hon. LLD: Buckingham, 1992; Bristol, 1992; London, 1993; Anglia Poly. Univ., 1994; Manchester Metropolitan, 1995. *Publications:* Protecting the Public: the new challenge (Hamlyn Lecture), 1990; (ed with J. Woolf) Declaratory Judgement, 2nd edn, 1993; (ed jtly) De Smith, Judicial Review of Administrative Action, 5th edn, 1995. *Address:* House of Lords, SW1A 0PW. *Clubs:* Garrick, Royal Automobile.

WOOLF, Geoffrey David; General Secretary, National Association of Teachers in Further and Higher Education, 1989–94; *b* 15 April 1944. *Educ:* Polytechnic of Central London (BSc Econ). Lecturer in History, Southgate Technical College, 1974–89. *Recreation:* politics. *Address:* 18 Selborne Road, Southgate, N14 7DH. *T:* 0181–882 0785.

WOOLF, Harry, PhD; Professor-at-Large, Institute for Advanced Study, Princeton, USA, since 1976 (Director, 1976–87); *b* 12 Aug. 1923; *s* of Abraham Woolf and Anna (*née* Frankman); *m* (marr. diss.); two *s* two *d*. *Educ:* Univ. of Chicago (BS Physics and Maths 1948; MA Physics and History 1949); Cornell Univ. (PhD Hist. of Science 1955). Served US Army, 1943–46. Instructor: Boston Univ., Mass, 1953–55; Brandeis Univ., Waltham, Mass, 1954–55; Univ. of Washington, Seattle: Asst Prof., Associate Prof., and Prof., 1955–61; Johns Hopkins University: Prof., Hist. of Science Dept, 1961–76 (Chm. of Dept, 1961–72); Provost, 1972–76; Princeton University: Mem. Adv. Council, Depts of Philosophy, 1980–84, and of Comparative Lit., 1982–86. Pres., Chm. of Bd, Johns Hopkins Program for Internat. Educn in Gynecology and Obstetrics, Inc., 1973–76, Trustee 1976–; Mem. Adv. Bd, Smithsonian Research Awards, 1975–79; Member: Vis. Cttee Student Affairs, MIT, 1973–77; Corporation Vis. Cttee, Dept of Linguistics and Philosophy, MIT, 1977–83; Nat. Adv. Child Health and Human Develt Council, NIH, 1977–80; Mem. Vis. Cttee, Research Center for Language Sciences, Indiana Univ., 1977–80; Trustee: Associated Universities Inc., Brookhaven Nat. Laboratories, Nat. Radio Astronomy Observatory, 1972–82; Hampshire Coll., Amherst, Mass, 1977–81; Merrill Lynch Cluster C Funds, 1982–; Reed Coll., 1992–; Dibner Inst. for the Hist. of Science, 1992–; Trustee-at-Large, Univs Research Assoc. Inc., Washington, DC (Fermi Nat. Accelerator Lab.), 1978–91, Chm. Bd 1979–89. Member: Corp. Visiting Cttee for Dept. of Physics, MIT, 1979–85; Council on Foreign Relations Inc., 1979–; Adv. Panel, WGBH, NOVA, 1979–; Internat. Research and Exchanges Bd, NY, 1980–; Scientific Adv. Bd, Wissenschaftskolleg zu Berlin, 1981–87; Board of Directors: Alex. Brown Mutual Funds, Inc., Baltimore, 1981–; W. Alton Jones Cell Science Center, 1982–86; Westmark Corp., 1987–92; Family Health Internat., 1992–; Advanced Technology Labs, 1992–; Spacelabs Medical, 1992–. Member: Adv. Council, Dept of Comparative Literature, Princeton Univ., 1982–; Adv. Council, Nat. Science Foundn, 1984–89; Bd of Trustees, Rockefeller Foundn, 1984–94; Dir-at-large, Amer. Cancer Soc., 1982–86. Member: Académie Internat. d'Histoire des Sciences; Amer. Philosoph. Soc.; Phi Beta Kappa; Sigma Xi (also Bicentennial Lectr, 1976). Editor, ISIS Internat. Review, 1958–64; Associate Editor, Dictionary of Scientific Biog., 1970–80; Mem. Editl Bd, Interdisciplinary Science Revs, 1975–; Mem. Editl Adv. Bd, The Writings of Albert Einstein, 1977–. Fellow, Amer. Acad. of Arts and Scis; FAAAS. Hon. DSc: Whitman Coll., 1979; Amer. Univ., Washington DC, 1982; Hon. LHD: Johns Hopkins Univ., 1983; St Lawrence Univ., 1986. *Publications:* The Transits of Venus: a study in eighteenth-century science, 1959, repr. 1981; (ed) Quantification: essays in the history of measurement in the natural and social sciences, 1961; (ed) Science as a Cultural Force, 1964; (ed and contrib.) Some Strangeness in the Proportion: a centennial symposium to celebrate the achievements of Albert Einstein, 1980; (ed) The Analytic Spirit: essays in the history of science, 1981. *Address:* Institute for Advanced Study, Princeton, NJ 08540, USA. *T:* (609) 7348018. *Club:* Century Association (New York).

WOOLF, Sir John, Kt 1975; film and television producer; Founder and Chairman, Romulus Films Ltd, since 1948; Managing Director, since 1967 and Chairman, since 1982, British & American Film Holdings Plc; Director, First Leisure Corporation Plc, since 1982; *s* of Charles M. and Vera Woolf; *m* 1955, Ann Saville; one *s* (and one *s* decd). *Educ:* Institut Montana, Switzerland. War of 1939–45 (Bronze Star (USA), 1945): Asst Dir, Army Kinematography, War Office, 1944–45. Co-founder and Executive Director, Anglia TV Group PLC (responsible for Drama Dept), 1958–83. Member: Cinematograph Films Council, 1969–79; Bd of Governors, Services Sound & Vision Corp. (formerly Services Kinema Corp.), 1974–83; Trustee and Mem. Exec. Cttee, Cinema and Television Benevolent Fund. Freeman, City of London, 1982. FRSA 1978. Films produced by Romulus Group include: The African Queen, Pandora and the Flying Dutchman, Moulin Rouge, I am a Camera, Carrington VC, Beat the Devil, Story of Esther Costello, Room at the Top, Wrong Arm of the Law, The L-Shaped Room, Term of Trial, Life at the Top, Oliver!, Day of the Jackal, The Odessa File (Romulus prodns have won 13 Oscars in various categories). TV productions for Anglia include over 100 plays and the series Orson Welles' Great Mysteries, and Tales of the Unexpected. Personal awards include: British Film Academy Award for Best Film of 1958: Room at the Top; Oscar and Golden Globe for Best Film of 1969: Oliver!; nominated Producer of the Year, Producers Guild of America, 1968; special awards for contribution to British film industry from Cinematograph Exhibitors Assoc., 1969, Variety Club of GB, 1974. *Address:* 214 The Chambers, Chelsea Harbour, SW10 0XF. *T:* 0171–376 3791, *Fax:* 0171–352 7457.

WOOLF, John Moss, CB 1975; Deputy Chairman of the Board of Customs and Excise, and Director-General (Customs and Establishments), 1973–78; *b* 5 June 1918; *o s* of Alfred and Maud Woolf; *m* 1940, Phyllis Ada Mary Johnson (*d* 1990); one *d*. *Educ:* Drayton Manor Sch.; Honourable Society of Lincoln's Inn. Barrister-at-law, 1948. War Service, 1939–46 (Captain, RA). Inland Revenue, 1937. Asst Principal, Min. of Fuel and Power, 1948; HM Customs and Excise, 1950: Principal, 1951; Asst Sec., 1960; Chm., Valuation Cttee, Customs Cooperation Council, Brussels, 1964–65; National Bd for Prices and Incomes, 1965; Under-Secretary, 1967; Asst Under-Sec. of State, Dept of Employment and Productivity, 1968–70; HM Customs and Excise: Comr, 1970; Dir of Establishments and Organisation, 1971–73. Advr on Price Problems, Govt of Trinidad & Tobago, 1968. Assoc. of First Div. Civil Servants: Mem. of Exec. Cttee, 1950–58 and 1961–65; Hon. Sec., 1952–55; Chm., 1955–58 and 1964–65; Mem., Civil Service National Whitley Council (Staff Side), 1953–55. Leader of Review Team to examine responsibilities of the Directors of the Nat. Museums and Galleries, 1978–79; Review of Organisation and Procedures of Chancery Div. of High Court, 1979–81; Overseas Adviser to CEGB, 1979–82. Commandeur d'Honneur, Ordre du Bontemps de Médoc et des Graves, 1973; Hon. Borgenerális (Hungary), 1974. *Publications:* Report on Control of Prices in Trinidad and Tobago (with M. M. Eccleshall), 1968; Report of the Review Body on the Chancery Division of the High Court (with Lord Oliver of Aylmerton and R. H. H. White), 1981. *Recreations:* reading, gardening. *Address:* West Lodge, 113 Marsh Lane, Stanmore, Mddx HA7 4TH. *T:* 0181–952 1373. *Club:* Civil Service.

WOOLFORD, Harry Russell Halkerston, OBE 1970; Consultant, formerly Chief Restorer, National Gallery of Scotland; *b* 23 May 1905; *s* of H. Woolford, engineer; *m* 1932, Nancy Philip; one *d*. *Educ:* Edinburgh. Studied art at Edinburgh Coll. of Art (Painting and Drawing) and RSA Life School (Carnegie Travelling Scholarship, 1928), London, Paris and Italy; afterwards specialized in picture restoration. FMA; FIIC. Hon. Mem., Assoc. of British Picture Restorers, 1970. Hon. MA Dundee, 1976. *Address:* 7a Barntongate Avenue, Barnton, Edinburgh EH4 8BD. *T:* 0131–339 6861. *Club:* Scottish Arts.

WOOLFSON, Mark; Consultant and Director of Consortium, Pollution Control Consultants, 1972–87; a Partner, Posford Duvivier (formerly Posford Pavry & Partners), 1972–90, retired; *b* 10 Nov. 1911; *s* of Victor Woolfson and Sarah (*née* Kixman); *m* 1940, Queenie Carlis; two *d*. *Educ:* City of London. Student Engr, Lancashire Dynamo & Crypto, until 1936; Engr, ASEA Electric Ltd, 1936–40; War Service, RNVR, 1940–46 (Lt-Comdr); MPBW, later DoE, 1946–71, Chief Mech. and Electr. Engineer, 1969–71. FIMechE, FIEE. *Publications:* papers in Jls of Instns of Civil, Mechanical and Elect. Engrs. *Recreations:* tennis, gardening, golf. *Address:* 1 Highlawn House, Sudbury Hill, Harrow-on-the-Hill HA1 3NY. *T:* 0181–422 1599.

WOOLFSON, Prof. Michael Mark, FRS 1984; FRAS; FInstP; Emeritus Professor of Theoretical Physics, University of York; *b* 9 Jan. 1927; *s* of Maurice and Rose Woolfson; *m* 1951, Margaret (*née* Frohlich); two *s* one *d*. *Educ:* Jesus College, Oxford (MA); UMIST (PhD, DSc). Royal Engineers, 1947–49. Research Assistant: UMIST, 1950–52; Cavendish Lab., Cambridge, 1952–54; ICI Fellow, Univ. of Cambridge, 1954–55; Lectr, 1955–61, Reader, 1961–65, UMIST; Prof. of Theoretical Physics, 1965; Head of Dept. of Physics, 1982–87, Univ. of York. Hughes Medal, Royal Soc., 1986; Patterson Award, Amer. Crystallographic Assoc., 1990; Aminoff Medal, Royal Swedish Acad. of Scis, 1992. *Publications:* Direct Methods in Crystallography, 1961; An Introduction to X-Ray Crystallography, 1970; The Origin of the Solar System, 1989; Physical and Non-Physical Methods of Solving Crystal Structures; papers in learned jls. *Recreation:* wine making. *Address:* 24 Sandmoor Green, Leeds LS17 7SB. *T:* Leeds (0113) 266 2166.

WOOLHOUSE, Prof. Harold William; Director, Waite Agricultural Research Institute, and Dean, Faculty of Agricultural and Natural Resource Sciences, University of Adelaide, since 1990; *b* 12 July 1932; *s* of William Everson Woolhouse and Frances Ella Woolhouse; *m* 1959, Leonie Marie Sherwood; two *s* one *d*. *Educ:* Univ. of Reading (BSc); Univ. of Adelaide (PhD). Lecturer and Sen. Lectr, Sheffield Univ., 1960–69; Professor of Botany, Leeds Univ., 1969–80; Dir, John Innes Inst., and Prof. of Biological Scis, UEA, 1980–86; Dir of Res., AFRC Inst. of Plant Sci. Res., and Hon. Prof., UEA, 1987–90. Vis. Professor, USC, Los Angeles, 1968; Andrew D. White Professor at Large, Cornell Univ., 1983–89. Hon. DSc UEA, 1990. *Publications:* research papers on plant senescence, photosynthesis, metal toxicity and tolerance, and physiology of adaptation. *Recreations:* poetry, music, poultry breeding, gardening. *Address:* Old Sun House, 65 Damgate Street, Wymondham, Norfolk NR18 0BH; Waite Agricultural Research Institute, University of Adelaide, Glen Osmond, SA 5064, Australia. *T:* (8) 3722201.

WOOLHOUSE, Prof. John George, CBE 1988; Professor of Education, and Director of Centre for Education and Industry, University of Warwick, since 1988; *b* 17 June 1931; *s* of George Francis Woolhouse and Doris May Woolhouse (*née* Webber); *m* 1958, Ruth Carolyn Harrison; two *s* one *d*. *Educ:* Chichester High Sch. for Boys; Ardingly Coll; Brasenose Coll., Univ. of Oxford (MA). FIMgt. Rolls-Royce Ltd, 1954–72: Dir, Rolls-Royce and Associates, 1965–68; Co. Educn and Trng Officer, 1968–72; Asst Dir, Kingston Polytechnic and Dir, Kingston Regl Management Centre, 1972–78; Dir Atkins Planning, W. S. Atkins Gp Consultants, and Hd of Human Resources Develt, 1978–82; Dir, Technical and Vocational Educn Initiative, MSC, 1983–86; Dir of Educn Progs,

MSC, 1986–87. Chm., Assoc. of Regional Management Centres, 1977–78. *Publications:* chapters in: The Training of Youth in Industry, 1966; The Management Development Handbook, 1973; Gower Handbook of Management, 1983; Reform of Post-16 Education and Training in England and Wales, 1993. *Recreations:* travel, music, boating, fishing. *Address:* Ivy Farm House, Ivy Farm Lane, Coventry CV4 7BW. *Club:* Royal Air Force.

WOOLLAM, John Victor; Barrister-at-Law; *b* 14 Aug. 1927; *s* of Thomas Alfred and Edie Moss Woollam; *m* 1964, Lavinia Rosamond Ela, *d* of S. R. E. Snow; two *s*. *Educ:* Liverpool Univ. Called to the Bar, Inner Temple. Contested (C) Scotland Div. of Liverpool, 1950; MP (C) W Derby Div. of Liverpool, Nov. 1954–Sept. 1964; Parliamentary Private Sec. to Minister of Labour, 1960–62. *Recreation:* philately. *Address:* Old Ruggs Cottage, The Street, Kilmington, Devon EX13 7RW. *T:* Axminster (01297) 33336.

WOOLLASTON, Sir (Mountford) Tosswill, Kt 1979; painter (abandoned other occupations, 1966); *b* 11 April 1910; *s* of John Reginald Woollaston and Charlotte Kathleen Frances (*née* Tosswill); *m* 1936, Edith Winifred Alexander; three *s* one *d*. *Educ:* Huinga Primary; Stratford (NZ) Secondary; brief brushes with art schools, Christchurch, 1931; King Edward Technical Coll., Dunedin, 1932. Member, The Group, Christchurch, 1935–; a few private but enthusiastic supporters; work featured in Art in New Zealand, 1937. Doldrums, 1950s; Auckland City Art Gallery began purchasing work, 1958, other galleries followed; overseas travel grant, NZ Arts Council, 1961; reputation increased. Govt purchases for embassies overseas, early sixties; Peter McLeavey, Dealer, Wellington, took over selling, 1967. *Publications:* The Faraway Hills (Auckland City Art Gall. Associates), 1962; ERUA (48 drawings of a boy, with text—Paul), 1966; Sage Tea (autobiog.), 1981. *Recreation:* gardening. *Address:* Kelling Road, Upper Moutere, Nelson, New Zealand.

WOOLLCOMBE, Rt. Rev. Kenneth John; an Assistant Bishop, Diocese of Worcester, since 1989; *b* 2 Jan. 1924; *s* of late Rev. E. P. Woollcombe, OBE, and Elsie Ockenden Woollcombe; *m* 1st, 1950, Gwendoline Rhona Vyvien Hodges (*d* 1976); three *d*; 2nd, 1980, Rev. Juliet Dearmer; one *d*. *Educ:* Haileybury Coll., Hertford; St John's Coll., Oxford; Westcott House, Cambridge. Sub-Lieut (E) RNVR, 1945. Curate, St James, Grimsby, 1951; Fellow, Chaplain and Tutor, St John's Coll., Oxford, 1953, Hon. Fellow, 1971; Professor of Dogmatic Theology, General Theological Seminary, New York, 1960; Principal of Episcopal Theological Coll., Edinburgh, 1963; Bishop of Oxford, 1971–78; Asst Bishop, Diocese of London, 1978–81; Canon Residentiary of St Paul's, 1981–89, Precentor 1982–89. Chm., SPCK, 1973–79; Mem., Central Cttee, World Council of Churches, 1975–83; Chm., Churches' Council for Covenanting, 1978–82; Co-Chm., English Anglican-RC Cttee, 1985–88; Judge in Court of Ecclesiastical Causes Reserved, 1984–89. Hon. Chaplain, 1978–87, Hon. Liveryman, 1986, Glass Sellers' Co. STD Univ. of the South, Sewanee, USA, 1963; Hon. DD Hartford, Conn, 1975. *Publications:* (contrib.) The Historic Episcopate, 1954; (jointly) Essays on Typology, 1957. *Address:* 19 Ashdale Avenue, Pershore, Worcs WR10 1PL.

WOOLLETT, Maj.-Gen. John Castle, CBE 1957 (OBE 1955); MC 1945; MA Cantab; FICE; Principal Planning Inspector, Department of the Environment, 1971–81; *b* 5 Nov. 1915; *o s* of John Castle Woollett and Lily Bradley Woollett, Bredgar, Kent; *m* 1st, 1941, Joan Eileen Stranks (marr. diss., 1957); two *s* (and one *s* decd); 2nd, 1959, Helen Wendy Willis; two step *s*. *Educ:* St Benedict's Sch.; RMA Woolwich; St John's Coll., Cambridge. Joined RE, 1935; 23 Field Co., 1938–40 (BEF, 1939–40); 6 Commando, 1940–42; Major Comdg 16 Field Sqdn and 16 Assault Sqdn RE, 1942–45 (BLA, 1944–45); Student, Staff Coll., Camberley, 1946; DAAG and GSO2, Brit. Service Mission to Burma, 1947–50; Major Comdg 51 Port Sqdn RE, 1950; Instructor, Staff Coll., Camberley, 1950–53; Lt-Col Comdg 28 Field Engr Regt, 1954–55 (Korea); Bt Lt-Col 1955; Comdr Christmas Is, 1956–57; GSO1, Northern Army Gp, 1957–59; Col GS, US Army Staff Coll., Fort Leavenworth, 1959–61; DQMG (Movements), BAOR, 1962–64; Brig. Comdg Hants Sub District and Transportation Centre, RE, 1964–65; Sch. of Transport, 1965–66; Dep. Engr-in-Chief, 1966–67; Maj.-Gen., Chief Engineer, BAOR, 1967–70, retired. Col Comdt, RE, 1973 78. Pres., Instn of RE, 1974–79. *Recreation:* cruising. *Address:* 42 Rhinefield Close, Brockenhurst, Hants SO42 7SU. *Clubs:* Army and Navy, Royal Ocean Racing, Royal Cruising; Island Sailing (Cowes), Royal Lymington Yacht.

WOOLLEY, David Rorie, QC 1980; barrister-at-law; a Recorder of the Crown Court, 1982–94; *b* 9 June 1939; *s* of Albert and Ethel Woolley; *m* 1988, Mandy, *d* of Donald and Barbara Hutchison, Upper Dicker, Sussex. *Educ:* Winchester Coll.; Trinity Hall, Cambridge (BA Hons Law). Called to the Bar, Middle Temple, 1962, Bencher, 1988. Vis. Scholar, Wolfson Coll., Cambridge, 1982–87. Inspector, DoE inquiry into Nat. Gall. extension, 1984. *Publications:* Town Hall and the Property Owner, 1965; contribs to various legal jls. *Recreations:* opera, mountaineering, real tennis. *Address:* 1 Sergeants' Inn, EC4Y 1NH. *T:* 0171–583 1355. *Clubs:* MCC; Swiss Alpine.

WOOLLEY, John Maxwell, MBE 1945; TD 1946; Clerk, Merchant Taylors' Company, and Clerk to The Governors, Merchant Taylors' School, 1962–80; *b* 22 March 1917; *s* of Lt-Col Jasper Maxwell Woolley, IMS (Retd) and Kathleen Mary Woolley (*née* Waller); *m* 1952, Esme Adela Hamilton-Cole; two *s*. *Educ:* Cheltenham College; Trinity College, Oxford. BA (Oxon) 1938, MA (Oxon) 1962. Practising Solicitor, 1950–55; Asst Clerk, Merchant Taylors' Company, 1955–62. Hon. Mem. CGLI, 1991. *Address:* Flat 27, 15 Grand Avenue, Hove, E Sussex BN3 2NG. *T:* Brighton (01273) 733200. *Club:* Hove.

WOOLLEY, (John) Moger; Chairman: Dolphin Packaging, since 1990; API plc, since 1992; BM Group, since 1992; *b* 1 May 1935; *s* of Cyril Herbert Steele Woolley and Eveline Mary May Woolley; *m* 1960, Gillian Edith Millar; one *s* one *d*. *Educ:* Taunton Sch.; Bristol Univ., 1956–59 (BSc). National Service, 1954–56. Various management positions, DRG plc, 1959–89, Chief Exec., 1985–89. Non-Executive Director: Staveley Industries, 1990–; Bristol Water Hldgs, 1990–; United Bristol Hosp. Trust, 1991–93; Avon Rubber, 1992–. *Recreations:* cricket, hockey, golf, gardening. *Address:* Matford House, Northwoods, Winterbourne, Bristol BS17 1RS. *T:* Winterbourne (01454) 772180. *Clubs:* MCC; Merchant Venturers' (Bristol).

WOOLLEY, His Honour Roy Gilbert; a Circuit Judge, 1976–93; *b* 28 Nov. 1922; *s* of John Woolley and Edith Mary Woolley; *m* 1953, Doreen, *d* of Humphrey and Kathleen Morris; two *s* two *d*. *Educ:* Overton and Marchwiel Primary Schs; Deeside Secondary Sch.; UCL (LLB Hons 1949). Served War, 1939–45, Air Gunner, RAF. Christopher Tancred Student, Lincoln's Inn, 1948; called to the Bar, 1951; Wales and Chester Circuit; Recorder, 1975. Reader: Diocese of Chester, 1955–; Diocese of Lichfield, 1977–. Member: Lichfield Diocesan Synod, 1988–; General Synod of C of E, 1990–; Legal Adv. Commn of C of E, 1991–. *Recreations:* outdoor pursuits, incl. horse riding, gardening; interested in music, poetry, art and antique furniture. *Address:* Henlle Hall, St Martins, Oswestry, Salop SY10 7AX. *T:* Oswestry (01691) 661257.

WOOLLEY, Russell; *see* Woolley, A. R.

WOOLMAN, (Joseph) Roger; Deputy Secretary, and Legal Adviser and Solicitor to Ministry of Agriculture, Fisheries and Food, Forestry Commission and Intervention Board for Agricultural Produce, since 1993; *b* 13 Feb. 1937; *s* of late Maurice Wollman and Hilda Wollman; *m* 1973, Elizabeth, *d* of late Eric Ingham; one *s* one *d*. *Educ:* Perse School, Cambridge; Trinity Hall, Cambridge (Exhibnr; MA). Solicitor, 1974. DTI and OFT Legal Departments, 1976–93: Under Sec., DTI, 1985–88 and 1991–93; Legal Dir, OFT, 1988–91. *Address:* 55 Whitehall, SW1A 2EY. *T:* 0171–270 8379. *Clubs:* Reform; Hampstead Golf.

WOOLMER, Kenneth John; Director of MBA Programmes, School of Business and Economic Studies, Leeds University, since 1991; Principal in Halton Gill Associates, consultants on central and local government relations, since 1979; *b* 25 April 1940; *s* of Joseph William and Gertrude May Woolmer; *m* 1961, Janice Chambers; three *s*. *Educ:* Gladstone Street County Primary, Rothwell, Northants; Kettering Grammar Sch.; Leeds Univ. (BA Econs). Research Fellow, Univ. of West Indies, 1961–62; Teacher, Friern Rd Sec. Mod. Sch., London, 1963; Lecturer: Univ. of Leeds (Economics), 1963–66; Univ. of Ahmadu Bello, Nigeria, 1966–68; Univ. of Leeds, 1968–79. Councillor: Leeds CC, 1970–78; West Yorkshire MCC, 1973–80 (Leader, 1975–77; Leader of Opposition, 1977–79). Chairman, Planning and Transportation Cttee, Assoc. of Metropolitan Authorities, 1974–77. Contested (Lab) Batley and Spen, 1983, 1987. MP (Lab) Batley and Morley, 1979–83; Opposition spokesman on trade, shipping and aviation, 1981–83; Mem., Select Cttee on Treasury and Civil Service, 1980–81; Chm., 1981, Vice-Chm., 1982, PLP Economics and Finance Gp. Dir, Leeds United AFC, 1991–. *Address:* 8 Ancaster Crescent, Leeds LS16 5HS.

WOOLRYCH, Prof. Austin Herbert, FBA 1988; Professor of History, University of Lancaster, 1964–85, now Emeritus; *b* 18 May 1918; *s* of Stanley Herbert Cunliffe Woolrych and May Gertrude (*née* Wood); *m* 1941, Muriel Edith Rolfe (*d* 1991); one *s* one *d*. *Educ:* Westminster Sch.; Pembroke Coll., Oxford (BLitt, MA). Served War, RAC, 1939–46: commnd RTR, 1940; Captain 1943. Lectr in History, subseq. Sen. Lectr, Univ. of Leeds, 1949–64; Pro-Vice-Chancellor, Univ. of Lancaster, 1971–75. Vis. Fellow, All Souls Coll., Oxford, 1981–82; Commonwealth Vis. Fellow to univs in Australia and NZ, 1983. Hon. DLitt Lancaster, 1986. *Publications:* Battles of the English Civil War, 1961, rev. edn 1991; Oliver Cromwell, 1964; (introd) Complete Prose Works of John Milton, vol 7, 1980; Commonwealth to Protectorate, 1982; England without a King, 1983; Soldiers and Statesmen, 1987; articles and reviews in jls and symposia. *Recreations:* walking, travel, opera. *Address:* 9 Hollowrayne, Burton-in-Kendal, Carnforth LA6 1NS. *T:* Burton (01524) 782471.

WOOLSEY, Rt. Rev. Gary Frederick; Assistant Bishop of Calgary, since 1992, and Rector of St Peter's, Calgary, since 1991; *b* 16 March 1942; *s* of William and Doreen Woolsey; *m* 1967, Marie Elaine Tooker; two *s* two *d*. *Educ:* Univ. of Western Ontario (BA); Huron Coll., London, Ont. (BTh); Univ. of Manitoba (Teacher's Cert.). Deacon, 1967; Priest-pilot, Diocese of Keewatin, 1967–68; Rector: St Peter's, Big Trout Lake, Ont., 1968–72; St Mark's, Norway House, Manitoba, 1972–76; St Paul's, Churchill, Man., 1976–80; Program Director and Archdeacon of Keewatin, 1980–83; Bishop of Athabasca, 1983–91. *Recreations:* fishing, hunting, boating, camping, photography, flying. *Address:* 919 75 Avenue SW, Calgary, Alta T2V 0S7, Canada. *T:* (home) (403) 2580143, (office) (403) 2520393.

WOOLTON, 3rd Earl of, *cr* 1956; **Simon Frederick Marquis;** Baron Woolton, 1939; Viscount Woolton, 1953; Viscount Walberton, 1956; *b* 24 May 1958; *s* of 2nd Earl of Woolton and of Cecily Josephine (now Countess Lloyd George of Dwyfor), *e d* of Sir Alexander Gordon Cumming, 5th Bt; *S* father, 1969; *m* 1987, Hon. Sophie Frederika, *o d* of Baron Birdwood, *qv*; three *d*. *Educ:* Eton College; St Andrews Univ. (MA Hons). Merchant banker, S. G. Warburg & Co. Ltd, 1982–88; Director: Woolton Elwes Ltd, 1994–; Rockbrook Hldgs, 1994–; Fiortho plc, 1995–. Trustee, Woolton Charitable Trust. Freeman, Skinners' Co. *Recreations:* gardening, golf, field sports. *Address:* Auchnacree House, Glenogil, by Forfar, Angus DD8 3SX; 18 Lower Addison Gardens, W14 8BQ. *Clubs:* White's, Brooks's, Pratt's, MCC; New (Edinburgh); Royal and Ancient.

WOOLVERTON, Kenneth Arthur; Head of Latin America, Caribbean and Pacific Department, Overseas Development Administration of the Foreign and Commonwealth Office, 1985–86; *b* 4 Aug. 1926; *s* of Arthur Eliott Woolverton and Lilian Woolverton; *m* 1957, Kathleen West; one *s*. *Educ:* Orange Hill Grammar Sch. Colonial Office, 1950–61; CRO, 1961–66 (2nd Sec., Jamaica); Min. of Overseas Development, 1966–79; Hd of Middle East Develt Div., ODA, 1979–81; Hd of British Develt Div. in the Caribbean, ODA, 1981–84. ARPS 1992. *Recreations:* photography, archaeology, sailing. *Address:* 47 Durleston Park Drive, Great Bookham, Surrey KT23 4AJ. *T:* Bookham (01372) 454055.

WOOLWICH, Area Bishop of; Rt. Rev. (Albert) Peter Hall; appointed Bishop Suffragan of Woolwich, 1984; *b* 2 Sept. 1930; *s* of William Conrad Hall and Bertha Gladys Hall; *m* 1957, Valerie Jill Page; two *s*. *Educ:* Queen Elizabeth Grammar School, Blackburn; St John's Coll., Cambridge (MA Mod. Langs); Ridley College, Cambridge. Deacon 1955, priest 1956; Curate: St Martin, Birmingham, 1955–60; St Mary Magdalene, Avondale, Zimbabwe, 1960; Rector of Avondale, Zimbabwe, 1963–70; Rector of Birmingham, 1970–84. *Recreation:* mountain walking. *Address:* 8B Hillyfields Crescent, Brockley, SE4 1QA. *T:* 0181–469 0013, *Fax:* 0181–694 8309.

WOON, Peter William; Editor, BBC TV News, 1980–85; *b* 12 Dec. 1931; *s* of Henry William Woon and Gwendoline Constance Woon; *m* 1st, 1956, Elizabeth Hird (marr. diss. 1974); one *s*; 2nd, 1974, Diana Ward (marr. diss. 1993). *Educ:* Christ's Hospital. 2nd Lieut Royal Signals, 1954–56; Reporter, Bristol Evening Post, 1949–54 and 1956–58; air corresp., Daily Express, 1958–61; BBC: reporter, 1961–66; Asst Editor, TV News, 1966–69; Editor, Radio News, 1969–75; Head of Information, 1975–77; Editor, News and Current Affairs, radio, 1977–80; Head, Ops, N America, 1985–88. *Address:* 8 Mulberry Close, Rosslyn Hill, Hampstead, NW3 5UP. *T:* 0171–794 1454.

WOOSNAM, Charles Richard, CBE 1993; a Forestry Commissioner, 1986–95; *b* 4 Aug. 1925; *s* of late Ralph William Woosnam and Kathleen Mary Woosnam (*née* Evan-Thomas); *m* 1950, Patricia Rodney Carruthers; two *s* two *d*. *Educ:* Winchester; Pembroke Coll., Cambridge. BA Estate Management. FRICS. Commissioned 15th/19th The King's Royal Hussars, 1943–47, served Europe and Palestine; with Land Agents Strutt and Parker, Builth Wells office, 1950–63; set up own Land Agency partnership, Woosnam & Tyler, 1964. Consultant, 1988–. Member: Welsh Water Authy, 1973–76 (Chm., Fisheries Adv. Cttee); Exec. Cttee, Timber Growers UK (formerly Timber Growers England & Wales), 1976–86 (Dep. Chm., England and Wales; Chm., Finance Cttee); Chm., CLA Game Fair Local Cttee, 1976; Pres., Royal Forestry Soc. of England, Wales and NI, 1995–. High Sheriff, Powys, 1985–86. *Recreations:* shooting, fishing. *Address:* Cefnllysgwynne, Builth Wells, Powys LD2 3HN. *T:* Builth Wells (01982) 552237. *Club:* Army and Navy.

WOOSNAM, Ian Harold, MBE 1992; professional golfer since 1976; *b* 2 March 1958; *s* of Harold and Joan Woosnam; *m* 1983, Glendryth Mervyn Pugh; one *s* two *d*. *Educ:* St Martin's Modern Sch. Numerous championship wins, 1987–, including: World Cup (individual), 1987 and 1991; World Match Play, 1987 and 1990; PGA, 1988; PGA Grand Slam of Golf, 1991; US Masters, 1991; British Masters, 1994. Hon. Mem., PGA European tour. *Publications:* Ian Woosnam's Golf Masterpieces, 1988; Power Golf, 1989, new edn

1991. *Recreations:* snooker, water-skiing, shooting. *Address:* c/o IMG, Pier House, Strand on the Green, W4 3NN. *Clubs:* Oswestry Golf; Wentworth Golf.

WOOSTER, Clive Edward Doré; consultant; *b* 3 Nov. 1913; *s* of Edward Doré Wooster; *m*; two *s*; *m* 1970, Patricia Iris (formerly Dewey). *Educ:* Private School, Southend-on-Sea. Private offices, 1930–40; War Service, Captain RA, 1940–46. Local Authority Offices and LCC, 1946–51; Ministry of Education, 1951–58; University Grants Cttee, 1958–59; Works Directorate, War Office, 1959–63; Dir of Building Management, MPBW, 1963–69; Dep. Chief Architect, Min. of Housing and Local Govt, 1969; Dir, Housing Develt, DoE, 1972–74, retired. RIBA Technical Standards Cttee, 1960–64; RIBA Building Controls Panel Chairman, 1960–63; RIBA Management Handbook Cttee, 1963–67; RIBA Council, 1970–72. *Publications:* Lectures on architectural and building management subjects; contrib. to professional journals. *Address:* 141 Harefield Road, Rickmansworth, Herts WD3 1PB. *T:* Rickmansworth (01923) 775401.

WOOTTON, Adrian; Head, British Film Institute, South Bank, since 1993; *b* 18 May 1962; *s* of Ronald Oliver Wootton and Unity Wootton; *m* 1986, Karen Sarah Goodman. *Educ:* Univ. of East Anglia (BA Hons English and Amer. Studies, MA Film Studies). Director: Bradford Playhouse and Film Theatre, 1986–89; Nottingham Media Centre Ltd, 1989–93; Shots in the Dark, Internat. Crime, Mystery and Thriller Fest., Nottingham, 1991–; Head of BFI on South Bank, incl. NFT, MOMI and London Film Fest., 1993–. *Publications:* (contrib.) 100 Great Detectives, 1992; (ed jtly) Celluloid Jukebox, 1995; contribs to arts magazines. *Recreations:* film, literature, music, theatre. *Address:* BFI on the South Bank, Waterloo, SE1 8XT. *T:* 0171–815 1300. *Club:* Groucho.

WOOTTON, Godfrey; *see* Wootton, N. G.

WOOTTON, (Harold) John, CEng, FCIT; FBCS; FIHT; Chief Executive, Transport (formerly Transport and Road) Research Laboratory, since 1991; *b* 17 Nov. 1936; *s* of Harold Wootton and Hilda Mary (*née* Somerfield); *m* 1960, Patricia Ann Riley; two *s*. *Educ:* Queen Mary's Grammar Sch., Walsall; QMC, Univ. of London; Univ. of Calif, Berkeley. FIHT 1980; FBCS 1985; FCIT 1987; CEng 1990. Lectr, Dept of Civil Engrg, Univ. of Leeds, 1959–62; Technical Dir, Freeman Fox Wilbur Smith, 1963–67; Jt Man. Dir, SIA Ltd, 1967–71; Chm., Wootton Jeffreys Consultants Ltd, 1971–91. Visiting Professor in: Computing, KCL, 1987–89; Transport Studies, UCL, 1989–92. *Publications:* numerous papers on transport, planning and computer topics. *Recreations:* cricket, golf, Rotary, photography, travel. *Address:* Transport Research Laboratory, Old Wokingham Road, Crowthorne, Berks RG45 6AU. *T:* Crowthorne (01344) 770001. *Club:* Royal Automobile.

WOOTTON, Ian David Phimester, MA, MB, BChir, PhD, FRSC, FRCPath, FRCP; Professor of Chemical Pathology, Royal Postgraduate Medical School, University of London, 1963–82; *b* 5 March 1921; *s* of D. Wootton and Charlotte (*née* Phimester); *m* 1946, Veryan Mary Walshe; two *s* two *d*. *Educ:* Weymouth Grammar School; St John's College, Cambridge; St Mary's Hospital, London. Research Assistant, Postgraduate Med. School, 1945; Lecturer, 1949; Sen. Lecturer, 1959; Reader, 1961. Consultant Pathologist to Hammersmith Hospital, 1952. Member of Medical Research Council Unit, Cairo, 1947–48; Major, RAMC, 1949; Smith-Mundt Fellow, Memorial Hosp., New York, 1951. Chief Scientist (Hosp. Scientific and Technical Services), DHSS, 1972–73. *Publications:* Microanalysis in Medical Biochemistry, 1964, ed 6th edn, 1982; Biochemical Disorders in Human Disease, 1970; papers in medical and scientific journals on biochemistry and pathology. *Recreations:* carpentry, boating, beekeeping. *Address:* Cariad Cottage, Cleeve Road, Goring, Oxon RG8 9DB. *T:* Goring-on-Thames (01491) 873050.

WOOTTON, John; *see* Wootton, H. J.

WOOTTON, (Norman) Godfrey; Stipendiary Magistrate for Merseyside, 1976–94; *b* 10 April 1926; *s* of H. N. and E. Wootton, Crewe, Cheshire. *Educ:* The Grammar Sch., Crewe; Liverpool Univ. (LLB). Called to Bar, Gray's Inn, 1951. Joined Northern Circuit, 1951. A Recorder of the Crown Court, 1972. *Recreations:* travel, photography. *Club:* Athenæum (Liverpool).

WOOTTON, Ronald William, CBE 1991; Head of West and North Africa and Mediterranean Department, Overseas Development Administration, 1986–91; *b* 7 April 1931; *s* of William George and late Lilian Wootton; *m* 1954, Elvira Mary Gillian Lakeman; one *s* one *d*. *Educ:* Christ's College, Finchley. Served Royal Signals, 1950–52. Colonial Office, 1952–63; Commonwealth Relations Office, 1963–65; ODM/ODA, 1965–91: Head of Overseas Manpower and Consultancies Dept, 1976–79; Head of UN Dept, 1979–82; Head of British Develt Div. in the Pacific, 1982–85. Mem., Internat. Cttee, Leonard Cheshire Foundn, 1992–. *Address:* 16 The Heath, Chaldon, Surrey CR3 5DG. *T:* Caterham (01883) 344903.

WOOZLEY, Prof. Anthony Douglas, MA; University Professor Emeritus of Philosophy and Law, University of Virginia, since 1983; *b* 14 Aug. 1912; *o s* of David Adams Woozley and Kathleen Lucy Moore; *m* 1st, 1937, Thelma Suffield (marr. diss. 1978), *e d* of late Frank Townshend, Worcester; one *d*; 2nd, 1995, Cora, *e d* of late Abraham Diamond, New York. *Educ:* Haileybury College; Queen's College, Oxford. Open Scholar, Queen's College, 1931–35; 1st Cl. Class. Hon. Mods, 1933; 1st Cl. Lit. Hum., 1935; John Locke Schol., 1935. Served War, 1940–46 (despatches); commissioned King's Dragoon Guards, 1941; served N Africa, Italy, Greece, Egypt, Syria, Palestine; Major. Fellow of All Souls College, 1935–37; Fellow and Praelector in Philosophy, Queen's Coll., 1937–54; Librarian, 1938–54; Tutor, Queen's College, 1946–54; University Lecturer in Philosophy, 1947–54; Senior Proctor, 1953–54; Prof. of Moral Philosophy, Univ. of St Andrews, 1954–67; University of Virginia: Prof. of Philosophy, 1966; Commonwealth Prof. of Philosophy, 1974–77; Commonwealth Prof. and Univ. Prof. of Philosophy and Law, 1977–83. Editor of The Philosophical Quarterly, 1957–62; Editor, Home University Library, 1962–68. Visiting Professor of Philosophy: Univ. of Rochester, USA, 1965; Univ. of Arizona, 1972. *Publications:* (ed) Thomas Reid's Essays on the Intellectual Powers of Man, 1941; Theory of Knowledge, 1949; (with R. C. Cross) Plato's Republic: a Philosophical Commentary, 1964; (ed) John Locke's Essay Concerning Human Understanding, 1964; Law and Obedience, 1979; articles and reviews in Mind, etc. *Address:* 655 Kearsarge Circle, Charlottesville, VA 22903, USA.

WORCESTER, Marquess of; Henry John Fitzroy Somerset; FRICS; *b* 22 May 1952; *s* and *heir* of 11th Duke of Beaufort, *qv*; *m* 1987, Tracy Louise, *yr d* of Hon. Peter Ward and Hon. Mrs Claire Ward; two *s* one *d*. *Educ:* Eton; Cirencester Agricultural College. With Morgan Grenfell Laurie Ltd (formerly Michael Laurie & Partners), London, 1977; subseq. with Franc Warwick. *Recreations:* hunting, shooting, golf, tennis, skiing, rock music. *Heir:* *s* Earl of Glamorgan, *qv*. *Club:* Turf.

WORCESTER, Bishop of, since 1982; **Rt. Rev. Philip Harold Ernest Goodrich;** *b* 2 Nov. 1929; *s* of late Rev. Canon Harold Spencer Goodrich and Gertrude Alice Goodrich; *m* 1960, Margaret Metcalfe Bennett; four *d*. *Educ:* Stamford Sch.; St John's Coll., Cambridge (MA); Cuddesdon Theological Coll. Curate, Rugby Parish Church, 1954–57; Chaplain, St John's Coll., Cambridge, 1957–61; Rector of the South Ormsby Group of Parishes, 1961–68; Vicar of Bromley, 1968–73; Diocesan Director of Ordinands, Rochester, 1974–82; Bishop Suffragan of Tonbridge, 1974–82. *Recreations:* gardening, music, walking, looking at buildings. *Address:* Bishop's House, Hartlebury Castle, Kidderminster, Worcs DY11 7XX. *Club:* United Oxford & Cambridge University.

WORCESTER, Dean of; *see* Jeffery, Very Rev. R. M. C.

WORCESTER, Archdeacon of; *see* Bentley, Ven. F. W. H.

WORCESTER, Robert Milton; Chairman, Market & Opinion Research International (MORI) Ltd, since 1973 (Managing Director, 1969–94); *b* 21 Dec. 1933; *s* of late C. M. and Violet Ruth Worcester, of Kansas City, Mo, USA; *m* 1st, 1958, Joann (*née* Ransdell); two *s*; 2nd, 1982, Margaret Noel (*née* Smallbone). *Educ:* Univ. of Kansas (BSc). Consultant, McKinsey & Co., 1962–65; Controller and Asst to Chm., Opinion Research Corp., 1965–68. Past Pres., World Assoc. for Public Opinion Research. Vice Pres., Internat., Social Science Council, UNESCO, 1989–94. Visiting Professor: City Univ., 1990–; LSE, 1992–. Member: Exec. Cttee, Pilgrims' Soc. of GB (Chm., 1993–); Programme Cttee, Ditchley Foundn. Comr, US-UK Fulbright Commn, 1995–. Consultant: The Times; Economist. Frequent broadcaster and speaker on British and Amer. politics. FRSA; MIMgt. Co-Editor, Internat. Jl of Public Opinion Research. *Publications:* edited: Consumer Market Research Handbook, 1971, 3rd edn 1986; (with M Harrop) Political Communications, 1982; Political Opinion Polling: an international review, 1983; (with Lesley Watkins) Private Opinions, Public Polls, 1986; (with Eric Jacobs) We British, 1990; British Public Opinion: history and methodology of political opinion polling in Great Britain, 1991; (with Eric Jacobs) Typically British, 1991; (with Samuel Barnes) Dynamics of Societal Learning about Global Environmental Change, 1992; contrib. The Times; papers in tech. and prof. jls. *Recreations:* choral music (St Bartholomew's Hospital Choir), gardening, scuba diving. *Address:* 32 Old Queen Street, SW1H 9HP. *T:* 0171–222 0232. *Club:* Reform.

WORDIE, Sir John (Stewart), Kt 1981; CBE 1975; VRD 1963; barrister-at-law; *b* 15 Jan. 1924; *s* of late Sir James Mann Wordie, CBE, Hon. LLD, and of Lady Wordie (*née* Henderson); *m* 1955, Patricia Gladys Kynoch, Keith, Banffshire, *d* of Lt-Col G. B. Kynoch, CBE, TD, DL; four *s*. *Educ:* Winchester Coll.; St John's Coll., Cambridge (MA; LLM). Served RNVR, 1942–46. Comdr RNR, 1967; Comdr London Div. RNR, 1969–71. Cambridge, 1946–49; Called to the Bar, Inner Temple, 1950; in practice at the Bar, 1951–86. Chairman: Burnham and Pelham Cttees, 1966–87; Soulbury Cttee, 1966–; Wages Councils, 1956–93; Mem., Agricultural Wages Bd for England and Wales, 1974–95; Dep. Chm. and Mem., Central Arbitration Cttee, 1976–91; Mem. Council, ACAS, 1986–90. Chm., Nat. Jt Council for Lectures in Further Educn, 1980–93. Mem. Court of Assistants, Salters' Co., 1971–, Master, 1975. *Recreations:* shooting, sailing and boating, athletics, tennis. *Address:* Dodington House, Breamore, Fordingbridge, Hants SP6 2EH. *T:* Downton (01725) 512317. *Clubs:* Travellers, Army and Navy, Royal Ocean Racing; Hawks (Cambridge); Royal Tennis Court (Hampton Court); Clyde Corinthian Yacht.

WORDLEY, Ronald William; Chairman, The Buckingham Group (Winslow Press) Ltd, 1987–93; Director, BCS Developments Ltd, since 1989; Managing Director, 1978–87, Chairman, 1985–86, HTV Ltd; *b* 16 June 1928; *s* of William Wordley and Elizabeth Anne Hackett; *m* 1953, Pamela Mary Offord; two *s* one *d* (and one *s* decd). *Educ:* Barnet Grammar Sch.; City of London Coll.; RMA, Sandhurst. Regular Army Officer: 2/Lieut RA, 1948; regtl duty, UK, Far East and Europe; Liaison Officer, RM Commando Bde, 1951, Captain; Air OP Pilot, 1953; Army Light Aircraft Sch., 1955; seconded Army Air Corps Cadre, 1957; resigned commn, 1958. Unilever (United Africa Co.), 1958–59; Anglia Television Ltd: Sales Exec., 1959; Gen. Sales Manager, 1962; Dep. Sales Controller, 1964; joined Harlech Consortium as Sales Controller, 1967; Sales Dir on bd of HTV Ltd, 1971. Director: Instock Ltd; Independent Television Publications Ltd; (also Mem. Council), Independent Television Cos Assoc. Ltd; HTV Gp plc; HTV Equipment Ltd; HTV Property Ltd., 1971–87. Hon. Patron, Royal Regt of Wales, 1986–91. Mem., Inst. of Marketing; FRSA 1983; FInstD 1986. *Recreations:* music, travel, golf, swimming. *Address:* 6 Spring Leigh, Leigh Woods, Bristol, Avon BS8 3PG. *T:* Bristol (0117) 973 9256; TSDY Tirion II, Quay 11, Berth 14, Port de La Rague, Theoule-sur-Mer 06590, France. *Clubs:* Clifton (Bristol); Bristol and Clifton Golf.

WORDSWORTH, Barry; conductor; Music Director of Covent Garden Royal Ballet and of Birmingham Royal Ballet, since 1990; *b* 20 Feb. 1948; *s* of Ronald and Kathleen Wordsworth; *m* 1970, Ann Barber; one *s*. *Educ:* Royal College of Music. Conductor, Royal Ballet, 1974–84; Music Dir, New Sadler's Wells Opera, 1982–84; Musical Dir and Prin. Conductor, Brighton Philharmonic Orch., 1989–; Prin. Conductor, BBC Concert Orch., 1989–. Joint winner, Sargent Conductor's Prize, 1970; Tagore Gold Medal, RCM, 1970. *Recreations:* swimming, photography, cooking. *Address:* c/o Manygate Management, 13 Cotswold Mews, 30 Battersea Square, SW11 3RA.

WORKMAN, Charles Joseph, TD 1966; Part-time Chairman: Industrial Tribunals for Scotland, 1986–92; Social Security Appeal Tribunals, 1986–94; Disability Appeal Tribunals, 1992–94; *b* 25 Aug. 1920; *s* of Hugh William O'Brien Workman and Annie Shields; *m* 1949, Margaret Jean Mason; one *s* two *d*. *Educ:* St Mungo's Acad., Glasgow; Univ. of Glasgow (MA 1950, LLB 1952). Admitted solicitor, 1952. Served War, 1939–45: France, Belgium, Holland, Germany; commnd Second Fife and Forfar Yeomanry, RAC, 1942; Captain, 1945; served Intell. Corps TA and TAVR, 1954–69; Bt Lt-Col 1969; Hon. Col, Intell. and Security Gp (V), 1977–86. Entered Office of Solicitor to Sec. of State for Scotland as Legal Asst, 1955; Sen. Legal Asst, 1961; Asst Solicitor, 1966; Dep. Solicitor to Sec. of State, 1976; Dir, Scottish Courts Administration, 1978–82; Senior Dep. Sec. (Legal Aid), Law Soc. of Scotland, 1982–86. Chm., Public Service and Commerce Gp, Law Soc. of Scotland, 1977–78. Founder Mem., Edinburgh Chamber Music Trust, 1977–. *Publication:* (contrib.) The Laws of Scotland: Stair Memorial Encyclopaedia, vol. 2, 1987. *Recreations:* hill walking, swimming, music. *Address:* Green Lane Cottage, Lasswade, Midlothian EH18 1HE. *Club:* New (Edinburgh).

WORKMAN, Timothy (Henry); a Metropolitan Stipendiary Magistrate, since 1986; a Chairman, Inner London Juvenile Panel, since 1989, and Family Proceeding Court, since 1992; a Recorder, since 1994; *b* 18 Oct. 1943; *s* of Gordon and late Eileen Workman; *m* 1971, Felicity Ann Caroline Western; one *s* one *d*. *Educ:* Ruskin Grammar Sch., Croydon. Probation Officer, Inner London, 1967–69; admitted Solicitor, 1969; Solicitor, subseq. Partner, C. R. Thomas & Son, later Lloyd Howorth & Partners, Maidenhead, 1969–85. *Recreations:* ski-ing, pottery. *Address:* Orchard House, Fleet Hill, Finchampstead, Berks RG11 4LA. *T:* Eversley (01734) 733315. *Club:* Medico-Legal.

WORLOCK, Most Rev. Derek John Harford; *see* Liverpool, Archbishop of, (RC).

WORMALD, Brian Harvey Goodwin, MA; University Lecturer in History, Cambridge, 1948–79; Fellow of Peterhouse, 1938–79, Emeritus Fellow 1979; *b* 24 July 1912; *s* of late Rev. C. O. R. Wormald and Mrs A. W. C. Wormald (*née* Brooks); *m* 1946, Rosemary, *d* of E. J. B. Lloyd; four *s*. *Educ:* Harrow; Peterhouse, Cambridge (Scholar). BA 1934 (1st Class Hons Hist. Tripos, Parts I and II); Members Prize (English Essay), 1935; Strathcona

Research Student, St John's College, 1936–38; Prince Consort Prize, 1938; MA 1938. Chaplain and Catechist, Peterhouse, 1940–48; Dean, 1941–44; Tutor, 1952–62. Select Preacher, Cambridge, 1945 and 1954. Junior Proctor, 1951–52. Received into Catholic Church, 1955. *Publications:* Clarendon: Politics, History and Religion, 1951; Francis Bacon: History, Politics, Science, 1993. *Address:* c/o Peterhouse, Cambridge CB2 1RD. *Club:* Travellers'.

WORMALD, Peter John, CB 1990; Director, Office of Population Censuses and Surveys, and Registrar General for England and Wales, 1990–March 1996; *b* 10 March 1936; *s* of late H. R. and G. A. Wormald; *m* 1962, Elizabeth North; three *s*. *Educ:* Doncaster Grammar Sch.; The Queen's Coll., Oxford (MA). Assistant Principal, Min. of Health, 1958, Principal, 1963; HM Treasury, 1965–67, Asst Sec., 1970; Under Sec., DHSS, 1978; Dep. Sec., Dept of Health (formerly DHSS), 1987. *Recreations:* music, golf, contract bridge. *Address:* c/o Office of Population Censuses and Surveys, St Catherine's House, 10 Kingsway, WC2B 6JP. *Club:* United Oxford & Cambridge University.

WORRALL, Anna Maureen, (Mrs G. H. G. Williams); QC 1989; a Recorder, since 1987; *m* 1964, G. H. Graeme Williams, *qv*; two *d*. *Educ:* Hillcrest Sch., Bramhall; Loreto Coll., Llandudno; Manchester Univ. Called to the Bar, Middle Temple, 1959; in practice, 1959–63 and 1971–; Lectr in Law, Holborn Coll. of Law, Language and Commerce, 1964–69; Dir, ILEA Educnl Television Service, 1969–71. *Recreations:* theatre, music, cooking, walking, travel. *Address:* Cloisters, Pump Court, Temple, EC4Y 7AA. *T:* 0171–583 0303. *Clubs:* Reform, Network.

WORRALL, Denis John, PhD; Chief Executive, Omega Investment Research Ltd, since 1990; *b* 29 May 1935; *s* of Cecil John Worrall and Hazel Worrall; *m* 1965, Anita Ianco; three *s*. *Educ:* Univ. of Cape Town (BA Hons, MA); Univ. of South Africa (LLB); Cornell Univ. (PhD). Teaching and research positions, Univs of Natal, S Africa, Ibadan, Witwatersrand, California, Cornell; Rearch Prof. and Dir, Inst. of Social and Economic Research, Rhodes Univ., 1973. Senator, 1974; elected to Parlt, 1977; Chm., Constitutional Cttee, President's Council, 1981; Ambassador: to Australia, 1983–84; to the UK, 1984–87; Co-Leader, Democratic Party, 1988–90; MP (Democratic Party) Berea (Durban), South Africa, 1989–94. Advocate of Supreme Court of S Africa. *Publication:* South Africa: government and politics, 1970. *Recreations:* tennis, reading, music. *Address:* PO Box 5455, Cape Town, 8000, South Africa.

WORSFOLD, Reginald Lewis, CBE 1979; Member for Personnel, British Gas Corporation (formerly Gas Council), 1973–80, retired; *b* 18 Dec. 1925; *s* of Charles S. and Doris Worsfold; *m* 1st, 1952, Margot Kempell (marr. diss. 1974); one *s* one *d*; 2nd, 1982, Christine McKeown. *Educ:* School of Technology, Art and Commerce, Oxford; London Sch. of Economics. MIPM. Served War of 1939–45: Lieut 44 Royal Marine Commandos, 1943–46. Organising Commissioner, Scout Council of Nigeria, 1947–49; Personnel Manager: British European Airways, 1953–65; W Midlands Gas Bd, 1965–69; Gas Council: Dep. Personnel Dir, 1969–70; Personnel Dir, 1970–72. *Recreations:* sailing, camping, music. *Address:* Beck House, 43 Wychwood Grove, Chandler's Ford, Hants SO5 1FQ. *T:* Chandler's Ford (01703) 269873.

WORSKETT, Prof. Roy, RIBA; MRTPI; consultant architect and town planner; Partner, Architectural Planning Partnership, Horsham, 1982–85; *b* 3 Sept. 1932; *s* of Archibald Ellwood Worskett and Dorothy Alice Roffey; two *s* one *d*. *Educ:* Collyer's Sch., Horsham; Portsmouth Sch. of Architecture. MRTPI 1975; RIBA 1955. Architect's Dept, LCC, 1957–60; Architect, Civic Trust, London, 1960–63; Historic Areas Div., DoE (formerly MPBW), 1963–74; City Architect and Planning Officer, Bath City Council, and Prof. of Urban Conservation, Sch. of Architecture, Bath Univ., 1974–79; Consultant Head, Conservation Section, Crafts Council, 1979–82. Consultant Architect: Bath CC, 1979–83; Salisbury DC, 1980–; Brighton Palace Pier, 1987–; London borough of Greenwich, 1988–93; London boroughs of Lambeth, Kensington and Chelsea, and Richmond, 1988–; Consultant: Ford Foundn in India, 1982–; Council of Europe, 1984–; Nat. Audit Office, 1987; evidence to Public Inquiries at Mansion House, for City of London, and at County Hall, London, 1984–; Advr, Urban Redevelt Authority, Singapore, 1992–; Conservation Advr, Union Rlys and British Land, 1993–. Chairman: Conservation Cttees, Crafts Adv. Cttee, 1974–79; Design Panel, Spitalfields Develt Gp, 1990–; Member: Heritage Educn Group, 1976–88; Council for Urban Study Centres, TCPA, 1977–80; Council of Management, Architectural Heritage Fund, 1977–. Pres., Urban Design Gp, 1983–84. Vis. Prof., Internat. Centre for Conservation, Rome, 1972–. *Publications:* The Character of Towns, 1968; articles in architect. and planning magazines. *Recreation:* looking and listening in disbelief. *Address:* 1 Hampers Lane, Horsham, West Sussex RH13 6HB. *T:* Horsham (01403) 254208.

WORSLEY, Lord; George John Sackville Pelham; *b* 9 Aug. 1990; *s* and *heir* of 8th Earl of Yarborough, *qv*.

WORSLEY, Francis Edward, (Jock); Complaints Commissioner, Securities and Investment Board, since 1994; *b* 15 Feb. 1941; *s* of late Francis Arthur Worsley and Mary Worsley; *m* 1962, Caroline Violet (*née* Hatherell); two *s* two *d*. *Educ:* Stonyhurst College. FCA. Articled, Barton, Mayhew & Co., 1959–64; with Anderson Thomas Frankel, Chartered Accountants, 1964–69; Financial Training Co., 1969–93 (Chm., 1972–92). Dir, 1990–94, Dep. Chm., 1992–94, Lautro. Non-executive Director: Cleveland Trust PLC, 1993–; Reece Plc; non-exec. Chm., Lloyds Members Agency Services Ltd, 1994–. Pres., Inst. of Chartered Accountants in England and Wales, 1988–89. Mem., Building Socs Commn, 1991–. *Recreations:* tennis, wine, cooking. *Address:* 136/142 Bramley Road, W10 6SR. *T:* 0181–960 4421.

WORSLEY, Air Cdre Geoffrey Nicolas Ernest T. C.; *see* Tindal-Carill-Worsley.

WORSLEY, Giles Arthington, PhD; FSA; Editor, Perspectives on Architecture, since 1994; Member, Royal Fine Art Commission, since 1994; *b* 22 March 1961; *s* of Sir (William) Marcus (John) Worsley, *qv*. *Educ:* Eton; New Coll., Oxford; Courtauld Inst., Univ. of London (PhD 1989). Country Life: architectural writer, 1985–88; Architectural Editor, 1989–94; Editor, Georgian Group Jl, 1991–94. Member: Historic Buildings and Areas Adv. Cttee, English Heritage, 1995–; Exec. Cttee, Save Britain's Heritage, 1985–; Exec. Cttee, Georgian Gp, 1990–. Prizes incl. Alexander Prize, RHistS, 1992. *Publications:* Architectural Drawings of the Regency Period, 1991; Classical Architecture in Britain: the heroic age, 1995. *Recreations:* walking, reading, buildings. *Address:* 70 Eccleston Square, SW1V 1PJ. *T:* and *Fax:* 0171–821 1993.

WORSLEY, Jock; *see* Worsley, F. E.

WORSLEY, Sir Marcus; *see* Worsley, Sir W. M. J.

WORSLEY, Michael Dominic Laurence; QC 1985; *b* 9 Feb. 1926; *s* of Paul Worsley and Magdalen Teresa Worsley; *m* 1962, Pamela (*née* Philpot) (*d* 1980); one *s* (and one *s* decd); *m* 1986, Jane, *d* of Percival and Mary Sharpe. *Educ:* Bedford School; Inns of Court School of Law. RN 1944–45. Lived in Africa, 1946–52; called to the Bar, Inner Temple, 1955, Bencher, 1980; Standing Prosecuting Counsel to Inland Revenue, 1968–69; Treasury Counsel at Inner London Sessions, 1969–71; Junior Treasury Counsel, 1971–74, Senior Treasury Counsel, 1974–84, CCC. *Recreations:* music, travelling. *Address:* 6 King's Bench Walk, Temple, EC4Y 7DR. *T:* 0171–583 0410. *Clubs:* Garrick, Lansdowne; Thomas More Society.

WORSLEY, Nicholas Jarvis; QC 1993; a Recorder, since 1985; *b* 21 July 1943; *s* of Edgar Taylor Worsley and Vida Worsley (*née* McCormick); *m* 1967, Anna Maxine Bekenn; two *d*. *Educ:* Clifton Coll., Bristol; Fitzwilliam House, Cambridge. Called to the Bar, Inner Temple, 1966. Chm., Agricl Lands Tribunal, 1976–. *Recreations:* contemporary art and design, architecture. *Address:* Lansdowne Crescent, Worcester.

WORSLEY, Paul Frederick; QC 1990; a Recorder, since 1987; *b* 17 Dec. 1947; *s* of Eric Worsley, MBE, GM and Sheila Mary Worsley (*née* Hoskin); *m* 1974, Jennifer Ann, JP, *d* of late Ernest Avery; one *s* one *d*. *Educ:* Hymers College, Hull; Mansfield College, Oxford (MA). Called to the Bar, Middle Temple, 1970 (Astbury Scholar); practised NE Circuit, 1970–. *Recreations:* Spy prints, Whitby, opera, sailing. *Address:* Park Court Chambers, 40 Park Cross Street, Leeds LS1 2QH. *T:* Leeds (0113) 244 3277; 1 Hare Court, EC4Y 7BE. *T:* 0171–353 5324. *Club:* Yorkshire (York).

WORSLEY, Gen. Sir Richard (Edward), GCB 1982 (KCB 1976); OBE 1964; Pilkington Brothers, 1982–86; Chairman: Western Provident Assoc., since 1989; Electro-Optical Division, Pilkington Group, 1984–86 (Chief Executive, 1982–86); Barr and Stroud, 1982–86; Pilkington PE, 1982–86; *b* 29 May 1923; *s* of H. H. K. Worsley, Grey Abbey, Co. Down; *m* 1st, 1959, Sarah Anne Mitchell; one *s* one *d*; 2nd, 1980, Caroline, Duchess of Fife, *er d* of 3rd Baron Forteviot, MBE. *Educ:* Radley Coll. Served War: commissioned into Rifle Bde, 1942, Middle East and Italian Campaigns, 1942–45. Instr, RMA Sandhurst, 1948–51; Malayan Emergency, 1956–57; Instr, Staff Coll., Camberley, 1958–61; CO, The Royal Dragoons, 1962–65; Comdr, 7th Armoured Bde, 1965–67; Imperial Defence Coll., 1968; Chief of Staff, Far East Land Forces, 1969–71; GOC 3rd Div., 1972–74; Vice-QMG, MoD, 1974–76; GOC 1 (Br) Corps, 1976–78; QMG, 1979–82. Freeman: City of London, 1983; Glass Sellers' Co., 1984. *Recreations:* shooting, ornithology. *Club:* Cavalry and Guards.

WORSLEY, Sir (William) Marcus (John), 5th Bt *cr* 1838; JP; Lord-Lieutenant of North Yorkshire, since 1987; *b* 6 April 1925; *s* of Colonel Sir William Arthington Worsley, 4th Bt, and Joyce Morgan (*d* 1979), *d* of Sir John Fowler Brunner, 2nd Bt; *S* father, 1973; *m* 1955, Hon. Bridget Assheton, *d* of 1st Baron Clitheroe, PC, KCVO; three *s* one *d*. *Educ:* Eton; New Coll., Oxford. Green Howards, 1943–47 (Lieut seconded to Royal West African Frontier Force). BA Hons (Oxford) Modern History, 1949. Programme Assistant, BBC European Service, 1950–53. Contested (C) Keighley, 1955; MP (C) Keighley, 1959–64, Chelsea, 1966–Sept. 1974; Parliamentary Private Secretary: to Minister of Health, 1960–61; to Minister without Portfolio, 1962–64; to Lord President of the Council, 1970–72. Second Church Estates Commissioner, 1970–74; a Church Commissioner, 1976–84. Pres., Royal Forestry Soc. of England, Wales and N Ireland, 1980–82 (Vice-Pres., 1976–80); National Trust: Dep. Chm., 1986–92; Chm., Yorks Reg. Cttee, 1969–80; Chm., Properties Cttee, 1980–90. Hon. Col, 2nd Bn, Yorkshire Volunteers, 1988–93. JP 1957 (Chm., Malton Bench, 1983–90), DL 1978–87, North Yorks; High Sheriff of North Yorks, 1982. KStJ 1987. *Recreations:* walking, reading. *Heir:* *s* William Ralph Worsley, FRICS [*b* 12 Sept. 1956; *m* 1987, Marie-Noëlle, *yr d* of Bernard H. Dreesmann; two *d*]. *Address:* Hovingham Hall, York YO6 4LU. *T:* Hovingham (01653) 628206. *Club:* Boodle's.

WORSTHORNE, Sir Peregrine (Gerard), Kt 1991; writer; Editor, Comment Section, Sunday Telegraph, 1989–91; *b* 22 Dec. 1923; *s* of Col Koch de Gooreynd, OBE (who assumed surname of Worsthorne by deed poll, 1921), and Baroness Norman, CBE; *m* 1st, 1950, Claude Bertrand de Colasse (*d* 1990); one *d*; 2nd, 1991, Lady Lucinda, *d* of Viscount Lambton, *qv*. *Educ:* Stowe; Peterhouse, Cambridge (BA); Magdalen Coll., Oxford. Commnd Oxf. and Bucks LI, 1942; attached Phantom, GHQ Liaison Regt, 1944–45. Sub-editor, Glasgow Herald, 1946; Editorial staff: Times, 1948–53; Daily Telegraph, 1953–61; Deputy Editor, Sunday Telegraph, 1961–76, Associate Editor, 1976–86, Editor, 1986–89. *Publications:* The Socialist Myth, 1972; Peregrinations: selected pieces, 1980; By the Right, 1987; Tricks of Memory (autobiog.), 1993. *Recreations:* tennis, reading. *Address:* The Old Rectory, Hedgerley, Bucks SL2 3UY. *T:* Slough (01753) 646167. *Clubs:* Beefsteak, Garrick, Pratt's.

See also Sir S. P. E. C. W. Towneley.

WORSWICK, (George) David (Norman), CBE 1981; FBA 1979; Director, National Institute of Economic and Social Research, 1965–82; *b* 18 Aug. 1916; *s* of Thomas Worswick, OBE, and Eveline (*née* Green); *m* 1940, Sylvia, *d* of A. E. Walsh, MBE; one *s* two *d* (and one *s* decd). *Educ:* St Paul's Sch.; New Coll., Oxford (Scholar). Final Hons (Maths), 1937; Dipl. in Economics and Political Science, 1938. Research staff, Oxford Univ. Institute of Statistics, 1940–60; Fellow and Tutor in Economics, Magdalen Coll., Oxford, 1945–65 (Sen. Tutor, 1955–57; Vice-President, 1963–65; Emeritus Fellow, 1969). Vis. Prof. of Economics, MIT, 1962–63. Mem., SSRC, 1966–70. President: Sect. F, British Assoc., 1971; Royal Econ. Soc., 1982–84. Hon. DSc City, 1975. *Publications:* (ed jtly) The British Economy 1945–50, 1952; (ed jtly) The British Economy in the 1950's, 1962; (ed) The Free Trade Proposals, 1960; (jtly) Profits in the British Economy 1909–1938, 1967; (ed) Uses of Economics, 1972; (ed jtly) The Medium Term, 1974; (ed) The Concept and Measurement of Involuntary Unemployment, 1976; (ed jtly) Keynes and the Modern World, 1983; (ed) Education and Economic Performance, 1985; Unemployment: a problem of policy, 1991; articles in academic jls. *Address:* 25 Beech Croft Road, Oxford OX2 7AY. *T:* Oxford (01865) 52486. *Club:* United Oxford & Cambridge University.

See also R. D. Worswick.

WORSWICK, Dr Richard David, CChem, FRSC; Government Chemist and Chief Executive, Laboratory of the Government Chemist, since 1991; *b* 22 July 1946; *s* of (George) David (Norman) Worswick, *qv*; *m* 1970, Jacqueline Brigit Isobel Adcock; three *d*. *Educ:* New College, Oxford (BA Hons Nat. Sci. 1969; MA 1972; DPhil 1972). CChem, FRSC 1991. SRC post-doctorate res. asst, Inorganic Chem. Lab., Oxford, 1972–73; Res. Admin, Boots Co., Nottingham, 1973–76; Harwell Lab., UKAEA, 1976–91: marketing and planning, 1976–85; Head, Res. Planning and Inf. Services, 1985–87; Head, Safety Branch, 1988; Head, Envtl and Med. Scis Div., 1988–90; Dir, Process Technology and Instrumentation, AEA Industrial Technology, 1990–91. *Publications:* research papers in sci. jls. *Recreations:* listening to music, playing the violin, gardening. *Address:* Laboratory of the Government Chemist, Queen's Road, Teddington, Middx TW11 0LY. *T:* 0181–943 7300.

WORTH, Irene, Hon. CBE 1975; actress; *b* 23 June 1916. *Educ:* University of California, Los Angeles (BE). Antoinette Perry Award for distinguished achievement in the Theatre, 1965. First appeared as Fenella in Escape Me Never, New York, 1942; debut on Broadway as Cecily Harden in The Two Mrs Carrolls, Booth Theatre, 1943. Studied for six months with Elsie Fogerty, 1944–45. Subsequently appeared frequently at Mercury, Bolton's, Q, Embassy, etc. Parts include: Anabelle Jones in Love Goes to Press, Duchess Theatre, 1946 (after Embassy); Ilona Szabo in The Play's the Thing, St James's, 1947 (after tour and Lyric, Hammersmith); Eileen Perry in Edward my Son, Lyric, 1948; Lady Fortrose in Home is Tomorrow, Cambridge Theatre, 1948; Olivia Raines in Champagne for Delilah, New, 1949; Celia Coplestone in The Cocktail Party, New, 1950 (after Edinburgh Festival, 1949; Henry Miller Theatre, New York, 1950); Desdemona in Othello, Old Vic, 1951; Helena in Midsummer Night's Dream, Old Vic, 1952; Catherine de Vausselles in The Other Heart, Old Vic, 1952; Lady Macbeth in Macbeth, Desdemona in Othello, Helena in Midsummer Night's Dream, Catherine de Vausselles in The Other Heart, Old Vic tour of S Africa, 1952; Portia in The Merchant of Venice, Old Vic, 1953; Helena in All's Well That Ends Well and Queen Margaret in Richard III, First Season Shakespeare Festival Theatre, Stratford, Ont, Canada, 1953; Frances Farrar in A Day By The Sea, Haymarket, 1953–54; Alcestis in A Life in the Sun, Edinburgh Festival, 1955; leading rôles in: The Queen and the Rebels, Haymarket, 1955; Hotel Paradiso, Winter Garden, 1956; Mary Stuart, Phœnix Theatre, NY, 1957, Old Vic, 1958; The Potting Shed, Globe Theatre, London, 1958; Rosalind in As You Like It, Shakespeare Festival Theatre, Stratford, Ont, 1959; Albertine Prine in Toys in the Attic, Hudson Theatre, New York, 1960 (NY Newspaper Guild Page One Award); Season at Royal Shakespeare Theatre, Stratford, 1962; Goneril in King Lear, Aldwych, 1962; Doctor Mathilde von Zahnd in The Physicists, Aldwych, 1963; Clodia Pulcher in The Ides of March, Haymarket, 1963; World tour of King Lear for Royal Shakespeare Company, 1964; Alice in Tiny Alice, Billy Rose Theatre, New York, 1965 (Tony award 1965), Aldwych, 1970; Hilde in A Song at Twilight, Anne in Shadows of the Evening, Anna-Mary in Come into the Garden Maud (Noël Coward Trilogy), Queen's, 1966 (Evening Standard Award); Hesione Hushabye in Heartbreak House, Chichester and Lyric, 1967 (Variety Club of GB Award, 1967); Jocasta in Seneca's Oedipus, National Theatre, 1968; Hedda in Hedda Gabler, Stratford, Ont, 1970; worked with internat. Co. for Theatre Res., Paris and Iran, 1971; Notes on a Love Affair, Globe, 1972; Madame Arkadina, The Seagull, Chichester, 1973; Hamlet, Ghosts, The Seagull, Greenwich, 1974; Sweet Bird of Youth, Lake Forest, Washington, New York, 1975 (Tony Award, 1975; Jefferson Award, 1975); The Cherry Orchard, NY, 1977 (Drama Desk Award, 1977); Happy Days, NY, 1979; The Lady from Dubuque, NY, 1980; L'Olimpiade, Edinburgh Fest., 1982; The Chalk Garden, NY, 1982; The Physicists, Washington, 1983; The Golden Age, NY, 1984; Coriolanus, Nat. Theatre, 1984; The Bay at Nice, Nat. Theatre, 1986; You Never Can Tell, Haymarket, 1987; Volumnia in Coriolanus, Public Theatre, NY, 1988–89; Lake Forest, Ill, productions: Misalliance, 1976; Old Times, 1977; After the Season, 1978; Lost in Yonkers, NY, 1991 (Tony Award, 1991). *Films:* Orders to Kill, 1957 (British Film Academy Award for Best Woman's Performance, 1958); The Scapegoat, 1958; King Lear (Goneril), 1970; Nicholas and Alexandra, 1971; Eye Witness, 1980; Deathtrap, 1982; Fast Forward, 1985; Lost in Yonkers, 1993. *Television:* The Lady from the Sea, BBC, 1953; The Lake, BBC, 1953 (Daily Mail National Television Award, 1953–54), and has subseq. appeared on television and acted with CBC Television in NY and Canada; Coriolanus (BBC Shakespeare series), 1984. Hon. Dr Arts Tufts Univ., 1980; Hon. DFA Queen's Coll., NY, 1986. Whitbread Anglo-American Award for Outstanding Actress, 1967; NY Theatre Hall of Fame, 1979; Obie Award for outstanding achievement in the theatre, 1989. *Recreation:* music. *Address:* c/o ICM, Sam Cohn, 40 West 57th Street, New York, NY 10019, USA.

WORTH, Prof. Katharine Joyce; Professor of Drama and Theatre Studies in the University of London at Royal Holloway and Bedford New College, 1985–87, now Emeritus (at Royal Holloway College, 1978–85); *b* 4 Aug. 1922; *d* of George and Elizabeth Lorimer; *m* 1947, George Worth; two *s* one *d*. *Educ:* Bedford Coll., Univ. of London (BA English, MA res. degree, PhD). Lectr in drama and theatre history (pt-time), Central Sch. of Speech and Drama and for Univ. of London Dept of Extra-Mural Studies, 1948 intermittently until 1963; Lectr 1964–74, Reader 1974–78, in English Lit., RHC; Hon. Fellow, RHBNC, 1990. Leverhulme Professorial Fellowship, 1987–89. Vis. Prof., KCL, 1987–. Hon. Pres., Consortium for Drama and Media in Higher Educn, 1987–; Co-editor, Theatre Notebook, 1987–; Editorial Board: Yeats Annual, 1985–; Modern Drama, 1985–; Univ. of Michigan Press, 1988–. Prodns of Beckett's TV play, Eh Joe, and his radio plays, Words and Music, Embers and Cascando, 1972–84 (music for Words and Music and Cascando by Humphrey Searle); stage adaptation of Samuel Beckett's Company, perf. Edinburgh, Belfast, London and NY, 1987–88. *Publications:* Revolutions in Modern English Drama, 1973; (ed) Beckett the Shape Changer, 1975; The Irish Drama of Europe: from Yeats to Beckett, 1978; Oscar Wilde, 1983; Maeterlinck's Plays in Performance, 1985; (critical edn): W. B. Yeats: Where There is Nothing, and, W. B. Yeats and Lady Gregory: The Unicorn from the Stars, 1987; Waiting for Godot and Happy Days: text and performance, 1990; Sheridan and Goldsmith, 1992; many articles and reviews on modern drama in symposia and in English, Irish and Amer. jls, incl. Modern Drama, TLS, Irish Univ. Rev., Th. Notebook, etc. *Recreations:* foreign travel, theatre, art galleries, walking in the country. *Address:* 48 Elmfield Avenue, Teddington, Mddx TW11 8BT. *T:* 0181–977 5778.

WORTHINGTON, Anthony, (Tony); MP (Lab) Clydebank and Milngavie, since 1987; *b* 11 Oct. 1941; *s* of Malcolm and Monica Worthington; *m* 1966, Angela Oliver; one *s* one *d*. *Educ:* LSE (BA Hons); Univ. of Glasgow (MEd). Lecturer, Social Policy and Sociology: HM Borstal, Dover, 1962–66; Monkwearmouth Coll. of Further Educn, Sunderland, 1967–71; Jordanhill Coll. of Educn, Glasgow, 1971–87. Councillor, Strathclyde Region, 1974–87 (Chm., Finance Cttee, 1986–87). Opposition front bench spokesman: on educn and employment in Scotland, 1989–92; on overseas develt, 1992–93; on foreign affairs, 1993–94; on Northern Ireland, 1995–. Mem., Home Affairs Select Cttee, 1987–89; Sec., All Party Population and Develt Gp, 1989–. Chm., Labour Campaign for Criminal Justice, 1987–89. *Recreations:* sailing, running, gardening. *Address:* 24 Cleddans Crescent, Hardgate, Clydebank G81 5NW. *T:* Duntocher (01389) 873195. *Clubs:* Royal Gourock Yacht; Radnor Park Bowling.

WORTHINGTON, Edgar Barton, CBE 1967; MA, PhD; environmental consultant; *b* 13 Jan. 1905; *s* of Edgar Worthington and Amy E. Beale; *m* 1st, 1930, Stella Desmond Johnson (*d* 1978); three *d*; 2nd, 1980, Harriett Stockton, Cape Cod. *Educ:* Rugby; Gonville and Caius Coll., Cambridge. Expeditions to African Lakes, 1927–31; Balfour Student, 1930–33, and Demonstrator in Zoology, Cambridge Univ., 1933–37; Scientist for the African Research Survey, 1934–37; Mungo Park Medal, RSGS, 1939; Director of Laboratories and Secretary of Freshwater Biological Assoc., Windermere, 1937–46; Scientific Adviser to Middle East Supply Centre, 1943–45; Development Adviser, Uganda, 1946; Scientific Secretary to Colonial Research Council, 1946–49, to E Africa High Commission, 1950–51; Secretary-General to Scientific Council for Africa South of the Sahara, 1951–55; Deputy Director-General (Scientific) Nature Conservancy, 1957–65; Scientific Dir, Internat. Biological Programme, 1964–74; Pres., Cttee on Water Res. of Internat. Council of Scientific Unions, 1973–77. Mem. of Honour, IUCN, 1978; Mem. (*hc*), Linnean Soc., 1991. Avicenne Medal, UNESCO, 1993. Order of Golden Ark (Netherlands), 1976. *Publications:* (with Stella Worthington) Inland Waters of Africa, 1933; Science in Africa, 1938; Middle East Science, 1946; Development Plan for Uganda, 1947; (with T. T. Macan) Life in Lakes and Rivers, 1951, rev. edn 1973; Science in the Development of Africa, 1958 (trans. French, 1960); (ed) Man-made Lakes: problems and environmental effects, 1973; Evolution of the IBP, 1975; (ed) Arid Land Irrigation: problems and environmental effects, 1976; The Nile, 1978; The Ecological Century, 1983; official reports and papers in scientific journals. *Recreations:* nature conservation, field sports and farming. *Address:* Colin Godmans, Furner's Green, Uckfield, East Sussex TN22 3RR. *T:* Chelwood Gate (01825) 740322. *Clubs:* Athenæum, Farmers'.

WORTHINGTON, His Honour George Noel; a Circuit Judge, 1979–94; *b* 22 June 1923; *s* of late George Errol Worthington and Edith Margaret Boys Worthington; *m* 1954, Jacqueline Kemble Lightfoot, 2nd *d* of late G. L. S. Lightfoot and Mrs Lightfoot; one *s* one *d* (and one *s* decd). *Educ:* Rossall Sch., Lancashire. Served War of 1939–45 in Royal Armoured Corps, 1941–46. Admitted a solicitor, 1949; a Recorder of the Crown Court, 1972–79. Liveryman, Wax Chandlers' Co. *Recreations:* gardening, theatre. *Club:* Athenæum.

WÖSSNER, Dr Mark Matthias; President and Chief Executive Officer, Bertelsmann AG, since 1983. *Educ:* Stuttgart Technical University (DrIng). Management Asst, Bertelsmann AG, Gütersloh, 1968; Mohndruck (Bertelsmann largest printing operation): Production Manager, 1970; Technical Dir, 1972; Gen. Manager, 1974; Mem. Exec. Bd, Bertelsmann, 1976; Dep. Chm. of Bd, 1981, Chm., 1983. *Address:* Bertelsmann AG, Postfach 111, 33311 Gütersloh, Germany. *T:* 05241800.

WOUK, Herman; author, US; *b* New York, 27 May 1915; *s* of Abraham Isaac Wouk and Esther Wouk (*née* Levine); *m* 1945, Betty Sarah Brown; two *s* (and one *s* decd). *Educ:* Townsend Harris High Sch.; Columbia Univ. (AB). Radio script writer, 1935–41; Vis. Professor of English, Yeshiva Univ., 1952–57; Presidential consultative expert to the United States Treasury, 1941. Served United States Naval Reserve, 1942–46, Deck Officer (four campaign stars). Member Officers' Reserve Naval Services. Trustee, College of the Virgin Islands, 1961–69. Hon. LHD Yeshiva Univ., New York City, 1954; Hon. DLit: Clark Univ., 1960; American Internat. Coll., 1979; Hon. PhD Bar-Ilan, 1990. Columbia University Medal for excellence, 1952; Alexander Hamilton Medal, Columbia Univ., 1980; Berkeley Medal, Univ. of Calif, 1984; Golden Plate Award, Amer. Acad. of Achievement, 1986; Lone Sailor Award, US Navy Meml Foundn, 1987; Kazetnik Award, Yad Vashem, 1990. *Publications: novels:* Aurora Dawn, 1947; The City Boy, 1948; The Caine Mutiny (Pulitzer Prize), 1951; Marjorie Morningstar, 1955; Youngblood Hawke, 1962; Don't Stop The Carnival, 1965; The Winds of War, 1971 (televised 1983); War and Remembrance, 1978 (televised 1989); Inside, Outside (Washington Book Award), 1985; The Hope, 1993; The Glory, 1994; *plays:* The Traitor, 1949; The Caine Mutiny Court-Martial, 1953; Nature's Way, 1957; *non-fiction:* This Is My God, 1959. *Address:* c/o BSW Literary Agency, 303 Crestview Drive, Palm Springs, CA 92264, USA. *Clubs:* Cosmos, Metropolitan (Washington); Bohemian (San Francisco); Century (New York).

WRAGG, Prof. Edward Conrad; Professor of Education, Exeter University, since 1978 (Director, School of Education, 1978–94); *b* 26 June 1938; *s* of George William and Maria Wragg; *m* 1960, Judith (*née* King); one *s* two *d*. *Educ:* King Edward VII Grammar Sch., Sheffield; Durham Univ. (BA Hons German Cl. 1; Postgrad. CertEd, Cl. 1); Leicester Univ. (MEd); Exeter Univ. (PhD). Asst Master, Queen Elizabeth Grammar Sch., Wakefield, 1960–64; Head of German, Wyggeston Boys' Sch., Leicester, 1964–66; Lectr in Education, Exeter Univ., 1966–73; Prof. of Educn, Nottingham Univ., 1973–78. Pres., British Educnl Research Assoc., 1981–82; Specialist Adviser, Parliamentary Select Cttee, 1976–77; Chairman: School Broadcasting Council for UK, 1981–86; Educnl Broadcasting Council for UK, 1986–87; BBC Regl Adv. Council for South and West, 1989–92, for South, 1992–; Member: Educnl Res. Bd, SSRC, 1974–78; Educn Sub-Cttee, UGC, 1981–89. Specialist Advr in Educn, UFC, 1989–. Presenter of radio and TV series and items on education, including Chalkface (Granada), Crisis in Education (BBC), The Education Roadshow (BBC), The Education Programme (BBC), Pebble Mill at One (BBC), Teaching Today (BBC). Editor, Research Papers in Education, 1986–. FCP 1988. DUniv: Open, 1989; Strathclyde, 1993. *Publications:* Teaching Teaching, 1974; Teaching Mixed Ability Groups, 1976; Classroom Interaction, 1976; A Handbook for School Governors, 1980; Class Management and Control, 1981; A Review of Teacher Education, 1982; Swineshead Revisited, 1982; Classroom Teaching Skills, 1984; Pearls from Swineshire, 1984; The Domesday Project, 1985; Education: an action guide for parents, 1986; Teacher Appraisal, 1987; Education in the Market Place, 1988; The Wragged Edge, 1988; Parents and Schools, 1989; Riches from Wragg, 1990; Mad Curriculum Disease, 1991; Class Management, 1993; Questioning, 1993; Explaining, 1993; Primary Teaching Skills, 1993; The Parents' File, 1993; No, Minister!, 1993; An Introduction to Classroom Observation, 1994; Flying Boot, 1994; Effective Teaching, 1994; frequent contributor to Guardian, Times Educnl Supp. (regular columnist), Times Higher Educn Supp., Observer, Independent, Good Housekeeping. *Recreations:* football playing, watching and coaching; cooking, running, writing, music. *Address:* 14 Doriam Close, Exeter EX4 4RS. *T:* Exeter (01392) 491052.

WRAGG, John, RA 1991 (ARA 1983); sculptor; *b* 20 Oct. 1937; *s* of Arthur and Ethel Wragg. *Educ:* York Sch. of Art; Royal Coll. of Art. *Work in Public Collections:* Israel Mus., Jerusalem; Tate Gall.; Arts Council of GB; Arts Council of NI; Contemp. Art Soc.; Wellington Art Gall., NZ; work in private collections in GB, America, Canada, France and Holland. *One-man Exhibitions:* Hanover Gall., 1963, 1966 and 1970; Galerie Alexandre Iolas, Paris, 1968; York Fest., 1969; Bridge Street Gall., Bath, 1982; Katherine House Gall., Marlborough, 1984; Quinton Green Fine Art, London, 1985; Devizes Mus. Gall., 1994; England & Co., London, 1994; L'Art Abstrait, London, 1995; *Exhibitions:* Lords Gall., 1959; L'Art Vivant, 1965–68; Arts Council Gall., Belfast, 1966; Pittsburgh Internat., 1967; Britische Kunst heute, Hamburg, Fondn Maeght, and Contemp. Art Fair, Florence, 1968; Bath Fest. Gall., 1977 and 1984; Artists Market, 1978; Biennale di Scultura di Arese, Milan, and King Street Gall., Bristol, 1980; Galerie Bollhagen Worpswede, N Germany, 1981 and 1983; Quinton Green Fine Art, London, 1984, 1985, 1986 and 1987; Best of British, Simpsons, 1993; Connought Brown, 1993. Sainsbury Award, 1960; Winner of Sainsbury Sculpture Comp., King's Road, Chelsea, 1966; Arts Council Major Award, 1977; Chantry Bequest, 1981. *Relevant Publications:* chapters and articles about his work in: Neue Dimensionen der Plastic, 1964; Contemporary British Artists, 1979; British Sculpture in the Twentieth Century, 1981; Studio Internat., Art & Artiste, Sculpture Internat., Arts Rev., and The Artist. *Recreation:* walking. *Address:* 6 Castle Lane, Devizes, Wilts SN10 1HJ. *T:* Devizes (01380) 727087.

WRAIGHT, Sir John (Richard), KBE 1976; CMG 1962; HM Diplomatic Service, retired; company consultant and company director, since 1976; *b* 4 June 1916; *s* of late Richard George Wraight; *m* 1947, Marquita Elliott. *Educ:* Selhurst Grammar Sch.; London Univ. extension courses at SSEES. Served War of 1939–45 with Honourable Artillery Company and RHA, Western Desert and Libya; Balkans Section, Ministry of Economic Warfare Mission in the Middle East, Cairo, 1944. Economic Warfare Adviser, HQ Mediterranean Allied Air Forces, Italy, June-Dec. 1944. Worked in City of London, 1933–39; Foreign Office, 1945; Special Assistant to Chief of UNRRA Operations in Europe, 1946 (special missions to Vienna, Prague and Belgrade). Entered Foreign (subseq. Diplomatic) Service, 1947; British Embassy: Athens, 1948; Tel Aviv, 1950 (negotiated first British financial agreement with new state); Washington, 1953; Asst Head of Economic Relations Dept, Foreign Office, 1957; Counsellor (Commercial): Cairo, 1959 (helped to restore trade links after Suez); Brussels and Luxembourg, 1962 (UK Comr on Tripartite Commn for Restitution of Monetary Gold, Brussels, 1962–68); Minister and Consul-General, Milan, 1968–73; Ambassador to Switzerland, 1973–76. Internat. consultant to Phillips & Drew, 1976–88. Pres., Greater London SW Scout County, 1977–. Commander of the Order of the Crown (Belgium), 1966. *Publications:* The Food Situation in Austria, 1946; The Swiss and the British, 1987; The Swiss in London, 1991. *Recreations:* music, gardening, birdwatching. *Address:* 35 Jameson Street, W8 7SH.

WRAN, Hon. Neville Kenneth, AC 1988; QC (NSW) 1968; Premier of New South Wales, 1976–86. *Educ:* Fort Street Boys' High Sch., Sydney; Sydney Univ. (LLB). Solicitor before admission to Bar of NSW, 1957. Joined Australian Labor Party, 1954, Nat. Pres., 1980–86. Elected to Legislative Council, 1970; Dep. Leader of Opposition, 1971; Leader of Opposition, Legislative Council, 1972; MLA for Bass Hill, Nov. 1973–1986; Leader of Opposition, Dec. 1973–76. Chm., CSIRO, 1986–91. Is especially interested in law reform, civil liberties, industrial relations, conservation and cultural matters. Chm., Turnbull and Partners, investment bankers, 1987–. Chm., Lionel Murphy Foundn. Australian Mem., Eminent Persons' Gp, Asia-Pacific Econ. Co-operation, 1993–. Dep. Chancellor, Bond Univ., 1992–. FRSA 1990. Hon. LLD, 1995. *Recreations:* reading, walking, swimming, tennis. *Address:* GPO Box 4545, Sydney, NSW 2001, Australia. *Clubs:* Sydney Labor (Hon. Life Mem.), University and Schools (Sydney).

WRATTEN, Donald Peter; Director, National Counties Building Society, since 1985; *b* 8 July 1925; *er s* of late Frederick George and Marjorie Wratten; *m* 1947, Margaret Kathleen (*née* Marsh); one *s* one *d*. *Educ:* Morehall Elem. Sch. and Harvey Grammar Sch., Folkestone; London Sch. of Economics. Storehand, temp. clerk, meteorological asst (Air Min.), 1940–43; service with RAF Meteorological Wing, 1943–47. LSE, 1947–50. Joined Post Office, 1950; Private Sec. to Asst Postmaster Gen., 1955–56; seconded to Unilever Ltd, 1959; Private Sec. to Postmaster Gen., 1965–66; Head of Telecommunications Marketing Div., 1966–67; Director: Eastern Telecommunications Region, 1967–69; Exec. Dir, Giro and Remittance Services, 1969–74 (Sen. Dir, 1970–74); Sen. Dir, Data Processing Service, 1974–75; Sen. Dir, Telecom Personnel, 1975–81. Member: Industrial Adv. Panel, City Univ. Business Sch., 1974–81 (Chm., 1977–81); Court, Cranfield Inst. of Technology, 1976–81; Business Educn Council, 1977–83; Council: Intermediate Technology Develt Gp, 1982–85; Internat. Stereoscopic Union, 1987–; Chm., Stereoscopic Soc., 1993– (Vice-Chm., 1990–92). Chm., Radlett Soc. & Green Belt Assoc., 1989–. *Publication:* The Book of Radlett and Aldenham, 1990. *Recreations:* 3-D photography, social history. *Address:* 10 Homefield Road, Radlett, Herts WD7 8PY. *T:* Radlett (01923) 854500.

WRATTEN, Air Chief Marshal Sir William (John), KBE 1991 (CBE 1982); CB 1991; AFC 1973; FRAeS; Air Officer Commanding-in-Chief Strike Command, and Commander Allied Air Forces Northwestern Europe, since 1994; Air Aide-de-Camp to the Queen, since 1995; *b* 15 Aug. 1939; *s* of William Wellesley Wratten and Gwenneth Joan (*née* Bourne); *m* 1963, Susan Jane Underwood; two *s* two *d*. *Educ:* Chatham House Grammar Sch., Ramsgate; RAF Coll., Cranwell. FRAeS 1991. OC, RAF Coningsby, 1980–82; Sen. RAF Officer, Falkland Is, 1982; RCDS, 1983; Dir, Operational Requirements (RAF), MoD, 1984–86; SASO, HQ 1 Gp, 1986–89; AOC No 11 Gp, 1989–91; Air Comdr British Forces ME, and Dep. to Comdr (on attachment), Nov. 1990–March 1991; Dir Gen., Saudi Armed Forces Project, 1992–94. Legionnaire, Legion of Merit (USA), 1993. *Recreation:* golf. *Club:* Royal Air Force.

WRAXALL, 2nd Baron, *cr* 1928, of Clyst St George, Co. Devon; **George Richard Lawley Gibbs;** DL; landowner, farmer and forester, since 1954; *b* 16 May 1928 (for whom Queen Mary was sponsor); *er s* of 1st Baron and Hon. Ursula Mary Lawley, OBE 1945, RRC (*d* 1979), *e d* of 6th Baron Wenlock; *S* father 1931. *Educ:* Eton; RMA Sandhurst. Coldstream Guards, 1946–53; 2nd Lieut, 1948; Actg Captain, 1953; Captain, RARO, 1954; Lieut North Somerset Yeomanry/44 Royal Tank Regt (TA), Dec. 1958; Captain, 1962; Major, 1965; retired 1967. Chairman: N Somerset Conservative Assoc., 1970–74; Avon County Scout Council, 1976–; N Somerset Yeo. Regtl Assoc., 1989– (Trustee, 1970–); President: Assoc. of Professional Foresters, 1991–95; Woodspring Cons. Assoc., 1992– (Life Vice-Pres. and Trustee, 1984–); Council Mem., Royal Bath and West Show, 1955–89. Mem., Exec. Cttee, Woodard Corporation, 1983–92; Chm. Governors, St Katherine's Sch., Avon, 1976 81; Fellow, Woodard Schs (Western Div.), 1979–92. Patron, N Somerset Agricl Soc., 1988–. Patron of benefices: Flax Bourton, dio. Bath and Wells; Exwick, and Clyst St George, dio. Exeter. DL Avon, 1974. *Heir: b* Hon. Sir Eustace Hubert Beilby Gibbs, *qv*. *Address:* Tyntesfield, Wraxall, Bristol, Avon BS19 1NU. *T:* Flax Bourton (01275) 462923. *Clubs:* Royal Automobile, Cavalry and Guards; Clifton (Bristol).

WRAXALL, Sir Charles (Frederick Lascelles), 9th Bt *cr* 1813; Assistant Accountant, 1987–89; *b* 17 Sept. 1961; *s* of Sir Morville William Lascelles Wraxall, 8th Bt, and of Lady (Irmgard Wilhelmina) Wraxall; *S* father, 1978; *m* 1983, Lesley Linda, *d* of William Albert and Molly Jean Allan; one *s* one *d*. *Educ:* Archbishop Tenison's Grammar School, Croydon. *Recreations:* stamp and postcard collection, watching football. *Heir: s* William Nathaniel Lascelles Wraxall, *b* 3 April 1987.

WRAY, Prof. Gordon Richard, FRS 1986; FEng 1980; Eur Ing; Royal Academy of Engineering Professor in Principles of Engineering Design, Engineering Design Institute, Loughborough University of Technology, 1988–93, now Professor Emeritus; *b* 30 Jan. 1928; *s* of Joseph and Letitia Wray (*née* Jones); *m* 1954, Kathleen Senior; one *s* one *d*. *Educ:* Bolton Tech. Coll., Univ. of Manchester (BScTech, MScTech, PhD); DSc Loughborough; FIMechE, FTI; FRSA. Engineering apprentice, Bennis Combustion, Bolton, 1943; Design draughtsman, Dobson & Barlow, Bolton, 1946; Sir Walter Preston Scholar, Univ. of Manchester, 1949; Develt Engineer, Platts (Barton), 1952; Lectr in Mech. Engrg, Bolton Tech. Coll., 1953; Lectr in Textile Engrg, UMIST, 1955; Loughborough University of Technology: Reader, 1966–70, Prof. and Hd of Dept, 1970–88, Dept of Mech. Engrg; Dir, Engrg Design Inst., 1988–91. Springer Vis. Prof., Univ. of California, Berkeley, 1977. Lectures: Brunel, BAAS, 1980; Thomas Hawksley Meml, IMechE, 1989. Member: DoI Chief Scientist's Requirements Bd, 1974–75; CEI/CSTI Interdisciplinary Bd, 1978–83; SEFI Cttee on Innovation, Brussels, 1980–82; Royal Soc. Working Gp on Agricl Engrg, 1981–82; SERC Applied Mechanics Cttee, 1982–85; Fellowship of Engrg Working Party on DoI Requirements Bds, 1982; SERC Working Party on Engrg Design, 1983; Royal Soc. Sectional Cttee 4 (i), 1986–89; Cttee, Engrg Profs Conf., 1986–88; Royal Soc. Mullard Award Cttee, 1986–92; Royal Soc./SERC Industrial Fellowships Panel, 1986–89; Royal Soc. Technology Activities Cttee, 1989–93; Chm., Engrg Council/Design Council Wkg Party on Attaining Competences in Engrg Design, 1989–91. First recipient of title European Engineer (Eur Ing), Paris, 1987. Mem. Council, IMechE, 1964–67 (Chm., Manip. and Mech. Handling Machinery Gp, 1969–71). Chm., Judging Panel, William Lee Quatercentenary Technology Prize, 1989. Hon. MIED 1990. IMechE Prizes: Viscount Weir, 1959; Water Arbitration, 1972; James Clayton, 1975; Warner Medal, Textile Inst., 1976; S. G. Brown Award and Medal, Royal Soc., 1978; Engrg Merit Award, ASME, 1977. *Publications:* (contrib.) Textile Engineering Processes, ed Nissan, 1959; Modern Yarn Production from Man-made Fibres, 1960; Modern Developments in Weaving Machinery, 1961; An Introduction to the Study of Spinning, 3rd edn 1962; (contrib.) Contemporary Textile Engineering, ed Happey, 1982; numerous papers to learned jls. *Recreations:* fell-walking, photography, steam traction engines, theatre, music, gardening, DIY. *Address:* Stonestack, Rempstone, Loughborough, Leics LE12 6RH. *T:* Wymeswold (01509) 880043.

WRAY, James; MP (Lab) Glasgow, Provan, since 1987; *b* 28 April 1938; *m*; one *s* two *d*. Heavy goods vehicle driver. Mem., Strathclyde Regl Council, 1976. President: Scottish Fedn of the Blind, 1987 (Vice Pres., 1986); St Enoch's Drug Centre; Scottish Ex-Boxers' Assoc.; Gorbals United FC. Mem., TGWU. *Address:* Robin Hill Cott, Hazelden Road, Newton Mearns, Glasgow G77 6RR; House of Commons, SW1A 0AA.

WRAY, (Karen) Prudence Patricia, (Mrs B. H. Wray); *see* Skene, K. P. P.

WRENBURY, 3rd Baron, *cr* 1915; **Rev. John Burton Buckley;** Non-Stipendiary Minister, Brightling, Dallington, Mountfield and Netherfield, diocese of Chichester, since 1990; *b* 18 June 1927; *s* of 2nd Baron and Helen Malise (*d* 1981), 2nd *d* of late His Honour John Cameron Graham of Ballewan, Stirlingshire; *S* father, 1940; *m* 1st, 1956, Carolyn Joan Maule (marr. diss., 1961), *o d* of Lt-Col Ian Burn-Murdoch, OBE, of Gartincaber, Doune, Perthshire; 2nd, 1961, Penelope Sara Frances, *o d* of Edward D. Fort, The White House, Sixpenny Handley, Dorset; one *s* two *d*. *Educ:* Eton Coll.; King's Coll., Cambridge. Deputy Legal Adviser to the National Trust, 1955–56; Partner: Freshfield's, Solicitors, 1956–74; Thomson Snell and Passmore, 1974–90. Ordained deacon in Church of England, 1990, priest, 1991. *Recreations:* golf, campanology, bagpipes. *Heir: s* Hon. William Edward Buckley, *b* 19 June 1966. *Address:* Oldcastle, Dallington, near Heathfield, East Sussex TN21 9JP. *T:* Rushlake Green (01435) 830400. *Club:* Oriental.

WREXHAM, Bishop of, (RC), since 1994; **Rt Rev. Edwin Regan;** *b* 31 Dec. 1935; *s* of James Regan and Elizabeth Ellen Regan (*née* Hoskins). *Educ:* St Joseph's RC Primary Sch., Aberavon; Port Talbot County Grammar Sch.; St John's Coll., Waterford, Eire; Corpus Christi Coll., London. Priest, 1959; Curate, Neath, 1959–66; Adviser in RE, Archdio. Cardiff, 1967–89; Chaplain, St Clare's Convent, Porthcawl, 1967–71; Administrator, St David's Cathedral, Cardiff, 1971–84; Parish Priest: St Helen's, Barry, 1984–89; St Mary's, Bridgend, 1989–94. *Recreation:* hill-walking. *Address:* Bishop's House, Sontley Road, Wrexham, Clwyd LL13 7EW. *T:* Wrexham (01978) 262726.

WREY, Benjamin Harold Bourchier; Chairman, Henderson Administration Group, since 1992; *b* 6 May 1940; *s* of Christopher B. Wrey and Ruth Wrey (*née* Bowden); *m* 1970, (Anne) Christine (Aubrey) Cherry; one *d*. *Educ:* Blundell's Sch.; Clare Coll., Cambridge (Hons in Econs; MA). Legal and General Assurance Soc., 1963–66; Investment Dept, Hambros Bank, 1966–69; Henderson Administration, 1969–: Director, 1971; Jt Man. Dir/Dep. Chm., 1982. Dep. Chm., Institutional Fund Managers' Assoc., 1994. *Publications:* articles on investment. *Recreations:* shooting, fishing, travel, ballet, photography. *Address:* Henderson Administration Group, 3 Finsbury Avenue, EC2M 2PA. *T:* 0171–638 5757. *Clubs:* Boodle's, City of London; Hurlingham.

WREY, Sir (George Richard) Bourchier, 15th Bt *cr* 1628, of Trebitch, Cornwall; *b* 2 Oct. 1948; *s* of Sir Bourchier Wrey, 14th Bt and of Sybil Mabel Alice Wrey, *d* of Dr George Lubke, S Africa; *S* father, 1991; *m* 1981, Lady Caroline Lindesay-Bethune, *d* of 15th Earl of Lindsay; two *s* one *d*. *Educ:* Eton. *Recreation:* shooting. *Heir: s* Harry David Bourchier Wrey, *b* 3 Oct. 1984. *Address:* 60 The Chase, SW4 0NH. *T:* 0171–622 6625. *Club:* Turf.

WRIGGLESWORTH, Sir Ian (William), Kt 1991; Deputy Chairman, John Livingston & Sons Ltd, since 1987; *b* Dec. 1939; *s* of Edward and Elsie Wrigglesworth; *m* Patricia Truscott; two *s* one *d*. *Educ:* Stockton Grammar Sch.; Stockton-Billingham Technical Coll; Coll. of St Mark and St John, Chelsea. Formerly: Personal Assistant to Gen. Sec., NUT; Head of Research and Information Dept of Co-operative Party; Press and Public Affairs Manager of National Giro. Contested (SDP/Alliance) Stockton South, 1987. MP (Lab and Co-op, 1974–81, SDP, 1981–87) Teesside, Thornaby, Feb. 1974–1983, Stockton South, 1983–87. PPS to Mr Alec Lyon, Minister of State, Home Office, 1974; PPS to Rt Hon. Roy Jenkins, Home Secretary, 1974–76; Opposition spokesman on Civil Service, 1979–80; SDP spokesman on industry, 1981, on industry and economic affairs, 1983–87. Pres., Liberal Democrats, 1988–90. Director: Fairfield Industries Ltd, 1987–; CIT Research Ltd, 1987–; Northern Develt Co., 1993–; Crabtree Gp Plc, 1994–; Divl Dir, Smiths Industries PLC, 1976–. Chm., Northern Reg., CBI, 1992–94. Gov., Univ. of Teesside, 1993–. Freeman, City of London; Liveryman, Co. of Founders. *Address:* Fairfield Industries Ltd, 24 Buckingham Gate, SW1E 6LB. *T:* 0171–828 8323. *Clubs:* Reform, National Liberal.

WRIGHT, family name of **Baron Wright of Richmond.**

WRIGHT OF RICHMOND, Baron *cr* 1994 (Life Peer), of Richmond-upon-Thames in the London Borough of Richmond-upon-Thames; **Patrick Richard Henry Wright,** GCMG 1989 (KCMG 1984; CMG 1978); HM Diplomatic Service, retired; *b* 28 June 1931; *s* of late Herbert H. S. Wright and of Rachel Wright (*née* Green), Haslemere, Surrey; *m* 1958, Virginia Anne Gaffney; two *s* one *d*. *Educ:* Marlborough; Merton Coll. (Postmaster), Oxford (MA; Hon. Fellow, 1987). Served Royal Artillery, 1950–51; joined Diplomatic Service, 1955; Middle East Centre for Arabic Studies, 1956–57; Third Secretary, British Embassy, Beirut, 1958–60; Private Sec. to Ambassador and later First Sec., British Embassy, Washington, 1960–65; Private Sec. to Permanent Under-Sec., FO, 1965–67; First Sec. and Head of Chancery, Cairo, 1967–70; Dep. Political Resident, Bahrain, 1971–72; Head of Middle East Dept, FCO, 1972–74; Private Sec. (Overseas Affairs) to Prime Minister, 1974–77; Ambassador to: Luxembourg, 1977–79; Syria, 1979–81; Dep. Under-Sec. of State, FCO, 1982–84; Ambassador to Saudi Arabia, 1984–86; Permanent Under-Sec. of State and Head of Diplomatic Service, 1986–91. Mem., Security Commn, 1993–. Director: Barclays Bank plc, 1991–; British Petroleum Co., 1991–; De La Rue, 1991–; Unilever, 1991–; BAA, 1992–. Vice Pres., Home Start, 1991–. Chm., RIIA, 1995– (Mem. Council, 1992–); Member: Council, RCM, 1991– (FRCM 1994); Atlantic Coll., 1993–; ICRC Consultative Gp of Internat. Experts, 1992–95. Governor: Ditchley Foundn, 1986–; Wellington Coll., 1991–. KStJ 1990; Registrar OStJ, 1991–95. *Recreations:* music, philately, walking. *Address:* c/o House of Lords, Westminster, SW1A 0PW. *Club:* United Oxford & Cambridge University.

WRIGHT, Alan John; a Master of the Supreme Court, Supreme Court Taxing Office, 1972–91; *b* 21 April 1925; *s* of late Rev. Henry George Wright, MA and Winifred Annie Wright; *m* 1952, Alma Beatrice Ridding; two *s* one *d*. *Educ:* St Olave's and St Saviour's Grammar Sch., Southwark; Keble Coll., Oxford. BA 1949, MA 1964. Served with RAF, India, Burma and China, 1943–46. Solicitor 1952; in private practice with Shaen Roscoe & Co., 1952–71; Legal Adviser to Trades Union Congress, 1955–71. Lay Reader, Southwark dio., 1989–. *Recreations:* Germanic studies, walking, travel, youth work, foreign languages. *Address:* 21 Brockley Park, Forest Hill, SE23 1PT.

WRIGHT, Alec Michael John, CMG 1967; *b* Hong Kong, 19 Sept. 1912; *s* of Arthur Edgar Wright and Margery Hepworth Chapman; *m* 1948, Ethel Surtees; one *d*. *Educ:* Brentwood Sch. ARICS 1934; ARIBA 1937. Articled pupil followed by private practice in London. Joined Colonial Service, 1938; appointed Architect in Hong Kong, 1938. Commissioned Hong Kong Volunteer Defence Force, 1941; POW in Hong Kong, 1941–45. Chief Architect, Public Works Dept, Hong Kong, 1950; Asst Director of Public Works, 1956; Dep. Director, 1959; Director, 1963–69; Commissioner for Hong Kong in London, 1969–73. *Address:* 13 Montrose Court, Exhibition Road, SW7 2QG. *T:* 0171–584 4293. *Club:* Hong Kong (Hong Kong).

See also Sir Denis Wright.

WRIGHT, Hon. Alison Elizabeth, JP; Director General, British Invisibles, since 1991; *b* 5 Jan. 1945; *d* of Baron Franks, OM, GCMG, KCB, KCVO, CBE, FBA and late Barbara Mary Tanner; *m* 1973, Stanley Harris Wright, *qv*. *Educ:* Headington School, Oxford; Downe House, Newbury; St Anne's College Oxford (BA PPE). Research Officer, Overseas Development Institute, 1965–69; research in Spain, 1970–72; business advr on Spain and Portugal, 1972–87; Managing Consultant, Ernst & Whinney, then Ernst & Young, 1988–90. Member: Heilbron Cttee on Law of Rape, 1975; Top Salaries Review Body, Nov. 1984, resigned April 1985; Commonwealth Develt Corp., 1984–94; Council, Overseas Develt Inst., 1988–; Council, British Consultants Bureau, 1993–; CSO Adv. Cttee, 1992–; Adv. Council, NCVO, 1994–; Council, City Univ., 1994–. JP Inner London 1978; Mem., Inner London Exec. Cttee, Magistrates' Assoc., 1980–82. Trustee, Marshall Plan of the Mind, BBC, 1992–. *Publications:* The Less Developed Countries in World Trade (with M. Zammit Cutajar), 1969; The Spanish Economy 1959–1976, 1977; contribs to Economist Intelligence Unit and other publications. *Recreations:* reading, theatre. *Address:* British Invisibles, Windsor House, 39 King Street, EC2V 8DQ. *T:* 0171–600 1198.

WRIGHT, Sir Allan Frederick, KBE 1982; farmer; Chairman: Alliance Textiles Ltd; R. G. Robinson Produce Ltd; Farmers' Mutual Insurance Group; Mair Astley Hldgs; Director: NZ Skin Pool Co-operative; Southpower; Earnscleugh Orchards; Trigon Industries Ltd; *b* Darfield, 25 March 1929; *s* of Quentin A. Wright; *m* 1953, Dorothy June Netting; three *s* two *d*. *Educ:* Christ's Coll., Christchurch. Nat. Pres., Young Farmers' Clubs, 1957–58; President: N Canterbury Federated Farmers, 1971–74; Federated Farmers of NZ, 1977–81 (formerly Sen. Nat. Vice-Pres.). Mem., NZ Cricket Bd of Control, 1967–90; Manager, NZ Cricket Team to England, 1983; Pres., NZ Cricket, 1993–94. Chancellor, Lincoln Univ., 1990–94 (Chm. Council, Lincoln Coll., 1985–89, Mem., 1974–89). *Recreations:* cricket (played for N Canterbury), rugby, golf. *Address:* Annat, RD Sheffield, Canterbury, New Zealand.

WRIGHT, Dr Anne Margaret; Vice Chancellor, University of Sunderland, since 1992 (Rector and Chief Executive, Sunderland Polytechnic, 1990–92); *b* 26 July 1946; *d* of Herbert and Florence Holden; *m* 1970, Martin Wright; one *d*. *Educ:* Holy Trinity Indep. Grammar Sch., Bromley; King's Coll., London (BA Hons English I, 1967; Inglis Teaching Studentship, 1967–68; PhD 1970). Lectr in English, Lancaster Univ., 1969–71; Lectr, then Sen. Lectr, Principal Lectr and Reader in Modern English Studies, Hatfield Poly., 1971–84; British Acad. Res. Award, Univ. of Texas at Austin, 1979; Registrar for Arts and Humanities, CNAA, 1984–86; Dep. Rector (Academic), Liverpool Poly, 1986–90. Member: English Studies Bd, 1978–84, Arts and Humanities Res. Sub-Cttee, 1979–84, CNAA; Cttee I of Cttee for Internat. Co-op. in Higher Educn, British Council, 1990–; Council for Industry and Higher Educn, 1993–; Director: Higher Educn Quality Council, 1992–; Further Educn Funding Council, 1992–; Hong Kong UPGC, 1992–. Chm., City of Sunderland Common Purpose, 1990–; Director: Everyman Theatre, Liverpool, 1988–90; The Wearside Opportunity, 1991–; Northern Sinfonia, 1991–; Northern Arts, 1991–; Wearside TEC, 1993–. *Publications:* (ed jtly) Heartbreak House: a facsimile of the revised typescript, 1981; Literature of Crisis 1910–1922, 1984; Bernard Shaw's Saint Joan, 1984; articles in jls and entries in dictionaries of lit. biog. *Recreations:* singing, theatre, opera, the arts. *Address:* Langham Tower, Ryhope Road, Sunderland SR2 7EE. *T:* 0191–515 2000.

WRIGHT, Prof. Anthony, DM; FRCSE; Professor of Otorhinolaryngology, and Director, Institute of Laryngology and Otology, University College London, since 1991; *b* 21 Nov. 1949; *s* of Arthur Donald and Hilda Wright; *m* 1989, Linda Steele; two *d*. *Educ:* Mill Hill Sch.; Emmanuel Coll., Cambridge (Sen. Schol.; Captain, Univ. Boxing Team, 1970); Lincoln Coll., Oxford (Full Blue, Boxing, 1972). DM Oxon 1986; LLM UWC Cardiff, 1995; FRCSE 1979. Sen. Lectr in ENT Surgery, Inst. of Laryngology and Otology, 1984–89; Consultant ENT Surgeon, Royal Free Hosp., 1989–91. *Publications:* Dizziness: a guide to disorders of balance, 1988; scientific articles on the structure and function of the inner ear. *Recreation:* attempting to make coffee that tastes as good as it smells. *Address:* 1 Milton Park, Highgate, N6 5QB. *T:* 0181–340 5593. *Clubs:* Athenæum; Hawks (Cambridge).

WRIGHT, Dr Anthony Wayland; MP (Lab) Cannock and Burntwood, since 1992; *b* 11 March 1948; *s* of Frank and Maud Wright; *m* 1973, Moira Elynwy Phillips; three *s* (and one *s* decd). *Educ:* Desborough County Primary Sch.; Kettering Grammar Sch.; LSE (BSc Econ 1st Cl. Hons); Harvard Univ. (Kennedy Schol.); Balliol Coll., Oxford (DPhil). Lectr in Politics, UCNW, Bangor, 1973–75; Lectr 1975, Sen. Lectr 1987, Reader 1989, in Politics, Sch. of Continuing Studies, Univ. of Birmingham. Educnl Fellowship, IBA, 1979–80; Chm., S Birmingham CHC, 1983–85. Jt Editor, Political Qtly. *Publications:* G. D. H. Cole and Socialist Democracy, 1979; Local Radio and Local Democracy, 1982; British Socialism, 1983; Socialisms: theories and practices, 1986; R. H. Tawney, 1987; (ed jtly) Party Ideology in Britain, 1989; (ed jtly) The Alternative, 1990; (ed jtly) Consuming Public Services, 1990; (ed jtly) Political Thought since 1945, 1992; Citizens and Subjects, 1993; (ed with G. Brown) Values, Visions and Voices, 1995; contribs to learned jls. *Recreations:* tennis, walking, gardening. *Address:* House of Commons, SW1A 0AA. *T:* 0171–219 5029.

WRIGHT, Arthur Francis Stevenson, MBE 1945; FRIBA, FRIAS; architect principal in private practice, since 1949, consultant, since 1983; *b* 15 Feb. 1918; *s* of Arthur and Alice Wright; *m* 1946, Catherine Grey Linton; one *d*. *Educ:* Morgan Academy; College of Art, Dundee (DipArch 1948). Served War, Royal Engineers (Major), 1940–46. FRIBA 1956; FRIAS 1954 (Pres., 1975–77); FCIOB (FIOB 1974); FCIArb (FIArb 1976). Chm., Jt Standing Cttee of Architects, Surveyors and Builders in Scotland, 1973–75. *Recreations:* fishing, golf. *Address:* Thorvale, Castlegate, Ceres, Fife KY15 5NG. *T:* Ceres (01334) 82540.

WRIGHT, (Arthur Robert) Donald, OBE 1984; *b* 20 June 1923; *s* of late Charles North Wright and Beatrice May Wright; *m* 1948, Helen Muryell Buxton; two *s* three *d*. *Educ:* Bryanston Sch.; Queens' Coll., Cambridge. War Service (commnd 1943), NW Europe (despatches) and India, 1942–46. Taught at: University Coll. Sch., 1948–50; The Hill School, Pennsylvania, 1950; Leighton Park School, 1951–52; Marlborough College (Housemaster), 1953–63; Headmaster, Shrewsbury Sch., 1963–75. Chm., HMC, 1971. Appointments' Sec. to Archbishops of Canterbury and York, 1975–84 and Sec., Crown Appointments Commn, 1977–84. A Chm., Civil Service Comrs' Interview Panel, 1984–91. Chm., William Temple Foundn, 1976–85. Chm., Council, Benenden Sch., 1976–86; Governor, King's Coll. Sch., Wimbledon, 1981–93. *Publications:* (ed) Neville Cardus on Music: a centenary collection, 1988; (ed and contrib.) Walter Hamilton: a portrait, 1991. *Address:* Mill Barn, Coulston, near Westbury, Wilts BA13 4NY.

WRIGHT, Beatrice Frederika, (Lady Wright); Vice-President, Royal National Institute for the Deaf, since 1978; Co-Founder, Hearing Dogs for the Deaf, 1982 (President, 1983–88); *b* New Haven, Connecticut; *d* of Mr and Mrs F. Roland Clough; *m* 1st, 1932, John Rankin Rathbone (Flight Lieut, RAFVR, MP, killed in action, 1940); one *s* one *d*; 2nd, 1942, Paul Hervé Giraud Wright (*see* Sir Paul Wright); one *d*. *Educ:* Ethel Walker School, Simsbury, Conn; Radcliffe College, Oxford. MP (U) Bodmin Div. of Cornwall, 1941–45. *Address:* 62 Westminster Gardens, Marsham Street, SW1P 4JG.

See also J. R. Rathbone.

WRIGHT, Rt. Rev. Benjamen; Rector of Busselton, Western Australia, since 1993; *b* 15 March 1942; *s* of Clarice and Herbert Wright; *m* 1966, Annette Jennifer Dunne; two *s* one *d*. *Educ:* Slade Sch., Warwick, Qld; Murdoch Univ., Perth (ThL, BA). Ordained deacon, 1964, priest, 1965; Asst Curate, Applecross, 1964–67; Priest-in-charge, 1967–69, Rector, 1969–71, Narembeen; Army Reserve Chaplain, 1971–76; Rector, Alice Springs and Chaplain, St Mary's Child and Welfare Services, dio. of NT, 1976–80; Rector, Scarborough, 1980–88; Archdeacon of Stirling, 1986–88; Rector, Kalgoorlie, Boulder, 1988; Asst Bishop, dio. of Perth (Goldfields Region), 1988–91; Archdeacon of Goldfields, 1988–89; Archdeacon of O'Connor, 1990; Bishop of Bendigo, 1992–93. Hon. Canon of Christ Church Cathedral, Darwin, 1979–80. *Recreations:* fishing, gardening. *Address:* The Rectory, 43 Peel Terrace, Busselton, WA 6280, Australia.

WRIGHT, Brian; *see* Wright, G. B.

WRIGHT, Charles Christopher; Taxing Master of the Supreme Court, since 1992; *b* 15 July 1938; *s* of late Charles Gordon Wright, LDS RCS and of Gwendoline Margaret Wright; *m* 1969, Angela Whitford. *Educ:* Emscote Lawn, Warwick; Rugby Sch.; New Coll., Oxford (MA 2nd Cl. Hons Jurisp. 1961). Solicitor of the Supreme Court, 1965; Partner, Lee & Pembertons, 1967–92. Sen. Vice-Pres., West London Law Society, 1991–92. *Recreations:* walking, swimming, holiday golf, reading. *Address:* Supreme Court Taxing Office, Cliffords Inn, Fetter Lane, EC4A 1DQ. *Club:* Royal Automobile.

WRIGHT, Christopher Norman; Chairman, Chrysalis Group plc (formerly Chrysalis), since 1969; *b* 7 Sept. 1944; *s* of Walter Reginald Wright and Edna May (*née* Corden); *m* 1972, Carolyn Rochelle Nelson; two *s* one *d*. *Educ:* King Edward VI Grammar Sch., Louth; Manchester Univ. (BA Hons 1966); Manchester Business Sch. Co-Founder, Ellis Wright Agency, 1967; name changed to: Chrysalis, 1968; Chrysalis Gp plc, 1985. Chm., British Phonographic Industry, 1980–83; Director: Phonographic Performance Ltd, 1980–; Internat. Fedn of Phonographic Industry, 1981– (Vice-Pres., 1981–91). *Recreations:* playing tennis, breeding race horses, music, watching sport of all kinds. *Address:* c/o Chrysalis Group plc, 13 Bramley Road, W10 6SP. *T:* 0171–221 2213. *Club:* Turf.

WRIGHT, Claud William, CB 1969; Deputy Secretary, Department of Education and Science, 1971–76; *b* 9 Jan. 1917; *s* of Horace Vipan Wright and Catherine Margaret Sales; *m* 1947, Alison Violet Readman; one *s* four *d*. *Educ:* Charterhouse; Christ Church, Oxford (MA). Assistant Principal, War Office, 1939; Private, Essex Regiment, 1940; 2nd Lieut, KRRC, 1940; War Office, rising to GSO2, 1942–45; Principal, War Office, 1944; Min. of Defence: Principal, 1947; Asst Sec., 1951; Asst Under-Sec. of State, 1961–68; Dep. Under-Sec. of State, 1968–71. Chm., Cttee on Provincial Museums and Galleries, 1971–73. Research Fellow, Wolfson Coll., Oxford, 1977–83. Lyell Fund, 1947, R. H. Worth Prize, 1958, Prestwich Medal, 1987, Geological Society of London; Foulerton Award, Geologists Association, 1955; Stamford Raffles Award, Zoological Society of London, 1965; Phillips Medal, Yorks Geol. Soc., 1976; Strimple Award, Paleontol Soc., USA, 1988. President, Geologists Assoc., 1956–58. Hon. Associate, British Museum (Nat. Hist.), 1973; fil.Dr *hc* Uppsala, 1979; Hon. DSc Hull, 1987. *Publications:* (with W. J. Arkell *et al*) vol. on Ammonites, 1957, 2nd edn 1995, (with W. K. Spencer) on Starfish, 1966, in Treatise on Invertebrate Palaeontology; (with J. S. H. Collins) British Cretaceous Crabs, 1972; (with W. J. Kennedy) Ammonites of the Middle Chalk, 1981; (with W. J. Kennedy) Ammonites of the Lower Chalk, pt I, 1984, pt II, 1987, pt III, 1990, pt IV, 1995; (with A. B. Smith) British Cretaceous Echinoidea, pt I, 1988, pt II, 1990, pt III, 1993; papers in geological, palaeontological and archaeological journals. *Recreations:* palaeontology, natural history, gardening, archæology. *Address:* Old Rectory, Seaborough, Beaminster, Dorset DT8 3QY. *T:* Broadwindsor (01308) 868426. *Club:* Athenæum.

WRIGHT, Prof. Crispin James Garth, PhD, DLitt; FBA 1992; Professor of Logic and Metaphysics, University of St Andrews, since 1978; *b* 21 Dec. 1942; *s* of Geoffrey Joseph Wright and Jean Valerie Holford; *m* 1985, Catherine Steedman (*née* Pain); two *s*, and one step *s* one step *d*. *Educ:* Birkenhead Sch.; Trinity Coll., Cambridge (BA Hons 1964; MA, PhD 1968); BPhil 1969, DLitt 1988, Oxon. Oxford University: Jun. Res. Fellow, Trinity Coll., 1967–69; Prize Fellow, All Souls Coll., 1969–71; Lectr, Balliol Coll., 1969–70; Lectr, UCL, 1970–71; Res. Fellow, All Souls Coll., Oxford, 1971–78; Prof. of Phil., 1987–92, Nelson Prof. of Phil., 1992–94, Univ. of Michigan, Ann Arbor. *Publications:* Wittgenstein on the Foundations of Mathematics, 1980; Frege's Conception of Numbers as Objects, 1983; Realism, Meaning and Truth, 1986; Truth and Objectivity, 1993. *Recreations:* gardening, squash, mountain-walking, running, P. G. Wodehouse. *Address:* Department of Logic and Metaphysics, University of St Andrews, Fife KY16 9AL. *T:* St Andrews (01334) 76161.

WRIGHT, David John, CMG 1992; LVO 1990; HM Diplomatic Service; Deputy Under-Secretary of State, Foreign and Commonwealth Office, since 1994; *b* 16 June 1944; *s* of J. F. Wright; *m* 1968, Sally Ann Dodkin; one *s* one *d*. *Educ:* Wolverhampton Grammar Sch.; Peterhouse, Cambridge (MA). Third Secretary, FO, 1966; Third Sec., later Second Sec., Tokyo, 1966–72; FCO, 1972–75; Ecole Nationale d'Administration, Paris, 1975–76; First Sec., Paris, 1976–80; Private Sec. to Secretary of the Cabinet, 1980–82; Counsellor (Economic), Tokyo, 1982–85; Head of Personnel Services Dept, FCO, 1985–88; Dep. Private Sec. to HRH the Prince of Wales, 1988–90 (on secondment); Ambassador to Republic of Korea, 1990–94. *Recreations:* running, golf, cooking, military history. *Address:* c/o Foreign and Commonwealth Office, SW1A 2AH. *Club:* United Oxford & Cambridge University.

WRIGHT, David Stephen, FRCP, FFOM; Chief Medical Officer, British Petroleum Co. plc, since 1989; Dean, Faculty of Occupational Medicine, 1991–94 (Vice-Dean, 1988–91); *b* 4 Aug. 1935; *s* of Edward Alfred Wright and Winifred May Wright (*née* Oliver); *m* 1966, Caroline Auza; two *s* one *d*. *Educ:* Epsom Coll.; St Bartholomew's Hosp. Med. Coll. (MB BS 1959); MSc Salford 1973; DPH, DIH. FFOM 1983; FRCP 1989. MO, RN, 1960–85; Prof. of Naval Occupational Medicine, 1982–85; Head, BP Gp Occupational Health Centre, 1985–91. British Medical Association: Member: Armed Forces Cttee, 1966–88 (Chm., 1985–88); Council, 1985–88. OStJ 1984. *Publications:* contribs on asbestos and noise to learned jls. *Recreations:* gardening, walking. *Address:* 9 Ashburton Road, Alverstoke, Gosport, Hants PO12 2LH. *T:* Gosport (01705) 582459.

WRIGHT, Sir Denis (Arthur Hepworth), GCMG 1971 (KCMG 1961; CMG 1954); HM Diplomatic Service, retired; *b* 23 March 1911; *s* of late A. E. Wright, Hong Kong, and Margery Hepworth Chapman, York; *m* 1939, Iona Craig, Bolney, Sussex; no *c*. *Educ:* Brentwood School; St Edmund Hall, Oxford, Hon. Fellow 1972. Asst Advertising Manager to Gallaher & Co. (Tobacco Manufacturers), 1935–39. Employed from outbreak of war as Vice-Consul on economic warfare work at HM Consulate at Constantza (Roumania), 1939–41. Vice-Consul-in-charge of HM Consulate at Trebizond (Turkey), 1941–43; Acting-Consul-in-charge of HM Consulate, Mersin (Turkey), 1943–45; First Secretary (Commercial) to HM Embassy, Belgrade, 1946–48; Superintending Trade Consul at Chicago for Middle-Western Region of USA, 1949–51; Head of Economic Relations Department in the Foreign Office, 1951–53; appointed Chargé d'Affaires, Tehran, on resumption of diplomatic relations with Persia, Dec. 1953; Counsellor, HM Embassy, Tehran, 1954–55; Asst Under-Sec., FO, 1955–59; Ambassador to Ethiopia, 1959–62; Asst Under-Sec., FO, 1962; Ambassador to Iran, 1963–71. Dir, Shell Transport & Trading Co., Standard Chartered Bank, and Mitchell Cotts Gp, 1971–81. Governor, Oversea Service, Farnham Castle, 1972–86; Mem. Council, British Inst. of Persian Studies, 1973– (Pres., 1978–87); Pres., Iran Soc., 1989–95 (Chm., 1976–79). Hon. Fellow St Antony's Coll., Oxford, 1976. Sir Percy Sykes Meml Medal, RSAA, 1990. *Publications:* Persia (with James Morris and Roger Wood), 1969; The English Amongst the Persians, 1977; The Persians Amongst the English, 1985. *Address:* Duck Bottom, 15 Flint Street, Haddenham, Aylesbury, Bucks HP17 8AL. *Club:* Travellers'.

See also A. M. J. Wright.

WRIGHT, Desmond Garforth, QC 1974; *b* 13 July 1923; *s* of late Arthur Victor Wright and Doris Greensill; *m* 1952, Elizabeth Anna Bacon; one *s* one *d*. *Educ:* Giggleswick; Royal Naval Coll., Greenwich; Worcester Coll., Oxford (MA). Cholmondley Scholar of Lincoln's Inn. Served War of 1939–45: RNVR, 1942–46. Staff of Flag Officer Malaya Forward Area, 1946. Called to Bar, Lincoln's Inn, 1950, Bencher, 1981. *Publication:* Wright on Walls, 1954. *Recreations:* cartology, conversation, skiing on snow. *Address:* 1 Atkin Building, Gray's Inn, WC1R 5BQ. *T:* 0171–404 0102.

WRIGHT, Donald; *see* Wright, A. R. D.

WRIGHT, Mrs Edmund Gordon; *see* Cross, H. M.

WRIGHT, Sir Edward (Maitland), Kt 1977; MA, DPhil, LLD, DSc; FRSE; Research Fellow, University of Aberdeen, 1976–83; *b* 1906; *s* of M. T. Wright, Farnley, Leeds; *m* 1934, Elizabeth Phyllis (*d* 1987), *d* of H. P. Harris, Bryn Mally Hall, N Wales; one *s*. *Educ:* Jesus Coll. and Christ Church, Oxford; Univ. of Göttingen. Master, Chard School, Somerset, 1923–26; Scholar, Jesus College, Oxford, 1926–30; Senior Scholar, Christ Church, 1930–33; Lecturer, King's College, London, 1932–33; Lecturer, Christ Church, 1933–35; Flt Lieut, RAFVR, 1941–43; Principal Scientific Officer, Air Ministry, 1943–45; Prof. of Mathematics, 1935–62, Vice-Principal, 1961–62, Principal and Vice-Chancellor, 1962–76, Univ. of Aberdeen. Member: Anderson Cttee on Grants to Students, 1958–60; Hale Cttee on Univ. Teaching Methods, 1961–64; Scottish Universities Entrance Bd, 1948–62 (Chm. 1955–62); Royal Commission on Medical Education, 1965–67. Vice-Pres., RUSI, 1969–72. Associate Editor, Math. Abstracts, 1950–; Hon. Editor, Jl Graph Theory, 1983–. Hon. LLD: St Andrews, 1963; Pennsylvania, 1975; Aberdeen, 1978; Hon. DSc Strathclyde, 1974. Hon. Fellow, Jesus College, Oxford, 1963. Macdougall-Brisbane Prize, RSE, 1952; Sen. Berwick Prize, London Math. Soc., 1978. Gold Medal of the Order of Polonia Restituta of the Polish People's Republic, 1978. *Publications:* Introduction to the Theory of Numbers (with Professor G. H. Hardy), 1938, 5th edn 1979; mathematical papers in scientific journals. *Address:* 16 Primrosehill Avenue, Cults, Aberdeen. *T:* Aberdeen (01224) 861185. *Club:* Caledonian.

WRIGHT, Eric; Chairman, Yorkshire and Humberside Development Agency (formerly Association), since 1993; *b* 17 Nov. 1933; *s* of Alec Wright and Elsie (*née* Worthington); *m* 1st, 1955, Pauline Sutton (marr. diss. 1993); three *s* (and one *s* decd); 2nd, 1993, Hazel Elizabeth Story. *Educ:* Wolstanton Grammar Sch.; Keble Coll., Oxford (BA 1st Cl. Hons Mod. Hist.). 2nd Lieut RASC, 1955–57. Ministry of Fuel and Power, 1957–65; Civil Service Commission, 1965–67; Min. of Technology, 1968–70; Sloan Fellow, London Business Sch., 1970–71; Principal Private Sec. to Secretary of State, DTI, 1971–72; Dept of Trade, 1972–77; Dept of Industry, 1977–83; Under-Sec., 1979–; DTI, 1983–93 (Regl Dir, Yorks and Humberside, 1985–93). *Recreations:* music, tennis, chess. *Address:* Westgate House, 100 Wellington Street, Leeds LS1 4LT. *T:* Leeds (0113) 243 9222.

WRIGHT, Eric David, CB 1975; Deputy Under-Secretary of State, Home Office, and Director-General, Prison Service, 1973–77; *b* 12 June 1917; *s* of Charles Henry and Cecelia Wright; *m* 1944, Doris (*née* Nicholls); one *s*. *Educ:* Ealing County Grammar School. Joined War Office, 1935; Principal, 1945; seconded to Dept of the Army, Australia, 1951; Asst Secretary, 1955; Command Secretary, BAOR, 1955–58; Imperial Defence College, 1964; Asst Under-Sec. of State, MoD, 1965; on loan to Home Office, Police Dept, 1970–73. Mem., Parole Bd, 1978–83. Chm., Hillingdon CHC, 1988–90. *Address:* 32 Valley Road, Rickmansworth, Herts WD3 4DS.

WRIGHT, Prof. Esmond; Emeritus Professor of American History, University of London, since 1983; Vice-President, Automobile Association, since 1985 (Vice-Chairman and Hon. Treasurer, 1971–85; Chairman, Drive Publications, 1980–85); *b* 5 Nov. 1915; *m* 1945, Olive Adamson. *Educ:* University of Durham (Open Entrance Schol.); Univ. of Virginia (Commonwealth Fund Fellow). War Service, 1940–46, demobilised as Lt-Col, 1946. Glasgow Univ., 1946–67; Prof. of Modern History, 1957–67. MP (C) Glasgow, Pollok, March 1967–1970; Dir, Inst. of US Studies and Prof. of American History, Univ. of London, 1971–83; Principal, Swinton Cons. Coll., 1972–76. Chm., Border TV, 1981–85 (Vice-Chm., 1976–81). Founder-Mem., British Association for American Studies (Chm., 1965–68). Mem., Marshall Aid Commemoration Commn, 1966–83; Vice-Chm., British Road Fedn, 1981–85. For. Mem., Amer. Philosophical Soc., 1990–. FRHistS; FRSA (Franklin Medal, 1988). Hon. LHD Pennsylvania, 1983; Hon. DLitt New Brunswick, 1984. *Publications:* A Short History of our own Times, 1951; George Washington and the American Revolution, 1957; The World Today, 1961, 4th edn 1978; Fabric of Freedom, 1961, 2nd edn 1978; (ed) Illustrated World History, 1964; Benjamin Franklin and American Independence, 1966; (ed) Causes and Consequences of the American Revolution, 1966; (ed) American Themes, 1967; American Profiles, 1967; (ed) Benjamin Franklin, a profile, 1970; A Time for Courage, 1971; A Tug of Loyalties, 1974; Red, White and True Blue, 1976; (with A. G. Nicolson) Europe Today, 1979; The Great Little Madison (British Academy Lecture), 1981; The Fire of Liberty, 1983; (ed) History of the World: Pre-History to Renaissance, 1985, The Last Five Hundred Years, 1986; Franklin of Philadelphia, 1986; Franklin: his life as he wrote it, 1989; The Sayings of Benjamin Franklin, 1995; The Search for Liberty, 1995; An Empire for Liberty, 1995; The American Dream, 1995; articles in periodicals. *Address:* Radleigh House, Masham, N Yorks HG4 4EF. *Club:* Athenæum.

WRIGHT, Georg Henrik von, GCVO (Hon.); MA; Research Professor in the Academy of Finland, 1961–86; *b* Helsingfors, 14 June 1916; *s* of Tor von Wright and Ragni Elisabeth Alfthan; *m* 1941, Maria Elisabeth von Troil, CVO (Hon.); one *s* one *d*. *Educ:* Svenska Normallyceum, Helsingfors; Helsingfors Univ. Helsingfors University: Lectr and Acting Prof. of Philosophy, 1943–46; Prof. of Philosophy, 1946–61 (also in Univ. of Cambridge, 1948–51); Prof. at Large, Cornell Univ., 1965–77; Chancellor of Abo Academy, 1968–77; Visiting Professor: Cornell Univ., 1954 and 1958; Univ. Calif, Los Angeles, 1963; Univ. Pittsburg, 1966; Univ. Karlsruhe, 1975; Univ. Leipzig, 1994–95; Lectures: Shearman Meml, University Coll., London, 1956; Gifford, Univ. of St Andrews, 1959–60; Tarner, Trinity Coll., Cambridge, 1969; Woodbridge, Columbia Univ., 1972; Nellie Wallace, Univ. of Oxford, 1978; Tanner, Helsingfors Univ., 1984. President: Internat. Union of History and Philosophy of Science, 1963–65; Acad. of Finland, 1968–69; Philosophical Soc. of Finland, 1962–73; Institut International de Philosophie, 1975–78. Fellow: Finnish Soc. of Sciences (Pres., 1966–67, Hon. Fellow 1978); New Soc. of Letters, Lund; Royal Swedish Academy of Sciences; Royal Soc. of Letters, Lund; British Academy; Royal Swedish Academy of Letters, History and Antiquities; Finnish Acad. of Sciences; Royal Danish Acad. of Sciences and Letters; Royal Acad. of Arts and Sciences, Uppsala; Norwegian Acad. of Science and Letters; Royal Acad. of Science, Trondheim; European Acad. of Arts, Sciences and Humanities; World Acad. of Arts and Scis; Serbian Acad. of Scis and Arts; Hon. Foreign Mem., Amer. Acad. of Arts and Sciences. Sometime Fellow, Trinity College, Cambridge, Hon. Fellow 1983. Hon. degrees: Helsingfors Univ. (doctor of pol. sci.); Univ. of Liverpool (DLitt); doctor of philosophy: Univ. of Lund; Univ. of Bologna; Abo Acad.; Univ. of Tromsø; Turku Univ. (doctor of philosophy, doctor of law); Saint Olaf Coll., Northfield, Minn. (doctor of humane letters); Tampere Univ. (doctor of soc. sci.); Univ. of Stockholm (doctor of law); Univ. of Buenos Aires; Univ. of Salta. Wilhuri Foundn Internat. Prize, 1976; Alexander von Humboldt Foundn Forschungspreis, 1986; Gold Medal, Swedish Acad., 1986; Selma Lagerlöf Literature Prize, 1993. *Publications:* The Logical Problem of Induction, 1941, rev. edn 1957; Den logiska Empirismen, 1943; Über Wahrscheinlichkeit, 1945; A Treatise on Induction and Probability, 1951; An Essay in Modal Logic, 1951; Logical Studies, 1957; The Varieties of Goodness, 1963; The Logic of Preference, 1963; Norm and Action, 1963; An Essay in Deontic Logic, 1968; Time, Change, and Contradiction, 1969; Explanation and Understanding, 1971; Causality and Determinism, 1974; Freedom and Determination, 1980; Wittgenstein, 1982; Philosophical Papers I–III, 1983–84; Vetenskapen och förnuftet, 1986; (contrib.) The Philosophy of Georg Henrik von Wright, 1989; The Tree of Knowledge, 1993. *Address:* 4 Skepparegatan, Helsingfors, Finland.

WRIGHT, (George) Brian; JP; Head of Educational Broadcasting Services, BBC, 1989–93; *b* 9 April 1939; *s* of George Wright and Martha Blair Wright (*née* Dundee); *m* 1963, Joyce Avril Frances Camier; two *s*. *Educ:* Trinity Coll., Dublin (MA, HDipEd). Schoolmaster, 1961–67; Local Govt Administrator, 1967–69; BBC Educn Officer, Belfast, Nottingham, Birmingham, 1969–81; Chief Educn Officer, BBC, 1981–89. Occasional Lectr, Henley Management Coll., 1994–95. JP Ealing, 1992–93, Nottingham, 1993. *Publications:* How Britain Earns Its Living, 1980; (with John Cain) In a Different Class, 1994. *Recreations:* reading, crosswords, watching Rugby, dabbling at being a writer. *Address:* Oliver House, Nicker Hill, Keyworth, Nottingham NG12 5ED. *T:* Nottingham (0115) 937 3023.

WRIGHT, George Henry, MBE 1977; Regional Secretary, Wales, Transport and General Workers Union, since 1972; Vice-Chairman, Wales Co-operative Development Centre, since 1985 (Chairman, 1983–85); *b* 11 July 1935; *s* of William Henry and Annie Louisa Wright; *m* 1956, Margaret Wright; two *d*. *Educ:* Tinkers Farm Sch., Birmingham. Car worker, 1954–65. T&GWU: District Officer, West Bromwich, 1966–68; District Secretary, Birmingham, 1968–72. Gen. Sec., Wales TUC, 1974–84 (Chm., 1989–90). Member: MSC Wales, 1976–88; Employment Appeal Tribunal, 1985–; Welsh Trng Adv. Gp, 1989–; Bd, Welsh Develt Agency, 1994–; Central Arbitration Cttee, Dept of Employment, 1994–; Econ. and Social Cttee, EC, 1994–. *Recreations:* fishing, gardening. *Address:* 5 Kidwelly Court, Caerphilly, Mid Glamorgan, Wales CF8 2TY. *T:* Caerphilly (01222) 885434.

WRIGHT, George Paul; Chief Superintendent, Royal Signals and Radar Establishment, Ministry of Defence, Baldock, 1976–80; *b* 27 April 1919; *s* of late George Maurice Wright, CBE, and of late Lois Dorothy Wright (*née* Norburn); *m* 1957, Jean Margaret Reid, *d* of Lt-Col Charles Alexander Reid Scott, DSO and Marjorie Reid Scott (*née* Mackintosh); one *s* one *d*. *Educ:* Bishops Stortford Coll.; Magdalen Coll., Oxford. BA 1948, MA 1951; FInstP. Admty Signal Estabt, 1939–45; Services Electronics Research Lab., 1945–57; Dept of Physical Research, Admty, 1957–63; Services Electronics Research Lab., 1963–76 (Dir, 1972–76). *Recreations:* music, sailing, gardening. *Address:* Tilekiln Farmhouse, Earls Colne, Colchester, Essex CO6 2JR. *T:* Earls Colne (01787) 222432. *Clubs:* United Oxford & Cambridge University, Civil Service; Blackwater Sailing (Maldon).

WRIGHT, Gerard, QC 1973; *b* 23 July 1929; *s* of Leo Henry and Catherine M. F. Wright; *m* 1950, Betty Mary Fenn; one *s* two *d*. *Educ:* Stonyhurst Coll.; Lincoln Coll., Oxford (BA, BCL). Served in Army, 1947–49, rank T/Captain. Called to Bar, Gray's Inn, 1954 (Arden Scholar, Barstow Scholar); Northern Circuit. KHS 1974; KCHS 1979; KCSHS 1992; Auxiliaire de l'Hospitalité de Notre Dame de Lourdes, 1982, Titulaire 1985. *Publication:* Test Tube Babies—a Christian view (with others), 1984. *Recreations:* skiing, sailing. *Address:* 1 King's Court, Hoylake, Merseyside L47 1JE. *T:* 0151–632 5566; 25–27 Castle Street, First Floor, Liverpool L2 4TA.

WRIGHT, Graeme Alexander; Editor, Wisden Cricketers' Almanack, 1986–92; cricket writer, Independent on Sunday, since 1990; *b* 23 April 1943; *s* of Alexander John Wright and Eileen Margaret (*née* Hanlon). *Educ:* St Patrick's Coll., Wellington, NZ; St Patrick's High Sch., Timaru, NZ; Univ. of Canterbury, Christchurch, NZ. Copywriter, NZ Broadcasting Corp., 1965–67; Sub-editor, BSI, 1968–69; Editor and writer, Publicare Ltd, 1969–72; Managing Editor, Queen Anne Press, 1973–74; freelance editor and writer, 1974–; Dir, John Wisden & Co. Ltd, 1983–86. *Publications:* (with Phil Read) Phil Read, 1977; The Illustrated Handbook of Sporting Terms, 1978; Olympic Greats, 1980; (with George Best) Where do I go from here?, 1981; (with Patrick Eagar): Test Decade 1972–1982, 1982; Botham, 1985; (with Joe Brown) Brown Sauce, 1986; Merrydown: forty vintage years, 1988; Betrayal: the struggle for cricket's soul, 1993. *Recreations:* reading, music, letter-writing, travelling. *Address:* 14 Field End Road, Eastcote, Pinner, Middx HA5 2QL. *Club:* MCC.

WRIGHT, Prof. H(enry) Myles; RIBA; RTPI; Lever Professor of Civic Design, University of Liverpool, 1954–75; now Emeritus Professor; University Planning Consultant, 1957–77; *b* 9 June 1908; *s* of H. T. Wright, Gosforth, Newcastle upon Tyne; *m* 1939, Catharine Noble (*d* 1981), *y d* of Very Rev. H. N. Craig, Dean of Kildare; two *d*. *Educ:* Fettes College, Edinburgh (Foundationer); King's College, Newcastle upon Tyne; St John's College, Cambridge. Assistant in various private offices, 1930–35; Asst Editor, The Architects' Journal, and in private practice, 1935–40; Partner in firm of Sir William Holford, 1948–54; principally engaged on planning proposals for Cambridge and Corby New Town. Member British Caribbean Federal Capital Commn, 1956. *Publications:* The Planner's Notebook, 1948; Cambridge Planning Proposals, 1950, and Corby New Town (with Lord Holford), 1952; Land Use in an Urban Environment (Editor and contributor), 1961; The Dublin Region: Preliminary and Final Reports, 1965 and 1967; Lord Leverhulme's Unknown Venture, 1982; other technical publications. *Recreations:* walking, reading. *Address:* 9 Pine Hey, Neston, S Wirral, Cheshire L64 3TJ.

WRIGHT, Hugh Raymond, MA; Chief Master, King Edward's School, Birmingham, since 1991; *b* 24 Aug. 1938; *s* of Rev. Raymond Blayney Wright and Alice Mary Wright (*née* Hawksworth); *m* 1962, Jillian Mary McIldowie Meiklejohn; three *s*. *Educ:* Kingswood Sch., Bath; The Queen's Coll., Oxford (Bible Clerk; MA Lit. Hum.). Asst Master, Brentwood Sch., 1961–64; Cheltenham Coll., 1964–79: Hd of Classics, 1967–72; Housemaster, Boyne House, 1971–79; Headmaster: Stockport Grammar Sch., 1979–85; Gresham's School, Holt, 1985–91. Headmasters' Conference: Chm., 1995; Chm., NW Dist, 1983; Chm., Community Service Sub-Cttee, 1985–90 (Mem., 1980–90); Rep. on ISJC Europe Cttee, 1991–; Mem., Assisted Places Wking Pty, 1992–. Member: Bloxham Project Steering Cttee, 1993–; Admty Interview Bd Panel, 1982–. Mem., Court, 1992–, Council, 1995–, Birmingham Univ. FRSA 1984. *Publication:* film strips and notes on The Origins of Christianity and the Medieval Church, 1980. *Recreations:* music, theatre, hill walking, wildfowl, gardening, Rugby football, tennis. *Address:* King Edward's School, Birmingham B15 2UA. *T:* 0121–472 1672. *Club:* East India.

WRIGHT, Prof. Jack Clifford, MA, BA; Professor of Sanskrit in the University of London, at the School of Oriental and African Studies, since 1964; *b* 5 Dec. 1933; *s* of late Jack and Dorothy Wright, Aberdeen; *m* 1958, Hazel Chisholm (*née* Strachan), Crathes, Banchory; one *s*. *Educ:* Robert Gordon's Coll., Aberdeen; Univ. of Aberdeen (MA Hons in French and German, 1955); University of Zürich; Univ. of London (BA Hons in Sanskrit, 1959). Lectr in Sanskrit, 1959–64, Head, Dept of Indology and Mod. Langs and Lits of S Asia, 1970–83, SOAS, Univ. of London. *Address:* School of Oriental and African Studies, University of London, Thornhaugh Street, Russell Square, WC1H 0XG.

WRIGHT, Hon. James Claude, Jr; Speaker, US House of Representatives, 1987–89; Senior Political Consultant, American Income Life Insurance Co., since 1989; *b* 22 Dec. 1922; *s* of James C. Wright and Marie Wright (*née* Lyster); *m* 1972, Betty Hay; one *s* three *d* by former marr. *Educ:* Weatherford College, Univ. of Texas. Served US Army Air Force, 1941–45 (DFC, Legion of Merit). Mem., Texas Legislature, 1947–49; Mayor of Weatherford, Texas, 1950–54; Mem., US House of Representatives for Fort Worth, 1955–89; Dep. Democratic Whip to 1976; Majority Leader, 1976–87; former Mem. of Committees: Budget, Public Works and Transportation; Govt Operations; Highway Beautification (Chm.). Vis. Prof., Texas Christian Univ., 1991–. Former lay minister, Presbyterian Church. Columnist, Fort Worth Star-Telegram, 1992–. *Publications:* You and Your Congressman, 1965; The Coming Water Famine, 1966; Of Swords and Plowshares, 1968; (jtly) Congress and Conscience, 1970; Reflections of a Public Man, 1984; Worth It All, 1993. *Address:* 9A10 Federal Building, 819 Taylor Street, Fort Worth, TX 76102, USA.

WRIGHT, James Robertson Graeme; DL; Vice-Chancellor, University of Newcastle upon Tyne, since 1992; *b* 14 June 1939; *s* of John Wright and Elizabeth Calder (*née* Coghill); *m* 1966, Jennifer Susan Greenberg; two *d*. *Educ:* Inverness Royal Acad.; Dundee High Sch.; Univ. of Edinburgh (MA 1st cl. Hons Classics 1961, Guthrie Fellowship in Classical Lit., C. B. Black Scholarship in New Testament Greek); St John's Coll., Cambridge (Major Scholar, BA 1st cl. Classical Tripos Pt II 1963, MA 1968, Henry Arthur Thomas Studentship, Denney Studentship, Ferguson Scholarship in Classics, 1962). University of Edinburgh: Asst Lectr in Humanity (Latin), 1965; Lectr, 1966–78; Sen. Warden, Pollock Halls of Residence, 1973–78; Mem., Univ. Court, 1975–78; St Catharine's College, Cambridge: Fellow, 1978–87; Professorial Fellow, 1987–91; Hon. Fellow, 1992–; Dir, Studies in Classics, 1978–87; Bursar, 1979–87; Cambridge Bursar's Committee: Sec., 1983–86; Chm., 1986–87; Sec.-Gen. of Faculties, Univ. of Cambridge, 1987–91. Non-executive Member: Cambridge Dist HA, 1990–91; Northern and Yorks RHA, 1994–; Mem., SHEFC, 1992–; Associate Comr, Hamlyn Nat. Commn on Educn, 1992–93. British Council: Mem., CICHE, 1993–; Mem., CICHE Cttee 2 (Asia and Oceans Reg.), 1992–94. Dir, Newcastle Initiative, 1993–. Mem., Governing Body, Shrewsbury Sch., 1986–. DL Tyne and Wear, 1995. *Publications:* articles and reviews in classical jls. *Recreations:* walking, travel in France, food, wine. *Address:* 6 Kensington Terrace, Newcastle upon Tyne NE1 7RU. *T:* 0191–222 6064. *Clubs:* Athenæum; Northern Counties (Newcastle upon Tyne).

WRIGHT, Joe Booth, CMG 1979; HM Diplomatic Service, retired; Ambassador to Ivory Coast, Upper Volta and Niger, 1975–78; *b* 24 Aug. 1920; *s* of Joe Booth Wright and Annie Elizabeth Wright; *m* 1st, 1945, Pat (*née* Beaumont); one *s* two *d*; 2nd, 1967, Patricia Maxine (*née* Nicholls). *Educ:* King Edward VI Grammar Sch., Retford; Univ. of London. BA Hons, French. GPO, 1939–47. Served War, HM Forces: RAOC, Intelligence Corps, 1941–46. Entered Foreign Office, 1947; FO, 1947–51; Vice-Consul, Jerusalem, 1951; Consul, Munich, 1952, and Basra, 1954; Dep. Consul, Tamsui, 1956; FO, 1959–64; Consul, Surabaya, 1964; Consul, Medan, 1965–67; First Sec. (Information), Nicosia, 1968; Head of Chancery and Consul, Tunis, 1968–71; Consul-General: Hanoi, 1971–72; Geneva, 1973–75. Mem., Inst. of Linguists and Translators' Guild, 1982–. FRSA 1987. *Publications:* Francophone Black Africa Since Independence, 1981; Zaire Since Independence, 1983; Paris As It Was, 1985; Who Was the Enemy?, 1993; Security and Cooperation in Europe: the view from the East, 1993. *Recreations:* cricket, film-going, music, Chinese painting. *Address:* 29 Brittany Road, St Leonards-on-Sea, East Sussex TN38 0RB. *Club:* Royal Over-Seas League.

WRIGHT, Captain John, DSC 1944; RN (retd); General Manager, HM Dockyard, Devonport, 1972–77; *b* 30 April 1921; *s* of Percy Robert and Lucy Ada Wright; *m* 1946, Ethel Lumley Sunderland; one *s* two *d*. *Educ:* Liverpool Univ. (Part I for BSc). MIEE; Silver Medal, City and Guilds. Served War: RNVR, 1942; 16th Destroyer Flotilla, 1942; HMS Birmingham, 1943; HMS Diadem, 1943. Devonport Gunnery Sch., 1946; HMS Collingwood, 1948; BJSM, USA, 1951; Admiralty Surface Weapons Estabt, 1952; HMS Cumberland, 1956; Naval Ordnance Div., 1958; British Naval Staff, USA, 1960; Polaris Technical Dept, 1964; HM Dockyard, Chatham, 1968; RN retd 1972. Gen. Manager, Marconi Space and Defence Systems Ltd, Portsmouth, 1981–82; Asst Man. Dir and Gen. Manager, Marconi Underwater Systems, 1982–84. *Recreations:* fishing, gardening, golf. *Address:* The Ferns, 15 Brook Meadow, Fareham, Hants PO15 5JH. *T:* Fareham (01329) 280512.

WRIGHT, John Hurrell C.; *see* Collier-Wright.

WRIGHT, Hon. Sir (John) Michael, Kt 1990; **Hon. Mr Justice Wright;** a Judge of the High Court of Justice, Queen's Bench Division, since 1990; Presiding Judge, South Eastern Circuit, since 1995; *b* 26 Oct. 1932; *s* of Prof. John George Wright, DSc, MVSc, FRCVS, and Elsie Lloyd Razey; *m* 1959, Kathleen, *er d* of F. A. Meanwell; one *s* two *d*. *Educ:* King's Sch., Chester; Oriel Coll., Oxford. BA Jurisprudence 1956, MA 1978. Served Royal Artillery, 1951–53; TA, 1953–57. Called to Bar, Lincoln's Inn (Tancred Student), 1957, Bencher 1983; QC 1974; a Recorder, 1974–90; Leader, SE Circuit, 1981–83; Chm. of the Bar, 1983–84 (Vice-Chm., 1982–83). Member: Bar Council, 1972–73; Senate of the Four Inns of Court, 1973–74; Senate of the Inns of Court and the Bar, 1975–84. Mem. Supreme Court Rules Cttee, 1973–74. Legal Assessor to the Disciplinary Cttee, RCVS, 1983–90; Vice-Chm., Appeal Cttee, ICA, 1989–90. Hon. Member: American Bar Assoc.; Canadian Bar Assoc. *Recreations:* books, music. *Address:* c/o Royal Courts of Justice, Strand, WC2A 2LL.

WRIGHT, Sir (John) Oliver, GCMG 1981 (KCMG 1974; CMG 1964); GCVO 1978; DSC 1944; HM Diplomatic Service, retired; King of Arms, Most Distinguished Order of St Michael and St George, since 1987; *b* 6 March 1921; *m* 1942, Lillian Marjory Osborne; three *s*. *Educ:* Solihull School; Christ's College, Cambridge (MA; Hon. Fellow 1981; pre-elected Master, May 1982, resigned July 1982). Served in RNVR, 1941–45. Joined HM Diplomatic Service, Nov. 1945; served: New York, 1946–47; Bucharest, 1948–50; Singapore, 1950–51; Foreign Office, 1952–54; Berlin, 1954–56; Pretoria, 1957–58. Imperial Defence College, 1959. Asst Private Sec. to Sec. of State for Foreign Affairs, 1960; Counsellor and Private Sec., 1963; Private Sec. to the Prime Minister, 1964–66 (to Rt Hon. Sir Alec Douglas-Home, and subseq. to Rt Hon. Harold Wilson); Ambassador to Denmark, 1966–69; seconded to Home Office as UK Rep. to NI Govt, Aug. 1969–March 1970; Chief Clerk, HM Diplomatic Service, 1970–72; Dep. Under-Sec. of State, FCO, 1972–75; Ambassador to Federal Republic of Germany, 1975–81; retired, then re-apptd, Ambassador to Washington, 1982–86. Director: Siemens Ltd, 1981–82; Amalgamated Metal Corp., April-July 1982; Savoy Hotel plc, 1987–94; Berkeley Hotel, 1994–; General Technology Systems Inc., 1990–95; Enviromed plc, 1993–. Distinguished Vis. Prof., Univ. of S Carolina, 1986–90; Clark Fellow, Cornell Univ., 1987; Lewin Vis. Prof., Washington Univ., St Louis, 1988. Pres., German Chamber of Industry and Commerce, London, 1989–92. Bd Mem., British Council, 1981–82, 1986–90. Trustee: British Museum, 1986–91; Internat. Shakespeare Globe Centre, 1986–; Chm., British Königswinter Conf. Steering Cttee, 1987–; Co-Chm., Anglo-Irish Encounter, 1986–91. Gov., Reigate Grammar Sch., 1987– (Chm., 1990–). Hon. DHL Univ. of Nebraska, 1983; Hon. DL Rockford Coll., Ill, 1985. Grand Cross, German Order of Merit, 1978. *Recreations:* theatre, gardening. *Address:* Burstow Hall, near Horley, Surrey RH6 9SR. *T:* Horley (01293) 783494. *Club:* Travellers.

WRIGHT, (John) Stephen; Managing Director and Senior International Vice-President, IMG Artists, since 1991; *b* 12 Feb. 1946; *s* of Eustace McDonald Wright and Hilde Wright; *m* 1977, Jadwiga Maria Rapf; two *s* one *d*. *Educ:* Dragon Sch., Oxford; Westminster; Magdalene Coll., Cambridge (Hons Mod. Langs and Law). Co-founder and Dir, Oxford and Cambridge Shakespeare Co., 1969–71; Dir, Shawconcerts Ltd, 1971–75; Dir, later Jt Man. Dir, Harold Holt, 1975–90. *Recreations:* cricket, wine, classic cars. *Address:* 19 Shaa Road, W3 7LW. *Club:* Garrick.

WRIGHT, Joseph, OBE 1978; FRPharmS; FCIS; Secretary (Chief Executive), National Pharmaceutical Association (formerly National Pharmaceutical Union), 1961–81; *b* 7 Jan. 1917; *s* of late Thomas Wright and Margaret (*née* Cardwell); *m* 1942, Margaretta May Hart Talbot, BA, MRPharmS; two *s* two *d*. *Educ:* Blackpool Boys' Grammar Sch.; Chelsea Polytechnic. Dip., Chem. and Druggist and PhC examinations. Called to the Bar, Middle Temple, 1952. In retail pharmacy, 1933–47, incl. 4 years apprenticeship in Blackpool, with subseq. experience in London. Served war, RAF, commnd wireless navigator, Coastal Comd. On staff, Pharm. Section, Min. of Health, 1947–48; joined NPU, 1948: Asst Sec., 1949, Dep. Sec., 1955, Sec. and Manager, 1961; Dir, NPA Gp, 1971 (Gp comprises Nat. Pharm. Assoc. Ltd, Chemists' Def. Assoc. Ltd, Pharmacy Mutual Insce Co. Ltd, Pharm. and Gen. Prov. Soc., NPU Ltd (t/a NPA Sces), NPU Holdings Ltd). Director: NPU Holdings Ltd, 1965–81; NPU Ltd, 1971–81; Indep. Chemists Marketing Ltd, 1972–81; NPU Marketing Ltd, 1966–81; Member: Standing Pharm. Adv. Cttee, 1964–82; Poisons Bd, 1963–84; Panel of Fellows of Pharm. Soc., 1965–82; Gen. Practice Sub-Cttee, PSGB, 1963–81; Bd, Nat. Chamber of Trade, 1973–82; Trade & Professional Alliance, 1975–81; Legislation & Taxation Cttee, Nat. Ch. of Trade, 1964–81; Adviser to Pharm. Services Negotiating Cttee, 1977–81. Hon. Life Mem., S African Retail Chem. and Druggists Assoc., 1974; Distinguished Service Award, Pharmacy Guild of Aust., 1978. Charter Gold Medal of Pharmaceutical Soc. of GB, 1980. Liveryman, Worshipful Soc. of Apoth. of London, 1978–. Freedom of City of London. *Recreations:* reading, travel, amateur radio (G0AJO) and—intermittently—grandchildren. *Address:* 116 Wynchgate, Winchmore Hill, N21 1QU. *T:* 0181–886 1645.

WRIGHT, Judith, (Mrs J. P. McKinney); writer; *b* 31 May 1915; *d* of late Phillip Arundell Wright, CMG, and Ethel Mabel (*née* Bigg); *m* J. P. McKinney; one *d*. *Educ:* NSW Correspondence Sch.; New England Girls' Sch.; Sydney Univ. Secretarial work, 1938–42; Univ. Statistician (Univ. of Queensland), 1945–48. Creative Arts Fellow, ANU, 1974; Australia Council Senior Writers' Fellowship, 1977. FAHA 1970. Dr of Letters (Hon.): Univ. of New England, 1963; Univ. of Sydney, 1976; Monash Univ., 1977; ANU, 1981; Univ. of NSW, 1985; Griffith Univ., 1988; Univ. of Melbourne, 1988. Encyclopædia Britannica Writer's Award, 1965; Robert Frost Medallion, Fellowship of Australian Writers, 1975; Asan World Prize, Asan Meml Assoc., 1984; NSW Premier's Special Prize for Poetry, 1991; Queen's Gold Medal for Poetry, 1992; Human Rights Poetry Award, 1994;. *Publications: verse:* The Moving Image, 1946; Woman to Man, 1950; The Gateway, 1953; The Oxford Book of Australian Verse, 1954; New Land New Language (anthology), 1956; The Two Fires, 1955; Birds, 1960; Five Senses, 1963; The Other Half, 1966; Collected Poems, 1971; Alive, 1972; Fourth Quarter, 1976; The Double Tree, 1978; Phantom Dwelling, 1985; A Human Pattern, 1990; Collected Poems 1942–1985, 1994; *prose:* The Generations of Men, 1955; Preoccupations in Australian Poetry, 1964; The Nature of Love, 1966; Because I Was Invited, 1975; Charles Harpur, 1977; The Coral Battleground, 1977; The Cry for the Dead, 1981; We Call for a Treaty, 1985; Born of The Conquerors, 1991; Going on Talking, 1992; four books for children; also critical essays and monographs. *Recreation:* gardening. *Address:* PO Box 93, Braidwood, NSW 2622, Australia.

WRIGHT, Kenneth Campbell, CMG 1987; OBE 1973; PhD; HM Diplomatic Service, retired; Political Affairs Adviser, Saferworld Foundation, since 1992; with Research Department, The Economist, since 1992; *b* 31 May 1932; *s* of James Edwin Wright and Eva Rebecca Wright (*née* Sayers) *m* 1958, Diana Yolande Binnie; one *s* two *d*. *Educ:* George Heriot's Sch., Edinburgh; Univs of Edinburgh (MA 1st Cl. Hons Mod Langs, PhD) and Paris (LèsL). Short-service commission, Royal Air Force, 1957–60. Lecturer, Inst. Politique Congolais and Lovanium Univ., Congo (Zaire), 1960–63; Lectr, later Sen. Lectr, Dept of Modern Languages, Univ. of Ghana, 1963–65; entered HM Diplomatic Service, 1965; FO, 1965–68; First Sec., Bonn, 1968–72; FCO, 1972–75; First Sec., later Counsellor, UK Permanent Representation to the European Communities, Brussels, 1975–79; FCO, 1979–82; Counsellor, Paris, 1982–85; Asst Under-Sec. of State, FCO, 1985–89. Dir, BIEC, subseq. BI, 1989–91. *Recreations:* people, places, books. *Address:* c/o Royal Bank of Scotland, Drummonds Branch, 49 Charing Cross, SW1A 2DX. *Club:* Athenæum.

WRIGHT, Lance Armitage, RIBA; Associate Director, International Committee of Architectural Critics, since 1978; *b* 25 Dec. 1915; *s* of Edmund Lancelot Wright and Elizabeth Helen (*née* Bonser); *m* 1942, Susan Melville Foster; two *s* two *d*. *Educ:* Haileybury; University Coll. London; Architectural Assoc. Sch. Architect in private practice, 1946–73; Registrar, Royal West of England Academy Sch. of Architecture, 1950–53; Technical Editor, The Architects Journal, 1954; Editor, The Architectural

Review, 1973–80. Exhibn of drawings, Hot Bath Gall., Bath, 1995. Chevalier, Order of St Gregory the Great, 1971. *Publication:* (with D. A. C. A. Boyne) Architects Working Details, vols 4–15, 1953–69. *Address:* The White House, Summerside, Buckland, near Faringdon, Oxon, OX7 8RB.

WRIGHT, Lester Paul; Under Secretary, Department of National Heritage, since 1992; *b* 2 July 1946; *s* of late Christopher Percy Wright and of Mary Wright (*née* Sutton); *m* 1969, Jill Wildman; one *s* (and one *s* decd). *Educ:* Bedford Sch.; Gonville and Caius Coll., Cambridge (MA, PhD); Harvard Univ. Lectr in History, Univ. of Reading, 1970–71; Home Office, 1971; Asst Private Sec. to Home Sec., 1972; Harkness Fellow, Harvard Univ. and Univ. of California at Berkeley, 1976–77; Private Sec. to Perm. Under Sec., 1980–82; Asst Sec., 1983–92. *Recreations:* music, theatre, walking, looking at pictures. *Address:* Department of National Heritage, 2–4 Cockspur Street, SW1Y 5DH.

WRIGHT, Margaret; Development Executive, The Law Society, 1988–91; *b* 18 Oct. 1931; *d* of Harry Platt and Edith Baxter; *m* 1991, Bill Wright. *Educ:* Bedford College, Univ. of London (BA Hons 1st Cl., History). Called to the Bar, Gray's Inn, 1956. Estate Duty Officer, Inland Revenue, 1952–63; Inst. of Professional Civil Servants, 1963–87 (Dep. Gen. Sec., 1980–87); Gen. Sec., Clearing Bank Union, 1987–88. Mem., Industrial Disputes Panel, Jersey, 1989–. *Recreations:* renovating old houses, travel, reading. *Address:* Brickwall Farm, Broad Road, Bacton, Stowmarket, Suffolk IP14 4HP. *T:* Bacton (01449) 780197.

WRIGHT, Prof. Margaret S.; *see* Scott Wright.

WRIGHT, Martin; Visiting Research Fellow, Centre for Legal Studies, University of Sussex, since 1995; Policy Development Officer, Victim Support, 1988–94; *b* 24 April 1930; *s* of late Clifford Kent Wright and Rosalie Wright, Stoke Newington; *m* 1957, Louisa Mary Nicholls; three *s* two *d*. *Educ:* Repton; Jesus Coll., Oxford; PhD LSE, 1992. Librarian, Inst. of Criminology, Cambridge, 1964–71; Dir, Howard League for Penal Reform, 1971–81; NAVSS, later Victim Support, 1985–, Information Officer, 1985–88. Chm., Lambeth Mediation Service, 1989–92; Vice-Chm., Forum for Initiatives in Reparation and Mediation, 1988–89. Vis. Scholar, Centre for Criminological and Legal Res., Univ. of Sheffield, 1994–95. ALA 1960. *Publications:* (ed) The Use of Criminological Literature, 1974; Making Good: Prisons, Punishment and Beyond, 1982; (ed jtly) Mediation and Criminal Justice, 1988; Justice for Victims and Offenders: a restorative response to crime, 1991. *Recreation:* suggesting improvements. *Address:* 19 Hillside Road, SW2 3HL. *T:* 0181–671 8037.

WRIGHT, Hon. Sir Michael; *see* Wright, Hon. Sir J. M.

WRIGHT, Michael Thomas; writer and lecturer on architecture, fine arts and conservation; *b* 10 Dec. 1936; *o c* of Thomas Manning Wright and Hilda Evelyn Wright (*née* Whiting); *m* 1st, 1964, Jennifer Olga Angus (marr. diss. 1990), 2nd *d* of C. B. Angus, Singapore; two *s*; 2nd, 1990, Wendelina Elisabeth Pascall (*née* van Manen). *Educ:* Bristol Grammar Sch.; Gonville and Caius Coll., Cambridge (MA); Trinity Coll., Dublin. Formerly: Financial Analyst, Ford Motor Co. Asst Sec., Town Planning Inst.; Editor, Town Planning Inst. Jl; Asst Editor, Country Life; Managing Editor, Journal of Royal Inst. of British Architects; Dep. Editor, Country Life; Publisher: Country Life, 1984–87 (Editor, 1973–84, Editor in Chief, 1980–84); Practical Woodworking, 1985–87; Television, 1985–87; Editor in Chief and Publisher, Antique Dealer and Collectors' Guide, 1982–87; Dir, Nat. Heritage Meml Fund, 1987–88; Editorial Consultant, Country Life Books, 1978–86. Vis. Lectr in British Architecture, Roger Williams Univ., USA, 1995. Member, Honourable Society of Gray's Inn. Churchwarden, St Michael's Parish Church, Highgate, 1974–79; Chm., Highgate Soc., 1985–87. Judge, RICS (formerly RICS/The Times) Conservation Awards, 1976–89, 1991–. Lectr, NADFAS, 1989–; Tutor, Dept of Continuing Educn, Univ. of Bristol. Chairman: Lutyens Trust, 1993–95 (Trustee, 1986–95); Friends of Bristol Art Gall., 1993–; Member: DoE Working Party on Rural Settlements; Cttee, SPAB, 1987–. FRSA 1980. JP Haringey, 1986–89. *Publications:* Explore Britain's Country Gardens, 1993; contrib. articles to: TPI Jl; RIBA Jl; Water Space; Country Life; Homes and Gardens. *Recreations:* music, tennis, walking; participation in local amenity society work. *Address:* Doverhay, Woollard Lane, Whitchurch, near Bristol, Avon BS14 0QS. *T:* Whitchurch (01275) 838201. *Club:* Travellers'.

WRIGHT, Prof. Michael Thomas, FEng 1988; Professor of Mechanical Engineering, since 1990, and Senior Pro-Vice Chancellor, 1994, Aston University; *b* 11 April 1947; *s* of William George and Lilly May Wright; *m* 1970, Patricia Eunice Cox; one *d*. *Educ:* Sheldon Heath Sch., Birmingham; Aston Univ. (BSc 1st Cl. Hons, PhD). Sen. Mem., IEEE 1980; FIEE 1981; FIMechE 1989; FIMA 1994. Apprentice, Electrical Power Engineering Co.; 1969–82: Redman Heenan Froude, Heenan Drives, Linear Motors, Parsons Peebles Motors and Generators, NEI Peebles, Scottish Engineering Training Scheme; Engrg Dir, GEC Large Machines, 1982–85; Man. Dir, Molins Tobacco Machinery, 1985–87; Man. Dir, 1988–90, non-Exec. Dir, 1990–, Molins; Aston University: Vis. Prof. of Electrical Engrg, 1986–90; Head, Dept of Mech. and Elect. Engrg, 1990–92. Chairman: Aston Business Sch., 1992–93; 600 Group, 1993–. *Publications:* numerous papers on electrical machines and drives in learned jls; articles on shooting and ballistics. *Recreations:* shooting, history of film, travelling, reading. *Address:* Aston University, Aston Triangle, Birmingham B4 7ET. *T:* 0121–359 3611.

WRIGHT, Prof. Nicholas Alcwyn, MD, PhD, DSc; FRCPath; Professor of Histopathology, Royal Postgraduate Medical School, since 1980; Director of Clinical Research, Imperial Cancer Research Fund, since 1991; *b* 24 Feb. 1943; *s* of late Glyndwr Alcwyn Wright and Hilda Lilian (*née* Jones); *m* 1966, Vera, (Ned), Matthewson; one *s* one *d*. *Educ:* Bristol Grammar Sch.; Durham Univ. (MB BS 1965); Newcastle Univ. (MD 1974; PhD 1975; DSc 1984); MA (Oxon) 1979. FRCPath 1986. University of Newcastle upon Tyne: Demonstrator in Pathology, 1966–71; Res. Fellow, 1971–74; Lectr in Pathology, 1974–76; Sen. Lectr, 1976–77; Clinical Reader in Pathology, Univ. of Oxford, 1977, Nuffield Reader, 1978; Fellow, Green Coll., Oxford, 1979–80; Dir of Histopathology, Hammersmith Hosp., 1980–; Clin. Dir of Path., Hammersmith Hosps Trust, 1994–; Imperial Cancer Research Fund: Asst Dir, 1988; Associate Dir, 1989; Dep. Dir, 1990; Dir, Histopathology Unit, 1988–. Chm., Research for Health Charities Gp, 1994–. Mem. Council: RCPath, 1982, 1986, 1990; British Soc. for Gastroenterology, 1986, 1990. Editor, Cell and Tissue Kinetics, 1980–87. Lectures: Avery Jones, Central Middx Hosp., 1989; Kettle, RCPath, 1990; Showering, Southmead Hosp., 1991; Morson, British Soc. Gastroenterology, 1991; Burroughs Wellcome, Yale Univ., 1993. *Publications:* Introduction to Cell Population Kinetics, 1977; (ed) Psoriasis: cell proliferation, 1982; The Biology of Epithelial Cell Populations, 1984; (ed) Colorectal Cancer, 1989; (ed) Oxford Textbook of Pathology, 1991; (ed) Clinical Aspects of Cell Proliferation, 1991; (ed) Molecular Pathology of Cancer, 1993. *Recreations:* Rugby football, cricket, squash, military history, cooking. *Address:* Department of Histopathology, Royal Postgraduate Medical School, Hammersmith Hospital, Du Cane Road, W12 0NN. *T:* 0181–740 3292; Imperial Cancer Research Fund, Lincoln's Inn Fields, WC2A 3PX. *T:* 0171–242 0200. *Club:* Athenæum.

WRIGHT, Very Rev. (Nicholas) Thomas, DPhil; Dean of Lichfield, since 1994; *b* 1 Dec. 1948; *s* of Nicholas Irwin Wright and Rosemary (*née* Forman); *m* 1971, Margaret Elizabeth Anne Fiske; two *s* two *d*. *Educ:* Sedbergh Sch.; Exeter Coll., Oxford (BA 1st cl. Hons LitHum 1971; MA 1975; DPhil 1981); Wycliffe Hall, Oxford (BA 1st cl. Hons Theology 1973). Ordained deacon, 1975, priest 1976; Jun. Res. Fellow, 1975–78, Jun. Chaplain, 1976–78, Merton Coll., Oxford; Fellow and Chaplain, Downing Coll., Cambridge, 1978–81; Asst Prof. of New Testament Studies, McGill Univ., Montreal, and Hon. Prof., Montreal Dio. Theol Coll., 1981–86; Lectr in Theology, Oxford Univ., and Fellow, Tutor and Chaplain, Worcester Coll., Oxford, 1986–93. Fellow, Inst. for Christian Studies, Toronto, 1992–; Canon Theologian, Coventry Cathedral, 1992–. Mem., Doctrine Comn of C of E, 1979–81, 1989–. *Publications:* Small Faith, Great God, 1978; The Work of John Frith, 1983; The Epistles of Paul to the Colossians and to Philemon, 1987; The Glory of Christ in the New Testament, 1987; The Interpretation of the New Testament 1861–1986, 1988; The Climax of the Covenant, 1991; New Tasks for a Renewed Church, 1992; The Crown and the Fire, 1992; The New Testament and the People of God, 1992; Who Was Jesus?, 1992; Following Jesus, 1994; Jesus and the Victory of God, 1995. *Recreations:* music, hill walking, poetry, cricket, golf. *Address:* The Deanery, Lichfield, Staffs WS13 7LD. *T:* Lichfield (01543) 256120.

WRIGHT, Sir Oliver; *see* Wright, Sir J. O.

WRIGHT, Sir Paul (Hervé Giraud), KCMG 1975 (CMG 1960); OBE 1952; FRSA; HM Diplomatic Service, retired; Chairman: Irvin Great Britain Ltd, 1979–88; British American Arts Association, 1983–88; Member Council, Forte plc (formerly Trusthouse Forte), since 1987; *b* 12 May 1915; *o s* of late Richard Hervé Giraud Wright; *m* 1942, Beatrice Frederika Rathbone (*see* Beatrice Wright), *widow* of Flt-Lt J. R. Rathbone, MP; one *d*. *Educ:* Westminster Sch. (Hon. Fellow, 1992). Employed by John Lewis Partnership Ltd, 1933–39. Served HM Forces, War of 1939–45; Major, KRRC; HQ 21 Army Group, 1944–45 (despatches). Contested (L) NE Bethnal Green, 1945. Asst Dir, Public Relations, National Coal Bd, 1946–48; Dir, Public Relations, Festival of Britain, 1948–51. HM Foreign Service: Paris and New York, 1951–54; Foreign Office, 1954–56; The Hague, 1956–57; Head of Information, Policy Dept in FO, 1957–60; Cairo, 1960–61; UK Delegn to N Atlantic Council, 1961–64; Minister (Information), Washington, 1965–68, and Dir-Gen., British Inf. Services, NY, 1964–68; Ambassador to Congo (Kinshasa) and to Republic of Burundi, 1969–71; Ambassador to the Lebanon, 1971–75. Special Rep. of Sec. of State for Foreign and Commonwealth Affairs, 1975–78. Chm., British Lebanese Assoc., 1987–90. Hon. Sec. Gen., London Celebrations Cttee for Queen's Silver Jubilee, 1977; Vice-Chm., The American Fest., 1985; Pres., Elizabethan Club, 1988–; Governor, Westminster Cathedral Choir School, 1981– (Chm., 1993–); Chm., Westminster Sch. Develt Council, 1994–. Hon. RCM 1990. Kt of the Order of the Cedar of Lebanon, 1990. *Publication:* A Brittle Glory (autobiog.), 1986. *Address:* 62 Westminster Gardens, Marsham Street, SW1P 4JG. *Clubs:* Garrick, Beefsteak.

WRIGHT, Penelope Ann, (Mrs D. C. H. Wright); *see* Boys, P. A.

WRIGHT, Peter, CBE 1988 (OBE 1982); Chief Constable, South Yorkshire Police, 1983–90; *b* Stockport, 21 July 1929; *s* of late Henry Wright and Elizabeth (*née* Burton); *m* 1950, Mary Dorothea (*née* Stanway); one *s*. *Educ:* Edgeley Roman Catholic Sch.; Stockport Technical School. RN, 1947–49. Manchester City Police, 1954, to Chief Superintendent, Greater Manchester, 1975; Asst Chief Constable, 1975–79, Dep. Chief Constable, 1979–82, Merseyside. Police Advr, MoD, 1990–93. Mem., Parole Review Cttee, 1987–88. Pres., ACPO, 1988–89. Freeman, City of London, 1992. *Recreations:* walking, gardening. *Address:* c/o South Yorkshire Police, Snig Hill, Sheffield S3 8LY. *T:* Sheffield (01742) 78522. *Club:* Commonwealth Trust.

WRIGHT, Peter, FRCP, FRCS, FRCOphth; Consultant Ophthalmic Surgeon, Moorfields Eye Hospital, 1973–94, Consulting Ophthalmic Surgeon, 1994; President, Royal College of Ophthalmologists, 1991–94; *b* 7 Sept. 1932; *s* of late William Victor Wright and Ada Amelie (*née* Craze); *m* 1960, Elaine Catherine Donoghue (marr. diss. 1992); two *d* (one *s* decd). *Educ:* St Clement Danes; King's Coll. London; King's Coll. Hosp. (MB BS 1955). AKC 1955; MRCS, LRCP 1955; FRCS 1964; DO 1959; FCOphth 1988; FRCP 1994. Resident appts, KCH and Guy's Hosp., 1955–57; ophthalmic specialist, RAF Med. Br., 1957–59; Lectr in Anatomy and Physiology, Guy's Hosp. Med. Sch., 1959–61; House Surgeon and Sen. Resident, Moorfields Eye Hosp., 1961–65; Lectr in Physiology, Inst. of Ophthalmology, 1965–68; Consultant Ophthalmic Surgeon: KCH, 1966–78; Sydenham Children's Hosp., 1967–73; Clinical Sub-Dean, Inst. Ophthalmology, 1980–86; Surgical Tutor, Moorfields Eye Hosp., 1981–86; Cons. Advr in Ophthalmology, DoH, 1988–. Cons. Advr, Royal Soc. of Musicians, 1986–. Examiner: Dip. in Ophthalmology, 1967–73; Ophthalmic Nursing Bd, 1973–78 (Mem., 1974–87); Mem., Court of Examnrs, RCS, 1977–83. Ophthalmic Section, Royal Society of Medicine: Mem. Council and Vice-Pres., 1968–75; Pres., 1988–90; Ophthalmological Society of UK: Sec., 1968–70; Mem. Council, 1970–74; Vice-Pres., 1985–87; Pres., 1987–88; Southern Ophthalmic Society: Mem. Council, 1970–74; Pres., 1984–85; Sen. Vice-Pres., Coll. of Ophthalmologists, 1988–92; Mem. Council, RCS, 1992–; Trustee and Mem. Council, Assoc. for Eye Res., 1966– (Treas. 1966–82). Lectures: Charnwood, 1977; Doyne (and Medal), 1986; Mauerberger Meml, 1987. Hon. Mem., NZ Ophthalmol Soc.; Mem., French and German Ophthalmol Socs; Internat. Mem., Amer. Acad. Ophthal. Freeman, City of London; Liveryman, Soc. of Apothecaries. *Publications:* chapters in: Clinical Aspects of Immunology, 1981; Clinical Ophthalmology, 1987; Relationships in Dermatology, 1988; contribs on external eye disease and immunology to med. jls. *Recreations:* playing the piano, gardening. *Address:* Southbrook Court, Southbrook Lane, Bovey Tracey, Devon TQ13 9NB.

WRIGHT, Peter Michael, FRCO(CHM); Organist and Director of Music, Southwark Cathedral, since 1989; *b* 6 March 1954; *s* of Dudley Cyril Brazier Wright and Pamela Deirdre (*née* Peacock). *Educ:* Highgate Sch. (Music Schol.); Royal Coll. of Music (Exhibnr; ARCM); Emmanuel Coll., Cambridge (Organ Schol.; MA). LRAM. Sub-Organist, Guildford Cathedral, and Music Master, Royal Grammar Sch., Guildford, 1977–89. Conductor: Guildford Chamber Choir, 1984–94; Surrey Festival Choir, 1987–. Freelance conductor, recitalist (organ), adjudicator and broadcaster. Mem. Council, RCO, 1990–. *Recreations:* travel, theatre, reading, good food. *Address:* 52 Bankside, SE1 9JE. *T:* 0171–261 1291.

WRIGHT, Sir Peter (Robert), Kt 1993; CBE 1985; Director, The Birmingham (formerly Sadler's Wells) Royal Ballet, 1977–95; *b* 25 Nov. 1926; *s* of Bernard and Hilda Mary Wright; *m* 1954, Sonya Hana; one *s* one *d*. *Educ:* Bedales School; Leighton Park Sch. Dancer: Ballet Jooss, 1945–47, 1951–52; Metropolitan Ballet, 1947–49; Sadler's Wells Theatre Ballet, 1949–51, 1952–56; Ballet Master, Sadler's Wells Opera, and Teacher, Royal Ballet Sch., 1956–58; freelance choreographer and teacher, 1958–61; Ballet Master and Asst Dir, Stuttgart Ballet, 1961–63; BBC Television Producer, 1963–65; freelance choreographer, 1965–69; Associate Dir, Royal Ballet, 1969–77. Special Prof., Sch. of Performance Studies, Birmingham Univ., 1990–. Governor: Royal Ballet Sch., 1976–; Sadler's Wells Theatre, 1987–. Pres., Benesh Inst., 1993–. *Creative Works:* Ballets: A Blue

Rose, 1957; The Great Peacock, 1958; Musical Chairs, 1959; The Mirror Walkers, 1962; Quintet, 1962; Namouna, 1963; Designs for Dancers, 1963; Summer's Night, 1964; Danse Macabre, 1964; Variations, 1964; Concerto, 1965; Arpege, 1974; El Amor Brujo, 1975; Summertide, 1976; own productions of classics: Giselle: Stuttgart, 1966; Cologne, 1967; Royal Ballet, 1968 and 1985; Canadian National Ballet, 1970; Munich, 1976; Dutch National Ballet, 1977; Houston, Texas, 1979; Frankfurt, 1980; Rio de Janeiro, Brazil, 1982; Winnipeg, 1982; Tokyo, 1989; The Sleeping Beauty: Cologne, 1968; Royal Ballet, 1968; Munich, 1974; Dutch National Ballet, 1981; Sadler's Wells Royal Ballet, 1984; Vienna State Opera Ballet, 1995; Coppelia: Royal Ballet, 1976; Sadler's Wells Royal Ballet, 1979; Scottish Ballet, 1992; Birmingham Royal Ballet, 1995; Swan Lake: Sadler's Wells Royal Ballet, 1981; Munich, 1984; Birmingham Royal Ballet, 1991; Nutcracker: Royal Ballet, 1984, Birmingham Royal Ballet, 1990. FBSM (Conservatoire Fellow), 1991; Fellow, Birmingham Soc., 1995. Hon. DMus London, 1990; Hon. DLitt Birmingham, 1994. Evening Standard Award for Ballet, 1982; Queen Elizabeth II Coronation Award, Royal Acad. of Dancing, 1990; Digital Premier Award, 1991. *Recreations:* ceramics, gardening. *Address:* c/o Birmingham Royal Ballet, Birmingham Hippodrome, Thorp Street, Birmingham B5 4AU.

WRIGHT, Maj.-Gen. Richard Eustace John G.; *see* Gerrard-Wright.

WRIGHT, Sir Richard (Michael) C.; *see* Cory-Wright.

WRIGHT, Robert Anthony Kent, QC 1973; *b* 7 Jan. 1922; *s* of Robert and Eva Wright; *m* 1956, Gillian Elizabeth Drummond Hancock. *Educ:* Hilton Coll., Natal, S Africa; St Paul's Sch., London; The Queen's Coll., Oxford (MA). Indian Army, 1942–46, Major. Oxford, 1946–48. Called to Bar, Lincoln's Inn, 1949, Bencher 1979. Hon. Fellow, Univ. of Central England. *Recreations:* music, sailing, golf, walking. *Address:* Erskine Chambers, 30 Lincoln's Inn Fields, WC2A 3PF. *T:* 0171–242 5532. *Clubs:* National Liberal; Bosham Sailing (Bosham); Island Sailing (Cowes); Royal Wimbledon Golf (Wimbledon).

WRIGHT, Rt. Rev. Roderick; *see* Argyll and the Isles, Bishop of, (RC).

WRIGHT, Very Rev. Ronald (William Vernon) Selby, CVO 1968; TD; DD; FRSE; FSA Scotland; JP; Minister Emeritus of the Canongate (The Kirk of Holyroodhouse), Edinburgh, and of Edinburgh Castle (Minister, 1936–77); Extra Chaplain to the Queen in Scotland, 1961–63 and since 1978 (Chaplain, 1963–78); Chaplain to The Queen's Body Guard for Scotland, Royal Company of Archers, 1973–93, Hon. Member, since 1994; *b* 12 June 1908; *s* of late Vernon O. Wright, ARCM, and late Anna Gilberta, *d* of Major R. E. Selby; unmarried. *Educ:* Edinburgh Academy; Melville Coll.; Edinburgh Univ. (MA; Hon. DD 1956); New Coll. Edinburgh. Warden, St Giles' Cathedral Boys' Club, 1927–36, and Canongate Boys' Club (formerly St Giles'), 1937–78. Cadet Officer, The Royal Scots, 1927–31; Student-Asst at St Giles' Cathedral, 1929–36; Asst Minister of Glasgow Cathedral, 1936; Warden of first Scottish Public Schools' and Clubs' Camp, 1938; Chaplain to 7th/9th (Highlanders) Bn The Royal Scots, 1938–42 (France, 1940), 1947–49; Senior Chaplain to the Forces: 52nd (Lowland) Div., 1942–43; Edinburgh Garrison, 1943; Middle East Forces, 1943–44; NE London, 1944; 10th Indian Div., CMF, 1944–45 (despatches); Hon. SCF, 1945–. Special Preacher, Oxford Univ., 1944; Select Preacher, Cambridge Univ., 1947; Visiting Preacher: Aberdeen Univ., 1946, 1953, 1965, 1973; St Andrews Univ., 1951, 1956, 1967, 1973; Glasgow Univ., 1955, 1973; Edinburgh Univ., 1959; Birmingham Univ., 1959; Hull Univ., 1967; Dundee Univ., 1973. Chaplain to, the Lord High Comr, 1959, and 1960. Conducted numerous series of religious broadcasts for BBC as Radio Padre, toured for War Office and BBC all Home Comds in 1942 and 1943 and MEF, 1943–44; toured transit camps etc in Italy, Austria, S Germany, etc, 1945; toured, for Church of Scotland: India, 1972; for HM Forces: Hong Kong 1973; Singapore, 1973. Moderator, Presbytery of Edinburgh, 1963; Moderator, Gen. Assembly of the Church of Scotland, 1972–73. Chm., Edinburgh and Leith Old People's Welfare Council, 1956–69; Extraordinary Dir, The Edinburgh Academy, 1973–; Hon. Church of Scotland Chaplain to: Fettes Coll., 1957–60, 1979–93 (Hon. Mem., 1994); Loretto Sch., 1960–84 (Hon. Old Lorettonian, 1976); Edinburgh Acad., 1966–73; Hon. Mem. Cargilfield Sch., 1985; Chaplain to: Governor of Edinburgh Castle, 1937–91; Merchant Co. of Edinburgh, 1973–82; ChStJ 1976; President: Scottish Church Soc., 1971–74; Scottish Assoc. of Boys Clubs; Vice-Pres., Old Edinburgh Club; Hon. Pres. Scottish Churches FA; Patron, Lothian Amateur FA. Mem. Edinburgh Educn Cttee, 1960–70. JP Edinburgh, 1963. Cross of St Mark, 1970. *Publications:* Asking Why (with A. W. Loos), 1939; The Average Man, 1942; Let's Ask the Padre, 1943; The Greater Victory, 1943; The Padre Presents, 1944; Small Talks, 1945; Whatever the Years, 1947; What Worries Me, 1950; Great Men, 1951; They Looked to Him, 1954; Our Club, 1954; The Kirk in the Canongate, 1956; The Selfsame Miracles, 1957; Our Club and Panmure House, 1958; Roses in December, 1960; The Seven Words, 1964; An Illustrated Guide to the Canongate, 1965; Take up God's Armour, 1967; The Seven Dwarfs, 1968; Haply I May Remember, 1970; In Christ We Are All One, 1972; Seven Sevens, 1977; Another Home, 1980; The Shadow on the Wall, 1992; *edited and contributed to:* Asking Them Questions, 1936; A Scottish Camper's Prayer Book, 1936; I Attack, 1937; Asking Them Questions-Second Series, 1938; Front Line Religion, 1941; Soldiers Also Asked, 1943; Asking Them Questions-Third Series, 1950; Asking Them Questions (a Selection), 1953; The Beloved Captain: Essays by Donald Hankey, 1956; (with L. Menzies and R. A. Knox) St Margaret, Queen of Scotland, 1957; A Manual of Church Doctrine (with T. F. Torrance), 1960; Fathers of the Kirk, 1960; Asking Them Questions, a new series, 1972, 1973; The Wind on the Heath, 1994; contrib. to Chambers's Encyclopædia, DNB, etc. Editor, Scottish Forces' Magazine (quarterly), 1941–76. *Recreation:* after trying to run Boys' Clubs and Camps, 1927–78 and a busy parish, now enjoying a busy retirement. *Address:* The Queen's House, 36 Moray Place, Edinburgh EH3 6BX. *T:* 0131–226 5566. *Clubs:* Athenæum; New (Hon. Mem.) (Edinburgh).

WRIGHT, Roy Kilner; Deputy Editor, The London Standard (formerly Evening Standard), 1979–88; *b* 12 March 1926; *s* of Ernest Wright and Louise Wright; *m* 1st (marr. diss.); two *d*; 2nd, 1969, Jane Barnicoat (*née* Selby). *Educ:* elementary sch., St Helens, Lancs. Jun. Reporter, St Helens Reporter, 1941; Army Service; Sub-Editor: Middlesbrough Gazette, 1947; Daily Express, Manchester, 1951; Daily Mirror, London, 1952; Features Editor, Daily Express, London; Dep. Editor, Daily Express, 1976, Editor, 1976–77; Dir, Beaverbrook Newspapers, 1976–77; Senior Asst Editor, Daily Mail, 1977. *Address:* Girards, Broadchalke, Salisbury, Wilts SP5 5HL. *T:* Salisbury (01722) 780385.

WRIGHT, Rt. Rev. Royston Clifford; Bishop of Monmouth, 1986–92; *b* 4 July 1922; *s* of James and Ellen Wright; *m* 1945, Barbara Joyce Nowell; one *s* one *d*. *Educ:* Univ. of Wales, Cardiff (BA 1942); St Stephen's House, Oxford. Deacon 1945, priest 1946; Curate: Bedwas, 1945–47; St John Baptist, Newport, 1947–49; Walton-on-the-Hill, Liverpool, 1949–51; Chaplain RNVR, 1950; Chaplain RN, 1951–68; Vicar of Blaenavon, Gwent, 1968–74; RD of Pontypool, 1973–74; Canon of Monmouth, 1974–77; Rector of Ebbw Vale, Gwent, 1974–77; Archdeacon of Monmouth, 1977; Archdeacon of Newport, 1977–86. *Recreations:* four grandchildren; listening to Baroque music. *Address:* 23 Rupert Brooke Drive, Newport, Gwent NP9 3HP. *T:* Newport (01633) 250770.

WRIGHT, Hon. Ruth Margaret; *see* Richardson, Hon. R. M.

WRIGHT, Sheila Rosemary Rivers; *b* 22 March 1925; *d* of Daniel Rivers Wright and Frances Grace Wright; *m* 1949, Ronald A. Gregory; two *c*. Social Science Cert. 1951; BScSoc London External 1956. Personnel Officer, 1951–57; Social Worker, 1957–74. Councillor: Birmingham CC, 1956–78; West Midlands CC, 1973–81. MP (Lab) Birmingham, Handsworth, 1979–83. Member, Birmingham Reg. Hosp. Bd and W Midlands RHA, 1966–80. *Address:* 41 Beaudesert Road, Birmingham B20 3TQ. *T:* 0121–554 9840.

WRIGHT, Shirley Edwin McEwan; corporate consultant; *b* 4 May 1915; *s* of Alfred Coningsby Wright and Elsie Derbyshire; *m* 1939, Dora Fentem; one *s* three *d*. *Educ:* Herbert Strutt Sch., Belper; Coll. of Technology, Manchester; Univ. of Sheffield. BEng, CEng, FIMechE. Metropolitan Vickers, 1932, ICI Explosives Div., 1938; Asst Chief Engr, ICI Nobel Div., 1955; Dir, Irvine Harbour Bd, 1962; Engrg and Techn Dir, ICI Nobel Div., 1965; Pres., Philippine Explosives Corp., 1970; Chief Exec., Livingston Develt Corp., 1972–77; Dir, Premix-Fibreglass, 1978–80. *Recreations:* cricket, golf. *Address:* 33 St Juliens Way, Cawthorne, near Barnsley S75 4ES. *T:* Barnsley (01226) 792030.

WRIGHT, Stanley Harris; Director: Stadium Ltd, since 1989; *b* 9 April 1930; *er s* of John Charles Wright and Doris Wright; *m* 1st, 1957, Angela Vivien Smith (marr. diss. 1973); one *s*; 2nd, 1973, Alison Elizabeth Franks (*see* Hon. A. E. Wright). *Educ:* Bolton Sch.; Merton Coll., Oxford (Postmaster); 1st cl. hons PPE. Nat. Service, Manchester Regt, 1948–49. Asst Principal, BoT, 1952–55; 2nd Sec., UK Delegn to OEEC, Paris, 1955–57; Principal, HM Treasury, 1958–64; 1st Sec. (Financial), British Embassy, Washington, 1964–66; Asst Sec., HM Treasury, 1966–68; Lazard Bros & Co. Ltd, 1969 and 1970 (Dir 1969); Under-Sec., HM Treasury, 1970–72. Exec. Dir, Lazard Bros & Co. Ltd, 1972–81; Exec. Chm., International Commercial Bank Plc, 1981–83; Non-Executive Director: Wilkinson Match Ltd, 1974–81; Scripto Inc., 1977–81; Law Land Co., 1979–81; Wolstenholme Rink, 1980–93 (Chm., 1982–91); Royal Trust Bank, 1984–88; Royal Trust Asset Management (UK Holdings) Ltd, 1987–88 (Chm.); James Ferguson Holdings Plc, 1987–88; Partner, Price Waterhouse and Partners, 1985–88. Business consultant, 1989–93. Chm., British Bankers Assoc. Fiscal Cttee, 1974–80; Member: Layfield Cttee on Local Government Finance, 1974–76; Armstrong Cttee on Budgetary Reform, 1979–80; (and Dir of Studies), CBI Wkg Pty on Tax Reform, 1984–85; CS Commn Final Selection Bd, 1986–; Panel for Financial Services Tribunal, 1988–91; Mem. Council, and Treas., QMW, London, 1989– (Mem. Council, 1977–89, Hon. Treas., 1987–89, Westfield Coll.). *Publications:* Two Cheers for the Institutions, 1994; articles on financial and fiscal matters. *Recreations:* various. *Address:* 6 Holly Place, NW3 6QU. *Clubs:* Reform, MCC.

WRIGHT, Stephen; *see* Wright, J. S.

WRIGHT, Stephen John Leadbetter; HM Diplomatic Service; Assistant Under Secretary of State (European Union affairs), Foreign and Commonwealth Office, since 1994; *b* 7 Dec. 1946; *s* of late J. H. Wright, CBE and Joan Wright; *m* 1970, Georgina Susan Butler; one *s* one *d*. *Educ:* Shrewsbury Sch.; The Queen's Coll., Oxford (BA Mod. History, 1968). HM Diplomatic Service, 1968; Havana, 1969–71; CS Coll., 1971–72; FCO, 1972–75; British Information Services, NY, 1975–80; UK Permanent Repn to EC, Brussels, 1980–84; FCO, 1984–85; seconded to Cabinet Office, 1985–87; Counsellor and Hd of Chancery, New Delhi, 1988–91; Counsellor (Ext. Relations), UK Perm. Repn to EC, Brussels, 1991–94. *Recreations:* photography, birdwatching, books. *Address:* c/o Foreign and Commonwealth Office, King Charles Street, SW1A 2AH.

WRIGHT, Very Rev. Thomas; *see* Wright, Very Rev. N. T.

WRIGHT, Prof. Verna, FRCP; Professor of Rheumatology, University of Leeds, 1970–94, now Emeritus; Consultant Physician in Rheumatology, Leeds Area Health Authority (A) Teaching, and Yorkshire Regional Health Authority, 1964–94; Co-Director, Bioengineering Group for Study of Human Joints, University of Leeds, 1964–94; *b* 31 Dec. 1928; *s* of Thomas William and Nancy Eleanor Wright; *m* 1953, Esther Margaret Brown; five *s* four *d*. *Educ:* Bedford Sch.; Univ. of Liverpool (MB ChB 1953, MD 1956). FRCP 1970 (MRCP 1958). House Officer, Broadgreen Hosp., Liverpool, 1953–54; Sen. Ho. Officer, Stoke Mandeville Hosp., 1954–56; Research Asst, Dept of Clin. Medicine, Univ. of Leeds, 1956–58; Research Fellow, Div. of Applied Physiology, Johns Hopkins Hosp., Baltimore, 1958–59; Lectr, Dept of Clin. Med., Univ. of Leeds, 1960–64; Sen. Lectr, Dept of Medicine, Univ. of Leeds, 1964–70. Adv. Fellow to World Fedn of Occupational Therapists, 1980–. President: Heberden Soc., 1976–77; British Assoc. for Rheumatology and Rehabilitation, 1978–80; Soc. for Research in Rehabilitation, 1978; Soc. for Back Pain Research, 1977–79; Arthritis and Rheumatism Council: Chairman: Standing Cttee for Academic Develt and Res., 1989–93; Exec. and Finances Cttee, 1993–. Member, Johns Hopkins Soc. for Scholars, USA, 1978–. Lectures: Casson Meml, Assoc. of Occupational Therapists, 1979; John Gibson Flemming, Royal Infirmary, Glasgow, 1984; Phillip Ellman, RSocMed, 1985; Kodama Meml, Japanese Rheumatism Assoc., Tokyo, 1986; C. W. Stewart Meml, Maryland Univ., 1988; John Matheson Shaw, RCPE, 1988; Heberden Oration, British Soc. of Rheumatology, 1985. Hon. Member: Canadian Rheumatism Assoc., 1978; Brazilian Soc. for Rheumatology, 1978; Hellenic Soc. of Rheumatology, 1981; Amer. Rheumatism Assoc., 1985. Elizabeth Fink Award, Nat. Ankylosing Spondylitis Soc., 1987. *Publications:* Lubrication and Wear in Joints, 1969; (with J. M. H. Moll) Seronegative Polyarthritis, 1976; Clinics in Rheumatic Diseases: Osteoarthrosis, 1976; (with I. Haslock) Rheumatism for Nurses and Remedial Therapists, 1977; (with D. Dowson) Evaluation of Artificial Joints, 1977; (with D. Dowson) Introduction to the Biomechanics of Joints and Joint Replacement, 1981; The Relevance of Christianity in a Scientific Age, 1981; (with H. A. Bird) Applied Drug Therapy of the Rheumatic Diseases, 1982; Topical Reviews in Rheumatic Disorders, vol. 2, 1982; Clinics in Rheumatic Diseases: osteoarthritis, 1982; Clinics in Rheumatic Diseases: measurement of joint movement, 1982; Bone and Joint Disease in the Elderly, 1983; (with R. A. Dickson) Integrated Clinical Science: musculo-skeletal disease, 1984; Personal Peace in a Nuclear Age, 1985; Arthritis and Joint Replacement (family doctor bklt), 1987; Pain, Clinical Rheumatology, International Practice and Research, 1987; (jtly) Diagnostic Picture Tests in Rheumatology, 1987; (with E. L. Radin) Mechanics of Human Joints: physiology, pathophysiology and treatment, 1993; (with P. S. Helliwell) Psoriatic Arthritis, 1994. *Recreations:* interdenominational Christian youth work, voracious reader. *Address:* Inglehurst, Park Drive, Harrogate HG2 9AY. *T:* Harrogate (01423) 502326, *Fax:* (01423) 521981.

WRIGHT, Vincent, PhD; FBA 1995; Fellow of Nuffield College, Oxford, since 1977; *b* 6 Aug. 1937; *s* of Walter Hogarth Wright and Mary Teresa Kinsella. *Educ:* London Sch. of Economics (BSc Econ; PhD 1965); Inst d'Etudes Politiques, Paris. Lectr, Newcastle Univ., 1965–69; Vis. Fellow, St Antony's Coll., Oxford, 1969–70; Lectr, Sen. Lectr, and Reader, LSE, 1970–79; Prof., Eur. Univ. Inst., Florence, 1980–82 (on leave of absence); Einaudi Prof., Cornell Univ., 1988–89. Vis. Prof., Amer. and Eur. univs. Member, Academic Board: Inst d'Etudes Politiques, Bordeaux, 1993–; Res. Centre, Juan March Inst., Madrid, 1995–. Chairman: Hist. Gp, Internat. Inst. of Admin. Scis, 1993–; Scientific Bd, Centre d'Etude de la Vie Politique Française, CNRS, Paris, 1994–. Officier, Ordre

Nat. du Mérite (France), 1995. *Publications:* Le Conseil d'Etat sous le Second Empire, 1972; (jtly) Les Préfets du Second Empire, 1973; (jtly) Les Universités Britanniques, 1973; The Government and Politics of France, 1978, 3rd edn 1989; *edited:* (jtly) Local Government in Britain and France: problems and prospects, 1979 (trans. French 1982); (also contrib.) Continuity and Consensus in France, 1979; (also contrib.) Continuity and Change in France, 1984; (jtly) La Crise de la sidérurgie européenne 1974–1984, 1985; (jtly) Economic Policy and Policy Making under the Mitterrand Presidency, 1985; (jtly) The Political Management of Industrial Crisis: the case of steel 1974–1984, 1986; (jtly) Tensions in the Territorial Politics of Western Europe, 1987; (jtly) The Politics of Privatization in Western Europe, 1989; (also contrib.) The Representativity of Public Administration, 1991; Les privatisations en Europe: programmes et problèmes, 1993, rev. edn as Privatization in Western Europe, 1994; (jtly) La Riforma Administrativa in Europa, 1994; (jtly) The State in Western Europe: retreat or redefinition?, 1994. *Address:* Nuffield College, Oxford OX1 1NF.

WRIGHT, Prof. William David, ARCS, DIC, DSc; Professor of Applied Optics, Imperial College of Science and Technology, 1951–73; *b* 6 July 1906; *s* of late William John Wright and Grace Elizabeth Ansell; *m* 1932, Dorothy Mary Hudson (*d* 1990); two *s*. *Educ:* Southgate County Sch.; Imperial Coll. Research engineer at Westinghouse Electric and Manufacturing Co., Pittsburgh, USA, 1929–30; research and consultant physicist to Electric and Musical Industries, 1930–39. Lecturer and Reader in Technical Optics Section, Imperial Coll., 1931–51. Kern Prof. of Communications, Rochester Inst. of Technol., USA, 1984–85. Chm. Physical Soc. Colour Group, 1941–43; Vice-Pres., Physical Soc., 1948–50; Sec., International Commn for Optics, 1953–66; Chairman: Physical Soc. Optical Group, 1956–59; Colour Group (GB), 1973–75; Pres., International Colour Assoc., 1967–69. Hon. DSc: City Univ., 1971; Waterloo, Canada, 1991. *Publications:* The Perception of Light, 1938; The Measurement of Colour, 4th edn, 1969; Researches on Normal and Defective Colour Vision, 1946; Photometry and the Eye, 1950; The Rays are not Coloured, 1967. About 80 original scientific papers, mainly dealing with colour and vision. *Address:* 25 Craig Mount, Radlett, Herts WD7 7LW. *T:* Radlett (01923) 855306.

WRIGHTSON, Sir (Charles) Mark (Garmondsway), 4th Bt *cr* 1900; Director, Hill Samuel & Co. Ltd, since 1984; *b* 18 Feb. 1951; *s* of Sir John Garmondsway Wrightson, 3rd Bt, TD, and of Hon. Rosemary, *y d* of 1st Viscount Dawson of Penn, GCVO, KCB, KCMG, PC; *S* father, 1983; *m* 1975, Stella Virginia, *d* of late George Dean; three *s*. *Educ:* Eton; Queens' Coll., Cambridge (BA 1972). Called to the Bar, Middle Temple, 1974. Joined Hill Samuel & Co. Ltd, 1977. *Heir:* *s* Barnaby Thomas Garmondsway Wrightson, *b* 5 Aug. 1979. *Address:* 39 Westbourne Park Road, W2 5QD.

WRIGLEY, Prof. Edward Anthony, (Tony), PhD; FBA 1980; Master of Corpus Christi College, Cambridge, since 1994; Professor of Economic History, University of Cambridge, since 1994; *b* 17 Aug. 1931; *s* of Edward Ernest Wrigley and Jessie Elizabeth Wrigley; *m* 1960, Maria Laura Spelberg; one *s* three *d*. *Educ:* King's Sch., Macclesfield; Peterhouse, Cambridge (MA, PhD). William Volker Res. Fellow, Univ. of Chicago, 1953–54; Lectr in Geography, Cambridge, 1958–74; Peterhouse, Cambridge: Fellow, 1958–74; Emeritus Fellow, 1974–; Tutor, 1962–64; Sen. Bursar, 1964–74; Co-Dir, Cambridge Gp for History of Population and Social Structure, 1974–94; Prof. of Population Studies, LSE, 1979–88; Sen. Res. Fellow, 1988–94, Academic Sec., 1992–94, All Souls Coll., Oxford. Pres., Manchester Coll., Oxford, 1987–. Mem., Inst. for Advanced Study, Princeton, 1970–71; Hinkley Vis. Prof., Johns Hopkins Univ., 1975; Tinbergen Vis. Prof., Erasmus Univ., Rotterdam, 1979. President: British Soc. for Population Studies, 1977–79; Econ. History Soc., 1995–; Chm., Population Investigation Cttee, 1984–90; Treas., British Acad., 1989–95. Editor, Economic History Review, 1986–92. *Publications:* Industrial Growth and Population Change, 1961; (ed) English Historical Demography, 1966; Population and History, 1969; (ed) Nineteenth Century Society, 1972; (ed) Identifying People in the Past, 1973; (ed with P. Abrams) Towns in Societies, 1978; (with R. S. Schofield) Population History of England, 1981; (ed jtly) The Works of Thomas Robert Malthus, 1986; People, Cities and Wealth, 1987; Continuity, Chance and Change, 1988; (ed with R. A. Church) The Industrial Revolutions, 1994. *Recreations:* gardening, violin making. *Address:* 13 Sedley Taylor Road, Cambridge CB2 2PW. *T:* Cambridge (01223) 247614.

WRIGLEY, Air Vice-Marshal Henry Bertram, CB 1962; CBE 1956; DL; Senior Technical Staff Officer, Royal Air Force Fighter Command, 1960–64, retired; Sales Manager Air Weapons, Hawker Siddeley Dynamics, 1964–76; *b* 24 Nov. 1909; *s* of Frederick William Wrigley and Anne Jeffreys, Seascale, Cumberland; *m* 1935, Audrey (*d* 1987), *d* of C. S. Boryer, Portsmouth; one *d*. *Educ:* Whitehaven Grammar Sch.; RAF Coll., Cranwell. 33 Squadron, 1930; HMS Glorious 1931; HMS Eagle, 1933; long Signals Course, 1934; various signals appointments until 1937; RAF Signals Officer, HMS Glorious, 1938; served War of 1939–45, X Force, Norway, 1940; Fighter Command, 1940–43; HQ South East Asia, 1943–46; RAF Staff Coll., 1946; comd Northern Signals Area, 1947–50; jssc 1950; Inspector, Radio Services, 1950–52; Chief Signals Officer, 2nd TAF, 1952–54; Director of: Signals (I), Air Ministry, 1954–57; Guided Weapons (Air), Min. of Aviation, 1957–60. DL, Hertfordshire, 1966. *Recreation:* gardening. *Address:* Boonwood, Turpin's Chase, Oaklands Rise, Welwyn, Herts AL6 0RA. *T:* Welwyn (01438) 715231. *Club:* Royal Air Force.

WRIGLEY, Prof. Jack, CBE 1977; Professor of Education, 1967–88, and Deputy Vice-Chancellor, 1982–88, University of Reading, now Professor Emeritus; *b* 8 March 1923; *s* of Harry and Ethel Wrigley; *m* 1946, Edith Baron; two *s*. *Educ:* Oldham High Sch.; Manchester Univ. BSc, MEd (Manch.); PhD (Queen's, Belfast). Asst Mathematics Teacher: Stretford Grammar Sch., 1946–47; Chadderton Grammar Sch., 1948–50; Research Asst, Manchester Univ., 1950–51; Lectr in Educn: Queen's Univ., Belfast, 1951–57; Univ. of London Inst. of Educn, 1957–62; Research Adviser, Curriculum Study Gp in Min. of Educn, 1962–63; Prof. of Educn, Univ. of Southampton, 1963–67; Dir of Studies, Schools Council, 1967–75. Member: Bullock Cttee on Teaching of Reading and other uses of English, 1972–74; SSRC, Mem. Council and Chm. Educnl Res. Bd, 1976–81. Specialist Adviser, H of C Select Cttee on Educn, Sci., and Arts, 1989–90. *Publications:* (ed) The Dissemination of Curriculum Development, 1976; Values and Evaluation in Education, 1980; contrib. learned jls. *Recreations:* chess (Ulster Chess Champion, 1957), theatre, foreign travel. *Address:* Valley Crest, Thrushwood, Keswick, Cumbria CA12 4PG. *T:* Keswick (017687) 71146.

WRIGLEY, Tony; *see* Wrigley, E. A.

WRINTMORE, Eric George; His Honour Judge Wrintmore; a Circuit Judge, since 1984; *b* 11 June 1928; *s* of Rev. F. H. and Muriel Wrintmore; *m* 1951, Jean Blackburn; two *s* one *d*. *Educ:* Stationers' Company's Sch.; King's Coll. London (LLB Hons). Called to Bar, Gray's Inn, 1955; full-time Chm., Industrial Tribunals, 1971; Regional Chm., Industrial Tribunals, 1976–84; a Dep. Circuit Judge, 1980–83; a Recorder, 1983–84. *Recreations:* sailing, squash, golf. *Address:* The Crown Court, The Court House, Southgate, Chichester, Sussex PO19 1SX. *Club:* Chichester Yacht.

WRIXON-BECHER, Major Sir William F.; *see* Becher.

WROATH, John Herbert; His Honour Judge Wroath; a Circuit Judge, since 1984; *b* 24 July 1932; *s* of Stanley Wroath and Ruth Ellen Wroath; *m* 1959, Mary Bridget Byrne; two *s* one *d*. *Educ:* Ryde Sch., Ryde, IoW. Admitted Solicitor, 1956; private practice, 1958–66; Registrar, Isle of Wight County Court, 1965; County Prosecuting Solicitor, 1966; full-time County Court Registrar, 1972; a Recorder of the Crown Court, 1978–84. *Recreations:* sailing, bowling, reading, painting. *Address:* 8 Tides Reach, Birmingham Road, Cowes, Isle of Wight PO31 7NU. *T:* Isle of Wight (01983) 293072. *Clubs:* Royal London Yacht; Cowes Island Sailing (Cowes).

WROE, David Charles Lynn, CB 1995; Deputy Director, Central Statistical Office, since 1991; *b* 20 Feb. 1942; *m* 1966, Susan Higgitt; three *d*. *Educ:* Reigate Grammar Sch.; Trinity Coll., Cambridge (MA); Trinity Coll., Oxford (Cert. Statistics); Birkbeck Coll., London (MSc). Min. of Pensions and National Insurance, 1965–68; Central Statistical Office, 1968–70, 1973–75, 1976–82; secondment to Zambian Govt, 1971–72; Secretariat of Royal Commission on Distribution of Income and Wealth, 1975–76; Under Sec., Regional Policy Directorate, 1982–86, Dir of Stats, 1982–91, Under Sec., Housing Monitoring and Analysis, 1986–91, DoE. Non-exec. Dir, John Laing Construction Ltd, 1994–. Mem. Council, Royal Statistical Soc., 1993–. *Recreation:* sailing. *Address:* Central Statistical Office, Great George Street, SW1P 3AQ.

WRONG, Henry Lewellys Barker, CBE 1986; Director, European Arts Foundation, since 1990; *b* Toronto, Canada, 20 April 1930; *s* of Henry Arkel Wrong and Jean Barker Wrong; *m* 1966, Penelope Hamilton Norman; two *s* one *d*. *Educ:* Trinity Coll., Univ. of Toronto (BA). Stage and business administration, Metropolitan Opera Assoc., New York, 1952–64; Director Programming, National Arts Center, Ottawa, 1964–68; Director: Festival Canada Centennial Programme, 1967; Barbican Centre, 1970–90; Chm., Spencer House (St James's) Ltd, 1989–91. Member: Royal Opera House Trust, 1989–; Adv. Cttee, ADAPT (Access for Disabled People to Arts Premises Today); Royal Fine Art Commn, 1995–. Trustee: Henry Moore Foundn, 1990–; LSO, 1990–. Liveryman, Fishmongers' Co., 1987. FRSA 1988. Hon. DLitt City, 1985. Pro cultura Hungarica, 1989. Centennial Medal, Govt of Canada, 1967; Officier, Ordre Nat. du Mérite (France), 1985. *Address:* Yew Tree House, Much Hadham, Herts SG10 6AJ. *T:* Much Hadham (01279) 842106. *Clubs:* White's; Badminton and Rackets (Toronto).

WRONG, Prof. Oliver Murray, DM; FRCP, FRCPE; Professor of Medicine, University College London, 1972–80, now Emeritus Professor; *b* 7 Feb. 1925; *s* of Edward Murray Wrong and Rosalind Grace Wrong (*née* Smith); *m* 1956, Marilda Musacchio; two *d* (and one *d* decd). *Educ:* Upper Canada Coll., Toronto; Edinburgh Acad.; Magdalen Coll., Oxford (BM BCh 1947; DM 1964). FRCP 1968; FRCPE 1970. Junior hosp appts, Oxford, 1947–51; RAMC, MO Singapore and Malaya, 1948–50; Toronto Gen. Hosp., 1951–52; Mass. Gen. Hosp., Boston, 1952–53; Univ. Tutor in Medicine, Manchester, 1954–58; Lectr and Sen. Lectr in Medicine, RPMS, 1961–69; Prof. of Medicine, Univ. of Dundee, 1969–72; Dir, Dept of Medicine, UCL, 1972–82. Teale Lectr, RCP, 1971; James Howard Means Vis. Physician, Mass. Gen. Hosp., 1974; Vis. Prof., Harvard and Sherbrooke Med. Schs, 1974; Toronto and McGill Med. Schs, 1976. Chm., Nat. Kidney Res. Fund, 1976–80. *Publications:* (with C. J. Edmonds and V. S. Chadwick) The Large Intestine: its role in mammalian nutrition and homeostasis, 1981; articles in med. jls on salt and water metabolism, kidney function, the large intestine in health and disease. *Recreations:* nature, travel, music (esp. baroque). *Address:* Flat 8, 96–100 New Cavendish Street, W1M 7FA. *T:* 0171–637 4740.

WROTTESLEY, family name of **Baron Wrottesley.**

WROTTESLEY, 6th Baron *cr* 1838; **Clifton Hugh Lancelot de Verdon Wrottesley;** Bt 1642; *b* 10 Aug. 1968; *s* of Hon. Richard Francis Gerard Wrottesley (*d* 1970) (2nd *s* of 5th Baron) and of Georgina Anne (who *m* 1982, Lt-Col Jonathan L. Seddon-Brown), *er d* of Lt-Col Peter Thomas Clifton, *qv*; *S* grandfather, 1977. *Educ:* Eton; Edinburgh Univ. Commnd 1st Bn Grenadier Guards, 1990; Lieut, 1993, Capt. 1994; retd, 1995. *Heir:* half-uncle Hon. Stephen John Wrottesley [*b* 21 Dec. 1955; *m* 1982, Mrs Roz Fletcher (*née* Taylor); two *d*]. *Address:* c/o C. Hoare & Co., 32 Lowndes Street, SW1X 9HZ. *Clubs:* Carlton, Cavalry and Guards, Lansdowne.

WROUGHTON, Philip Lavallin, Lord-Lieutenant of Berkshire, since 1995; Chairman and Chief Executive, C. T. Bowring & Co. Ltd, since 1988; Vice Chairman, Marsh & McLennan Companies, Inc., since 1994 (Director, since 1988); *b* 19 April 1933; *s* of Michael Lavallin Wroughton and Elizabeth Angela Wroughton (*née* Rate); *m* 1957, Catriona Henrietta Ishbel MacLeod; two *d*. *Educ:* Eton Coll. Nat. Service, 1951–53, 2nd Lieut KRRC. Price Forbes & Co. Ltd, 1954–61; C. T. Bowring & Co. Ltd, 1961–. Mem., Council of Lloyds, 1992–. High Sheriff, Berks, 1977; DL Berks, 1994. *Recreations:* shooting, racing. *Address:* Woolley Park, Wantage, Oxon OX12 8NJ. *T:* Chaddleworth (01486) 638214. *Club:* White's.

WU Shu-Chih, Hon. Alex, CBE 1983 (OBE 1973); JP; company director; Chairman, Fidelity Management Ltd, since 1965; Vice-Chairman, Dai Nippon Printing Co. (HK) Ltd, since 1973 (Managing Director, 1964–73); *b* 14 Sept. 1920; *s* of Wu Chao-Ming and Yeh Huei-Cheng; *m* 1946; three *s* three *d*. *Educ:* National South West Associated Univ., Kunming, China. Director: Hong Kong Ferry Co. Ltd, 1976–; Hong Kong Aircraft Engineering Co. Ltd, 1983–; Longman Group (Far East) Ltd, 1984–; Nat. Electronics (Consolidated) Ltd, 1984–; K. Wah Stones (Holdings) Ltd, 1986–; Consultant: General Association Hong Kong Ltd, 1980–; Austdairy Ltd, 1987– (Dir, 1983–87); Omisa Oil Management, SA, 1987–90; China Daily, 1988–; Proprietor, Sino-Scottish Trading Co., 1960–; Publisher, Sino-American Publishing Co., 1960–. Chairman: Supplementary Med. Professions Council, 1981–89; Printing Industry Trng Bd, 1967–89; Council for the Performing Arts, 1982–89; Council, Hongkong Acad. for Performing, 1982–86; Vice-Chairman: Hong Kong Trade Develt Council, 1974–83; Vocational Trng Council, 1982–89; Nominating Cttee, Stock Exchange of Hong Kong Ltd, 1992– (Chm., 1989–91); Member: Hong Kong Heart Foundn Ltd, 1975–; Aviation Adv. Bd, 1980–89; Med. Sub-Cttee, Univ. and Polytechnic Grants Cttee, 1983–89; Hong Kong Indust. Estates Corp., 1984–89; Adv. Cttee on China–Hong Kong Trade Develt Council, 1985–; Hong Kong Inst. for Promotion of Chinese Culture, 1985–; Bd of Governors, Hong Kong Philharmonic Soc. Ltd, 1978–. Pres., Hongkong Jun. Chamber of Commerce, 1960; Hon. Pres., Hong Kong Printers Assoc., 1983–. MLC Hong Kong, 1975–85. JP Hong Kong, 1973. Fellow, Hong Kong Management Assoc., 1983; FIMgt (FBIM 1979); FInstD 1980; FIOP 1984. Hon. LLD Hong Kong, 1992. *Recreations:* classical music, Western and Peking opera, tennis, soccer, swimming, contract bridge. *Address:* 14/F, Hart House, 12–14 Hart Avenue, Tsimshatsui, Kowloon, Hong Kong. *T:* 668789. *Clubs:* Hong Kong, Rotary of Hong Kong; Royal Hong Kong Jockey; Royal Hong Kong Golf.

WULF-MATHIES, Dr Monika; Member, European Commission, since 1995; *b* 17 March 1942; *d* of Carl-Hermann Baier and Margott Heisser; *m* 1968, Dr Carsten Wulf-Mathies. *Educ:* Univ. of Hamburg (DrPhil 1968). Br. Asst, Federal Ministry of Econs, Germany, 1968–71; Hd, Dept for Social Policy, Federal Chancery, 1971–76; joined ÖTV,

1971; Mem., Man. Exec, Cttee, 1976–95; Chm., 1982–95. *Recreation:* garden. *Address:* European Commission, 200 rue de la Loi, 1049 Brussels, Belgium. *T:* (2) 993870.

WULSTAN, Prof. David; Research Professor, University of Wales, Aberystwyth, since 1990; *b* 18 Jan. 1937; *s* of Rev. Norman and (Sarah) Margaret Jones; *m* 1965, Susan Nelson Graham; one *s*. *Educ:* Royal Masonic Sch., Bushey; Coll. of Technology, Birmingham; Magdalen Coll., Oxford (Academical Clerk, 1960; Burrowes Exhibr, 1961; Mackinnon Sen. Schol., 1963; Fellow by examination, 1964). MA, BSc, BLitt; ARCM. Lectr in History of Music, Magdalen Coll., Oxford, 1968–78; also at St Hilda's and St Catherine's Colls; Vis. Prof., Depts of Near Eastern Studies and Music, Univ. of California, Berkeley, 1977; Statutory (Sen. Lectr), University Coll., Cork, 1979, Prof. of Music, 1980–83; Gregynog Prof. of Music, UCW, Aberystwyth, 1983–90. Dir, Clerkes of Oxenford (founded 1961); appearances at Cheltenham, Aldeburgh, York, Bath, Flanders, Holland, Krakow, Zagreb, Belgrade Fests, BBC Proms; many broadcasts and TV appearances, gramophone recordings; also broadcast talks, BBC and abroad. *Publications:* Septem Discrimina Vocum, 1983; Tudor Music, 1985; Musical Language, 1992; The Emperor's Old Clothes, 1994; editor: Gibbons, Church Music, Early English Church Music, vol. 3, 1964, vol. 27, 1979; Anthology of Carols, 1968; Anthology of English Church Music, 1971; Play of Daniel, 1976; Victoria, Requiem, 1977; Tallis, Puer Natus Mass, 1977; Coverdale Chant Book, 1978; Sheppard, Complete Works, 1979–; Weelkes, Ninth Service, 1980; many edns of anthems, services etc; entries in Encyclopédie de Musique Sacrée, 1970; chapter in A History of Western Music, ed Sternfeld, 1970; articles and reviews in learned jls. *Recreations:* badminton, tennis, cooking, eating. *Address:* Tŷ Isaf, Llanilar, near Aberystwyth, Dyfed SY23 4NP. *T:* Llanilar (01974) 241229.

WUTTKE, Hans A., Dr jur; German banker, retired; Executive Vice President and Chief Executive, International Finance Corporation (World Bank Group), 1981–84; *b* Hamburg, 23 Oct. 1923; *m*; two *s* two *d*; *m* 1982, Jagoda M. Buić. *Educ:* Univs of Cologne and Salamanca. Dresdner Bank AG, 1949–54; Daimler-Benz AG, 1954–61; Partner, M. M. Warburg-Brinckmann, Wirtz and Co., Hamburg, 1961–75; Executive Director, S. G. Warburg and Co. Ltd, London, 1962–75; Man. Dir, Dresdner Bank AG, Frankfurt, 1975–80; Chm., Deutsch-Süd-Amerikanische Bank AG, 1975–80. Mem. Board several European companies; Mem. Bd, German Development Co., Cologne, 1962–80; Chairman: East Asia Assoc., 1963–73; Comité Européen pour le Progrès Economique et Social (CEPES), 1976–80. *Address:* 77 Cadogan Square, SW1X 0DY; (office) 6 Edith Grove, SW10 0NW. *T:* 0171–376 5163, *Fax:* 0171–376 5643; 38 Quai d'Orléans, Paris 75004, France. *T:* 43299399, *Fax:* 43299332.

WYATT, family name of **Baron Wyatt of Weeford**.

WYATT OF WEEFORD, Baron *cr* 1987 (Life Peer), of Weeford in the county of Staffordshire; **Woodrow Lyle Wyatt;** Kt 1983; Chairman, Horserace Totalisator Board, since 1976; *b* 4 July 1918; *y s* of late Robert Harvey Lyle Wyatt and Ethel Morgan; *m* 1957, Lady Moorea Hastings (marr. diss., 1966), *e d* of 15th Earl of Huntingdon and Cristina, *d* of the Marchese Casati, Rome; one *s*; *m* 1966, Veronica, *widow* of Baron Dr Laszlo Banszky Von Ambroz; one *d*. *Educ:* Eastbourne Coll.; Worcester Coll., Oxford, MA. Served throughout War of 1939–45 (despatches for Normandy); Major, 1944. Founder and Editor, English Story, 1940–50; Editorial Staff, New Statesman and Nation, 1947–48; Weekly Columnist: Reynolds News, 1949–61; Daily Mirror, 1965–73; Sunday Mirror, 1973–83; News of the World, 1983–; fortnightly columnist, The Times, 1983–. Began Panorama with Richard Dimbleby, 1955; under contract BBC TV, 1955–59; introduced non-heat-set web offset colour printing to England, 1962. MP (Lab) Aston Div. of Birmingham, 1945–55, Bosworth Div. of Leicester, 1959–70; Member of Parly Delegn to India, 1946; Personal Asst to Sir Stafford Cripps on Cabinet Mission to India, 1946; Parly Under-Sec. of State, and Financial Sec., War Office, May-Oct. 1951. Contested (Lab) Grantham Div. of Lincolnshire, 1955. Mem. Council, Zoological Soc. of London, 1968–71, 1973–77. *Publications:* (ed with introd.) English Story, 10 vols, 1940–50; The Jews at Home, 1950; Southwards from China, 1952; Into the Dangerous World, 1952; The Peril in Our Midst, 1956; Distinguished for Talent, 1958; (ed with introd.) 69 Short Stories by O'Henry, 1967; Turn Again, Westminster, 1973; The Exploits of Mr Saucy Squirrel, 1976; The Further Exploits of Mr Saucy Squirrel, 1977; What's Left of the Labour Party?, 1977; To the Point, 1981; Confessions of an Optimist (autobiog.), 1985; (ed with introd.) The Way We Lived Then: the English story in the 1940s, 1989; High Profiles (play), 1992. *Address:* House of Lords, SW1A 0PW.

WYATT, (Alan) Will; Managing Director, BBC Network Television, since 1991; *b* 7 Jan. 1942; *s* of Basil Wyatt and Hettie Evelyn (*née* Hooper); *m* 1966, Jane Bridgit Bagenal; two *d*. *Educ:* Magdalen College Sch., Oxford; Emmanuel Coll., Cambridge. Trainee reporter, Sheffield Telegraph, 1964; Sub-Editor, BBC Radio News, 1965; moved to BBC television, 1968; Producer: Late Night Line Up, In Vision, The Book Programme, B. Traven—a mystery solved, *et al*, 1970–77; Asst Hd of Presentation (Programmes), 1977; Hd of Documentary Features, 1981; Hd of Features and Documentaries Gp, 1987; Asst Man. Dir, BBC Network Television, 1988. Chm., BBC Guidelines on Violence, 1983, 1987; Director: BARB, 1989–91; BBC Subscription TV, 1990–93; BBC Enterprises, 1991–94; BBC Worldwide Television, 1994–. Governor, London Inst., 1990–. FRTS 1992. *Publication:* The Man Who Was B. Traven, 1980. *Recreations:* fell walking, horse racing. *Address:* c/o BBC Television Centre, W12 7RJ. *T:* 0181–743 8000.

WYATT, Arthur Hope, CMG 1980; HM Diplomatic Service, retired; re-employed in Foreign and Commonwealth Office, 1990–95; *b* 12 Oct. 1929; *s* of Frank and Maggie Wyatt, Anderton, Lancs; *m* 1957, Barbara Yvonne, *d* of Major J. P. Flynn, late Indian Army; two *d*. *Educ:* Bolton School. Army, 1947–50; FO, 1950–52; 3rd Sec., Ankara, 1952–56; 2nd Sec., Phnom Penh, 1956–58; 2nd Sec., Ankara, 1958–61; FO, 1962–66; 1st Sec., Bonn, 1966–70; FCO, 1970–72; Counsellor and Head of Chancery, Lagos, 1972–75; Dep. High Comr, Valletta, 1975–76; Diplomatic Service Inspector, 1977–79; Counsellor (Econ. and Comm.) and Consul-Gen., Tehran, 1979–80; Counsellor, Ankara, 1981–84; Minister, Lagos, 1984–86; High Comr to Ghana and Ambassador (non-resident) to Togo, 1986–89. *Recreations:* golf, football, bridge, stamp collecting. *Address:* 44 Baronsmede, W5 4LT. *T:* 0181–579 0782.

WYATT, (Christopher) Terrel, FEng, FICE, FIStructE; Chairman, W. S. Atkins Ltd, since 1987; *b* 17 July 1927; *s* of Lionel Harry Wyatt and Audrey Vere Wyatt; *m*; four *s*; *m* 1990, Patricia Perkins. *Educ:* Kingston Grammar Sch.; Battersea Polytechnic (BScEng); Imperial Coll. (DIC). FICE 1963; FIStructE 1963; FEng 1980. Served RE, 1946–48. Charles Brand & Son Ltd, 1948–54; Richard Costain Ltd, 1955–87: Dir, 1970–87; Gp Chief Exec., 1975–80; Dep. Chm., 1979–80; Chm., Costain Group PLC, 1980–87. *Recreation:* sailing. *Address:* The White House, St Martin's Avenue, Epsom, Surrey KT18 5HS.

WYATT, David Joseph, CBE 1977; Adviser on International Relations, British Red Cross Society, since 1992; HM Diplomatic Service, 1949–85; *b* 12 Aug. 1931; *s* of late Frederick Wyatt and Lena (*née* Parr); *m* 1st, 1957, Annemarie Angst (*d* 1978); two *s* one *d*; 2nd, 1990, Dr Wendy Baron, *qv*. *Educ:* Leigh Grammar Sch. National Service, RAF, 1950–52. Entered Foreign Service, 1949; Berne, 1954; FO, 1957–61; Second Sec., Vienna, 1961; First Sec., Canberra, 1965; FCO, 1969–71; First Sec., Ottawa, 1971; Counsellor, 1974; seconded Northern Ireland Office, Belfast, 1974–76; Counsellor and Head of Chancery, Stockholm, 1976–79; Under Sec. on loan to Home Civil Service, 1979–82; UK Mission to UN during 1982 General Assembly (personal rank of Ambassador); Minister and Dep. Comdt, British Mil. Govt, Berlin, 1983–85. Acting Dir Gen, Jan.–July 1990, Dir, Internat. Div., 1985–92, BRCS. FRSA 1991. *Address:* c/o British Red Cross Society, 9 Grosvenor Crescent, SW1X 7EJ.

WYATT, Derrick Arthur; QC 1993; Common University Fund Lecturer in Law, University of Oxford and Fellow, St Edmund Hall, Oxford, since 1978; *b* 25 Feb. 1948; *s* of Iris Ross (formerly Wyatt, *née* Thompson) and step *s* of Alexander Ross; *m* 1970, (Margaret) Joan Cunnington; one *s* one *d*. *Educ:* Alsop High Sch.; Emmanuel Coll., Cambridge (MA, LLB); Univ. of Chicago Law Sch. (JD). Lectr in law, Univ. of Liverpool, 1971–75; called to the Bar, Lincoln's Inn, 1972; Fellow, Emmanuel Coll., Cambridge, 1975–78. Vis. Prof., Florida State Univ., 1987. Consultant, Oxford Inst. of Legal Practice, 1993–. Member: Vale of White Horse DC, 1983–87; Abingdon Town Council, 1983–87. Mem. Editl Cttee, British Yearbook of Internat. Law, 1992–. *Publications:* Wyatt and Dashwood's European Community Law, 1980, 3rd edn 1993; (with B. Rudden) Basic Community Laws, 1980, 4th edn 1993; (ed with A. Barav) Yearbook of European Law, 1988–; articles and reviews in learned jls. *Recreations:* walking, camping. *Address:* St Edmund Hall, Oxford OX1 4AR. *T:* Oxford (01865) 279000.

WYATT, Gavin Edward, CMG 1965; Director of Projects Department, Europe, Middle East and North Africa Region, World Bank, 1975–76 (Assistant Director, 1973–75); *b* 12 Jan. 1914; *s* of Edward A. Wyatt and Blanche M. Muller; *m* 1950, Mary Mackinnon, *d* of John Macdonald, Oban; one *s* one *d*. *Educ:* Newton Abbot Grammar Sch. CEng, FIEE 1951; FIMechE 1962. Engineer and Manager, East African Power & Lighting Co. Ltd, Tanganyika and Kenya, 1939–57; Chief Exec. Officer and General Manager, Electricity Corp. of Nigeria, 1957–62; Man. Director, East Africa Power & Lighting Co. Ltd, 1962–64; World Bank, 1965–76. *Recreations:* gardening, viticulture, oenology. *Address:* Holne Bridge Lodge, Ashburton, South Devon TQ13 7NW.

WYATT, Terrel; *see* Wyatt, C. T.

WYATT, Wendy, (Mrs D. J. Wyatt); *see* Baron, O. W.

WYATT, Will; *see* Wyatt, A. W.

WYETH, Andrew Newell; artist; landscape painter; *b* 12 July 1917; *s* of Newell and Carolyn Wyeth; *m* 1940, Betsy Merle James; two *s*. *Educ:* privately. First one man exhibn, William Macbeth Gall., NY, 1937; subsequent exhibitions include: Doll & Richards, Boston, 1938, 1940, 1942, 1944; Cornell Univ., 1938; Macbeth Gall., 1938, 1941, 1943, 1945; Art Inst. of Chicago, 1941; Museum of Modern Art, NYC, 1943; M. Knoedler & Co., NYC, 1953, 1958; Dunn Internat. Exhibn, London, 1963; MIT, Cambridge, 1966; The White House, Washington, 1970; Tokyo, 1974, 1979; Metropolitan Museum, NY, 1976; RA, 1980 (first by living American artist); Arnot Museum, Elmira, NY, 1985; Seibu-Pisa, Tokyo, 1986; Moscow, Leningrad, 1987; Nat. Gall. of Art, Corcoran Gall. of Art, Washington, 1987; Milan, 1987; Fitzwilliam Mus., Cambridge, 1988. Member: Nat. Inst. of Arts and Letters (Gold Medal, 1965); Amer. Acad. of Arts and Sciences; Amer. Acad. of Arts and Letters (Medal of Merit, 1947); Académie des Beaux-Arts, 1977; Hon. Mem., Soviet Acad. of the Arts, 1978. Presidential Medal of Freedom, 1963; Einstein Award, 1967; Congressional Medal, USA, 1988. Hon. AFD: Colby Coll., Maine, 1954; Harvard, 1955; Dickinson, 1958; Swarthmore, 1958; Nasson Coll., Maine, 1963; Temple Univ., 1963; Maryland, 1964; Delaware, 1964; Northwestern Univ., 1964; Hon. LHD Tufts, 1963. *Publication:* The Helga Paintings, 1987. *Address:* c/o Frank E. Fowler, PO Box 247, Lookout Mountain, TN 37350, USA.

WYFOLD, 3rd Baron, *cr* 1919, of Accrington; **Hermon Robert Fleming Hermon-Hodge,** ERD 1990; 3rd Bt, *cr* 1902; Director, Robert Fleming Holdings, 1949–85, retired; formerly director other companies; *b* 26 June 1915; *s* of 2nd Baron and Dorothy (*d* 1976), *e d* of late Robert Fleming, Joyce Grove, Oxford; *S* father, 1942. *Educ:* Eton; Le Rosey, Switzerland. Captain, Grenadier Guards (RARO), 1939–65. *Heir:* none. *Address:* c/o Robert Fleming Holdings, 25 Copthall Avenue, EC2R 7DR. *T:* 0171–638 5858. *Clubs:* Carlton, Pratt's; Metropolitan (New York).

WYLD, Martin Hugh; Chief Restorer, National Gallery, since 1979; *b* 14 Sept. 1944; *s* of John Wyld and Helen Leslie Melville; one *s* one *d*. *Educ:* Harrow School. Assistant Restorer, National Gallery, 1966. *Recreation:* travel. *Address:* 21 Grafton Square, SW4 0DA. *T:* 0171–720 2627. *Clubs:* Colony Room, MCC.

WYLDBORE-SMITH, Maj.-Gen. Sir (Francis) Brian, Kt 1980; CB 1965; DSO 1943; OBE 1944; General Officer Commanding, 44th Division (TA) and Home Counties District, 1965–68; Director, Conservative Board of Finance, 1970–92; *b* 10 July 1913; *s* of Rev. W. R. Wyldbore-Smith and Mrs D. Wyldbore-Smith; *m* 1944, Hon. Molly Angela Cayzer, *d* of 1st Baron Rotherwick; one *s* four *d*. *Educ:* Wellington Coll.; RMA, Woolwich. Served Middle East, Italy, France and Germany, 1941–45; Military Adviser to CIGS, 1947–49; GSO1, 7 Armoured Div., 1951–53; Comd 15/19 King's Royal Hussars, 1954–56; IDC 1959; BGS Combat Development, 1959–62; Chief of Staff to Commander-in-Chief, Far East Command, 1962–64. Col, 15/19 Hussars, 1970–77. *Recreations:* hunting, shooting. *Address:* Grantham House, Grantham, Lincs NG31 6SS. *T:* Grantham (01476) 64705. *Clubs:* Buck's, Naval and Military.

WYLIE, Rt. Hon. Lord; Norman Russell Wylie, PC 1970; VRD 1961; a Senator of the College of Justice in Scotland, 1974–90; *b* 26 Oct. 1923; *o s* of late William Galloway Wylie and late Mrs Nellie Smart Wylie (*née* Russell), Elderslie, Renfrewshire; *m* 1963, Gillian Mary, *yr d* of late Dr R. E. Verney, Edinburgh; three *s*. *Educ:* Paisley Grammar Sch.; St Edmund Hall, Oxford (Hon. Fellow, 1975); Univs of Glasgow and Edinburgh. BA (Oxon) 1948; LLB (Glasgow) 1951. Admitted to Faculty of Advocates, 1952; QC (Scotland) 1964. Appointed Counsel to Air Ministry in Scotland, 1956; Advocate-Depute, 1959; Solicitor-General for Scotland, April-Oct. 1964. MP (C) Pentlands Div., Edinburgh, Oct. 1964–Feb. 1974; Lord Advocate, 1970–74. Mem., Parole Bd for Scotland, 1991–93. Justice of Appeal, Republic of Botswana, 1994–. Trustee, Carnegie Trust for Univs of Scotland, 1976–; Chm., Scottish Nat. Cttee, English-Speaking Union of the Commonwealth, 1978–84. Served in Fleet Air Arm, 1942–46; subseq. RNR; Lt-Comdr, 1954. *Recreations:* shooting, sailing. *Address:* 30 Lauder Road, Edinburgh EH9 2JF. *T:* 0131–667 8377. *Clubs:* New (Edinburgh); Royal Highland Yacht.

WYLIE, Alexander Featherstonhaugh; QC (Scot) 1991; *b* 2 June 1951; *s* of Ian Hamilton Wylie and Helen Jane Mearns or Wylie; *m* 1975, Gail Elizabeth Watson Duncan; two *d*. *Educ:* Edinburgh Univ. (LLB Hons). ACIArb 1977, FCIArb 1991. Qualified Solicitor in Scotland, 1976; called to the Scottish Bar, 1978; called to the Bar, Lincoln's Inn, 1990. Standing Junior Counsel in Scotland to Accountant of Court, 1986; Advocate Depute, 1989–92. Jt Chm., Discipline Cttee, Inst. of Chartered Accountants of Scotland, 1994–; Mem. (part-time), Scottish Legal Aid Bd. *Address:* Advocates' Library, Parliament House, Parliament Square, Edinburgh EH1 1RF. *T:* (clerk) 0131–226 2881.

WYLIE, Prof. Christopher Craig; Martin Lenz Harrison Professor of Developmental Biology and Genetics, University of Minnesota School of Medicine, since 1994; *b* 15 Sept. 1945; *s* of Joseph and Edna Wylie; *m* 1st, 1969, Christine Margaret Hall; 2nd, 1976, Janet Heasman; three *s* one *d*. *Educ:* Chislehurst and Sidcup County Grammar School for Boys; University College London (BSc, 1st cl. Hons Anatomy 1966; PhD 1971). Lectr in Anatomy, University College London, 1969; St George's Hospital Medical School: Sen. Lectr in Anatomy, 1975; Reader, 1983; Prof., 1985; F. J. Quick Prof. of Biol., Cambridge Univ., 1988–94, now Prof. Emeritus; Fellow, Darwin Coll., Cambridge, 1989–94. Vis. Asst Prof. in Biology, Dartmouth Coll., 1975; Vis. Associate Prof. of Anatomy, Harvard Med. Sch., 1981. Editor in Chief, Development (internat. jl of develt biol.), 1987–. *Publications:* numerous research articles in sci. jls of biology. *Recreations:* relaxing with the family, racket sports. *Address:* 7024 Lanham Lane, Edina, MN 55439, USA. *T:* (612) 9412841.

WYLIE, Derek; *see* Wylie, W. D.

WYLIE, Rt. Hon. Norman Russell; *see* Wylie, Rt Hon. Lord.

WYLIE, Sian Meryl, (Mrs Ian Wylie); *see* Griffiths, S. M.

WYLIE, (William) Derek, FRCP, FRCS, FRCA; Consulting Anaesthetist, St Thomas' Hospital, SE1; Consultant Anaesthetist, The Royal Masonic Hospital, 1959–82; Dean, St Thomas's Hospital Medical School, 1974–79; Adviser in Anaesthetics to the Health Service Commissioner, 1974–79; *b* 24 Oct. 1918; *s* of Edward and Mabel Wylie, Huddersfield; *m* 1945, Margaret Helen, 2nd *d* of F. W. Toms, Jersey, CI (formerly Dep. Inspector-Gen., Western Range, Indian Police); one *s* two *d* (and one *s* decd). *Educ:* Uppingham Sch.; Gonville and Caius Coll., Cambridge (MA; MB, BChir); St Thomas's Hosp. Med. Sch. MRCP 1945, FRCP 1967; FRCA (FFARCS 1953); FRCS 1972. Resident posts at St Thomas' Hosp., 1943–45. Served RAFVR, 1945–47, Wing Comdr. Apptd Hon. Staff, St Thomas' Hosp., 1946; Consultant, 1948; Sen. Cons. Anaesthetist, 1966–79; Cons. Anaesthetist, The National Hosp. for Nervous Diseases, 1950–67. Examiner: FFARCS, 1959–72; FFARCSI, 1966–78. Mem., Bd of Faculty of Anaesthetists, RCS, 1960–70 (Dean, 1967–69; Vice-Dean, 1965–66; Bernard Johnson Adviser in Postgraduate Studies, 1959–67; Faculty Medal, 1984); Mem. Council, RCS, 1967–69; FRSM (Mem. Council, 1962–72; Hon. Treas., 1964–70; Pres., Section of Anaesthetics, 1963); Mem., Bd of Governors, St Thomas' Hosp., 1969–74; Mem. Council, Med. Defence Union, 1962–92, Pres., 1982–88. Jenny Hartmann Lectr, Basle Univ., 1961; Clover Lectr and Medallist, RCS(Eng), 1974. Pres., Assoc. of Anaesthetists of GB and Ireland, 1980–82, Hon. Mem., 1984 (John Snow Silver Medal, 1988). Hon. Citizen of Dallas, USA, 1963; Hon. FFARCSI, 1971; Hon. FANZCA (Hon. FFARACS, 1984). Henry Hill Hickman Medal, RSM, 1983. *Publications:* The Practical Management of Pain in Labour, 1953; (ed with Dr H. C. Churchill-Davidson), A Practice of Anaesthesia, 1960, 3rd edn 1972; papers in specialist and gen. med. jls. *Recreations:* reading, travel, philately. *Address:* St John's Cottage, Nursery Lane, Fairwarp, Uckfield, East Sussex TN22 3BD. *T:* Nutley (0182571) 2822. *Club:* Royal Automobile.

WYLLIE, Very Rev. Hugh Rutherford; Moderator of the General Assembly of the Church of Scotland, 1992–93; Minister at the Old Parish Church of Hamilton, since 1981; *b* 11 Oct. 1934; *s* of late Hugh McPhee Wyllie and Elizabeth Buchanan; *m* 1962, Eileen Elizabeth Cameron, MA; two *d*. *Educ:* Shawlands Acad., Glasgow; Hutchesons' Grammar Sch., Glasgow; Univ. of Glasgow (MA; Pitcairn Miller Frame Awards, 1961, 1962). The Union Bank of Scotland, 1951–53 (MCIBS). RAF Nat. Service, 1953–55. Licensed and ordained by Presbytery of Glasgow, 1962; Asst Minister, Glasgow Cathedral, 1962–65; Minister: Dunbeth Church, Coatbridge, 1965–72; Cathcart South Church, Glasgow, 1972–81; Convener, General Assembly: Stewardship and Budget Cttee, 1978–83; Stewardship and Finance Bd, 1983–86; Assembly Council, 1987–91; Member, General Assembly: Bd of Nomination to Church Chairs, 1985–91, 1993–; Bd of Practice and Procedure, 1991–95; Moderator of the Presbytery of Hamilton, 1989–90; Convener, Business Cttee, 1991–95; Chaplain: Royal British Legion (Hamilton Br.), 1981–; Lanarks Burma Star Assoc., 1983–; Strathclyde Police 'Q' Div., 1983–. Master, Hamilton Hosp., 1982–. Established Centre for Information for the Unemployed, Hamilton, 1983; introduced Dial-a-Fact on drugs and alcohol, 1986; established Hamilton Church History Project, 1984–87; Pres., Glasgow Univ. SCM, 1958; Chm., SCM Scottish Council, 1958. Pres., Hamilton Burns Club, 1990. Freeman, Hamilton DC, 1992. Dr William Barclay Meml Lectr, 1994. Hon. DD Aberdeen, 1993. *Recreations:* gardening, DIY, two yellow Labradors. *Address:* Mansewood, 62 Union Street, Hamilton ML3 6NA.

WYLLIE, Prof. Peter John, PhD; FRS 1984; Professor of Geology, California Institute of Technology, since 1983 (Chairman, Division of Geological and Planetary Sciences, 1983–87); *b* 8 Feb. 1930; *s* of George William and Beatrice Gladys Wyllie (*née* Weaver); *m* 1956, Frances Rosemary Blair; two *s* one *d* (and one *d* decd). *Educ:* Univ. of St Andrews. BSc 1952 (Geology and Physics); BSc 1955 (1st cl. hons Geology); PhD 1958 (Geology). Glaciologist, British W Greenland Expdn, 1950; Geologist, British N Greenland Expdn, 1952–54; Asst Lectr in Geology, Univ. of St Andrews, 1955–56; Research Asst, 1956–58, Asst Prof. of Geochemistry, 1958–59, Pennsylvania State Univ.; Research Fellow in Chemistry, 1959–60, Lectr in Exptl Petrology, 1960–61, Leeds Univ.; Associate Prof. of Petrology, Pennsylvania State Univ., 1961–65 (Acting Head, Dept Geochem. and Mineralogy, 1962–63); University of Chicago: Prof. of Petrology and Geochem., 1965–77; Master Phys. Scis, Collegiate Div., Associate Dean of Coll. and of Phys. Scis Div., 1972–73; Homer J. Livingston Prof., 1978–83; Chm., Dept of Geophysical Scis, 1979–82. Louis Murray Vis. Fellow, Univ. of Cape Town, 1987. Pres., Internat. Mineralogical Assoc., 1986–90; Vice Pres., Internat. Union of Geodesy and Geophysics, 1991–95. Foreign Associate, US Nat. Acad. of Scis, 1981 (Chm. Cttee on Solid-Earth Sciences and Society, report published 1993); Fellow: Amer. Acad. of Arts and Scis, 1982; Amer. Geophys. Union; Geol Soc. Amer.; Mineral Soc. Amer., 1965; Corresponding Fellow, Edin. Geol Soc., 1985–; Foreign Fellow: Indian Geophys. Union, 1987; Indian Nat. Sci. Acad., 1991; Nat. Acad. of Scis, India, 1992; Foreign Mem., Russian (formerly USSR) Acad. of Scis, 1988. Hon. Member: Mineralogical Soc. of GB and Ireland, 1986–; Mineralogical Soc. of Russia, 1986–. Hon. DSc St Andrews, 1974. Polar Medal, 1954; Wollaston Medal, Geol Soc. of London, 1982; Abraham-Gottlob-Werner Medal, German Mineral Soc., 1987. *Publications:* Ultramafic and Related Rocks, 1967; The Dynamic Earth, 1971; The Way the Earth Works, 1976; numerous papers in sci. jls. *T:* (818) 791–9164. *Club:* Arctic (Cambridge).

WYLLIE, William Robert Alexander; Chairman and Chief Executive, Asia Securities Ltd, Hong Kong, since 1971; Chairman, Asia Securities International Ltd, since 1987; *b* 9 Oct. 1932; *s* of Robert Wyllie and Marion Margaret Rae (*née* McDonald); *m* 1988, Rhonda Noreen (*née* McGrath); two *s* one *d* from previous marr. *Educ:* Scarborough State Sch., Perth, W Australia; Perth Technical Coll. (qual. Automobile and Aeronautical Engrg). MIRTE. Sen. Exec./Br. Manager, Wearne Bros Ltd, Malaysia/Singapore, 1953–64; Man. Dir, Harpers Internat. Ltd, Hong Kong, 1964–73; Chm. and Chief Exec., China Engineers Holdings Ltd, Hong Kong, 1973–75; Deputy Chairman and Chief Executive: Hutchison Internat. Ltd, Hong Kong, 1975–Dec. 1977; Hutchison Whampoa Ltd, Hong Kong, Jan. 1978–June 1979 (Chm. and Chief Exec., 1979–80). FInstD 1980. *Recreations:* power boating, water skiing, Scuba diving, restoration of vintage cars. *Address:* Asia Securities International Ltd, 17/F One Pacific Place, 88 Queensway, Hong Kong. *T:* (office) 8105500; (home) 8094946. *Clubs:* Hong Kong, American, Shek O Country, Royal Hong Kong Jockey, Royal Hong Kong Yacht (Hong Kong); Clearwater Bay Golf and Country.

WYNDHAM, family name of **Baron Egremont and Leconfield.**

WYNDHAM-QUIN, family name of **Earl of Dunraven.**

WYNESS, James Alexander Davidson; Senior Partner, Linklaters & Paines, since 1994; *b* 27 Aug. 1937; *s* of late Dr James Alexander Davidson Wyness and of Millicent Margaret (*née* Beaton); *m* 1966, Josephine Margaret Worsdell; three *d*. *Educ:* Stockport Grammar Sch.; Emmanuel Coll., Cambridge (MA, LLB). National Service, 2 Lieut, RA. Articled Clerk, A. F. & R. W. Tweedie, 1964–66 (qualified 1965); Linklaters & Paines, 1966–: Partner, 1970–; Managing Partner, 1987–91; Jt Sen. Partner, 1991–93. Non-Exec. Dir, Bowthorpe plc, 1979–. Mem., Law Soc. Mem., Co. of City of London Solicitors. Pres., Saracens FC (RFU) (Captain, 1962–65); Mddx RFU; London Div. RFU. *Recreations:* visiting France, growing vegetables, Rugby football, reading. *Address:* Linklaters & Paines, Barrington House, 59–67 Gresham Street, EC2V 7JA. *T:* 0171–606 7080.

WYNFORD, 8th Baron, *cr* 1829; **Robert Samuel Best;** MBE 1953; DL; Lt-Col Royal Welch Fusiliers; *b* 5 Jan. 1917; *e s* of 7th Baron and Evelyn (*d* 1929), *d* of late Maj.-Gen. Sir Edward S. May, KCB, CMG; *S* father, 1943; *m* 1941, Anne Daphne Mametz, *d* of late Maj.-Gen. J. R. Minshull Ford, CB, DSO, MC; one *s* two *d*. *Educ:* Eton; RMC, Sandhurst. 2nd Lieut, RWF, 1937; served BEF; GHQ Home Forces; North Africa (Croix de Guerre); Egypt; Italy; wounded, 1944; Instructor, Staff College, 1945–46; War Office, 1947–49; OC Depot, RWF, 1955–57; Instructor Joint Service Staff Coll., 1957–60; RARO 1960. DL Dorset, 1970. *Heir: s* Hon. John Philip Robert Best [*b* 23 Nov. 1950; *m* 1981, Fenella Christian Mary, *o d* of Arthur Reginald Danks; one *s* one *d*]. *Club:* Army and Navy.

WYNGAARDEN, James Barnes, MD; FRCP; Foreign Secretary, National Academy of Sciences, Washington, 1990–94; *b* 19 Oct. 1924; *s* of Martin Jacob Wyngaarden and Johanna Kempers Wyngaarden; *m* 1946, Ethel Dean Vredevoogd (marr. diss. 1976); one *s* four *d*. *Educ:* Calvin College; Western Michigan University; University of Michigan. MD 1948; FRCP 1984. Investigator, NIH, 1953–56; Associate Prof. of Medicine, Duke Univ. Med. Center, 1956–61; Prof. of Medicine, Duke Univ. Med. Sch., 1961–65; Chairman, Dept of Medicine: Univ. of Pennsylvania Med. Sch., 1965–67; Duke Univ. Med. Sch., 1967–82; Dir, NIH, 1982–89; Assoc. Dir, Life Scis, Exec. Office of the President of USA, 1989–90. Hon. DSc: Michigan, 1980; Ohio, 1984; Illinois, 1985; George Washington, 1986; S Carolina, 1989; Western Michigan, 1989; Hon. PhD Tel Aviv, 1987. *Publications:*(ed jtly) The Metabolic Basis of Inherited Disease, 1960, 5th edn 1983; (with O. Sperling and A. DeVries) Purine Metabolism in Man, 1974; (with W.N. Kelley) Gout and Hyperuricemia, 1976; (with L. H. Smith) Review of Internal Medicine; a self-assessment guide, 1979, 3rd edn 1985; (ed jtly) Cecil Textbook of Medicine, 15th edn 1979 to 19th edn 1992. *Recreations:* tennis, ski-ing, painting. *Address:* National Academy of Sciences, 2101 Constitution Avenue, NW, Washington, DC 20418, USA. *T:* (202) 3342800.

WYNN, family name of **Baron Newborough.**

WYNN, Arthur Henry Ashford; Adviser on Standards, Department of Trade and Industry (formerly Ministry of Technology), 1965–71; *b* 22 Jan. 1910; *s* of late Prof. William Henry Wynn, MD, MSc; *m* 1938, Margaret Patricia Moxon; three *s* one *d*. *Educ:* Oundle Sch.; Trinity Coll., Cambridge (Entrance Scholar, Nat. Science and Mathematics; MA). Barrister-at-Law, Lincoln's Inn, 1939; Director of Safety in Mines Research Establishment, Ministry of Fuel and Power, 1948–55; Scientific Member of National Coal Board, 1955–65; Member: Advisory Council on Research and Development, Ministry of Power, 1955–65; Safety in Mines Research Advisory Board, 1950–65; Exec. Cttee, British Standards Institution, 1966–71; Advisory Council on Calibration and Measurement, 1967–71; Chairman: Standing Joint Cttee on Metrication, 1966–69; Adv. Cttee on Legal Units of Measurement, 1969–71. *Publications:* (with Margaret Wynn): The Protection of Maternity and Infancy in Finland, 1974; The Right of Every Child to Health Care in France, 1974; Nutrition Counselling in Canada, 1975; Prevention of Handicap of Perinatal Origin in France, 1976; Prevention of Preterm Birth, 1977; Prevention of Handicap and Health of Women, 1979; Prevention of Handicap of Early Pregnancy Origin, 1981; Lead and Human Reproduction, 1982; The Case for Preconception Care, 1991. *Address:* 9 View Road, N6 4DJ. *T:* 0181–348 1470.

WYNN, Sir (David) Watkin W.; *see* Williams-Wynn.

WYNN, Terence; Member (Lab) European Parliament, Merseyside East and Wigan, since 1994 (Merseyside East, 1989–94); *b* 27 June 1946; *s* of Ernest Wynn and Lily (*née* Hitchen); *m* 1967, Doris Ogden; one *s* one *d*. *Educ:* Leigh Technical Coll.; Riversdale Technical Coll., Liverpool (OND); Liverpool Polytechnic (Combined Chief Engrs Cert); Salford Univ. (MSc Manpower Studies and Industrial Relns 1984). Seagoing Marine Engr Officer, MN, 1962–74; Engr Surveyor, ICI, Runcorn, 1975–76; Ship Repair Man., Manchester Dry Docks, 1976–78; Trng Advr, Shipbuilding ITB, 1978–82; Sen. Trng Exec., Marine Trng Assoc., 1982–89. Methodist local preacher, 1978–. *Recreation:* Rugby League supporter. *Address:* 34 Holden Brook Close, Leigh, Lancs WN7 2HL. *Club:* Leigh Labour.

WYNN, Terence Bryan; Director, More Publicity, since 1990; Editor, Brentwood News, since 1990; *b* 20 Nov. 1928; *o s* of late Bernard Wynn and Elsie Wynn (*née* Manges); unmarried. *Educ:* St Cuthbert's Grammar Sch., Newcastle upon Tyne. Started as jun. reporter with Hexham Courant, Northumberland, 1945; Blyth News, 1947–48; Shields Evening News, 1948–50; Sunderland Echo, 1950–53; Reporter with Daily Sketch, 1953–58; News Editor, Tyne Tees Television, 1958, then Head of News and Current Affairs, 1960–66; Editorial Planning, BBC Television News, 1966–67; Sen. Press and Information Officer with Land Commn, 1967–71; Sen. Inf. Officer, HM Customs and Excise, 1971–72; Editor, The Universe, 1972–77; Editor, Liberal News, and Head of Liberal Party Orgn's Press Office, 1977–83; Regl Press Officer, MSC, COI, London and SE Region, 1983–85; Editor, Your Court (house jl of Lord Chancellor's Dept), 1985–88. Helped to found and first Editor of Roman Catholic monthly newspaper, Northern Cross. Chm., Catholic Writers' Guild, 1967–70 (Hon. Vice-Pres., 1970); Judge for British Television News Film of the Year Awards, 1961–64; Mem. Mass Media Commn, RC Bishops' Conf. of England and Wales, 1972–83. *Publication:* Walsingham, a modern mystery play, 1975. *Recreations:* reading, writing, talking. *Address:* Bosco Villa, 30 Queen's Road, South Benfleet, Essex SS7 1JW. *T:* South Benfleet (01268) 792033.

WYNNE, Prof. Charles Gorrie, FRS 1970; BA, PhD; Senior Visiting Fellow, Cambridge University Institute of Astronomy, since 1988; *b* 18 May 1911; *s* of C. H. and A. E. Wynne; *m* 1937, Jean Richardson; one *s* one *d* (and one *s* decd). *Educ:* Wyggeston Grammar Sch., Leicester; Exeter Coll., Oxford (Scholar). Optical Designer, Taylor Taylor

& Hobson Ltd, 1935–43; Wray (Optical Works) Ltd, 1943–60, latterly Director; Dir, Optical Design Gp, 1960–78, and Sen. Res. Fellow, 1978–87, Imperial Coll., London; Prof. of Optical Design, Univ. of London, 1969–78, now Emeritus. Vis. Prof. Univ. of Durham, 1987–90. Dir, IC Optical Systems, 1970– (Chm., 1975–88). Hon. Sec. (business), Physical Soc., 1947–60; Hon. Sec., Inst. of Physics and Physical Soc., 1960–66. Editor, Optica Acta, 1954–65. Thomas Young Medal, Inst. of Physics, 1971; Gold Medal, Royal Astronomical Soc., 1979; Rumford Medal, Royal Soc., 1982. *Publications:* scientific papers on aberration theory and optical instruments in Proc. Phys. Soc., Mon. Not. RAS, Astrophys. Jl, Optica Acta, etc. *Address:* 4 Holben Close, Barton, Cambs CB3 7AQ. *T:* Cambridge (01223) 263098.

WYNNE, David, OBE 1994; sculptor, since 1949; *b* Lyndhurst, Hants, 25 May 1926; *s* of Comdr Charles Edward Wynne and Millicent (*née* Beyts); *m* 1959, Gillian Mary Leslie Bennett (*née* Grant) (*d* 1990); two *s*, and one step *s* one step *d*. *Educ:* Stowe Sch.; Trinity Coll., Cambridge. FZS; FRSA. Served RN, 1944–47: minesweepers and aircraft carriers (Sub-Lieut RNVR). No formal art training. First exhibited at Leicester Galls, 1950, and at Royal Acad., 1952. One-man Exhibitions: Leicester Galls, 1955, 1959; Tooth's Gall., 1964, 1966; Temple Gall., 1964; Findlay Galls, New York, 1967, 1970, 1973; Covent Garden Gall., 1970, 1971; Fitzwilliam Museum, Cambridge, 1972; Pepsico World HQ, New York, 1976; Agnew's Gall., 1983; retrospective, Cannizaro House, 1980; also various mixed exhibns. Large works in public places: Magdalen Coll., Oxford; Malvern Girls' Coll.; Civic Centre, Newcastle upon Tyne; Lewis's, Hanley; Ely Cathedral; Birmingham Cath.; Church of St Paul, Ashford Hill, Berks; Ch. of St Thomas More, Bradford-on-Avon; Mission Ch., Portsmouth; Fountain Precinct, Sheffield; Bowood House, Wilts; Risen Christ and 2 seraphim, west front of Wells Cathedral, 1985; Abbey Gdns, Tresco, Isles of Scilly; Highgrove, Glos; London and environs: Albert Bridge; British Oxygen Co., Guildford; Cadogan Place Gardens and Cadogan Sq.; Crystal Palace Park; Guildhall; Longbow House; St Katharine-by-the-Tower; Taylor Woodrow; Wates Ltd, Norbury; also London Road, Kingston-upon-Thames; Elmsleigh Centre, Staines; IPC HQ, Sutton; St Raphael's Hospice, Cheam, Surrey; Central Park, Watford; Queen Elizabeth Gates, Hyde Park Corner; USA: Ambassador Coll., Texas, and Ambassador Coll., Calif; Atlantic Richfield Oil Co., New Mexico; Lakeland Meml Hosp., Wis; First Fed. Savings, Mass; Pepsico World HQ, Purchase, NY; Playboy Hotel and Casino, Atlantic City, NJ; Sarasota, Fla; Mayo Foundation, Minn; Sherman, Texas; Ritz Carlton, Rancho Mirage, Calif; Mayo Clinic, Rochester, Minn; Grayson Bank, Sherman, Texas; also Perth, WA, and Place Camelotti, Geneva, 1988. Bronze portrait heads include: Sir Thomas Beecham, 1956; Sir John Gielgud, 1962; Yehudi Menuhin, 1963; The Beatles, 1964; Kokoschka, 1965; Sir Alec Douglas-Home, 1966; Robert, Marquess of Salisbury, 1967; The Prince of Wales, 1969; Lord Baden-Powell, 1971; Virginia Wade, 1972; The Queen, 1973; King Hassan of Morocco, 1973; Air Chief Marshal Lord Dowding, 1974; The Begum Aga Khan, 1975; Pele, 1976; Lord Hailsham, 1977; Prince Michael of Kent, 1977; Earl Mountbatten of Burma, 1981; Paul Daniels, 1982; Jackie Stewart, 1982; Portrait Figures: Arnold Palmer, 1983; Björn Borg, 1984; Leonard Cheshire, for Stowe Sch., 1995; other sculptures: Fred Perry, AELTC, 1984; Shergar and jockey, 1981; Shareef Dancer and groom, 1984; Cresta Rider, St Moritz, 1985; Two Dolphins, Provence, France, 1986. Designed: Common Market 50 pence piece of clasped hands, 1973; King Hassan, for Moroccan coinage, 1973; the Queen's Silver Jubilee Medal, 1977 (with new effigy of the Queen wearing St Edward's Crown). *Publication:* The Messenger, a sculpture by David Wynne, 1982. *relevant publications:* T. S. R. Boase, The Sculpture of David Wynne 1949–1967, 1968; Graham Hughes, The Sculpture of David Wynne 1968–1974, 1974; Jonathan Stone (ed), The Sculpture of David Wynne 1974–92, 1993. *Recreations:* active sports, poetry, music. *Address:* 5 Burlington Lodge Studios, Buer Road, SW6 4LA. *T:* 0171–731 1071. *Clubs:* Garrick, Queen's, Hurlingham; Village (Wimbledon); Leander (Henley-on-Thames); 1st and 3rd Trinity Boat; St Moritz Tobogganing; The Royal Tennis Court (Hampton Court Palace).

WYNNE, Col J. F. W.; *see* Williams-Wynne.

WYNNE-EDWARDS, Vero Copner, CBE 1973; MA, DSc; FRS 1970; FRSE, FRSC; Regius Professor of Natural History, University of Aberdeen, 1946–74, Vice Principal, 1972–74; *b* 4 July 1906; 3rd *s* of late Rev. Canon John Rosindale Wynne-Edwards and Lilian Agnes Streatfeild; *m* 1929, Jeannie Campbell, *e d* of late Percy Morris, Devon County Architect; one *s* one *d*. *Educ:* Leeds Grammar Sch.; Rugby Sch.; New Coll., Oxford. 1st Class Hons in Natural Science (Zoology), Oxford, 1927; Senior Scholar of New Coll., 1927–29; Student Probationer, Marine Biological Laboratory, Plymouth, 1927–29; Assistant Lecturer in Zoology, Univ. of Bristol, 1929–30; Asst Prof. of Zoology, McGill Univ., Montreal, 1930–44; Associate Prof., 1944–46. Canadian representative, MacMillan Baffin Island expedition, 1937; Canadian Fisheries Research Board expeditions to Mackenzie River, 1944, and Yukon Territory, 1945; Baird Expedition to Central Baffin Island, 1950. Visiting Prof. of Conservation, University of Louisville, Kentucky, 1959, Commonwealth Universities Interchange Fellow New Zealand, 1962; Leverhulme Emeritus Fellowship, 1978–80. Jt Editor, Journal of Applied Ecology, 1963–68. Member: Nature Conservancy, 1954–57; Red Deer Commn (Vice-Chm.), 1959–68; Royal Commn on Environmental Pollution, 1970–74; President: British Ornithologists' Union, 1965–70; Scottish Marine Biological Assoc., 1967–73; Section D, British Assoc., 1974; Chairman: NERC, 1968–71; DoE and Scottish Office Adv. Cttees on Protection of Birds, 1970–78; Scientific Authority for Animals, DoE, 1976–77. For. Mem., Societas Scientiarum Fennica, 1965; Hon. Mem., British Ecological Soc., 1977; Hon. Fellow, Amer. Ornithologists' Union, 1991. Hon. FIBiol 1980. Hon. DUniv Stirling, 1974; Hon. LLD Aberdeen, 1976. Godman-Salvin Medal, British Ornithologists' Union, 1977; Neill Prize, RSE, 1977; Frink Medal, Zoological Soc., 1980. *Publications:* Animal Dispersion in relation to social behaviour, 1962; Evolution through Group Selection, 1986; (contrib.) Leaders in the Study of Animal Behaviour, ed D. A. Dewsbury, 1985; scientific papers on ornithology (esp. oceanic birds), animal populations. *Recreation:* natural history. *Address:* Ravelston, William Street, Torphins, via Banchory, Aberdeenshire AB31 4JR.

X

XENAKIS, Iannis; composer, architect, civil engineer; Professor, Université de Paris I (Panthéon-Sorbonne), 1973–89, now Emeritus; *b* Athens, 29 May 1922; *s* of Clearchos Xenakis and Fotini Pavlou; *m* 1953, Françoise Gargouïl; one *d*. *Educ:* Athens Polytechnic Inst.; Ecole Normale de Musique, Paris; Gravesano; Paris Conservatoire; studied with Milhaud, Scherchen, Messiaen; studied engineering, Athens. DèsL Sorbonne, 1976. Fought in Greek Resistance, war of 1939–45, sentenced to death; exile, France, 1947; with Le Corbusier as engineer and architect, 1947–60. Numerous musical compositions through introd. of mass concept of music, stochastic music, symbolic music, through probability calculus and set theory, including instrumental, electro-acoustic and computerized works; designer of pavilions and spectacles. Numerous academic appts, including Associate Prof., Indiana Univ., Bloomington, USA, 1967–72, and Gresham Prof. of Music, 1975. Member: Centre Nat. de Recherche Scientifique; Acad. des Beaux Arts, 1983; Akademie der Kunste, Berlin and Munich, 1983; For. Mem., Swedish Royal Acad. of Music, 1989; Hon. Member: Amer. Acad. of Arts and Letters, 1975; Scottish Soc. of Composers, 1987–. Hon. DMus: Edinburgh, 1989; Glasgow, 1990. Maurice Ravel Gold Medal, 1974; Beethoven Prize (FRG), 1977. Officier: Ordre National du Mérite (France), 1985; Légion d'Honneur (France), 1991 (Chevalier, 1982); Commandeur, Ordre des Arts et des Lettres (France), 1991 (Officier, 1981). *Compositions include: orchestral:* Métastasis, 1954; Pithoprakta, 1956; Stratégie, 1962; Terretektorh, 1966; Nomos Gamma, 1968; Kraanerg (ballet score), 1969; Antikhthon 1971; Erikhthon (pno and orch.), 1974; Noomena, 1974; Jonchaies, 1977; Lichens, 1984; Alax, 1985; Keqrops (pno and orch.), 1986; Horos, 1986; Ata, 1987; Kyania, 1990; Dox-Orkh (violin and orch.), 1991; Roaï, 1991; Krinoïdi, 1991; *vocal and orchestral:* Cendrées, 1973; Anemoessa, 1979; Aïs, 1979; Nekuïa, 1981; Kassandra: Oresteïa II, 1987; *choral:* Oresteïa, 1966; Medea, 1967; Pour la Paix, 1981; *instrumental ensemble:* Atrées, 1960; Eonta, 1963; N'Shima, 1975; Thallein, 1984; Jalons, 1986; Waarg, 1988; *solo instrumental:* Nomos Alpha ('cello), 1966; Persephassa (perc.), 1969; Gmeeoorh (organ), 1974; Psappha, 1975; Khoaï (hpchd), 1976; Pléïades (perc.), 1978; Komboï (hpchd and perc.), 1981; Tetras (strings), 1983; Naama (hpchd), 1984; Tetora (strings), 1990; *electro-acoustic:* Bohor, 1962; Hibiki Hana Ma, 1970; Persepolis, 1971; Polytope de Cluny, 1972; La Légende d'Eer, 1977; Voyage Absolu des Unari vers Andromède, 1989; Gendy 3, 1991. *Publications:* Musiques Formelles, 1963 (Formalized Music, 1970, rev. and enlarged edn, 1991); Musique Architecture, 1970; Xenakis, les Polytopes, 1975; Arts and Sciences: Alloys, 1979. *Address:* 17 rue Victor Massé, F-75009 Paris, France.

Y

YACOUB, Sir Magdi (Habib), Kt 1992; FRCS; British Heart Foundation Professor of Cardiothoracic Surgery, National Heart and Lung Institute (formerly Cardiothoracic Institute), at Royal Brompton (formerly Brompton) Hospital, since 1986; Consultant Cardiothoracic Surgeon, Harefield Hospital, Middlesex, since 1969; *b* Cairo, 16 Nov. 1935; *m*; one *s* two *d*. *Educ:* Cairo University, FRCS, FRCSE, FRCSGlas, 1962; LRCP 1966, MRCP 1986, Hon. FRCP 1990. Rotating House Officer, Cairo Univ. Hosp., 1958–59; Surgical Registrar, Postgrad. Surgical Unit, Cairo Univ., 1959–61; Resident Surgical Officer, 1962–63, Surgical Registrar, 1963–64, London Chest Hosp.; Rotating Sen. Surgical Registrar, Nat. Heart and Chest Hosps, 1964–68; Asst Prof. of Cardiothoracic Surgery, Chicago Univ., 1968–69; Consultant Cardiac Surgeon, Nat. Heart Hosp., 1973–89. Hon. Consultant: Royal Free Hosp. Med. Sch.; King Edward's Coll. of Medicine, Lahore, Pakistan; Hon. Prof. of Surgery, Univ. of Sienna; Hon. Prof. of Cardiac Surgery, Charing Cross and Westminster Hosp. Med. Schs. Has developed innovations in heart and heart-lung transplants. Mem., Soc. Thoracic Surgeons; FRSocMed. Hon. DSc: Brunel, 1985; Amer. Univ. at Cairo, 1989; Loughborough, 1990; Hon. MCh Cardiff, 1986; Hon. PhD Lund, 1988. Editor: Annual in Cardiac Surgery; Current Opinion in Cardiology: coronary artery surgery. *Publications:* papers on pulmonary osteoarthropath, aortic valve homografts, surgical treatment of ischaemic heart disease, valve repairs, and related subjects. *Address:* National Heart and Lung Institute, Dovehouse Street, SW3 6LY.

YALE, David Eryl Corbet, FBA 1980; Reader in English Legal History, Cambridge University, 1969–93, now Emeritus; Fellow, Christ's College, Cambridge, since 1950; *b* 31 March 1928; *s* of Lt-Col J. C. L. Yale and Mrs Beatrice Yale (*née* Breese); *m* 1959, Elizabeth Ann, *d* of C. A. B. Brett, Belfast; two *s*. *Educ:* Malvern Coll., Worcs; Queens' Coll., Cambridge (BA 1949, LLB 1950, MA 1953). Called to the Bar, Inner Temple, 1951; Asst Lectr and Lectr in Law, Cambridge Univ., 1952–69. Pres., Selden Soc., 1994–. *Publications:* various, mainly in field of legal history. *Recreation:* fishing. *Address:* Christ's College, Cambridge CB2 3BU. *T:* Cambridge (01223) 334900; Saethon, Porthmadog, Gwynedd LL49 9UR. *T:* Porthmadog (01766) 512129.

YALOW, Rosalyn Sussman, PhD; Senior Medical Investigator, Veterans Administration, later Veterans Affairs, 1972–92, Senior Medical Investigator Emeritus, since 1992; *b* 19 July 1921; *d* of Simon Sussman and Clara (*née* Zipper); *m* 1943, Aaron Yalow; one *s* one *d*. *Educ:* Hunter Coll., NYC (AB Physics and Chemistry, 1941); Univ. of Ill, Urbana (MS Phys. 1942, PhD Phys. 1945). Diplomate, Amer. Bd of Radiol., 1951. Asst in Phys., Univ. of Ill, 1941–43, Instr, 1944–45; Lectr and Temp. Asst Prof. in Phys., Hunter Coll., 1946–50. Veterans Admin Hospital, Bronx, NY: Consultant, Radioisotope Unit, 1947–50; Physicist and Asst Chief, Radioisotope Service, 1950–70 (Actg Chief, 1968–70); Chief, Nuclear Medicine Service, 1970–80; Dir, Solomon A. Berson Res. Lab., 1973–; Chm., Dept of Clin. Scis, Montefiore Hosp. and Med. Center, Bronx, NY, 1980–85; Chief, VA Radioimmunoassay Ref. Lab., 1969–. Consultant, Lenox Hill Hosp., NYC, 1952–62. Res. Prof., Dept of Med., Mt Sinai Sch. of Med., 1968–74, Distinguished Service Prof., 1974–79; Distinguished Prof.-at-Large, Albert Einstein Coll. of Med., Yeshiva Univ., NY, 1979–85, Prof. Emeritus, 1985–; Solomon A. Berson Distinguished Prof.-at-Large, Mt Sinai Sch. of Medicine, City Univ. of NY, 1986–. IAEA Expert, Instituto Energia Atomica, Brazil, 1970; WHO Consultant, Radiation Med. Centre, India, 1978; Sec., US Nat. Cttee on Med. Physics, 1963–67. Member: President's Study Gp on Careers for Women, 1966–67; Med. Adv. Bd, Nat. Pituitary Agency, 1968–71; Endocrinol. Study Sect., Nat. Insts of Health, 1969–72; Cttee for Evaluation of NPA, Nat. Res. Council, 1973–74; Council, Endocrine Soc., 1974–80 (Koch Award, 1972; Pres., 1978); Bd of Dirs, NY Diabetes Assoc., 1974–77. Member: Editorial Adv. Council, Acta Diabetologica Latina, 1975–77; Ed. Adv. Bd, Encyclopaedia Universalis, 1978–; Ed. Bd, Mt Sinai Jl of Medicine, 1976–79; Ed. Bd, Diabetes, 1976–79. Fellow: NY Acad. of Sciences (Chm., Biophys. Div., 1964–65; A. Cressy Morrison Award in Nat. Sci., 1975); Radiation Res. Soc.; Amer. Assoc. of Physicists in Med.; Biophys. Soc.; Amer. Diabetes Assoc. (Eli Lilly Award, 1961; Commemorative Medallion, 1972; Banting Medal, 1978; Rosalyn S. Yalow Res. and Develt Award estabd 1978); Amer. Physiol Soc.; Soc. of Nuclear Med. Associate Fellow in Phys., Amer. Coll. of Radiol. Member: Nat. Acad. of Sciences; Amer. Acad. Arts and Sciences; Foreign Associate, French Acad. of Medicine. Hon. DSc and Hon. DHumLett from univs and med. colls in the US, France, Argentina, Canada. Nobel Prize in Physiology or Medicine, 1977; VA Exceptional Service Award, 1975 and 1978; Nat. Medal of Sci., 1988. Has given many distinguished lectures and received many awards and prizes from univs and med. socs and assocs. *Publications:* over 500 papers and contribns to books, research reports, proceedings of conferences and symposia on radioimmunoassay of peptide hormones and related subjects, since 1950. *Address:* VA Medical Center, 130 West Kingsbridge Road, Bronx, NY 10468, USA. *T:* (718) 579 1644.

YAM, Yee-Kwan David; Hon. Mr Justice Yam; High Court Judge, Hong Kong, since 1994; *b* 4 Oct. 1948; *s* of Yam Fat-Shing Frank and Ng Yuet-Hing Nora; *m* 1977, Dr Stella T. P. Wong; two *s*. *Educ:* Hong Kong Univ. (BSc 1971; LLB 1975); Inns of Court Sch. of Law. Called to the Bar, Middle Temple, and to Hong Kong Bar, 1976; in practice, 1977–87; District Court Judge, 1987–94. *Recreations:* golf, badminton, music. *Address:* Supreme Court, 38 Queensway, Hong Kong. *T:* 8254421. *Clubs:* Royal Hong Kong Jockey, Shek O Golf and Country (Hong Kong); Honichi Golf (China).

YAMAZAKI, Toshio; President, Temple University, Japan, since 1991; Japanese Ambassador to the Court of St James's, 1985–88; retired; *b* 13 Aug. 1922; *s* of Takamaro Yamazaki and Konoe Yamazaki; *m* 1955, Yasuko Arakawa; one *s* one *d*. *Educ:* Tokyo University (Faculty of Law). 2nd Sec., Japanese Embassy, London, 1955–59; Dir, British Commonwealth Div., European and Oceanic Affairs Bureau, Min. of Foreign Affairs, 1962–64; Counsellor, Permt Mission to UN, New York; 1964–67; Dir, Financial Affairs Div., Minister's Secretariat, Min. of Foreign Affairs, 1967–70; Dep. Dir-Gen., Treaties Bureau, 1970; Minister, Washington, 1971–74; Dir-Gen., Amer. Affairs Bureau, Min. of Foreign Affairs, 1974–77; Dep. Vice-Minister for Admin, 1978–80; Ambassador to Egypt, 1980–82, to Indonesia, 1982–84. Chm., Japan-British Soc., Tokyo, 1988–94. Grand Cordon, Order of Sacred Treasure (Japan), 1994; Order of Republic, 1st cl. (Egypt), 1982; Banda 2nd cl., Orden del Aguila Azteca (Mexico), 1978; Grosses Verdienstkreuz mit Stern (FRG), 1979. *Recreation:* golf. *Address:* 9-1-506 Sanban-cho, Chiyoda-ku, Tokyo 102, Japan. *T:* (3) 32881458. *Clubs:* Tokyo (Tokyo); Tokyo Golf.

YAMEY, Prof. Basil Selig, CBE 1972; FBA 1977; Professor of Economics, University of London, 1960–84, now Emeritus; Member (part-time), Monopolies and Mergers Commission, 1966–78; *b* 4 May 1919; *s* of Solomon and Leah Yamey; *m* 1st, 1948, Helen Bloch (*d* 1980); one *s* one *d*; 2nd, 1991, Demetra Georgakopoulou. *Educ:* Tulbagh High Sch.; Univ. of Cape Town; LSE. Lectr in Commerce, Rhodes Univ., 1945; Senior Lectr in Commerce, Univ. of Cape Town, 1946; Lectr in Commerce, LSE, 1948; Associate Prof. of Commerce, McGill Univ., 1949; Reader in Economics, Univ. of London, 1950. Dir, Private Bank and Trust Co. Ltd, 1989–94. Managing Trustee, IEA, 1986–91. Trustee: National Gall., 1974–81; Tate Gall., 1979–81; Member: Council, National Trust, 1979–81; Museums and Galls Commn, 1983–84; Cinematograph Films Council, 1969–73. Mem. Committee of Management: Courtauld Inst., 1981–84; Warburg Inst., 1981–84; Mem., Governing Body, London Business Sch., 1965–84. *Publications:* Economics of Resale Price Maintenance, 1954; (jt editor) Studies in History of Accounting, 1956; (with P. T. Bauer) Economics of Under-developed Countries, 1957; (jt editor) Capital, Saving and Credit in Peasant Societies, 1963; (with H. C. Edey and H. Thomson) Accounting in England and Scotland, 1543–1800, 1963; (with R. B. Stevens) The Restrictive Practices Court, 1965; (ed) Resale Price Maintenance, 1966; (with P. T. Bauer) Markets, Market Control and Marketing Reform: Selected Papers, 1968; (ed) Economics of Industrial Structure, 1973; (jt editor) Economics of Retailing, 1973; (jt editor) Debits, Credits, Finance and Profits, 1974; (with B. A. Goss) Economics of Futures Trading, 1976; Essays on the History of Accounting, 1978; (jt editor) Stato e Industria in Europa: Il Regno Unito, 1979; Further Essays on the History of Accounting, 1983; Arte e Contabilità, 1986; Análisis Económico de los Mercados, 1987; Art and Accounting, 1989; (ed) Luca Pacioli, Exposition of Double Entry Book-keeping, Venice 1494, 1994; (jt editor) Accounting History: some British contributions, 1994; articles on economics, economic history and law in learned journals. *Address:* 27B Elsworthy Road, NW3 3BT. *T:* 0171–405 7686.

YAN, Hon. Manuel T.; Philippine Ambassador to the Court of St James's, 1991–92; *b* 24 Jan. 1920; *s* of Jose R. Yan and Romana Tecson; *m* 1st, 1944, Amelia D. Acab (*d* 1983); five *c*, 2nd, 1988, Eliosa Fernandez. *Educ:* Philippine Mil. Acad. (BS 1941); Engr Sch., US Army, Fort Belvoir, Va; Mapua Inst. of Technol. (BS Civil Engrg, 1951); Comd and Gen. Staff Coll., Fort Leavenworth, Kansas. Served World War II, Second Lieut (Battle of Bataan); CO 20th Bn Combat Team, 1953–55; Chief of Intelligence, Philippine Constabulary, 1956–59; Sec.-Gen. Staff, 1959–61, Chief, Intelligence Service, 1961–63, Armed Forces of the Philippines; Chief of Staff, First Philippine Constab. Zone, 1963–65; Zone Comdr, Second Philippine Constab. Zone, 1966–67 (Brig. Gen.); Chief of Philippine Constab., concurrently Vice Chief of Staff, Armed Forces of the Philippines, 1967; Chief of Staff, Armed Forces of the Philippines, 1968–72 (General); Chief of Mission and Ambassador: to Thailand, 1972–81; to Indonesia, 1981–87; Dep. Minister for Foreign Affairs, 1987; Actg Sec. of Foreign Affairs, Sept.–Oct. 1987; Under Sec. of Foreign Affairs, 1987–91. Knight Grand Cross (1st Class): Order of the Crown, Thailand; Order of White Elephant, Thailand; Bintang Jasa Utama Award, Indonesia; decorations from US, Vietnam, Korea. *Recreations:* badminton, hiking, reading. *Address:* No 16 La Salle Street, North East Greenhills, San Juan, Metro Manila, Philippines. *Clubs:* Filipino, Association of Generals and Flag Officers (Manila).

YANG, Chen Ning; physicist, educator; Einstein Professor and Director, Institute for Theoretical Physics, State University of New York at Stony Brook, New York, since 1966; *b* Hofei, China, 22 Sept. 1922; *s* of Ke Chuen Yang and Meng Hwa Lo; *m* 1950, Chih Li Tu; two *s* one *d*. Naturalized 1964. *Educ:* National Southwest Associated Univ., Kunming, China (BSc), 1942; University of Chicago (PhD), 1948. Institute for Advanced Study, Princeton, NJ: Member, 1949–55; Prof. of Physics, 1955–65; several DSc's from universities. Member of Board: Rockefeller Univ., 1970–76; AAAS, 1976–80; Salk Inst., 1978–; Ben Gurion Univ.; Member: Amer. Phys. Soc.; Nat. Acad. Sci.; Amer. Philos. Soc., Sigma Xi; Brazilian, Venezuelan and Royal Spanish Acads of Sci; Foreign Member: Royal Soc., 1992; Russian Acad. of Sciences, 1994. Nobel Prize in Physics, 1957; Rumford Prize, 1980; Nat. Medal of Science, 1986; Benjamin Franklin Medal, Amer. Phil Soc., 1993; Bower Prize, Franklin Inst., 1994. *Publications:* contrib. to Physical Review, Reviews of Modern Physics. *Address:* State University of New York at Stony Brook, NY 11794-3840, USA.

YANG SHANGKUN; President of the People's Republic of China, 1988–93; *b* Tongnan County, Sichuan Province, 1907; *m* Li Bozhao (decd), playwright. *Educ:* Sun Yat-sen Univ., Moscow. Joined Communist Youth League, 1925, and Communist Party, 1926; formerly: Head of Propaganda Department: All-China Fedn of Trade Unions, Shanghai (also Sec. of Party Orgn); Communist Party's Jiangsu Provincial Cttee; Communist Party's Central Cttee; Editor, Red China newspaper; Dep. Head, Communist Party's sch., Jiangxi; Dir, Political Dept, First Front Army of Red Army; Dep. Dir, Gen. Pol Dept, Red Army; Pol Commisar, Third Red Army Corps; Long March, Oct. 1934–Oct. 1935; Chinese Communist Party's Central Committee: successively: Sec., N Bureau, 1937; Sec.-Gen., Mil. Commn, 1945; Dir, Gen. Office; Dep. Sec.-Gen.; Alternate Mem. of Secretariat; Mem. Secretariat, Guangdong Provincial Party Cttee; removed from posts and imprisoned during Cultural Revolution, 1966–76; successively: Second Sec., Guangdong Provincial Party Cttee; Vice-Gov., Guangdong; First Sec., Guangzhou City Party Cttee;

Chm., Guangzhou City Revolutionary Cttee; Vice-Chm. and Sec.-Gen., Standing Cttee, Nat. People's Congress, 1980; Exec. Vice-Chm., 1982–, First Vice-Chm., 1989–, Mil. Commn of Party Central Cttee (Sec.-Gen., 1980–81); Mem., Pol Bureau, 1982–92. *Recreations:* sports, especially swimming.

YANG, Hon. Sir Ti Liang, Kt 1988; **Hon. Mr Justice Yang;** Chief Justice of Hong Kong, since 1988; *b* 30 June 1929; *s* of late Shao-nan Yang and Elsie (*née* Chun); *m* 1954, Eileen Barbara (*née* Tam); two *s*. *Educ:* The Comparative Law Sch. of China; Soochow Univ., Shanghai; UCL (LLB Hons 1953; Fellow 1989). FCIArb 1990. Called to the Bar (with honours), Gray's Inn, 1954, Hon. Bencher, 1988. Magistrate, Hong Kong, 1956; Sen. Magistrate, 1963; Rockefeller Fellow, London Univ., 1963–64; District Judge, Dist Court, 1968; Judge of the High Court, Hong Kong, 1975; Justice of Appeal, Hong Kong, 1980; Pres., Court of Appeal of Negara Brunei Darussalam, 1988–92. Chairman: Kowloon Disturbances Claims Assessment Bd, 1966, Compensation Bd, 1967; Commn of Inquiry into the Rainstorm Disasters, 1972; Commn of Inquiry into the Leung Wing-sang Case, 1976; Commn of Inquiry into the MacLennan Case, 1980; Mem., Law Reform Commn, 1980– (Chm., Sub-cttee on law relating to homosexuality, 1980). Mem., Chinese Lang. Cttee (Chm. Legal Sub-cttee), 1970. Patron, Soc. for Rehabilitation of Offenders, Hong Kong; Hon. President: Hong Kong Scouts Assoc.; Soc. Against Child Abuse. Chairman: University and Polytechnic Grants Cttee, 1981–84; Hong Kong Univ. Council, 1987–. Pres., Bentham Club. Hon. LLD: Chinese Univ. of Hong Kong, 1984; Hong Kong Poly., 1992; Hon. DLitt Hong Kong Univ., 1991. Order of Chivalry, First Class, SPMB, Negara Brunei Darussalam, 1990. *Recreations:* philately, reading, walking, oriental ceramics, travelling, music. *Address:* Supreme Court, 38 Queensway, Hong Kong. *T:* Hong Kong 8254601; Flat 8, Duchess of Bedford House, Duchess of Bedford's Walk, W8 7QL. *Clubs:* Athenæum; Hong Kong, Hong Kong Country, Royal Hong Kong Jockey (Hong Kong).

YAPP, Sir Stanley Graham, Kt 1975; Chairman, West Midlands County Council, 1983–84 (Leader, 1973–77; Vice-Chairman, 1982–83); Member, Birmingham City Council, later Birmingham District Council, 1961–77 (Leader, 1972–74); *s* of late William and of Elsie Yapp; *m* 1961, Elisbeth Wise (marr. diss.); one *d*; *m* 1974, Carol Matheson (marr. diss.); one *s*; *m* 1983, Christine Horton. Member, West Midlands Economic Planning Council (Chm., Transport Cttee); Member many bodies both local and national, inc.: Vice-Chm. LAMSAC; Member: Local Govt Trng Board; Nat. Jt Councils on pay and conditions; AMA; BR Adv. Bd, Midlands and N Western Reg., 1977–79; Chm., West Midlands Planning Authorities Conf., 1973–75, Vice-Chm. 1975–77. Governor, BFI, 1977–79. FIMgt. *Publications:* contribs to Local Government Chronicle, Municipal Journal, Rating and Valuation. *Recreations:* astronomy, reading walking. *Address:* 172 York Road, Hall Green, Birmingham B28 8LE.

YARBOROUGH, 8th Earl of, *cr* 1837; **Charles John Pelham;** Baron Yarborough, 1794; Baron Worsley, 1837; *b* 5 Nov. 1963; *o s* of 7th Earl of Yarborough and Ann, *d* of late John Herbert Upton; *S* father, 1991; *m* 1990, Anna-Karin Zecevic, *d* of George Zecevic; three *s*. *Heir:* *s* Lord Worsley, *qv*. *Address:* Brocklesby Park, Habrough, Lincs DN37 8PL.

YARBURGH-BATESON; *see* de Yarburgh-Bateson, family name of Baron Deramore.

YARD, John; Director, Business Services (Information Technology) Office, Inland Revenue, since 1993; *b* 29 July 1944; *s* of Ernest Alfred and Kathleen Lilian Yard; *m* 1st, 1967, Lynda Jennifer Gilbert; 2nd, 1992, Jean Pamela Murray; two *s* one *d*. *Educ:* St Marylebone Grammar Sch. Inland Revenue: Exec. Officer and PAYE Auditor, 1963–71; Inspector of Taxes, 1971–84; Dep. Dir (Systems and Policy), 1984–91; Head of Change Mgt Gp, 1992. *Recreations:* squash, property renovation. *Address:* Business Services Office, Board of Inland Revenue, 7th Floor Maltravers, c/o Somerset House, Strand, WC2R 1LB.

YARDE-BULLER, family name of **Baron Churston.**

YARDLEY, Sir David (Charles Miller), Kt 1994; Chairman, Commission for Local Administration in England, 1982–94; a Complaints Commissioner, Securities and Investments Board, since 1994; *b* 4 June 1929; *s* of late Geoffrey Miller Yardley and Doris Woodward Yardley (*née* Jones); *m* 1954, Patricia Anne Tempest Olver; two *s* two *d*. *Educ:* The Old Hall Sch., Wellington; Ellesmere Coll., Shropshire; Univ. of Birmingham (LLB, LLD); Univ. of Oxford (MA, DPhil). Called to Bar, Gray's Inn, 1952. RAF Flying Officer (nat. service), 1949–51. Bigelow Teaching Fellow, Univ. of Chicago, 1953–54; Fellow and Tutor in Jurisprudence, St Edmund Hall, Oxford, 1953–74, Emeritus Fellow, 1974–; CUF Lectr, Univ. of Oxford, 1954–74; Sen. Proctor, Univ. of Oxford, 1965–66; Barber Prof. of Law, Univ. of Birmingham, 1974–78; Head of Dept of Law, Politics and Economics, Oxford Poly., 1978–80; Rank Foundn Prof. of Law, University Coll. at Buckingham, 1980–82. Visiting Prof. of Law, Univ. of Sydney, 1971; Hon. Prof. of Law, Univ. of Buckingham, 1994; Vis. Prof., Oxford Brookes Univ., 1995–. Constitutional Consultant, Govt of W Nigeria, 1956. Chm., Thames Valley Rent Tribunal, 1963–82; Vice-Pres., Cambs Chilterns and Thames Rent Assessment Panel, 1966–82; Oxford City Councillor, 1966–74; Chairman: Oxford Area Nat. Ins. Local Appeal Tribunal, 1969–82; Oxford Preservation Trust, 1989–. Chm. of Governors, St Helen's Sch., Abingdon, 1967–81. FRSA 1991. Freeman, City of Oxford, 1989. *Publications:* Introduction to British Constitutional Law, 1960, 8th edn (as Introduction to Constitutional and Administrative Law), 1995; A Source Book of English Administrative Law, 1963, 2nd edn, 1970; The Future of the Law, 1964; Geldart's Elements of English Law, 7th edn, 1966–10th edn (as Geldart's Introduction to English Law), 1991, 11th edn 1995; Hanbury's English Courts of Law, 4th edn, 1967; Hanbury and Yardley, English Courts of Law, 5th edn, 1979; Principles of Administrative Law, 1981, 2nd edn, 1986; (with I. N. Stevens) The Protection of Liberty, 1982. *Recreations:* lawn tennis, opera, cats. *Address:* 9 Belbroughton Road, Oxford OX2 6UZ. *T:* Oxford (01865) 54831. *Club:* Royal Air Force.

YARMOUTH, Earl of; Henry Jocelyn Seymour; *b* 6 July 1958; *s* and *heir* of 8th Marquess of Hertford, *qv*; *m* 1990, Beatriz, *d* of Jorge Karam; two *s* one *d*. *Heir:* *s* Lord Conway, *qv*.

YARNOLD, Rev. Edward John, SJ; DD; Tutor in Theology, Campion Hall, Oxford, since 1964 (Master, 1965–72; Senior Tutor, 1972–74); *b* 14 Jan. 1926; *s* of Edward Cabré Yarnold and Agnes (*née* Deakin). *Educ:* St Michael's Coll., Leeds; Campion Hall, Oxford (MA); Heythrop College (STL). Taught classics at St Francis Xavier's Coll., Liverpool, 1954–57; ordained, 1960; taught classics at St Michael's Coll., Leeds, 1962–64; Res. Lectr, Oxford Univ., 1991–. Sarum Lectr, Univ. of Oxford, 1972–73; Lectr (part-time), Heythrop Coll., London, 1978–80; Vis. Prof., Univ. of Notre Dame, 1982–; Murray Prof. of Catholic Thought, Univ. of Toledo, Ohio, 1995. Gen. Sec., Ecumenical Soc. of Blessed Virgin Mary, 1994– (Associate Gen. Sec., 1975–94); Mem., Anglican-Roman Catholic Internat. Commn, 1970–81 and 1983–91; Pres., Catholic Theol. Assoc. of GB, 1986–88. Order of St Augustine, 1981. *Publications:* The Theology of Original Sin, 1971; The Awe-Inspiring Rites of Initiation, 1972; The Second Gift, 1974; (with H. Chadwick) Truth and Authority, 1977; (ed jtly and contrib.) The Study of Liturgy, 1978; They are in Earnest, 1982; Eight Days with the Lord, 1984; (ed jtly and contrib.) The Study of Spirituality, 1986; In Search of Unity, 1989; Time for God, 1991; (ed jtly and contrib.) Anglicans and Roman Catholics: the search for unity, 1994; articles in learned jls. *Recreations:* opera, cricket. *Address:* Campion Hall, Oxford OX1 1QS. *T:* Oxford (01865) 286111, *Fax:* (01865) 286148.

YARNOLD, Patrick; HM Diplomatic Service; Consul-General, Marseilles, since 1995; *b* 21 March 1937; *s* of late Leonard Francis Yarnold and Gladys Blanche Yarnold (*née* Merry); *m* 1961, Caroline, *er d* of late Andrew J. Martin; two *d*. *Educ:* Bancroft's School. HM Forces, 1955–57. Joined HM Foreign (now Diplomatic) Service, 1957; served: FO, 1957–60; Addis Ababa, 1961–64; Belgrade, 1964–66; FO (later FCO), 1966–70; 1st Sec., Head of Chancery, Bucharest, 1970–73; 1st Sec. (Commercial), Bonn, 1973–76; FCO, 1976–79; Counsellor (Economic and Commercial), Brussels, 1980–83; Consul-Gen., Zagreb, 1983–85; Counsellor and Head of Chancery, Belgrade, 1985–87; Hd of Defence Dept, FCO, 1987–90; Consul-Gen., Hamburg, 1990–94. *Recreations:* travel, photography, walking, genealogy, local history, Chinese cooking, etc. *Address:* c/o Foreign and Commonwealth Office, SW1A 2AH.

YARRANTON, Sir Peter (George), Kt 1992; Chairman: Sports Council, 1989–94; Sports Partner Ltd, 1990–95; *b* 30 Sept. 1924; *s* of late Edward John Yarranton and Norah Ellen (*née* Atkins); *m* 1947, Mary Avena (*née* Flowitt); one *s* one *d*. *Educ:* Willesden Technical Coll. Prelim. ARIBA. Joined RAF, 1942; commnd 1944; Flying Officer, 1945; Flt Lieut, 1949; voluntarily retd, 1957. Shell Mex & BP Ltd: management trainee, 1957–58; Ops Officer, Reading, 1958–61; UK Indust. Relations Officer, 1961–63; i/c Indust. Relations, 1963–66; Manager, Indust. Relations, 1966–69; Regional Ops Manager, SE Region, 1969–75; Manager, Plant and Engrg, Distbn Div., Shell UK Oil, 1975–77; Gen. Manager, Lensbury Club, 1978–92. Founder Dir, London Docklands Arena Ltd, 1984–93; non-exec. Dir, Drug Check UK Ltd, 1995–. Governor: Sports Aid Foundn, 1989–; London Marathon Ltd, 1989–94; Trustee, Golden Globe Charity Trust, 1990–93; Mem., Jet Heritage, 1994–. Fellow, Recreation Managers Assoc., 1979–; President: Rugby Football Union, 1991–92 (Public Relations Advr to the Union, 1983–); Mddx County RFU, 1986–88; Lensbury RFC; Wasps FC, 1982–85; England Internat. (5 caps), Rugby Union Football: *v* Ireland, New Zealand and Wales, 1954, Scotland and France 1955; played for and captained Barbarians, London, Mddx, Wasps, British Combined Services, and RAF Rugby Clubs; formerly: Mem., London and Mddx Premier Swimming and Water Polo Teams; Captain, RAF Swimming and Water Polo Teams. Gov., Queen's Coll., Taunton, 1993–. Freeman, City of London, 1977; Liveryman, Worshipful Co. of Gold and Silver Wyre Drawers, 1977 (Mem., Court of Assts, 1987). FIMgt (FBIM 1980); FIPM 1975. Mem. Editorial Bd, Rugby World and Post, 1983–93. Hon. DArts De Montfort, 1993. *Recreations:* all sports, indoor and outdoor, particularly Rugby, soccer, cricket, swimming, water polo and sub-aqua diving. *Address:* Broom Point, Broom Water West, Teddington, Mddx TW11 9QH; 2 Sunnydale Villas, Durlston Road, Swanage, Dorset BH19 2HY. *Clubs:* East India, Royal Air Force, Rugby, Cricketers.

YARROW, Dr Alfred, FFPHM; Honorary Member, Epidemiology Unit, Ministry of Health, Jerusalem, since 1987; *b* 25 May 1924; *s* of Leah and step *s* of Philip Yarrow; *m* 1953, Sheila Kaufman; two *d*. *Educ:* Hackney Downs Grammar Sch.; Edinburgh Univ. (MB, ChB); London Sch. of Hygiene and Trop. Medicine (Hons DPH). Foundn FFCM (now FFPHM) 1972. Dep. Area MO, Tottenham and Hornsey, 1955–60; Area MO, SE Essex, 1960–65; MOH, Gateshead, 1965–68; Dir, Scottish Health Educn Unit, 1968–73; SMO, 1973–77, SPMO, 1977–84, DHSS. Temp. Consultant, WHO, 1975–76. Brit. Council Lectr, 1975; Council of Europe Fellow, 1978. *Publications:* So Now You Know About Smoking, 1975; Politics, Society and Preventive Medicine, 1986; scientific papers on demography, epidemiology, preventive medicine and health educn. *Recreations:* lawn bowls, travelling, reading. *Address:* 9/4 Nof Harim, Jerusalem 96190, Israel. *T:* 438792.

YARROW, Sir Eric Grant, 3rd Bt, *cr* 1916; MBE (mil.) 1946; DL; Chairman, Clydesdale Bank PLC, 1985–91 (Director 1962–91, Deputy Chairman, 1975–85); Director: Standard Life Assurance Co., 1958–91; National Australia Bank Ltd, 1987–91; *b* 23 April 1920; *o s* of Sir Harold Yarrow, 2nd Bt and 1st wife, Eleanor Etheldreda (*d* 1934); *S* father, 1962; *m* 1st, 1951, Rosemary Ann (*d* 1957), *yr d* of late H. T. Young, Roehampton, SW15; (one *s* decd); 2nd, 1959, Annette Elizabeth Françoise (marr. diss. 1975), *d* of late A. J. E. Steven, Ardgay; three *s* (including twin *s*); 3rd, 1982, Mrs Joan Botting, *d* of late R. F. Masters, Piddinghoe, Sussex. *Educ:* Marlborough Coll.; Glasgow Univ. Served apprenticeship, G. & J. Weir Ltd. Served Burma, 1942–45; Major RE, 1945. Asst Manager Yarrow & Co., 1946; Dir, 1948; Man. Dir, 1958–67; Chm., 1962–85; Pres., Yarrow PLC, 1985–87. Mem. Council, RINA, 1957–; Vice-Pres., 1965; Hon. Vice-Pres., 1972. Mem., General Cttee, Lloyd's Register of Shipping, 1960–87; Prime Warden, Worshipful Co. of Shipwrights, 1970; Deacon, Incorporation of Hammermen of Glasgow, 1961–62; Retired Mem. Council, Institution of Engineers & Shipbuilders in Scotland; Mem. Council, Inst. of Directors, 1983–90; Mem., Glasgow Action, 1985–91. Pres., Scottish Convalescent Home for Children, 1957–70; Hon. Pres., Princess Louise Scottish Hospital at Erskine, 1986– (Chm., 1980–86). President: British Naval Equipment Assoc., 1982–90; Smeatonian Soc. of Civil Engineers, 1983; Marlburian Club, 1984; Scottish Area, Burma Star Assoc., 1990–; Vice President: RHAS, 1990–91; Glasgow Br., RNLI, 1988–; Chm., Blythe Sappers, 1989. DL Renfrewshire, 1970. OStJ. *Recreations:* golf, family life. *Heir:* *g s* Ross William Grant Yarrow, *b* 14 Jan. 1985. *Address:* Cloak, Kilmacolm, Renfrewshire PA13 4SD. *T:* Kilmacolm (01505) 872067. *Clubs:* Army and Navy; Royal Scottish Automobile; Royal & Ancient Golf (St Andrews).

YARWOOD, Michael Edward, OBE 1976; entertainer, since 1962; *b* 14 June 1941; *s* of Wilfred and Bridget Yarwood; *m* 1969, Sandra Burville (marr. diss. 1987); two *d*. *Educ:* Bredbury Secondary Modern Sch., Cheshire. First television appearance, 1963; *BBC TV:* Three of a Kind, 1967; Look—Mike Yarwood, and Mike Yarwood in Persons (series), 1971–82; *ATV:* Will the Real Mike Yarwood Stand Up? (series), 1968; *Thames:* Mike Yarwood in Persons, 1983–84; Yarwood's Royal Variety Show, the Yarwood Chat Show, and Mike Yarwood in Persons, 1986; *stage:* Royal Variety performances, 1968, 1972, 1976, 1981, 1987, 1993; One for the Pot, UK tour, 1988. Variety Club of Gt Britain award for BBC TV Personality of 1973; Royal Television Society award for outstanding creative achievement in front of camera, 1978. Mem., Grand Order of Water Rats, 1968. *Publications:* And This Is Me, 1974; Impressions of my life (autobiog.), 1986. *Recreations:* golf, tennis. *Address:* Oxshott, Surrey. *Club:* Lord's Taverners.

YASS, Irving, CB 1993; Director, Transport and Planning, London First, since 1995; *b* 20 Dec. 1935; *s* of late Abraham and Fanny Yass; *m* 1962, Marion Leighton; two *s* one *d*. *Educ:* Harrow County Grammar School for Boys; Balliol Coll., Oxford (Brackenbury Schol.; BA). Assistant Principal, Min. of Transport and Civil Aviation, 1958; Private Sec. to Joint Parliamentary Secretary, 1960; HM Treasury, 1967–70; Asst Secretary, Dept of the Environment, 1971; Secretary, Cttee of Inquiry into Local Govt Finance, 1974–76; Dept of Transport, 1976–94 (Under Sec., 1982); Dir, Planning and Transport, Govt Office for London, 1994–95. *Address:* London First, Caxton House, 6 Tothill Street, SW1H 9NA. *T:* 0171–222 1445.

YASSIN, Ali Mohamed Osman; Permanent Representative of the Republic of the Sudan to the United Nations, since 1994; *b* 7 Aug. 1943; *s* of Mohamed Osman and Mrs Mahdi

Nafisa Hamid; *m* 1st, Dr Fatima Mukhtar; one *s* three *d*; 2nd, Eiman Khalid; one *s* one *d*. *Educ:* Univ. of Khartoum (BA, LLB); Queen Mary Coll., Univ. of London (LLM). Dept of Govt Contracts and Internat. Agreements, Sudan, 1977; Legal Advr, Min. of Communications and Post and Telegraph Corp., 1978–79; Head, Legal Dept, Council of Ministers Secretariat-Gen., 1979–82; Commercial Registrar-Gen., 1982–83; Mem., Sudan Bar Assoc., and private practice, 1983–89; Under-Sec., Min. of Justice, and acting Attorney Gen., 1989; Ambassador and Perm. Under-Sec., Min. of Foreign Affairs, 1991; Ambassador to UK, 1992–94. *Recreations:* reading, films, videos, history. *Address:* Sudan Permanent Mission to UN, 733 Third Avenue, 9th Floor, New York, NY 10017, USA.

YASSUKOVICH, Stanislas Michael, CBE 1991; Chairman, Flextech plc, since 1989; Vice Chairman, Cragnotti & Partners Group, since 1991; *b* 5 Feb. 1935; adopted British nationality, 1993; *s* of Dimitri and Denise Yassukovich; *m* 1961, Diana (*née* Townsend); two *s* one *d*. *Educ:* Deerfield Academy; Harvard University. US Marine Corps, 1957–61. Joined White, Weld & Co., 1961: posted to London, 1962; Branch Manager, 1967; General Partner, 1969; Managing Director, 1969; European Banking Co. Ltd: Managing Director, 1973; Group Dep. Chm., 1983. Sen. Advr, Merrill Lynch & Co., 1989–90; Dir, Merrill Lynch Europe Ltd, 1985–90 (Chm., 1985–89); Chm., Hemingway Properties, 1993–; Vice-Chm., Bristol & West Building Soc., 1991–; Dep. Chm., ABC Internat. Bank, 1993–; Director: Casket Plc, 1991–; SW Water, 1992–. Jt Dep. Chm., Internat. Stock Exchange, 1986–89; Chm., Securities Assoc., 1988–91. Chairman: City Res. Project, 1991–; City Disputes Panel, 1994–. *Publications:* articles in financial press. *Recreations:* hunting, shooting, polo. *Address:* S. M. Yassukovich & Co. Ltd, 25 St James's Street, SW1A 1HA. *T:* 0171–839 3551. *Clubs:* Buck's, Turf; Travellers' (Paris); Brook, Union (New York).

YATES, Alfred, CBE 1983; FBPsS; Director, National Foundation for Educational Research in England and Wales, 1972–83; *b* 17 Nov. 1917; *s* of William Oliver Yates and Frances Yates; *m* 1st, 1943, Joan Mary Lawrence-Fellows (*d* 1987); one *s* one *d*; 2nd, 1989, Elsie Roberts. *Educ:* Farnworth Grammar Sch.; Sheffield Univ. (BA); Oxford Univ. (MA); QUB (MEd). FBPsS 1957. Served War, Army, 1940–46: Captain, REME. Schoolmaster, Launceston Coll., Cornwall, 1939–40; Lectr, QUB, 1946–51; Sen. Res. Officer, NFER, 1951–59; Sen. Tutor, Dept of Educnl Studies, Oxford Univ., 1959–72. FCP 1981. *Publications:* Admission to Grammar Schools, 1957; Grouping in Education, 1966; An Introduction to Educational Measurement, 1968; The Role of Research in Educational Change, 1971; The Organisation of Schooling, 1971. *Recreations:* reading, theatre, watching Association football and cricket. *Address:* 14 Craighall Road, Bolton BL1 7HH. *T:* Bolton (01204) 595642.

YATES, Anne; *see* Yates, E. A.

YATES, Brian Douglas; Chairman, Consumers' Association, since 1994; *b* 1 May 1944; *s* of Bertram Yates and Barbara (*née* Wenham); *m* 1971, Patricia, *d* of Arthur Hutchinson, DFC; one *s*. *Educ:* Uppingham Sch.; Clare Coll., Cambridge (MA); London Business Sch. (MBA). Chartered Engineer. RHP Bearings, 1973–81; Thorn EMI, 1981–85; Dexion, 1985–88; Morris Mechanical Handling, 1988–. Member: Northampton BC, 1979–83; Hampshire CC, 1985–89. Mem. Council, Consumers' Assoc., 1986–. *Recreations:* tennis, cross country ski-ing. *Address:* 19 Park Avenue, Harpenden AL5 2DZ. *T:* Harpenden (01582) 768484. *Clubs:* Royal Over-Seas League; Hatfield House Tennis.

YATES, Edgar; *see* Yates, W. E.

YATES, (Edith) Anne, (Mrs S. J. Yates), CBE 1972; *b* 21 Dec. 1912; *d* of William Blakeman and Frances Dorothea (*née* Thacker); *m* 1935, Stanley James Yates (*d* 1990); one *s* one *d* (and one *s* decd). *Educ:* Barrs' Hill Girls' Sch., Coventry. Nottinghamshire County Council: Mem., 1955–93; Alderman, 1966; Chm., 1968–74; Leader, Cons. Gp, 1991–92. Mem., BTEC Bd for Distribution, Hotel and Catering and Leisure Services, 1984–88. Chairman: E Midlands Tourist Bd, 1971–76; E Midlands Sports Council, 1972–77, Indep. Chm., Nat. Cttee on Recreation Management Trng, 1976–82 (Yates Report, 1984); Member: Sports Council, 1971–74; E Midlands Council of Sport and Recreation, 1977–82; MSC, 1974–76; E Midlands Regional MSC, 1977–82; English Tourist Bd, 1975–81; Nat. Water Council, 1973–79 (Chm., Water Training Cttee, 1973–79). Life Vice Pres., Inst. of Trading Standards Admin, 1965. Chm., Notts Internat. Rowing Regatta, 1987–90; Mem., Sports Aid Foundn, 1984–94; Chm., Sports Aid Foundn (E Midlands), 1990–94. *Recreations:* reading, music, theatre. *Address:* Manor Court, Rolleston, Newark, Notts NG23 5SE. *T:* Southwell (01636) 813362.

YATES, Ian Humphrey Nelson, CBE 1991; Director, 1989–90, Chief Executive, 1975–90, The Press Association Ltd; *b* 24 Jan. 1931; *s* of James Nelson Yates and Martha (*née* Nutter); *m* 1956, Daphne J. Hudson, MCSP; three *s*. *Educ:* Lancaster Royal Grammar Sch.; Canford Sch., Wimborne. Royal Scots Greys, Germany and ME (National Service Commn), 1951–53. Management Trainee, Westminster Press Ltd, 1953–58 (Westmorland Gazette, and Telegraph & Argus, Bradford); Asst to Man. Dir, King & Hutchings Ltd, Uxbridge, 1958–60; Bradford and District Newspapers: Asst Gen. Man., 1960; Gen. Man., 1964; Man. Dir, 1969–75; Dir, Westminster Press Planning Div., 1969–75. Chairman: Universal News Services Ltd, 1988–90; Tellex Monitors Ltd, 1988–90; CRG Communications Gp Ltd, 1990–. President: Young Newspapermen's Assoc., 1966; Yorks Newspaper Soc., 1968. Member: Council, Newspaper Soc., 1970–75; Council, Commonwealth Press Union, 1977–90; Pres., Alliance of European News Agencies, 1987–88 (Chm., New Media Cttee, 1984–89). FRSA 1989. *Recreations:* walking, reading, theatre. *Address:* Woodbury, 11 Holmwood Close, East Horsley, Surrey KT24 6SS. *T:* East Horsley (01483) 283873.

YATES, Ivan R., CBE 1982; FEng 1983; independent consultant; Deputy Chief Executive (Engineering), 1986–90, Director, 1981–90, British Aerospace PLC; *b* 22 April 1929; *m* 1967, Jennifer Mary Holcombe; one *s* one *d*. *Educ:* Liverpool Collegiate Sch.; Liverpool Univ. (BEng 1st Class Hons). FIMechE; FRAeS 1968; FAIAA 1984; CBIM. Graduate Apprentice, English Electric, Preston, 1950, Chief Project Engr, 1959; Project Manager, Jaguar, 1966; British Aircraft Corporation: Special Dir, Preston Div., 1970; Dir, Preston, Warton Div., 1973; Dir, Aircraft Projects, 1974; Director: SEPECAT SA, 1976; Panavia GmbH, 1977; Eurofighter GmbH, 1986–90; British Aerospace: Man. Dir, Warton, 1978; Dir of Engrg and Project Assessment, Aircraft Gp, 1981; Chief Exec., Aircraft Gp, 1982–85; Dep. Man. Dir (Aircraft), 1985–86. Vis. Prof. in Design, Cambridge Univ., 1991–; Industrial Fellow Commoner, Churchill Coll., Cambridge, 1992–. Mem., Technology Requirements Bd, 1985–; Advr, H of C Sci. and Technol. Cttee, 1993–94. Pres., 1988–89, Dep. Pres., 1989–90, SBAC; Mem. Council, RAeS, 1986–91. Member: Design Council, 1990–; Council, RUSI, 1989–93. Commissioner, Royal Commn for Exhibn of 1851, 1990–. Mem. Council, Imperial Coll., 1991–. FRSA 1985 (Mem., Manufacture and Commerce Cttee). Hon. DSc: Loughborough, 1989; City, 1991. British Silver Medal, 1979, Gold Medal, 1985, RAeS. *Publications:* Innovation, Investment and Survival of UK Economy, 1993; various papers and lectures. *Recreations:* walking, ski-ing, painting, music. *Fax:* (office) Lewes (01273) 480469. *Club:* Athenæum.

YATES, Rt. Rev. John; Bishop of Gloucester, 1975–91; *b* 17 April 1925; *s* of late Frank and late Edith Ethel Yates; *m* 1954, Jean Kathleen Dover; one *s* two *d*. *Educ:* Battersea Grammar School; Blackpool Grammar School; Jesus College, Cambridge (MA). RAFVR (Aircrew), 1943–47; University of Cambridge, 1947–49; Lincoln Theological College, 1949–51. Curate, Christ Church, Southgate, 1951–54; Tutor and Chaplain, Lincoln Theological College, 1954–59; Vicar, Bottesford-with-Ashby, 1959–65; Principal, Lichfield Theological College, 1966–72; Bishop Suffragan of Whitby, 1972–75; Head, Archbp of Canterbury's staff (with title of Bp at Lambeth), 1991–94. Chm., Gen. Synod Bd for Social Responsibility, 1987–91. Hon. DLitt CNAA, 1992. *Address:* 14 Belle Vue Road, Andover, Hants SP10 2DF.

YATES, Peter (James); film director/producer and theatre director; *b* 24 July 1929; *s* of Col Robert L. Yates and Constance Yates; *m* 1960, Virginia Pope; two *s* one *d* (and one *d* decd). *Educ:* Charterhouse; Royal Academy of Dramatic Art. Entered film industry, 1956. *Films directed:* Summer Holiday, 1962; One Way Pendulum, 1964; Robbery, 1966; Bullitt, 1968; John and Mary, 1969; Murphy's War, 1970; The Hot Rock, 1971; The Friends of Eddie Coyle, 1972; For Pete's Sake, 1973; Mother, Jugs and Speed, 1975; The Deep, 1976; Breaking Away (dir and prod.), 1979 (nominated 1980 Academy Awards, Director and Producer); The Janitor (dir and prod.), 1980; Krull, 1982; The Dresser (dir and prod.), 1983 (nominated 1984 Academy Awards, Dir and Producer); Eleni, 1985; The House on Carroll Street (dir and prod.), 1986; Suspect, 1987; An Innocent Man, 1989; Year of the Comet, 1991; Roommates, 1993. *Theatre directed:* The American Dream, Royal Court, 1961; The Death of Bessie Smith, (London) 1961; Passing Game, (New York) 1977; Interpreters, (London) 1985. *Recreations:* tennis, sailing, skiing. *Address:* c/o United Talent Agency, 9560 Wilshire Boulevard, Beverley Hills, CA 90212, USA. *Club:* Garrick.

YATES, William; The Administrator of Christmas Island, Indian Ocean, 1982–83; *b* 15 September 1921; *er s* of late William Yates and of Mrs John T. Renshaw, Burrells, Appleby, Westmorland; *m* 1st, 1946, Hon. Rosemary (marr. diss. 1955), *yr d* of 1st Baron Elton; two *d* (one *s* decd); 2nd, 1957, Camilla, *d* of late E. W. D. Tennant, Orford House, Ugley, Bishop's Stortford; four *s*. *Educ:* Uppingham; Hertford Coll., Oxford. Served War, 1940–45, North Africa and Italy; Captain The Bays, 1945. Shropshire Yeomanry, 1956–67. Appointed Legal Officer to report on State lands in Department of Custodian's Office in Tripoli, Libya, 1951. MP (C) The Wrekin Division of Shropshire, 1955–66. Myron Taylor Lectures in International Affairs, Cornell Univ., USA, 1958 and 1966. MP (L) Holt, Vic, Aust. Commonwealth, 1975–80; Mem. Liberal Party Parly Cttee for Defence and Foreign Affairs, 1975–80; Mem., Cttee of Privileges, House of Representatives, 1977–80. Mem., Inst. of Internat. Affairs, Victoria. *Address:* The Old House, Old Tallangatta, Vic 3700, Australia. *Clubs:* Cavalry and Guards; Commonwealth (Canberra).

YATES, Prof. (William) Edgar, MA, PhD; Professor of German, University of Exeter, since 1972; *b* 30 April 1938; *s* of Douglas Yates and Doris Yates (*née* Goode); *m* 1963, Barbara Anne Fellowes; two *s*. *Educ:* Fettes Coll. (Foundn Schol.); Emmanuel Coll., Cambridge (Minor Open Schol.; MA, PhD). 2nd Lieut, RASC, 1957–58. Lectr in German, Univ. of Durham, 1963–72; University of Exeter: Hd of Dept of German, 1972–86; Dep. Vice-Chancellor, 1986–89. Vice-Chm., Conf. of Univ. Teachers of German, 1991–93. Lewis Fry Meml Lectr, Univ. of Bristol, 1994. Vice Pres., Wiener Shakespeare-Ges., 1992–; Member: Cttee, MHRA, 1980–; Council, English Goethe Soc., 1984–; Council, Internat. Nestroy-Ges., 1986–. Germanic Editor, MLR, 1981–88; Editor, Nestroyana, 1992–. Corresp. Mem., Austrian Acad. of Scis, 1995. Gov., Exeter Sch., 1986– (Vice Chm., 1992–94, Chm., 1994–). J. G. Robertson Prize, Univ. of London, 1975. *Publications:* Grillparzer: a critical introduction, 1972; Nestroy: satire and parody in Viennese popular comedy, 1972; Humanity in Weimar and Vienna: the continuity of an ideal, 1973; Tradition in the German Sonnet, 1981; Schnitzler, Hofmannsthal, and the Austrian Theatre, 1992; Nestroy and the Critics, 1994; *edited:* Hofmannsthal: Der Schwierige, 1966; Grillparzer: Der Traum ein Leben, 1968; Nestroy: Stücke 12-14 (Hist.-krit. Ausgabe), 1981–82, Stücke 34, 1989, Stücke 18/1, 1991; (jtly) Viennese Popular Theatre, 1985; (jtly) Grillparzer und die europäische Tradition, 1987; Vom schaffenden zum edierten Nestroy, 1994; numerous articles on Austrian literary and cultural history, on German literature of the Biedermeier period, and on German lyric poetry. *Recreation:* music. *Address:* 7 Clifton Hill, Exeter EX1 2DL. *T:* Exeter (01392) 54713.

YATES, William Hugh; Senior Partner, Knight Frank & Rutley, since 1992; *b* 18 Dec. 1935; *s* of late Brig. Morris Yates, DSO, OBE and Kathleen Rosanna Yates (*née* Sherbrooke, later Mrs Hugh Cowan); *m* 1st, 1963, Celia Geraldine Pitman (marr. diss. 1972); one *s*; 2nd, 1979, Elizabeth Susan Mansel-Pleydell (*née* Luard); four step *s*. *Educ:* Lancing Coll.; RMA Sandhurst. FRICS. Commissioned, Royal Dragoons, 1955; ADC to Governor of Aden, 1959. Articled surveyor, Rylands & Co., 1961; Knight Frank & Rutley, 1964–: Man. Dir, Geneva, 1968–72; Partner, 1972; Man. Partner, 1978–82; Head of Residential Div., 1982–92. Director: INCAS SA, 1970–78; European Property Investment Co. NV, 1973–81; Ecclesiastical Insurance Group, 1985– (Dep. Chm., 1995–); Woolwich Building Soc., 1990–. Save the Children Fund: Chm., Fund Raising Cttee, 1980–86; Hon. Treasurer, 1986–92. *Recreations:* riding, gardening, golf, music. *Address:* Knight Frank & Rutley, 20 Hanover Square, W1R 0AH. *T:* 0171–629 8171. *Clubs:* Turf, Cavalry and Guards; Wentworth Golf.

YATIM, Datuk Rais, DSNS (Malaysia) 1978; Advocate and Solicitor of the High Court of Malaya; Minister of Foreign Affairs, Malaysia, 1986–87; *b* 15 April 1942; *s* of Yatim Tahir and Siandam Boloh; *m* 1975, Datin Masnah; two *s* one *d*. *Educ:* Language Inst., Kuala Lumpur; Northern Illinois Univ.; Univ. of Singapore. DipEd; LLB (Hons); DipPsych; PhD London, 1994. Language teacher, 1966–68. Parly Sec., Min. of Youth, 1974; Dep. Law Minister, 1976; Chief Minister, State of Negeri Sembilan, 1978–82; Minister of Land Regl Develt, 1982–84; Minister of Information, 1984–86. Dep. Pres., Parti Melayu, 1989–. Returned to law practice in Kuala Lumpur, 1988–. Pres., Malaysia's Anti-Drug Assoc., 1976–87. Mem., MG Owners' Club, Swavesey. *Publications:* Faces in the Corridors of Power: a pictorial depiction of Malaysians in power and authority, 1987; Freedom and Executive Power in Malaysia, 1995. *Recreations:* photography, jogging, travel. *Address:* (residence) 41 Road 12, Taman Grandview, Ampang Jaya, 68000 Ampang, Selangor Darul Ehsan, Malaysia. *T:* (3) 4569621. *Club:* Darul Ehsan Recreational (Kuala Lumpur).

YAXLEY, John Francis, CBE 1990; HM Overseas Civil Service, 1961–94, retired; *b* 13 Nov. 1936; *s* of late Rev. Canon R. W. and of Dorothy Yaxley; *m* 1960, Patricia Anne Scott; one *s*. *Educ:* Hatfield Coll., Durham Univ. (BA Hons). National Service, 1958–60. Joined HMOCS, 1961; posts in New Hebrides and Solomon Islands, 1961–75; seconded FCO, 1975–77; Hong Kong, 1977–89: posts included Dir of Industry, Sec. for Econ. Services, and Dep. Financial Sec.; Comr, Hong Kong Govt, London, 1989–93. Mem., Salvation Army Adv. Bd, 1990–. Chm., Oriental Mus. Develt Trust, 1994–, Mem., Council, 1995–, Durham Univ. Treas., W Mercia NADFAS, 1995–. Trustee, Triumph over Phobia UK, 1995–. *Publication:* The Population of the New Hebrides (with Dr Norma McArthur), 1968. *Recreations:* walking, birdwatching, history, gardening. *Address:*

Old Housing, Fifield, Oxon OX7 6HF. *Clubs:* Commonwealth Trust, Royal Over-Seas League.

YELLOWLEES, Sir Henry, KCB 1975 (CB 1971); Chief Medical Officer, Department of Health and Social Security, Department of Education and Science and Home Office, 1973–83; *b* 1919; *s* of late Henry Yellowlees, OBE, Psychiatrist of Bath. *Educ:* Stowe Sch.; University Coll., Oxford. MA, BM, BCh Oxon 1950. FRCP 1971 (MRCP 1966, LRCP 1950); FFCM 1972; FRCS 1983 (MRCS 1950); FRCPE 1993. Pilot, RAF, 1941–45. Resident Med. Officer, Mddx Hosp., London, 1951–54; Asst Senior Med. Officer, South West Regional Hosp. Bd, 1954–59; Dep. Sen. Admin. Med. Officer, North West Metropolitan Regional Hosp. Bd, 1959–63; Principal Med. Officer, Min. of Health, 1963–65 (seconded); Senior Principal Med. Officer, 1965–67 (established); Dep. Chief Med. Officer, 1967–72, 2nd Chief Med. Officer, 1972–73, Dept of Health and Social Security. Consultant, MoD, 1985; Occasional Consultant, European Reg., WHO, 1985–95. Chm., WHO Commn to investigate health care of Bulgarian citizens arriving in Turkey, 1989. Member: Medical Research Council, 1974–83; Gen. Medical Council, 1979–89; Health Services Supervisory Bd, 1983; Council, BMA, 1986–90; Council, British Nutrition Foundn, 1973–95. Hon. FRCP Glasgow, 1974; Hon. FRCPsych, 1977; Fellow Brit. Inst. of Management, 1974–83; Vice-Pres., Mental After-Care Assoc.; Hon. Mem., Nat. Assoc. of Clinical Tutors. *Address:* 70c Archway Street, Barnes, SW13 0AW.

YELTSIN, Boris Nikolayevich; President, Russian Federation, since 1991; *b* Sverdlovsk, 1 Feb. 1931. *Educ:* Urals Polytechnic Inst. Foreman, then chief of works, chief engr, head of construction admin, Yushgorstvoy trust, 1955–63; chief engr, dir, Sverdlovsk house building complex, 1963–68. Mem., CPSU, 1961–90: Sec., Sverdlovsk provincial cttee, 1968–76; First Sec., Dist Central Cttee, Sverdlosk, 1976–85; Mem., Party Central Cttee, 1981; Sec., Central Cttee, 1985–86; First Sec., Moscow Party Cttee, 1985–87; Candidate Mem., Politburo, 1986–88; First Dep. Chm., State Cttee for Construction, 1987–89; Chm., Cttee for Construction and Architecture, 1989–90; Mem., Congress of People's Deputies, 1989–91. Chm., Supreme Soviet, RSFSR, 1990–91. *Publications:* Against the Grain (autobiog.), 1990; Three Days, 1992; The View from the Kremlin, 1994. *Address:* c/o The Kremlin, Moscow, Russia. *Fax:* 206 3961.

YENTOB, Alan; Controller, BBC1, since 1993; *b* 11 March 1947; *s* of Isaac Yentob and Flora Yentob (*née* Khazam); one *s* one *d* by Philippa Walker. *Educ:* King's School, Ely; Univ. of Grenoble; Univ. of Leeds (LLB). BBC general trainee, 1968; producer/director, 1970–; arts features, incl. Omnibus; Editor, Arena, 1978–85; Co-Editor, Omnibus, 1985; Hd of Music and Arts, BBC TV, 1985–88; Controller, BBC2, 1988–93. Member: Bd of Directors, Riverside Studios, 1984–91; BFI Production Board, 1985–93; Council, English Stage Co., 1990–. Gov., Nat. Film School, 1988–; Trustee, Architecture Foundn, 1992–. FRTS; Hon. Fellow: RCA, 1987; RIBA, 1991. *Recreations:* swimming, books.

YEO, Diane Helen; Director, Malcolm Sargent Cancer Fund for Children, since 1995; *b* 22 July 1945; *d* of Brian Harold Pickard, FRCS and Joan Daisy Pickard; *m* 1970, Timothy Stephen Kenneth Yeo, *qv*; one *s* one *d*. *Educ:* Blackheath High Sch.; London Univ.; Institut Français de Presse. BBC Radio, 1968–74; Africa Educnl Trust, 1974–79; Girl Guides' Assoc., 1979–82; YWCA, 1982–85; Director: Inst. of Charity Fundraising Managers, 1985–88; Charity Appointments, 1985–; Charity Comr, 1989–95. Consultant: Centre for Voluntary Organisation, LSE, 1988–; Centre for Charity and Trust Research, South Bank Univ., 1995–; Chairman: Charity Standards Cttee, 1991–; Adv. Cttee on Trusteeship, 1993–; Member: Nathan Cttee on Effectiveness and the Voluntary Sector, 1989–90; Advertising Standards Authority Political Advertising Working Gp, 1991–; Adv. Council, NCVO, 1994–. Vice-Chm., NCVO/Charity Commn Cttee on Trng of Trustees, 1989– (report, On Trust, 1990). FRSA. *Publications:* contribs to professional jls. *Recreations:* tennis, swimming, photography, piano. *Address:* Malcolm Sargent Cancer Fund for Children, 14 Abingdon Road, W8 6AF. *T:* 0171–937 4548.

YEO, Douglas; Director, Shell Research Ltd, Thornton Research Centre, 1980–85; *b* 13 June 1925; *s* of Sydney and Hylda Yeo; *m* 1947, Joan Elisabeth Chell; two *d*. *Educ:* Secondary Sch., St Austell; University Coll., Exeter (BSc London). Expedn on locust control, Kenya, 1945. HMOCS, 1948–63; Tropical Pesticides Research Inst., Uganda and Tanzania, 1948–61 (Scientific Officer, 1948–51, Sen. Scientific Officer, 1951–57, Prin. Scientific Officer, 1957–61). Internat. African Migratory Locust Control Organisation, Mali: on secondment, 1958, 1960; Dir and Sec. Gen., 1961–63. Shell Research Ltd: Research Dir, Woodstock Agricultural Research Centre, 1963–69, Dir, 1969–76; Dir, Biosciences Lab., Sittingbourne, 1976–80. Mem. Council, RHBNC, London Univ., 1985–90. FIBiol. *Publications:* papers in Bulletin Ent. Res., Bull. WHO, Anti-Locust Bull., Qly Jl Royal Met. Soc., Jl Sci. Fd. Agric., Plant Protection Confs, etc. *Recreations:* sailing, hill walking, fishing. *Address:* Tremarne, Tremarne Close, Feock, Truro TR3 6SB. *Club:* Royal Corinthian Yacht (Burnham on Crouch).

YEO, Kok Cheang, CMG 1956; MD; MB; BS; DPH; DTM&H; *b* 1 April 1903; *s* of Yeo Kim Hong; *m* Florence, *d* of late Sir Robert Ho-tung, KBE; one *s* two *d*. *Educ:* Hong Kong University; Cambridge University; London School of Hygiene and Tropical Medicine. MB, BS, Hong Kong, 1925, MD, 1930; DTM&H (England) 1927; DPH, Cambridge, 1928. Assistant Medical Officer of Health, Hong Kong, 1928; Lecturer and Examiner in public health, Hong Kong University, 1936–37; Official JP 1938; Chinese Health Officer, senior grade, 1939–47; Deputy Director of Health Services, and Vice-Chairman of Urban Council, 1947–50; Deputy Director of Medical and Health Services, 1950–52; member of Legislative Council, Hong Kong, 1951–57; Director of Medical and Health Services, Hong Kong, 1952–58; Professor of Social Medicine, Hong Kong University, 1953–58; retd 1958. *Address:* White Gates, Westfield, Hastings, East Sussex TN35 4SB.

YEO, Timothy Stephen Kenneth; MP (C) Suffolk South, since 1983; *b* 20 March 1945; *s* of late Dr Kenneth John Yeo and Norah Margaret Yeo; *m* 1970, Diane Helen Pickard (*see* D. H. Yeo); one *s* one *d*. *Educ:* Charterhouse; Emmanuel Coll., Cambridge (Open Exhibnr; MA 1971). Asst Treas., Bankers Trust Co., 1970–73; Director, Worcester Engineering Co. Ltd, 1975–86. Dir, Spastics Soc., 1980–83, Mem., Exec. Council, 1984–86. PPS to Sec. of State for Home Dept, 1988–89, to Sec. of State for Foreign Affairs, 1989–90; Parly Under Sec. of State, DoE, 1990–92, DoH, 1992–93; Minister of State, DoE, 1993–94. Mem., Social Services Select Cttee, 1985–88; Jt Sec., Cons. Pty Finance Cttee, 1984–87. Captain, Parly Golfing Soc., 1991–95. Hon. Treasurer, International Voluntary Service, 1975–78. Trustee: African Palms, 1970–85; Tanzania Development Trust, 1980–; Chm., Tadworth Court Trust, 1983–90. *Publication:* Public Accountability and Regulation of Charities, 1983. *Recreation:* skiing. *Address:* House of Commons, SW1A 0AA. *T:* 0171–219 3000. *Clubs:* Carlton; Sudbury Conservative (Sudbury); Royal St George's (Sandwich).

YEOMAN, Maj.-Gen. Alan, CB 1987; Director, Army Sport Control Board, since 1988; *b* 17 Nov. 1933; *s* of George Smith Patterson Yeoman and Wilhelmina Tromans Elwell; *m* 1960, Barbara Joan Davies; two *s* one *d*. *Educ:* Dame Allan's School, Newcastle upon Tyne. Officer Cadet, RMA Sandhurst, 1952; commnd Royal Signals, 1954; served Korea, Malaysia, Singapore, Cyprus, UK, BAOR and Canada, 1954–70 (Staff Coll., 1963); CO 2 Div. Sig. Regt, BAOR, 1970–73; HQ 1 (BR) Corps, BAOR, 1973–74; MoD, 1974–77; Col AQ, HQLF Cyprus, 1978–79; Comd Trng Gp, Royal Signals and Catterick Garrison, 1979–82; Brig. AQ, HQ 1 (BR) Corps, BAOR, 1982–84; Comd Communications, BAOR, 1984–87; retd 1988. Col Comdt, Royal Corps of Signals, 1987–93. Hon. Col, 37th (Wessex and Welsh) Signal Regt, T&AVR, 1987–95. *Recreations:* golf, cricket, ski-ing. *Address:* c/o Lloyds Bank, Catterick Garrison, North Yorks DL9 3JE. *Clubs:* Army and Navy, MCC.

YEOMAN, Prof. Michael Magson, PhD; FRSE; Regius Professor of Botany, 1978–93, now Emeritus, and Curator of Patronage, 1988–93, University of Edinburgh; *b* 16 May 1931; *s* of Gordon Yeoman and Mabel Ellen (*née* Magson), Newcastle upon Tyne; *m* 1962, Erica Mary Lines; two *d*. *Educ:* Gosforth Grammar Sch.; King's Coll., Univ. of Durham (BSc 1952, MSc 1954, PhD 1960); FRSE 1980. National Service, Royal Corps of Signals, 1954–56. Demonstrator in Botany, King's Coll., Newcastle upon Tyne, 1957–59; Edinburgh University: Lectr in Botany, 1960; Sen. Lectr, 1968; Reader, 1973; Dean, Fac. of Science, 1981–84; Vice-Principal, 1988–91. Vis. Prof., NENU, Changchun, China, 1986–. Chm., Univs Council for Adult and Continuing Educn (Scotland), 1989–91. Member: Governing Bodies, Nat. Vegetable Res. Stn and Scottish Plant Breeding Stn, 1978–82; SERC Biological Scis Cttee, 1982–85; SERC Biotechnology Management Cttee, 1983–85; British Nat. Cttee for Biology, 1981–89. Chm., Edinburgh Centre for Rural Res., 1989–93; Governor: East of Scotland Coll. of Agriculture, 1984–93; Scottish Crops Res. Inst., 1986–89. Trustee: Edinburgh Botanic Gdn (Sibbald) Trust, 1986–; Royal Botanic Gdn, Edinburgh, 1992– (Chm., Scientific Adv. Bd, 1995–). Mem. Council, RSE, 1985–91 (Fellowship Sec., 1986–91). Gov. and Vice Chm., Ellingham C of E First Sch., 1993–. Member Editorial Board: Jl of Experimental Botany, 1981–85; Plant Science Letters, 1974–83; New Phytologist (Trustee); Botanical Jl of Scotland, 1992–. *Publications:* (ed) Cell Division in Higher Plants, 1976; (jtly) Laboratory Manual of Plant Cell and Tissue Culture, 1982; (ed) Plant Cell Technology, 1986; contrib. scientific jls; chapters, articles and revs in books. *Recreations:* military history, photography, gardening, walking. *Address:* Bremel Barn, Ellingham Glebe, Ellingham, Northumberland NE67 5EU. *T:* Chathill (01665) 589252.

YEOMAN, Philip Metcalfe, MD; FRCS; Consultant Orthopaedic Surgeon, Bath, 1964–88, retired; *b* 29 April 1923; *s* of William Yeoman, MD and Dorothy Young; *m* 1947, Idonea Evelyn Mary Scarrott; two *s* one *d*. *Educ:* Sedbergh; Cambridge (MA, MB BChir, MD); University Coll. Hosp. London. Flight Lieut, RAF Hosp., Ely, 1950–52. Lectr, Inst. of Orthopaedics, 1959–64. Member: Pensions Appeal Tribunals, 1986–; Professional and Linguistic Assessment Bd, 1987–. External Examr in Surg., Univ. of Liverpool. Mem. Council, RCS, 1984–92 (Mem., Court of Examrs, 1980–; Hunterian Prof., 1983); Vice-Pres., British Orthopaedic Assoc., 1984–85 (Robert Jones Gold Medal, 1963; North American Travelling Fellow, 1964; Mem. Council, 1981–84); President: Section of Orthopaedics, RSocMed, 1983; North American Travelling Fellows, 1981–83. Mem., Internat. Skeletal Soc. Hugh Owen Thomas Meml Lectr, Liverpool, 1988. *Publications:* chapters on peripheral nerve injuries, brachial plexus injuries, bone tumours, surgical management of rheumatoid arthritis of the cervical spine. *Recreations:* golf, gardening. *Address:* Broadmead, Monkton Combe, near Bath BA2 7JE. *T:* Limpley Stoke (0122122) 3294. *Club:* Army and Navy.

YEOMANS, Richard Millett, CEng, FIEE; FIMechE; Chief Executive, Scottish Nuclear Ltd, 1989–91; *b* 19 July 1932; *s* of late Maj. Richard J. Yeomans and Lillian (*née* Spray); *m* 1957, Jennifer Margaret Wingfield Pert; three *s* one *d*. *Educ:* Durban, SA; Cornwall Tech. Coll. CEng; FIEE; FIMechE. Student apprentice, CEGB, 1948. Lt, REME, 1953–55. CEGB power stations, 1955–67; South of Scotland Electricity Board: Dep. Manager, Longannet Power Stn, 1971–75; Manager, Inverkip Power Stn, 1975–77; Manager, Hunterston A&B Nuclear Power Stns, 1977–80; Generation Engineer (Nuclear), 1980–87; Chief Engineer, 1987–89. *Recreations:* sailing, golf, gardening. *Address:* Ashcraig, Skelmorlie, Ayrshire PA17 5HB. *T:* Greenock (01475) 520298.

YERBURGH, family name of **Baron Alvingham.**

YERBURGH, John Maurice Armstrong; Vice Lord-Lieutenant of Dumfries and Galloway (District of Stewartry), since 1990; President, Daniel Thwaites PLC, since 1993 (Director, since 1947; Chairman, 1966–93); *b* 23 May 1923; *e s* of late Major Guy Yerburgh (*d* 1926), OBE, Belgian Croix de Guerre, Italian Croce di Guerra and Lady (Hilda Violet Helena) Salisbury-Jones, *e d* of Rt Hon. Sir Maurice de Bunsen, Bt, GCMG, GCVO, CB; *m* 1973, Ann Jean Mary, *d* of N. P. Maclaren, Brooklands, Crocketford, Dumfries; one *s* four *d*. *Educ:* Eton; Magdalene College, Cambridge (BA). Commissioned Irish Guards 1943; served with 2nd Bn, France, Holland, Belgium, Germany; retired 1947 with rank of Captain. Contested (C) Blackburn, 1959 and 1963. Chm., S of Scotland Regional Adv. Cttee, Forestry Commn, 1972–87; Governor, Cumbria College of Agriculture and Forestry, 1975–89; Shire Horse Society: Pres., 1983–84; Dep. Pres., 1988. DL Dumfries and Galloway (Dist of Stewartry), 1989. *Recreations:* shooting, fishing, trees. *Address:* Barwhillanty, Parton, Castle Douglas, Kirkcudbrightshire DG7 3NS. *T:* Parton (016447) 237.

YEUNG, Kai-yin, CBE 1993; JP; Executive Director, Sino Land Company Ltd, since 1993; *b* 6 Jan. 1941; *s* of late K. F. Yeung and C. H. Lai; *m* 1964, Anna Lau; one *s* one *d*. *Educ:* Univ. of Hong Kong (BA Hons 1962). Joined Hong Kong Civil Service, 1962: staff appts, Hong Kong Admin. Service, 1962–73; Directorate rank, 1973–93; various appts at Asst and Dep. Head of Dept level, in trade, econ. develt and public finance, 1973–84; Comr, Hong Kong Export Credit Insce Corp., 1984–86; Dir Gen. of Industry, 1986–89; Sec. for Educn and Manpower, 1989–91; Sec. for the Treasury, 1991–93; Sec. for Transport, 1993, retd. JP Hong Kong, 1976. *Recreations:* serious music, racing. *Address:* Sino Land Company Ltd, Tsim Sha Tsui Centre, 11/F, Salisbury Road, Kowloon, Hong Kong. *Club:* Royal Hong Kong Jockey (Voting Mem.).

YEVTUSHENKO, Yevgeny Aleksandrovich; poet, novelist, film director, film actor, photographer; *b* 18 July 1933; *m*; five *s*; *m* 4th, 1986, Maria Novikova. *Educ:* Moscow Literary Inst., 1952–56 (expelled). Elected Mem., Congress of People's Deputies of USSR, 1989. Has visited 93 countries; Vice-Pres., Russian PEN, 1990–; Hon. Mem., Amer. Acad. of Arts and Scis, 1987; hon. degrees from numerous Univs. Film actor: Take Off, 1979 (silver prize, Moscow Internat. film fest.); film director: Kindergarten, 1984; Stalin's Funeral, 1990. *Publications: in Russian:* Scouts of the Future, 1952; The Third Snow, 1955; The Highway of Enthusiasts, 1956; The Promise, 1959; The Apple, 1960; A Sweep of the Arm, 1962; Tenderness, 1962; Mail Boat, 1966; Bratsk Power Station, 1967; Kazan's University, 1971; A Father's Hearing, 1975; Morning People, 1978; Talent is not a Miracle by Chance (essays), 1980; Wild Berries Places (novel), 1981; Mother and Neutron Bomb and other poems, 1983; Almost at the End, 1986; A Wind of Tomorrow (essays), 1987; Selected Poetry, 3 vols, 1987; words to Shostakovich's 13th Symphony and Execution of Stepan Razin Oratorio; *in English:* Zima Junction, 1961; A Precocious Autobiography, 1963; Bratsk Power Station, 1966; Stolen Apples, 1972; From Desire to Desire, 1976; The Face Behind the Face, 1979; Dove in Santiago, 1982; Invisible Threads (photography), 1981; Wild Berries (novel), 1984; Ardabiola (novel), 1985; Almost at the

End, 1987; Divided Twins (photography), 1987; Last Attempt, 1988; Politics—everybody's privilege (essays), 1990; Collected Poems 1952–90, 1991; Fatal Half Measures, 1991; (ed) Twentieth-Century Russian Poetry, 1993.

YOCKLUNN, Sir John (Soong Chung), KCVO 1977; Kt 1975; Associate Librarian (Gippsland), Monash University Library, since 1993 (Chief Librarian, Gippsland Institute of Advanced Education, then Monash University College, 1983–92); *b* Canton, China, 5 May 1933; *s* of late Charles Soong Yocklunn and Wui Sin Yocklunn, formerly of W Australia; *m* 1981, Patricia Ann Mehegan. *Educ:* Perth Modern Sch.; Northam High Sch., W Australia; Univ. of W Australia (BA); Aust. Nat. Univ. (BA); Univ. of Sheffield (MA). ALA; ALAA. Dept of the Treasury, Canberra, 1959–63; Nat. Library of Australia, Canberra, 1964–67; Librarian-in-Charge, Admin Coll. of Papua New Guinea, Port Moresby, 1967–69; Exec. Officer, Public Service Board of Papua New Guinea, 1969–70; Librarian, Admin Coll., 1970–72; Principal Private Sec. to Chief Minister, 1972–73; study in UK, under James Cook Bicentenary Schol., 1973–74; on return, given task of organising a national library; Sen. Investigation Officer, Public Services Commn, 1974–77; Asst Sec. (Library Services), Dept of Educn (National Librarian of PNG), 1978–83. Chm., PNG Honours and Awards Cttee, 1975–83; Advr on Honours to PNG Govt, 1984–85; Consultant on estabt of new honours system, 1985–86. Vice-Pres., Pangu Pati, 1968–72; Nat. Campaign Manager for Pangu Pati for 1972 general elections in Papua New Guinea; Treasurer, Pangu Pati, 1973–80. Asst Dir, Visit of Prince of Wales to PNG, 1975; Dir, Visits of the Queen and Prince Philip to PNG, 1977 and 1982. Australian Library and Information Association: Chm., Gippsland Regional Gp, 1984–; Mem., Vict. Br. Council, 1986–; rep. on Commonwealth Library Assoc., 1988–91; Mem. Exec. Cttee, Vict. Div., Aust. Council for Library and Inf. Servs, 1989–. Mem. Adv. Council, CARE Aust., 1988–. Trustee, 1986–, Chm. of Friends, 1985–88, Vice-Chm., 1992–, Mus. of Chinese Australian Hist. *Publications:* The Charles Barrett Collection of Books relating to Papua New Guinea, 1967, 2nd edn 1969; articles on librarianship, etc., in various jls. *Recreations:* book collecting, languages, cooking. *Address:* Monash University Gippsland Campus, Churchill, Victoria 3842, Australia. *T:* (office) (51) 226420; (home) (51) 348303.

YONG NYUK LIN; Member, Presidential Council for Minority Rights, Singapore, 1979–91; *b* Seremban, Malaya, 24 June 1918; *s* of late Yong Thean Yong and Chen Shak Moi; *m* 1939, Kwa Geok Lan; two *d. Educ:* Raffles Coll., Singapore. Science Master, King George V Sch., Seremban, Malaya, 1938–41; with Overseas Assurance Corp., Singapore, 1941 (resigned, as Gen. Manager, 1958). Legislative Assemblyman, Singapore, 1959–65, MP 1965–79; Minister for Educn, 1959–63; Chm., Singapore Harbour Bd, 1961–62; Minister for: Health, 1963–68; Communications, 1968–75; Minister without Portfolio, 1975–76; High Comr in London, 1975–76. Chm., Singapore Land/Marina Centre Development Private Ltd, 1980–86. *Address:* 50 Oei Tiong Ham Park, Singapore 1026.

YORK, Archbishop of, since 1995; **Most Rev. and Rt Hon. David Michael Hope;** PC 1991; DPhil; *b* 14 April 1940. *Educ:* Nottingham Univ. (BA Hons Theol); Linacre Coll., Oxford (DPhil; Hon. Fellow, 1993). Curate of St John, Tuebrook, Liverpool, 1965–70; Chaplain, Church of Resurrection, Bucharest, 1967–68; Vicar, St Andrew, Warrington, 1970–74; Principal, St Stephen's House, Oxford, 1974–82; Warden, Community of St Mary the Virgin, Wantage, 1980–87; Vicar of All Saints', Margaret Street, 1982–85; Bishop of Wakefield, 1985–91; Bishop of London, 1991–95. Examining Chaplain to: Bp of Bath and Wells, 1976–85; Bp of Wakefield, 1979–85; Bp of Norwich, 1981–85; Bp of London, 1984–85. Prelate, Order of British Empire, 1991–95; Dean of the Chapels Royal, 1991–95. *Publications:* The Leonine Sacramentary, 1971; Living the Gospel, 1993. *Address:* Bishopthorpe, York YO2 1QE. *T:* York (01904) 707021.

YORK, Dean of; *see* Furnell, Very Rev. R.

YORK, Archdeacon of; *see* Austin, Ven. G. B.

YORK, Christopher, DL; *b* 27 July 1909; *s* of late Col Edward York; *m* 1934, Pauline Rosemary, *d* of late Sir Lionel Fletcher, CBE; one *s* three *d. Educ:* Eton; RMC Sandhurst. Joined The Royal Dragoons, India, 1930; retired, 1934, on to Supplementary Reserve; rejoined Regt, 1939, rank Major; joined Land Agents Soc., 1934, and passed examinations, acting as Land Agent until elected MP; MP (U) Harrogate Division, 1950–54 (Ripon Division of the West Riding, 1939–50); DL West Riding of Yorkshire, later N Yorkshire, 1954; High Sheriff of Yorkshire, 1966. Pres., RASE, 1979. Hon. Fellow, Royal Veterinary Coll., 1971. *Recreation:* writing. *Address:* South Park, Long Marston, York YO5 8LL. *TA* and *T:* York (01904) 738357. *Clubs:* Boodle's, Carlton.

YORK, Michael, (Michael York-Johnson); actor; *b* 27 March 1942; *s* of Joseph Johnson and Florence Chown; *m* 1968, Patricia Frances McCallum. *Educ:* Hurstpierpoint College; Bromley Grammar School; University College, Oxford (BA). *Stage:* Dundee Repertory Theatre, 1964; National Theatre Co., 1965; Outcry, NY, 1973; Bent, NY, 1980; Cyrano de Bergerac, Santa Fe, 1981; Whisper in the Mind, Phoenix, 1991; The Crucible, NY, 1992; Someone Who'll Watch Over Me, NY, 1993; *films:* The Taming of the Shrew, Accident, 1966; Romeo and Juliet, 1967; Cabaret, England Made Me, 1971; The Three Musketeers, 1973; Murder on the Orient Express, 1974; Logan's Run, 1975; The Riddle of the Sands, 1978; Success is the Best Revenge, 1984; Dawn, 1985; Vengeance, 1986; The Secret of the Sahara, Imbalances, 1987; The Joker, Midnight Blue, The Return of the Musketeers, 1988; The Long Shadow, 1992; Rochade, 1992; Eline Vere, 1992; Wide Sargasso Sea, 1993; Discretion Assured, 1993; The Shadow of a Kiss, 1994; Gospa, 1995; *television* includes: Jesus of Nazareth, 1976; A Man Called Intrepid, 1978; For Those I Loved, 1981; The Weather in the Streets, The Master of Ballantrae, 1983; Space, 1984; The Far Country, 1985; The Four Minute Mile, The Heat of the Day, 1988; Till We Meet Again, 1989; The Night of the Fox, 1990; Fall from Grace, 1994; September. Chm., Calif Youth Theatre, 1987–. Hon. DFA S Carolina, 1988. *Publications:* (contrib.) The Courage of Conviction, 1986; (contrib.) Voices of Survival, 1987; Travelling Player (autobiog.), 1991. *Recreations:* travel, music, collecting theatrical memorabilia.

YORK, Susannah; actress and writer; *b* 9 Jan. 1942; *d* of William Fletcher and Joan Bowring; *m* 1960, Michael Wells (marr. diss. 1976); one *s* one *d. Educ:* Marr Coll., Troon, Scotland; RADA, London. *Films* include: The Greengage Summer, 1961; Freud, 1962; Tom Jones, 1963; A Man for All Seasons, 1966; The Killing of Sister George, 1968; They Shoot Horses, Don't They, 1969; X, Y and Zee, 1971; Images, 1972; Superman, 1978; Golden Gate Murders, 1979; Alice, 1980; Superman 2, 1984; A Christmas Carol, Mio My Mio, 1986; Bluebeard; Just Ask for Diamonds, 1988; Melancholia, 1989; Barbarblu Barbarblu; Little Women. *Theatre* includes: Wings of a Dove, 1964; A Singular Man, 1965; The Maids, 1974; Peter Pan, 1977; The Singular Life of Albert Nobbs, 1978; Hedda Gabler, New York 1981, London 1982; Agnes of God, 1983; The Human Voice (own trans. of Cocteau), 1984; Fatal Attraction, Haymarket, 1985; The Apple Cart, Haymarket, 1986; The Women, Old Vic, 1986; The Glass Menagerie (tour), 1989; A Streetcar Named Desire, Octagon, Bolton, 1990; Noonbreak (own trans. of Claudel), London and Manchester, 1991; September Tide, London, 1993. TV series: Second Chance, 1981; We'll Meet Again, 1982; The Prince Regent, 1983; Devices and Desires, 1990; Trainer, 1991, 1992. *Publications:* In Search of Unicorns, 1973, rev. edn 1984; Larks Castle, 1975, rev. edn, 1985; (ed) The Big One, 1984. *Recreations:* family, writing, gardening, reading, houses, riding, languages, travelling, theatre, cinema, walking. *Address:* c/o Jonathan Altaras Associates, 2 Goodwins Court, WC2N 4LL.

YORK-JOHNSON, Michael; *see* York, M.

YORKE, family name of **Earl of Hardwicke.**

YORKE, David Harry Robert, CBE 1993; FRICS; Consultant, Weatherall Green & Smith, Chartered Surveyors, since 1992; *b* 5 Dec. 1931; *s* of late Harry Yorke and of Marie Yorke, Minera, N Wales; *m* 1955, Patricia Gwynneth Fowler-Tutt; one *d. Educ:* Dean Close Sch., Cheltenham; College of Estate Management. FRICS 1966 (ARICS 1956); FCIArb 1994. Articled to Tregear & Sons, 1948–54. 2nd Lieut RA, 1955–56. Weatherall Green & Smith, 1960–: Partner, 1961–92; Sen. Partner, 1984–89; Gp Chm., 1989–92. Dir, London Auction Mart, 1981–92; Chm., Belgravia Property Co. Ltd, 1993–95. Mem., Bristol Develt Corp., 1988–; Dir, British Waterways Bd, 1988–. Royal Institution of Chartered Surveyors: Mem., Gen. Council, 1978–92; Pres., Gen. Practice Div., 1981–82; Pres., 1988–89; Chm., RICS Insurance Services, 1991–. Mem. Council, British Property Fedn, 1990–94. Pres., British Chapter, Internat. Real Estate Fedn, 1974. Freeman, City of London, 1979; Liveryman, Co. of Chartered Surveyors, 1979. *Recreations:* crosswords, boats, swimming, occasional cookery. *Address:* Penolva, St Mawes, Truro, Cornwall TR2 5DR. *T:* St Mawes (01326) 270235; 2 Chester Cottages, Bourne Street, SW1W 8HG. *T:* 0171–823 4015. *Club:* Buck's.

YORKE, Margaret, (Margaret Beda Nicholson); writer; *b* 30 Jan. 1924; *d* of John Peel Alexander Larminie and Alison Yorke (*née* Lyle); *m* 1945, Basil Nicholson (marr. diss. 1957, he *d* 1987); one *s* one *d. Educ:* Prior's Field, Surrey. WRNS, 1942–45. Bookseller; School Sec.; Asst Librarian, St Hilda's Coll., Oxford, 1959–60; Library Asst (cataloguer), Christ Church, Oxford, 1963–65. Chm., Crime Writers' Assoc., 1979–80. CWA Golden Handcuffs Award, 1993. *Publications:* Summer Flight, 1957; Pray Love Remember, 1958; Christopher, 1959; Deceiving Mirror, 1960; The China Doll, 1961; Once a Stranger, 1962; The Birthday, 1963; Full Circle, 1965; No Fury, 1967; The Apricot Bed, 1968; The Limbo Ladies, 1969; Dead in the Morning, 1970; Silent Witness, 1972; Grave Matters, 1973; Mortal Remains, 1974; No Medals for the Major, 1974; The Small Hours of the Morning, 1975; The Cost of Silence, 1977; The Point of Murder, 1978; Death on Account, 1979; The Scent of Fear, 1980 (Swedish Acad. of Detection Award, 1982); The Hand of Death, 1981; Devil's Work, 1982; Find Me a Villain, 1983; The Smooth Face of Evil, 1984; Intimate Kill, 1985; Safely to the Grave, 1986; Evidence to Destroy, 1987; Speak for the Dead, 1988; Crime in Question, 1989; Admit to Murder, 1990; A Small Deceit, 1991; Criminal Damage, 1992; Dangerous to Know, 1993; Almost the Truth, 1994; Pieces of Justice (short stories), 1994; Serious Intent, 1995. *Recreations:* theatre, reading, swimming, gardening, travel. *Address:* Oriel Cottage, High Street, Long Crendon, Bucks HP18 9AL. *Clubs:* Royal Over-Seas League, Detection, PEN.

YORKE, Very Rev. Michael Leslie; Provost of Portsmouth, since 1994; *b* 25 March 1939; *s* of Leslie Henry and Brenda Emma Yorke; *m* 1st, 1964, Michal Sara Dadd (*d* 1987); one *s* one *d*; 2nd, 1988, Frances Grace Archer. *Educ:* Midhurst Grammar Sch.; Brighton Coll.; Magdalene Coll., Cambridge (BA 1962; MA 1966); Cuddesdon Theol Coll., Oxford. Ordained deacon, 1964, priest, 1965; Curate, Croydon Parish Church, 1964–68; Precentor and Chaplain, 1968–73, Dep. Dir of Res. and Trng, 1972–74, Chelmsford Cathedral; Rector, Ashdon with Hadstock, 1974–78; Canon Residentiary, 1978–88, Vice Provost, 1984–88, Chelmsford Cathedral; Vicar, St Margaret's with St Nicholas, King's Lynn, 1988–94. *Recreations:* opera, 20th century military history, long country walks, contemporary art. *Address:* Provost's House, Pembroke Road, Old Portsmouth, Hants PO1 2NS. *T:* Portsmouth (01705) 824400; Westgate House, The Green, Burnham Market, Norfolk PE31 8HD.

YORKE, Robert Anthony; management consultant, since 1981; Commissioner, Royal Commission on the Historical Monuments of England, since 1991; *b* 27 June 1944; *s* of late Patrick Langdon Yorke and of Pamela Mary (*née* Rudgard; now Mrs Robert Michael Clive); *m* 1975, Morag, *d* of late J. S. M. Dow; one *s* one *d. Educ:* Marlborough Coll.; Clare Coll., Cambridge (MA); London Business Sch. (MSc). Financial Controller, Bowater Corp., 1975–77; Chief Exec., Ridham Freight Services, 1977–81; Director, Rotadata Ltd, 1981–; London and Devonshire Trust Ltd, 1987–. Chairman: Nautical Archaeol. Soc., 1987–91; Jt Nautical Archaeol. Policy Cttee, 1995– (Vice-Chm., 1988–95). *Publications:* contribs to learned jls. *Recreations:* nautical archaeology, tennis, ski-ing. *Address:* Silver Birches, Bashurst Hill, Itchingfield, Horsham, W Sussex RH13 7NY. *T:* Horsham (01403) 790311.

YORKSHIRE, EAST RIDING, Archdeacon of; *see* Buckingham, Ven. H. F.

YOUARD, Richard Geoffrey Atkin; The Investment Ombudsman (formerly Investment Referee), since 1989; *b* 27 Jan. 1933; *s* of Geoffrey Bernard Youard, MBE and Hon. Rosaline Joan Youard (*née* Atkin); *m* 1960, Felicity Ann Morton; one *s* two *d. Educ:* Bradfield Coll., Berks; Magdalen Coll., Oxford (BA Jurisprudence). Admitted Solicitor, 1959. Commnd (2nd Lieut) RA, 1952 (Nat. Service); Lieut TA, 1954. Slaughter and May, London: Articled Clerk, 1956–59; Asst Solicitor, 1959–68; Partner, 1968–89. Inspector, DTI, 1987–. Hon. Sen. Res. Fellow, KCL, 1988–. Chairman: Nat. Fedn of Consumers Groups, 1968; Cttee of Inquiry, Accountants Jt Disciplinary Scheme, 1989–; Mem., Home Office Cttee on London Taxicab and Car Hire Trade, 1967. Clerk to Governors, Bradfield Coll., 1968–89, Governor, 1989–95. *Publications:* (contrib.) Sovereign Borrowers, 1984; (contrib.) Current Issues of International Financial Law, 1985; (jtly) Butterworths Banking Documents, 1986; (contrib.) Butterworths Banking and Financial Law Review, 1987; contribs on legal aspects of internat. finance to Jl of Business Law, Euromoney and Internat. Financial Law Review. *Recreations:* gardening, electronics (holder of Amateur Transmitting Licence), beekeeping, map collecting, reading, jazz, playing the trumpet/cornet. *Address:* 12 Northampton Park, N1 2PJ. *T:* 0171–226 8055. *Club:* Garrick.

YOUDS, His Honour Edward Ernest; a Circuit Judge, Bedford, 1972–85; *b* 21 Nov. 1910; *s* of late Edward Youds. *Educ:* Birkenhead Sch.; Magdalene Coll., Cambridge. BA, LLB (Hons) Cantab. Called to Bar, Gray's Inn, 1936. Practised on Northern Circuit as Barrister-at-law. Served 1940–45, France and Germany (despatches, 1945). Dep. Chm., Lancs County Sessions, 1961–66; County Court Judge, 1966–69; Puisne Judge, High Court, Uganda, 1969–72.

YOUENS, Sir Peter (William), Kt 1965; CMG 1962; OBE 1960; *b* 29 April 1916; 2nd *s* of late Canon F. A. C. Youens; *m* 1943, Diana Stephanie (*d* 1990), *d* of Edward Hawkins, Southacre, Norfolk; two *d. Educ:* King Edward VII's School, Sheffield; Wadham College, Oxford. MA (Oxon), 1938. Joined Colonial Administrative Service; naval service, 1939–40. Sub-Lt, Cadet S. L., 1939; Asst Dist Comr, 1942; Dist Comr, 1948; Colony Comr and Member, Sierra Leone Legislative Council, 1950; Asst Sec., Nyasaland, 1951; Dep. Chief Sec., 1953–63; Secretary to the Prime Minister and to the Cabinet, Malawi, 1964–66 (Nyasaland, 1963–64); Mem., Nyasaland Legislative Council, 1954–61. Retired, 1966. Exec. Dir, Lonrho Ltd, 1966–69, Non-Exec. Dir, 1980–81, Exec. Dir, 1981–94;

Partner, John Tyzack & Partners Ltd, 1969–81. *Address:* Hill View, Primrose Hill Road, NW3 3AB. *Clubs:* East India, Devonshire, Sports and Public Schools; Vincent's (Oxford).

YOUNG, family name of **Baron Kennet, Baroness Young** and **Barons Young of Dartington** and **Young of Graffham.**

YOUNG; *see* Hughes-Young, family name of Baron St Helens.

YOUNG, Baroness *cr* 1971 (Life Peer), of Farnworth in the County Palatine of Lancaster; **Janet Mary Young;** PC 1981; DL; *b* 23 Oct. 1926; *d* of John Norman Leonard Baker and Phyllis Marguerite Baker (*née* Hancock); *m* 1950, Geoffrey Tyndale Young; three *d*. *Educ:* Dragon School Oxford, Headington School, and in America; St Anne's Coll., Oxford; MA (Politics, Philosophy and Economics); Hon. Fellow, 1978. Baroness in Waiting (Govt Whip), 1972–73; Parly Under-Sec. of State, DoE, 1973–74; Minister of State, DES, 1979–81; Chancellor, Duchy of Lancaster, 1981–82; Leader of House of Lords, 1981–83; Lord Privy Seal, 1982–83; Minister of State, FCO, 1983–87. A Vice-Chm., Cons. Party Organisation, 1975–83, Dep. Chm., 1977–79; Chm., Assoc. of Cons. Peers, 1995–. Co-Chm., Women's Nat. Commn, 1979–83. Councillor Oxford City Council, 1957; Alderman, 1967–72; Leader of Conservative Group, 1967–72. Director: UK Provident Instn, 1975–79; Nat. Westminster Bank, 1987–; Marks and Spencer Plc, 1987–. Mem., BR Adv. Bd, Western Reg., 1977–79. Chairman: ISJC, 1989–92; GBGSA, 1989–94. A Vice-President: W India Cttee, 1987–; Assoc. of Dist Councils, 1990–. Chancellor, Univ. of Greenwich, 1993–. Member: Council of Management, Ditchley Foundn, 1990–; Court, Cranfield Univ. (formerly Inst. of Technology), 1991–; Chm. Council, Headington Sch., Oxford, 1993–. DL Oxon, 1989. Hon. FICE. Hon. DCL Mt Holyoke Coll., 1982. *Recreation:* music. *Address:* House of Lords, SW1A 0PW.

YOUNG OF DARTINGTON, Baron *cr* 1978 (Life Peer), of Dartington in the County of Devon; **Michael Young,** BSc (Econ), MA, PhD; Director, Institute of Community Studies since 1953; Trustee, Dartington Hall, 1942–92; *b* 9 Aug. 1915; father a musician, mother a writer; *m* 1st, 1945, Joan Lawson; two *s* one *d*; 2nd, 1960, Sasha Moorsom (*d* 1993); one *s* one *d*. *Educ:* Dartington Hall Sch.; London Univ. Barrister, Gray's Inn. Dir of Political and Economic Planning, 1941–45; Sec., Research Dept, Lab. Party, 1945–51. Chairman: Social Science Research Council, 1965–68; Dartington Amenity Research Trust, 1967–; Internat. Extension Coll., 1970–; Nat. Consumer Council, 1975–77; Mutual Aid Centre, 1977–; Coll. of Health, 1983–90; Health Information Trust, 1987–; Argo Venture, 1984–; Open Coll. of the Arts, 1987–90; Open Sch., 1989–; Language Line, 1989–; Educn Extra, 1990–; Dir, Mauritius Coll. of the Air, 1972; Member: Central Adv. Council for Education, 1963–66; NEDC, 1975–78; Policy Cttee, SDP, 1981–83; President: Consumer's Assoc., 1965– (Chm., 1956–65); National Extension Coll., 1971– (Chm., 1962–71); Adv. Centre for Educn, 1976– (Chm., 1959–76); Birkbeck Coll., London Univ., 1989–92. Chm., Tawney Soc., 1982–84. Fellow, Churchill Coll., Cambridge, 1961–66; Vis. Prof. of Extension Educn, Ahmadu Bello Univ., Nigeria, 1974; Regents' Lectr, UCLA, 1985. Hon. FBA 1995. Hon. Fellow: LSE, 1978; Plymouth Polytechnic, 1980; QMC, 1983. Hon. LittD Sheffield, 1965; DUniv Open, 1973; Hon. DLitt: Adelaide, 1974; Keele, 1991; Hon. LLD Exeter, 1982. *Publications:* Family and Kinship in East London (with Peter Willmott), 1957; The Rise of the Meritocracy, 1958; (with Peter Willmott) Family and Class in a London Suburb, 1960; Innovation and Research in Education, 1965; (with Patrick McGeeney) Learning Begins at Home, 1968; (ed) Forecasting and the Social Sciences, 1968; (with Peter Willmott) The Symmetrical Family, 1973; (ed) The Poverty Report, 1974 and 1975; (with Marianne Rigge) Mutual Aid in a Selfish Society, 1979; (with others) Distance Teaching for the Third World, 1980; The Elmhirsts of Dartington—the creation of an Utopian Community, 1982; (with Marianne Rigge) Revolution From Within: co-operatives and co-operation in British industry, 1983; Social Scientist as Innovator, 1984; The Metronomic Society, 1988; (ed with Tom Schuller) The Rhythms of Society, 1988; (with Tom Schuller) Life After Work—the arrival of the ageless society, 1991; Your Head in Mine (poetry), 1994. *Recreation:* painting. *Address:* 18 Victoria Park Square, E2 9PF.

YOUNG OF GRAFFHAM, Baron *cr* 1984 (Life Peer), of Graffham in the County of W Sussex; **David Ivor Young;** PC 1984; Executive Chairman, Cable and Wireless, since 1990; *b* 27 Feb. 1932; *s* of late Joseph and of Rebecca Young; *m* 1956, Lita Marianne Shaw; two *d*. *Educ:* Christ's Coll., Finchley; University Coll., London (LLB Hons; Fellow, 1988). Admitted solicitor, 1956. Exec., Great Universal Stores Ltd, 1956–61; Chairman: Eldonwall Ltd, 1961–75; Manufacturers Hanover Property Services Ltd, 1974–84; Director: Town & City Properties Ltd, 1972–75; Salomon Inc., 1990–94. Chm., British ORT, 1975–80 (Pres., 1980–82); Pres., World ORT Union, 1990–93 (Chm., Admin. Cttee, 1980–84). Dir, Centre for Policy Studies, 1979–82 (Mem., Management Bd, 1977); Mem., English Industrial Estates Corp., 1980–82; Chm., Manpower Services Commn, 1982–84. Industrial Adviser, 1979–80, Special Adviser, 1980–82, DoI; Minister without Portfolio, 1984–85; Sec. of State for Employment, 1985–87; Sec. of State for Trade and Industry, 1987–89; Dep. Chm., Cons. Party, 1989–90. Mem., NEDC, 1982–89. Pres., Inst. of Directors, 1992–. Pres., Jewish Care, 1990–; Chairman: Internat. Council of Jewish Social and Welfare Services, 1981–84; Central Council for Jewish Community Services, 1993–; Bd of Govs, Oxford Centre for Postgrad. Hebrew Studies, 1989–93. Dir, Royal Opera House Trust, 1990–95; Chairman: London Philharmonic Trust, 1995–; Develt Bd, 1994–, Council, 1995–, UCL. Hon. FRPS 1981. *Publication:* The Enterprise Years: a businessman in the Cabinet, 1990. *Recreations:* golf, fishing, photography. *Address:* Cable and Wireless, 124 Theobalds Road, WC1X 8RX. *Clubs:* Savile; Royal & Ancient Golf (St Andrews); West Sussex Golf.

See also B. A. Rix.

YOUNG, Prof. Alec David, OBE 1964; MA; FRS 1973; FEng 1976; Professor and Head of the Department of Aeronautical Engineering, Queen Mary College, London University, 1954–78, now Emeritus; Vice-Principal, Queen Mary College, 1966–78; *b* 15 Aug. 1913; *s* of Isaac Young and Katherine (*née* Freeman); *m* 1st, 1937, Dora Caplan (*d* 1970); two *s* one *d*; 2nd, 1971, Rena Waldmann (*née* Szafer). *Educ:* Caius Coll., Cambridge. Wrangler, Mathematical Tripos, 1935. Research Student in Aeronautics, Cambridge, 1935–36; Mem. of staff, Aerodynamics Dept, Royal Aircraft Estab., 1936–46; College of Aeronautics: Senior Lectr and Dep. Head of Dept of Aerodynamics, 1946–50; Prof. and Head of Dept of Aerodynamics, 1950–54. Dean, Faculty of Engineering, Univ. of London, 1962–66; Mem. Senate, Univ. of London, 1970–78. Member: Fluid Dynamics Panel, AGARD, 1965–90; various Cttees of Aeronautical Research Council (Chm. of Council, 1968–71). Exec. Sec., Internat. Council of Aeronautical Scis, 1987–90. Chm., Bd of Direction, Von Karman Institute for Fluid Dynamics, 1964–93; Mem., Advisory Bd, RAF Coll., Cranwell, 1966. Gold Medal, 1972, Royal Aeronautical Soc. (Past Chm., Aerodynamics Data Sheets Cttee); FRAeS, 1951, Hon. FRAeS 1984. Ludwig Prandtl Ring, Deutsche Gesellschaft für Luft-und Raumfahrt, 1976; Von Karman Medal, AGARD, 1979. Commandeur de l'Ordre de Leopold, 1976. Fellow: QMC, 1980; AIAA, 1987. Editor, Progress in Aerospace Sciences, 1983–93. *Publications:* (jtly) An Elementary Treatise on the Mechanics of Fluids, 1960, 2nd edn 1970; (jtly) Aircraft Excrescence Drag, 1981; Boundary Layers, 1989; various, of Aeronautical Research Council, Coll. of Aeronautics Reports series, and in Proc. and Reports of AGARD; articles in Aeronautical Quarterly and Jl of Royal Aeronautical Soc., Quarterly Jl of Mechanics and Applied Mathematics, and Aircraft Engineering. *Recreations:* drama, sketching, etching. *Address:* 70 Gilbert Road, Cambridge CB4 3PD. *T:* Cambridge (01223) 354625.

YOUNG, Alexander, FRNCM; retired as free-lance concert and opera singer; Head of Department of Vocal Studies, Royal Northern College of Music, Manchester, 1973–86; *b* London; *m* 1948, Jean Anne Prewett; one *s* one *d*. *Educ:* secondary; (scholar) Royal Coll. of Music, London; studied in London with late Prof. Pollmann, of Vienna State Academy. FRNCM 1977. Served War, HM Forces, 1941–46. Has regular engagements with the BBC and has sung in the USA, Canada, and most European countries, as well as frequently in Britain. First operatic rôle (tenor), as Scaramuccio in Strauss' Ariadne, Edin. Fest., with Glyndebourne Opera, 1950; parts at Glyndebourne, and began broadcasting for BBC, 1951 (subseq. incl. opera, oratorio, recitals, light music, etc). First appearances: with English Opera Group, world Première of Lennox Berkeley's opera, A Dinner Engagement, 1954; also appeared at Royal Festival Hall, several times with Sir Thomas Beecham, in Mozart Requiem; at Sadler's Wells Opera, as Eisenstein in Die Fledermaus, 1959, and subsequently in many roles such as: Ramiro in La Cenerentola; title role in Count Ory; Almaviva in The Barber of Seville; notable roles include: Tom in Stravinsky's Rake's Progress (which he created for British audiences); David in Die Meistersinger; title role in Mozart's Idomeneo. At Covent Garden sang in: Strauss's Arabella; Britten's A Midsummer Night's Dream. Oratorio roles include: Evangelist in Bach Passions; Elgar's Dream of Gerontius; Britten's War Requiem. Was regularly engaged by Welsh National Opera and Scottish Opera. Many commercial recordings, especially of Handel oratorios and operas, as well as The Rake's Progress conducted by the composer. Lieder recitals a speciality. *Recreations:* railway modelling, stamp collecting, photography.

YOUNG, Andrew; Co-Chairman, Atlanta Committee for the Olympic Games; Vice Chairman, Law Companies Group, Inc., since 1993; *b* New Orleans, La, 12 March 1932; *s* of Andrew J. Young and Daisy Fuller; *m* 1954, Jean Childs; one *s* three *d*. *Educ:* Howard Univ., USA; Hartford Theological Seminary. Ordained, United Church of Christ, 1955; Pastor, Thomasville, Ga, 1955–57; Associate Dir for Youth Work, Nat. Council of Churches, 1957–61; Admin. Christian Educn Programme, United Church of Christ, 1961–64; Mem. Staff, Southern Christian Leadership Conf., 1961–70, Exec. Dir, 1964–70, Exec. Vice-Pres., 1967–70; elected to US House of Representatives from 5th District of Georgia, 1972 (first Black Congressman from Georgia in 101 years); re-elected 1974 and 1976; US Ambassador to UN, 1977–79; Mayor of Atlanta, 1982–89. Formerly Chm., Law Internat., Inc. Chairman: Atlanta Community Relations Commn, 1970–72; National Democratic voter registration drive, 1976; during 1960s organized voter registration and community develt programmes. Mem. Bd of Dirs, Martin Luther King, Jr Center. Holds numerous hon. degrees and awards, including: Presidential Medal of Freedom, 1980; Légion d'Honneur (France). *Address:* Atlanta Committee for the Olympic Games, PO Box 1996, Atlanta, GA 30301–1996, USA.

YOUNG, Dr Andrew Buchanan, FRCPE, FFPHM; Deputy Chief Medical Officer, Scottish Office Home and Health Department, since 1989; *b* 11 Aug. 1937; *s* of Alexander and Elizabeth Young; *m* 1965, Lois Lilian Howarth; one *s* one *d*. *Educ:* Falkirk High School; Edinburgh Univ. (MB ChB). DTM&H. Supt, Presbyterian Church of E Africa Hosps, Kenya, 1965–72; Fellow in Community Medicine, Scottish Health Service, 1972–75; Scottish Home and Health Department: MO 1975; SMO 1978; PMO 1985. Pres., Edinburgh Medical Missionary Soc. QHP, 1993–May 1996. *Recreations:* rambling, reading. *Address:* 53c Fountainhall Road, Edinburgh EH9 2LH.

YOUNG, Barbara Scott; Chief Executive, Royal Society for the Protection of Birds, since 1991; *b* 8 April 1948; *d* of George Young and Mary (*née* Scott). *Educ:* Perth Acad.; Edinburgh Univ. (MA Classics); Strathclyde Univ. (Diploma Sec. Sci.); DipHSM, 1971. Various posts, finally Sector Administrator, Greater Glasgow Health Bd, 1973–78; Dir of Planning and Develt, St Thomas' Health Dist, 1978–79; Dist Gen. Administrator, NW Dist, Kensington and Chelsea and Westminster AHA, 1979–82; Dist Administrator, Haringey HA, 1982–85; District General Manager: Paddington and N Kensington HA, 1985–88; Parkside HA, 1988–91. Member: BBC Gen. Adv. Council, 1985–88; Cttee, King's Fund Inst., 1986–90; Delegacy, St Mary's Hosp. Med. Sch., 1991–. Pres., Inst. of Health Services Management, 1987–88. Internat. Fellow, King Edward VII Hosp. Fund Coll., 1985–87 and 1990. Trustee, Wytham Hall, 1990–92; Mem. Trustee Bd, NCVO, 1993–. Patron, Inst. of Ecol and Envmt Management, 1993–. DUniv Stirling, 1995. FRSA. *Publications:* (contrib.) What Women Want, 1990; (contrib.) Medical Negligence, 1990; articles in Hosp. Doctor. *Recreations:* obsessive cinema going, gardening. *Address:* Royal Society for the Protection of Birds, The Lodge, Sandy, Beds SG19 2DL. *T:* Sandy (01767) 680551.

YOUNG, Bertram Alfred, OBE 1980; dramatic critic, 1964–91, and arts editor, 1971–77, The Financial Times; *b* 20 Jan. 1912; *y* (twin) *s* of Bertram William Young and Dora Elizabeth Young (*née* Knight); unmarried. *Educ:* Highgate. Served with Artists Rifles, 1930–35, and Lancs Fusiliers, KAR and Staff, 1939–48; Asst Editor, Punch, 1949–62; Dramatic Critic, Punch, 1962–64. Mem., British Council Drama Adv. Cttee, 1973–83; Pres., Critics' Circle, 1978–80. Hon. Kentucky Col, 1980. *Publications:* Tooth and Claw, 1958; How to Avoid People, 1963; Bechuanaland, 1966; Cabinet Pudding, 1967; Colonists from Space, 1979; The Mirror up to Nature, 1982; The Rattigan Version, 1986; author of about 20 radio plays broadcast 1938–49. *Recreation:* music (consumer only). *Address:* 1 Station Street, Cheltenham GL50 3LX. *T:* Cheltenham (01242) 581485. *Club:* Garrick.

YOUNG, Sir Brian (Walter Mark), Kt 1976; MA; Director General, Independent Broadcasting Authority (formerly Independent Television Authority), 1970–82; *b* 23 Aug. 1922; *er s* of late Sir Mark Young, GCMG and Josephine (*née* Price); *m* 1947, Fiona Marjorie, *o d* of late Allan, 16th Stewart of Appin, and Marjorie (*née* Ballance); one *s* two *d*. *Educ:* Eton (King's Schol.); King's College, Cambridge (Schol.). FSA 1994. Served in RNVR, mainly in destroyers, 1941–45. First class hons in Part I, 1946, and Part II, 1947, of Classical Tripos; Porson Prize, 1946; Winchester Reading Prize, 1947; BA 1947; MA 1952. Assistant Master at Eton, 1947–52; Headmaster of Charterhouse, 1952–64; Dir, Nuffield Foundn, 1964–70. Chm., Christian Aid, 1983–90. Member: Central Advisory Council for Education, 1956–59 (Crowther Report); Central Religious Adv. Cttee of BBC and ITA, 1960–64; Bd of Centre for Educn Develt Overseas, 1969–72; Arts Council of GB, 1983–88; Exec. Cttee, British Council of Churches, 1983–90; Chm., Associated Bd of the Royal Schs of Music, 1984–87. Pres., British and Foreign Sch. Soc., 1991–. A Managing Trustee, Nuffield Foundn, 1978–90; Trustee: Lambeth Palace Liby, 1984–; Imperial War Mus., 1985–92. Hon. RNCM, 1987. Hon. DLitt Heriot-Watt, 1980. *Publications:* Via Vertendi, 1952; Intelligent Reading (with P. D. R. Gardiner), 1964; The Villein's Bible: stories in Romanesque carving, 1990. *Recreations:* music, travel, history, problems. *Address:* Hill End, Woodhill Avenue, Gerrards Cross, Bucks SL9 8DJ. *T:* Gerrards Cross (01753) 887793.

See also T. M. S. Young.

YOUNG, Christopher Godfrey; His Honour Judge Young; a Circuit Judge, since 1980; *b* 9 Sept. 1932; *s* of the late Harold Godfrey Young, MB, ChB, and Gladys Mary

Young; *m* 1969, Jeanetta Margaret (*d* 1984), *d* of Halford and Dorothy Vaughan; one *s*. *Educ:* Bedford Sch.; King's Coll., Univ. of London (LLB Hons 1954). Called to the Bar, Gray's Inn, 1957; Midland and Oxford Circuit, 1959; a Recorder of the Crown Court, 1975–79. Mem., Parole Bd, 1990–93. Chm., Maidwell with Draughton Parish Council, 1973–76. *Recreations:* music, natural history, gardening. *Address:* Stockshill House, Duddington, near Stamford, Lincs PE9 3QQ.

YOUNG, Ven. Clive; Archdeacon of Hackney and Vicar of Guild Church of St Andrew, Holborn, since 1992; *b* 31 May 1948; *s* of William Alfred Young and Dorothy Young; *m* 1971, Susan Elizabeth Tucker. *Educ:* King Edward VI Grammar Sch., Chelmsford; St John's Coll., Durham (BA Hons); Ridley Hall, Cambridge. Ordained: deacon, 1972; priest, 1973; Assistant Curate: Neasden cum Kingsbury St Catherine, London, 1972–75; St Paul, Hammersmith, 1975–79; Priest-in-charge, 1979–82, Vicar, 1982–92, St Paul with St Stephen, Old Ford; Area Dean, Tower Hamlets, 1988–92. *Recreations:* music, gardening. *Address:* St Andrew's Vicarage, 5 St Andrew Street, EC4A 3AB. *T:* 0171–353 3544.

YOUNG, Colin, CBE 1994 (OBE 1976); Director: Ateliers du Cinéma Européen, since 1993; National Film and Television School of Great Britain, 1970–92; *b* 5 April 1927; *s* of Colin Young and Agnes Holmes Kerr Young; *m* 1st, 1960, Kristin Ohman; two *s*; 2nd, 1987, Constance Yvonne Templeman; one *s* one *d*. *Educ:* Bellahouston Academy, Glasgow; Univs of Glasgow, St Andrews and California (Los Angeles). Theatre and film critic, Bon Accord, Aberdeen, 1951; cameraman, editor, writer, director, 1953–; producer, 1967–; UCLA (Motion Pictures): Instructor, 1956–59; Asst Prof., 1959–64; Assoc. Prof., 1964–68; Prof., 1968–70, Head, Motion Picture Div., Theater Arts Dept, UCLA, 1964–65; Chm., Dept of Theater Arts, 1965–70. Res. Associate, Centre Nat. de Recherche Scientifique, Paris, 1984 and 1987; Andrew W. Mellon Vis. Prof. in Humanities, Rice Univ., Houston, Texas, 1985–86. Vice-Chm., 1972–76, Chm., 1976–91, Edinburgh Film Festival; Chm., Edinburgh Internat. Film and Television Council; Governor, BFI, 1974–80. Member: Arts Council Film Cttee, 1972–76; Public Media Panel, Nat. Endowment for Arts, Washington, 1972–77; Gen. Adv. Council, BBC, 1973–78; Council of Management, BAFTA, 1974–81; Exec. Cttee, Centre International de Liaison des Ecoles de Cinéma et de Télévision, 1974–94 (Pres., 1980–94); Nat. Film Finance Corp., 1979–85. Consultant, Goldcrest Films & Television Ltd, 1985–86. FBKS 1975. Chm., Cttee on Educational Policy, UCLA, 1968–69. London Editor, Film Quarterly, 1970–91 (Los Angeles Editor, 1958–68). Michael Balcon Award, 1983, Fellow, 1993, BAFTA. Chevalier de l'Ordre des Arts et des Lettres (France), 1987. *Publications:* various articles in collections of film essays including Principles of Visual Anthropology, 1975; experimental film essay for Unesco, 1963; ethnographic film essay for Unesco, 1966; contribs to Film Quarterly, Sight and Sound, Jl of Aesthetic Education, Jl of the Producers Guild of America, Kosmorama (Copenhagen), etc. *Address:* Ateliers du Cinéma Européen, 68 rue de Rivoli, 75004 Paris, France.

YOUNG, Sir Colville (Norbert), GCMG 1994; MBE 1986; JP; DPhil; Governor-General of Belize, since 1993; *b* 20 Nov. 1932; *s* of Henry Oswald Young and Adney Wilhelmina (*née* Waite); *m* 1956, Norma Eleanor Trapp; three *s* one *d*. *Educ:* Univ. of West Indies (BA 1961); Univ. of York (DPhil 1971). Principal, St Michael's Coll., Belize, 1974–76; Lectr in English and Gen. Studies, Belize Tech. Coll., 1976–86; University College of Belize: Pres., 1986–90; Lectr, 1990–93. JP Belize, 1985. *Publications:* Creole Proverbs of Belize, 1980, rev. edn 1988; From One Caribbean Corner (poetry), 1983; Caribbean Corner Calling, 1988; Language and Education in Belize, 1989; Pataki Full, 1990; contrib. poetry and drama in various anthologies; articles in Belizean Affairs, Jl Belizean Affairs, Belcast Jl, Caribbean Dialogue, Handbook on World Educn. *Recreations:* creative writing, playing and arranging steelband music. *Address:* Belize House, Belmopan, Belize, Central America. *T:* (8) 22521.

YOUNG, David Edward Michael, QC 1980; a Recorder, since 1987; *b* 30 Sept. 1940; *s* of George Henry Edward Young and Audrey Young; *m* 1968, Ann de Bromhead; two *d*. *Educ:* Monkton Combe Sch.; Hertford Coll., Oxford (MA). Called to the Bar, Lincoln's Inn, 1966, Bencher, 1989; practising at Chancery Bar, specialising in intellectual property work. Dep. Judge, Patent County Court, 1990–; a Dep. High Court Judge, 1993–. Chm., Plant Varieties and Seeds Tribunal, 1987–. *Publications:* (co-ed) Terrell on the Law of Patents, 12th edn 1971 to 14th edn 1994; Passing Off, 1985, 3rd edn 1994. *Recreations:* tennis, country pursuits, ski-ing. *Address:* 3 New Square, Lincoln's Inn, WC2A 3RS. *T:* 0171–405 1111.

YOUNG, (David) Junor; HM Diplomatic Service, retired; Director, Colchester and District Visual Arts Trust; *b* 23 April 1934; *m* 1954, Kathleen Brooks; two *s* two *d*. *Educ:* Robert Gordon's College. Joined Foreign Office, 1951; served Berlin, Ankara, South Africa, DSAO, Port Louis, Belgrade, 1951–75; Consul (Comm.), Stuttgart, 1978–81; First Sec., Kampala, 1981–84; Consul Gen., Hamburg, 1984–86; Counsellor (Commercial), Bonn, 1986–88; High Comr, Solomon Is, 1988–90; Dep. High Comr, Karachi, 1991–94. *Recreations:* fishing, shooting. *Address:* Pine Cottage, Hintlesham, Suffolk IP8 3NH.

YOUNG, Rt. Rev. David Nigel de Lorentz; *see* Ripon, Bishop of.

YOUNG, Lt-Gen. Sir David (Tod), KBE 1980; CB 1977; DFC 1952; GOC Scotland and Governor of Edinburgh Castle, 1980–82; *b* 17 May 1926; *s* of late William Young and Davina Tod Young; *m* 1st, 1950, Joyce Marian Melville (*d* 1987); two *s*; 2nd, 1988, Joanna Myrtle Oyler (*née* Torin). *Educ:* George Watson's Coll., Edinburgh. Commissioned, The Royal Scots (The Royal Regt), 1945 (Col, 1975–80). Attached Glider Pilot Regt, 1949–52; Bt Lt-Col, 1964; Mil. Asst to Dep. Chief of Gen. Staff, MoD, 1964–67; commanded 1st Bn The Royal Scots (The Royal Regt), 1967–69; Col Gen. Staff, Staff Coll., 1969–70; Comdr, 12th Mechanized Bde, 1970–72; Dep. Mil. Sec., MoD, 1972–74; Comdr Land Forces, NI, 1975–77; Dir of Infantry, 1977–80. Col Comdt: Scottish Div., 1980–82; UDR, 1986–91; Hon. Col, NI Regt AAC, 1988–93. Pres., ACFA, Scotland, 1984–. HM Comr, Queen Victoria Sch., Dunblane, 1984–93. Chm., Cairntech Ltd, Edinburgh, 1983–92 (Dir, 1992–). Chm., St Mary's Cathedral Workshop Ltd, 1986–92 (Hon. Pres., 1993–). Chm. Scottish Cttee, Marie Curie Meml Foundn, 1986– (Mem., 1983–); Vice Pres., Scottish Partnership Agency for Palliative and Cancer Care, 1993–; Governor, St Columba's Hospice, Edinburgh, 1986–. *Recreations:* golf, spectator of sports. *Address:* c/o Adam & Co. plc, 22 Charlotte Square, Edinburgh EH2 4DF. *Clubs:* Royal Scots, New (Edinburgh).

YOUNG, David Tyrrell; Chairman, GW Run Off Ltd, since 1993; *b* 6 Jan. 1938; *s* of Tyrrell F. Young and Patricia M. Young (*née* Spicer); *m* 1965, Madeline Helen Celia Philips; three *d*. *Educ:* Charterhouse. Trained as Chartered Accountant, Gérard van de Linde & Son, 1955–60; James Edward Dangerfield, 1961–65; joined Spicer & Pegler, later Spicer & Oppenheim, 1965 (merged with Touche Ross, 1990): Partner 1968; Managing Partner, 1982; Sen. Partner, 1988–90; Dep. Chm., 1990–93. Mem. Council, Inst. of Chartered Accountants in England and Wales, 1979–82. Director: Lombard Ins. Gp, 1993–; Asprey, 1993–; Wates City of London Properties, 1994–. Mem. Court, Fishmongers' Co., 1981–. FRSA 1992. *Recreations:* golf, tennis, limited gardening. *Address:* Overhall, Ashdon, Saffron Walden, Essex CB10 2JH. *T:* Saffron Walden (01799) 584556. *Clubs:* City of London, Honourable Artillery Company; Royal St George's Golf, Royal Worlington Golf.

YOUNG, David Wright; MP (Lab) Bolton South East, since 1983 (Bolton East, Feb. 1974–1983); teacher; *b* Greenock, Scotland. *Educ:* Greenock Academy; Glasgow Univ.; St Paul's Coll., Cheltenham. Head of History Dept; subseq. insurance executive. Joined Labour Party, 1955; contested: South Worcestershire, 1959; Banbury, 1966; Bath, 1970. PPS to Sec. of State for Defence, 1977–79. Mem., Select Cttee on Employment, 1982–. Formerly Alderman, Nuneaton Borough Council; Councillor, Nuneaton District Council. Chm., Coventry East Labour Party, 1964–68. Member: TGWU; Co-operative Party. Is especially interested in comprehensive educn, defence, pensions, economics. *Recreations:* reading, motoring. *Address:* House of Commons, SW1A 0AA.

YOUNG, Donald Anthony, CEng, FIGasE; Managing Director, National Transmission, British Gas plc, 1991–93, retired; *b* 23 June 1933; *s* of Cyril Charles Young and Sarah Young; *m* 1960, June (*née* Morrey); two *d*. *Educ:* Stockport Secondary Sch. FIGasE 1969. National Service, 2nd Lieut REME, 1953–55. North Western Gas Bd, 1949–60; E Midlands Gas Bd, 1960–68; Gas Council Terminal Manager, Bacton Natural Gas Reception Terminal, 1968–70; Gas Council Plant Ops Engr, 1970–73; Asst Dir (Ops), Prodn & Supply Div., British Gas HQ, 1973–77; Regional Dep. Chm., N Thames Gas, 1977–79; Dir (Operations), Prodn & Supply Div., British Gas HQ, 1979–83; Regional Chairman: Southern Reg., British Gas Corp., subseq. British Gas plc Southern, 1983–89; British Gas plc West Midlands, 1989–91. CIMgt (CBIM 1986). *Recreations:* gardening, walking. *Address:* Georgian House, Penn Lane, Tanworth in Arden, Warwickshire B94 5HH.

YOUNG, Edward Preston, DSO 1944; DSC 1943; writer and retired book designer; *b* 17 Nov. 1913; *m* 1st, 1945, Diana Lilian Graves (marr. diss.); two *d*; 2nd, 1956, Mary Reoch Cressall. *Educ:* Highgate Sch. Served War, 1940–45: RNVR; entered submarine service 1940 (despatches, DSC); first RNVR officer to command operational submarine, 1943 (DSO, Bar to DSC); temp. Commander RNVR, 1945. Man. Dir, Rainbird Publishing Gp Ltd, 1970–73. *Publications:* One of Our Submarines, 1952; Look at Lighthouses, 1961; The Fifth Passenger, 1962; Look at Submarines, 1964. *Address:* 15 Maple Walk, Rustington, W Sussex BN16 3QP.

YOUNG, Eric, OBE 1976; HM Diplomatic Service, retired; Editor, Control Risks Information Services, 1984–93; *b* 16 Nov. 1924; *s* of late Robert Young, MBE, and Emily Florence Young, Doncaster; *m* 1949, Sheila Hutchinson; three *s* one *d*. *Educ:* Maltby Grammar Sch.; Sheffield Univ. (BA 1948). Served War, RN, 1943–46. Editorial staff: Sheffield Telegraph, 1948; Western Morning News, 1951; Daily Dispatch, 1952; Manchester Guardian, 1953; PRO, NCB, Manchester, 1958; Dep. Dir, UK Inf. Office, Tanganyika and Zanzibar, 1960; First Secretary: (Inf.), Dar es Salaam, 1961; (Aid), Kaduna, 1963; Commonwealth Office (later FCO), 1967; Madras, 1969; Head of Chancery, Reykjavik, 1973 (Hd of Brit. Interests Section, French Embassy, during breach of diplomatic relations, 1976); Dep. High Comr, Bombay, 1977; High Comr, Seychelles, 1980–83. *Recreations:* music, books, hill walking in England and France. *Address:* 3 West Hall, Sudbourne Park, Orford, Woodbridge, Suffolk IP12 2AJ.

YOUNG, Rev. Prof. Frances Margaret, PhD; Edward Cadbury Professor of Theology, since 1986, and Dean, Faculty of Arts, since 1995, University of Birmingham; Methodist minister, since 1984; *b* 25 Nov. 1939; *d* of A. Stanley Worrall and Mary F. Worrall (*née* Marshall); *m* 1964, Robert Charles Young; three *s*. *Educ:* Bedford Coll., Univ. of London (BA); Girton Coll., Univ. of Cambridge (MA, PhD). Research Fellow, Clare Hall, Cambridge, 1967–68; University of Birmingham: Temp. Lectr, 1971–73; Lectr, 1973–82; Sen. Lectr, 1982–86; Hd, Dept of Theol., 1986–95. Hon. DD Aberdeen, 1994. *Publications:* Sacrifice and the Death of Christ, 1975; (contrib.) The Myth of God Incarnate, 1977; From Nicaea to Chalcedon, 1983; Face to Face, 1985, 2nd edn 1990; (with David Ford) Meaning and Truth in 2 Corinthians, 1987; The Art of Performance, 1990; The Theology of the Pastoral Epistles, 1994; numerous articles, etc. *Recreations:* outdoor pursuits, music. *Address:* Department of Theology, University of Birmingham, PO Box 363, Birmingham B15 2TT. *T:* 0121–414 5660; 142 Selly Park Road, Birmingham B29 7LH. *T:* 0121–472 4841.

YOUNG, Frieda Margaret, OBE 1969; HM Diplomatic Service, retired; *b* 9 April 1913; *d* of Arthur Edward Young. *Educ:* Wyggeston Grammar Sch., Leicester; Wycombe Abbey Sch., Bucks; and in France and Germany. Home Office, 1937–39; Min. of Home Security, 1939–41; MOI 1941–44; Paris 1944–48; Tehran 1948–51; Vienna 1951–54; FO 1954–57; First Secretary and Consul, Reykjavik, 1957–59; Consul, Cleveland, 1959–62; FO 1962–65; Consul, Bergen, 1965–68; Consul-General, Rotterdam, 1968–73. *Recreations:* travel, bird-watching. *Address:* 6 Lady Street, Lavenham, Suffolk.

YOUNG, Gavin David, FRSL, FRGS; author and traveller; *b* 24 April 1928; *s* of Lt-Col Gavin David Young and Daphne, *yr d* of Sir Leolin Forestier-Walker, Bt, KBE. *Educ:* Rugby; Trinity Coll., Oxford (MA). FRSL 1987; FRGS 1989. National Service, Lieut, Welsh Guards, 1946–48; served Palestine, 1947–48. Lived with Marsh Arabs of S Iraq, 1952–54; at large in SW Arabia (Hejaz, Tihama and Asir), with Desert Locust Control, 1954–56; foreign corresp. with The Observer, 1959–90, covering wars, etc, in Algeria, Cuba, Nagaland, Congo, Middle East, Kurdistan, Yemen, Bangladesh, Angola, Vietnam, Cambodia; Observer's corresp. in NY, 1962–63, Paris, 1967. *Publications:* Return to the Marshes, 1977; Iraq: land of two rivers, 1979; Slow Boats to China, 1981; Slow Boats Home, 1985; Worlds Apart, 1987; Beyond Lion Rock, 1988; In Search of Conrad, 1991 (jtly, Thomas Cook Travel Book Award, 1992); From Sea to Shining Sea: a present day journey through America's past, 1995; contribs to jls and magazines. *Recreations:* travel in remote places, reading, walking, music, talking late. *Address:* c/o Well, 49 Earls Court Road, W8 6EE. *T:* 0171–937 3538. *Clubs:* Brooks's, Beefsteak, Cavalry and Guards, Pratt's, Shikar; Foreign Correspondents' (Hong Kong).

YOUNG, Gavin Neil B.; *see* Barr Young.

YOUNG, George Bell, CBE 1976; Managing Director, East Kilbride Development Corporation, 1973–90 (and Stonehouse, 1973–77); *b* 17 June 1924; *s* of late George Bell Young and late Jemima Mackinlay; *m* 1946, Margaret Wylie Boyd (decd); one *s*; *m* 1979, Joyce Marguerite McAteer. *Educ:* Queens Park, Glasgow. MIEx 1958; FInstM 1984 (MInstM 1969); CBIM 1988 (FBIM 1982). RNVR, 1942–45, Lieut (destroyers and mine-sweepers). Journalist and Feature Writer, Glasgow Herald, 1945–48; North of Scotland Hydro-Electric Board, 1948–52; Chief Exec. (London), Scottish Council (Development and Industry), 1952–68 (Founder Fellow, 1986); Gen. Man., E Kilbride Develt Corp., 1968–73. Pres., Lanarks Br., BIM, 1985; Chm., BIM Scotland, 1988–91. Mem. Council, Nat. Trust for Scotland, 1974–79; Dir, Royal Caledonian Schools, 1957–85; Chm., East Kilbride and District National Savings Cttee, 1968–78; Trustee, Strathclyde Scanner Campaign; Scottish Chm., British Heart Foundn, 1975–79 (Mem., East Kilbride Cttee, 1970–; Pres., Scottish Appeal, 1980–). Hon. Vice-Pres., East Kilbride Dist Sports Council, 1984. Chm., E Kilbride Cttee, Order of St John, 1972–88 (CStJ 1979). Mem., Amer. Inst. of Corporate Asset Managers, 1985. Member: Saints and Sinners

Club of Scotland (Hon. Sec., 1982–89; Chm., 1990); Royal Glasgow Inst. of the Fine Arts; The Merchants House of Glasgow; Mem. Scotland Cttee, Nat. Children's Homes, 1980–88. FRSA 1968. Freeman, East Kilbride, 1990. *Recreations:* reading, travel. *Address:* 4 Newlands Place, East Kilbride, Lanarkshire G74 1AE. *Clubs:* Royal Scottish Automobile (Glasgow); Largs Kelburn Golf.

YOUNG, Rt. Hon. Sir George (Samuel Knatchbull), 6th Bt, *cr* 1813; PC 1993; MP (C) Ealing, Acton, since Feb. 1974; Secretary of State for Transport, since 1995; *b* 16 July 1941; *s* of Sir George Young, 5th Bt, CMG, and Elisabeth (*née* Knatchbull-Hugessen); *S* father 1960; *m* 1964, Aurelia Nemon-Stuart, *er d* of late Oscar Nemon, and of Mrs Nemon-Stuart, Boar's Hill, Oxford; two *s* two *d*. *Educ:* Eton; Christ Church, Oxford (Open Exhibitioner); MA Oxon, MPhil Surrey. Economist, NEDO, 1966–67; Kobler Research Fellow, University of Surrey, 1967–69; Economic Adviser, PO Corp., 1969–74. Councillor, London Borough of Lambeth, 1968–71; Mem., GLC, for London Borough of Ealing, 1970–73. An Opposition Whip, 1976–79; Parly Under Sec. of State, DHSS, 1979–81, DoE, 1981–86; Comptroller of HM Household, 1990; Minister of State, DoE, 1990–94; Financial Sec. to HM Treasury, 1994–95. Chm., Acton Housing Assoc., 1972–79. Dir, Lovell Partnerships Ltd, 1987–90. Trustee, Guinness Trust, 1986–90. *Publications:* Accommodation Services in the UK 1970–1980, 1970; Tourism, Blessing or Blight?, 1973. *Recreation:* bicycling. *Heir:* *s* George Horatio Young, *b* 11 Oct. 1966. *Address:* House of Commons, SW1A 0AA.

YOUNG, Gerard Francis, CBE 1967; DL; CEng, FIMechE; HM Lord-Lieutenant and Custos Rotolurum, for South Yorkshire, 1974–85; *b* 5 May 1910; *s* of Smelter J. Young, MICE, and Edith, *d* of Sir John Aspinall, Pres. ICE and Pres. IMechE; *m* 1937, Diana Graham Murray, MA, BSc, JP, *d* of Charles Graham Murray, MD; two *s* three *d*. *Educ:* Ampleforth College. Engrg Apprentice, LNER, Doncaster. Entered family firm, The Tempered Spring Co. Ltd (later Tempered Group Ltd), 1930; Dir, 1936; Man. Dir, 1942; Chm., 1954–78. Dir, 1958, Chm., 1967–80, Sheffield Area Board, Sun Alliance & London Insurance Group; Dir, National Vulcan Engineering Insce Group, 1962–79. Member: Nat. Bd for Prices and Incomes, 1968–71; Top Salaries Review Body, 1971–74; Armed Forces Pay Review Body, 1971–74; Gen. Comr of Income Tax, 1947–74 (Chm., Don Div., 1968–74). Dir, Crucible Theatre Trust Ltd, 1967–75; Sec., Assoc. of Christian Communities in Sheffield, 1940–46; Chm., Radio Hallam Ltd, 1973–79; Trustee, Sheffield Town Trust (Town Collector, 1978–81); Chm., J. G. Graves Charitable Fund, 1974–85; Chm., Freshgate Foundn, 1979–86; Mem., Finance Bd, RC Dio. of Hallam, 1981–95. President: Council of St John, South and West Yorks, 1979–85; Yorks Volunteers Council, 1980–81; TAVRA Yorks & Humberside, 1983–85 (Vice-Pres., 1974–82). Univ. of Sheffield: Mem. Council, 1943; Treas., 1947–51; Pro-Chancellor, 1951–67; Chm., 1956–67; Life Mem. of Court, 1983. Mem. Bd of Govs, United Sheffield Hosps, 1948–53 (Chm. of Finance Cttee, 1948–50); Chm., Royal Hosp., 1951–53. Master, Company of Cutlers in Hallamshire, 1961–62. JP Sheffield, 1950–85. (Last) High Sheriff of Hallamshire, 1973–74; DL West Riding of Yorks, 1974. Hon. LLD Sheffield, 1962. KStJ 1976; GCSG 1974. *Recreations:* gardening, 13 grandchildren. *Address:* 69 Carsick Hill Crescent, Sheffield S10 3LS. *T:* Sheffield (0114) 230 2834. *Club:* Sheffield (Sheffield).

See also H. J. S. Young.

YOUNG, Hon. Sir Harold (William), KCMG 1983; Senator for South Australia, 1967–83, President of the Senate, 1981–83, retired; *b* 30 June 1923; *s* of Frederick James Garfield Young and Edith Mabel Scott; *m* 1952, Eileen Margaret Downing; two *s* two *d*. *Educ:* Prince Alfred Coll., Adelaide. Farmer and grazier prior to entering Parliament; former Vice Pres., United Farmers' and Graziers' Assoc. of SA; served on SA Wheat Res. Cttee, and Federal Exporters and Overseas Transport Shipping Freight Negotiating Cttee; Mem., Australian Wool Industry Council. Government Whip in the Senate, 1971–72; Opposition Whip, 1972–75; Shadow Spokesman on the Media, 1975; Chm., Govt Members' Cttee on National Resources, Energy and Trade, 1976–81; Senate: Temp. Chm. of Cttees, 1976–81; Chm., Select Cttee on Offshore Petroleum Resources, 1971 (Mem., 1968); Member: Industry and Trade Cttee, 1970–75; Estimates Cttee, 1970–81; Parlt Publications Cttee; Standing Orders Cttee; Broadcasting of Parlt Proceedings; Jt Foreign Affairs and Defence Cttee; Library Cttee; Jt Statutory Cttee on Public Works; Jt House Cttee; Jt Chm., New Parlt House Cttee, 1981–83 (Mem., 1976–83); Leader Delegn to S America and Africa. International Parliamentary Union: Leader, Delegn to Madrid and Sofia, 1976–77, to European Parlt, 1977; Mem., Internat. Exec., 1976–77. Order of Diplomatic Service Merit (Korea), 1982. *Address:* 1C Kingsley Avenue, Glenunga, SA 5064, Australia.

YOUNG, Hugo John Smelter; journalist; *b* 13 Oct. 1938; *s* of Gerard Francis Young, *qv*; *m* 1st, 1966, Helen Mason (*d* 1989); one *s* three *d*; 2nd, 1990, Lucy Waring. *Educ:* Ampleforth Coll.; Balliol Coll., Oxford (MA Jurisprudence). Yorkshire Post, 1961; Harkness Fellow, 1963; Congressional Fellow, US Congress, 1964; The Sunday Times, 1965–84: Chief Leader Writer, 1966–77; Political Editor, 1973–84; Jt Dep. Editor, 1981–84. Political Columnist, The Guardian, 1984–; Dir, The Tablet, 1985–. Chairman: Scott Trust, 1989–; UK Adv. Cttee, Harkness Fellowships, 1993–95. Hon. DLitt Sheffield, 1993. Columnist of the Year: British Press Awards, 1980, 1983, 1985; Granada TV What the Papers Say Awards, 1985. *Publications:* (jtly) The Zinoviev Letter, 1966; (jtly) Journey to Tranquillity, 1969; The Crossman Affair, 1974; (jtly) No, Minister, 1982; (jtly) But, Chancellor, 1984; (jtly) The Thatcher Phenomenon, 1986; One of Us, 1989, rev. edn 1991. *Address:* c/o The Guardian, 119 Farringdon Road, EC1R 3ER.

YOUNG, Ian Robert, OBE 1985; PhD; FRS 1989; FEng 1988; Senior Research Fellow, Hirst Research Centre, GEC plc, since 1981; *b* 11 Jan. 1932; *s* of John Stirling Young and Ruth Muir Young (*née* Whipple); *m* 1956, Sylvia Marianne Whewell Ralph; two *s* one *d*. *Educ:* Sedbergh Sch., Yorkshire; Aberdeen Univ. (BSc, PhD). FIEE. Hilger & Watts Ltd, 1955–59; Evershed & Vignoles Ltd (and affiliates), 1959–76; EMI Ltd, 1976–81; GEC plc, 1981–. Vis. Prof. of Radiology, RPMS, 1986. Hon. FRCR, 1990; Hon. Mem., Amer. Soc. of Neuroradiology, 1995. Hon. DSc Aberdeen, 1992. *Publications:* over 100 papers in Proc. IEE, Magnetic Resonance in Medicine, Magnetic Resonance Imaging, Jl Magnetic Resonance, Computer Assisted Tomography, etc; 40 separate patents. *Recreations:* bird watching, hill walking, brick laying. *Address:* Church Hill Cottage, West Overton, near Marlborough, Wilts SN8 4ER. *T:* Marlborough (01672) 86615.

YOUNG, James Edward D.; *see* Drummond Young.

YOUNG, Jimmy; *see* Young, L. R.

YOUNG, John Adrian Emile; Partner, Cameron Markby Hewitt (formerly Markby, Stewart & Wadesons), 1965–95; *b* 28 July 1934; *s* of John Archibald Campbell Young and Irene Eugenie Young (*née* Bouvier); *m* 1959, Yvonne Lalage Elizabeth Bankes; three *s* one *d*. *Educ:* Cranbrook Sch., Kent; London Univ. (LLB). Admitted solicitor, 1958; Asst Sec., Law Soc., 1958–64. Nat Chm., Young Solicitors Gp, 1965–66; Pres., Assoc. Internat. des Jeunes Avocats, 1968–69; Law Society: Mem. Council, 1971–95; Dep. Vice-Pres., 1993–94; Vice-Pres., 1994–95; Mem. Council, Internat. Bar Assoc., 1983–94. FRSA 1989. Master, City of London Solicitors' Co., 1989–90. *Publications:* sundry legal articles. *Recreations:* music (runs local church choir), gardening, family! *Address:* Stonewold House, The Street, Plaxtol, Sevenoaks, Kent TN15 0QH. *T:* Sevenoaks (01732) 810289.

YOUNG, John Allen, CBE 1975; a Managing Director, since 1955, Chairman, since 1962, and Chief Executive, since 1989, Young & Co.'s Brewery; *b* 7 Aug. 1921; *e s* of late William Allen Young and of Joan Barrow Simonds; *m* 1951, Yvonne Lieutenant, Liège; one *s*. *Educ:* Nautical Coll., Pangbourne; Corpus Christi Coll., Cambridge (BA Hons Econs). Served War, 1939–45: Lt-Comdr (A) RNVR; comd 888 Naval Air Sqdn (despatches). Runciman Ltd, 1947; Moor Line, 1949; Young & Co.'s Brewery, 1954–. Chairman: Foster-Probyn Ltd; Cockburn & Campbell; RI Shipping Ltd. Gen. Comr of Taxes, 1965–91. President: London Carthorse Parade Soc., 1957–62; Shire Horse Soc., 1963–64 (Treas., 1962–73); Greater London Horse Show, 1972–74; Battersea Scouts, 1974–86; London Harness Horse Parade Soc., 1992–. Chm. Bd of Governors, Nat. Hosps for Nervous Diseases, 1982–86 (Mem. Bd, 1972–86; Chm. Finance, 1974–82); Dep. Chm., Inst. of Neurology, 1982–86 (Chm., Jt Res. Adv. Cttee, 1973–82); Pres., Nat. Hosps Develt Foundn, 1993– (Chm., 1984–93); Governor, Chalfont Centre for Epilepsy, 1983–; Mem. Bd of Management, Royal Hosp. and Home, Putney, 1990–95. Trustee: Licensed Trade Charities Trust, 1984–91; Clapham Junction Disaster Fund, 1989–. Freeman: City of London, 1986; Borough of Wandsworth, 1992. *Recreations:* music, sailing. *Address:* Moonsbrook Cottage, Wisborough Green, West Sussex RH14 0EG. *T:* Wisborough Green (01403) 700355. *Club:* Royal Yacht Squadron (Cowes).

YOUNG, Sir John (Kenyon Roe), 6th Bt *cr* 1821; Senior Buyer; *b* 23 April 1947; *s* of Sir John William Roe Young, 5th Bt, and Joan Minnie Agnes (*d* 1958), *d* of M. M. Aldous; *S* father, 1981; *m* 1977, Frances Elise, *o d* of W. R. Thompson; one *s* one *d*. *Educ:* Hurn Court; Napier College. Joined RN, 1963; transferred to Hydrographic Branch, 1970; qualified Hydrographic Surveyor, 1977; retired from RN, 1979; attended Napier Coll., 1979–80. Member: Hydrographic Soc.; Inst. of Purchasing Mgt. *Recreations:* Rugby, golf. *Heir:* *s* Richard Christopher Roe Young, *b* 14 June 1983. *Address:* Bolingey, 159 Chatham Road, Maidstone, Kent ME14 2ND.

YOUNG, Hon. Sir John (McIntosh), AC 1989; KCMG 1975; Lieutenant-Governor of Victoria, Australia, 1974–95; Chairman, Police Board of Victoria, since 1992; *b* Melbourne, 17 Dec. 1919; *s* of George David Young, Glasgow, and Kathleen Mildred Young, Melbourne; *m* 1951, Elisabeth Mary, *yr d* of late Dr Edward Wing Twining, Manchester; one *s* two *d*. *Educ:* Geelong Grammar Sch.; Brasenose Coll., Oxford (MA; Hon. Fellow, 1991); Inner Temple; Univ. of Melbourne (LLB). Served War: Scots Guards, 1940–46 (Captain 1943); NW Europe (despatches), 1945. Admitted Victorian Bar, 1948; Associate to Mr Justice Dixon, High Court of Australia, 1948; practice as barrister, 1949–74; Hon. Sec., Victorian Bar Council, 1950–60; Lectr in Company Law, Univ. of Melbourne, 1957–61; Hon. Treas., Medico Legal Soc. of Vic., 1955–65 (Vice-Pres., 1966–68; Pres., 1968–69). QC (Vic.) 1961; admitted Tasmanian Bar, 1964, QC 1964; NSW Bar, 1968, QC 1968; Consultant, Faculty of Law, Monash Univ., 1968–74; Chief Justice, Supreme Court of Victoria, 1974–91. Mem., Bd of Examiners for Barristers and Solicitors, 1969–72; Mem. Council, Geelong Grammar Sch., 1974; President: Victorian Council of Legal Educn and Victoria Law Foundn, 1974–91; Scout Assoc. of Australia, 1986–89 (Vice-Pres., 1985; Pres., Victorian Br., 1974–87); Chief Scout of Australia, 1989–; Pres., St John Council for Victoria, 1975–82; GCStJ 1991 (KStJ 1977); Chancellor, Order of St John in Australia, 1982–91. Hon. Colonel: 4th/19th Prince of Wales's Light Horse, 1978–; Royal Victoria Regt, 1994–; Rep. Hon. Col, RAAC, 1986–; Hon. Air Cdre, No 21 (City of Melbourne) Sqn, RAAF, 1986–. Hon. LLD: Monash, 1986; Melbourne, 1989. *Publications:* (co-author) Australian Company Law and Practice, 1965; articles in legal jls. *Recreation:* golf. *Address:* 17 Sorrett Avenue, Malvern, Victoria 3144, Australia. *T:* (3) 98226259. *Clubs:* Cavalry and Guards; Melbourne, Australian (Melbourne).

YOUNG, John Richard Dendy; Attorney of Supreme Court, South Africa, since 1984; *b* 4 Sept. 1907; 5th *s* of James Young and Evelyn Maud Hammond; *m* 1946, Patricia Maureen Mount; four *s* two *d*. *Educ:* Hankey, Cape Province, SA; Humansdorp, CP, SA; University, South Africa (External). Joined Public Service, S Rhodesia, 1926; resigned to practise at Bar, 1934; joined Military Forces, 1940; active service, North Africa, Sicily and Italy; commissioned in the field; demobilised, 1945. QC 1948; MP Southern Rhodesia, 1948–53; Member Federal Assembly, 1953–56; Judge of the High Court of Rhodesia, 1956–68; Chief Justice, Botswana, 1968–71; Advocate of Supreme Court of SA, 1971–84; Sen. Counsel, 1979–84; Judge of Appeal, Lesotho, Swaziland, Botswana, 1979–84. *Recreations:* swimming, walking. *Address:* 8 Tulani Gardens, Greenfield Road, Kenilworth, Cape, 7700, South Africa.

YOUNG, John Robert Chester, CBE 1992; Executive Director and Chief Executive, Securities and Investment Board, since 1993; *b* 6 Sept. 1937; *s* of Robert Nisbet Young and Edith Mary (*née* Roberts); *m* 1963, Pauline Joyce; one *s* one *d* (and one *s* decd). *Educ:* Bishop Vesey's Grammar Sch.; St Edmund Hall, Oxford Univ. (MA); Gray's Inn, London. Joined Simon & Coates, members of the Stock Exchange, 1961; Partner, 1965; Dep. Sen. Partner, 1976; London Stock Exchange (formerly Stock Exchange, subseq. Internat. Stock Exchange): Mem. Council, 1978–82; Dir of Policy and Planning, 1982–87; Vice-Chm. (non-exec.), Managing Bd, 1987–90. Chief Exec. and Dir, SFA (formerly Securities Assoc.), 1987–93. Non-exec. Dir, E Surrey Hosp. and Community Healthcare NHS Trust, 1992–. Formerly internat. athlete, Rugby player and England Rugby selector. FRSA 1995. *Recreations:* cooking, Rugby football. *Address:* Securities and Investments Board, Gavrelle House, 2–14 Bunhill Row, EC1Y 8RA. *T:* 0171–638 1240. *Clubs:* City of London; Vincent's (Oxford); Harlequins.

See also L. Botting.

YOUNG, John Robertson, (Rob), CMG 1991; HM Diplomatic Service; Deputy Under-Secretary of State, Foreign and Commonwealth Office, since 1994; *b* 21 Feb. 1945; *s* of late Francis John Young and of Marjorie Elizabeth Young; *m* 1967, Catherine Suzanne Françoise Houssait; one *s* two *d*. *Educ:* King Edward VI Sch., Norwich; Leicester Univ. (BA 1st Cl. Hons, French). Entered FCO, 1967; MECAS, Lebanon, 1968; Third Sec., Cairo, 1970; Second Sec., FCO, 1972; Private Sec. to Minister of State, 1975; First Sec., Paris, 1977; Asst Head, Western European Dept, FCO, 1982; Counsellor, Damascus, 1984; Head of Middle East Dept, FCO, 1987; Minister, Paris, 1991. *Recreations:* music, sailing, acting. *Address:* c/o Foreign and Commonwealth Office, SW1A 2AH. *Club:* Cruising Association.

YOUNG, John Zachary, MA; FRS 1945; Professor of Anatomy, University College, London, 1945–74, now Emeritus, Hon. Fellow, 1975; engaged in research at Oxford University, Marine Biology Station, Plymouth, and Duke Marine Laboratory, Beaufort, N Carolina; *b* 18 March 1907; *s* of Philip Young and Constance Maria Lloyd; *m* Phyllis Heaney; one *s* one *d*; *m* Raymonde Parsons; one *d*. *Educ:* Wells House, Malvern Wells; Marlborough Coll.; Magdalen Coll., Oxford (Demy). Senior Demy, Magdalen Coll., 1929, Christopher Welch Scholar, 1928, Naples Biological Scholar, 1928, 1929; Fellow of Magdalen Coll., Oxford, 1931–45 (Hon. Fellow, 1975); University Demonstrator in Zoology and Comparative Anatomy, Oxford, 1933–45; Rockefeller Fellow, 1936. Fullerton Professor of Physiology, Royal Institution, 1958–61. Pres., Marine Biol Assoc.,

1976–86. Foreign Member: Amer. Acad. of Arts and Scis; Amer. Philosophical Soc.; Accademia dei Lincei. Hon. FBA 1986. Hon. DSc: Bristol, 1965; McGill, 1967; Durham, 1969; Bath, 1973; Duke, 1978; Oxford, 1979; Hon. LLD: Glasgow, 1975; Aberdeen, 1980. Royal Medal, Royal Society, 1967; Linnean Gold Medal, 1973; Jan Swammerdam Medal, Amsterdam Soc. for Natural Scis and Medicine, 1980. *Publications:* The Life of Vertebrates, 1950, 3rd edn 1981; Doubt and Certainty in Science, 1951; The Life of Mammals, 1957; A Model of the Brain, 1964 (lectures); The Memory System of the Brain, 1966; An Introduction to the Study of Man, 1971; The Anatomy of the Nervous System of *Octopus vulgaris*, 1971; Programs of the Brain, 1978; Philosophy and the Brain, 1987; scientific papers, mostly on the nervous system. *Recreation:* walking. *Address:* 1 The Crossroads, Brill, Bucks HP18 9TL. *T:* Brill (01844) 237412; Department of Experimental Psychology, South Parks Road, Oxford OX1 3UD. *T:* Oxford (01865) 271444, *Fax:* (01865) 310447.

YOUNG, Joyce Jean, RGN, RMN; Regional Nursing Officer, Oxford, 1984–92; independent consultant and advisor to health services, since 1993; *b* 16 Nov. 1936; *d* of Leslie Cyril and Frances May Lyons. *Educ:* Cowes High School, Isle of Wight. General Nurse training, Essex County Hosp., Colchester, 1955–58; Mental Nurse training, Severalls Hosp., Colchester, 1959–60; Ward Sister posts, gen. and psych. hosps, 1960–70; Clinical Nurse Advr, Hosp. Adv. Service, 1970–72; Regl Nurse Advr, SE Metrop. Hosp. Bd for Mental Illness, Mental Handicap and Elderly Services, 1972–74; Dist Nursing Officer, Tunbridge Wells Health Dist., 1974–80; Chief Nursing Officer, Brighton HA, 1980–84. Nursing Advisor to Social Services Select Cttee, 1985–; Mem., Broadmoor Hosp. Management Bd, 1987–; Dir, NSQT, 1992–; Member: Prison Health Adv. Cttee, 1992–; (non-exec.), Bd, Special Hosps Service Authy, 1993–. *Publications:* (contrib.) Impending Crisis of Old Age (Nuffield Provincial Trust), 1981; articles in Nursing Times and Nursing Mirror. *Recreations:* gardening, wild life. *Address:* Skimbles, Swinbrook Road, Shipton-under-Wychwood, Oxfordshire OX7 6DX.

YOUNG, Junor; *see* Young, D. J.

YOUNG, Kenneth Middleton, CBE 1977; Chairman: Student Loans Co. Ltd, since 1992; Further Education Development Agency (formerly Association), since 1994; *b* 1 Aug. 1931; *s* of Cyril W. D. Young and Gwladys Middleton Young; *m* 1958, Brenda May Thomas; one *s* one *d*. *Educ:* Neath Grammar Sch.; University Coll. of Wales, Aberystwyth (Hon. Fellow, 1991); Coll. of Science and Technology, Univ. of Manchester. BA (Hons) 1952; Diploma in Personnel Management, 1954. Pilot Officer/Navigator, General Duties (Aircrew), RAF, 1952–54. Asst Personnel Manager, Elliott-Automation Ltd, 1955–59; Collective Agreements Manager, later Salary Administration Manager, Massey-Ferguson (UK) Ltd, 1959–64; Personnel Adviser, Aviation Div., Smiths Industries Ltd, 1964–66; Group Personnel Manager, General Electric Company Ltd, and Dir, GEC (Management) Ltd, 1966–71; Post Office Corporation, 1972–92: Bd Mem. for Personnel, 1972–84, for Personnel and Corporate Resources, 1984–90; Man. Dir, Royal Mail Parcels, 1987; Vice-Chm., 1986–90; Actg Chm., 1989; Dep. Chm., 1990–92; Chairman: Subscription Services, 1988–92; Girobank PLC, 1989–90; Post Office Counters, 1990–92, Director: Courage (formerly FBG) Pensions Ltd, 1993–; Courage (formerly FBG) Pensions Investments Ltd, 1993–. Member: Management Bd, Engineering Employers Fedn, 1971; CBI Employment Policy Cttee, 1978–84; Employment Appeal Tribunal, 1985–; BIC Target Team on Business/Educn Partnerships, 1988–89; Trustee, Post Office Pension Funds, 1989–. Chm., Rev. Gp, Further Educn Funding Councils for England and Wales, 1993–. Member: Council, Inst. of Manpower Studies, 1980–86; London Business Sch. Liaison Cttee, 1982–89; Chairman: Bd of Govs, SW London Coll., 1991; Roehampton Inst., 1992–95; Vice-Pres., St David's UC, Lampeter, 1993–; Mem. Council, Univ. of Wales, Aberystwyth, 1994–. CIMgt; FIPM. *Recreations:* photography; Wales Rugby; theatre. *Address:* Ingleton, Main Drive, Gerrards Cross, Bucks SL9 7PR. *Club:* East India, Devonshire, Sports and Public Schools.

YOUNG, Sir Leslie (Clarence), Kt 1984; CBE 1980; DL; Chairman, Hoskins Ltd, since 1992; *b* 5 Feb. 1925; *s* of late Clarence James Young and of Ivy Isabel Young; *m* 1949, Muriel Howard Pearson; one *s* one *d*. *Educ:* London School of Economics (DScEcon). Courtaulds Ltd: held range of senior executive appts, incl. chairmanship of number of gp companies, 1948–68; J. Bibby & Sons Ltd, 1968–86: Managing Director, J. Bibby Agriculture Ltd, 1968; Chm. and Man. Dir, J. Bibby Food Products Ltd, 1970; Gp Man. Dir, 1970, Dep. Chm. and Man. Dir, 1977, Chm., 1979–86, J. Bibby & Sons Ltd. Director: Bank of England, 1986–90; National Westminster Bank, 1986–90 (Regl Dir, 1979–90, Chm., 1986–90, Northern Regl Bd); Swiss Pioneer Life (formerly Pioneer Mutual Insce Co.), 1986–92; Sibec Developments PLC, 1988–91; Britannia Cable Systems Wirral plc, 1990–92. Chairman: NW Regional Council, CBI, 1976–78; NW Industrial Development Board, 1978–81; Merseyside Develt Corp., 1981–84; British Waterways Bd, 1984–87; Dir, Lancashire Enterprises Ltd, 1992–. Trustee, Civic Trust for the North West, 1978–83. Non-Exec. Dir, Granada Television Ltd, 1979–84. Chm. Trustees, Nat. Museums and Galls on Merseyside, 1986–95. Member Council: N of England Zoological Soc., 1979–85; Royal Liverpool Philharmonic Soc., 1980–. DL Merseyside, 1983. Hon. Col, Liverpool Univ. OTC, 1989–94. Hon. LLD Liverpool, 1988. *Recreations:* fly-fishing, walking, shooting. *Address:* Overwood, Vicarage Lane, Burton, South Wirral L64 5TJ. *T:* 0151–336 5224. *Club:* Royal Automobile.

YOUNG, Leslie Ronald, (Jimmy Young), CBE 1993 (OBE 1979); Presenter, Jimmy Young Programme, BBC Radio Two, since 1973 (Radio One, 1967–73); *b* 21 Sept.; *s* of Frederick George Young and Gertrude Woolford; *m* 1st, 1946, Wendy Wilkinson (marr. diss.); one *d*; 2nd, 1950, Sally Douglas (marr. diss.). *Educ:* East Dean Grammar Sch., Cinderford, Glos. RAF, 1939–46. First BBC radio broadcast, songs at piano, 1949; pianist, singer, bandleader, West End, London, 1950–51; first theatre appearance, Empire Theatre, Croydon, 1952; regular theatre appearances, 1952–; first radio broadcast introd. records, Flat Spin, 1953; BBC TV Bristol, Pocket Edition series, 1955; first introd. radio Housewives' Choice, 1955; BBC radio series, incl.: The Night is Young, 12 o'clock Spin, Younger Than Springtime, Saturday Special, Keep Young, Through Till Two, 1959–65; presented progs, Radio Luxembourg, 1960–68. BBC TV: series, Jimmy Young Asks, 1972; The World of Jimmy Young, 1973. First live direct BBC broadcasts to Europe from Soviet Union, Jimmy Young Programme, 16 and 17 May 1977; Jimmy Young Programmes broadcast live from Egypt and Israel, 9 and 12 June 1978, from Zimbabwe-Rhodesia, 9 and 10 Aug. 1979; Host for Thames TV of first British Telethon, 2nd and 3rd Oct. 1980; Jimmy Young Programmes live from Tokyo, 26th, 27th and 28th May 1981, from Sydney, 4–8 Oct. 1982, from Washington DC, 3–7 Oct. 1983. ITV series: Whose Baby?, 1973; Jim's World, 1974; The Jimmy Young Television Programme, 1984–87. Hit Records: 1st, Too Young, 1951; Unchained Melody, The Man From Laramie, 1955 (1st Brit. singer to have 2 consec. no 1 hit records); Chain Gang, More, 1956; Miss You, 1963. Weekly Column, Daily Sketch, 1968–71. Hon. Mem. Council, NSPCC, 1981–. Freeman, City of London, 1969. Variety Club of GB Award, Radio Personality of the Year, 1968; Sony Award, Radio Personality of the Year, 1985; Sony Radio Awards Roll of Honour, 1988; Jimmy Young Programme: BBC Current Affairs Prog. of the Year, Daily Mail Nat. Radio Awards, 1988; Radio Prog. of the Year, TV and Radio Inds Club Award, 1989. Silver Jubilee Medal, 1977. *Publications:* Jimmy Young Cookbook: No 1, 1968; No 2, 1969; No 3, 1970; No 4, 1972; (autobiogs) JY, 1973, Jimmy Young, 1982; contrib. magazines, incl. Punch, Woman's Own. *Address:* c/o Broadcasting House, Portland Place, W1A 1AA. *Club:* Wigan Rugby League Social.

YOUNG, Neil; *see* Young, R. N.

YOUNG, Sir Norman (Smith), Kt 1968; formerly Chairman: Pipelines Authority of South Australia; South Australian Brewing Co. Ltd; South Australian Oil and Gas Corporation Pty Ltd; News Ltd; Elder Smith Goldsbrough Mort Ltd; Bradmill Ltd; *b* 24 July 1911; *s* of Thomas and Margaret Young; *m* 1936, Jean Fairbairn Sincock; two *s* one *d*. *Educ:* Norwood High Sch.; University of Adelaide. Member: Adelaide City Council, 1949–60; Municipal Tramways Trust, 1951–67 (Dep. Chairman); Royal Commn on Television, 1953–54; Bankruptcy Law Review Cttee, 1956–62. Fellow, Inst. of Chartered Accountants, 1933; FASA, 1932; Associate in Commerce, University of Adelaide, 1930. *Publication:* Bankruptcy Practice in Australia, 1942. *Address:* 522 Greenhill Road, Hazelwood Park, SA 5006, Australia. *T:* 791684.

YOUNG, Priscilla Helen Ferguson, CBE 1982; Director, Central Council for Education and Training in Social Work, 1971–86; retired; *b* 25 Nov. 1925; *d* of Fergus Ferguson Young and Helen Frances Graham (*née* Murphy). *Educ:* Kingsley Sch., Leamington Spa; Univ. of Edinburgh (MA). Social Worker: London Family Welfare Assoc., 1947–51; Somerset CC Children's Dept, 1951–53; Oxford City Children's Dept, 1953–58 (Dep. Children's Officer); Child and Family Services, Portland, Me, USA, 1958–61; Lectr/Sen. Lectr, Sch. of Social Work, Univ. of Leicester, 1961–71. Nat. Chairperson, Family Service Units, 1987–93. Hon. Fellow, Sheffield City Polytechnic, 1977. Hon. DLitt Ulster, 1987.

YOUNG, Sir Richard (Dilworth), Kt 1970; BSc, FIMechE; Chairman, Boosey & Hawkes Ltd, 1979–84 (Deputy Chairman, 1978–79); Director: The Rugby Group PLC (formerly Rugby Portland Cement Co.), 1968–89; Commonwealth Finance Development Corp. Ltd, 1968–86; *b* 9 April 1914; *s* of Philip Young and Constance Maria Lloyd; *m* 1951, Jean Barbara Paterson Lockwood, *d* of F. G. Lockwood; four *s*. *Educ:* Bromsgrove; Bristol Univ. Joined Weldless Steel Tube Co. Ltd, 1934; served with Tube Investments companies in production and engineering capacities until 1944; Representative of TI in S America and Man. Dir of Tubos Britanicos (Argentina) Ltda, 1945–50; Man. Dir of TI (Export) Ltd, 1950–53; Sales Dir of TI Aluminium Ltd, 1953–56; Asst to Chm. of Tube Investments Ltd, 1957–60; Dir, 1958; Asst Man. Dir, 1959; Man. Dir, 1961–64; Chairman: Park Gate Iron & Steel Co., 1959–64; Raleigh Industries Ltd, 1960–64; Alfred Herbert Ltd: Dep. Chm., 1965–66; Chm., 1966–74; Director: Ingersoll Milling Machine Co., USA, 1967–71; Ingersoll Engineers Inc., 1976–86; Warwick Univ. Sci. Park Ltd, 1983–95; Retirement Securities Ltd, 1983–94. Member: Council BIM, 1960–65; Council, CBI, 1967–74; Council, IMechE, 1969–76; Adv. Cttee on Scientific Manpower, 1962–65; SSRC, 1973–75; Council, Warwick Univ., 1966–89; Central Adv. Council on Science and Technol., 1967–70; SRC Engineering Bd, 1974–76. Freeman, City of London, 1987. CIMgt. Hon. DSc Warwick, 1987. *Club:* Athenæum.

YOUNG, Rob; *see* Young, J. R.

YOUNG, Robert; Competition Policy Consultant, Coopers & Lybrand, since 1993; *b* 27 March 1944; *s* of Walter Horace Young and Evelyn Joan Young; *m* 1965, Patricia Anne Cowin; one *s* one *d* (and one *s* decd). *Educ:* Magdalen College, Oxford (BA Hons 1965). Graduate apprentice, Rolls-Royce, 1965; IBM UK, 1969–71; Rolls-Royce Motors, 1971–81: Man. Dir, Military Engine Div., 1977–79; Dir and Gen. Manager, Diesel Div., 1979–81; Vickers, 1981–85 (Group Commercial Dir, 1981–83); Man. Dir, Crane Ltd, 1985–88; Chief Exec., Plastics Div., McKechnie plc, 1989–90; Dir, Beauford plc, 1990–92. Member: Central Policy Review Staff, 1983; No 10 Policy Unit, 1983–84; CBI W Midlands Regional Council, 1980–81 (Chm., CBI Shropshire, 1981); Monopolies and Mergers Commn, 1986–92; Fulbright Commn, 1994–. FInstD. *Recreations:* Mozart, railways, cats, photography. *Address:* 54 Fordhook Avenue, Ealing, W5 3LR. *Club:* Institute of Directors.

YOUNG, Sir Robert Christopher M.; *see* Mackworth-Young.

YOUNG, Robert Henry; Consultant Orthopædic Surgeon, St George's Hospital, SW1, 1946–68; Hon. Consultant, St Peter's Hospital, Chertsey, 1939–68; *b* 6 Oct. 1903; *s* of James Allen Young and Constance Barrow Young; *m* 1st, 1929, Nancy Willcox; 2nd, 1961, Norma, *d* of Leslie Williams; two *s*. *Educ:* Sherborne Sch.; Emmanuel Coll., Cambridge; St Thomas' Hospital, SE1. *Publications:* numerous articles in leading medical journals. *Address:* Milestone Farm, Ash, near Martock, Somerset TA12 6PD. *Clubs:* United Oxford & Cambridge University, Buck's.

YOUNG, Robin Urquhart; Regional Director, Government Office for London, since 1994; *b* 7 Sept. 1948; *s* of Col Ian U. Young and Mary Young. *Educ:* Fettes Coll., Edinburgh; University Coll., Oxford (BA 1971). Joined DoE, 1973; Private Sec. to Parly Sec., Planning and Local Govt, 1976; Private Sec. to Minister of Housing, 1980–81; Local Govt Finance, 1981–85; Private Sec. to successive Secs of State, 1985–88; Under Secretary: Housing, 1988–89; Envmt Policy, 1989–91; Local Govt Review, 1991–92; Local Govt, DoE, 1992–94; Dep. Sec., 1994–. Dir (non-exec.), Bovis Construction Ltd, 1989–94. *Recreations:* squash, tennis, cinema. *Address:* Government Office for London, Podium 2, Room 023, 2 Marsham Street, SW1P 3EB.

YOUNG, (Roderic) Neil; Investment Consultant, since 1989; *b* 29 May 1933; *s* of late Dr F. H. Young and of S. M. Young (*née* Robinson); *m* 1962, Gillian Margaret Salmon; two *s* one *d*. *Educ:* Eton; Trinity College, Cambridge (MA). FCA. 2nd Lieut Queen's Own Royal West Kent Regt, 1952–53. Howard Howes & Co., 1956–59; Fenn & Crosthwaite, 1960–63; Brown Fleming & Murray, 1964–68; Director: Murray Johnstone, 1969–70; Kleinwort Benson, 1971–88. Director: Malvern UK Index Trust, 1990–; London and SE Bd, Bradford and Bingley Bldg Soc., 1990–. City of London: Mem., Court of Common Council, 1980; Alderman, Ward of Bread Street, 1982–94; Sheriff, 1991–92; Master, Gunmakers' Co., 1994–95. Adv. Cttee, Greenwich Hosp. *Recreations:* gardening, shooting, DIY, golf. *Address:* Pembury Hall, Pembury, Kent TN2 4AT. *T:* Pembury (01892) 822971. *Clubs:* City Livery; Rye Golf.

YOUNG, Roger; Chief Executive, Scottish Hydro-Electric plc, since 1988; *b* 14 Jan. 1944; *s* of Arnold and Margaret Young; *m* 1970, Susan Neilson; one *s* two *d*. *Educ:* Gordonstoun Sch.; Edinburgh Univ. (BSc Engrg); Cranfield Business Sch. (MBA). Rolls-Royce Ltd, 1961–72; Alidair Ltd, 1972–73; Wavin Plastics Ltd, 1973–76; Aurora Holdings Ltd, 1976–80; Low & Bonar plc, 1980–88. Non-executive Director: Ivory & Sime plc; Bank of Scotland, 1994–. *Recreations:* family, hill walking. *Address:* Scottish Hydro-Electric plc, 10 Dunkeld Road, Perth PH1 5WA. *Club:* Caledonian.

YOUNG, Roger Dudley; Director General, Institute of Management, since 1992; *b* 7 Jan. 1940; *s* of Henry G. Young and Winifred G. Young; *m* 1965, Jennifer J. Drayton; one *s* two *d*. *Educ:* Dulwich Coll. AIIMR; CIMgt. Drayton Group, 1958–69; Imperial Group, 1969–73; Robert Fleming, 1971–73; Director: Henry Ansbacher Group, 1973–82;

Touche Remnant Group, 1982–85; Chief Executive: Bank Julius Baer (London), 1985–89; March Group, 1989–91. Chairman: Clex Developments, 1976–; Winsade Finance, 1967–; Director: Foundn for Management Educn, 1992–; Nat. Forum for Management Educn and Develt, 1989–; European Inst. of Management Ltd, 1992–; Management Verification Consortium Ltd, 1992–; Ipswich Hosp. NHS Trust, 1992–; non-exec. appts. *Recreations:* small businesses, tennis, sculpture. *Address:* Ashbrook House, Layham Road, Layham, Ipswich IP7 5NB. *T:* (office) 0171–497 0580. *Clubs:* Athenæum, Honourable Artillery Company.

YOUNG, Sir Roger (William), Kt 1983; MA; STh, LHD, FRSE; Principal of George Watson's College, Edinburgh, 1958–85; *b* 15 Nov. 1923; *yr s* of late Charles Bowden Young and Dr Ruth Young, CBE; *m* 1950, Caroline Mary Christie; two *s* two *d. Educ:* Dragon Sch., Oxford; Westminster Sch. (King's Scholar); Christ Church, Oxford (Scholar). Served War of 1939–45, RNVR, 1942–45. Classical Mods, 1946, Lit Hum 1948. Resident Tutor, St Catharine's, Cumberland Lodge, Windsor, 1949–51; Asst Master, The Manchester Grammar Sch., 1951–58. 1st Class in Archbishop's examination in Theology (Lambeth Diploma), 1957. Participant, US State Dept Foreign Leader Program, 1964. Scottish Governor, BBC, 1979–84. Member: Edinburgh Marriage Guidance Council, 1960–75; Scottish Council of Christian Educn Movement, 1960–81 (Chm., 1961–67; Hon. Vice-Pres., 1981–85); Gen. Council of Christian Educn Movement, 1985–94 (Vice-Pres., 1989–); Management Assoc., SE Scotland, 1965–85; Educational Research Bd of SSRC, 1966–70; Court, Edinburgh Univ., 1967–76; Public Schools Commn, 1968–70; Consultative Cttee on the Curriculum, 1972–75; Adv. Cttee, Scottish Centre for Studies in Sch. Administration, 1972–75; Royal Soc. of Edinburgh Dining Club, 1972–; Scottish Adv. Cttee, Community Service Volunteers, 1973–78; Edinburgh Festival Council, 1970–76; Independent Schs Panel of Wolfson Foundn, 1978–82; Gen. Adv. Council of BBC, 1978–79; Scottish Council of Independent Schs, 1978–85; Royal Observatory Trust, Edin., 1981–93; Council, RSE, 1982–85; ISJC, 1988–94. Hon. Sec., Headmasters' Assoc. of Scotland, 1968–72, Pres., 1972–74; Chairman: HMC, 1976; BBC Consult. Gp on Social Effects of TV, 1978–79; Bursary Bd, Dawson International Ltd, 1977–85; Bath Film Soc., 1990–93; Dep. Chm., GBA, 1988–94. Trustee: Campion Sch., Athens, 1984–91; Wells Cathedral Sch., 1987–; Chm. Council, Cheltenham Ladies' Coll., 1986–93; Member, Governing Body: Westminster Sch., 1986–; Royal Sch., Bath, 1987–; Mem. Council, Bath Univ., 1993–. Conducted Enquiry on Stirling Univ., 1973. Hon. LHD, Hamilton Coll., Clinton, NY, 1978. *Publications:* Lines of Thought, 1958; Everybody's Business, 1968; Everybody's World, 1970; Report on the Policies and Running of Stirling University 1966–1973, 1973. *Recreations:* gardening, films, photography, climbing, golf, knitting. *Address:* 11 Belgrave Terrace, Bath, Avon BA1 5JR. *T:* Bath (01225) 336940. *Club:* East India.

YOUNG, Sheriff Sir Stephen Stewart Templeton, 3rd Bt, *cr* 1945; Sheriff of North Strathclyde at Greenock, since 1984; advocate; *b* 24 May 1947; *s* of Sir Alastair Young, 2nd Bt, and Dorothy Constance Marcelle (*d* 1964), *d* of late Lt-Col Charles Ernest Chambers, and *widow* of Lt J. H. Grayburn, VC, Parachute Regt; *S* father, 1963; *m* 1974, Viola Margaret Nowell-Smith, *d* of Prof. P. H. Nowell-Smith, *qv* and Perilla Thyme (she *m* 2nd, Lord Roberthall, KCMG, CB); two *s. Educ:* Rugby; Trinity Coll., Oxford; Edinburgh Univ. Voluntary Service Overseas, Sudan, 1968–69. Sheriff of Glasgow and Strathkelvin, March-June 1984. *Heir: s* Charles Alastair Stephen Young, *b* 21 July 1979. *Address:* Glen Rowan, Shore Road, Cove, Dunbartonshire G84 0NU.

YOUNG, Thomas Nesbitt; HM Diplomatic Service; Ambassador to Azerbaijan, since 1993; *b* 24 July 1943; *s* of Sir Frank Young, FRS and Lady Young; *m* 1971, Elisabeth Ann Shepherdson Hick; one *s* one *d. Educ:* The Leys Sch., Cambridge; Pembroke Coll., Oxford (BA Hons Chem., MA). Teaching, Kigezi Coll., Kabale, Uganda, 1962; joined HM Diplomatic Service, 1966; Ankara, 1969–71; Madrid, 1972–76; Head of Chancery, Ankara, 1979–80; Dep. Dir of Trade Develt, NY, 1981; First Sec., Washington, 1981–84; Asst Head, Nuclear Energy Dept, FCO, 1984–86; Dep. High Comr, Accra, 1987–90; Dir of Trade Promotion, British High Commn, Canberra, 1990–93. *Recreations:* hill-walking, sailing, Renaissance music, reaching inaccessible places. *Address:* c/o Foreign and Commonwealth Office, King Charles Street, SW1A 2AH.

YOUNG, Timothy Mark Stewart; Headmaster, Royal Grammar School, Guildford, since 1992; *b* 6 Oct. 1951; *s* of Sir Brian Walter Mark Young, *qv*; *m* 1990, Dr Alison Mary Keightley, MRCP, FRCR; two *s. Educ:* Eton (King's Schol.); Magdalene Coll., Cambridge (BA 1974; MA 1978); Bristol Univ. (PGCE 1975). Asst Master, Eton, 1975–83 and 1985–87; Asst Master, Wanganui Collegiate Sch., NZ, 1984; Teacher, Harvard Sch., Los Angeles, 1987–88; Housemaster, Eton, 1988–92. FRSA. *Recreations:* music, cinema, travel, Watford FC. *Address:* Cobbetts, Mavins Road, Farnham, Surrey GU9 8JS. *Club:* County (Guildford).

YOUNG, Wayland; *see* Kennet, Baron.

YOUNG, William Hilary, CMG 1957; HM Diplomatic Service, retired; Ambassador to Colombia 1966–70; *b* 14 Jan. 1913; *s* of late Rev. Arthur John Christopher Young and Ethel Margaret (*née* Goodwin); *m* 1st, 1946, Barbara Gordon Richmond, *d* of late Gordon Park Richmond; one *s* one *d*; 2nd, 1986, Virginia, *widow* of Sir Ivo Stourton, CMG, OBE, KPM. *Educ:* Marlborough Coll.; Emmanuel Coll., Cambridge. Entered Consular Service, 1935; served HM Legation, Tehran, 1938–41; Foreign Office, 1941–45; 1st Secretary, 1945; Berlin (Political Division, Control Commission), 1945–48; HM Legation, Budapest, 1948–50; attached to IDC, 1951; Counsellor: UK High Commn, New Delhi, 1952–54; Foreign Office, 1954–57; Minister, Moscow, 1957–60; Senior Civilian Instructor, IDC, 1960–62; Minister, British Embassy, Pretoria and Cape Town, 1962–65; Fellow, Harvard University Center for Internat. Affairs, 1965–66. *Address:* The Old Bakery, Kimpton, Andover, Hants SP11 8NU.

YOUNG, Hon. William Lambert, CMG 1992; JP; High Commissioner for New Zealand in UK, 1982–85; concurrently Ambassador to Ireland and High Commissioner in Nigeria, 1982–85; *b* 13 Nov. 1913; *s* of James Young and Alice Gertrude Annie Young; *m* 1946, Isobel Joan Luke; one *s* four *d. Educ:* Wellington Coll. Commenced work, 1930; spent first 16 yrs with farm servicing co., interrupted by War Service, N Africa with Eighth Army, 1940–43; took over management of wholesale distributing co. handling imported and NZ manufactured goods; Gen. Man. of co. manufg and distributing radios, records, electronic equipment and owning 32 retail stores, 1956; purchased substantial interest in importing and distributing business, 1962. MP (National) Miramar, 1966–81; Minister of Works and Develt, 1975–81; introduced Women's Rights of Employment Bill, 1975; Pres., Assoc. of Former MPs of NZ, 1993–. Formerly Chairman: National Roads Bd; National Water and Soil Authority; NZ Fishing Licensing Authority. Formerly Director: Johnsons Wax of NZ Ltd (subsid. of USA Co.); Howard Rotovator Co. Ltd; AA Mutual Insurance Co.; J. J. Niven Ltd; NZ Motor Bodies Ltd; Trustee, Wellington Savings Bank. Pres., Star Boating Club, 1981–; Mem. Council, NZ Amateur Rowing Assoc., 1984–87. Life Mem., AA of Wellington (Mem. Council, 1976–). JP 1962. *Address:* 3/28 Oriental Terrace, Oriental Bay, Wellington 6001, New Zealand. *T:* (4) 8018030. *Club:* Wellington (Wellington, NZ).

YOUNG, Sir William Neil, 10th Bt, *cr* 1769; Head of Middle East, Barclays International Private Banking, since 1994; *b* 22 Jan. 1941; *s* of Captain William Elliot Young, RAMC (killed in action 27 May 1942), and Mary, *d* of late Rev. John Macdonald; *S* grandfather, 1944; *m* 1965, Christine Veronica Morley, *o d* of late R. B. Morley, Buenos Aires; one *s* one *d. Educ:* Wellington Coll.; Sandhurst. Captain, 16th/5th The Queen's Royal Lancers, retired 1970. Dir, Kleinwort Benson International Investment Ltd, 1982–87; Head: Investment Management, Saudi Internat. Bank, 1987–91; ME Dept, Coutts & Co., 1991–94. *Recreations:* ski-ing, sailing, tennis, shooting. *Heir: s* William Lawrence Elliot Young, *b* 26 May 1970. *Address:* Penchrise Peel, Hawick, Roxburghshire TD9 9UA. *Clubs:* Cavalry and Guards; Hong Kong (Hong Kong).

YOUNGER, family name of **Viscount Younger of Leckie** and **Baron Younger of Prestwick.**

YOUNGER OF LECKIE, 3rd Viscount, *cr* 1923; **Edward George Younger;** OBE 1940; 3rd Bt of Leckie, *cr* 1911; Lord-Lieutenant, Stirling and Falkirk (formerly of County of Stirling), 1964–79; Colonel, Argyll and Sutherland Highlanders (TA); *b* 21 Nov. 1906; *er s* of 2nd Viscount and Maud (*d* 1957), *e d* of Sir John Gilmour, 1st Bt; *S* father 1946; *m* 1930, Evelyn Margaret, MBE (*d* 1983), *e d* of late Alexander Logan McClure, KC; three *s* one *d. Educ:* Winchester; New Coll., Oxford. Served War of 1939–45 (OBE). *Heir: s* Baron Younger of Prestwick, *qv. Address:* Leckie, Gargunnock, Stirling FK8 3BN. *T:* Gargunnock (01786) 860281. *Club:* New (Edinburgh).

See also Hon. R. E. G. Younger.

YOUNGER OF PRESTWICK, Baron *cr* 1992 (Life Peer), of Ayr in the District of Kyle and Carrick; **George Kenneth Hotson Younger,** KCVO 1993; TD 1964; PC 1979; DL; FRSE; Chairman: Royal Bank of Scotland, since 1990 (Director, since 1989; Deputy Chairman, 1990); Royal Bank of Scotland Group, since 1991; *b* 22 Sept. 1931; *e s* and *heir* of 3rd Viscount Younger of Leckie, *qv*; *m* 1954, Diana Rhona, *er d* of Captain G. S. Tuck, RN, Little London, Chichester, Sussex; three *s* one *d. Educ:* Cargilfield Sch., Edinburgh; Winchester Coll. (Fellow, 1992–); New Coll., Oxford. Commnd in Argyll and Sutherland Highlanders, 1950; served BAOR and Korea, 1951; 7th Bn Argyll and Sutherland Highlanders (TA), 1951–65; Hon. Col, 154 (Lowland) Transport Regt, RCT, T&AVR, 1977–85. Chairman: Siemens Plessey Electronic Systems, 1990–; SPEED plc, 1992–; Murray Johnston Trusts, 1993– (Dir, 1989–; Dep. Chm., 1992–93); Director: George Younger & Son Ltd, 1958–68; J. G. Thomson & Co. Ltd, Leith, 1962–66; Maclachlans Ltd, 1968–70; Tennant Caledonian Breweries Ltd, 1977–79; Scottish Equitable Life Assurance Soc., 1990–; PIK Ltd (formerly Ayrshire Community Airport Project), 1991–. Contested (U) North Lanarkshire, 1959; Unionist Candidate for Kinross and West Perthshire, 1963, but stood down in favour of Sir A. Douglas-Home. MP (C) Ayr, 1964–92; Scottish Conservative Whip, 1965–67; Parly Under-Sec. of State for Develt, Scottish Office, 1970–74; Minister of State for Defence, 1974; Sec. of State for Scotland, 1979–86; Sec. of State for Defence, 1986–89. Chm., Conservative Party in Scotland, 1974–75 (Dep. Chm., 1967–70); Pres., Nat. Union of Cons. and Unionist Assocs, 1987–88. Chancellor, Napier Univ., 1993–. Pres., Royal Highland and Agricl Soc., 1990; Chairman: Royal Anniversary Trust, 1990–; Romanian Orphanage Trust, 1990; Edinburgh Festival (formerly Empire) Theatre Trust, 1991–; Royal Armouries, 1994–. Brig., Queen's Body Guard for Scotland (Royal Company of Archers). DL Stirlingshire, 1968. Hon. LLD Glasgow, 1992; Dr *hc* Edinburgh, 1992; Hon. DLitt Napier, 1992. *Recreations:* music, tennis, sailing, golf. *Address:* 67 Lombard Street, EC3P 3DL. *Clubs:* Caledonian; Highland Brigade.

See also Hon. R. E. G. Younger.

YOUNGER, Maj.-Gen. Allan Elton, DSO 1944; OBE 1962; MA; Director-General, Royal United Services Institute for Defence Studies, 1976–78; *b* 4 May 1919; *s* of late Brig. Arthur Allan Shakespear Younger, DSO, and late Marjorie Rhoda Younger (*née* Halliley); *m* 1942, Diana Lanyon; three *d. Educ:* Gresham's; RMA Woolwich; Christ's Coll., Cambridge. Commnd RE, 1939; France and Belgium, 1940; France, Holland and Germany, 1944–45; Burma, 1946–47; Malaya, 1948; Korea, 1950–51; RMA Sandhurst, 1954–57; Bt Lt-Col 1959; comd 36 Corps Engineer Regt in UK and Kenya, 1960–62; Instructor US Army Comd and Gen. Staff Coll., Fort Leavenworth, 1963–66; Programme Evaluation Gp, 1966–68; Chief Engr, Army Strategic Comd, 1968–69; COS, HQ Allied Forces Northern Europe, Oslo, 1970–72; Sen. Army Mem., Directing Staff, RCDS, 1972–75. Col Comdt, RE, 1974–79. Mem. Council, Lord Kitchener Nat. Meml Fund. Silver Star (US), 1951. *Publications:* contribs to RUSI Jl, Military Review (USA). *Recreation:* gardening.

YOUNGER, David; *see* Younger, J. D. B.

YOUNGER, (James) Samuel; Managing Director, BBC World Service, since 1994; *b* 5 Oct. 1951; *s* of Rt Hon. Sir Kenneth Gilmour Younger, KBE, PC and Elisabeth Kirsteen (*née* Stewart); *m* 1984, Katherine Anne Spencer; one *s. Educ:* Westminster Sch.; New Coll., Oxford (BA Hons). Asst Editor, Middle East International, 1972–78; BBC World Service: Sen. Asst, Central Current Affairs Talks, 1979–84; Sen. Producer and Exec. Producer, Current Affairs, 1984–86; Asst Head, Arabic Service, 1986–87; Head, Current Affairs, 1987–89; Head, Arabic Serivce, 1989–92; Controller, Overseas Services, 1992–94; Director of Broadcasting, 1994. *Recreations:* sport, choral singing. *Address:* 28 Rylett Crescent, W12 9RL. *T:* 0181–743 4449.

YOUNGER, Captain (John) David (Bingham); Lord-Lieutenant of Tweeddale, since 1994 (Vice Lord-Lieutenant, 1992–94); Managing Director, Broughton Brewery, since 1979; *b* 20 May 1939; *s* of Major Oswald Bingham Younger, MC, A and SH, and Dorothea Elizabeth Younger (*née* Hobbs); *m* 1962, Anne Rosaleen Logan; one *s* two *d. Educ:* Eton Coll.; RMA Sandhurst. Regular Army, Argyll and Sutherland Highlanders, 1957–69; Scottish and Newcastle Breweries, 1969–79. Chairman: Belhaven Hill Trust, 1986–94; Scottish Borders Tourist Board, 1989–91; Dir, Queen's Hall (Edinburgh) Ltd, 1992–. Mem., Royal Company of Archers, Queen's Body Guard for Scotland, 1969– (Sec., 1993–). DL Borders, 1988. *Recreations:* country pursuits. *Address:* Kirkurd House, Blyth Bridge, Peeblesshire EH46 7AH. *T:* Peebles (01721) 752223.

YOUNGER, Maj.-Gen. Sir John William, 3rd Bt *cr* 1911; CBE 1969 (MBE 1945); Commissioner-in-Chief, St John Ambulance Brigade, 1980–85; *b* 18 Nov. 1920; *s* of Sir William Robert Younger, 2nd Bt, and of Joan Gwendoline Johnstone (later Mrs Dennis Wheatley; she *d* 1982); *S* father, 1973; *m* 1st, 1948, Mrs Stella Jane Dodd (marr. diss. 1952), *d* of Rev. John George Lister; one *s* one *d*; 2nd, 1953, Marcella Granito, Princess Pignatelli Di Belmonte (*d* 1989), *d* of Prof. Avv. R. Scheggi; 3rd, 1991, Anne Henrietta Maria St Paul Seely, *o d* of Horace George St Paul Butler. *Educ:* Canford Sch.; RMC Sandhurst. Served War 1939–45, Middle East (PoW) (MBE); 2nd Lt, Coldstream Gds, 1939; staff coll., Camberley, 1949; Lt Col 1959; Comd, 1st Bn Coldstream Guards; AQMG, HQ London Dist, 1961–63; Col 1963; AAG, War Office, 1963–65; NDC, New Delhi, 1966; Brig. 1967; Dep. Dir, Army Staff Duties, MoD, 1967–70; Dir of Quartering (A), MoD, 1970–73; Maj.-Gen. 1971; Dir, Management and Support of Intelligence, 1973–76. Chm. or Mem., various Civil Service Commn and Home Office Interview Bds. Dep. Comr, St John Ambulance Bde, London (Prince of Wales's) Dist, 1978. KStJ 1980.

Recreations: reading, photography, travel. *Heir:* *s* Julian William Richard Younger, [*b* 10 Feb. 1950; *m* 1981, Deborah Ann Wood; one *s*]. *Address:* 23 Cadogan Square, SW1X 0HU. *Club:* Boodle's.

YOUNGER, Hon. Robert Edward Gilmour; Sheriff of Tayside, Central and Fife, since 1982; *b* 25 Sept. 1940; third *s* of 3rd Viscount Younger of Leckie, *qv*; *m* 1972, Helen Jane Hayes; one *s* one *d*. *Educ:* Cargilfield Sch., Edinburgh; Winchester Coll.; New Coll., Oxford (MA); Edinburgh Univ. (LLB); Glasgow Univ. Advocate, 1968; Sheriff of Glasgow and Strathkelvin, 1979–82. *Recreation:* out of doors. *Address:* Old Leckie, Gargunnock, Stirling, Scotland FK8 3BN. *T:* Gargunnock (01786) 860213.

See also Baron Younger of Prestwick.

YOUNGER, Samuel; *see* Younger, J. S.

YOUNGSON, Prof. Alexander John, CBE 1987; Emeritus Professor, Australian National University, since 1980; *b* 28 Sept. 1918; *s* of Alexander Brown, MA, MB, ChB and Helen Youngson; *m* 1948, Elizabeth Gisborne Naylor; one *s* one *d*. *Educ:* Aberdeen Grammar Sch.; Aberdeen Univ. Pilot, Fleet Air Arm, 1940–45. MA Aberdeen Univ., 1947; Commonwealth Fellow, 1947–48. Lecturer, University of St Andrews, 1948–50; Lecturer, University of Cambridge, 1950–58; Prof. of Political Economy 1963–74, and Vice-Principal, 1971–74, Univ. of Edinburgh; Dir, Res. Sch. of Social Scis, ANU, 1974–80; Prof. of Econs, Univ. of Hong Kong, 1980–82. Chm., Royal Fine Art Commn for Scotland, 1983–90 (Mem., 1972–74). Hon. FRIAS 1984. DLitt Aberdeen, 1952; DUniv York, 1993. *Publications:* The American Economy, 1860–1940, 1951; Possibilities of Economic Progress, 1959; The British Economy, 1920–1957, 1960; The Making of Classical Edinburgh, 1966; Overhead Capital, 1967; After the Forty-Five, 1973; Beyond the Highland Line, 1974; Scientific Revolution in Victorian Medicine, 1979; (ed) China and Hong Kong: the economic nexus, 1983; The Prince and the Pretender, 1985; Urban Development and the Royal Fine Art Commission, 1990; Edinburgh and the Border Country, 1993; contrib. to various journals devoted to economics and economic history. *Recreation:* gardening. *Address:* 17 The Horseshoe, York YO2 2LY.

YOUNIE, Edward Milne, OBE 1978; HM Diplomatic Service, retired; Consultant, Trefoil Associates, since 1983; *b* 9 Feb. 1926; *s* of John Milne and Mary Dickie Younie; *m* 1st, 1952, Mary Groves (*d* 1976); 2nd, 1979, Mimi Barkley (marr. annulled 1991); 3rd, 1994, Mrs Alyn Denholm. *Educ:* Fettes Coll. (Scholar); Gonville and Caius Coll., Cambridge (Scholar) (BA Hons). RN, 1944–46. HM Colonial Service, Tanganyika, 1950–62; FCO, 1963; Johannesburg, 1964–67; Blantyre, 1967–69; First Secretary: Lagos, 1972–76; Nairobi, 1977–79; Salisbury, 1979–81 (Counsellor, 1980); FCO, 1981–82. *Recreations:* golf, tennis, music. *Address:* Wester Corsehill, Thornhill, Stirling FK8 3QD. *Club:* Brooks's.

YOUNSON, Maj.-Gen. Eric John, OBE 1952; Eur Ing; CEng, FRAeS, FIMgt; *b* 1 March 1919; *o s* of late Ernest M. Younson, MLitt, BCom, Jarrow; *m* 1946, Jean Beaumont Carter, BA; three *d*. *Educ:* Jarrow Grammar Sch.; Univ. of Durham (BSc); Royal Military Coll. of Science. Served War of 1939–45: commissioned, RA, 1940; UK and NW Europe (despatches). Directing Staff, RMCS, 1953–55; Atomic Weapons Research Estab., 1957–58; Attaché (Washington) as rep. of Chief Scientific Adviser, 1958–61; Head of Defence Science 3, MoD, 1961–63; Dep. Dir of Artillery, 1964–66; Dir of Guided Weapons Trials and Ranges, Min. of Technology, 1967–69; Vice-Pres., Ordnance Board, 1970–72, Pres., 1972–73, retired 1973; Sen. Asst Dir, Central Bureau for Educnl Visits and Exchanges, 1973–74; Dep. Dir, SIMA, 1974–78; Sec.-Gen., EUROM, 1975–77; Clerk to Worshipful Co. of Scientific Instrument Makers, 1976–87 (Hon. Liveryman and Clerk Emeritus, 1987). FRSA. Freeman, City of London, 1981. *Publications:* The Worshipful Company of Scientific Instrument Makers: history, 1988; articles on gunnery and scientific subjects in Service jls; occasional poetry. *Recreations:* photography, electronics. *Address:* 7 Pondwick Road, Harpenden, Herts AL5 2HG. *T:* Harpenden (01582) 621691.

YURKO, Allen Michael; Managing Director and Chief Executive Officer, SIEBE plc, since 1994; *b* 25 Sept. 1951; *s* of Mike Yurko and Catherine (*née* Ewanishan); *m* 1991, Gayle Marie Skelley. *Educ:* Lehigh Univ. (BA Bus. and Econs); Baldwin-Wallace Coll., USA (MBA). Divl Controller, Joy Mfg, 1978–81; Gp Controller, Eaton Corp., 1981–83; Chief Financial Officer and Gp Vice-Pres., Mueller Hldgs, 1983–89; Robertshaw Controls: Vice-Pres. of Finance, 1989–90; Pres., 1990–91; Pres. and Chief Operating Officer, Siebe T. & A. Controls, 1991–92; Man. Dir and Chief Operating Officer, SIEBE plc, 1992–93. *Recreations:* boating, golf, sports cars, theatre. *Address:* SIEBE plc, Saxon House, Victoria Street, Windsor, Berks SL4 1EN. *T:* Windsor (01753) 855411. *Clubs:* Annabel's; Sunningdale Golf.

YUSUF, Dr Abul Faiz Mohammad, FRCPE; High Commissioner for People's Republic of Bangladesh in London, since 1992 and Ambassador to Portugal, since 1993; *b* 1 Nov. 1926; *s* of late Dr M. D. Omar and Mahmuda Omar; *m* 1952, Rokeya Yusuf (*d* 1991); one *s* two *d*. *Educ:* Univ. of Dhaka (MB BS); Univ. of Edinburgh (DTM&H). General practice in Medicine, 1952–63; Consultant Physician, 1967–91. *Recreations:* fishing, gardening, reading, travels. *Address:* 7 Spaniards Close, Hampstead, NW11. *T:* 0181–209 0169; Bangladesh High Commission, 28 Queen's Gate, SW7 5JA. *Clubs:* Chittagong, Lions International (Chittagong).

Z

ZACHARIAH, Joyce Margaret; Secretary of the Post Office, 1975–77; *b* 11 Aug. 1932; *d* of Robert Paton Emery and Nellie Nicol (*née* Wilson); *m* 1978, George Zachariah. *Educ:* Earl Grey Sch., Calgary, Canada; Hillhead High Sch., Glasgow; Glasgow Univ. (MA 1st cl. Hons French and German, 1956). Post Office: Asst Principal, 1956; Private Sec. to Dir Gen., 1960; Principal, 1961; Asst Sec., 1967; Dir, Chairman's Office, 1970. *Address:* Kelvinbrae, Wisborough Lane, Storrington, W Sussex RH20 4ND.
See also E. J. Emery.

ZACHAROV, Prof. Vasilii, (Basil), PhD, DSc; consultant; Director of Information Processing, International Organization for Standardization, Geneva, 1990–95 (Head of Information Processing, 1989–90); *b* 2 Jan. 1931; *s* of Viktor Nikiforovich Zakharov and Varvara Semyenovna (*née* Krzak); *m* 1959, Jeanne (*née* Hopper) one *s* one *d*. *Educ:* Latymer Upper Sch.; Univ. of London (BSc: Maths 1951, Phys 1952; MSc 1958; PhD 1960; DIC 1960; DSc 1977). Research in Computer systems and applications, Birkbeck Coll., 1953–56; digital systems development, Rank Precision Instruments, 1956–57; Research Fellow, Imperial Coll., 1957–60; Physicist, European Organisation for Nuclear Res. (CERN), Geneva, 1960–65; Reader in Experimental Physics, Queen Mary Coll., London, 1965–66; Head of Computer Systems and Electronics Div., as Sen. Principal Sci. Officer, SRC Daresbury Laboratory, 1966–69, Dep. Chief Sci. Officer, 1970–78; Dir, London Univ. Computing Centre, 1978–80, and Prof. of Computing Systems, 1979–80; Sen. Associate, CERN, Geneva, 1981–83; Invited Prof., Univ. of Geneva, 1984–87. Vis Scientist: JINR Dubna, USSR, 1965; CERN, 1971–72; Consultant to AERE Harwell, 1965; Vis. Prof. of Physics, QMC London, 1968; Vis. Prof., Westfield Coll., 1974–78. Member, SRC Comp. Sci. Cttee, 1974–77. *Publications:* Digital Systems Logic, 1968, and other books; scientific papers in professional jls on photoelectronics, computer systems, elementary particle physics and computer applications. *Recreations:* collecting Russian miscellanea, skiing, shooting, amateur radio; grape growing, wine making, wine drinking. *Address:* The Firs, Oldcastle, Cheshire SY14 7NE.

ZAHIRUDDIN bin Syed Hassan, Tun Syed, SPCM 1987; SMN, PSM, DUNM; SPMP 1970; JMN, PJK; Hon. GCVO 1974; Orang Besat Empat, Perak, since 1984; a Pro-Chancellor, University of Malaya, since 1987; *b* 11 Oct. 1918; *m* 1949, Toh Puan Halimah, *d* of Haji Mohamed Noh; five *s* five *d*. *Educ:* Malay Coll., Kuala Kangsar; Raffles Coll., Singapore (Dip.Arts). Passed Cambridge Sch. Cert. Malay Officer, Tanjong Malim, etc, 1945–47; Dep. Asst Dist Officer, 1948; Asst Dist Officer, 1951–54; 2nd Asst State Sec., Perak, 1955; Registrar of Titles and Asst State Sec. (Lands), Perak, 1956; Dist Officer, Batang Padang, Tapah, 1957; Dep. Sec., Public Services Commn, 1958; Principal Asst Sec. (Service), Fedn Estabt Office, Kuala Lumpur, 1960; State Sec., Perak, 1961; Permanent Sec.: Min. of Agric. and Co-operatives, Kuala Lumpur, 1963; Min. of Educn, Kuala Lumpur, 1966; Dir-Gen., Public Services Dept, Kuala Lumpur, 1969; retd, 1972. Chm., Railway Services Commn, Kuala Lumpur, 1972–73. High Comr for Malaysia in London, 1974–75; Governor of Malacca, 1975–84. Chairman: Special Cttee on Superannuation in the Public Services, 1972, and Statutory Bodies; Bd of Governors, Malay Coll., Kuala Kangsar; Interim Council of Nat. Inst. of Technology; Central Bd. Vice-Pres., Subang Nat. Golf Club, 1972–74. *Recreation:* golf. *Address:* Rumah Keledong, No 10 Jalan Tun Dr Ismail, 30350 Ipoh, Malaysia.

ZAMBONI, Richard Frederick Charles, FCA; Managing Director, 1979–89 and a Vice-Chairman, 1986–89, Sun Life Assurance Society plc; Chairman, Avon Enterprise Fund PLC, since 1990 (Director, since 1984); *b* 28 July 1930; *s* of Alfred Charles Zamboni and Frances Hosler; *m* 1960, Pamela Joan Marshall (*d* 1993); two *s* one *d*. *Educ:* Monkton House Sch., Cardiff. Gordon Thomas & Pickard, Chartered Accountants, 1948–54; served Royal Air Force, 1954–56; Peat Marwick Mitchell & Co., 1956–58; British Egg Marketing Board, 1959–70, Chief Accountant, from 1965; Sun Life Assurance Society plc, 1971–89, Director, 1975–89; Chairman: Sun Life Investment Management Services, 1985–89; Sun Life Trust Management, 1985–89; Sun Life Direct Marketing, 1986–89. Deputy Chairman: Life Offices' Assoc., 1985 (Mem., Management Cttee, 1981–85); Assoc. of British Insurers, 1986–88 (Dep. Chm., 1985–86, Chm., 1986–88, Life Insurance Council); Member: Council, Chartered Insurance Inst., 1983–85; Life Assurance and Unit Trust Regulatory Orgn's steering gp, 1985–86; Hon. Treasurer, Insurance Institute of London, 1982–85. Member, Management Cttee, Effingham Housing Assoc. Ltd, 1980–86; Chm., Council of Management, Grange Centre for the Handicapped, 1991–. Pres., Insurance Offices RFU, 1985–87. *Recreations:* ornithology, gardening, golf. *Address:* Long Meadow, Beech Avenue, Effingham, Leatherhead, Surrey KT24 5PH. *T:* Bookham (01372) 458211.

ZAMYATIN, Leonid Mitrofanovich; Soviet Ambassador to the Court of St James's, 1986–91; *b* Nizhni Devitsk, 9 March 1922; *m* 1946; one *d*. *Educ:* Moscow Aviation Inst.; Higher Diplomatic School. Mem., CPSU, 1944–91 (apptd Mem. Central Cttee, 1976); Min. of Foreign Affairs, 1946; First Sec., Counsellor on Political Questions, USSR Mission to UN, 1953–57; Soviet Dep. Rep., Preparatory Cttee, later Bd of Governors, IAEA, 1957–59; Soviet Rep., IAEA, 1959–60; Dep. Head, American Countries Dept, Min. of Foreign Affairs, 1960–62; Head of Press Dept, 1962–70; Mem., Collegium of Ministry, 1962–70; Dir-Gen., TASS News Agency, 1970–78, Govt Minister, 1972; Dep. to USSR Supreme Soviet, 1970–89; Chief, Dept of Internat. Inf., Central Cttee, CPSU, 1978–86. Mem., Commn for Foreign Relations, Soviet of Nationalities, 1974. Lenin Prize 1978; USSR Orders and medals incl. Order of Lenin (twice).

ZANDER, Prof. Michael; Professor of Law, London School of Economics, since 1977; *b* 16 Nov. 1932; *s* of late Dr Walter Zander and Margaret Magnus; *m* 1965, Betsy Treeger; one *d* one *s*. *Educ:* Royal Grammar Sch., High Wycombe; Jesus Coll., Cambridge (BA Law, double 1st Cl. Hons; LLB 1st Cl. Hons; Whewell Scholar in Internat. Law); Harvard Law Sch. (LLM). Solicitor of the Supreme Court. National Service, RA, 1950–52, 2nd Lieut. Cassel Scholar, Lincoln's Inn, 1957, resigned 1959; New York law firm, 1958–59; articled with City solicitors, 1959–62; Asst Solicitor with City firm, 1962–63; London Sch. of Economics: Asst Lectr, 1963; Lectr, 1965; Sen. Lectr, 1970; Reader, 1970; Convener, Law Dept, 1984–88. Legal Correspondent, The Guardian, 1963–87. Mem., Royal Commn on Criminal Justice, 1991–93. *Publications:* Lawyers and the Public Interest, 1968; (ed) What's Wrong with the Law?, 1970; (ed) Family Guide to the Law, 1971 (2nd edn 1972); Cases and Materials on the English Legal System, 1973 (6th edn 1992); (with B. Abel-Smith and R. Brooke) Legal Problems and the Citizen, 1973; Social Workers, their Clients and the Law, 1974 (3rd edn 1981); A Bill of Rights?, 1975 (3rd edn 1985); Legal Services for the Community, 1978; (ed) Pears Guide to the Law, 1979; The Law-Making Process, 1980 (4th edn 1994); The State of Knowledge about the English Legal Profession, 1980; The Police and Criminal Evidence Act 1984, 1985 (3rd edn 1995); A Matter of Justice: the legal system in ferment, 1988 (rev. edn 1989); articles in Criminal Law Rev., Mod. Law Rev., Law Soc.'s Gazette, New Law Jl, Solicitors' Jl, Amer. Bar Assoc. Jl, New Society, etc. *Recreations:* swimming, the cello. *Address:* 12 Woodside Avenue, N6 4SS. *T:* 0181–883 6257, *Fax:* 0181–444 3348.

ZANZIBAR AND TANGA, Bishop of; *see* Tanzania, Archbishop of.

ZARNECKI, Prof. George, CBE 1970; MA, PhD; FSA; FBA 1968; Professor of History of Art, University of London, 1963–82, now Emeritus Professor (Reader, 1959–63); Deputy Director, Courtauld Institute of Art, 1961–74; *b* 12 Sept. 1915; *m* 1945, Anne Leslie Frith; one *s* one *d*. *Educ:* Cracow Univ. MA Cracow Univ., 1938; PhD Univ. of London, 1950. Junior Asst, Inst. of History of Art, Cracow Univ., 1936–39. Served war of 1939–45 as lance-corporal in Polish Army; in France, 1939–40 (Polish Cross of Valour and Croix de Guerre, 1940); prisoner of war, 1940–42; interned in Spain, 1942–43; in Polish Army in UK, 1943–45. On staff of Courtauld Institute of Art, Univ. of London, 1945–82, Hon. Fellow, 1986. Slade Professor of Fine Art, Univ. of Oxford, 1960–61. Vice-President: Soc. of Antiquaries of London, 1968–72; British Soc. of Master Glass Painters, 1976–90; British Archaeol Assoc., 1979–; British Academy: Member: Corpus Vitrearum Medii Aevi Cttee, 1956–85; Publications Cttee, 1978–84; Corpus of Romanesque Sculpture in Britain and Ireland, 1988–; Chm., Corpus of Anglo-Saxon Sculpture Cttee, 1979–84. Member: Conservation Cttee, Council for Places of Worship, 1969–75; Royal Commn on Historical Monuments, 1971–84; Arts Sub-Cttee of UGC, 1972–77; Sub-Cttee for Higher Doctorates, CNAA, 1978–82; Chm., Working Cttee organizing Arts Council exhibition, English Romanesque Art 1066–1200, 1984. Mem., Inst. for Advanced Study, Princeton, 1966; Foreign Member: Polish Acad. of Learning, 1992; Polish Acad. of Scis, 1994. Hon. Mem., Royal Archaeol Inst., 1985. Hon. DLitt: Warwick, 1978; East Anglia, 1981; Hon. LittD Dublin, 1984. Gold Medal, Soc. of Antiquaries, 1986. Gold Medal of Merit (Poland), 1978. *Publications:* English Romanesque Sculpture 1066–1140, 1951; Later English Romanesque Sculpture 1140–1210, 1953; English Romanesque Lead Sculpture, 1957; Early Sculpture of Ely Cathedral, 1958; Gislebertus, sculpteur d'Autun, 1960 (English edn, 1961); Romanesque Sculpture at Lincoln Cathedral, 1964; La sculpture à Payerne, Lausanne, 1966; 1066 and Architectural Sculpture (Proceedings of Brit. Acad.), 1966; Romanik (Belser Stilgeschichte, VI), 1970 (English edn, Romanesque Art, 1971); The Monastic Achievement, 1972; (contrib.) Westminster Abbey, 1972; Art of the Medieval World, 1975 (trans. Chinese, 1991); Studies in Romanesque Sculpture, 1979; Romanesque Lincoln, 1988; Further Studies in Romanesque Sculpture, 1992; articles in archaeological journals. *Address:* 22 Essex Park, N3 1NE. *T:* 0181–346 6497.

ZEALLEY, Christopher Bennett; *b* 5 May 1931; *s* of Sir Alec Zealley and Lady Zealley (*née* King); *m* 1966, Ann Elizabeth Sandwith; one *s* one *d*. *Educ:* Sherborne Sch.; King's Coll., Cambridge (MA Law). Commnd RNVR, 1953; ICI Ltd, 1955–66; IRC, 1967–70; Chairman: Public Interest Res. Centre, 1972–; Social Audit Ltd, 1972–; Director: Dartington Hall Trust, 1970–88; Charity Appointments, 1988– (Chm., 1988–92). Association for Consumer Research (formerly Consumers' Association): Chm., 1991–92; Mem. Council, 1976–92, 1994– (Chm., 1977–82). Trustee: Charities Aid Foundn, 1982–90; Res. Inst. for Consumer Affairs. Director: JT Group Ltd; Grant Instruments Ltd; Good Food Club Ltd. Chairman: Dartington Coll. of Art, 1973–91; Dartington Summer Sch. of Music, 1980–. *Publication:* Creating a Charitable Trust, 1994. *Recreation:* music. *Address:* Sneydhurst, Broadhempston, Totnes, Devon TQ9 6AX. *Club:* Naval.

ZEALLEY, Dr Helen Elizabeth, MD; FRCPEd, FFPHM; Director of Public Health and Chief Administrative Medical Officer, since 1988, Executive Director, since 1991, Lothian Health Board; *b* 10 June 1940; *d* of late Sir John Howie Flint Brotherston and of Lady Brotherston; *m* 1965, Dr Andrew King Zealley; one *s* one *d*. *Educ:* St Albans High Sch. for Girls; Edinburgh Univ. (MB, ChB 1964; MD 1968). FRCPEd 1987; FFPHM 1980. Virologist, City Hosp., Edinburgh, 1965–70; Consultant in Public Health Medicine, Lothian Health Bd, 1974–88, with a special interest in the health of children. Member: Council, RCPE, 1989–; Bd, Faculty of Public Health Medicine, 1989–. Mem. Court, Edinburgh Univ., 1992–. Kentucky Colonel, 1961. Hon. DCCH 1993. *Recreations:* family, sailing, ski-ing, WHO Health for All movement. *Address:* Viewfield House, 12 Tipperlinn Road, Edinburgh EH10 5ET. *T:* 0131–447 5545.

ZEEMAN, Sir (Erik) Christopher, Kt 1991; PhD; FRS 1975; Principal, Hertford College, Oxford, 1988–95; *b* 4 Feb. 1925; *s* of Christian Zeeman and Christine Zeeman (*née* Bushell); *m* 1960, Rosemary Gledhill; three *s* two *d*. *Educ:* Christ's Hospital; Christ's Coll., Cambridge (MA, PhD; Hon. Fellow, 1989). Commonwealth Fellow, 1954; Fellow of Gonville and Caius Coll., Cambridge, 1953–64; Lectr, Cambridge Univ., 1955–64; Prof., and Dir of Maths Res. Centre, Warwick Univ., 1964–88. Sen. Fellow, SRC, 1976–81. Visiting Prof. at various institutes, incl.: IAS; Princeton; IHES, Paris; IMPA, Rio; Royal Instn; also at various univs, incl.: California, Florida, Pisa. Hon. Dr, Strasbourg. *Publications:* numerous research papers on topology, dynamical systems, and applications to biology and the social sciences, in various mathematical and other jls. *Recreation:* family. *Address:* 23 High Street, Woodstock, Oxon OX20 1TE. *T:* Woodstock (01993) 813402.

ZEFFIRELLI, G. Franco (Corsi); opera, film and theatrical producer and designer since 1949; *b* 12 February 1923. *Educ:* Florence. Designer: (in Italy): A Streetcar Named Desire; Troilus and Cressida; Three Sisters. Has produced and designed numerous operas at La Scala, Milan, 1952–, and in all the great cities of Italy, at world-famous festivals, and in UK and USA; *operas include:* Lucia di Lammermoor, Cavalleria Rusticana, and Pagliacci (Covent Garden, 1959, 1973); Falstaff (Covent Garden, 1961); L'Elisir D'Amore (Glyndebourne, 1961); Don Giovanni, and Alcina (Covent Garden, 1962); Tosca, Rigoletto (Covent Garden, 1964, 1966, 1973, Metropolitan, NY, 1985); Don Giovanni (Staatsoper-Wien, 1972); Otello (Metropolitan, NY, 1972); Antony and Cleopatra (Metropolitan, NY, 1973); Otello (La Scala, 1976); La Bohème (Metropolitan, NY, 1981); Turandot (La Scala, 1983, 1985, Metropolitan, NY, 1987); Don Carlos (La Scala, 1992); *stage:* Romeo and Juliet (Old Vic, 1960); Othello (Stratford-on-Avon), 1961; Amleto (National Theatre), 1964; After the Fall (Rome), 1964; Who's Afraid of Virginia Woolf (Paris), 1964, (Milan), 1965; La Lupa (Rome), 1965; Much Ado About Nothing (National Theatre), 1966; Black Comedy (Rome), 1967; A Delicate Balance (Rome), 1967; Saturday, Sunday, Monday (Nat. Theatre), 1973; Filumena, Lyric, 1977; Six Characters in Search of an Author (Nat. Theatre), 1992; *films:* The Taming of the Shrew, 1965–66; Florence, Days of Destruction, 1966; Romeo and Juliet, 1967; Brother Sun, Sister Moon, 1973; Jesus of Nazareth, 1977; The Champ, 1979; Endless Love, 1981; La Traviata, 1983; Cavalleria Rusticana, 1983; Otello, 1986; The Young Toscanini, 1988; Hamlet, 1991; The Sparrow, 1993. Produced Beethoven's Missa Solemnis, San Pietro, Rome, 1971. *Publication:* Zeffirelli (autobiog.), 1986. *Address:* c/o Ken McReddie Ltd, 91 Regent Street, W1R 7TB.

ZEHETMAYR, John Walter Lloyd, OBE 1991; VRD 1963; FICFor; Senior Officer for Wales and Conservator South Wales, Forestry Commission, 1966–81, retired; *b* 24 Dec. 1921; *s* of late Walter Zehetmayr and late Gladys Zehetmayr; *m* 1945, Isabell (Betty) Neill-Kennedy; two *s* one *d. Educ:* St Paul's, Kensington; Keble Coll., Oxford (BA). Served RNVR, 1942–46 (despatches); now Lt Cdr RNR retired. Forestry Commission: Silviculturist, 1948–56; Chief Work Study Officer, 1956–64; Conservator West Scotland, 1964–66. Chm., Forestry Safety Council, 1986–92. Member: Prince of Wales' Cttee, 1970–89; Brecon Beacons Nat. Park Cttee, 1982–91. Vice-Pres., Glamorgan Wildlife Trust, 1992. *Publications:* Experiments in Tree Planting on Peat, 1954; Afforestation of Upland Heaths, 1960; The Gwent Small Woods Project 1979–84, 1985; Forestry in Wales, 1985; The Effectiveness of Health and Safety Measures in Forestry, 1992. *Recreations:* garden, conservation, skiing. *Address:* The Haven, Augusta Road, Penarth, S Glam CF64 5RH.

ZEIDLER, Sir David (Ronald), AC 1990; Kt 1980; CBE 1971; FAA 1985; FRACI; FIChemE; FIEAust; FTS; Chairman and Managing Director, ICI Australia, 1973–80, retired; *s* of Otto William and Hilda Maude Zeidler; *m* 1943, June Susie Broadhurst; four *d. Educ:* Scotch Coll., Melbourne; Melbourne Univ. (MSc). FTS 1976; FIEAust 1988. CSIRO, 1941–52; joined ICI Australia, 1952: Research Manager, 1953; Development Manager, 1959; Controller, Dyes and Fabrics Gp, 1962; Dir, 1963; Man. Dir, 1971; Dep. Chm., 1972. Chm., Metal Manufactures Ltd, 1980–88; Director: Amatil Ltd, 1979–89; Broken Hill Pty Co. Ltd, 1978–88; Commercial Bank of Australia Ltd, 1974–82; Westpac Banking Corp., 1982–91 (Dep. Chm., 1989–91); Australian Foundation Investment Co. Ltd, 1982–90; past Director: ICI New Zealand Ltd; IMI Australia Ltd. Vice-Pres., Walter and Eliza Hall Inst. of Med. Res., 1972–89; Dep. Chm., Queen's Silver Jubilee Trust, 1977–88. Chairman: Govt Inquiry into Elec. Generation and Power Sharing in SE Aust., 1980–81; Defence Industry Cttee, 1981–84; Member, or past Mem., cttees concerned with prof. qualifications, defence industry, educn and trng, internat. business co-operation. Member: Aust.-Japan Businessmen's Co-operation Cttee, 1978–80; Aust.-NZ Businessmen's Council Ltd, 1978–80; Sir Robert Menzies Meml Trust, 1978–80; Council, Aust. Acad. of Technol Scis, 1979–88 (Vice-Pres., 1970–71; Pres., 1983–88); Council, Science Museum of Victoria, 1964–82; Commerce and Industry Cttee, 1978–85, and Defence Industry Cttee, 1977–84 (Chm., 1981–84), Victorian Div. of Aust. Red Cross Soc.; Inst. of Dirs; Royal Society, Victoria; Royal Soc. for Encouragement of Arts Manuf. and Commerce in London; Cook Society. Director: Schizophrenia Aust. Foundn, 1986–; Aust. Bicentennial Multicultural Foundn, 1988–; Vict. Govt Strategic Res. Foundn, 1988– (Dep. Chm., 1990–). Governor, Ian Clunies Ross Meml Foundn, 1984–. *Recreations:* tennis, ski-ing, golf. *Address:* 45/238 The Avenue, Parkville, Victoria 3052, Australia. *T:* 387 5720. *Clubs:* Melbourne, Australian (Melb. and Sydney); Sciences.

ZEKI, Prof. Semir, FRS 1990; Professor of Neurobiology, University College London, since 1981; *b* 8 Nov. 1940; *m* 1967, Anne-Marie Claire Blestel; one *d* one *s. Educ:* University College London (BSc Anat. 1964; PhD 1967). Asst Lectr, UCL, 1966–67; Res. Associate, St Elizabeth's Hosp., Washington DC, 1967–68; Asst Prof., Univ. of Wisconsin, 1968–69; Lectr in Anatomy, UCL, 1969–75; Henry Head Res. Fellow, Royal Soc., 1975–80; Reader in Neurobiology, UCL, 1980–81. Visiting Professor: Duke Univ., 1977; Ludwig Maximillians Univ., Munich, 1982–87; Univ. of California, Berkeley, 1984; St Andrews, 1985; Vis. Professorial Fellow, RPMS, Hammersmith Hosp., 1991–. Lectures: Edridge Green, RCS, 1987; G. L. Brown, Physiol Soc., 1988; first Dist. in Neurosci., Edinburgh Univ., 1989; David Marr, Cambridge Univ., 1989; Perception, European Conf. of Visual Perception, 1990; Halliburton, KCL, 1991; Philip Bard, Johns Hopkins Univ., 1992; Siemens Foundn, Munich, 1992; Newton, Colour Gp of GB; Donders, Nijmingen Univ., 1994; Paul Broca, French Neurol Assoc., and Ferrier, Royal Soc., 1995. Member: Neuroscience Res. Program and Neurosci. Inst., NY, 1985–; Wellcome Trust Vision Panel, 1985–93 (Chm., 1987–93); Bd of Scientific Govs, Scripps Res. Inst., Calif., 1992–. Trustee, Fight for Sight, 1992–; Guarantor, Brain, 1994–. MRI, 1985; Member: Academia Europaea, 1990; Eur. Acad. of Scis and Arts, 1992. . Hon. Mem., Italian Primatological Assoc., 1988. Hon. DSc Aston, 1994. Minerva Foundn Prize, USA, 1985; Prix Science pour l'Art, LVMH, Paris, 1991; Rank Prize, 1992; Zotterman Prize, Swedish Physiol Soc., 1993. *Publications:* A Vision of the Brain, 1993; (with Balthus) La Quête de l'Essential, Paris, 1995; articles on vision and the brain in professional jls. *Recreations:* reading (esp. about the darker side of man), music, deep sleep. *Address:* Anatomy Department, University College London, WC1E 6BT. *T:* 0171–380 7187.

ZELLICK, Prof. Graham John, PhD; Principal, Queen Mary and Westfield College, University of London, and Professor of Law in the University of London, since 1991; Deputy Vice-Chancellor, University of London, since 1994; *b* 12 August 1948; *s* of R. H. and B. Zellick; *m* 1975, Jennifer Temkin, *qv*; one *s* one *d. Educ:* Christ's Coll., Finchley; Gonville and Caius Coll., Cambridge (MA, PhD); Stanford Univ. Called to the Bar, Middle Temple, 1992. Ford Foundn Fellow, Stanford Law Sch., 1970–71; Queen Mary College, later Queen Mary and Westfield College, London: Lectr, 1971–78; Reader in Law, 1978–82; Prof. of Public Law, 1982–88; Dean of Faculty of Laws, 1984–88; Head, Dept of Law, 1984–90; Drapers' Prof. of Law, 1988–91; Sen. Vice-Principal and Acting Principal, 1990–91; University of London: Dean, Faculty of Laws, 1986–88; Dep. Chm., Academic Council, 1987–89. Vis. Fellow, Centre of Criminology, 1978–79, and Vis. Prof. of Law, 1975, 1978–79, Toronto Univ.; Vis. Scholar, St John's Coll., Oxford, 1989. Lectures: Noel Buxton, NACRO, 1983; Webber, Jews' Coll., London, 1986; Sir Gwilym Morris, UWIST, Cardiff, 1986; Wythe, Coll. of William and Mary, Va, 1989. Member: Council and Exec. Cttee, Howard League for Penal Reform, 1973–82; Jellicoe Cttee on Bds of Visitors of Prisons, 1973–75; Sub Cttee on Crime and Criminal Justice, 1984–88, and Sub Cttee on Police Powers and the Prosecution Process, 1985–88, ESRC; Lord Chancellor's Legal Aid Adv. Cttee, 1985–88; Newham Dist Ethics Cttee, 1985–86; Data Protection Tribunal, 1985–95; Lord Chancellor's Adv. Cttee on Legal Educn, 1988–90; S Thames RHA, 1994–95; E London and the City HA, 1995–; Chairman: Prisoners' Advice and Law Service, 1984–89; Legal Cttee, All-Party Parly War Crimes Gp, 1988–91; Dep. Chm., Justice Cttee on Prisoners' Rights, 1981–83. Dir, UCAS, 1994–. Chairman: Cttee of Heads of Univ. Law Schs, 1988–90; E London Strategic Forum for Nat. Educn and Trng Targets, 1993– (Chm., Educn Cttee, 1990–93); Vice-Chm., Acad. Study Gp for Israel and ME, 1995–; Mem. Council, CVCP, 1993–95. Member: Council: UCS, 1983–92; West London Synagogue, 1990–93; City and East London Confedn for Medicine and Dentistry, 1991–; St Bartholomew's Hosp. Med. Coll., 1991–; Council of Govs, London Hosp. Med. Coll., 1991–; Court of Governors: Polytechnic of Central London, 1973–77; Polytechnic of N London, 1986–89; Univ. of Greenwich, 1994–; Gov., Pimlico Sch., 1973–77; Chm., Lawyers' Gp, 1984–89, and Trustee, 1985–87, Tel Aviv Univ. Trust.; Mem. Council, Spitalfields Heritage Centre, 1992–; Patron, Redress Trust, 1993–. Freeman, City of London, 1992; Liveryman, Drapers' Co., 1995– (Freeman, 1992). FIMgt (FBIM 1991); FRSA 1991. JP Inner London (N Westminster), 1981–85. Editor: European Human Rights Reports, 1978–82; Public Law, 1981–86; Member of Editorial Board: British Jl of Criminology, 1980–90; Public Law, 1981–91; Howard Jl of Criminal Justice, 1984–87; Civil Law Library, 1987–. *Publications:* Justice in Prison (with Sir Brian MacKenna), 1983; (ed) The Law Commission and Law Reform, 1988; (contrib.) Halsbury's Laws of England, 4th edn 1982; contribs to collections of essays, pamphlets, the national press, and professional and learned periodicals incl. British Jl of Criminology, Civil Justice Quarterly, Criminal Law Rev., Modern Law Rev., Public Law, Univ. of Toronto Law Jl, William and Mary Law Rev. *Address:* Queen Mary and Westfield College, E1 4NS. *T:* 0171–975 5001, *Fax:* 0181–981 2848. *Club:* Reform.

ZELLICK, Jennifer, (Mrs G. J. Zellick); *see* Temkin, J.

ZEMAN, Prof. Zbyněk Anthony Bohuslav; Research Professor in European History, since 1982, and Professorial Fellow of St Edmund Hall, since 1983, Oxford University; *b* Prague, 18 Oct. 1928; *s* of late Jaroslav and Růžena Zeman; *m* 1956, Sarah Anthea Collins (separated); two *s* one *d. Educ:* London and Oxford Universities. BA (Hons) London, DPhil Oxon. Research Fellow, St Antony's Coll., Oxford, 1958–61, and Mem. editorial staff, The Economist, 1959–62; Lectr in Modern History, Univ. of St Andrews, 1962–70; Head of Research, Amnesty International, 1970–73; Director, East-West SPRL (Brussels) and European Cooperation Research Gp, 1974–76; Prof. of Central and SE European Studies and Dir, Comenius Centre, Lancaster Univ., 1976–82. Vis. Prof. of Hist., Charles Univ., Prague, 1990–91. Hon. Fellow: Österreichisches Ost-und Südosteuropa-Institut, 1988–89; Inst. of History of Czech Army, Prague, 1994–95. *Publications* include: The Break-up of the Habsburg Empire 1914–1918, 1961; Nazi Propaganda, 1964; (with W. B. Scharlau) The Merchant of Revolution, A Life of Alexander Helphand (Parvus), 1965; Prague Spring, 1969; A Diplomatic History of the First World War, 1971; (ed jtly) International Yearbook of East West Trade, 1975; The Masaryks, 1976; (jtly) Comecon Oil and Gas, 1977; Selling the War: art and propaganda in the Second World War, 1978; Heckling Hitler: caricatures of the Third Reich, 1984; Pursued by a Bear: the making of Eastern Europe, 1989; The Making and Breaking of Communist Europe, 1991. *Address:* St Edmund Hall, Oxford OX1 4AR.

ZENINED, Abdesselam, Hon. GCVO 1987; Moroccan Ambassador, Moscow, since 1991; *b* 15 Dec. 1934; *m* 1960; one *s* two *d. Educ:* Bordeaux Univ.; Sorbonne. Carnegie scholarship, Inst. des Hautes Etudes Internat., Geneva, 1962. Ministry of Foreign Affairs, Morocco, 1959; Min. of Information, 1967; Under-Sec., Prime Minister's Office, 1974–77; MP 1977–80; Minister of Tourism, 1979–80; Ambassador: to Iraq, 1980–85; to UK, 1987–91. *Address:* 8 pērēoulok Ostrovskogo, Moscow 119034, Russia. *Club:* Ambassadors'.

ZETLAND, 4th Marquess of, *cr* 1892; **Lawrence Mark Dundas;** Bt 1762; Baron Dundas, 1794; Earl of Zetland, 1838; Earl of Ronaldshay (UK), 1892; DL; *b* 28 Dec. 1937; *e s* of 3rd Marquess of Zetland, DL and of Penelope, *d* of late Col Ebenezer Pike, CBE, MC; *S* father, 1989; *m* 1964, Susan, 2nd *d* of late Guy Chamberlin, Oatlands, Wrington Hill, Wrington, Bristol, and late Mrs Chamberlin; two *s* two *d. Educ:* Harrow School; Christ's College, Cambridge. Late 2nd Lieut, Grenadier Guards. DL N Yorks, 1994. *Heir: s* Earl of Ronaldshay, *qv*. *Address:* Aske, Richmond, N Yorks DL10 5HJ. *T:* Richmond (01748) 823222. *Clubs:* All England Lawn Tennis and Croquet, Jockey (Steward, 1992–94).

ZETTER, Paul Isaac, CBE 1981; Chairman, Zetters Group Ltd, since 1972; *b* 9 July 1923; *s* of late Simon and Esther Zetter; *m* 1954, Helen Lore Morgenstern; one *s* one *d. Educ:* City of London Sch. Army, 1941–46. Family business, 1946–; became public co., 1965. Chm., Southern Council for Sport and Recreation, 1985–87; Member: Sports Council, 1985–87; National Centres Bd, Sports Council, 1987–88; Governor, 1975–, and Hon. Vice-Pres., 1985–, Sports Aid Foundation (Chm., 1976–85); Vice-Chm., World Ice Skating Championships, 1994–95. Trustee: Thames Salmon Trust, 1988–92; Foundn for Sports and Arts, 1991– (Chm., Sports Working Party, 1991–94). President: John Carpenter Club, 1987–88; Restricted Growth Assoc., 1993–. Liveryman, Glovers' Co., 1981–; Freeman, City of London, 1981. *Publications:* It Could Be Verse, 1976; Bow Jest, 1992. *Recreations:* varied water sports, walking, writing. *Address:* 86 Clerkenwell Road, EC1P 1ZS. *Clubs:* Royal Automobile, East India.

ZETTERBERG, Christer; President and Chief Executive Officer, AB Volvo, since 1990; *b* 2 Nov. 1941; *m* 1966, Inger Mathson; three *d*. MBA 1967. Officer, Royal Swedish Navy Reserve, 1964. Svenska Cellulosa AB, 1968–76 (Manager, Pulp Sales and Head, Pulp Div.); President: Calor-Celsius, 1976–80; Tibnor, 1980–83; Holmens Bruk, 1983–88; Pres. and Chief Exec. Officer, PKBanken, 1988–90. *Address:* AB Volvo, S-405 08 Gothenburg, Sweden. *T:* (31) 590090.

ZHAO ZIYANG; General Secretary, Central Committee, Chinese Communist Party, 1987–89; *b* Huaxian County, Henan Prov., 1919; *m*; four *s* one *d*. Joined Chinese Communist Youth League, 1932, Chinese Communist Party, 1938; held various posts, S China Sub-Bureau of Central Cttee, Guangdong Provincial Cttee, and Cttee of Inner Mongolia Autonomous Reg., 1950–74; First Sec. of Provincial Cttee and Chm. of Revolutionary Cttee, Guangdong, 1974, Sichuan, 1975–80; First Political Commissar, Chengdu Mil. Reg., Chinese People's Liberation Army, 1976–80; Vice-Chm., 5th Nat. Cttee, Chinese People's Political Consultative Conf., 1978–80; Vice Premier, State Council, 1980, Premier, 1980–87. Mem., 10th Central Cttee, Chinese Communist Party, 1973; Alternate Mem., 1977, Mem., 1979, Mem. Standing Cttee, 1980, Political Bureau, and Vice Chm., 1981, 11th Central Cttee; Mem., 1982, and Mem. Standing Cttee, 1982,

Political Bureau, 12th Central Cttee. *Address:* 6 Fuqiang Alley, Beijing, People's Republic of China.

ZHUKOV, Georgi Alexandrovich; Hero of Socialist Labour (1978); Orders of: Lenin (2); October Revolution; Red Banner of Labour (2); Red Star; Great Patriotic War, Grade 2; Friendship of Peoples; Joliot-Curie Medal; Columnist of Pravda, since 1962; Member Presidium, World Peace Council, since 1974; Vice-President, Soviet-American Institute, since 1961; President, Society USSR-France, since 1958; Secretary, Moscow writing organization, since 1970; *b* 1908. *Educ:* Lomonosov Inst., Moscow. Corresp.: local papers in Lugansk, Kharkov, 1927–32; Komsomolskaya Pravda, 1932–46 (Mem. Editorial Bd); Pravda in Paris, 1947–52; Foreign Editor of Pravda, 1952–57; Chairman, USSR Council of Ministers' State Committee for Cultural Relations with Foreign Countries, 1957–62. Mem., Central Auditing Cttee of CPSU, elected by XX, XXII, XXIII and XXIV Congresses of CPSU, 1956–89; Alternate Mem., Central Cttee of CPSU, elected by XXV, XXVI and XXVII Congresses of CPSU, 1976–89; Mem., Foreign Relations Cttee, USSR Supreme Soviet, 1966–89; MP, 1962–89; Chm., Soviet-French Parly Gp, 1966–89. Prizes: Lenin (for Journalism); Vorovsky; Union of Soviet Journalists; internat. organization of journalists. *Publications:* Border, 1938; Russians and Japan, 1945; Soldier's Life, 1946; American Notes (essays), 1947; The West After War, 1948; Three Months in Geneva, 1954; Taming Tigers, 1961; Japan, 1962; Meetings in Transcarpathia, 1962; One MIG from a Thousand, 1963, 2nd edn 1979; These Seventeen Years, 1963; Silent Art, 1964; The People of the Thirties, 1964; Vietnam, 1965; America, 1967; The People of the Forties, 1968, 2nd edn 1975; From Battle to Battle: letters from the ideological front, 1970; Chilean Diary, 1970; The USA on the Threshold of the Seventies, 1970; The People in the War (about Vietnam), 1972; 33 Visas, 1972; Times of Great Changes, 1973; Alex and others, 1974; Poisoners, 1975; The War: the beginning and the end, 1975; Letters from Rambouillet, 1975; European Horizons, 1975; Thirty Conversations with TV Viewers, 1977; Town's Beginning, 1977; Thoughts of Unthinkable, 1978; Society without Future, 1978; The Tale of Dirty Tricks, 1978; Roots, 1980; Pioneer Builders, 1982; Steep Steps, 1983 (English edn 1987); Journey through Indo-China, 1984; Journalists, 1984 (Chinese edn 1988); Where is peace—there life, 1985; Lack of Spirit, 1985; Dogs of War, 1986; Soldier's Thoughts, 1987; USSR–USA: the seventy years long way, 1988; Selected Works in Two Volumes, 1989.

ZIA, Khaleda; Prime Minister of Bangladesh, since 1991; *b* 15 Aug. 1945; *m* 1960, Gen. Ziaur Rahman (*d* 1981), President of Bangladesh; two *s*. *Educ:* Surendranath Coll., Dinajpur. Vice-Chm., 1982–84, Chm., 1984–, Bangladesh Nat. Party. *Address:* Office of the Prime Minister, Tejgaon, Dhaka, Bangladesh.

ZIEGLER, Henri Alexandre Léonard, Ingénieur Général Air; Grand Officier, Légion d'Honneur; Croix de Guerre (1939–45); Rosette de la Résistance; Hon. CBE; Hon. CVO; Legion of Merit (US); French Aviation Executive; *b* Limoges, 18 Nov. 1906; *s* of Charles Ziegler and Alix Mousnier-Buisson; *m* 1932, Gillette Rizzi; three *s* one *d*. *Educ:* Collège Stanislas, Paris; Ecole Polytechnique (Grad.); Ecole Nationale Supérieure de l'Aéronautique. Officer-Pilot in French Air Force, 1928 (5000 hours); Tech. Officer, Min. of Aviation, 1929; Dep. Dir of Flight Test Centre, 1938; Foreign Missions: Gt Britain, USA, Germany, Poland, USSR. War of 1939–45: Dep. Buying Mission, USA, Dec. 1939; French Resistance, 1941–44; Col and Chief of Staff, Forces Françaises de l'Intérieur (London), 1944. Dir-Gen., Air France, 1946–54. Dir of Cabinet: of J. Chaban-Delmas (Min. of Public Works, Transport and Tourism), 1954; of Gen. Cornuglion-Molignier (Min. of Public Works), 1955–56; Admin. Dir-Gen., Ateliers d'aviation Louis Breguet, 1957–67. Pres. Dir-Gen., Sud Aviation, 1968; Pres. Dir-Gen., Soc. Nationale Industrielle Aérospatiale, 1970–73; Pres., Airbus Industrie, 1970–74. Pres., Air Alpes, 1961–76; Pres., Forum Atomique Européen, 1956–60; Admin. Inst. du Transport Aérien, 1969–77; Pres., Union Syndicale des Industries Aérospatiales, 1971–74. Mem., Amicale des anciens des essais en vol. Hon. Fellow, Soc. of Experimental Test Pilots; Hon. FRAeS. *Publication:* La Grande Aventure de Concorde, 1976. *Recreation:* alpinism. *Address:* 55 boulevard Lannes, 75116 Paris, France. *T:* 45046153. *Club:* Aéro-Club de France (Paris).

ZIEGLER, Philip Sandeman, CVO 1991; author; *b* 24 Dec. 1929; *s* of Major Colin Louis Ziegler, DSO, DL, and Mrs Dora Ziegler (*née* Barnwell); *m* 1st, 1960, Sarah Collins; one *s* one *d*; 2nd, 1971, (Mary) Clare Charrington; one *s*. *Educ:* Eton; New Coll., Oxford (1st Cl. Hons Jurisprudence; Chancellor's Essay Prize). Entered Foreign Service, 1952; served in Vientiane, Paris, Pretoria and Bogotá; resigned 1967; joined William Collins and Sons Ltd, 1967, Editorial Dir 1972, Editor-in-Chief, 1979–80. Chairman: The London Library, 1979–85; Soc. of Authors, 1988–90; Public Lending Right Adv. Cttee, 1994–. FRSL 1975; FRHS 1979. Hon. DLitt Westminster Coll., Fulton, 1988. *Publications:* Duchess of Dino, 1962; Addington, 1965; The Black Death, 1968; William IV, 1971; Omdurman, 1973; Melbourne, 1976 (W. H. Heinemann Award); Crown and People, 1978; Diana Cooper, 1981; Mountbatten, 1985; Elizabeth's Britain 1926 to 1986, 1986; The Sixth Great Power: Barings 1762–1929, 1988; King Edward VIII, 1990; Wilson: the authorised life, 1993; London at War 1939–45, 1995; *edited:* the Diaries of Lord Louis Mountbatten 1920–1922, 1987; Personal Diary of Admiral the Lord Louis Mountbatten 1943–1946, 1988; From Shore to Shore: the diaries of Earl Mountbatten of Burma 1953–1979, 1989; (with Desmond Seward) Brooks's: a social history, 1991. *Address:* 22 Cottesmore Gardens, W8 5PR. *T:* 0171–937 1903, *Fax:* 0171–937 5458. *Club:* Brooks's.

ZIENKIEWICZ, Prof. Olgierd Cecil, CBE 1989; FRS 1979; FEng 1979; Professor and Head of Civil Engineering Department, 1961–88, and Director, Institute for Numerical Methods in Engineering, 1976–88, University of Wales at Swansea, now Professor Emeritus; UNESCO Professor of Numerical Methods in Engineering, Universidad Politécnica de Cataluña, Barcelona; J. Walter Professor of Engineering, University of Texas, Austin; *b* Caterham, 18 May 1921; *s* of Casimir Zienkiewicz and Edith Violet (*née* Penny); *m* 1952, Helen Jean (*née* Fleming), Toronto; two *s* one *d*. *Educ:* Katowice, Poland; Imperial Coll., London (FIC 1993). BSc (Eng); ACGI; PhD; DIC; DSc (Eng); DipEng; FICE; FASCE. Consulting engrg, 1945–49; Lectr, Univ. of Edinburgh, 1949–57; Prof. of Structural Mechanics, Northwestern Univ., 1957–61. Naval Sea Systems Comd Res. Prof., Monterey, Calif, 1979–80; Chalmers Jubilee Prof., Gothenburg, 1990, 1992. Hon. Founder Mem., GAMNI, France. Chairman: Cttee on Analysis and Design, Internat. Congress of Large Dams; Jt Computer Cttee, Instn of Civil Engineers. Mem. Council, ICE, 1972–75 (Chm., S Wales and Mon. Br.); Telford Premium, ICE, 1963–67. Pres., Internat. Assoc. Computational Mechanics, 1986–90. General Editor, Internat. Jl Numerical Methods in Engineering; Member Editorial Board: Internat. Jl Solids and Structures; Internat. Jl Earthquakes and Structural Mechanics; Internat. Jl Rock Mechanics, Numerical and Analytical Methods in Geomechanics. For. Associate, US Nat. Acad. of Engrg, 1981; For. Mem., Polish Acad. of Sci., 1985. Hon. Prof., Dalian Inst. of Technology, China, 1987; Hon. Dr, Lisbon, 1972; Hon. DSc: NUI, 1975; Northwestern Univ., Illinois, 1984; Chalmers Univ. of Technology, Gothenburg, 1987; Univ. of Technol., Warsaw, 1989; Technical Univ., Krakow, 1989; Technical Univ., Budapest, 1992; Univ. of Hong Kong, 1992; Univ. of Padua, 1992; Aristotelian Univ. of Thessaloniki, 1993; Brunel Univ., 1993; Univ. of Wales, 1993; Hon. DTech: Norwegian Inst. of Technol., Trondheim, 1985; Technische Univ., Vienna, 1993; Hon. DSci Free Univ., Brussels, 1982; Hon. LLD Dundee, 1987. FCGI 1979. James Clayton Fund Prizes, IMechE, 1967, 1973; James Alfred Ewing Medal, ICE, 1980; Newmark Medal, ASCE, 1980; Worcester Reed Warner Medal, ASME, 1980; Gauss Medal, Acad. of Science, Braunschweig, West Germany, 1987; Royal Medal, Royal Soc., 1990; Gold Medal, IStructE, 1992. *Publications:* Stress Analysis, 1965; Rock Mechanics, 1968; Finite Element Method, 1967, 4th edn 1989; Optimum Design of Structures, 1973; Finite Elements in Fluids, 1975; Numerical Methods in Offshore Engineering, 1977; Finite Elements and Approximation, 1983; numerous papers in Jl ICE, Jl Mech. Sci., Proc. Royal Soc., Internat. Jl of Num. Methods in Engrg, etc. *Recreations:* sailing, skin-diving. *Address:* 29 Somerset Road, Langland, Swansea SA3 4PG. *T:* Swansea (01792) 368776. *Clubs:* Athenæum; Rotary (Mumbles); Mumbles Yacht.

ZIJLSTRA, Jelle; Central Banker; President, Netherlands Bank, 1967–81; Member, Supervisory Board, Royal Dutch Petroleum, since 1982; *b* 27 Aug. 1918; *s* of Ane Zijlstra and Pietje Postuma; *m* 1946, Hetty Bloksma; two *s* three *d*. *Educ:* Netherlands Sch. of Economics. Asst, Netherlands Sch. of Economics, 1945; Prof., Theoretical Economics, 1948–52; Prof., Public Finance, 1963–66, Free Univ. of Amsterdam; Minister of Economic Affairs, 1952–58; of Finance, 1959–63; Prime Minister, 1966–67. Mem., Chm. Board, and Pres., BIS, 1967–82; Governor, IMF, 1967–81. *Publications:* Planned Economy, 1947; The Velocity of Money and its Significance for the Value of Money and for Monetary Equilibrium, 1948; Economic Order and Economic Policy, 1952. *Recreations:* sailing, skiing. *Address:* Park Oud Wassenaar, flat 44, 2243 BX Wassenaar, Netherlands.

ZILKHA, Selim Khedoury; Chairman and Chief Executive Officer, Zilkha Energy Co., Houston, Texas, since 1987; *b* 7 April 1927; *s* of Khedoury Aboodi Zilkha and Louise (*née* Bashi); *m* (marr. diss.); one *s* one *d*. *Educ:* English Sch., Heliopolis, Egypt; Horace Mann Sch. for Boys, USA; Williams Coll., USA (BA Major Philos.). Dir, Zilkha & Sons Inc., USA, 1947–87; Chm. and Man. Dir, Mothercare Ltd and associated cos, 1961–82; Dir, Habitat Mothercare Gp, 1982; Chairman: Amerfin Co. Ltd, GB, 1955–68; Spirella Co. of Great Britain Ltd, 1957–62; Chm./Jt Man. Dir, Lewis & Burrows Ltd, 1961–64; Chairman and Chief Executive Officer: Towner Petroleum Co., Houston, 1983–85; SKZ Inc., Houston, 1986. *Recreations:* bridge, backgammon, golf, tennis. *Address:* 750 Lausanne Road, Los Angeles, CA 90077, USA. *Clubs:* Portland; Sunningdale Golf; Travellers' (Paris).

ZIMAN, Prof. John Michael, FRS 1967; Emeritus Professor of Physics, University of Bristol, 1988; *b* 16 May 1925; *s* of late Solomon Netheim Ziman, ICS, retired, and Nellie Frances Ziman (*née* Gaster); *m* 1951, Rosemary Milnes Dixon; two adopted *s* two adopted *d*. *Educ:* Hamilton High Sch., NZ; Victoria University Coll., Wellington, NZ; Balliol Coll., Oxford. Junior Lectr in Mathematics, Oxford Univ., 1951–53; Pressed Steel Co. Ltd Research Fellow, Oxford Univ., 1953–54; Lectr in Physics, Cambridge Univ., 1954–64; Fellow of King's Coll., Cambridge, 1957–64; Editor of Cambridge Review, 1958–59; Tutor for Advanced Students, King's Coll., Cambridge, 1959–63; University of Bristol: Prof. of Theoretical Physics, 1964–69; Melville Wills Prof. of Physics, 1969–76; Dir, H. H. Wills Physics Lab., 1976–81; Henry Overton Wills Prof. of Physics, 1976–82. Vis. Prof., Dept of Social and Economic Studies, 1982–87, Dept of Humanities, 1982–, Imperial Coll., London. Rutherford Memorial Lectr in India and Pakistan, 1968. Dir, Sci. Policy Support Gp, 1986–91; Chairman: Council for Science and Society, 1976–90; European Assoc. for Study of Science and Technology, 1982–86; Member: Scientific Council, Internat. Centre for Theoretical Physics, Trieste, 1970–79; CNAA, 1982–87. Hon. DSc Victoria Univ. of Wellington, NZ, 1985. Jt Editor, Science Progress, 1965–92. *Publications:* Electrons and Phonons, 1960; Electrons in Metals, 1963; (with Jasper Rose) Camford Observed, 1964; Principles of the Theory of Solids, 1965; Public Knowledge, 1968; Elements of Advanced Quantum Theory, 1969; The Force of Knowledge, 1976; Reliable Knowledge, 1978; Models of Disorder, 1979; Teaching and Learning about Science and Society, 1980; Puzzles, Problems and Enigmas, 1981; An Introduction to Science Studies, 1984; (with Paul Sieghart and John Humphrey) The World of Science and the Rule of Law, 1986; Knowing Everything about Nothing, 1987; Prometheus Bound, 1994; Of One Mind, 1995; numerous articles in scientific jls. *Address:* 27 Little London Green, Oakley, Aylesbury, Bucks HP18 9QL. *T* and *Fax:* Brill (01844) 237464.

ZINNEMANN, Fred; Film Director since 1934; *b* Austria, 29 April 1907; *s* of Dr Oskar Zinnemann, Physician and Anna F. Zinnemann; *m* 1936, Renée Bartlett; one *s*. *Educ:* Vienna Univ. (Law School). First film, The Wave (documentary) directed for Mexican Govt, 1934; initiated, with others, school of neo-realism in American cinema, directing among other films: The Seventh Cross, 1943; The Search, 1948; The Men, 1949; Teresa, 1950; High Noon, 1951; Member of the Wedding, 1952; From Here to Eternity, 1953. Later films include: Oklahoma!, 1956; The Nun's Story, 1959; The Sundowners, 1960; Behold a Pale Horse, 1964; A Man for All Seasons, 1966; The Day of the Jackal, 1973; Julia, 1977; Five Days One Summer, 1982. Exhibn of photographs of NY taken in 1932, V&A Mus., 1992. Member: Amer. Film Inst. (co-founder and ex-trustee); Acad. of Motion Picture Arts; Directors' Guild of America (2nd Vice-Pres., 1960–64); Hon. Pres., Directors' Guild of Great Britain, 1983–87. Fellow: BAFTA, 1978; BFI, 1990. Hon. DLitt Durham, 1994. Awards include: Academy Award, Los Angeles, 1951, 1954, 1967; Film Critics' Award, NY, 1952, 1954, 1960, 1967; Golden Thistle Award, Edinburgh, 1965; Moscow Film Festival Award, 1965; D. W. Griffith Award, 1970; Donatello Award, Florence, 1978; US Congressional Lifetime Achievement Award, 1987; John Huston Award (1st recipient), Artists' Rights Foundn, LA, 1994. Gold Medal of City of Vienna, 1967. Order of Arts and Letters, France, 1982. *Publications:* Fred Zinnemann: an autobiography, 1992; article on directing films, Encyclopædia Britannica. *Recreations:* mountain climbing, chamber music. *Address:* 98 Mount Street, W1Y 5HF. *Club:* Sierra (San Francisco).

ZOBEL de AYALA, Jaime; Chairman and President, Ayala Corporation, since 1983; Chairman, Bank of the Philippine Islands, since 1985; *b* 18 July 1934; *s* of Alfonso Zobel de Ayala and Carmen Pfitz y Herrero; *m* 1958, Beatriz Miranda; two *s* five *d*. *Educ:* La Salle, Madrid; Harvard Univ. (BA, Arch. Scis). Lt Col, Philippine Air Force (Res.). Philippine Ambassador to the Court of St James's and concurrently to Scandinavian countries, 1970–74. Mem., Camera Club of the Philippines, 1978–; Associate, RPS, 1984. Hon. Dr of Business Management De La Salle Univ., 1985; Hon. LLD Univ. of Philippines, 1991. Comendador de la Orden del Mérito Civil, Spain, 1968; Chevalier des Arts et des Lettres, 1980. *Recreation:* photography. *Address:* Ayala Corporation, Makati, Metro Manila 1200, Philippines. *Clubs:* White's; Fox (Harvard).

ZOLEVEKE, Sir Gideon (Asatori Pitabose), KBE 1983 (MBE 1968); retired as public servant, 1973 and as politician, 1980; farmer since 1980; *b* 3 Aug. 1922; *s* of Pita Pitabose and Mata Taburana; *m* 1954, Melody Sukuluta'a Watanamae; three *s* three *d* (and one *s* decd). *Educ:* primary schs, Solomon Is; secondary sch. and tertiary educn, Fiji. Dip. in Surgery and Medicine, Fiji Sch. of Medicine, Suva; DCMHE London. Served British Solomon Is Protectorate Defence Force, 1942–45 (Pacific Stars). Govt MO, 1951–62; Sen. Health Educn Officer, 1962–73; Mem., Governing Council, 1973–74 (Chm., Works and Public Utilities); MLA, 1974–78 (Backbencher, 1975–76); Minister of: Works and Public Utilities, 1974–75; Home Affairs, April-July 1975; Educn, July-Nov. 1975;

Agriculture and Lands, 1976–78; Health and Med. Services, 1978–80. Mem. and leader, various govt delegns, 1953–. Mem., Solomon Is Public Service Commn, 1981–; Chairman: Solomon Is Electricity Authy Bd of Management, 1983–; Solomon Is Water Authy, 1994–. Dir, Boral Gas (SI), 1983–. Founder and first Pres., Solomon Is Med. Officers Assoc., 1952–69; President: W Pacific Br.,BMA, 1961–70; Choiseul People's Assoc., 1955–71; Civil Servants Assoc., British Solomon Is Protectorate, 1966–67; Solomon Is Br., BRCS, 1974–78 (BRCS award, 1978; Life Mem., 1982); Solomon Is Red Cross, 1978–82; St John's Primary Sch., Rove, Honiara, 1968–76; Honiara Club, 1963–68; Foundn Mem., 1967–, Pres. and Chm., 1980–, Sir Winston Churchill Trust Fund, Solomon Is. *Publications:* A Man from Choiseul (autobiog.), 1980; (contrib.) Lands in the Solomon Islands, 1982; (contrib.) Solomon Island Politics, 1983. *Recreations:* writing, reading. *Address:* Kaiti Hill, PO Box 243, Honiara, Solomon Islands. *T:* Honiara 22927.

ZOUCHE, 18th Baron, *cr* 1308, of Haryngworth; **James Assheton Frankland;** Bt 1660; company director; President, Multiple Sclerosis Society of Victoria, 1981–84; *b* 23 Feb. 1943; *s* of Major Hon. Sir Thomas William Assheton Frankland, 11th Bt, and Mrs Robert Pardoe (*d* 1972), *d* of late Captain Hon. Edward Kay-Shuttleworth; *S* to father's Btcy 1944; *S* grandmother, 17th Baroness Zouche, 1965; *m* 1978, Sally Olivia, *y d* of R. M. Barton, Bungay, Suffolk; one *s* one *d*. *Educ:* Lycée Jaccard, Lausanne. Served 15/19th the King's Royal Hussars, 1963–68. *Heir: s* Hon. William Thomas Assheton Frankland [*b* 23 July 1984]. *Address:* The Abbey, Charlton Adam, Somerton, Somerset TA11 7BE. *Clubs:* Cavalry and Guards; Melbourne (Melbourne).

ZUCKER, Kenneth Harry, QC 1981; **His Honour Judge Zucker;** a Circuit Judge, since 1989; *b* 4 March 1935; *s* of Nathaniel and Norma Zucker; *m* 1961, Ruth Erica, *y d* of Dr H. Brudno; one *s* one *d*. *Educ:* Westcliff High Sch.; Exeter Coll., Oxford, 1955–58 (MA). Served in Royal Air Force, 1953–55. Bacon Scholar, Gray's Inn, 1958; called to Bar, Gray's Inn, 1959; Atkin Scholar, Gray's Inn, 1959. A Recorder, 1982–89. *Recreations:* reading, walking, photography, bookbinding.

ZUCKERMAN, Prof. Arie Jeremy, MD, DSc; FRCP, FRCPath; Professor of Medical Microbiology in the University of London, since 1975, and Dean, Royal Free Hospital School of Medicine, since 1989; *b* 30 March 1932. *Educ:* Birmingham Univ. (BSc 1953; MSc 1962; DSc 1973); London Univ. (MB BS 1957; MD 1963; DipBact 1965). MRCS, LRCP, 1957; DObst, RCOG, 1958; MRCPath 1965, FRCPath 1977; MRCP 1977, FRCP 1982. Ho. Surg., Royal Free Hosp., 1957–58; Ho. Phys., 1958, Casualty Surg. and Admissions Officer, 1958–59, Whittington Hosp.; Flt Lieut, then Sqn Leader, Medical Branch, RAF, 1959–62: Unit MO and Tutor in Aviation Medicine, Advanced Flying Sch., 1959–60; Epidemiol Res. Lab., PHLS, 1960–62; seconded to Dept of Pathol., Guy's Hosp. Med. Sch., 1962–63; Sen. Registrar, PHLS, 1963–65; London School of Hygiene and Tropical Medicine: Sen. Lectr, Dept of Bacteriol. and Immunol., 1965–68; Reader in Virology, 1968–72; Prof. of Virology, 1972–75; Dir, Dept of Med. Microbiol., 1975–88. Chm., Conf. of Metropolitan Deans, 1992–; Mem., Court, Univ. of London, 1992–. Hon. Consultant Microbiologist: UCH, 1982–89; Royal Free Hosp., 1989–; Hon. Consultant Virologist: Charing Cross Hosp., 1982–; NE Thames Regl Blood Transfusion Centre, Brentwood, 1970–. World Health Organisation: Consultant on hepatitis, 1970–; Mem., Expert Adv. Panel on Virus Diseases, 1974–; Dir, Collaborating Centre for Ref. and Res. on Viral Diseases, 1990–; Dir, Collaborating Centre for Ref. and Res. on Viral Hepatitis, London, 1974–89. Non-exec. Dir, Royal Free Hampstead NHS Trust, 1990–; Dir, Anthony Nolan Bone Marrow Trust, 1990–. Mem. Council, Zool Soc. of London, 1989–92. Stewart Prize, BMA, 1981; James Blundell Medal and Award, British Blood Transfusion Soc., 1992. Editor: Jl of Med. Virology, 1976–; Jl of Virological Methods, 1979–. *Publications:* Virus Diseases of the Liver, 1970; Hepatitis-associated Antigen and Viruses, 1972, 2nd edn as Human Viral Hepatitis, 1975 (trans. Japanese, 1980); (with C. R. Howard) Hepatitis Viruses of Man, 1979 (trans. Japanese, 1981); A Decade of Viral Hepatitis: abstracts 1969–1979, 1980; (ed) Viral Hepatitis: clinics in tropical medicine and communicable diseases, 1986; (ed jtly) Principles and Practice of Clinical Virology, 1987 (trans. Italian, 1992), 3rd edn 1994; (ed) Viral Hepatitis and Liver Disease, 1988; (ed) Recent Developments in Prophylactic Immunization, 1989; (ed) Viral Hepatitis, 1990 (trans. Spanish, 1991); (ed with H. Thomas) Viral Hepatitis: scientific basis and clinical management, 1993; contribs to many learned jls. *Address:* Royal Free Hospital School of Medicine, Rowland Hill Street, Hampstead, NW3 2PF. *T:* 0171–794 0500.

ZUKERMAN, Pinchas; conductor, concert violinist and violist; *b* Tel Aviv, Israel, 16 July 1948; *s* of Jehuda and Miriam Zukerman; *m* 1985, Tuesday Weld, actress; two *d* by previous *m*. *Educ:* Juilliard School of Music. Début, USA, 1963, Europe, 1970. Violin soloist with every major orchestra in USA and Europe; tours of USA, Europe, Israel, Scandinavia, Australia; extensive recordings. Music Director: South Bank Festival, 1978–80; St Paul Chamber Orch., 1980–87; Principal Guest Conductor, Dallas Symph. Orch., 1993–95 (Principal Conductor, Internat. Summer Music Fest., 1990–95). First prize, Leventritt Internat. Violin Competition, 1967. *Recreation:* tennis. *Address:* c/o Shirley Kirshbaum & Associates, 711 West End Avenue, New York, NY 10025, USA. *T:* (212) 222–4843.

ZUNZ, Sir Gerhard Jacob, (Sir Jack), Kt 1989; FEng 1983; consulting engineer; *b* 25 Dec. 1923; *s* of Wilhelm Zunz and Helene (*née* Isenberg); *m* 1948, Babs Maisel; one *s* one *d* (and one *d* decd). *Educ:* Athlone High Sch., Johannesburg; Univ. of the Witwatersrand (BScCivEng); FICE, FIStructE. War service, Egypt and Italy, with SA Artillery, 1943–46. Asst Engr, Alpheus, Williams & Dowse, 1948–50; Structural and Civil Engr with Ove Arup & Partners, London, 1950–54; Co-founder and Partner, Ove Arup & Partners (S Africa), 1954–61; Ove Arup & Partners: Associate Partner, 1961–65; Sen. Partner, and Partner in all overseas partnerships, 1965–77; Dir and Chm., 1977–84; Co-Chm., Ove Arup Partnership, and Dir, Ove Arup & Partners, 1984–89, Consultant, 1989–95. Chairman: Ove Arup Foundn, 1992–; AA Foundn, 1993–. Industrial Fellow Commoner, Churchill Coll., Cambridge, 1967–68; former mem., various cttees associated with the construction industry. Hon. FRIBA 1990; FCGI 1990. Hon. DSc W Ontario, 1993; Hon. DEng Glasgow, 1994. Oscar Faber Silver Medal (jtly, with Sir Ove Arup), 1969; IStructE Gold Medal, 1988. *Publications:* (some jtly) number of technical papers to learned socs, incl. papers on Sydney Opera House and Hongkong & Shanghai Bank. *Recreations:* theatre, music, golf, tribal art. *Address:* 2A Drax Avenue, Wimbledon, SW20 0EH. *T:* 0181–947 1537.